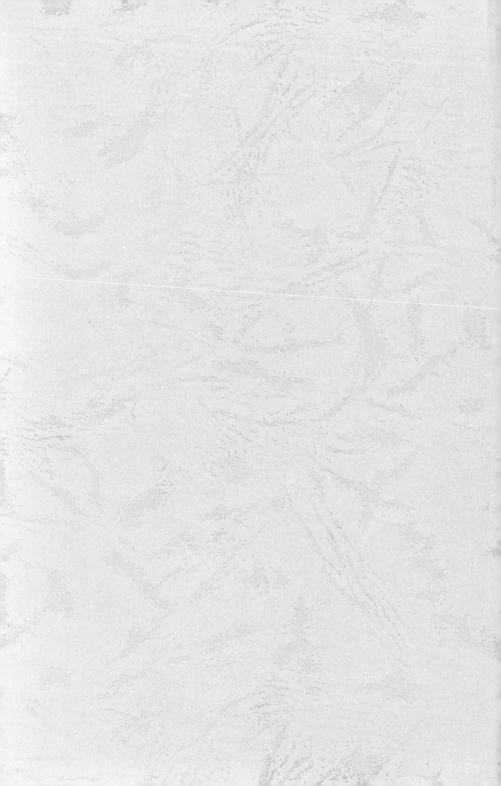

英华大词典

修订第三版

A NEW ENGLISH-CHINESE DICTIONARY

Third Revised Edition

原　编　者　　郑易里　曹成修

第二版修订者　　郑易里　党凤德　徐式谷

胡学元　刘邦琛　沈凤威

第三版修订者　　商务印书馆辞书研究中心

（徐式谷　王良碧　朱　原　任永长）

商　务　印　书　馆

2002年·北京

此扉页用含有商务印书馆注册商标的水印防伪纸印制，有这种扉页的《英华大词典》最新修订本是正版图书。请注意识别。

第三版修订者前言

《英华大词典》自五十年代初问世，迄今已近半个世纪。在七十年代以前的二十余年中，它曾是我国市场上唯一的一本由国人自编的中型偏大的英汉词典，对当时的英语翻译与教学发挥了重要的作用。七十年代以来，各种英汉词典的编纂出版日渐繁多，而《英华大词典》也在70年代末和80年代初作了全面的修订，于1984年出了修订第二版(修订经过详见后文"修订第二版前言")。经过修订的《英华大词典》第二版的篇幅比初版几乎扩大一倍，面目焕然一新，它作为一本语词和百科条目兼收的"大学版"词典，由于其篇幅适中，选词精当，词汇量大，释义和例证的译文使用规范的现代汉语，特别是中国人学习和使用英语中难度很大的英语习语、口语和俚语在词典中收集得非常丰富而实用，因而仍然是深受读者欢迎的一部中型英语工具书，出版后多次重印，已在内地和香港地区销行近七十万册，并曾被作为官方正式礼品赠送给于1984年访问北京的英国首相撒切尔夫人。

然而，《英华大词典》自第二次修订至今又已十余年，因此出版者利用这次重排繁体汉字本的机会邀请我们对全书再进行一次修订。我们所做的修订工作有以下几个方面：一，改正了若干文字内容和技术上的疏漏和错讹；二，增收了近年来涌现的英语新词近三千条以及若干新的词义和短语；三，鉴于国际上美国英语使用日益广泛，故而在原有的英国英语注音之外，我们又增加了K. K. 音标的美语注音；四，一部分科技术语与地名词条增加了香港、台湾等地的流行译法；五，改进了规格体例，使符号和字体更加醒目，便于读者查阅。

在修订过程中，原台湾辅仁大学英语研究所教授刘佑知先生给予了我们很大的帮助，他所提出的许多真知灼见都被一一吸收，融进了我们的修订内容。在此谨对刘先生表示衷心的感谢。商务印书馆的张月中先生和王小甦女士统管本次修订版的校对工作，任务重，时间紧，如果没有他们二位高度的工作责任感和细致的工作作风，本书的如期出版是不可能的。不言而喻，在校对过程中，该馆编校质量部的其他先生和女士们也都出了大力。商务印书馆的胡龙彪先生对本书的电子文本进行了认真细致的审核，提出了多条改进意见。我们在此一并致谢。

修订者学养有限，绠短汲深，疏漏之处在所难免，恳请读者及同行不吝赐教。

商务印书馆辞书研究中心

(徐式谷　王良碧　朱原　任永长)　谨识

公元1999年5月于北京

修订第二版前言

《英华大词典》(修订第二版)是在1957年修订第一版的基础上,先经原编者作初步修订,后又由商务印书馆编辑部组织馆内外力量再作加工,于1981年初完成初稿陆续发排的。在发排过程中,又对初稿作了一次全面的修改和增补。现将新版增补修订的内容以及修订过程分别简述如下。

一、新版《英华大词典》增补修订的内容

增收大量新词:新版《英华大词典》在收词上,除保留旧版百科性条目和俚俗语词较多的优点外,并对旧版作了大量补充。新版增收了《英语新词词典》(杨志达译,1978)的全部三万词条,又参照国内外同类型的词典,另行增补一批新词,并特别注意补收了旧版所忽视的"构词成分"(combining form)。这样,本词典的词目,包括缩略语、复合词和派生词在内,在删除旧版中个别过于冷僻的词目后,总数已达到十二万条以上,总字数约六百万字。

词目划分音节:新版的全部词目和绝大部分派生词都划分音节,以利于读者掌握读音和移行规则,这也是目前国外大部分英语词典的通行做法。

调整异源同形词:旧版中词源不同而拼写形式相同的词目,均放在一个条目词内处理,往往造成词义混淆和例证张冠李戴;新版中的这些词均分立条目。

更新、补充注音:新版在注音方面仍采用国内通行的国际音标,但是按丹尼尔·琼斯氏的《正音词典》第十三版作了一定的更新,如以标音符号 əu 代替 ou 等。同时,旧版在处理条目词的注音时,凡认为与上条词目有相同的,该相同部分就略而不标;新版则全部标音,读者查阅时可以一目了然。

释义有较大的修订、补充:新版注意保持旧版释义译文表达方式丰富和生动活泼的特色,但对释义的义项作了大量修订和补充,若干重点词全部改写。旧版时常将动词的及物与不及物释义混杂在一起,有碍于读者辨别和理解词义,新版则力求区别处理。旧版对介词与形容词和动词的搭配关系未加注意,新版则尽量在汉语释义后用圆括号注明搭配的介词。旧版中某些词的多项释义含糊地并列,新版则尽量用①②③……符号加以分隔,按不同意义分项归并。此外,新版还有选择地在某些释义之后举出其反义词(置于圆括号内),以利于读者从对照中加深理解。

对例证、习语和复合词作一定的增补与调整:新版对例证、习语和复合词均有所补充,对习语的增补尤为注意,放宽界限,力求多收,以利于读者查阅。对旧版中例证、习语和复合词三者

目　次

相互混淆的缺点,新版尽可能予以分类归并,务使界限分明,便于检索。

此外,在编排方式和规格体例方面,新版也作了一些方便读者的改动,详见“用法说明”,此处不再赘言。

二、新版《英华大词典》的修订过程

《英华大词典》原系郑易里、曹成修两先生所编,成稿于 1949 年以前;1950 年由三联书店在上海出版。1957 年,由当时的时代出版社约请尚永清、张景明、陈羽纶三位先生就原纸型进行过挖改修订。后来,词典改由商务印书馆出版。六十年代,商务印书馆委托原编者郑易里先生根据国外同类型的词典做过一番修订工作,但由于种种原因,未能付排问世。1978 年,商务印书馆编辑部根据少量增补、小规模修订的原则,又请郑易里、胡学元、刘邦琛、沈凤威四位先生在郑的修订稿的基础上分别负责 A－D 字母、E－L 字母、M－R 字母和 S－Z 字母四个部分的增补修订工作。1980 年初,商务印书馆重新组织力量,对该稿进行增补、审订和加工整理工作,至 1981 年初完成初稿后陆续发排。在发排过程中,考虑到国内外英语词典发展的新形势,又由党凤德、徐式谷两位先生对校样作了一次全面的修改和增补。

这几年中,先后参加过本词典部分审订加工和整理定稿工作的,有王良碧、刘邦琛、刘秀英、任永长、沈凤威、李华驹、陈少衡、陈羽纶、陈作卿、林光、费致德、姚乃强、欧阳达、徐式谷、党凤德、曹丽顺、戴钢、杨枕旦、薛琪等诸位女士和先生。本书在校对改版过程中,内容改动较大,承北京第二新华印刷厂排版改版人员和商务印书馆校对科同仁积极热心协助配合,使增订工作得以顺利进行。对本词典的修订出版予以支持协助的还有其他单位的和商务印书馆出版部及外语编辑室的许多热心人士。对这些女士和先生,我们谨在此致以衷心的感谢。

本词典的责任编辑是徐式谷先生。

本词典修订、审读、定稿的总负责人是党凤德先生。

词典反映多人多方面知识的积累,它是几代人长期呕心沥血的精神产品。随着科学文化的迅速发展,反映新事物的词义和词汇不断增加;在技术设备等条件不很理想的情况下,词典的编纂和修订工作十分艰巨。有机会从事此项工作并且愿意在这方面努力的人,都是在前人已有成果的基础上起步的,但同时也在不断创新,从而使词典达到新的水平和具有新的特色。我们经验不多,学识浅薄,疏漏谬误之处,势所难免,希望读者和同行多提宝贵意见,以便下次修订时参考改正。

《英华大词典》修订小组

1983 年 6 月

1989 年重印本说明

《英华大词典》(修订第二版)于 1984 年 10 月出书后,蒙各界读者厚爱,迄今已印行 52 万余册(两种开本合计印数,不包括香港版)。此次重印前,我们在条件允许的情况下对书中的一些印刷错讹和技术疏忽作了挖改处理,并借此机会向曾经在这方面给我们提供过宝贵意见的读者和专家们表示衷心的感谢。

《英华大词典》修订小组

1989 年 2 月

用法说明

一、词目

(1)一般词目排黑正体;外来语词目排黑斜体。

(2)同一词而拼法不同的,合并为一个词目,中以逗号分开,例如:**mac·ca·boy, mac·ca-baw.**

(3)语源不同而拼法相同的词分立词目,例如:**lay·er**[1], **lay·er**[2].

(4)词目一律划分音节。

二、读音

(1)国际音标和 K.K. 音标套以方括号,国际音标在前,K.K. 音标在后,用分号";"隔开。重音和次重音符号打在重读音节之前,例如:**ab·o·li·tion** [ˌæbəˈliʃən; ˏæbəˋlɪʃən].

(2)同一词目有两个或两个以上读音时,音标相同的部分用"-"符号省略,例如:**mac·ca-boy, mac·ca·baw** [ˈmækəbɔi, -bɔː; ˋmækəbɔɪ, -bɔ].

(3)可不发音的音标用斜体字表示,例如:**na·tion** [ˈneiʃən; ˋneʃən]。元音的长音符号可有可无时,用圆括号表示,例如:**cross** [krɔ(ː)s; krɔs].

三、词类

词类按名词、代词、形容词、冠词、数词、动词、副词、连接词、前置词和感叹词划分为十类,在释义时使用各自的英语略语词,如 ***n.*** 指替名词,***a.*** 指替形容词等(详见"缩略语表")。

四、词形变化

(1)名词、代词、形容词、副词和动词等的不规则词形变化排黑斜体,套以圆括号,并视需要加注读音。

(2)变形词同一级别而拼法不同的,用逗号","分开;级别不同的,用分号";"分开。例如:**gnaw** 的词形变化为:(~***ed***; ~***ed***, ***gnawn*** [nɔːn; nɔn]).

五、释义

(1)词类不同并需要分开释义时,在第一个和以后的词类变换前加罗马数字,及物动词和不及物动词变换时,后者变换前加破折号"—"。

(2)同词类有多项释义时,用 **1.**, **2.**, **3.**, …分开。某分义项需要再往下分时,用(a), (b), (c), ... 分开。

(3)同一义项用一个以上汉语对等词释义时,凡意思相近的,用逗号分开,意思较远的,用分号分开,例如:**a·bout** ***ad.*** ... **1.** 大约,差不多;前后,左右。

(4)释义之后所列搭配用词排白斜体,套以圆括号,例如:**look** ***vi.*** ... **1.** 看,注视 (*at*).

(5)可以互相替换用的词,不论英语或汉语,一律用方括号表示,例如:*a bird in the hand* [*bush*] 现实[不现实]的、有[无]把握的事物。

(6)释义时所用各种门类词缩略语见“缩略语表”。

(7)释义中有关词目词的用法套以六角括号,例如:**a·ware ...** 〔用作表语〕知道。

(8)释义时需要进一步注明用法、注意事项及其他语言和文化信息时,前面冠以“★”符号。

六、例证

(1)例词例句基本上按不同词类分列,一律排白斜体。

(2)词目词的例证不套括号;复合词和派生词的例证套以圆括号。

七、成语词组

(1)成语词组集中在释义之后,基本上按其中心词的不同词类分列,其先后次序以成语首词的字母次序为准。

(2)成语词组排黑斜体。

八、复合词

(1)复合词排黑正体。

(2)复合词需要分词类释义时,用**1.**,**2.**,…分开,例如:**mad** 的复合词 **~cap 1.** ***n.*** 狂妄的人,…。**2.** ***a.*** 鲁莽的,…。

九、派生词

(1)不立词条的简单派生词排黑正体,放在词条最后,并划分音节,酌情注音。

(2)派生词前一律冠以“**-**”符号。此处“**-**”符号可代表本词目的全部拼法,例如:**-ly**,**-ness**;也可代表本词目的部分拼法,例如:**mac·ro·cyte** 的派生词写成 **-cyt·ic**.

十、其他符号

(1)“~”符号代表词目词的全部拼法。

(2)“-”符号代表词目词的部分拼法,但在简单派生词中也可代表词目词的全部。

缩略语表

a. ………… adjective（形容词）
ad. ………… adverb（副词）
art. ………… article（冠词）
c. *f*. ………… confer（参看）
comb. *f*. ………… combining form（构词成分）
conj. ………… conjunction（连接词）
fem. ………… feminine（阴性）
int. ………… interjection（感叹词）
mas. ………… masculine（阳性）
n. ………… noun（名词）
neg. ………… negative（否定词）
nom. ………… nominative（主格）
num. ………… numeral（数词）
obj. ………… objective（宾格）
p. ………… past（过去）
pl. ………… plural（复数）
poss. ………… possessive（所有格）
p. *p*. ………… past participle（过去分词）
pref. ………… prefix（前缀）
prep. ………… preposition（前置词）
pres. ………… present（现在）
pres. *p*. ………… present participle（现在分词）
pro. ………… pronoun（代词）
rel. *pro*. ………… relative pronoun（关系代词）
sing. ………… singular（单数）
suf. ………… suffix（后缀）
v. ………… verb（动词）
v. *aux*. ………… auxiliary verb（助动词）
vi. ………… intransitive verb（不及物动词）
vt. ………… transitive verb（及物动词）

*　　*　　*

〔Am.〕………… 美国英语
〔Ar.〕………… 阿拉伯语
〔Aus.〕………… 澳大利亚英语
〔Ban.〕………… 班图语
〔Can.〕………… 加拿大用语
〔Chin.〕………… 汉语
〔D.〕………… 荷兰语
〔Egy.〕………… 埃及语
〔Eng.〕………… 英语
〔F.〕………… 法语
〔G.〕………… 德语
〔Gr.〕………… 希腊语
〔Haw.〕………… 夏威夷语
〔Heb.〕………… 希伯来语
〔Hind.〕………… 印地语
〔Ind.〕………… 印度用语
〔Ir.〕………… 爱尔兰语
〔It.〕………… 意大利语
〔Jap.〕………… 日语
〔Jav.〕………… 爪哇语
〔Kor.〕………… 朝鲜语
〔L.〕………… 拉丁语
〔Ma.〕………… 马来语
〔Maor.〕………… 毛利语
〔Per.〕………… 波斯语
〔Pg.〕………… 葡萄牙语
〔Phil.〕………… 菲律宾用语
〔Pol.〕………… 波兰语
〔Russ.〕………… 俄语
〔S. Afr.〕………… 南非用语
〔Sans.〕………… 梵语
〔Scot.〕………… 苏格兰语
〔Slav.〕………… 斯拉夫语
〔Sp.〕………… 西班牙语
〔Teut.〕………… 条顿语
〔Thai.〕………… 泰语

〔Turk.〕………… 土耳其语

* * *

(照笔画次序)

〔大洋〕……………… 大洋洲
〔中〕………………… 中国
〔日〕………………… 日本
〔印〕………………… 印度
〔希〕………………… 希腊
〔英〕………………… 英国
〔拉美〕……………… 拉丁美洲
〔非〕………………… 非洲
〔法〕………………… 法国
〔美〕………………… 美国
〔秘〕………………… 秘鲁
〔爱〕………………… 爱尔兰
〔欧〕………………… 欧洲
〔意〕………………… 意大利
〔德〕………………… 德国
〔澳〕……… 澳大利亚,澳洲

* * *

(照笔画次序)

〔口〕………………… 口语
〔反〕………………… 反意语
〔方〕………………… 方言
〔古〕………………… 古语
〔罕〕………………… 罕用语
〔儿〕………………… 儿语
〔卑〕………………… 下流语
〔俚〕………………… 俚语
〔弱〕………………… 弱音
〔贬〕………………… 贬义
〔书〕………………… 书面语
〔婉〕………………… 委婉语
〔喻〕………………… 比喻
〔强〕………………… 强音
〔蔑〕………………… 蔑称
〔学〕………………… 学生用语
〔旧〕………………… 旧用
〔废〕………………… 废语
〔讽〕………………… 讽刺语
〔谚〕………………… 谚语
〔谑〕………………… 戏谑语
〔缩〕………………… 缩略语

* * *

(照笔画次序)

【工】………………… 工业
【天】………………… 天文学
【天主】……………… 天主教
【化】………………… 化学
【化纤】……………… 化学纤维
【心】………………… 心理学
【水】……………… 水利;水文
【占】………………… 占星术
【古生】……………… 古生物学
【史】………………… 历史
【印】………………… 印刷
【生】………………… 生物学
【生化】……………… 生物化学
【地】……… 地质学;地理学
【光】………………… 光学
【自】………………… 自动化
【交】………………… 交通
【宇】………… 宇宙空间技术
【贝】………………… 贝类
【佛】………………… 佛教
【希神】……………… 希腊神话
【冶】………………… 冶金
【社】………………… 社会学
【林】………………… 林业
【物】………………… 物理学
【股】………………… 股票
【法】………………… 法律
【宗】………………… 宗教
【空】………………… 航空
【美】………………… 美术
【建】………………… 建筑
【政】………………… 政治学
【计】………………… 计算机
【胚】………………… 胚胎学
【军】………………… 军事
【神】………………… 神学
【鸟】………………… 鸟类
【纹】………………… 纹章

【讯】…………………… 电讯
【伦】…………………… 伦理学
【气】…………………… 气象学
【邮】…………………… 邮政
【纺】…………… 纺织;印染
【修】…………………… 修辞学
【核】…………………… 核物理学
【拳】…………………… 拳击
【海】…………………… 航海
【病】…………………… 病理学
【原】…………………… 原子能
【哲】…………………… 哲学
【畜】…………………… 畜牧
【教】…………………… 教育
【动】………… 动物;动物学
【鱼】…………………… 鱼类
【船】…………………… 造船
【商】…………………… 商业
【植】………… 植物;植物学
【无】…………………… 无线电
【犹】…………………… 犹太教
【犹神】………………… 犹太神话
【统】…………………… 统计学
【基督】………………… 基督教
【电】…………………… 电学
【圣】…………………… 圣经
【农】…………………… 农业
【经】…………………… 经济学
【解】…………………… 解剖学
【微】…………………… 微生物学
【韵】…………………… 音韵学
【语】…………………… 语言学
【牌】…………………… 牌戏
【数】…………………… 数学
【精】…………………… 精神病学
【乐】…………………… 音乐
【剑】…………………… 击剑
【剧】…………………… 戏剧
【影】…………………… 电影
【机】…………………… 机械工程
【徽】…………………… 徽章
【雕】…………………… 雕刻
【虫】…………………… 虫类
【医】…………………… 医学
【药】…………………… 药学
【猎】…………………… 打猎
【绘】…………………… 绘画
【矿】…………… 矿物;采矿
【罗神】………………… 罗马神话
【逻】…………………… 逻辑学
【摄】…………………… 摄影
【体】…………………… 体育

Jones 音标与 K. K. 音标对照表

元音与双元音

符号		范例	符号		范例
Jones	K. K.		Jones	K. K.	
iː	i	bee[biː; bi]	ʌ	ʌ	cut[kʌt; kʌt]
i	ɪ	sit[sit; sɪt]	əː	ɝ	fur[fəː; fɝ]
e	ɛ	ten[ten; tɛn]	ə	ə	ago[ə'gəu; ə`go]
æ	æ	hat[hæt; hæt]		ɚ	never['nevə; `nɛvɚ]
ɑː	ɑr	barn[bɑːn; bɑrn]	ei	e	page[peidʒ; pedʒ]
	ɑ	palm[pɑːm; pɑm]	əu	o	no[nəu; no]
	æ	ask[ɑːsk; æsk]	ai	aɪ	five[faiv; faɪv]
ɔ	ɑ	got[gɔt; gɑt]	au	aʊ	now[nau; naʊ]
	ɔ	long[lɔŋ; lɔŋ]	ɔi	ɔɪ	join[dʒɔin; dʒɔɪn]
ɔː	ɔ	saw[sɔː; sɔ]	iə	ɪr	near[niə; nɪr]
	ɔr	born[bɔːn; bɔrn]	ɛə	ɛr	pair[pɛə; pɛr]
u	ʊ	put[put; pʊt]	uə	ʊr	pure[pjuə; pjʊr]
uː	u	tool[tuːl; tul]			

辅　音

符号		范例	符号		范例
Jones	K. K.		Jones	K. K.	
p	p	pen[pen; pɛn]	s	s	so[səu; so]
b	b	bag[bæg; bæg]	z	z	zoo[zuː; zu]
t	t	tea[tiː; ti]	ʃ	ʃ	ship[ʃip; ʃɪp]
d	d	did[did; dɪd]	ʒ	ʒ	vision['viʒn; `vɪʒən]
k	k	cat[kæt; kæt]	h	h	how[hau; haʊ]
g	g	game[geim; gem]	m	m	man[mæn; mæn]
tʃ	tʃ	chin[tʃin; tʃɪn]	n	n	no[nəu; no]
dʒ	dʒ	June[dʒuːn; dʒun]	ŋ	ŋ	sing[siŋ; sɪŋ]
f	f	fall[fɔːl; fɔl]	l	l	leg[leg; lɛg]
v	v	voice[vɔis; vɔɪs]	r	r	red[red; rɛd]
θ	θ	thin[θin; θɪn]	j	j	yes[jes; jɛs]
ð	ð	then[ðen; ðɛn]	w	w	wet[wet; wɛt]

A

A

A, a [ei; e] **n.** (*pl.* ***A's***, ***As***, ***a's***, ***as*** [eiz; ez]) **1.** 英文字母表的第一字母。**2.** 〔A〕A 字形(物)。**3.** 〔A〕【乐】A 音;A 调 **4.** 【数】第一已知数。**5.** 〔美〕〔A〕(学业成绩的)优等。**6.** 表示"第一"的符号。*A1* = *A one* [ˈei ˈwʌn] 头等的,极好的。*A major* [*minor*] A 大调[小调]。*straight A's* 全优。A (*No.*) *1 tea* 一级茶。*an A tent* A 字形帐篷。*He is A* (*No.*) *1*. 他是头号人物。***from A to Z*** 自始至终;完全。***not know A from B*** 一字不识。

a [强 ei, 弱 ə; 强 e, 弱 ə], **an** [强 æn, 弱 ən; 强 æn, 弱 ən] 〔an 用在以元音音素开始的词前〕 *indefinite art*. **1.** 〔普通可数名词第一次提到时,冠以不定冠词主要表示类别,有时则兼含"一"的概念〕: *This is a transformer*. 这是变压器。*Ours is a developing country*. 我国是个发展中的国家。*a house* 一所住宅。*an army* 一支军队。**2.** 〔在数量概念上,说明表示时间、距离、重量及数目的名词〕一。*a thousand* 一千。*an hour* 一小时。*a mile* 一英里。*a pound* 一磅。**3.** 〔与数量形容词、数词等连用而表示一个整体单位〕: *a dozen times* 十二次。*a great many years* 许多年。*A ten years is not so long*. 十年的时间并不算怎么长。**4.** 〔与某些复数名词连用而仍表示一个单位〕: *a glassworks* (一家)玻璃厂。*a falls in the river* 河中的瀑布。**5.** 〔与序数词或形容词最高级结合共同限定所修饰的名词〕: *He tried to jump up a third time*. 他试图作第三次的跳高动作。*It was a most beautiful sight*. 这是一个最美丽的景致。**6.** 〔表示同类事物中的代表〕任何一个[种]。*A horse is useful*. 马是有用的。**7.** 同一的,相同的: *We are all of a mind*. 我们大家一条心。*of a size* (属于)同一大小。*birds of a feather* 同一毛色的鸟。**8.** 〔两件成套的东西,用 and 连接,仍视为一个单位〕一(副)。*a cup and saucer* 带茶托的茶杯。**9.** 〔抽象名词用作普通名词,表示类别,例证〕: *Would you do me a kindness*? 你能帮我一下忙吗? *a virtue* 一种美德。**10.** 〔用于专有名词前,以整体概括个体,表示类似的一个或某一个〕: *a Mr. Smith* 一位叫史密斯的人。*a Newton* 像牛顿那样的人。*a Ford* 一辆福特汽车。**11.** 〔与 how, what, such, too, so, quite, rather 以及 half 等搭配使用时,常置于各该词的后面〕: *So beautiful a jewel*! 多么好看的宝石! *How great a man he is*! 他真是伟人! *rather a queer fellow* 十分古怪的家伙。*half an hour* 半小时。**12.** 〔在习惯用法上,相当于介词 in, for, on 的作用〕每(…),在…内,按(…而论),换(得)。*three times a day* 每天三次。*five dollars a catty* 五元美金(买)一斤。*twice a year* 一年内两次。**13.** 〔口〕一客: *an ice* 一客冰淇淋。

A. = **1.** 【化】argon 氩。**2.** 【物】angstrom (unit) 埃(Å)。

A. = **1.** absolute (temperature). **2.** Academy. **3.** Admiral. **4.** adult (= for adults only). **5.** America(n).

a. = **1.** about. **2.** accepted. **3.** acre. **4.** acting. **5.** active. **6.** adjective. **7.** after. **8.** afternoon. **9.** aged. **10.** alto. **11.** ampere. **12.** *anno* (= in the year of). **13.** answer. **14.** *ante* (= before). **15.** approved.

a- *pref*. **1.** 表示加强: *a*bide, *a*rise, *a*wake. **2.** 表示"on", "in", "to", "into" 的意思: *a*foot = on foot. *a*side = to one side. *a*back = backward. *a*bed = in bed. *a*sunder = into pieces. *a*sleep = in sleep. **3.** 表示"of"的意思: *a*kin (of kin); *a*new (of new). **4.** 表示"from" 的意思: *a*bridge. **5.** 表示 "out" 的意思: *a*mend. **6.** 表示 "not" 的意思: *a*chromatic, *a*moral, *a*sexual.

A.A., AA = **1.** antiaircraft: *an A.A. artillery unit* 高射炮部队。**2.** ack-ack. **3.** Alcoholics Anonymous.

AAAL = American Academy of Arts and Letters 美国艺术和文学学会。

AAAS = **1.** American Association for the Advancement of Science 美国科学促进会。**2.** American Academy of Arts and Sciences 美国艺术和科学研究院。

AAF = Army Air Forces 〔美〕陆军航空队。

aah [ɑː; ɑ] **n.** 啊〔喊叫声〕。—**vi.** "啊,啊"地喊叫〔出于惊喜、意外等〕。

AAM = air-to-air missile 空对空导弹。

aard·vark [ˈɑːdvɑːk; ˋɑrd͵vɑrk] **n.** 【动】土豚〔非洲食蚁兽〕。

aard·wolf [ˈɑːdwulf; ˋɑrd͵wʊlf] **n.** 【动】土狼〔非洲南部产〕。

Aar·hus [ˈɔːhuːs; ˋɔr͵hus] **n.** 阿尔路斯〔丹麦港市〕。

Aar·on [ˈɛərən; ˋɛrən] **n.** **1.** 艾伦〔男子名〕。**2.** 亚伦〔基督教《圣经》中人物,摩西之兄,犹太教第一祭司长〕。**~'s beard** 【植】黄栌,虎耳草(之类)。**~'s rod** **1.** 【植】麒麟草。**2.** 【圣】(缠有蛇的)亚伦魔杖。**3.** 【建】缠蛇杆式装饰。

AAS = American Academy of Sciences 美国科学院。

AAUP = American Association of University Professors 美国大学教授联合会。

AAWB = Afro-Asian Writers' Bureau 亚非作家常设局。

A.B., AB = **1.** able-bodied seaman 【英军】二等水兵; 【海】一等水手。**2.** 〔L.〕 *Artium Baccalaureus* (= Bachelor of Arts) 文学士。**3.** airborne. **4.** Atomic Bomb 原子弹。

ab. = **1.** abbreviation. **2.** about. **3.** absent. **4.** absolute. **5.** (times) at bat 【棒球】打球的次数。

ab- [æb-, əb-; æb-, əb-] ***pref*.** **1.** = away, (away) from, off, apart: *ab*normal; *ab*duct 等。**2.** 【物】= absolute. ★在 c, t 前作 abs-, 如: *abs*cond, *abs*tract; 在 m, p, v 前作 a-, 如: *a*mentia, *a*perient, *a*vert.

ab [æb; ɑb] ***prep*.** 〔L.〕从(= from, away)。~ ***extra*** [ˈekstrə; ˋɛkstrə] 自外,从外部,外来。~ ***initio*** [iˈniʃiəu; ɪˋnɪʃɪo] 从开头,从开始〔略 ab init〕。~ ***intra*** [ˈintrə; ˋɪntrə] 从内部。~ ***origine*** [əuˈridʒiniː; oˋrɪdʒɪni] 从起源。~ ***ovo*** [ˈəuvəu; ˋovo] 从开始。~ ***uno disce omnes*** [ˈjuːnəu ˈdisiː ˈɔmniːz; ˋjuno ˋdɪsi ˋɔmniz] 由一斑而知全豹,闻一而知十。~ ***urbe condita*** [ˈəːbi ˈkɔnditə; ˋɜbɪ ˋkɑndɪtə] 由罗马建都(公元前 753 年)起算〔略 A.U.C.〕。

a·ba [ˈæbə; ˋɑbə] **n.** **1.** 驼毛[山羊毛等]原色粗呢;粗厚农民呢。**2.** 阿拉伯式斗篷。

ab·a·ca [ˌɑbəˈkɑː; ˌɑbəˋkɑ] **n.** 马尼拉麻;麻蕉。

ab·a·ci [ˈæbəsai; ˋæbə͵saɪ] abacus 的复数。

A

a·back [ə'bæk; ə`bæk] ***ad.*** 向后;【海】逆帆。***be taken ~*** **1.** (突遇逆风)成逆帆。**2.** 吓了一跳(*He was taken ~ by the news.* 他被这消息吓了一跳)。

ab·a·cus ['æbəkəs; `æbəkəs] ***n.*** (*pl.* **~*es***, **-*ci*** [-sai; -saɪ]) **1.** 算盘。**2.** 【建】(圆柱顶部的)顶板,冠板。*learn to use [work] an ~* 学打算盘。

A·ba·dan [ˌæbə'dɑːn; ˏɑbɑ`dɑn] ***n.*** **1.** 阿巴丹岛〔伊朗〕。**2.** 阿巴丹〔伊朗港市〕。

A·bad·don [ə'bædən; ə`bædən] ***n.*** **1.** 无底洞,地狱。**2.** 地狱恶魔(= Apollyon)。

a·baft [ə'bɑːft; ə`bæft] ***ad.***, ***prep.*** 【海】在船尾,向船尾;在…后面。~ *the beam* 在船的横梁之后。

ab·a·lo·ne [ˌæbə'ləuni; ˏæbə`lonɪ] ***n.*** 【动】石决明〔旧称鲍鱼〕。

ab·am·pere [æb'æmpɛə; æb`æmpɛr] ***n.*** 【物】绝对安培,电磁制安培。

a·ban·don [ə'bændən; ə`bændən] **I** ***vt.*** **1.** 扔弃(地位等),离弃(家园);断绝(念头等),戒除(恶习等)。**2.** 【法】遗弃(妻子),放弃(权利等)。**3.** 【保险】投保(货物等)。~ ***oneself to*** 恣意,沉迷(酒,色)(~ *oneself to pleasure(s)* 恣意享乐。~ *oneself to despair* 悲观失望。~ *oneself to emotion* 感情用事)。**II** ***n.*** 放肆;任性(*opp.* restraint, constraint)。***with ~*** 尽情地(唱等)。**-er** ***n.*** 放弃者,遗弃者;【保险】投保人。

a·ban·doned [ə'bændənd; ə`bændənd] ***a.*** **1.** 被放弃[扔弃,遗弃]了的。**2.** 心灰意懒的,自暴自弃的,放荡的,堕落的,无耻的。*an ~ character* 荡子;无赖;无可救药的人。*an ~ child* 弃儿。

a·ban·don·ee [əˌbændə'niː; əˏbændə`ni] ***n.*** **1.** 【保险】承保人。**2.** 【法】被遗弃人。

a·ban·don·ment [ə'bændənmənt; ə`bændənmənt] ***n.*** **1.** 放弃,断念。**2.** 放肆。**3.** 【保险】投保;委付。~ *of an action* 【法】放弃诉讼。~ *of a right* 弃权。

à bas [ɑː 'bɑː; ɑ `bɑ] 〔F.〕打倒…(= down with)。

a·base [ə'beis; ə`bes] ***vt.*** 贬,降低(地位、价值、身分)。~ *oneself* 自贬,自卑。**-ment** ***n.*** 失意;屈辱;败落。

a·bash [ə'bæʃ; ə`bæʃ] ***vt.*** 使…羞愧,使…脸红。*Nothing can ~ him.* 什么也不会使他脸红[羞愧],他的脸皮很厚。*be [feel] ~ed* 局促不安。**-ment** ***n.***

a·bask [ə'bɑːsk; ə`bæsk] ***ad.*** 晒着太阳,靠近炉火(取暖)。

a·bate [ə'beit; ə`bet] ***vt.*** **1.** 减少,减轻(痛苦等);降低,减(价);缓和。**2.** 【法】取消(法令),中止(诉讼);排除(障碍)。**3.** 除掉;夺去。~ *a tax* 减税。~ *sb.'s pain* 减轻某人的痛苦。~ *sb. of sth.* 夺取某人的东西。~ *a nuisance* 排除骚扰。— ***vi.*** **1.** (洪水、风暴、病痛等)减少,减轻,减退。*The storm has ~d.* 风暴减弱了。**2.** 【法】中止,作废。

a·bate·ment [ə'beitmənt; ə`betmənt] ***n.*** **1.** 减少,减轻,减退。**2.** 【法】(遗产的)非法占有;中断;失效。~ *of penalty* 减刑。~ *of taxes* 减税。***plea in ~*** 【法】妨诉抗辩。

ab·a·t(t)is ['æbətis; `æbətɪs] ***n.*** (*pl.* ~ ['æbətiːz; `æbətiz])【军】鹿砦,拒木,障碍物。

ab·at·toir ['æbətwɑː; ˏæbə`twɑr] ***n.*** 〔F.〕屠宰场。

ab·ax·i·al [æb'æksiəl; æb`æksɪəl] ***a.*** 【植】背轴的,远轴的(*opp. adaxial*)。

abb [æb; æb] ***n.*** **1.** 粗羊毛。**2.** 粗毛线。**3.** 纬纱(= woof; *opp.* warp)。

Abb. = **1.** Abbess. **2.** Abbey. **3.** Abbot.

Ab·ba ['æbə; `æbə] ***n.*** **1.** 圣父〔东正教冠于主教和大主教名字前的尊称〕。**2.** 天父〔基督教祈祷时用于称呼上帝〕。

ab·ba·cy ['æbəsi; `æbəsɪ] ***n.*** 修道院院长的职位[管区、任期]。

Ab·bas·sid [ə'bæsid, 'æbəsid; ə`bæsɪd, `æbəsɪd] **I** ***n.*** (阿拉伯帝国)阿巴斯王朝(750—1258)的统治者。**II** ***a.*** 阿巴斯王朝的。

ab·ba·tial [ə'beiʃəl; ə`beʃəl] ***a.*** 男[女]修道院长的;修道院的。

ab·bé ['æbei, F. 'æbei; `ɑbə] ***n.*** 〔F.〕(*pl.* **~*s***) 修道院院长;神父。

ab·bess ['æbis; `æbɪs] ***n.*** 女修道院院长。

Ab·be·vil·li·an [ˌæbi'viliən, -ljən; ˏæbɪ`vɪlɪən, -ljən] ***a.*** 【考古】阿贝维尔期的〔阿贝维尔为法国城市名,阿贝维尔期指旧石器时代晚期文化,特点是使用石手斧〕。

Ab·bey ['æbi; `æbɪ] ***n.*** 阿比〔姓氏〕。

ab·bey ['æbi; `æbɪ] ***n.*** **1.** 修道院,大教堂,大寺院。**2.** 全院修道士[修道女]。*the Abbey* 伦敦威斯敏斯特(Westminster)大教堂。

Ab·bot(t) ['æbət; `æbət] ***n.*** 阿博特〔姓氏〕。

ab·bot ['æbət; `æbət] ***n.*** 男修道院院长。***the Abbot of Misrule [Unreason]*** (英国指十五、十六世纪时)圣诞节狂欢会的主持人。

abbr(ev). = **1.** abbreviated. **2.** abbreviation.

ab·bre·vi·ate [ə'briːvieit; ə`brivɪˏet] ***vt.*** **1.** 节略,省略,缩写。**2.** 缩短(行期等)。**3.** 【数】约分。*New York is ~d to N. Y.* New York 缩写为 N.Y.

ab·bre·vi·a·tion [əˌbriːvi'eiʃən; əˏbrivɪ`eʃən] ***n.*** **1.** 省略,缩写。**2.** 缩写词,略语。**3.** 【数】约分。**4.** 【乐】略号。

ab·bre·vi·a·tor [ə'briːviˌeitə; ə`brivɪˏetɚ] ***n.*** 缩写者;节略者。

Abby ['æbi; `æbɪ] ***n.*** 阿比〔女子名, Abigai 的昵称〕。

ABC ['eibiː'siː; `ebi`si] ***n.*** (*pl.* ***ABC's***) 字母表;初步,入门;基础知识。*the ~ of finance* 财政初步。~ *book* 初学书,入门书。~ *method* (由字母教起的)初级语文教授法。***as easy as ~*** 极其容易。***the ~ (guide)*** 〔英〕(按字母顺序编排的)铁路旅行指南。~ ***art*** (排斥任何形式的装饰、将线条和图形压缩至最低限度的)ABC 艺术。

ABC = **1.** American Broadcasting Company 美国广播公司。**2.** Australian Broadcasting Corporation 澳大利亚广播公司。**3.** Asian Badminton Confederation 亚洲羽毛球联合会。**4.** Advance(d) Booking Charter (美)预订章程(一种在动身前一定日期预订可享受优惠票价的规定)。

ABC warfare = atomic, biological, chemical warfare 原子、生物、化学战。

ab·cou·lomb [æb'kuːlɔm; æb`kulɑm] ***n.*** 【物】绝对库伦;电磁制库伦。

ABD = All But Dissertation (已完成课程及考试但尚缺论文的)准博士。

ab·di·cate ['æbdikeit; `æbdəˏket] ***vt.*** **1.** 弃,放弃(权利)。**2.** 退(位);让(位);辞(职);【法】废(嫡)。— ***vi.*** (国王)退位。~ ***the throne in sb.'s favour [in favour of sb.]*** 让位给某人。

ab·di·ca·tion [ˌæbdi'keiʃən; ˏæbdə`keʃən] ***n.*** **1.** 弃权;让位;辞职。**2.** 【法】废嫡。

ab·di·ca·tor ['æbdikeitə; `æbdɪˏketɚ] ***n.*** 弃权人;让位者。

ab·do·men ['æbdəmen, æb'dəumen; `æbdəmən, æb`domən] ***n.*** 腹,下腹部;【虫】腹部。

ab·dom·i·nal [æb'dɔminl; æb`dɑmənl] ***a.*** **1.** 腹部的,腹腔的。**2.** 【鱼】有腹鳍的。~ **breathing** 腹式呼吸。~ **catarrh** 肠炎。~ **cavity** 腹腔。~ **dropsy** 腹水病。~ **operation** 剖腹手术。~ **region** 腹部。~ **typhus** 肠伤寒。

ab·dom·i·nous [æb'dɔminəs; æb`dɑmənəs] ***a.*** 大肚皮的,肥胖的。

ab·duce [æb'djuːs; æb`djus] ***vt.*** 【解】使外展。

ab·du·cent [æb'djuːsnt; æb`djusənt] ***a.*** 【解、动】外展的(*opp.* adducent)。~ **muscles** 外展肌。

ab·duct [æb'dʌkt; æb`dʌkt] ***vt.*** **1.** 诱拐,拐走。**2.** 【生理】使外展(*opp.* adduct)。

ab·duc·tion [æbˈdʌkʃən; æbˋdʌkʃən] ***n***. **1.** 诱拐。**2.** 外展(作用)。

ab·duc·tor [æbˈdʌktə; æbˋdʌktɚ] ***n***. **1.** 诱拐者,拐子。**2.**【解】外展肌 (*opp*. adductor)。

Abe [eib; eb] ***n***. 埃布〔男子名, Abraham 的昵称〕。

a·beam [əˈbiːm; əˋbim] ***ad***. 正横〔与船的龙骨或飞机机身成直角〕。

a·be·ce·dar·i·an [ˌeibi(ː)si(ː)ˈdɛəriən; ˏebɪsɪˋdɛrɪən] **I** ***a***. **1.** 照 ABC 顺序的。**2.** 初学的,初步的,基本的。**II** ***n***.〔美〕**1.** 初学者。**2.** 启蒙老师。

a·bed [əˈbed; əˋbɛd] ***ad***.〔古〕在床上。*be ill* [*sick*] ~ 病倒床上。*lie* ~ 躺在床上,坐月子。

A·bel [ˈeibəl; ˋe bl] ***n***. **1.** 埃布尔〔姓氏,男子名〕。**2.**【圣】亚伯〔亚当和夏娃的次子〕。

a·bele [əˈbiːl, ˈeibl; əˋbil, ˋebl] ***n***.【植】银白杨。

a·be·lian [əˈbiːljən; əˋbiljən] ***a***.【数】能成立可换定律的。*an A-group*【数】可换群。

Ab·er·crom·bie, Ab·er·crom·by [ˈæbəkrʌmbi; ˋæbɚˏkrʌmbɪ] ***n***. 阿伯克龙比〔姓氏〕。

Ab·er·deen [ˌæbəˈdiːn; ˏæbɚˋdin] ***n***. **1.** 阿伯丁〔英国港市〕。**2.** 阿伯丁郡〔英国郡名〕(= ~shire)。**3.** 苏格兰粗毛猎狐狗(= ~ terrier)。~ **Angus** [ˈæŋgus; ˋæŋgəs] ***n***. (苏格兰肉用)无角黑牛。

ab·er·de·vine [ˌæbədəˈvain; ˏæbɚdɪˋvaɪn] ***n***.【鸟】金雀类。

a·ber·glau·be [ˌɑːbəˈglaubə; ˏɑbɚˋglaʊbə] ***n***.〔G.〕迷信。

ab·er·rance [æˈberəns; æbˋɛrəns], **-ran·cy** [-si; -sɪ] ***n***. 离开正道,越轨。

ab·er·rant [æˈberənt; æbˋɛrənt] ***a***. **1.** 离开正路的,脱离常规的。**2.**【生】畸变的,异常的。~ **form**【生】畸变型。

ab·er·ra·tion [ˌæbəˈreiʃən; ˏæbəˋreʃən] ***n***. **1.** 偏差,越轨,错乱;一时的记错;【法】过失。**2.**【医】乖常,失常;【生】畸变,变型。**3.**【物】像差;【天】光行差。*mental* ~ 精神失常。

a·bet [əˈbet; əˋbɛt] ***vt***. 唆使,鼓动,怂恿;助长 (*opp*. hinder)。***aid and*** ~【法】教唆,煽动。~ ***an evil-doer*** 助桀为虐。**-ment** ***n***. 煽动,教唆。

a·bet·ter, -tor [əˈbetə; əˋbɛtɚ] ***n***. 煽动者,教唆者。

a·bey·ance [əˈbeiəns; əˋbeəns] ***n***. 中止,暂搁,保留,缓议,缓办,停止;未定;【法】(所有权等的)未定。***be in*** ~ 暂停;未定。***fall into*** ~ (世袭爵位等)即行中止;(法规等)暂时失效。***hold*** [***leave***] ***in*** ~ 暂搁。

ab·hor [əbˈhɔː; əbˋhɔr] ***vt***. (***-hor·red***; ***-hor·ring***) 憎恶,厌恶,嫌弃。

ab·hor·rence [əbˈhɔrəns; əbˋhɔrəns] ***n***. 嫌恶,厌恶,痛恨;极其讨厌的人[物]。***have an*** ~ ***of*** = ***hold in*** ~ 厌恶,痛恨。

ab·hor·rent [əbˈhɔrənt; əbˋhɔrənt] ***a***. **1.** 可恶的,讨厌的。**2.** 不相容的,跟…不(投)合的 (*to*; *from*);〔古〕嫌厌 (*of*)。***be*** ~ ***to*** (*sb*.; *sb*.'*s idea*) 和(某人)不相投,和(某人意见)不合。

ab·hor·rer [əbˈhɔːrə; əbˋhɔrɚ] ***n***. 嫌恶者,反对者。

a·bid·ance [əˈbaidəns; əˋbaɪdns] ***n***. **1.** 继续。**2.** 留在 (*in*)。**3.** 遵守。~ *by rules* [*terms*] 遵守规章[条例]。

a·bide [əˈbaid; əˋbaɪd] ***vi***. (***a·bode*** [əˈbəud; əˋbod], ***a·bid·ed***; ***a·bode***, ***a·bid·ed***) **1.**〔古〕住,居住,逗留。**2.** 保持,继续。**3.** 遵守。~ *in Paris* 住在巴黎。~ *in one's father's house* 住在自己父亲家里。~ *in sin* 怙恶不悛。~ *with one's father* 和父亲同住。— ***vt***. **1.** 等待。**2.** 忍受,忍耐〔用于否定和疑问〕: *I can not* ~ *him*. 我对他忍无可忍。~ ***by*** 坚持,遵守(法律、契约、诺言等);依从,服从(~ *by one's opinion* 固执己见。~ *by the inevitable* 迫于不得已)。

a·bid·ing [əˈbaidiŋ; əˋbaɪdɪŋ] ***a***.〔书〕持久的,不变的。~ *friendship* 持久的友谊。~ *place* 住宅,家。

Ab·i·djan [ˌæbiˈdʒɑːn; ˋæbɪˏdʒɑn] ***n***. 阿比让(阿比尚)〔象牙海岸共和国首都〕。

Ab·i·gail [ˈæbigeil; ˋæbɪgel] ***n***. **1.** 阿比盖尔〔女子名〕。**2.** [a-] (贵妇人的)使女。

a·bil·i·ty [əˈbiliti; əˋbɪlətɪ] ***n***. 能,能力,本领,技能;〔*pl*.〕才,才能,才干。*financial abilities* 财力。*a man of* ~ 有本事的人。***to the best of one's*** ~ 竭力,尽力,尽量。

-a·bil·i·ty *suf*. 由 -able 转成的名词词尾,表示"可能性": cur*ability*.

ab in·i·tio [ˌæbiˈniʃiəu; ˏæbɪˋnɪʃɪo]〔L.〕从开始起。

a·bi·o·gen·e·sis [ˌeibaiəuˈdʒenisis; ˏæbɪəˋdʒɛnɪsɪs] ***n***.【生】自然发生(论);无生源说。

ab·i·o·ge·net·ic [ˌeibaiəudʒiˈnetik; ˏæbɪodʒɪˋnɛtɪk] ***a***. 自然发生(论)的,无生源(说)的。

ab·i·og·e·nist [ˌeibaiˈɔdʒinist; ˏæbɪˋɑdʒɪnɪst] ***n***. 自然发生论者,偶发论者,无生源说者。

a·bi·o·sis [ˈeibaiˈəusis; ˏæbɪˋosɪs] ***n***.【医】生活力缺失。

abi·ot·ic [ˌeibaiˈɔtik; ebaɪˋɑtɪk] ***a***. 无生命的,非生物的。

ab·ject [ˈæbdʒekt; æbˋdʒɛkt] **I** ***a***. **1.** 卑鄙的,下贱的,下流的。**2.** 不幸的,悲惨的。*an* ~ *time-server* 卑鄙的趋炎附势者。*make an* ~ *apology* 告饶。~ *poverty* 赤贫。**II** ***n***.〔古〕小人,下流人。**-ly** *ad*. **-ness** *n*.

ab·jec·tion [æbˈdʒekʃən; æbˋdʒɛkʃən] ***n***. **1.** 落魄。**2.** 卑劣。

ab·ju·ra·tion [ˌæbdʒuəˈreiʃən; ˏæbdʒʊˋreʃən] ***n***. 发誓断绝,公开放弃。

ab·jure [əbˈdʒuə; əbˋdʒʊr] ***vt***. 发誓弃绝(信仰等);公开放弃(国籍、权利等)。~ *the realm* 宣誓离开本国。

ab·lac·ta·tion [ˌæblækˈteiʃən; ˏæblækˋteʃən] ***n***. 断奶。

ab·late [æbˈleit; æbˋlet] ***vt***., ***vi***. 切除、融化、消散、腐蚀。

ab·la·tion [æbˈleiʃən; æbˋleʃən] ***n***. **1.**【医】部分切除(术);【医】脱落。**2.**【地】消融,冰面融化;【化】烧蚀。

ab·la·ti·val [ˌæbləˈtaivəl; ˏæbləˋtaɪvəl] ***a***.【语法】夺格的。

ab·la·tive[1] [ˈæblətiv; ˋæblətɪv] ***a***., ***n***.【语法】(拉丁语的)夺格(的)。~ **absolute** 独立夺格(结构)。

ab·la·tive[2] [ˈæblətiv; ˋæblətɪv] ***a***. 易切除的,易烧蚀的。~ *plastics* 烧蚀性塑料。

ab·la·tor [æbˈleitə; æbˋletɚ] ***n***. 防烧蚀材料。

ab·laut [ˈæblaut, G. ˈæplaut; ˋæblaʊt, G. ˋæplaʊt] ***n***.【语音】母音交替〔*cf*. gradation〕。(例: s*i*ng — s*a*ng — s*u*ng)。

a·blaze [əˈbleiz; əˋblez] **I** ***a***.〔常用作表语〕。**II** ***ad***. **1.** 燃烧,着火。**2.** 发光,烧起,炽燃,(东西)闪耀。**3.** (人心)激昂。***be*** ~ ***with anger*** 发火,动怒。***set*** ~ 烧起,燃起。

a·ble [ˈeibl; ˋe bl] ***a***. (***a·bler***; ***a·blest***) **1.**〔接不定式〕能;会。**2.** (人)有才能的,有本事的,能干的 (*opp*. incompetent)。**3.** (行为等)显示出才华的。**4.**【法】有法定资格的。*be* ~ *to swim* 会游泳。*an* ~ *man* 能干人。*an* ~ *speech* 漂亮的演说。★ can 没有不定式,也没有将来式,过去式等变化,故必要时可说作 shall [will, may] be ~ to 或 have [has, had] been ~ to. ~-**bodied** ***a***. 强壮的,健全的 (*an* ~-*bodied seaman* 一级水手,二等水兵。*an* ~-*bodied man* [*woman*] 男子[女子]全劳动力)。~-**minded** ***a***. 能干的,能力强的。

-a·ble *suf*.〔附在动词或名词后构成形容词〕**1.** 能…的,适于…的。bear*able*, sal*able*. **2.** 易…的: change*able*. ★以 -ate 结尾的、三音节以上的拉丁系动词,应先略去 -ate 再加用 -able: educ*ate* — educ*able*. 与 -able 相对应的副词词尾是 -ably: not*able* — not*ably*.

a·blings [ˈeiblinz; ˋeblɪnz], **a·blins** [ˈeiblinz; ˋeblɪnz] ***ad***.〔Scot.〕多半,大概,也许。

a·bloom [əˈbluːm; əˋblum] ***a***.〔多作表语〕, ***ad***. (花)盛开,开着花。

ab·lu·ent [ˈæbluənt; ˋæbljʊənt] **I** ***a***. 洗涤的。**II** ***n***. 洗

A

涤剂。

a·blush [əˈblʌʃ; əˋblʌʃ] **I** *a*. 〔常作表语〕。**II** *ad*. (因羞愧而)脸红。

ab·lu·tion [əˈbluːʃən; əbˈljuʃən] *n*. **1.** 洗净,沐浴。**2.** 〔主 *pl*.〕【宗】斋戒沐浴,洗礼。**3.** 净水,洗净液。**4.** 〔*pl*.〕〔英〕〔用作复数〕兵营内的洗浴设备;〔用作单数〕有洗浴设备的房间[建筑]。**-a·ry** [-əri; -ərɪ] *a*.

a·bly [ˈeibli; ˋeblɪ] *ad*. 巧妙地,适宜地,能干地。

-a·bly *suf*. 可…地。

ABM = **1.** antiballistic missile 反弹道导弹。**2.** Atomic Bomb Mission 〔美〕原子弹爆炸调查团。

Ab·na·ki [æbˈnɑːki; æbˋnɑkɪ] *n*. 〔*pl*.〕阿布纳基人〔早先聚居在美国缅因州的阿尔衮琴部落联盟的一支印第安人〕。

ab·ne·gate [ˈæbnigeit; ˋæbnɪˏget] *vt*. **1.** 放弃(权利等)。**2.** 克制。

ab·ne·ga·tion [ˌæbniˈgeiʃən; ˏæbnɪˋgeʃən] *n*. **1.** 放弃。**2.** 克制。

ab·ne·ga·tor [ˈæbnigeitə; ˋæbnɪˏgetɚ] *n*. **1.** 克制者。**2.** 弃权者。

ab·nor·mal [æbˈnɔːməl; æbˋnɔrml̩] *a*. 反常的,变态的,不规则的。~ *condition* 非常状态。~ *psychology* 变态心理学。**-ly** *ad*.

ab·nor·mal·i·ty [ˌæbnɔːˈmæliti; ˏæbnɔrˋmælətɪ] *n*. **1.** 反常,变态,不规则。**2.** 变体,畸形,反常事物。

ab·nor·mi·ty [æbˈnɔːmiti; æbˋnɔrmətɪ] *n*. 反常,不规则,畸形。

abo [ˈæbəu; ˋæbo] *n*. 〔Aus.〕〔蔑〕土人,土著。

a·board [əˈbɔːd; əˋbord] **I** *ad*. **1.** 在船[飞机、车]上,上船[飞机、车]。**2.** 靠船边。*climb* ~ *a train* [*plane*] 上车[飞机]。*keep the land* ~ (船)靠岸开。**II** *prep*. 在船[飞机、车]上。*go home* ~ *a train* 坐火车回家。***All*** ~! 各位上船!〔美〕各位上车[飞机]! ***close*** [***hard***] ~ 紧靠船边。***fall*** ~ (***of***) (*another ship*) 与(他船)船边相撞。***go*** ~ (of) a ship 乘船。lay (*enemy's ship*) ~ 靠近(敌船)。***step*** ~ 上(船、飞机等)。***take*** ~ 装入。

a·bode[1] [əˈbəud; əˋbod] abide 的过去式及过去分词。

a·bode[2] [əˈbəud; əˋbod] *n*. **1.** 住所。**2.** 居住,寄住。***make one's*** ~ 居住。***take up one's*** ~ 住到,住进。

ab·ohm [æˈbəum; æˋbom] *n*. 【物】绝对欧姆。

a·boi·deau [ˌɑːbwɑːˈdəu; ˏɑbwɑˋdo] *n*. 〔Can.〕堰。

a·boil [əˈbɔil; əˋbɔɪl] *ad*., *a*. 沸腾,滚(水)。

a·bol·ish [əˈbɔliʃ; əˋbɑlɪʃ] *vt*. 取消,废除(制度等) (*opp*. establish)。**-able** *a*. 可废除的。**-er** *n*. 取消者,废除者。**-ment** *n*. 取消,废除。

ab·o·li·tion [ˌæbəˈliʃən; ˏæbəˋlɪʃən] *n*. 废除,废弃;取消 (*opp*. establishment);废除死刑;〔美〕废除黑奴制度。**-ism** *n*. 奴隶制度[死刑]废除论。**-ist** *n*. (奴隶制度)废除论者。

ab·o·ma·sum [ˌæbəˈmeisəm; ˏæbəˋmesəm], **-sus** [-səs; -səs] *n*. 皱胃〔反刍动物的第四胃〕。

A-bomb [ˈeibɔm; ˋebɑm] **I** *n*. 原子弹。**II** *vt*. 用原子弹轰炸。

a·bom·i·na·ble [əˈbɔminəbl; əˋbɑmnəbl̩] *a*. 讨厌的,可恶的,可鄙的;〔口〕(天气等)极坏的。*an* ~ *affair* 丑事。**A- Snowman** (喜马拉雅山的)雪人。**-bly** *ad*. **1.** 讨厌,可恶,可鄙。**2.** 〔口〕极坏,丑。

a·bom·i·nate [əˈbɔmineit; əˋbɑməˏnet] *vt*. 厌恶,痛恨,憎恨,嫌恶。

a·bom·i·na·tion [əˌbɔmiˈneiʃən; əˏbɑməˋneʃən] *n*. 厌恶,憎恨,可恶;令人憎恶的[讨厌的]事物[行为]。***hold ... in*** ~ 厌恶…,憎恶…。

a·bom·i·na·tor [əˈbɔmineitə; əˋbɑməˏnetɚ] *n*. 嫌恶者。

à bon mar·ché [ɑ bɔːŋ marʃéi; ɑ bɔŋ marʃé] 〔F.〕廉价,便宜。

ab·o·rig·i·nal [ˌæbəˈridʒənl; ˏæbəˋrɪdʒənl̩] **I** *a*. 原来的;土著的;原住的,原生的。**II** *n*. 土著住民,土生动[植]物。**-ly** *ad*. 原来,本来,从最初。**-i·ty** [-næliti; -ˋnælətɪ] *n*. 原生状态,原始性。

ab·o·rig·i·nes [ˌæbəˈridʒiniːz; ˏæbəˋrɪdʒəniz] *n*. 〔*pl*.〕土著住民,土生动[植]物。

a·born·ing [əˈbɔːniŋ; əˋbɔrnɪŋ] **I** *ad*. 在诞生[产生]过程中。**II** *a*. 〔用作表语〕诞生[产生]过程中的。

a·bort [əˈbɔːt; əˋbɔrt] *vi*. **1.** 流产,小产,堕胎。**2.** (计划等)失败。**3.** 【生理】发育不全,退化。**4.** 〔空俚〕飞行中断。—*vt*. **1.** 使流产。**2.** 抑止(将发之病)。**3.** 使(计划)夭折。

a·bor·ti·cide [əˈbɔːtisaid; əˋbɔrtəˏsaɪd] *n*. 堕胎,堕胎药。

a·bor·ti·fa·cient [əˌbɔːtiˈfeiʃənt; əˏbɔrtəˋfeʃənt] **I** *a*. 引起流产的。**II** *n*. 堕胎药或器械。

a·bor·tion [əˈbɔːʃən; əˋbɔrʃən] *n*. **1.** 流产,小产。**2.** 流产的胎儿,不足月婴儿。**3.** 【生】发育不全;畸形;败育。**4.** 失败,夭折。*an induced* ~ 人工流产。*have an* ~ 流产,打胎。*prove an* ~ (事情)结果流产[失败]。~ **pill** 止孕药片〔特指法国药 RU-486〕。**-ist** *n*. 为人进行人工流产者。

a·bor·tive [əˈbɔːtiv; əˋbɔrtɪv] **I** *a*. **1.** 流产的。**2.** (药)打胎的。**3.** 【生】发育不全的,败育的。**4.** 【医】使病程中断的。**5.** 失败的,夭折的。*an* ~ *egg* 败育卵。*prove* ~ 归于失败。*apply* ~ *treatment to a disease* 对疾病采取预防措施。**II** *n*. **1.** 早产婴儿。**2.** 堕胎药。**-ly** *ad*.

ABO system [ˌei ˌbiː ˈəu ˈsistim; e ˏbi ˋo ˋsɪstəm] ABO 血型制。

a·bou·li·a [əˈbuːliə; əˋbulɪə] *n*. = abulia.

a·bound [əˈbaund; əˋbaʊnd] *vi*. **1.** 大量存在。**2.** 充满,富有 (*in*, *with*)。*Wild animals* ~*s in this park*. 这个公园里野兽很多。*He* ~*s in courage*. 他很有胆量。*This country* ~*s with tigers*. 这里老虎很多。

a·bout [əˈbaut; əˋbaʊt] **I** *ad*. **1.** 大约,差不多;前后,左右。~ *a mile* 大约一英里。*That's* ~ *right*. 大致不差。*That's* ~ (*the size of*) *it*. 就是那么一回事;大概如此。*It is* ~ *finished* 差不多要完成[终结]。**2.** 周围,四面;到处。*look* ~ 四顾。**3.** 活动;盛行,到处散布,传布。*The news is going* ~. 消息正在传开。**4.** 绕着,围着,倒转,掉转。*round* ~ 掉转,回头,倒过来。*face* ~ (使)转过来。*put the ship* ~ 把船倒过头来。*the wrong way* ~ 相反,倒转过来。**5.** 附近;〔古〕周围。*Is the manager* ~? 经理在吗? *There is no one* ~. 附近无人。*a mile* ~ 周围一英里。**6.** 〔接带 to 的不定式〕将要。**II** *prep*. **1.** 在…周围。~ *the neck* 绕着脖子,围在颈上。**2.** 在…附近,在…身边,手头。*somewhere* ~ *here* 在此地附近。*I have no money* ~ *me*. 我身边无钱。**3.** 前后,左右;大概。~ *noon* 正午前后。**4.** 对于,关于。*talk* ~ *sb*. 谈论某人。*He is most particular* ~ *being conscientious*. 他最讲究认真。**5.** 从事于。*What are you* ~? 你在干什么? **III** *a*. 〔用作表语〕传播,流行。*Rumour is* ~. 谣言纷纷。~ ***and*** ~ 〔美俚〕差不多,大致相同。(***Right***) ~ ***face*** 〔美〕向后转! ~ ***turn*** 〔英〕向后转。***be*** ~ **1.** 起来;活动;动手,做事 (*Butterflies are* ~ *early this year*. 今年蝴蝶活动得早。*He is not yet* (*up and*) ~. 他还没有起来,还未动手。*Mind what you are* ~! 当心! 注意!) **2.** 散布,传播,流行。***be*** ~ ***to*** 准备,将要,正打算 (*He is* ~ *to speak*. 他正打算说话)。***go*** ~ **1.** 正要,将要。**2.** 使(船)掉头。***go a long way*** ~ 绕很多路。***much*** ~ 几乎。***out and*** ~ 从事日常工作,(病后等)起来做事。***set*** ~ 动手,着手。***take turns*** ~ 轮流。***turn and turn*** ~ 交互。~**-face 1.** *n*. 【美军】向后转(的命令);改变观点[立场、主意]。**2.** *vi*. 改变立场[态度]。~**-ship** *vi*. 【海】改变航向。~**-sledge** *n*. 大铁锤。~**-turn** *n*., *vi*. = ~**-face**.

a·bove [əˈbʌv; əˋbʌv] **I** *ad*. **1.** 在上面;在头上;【宗】在

天上。*in the room* ～ 在楼上房间里。**2.** 上级;(河)上流;以上。*appeal to the court* ～ 告到上级法院。*persons of fifty and* ～ 五十岁以上的人们。**3.** 上述,上文。*as is stated* ～ 如上所说。**II** ***prep*.** **1.** 在…之上,在…上面。**2.** 所不及,难于。**3.** 超过,高过,多过,以上,以外。*500 feet* ～ *sea level* 海拔500英尺。*He is* ～ *doing such things*. 他不是做这种事的人。*I am not* ～ *asking questions*. 我不以发问为耻。*It is* ～ *comprehension*. 那是难于理解的。*persons* ～ *fifty* 五十岁以上的人们。*to rise* ～ *self* 不为私利所蔽。*to tower* ～ *the rest* 高过其他,超群,出类拔萃。～ ***all*** 尤其是,最重要的是。～ ***all things*** 第一是。～ ***oneself*** 〔口〕趾高气扬,得意忘形。～ ***price*** 无价之(宝)。～ ***the rest*** 特别,格外。**III** ***a*.** 上记,前述。*the* ～ *facts* 上述事实。**IV** ***n*.** **1.** 上;天,天上。**2.** 上记,前述。*The* ～ *shows a loss*. 以上表示亏损。*from* ～ 从天上。～**board** ***ad*.**, ***a*.** 公开,光明正大,光明磊落(*open and* ～ *board* 光明正大)。～**-ground** ***ad*.**, ***a*.** **1.** 在地上;在世,活着(的),未死(的)。**2.** 正统的;官方的。～**-mentioned** ***a*.** 上述的。

abr. = abridged; abridg(e)ment.

ab·ra·ca·dab·ra [ˌæbrəkəˈdæbrə; ˏæbrəkəˋdæbrə] ***n*.** **1.** 三角形驱病符〔用 **ABRACADABRA** 一字每行递减末尾一字母排成的三角形[符箓,咒文]〕。**2.** 胡言乱语。

a·brad·ant [əˈbreidənt; əˋbredənt] **I** ***a*.** 磨损的。**II** ***n*.** 研磨料,腐蚀剂,研磨剂。

ab·rade [əˈbreid; əˋbred] ***vt*.**, ***vi*.** 刮擦,擦伤,磨损。**-r** ***n*.** 研磨器。

A·bra·ham [ˈeibrəhæm, ˈeibrəhəm; ˋebrəˏhæm, ˋebrəhəm] ***n*.** **1.** 亚伯拉罕〔男子名〕。**2.** 亚伯拉罕〔基督教《圣经》中犹太人的始祖〕。***in*** ～***'s bosom*** **1.** 同死去的祖先一道安息。**2.** 处于极乐境界。***sham*** ～ 装病。～**man** ***n*.** (十六、七世纪时流浪英国各地的)装疯乞丐。

a·bran·chi·al [æˈbræŋkiəl; əˋbræŋkɪəl] ***a*.** 【动】无鳃的。

ab·rase [əˈbreiz; əˋbrez] ***vt*.** = abrade.

ab·ra·sion [əˈbreiʒən; əˋbreʒən] ***n*.** **1.** 磨去;擦去。**2.** 擦伤,磨损。**3.** 磨蚀;【地】冲蚀,海蚀。～ **resistance** 耐磨度。

ab·ra·sive [əˈbreisiv; əˋbresɪv] **I** ***a*.** **1.** 有磨损力的,有剥蚀作用的。**2.** 引起摩擦的,招人讨厌的。**II** ***n*.** 琢料,磨料,金刚砂。～ **fabric** 金刚砂布。

a·bra·zo [ɑːˈbrɑːðəu; ɑˋbraso] ***n*.** (*pl*. ～**s** [-ðəus; -sos]) (Sp.) 拥抱〔尤指欢迎某人时的拥抱〕。

ab·re·act [æbri(ː)ˈækt; ˏæbrɪˋækt] ***vt*.** 【精】对…使用精神发泄疗法,发泄(受压抑的感情)。

ab·re·ac·tion [æbriˈækʃən; æbrɪˋækʃən] ***n*.** 【精】精神发泄疗法。

a·breast [əˈbrest; əˋbrɛst] ***ad*.** 相并,并肩;并列。***keep*** ～ ***of*** [***with***] (*the times*) 跟着(时代)跑。***line*** ～ (舰队)横排成一线。***walk*** (*three*) ～ (三人)并排着走。

a·bridge [əˈbridʒ; əˋbrɪdʒ] ***vt*.** **1.** 省略,摘要,节略(*opp*. lengthen);短缩(寿命)。**2.** 削,夺,剥夺。*an* ～*d edition* 节略版,节本。～*d notation* 【数】简记法。～ (*sb*.) ***of*** (*his liberty*) 剥夺(某人)(自由)。

a·bridge·ment, a·bridg·ment [əˈbridʒmənt; əˋbrɪdʒmənt] ***n*.** **1.** 概略,节略,摘要;节本。**2.** 削减,剥夺。

abrim [əˈbrim; əˋbrɪm] ***ad*.** 满满地,满边儿。

a·broach [əˈbroutʃ; əˋbrotʃ] **I** ***a*.** 〔常用作述语〕**II** ***ad*.** **1.** (酒桶)开着口(使酒可以流出)。**2.** 传播。***set*** ～ **1.** 开(桶)口。**2.** 发泄(感情);发表,吐露;倡导,传播。

a·broad [əˈbrɔːd; əˋbrɔd] ***ad*.** **1.** 到处;四处传开,流行。**2.** 到国外,在海外。*He's never been* ～ *in his life*. 他有生以来没有出过国。*A lion at home, a mouse* ～. 在家如狮,在外如鼠。*He was sent* ～. 他被派到海外。***at home and*** ～ 在国内外。***be all*** ～ **1.** 〔口〕〔常作述语〕满不是这么回事,离题万里,猜错。**2.** 〔口〕简直莫名其妙。***be all*** ～ ***to do anything with*** 对…一窍不通。***from*** ～ 从国外,从海外;舶来的。***get*** ～ **1.** 出去,出门。**2.** (谣言)传出去,传开。***go*** [***travel***] ～ 到外国,出洋。

ab·ro·gate [ˈæbrəugeit; ˋæbrəˏget] ***vt*.** 废除(法令等);取消,结束。**-ga·tion** [-ˈgeiʃən; -ˋgeʃən] ***n*.**

ab·ro·ga·tor [ˈæbrəugeitə; ˋæbrəˏgetɚ] ***n*.** 废除者。

ab·rupt [əˈbrʌpt; əˋbrʌpt] ***a*.** **1.** 突然的,猝然的。**2.** 粗暴的,没礼貌的,(态度)生硬的。**3.** 陡的,险峭的;急转的。**4.** (讲话、文章等)不连贯的,支离的。**5.** 【地】断裂的;【植】裂状的。*an* ～ *turn* 急转弯。*an* ～ *manner* 无礼的态度。*an* ～ *entrance* 闯入。**-ly** ***ad*.** **-ness** ***n*.**

ab·rup·tion [əˈbrʌpʃən; əˋbrʌpʃən] ***n*.** 突然分离,分裂,断裂。

A.B.S. = **1.** American Bible Society 【宗】美国圣经学会。**2.** American Bureau of Shipping 美国船舶局。

abs. = **1.** absent. **2.** absolutely. **3.** abstract.

abs- ***pref*.** 〔与 ab- 同,用于字母 c, t 前〕。

Ab·sa·lom [ˈæbsələm; ˋæbsələm] ***n*.** **1.** 押沙龙〔基督教《圣经》中人物,大卫王之宠儿,后因反叛其父被杀〕。**2.** 阿布萨洛姆〔男子名〕。

ab·scess [ˈæbsis; ˋæbˏsɪs] ***n*.** 脓肿。

ab·scind [æbˈsind; æbˋsɪnd] ***vt*.** 切断,切开。

ab·scise [æbˈsaiz; æbˋsaɪz] **I** ***vt*.** 切除,割断。**II** ***n*.** 【植】脱落。

ab·scis·sa [æbˈsisə; æbˋsɪsə] ***n*.** (*pl*. ～**s**, **-sae** [-siː; -si]) 【数】横坐标,横轴。

ab·scis·sion [æbˈsiʒən; æbˋsɪʒən] ***n*.** **1.** 【医】切除;【植】脱离,(幼果)脱落。**2.** 【修】顿断法。

ab·scond [əbˈskɔnd; æbˋskɑnd] ***vi*.** 潜逃,隐匿;失踪;潜伏。～ *with the money* 卷款潜逃。

ab·scond·ence [əbˈskɔndəns; æbˋskɑndns] ***n*.** 逃亡,逃走;失踪;潜伏。

ab·sence [ˈæbsəns; ˋæbsns] ***n*.** **1.** 不在,缺席,缺勤(*opp*. presence)。**2.** 缺乏,缺少,无。**3.** 心不在焉,不注意。～ ***from*** (*school, office*) 缺(课),缺(席),缺(工),缺(勤),不在。～ ***in*** (*London*) 暂离某地而在(伦敦)。～ ***of mind*** 心不在焉,心神不定。～ ***of reason*** 发狂。***in sb.'s*** ～ 当某人不在时,背地里。***in the*** ～ ***of*** 无…时,缺少…时。***leave of*** ～ 请假,准假。～ ***without leave*** 擅离职守。

ab·sent [ˈæbsənt; ˋæbsnt] **I** ***a*.** **1.** 不在的,缺席的,缺勤的(*opp*. present)。**2.** 缺少的,无。**3.** 不在意的,茫然的,恍惚的。*He is* ～ *on business*. 他因事外出。*to be* ～ *from a friend* 和朋友分离。*Long* ～ *soon forgotten*. 离久情疏。*an* ～ *air* 发呆,茫然,恍惚。*He was* ～ *in his mind then*. 当时他心不在焉。～ ***over leave*** 【军】超假不归。～ ***treatment*** 〔美口〕顾客少,卖座少。***be*** ～ ***from*** (*home, school, office*) 不在(家),缺(课),缺(席),缺(勤);缺(工)。***be*** ～ ***in*** (*Paris*) 不在某地而在(巴黎)。***be*** ～ ***without excuse*** [***leave***] 擅自缺席。***in an*** ～ ***sort of way*** 心不在焉地,茫然。**II** [æbˈsent; æbˋsɛnt] ***vt*.** 使缺席。～ ***oneself from*** 不在,不到,缺席,缺勤;擅自离开。**-ly** ***ad*.** 心不在焉地,茫然,心神不定地。

ab·sen·tee [ˌæbsənˈtiː; ˏæbsnˋti] ***n*.** **1.** 不在者;缺席者,缺勤者。**2.** 在外者,外住者;(不居于产权所在地的)不在地主。**3.** 【讯】空号。*an* ～ *without leave* 擅自缺席[外出]者。～ **ballot** 缺席选举人票〔指缺席者预先交给选举机构的票〕。～ **vote** 缺席投票〔因病等而通过邮寄投票〕。**-ism** ***n*.** **1.** 不在外出地主的身分。**2.** 旷工,旷课;缺勤。

ab·sen·te reo [æbˈsentiˈriːəu; æbˋsɛntɪˋrio] ***ad*.** 〔L.〕【法】被告缺席。

ab·sent-mind·ed [ˌæbsəntˈmaindid; ˋæbsntˋmaɪndɪd] ***a*.** 心不在焉的,茫然的,心神恍惚的(*opp*. attentive)。**-ly** ***ad*.** **-ness** ***n*.**

A

ab·sinth(e) [ˈæbsinθ; ˋæbsɪnθ] ***n*. 1.** 苦艾酒。**2.**【植】苦艾;〔美〕山艾树。(= sagebrush)。**-ism *n*.** 苦艾酒中毒。

ab·sit o·men [ˌæbsitˈəumən; ˋæbsɪtˋomən]〔L.〕大吉大利〔迷信语,原意是愿无不祥的征兆!〕。

ab·so·lute [ˈæbsəljuːt; ˋæbsəˏlut] ***a*. 1.** 绝对的 (*opp*. relative, comparative); 完全的,纯粹的。**2.** 无条件的,无限制的。**3.** 专制的,独裁的,独行的,独断的。**4.** 确实的,肯定的。**5.**【语法】独立的,游离的。~ *truth* 绝对真理。~ *liberty* 无限自由。*an* ~ *ruler* 专制君主。~ *proofs* 确实的证据。~ *refusal* 断然拒绝。***by*** **~ *necessity*** 万不得已。***the A-*** **1.**【哲】绝对。**2.** 上帝,神。~ **adjective** 独立形容词〔略去后续的名词,如:the rich, the poor〕。~ **alcohol**【化】无水酒精,纯酒精。~ **altitude**【空】(由地面起算的)绝对高度,离地高度。~ **ceiling** 理论升限,绝对升限。~ **construction**【语法】独立结构。~ **dry wood**【林】全干材。~ **magnitude**【天】绝对星等。~ **majority**〔英〕绝对多数。~ **monarchy** 君主专制国[政体]。~ **music** 纯音乐,无标题音乐。~ **pitch 1.** 绝对音高,标准音高;绝对音调。**2.** 音高辨音力。~ **temperature** 绝对温度〔用 K 或 R 为记号〕。~ **value**【数】绝对值。~ **verb** 省去宾语的动词。(例:He *gives* largely to hospitals. 他向医院大量捐钱)。~ **zero**【物】绝对零度〔-273.16℃〕。**-ness *n*.** 绝对;完全;专制。

ab·so·lute·ly [ˈæbsəljuːtli; ˋæbsəlutlɪ] **I *ad*. 1.** 绝对地;完全地。**2.** 确实地。**3.** 专制地,独裁地。**4.**【语】独立地。*an adjective used* ~ 略去后续名词而独立使用的形容词(例:The blind cannot see. 盲人不能看东西。) **II *int*.**〔表示完全同意、赞成〕〔口〕是,是那样,当然。"*Do you think it will work well?*" "*A-!*" "这样做行不行?""当然行!"

ab·so·lu·tion [ˌæbsəˈljuːʃən; ˏæbsəˋluʃən] ***n*. 1.** 免除(罪责);解除(责任);赦免 (*from*; *of*)。**2.**【宗】忏悔式,赦罪文。*pronounce the* ~ 宣读赦罪文。

ab·so·lut·ism [ˈæbsəljuːtizm; ˋæbsəlutˏɪzəm] ***n*. 1.** 专制主义。**2.** 绝对主义,绝对论。

ab·so·lut·ist [ˈæbsəljuːtist; ˋæbsəˏlutɪst] ***n*. 1.** 专制主义者。**2.** 绝对主义者,绝对论者。

ab·sol·u·to·ry [əbˈsɔljutəri; æbˋsɑljəˏtorɪ] ***a*.** 免罪的,赦免的。

ab·solve [əbˈzɔlv; æbˋzɑlv] ***vt*. 1.** 免除,解除。**2.** 赦免,宽恕 (*opp*. blame)。**3.** 某学科考试及格取得(学分)。~ (*sb*.) ***from*** (*a promise*; *blame*)。**1.** 解(约)。**2.** 替…开脱(罪责)。~ (*sb*) of (*sin*) 赦免(罪状)。

ab·so·nant [ˈæbsənənt; ˋæbsənənt] ***a*. 1.** 不合拍的,不谐和的。**2.** 不合理的,背理的,悖理的。~ ***from*** [*to*] (*nature*) 违反(自然)。

ab·sorb [əbˈsɔːb, -ˈzɔːb; əbˋsɔrb, -ˋzɔrb] ***vt*. 1.** 吸收。**2.** 并吞;合并;同化。**3.** 吸引(注意),使(精神)贯注。**4.** 忍受;承担(费用)。**5.** 占用(时间)。**6.** 理解(含义)。*A blotter* ~*s ink*. 吸墨纸吸收墨水。~ *sb.'s attention* 吸引某人注意。***be*** **~*ed by*** 被…并吞;为…所吸收。***be*** **~*ed in*** [***with***] 全神贯注在…,一心从事;热衷于 (*be* ~*ed in the pursuit of knowledge* 一心研究学问)。**-a·bil·i·ty** [-əˈbiliti; -əˋbɪlətɪ] ***n*.** 吸收性。**-a·ble** [-ˈsɔːbəbl; -ˋsɔrbəbl] ***a*.** 可吸收的,易吸收的。

ab·sorbed [əbˈsɔːbd; əbˋsɔrbd] ***a*.** 注意集中的,一心一意的。*with* ~ *interest* 充满兴趣地。**-ly *ad*.** 一心,专心一意地,一心不乱地。

ab·sor·be·fa·cient [əbˌsɔːbiˈfeiʃənt; əbˏsɔrbəˋfeʃənt] ***a*.** 吸收性的。— ***n*.**【医】吸收剂。

ab·sorb·en·cy [əbˈsɔːbənsi; əbˋsɔrbənsɪ] ***n*.** 吸收力。

ab·sorb·ent [əbˈsɔːbənt; əbˋsɔrbənt] **I *a*.** 吸收的,有吸收力的,吸收性的。**II *n*. 1.** 吸收质,吸收体;【医】吸收剂,解酸剂,中和剂。**2.**【解】淋巴管;吸收管。~ *cotton* 脱脂棉,药棉。~ *of* (*heat*) 能吸收(热)。

ab·sorb·er [əbˈsɔːbə; əbˋsɔrbɚ] ***n*. 1.** 吸收者,吸收器,吸收装置。**2.** 减震器。*acoustic* ~ 消声器。

ab·sorb·ing [əbˈsɔːbiŋ; əbˋsɔrbɪŋ] ***a*. 1.** 吸收的。**2.** 非常有趣的,引人入胜的。*a shock-*~ *device* 减震装置。*an* ~ *well* 吸水井,渗井。

ab·sorp·tance [əbˈsɔːptəns; əbˋsɔrptəns] ***n*.**【物】吸收比。

ab·sorp·tion [əbˈsɔːpʃən; əbˋsɔrpʃən] ***n*. 1.** 吸收,合并。**2.** 专心,一心不乱,热中 (*in*)。**3.**〔口〕饮食。~ *in one's work* 埋头工作。~ *of heat* 吸收热量。~ *of nourishment* 吸收营养。*the* ~ *of smaller tribes* 兼并[吸收]小部落。

ab·sorp·tive [əbˈsɔːptiv; əbˋsɔrptɪv] ***a*.** 有吸收力的,吸收性的。**-ness *n*.**

ab·sorp·tiv·i·ty [ˌæbsɔːpˈtiviti; ˏæbsɔrpˋtɪvətɪ] ***n*.** 吸收性,吸收率[系数],吸收能力。

ab·squat·u·late [æbˈskwɔtjuleit; æbˋskwɑtʃəˏlet] ***vi*.**〔美俚〕逃走,逃跑,〔谑〕溜掉。

ab·stain [əbˈstein; əbˋsten] ***vi*. 1.** 戒,断(烟等),慎(行)。**2.** 弃权。~ ***from*** (*wine*) [*luxury*, *doing*, *voting*] 戒(酒)[避免奢华,不做,放弃投票]。

ab·stain·er [əbˈsteinə; əbˋstenɚ] ***n*. 1.** 戒酒的人。**2.** 弃权者。*a total* ~ 绝对戒酒的人。

ab·ste·mi·ous [æbˈstiːmjəs; æbˋstimɪəs] ***a*. 1.** 有节制的,饮食有度的。**2.** 节俭的。*an* ~ *diet* 适度的饮食。*an* ~ *meal* [*life*] 简朴的膳食[生活]。**-ly *ad*.** 有节制地,适度。**-ness *n*.** 饮食有度,节制。

ab·sten·tion [æbˈstenʃən; æbˋstɛnʃən] ***n*. 1.** 戒绝;克制;回避。**2.** 弃权;投票弃权者。~ *from exerting pressures on* 不对…施加压力。~ *from voting* 弃权不投票。~ *from smoking* 戒烟。

ab·sterge [æbˈstəːdʒ; æbˋstɝdʒ] ***vt*.** 擦去,洗净;使净化。

ab·ster·gent [æbˈstəːdʒənt; æbˋstɝdʒənt] **I *a*. 1.** 洗去的,洗净的,去垢的。**2.** 清泻的。**II *n*. 1.** 去垢剂,洗涤剂(肥皂、洗衣粉等);去污粉。**2.**【医】洗涤药,泻药。

ab·ster·sion [æbˈstəːʃən; æbˋstɝʃən] ***n*.** 洗净,净化。

ab·ster·sive [æbˈstəːsiv; æbˋstɝsɪv] ***a*.** 去垢的,使清洁的。

ab·sti·nence [ˈæbstinəns; ˋæbstənəns] ***n*. 1.** 禁欲,节制;戒酒。**2.**【经】节约。

ab·sti·nen·cy [ˈæbstinənsi; ˋæbstənənsɪ] ***n*.** 节制;禁欲。

ab·sti·nent [ˈæbstinənt; ˋæbstənənt] ***a*.** 禁欲的,有节制的。**-ly *ad*.** 有节制地;适度地。

ab·stract [ˈæbstrækt; ˋæbstrækt] **I *a*. 1.** 抽象的 (*opp*. concrete); 理论上的 (*opp*. applied); 观念的,空想的 (*opp*. practical)。**2.** 难解的,深奥的。**3.** 茫然的,恍恍惚惚的。**4.**【数】不名的。**5.**【美】抽象派的 (*opp*. representational)。~ *expressionism* 抽象表现主义(派)。~ *mathematics* 理论数学。~ *noun* 抽象名词。~ *number* 不名数。**II *n*. 1.** 抽象,【逻】抽象概念,抽象名词。**2.**【化】萃取物,提出物;提要,摘要。~ *of title* 财产权归属说明书。***in the*** **~** 抽象地,观念上,理论上。***make an*** **~ *of*** 把…的要点摘录下来。**III** [æbˈstrækt; æbˋstrækt] ***vt*. 1.** 提取,抽取;析离,分离;转移(注意等)。**2.**〔婉〕偷窃。**3.** 概括,摘录。**4.** 使(概念等)抽象化。~ (*somewhat*) *from sb.'s enjoyment* 使某人扫兴。~ *sb.'s attention from* 从…上转移开某人的注意。**-ly *ad*.** 抽象地,理论上,观念上。**-ness *n*.** 抽象性。

ab·stract·ed [æbˈstræktid; æbˋstræktɪd] ***a*. 1.** 分了心的。**2.** 分离了的,脱离了的。**3.** 抽象了的。***with an*** **~ *air*** 出神地,茫然,心不在焉。**-ly *ad*.** 呆呆地,茫然;抽象地。**-ness *n*.** 出神,发呆。

ab·strac·tion [æbˈstrækʃən; æbˋstrækʃən] ***n*. 1.** 抽象(作用);抽象概念;提取,抽出。**2.** 出神,发呆。**3.**〔婉〕偷窃。**4.** 不切实际的观念。***with an air of*** **~** 茫然,呆呆地,心不在焉。**-ism *n*.**【美】抽象主义;抽象派艺术。**-ist *n*.** 抽象派画家[艺术家]。

ab·strac·tive [æbˈstræktiv; æbˋstræktɪv] ***a*. 1.** 有提取

力的。2. 抽象的。3. 摘要的。**-ly** *ad*.

ab·strict [æb'strikt; æb`strɪkt] *vt*., *vi*.【植】(使)分离,(使)脱落。

ab·stric·tion [æb'strikʃən; æb`strɪkʃən] *n*.【植】分离,脱落。

ab·struse [æb'struːs; æb`strus] *a*. 难解的;深奥的。**-ly** *ad*. **-ness** *n*.

ab·surd [əb'səːd; əb`sɝd] *a*. 不合理的;荒谬的,荒诞的,荒唐无稽的;荒唐可笑的。*Don't be* ~. 不要胡闹[搞,说]。**-ly** *ad*. **-ness** *n*.

ab·surd·ism [əb'səːdizəm; əb`sɝdɪzəm] *n*. (哲学和文艺方面的)荒诞主义。

ab·surd·ist [əb'səːdist; əb`sɝdɪst] **I** *n*. 荒诞主义者;荒诞派作家。**II** *a*. 荒诞主义的,荒诞派的。~ *theatre* 荒诞派戏剧。

ab·surd·i·ty [əb'səːditi; əb`sɝdətɪ] *n*. 荒谬;谬论;荒唐事[话等]。*the height of* ~ 荒唐透顶。

abt., **abt** = about.

ABU = Asian Broadcasting Union 亚洲广播联盟。

A·bu Dha·bi [ˌæbuː 'dæbiː;ˏæbu `dæbi] **1.** 阿布扎比〔组成阿拉伯联合酋长国的酋长国之一〕。**2.** 阿布扎比〔阿拉伯联合酋长国首都〕。

a·bu·li·a [ə'bjuːliə; ə`bjulɪə] *n*.【心、医】意志力丧失。

a·bun·dance [ə'bʌndəns; ə`bʌndəns] *n*. 丰富,充裕,富裕 (*opp*. scarcity)。*a year of* ~ 丰年。~ ***of*** 丰富,充裕,富足。(*A- of instances are cited*. 引用了大量例子。*He has* ~ *of time to himself*. 他时间充裕。) ***in*** ~ 丰富,充裕,(生活)优裕。

a·bun·dant [ə'bʌndənt; ə`bʌndənt] *a*. 丰富的,大量的。*an* ~ *harvest* 丰收。*an* ~ *year* 丰年。***be*** ~ ***in*** (*minerals*) 富有(矿产),(矿产)丰富。**-ly** *ad*. 丰富地,多。

a·buse [ə'bjuːz; ə`bjuz] **I** *vt*. **1.** 滥用(职权等),妄用,误用(才能等)。**2.** 骂;讲…坏话,污蔑。**3.** 虐待,酷待;凌辱;〔古〕欺骗。~ *one's privilege* 滥用特权。**II** [ə'bjuːs; ə`bjus] *n*. **1.** 滥用,妄用,乱用,误用。**2.** 骂,讲坏话。**3.** 〔常 *pl*.〕弊病,弊端,恶习。**4.** 虐待,侮辱。*a crying* ~ 急应革除的恶习或弊病。*a word of* ~ 骂人话。*drug* ~吸毒上瘾。

a·bu·sive [ə'bjuːsiv; ə`bjusɪv] *a*. **1.** 骂人的,说人坏话的。**2.** 滥用的,妄用的,误用的。~ *language* 骂人话。*become* ~ 嘴变坏。**-ly** *ad*. 滥,妄;刻薄;侮辱地,无礼地。**-ness** *n*. 滥用;骂詈;虐待;弊害。

a·but [ə'bʌt; ə`bʌt] *vi*., *vt*. 邻接,毗连,贴近,靠紧,接近。~ ***against*** 紧靠着。~ ***on*** [***upon***] 接连,邻接;靠在…上。

a·bu·ti·lon [ə'bjuːtilən; ə`bjutɪˏlɑn] *n*.【植】苘麻属;苘麻,白麻(等)。

a·but·ment [ə'bʌtmənt; ə`bʌtmənt] *n*. **1.** 邻接,接界;接合(点)。**2.**【建】桥台,桥座,支柱。

a·but·tal [ə'bʌtl; ə`bʌtl] *n*. **1.** 接界,邻接。**2.** 〔常 *pl*.〕地界。

a·but·ter [ə'bʌtə; ə`bʌtɚ] *n*. 〔美〕接邻房地产的业主。

a·buzz [ə'bʌz; ə`bʌz] *a*. 〔用作表语〕**1.** 嗡嗡叫的。**2.** 嘈杂,扰嚷;活跃,热闹。*The class is* ~ *with discussion*. 课堂讨论很热烈。

ab·volt [æb'vəult; æb`volt] *n*.【物】绝对伏特;电磁制伏特。

aby(e) [ə'bai; ə`baɪ] *vt*. (***a·bought*** [ə'bɔːt; ə`bɔt]; ***a-bought***) 〔古〕偿,赔,赎(罪)。

a·bysm [ə'bizəm; ə`bɪzəm] *n*. 〔诗〕= abyss.

a·bys·mal [ə'bizməl; ə`bɪzml] *a*. **1.** 深不可测的,无底的,地狱(似)的。**2.** 极度悲惨[恶劣,卑下]的。~ *ignorance* 极端愚昧。~ *poverty* 赤贫。

a·byss [ə'bis; ə`bɪs] *n*. **1.** 深渊,无底洞。**2.** 〔古〕地狱,阴间;浑沌。*an* ~ *of disgrace* [*ignominy*] 丢脸已极。*an* ~ *of despair* 绝望。*the* ~ *of time* 无限之时,永远。*the horror of an* ~ 看深渊时引起的恐怖心。

a·bys·sal [ə'bisəl; ə`bɪsl] *a*. 深海的,深渊的。~ **rock**【地】深成岩。~ **zone**【地】深渊带。

Ab·ys·sin·i·a [ˌæbi'sinjə; ˏæbə`sɪnɪə] *n*. 阿比西尼亚〔埃塞俄比亚 (Ethiopia) 的旧名〕〔非洲〕。

ab·zy·me ['æbzaim; `æbzaɪm] *n*.【生化】抗体酶。

AC, A.C. = **1.** air controlman 美海军航空兵的空中交通管制员。**2.** alternating current【电】交变电流,交流电。**3.** aircraft(s)man 空军士兵。**4.** 〔L.〕*Ante Christum* (= before Christ) 公元前。

a/c, A/C = **1.** account. **2.** account current, current account 往来账户;活期存款账户。

-ac *suf*. 〔用以构成形容词,由此构成的形容词常用作名词〕**1.** 表示"有…性质的": elegi*ac*, demoni*ac*. **2.** 表示"关于…的": cardi*ac*, coeli*ac*, ili*ac*. **3.** 表示"有…病的": mani*ac*.

A·ca·cia [ə'keiʃə; ə`keʃə] *n*.【植】金合欢属;〔a-〕金合欢,银叶相思树;洋槐,刺槐;阿拉伯树胶。

Acad. = **1.** Academic. **2.** Academy.

ac·a·deme [ˌækə'diːm; ˏækə`dim] *n*. 〔诗〕= academy.

ac·a·de·mia [ˌækə'diːmjə; ˏækə`dimɪə] *n*. **1.** 学术界。**2.** 学术生活和兴趣;学术环境。

ac·a·dem·ic [ˌækə'demik; ˏækə`dɛmɪk] **I** *a*. **1.** 学院的;大学的;学会的,(学术、文艺)协会的。**2.** 学究的;学理上的;空谈的,非实用的。**3.** 〔A-〕柏拉图学派的。**4.** 〔美〕文科的,文学的。*an* ~ *curriculum* 大学课程。*an* ~ *degree* 学位。~ *interests* 校董。*an* ~ *discussion* 学术讨论。~ *freedom* 学术自由。~ *front* 学术战线。~ *rank* 学衔。~ *research* 学术研究。**II** *n*. **1.** 大学教师,大学生,学会会员。**2.** 〔*pl*.〕纸上空论,空论。**3.** 〔A-〕柏拉图学派的人。

ac·a·dem·i·cal [ˌækə'demikəl; ˏækə`dɛmɪkl] **I** *a*. = academic. *an* ~ *clique* 学阀。*an* ~ *year* 学年。**II** *n*. 〔*pl*.〕大学礼服。***in full*** ~***s*** 穿着大学礼服。**-ly** *ad*. 学问上;理论上;用学究态度。

a·cad·e·mi·cian [əˌkædə'miʃən; əˏkædə`mɪʃən] *n*. 学会会员,院士。

ac·a·dem·i·cism [ˌækə'demisizəm; ˏækə`dɛməsɪzəm] *n*. 学院风气 (= academism [ə'kædəmizəm; ə`kædəmɪzəm])。

a·cad·e·my [ə'kædəmi; ə`kædəmɪ] *n*. **1.** 学会,研究院,学术协会,文艺协会。**2.** 中等学校;专科院校。**3.** 〔A-〕柏拉图学园,柏拉图哲学。*an* ~ *of music* 音乐学校。*a military* ~ 〔美〕军事学院。*the Military Academy*陆军军官学校;〔英〕陆军炮工兵军官学校。*the naval* ~ 海军学校。*the Royal Academy of Arts* 〔英〕皇家美术院。*the Royal Military Academy* 英国陆军军官学校。~ **board** 油画纸。

ac·a·jou ['ækəʒuː; `ækəʒu] *n*. = cashew.

-acal *suf*. 〔用以构成形容词;特别在由 -ac 构成的形容词转为名词时,用以代替 -ac,再构成形容词〕: demoni*acal*, mani*acal*.

ac·a·leph ['ækəlef; `ækəlɛf], **ac·a·lephe** ['ækəliːf; `ækəlif] *n*.【动】水母。

a·can·thine [ə'kænθin; ə`kænθɪn] *a*.【植】(似)老鼠簕属植物的。

a·can·tho·ceph·a·lan [əˌkænθə'sefələn; əˏkænθə`sɛfələn] *n*.【动】棘头网动物。

a·can·thoid [ə'kænθɔid; ə`kænθɔɪd] *a*. 多刺的,棘状的 (= acanthous)。

ac·an·thop·ter·yg·i·an [ˌækənˌθɔptə'ridʒiən; ˏækənˏθɑptə`rɪdʒɪən] **I** *n*.【鱼】棘鳍类鱼。**II** *a*. 棘鳍类的。

A·can·thus [ə'kænθəs; ə`kænθəs] *n*. (*pl*. ~***es***, ***-thi*** [-θai; -θaɪ]) **1.**【植】老鼠簕属。**2.** 〔a-〕莨苕;【建】(柱头上)莨苕叶形装饰,叶板。

a·cap·pel·la [ˌɑːkə'pelə; ˏɑkə`pɛlə] *a*. 〔It.〕【乐】无伴奏的〔指合唱〕。

A

a ca·pric·cio [ˌɑːkɑːˈpriːtʃəː; ˏɑkɑˋpritʃo] [It.]【乐】随想曲。

ac·a·ri·a·sis [ˌækəˈraiəsis; ˏækəˋraɪəsɪs] ***n.***【医】螨病,(壁虱病)。

a·car·i·cide [əˈkærisaid; əˋkærɪˏsaɪd] ***n.***【药】杀螨剂。

ac·a·rid [ˈækərid; ˋækərɪd] ***n.***【动】螨。

ac·a·roid [ˈækərɔid; ˋækəˏrɔɪd] ***a.***【动】螨类的,螨状的。

ac·a·rol·o·gy [ˌækəˈrɔlədʒi; ˏækəˋrɑlədʒɪ] ***n.*** 螨虫学。**-gist** ***n.*** 螨虫研究专家。

a·car·pel·ous, a·car·pel·lous [æˈkɑːpələs; eˋkɑrpələs] ***a.***【植】无心皮的;无果爿的。

a·car·pous [æˈkɑːpəs; eˋkɑrpəs] ***a.***【植】不结果实的。

ACAS = Advisory, Conciliation and Arbitration Service (英国)咨询调节和仲裁局。

a·cat·a·lec·tic [eiˌkætəˈlektik; eˏkætˋlɛktɪk] **I** ***a.*** 〔诗〕(音节数)完全的。**II** ***n.*** 完整的诗行。

a·cau·dal [eiˈkɔːdəl; eˋkɔdl] ***a.***【动】无尾的(= acaudate)。

a·cau·les·cent [ˌeikɔːˈlesənt; ˏækɔˋlɛsənt] ***a.***【植】无茎的,短茎的。

ACC = **1.** Air Coordinating Committee (美国)航空协调委员会。**2.** anodal [anodic] closure contraction【医】(肌肉的)阳极通电收缩。

acc. = **1.** acceptance. **2.** according. **3.** account(ant). **4.** accusative.

ac·cede [ækˈsiːd; ækˋsid] ***vi.*** **1.** 同意,依从,答应,允诺。**2.** 即(位),就(职),继承。**3.** 加入,参加。~ *to a request* 答应要求。~ *to a party* 加入政党。~ *to the throne* 继承王位。

ac·cel·er·an·do [ækˌseləˈrændəu; ækˏsɛləˋrændo] ***ad.*** [It.]【乐】渐快。

ac·cel·er·ant [ækˈselərənt; ækˋsɛlərənt] ***n.*** 促进物;【化】触媒,促进剂,催化剂;【冶】捕集剂。

ac·cel·er·ate [ækˈseləreit; ækˋsɛləˏret] **I** ***vt.*** 加速;催促,促进。~ *measure* [*the pace*] 加速步调。— ***vi.*** 速度增加。**II** ***n.*** 接受速成教育的学生。**-d** ***a.***【物】加速的。

ac·cel·er·a·tion [ækˌseləˈreiʃən; ækˏsɛləˋreʃən] ***n.*** **1.** 加速;促进。**2.**【物】加速度;变速。**3.**【教】加速升级。*uniform* [*variable*] ~ 等[不等]加速度。*lightning* ~【汽车】瞬间加速度。*brief* ~ 瞬时有效加速度。~ *of gravity* 重力加速度。

ac·cel·er·a·tive [ækˈselərətiv; ækˋsɛləˏretɪv] ***a.*** 加速的,催促的。

ac·cel·er·a·tor [ækˈseləreitə; ækˋsɛləˏretɚ] ***n.*** **1.** 加速者;加速器;催速剂。**2.**【汽车】加速踏板。**3.**【摄】催显剂。

ac·cel·er·o·graph [ækˈselərəgrɑːf; ækˋsɛlərəgræf] ***n.***【空】自动加速仪。

ac·cel·er·om·e·ter [ækˌseləˈrɔmitə; ækˏsɛləˋrɑmɪtɚ] ***n.*** 加速表,加速计,加速仪;过荷指示器。

ac·cent [ˈæksənt; ˋæksənt] **I** ***n.*** **1.** 重音,扬音,强音;重音符号;韵符;抑扬。**2.** 强调 (*on*)。**3.** 音调,声调,口音,腔,土腔。**4.** 特征,特色。**5.** 〔*pl.*〕〔诗〕词句。*a primary* [*secondary*] ~ 第一[第二]重音,主[次]强音。*an acute* ~ 重音[扬音]符号(ˊ)。*a grave* ~ 抑音符号(ˋ)。*a circumflex* ~ 抑扬音符号(ˆ)。*an Irish* ~ 爱尔兰腔调。~ *of grief* 悲调。*in tender* ~*s* 用柔和的声调。**II** [ækˈsent; ækˋsɛnt] ***vt.*** **1.** 重读;给…加上重音符号。**2.** 〔美〕着重说,强调。

ac·cen·tu·al [ækˈsentjuəl; ækˋsɛntʃuəl] ***a.*** **1.** 重音的,强音的。**2.** 〔诗〕按照音节抑扬作成的 (*opp.* quantitative)。**-ly** ***ad.***

ac·cen·tu·ate [ækˈsentjueit; ækˋsɛntʃuˏet] ***vt.*** **1.** 着重说,着重指出,强调。**2.** 重读;给…加上重音符号。

ac·cen·tu·a·tion [ækˌsentjuˈeiʃən; ˋækˏsɛntʃuˋeʃən] ***n.*** **1.** 重读;重音符号。**2.** (音的)抑扬。**3.** 强调;加重。

ac·cept [əkˈsept; əkˋsɛpt] ***vt.*** **1.** 受,接受,收(礼等),领(情等)。**2.** 承担(职位等),答应,应(聘等),顺应(形势)。**3.** 同意,承认;信(教等),容纳;理解。**4.**【商】承兑,认付(汇票等)。*She did not* ~ *his hand in marriage.* 她不肯和他结婚。~ *the situation* 听天由命。~...(*as*) *true* 信…以为真。*the* ~*ed meaning* 普通意义,众所公认的意义。~ *of* 〔古〕= accept ★目前在商业上、法律上均不接用 *of*. ~ ***the person*** [***face***] ***of*** 〔古〕偏袒,偏爱,宠。**-er** ***n.*** 领受人;接受者。

ac·cept·a·bil·i·ty [əkˌseptəˈbiliti; əkˏsɛptəˋbɪlətɪ] ***n.*** 接受;承诺;适意,合意。

ac·cept·a·ble [əkˈseptəbl; əkˋsɛptəbl] ***a.*** 可接受的;合意的,(礼物等)令人满意的。

ac·cept·ance [əkˈseptəns; əkˋsɛptəns] ***n.*** **1.** 接受;验收 **2.** 答应,承认;(政党候选人)接受提名。**3.**【商】承兑,认付(期票)。~ ***for honour*** 参加承兑。***find*** ~ ***with*** [***in***] 得…答应。~ **house** 期票承兑行。~ **market** 证券市场。~ **supraprotest** 参加承兑。~ **speech** 受命演说。~ **test** 验收试验。

ac·cept·ant [əkˈseptənt; əkˋsɛptənt] ***a.*** 容易接受的。

ac·cep·ta·tion [ˌæksepˈteiʃən; ˏæksɛpˋteʃən] ***n.*** **1.** (字、句的)意义;通义。**2.** 〔古〕承认。*formal* ~【逻】第一义,意义。*material* ~ 字义。

ac·cept·ed [əkˈseptid; əkˋsɛptɪd] ***a.*** 常规的;认可的;公认为真实的;有效的;正常的。

ac·cep·tor [əkˈseptə; əkˋsɛptɚ] ***n.*** **1.** 领受人,接受者;承兑(票据)人。**2.**【生】受体。**3.**【无】接收器,接受体;受主;谐振电路。*electron* ~ 电子接受体。

ac·cess [ˈækses; ˋæksɛs] ***n.*** **1.** 接近;会面。**2.** 捷径,门路〔指方法、手段〕;检查孔;进路,入口;【自】(存贮器的)存取。**3.** (病的)发作;(怒气等的)爆发。**4.** 增加。*a man of difficult* ~ 难接近的人,难会见的人。~ *and recess* (病的)发作和静止。*an* ~ *of anger* 发怒,动怒。*an* ~ *of fever* 发热。*an* ~ *of territory* 领土的增加。~ *to books* 接触书籍的机会。***be easy*** [***hard, difficult***] ***of*** ~ 容易[难]接近的;容易[难]进去的;容易[难]会见的。***gain*** ~ ***to*** 接近;会见,谒见;接通(计算机)。***give*** ~ ***to*** 接见;准许出入。***have*** ~ ***to*** 得接近;得会见;得进入。***within easy*** ~ ***of*** (*London*) 容易去到(伦敦)的地方。~ ***channel*** "向公众开放"专栏节目频道。~ **clerk** 贵重物品保管员。~ **program** **1.** (美)(电视网分台于每周特定时间内播放的)每周特别电视节目。**2.** (英)"向公众开放"专栏节目播送〔供独立团体使用电台、电视台播送临时性节目〕。~ **time**【自】存取时间。

ac·ces·sa·ry [əkˈsesəri; ækˋsɛsərɪ] ***n.*** = accessory.

ac·ces·si·bil·i·ty [ækˌsesiˈbiliti; ækˏsɛsəˋbɪlətɪ] ***n.*** **1.** 可近,易接近,可亲。**2.** 易受影响。

ac·ces·si·ble [əkˈsesəbl; ækˋsɛsəbl] ***a.*** **1.** 能接近的,容易会见的。**2.** 可以进入的;容易理解的。**3.** 易受影响的。**4.** 好相处的。*an* ~ *path* 通路。*an* ~ *person* 温和的人。*minds* ~ *to reason* 通情达理的人们。**-bly** ***ad.***

ac·ces·sion [ækˈseʃən; ækˋsɛʃən] **I** ***n.*** **1.** 能接近,接近,到达。**2.** 就任;继承。**3.** 增加;增加物。**4.** 〔美〕新添的图书[作品]。**5.** 参加(某团体)。**6.**【法】财产自然增益的所有权。**7.**【医】发作。**8.** 同意。*a list of* ~*s to a library* 图书馆的新书目录。*the* ~(*s*) *book* [*number*] 新书登记簿[号码]。~ ***to manhood*** 成年。~ ***to the throne*** 即位。~ ***to a treaty*** 加盟,加入条约。~ **book** (图书馆的)新书目录,入藏新书(期刊等)登记簿。**II** ***vt.*** 〔美〕把(新书)编入目录。

ac·ces·so·ry [ækˈsesəri; ækˋsɛsərɪ] **I** ***a.*** **1.** 附属的,附带的,辅助的。**2.** 从犯的,同谋的。*an* ~ *bud* [*shoot*] 副芽。~ *fruits* 假果。**II** ***n.*** **1.** 零件,附件,附属品。**2.** 〔*pl.*〕(妇女)全套衣饰中的小配件。**3.** 〔美〕从犯 (*opp.* principal)。*the accessories* (*of a motorcar*)【汽车】附件,零件。~ ***before*** [***after***] ***the fact*** 事前[后]从犯。~

bud【植】副芽。~ **fruit**【植】副果。~ **nerve**【解】副神经。~ **road** 干道的支路。~ **television**“向公众开放”电视(节目)。

ac·ci·dence [ˈæksidəns; ˋæksədəns] ***n*.** **1.**【语法】词法,词形变化(的研究)。**2.** 初步,入门。

ac·ci·dent [ˈæksidənt; ˋæksədənt] ***n*.** **1.** 故障,事故,偶发事件;偶然。**2.** 灾难,灾害,不幸,不测,意外,横祸。**3.** 附带事件,附属品。**4.**【哲】偶然性(*opp*. necessity)。**5.**【地】褶皱;起伏,高低。*a happy* ~ 巧事。*a chapter of* ~*s* 许多不幸;命途多舛。*an aeroplane* ~ 飞机失事。*a tram* ~ 电车事故。~*s of the ground*【地】地表的高低起伏。***by*** ~ 偶然(*opp*. on purpose)。***have an*** ~ 遭受意外。***meet with an*** ~ 遭不测。***without*** ~ 平安,无恙。~ **insurance** 伤亡保险。~ **- prone** ***a*.** (因粗枝大叶而)特别易出事故的。

ac·ci·den·tal [ˌæksiˈdentl; ˏæksəˋdɛntl̩] **I** ***a*.** **1.** 偶然的,不测的;意外的(*opp*. planned)。**2.** 非本质的(*opp*. essential)。**3.** 附带的,附属的。~ *death* 意外死亡。**II** ***n*.** **1.** 偶然事;偶然;附带事物。**2.**【乐】临时符。~ **colours**【物】偶生色。~ **notation**【乐】升降符号。~ **president** 意外总统〔指因美国总统死亡或辞职等而由副总统接任的总统〕。

ac·ci·den·tal·ly [ˌæksiˈdentəli; ˏæksəˋdɛntlɪ] ***ad*.** 偶然,意外,附带。*to meet* ~ 偶然碰到。

ac·ci·die [ˈæksidiː; ˋæksədi] ***n*.** = acedia.

Ac·cip·i·ter [ækˈsipitə; ækˋsɪpɪtɚ] ***n*.** (*pl*. *-tres* [-triːz; -triz]) **1.**【动】鹰属。**2.**〔a-〕鹰。

ac·cip·i·tral [ækˈsipitrəl; ækˋsɪpɪtrəl], **ac·cip·i·trine** [-train; -traɪn] ***a*.** 鹰(样)的;眼光敏锐的;贪婪的。

ac·claim [əˈkleim; əˋklem] **I** ***n*.** 〔诗〕喝采,欢呼。**II** ***vt*.**, ***vi*.** (为…)喝采,欢呼着欢迎(某人),欢呼着同意(某事)。

ac·cla·ma·tion [ˌækləˈmeiʃən; ˏækləˋmeʃən] ***n*.** 喝采,称赞,欢呼;鼓掌通过。*amidst the loud* ~ *of* 在欢声雷动中。*carry* (*a motion*) *by* ~ 鼓掌通过(议案)。

ac·clam·a·to·ry [əˈklæmətəri; əˋklæməˏtorɪ] ***a*.** 喝采的,欢呼的,全场一致的。

ac·cli·mate [əˈklaimit; əˋklaɪmɪt] ***v*.** 〔美〕= acclimatize.

ac·cli·ma·tion [ˌæklaiˈmeiʃən; ˏæklaɪˋmeʃən] ***n*.** 〔美〕= acclimatization.

ac·cli·ma·ti·za·tion [əˌklaimətaiˈzeiʃən; əˏklaɪmətəˋzeʃən] ***n*.** 服水土,适应气候。~ **fever** 水土病。

ac·cli·ma·tize [əˈklaimətaiz; əˋklaɪməˏtaɪz] ***vt*.**, ***vi*.** (使)服水土,(使)适应新环境。~ *oneself to* 适应(新环境)。

ac·cliv·i·ty [əˈkliviti; əˋklɪvətɪ] ***n*.** 倾斜,斜坡,上斜(*opp*. declivity)。

ac·cli·vous [əˈklaivəs; əˋklaɪvəs] ***a*.** 向上倾斜的。

ac·co·lade [ˈækəleid; ˏækəˋled] ***n*.** **1.** 武士爵位的授与(礼)。**2.** 嘉奖,表扬;(见面问好的)接吻[拥抱]。**3.**【乐】达谱号。

ac·com·mo·date [əˈkɔmədeit; əˋkɑməˏdet] ***vt*.** **1.** 适应,顺应,调节;迁就,迎合。**2.** 劝息,调停,调解,排解。**3.** 供应,供给,通融,借给,贷。**4.** 留宿;收容(病人),装载(乘客);照应,招待。*The hotel is well* ~*d*. 这旅馆设备周全。~ (*sb*.) *for the night* 留(某人)住一夜。*The guests are well* ~*d*. 招待周到。~ ***oneself to*** (*circumstances*) 适应(环境),随遇而安。~ (*sb*.) ***with*** (*money*, *lodging*) 通融(某人款项),招待(某人住宿)。

ac·com·mo·dat·ing [əˈkɔmədeitiŋ; əˋkɑməˏdetɪŋ] ***a*.** 亲切的,爽气的;易打交道的。*an* ~ *person* 爽快人,好人。**-ly** ***ad*.**

ac·com·mo·da·tion [əˌkɔməˈdeiʃən; əˏkɑməˋdeʃən] ***n*.** **1.** 适应(性),顺应,迁就;调节(作用)。**2.** 和解,调解,排解,调停。**3.**〔美,常 *pl*.〕供应,供给,通融,将就;便利;设备;膳宿;接待。**4.**【商】贷款;通融资金。~*s at a hotel* 旅馆设备。***as a matter of*** ~ 为…便利计。~ **bill**〔英〕通融票据。~ **bridge** 专用[特设]桥梁。~ **ladder** 舷梯。~ **payment** 回扣式付款〔一种先多收顾客款再暗中退还从而掩盖贿赂的付款方式〕。~ **road** 专用道路。~ **sale**【商】转批。~ **train**〔美〕慢车(*opp*. express train)。**-ism** ***n*.** 迁就主义。

ac·com·mo·da·tor [əˈkɔmədeitə; əˋkɑmədetɚ] ***n*.** **1.** 调节者。**2.** 调解人。**3.** 贷款人。**4.** 临时的用人。

ac·com·pa·ni·ment [əˈkʌmpənimənt; əˋkʌmpənɪmənt] ***n*.** **1.** 伴随物,附属物。**2.**【乐】伴奏,和奏,助音。*to the* ~ *of* 伴和着,随着。~ *of the scale*【乐】陪音。*play an* ~ 伴奏。

ac·com·pa·nist [əˈkʌmpənist; əˋkʌmpənɪst] ***n*.**【乐】伴奏者,伴唱者。

ac·com·pa·ny [əˈkʌmpəni; əˋkʌmpənɪ] ***vt*.** **1.** 陪,伴,陪着;陪衬,衬,兼带。**2.** 给…伴奏,与…和奏。~ *one's word with a blow* 边说边打。*an* ~*ing letter* 附函。*Accompanied by Miss X*. 由某某小姐伴奏。***be accompanied by*** 有(某人)陪伴;伴有,附有,带着。***be accompanied with*** (*a thing*) 带着,带有,兼有。—***vi*.** 伴奏。

ac·com·plice [əˈkɔmplis; əˋkɑmplɪs] ***n*.** 同谋,同犯;帮凶。

ac·com·plish [əˈkɔmpliʃ; əˋkɑmplɪʃ] ***vt*.** 成就,完成,贯彻(计划等),达到(目的);实行。~ *one's object* 达到目的。~ *one's mission* 完成使命。

ac·com·plished [əˈkɔmpliʃt; əˋkɑmplɪʃt] ***a*.** **1.** 已完成的。**2.** 有教养的,有才能的,学识渊博的。~ *facts* 既成事实。*an* ~ *villain* 臭名昭彰的坏蛋。*an* ~ *lady* 才女。***be*** ~ ***in*** 专长,擅长,精通。

ac·com·plish·ment [əˈkɔmpliʃmənt; əˋkɑmplɪʃmənt] ***n*.** **1.** 成就,完成,履行,贯彻,实行。**2.**〔*pl*.〕才能,技能,教养。*difficult of* ~ 实行起来困难的。*a girl of many* ~*s* 多才多艺的姑娘。

ac·cord [əˈkɔːd; əˋkɔrd] **I** ***vi*.** 一致,与…符合(*with*)。*His actions* ~ *with his words*. 他言行一致。—***vt*.** **1.** 使一致。**2.** 给予(礼遇等)。*They* ~*ed a warm welcome to me*. 他们对我热烈欢迎。**II** ***n*.** **1.** 一致,调和;和谐;和解,协定。**2.** 自顾,自动。**3.**【乐】和音,和弦(*opp*. discord)。***be in*** ~ ***with*** 与…一致的,符合…的。***be of one*** ~ 一致。***full*** ~ ***with*** 完全同意。***of its own*** ~ 自然,自行,自动。***of one's own*** ~ 自愿地,主动地。(*They won't do it of their own* ~. 他们不会自动去干这事的。) ***out of*** ~ ***with*** 不符合…的,同…不一致。***with one*** ~ 一致地。

ac·cord·ance [əˈkɔːdəns; əˋkɔrdns] ***n*.** **1.** 一致,协调。**2.** 给予。***in*** ~ ***with*** 照,据,依照;与…一致,合乎(*in* ~ *with the form provided* 照格式)。

ac·cord·ant [əˈkɔːdənt; əˋkɔrdnt] ***a*.** 一致的,相合的;成谐音的;调和的(*with*; *to*)。

ac·cord·ing [əˈkɔːdiŋ; əˋkɔrdɪŋ] ***ad*.** 照,依,据,按。~ ***as*** 照,依照,据,随。~ ***to*** 照,依照,据,据…所说(~ *to his account* 照他的话。~ *to all accounts* 照大家的话。*act* ~ *to circumstances* 随机应变。*from each* ~ *to his ability, to each* ~ *to his work* 各尽所能,按劳分配)。

ac·cord·ing·ly [əˈkɔːdiŋli; əˋkɔrdɪŋlɪ] ***ad*.** **1.** 因此,于是,所以。**2.** 随着;相应地。*You may arrange* ~. 你可以权宜处理。~ ***as*** = according as.

ac·cor·di·on [əˈkɔːdjən; əˋkɔrdɪən] **I** ***n*.** 手风琴。**II** ***a*.** (如手风琴般)可折叠的。**-ist** [-ist; -ɪst] ***n*.** 手风琴演奏者。

ac·cost [əˈkɔst; əˋkɔst] ***vt*.** **1.** (接近…)搭话;招呼(不认识的人)。**2.** (娼妓等)引诱,勾引。

ac·couche·ment [əˈkuːʃmɑ̃ː, -mənt; əˋkuʃmɑ̃, -mənt] ***n*.** 〔F.〕分娩,生产。

ac·cou·cheur [ˌækuːˈʃəː; ˏækuˋʃɝ] ***n*.** 〔F.〕(男)产科医士。

A

ac·cou·cheuse [ˌæku:ˈʃə:z; ˏækuˋʃɜz] ***n***. 〔F.〕女助产士。

ac·count [əˈkaunt; əˋkaʊnt] **I** ***n***. **1**. 计算;账;账目;账户;计算书,账单;报告书,报表。**2**. 说明,解释;记事,故事。**3**. 理由,原因。**4**. 重要性;考虑;价值;利益。*an open* ~ 来往账目,未结算账目。*Bad things can be turned to good* ~ . 坏事可以变成好事。***Accounts differ***. 言各不同。***ask an*** ~ 请求付账;请求回答。***balance*** ~***s with*** 与…结清各账。***bring*** [***call***] ***to*** ~ 责问,质问,要求说明。***by all*** ~***s*** 据大家所说。***cast*** ~ 计算。***charge*** (*a sum*) ***to sb.'s*** ~ 记某人账。***close an*** ~ ***with*** 与…停止交易。***find no*** ~ ***in*** 不合算。***find one's*** ~ ***in*** 因…得利[好处]。***for*** ~ ***of*** 为…代销。***from all*** ~***s*** 从各种说法来估计。***give a bad*** [***poor***] ~ ***of*** 〔俚〕贬责。***give a good*** ~ ***of*** **1**. 夸奖。**2**. 〔口〕打败;【猎】打死。***give a good*** [***bad***] ~ ***of oneself*** **1**. 付[未]清欠账。**2**. 表现好[糟],做成功[失败] (*He has not given a good* ~ *of himself in battle*. 他在战场上表现得不英勇)。***give an*** ~ ***of*** 报告,叙述,记述,说明。***go to one's*** (***long***) ~ 死。***hand in one's*** ~ ***s*** 死。***hold ... in great*** ~ 极重视。***hold ... of much*** ~ 看重,重视。***hold ... of no*** ~ 看轻,藐视。***in*** ~ ***with*** 与…有生意来往。***joint*** ~ 共同计算。***keep*** ~***s*** **1**. 记账,入账,登账。**2**. 做会计员。***keep*** ~ ***with*** 与…继续交易。***lay one's*** ~ ***with*** 预期,期望;考虑,斟酌。***leave*** (*it*) ***out of*** ~ 不把…打在数内,不顾,不考虑。***make*** (***much***) ~ ***of*** 重视,看重。***make little*** [***no***] ~ ***of*** 轻视,看轻。***of*** (***much***) ~ 重要的 (*man of* ~ 要人)。***of no*** ~ 不重要的,无价值的。***on*** ~ 先付,暂付 (*pay five pounds on* ~ 先付五镑)。***on*** ~ ***of*** 因为,因。***on all*** ~***s*** = ***on every*** ~ 无论如何,总之。***on any*** ~ 无论如何。***on no*** ~ = ***not ... on any*** ~ 决不,总不。***on a person's*** [***one's***] ~ **1**. 以某人[自己]费用。**2**. 为了某人[自己]。***on one's own*** ~ **1**. 为自己(利益)打算。**2**. 依靠自己;自行负责。***on this*** [***that***] ~ 因此,于是。***open an*** ~ ***with*** 与…开一往来户头;开了…的头。***pay ... on*** ~ 把…付作定钱。***place*** [***pass***] ***to the*** ~ ***of*** 并入…账内。***render an*** ~ **1**. 分辩,辩解。**2**. 决算报告。***sale on*** ~ 赊销。***send in an*** ~ 报账。***send in*** ~***s*** 报销。***settle*** [***square***] ~***s*** 结算,清算。***Short*** ~***s make long friends***. 账目常清,友谊长存。***take*** ~ ***of*** = ***take into*** ~ 考虑,斟酌,计及 (*take the interests of the whole into* ~ 顾全大局。*take the whole situation into* ~ 统筹全局)。***take no*** ~ ***of*** 不考虑,不计及,无视。***the great*** [***last***] ~ 最后的审判。***turn ... to*** (***good***) ~ 利用。**II** ***vt***. 认为…如何〔后接受词及补语〕。*be much* [*little*] ~*ed of* 被重[轻]视。*He* ~*s himself well paid*. 他认为自己的报酬不坏。~ *oneself happy* 自以为幸福。—***vi***. 说明。~ ***for*** **1**. 证明,说明;由于 (*How do you* ~ *for it*? 你如何说明它呢? *There is no* ~*ing for taste*(*s*). 人各有所好)。**2**. 说明(银钱等的)用途。**3**. 打死,打落(敌机);【体】得(几)分。~ **book** 账簿。~ **current** = **current** ~ 往来账户〔略 a/c.〕。~ **executive** (广告公司等的)客户业务经理。~ **note** 账单。~**s payable** [**receivable**] 应付[应收]账。~ **purchase** 赊买。~ **rendered** (贷方交给借方审查和清算的)借贷细账。~ **sales** **1**. 销货账 **2**. 赊销。~ **settled** 决算,清算。~ **stated** (借贷双方都认可的)细账。

ac·count·a·bil·i·ty [əˌkauntəˈbiliti; əˏkaʊntəˋbɪlətɪ] ***n***. 有责任,有义务。

ac·count·a·ble [əˈkauntəbl; əˋkaʊntəbl] ***a***. 有责任的,有解说义务的;可说明的。*Every person is* ~ *for his own work*. 每个人都要对自己的工作负责。

ac·count·an·cy [əˈkauntənsi; əˋkaʊntənsɪ] ***n***. 会计工作,会计的职位。

ac·count·ant [əˈkauntənt; əˋkaʊntənt] ***n***. 会计员,账房,出纳。~ *general* 会计主任。*a chartered* ~ 会计师。

ac·count·ing [əˈkauntiŋ; əˋkaʊntɪŋ] ***n***. **1**. 会计;会计学。**2**. 账;记账;清算账目。*business* ~ *at different levels* 分级核算。***There's no*** ~ ***for tastes***. 〔口〕人各有所好。

ac·cou·ple·ment [əˈkʌplmənt; əˋkʌplmənt] ***n***. **1**. 拼凑。**2**. 【建】圆柱成对密立。**3**. 拼凑在一起的木材。

ac·cou·tre, -ter [əˈku:tə; əˋkutɚ] ***vt***. 穿;【军】装备。***be*** ~***d with*** [***in***] 穿着。**-ment** ***n***. **1**. 衣服。**2**. 〔*pl*.〕(武器,军服以外的)装备,配备。

Ac·cra [əˈkrɑ:; əˋkrɑ] ***n***. 阿克拉〔加纳首都〕。

ac·cred·it [əˈkredit; əˋkrɛdɪt] ***vt***. **1**. 相信,听信;认可。**2**. 授权,委派,任命。**3**. 认(某事)为(某人所为),归在 (*to*, *with*)。**4**. 鉴定…为合格。*an* ~*ed journalist* 特派记者。*an* ~*ed school* 立案学校。*They* ~ *these remarks to him*. = *He is* ~*ed with these remarks*. 他们认为那些话是他说的。

ac·crete [æˈkri:t; əˋkrit] **I** ***vi***. **1**. 增大,生长。**2**. 合生;连生。—***vt***. 使附着,使与…相联合。**II** ***a***. 【植】合生的。

ac·cre·tion [æˈkri:ʃən; əˋkriʃən] ***n***. **1**. 增大。**2**. 【地】冲积层。**3**. 增加物;生长。**4**. 连生,合生。**5**. 【法】(财产的)自然增加。~ ***cutting*** = ~ ***thinning*** 【林】促进生长的采伐。~ ***of population*** 人口增加率。

ac·cru·al [əˈkru:əl; əˈkruəl] ***n***. 增加,增殖;增加物;增加额。

ac·crue [əˈkru:; əˋkru] ***vi***. **1**. 增长。**2**. (利息等)自然增殖。**3**. 【法】(诉讼)发生。*A profit* ~*s to the government from* ... 政府由…得到利益。*pay the interest* ~*d* 支付所生利息。*Knowledge will* ~*s to you from reading*. 读书能增智。

acct. = account(ant).

ac·cul·tu·rate [əˈkʌltʃəˌreit; əˋkʌltʃəˏret] ***vi***., ***vt***. (使)受同化,(使)受融化。

ac·cul·tu·ra·tion [əˌkʌltʃəˈreiʃən; əˏkʌltʃəˋreʃən] ***n***. 文化移入;文化适应;文化交流。

ac·cum·bent [əˈkʌmbənt; əˋkʌmbənt] ***a***. **1**. 依着的,横卧的。**2**. 【植】依伏的。

ac·cu·mu·late [əˈkju:mjuleit; əˋkjumjəˏlet] ***vt***. **1**. 积累,存储,蓄积(财产等),堆积。**2**. 〔英大学〕同时取得(高的和低的学位)。—***vi***. **1**. 积,贮,累积,积聚。**2**. 〔英大学〕同时取得高的和低的学位。~*d funds* 积累的资金。

ac·cu·mu·la·tion [əˌkju:mjuˈleiʃən; əˏkjumjəˋleʃən] ***n***. **1**. 积累,堆积;累积物。**2**. 〔英大学〕高低学位的同时获得。*the* ~ *of knowledge* 知识的积累。

ac·cu·mu·la·tive [əˈkju:mjulətiv; əˋkjumjəˏletɪv] ***a***. **1**. 积累的,堆积的。**2**. 热心贮蓄的。**-ly** ***ad***.

ac·cu·mu·la·tor [əˈkju:mjuleitə; əˋkjumjəˏletɚ] ***n***. **1**. 累积者;积聚者。**2**. 【机】蓄力器;【电】蓄电池;【计】累加器,记存器;【无】贮能电路;缓冲器。*a binary* ~ 二进位累加器。

ac·cu·ra·cy [ˈækjurəsi; ˋækjərəsɪ] ***n***. 正确,准确(度);精确。*firing* ~ 命中率。***with*** ~ 正确地。

ac·cu·rate [ˈækjurit; ˋækjərɪt] ***a***. 准确的,精密的。**-ly** ***ad***.

ac·curs·ed [əˈkə:sid; əˋkɝsɪd], **ac·curst** [əˈkə:st; əˋkɝst] ***a***. **1**. 被咒的,不幸的,倒楣的。**2**. 可恶的,讨厌的。**-ly** ***ad***. **-ness** ***n***.

ac·cus·a·ble [əˈkju:zəbl; əˋkjuzəbl] ***a***. 可指责的,可指控的。

ac·cus·al [əˈkju:zəl; əˋkjuzəl] ***n***. = accusation.

ac·cus·ant [əˈkju:zənt; əˋkjuzənt] ***n***. 指责者;控诉者。

ac·cu·sa·tion [ækju(:)ˈzeiʃən; ˏækjəˋzeʃən] ***n***. **1**. 非难,谴责。**2**. 告发,控告。**3**. (被指控的)罪状,罪名。*a false* ~ 诬告。***be under an*** ~ 受指责,被控告。***bring an*** ~ ***against*** 对…起诉,控告;指责;攻击(某人)。

ac·cu·sa·ti·val [əˌkju:zəˈtaivəl; əˏkjuzəˋtaɪvəl] ***a***. 【语法】直接受格的。

ac·cu·sa·tive [əˈkjuːzətiv; əˋkjuzətɪv] ***n.***, ***a.*** 【语法】直接受格(的)。★objective 较此词更常用。

ac·cu·sa·to·ri·al [əˌkjuːzəˈtɔːriəl; əˏkjuzəˋtorɪəl] ***a.*** **1.** 弹劾性的,非难的,声讨性的。**2.** 公诉人的,告发人的。

ac·cu·sa·to·ry [əˈkjuːzətəri; əˋkjuzəˏtorɪ] ***a.*** **1.** 非难的,责问的,问罪的。**2.** 控告的,告发的。

ac·cuse [əˈkjuːz; əˋkjuz] ***vt.*** **1.** 非难,谴责。**2.** 因某事而谴责[指控]某人 (*for*);把某事归罪于某人 (*for*)。**3.** 控告[告发]某人犯某罪 (*of*)。~ *the times* 说时世不好。*Man often ~s nature for his own misfortunes.* 人类常把自身的不幸归咎于天。*They ~d him of taking bribes.* 他们控告他受贿。***the ~ed*** 【法】被告,刑事被告。— ***vi.*** 控诉;起诉。

ac·cus·er [əˈkjuːzə; əˋkjuzɚ] ***n.*** 上诉人,原告;责难者。

ac·cus·ing [əˈkjuːziŋ; əˋkjuzɪŋ] ***a.*** 非难的,谴责的。*point an ~ finger at a person* 指着某人责骂。**-ly** ***ad.***

ac·cus·tom [əˈkʌstəm; əˋkʌstəm] ***vt.*** 使习惯。*one's ~ed hour* 惯常的时间。~ ***oneself to*** 使自己惯于。***be ~ed to*** (*hard work, early rising*) 惯于(苦干,早起)。

ac·cu·tron [ˈækjutrɔn; ˋækjʊtrɑn] ***n.*** 电子手表。

ACD solution 【医】ACD 溶液,(血库中用于防止全血凝结的)酸-枸橼酸盐-葡萄糖溶液。

ace [eis; es] **I** ***n.*** **1.** (纸牌、骰子等的)么,一 (*cf.* deuce 二, trey 三, cater 四, cinq 五, sice 六)。**2.** 同花色中最大的牌。**3.** (网球赛等的)发球得分。**4.** 少许,毫厘。**5.** (击落五架以上敌机的)飞行勇士,空中英雄;(棒球等的)优秀选手,能手,专家。**6.** 〔美口〕一元的钞票。~ ***in the hole*** 暗藏的"A"牌;备用的论点或手段。~ ***of ~s*** 〔美〕空中英雄之英雄,能手中之能手,强中之强。***have*** [***keep***] ***an ~ up one's sleeve*** 持有最重要的情报,手中有大牌[良策]。***not an*** ~ 毫无。***within an ~ of …*** 差点儿,几乎,险些儿 (*He came within an ~ of winning.* 他差点儿获胜)。**II** ***a.*** 第一流的;能干的。**III** ***vt.*** **1.** (网球赛等)以发球赢(对方)一分。**2.** 在(考试)中得满分。**~-high** ***a.*** 〔口〕**1.** 极好的 (*feel ~-high* (身体)顶好)。**2.** 有威望的;受敬重的 (*He is ~-high with me.* 我尊敬他)。

a·ce·di·a [əˈsiːdiə; əˋsidɪə] ***n.*** **1.** 懒惰;麻痹,不关心。**2.** 【医】淡漠忧郁症。

A·cel·da·ma [əˈkeldəmə, əˈsel-; əˋkɛldəmə, əˋsɛl-] ***n.*** **1.** 【圣】血田〔以出卖耶稣所得之钱购买的土地〕。**2.** 流血之地。

a·cel·lu·lar [eiˈseljulə; eˋsɛljələ] ***a.*** 非细胞组成的。

ace·naph·thene [ˌæsəˈnæpθiːn; ˏæsəˋnæpθin] ***n.*** 【化】苊。

a·cen·tric [æˈsentrik; eˋsɛntrɪk] ***a.*** 无中心的;偏心的,离心的。

-a·ce·ous *suf.* 【生】…类的,…科的:crust*aceous* 甲壳类的;ros*aceous* 蔷薇科的。

a·ceph·a·lous [æˈsefələs; eˋsɛfələs] ***a.*** **1.** 无头的。**2.** 没有首领的。**3.** 〔诗〕一行诗中缺少第一音步的。

a·ce·qui·a [əˈseikjə, -ˈseikiə; əˋsekjə, -ˋsekɪə] ***n.*** 水沟,水渠。

ac·er·ate [ˈæsərit; ˋæsəˏret] ***a.*** 【植】针状的。

a·cerb [əˈsəːb; əˋsɝb] ***a.*** **1.** 酸(味)的。**2.** (性情,言语等)尖刻的,厉害的,粗暴的。

ac·er·bate [ˈæsəbeit; ˋæsɚˏbet] ***vt.*** **1.** 使变酸;使变苦。**2.** 激怒;使不痛快。

a·cer·bic [əˈsəːbik; əˋsɝbɪk] ***a.*** = acerb.

a·cer·bi·ty [əˈsəːbiti; əˋsɝbətɪ] ***n.*** **1.** 苦酸,苦涩。**2.** (语言等的)刻薄,辛辣。

ac·er·ose [ˈæsərəus; ˋæsəˏros] ***a.*** 【植】针状的。

a·cer·vate [əˈsəːvit; əˋsɝvet] ***a.*** 【植】成堆生长的,丛生的,簇生的。**-ly** ***ad.***

a·ces·cent [əˈsesənt; əˋsɛsənt] ***a.*** 容易变酸的;有酸味的,发酸的,微酸的。

a·cet- *comb. f.* = aceto-〔acet- 用于母音前〕:*acet*aldehyde, *acet*amide.

ac·e·tab·u·lum [ˌæsəˈtæbjuləm; ˏæsəˋtæbjʊləm] ***n.*** (*pl.* *-la* [-lə; -lə]) **1.** (古罗马餐桌上用的)醋罐。**2.** 【解】髋臼。**3.** 【动】吸盘,碟状体。

ac·e·tal [ˈæsitæl; ˋæsəˏtæl] ***n.*** 乙缩醛,乙醛缩二乙醇。

ac·et·al·de·hyde [æsiˈtældəhaid; ˏæsəˋtældəˏhaɪd] ***n.*** 【化】乙醛。

ac·et·am·ide [ˌæsiˈtæmaid; ˏæsəˋtæmaɪd] ***n.*** 【化】乙酰胺。

ac·et·an·i·lide, ac·et·an·i·lid [ˌæsiˈtænilaid, -lid; ˏæsəˋtænḷˏaɪd, -ḷɪd] ***n.*** 【化】乙酰(替)苯胺;退热冰。

ac·e·tar·i·ous [ˌæsiˈtɛəriəs; ˏæsəˋtɛrɪəs] ***a.*** 拌生菜用的,拌色拉 (salad) 用的;(蔬菜等)凉拌用的。

ac·e·tate [ˈæsiteit; ˋæsəˏtet] ***n.*** 【化】醋酸盐;醋酸酯;醋酸根,醋酸基;醋酸纤维素。

a·ce·tic [əˈsiːtik, əˈsetik; əˋsitɪk, əˋsɛtɪk] ***a.*** 醋的;酸的。~ **acid** 醋酸,乙酸。

a·cet·i·fi·ca·tion [əˌsetifiˈkeiʃən; əˏsɛtəfɪˋkeʃən] ***n.*** 【化】醋化(作用)。

a·cet·i·fy [əˈsetifai; əˋsɛtəˏfaɪ] ***vt.***, ***vi.*** (使)醋化,(使)变酸。

ac·e·tim·e·ter [ˌæsiˈtimitə; ˏæsɪˋtɪmɪtɚ] ***n.*** 醋酸(比重)计(= acetometer)。

ac·e·tin [ˈæsitn; ˋæsɪtn̩] ***n.*** 醋精,甘油醋酸酯。

aceto- *comb. f.* 乙酰,乙川〔用于子音前〕:*aceto*benzoic.

ac·e·tom·e·ter [ˌæsiˈtɔmitə; ˏæsɪˋtɑmɪtɚ] ***n.*** 醋酸(比重)计。

ac·e·tone [ˈæsitəun; ˋæsəˏton] ***n.*** 【化】丙酮。

ac·e·tose [ˈæsitəus; ˋæsətos] ***a.*** = acetous.

ac·e·tous [ˈæsitəs; ˋæsɪtəs] ***a.*** 醋(一样)的,酸的;醋酸的。

a·ce·tum [əˈsiːtəm; əˋsitəm] ***n.*** 【药】醋。

ac·e·tyl [ˈæsitil; ˋæsəˏtɪl] ***n.*** 【化】乙酰(基)。

a·cet·y·lene [əˈsetiliːn; əˋsɛtḷˏin] ***n.*** 【化】乙炔;电石气。~ **lamp** 电石气灯,矿灯。

ACGB = Arts Council of Great Britain 大不列颠艺术委员会。

achar·ne·ment [F. ɑʃarnəmɑ̃; ɑˏʃarnəˋmɑ̃] ***n.*** 〔F.〕凶猛,残暴。

A·cha·tes [əˈkeitiːz; əˋketiz] ***n.*** 忠实的朋友〔Achates 原为 Virgil 所著史诗中忠于友情的英雄〕。

ache [eik; ek] **I** ***vi.*** **1.** 痛,疼痛。**2.** 〔口〕渴望 (*to* do),怀想,想念 (*for*)。*His heart ~s.* 他心口痛。*I am aching to join in the game.* 我渴望参加比赛。**II** ***n.*** 痛,疼痛。

a·chene [æˈkiːn; æˋkin] ***n.*** (*pl.* *-nia* [-niə; -nɪə]) 【植】瘦果。

Ach·er·on [ˈækərɔn; ˋækəˏrɑn] ***n.*** 【希、罗神】冥河;阴间,地狱。

Acheson [ˈætʃisn; ˋætʃɪsn] ***n.*** 艾奇逊〔姓氏〕。

a che·val [F. ɑ ʃəvˈɑl; F. ɑ ʃəvˋɑl] 〔F.〕 **1.** 在马上;跨。**2.** (对一场争论所持的)骑墙态度。

a·chiev·a·ble [əˈtʃiːvəbl; əˋtʃivəbḷ] ***a.*** 做得成的,可完成的。

a·chieve [əˈtʃiːv; əˋtʃiv] ***vt.*** 完成,做到;获得(胜利等);达到(目的),实现。*to ~ a great deal in one's work* 工作很有成绩。— ***vi.*** 取得预期效果。

a·chieve·ment [əˈtʃiːvmənt; əˋtʃivmənt] ***n.*** **1.** 完成;达到。**2.** 成绩,成就;功绩;造诣。**3.** 【徽】纹章。~ **age** 智力成就年龄。~ **quotient** 【心】造诣指数〔受教育年限与智力发展年限的比值〕。

Ach·il·le·an [ˌækiˈliːən; ˏækɪˋliən] ***a.*** 阿基里斯(一样)的;勇敢的;刀枪不入的。

A·chil·les [əˈkiliːz; əˋkɪliz] ***n.*** 【希神】阿基里斯。~ (') ***heel*** 唯一致命的弱点〔传说阿基里斯除脚踵外全身刀枪

A

不入]。

aching [ˈeikiŋ; ˋekɪŋ] *a*. 痛的，疼痛的；心痛的。*an* ～ *tooth* 作痛的牙齿。*an* ～ *void* 悲痛空虚的感觉。

ach·la·myd·e·ous [ˌækləˈmidiəs; ˏækləˋmɪdɪəs] *a*. 【植】无被的；裸花的。

a·chlor·hy·dri·a [ˌeikloːˈhaidriə; ˏekloˋhaɪdrɪə] *n*. 【医】胃酸缺乏。**-hy·dric** [-haidrik; -haɪdrɪk] *a*.

a·chon·drite [eiˈkɔndrait; eˋkɑndraɪt] *n*. 无球粒陨石。**-drit·ic** [-draitik; -draɪtɪk] *a*.

a·chon·dro·pla·sia [eikɔndrəˈpleiʒə; eˏkɑndrəˋpleʒə] *n*. 【医】软骨发育不全。**-plas·tic** [-ˈplæstik; -ˋplæstɪk] *a*.

a·chro·mate [ˈækrəumeit; ˋækrəˏmet] *n*. 全色盲者，色盲患者。

achro·mat·ic [ˌækrəuˈmætik; ˏækrəˋmætɪk] *a*. 无色的；【生】非染色质的；【物】消色差的；非彩色的(指黑、白、灰色的)。～ **lens** 消色差透镜。～ **vision** 全色盲。

a·chro·ma·tic·i·ty, a·chro·ma·tism [əˌkrəuməˈtisiti, -izəm; əˏkroməˋtɪsətɪ, -ɪzm̩] *n*. 【物】无色；消色差。

a·chro·ma·tin [əˈkrəumətin; əˋkromətɪn] *n*. 【生】(细胞核内的)非染色质。

a·chro·ma·tize [əˈkrəumətaiz; əˋkroməˏtaɪz] *vt*. 使无色，灭色；【物】消…色差；使成非彩色。

a·chro·ma·top·sia [əˌkrəuməˈtɔpsiə; əˏkroməˋtɑpsɪə] *n*. 【医】色盲，全色盲。

a·chro·ma·tous [əˈkrəumətəs; eˋkromətəs] *a*. 无色的，颜色不足的。

a·chro·mic [əˈkrəumik; eˋkromɪk] *a*. 无色的。

A·chro·my·cin [ˌækrəuˈmaisin, Am. ˌeikrəˈmaisin; ˏækrəˋmaɪsɪn, ˏekrəˋmaɪsɪn] *n*. 【药】阿克洛密辛四环素〔tetracycline 的商标名〕；〔a-〕四环素。

a·cic·u·la [əˈsikjulə; əˋsɪkjʊlə] *n*. (*pl*. *-lae* [-iː; -i]) *n*. 【生】针，刺；【地】针状结晶。

ac·id [ˈæsid; ˋæsɪd] **I** *a*. **1.** 酸味的。**2.** 【化】酸的，酸性的。**3.** 〔喻〕尖酸刻薄的，易怒的。**II** *n*. **1.** 酸味物。**2.** 【化】酸。**3.** 〔美俚〕麻醉药物 LSD (麦角酸二乙基醯胺)。～ **cloud** 酸云〔含高浓度硫酸等的低云区〕。～ **fog** 酸雾〔指酸度远超过酸雨的雾〕。～**-head** 经常服用 LSD 的人。～ **looks** 苦脸，易怒的面孔。～ **mist** 酸性雾，酸性霭。～ **pad** **1.** (供瘾君子光顾的)毒品注射窝。**2.** 瘾君子毒品注射聚会。～ **number** [**value**] 酸值。～**-proof** *a*. 耐酸的。～ **radical** 酸根[基]。～ **rain**(工业污染造成的)酸雨。～ **reaction** 酸性反应。～**-resistant** **1.** 耐酸的，抗酸的。**2.** 耐酸物，抗酸物。～ **rock** (引起吸毒幻觉似的)疯狂摇摆舞歌曲。～ **test** 酸性试验；〔喻〕严峻的考验。～ **trip** 〔俚〕因吸毒而引起的幻觉经历。～ **wash** 酸洗〔一种用氯溶液洗涤牛仔裤等的方法〕。**-ly** *ad*. **-ness** *n*.

ac·i·d(a)e·mia [ˌæsiˈdiːmiə; ˏæsɪˋdimɪə] *n*. 【医】酸血症。

ac·id-fast [ˈæsid-fɑːst; ˋæsɪd-fæst] *a*. 抗酸的。～ *bacteria* 抗酸细菌。

ac·id-form·ing [ˈæsidˌfɔːmiŋ; ˋæsɪdˏfɔrmɪŋ] *a*. **1.** 成酸的；酸的。**2.** (食物)消化时产生大量酸性物质的。

a·cid·ic [əˈsidik; əˋsɪdɪk] *a*. **1.** 【化】酸性的。**2.** 【矿】硅石多的。

ac·i·dif·er·ous [ˌæsiˈdifərəs; ˏæsɪˋdɪfərəs] *a*. 生酸的，含酸的。

a·cid·i·fi·ca·tion [əˌsidifiˈkeiʃən; əˏsɪdəfɪˋkeʃən] *n*. 酸化(作用)，成酸性，发酸。

a·cid·i·fi·er [əˈsidifaiə; əˋsɪdəˏfaɪr] *n*. **1.** 酸化器。**2.** 酸化剂。

a·cid·i·fy [əˈsidifai; əˋsɪdəˏfaɪ] *vt*., *vi*. (使)变酸，(使)酸化。

ac·i·dim·e·ter [ˌæsiˈdimitə; ˏæsɪˋdɪmətə] *n*. 【化】酸(液)比重计，酸度计。

a·cid·i·ty [əˈsiditi; əˋsɪdətɪ] *n*. 酸味；酸性，酸度。

ac·id·ize [ˈæsidaiz; ˋæsəˏdaɪz] *vt*. 酸处理，酸化。

ac·i·doid [ˈæsidɔid; ˋæsɪdɔɪd] **I** *a*. (土壤等)似酸的；有变酸倾向的。**II** *n*. 可能变酸的物质。

ac·i·dom·e·ter [æˈsidɔmitə; æˋsɪdɑmətə] *n*. 酸度计；pH 计。

a·cid·o·phil [əˈsidəfil; ˋæsɪdoˏfɪl] *n*. 嗜酸细胞；嗜酸物。

ac·i·doph·i·lus milk [ˈæsiˈdɔfiləs milk; ˏæsɪˋdɑfɪləs mɪlk] 酸(牛)奶。

ac·i·do·sis [ˌæsiˈdəusis; ˏæsɪˋdosɪs] *n*. 【医】酸中毒。

a·cid·u·late [əˈsidjuleit; əˋsɪdʒəˏlet] *vt*. 使带酸性，酸化。

a·cid·u·lat·ed [əˈsidjuleitid; əˋsɪdʒəˏletɪd] *a*. **1.** 带酸味的。**2.** 易怒的，尖刻的。

a·cid·u·lous [əˈsidjuləs; əˋsɪdʒələs] *a*. **1.** 有酸味的，带酸的。**2.** 脾气坏的，别扭的。

ac·i·er·ate [ˈæsiəreit; ˋæsɪəˏret] *vt*. 化(铁)为钢。

ac·i·form [ˈæsifɔːm; ˋæsɪˏfɔrm] *a*. 针状的；锐利的。

ac·i·nac·i·form [ˌæsiˈnæsifɔːm; ˏæsɪˋnæsɪˏfɔrm] *a*. 【植】短剑状的。

a·cin·i·form [əˈsinifɔːm; əˋsɪnəˏfɔrm] *a*. 腺泡状的，葡萄状的；多核的。

ac·i·nus [ˈæsinəs; ˋæsɪnəs] *n*. (*pl*. *-ni* [-nai; -ˏnaɪ]) 【植】小果；葡萄核；【动】腺泡；粒体。

-a·cious *suf*. 有…倾向的，爱…的，…多的：loqu*acious*，pugn*acious*.

-ac·i·ty *suf*. 有…倾向：loqu*acity*，pugn*acity*.

ack-ack [ˈæk ˈæk; ˋæk ˋæk] *a*. 〔俚〕防空炮火的，高射炮的。— *n*. 高射炮，防空炮火。

ack em·ma [ækˈemə; ækˋɛmə] **1.** 〔英口〕午前〔报务员间通用〕。**2.** 〔英军俚〕飞机修理工人。*at 10* ～ 上午十时。

Ackerman(n) [ˈækəmən; ˋækərmən] *n*. 阿克曼〔姓氏〕。

ac·knowl·edge [əkˈnɔlidʒ; əkˋnɑlɪdʒ] *vt*. **1.** 认，承认；供认。**2.** 感谢，答谢。**3.** 告知收到(信等)。**4.** 对(人)打招呼。**5.** 【法】公证。～ *one's defeat* 认输。～ *one's fault* 认错，赔不是，道歉。～ *a man as* [*to be*] *one's superior* 自认不如某人。～ (*the receipt of*) *a letter* 表示收到来信。～ *a statement* 声明已经注意到。～ *a deed* 公证一项契约。～ ***oneself to be*** 自认是。～ ***the applause*** 谢幕。

ac·knowl·edged [əkˈnɔlidʒid; əkˋnɑlɪdʒd] *a*. 世所公认的，已有定评的。*the* ～ *leader* 公认的领袖。

ac·knowl·edge·ment, ac·knowl·edg·ment [əkˈnɔlidʒmənt; əkˋnɑlɪdʒmənt] *n*. **1.** 承认；自认，供认。**2.** 感谢；谢意。**3.** 收条。**4.** 【法】承认书。*bow one's* ～*s* (*of applause*) (对欢呼)点头答礼。*in* ～ *of* 领谢，答谢。

a·clin·ic [æˈklinik; eˋklɪnɪk] *a*. 【物】无倾角的。～ **line** 【物】无倾线，(地)磁赤道(线)。

ACLS = **1.** Automatic Carrier Landing System 【军】舰载机自动着陆装置。**2.** American Council of Learned Societies 美国学术团体理事会。

A.C.M. = Air Chief Marshal 空军上将。

ACM **1.** = automated checkout machine 自动收款机。**2.** = Association for Computing Machinery (美国)计算机协会。

ac·me [ˈækmi; ˋækmɪ] *n*. 顶点，极点；极致。～ *of science* 科学尖端。***be the*** ～ ***of perfection*** 十全十美。

ac·ne [ˈækni; ˋæknɪ] *n*. 【医】脂肪腺炎；痤疮；粉刺，酒刺。～ **rosacea** 酒糟鼻。～ **sebacea** 皮脂溢。

a·cock [əˈkɔk; əˋkɑk] *ad*. (帽边)反卷。*set one's hat* ～ 反卷着帽边。

AC of S = Assistant Chief of Staff. 〔美〕助理参谋长。

ac·o·lyte [ˈækəlait; ˋækəˏlaɪt] *n*. **1.** 侍僧。**2.** 【天主】侍祭。**3.** 侍者；助手；【天】陪星，卫星。

A. Com. = Associate in (或 of) Commerce 商业准学士。

ac·o·nite [ˈækənait; ˋækəˏnaɪt] ***n.*** 【植】附子，草乌，乌头。**-nit·ic** [ˌækəˈnitik; ˏækəˋnɪtɪk] ***a.***

a·con·i·tine [əˈkɔnitiːn; əˋkɑnɪtin] ***n.*** 【药】乌头碱。

a·corn [ˈeikɔːn; ˋekɔrn] ***n.*** 栎子，橡子，槲果。***come to the*** ～s〔美〕处境困难。～ **cup** 壳斗。～ **shell** 1. 橡子壳。2.【贝】藤壶。～ **tube**,〔英〕～ **valve**【无】橡实形(电子)管。

a·cot·y·le·don [æˌkɔtiˈliːdən; ˏekɑtɪˋlidn] ***n.*** 【植】无子叶植物。**-ous** [-əs; -əs] ***a.*** 【植】无子叶的。

a·cou·me·ter [əˈkuːmitə; əˋkumɪtɚ] ***n.*** 测听计，听力计，测声器。

a·cous·tic(al) [əˈkuːstik(əl); əˋkustɪk(əl)] ***a.*** 1. 听觉的；声学的。2. 助听的；传音的。3. 原声的，不经过电子设备传声的。～ **phonogram** 传音唱片。～ (**magnetic**) **mine** 感音(磁性)水雷。～ **meter** 比声计。～ **nerves** 听神经。～ **wave** 声波。**-ti·cal·ly** ***ad.*** 在听觉上；在声学上。

ac·ous·ti·cian [ˌækuːsˈtiʃən; ˏækusˋtɪʃən] ***n.*** 声学家。

a·cous·ti·con [əˈkuːstikən; əˋkustɪkən] ***n.*** 助听器。

a·cous·tics [əˈkuːstiks; əˋkustɪks] ***n.*** 1.〔用作 *sing.*〕声学。2.〔用作 *pl.*〕(剧院等的)音响装置，音响效果。*The ～ of this theater are faulty* [*admirable*]. 这个剧院的音响效果不好[很好]。

a·cous·to-e·lec·tron·ics [æˌkuːstəuiˈlektrɔniks; ˏækustoɪˋlɛktrɑnɪks] ***n.*** 电子声学。

a cou·vert [aːkuːˈvɛə; akuˋvɛr]〔F.〕安全；受庇护。

ACP = 1. African, Caribbean and Pacific Associables 非洲、加勒比、太平洋地区国家集团。2. American College of Physicians 美国内科医师协会。

ac·quaint [əˈkweint; əˋkwent] ***vt.*** 1. 使熟悉，了解(*with*)〔多用被动语态〕。2. 把某事告知[通知，介绍]给某人。*I am already ～ed with the facts*. 我已经了解这些事实。*Let me ～ you with the facts*. 让我把事实告诉你。*She ～ed her roommates with my husband*. = *She made my husband ～ed with her roommates*. 她把我丈夫介绍给她的同室伙伴。～ *each other with their views* 互通声气。～ (*sb.*) ***with*** (*a fact*) 把(事实)告知(某人)。～ ***oneself with*** 知道，通晓。***be*** [***get***] ～***ed with*** 1. 了解，熟知。2. 与…相识 (*We are ～ed with eath other*. 我们互相认识，彼此是熟人)。***make*** (*sb.*) ～***ed with*** 1. 把…通知[告知](某人)。2. 把…介绍给(某人)。

ac·quaint·ance [əˈkweintəns; əˋkwentəns] ***n.*** 1. 相识，相熟；熟人。2. 知识，心得。*a nodding ～* 点头之交。*a speaking ～* 搭话朋友，初交。*He is not a friend, only an ～*. 他不是朋友，只是相识。*have a large circle of ～s* 交游甚广。*He has a slight ～ with astronomy*. 他懂一点儿天文学。***cut*** [***drop***] ***sb.'s*** ～ 和某人绝交。***have*** [***no***] ～ ***with*** 和…[不]认识。***make*** ～ ***with*** [***of***] 接近，结识。***pick*** ～ ***with*** 结识，和…相识。***scrape*** ～ ***with*** 设法结识。**-ship** ***n.*** 相识，相熟；认识。

ac·quest [əˈkwest; əˋkwɛst] ***n.*** 1. 取得物。2.【法】继承方法以外取得的财产。

ac·qui·esce [ˌækwiˈes; ˏækwɪˋɛs] ***vi.*** 默许，默认，勉强同意(*opp.* protest)。～ ***in*** (*a plan*; *proposal*) 勉强同意(计划；提议)。

ac·qui·es·cence [ˌækwiˈesns; ˏækwɪˋɛsns] ***n.*** 默认，默许。*He smiled ～*. 他笑了一笑表示同意。

ac·qui·es·cent [ˌækwiˈesnt; ˏækwɪˋɛsnt] ***a.*** 默许的，默认的，勉强顺从的。**-ly** ***ad.***

ac·quire [əˈkwaiə; əˋkwaɪr] ***vt.*** 1. 得，取得，获得；招致。2. 学得(知识等)，养成(习惯等)。3. (在探测器上)捕捉住(目标)。～ *a bad habit* 养成不良习惯。～ *a good reputation* 得了好名。～ *currency* 流传，散布。**-ment** ***n.*** 取得，获得；学得；〔*pl.*〕学识，技艺。

ac·quired [əˈkwaiəd; əˋkwaɪrd] ***a.*** 1. 已得到的，已获得的。2. 已成习惯的。3.【生】习得的，后天的(*opp.* natural)。*an ～ taste* 学会的嗜好。～ [illegible] 性。～ **immunity** 后天免疫(性)。～ **immune** [illegible]获得 **syndrome** 艾滋病，爱滋病，获得性免疫缺损综合征。

ac·qui·si·tion [ˌækwiˈziʃən; ˏækwəˋzɪʃən] ***n.*** 1. 取得，获得；习得。2. 取得物，获得物[人]。3.【无】探测。

ac·quis·i·tive [əˈkwizitiv; əˋkwɪzətɪv] ***a.*** 可以得到的，可以学得的；想获得的(*of*)；贪得无厌的。*an ～ mind* 好学心，利欲心(等)。**-ly** ***ad.*** **-ness** ***n.***

ac·quit [əˈkwit; əˋkwɪt] ***vt.*** 1. 使(某人)卸去(责任、义务等)(*of*)。2. 宣判无罪(*opp.* convict)。3. 表现(*oneself*)；完成，履行(*oneself of*)。4.〔古〕付清，还清。～ *a person of his responsibility* [*duty*] 解除某人的责任[义务]。*She ～ted herself well of* [*in*] *her promise*. 她很好地履行了自己的诺言。～ ***oneself*** (*bravely*) 表现(勇敢)，行动(勇敢)。～ ***oneself of*** (*one's duty*) 尽(责)。***be ～ted of*** (*a crime*) 被宣告无罪。～**tal** [-l; -l̩] ***n.*** 1. 宣告无罪。2. 付清，还清。3. 尽责。～**tance** [-təns; -tn̩s] ***n.*** 1. 免除，解除。2. 还清；(清欠)收据。

ac·quitt·al, ac·quit·ment [əˈkwitəl, -mənt; əˋkwɪtl̩, -mənt] ***n.*** 1. 宣判无罪。2. (义务的)履行。3. (债务的)清偿。

a·cre [ˈeikə; ˋekɚ] ***n.*** 1. 英亩(= 40.4687 ares)〔约中国六亩〕。2.〔*pl.*〕土地，耕地。3.〔*pl.*〕〔口〕大量。*broad ～s* 宽广的土地。*a lord of broad ～s* 土地主。*a library with ～s of books*. 有大量藏书的图书馆。***God's*** ～ 墓地。

a·cre·age [ˈeikəridʒ; ˋekərɪdʒ] ***n.*** 1. 英亩数；面积。2. 按英亩出售[分配]的土地。*the ～ under cultivation* 耕地面积。

a·cred [ˈeikəd; ˋekɚd] ***a.*** 1. 英亩的。2. 拥有许多地产的。*a many-～ estate* 许多英亩的地产。

ac·rid [ˈækrid; ˋækrɪd] ***a.*** 1. 辣的，苦的；腐蚀性的。2. 毒辣的，刻毒的；泼辣的。**-ness** ***n.*** = acridity.

a·crid·i·ty [æˈkriditi; æˋkrɪdətɪ] ***n.*** 1. 辣，苦。2. 狠毒，刻毒。

ac·ri·dine [ˈækridin; ˋækrəˏdin] ***n.*** 【化】吖啶，氮蒽，氮杂蒽，夹氮蒽。

ac·ri·fla·vine [ˈækriˈfleiviːn; ˋækrɪˋflevin] ***n.*** 【化】吖啶黄。

ac·ri·mo·ni·ous [ˌækriˈməunjəs; ˏækrəˋmonɪəs] ***a.*** 1. 恶毒的，毒辣的。2. 剧烈的，厉害的。**-ly** ***ad.*** **-ness** ***n.***

ac·ri·mo·ny [ˈækriməni; ˋækrəmonɪ] ***n.*** (态度、语言等的)毒辣，激烈，刻毒。

a·crit·i·cal [eiˈkritikəl; eˋkrɪtəkəl] ***a.*** 1. 不批评的，不吹毛求疵的，不打算批评或品评的。2.【医】没有危险征兆的。

ac·ro- *comb. f.* 肢端，尖端；最高，顶上：*acro*phobia.

ac·ro·bat [ˈækrəbæt; ˋækrəˏbæt] ***n.*** 1. 杂技演员，走钢丝的演员。2. (主张、政见等的)善变者，翻云覆雨者。

ac·ro·bat·ic [ˌækrəuˈbætik; ˏækrəˋbætɪk] ***a.*** 杂技的，走钢丝的。～ **feats** 杂技。～ **flight** 特技飞行。**-i·cal·ly** ***ad.***

ac·ro·bat·ics [ˌækrəuˈbætiks; ˏækrəˋbætɪks] ***n.*** 〔*pl.*〕〔用作单或复〕杂技【军】特技飞行。

ac·ro·bat·ism [ˈækrəubætizəm; ˋækrəˏbætɪzəm] ***n.*** 杂技。

ac·ro·car·pous [ˌækrəuˈkɑːpəs; ˏækrəˋkɑrpəs] ***a.*** 【植】茎端结实的〔如某些藓苔〕；顶(生)蒴的。

ac·ro·gen [ˈækrəudʒen; ˋækrədʒən] ***n.*** 【植】顶生植物。

a·cro·le·in [əˈkrəuliːin; əˋkrolɪɪn] ***n.*** 【化】丙烯醛。

ac·ro·lect [ˈækrəulekt; ˋækrolɛkt] ***n.*** (流行于一个社区内最体面的)标准方言。

ac·ro·lith [ˈækrəuliθ; ˋækrəlɪθ] ***n.*** 石首石肢木身像。

ac·ro·meg·a·ly [ˌækrəuˈmegəli; ˏækrəˋmɛgəlɪ] ***n.*** 【医】肢端肥大症。**-me·gal·ic** [-məˈgælik; -məˋgælɪk] ***a.***, ***n.*** 有肢端肥大症的(人)。

a·cron·y·c[illegible] krɔnikəl; ə`krɑnɪkḷ] *a*.【天】日落[illegible]的天体〕。

[illegible]ro·nym [ˈækrənim; `ækrənɪm] *n*. 首字母缩略词〔如 loran = *lo*ng-*ran*ge *n*avigation〕。

a·crop·e·tal [əˈkrɔpitl; ə`krɑpətəl] *a*.【植】向顶的。**-ly** *ad*.

ac·ro·pho·bi·a [ˌækrəuˈfəubiə; ˏækrə`fobɪə] *n*.【医】高处恐怖(症)。

ac·rop·o·lis [əˈkrɔpəlis; ə`krɑpəlɪs] *n*. **1**. (古希腊都城的)卫城。**2**. 〔the A-〕雅典的卫城。

a·cross [əˈkrɔs; ə`krɔs] **I** *ad*. **1**. 横切,横断,越过,横过;(走)过。**2**. 交叉,成十字地;对过,斜对面。**3**. 宽,阔。*What is the distance* ~ ? 到对面有多少距离? *come* ~ *in a steamer* 乘船渡过(河等)。*The channel is 20 miles* ~. 海峡宽20英里。*stand with two arms* ~ 叉手站立着。**II** *prep*. **1**. 横过,横断,越过;(走)过。**2**. 与…交叉,与…成十字;在横过…处,在…对面。**3**. 经过(一段时间)。*walk* ~ *the street* 穿过街道。*He lives* ~ *the road*. 他住在马路对面。*lay* (*two sticks*) ~ *each other* 把(二棍)交叉放置。~ *the nineteenth century* 在十九世纪整整一百年间。*all* ~ *China* 全中国。~ ***from*** 〔美口〕在…的正对面。~ (***the***) ***country*** 全国各地。***be*** ~ ***a horse's back*** 骑马。***come*** [***run***] ~ 发现;碰见 (*I came* ~ *an old friend*. 我碰见了一个老朋友。*I have come* ~ *a curious plant*. 我发现一种珍奇植物)。***come*** ~ (***one's***) ***mind*** 忽然想起。***get*** ~ **1**. 使了解 (*get the idea* ~ *to the class* 使学生了解这一思想)。**2**. 与(人)冲突。**3**. (计划)成功。***go*** ~ **1**. 渡过,越过。**2**. 不顺 (*go* ~ *a bridge* 过桥。*Things go* ~. 诸事不顺)。***It's*** ~ ***to you***. 〔口〕那是你的事了。***put*** (*a business deal*) ~ 使生意成交。***put it*** ~ ***a person*** 〔口〕向某人报仇;欺骗某人。~**-the-board** *a*. **1**. 全面的 (*an* ~*-the-board tax cut* 普遍减税)。**2**. 定时播送的。

a·cros·tic [əˈkrɔstik; ə`krɔstɪk] **I** *a*. 藏头诗的;离合体的。**II** *n*. (各行首词首字母能联成句子的)藏头诗,(各行首词末字母能联成句子的)离合体诗。

ACRR = American Council on Race Relations 美国种族关系理事会。

a·cryl·ic [əˈkrilik; ə`krɪlɪk] *a*.【化】丙烯酸的。~ **acid** 丙烯酸。~ **fibre** 丙烯酸系纤维。~ **plastic** 丙烯酸塑料。~ **resin** 丙烯酸(类)树脂。

ACS = **1**. antireticular cytotoxic serum【医】抗网状细胞毒血清。**2**. American College of Surgeons 美国外科医师学会。**3**. American Chemical Society 美国化学学会。

ACT = **1**. Association of Classroom Teachers (美国)任课教师协会。**2**. American College Test 美国大学测验。**3**. Australian Capital Territory (澳大利亚)首都直辖区。

act [ækt; ækt] **I** *n*. **1**. 行为;举动;动作。**2**. 决议,决议书;法令,条例。**3**. (戏剧的)幕,段;简短的节目。**4**. (牛津;剑桥等大学的)学位论文答辩。*an* ~ *of hostility*【法】敌对行为。*Act III, Scene ii* 第三幕,第二场。~ *and deed* 有约束力的契约;文据。~ *of God* [*Providence, Nature*]【法】不可抗力,天灾。~ *of grace* 恩典,特典;〔A-〕大赦令。~ *of Parliament* [*Congress*] 法令。*The Acts* (*of the Apostles*) (基督教《圣经·新约全书》中的)《使徒行传》。***get into the*** ~ 插手,参加。***have*** ~ ***or part in*** 参与,是…的同谋犯。***in the*** (***very***) ~ (***of***) 正在动作时;当场 (*be caught in the* ~ 当场被捕)。***put on an*** ~ 〔口〕装腔;炫耀自己。***to be in*** ~ ***to*** 〔古〕将要。**II** *vt*. **1**. 演(戏);扮演(角色)。**2**. 学,仿效,装。~ *the lord* 装阔。*He* ~*ed his part well*. 他演得不错;他做得不错。—*vi*. **1**. 作,干,实行,举止。**2**. 生效,发生作用。**3**. 当演员;充当,装作。~ *the fool* 做傻事情;出洋相。*How ought I to* ~ ? 我应该怎么办呢? *The medicine* ~*s well*. 药效不错。*The brake did not* ~. 煞车不灵了。~ ***against*** 违反(法律等);作不利于…的事。~ ***a part*** 扮演;装作,做戏。~ ***as*** (*guide*) 做(向导)。~ ***for*** 代理。~ ***on*** **1**. 遵行,奉行,按照…行动。**2**. 作用于,对…起作用[反应],影响到,有效验 (*Mind* ~*s upon mind*. 心心相印)。~ ***one's age*** 〔美口〕行为聪明有礼,有大人气了,不再顽皮了。~ ***the part of*** (*Hamlet*; *benefactor*), 演(哈姆雷特);做(保护人)。~ ***towards*** (*a person*) 待人。~ ***up*** 〔美口〕**1**. 开玩笑,调皮。**2**. (机器等)出毛病。~ ***up to*** 实行,遵守,遵照。~ ***upon*** = ~ on (*We must heed the correct views, and* ~ *upon them*. 对正确的意见必须听,并且照它做)。~***ing in the spirit of*** 本着…的精神。

act·a·ble [ˈæktəbl; `æktəbḷ] *a*. (戏本、角色等)可上演的,可扮演的。

Ac·ta Sanc·to·rum [ˈɑːktɑː sɑŋkˈtəurəm; `ɑkta sɑŋk`torəm] 〔L.〕【宗】圣徒行传〔圣徒和殉教者言行录集〕。

ac·tin [ˈæktin; `æktɪn] *n*.【生】肌动朊,肌纤朊。

act·ing [ˈæktiŋ; `æktɪŋ] **I** *n*. **1**. 行为。**2**. 演技,演出。**3**. 装假,做戏。*a play suitable for* ~ 适合上演的剧本。**II** *a*. **1**. 活动着的。**2**. 代理的,临时的。**3**. (供)演出的。*an* ~ *principal* 代理校长。*an* ~ *copy* [*script*]【剧】台本,脚本。*an* ~ *volcano* 活火山。

Ac·tin·i·a [ækˈtiniə; æk`tɪnɪə] *n*. (*pl*. ~*s*, *-ae* [-iː; -i])【动】红海葵属;〔a-〕红海葵。

ac·tin·ic [ækˈtinik; æk`tɪnɪk] *a*.【化】(有)光化(性)的。~ **ray** 光化射线。

ac·ti·nide [ˈæktinaid; `æktɪnaɪd] **series** 锕系。

ac·tin·ism [ˈæktinizəm; `æktɪnˏɪzəm] *n*.【化】射线作用,光化作用,光化度,光化性。

ac·tin·i·um [ækˈtiniəm; æk`tɪnɪəm] *n*.【化】锕〔元素名,符号为 Ac〕。

ac·ti·no- *comb.f*.【物】放射线的,【动】放射状的。

ac·tin·o·graph [ækˈtinəugrɑːf; æk`tɪnəˏgræf] *n*.【摄】曝光计;【物】辐射仪,日射计。

ac·ti·noid [ˈæktinɔid; `æktənɔɪd] *a*. 射线状的。

ac·ti·nol·o·gy [ˌæktiˈnɔlədʒi; ˏæktɪ`nɑlədʒɪ] *n*. 放射线学。

ac·ti·nom·e·ter [ˌæktiˈnɔmitə; ˏæktə`nɑmɪtə] *n*. 光量计;露光仪;光化线强度记录器,曝光计。

ac·ti·no·mor·phic [ˌæktinəuˈmɔːfik; ˏæktɪnə`mɔrfɪk] *a*.【生】辐射对称的。

ac·ti·no·my·ces [ˌæktinəuˈmaisiːz; ˏæktɪnə`maɪsiz] *n*.【微】放线菌。

ac·ti·no·my·cin [ˌæktinəuˈmaisin; ˏæktɪnə`maɪsɪn] *n*.【微】放线菌素。

ac·ti·no·my·co·sis [ˌæktinəumaiˈkəusis; ˏæktɪnomaɪ`kosɪs] *n*.【微】放线菌病。

ac·ti·non [ˈæktinɔn; `æktɪˏnɑn] *n*.【化】锕射气〔An〕。

ac·ti·no·ther·a·py [ˈæktinəuˈθerəpi; ˏæktɪnə`θɛrəpɪ] *n*.【医】(放射线、紫外线的)射线疗法。

ac·ti·no·u·ra·ni·um [ˌæktinəujuəˈreinjəm; ˏæktɪnoju`renɪəm] *n*.【化】锕铀〔AcU, 即铀[235]〕。

ac·tion [ˈækʃən; `ækʃən] **I** *n*. **1**. 动作,活动;行为,行动。★ act 指一次所作的行为;action 虽与 act 同义,但多半指某一期间内出现数次的行动;累积而成的 action 叫做 conduct. **2**. 举动,态度,姿势。**3**. 主动力,作用,机能。**4**. (机械装置中)有动作的部分;机械装置[作用]。**5**. 措施,手段。**6**. (演员的)表演;(小说等中的)情节。**7**.【法】诉讼。**8**.【军】战斗,战事。**9**. 某一地区[场合]内最热闹盛行的活动。**10**. 〔美口〕刺激性的活动;赌博。*a chemical* ~ 化学作用[反应]。*take* (*prompt*) ~ 采取(快速)措施。*accept* ~ 应战。*an encounter* ~ 遭遇战。*a defensive* [*an offensive*] ~ 防御[攻击]战。***A-!*** 【影】开演! ***A- stations!*** 【军】各就各位! ~ ***of the bowels***【医】通便(作用)。~ ***of the first impression***【法】新诉〔无以前判例可循的诉讼〕。***be in*** ~ 行动中。***be put out of*** ~ 失掉战斗力;(机械等)出毛病,不灵。***break off an*** ~ 停战。***bring*** [***take***] ***an*** ~ ***against*** 对…提起诉讼,控告。***bring*** [***come***] ***into*** ~ 使…参加战斗,参

战,使开始战斗,开战。**by** [**under**] **the** ～ **of** 在…作用下。**clear** (*a ship, or the decks*) **for** ～ (军舰)准备战斗。**go into** ～ 开始行动;投入战斗。**line of** ～【物】作用线;〔喻〕活动的形式[方针]。**man of** ～ 活动家,实行家。**out of** ～ 损坏;有故障。**put into** [**in**] ～ 实行,实施;开动。**see** ～ 加入战斗。**suit the** ～ **to the word** 见 suit 条。**take** ～ (**in**) **1.** 着手,动手,开始。**2.** 提起诉讼(*against*)。**II** *vt*.〔古〕对…提起诉讼。～ **committee** 行动委员会。～ **figure**(模仿真人、外星人或机器人等的)玩具人,活动人。～ **film**(电影的)动作片,打斗片。～ **group** 行动小组。～ **level** 禁售程度〔食物中有害物质含量足以危害公众健康,以致政府采取行动阻止其出售的食品的含毒浓度级〕。～ **painting** 洒泼画〔抽象派画,以乱洒颜料等为特征〕。～ **radius**【军】行动半径。～ **replay** 动作重放(体育比赛项目等精彩场面的录像磁带的重放)。～ **shot** 动态照片。～ **stations** (投入战斗前的)作战岗位。**-er** *n*.(电影的)动作片,打斗片。

ac·tion·a·ble [ˈækʃənəbl; ˋækʃənəbl] *a*. 可控告的。

ac·ti·va·ble [ˈæktivəbl; ˋæktɪvəbl] *a*.【化】能被活化的。

ac·ti·vate [ˈæktiveit; ˋæktə͵vet] *vt*. **1.** 使活动,开动,起动,触发;创设,成立(机构等)。**2.**【化】激活;活化。**3.**【物】赋能;使产生放射性。**4.** 使(阴沟)产生微生物(而加以净化)。～*d charcoal* 活性碳。～*d sludge process* 用活性污泥加速阴沟污物的分解。～ *analysis* 活化[激活]分析。**-va·tion** [-ˈveiʃən; -ˋveʃən] 激活,活化(作用)。

ac·ti·va·tor [ˈæktiveitə; ˋæktɪvetɚ] *n*.【化】活化剂;催化剂。～ **RNA**【生化】激活核糖核酸。

ac·tive [ˈæktiv; ˋæktɪv] *a*. **1.** 活动的,有活动力的;【生】活性的;【电】有功的;【无】有源的;【物】放射性的。**2.** 有生气的,活泼的,灵敏的,敏捷的;主动的,能动的,积极的;有力的,勤勉的;【医】有特效的。**3.** 现行的,活动中的;【军】现役的。*an* ～ *demand* 畅销。*an* ～ *volcano* 活火山。*The market is* ～. 市场活跃。～ *measures* 积极手段。**on** ～ **service**【军】现役,现役中的。**take an** ～ **part** [**interest**] **in** 积极参加。～ **antenna** 有源天线。～ **capital** 流动资本。～ **carbon**【化】活性碳。～ **current**【物】有功电流。～ **defense**【军】积极防御。～ **duty** 现役。～ **euthanasia** 积极式安乐死〔为使患不治之症者减少痛苦而用致死药物等手段促其安然死去的做法〕。～ **immunity** 自动免疫性。～ **list**【军】现役名册。～ **service** **1.** 现役。**2.** 战时服役。～ **title** (出版者认为继续有销路的)热门书。～ **voice**【语法】主动语态。～-**wear** 运动服。～ **weapon**【军】在编(制)武器。**-ly** *ad*. 活跃地;积极地,能动地;【语法】主动地。**-ness** *n*. 活跃,积极性。

ac·tiv·ism [ˈæktivizəm; ˋæktəvɪzəm] *n*. **1.** 积极精神。**2.**【哲】能动性。**3.** 积极行动主义。

ac·tiv·ist [ˈæktivist; ˋæktɪvɪst] *n*. 积极分子;积极行动者;行动主义分子。

ac·tiv·i·ty [ækˈtiviti; ækˋtɪvətɪ] *n*. **1.** 活动;活跃;动作;活动力;能动性。**2.** 活性;放射性。**3.** 机能,功能。**4.**〔美〕机构。**5.**〔*pl*.〕活动范围。*conscious* ～ 主观能动性。*recreational activities* 文娱活动。**be in** ～ (火山等)在活动中。**with** ～ 精神充沛的。

ac·tiv·ize [ˈækti͵vaiz; ˋæktə͵vaɪz] *vt*. 使活动,使行动,激起。

ac·to·my·o·sin [͵æktəuˈmaiəsin; ͵æktoˋmaɪəsɪn] *n*.【生化】肌纤凝蛋白。

Ac·ton [ˈæktən; ˋæktən] *n*. 阿克顿〔姓氏〕。

ac·ton [ˈæktən; ˋæktən] *n*. 锁子甲,衬甲的衣服,铠衣。

ac·tor [ˈæktə; ˋæktɚ] *n*. **1.** 男演员。**2.** 行动者,行为者。**3.** 原告。**4.**【化】原动质。**a bad** ～〔美〕坏蛋(*He's a bad* ～ *when he's drunk*. 他喝醉时,行为不检点)。

ac·tress [ˈæktris; ˋæktrɪs] *n*. 女演员。

ACTU = Australian Council of Trade Unions 澳大利亚工会理事会。

ac·tu·al [ˈæktjuəl; ˋæktʃuəl] *a*. 现实的,实际的,真实的,现行的,现在的。**the** ～ **state** 现状。～ **cost** 实际成本。～ **range**【军】实际投弹距离;(火炮)实际射程。～ **sin**【神】自罪。(*opp*. original sin). **in** ～ **existence** 现存。**in** ～ **life** 在现实生活中。**-ist** *n*. 实际家,现实家;现实论者。**-i·ty** [͵æktjuˈæliti; ͵æktʃuˋælətɪ] *n*. 现实,现存;现实性;〔*pl*.〕现状。**-i·za·tion** [͵æktjuəlaiˋzeiʃən; ͵æktʃuəlɪˋzeʃən] *n*. 实现,现实化。**-ize** [ˈæktjuəlaiz; ˋæktʃuəl͵aɪz] *vt*. 使现实化,实行,实现。**-ly** *ad*. **1.** 现在,如今;实际上;真。**2.** 竟然(*Believe it or not, he* ～*ly won*. 信不信由你,他居然胜利了。)

ac·tu·ar·i·al [͵æktjuˈɛəriəl; ͵æktʃuˋɛrɪəl] *a*. **1.**〔古〕(法院)记录员的。**2.** 保险统计师的;保险统计的。

ac·tu·ar·y [ˈæktjuəri; ˋæktʃu͵ɛrɪ] *n*. **1.**〔古〕(法院的)记录员;登记官。**2.** 保险统计师;计算员。

ac·tu·ate [ˈæktjueit; ˋæktʃu͵et] *vt*. 开动(机械等);驱使,激励(人等)。**be** ～**d by** (*love*) 为(爱情)所驱使。

ac·tu·a·tion [͵æktjuˈeiʃən; ͵æktʃuˋeʃən] *n*. 开动;驱使,激励。

ac·tu·a·tor [ˈæktʃueitə; ˋæktʃuetɚ] *n*.【机】促动器;【电】(电磁铁)螺线管;【自】执行元件;激励器。

ac·u·ate [ˈækjuit; ˋækjuɪt] *a*. 尖锐的。

a·cu·i·ty [əˈkju(:)iti; əˋkjuətɪ] *n*. **1.** 尖锐。**2.** (思想、视力的)敏锐。**3.** (疾病的)剧烈。～ *of wit* 才思敏锐。

a·cu·le·ate [əˈkju:liit; əˋkjulɪ͵et] *a*. **1.**【虫】有螯刺的。**2.**【植】有皮刺的。**3.** (语言)尖锐的。

a·cu·le·us [əˈkju:liəs; əˋkjulɪəs] *n*. (*pl*. **-le·i** [-ai; -aɪ]) **1.**【植】皮刺。**2.**【动】螯针;螯刺;刺状产卵器。

a·cu·men [əˈkju:men; əˋkjumɪn] *n*. **1.** 敏锐,聪明。**2.**【植】尖头〔如叶子的尖端〕。*political* ～ 政治才干。*business* ～ 业务手腕。

a·cu·mi·nate [əˈkju:minit; əˋkjumɪnɪt] **I** *a*. 尖的;有尖头的。**II** [əˈkju:mineit; əˋkjumɪnet] *vt*., *vi*. (使)变尖。

a·cu·mi·na·tion [ə͵kju:miˈneiʃən; ə͵kjumɪˋneʃən] *n*. 尖锐;尖头。

ac·u·punc·ture [ˈækjupʌŋktʃə; ˋækju͵pʌŋktɚ] **I** *n*. 针刺(法)。～ *and moxibustion* 针灸。～ *points* 穴位。**II** *vt*. 对…施行针刺疗法。

a·cush·la [əˈkuʃlə; əˋkuʃlə] *n*. 〔Ir.〕爱人,意中人。

a·cute [əˈkju:t; əˋkjut] *a*. **1.** 锐,尖(*opp*. blunt; obtuse);【植】急尖的。**2.** 敏锐的,精明的,深刻的。**3.** 剧烈的,厉害的。**4.**【乐】尖锐的,高音的;【语音】锐音的;【医】急性的(*opp*. chronic)。～ *pain* 剧痛。～ **accent** 撇形重音符号。～ **angle** 锐角。～ **appendicitis** 急性阑尾炎。**-ly** *ad*. 尖锐地;剧烈地。**-ness** *n*. 锐利;敏锐;剧烈。

ACV = Air Cushion Vehicle 气垫运载工具。

-acy *suf*. 〔构成抽象名词〕表示"性质"、"状态"、"职位": accur*acy*, fall*acy*, magistr*acy*.

a·cy·clic [eiˈsaiklik; əˋsaɪklɪk] *a*. 非周期性的;【化】非环式的;【植】非轮生的。

ac·yl [ˈæsil; ˋæsəl] *n*.【化】酰(基)。

AD, A. D. = **1.** active duty 现役。**2.** assembly district (美国某些州的)选区。**3.**〔L.〕*Anno Domini* 公元。

ad. = add; adverb; advertisement.

a.d. = 〔L.〕*ante diem* (= before the day).

ad[1] [æd; æd] *n*.〔美俚〕广告。*an* ～ *balloon* 广告气球。*an* ～ *police* 对竞选宣传进行监督的人[机构]。

ad[2] [æd; æd] *n*.【网球】打成平局后得分 = advantage. ～ *in* (打成平局后)发球人得分。～ *out* (打成平局后)接球人得分。

ad- *pref*. 向…;接近〔表示运动、方向、变化、添加等意义〕。★在元音或在 b, d, h, m, v 之前,仍为 ad- 不变;在 c, f, g, l, n, p. q. r, s, t, 之前, ad- 的 d 因受同化而变为 ac-, af-, ag-, al-, an-, ap-, ac -,〔在 q 前〕ar-, as-, at-.

A

-ad *suf*. **1.** (a)集合名词的词尾: mon*ad* 一价元素。dy*ad* 二价元素, tri*ad* 三价元素, chili*ad* 一千, myri*ad* 一万。(b)女妖名: Dry*ad* 树精。(c) 诗名: Illi*ad*, *Dunciad*. (d) 植物科名: lili*ad* 百合花科。**2.** = -ade: ball*ad*, sal*ad*, etc.

A/D = analogue-to-digital【计】模(拟)-数(字)。

ad [æd; æd] ***prep***. [L.] **1.** 达,到(= *to*; *towards*)。**2.** 根据(= *up to*; *according to*)。~ ***ar·bi·tri·um*** [ɑːˈbitriəm; ɑrˋbɪtrɪəm] 随意。~ ***cap·tan·dum*** [kæpˈtændəm; kæpˋtændəm] (***vul·gus***) [ˈvʌlgəs; ˋvʌlgəs]讨好众人的。~ ***e·un·dem*** [iːˈʌndəm; iˋʌndəm] 按同等学历。~ ***fi·nem*** [ˈfainem; ˋfaɪnɛm] 到[在]最后。~ ***hoc*** [ˈhɔk; ˋhɑk] 特定,特别 (*an ~ hoc committee* 特设委员会)。~ ***in·fi·ni·tum*** [ˌinfiˈnaitəm; ˏɪnfəˋnaɪtəm] 永远,无限,无穷(略 *ad inf*.)。~ ***i·ni·ti·um*** [iniˈʃiːəm; ɪnɪˋʃiəm] 在开始。~ ***in·te·rim*** [ˈintərim; ˋɪntərɪm] 暂时的,临时的(略 *ad int*.] (*chargé d'affaires ~ interim* 临时代办)。~ ***lib·i·tum*** [ˈlibitəm; ˋlɪbɪtəm] 随意,任意(略 *ad lib*.);【乐】自由演唱。~ ***loc·um*** [ˈlɔkəm; ˋlɑkəm] 在这里。~ ***nau·se·am*** [ˈnɔːsiæm; ˋnɔʃɪˏæm] 令人作呕,讨厌。~ ***ref·er·en·dum*** [refəˈredəm; ˏrɛfəˋrɛndəm] 还要斟酌,尚须考虑 (~ *referendum contract* 暂定契约书,草约)。~ ***rem*** [ˈrem; ˋrɛm] 得要领,中肯,适宜。~ ***un·guem*** (***factus***) [ˈʌŋgwem; ˋʌŋgwɛm]; [ˈfæktəs; ˋfæktəs] 完善。~ ***va·lor·em*** [vəˈlɔrem; vəˋlorəm] 按价(~ *valorem duty* 按价收税)。~ ***ver·bum*** [ˈvəːbəm; ˋvɝbəm] 逐字。

A·da [ˈeidə; ˋedə] ***n***. 埃达[女子名]。

a·dac·ty·lous [əˈdæktiləs; eˋdæktɪləs] ***a***. 生来无指或缺趾的。

ad·age [ˈædidʒ; ˋædɪdʒ] ***n***. 格言,箴言;古话,谚语。

a·da·gio [əˈdɑːdʒiəu; əˋdɑdʒɪo] **I** ***ad***., ***a***. [It.]【乐】缓慢地(的),悠闲地(的)。**II** ***n***. **1.**【乐】柔板。**2.** 悠闲的双人芭蕾舞。

Ad·am[1] [ˈædəm; ˋædəm] ***n***. 亚当[姓氏,男子名]。

Ad·am[2] [ˈædəm; ˋædəm] ***n***.【圣】亚当;最初的人。(***as***) ***old as*** ~ 古老;陈旧。***from*** ~ ***on down*** 自从开天辟地以来。***not know*** (*a person*) ***from*** ~ 全然不知,从未见过。***the old*** ~【宗】人类本性之恶,原罪。~ **and Eve** [美口]两个鸡蛋 (~ *and Eve on a raft* [美口]烤面包上加两个鸡蛋)。~**'s ale** [**wine**] [口]水。~**'s apple 1.**【解】喉结,喉核。**2.**【植】车前属;柚;冠状狗牙花。~**'s needle**【植】丝兰属。

Ad·am[3] [ˈædəm; ˋædəm] ***a***. (家具和建筑)亚当式的[亚当是指十八世纪英国建筑师 Robert 和 James Adam 兄弟]。

ad·a·mant [ˈædəmənt; ˋædəˏmɑnt] **I** ***n***. 坚硬无比的东西;【地】硬石(指金刚石等)。**II** ***a***. **1.** 坚硬的。**2.** 坚决的。*Once he had made his decision, he was ~ and would not change his mind*. 他一旦做出决定,就坚决不改变主意。

ad·a·man·tine [ˌædəˈmæntain; ædəˋmæntɪn] ***a***. **1.** 金刚石似的;坚硬无比的。**2.** (牙齿)珐琅质的。**3.** 坚决的,断然的。~ *chains* 极坚固的铁链。~ **lustre** 金刚光泽。~ **spar**【地】刚玉。

Ad·am·ite [ˈædəmait; ˋædəmˏaɪt] **I** ***n***. **1.** 亚当的后裔,人。**2.** 裸体的人;【宗】裸体生活宗派。**II** ***a***. 亚当后裔的,人的。

Ad·ams [ˈædəmz; ˋædəmz] ***n***. 亚当斯[姓氏]。

ad·ams·ite [ˈædəmzait; ˋædəmzˏaɪt] ***n***. **1.**【化】二苯胺氯胂(毒气)。**2.**【矿】暗绿云母。

Ad·ams·town [ˈædəmzˈtaun; ˋædəmzˋton] ***n***. 亚当斯敦[皮特凯恩岛(英)首府]。

a·dapt [əˈdæpt; əˋdæpt] ***vt***. **1.** 使适应,使适合,使适于。**2.** 改,修改,改编,改写(剧本等)。~ (*one's behaviour*) *to* (*the company*) 使(自己行动)配合(同伴)。~ *oneself to* (*circumstances*) 适应(环境),随遇而安,通权达变。**-ed** ***a***. 适合…的;改编成…的。*This book is ~ed to children*. 这书是为适合儿童需要而改写的。*The novel was ~ed for the stage*. 这部小说改编成剧本了。*The play is ~ed from a novel*. 这是一部由小说改编成的戏剧。—***vi***. 适应不同环境[情况等]。

a·dapt·a·bil·i·ty [əˌdæptəˈbiliti; əˏdæptəˋbɪlətɪ] ***n***. 适应性,顺应性。

a·dapt·a·ble [əˈdæptəbl; əˋdæptəbl] ***a***. **1.** 可以适应的。**2.** 能改编的。

ad·ap·ta·tion [ˌædæpˈteiʃən; ˏædəpˋteʃən] ***n***. **1.** 适合,适应,顺应 (*to*)。**2.** 改编(的作品) (*from*)。**3.**【生】适应性的改变;感官适应性调节。**4.** 同化。*the principle of ~ to local conditions* 因地制宜的原则。

a·dapt·er, -or [əˈdæptə; əˋdæptɚ] ***n***. **1.** 改编者。**2.**【机】转接器,接头;插座;衬套。**3.**【无】拾音器。

a·dap·tion [əˈdæpʃən; əˋdæpʃən] ***n***. [美] = adaptation.

a·dap·tive [əˈdæptiv; əˋdæptɪv] ***a***. 适合的,适应的。

ADAPTS [əˈdæpts; əˋdæpts] ***n***. 空投式海面油污清除装置。

ADAS = Agricultural Development and Advisory Service (英国)农业发展与咨询服务处。

A·dar [əˈdɑː; əˋdɑr] ***n***. [Heb.] (犹太历)六月。

ad·ax·i·al [æˈdæksiəl; æˋdæksɪəl] ***a***.【植】近轴的。

ADB = **1.** Asian Development Bank 亚洲开发银行。**2.** African Development Bank 非洲开发银行。

ADC = **1.** [F.] *aide-de-camp*. **2.** Aerospace Defense Command (美国)航空空间防御司令部。**3.** Aid to Dependent Children (美国)对贫困儿童补助计划。**4.** Air Defense Command (美国)防空司令部。**5.** Assistant Division Commander 副师长。

ad·col·umn [ˈædkələm; ˋædˏkɑləm] ***n***. [美口]广告栏。

ad-craft [ˈædkrɑːft; ˋædˏkræft] ***n***. [美口]广告业。

ADD = American Dialect Dictionary 美国方言词典。

add [æd; æd] ***vt***. **1.** 加,增,添,追加,附加;获得。**2.** 又说;补充说。**3.** 加算,累积。~ *some water to the tea* 给茶里加些开水。~ *one thing to another* 加一物于另一物。*Add three and seven and you will have ten*. 7 加 3 等于 10。—***vi***. **1.** 增加。**2.** 作加法。**3.** 加算,合计。*learn to* ~ 学做加法。~ ***in*** 算入。~ ***it on*** [口]浮报,虚报。~ ***to*** 增加 (*This ~ed to our difficulties*. 这增加了我们不少困难)。~ ***up*** 合计;符合预期的数目 (*The figures don't ~ up right*. 这些数字加起来不对)。~ ***up to*** 总计共达;[口]总之就是 (*The evidence ~s up to a case of theft*. 证据显示出是一起盗窃案)。***to*** ~ ***to*** 更加,又加 (*To ~ to the danger, darkness fell upon the water*. 更加危险的是,夜幕又降临水面)。**-ed** ***a***. 附加的,增加的;更多的。

add·a·ble, add·i·ble [ˈædəbl; ˋædəbl] ***a***. **1.** 可加上的。**2.** 被加上的。

add. = addenda; addendum; addition(al); address.

ad·dax [ˈædæks; ˋædæks] ***n***.【动】曲角羚羊。

ad·dend [ˈædend, əˈdend; ˋædɛnd, əˋdɛnd] ***n***.【数】加数。

ad·den·dum [əˈdendəm; əˋdɛndəm] ***n***. (*pl*. *-da*) **1.** 附录,补遗。**2.** 追加物,附加物。**3.** (齿轮的)齿头高度,齿顶高。

ad·der[1] [ˈædə; ˋædɚ] ***n***. 加法器;加法电路。

ad·der[2] [ˈædə; ˋædɚ] ***n***. 小毒蛇,蝰蛇。***deaf as an*** ~ 完全耳聋。

ad·der's-mouth [ˈædəzmauθ; ˋædɚzˏmauθ] ***n***.【植】沼兰属植物。

ad·der's-tongue [ˈædəzˌtʌŋ; ˋædɚzˏtʌŋ] ***n***.【植】**1.** 山慈姑(= dog's tooth violet)。**2.** 瓶尔小草属植物。

ad·dict [əˈdikt; əˋdɪkt] **I** ***vt***. **1.** 使沉溺,使嗜好;热中于。**2.** 使吸毒成瘾。~ ***oneself to*** 沉溺于,热中于,一心在。

be ～*ed to* 嗜好，嗜爱。— *vi*. 使人上瘾。*Drugs are ～ing*. 麻醉品会使人上瘾。II [ˈædikt, ˋædɪkt] *n*. 〔俚〕有(毒)瘾的人。*a drug* ～ 吸毒成瘾者。

ad·dic·tion [əˈdikʃən; əˋdɪkʃən] *n*. 热中，沉溺，嗜好；吸毒成瘾。

ad·dic·tive [əˈdiktiv; əˋdɪktɪv] *a*. 沉溺的；使成瘾的；上瘾的。

add-in [ˈædin; ˋædɪn] *n*. 【自】(电子计算机的)附件，附加物。

adding [ˈædiŋ; ˋædɪŋ] *n*. 计算，加算。～ *machine* 计算器，加算器。

Ad·dis [ˈædis; ˋædɪs] *n*. 阿迪斯〔姓氏〕。

Ad·dis A·ba·ba [ˈædisˈæbəbə; ˋædɪs ˋæbəbə] 亚的斯亚贝巴(亚底斯亚贝巴)〔埃塞俄比亚(衣索比亚)首都〕。

Ad·di·son [ˈædisn; ˋædəsn] *n*. 阿迪森〔姓氏〕。～**'s disease** 阿迪森氏病，(肾上腺性)青铜色皮病，类青铜色皮病。

ad·dit·a·ment [əˈditəmənt; əˋdɪtəmənt] *n*. 增加物，附加物。

ad·di·tion [əˈdiʃən; əˋdɪʃən] *n*. **1.** 附加，追加；附加物。**2.** 【数】加法，加算。**3.** 【法】(加在姓名后的)头衔，官衔；称号。**4.** (建筑物的)附加部分。*have an* ～ (*to one's family*) 生孩子，添人口。*in* ～ 加之，又，另外。*in* ～ *to* 加之，除…外又。～ **compound** 【化】加成化合物。

ad·di·tion·al [əˈdiʃənl; əˋdɪʃənl] *a*. 附加的，追加的，另外的。*an* ～ *tax* 附加税。*the* ～ *regulation* 补充规定。**-ly** [əˈdiʃənəli; əˋdɪʃənəlɪ] *ad*. 加之，另外，又。

ad·di·tive [ˈæditiv; ˋædətɪv] I *a*. **1.** 附加的，增加的。**2.** 【化】加成的，加和的。**3.** 【数】加法的；加性的。II *n*. **1.** 添加剂；添加物。**2.** 【数】加法。～ **group** 【数】加法群。～ **reaction** 【化】加成反应。

ad·dle [ˈædl; ˋædl] I *a*. **1.** 变质腐败的，坏的；混乱的。**2.** (思想)糊涂的，空虚的。～ *eggs* 臭蛋。II *vt*., *vi*. **1.** (使)腐坏。**2.** (使)变混乱。～ *one's brain over figures* 给数字弄昏头脑。～**brained**, ～**headed**, ～**pated** *a*. 思想糊涂的，昏头昏脑的。～**head**, ～**pate** 昏愦的人，糊涂虫。

ad·dled [ˈædld; ˋædld] *a*. **1.** 腐败了的，坏了的。**2.** (头脑等)混乱的；昏愦的。

ad·do·me·ter [əˈdɔmitə; əˋdɑmɪtɚ] *n*. 加算器。

add-on [ˈædˈɔn; ˋædˋɑn] *n*. 〔口〕分期付款方式。

ad·dress [əˈdres, Am. ˈædres; əˋdrɛs, ˋædrɛs] I *n*. **1.** (信上的)称呼，姓名；地址。**2.** 致辞；寒暄；演说；正式请愿。**3.** 谈吐，风度。**4.** 〔*pl*.〕求爱，献殷勤。**5.** 灵巧，娴熟。*change one's* ～ 改变住址。*an inside* ～ 信纸左上角的收信人姓名、地址。*an inaugural* ～ 就任致辞[演说]。*a man of pleasing* [*good*] ～ 谈吐流利的人。*an* ～ *of thanks* 谢辞。*show great* ～ *in* (*doing sth*.) 在(做某事上)显示出有本领。*pay one's* ～*es to a lady* 向某女士大献殷勤。*opening* [*closing*] ～ 开[闭]幕辞。*the A-* **1.** 〔英〕议院答辞；〔美〕总统咨文。**2.** 【法】撤职请求。*with* ～ 巧妙地。II *vt*. **1.** 在…上写姓名住址；称呼；向…致意。**2.** 【商】交，委托。**3.** 给…讲话；向…演说，向…求爱，向…献殷勤。**4.** 【法】(立法部门)请求撤销(不适任法官的)职务。**5.** 引导，引见。**6.** 应付，处理(问题等)。**7.** 满足(需求等)。**8.** 【高尔夫球】瞄准。～ *a letter to sb*. 写信给某人。～ *an audience* 对听众演说。～ *sb*. 跟人攀谈。～ *a meeting* 向会众演说。～ *a protest to sb*. 对某人提抗议。～ *the ball* 【高尔夫球】用棒碰球作瞄准准备。～ *oneself to* **1.** 专心(工作)。**2.** 向…讲话，和…通信。**3.** (在演说时)述及，讲到。～ **book** 通讯花名册。～**ing machine** 姓名住址印刷机。

ad·dress·ee [ˌædreˈsiː; ˏædrɛˋsi] *n*. 收信人，收件人。

ad·dress·er, -or [əˈdresə; əˋdrɛsɚ] *n*. **1.** 发言人，陈述人。**2.** 发信人；署名人。

ad·dress·o·graph [əˈdresəgrɑːf; əˋdrɛsəˏgræf] *n*. 姓名住址印刷机〔原商标名〕。

ad·duce [əˈdjuːs; əˋdjus] *vt*. 引用，引证，举出。～ *reasons in support of one's case*. 提出理由来支持自己的论证。

ad·du·cent [əˈdjuːsnt; əˋdjusənt] *a*. 【生理】内转的；(肌肉)内收的。

ad·duc·i·ble [əˈdjuːsibl; əˋdjusəbl] *a*. 可以引用的。

ad·duct [əˈdʌkt; əˋdʌkt] I *vt*. 【生理】使内收 (*opp*. abduct)。II [ˈædʌkt; ˋædʌkt] *n*. 【化】加合物。

ad·duc·tion [əˈdʌkʃən; əˋdʌkʃən] *n*. **1.** 引用，引证。**2.** 【解】内收(作用)。

ad·duc·tor [əˈdʌktə; əˋdʌktɚ] *n*. 【解】内收肌 (*opp*. abductor)；【动】闭谷肌。

Ade [eid; ed] *n*. 埃德〔姓氏〕。

ade [eid; ed] *n*. 〔美〕果汁水。*grape* ～ 葡萄水。

-ade *suf*. 〔构成表示下列意义的名词〕**1.** 动作：block*ade* 堵塞。**2.** 行动中的集团：cavalc*ade* 马队。**3.** 动作的结果或成品：masquer*ade* 化装舞会；pom*ade* 发油。**4.** 某些饮料：lemon*ade* 柠檬水。

Ad·e·la [ˈædilə; ˋædḷə] *n*. 阿迪拉〔姓氏，女子名〕。

Ad·e·laide[1] [ˈædəleid; ˋædḷˏed] *n*. 阿德莱德〔女子名〕。

Ad·e·laide[2] [ˈædəleid; ˋædḷˏed] *n*. 阿德莱德〔澳大利亚港市〕。

A·dele [əˈdel; əˋdɛl] *n*. 阿黛尔〔女子名〕。

Ad·e·li·ne [ˈædiliːn, ˈædəlain; ˋædɪlin, ˋædəlaɪn] *n*. 阿德琳〔女子名〕。

a·demp·tion [əˈdempʃən; əˋdɛmpʃən] *n*. 【法】(遗产的)取消；〔因立遗嘱人亡故时，遗产产权已非其所有〕。

A·den [ˈeidn; ˋedn] *n*. 亚丁〔民主也门首都〕。

ad·e·nine [ˈædiniːn; ˋædənɪn] *n*. 【生化】腺嘌呤。

ad·e·ni·tis [ˌædiˈnaitis; ˏædəˋnaɪtɪs] *n*. 【医】(淋巴)腺炎。

ad·e·no·car·ci·no·ma [ˈædinəuˌkɑːsiˈnəumə; ˋædinəuˏkɑːsɪˋnəumə] *n*. 【医】腺癌。

ad·e·noid [ˈædinɔid; ˋædnˏɔɪd] I *a*. 【医】腺样(的)。II *n*. **1.** 【植】腺状物。**2.** 〔*pl*.〕【医】腺样增殖(症)。**3.** 〔美俚〕声音微弱的电台歌手。～ **growth** 腺样增殖(体)。

ad·e·noi·dal [ˈædinɔidl; ˋædnˋɔɪdl] = adenoid (*a*.).

ad·e·nol·o·gy [ˌædiˈnɔlədʒi; ˏædəˋnɑlədʒɪ] *n*. 【医】腺学。

ad·e·no·ma [ˌædiˈnəumə; ˏædəˋnomə] *n*. 【医】腺瘤。

a·den·o·sine [əˈdenəsiːn; əˋdɛnəsin] *n*. 【生化】腺甙。

ad·e·no·vi·rus [æˌdinəuˈvaiərəs; ˏædinoˋvaɪrəs] *n*. 呼吸系统病毒。

ad·e·nyl·ic [ˌædəˈnilik; ˏædəˋnɪlɪk] *a*. ～ *acid* 【生化】腺甘酸。

ad·ept [ˈædept, əˈdept; ˋædɛpt, əˋdɛpt] I *a*. 熟练的；内行的。*be* ～ *in* [*at*] 善于，擅长，精通。II *n*. 内行，熟手。*an* ～ *in philosophy* 哲学大家。*a musical* ～ 音乐名手。**-ly** *ad*. **-ness** *n*.

ad·ep·tism [əˈdeptizm; əˋdɛptizm] *n*. 重用专家的作风，用人唯贤 (*opp*. nepotism)。

ad·e·qua·cy [ˈædikwəsi; ˋædəkwəsɪ] *n*. 适当，恰当；足够。

ad·e·quate [ˈædikwit; ˋædəkwɪt] *a*. **1.** 适当的；足够的，充分的。**2.** 恰当，胜任的。**3.** 尚可的，差强人意的。*give only an* ～ *performance* 演出仅差强人意。～ **for** 适合；足够。～ **to** (*one's needs*) 敷(用)，够(用)。～ *to* (*one's post*) 胜(任)。*The supply is not* ～ *to the demand*. 供不应求。**-ly** *ad*. **-ness** *n*.

a·der·min [əˈdəːmin; eˋdɝmɪn] *n*. 维生素 B_6 (= pyridoxine)。

a deux [F. a dø] 〔F.〕〔介词片语〕两人一起；两人之间。

A.D.F. = **1.** automatic direction finder 【无】自动测向器。**2.** African Development Fund 非洲开发基金。**3.** Aircraft direction finder 飞机测向仪。

ADGB = Air Defence of Great Britain 英国防空部队。

ADH = antidiuretic hormone 【生化】抗利尿激素。

ad·here [ədˈhiə; ədˋhɪr] *vi*. **1.** 黏附；固着 (*to*)。**2.** 追

随;依附。3. 遵循;坚持(*to*)。*the mud adhering to our shoes* 黏在鞋子上的泥。~ *to neutrality* 严守中立。—*vt*. 使黏附。

ad·her·ence [ad'hiərəns; əd`hɪrəns] *n*. 1. 黏附。2. 固执;坚持,依附〔指精神方面的; adhesion 则是物质上的〕。

ad·her·ent [əd'hiərənt; əd`hɪrənt] I *a*. 1. 黏附…的,依附…的。2.【植】骈生的,连生的(*to*)。3.【语法】(在名词之前的)修饰语的。II *n*. 追随者,支持者,拥护者,信徒〔其后通常接 of, 偶尔也接 to〕。*an enthusiastic* ~ *of the theory* 该学说的热情支持者。

ad·he·sion [əd'hiːʒən; əd`hiʒən] *n*. 1. 黏附,附着,胶着。2. 黏附力;黏附(现象)。3. 追随;皈依;信奉;同意,加入。4.【医】黏连(物)。***give in one's*** ~ 表示同意,声明加入。

ad·he·sive [əd'hiːsiv; əd`hisɪv] I *a*. 黏附性的,胶黏的。II *n*. 胶合剂,黏合剂。~ **disc**【植】吸盘。~ **envelope** 胶口信封。~ **plaster** 橡皮膏。~ **stamp** 带胶邮票。~ **tape** 胶带。**-ly** *ad*. **-ness** *n*.

ad·hib·it [æd'hibit; æd`hɪbɪt] *vt*. 1. 贴,黏。2.〔古〕用,服(药等)。3. 容许(进入)。

ad hoc [æd'hɔk; `æd`hαk]〔L.〕1.〔介词片语〕特别是。2.〔用作修饰语〕特别的。*an* ~ *commission of inquiry* 特别调查委员会。

ad ho·mi·nem [ˌæd'hɔmiˌnem; `æd`hαməˏnɛm]〔L.〕〔介词片语〕1. 怀有偏见地;感情用事地。2. 矛头指向个人地。

ADI = acceptable daily intake (辐射线、药物等)每日允许摄入量。

ad·i·a·bat ['ædiəbæt; `ædɪəbæt] *n*.【物】绝热线。

ad·i·a·bat·ic [ˌædiə'bætik; ˏædɪə`bætɪk] *a*.【物】绝热的;不传热的。*an* ~ *curve* 绝热曲线。

Ad·i·an·tum [ˌædi'æntəm; ˏædɪ`æntəm] *n*.【植】1. 石长生属。2.〔a-〕= maidenhair.

ad·i·aph·o·re·sis [ˌædai'æfəriːsis; ˏædɪ`æfərisɪs] *n*.【医】无汗症。

ad·i·aph·o·ret·i·c [ˌædi'æfəretik; ˏædɪ`æfərɛtɪk] I *a*. 无汗的。II *n*. 止汗剂。

ad·i·aph·o·rous [ˌædi'æfərəs; ˏædɪ`æfərəs] *a*. 1. 不偏不倚,中立,无可无不可。2.【医】无反应的,无活动的。

ad·i·a·ther·man·cy [ˌædiə'θəːmənsi; ˏædɪə`θɝmənsɪ] *n*.【物】不透红外线性。**-ma·nous** *a*.

a·dieu [ə'djuː; ə`dju] I *int*. 再会,一路平安。II *n*. (*pl*. ~*s*, ***a·dieux*** [ə'djuːz; ə`djuz]) 告别,辞别。***bid*** ~ ***to*** (*sb*.) 向某人告别。***make*** [***take***] ***one's*** ~ 辞行。

ad·i·os [αː'djəus; ˏædɪ`os]〔Sp.〕*int*. 再见。

a·dip·ic [ə'dipik; ə`dɪpɪk] *a*. ~ **acid**【化】己二酸。

ad·i·po·cere [ˌædipəu'siə; ˏædəpə`sɪr] *n*. 尸蜡,尸油。

ad·i·pose ['ædipəus; `ædəˏpos] I *a*. 脂肪质的,脂肪多的。II *n*. 动物脂肪。~ *tissue*【生】脂肪组织。

ad·i·pos·i·ty [ˌædi'pɔsiti; ˏædə`pαsətɪ] *n*. 多脂,肥胖。

ad·it ['ædit; `ædɪt] *n*. 1. 入口。2.【矿】横坑,平峒。

ADIZ = air defence identification zone【空】防空识别区。

adj. = adjacent; adjective; adjunct; adjustment.

ad·ja·cen·cy [ə'dʒeisənsi; ə`dʒesnsɪ] *n*. 1. 接近,毗邻。2. 邻接物。3. 紧接在某一节目之前或之后的电视[广播]节目。

ad·ja·cent [ə'dʒeisənt; ə`dʒesnt] *a*. 1. 毗邻的,邻近的。2. (时间上)紧接着的。~ *angle* 邻角。~ *towns and villages* 附近的城市和乡村。***be*** ~ ***to*** 接近…。

ad·jec·ti·val [ˌædʒek'taivəl; ˏædʒɪk`taɪvəl] *a*.【语法】形容词的,形容词性的。**-ly** *ad*.

ad·jec·tive ['ædʒiktiv; `ædʒɪktɪv] I *n*.【语法】形容词。II *a*. 1. 形容词(性)的。2. 附属的。3.【法】有关程序的。~ **clause** [**phrase**] 形容从句[短语]。~ **colours** 间接色素,媒染染料。~ **law**【法】附属法,程序法(*opp*. substantive law)。

ad·join [ə'dʒɔin; ə`dʒɔɪn] *vi*. 接,贴连,毗连,邻接;临。*The two houses* ~. 这两座房子相连。—*vt*. 1. 接,邻;临。2. 附上,加上,使结合。*Canada* ~*s the United States*. 加拿大与美国接壤。

ad·join·ing [ə'dʒɔiniŋ; ə`dʒɔɪnɪŋ] *a*. 邻,邻接的,隔壁。*an* ~ *room* 邻室。~ **rock** 围岩。

ad·journ [ə'dʒəːn; ə`dʒɝn] *vt*. 使延期;使中止,休(会)。~ *the debate* 暂停辩论。—*vi*. 1. 延会,休会,散会。2.〔俚〕搬会场,移座位。~ *without day* [*sine die*] 无限期休会。~ *to the dining room* 移到餐室。**-ment** *n*. 1. 延期,闭会,休会,延会。2. 休会时期。

Adjt. = Adjutant.

ad·judge [ə'dʒʌdʒ; ə`dʒʌdʒ] *vt*. 1. 判决,宣判;裁定。2. 判给,断与。3. 断定,认为。~ *a man* (*to be*) *guilty* 判决某人有罪。*be* ~*d wise to do sth*. 去做某事被视为明智。

ad·judge·ment, ad·judg·ment [ə'dʒʌdʒmənt; ə`dʒʌdʒmənt] *n*. 判决;宣告;判定;定罪;判归。

ad·ju·di·cate [ə'dʒuːdikeit; ə`dʒudɪˏket] *vt*. 判决,裁断,裁定。—*vi*. 审断,判决(*on*; *upon*)。~ *in a case* [*on a matter*] 判决案子[事件]。

ad·ju·di·ca·tion [əˌdʒuːdi'keiʃən; əˏdʒudɪ`keʃən] *n*. 1. 判决,宣告。2. 破产宣告。

ad·ju·di·ca·tive [ə'dʒuːdikeitiv; ə`dʒudɪˏketɪv] *a*. 判决的。

ad·ju·di·ca·tor [ə'dʒuːdikeitə; ə`dʒudɪˏketɚ] *n*. 判决者,裁定者,审判者,评判人。

ad·junct ['ædʒʌŋkt; `ædʒʌŋkt] I *n*. 1. 附属物,附件。2. 助手,副手。3.【语法】附加语,修饰语。4.【逻】附属性质,非本质属性。II *a*. 附属的(*to*; *of*)。~ **professor**〔美〕副教授。

ad·junc·tion [æ'dʒʌŋkʃən; ə`dʒʌŋkʃən] *n*. 1.【数】附益,附加。2. 添加,附加。

ad·junc·tive [ə'dʒʌŋktiv; ə`dʒʌŋktɪv] *a*. 附属的;附加语的。**-ly** *ad*.

ad·ju·ra·tion [ˌædʒuə'reiʃən; ˏædʒʊ`reʃən] *n*. 1. 严令。2. 恳请。

ad·jure [ə'dʒuə; ə`dʒʊr] *vt*. 1. (以发誓或诅咒威迫的方式)严令。2. 恳求,恳请。~ *sb*. *to tell the truth* 要某人务必说实话。

ad·just [ə'dʒʌst; ə`dʒʌst] *vt*. 1. 调准(望远镜等),对准,校正,校准(机械等)。2. 调整;整理,整顿。3. 核算(盈亏)。4.【保险】评定(赔偿要求)。5. 调停,排解(纠纷等)。6. 使适应(环境)。~ *a camera* 校准镜头。~ *accounts* 清理帐目;核算。~ *one's clothes* 整顿装束。~ *differences* 调解分歧。~ *oneself* 整装。~ *oneself to one's environment* 使自己适应环境。—*vi*. 1. 获得校准。2. 适应于(*to*)。~**ing plane**【空】调节翼。~**ing points** (炮兵的)试射点。

ad·just·a·ble [ə'dʒʌstəbl; ə`dʒʌstəbl] *a*. 可校准的,可调整的。*an* ~ *wrench* 活动扳手。

ad·just·er [ə'dʒʌstə; ə`dʒʌstɚ] *n*. 1. 调整者;调解者。2.【机】调整器。3. (赔偿财产损失等的)核算人。

ad·just·ment [ə'dʒʌstmənt; ə`dʒʌstmənt] *n*. 1. 调整;调节(装置);校正。2. 调节。3. (赔偿损失的)清算。

ad·ju·tage ['ædʒutidʒ; `ædʒʊtɪdʒ] *n*. 喷射管。

ad·ju·tan·cy ['ædʒutənsi; `ædʒətənsɪ] *n*. 副官职位。

ad·ju·tant ['ædʒutənt; `ædʒətənt] I *a*. 补助的。II *n*. 1.【军】副官。2.【鸟】鹳(= ~ bird [crane, stork])。~ **general** (*pl*. ~**s general**) 副官长;〔the A- General〕〔美〕陆军副官;副官署署长。**A- General's Department**【美陆军】军务局。

ad·ju·vant ['ædʒuvənt; `ædʒəvənt] I *a*. 辅助的。II *n*. 1. 助理员,助手。2.【医】辅药,佐药。

Ad·ler ['ædlə; `ædlɚ] *n*. 阿德勒〔姓氏〕。

ad-lib [æd'lib; æd`lɪb] I *vt*., *vi*. (***ad-lib·bed***; ***ad-lib-***

A

bing)〔美口〕**1.** (演奏时)临时穿插;即兴撰造(词句、乐曲等)。**2.** 临时拼凑。**II** *n.* **1.** 即兴[即席]演奏,临时穿插。**2.** 权宜措施。**III** *a.*, *ad.* **1.** 临时穿插的[地],临时拼凑的[地]。**2.** 随意的[地]。*an ~ organization* 临时拼凑的组织。**-libber** *n.* 即兴表演的人;即兴讲演者。

ad loc 〔L.〕在那地方;去那地方(= ad locum)。

adm. = administration; administrative; administrator; administratrix.

Adm. = Admiral; Admiralty.

ad·man [ˈædmæn; ˋædmæn] *n.* (*pl.* **-men** [-men; -mɛn])〔美俚〕**1.** 广告员。**2.** 写广告的人。

ad·mass [ˈædmæs; ˋædmæs] **I** *n.* **1.** (依靠各种宣传工具企图影响广大消费者的)广告推销制度。**2.** 受广告影响的社会。**II** *a.* 广告推销性质的;受广告推销影响的。

ad·meas·ure [ædˈmeʒə; ædˋmɛʒɚ] *vt.* 分配,配给。**-ment** *n.* **1.** 分配,配给。**2.** 测量;尺寸。

ad·min·i·cle [ædˈminikl; ædˋmɪnɪkl] *n.* **1.** 补助物。**2.** 【法】副证,补充证据。

ad·mi·nic·u·lar [ˌædmiˈnikjulə; ˏædmiˋnɪkjəlɚ] *a.* 补助的;补充的。

ad·min·is·ter [ədˈministə; ədˋmɪnəstɚ] *vt.* **1.** 管理,管制,掌管,统制;处理,支配;治理。**2.** 施行,实施。**3.** 给与,供给;下药,使…吃药。**4.** 使…发誓,使…保证。~ *justice* 执行法律,审判。~ *medicine to sb.* 给某人吃药,下药。~ *a rebuke* 责备。~ *fuel to the fire of ...* 煽动,使…火上加油。~ *sb. a box on the ear* 给某人一个耳光。~ *an oath to sb.* 使某人发誓。—*vi.* **1.** 管理;承办,代办;【法】管理遗产。**2.** 补助,辅助。~ **to** 有助于 (Health ~*s to peace of mind.* 健康有助于身心的安宁)。

ad·min·is·trate [ədˈministreit; ədˋmɪnəˏstret] *vt.* 〔美〕管理;支配。

ad·min·is·tra·tion [ədˌminisˈtreiʃən; ədˏmɪnəˋstreʃən] *n.* **1.** 管理,掌管,经营;〔英〕行政,施政。**2.** 行政机关,局[处、署];〔A- 主美〕政府。**3.** 给与;施行。**4.** 给药,(药的)服法。**5.** 【军】后方勤务。**6.** 【法】遗产管理。**7.** (官员的)任职期。*an ~ journal* 〔美〕当权派报纸。*an ~ senator* 〔美〕支持政府的参议院议员。*a board of ~* 董事会。*Fewer and better troops and simple ~* 精兵简政。~ *chief* 行政处长,总务处长。*civil ~* 民政。*military ~* 军政。~ *of justice* 处罚。*oral ~* 【医】口服。

ad·min·is·tra·tive [ədˈministrətiv; ədˋmɪnəˏstretɪv] *a.* **1.** 管理的;行政的。**2.** 非战斗性行政勤务的。*the Broadcasting A- Bureau* 广播事业局。~ *ability* 行政手腕;管理[经营]才能。*an ~ district* 行政区划。~ **services** **1.** 非战斗性行政勤务。**2.** 行政勤务部队。

ad·min·is·tra·tor [ədˈministreitə; ədˋmɪnəˏstretɚ] *n.* **1.** 管理人;理事;行政官员。**2.** 【法】遗产管理人。**3.** 给药人。**4.** 代管教区的牧师。**-ship** [-ʃip; -ʃɪp] *n.* 管理人[行政官等]之职。

ad·min·is·tra·trix [ədˈministreitriks; ədˏmɪnəˋstretrɪks] *n.* (*pl.* **~es**; **-trices** [-trisiːz; -trɪˏsiz]) **1.** 女管理员。**2.** 【法】女遗产管理人。

ad·mi·ra·ble [ˈædmərəbl; ˋædmərəbl] *a.* **1.** 可钦佩的,可佩服的,可惊叹的。**2.** 美妙的,极好的。**-bly** *ad.* 可赞叹地,美妙地。**-ness** *n.* 美妙。

ad·mi·ral [ˈædmərəl; ˋædmərəl] *n.* **1.** 海军上将;海军将官;舰队司令。**2.** (海军上将所乘的)旗舰。**3.** 渔船队长,商船队长。**4.** 【虫】红[白]纹蝶。*an ~ of the fleet* 〔英〕海军元帅。*a fleet ~* (美海军)五星上将。*an ~ of the navy* 〔苏联〕海军元帅。*a full ~* 海军大将。*a vice ~* 海军中将。*a rear ~* 海军少将。***~'s watch*** 〔美俚〕熟睡一晚(的机会);充分的休息。**-ship** 海军上将[将官]之职。

ad·mi·ral·ty [ˈædmərəlti; ˋædmərəltɪ] *n.* **1.** 海军大将之职。**2.** 〔A-〕〔英〕海军部。**3.** 海事法;海事法庭。**4.** 制海权。*the Board of A-* 〔英〕海军部委员会。*First Lord of the A-* 〔英〕海军大臣。*Lords Commissioners of the A-* 〔英〕海军部委员。~ **cloth** 海军呢。~ **council** 海军将官会议。**A- Court** 〔英〕海事法庭。~ **creeper** 探海锚。~ **mile** 〔英〕海里 = nautical mile. ~ **port** 海军要塞。

ad·mi·ra·tion [ˌædməˈreiʃən; ˏædməˋreʃən] *n.* **1.** 赞美,钦佩,羡慕,佩服 (*for*)。**2.** 人人赞美的人[物]。*a note of ~* 感叹号(!) ***be struck with*** ~ 惊叹,赞叹。***do sth. to*** ~ 把某事做得极好。***in*** ~ ***of*** 赞美,赏识。***to*** ~ 美满地 (*He has succeeded to ~.* 他已美满地成功了)。***with*** ~ 用惊叹[羡慕]的神气。

ad·mire [ədˈmaiə; ədˋmaɪr] *vt.* **1.** 赞美,称赞,钦佩,羡慕;崇拜。**2.** 〔口〕夸奖,褒奖。**3.** 〔美口〕想要,喜欢;欣赏。*I'd ~ to go.* 我很想去。*He ~s her for her finished manner.* 他羡慕她的文明礼貌。*I ~ his impudence.* 〔反〕我佩服他的脸厚。—*vi.* 〔古〕惊异 (*at*)。

ad·mir·er [ədˈmaiərə; ədˋmaɪrɚ] *n.* 赞美者,敬慕者;情人。

ad·mir·ing [ədˈmaiəriŋ; ədˋmaɪrɪŋ] *a.* 赞美的,羡慕的。**-ly** *ad.*

ad·mis·si·bil·i·ty [ədˌmisəˈbiliti; ədˏmɪsəˋbɪlətɪ] *n.* **1.** 许入;许进。**2.** 准许;可接受。

ad·mis·si·ble [ədˈmisəbl; ədˋmɪsəbl] *a.* **1.** 许进的。**2.** 可采纳的,可接受的。**3.** 有资格加入的 (*to*): *an ~ piece of evidence* 可接受的证据。~ *to an office* 有资格担任某职务。**-bly** *ad.*

ad·mis·sion [ədˈmiʃən; ədˋmɪʃən] *n.* **1.** 允许进入,许可入场[入学、入会];入场[入会]费。**2.** 承认;招认,坦白;首肯。*A- by ticket only.* 凭票入场。*grant sb. ~* 允许某人进入。~ *of blame* 承认罪过。**by** [**on**] **sb.'s own** ~ 据某人自己承认[供认]。***gain*** [***obtain***] ~ ***to*** [***into***] 获准进入。***grant sb.*** ~准许进入。~ ***free*** 免费入场,自由入场。***A- Day*** 〔美〕加邦节〔各州加入联邦的纪念日〕。~ **tickets** 入场券。~ **valves** 进气阀。

ad·mis·sive [ədˈmisiv; ædˋmɪsɪv] *a.* 许入的,入场的;容许有…的(*of*)。

ad·mit [ədˈmit; ədˋmɪt] *vt.* (**-mit·ted**; **-mit·ting**) **1.** 接受,许可入场〔入会、入学、入院〕。**2.** 承认,容许(辩解)。**3.** 收容,容纳。~ *sb. to the third year class* 许某人入三年级。*I ~ that I was wrong.* 我承认我错了。*To ~ one.* (门票)只许一人入场。— *vi.* **1.** 容许 (*of*)。**2.** 通向,通到 (*to*)。**3.** 承认 (*to*)。*This, I ~, is true.* 这的确是真的。*This key ~s to the house.* 这把钥匙能进这间屋子。~ **of** 容许,有…可能,容有…的余地 (~ *of improvement* 有改良的余地。~ *of no reply* 无从答覆。~ *of no excuse* 无可推诿,无可宽恕)。***be ~ted to bail*** 【法】准许保释。***be ~ted to the bar*** 〔美〕取得律师资格。(***while***) ~***ting that ...***, 虽说,即使。

ad·mit·ta·ble [ədˈmitəbl; ədˋmɪtəbl] *a.* 可接受的;可容许的。

ad·mit·tance [ədˈmitəns; ədˋmɪtns] *n.* **1.** 许可入场[入校等]。**2.** 【建】通道。**3.** 【物】导纳。*have free ~ to the theatre* 可免费进入剧场。***gain*** [***get***] ~ ***to*** 准入…,进入…。***No*** ~ (***except on business***) (闲人)免进,(非公)莫入。~ **function** 【物】导纳函数。

ad·mit·ted [ədˈmitid; ədˋmɪtɪd] *a.* 被承认了的;(事实)公认的,明白的。**-ly** *ad.* 明白地 (*I am admittedly afraid.* 我公开表示害怕了)。

ad·mix [ədˈmiks; ædˋmɪks] *vt.*, *vi.* 搀合,混合 (*with*)。

ad·mix·ture [ədˈmikstʃə; ædˋmɪkstʃɚ] *n.* **1.** 混合,搀合。**2.** 混合物,搀合料[剂];外加物。

ad·mon·ish [ədˈmɔniʃ; ədˋmɑnɪʃ] *vt.* **1.** 忠告[劝告](某人做某事)〔后接不定式;劝告不做某事后接 not 加不定式或接 against 加动名词〕。**2.** 为某事 (*for*, *of*) 告诫某人。**3.** 警告某人(有危险等) (*of*)。**4.** 敦促、提醒某人

A

(尽义务等)(*of*, *about*)。**5.** 要求、催办(某事)。*The teacher* ~*ed the students against being late*. 老师劝告学生不要迟到。~ *sb. of a danger* 警告某人注意危险。~ *silence* 安静一点。**-ment** ***n.***

ad·mo·ni·tion [ˌædməuˈniʃən; ˏædməˋnɪʃən] ***n.*** **1.** 训诫,忠告。**2.** 温和的责备。

ad·mon·i·tor [ədˈmɔnitə; ədˋmɑnətɚ] ***n.*** 劝告者,忠告者,训诫者。

ad·mon·i·to·ry [ədˈmɔnitəri; ədˋmɑnəˏtorɪ] ***a.*** **1.** 劝告的,忠告的。**2.** 责备的。

A.D.M.S. = Assistant Director of Medical Services 〔英〕助理军医局长。

ADN = 〔G.〕*Allgemeine Deutsche Nachrichtendienst* 德意志通讯社。

ad·noun [ˈædnaun; ˋædˏnaun] ***n.*** 【语法】作名词用的形容词〔例: *The new* supersedes *the old*. 新陈代谢〕。

a·do [əˈduː; əˋdu] ***n.*** 骚扰,无谓的纷扰,忙乱;费力,艰难。***make* [*have*] *much* ~** 大忙一阵,费尽心力(*He had much* ~ *in finding out his lodging*. 他费尽力气才找到住处)。***make much* ~ *about nothing*** 无事生非,小题大作。***once for* ~** 只一次,一劳永逸。***with much* ~** 煞费苦心,费尽心血,好容易才。***without more* [*future*] ~** 以后毫不费力,以后立即(*He paid up without any more* ~. 他不再啰嗦就付了钱)。

-a·do *suf.* 来自西班牙语的名词的词尾: brav*ado*, desper*ado*.

a·do·be [əˈdəubi; əˋdobɪ] **I** ***n.*** **1.** 砖坯。**2.** 土砖砌成的房子[土墙]。**3.** (制)砖(黏)土。**II** ***a.*** 用砖坯砌的。~ **dollar** 〔口〕墨西哥银币。~ **soil** 龟裂土。

ad·o·les·cence [ˌædəuˈlesns; ˏædlˋɛsns], **-cen·cy** [-si; -sɪ] ***n.*** 青年期,青春期,青春。

ad·o·les·cent [ˌædəuˈlesnt; ˏædlˋɛsnt] **I** ***a.*** 青年期的,青春期的。**II** ***n.*** 少年,少女。

Ad·olf, Ad·olph [ˈædɔlf; ˋædɑlf] ***n.*** 阿道夫〔男子名〕。

Ad·ol·phus [əˈdɔlfəs; əˋdɑlfəs] ***n.*** 阿道弗斯〔男子名〕。

ad·o·nai [ˌædəuˈneii; ˏadoˋnaɪ] 〔Heb.〕上帝,天主〔在希伯来语的著述中为"耶和华"的代用词〕。

A·don·is [əˈdəunis; əˋdonɪs] ***n.*** **1.** 【希神】阿多尼斯;爱神〔Venus 钟爱的美貌猎人〕;美男子。**2.** 【植】侧金盏花。**3.** 〔英〕一种蝶。

ad·o·nize [ˈædənaiz; ˋædəˏnaɪz] ***vt.***, ***vi.*** 打扮,装饰〔指男人〕。~ *oneself* (男人)打扮,装扮。

a·dopt [əˈdɔpt; əˋdɑpt] ***vt.*** **1.** 采用,采纳;正式通过。**2.** 选定(道路、职业等);采取(立场等)。**3.** 【语】沿用,借用(别国语言等)。**4.** 收养,立嗣,过继。~ *a proposal* 采纳提议。*words* ~*ed from a foreign language* 外来语。~ **out** 〔美〕将(孩子)给人收养。**-a·ble** ***a.*** 可采用的;可沿用的;可收养的。**-er** ***n.*** 采纳者;接受器。

a·dopt·ed [əˈdɔptid; əˋdɑptɪd] ***a.*** 收养的,过继的。*an* ~ *son* [*daughter*] 养子[女],义子[女]。*my* ~ *country* 我所入籍的国家。~ *words* 外来语。

a·dop·tion [əˈdɔpʃən; əˋdɑpʃən] ***n.*** **1.** 接受,采用。**2.** 继嗣,过继。**3.** (外国语的)借用。**4.** (候选人的)指定。

a·dop·tive [əˈdɔptiv; əˋdɑptɪv] ***a.*** **1.** 采用的。**2.** 收养的,继嗣的,过继的。**3.** 倾向于采用的。**4.** 假冒的。*an* ~ *father* [*son*] 养父[子],义父[子]。*an* ~ *disposition* 耳朵根子软的人。*an* ~ *courage* 假充勇敢。

a·dor·a·ble [əˈdɔːrəbl; əˋdorəbl] ***a.*** 值得崇拜的,值得敬慕的;〔口〕可爱的。**-a·bly** [-bli; -blɪ] ***ad.*** 崇拜,敬重;可爱。

ad·o·ra·tion [ˌædɔːˈreiʃən; ˏædəˋreʃən] ***n.*** **1.** 崇拜,崇敬;礼拜。**2.** 敬爱,爱慕。***in*** ~ 赞叹着,崇拜着,颂扬着。

a·dore [əˈdɔː; əˋdor] ***vt.*** **1.** 崇拜,崇敬。**2.** 敬慕,爱慕;〔口〕很欢喜。

a·dor·er [əˈdɔːrə; əˋdorɚ] ***n.*** 崇拜者;爱慕者。

a·dor·ing [əˈdɔriŋ; əˋdorɪŋ] ***a.*** 崇拜的;敬慕的,爱慕的。**-ly** ***ad.***

a·dorn [əˈdɔːn; əˋdɔrn] ***vt.*** 装饰,修饰,佩戴。~ (*a room*) ***with*** (*flowers*) 用(花)装饰(屋子),~ ***oneself with*** (*jewels*) 佩戴(宝石)。

a·dorn·ment [əˈdɔːnmənt; əˋdɔrnmənt] ***n.*** **1.** 装饰。**2.** 〔有时可用 *pl.*〕装饰品。*personal* ~ 装饰。

ad·os·cu·la·tion [əˌdɔskjuˈleiʃən; əˏdɑskjʊˋleʃən] ***n.*** 【医】体外受精。

a·down [əˈdaun; əˋdaun] ***ad.***, ***prep.*** 〔诗〕= down.

ADP = 【化】Adenosine diphosphate 二磷酸腺苷。

ad·person [ˈædpəsn; ˋædpɝsn] ***n.*** (*pl.* ***ad·people*** [ˈædpiːpl; ˋædpipl]) 广告商。

ADPS = automatic data-processing system 自动数据处理系统。

ad·re·nal [əˈdriːnl; əˋdrinl] **I** ***n.*** 肾上腺。**II** ***a.*** 肾脏附近的;肾上腺的。~ **gland** 肾上腺。

ad·ren·al·in(e) [əˈdrenəlin; æˋdrɛnlɪn] ***n.*** 【生】肾上腺素。

ad·ren·er·gic [ˌædriˈnəːdʒik; ˏædrɪˋnɝdʒɪk] ***a.*** 【医】肾上腺素能的。

ad·re·no·cor·ti·cal [əˌdriːnəuˈkɔːtikl; əˏdrinoˋkɔrtəkl] ***a.*** 肾上腺皮质的。

ad·re·no·cor·ti·co·tro·phic [əˌdriːnəuˌkɔːtikəuˈtrɔfik; əˏdrinoˏkɔrtəkoˋtrɑfɪk], **-tro·pic** [-pik; -pɪk] ***a.*** 【医】促肾上腺皮质的。

A·dri·an [ˈeidriən; ˋedrɪən] ***n.*** 埃德里安〔姓氏,男子名〕。

A·dri·at·ic [eidriˈætik; ˏedrɪˋætɪk] ***a.*** 亚得里亚海的。***the*** ~ (***sea***) 亚得里亚海。

A·dri·enne [ˈeidrien; ˋedrɪɛn] ***n.*** 埃德里安娜〔女子名〕。

a·drift [əˈdrift; əˋdrɪft] **I** ***a.*** 〔作述语用〕**II** ***ad.*** **1.** 飘浮,漂流无定〔指船〕。**2.** 〔喻〕飘泊(无定);无定职。**3.** 〔口〕孤陋寡闻 ***be all*** ~ 莫名其妙的;茫然失措的。***get*** ~ (随风)漂流。***go*** ~ 漂流;〔喻〕脱节。***set*** ~ 使(船)随风飘流。***turn*** (*sb.*) ~ 逐出(某人),使漂泊无依,免职,辞退。

a·droit [əˈdrɔit; əˋdrɔɪt] ***a.*** 熟练的,灵巧的,敏捷的,机灵的。~ *handling of an awkward situation* 巧妙地处理尴尬的局面。***be*** ~ ***in*** [***at***] 善于。**-ly** ***ad.*** **-ness** ***n.***

a·dry [əˈdrai; əˋdraɪ] ***a.***, ***ad.*** 〔古〕干;渴。

ad·sci·ti·tious [ˌædsiˈtiʃəs; ˏædsɪˋtɪʃəs] ***a.*** 追加的,附加的,补充的;外来的。*an* ~ *habit* 后天的习性。~ *remarks* 补充发言。

ad·script [ˈædskript; ˋædskrɪpt] ***a.*** 〔L.〕书写于后的。

ad·scrip·tion [ædˈskripʃn; ædˋskrɪpʃn] ***n.*** 隶属(= ascription)。

ad·scrip·tus gle·bae [ædsˈkriptəs ˈgliːbi; ædˋskrɪptəs ˋglibɪ] 〔L.〕(农奴)附属在土地上的。

ADSL = asynchronous digital subscriber line 【自】异步数字用户专线。

ad-smith [ˈædsmiθ; ˋædsmɪθ] ***n.*** 〔美谑〕广告写作者。

ad·sorb [ædˈsɔːb; ædˋsɔrb] ***vt.*** 【化】吸附。

ad·sor·bate [ædˈsɔːbeit; ædˋsɔrbet] ***n.*** 【化】被吸附物。

ad·sor·bent [ædˈsɔːbənt; ædˋsɔrbənt] **I** ***a.*** 有吸附力的。**II** ***n.*** 吸附剂。

ad·sorp·tion [ædˈsɔːpʃən; ædˋsɔrpʃən] ***n.*** 【化】吸附(作用)。

ad·su·ki bean [ædˈzuːki biːn; ædˋzukɪ bin] ***n.*** 小豆,赤豆(= adzuki bean)。

ad·sum [ˈædsʌm; ˋædsʌm] ***int.*** 〔L.〕到,有〔点名时的回答〕。

ad·u·lar·i·a [ˌædjuˈlɛəriə; ˏædʒəˋlɛrɪə] ***n.*** 【地】冰长石。

ad·u·late [ˈædjuleit; ˋædʒəˏlet] ***vt.*** 谄媚,奉承,拍…的马屁。**ad·u·la·tion** [ˌædjuˈleiʃən; ˏædʒəˋleʃən] ***n.***

ad·u·la·tor [ˈædjuleitə; ˋædʒəletɚ] ***n.*** 拍马屁的人。**-y** [-ri; -rɪ] ***a.*** 奉承的。

A·dul·lam·ite [əˈdʌləmait; əˋdʌləmaɪt] ***n.*** 【英史】转党

党员;退党议员〔指1886年英国下议院中因议会改革问题而退出自由党并加入保守党的议员〕。

a·dult [ˈædʌlt; ˋædʌlt] **I** *a*. **1**. 已成人的,成年人的。**2**. 老成的,已成熟的。**3**. 适合成年人阅读[观看]的。**II** *n*. **1**. 成年人。**2**.【生】成体;成虫。~ **day care** (为老人等提供的)成人日托服务。~ **education** 成人教育。~ **tooth** 固齿。**-hood** *n*. 成年。**-ly** *ad*.

a·dul·ter·ant [əˈdʌltərənt; əˋdʌltərənt] **I** *a*. 搀杂用的。**II** *n*. 搀杂物,搀杂剂。

a·dul·ter·ate [əˈdʌltəreit; əˋdʌltəˏret] **I** *vt*. 搀,兑,搀杂。~ *milk with water* 奶中兑水。**II** *a*. **1**. 私通的,通奸的。**2**. 搀假的;伪的,假的。~ *coin* 伪币。

a·dul·ter·a·tion [əˌdʌltəˈreiʃən; əˏdʌltəˋreʃən] *n*. 搀杂;伪造;冒牌货。

a·dul·ter·at·or [əˈdʌltəreitə; əˋdʌltəˏretɚ] *n*. 搀假者;伪造者。

a·dul·ter·er [əˈdʌltərə; əˋdʌltərɚ] *n*. 奸夫。

a·dul·ter·ess [əˈdʌltəris; əˋdʌltərɪs] *n*. 奸妇。

a·dul·ter·ine [əˈdʌltərain; əˋdʌltərɪn] **I** *a*. **1**. 苟合的,通奸的,通奸所生的。**2**. 不正当的,非法的。**3**. 伪造的;不纯的。*an* ~ *child* 私生子。~ *drugs* 伪劣药品。**II** *n*. 私生子。

a·dul·ter·ous [əˈdʌltərəs; əˋdʌltərəs] *a*. **1**. 私通的,通奸的;不正当的。**2**. 〔古〕搀过假的。

a·dul·ter·y [əˈdʌltəri; əˋdʌltərɪ] *n*. 通奸,私通。

a·dul·toid [ˈædʌltɔid; ˋædʌltɔɪd] *n*.【生】未熟成虫[体]。

ad·um·bral [æˈdʌmbrəl; æˋdʌmbrəl] *a*. 荫蔽的;在阴影里的,在暗处的。

ad·um·brate [ˈædʌmbreit; ˋædʌmbret] *vt*. **1**. 画…的轮廓,勾画。**2**. 暗示;预示。**3**. 遮蔽,遮暗,在…上投下阴影。

ad·um·bra·tion [ˌædʌmˈbreiʃən; ˏædəmˋbreʃən] *n*. **1**. 勾画;草图,轮廓。**2**. 阴影。**3**. 预示,预兆。

ad·um·bra·tive [æˈdʌmbrətiv; æˋdʌmbrətɪv] *a*. 轻描淡写的;暗示的;投影的。

a·dunc [əˈdʌŋk; əˋdʌŋk] *a*. 向内弯曲的〔如鹦鹉嘴〕。

a·dust [əˈdʌst; əˋdʌst] *a*. **1**. 烘焦了的,晒黑了的。**2**. 忧郁的,阴沉的。

adv. = *ad valorem* (= according to the price); advance; adverb; adverbial; advertisement; advocate.

ad·vance [ədˈvɑːns; ədˋvæns] **I** *vt*. **1**. 进,推进;促进(生长),助长;拨进(时针),增进;提早,提前。**2**. 使升级,提升。**3**. 提高,抬高,涨,加(价等)。**4**. 提出(意见等),提倡。**5**. 预付,预支;借贷。**6**. 前去(某地)做先遣工作。~ *the hour hand* 向前拨动时针。~ *sb. to the rank of colonel* 提升某人为上校。~ *sb. a month's salary* 预支给某人一个月的薪水。— *vi*. **1**. 推进,上进,前进,向前发展,进步。**2**. 提高,晋升。**3**. 涨价,腾贵。**4**.【军】前进,进攻 (*against*; *on*; *upon*)。**5**. 从事先遣工作。**6**. (颜色等)醒目。~ *in price* 涨价。~ *in knowledge* 增进知识。~ *in rank* 升级。*deep colours* ~ 深的颜色醒目。~ ***by rushes*** 突飞猛进。~ ***in the world*** 发迹,出头。~ ***on*** [***toward***] ***a place*** 向某地推进。**II** *n*. **1**. 前进,进展;增进,进步;向上,晋升 (*in rank*)。**2**. 腾贵,昂贵,上涨。**3**. 预付;垫款,贷出款项。**4**. 〔常 *pl*.〕接近;友好的表示;求爱。**5**.【军】前进,进攻。**6**. 事先写好的新闻报导。*encourage* [*repel*] *sb's* ~*s* 鼓励[阻碍]某人接近自己。*academic* ~*s* 学术成就。*an* ~ *sample* 订货小样。*His* ~*s were rejected*. 他的友好的表示被拒绝了。*Sound the* ~. 奏进行曲,吹前进号。*a temporary* ~ 暂垫款。***be in*** ~ ***of*** 在…之前;比…进步;高出,优于,胜过 (*He is far in* ~ *of his class*. 他在班上是尖子)。***be on the*** ~ 渐涨。***in*** ~ **1**. 预先,事先。**2**. 在先头,在前面 (*pay in* ~ 预付。*receive in* ~ 预收)。***make*** ~ **1**. 垫款,先付,预付。**2**. 接近(某人);表示友好;求爱 (*to*)。***with the*** ~ ***of*** 与…俱进地,因(年)老而,因(夜)深而。**III** *a*. 〔只作修饰语〕前进的;先头的;预先的。~ **copy** (征求意见的)新书样本。~ **guard**【军】前卫,先锋。~ **man** (为政界候选人到某地前进行联系和做好安排的)先遣人员;〔美〕(剧团等的)先遣宣传员。~ **sheets** 样本,样页,样张。

ad·vanced [ədˈvɑːnst; ədˋvænst] *a*. **1**. 前进的,先驱的;高等的,高深的。**2**. 先进的。**3**. (年纪)老的,(夜)深的。*most* ~ *branches of science and technology* 尖端科学技术。*rather an* ~ *young woman* 较先进的妇女。*a man* ~ *in years* 老年人。~ *age* 高龄。~ *grammar* 高等语法。~ *ideas* 进步思想。~ *post* 前哨。~ *studies* 高等[先进]的学术研究。*a culturally* ~ *country* 高度文明的国家。

ad·vance·ment [ədˈvɑːnsmənt; ədˋvænsmənt] *n*. **1**. 前进;促进;进步,发达。**2**. 升级;发迹;出头。**3**. 预付;垫付。

ad·vance-trenches [ədˈvɑːnstrenʧiz; ədˋvænstrenʧɪz] *n*. 〔*pl*.〕火线上的战壕,前哨壕沟。

ad·van·tage [ədˈvɑːntidʒ; ədˋvæntɪdʒ] **I** *n*. **1**. 利益,裨益;好处。**2**. 优点,长处,优越性,有利方面;优胜,优势。**3**.【网球】打成平手 (deuce) 而延长比赛后一方先得的一分(= vantage)。*personal* ~*s* 美貌。***be of great*** [***no***] ~ ***to*** 对…大大有利[毫无裨益]。***gain*** [***get, have, win***] ***an*** ~ ***over*** [***of***] 胜过,优于。***have the*** ~ 有…的利益;比…强,胜过;占上风,较…有利 (*You have the* ~ *of me*. **1**. 你比我强。**2**. 您还认识我,我不认识您了,您是哪一位?)。***take*** ~ ***of*** **1**. 乘,趁;利用。**2**. 欺骗;引诱(女人)。***take*** (***sb.***) ***at*** ~ 乘(人)不备,乘(人之)虚而抢先。***to*** ~ (因比较或衬托而)更加,越发 (*Her dress showed her beautiful figure to* ~. 她的衣服使她显得更加苗条)。***to sb.'s*** ~ = ***to the*** ~ ***of*** 对…有利地。***turn out to sb.'s*** ~ 变得对某人有利。***turn to*** ~ 使转化为有利。***with*** ~ 有利地,有效地。**II** *vt*. 有利于,有益于,有助于。*Such action will* ~ *our cause*. 这样的行动有益于我们的事业。~ **law** 有利规则〔在橄榄球等比赛中,一方犯规时裁判可因场上形势对被侵犯一方有利而不裁定停判罚的规定〕。**-d** *a*. 占优势的,处于有利地位的。

ad·van·ta·geous [ˌædvənˈteidʒəs; ˏædvənˋtedʒəs] *a*. 有利的。**-ly** *ad*. **-ness** *n*.

ad·vec·tion [ədˈvekʃən; ædˋvɛkʃən] *n*. (热的)对流;(空气的)平流。**-vec·tive** [-tiv; -tɪv] *a*.

ad·vent [ˈædvənt; ˋædvənt] *n*. **1**. (季节、事件等的)到来,出现。**2**. 〔A-〕耶稣降临;降临节。***since the*** ~ ***of*** 自…出现以来。**Ad·vent·ism** *n*. 耶稣再生论。**Ad·ventist** *n*. 耶稣再生论者。

ad·ven·ti·tia [ˌædvenˈtiʃjə, -ʃiə, -ʃə; ædvenˋtɪʃjə, -ʃɪə, -ʃə] *n*.【解】外膜。

ad·ven·ti·tious [ˌædvenˈtiʃəs; ˏædvenˋtɪʃəs] *a*. **1**. 偶然的;外来的。**2**.【生】不定的,偶生的;获得的,非遗传的。**3**.【医】偶发的。~ **buds** 不定芽。~ **root** 不定根。~ **plants** 新引种植物,外来植物。**-ly** *ad*.

ad·ven·tive [ædˈventiv; ædˋvɛntɪv] **I** *a*. 非本土的,外来的,引进的。**II** *n*. (动植物的)非本地生物,引进品种。

ad·ven·ture [ədˈventʃə; ədˋvɛntʃɚ] **I** *n*. **1**. 冒险。**2**. 奇遇。**3**.【商】投机。**4**. 冒险性格。*What an* ~! 啊呀,真了不得。*a singular* ~ 怪事。*go through strange* ~*s* 遍历奇险。**II** *vt*. **1**. 以…冒险。**2**. 大胆提出,大胆进行。~ *one's life on it* 拼着性命去干。~ *a proposal* 大胆提出建议。—*vi*. 冒险。**-tur·er** *n*. 冒险家;投机分子。**-tur·ism** *n*. 冒险主义。

ad·ven·ture·some [ədˈventʃəsəm; ədˋvɛntʃɚsəm] *a*. 冒险的。

ad·ven·tur·ess [ədˈventʃəris; ədˋvɛntʃərɪs] *n*. 女冒险家,女投机分子。

ad·ven·tur·ous [ədˈventʃərəs; ədˋvɛntʃərəs] *a*. **1**. 爱冒险的;胆大的。**2**. 冒险的;危险的。**-ly** *ad*. **-ness** *n*.

A

ad·verb [ˈædvəːb; ˋædvɚb] ***n*.**【语法】副词。*relative* [*interrogative*] ~ 关系[疑问]副词。

ad·ver·bi·al [ədˈvəːbjəl; ædˋvɚbɪəl] **I** ***a*.** 副词的;状语的。*an* ~ *clause* [*phrase*] 副词子句[片语]。~ *equivalents* 副词同等词。**II** ***n*.** 副词类。**-ly** ***ad*.**

ad·ver·sar·y [ˈædvəsəri; ˋædvɚˌsɛrɪ] ***n*.** **1.** 敌手,对手,反对者。**2.** 〔*the* A-〕魔鬼。*an imaginary* ~ 假想敌。

ad·ver·sa·tive [ədˈvəːsətiv; ədˋvɚsətɪv] **I** ***a*.** (词等)意义相反的。**II** ***n*.**【语法】反意语〔如 but, yet 等〕。**-ly** ***ad*.**

ad·verse [ˈædvəːs; ˋædvɚs] ***a*.** **1.** 逆的 L 反对的,相反的。**2.** 不利的,有害的,不幸的。**3.** 对面的。**4.**【植】对生的。~ *circumstances* 逆境。~ *criticisms* 恶评,非难。~ *fate* [*fortune*] 倒霉。*the* ~ *page* 对面的一页。~ *trade balance* 入超。~ *wind* 逆风。**be ~ to** 反对;不利于。**-ly** ***ad*.** 逆,反对地,相反地;不利,不幸(*act* ~ *to sb.'s interests* 举动对某人不利)。**-ness** ***n*.** 逆,反对;不利,不幸。

ad·ver·si·ty [ədˈvəːsiti; ədˋvɚsətɪ] ***n*.** 逆境,苦难,不幸。*Sweet are the uses of* ~. 常常是苦尽甘来。*the prosperities and adversities of this life* 人生的荣辱盛衰。**in** [**under**] ~ 在艰难中,在患难中,倒霉时候。

ad·vert[1] [ədˈvəːt; ədˋvɚt] ***vi*.** 留意,注意;提到,谈到(*to*)。*He* ~*ed briefly to the news of the day*. 他简短地谈到当天的消息。

advert[2] [ˈædvəːt; ˋædvɚt] ***n*.** 〔英口〕= advertisement.

ad·ver·tise [ˈædvətaiz, Am. ˌædvəˈtaiz; ˋædvɚˌtaɪz, ˏædvɚˋtaɪz] ***vt*.** **1.** 为…做广告。**2.** 通告,通知(*of*)。**3.** 宣扬。~ *a reward* 登悬赏广告。~ (*sth*.) *by posters* 用招贴为某物做广告。— ***vi*.** 登广告,做广告。~ ***for*** 登招请[待聘等]广告。~ ***oneself*** (***as***) 自吹(是)。

ad·ver·tise·ment [ədˈvəːtismənt, Am. ˌædvəːˈtaizmənt; ədˋvɚtɪzmənt, ˏædvɚˋtaɪzmənt] ***n*.** **1.** 做广告,登广告。**2.** 广告,公告;告示。

ad·ver·tis·er [ˈædvətaizə; ˋædvɚˌtaɪzɚ] ***n*.** **1.** 登广告的人,广告客户。**2.** 〔A-〕(以广告为主的)…报。*the Japan A-*《日本广告报》。

ad·ver·tis·ing [ˈædvətaiziŋ; ˋædvɚˌtaɪzɪŋ] **I** ***a*.** 广告(业)的。*an* ~ *agency* 广告公司。*the* ~ *pages* (报上的)广告版。**II** ***n*.** **1.** 〔集合词〕广告。**2.** 做广告,登广告。**3.** 广告业[技术]。~ **man** = adman.

ad·ver·tize = advertise.

ad·vice [ədˈvais; ədˋvaɪs] ***n*.** **1.** 忠告,劝告;建议;指教。**2.** (医生等的)诊察,意见。**3.** 〔常 *pl*.〕(政治、外交上的)报导,报告。**4.**【商】通知。*an* ~ *note* 通知单。*a remittance* ~ 汇款通知。~*s from foreign countries* 来自国外的报导。*a written* ~ 劝告书。***act on*** ~ 依劝。***ask*** ~ ***of*** 向…征求意见,请教,领教。***by*** [***on***] ***sb.'s*** ~ 依某人劝告。***follow sb.'s*** ~ 接受某人意见。***give*** [***tender***] ~ 劝告,忠告。***take*** ~ 征求意见,请教,领教(*take medical* ~ 请医生诊视)。***take sb.'s*** ~ = follow sb.'s ~.

ad·vis·a·bil·i·ty [ədˌvaizəˈbiliti; ədˏvaɪzəˋbɪlətɪ] ***n*.** 可劝告;适当,得当。

ad·vis·a·ble [ədˈvaizəbl; ədˋvaɪzəbl] ***a*.** 能劝告的,适当的,可取的。*an* ~ *course* 可取的方针。*Is it* ~ *for me to write to him?* 我给他写信合适吗? **-ness** ***n*.**

ad·vis·a·bly [ədˈvaizəbli; ədˋvaɪzəblɪ] ***ad*.** 得当,适当。

ad·vise [ədˈvaiz; ədˋvaɪz] ***vt*.** **1.** 忠告,劝告,建议。**2.**【商】通告,通知。~ *sb. against smoking* = ~ *sb. not to smoke* 劝告某人不要吸烟。— ***vi*.** **1.** 商量。**2.** 提出劝告。~ ***each other*** 互提意见。~ (*sb*.) ***of*** (*sth*.) 把(某事)通知[报告](某人)。~ ***with*** (*sb*.) ***on*** [***about***] (*sth*.) 和(某人)商量(某事)。***A- with your pillow***. 好好考虑一宵。

ad·vised [ədˈvaizd; ədˋvaɪzd] ***a*.** **1.** 考虑过的,细想过的〔今多用于构成复合词〕。**2.** 消息灵通的。*well-* ~ 深思熟虑的,明智的。*ill-* ~ 失策的,愚蠢的。*be kept thoroughly* ~ 消息十分灵通。

ad·vis·ed·ly [ədˈvaizidli; ədˋvaɪzɪdlɪ] ***ad*.** 深思熟虑地;故意地。

ad·vise·ment [ədˈvaizmənt; ədˋvaɪzmənt] ***n*.** **1.** 劝告,意见,忠告。**2.** 考虑;深思熟虑。*take the application under* ~ 仔细考虑该项申请。

ad·vis·er, ad·vi·sor [ədˈvaizə; ədˋvaɪzɚ] ***n*.** **1.** 劝告者,顾问。**2.** (美大学)指导教授,导师。*a legal* ~ 法律顾问。*an* ~ *to the President* 总统顾问。

ad·vi·so·ry [ədˈvaizəri; ədˋvaɪzərɪ] ***a*.** **1.** 劝告的,忠告的。**2.** 顾问的,咨询的。*an* ~ *body* 咨询机关,顾问团。*an* ~ *committee* 咨询委员会。*He accompanied the President in an* ~ *capacity*. 他以顾问身份做总统随行人员。

ad·vo·ca·cy [ˈædvəkəsi; ˋædvəkəsɪ] ***n*.** 拥护;鼓吹;主张,辩护。*speak in* ~ *of* 为…辩护。

ad·vo·cate [ˈædvəkit; ˋædvəkɪt] **I** ***n*.** **1.** 拥护者,鼓吹者,提倡者。**2.** 律师。*an* ~ *of* [*for*] *peace* 和平的鼓吹者。~*s of military gambles* 军事冒险分子。***the devil's*** ~ **1.** 〔罗马天主教会〕负责指出加入圣列的死者的缺点的教吏。**2.** 明知不对而争论不休的人。***the Judge A-***【陆军】军法官。***the Lord A-*** 〔Scot.〕检察长。**II** [ˈædvəkeit; ˋædvəket] ***vt*.** 拥护;鼓吹;提倡;主张;辩护。

ad·vo·ca·tion [ˌædvəˈkeiʃən; ˏædvəˋkeʃən] ***n*.** **1.** 〔废〕辩护。**2.** (苏格兰和罗马教庭)高级法院从初级法院提取自行审理的悬案。

ad·vo·ca·tor [ˈædvəkeitə; ˋædvəˏketɚ] ***n*.** 拥护者,鼓吹者,提倡者,辩护者。

ad·voc·a·to·ry [ædˈvɔkəˌtəri; ædˋvɑkəˏtorɪ] ***a*.** **1.** 辩护士的。**2.** 辩护的;鼓吹的。

ad·vo·ca·tus di·a·bo·li [ˌædvəˈkeitəs daiˈæbəlai; ˏædvəˋketəs daɪˋæbəlaɪ] 〔L.〕= devil's advocate.

ad·y·na·mia [ˌædiˈneimiə; ˏædɪˋnemɪə] ***n*.**【医】虚弱,无力,衰竭。

ad·y·nam·ic [ˌædaiˈnæmik; ˏædaɪˋnæmɪk] ***a*.** 衰弱的,虚弱的。

ad·y·tum [ˈæditəm; ˋædɪtəm] ***n*.** (*pl*. ***-ta*** [-tə; -tə]) (古代庙宇中的)内殿,内院;密室,私室。

adz, adze [ædz; ædz] **I** ***n*.** 手斧,锛子。**II** ***vt*.** 用锛子锛,用手斧劈。

ad·zu·ki bean [ædˈzuːki biːn; ædˋzukɪ bin] ***n*.** 小豆,赤豆。

æ 拉丁语和拉丁化了的希腊语中常见的连体字 (ligature);英语中,除固有名词(如 Cæsar, Æsop)而外,常写作 ae,有时略为 e.

***ae*.** = *aetatis*.

ae [ei; e] ***a*.** 〔Scot〕. = one.

A.E.A. = Atomic Energy Authority 〔英〕原子能管理局。

A. E. and P. = Ambassador Extraordinary and Plenipotentiary 特命全权大使。

AEC = Atomic Energy Commission 〔美〕原子能委员会。

ae·cid·i·um [iːˈsidiəm; iˋsɪdɪəm] ***n*.** (*pl*. ***-cid·i·a*** [-ˈsidiə; -ˋsɪdɪə])【植】锈孢子器。**-cid·i·al** ***a*.**

ae·ci·o·stage [ˈiːsiəsteidʒ; ˋisɪəstedʒ] ***n*.** 锈孢子器产生期。

ae·ci·um [ˈiːsiəm; ˋisɪəm] ***n*.** (*pl*. ***-ci·a*** [-iə; -ɪə])【植】锈孢子器。**ae·ci·al** ***a*.**

a·ë·des [eiˈiːdiːz; eˋidiz] ***n*.** (*pl*. ~) 伊蚊属蚊子,〔尤指埃及伊蚊〕。

***aeg*.** = 〔L.〕*aeger* (= *ill*).

Ae·ge·an [i(ː)ˈdʒiːən; iˋdʒiən] ***a*.** 爱琴海的。***the*** ~ ***Sea*** 爱琴海。

ae·ger [ˈiːdʒə; ˋidʒɚ] ***n*.** (若干英国与加拿大大学证明学

生因病不能考试的)诊断证明书。

ae·gis [ˈiːdʒis; ˋidʒɪs] ***n*.** **1.** 保护,掩护,庇护。**2.**【希神】(Zeus 神的)神盾。**3.** 赞助,主办。***under the* ～ *of*** 在…保佑[掩护]下。

A.E.I. = Atomic Energy Institute〔英〕原子能学会。

-aemia *suf*.〔构成名词〕表示"血的状态","血质"。*anaemia*.

Ae·ne·id [ˈiːniid; iˋniɪd] ***n*.**《埃涅伊德》〔罗马诗人 Virgil 所著史诗〕。

a·ë·ne·ous [eiˈiːniəs; eˋinɪəs] ***a*.** 青铜色泽的。

A-en·er·gy [ˈeiˈenədʒi; ˋeˋɛnə·dʒɪ] ***n*.**〔美俚〕原子能(= atomic energy)。

ae·o·li·an [i(ː)ˈəuljən; iˋolɪən] ***a*.** **1.** 风神伊俄勒斯(Aeolus)的。**2.**【地】风成的(= eolian)。**3.** 飕飕作响的。～ **harp** [**lyre**] 风奏琴〔风吹自鸣之琴〕。～ **rock** 风成岩。

Ae·ol·ic [iːˈɔlik; iˋɑlɪk] **I** ***a*.** 伊奥里斯地方的;伊奥里斯人的。**II** ***n*.** 伊奥里斯语。

Ae·o·lis [ˈiːəlis; ˋiəlɪs] ***n*.** 伊奥里斯〔古希腊在小亚细亚西北海岸地区的殖民地〕。

ae·o·lo·trop·ic [ˌiːələuˈtrɔpik; ˏiələˋtrɑpɪk] ***a*.**【物】各向异性的。

ae·o·lot·ro·py [ˌiːəˈlɔtrəpi; ˏiəˋlɑtrəpɪ] ***n*.**【物】各向异性,偏等性。

Ae·o·lus [ˈi(ː)əuləs; ˋiələs] ***n*.**【希神】伊俄勒斯〔风神〕。

ae·on [ˈiːən; ˋiən] = eon.

ae·o·ni·an [iːˈəunjən; iˋonɪən] = eonian.

ae·py·or·nis [ˌiːpiːˈɔːnis; ˏipiˋɔrnɪs] ***n*.** (古时栖于马达加斯加岛的)隆鸟。

aer- *pref*. = aero-

aer·ate [ˈeiəreit; ˋeəˏret] ***vt*.** **1.** 使暴露空气中,使通气。**2.** 使充以空气,打进空气[碳酸气等];向(血液等)供氧。～*d breads* 用二氧化碳发的面包。～*d waters* 汽水。

aer·a·tion [eiəˈreiʃən; ˏeəˋreʃən] ***n*.** **1.** 通风,通气。**2.** (饮料等的)充气,吹风。**3.** (肺中)换气。

aer·a·tor [ˈeiəreitə; ˋeəˏretə] ***n*.** **1.** 充气器,充气装置。**2.** 熏蒸(杀虫)装置。

aeri- *pref*. 表示"空气"= *aeri*form.

aer·i·al [ˈɛəriəl; ˋɛrɪəl] **I** ***a*.** **1.** 空气的,大气的,气体的。**2.** 航空的,空中的。**3.** 空气一样的,空气一样轻的;无形的,空想的。**4.** 高耸空中的;生存在空中的,【植】气生的。～ *music* 梦幻般的音乐。～ *spires* 高耸入云的塔尖。**II** ***n*.** **1.**【无】天线。**2.** 救火云梯。～ **attack** 空袭。～ **barrage** 气球空防。～ **blitz(krieg)** 空中闪击战。～ **bomb** 空投炸弹。～ **cable** 架空电缆。～**-cable way** 索道。～ **camera** 空中摄影照相机。～ **car** 气球吊篮;高架铁道车。～ **cascade** 大气瀑流,急风。～ **chart** 航空图。～ **current** 气流;天线电流。～ **defence** 防空。～ **Derby** 飞行竞赛。～ **farming** 飞机播种[喷药(等)]。～ **fight** 空战。～ **flare** 照明弹。～ **fleet** 空中舰队,航空机队。～ **ladder** 天梯,消防梯。～ **light-house** 航空灯塔。～ **line** 航空线。～ **liner** 定期民航机。～ **mail** [**post**] 航空邮寄。～ **manoeuvre** 空中演习。～ **mine** (用降落伞投下的)空雷。～ **mosaic** 航空照片镶嵌图。～ **navigation** 航空术。～ **navigator** 飞机师,飞行员。～ **parts**【植】地上部分。～ **perspective** 浓淡远近透视法。～ **plant** 气生植物。～ **potato** 马铃薯叶瘤。～ **railway** 架空铁道。～ **root**【植】气生根。～ **ropeway** (架空)索道。～ **route** 空中航线。～ **scout** 空中侦察(者)。～ **sickness** 航空病,晕机。～ **telegraphy** 无线电信术。～ **survey** 航空测量。～ **torpedo** 空投鱼雷。～ **train** 空中列车。～ **transport** 空运。～ **unit** 飞行部队。～ **wire**【无】天线。

aer·i·al·ist [ˈɛəriəlist; ˋɛrɪəlɪst] ***n*.** 空中飞人,(走钢丝等)高空杂技演员。

aer·i·al·i·ty [ˌɛəriˈæliti; ˏɛrɪˋælətɪ] ***n*.** 空气的性质[状态],空虚。

aer·i·al·ly [ˈɛəriəli; ˋɛrɪəlɪ] ***ad*.** 在空中;空气似地,空想地。

aer·ie [ˈɛəri, ˈiəri; ˋɛrɪ, ˋɪrɪ] ***n*.** **1.** (鹰等的)巢。**2.** 集中的雏群。**3.** 高山住屋[城堡等]。**4.**〔古〕孩子。

aer·if·er·ous [ˌɛəˈrifərəs; ɛˋrɪfərəs] ***a*.** 通气的。

aer·i·fi·ca·tion [ˌɛərifiˈkeiʃən; ˏɛrɪfɪˋkeʃən] ***n*.** **1.** 气(体)化。**2.** 充满气体,充气状态。

a·er·i·form [ˈɛərifɔːm; ˋɛrəˏfɔrm] ***a*.** **1.** 气态的;气体的。**2.** 无形的,无实体的;难捉摸的。

aer·i·fy [ˈɛərifai; ˋɛrəˏfaɪ] ***vt*.** **1.** 在…中充注空气(= aerate)。**2.** 使气体化,使与空气化合。

aer·o [ˈɛərəu; ˋɛro] **I** ***a*.** **1.** 飞机的;航空的,飞行的。**2.**〔口〕(指汽车等)流线型的。*an* ～ *club* 飞行俱乐部。**II** ***n*.**〔口〕飞机;飞船;飞行。～ **lens** (空中照相机所用)航空透镜。

aer·o- *pref*. 表示"空气","空中";"航空";"飞机","飞船"等,如,*aero*lite, *aero*batics, *aero*dynamics.

aer·o·am·phib·i·ous [ˈɛərəuæmˈfibiəs; ˋɛroæmˋfɪbɪəs] ***a*.** 海陆空(联合)的。

aer·o·bac·ter [ˌɛərəuˈbæktə; ˏɛroˋbæktə] ***n*.**【生】气杆菌。

aer·o·bal·lis·tics [ˌɛərəubəˈlistiks; ˏɛrobəˋlɪstɪks] ***n*.** 〔*pl*.〕航空弹道学。

aer·o·bat·ic [ˌɛərəuˈbætik; ˏɛərəˋbætɪk] ***a*.**【空】特技的。*an* ～ *flight* 特技飞行。

aer·o·bat·ics [ˌɛərəuˈbætiks; ˏɛərəˋbætɪks] ***n*.** 特技飞行,特技飞行术;特技飞行表演。

aer·obe [ˈɛərəub; ˋɛərob] ***n*.** 好气生物,需氧菌,需氧(气)微生物。

aer·o·bic [eiəˈrəubik; eəˋrobɪk] ***a*.** **1.** 需氧的,需气的。**2.** 需氧菌的;需氧菌产生的。**-ize** ***vi*.** 做增氧健身操。**-s** ***n*.** 增氧健身术。

aer·o·bi·ol·o·gy [ˌɛərəubaiˈɔlədʒi; ˏɛərobaɪˋɑlədʒɪ] ***n*.** 大气生物学。**-bi·o·log·ic(al)** [-ˌbiəˈlɔdʒik(əl); -ˏbɪəˋlɑdʒɪk(əl)] ***a*.**

aer·o·bi·um [ˌeiəˈrəubiəm; ˏeəˋrobɪəm] ***n*.** (*pl*. **-bi·a** [-biə; -bɪə]) 需氧菌。

aer·o·boat [ˈɛərəubəut; ˋɛərəˏbot] ***n*.** 水上飞机。

aer·o·bus [ˈɛərəubʌs; ˋɛərəˏbʌs] ***n*.** 客机,班机。

aer·o·cade [ɛərəuˈkeid; ˏɛroˋked] ***n*.** 飞行队,飞机队。

aero·cam·er·a [ˈɛərəukæmərə; ˏɛərəˋkæmərə] ***n*.** 航空照相机。

aer·o·craft [ˈɛərəkrɑːft; ˋɛrəˏkrɑft] ***n*.** 航空器,飞行器,飞机(= aircraft)。

aero·curve [ˈɛərəukəːv; ˋɛrəˏkɝv] ***n*.**【空】曲翼面。

aero·done [ˈɛərəudəun; ˋɛrəˏdon] ***n*.** 滑翔机。

aer·o·do·net·ics [ˌɛərəudəˈnetiks; ˏɛrədəˋnɛtɪks] ***n*.** 滑翔力学。

aer·o·drome [ˈɛərədrəum; ˋɛrəˏdrom] ***n*.**〔英〕飞机场(= airdrome)。

aer·o·drom·ics [ˈɛərəudrɔmiks; ˋɛrodrɔmɪks] ***n*.** = aerodonetics.

aer·o·dro·mo·me·ter [ˌɛərəudrəuˈmɔmitə; ˏɛrəˋdroˋmɑmɪtə] ***n*.** 气流速度表。

aer·o·dy·nam·ic [ˌɛərəudaiˈnæmik; ˏɛrodaɪˋnæmɪk] ***a*.** 空气动力学的。*an* ～ *missile* 飞航式导弹,有翼导弹。**-s** ***n*.** 空气动力学,气体力学。

aer·o·dyne [ˈɛərəudain; ˋɛrəˏdaɪn] ***n*.** 重航空器,重于空气的飞行器。

aer·o·em·bol·ism [ˌɛərəuˈembəlizm; ˏɛrəˋɛmbəlɪzəm] ***n*.**【医】**1.** 航空气(泡)栓(塞)症。**2.** 高空病。

aer·o·foil [ˈɛərəufɔil; ˋɛrəˏfɔɪl] ***n*.**【空】机翼;翼型;翼剖面。

aer·o·gel [ˈɛərədʒəl; ˋɛrəˏdʒəl] ***n*.** 气凝胶。

aer·o·gram(me) [ˈɛərəgræm; ˋɛrəˏgræm] ***n*.** **1.** 航空信件。**2.** 无线电报。**3.** 高空图解。

aer·o·graph [ˈɛərəgrɑːf; ˋɛrəˏgræf] ***n*.** 高空气象计。

aer·og·raph·er [ɛəˈrɔgrəfə; eəˋrɑgrəfə] ***n*.**【军】高空气

A

象侦察员。

aer·og·ra·phy [ɛə'rɔgrəfi; eə`rɑgrəfɪ] *n*. 高空气象学。

aero·lite ['ɛərəlait; `ɛrə,laɪt], **aer·o·lith** ['ɛərəliθ; `ɛərəlɪθ] *n*. 陨石。

aer·ol·o·gist [ɛə'rɔlədʒist; eə`rɑlədʒɪst] *n*. 高空气象学家。

aer·ol·o·gy [ɛə'rɔlədʒi; eə`rɑlədʒɪ] *n*. **1.** (高空)气象学。**2.**【美海军】= meteorology.

aer·o·man·cy ['ɛərəmænsi; `eəromænsɪ] *n*. 天气预报。

aer·o·ma·rine [ˌɛərəuməˈriːn; ˏɛərəmə`rin] *a*. 海上飞行的。

aer·o·me·chan·ic [ˌɛərəu miˈkænik; ˏɛromɪ`kænɪk] **I** *a*. 空气力学的。**II** *n*. 航空机械士。**-s** *n*. 空气力学，航空力学。

aer·o·med·i·cal [ˌɛərəuˈmedikəl; ˏeəro`mɛdɪkl] *a*. 航空医学的。

aer·o·med·i·cine [ˌɛərəˈmedsin; ˏɛrə`mɛdsn] *n*. 航空医学。

aer·o·me·te·or·o·graph [ˌɛərəu ˌmiːtiˈɔrəgrɑːf; ˏɛrə`mitɪərəgrɑf] *n*. 高空气象计。

aer·om·e·ter [ɛəˈrɔmitə; eə`rɑmətɚ] *n*. 气体比重计。

aer·om·e·try [ɛəˈrɔmitri; ˏeə`rɑmɪtrɪ] *n*. 气体测量。

aer·o·mo·bile [ˈɛərəu məbiːl; `ɛrə,məbil] *n*. 气垫汽车。

aer·o·naut [ˈɛərənɔːt; `ɛrə,nɔt] *n*. 气球[飞艇]驾驶员；气球[飞艇]乘客。

aer·o·nau·tic, -i·cal [ˌɛərəˈnɔːtik, -əl; ˏɛrə`nɔtɪk; -əl] *a*. 航空的。*an* ～ *station* 航空无线电站。

aer·o·naut·ics [ˌɛərəˈnɔːtiks; ˏɛrə`nɔtɪks] *n*. 航空学，航空术。*the space* ～ 宇宙航空学(或航天学)。

aer·o·neu·ro·sis [ˈɛərəunjuəˈrəusis; `ɛrənjʊ`rosɪs] *n*. (飞行员的)神经机能病。

ae·ron·o·my [ɛəˈrɔnəmi; ɛ`rɑnəmɪ] *n*. 高层大气物理与化学研究。

aer·o·pause [ˈɛərəu pɔːz; `ɛrə,pɔz] *n*. 大气的航空边界，大气上界。

aer·o·pha·gi·a [ˌɛərəuˈfeidʒiə; ˏɛrə`fedʒɪə] *n*.【医】吞气症。

aer·o·phare [ˈɛərəfɛə; `ɛrə,fɛr] *n*. (空中导航用的)无线电信标。

aer·o·pho·bi·a [ɛərəuˈfəubiə; ˏɛrə`fobɪə] *n*.【医】高空恐怖；气流恐怖。

aer·o·phone [ˈɛərəfəun; `ɛrə,fon] *n*. **1.** 管乐器。**2.** 助听器。**3.** (空袭时用的)探音机。**4.** (空中)无线电话机。～ *listening device* 空中听音机。

aer·o·phore [ˈɛərəfɔː; `ɛrə,fɔr] *n*. 呼吸器〔供停止呼吸的初生婴儿或矿井、水下工人使用〕。

aer·o·pho·tog·ra·phy [ˌɛərəu fəˈtɔgrəfi; ˏeərofə`tɑgrəfɪ] *n*. 空中照相术，航空摄影术。

aero·phyte [ˈɛərəfait, ˈɛːr-; `ɛrə,faɪt, `ɛr-] *n*. 气生植物 (= epiphyte)。

aer·o·plane [ˈɛərəplein; `ɛrə,plen] *n*. 〔英〕飞机。*a ship* ～ 舰上飞机。*a tractor* ～ 牵引式飞机。**by** ～ 乘飞机；用飞机。*take* ～ 坐飞机。～ **carrier** 航空母舰。～ **hangar** 飞机库。～ **spotting** 飞机着弹观测。

aer·o·plank·ton [ˌɛərəuˈplæŋktən; ˏɛrə`plæŋktn] *n*. 空中浮游微生物。

aer·o·pulse [ˈɛərəpʌls; `ɛrə,pʌls] *n*. 脉动式空气喷气发动机(= pulsejet)。

aer·o·scope [ˈɛərəskəup; `ɛrə,skop] *n*. 空气纯度检查器；细菌灰尘收检器。**-scop·ic** [-ˈskɔpik; -`skɑpɪk] *a*.

aer·o·sid·er·ite [ˌɛərəuˈsidərait; ˏɛro`sɪdəraɪt] *n*.【天】陨铁。

aer·o·sid·er·o·lite [ˌɛərəuˈsidərəlait; ˏɛro`sɪdərəlet] *n*.【天】陨铁石。

aer·o·si·nus·i·tis [ˌɛərəusainəˈsaitis; ˏɛrosaɪnə`saɪtɪs] *n*.【医】高空鼻窦炎，飞行员鼻窦炎。

aer·o·sol [ˈɛərəsɔl; `ɛrə,sɑl] *n*. **1.**【化】气溶胶；烟雾剂。**2.** 悬浮微粒。～ **bomb** 喷射烟雾剂的小容器。～ **insecticide** 喷雾刹虫剂。～ **shaving cream** 喷雾刮脸膏。

aer·o·space [ˈɛərəuspeis; `ɛrə,spes] **I** *n*. 大气圈及其以外的宇宙空间。**II** *a*. 宇宙空间的，宇宙航行的。

aer·o·sphere [ˈɛərəusfiə; `ɛro,sfɪr] *n*. (地球周围的)大气，气圈。

aer·o·stat [ˈɛərəustæt; `ɛrə,stæt] *n*. **1.** 浮空器，高空气球。**2.**【虫】气囊。

aer·o·stat·ic [ˌɛərəuˈstætik; ˏɛrə`stætɪk] *a*. 空气静力学的；航空术的；空中平衡的。

aer·o·stat·ics [ˌɛərəuˈstætiks; ˏɛrə`stætɪks] *n*. 空气静力学，气体静力学。

aer·o·sta·tion [ˌɛərəuˈsteiʃən; ˏɛro`steʃən] *n*. 气球[飞船]操纵术[学]。

aer·o·ther·a·peu·tics [ˌɛərəu ˌθerəˈpjuːtiks; ˏɛro,θɛrə`pjutɪks] *n*. 〔*pl*.〕空气疗法。

aer·o·ther·mo·dy·nam·ics [ˌɛərəu ˈθəːməuˈdainæmiks; ˏɛro`θɝmo`daɪnæmɪks] *n*. 〔*pl*.〕空气热力学。

aer·o·tow [ˈɛərətəu; `ɛrə,to] **I** *vt*. 空中牵引(飞机)。**II** *n*. 空中牵引。

aer·o·train [ˈɛərəutrein; `ɛrə,tren] *n*. 悬浮火车，单轨气垫火车。

aer·o·trans·port [ˈɛərəuˈtrænspɔːt; `ɛrə`trænspɔrt] *n*. 运输机。

aer·ugi·nous [iəˈruːdʒinəs; ɪ`rudʒɪnəs] *a*. 铜绿(色)的。

aer·y[1] [ˈeiəri; `ɛrɪ] *a*. 〔诗〕= aerial.

aer·y[2] [ˈɛəri, ˈɛrɪ; ˈiəri, `ɪrɪ] *n*. = aerie.

AES = Army Exchange Service〔美〕陆军商品零售部。

AESC = American Engineering Standards Committee 美国工程标准委员会。

Aes·cu·la·pi·an [ˌiːskjuˈleipjən; ˏɛskjə`lepɪən] *a*. **1.** 医神艾斯库累普(Aesculapius)的。**2.** 医术的；药的。

Aes·cu·la·pi·us [ˌiːskjuˈleipjəs; ˏɛskjə`lepɪəs] *n*. **1.**【罗神】艾斯库累普〔医神〕。**2.**〔喻〕医师。

Ae·sop [ˈiːsɔp; `isəp] *n*. 伊索〔希腊寓言作者，公元前620? —560?〕。～ *'s Fables*《伊索寓言》。**-i·an** [iːˈsəupiən; i`sopɪən] *a*. 伊索寓言式的，伊索的。

aes·the·si·a [iːsˈθiːziə; ɛs`θiʒə] *n*. 知觉；感觉；感觉力，知觉性 (= esthesia)。

aes·thete [ˈiːsθiːt, Am. ˈesθiːt; `isθit, `ɛsθit] *n*. **1.** 审美家。**2.** 唯美主义者。

aes·thet·ic(al) [iːsˈθetik(əl), Am. es-; is`θɛtɪk(əl), ɛs-] *a*. **1.** 审美的。**2.** 美的，艺术的。**3.** 美学的。

aes·thet·i·cal·ly [iːsˈθetikəli, Am. es-; is`θɛtɪkəlɪ, ɛs-] *ad*. **1.** 审美地。**2.** 从美学观点上。

aes·the·ti·cian [ˌiːsθiˈtiʃən, Am. es-; ˏisθə`tɪʃən, ɛs-] *n*. 审美学者；审美学家。

aes·thet·i·cism [iːsˈθetisizəm, Am. es-; is`θɛtəsɪzəm, ɛs-] *n*. **1.** 唯美主义。**2.** 艺术感，美感；艺术感的培养。

aes·thet·ics [iːsˈθetiks, Am. es-; is`θɛtɪks, ɛs-] *n*. 〔动词用单数〕美学；审美学；美的哲学。

aes·tho-phys·i·ol·ogy [ˈiːsθəuˌfiziˈɔlədʒi, Am. ˈesθəuˌfiziˈɔlədʒi; `ɛsθo,fɪzɪ`ɑlədʒɪ] *n*. 感觉生理学。

aes·ti·val [iːsˈtaivəl; ɛs`taɪvl] *a*. 夏天的，适于夏季的。～ *diseases* 夏天的疾病。

aes·ti·vate [ˈiːstiveit; `ɛstə,vet] *vi*. **1.** 过夏，消夏。**2.**【动】(蜗牛等)夏眠，夏蛰。

aes·ti·va·tion [ˌiːstiˈveiʃən; ˏɛstɪ`veʃən] *n*. **1.** 消夏。**2.**【动】夏蛰，夏眠 (*opp*. hibernation)。**3.**【植】花被卷叠式。

aet., **aetat.** = 〔L.〕*aetatis*.

ae·ta·tis [iːˈteitis; i`tetɪs] *a*. 〔L.〕…岁的；在…岁时。(= at the age of)〔一般都用其缩略形式。例：*aet*. [*aetat*.] 30 年龄为 30 岁〕。

ae·ther [ˈiːθə; `iθɚ] = ether. **-the·re·al** [iˈθiəriəl; ɪ-

`θɪrɪəl] *a*. = etherial.

ae·ti·ol·o·gi·cal [ˌi:tiəˈlɔdʒikəl;ˏitɪəˋlɑdʒɪkəl] *a*. **1**. 原因论的。**2**. 病原学的,病因论的。

ae·ti·ol·o·gy [ˌi:tiˈɔlədʒi;ˏitɪˋɑlədʒɪ] *n*. **1**. 原因论。**2**. 病原学,病因论。*the* ～ *of a folkway* 民间习俗的起因。*a headache of unknown* ～ 原因不明的头痛。

AEW = airborne early warning【军】空中预先警报。

Af. = **1**. Africa. **2**. African.

AF = **1**. Air France 法国航空公司。**2**. air force 空军。**3**. Admiral of the Fleet〔英〕海军元帅。**4**. audio frequency【无】音频。**5**. automatic following【无】自动跟踪。**6**. Allied Forces 盟军。

af- *pref*. = ad-.〔用于 f 前〕; *af*fect.

AFA = **1**. Air Force Association〔美〕空军协会。**2**. American Federation of Arts 美国艺术联合会。

A.F.A.C. = Air Force Armament Centre〔美〕空军军械中心。

a·far [əˈfɑ:; əˋfɑr] *ad*. 由远方;在远处;到远方;遥远。～ ***off*** 遥远地,在远方。***from*** ～ 从远方(来等)。

AFB = Air Force Base〔美〕空军基地。

AFBMC = Air Force Ballistic Missile Committe〔美〕空军弹道导弹委员会。

AFC, A.F.C. = **1**. automatic frequency [flight] control 自动频率[飞行]控制。**2**. Air Force Cross (英国)空军十字章。**3**. Association Football Club (英国)足球俱乐部。

A.F.C.E. = automatic flight control equipment 飞行自动控制设备。

AFD = accelerated freeze-drying (生肉等的)加速冷冻干燥。

AFDC = Aid to Families with Dependent Children (美国)对有子女家庭补助计划。

a·feard, a·feared [əˈfiəd; əˋfɪrd] *a*.〔方、古〕恐惧的;担忧的。

a·fe·brile [əˈfi:brəl, -ˈfebrəl; eˋfibrəl, -ˋfɛbrəl] *a*.【医】不发烧的,无热的。

aff. = **1**. affectionate. **2**. affirmative. **3**. affirming.

af·fa·bil·i·ty [ˌæfəˈbiliti;ˏæfəˋbɪlətɪ] *n*. 殷勤,温柔,和蔼。

af·fa·ble [ˈæfəbl; ˋæfəbl] *a*. **1**. 殷勤的,和蔼的,友好的。**2**. (天气等)宜人的。*an* ～ *smile* 笑容可掬。**-bly** *ad*.

af·fair [əˈfɛə; əˋfɛr] *n*. **1**. 事,事情,事件。**2**.〔常 *pl*.〕事务;事态。**3**. 不正常的恋爱事件,男女间的暧昧关系。**4**.〔口〕东西,物品。*Mind your own* ～! [*That is none of your* ～. *That's my own* ～.] 莫管闲事。*a got-up* ～ 预谋事件;圈套。*one's private* ～*s* 私事。*public* ～*s* 公事,公务。*family* ～*s* 家务,家事。*material* ～ 物质生活。*political* ～*s* 政治事务。*the* ～*s of state* 国事,政务。*a man of* ～*s* 事务家。*the state of* ～*s* 形势,事态。*a wonderful* ～ 奇异物品,珍品。***an*** ～ ***of honour*** 决斗。***be at the head of*** ～***s*** 总理政务。***have an*** ～ ***with...*** 与…搞不正当的恋爱。***wind up one's*** ～***s*** 料理事务,了结事务。

af·faire d'a·mour [ɑˈfɛ:r dɑˈmu:r; əˋfɛr dəˋmur], ***affaire de cœur*** [ɑˈfɛ:r də ˈkə:r; əˋfɛr dəˋkɚ]〔F.〕恋爱事件,桃色事件。

af·faire d'hon·neur [ɑfɛ:r dɔˈnə:; æfɛr dɔˋnɚ]〔F.〕决斗。

af·fect[1] [əˈfekt; əˋfɛkt] **I** *vt*. **1**. 影响,作用;感受,感染。**2**. 害(病),伤(风),中(暑)。**3**. 感动。*be* ～*ed by heat* [*cold*] 中暑[着凉]。*His lungs are* ～*ed*. 他患肺病了。*His death* ～*ed us deeply*. 他的死使我们深为感伤。**II** *n*. [ˈæfekt; ˋæfɛkt] **1**.【心】情感,感情。**2**.【数】偏差。

af·fect[2] [əˈfekt; əˋfɛkt] *vt*. **1**. 假装,佯装,假冒,冒充。**2**. 爱,好,爱用,爱穿。**3**. 成(某种形状)。**4**. 常去,常在(某处)。～ *composure* 假充沉着。～ *ignorance* 假装不知。～ *the scholar* 冒充学者。～ *loud neckties* 爱用花哨的领带。*Drops of water* ～ *roundness*. 滴水成珠。*Moss* ～*s the northern slopes*. 北坡常长青苔。

af·fec·ta·tion [ˌæfekˈteiʃən;ˏæfɪkˋteʃən] *n*. 假装;做作,矫揉造作,装模作样(的态度)。*an* ～ *of kindness* 假慈悲。***without*** ～ 老老实实地,直率地。

af·fect·ed[1] [əˈfektid; əˋfɛktɪd] *a*. **1**. 受了影响的,感染了的。**2**. 感动的。*the* ～ *part* 患部。

af·fect·ed[2] [əˈfektid; əˋfɛktɪd] *a*. **1**. 装模作样的,做作的。**2**. 觉得…的。*His manners are* ～. 他的态度不自然。*How is he* ～ *towards us?* 他觉得我们怎么样? ***ill*** ～ (*to*) 对…不友好的。***well*** ～ (*to*) 对…怀好意的。～ ***airs*** 装模作样。～ ***laugh*** 装笑,假笑。**-ly** *ad*. 装模作样地,不自然地。

af·fect·ing [əˈfektiŋ; əˋfɛktɪŋ] *a*. 令人感动的,动人的,引起同情的。*an* ～ *scene* 惨状。*an* ～ *sight* 动人的情景。**-ly** *ad*.

af·fec·tion [əˈfekʃən; əˋfɛkʃən] *n*. **1**. 爱;〔*pl*.〕爱慕。**2**. 心情;【心】感情。**3**.〔古〕性情。**4**. 作用,影响。**5**. 疾病。*the object of one's* ～*s* 所钟爱的人[物],意中人。～ *of the skin* 皮肤病。*the reciprocal* ～ *of moving bodies* 运动物体的相互作用。***have an*** ～ ***for*** [***towards***] 深爱着。***set one's*** ～***s on*** [***upon***] 钟爱。

af·fec·tion·al [əˈfekʃənl; əˋfɛkʃənəl] *a*. 爱情的;感情的。

af·fec·tion·ate [əˈfekʃənit; əˋfɛkʃənɪt] *a*. 感情深厚的,有感情的,慈爱的。*He is* ～ *to me*. 他爱我。*an* ～ *mother* 慈母。*be on* ～ *terms with* 和…交情极好。**-ness** *n*.

af·fec·tion·ate·ly [əˈfekʃənitli; əˋfɛkʃənətlɪ] *ad*. *Yours* ～ = *A- yours* 你的亲爱的〔写家信时结尾用语〕。

af·fec·tive [əˈfektiv; əˋfɛktɪv] *a*. 感动的,感情的。*an* ～ *state* 激动状态。

af·fer·ent [ˈæfərənt; ˋæfərənt] *a*.【生理】传入的,输入的。～ **nerve** 传入神经。

af·fet·tu·o·so [əˌfetjuˈəuzəu; əˏfɛtʃuˋozo] *a*., *ad*.〔It.〕【乐】哀婉动人的[地]。

af·fi·ance [əˈfaiəns; əˋfaɪəns] **I** *n*.〔古〕**1**. 信用,信托(*in*)。**2**. 婚约;誓约。**II** *vt*.〔古〕订婚。*one's* ～*d husband* [*wife*] 某人的未婚夫[妻]。***be*** ～***d to*** 是…的未婚夫[妻],和…订婚。

af·fi·ant [əˈfaiənt; əˋfaɪənt] *n*.【法】宣誓作证者;写口供书者。

af·fiche [æˈfi:ʃ; æˋfiʃ] *n*.〔F.〕布告,招贴。

af·fi·da·vit [ˌæfiˈdeivit;ˏæfəˋdevɪt] *n*.【法】宣誓口供,宣誓书。

af·fil·i·ate [əˈfilieit; əˋfɪlɪˏet] **I** *vt*. **1**. 把…收作会员;使隶属于,使成为…的分支机构。**2**.〔～ oneself〕使加入。**3**. 把…收为养子;【法】认定(私生子的)父亲为(某人)(*to, upon*)。**4**. 源自(*to*),来自(*upon*)。*the* ～*d middle school* 附属中学。～*d societies* 支部,分会。～ *sth. to* [*upon*] *its author* 认定某事为某人所为。～ ***oneself with*** 加入。***be*** ～***d with*** 与…有关系;与…结合;和…来往;加入。—*vi*. 参加;与…密切联系(*with*)。*She* ～*s with an academic society*. 她是某学术团体的成员。**II** [əˈfilieit; əˋfɪlɪet] *n*. **1**.〔美〕分支机构,分会。**2**. 会员。

af·fil·i·a·tion [əˌfiliˈeiʃən; əˏfɪlɪˋeʃən] *n*. **1**. 加入,入会。**2**.〔美〕亲密关系。**3**.【法】私生子父亲的认定。**4**. 追溯由来,溯源。*democrats with no party* ～ 无党派民主人士。*a sister city* ～ 姐妹城市的亲善关系。

af·fine [əˈfain; əˋfaɪn] *a*.【数】远交的,仿射的。

af·fined [əˈfaind; əˋfaɪnd] *a*. **1**. 有密切关系的,姻亲的。**2**. 有义务约束的。

af·fin·i·ty [əˈfiniti; əˋfɪnətɪ] *n*. **1**. 姻亲关系〔*cf*. consanguinity〕; 密切关系。**2**. (语言等的)类似,近似。**3**.

A

(男女之间的)吸引力,吸引人的异性。4.【数】仿射性。5.【化】亲和力。6.【生】类缘,亲缘,类同。*have an ~ for children* 喜欢小孩。*the close ~ of German with English* 德语与英语的密切近似。~ **card** 亲和卡〔供小团体内部使用的一种信用卡〕。

af·firm [ə'fəːm; ə`fɝm] *vt*. 1. 断言,肯定。2. 使(法律等)生效,批准。3.【法】不经宣誓而庄严宣布;证实。4. (上级法院)维持(下级法院的判决)。~ *one's loyalty to one's country* 声言忠于祖国。~ *a judgement of the lower court* 维持下级法庭的判决。—*vi*. 证明,证实(事实等) (*to*)。

af·firm·a·ble [ə'fəːməbl; ə`fɝməbl] *a*. 可断言的,可确定的。

af·firm·ance [ə'fəːməns; ə`fɝməns] *n*. 断言,确认。

af·firm·ant [ə'fəːmənt; ə`fɝmənt] *n*. 断言者;确认者。

af·fir·ma·tion [ˌæfəː'meiʃən;ˏæfɚ`meʃən] *n*. 1. 断言;肯定。2. 证实;批准。3.【法】不经宣誓而作出的证词。*The desirability of peace needs no ~* . 和平的可取无容赘言。

af·firm·a·tive [ə'fəːmətiv; ə`fɝmətɪv] I *a*. 确言的;肯定的,正面的;赞成的。*an ~ answer* 肯定的答覆。*an ~ approach to the problem* 正面解决问题。*an ~ vote* 赞成票。II *n*. 1. 确言;赞成。2. 肯定词,肯定语。3.【逻】肯定;肯定命题。*an ~ proposition* 肯定命题。*Two negatives make an ~*. 两个否定构成肯定。*an ~ sign*【数】正号。***answer* [*reply*] *in the ~*** 肯定答覆。**-ly** *ad*. 肯定地;断然。

af·fix [ə'fiks; ə`fɪks] I *vt*. 1. 附加上。2. 贴上,黏上。3. 签署;盖(章)。~ *a label to a bottle* 给瓶子贴上标签。~ *one's signature* 署名,签名。~ *a seal* 打上图章。II ['æfiks; `æfɪks] *n*. 1. 附加物,附件。2.【语法】词缀〔词首、词尾、词腰〕。

af·fix·a·tion [ˌæfik'seiʃən;ˏæfɪk`seʃən] *n*. 1. 附加物。2.【语】缀合法〔加词首或词尾〕。

af·fix·ture [ə'fikstʃə; ə`fɪkstʃɚ] *n*. 附加物,附添;贴。

af·fla·tus [ə'fleitəs; ə`fletəs] *n*. 〔诗〕神感;(诗人等的)灵感。

af·flict [ə'flikt; ə`flɪkt] *vt*. 使苦恼,折磨。***be ~ed with*** 患(病),为…所苦(*be ~ed with gout* 害痛风病。*be ~ed with a conscience* 受良心的苛责)。

af·flic·tion [ə'flikʃən; ə`flɪkʃən] *n*. 痛苦(*opp*. relief);哀伤,忧伤;苦恼;困苦,不幸。***to bear up under ~*** 忍受苦难,不屈不挠。

af·flic·tive [ə'fliktiv; ə`flɪktɪv] *a*. 苦恼的,悲伤的;悲惨的。

af·flu·ence ['æfluəns; `æflʊəns] *n*. 1. 丰富;富裕,富足。2. 流入;汇集。*live in ~* 生活优裕。*an ~ of youths* 青年汇集。

af·flu·ent ['æfluənt; `æflʊənt] I *a*. 1. 丰富的;富足的。2. 流入的;畅流的,滔滔的。*the ~ society* 富足的社会。*land ~ in natural resources* 自然资源丰富的土地。*an ~ fountain* 滔滔不断的泉水。II *n*. 支流。**-ly** *ad*.

af·flux ['æflʌks; `æflʌks] *n*. 1. 流入,汇集。2. 充血。*an ~ of blood to the head* 脑充血。

af·ford [ə'fɔːd; ə`ford] *vt*. 1. (财力、时间等)足以承担(损失、后果等),花费得起,经受得住。〔与 *can*, *may* 连用〕。2. 给与,供给;产,生产,出产。*I cannot ~ the expense* [*time*]. 我花不起这笔费用[腾不出工夫来]。*I cannot ~ to be critical*. 我不能苛求。~ *sb. an opportunity* 给予某人(…)机会。*The earth ~s grain*. 土地出产粮食。

af·for·est [æ'fɔrist; æ`fɔrɪst] *vt*. 在…植树造林。

af·for·est·a·tion [æˌfɔris'teiʃən; əˏfɑrəs`teʃən] *n*. 造林,绿化。*reclamative ~* 农业造林。*an ~ plan* 绿化规划。

af·fran·chise [ə'frænt*ʃ*aiz; ə`frænˏt*ʃ*aɪz] *vt*. 使(某人)摆脱奴役状态[义务等]〔*cf*. enfranchise〕。

af·fray [ə'frei; ə`fre] I *n*. (在公共场所)吵架,打架;纷争,闹事,骚扰,滋扰。II *vt*. 〔古〕吓唬。

af·freight [ə'freit; ə`fret] *vt*. 租用(船只)〔由船主负责行驶〕,包租(船只)。

af·freight·ment [ə'freitmənt; ə`fretmənt] *n*. 租船(运货)。

af·fri·cate ['æfrikit; `æfrɪkɪt] *n*.【语音】破擦音〔如 church 中的 ch〕— [-keit; -ket] *vt*. 使发破擦音。

af·fri·ca·tion [ˌæfri'keiʃən;ˏæfrɪ`keʃən] *n*.【语】(音的)破擦,塞擦。

af·fright [ə'frait; ə`fraɪt] I *vt*. 〔古、诗〕恐吓,吓。II *n*. 恐怖,惊吓。

af·front [ə'frʌnt; ə`frʌnt] I *vt*. 1. 侮辱,冒犯。2. 毅然对抗,泰然面对。*look ~ed* (受辱后)愤愤不平。~ *death* 临死不惧。II *n*. 当众侮辱。***offer an ~ to* [*upon*] = *put an ~ to* [*upon*]** 侮辱。

af·fron·tive [ə'frʌntiv; ə`frʌntɪv] *a*. 〔古〕侮辱的;公然冒犯的。

af·fu·sion [ə'fjuːʒən; ə`fjuʒən] *n*. 1.【宗】洗礼时的浇水。2.【医】泼水疗法。*cold ~* 冷泼疗法〔降发热病人的体温〕。

AFGE = American Federation of Government Employees 美国政府雇员联合会。

Af·ghan ['æfgæn; `æfgæn] I *a*. 阿富汗的;阿富汗人的;阿富汗语的。II *n*. 1. 阿富汗人;阿富汗语。2. 〔a-〕一种针织软毛毯,一种针织羊毛头巾。

Af·ghan·i·stan [æf'gænistæn; æf`gænəˏstæn] *n*. 阿富汗〔亚洲〕。

Afgh. = Afghanistan.

a·fi·cio·na·do [əːˌfiːsjə'nɑːdəu; əˏfisjə`nɑdo] *n*. (*fem*. ***a·fi·cio·na·da*** [-də; -də]) 〔Sp.〕热爱者,迷。*a football ~* 足球迷。

a·field [ə'fiːld; ə`fild] *ad*. 1. 在野外,在田中。2. 在战场上。3. 远离(家园、常道)。***far ~*** 远离;迷路 (*His remarks are far ~*. 他的话离题太远了)。***go* [*lead*] *too far ~*** 走入[使走入]歧途。

AFIPS = American Federation of Information Processing Societies 美国信息处理学会联合会。

a·fire [ə'faiə; ə`faɪr] *a*. 〔多作表语〕, *ad*. 1. 燃着,燃烧。2. 大为激动。*with heart ~* 热血沸腾,大为激动。*set a house ~* 放火烧房。

AFL = American Football league 美国橄榄球联盟。

a·flame [ə'fleim; ə`flem] *a*. 〔多作表语〕, *ad*. 1. 燃烧着,冒火焰。2. 涨红了脸;发亮。3. 大为激动。*His face is ~ with blushes*. 他的脸羞得通红。*I was ~ with curiosity*. 我好奇得要命。

af·la·tox·in [ˌæflə'tɔksin;ˏæflə`tɑksɪn] *n*. 黄曲霉毒素〔尤指花生所含者〕。

AFL-CIO = American Federation of Labor and Congress of Industrial Organizations 美国劳工联合会-产业工会联合会〔略作劳联-产联〕。

a·float [ə'fləut; ə`flot] *a*. 〔多作表语〕, *ad*. 1. 浮,漂浮。2. 在海上;在船上。3. (甲板等)浸在水中。4. 流行,传播,散播。5.【商】(票据)流通,(经济上)不困难。6. (计划等)尚未定案。*all the shipping ~* 航行中的所有船只。*cargo ~* 海上货物。*life ~* 海上生活。*get* (*a newspaper*) ~ 发行(一份报纸)。***keep ~*** 使…漂浮不沉;使…流通,使…不致负债。***set*** (*rumours*) ~ 散布(谣言)。

a·flut·ter [ə'flʌtə; ə`flʌtɚ] *a*. 〔多作表语〕, *ad*. 1. (旗等)飘扬;(翅膀)鼓动。2. 激动。3. 有动静。*All are ~ at the thought of his return*. 想到他的归来,大家都很激动。*The woods were ~ with unknown birds*. 树林里因有不知名的小鸟而有动静。

AFM = 1. American Federation of Musicians 美国音乐家联合会。2. Air Force Medal (英国)空军奖章。

AFMTC = Air Force Missile Test Centre 〔美〕空军导弹

试验中心。

A.F. of L. = **AFL.**

a fond [ɑːˈf ɔ̃ːŋ; ɑˋf ɔ̃] 〔F.〕完全，彻底。*supporting their party's principles* ～ 完全支持他们的党的原则。

a·foot [əˈfut; əˋfʊt] *a*.〔多作表语〕, *ad*. **1.** 徒步，步行。**2.** 进行中，活动中。*go* ～ 走路去。*A plot is* ～. 阴谋在酝酿中。*be early* ～ 早在进行。***get*** ～ 要走，会走；开始，实施。***set*** ～ 建立，建设；引起；施行。

a·fore [əˈfɔː, əˈfɔə; əˋfor, əˋfɔr] ***ad*.**, ***prep*.**, ***conj*.** 〔古、方〕**1.** 在…之前(= before)。**2.** 以前，早先。*serve* ～ *the mast* 做普通水手。～**cited** ***a*.** 上述，前举。～**hand** ***a*.**, ***ad*.**〔古〕事先，预先。～**mentioned** ***a*.** 前述，该。～**named** ***a*.** 前举，上举。～**said** ***a*.** 前述的，该。～**thought** ***a*.**〔多用于被修饰的名词之后〕预谋的，故意的 (*malice* ～*thought*【法】预谋)。～**time** ***ad*.** 从前；早先。

a for·ti·o·ri [ˈei ˌfɔːtiˈɔːrai; ˋe ˏforʃɪˋoraɪ]〔L.〕更不必说，更加，何况。*If no major country has the resources for the enterprise*, ～ *neither has any lesser power*. 如果大国没有人力物力来进行这项事业，小国就更加没有了。

a·foul [əˈfaul; əˋfaʊl] ***ad*.**〔美〕碰撞，冲突；缠住。***run*** [***fall***] ～ ***of*** 和…碰撞[冲突、纠缠] (*run* ～ *of the law* 和法律抵触。*The ship ran* ～ *of the floating seaweed*. 船只和漂浮的海草纠缠在一起)。

AFP = **1.** 〔F.〕*Agence France Presse* (= French Press Agency) 法国新闻社，法新社。**2.** alphafetoprotein 甲胎蛋白。

Afr. = **1.** Africa. **2.** African.

a·fraid [əˈfreid; əˋfred] ***a*.**〔常用作表语〕**1.** 畏惧，害怕。**2.** 恐怕，担心，愁着，担忧。*Who's* ～？谁怕？一点不怕。*Don't be* ～. 别怕，不要怕。*This is nothing to be* ～ *of*. 这没有什么了不起。*He is* ～ *for* [*about*] *his own safety* [*what will happen*]. 他担心自己的安全[将来发生的事]。***be afraid of*** [***to*** (*do*), ***that***] 怕，害怕 (*He is not* ～ *of anything*. 他肆无忌惮。*He is* ～ *of his own shadow*. 他提心吊胆，连自己的影子都害怕)。***I'm*** ～ ***...***〔口〕恐怕(是)，我看(是)…。*I'm* ～ *we can't go on Monday*. 星期一恐怕去不了。***I am*** ～ that... 不瞒你说，我看是这样。

A-frame [ˈeiˌfreim; ˋeˏfrem] **I** ***a*.** A 字形架的；(屋顶)A 字形结构的。**II** ***n*.** A 字形屋顶，A 形架。

Afr·a·mer·i·can [ˌæfrəˈmerikən; ˏæfrəˋmɛrɪkən] ***n*.**, ***a*.** 美国黑人(的)(= Afro-American)。

AFRASEC = Afro-Asian Organization for Economic Cooperation 亚非经济合作组织。

af·reet, af·rit(e) [ˈæfriːt; ˋæfrit] ***n*.**【阿神】恶魔。

a·fresh [əˈfreʃ; əˋfrɛʃ] ***ad*.** 从新，重行，再，另外。***start*** ～ 再从头开始。

Af·ric [æˈfrik; ˋæfrɪk] ***a*.**〔诗〕= African.

Af·ri·ca [ˈæfrikə; ˋæfrɪkə] ***n*.** 非洲。

Af·ri·can [ˈæfrikən; ˋæfrɪkən] **I** ***a*.** 非洲的；非洲人的。**II** ***n*.** 非洲人。～ **golf**〔美〕掷双骰儿。～ **lily**【植】百子莲。～ **mahogany**【植】非洲桃花心木。～ **sleeping sickness**【医】昏睡病，非洲锥虫病。

Af·ri·can·der [ˌæfriˈkændə; ˋæfrɪˋkændɚ] ***n*.** (一种)南非牛。

Af·ri·can·ist [ˈæfrikənist; ˋæfrɪkənɪst] ***n*.** **1.** 研究非洲文化语言的学者[专家]。**2.** 非洲民族主义者；泛非主义者。

Af·ri·can·ize [ˈæfrikənaiz; ˋæfrɪkəˏnaɪz] ***vt*.** **1.** 使非洲化。**2.** 使…带有非洲观点、性质等。**-i·za·tion** [ˌæfrikənaiˈzeiʃən; ˏæfrɪkənaɪˋzeʃən] ***n*.**

Af·ri·kaans [ˌæfriˈkɑːns; ˏæfrɪˋkɑns] ***n*.** 布尔语〔南非通用的荷兰语〕。

Af·ri·kan·der [ˌæfriˈkændə; ˏæfrɪˋkændɚ] ***n*.** **1.** 南非生长大的白人。**2.** 南非牛；南非羊。

Af·ri·ka·ner [ˌæfriˈkɑːnə; ˏæfrɪˋkɑnɚ] ***n*.**〔D.〕祖籍欧洲(尤其是荷兰)的南非人；布尔人。

Af·ro [ˈæfrəu; ˋæfro] **I** ***a*.** **1.** (仿效黑人留的)蓬松发型的。**2.**〔口〕美洲黑人的。**II** ***n*.** 蓬松发型。～**-rock** 非洲摇滚乐。

Afro- *comb. f.* 表示"非洲(的)"。

Af·ro-A·mer·i·can [ˌæfrəuəˈmerikən; ˋæfroəˋmɛrɪkən] ***n*.**, ***a*.** = Aframerican.

Af·ro-A·sian [ˌæfrəuˈeiʃən; ˏæfroˋeʃən] ***a*.** 亚非的。*an* ～ *conference* 亚非会议。

Af·ro-A·si·at·ic [ˌæfrəuˌeiʃiˈætik; ˏæfroˏeʃɪˋætɪk] ***a*.** (包括柏柏尔语、埃塞俄比亚语、闪语、乍得语和古埃及语的)亚非语系的。

a·front [əˈfrʌnt; əˋfrʌnt] ***ad*.** 在前面，在对面。

A.F.S. = Auxiliary Fire Service〔英〕辅助消防队。

AFSWC = Air Force Special Weapons Centre〔美〕空军特种武器中心。

AFT = American Federation of Teachers 美国教师联合会。

aft [ɑːft; æft] ***a*.**, ***ad*.**【海】在船尾，近船尾，向船尾。***fore and*** ～ 从船头到船尾。***right*** ～ 正在(船)后。

aft. = after(noon).

af·ter [ˈɑːftə; ˋæftɚ] **I** ***ad*.** 在后；继后；后来。*follow* ～ 跟着。*look before and* ～ 瞻前顾后，前思后想。***soon*** ～ 不久。*three days* ～ 三日后。**II** ***prep*.** **1.**〔表示时间关系〕在…以后(*opp*. before)；〔美〕(…点)过(…分)〔= past〕。**2.**〔位置地点〕在…后面 (*opp*. before)。**3.**〔表示次第顺序〕位于…之后；(地位、规模、重要性等)次于；(仅)低于。**4.**〔表示事件或时间的连续性〕紧挨着；(一个)接(一个)；相继。**5.**〔原因〕由于，因为；既然。**6.**〔表示让步关系，介词受词前常冠以强义限定词 all〕虽然，尽管。**7.** 追求，寻找；追捕〔常与 be, go, run 等词连用〕。**8.** 仿照，模仿；依据…(而改写、命名等)。**9.** 符合，一致；(很)像。**10.** 关注，关照。～ *four days* 四天以后。～ *supper* 晚饭后。～ *school* 放学后。*It's twenty* ～ *six*.〔美〕现在是六点二十分。*Shut the door* ～ *you when you leave the room*. 离开房间时请随手关门。*A-you, please*! 请您先走。*A- you*! 您先走!〔回答前一礼让语时的用语，you 应重读〕。*A- you with the paper, please*. 您看过这报纸后给我看看。*the largest city* ～ *London* 仅次于伦敦的一个大城市。*A colonel comes* ～ *a general*. 上校的地位低于将军的地位。*Please line up one* ～ *another*. 请按顺序排队。*day* ～ *day* 一天又一天。*time* ～ *time* 再三，常常。*She was very hungry* ～ *her long morning walk*. 她因为早晨散步很久，所以感到饿得很。*I shall never speak to him* ～ *what has happened*. 既然发生了这样的情况，我就永远不再跟他说话了。*A- all warnings, he persisted*. 尽管有各方警告，他仍坚持到底。*A- all my care in packing it the clock arrived broken*. 尽管我把这座时钟小心包装，可是运来时它还是被损坏了。*John is* ～ *you*. 约翰在找你。*He is much run* ～. 他是众所欢迎的人。*I don't go* ～ *fame or money*. 我不追名逐利。*The police ran* ～ *the burglars*. 警察追捕窃贼。*long* ～ *home* 怀念家乡。*hunt* ～ *novelty* 猎奇。*He was named* ～ *his uncle*. 他是依照叔父的名来命名的。*a play* ～ *Shakespeare* 模仿莎士比亚的剧作编写成的剧本。*He takes* ～ *his mother*. 他的长相和母亲一模一样。*You are a man* ～ *my heart*. 你这人很合我的心意。*look* ～ *one's child* 照料孩子。*Somebody asked* ～ *you this morning*. 今天上午有人打听你来着。～ ***all*** 毕竟；终于 (*He succeeded* ～ *all*. 他终于胜利了)。***be*** ～ ***doing***〔英方〕刚…了(*I am* ～ *having my dinner*. 我刚刚吃了晚饭)。***one*** ～ ***another*** 陆续，相继，挨次。***one*** ～ ***the other*** 轮流。**III** ***conj*.** 在…后。*He arrived* ～ *I did*. 他在我到后就到了。～ ***all is said and done*** 终归。**IV** ***a*.** 后，后来的；后面的。*the* ～ *results* 后果。***in*** ～

years 在后来的年月里。in ~ life 晚年。V n.〔英俚〕正餐的最后一道食品(如点心、水果等)。~birth【医】胞衣,胎胞;遗腹子的生产。~ body 船体后部。~ brain【解】后脑。~burner【空】补燃器,加力燃烧室。~ cabin 后舱。~care ① n.病后调养;罪犯释放后的安置。② a.售后服务的。~clap 意外变动,意外结果。~ cooler【机】后冷却机。~crop 第二次收获。~culture 补种。~-damp 矿山爆炸后的毒气。~deck 后甲板。~-dinner a.餐后的。~effect【物】后效应,后效;副作用;余功。~glow 晚霞;余辉。~grass 再生草。~heat【物】余热。~hours a.公余的,业余的。~image【心】遗像;余像;余味;余音。~life 1. 后世,来世。2. 后半生,晚年。~-light 1. 夕照。2. 事后的领悟。~-market (汽车)零件市场。~math 1. (牧草的)第二次刈割;再生草。2. 余波,余殃,余累;结果,后果(the ~math of war 战后余殃)。~most a. 1. 最后头的。2.【船】靠近船尾的。~-pains〔pl.〕【医】产后痛。~piece 1.【剧】剧终余兴。2.【船】舵盘脚。~-product 副产物。~ripening 后熟。~-sales a. 出售以后的(~sales services 售后服务)。~-sensation【心】后觉。~shock (地震的)余震。~taste 回味,余味;,余韵。~thought 1. 事后的想法。2. 计划外的加添物。~-treatment (印染物品等的)第二次处理。~wit 事后聪明。~word 跋,编后记。~years n. 事后的岁月。

af·ter·noon [ˈɑːftəˈnuːn; ˌæftɚˋnun] n. 1. 下午,午后。2.〔书〕后半期,后半。this ~ 今天下午。Good ~! 1. 您好〔下午见面时招呼语〕。2. 再见〔下午分手时用语〕。an ~ farmer 懒人。of an ~ 常常在下午。the ~ of life 后半生,晚年。-s ad.〔美〕每天下午(He slept late and worked afternoons. 他每天睡得晚,总在午后工作)。

af·ter·wards [ˈɑːftəwədz; ˋæftɚwɚdz], 美 **-ward** [-wəd;-wɚd] ad. 其后,后来,继后,然后,以后。I left there ~. 后来我就离开那里了。

A.G., AG = 1. adjutant general. 2. air gunner. 3. attorney general.

Ag【化】元素 argentum (银)的符号。

Ag. = August.

ag. = agriculture.

ag [æg; æg] a. 农业的,农用的。

ag- pref. = ad-〔在 g 前用 ag-: agglutinate〕.

a·ga [ˈɑːgə; ˋɑgə] n. (奥托曼帝国时代穆斯林国家的)统帅。

a·gain [əˈgeɪn; əˋgen] ad. 1. 又,再;再一次;加一倍。2. 此外,另外;而且,加之。3. (信息等)返回来。4. 而,但,抑或。Come ~. 请再来。be home ~ 回到家。Bring us word ~. 带回音来。A- we must remember that ... 而且我们得考虑考虑…。This is better, but then ~ it costs much. 这个好些,就是太贵。Then ~, why did he go? 那么,他为什么要走呢? ~ and ~ 再三再四,一再,三番五次。as large ~ as …之两倍大的。as many [much] ~ as 多一倍,加倍,二倍于。back ~ 复原,照旧,照样。be oneself ~ 病好了,复原了。echo [ring] ~ 反响,响应。ever and ~ = now and ~ 时时。once ~ 再一次。once and ~ = ~ and ~. over ~ 再一次。over and (over) ~ 翻来覆去,多次。time and ~ 好几次。

a·gainst [əˈgeɪnst; əˋgenst] I prep. 1. 对,对着,冒着;反对,敌对,逆;相反,不利于;违反,违背,犯。2. 撞着,碰,触;靠近;靠,倚。3. 防,御,以防,以备。4. 以…为背景;对照。5.〔表示方向,常同 over 连用〕在…的对面。6.〔表示对比关系,有时可同 as 连用〕…而…。7.〔表示交换关系〕以…抵付;凭…换取。Are you for or ~ the plan? 那个计划你是赞同呢还是反对? Her age is ~ her. 她的年龄不行了。Luck is ~ him. 他运气不好。talk ~ sb. 说(人)坏话。~ rule 犯规。fight for the weak ~ the strong 扶弱抑强。inform ~ sb. 告发(某人)。set a chair ~ the wall 把椅子靠在墙上。Caution ~ fire. 小心火烛。~ the famine 防饥荒。~ the evening sky 以黄昏的天空为背景。a matter of reason as ~ emotion 与感情相对立的理智问题。The park opens five hours a day this year ~ three hours a day last year. 这公园今年每天开放五小时,而去年每天开放三小时。Document ~ Acceptance. 承兑后交单。the rates ~ pounds sterling 英镑兑换率。~ a rainy day 未雨绸缪,以备不时之需。~ all chances 无望。~ one's will 无可奈何地,无奈。~ the stream 逆流;(在逆境中)奋斗。~ time [the clock] 准时,按时,尽快;加油,使劲儿。be ~ 反对。be up ~ (it) 遇到(经济上的)巨大困难。over ~ (the cinema) 在(电影院)正对面,正对电影院。run up ~ 忽然碰上[碰到]。II conj.〔古、方〕在…之时,在…之前。

ag·a·lite [ˈægəlait; ˋægəlaɪt] n.【矿】纤滑石。

ag·a·ma [ˈægəmə; ˋɑgəmə] n. (欧洲)蜥蜴。

Ag·a·mem·non [ˌægəˈmemnən; ˌægəˋmɛmnən] n.【希神】阿加迈农〔围攻 Troy 城的联军统帅〕。

a·ga·mete [ˈeigəmiːt, əˈgæmiːt; ˋegəmit, əˋgæmit] n.【生】非配偶子。

ag·a·mi [ˈægəmi; ˋægəmɪ] n.【鸟】鸨类。

a·gam·ic [əˈgæmik; əˋgæmɪk] a. 1.【生】无配子的;无性生殖的(= asexual)。2.【植】隐花的(= agamous)。

ag·a·mo·gen·e·sis [ˌægəməuˈdʒenisis; ˌægəməˋdʒɛnɪsɪs] n.【生】无配生殖;出芽生殖;单性生殖。

ag·a·mous [ˈægəməs; ˋægəməs] a.【生】无性(生殖)的,【植】隐花的。

A·ga·ña [ɑːˈgɑːnjə; ɑˋgɑnjɑ] n. 阿加尼亚〔关岛(美)首府〕。

ag·a·pan·thus [ˌægəˈpænθəs; ˌægəˋpænθəs] n.【植】百子莲(= African lily)。

a·gape[1] [əˈgeip; əˋgep] a.〔用作表语〕, ad. 目瞪口呆,哑然;大开着,张着。The wind set the window ~. 风把窗吹开。

ag·a·pe[2] [ˈægəpiː; ˋægəpi] n. (pl. -pae [-piː; -pi]) 1. 神对人的爱;教友之爱;自发之爱。2. 早期基督教徒的会餐(cf. love feast)。

ag·a·pe·mo·ne [ˌægəˈpiːməni; ˌægəˋpimənɪ] n. 温柔角〔搞自由恋爱的地方,常有贬意〕。

a·gar [ˈeigɑː; ˋɑgɑr] n. 1. 洋菜,琼脂,石花菜。2. 细菌培养基。

a·gar-agar [ˈeigɑːˈeigɑː; ˋegɑrˋegɑ] = agar 1.

ag·a·ric [ˈægərik, əˈgærik; ˋægərɪk, əˋgærɪk] n.【植】伞菌,蘑菇;木耳。~ mineral 岩乳(= rock milk)。

Ag·ate [ˈeigət; ˋegət] n. 埃格特〔姓氏〕。

ag·ate [ˈægət; ˋægət] n. 1. 玛瑙;〔美〕5½点铅字〔英国叫 ruby;〔美〕(小孩玩的)石子。2. [ˈægit; ˋægɪt]〔喻〕矮子。~ jasper 碧玉玛瑙。~ line 报纸上一栏宽、十四分之一英寸长的广告面积。

ag·ate·ware [ˈægətˌwɛə; ˋægɪtˌwɛr] n. 1. 玛瑙彩釉的铁器皿。2. 玛瑙彩纹的陶器。

Ag·a·tha [ˈægəθə; ˋægəθə] n. 阿格莎〔女子名〕。

A·ga·ve [əˈgeivi; əˋgevɪ] n.【植】龙舌兰属;〔a-〕龙舌兰。

a·gaze [əˈgeiz; əˋgez] ad. 注视,凝视。

AGC = 1. automatic ga(u)ge controller【无】自动测量调整装置。2. advanced graduate certificate 高级研究生证书。3. automatic gain control【无】自动增益控制。

age [eidʒ; edʒ] I n. 1. 年龄。2. 成年〔满廿一岁〕。3. 老年,晚年。4. 寿命;终生,一生。5. 时代,时期,年代。6.〔口〕很长的时间 a man in his green old ~ 童颜老者。full ~ 成年。A- before honesty. 小孩必须礼让老人。the ~ to come 后世。of the ~ 现代的。the present ~ 现代。It is ~s since I saw you last. 好久不见了。~s ago 从前;〔口〕老早,早就。an ~ ago 一代人以前,多年以前。at the ~ of 在…岁时。be of ~ 成年。be over [under] ~ 超过[未达]适龄年限。come of ~ 达

成人年龄。**from ～ =** with ～. **from ～ to ～** 世世,代代。**from an ～ =** for ～s 久远,长久。(**in**) **all ～s** 今昔(皆然)。**in one's ～** 在老年。**of all ～s** 古往今来的(事情);老老少少的(人)。**to all ～s** 直到千秋万代。**with ～** 因年老而…。**II** *vi*. **1.** 上年纪,显老,变老,苍老。**2.**【化】老化,陈化。—*vt*. **1.** 催人老,使人老。**2.**【化】使老化,使陈化。*Grief ～s us*. 忧伤逼人老。

-age *suf*. 〔名词词尾〕**1.** 集体: cellar*age*, bagg*age*. **2.** 地位、身份、状态: baron*age*, bond*age*. **3.** 动作: break*age*, pass*age*. **4.** 费用、租金: cart*age*, post*age*.

a·ged [ˈeidʒid; ˋedʒɪd] **a**. **1.** 老,老年的 (*opp*. young); 陈年的。*an ～ man* 老人。*the ～* 老人,老者。*～ wine* 陈年老酒。**2.**【物】被老化的。**3.** [ˈeidʒid; ˋedʒɪd] …岁的,(动物)达到几岁龄的〔通常,马 7 岁龄,牛 3 岁龄,猪 2 岁龄,羊 1 岁龄〕。*a man ～ forty* (*years*) 四十岁的人。**-ness** *n*. 老年,高龄。

age·ing [ˈeidʒiŋ; ˋedʒɪŋ] **n**. **1.** 变陈;成熟;【化】老化。**2.**【冶】时效。

age·ism [ˈeidʒizəm; ˋedʒɪzəm] **n**. 对老年人的歧视。

age·less [ˈeidʒlis; ˋedʒlɪs] **a**. 不会老的,长生不老的;永远的。

a·gen·cy [ˈeidʒənsi; ˋedʒənsɪ] **n**. **1.** 动作,作用;行为;动力,力量;媒介。**2.** 经办,代理,代办;代销处。**3.** 机构;(党、政)机关,厅,局。**4.**〔美〕印第安人事务局(= Indian ～)。*the free ～ of the citizens* 市民的自由行动。*the ～ of the wind* 风力。*a detective ～* 秘密侦察所。*a general ～* 总代理店。*an employment ～* 职业介绍所。*French Press A-* 法国新闻社。*A- for International Development* 国际开发署。**through** [**by**] **the ～ of** (某人)经手,经(某人)斡旋。

a·gen·da [əˈdʒendə; əˋdʒɛndə] **n**. 〔*pl*.〕(*sing*. **-dum** [-dəm; -dəm]) **1.** 议事日程,会议事项。**2.** 记事册。**3.**【神学】实际行为〔相对于信仰而言〕。*the first item on the ～* 议程的第一项。**place** [**put**] **sth. on the ～** 把某事提到日程上来。

a·gen·dum [əˈdʒendəm; əˋdʒɛndəm] **n**. agenda 的单数〔一般用其复数形式〕。

a·gen·e·sis [eiˈdʒiːnisis; eˋdʒinɪsɪs] **n**. 发育不全;阳萎,无生殖力。

a·gent [ˈeidʒənt; ˋedʒənt] **n**. **1.** 行为者,动作者;【语法】主动者。**2.** 原因;动因;作用物,(作用)药剂。**3.** 代理人,代办人;代理商,经理人。**4.** 事务官,总办,总管;〔美〕印第安人事务官(= *Indian ～*)。**5.**〔美口〕行商。**6.**〔英〕选举干事。**7.** 间谍,密探,特务。*advance ～* (剧团等的)先遣人员。**8.**【自】(电子计算机中的)代理人程序〔一种可执行繁杂任务的软件程序〕。*biological* [*chemical*] *～* 生物[化学]制剂。*a commercial ～* 商务总管。*a consular ～* 代理领事。*enemy ～s* 奸细,敌特。*a forwarding ～* 运输商,运输行。*a general ～* 总代理。*a house* [*land*] *～* 房屋[地产]经理人。*natural ～s* 自然力。*a road ～* 〔美〕(驿站道路的)拦路强盗。*a secret ～* 特务,侦探。*a sole ～* 包销人。*a station ～* 〔美〕站长。*a ticket ～* 〔美〕售票员。

a·gen·tial [eiˈdʒenʃəl; eˋdʒɛnʃəl] **a**. **1.** 代理人的。**2.**【语法】主动者的。

a·gen·tive [ˈeidʒintiv; ˋedʒəntɪv] **I** *a*.【语法】表示动作主体的词尾的。**II** *n*. 动作主体词尾〔如 *defendant* 的 *-ant*〕。**-tival** [-ˈtaivl; -ˋtaɪvl] **a**.

a·gent pro·vo·ca·teur [aʒɑ̃prɔˌvɔkaˈtəː; aˌʒɑ̃ˌprɔˌvɔˌkaˋtɝ] (*pl*. ***agents provocateurs***)〔F.〕(打入革命组织等内部、并故意诱使其成员触犯刑律而被捕的)密探,内奸,坐探。

ag·er·a·tum [ˌædʒəˈreitəm; ˌædʒəˋretəm] **n**.【植】藿香,藿香蓟。

ag·gie [ˈægi; ˋægɪ] **n**. **1.**〔美俚〕农科(大学)学生;农业学校[大学]。**2.** (小孩玩的)弹球。

ag·gior·na·men·to [ɑːdʒɔːnɑːˈmentɔː; ɑˌdʒɔrnɑˋmento] **n**. 〔It.〕(使罗马天主教的教义、制度等)现代化。

ag·glom·er·ate [əˈglɔməreit; əˋglɑməˌret] **I** *vt*., *vi*. (使)成团,(使)成块,(使)凝聚。**II** [əˈglɔmərit; əˋglɑmərɪt] *a*. **1.** 团集的,凝聚的,成块的。**2.**【植】群生的,密集的。**III** *n*. **1.** 附聚物,凝聚物;团块。**2.** 集块岩;烧结矿,烧结块。

ag·glom·er·a·tion [əˌglɔməˈreiʃən; əˌglɑməˋreʃən] **n**. 团聚作用,凝聚;团块。**be an ～ of** 是集…之大成。

ag·glom·er·a·tive [əˈglɔməreitiv; əˋglɑməˌretɪv] **a**. 凝聚的,附聚的;烧结的。

ag·glu·ti·nant [əˈgluːtinənt; əˋglutənənt] **I** *a*. 黏聚的;凝集的。**II** *n*. 黏聚物;凝集物;烧结剂;凝集剂。

ag·glu·ti·nate [əˈgluːtineit; əˋglutnˌet] **I** *vt*., *vi*. **1.** 胶合,黏上;黏合,接合。**2.** (使)胶质[胶状]化。**3.** (使)(细菌)凝聚。**II** [-nit; -nɪt] *a*. 胶合的;胶着性的。**III** *n*.【矿】黏合集块岩。

ag·glu·ti·na·tion [əˌgluːtiˈneiʃən; əˌglutnˋeʃən] **n**. **1.** 胶合,黏合。**2.** (伤口)愈合。**3.** 凝集(作用,现象)。

ag·glu·ti·na·tive [əˈgluːtinətiv; əˋglutnˌetɪv] **a**. 黏着的,胶合的。

ag·glu·ti·nin [əˈgluːtinin; əˋglutɪnɪn] **n**.【微、医】(使细菌、血球等起凝结作用的)凝集素。

ag·glu·tin·o·gen [ˌægluˈtinədʒən; ˌægluˋtɪnədʒən] **n**.【微、医】(产生凝集素的)凝集原。**-ic** *a*.

ag·grade [əˈgreid; əˋgred] *vt*. 使(河床或河谷)填积,加积。**-gra·da·tion** *n*.

ag·gran·dize [əˈgrændaiz; əˋgrænˌdaɪz] *vt*. **1.** 加大,扩大 (*opp*. reduce)。**2.** 提高(权利、地位)。**3.** 夸张 (*opp*. minimize)。*The king sought to ～ himself at the expense of his people*. 国王以牺牲百姓为代价来扩大自己的权势。**-ment** *n*.

ag·gra·vate [ˈægrəveit; ˋægrəˌvet] *vt*. **1.** 加重(病情等);使恶化。**2.**〔口〕惹恼,激怒。

ag·gra·vat·ing [ˈægrəveitiŋ; ˋægrəˌvetɪŋ] **a**. **1.** 使…恶化的。**2.**〔口〕可恼的,可厌的,惹人生气的。*How ～!* 多令人生气呀!

ag·gra·va·tion [ˌægrəˈveiʃən; ˌægrəˋveʃən] **n**. **1.** 加重;恶化。**2.**〔口〕激怒,惹恼。

ag·gre·gate [ˈægrigeit; ˋægrɪˌget] **I** *vt*. **1.** 集合,(使)聚集。**2.** 总计,共计,合计。*The sum will ～ a thousand dollars*. 总额共计一千元。**II** [ˈægrigit; ˋægrɪgɪt] *a*. **1.** 聚合的;(花)聚生的。**2.**【地】聚成岩的。**3.** 合计的,总。*an ～ flower* 聚生花。**III** *n*. **1.** 聚集,集合。**2.** 总数。**3.** 聚集体;凝聚体;团粒。**4.**【建】混凝料。**in the ～** 总计,合计。**～ animals** 群体动物。**～ motion** 集成运动。**～ power** 总力。**～ tonnage** (船的)总吨位。**～ unit** 联合机组;联动装置[机构]。

ag·gre·ga·tion [ˌægriˈgeiʃən; ˌægrɪˋgeʃən] **n**. **1.** 聚合,集合,凝聚,集成。**2.**【植】族聚;【动】群聚。**3.** 集团,聚合体,集成体。**-ga·tive** [ˈægrigeitiv; ˋægrɪˌgetɪv] **a**.

ag·gress [əˈgres; əˋgrɛs] *vi*. 攻击;侵略,挑衅 (*on*, *upon*, *against*)。*～ upon the public property* 侵占公共财产。

ag·gres·sion [əˈgreʃən; əˋgrɛʃən] **n**. 攻击;侵略,侵犯。*cultural ～* 文化侵略。*economic ～* 经济侵略。**commit ～ against** (对…)进行侵略。

ag·gres·sive [əˈgresiv; əˋgrɛsɪv] **a**. **1.** 侵略的,侵犯的;攻势的。**2.** 借故生端的;爱打架的,要打架的。**3.**〔美〕有进取心的,积极行动的 (*opp*. retiring)。*an ～ policy* 侵略政策。**assume** [**take**] **the ～** 挑战,取攻势。**-ly** *ad*.

ag·gres·sor [əˈgresə; əˋgrɛsɚ] **n**. 攻击者,侵略者;侵略国(= *～ nation*)。

ag·grieve [əˈgriːv; əˋgriv] *vt*. **1.**〔常用被动语态〕使烦恼;使悲伤。**2.** 侵害,使受委屈。**fee** [**be**] **～d at** [**by**] 感到受屈。

A

ag·gro [ˈægrəu; ˋægro] **n.** 〔英俚〕挑衅(性)。

a·gha [ˈɑːgə, ˈægə; ˋɑgə, ˋægə] **n.** 大人;统帅;老总〔土耳其和其他穆斯林国家对大官吏的尊称〕(= aga)。

a·ghast [əˈgɑːst; əˋgæst] **a.** 〔常用作表语〕吃惊的,吓呆的。***stand ~ at*** 被…吓一跳;被…吓呆。

ag·ile [ˈædʒail; ˋædʒaɪl] **a.** 轻快的,灵便的,敏捷的,灵活的。*an ~ mind* [*wit*] 头脑灵活[才思敏捷]。**-ly** ***ad.***

a·gil·i·ty [əˈdʒiliti; əˋdʒɪlətɪ] **n.** 轻快,敏捷;机敏。

a·gin [əˈgin; əˋgɪn] 〔方〕= again, against.

ag·ing [ˈeidʒiŋ; ˋedʒɪŋ] age 的现在分词。**n.** **1.** 陈酿。**2.** 熟化。**~ gene**【生】致衰老基因。

ag·i·o [ˈædʒiəu; ˋædʒo] **n.** (*pl.* **~s**) **1.**【商】贴水,扣头,折扣。**2.** 汇兑,兑换。

ag·i·o·tage [ˈædʒətidʒ; ˋædʒətɪdʒ] **n.** **1.** 汇兑(业务);兑换。**2.** 〔罕〕股票买卖。

ag·ism [ˈeidʒizəm; ˋedʒɪzəm] **n.** = ageism.

ag·i·ta [ˈædʒitə; ˋædʒɪtə] **n.** **1.** 胃灼热,消化不良。**2.** = agitation.

ag·i·tate [ˈædʒiteit; ˋædʒəˏtet] **vt.** **1.** 搅动,摇动。**2.** 激动,鼓励,煽动。**3.** 搅乱(人心),使不安,使谋虑。**4.** 热烈讨论。**5.** 思考。**6.** (通过演说或文章)使人注意。*The wind ~d the sea.* 风使海浪翻滚。*~ a fan* 摇扇。*be ~d by the bad news* 为听到坏消息而不安。*~ a question* 热烈讨论问题。—**vi.** 鼓吹,游说。***~ for*** (*reform*) 倡导(改革),鼓吹(改革)运动。**-d a.** **1.** 表现出不安的。**2.** 颤抖的。**3.** (问题等)被热烈讨论的,被激烈辩论的。

ag·i·ta·tion [ˌædʒiˈteiʃən; ˏædʒəˋteʃən] **n.** **1.** 搅动,搅拌。**2.** 激动;焦虑。**3.** 议论;鼓动。**4.** (民众的)骚动。**5.**【医】兴奋。*an anti-slavery ~* 废除奴隶运动。***be all ~*** 异常焦虑。**-al a.** 鼓动性的。

a·gi·ta·to [ˌædʒiˈtɑːtəu; ˏɑdʒɪəˋtɑto] **ad.** 〔It.〕【乐】快速而又激动地。

ag·i·ta·tor [ˈædʒiteitə; ˋædʒəˏtetəˑ] **n.** **1.** 鼓动者,鼓吹者。**2.** 搅拌器。

ag·it·prop [ˈædʒitprɔp; ˋædʒɪtˏprɑp] **I a.** (戏剧、传单等)宣传鼓动性的。**II n.** **1.** 宣传鼓动。**2.** 宣传鼓动机关;宣传鼓动者。

a·gleam [əˈgliːm; əˋglim] **a.** 〔用作表语〕,**ad.** 发光地;发光的。*a city ~ with lights* 灯火辉煌的城市。

ag·let [ˈæglit; ˋæglɪt] **n.** **1.** (带端)金属箍,带扣。**2.** (服装上装饰用的)挂襻[饰钮、带子、别针]。

a·gley [əˈgliː, əˈglai; əˋgli, əˋglaɪ] **ad.** 〔Scot.〕斜,歪。

a·glit·ter [əˈglitə; əˋglɪtəˑ] **a.** 〔用作表语〕, ad. 闪耀的[地]。

a·glow [əˈgləu; əˋglo] **a.** 〔用作表语〕,**ad.** 发亮,发红;兴奋。***be ~ with*** (点)得通红,(烧)得发红 (*He is ~ with health.* 他气色好。他容光焕发。*The garden is ~ with many flowers.* 园中百花盛开)。

AGM = **1.** annual general meeting [英]年会,每年一度的全会。**2.** air-to-ground missile 空对地导弹。

ag·nail [ˈægneil; ˋægˏnel] **n.** **1.** (指甲旁的)倒刺。**2.** 甲沟炎。**3.** (脚趾上的)鸡眼。

ag·nate [ˈægneit; ˋægnet] **I a.** **1.** 父方的,男系的 (*cf.* cognate)。**2.** 同族的,同种族的。**II n.** **1.** 男系亲属。**2.** 同族;同种。

ag·nat·ic [ægˈnætik; ægˋnætɪk] **a.** 男系亲属的。

ag·na·tion [ægˈneiʃən; ægˋneʃən] **n.** 男系亲属,宗族关系。

Ag·nes [ˈægnis; ˋægnɪs] **n.** 阿格尼丝〔女子名〕。

ag·no·men [ægˈnəumen; ægˋnomen] **n.** (*pl.* **~s**, ***ag·nom·i·na*** [ægˈnɔminə; ægˋnɑmɪnə]) **1.** 〔古罗马〕(因功授与的)附名,第四名〔如 *P. Cornelius Scipio Africanus* 即因出征阿非利加有功而被授与第四名 *Africanus*〕。**2.** 浑名,绰号。

ag·nos·tic [ægˈnɔstik; ægˋnɑstɪk] **I a.**【哲】不可知论的。**II n.** 不可知论者。

ag·nos·ti·cism [ægˈnɔstisizəm; ægˋnɑstəˏsɪzəm] **n.**【哲】不可知论。

Ag·nus De·i [ˈɑːgnusˈdeiiː; ˋægnəsˋdiaɪ] 〔L.〕神羔;神羔像;神羔诵,神羔祈祷式。

a·go [əˈgəu; əˋgo] **ad.** 以前,前。*ten years ~* 十年前。*How long ~ did you see him?* 你多久以前见过他? ***long ~*** 很久以前,从前。***not long ~*** 前不久。***some time ~*** 不久前。

a·gog [əˈgɔg; əˋgɑg] **a.** 〔常用作表语〕,**ad.** **1.** 急着要,渴望。**2.** 极度兴奋。*set the whole town ~* 轰动全城。***all ~ for*** 热望,急待。***all ~ to*** (*do*) 急着要,急待。

ago·go [əˈgəugəu; əˋgoˏgo] **a.** **1.** 活泼的,精力充沛的。**2.** 最时髦的。**3.** 摇摆舞的,跳摇摆舞者的,摇摆舞音乐唱片的,摇摆舞厅的。

a·gon [ˈɑːgɔn; ˋægon] **n.** (*pl.* **~s**, ***a·go·nes*** [əˈgɔniːz; əˋgɑniz]) **1.** (古希腊的运动、文学等的)锦标赛。**2.** (古希腊戏剧中的)人物之间的冲突。

ag·o·nal [ˈægənl; ˋgɑnl̩] **a.** 垂死痛楚的;呻吟待毙的;濒死的。

a·gone [əˈgɔn; əˋgɑn] **a.**, **ad.** 〔古〕以前,过去,往昔。

a·gon·ic [əˈgɔnik; eˋgɑnɪk] **a.** 不成角的;【物】无偏差的。**~ line**【物】零磁偏线。

ag·o·nist [ˈægənist; ˋægənɪst] **n.**【解】主动肌。

ag·o·nis·tic [ˌægəuˈnistik; ˏægəˋnɪstɪk] **a.** **1.** 〔古希腊〕运动比赛的。**2.** 争辩的,论战的。**3.** 紧张的,不自然的。*~ poses* 做作的姿态。**-s n.** 运动比赛学。

ag·o·nize [ˈægənaiz; ˋægəˏnaɪz] **vi.** 苦闷;挣扎。— **vt.** 使烦恼,使苦恼。*an ~d look* 愁眉苦脸,苦相。**-d a.** 烦恼的,痛苦的。

ag·o·niz·ing [ˈægənaiziŋ; ˋægəˏnaɪzɪŋ] **a.** 使人苦恼的。*an ~ pain* [*feeling*] 令人坐卧不安的痛苦[感觉]。**-ly** ***ad.***

ag·o·ny [ˈægəni; ˋægənɪ] **n.** **1.** 苦恼,烦闷。**2.** 死的痛苦。**3.** (感情的)迸发。**4.** 挣扎。***~ of mind*** 苦闷,苦恼。***in ~*** 在苦恼中。***in an ~ of joy*** 喜极,乐极。**~ column** (寻物、寻人、离婚等的)广告栏。

ag·o·ra[1] [ˈægərə; ˋægərə] **n.** (*pl.* ***-rae*** [-riː; -ri], **~s** [-rəz; -rəz]) 古希腊的大会场〔尤指集市〕。

a·go·ra[2] [ˌɑːgəuˈrɑː; ˏagoˋrɑ] **n.** (*pl.* ***-rot*** [-rəut; -rot]) 阿高拉〔以色列货币名,等于一(以色列)镑的 1/100〕。

ag·o·ra·pho·bi·a [ˌægərəˈfəubiə; ˏægərəˋfobɪə] **n.**【医】广场恐怖;旷野恐怖。

a·gou·ti [əˈguːti; əˋgutɪ] **n.** (*pl.*)【动】刺鼠。

a·gou·ty [əˈguːti; əˋgutɪ] **n.** (*pl.* ***-ties***) = agouti.

a·graffe [əˈgræf; əˋgræf] **n.** 钩钮,搭扣;搭钩。

a·gran·u·lo·cy·to·sis [əˌgrænjuˌləusaiˈtəusis; eˏgrænjəˏlosaɪˋtosɪs] **n.**【医】粒性白血球缺乏症。

ag·ra·pha [ˈægrəfə; ˋægrəfə] **n.** [*pl.*] 〔Gr.〕未载于福音书中的耶稣的言论。

a·graph·i·a [æˈgræfiə; æˋgræfɪə] **n.**【医】(因脑受损而不能写字的)失写症。**-ic a.**

a·grar·i·an [əˈgrɛəriən; əˋgrɛrɪən] **I a.** **1.** 土地的,耕地的。**2.** 农民的;农业的。**3.** 生于田野间的,野生的。*an ~ outrage* 农民暴动。*~ reforms* 土地改革。*~ revolution* 土地革命。*~ plants* 野生植物。**II n.** 土地均分论者。**-ism n.** 土地均分论,土地均分运动。

a·grav·ic [əˈgrævik; əˋgrævɪk] **n.**【宇】无动力区,无重力状况。

a·gree [əˈgriː; əˋgri] **vi.** **1.** 同意,赞成,承认,答应。**2.** 意见相合[相投];(气候、饮食等)适合,合适,合;调合。**3.** 约定,商定。**4.** 符合;【语法】(人称、数、格、性等前后)一致。*I ~.* 好,我赞成。*Brothers and sisters should ~.* 兄弟姐妹应当和好相处。— **vt.** 同意(某事);使…达到一致;认为正确无误。*We all agreed that the plan is a good one.* 我们一致认为这个计划很好。***~ in*** (*opinion*; *thinking*) (意见)相合;(想法)一致。***~ like***

cats and dogs 像猫狗一样处不好。～ ***on*** [***upon***, ***as to***] 对…意见一致。～ ***to*** (*a proposal*; *terms*) 答应,承认(提议;条件)。～ ***to differ*** [***to disagree***] 彼此同意保留不同意见。～ ***with*** 1. 赞同,与…意见相同,与…符合,与…相投。2. 与…一致。3. 适合,合(口胃),相宜。

a·gree·a·ble [ə'griəbl; ə`griəbl] ***a***. 1. 适意的,愉快的。2. 有礼貌的,会处人的。3. 欣然赞同的,可答应的。4. 适合…的,一致的。*I am quite* ～. 〔口、俚〕很好,我很同意。～ *to the taste* 可口,味道好。*be* ～ *to ear* 动听。*be* ～ *to a proposal* 欣然赞同一项建议。*be* ～ *to reason* 合乎道理。～ ***to*** 依,从,遵,照,如 (*A- to my promise, I have come*. 如约而来)。***do the*** ～ 亲切款待。***make oneself*** ～ ***to*** 尽量迎合,亲切待人。**-ness** ***n***. 适合,一致;适意,愉快。

a·gree·a·bly [ə'griəbli; ə`griəblɪ] ***ad***. 1. 欢然,欣然。2. 依照,一致,一样。～ ***to*** 照,应,依 (～ *to your request* 遵照您的要求)。

a·greed [ə'griːd; ə`grid] ***a***. 已一致[同意]的。(*It is*) ～! 好! 行! *They met at the* ～ *time*. 他们按约定时间见面。

a·gree·ment [ə'griːmənt; ə`grimənt] ***n***. 1. 一致,同意。2. 契约;协约,协定。3. 【语法】一致,呼应。***a gentleman's*** [***gentlemen's***] ～ 君子协定。***by*** ～ 同意,依约。***arrive at*** [***come to***] ***an*** ～ 达成协议。***bring about an*** ～ 商妥。***conclude*** [***enter into***] ***an*** ～ 订约。***in*** ～ ***with*** 符合…照…。***make an*** ～ ***with*** 与…达成协议。

a·gré·ment [ɑgremɑ̃; ɑgre`mɑ̃] ***n***. 〔F.〕1. (驻在国政府对派遣外交使节的)同意。2. 〔*pl*.〕(环境的)舒适,惬意。3. 〔*pl*.〕【乐】装饰音。*the* ～ *of social life* 社交生活上令人愉快的礼仪举止。

a·gres·tic [ə'grestik; ə`grɛstɪk] ***a***. 1. 乡土(气)的。2. 粗野的。

ag·ri·bar·on ['ægribærən; `ægrɪbærən] ***n***. 〔美〕农业综合企业界巨头。

ag·ri·busi·ness ['ægriˌbiznis; `ægrɪˏbɪznɪs] ***n***. 农业综合企业〔其业务包括农产品的加工,农业机械的制造以及化肥的生产等〕。

agric. = 1. agricultural. 2. agriculture. 3. agriculturist.

ag·ri·cul·tur·al [ˌægri'kʌltʃurəl; ˏægrɪ`kʌltʃərəl] ***a***. 农业的,耕种的,农学(上)的。*an* ～ *experimental station* 农业试验场。～ *products* 农产品。*an* ～ *school* 农业学校。*an* ～ *show* 农业展览会。

ag·ri·cul·ture ['ægrikʌltʃə; `ægrɪˏkʌltʃɚ] ***n***. 农业,农耕;农业生产;农学。

ag·ri·cul·tur·ist [ˌægri'kʌltʃərist; ˏægrɪ`kʌltʃərɪst] **-tur·al·ist** [-tʃurəlist; -tʃərəlɪst] ***n***. 农民,农场经营者;农学家。

ag·ri·mo·ny ['ægriməni; `ægrəˏmonɪ] ***n***. 【植】龙芽草。

ag·ri·mo·tor ['ægriməutə; `ægrɪˏmotɚ] ***n***. 农用拖拉机。

ag·ri·ol·o·gy [ˌægri'ɔlədʒi; ˏægrɪ`ɑlədʒɪ] ***n***. 无文字民族的风俗研究。

ag·ro ['ægrəu; `ægro] ***n***. = aggro.

ag·ro- *comb. f*. 土地,田地;农业。

ag·ro·bi·ol·o·gy [ˌægrə*u*bai'ɔlədʒi; ˏægrəbaɪ`ɑlədʒɪ] ***n***. 农业生物学。

ag·ro·chem·i·cal [ˌægrə*u*'kemikl; ˏægro`kɛmɪkl] ***n***. 1. 农业化学制品;农业化学药品。2. 从农产品中提取的化学药品(如糠醛)。

ag·rol·o·gy [ə'grɔlədʒi; ə`grɑlədʒɪ] ***n***. 农业土壤学。

ag·ro·nom·ic, -i·cal [ˌægrə*u*'nɔmik(əl); ˏægro`nɑmɪk(əl)] ***a***. 农业的,农艺的。～ *practices* 农业技术。～ *characters* 农艺性状。

ag·ro·nom·ics [ˌægrə*u*'nɔmiks; ˏægro`nɑmɪks] ***n***. 耕作学,农学;农业经营。

ag·ron·o·mist [æ'grɔnəmist, æ`grɑnəmɪst] ***n***. 耕作学家,农学家。

ag·ron·o·my [ə'grɔnəmi; ə`grɑnəmɪ] ***n***. 农学;作物学。

ag·ros·tol·o·gy [ˌægrəu*s*'tɔlədʒi; ˏægros`tɑlədʒɪ] ***n***. 【植】草本学。

ag·ro·tech·ni·cal ['ægrə*u*'teknikəl; `ægro`tɛknɪkəl] ***a***. 农业技术的。

ag·ro·tech·nic·i·an ['ægrə*u*tek'niʃən; `ægrotɛk`nɪʃən] ***n***. 农业技术员,农技师。

ag·ro·tech·nique ['ægrə*u*tek'niːk; `ægrotɛk`nik] ***n***. 农业技术。

ag·ro·tech·ny ['ægrə*u*tekni; `ægroˏtɛknɪ] ***n***. 农业品加工学。

ag·ro·town ['ægrə*u*taun; `ægrotaʊn] ***n***. 农业地区的城镇。

ag·ro·type ['ægə*u*taip; `ægrotaɪp] ***n***. 1. 农田类型。2. 作物类型。

a·ground [ə'graund; ə`graʊnd] ***a***. 〔用作表语〕, ***ad***. 1. 在地上。2. 搁浅,触礁。***get*** [***go***, ***run***, ***strike***] ～ (船)搁浅,触礁。

a·guar·dien·te [ɑːgwɑːdi'entei; ɑgwɑrdɪ`ɛnte] ***n***. 〔Sp.〕次白兰地酒;〔美西部〕甘蔗做的酒。

a·gue ['eigjuː; `egju] ***n***. 1. 疟疾。2. 打冷颤,发冷。

a·gued ['eigjuːd; `egjud] ***a***. 患冷热病的,害疟疾的。

a·gue·weed ['eigjuːwiːd; `egjuwid] ***n***. 1. 五叶龙胆。2. 贯叶泽兰(= boneset)。

a·gu·ish ['eigju(ː)iʃ; `egjʊɪʃ] ***a***. 1. 容易产生疟疾的;易患疟疾的;疟疾引起的。2. 打冷颤的,发冷的。

a·gu·ti [ə'guːti; ə`gutɪ] ***n***. = agouti.

ah [ɑː; ɑ] ***int***. 啊! 呀! 嗳! 〔表现痛苦、惊奇、怜惜、厌弃、欢喜等〕*Ah me*! 嗳呀!

A.H. = 〔L.〕*anno Hegirae* (= in the year of the Hegira) 穆罕默德纪元。

a.h. = ampere-hour 安培小时,安时。

a·ha [ɑ(ː)'hɑː; ɑ`hɑ] ***int***. 嗳呀! 哎嘿! 〔表现喜悦、轻蔑、惊愕等〕。

à haute voix [ɑː'əut'vwɑ; ɑ`ot`vwɑ] 〔F.〕高声地。

a·head [ə'hed; ə`hɛd] ***a***. 〔常作表语〕, ***ad***. 1. 在前;向前;提前。2. 〔美〕赢得;领先。*set the clock* ～ 把钟朝前拨。*He is* ～ *of his times*. 他走在时代前面。*be* ～ *of the other students in the class* 在班上名列前茅。～ ***of*** 在…前面;比…进步;优于;胜于 (*walk* ～ *of sb*. 走在某人前面)。***be*** ～ 〔口〕赢;赚。***be*** ～ ***of*** …比…好。***Breakers*** ～! 前面有碎浪[暗礁]! 前途危险! ***Full speed*** ～ 全速前进。***get*** ～ 前进,抢先。***get*** ～ ***in the world*** 出头,发迹。***go*** ～ 上前;前进;继续下去;进步 (*Things were going* ～. 事事顺畅)。***Go*** ～! 1. 【海】前进! 冲啊! (*opp*. go astern!); 开呀! 〔美国对火车的口令〕;动手! 干呀! 〔工作口令〕。2. 那末,还有呢〔提话口气〕。***Right*** [***straight***] ～ 1. 就在眼前。2. 勇往直前 (*They saw it right* ～. 他们看见那东西就在眼前。*galloping straight* ～ 驰骋向前)。***wind*** ～ 顶头风,迎面风。

a·heap [ə'hiːp; ə`hip] ***ad***. 〔英〕重叠,堆积。

a·hem [ə'hem, hm; ə`hɛm, hm] ***int***. 1. 啊嗨! 〔引起注意〕。2. 嗯〔语塞时发音〕。

a·him·sa [ə'himsə; ə`hɪmsə] ***n***. 【佛】不伤生;杀戒。

a·his·tor·ic(al) [ˌeihis'tɔːrik(əl); ˏehɪs`tɑrɪk(əl)] ***a***. 稗史的;与历史无关的;无历史记载的。**-al·ly** ***ad***.

A.H.M.S. = American Home Missionary Society 美国国内传教会。

A-ho·ri·zon ['eihə'raizn; `ehə`raɪzn̩] ***n***. 【地】表土,上层(甲层)土壤(腐植土)。

a·hoy [ə'hɔi; ə`hɔɪ] ***int***. 【海】喂! 啊嗬! 〔呼叫他船之声〕。*Ship* ～! 船呀! 喂!

AHQ = army headquarters 集团军司令部。

Ah·ri·man ['ɑːrimən; `ɑrɪmən] ***n***. 【祆教】鬼,邪神。

à huis clos [ɑː'wiː'kləu; aˏwi`klo] 〔F.〕关着门;秘密。

A

a·hull [əˈhʌl; əˋhʌl] *ad*.【海】卷帆并转舵于下风。

A·hu·ra Maz·da [ˈɑːhurəˈmæzdə; ˋɑhʊrəˋmæzdə]【袄教】最高的神,创世主,善灵(= Ormazd)。

Ah·waz [ɑːˈwɑːz; ɑˋwɑz] *n*. 阿瓦士〔伊朗城市〕。

a·i[1] [ˈɑːiː; ˋaɪ] *n*.【动】三趾树懒〔南美产〕。

ai[2] [ai; ɑɪ] *int*. 唉!〔痛苦、悲伤、怜悯等的感叹词〕。

AIAA = 1. American Institute of Aeronautics and Astronautics 美国航空和星际航空协会。2. Aircraft Industries Association of America 美国飞机工业协会。

AIC = ammunition identification code 弹药识别代字。

AICE = 1. American Institute of Chemical Engineers 美国化学工程师协会。2. American Institute of Consulting Engineers 美国顾问工程师协会。

AIChE = American Institute of Chemical Engineers 美国化学工程师协会。

AID = Agency for International Development〔美〕国际开发署。

aid [eid; ed] **I** *n*. 1. 帮助,援助。2. 帮助者,助手。3. 辅助设备。4.【海】航标。5.〔美〕副官(= aide-de-camp)。6.【英史】(国会允许的)国王特享税。*a deaf* ~ 助听器。*audio-visual* ~*s* 视听教具。*short-range* ~*s*【无】近程导航设备。***by*** [***with***] ***the*** ~ ***of*** 借…的帮助。***call in sb.'s*** ~ 求某人援助。***call*** (*sb.*) ***to one's*** ~ 求助于(人),向(人)求援。***give first*** ~ 急救。***go to sb.'s*** ~援助(某人)。***in*** ~ ***of*** 以助…,来帮助…。***What's*** (***all***) ***this in*** ~ ***of***? 〔口〕你的用意何在? **II** *vt*., *vi*. 助,帮助,援助;协助;接济。~ ***and abet***【法】同谋,教唆。~ (*sb.*) ***in*** (*doing*; *one's work*) 帮助(某人做),帮忙。~**man** 战地医务急救员。~**post**, ~***station*** 救护所。

A·i·da [ɑːˈiːdə; ɑˋidə]《阿伊达》〔意大利歌剧家威尔第的一部歌剧〕。

aid-de-camp [ˈeiddəˈkæmp; ˋeddəˋkæmp] *n*. (*pl*. ***aids-*** [ˈeidz-; ˋedz-])〔美〕= aide-de-camp.

aide [eid; ed] *n*. 1. = aide-de-camp. 2. 助手。

aide-de-camp [eidəˈkɑ̃ːŋ; edəˋkɑ̃] *n*. (*pl*. ***aides-*** [ˈeidz-; ˋedz-])〔F.〕【军】随从武官[参谋];副官;幕僚。

aide-mé·moire [ˈeidˈmemwɑː; ˌɛdˌmeˋmwɑr] *n*.〔F.〕(外交上的)备忘录。

aid·man [ˈeidmən; ˋedˌmæn] *n*. (*pl*. ***-men*** [-men; -men])【军】战斗部队医务员。

AIDS, Aids [eidz; edz] = acquired immune deficiency syndrome 艾滋病,爱滋病,获得性免疫缺损综合症。~**-related complex** 艾滋病相关症〔如:腹泻、发烧、消瘦、乏力等多为前期症状〕。

AIEE = American Institute of Electrical Engineers 美国电气工程师协会。

ai·glet [ˈeiglit; ˋeglɪt] *n*. = aglet.

ai·grette [ˈeigret, eiˈgret; ˋegrɛt, eˋgrɪt] *n*. 1.【鸟】白鹭。2.【植】冠毛。3. 鹭鸶毛帽饰。4.(宝石的)枝状饰。

ai·guille [ˈeigwiːl, ˈeigwiː; eˋgwil, eˋgwi] *n*. 1. 尖峰,锥岩。2.(岩石的)钻孔器。

ai·guil·lette [ˌeigwiˈlet; ˌegwɪˋlɛt] *n*.【军】饰带,肩带。

AIIE = American Institute of Industrial Engineers 美国工业工程师协会。

Ai·ken [ˈeikin; ˋekɪn] *n*. 艾肯〔姓氏〕。

ai·ki·do [aiˈkiːdəu; aɪˋkido] *n*.〔Jap.〕合气道〔一种自卫角斗术〕。

ail [eil; el] *vt*. 使苦恼,使烦恼。*What* ~*s you*? 你怎么啦? 哪里不舒服? — *vi*. 不舒服,生病(= ill)。*The child is* ~*ing*. 小孩生病了。

ai·lan·thus [eiˈlenθəs; eˋlænθəs] *n*. (*pl*. ~*es*) 臭椿属植物,樗树属植物。**-lanth·ic** [-θik; -θɪk] *a*.

Ai·leen [ˈeiliːn; ˋelin] *n*. 艾琳〔女子名, Helen 的异体〕。

ai·ler·on [ˈeilərɔn; ˋeləˌrɑn] *n*.〔常 *pl*.〕【空】副翼,辅(助)翼。

ail·ing [ˈeiliŋ; ˋelɪŋ] *a*. 不舒服的,害病的。

ail·ment [ˈeilmənt; ˋelmənt] *n*. 小病,失调。

ai·lu·ro·pho·bi·a [aiˌluərəˈfəubiə; eˌlʊrəˋfobɪə] *n*. 恐猫病,畏猫。**-phobe** *n*.

AIM = 1. American Indian Movement 美国印第安人运动。2. air intercept missile 空中截击导弹。

aim [eim; em] **I** *vi*. 1. 瞄准,针对。2. 指望,企图,旨在(*at*)。~ *at a mark* 瞄准目标。~ *at success* 指望成功。★英国说 ~ at doing, 美国则说 ~ to do. ~ ***at the moon***〔口〕妄想。~ ***high*** 胸怀大志,有志气,力争上游。~ ***too low*** 胸无大志。—*vt*. 把…瞄准,把…指向;把…掷向(*at*)。~ *a pistol at sb*. 以手枪瞄准某人。~ *a book at sb.'s head* 拿起一本书向某人的头上扔去。**II** *n*. 1. 照准,瞄准;靶子,目标。2. 目的,志向;宗旨。*achieve* [*attain*] *one's* ~ 达到目的。*miss one's* ~ 瞄歪;(希望)落空,失败。*the* ~ *and end of art* 艺术的终极目的。***take*** ~ (***at***)(对…)瞄准。***without*** ~无目的地,乱,瞎。

aim·less [ˈeimlis; ˋemlɪs] *a*. 无目的的,无目标的。**-ly** *ad*. **-ness** *n*.

ain [ein; en] *a*.〔英方〕自己的。

aî·né [eˈnei; ˌɛˋne] *a*.〔F.〕长子的,兄的(*cf*. cadet)。

aî·née [eˈnei; ɛˋne] *a*.〔F.〕姊的。

Ai·no [ˈainəu; ˋaɪno] **I** *a*.〔日〕阿伊努族的,虾夷人的。**II** *n*. (*pl*. ~ (*s*))〔日〕阿伊努人,虾夷人。

ain't [eint; ent]〔口〕= am not, are not, is not, has not, have not. *A- we got fun*?〔美〕不愉快吗?

A Int = Air Intelligence 航空情报。

Ai·nu [ˈainuː; ˋaɪnu] **I** *n*. (*pl*. ~ (*s*)) = Aino (*n*.) **II** *a*. = Aino (*a*.)。

air [ɛə; ɛr] **I** *n*. 1. 空气,大气。2. 天空,空中。3. 微风,和风。4. 态度,样子,风度,气派;〔*pl*.〕高傲的架子。5. 传播,公开。6.【乐】曲调,主调。*fresh* [*foul*] ~ 新鲜的[污浊的]空气。*open* ~ 户外。(*a*) *change of* ~ 转地(疗养)。*noxious* ~ 毒气。*a slight* ~ 微风。*a vernal* ~ 春风。*a national* ~ 国歌。*sing an* ~ 唱一曲。*have an* ~ *of importance* 摆架子。~***s and graces*** 装腔作势。***assume*** ~***s*** = put on ~s. ***be on the*** ~ 正在广播。***beat the*** ~ 徒劳,白劳。***by*** ~ 用[坐]飞机;用无线电。***clear the*** ~ 通通空气;澄清事实;消除误会。***fan the*** ~打空,扑空。***fish in the*** ~ = plough the ~. ***get the*** ~〔美俚〕被辞退,被解聘;被朋友[情人等]抛弃。***give*** ~ ***to one's view*** 说出自己意见。***give oneself*** ~***s*** 充气派,自大,摆架子。***give*** (*sb.*) ***the*** ~〔美俚〕辞退,解聘,撵走(某人);抛弃朋友[情人等]。***go off the*** ~【无】停止播送。***go on the*** ~【无】开始播送。***go up in the*** ~〔美俚〕1. 忿激,突然生气。2.(演员)突然忘记台词。***hot*** ~〔口〕吹牛,夸夸其谈。***in the*** ~ 1. 在空中。2.(谣言等)流传。3.(计划等)悬着,未决,渺茫(*His plans are still in the* ~. 他的计划还很渺茫)。4.【军】无掩护的,未设防的。***live on*** ~ 靠喝风过日子。***make the*** ~ ***blue*** 诅咒。***on the*** ~ 广播中,播送中。***out of thin*** ~ 无中生有地。***plough the*** ~ 白费气力。***put on*** ~***s*** 傲慢,摆架子,装气派。***put*** [***sent***] (*sb.*) ***on the*** ~〔口〕传播,宣扬。***speak on the*** ~ 发表广播演说。***take*** ~ 传开,泄露。***take the*** ~ 1. 出外兜风,散步。2.【空】离地,腾空,飞起来。3.【无】开始播送。4.〔俚〕离开,走开。***take to the*** ~ 做飞行家。***tread*** (***up***) ***on*** ~ 扬扬得意。***up in the*** ~ (计划等)未决,渺茫。***walk on*** ~ 扬扬得意。***with word and*** ~ 演唱皆备。**II** *vt*. 1. 晾,吹吹,使通风;烘干;烤干;风干。2. 宣扬,显示;夸示。3. 播送。~ *one's clothes on the roof* 在屋顶晾衣服。~ *the dog* 牵着狗散步。~ *a room* 让房间通通风。~ *oneself* 出外兜风,散步。~ *costly jewels* 夸示贵重宝石。~ *one's opinion* 发表己见。*The game was* ~*ed to all parts of the country*. 比赛实况向全国广播。— *vi*. 1. 散步,兜风。2. 晾着。3. 播送。~ **action** 空战。~ **alarm** 空袭警报。~ **alert** 1. 空袭警报(期间)。

2.【军】空中待机。~ **attack** 空中攻击,空袭。~ **base** 航空[空军]基地。~ **bath** 空气浴(装置);空气干燥器。~ **battery** (可以再充电的)空气电池。~ **bearing** 空气轴承。~ **bed** 气垫,气床。~ **bladder**【动】气泡;鳔。~ **blast** 鼓风,空气喷射。**Air Board** 航空局。~ **boat** 用在空气中旋转的螺旋桨推进的平底船。~**borne** *a*. 空运的,机载的;空降的;空中传播的;用空气运送的;通过无线电[电视]播送的(~*borne bacteria* 空气传播的细菌。~*borne troops* 空运部队)。~**borne soccer** 飞碟运动,飞盘运动。~ **brake** 空气制动器;减速板。~ **breather** 以吸入的大气助燃推进的导弹。~ **brick** 多孔砖,空心砖。~**-bridge** 空运线。~**brush** 1. *n*. 喷枪。2. *vt*. 用喷枪喷。~**bus**〔口〕(短程或中程)大型客机。~**cast** 1. *n*.〔美〕无线电广播。2. *vt*. 用无线电广播。~**caster**〔美〕无线电广播员。~ **castle** 空中楼阁,妄想。~ **cell**【解】气胞,气囊。~ **chamber** 气胞;气腔;气室。~ **coach** 二等客机。~ **cock** 气旋塞。**Air Commodore**〔英〕空军准将。~**compressor** 空气压缩机。~ **condenser** 空气冷却机。~**-condition** *vt*.〔美〕在…装设空气调节器;调节…的空气湿度和温度。~**-conditioned** *a*. 装有空气调节器的。~ **conditioner** 空气调节器。~**-conditioning** 空气调节。~ **control** 空中交通管制。~**-cooled** *a*. 气冷(式)。~ **cooler** 空气冷却器,气冷装置,气冷机。~ **corps**〔美〕(陆军中的)飞行大队。~ **corridor** 空中走廊。**Air Council**〔英〕空军最高会议。~ **cover** = ~ umbrella. ~ **craft** 航空器,飞行器,飞机。~**-craft(s)man**〔英〕空军下级士兵。~**craftwoman** 空军下级女士兵。~ **crew** 飞机乘务员,空勤人员。~**-cure** *vt*. 晾,用空气处理。~ **current** 气流。~ **cushion** 气垫;气褥;气枕;气室。~**-cushioned** *a*. 气垫的(~*-cushioned vehicle* 气垫运载工具)。~ **defence** 防空。~**dent** 气喷磨牙机。~ **division**〔美〕空军师。~ **drain** 气眼,气门,通气管,气道;防湿沟。~ **drill** 风钻。~**drome**〔美〕飞机场。~**-drop** *n*., *vt*. 空投。~**-dry** *vt*. 风干。~ **engine** 空气发动机。~ **express** 空运包裹。~**field** 飞机场。~ **fight** *n*. 空战。~ **fleet** 航空机队。~**flow** 气流。~**-flue** 气道,风道,烟道。~**foil**【空】机翼;翼形,翼剖面。~ **force** 空军。**Air Force blue** 空军蓝〔在美国指中等蓝色,为空军制服颜色;在英国为中等灰蓝色;为皇家空军制服颜色〕。**Air Force One** 空军一号〔美国总统的专用座机〕。~**frame** 机架;导弹弹体;(火箭等的)构架。**Air France** 法国航空公司。~ **freight** 空中货运(费)。~ **freighter** 货机。~ **ga(u)ge** 气压计。~**glow**【气】气辉。~**graph**〔英〕缩印航空邮件。~**-ground** *a*. 陆空的。~ **group** 空军大队。~ **gun** 气枪。~ **hammer** 气锤。~ **harbour** 航空港。~**-head** (伞兵的)着陆阵地。~ **hole** 通气孔,风眼;气门,(船舱等的)风窗;冰孔,不冻水面;【空】= airpocket. ~**hop** 1. *n*. 短程空中旅行。2. *vi*. 经常作空中短程旅行。~ **hostess** 客机女服务员,空中小姐。~ **jacket** 空气救生衣(= life belt);气套。~ **land** *vt*.【军】空降。~ **lane**【空】空中航线。~**-launch** *vt*. 空中发射。~ **letter** 航空信;航空邮笺。~**lift** 1. *vt*. 空运。2. *n*. 空运;空中补给线;空气升液器。~**line**〔美〕直路,近路;空中航线;定期航空,定期航空公司;最短距离;(潜水用)送气管。~**-line** 1. *a*. 直(*an* ~*-line road* 直路);飞行的;直线的。2. *n*. 两点间的直线;航线;航空系统;航空公司。~ **liner** 客机,班机。~ **lock** 气塞,气闸。~**-mail** 航空邮件,航空信。~**-man** 飞行员,飞机师;空军士兵。~**manship** 飞行术。~ **map** 空摄地图。**Air Marshal**〔英〕空军中将。~ **mass** 气团。~**-minded** *a*. 热心航空的。~**ometer** 风速计;气流计。~**-park** 小型飞机场。~ **patrol** 空中侦察;侦察飞行队。~**pipe** 通风管,通气管。~ **piracy** 空中劫持,劫机。~ **pirate** 空中劫机者。~**plane** 1. *n*.〔美〕飞机〔英国说 aeroplane〕。2. *vi*. 坐飞机。~ **play** (电台)播放唱片。~ **pocket**【空】空中陷阱,垂直气流。~ **pollution** 大气污染。~**port** 飞机场,航空站。~**porter** 机场接送乘客的专车。~ **post** = air-mail. ~ **power** 空军威力;制空权;空军部。~ **pressure** 风压;气压。~**proof** 1. *a*. 不透气的,密封的,气密的。2. *vt*. 使不透气。~ **propeller** 扇风机。~ **pump** 气泵。~**-raid** 空袭(*an* ~*-raid alarm* 空袭紧急警报。*an* ~*-raid precaution* 空袭预备警报。*an* ~ *-raid shelter* 防空洞,防空壕。*an* ~*-raid warning* 空袭警报)。~ **raider** 空袭机,空袭兵。~ **rifle** 气枪。~ **route** 航空路线。~**sac**【生】气囊。~**-scape** 空瞰图。~ **scoop**【空】进气口。~ **scout**【空】侦察机。~**screw** 飞机螺旋桨。~**-sea** *a*. 海空的。~ **shaft**【矿】通风井。~**shed** 飞机仓库。~**ship** 飞船。~**shipper** 空运企业。~**sickness** 航空病,晕机。~**-slaked** *a*. 风化了的。~ **sleeve**, ~ **sock** 锥形风标。~ **space** 1. 空域,领空。2. 广播时间。~ **speed** (飞机与空气相对的)飞行速度,空速(*cf*. *ground speed*)。~ **speedometer** 空速表。~**spring** 气褥,气垫(= ~ cushion)。~ **station** 航空站。~**stop** 直升机航空站。~ **stream** 气流。~**strip** (速成)机场跑道,简易机场。~**-taxi** (来往于无固定航线小城镇之间的)短程飞机。~ **thread** 游丝;蜘蛛丝;〔*pl*.〕= gossamer. ~**tight** *a*. 不透气的,密闭的;严密的;无懈可击的(*an* ~*tight test* 气密试验)。~**time** (电台或电视台的)广播时间;(无线电话等的)通话时间。~**-to-**~ *a*. 空对空的。~ **turbulence** 晴空湍流颠簸。~ **umbrella** 空中掩护。~ **vehicle** 空中运载工具。~**-waves**〔美俚〕无线电广播。~**way** 1.【矿】通风道。2. 空中航线;航空公司。3.〔*pl*.〕(电视台的)频道。~**-wise** *a*. 熟悉航空的。~**woman** 女飞行员,女飞机师。~**worthiness** 航空适宜性,耐飞性。~**worthy** *a*. 耐飞的,适宜飞行的。**-er** *n*.〔英口〕晒衣架。

AIRBM = Anti-intermediate range ballistic missile 反中远程弹道导弹。

Air·cav [ˈɛəkæv; ˋɛrˏkæv] *n*.〔美〕空降部队。

Aire·dale [ˈɛədeil; ˋɛrˏdel] *n*. 1. 硬毛杂种猎犬(= ~ terrier)。2. 〔a-〕〔美〕飞机师;飞机机务员;航空母舰飞机管理员。

air·i·ly [ˈɛərili; ˋɛrəlɪ] *ad*. 轻快地;活泼地,快活地。

air·i·ness [ˈɛərinis; ˋɛrɪnɛs] *n*. 1. 通风。2. 空虚。3. 轻快,快活。

air·ing [ˈɛəriŋ; ˋɛrɪŋ] *n*. 1. 晾,晒;烘干。2. 散步;(用汽车)兜风。3. 表态。4. 广播。*give the clothes an* ~ 晾干衣服。*give a scandal an* ~ 把丑事传开。*take an* ~ 散步。

air·less [ˈɛəlis; ˋɛrlɪs] *a*. 1. 空气不流通的,缺少新鲜空气的。2. 没有风的。

air·tel [ˈɛətel; ˋɛrtel] *n*. 机场旅馆。

air·y [ˈɛəri; ˋɛrɪ] *a*. (*-i·er*; *-i·est*) 1. 空气(一样)的,无形的。2. 航空的。3. 空中的,耸立空中的。4. 通风的。5. 空虚的;空想的。6. 轻浮的,轻佻的。7. 袅娜的,优美的;轻柔的。8. 快活的,轻快的。9. 〔口〕装阔的,做作的。~ *dreams* 幻梦。*an* ~ *tone* 做作的声调。

AIS = Artillery Intelligence Service 炮兵情报勤务,炮兵情报勤务处。

aisle [ail; aɪl] *n*. 1. (教堂的)走廊;耳堂。2. 〔美〕(戏院、客车等内的)过道,通道。3. 任何狭长的通路。***down the*** ~ 走向神坛去举行婚礼。(***roll***) ***in the*** ~ (观众)捧腹大笑。

ait [eit; et] *n*. 〔英方〕(河、湖中的)小岛。

aitch [eitʃ; etʃ] **I** *n*. H(h)字; h 音。*drop one's* ~*es* 不发 [h] 音(如把 ham [hæm; hæm] 读作 'am [æm; æm] 等)。**II** *a*. H 形的。~ **bone** 〔英〕牛的臀骨;牛臀部净肉。

Ait·ken [ˈeitkin; ˋetkən] *n*. 艾特肯〔姓氏〕。

a·jar[1] [əˈdʒɑː; əˋdʒɑr] *a*. 〔多作表语〕, *ad*. (门)微开,半开。*The door stood* ~. 门半开半掩。

a·jar[2] [əˈdʒɑː; əˋdʒɑr] *a*. 〔常用作表语〕, *ad*. 不协调。*He is* ~ *with the world*. 他与人处事总是格格不入。

a·kim·bo [əˈkimbəu; əˋkɪmbo] *a*. 〔多作表语〕, *ad*. 两

A

手叉腰。*with arms* ～ 两手叉腰。

a·kin [ə'kin; ə`kɪn] **a**.〔常用作表语〕1. 血族的,同族的。2. 同种的,同样的,类似的。**be** ～ **to** 是…的同族[近亲];类似,近似(*Pity is* ～ *to love*. 怜悯生爱情)。

Ak·kad ['ækæd; `ækæd] **n**. 1. 古巴比伦阿卡德区。2. 古巴比伦首都阿卡德;古巴比伦的阿卡德人。3. = Akkadian.

Ak·ka·di·an [ə'keidiən, -'kɑː-; ə`kedɪən, -`kɑ-] **I a**. 古阿卡德的;古阿卡德人的;古阿卡德语的。**II n**. 古阿卡德语〔美索不达米亚地区已消亡的闪语〕。

ak·va·vit ['ɑːkvəvit, 'æk-; `ɑkvəvɪt, `æk-] **n**. 阿瓜维特酒〔北欧出产的一种粮食酒,有香菜子味,通常作开胃酒饮用〕(= aquavit)。

AL = 1. Arab League 阿拉伯联盟。2. American Legion 美国军团。

al- *pref*.〔用于1前〕= ad-: *al*lude.

-al[1] *suf*. 1. 造成"…的,有…性质的,…特有的"等意义的形容词: post*al*, sensation*al*, tropic*al*. 2. 由动词造成表示该动作的名词 arriv*al*, refus*al*.

-al[2] *suf*.【化】醛: acet*al* 乙缩醛, chlor*al* 氯醛。

à la [ɑː lɑː; ɑ lə]〔F.〕1. …派的,…式的。2.【烹】…风味的。*chou à la crème* 奶油馅包。

a·la ['eilə; `elə] (*pl*. **a·lae** ['eiliː; `eli]) **n**.【生】翼,翅;翼状部。

Ala. = Alabama.

Al·a·bam·a [ˌælə'bæmə; ˏælə`bæmə] **n**. 阿拉巴马〔美国州名〕。**-bam·an** 1. **a**. 阿拉巴马州的。2. **n**. 阿拉巴马州人。

al·a·bas·ter ['æləbɑːstə; `æləˏbæstɚ] **I n**. 雪花石膏。**II a**. 雪花石膏制的;雪花石膏一样的,雪白的。～ *glass* 乳色玻璃。

à la bonne heure [ˌɑːlɑː'bɔ'nəː; ˏɑlɑˏbɑ`nɝ]〔F.〕好极了!巧极了!做得好!好!

à la carte [ɑːlɑː'kɑːt; ɑlɑ`kɑrt]〔F.〕照菜单点的。*à la carte meal* 点菜(*cf*. table d'hôte meal 客饭,份菜)。

a·lack [ə'læk; ə`læk], **a·lack·a·day** [ə'lækədei; ə`lækəde] **int**.〔古〕呜呼!哀哉!

a·lac·ri·ty [ə'lækriti; ə`lækrətɪ] **n**. 1. 乐意。2. 敏捷。**with** ～ 快;敏捷,踊跃,欣然。*He accepted my invitation with* ～. 他欣然接受我的邀请。

Aladdin [ə'lædin; ə`lædɪn] **n**. 阿拉丁〔《天方夜谭》(*Arabian Nights*)中获得神灯的青年名〕。～***'s lamp*** 如意灯,神灯;〔喻〕能满足一切愿望的东西。

a·lae ['eiliː; `eli] ala 的复数。

à la fran·çaise [a la frɑ̃'sez; a la frɑ̃`sɛz]〔F.〕法国式(的)。

à la king [ˌɑːlə'kiŋ; ˏɑlə`kɪŋ]〔F.〕【烹】切成小粒泡在有蘑菇、胡椒和青椒的奶油汁内的。*chicken* ～ 奶油鸡丁。

a·la·li·a [ə'leiliə; ə`lelɪə] **n**.【医】语言不清,哑。

al·a·me·da [ˌælə'meidə, -miːdə; ˏælə`medə, -midə] **n**.〔美〕林荫走道。

al·a·mo ['ɑːləməu, 'ælə-; `ɑləˏmo, `ælə-] **n**. (*pl*. ～*s*)杨树,三角叶杨〔美国西南部产〕。

al·a·mode ['æləməud; `æləˏmod] **I n**. 阿拉莫德薄黑绸〔又名 ～ silk〕。**II ad**., **a**. = *à la mode*.

à la mode [ɑːləː'məud; ˏɑlə`mod] **I ad**. 时髦地。**a**.〔F.〕1. 流行的,时新的。2. 加奶油[冰淇淋(等)]的。***beef*** ～ 蔬菜炖牛肉。***pie*** ～ 奶油馅饼。

à la mort [ˌælə'mɔːr; ælə`mɔr]〔F.〕1. 病危,濒死。2. 无精打采;忧郁。3. 致命地。

Al·an ['ælən; `ælən] **n**. 阿伦〔男子名〕。

à l'an·glaise [ɑlɑ̃ŋ'lez; ɑlɑ̃ŋ`glɛz]〔F.〕英国式(的)。

al·a·nine ['æləni(ː)n; `ælənin] **n**.【化】丙氨酸。

à la page [ɑːlɑːpaʒ; ɑ lɑ paʒ]〔F.〕时髦的,跟上时代的,新式的。

a·lar ['eilə; `elɚ] **a**. 1. (有)翼的,(有)翅的。2.【植】腋生的。3.【解】腋下的。

a·larm [ə'lɑːm; ə`lɑrm] **I n**. 1. 惊慌,恐慌。2. 警报,急报。3. 警报器,警铃。*The fire caused much* ～. 火灾引起很大恐慌。*a fire* ～ 火警。*a false* ～ 虚惊一场。***give the*** ～ = ***raise an*** ～ 发警报,向…告急。***in*** ～ 惊慌;担心。***sound the*** ～ 响警报,吹警号[笛]。***take*** (***the***) ～ ***at*** 对…感到吃惊。**II vt**. 1. 向…告急,向…报警,警戒。2. 吓,惊动;使放心不下。*Don't* ～ *yourself*. 不要惊慌。***be*** ～***ed at*** (*the news*)被(那消息)吓一跳。***be*** ～***ed for*** (*the safety of* ...)放心不下,担心(…的安全)。～ **bell** 警钟;警铃。～ **clock** 闹钟(*set the* ～ *clock for half past seven* 把闹钟拨到七点半)。～ **gauge** (锅炉上的)气压报警器。～ **gun** 信号炮。～ **post**【军】紧急集合处。～ **signal** 警报信号。～ **whistle** 警笛。～**-word** 暗号,口令。

a·larm·ing [ə'lɑːmiŋ; ə`lɑrmɪŋ] **a**. 使人惊慌的;引起惊慌的;告急的,危言耸听的。

a·larm·ism [ə'lɑːmizm; ə`lɑrmɪzm] **n**. 危言耸听;慌报军情。

a·larm·ist [ə'lɑːmist; ə`lɑrmɪst] **n**. 危言耸听者;慌报情况夸大事实者。

a·lar·um [ə'lɛərəm; ə`lærəm] **n**.〔古,诗〕= alarm.

a·la·ry ['eiləri; `elərɪ] **a**. 翼的,翅的,翅状的。

Alas. = Alaska.

a·las [ə'lɑːs; ə`lɑs] **int**. 哎呀!哎哟!〔表示悲痛、遗憾等〕。***Alas the day***!〔古〕嗳呀!天哪!

A·las·ka [ə'læskə; ə`læskə] **n**. 阿拉斯加〔美国州名〕。

A·las·kan [ə'læskən; ə`læskən] **I a**. 阿拉斯加州的。**II n**. 阿拉斯加州人。

a·late ['eileit; `elet], **alat·ed** [-id; -ɪd] **a**. 有翼(状物)的。

alb [ælb; ælb] **n**. (牧师、神父穿的)白麻布长袍。

Alb. = 1. Albania(n). 2. Albany. 3. Albert. 4. Alberta.

al·ba ['ɑːlbə, 'æl-; `ɑlbə, `æl-] **n**. (法国普罗旺斯人的)晨歌;朝曲。

al·ba·core ['ælbəkɔː; `ælbəˏkor] **n**. (*pl*. ～(*s*))长鳍金枪鱼。

Al·ba·ni·a [æl'beinjə; æl`benɪə] **n**. 阿尔巴尼亚〔欧洲〕。

Al·ba·ni·an [æl'beinjən; æl`benɪən] **I a**. 阿尔巴尼亚的;阿尔巴尼亚人的;阿尔巴尼亚语的。**II n**. 1. 阿尔巴尼亚人。2. 阿尔巴尼亚语。

Al·ba·ny ['ɔːlbəni; `ɔlbənɪ] **n**. 阿尔巴尼〔1. 美国纽约州首府。2. 加拿大中南部河名。3. 美国佐治亚州西南部城市〕。

al·ba·ta [æl'beitə; æl`betə] **n**. 洋银(= German silver)。

al·ba·tross ['ælbətrɔs; `ælbəˏtrɔs] **n**. (*pl*. ～*es*) 1.【动】信天翁。2.〔喻〕引起忧虑的事物〔源出英国诗人柯立芝兹 (Coleridge)所著长诗《老水手》,该诗叙述水手误杀信天翁以致全船遭难〕。

al·be·do [æl'biːdəu; æl`bido] **n**. 1.【天】反照率。2.【物】反射率,反照率。

al·be·it [ɔːl'biːit; ɔl`biɪt] **conj**.〔古〕纵令,虽然。

Al·bert ['ælbət; `ælbɚt] **n**. 艾伯特〔男名〕。

al·bert ['ælbət; `ælbɚt] **n**. 挂在背心上的表链(= ～ chain)。***The A- Hall*** (伦敦)艾伯特纪念堂〔常作音乐会和其他集会的会场〕。

Al·ber·ta [æl'bəːtə; æl`bɝtə] **n**. 艾伯塔〔男子名〕。

al·bert·ite ['ælbə'tait; `ælbɚtaɪt] **n**. (加拿大 Albert 矿所出的)一种黑沥青。

al·bes·cent [æl'besənt; æl`bɛsənt] **a**. 发白的,正在变白的。

Al·bi·gen·ses [ˌælbi'dʒensiːz; ˏælbɪ`dʒɛnsiz] **n**.〔*pl*.〕阿尔比教派〔大约在公元1020—1250年在法国南部兴盛的教派,后被视为异端而被镇压〕。**-gen·si·an a**., **n**.

Al·bin ['ælbin; `ælbɪn] **n**. 阿尔宾〔男子名〕。

al·bi·nism [ˈælbinizəm; ˋælbəˏnɪzəm] *n*.【医】白化病。

al·bi·no [ælˈbiːnəu; ælˋbino] *n*. (*pl*. ～*s*) **1.** 患白化病的人[动植物]。**2.**【生】白化体,白变种。～ **rat** (生物试验用的)天竺鼠。

Al·bi·on [ˈælbjən; ˋælbjən] *n*. **1.** 〔诗〕英格兰。**2.**【希神】阿尔比安〔海神之子〕。

al·bite [ˈælbait; ˋælbaɪt] *n*.【矿】钠长石。

al·biz·zi·a [ælˈbiziə; ælˋbɪzɪə] *n*.【植】合欢属植物。

ALBM = Air-launched ballistic missile 空中发射的弹道导弹。

al·bo·my·cin [ˌælbəˈmaisin; ˏælbəˋmaɪsɪn] *n*.【药】白霉素。

al·bu·gin·e·ous [ˌælbjuˈdʒiniəs; ˏælbjuˋdʒɪnɪəs] *a*. 眼白的;似眼白的。

al·bum [ˈælbəm; ˋælbəm] *n*. **1.** 相片簿,邮票簿。**2.** 〔古〕来宾签名簿(= visitor's book)。**3.** 文集;歌曲集。**4.** 唱片套;唱片集。

al·bu·men [ˈælbjumin; ælˋbjumən] *n*. **1.** 蛋白。**2.**【生化】清蛋白,白蛋白(= albumin)。**3.**【植】胚乳。

al·bu·men·ize [ælˈbjuːmənaiz; ælˋbjumənˏaɪz] *vt*. **1.** 使蛋白质化。**2.**【摄】在…上涂蛋白。～**d paper** 蛋白感光纸。

al·bu·min [ælˈbjumin; ælˋbjumɪn] *n*.【生化】清蛋白,白蛋白。

al·bu·mi·nate [ælˈbjuːmineit; ælˋbjumɪnɪt] *n*. 清蛋白盐。

al·bu·mi·noid [ælˈbjuːminɔid; ælˋbjumɪˏnɔɪd] *a*. 硬朊的,硬蛋白的。*n*.【生化】硬朊,硬蛋白质。

al·bu·mi·nose [ælˈbjuːminəus; ælˋbjumɪnos], **-nous** [-nəs; -nəs] *a*. (含)蛋白质的;多胚乳的。

al·bu·mi·nu·ri·a [ælˌbjuːmiˈnjuəriə; ælˏbjumɪˋnjurɪə] *n*.【医】蛋白尿(病)。

al·bu·mose [ˈælbjuməus; ˋælˏbjumos] *n*.【生化】(蛋白)脲。

al·bur·num [ælˈbəːnəm; ælˋbɝnəm] *n*. 边材,白木质(= sapwood)。

al·ca·hest [ˈælkəhest; ˋælkəˏhest] *n*. = alkahest.

al·cai·de, al·cay·de [ɑːlˈkaidi; ɑlˋkaɪdɪ] *n*. **1.** (西班牙等地)要塞司令;督军。**2.** (西班牙等地监狱的)看守;监狱长。

al·cal·de [ɑːlˈkɑːldei; ælˋkældɪ] *n*. (西班牙等地的)市长,镇长,村长。

al·caz·ar [ælˈkæzə; ælˋkæzɚ] *n*. (西班牙等地的)宫殿,堡垒。

al·chem·ic, al·chem·i·cal [ælˈkemik(əl); ælˋkɛmɪk-(ə)l] *a*. 炼金术的。

al·che·mist [ælˈkemist; ælˋkɛmɪst] *n*. 炼金术士。

al·che·mis·tic, al·che·mist·i·cal [ˌælkiˈmistik(əl); ˏælkɪˋmɪstɪk(əl)] *a*. 炼金术的;炼金术士的。**-i·cal·ly** *ad*.

al·che·my [ˈælkimi; ˋælkəmɪ] *n*. **1.** 炼金术;(中国古代的)炼丹术。**2.** 魔力,秘法。*convince the public of one's innocence by alchemies of eloquence* 用雄辩的口才让人相信自己无罪。

al·ci·dine [ˈælsidain; ˋælsɪdaɪn] *a*.【动】海雀科的。

ALCM = air-launched cruise missile 空中发射的巡航导弹。

al·co·hol [ˈælkəhɔl; ˋælkəˏhɔl] *n*. **1.**【化】醇;乙醇,酒精。**2.** 含酒精饮料。*absolute* ～ 无水酒精。*He does not touch* ～. 他不喝酒。

al·co·hol·ic [ˌælkəˈhɔlik; ˏælkəˋhɔlɪk] **I** *a*. **1.** 酒精的,含酒精的。**2.** 酒精中毒的。～ *drinks* 含酒精的饮料。**II** *n*. 酒鬼。**Alcoholics Anonymous** 嗜酒者互诫协会〔美国的戒酒团体,略作 AA, A.A.〕。～ **poisoning** 酒精中毒。

al·co·hol·ism [ˈælkəhɔlizəm; ˋælkəhɔˏlɪzəm] *n*. 酒精中毒。

al·co·hol·ize [ˈælkəhɔlaiz; ˋælkəhɔlˏaɪz] *vt*. **1.** 用酒精泡[浸、渍]。**2.**【化】醇化。**3.** 使醉。

al·co·hol·om·e·ter [ˌælkəhɔˈlɔmitə; ˏælkəhɔˋlɑmɪtɚ] *n*. 酒精比重计。

Al·co·ran [ælkɔˈrɑːn, -ˈræn; ˏælkoˋrɑn, -ˋræn] *n*. 〔古〕(伊斯兰教的)《古兰经》(一译《可兰经》)(= Koran)。

Al·cott [ˈɔːlkət; ˋɔlkət] *n*. 奥尔科特〔姓氏〕。

al·cove [ˈælkəuv; ˋælkov] *n*. **1.** 壁橱;壁龛;凹室;洞穴中凹处。**2.** 林中空地;园中凉亭。*dining* ～ (客厅或起居室一部分凹入的)餐室。*coat* ～ 衣帽间。

Al·cuin [ˈælkwin; ˋælkwɪn] *n*. 阿尔昆〔姓氏〕。

Al·cy·o·ne [ælˈsaiəni; ælˋsaɪənɪ] *n*.【天】昴宿六〔金牛座〕。

Ald., aldm. = Alderman.

al·de·hyde [ˈældihaid; ˋældəˏhaɪd] *n*.【化】乙醛;醛。

Al·den [ˈɔːldən; ˋɔldən] *n*. 奥尔登〔男子名〕。

al den·te [ælˈdentiː; ælˋdɛnti] 〔It.〕咬起来硬的;耐嚼的。

al·der [ˈɔːldə; ˋɔldɚ] *n*.【植】桤木。*the black* ～ 冬青。*the red* [*white*] ～ 赤[白]杨。

al·der·man [ˈɔːldəmən; ˋɔldɚmən] *n*. (*pl*. **-men**) **1.** 〔美〕市参议员。**2.** 〔英〕(仅次于市长的)高级市政官;副市长。**3.**【英史】郡长。**-ic** *a*. (像) alderman 的。

Al·dine [ˈɔːldain, -diːn; ˋɔldaɪn, -din] *a*. 阿尔杜斯版的〔指 Aldus Manutius 及其家人于 1494—1597 年在威尼斯和罗马印行的精装古籍〕;精装本的。

Al·ding·ton [ˈɔːldiŋtən; ˋɔldɪŋtən] *n*. 奥尔丁顿〔姓氏〕。

al·dol [ˈældɔːl; ˋældɔl] *n*.【化】丁间醇醛。

al·dose [ˈældəus; ˋældos] *n*.【化】醛(式)醣。

al·do·ste·rone [ælˈdɔstərəun, ˈældəus-; ælˋdɑstəˋron, ˋældos-] *n*.【生化】醛甾酮。

al·do·ste·ron·ism [ˈældɔstərəunizm; ˋældɑstəronɪzm] *n*.【医】醛甾酮增多症。

Al·dous [ˈɔːldəs, ˈældəs; ˋɔldəs, ˋældəs] *n*. 奥尔德斯〔男子名〕。

Al·dridge [ˈɔːldridʒ; ˋɔldrɪdʒ] *n*. 奥尔德里奇〔姓氏〕。

al·drin [ˈɔːldrin; ˋɔldrɪn] *n*.【化】艾氏剂〔一种剧毒杀虫剂〕;氯甲桥萘。

ale [eil; el] *n*. **1.** (淡色)浓啤酒。**2.** 乡下啤酒节。★ale 与 beer 同义,但较高级。*Good* ～ *will make a cat speak*. 好酒能使人说真话。*small* ～ 淡啤酒。***Adam's*** ～ 水。～**house** 酒馆;啤酒店。～**wife** **1.** 啤酒店老板娘。**2.** 〔美〕鳍白鱼类。

a·le·a·to·ric [ˌeiliəˈtɔrik; ˏelɪəˋtɑrɪk] *a*. **1.** 碰运气的。**2.** (音乐)胡乱凑成的,噪乐的。～ *music* (信手胡乱演来的)任意音乐。

a·le·a·to·ry [ˈeiliətəri; ˋelɪətorɪ] *a*. 碰运气的,侥幸的。*the* ～ *element in life* 人生中不可预测的因素。

Alec(k) [ˈælik; ˋælɪk] *n*. 亚历克〔男子名, Alexander 的昵称〕。

ale·con·ner [ˈeilkɔnə; ˋelˏkɑnɚ] *n*.【英史】酒类检查官;市镇挂名官员。

a·lee [əˈliː; əˋli] **I** *a*. 〔常用作表语〕。**II** *ad*.【海】在背风处;向下风(*opp*. aweather)。

ale·gar [ˈeiligə; ˋelɪgɚ] *n*. 〔英方〕发酸的啤酒;啤酒醋。

Al·e·man·ni [ˌæliˈmænai; ˏæləˋmænaɪ] *n*. 〔*pl*.〕阿勒曼尼人〔公元五世纪初侵入阿尔萨斯和瑞士部分领土,并在该地区定居,后于 496 年被克洛维斯所征服〕。

Al·e·man·nic [ˌæliˈmænik; ˏæləˋmænɪk] **I** *n*. 阿勒曼尼语〔在德国西南部、阿尔萨斯和瑞士所讲的任何一种日耳曼方言〕。**II** *a*. 阿勒曼尼的。

a·lem·bic [əˈlembik; əˋlɛmbɪk] *n*. **1.** 蒸馏器,(古代炼金术士用的)升华锅。**2.** 任何起净化作用的事物。

A·len·çon [əˈlensən; əˋlɛnsən] *n*. 阿郎松针绣花边。

a·leph [ˈɑːlif; ˋɑlɪf] *n*. 希伯来语字母表的第一个字母。

a·leph·null [ˈɑːlifˈnʌl; ˋɑlɪfˋnʌl] *n*.【数】阿列夫零。

A

A·lep·po [əˈlepəu; əˋlɛpo] ***n.*** 阿勒颇〔叙利亚城市〕。

a·lert [əˈləːt; əˋlɝt] **I** ***a.*** **1.** 警惕的,警觉的。**2.** 机警的,机灵的。**II** ***n.*** **1.** 警戒;警报。**2.** 警戒期间。**3.** 【军】紧急待命。*No. one* ～ 一级战备。***on the*** ～ 警惕,提防。**III** ***vt.*** 使警戒。*The troops were* ～*ed*. 部队在待命中。**-ly** ***ad.*** **-ness** ***n.***

a·leu·k(a)e·mi·a [ˌeiljuˈkiːmiə; ˏeljʊˋkimɪə] ***n.*** 【医】白血球缺乏症。**-mic** [-mik; -mɪk] ***a.***

a·leu·rone [əˈljuərən, -rəun; əˋljurɑn, -ron] ***n.*** 【化】糊粉。**-ron·ic** [-ˈrɔnik; -ˋrɑnɪk] ***a.***

Al·eut [ˈæliuːt; ˋælɪˏut] ***n.*** **1.** 阿留申岛人。**2.** 阿留申语。

A·leu·tian [əˈluːʃjən; əˋluʃjən] **I** ***a.*** **1.** 阿留申群岛的。**2.** 阿留申群岛人的。**II** ***n.*** **1.** 阿留申人。**2.** 〔*pl.*〕阿留申群岛(= ～ Islands)。

Alex [ˈæliks; ˋælɪks] ***n.*** 亚历克斯〔男子名, Alexander 的昵称〕。

Al·ex·an·der [ˌæligˈzɑːndə; ˏælɪgˋzændɚ], **the Great** 亚历山大大帝〔古马其顿国王,公元前 356—323〕。

Al·ex·an·dra [ˌæligˈzɑːndrə; ˏælɪgˋzɑndrə] ***n.*** 亚历山德拉〔女子名〕。

Al·ex·an·dri·a [ˌæligˈzɑːndriə; ˏælɪgˋzændrɪə] ***n.*** 亚历山大〔埃及港市〕。

Al·ex·an·dri·an [ˌæligˈzɑːndriən; ˏælɪgˋzændrɪən] ***a.*** **1.** 亚历山大港 (Alexandria) 的。**2.** 古代亚历山大文化时期的〔指古代亚历山大地区发展的古希腊文化,亦称古希腊后期文化〕。**3.** (马其顿)亚历山大大帝的。**4.** (诗歌)亚历山大格式的(= Alexandrine)。

Al·ex·an·drine [ˌæligˈzændrain; ˏælɪgˋzændrɪn] ***n.*** 亚历山大格式(的诗),英雄体(的诗)〔指六音步十二音节为一行抑扬格式诗〕。

al·ex·an·drite [ˌæligˈzɑːndrait; ˏælɪgˋzændraɪt] ***n.*** 变色宝石〔日光下呈深绿色,灯光下呈深红色〕。

a·lex·i·a [əˈleksiə; əˋlɛksɪə] ***n.*** 【医】失读症;无读字能力。

a·lex·in [əˈleksin; əˋlɛksɪn] ***n.*** 【医】(体液内的)补体,杀菌素。

A·lex·is [əˈleksis; əˋlɛksɪs] ***n.*** 亚历克西斯〔男子名〕。

a·lex·i·phar·mic [əˌleksiˈfɑːmik; əˏlɛksɪˋfɑrmɪk] **I** ***a.*** 消毒的,解毒的。**II** ***n.*** 解毒剂。

Alf. = Alfonso; Alfred.

'alf = half.

al·fal·fa [ælˈfælfə; ælˋfælfə] ***n.*** 【植】紫花苜蓿。

al·fil·a·ri·a, al·fil·e·ri·a [ælˌfiləˈriə; ælˏfɪləˋrɪə] ***n.*** 【植】芹叶太阳花。

al fine [ɑːlˈfiːnei; ɑlˋfine] 〔It.〕【乐】复唱[奏]到结尾。

Al·fon·so [ælˈfɔnsəu; ælˋfɑnso] ***n.*** 阿方索〔男子名〕。

al·for·ja [ælˈfɔːdʒə; ælˋfɔrdʒə] ***n.*** 帆布鞍囊,皮鞍囊。

Al·fred [ˈælfrid; ˋælfrɪd] ***n.*** 阿尔弗雷德〔男子名〕。

al·fres·co [ælˈfreskəu; ælˋfrɛsko] ***ad.***, ***a.*** 在户外,户外的。*dine* ～ 吃野餐。*an* ～ *luncheon* 野餐。★作副词用时常分写作 al fresco.

Alg. = **1.** Algeria(n). **2.** Algernon. **3.** Algiers.

alg. = **1.** algebra. **2.** algebraical.

al·ga [ˈælgə; ˋælgə] ***n.*** (*pl.* ***-gae*** [-dʒiː; -dʒi]) 【植】〔常 *pl.*〕藻;藻类。**-al** ***a.***, ***n.*** 藻(的)。

al·gae·cide [ˈældʒiːsaid; ˋældʒəsaɪd] ***n.*** (游泳池等处用的)除藻剂。

al·gar·ro·ba, al·ga·ro·ba [ˌælgəˈrəubə; ˏælgəˋrobə] ***n.*** **1.** 角豆树,角豆荚。**2.** 牧豆树,牧豆荚。

al·ge·bra [ˈældʒibrə; ˋældʒəbrə] ***n.*** 代数学。

al·ge·bra·ic, -i·cal [ˌældʒiˈbreiik(əl); ˏældʒəˋbreɪk(əl)] ***a.*** 代数的,代数学(上)的。**-i·cal·ly** ***ad.*** 代数学上。

al·ge·bra·ist [ˈældʒiˌbreiist; ˋældʒəˏbreɪst], **al·ge·brist** [ˈældʒibrist; ˋældʒəbrɪst] ***n.*** 代数学家。

Al·ger [ˈældʒə; ˋældʒɚ] ***n.*** 阿尔杰〔姓氏〕。

Al·ge·ri·a [ælˈdʒiəriə; ælˋdʒɪrɪə] ***n.*** 阿尔及利亚〔非洲〕。

Al·ge·ri·an [ælˈdʒiəriən; ælˋdʒɪrɪən] **I** ***a.*** **1.** 阿尔及利亚的;阿尔及利亚人的。**2.** 阿尔及利亚语的。**II** ***n.*** **1.** 阿尔及利亚人。**2.** 阿尔及利亚语。

Al·ge·rine [ˌældʒiˈriːn; ˏældʒəˋrin] **I** ***a.*** 阿尔及利亚的。**II** ***n.*** **1.** 阿尔及利亚人(尤指柏柏尔人的后裔)。**2.** 〔a-〕阿尔及利亚横条纹毛呢〔薄的做头巾,厚的做帐篷〕。**3.** 古代的北非海盗。

Al·ger·non [ˈældʒənən; ˋældʒənən] ***n.*** 阿尔杰农〔男子名〕。

-al·gi·a *suf.* 〔L〕痛:neur*algia*.

al·gid [ˈældʒid; ˋældʒɪd] ***a.*** 寒冷的,打寒颤的。

al·gid·i·ty [ælˈdʒiditi; ælˋdʒɪdətɪ] ***n.*** 寒冷,严寒。

Al·giers [ælˈdʒiəz; ælˋdʒɪrz] ***n.*** 阿尔及耳〔阿尔及利亚首都〕。

al·gin [ˈældʒin; ˋældʒɪn] ***n.*** 【化】**1.** 褐藻酸。**2.** 褐藻胶。

al·gin·ic [ælˈdʒinik; ælˋdʒɪnɪk] ***a.*** ～ **acid** 【化】褐藻酸。

al·goid [ˈælgɔid; ˋælgɔɪd] ***a.*** 藻的,藻质的。

Al·gol [ˈælgɔl; ˋælgɑl] ***n.*** 【天】大陵五〔英仙座β〕。

ALGOL = **1.** algebraic-oriented language 【计】代数排列语言。**2.** algorithmic language 【计】算法语言。

al·go·lag·ni·a [ˌælgəˈlægniə; ˏælgəˋlægnɪə] ***n.*** 【精】变态淫乐;性(被)虐待狂。

al·gol·o·gist [ælˈgɔlədʒist; ælˋgɑlədʒɪst] ***n.*** 藻类学家。

al·gol·o·gy [ælˈgɔlədʒi; ælˋgɑlədʒɪ] ***n.*** 藻类学。

al·gom·e·ter [ælˈgɔmitə; ælˋgɑmətɚ] ***n.*** 痛觉计。**-met·ric, -met·ri·cal** ***a.*** **-me·try** ***n.*** 痛觉测验。

Al·gon·ki·an [ælˈgɔŋkiən; ælˋgɑŋkɪən] ***a.*** 【地】元古代的(= Late Precambrian)。

Al·gon·quin, Al·gon·kin [ælˈgɔŋkwin; ælˋgɑŋkwɪn] ***n.*** 北美阿尔贡金族印第安人[语]。

al·go·pho·bi·a [ˌælgəˈfəubiə; ˏælgəˋfobɪə] ***n.*** 疼痛恐怖。

al·go·rism [ˈælgərizəm; ˋælgəˏrɪzəm] ***n.*** **1.** 十进制,十进位计数法。**2.** 算法;算术。**3.** 阿拉伯数字系统。***a cipher in*** ～ "0"(零);有名无实的人,傀儡。

al·go·rithm [ˈælgəriðəm; ˋælgərɪðəm] ***n.*** 【数】算法;规则系统;演段。

al·gua·zil, al·gua·cil [ˌælgwəˈziːl; ˏælgwəˋzil] ***n.*** (西班牙)警察。

al·gum [ˈælgəm; ˋælgəm] ***n.*** 【植】檀香树。

Al·ham·bra [ælˈhæmbrə; ælˋhæmbrə] ***n.*** 中古西班牙摩尔人 (Moor)诸王的宫殿〔以装饰豪华著称〕。

Al·ham·bresque [ˌælhæmˈbresk; ˏælhæmˋbrɛsk] ***a.*** (中古西班牙)摩尔诸王所建宫殿式的。

a·li·as [ˈeiliæs, ˈeiliəs; ˋelɪæs, ˋelɪəs] **I** ***ad.*** 别名。*Smith* ～ *Simpson* 史密斯别名辛普森。**II** ***n.*** 化名,别名。*go by the* ～ *Johnson* 化名约翰逊。

al·i·bi [ˈælibai; ˋæləˏbaɪ] **I** ***n.*** (*pl.* ～*s* [-z; -z]) **1.** 【法】不在犯罪现场的抗辩[事实]。**2.** 〔美口〕辩解,托辞。***set up*** [***prove***] ***an*** ～ 证明被告当时不在犯罪场所。**II** ***vi.*** 〔美口〕辩解,托词闪避。—***vt.*** 为(某人)提供不在现场的证词。

al·i·ble [ˈælibl; ˋæləbl̩] ***a.*** 有营养价值的。

Al·ice [ˈælis; ˋælɪs] ***n.*** 艾丽斯〔女子名, Adelaide 的异体〕。

A·li·ci·a [əˈliʃə; əˋlɪʃə] ***n.*** 艾丽西亚〔女子名, Adelaide 的异体〕。

Alick [ˈælik; ˋælɪk] ***n.*** 亚历克〔男子名, Alexander 的昵称〕。

al·i·cy·clic [ˌæliˈsaiklik; ˏælɪˋsaɪklɪk] ***a.*** 【化】脂环(族)的。

al·i·dad(e) [ˈælideid; ˋælɪded] ***n.*** 旋标装置;测高仪;照准仪。

al·ien [ˈeiljən; ˋelɪən] **I** ***a.*** **1.** 外国(人)的;异己的。**2.** (与…)相异 (*from*);(与…)相反,不合 (*to*)。*an* ～

enemy 敌侨。~ *friends* 友邦侨民。~ ***to the subject*** 不合题目。**II** ***n***. 外国人;外侨;外来人。**III** ***vt***. **1**.〔诗〕疏远;离间。**2**.【法】(所有权的)让渡,转让。

a·lien·a·bil·i·ty [ˌeiljənəˈbiliti;ˏeljənəˋbɪlətɪ] ***n***. **1**. 让渡的可能性。**2**. 疏远的可能性。

al·ien·a·ble [ˈeiljənəbl; ˋeljənəbl̩] ***a***. **1**. 可让渡的。**2**. 能疏远的。

al·ien·age [ˈeiljənidʒ; ˋeljənɪdʒ] ***n***. 外侨的法律地位。

al·ien·ate [ˈeiljəneit, -liən-; ˋeljəˏnet, -lɪən-] ***vt***. **1**. 疏远;离间,挑拨,使…不和。**2**.【法】让渡,转让(所有权)。**3**. 把(资金等)移作他用 (*from*)。~ *him from his friend* 离间他和他的朋友。~ *lands to another* 把土地转让给别人。~ ***oneself from*** 使自己脱离。***be ~d from*** 与…不和。

al·ien·a·tion [ˌeiljəˈneiʃən;ˏeljəˋneʃən] ***n***. **1**. 疏远;离间。**2**. 让渡,转让。**3**. 精神错乱。**4**.【哲】异化。~ *of affection* 爱情的转移。~ *of mind* 精神错乱。

al·ien·a·tor [ˈeiljəneitə; ˋeljənˏetɚ] ***n***. 让渡人;离间者。

a·lien·ee [ˌeiljəˈniː;ˏeljəˋni] ***n***.【法】受让人。

al·ien·ism [ˈeiljənizəm; ˋeljənˏɪzəm] ***n***. **1**. 外侨身份。**2**. 异国情调。**3**. 精神病学;精神病治疗;神经错乱。

al·ien·ist [ˈeiljənist; ˋeljənɪst] ***n***. 精神病学家,精神病医生。

al·ien·or [ˈeiljəˌnə; ˋeljənɚ] ***n***. (财产)转让者。

a·lif [ˈɑːlif; ˋɑlɪf] ***n***. 阿拉伯语的第一个字母。

al·i·form [ˈælifɔːm; ˋælɪˏfɔrm] ***a***. 翼状的,翅状的。

a·light[1] [əˈlait; əˋlaɪt] ***vi***. (~***ed***,〔罕〕***a·lit*** [əˈlit; əˋlɪt]) **1**. 降;下车[马] (*from*);【空】降落;(鸟)飞落(在树上) (*on*)。**2**. 偶然发现,碰见,遇见(*on*, *upon*)。~ *at Shanghai* 在上海下车。~ ***on one's feet*** 跳下站住;没有受伤。~**ing deck** (航空母舰上的)降落甲板。

alight[2] [əˈlait; əˋlaɪt] ***a***.〔常作表语〕**1**. 烧着,烧起。**2**. 照亮,照着。***be ~ with*** 给…烧起来[烧着];给…照着(*The room was ~ with lamps*. 房间里灯光明亮)。***get*** [***set***] ~ 使烧着…,把…烧起来(*get the wood ~* 把木柴点燃)。

a·lign [əˈlain; əˋlaɪn] ***vt***. **1**. 使排成一线[一行];校直。**2**. 使结盟,使密切合作。**3**.【物】匹配;调准。*He ~ed himself with the liberals*. 他与自由党人结成联盟。~ *the television receiver* 调整电视机。— ***vi***. **1**. 成一行,成一线;校直。**2**. 结盟,参加。*The troops ~ed*. 士兵们排成一行。**-er** ***n***. 校准器。

a·lign·ment [əˈlainmənt; əˋlaɪnmənt] ***n***. **1**. 列队,成直线。**2**. 校直;调整,调准。**3**.【工】准线。**4**.【政】结盟。(公路或铁路的)线路平面图。

a·like [əˈlaik; əˋlaɪk] **I** ***a***.〔常作表语〕相同,一样,相似。*The two brothers look very much ~*. 兄弟俩长得一模一样。**II** ***ad***. 一样,相等,相似。*We think ~*. 我们想法一样。***share and share ~*** 等分。***young and old ~*** 老少一样。

al·i·ment [ˈælimənt; ˋæləmənt] **I** ***n***. **1**. 食物;滋养品。**2**. 生活必需品。**3**. 抚养(费)。**II** [-ment; -mɛnt] ***vt***. **1**. 给与…食物[养料]。**2**. 抚养。

al·i·men·tal [ˌæliˈmentəl;ˏæləˋmɛntl̩] ***a***. 食物的,营养的,富有养分的。

al·i·men·ta·ry [ˌæliˈmentəri;ˏæləˋmɛntərɪ] ***a***. **1**. 有关食物的,有关营养的。**2**. 富有养分的。~ *canal* 消化管。**3**. 给予资助的,抚养的。*an ~ endowment* 资助金。~ **canal** (或 *tract*)消化道。

al·i·men·ta·tion [ˌælimenˈteiʃən;ˏæləmɛnˋteʃən] ***n***. **1**. 供给食物;营养。**2**. 扶养。

al·i·men·to·ther·a·py [ˌæliˈmentəuˈθerəpi;ˏæləˋmɛntəˋθɛrəpɪ] ***n***. 食物疗法。

al·i·mo·ny [ˈæliməni; ˋæləmonɪ] ***n***.【法】赡养费;抚养费;生活费。

A-line [ˈeiˈlain; ˋelaɪn] ***a***. (服装)A 字型的,上窄下宽的。

a·line [əˈlain; əˋlaɪn] = align. **-ment** = alignment.

Al·i·oth [ˈæliːɔθ; ˋæliɑθ] ***n***.【天】玉衡,北斗五〔大熊座ε〕。

al·i·ped [ˈæliped; ˋæləˏpɛd] **I** ***a***. 有翼肢的。**II** ***n***. 翼肢动物。

al·i·phat·ic [ˌæliˈfætik;ˏælɪˋfætɪk] ***a***.【化】脂肪的,脂(肪)族的。

al·i·quant [ˈælikwənt; ˋæləkwənt] **I** ***a***.【数】除不尽的。**II** ***n***. 除不尽的数。

al·i·quot [ˈælikwɔt; ˋælɪkwət] **I** ***a***.【数】除得尽的。**II** ***n***. 除得尽的数。

Al·i·son [ˈælisn; ˋælɪsn̩] ***n***. 艾丽森〔女子名, Alice 的昵称〕。

A-list [ˈeiˈlist; ˋeˋlɪst] **I** ***n***. 名流[要员]名单;重要项目清单。**II** ***a***. 重要的。

a·lit [əˈlit; əˋlɪt] alight[1]的过去式及过去分词。

-al·i·ty *suf*.〔构成名词〕表示"性质"; gener*ality*, speci*ality*, mor*ality*.

a·li·un·de [ˌeiliːˈʌndiː;ˏelɪˋʌndɪ] ***ad***., ***a***.〔多置于被修饰语之后〕【法】出于别的来源地[的],非由本文引证地[的]。*evidence* ~ 引自别处的证据。

a·live [əˈlaiv; əˋlaɪv] ***a***.〔多作表语〕**1**. 活着的;活动的,活泼的,精神抖擞的。**2**. 热闹的 (*with*)。**3**. 注意到的,敏感的 (*to*)。**4**.〔口〕生满(虱子等)的。**5**.【电】通有电流的,加有电压的。*be caught* ~ 被活捉,被生擒。*the happiest man* ~ 世上最幸福的人。~ ***and kicking*** 生气勃勃,活蹦乱跳。***all*** ~〔口〕活蹦乱跳;精神抖擞。***any man*** ~ 任何人。***as sure as I am*** ~ 极确实地。***be ~ to*** 注意,对…有敏感(*He is ~ to his own interests*. 他斤斤计较自己利益)。***be ~ with*** 勃勃,洋洋,兴旺,拥挤,(热情)洋溢 (*He is ~ with ambition*. 他雄心勃勃。*The hive is ~ with bees*. 蜂房里蜜蜂闹闹嚷嚷)。***bury*** ~ 活埋。***come*** ~ 活跃起来;觉悟起来;显得像真的一样。***Heart*** ~! 什么,哎呀。〔强烈的感叹句〕。***keep*** ~ 使活着,把(鱼)养着;让(火)烧着;使继续下去 (*keep old memories* ~ 永志不忘)。***Look*** ~!〔口〕赶快! 加油! ***Man*** ~! = Sakes ~! = Heart ~! ***skin*** ~ 活活剥去…的皮;〔口〕严厉谴责;〔口〕彻底击败。

a·li·yah [ˌɑːliːˈjɑː;ˏɑlɪˋjɑ] ***n***.〔Heb.〕犹太人往以色列移民。

a·liz·a·rin(e) [əˈlizərin; əˋlɪzərɪn] ***n***. 茜(草色)素,茜草红。

alk. = alkali.

al·ka·hest [ˈælkəhest; ˋælkəˏhɛst] ***n***.〔古〕(炼金术师探求的)万能溶剂。

al·ka·les·cence [ˌælkəˈlesns;ˏælkˋlɛsn̩s] ***n***. 微碱性。

al·ka·les·cent [ˌælkəˈlesnt;ˏælkəˋlɛsn̩t] ***a***. 微碱性的。

al·ka·li [ˈælkəlai; ˋælkəˏlaɪ] ***n***. (*pl*. ~(*e*)*s*)【化】碱;强碱。~ **blue** 碱性蓝。~ **metals** 碱金属。~ **rock**【矿】碱性(火成)岩。~ **soil** 碱土。

al·kal·ic [ælˈkælik; ælˋkælɪk] ***a***.【地】**1**. 碱性的;强碱性的。**2**. (岩石)含大量钠和钾盐的。

al·ka·li·fy [ˈælkælifai; ˋælkələˏfaɪ] ***vt***. 使碱化;给…加碱。

al·ka·lim·e·ter [ˌælkəˈlimitə;ˏælkəˋləmɪtɚ] ***n***. 碱量计;碳酸定量计。

al·ka·line [ˈælkəlain; ˋælkəˏlaɪn] **I** ***a***. 碱的,含碱的,碱性的;强碱的。**II** ***n***. 碱性。~ **earth**【化】碱土。~ **soil** 含碱土壤。~ **reaction**【化】碱性反应。

al·ka·line-earth metals [ˈælkəlinˈəːθ, -lain- ˈmetlz; ˋælkəlɪnˋɝθ, -laɪn- ˋmɛtl̩z]【化】碱土金属。

al·ka·lin·i·ty [ˌælkəˈliniti;ˏælkəˋlɪnətɪ] ***n***. 碱性,碱度。

al·ka·lin·ize [ˈælkəliˌnaiz; ˋælkəlɪnˏaɪz] ***vt***. 使碱化。**-i·za·tion** ***n***.

al·ka·lize [ˈælkəˌlaiz; ˋælkəˏlaɪz] ***vt***. 碱化。**-li·za·tion** ***n***.

A

al·ka·loid [ˈælkəlɔid; ˋælkə͵lɔɪd] **I** *a*. 碱的,碱一样的,含碱的。**II** *n*. 生物碱,植物碱基。

al·ka·loid·al [ˌælkəˈlɔidəl; ͵ælkəˋlɔɪd(ə)l] *a*. 生物碱的。

al·ka·lo·sis [ˌælkəˈləusis; ͵ælkəˋlosɪs] *n*. 碱中毒。

al·kane [ˈælkein; ˋælken] *n*. 【化】链烷,烷(属)烃。

al·ka·net [ˈælkənet; ˋælkə͵nɛt] *n*. 【植】朱草;朱草染料。

al·kene [ˈælkiːn; ˋælkin] *n*. 【化】链烯,烯烃。

al·kine [ˈælkain; ˋælkaɪn] *n*. = alkyne.

Al·ko·ran [ælkɔˈrɑːn, -ˈræn; ͵ælkoˋrɑn, -ˋræn] *n*. (伊斯兰教的)《古兰经》(= Koran)。

al·ky [ˈælki; ˋælkɪ] *n*. 〔美俚〕酒精。

al·kyd [ˈælkid; ˋælkɪd] *n*. 醇酸树脂。

al·kyl [ˈælkil; ˋælkɪl] *n*. 【化】烷基;烃基(= ~ radical)。**-lic** *a*.

al·ky·la·tion [ˌælkiˈleiʃən; ͵ælkəˋleʃ(ə)n] *n*. 烷基取代,烷化。**-late** [-ˌleit; -͵let] *n*., *vt*.

al·kyne [ˈælkain; ˋælkaɪn] *n*. 【化】炔。

all [ɔːl; ɔl] **I** *a*. **1.** 所有的,全部的,整个的,一切的。**2.** 非常的,极度的,尽可能的。**3.** 〔口〕用尽,用完。~ *night* 终夜,一夜。~ *place* 处处,到处。~ *one's life* 终生,毕生。~ *round* 周围。~ *the world over* 世界各地。~ *the year* (*round*) 一年到头。*He is* ~ *eyes*. 他只是看。*She is* ~ *smiles*. 她只管笑。*What is* ~ *this noise*? 这么吵嚷究竟是怎么回事? *The storm raged in* ~ *its fury*. 暴风雨猛烈极了。*Life is not* ~ *pleasure*. 生活不光是享乐。*The bread is* ~. 面包吃完了。*All men cannot be masters*. = *We cannot* ~ *be masters*. 并非人人都能当头头。***All Fools' Day*** 愚人节〔4月1日〕。~ ***fours*** **1.** (兽的)四足,(人的)手足。**2.** 一种纸牌玩法 (*go* [*run*] *on* ~ *fours* 爬着走。*be on* ~ *fours with* 〔英方〕与…相一致[吻合])。***All Hallows*** 〔古〕= *All Saints' Day*. ~ ***hours*** 有便的时候;深夜。~ ***jolly fine*** 极好的,极漂亮的。~ ***kind***(*s*) ***of*** 种种。***All Saints' Day*** 万圣节。~ ***sort***(*s*) ***of*** 种种。~ ***the go*** [***mode***, ***rage***] 〔美〕非常流行。~ ***the world and his wife*** 〔谑〕谁都,人人都。~ ***things to*** ~ ***men*** 八面玲珑。~ ***this*** 这一切。~ ***wool and a yard wide*** 〔美〕顶好的;真的,靠得住的。***and*** ~ ***that*** 及其他各物,…等等。***at*** ~ ***events*** 总之。***at*** ~ ***times*** 时时。***by*** ~ ***means*** 一定。***for*** ~ 虽有[无论]…仍然 (*For* ~ *you say, I still like him*. 虽然你说了这一番话,我还是喜欢他)。***for*** ~ ***that*** = ***for all***. ***in*** ~ ***directions*** 四面八方。***in*** ~ ***its splendour*** [***glory***] 荣耀之极,趾高气扬。***of*** ~ 有的是… (*Why go to Norway, of* ~ *countries*? 有的是国家,为什么偏要去挪威呢?) ***not*** ~ 不一定都 (*Not* ~ *men are wise*. 人不一定都聪明)。***with*** ~ = ***for*** ~. ***with*** ~ ***speed*** 尽快,赶快。**II** *n*., *pro*. 全部;全体;一切。*All are agreed*. 全体赞成。*All is still*. 万籁俱寂。*He lost his* ~. 他已倾家荡产。*He's* ~ *we got to go on*. 他是我们探寻的唯一线索。*That is* ~ *that there is to it*. 不过如此。*That's* ~. 就只这些,没有了,只此而已。~ ***in*** ~ **1.** 完全 (*trust me not at* ~, *or* ~ *in* ~. 毫不信任我或完全信任我)。**2.** 全部,一切。**3.** 最心爱的,第一 (*Study is* ~ *in* ~ *to me*. 在我是学习第一)。***All is lost*** [***over***] 已无望,全完了。***A- is not gold that glitters***. 发光的东西并不都是金子。~ ***of ...*** 全体,大家,一齐,都,各自;〔美〕足足,整整(~ *of 100 dollars* 整整一百元)。~ ***of a doodah*** [ˈduːdə; ˋdudə] 〔美俚〕兴奋,神经过敏。***All's well***. 都好了。***All's well that ends well***. 〔谚〕结果好就一切都好。~ ***told*** 合计,总计。***above*** ~ 尤其,最,最主要的。***and*** ~ 及其他一切;等等;连…都 (*He ate it, bone and* ~. 他连骨头都吃掉了)。***at*** ~ 全然;既然,究竟 (*No danger at* ~. 毫无危险。*Do you know at* ~? 你究竟知不知道? *If you do it at* ~, *do it well*. 既做就得好好地做。*very little, if any at* ~ 就是有也很有限)。***after*** ~ 终归,到底。***be*** ~ ***one*** 全是一样;怎么都好 (*to*)。***for*** ~ ***I care*** 与我何干。***for*** ~ ***I know*** 也未可知。***for good and*** ~ 永远。***in*** ~ 总计。***not at*** ~ 毫不,毫无 (*He is not at* ~ *stupid*. 他一点不傻。*Oh, not at* ~. 啊,一点也不。*Thank you so much*. —*Not at* ~. 多谢多谢。—不谢不谢)。***once for*** ~ 只此一次;断然。***one and*** ~ = ~ ***and sundry*** 全都,尽都,无论谁都。***That's*** ~. 没有了,完了;全有了。***when*** ~ ***comes to*** ~ 〔古〕结果。***when*** ~ ***is said*** (***and done***) 毕竟,到底,终于。**III** *ad*. **1.** 完全,全然,都;〔口〕极;简直。**2.** 〔诗〕正当,正在。**3.** 【体】各,彼此。~ *as the day began to break* 正当破晓时。*The score is two* ~. 比赛成绩彼此两分。*love* ~ 彼此零分。~ ***alone*** 仅仅一个人;独力。~ ***along*** 始终,一直都;一路,沿途。~ ***around*** 遍处;一一。~ ***at once*** 突然。~ ***but*** 简直是,几乎跟…一样 (*He is* ~ *but dead*. 他简直是死人[行尸走肉])。~ ***gone*** 〔口〕完了,没有了。~ ***in*** 疲倦极了 (*I'm* ~ *in*. 我疲倦极了)。~ ***out*** 竭尽全力(*go* ~ *out* 全力以赴)。~ ***over*** **1.** 遍身;〔美〕到处,处处。**2.** 全完了 (*The meeting was* ~ *over*. 会开完了)。**3.** 〔口〕完全,完全像(*He is his father* ~ *over*. 他完全像他父亲)。~ ***over with*** 全完了,不行了(*It is* ~ *over with him*. 他完全完了[无希望了])。~ ***quiet*** 十分平静,无问题。~ ***ready*** 一切就绪。~ ***right*** 〔俚〕不错;好,行;没关系,没有什么(*All right*! 可以可以! 晓得了! 好! 〔反〕好! 看! *All right*! *You shall repent this*. 好! 以后不要懊悔)。~ ***square*** 〔美俚〕**1.** 付清款项,完成应作的工作。**2.** (运动)比分拉平。~ ***the better*** [***more***] 反而更(好),却更。~ ***the farther*** 〔美俚〕尽…所有,尽…所能(*That is* ~ *the farther I got*. 那是尽我所有了)。~ ***the same*** 依然。~ ***there*** 头脑清醒(*He is not* ~ *there*. 他头脑不清)。~ ***too*** 总是太,过。~ ***too often*** 再三再四。~ ***too soon*** 总是太早。~ ***up*** (*with*) 全完了[无望、失败]。~ ***very fine*** [***well***] 〔口、反〕很好,顶好(~ *very well, but* ... 固然很好,但是…)。~ ***wet*** 〔美俚〕完全弄错。**All-American** *n*., *a*. 全美代表选手;全美(国)的。~**-around** *a*. 〔美〕= all-round. ~ **clear** 解除警报。~**-fired** *a*., *ad*. 非常的(地)(*Don't be so* ~*-fired sure of yourself*. 不要过分自信)。~**-important** *a*. 最重要的,重大的。~**-in** *a*. 〔英〕**1.** 包含全部的 (*an* ~*-in 10-day tour* 包括一切的十日游)。**2.** 竭尽全力的 (*an* ~*-in effort* 全力以赴)。**3.** 【摔交】自由式的,无限制的。~**-inclusive** *a*. 包括一切的。~**-in-one** (妇女胸罩和腰带连在一起的)紧身胸衣。~**-mains** *a*. (收音机等)适应各种电压的〔仅作表语〕。~**-night** *a*. 通宵的,整夜营业的。~**-or-none** *a*. 全有或全无的。~**-or-nothing** *a*. 获得一切或一无所有的,不全则无的,孤注一掷的。~**-out** *a*. 〔俚〕全力的;全面的;彻底的(*an* ~*-out conflict* 全面战争。*an* ~*-out effort* 全力以赴。*an* ~*-out reform* 彻底改革)。~ **over** **1.** *a*. 全,满。**2.** *n*. 全花织物。~**-overish** *a*. 〔俚〕浑身难过的;说不出地不舒服的(*feel* ~*-overish* 觉得不舒服)。~**-possessed** 〔美俚〕着了魔的,入了迷的(*like* ~*-possessed* 仿佛中了邪)。~**-powerful** *a*. 全能的,力量无限的。~**-purpose** *a*. 通用的,可作各种用途的。~**-red** [**All-Red**] *a*. (航线等)在全英国的,英联邦范围内的。~**-round** *a*. 广博的,多方面的;万能的,多才多艺的(*an* ~*-round athlete* 全能运动选手。~*-round education* 圆满的教育。*an* ~*-round magazine* 综合杂志。*an* ~*-round price* 各费在内的价钱)。~**-rounder** 多面手;全能运动员。~**seed** 多种子植物。~**-sided** *a*. 全面的。~**-spice** 【植】多香果。~**-star** *a*. 名角全体的(*an* ~*-star cast* [*team*] 名角会演,一流选手[队])。~**-time** *a*. 一时不闲的;专职的,全时工作的。空前的(*an* ~*-time record* 空前的纪录)。~**-up weight** 空中总重量〔包括飞机和机载客货在内〕。~**-way** *a*. (飞机场)具有各向跑道

的。～**ways fuze** 不论落地角度如何均可引爆的炸弹触爆雷管。～**-weather** *a*. 全天候的；任何天候皆能应用［适应］的。～**-year** *a*. 全年的。

Al·lah [ˈælə, ˈælɑː; ˋælə, ˋælɑ] *n*. (伊斯兰教的)真主。～ *is* ～. 真主之外无真主。

Al·lan [ˈælən; ˈælən] *n*. 阿伦[男子名, Alan 的异体]。

al·lan·to·ic [ˌælənˈtəuik; ˏælənˋtoɪk] *a*. 尿囊的；有尿囊的。

al·lan·toid [əˈlæntɔid; əˋlæntɔɪd] *a*. 尿囊的；尿囊状的；腊肠状的。

al·lan·to·in [æˈlæntəin; æˋlæntoɪn] *n*. 尿囊素。

al·lan·to·is [æˈlæntəuis; æˋlæntoɪs] *n*. 【解】尿囊。

al·lar·gan·do [ˌɑːlɑːˈgɑːndəu; ˏɑlɑrˋgɑndo] *a*., *ad*. 【乐】渐慢和渐强。

al·lay [əˈlei; əˋle] *vt*. 减轻, 压(惊), 止(渴), 消(痛), 解(忧)。

al·lée [əˈlei; əˋle] *n*. 〔林荫〕小径。

al·le·ga·tion [ˌæliˈgeiʃən; ˏæləˋgeʃən] *n*. 断言, 主张；陈述, 辩解。

al·lege [əˈledʒ; əˋlɛdʒ] *vt*. **1**. 断言, 宣称。**2**. 提出…作为理由。*It is* ～*d that* ... 据说。

al·leg·ed [əˈledʒd; əˋlɛdʒd] *a*. **1**. 被提出而尚未证实的, 有嫌疑的。**2**. 声称的, 宣称的。**3**. 作为理由[辩解等]的。*the* ～ *thief* 嫌疑盗窃犯。*the* ～ *reason* 举出来的理由。

al·le·giance [əˈliːdʒəns; əˋlidʒəns] *n*. **1**. 忠诚, 归顺, 忠心 (*opp*. treason)。**2**. (封建)臣道, 忠节。*in* ～ *to science* 献身科学。

al·le·gor·ic, -i·cal [ˌæliˈgɔrik, -ikəl; ˏæləˋgɔrɪk, -ɪkəl] *a*. 比喻的, 寓言的。**-i·cal·ly** *ad*.

al·le·go·rist [ˈæligərist; ˋæləˏgorɪst] *n*. 讽喻家, 寓言作者。

al·le·go·rize [ˈæligəraiz; ˋæləgəˏraɪz] *vt*. 用比喻讽喻的方式说；以讽喻的含义解释。—*vi*. 作寓言；使用讽喻。

al·le·go·ry [ˈæligəri; ˋæləgorɪ] *n*. 比喻；寓言；象征。

al·le·gret·to [ˌæliˈgretəu; ˏæləˋgrɛto] **I** *ad*. 〔It.〕【乐】稍快, 稍急。**II** *n*. 小快板。

al·le·gro [əˈleigrəu; əˋlegro] **I** *ad*. 〔It.〕【乐】轻快地, 活泼地。**II** *n*., *a*. 快板(的)。

al·lel(e) [əˈliːl; əˋlil], **al·lelo·morph** [əˈliːləmɔːf; əˋliləˏmɔrf] *n*. 【遗】等位基因, 对偶基因。

al·le·lu·ia [ˌæliˈluːjə; ˏæləˋlujə] *n*., *int*. = hallelujah.

al·le·mande [ˌæliˈmɑːnd; ˏæləˋmænd] *n*. **1**. 阿列曼达舞〔德国十七和十八世纪的一种舞蹈〕。**2**. 阿列曼达舞曲。**3**. 四对方阵舞。

Al·len [ˈælin, ˈælən; ˋælɪn, ˋælən] *n*. 阿伦[姓氏, 男子名]。

Al·len·by [ˈælənbi; ˋælənbɪ] *n*. 阿伦比〔姓氏〕。

al·ler·gen [ˈælədʒən; ˋæləˏdʒɛn], **-gin** [-dʒin; -dʒɪn] *n*. 【医】变应素, 变应原, 过敏原〔如药物、食物、花粉等〕。

al·ler·gic [əˈləːdʒik; əˋlɜdʒɪk] *a*. **1**. 过敏症的, 变(态反)应性的。**2**. 〔俚〕神经过敏的, 敏感的；憎恶的。*an* ～ *reaction to wool* 对羊毛的过敏反应。～ *to studying* 不喜欢念书。

al·ler·gist [ˈælədʒist; ˋælədʒɪst] *n*. 治疗过敏症专家, 变态反应症专家。

al·ler·gy [ˈælədʒi; ˋælədʒɪ] *n*. **1**. 【医】变(态反)应性, 过敏。**2**. 憎恶, 反感。*have an* ～ *to hard work* 厌恶做辛苦的工作, 好逸恶劳。

al·le·thrin [ˈæliθrin; ˋælɪθrɪn] *n*. 丙烯除虫菊(酯), 丙烯菊酯。

al·le·vi·ate [əˈliːvieit; əˋlivɪˏet] *vt*. 减轻(痛苦等), 缓和(愁苦等)。

al·le·vi·a·tion [əˌliːviˈeiʃən; əˏlivɪˋeʃən] *n*. **1**. 减轻, 缓和。**2**. 起缓和作用的东西, 解痛物, 慰藉物。

al·le·vi·a·tive [əˈliːviətiv; əˋlivɪˏetɪv], **-to·ry** [-təri; -tərɪ] *a*. 减轻的, 缓和的, 解痛的, 解忧的。

al·le·vi·a·tor [əˈliːvieitə; əˋlivɪˏetɚ] *n*. 减轻者, 安慰者, 缓和物, 解痛品。

al·ley [ˈæli; ˋælɪ] *n*. **1**. 小街, 小巷, 胡同, 弄堂。**2**. 公园[庭园]中的小径。**3**. 【网球】双打时球场两边留出的空地。*an* ～ *off Fleet Str*. 从弗利特街分出的小巷。*a blind* ～ 死巷, 死胡同；无发展前途的职业。***down*** [***up***] ***one's*** ～ 〔俚〕拿手, 专长。～**way** *n*. 〔美〕窄街, 通道。

al·ley-oop [ˌæliˈuːp; ˏælɪˋup] *int*. 杭育〔劳动呼声[号子]〕。

All·fa·ther [ˈɔːlˈfɑːðə; ˋɔlˋfɑðɚ] *n*. 神, 上帝。

all hail [ˈɔːlˈheil; ˋɔlˋhel] 〔古〕身体好! 〔招呼语〕。

All·hal·low·mas [ˈɔːlˈhæləuməs; ˋɔlˋhæloməs] = Allhallows.

All·hal·low·tide [ˌɔlˈhæləutaid; ˏɔlˋhælotaɪd] *n*. 〔古〕万圣节日。

al·li·a·ceous [ˌæliˈeiʃəs; ˏælɪˋeʃəs] *a*. **1**. 葱属的, 葱的, 韭的, 大蒜的。**2**. 有葱味[蒜味等]的。

al·li·ance [əˈlaiəns; əˋlaɪəns] *n*. **1**. 同盟, 联盟。**2**. 联姻。**3**. 同盟条约。**4**. 同盟者。**5**. 近似, 共同点。**6**. 【植】群落属。*a dual* [*triple*, *quadruple*] ～ 二国[三国、四国]同盟。*an offensive and defensive* ～ 攻守同盟。***enter into*** [***form an***] ～ ***with*** 与…联盟[结盟]。***in*** ～ ***with*** 与…联合。

al·li·cin [ˈælisin; ˋæləsɪn] *n*. 蒜素。

al·lied [əˈlaid, ˈælaid; əˋlaɪd, ˋælaɪd] *a*. **1**. 同盟的, 同盟国的。**2**. 姻亲的。**3**. 同源的；类似的。**4**. 〔A-〕(第一次世界大战中)协约国的；(第二次世界大战中)同盟国的。*the A- and Associated Powers* (第一次世界大战的)协约国。*the A- Military Government* (第二次世界大战中的)同盟国军政府〔略 AMG〕。

Al·lies [ˈælaiz, əˈlaiz; ˋælaɪz, əˋlaɪz] *n*. 〔*pl*.〕**1**. (第一次世界大战的)协约国。**2**. (第二次世界大战的)同盟国。

al·li·ga·tor [ˈæligeitə; ˋæləˏgetɚ] *n*. **1**. 短吻鳄, 鳄(鱼)。**2**. 鳄皮。**3**. 水陆两用平底军用车。**4**. 鳄式碎石机。**5**. 摇摆舞音乐爱好者。～ **bait** 〔美口〕鳄饵；难吃之物。～ **ring** 齿环。～ **tortoise** 甲鱼, 水鱼, 团鱼。～ **wrench** 鳄式扳手。

al·lit·er·ate [əˈlitəreit; əˋlɪtəˏret] *vi*. **1**. 押头韵(*with*)。**2**. 用头韵体作诗。—*vt*. 使成头韵体。

al·lit·er·a·tion [əˌlitəˈreiʃən; əˏlɪtəˋreʃən] *n*. 头韵(法)。

al·lit·er·a·tive [əˈlitərətiv; əˋlɪtəˏretɪv] *a*. 头韵法的, 头韵体的。

al·li·um [ˈæliəm; ˋælɪəm] *n*. 葱属植物。

al·lo [ˈæləu; ˋælo] *a*. 紧密相联的；【化】同分异构的。

allo- *comb*. *f*. 异, 他：*allo*nym, *allo*morph.

al·lo·cate [ˈæləukeit; ˋæloket] *vt*. **1**. 分派, 配给。**2**. 配置；部署。**3**. 划拨(经费等)。～ *funds for housing* 拨款盖房子。～ *sb*. *to a certain duty* 派某人担任某职务。

al·lo·ca·tion [ˌæləuˈkeiʃən; ˏæloˋkeʃən] *n*. **1**. (原料等的)分配, 配给。**2**. 配给物, 配给量。**3**. 定位置, 部署。**4**. 【会】(经费、收入等的)分配法。***be under*** ～ 作为配售品。***put on*** ～ 实行配销。

al·lo·chro·ic [ˌæləˈkrəuik; ˏæləˋkroɪk] *a*. 【医】变色的。

al·loch·tho·nous [əˈlɔkθənəs; əˋlɑkθənəs] *a*. 外来的；非本土的。

al·lo·cu·tion [ˌæləuˈkjuːʃən; ˏæloˋkjuʃən] *n*. (罗马教皇、将军等的)训谕, 面谕。

al·lod [ˈælɔd; ˋælɑd] *n*. 封建地产, 自主地产。

al·lo·di·al [əˈləudjəl; əˋlodɪəl] *a*. 自主地产的。

al·lo·di·um [əˈləudjəm; əˋlodɪəm] *n*. (*pl*. *-di·a* [-diə; -dɪə])【法】(封建时代的)自主地产。

al·log·a·my [əˈlɔgəmi; əˋlɑgəmɪ] *n*. 【植】异花受粉；【动】异体受精。

al·lom·er·ism [əˈlɔmərizəm; əˋlɑməˏɪzəm] *n*. 【化】异质同晶(现象)。

A

al·lom·e·try [ə'lɔmitri; ə`lɑmətrɪ] *n*.【生】体形变异(学)。

al·lo·morph ['æləmɔːf; `ælə͵mɔrf] *n*. 1.【矿】同质异晶。2.【语】同词素的异形词。**-ic** [͵ælə'mɔːfik; ͵ælə`mɔrfɪk], **-ous** [͵ælə'mɔːfəs; ͵ælə`mɔrfəs] *a*. **-ism** [͵ælə'mɔːfizəm; ͵ælə`mɔrfɪzəm] *n*. 同质异晶(现象)。

al·lo·nym ['ælənim; `ælənɪm] *n*. 1.(著作者假托的)别名;假名。2. 假托伪名的著作。

al·lo·path, al·lop·a·thist ['æləupæθ, æ'lɔpəθist; `æləpæθ, æ`lɑpəθɪst] *n*. 对抗疗法医师。**-path·ic** [-'pæθik; -`pæθɪk] *a*.

al·lop·a·thy [æ'lɔpəθi; æ`lɑpəθɪ] *n*. 对抗疗法(说)。

al·lo·pat·ric [͵ælə'pætrik; ͵ælə`pætrɪk] *a*.【生】在各区生长的;分布区不重叠的;孤立地发生的。**-cal·ly** *ad*. **-lop·a·try** *n*.

al·lo·phane ['æləfein; `ælə͵fen] *n*.【矿】水铝英石。

al·lo·phone ['æləfəun; `æləfon] *n*.【语音】音素的变形。*The relatively short* (æ) *of mat and the relatively long* (æ) *of mad are ~s*. 单词 mat 中较短的 æ 和单词 mad 中较长的 æ 是音素的变形。

al·lo·plasm ['æləplæzm; `æləplæzm̩] *n*.【生】异质。**-plas·mic** [͵ælə'plæzmik; ͵ælə`plæzmɪk], **-plas·mat·ic** [͵æləplæz'mætik; ͵æləplæz`mætɪk] *a*.

al·lo·pol·y·ploi·dy [͵ælə'pɔli͵plɔidi; ͵ælə`pɑlɪ͵plɔɪdɪ] *n*.【生】异源多倍性。**-poly·ploid** [-͵plɔid; -͵plɔɪd] *n*., *a*. 异源多倍体(的)。

al·lo·sau·rus [͵ælə'sɔːrəs; ͵ælə`sɔrəs] *n*. 侏罗纪的恐龙,异龙。

al·lot [ə'lɔt; ə`lɑt] *vt*. 1. 分配,摊派给,发给;把…拨给(*to*)。2. 指定[拨出](款项等)作某种用途(*for*)。3. 规定,派定。~ *the profits* 分配红利。~ *shares* 分摊股分。~ *money for a school* 拨款办学。*Each speaker is ~ted five minutes*. 每个发言人规定发言五分钟。~ ***upon*** ...〔美俚〕打算,正想。

al·lo·the·ism ['æləθiːizəm; `æləθiɪzəm] *n*. 异神崇拜;异神教。

al·lot·ment [ə'lɔtmənt; ə`lɑtmənt] *n*. 1. 分配,分派;份额。2.〔英〕(划成小块出租的)副业生产地。3.【美军】从工资中扣除的费用(如扣除亲属赡养费,人寿保险费)。4. 命运,天命。

al·lo·trope ['ælətrəup; `ælə͵trop] *n*.【化】同素异形体。

al·lo·trop·ic, al·lo·trop·i·cal [͵ælə'trɔpik, -ikəl; ͵ælə`trɑpɪk, -ɪkəl] *a*.【化】同素异形的。**-i·cal·ly** *ad*.

al·lot·ro·pism [ə'lɔtrəpizəm; ə`lɑtrəpɪzm̩], **al·lot·ro·py** [ə'lɔtrəpi; ə`lɑtrəpɪ] *n*.【化】同素异形(现象),同素异性(作用)。

all' ot·ta·va [͵ɑːlə'tɑːvə, It. ͵ɑːlɔ'tɑːvɑː; ͵ɑlə`tɑvə, It. ͵ɑlɑ`tɑvɑ]【乐】高或低八度演奏。

al·lot·tee [͵ɔlɔ'tiː; ə͵lɑ`ti] *n*. 接受配给的人。

al·low [ə'lau; ə`laʊ] *vt*. 1. 准许(做某事),许可(某现象存在)。2. 容许,听任,任,由,允许,让(某人做某事)〔接不定式〕。3. 承认(某事)(*that*);承认(某人如何)〔接不定式〕。4. 给予…以,让…得到。5. 沉溺,放纵〔用反身代词〕。6. 酌量;酌情增[减]。7.〔美口〕想要〔接不定式〕。8.(由于不小心而)让(某事)得以发生。*Allow me to introduce to you my friend Johnson*. 请允许我把我的朋友约翰逊介绍给你。~ *a free passage* 准许自由通行。*Dogs are not ~ed in the park*. 不许带狗进入公园。*No smoking* (~*ed*). 禁止吸烟。*We ~ that we are wrong*. 我们承认自己错了。*They all ~ him to be a good football player*. 他们都承认他是一位优秀足球运动员。~ *three percent of our profits for tear and wear* 少算百分之三的利润作为损耗费。~ *a bread to burn* (不小心)让面包烤焦。—*vi*. 1. 承认(*of*)。2. 容许(*of*)。3. 原谅,体谅;考虑到,酌量(*for*)。4. 为…酌留余地,以防(*for*)。*The question ~s of no dispute*. 问题无争论余地。~ *of sb's authority* 承认某人的权威。*We must ~ for his youth*. 我们得体谅他年轻。~ *for the circumstances* 考虑到具体情况。~ *oneself in* 耽溺。~***ing that*** 即令是…也[仍]。

al·low·a·ble [ə'lauəbl; ə`laʊəbl̩] *a*. 可容许的,可承认的,不碍事的,正当的。*Two mistakes are ~ in this game*. 这种游戏允许犯规两次。**-bly** *ad*.

al·low·ance [ə'lauəns; ə`laʊəns] I *n*. 1. 零用钱,给与额,津贴,补助,零用钱。2.【机】(加工)留量;配合公差。3. 斟酌,酌量;预留;容差;【商】折扣。4. 默许,默认;承认。5.【体】给对方的让步。*an ~ of rice* 给予一份大米。*a clothing* [*traveling*] ~ 服装[旅]费。*short ~* 给予量不足。*a time ~* (给对方的)时间的宽限。*By your ~ I'd like to leave before you*. 对不起,我要先走了。***at no ~*** 无限制,尽性(*plunder at no ~* 大肆掠夺)。***make ~ for*** 1. 留有余地;斟酌,酌量,估量。2. 原谅,体谅。3. 扣除(*make an ~ of 10% for cash payment* 现款九折)。II *vt*. 1. 给…发津贴。2. 按定量供给。

al·low·ed·ly [ə'lauidli; ə`laʊɪdlɪ] *ad*. 1. 被许可。2. 当然,肯定。

al·loy ['ælɔi; `ælɔɪ] I *n*. 1. 合金。2.(合金中的)劣等金属。3.(金银的)成色,成份。4.〔喻〕搀杂品。*Brass is an ~ of copper and zinc*. 黄铜是铜和锌的合金。*pleasure without ~* 玩得痛快。II [ə'lɔi; ə`lɔɪ] *vt*. 1. 合铸,熔合(金属)。2. 在…中搀以杂质;使(金属)减低成色。3. 减损(兴趣等)。— *vi*. 熔合,搀。~ **steel** 合金钢,特种钢。

all·spice ['ɔːl͵spais; `ɔl͵spaɪs] *n*.【植】多香果。

al·lude [ə'ljuːd; ə`lud] *vi*. 暗指,暗示;(婉转)提到;指…说(*to*)。*Were you alluding to me?* 是指我说吗?

al·lure [ə'ljuə; ə`lɪʊr] I *vt* 引诱,勾引,诱惑。*Rewards ~ men to brave danger*. 重赏之下必有勇夫。~***d by hopes*** 被希望引诱着。~ (*sb*.) ***from*** 诱使(某人)离开…。~ (*sb*.) ***into*** [***to***] 把(某人)诱进,骗入。II *n*. 诱惑力,魅力。

al·lure·ment [ə'ljuəmənt; ə`lʊrmənt] *n*. 引诱,诱惑;诱惑力,诱惑物。

al·lur·ing [ə'ljuriŋ; ə`ljurɪŋ] *a*. 诱惑的,迷人的,引人的,媚人的。*Circuses are ~ both to children and to adults*. 马戏既吸引小孩,也吸引大人。**-ly** *ad*. 诱人地,妩媚地。

al·lu·sion [ə'ljuːʒən; ə`luʒən] *n*. 暗示,暗指,提及,引喻。***in ~ to*** 暗指。***make ~ to*** 提及。

al·lu·sive [ə'ljuːsiv; ə`lusɪv] *a*. 1. 暗指的。2.(文章、谈话等)多用典故的,引喻的。*a story ~ to her history* 影射她的身世的故事。

al·lu·vi·al [ə'ljuːvjəl; ə`luvɪəl] I *a*.【地】冲积的。~ *deposits* 冲积物。~ *gold* 沙金。II *n*. 冲积土[层,矿床],淤积土。

al·lu·vi·on [ə'ljuːvjən; ə`luvɪən] *n*. 1. 波浪的冲击。2. 泛滥,洪水。3.【法】(冲积造成的)土地增加。4. 沙滩,沙洲,冲积地;冲积物。

al·lu·vi·um [ə'ljuːvjəm; ə`luvɪəm] *n*. (*pl*. ~*s*, *-vi·a* [-viə; -vɪə])【地】冲积层;冲积土。

Al·ly ['æli; `ælɪ] *n*. 艾丽〔女子名, Alice 的昵称〕。

al·ly[1] I [ə'lai, æ'lai; ə`laɪ, æ`laɪ] *vt*., *vi*. (使)结盟;(使)联姻。~ ***oneself with*** [***to***] 与…结盟[联合];与…联姻。***be allied to*** 类似,与…是同类。II ['ælai, ə'lai; `ælaɪ, ə`laɪ] *n*. 1. 同盟者,同盟国。2. 伙伴;助手。3. 同类的动植物。*the Allies* 1.(第一次世界大战中的)协约国。2.(第二次世界大战中的)同盟国。

al·l(e)y[2] ['æli; `ælɪ] *n*. 弹球〔游戏用〕。

al·lyl ['ælil; `æləl] *n*.【化】烯丙基。

alm [ælm; ælm] *n*. 捐赠,施舍。

Al·ma ['ælmə; `ælmə] *n*. 阿尔玛〔女子名〕。

Al·ma-A·ta [͵ɑːlmə'ɑːtə; ͵ɑlmə`ɑtə] *n*. 阿拉木图〔哈萨克城市〕。

al·ma(h) ['ælmə; `ælmə] *n*. 埃及舞女。

A

Al·ma·gest [ˈælmədʒest; ˋælmədʒɛst] ***n*. 1.**《天文学大成》〔公元二世纪时托勒密作的天文学数学名著〕。**2.** 〔a-〕(中古时代)占星学书;点金术书。

Al·ma Ma·ter [ˈælməˈmeitə; ˋɑlməˋmɑtɚ] 〔L.〕 **1.** 母校。**2.** 〔美〕校歌。

al·ma·nac [ˈɔːlmənæk; ˋɔlmənæk] ***n*.** 历书,日历,月份牌;年鉴。

al·man·dine [ˈælməndain; ˋælmənˏdin], **al·man·dite** [ˈælməndait; ˋælməndaɪt] ***n*.**【矿】铁铝榴石,贵榴石。

al·might·i·ness [ɔːlˈmaitinis; ɔlˋmaɪtɪnɪs] ***n*.** 全能。

al·might·y [ɔːlˈmaiti; ɔlˋmaɪtɪ] **I *a*. 1.** 全能的。**2.** 〔口〕非常的,无比的,可怕的。**II *ad*.** 非常;…得够呛[要命]。*It's ~ hot*. 热得要命。***A- God* = *God A-* = *the A-*** 全能之神。*in an ~ fix* 处境万分狼狈。

al·mond [ˈɑːmənd; ˋɑmənd] ***n*. 1.** 巴旦杏,扁桃;杏仁。**2.** 〔古〕扁桃腺。~**-eyed *a*.** 杏眼的。~ **oil** 杏仁油。

al·mon·er [ˈɑːmənə; ˋɑmənɚ] ***n*. 1.** 救济品分发员,施赈人员。**2.** 〔英〕医院的社会服务员。

al·mon·ry [ˈɑːmənri; ˋɑmənrɪ] ***n*.** 救济品分发处,施赈所。

al·most [ˈɔːlməust, ˈɔːlməst; ˋɔlmost, ˋɔlməst] **I *ad*.** 差不多,几乎,将近,快要。*It's ~ two o'clocks now*. 现在快两点了。~ *never* [*no*, *nothing*] 〔美〕难得,几乎从不[没有]。**II *a*.** 〔罕〕近似的。*his ~ impudence* 他近似无礼的态度。

alms [ɑːmz; ɑmz] ***n*.** 〔*sing*., *pl*.〕 **1.** 施舍。**2.** 施舍物,救济品。*ask for ~* 募捐。~ **deed** 乐善好施的行为。~**giver** 慈善家,施主。~**giving** 施舍,赈济。~**house** 济贫院。~**man** 受救济的人。

al·mu·can·tar [ˌælmjuːˈkæntə; ˏælmjuˋkæntɚ] ***n*.**【天】(地)平纬圈,高度方位仪。

al·muce [ˈælmjuːs; ˋælmjus] ***n*.** 皮兜帽〔原为牧师帽〕。

al·mug [ˈælməg; ˋælməg] ***n*.** = algum.

al·ni·co [ˈælnikəu; ˋælnɪˏko] ***n*.**【冶】铝镍钴合金。

al·od [ˈæləd; ˋælɑd] ***n*.** (封建时代的)自主地产,自由地产。

a·lo·di·um [əˈləudiəm; əˋlodɪəm] ***n*.** 封建地产,自主地产。**a·lo·di·al *a*.**

al·oe [ˈæləu; ˋælo] ***n*. 1.**【植】芦荟;沉香,伽南香。**2.** 〔*pl*.〕芦荟油〔泻药〕。**3.** 〔美〕龙舌兰〔亦作 American ~〕。~**swood** [-zwud; -zwʊd] 伽罗木,沉香。

A·lo·fi [əˈlɔfi; əˋlɑfɪ] ***n*.** 阿洛菲〔纽埃岛(新)首府〕。

a·loft [əˈlɔft; əˋlɔft] ***ad*. 1.** 高高地;在上面。**2.** 在空中。**3.**【海】桅上,桅杆高处,帆索高处。*be sent ~ to bed* 被打发上楼睡觉。*climb ~* 爬到桅杆高处。***go ~*** 〔俚〕升天,死。

a·lo·ha [əˈləuə, ɑːˈləuhɑː, əˈləuə; əˋloə, ɑˋlohɑ, əˋloə] ***int*.** 〔Haw.〕阿洛哈〔问候或告别时用语〕。~ **shirt** 夏威夷式的运动衫。**A- State** 美国夏威夷州的别名。

al·o·in [ˈæləuin; ˋæloɪn] ***n*.**【化】芦荟素。

a·lone [əˈləun; əˋlon] **I *ad*. 1.** 单独地;独自;孤独地。**2.** 〔用在名词或代词后,起限定的作用〕只,只有;仅仅。*He walked on ~ to the bookstore*. 他一个人走着到书店去。*She ~ can speak French*. 只有她会讲法语。**II *a*.** 〔用作述语〕单独的;独一无二的。*I want to be ~*. 我愿意一个人生活。*I am not ~ in this opinion*. 不单是我意见这样。*He was all ~*. 他只一个人。***leave ~*** 不要管,不要动 (*Leave my book ~*. 不要动我的书)。***let ~* 1.** 听,由,任随 (*Let me ~ to do it*. 由我做吧)。**2.** 莫说…(连) (*I know the whole tune, let ~ the words*. 莫说歌词,连整个歌曲我都知道的。*let-alone policy* 放任政策)。***let well enough ~*** 满足于现状。***not ~ ... but*** 不仅…又。

a·long [əˈlɔŋ; əˋlɔŋ] **I *ad*. 1.** 成一行地,纵长地;沿,循。**2.** 一块儿,一道(去)。**3.** 上前,在前。**4.** 〔美口〕(时间)晚,一直到,过去。**5.** 在手头。*All the cars parked ~ by the station*. 所有的汽车都沿着车站停放一行。*Come ~*. 跟我来。*walk ~* 向前走。*~ toward evening* 一直到傍晚。*The afternoon was well ~*. 下午又快过去[快完]了。***all ~* 1.** 始终;一直;一贯。**2.** 从左到右;从上到下。***~ about*** 大约在(= *about two o'clock* 接近两点钟时)。***~ back*** 〔美口〕刚才,近来。(***all***) ***~ of*** 〔俚〕因,由于。***~ with*** 与…一道;以外(*~ with other advantages* 其他利益以外)。***be ~*** 〔俚〕来到;赶上 (*He will be ~ soon*. 他一会儿就来)。***Get*** [***Go***] ***~!*** 〔俚〕向前走,走开。***get ~* 1.** 生活,过日子。**2.** 上年纪。***get ~ with*** (工作)进行,进步。***right ~*** 〔口〕不停,不断,一直,始终。**II *prep*.** 沿着。*The road runs ~ the river*. 公路与河并行。~**-shore 1. *ad*.**, ***a*.** 沿海,沿岸。**2. *n*.** 岸;码头。

a·long·side [əˈlɔŋˈsaid; əˋlɔŋˋsaɪd] **I *ad*.** 在…的侧面;与…并排。*The two ships lay ~ of each other*. 两条船并排靠着。*sit ~ of sb*. 和某人并肩坐着。**II *prep*.** 横靠,傍着。*The ship lies ~ the pier*. 船横靠着码头停泊。

a·loof [əˈluːf; əˋluf] **I *ad*. 1.** 离开,避开,隔开。**2.**【海】向上风方向。***keep*** [***hold***, ***stand***] ***~*** (***from***) 离开(…);对(…)敬而远之。***stand ~ over*** 对…采取超然态度。**II *a*.** 〔多作述语〕**1.** 冷淡的。**2.** 孤零零的。*an ~ church* 一座孤零零的教堂。*The girl's manner was ~*. 姑娘的态度是冷淡的。**-ness *n*.**【医】超然,冷淡。

al·o·pe·ci·a [ˌæləˈpiːʃiə; ˏæləˋpiʃɪə] ***n*.** 脱发(症)。

a·lors [æˈlɔː; æˋlɔr] ***int*.** 〔F.〕那么;那就〔一般化的口头语〕。

a·loud [əˈlaud; əˋlaʊd] ***ad*.** 高声,响亮。*shout ~* 大叫。**It reeks ~.** 〔俚〕臭极了。**think ~** 自言自语。

a·low [əˈləu; əˋlo] ***ad*.** 向下,在下;在船内。~ *and aloft* 上上下下都;无处不。

A.L.P. = American Labor Party 美国劳工党。

alp [ælp; ælp] ***n*. 1.** 高山,高峰。**2.** (阿尔卑斯)山地牧场。***~s on ~s*** 重重高山;重重难关。

al·pac·a [ælˈpækə; ælˋpækə] ***n*. 1.**【动】(南美)羊驼。**2.** 羊驼毛;羊驼呢。

al·pen·glow [ˈælpingləu; ˋælpənˏglo] ***n*.** (高山上见到的)早霞,晚霞。

al·pen·horn [ˈælpinhɔːn; ˋælpɪnˏhɔrn] ***n*.** (瑞士阿尔卑斯牧民用的)长柄木号角。

al·pen·stock [ˈælpinstɔk; ˋælpənˏstɑk] ***n*.** 登山杖。

al·pes·trine [ælˈpestrin; ælˋpɛstrɪn] ***a*. 1.** 阿尔卑斯山脉和山区的。**2.**【植】生长于亚高山区的。

al·pha [ˈælfə; ˋælfə] ***n*. 1.** 阿尔法〔希腊语字母表首字母 α,相当于英语的 a〕。**2.** 最初。**3.**【天】α 星,主星。***~ and omega*** 首尾,始终;全体。~ **decay**【原】α 衰变,~ **female** 女性至上主义者。~ **male** 大男子主义者。~ **plus** 最高级的,最好的。~ **rays**【物】α 射线。~ **rhythm** [**wave**] 脑中每秒钟约十下的波动。~**scope** 计算机屏幕显示器。~ **test** α 测试〔对电脑软件等试制品进行的初级测试〕。

al·pha·bet [ˈælfəbit; ˋælfəˏbɛt] ***n*. 1.** 字母表。**2.** 初步。*a phonetic ~* 音标文字。*the ~ of law* 法学入门。

al·pha·bet·ic, -i·cal [ˌælfəˈbetik(əl); ˏælfəˋbɛtɪk(əl)] ***a*.** ABC 的,字母的;照字母表次序的。*in ~ order* 按照字母顺序。**-i·cal·ly *ad*.** 用字母表,照字母次序。

al·pha·bet·ize [ˈælfəbitaiz; ˋælfəbəˏtaɪz] ***vt*. 1.** 照字母表次序排列。**2.** 用字母标记,使拼音化。

al·pha·nu·mer·ic [ˌælfənjuːˈmerik; ˏælfənuˋmɛrɪk] ***a*.** 字母数字式的。

al·pha·tron [ˈælfətrɔn; ˋælfətrɑn] ***n*.**【空】α 粒子电离压强计。

Al·phon·so [ælˈfɔnzəu; ælˋfɑnzo] ***n*.** 阿方索〔男子名〕。

alp·horn [ˈælphɔːn; ˋælpˏhɔrn] ***n*.** 长柄木号角(= alpenhorn)。

al·pho·sis [ælˈfəusis; ælˋfosɪs] ***n*.** 白化症状。

A

al·pine [ˈælpain; ˋælpaɪn] **I** *a*. **1.** 高山(性)的。**2.** 〔A-〕阿尔卑斯山的;阿尔卑斯山区居民的。**II** *n*. **1.** 高山植物。**2.** 高山型的白种人〔不同于地中海型和北欧型的白种人〕。~ **club** 登山俱乐部。~ **garden** 奇石园。~ **hat** 登山帽。~ **light** 紫外线。~ **plants** 高山植物。

al·pin·ism [ˈælpinizəm; ˋælpɪnˏɪzəm] *n*. 登山。

al·pin·ist [ˈælpinist; ˋælpɪnɪst] *n*. 〔常 A-〕登山运动员,登山家。

Alps [ælps; ælps] *n*. 〔the ~ 〕阿尔卑斯山脉。

al·read·y [ɔːlˈredi; ɔlˋrɛdɪ] *ad*. **1.** 〔表示现在或过去某时发生的事实〕已经,早已。**2.** 〔问句或否定句中表示惊愕、意外时〕还(没有吗?),已经…(吗?) *I have ~ met him*. 我已经同他会面了。*When we came in, we found they had ~ arrived*. 我们来时,发现他们已经到了。*Have you finished supper ~?* 你吃完晚饭了吗? *You haven't ~ done your washing, have you?* 你的衣服还没有洗完吗?

al·right [ɔːlˈrait; ɔlˋraɪt] *ad*. 〔俚〕= all right.

a.l.s. = autograph letter signed 亲笔签署的信。

Al·sace [ˈælsæs; ˋælsæs] *n*. 阿尔萨斯〔法国一地区〕。

Al·sa·tia [ælˈseiʃjə; ælˋseʃə] *n*. **1.** 法国 Alsace 地区的旧名。**2.** 阿尔塞西区〔伦敦市中央的一区,昔为债务人和罪犯的藏匿地〕。**3.** 〔喻〕避难所。

al·sike (clo·ver) [ˈɔːlsaik (kləuvə); ˋɔlsaɪk (klovɚ)] *n*. 【植】杂三叶草。

Al Si·rat [ˌælsiˈrɑːt; ˏælsɪˋrɑt] **1.** 《古兰经》的真谛。**2.** 【穆斯林】(架于地狱火上)通向天堂的窄桥。

Al·sop(p) [ˈɔːlsəp; ˋɔlsəp] *n*. 奥尔索普〔姓氏〕。

al·so [ˈɔːlsəu; ˋɔlso] **I** *ad*. 亦,也,同样;〔口〕而且,还。*Tom has been to Canada. Harry has ~ been to Canada*. 汤姆去过加拿大。哈里也去过。★在口语中,多用 *as well* 或 *too*;在否定句中,则用 *either*. **II** *conj*. = and. *She was noble, ~ beautiful*. 她很高尚,而且长得美。***not only ... but ~ ...***不但…并且…。**~-ran** *n*. **1.** 【赛马】落选的马。**2.** (比赛、竞争、竞选等的)失败者。**3.** 无足轻重的人。**~-runner** *n*. (比赛、竞争的)失败者。

alt [ælt; ælt] *n*., *a*. 【乐】中高音(的)。***in ~*** **1.** 高音的。**2.** 〔俚〕得意洋洋,趾高气扬。

alt. = alternate; altitude.

Al·ta [ˈæltə; ˋæltə] *n*. 阿尔塔〔女子名〕。

Al·tai [ælˈtai; ælˋtaɪ] *n*. 〔the ~〕阿尔泰山。

Al·tai·an [ælˈteiən; ælˋteən] *a*., *n*. 阿尔泰山 (Altai) 的(人)。

Al·ta·ic [ælˈteiik; ælˋte·ɪk] **I** *a*. **1.** 阿尔泰山脉的,阿尔泰山人的。**2.** 阿尔泰语系的。**II** *n*. 阿尔泰语系〔包括突厥语,蒙语和通古斯语〕。

Al·ta·ir [ælˈtɛə; ælˋtɑ·ɪr] *n*. 【天】河鼓二,牛郎星。

al·tar [ˈɔːltə; ˋɔltɚ] *n*. **1.** 祭坛;圣餐台;圣坛。**2.** (干船坞的)台阶。***lead (a woman) to the ~*** 娶(某女),与(某女)结婚。~ **boy** 祭坛小厮,祭坛侍者。~ **cloth** 祭坛罩。~ **piece** 祭坛背后的绘画[雕刻,屏风]。

alt·az·i·muth [æltˈæzimәθ; æltˋæzəməθ] *n*. 【天】(地平)经纬仪。

al·ter [ˈɔːltə; ˋɔltɚ] *vt*. **1.** 变更;改变,改换;改建(房屋),改做(衣服)。**2.** 〔美方〕阉割,给(雄性动物)去势,给(雌性动物)割去卵巢。— *vi*. 变,改;(人)变老。~ ***for the better [worse]*** 改好[坏],变好[坏]。**-a·bil·i·ty** *n*. 可变性。**-a·ble** *a*. 可改变的。**-a·bly** *ad*.

al·ter·ant [ˈɔːltərənt; ˋɔltərənt] **I** *a*. 引起变化的。**II** *n*. 引起变化的东西;变质[色]剂。

al·ter·a·tion [ˌɔːltəˈreiʃən; ˏɔltəˋreʃən] *n*. **1.** 变更,改变,变化。**2.** 【地】蚀变。**3.** 〔美方〕阉割。

al·ter·a·tive [ˈɔːltərətiv; ˋɔltəˏretɪv] **I** *a*. **1.** 引起改变的。**2.** 【医】增强体质的。**II** *n*. 【医】体质改变药;体质改变疗法。

al·ter·cate [ˈɔːltəːkeit; ˋɔltɚˏket] *vi*. 争辩;口角,吵嘴。~ *with sb. about a trifle* 与某人因细故口角。

al·ter·ca·tion [ˌɔːltəːˈkeiʃən; ˏɔltɚˋkeʃən] *n*. 争辩,吵嘴,口角。

al·ter e·go [ˈæltərˈegəu; ˋæltɚˋɛgo] 〔L.〕 **1.** 他我,另一个我;个性中的另一面。**2.** 心腹朋友,知己。

al·ter·nant [ɔːlˈtəːnənt; ɔlˋtɝnənt] **I** *a*. **1.** 交替的,互换的。**2.** 【地】(砂与泥等的)互隔层的。**II** *n*. 【数】交替函数。

al·ter·nate [ɔːlˈtəːnit; ɔlˋtɝnɪt] **I** *a*. **1.** 交替的,轮流的。**2.** 隔一的,间隔的。**3.** 备用的,补充的;预备的,候补的。**4.** 【植】交错的,互生的。**5.** 〔美俚〕副,代理的。*an ~ member of the committee* 候补委员。~ *angles* 【数】(一对)错角。~ *hope and fear* 一喜一忧。~ *layout* 另一方案。~ *leaves* 【植】互生叶。***each ~ day*** 每隔一日。***in ~ lines*** 隔一行。***on ~ days*** 隔日。**II** *n*. **1.** 替换物。**2.** 〔美〕(委员)代理人。*delegates and ~s* 代表们和代理人们。[ˈɔːltəːneit; ˋɔltɚˏnet] *vt*. 使交替,使轮流。*The sentries ~d their watch*. 哨兵轮流站岗。*He ~s joy with grief*. 他时喜时忧。— *vi*. **1.** 交替,轮流。**2.** 【电】交流。~ *between joy and grief* 悲喜交集。*alternating current* 【电】交流(电流)。*alternating personality* 【心】多重人格。*alternating series* 【数】交错级数。*alternating temperature* 变温。

al·ter·na·tion [ˌɔːltəːˈneiʃən; ˏɔltɚˋneʃən] *n*. **1.** 交替,更迭,变换;间隔。**2.** 【数】错列。**3.** 【植】交错。**4.** 【农】轮种。*the ~ of crops* 作物的轮种。*the ~ of the seasons* 四季的循环。~ ***of generations*** 【生】世代交替。

al·ter·na·tive [ɔːlˈtəːnətiv; ɔlˋtɝnətɪv] **I** *a*. **1.** 随便一个的,二中择一的,交替的。**2.** 非传统[正统]的,另类的。~ *conjunctions* 选择连接词(如: *or*, *nor*)。~ *courses* (或死或降的)两条路。*an ~ question* 选择疑问句(如: Is the baby a boy or a girl?) **II** *n*. 二者之一,二中选一;交替;可采用的方法;替换物。*That's the only ~*. 那是唯一可取的办法。*There are three ~s*. 如上[如下]三者任择其一。*There is no other ~*. 别无他法。*The ~s are death and submission* 或死或降,任选其一。***no ~ but ...*** 除…外别无他法(无可奈何,只好…)。**-ly** *ad*. 二中择一地;替换着。

al·ter·na·tor [ˈɔːltə(ː)neitə; ˋɔltɚˏnetɚ] *n*. 交流发电机。*a radio frequency ~* 射频振荡器;高频发生器。

al·th(a)e·a [ælˈθiːə; ælˋθiə] *n*. 【植】**1.** 蜀葵属植物。**2.** 木槿(= rose of sharon)。

al·tho [ɔːlˈðəu; ɔlˋðo] *conj*. 〔美〕= although.

alt·horn [ˈælthɔːn; ˋæltˏhɔrn] *n*. 【乐】中音萨克号。

al·though [ɔːlˈðəu; ɔlˋðo] *conj*. 尽管,虽然〔引导让步副词子句,主句中不用 but, 可用 yet〕。*A- I believe it, yet I must consider*. 我虽然相信,但还要考虑一下。*A- many difficulties and obstacles are still ahead, nevertheless, we are certain to make still greater achievements*. 仅管在前进道路上还存在着许多困难和障碍,但是,我们一定能够取得更加伟大的成就。

al·ti·graph [ˈæltigrɑːf; ˋæltəgræf] *n*. 高度自记仪,高度记录器;气压计。

al·tim·e·ter [ˈæltimiːtə; ˋæltɪmitɚ] *n*. 测高计,高度表。

al·tim·e·try [ælˈtimitri; ælˋtɪmɪtrɪ] *n* 高度测量术。

al·ti·tude [ˈæltitjuːd; ˋæltəˏtjud] *n*. **1.** 高,高度;海拔(高度)。**2.** 【天】地平纬度。**3.** 〔常 *pl*.〕高处。**4.** 高位,高等。**5.** 【数】顶垂线,高线。*the ceiling ~* 升限。*high [low] ~* 【空】高[低]空。*(an) ~ sickness* 高空病。*grabbing for ~* (空战中)抢占高度;〔喻〕渐渐发怒。*In these ~s, snow never melts*. 在这么高的地方,积雪终年不化。~ **flight** 高空飞行。

al·to [ˈæltəu; ˋælto] *n*. 〔It.〕 **1.** 【乐】男声最高音;中高音,女低音。**2.** 中提琴(= viola)。**3.** 唱男声最高音[中高音,女低音]的歌手。

al·to·cu·mu·lus [ˈæltəuˈkjuːmjuləs; ˏæltoˋkjumjələs] (*pl*. ***al·to·cu·mu·li*** [-mjəˌlai; -mjəˏlaɪ]) *n*. 【气】

高积云〔略 Ac〕。

al·to·geth·er [ˌɔːltəˈgeðə;ˏɔltəˋgeðɚ] **I** *ad*. **1.** 全然,全,完全。**2.** 一共。**3.** 总之。*not ~ wrong* 不完全错。*He wrote six books ~*. 他一共写了六本书。A-, *it's a great success*. 总的说来是巨大的成功。***taken ~*** 总而言之。**II** *n*. 〔口〕〔the ~〕裸体。***in the ~*** 〔口〕赤身露体。

Al·ton [ˈɔːltən; ˋɔltən] *n*. 奥尔顿〔姓氏,男子名〕。

al·to-re·lie·vo [ˈæltəuriˈliːvəu; ˋælto·rɪˋlivo] *n*. 高凸浮雕〔*cf*. basso-relievo〕。

al·to-ri·lie·vo [ˈɑːltɔːriˈljevɔː; ˋɑltorɪˋlɪevo] *n*. (*pl*. ***alti-rilievi*** [ˈɑːltiriˈljɛvi; ˋɑltɪrɪˋlɪevɪ]) 〔It.〕= alto-relievo.

al·to·stra·tus [ˈæltəuˈstreitəs; ˋæltoˋstretəs] *n*. 【气】高层云〔略 As〕。

al·tri·cial [ælˈtriʃəl; ælˋtrɪʃəl] *a*. 守巢的,守雏的〔指某些幼鸟出生时眼盲,需双亲照料〕。

al·tru·ism [ˈæltruizəm; ˋæltrʊˏɪzəm] *n*. 利他主义,爱他主义。

al·tru·ist [ˈæltruist; ˋæltrʊˏɪst] *n*. 利他主义者,爱他主义者。

al·tru·is·tic [ˌæltruˈistik;ˏæltrʊˋɪstɪk] *a*. 利他的,利他主义的。**-ti·cal·ly** *ad*

al·u·del [ˈæljudel; ˋæljʊdel] *n*. 【化】梨状升华器〔回收升华作物时使用的陶制或玻璃制的梨状器皿,使用时打开上下口并按次序接上管子的插口〕。

al·u·la [ˈæljulə; ˋæljulə] *n*. (*pl*. *-lae* [-liː; -li]) **1.** 【动】角翼,小翼。**2.** (昆虫的)翼膜,翅瓣。

al·um[1] [ˈæləm; ˋæləm] *n*. 明矾 *basic* [*cubic*] ~ 明矾石。

a·lum[2] [əˈlʌm; əˋlʌm] *n*. 〔口〕校友(= alumnus 或 alumna)。

a·lu·mi·na [əˈljuːminə; əˋlumɪnə] *n*. 【化】矾土,铝氧土。

a·lu·mi·nate [əˈluːmineit; əˋlumɪˏnet] *n*. 铝酸盐。

a·lu·mi·ni·fer·ous [əˌljuːmiˈnifərəs; əˏljumɪˋnɪfərəs] *a*. 含铝的;含铝土的;含矾的。

a·lu·min·ium [ˌæljuˈminjəm;ˏæljəˋmɪnɪəm] *n*. 【化】铝。~ **acetate** 醋酸铝。~ **bronze** 铝铜,矾铜。~ **foil** 铝箔。~**ware** 铝制厨房用具,铝制器皿。

a·lu·mi·nize [əˈluːminaiz; əˋluməˏnaɪz] *vt*. 给…镀铝;在…涂铝;对…进行铝处理。

a·lu·mi·no·ther·my [əˈluːminəuˌθəːmi; əˋljumənoˏθɝmɪ] *n*. 铝热(法)。

a·lu·mi·nous [əˈljuːminəs; əˋlumɪnəs] *a*. **1.** 明矾的,含明矾的。**2.** 矾土的,含矾土的。**3.** 铝的,含铝的。

a·lu·mi·num [əˈljuːminəm; əˋlumɪnəm] *n*. 〔美〕= aluminium.

a·lum·na [əˈlʌmnə; əˋlʌmnə] *n*. (*pl*. ***-nae*** [-niː; -ni]) 〔L〕女毕业生;女校友。

a·lum·nus [əˈlʌmnəs; əˋlʌmnəs] *n*. (*pl*. ***-ni*** [-nai; -naɪ]) 〔L〕男毕业生,男校友。*an alumni association* 〔美〕校友会,同学会(= old boys' association)。

al·um·root [ˈæləmruːt; ˋæləmˏrut] *n*. 【植】矾根草〔虎耳草属〕。

A·lun·dum [əˈlʌndəm; əˋlʌndəm] *n*. **1.** 【商标】钢铝石,钢玉石,人造磨石。**2.** 〔a-〕铝氧粉。

al·u·nite [ˈæljunait; ˋæljʊnaɪt] *n*. 明矾石。

Al·va [ˈælvə; ˋælvə] *n*. 阿尔瓦〔男子名,女子名〕。

al·ve·o·lar [ælˈviələ, ˌælviˈəulə; ælˋvɪələ˞,ˏælvɪˋolə˞] **I** *a*. **1.** 【解】齿槽的。**2.** 【解】肺泡的,气泡的。**3.** 【语音】齿龈的。**II** *n*. 【语音】齿龈音 (如 t, d, s 等)。

al·ve·o·late [ælˈviəlit; ælˋvɪəlɪt] *a*. 蜂窝状的,有小窝的;【动】具有气泡的。

al·ve·o·lus [ælˈviələs; ælˋvɪələs] *n*. (*pl*. *-li* [-lai; -laɪ]) **1.** 蜂窝;小窝。**2.** 【解】齿槽。**3.** 【解】肺泡,【动】气泡。

Al·vin [ˈælvin; ˋælvɪn] *n*. 阿尔文〔男子名〕。

al·vine [ˈælvain; ˋælvaɪn] *a*. **1.** 小肠的;肠的。**2.** 腹部的。

al·way [ˈɔːlwei; ˋɔlwe] *ad*. 〔古、诗〕= always.

al·ways [ˈɔːlweiz, -wiz; ˋɔlwez, -wɪz] *ad*. **1.** 永远,始终。**2.** 经常,老是,总是,一直。**3.** 不断地。*She is ~ busy*. 她总是忙。*You must ~ bear this in mind*. 这一点你要经常记在心里。*Near, ~ near, he came*. 他一步步走过来,愈来愈近了。***almost ~*** 通常。***not ~*** 未必,不一定。

a·lys·sum [əˈlisʌm; əˋlɪsʌm] *n*. 【植】庭荠属植物。*sweet ~* 香雪球。

AM = amplitude modulation 调幅。

Am 【化】元素镅 (americium) 的符号。

Am. = **1.** America. **2.** American. **3.** Ammunition.

am = **1.** ammeter. **2.** ampere-meter.

a. m. = 〔L.〕*anno mundi* (= in the year of the world).

A.M. = **1.** *Artium Magister* 文科硕士(= Master of Arts)。

a.m., A.M. [ˈeiˈem; ˋeˋɛm] **1.** = 〔L〕ante meridiem 午前,上午(= before noon)。**2.** 由午夜至中午。★此词常为小写,但在时间表中或作标题时则为大写。*from 8 to 10 a. m*. 上午 8 时至 10 时。

am [强 æm,弱 əm; æm, əm] be 的第一人称、单数、直陈式、现在时。

Am·a·bel [ˈæməbel; ˋæməbel] *n*. 阿玛贝尔〔女子名〕。

am·a·da·vat [ˌæmədəˈvæt;ˏæmədəˋvæt] *n*. 【动】莓莺〔印度的一种观赏鸣禽〕。

am·a·dou [ˈæməduː; ˋæməˏdu] *n*. (止血和引火用的)火绒〔取自树上菌类的一种海绵状物质〕。

a·mah [ˈɑːmə; ˋɑmə] *n*. (东方国家的)保姆,女仆,阿妈。

a·main [əˈmein; əˋmen] *ad*. 〔古、诗〕**1.** 全力地。**2.** 全速地。**3.** 突然地,急忙地。**4.** 非常地。

a·mal·gam [əˈmælgəm; əˋmælgəm] *n*. **1.** 【冶】汞合金,汞齐。**2.** 混合物。

a·mal·gam·a·ble [əˈmælgəməbl; əˋmælgəməbl̩] *a*. 可汞合的;可汞齐化的。

a·mal·ga·mate [əˈmælgəmeit; əˋmælgəˏmet] *vt*., *vi*. **1.** 【冶】使(金属)与水银混合,使(金属)汞齐化。**2.** 混合;合并;融合。~*d union* 联合工会。

a·mal·ga·ma·tion [əˌmælgəˈmeiʃən; əˏmælgəˋmeʃən] *n*. **1.** 【冶】汞合,汞齐化。**2.** 混,合并。**3.** 〔美〕(种族等的)融合 **-tive** *a*.

a·mal·ga·mat·or [əˈmælgəmeitə; əˋmælgəˏmetɚ] *n*. **1.** 混汞机。**2.** 混合物;合并者。**3.** 【冶】(混汞)提金器。

A·man·da [əˈmændə; əˋmændə] *n*. 阿曼达〔女子名〕。

am·a·ni·ta [ˌæməˈnaitə;ˏæməˋnaɪtə] *n*. 【植】蛤蟆菌属菌类。

a·man·u·en·sis [əˌmænjuˈensis; əˏmænjʊˋɛnsɪs] *n*. (*pl*. *-ses* [-siːz; -siz]) 抄写员,听写员,秘书。

am·a·ranth [ˈæmərænθ; ˋæməˏrænθ] *n*. **1.** (传说中的)不凋花。**2.** 【植】苋;〔A-〕苋属。**3.** 苋菜红,深紫红。

am·a·ran·thine [ˌæməˈrænθain;ˏæməˋrænθaɪn] *a*. **1.** 不凋的。**2.** 似苋的。**3.** 深紫红的。

am·a·relle [ˌæməˈrel;ˏæməˋrɛl] *n*. 酸樱桃。

Am·a·ryl·lis [ˌæməˈrilis;ˏæməˋrɪlɪs] *n*. **1.** 〔诗〕女牧羊人。**2.** 孤挺花属;〔a-〕孤挺花。

a·mass [əˈmæs; əˋmæs] *vt*. 积累,积聚;收集。*~ great fortunes* 发大财。—*vi*. 集合。**-er** *n*. 积聚者。

a·mass·ment [əˈmæsmənt; əˋmæsmənt] *n*. 积聚,积累,收集。

am·a·teur [ˈæmətə(ː), ˈæmətjuə; ˋæməˏtʊr, ˋæmətʃʊr] **I** *a*. 爱好…的,业余的。*an ~ performance* 游艺会。*an ~ dramatic club* 业余剧社。**II** *n*. 业余者,爱好者 (*opp*. professional)。*an ~ in boxing* 业余拳击爱好者。*a radio ~* 业余无线电爱好者。

am·a·teur·ish [æməˈtəːriʃ, -ˈtjuər-; ˌæməˋtɝɪʃ, -ˋtjʊrɪ-] *a*. 1. 业余的。2. 不熟练的。

am·a·teur·ism [ˈæmətəːrizəm; ˌæməˋtɝɪzm̩] *n*. 业余活动,业余性质[方式、身份、技艺]。

am·a·tive [ˈæmətiv; ˋæmətɪv] *a*. 恋爱的;色情的。

am·a·tol [ˈæmətɔl; ˋæməˌtɑl] *n*. 硝铵、三硝基甲苯炸药,阿马图炸药。

am·a·to·ri·al [ˌæməˈtɔːriəl; ˌæməˋtorɪəl], **am·a·to·ry** [ˈæmətəri; ˋæməˌtorɪ] *a*. 恋爱的;色情的。~ *poems* 情诗。

am·au·ro·sis [ˌæmɔːˈrəusis; ˌæmɔˋrosɪs] *n*. 【医】黑内障,黑蒙,青光瞎。**-rot·ic** [-ˈrɔtik; -ˋrɑtɪk] *a*.

a·maze [əˈmeiz; əˋmez] I *vt*. 使惊奇,使吃惊。*be* ~*d at* [*by*] 对…大为惊异。*be* ~*d to see* [*hear*, *find*] 看到[听到,发现]…大为吃惊。II *n*. 〔诗〕= amazement.

a·mazed·ly [əˈmeizidli; əˋmezɪdlɪ] *ad*. 愕然。

a·maze·ment [əˈmeizmənt; əˋmezmənt] *n*. 惊奇,诧异,惊异。*be filled with* ~ 大为惊异。*in* ~ 骇然。*to sb.'s* ~ 使某人惊异的是…。

a·maz·ing [əˈmeiziŋ; əˋmezɪŋ] *a*. 令人惊异的。**-ly** *ad*. 可惊地,非常。

Am·a·zon[1] [ˈæməzən; ˋæməˌzɑn] *n*. 〔the ~〕〔南美〕亚马逊河。

Am·a·zon[2] [ˈæməzən; ˋæməzən] *n*. 1.【希神】亚马逊族女战士。2.〔a-〕女战士。3.〔a-〕彪形妇女。4.〔a-〕中美和南美产的绿色小鹦鹉。5.〔a-〕【动】悍蚁〔这种蚂蚁奴役其他的蚂蚁〕。6.〔a-〕亚马逊毛呢。

A·ma·zo·nas [ˌæməˈzəunəs; ˌæməˋzonəs] *n*. 亚马逊〔巴西州名〕。

Am·a·zo·ni·an[1] [ˌæməˈzəunjən; ˌæməˋzonɪən] I *a*.〔南美〕亚马逊河流域的。II *n*. 亚马逊河区的印第安人。

Am·a·zo·ni·an[2] [ˌæməˈzəunjən; ˌæməˋzonɪən] *a*. 1. 亚马逊族女战士一样的。2.〔常 a-〕刚勇的(女人)。

am·a·zon·ite [ˈæməzənait; ˋæməzəˌnaɪt] *n*.【矿】天河石,微斜长石。

am·bag·es [æmˈbeidʒiːz; æmˋbedʒiz] *n*.〔古〕〔*pl*.〕1. 迂回的道路。2. 转弯抹角的说法[做法]。3. 诡秘行为。

am·ba·gious [æmˈbeidʒəs; æmˋbedʒəs] *a*.〔古〕迂回曲折的。~ *reasoning* 迂回曲折的推理。

am·ba·ri, -ry [æmˈbɑːri; æmˋbɑrɪ] *n*. 1. 洋麻,槿麻。2. 洋麻[槿麻]纤维(= kenaf)。

am·bas·sa·dor [æmˈbæsədə; æmˋbæsədɚ] *n*. 1. 大使;使节。2. 专使,特使。3. 代表。*an* ~*-at-large* 巡回大使,无任所大使。*an* ~ *extraordinary* 特派大使。*A tourist abroad can be an* ~ *of good-will for his country*. 国外旅游者可以做本国的亲善代表。*an* ~ *plenipotentiary* 全权大使。***The*** ~ ***to the Court of St. James's*** 驻英大使。

am·bas·sa·do·ri·al [æmˌbæsəˈdɔːriəl; æmˌbæsəˋdorɪəl] *a*. 大使的。*an* ~*-level meeting* 大使级会议。

am·bas·sa·dress [æmˈbæsədris; æmˋbæsədrɪs] *n*. 女大使;大使夫人。

am·ber [ˈæmbə; ˋæmbɚ] I *n*. 1. 琥珀。2. 琥珀色。3.【军】线状无烟火药(弹)。II *a*. 1. 琥珀制的。2. 琥珀色的。III *vt*. 使成琥珀色。

am·ber·gris [ˈæmbəgri(ː)s; ˋæmbɚˌgrɪs, -gris] *n*. 龙涎香。

am·ber·jack [ˈæmbədʒæk; ˋæmbɚdʒæk] *n*.【鱼】1. 环带鰤。2. 杜氏鰤。3. 长背鰤。

Am·ber·ite [ˈæmbərait; ˋæmbəraɪt] *n*. 琥珀炸弹〔一种无烟炸药〕。

Am·ber·lite [ˈæmbəlait; ˋæmbɚlaɪt] *n*. 安珀莱特〔离子交换树脂的商标名称〕;〔a-〕离子交换树脂。

am·ber·oid [ˈæmbərɔid; ˋæmbɚˌɔɪd] *n*. 人造琥珀;安伯罗合成琥珀。

am·bi- *comb. f*. 表示"二","二者":*ambi*dextrous.

am·bi·ance [ˈæmbiəns; ˋæmbɪəns] *n*. 环境;气氛(= ambience)。

am·bi·dex·ter [ˈæmbiˈdekstə; ˌæmbəˋdɛkstɚ] I *n*. 1. 两双手都很灵巧的人。2. 两面讨好的人,怀二心的人。II *a*. 1. 两双手都很灵巧的。2. 有二心的,口是心非的,表里不同的。

am·bi·dex·trous [ˈæmbiˈdekstrəs; ˌæmbəˋdɛkstrəs] *a*. 1. 两只手都很灵巧的。2. 表里不同的,怀有二心的。3. 非常熟练的。*A- tennis players are rare*. 能用左右手打网球的人很少。

am·bi·ence [ˈæmbiəns; ˋæmbɪəns] *n*. = ambiance.

am·bi·ent [ˈæmbiənt; ˋæmbɪənt] *a*. 包围着的,周围的。~ *temperature* 室温。

am·bi·gu·i·ty [ˌæmbiˈgjuːiti; ˌæmbɪˋgjuətɪ] *n*. 1. 可作两种或多种解释;含糊;意义不明确。2. 模棱两可的话,含糊的话。

am·big·u·ous [æmˈbigjuəs; æmˋbɪgjʊəs] *a*. 1. 有两种或多种意思的。2. 含糊的,不明确的。*an* ~ *answer* 模棱两可的答覆。*an* ~ *future* 前途未卜。~ **case**【数】歧例。**-ly** *ad*. 含糊地。**-ness** *n*. 含糊。

am·bi·sin·is·ter [ˌæmbiˈsinistə; ˌæmbəˋsɪnɪstɚ] *a*. 两双手都很笨拙的。

am·bi·syl·lab·ic [ˌæmbisiˈlæbik; ˌæmbəsɪˋlæbɪk] *a*. (子音)与前后元音都有关系的〔如 cynic 中的 n〕。

am·bit [ˈæmbit; ˋæmbɪt] *n*. 界限;范围;周围。

am·bi·tend·en·cy [ˌæmbiˈtendənsi; ˌæmbəˋtɛndənsɪ] *n*.【心】自我矛盾倾向。

am·bi·tion [æmˈbiʃən; æmˋbɪʃən] I *n*. 1. 抱负,志气,雄心。2. 野心,奢望。3.〔俚〕锐气,精力。*Until all is over* ~ *never dies*. 不到黄河心不死。*burn with an* ~ 野心勃勃。*the height of one's* ~ 最高志向。II *vt*. 热望,想望得到。

am·bi·tious [æmˈbiʃəs; æmˋbɪʃəs] *a*. 1. 野心勃勃的,有雄心的,抱负不凡的;心怀奢望的。2. 热望的。3. 炫耀的,矫饰的。*be* ~ *of* 热望着,渴望着。*an* ~ *style* 矫饰的文体。**-ly** *ad*. **-ness** *n*.

am·biv·a·lence [ˈæmbiˈveiləns; ˋæmbɪˋveləns] *n*. (对同一人、物、事的)矛盾心理(如又爱又憎)。

am·biv·a·lent [ˌæmbiˈveilənt; ˌæmˋbɪvələnt] I *a*. (对人或事务)有矛盾感情的。II *n*. 两性人。**-ly** *ad*.

am·bi·ver·sion [ˌæmbiˈvəːʃən; ˌæmbɪˋvɝʃən] *n*.【心】中向性格。

am·bi·vert [ˈæmbivəːt; ˋæmbɪvɝt] *n*.【心】具有合乎内向和外向之间性格的人;具有中向性格的人。

am·ble [ˈæmbl; ˋæmbl̩] I *n*. 1. (马的)慢步,溜蹄。2. (人的)漫步,缓步。II *vi*. (马)溜花蹄;(人)慢慢走。

am·blyg·o·nite [æmˈbligənait; æmˋblɪgəˌnaɪt] *n*.【矿】磷铝石。

am·bly·o·pi·a [ˌæmbliˈəupiə; ˌæmblɪˋopɪə] *n*.【医】弱视,视力不足。**-op·ic** *a*.

am·bo [ˈæmbəu; ˋæmbo] *n*. (*pl*. ~*s*, ~*nes* [-ˈbəuniːz; -ˋboniz])(早期教堂的)读经台,讲道台。

am·bo·cep·tor [ˈæmbəˌseptə, -bəu-; ˋæmbəˌseptɚ, -bo-] *n*.【微】介体。

Am·boi·na (wood) [æmˈbɔinə; æmˋbɔɪnə] 青龙木,蔷薇木,黄柏木〔产于亚洲,为家具用材〕。

am·broid [ˈæmbrɔid; ˋæmbrɔɪd] *n*. = amberoid.

Am·brose [ˈæmbrəuz; ˋæmbroz] *n*. 安布罗斯〔男子名〕。

am·bro·sia [æmˈbrəuzjə; æmˋbrozɪə] *n*. 1.【希、罗神】神仙的食物。2. 美味芳香的食品[饮料]。3. 蜜蜂的食料。~ **beetle** 粉蠹虫。

am·bro·sial [æmˈbrəuzjəl; æmˋbrozɪəl], **am·bro·sian** [-zjən; -zɪən] *a*. 1. 上天诸神食用的。2. 美味的。3. 芬芳的。4. 美妙的。

am·bro·type [ˈæmbrətaip; ˋæmbrəˌtaɪp] *n*. (老式的)玻璃版照相。

am·bry [ˈæmbri; ˋæmbrɪ] *n*. 1.〔古〕橱柜,壁橱;神器柜;食品柜。2. 教堂内的壁龛。

ambs·ace [ˈeimzeis; ˋemzˏes] ***n*. 1.** (骰子的)双幺,最低的点数。**2.** 厄运,倒霉。**3.** 最无价值的东西,最不重要的东西。***within ~ of*** 〔古〕快要,濒于,差点儿…(= *within an ace of*)。

am·bu·la·crum [ˌæmbjuˈleikrəm; ˏæmbjʊˋlekrəm] ***n*.** (*pl*. *-cra* [-krə; -krə])【动】(昆虫的)步行足;步带。**-la·cral** ***a*.**

am·bu·lance [ˈæmbjuləns; ˋæmbjələns] ***n*. 1.** 野战医院。**2.** 救护车[船、飞机],红十字车。**3.** (旧时美国西部)旅客乘坐的旅行车。~ **chaser** [lawyer]〔美俚〕(交通)事故律师〔指鼓动(交通)事故受害者起诉要求赔偿的律师〕。~ **corps** 野战卫生队。~ **man** 救护车[船、飞机]上的救护人员。

am·bu·lant [ˈæmbjulənt; ˋæmbjələnt] ***a*. 1.** 走动的,移动的。**2.**【医】能走动的,不卧床的。*an ~ radio station* 流动电台。*an ~ blacksmith* 走街串巷的铁匠。

am·bu·late [ˈæmbjuleit; ˏæmbjəˋlet] ***vi*.** 步行,走动,移动。*The patient was allowed to ~ in his room*. 病人被允许在屋里走动。**-tion** ***n*.**

am·bu·la·to·ry [ˈæmbjulətəri; ˋæmbjələˏtorɪ] **I** ***a*. 1.** 步行的,(适于)走动的。**2.** 流动的。**3.**【医】= ambulant. **4.**【法】可变更的,未确定的。*an ~ court* 流动法庭。*an ~ will* 可变更的遗嘱。**II** ***n*.** (有顶的)回廊,走廊。

am·bu·let [ˈæmbjulit; ˋæmbjʊlɪt] ***n*.** (长途)救护车。

am·bur·y [ˈæmbəri; ˋæmbərɪ] ***n*. 1.** (牛马的)软瘤。**2.**【植】根肿病(= anbury)。

am·bus·cade [ˌæmbəsˈkeid; ˏæmbəsˋked] **I** ***n*. 1.** 伏击。**2.** 埋伏地点。**3.** 伏兵。**II** ***vt*.** 伏击。—***vi*.** 打埋伏。

am·bush [ˈæmbuʃ; ˋæmbʊʃ] **I** ***n*.** 伏击;埋伏(处);伏兵。***fall into an ~*** 中埋伏。***lay*** [***make***] ***an ~*** (***for***) 打埋伏,埋伏着等…;设置伏兵。***lie*** [***hide***] ***in ~*** 打埋伏,埋伏着等。**II** ***vt*. 1.** 自埋伏处出击。**2.** 伏(兵)于(隐处等)(*in*)。*We were ~ed*. 我们遭到伏击。~ *troops in the woods* 设伏兵于林中。—***vi*.** 设置伏兵;埋伏;伏击。**-ment** ***n*.**

a·me·ba [əˈmiːbə; əˋmibə], **a·me·boid** [-bɔid -bɔɪd] ***n*.** = amoeba, amoeboid.

am·e·bi·a·sis [æmiˈbaiəsis; æmɪˋbaɪəsɪs] ***n*.** 变形虫病,内变形虫病

a·me·bo·cyte [əˈmibəˌsait; əˋmibəˏsaɪt] ***n*.** 变形细胞(= amoebocyte)。

âme dam·née [ɑm dɑːˈnei; ɑm dɑˋne] ***n*.** 〔F.〕(*pl*. ***âmes damnées***)甘心当工具的人;奴才。

a·meer [əˈmiə; əˋmɪr] ***n*.** (伊斯兰教国家的)亲王,贵族;司令官;元首 = amir, emir. **-ate** ***n*.** = amirate, emirate.

A·me·lia [əˈmiːljə; əˋmiljə] ***n*.** 阿米莉亚〔女子名〕。

a·mel·io·rant [əˈmiːljərənt; əˋmiljərənt] ***n*.** 起改良作用的东西;土壤改良剂。

a·mel·io·rate [əˈmiːljəreit; əˋmiljəˏret] ***vt*.** 改善,改良。~ *housing conditions* 改善住房条件。— ***vi*.** 改良,变好。*The situation has ~ed*. 情况好转。**-tion** ***n*.** **-tive** ***a*.** **-tor** ***n*.** 改良者,改良物。

A·men [ˈɑːmən; ˋɑmən] ***n*.** (古埃及的)太阳神〔生命与生殖之神〕。

a·men [ˈɑːˈmen, ˈeiˈmen; ˋɑˋmɛn; ˋeˋmɛn] **I** ***int*.** 阿门〔= So be it. 但愿如此,基督教祈祷结尾语〕。**II** ***n*.** 〔美口〕认可,批准(的表示)。***give one's*** [***say***] ***~ to*** 核准。**III** ***vt*.** 〔美口〕**1.** 批准,核准。**2.** 完成。~ [ˈei-; ˋe-] **corner** 〔美〕教堂前座〔领着说阿门的人的座位〕。~ **seat** 〔美〕教堂前座的座位。

a·me·na·ble [əˈmiːnəbl; əˋminəbl̩] ***a*. 1.** 有服从义务的,应服从(法律等)的。**2.** 可依照的;顺从的,肯听话的,(人)服理的。**3.** 经得起检验的,可以由…处理的(*to*)。*a person easily ~ to flattery* 易为谗言所动的人,耳朵软的人。*be ~ to law* 服从(法律), *be ~ to reason* 讲(理);通达(情理)。*He is ~ to counsel*. 他这人听劝。*an ~ servant* 俯首贴耳的奴仆。*These data are ~ to checking*. 这些资料经得起检查。**-bil·i·ty** [əˌmiːnəˈbiliti; əˏminəˋbɪlətɪ] ***n*.** **-ness** ***n*.** **-bly** ***ad*.**

a·mend [əˈmend; əˋmɛnd] ***vt*. 1.** 订正,改正,修正(议案等)。**2.** 改变(行为等)。—***vi*.** 改良;改过。*an ~ed bill* 修正案。~ *one's ways* 改过自新。**-a·ble** ***a*.** **-er** ***n*.** 订正者,改正者,修正者。

a·mend·a·ble [əˈmendəbl; əˋmɛndəbl̩] ***a*.** 能改正的。

a·mend·a·to·ry [əˈmendətəri; əˋmɛndəˏtorɪ] ***a*.** 〔美〕改正的;修正的;矫正的,纠正的。

a·mende [æˈmɑ̃ːnd, F. amɑ̃ːd; ˏæˋmɑ̃nd, F. ˏaˋmɑ̃d] ***n*.** 〔F.〕罚款;道歉;赔偿。~ ***honorable*** [F. aˈmɑːŋ dɔnɔːˈrɑbl; amɑŋ dɑnɑˋrɑbl̩] 正式道歉,赔偿。

a·mend·ment [əˈmen*d*mənt; əˋmɛn*d*mənt] ***n*. 1.** 改善,改进。**2.** 改正,修正。**3.** 修正草案,修正建议。**4.** 改良土壤的物质(如石灰)。*propose* [*move*] *an ~* 提修改建议。

a·mends [əˈmendz; əˋmɛndz] ***n*. 1.** 赔偿;赎罪。**2.** 〔古〕(健康的)恢复,复原。***make ~*** (***for***) 赔偿(损失);道歉;赎罪。★原为复数形,现作单数用。

A·men·ho·tep [ˌɑːmənˈhəutep; ˏɑmənˋhotɛp] 阿孟和蒂〔公元前十六至十四世纪古埃及四法老中的任何一个〕。

a·men·i·ty [əˈmiːniti; əˋmɛnətɪ] ***n*. 1.** (环境、房屋等的)适意,舒适,快感。**2.** 优雅,温厚。**3.** 〔*pl*.〕愉快,快事,乐事;(社交上令人愉快的)举止,礼仪。*amenities of home life* 家庭乐趣。*an exchange of amenities* 相互问好,寒暄。

a·men·or·rhe·a, a·men·or·rhoe·a [eiˌmenəˈriːə; eˏmɛnəˋriə] ***n*.** 月经不调,经闭。

A·men-Ra [ˈɑːmənˈrɑː; ˋɑmənˋrɑ] ***n*.** 古埃及太阳神(= Amon-Re)。

a men·sa et tho·ro [ei ˈmensə et ˈθɔːrəu; ə ˋmɛnsə ɛt ˋθoro] 〔L.〕【法】夫妻未解除婚约但不共寝食的分居(关系)。

am·ent[1] [ˈæmənt; ˋæmənt] ***n*.**【植】葇荑花序。

a·ment[2] [ˈeimənt; ˋemənt] ***n*.** 〔英〕智力欠缺的人;呆子,白痴。

am·en·ta·ceous [ˌæmənˈteiʃəs; ˏæmənˋteʃəs] ***a*.** 葇荑花的,葇荑花状的,像葇荑花的。

a·men·tia [eiˈmenʃiə; eˋmɛnʃɪə] ***n*.**【医】智力缺陷,精神错乱。

am·en·tif·er·ous [ˌæmənˈtifərəs; ˏæmənˋtɪfərəs] ***a*.**【植】葇荑花的;葇荑花序的。

a·merce [əˈməːs; əˋmɝs] ***vt*. 1.** 对…罚款。**2.** 惩罚。~ *the criminal in the sum of eighty dollors* 对该犯课以罚金八十元。~ *sb. of a month's salary* 罚某人扣薪一个月。**-ment** ***n*.** 罚金,罚款。

a·mer·ci·a·ble [əˈməːsiəbl; əˋmɝsɪəbl̩] ***a*.** 应罚款的。

A·mer·i·ca [əˈmerikə; əˋmɛrɪkə] ***n*. 1.** 美洲。**2.** 美国。**3.** 〔*pl*.〕南北美洲,西半球。*North* [*South*] ~ 北〔南〕美洲。*Central ~* 中美洲。*Latin ~* 拉丁美洲。*the United States of ~* 美利坚合众国〔略作 U.S.A.〕。

A·mer·i·can [əˈmerikən; əˋmɛrɪkən] **I** ***a*. 1.** 美洲的。**2.** 美国的。*an ~ citizen* 美国公民。*the Amazon and other ~ rivers* 亚马逊河和美洲的其他河流。**II** ***n*. 1.** 美洲人;美国人。**2.** 美国英语。**3.** 美洲印第安人。~ **Beauty**【植】美国月月红。~ **cheese** = cheddar. ~ **cloth** [**leather**] (做桌布用的)漆布。~ **crawl** 自由式游泳法。~ **English** 美国英语。~ **Indians** 美洲印第安人。~ **organ** 小风琴。~ **plan** (旅馆的)供膳制〔不供膳的叫 European plan〕。~ **Revolution** 美国独立战争。~ **Sign Language** (北美聋人用的一种)北美手势语。

A·mer·i·ca·na [əˌmeriˈkɑːnə; əˏmɛrəˋkɑnə] ***n*.** 〔*pl*.〕美国志书;有关美国[美洲]的史料[文物]。

A·mer·i·can·ese [əˌmerikəˈniːz; əˏmɛrɪkəˋniz] ***n*.** 〔贬〕美国英语。

A

A·mer·i·can·ism [əˈmerikənizəm; əˋmɛrəkən͵ɪzəm] ***n.*** **1.** 美国英语,美国腔;美国语法。**2.** 美国派,美式;美国习惯[想法]。**3.** 崇尚美国,效忠美国。

A·mer·i·can·ist [əˈmerikənist; əˋmɛrəkənɪst] ***n.*** **1.** 美国[美洲]事务[史地等]的研究者[生]。**2.** 研究美洲印第安人及其文化的人类学者。**3.** 亲美国者。

A·mer·i·can·i·za·tion [əˌmerikənaiˈzeiʃən; ə͵mɛrɪkənɪˋzeʃən] ***n.*** 美国化。

A·mer·i·can·ize [əˈmerikənaiz; əˋmɛrəkən͵aɪz] ***vt.***, ***vi.*** **1.** (使)美国化。**2.** (使)带美国腔。

am·er·ic·i·um [ˌæməˈrisiəm; ͵æməˋrɪsɪəm] ***n.*** 【化】镅〔1944 年美国发现超铀新元素之一,符号 Am, 因发现地取名〕。

Am·er·ind [ˈæmərind; ˋæmə͵rɪnd] ***n.*** 美洲印第安人;爱斯基摩人。

Am·er·in·di·an [ˌæmərˈindjən; ͵æməˋrɪndɪən] **1.** ***n.*** = Amerind. **2.** ***a.*** 美洲印第安人(文化)的,爱斯基摩人(文化)的。

a·mes·ace [ˈeimzeis; ˋemzes] ***n.*** = ambsace.

a·met·a·bol·ic [ˌeimetəˈbɔːlik; ͵emɛtəˋbɔlɪk], **a·me·tab·o·lous** [ˌeiməˈtæbələs; ͵eməˋtæbələs] ***a.*** 【动】(昆虫在发育中)无变态的。

am·e·thyst [ˈæmiθist; ˋæməθɪst] ***n.*** **1.** 【矿】紫石英,紫晶;紫蓝色青玉。**2.** 紫色。

am·e·thys·tine [ˌæmiˈθistain; ͵æmɪˋθɪstaɪn] ***a.*** 紫晶质的,紫色的。

am·e·tro·pi·a [ˌæmiˈtrəupiə; ͵æmɪˋtropɪə] ***n.*** 屈光不正;变常眼。**-trop·ic** [-ˈtrəupik, -ˈtrɔpik; -ˋtropɪk, -ˋtrɑpɪk] ***a.***

Am·ex [ˈæmeks; ˋæmɛks] ***n.*** **1.** 美国股票交易所(= American Stock Exchange)。**2.** (第一次世界大战中派赴欧洲的)美国远征军(= American Expeditionary Force)。

AMG = Allied Military Government 盟国军政府。

Am·ha·ra [ɑːmˈhɑːrɑː; ɑmˋhɑrə] ***n.*** **1.** 阿姆哈拉〔埃塞俄比亚一地区〕。**2.** 阿姆哈拉族;阿姆哈拉人。

Am·har·ic [æmˈhærik; æmˋhærɪk] **I** ***a.*** **1.** 阿姆哈拉的。**2.** 阿姆哈拉语的。**3.** 阿姆哈拉人的。**II** ***n.*** 阿姆哈拉语〔一种闪族语,旧时为埃塞俄比亚宫廷贵族语言〕。

Am·herst [ˈæməst, ˈæmhəːst; ˋæməst, ˋæmhɝst] ***n.*** 阿默斯特〔姓氏〕。

a·mi [ɑˈmiː; ɑˋmi] ***n.*** (*pl.* ~*s* [æˈmiː; æˋmi]) 〔F.〕 **1.** 男朋友 (*opp.* amie)。**2.** 〔欧洲人口语〕美国人。

a·mi·a·bil·i·ty [ˌeimjəˈbiliti; ͵emɪəˋbɪlətɪ] ***n.*** 亲切,和蔼;温和,和气;可爱。

a·mi·a·ble [ˈeimjəbl; ˋemɪəbl] ***a.*** 可爱的,和蔼可亲的,亲切的;温和的。**-ness** ***n.*** **-a·bly** ***ad.***

am·i·an·thus [ˌæmiˈænθəs; ͵æmɪˋænθəs], **-an·tus** [-ˈæntəs; -ˋæntəs] ***n.*** 【矿】(优质)细丝型石绵,石麻,石绒。

am·i·ca·bil·i·ty [ˌæmikəˈbiliti; ͵æmɪkəˋbɪlətɪ] ***n.*** 友好,和睦,亲善;温和。

am·i·ca·ble [ˈæmikəbl; ˋæmɪkəbl] ***a.*** 亲切的,和蔼的,友好的,和睦的。~ *relations* 友好关系。~ *settlement* 和解。~ **number** 【数】互满数。**-ness** ***n.*** **-bly** ***ad.***

am·ice[1] [ˈæmis; ˋæmɪs] ***n.*** 【天主】**1.** (僧侣做弥撒时围在颈后肩头上的)长方形白麻布。**2.** 僧侣带头巾的披肩。

am·ice[2] [ˈæmis; ˋæmɪs] ***n.*** 皮头巾;皮帽;(连在外套上的)兜帽。

ami·cron [eiˈmaiˌkrɔn; eˋmaɪ͵krɑn] ***n.*** 【化】次微(胶)粒,超微粒〔超倍显微镜不可见的,直径小于 10^{-7}厘米〕。

a·mi·cus cu·ri·ae [əˈmaikəsˈkjuəriiː; əˋmaɪkəsˋkjʊrɪ͵i] 【法】法庭之友〔审理某些案件时前往提供或被传去提供情况,或提醒法庭在审理时加以注意的人〕。

a·mid [əˈmid; əˋmɪd] ***prep.*** = amidst.

am·ide [ˈæmaid; ˋæmaɪd] ***n.*** 【化】**1.** 酰胺。**2.** 氨化物。

am·i·din [ˈæmidin; ˋæmɪdɪn] ***n.*** 【化】淀粉在水中的透明溶液。

am·i·dine [ˈæmiˌdiːn; ˋæmɪ͵din] ***n.*** 【化】脒。

a·mi·do·gen [əˈmiːdədʒən, əˈmidədʒən; əˋmidədʒən, əˋmɪdədʒən] ***n.*** 【化】(酰)胺基;氨基。

am·i·dol [ˈæmidɔl; ˋæmə͵dɑl] ***n.*** 【摄】二氨酚显影剂。

am·i·done [ˈæmidəun; ˋæmɪ͵don] ***n.*** 【化】阿米酮,美沙酮(= methadone)。

a·mid·ship(s) [əˈmidʃip(s); əˋmɪdʃɪp(s)] ***ad.*** 在船中部,在船腹。

a·midst [əˈmidst; əˋmɪdst] ***prep.*** 在…的当中,在…的包围中。~ *enemies* [*dangers*] 在敌人[危险]包围中。

a·mie [ɑˈmiː; ɑˋmi] ***n.*** (*pl.* ~*s* [ɑˈmiː; ͵ɑˋmi]) 〔F.〕 女朋友。

a·mi·go [əˈmiːgəu; əˋmigo] ***n.*** (*pl.* ~*s* [-gəuz; -goz]) 〔Sp.〕 **1.** 朋友。**2.** 对美国人友好的西班牙语系人。

amil [ˈɑːmil; ˋɑmɪl] ***n.*** 【史】(印度)收税员;税款包收员。**-ar** ***n.*** = amil.

am·i·nate [ˈæmineit; ˋæmənet] ***vt.*** 【化】使胺化。

am·i·na·tion [ˌæmiˈneiʃən; ͵æmɪˋneʃən] ***n.*** 【化】胺化作用。

a·mine [ˈæmiːn; əˋmin] ***n.*** 【化】胺。

a·mi·no [ˈæminəu, əˈmiːnəu; ˋæmɪno, əˋmino] ***a.*** 【化】氨基的。~ **acid** 氨基酸;氨酸。

A·mi·no·bu·tene [əˌmiːnəuˈbjuːtiːn; ə͵minoˋbjutin] ***n.*** 【化】氨基丁烯〔一种解痛剂〕。

a·mi·no·phe·nol [əˌmiːnəuˈfiːnəul; ə͵minoˋfinol] ***n.*** 【化】氨基(苯)酚〔用作染料、显影剂〕。

a·mi·no·plast [əˈmiːnəuplæst; əˋminəplæst] ***n.*** 氨基塑料。

a·mi·no·py·rine [əˌmiːnəuˈpairiːn, ˌæmənəu-; ə͵minoˋpaɪrin, ͵æməno-] ***n.*** 氨基比林;匹拉米董〔用做退烧剂、减痛剂〕。

a·mi·no·tri·a·zole [əˌmiːnəuˈtraiəˌzəul; ə͵minoˋtraɪə͵zol] ***n.*** 氨基三唑〔除草药〕。

a·mir [əˈmiə; əˋmɪr] ***n.*** = ameer. **-ate** ***n.*** 酋长国(= ameerate)。

A·mis [ˈeimis; ˋemɪs] ***n.*** 埃米斯〔姓氏〕。

Am·ish [ˈɑːmiʃ, ˈæmiʃ; ˋɑmɪʃ, ˋæmɪʃ] **I** ***n.*** 〔*pl.*〕【宗】阿门宗派〔十七世纪成立的一个教规严格的孟诺教派,因创此教派的雅可布·阿门而得名〕。**II** ***a.*** 阿门宗派的。

a·miss [əˈmis; əˋmɪs] **I** ***ad.*** **1.** 差错,错。**2.** 不顺当,不合,不适当。*Nothing happened* ~. 没有错,无不顺当。*speak* ~ 说错。**come** ~ 不称心,有妨碍(*Nothing comes* ~ *to him.* 他事事顺当。*Nothing comes* ~ *to a hungry man.* 饥不择食)。**do** ~ 做错,犯错误。**go** ~ 不顺当,别扭(*all went* ~ 事事别扭)。**take** (*sth.*) ~ 见怪,见责;生气;误会(*Don't take my words* ~. 请不要介意我的话)。**II** ***a.*** 不顺当,别扭,有毛病。*What's* ~ *with it?* 那怎么啦? *There is something* ~ *with him.* 他有点失常;他有点不对头。**not** ~ 不错,不坏(*It is not* ~ *to ask advice.* 求教总没错,不妨商量。*She is not* ~. 她(容貌)不坏)。

A·mi·ta·bha [ˌʌmiˈtɑːbə; ͵ʌmɪˋtɑbə] ***n.*** 〔Sans.〕 阿弥陀佛。

a·mi·to·sis [ˌæmiˈtəusis; ͵æməˋtosɪs] ***n.*** 【生】无丝分裂。

am·i·trol [ˈæmitrɔːl; ˋæmɪtrəl] ***n.*** 氨基三唑〔一种除草药〕(= aminotriazole)。

am·i·ty [ˈæmiti; ˋæmətɪ] ***n.*** 亲睦,友好,和好。*a treaty of* ~ *and peace* 友好和平条约。*live* [*be*] *in* ~ *with* 和…友好相处。

AMM = antimissile missile 反导弹导弹。

Am·man [əˈmɑːn; əˋmɑn] ***n.*** 安曼〔约旦首都〕。

am·me·ter [ˈæmitə; ˋæ͵mitɚ] ***n.*** 电流表,安培计。

am·mine [ˈæmiːn; ˋæmin] ***n.*** 【化】氨(络);氨络物。

am·mo [ˈæməu; ˋæmo] ***n.*** 〔军俚〕弹药〔由 ammunition 一词缩成〕。

Am·mon [ˈæmən; ˋæmən] *n*. (古埃及的)太阳神。

am·mo·nal [ˈæmənæl; ˋæməˏnæl] *n*. 阿芒拿〔硝铵、铝、炭炸药〕。

am·mo·nia [əˈməunjə; əˋmonjə] *n*. 【化】氨〔NH_3〕;氨水。

am·mo·ni·ac [əˈməuniæk; əˋmoniˏæk] **I** *a*. 氨(性)的,含氨的。**II** *n*. 氨草胶(= gum ～)。～ *nitrogen* 氨态氮。*sal* ～ 硇砂。

am·mo·ni·a·cal [ˌæməuˈnaiəkəl; ˏæmoˋnaɪəkl] *a*. = ammoniac.

am·mo·ni·at·ed [əˈməunieitid; əˋmoniˏetɪd] *a*. 充氨的,含氨的。

am·mo·nic [əˈməunik; əˋmonɪk] *a*. 氨的,铵的。

am·mo·ni·fi·ca·tion [əˌmɔnifiˈkeiʃən; əˏmɑnəfəˋkeʃən] *n*. **1.** 加氨(作用)。**2.** (分解)成氨(作用)。

am·mo·ni·fy [əˈməunifai; əˋmonɪfaɪ] *vt*. 使生氨;给…加氨。—*vi*. 进行氨处理,成氨。

am·mo·nite [ˈæmənait; ˋæməˏnaɪt] *n*. **1.** 【古生】菊石,鹦鹉螺化石。**2.** 硝石炸药。**3.** 干肉粉〔作肥料用〕。

am·mo·ni·um [əˈməunjəm; əˋmonɪəm] *n*. 【化】铵。～ **chloride** 氯化铵。～ **nitrate** 硝酸铵。～ **sulphate** 硫酸铵。

am·mo·no [ˈæmənəu; ˋæmәno] *a*. **1.** 氨的;含氨的。**2.** 氨衍生的。

am·mo·no·tel·ic [ˌæmənəuˈtelik; ˏæmənoˋtɛlɪk] *a*. 排氨代谢的。**-not·el·ism** [-ˈnɔtlizəm; -ˋnɑtlɪzəm] *n*.

am·mu·ni·tion [ˌæmjuˈniʃən; ˏæmjəˋnɪʃən] **I** *n*. **1.** 弹药。**2.** 〔废〕军需品。**3.** 〔喻〕战斗手段。～ **boots** 〔英〕军用鞋。～ **box** [**chest**] 弹药箱。～ **clip** 子弹夹。～ **depot**, ～ **dump** 军火库。～ **industry** 军需工业。～ **wagon** 弹药车。**II** *vt*. 供给…弹药,给…装弹药。

am·ne·sia [æmˈniːzjə; æmˋniʒɪə] *n*. 【医】健忘症。

am·nes·tic [æmˈnestik; æmˋnɛstɪk] *a*. 引起遗忘(症)的。

am·nes·ty [ˈæmnesti; ˋæmˏnɛstɪ] **I** *n*. **1.** 大赦,特赦。**2.** 〔古〕故意忽视(某人的过失)。**II** *vt*. 大赦,赦免。

am·ni·o·cen·te·sis [ˌæmniəusenˈtisis; ˏæmnɪosɛnˋtɪsɪs] *n*. 羊膜穿刺术。

am·ni·on [ˈæmniən; ˋæmnɪən] *n*. (*pl*. *-nia* [-niə; -nɪə]) 【解】羊膜。

am·ni·o·tin [æmˈniːətin; æmˋnɪətɪn] *n*. 【药】安尼奥廷〔含雌性激素物质的油剂,用如雌酮〕。

am·o·bar·bi·tal [ˌæməuˈbɑːbitɔːl; ˏæmoˋbɑrbɪtɔl] *n*. 【药】异戊巴比妥〔一种镇静剂和安眠药〕。

am·o·di·a·quin [ˌæməuˈdaiəkwin; ˏæmoˋdaɪəkwɪn] *n*. 【药】安双喹〔疟疾药〕。

a·moe·ba [əˈmiːbə; əˋmibə] *n*. (*pl*. *-bae* [-biː; -bi], ～*s*) 阿米巴,变形虫。

am·oe·b(a)e·an [ˌæmiˈbiːən; ˏæmɪˋbiən] *a*. (诗歌等)对话体的,应答的。～ **strains** 对话体的诗歌。

am·oe·bi·a·sis [ˌæmiˈbaiəsis; ˏæmɪˋbaɪəsɪs] *n*. 变形虫病,内变形虫病(= amebiasis)。

a·moe·bic [əˈmiːbik; əˋmibɪk] *a*. 变形虫的,变形虫性的。

a·moe·bo·cyte [əˈmiːbəsait; əˋmibəˏsaɪt] *n*. 变形细胞。

a·moe·boid [əˈmiːbɔid; əˋmiˏbɔɪd] *n*. 【医】变形虫状的,变形虫似的。

a·mok [əˈmɔk; əˋmʌk] *a*., *ad*. = amuck.

a·mo·le [əˈməulei; əˋmole] *n*. **1.** (产生美国西南部和墨西哥的)代皂植物的根。**2.** 代皂植物。

A·mon [ˈɑːmən; ˋɑmən] *n*. 亚蒙神〔原义司生殖力的神〕;埃及主神(= Ammon)。

a·mong [əˈmʌŋ; əˋmʌŋ] *prep*. 在(多数)之中,在…中间。★between 一般指"在两者之间", among 一般指"在三者或三者以上之中"。～ *us Chinese* 在我们中国人中间。～ *the Greeks* 在希腊时代。*life* ～ *the Arabs* (别国人的)阿拉伯生活。*a house* ～ *the trees* 树木环绕着的屋子。*fall* ～ *thieves* 沦落到与盗贼为伍。*quarrel* ～ *themselves* 内部相互争吵。*be* ～ *the best books* 是最优秀的作品之一。～ ***others*** [***other things***] 其中,就中,尤其,格外,加上[以及]其他种种事实[问题]。～ ***the missing*** 〔美〕失踪中,下落不明。～ ***themselves*** [***ourselves***, ***yourselves***] 在自己人中间。～ ***the rest*** 其中之一,也在其中(*myself* ～ *the rest* 我也是其中的一个)。***from*** ～ 从…中。***one*** ～ ***a thousand*** 千中挑一的人;奇人。

a·mongst [əˈmʌŋst; əˋmʌŋst] *prep*. 〔书〕 = among.

A·mon-Re [ˈɑːmənˈrei; ˋɑmənˋre], **Amon-Ra** [-ˈrɑː; -ˋrɑ] *n*. 古埃及太阳神。

a·mon·til·la·do [əˌmɔntiˈlɑːdəu; əˏmɑntəˋlɑdo] *n*. (*pl*. ～*s*) (西班牙产的)白葡萄酒;〔喻〕平淡无味,态度冷淡。

a·mor·al [eiˈmɔrəl; eˋmɔrəl] *a*. 非道德的,超道德的,与道德无关的,没有道德意识的。*Infants are* ～. 婴儿没有道德意识。

a·morce [əˈmɔːs; əˋmɔrs] *n*. 起爆剂。

am·o·ret·to [ˈɑːməˈretəu; ˏæməˋrɛto] *n*. (*pl*. *-ret·ti* [-reti; -rɛtɪ]) (意大利十六世纪艺术作品中的)小爱神。

am·o·rist [ˈæmərist; ˋæmərɪst] *n*. **1.** 情人;好色之徒。**2.** 恋爱文学作家。

am·o·rous [ˈæmərəs; ˋæmərəs] *a*. **1.** 好色的;色情的。**2.** 多情的,脉脉含情的。**2.** 恋爱的;有关爱情的。～ *songs* 恋歌,情歌。～ *glances* (女人传情的)眼神,秋波。*be* ～ *of* 爱慕。**-ly** *ad*. 好色地,情意脉脉地。**-ness** *n*. 好色。

a·mor pa·tri·ae [ˈeimɔː ˈpeitriiː; ˋemɔr ˋpetrɪi] 〔L.〕爱国心。

a·mor·phism [əˈmɔːfizəm; əˋmɔrfɪzəm] *n*. **1.** 无定形(现象)。**2.** 【化】无晶形,非晶性。**3.** 无组织;无定向;虚无主义。**4.** 乱七八糟,杂乱无章。**-phous** [əˈmɔːfəs; əˋmɔrfəs] *a*. **-phous·ly** *ad*.

a·mort [əˈmɔːt; əˋmɔrt] *a*. 死了似的,死气沉沉的,意气消沉的。

am·or·tise, -tize [əˈmɔːtaiz; əˋmɔrtaɪz] *vt*. **1.** 【法】把(不动产)转让(尤指让与教会永久管理);把(不动产)让与法人。**2.** 分期偿还(债务等);分期注销(费用等),摊提(资产)。

am·or·ti·za·tion [əˌmɔːtiˈzeiʃən; əˏmɔrtəˋzeʃən] *n*. **1.** 【法】不动产的让渡[捐赠]。**2.** 分期偿还,摊提(资产等)。

A·mos [ˈeimɔs; ˋeməs] *n*. **1.** 【圣】阿摩司〔公元前八世纪的希伯来先知〕。**2.** 【圣】(旧约中的)《阿摩司书》。**3.** 埃莫斯〔男子名〕。

am·o·site [ˈæməsait; ˋæməsaɪt] *n*. 铁石棉。

a·mount [əˈmaunt; əˋmaunt] **I** *vi*. **1.** 总计,共计,合计(*to*)。**2.** 相当于,等于。**3.** 成为(*to*)。*Their expenses* ～ *to fifty dollars*. 他们的消费共计五十元。*His answer* ～*s to a threat*. 他的回答等于恐吓。*What, after all, does it* ～ *to*? 结果怎么样? ～ ***to little*** = ***not*** ～ ***to much*** 没有什么了不起,有限得很,无多大道理。～ ***to much*** 大起来,变伟大。～ ***to something*** (人)成器,成才。**II** *n*. **1.** 总和,总额。**2.** 数值,量,金额。**3.** 结果,效果;要旨。*a lethal* ～ 致死剂量。*a trace* ～ 微量。*the gross* ～ 约计,概数。*the net* ～ 细数。*the* ～ 总数。*What is the* ～? 一共多少? *a large* ～ *of money* 巨额的钱。*This is the* ～ *of what he said*. 这是他所说的要点。***an*** ～ ***of*** (*work*) 相当数量的(工作),适量[度]的。***any*** ～ (***of***) 任何数量(的);大量(的)。***in*** ～ 总之,结局;总计。

a·mour [əˈmuə; əˋmur] *n*. 〔F.〕私通;不正当的恋爱事件。*have an* ～ *with* ... 同…有不正当的男女关系。

a·mour-pro·pre [ˈæmuəˈprɔpr; ˋɑmurˋprɔpr] *n*. 〔F.〕自尊,自负。

A·moy [əˈmɔi; əˋmɔɪ] *n*. (旧时欧美人所习称的)厦门〔中国〕。

amp. = ampere; amperage.

AMP = **1.** adenosine monophosphate 腺苷酸。**2.** amplification 放大。**3.** amplifier 放大器。

AMPAS = Academy of Motion Picture Arts and Sciences〔美〕电影艺术和科学研究院。

am·pe·lop·sis [ˌæmpəˈlɔpsis; ˏæmpəˋlɑpsɪs] *n*.【植】**1.**〔A-〕白蔹属。**2.** 蛇葡萄科植物。

am·per·age [ˈæmpεəridʒ; æmˋpɪrɪdʒ] *n*. 安培数，电流量。

Am·père [ˈæmpεə; ˋæmˋpεr] **A. M.** 安培〔1775—1836，法国物理学家〕。

am·pere, am·père [ˈæmpεə; ˋæmpɪr] *n*.【电】安培。～**-hour** 安培时。～**meter** [-miːtə; -mitɚ] 电流表，安培表。～**'s law**【物】安培定律。～ **turn** 安匝(数)。

am·per·sand [ˈæmpəsænd; ˋæmpɚsˏænd] *n*. '&'(= and) 的名称〔原为 *and per se and*〕。

am·phet·a·mine [æmˈfetəmiːn; æmˋfεtəˏmin] *n*.【药】氨基丙苯，苯基丙胺，安非他命〔解除忧郁、疲劳的药〕。

am·phi- *comb. f.*〔*Gr.*〕**1.** 两侧，两端：*amphi*stylar. **2.** 周围。**3.** 两类：*amphi*biotic.

am·phi·ar·thro·sis [ˌæmfiɑːˈθrəusis; ˏæmfɪɑrˋθrosɪs] *n*.【解】微动关节。

am·phi·as·ter [ˈæmfiˌæstə; ˋæmfɪˏæstɚ] *n*.【医】双星体。

Am·phib·i·a [æmˈfibiə; æmˋfɪbɪə] *n*.〔*pl*.〕【动】两栖纲。

am·phib·i·an [æmˈfibiən; æmˋfɪbɪən] **I** *a*. 两栖类的。**II** *n*. **1.** 两栖动物[植物]。**2.** 水陆两用飞机[战车]。**3.** 双重性格的人。

am·phi·bi·ot·ic [ˌæmfibaiˈɔtik; ˏæmfɪbaɪˋɑtɪk] *a*.【动】(一成长阶段在水，一成长阶段在陆的)水陆先后两栖的；水生陆栖的；水陆两生的。

am·phib·i·ous [æmˈfibiəs; æmˋfɪbɪəs] *a*. **1.** 两栖的。**2.** 水陆两用的。**3.** 有双重性格的。～ *forces* 海陆空军。～ *operations* 海陆空军协同作战。**-ly** *ad*.

am·phi·bole [ˈæmfibəul; ˋæmfɪˏbol] *n*.【矿】闪石。

am·phib·o·lite [æmˈfibəlait; æmˋfɪbəlaɪt] *n*.【矿】闪岩。

am·phi·bol·o·gy [ˌæmfiˈbɔlədʒi; ˏæmfɪˋbɑlədʒɪ] *n*. 含糊语句；意义含糊，文意不明。

am·phib·o·lous [æmˈfibələs; æmˋfɪbələs] *a*. 含糊的，模棱两可的。

am·phi·brach [ˈæmfibræk; ˋæmfɪˏbræk] *n*.〔古诗〕抑扬抑格〔弱强弱的三音节诗格〕。

am·phi·chro·ic [ˌæmfiˈkrəuik; ˏæmfɪˋkroɪk] *a*.【化】两变色的。

am·phi·coe·lous [ˌæmfiˈsiːləs; ˏæmfɪˋsiləs] *a*.【解】两凹形的；两边内陷的。

am·phic·tyon [æmˈfiktiən; æmˋfɪktɪən] *n*. **1.** (古希腊的近邻同盟会议)代表。**2.**〔*pl*.〕(古希腊)近邻同盟会议。

am·phic·ty·o·ny [æmˈfiktiəni; æmˋfɪktɪənɪ] *n*. (*pl*. *-nies*) 邻邦同盟〔古希腊近邻诸邦以保护神庙为名而结成的联盟〕。**-o·nic** [-ˈɔnik; -ˋɑnɪk] *a*.

am·phi·go·ry, am·phi·gou·ri [ˈæmfigəri; ˋæmfɪgorɪ] *n*. 打油诗；胡乱诌成的诗文。

am·phim·a·cer [æmˈfiməsə; æmˋfɪməsɚ] *n*.〔古诗〕扬抑扬格〔强弱强的三音节诗格〕。

am·phi·mix·is [ˌæmfiˈmiksis; ˏæmfɪˋmɪksɪs] *n*.【生】两性融合；杂交繁育。

am·phi·ox·us [ˌæmfiˈɔksəs; ˏæmfɪˋɑksəs] *n*.【动】蛞蝓鱼，文昌鱼。

am·phi·pod [ˈæmfipɔd; ˋæmfɪpɑd] **I** *n*.【动】片脚动物。**II** *a*.【动】片脚类的。

am·phi·pro·style [æmˈfiprəustail; æmˋfɪprostaɪl] *n*.【建】两向拜式〔前后有排柱而两侧无柱的建筑〕。

am·phis·bae·na [ˌæmfisˈbiːnə; ˏæmfɪsˋbinə] *n*. **1.**【希，罗神】两头蛇。**2.**【动】无足蜥蜴。**3.**〔A-〕蜥蜴属。

am·phis·bae·ni·an [ˌæmfisˈbiːniən; ˏæmfɪsˋbinɪən] *n*. 蚓蜥属动物。

am·phi·sty·lar [ˌæmfiˈstailə; ˏæmfɪˋstaɪlɚ] *a*.【建】两侧或前后有圆柱的。

am·phi·the·a·tral [ˌæmfiˈθiətrəl; ˏæmfɪˋθɪətrəl] *a*. = amphitheatrical.

am·phi·the·a·tre, am·phi·the·a·ter [ˈæmfiˌθiətə; ˋæmfəˏθɪətɚ] *n*. **1.** (古罗马时代的)圆形剧场，竞技场。**2.** 阶式剧场[教室]。**3.** 盆状地形。**-the·at·ric** [ˌæmfiθiˈætrik; ˏæmfɪθɪˋætrɪk] *a*.

am·pho·ra [ˈæmfərə; ˋæmfərə] *n*. (*pl*. *-rae* [-riː; -ri], ～*s*) (古希腊的)双耳酒罐[油罐]。

am·phor·ic [æmˈfɔrik; æmˋfɑrɪk] *a*.【医】瓮音的，空瓮性的。

am·pho·ter·ic [ˌæmfəˈterik; ˏæmfəˋtεrɪk] *a*. 有酸碱两性的。

am·pho·ter·i·cin B [ˌæmfəˈterəsin ˈbiː; ˏæmfəˋtεrəsɪn ˋbi] 两性霉素乙。

am·ple [ˈæmpl; ˋæmpl] *a*. (*-pler*; *-plest*) **1.** (房屋)广大的，宽敞的。**2.** 丰富的，充足的，富裕的。(*opp*. *scanty*, *meager*)。～ *evidences* 充足的证据。*of* ～ *means* 富有的。*do* ～ *justice to a meal* 大吃，饱餐。**-ness** *n*. 广大；丰富，充足。

am·plex·i·caul [æmˈpleksikɔːl; æmˋplεksɪkɔl] *a*.【植】抱茎的。

am·pli·a·tion [ˌæmpliˈeiʃən; ˏæmplɪˋeʃən] *n*.〔古〕扩大，扩张；(加某物以)增大。

am·pli·a·tive [ˈæmplieitiv; ˋæmplɪˏetɪv] *a*.【逻】扩充的，扩张(性)的。

am·pli·dyne [ˈæmplidain; ˋæmpləˏdaɪn] *n*. (微场)电机放大器，交磁放大机。

am·pli·fi·ca·tion [ˌæmplifiˈkeiʃən; ˏæmpləfəˋkeʃən] *n*. **1.** 扩大；扩充。**2.**【电】增幅，放大(率)。**3.** (声明等的)补充材料。

am·pli·fi·er [ˈæmplifaiə; ˋæmpləˏfaɪɚ] *n*. **1.**【电】扩大器；扩音器。**2.** 放大镜；放大器。*a sight* ～ 雷达瞄准放大器。*speech* ～ 音频放大器。

am·pli·fy [ˈæmplifai; ˋæmpləˏfaɪ] *vt*. **1.** 扩大，放大。**2.** 引申，详述。**3.**【电】增强(电流等)。**4.** 夸大。—*vi*. 引申，详说，作进一步阐述 (*on*)。*There is no need to* ～. 无详述之必要。～ *on a certain subject* 详细阐述某一问题。

am·pli·tude [ˈæmplitjuːd; ˋæmpləˏtjud] *n*. **1.** 广阔，广大。**2.** 丰富，充足。**3.** (思想的)广度。**4.** (天体出没时偏离正东或正西的)角度距离。**5.**【物，电】振幅。～ **modulation**【无】振幅调制。

am·ply [ˈæmpli; ˋæmplɪ] *ad*. 广大地，广泛地；充足地；详细地。*He apologized* ～ *for his error*. 他因自己的过失而大为抱歉。*They were* ～ *supplied with food*. 他们有充足的食物供应。

am·poule, am·pul(e) [ˈæmpuːl; ˋæmpul] *n*. **1.** (装针药水的)小玻璃管，安瓿。**2.** = ampulla.

AMPS = advanced mobile phone service 高级移动电话服务系统。

am·pul·la [æmˈpulə; æmˋpulə] *n*. (*pl*. *-lae* [-liː; -li]) **1.** (古罗马的)细劲坛。**2.** 神酒瓶；圣油瓶。**3.**【解】壶腹。**4.**【生】坛状体。

am·pul·la·ceous [ˌæmpəˈleiʃəs; ˏæmpəˋleʃəs] *a*. 细颈坛状的，坛形的。

am·pu·tate [ˈæmpjuteit; ˋæmpjəˏtet] *vt*. 切断，截除，截(肢)。

am·pu·ta·tion [æmpjuˈteiʃən; ˏæmpjəˋteʃən] *n*.【医】截肢(术)。

am·pu·ta·tor [ˈæmpjuteitə; ˋæmpjuˏtetɚ] *n*. 施行截肢手术者。

am·pu·tee [ˌæmpjuˈtiː; ˏæmpjuˋti] *n*. 被截肢者。

am·ri·ta [əmˈriːtə; ʌmˋritə] *n*.【印度神】**1.** 长生不老

酒。2. 长生不老。

Am·ster·dam [ˈæmstəˈdæm; ˋæmstə ˏdæm] *n*. 阿姆斯特丹〔荷兰首都,海牙为政府所在地〕。

amt. = amount.

am·trac [æmˈtræk; æmˋtræk], **am·track** [ˈæmtræk; ˋæmtræk] *n*. (第二次世界大战中使用的)小型水陆两用登陆车。

amu, AMU = atomic mass unit 原子质量单位。

a·muck [əˈmʌk; əˋmʌk] **I** *ad*., *a*. 狂暴;狂怒;杀气腾腾。***run*** ~ 乱斩乱杀,横行霸道;乱窜。***run*** ~ ***at society*** 胡作非为。**II** *n*. (马来人常患的)神经错乱。

am·u·let [ˈæmjulit; ˋæmjəlɪt] *n*. 护身符,驱邪符。

A·mur [ɑːˈmuə; ɑˋmʊr] *n*. (旧时欧美人所习称的)阿穆尔河〔中国黑龙江〕。

a·muse [əˈmjuːz; əˋmjuz] *vt*. 娱乐,使…喜欢[高兴],逗…笑。*You* ~ *me!* 傻气! 多好笑! ~ ***oneself by*** [***with***] 以…自娱[消遣]。***be*** ~***d at*** [***by, with***] 觉得;有趣[好笑]! 以…为乐。**a·mus·a·ble** *a*. **-r** *n*.

a·muse·ment [əˈmjuːzmənt; əˋmjuzmənt] *n*. **1.** 娱乐,消遣;乐趣。**2.** 娱乐品;娱乐活动。*an* ~ *park* 露天游艺场。*find much* ~ *in* 最爱…,对…最有兴趣。~ **tax** 娱乐捐。

a·mu·si·a [ˌeiˈmjuːziə; ˏeˋmjuzɪə] *n*.【医】(失去唱歌能力的)失歌症。

a·mus·ing [əˈmjuːziŋ; əˋmjuzɪŋ] *a*. 有趣的! 好笑的。*How* ~ *!* 多有趣! 多好笑! **-ly** *ad*.

a·mu·sive [əˈmjuːziv, əˈmjuːsiv; əˋmjuzɪv, əˋmjusɪv] *a*. 有趣的;引人发笑的。

AMVETS = American Veterans of World War II 美国第二次世界大战退伍军人协会。

Am·vets [ˈæmvets; ˋæmˏvets] *n*. *pl*. = AMVETS.

A·my [ˈeimi; ˋemɪ] *n*. 埃米〔女子名〕。

a·myg·da·la [əˈmigdələ; əˋmɪgdələ] *n*. (*pl*. ***-lae*** [-liː; -li]) **1.** 杏仁。**2.**【解】扁桃(腺)。

a·myg·da·la·ceous [əˌmigdəˈleiʃəs; əˏmɪgdəˋleʃəs] *a*. 樱属植物的〔如桃、杏、樱桃等多肉的坚果植物〕。

a·myg·da·late [əˈmigdəlit; əˋmɪgdəlɪt] *a*. **1.** 杏仁(似)的。**2.** 扁桃(腺)的。

a·myg·dale [əˈmigdeil; əˋmɪgdel], **a·myg·dule** [-duːl, -djuːl; -dul, -djul] *n*.【矿】杏仁石;杏仁孔。

a·myg·da·lin [əˈmigdəlin; əˋmɪgdəlɪn] *n*.【化、药】苦杏仁苷,苦扁桃仁苷〔用作去痰药或调味剂〕。

a·myg·da·loid [əˈmigdəˌlɔid; əˋmɪgdəˏlɔɪd] **I** *n*.【矿】杏仁岩。**II** *a*. **1.** 杏仁状的。**2.** 杏仁岩的。**3.** 扁桃状的。

a·myg·da·loid·al [əˌmigdəˈlɔidl; əˏmɪgdəˋlɔɪdl̩] *a*. 杏仁状的(= amygdaloid)。

am·yl [ˈæmil; ˋæmɪl] *n*.【化】戊基,戊烷基。

am·y·la·ceous [ˈæmiˈleiʃəs; ˏæmɪˋleʃəs] *a*. 淀粉(状)的,淀粉质的。

am·yl·ase [ˈæmileis; ˋæmɪˏles] *n*.【生化】淀粉(糖化)酶。

am·yl·ene [ˈæmiˌliːn; ˋæmɪˏlin] *n*.【化】戊烯。

a·myl·ic [əˈmilik; əˋmɪlɪk] *a*. 淀粉的。

amyl(o)- *comb.f*. = amyl, amylum.

a·myl·o·gen [əˈmilədʒən; əˋmɪlədʒən] *n*. 可溶性淀粉。

am·y·loid [ˈæmilɔid; ˋæmɪˏlɔɪd] **I** *a*. 淀粉状的,淀粉质的。**II** *n*. **1.**【生化】淀粉状蛋白。**2.**【造纸】(硫酸)胶化纤维素。

am·y·lol·y·sis [ˌæmiˈlɔlisis; ˏæmɪˋlɑləsɪs] *n*.【生化】淀粉分解。**am·y·lo·ly·tic** [ˌæmiləuˈlitik; ˏæmɪloˋlɪtɪk] *a*.

am·y·lo·pec·tin [ˌæmiləuˈpektin; ˏæmɪloˋpɛktɪn] *n*.【生化】支链淀粉;胶淀粉。

am·y·lop·sin [ˌæmiˈlɔpsin; ˏæmɪˋlɑpsɪn] *n*.【生化】胰淀粉酶。

am·y·lose [ˈæmiləus; ˋæmɪˏlos] *n*.【生化】直链淀粉;糖淀粉。

am·y·lum [ˈæmiləm; ˋæmɪləm] *n*.【化】淀粉 (starch) 的拉丁名称。

a·my·o·to·ni·a [eiˌmaiəˈtəuniə; ˏemaɪəˋtonɪə] *n*.【医】肌弛缓。

Am·y·tal [ˈæmitəl, -tæl; ˋæmɪtɑl, -tæl] *n*.【药】阿米他,异戊巴比妥〔用作镇静剂,安眠药〕(= amobarbital)。

an[1] [强 æn, 弱 ən, n; æn, ən, n] indef. art. 见 **a** 条。

an[2], **an'** [强 æn, 弱 ən; æn, ən] *conj*. **1.** 〔方、口〕= and. **2.** 〔古、方〕= (and) if.

an. = **1.** *anno*. **2.** anonymous. **3.** answer. **4.** *ante*.

an- *pref*. **1.** = 〔L.〕 *ad-*: *an*nex. **2.** = 〔Gr.〕 *a-*: *an*archy (*cf*. a-[3]). **3.** = 〔Gr.〕 *ana-*: *an*ode.

-an *suf*. **1.** 〔构成形容词〕表示"…的,有…性质;属于…的;【动】…纲[类]的": Mahomet*an*, Elizabeth*an*, Mammali*an*. **2.** 〔常构成与形容词同形的名词〕表示"…地方的人;精通…的人,信奉…的人": histori*an*, Americ*an*.

A.N., **A-N** = Anglo-Norman 英格兰和诺曼底的;英格兰诺曼底人(的);英格兰诺曼底语(的)。

ANA = **1.** All Nippon Airways 全日本航空公司。**2.** American Nurse Association 全美护士协会。

a·na[1] [ˈɑːnə; ˋɑnə] *n*. (*pl*. ~ (***s***)) 丛谈,语录;轶事谈;回忆录。

an·a[2] [ˈænə; ˋænə] *ad*.【处方】= āā 等量;各。*wine and honey* ~ *two ounces* 酒和蜂蜜各二英两。

ana- *pref*. **1.** 表示"向上": *ana*dromous. **2.** 表示"向后": *ana*gram. **3.** 表示"再一次": *ana*baptist. **4.** 表示"贯穿": *ana*lysis. **5.** 表示"类似": *ana*logy.

-ana *suf*. 〔附在人名地名后〕表示"语录,逸话,杂记,集": Shakespeari*ana* 莎士比亚轶事集。

an·a·bae·na [ˌænəˈbiːnə; ˏænəˋbinə] *n*.【植】**1.** 念珠藻科的水藻〔常生于蓄水池,可使水发腥味〕。**2.** 念珠藻团。

an·a·bap·tism [ˌænəˈbæptizəm; ˏænəˋbæptɪzəm] *n*. **1.**【宗】再洗礼;再浸礼论。**2.** 〔A-〕再浸礼教。**-tist** *n*. 再浸礼教徒。

an·a·bas [ˈænəbæs; ˋænəˏbæs] *n*.【动】攀鲈亚目鱼;攀鲈属鱼〔因此种鱼有攀登习性,故名〕。

a·nab·a·sis [əˈnæbəsis; əˋnæbəsɪs] *n*. (*pl*. ***-ses*** [-siːz; -siz]) **1.** 进军,远征。**2.** 〔A-〕(色诺芬 (Xenophon) 所写的)《希腊远征波斯记》。**3.**【医】病加重(期)。**4.** 艰险撤军。

an·a·bat·ic [ˌænəˈbætik; ˏænəˋbætɪk] *a*.【气】(风、气流等)上升的。

an·a·bi·o·sis [ˌænəbaiˈəusis; ˏænəbaɪˋosɪs] *n*.【医】复苏,回生。

a·nab·o·lism [əˈnæbəlizəm; əˋnæblˏɪzəm] *n*. **1.** (食物的)吸收和同化。**2.**【生】组成[合成]代谢。

an·a·branch [ˈænəbrɑːntʃ; ˋænəˏbræntʃ] *n*.【地】再会流侧流;再流入主流的支流。

a·nach·ro·nism [əˈnækrənizəm; əˋnækrəˏnɪzəm] *n*. **1.** 时代错误,弄错年代。**2.** 与时代不合的事物。*Contemporary monarchy is an* ~. 现代的君主政体是不合时宜的事物。**-nis·tic**, **-nis·ti·cal** [əˌnækrəˈnistik(əl); əˏnækrəˋnɪstɪk(əl)], **-nous** [əˈnækrənəs; əˋnækrənəs] *a*.

an·a·clas·tic [ˌænəˈklæstik; ænəˋklæstɪk] *a*.【光】屈折的,由折射引起的。

an·a·cli·nal [ˌænəˈklainl; ˏænəˋklaɪnl̩] *a*.【地】正倾型的,逆地层下倾的方向而活动的。

an·a·clit·ic [ˌænəˈklitik; ˏænəˋklɪtɪk] *a*. **1.** 依靠的,依赖的。**2.**【心】情感依附的。

an·a·co·lu·thon [ˌænəkəuˈluːθɔn; ˏænəkəˋluθɑn] *n*. (*pl*. ***-tha*** [-θə; -θə]) **1.** 错格(指同一句子中结构的前后不一致或不连贯)。**2.** 错格句〔如: As a regular reader of your papers—Why does it give so little space to science? 作为贵报的一名忠实读者——(我想提的意见是)

贵报给予科学问题的版面为什么这样少?〕

an·a·con·da [ˌænəˈkɔndə; ˏænəˋkɑndə] *n*.【动】(南美产的)蟒蛇。

A·nac·re·on [əˈnækriən; əˋnækrɪən] *n*. 安纳克里昂〔纪元前约 570—480 年间希腊抒情诗人,特嗜歌颂爱情和欢宴〕。

a·nac·re·on·tic [əˌnækriˈɔntik; əˏnækrɪˋɑntɪk] **I** *a*. (古希腊抒情诗人)安纳克里昂(Anacreon)派的;歌颂爱情和欢宴的;酒色的。**II** *n*. 〔*pl*.〕安纳克里昂风格的诗,专写醇酒妇人的诗。

an·a·cru·sis [ˌænəˈkruːsis; ˏænəˋkrusɪs] *n*. 行首额外音节〔以重音开始的诗句前额外加上的轻音节,但不作为该诗句的第一音步〕。

an·a·cul·ture [ˈænəkʌltʃə; ˋænəkʌltʃɚ] *n*.【微】细菌的混合培养(尤指为生产自体疫苗用的)。

an·a·dem [ˈænədem; ˋænəˏdɛm] *n*. 〔诗〕花冠,花环。

an·a·di·plo·sis [ˌænədiˈpləusis; ˏænədɪˋplosɪs] *n*.【修】反覆法,蝉联法〔为了强调反覆使用句中关键性字眼,特别是把末一词用于下句之首: *He gave his life; life was all he could give*〕。

a·nad·ro·mous [əˈnædrəməs; əˋnædrəməs] *a*. (海鱼)溯河产卵的,溯河(性)的。~ **fish** 溯河性海鱼。~ **migration** 溯河回游。

a·nae·mi·a [əˈniːmjə; əˋnimɪə] *n*.【医】贫血症(= anemia)。

a·nae·mic [əˈniːmik; əˋnimɪk] *a*. 贫血(症)的(= anemic)。

an·aer·obe [əˈneiərəub; æˋneəˏrob] *n*.【微】厌氧微生物,厌气微生物(*opp*. *aerobe*)。**-bic** [əˌneiəˈrəbik; ænˏeəˋrobɪk] *a*.【微】厌气性的。

an·aer·o·bi·um [ˌænəˈrəubiəm; ˏænəˋrobɪəm] *n*. (*pl*. **-bia** [-biə; -bɪə]) 厌氧菌。

an·aes·the·si·a [ˌænisˈθiːzjə; ˏænəsˋθiʒə] *n*.【医】**1**. 感觉缺失,麻木。**2**. 麻醉。*local* ~ 局部麻醉。*general* ~ 全身麻醉。

an·aes·thet·ic [ˌænisˈθetik; ˏænəsˋθɛtɪk] **I** *a*. 麻醉的。**II** *n*. 麻醉药[剂]。

an·aes·the·tist [æˈniːsθitist; əˋnɛsθətɪst] *n*. 麻醉医师。

an·aes·the·ti·za·tion [æˌniːsθitaiˈzeiʃən; æˏnisθɪtaɪˋzeʃən] *n*. 麻醉;麻木。

an·aes·the·tize [æˈniːsθitaiz; əˋnɛsθəˏtaɪz] *vt*. 使麻醉;使麻木。

an·a·glyph [ˈænəglif; ˋænəˏglɪf] *n*. **1**. 浅浮雕。**2**. 立体照片[影片]。

an·a·glyph·ic [ˌænəˈglifik; ˏænəˋglɪfɪk] *a*. **1**. 浮雕(装饰)的。**2**. 立体照片的。

an·ag·no·ri·sis [ˌænægˈnɔːrisis; ˏænægˋnɔrɪsɪs] *n*. (戏剧的)大团圆〔如:剧中人终于认出自己的亲人或自己的真实处境〕。

an·a·go·ge [ˌænəˈgəudʒi; ˏænəˋgodʒɪ] *n*. (对《圣经》的)神秘解释〔旨在揭示隐晦的含义〕。

an·a·gog·ic, an·a·gog·i·cal [ˌænəˈgɔdʒik(əl); ˏænəˋgɑdʒɪk(əl)] *a*. (对《圣经》的解释)神秘的。*an* ~ *interpretation* 神秘的解释。

an·a·gram [ˈænəgræm; ˋænəgræm] *n*. **1**. 颠倒字母而成的词句〔如 *emit* 作 *mite*, lived 作 devil 等〕。**2**. 〔*pl*. 作单数用〕字谜游戏。**-mat·ic, -mat·i·cal** *a*. **-ma·tism** *n*. 字谜作法。**-mat·ize** *vt*. 把…作字谜。

a·nal [ˈeinəl; ˋenəl] *a*. 肛门的,直肠的;【昆】臀的,尾端的。~ **fistula** 痔瘘。~ **length** (鱼的)吻至肛门长度。

anal. = **1**. analogy. **2**. analysis. **3**. analytic.

an·al·cite [əˈnælsait; æˋnælsaɪt], **an·al·cime** [-saim, -siːm; -saɪm, -sim] *n*.【矿】方沸石。

an·a·lec·ta [ˌænəˈlektə; ˏænəˋlɛktə] *n*. *pl*. = *analects*.

an·a·lec·tic [ˌænəˈlektik; ˏænəˋlɛktɪk] *a*. 选集的,拔萃的。

an·a·lects [ˈænəlekts; ˋænəˏlɛkts] *n*. *pl*. 文选,选集,言论集。*the A- of Confucius*《论语》。

an·a·lem·ma [ˌænəˈlemə; ˏænəˋlɛmə] *n*. (地球仪上表示)太阳的日倾斜度的刻度〔通常穿过赤道,呈延长了的 8 字形〕。

an·a·lep·tic [ˌænəˈleptik; ˏænəˋlɛptɪk] **I** *a*. 提神的;强身的。**II** *n*. **1**. 回苏剂,兴奋剂。**2**. 强壮剂,复原剂。

an·al·ge·si·a [ˌænælˈdʒiːzjə; ˏænælˋdʒizɪə] *n*.【医】**1**. 痛觉缺失。**2**. 无痛法,止痛法。

an·al·ge·sic [ˌænælˈdʒesik; ˏænælˋdʒɛsɪk], **an·al·get·ic** [-ˈdʒetik; -ˋdʒɛtɪk] **I** *a*. 止痛的。**II** *n*. 止痛药。

an·a·log [ˈænəlɔg; ˋænlˏɑg] *n*. = analogue.

an·a·log·ic, -i·cal [ˌænəˈlɔdʒik(əl); ˏænlˋɑdʒɪk(əl)] *a*. **1**. 类似的,相似的。**2**. 类推的,对比的。**-i·cal·ly** *ad*.

a·nal·o·gism [əˈnælədʒizəm; əˋnælədʒɪzəm] *n*.【逻】推论,类推。

a·nal·o·gist [əˈnælədʒist; əˋnælədʒɪst] *n*. 进行类推的人;类比推理者。

a·nal·o·gize [əˈnælədʒaiz; əˋnæləˏdʒaɪz] *vt*. 用类推法说明,类推,推论。— *vi*. 使用类推法作推理。

a·nal·o·gous [əˈnæləgəs; əˋnæləgəs] *a*. **1**. 类似的,相似的。**2**.【生】同功的,功能相同的。**be ~ to** 类似。~ **organ** 同功器官。~ **pole** 热正极。**-ly** *ad*. **-ness** *n*.

an·a·logue [ˈænəlɔg; ˋænlˏɑg] *n*. **1**. 类似物。**2**. 同源语。**3**.【生】相似体。**4**. 相对应的人;对手方。*The gill of a fish is the ~ of the lung of a cat*. 鱼的鳃和猫的肺是类似物。~ **computer** 模拟计算机。

a·nal·o·gy [əˈnælədʒi; əˋnælədʒɪ] *n*. **1**. 类比,相似(*between*; *to*; *with*)。**2**.【逻】类推。**3**.【语】类同。**4**.【生】异体同功,同功器官〔*cf*. homology〕。**5**. 模拟,比拟。*a false* ~ 似是而非的对比。*a forced* ~ 勉强的类推,牵强附会。**by ~** 照此类推。**by ~ with** 由…类推。**by way of ~** 比方。**have** [**bear**] **~ to** [**with**] 类似。**on the ~ of** = by ~ with. **trace an ~ between** 在(二者)间寻求类似点。

an·al·pha·bet·ic [ænˌælfəˈbetik; ˏænælfəˋbɛtɪk] *a*. **1**. 不按字母顺序的。**2**. 不识字的,文盲的。**3**. 非字母注音的。

an·a·lys·a·ble [ˈænəlaizəbl; ˋænəlaɪzəbl] *a*. 可以分析的,分解得了的。

a·nal·y·sand [əˈnælisænd; əˋnælɪˏsænd] *n*. 精神分析对象〔正在接受精神分析疗法治疗的患者〕。

an·a·lyse [ˈænəlaiz; ˋænlˏaɪz] *vt*. **1**. 分解;分析;解析。**2**. 〔美〕= psychoanalyse. ~ ... **into** 把…分解成。

a·nal·y·sis [əˈnælisis; əˋnæləsɪs] *n*. (*pl*. **-ses** [-siːz; -siz]) **1**. 分解,分析;【数】解析。**2**. 梗概,要略。**3**. 〔美〕用精神分析法治疗(= psychoanalysis)。**in the last ~** = **on** (**the last**) ~ 归根结底,总之。**under ~** 在精神分析治疗下。~ **situs**【数】拓朴(学)。

an·a·lyst [ˈænəlist; ˋænlɪst] *n*. **1**. 分解者,分析者;化验员。**2**. 〔美〕精神病医师(= psychoanalyst)。

an·a·lyt·ic, an·a·lyt·i·cal [ˌænəˈlitik(əl); ˏænlˋɪtɪk(əl)] *a*. 分解的,分析的。*The analytical method is dialectical*. 分析的方法就是辩证的方法。~ **balance** 分析天平〔一种极精密的天平,供化学分析用〕。~ **chemistry** 分析化学。~ **geometry** 解析几何学。**-i·cal·ly** *ad*.

an·a·lyt·ics [ˌænəˈlitiks; ˏænlˋɪtɪks] *n*. *pl*. 〔用作单或复〕分析学,解析学。

an·a·lyze [ˈænəlaiz; ˋænlˏaɪz] *vt*. 〔美〕= analyse.

an·am·ne·sis [ˌænæmˈniːsis; ˏænæmˋnisɪs] *n*. **1**. 回想,回忆(尤指对假想的前世生活的回忆)。**2**.【医】既往症;既往病历。

an·a·mor·phism [ˌænəˈmɔːfizəm; ˏænəˋmɔrfɪzəm] *n*.【地】合成变质。

an·a·mor·pho·scope [ˌænəˈmɔːfəskəup; ˏænəˋmɔrfəˏskop] *n*. 歪像(变正)镜〔一种改变歪像为正像的曲面

镜〕。

an·a·mor·pho·sis [ˌænəˈmɔːfəsis; ˏænəˋmɔrfəsɪs] *n*. 1. 歪像,畸态。2.【植】畸形,变体。3.【生】渐进变化,渐变。4.【虫】增节变态。

a·na·nas [əˈnɑːnəs; əˋnɑnəs] *n*. 〔罕〕【植】凤梨(= pineapple)。

an·an·drous [ænˈændrəs; ænˋændrəs] *a*. 【植】无雄蕊的,隐花的。

An·a·ni·us [ænəˈnaiəs; ænəˋnaɪəs] *n*. 1.【圣】亚拿尼亚〔把应该献给使徒的钱私藏了一部分的信士,见《圣经·使徒行传》第五章〕。2.〔转义〕〔a-〕撒谎的人。

an·a·nym [ˈænənim; ˋænənɪm] *n*. 倒拼的名字〔如将 Smiles 写作 Selims〕。

an·a·paest [ˈænəpiːst; ˋænəˏpɛst] *n*. 〔诗〕1. 抑抑扬[短短长]格。2. 抑抑扬格的诗句〔如: And the ˈsheen of their ˈspears was like ˈstars on the ˈsea〕。**-ic** [-ik; -ɪk] *a*.

an·a·phase [ˈænəfeiz; ˋænəˏfez] *n*. 【生】(细胞分裂的)后期。

a·naph·o·ra [əˈnæfərə; əˋnæfərə] *n*. 1.【语】首语重复(法)(*opp*. epistrophe)〔指一个单词或片语出现在连续数句的开头〕。2. 指代法〔使用代替词来指代前面的语词,如: Mary dances better than June does 中,用 does 代替 dances〕。

an·aph·ro·dis·i·ac [ænˌæfrəˈdiziæk; ænˏæfrəˋdɪzɪæk] **I** *a*. 平性欲的,制性欲的。**II** *n*. 平性欲剂,制性欲剂。

an·a·phy·lac·tic [ˌænəfiˈlæktik; ˏænəfɪˋlæktɪk] *a*. 【医】过敏反应的。

an·a·phy·lac·tin [ˌænəfiˈlæktin; ˏænəfɪˋlæktɪn] *n*. 【医】过敏素。

an·a·phy·lax·is [ˌænəfiˈlæksis; ˏænəfəˋlæksɪs] *n*. 【医】过敏性(反应)。

an·a·plas·tic [ˌænəˈplæstik; ˏænəˋplæstɪk] *a*. 1.【医】整形手术的;整形的。2. (细胞)退化的;(肿瘤)恶性的。

an·a·plas·ty [ˈænəplæsti; ˋænəplæstɪ] *n*. 【医】整形(外科)术。

an·ap·tyx·is [ˌænæpˈtiksis; ˏænæpˋtɪksɪs] *n*. (*pl*. -tyx·es [-tiksiːz; -tɪksiz])【语】加母音现象〔为发音的方便而外加一元音,如 athlete 读成 [ˈæθəliːt; ˋæθəlit]〕。**an·ap·tyc·tic** [ˌænæpˈtiktik; ˏænæpˋtɪktɪk] *a*.

an·arch [ˈænɑːk; ˋænɑrk] *n*. = anarchist.

an·ar·chic, -i·cal [æˈnɑːkik(əl); ænˋɑrkɪk(l)] *a*. 无政府(主义)的。

an·ar·chism [ˈænəkizəm; ˋænəˑkɪzəm] *n*. 无政府主义;无政府(状态)。

an·ar·chist [ˈænəkist; ˋænəˑkɪst] *n*. 无政府主义者。

an·ar·cho- *comb*. *f*. 表示"无政府主义的": *anarcho-socialist*.

an·ar·cho-so·cial·ist [ˈænəkəuˈsəuʃəlist; ˋænəkoˋsoʃəlɪst] *n*. 无政府社会主义者。

an·na·cho-syn·dic·a·lism [ˈænəkəuˈsindikəlizəm; ˋænəko-ˋsɪndɪkəlɪzəm] *n*. 无政府工团主义。

an·ar·chy [ˈænəki; ˋænəˑkɪ] *n*. 无政府(状态);混乱。

an·ar·thri·a [æˈnɑːθriə; æˋnɑrθrɪə] *n*. 【医】(因大脑受伤引起的)口齿不清,口吃。

an·a·sar·ca [ˌænəˈsɑːkə; ˏænəˋsɑrkə] *n*. 【医】全身水肿,普遍性水肿。

An·a·sta·sia [ˌænəˈsteizjə; ˏænəˋstezɪə] *n*. 阿纳斯塔西娅〔女子名〕。

an·a·stat·ic [ˌænəˈstætik; ˏænəˋstætɪk] *a*. 【印】凸版的。～ **printing** 凸版印刷。

an·as·tig·mat [æˈnæstigmæt; æˋnæstɪgˏmæt] *n*. 【摄】去像散透镜。**-ic** [æˌnæstigˈmætik; æˏnæstɪgˋmætɪk] *a*. 去像散的。

an·as·to·mose [əˈnæstəməuz; əˋnæstəˏmoz] *vt*., *vi*. 1. (使)(血管)吻合。2. (使)(河流)汇合。

an·as·to·mo·sis [ˌænəstəˈməusis; ˏænæstəˋmosɪs] *n*. (*pl*. -ses [-siːz; -siz]) 1. (筋脉等的)吻合(术)。2. (运河等的)交叉合流。

a·nas·tro·phe [əˈnæstrəfi; əˋnæstrəfɪ] *n*. 【修】倒装法〔如 Homeward directly he went〕。

anat. = 1. anatomical. 2. anatomist. 3. anatomy.

an·a·tase [ˈænəteiz; ˋænətez] *n*. 【矿】八面石(锐钛矿)。

a·nath·e·ma [əˈnæθimə; əˋnæθəmə] *n*. 1. 咒,诅咒。2.【宗】咒逐〔用诅咒逐出教会〕。3. 被诅咒的人[物]。4. 极其讨厌的人[物]。

An·a·to·li·a [ˌænəˈtəuljə; ˏænəˋtolɪə] *n*. 1. 小亚细亚古名。2. 安那托力亚〔土耳其的亚洲部分〕。

an·a·tom·ic, -i·cal [ˌænəˈtɔmik(əl); ˏænəˋtɑmɪk(əl)] *a*. 1. 解剖的,解剖(学)上的。2. 组织的,构造上的。～ *terms* 解剖学术语。**-i·cal·ly** *ad*. 解剖地;在解剖上。

a·nat·o·mist [əˈnætəmist; əˋnætəmɪst] *n*. 解剖学者。

a·nat·o·mize [əˈnætəmaiz; əˋnætəˏmaɪz] *vt*. 1. 解剖。2. 分析,解析。

a·nat·o·my [əˈnætəmi; əˋnætəmɪ] *n*. 1. 解剖术;解剖学。2. 解剖体;组织,构造。3. 解剖,分解,分析。4. 〔俚、古〕骨骼。5. 瘦得仅剩皮包骨头的人。*human* ～ 人体解剖学。*morbid* ～ 病理解剖学。

a·nat·ro·pous [əˈnætrəpəs; əˋnætrəpəs] *a*. 【植】(胚珠)倒生的。

a·nat·to [ɑˈnɑːtəu; ɑˋnɑto] *n*. 胭脂树红,果红〔用来给食品着色〕。

an·bur·y [ˈænbəri; ˋænbərɪ] *n*. 1. (牛马的)软瘤,血痔。2. (植物的)根肿病。

-ance *suf*. 1. 表示行动、状态、性质等的名词词尾〔相对应的形容词词尾为 -ant〕: brilli*ance*, dist*ance*. 2. 附于动词后形成名词: assist*ance*.

an·ces·tor [ˈænsistə; ˋænsɛstəˑ] *n*. 1. 祖先,祖宗。2.【生】先祖,原种。3.【法】被继承人。

an·ces·tral [ænˈsestrəl; ænˋsɛstrəl] *a*. 祖先的;祖传的。～ *forms of life* 生物的原始形态。～ *features* 遗传性状。

an·ces·tress [ˈænsistris; ˋænsɛstrɪs] *n*. 女祖先〔*cf*. ancestor〕。

an·ces·try [ˈænsistri; ˋænsɛstrɪ] *n*. 1. 〔集合词〕祖先。2. 家世,世系。3. 世家,名门。4.【生】系谱。*He is of good* ～. 他出身名门。

an·chi·there [ˈæŋkiθiə; ˋæŋkɪθɪr] *n*. 【古生】化石马。

an·chor [ˈæŋkə; ˋæŋkəˑ] **I** *n*. 1. 挂锚;锚状物。2. 桩,支架。3. 〔喻〕依靠。4.【体】一队运动员中最后参加比赛的人;殿后的人〔如接力赛中跑最后一棒的人〕。5. 〔美俚〕(卡车的)紧急煞车器。*a bower* [*kedge*] ～ 中[小]锚。*a sheet* ～ 1. 〔古〕主锚。2. 〔喻〕希望,靠山。***be*** [***lie***, ***ride***] ***at*** ～ 停泊着,抛着锚。***back an*** ～ 抛副锚。***cast*** [***drop***] ～ 抛锚。***cat the*** ～ 挂锚。***come to*** (***an***) ～ 抛锚;〔喻〕住下来,住定。***lay out an*** ～ ***to windward*** 为安全打算。***Stand by the*** ～ ! 〔命令〕准备抛锚! ***swallow the*** ～ 摆脱航海生活。***The*** ～ ***comes home***. 1. 脱锚了。2. 事情失败了。***weigh*** ～ 起锚,开船。**II** *vi*. 1. 抛锚。2. 停泊;固定。— *vt*. 1. 抛锚泊(船)。2. 把…固定住。～ ***one's hope in*** [***on***] 把希望寄托在…上。～ **and collar** (门上的)铰链。～ **escapement** (钟表的)卡摆擒纵机。～ **gear**【海】抛[起]锚设备。～ **ground**【海】锚地。～ **ice**【海】底冰。～ **light** 船首夜间指示灯。～**man** 1. (电台或电视台新闻节目中的)现场报导员。2. (电台或电视台讨论节目中的)主持人。～ **ring**【数】环面。～ **watch**【海】锚更。

An·chor·age [ˈæŋkəridʒ; ˋæŋkərɪdʒ] *n*. 安克雷奇〔美国阿拉斯加州港市〕。

an·chor·age [ˈæŋkəridʒ; ˋæŋkərɪdʒ] *n*. 1. 抛锚;停泊。2. 抛锚地。3. 停泊税。4. 〔喻〕寄托。

an·cho·ress [ˈæŋkəris; ˋæŋkərɪs] *n*. 女隐士;女修道者。

an·cho·ret [ˈæŋkərit; ˋæŋkərɪt], **-rite** [-rait; -raɪt] *n*. 隐士。

an·cho·ret·ic [ˌæŋkəˈretik; ˏæŋkəˋretɪk] ***a*.** 隐士的,隐居的。

an·cho·rette[ˈæŋkəret; ˋæŋkərɛt] ***n*.** 〔电台或电视台〕新闻节目女主持人。

an·cho·vy [ˈæntʃəvi; ˋæntʃəvɪ] ***n*.** (*pl*. ~(*s*)) 【鱼】鳀。~ *sauce* 鳀制酱油,鳕鱼汁。

an·chu·sa [ænˈkjuːzə; ænˋkjuzə] ***n*.** 【园艺】毛茎植物,阿看草。

an·chu·sin [æŋˈkjuːsn, -zn; æŋˋkjusən, -zən] ***n*.** 阿看草染料。

an·chy·lose [ˈæŋkiləuz; ˋæŋkɪˏloz] ***vt*., *vi*. 1.** (使)(关节)僵硬(起来)。**2.** (使)(骨与骨)胶合,黏连。**-d** [-zd; -zd] ***a*.** 关节僵硬的。

an·chy·lo·sis [ˌæŋkaiˈləusis; ˏæŋkaɪˋlosɪs] ***n*. 1.** 关节僵硬。**2.** 骨骼胶合。

an·cien ré·gime [ɑːnˈsjeŋ reiˈʒiːm; ɑ̃ˋsjæ reˋʒim] 〔F.〕(特指法国1789年革命前的)旧制度。

an·cient[1] [ˈeinʃənt; ˋenʃənt] **I *a*. 1.** 已往的,古代的。**2.** 古来的,古老的,旧式的。**3.** 〔古〕年老的。*an* ~ *city* 古城。~ *relics* 古代遗物。**II *n*. 1.** 古(代的)人。**2.** 〔古〕高龄老人,老者。**3.** 〔*the* ~s〕古文明国的国民;(希腊、罗马时代的)古典作家[艺术家]。***A- of Days*** 上帝,神。~ **lights** 【法】(他人无权遮蔽其光线的)二十年以上的老窗户。~ **regime** = *ancien régime*. **-ly *ad*.** 从前,古时候,在古代。**-ness *n*.** 旧;古代。

ancient[2] [ˈeinʃənt; ˋenʃənt] ***n*.** 〔古〕旗;旗手。

an·cient·ry [ˈeinʃəntri; ˋenʃəntrɪ] ***n*. 1.** 古旧;古风。**2.** 古代。**3.** 〔废〕世家。

an·cil·lar·y [ænˈsiləri; ænˋsələrɪ] **I *a*.** 辅助的,附属的,副 (*to*)。*an* ~ *science* 辅助科学。**II *n*.** 〔英〕助手,随从。

an·cip·i·tal [ænˈsipitl; ænˋsɪpətl̩], **an·cip·i·tous** [-təs; -təs] ***a*.** 【植】(茎)有两棱的。

an·cle [ˈæŋkl; ˋæŋkl̩] ***n*.** = ankle.

an·con [ˈæŋkɔn; ˋæŋkɑn] ***n*. 1.** 肘。**2.** 【建】肘托。**A- sheep** 长身短腿的羊。

an·cress [ˈæŋkris; ˋæŋkrɪs] ***n*.** = anchoress.

-ancy *suf*. = -ance: ascen*dancy*.

an·cy·los·to·mi·a·sis [ˌæŋsiˌlɔstəˈmaiəsis; ˏæŋsɪˏlɑstəˋmaɪəsɪs] ***n*.** 钩虫病。

and [强 ænd, 弱 ənd, ; ɛnd, ənd] **I *conj*. 1.** 〔表示并列或对称关系〕及,和,与,同;又,兼。*a statesman* ~ *writer* 政治家兼作家。*I went to his house*, ~ *he came to mine*. 我去他家,他也来我家。**2.** 〔表示配合,整体〕*a carriage* ~ *four* 四马马车。*a cup* ~ *saucer* 连碟茶杯。*brandy* ~ *water* 兑水的白兰地。**3.** 〔表示连续、反覆〕*They walked two* ~ *two* 一双一双地走。*many* ~ *many a time* 屡次,多次。*talked* ~ *talked* 说了又说。**4.** 〔表示种种不一〕*There are books* ~ *books* [*men* ~ *men*] 书[人]有种种,好坏不一。**5.** 〔表示结果〕那么;就会;一…就…。*The sun came out* ~ *the grasses dried*. 日出草干。*He spoke* ~ *all was still*. 他一讲话,全体立即肃静无声。**6.** 〔用于祈使语气引导出条件句〕假如…那就…。*Stir* ~ *you are a dead man*. 你要动就要你的命。*Speak the truth* [*If you speak the truth*], ~ *you need have no shame*. (假如)你说真话,就不必害羞。**7.** 〔口〕〔用于 go, come, try 等动词间〕*Try* ~ (= *try to*) *do* 试着做一做。*Go* ~(= *go to*) *see* 去看看吧。**8.** 〔连接数词〕*One* ~ *twenty is* [*are*] *21*. *Two hundred* ~ *twenty-three is* [*are*] *223* 〔百位数之后美国常不加用 and〕。*seven* ~ *six* 〔英币〕7先令6便士〔略作7/6〕。**9.** 〔表示转折〕但,却。*So able*, ~ *he is very modest*. 他这样能干,但很谦虚。**10.** 〔强调进一步,加重语气〕而且,又。*He did it*, ~ *did it well*. 他做了,而且做得很好。**11.** 〔用于二形容词之间,使前一形容词带有副词性质〕*nice* ~ *warm* 暖和得舒服。*fine* ~ *thin* 纤细的。*rare* ~ *hungry* 饥肠辘辘。*fine* ~ *startled* = *extremely startled* 大吃一惊。**12.** 〔惊异,得知真情时〕*A- are you really going*? 嘿,你真要走吗? **13.** 〔表示动作的连续〕于是,然后。*She read for half an hour* ~ *went to bed*. 她读了半小时书,然后就睡觉了。**14.** 〔表示同时〕又。*eat* ~ *drink* 又吃又喝。**15.** 〔表示目的〕*Go* ~ *tell her the news*. 去把消息告诉她。**16.** 〔用于句首起承接作用〕于是,因此,接着。*A- he said unto Moses*. 接着他对摩西说。*A- you may now tell us all about it*. 因此,现在你可以把这件事情的原委讲给我们听了。**17.** 〔连接两个名词使后一名词具有形容词意义的特殊用法〕*dance* ~ *delight* = *delightful dance* 愉快的跳舞。~ ***all* 1.** 〔口〕连…都一齐 (*He ate the fish, bone* ~ *all*. 他吃鱼连骨头都一齐吃了)。**2.** 〔方〕此外;的确。~ ***all that*** = ~ so on. ~ ***all this*** = ~ that. ~ ***as well*** 以及,又。~ ***... at that*** 而且。~ **Co.** [ənˈko] = **& Co. ...**公司。~ ***how*** 〔美〕非常,很,真(*He was a miser* —~ *how*! 他是吝啬鬼——可不是吗!)。~ ***no wonder*** 也难怪。~ ***now*** 那么。~ / *or* [ænd ɔr] 及(或) (*Contributions in money* ~ / *or garments are welcome*. 欢迎捐助现金及(或)衣服)。~ ***others*** 其他等等。~ ***so*** 所以。~ ***so forth*** = ~ ***so on*** 等等,云云。~ ***that*** 而且 (*You must tell him*, ~ *that at once*. 你必须告诉他,而且要立刻告诉他)。~ *the like* 等等,云云。~ ***the rise*** 〔美〕还多(*a hundred* ~ *the rise* 一百以上)。~ ***then*** 其次,然后,于是就。~ ***what not*** 等等,云云。~ ***with reason*** 也难怪。~ ***yet*** 然而,但。***by twos*** ~ ***threes*** 三两成群。**II *n*. 1.** 附加条件。**2.** 〔常 *pl*.〕附加细节。*He accepted the job, no* ~ *about it*. 他接受了这项工作,没有附加条件。*It was a long story, with many* ~*s*. 这故事说来话长,有许多细节。**"and" gate** 【计】"与"门。

and*.** = ***an·dan·te [ænˈdænti; ænˋdæntɪ] **I *ad*.** 〔It.〕【乐】缓慢地,温和地,用行板。**II *n*.** 【乐】行板。

An·da·lu·sia [ˌændəˈluːzjə; ˏændəˋluʒə] ***n*.** 安达卢西亚〔西班牙南部一区域〕。

An·da·lu·sian [ˌændəˈluːziən; ˏændəˋluʒɪən] **I *n*.** 安达卢西亚;安达卢西亚人;安达卢西亚鸡。**II *a*.** 安达卢西亚(人)的。

an·da·lu·site [ˌændəˈluːsait; ˏændəluˋsaɪt] ***n*.** 【矿】红柱石。

An·da·man(s) [ˈændəmæn(z); ˋændəmæn(z)] ***n*.** 安达曼群岛〔印度〕(= Andaman Islands)。**-ese** [ˌændəmænˈniːz; ˏændəməˋniz] ***n*. 1.** 安达曼群岛上的当地居民。**2.** 安达曼语。

an·dan·ti·no [ˌændænˈtiːnəu; ˏændænˋtino] **I *ad*.** 〔It.〕【乐】用小行板。**II *n*.** 【乐】小行板。

An·de·an [ænˈdiːən; ænˋdiən] **I *a*.** (南美)安第斯山脉的。**II *n*.** 安第斯山人。

An·der·son [ˈændəsn; ˋændɚsn̩] ***n*. 1.** 安德森〔姓氏〕。**2. H.C.** ~ 安徒生〔1805—1875,丹麦童话作家〕。**3. C. D.** ~ 安德森〔1905—,美国物理学家,阳电子的发现者〕。~-*shelter* 〔英〕家庭防空壕。

An·des [ˈændiːz; ˋændiz] ***n*. *pl*.** 〔*the* ~〕安第斯山脉〔南美〕。

an·des·ite [ˈændizait; ˋændɪˏzaɪt] ***n*.** 【矿】安山岩。

and·i·ron [ˈændaiən; ˋændˏaɪɚn] ***n*.** (壁炉的)柴架。

An·dor·ra [ænˈdɔrə; ænˋdɔrə] ***n*.** 安道尔〔欧洲〕。~ *La Vella* 安道尔(市)〔安道尔首都〕。

an·dr- *comb*. *f*. 〔用于母音前〕= andro-.

an·dra·dite [ˈændrədait; ˋændrədaɪt] ***n*.** 【矿】钙铁榴石。

An·dre [ˈændri, ˈɑːndrei; ˋændrɪ, ˋɑndre] ***n*.** 安德烈〔男子名, Andrew 的异体〕。

An·drew [ˈændruː; ˋændru] ***n*.** 安德鲁〔男子名〕。

An·drews [ˈændruːz; ˋændruz] ***n*.** 安德鲁斯〔姓氏〕。

an·dro- *comb*. *f*. 表示"男性的","雄性的": *andro*gynous, *andro*sphinx.

an·droe·ci·um [æn'dri:ʃiəm; æn`driʃɪəm] *n*.【植】雄蕊。

an·droc·ra·cy [æn'drɔkrəsi; ˏæn`drɑkrəsɪ] *n*. 男性中心社会。

an·dro·gen ['ændrədʒən; `ændrədʒən] *n*. 雄性激素。

an·drog·e·nous [æn'drɔdʒinəs; æn`drɑdʒɪnəs] *a*.【生】产雄的。

an·dro·gyne ['ændrɔdʒain; `ændrəˏdʒaɪn] *n*. 雌雄同序植物。

an·drog·y·nous [æn'drɔdʒinəs; æn`drɑdʒənəs] *a*. **1.** 兼两性的,雌雄同体的。**2.**【植】雌雄同丝的;雌雄同序的。

an·drog·y·ny [æn'drɔdʒini; æn`drɑdʒɪnɪ] *n*.【植】雌雄同体。

an·droid ['ændrɔid; `ændrɔɪd] *n*. (科学幻想小说中的)机器人;似人自动机 (*cf*. robot)。

An·drom·e·da [æn'drɔmidə; æn`drɑmɪdə] *n*. **1.**【希神】安德罗米达〔埃塞俄比亚公主,其母夸其美貌而得罪海神,致使全国遭殃〕。**2.**〔the ~ 〕【天】仙女座。

an·dro·pause ['ændrəpɔz; `ændrəpɑz] *n*. 男性更年期。

an·dro·sphinx ['ændrɔsfiŋks; `ændrəˏsfɪŋks] *n*. 男面狮身像。

an·dros·ter·one [æn'drɔstərəun; æn`drɑstəˏon] *n*.【化】雄甾酮。

An·dy ['ændi; `ændɪ] *n*. 安迪〔男子名, Andrew 的昵称〕。

ane [ein; en] *a*., *n*.〔Scot.〕= one.

-ane *suf*. **1.** -an 的变体,但所表意义与 -an 不同: hum*ane* —hum*an*. **2.**【化】烷: meth*ane* (甲烷), eth*ane* (乙烷)。

a·near [ə'niə; ə`nɪr] *ad*., *prep*.〔方、诗〕近,在近旁;接近。

an·ec·dot·age ['ænikdəutidʒ; `ænɛkˏdotɪdʒ] *n*. **1.** 轶事集,逸话集。**2.**〔谑〕好谈逸事的老年时代。*Grandfather is in his* ~. 爷爷年老话多,爱谈往事。

an·ec·dot·al [ˌænek'dəutl; ˏænɪk`dotl] *a*. 逸事(多)的。

an·ec·dote ['ænikdəut; `ænɪkˏdot] *n*. 逸话,轶事,掌故,奇闻;〔*pl*.〕秘史。

an·ec·dot·ic, -i·cal [ˌænek'dɔtik(əl); ˏænɪk`dɑtɪk(əl)] *a*. 逸事(多)的,爱讲逸事的。

an·e·cho·ic [ˌæne'kəuik; ˏænɛ`koɪk] *a*. 无回声的;无反响的。~ **chamber** 无回声室。

a·nele [ə'ni:l; ə`nil] *vt*.〔古〕给…行临终涂油礼。

a·ne·mi·a [ə'ni:miə; ə`nimɪə] *n*. = anaemia.

a·ne·mic [ə'ni:mik; ə`nimɪk] *a*. = anaemic.

a·nem·o·graph [ə'neməgrɑ:f; ə`nɛməˏgræf] *n*. 风速计。**-ic** [əˌnemə'grɑ:fik; əˏnɛmə`græfɪk] *a*.

an·e·mol·o·gy [ˌænə'mɔlədʒi; ˏænə`mɑlədʒɪ] *n*. 测风学。

an·e·mom·e·ter [ˌæni'mɔmitə; ˏænə`mɑmətɚ] *n*. 风速表。

an·e·mo·met·ric(al) [ˌænimə*u*'metrik(əl); ˏænəmə`metrɪk(əl)] *a*. 测定风速和风向的。

an·e·mom·e·try [ˌæni'mɔmitri; ˏænɪ`mɑmɪtrɪ] *n*. 风速测定(法)。

a·nem·o·ne [ə'neməni; ə`nɛməˏni] *n*. **1.**【植】银莲花,白头翁。**2.**【动】海葵(= sea ~)。

an·e·moph·i·lous [ˌæni'mɔfiləs; ˏænə`mɑfələs] *a*.【植】风媒的〔*cf*. entomophilous〕。~ **flower** 风媒花。

a·nem·o·scope [ə'neməskəup; ə`nɛməˏskop] *n*. 风向仪。

an·e·mo·sis [ˌæni'məusis; ˏænə`mosɪs] *n*. (树木因风吹而在年轮之间发生的)轮裂。

a·nent [ə'nent; ə`nɛnt] *prep*.〔古〕关于,论及;在…方面。

-a·neous *suf*. 属于…的: extr*aneous*.

an·er·gy ['ænədʒi; `ænədʒɪ] *n*.【医】**1.** 无反应性。**2.** 无力。**-er·gic** *a*.

an·er·oid ['ænərɔid; `ænəˏrɔɪd] **I** *a*. (晴雨表等)不用液体的,不装水银的。**II** *n*. 无液[空盒]气压表,无液晴雨表(= ~ barometer)。

an·es·the·sia [ˌænis'θi:zjə; ˏænəs`θiʒə] *n*. = anaesthesia.

an·es·the·si·ol·o·gist [ˌænisˌθizi'ɔlədʒist; ˏænəsˏθɪzɪ`ɑlədʒɪst] *n*. 麻醉学医师,麻醉学专家。

an·es·the·si·ol·o·gy [ˌænisθizi'ɔlədʒi; ˏænəsˏθɪzɪ`ɑlədʒɪ] *n*. 麻醉学。

an·es·thet·ic [ˌænis'θetik; ˏænəs`θɛtɪk] *a*. = anaesthetic.

an·es·the·tist [æ'ni:sθətist; ə`nɛsθətɪst] *n*. = anaesthetist.

an·es·the·tize [æ'nisθətaiz; ə`nɛsθəˏtaɪz] *a*. = anaesthetize.

a·nes·trus [æ'nestrəs; æ`nɛstrəs] *n*.【动】乏情期,不动情期。

an·e·thole ['ænəθəul; `ænəˏθol] *n*.【化】茴香脑。

An·eu·rin [ə'naiərin; ə`naɪrɪn] *n*. 阿奈林〔男子名〕。

an·eu·rin ['ænjuərin; `ænjʊrɪn] *n*.【化】维生素 B_1,盐酸硫胺素;抗神经炎素。

an·eu·rism, an·eu·rysm ['ænjuərizəm; `ænjəˏrɪzəm] *n*.【医】动脉瘤。**-ris·mal, -rys·mal** [-'rizməl; -`rɪzməl] *a*.

a·new [ə'nju:; ə`nju] *ad*. 重新,再,另。*begin one's life* ~ 重新做人。*edit* ~ 改订。

an·frac·tu·os·i·ty [ænˌfræktju'ɔsiti; ænˏfræktʃʊ`ɑsətɪ] *n*. **1.** 弯曲;曲折,错综。**2.**〔*pl*.〕弯曲的路[沟渠等]。

an·frac·tu·ous [æn'fræktjuəs; æn`fræktʃʊəs] *a*. 弯曲的,迂回的;错综的。

A.N.G. = American Newspapers Guild 美国报业公会。

an·ga·kok ['æŋgəkɔk; `æŋgəˏkɑk] = angekok.

an·ga·ry ['æŋgəri; `æŋgərɪ] *n*.【国际法】战时征用权〔指交战国征用或毁坏中立国财产的权利,但负有赔偿义务〕。

an·ge·kok ['æŋgəkɔk; `æŋgəˏkɑk] *n*. 爱斯基摩巫医。

an·gel ['ein*d*ʒəl; `endʒəl] **I** *n*. **1.** 天使;守护神。**2.** 安琪儿,可爱的人。**3.** 英国古金币名。**4.**〔美口〕后台老板。*an* ~ *of a child* 天使一样的小孩。*an evil* [*a fallen*] ~ 恶魔,凶神。*a good* [*guardian*] ~ 吉神,守护神。~*'s visit* 不常有的事。***entertain an* ~ *unawares*** 无意中接待了要人[名人]而不知其身分,无意中有恩惠于微服私行的要人[名人]。***Speak of* ~*s, and you will hear their wings***. 说到某人,某人就到。~ **cake** [**food**]〔美〕(面粉、糖、蛋白做的)白蛋糕。~ **fish** *n*.【鱼】鳐乌鲂。~**-on-horse-back** 熏肉夹牡蛎。~ **puss** *n*.〔美俚〕天使面孔。~ **shark** *n*. 扁鲨。**II** *vt*.〔美口〕做…的后台老板,出钱资助(演出等)。~ **investor** 天使投资人〔指对一家或多家新兴科技企业投资的个人〕。

An·ge·la ['æn*d*ʒilə; `æn*d*ʒələ] *n*. 安吉拉〔女子名〕。

An·gel·e·no [ˌændʒi'li:nə*u*; ˏændʒɪ`lino] *n*. (*pl*. ~*s*) 洛杉矶人。

an·gel·ic, -i·cal [æn'dʒelik(əl); æn`dʒɛlɪk(əl)] *a*. 天使(似)的,有天使性质的。

an·gel·i·ca [æn'dʒelikə; æn`dʒɛlɪkə] *n*. **1.**【植】白芷。**2.**〔A-〕白芷属;白芷味白葡萄酒。~ **tree** *n*.【植】楤木。

An·ge·li·na [ˌændʒi'li:nə; ˏændʒɪ`linə] *n*. 安吉利娜〔女子名, Angela 的昵称〕。

An·gell ['eindʒəl; `endʒəl] *n*. 安吉尔〔姓氏〕。

An·ge·lo ['ændʒiləu; `ændʒɪlo] *n*. 安吉洛〔男子名〕。

an·ge·lus ['ændʒiləs; `ændʒələs] *n*. **1.**【天主】(早晨、中午、晚上为纪念耶稣降临人世而做的)祈祷。**2.** 祈祷钟(= Angelus bell)。

an·ger ['æŋgə; `æŋgɚ] **I** *n*. **1.** 怒,忿怒。**2.**〔方〕(伤口处的)发炎,炎症。*He is easily moved to* ~. 他动辄发怒。*be furious* [*filled*] *with* ~ 满腔怒火。***in a fit of* ~**

A

勃然大怒。*in a moment of* ～ 一时之气,一阵气恼。*in* ～ 动怒,生气。II *vt*. 激怒,触怒,使发怒,使生气。*He was ～ed at the insult*. 他因受辱而恼怒。—*vi*. 发怒,恼火。*She ～s with little or no provocation*. 她无缘无故就发怒。

an·gi·na [æn'dʒainə; æn`dʒaɪnə] *n*.【医】1. 咽喉痛,咽峡炎。2. 心绞痛(= ～ pectoris)。

an·gi·og·ra·phy [ˌændʒi'ɔgrəfi; ˏændʒɪ`ɑgrəfɪ] *n*. 1. 血管照相术。2. 血管学。

an·gi·ol·o·gy [ˌændʒi'ɔlədʒi; ˏændʒɪ`ɑlədʒɪ] *n*. 血管学,血管淋巴管学。

an·gi·o·ma [ˌændʒi'əumə; ˏændʒɪ`omə] *n*. (*pl*. **-mata** [-mətə; -mətə], ～*s*) 血管瘤。**-tous** [-'ɔmətəs, -'əumətəs; -`ɑmətəs, -`omətəs] *a*.

an·gi·o·plas·ty [ˌændʒi'əuplæsti; ˏændʒɪ'oplæstɪ] *n*.【医】血管成型术,血管清理术。

an·gi·o·sperm ['ændʒiəuspəːm; `ændʒɪoˏspɝm] *n*. 被子植物。

Ang·kor ['æŋkɔː; `æŋkɔr] *n*. 吴哥〔柬埔寨古城〕。～ **Wat** [**Vat**] 吴哥窟,吴哥庙〔古高棉王朝庞大的宫殿遗址〕。

Angl. = 1. Anglican. 2. Anglice.

An·gle ['æŋgl; `æŋgḷ] *n*.【英史】盎格鲁人〔*cf*. *Angles*〕。

an·gle[1] ['æŋgl; `æŋgḷ] I *n*. 1. 角,隅,角落;棱,嫱角。2.【数】角,角位,角的度数。3.【机】角铁。4. 见地,观点。5. (事物的)方面,角度。6. 〔口〕隐蔽的个人动机;诡计。7. 〔口〕(新闻报导的)偏见,歪曲。*an auxiliary* [*subsidiary, supplementary*] ～ 补角。*an external* [*exterior*] ～ 外角。*an internal* [*interior*] ～ 内角。*an obtuse* ～ 钝角。*a vertical* ～ 对顶角。*a right* ～ 直角。*a straight* ～ 平角。*an optical* [*a visual*] ～ 视角;【矿】光轴角。～ *of attack*【空】气压角,迎角。～ *of bank* [*roll*]【空】转角。***meet at right ～s*** 相交成直角。***take the ～*** 测角度。***view from various ～s*** 由各方面观察。II *vt*. 1. 使(摄影机等)偏成[转向]某一角度。2. 使(新闻报导等)带上色彩[倾向性]。*She ～d her column of chitchat towards teen-agers*. 她的闲话专栏着眼于青少年。～ *one's camara* (摄影时)对角度。～ *a report* 使报告搀杂偏见。—*vi*. 1. 转变角度;突然朝某方向转去。2. 以一个角度移动。～**-dozer** 铲土机,侧铲推土机。～ **iron** [**bar**] 角铁,L 形铁。～**-site** 硫酸铅矿。～**-table**【建】托架,斜撑铁。

an·gle[2] ['æŋgl; `æŋgḷ] I *n*. 〔古〕钓钩;钓具。*a brother of the* ～ 钓鱼者。II *vi*. 1. 钓鱼。2. 〔美俚〕钓(誉),贪图,图谋。～ *for carp* 钓鲤鱼。～ *for praise* 沽名钓誉。—*vt*. 在…钓鱼。～**worm** *n*. 蚯蚓(= earthworm)。

an·gled ['æŋgld; `æŋgld] *a*. 有角的;成角度的。

an·gle·pod ['æŋglpɔd; `æŋglpɑd] *n*. 萝藦科属植物。

an·gler ['æŋglə; `æŋglɚ] *n*. 1. 钓鱼者。2. 沽名钓誉者,追逐(名利等)的人 (*for*)。3.【鱼】鮟鱇。

An·gles ['æŋglz; `æŋgḷz] *n*. [*pl*.] 盎格鲁族〔五世纪由 Schleswig (今德国北部)移住英国的条顿族的一支,其居住地即称 Angle-land, 后转为今名 England〕。

An·gli·a ['æŋgljə; `æŋglɪə] 〔L.〕= England.

An·gli·an ['æŋgljən; `æŋglɪən] I *a*. 盎格鲁的,盎格鲁人的。II *n*. 盎格鲁人[语]。

An·glic ['æŋglik; `æŋglɪk] *n*. (瑞典语言学家 R. E. Zachrisson 氏所创的)简易英语。

An·gli·can ['æŋglikən; `æŋglɪkən] I *a*. 1. 英国国教的,英国圣公会的。2. 〔美〕英国的。*the* ～ *Church* 英国国教。II *n*. 英国国教徒,英国圣公会教徒。**-ism** *n*. 1. 英国国教(教义),英国圣公会(教义)。2. 英国风度;英国方式。

An·gli·ce [æŋ'glasi; `æŋglɪsɪ] *ad*. 〔L.〕用英语,照英语说。

An·gli·cism ['æŋglisizəm; `æŋgləsɪzəṃ] *n*. 1. 英国风格。2. 英国说法[语法、语义],英国惯用语。3. 〔美〕英国语法。**-gli·cist** *n*. 英国语言和文学的研究者。

An·gli·cize ['æŋglisaiz; `æŋgləˏsaɪz], **An·gli·fy** [-fai; -faɪ] *vt*., *vi*. (使)变为英国派;(在语言习惯等方面)(使…)英语化。★亦可作 a-.

an·gling ['æŋgliŋ; `æŋglɪŋ] *n*. 钓鱼(术)。

An·glist ['æŋglist; `æŋglɪst] *n*. 英国通。

An·glis·tics [ˌæŋ'glistiks; æŋ`glɪstɪks] *n*. 英语学。

An·glo ['æŋgləu; `æŋglo] *n*. (*pl*. ～*s*) (住美国西南地区讲英语的)北欧裔美国人。

An·glo- ['æŋgləu-; `æŋglo] *comb*. *f*. 〔English 一词的构词形式〕表示"英国,英裔,英国的": *Anglo*-African.

An·glo-Af·ri·can ['æŋgləu'æfrikən; `æŋglo`æfrɪkən] *n*., *a*. 英裔非洲人的。

An·glo-A·mer·i·can ['æŋgləuə'merikən; `æŋgloəˏmɛrəkən] 1. *n*. 英裔美国人;住在美国的英国人。2. *a*. 英美的;英裔美国人的。

An·glo-Cath·o·lic ['æŋgləu'kæθəlik; `æŋglo`kæθəlɪk] *n*., *a*. 英国国教高教会派的。

An·glo-French ['æŋgləu'frentʃ; `æŋglo`frɛntʃ] *n*. 1. 英法的;英国法语的。2. 英国法语。

An·glo·ma·ni·a ['æŋgləu'meiniə; `æŋglo`menɪə] *n*. 英国狂,亲英。**-c** [-niæk; -nɪˏæk] *n*. 醉心英国的人,亲英分子。

An·glo-Nor·man ['æŋgləu'nɔːmən; `æŋglo`nɔrmən] 1. *a*. 英格兰和诺尔曼(人、语)的;诺尔曼系英国人的。2. *n*. 诺尔曼系英国人;盎格鲁诺尔曼语。

An·glo·phil(e) ['æŋgləufail; `æŋgləˏfaɪl] 1. *a*. 亲英派的。2. *n*. 亲英分子,亲英派。

An·glo·phobe ['æŋgləufəub; `æŋgləˏfob] *n*. 反对[憎恶]英国者,恐英者。

An·glo·pho·bi·a [ˌæŋgləu'fəubiə; ˏæŋglo`fobɪə] *n*. 反对[憎恶]英国;恐英病。

An·glo·phone ['æŋgləufəun; `æŋglofon] *n*. (在有包括英语在内的多种语言的国家中)以英语为母语的人。

An·glo-Sax·on ['æŋgləu'sæksən; `æŋglo`sæksn] 1. *n*. 五世纪左右移居英国的日耳曼族人民;〔*pl*.〕盎格鲁撒克逊族;盎格鲁撒克逊语〔又名 Old English〕;简易英语;英国人。2. *a*. 盎格鲁撒克逊族[语]的;古代英语的;英国的。**-ism** 盎格鲁撒克逊风格[腔调];英人气质。

An·go·la [æŋ'gəulə; æŋ`golə] *n*. 安哥拉〔非洲〕;〔a-〕= Angora. **-lan** [-lən; -lən] *n*. 安哥拉人。*a*. 安哥拉(人)的。

an·gor ['æŋgəː; `æŋgɔr] *n*. 1. 剧痛。2. 心绞痛(= angina pectoris)。

An·go·ra [æŋ'gɔːrə; æŋ`gorə] *n*. 1. 安哥拉棉毛呢。2. 安哥拉猫(= ～ cat)。3. 安哥拉兔(= ～ rabbit)。4. = Ankara. ～ **cloth** 安哥拉绣花布;马海毛呢。～ **goat** 安哥拉山羊。

an·gos·tu·ra [ˌæŋgəs'tjuərə; ˏæŋgəs`tjʊrə] *n*. (南美)安哥斯图拉苦味树皮〔可解热滋补〕。

an·gri·ly ['æŋgrili; `æŋgrəlɪ] *ad*. 怒,忿怒。

an·gry ['æŋgri; `æŋgrɪ] *a*. 1. 发怒的,忿怒的。2. (风雨等)凶猛的。3. (颜色等)刺目的。4. (伤口等)肿痛的,发炎的。～ *waves* 怒涛。～ *winds* 烈风。*an* ～ *wound* 发炎的伤口。～ **red** 鲜红。***be*** [***get***] ～ ***at*** (***about***) 因…而发怒,生…的气。***be*** [***get***] ～ ***with*** (*sb*.) 生(某人)的气。***have ～ words with...*** 和…吵嘴。***make*** (*sb*.) ～ 惹(某人)发火[发怒,生气]。

angst [ɑːŋst; ɑŋkst] *n*. 担心;焦虑;苦恼。

ang·strom ['æŋstrəm; `æŋstrəm] *n*.【物】埃〔一亿分之一厘米,用做测量波长的单位〕。

an·guine ['æŋgwin; `æŋgwɪn] *a*. (像)蛇的。

an·guish ['æŋgwiʃ; `æŋgwɪʃ] I *n*. (极度)痛苦,苦闷,烦恼。*in* ～ 极度痛苦。II *vt*., *vi*. (使)痛苦;(使)苦恼。**-ed** *a*. 痛苦的。

an·gu·lar ['æŋgjulə; `æŋgjəlɚ] *a*. 1. 有角的,角形的;

尖锐的。2. 用角度量的;角的。3. 瘦骨嶙峋的。4. 不灵活的,生硬的。*in an* ~ *manner* (态度)生硬。~ **bone** 隅骨。~ **leaf spot** 叶角斑病。~ **process** 隅骨突起。**-ly** *ad*.

an·gu·lar·i·ty [ˌæŋgjuˈlæriti; ˏæŋgjəˋlærətɪ] *n*. 1. 有角,角弯曲度。2. 〔*pl*.〕角状部分,棱角 3. (样子、衣着等)难看,生硬。4. 【机】斜度。*soften down* [*round off*] *awkward angularities* 磨去笨拙的棱角。

an·gu·late [ˈæŋgjuleit; ˋæŋgjəlɪt] **I** *a*. 有角的,成角的。**II** *vt*., *vi*. (使)具棱角。

an·gu·la·tion [ˌæŋgjuˈleiʃən; ˏæŋgjəˋleʃən] *n*. 1. 作角,作成角度。2. 角的形状;部分或位置。

An·gus [ˈæŋgəs; ˋæŋgəs] *n*. 1. 安格斯〔男子名〕。2. 苏格兰东部郡名。

ang·wan·ti·bo [æŋˈgwɑːntibəu; æŋˋgwɑntɪbo] *n*. (*pl*. ~*s*)【动】金熊猴。

an·har·mon·ic [ˌænhɑːˈmɔːnik; ˏænhɑrˋmɑnɪk] *a*. 【物】非谐的。~ **force** 非谐力。~ **ratio**【物】交比,非调和比。

an·hin·ga [ænˈhiŋgə; ænˋhɪŋgə] *n*.【动】蛇鸟。

an·hy·drid(e) [ænˈhaidraid; ænˋhaɪdraɪd] *n*.【化】酐。

an·hy·drite [ænˈhaidrait; ænˋhaɪdraɪt] *n*.【矿】硬石膏,无水石膏。

an·hy·drous [ænˈhaidrəs; ænˋhaɪdrəs] *a*.【化】无水的。

an·i·co·nic [ˌænaiˈkɔnik; ˏænaɪˋkɑnɪk] *a*. 不把崇拜的神做成人形[兽形]的,不使用偶像(作崇拜对象)的;反对偶像的;只崇拜象征性的神的。

a·nigh [əˈnai; əˋnaɪ] *ad*., *prep*.〔英方〕近。

an·il [ˈænil; ˋænɪl] *n*. 1.【植】木蓝。2. 靛蓝。

an·ile [ˈeinail; ˋenaɪl] *a*. 1. 衰老的;老太婆似的。2. 糊涂的。

an·i·lin(e) [ˈæniliːn; ˋænlˏin] *n*.【化】苯胺。~ **printing** 曲面双色印刷,阿尼林印刷(= flexographic printing)。

an·il·i·ty [æˈniliti; æˋnɪlətɪ] *n*. 1. 衰老,老年昏聩。2. 〔常 *pl*.〕糊涂言行。

an·i·ma [ˈænimə; ˋænɪmə] *n*. 〔L.〕人生之本;灵魂。

an·i·mad·vert [ˌænimædˈvəːt; ˏænəmædˋvɝt] *vi*. 谴责,责备,苛责(*on*, *upon*)。~ ***on sb.'s shortcomings*** 揭人缺点[疮疤]。**-ver·sion** [-ˈvəːʃən; -vɝʃən] *n*.

an·i·mal [ˈæniməl; ˋænəml] **I** *n*. 1. 动物;兽;牲畜。2. 〔俚〕家畜,牲口。3. 〔俚〕畜生(一般的人)〔骂人语〕。*domestic* ~*s* 家畜。*wild* ~*s* 野生动物。**II** *a*. 动物的;肉欲的。~ **appetites** [**desires**] 兽欲。~ **courage** 蛮勇。~ **food** 肉食。~ **heat** 体温。~ **husbandry** 畜牧业,家畜学。~ **kingdom** 动物界。~ **life** 动物的生态。~ **magnetism** 魅力。~ **passion** 肉欲,兽欲。~ **spirits** 血气,元气。**-ly** *ad*. 肉体上。

an·i·mal·cule [ˌæniˈmælkjuːl; ˏænəˋmælkjʊl] *n*. 微动物;微生物。

an·i·mal·cu·lum [ˌæniˈmælkjuləm; ˏænəˋmælkjələm] *n*. (*pl*. *-la* [-lə; -lə]) 极微动物(= animalcule)。

an·i·mal·ism [ˈæniməlizəm; ˈænəməlˏɪzəm] *n*. 1. 动物的生活[活动、性状]。2. 兽性,兽欲。3. 人即动物的学说。

an·i·mal·ist [ˈæniməlist; ˋænəməlɪst] *n*. 1. 兽欲主义者。2. 动物画家[雕刻家]。3.动物权益保护者。

an·i·mal·i·ty [ˌæniˈmæliti; ˏænəˋmælətɪ] *n*. 1. 兽性。2. 动物生态。3. 动物界。

an·i·mal·i·za·tion [ˌæniməlaiˈzeiʃən; ˏænəməlɪˋzeʃən] *n*. 1. 动物化,兽性化。2. (食物等)动物质化。

an·i·mal·ize [ˈæniməlaiz; ˋænəməlˏaɪz] *vt*. 1. 使动物化;使像野兽一样。2. 使耽于兽欲。3. 使变成动物质。*to* ~ *food through digestion* 通过消化使食物变成动物质。*men that were* ~*d by war* 由于战争而变得和野兽一样的人。

an·i·mate [ˈænimeit; ˋænəˏmet] **I** *vt*. 1. 使活起来,赋与…以生命。2. 给与…以生气;使有生气;使活泼。3. 鼓舞,激励,激发。4. 绘制(动画片)。**II** *a*. [ˈænimit; ˋænəmɪt] 1. 有生命的;有生气的。2. 生气蓬勃的,活泼的。~ *nature* 生物界,动物界。

an·i·mat·ed [ˈænimeitid; ˋænəˏmetɪd] *a*. 1. 精力旺盛的,生气蓬勃的。2. 栩栩如生的。3. 热闹的,热烈的。*an* ~ *bust* 栩栩如生的胸像。*an* ~ *cartoon* [*drawing*] 动画片。*an* ~ *description* 生动的描写。*an* ~ *discussion* 热烈的讨论。~ *pictures* 走马灯;〔古〕电影。*an* ~ *talk* 畅谈。

an·i·mat·er [ˈæniˌmeitə; ˋænɪˏmetɚ] *n*. 1. 赋予生气者,鼓舞者。2.【影】画动画片的人。

an·i·mat·ing [ˈænimeitiŋ; ˋænəˏmetɪŋ] *a*. 使有生气的,令人兴奋的,活泼的。

an·i·ma·tion [ˌæniˈmeiʃən; ˏænəˋmeʃən] *n*. 1. 生气;生机。2. 生动,活泼。3. 动画片(制作)。*a face devoid of* ~ 死人(一样的)面孔。*suspended* ~ 假死,晕厥。***with*** ~ 活泼地,生动地。

an·i·ma·tism [ˈænimətizəm; ˋænɪmətɪzəm] *n*. 物活论〔指非生物的东西具有意识或个性〕。

an·i·ma·tor [ˈænimeitə; ˋænɪˏmetɚ] *n*. = animater.

an·i·mé [ˈænimei; ˋænɪˏme] **I** *n*. 〔F.〕芳香树脂。**II** *a*. 有生命的。

an·i·mism [ˈænimizəm; ˋænəˏmɪzəm] *n*. 万物有灵论;泛灵论;精灵崇拜。**an·i·mist** *n*. 泛灵论者;精灵崇拜者。

an·i·mos·i·ty [ˌæniˈmɔsiti; ˏænəˋmɑsətɪ] *n*. 怨恨,仇恨,敌视,憎恶。*animosities between classes* 阶级间的仇恨。***have*** ~ ***against*** [***towards***] 仇视,敌视。

an·i·mus [ˈæniməs; ˋænəməs] *n*. 1. 意图,宗旨,主导思想。2. 敌意,恶意。

an·i·on [ˈænaiən; ˋænˏaɪən] *n*.【化】阴离子,阳向离子。

an·ise [ˈænis; ˋænɪs] *n*.【植】大茴香。

an·i·seed [ˈænisiːd; ˋænɪˏsid] *n*. 大茴香子,八角子。

an·i·sei·ko·ni·a [ˌænaisəˈkəunjə; ˏænaɪsəˋkonɪə] *n*. (眼睛的)左右异像症;【医】(两眼)物像不等。

an·i·sette [ˌæniˈzet; ˏænɪˋzɛt] *n*. 〔F.〕大茴香酒。

aniso- *comb. f*. 不等的;不同的,异(*opp*. *iso-*): *aniso*tropic.

an·i·sole [ˈænisəul; ˋænəsol] *n*.【化】茴香醚,苯甲醚,甲氧基苯。

an·i·so·mer·ic [æˌnaisəuˈmerik; æˏnaɪsoˋmɛrɪk] *a*. 【化】非异构的。

an·i·som·er·ous [ˈænaiˈsɔmərəs; ˏænaɪˋsɑmərəs] *a*. 【植】(花部的)不齐数的。

an·i·so·met·ric [ænˌaisəuˈmetrik; ænˏaɪsoˋmɛtrɪk] *a*. 不等轴的。

an·i·so·me·tro·pi·a [ænˌaisəumiˈtrəupiə; ænˏaɪsoməˋtropɪə] *n*.【医】屈光参差。**-trop·ic** [-trɔpik; -trɑpɪk] *a*.

an·i·so·trop·ic [ænˌaisəuˈtrɔpik; ænˏaɪsoˋtrɑpɪk] *a*. 1.【植】对外界刺激有不同反应的。2.【物】各向异性的。**an·i·sot·ro·py** [ˌænaiˈsɔtrəpi; ˏænaiˋsɑtrəpɪ], **an·i·sot·ro·pism** [-pizm; -pɪzm] *n*. **an·i·so·trop·i·cal·ly** *ad*.

A·ni·ta [əˈniːtə; əˋnitə] *n*. 安妮塔〔女子名, Ann 的昵称〕。

An·ka·ra [ˈæŋkərə; ˋɑŋkərə] *n*. 安卡拉〔土耳其首都〕。

an·ker [ˈæŋkə; ˋæŋkɚ] *n*. 安克〔荷兰液量名,约 10 加仑〕。

an·ker·ite [ˈæŋkərait; ˋæŋkəˏraɪt] *n*.【矿】铁白云石。

ankh [æŋk; æŋk] *n*. T 型十字(章)〔古埃及生命的象征〕。

an·kle [ˈæŋkl; ˋæŋkl] **I** *n*. 踝;踝节部,脚脖子。**II** *vi*. 〔美俚〕走,走路。~ **bone** 踝骨。~ **boot** 高帮鞋。~**-deep** *a*., *ad*. 深及踝部的〔地〕。

an·klet [ˈæŋklit; ˋæŋklɪt] *n*. 1. 踝环,脚镯。2. 〔*pl*.〕翻

A

口短袜,套袜。3. 带踝襻的女鞋。

an·kus [ˈæŋkəs; ˋæŋkəs] ***n.*** (有尖钉和钩的)驱象刺棒。

an·ky·lo·saur [ˈæŋkələuˌsɔː; ˋæŋkəloˏsɔr] ***n.*** 甲龙亚目动物。

an·ky·lose [ˈæŋkiləus; ˋæŋkəˏlos] ***vt.*** **1.** 使(骨)长合。**2.** 使(关节)僵硬。—***vi.*** **1.** (骨与骨)长合。**2.** (关节)变僵硬。

an·ky·lo·sis [ˌæŋkaiˈləusis; ˏæŋkəˋlosɪs] ***n.*** = anchylosis.

an·ky·los·to·mi·a·sis [ˌæŋkaiˌlɔstəˈmaiəsis; ˏæŋkəˏlɑstəˋmaɪəsɪs] ***n.*** 钩虫病。

an·lace [ˈænlis; ˋænlɪs] ***n.*** (中世纪的)双刃短剑。

an·la·ge [ˈɑːnlɑːgə; ˋɑnlɑgə] ***n.*** (*pl.* ***-gen*** [-gən; gən], ~***s*** [-gəz; -gəz]) **1.** 后期发展的基础;基础。**2.**【胚】原基。

Ann [æn; æn] ***n.*** 安〔女子名〕。

ann. = **1.** 〔L.〕*anni* (= years). **2.** annals. **3.** annual. **4.** annuity.

An·na [æˈnə; ˋænə] ***n.*** 安娜〔女子名,Ann 的异体〕。

an·na [æˈnə; ˋænə] ***n.*** 安娜〔印度旧币名,一卢比(rupee) 的十六分之一〕。*have eight ~s of dark blood* 〔口〕对半混血。

An·na·bel·la [ˌænəˈbelə; ˏænəˋbɛlə] ***n.*** 安娜贝拉〔女子名〕。

an·na·berg·ite [ˈænəˈbəːgait; ˋænəˋbɝgaɪt] ***n.*** 镍华。

an·nal [ˈænəl; ˋænl] ***n.*** 〔古〕纪要,纪事录。

an·nal·ist [ˈænəlist; ˋænlɪst] ***n.*** 编年史作者,年表编者。

an·nal·ist·ic [ˌænəˈlistik; ˏænəˋlɪstɪk] ***a.*** 编年史的;按年代编辑的。

an·nals [ˈænəlz; ˋænlz] ***n.*** *pl.* **1.** 编年史。**2.** 年代记,年表,年鉴,年刊。**3.** 历史记载。*the ~ of war* 战史。*the ~ of the publisher's association* 出版家协会的年刊。

An·nap·o·lis [əˈnæpəlis; əˋnæpəlɪs] ***n.*** 安纳波利斯〔美国港市〕。

an·nat·to [əˈnɑːtəu; əˋnɑto] ***n.*** 胭脂树红,果红〔用做食品着色剂〕。

Anne [æn; æn] ***n.*** **1.** 安妮〔女子名〕。**2.** 英国女王〔1702—1714 年在位〕。*Queen ~ is dead.* 〔古〕陈旧的消息。

an·neal [əˈniːl; əˋnil] ***vt.*** **1.**【冶】使韧化,使退火,使焖火。**2.** 〔喻〕锻炼(意志)。**3.** 〔古〕(在窑里)烧,给…上釉。

an·nec·tent, an·nec·tant [əˈnektənt; əˋnɛktənt] ***n.*** 【生】连接的。

an·ne·lid [ˈænəlid; ˋænlɪd] ***n.***【动】环虫,蠕虫,环节动物。

An·nel·i·da [əˈnelidə; əˋnɛlɪdə] ***n.*** *pl.*【动】环节动物门。

an·nel·i·dan [əˈnelidən; əˋnɛlɪdən] ***n.***, ***a.*** 环节动物(的)。

An·net·ta [əˈnetə; əˋnɛtə] ***n.*** 安妮塔〔女子名, Ann 的昵称〕。

An·nette [əˈnet; əˋnɛt] ***n.*** 安妮特〔女子名, Ann 的昵称〕。

an·nex [əˈneks; əˋnɛks] **I** ***vt.*** **1.** 附加,添加,追加;附带(条件) (*to*)。**2.** 签署,盖(印)。**3.** 合并,并吞,兼并(领土) (*to*)。**4.** 获得,得到。**5.** 擅自拿走,偷。*a protocol ~ed to the treaty* 附加于条约的议定书。*The manager ~ed his seal to the document.* 经理在文件上盖印。*~ the honors* [*laurels*] 〔美〕竞赛获胜,得锦标。**II** [ˈæneks; ˋænɛks] ***n.*** **1.** 附录,附件;附属品。**2.** 附属建筑。*an ~ to a hotel* 旅馆的增建部分。

an·nex·a·tion [ˌænekˈseiʃən; ˏænɛkˋseʃən] ***n.*** **1.** 附加。**2.** 合并,归并,吞并。**3.** 附加物,吞并物。

An·nie [ˈæni; ˋænɪ] ***n.*** 安妮〔女子名, Ann 的昵称〕。~ **Oakley** [ˈəukli; ˋoklɪ] 〔口〕优待券,免费入场券。

an·ni·hi·la·ble [əˈnaiələbl; əˋnaɪələbl] ***a.*** 可歼灭的;可消灭的。

an·ni·hi·late [əˈnaiəleit; əˋnaɪəˏlet] ***vt.*** **1.** 消灭,歼灭。**2.** 废止(法律)。**3.** 彻底打败。**4.**【物】使(一个核粒子及另一反粒子)湮灭。*annihilating operation* 歼灭战。*The home basketball team ~d the visiting team.* 本地篮球队大败客队。

an·ni·hi·la·tion [əˌnaiəˈleiʃən; əˏnaɪəˋleʃən] ***n.*** **1.** 绝灭,消灭,歼灭。**2.**【物】湮灭。**3.**【神学】灵魂与肉体的毁灭。**-ism** ***n.***【宗】灵魂寂灭论〔认为作恶者死后灵魂必归毁灭〕。

an·ni·hi·la·tor [əˈnaiəleitə; əˋnaɪəˏletɚ] ***n.*** **1.** 消灭者,歼灭者。**2.** 灭火器。**3.**【数】零化子。**4.**【空】减震器,阻尼器。

an·ni·ver·sa·ry [ˌæniˈvəːsəri; ˏænəˋvɝsərɪ] **I** ***a.*** **1.** 年年的,每年的。**2.** 周年的;周年纪念的。*The celebration is an ~ affair.* 庆祝会年年举行。*an ~ gift* 周年纪念礼物。**II** ***n.*** 周年纪念(日)。*a wedding ~* 结婚周年纪念。~ ***of sb.'s birth*** 生日。~ ***of sb.'s death*** 忌日,逝世纪念日。

An·no Do·mi·ni [ˈænəu ˈdɔminai; ˋænoˋdɑmənaɪ] 〔L.〕**1.** 公元〔略 A.D.〕〔*cf. B.C.*〕。**2.** 〔口、谑〕衰龄,老年。*A.D. is his trouble.* 他衰老了。*the Anno Domini clause* 〔谑〕年老退职制度。

An·no He·gi·rae [ˈænəu hiˈdʒairiː; ˋæno hɪˋdʒaɪri] 〔L.〕伊斯兰教纪元。

an·no mun·di [ˈænəu ˈmʌndai; ˋæno ˋmʌndaɪ] 〔L.〕开天辟地以来,世界纪元〔略 A.M.〕。

an·no·tate [ˈænəuteit; ˋænoˏtet] ***vt.***, ***vi.*** 注解,注释。*an ~d edition* 注释版。**-ta·tion** [-ˈteiʃən; -ˋteʃən] ***n.*** **-ta·tor** ***n.*** 注释者。

an·nounce [əˈnauns; əˋnaʊns] ***vt.*** **1.** 告知,报知,通告。**2.** 宣布,宣告,发表;唱名报(客等);通知(开宴等)。**3.** 预告;显示。**4.** 当(节目的)报幕员[广播员]。*~ a call* (长途电话)接通通知。*~ a new edition* 登新书广告。*~ a visitor* 通报有客。*It has been semiofficially ~d that ...* 据半官方消息。*~ a lecture series* 宣告有一系列讲演。*The servant ~d Mr. and Mrs. Smith.* 仆人唱名报告"史密斯先生和夫人到"。*~ dinner* 通知开宴[饭]。*He ~s three programmes a week.* 他每星期播送三个节目。— ***vi.*** **1.** 做报幕员[广播员]。**2.** 宣布参加竞选 (*for*)。**3.** 宣布支持某人 (*for*)。*He ~d for governor.* 他宣布竞选州长。

an·nounce·ment [əˈnaunsmənt; əˋnaʊnsmənt] ***n.*** **1.** 通告,布告,宣告,预告,声明。**2.** 宣布的行动[过程]。**3.** 言谈。*Every new ~ of hers was greeted with shouts of laughter.* 她说的每一句话都引起哄堂大笑。*an ~ of marriage* 结婚通告。

an·nounc·er [əˈnaunsə; əˋnaʊnsɚ] ***n.*** **1.** 宣告者。**2.** (电视,电台)播音员;(戏剧等的)报幕员;(比赛等的)解说员。

an·noy [əˈnɔi; əˋnɔɪ] **I** ***vt.*** 惹恼,打搅;使烦恼。*A fly keeps ~ing me.* 一个苍蝇老在打搅我。*I was much ~ed with him.* 我被那家伙缠死了。**II** ***n.*** 〔诗、罕〕= annoyance.

an·noy·ance [əˈnɔiəns; əˋnɔɪəns] ***n.*** **1.** 烦恼,为难;麻烦。**2.** 烦恼的事情。***put*** (*sb.*) ***to ~*** 使(人)烦恼,为难,打搅。***to one's ~*** 为难的是,烦恼的是。

an·noy·ing [əˈnɔiiŋ; əˋnɔɪɪŋ] ***a.*** 令人烦恼的,令人厌烦的,令人讨厌的。*How ~!* 多讨厌! 真讨厌! **-ly** ***ad.***

an·nu·al [ˈænjuəl; ˋænjʊəl] **I** ***a.*** **1.** 每年的;年度的;一年(一次)的。**2.** (植物)一年一生的,一季生的。*an ~ report* 年报。**II** ***n.*** **1.** 一年生[一季生]植物。**2.** 年刊,年报,年鉴。~ **expenditure** [**revenue**] 岁出[入]。~ **ring**【植】年轮。~ **plant** 一年生植物。**-ly** ***ad.*** 年年,每年。

an·nu·i·tant [əˈnju(ː)itənt; əˋnjuətənt] ***n.*** 领年金者。

an·nu·i·ty [əˈnju(ː)iti; əˋnuətɪ] ***n.*** 年金。*a contingent* [*life, terminable*] ~ 临时[终身、定期]年金。

an·nul [əˈnʌl; əˋnʌl] *vt*. 取消(命令),废除,注销。*The treaty was annulled*. 条约废除了。

an·nu·lar [ˈænjulə; ˋænjələ˞] *a*. 环的;环状的,轮状的,有环纹的。~ **eclipse**【天】环蚀。~ **saw** 圆锯,钢丝锯。**-ly** *ad*. 环状地。

an·nu·late, an·nu·lat·ed [ˈænjuleit(id); ˋænjə͵let(ɪd)] *a*. **1**. 有环的,有环纹的。**2**. 由环构成的。

an·nu·la·tion [ˌænjuˈleiʃən; ͵ænjəˋleʃən] *n*. **1**. 成环,成环状。**2**. 环,环状物。

an·nu·let [ˈænjulit; ˋænjəlɪt] *n*. **1**. 小环。**2**.【动】小节。**3**.【建】圆箍线。

an·nul·ment [əˈnʌlmənt; əˋnʌlmənt] *n*. 取消,废止,作废,注销。

an·nu·loid [ˈænjulɔid; ˋænjulɔɪd], **an·nu·lose** [ˈænjuləus; ˋænju͵los] *a*. 有环的,有环节的。

an·nu·lus [ˈænjuləs; ˋænjələs] *n*. (*pl*. *-li* [-lai; ͵laɪ], *~es*) **1**. 环(带),环节,环轮。**2**.【动】体环;菌环。**3**.【天】环食带。**4**.【数】圆环域。

an·num [ˈænəm; ˋænəm] *n*. [L.]年。*per* ~ 每年。

an·nun·ci·ate [əˈnʌnʃieit; əˋnʌnʃɪ͵et] *vt*. [罕]公布,通告。

an·nun·ci·a·tion [əˌnʌnsiˈeiʃən; ə͵nʌnsɪˋeʃən] *n*. **1**. 通告,公布。**2**. [the A-]【宗】天使报喜[指天使加布里埃尔预告圣母玛利亚,她将生育耶稣]。**3**. 天使报喜节[三月二十五日]。~ **lily** 白百合花。

an·nun·ci·a·tor [əˈnʌnʃieitə; əˋnʌnʃɪ͵etə˞] *n*. **1**. 通告者。**2**. [美]信号器。*alarm* ~ 警报信号器。

a·no·a [əˈnəuə; əˋnoə] *n*. (印度尼西亚西里伯岛上的)小野牛。

an·ode [ˈænəud; ˋænod] *n*.【电】阳极,正极,板极。**a·nod·ic** [əˈnɔdik; ænˋɑdɪk] *a*.

an·o·dize [ˈænəudaiz; ˋæno͵daɪz] *vt*. 对…作阳极化处理,阳极电镀。

an·o·dyne [ˈænəudain; ˋænə͵daɪn] **I** *a*. 止痛的。**II** *n*. 止痛药[剂]。

an·o·e·sis [ˌænəuˈiːsis; ͵ænəˋisɪs] *n*. 纯被动的意识。

an·oes·trum [ænˈestrəm; ænˋestrəm] *n*.【动】非发情期间(*opp*. oestrum)。

a·noint [əˈnɔint; əˋnɔɪnt] *vt*. **1**. 给…涂油,在(伤口上)涂油。**2**.【宗】涂油使神圣化。**3**. 照天意选定。***the (Lord's) Anointed*** **1**. 救世主,基督。**2**. 神权国王,古犹太王。**-ment** *n*. 涂油。

an·o·lyte [ˈænəlait; ˋænəlaɪt] *n*. 阳极电解液。

a·nom·a·lism [əˈnɔməlizəm; əˋnɑml͵ɪzəm] *n*. [罕] = anomaly.

a·nom·a·lis·tic [əˌnɔməˈlistik; ə͵nɑmlˋɪstɪk] *a*. **1**. 异常的,不规则的。**2**.【天】近点的。~ **month**【天】近点月[约 27½ 日]。~ **year**【天】近点年[365 日 6 时 13 分 53 秒]。**-cal·ly** *ad*.

a·nom·a·lous [əˈnɔmələs; əˋnɑmələs] *a*. 不规则的,异常的,反常的。~ **(finite) verb**【语法】特殊既定式动词[指 be, ought, dare, can, shall 等在否定句和疑问句中用法与助动词相同的二十四个动词形式]。**-ly** *ad*. **-ness** *n*.

a·nom·a·lure [əˈnɔməljuə; əˋnaməljur] *n*.【动】鳞尾松鼠(= scaletailed squirrel)。

a·nom·a·ly [əˈnɔməli; əˋnɑməlɪ] *n*. **1**. 不规则,反常(现象),异常,破格。**2**. 畸形物。【天】近点角[指行星偏离近日点的角度距离]。*the* ~ *of English spelling* 英语拼写法的不规则。*gravity* ~【物】重力异常。*A hare-lipped monkey is an* ~. 豁嘴的猴子是异常的东西。

an·o·mie, an·o·my [ˈænəmi; ˋæməmɪ] *n*. (社会)反常状态;混乱;(不顾准则和法纪的)无法无天行为。

an·o·mite [ˈænəmait; ˋænəmaɪt] *n*.【矿】褐云母。

anomo- *comb*. *f*. 表示"不规则的"。

a·non [əˈnɔn; əˋnɑn] *ad*. [古] **1**. 即刻,立即。**2**. 不久。**3**. 下次再。*and* ~ 时或。*ever and* ~ 时时。*About that, more* ~. 关于此事,容当他日言及。

anon. = anonymous.

an·o·nym [ˈænənim; ˋænə͵nɪm] *n*. **1**. 匿名(作)者,无名氏。**2**. 假名。

an·o·nym·i·ty [ˌænəˈnimiti; ͵ænəˋnɪmətɪ] *n*. 匿名,无名。*men hiding behind* ~ 隐姓埋名的人。

a·non·y·mous [əˈnɔniməs; əˋnɑnəməs] *a*. **1**. 匿名的;无名的;假名的。**2**. 无个性特征的。*an* ~ *author* 无名氏作者。*an* ~ *letter* 匿名信。*an* ~ *placard* 无名告示。~ *faces* 生面孔。**-ly** *ad*. **-ness** *n*.

a·noph·e·les [əˈnɔfiliːz; əˋnɑfə͵liz] *n*.【动】疟蚊属。~ **mosquito** 疟纹。

a·no·rak [ˈɑːnərɑːk; ˋɑnə͵rɑk] *n*. (严寒地带人所穿)带风帽的厚茄克,皮猴。

an·o·rex·i·a [ˌænəuˈreksiə; ͵ænəˋrɛksɪə] *n*.【医】食欲缺乏,厌食。~ **nervosa** 神经性食欲缺乏。

an·or·thite [əˈnɔːθait; əˋnɔrθaɪt] *n*. 钙长石。**-thit·ic** [-ˈθitik; -ˋθɪtɪk] *a*.

an·os·mi·a [æˈnɔsmiə; ænˋɑsmɪə] *n*.【医】嗅觉缺失。

an·oth·er [əˈnʌðə; əˋnʌðə˞] **I** *a*. **1**. 又一,另一。**2**. 别的,另外的。**3**. 类似的。*Will you have* ~ *cup*? 再来一杯好吗? *One man's meat is* ~ *man's poison*. [谚]利于甲者(可能)不利于乙。*I'll come to see you at* ~ *time*. 改日再来看你。*He may be* ~ *Edison*. 他可能成为爱迪生那样的人物。**II** *pron*. **1**. 另一件东西,另一个人。**2**. 别的东西,别的人。**3**. 那样的人[东西],同样的人[东西] *X versus Y and* ~【法】某甲对某乙及另外一人的案件[不指出第三者真名时的说法]。*Have* ~, *please*. 请再吃一个。*Liar! — You're* ~! 撒谎的家伙!——你就是这种人! ~ ***day*** 他日,改天。~ ***day or two*** 再过一两天。~ ***place*** 别处,另外一处[(英)在下院时是指上院、在上院时是指下院而言]。~ ***thing*** [***question***] 另一回事,另一个(问题)。~ ***time*** 下次。~ ***world*** 来世;天国。***in*** ~ ***moment*** 过一会儿。***one after*** ~ 相继,顺次。***one*** ~ 相互。***one way and*** ~ 用种种方法。***one way or*** ~ 设法,无论如何。***such*** ~ (另一个)那样的人或东西;无独有偶的人[事、物](*You will never see such* ~. 那样的人恐怕再看不到了。*It's just such* ~. 这真是无独有偶)。***taken one with*** ~ 从大体上说,大体上,总的看来。

an·our·ous, an·u·rous [əˈnuərəs; əˋnorəs] *a*.【动】无尾的。

an·ox·e·mi·a [ˌænɔkˈsiːmiə; ͵ænɑksˋimɪə] *n*.【医】血缺氧,缺氧血症。**-mic** [-mik; -mɪk] *a*.

an·ox·i·a [æˈnɔksiə; æˋnɑksɪə] *n*.【医】缺氧症。

an·ox·ic [æˈnɔksik; ænˋɑksɪk] *a*.【医】缺氧的。

ans. = answer.

ANSA = [It.] *Agenzia Nazionale Stampa Associata* [意]安莎通讯社(= Associated National Press Agency)。

an·sa [ˈænsə; ˋænsə] *n*. (*pl*. ***an·sae*** [-siː; -si])【解】襻,脊神经。

an·sate [ˈænseit; ˋænset] *a*. 有柄的,有把手的。

An·schluss [ˈɑːnʃlus; ˋɑnʃlus] *n*. [G.] **1**. (政治或经济的)联合,结合。**2**. (1938 年纳粹德国对奥地利的)吞并。

An·selm [ˈænselm; ˋænsɛlm] *n*. 安塞尔姆[男子名]。

an·ser·ine [ˈænsərain; ˋænsə͵raɪn], **an·ser·ous** [ˈænsərəs; ˋænsərəs] **I** *a*. **1**. 鹅(似)的。**2**. 愚蠢的。**II** *n*.【化】鹅肌肽。

an·swer [ˈɑːnsə; ˋænsə˞] **I** *n*. **1**. 回答,答复。**2**. 解答,答案。**3**. 答辩,抗辩。**4**. 报复。*an* ~ *to a question* 某问题的解答。*have no* ~ *to* (*sb*.*'s letter*) 无回音[回信]。***in*** ~ ***to*** …以回答,为答复(抗议等)而。***one who knows all the*** ~***s*** [美俚]万事通;老世故。***The*** ~***'s a lemon***. [回答荒唐提问时用语]你这个(可笑的)问题,无法回答;废话! **II** *vt*. **1**. 答,回答,答复;答应。**2**. 解答,答辩。**3**. 报复。**4**. 适合;符合。**5**. 尽(责),偿(债)。**6**. 响应。~ *a*

A

charge 对控告做出答辩。～ *a debt* 偿还债务。～ *a letter* 回信。～ *a riddle* 解谜。～ *blows with blows* 以眼还眼,以牙还牙。～ *the bell* [*door*] 应声开门。— ***vi***. **1.** 回答;答辩,辩解。**2.** 负责,保证;抵偿。**3.** 适合;符合,一致。**4.** 见效,成功。～ (*to*) *the purpose of*... 可用作…。*Gypsum ～s as manure*. 石膏可作肥料。*Everything ～ed*. 事事顺利[如愿]。～ **back** 〔卑〕顶嘴,还口。～ ***for*** 负…的责任,保证;偿(罪),负责(受处分);代(被问人)回答(*I'll ～ for her safety*. 我将为她的安全负责。～ *for a crime* 负罪责。*I won't ～ for what I'll be doing*. 我就老实不客气了)。～ ***to*** 回答;符合。～ ***to the name of*** 叫做,名叫(*The dog ～s to the name of John*. 这只狗叫做约翰)。～ ***up*** 应答快(～ *up to a question* 立刻回答问题)。～**phone**〔主英〕电话答录机。

an·swer·a·ble [ˈɑːnsərəbl; ˋænsərəbl] ***a***. **1.** 可答复的;应答辩的。**2.** 应负责的;应抵偿的。**3.** 适合的,相当的。～ *for an act* 为某行为负责。～ *for damages* 有赔偿损害的责任。～ ***to*** 对(某人)有责任;适合(目的)(*the government ～ to the people* 对人民负责的政府。*achievements ～ to expectation* 与希望相符的收获)。

an·swer·ing [ˈɑːnsəriŋ; ˋænsərɪŋ] **I** ***a***. 回答的;适当的;符合…的。*a person ～ to this description* 和相貌说明书相符的人。*an ～ pennant* 应答旗〔国际船舶用以表示已收到信号〕。**II** ***n***. 回答。～ **machine** 电话答录机。～ **service** 代客接听电话服务。

ant [ænt; ænt] ***n***. 蚂蚁。***have ～s in one's pants*** (因焦急,气愤等而)坐立不安,急于采取行动。～ **bear**【动】大食蚁兽。～ **cow** 蚜虫。～ **eater** 食蚁兽(*the scaly ～ eater* 穿山甲)。～ **hill** 蚁冢;人口稠密的地方。～ **lion**【虫】沙挼子,蚁狮〔蛟蜻蛉科幼虫〕。

ant- *pref*. 用于母音前。= *anti-*.

an't [ɑːnt; ænt] **1.** 〔口〕= are not. **2.** 〔英口〕am not. **3.** 〔方、卑〕= is not, has not, have not.

ant. = **1.** antenna. **2.** antiquarian. **3.** antiquities. **4.** antonym.

-ant *suf*. **1.** …性的: stimul*ant*. **2.** …的人〔物〕; serv*ant*. stimul*ant*.

an·ta [ˈæntə; ˋæntə] ***n***. (*pl*. **-tae** [-tiː; ti], **～s**) 〔L.〕【建】壁端柱。

ant·ac·id [ˈæntˈæsid; æntˋæsɪd] **I** ***a***. 中和酸的,解酸的。**II** ***n***. 【医】解酸剂;抗酸剂。

An·tae·us [ænˈtiəs; ænˋtɪəs] ***n***. 【希神】安泰〔大力士,大地之子,只要不离开其母大地就不能战胜〕。**-tae·an** ***a***.

an·tag·o·nism [ænˈtægənizəm; ænˋtægə͵nɪzəm] ***n***. **1.** 敌对,对立。**2.** 相克作用,对抗(作用),对抗性。～ *of the oppressed against* [*to*] *the oppressor* 被压迫者对压迫者的敌视[仇视]。*the ～ between capital and labor* 劳资间的对立。***be brought into ～ with = come into ～ with*** 和…闹翻脸。***in ～ to*** 反对,对抗。

an·tag·o·nist [ænˈtægənist; ænˋtægənɪst] ***n***. **1.** 敌手,反对者;对抗者。**2.**【解】对抗肌,拮抗肌。**3.**【医】对抗剂。**4.**【解】对合牙。**5.** (戏剧、小说等的)反面人物(*opp*. protagonist)。

an·tag·o·nis·tic, -ti·cal [æn͵tægəˈnistik, -tikəl; æn͵tægəˋnɪstɪk, -tɪkəl] ***a***. 对抗(性)的,敌对的,相反的,不相容的。*Cats and dogs are ～*. 狗和猫是敌对的。**-ti·cal·ly *ad***. 反对地,敌对地,翻起脸来。

an·tag·o·nize [ænˈtægənaiz; ænˋtægə͵naɪz] ***vt***. **1.** 反抗,对抗。**2.** 引起…的对抗。**3.** 中和,抵销。**4.** 招…的怨。*His speech ～d many voters*. 他的发言引起许多投票者的不满。～ *a bill* 反对某项议案。— ***vi***. 引起对抗,招怨。

ant·al·ka·li [æntˈælkəlai; æntˋælkə͵laɪ] ***n***. (*pl*. **-li(e)s**) 解碱剂。

ant·aph·ro·dis·i·ac [͵æntæfrəˈdiziæk; ͵æntæfrəˋdɪzɪæk] ***a***. 抑制性欲的,制欲的。**II** ***n***. 【医】制欲药。

ant·arc·tic [ænˈtɑːktik; æntˋɑrktɪk] **I** ***a***. 南极(地方)的。**II** ***n***. 南极(地带)。*the A- Circle* 南极圈。*the A- Ocean* 南冰洋。*the A- Zone* 南极地带。

Ant·arc·ti·ca [ænˈtɑːktikə; æntˋɑrktɪkə] ***n***. 南极洲。

An·tar·es [ænˈtɛəriːz; ænˋtɛriz] ***n***. 【天】心宿二,大火〔天蝎座 α〕。

an·te [ˈænti; ˋæntɪ] **I** ***n***. **1.**【牌】预下的赌注。**2.**〔口〕(应摊的)份子。**II** ***vt***. (**-ted**, **-teed**; **-te·ing**) **1.** 预下(赌注)。**2.**〔口〕拿出(钱,意见等);出(份子) (*up*)。*He ～d up his half of the bill*. 他付了该他分担的一半账单。～ *up ideas* 提出想法。

an·te- *pref*. …前的,较…前的: *ante*cedent, *ante*room.

an·te·bel·lum [͵æntiˈbeləm; ˋæntɪˋbɛləm] ***a***. 〔L.〕战前的;〔美〕南北战争前的。～ *days* 战前时代。*the ～ South* 战前的南方。

an·te·cede [͵æntiˈsiːd; ͵æntəˋsid] ***vt***. 在…之前;居…之先。*Shakespeare ～s Milton*. 莎士比亚在密尔顿之前。

an·te·ced·ence [͵æntiˈsiːdəns; ͵æntəˋsidəns] ***n***. **1.** 先行,居先。**2.**【天】逆行。

an·te·ced·ent [͵æntiˈsiːdənt; ͵æntəˋsidənt] **I** ***a***. **1.** 先行的,先前的。**2.**【逻】假定的,前提的。**3.**【地】先成的。**II** ***n***. **1.** 先例,前例。**2.**〔*pl*.〕经历,履历,学历。**3.**〔*pl*.〕祖先。**4.**【语法】先行词。**5.**【逻】前提,前件。**6.**【数】(比例的)前项〔如 a:b 中的 a〕。*inquire into sb.'s ～s* 调查某人履历。*a man of shady ～s* 来历可疑的人。*～s and consequences of the war* 战争的前因和后果。*of English ～s* 祖籍英国。**-ly *ad*** 在前,在先。

an·te·ces·sor [͵æntiˈsesə; ͵æntəˋsesɚ] ***n***. **1.** 先行者,先驱者,前任。**2.**〔罕〕祖先。

an·te·cham·ber [ˈæntiˌtʃeimbə; ˋæntɪ͵tʃembɚ] ***n***. 接待室;前堂,前厅。

an·te·chap·el [ˈæntiˌtʃæpəl; ˋæntɪ͵tʃæpl] ***n***. 教堂门厅。

an·te·choir [ˈæntiˌkwaiə; ˋæntɪ͵kwaɪr] ***n***. (教堂的)唱诗台。

an·te·date [ˈæntiˈdeit; ˋæntɪ͵det,͵æntɪˋdet] **I** ***n***. 比实际早些的日期。**II** ***vt***. **1.** 把…上的日期填早(若干时间)。**2.** 把…说早;使提前。**3.** 前于,先于。～ *a letter by a week* 把信上日期填早一星期。*The cold weather ～d their departure*. 寒冷的天气使他们提前离开。*His death ～d his brother's*. 他去世先于他的兄弟。

an·te·di·lu·vi·an [͵æntidiˈljuːviən; ͵æntɪdɪˋljuvɪən] **I** ***a***. **1.** (《圣经》所说的)大洪水以前的。**2.** 上古的,古风的,古老的,原始的。*an ～ automobile* 古老的汽车。**II** ***n***. **1.** 大洪水以前的人。**2.** 老朽,时代落伍者。

an·te·fix [ˈæntiˈfiks; ˋæntɪˋfɪks] ***n***. (*pl*. **～es**)【建】檐口饰。**-al *a***.

an·te·lope [ˈæntiləup; ˋæntl͵op] ***n***. (*pl*. **～(s)**) **1.** 羚羊。**2.** 羚羊皮。**3.**〔美〕叉角羚(= pronghorn)。

an·te·me·rid·i·an [ˈæntiməˈridiən; ͵æntɪməˋrɪdɪən] ***a***. 午前的。

an·te me·ri·di·em [ˈænti meˈridiem; ˋæntɪ məˋrɪdɪ͵ɛm] 〔L.〕午前,上午〔略 A.M. 或 a. m.〕〔*cf*. P.M.〕。

an·te·mor·tem [ˈæntiˈmɔːtəm; ˋæntɪˋmɔrtəm] ***a***. 〔L.〕死前的。*an ～ confession* 临终忏悔。

an·te·mun·dane [͵æntiˈmʌndein; ˋæntɪˋmʌnden] ***a***. 世界创造前的,开天辟地以前的。

an·te·na·tal [ˈæntiˈneitl; ͵æntɪˋnetl] ***a***. 胎儿的,出生前的,产前的。～ *training* 胎教。*an ～ life* 母胎内的生命。

an·ten·na [ænˈtenə; ænˋtɛnə] ***n***. (*pl*. **-nae** [-niː; -ni], **～s**) **1.**【动】触角。**2.**【无】天线〔英国常用 aerial〕。～ **array**【无】天线阵。**-l** [-nəl; -nəl], **-ry** [-ri; -rɪ] ***a***.

an·te·nup·tial [ˈæntiˈnʌpʃəl; ͵æntɪˋnʌpʃəl] ***a***. 结婚前的。

an·te·pen·di·um [͵æntiˈpendiəm; ͵æntɪˋpɛndɪəm] ***n***. **1.** (教堂祭坛前的)帷幔,缎帐。**2.** (教堂布道讲坛上的)

A

桌布。

an·te·pe·nult [ˈæntipiˈnʌlt; ˌæntɪpɪˋnʌlt] ***n.***, ***a.*** 倒数第三音节(的)〔如 accumulate 中的 cu〕。

an·te·pe·nul·ti·mate [ˈæntipiˈnʌltimit; ˌæntɪpɪˋnʌltəmɪt] ***n.***, ***a.*** **1.** 倒数第三音节(的)。**2.** 倒数第三个(的)。

an·te·pran·di·al [ˈæntiˈprændjəl; ˌæntɪˋprændɪəl] ***a.*** 正餐前的,饭前的。

an·te·ri·or [ænˈtiəriə; ænˋtɪrɪɚ] ***a.*** (*opp.* posterior) **1.** 以前的,先前的;先存在的 (*to*)。**2.** 前面的,前部的 (*to*). *an ~ age* 早期。*age ~ to the flood* 洪水以前的时期。**-i·ty** [ænˌtiəriˈɔriti; ænˌtɪrɪˋɔrətɪ] ***n.*** 先前;原先。**-ly** ***ad.*** 在以前;在前面。

an·te·room [ˈæntirum; ˋæntɪˌrʊm] ***n.*** 接待室,休息室,前室。

an·te·ty·pe [ˈæntitaip; ˋæntɪˌtaɪp] ***n.*** 前型,原型。

an·te·ver·sion [ˌæntiˈvəːʃən, -ʒən; ˌæntɪˋvɝʃən, -ʒən] ***n.*** 【医】子宫前倾。

an·te·vert [ˌæntiˈvəːt; ˌæntɪˋvɝt] ***vt.*** 【医】引起…前倾。

ant·he·li·on [ænˈθiːljən; ænˋθilɪən] ***n.*** 【气】反假日,幻日。

ant·hel·min·tic [ˌænθelˈmintik; ˌænθəlˋmɪntɪk] **I** ***a.*** 驱肠虫的。**II** ***n.*** 驱肠虫剂。

an·them [ˈænθəm; ˋænθəm] ***a.*** **1.** 圣歌,赞歌。**2.** 国歌。**3.** 校歌。*a national ~* 国歌。*the Royal Anthem* 英国国歌。

an·the·mi·on [ænˈθiːmiən; ænˋθɪmɪən] ***n.*** (*pl.* ***-mi·a*** [-ə; -ə]) 花状平纹,叶状平纹〔绘画、雕刻中的装饰〕。

an·ther [ˈænθə; ˋænθɚ] ***n.*** 【植】花药,花粉囊。~ **dust** 花粉。~ **sac** 花粉囊。~ **stalk** 花丝。

an·ther·id·i·um [ˌænθəˈridiəm; ˌænθəˋrɪdɪəm] ***n.*** (*pl.* ***-idi·a*** [-ə; -ə])【植】(隐花植物如苔,蕨等的)精子囊,雄器;精子器。**-id·i·al** ***a.***

an·ther·o·zo·id [ˌænθərəˈzəuid; ˌænθərəˋzoɪd] ***n.*** 【植】(隐花植物如苔、蕨等的)游动精子。

an·the·sis [ænˈθiːsis; ænˋθisɪs] ***n.*** 开花;开花期。

an·tho·car·pous [ˌænθəˈkɑːpəs; ˌænθəˋkɑrpəs] ***a.*** 【植】副生的;掺花果的。~ *fruit* 副果。

an·tho·cy·a·nin [ˌænθəˈsaiənin; ˌænθəˋsaɪənɪn], **an·tho·cy·an** [-ˈsaiən; -ˋsaɪən] ***n.*** 【化】花青苷,花色苷。

an·tho·di·um [ænˈθəudiəm; ænˋθodɪəm] ***n.*** (*pl.* ***-di·a*** [-ə; -ə]) 【植】集合花。

an·thol·o·gist [ænˈθɔlədʒist; ænˋθɑlədʒɪst] ***n.*** 文集编者;文选编者。

an·thol·o·gy [ænˈθɔlədʒi; ænˋθɑlədʒɪ] ***n.*** (诗、文、曲、画等)选集。

An·tho·ny [ˈæntəni, Am. -θəni; ˋæntənɪ, -θənɪ] ***n.*** 安东尼〔男子名〕。***St.*** ~ 圣安东尼〔猪倌的保护神〕。***St.*** *~'s fire* 【医】丹毒。~ **pig** 一胎中最小的仔猪。

an·thoph·i·lous [ænˈθɔfiləs; ænˋθɑfələs] ***a.*** (虫等)爱花的,栖息花上的,以花为食的。

an·tho·phore [ˈænθəˈfɔː; ˋænθəˌfɔr] ***n.*** 【植】花冠柄。

An·tho·zo·a [ˌænθəˈzəuə; ˌænθəˋzoə] ***n.*** 〔*pl.*〕【动】珊瑚虫纲。

an·tho·zo·an [ˌænθəˈzəuən; ˌænθəˋzoən] **I** ***n.*** 【动】珊瑚虫〔包括珊瑚、海葵、海团扇等〕。**II** ***a.*** 珊瑚虫的。~ **polyp** 珊瑚虫〔珊瑚水螅〕。

an·thra·cene [ˈænθrəsiːn; ˋænθrəsin] ***n.*** 【化】蒽。

an·thra·cite [ˈænθrəsait; ˋænθrəˌsaɪt] ***n.*** 无烟煤,硬煤。

an·thra·cit·ic [ˌænθrəˈsitik; ˌænθrəˋsɪtɪk] ***a.*** 无烟煤的;无烟煤似的。

an·thra·cit·ous [ˈænθrəsaitəs; ˋænθrəˌsaitəs] ***a.*** 含无烟煤的。

an·thrac·nose [ænˈθræknəus; ænˋθræknos] ***n.*** 【植】炭疽病。

an·thra·coid [ˈænθrəkɔid; ˋænθrəˌkɔɪd] ***a.*** 似炭疽的。

an·thrax [ˈænθræks; ˋænθræks] ***n.*** (*pl.* ***an·thra·ces*** [ˈænθrəsiːz; ˋænθrəsiz]) 【医】炭疽(病)。~ **bacillus** 炭疽杆菌。

an·thro·p(o)- *comb. f.* 表示"人,人类,人类学": *anthropo*geny.

an·thro·po·cen·tric [ˌænθrəpəuˈsentrik; ˌænθrəpəˋsɛntrɪk] ***a.*** **1.** 以人类为宇宙中心的。**2.** 按人类标准判断宇宙万物的。**-trism** [-trizəm; -trɪzəm] ***n.*** 人类中心说,人类本位说。

an·thro·po·gen·e·sis [ˌænθrəpəuˈdʒenisis; ˌænθrəpoˋdʒɛnəsɪs] ***n.*** 人类起源和发展学。

an·thro·pog·e·ny [ˌænθrəˈpɔdʒini; ˌænθrəˋpɑdʒənɪ] ***n.*** = anthropogenesis.

An·thro·pog·ra·phy [ˌænθrəˈpɔgrəfi; ˌænθrəˋpɑgrəfɪ] ***n.*** 人类地理分布学。

an·thro·poid [ˈænθrəupɔid; ˋænθroˌpɔɪd] **I** ***a.*** (猿等)似人类的。**II** ***n.*** 类人猿。

an·thro·po·log·ic, an·thro·po·log·i·cal [ænθrəpəˈlɔdʒik(əl); ænθrəpəˋlɑdʒɪk(əl)] ***a.*** 人类学(上)的。**-i·cal·ly** ***ad.*** 人类学上。

an·thro·pol·o·gist [ˌænθrəˈpɔlədʒist; ˌænθrəˋpɑlədʒɪst] ***n.*** 人类学者。

an·thro·pol·o·gy [ˌænθrəˈpɔlədʒi; ˌænθrəˋpɑlədʒɪ] ***n.*** 人类学。

an·thro·pom·e·try [ˌænθrəˈpɔmitri; ˌænθrəˋpɑmətrɪ] ***n.*** 人体测量(学)。

an·thro·po·mor·phism [ˌænθrəupəuˈmɔːfizəm; ˌænθrəpəˋmɔrfɪzəm] ***n.*** 拟人说,人格化〔使神仙、动物、非生物具有人的形状或特点〕。**-phic, -phic·al** ***a.***

an·thro·po·mor·phize [ˌænθrəupəuˈmɔːfaiz; ˌænθrəpəˋmɔrfaɪz] ***vt., vi.*** 赋与(…)人性[人形],(使)人格化。

an·thro·po·mor·phous [ˌænθəupəuˈmɔːfəs; ˌænθrəpəˋmɔrfəs] ***a.*** 有人形的,似人的。

an·thro·pop·a·thy [ˈænθrəˈpɔpəθi; ˋænθrəˋpɑpəθɪ] ***n.*** 神人同感论;神人同情说;上帝有人情之说。

an·thro·poph·a·gi [ˌænθrəuˈpɔfədʒai; ˌænθrəˋpɑfədʒaɪ] ***n.*** *pl.* (*sing.* ***-agus*** [-əgəs; -əgəs]) 食人肉的人。

an·thro·poph·a·gite [ˌænθrəuˈpɔfədʒait; ˌænθrəˋpɑfədʒaɪt] ***n.*** 吃人肉者;吃同类之肉的动物。

an·thro·poph·a·gous [ˌænθrəuˈpɔfəgəs; ˋænθrəˋpɑfəgəs] ***a.*** 吃人肉的。

an·thro·poph·a·gus [ˌænθrəuˈpɔfəgəs; ˌænθroˋpɑfəgəs] ***n.*** (*pl.* ***-gi*** [-dʒai; -dʒaɪ]) 食人肉的人〔此词一般多用其复数形式〕。

an·thro·poph·a·gy [ˌænθrəuˈpɔfədʒi; ˌænθrəˋpɑfədʒɪ] ***n.*** 嗜吃人肉,吃人习俗。

an·thro·po·so·ci·ol·o·gy [ˈænθrəuˌpəuˌsəusiˈɔlədʒi; ˋænθroˌpoˌsosɪˋɑlədʒɪ] ***n.*** 人类社会学。

an·thro·pot·o·my [ˌænθrəuˈpɔtəmi; ˌænθrəˋpɑtəmɪ] ***n.*** 人体解剖学。

an·thu·ri·um [ænˈθjuriəm; ænˋθjʊrɪəm] ***n.*** 天南星科,安修里昂属植物。

an·ti [ˈænti, ˈæntai; ˋæntɪ, ˋæntaɪ] **I** ***n.*** (*pl.* *~s*) 〔口〕反对者,反对派。*pros and ~s* 赞成派和反对派。*the ~ group* 反对派。**II** ***a.*** 唱反调,反对。*He is terribly ~.* 他爱唱反调。**III** ***prep.*** 反对。*He was ~ all that.* 凡此种种他都反对。

anti- *pref.* **1.** 反,排: *anti*alien, *anti*militarism. **2.** 伪,假: *anti*pope **3.** 对: *anti*type, *anti*thesis. **4.** 非: *anti*grammatical. **5.** 抗,阻,防: *anti*toxin, *anti*aircraft. **6.** 逆,正反对: *anti*cyclone, *anti*pole.

an·ti·air [ˈæntiˈɛə; ˋæntɪˋɛr] ***a.*** 〔口〕~ antiaircraft.

an·ti·air·craft [ˈæntiˈɛəkrɑːft; ˌæntɪˋɛrˌkræft] **I** ***a.*** 防空(用)的。**II** ***n.*** **1.** 高射炮。**2.** 高射炮部队。**3.** 高射炮炮火。~ **artillery** 高射炮队〔略 AAA〕。~ **control** 防空管制。~ **devices** 防空设备。~ **dug-out** 防空壕。~

A

gun 高射炮。

an·ti-alien [ˈæntiˈeiljən; ˏæntɪˋeljɛn] *a*. 排外的。

an·ti·a·part·heid [ˈæntiəˈpɑːthaid; ˏæntɪəˋpɑrthaɪd] *a*. 反(南非)种族隔离的。

an·ti·ar [ˈæntiɑː; ˋæntɪɑr] *n*. **1**. 见血封喉〔爪哇产植物〕。**2**. 见血封喉毒汁〔用来涂在箭头上〕。

an·ti·aux·in [ˈæntiˈɔːksin; ˋæntɪˋɔksɪn] *n*. 【生】抗生长素。

an·ti·bac·te·ri·al [ˈæntibækˈtiəriəl; ˏæntɪbækˋtɪrɪəl] **I** *a*. 抗细菌的。**II** *n*. 抗菌剂,抗菌物。

an·ti-bal·lis·tic [ˈæntibəˈlistik; ˏæntɪbəˋlɪstɪk] *a*. 反弹道的。~ **missile** 反弹道导弹。

an·ti·bar·y·on [ˈæntiˈbæriən; ˏæntɪˋbærɪən] *n*. 【物】反重子。

an·ti·bil·ious [ˈæntiˈbiljəs; ˋæntɪˋbɪljəs] *a*. 【医】抗胆病的。

an·ti·bi·o·sis [ˈæntibaiˈəusis; ˏæntɪbaɪˋosɪs] *n*. (*pl*. *-ses* [-siːz; -siz]) 【生】抗菌,抗生(现象)。

an·ti·bi·ot·ic [ˈæntibaiˈɔtik; ˏæntɪbaɪˋɑtɪk] **I** *a*. **1**. 破坏[伤害]生命的。**2**. 抗生的,抗菌的。**II** *n*. 抗生素。

an·ti·black [ˌæntiˈblæk; ˏæntɪˋblæk] *n*. 反黑人的。

an·ti·bod·y [ˈæntiˌbɔdi; ˋæntɪˏbɑdɪ] *n*. 【医】抗体。

an·tic [ˈæntik; ˋæntɪk] **I** *a*. **1**. 滑稽的,诙谐的。**2**. 〔古〕奇异的,古怪的。**II** *n*. 〔常 *pl*.〕 **1**. 滑稽动作,古怪行径。**2**. 〔古〕小丑。**III** *vi*. (*-ticked*; *-ticking*) 做滑稽动作。

an·ti·cat·a·lyst [ˈæntiˈkætəlist; ˏæntɪˋkætəlɪst] *n*. 【化】反催化剂。

an·ti·ca·thode [æntiˈkæθəud; ˏæntɪˋkæθod] *n*. 【物】对阴极。

an·ti·christ [ˈæntikraist; ˋæntɪˏkraɪst] *n*. **1**. 反对基督者。**2**. 〔the A-〕假耶稣。

an·ti·chris·tian [ˈæntiˈkristjən; ˏæntɪˋkrɪstʃən] *a*., *n*. 反对基督(教)的(人)。**-ism** *n*. 反基督(教)。

an·tic·i·pant [ænˈtisipənt; ænˋtɪsəpənt] **I** *a*. 预期的,期望的 (*of*)。*We were eagerly* ~ *of her arrival*. 我们热切地期望她的到来。**II** *n*. 期待者。

an·tic·i·pate [ænˈtisipeit; ænˋtɪsəˏpet] *vt*. **1**. 预期,预料,预测;指望,期待。**2**. 预行讨论[考虑,处置];预先挪用;预支,预付。**3**. 抢先于,占…之先。**4**. 促进,提早,使提前发生。*I* ~ (*that there will be*) *trouble*. 我预料会有麻烦。~ *a story* 为某个故事埋下伏笔。~ *one's wages* 预支工资。~ *the enemy* 先发制敌。~ *the question* 预先估定问题。~ *one's ruin* 促其灭亡。*Did the Vikings* ~ *Columbus in discovering America*? 北欧海盗是在哥伦布之前发现美洲的吗? —*vi*. 预测,预言,预感。

an·tic·i·pa·tion [ænˌtisiˈpeiʃən; ænˏtɪsəˋpeʃən] *n*. **1**. 预期,预测,预料;期待。**2**. 预先挪用,预支。**3**. 预感;预言。**4**. 占先,抢先。**5**. 【法】提前提取信托金的收益。**6**. 【医】提前出现。**7**. 【乐】先取音。**8**. 【修】预期描写法,预辩法(= prolepsis)。*The children waited with eager* ~ *for Christmas*. 孩子们热切期待圣诞节的到来。**by** ~ = **in** ~ 先,预先 (*Thanking you in* ~. 预先致谢)。**in** ~ **of** 期待 (*in* ~ *of an increase in salary* 期待加薪)。

an·tic·i·pa·tive [ænˈtisipeitiv; ænˋtɪsəˏpetɪv] *a*. **1**. 预期的,预想的。**2**. 抢先的,先发制人的。**-ly** *ad*.

an·tic·i·pa·tor [ænˈtisipeitə; ænˋtɪsəˏpetɚ] *n*. **1**. 先见者,预想者;期望者。**2**. 抢先者,占先者,先发制人者。**3**. 【无】预感器,预测器。

an·tic·i·pa·to·ry [ænˈtisipeitəri; ænˋtɪsəpəˏtorɪ] *a*. **1**. 预期的,期望着的。**2**. 提前发生的。**3**. 因预想将来而有所表示的。**4**. 【语法】先行的。**-to·ri·ly** *ad*.

an·ti·cler·i·cal [æntiˈklerikəl; ˏæntɪˋklɛrɪkəl] *a*. 反教权的。

an·ti·cli·max [ˈæntiˈklaimæks; ˏæntɪˋklaɪmæks] *n*. **1**. 【修】突降法 (*opp*. climax)。**2**. (重要性、兴趣等的)突降;(命运等的)突然衰败,虎头蛇尾。

an·ti·cli·nal [ˈæntiˈklainəl; ˏæntɪˋklaɪnəl] *a*. 【地】逆斜的,背斜的〔*cf*. synclinal〕。

an·ti·cline [ˈæntiˈklain; ˋæntɪˏklaɪn] *n*. 【地】背斜。

an·ti·cli·no·ri·um [ˈæntiklaiˈnɔːriəm; ˏæntɪklaɪˋnorɪəm] *n*. 【地】复背斜。

an·ti·clock·wise [ˈæntiˈklɔkwaiz; ˏæntɪˋklɑkwaɪz] *a*., *ad*. 逆时针方向的[地],反时针方向旋转的[地] (= counterclockwise)。

an·ti·co·ag·u·lant [ˈæntikəuˈægjulənt; ˏæntɪkoˋægjələnt] *n*. 抗凝(血)剂。

an·ti·co·ag·u·late [ˌæntikəuˈægjuleit; ˏæntɪkoˋægjəlet] *vt*. (用抗凝剂)抗(血凝)。

an·ti·co·don [ˌæntiˈkəudən; ˏæntɪˋkodɑn] *n*. 【生】反密码子。

an·ti-co·her·er [ˈæntikəuˈhiərə; ˏæntɪkoˋhirɚ] *n*. 【电】散屑器。

an·ti·cy·clone [ˈæntiˈsaikləun; ˏæntɪˋsaɪklon] *n*. 【气】反气旋;高气压。

an·ti·de·pres·sant [ˈæntidiˈpresənt; ˏæntɪdɪˋprɛsənt] **I** *a*. 【精】抗抑郁症(药物)的。**II** *n*. 抗抑郁症药。

an·ti·diph·the·rit·ic [ˈæntiˌdifθəˈritik; ˏæntɪˏdɪfθəˋrɪtɪk] **I** *a*. 预防白喉的。**II** *n*. 抗白喉血清。

an·ti·dot·al [ˈæntidəutl; ˋæntɪˏdotl] *a*. 解毒的。

an·ti·dote [ˈæntidəut; ˋæntɪˏdot] *n*. **1**. 解毒剂 (*for*; *against*; *to*)。**2**. 〔喻〕矫正法,防止法。~ *against arsenic* 解砷毒剂。*Hard work is the best* ~ *to mischief*. 繁忙的工作是防止为非作歹的最好方法。

an·ti·draft [ˈæntiˈdrɑːft; ˏæntɪˋdræft] **I** *a*. 反征兵的。**II** *n*. 反征兵,抗拒征兵。

an·ti·drom·ic [ˌæntiˈdrɔmik; ˏæntɪˋdrɑmɪk] *a*. 【生理】(神经作用)逆向的,逆行的。

an·ti·dump·ing [ˈæntiˈdʌmpiŋ; ˏæntɪˋdʌmpɪŋ] *a*. 反倾销政策的。

an·ti·e·lec·tron [ˈænti-iˈlektrɔn; ˏæntɪ-ɪˋlɛktrɑn] *n*. 阳电子,正电子,正子。

an·ti·e·met·ic [ˈæntiiˈmetik; ˏæntɪɪˋmɛtɪk] **I** *n*. 止呕剂,抗吐剂。**II** *a*. 止呕的,抗吐的。

an·ti·fat [ˈæntiˈfæt; ˏæntɪˋfæt] *a*. 减肥的。

an·ti·fe·brile [ˈæntiˈfiːbrail; ˏæntɪˋfibrɪl] **I** *a*. 退热的。**II** *n*. 退热剂。

an·ti·fe·brin(e) [ˌæntiˈfebrin; ˏæntɪˋfɛbrɪn] *n*. 【药】退热冰,乙酰苯胺。

an·ti·fed·er·al [ˈæntiˈfedərəl; ˏæntɪˋfɛdərəl] *a*. 【美史】反联邦制度的。**-ism** *n*. 反联邦制度。**-ist** *n*. 反联邦制度者。

an·ti·fer·til·i·ty [ˈæntifəːˈtiliti; ˏæntɪfɚˋtɪlətɪ] *a*. 避孕的,防止生殖的。

an·ti·for·eign [ˈæntiˈfɔrin; ˏæntɪˋfɑrɪn] *a*. 排外的。

an·ti·freeze [ˈæntiˈfriːz; ˏæntɪˋfriz] *n*. 防冻剂,防冻液,抗凝剂〔用于汽车散热器的水中或坦克的汽油中〕。

an·ti·fric·tion [ˈæntiˈfrikʃən; ˏæntɪˋfrɪkʃən] **I** *a*. 减少摩擦的。**II** *n*. 减摩剂,润滑剂。~ *bearing* 滚动轴承。

an·ti·fun·gal [ˈæntiˈfʌŋgəl; ˏæntɪˋfʌŋgəl] *a*. 杀真菌的。

an·ti·gas [ˈæntiˈgæs; ˏæntɪˋgæs] *a*. 防毒(气)的。*an* ~ *kit* 单人防毒装备。*an* ~ *mask* 防毒面具。

an·ti·gen [ˈæntidʒən; ˋæntədʒən] *n*. 【医】抗原。

an·ti·gen·i·ci·ty [ˈæntidʒəˈnisiti; æntɪdʒəˋnɪsətɪ] *n*. 抗原性。

an·ti·grop·e·los [ˈæntiˈgrɔpiləuz; ˏæntɪˋgrɑpəˏloz] *n*. 〔单复同〕〔谑〕防水绑腿。

an·ti-G suit [ˈæntidʒiːsjuːt; ˏæntɪˋdʒisjut] (飞行员穿的)加压服。

An·ti·gua [ænˈtigə; ænˋtigə] *n*. 安提瓜(岛)〔拉丁美洲〕。

Antigua And Barbuda [æn'tiːgə ən ˋbɑːbuːdə; ænˋtɪgə ən ˋbɑrbudə] 安提瓜和巴布达〔拉丁美洲〕。

an·ti·he·lix ['ænti'hiːliks; ˏæntɪˋhilɪks] ***n***. (*pl*. ***-hel·i·ces***[-'helisiːz; -ˋhiləsiz], ~*es* [-siz; -sɪz])【解】对耳轮。

an·ti·he·ro ['ænti'hiərəu; ˏæntɪˋhɪro] ***n***. (小说等)不按传统主角品格塑造的主角,非正统派主角。

an·ti·his·ta·mine ['ænti'histəmi(:)n; ˋæntɪˋhɪstəmɪ(i)n] ***n***.【药】抗组胺剂〔用以治疗过敏反应〕。**-his·ta·min·ic** [-ˌhistə'minik; -ˏhɪstəˋmɪnɪk] ***a***.

an·ti·hy·per·on [ˌænti'haipərɔn; ˏæntɪˋhaɪpərɑn] ***n***.【物】反超子。

an·ti-ic·er ['ænti'aisə; ˏæntɪˋaɪsɚ] ***n***.【空】防冰[防冻]装置。

an·ti·il·lit·er·a·cy ['æntii'litərəsi; ˏæntɪɪˋlɪtərəsɪ] ***n***. 扫除文盲。~ *campaign* 扫盲运动。

an·ti-im·pe·ri·al·ism ['æntiim'piəriəlizəm; ˏæntɪɪmˋpɪrɪəlˏɪzəm] ***n***. 反帝国主义。

an·ti·knock ['ænti'nɔk; ˏæntɪˋnɑk] **I** ***n***. 减震,消震;(内燃机减低燃料爆音的)减震剂。**II** ***a***. 减震的。

an·ti·la·bor [ˌænti'leibə; ˏæntɪˋlebɚ] ***a***. 反工会的,反工人利益的。

an·ti·lep·ton [ˌænti'leptən; ˏæntɪˋlɛptən] ***n***.【物】反轻子。

an·ti·leu·ke·mic ['æntilju:'kemik; ˏæntɪljuˋkɛmɪk] ***a***. 抗白血病的。

an·ti·lith·ic ['ænti'liθik; ˏæntɪˋlɪθɪk] **I** ***n***.【医】(泌尿器的)抗结石剂。**II** ***a***.【医】抗结石的。

An·til·les [æn'tiliːz ; ænˋtɪlɪz] ***n***. *pl*. 安的列斯群岛〔西印度群岛的组成部分〕。**Greater and Lesser** ~ 大、小安的列斯群岛。

an·ti-lock ['æntilɔk; ˋæntɪlɑk] ***a***.【机】(制动系统)防抱死的。~ **brake system** 防抱死制动装置。

an·ti·log·a·rithm ['ænti'lɔgəriθəm; ˏæntɪˋlɔgəˏrɪθəm] ***n***.【数】逆对数,真数。

an·til·o·gy [æn'tilədʒi; ænˋtɪlədʒɪ] ***n***. (观念,言语等的)前后矛盾,自相矛盾。

an·ti·ly·sin ['ænti'laisin; ˏæntɪˋlaɪsɪn] ***n***.【医】抗溶素。

an·ti·lys·sic ['ænti'lisik; ˏæntɪˋlɪsɪk] ***a***.【医】抗狂犬病的,防治狂犬病的。

an·ti·ma·cas·sar ['æntimə'kæsə; ˏæntɪməˋkæsɚ] ***n***. (椅子或沙发等的)背套,扶手套。

an·ti·mag·net·ic [ˌæntimæg'netik; ˏæntɪmægˋnɛtɪk] ***a***. (手表)防磁的。*an* ~ *watch* 防磁手表。

an·ti·ma·lar·i·al [ˌæntimə'lɛəriəl; ˏæntɪməˋlɛrɪəl] **I** ***a***. 抗疟的。**II** ***n***. 抗疟药。

an·ti·masque, an·ti·mask ['æntimɑːsk; ˋæntɪˏmæsk] ***n***. (假面戏幕间的)滑稽穿插。

an·ti·mat·ter [ˌænti'mætə; ˏæntɪˋmætɚ] ***n***.【物】反物质。

an·ti·mech·a·nized ['ænti'mekənaizd; ˏæntɪˋmɛkəˏnaɪzd] ***a***.【军】反装甲的。~ *weapons* 反装甲武器。

an·ti·mere ['æntimiə; ˋæntɪmɪr] ***n***.【动】体辐。**-mer·ic** [-'merik; -ˋmɛrɪk] ***a***. 体辐的。

an·ti·me·tab·o·lite ['æntiˌme'tæbəlait; ˋæntɪˏmɛˋtæbəlaɪt] ***n***.【生化】抗代谢物。

an·ti·mil·i·ta·rism [ˌænti'militərizəm; ˏæntɪˋmɪlətəˏrɪzəm] ***n***. 反军国主义,反黩武主义。

an·ti·mis·sile ['ænti'misail; ˏæntɪˋmɪsaɪl] ***a***. 反导弹的。

an·ti·mo·nar·chi·cal ['æntimɔ'nɑːkikəl; ˏæntɪməˋnɑrkɪkəl] ***a***. 反君主政体的,反君主制的。**-chist** ***n***. 反君主政体者。

an·ti·mo·ni·al [ˌænti'məunjəl; ˏæntɪˋmonɪəl] **I** ***a***. 锑的,含锑的。**II** ***n***. 含锑药剂。

an·ti·mon·ic [ˌænti'məunik; ˏæntɪˋmonɪk] ***a***. **1.** 锑的,含锑的。**2.**【化】五价锑的,五价锑的化合物的。

an·ti·mo·nous ['æntiməunəs; ˋæntɪmonəs], **an·ti·mo·ni·ous** [-'məuniəs; -ˋmonɪəs] ***a***. **1.** 有锑的,似锑的。**2.**【化】亚锑的,三价锑的;含锑的。

an·ti·mon·soon [ˌæntimən'suːn; ˏæntɪmɑnˋsun] ***n***.【气】反季风。

an·ti·mo·ny ['æntiməni; ˋæntɪˏmonɪ] ***n***.【化】锑。

an·ti·morph ['æntimɔːf; ˋæntɪˏmɔrf] ***n***.【生】反效等位基因。

an·ti·my·cin ['ænti'maisin; ˋæntɪˏmaɪsɪn] ***n***.【药】抗霉素。

an·ti·neu·tri·no ['æntinjuː'triːnəu; ˏæntɪnjuˋtrino] ***n***.【物】反中微子。

an·ti·neu·tron ['ænti'njuːtrɔn; ˋæntɪˋnjutrɑn] ***n***.【物】反中子。

an·ti·node ['æntinəud; ˋæntɪnod] ***n***.【物】(波)腹、腹点。

an·ti·noise ['ænti'nɔiz; ˋæntɪˋnɔɪz] ***a***. 抗噪音的,减少噪音的。

an·ti·no·mi·an [ˌænti'nəumiən; ˏæntɪˋnomɪən] **I** ***a***.【宗】反对遵从道德律的,唯信仰论的〔指单纯依靠信仰而不必遵从道德法规就能得到拯救〕。**II** ***n***. 道德律废弃论者,唯信仰论者。**-ism** ***n***.【宗】唯信仰主义。

an·tin·o·my [æn'tinəmi; ænˋtɪnəmɪ] ***n***. **1.** (某一法律与另一法律的)对立。**2.** (两个显然都合理的原则或法律之间的)矛盾,不一致。**3.**【哲】二律背反。

an·ti·nov·el ['ænti'nɔvəl; ˋæntɪˏnɑvəl] ***n***. (不按传统格式写成的)非传统小说(如不以情节为主,运用意识手法等)。

an·ti·nu·cle·on ['ænti'njuːkliɔn; ˋæntɪˋnjuklɪɑn] ***n***.【物】反核子。

an·ti·ox·i·dant [ˌænti'ɔksidənt; ˏæntɪˋɑksədənt] **I** ***n***. 防氧化剂,抗氧化剂〔用做食物防腐剂〕。**II** ***a***. 防氧化的。

an·ti·par·ti·cle ['ænti'pɑːtikl; ˋæntɪˋpɑrtɪkl] ***n***.【物】反粒子。

an·ti·pas·to [ˌænti'pɑːstəu; ˏɑntɪˋpɑsto] ***n***. (*pl*. ~*s*) 〔It.〕饭前小菜,开胃食物。

an·ti·pa·thet·ic, -i·cal [ænˌtipə'θetik(əl); ænˏtɪpəˋθɛtɪk(əl)] ***a***. **1.** 生来厌恶的,不合天性的,格格不入的。**2.** 引起反感的。*He was* ~ *to any change*. 他素来厌恶任何变革。

an·ti·path·ic [ˌænti'pæθik; ˏæntɪˋpæθɪk] ***a***. **1.** 不相容的,反对的。**2.**【医】相克症状的。

an·tip·a·thy [æn'tipəθi; ænˋtɪpəθɪ] ***n***. **1.** 嫌忌;厌恶;反感,憎恶;不相容性。**2.** 被人厌恶的事物。***have an*** ~ ***to*** 对…有反感,生性不爱…(*Some people have an* ~ *to cats*. 有的人讨厌猫)。

an·ti·pe·ri·od·ic ['æntiˌpiəri'ɔdik; ˏæntɪˏpɪrɪˋɑdɪk] **I** ***a***. 抗周期性病的。**II** ***n***. 抗疟剂。

an·ti·per·i·stal·sis ['æntiˌperi'stælsis; ˏæntɪˏpɛrɪˋstælsɪs] ***n***.【生理】(肠壁的)逆蠕动。

an·ti·per·se·cu·tion ['æntiˌpəːsi'kjuːʃən; ˏæntɪˏpɝsɪˋkjuʃən] ***a***. 反迫害的。

an·ti·per·son·nel ['æntiˌpəːsə'nel; ˏæntɪˏpɝsəˋnɛl] ***a***. 杀伤(性)的〔旨在杀伤人而不在摧毁物资〕。~ *bombs* 杀伤炸弹。

an·ti·per·spir·ant ['ænti'pəːspirənt; ˏæntɪˋpɝspərənt] ***n***. 止汗药。

an·ti·phlo·gis·tic ['æntiflәu'dʒistik; ˏæntɪfloˋdʒɪstɪk] **I** ***a***.【医】消炎的。**II** ***n***. 消炎剂。

an·ti·phlo·gis·tine ['æntiflәu'dʒistin; ˏæntɪfloˋdʒɪstɪn] ***n***.【医】消炎膏,消肿膏。

an·ti·phon, an·tiph·o·ny ['æntifən(i); ˋæntɪˏfɑn(ɪ)] ***n***. **1.** 唱和的诗歌。**2.** 应答轮唱的赞美诗。**3.** 在唱赞歌前(或后)朗读的诗句。

an·tiph·o·nal [æn'tifənl; ænˋtɪfənl] **I** ***a***. 应答轮唱的,对唱的。**II** ***n***. 唱和歌集。

an·tiph·o·nar·y [æn'tifənəri; ænˋtɪfənərɪ] ***n***. 唱和歌集。

A

an·tiph·ra·sis [æn'tifrəsis; æn`tɪfrəsɪs] *n*. 词义反用法;反语,反话〔表示幽默或讽刺,如: a giant of three feet, four inches 中的 giant〕。

an·tip·o·dal [æn'tipdl; æn`tɪpədl], **an·tip·o·de·an** [æn,tipə'di(:)ən; æn,tɪpə`dɪ(i)ən] *a*. **1.**【地】对蹠的,在地球上正相反面的。**2.** 恰恰相反的。**3.**【生】反足的。*twin brothers with ~ personalities* 性格恰恰相反的孪生兄弟。

an·ti·pode ['æntipəud; `æntɪ,pod] *n*. **1.** 恰恰相反的事务。**2.**【化】对映体。**3.**【无】对蹠点。

an·tip·o·de·an [æn,tipə'di:ən; æn,tɪpə`diən] *a*. = antipodal.

an·tip·o·des [æn'tipədi:z; æn'tɪpə,diz] *n*. *pl*. **1.** 对蹠地,地球上相反的地区。**2.**〔英〕〔A-〕新西兰和澳大利亚。**3.**〔罕〕对蹠人。**4.**〔也用作单数〕恰恰相反的事物。*The South Pole is the antipode of the North Pole*. 南极是北极的对蹠地。*Our ~ sleep while we wake*. 我们醒着的时候,我们地球背面的人却在睡觉。*The ~ of love is hatred*. 爱的反面是恨。

an·ti·pole ['æntipəul; `æntɪ,pol] *n*. **1.** 相反极。**2.** 恰恰相反的事物 (*of, to*)。

an·ti·pol·lu·tion ['æntipə'lju:ʃən; ,æntɪpə`ljuʃən] *n*., *a*. 反污染(的)。

an·ti·pope ['æntipəup; `æntɪpop] *n*. 伪教皇。

an·ti·pro·ton ['æntiprəutən; `æntɪprotɑn] *n*.【物】反质子。

an·ti·py·ret·ic ['æntipai'retik; ,æntɪpai`retɪk] **I** *a*. 退热的。**II** *n*. 退热药。

an·ti·py·rin(e) [,ænti'paiərin; ,æntɪ`paɪərɪn] *n*.【药】安替比灵〔退热药〕。

an·ti·quar·i·an [,ænti'kwɛəriən; ,æntɪ`kwɛrɪən] **I** *a*. **1.** 古物的,文物的。**2.** 研究文物的,搜集古物的。**3.** 搜集古籍的。**II** *n*. **1.** 文物工作者,古物收藏者。**2.** 古籍商,古玩商。**3.** 大幅图画纸〔31×53 英寸〕。**-ism** *n*. 古物癖,好古癖;对古物的研究。

an·ti·quar·i·um [,ænti'kwɛəriəm; ,æntɪ`kwɛrɪəm] *n*. 古物陈列馆。

an·ti·quark ['ænti'kwɑ:k; ,æntɪ`kwɑrk] *n*.【物】反夸克。

an·ti·quar·y ['æntikwəri; `æntɪkwɛrɪ] *n*. 文物工作者,古物收藏者。

an·ti·quate ['æntikwit; `æntəkwet] *vt*. **1.** 使变旧;使过时。**2.** 使具有古风,把…设计得古色古香。~ *a building* 设计一座古代风格的建筑物。

an·ti·quat·ed ['æntikweitid; `æntə,kwetɪd] *a*. **1.** 陈旧的,旧式的,过时的。**2.** 古色古香的,有古风的。**3.** 年老的。

an·tique [æn'ti:k; æn`tik] **I** *a*. **1.** 古代的;古风的。**2.** 旧式的,过时的。**II** *n*. **1.** 古物,古董。**2.** 古(代)式(样),古风。**3.** 一种黑体字。*an ~ dealer* 古董商。**III** *vi*. 购买古玩。**an·tiqu·er** *n*. 古物收藏家。**-ly** *ad*. **-ness** *n*.

an·tiq·ui·ty [æn'tikwiti; æn`tɪkwətɪ] *n*. **1.** 古旧。**2.** 古代。**3.**〔集合词〕古人。**4.**〔*pl*.〕古代的风俗[制度等]。**5.**〔*pl*.〕古物,古迹,古代文物。*of ~* 太古的。

an·ti·rab·ic ['ænti'ræbik; ,æntɪ`ræbɪk] *a*. 抗狂犬病的。

an·ti·rac·ism ['ænti'reisizəm; ,æntɪ`resɪzəm] *n*. 反种族主义,反种族歧视。

an·ti·rat·tler ['ænti'rætlə; ,æntɪ`rætlɚ] *n*. (车辆等的)防震音装置。

an·tir·rhi·num [,ænti'rainəm; ,æntɪ`raɪnəm] *n*.【植】金鱼草;〔A-〕金鱼草属。

an·ti·sab·ba·tar·ian ['æntisæbə'tɛəriən; ,æntɪ,sæbə`tɛrɪən] **I** *a*. 反对安息日的。**II** *n*. 不守安息日的人,反对安息日者。

an·ti·sa·loon ['æntisə'lu:n; ,æntɪsə`lun] *a*.〔美〕反对卖酒的。*A- League* 主张关闭酒店的同盟〔成立于 1893 年〕。

an·ti·scor·bu·tic ['æntiskɔ:'bju:tik; ,æntɪskɔr`bjutɪk] **I** *a*. 抗坏血病的。**II** *n*. 抗坏血病药。

an·ti·scrip·tur·al [ænti'skriptʃərəl; ,æntɪ`skrɪptʃʊrəl] *a*. 反对圣经的,违反圣经的。

an·ti-seis·mic ['ænti'saizmik; `æntɪ`saɪzmɪk] *a*. 抗地震的。

an·ti-Sem·ite ['ænti'si:mait; ,æntɪ`sɛmaɪt] *n*. 排犹(太)分子,反犹分子。

an·ti-Se·mit·ic ['æntisi'mitik; æn,tɪsɪ`mɪtɪk] *a*. 反犹太人的。

an·ti-Sem·i·tism [,ænti'semitizəm; ,æntɪ`sɛmɪtɪzəm] *n*. 排犹主义,反犹太主义。

an·ti·sep·sis [,ænti'sepsis; ,æntə`sɛpsɪs] *n*. 防腐(法),消毒(法),灭菌(法)。

an·ti·sep·tic [,ænti'septik; ,æntə`sɛptɪk] **I** *a*. **1.** 防腐的,有消毒力的。**2.** 消过毒的,无菌的。**3.** 异常整洁的。**4.** 冷静的;客观的。**II** *n*. 防腐剂;杀菌剂〔如碘酒、酒精、硼酸等〕。~ **finish** 防腐加工。~ **gauze** 消毒纱布。**-tically** *ad*.

an·ti·sep·ti·cize [,ænti'septisaiz; ,æntɪ`sɛptə,saɪz] *vt*. 使起防腐作用,以防腐剂处理。

an·ti·se·rum ['ænti'siərəm; ,æntɪ`sɪrəm] *n*.【医】抗血清。

an·ti·skid ['ænti'skid; ,æntɪ`skɪd] *a*. 防滑的。

an·ti·slav·er·y ['ænti'sleivəri; ,æntə`slevrɪ] *n*., *a*. 反对奴隶制度(的)。

an·ti·smut ['æntismʌt; `æntɪsmʌt] *a*. 禁淫秽书报的。

an·ti·so·cial ['ænti'səuʃəl; ,æntɪ`soʃəl] *a*. **1.** 厌恶社交的。**2.** 反社会(组织)的,反社会福利的。**-ist** *n*. **1.** 厌恶社交的人。**2.** 反社会主义者。

an·ti·spas·mod·ic ['æntispæz'mɔdik; ,æntɪspæz`mɑdɪk] **I** *a*. 治痉挛的,防痉挛的。**II** *n*. 镇痉药。

an·ti·stat·ic [,ænti'stætik; ,æntɪ`stætɪk] *a*. 抗静电的。

an·tis·tro·phe [æn'tistrəfi; æn`tɪstrəfɪ] *n*. **1.** (古希腊戏剧中)歌咏队在舞台上从左向右的舞动;从左向右舞动时唱的歌。**2.**【乐】对照乐节;对唱乐节。**3.**【修】同语溯用法〔如: the glory of success and the success of glory〕;反唇相讥〔用对方原语反击对方〕。**-stroph·ic** [-'strɔfik; -`strɑfɪk] *a*.

an·ti·sub·mar·ine ['ænti,sʌbmə'ri:n; ,æntɪsʌbmərin] *a*. 反潜(艇)的,防潜(艇)的。~ **bomb** 深水炸弹。~ **gun** 反潜艇炮。

an·ti·tank ['ænti'tæŋk; ,æntɪ`tæŋk] *a*. 反坦克的〔略 A. T. 或 AT〕。*an ~ gun* 反坦克炮。

an·ti·tech·nol·o·gy ['ænti,tek'nɔlədʒi; ,æntɪ,tɛk`nɑlədʒɪ] *n*. 反技术化〔一种出于所谓人道主义考虑而反对进行技术研究的观点〕。

an·ti·the·ism ['ænti'θi:izəm; ,æntɪ`θiɪzəm] *n*. 无神论。

an·ti·the·ist ['ænt'θi:ist; ,æntɪ`θiɪst] *n*. 无神论者。

an·tith·e·sis [æn'tiθisis; æn`tɪθəsɪs] *n*. (*pl*. *-ses* [-si:z; -siz]) **1.**【修】对语,对句〔如: Man proposes, God disposes〕。**2.** 对语的后半部。**3.** 对照,对立(面)。**4.**【乐】对应乐节。*Joy is the ~ of sorrow*. 欢乐是苦恼的对立面。

an·ti·thet·ic, an·ti·thet·i·cal [,ænti'θetik(əl); ,æntɪ`θɛtɪk(əl)] *a*. **1.** 对立的,对照的。**2.** 正相反的。**-i·cally** *ad*.

an·ti·tox·ic [,ænti'tɔksik; ,æntɪ`tɑksɪk] *a*. 抗毒(性)的。

an·ti·tox·in(e) ['ænti'tɔksin; ,æntɪ`tɑksɪn] *n*.【生】抗毒素。

an·ti·trades ['ænti'treidz; `æntɪ,tredz] *n*.〔*pl*.〕反贸易风,反信风。

an·ti·tra·gus [æn'titrəgəs; æn`tɪtrəgəs] *n*. (*pl*. *-gi* [-dʒai; -dʒaɪ])【解】对耳屏。

an·ti-Trin·i·tar·i·an ['æntitrini'tɛəriən; ,æntɪ,trɪnə-

ˋtɛrɪən] I *a*. 【神】反对三位一体说的。II *n*. 反三位一体论者。**-ism** [-izm; -ˏɪzəm] *n*. 反三位一体说。

an·ti·trust [ˈæntiˈtrʌst; ˏæntɪˋtrʌst] *a*. 反托拉斯的,反垄断的。

an·ti·tus·sive [ˈæntiˈtʌsiv; ˋæntɪˋtʌsɪv] I *a*. 镇咳的。II *n*. 镇咳药。

an·ti·type [ˈæntitaip; ˋæntəˏtaɪp] *n*. **1.** 模型[典型]所代表的原型,象征所代表的事物。**2.** 【神】《圣经》《旧约》中所预示的《新约》中的事物。

an·ti·u·ni·verse [ˈæntiˈjuːnivəːs; ˏæntɪˋjunɪvɚs] *n*. 【物】反宇宙。

an·ti·ven·in [ˈæntiˈvenin; ˏæntɪˋvɛnɪn] *n*. 抗蛇毒素。

an·ti·vi·ral [ˈæntiˈvairəl; ˏæntɪˋvaɪrəl] *a*. 【医】抗病毒的。

an·ti·vi·rus [ˈæntiˈvairəs; ˋæntɪˋvaɪrəs] *n*. 【自】(电子计算机的)抗病毒疫苗软件。

an·ti·vi·ta·min [ˌæntiˈvitəmin; ˏæntɪˋvɪtəmɪn] *n*. **1.** 抗维生素。**2.** 破坏维生素的酶。

an·ti·viv·i·sec·tion [ˈæntiˌviviˈsekʃən; ˋæntɪˏvɪvɪˋsɛkʃən] *n*. 反对活体实验〔反对在活的动物身上作医学实验的主张〕。**-ist** *n*., *a*.

an·ti·war [ˈæntiˈwɔː; ˏæntɪˋwɔr] *a*. 反战的。

an·ti·world [ˈæntiˈwəːld; ˏæntɪˋwɝld] *n*. 反物质世界〔由所谓反物质组成的假想世界〕。

an·ti·yan·kee·ism [ˈæntiˈjæŋkiːizəm; ˏæntɪˋjæŋkizəm] *n*. **1.** 反美国佬主义。**2.** 反美国腔,反美国式。

ant·ler [ˈæntlə; ˋæntlɚ] *n*. 多叉鹿角。

An·toi·nette [ˌæntwɑːˈnet; ˏæntwɑˋnɛt] *n*. 安托万内特〔女子名, Antonia 的昵称〕。

An·ton [ˈæntən; ˋæntən] *n*. 安东〔男子名, Ant(h)ony 的异体〕。

An·to·ni·a [ænˈtəunjə; ænˋtonɪə] *n*. 安东尼娅〔女子名〕。

An·to·ni·o [ænˈtəuniəu; ænˋtonɪˏo] *n*. 安东尼奥〔男子名, Ant(h)ony 的异体〕。

an·to·no·ma·sia [ˌæntənəuˈmeiʒə; ˏæntənoˋmeʒə] *n*. 【修】代称,换称〔如:称法官为 his honor, 称 a wise man 为 a Solomon〕。

an·to·nym [ˈæntəunim; ˋæntoˏnɪm] *n*. 反义词 (*opp*. synonym)。'*Bad' is the* ~ *of* '*good*'. "坏"是"好"的反义词。

an·ton·y·mous [ænˈtɔniməs; ænˋtɑnɪməs] *a*. 反义的,反义词的。

an·tre [ˈæntə; ˋæntɚ] *n*. 〔诗〕洞窟。

an·trorse [ænˈtrɔːs; ænˋtrɔrs] *a*. 【生】向上的,向前的。**-ly** *ad*.

an·trum [ˈæntrəm; ˋæntrəm] *n*. (*pl*. **-tra** [-trə; -trə]) 【解】窦,房。*dental* ~ 牙窦。

ANTU, an·tu [ˈæntuː; ˋæntju] *n*. 安妥〔杀鼠药 alpha-naph-thyl-thiourea 的商标名称〕。

Ant·werp [ˈænt-wəːp; ˋænt-wɝp] *n*. 安特卫普〔比利时港市〕

A·nu·bis [əˈnjuːbis, -ˈnuː-; əˋnjubɪs, -ˋnu-] *n*. 亡灵接引神〔埃及的豺面神,引领亡灵前去接受审判〕。

a·nu·cle·ar [eiˈnuːkliə, -njuː-; eˋnjuklɪɚ, -nju-] *a*. 【生】无细胞核的。

an·u·ran [əˈnjurən; əˋnjurən] *n*., *a*. 【动】无尾目动物(的)〔包括蛙、蟾蜍等〕

an·u·re·sis [ˌænjuˈriːsis; ˋænjuˋrisɪs] *n*. 尿闭,无尿症。**-ret·ic** [-ˈretik; -ˋrɛtɪk] *a*.

an·u·ri·a [əˈnjuəriə; əˋnjurɪə] *n*. 无尿(症)。**an·ur·ic** [-rik; -rɪk] *a*.

an·u·rous [əˈnjuːrəs; əˋnjurəs] *a*. (蛙,蟾蜍等)无尾的。

a·nus [ˈeinəs; ˋenəs] *n*. (*pl*. ~(*es*)) 〔L.〕【解】肛门。

an·vil [ˈænvil; ˋænvɪl] *n*. **1.** (铁)砧。**2.** 【解】(耳朵里的)砧骨。**3.** (电键的)下接点。**4.** 砧琴〔一种敲击乐器〕。*on the* ~ 在讨论中,在制作中,在编辑中。(*We have now another scheme on the* ~. 我们正在准备另一个计划)。

anx·i·e·ty [æŋˈzaiəti; æŋˋzaɪətɪ] *n*. **1.** 悬念,挂虑,忧虑。**2.** 切望,渴望。**3.** 【病】(精神)不安,苦闷。*cause sb. much* ~ 使人极不放心。***be all*** [***in great***] ~ 担忧。***feel no*** ~ ***about*** 对…不愁,不着急[关心]。***give*** ~ ***to*** 使…担心。***with great*** ~ 非常担忧、焦急。**~-ridden** *a*. 忧心忡忡的。

anx·ious [ˈæŋkʃəs; ˋæŋkʃəs] *a*. **1.** 忧虑的,担心的;挂念的,焦急的。**2.** 切望的,渴望的;急想。**3.** 使人不安的。*He is* ~ *to see you*. 他急想见你。~ ***seat*** [***bench***] 〔美〕忏悔者座位 (*on the* ~ *seat* 坐立不安)。***be*** ~ ***about*** (*sb.'s health*; *the consequences*) 担忧(某人健康);害怕(结果)。***be*** ~ ***for*** 切望,急欲,急着,愁着。(*The boy was* ~ *for a radio*. 那孩子渴望有一个收音机。*be* ~ *for sb.'s safety* 为某人的安全担心)。**-ly** *ad*.

an·y [ˈeni; ˋɛnɪ] I *a*. **1.** 〔用于疑问句、否定句、条件子句中,或用于肯定句但与含有疑问、否定意义的词连用〕什么,一些,一点。*Have you* ~ *book to read*? 你有什么可读的书吗? *If there arise* ~ *difficulty, send for me*. 有什么麻烦找我好了。*I cannot see* ~ *difference*. 我一点差别也看不出。**2.** 〔通常重读,多用于肯定句〕任何,随便哪一个,每一个。*Any child knows that* ... 任何孩子都知道…。*You may call* ~ *day you please*. 随便哪天来都可以。**3.** 一般的,普通的。*We don't accept just* ~ *students*. 我们并不收一般的学生〔只收高材生〕。*You are not just* ~ *girl*. 你和一般女子就是不一样。**4.** 〔与单数名词连用,代替 a, an, one〕一个。*This bucket is useless — it hasn't* ~ *handle*. 这桶没啥用场——它没有桶柄。II ***pron***. 〔*sing*., *pl*.〕哪个,无论哪个,任何,(无论)多少。*Choose* ~ *of these books*. 这些书随便挑哪本好了。*Do* ~ *of you know*? 你们当中,有谁知道吗? *Keep the apple, I don't want* ~. 把苹果收起来,我不要吃。*A- is better than none*. 有总比没有好。III ***ad***. 一些,少许,略微,稍微。〔常与比较级连用〕。*Is he* ~ *better today*? 他今天好些吗? *Did she cry* ~? 她一点没有哭吗? ~ ***and every*** 统统,全体 (~ *and every book in this library* 这个图书馆里的全部藏书)。~ ***amount*** [***number***] 许多,很多 ("*Have you* ~ *salt*?" 你有盐吗? "*Any amount*." 啊,有的是)。~ ***longer*** 再 (*I don't drink* ~ *longer*. 我不再喝酒了)。~ ***more*** 再;更 (*I won't smoke* ~ *more*. 我不再抽烟了)。~ ***old*** 任何…都 (*A- old colour will do*. 任何颜色都好)。~ ***one*** 随便哪一个 (*You may take* ~ *one of these*. 任择其一)。~ ***time*** 无论何时,随便什么时候 (*You are welcome* ~ *time*. 无论何时,你都受欢迎)。***at*** ~ ***cost*** 无论如何,必得,非要 (*The stolen painting must be recovered at* ~ *cost*. 无论如何要把被盗的画找回来)。***at*** ~ ***rate*** 好歹,总之,无论如何;至少 (*The firm has done much better this year than last*; *at* ~ *rate, so I am told by one of the staff*. 这家公司今年比去年好,至少我是听一位职工这样说的)。***if*** ~ 若有;即使有也(极少) (*There is little* (*water*), *if* ~. 水吗大概没有)。***in*** ~ ***case*** 横竖,总之 (*In* ~ *case you had better hear what your wife has to say*. 总之,你最好听你妻子的话)。***of*** ~ 在所有的…之中 (*the biggest war of* ~ *since 1946* 1946 年以来最大的一次战争)。***scarcely*** [***hardly***] ~ 几乎没有,少有。

an·y·bod·y [ˈeniˌbɔdi; ˋɛnɪˏbɑdɪ] I ***pron***. **1.** 〔用于疑问句、否定句、条件子句中〕任何人。*Is* ~ *here*? 有人吗? *I haven't seen* ~. 我没有看到任何人。**2.** 〔用于肯定句中〕随便哪一个人。*You may ask* ~ *here for help*. 这里随便哪一个人都可以为你效劳。*He doesn't lend his book to* ~. 他不借书给任何人;〔但 anybody 用降调读,则 anybody 便等于 everybody〕他的书不一定谁都借。

A

~ *else* 别人(*Does* ~ *else want it*? 还有别人要吗?)。~*'s game* 〔美〕输赢不能预测的比赛。~*'s guess* 谁也预料不到的事情[问题]。*if* ~ 如果有人的话(*She can do it if* ~. 要是有人能做的话,她就能)。**II** *n*. **1.** 有声名的人,重要人物。**2.** 平常人。*Is he* ~? 他是要人吗? *If you wish to be* ~. 你要是想出名的话。*Everybody was invited who is* ~. 重要人物都被邀请了。*two or three anybodies* 两三个普通人。

an·y·how [ˈenihau; ˋɛnɪˏhau] *ad*. **1.** 总之,无论如何,不管怎样(= in any case)。**2.** 无论用什么方法(= in any possible way)。**3.** 马马虎虎,随随便便。A-, *let us try*. 好歹试试看。*The door was locked; we couldn't get into the room* ~. 门锁着,我们不论用什么办法也进不了房间。*all* ~ 〔美口〕草率,潦草,马虎(*Things are all* ~. 事事都很马虎)。*feel* ~ (身体)不舒服。

an·y·more [ˈeniˈmɔː; ˋɛnɪmɔr] *ad*. 再也(不),(不)再〔用于含有否定意义的结构〕。*He doesn't live here* ~. 他(现在)不再住在这里了。*That's hard to get* ~. 那个已经难弄到了。

an·y·one [ˈeniwʌn; ˋɛnɪˏwʌn] *pron*. 任何人(= anybody)。

an·y·place [ˈenipleis; ˋɛnɪˏples] *ad*. 〔美口〕在任何地方,无论哪里(= anywhere)。

an·y·thing [ˈeniθiŋ; ˋɛnɪˏθɪŋ] *pron*. **1.** 〔用于疑问句、否定句、条件子句中,或用于肯定句但与含有疑问、否定意义的词连用〕任何事[物],什么事[物]。**2.** 〔用于肯定句〕随便哪件事[东西]。*Is there* ~ *for me*? 有东西给我吗? *Tell me if there is* ~ *wrong with this watch*. 请告诉我这块表有什么毛病。A- *will do*. 什么东西都可以。*I can't do* ~. 我什么也不能做;〔*anything* 用降升调读时〕我不是什么事都能做。~ **but** **1.** 决不是(*He is* ~ *but a statesman*. 他决不是一位政治家)。**2.** 除…外什么都,只不,单单不(*I will do* ~ *but that*. 除那个而外,我什么都干)。~ **like** **1.** 像…那样的。**2.** 全然(没有)(*Can the student use his dictionary with* ~ *like efficiency*. 这个学生能多多少少有效地使用字典吗? *I have not* ~ *like finished it*. 我还一点都没完成呢)。~ **of** **1.** 很少,一点,多少。**2.** 有…气派(*Do you see* ~ *of him*? 你不常看见他吗? *Is he* ~ *of a scholar*? 他有学者气派吗?)。**as...as** ~ 〔口〕无比地,非常(*He is as proud as* ~. 他非常骄傲)。**for** ~ 给什么都(不干),决(不)(*I would not do it for* ~. 我绝对不干)。**for ~ I care** 管不着,与我无关(*He may die for* ~ *I care*. 他死与我无关[我管不着])。**for ~ I know** [**to the contrary**] 据我所知,总之,大概(*He may be a good man for* ~ *I know*. 据我所知,他可能是好人)。**if** ~ 要说呢,只是…罢了(*He is, if* ~, *a little taller than I*. 要说呢,只是他比我高一点罢了)。**like** ~ 〔口〕极,非常(*He worked like* ~. 他非常勤勉)。**not come to** ~ 落空了(*His plan did not come to* ~. 他的计划落空了)。**unable to do ~ with** 对…无可奈何。

an·y·time [ˈenitaim; ˋɛnɪˏtaɪm] *ad*. **1.** 在任何时候。**2.** 总是,无例外地,一定。*You can get a job* ~. 你无论什么时候都能找到工作。*I can do better than that* ~. 我一定会做得比这还好〔如果去做的话〕。

an·y·way [ˈeniwei; ˋɛnɪˏwe] *ad*. = anyhow.

an·y·ways [ˈeniweiz; ˋɛnɪˏwez] *ad*. 〔口〕从任何观点来看,不管怎样。*It doesn't see* ~ *good for him*. 不论从哪个方面看,这对他都没有好处。

an·y·where [ˈenihwɛə; ˋɛnɪˏhwɛr] *ad*. **1.** 无论何处,任何地方。**2.** 〔口〕(用于否定句)根本(不)。**3.** 〔表示数字的不能确定〕大概在…之间。*You can go* ~ *you like*. 你爱到什么地方去都可以。*She never came* ~ *near to knowing the value of life*. 她根本不懂得人生意义。~ *from 800 to 1200 men* 大致是八百至一千二百人。~ *you go* 到处。**get** ~ 〔口〕吃得开,成功(*You'll never get* ~ *with that attitude*! 你那种态度可不行)。**not** [**never**] **go** ~ 哪里也不去,隐居。

an·y·wise [ˈeniwaiz; ˋɛnɪˏwaɪz] *ad*. 无论如何,决(不),总(不)。*He couldn't finish reading it* ~. 他无论如何也读不完。

Anzus, ANZUS [ˈænzəs; ˋænzʊs] = Australia, New Zealand and the United States (Mutual Security Pact) 澳新美(安全条约): the ~ Council 澳新美理事会。

A.O. = Army Order 军令。

a/o, A/O = account of …账上。

A.O.C., AOC = Air Officer Commanding 〔英〕空军指挥官。

A.O.D. = Army Ordnance Department 〔美〕陆军军械部。

A. of F. = Admiral of the Fleet 〔英〕海军元帅。

A-OK [ˌeiəuˈkei; ˋeˏoˋke] **I** *a*. 〔口〕极好,妙。*an A-OK rocket launching* 一次完美的火箭发射。**II** *int*. 妥了,一切就绪。

AOL = absent over leave 逾假未归。

Aomori [ˈaumɔri; ˋaʊmɔrɪ] *n*. 青森〔日本港市〕。

AONB, A. O. N. B. = Area of Outstanding Natural Beauty 〔英〕国家保护的自然风景区。

A one [ˈeiˈwʌn; ˋeˋwʌn] *a*. 〔口〕第一流的。*The meals there are* ~. 那里的饭菜是第一流的。

aor. = aorist.

a·o·rist [ˈɛərist; ˋeərɪst] *n*. (希腊动词的)不定过去式。

a·or·ta [eiˈɔːtə; eˋɔrtə] *n*. (*pl*. *-tae* [-tiː; -tɪ]) 【解】主动脉;【虫】大血管。**a·or·tic** [-tik; -tɪk] *a*.

a·ou·dad [ˈaudæd; ˋɑuˏdæd] *n*. 【动】鬣羊。

à out·rance [ɑːuːˈtrɑːns; aˏuˋtrɑ̃s] 〔F.〕(战斗)至死。*a war waged à outrance* 一场打到底的战争。

AP, A.P. = **1.** Associated Press 〔美〕联合通讯社〔简称美联社〕。**2.** airplane.

Ap. = **1.** Apostle. **2.** April.

ap- *pref*. **1.** 〔用于 p 前〕 = ad-: *ap*pear. **2.** = apo-.

a·pace [əˈpeis; əˋpes] *ad*. 飞快地,迅速地。*Old age comes on* ~. 老来日子快。*Ill news runs* ~. 恶事传千里。

A·pach·e [əˈpætʃi; əˋpætʃɪ] *n*. 阿帕切人〔美国西南部印第安人的一族〕。

a·pache [əˈpæʃ; əˋpæʃ] *n*. (巴黎等地的)流氓。~ *dance* 巴黎下层社会狂乱的双人舞。

ap·a·nage [ˈæpənidʒ; ˋæpənɪdʒ] *n*. **1.** 王子的封地[封禄]。**2.** 合法的额外收入。**3.** 属性,附属物。**4.** 属地。

a·pa·re·jo [ˌæpəˈreihəu; ˏæpəˋreho] *n*. (*pl*. ~*s*) 〔Sp.〕皮驮鞍。

a·part [əˈpɑːt; əˋpɑrt] **I** *ad*. **1.** 分,离。**2.** 分别,各别。**3.** 相距,相隔。**4.** 撇开,除去。**5.** 拆开,卸开。*fall* ~ *from decay* 因腐朽而崩溃。*New York and Tokyo are thousands of miles* ~. 纽约和东京相距几千英里。*Consider a question* ~ *from the others*. 撇开其他问题而单独考虑某一问题。~ **from** 且莫说,除了…以外。**come** ~ (精神)错乱,涣散。**jesting** [**joking**] ~ 笑话且莫讲,说正经的。**lay** [**put**, **set**] (*sth*.) ~ **for** 把(某物)留给…。**take** (*the machine*) ~ 把(机械等)拆开。**II** *a*. 〔置于名词后〕(与众)不同的。*a race* ~ 与众不同的人种。

a·part·heid [əˈpɑːtheit, əˈpɑːthaid; əˋpɑrthet, əˋpɑrthaɪd] *n*. **1.** (南非的)种族隔离(政策)。**2.** 孤傲。

a·part·ment [əˈpɑːtmənt; əˋpɑrtmənt] *n*. **1.** 〔美〕(一座房屋隔成数家的)公寓住宅。★英国称 block of flats; (公寓住宅,一家分得的)一套房间。**2.** 〔*pl*.〕〔英〕(备有家具的)出租房间。**3.** (宫殿等的)房间。**He's got ~s to let**. 〔俚〕他脑筋有点差[傻]。~ **complex** 〔美〕公寓大楼。~ **hotel** 〔美〕公寓饭店。~ **house** [**building**] 〔美〕公寓,公共住宅。

a·part·o·tel [əˌpɑːtəˈtel; əˏpɑrtəˋtɛl] *n*. = apartment hotel.

ap·a·tet·ic [ˌæpəˈtetik; ˏæpəˋtɛtɪk] *a*.【动】保护色的,保护形态的。*the ~ coloration or form of some animals* 某些动物的保护色或保护形态。

ap·a·thet·ic(al) [ˌæpəˈθetik(əl); ˏæpəˋθɛtɪk(əl)] *a*. **1.** 无动于衷的,麻木不仁的,感觉迟钝的 (*opp*. emotional)。**2.** 无表情的,冷淡的 (*opp*. concerned)。*~ airs* 暮气。**-i·cal·ly** *ad*.

ap·a·thy [ˈæpəθi; ˋæpəθɪ] *n*. 无感情,冷淡,漠不关心 (*opp*. ardor, fervor)。***have an ~ to*** 对…冷淡。

ap·a·tite [ˈæpətait; ˋæpəˏtaɪt] *n*.【矿】磷灰石。

APC = **1.** aspirin, phenacetin, and caffeine compound【药】复方阿司匹林。**2.** automatic phase control【无】自动相位控制。

A.P.D. = Army Pay Department. 陆军军饷署。

ape [eip; ep] **I** *n*. **1.** 猿;无尾猿,短尾猿,类人猿。**2.** 学样的人。**3.** 无教养的人,粗笨的人。**4.** 失去自制,狂热。***an ~ leader*** 老处女。***a God's ~*** 生来的傻子。***lead ~s in hell***〔谑〕终身不嫁。***play the ~*** 模仿,学样。***say an ~'s paternoster*** (吓得,冷得)牙齿打战。***go ~*** 失去自制,变狂热。***go ~ over [for]***〔美口〕热衷于,迷住,爱上。**II** *vt*. 仿效。*~ it* 仿效。*~* **hanger**〔美〕(自行车的)高把手;(电车等的)高扶手。*~* **man** 猿人。

a·peak [əˈpiːk; əˋpik] *a*.〔用作表语〕, *ad*.【海】(锚、桨等)竖着。

Ap·en·nine [ˈæpinain; ˋæpɪˏnaɪn] *a*. 亚平宁山的。

Ap·en·nines [ˈæpinainz; ˋæpəˏnaɪnz] *n*. *pl*. (意大利的)亚平宁山脉。

a·pep·sia [əˈpepsiə; eˋpɛpsɪə], **a·pep·sy** [-si; -sɪ] *n*.【医】消化停止,不消化。

a·per·çu [ˌæpəːˈsjuː; ˏɑpɛrˋsju] *n*.〔F.〕**1.** 一瞥,一瞥的印象。**2.** 洞察,敏悟。**3.** 摘要,梗概。

a·per·i·ent [əˈpiəriənt; əˋpɪrɪənt] **I** *a*.【医】轻泻的。**II** *n*. 轻泻剂。

a·pe·ri·od·ic [ˌeipiəriˈɔdik; ˏepɪrɪˋɑdɪk] *a*. **1.** 非周期的。**2.**【物】非周期性(振动)的。**-o·dic·i·ty** [-ˈdisiti; -ˋdɪsətɪ] *n*. 无周期性。

a·pé·ri·tif [əˌperiˈtiːf; ɑˏperɪˋtif] *n*.〔F.〕开胃酒。

a·per·i·tive [əˈperitiv; əˋpɛrətɪv] *a*., *n*. = aperient; apéritif.

ap·er·ture [ˈæpətjuə; ˋæpə·tʃɚ] *n*. **1.** 孔,隙缝。**2.** (照相机的)光圈;孔径,口径。*~* **card** 穿孔卡片;(镶有缩微胶片的)窗孔卡片。

ap·er·y [ˈeipəri; ˋepərɪ] *n*. **1.** 学样,摹仿。**2.** 猴房。**3.** 愚蠢的行为,恶作剧的行为。

a·pet·a·lous [eiˈpetələs; eˋpɛtələs] *a*.【植】无花瓣的。

APEX, Apex = Advance Purchase excursion 优惠价机票预订〔在 3-5 周前预订,可享受价格低廉的机票预购法〕。

a·pex [ˈeipeks; ˋepɛks] *n*. (*pl*. *~es* [-iz; -ɪz], ***a·pi·ces*** [ˈeipisiːz; ˋepɪsiz]) **1.** (山)顶;尖端,顶点,绝顶。**2.**【天】奔赴点,向点。**3.**【无】(电波由电离层反射时的)反射点。**4.**【矿】矿脉顶〔指离地面最近的矿脉〕。*the ~ of a mountain* 山顶。*His election to the presidency was the ~ of his career*. 当选总统是他一生事业的顶峰。

APF = animal protein factor【生化】动物蛋白因子。

aph- *pref*. = apo-.

aph·a·nite [ˈæfənait; ˋæfənaɪt] *n*.【矿】隐晶岩,非显晶岩。

a·ph(a)er·e·sis [əˈfiərisis; əˋfɛrəsɪs] *n*.【语法】头音节省略〔advantage 转变为 vantage; It is 转变为 'tis 等〕。**-re·tic** [-ˈretik; -ˋrɛtɪk] *a*.

a·pha·si·a [æˈfeizjə; əˋfeʒə] *n*.【医】无语言能力,失语(症)。

a·phe·li·on [æˈfiːljən; æˋfilɪən] *n*. (*pl*. *-lia* [-liə; -lɪə])【天】远日点〔指星体轨道上离日最远的点, *opp*. perihelion〕。

a·phe·li·ot·ro·pism [əˌfiːliˈɔtrəpizəm; əˏfilɪˋɑtrəpɪzm] *n*. (植物的)背光性,背日性。**-o·trop·ic** [-əuˈtrɔpik; -oˋtrɑpɪk] *a*.

aph·e·sis [ˈæfisis; ˋæfəsɪs] *n*.【语】词首母音脱落〔esquire 转变为 squire 等〕。

aph·i·cide [ˈæfisaid; ˋefəsaɪd] *n*.〔农〕杀蚜虫剂。

a·phid [ˈeifid; ˋefɪd] *n*. = aphis.

a·phis [ˈeifis; ˋefɪs] *n*. (*pl*. ***aph·i·des*** [ˈeifidiːz; ˋæfədiz]) 蚜虫;〔*A*-〕蚜虫属。

a·pho·ni·a [æˈfəunjə; æˋfonɪə] *n*.【医】失音(症),无发音能力。

a·phon·ic [ˌeiˈfɔnik; əˋfɑnɪk] **I** *a*. **1.** 无发音能力的,失音的。**2.**【语音】不发音的;无声的。**II** *n*. 失音症患者。

aph·o·rism [ˈæfərizəm; ˋæfəˏrɪzəm] *n*. 格言,警句。

aph·o·rist [ˈæfərist; ˋæfərɪst] *n*. 警句家。

aph·o·ris·tic(al) [ˌæfəˈristik(əl); ˏæfəˋrɪstɪk(əl)] *a*. **1.** 格言式的。**2.** 富于警句的;爱引用格言的。

a·pho·tic [eiˈfəutik; eˋfotɪk] *a*. 无光的〔尤指 aphotic zone (无光带)和 aphotic region (无光区),即海洋中三百英尺以下的地方〕。*~ depths* 无光的深处。

aph·ro·dis·i·a [ˌæfrəuˈdiziə; ˏæfrəˋdɪʒə] *n*. 性欲。

aph·ro·dis·i·ac [ˌæfrəuˈdiziæk; ˏæfrəˋdɪzɪˏæk] **I** *a*. 刺激性欲的。**II** *n*. 催欲剂,春药。

Aph·ro·di·te [ˌæfrəuˈdaiti; ˏæfrəˋdaɪtɪ] *n*. **1.**【希神】阿芙罗狄蒂〔爱与美的女神,相当于 Venus〕。**2.**〔a-〕黑斑褐色蝴蝶。

aph·tha [ˈæfθə; ˋæfθə] *n*. (*pl*. *-thae* [-θiː; -θi])【医】**1.** 口疮。**2.** 小溃疡。

a·phyl·lous [eiˈfiləs; eˋfɪləs] *a*.【植】无叶(性)。

A·pi·a [ɑːˈpi(ː)ə; ɑˋpiɑ] *n*. 阿比亚〔西萨摩亚首都〕。

a·pi·an [ˈeipjən; ˋepɪən] *a*. 关于蜜蜂的。

a·pi·ar·i·an [ˌeipiˈɛəriən; ˏepɪˋɛrɪən] **I** *a*. 蜜蜂的;养蜂的。**II** *n*. 养蜂人。

a·pi·a·rist [ˈeipiərist; ˋepɪərɪst] *n*. 养蜂家,养蜂人。

a·pi·ar·y [ˈeipjəri; ˋepɪˏɛrɪ] *n*. 养蜂场;蜂房。

ap·i·cal [ˈæpikəl; ˋæpɪkl] **I** *a*. **1.** 顶点的,顶端的。**2.**【语】用舌尖发音的。**II** *n*. 舌尖音〔如 t, d, s, l 等〕。

ap·i·ces [ˈeipisiːz; ˋepɪˏsiz] apex 的复数。

a·pi·cul·ture [ˈeipikʌltʃə; ˋepɪˏkʌltʃɚ] *n*. 养蜂(学)。

a·pi·cul·tur·ist [ˌeipiˈkʌltʃərist; ˏepɪˋkʌltʃʊrɪst] *n*. 养蜂家。

a·piece [əˈpiːs; əˋpis] *ad*. 每人,每个,各。*The cakes cost a dollar ~*. 蛋糕每块一元。★主语是单数名词时应作 The *cake* cost a dollar *a piece*.

à pied [aˈpjei; ɑˋpje]〔F.〕徒步,步行。

A·pis [ˈeipis; ˋepɪs] *n*. 神牛〔古埃及人信奉为神的化身的公牛〕。

ap·ish [ˈeipiʃ; ˋepɪʃ] *a*. **1.** 猿一样的。**2.** 学人样的;乱模仿的。**3.** 傻气的。

a·piv·o·rous [eiˈpivərəs; eˋpɪvərəs] *a*. 食蜂的〔如某些鸟类〕。

a·pla·cen·tal [ˌeipləˈsentl; ˏepləˋsɛntl] *a*. 无胎盘的〔如袋鼠〕。

ap·la·nat [ˈæplənæt; ˋæplənæt] *n*.【光】消球差透镜;齐明镜。**-ic** [ˌæpləˈnætik; ˏæpləˋnætɪk] *a*. 消球差的。**-ism** *n*. 消球差;等光程。

a·plen·ty [əˈplenti; əˋplɛntɪ] **I** *ad*.〔美口〕**1.** 丰富,很多。**2.** 极。*There's water ~ there*. 那里水很多。*be scared ~* 吓得要死。**II** *a*. 丰富的〔多置于被修饰的名词之后〕。*money ~ for one's needs* 足够花的钱。**III** *n*.〔美〕丰富,大量(= a plenty)。

ap·lite [ˈæplait; ˋæplaɪt] *n*. 细晶岩,半花岗岩。

a·plomb [ˈæplɔ̃ːŋ; ˋæplɔ̃ŋ] *n*.〔F.〕**1.** 垂直。**2.** 冷静,沉着;自信,自恃。*with ~* 沉着地。

ap·neu·sis [æpˈnjuːsis; æpˋnjusɪs] *n*.【医】长吸式呼吸。

ap·n(o)e·a [æpˈniːə; æpˋniə] *n*.【医】呼吸暂停,窒息。

apo. = apogee.

APO = Army Post Office 军用邮局。

A

Apoc. = Apocalypse; Apocrypha 1.

a·poc·a·lypse [əˈpɔkəlips; əˋpɑkəˏlɪps] *n*. 【基督教】天启,启示;〔the A-〕【圣】《启示录》。**-lyp·tic, -lyp·ti·cal** [-ˈliptik(l); -ˋlɪptɪk(l)] *a*. **1.** 天启的,启示的。**2.**《圣经》《启示录》中恐怖场景的,预示世界末日情景的。

a·po·car·pous [ˌæpəˈkɑːpəs; ˏæpəˋkɑrpəs] *a*. 【植】离心皮的。

apo·chro·mat [ˈæpəkrəumæt; ˋæpəkroˏmæt] *n*. 【光】高度消色镜。

a·po·chro·mat·ic [ˌæpəkrəuˈmætik; ˏæpəkroˋmætɪk] *a*. 高度消色的。

a·poc·o·pate [əˈpɔkəpeit; əˋpɑkəˏpet] *vt*. 删除(词尾字母或音节)〔如: mos' 代替 most〕。**-pa·tion** *n*.

a·poc·o·pe [əˈpɔkəpi; əˋpɑkəpɪ] *n*. 【语法】词尾省略,词尾消失〔例 mine 变化为 my; cinematograph 变化为 cinema〕。

a·poc·ry·pha [əˈpɔkrifə; əˋpɑkrəfə] *n*. 〔*sing*., *pl*.〕 **1.** 〔A-〕【宗】伪经,经外书。**2.** 不足凭信的书;著者不明的书。**-phal** [-fəl; -fəl] *a*.

a·poc·y·na·ceous [əˌpɔsiˈneiʃəs; əˏpɑsɪˋneʃəs] *a*. 【植】夹竹桃科的。

a·poc·y·num [əˈpɔsinəm; əˋpɑsɪnəm] *n*. 罗布麻,红野麻。

ap·od [ˈæpəd; ˋæpɑd] **I** *n*. **1.** 无足动物。**2.** 无腹鳍鱼。**II** *a*. **1.** 无足的。**2.** 无腹鳍的。**-al** *a*.

ap·o·deic·tic [ˌæpəuˈdaiktik; ˏæpoˋdaɪktɪk], **ap·o·dic·tic** [-ˈdiktik; -ˋdɪktɪk] *a*. **1.** 可以明确表示[证实]的。**2.** 绝对肯定的;必然真实的。**3.**【逻】具有[表达]必然真理的;【哲】必然的。

a·pod·o·sis [əˈpɔdəsis; əˋpɑdəsɪs] *n*. (*pl*. **-ses** [-siːz; -ˏsiz])【语法】条件句的结论句〔如: If I could go, I would go. 里的 I would go〕。

ap·o·en·zyme [ˌæpəuˈenzaim; ˏæpoˋɛnzaɪm] *n*. 【生化】酶蛋白。

a·pog·a·my [əˈpɔgəmi; əˋpɑgəmɪ] *n*. 【植】无配子生殖。

ap·o·gee [ˈæpəudʒiː; ˋæpoˏdʒi] *n*. **1.**【天】远地点〔指月亮、人造卫星轨道上离地球最远的点, *opp*. perigee〕。**2.** 最高点,最远点;极点。*the* ~ *of Renaissance art* 文艺复兴时代艺术的最高峰。**-ge·an** [ˌæpəuˈdʒiːən; ˏæpəˋdʒiən] *a*.

ap·o·ge·ot·ro·pism [ˌæpəudʒiˈɔtrəpizm; ˏæpədʒəˋɑtrəpɪzm] *n*. 【植】(植物器官的)背地性;负向地性。

ap·o·laus·tic [ˌæpəˈlɔːstik; ˏæpəˋlɔstɪk] *a*. 恣意享乐的;放纵的。

a·po·lit·i·cal [ˌeipəˈlitikəl; ˏepəˋlɪtɪkl] *a*. **1.** 非政治的,无关政治的。**2.** 不关心政治的。**-ly** *ad*.

A·pol·lo [əˈpɔləu; əˋpɑlo] *n*. **1.**【希神】阿波罗〔太阳、音乐、诗、健康等的守护神〕。**2.** 〔诗〕太阳。**3.** 美男子。~ **Program** 阿波罗计划〔包括登月行动的美国宇航计划〕。

A·pol·lyon [əˈpɔljən; əˋpɑljən] *n*. (地狱中的)魔王。

a·pol·o·get·ic, a·pol·o·get·i·cal [əˌpɔləˈdʒetik(əl); əˏpɑləˋdʒɛtɪk(əl)] **I** *a*. **1.** 辩护的,辩解的。**2.** 谢罪的,道歉的,认错的。*He was very* ~. 他已表示十分道歉了。**II** *n*. 〔常 *pl*.〕辩解;辩护;护教学〔指神学中为基督教教条进行辩护的一个分支〕。**-i·cal·ly** *ad*. 辩解,道歉,认错。

ap·o·lo·gi·a [ˌæpəˈləudʒiə; ˏæpəˋlodʒɪə] *n*. **1.** (口头或书面的)正式辩解,辩解书。**2.** 道歉。

a·pol·o·gist [əˈpɔlədʒist; əˋpɑlədʒɪst] *n*. **1.** 辩解者,辩护者。**2.** 护教学专家(指为基督教信仰进行辩护的人)。

a·pol·o·gize [əˈpɔlədʒaiz; əˋpɑləˏdʒaɪz] *vi*. **1.** 辩解,辩护。**2.** 道歉,认错,赔不是。*A- to him for your rudeness*. 你对人不礼貌,向他赔个不是。~ *for oneself* 替自己辩护。

ap·o·logue [ˈæpəlɔg; ˋæpəˏlɔg] *n*. 寓言,富有教育意义的故事。

a·pol·o·gy [əˈpɔlədʒi; əˋpɑlədʒɪ] *n*. **1.** 辩解,辩护。**2.** 道歉,赔不是。**3.** 〔口〕临时凑合的代用品。*a lame* ~ 蹩脚的辩解。*a letter of* ~ 道歉信。**an** [*a mere*] ~ *for* (*a dinner*) 勉强充作(正餐)的(食物)。*in* ~ *for* 为…辩解,为…赔不是。***make an*** ~ ***for*** 为…道歉。***owe someone an*** ~ 得向某人道歉。

a·po·lune [ˈæpəuljuːn; ˏæpoˏljun] *n*. 月(球)轨(道)最远点,远月点。

ap·o·mict [ˈæpəumikt; ˋæpəˏmɪkt] *n*. 无配偶生殖植物。**-ic** *a*.

ap·o·mix·is [ˌæpəuˈmiksis; ˏæpəˋmɪksɪs] *n*. 无融合生殖,无精生殖。

ap·o·mor·phine [ˌæpəuˈmɔːfiːn; ˏæpəˋmɔrfin] *n*. 阿朴吗啡〔用做呕吐剂、祛痰剂的缩水吗啡〕。

ap·o·neu·ro·sis [ˌæpəunuˈrəusis; ˏæponuˋrosɪs] *n*. (*pl*. **-ses** [-siːz; -siz]) 腱膜。**-rot·ic** [-ˈrɔtik; -ˋrɑtɪk] *a*.

ap·o·pemp·tic [ˈæpəuˈpemptik; ˏæpəˋpɛmptɪk] *a*. 〔古〕告别的,送别的;临别所言的。*an* ~ *song* 离歌。

ap·o·phthegm [ˈæpəuθem; ˋæpəˏθɛm] *n*. 格言,箴言 (= apothegm)。**-atic** [ˌæpəuθegˈmætik; ˏæpəθɛgˋmætɪk] *a*.

a·poph·y·ge [əˈpɔfidʒiː; əˋpɑfɪdʒi] *n*. (古典建筑物的)蜗牛形柱墩。

a·poph·yl·lite [əˈpɔfilait; əˋpɑfɪlaɪt] *n*. 【矿】鱼眼石。

a·poph·y·sis [əˈpɔfisis; əˋpɑfəsɪs] *n*. (*pl*. **-ses** [-siːz; -siz]) **1.**【解】骨突;表皮层。**2.**【植】蒴托;鳞质〔指球果鳞片〕。**-y·se·al** [-ˈsiəl; -ˋsɪəl] *a*.

ap·o·plec·tic, ap·o·plec·ti·cal [ˌæpəuˈplektik(əl); ˏæpəˋplɛktɪk(əl)] *a*. 中风的,易患中风病的。*an* ~ *fit* [*stroke*] 中风。

ap·o·plex·y [ˈæpəupleksi; ˋæpəˏplɛksɪ] *n*. 【医】中风,卒中。*cerebral* ~ 脑溢血。*be seized with* ~ 中风。

a·port [əˈpɔːt; əˋport] *ad*. 【海】在左舷。*put the helm* ~ 使舵柄靠左。***Hard*** ~ ! 尽力使舵柄靠左! 左满舵!

ap·o·se·mat·ic [ˌæpəusiˈmætik; ˏæposɪˋmætɪk] *a*. 【动】警戒色的。**-i·cal·ly** *ad*.

a·po·si·o·pe·sis [ˌæpəuˌsaiəuˈpiːsis; ˏæpəˏsaɪəˋpisɪs] *n*. 【修】说话中断法〔如: The first thing I saw — but I dare not describe the dreadful sight. 我一眼看到的是——啊,太可怕了,我简直不敢去形容〕。

a·po·spor·y [ˈæpəuˌspɔːri; ˋæpəˏsporɪ] *n*. 无孢子生殖。

a·pos·ta·sy [əˈpɔstəsi; əˋpɑstəsɪ] *n*. 背教;脱党;变节;放弃信仰。

a·pos·tate [əˈpɔseit; əˋpɑstet] **I** *a*. 背教的;脱党的;变节的;放弃信仰的。**II** *n*. 背教者,脱党者;背信者,变节者,叛徒。**-ta·tic** [ˌæpəuˈstætik; ˏæpoˋstætɪk] *a*.

a·pos·ta·tize [əˈpɔstətaiz; əˋpɑstəˏtaɪz] *vi*. 弃教;脱党;变节。

a pos·te·ri·o·ri [ˈei pɔsˌteriˈɔːrai; ˋepɑsˏtɪrɪˋoraɪ] 〔L.〕【逻】**1.** 由结果追溯到原因的;由特殊推论出一般的;归纳的。**2.** 凭经验的 (*opp*. a priori)。~ ***reasoning*** 归纳推理。

a·pos·til(le) [əˈpɔstil; əˋpɑstɪl] *n*. 旁注,注。

a·pos·tle [əˈpɔsl; əˋpɑsl] *n*. **1.** 〔A-〕【基督教】(《圣经》中所讲的)使徒。**2.** 最初的传教士。**3.** (主义、政策等的)提倡者,鼓吹者。**4.**【海】船头系缆柱。~ **spoon** (柄端刻成使徒像的)使徒匙。**-ship** *n*. 使徒的职位[身分]。

a·pos·to·late [əˈpɔstəulit; əˋpɑstlɪt] *n*. 使徒的职务[身分、任期]。

ap·os·tol·ic [ˌæpəsˈtɔlik; ˏæpəsˋtɑlɪk] *a*. **1.** 使徒的。**2.** 适合使徒教义的。**3.** 使徒传来的。**4.** 罗马教皇的。~ **age** 使徒时代〔即基督教创立的最初时期〕。~ **delegate** 教皇代表〔教皇派往与梵蒂冈无外交关系的国家的代表〕。~ **indulgence** 教皇的赦免。~ **succession** 使徒传统〔指耶稣交给圣彼得等使徒的宗教权力,由各代主教相传下来〕。

a·pos·tro·phe[1] [ə'pɔstrəfi; ə`pɑstrəfɪ] *n*. **1.** 撇号,省字号〔例 can't(= can not),'55(= 1955)〕。**2.** 所有格符号〔例 boy's, boys'〕。**3.** 复数符号〔例 many M.P.'s〕。**4.** 表示一字中的某一音不发〔如:'lectric(= electric)〕。**-troph·ic** [ˌæpəs'trɔfik; ˏæpəs`trɑfɪk] *a*. 使用撇号的。

a·pos·tro·phe[2] [ə'pɔstrəfi; ə`pɑstrəfɪ] *n*. 【修】顿呼法〔叙述中忽然对不在场的第三者所发出的直接呼语;或对无生命物发出呼唤,如: Frailty, thy name is woman. 脆弱啊,你的名字就是女人〕。**-troph·ic** [ˌæpəs'trɔfɪk; ˏæpəs`trɑfɪk] *a*. 使用顿呼法的。

a·pos·tro·phize[1] [ə'pɔstrəfaiz; ə`pɑstrəˏfaɪz] *vt*., *vi*. 加省字号以缩短(单词的拼写形式);(给…)记上省字符号[所有格符号]。

a·pos·tro·phize[2] [ə'pɔstrəfaiz; ə`pɑstrəfaɪz] *vt*., *vi*. (对…)发出呼语。

a·poth·e·car·y [ə'pɔθikəri; ə`pɑθəˏkɛrɪ] *n*. **1.** 药剂师;药房老板。**2.** 药房。*apothecaries' measure* 药用容量单位。*apothecaries' weight* 药用重量单位。

ap·o·the·ci·um [ˌæpə'θisiəm; ˏæpə`θɪsɪəm] *n*. (*pl*. *-cia* [-siə; -sɪə])【植】子囊盘。**-the·ci·al** [-siəl; -sɪəl] *a*.

ap·o·thegm ['æpə*u*θem; `æpəˏθɛm] *n*. 格言。**-at·ic** *a*.

ap·o·them ['æpə*u*ˌθem; `æpəˏθɛm] *n*. 【数】边心距,垂幅。

a·poth·e·o·sis [əˌpɔθi'əusis; əˏpɑθɪ`osɪs] *n*. (*pl*. *-ses* [-si:z; -siz]) **1.** 尊为神,封为神,神化。**2.** 礼赞,崇拜。**3.** 极点,顶峰。

a·poth·e·o·size [ə'pɔθiə*u*saiz; ə`pɑθɪəˏsaɪz] *vt*. **1.** 把,尊为神,神化。**2.** 尊崇,崇拜,颂扬。

app. = apparatus; apparent(ly); appended; appendix; appointed; apprentice; approved; approximate.

app [æp; æp] *n*.【自】应用程序(= application)。

Ap·pa·la·chi·an [ˌæpə'leitʃiən; ˏæpə`letʃɪən] *a*. 阿帕拉契山脉的。

Ap·pa·la·chi·ans [ˌæpə'leitʃjənz; ˏæpə`letʃɪənz] *n*. *pl*. 〔the ~〕阿帕拉契山脉〔北美洲〕。

ap·pal(l) [ə'pɔ:l; ə`pɔl] *vt*. 吓坏,使惊骇,使胆寒。*be ~ed at* 被…吓坏,弄得毛骨悚然。

ap·pal·ling [ə'pɔ:liŋ; ə`pɔlɪŋ] *a*. **1.** 骇人的,可惊的。**2.** 〔口〕(愚笨等)过分的。*an ~ accident* 骇人听闻的事故。~ *ignorance* 过分愚蠢。**-ly** *ad*. 可惊地。

ap·pa·loo·sa [ˌæpə'lu:sə; ˏæpə`lusə] *n*. 阿巴鲁萨马〔北美西部骑用马〕。

ap·pa·nage ['æpənidʒ; `æpənɪdʒ] *n*. = apanage.

ap·pa·rat [ˌɑ:pɑ:'rɑ:t; ˏɑpɑ`rɑt] *n*. 〔Russ.〕 = apparatus 3.

ap·pa·ra·tus [ˌæpə'reitəs; ˏæpə`retəs] *n*. (*pl*. ~-(*es*)) **1.** 器具,装置,设备,机器,器械,仪器。**2.** (身体上的)器官。**3.** 政治机构,机关,政党的基层组织,地下活动组织。**4.** (学术著作中的)注释(或索引等)。*a chemical ~* 化学仪器。*a feeding ~* 给水装置。*a fire ~* 灭火器。*a radio* [*wireless*] ~ 无线电信机,无线电装置。*the respiratory ~* 呼吸器官。*the state ~* 国家机构。~ **criticus** 书中所附的参考资料。

ap·par·el [ə'pærəl; ə`pærəl] **I** *vt*. 〔书〕使穿衣;装饰。*a girl gaily ~(l)ed* 衣着漂亮的少女。*a book tastefully ~(l)ed* 装饰雅致的书。**II** *n*. **1.** 服装。**2.** (衣服上的)装饰。**3.** 法衣的长方形绣花装饰。**4.** 外表,外观。**5.** 船具〔如:桅、帆、索具和锚〕。*the queen's ~* 女王的服饰。*the gay ~ of spring* 明媚的春光。

ap·par·ent [ə'pærənt; ə`pærənt] *a*. **1.** 明显的,显而易见的 (*to*)。**2.** 貌似的;表面的,外观上的。**3.**【物】表观的;视在的,外显的。*His reluctance was only ~*. 他不过是表面上不愿意罢了。*The solution to the problem was ~ to all*. 问题的解决方法是显而易见的。~ **angle**【地】视角。~ **dip**【地】视倾角。~ **expansion**【物】表观膨胀。~ **load**【物】视载荷。~ **solar time**【天】视太阳时。**-ly** *ad*. 显然地,表面上。

ap·pa·ri·tion [ˌæpə'riʃən; ˏæpə`rɪʃən] *n*. **1.** 鬼,幽灵,妖怪。**2.** 幻象,幻影。**3.** (星等的)出现。

ap·par·i·tor [ə'pæritɔ:; ə`pærətɔr] *n*. **1.** (古罗马行政官的)执行吏。**2.** (宗教裁判所的)命令送达官。

ap·pas·si·o·na·ta [əˌpɑ:siə'nɑ:tə; əˏpɑsɪə`nɑtə] *a*. 〔It.〕【乐】热情的。

ap·peal [ə'pi:l; ə`pil] **I** *vi*. **1.** 呼吁;要求。**2.** 诉诸于;向…求助 (*to*)。**3.** 投合…心意,对…有吸引力 (*to*)。**4.** 【法】控诉,上诉 (*to*)。~ *for aid* 请求援助。~ *for sympathy* 吁请同情。*They ~ed to the public to help the distressed children*. 他们呼吁公众帮助那些受难的儿童。~ *to a higher court* 上诉。~ *against the judge's decision* 不服判决而上诉。*These pictures do not ~ to me*. 这些画不合我意[我不欣赏]。~ **to the country** (解散议会)请国民公断。~ **to force** 诉诸武力。~ **to reason** 讲理。**II** *n*. **1.** 呼吁(书),恳求。**2.** 控诉;起诉,上诉。**3.** 魅力,吸引力。*an ~ for help to the public* 向公众求援的呼吁。*a court of ~* 上级法院。**lodge** [**enter**] **an ~** 提出上诉。**make an ~ to** 诉诸。

ap·peal·ing [ə'pi:liŋ; ə`pilɪŋ] *a*. **1.** 恳求的,哀求的。**2.** 有感染力的,吸引人的。*an ~ smile* 动人心弦的微笑。**-ly** *ad*. **-ness** *n*.

ap·pear [ə'piə; ə`pɪr] *vi*. **1.** 出现,露出,显现。**2.** 出庭,出场,演出,(在公开场合)露面。**3.** (书等)出版;发表。**4.** 变得明显。**5.** 显得,好像。~ *in public* 露面。~ *in court* 出庭,到案。*for reasons that do not ~* 用含糊的理由。~ *on the stage* 上台,演出。*He ~s to have caught cold*. 他似乎是受凉了。*He ~s (to be) very young*. 他显得很年轻。*It ~s to me that you are right*. 我觉得你是对的。***It ~s that …*** 似乎是…。***strange as it may ~*** 虽似奇怪[插入语]。

ap·pear·ance [ə'piərəns; ə`pɪrəns] *n*. **1.** 出现;露面,出场,登台。**2.** 出版,刊行。**3.** 外貌,外观;〔*pl*.〕表面的迹象[征兆]。**4.** 〔古〕幻想;幽灵。**5.**【法】出庭。**6.**【哲】现象 (*opp*. essence)。*Appearances are deceptive*. 外表是靠不住的。*Never judge by ~*. 不要以貌取人。*personal ~* 容貌,风采。***at first ~*** 乍一看,初看起来。***at the ~ of*** 看见…而,与…的出现同时,…公布后即。***enter an ~*** 出庭,出面。***for ~ sake*** 为了装门面,为了体面。***give the ~ of*** (*honesty*) 假装(老实)。***in ~*** 看上去,外表上。***keep up ~s*** 装场面,保全体面,维持面子。***make a good*** [***an ill***] ~ 以壮[有碍]观瞻。***make an ~*** 出面,出庭,到案。***make its first ~*** (书)初版,(杂志)创刊。***make one's ~*** 露面。***make one's first*** [***last***] ***~ on the stage*** 初次[末次]登台。***put in an ~*** 出面,出庭。***put on the ~ of*** (*innocence*) 假装(清白)。***save ~s*** = keep up ~s. ***There is every ~ of…*** 无一处不像…。***There is no ~ of*** (***him***; ***rain***). 简直不见(他的影子); 一点没有(下雨的样子)。***to all ~(s)*** 显然;没有不像…的,看着都…。

ap·peas·a·ble [ə'pi:zəbl; ə`pizəbl̩] *a*. 平息得了的,缓和得了的;劝解得了的。

ap·pease [ə'pi:z; ə`piz] *vt*. **1.** 平息(愤怒),缓和(情绪),劝慰,抚慰。**2.** 对…让步,安抚,姑息;绥靖。**3.** 充(饥),果(腹),解(渴),满足(欲望)。~ *the king's anger* = ~ *the angry king* 劝使国王息怒。~ *one's hunger with cake* 吃饼充饥。~ *sb's curiosity* 满足某人的好奇心。*Hitler was ~d at Munich*. 在慕尼黑对希特勒实行了绥靖政策。

ap·pease·ment [ə'pi:zmənt; ə`pizmənt] *n*. 姑息,迁就;抚慰;缓和,绥靖;满足。~ **policy** 绥靖政策,姑息政策。

ap·pel [ə'pel; ə`pɛl] *n*.【剑】垫步。

ap·pel·lant [ə'pelənt; ə`pɛlənt] **I** *n*.【法】控诉人;上诉人,请求人。**II** *a*.【法】有关上诉的,上诉的。

ap·pel·late [ə'pelit; ə`pɛlɪt] *a*.【法】受理上诉的。*an ~ court* 受理上诉的法院。

A

ap·pel·la·tion [ˌæpəˈleiʃən; ˏæpəˋleʃən] *n*. 1. 称呼。2. 名称,称号。

ap·pel·la·tive [əˈpelətiv; əˋpɛlətɪv] I *a*. 1. 命名的;名称的。2.【语法】通称的(*opp*. proper);普通名词的。II *n*. 1. 称号,名称;通称。2.【语法】普通名词。

ap·pel·lee [ˌæpəˈliː; ˏæpəˋli] *n*. 被告。

ap·pel·lor [əˈpelə; əˋpɛlɔr] *n*. 控诉人,上诉人,原告。

ap·pend [əˈpend; əˋpɛnd] *vt*. 1. (用线等)挂上。2. 附上,添上,加上;追加,增补。~ *a label to a trunk* 给行李挂上标签。~ *an index to a book* 给书籍加上索引。~ *one's signature* 签名,署名。~ *a seal to a contract* 在合同上盖章。

ap·pend·age [əˈpendidʒ; əˋpɛndɪdʒ] *n*. 1. 附属物,配件。2.【生】附器;附肢〔如:树的枝,狗的尾等〕。

ap·pend·ant [əˈpendənt; əˋpɛndənt] I *a*. 附加的,附属的(*to*)。*the salary ~ to a position* 随着职务而来的薪水。II *n*. 1. 附属物。2.【法】附带的遗产(或权利)。

ap·pen·dec·to·my [ˌæpənˈdektəmi; ˏæpənˋdɛktəmɪ] *n*.【医】阑尾截除术。

ap·pen·di·ci·tis [əˌpendiˈsaitis; əˏpɛndəˋsaɪtɪs] *n*.【医】阑尾炎。

ap·pen·di·cle [əˈpendikl; əˋpɛndəkl] *n*. 小附属物。

ap·pen·dic·u·lar [ˌæpənˈdikjulə; ˏæpənˋdɪkjələ˞] *a*. 附属物的,有附属物的(尤指脊椎动物的四肢)。

ap·pen·dix [əˈpendiks; əˋpɛndɪks] *n*. (*pl*. **~es**; **-dices** [-disiːz; -dɪsiz]). 1. 附属物;附庸。2. 附录,附言,补遗。3.【解】阑尾(= vermiform ~)。3. (飞船充气和放气用的)气量调节管。II *vt*. 附加于。

ap·pen·tice [əˈpentis; əˋpɛntɪs] *n*.【建】厢房;耳房。

ap·per·ceive [ˌæpə(ː)ˈsiːv; ˏæpə(ɚ)ˋsiv] *vt*. 1.【心】(借助老经验来)阐明(新概念)。2.【哲】统觉,明觉。3.【废】领悟,知觉。

ap·per·cep·tion [ˌæpə(ː)ˈsepʃən; ˏæpɚ(ɚ)ˋsɛpʃən] *n*. 1.【哲】统觉;明觉(作用)。2.【心】借助老经验来理解新概念;触类旁通。

ap·per·tain [ˌæpə(ː)ˈtein; ˏæpɚˋten] *vi*. 属于;和…有关(*to*)。*a house and everything ~ing to it*. 房屋及其附属物。*Forestry ~s to agriculture*. 森林学和农学有关。

ap·pe·tence, ap·pe·ten·cy [ˈæpitəns(i); ˋæpətəns(ɪ)] *n*. 1. 强烈的欲望。2. 本能的倾向,习性。3.【化】亲和力(*for*)。*an ~ for* [*after*] *knowledge* 强烈的求知欲。**-tent** *a*.

ap·pe·tite [ˈæpitait; ˋæpəˏtaɪt] *n*. 1. 欲望,(特指)胃口,食欲。2. 嗜好,爱好。*the sexual ~* 性欲。*Fit the ~ to the dishes and dress to the figure*. 看菜吃饭,量体裁衣。***A good ~ is a good sauce***.〔谚〕饥不择食。***give ~*** 促进食欲。***have a good*** [***poor***] ***~*** 食欲旺盛[不振]。***have an ~ for*** (*music*) 爱好(音乐)。***to one's ~*** 合口味,正合…胃口。***with a good ~*** 胃口好,大大(吃了一顿)。

ap·pe·ti·tive [əˈpetitiv; əˋpɛtɪtɪv] *a*. 食欲上的,增进食欲的,开胃的。

ap·pe·tiz·er, -tis·er [ˈæpitaizə; ˋæpəˏtaɪzɚ] *n*. 1. 开胃菜,开胃酒。2. 刺激欲望的事物。*Hunger* [*Exercise*] *is a good ~*. 饥饿[运动]是最好的开胃物。

ap·pe·tiz·ing, -tis·ing [ˈæpitaiziŋ; ˋæpəˏtaɪzɪŋ] *a*. 1. 刺激食欲的。2. 美味的。*the ~ smell of cakes* 蛋糕那令人馋涎欲滴的香味。

Ap·pi·an [ˈæpiən; ˋæpɪən] **way** 阿庇乌大道〔古罗马皇帝 Appius 所建军用大道,从罗马经过加普亚通到布朗迪西恩(今布林迪西),长 350 英里〕。

ap·plaud [əˈplɔːd; əˋplɔd] *vt*., *vi*. 1. 鼓掌欢迎[喝采],欢呼。2. 赞美,夸奖,称赞。*I ~ (you for) your decision*. 我赞佩你的决心。~ (*sb*.) *for* (*his courage*) 夸奖(某人勇敢)。

ap·plause [əˈplɔːz; əˋplɔz] *n*. 1. 喝采,热烈鼓掌。2. 夸奖,称赞。*a storm of ~* 掌声雷动,暴风雨般的掌声。*unanimous ~* 全场鼓掌。*win ~* 博得喝采,受到赞扬。**ap·plaus·ive** *a*.

ap·ple [ˈæpl; ˋæpl] *n*. 1. 苹果,苹果树。2. 苹果状的东西。3.〔美俚〕(棒球的)球;炸弹;手榴弹。4.〔美俚〕人,家伙。*a cherry ~* 棠梨。*a mad ~* 茄子。*a Persian ~* 枸橼。***Adam's ~*** 喉结。~ ***of discord***【希神】(各女神争夺的、作为最美丽者象征的)金苹果,纷争之果;〔喻〕争端,祸根。~ ***of love*** 蕃茄。~ ***of Sodom = Dead Sea ~*** (传说中的)一摘就冒烟成灰的美丽的苹果;〔喻〕华而不实的事物。~ ***of the*** [***one's***] ***eye*** 瞳孔,眼珠,珍爱之物,掌中珠。***throw away the ~ because of the core*** 因噎废食。***upset the*** [或 ***sb.'s***] ***~ cart*** 打破(某人)计划。~ **butter** 1. 苹果酱。2.〔美方〕聊天。~ **green** 苹果绿。~**-head** 1.〔美俚〕笨蛋。2. (玩具狗的)圆脑袋。~ **jack**〔美〕苹果白兰地。~ **knocker**〔美口〕1. 苹果采摘人。2. 农夫,庄稼汉。3. 生手。~**-pie** 1. *n*. 苹果馅饼。2. *a*. 典型美国式的。~**-pie bed** (学生恶作剧)故意把被褥叠得使人睡下伸不直脚的卧铺。~ **pie order**〔口〕井然有序(*in* [*into*] *~-pie order* 秩序井然,整整齐齐。*put things into ~-pie order* 把东西收拾得整整齐齐)。~ **polisher**〔美俚〕拍马屁的人(尤指学生)。~ **polishing**〔美俚〕巴结(教授)。~ **sauce** 1. 苹果酱。2. 不诚恳的奉承。3. 胡说。~**wife**, ~**woman** 卖苹果的女人。~**wood** 苹果木。

Ap·ple·ton [ˈæpltən; ˋæpltən] *n*. 阿普尔顿〔姓氏〕。

ap·pli·ance [əˈplaiəns; əˋplaɪəns] *n*. 1. 器具,用具;器械;装置,设备。2. 适用,应用。*Stoves, irons, etc. are household ~s*. 炉子、熨斗等是家庭用具。~ *of* (*a principle*) *to*... 把(原理)应用到…上。~ **garage**〔厨房中的〕电厨具库;厨房用品专柜。

ap·pli·ca·bil·i·ty [ˌæplikəˈbiliti; ˏæplɪkəˋbɪlətɪ] *n*. 适用性,应用性;适当。

ap·pli·ca·ble [ˈæplikəbl; ˋæplɪkəbl] *a*. 1. (规则)可适用的,能应用的。2. 合适的,适当的(*to*)。*an ~ rule* 切实可行的规则。*a solution that is ~ to the problem* 适合于这个问题的解决方法。**-bly** *ad*. 适当。**-ness** *n*. 适切,剀切。

ap·pli·cant [ˈæplikənt; ˋæpləkənt] *n*. 请求人,申请人。*an ~ for a situation* 找事的,求职者。*an ~ for admission to a school* 入学申请者。

ap·pli·ca·tion [ˌæpliˈkeiʃən; ˏæpləˋkeʃən] *n*. 1. 适用,应用;运用。2. 申请,请求;申请表格。3. 勤勉,用功。4. 敷用;敷用药。*a written ~* 申请书。*an ~ for admission* (*to a school*) 入学申请。*fill out an ~* 填写申请表。*He shows very little ~ to his study*. 他不用功,不勤学。*a man of close ~* 勤奋的人,专心一意的人。*a point of ~* 作用点,施力点。*for external* [*internal*] *~* 外用[内用](药)。***make an for*** (*help*) ***to*** (*sb*.) 请求(某人)(帮助)。***on ~*** (***to***) (向…)提出要求(*A list of new books will be sent on ~ to the publisher*. 新书目录,可向出版者函索)。~ **blank** [**form**] 空白申请书。

ap·pli·ca·tive [ˈæplikeitiv; ˋæpləˏketɪv] *a*. 可适用的,合用的;实用的。

ap·pli·ca·tor [ˈæplikeitə; ˋæpləˏketɚ] *n*. (耳鼻科用的)棒状涂药器,棉棍。

ap·pli·ca·to·ry [ˈæplikətəri; ˋæpləkəˏtorɪ] *a*. 可适用的,适宜的;实用的。

ap·plied [əˈplaid; əˋplaɪd] *a*. 适用的,应用的,实用的(*opp*. pure, abstract, theoretical)。~ **art** 实用美术。~ **chemistry** 应用化学。~ **mathematics** 应用数学。

ap·pli·qué [æˈpliːkei; æpliˋke] I *a*.〔F.〕(花纹)缝上的;贴补的。~ *lace* 补贴的花边。II *n*. (服装等的)补花,贴花,嵌花。III *vt*. (***-quéd***; ***-quéing***) 缝饰,镶饰在…上贴花。~ *a satin blouse with wool of the same colour* 用同色毛线在一件缎衫上贴花。

ap·ply [əˈplai; əˋplaɪ] *vt*. 1. 运用,应用(原则),把…运

用于。**2.** 用(药)敷,搽;用(火)点(灯);用(…)做(…)。**3.** 专心,致力。~ *the rule to each situation* 把该法则应用于每一种具体情况。~ *scientific discoveries to the industrial production* 把科学发现应用于工业生产。~ *a plaster to a wound* 用膏药贴伤口。*A- at the office.* 请在办事处接洽。~ *paint to a house* 油漆房屋。—*vi.* **1.** 适合;适用。**2.** 申请,请求。**3.** 专心,努力。~ *to the Danish Consul for a visa* 向丹麦领事馆申请签证。*For particulars* ~ *to the office.* 详情请问办事处。~ *for a position* 求职。~ ***oneself to*** 专心(做事)。~ ***one's mind to*** (*one's lessons*) 专心致志于,热心于(学习)。~ ***to*** (*a person*) ***for*** (*help*) 向(某人)求(援)。

ap·pog·gia·tu·ra [əˌpɒdʒəˈturə; əˌpɑdʒəˋturə] ***n.*** [It.]【乐】倚音,花音。

ap·point [əˈpɔint; əˋpɔɪnt] ***vt.*** **1.** 委派,任命(*opp.* dismiss)。**2.** 指定,约定(时间、地点等)。**3.** 给…提供装备[设备]。**4.**【法】处置(财产)。**5.** 命令。**6.** 规定。*He was ~ed ambassador.* 他已被任命为大使。~ *a new secretary* 委派一名新秘书。~ *a time for a meeting* 约定开会的时间。*The house is well ~ed.* 这房子设备齐全。*The law was ~ed by the king.* 这项法律是由国王规定的。

ap·point·ed [əˈpɔintid; əˋpɔɪntɪd] ***a.*** **1.** 指定的,约定的。**2.** 设备…的。*at the* ~ *time* 在约定的时间。*one's* ~ *lot* 宿命。*one's* ~ *task* 指定的工作,本职工作。*a well* [*poorly*] ~ *guest-room* 设备完美的[简陋的]客房。

ap·point·ee [æpɔinˈtiː; ˌæpɔɪnˋti] ***n.*** **1.** 被任命者,被指定者。**2.**【法】被指定为财产的受益者。**ap·point·er** ***n.*** 任命者。

ap·point·ive [əˈpɔintiv; əˋpɔɪntɪv] ***a.*** **1.** (官职等)委任的,任命的。**2.** 有任命[指定]权的。*an* ~ *office* 委任的职务。*the president's* ~ *power* 总统的委任权。

ap·point·ment [əˈpɔintmənt; əˋpɔɪntmənt] ***n.*** **1.** 任命,委派,任用。**2.** 任职,官职,职位。**3.** 法令,命令;天意。**4.** 指定;约定,约会;【医】(门诊)预约。**5.** [*pl.*]设备;家具。**6.**【法】指定(财产受益人)。*obtain a good* ~ 获得一项好差事。*an* ~ *for* [*to meet at*] *six o'clock* 六点钟的约会。***by a natural*** ~ 由于自然的巧合。***by*** ~ 照章,按约。***have an*** ~ ***with sb.*** 和某人有约会。***keep*** [***break***] ***one's*** ~ 守[违]约。***make an*** ~ ***with sb.*** 和某人定下约会时间。***take up an*** ~ 就职,上任。~ **call**【讯】定人定时呼叫。

ap·point·or [əˈpɔintə; əˋpɔɪntɚ] ***n.*** **1.** = appointer. **2.**【法】指定人(有权用证书或遗嘱指定财产归属的人)。

ap·port [əˈpɔːt; əˋpɔrt] **I** ***n.*** 幻姿(指在招魂会或降神会上用幻术来产生有形的东西)。**II** ***vt.*** 使生幻姿。

ap·por·tion [əˈpɔːʃən; əˋpɔrʃən] ***vt.*** 分派,分摊;分配(*among*)。*an ~ed task* 所分担的工作。~ *time among various employments* 为做各项不同的工作分配时间。**-ment** ***n.*** 分配,分摊。

ap·pos·a·ble [əˈpəuzəbl; əˋpozəbl] ***a.*** 可并置的,可置于附近的。*The human thumb is* ~. 人类的拇指与其他四指对置。

ap·pose [əˈpəuz; əˋpoz] ***vt.*** (***-posed***; ***-pos·ing***) **1.** 并列;把…置于对面或附近。**2.** [古]把某物置于[应用于]他物上。~ *food before a guest* 把食物放在客人面前。~ *a seal to a document* 在文件上盖章。

ap·po·site [ˈæpəzit; ˋæpəzɪt] ***a.*** **1.** 适当的,合适的。**2.**【植】并生的;附着的。*an* ~ *answer* 得当的答覆。*be* ~ *to the case* 切合实情的。**-ly** ***ad.*** **-ness** ***n.***

ap·po·si·tion [ˌæpəˈziʃən; ˌæpəˋzɪʃən] ***n.*** **1.** 并置;并列。**2.**【植】敷着,附着生长。**3.**【语法】同格,同位。*growth by* ~ (细胞膜的)附着生长。*the* ~ *of thumb and forefinger* 大拇指与食指并列。*a noun in* ~ 同格名词。***in*** ~ ***to*** 与…同格。**-al** ***a.***

ap·pos·i·tive [əˈpɔzitiv; əˋpɑzətɪv] **I** ***a.***【语法】同位的,同格的。**II** ***n.***【语法】同位语。~ **adjective** 同位形容词。~ **construction** 同位结构。~ **noun** 同位名词。**-ly** ***ad.***

ap·prais·a·ble [əˈpreizəbl; əˋprezəbl] ***a.*** 可估价的,可评价的。

ap·prais·al [əˈpreizəl; əˋprezl] ***n.*** 评价,估价,估计,鉴定。*make* [*give*] *an objective* ~ *of* 对…作出客观的评价。

ap·praise [əˈpreiz; əˋprez] ***vt.*** **1.** 评价,估价。**2.** 鉴定,品定。*Property is ~d for taxation.* 估产定税。**-ment** ***n.*** 评价;估价,估计价额;鉴定,评定。

ap·prais·er [əˈpreizə; əˋprezɚ] ***n.*** 估价人,评价人,鉴定人。

ap·pre·ci·a·ble [əˈpriːʃiəbl; əˋprɪʃɪəbl] ***a.*** **1.** 可估价的。**2.** 可察觉的。*There is no* ~ *difference.* 大致相同。

ap·pre·ci·ate [əˈpriːʃieit; əˋprɪʃɪˌet] ***vt.*** **1.** 估价,评价,鉴别。**2.** 体会;了解,意识到,懂得。**3.** 欣赏,鉴赏,赏识。**4.** 感激,感谢。**5.** 使提价。~ *the difficulties of the situation* 意识到局势困难。*I* ~ *your kindness.* 多谢厚意。~ *good food* 欣赏美味。~ *sb.'s friendship* 珍视某人的友谊。*New buildings ~s the value of land.* 新建筑物提高了土地的价值。—***vi.*** 涨价,腾贵(*opp.* depreciate)。*Things* ~ *as time goes on.* 货物逐日腾贵。

ap·pre·ci·a·tion [əˌpriːʃiˈeiʃən; əˌprɪʃɪˋeʃən] ***n.*** **1.** 评价,鉴别。**2.** 知道,了解。**3.** 鉴赏,欣赏。**4.** 感谢;感激。**5.** (地价等的)上涨,腾贵(*opp.* depreciation)。~ *of literature* 文学鉴赏。*She has an* ~ *of art and music.* 她对于美术和音乐有了解。*in* ~ *of* 因赏识…而,因感激…而。*We offer this small token by way of* ~. 我们赠送这个小纪念品作为酬谢。

ap·pre·ci·a·tive [əˈpriːʃjətiv; əˋprɪʃɪˌetɪv] ***a.*** **1.** 能评价的,有鉴别力的,有眼力的;有欣赏力的。**2.** 感谢的。*an* ~ *audience* 有欣赏力的观众。*I am very* ~ *of your kindness.* 我很感激你的厚意。

ap·pre·ci·a·tor [əˈpriʃiˌeitə; əˋprɪʃɪˌetɚ] ***n.*** 鉴别者;赏识者;鉴赏者。

ap·pre·ci·a·to·ry [əˈpriːʃjətəri; əˋprɪʃɪəˌtorɪ] ***a.*** = appreciative.

ap·pre·hend [ˌæpriˈhend; ˌæprɪˋhɛnd] ***vt.*** **1.** 理解,领悟。**2.** 逮捕,捉拿;拘押。**3.** 怕,忧虑。*I don't* ~ *his meaning.* 我不理解他的意思。~ *danger in every sound* 风声鹤唳,草木皆兵。*It is ~ed that ...* 恐怕会…。~ *a hot summer* 担心会有一个炎热的夏季。~ *a criminal* 捕捉罪犯。—***vi.*** **1.** 理解,领悟。**2.** 忧虑,害怕。

ap·pre·hen·si·bil·i·ty [ˈæpriˌhensiˈbiliti; ˌæprɪhɛnsəˋbɪlətɪ] ***n.*** 可理解。

ap·pre·hen·si·ble [ˌæpriˈhensəbl; ˌæprɪˋhɛnsəbl] ***a.*** 可理解的。*not* ~ *even to professional men* 连专门家都难以理解的(东西)。

ap·pre·hen·sion [ˌæpriˈhenʃən; ˌæprɪˋhɛnʃən] ***n.*** **1.** 理解(力);领悟。**2.** 见解。**3.** 逮捕(*opp.* release)拘押。**4.** [常 *pl.*]不安,忧虑。***be dull*** [***quick***] ***of*** ~ 头脑敏捷[迟钝]。***entertain*** [***have***] ***some ~s for*** [***of***] 恐怕,深怕。***in my*** ~ 我以为,在我想来。***under the*** ~ ***that*** …唯恐,就怕。

ap·pre·hen·sive [ˌæpriˈhensiv; ˌæprɪˋhɛnsɪv] ***a.*** **1.** 忧虑的,担心的。**2.** 有理解力的,善于领会的,聪明的,敏捷的。*an* ~ *mind* 敏捷的头脑。**3.** 有关理解力的。**4.** 意识到…的(*of*)。***be*** ~ ***for sb.'s safety*** 担心某人的安全。***be*** ~ ***of danger*** 害怕有危险。***be*** ~ ***of one's folly*** 意识到自己的愚蠢。***be*** ~ ***that ... may*** 怕…会。**-ly** ***ad.***

ap·pren·tice [əˈprentis; əˋprɛntɪs] **I** ***n.*** **1.** 徒弟,学徒;学徒工。**2.** 见习生,生手,初学者。*an ~'s indenture* 学

A

徒契约。an ~s' school 艺徒学校。**be bound ~ to** 做…的学徒。**go ~** 做学徒。**II** *vt*. 使做学徒。~ **oneself to** (*a tailor*) 做(裁缝)学徒。**be ~ to** 做…的学徒[徒弟]。**-ship** 徒弟的身分[年限] (*the period of apprenticeship* 见习期限,学徒年限。*serve one's apprenticeship at* ... [*with sb*.] 在…[跟某人]做学徒)。~ **seaman** 〔美〕三等水手。

ap·pressed [ə'prest, æ-; ə`prest, æ-] *a*. 紧贴的;紧靠的;平贴着的。

ap·prise [ə'praiz; ə`praɪz] *vt*. 〔书〕报告,通知,告知。~ **sb. of** (**sth.**) 告知某人某事 (~ *him of my arrival* 通知他我已到达)。

ap·prize [ə'praiz; ə`praɪz] *vt*. = apprise.

appro. = approval.

ap·pro ['æprəu; `æpro] *n*. 〔仅用于下列成语〕: **on ~** 〔俚〕(商品)供试用的,包退包换的。

ap·proach [ə'prəutʃ; ə`protʃ] **I** *vt*. **1.** 向…接近,走近;使接近。**2.** 探讨;看待,对待,处理。**3.** 向…接洽[提议]。**4.** 〔美〕企图收买。~ *one's home* 快到家。~ *completion* 将近完成。*It is wrong to ~ a problem from a metaphysical point of view*. 用形而上学的观点来看待问题是错误的。~ *Shakespeare as a poet* 诗才堪与莎士比亚相比拟。~ *the manager with a suggestion* 向经理提出建议。~ *the manager on a business* 为一项事务与经理接洽。~ *a government officer* 企图向政府官员行贿。—*vi*. 临近,靠近,近似。*Winter ~es*. 冬天快到了。**II** *n*. **1.** 走近,接近,逼近。**2.** 近似,类似。**3.** 进路,入口;门径,接近[处理]的方法,手段。**4.** 探索,探讨。**5.** 看法,观点。**6.** 〔*pl*.〕亲近;打交道。**7.** 【军】(为逼近敌方工事而挖的)战壕。**8.** 【空】进场(飞行),进入(投弹点)。**9.** 【军】战斗前进。**10.** 〔*pl*.〕提议,建议。*the best ~ to study a foreign language* 学习外国语的最佳方法。*the blind ~* 【空】盲目(按仪表)进场。*the instrument ~* 【空】按仪表进场。*a scientific ~* 科学态度。*his nearest ~ to a smile* 他的似笑非笑的笑容。*an ~ to the bridge* 桥畔,引桥。*the ~ to the village* 到村庄去的路。**make ~es to** (**sb.**) 同(某人)亲近;和(某人)打交道。~ **light** 【空】着陆信号灯。

ap·proach·a·bil·i·ty [əˌprəutʃə'biliti; əˌprotʃə`bɪlətɪ] *n*. 可接近,易接近。

ap·proach·a·ble [ə'prəutʃəbl; ə`protʃəbl̩] *a*. **1.** 可进入的。**2.** 易接近的;易交谈的,平易近人的。

ap·pro·bate ['æprəubeit; `æprəˌbet] *vt*. 〔美〕认可,批准。~ *an act* 通过议案。~ *the applicant to keep a shop* 批准申请人开业。

ap·pro·ba·tion [ˌæprə'beiʃən; ˌæprə`beʃən] *n*. **1.** 认可,批准。**2.** 嘉奖,称赞。*meet with one's ~* 得某人同意。*on ~* (略 *on appro*.) (商品)供试用的 〔*cf*. on approval〕。

ap·pro·ba·to·ry ['æprəbeitəri; ə`probəˌtorɪ] *a*. 表示赞许的,表示同意的。

ap·pro·pri·a·ble [ə'prəupriəbl; ə`proprɪəbl] *a*. **1.** 可作专用的。**2.** 可挪用的,可盗取的。**3.** 可拨作…经费的。

ap·pro·pri·ate [ə'prəuprieit; ə`proprɪet] **I** *vt*. **1.** 擅用,挪用,占用,盗用。**2.** 〔美口〕盗取(少量公物)。**3.** 充用,充当,拨作…费用。**4.** 〔美〕(州议会)认可(某项)经费。~ *money for the navy* 拨款作海军费用。~ *the building for storage* 拨房子当仓库。~ *public funds for one's own private use* 挪用公款。~ *public property to oneself* 私拿公物。**II** [-priit; -prɪɪt] *a*. **1.** 适当的,合适的 (*to*)。**2.** 特定的,专属的。*an ~ example* 适当的例子。*Each played his ~ part*. 每个人都起了他所特有的作用[各得其所]。**be ~ for** [**to**] 适于,合乎。**-ly** *ad*. 适当地。**-ness** *n*. 适当。

ap·pro·pri·a·tion [əˌprəupri'eiʃən; əˌproprɪ`eʃən] *n*. **1.** 专用。**2.** 私用;挪用,擅用,盗用。**3.** 充当,充用。**4.** 经费。**5.** 【宗】圣俸的转让;转让的圣俸;拨款;拨款的立法行动。*The ~ of the land made it possible to have a new building*. 该块土地的拨用使得建造新楼成为可能。~ *of public fund* 盗用公共基金。*a large ~ for aid to the homeless children* 用来抚养无家可归儿童的巨额拨款。**the Appropriations Committee** 〔美〕岁出委员会;拨款委员会。~ **bill** 〔美〕(提交议会的)岁出预算案,拨款预算案。

ap·pro·pri·a·tive [ə'prəupriətiv; ə`proprɪˌetɪv] *a*. **1.** 专用[私用]的。**2.** 盗用的,挪用的,占用的。**3.** 充作…用的,政府支出的。

ap·pro·pri·a·tor [ə'prəuprieitə; ə`proprɪetɚ] *n*. **1.** 拨给者。**2.** 专用者。**3.** 擅用者;盗用者。

ap·prov·a·ble [ə'pruːvəbl; ə`pruvəbl̩] *a*. 可批准的;可赞同的。

ap·prov·al [ə'pruːvəl; ə`pruvəl̩] *n*. **1.** 赞成,同意。**2.** 批准;认可。*Do not lightly express your ~ or disapproval*. 不可轻易表示赞成或反对。*meet with sb.'s ~* 得某人赞成。**for** (**sb.'s**) **~** 提请(某人)批准[承认];求(某人)指正。**on ~** 〔俚〕(商品)供试用的,包退包换的。**with ~ of the authorities** 经当局批准。

ap·prove [ə'pruːv; ə`pruv] *vt*. **1.** 批准,认可 (*opp*. reject)。**2.** 赞成,满意。**3.** 〔 ~ oneself〕〔古〕显示,证明,证实。~ *the work of a student* (老师)赞许学生的作业。*Congress ~d the bill*. 国会批准了该项法案。*The plan ~d itself to me*. 我认为这个计划已证实是好的。*the most ~d method* 最好的办法。—*vi*. 赞成,满意 (*of*)。~ **of** 赞成 (*I quite ~ of your plan*. 我十分赞成你的计划)。~ **oneself** 证实自己是… (*He ~d himself ripe for the military command*. 他显现得已经可以做司令官了。*He ~d himself a good man*. 他证实自己是好人)。**be ~d for distribution** 批转,批发。

ap·proved [ə'pruːvd; ə`pruvd] *a*. 已被承认的;良好的;有效的。*an ~ tenderer* 指定投标人。~ **school** 〔英〕少年罪犯教养院,工读学校。

ap·prov·er [ə'pruːvə; ə`pruvɚ] *n*. **1.** 赞成者,批准者。**2.** 【法】自首告发同犯的人。

approx. = approximate(ly)。

ap·prox·i·mal [ə'prɔksiməl; ə`prɑksɪməl] *a*. 【解】邻近的;邻接的。

ap·prox·i·mate [ə'prɔksimeit; ə`prɑksəˌmet] **I** *vt*. **1.** 使接近。**2.** 接近;走近。**3.** 近似,约计。**4.** 模拟。**5.** 估计。~ *a solution to a problem* 使问题近于解决。~ *something to perfection* 使某物臻于完善。*The total income this year ~s 10,000 dollors*. 今年总收入接近一万元。~ *the motions of the stars in a planetarium* 在天文馆中模拟行星的运行情况。*We ~d the distance at 100 miles*. 我们估计行程距离为100英里。—*vi*. 近于。*His income this year ~s to 8,000 dollars*. 他今年的收入接近八千元。**II** [ə'prɔks*i*mit; ə`prɑksɪmɪt] *a*. 近似的,大概的。*an ~ account* 简要的说明。*an ~ date* 大约的日期。*the ~ estimate* 大概的估计。*an ~ number* 概数。*an ~ value* 近似值。**-ly** *ad*. 大体,大致。

ap·prox·i·ma·tion [əˌprɔksi'meiʃən; əˌprɑksə`meʃən] *n*. **1.** 接近;近似。**2.** 【数】近似值。**3.** 概算,略计。*successive ~s* 逐次近似计算法。**be a very close ~ to** 很接近于…。

ap·pur·te·nance [ə'pəːtinəns; ə`pɝtnəns] *n*. **1.** 〔常 *pl*.〕附属物,从属物。**2.** 【法】(财产上的)附属[附带]权利〔如:道路通行权、果园所有权等〕。**3.** 〔*pl*.〕(附属)装置,设备。*a house and all its ~s* 房子及其一切附属物。

ap·pur·te·nant [ə'pəːtinənt; ə`pɝtnənt] **I** *a*. **1.** 附属的,从属的 (*to*)。**2.** 贴切的,恰当的。*a right-of-way ~ to land* [*buildings*] 随着土地[房子]而来的道路通行权。*a note ~ to the subject* 切合主题的注解。**II** *n*. 附属物。

Apr. = April.

a·prax·i·a [ə'præksiə; ə`prækʃɪə] *n*.【医】(精神性)失用症。

a·prax·ic [ə'præksik; ə`præksɪk], **a·prac·tic** [-'præktik; -`præktɪk] *a*.【医】患精神性失用症的。

a·près [æprei; æpre] *prep*.〔F.〕在…之后;〔用在带连字符的复合词中〕在…之后的: ~ *moi le déluge* 死后(洪)大水,与我何干,身后事与我何干。*an ~-ski party* 滑雪运动后举行的茶会。

a·pri·cot ['eiprikɔt; `eprɪˏkɑt] *n*. **1**.【植】杏,杏树。**2**. 杏黄色。**3**.〔A-〕【植】李属。~ *plum* 红李。*Japanese* ~ 梅。

A·pril ['eiprəl; `eprəl] *n*. **1**. 四月。**2**. 埃普丽尔〔女子名〕。~ **fool** 四月傻瓜〔愚人节中受愚弄的人〕。~ **Fools' Day** 愚人节〔每年 4 月 1 日〕。~ **shower** 忽下忽停的春雨。

a pri·o·ri ['ei prai'ɔ:rai; `epraɪ`oraɪ] **I** *a*.〔L.〕由原因推及结果的;演绎的;先验的;推测的(*opp*. a posteriori)。*an ~ judgment* 忆测的判断。**II** *ad*. 演绎地,先验地。

a·pri·o·rism [ˌeiprai'ɔ:rizəm; ˏeprɪ`orɪzəm] *n*. 先验论,先验的原理;演绎推理。

a·pri·or·i·ty [ˌeiprai'ɔriti; ˏepraɪ`ɔrətɪ] *n*. **1**. 演绎性,推论性,先验性。**2**. 演绎推论法的运用。

a·pron ['eiprən; `eprən] **I** *n*. **1**. 围裙。**2**. (炮的)旋转保护罩。**3**.【船】(船头的)护船木。**4**.【机】(防护)挡板;(机床刀座下的)拖板箱。**5**.【地】冰川沉积堆。**6**.【剧】舞台幕前的突出部分,台口(= ~ *stage*)。**7**.【空】(飞机的)库前跑道,停机坪。**8**.〔美口〕铁丝网,伪装天幕。**II** *vt*. 用围裙围住。~ **stage** 台口。~ **string** 围裙带(*be tied to one's mother's* [*wife's*] ~ *string* 为母亲[妻子]所左右,受裙带影响)。**-ful** *n*. 满满一围裙(的)东西(*an apronful of hazelnuts*)满满一围裙的榛子。

ap·ro·pos ['æprəpəu; ˏæprə`po] **I** *a*., *ad*. **1**. 适当的[地],恰好,凑巧。**2**. 顺便说一说(= by the way)。*Your telegram comes* ~. 你的电报来得正是时候。*A-, I have something to tell you*. 顺便跟你说个事。**II** *prep*.〔口〕关于。~ ***of*** 关于,就…说,至于,说到。~ ***of nothing*** 突然地;毫无理由地。

APS, A.P.S. = **1**. American Peace Society 美国和平协会。**2**. American Philosophical Society 美国哲学学会。**3**. American Physical Society 美国物理学会。**4**. American Philatelic Society 美国集邮学会。

apse [æps; æps] *n*. (*pl*. ***ap·ses*** ['æpsəz, -siz; `æpsəz, -sɪz]) **1**. (教堂东端的)半圆室。**2**.【天】拱点(= apsis)。

ap·si·dal ['æpsidl; `æpsidl] *a*. **1**.【天】拱点的。**2**.【建】半圆室的。~ **motion** 拱线运动。~ **surface**【数】长短径曲面。

ap·sis ['æpsis; `æpsɪs] *n*. (*pl*. ***ap·si·des*** [æp'saidi:z; æp`saɪdiz]) **1**.【天】近日点(= lower ~), 远日点(= higher ~), 拱点。**2**.【建】= apse.

AP star ['eipi: stɑ:; `epi stɑr]【天】特一级星〔光度属一级而光谱自具特点的星〕。

APT = **1**. automatically programmed tool【计】自动数控程序。**2**. automatic picture transmission (人造卫星)自动图像传输。**3**. advanced passenger train 先进型旅客特快列车。

apt [æpt; æpt] *a*. **1**. 易于…的,有…倾向的,好…的〔后接不定式〕〔美〕有…可能的。**2**. 适当的,恰当的。**3**. 灵敏的,灵巧的;擅长的;(学生等)有希望的。*He is ~ at teaching*. 他善于教书。*He is ~ to succeed*. 他很可能成功。*We are ~ to think ill of others*. 我们往往从坏的方面考虑人。*Iron is ~ to rust*. 铁易生锈。*an ~ comment* 恰当的评论。

apt(s) = apartment(s).

ap·ter·al ['æptərəl; `æptərəl] *a*. **1**.【动】无翅的。**2**.【建】无侧柱的。

ap·ter·ous ['æptərəs; `æptərəs] *a*.【动】无翅的,无翼的。

ap·ter·yg·i·al [ˌæptə'ridʒiəl; ˏæptə`rɪdʒɪəl] *a*.【动】缺少对鳍或对肢的。

ap·ti·tude ['æptitju:d; `æptəˏtjud] *n*. **1**. 适合性。**2**. 倾向。**3**. 天资;才能。**4**. 颖悟,聪颖。*an ~ test* 能力倾向测验,性向测验(*cf*. intelligence test)。*a boy of remarkable* ~ 神童。***have an ~ for*** 有…的才能。***have an ~ to*** (*vices*) 易染(恶习)。

apt·ly ['æptli; `æptlɪ] *ad*. 适当地,善,巧。*It has ~ been said that* .... 说得对[好]。

apt·ness ['æptnis; `æptnɛs] *n*. **1**. 适合性。**2**. 性情,倾向。**3**. 才能。

A·pus ['eipəs; `epəs] *n*.【天】天燕(星)座。

a·py·ret·ic [ˌeipai'retik; ˏepaɪ`retɪk] *a*.【医】无热的,不发热的。

AQ, A.Q. = achievement quotient.

aq. = 〔L.〕*aqua* (= *water*).

AQI = air quality index 空气质量指数。

aq·ua ['ækwə; `ækwə] *n*.〔L.〕水;溶液。~ ***ammoniae*** [ə'məunii:; ə`monii]【化】氨水。~ ***fortis*** ['fɔ:tis; `fɔrtɪs]【化】硝酸。~ ***pura*** ['pjuərə; `pjurə] 纯水,蒸馏水。~ ***regia*** ['ri:dʒiə; `ridʒɪə]【化】王水。~ ***vitae*** ['vaiti:; `vaɪtɪ] 烧酒;酒精。

aq·ua·cade ['ækwəkeid; `ækwəˏked] *n*.〔美〕水技会演大会。

aq·ua·cul·ture ['ækwəkʌltʃə; `ækwəˏkʌltʃɚ] *n*. 水产养殖。**-tur·al** *a*.

aq·ua·fer ['ækwəfə; `ækwəˏfɚ] *n*. 含水层(= aquifer)。

aq·ua·gun ['ækwəgʌn; `ækwəˏgʌn] *n*. (潜水员用的)水枪。

aq·ua-lung ['ækwəlʌŋ; `ækwəˏlʌŋ] *n*. (潜水员用的)水中呼吸器。

aq·ua·ma·rine [ˌækwəmə'ri:n; ˏækwəmə`rin] *n*. **1**.【矿】海蓝宝石,蓝晶。**2**. 海蓝色。

aq·ua·naut ['ækwənɔ:t; `ækwəˏnɔt] *n*. **1**. 海底科学工作者,深水操作人员。**2**. 穿紧身潜水服的潜泳者。

aq·ua·plane ['ækwəplein; `ækwəˏplen] **I** *n*. (由小汽艇拖行的)滑水板。**II** *vi*. 站在滑水板上滑行。

aq·ua·relle [ˌækwə'rel; ˏækwə`rɛl] *n*.〔F.〕透明水彩画(法);套色版画(法)。

A·quar·i·an [ə'kweəriən; ə`kwɛrɪən] *a*. 宝瓶座时代的;太空时代的。

a·quar·ist [ə'kweərist; ə`kwɛrɪst] *n*. **1**. (室内)养鱼爱好者,爱养水生动植物者。**2**. 水族馆馆长,水族馆的领导人。

a·quar·i·um [ə'kweəriəm; ə`kwɛrɪəm] *n*. (*pl*. ***~s, ~ria*** [-riə; -rɪə]) **1**. 水族馆。**2**. 水族槽;养鱼缸;玻璃鱼池。

A·quar·i·us [ə'kweəriəs; ə`kwɛrɪəs] *n*. **1**.【天】宝瓶(星)座。**2**.【天】宝瓶宫〔黄道第十一宫〕。

a·qua·tel [ˌækə'tel; ˏækə`tɛl] *n*.〔英口〕水上旅店〔供应住宿设备的系船池〕。

a·quat·ic [ə'kwætik; ə`kwætɪk] **I** *a*. **1**. 水的;水生的,水栖的。**2**. 水上的,水中的。*an ~ bird* 水鸟。~ *plant* 水生植物。~ *products* 水产物。~ *sports* 水上运动。**II** *n*. **1**. 水生动植物。**2**.〔*pl*.〕水上运动。

aq·ua·tint ['ækwətint; `ækwəˏtɪnt] *n*. 蚀刻凹板(画)

aq·ua·vit ['ækwəvit; `ækwəˏvɪt] *n*. 阿瓜维特酒〔北欧产开胃酒〕。

aq·ue·duct ['ækwidʌkt; `ækwɪˏdʌkt] *n*. **1**. 渠道;渡槽,导水管。**2**.【解】导管。

a·que·ous ['eikwiəs; `ekwɪəs] *a*. **1**. 水的;水样的;水多的。**2**. 水成的。~ **solution** 水溶液。~ **humor**【解】(眼球水晶体的)水状液。~ **rock** 水成岩。~ **tint** 水彩,水色。~ **tissue**【植】储水组织。

aq·ui·cul·ture ['ækwikʌltʃə; `ækwəˏkʌltʃɚ] *n*. 水产养殖;(植物的)溶液培养。**-tur·al** *a*.

A

aq·ui·fer [ˈækwifə; ˋækwəfɚ] *n*. (其含水量足可成为泉或井的)蓄水层。
Aq·ui·la [ˈækwilə; ˋækwələ] *n*. 【天】天鹰(星)座。
aq·ui·le·gi·a [ˌækwiˈlidʒiə; ˏækwəˋlidʒɪə] *n*. 毛茛科耧斗菜属植物。
aq·ui·line [ˈækwilain; ˋækwəˏlaɪn] *a*. **1**. 鹰的,似鹰的。**2**. (像鹰嘴那样)弯曲的。*an* ～ *nose* 鹰钩鼻。
a quo [ei kwəu; e kwo] 〔L.〕从此。
AR = **1**. account receivable 应收账。**2**. annual return 年度报告。**3**. all risks【保险】综合险。**4**. 〔L.〕*anno regni* (= in the year of the reign) …朝代。**5**. armed robbery〔美俚〕(警察用语)武装抢劫。**6**. all rail 全程铁路(运输)。
AR. = 〔美〕Army Regulations 军政法规汇编。
Ar【化】= **1**. 元素氩 (argon) 的符号。**2**. aryl radical.【化】芳基。
Ar. = **1**. Arabic. **2**. Aramaic. **3**. argentum.
ar. = **1**. argent. **2**. aromatic. **3**. arrival. **4**. arrive.
ar- *pref*. 〔用于 r 前〕= ad-: *ar*rest.
-ar *suf*. **1**. …的,…性的,…似的: famili*ar*, simil*ar*. **2**. …的人[物]: schol*ar*, alt*ar*. **3**. = -er, -or: begg*ar*, li*ar*.
A.R.A. = **1**. American Railway Association 美国铁路协会。**2**. Associate of the Royal Academy 〔英〕皇家艺术院准会员。
Ar·ab [ˈærəb; ˋærəb] **I** *n*. **1**. 阿拉伯人。**2**. 阿拉伯马。**3**. 街头流浪儿(= street ～)。**II** *a*. 阿拉伯的,阿拉伯人的。**-dom** *n*. 阿拉伯世界。
Arab. = Arabia; Arabian; Arabic.
Ar·a·bel·(l)a [ˌærəˈbelə; ˏærəˋbɛlə] *n*. 阿拉贝拉〔女子名〕。
ar·a·besque [ˌærəˈbesk; ˏærəˋbɛsk] **I** *a*. **1**. 阿拉伯式的。**2**. 精致的;奇异的。**3**. 蔓藤花纹的。**4**. (文句)复杂难懂的。**II** *n*. **1**. 蔓藤花纹。**2**. 芭蕾舞的一种姿势〔身体向前,一足落地,一足后伸,两手前后平伸〕。**3**. 轻松的狂想乐曲。**4**. 复杂难懂的文句。
A·ra·bi·a [əˈreibjə; əˋrebɪə] *n*. 阿拉伯半岛〔亚洲〕。
A·ra·bi·an [əˈreibjən; əˋrebɪən] **I** *a*. 阿拉伯(半岛)的;阿拉伯人的。***the*** ～ ***bird*** 凤凰。***the A- Nights' Entertainments*** = *the Thousand and One Nights* 〈一千零一夜〉〔旧译〈天方夜谭〉,古代阿拉伯民间故事集〕。**II** *n*. 阿拉伯人。
Ar·a·bic [ˈærəbik; ˋærəbɪk] **I** *a*. 阿拉伯的;阿拉伯人[语]的。**II** *n*. 阿拉伯语。～ **figures** [**numerals**] 阿拉伯数字。
Ar·ab·ist [ˈærəbist; ˋærəˏbɪst] *n*. 阿拉伯(语)学者,阿拉伯研究专家。
A·rab·i·za·tion [ˌærəbaiˈzeiʃən; ˏærəbaɪˋzeʃən] *n*. 阿拉伯化。
A·rab·i·ze [ˈærəbaiz; ˋærəˏbaɪz] *vt*. 使阿拉伯化。
ar·a·ble [ˈærəbl; ˋærəbl̩] **I** *a*. **1**. 适于耕种的,可耕的。**2**. 〔英〕从事农作物栽培的。**II** *n*. (可)耕地(= ～ land)。～ *farming* 作物栽培。～ *soil* 适于耕种的土壤。
Ar·a·by [ˈærəbi; ˋærəbɪ] *n*. 〔诗〕= Arabia.
a·rach·nid [əˈræknid; əˋræknɪd] *n*. 蜘蛛网动物〔包括蝎子、蜘蛛、虱子等〕。
a·rach·noid [əˈræknɔid; əˋræknɔɪd] **I** *a*. **1**. 蛛网状的。**2**. 【解】蛛网膜的。**II** *n*. 【解】蛛网膜。～ *of brain* 脑蛛网膜。
a·rae·o·style [əˈriːəstail; əˋriəˏstaɪl] **I** *n*. 【建】疏柱式建筑物。**II** *a*. 【建】疏柱式的。
a·rae·o·sys·tyle [əˌriːəˈsistail; əˏriəˋsɪstaɪl] **I** *n*. 【建】对柱式建筑物。**II** *a*. 【建】对柱式的。
A·ra·gon [ˈærəgən; ˋærəˏgən] *n*. 阿拉贡〔西班牙东北部地名,古为一王国〕。
Ar·a·go·nese [ˌærəgəˈniːz; ˏærəgəˋniz] **I** *a*. 阿拉贡的,阿拉贡人的;阿拉贡语的。**II** *n*. **1**. (*pl*. ～) 阿拉贡人。**2**. 阿拉贡西班牙方言。
a·rag·o·nite [əˈrægənait, ˈærəgə-; əˋrægəˏnaɪt, ˋærəgə-] *n*. 【矿】霰石,文石。
ar·ak, ar·rack [ˈærək; ˋærɪk] *n*. 亚力酒〔椰子、大米、糖汁等酿成的一种烧酒〕。
Ar·al [ˈɑːrəl; ˋɛrəl] *n*. **Lake** ～ 咸海〔苏联〕〔亦作 ～ **Sea**〕。
ARAM = Associate of the Royal Academy of Music (英国)皇家音乐院准会员。
Ar·am [ˈɛərəm; ˋɛrəm] *n*. 阿拉姆〔姓氏〕。
Ar·a·mae·an, Ar·a·me·an [ˌærəˈmiən; ˏærəˋmɪən] **I** *n*. **1**. 阿拉米人〔古叙利亚和美索不达米亚人〕。**2**. = Aramaic. **II** *a*. **1**. 阿拉米人的。**2**. 阿拉米语的。
Ar·a·ma·ic [ˌærəˈmeiik; ˏærəˋmeɪk] *n*. 阿拉米语〔古代西南亚的通用语言〕(略 **Aram.**)。
Aramco, ARAMCO = Arabian-American Oil Company 阿拉伯-美国石油公司。
a·ra·ne·id [əˈreiniid; əˋrenɪˏɪd] *n*. 【动】真蜘蛛类动物,蜘蛛。
A·rap·a·ho [əˈræpəhəu; əˋræpəho] *n*. (*pl*. ～) **1**. 阿拉帕荷人〔原住北美北普拉特和阿肯色河,现住怀俄明和俄克拉荷马的一支印第安人部落〕。
ar·a·pai·ma [ˌærəˈpaimə; ˏærəˋpaɪmə] *n*. 巨骨舌鱼〔产于南美,长达 3.5m. 的一种大淡水鱼〕。
ar·a·ro·ba [ˌærəˈrəubə; ˏærəˋrobə] *n*. **1**. 柯桠粉〔来自柯桠树,用以制药〕。**2**. 柯桠树〔巴西的一种树〕。
Ar·au·ca·ni·an [ˌærɔːˈkeiniən; ˏærɔˋkenɪən], **A·rau·can** [əˈrɔːkən; əˋrɔkən] **I** *n*. **1**. 阿洛柯人〔智利和阿根廷的一支印第安人〕。**2**. 阿洛柯语。**II** *a*. 阿洛柯人的;阿洛柯语的。
Ar·au·car·i·a [ˌærɔːˈkɛəriə; ˏærɔˋkɛrɪə] *n*. 【植】**1**. 南洋杉属。**2**. 〔a-〕南洋杉。
A·ra·wak [ˈɑːrɑːˌwɑːk, ˈærəˌwæk; ˋɑrɑˏwɑk, ˋærəˏwæk] *n*. 阿拉瓦人〔南美洲的一支印第安人〕。
A·ra·wa·kan [ˌɑːrɑːˈwɑːkən; ˏɑrɑˋwɑkən] **I** *a*. 阿拉瓦语系的。**II** *n*. **1**. 阿拉瓦部落人。**2**. 阿拉瓦语系。
ar·ba·lest, ar·ba·list [ˈɑːbəlist; ˋɑrbəlɪst] *n*. (中世纪的)劲弩。
ar·bi·ter [ˈɑːbitə; ˋɑrbɪtə] *n*. **1**. 仲裁人,调停人,公断人。**2**. 裁决者,决定者。
ar·bi·tra·ble [ˈɑːbitrəbl; ˋɑrbətrəbl̩] *a*. 可调停的,可仲裁的;委诸仲裁的。
ar·bi·trage [ˈɑːbitridʒ; ˏɑrbɪˋtrɪdʒ] *n*. **1**. 〔古〕裁判;仲裁。**2**. [ˌɑːbiˈtrɑːʒ; ˏɑrbəˋtrɑʒ]【商】套利,套汇〔指在一个市场购进汇票,股票,而在另一市场卖出,以赚取价格的差额〕。*an* ～ *house* 套利公司。
ar·bi·tral [ˈɑːbitrəl; ˋɑrbətrəl] *a*. 仲裁(人)的,公断(人)的。
ar·bit·ra·ment [ɑːˈbitrəmənt; ɑrˋbɪtrəmənt] *n*. **1**. 仲裁。**2**. 仲裁做出的决定,裁决。**3**. 仲裁的权力。
ar·bi·trar·i·ly [ˈɑːbitrərili; Am. ˌɑːbiˈtrerili; ˋɑrbətrerəlɪ, ˏɑrbəˋtrerəlɪ] *ad*. **1**. 任意;姿意,擅自。**2**. 专横地。
ar·bi·trar·i·ness [ˈɑːbitrərinis; ˋɑrbətrərˏɪnɪs] *n*. **1**. 任意;任性。**2**. 霸道;专横,独断,武断。*In criticism, it is essential to guard against subjectivism and* ～. 批评要防止主观武断。
ar·bi·trar·y [ˈɑːbitrəri; ˋɑrbəˏtrerɪ] *a*. **1**. 任意的;任性的,随心所欲的。**2**. 霸道的,专横的,独断独行的。～ *and unreasonable* 蛮横无理。～ *arguments* 强词夺理的议论。
ar·bi·trate [ˈɑːbitreit; ˋɑrbəˏtret] *vt*. **1**. 仲裁;公断。**2**. 把…交付仲裁,使…听任公断。～ *quarrels* 仲裁争端。— ***vi***. 进行仲裁。～ *between two parties* 在双方间进行仲裁。～ *in a dispute* 就某争端进行仲裁。
ar·bi·tra·tion [ˌɑːbiˈtreiʃən; ˏɑrbəˋtreʃən] *n*. 仲裁,公

断,调解。~ ***of exchange*** 汇兑的套利〔指在两个或两个以上的市场上,同时买进和卖出外汇,以赚取价格的差额〕。***refer*** [***submit***] ***to*** ~ 交付公断。

ar·bi·tra·tor [ˈɑːbitreitə; ˋɑrbəˏtretɚ] ***n***. 仲裁人,裁决者。

ar·bi·tress [ˈɑːbitris; ˋɑrbətrɪs] ***n***. 女仲裁人。

ar·bor[1] [ˈɑːbə; ˋɑrbɚ] ***n***.【机】轴;(机床的)心轴,刀轴。

ar·bor[2] [ˈɑːbɔː; ˋɑrbɔr] ***n***. (*pl*. ~***es*** [ˈɑːbəriːz; ˋɑrbəˏriz]) 树木,乔木。**A- Day**〔美〕植树节。

ar·bor[3] [ˈɑːbə; ˋɑrbɚ] ***n***.〔美〕= arbour.

ar·bo·ra·ceous [ˌɑːbəˈreiʃəs; ˏɑrbəˋreʃəs] ***a***. **1**. 树状的。**2**. 树木繁茂的。

ar·bo·re·al [ɑːˈbɔːriəl; ɑrˋbɔrɪəl] ***a***. **1**. 树的,乔木的;木本的。**2**. 栖息在树上的,生活在树上的。

ar·bo·re·ous [ɑːˈbɔːriəs; ɑrˋborɪəs] ***a***. **1**. 树木繁茂的,森林多的。**2**. 树木的。**3**. 树状的。

ar·bo·res·cence [ˌɑːbəˈresns; ˏɑrbəˋrɛsns] ***n***. **1**. 树状。**2**. (矿物等的)枝状。

ar·bo·res·cent [ˌɑːbəˈresnt; ˏɑrbəˋrɛsnt] ***a***. **1**. 树状的。**2**. 树枝状的。

ar·bo·re·tum [ˌɑːbəˈriːtəm; ˏɑrbəˋritəm] ***n***. (*pl*. ~***s***, ***-ta*** [-tə; -tə]) 树木园,植物园。

ar·bor·i·cul·tur·al [ˌɑːbəriˈkʌltʃərəl; ˏɑrbərɪˋkʌltʃərəl] ***a***. 培植树木的;树木栽培学的,林学的。

ar·bor·i·cul·ture [ˈɑːbərikʌltʃə; ˋɑrbərɪˏkʌltʃɚ] ***n***. 栽树,造林;林学,树木栽培学。

ar·bor·i·cul·tur·ist [ˌɑːbəriˈkʌltʃərist; ˏɑrbərɪˋkʌltʃərɪst] ***n***. 造林专家,树木栽培家。

ar·bor·ist [ˈɑːbɔːrist; ˋɑrbɔrɪst] ***n***. 树艺家,树木栽培家,树木研究者。

ar·bor·i·za·tion [ˌɑːbəraiˈzeiʃən; ˏɑrbəraɪˋzeʃən] ***n***. (结晶、血管等的)树枝状。

ar·bor·ize [ˈɑːbəraiz; ˋɑrbəˏraɪz] ***vt***., ***vi***. (使)(血管等)形成树枝状,(使)分叉。

ar·bor·ous [ˈɑːbərəs; ˋɑrbərəs] ***a***. 树的,乔木的;由树木组成的。

ar·bor·vi·tae [ˈɑːbəvaiti; ˋɑrbɚvaɪtɪ] ***n***. **1**.【植】侧柏;〔A-〕金钟柏属。**2**.【解】(小脑)活树。

ar·bour [ˈɑːbə; ˋɑrbɚ] ***n***. **1**. (树枝交叉形成的)棚架,藤架,凉亭。**2**.〔废〕草地;花园。

ar·bo·vi·rus [ˈɑːbəˈvaiərəs; ˋɑrbəˋvaɪərəs] ***n***.【微】树木病毒。

Ar·buth·not [ɑːˈbʌθnət; ɑrˋbʌθnət] ***n***. **1**. 阿巴斯诺特〔姓氏〕。**2**. **John** ~ 阿巴斯诺特(1667—1735),苏格兰讽刺作家,医生。★英国人绰号 John Bull 即出自其所著 *The History of John Bull* 一书。

Ar·bu·tus [ɑːˈbjuːtəs; ɑrˋbjutəs] ***n***.【植】杨梅属〔石南科〕;〔a-〕杨梅树;岩梨。

ARC, A.R.C. = American Red Cross 美国红十字会。

arc [ɑːk; ɑrk] ***n***. **1**. 弧;弓形,拱(洞)。**2**. 电弧,弧光。~ **de triomphe** 凯旋门。~ **furnace** 电弧炉。~ **lamp** 弧光灯。~ **light** **1**. 弧光。**2**. 弧光灯。~**-over** ***n***.【物】电弧放电。~ **welding** (电)弧焊。

ar·cade [ɑːˈkeid; ɑrˋked] ***n***. **1**.【建】拱廊,连拱廊。**2**. 有拱廊[骑楼]的街道〔两边多有店铺〕。

ar·cad·ed [ɑːˈkeidid; ɑrˋkedɪd] ***a***. 连拱式的;拱廊式的,有骑楼的。

Ar·ca·di·a [ɑːˈkeidjə; ɑrˋkedɪə] ***n***. **1**. 阿卡狄亚〔古希腊一山地牧区,以境内居民生活淳朴与宁静著称〕。**2**.〔喻〕世外桃源。

Ar·ca·di·an [ɑːˈkeidjən; ɑrˋkedɪən] **I** ***a***. **1**. 阿卡狄亚的。**2**. 田园的;淳朴的;牧歌的。**II** ***n***. **1**. 阿卡狄亚人。**2**. 淳朴的人。**-ism** ***n***. 淳朴的田园风趣,牧歌似的情调。

Ar·ca·dy [ˈɑːkədi; ˋɑrkədɪ] ***n***.〔诗〕= Arcadia.

ar·ca·num [ɑːˈkeinəm; ɑrˋkenəm] ***n***. (*pl*. ~***s***, ***-na*** [-nə; -nə]) **1**. 秘密的知识。**2**. 秘密,神秘。**3**. 秘方,秘药。

ar·ca·ture [ˈɑːkətʃə; ˋɑrkətʃɚ] ***a***.【建】**1**. 小拱廊,小连环拱廊。**2**. 封闭式拱廊,假拱廊〔作为装饰用〕。

arc-bou·tant [ɑːbuːˈtaːn; ˏɑrbuˋtɑn] ***n***. (*pl*. ***-tants*** [-ˈtaːn; -ˋtɑn]) 〔F.〕【建】飞拱。

arch[1] [ɑːtʃ; ɑrtʃ] **I** ***n***. **1**.【建】弓架结构;拱廊;拱门;弓形门;穹窿,拱洞,拱顶。**2**. 弓形,半圆形。*a memorial* ~ 纪念门,牌坊。*a triumphal* ~ 凯旋门。~ *of the foot* 足底弓。*the* ~ *of the heavens* 苍穹。***the Court of Arches*** (坎特伯雷的)宗教裁判上诉院。**II** ***vi***. **1**.【建】作(成)拱。**2**. 成弓形,弓着。— ***vt***. **1**.【建】把…作成拱形;使弯作弓形。**2**. 用拱连接,用拱覆盖。*The rainbow ~es the heaven*. 彩虹在天上成弓形。*A cat ~es its back*. 猫弓着背。

arch[2] [ɑːtʃ; ɑrtʃ] ***a***. 首要的;总的。*the* ~ *villain* 流氓头子。

arch[3] [ɑːtʃ; ɑrtʃ] ***a***. 诡诈的;淘气的。*an* ~ *smile* 顽皮的微笑。

arch. = archaic; archaism; archery; archipelago; architect; architecture.

arch- *pref*. 首位的,最高的,主要的: *arch*duke, *arch*bishop.

-arch ***n***. suf. 统治者,王,皇帝: matri*arch*, mon*arch*.

Ar·chae·an [ɑːˈki(ː)ən; ɑrˋkiən] ***n***., ***a***.【地】太古代(的);太古代岩石(的)。

ar·chae·o-, ar·che·o- *comb. f*. 古代的,原始的: *archaeo*logy.

ar·chae·o·log·i·cal [ˌɑːkiəˈlɔdʒikəl; ˏɑrkɪəˋlɑdʒɪkəl] ***a***. 考古学(上)的。**-ly** ***ad***.

ar·chae·ol·o·gist [ˌɑːkiˈɔlədʒist; ˏɑrkɪˋɑlədʒɪst] ***n***. 考古学家。

ar·chae·ol·o·gy [ˌɑːkiˈɔlədʒi; ˏɑrkɪˋɑlədʒɪ] ***n***. **1**. 考古学,古物学。**2**.〔罕〕古代史。**3**. 文化遗物。

ar·chae·op·ter·yx [ˌɑːkiˈɔptəriks; ˏɑrkɪˋɑptərɪks] ***n***.【古生】始祖鸟。

Ar·chae·o·zo·ic [ˌɑːkiəˈzəuik; ˏɑrkɪəˋzoɪk] **I** ***a***. 太古代的。**II** ***n***. 〔the ~〕太古代(= the ~ era)。

ar·cha·ic [ɑːˈkeiik; ɑrˋkeɪk] ***a***. **1**. 古代的;古风的。**2**. (语言等)古体的,陈旧的。*the* ~ 古代,古物。*Thou is an ~ form of you*. "Thou" 是"you" 的古体。**-al·ly** ***ad***.

ar·cha·ism [ˈɑːkeiizəm; ˋɑrkɪˏɪzəm] ***n***. **1**. 古语,古体,古风。**2**. (语言等的)拟古主义。

ar·cha·ist [ˈɑːkeiist; ˋɑrkeɪst] ***n***. **1**. 拟古主义者,摹仿古风的人。**2**. 古物研究家。

ar·cha·is·tic [ˌɑːkeiˈistik; ˏɑrkɪˋɪstɪk] ***a***. 古风的,拟古的。

ar·cha·ize [ˈɑːkeiaiz; ˋɑrkɪˏaɪz] ***vt***. 使(文章等)有古风。— ***vi***. 用古词古语;仿古。

arch·an·gel [ˈɑːkˌeindʒəl; ˋɑrkˋendʒəl] ***n***. **1**. 天使长,大天使。**2**.【植】白芷属植物。

ar·chan·thro·pine [ɑːˈkænθrəpain; ɑrˋkænθrəpaɪn] ***n***. 猿人。

arch·bish·op [ˈɑːtʃˈbiʃəp; ˋɑrtʃˋbɪʃəp] ***n***. 大主教。**-ric** ***n***. 大主教的职位[任期、管区]。

arch·dea·con [ˈɑːtʃˈdiːkən; ˋɑrtʃˋdikən] ***n***. 副主教。**-ry** ***n***. 副主教的职权[地位、管区、宅邸]。

arch·di·o·cese [ˈɑːtʃˈdaiəsis; ˋɑrtʃˋdaɪəˏsɪs] ***n***. 大主教管区。

arch-dove [ˈɑːtʃˈdʌv; ˋɑrtʃˋdʌv] ***n***. (政治上的)鸽派首脑。

arch·du·cal [ˈɑːtʃˈdjuːkəl; ˏɑrtʃˋdjukəl] ***a***. **1**. 大公的。**2**. 大公领地的,大公国的。

arch·duch·ess [ˈɑːtʃˈdʌtʃis; ˋɑrtʃˋdʌtʃɪs] ***n***. **1**. 大公夫人。**2**. (从前奥地利皇家的)公主。

arch·duch·y [ˈɑːtʃˈdʌtʃi; ˋɑrtʃˋdʌtʃɪ] ***n***. 大公领地,大公国。

arch·duke [ˈɑːtʃˈdjuːk; ˋɑrtʃˋdjuk] ***n***. 大公〔1918 年前奥

A

国皇太子的称呼)。

Ar·che·an [ɑːˈkiən; ɑrˋkiən] ***n.*** , ***a.*** = Archaean.

arched [ɑːtʃt; ɑrtʃt] ***a.*** 拱形的,半圆形的;弓架结构的。*an* ~ *bridge* 拱桥。

arch·en·e·my [ˈɑːtʃˈenimi; ˋɑrtʃˋɛnəmi] ***n.*** **1.**【基督教】(魔王)撒旦。**2.** 主敌,大敌。

Arch·er [ˈɑːtʃə; ˋɑrtʃɚ] ***n.*** 阿彻(姓氏)。

arch·er [ˈɑːtʃə; ˋɑrtʃɚ] ***n.*** **1.** 射手,弓箭手。**2.** (A-)【天】射手座;人马宫。~**-fish** 射手鱼(东南亚淡水鱼,嘴能喷水)。

arch·er·y [ˈɑːtʃəri; ˋɑrtʃəri] ***n.*** **1.** 射箭,箭术。**2.** (弓、箭等)射箭用具。**3.** (集合词)弓箭手;射箭运动员。

ar·che·typ·al [ˈɑːkitaipəl; ˋɑrkɪˏtaɪpl̩] ***a.*** **1.** 原始模型的。**2.** 典范的。

ar·che·type [ˈɑːkitaip; ˋɑrkəˏtaɪp] ***n.*** **1.** 原始模型。**2.** 典型。

arch·fiend [ˈɑːtʃˈfiːnd; ˋɑrtʃˋfind] ***n.*** 魔王;【基督教】撒旦。

ar·chi- *pref.* **1.** = arch-. **2.**【生】原: *archi*plasm.

Ar·chi·bald [ˈɑːtʃibəld, ˈɑːtʃibɔːld; ˋɑrtʃɪbəld, ˋɑrtʃɪˏbɔld] ***n.*** 阿奇博尔德(男子名)。

ar·chi·bald [ˈɑːtʃibəld, ˈɑːtʃbɔːld; ˋɑrtʃɪbəld, ˋɑrtʃəbɔld] ***n.*** (俚)高射炮。

ar·chi·cer·e·brum [ˈɑːkiˈseribrəm; ˋɑrkiˋsɛrɪbrəm] ***n.*** 【动】原脑。

ar·chi·di·ac·o·nal [ˌɑːkidaiˈækənəl; ˏɑrkɪdaɪˋækənl̩] ***a.*** 副主教的。

Ar·chie [ˈɑːtʃi; ˋɑrtʃɪ] ***n.*** 阿奇(男子名, Archibald 的昵称)。

ar·chie [ˈɑːtʃi; ˋɑrtʃɪ] ***n.*** (俚)高射炮。

ar·chi·e·pis·co·pal [ˌɑːkiiˈpiskəpəl; ˏɑrkɪəˋpɪskəpl̩] ***a.*** 大主教的。

ar·chil [ˈɑːkil; ˋɑrkɪl] ***n.*** **1.** 紫色地衣染;,苔色素。**2.** 石蕊地衣,海石蕊。

ar·chi·mage [ˈɑːkiˌmeidʒ; ˋɑrkəˏmedʒ] ***n.*** 大魔法师,大巫师。

Ar·chi·me·des [ɑːkiˈmiːdiːz; ˏɑrkəˋmidiz] ***n.*** 阿基米德(古希腊数学家 287? —212 B. C.)。**-me·de·an** [-ˈmiːdjən; -ˋmidɪən] ***a.***

ar·chin, ar·chine [ɑːˈʃiːn; ɑrˋʃin] ***n.*** (苏联)俄尺(等于28英寸)。

ar·chi·pel·a·go [ˌɑːkiˈpeligəu; ˏɑrkəˋpɛləgo] ***n.*** (*pl.* ~*es*, ~*s*) **1.** 多岛海。**2.** 群岛。**3.** (the A-)爱琴海及其岛屿。**-lag·ic** ***a.***

ar·chi·plasm [ˈɑːkiplæzəm; ˋɑrkɪˏplæzəm] ***n.*** 【生化】原形质。

ar·chi·tect [ˈɑːkitekt; ˋɑrkəˏtɛkt] ***n.*** **1.** 建筑师,设计师;创制者。**2.** (A-)造物主。*a naval* ~ 造船技师。*the* ~ *of one's own fortunes* 掌握自己命运的人。*the* ~*s of the Constitution* 宪法起草者。*the Great A- (of the Universe)* 造物主,上帝。

ar·chi·tec·ton·ic(al) [ˌɑːkitekˈtɔnik(əl); ˏɑrkɪtɛkˋtɑnɪk(əl)] ***a.*** **1.** 建筑术的。**2.** 构造的,结构的。**3.** (知识)成体系的,系统化的。~**s** ***n.*** *pl.* (用作 *sing.*) **1.** 建筑学。**2.** 建筑设计;结构设计。**3.**【哲】(认识)体系论,(知识)系统化。*the* ~*s of a symphony* 交响音乐的结构设计。

ar·chi·tec·tur·al [ˌɑːkiˈtektʃərəl; ˏɑrkɪˋtɛktʃərəl] ***a.*** 建筑学的;建筑上的。**-ly** ***ad.*** 建筑(学)上。

ar·chi·tec·ture [ˈɑːkitektʃə; ˋɑrkəˏtɛktʃɚ] ***n.*** **1.** 建筑学。**2.** 建筑(样式、风格);建筑物。**3.** 构造,结构;【自】(电子计算机的)架构,体系结构。*civil* ~ 民用建筑。*domestic* ~ 住宅建筑。*naval* ~ 造船术,造船学。*the* ~ *of a beehive* 蜂窝的结构。

ar·chi·trave [ˈɑːkitreiv; ˋɑrkəˏtrev] ***n.*** 【建】**1.** 框缘。**2.** (柱的)下楣。**3.** (窗等的)嵌线。**4.** 额枋。

ar·chi·val [ɑːˈkaivəl; ɑrˋkaɪvl̩] ***a.*** 档案的;档案里的;包括有档案的。

ar·chives [ˈɑːkaivz; ˋɑrkaɪvz] ***n.*** *pl.* **1.** 档案馆[室],档案处。**2.** 档案。*the State A- Bureau* 国家档案局。*family* ~ 家谱。

ar·chi·vist [ˈɑːkivist; ˋɑrkəvɪst] ***n.*** 档案保管人。

ar·chi·volt [ˈɑːkivəult; ˋɑrkɪˏvolt] ***n.*** 【建】**1.** 拱门饰(拱门沿边的嵌线或其他饰物)。**2.** 拱门内侧的穹窿。

ar·chon [ˈɑːkən; ˋɑrkɑn] ***n.*** **1.** 古希腊雅典九人执政官之一;执政官。**2.** 主要官员。

ar·cho·saur [ˈɑːəsɔ; ˋɑrəsɑ] ***n.*** 【考古】祖龙。

arch·priest [ˈɑːtʃˈpriːst; ˋɑrtʃˋprist] ***n.*** **1.**【宗】(原义为主教的)主助祭;副主教。**2.** 主祭。

arch·way [ˈɑːtʃwei; ˋɑrtʃˏwe] ***n.*** 拱道;拱洞。

arch·wise [ˈɑːtʃwaiz; ˋɑrtʃˏwaɪz] ***ad.*** 拱状地;拱廊似地;成弓形。

-ar·chy *suf.* 政治,政体。matri*archy*, mon*archy*.

ar·ci·form [ˈɑːsifɔːm; ˋɑrsɪfɔrm] ***a.*** 拱形的,弓状的。

arc·o·graph [ˈɑːkəgrɑːf; ˋɑrkəˏgræf] ***n.*** (不用中心点画圆的)圆弧规。

arc·ol·o·gy [ɑːˈkɔlədʒi; ɑrˋkɑlədʒɪ] ***n.*** 生态建筑(在单一建筑内达到完整的计划城市或环境)。

ARCS = **1.** Associate of the Royal College of Surgeons (英国)皇家外科医师协会准会员。**2.** Associate of the Royal College of Science (英国)皇家科学协会准会员。**3.** Australian Red Cross Society 澳大利亚红十字会。

arc·tic [ˈɑːktik; ˋɑrktɪk] **I** ***a.*** **1.** 北极的;寒带的 (*opp.* antarctic)。**2.** 极冷的,(态度等)冷淡的。**II** ***n.*** **1.** 北极圈;北极地方。**2.** (*pl.*)(美)橡皮套靴。*the A- Circle* 北极圈。*an* ~ *expedition* 北极探险。*the A- pole* 北极 (= North Pole)。*the A- Ocean* 北冰洋。*an* ~ *smile* 冷笑。

Arc·tu·rus [ɑːkˈtjuərəs; ɑrkˋtjurəs] ***n.*** 【天】大角(牧夫座 α)。

ar·cu·ate [ˈɑːkjuit; ˋɑrkjuɪt], **ar·cu·at·ed** [ˈɑːkjueitid; ˋɑrkjuˏetɪd] ***a.*** **1.** 弓形的。**2.**【建】拱式的。~ *islands* 弓形列岛。

ARD = acute respiratory disease 急性呼吸系统疾病。

-ard *suf.* 做…的人,…的人,沉湎…的人: drunk*ard*, Spani*ard*, slugg*ard*.

ar·deb [ˈɑːdeb; ˋɑrdɛb] ***n.*** 阿德布(埃及干品容量单位,等于5.6189(美制蒲式耳))。

Ar·dell(e) [ɑːˈdel; ɑrˋdɛl] ***n.*** 阿黛尔(女子名。Adele 的异体)。

Ar·den [ˈɑːdn; ˋɑrdn] ***n.*** **1.** 阿登(姓氏,男子名)。**2.** 阿尔丁(英国沃里克郡的小林区,原系大森林。莎士比亚以该地作为《皆大欢喜》一剧的背景)。

ar·den·cy [ˈɑːdənsi; ˋɑrdnsɪ] ***n.*** 热心,热情;热烈。

ar·dent [ˈɑːdənt; ˋɑrdnt] ***a.*** **1.** 热心的;热烈的。**2.** 炽热的。**3.** 强烈的。*an* ~ *admirer* 热烈的赞美者。~ *passion* 热情。*an* ~ *protest* 强烈的抗议。~ *hate* 愤恨。~ *spirits* 烧酒。**-ly** ***ad.*** **-ness** ***n.***

Ar·dis [ˈɑːdis; ˋɑrdɪs] ***n.*** 阿迪丝(女子名)。

ar·do·me·ter [ɑːˈdɔmitə; ɑrˋdɑmɪtɚ] ***n.*** 光测高温计。

ar·dour, (美)**ar·dor** [ˈɑːdə; ˋɑrdɚ] ***n.*** **1.** 热情,热心。**2.** (罕)灼热。*patriotic* ~ 爱国热情。*with* ~ 热心地。*with enthusiastic* ~ 轰轰烈烈地。

ar·du·ous [ˈɑːdjuəs; ˋɑrdʒuəs] ***a.*** **1.** 费力的,艰巨的。**2.** 奋斗的,努力的。**3.** 险峻的。~ *paths* 陡峭的道路。*an* ~ *task* 艰难的工作。*an* ~ *winter* 严冬。*an* ~ *worker* 勤奋的工人。**-ly** ***ad.*** 艰苦地。**-ness** ***n.*** 艰难,艰苦,奋斗。

are[1] [强 ɑː, 弱 ɑ, ə; 强 ɑr, 弱 ɑ, ə] be 的第二人称单、复数。第一、三人称复数现在陈述语气。*Are you there?* (电话用语)喂! 喂!

are[2] [ɑː; ɑr] ***n.*** 公亩(等于100平方米)。

ar·e·a [ˈɛəriə; ˋɛrɪə] ***n.*** **1.** 面积;平地;地面。**2.** 空地;(英)地下室前的空地。**3.** 地区,地方;(喻)区域;范围。*a* *vast uncultivated* ~ 广阔的未开垦地。*a mountainous* ~ 山区。*a fortified* ~ 要塞地带。*an* ~ *of investigation* 研究范围。*the liberated* ~*s* 解放区。*an* ~ *of fire*【军】射界。*This room is 16 square metres in* ~. 这个房间的面积为 16 平方米。~ **bombing**【军】(无特定目标的全区性)区域轰炸。~ **bell** 地下室门铃。~ **bombing** 大面积轰炸(= carpet bombing)。~ **code** (美国、加拿大)电话分区的三位数代号。~ **rug** (房间内只遮住部分地面的)小地毯。~**way** 1.〔英〕地下室前的空地。2.(建筑物之间的)通道。

Ar·e·ca [ˈærikə; ˋærɪkə] *n*. 1.【植】槟榔属。2.〔a-〕槟榔;槟榔树〔又称 betel palm〕。~ **nut** 槟榔果。~ **palm** 槟榔树。

a·re·na [əˈriːnə; əˋrinə] *n*. 1. 古罗马圆形剧场中央的竞技场;(一般的)竞技场所。2. 活动场所,竞争场所。*an* ~ *of warfare* 战场。*the* ~ *of politics* 政治舞台。*a boxing* ~ 拳击比赛场地。*a circus* ~ 马戏场。~ **theater** 舞台设在观众座席中央的剧场,圆形剧场。

ar·e·na·ceous [ˌæriˈneiʃəs; ˏærɪˋneʃəs] *a*. 1. 砂(质)的,多砂的。2. 似砂的,枯燥无味的。3.(植物)砂中生长的。

ar·e·nic·o·lous [ˌæriˈnikələs; ˏærəˋnɪkələs] *a*. 生活在沙中的,生长在沙中的。

ar·e·nite [ˈærinait; ˋærɪˏnaɪt] *n*.【矿】粗屑岩。

aren't [ɑːnt; ɑrnt] 1. = are not. 2.〔英口〕= an't, am not: *I am good*, ~ *I* (= am I not)?

a·re·o·la [æˈriələ; æˋrɪələ] *n*. (*pl*. ~*s*, *-lae* [-liː; -li]) 1. 小空隙。2.【生】(叶脉间、翅脉间的)网隙。3.【解】乳头晕。4.【植】果脐。**-r** *a*.

ar·e·om·e·ter [ˌæriˈɔmitə; ˏærɪˋɑmɪtɚ] *n*. 液体比重计,浮秤。

Ar·e·op·a·gite [ˌæriˈɔpəgait; ˏærɪˋɑpəˏdʒaɪt] *n*. 古希腊雅典最高法院的法官。

Ar·e·op·a·gus [ˌæriˈɔpəgəs; ˏærɪˋɑpəgəs] *n*. 1. 雅典一小丘名〔雅典最高法院在该处断案〕。2.(古希腊)雅典最高法院。

A·re·qui·pa [ˌæriˈkiːpə; ˏɑreˋkipɑ] *n*. 阿雷基帕〔秘鲁城市〕。

Ar·es [ˈɛəriːz; ˋɛriz] *n*.【希神】阿瑞斯〔战神,相当于罗马神话中的 Mars〕。

a·rête [æˈreit; æˋret] *n*.〔F.〕险峻的山脊;【地】刃嵴。

arg. = 1. argent. 2. argentum.

ar·gal, ar·gol [ˈɑːgəl; ˋɑrgəl] *n*. 粗酒石〔酒桶里酒变陈时的沉淀〕。

ar·ga·la [ˈɑːgələ; ˋɑrgələ] *n*.【鸟】(印度)鹳。

ar·ga·li [ˈɑːgəli; ˋɑrgəlɪ] *n*.【动】(亚洲)大角野羊。

ar·gand [ˈɑːgænd; ˋɑrgænd] *n*. 管状灯芯的灯。

ar·gent [ˈɑːdʒənt; ˋɑrdʒənt] I *n*. 1.〔古、诗〕银。2.〔诗〕银白色。3.〔废〕银币;货币。II *a*. 1. 银的;银似的。2. 银制的。3. 银色的。

ar·gen·tic [ɑːˈdʒentik; ɑrˋdʒɛntɪk] *a*. 银的,含银的〔尤指含二价银的化合物而言〕。

ar·gen·tif·er·ous [ˌɑːdʒənˈtifərəs; ˏɑrdʒənˋtɪfərəs] *a*. (矿砂等)含银的;产银的,有银的。

Ar·gen·ti·na [ˌɑːdʒənˈtiːnə; ˏɑrdʒənˋtinə] *n*. 阿根廷〔拉丁美洲〕。

ar·gen·tine [ˈɑːdʒəntain; ˋɑrdʒəntaɪn] I *a*. 银的;像银的;银色的。II *n*. 1. 银,银色金属。2.【矿】珠光石,银白色页状方解石。3. 银色素〔取自鱼鳞,用来做人造珍珠〕。

Ar·gen·tine [ˈɑːdʒəntain; ˋɑrdʒənˏtain] I *a*. 阿根廷的;阿根廷人的。II *n*. 1. 阿根廷人。2.〔the ~〕阿根廷。

Ar·gen·tin·e·an [ˌɑːdʒənˈtiniən; ˏɑrdʒənˋtɪnɪən] I *n*. 阿根廷人。II *a*. 阿根廷的;阿根廷人的。

ar·gen·tite [ˈɑːdʒənˌtait; ˋɑrdʒənˏtaɪt] *n*. 辉银矿。

ar·gen·tous [ɑːˈdʒentəs; ɑrˋdʒɛntəs] *a*.【化】亚银的,含亚银的〔指含一价银的化合物而言〕。

ar·gil [ˈɑːdʒil; ˋɑrdʒɪl] *n*. 1. 白黏土,陶土。2. 矾土。

ar·gil·la·ceous [ˌɑːdʒiˈleiʃəs; ˏɑrdʒɪˋleʃəs] *a*. 1. 黏土的。2. 含黏土的。3. 黏土似的。

ar·gil·lite [ˈɑːdʒilait; ˋɑrdʒɪˏlaɪt] *n*.【地】1. 厚层泥岩。2. 泥质板岩。

ar·gi·nase [ˈɑːdʒineis; ˋɑrdʒɪˏnes] *n*.【生化】(肝脏里的)精氨酸酶,胍基戊氨酸酶。

ar·gi·nine [ˈɑːdʒinain; ˋɑrdʒɪˏnaɪn] *n*.【生化】精氨酸。

Ar·give [ˈɑːgaiv; ˋɑrgaɪv] *n*., *a*.〔诗〕希腊人(的)。

ar·gle-bar·gle [ˈɑːglˈbɑːgl; ˋɑrglˋbɑrgl] *n*., *vi*.〔英口〕1. 争论,辩论,热烈讨论。2. 讨价还价。

Ar·go [ˈɑːgəu; ˋɑrgo] *n*. 1.【希神】亚尔古舟〔贾森找金羊毛所乘的船〕。2.【天】南船座。

ar·gol [ˈɑːgəl; ˋɑrgəl] *n*. 粗酒石〔酒桶里酒变陈时的沉淀〕。

ar·gon [ˈɑːgɔn; ˋɑrgɑn] *n*.【化】氩〔元素名,符号为 A〕。

Ar·go·naut [ˈɑːgənɔːt; ˋɑrgəˏnɔt] *n*. 1.【希神】亚尔古英雄〔随同贾森乘亚尔古舟,去海外寻找金羊毛的英雄〕。2.【美史】1849 年左右到加利福尼亚去淘金的人。3.〔a-〕舡鱼(= paper nautilus)。**-ic** [-tik; -tɪk] *a*. 亚尔古船上人的,乘亚尔古船远行的。

ar·go·sy [ˈɑːgəsi; ˋɑrgəsɪ] *n*.〔诗〕1. 大商船。2. 大商船队。3. 丰富的贮藏,丰富的供应。

ar·got [ˈɑːgəu; ˋɑrgo] *n*.〔F.〕1.(某一职业或团体惯用的)行话。2.(盗贼等的)暗语,黑话。

ar·gu·a·ble [ˈɑːgjuəbl; ˋɑrgjuəbl] *a*. 可论证的,可争辩的,有疑义的。

ar·gue [ˈɑːgju; ˈɑrgjʊ] *vt*. 1. 辩论,争论,争辩(某事、某论点等),为(某事,某论点等)作辩解,(找理由)把(某事等)辩解[搪塞]过去(*away*, *off*)。2. 说服,劝说,劝服(某人)做[不做]某事(*into* [*out of*])。3. 主张,认为。论证(*that*)。4.(事实、行为等)证明,表明。~ *a point* [*a matter*] 就一个论点[问题]进行辩论。*He* ~*d me into joining the party*. 他说服我参加舞会。*She* ~*d herself into going back*. 她经过多次反复考虑后决定返回去了。*Columbus* ~*s that the world is round*. 哥伦布提出地球是圆的。*Her clothes* ~ *poverty*. 她的衣着表明她家境清寒。*It* ~*s him to be a rogue*. 那证明他是一个无赖。—*vi*. 争论,辩论。~ ***against*** 反对…,成为…的反证。~ ***down*** 说服(某人)。~ ***for*** 赞成,力主,为…作争辩。~ (*sb*.) ***into*** (*consent*) [***out of*** (*his opinion*)] 劝(某人)使其(答应)[放弃(其意见)]。~ ***it away*** [***off***] 用话把它搪塞过去。~ ***on*** [***upon***] 论及。~ ***with*** (*sb*.) ***about*** [***on***] 与(某人)讨论,议论(某事)。

ar·gu·er [ˈɑːgjuə; ˋɑrgjuɚ] *n*. 辩论者,争论者。

ar·gu·fy [ˈɑːgjufai; ˋɑrgjuˏfaɪ] *vi*., *vt*.〔美俚〕啰哩啰嗦地辩论;纠缠不休地争论。

ar·gu·ment [ˈɑːgjumənt; ˋɑrgjəmənt] *n*. 1. 争论,辩论,论证。2. 论据,论点。3.(书籍等的)梗概,摘要,大纲;(剧本等的)情节。4.【数】幅角;宗量,宗数,自变数。5.【逻】(三段论中的)中项,中词。6.〔废〕证据。*an artificial* ~ 巧辩,诡辩。*start* [*put forward*] *an* ~ 开始[挑起]争论。~ ***against*** [***for***, ***in favour of***] 反对[赞成]…的论点。***get*** [***fall***] ***into an*** ~ ***with*** 与…发生争论。***ram an*** ~ ***home*** 反覆说明论点使对方接受。***without*** ~ 无异议。

ar·gu·men·ta·tion [ˌɑːgjumenˈteiʃən; ˏɑrgjəmɛnˋteʃən] *n*. 1. 立论,推论,论证。2. 辩论,争论。3.(有别于描写、叙述和说明的)论说;论说文;辩论性的演说。

ar·gu·men·ta·tive [ˌɑːgjuˈmentətiv; ˏɑrgjəˋmɛntətɪv] *a*. 1. 争辩的,辩论的。2. 好争辩的。**-ly** *ad*. **-ness** *n*.

ar·gu·men·tum [ˌɑːgjuˈmentəm; ˏɑrgjʊˋmɛntəm] *n*.〔L.〕= argument. ~ ***ad hominem*** (= to the man) 1. 向辩论对手作人身攻击而不回答其论点。2. 辩论时以迎合听众特殊的情绪、偏见或利益取胜,使用哗众取宠的手法。

Ar·gus [ˈɑːgəs; ˋɑrgəs] *n*. 1.【希神】百眼巨人。2. 机警的看守(人)。~**-eyed** [-aid; -aɪd] *a*. 眼光锐利的;机警的。

A

ar·gute [ɑːˈgjuːt; ɑrˋgjut] ***a*.** **1.** 锐利的;伶俐的,机警的。**2.** (声音)尖锐的。**3.** (叶边等)锯齿形的。

ar·gy-bar·gy [ˈɑːgiˈbɑːgi; ˋɑrgɪˋbɑrgɪ] ***n*.** 〔方、口〕争争吵吵,抬杠,讨价还价。

ar·gyle [ˈɑːgail; ˋɑrgaɪl] **I** ***a*.** 阿盖尔(图案)的〔阿盖尔图案是不同颜色的斜方形或菱形拼成的图案,用于针织品〕。**II** ***n*.** **1.** 针织品的多角菱形图案,阿盖尔图案。**2.** 〔*pl*.〕花格短袜。

Ar·gyll [ɑːˈgail; ɑrˋgaɪl] ***n*.** 阿盖尔〔苏格兰郡名〕。

ar·gyr·i·a [ɑːˈdʒiriə; ɑrˋdʒɪrɪə] ***n*.** 银中毒,银质沉着病。

ar·gyr·o·dite [ɑːˈdʒirədait; ɑrˋdʒɪrədaɪt] ***n*.** 硫银锗矿。

a·ri·a [ˈɑːriə; ˋɑrɪə] ***n*.** 〔It.〕【乐】咏叹调;唱腔;唱段。

-aria *suf*. 【动】…目: actini*aria* 海葵目。

-arian *suf*. …派的(人),…岁的(人): veget*arian* sexagen*arian*.

Ar·i·an[1] [ˈɛəriən; ˋɛrɪən] **I** ***a*.** 阿里乌斯(教)的。**II** ***n*.** 阿里乌斯教徒。**-ism** ***n*.** 阿里乌斯教〔亚历山大神学家阿里乌斯 (Arius) 的教义,认为耶稣不是神,但比凡人高超〕。

Ar·i·an[2] [ˈɛəriən; ˋɛrɪən] ***a*., *n*.** = Aryan.

ARIBA = Associate of the Royal Institute of British Architects 英国皇家建筑师协会准会员。

ar·id [ˈærid; ˋærɪd] ***a*.** **1.** 干旱的;贫瘠的,荒芜的。**2.** 枯燥无味的。*an* ~ *land* 旱地。**-ly** ***ad*.**

a·rid·i·ty [æˈriditi; əˋrɪdətɪ] ***n*.** **1.** 无旱;贫瘠,荒芜。**2.** 枯燥,乏味。

ar·i·el [ˈɛəriəl; ˋɛrɪˏɛl] ***n*.** 【动】(阿拉伯)羚羊。

Ar·i·el [ˈɛəriəl; ˋɛrɪəl] ***n*.** **1.** (莎士比亚剧本《暴风雨》中的)空气般的精灵。**2.** 【天】天王星的第一卫星,天(王)卫一。

Ar·i·es [ˈɛəriːz; ˋɛriz] ***n*.** 【天】白羊(星)座。

ar·i·et·ta [ˌæriˈetə; ˏærɪˋɛtə] ***n*.** 〔It.〕【乐】小咏叹调。

a·ri·ga·to [ˌɑːriːˈgɑːtəu; ˏɑrɪˋgɑto] ***n*.** 〔Jap.〕谢谢。

a·right [əˈrait; əˋraɪt] **I** ***ad*.** 〔书〕正确地,不错。*if I remember* ~ 如果我没记错。*He guessed* ~. 他猜对了。**II** ***vt*.** 〔书〕改正,纠正。

A·ri·ka·ra [əˈriːkərə; əˋrikərə] ***n*.** **1.** 阿里卡拉人〔美国密苏里河平原的一支印第安人〕。**2.** 阿里卡拉人讲的卡多恩语。

ar·il [ˈæril; ˋærɪl] ***n*.** 【植】假种皮,子衣,子壳。

ar·i·ose [ˈæriəus, ˌɛəriˈəus; ˋærɪˏos, ɛrɪˋos] ***a*.** 如歌的;旋律的。

a·ri·o·so [ˌɑːriəˈəuzəu; ˏɑrɪˋozo] **I** ***a*.** 〔It.〕悦耳的,宛如咏叹调的。**II** ***ad*.** 悦耳地,宛如咏叹调地。**III** ***n*.** 咏叹调。

-arious *suf*. …性的: greg*arious*.

a·rise [əˈraiz; əˋraɪz] ***vi*.** (***a·rose*** [əˈrəuz; əˋroz]; ***a·ris·en*** [əˈrizn; əˋrɪzn]) **1.** 起,兴起;出现;发生。**2.** (人早上)起来,起身。**3.** (太阳)上升。**4.** 产生于,起因于,出身于 (~ *from*, ~ *out of*)。*Questions arose*. 问题发生了。*Accidents* ~ *from carelessness*. 事故往往起因于疏忽。

a·ris·ta [əˈristə; əˋrɪstə] ***n*.** (*pl*. ***-tae*** [-tiː; -ti]) (谷)芒;(蝇类的)口刺;触角芒。

a·ris·tate [əˈristeit; əˋrɪstet] ***a*.** 有芒的,有刺的;有触角芒的。

ar·is·toc·ra·cy [ˌærisˈtɔkrəsi; ˏærɪsˋtɑkrəsɪ] ***n*.** **1.** 贵族政治[政府],贵族统治的国家。**2.** 〔the ~〕(集合词)贵族,贵族阶层,上层阶级,第一流人物。**3.** 贵族的派头。*the* ~ *of wealth* 富豪。*an* ~ *of scientists* 科学家的佼佼者。

a·ris·to·crat [ˈæristəkræt; ˋærɪstəˏkræt] ***n*.** **1.** 贵族。**2.** 贵族政治论者。**3.** 有贵族派头的人。*a struggle between the* ~*s and the plebeians* 贵族与平民之间的纷争。

a·ris·to·crat·ic, a·ris·to·crat·i·cal [ˌæristəˈkrætik(əl); ˏærɪstəˋkrætɪk(əl)] ***a*.** **1.** 贵族的,(主张)贵族掌政的。**2.** 贵族气派的。~ *bearing* 贵族派头。~ *snobbishness* 媚上骄下。**-i·cal·ly** ***ad*.**

ar·is·toc·rat·ism [ˌærisˈtɔkrətizəm; ˏærɪsˋtɑkrətɪzəm] ***n*.** 贵族主义;贵族气派[作风]。

Ar·is·tot·le [ˈæriˌstɔtl; ˋærɪˏstɑtl] ***n*.** 亚里士多德〔公元前 384—322 年,古希腊哲学家〕。~*'s lantern* (海胆的)咀嚼器。

Ar·is·to·te·li·an (亦作 **Ar·is·to·te·le·an**) [ˌæristəˈtiːljən, -tiˈliːən; ˏærɪstəˋtilɪən, -tɪlɪən] **I** ***a*.** **1.** 亚里士多德的。**2.** 亚里士多德学派的。**II** ***n*.** **1.** 亚里士多德学派的人。**2.** 求实者〔思想上倾向于注重经验和实际的人〕。

a·rith·me·tic [əˈriθmətik; əˋrɪθməˏtɪk] ***n*.** **1.** 算术,算法;计算。**2.** 算术书。*I challenge your* ~. 你的算法靠不住。*mental* ~ 心算。~ *device* 运算装置,运算器。~ *speed* 运算速度。

ar·ith·met·i·cal [ˌæriθˈmetikəl; ˏærɪθˋmɛtɪkəl] ***a*.** 算术(上)的。~ **complement** 馀数。~ **progression** 算术级数,等差级数。**-ly** ***ad*.** 用算术,算术上。

a·rith·me·ti·cian [əˌriθməˈtiʃən; əˏrɪθməˋtɪʃən] ***n*.** 算术家。

ar·ith·mom·e·ter [ˌæriθˈmɔmitə; ˏærɪθˋmɑmɪtɚ] ***n*.** (初期的)加算器,四则计算机。

-arium 〔L.〕 *suf*. 关于…的物,…的场所: aqu*arium*, honor*arium*.

a ri·ve·der·ci [ɑːˌriveiˈdeətʃi; ɑˏrɪveˋdɚtʃɪ] 〔It.〕〔古〕回头见! 再见〔暂时分别时用语〕。

Ariz. = Arizona.

Ar·i·zo·na [ˌæriˈzəunə; ˏærəˋzonə] ***n*.** 亚利桑那〔美国州名〕。

Ark. = Arkansas [ˈɑːkənsɔː, Am. ˈɑrkənsɔ, ɑrˈkænzəs; ˋɑrkənsɔ, Am. ˋɑrkənsɑ, ɑrˋkænzəs] ***n*.** 阿肯色〔美国州名〕

ark [ɑːk; ɑrk] ***n*.** **1.** 【圣】方舟;〔喻〕避难所。**2.** 〔方、诗〕箱,柜;【圣】约柜。**3.** 犹太教堂中贮存圣经和犹太教法典卷轴的地方。**4.** 〔美〕大平底船,河船。***Noah's*** ~ 挪亚方舟〔《圣经》中挪亚为避洪水而造的方舟,舟中载有成对的各类动物〕;装有各种动物的玩具船。~ ***of the covenant*** 约柜〔装有两块十诫碑的箱子〕。

Ar·kan·sas [ˈɑːkənsɔː, Am. ˈɑrkənsɔ, ɑrˈkænzəs; ˋɑrkənˏsɔ, ɑrˋkænzəs] ***n*.** **1.** 阿肯色〔美国州名〕。**2.** 〔the ~〕阿肯色河〔美国〕。

Ar·kan·san [ɑːˈkænzən; ɑrˋkænzən], **Ar·kan·si·an** [ɑːˈkænziən; ɑrˋkænzɪən] **1.** ***a*.** 阿肯色州(人)的。**2.** ***n*.** 阿肯色州人。

Ar·kan·saw·yer [ˌɑːkənˈsɔːjə; ˏɑrkənˋsɔjə] ***n*.** 〔美〕阿肯色州人〔用做绰号〕。

Ar·kie [ˈɑːkiː; ˋɑrki] ***n*.** 〔美〕(从阿肯色州来的)临时雇农。

ar·kose [ˈɑːkəus; ˋɑrkos] ***n*.** 〔F.〕长石砂岩。

Ark·wright [ˈɑːkrait; ˋɑrkˏraɪt] ***n*.** **1.** 阿克赖特〔姓氏〕。**2.** **Sir Richard** ~ 阿克赖特〔1732—1792,英国纺织机发明人〕。**3.** 〔a-〕(能制箱、柜等的)木匠。

Ar·len [ˈɑːlən; ˋɑrlən] ***n*.** 阿伦〔姓氏,男子名〕。

Ar·lene [ɑːˈliːn; ɑrˋlin] ***n*.** 阿琳〔女子名〕。

arles [ɑːlz; ɑrlz] ***n*. *pl*.** 〔用作单〕〔Scot.〕定钱(尤指雇用仆人时先付的钱)。

Ar·lo [ˈɑːləu; ˋɑrlo] ***n*.** 阿洛〔男子名〕。

arm[1] [ɑːm; ɑrm] ***n*.** **1.** 臂,【动】前肢。**2.** 【机】(轮)辐;【电】线担,支路,支架。**3.** 臂状物;衣袖;电唱头臂;(椅子)扶手。**4.** 树枝,枝干。**5.** 港湾,海湾。**6.** 力,权力。**7.** 【棒球】投球能力。*the right* ~ 右臂;得力的助手。*Justice has long* ~*s*. 天网恢恢,疏而不漏。*an* ~ *of the sea* 海湾,河口。*the* ~ *of the government* 政府的分支机构。*the strong* ~ *of the law* 法律的威力。*the* ~ *of a record player* 唱机的唱头臂。*lose one's* ~ 【棒球】失去投球能力。~ ***in*** ~ 臂挽着臂。***by the strong*** ~ 强

制地。**chance one's ～**〔英口〕冒险一试。**child in ～s** 怀抱中的婴儿。**cost** (*sb.*) **an ～ and a leg**〔俚〕使付出一大笔钱。**give one's ～** 伸手臂给(同行女人挽);〔喻〕提携。**in the ～s of Morpheus** 进入梦乡。**keep** (*sb.*) **at ～'s length** 疏远,不使接近。**make a long ～** 伸臂(攫取)。**offer one's ～** = give one's ～. **put the ～ on sb.** 向某人讨钱;抢劫某人。**take** (*sb.'s*) **～s** 拉伸出之臂。**take** (*a child*) **in one's ～s** 抱(孩子)。**talk sb.'s ～ off**〔俚〕对某人唠叨个没完。**the ～ of flesh** 人力,人的努力。**twist sb.'s ～** 倒扭某人手臂;向某人施加压力。**throw one's ～s around another's neck** 搂住脖子。**under the ～** 挟在腋下。**with folded ～s** 两臂交叉于胸前(*look on with folded ～s* 袖手旁观)。**within ～'s reach** 在左右,近在咫尺。**with open ～s** 伸开双手,真心诚意地(欢迎)。**would give one's right ～ for**〔口〕愿意为…付出巨大代价。～**band** 臂章。～**hole** 袖孔。～**pad** 椅子扶手上的小垫子。～**pit** 腋窝。～**rest** (靠椅、拐杖等的)扶手。～**'s-length** *a.* 不友好的,不亲密的。～**-twisting** *n.*, *a.* 强大压力(的)。～ **wrestling** 臂力,拗手腕。

arm² [ɑːm; ɑrm] **I** *n.* **1.** 〔*pl.*, 罕 *sing.*〕军械,武器。**2.** 〔喻〕军事。**3.** (步、骑等的)兵种。**4.** (盾、旗等上的)纹章。*a man at ～s* 战士。*a passage of* [*at*] *～s* 比武,两人对打。*a stand of ～s* (一名士兵的)全副武装。*deed of ～s* 战功。*force of ～s* 武力,兵力。*small ～s* 轻兵器(指手枪、步枪、机枪等)。*the suspension of ～s* 休战。**appeal to ～s** 诉诸武力。**bear ～s** 服兵役。**bred to ～s** 自幼习武。**by ～** 用武力。**carry ～s** 携带武器;服兵役。**go to ～s** 诉诸武力。**lay down ～s** 缴械;投降。**Order ～s!** 枪放下! **Pile ～s!** 架枪! **Present ～s!** 举枪(敬礼)! **rest on one's ～s** (战斗中的)暂时休息。**rise in ～s** 动武,起兵。**Shoulder ～s!** 枪上肩! **take up ～s** 拿起武器。**To ～s!** 快拿武器! 准备战斗! **turn one's ～s against** 攻击。**under ～s** **1.** 备战。**2.** 在服兵役期间。**up in ～s** 武装反抗。**II** *vt.* **1.** 供给…武器,武装(军队等)。**2.** 供给;发给 (*with*)。**3.** 打开(雷等)的保险;给…装上导火线。**4.** 给…装甲。*an ～ed mediation* 武装调解。*I ～ed my men with guns.* 我发枪给部下。*be ～ed at all points* 全身武装,周身披甲;戒备严密。*be ～ed to the teeth* 全副武装,武装到牙齿。*be ～ed with* 用…武装着;装备着。*be ～ed with a letter of introduction* 带着介绍信。—*vi.* 拿起武器,武装起来。

ar·ma·da [ɑːˈmɑːdə; ɑrˋmɑdə] *n.* **1.** 舰队。**2.** (飞机、汽车等的)大队。**3.** 〔the A-〕(1588 年西班牙进攻英国时的)无敌舰队(= the Invincible [Spanish] Armada)。*an ～ of planes* 飞机机群。*an ～ of buses* 汽车队。

ar·ma·dil·lo [ˌɑːməˈdiləu; ˏɑrməˋdɪlo] *n.* 【动】犰狳。

Ar·ma·ged·don [ˌɑːməˈgedn; ˏɑrməˋgɛdn] *n.* **1.** 【圣】世界末日善恶决战的战场。**2.** (国际间的)大决战。

Ar·ma·gnac [ˈɑːmənjæk; ˏɑrməˋnjæk] *n.* 〔有时作 a-〕阿马涅克白兰地〔法国加斯柯尼的阿马涅克所产的一种酒〕。

ar·ma·ment [ˈɑːməmənt; ˋɑrməmənt] *n.* **1.** 军队。**2.** (一国的)武装力量。**3.** (军舰、要塞等的)火炮;一个作战单位的武器,装备。**4.** 武装(过程)。**5.** (动植物的)防护器官。**6.** 战斗部〔指导弹的弹头、引信和保险装置系统的结合部〕。*the reduction of ～s* 裁(减)军(备)。*an anti-torpedo ～* 水雷防御炮。*a main* [*secondary*] *～* 主[副]炮。*the vast ～ sent by the Rome emperor* 罗马皇帝派遣的大批军队。*planes with the newest ～* 配备有最新武器的飞机。*The country's ～ will take years.* 国家的武装过程需要几年。

ar·ma·men·tar·i·um [ˌɑːmənənˈtɛəriəm; ˏɑrməmen-ˋtɛrɪəm] *n.* (*pl.* ～s, **-ia** [-ə; -ə]) 物资、器械装备(尤指医疗物资和器械)。

Ar·mand [ˈɑːmɔnd; ˋɑrmɑnd] *n.* 阿曼德〔男子名, Herman(n) 的异体〕。

ar·ma·ture [ˈɑːmətjuə; ˋɑrmətʃɚ] *n.* **1.** 【电】转子,电枢;衔铁;引铁。**2.** 甲胄。**3.** 【生】防护器官;【虫】体刺。**4.** 【建】加强料;钢筋。**5.** (塑像的)骨架。*a small animal having sharp teeth for its ～* 有利齿当武器的小动物。

arm·chair [ˈɑːmˈtʃɛə; ˋɑrmˏtʃɛr] **I** *n.* 扶手椅子。**II** *a.* **1.** 安逸的,舒适的。**2.** 理论性的,不切实际的。*an ～ travel* 舒适的旅行。*an ～ soldier* 不上前线的士兵。*an ～ strategist* 纸上谈兵者。

arme blanche [ɑːmˈblɑːŋʃ; ˋɑrmˋblɑ̃ʃ] 〔F.〕 **1.** (骑兵用的)大刀,标枪。**2.** 骑兵。

armed [ɑːmd; ɑrmd] *a.* **1.** 武装了的。**2.** 【动、植】有(刺、齿等)防护器官的。**3.** (炮弹等)装上导火线的。**4.** 有装甲的。**5.** 有扶手的。*an ～ merchantman* 武装商船。*～ neutrality* 武装中立。*～ peace* 武装和平。*～ robbery* 武装抢劫,持械抢劫。*～ forces* [*services*] 军队;海陆空三军。*～ eyes* 戴着眼镜的眼睛〔*cf.* naked eye〕。*～ glass* 铁丝网夹心玻璃。*long-～* 长胳膊的。

Ar·me·ni·a [ɑːˈmiːnjə; ɑrˋminɪə] *n.* 亚美尼亚。

Ar·me·ni·an [ɑːˈmiːnjən; ɑrˋminɪən] **I** *a.* 亚美尼亚(人)的。**II** *n.* 亚美尼亚人[语]。

ar·met [ˈɑːmet; ˋɑrmɛt] *n.* (中世纪的)铁盔。

arm·ful [ˈɑːmful; ˋɑrmˏfʊl] *n.* 一抱。*an ～ of wood* 一抱柴。

ar·mi·ger [ˈɑːmidʒə; ˋɑrmɪdʒɚ] *n.* (*pl.* **-ge·ri** [-ri; -rɪ]) (中世纪)骑士的扈从;(骑士与自由民之间的)乡绅。

ar·mil·lar·y [ɑːˈmiləri; ˋɑrmɪˏlɛrɪ] *a.* 环的,手镯的;环形的。～ **sphere** 浑天仪。

ar·mip·o·tent [ɑːˈmipətənt; ɑrˋmɪpətənt] *a.* 〔罕〕兵力强大的。

ar·mi·stice [ˈɑːmistis; ˋɑrməstɪs] *n.* **1.** 停战,休战。**2.** 休战条约,停战协定。**A- Day** 第一次世界大战的停战纪念日〔1918 年 11 月 11 日〕。

arm·less [ˈɑːmlis; ˋɑrmlɪs] *a.* **1.** 无臂的。**2.** 无武装[战备]的。**3.** (动植物)无防护器官的。

arm·let [ˈɑːmlit; ˋɑrmlɪt] *n.* **1.** 小海湾。**2.** 臂饰,臂环,臂章。

arm·load [ˈɑːmləud; ˋɑrmˏlod] *n.* 〔美口〕一抱(量)。

arm·lock [ˈɑːmˌlɔk; ˋɑrmˏlɑk] *n.* 【摔跤】锁臂勾腿。

ar·moire [ɑːˈmwɑːr; ɑrˋmwɑr] *n.* 〔F.〕大型衣橱。

ar·mor [ˈɑːmə; ˋɑrmɚ] *n.* 〔美〕= armour.

ar·mo·ri·al [ɑːˈmɔːriəl; ɑrˋmorɪəl] **I** *a.* 纹章的,盾徽的。**II** *n.* 纹章集。～ **bearings** 纹章。

Ar·mor·ic, Ar·mor·i·can [ɑːˈmɔrik, ɑːˈmɔrikən; ɑr-ˋmɔrɪk, ɑrˋmɔrɪkn] **I** *a.* 阿莫里卡(法国布列塔尼之旧名)的,阿莫里卡人的,阿莫里卡语的。**II** *n.* **1.** 阿莫里卡人,布列塔尼人。**2.** 阿莫里卡语;布列塔尼语。

ar·mor·y [ˈɑːməri; ˋɑrmərɪ] *n.* 〔美〕= armoury.

ar·mour [ˈɑːmə; ˋɑrmɚ] **I** *n.* **1.** 甲胄,盔甲。**2.** 铠板;装甲用钢板。**3.** (动植物的)防护器官。**4.** 潜水服。**5.** 装甲部队。**6.** (覆盖在电线外的)铠装。～*-piercing projectile* 穿甲弹。**be clad in ～** 穿着盔甲的,武装着的;装甲的。**II** *vt.* 为…装甲;为…穿上铠甲。～**-bearer** 武士的扈从。～**-clad** **1.** *a.* 武装的,装甲的。**2.** *n.* 装甲舰。～ **plate** 装甲用钢板。**-ing** *n.* 武装;铠装。

ar·mo(u)red [ˈɑːməd; ˋɑrmɚd] *a.* **1.** 武装的;装甲的。**2.** 穿戴铠甲的;(电缆等)铠装的。*～ cable* 铠装电缆。*～ concrete* 钢筋混凝土。*an ～ cruiser* 装甲巡洋舰。*～ forces* 装甲部队。*an ～ seat* 【空】装甲座位。*an ～ train* 铁甲列车。

ar·mo(u)r·er [ˈɑːmərə; ˋɑrmərɚ] *n.* **1.** (从前的)盔甲,兵器制造者。**2.** 武器制造者。**3.** (部队里,战舰上维修武器的)军械士。

ar·mo(u)r·y [ˈɑːməri; ˋɑrmərɪ] *n.* **1.** 军械库。**2.** 〔美〕国民警卫队训练场。**3.** 〔美〕兵工厂。**4.** 〔集合词〕武器,军械。**5.** 〔古〕纹章。**6.** 纹章学。

A

arms [ɑːmz; ɑrmz] ***n***. 〔*pl*.〕**1**. 见 arm²条。**2**. (手枪等)小武器。**3**. 纹章(= coat of ~)。

Arm·strong [ˈɑːmstrɔŋ; ˋɑrmstrɔŋ] ***n***. 阿姆斯特朗〔姓氏〕。

ar·mure [ˈɑːmjuə; ˋɑrmjʊr] ***n***. **1**. 小卵石纹织物。**2**. 〔废〕盔甲。

ar·my [ˈɑːmi; ˋɑrmɪ] ***n***. **1**. 陆军;军队。**2**. 军;集团军;兵团;野战军。**3**. 大群;团体。~ *and navy* 陆海军。*a regular* ~ 正规军。*a reserve* ~ 后备军。*a standing* [*conventional*] ~ 常备军。*an* ~ *of ants* 大群蚂蚁。*the* ~ *of the unemployed* 失业大军。~ ***act*** 陆军刑法,军法。***A- Air Forces*** 〔美〕陆军航空部队。***A- and Navy Store*** 〔英〕军人消费合作社。~ ***of operation*** 野战军。***A- Service Corps*** 辎重队。***join the*** ~ 入伍,参军。***raise an*** ~ 招兵,募兵。***serve in the*** ~ 服兵役,在军队中工作。~ **act** 陆军刑法,军法。~ **brat** 〔美俚〕(随营长大的)陆军官或士兵的儿子。~ **brown** 军服黄色。~ **corps** 军。~ **corps commander** 军长。**A- Day** 陆军节。~ **group** 集团军。~**-list** 陆军军官名册。~ **register** = ~**-list**. ~ **surplus** 陆军剩余物资。~ **worm** (成群结队毁坏庄稼的)黏虫。

Arne [ɑːn; ɑrn] ***n***. 阿恩〔姓氏,男子名〕。

ar·ni·ca [ˈɑːnikə; ˋɑrnɪkə] ***n***. **1**. 【植】山金车花。**2**. 【药】阿尼卡酊剂〔用以治疗扭伤〕。

Ar·nold [ˈɑːnld; ˋɑrnld] ***n***. 阿诺德〔姓氏,男子名〕。

ar·oid [ˈærɔid, ˈɛər-; ˋærɔɪd, ˋɛr-] ***n***. 天南星科植物。

a·roint [əˈrɔint; əˋrɔɪnt] ***int***. 〔古〕去! *A- thee*! 去! 滚!

a·ro·ma [əˈrəumə; əˋromə] ***n***. **1**. 芳香,香味。**2**. 气派,风格,风味。*a city with the* ~ *of Paris* 具有巴黎风格的城市。

ar·o·mat·ic [ˌærəuˈmætik; ˏærəˋmætɪk] **I** ***a***. **1**. 香气浓的,芳香的。**2**. 【化】芳香族的。**II** ***n***. **1**. 芳香植物。**2**. 〔常 *pl*.〕香料,芳香剂。~ **crops** 香料作物。~ **compounds** 芳香族化合物。

a·ro·ma·tize [əˈrəumətaiz; əˋroməˏtaɪz] ***vt***. **1**. 使芳香,在…中加香味。**2**. 【化】使芳构化。

a·rose [əˈrəuz; əˋroz] arise 的过去式。

a·round [əˈraund; əˋraʊnd] **I** ***ad***. **1**. 周围,四面。**2**. 〔美口〕各处,四处。**3**. 左近,在附近。**3**. 围着,环绕。**4**. 向相反方向。**5**. 循环重现;旋转。**6**. 恢复知觉。**7**. 活跃着。**8**. 到(谈话双方都熟悉的)某地。*Travel* ~ *from place to place* 周游。*look* ~ 环视,四顾。*sit* ~ *a table* 围着桌子坐。*a car circling* ~ 一辆在兜着圈子的车。*Will you please wait* ~ *for me*? 请在附近等我好吗? *Turn* ~! *You're going the wrong way*. 转回来,你走错路了! *The column measures two feet* ~. 这根柱子周长2英尺。*She hasn't been* ~ *lately*. 她最近不活跃了。*He came* ~ *to see me*. 他到这里来看我。*bring sb*. ~ 使某人恢复知觉。***all*** ~ 四处,到处;全面地(*shook hands all* ~ 一一握手)。***all the year*** ~ 整年(*mild all the year* ~ 一年四季都很温暖)。***be*** ~ 〔美口〕起床;走动(*He's up and* ~ *now*. 他起来走动了)。***fool*** ~ 〔口〕吊儿郎当。***hang*** ~ 在附近徘徊。***have been*** ~ (***a lot***) 〔口〕见识(很)多;世故(很)深。***the other way*** ~ 〔美〕从相反方向;用相反方式。**II** ***prep***. **1**. 在周围,围着;绕过。**2**. 〔美口〕在近处,在附近;前后,左右,差不多。**3**. 〔美口〕到处。**4**. 在那边。**5**. 朝着各个方向。**6**. 在(某人)身边。~ *here* 在这边。~ *the corner* 〔美〕在拐角那里(=〔英〕*round the corner*)。*roam* ~ *the country* 漫游全国。*stay* ~ *the house* 总不离家。~ *four o'clock* 四点前后。*travel* ~ *the world* 作环球旅行。*leave the books* ~ *the house* 在房子里到处乱丢书。*the few men* ~ *the despot* 暴君身边寥寥可数的几个人。***get*** ~ 绕过(障碍),解决(困难),回避(事实)。~**-the-clock** ***a***. 连续二十四小时的;连续不停的(*an* ~*-the-clock operation* 连续二十四小时的作业)。

a·rous·al [əˈrauzəl; əˋraʊzl] ***n***. 〔罕、古〕觉醒;激励,唤起。

a·rouse [əˈrauz; əˋraʊz] ***vt***. **1**. 唤醒。**2**. 唤起,引起。**3**. 鼓励,激发。~ *suspicion* 引起猜疑。~ *sb*. *from sleep* 唤醒某人。— ***vi***. 睡醒。

a·row [əˈrəu; əˋro] ***ad***. 〔诗〕一列,一排。

A.R.P., **ARP** = air raid precautions 空袭预防措施。**ARP post** 防空哨。**ARP shelter** 防空洞。~ **warden** 防空监视员。

ar·peg·gio [ɑːˈpedʒiəu; ɑrˋpɛdʒɪˏo] ***n***. 〔It.〕(*pl*. ~*s*) 【乐】琶音,急速和弦。

ar·pent [ˈɑːpənt; ˋɑrpənt] ***n***. 阿邦〔法国旧地积度量单位,现仍在加拿大的魁北克和美国的路易斯安那部分地区使用,约等于5/6英亩〕。

ar·que·bus [ˈɑːkwibəs; ˋɑrkwɪbəs] ***n***. 火绳钩枪。

arr. = **1**. arrival. **2**. arrive. **3**. arrived. **4**. arranged. **5**. arrangements.

ar·rack [ˈærək; ˋærək] ***n***. (大米、糖蜜或椰汁制成的)烧酒(= arak)。

ar·rah [ˈærə; ˋærə] ***int***. 啊呀〔表示惊愕、愤怒等的声音〕。

ar·raign [əˈrein; əˋren] ***vt***. **1**. 【法】传讯,提审,审问。**2**. 弹劾,责难,控告。**-ment** ***n***.

ar·range [əˈreindʒ; əˋrendʒ] ***vt***. **1**. 整理,整顿;布置。**2**. 商定,商妥。**3**. 准备,安排。**4**. 调停(纠纷)。**5**. 【乐】改编。~ *one's collections* 整理搜集品。*The meeting is* ~*d for Saturday afternoon*. 会议安排在星期六下午。*Everything is so far* ~*d*. 样样都准备好了。~ *a dispute* 调解纠纷。~ *a novel for the stage* 改编小说为剧本。—***vi***. **1**. 商定,商妥。**2**. 准备,设法,安排。*I will* ~ *somehow*. 我终归会想好办法的。*We have* ~*d for him to live near us*. 我们已安排他住在附近。~ *for* (*an appointment*) 约(会面时间)。~ (*things*) ***in order*** 整顿(东西)。~ ***with*** (*sb*.) ***about*** (*sth*.) 与(某人)商定(某事)。

ar·range·ment [əˈreindʒmənt; əˋrendʒmənt] ***n***. **1**. 整顿,整理;排列,布置,分类。**2**. 〔*pl*.〕安排,料理,筹备,预备。**3**. 商定,约定。**4**. 调解,和解。**5**. 改作,改编;改编的乐曲。*Arrangements have been made for the party*. 为聚会做了安排。***come to an*** ~ 谈妥。***make*** ~***s for*** 为…做准备。***make*** ~***s with*** 与…达成协议。***make business*** ~ 接洽事务。~ **committee** 筹备委员(会)。

ar·rant [ˈærənt; ˋærənt] ***a***. 彻头彻尾的;臭名远扬的。*an* ~ *fool* 大傻瓜。*an* ~ *hypocrite* 彻头彻尾的伪君子。*an* ~ *lie* 弥天大谎。**-ly** ***ad***.

ar·ras [ˈærəs; ˋærəs] ***n***. (壁上装饰的)挂毯。

ar·ray [əˈrei; əˋre] **I** ***vt***. **1**. 打扮,装饰。**2**. 使…列队,排列。**3**. 提出(陪审官)名单,使(陪审官)列席,召集(陪审官)。*The general* ~*ed his troops for battle*. 将军使军队列队准备战斗。*The girl* ~*ed herself in her finest clothes*. 这女孩打扮得花枝招展。*The count and his men* ~*ed themselves against the king*. 伯爵举兵对抗国王。**II** ***n***. **1**. 整列,队列,阵(列);阵容。**2**. 〔诗〕衣裳,装扮,打扮。**3**. 陪审官名单。**4**. 一大批,一大群,一连串。**5**. 【数】排列。*a battle* ~ 战斗队形,列阵。*holiday* ~ 节日盛装。*be in fine* ~ 盛装。*an* ~ *of actors* 演员的阵容。*a window* ~ 橱窗陈列品。***an*** ~ ***of*** (*umbrellas*) 一排(伞)。***in battle*** ~ 列阵,严阵。***in proud*** ~ 堂堂正正。

ar·ray·al [əˈreiəl; əˋreəl] ***n***. **1**. 列阵,军容。**2**. 排列。

ar·rear [əˈriə; əˋrɪr] ***n***. **1**. 〔*pl*.〕欠款,尾数;欠工,尾活。**2**. (工作的)耽搁,延误,落后。**3**. 剩余品。~*s of stock* 滞销货。~*s of rent* 欠租,拖欠未交的租金。~*s of correspondence* 待覆的信件。***in*** ~(*s*) 拖欠,下欠(*fall in*(*to*) ~(*s*) 拖欠款项)。***in*** ~ ***of*** 赶不上,不及。***in*** ~(*s*) ***with*** (*payments*) 拖延(交款)。***work off*** ~***s*** 补做尾活;陆续补还欠款。

ar·rear·age [əˈriəridʒ; əˋrɪrɪdʒ] ***n***. **1**. 〔*pl*.〕欠款。**2**.

落后,拖延,延误。3. 备用品。

ar·rect [ə'rekt; ə`rɛkt] **a**. **1**. (耳朵)竖着的。**2**. 仔细听着的,警觉的。*a rabbit with ears* ~ 竖着耳朵的兔子。

ar·rest [ə'rest; ə`rɛst] **I** **vt**. **1**. 逮捕,拘捕,扣留。**2**. 止住,阻止,抑制。**3**. 吸引(注意)。*The policeman ~ed the thief*. 警察逮捕了窃贼。*The doctor ~ed the growth of the disease*. 医生止住了病情的恶化。*The bright colours of the flowers ~ed the girl's attention*. 花的艳丽色彩引起了女孩的注意。*She ~ed herself in the act of sitting*. 她要坐而没坐下来。~ (*sb*.) **for** (*a crime*) 因(罪嫌)逮捕(某人)。~ **sb.'s eye** 惹人注目。**II** **n**. **1**. 停止,阻止,抑制;制动(装置)。**2**. 逮捕,拘留,收押。~ **of judgement** 暂缓判决〔陪审团宣布有罪或无罪后;法官因某种法律的原因而暂不作判决〕, **be put** [**held, placed**] **under** ~ 在拘留中。**under house** ~ 软禁。

ar·rest·er [ə'restə; ə`rɛstɚ] **n**. **1**. 逮捕者。**2**. 防止装置。**3**. 避雷器。*a lightning* ~ 避雷针。*a spark* ~ 火花制止器〔防止火花外射的装置〕。

ar·rest·ing [ə'restiŋ; ə`rɛstɪŋ] **a**. **1**. 引人注意的,显著的。**2**. 制动的。*an ~ work of art* 引人注意的艺术品。

ar·rest·ment [ə'restmənt; ə`rɛstmənt] **n**. **1**. 阻止;制动。**2**. 逮捕,拘捕;扣留,扣押。

ar·ret [ə'rei; ə`re] **n**. 〔F.〕 **1**. 命令。**2**. 裁判,判决。**3**. 逮捕;扣押。

ar·rhyth·mi·a [ə'riðmiə, ə'riθ-; ə`rɪðmɪə, ə`rɪθ-] **n**. 【医】心律不齐。**ar·ryth·mic, -rhyth·mi·cal** [ə'riðmik(əl), ə'riθ-; ə`rɪðmɪk(əl), ə`rɪθ-] **a**. **-rhyth·mi·cal·ly** **ad**.

ar·ride [ə'raid; ə`raɪd] **vt**. 〔古〕使喜欢,使满足。

ar·rière-ban [æriɛə'bæn; `ærɪɚ`bæn] **n**. 〔F.〕 **1**. 【史】(中世纪法国国王召集臣下的)总动员令。**2**. 对国王有应召服军役义务的诸侯。

ar·rière-pen·sée ['æriɛəpɑːn'sei; ˏaˏrjɛrˏpɑ̃`se] **n**. 〔F.〕心事,心思;隐蔽的意图。

ar·ris ['æris; `ærɪs] **n**. 【建】棱(角)。~ **gutter** V 形檐槽。

ar·ri·val [ə'raivəl; ə`raɪvəl] **n**. **1**. 到达,抵达。**2**. 到达者;到达物。**3**. 出现,登场。**4**. 新生婴儿。*The new ~ was a daughter*. 新生婴儿是一个女孩。*a new* ~ 新来者;新到货;新生儿。~ *at a conclusion* 得出结论。*on his ~ at sixty* 年满六十。**cash on** ~ 【商】货到付款。**delivery on** ~ 【商】货到即交。~ **list** 抵埠乘客名单。~ **station** 末站,终点站。

ar·rive [ə'raiv; ə`raɪv] **vi**. **1**. 到达,抵,到,达。**2**. (时间、事件等)到来,发生。**3**. 达到(结果),得出(结论等)(*at*)。**4**. (艺术家等)成功,成名。~ *at a place* 到达某地。~ *in England* 到英国。~ *at a conclusion* 得到结论。~ *at manhood* 达成年。~ *upon the scene* 到场。*The time has ~d for action*. 采取行动的时刻到来了。*He has ~d professionally*. 他在职业上功成名就。★指到达的时间或地点用 at, 到某大都会时用 in.

ar·ri·ve·der·ci [ɑːriveˈdɛətʃiː; ɑˏrive`dɛrtʃi] **int**. 〔It.〕回头见! 再见! 〔暂时分别时用语〕。

ar·ri·viste [æriː'vist; ɑri`vist] **n**. 〔F.〕暴发户,野心家,钻营者,名利狂。

ar·ro·ba [ə'rɔːbə; ə`rɔbə] **n**. 〔Sp.〕阿罗瓦〔**1**. 西班牙重量单位,用于南美某些国家,合 25.36 磅。**2**. 葡萄牙重量单位,用于巴西,合 32.38 磅。**3**. 液量单位用于某些操西班牙语的国家,相当于13到17夸脱。〕

ar·ro·gance, ar·ro·gan·cy ['ærəgəns, -si; `ærəgəns, -sɪ] **n**. 自大,傲慢 (*opp*. humility)。~ **of power** (大国的)炫耀武力。

ar·ro·gant ['ærəgənt; `ærəgənt] **a**. 自大的,傲慢的,妄自尊大的。~ *airs* 骄气。~ *and unreasonable demands* 蛮横无理的要求。**-ly** **ad**.

ar·ro·gate ['ærəugeit; `æroˏget] **vt**. **1**. 僭称,冒称;霸占,擅取。**2**. 不当地把…归于 (*to*)。~ *the right to make decisions* 冒称有权做出决定。~ *to oneself some importance* 妄自尊大。~ *bad motives to sb*. 无根据地认为某人别有用心。

ar·ro·ga·tion [ˌærəu'geiʃən; ˏæro`geʃən] **n**. 僭称;霸占;僭越。

ar·ron·disse·ment [ærɔn'diːs'mɑ̃ːŋ; ˏaˏrɔ̃ˏdis`mɑ̃] **n**. 〔F.〕县,(大城市的)区。

ar·row ['ærəu; `æro] **n**. **1**. 矢,箭。**2**. 箭状物,箭头记号〔→〕。**3**. 〔the A-〕【天】天箭座。*shoot an* ~ 射箭。*a spent* ~ 强弩之末。*a traffic* ~ 交通箭头标志。**a broad** ~ 宽矢形戳记〔标明英国政府财产的官印〕。**as straight as an** ~ 笔直。**have an** ~ **left in one's quiver** 还有资本;还有对策。~**head** ['ærəuhed; `æroˏhɛd] **n**. **1**. 箭头镞。**2**. = broad ~. **3**. 【植】慈菇。~**-headed** **a**. 箭头形的,镞状的。~**-headed characters** 楔形文字。~**root** ['ærəuruːt; `æroˏrʊt] **n**. 【植】**1**. 竹竽,葛。**2**. 竹竽粉,葛粉。~ **wood** ['ærəuwud; `æroˏwʊd] **n**. 【植】弓木,荚蒾〔北美印第安人用以制箭〕。

ar·row·worm ['ærəuˌwəːm; `æroˏwɝm] **n**. 【虫】箭虫。

ar·row·y ['ærəui; `æroɪ] **a**. **1**. 矢的,箭一样的;笔直的。**2**. 像箭一样迅速的。

ar·roy·o [ə'rɔiəu; ə`rɔɪo] **n**. (*pl*. ~**s**) 〔美〕 **1**. 小河,小溪。**2**. 旱谷,干涸的沟壑。

ARS = **1**. American Rocket Society 美国火箭学会。**2**. Agricultural Research Service 农业研究服务处〔美国农业部一机构〕。

arse [ɑːs; ɑrs] **n**. 〔卑〕屁股。

ar·se·nal ['ɑːsinl; `ɑrsnəl] **n**. **1**. 军械库,武器库。**2**. 兵工厂。**3**. 〔喻〕(思想等的)武库。*a naval* ~ 海军军工厂。

ar·se·nate ['ɑːsinit; `ɑrsnˏet] **n**. 【化】砷酸盐。

ar·se·nic ['ɑːsnik; `ɑrsnɪk] **I** **n**. 【化】砷,信石,砒霜。**II** **a**. 砷的。~ *acid* 砷酸。*white* ~ 砒霜。

ar·sen·i·cal [ɑː'senikəl; ɑr`sɛnɪkl] **I** **a**. 砷的,含信石的。~ *poisoning* 砷中毒。**II** **n**. 砷化物。

ar·se·nide ['ɑːsinaid; `ɑrsnˏaɪd] **n**. 砷化物。

ar·se·ni·ous, -nous [ɑː'siːnjəs, -nəs; ɑr`sinɪəs, -nəs] **a**. (含)砷的;亚砷的。~ **acid** 亚砷酸。

ar·se·nism ['ɑːsinizəm; `ɑrsɪnɪzəm] **n**. 慢性砷中毒。

ar·se·nite ['ɑːsinait; `ɑrsnˏaɪt] **n**. 【化】砷华,亚砷酸盐。

ar·se·niu·ret·ed, ar·se·niu·ret·ted [ɑː'siːnjə'retid, -'sen-; ɑr`sinjəˏrɛtɪd, -`sɛn-] **a**. 砷化的。

ar·se·no·py·rite [ˌɑːsinəu'pairait; ˏɑrsno`paɪraɪt] **n**. 【矿】含砷黄铁矿,毒砂。

ars gra·ti·a ar·tis ['ɑːz'greiʃjə'ɑːtis; ɑrz`greʃɪə`ɑrtɪs] 〔L.〕为艺术而艺术。

ar·shin [ɑː'ʃiːn; ɑr`ʃin] **n**. 俄尺〔= 28 英寸〕。

ar·sine [ɑː'siːn, 'ɑːsiːn; ɑr`sin, `ɑrsin] **n**. **1**. 胂。**2**. 砷化三氢。

ar·sis ['ɑːsis; `ɑrsɪs] **n**. (*pl*. **-ses** [-siːz; -siz]) **1**. (古典诗的)弱音节。**2**. (英国诗的)强音节〔因误解 arsis 的希腊文原义,而讹传为强音节〕。**3**. 【乐】弱拍。

ARSL = Associate of the Royal Society of Literature (英国)皇家文学学会准会员。

ar·son ['ɑːsn; `ɑrsn] **n**. (故意)放火,纵火(罪)。

ars·phen·a·mine [ˌɑːsfenə'miːn, ɑːs'fenəmiːn; ˏɑrsfenə`min, ɑrs`fenəmin] **n**. 【药】胂凡纳明,六〇六(药)〔用以治疗梅毒〕。

art[1] [ɑːt; ɑrt] **I** **n**. **1**. 艺术,美术。**2**. 〔*pl*.〕(中世纪大学的)文科(= liberal arts)。**3**. 技术,技巧;技艺。**4**. 策略,诡计,奸计。**5**. 〔美口〕(新闻、杂志上的)插图。**6**. 〔古〕学问。**7**. 做作,装模作样。*the ~ for ~ school* 艺术至上派,唯美派。*an ~ gallery* 美术馆;画廊。*the ~ of agriculture* 农艺。*the ~ preservative of all ~s* 印刷术。*the black* ~ 魔术。*the fine ~s* 美术〔包括绘画、雕塑、建筑、文学、音乐、戏剧等〕。*the industrial ~s* 工艺。

A

the healing [*benevolent*] ~ 医术。*the liberal* ~*s* 文科〔包括文学、音乐、哲学等〕。*the manly* [*noble, self-defence*] ~ 拳术。*the mechanical* [*useful*] ~*s* 手工工艺。*a bachelor of* ~*s* 文学士。*a master of* ~*s* 文学硕士。*a smile without* ~ 自然的[天真的]微笑。~ *of strategy* 战略。~ ***and part*** 策划并参与 (*He is* ~ *and part in the crime*. 他是这个罪案的共犯;他策划并参与犯罪活动)。~ ***for*** ~***'s sake*** 为艺术而艺术。**II** ***vt***. 使艺术化〔仅用于下列成语〕。~ ***up*** 使艺术化。~ **deco** [**A- D-**]艺术装饰。~ **director 1.** (电影、电视的)美术设计人。**2.** 美术编辑。~ **form** 艺术形式。~ **glass** 彩色艺术玻璃;艺术玻璃花瓶[灯等]。~ **rock** (指在演奏风格上使用传统或古典音乐的)艺术摇滚乐。~ **store** 艺术用品商店。~ **ware** 工艺品。~ **work** 书刊、杂志上的图片。

art[2] [ɑːt; ɑrt] ***vi***. 〔古、诗〕〔主语为 thou 时〕be 的第二人称、单数、现在、陈述语气。

art. = **1.** article. **2.** artist. **3.** artillery. **4.** artificial.

-art *suf*. = -ard: bragg*art*.

ar·tal [ˈɑːtɑːl; ˋɑrtɑl] ***n***. 〔rotl 的复数形〕穆斯林地区的重量名〔相当于 1—5 磅不等〕。

ar·te·fact [ˈɑːtifækt; ˋɑrtɪˏfækt] ***n***. = artifact.

ar·tel [ɑːˈtel; ɑrˋtɛl] ***n***. (旧俄时代的)劳动组合,(生产)合作社。

Ar·te·mis [ˈɑːtimis; ˋɑrtəmɪs] ***n***. 【希神】阿特米丝〔月亮女神〕。

ar·te·mis·i·a [ˈɑːtiˈmiziə; ˏɑrtɪˋmɪzɪə] ***n***. 【植】艾;〔A-〕艾属。

ar·te·ri·al [ɑːˈtiəriəl; ɑrˋtɪrɪəl] ***a***. **1.** 动脉的,动脉状的。**2.** 干线的。*an* ~ *road* [*highway*] 公路干线。

ar·te·ri·al·ize [ɑːˈtiəriəlaiz; ɑrˋtɪrɪəlˏaɪz] ***vt***. 使(静脉血)转变为动脉血。

ar·te·ri·og·ra·phy [ɑːˌtiəriˈɔgrəfi; ɑrˏtɪrɪˋagrəfɪ] ***n***. **1.** 动脉搏描记法。**2.** 动脉照相术。

ar·te·ri·ole [ɑːˈtiəriəul; ɑrˋtɪrɪˏol] ***n***. 小动脉。**-ri·o·lar** [-ˈəulə; -ˋolɚ] ***a***.

ar·te·ri·ol·o·gy [ɑːtiːriˈɔlədʒi; ɑrˏtirɪˋalədʒɪ] ***n***. 【医】动脉学。

ar·te·ri·o·scle·ro·sis [ɑːˌtiəriəuskliəˈrəusis; ɑrˋtɪrɪˏosklɪˋrosɪs] ***n***. 【医】动脉硬化(症)。

ar·te·ri·ot·o·my [ɑːˌtiəriˈɔtəmi; ˋɑrtɪrɪˋatəmɪ] ***n***. 【医】动脉切开术。

ar·te·ri·o·ve·nous [ɑːˌtiəriəuˈviːnəs; ɑrˏtɪrɪoˋvinəs] ***a***. 动静脉的。

ar·te·ri·tis [ˌɑːtəˈraitis; ˏɑrtəˋraɪtɪs] ***n***. 【医】动脉炎。

ar·ter·y [ˈɑːtəri; ˋɑrtərɪ] ***n***. **1.** 【解】动脉。**2.** 干线,要道;中枢。*the brachial* [*carotid, pulmonary*] ~ 上膊[颈、肺]动脉。*the main* ~ 大动脉。*a traffic* ~ 交通干线。

ar·te·sian [ɑːˈtiːzjən; ɑrˋtiʒɪən] ***a***. 自流的。~ **well** 自流井,喷水井。

art·ful [ˈɑːtful; ˋɑrtfəl] ***a***. **1.** 狡猾的。**2.** 有手腕的;机灵的,巧妙的。**3.** 〔古〕不自然的,人为的。*an* ~ *swindle* 诈骗。*an* ~ *trick* 妙计。**-ly** ***ad***. **-ness** ***n***. 狡猾,巧妙。

ar·thral·gia [ɑːˈθrældʒiə; ɑrˋθrældʒə] ***n***. 关节痛。

ar·thrit·ic [ɑːˈθritik; ɑrˋθrɪtɪk] **I** ***a***. 关节炎的。**II** ***n***. 关节炎患者。

ar·thri·tis [ɑːˈθraitis; ɑrˋθraɪtɪs] ***n***. 【医】关节炎。

Ar·thro·gastra [ˌɑːθrəˈgæstrə; ˏɑrθrəˋgæstrə] ***n***. 〔*pl*.〕【动】腹节类〔如蝎子等〕。

ar·throp·a·thy [ɑːˈθrɔpəθi; ɑrˋθrapəθɪ] ***n***. 关节病。

ar·thro·pod [ˈɑːθrəpɔd; ˋɑrθrəpad] **I** ***a***. 节肢动物的。**II** ***n***. 节肢动物。

Ar·throp·o·da [ɑːˈθrɔpədə; ɑrˋθrapədə] ***n***. 〔*pl*.〕【动】节肢动物门。

ar·thro·sis [ɑːˈθrəusis; ɑrˋθrosɪs] ***n***. **1.** 关节。**2.** 关节病。

ar·thro·spore [ˈɑːθrəspɔː; ˋɑrθrəspɔr] ***n***. 【生】分节孢子。

Ar·thros·tra·ca [ɑːˈθrɔstrəkə; ɑrˋθrastrəkə] ***n***. 〔*pl*.〕【动】节甲类。

Ar·thur [ˈɑːθə; ˋɑrθɚ] ***n***. 亚瑟〔男子名〕。***King*** ~ 亚瑟王〔传说中的六世纪前后英国国王〕。

Ar·thuri·an [ɑːˈθjuəriən; ɑrˋθjərɪən] ***a***. 亚瑟王的,有关亚瑟王及其圆桌骑士的传奇的。

Ar·ti·choke [ˈɑːtitʃəuk; ˋɑrtɪˏtʃok] ***n***. 【植】**1.** 朝鲜蓟,洋蓟。**2.** 菊芋(= Jerusalem ~)。*Chinese* ~ 【植】甘露子,宝塔菜。

ar·ti·cle [ˈɑːtikl; ˋɑrtɪkl] **I** ***n***. **1.** 物品;制品,商品。**2.** 项目,条款。**3.** 【动】节。**4.** (报章杂志中的)文章,论文。**5.** 【语法】冠词。**6.** 〔古〕(之)际,刹那。**7.** 〔俚〕人,家伙。*an* ~ *of food* 一种食品。*a smooth* ~ 圆滑的人。~*s of trade* 商品。~*s of luxury* 奢侈品。*And the next* ~? 〔店员用语〕还要别的吗? ~*s and clauses* 条款。*an editorial* ~ 〔美〕= *a leading* ~ 〔英〕社论。~*s of apprenticeship* 学徒合同。*the definite* [*indefinite*] ~ 定[不定]冠词。~ ***by*** ~ 逐条。~***s of association*** 公司章程。***Articles of Confederation*** 美国建国初期十三州的第一部宪法。~***s of war*** 陆军法规。***in the*** ~ ***of death*** 临终,弥留之际。**II** ***vt***. **1.** 把…逐条登载,分条解释。**2.** 列举(罪状);控告。**3.** 用条款约束;定契约把…收为学徒。~ *an apprentice* 收学徒。*be* ~*d to a printer* 在印刷厂当学徒。*an* ~*d clerk* 〔美〕定有年限契约的店员。*an* ~*d apprentice* 定有年限契约的徒弟。—***vi***. **1.** 订契约。**2.** 约定 (*with*)。

ar·tic·u·lar [ɑːˈtikjulə; ɑrˋtɪkjəlɚ] ***a***. 关节的。*an* ~ *inflammation* 关节炎。

ar·tic·u·late [ɑːˈtikjulit; ɑrˋtɪkjəlɪt] **I** ***a***. **1.** 明了的,明白的;发音清晰的,音节分明的。**2.** 能说话的;口齿清晰[伶俐]的。**3.** 有关节的;有节的;接合起来的。*an* ~ *system of philosophy* 一套说得头头是道的哲学体系。*A baby can not use* ~ *speech*. 婴儿说话口齿不清。*The backbone is an* ~ *structure*. 脊椎骨是一种关节相连的结构。**II** ***n***. 节体动物。**III** [-leit; -let] ***vt***., ***vi***. **1.** 发音清晰地说,清晰认真地发音。**2.** 【语】形成(声音)。**3.** 表现(思想)。**4.** (用关节)接合。*A- your words carefully*. 请仔细咬清字眼说吧。*a full* ~*d system* 完整的体系。~ *distinctly* 发音清晰。*The injured bone didn't* ~ *well*. 受伤的骨头没有连接好。

ar·tic·u·la·tion [ɑːˌtikjuˈleiʃən; ɑrˏtɪkjəˋleʃən] ***n***. **1.** 发音;发音的方法。**2.** 发出的音,子音。**3.** 接合,连接。**4.** (骨头的)关节,(植物的)节。**5.** 【无】清晰度。**6.** (假牙的)咬合。

ar·tic·u·la·tor [ɑːˈtikjuleitə; ɑrˋtɪkjəˏletɚ] ***n***. **1.** 发音清楚的人。**2.** 发音器官。**3.** (假牙的)咬合器。**4.** 接骨的人。

ar·tic·u·la·to·ry [ɑːˈtikjuleitəri; ɑrˋtɪkjəleˏtɔrɪ] ***a***. 有音节的;关节的。

ar·ti·fact [ˈɑːtifækt; ˋɑrtɪˏfækt] ***n***. **1.** 人工制品〔尤指原始工具〕。**2.** 【生】(组织结构的)人为现象。**3.** 脑电波图中不是来源于人脑的电波。

ar·ti·fice [ˈɑːtifis; ˋɑrtəfɪs] ***n***. **1.** 技巧,技能。**2.** 诡计,巧计;策略,谋略,手段。*by* ~ 用手段,用计。

ar·tif·i·cer [ˈɑːtifisə; ɑrˋtɪfəsɚ] ***n***. **1.** 技工;工匠。**2.** 【军】技术兵。**3.** 设计者,发明家。*the A- of the Universe* = *the Great A-* 造物主。

ar·ti·fi·cial [ˌɑːtiˈfiʃəl; ˏɑrtəˋfɪʃəl] **I** ***a***. **1.** 人工的,人造的;人为的 (*opp*. natural)。**2.** 摹拟的 (*opp*. genuine, real);不自然的,矫揉造作的,虚假的。**3.** 武断的,随意决定的。~ *rules for dormitory residents* (不考虑居住者实际情况的)武断的宿舍管理规则。*an* ~ *system of classification* 人为的分类系统。~ *daylight* 太阳灯。*an* ~ *eye* 人造眼,假眼。*an* ~ *tooth* 假牙。~ *flowers* 假花。~ *ice* 人造冰。*an* ~ *smile* 假笑。**II**

n. 人造肥料;〔美〕假花。~ **aids** 骐。~ **blood** 人造血。~ **daylight** 太阳灯。~ **fertilizer** 化肥。~ **gene** 人工基因。~ **horizon** 飞行水平差。~ **inoculation** 人工接种。~ **intelligence** 人工智能。~ **person**【法】法人[团体、学校、公司等]。~ **reality**(由电子计算机三维图像显示的)虚拟现实。~ **respiration** 人工呼吸。~ **satellite** 人造卫星。~ **selection**【生】人为淘汰。~ **sight** 人工视力〔指盲人经视皮质电刺激而获得的感知物体的能力。~ **skin** 人造皮肤。**-i·ty** [-ˈæliti; -ˋælətɪ] *n*. 人工,人造,人为;人造物,人为之事;不自然。**-ly** *ad*. 人工地,人为地,不自然地,虚伪地。**-ness** *n*. 人工,人为,矫揉造作,不自然。

ar·til·ler·ist [ɑːˈtilərist; ɑrˋtɪlərɪst] *n*. **1**. 炮兵,炮手。**2**. 炮术家。

ar·til·ler·y [ɑːˈtiləri; ɑrˋtɪlərɪ] *n*. **1**. 大炮。**2**. 〔the ~〕炮兵,炮队。**3**. 炮术;炮学。**4**. 〔美俚〕防身武器。**5**. 〔美俚〕(注射麻醉剂的)皮下注射器。**6**. 〔喻〕口才,辩才。~ **duel** 炮战。~ **escort** 炮兵掩护。~ **fire** 炮火,炮击。~**man** 炮兵,炮手。~ **park** 放炮场地。~ **preparation** 准备炮击。~ **train** 炮兵纵列。

ar·ti·o·dac·tyl [ˌɑːtiəuˈdæktil; ˏɑrtɪəˋdæktɪl] *n*. 偶蹄动物〔如骆驼、鹿〕。

Ar·ti·o·dac·ty·la [ˌɑːtiəuˈdæktilə; ˏɑrtɪəˋdæktɪlə] *n*. 〔*pl*.〕【动】偶蹄目。

ar·ti·san [ˌɑːtiˈzæn; ˋɑrtəzn̩] *n*. 工匠,手工业工人。

art·ist [ˈɑːtist; ˋɑrtɪst] *n*. **1**. 美术家,艺术家。**2**. 能手。*a commercial* ~ 商业美术家。*He is an* ~ *with cards*. 他是打牌能手。

ar·tiste [ɑːˈtiːst; ɑrˋtist] *n*. 〔F.〕职业艺术家,艺人;〔谑〕大师。

ar·tis·tic, -ti·cal [ɑːˈtistik(əl); ɑrˋtɪstɪk(əl)] *a*. **1**. 美术(家)的,艺术(家)的。**2**. (爱好)艺术的,风雅的。**-ti·cal·ly** *ad*.

art·ist·ry [ˈɑːtistri; ˋɑrtɪstrɪ] *n*. **1**. 艺术的手腕[技巧,才干]。**2**. 艺术效果,艺术性。**3**. 艺术作品;艺术(工作)。

art·i·zan [ˌɑːtiˈzæn; ˋɑrtəzən] *n*. = artisan.

art·less [ˈɑːtlis; ˋɑrtlɪs] *a*. **1**. 无虚饰的,天真的,朴实的(*opp*. cunning)。**2**. 粗笨的,拙劣的。**-ly** *ad*. **-ness** *n*. 质朴,率直;拙劣。

art·mo·bile [ˈɑːtməbiːl; ˋɑrtməbil] *n*. 流动艺术展览;巡回画廊;流动艺术展览车。

ar·to·type [ˈɑːtəutaip; ˋɑrtəˏtaɪp] *n*. 【印】= collotype.

art·sy [ˈɑːtsi; ˋɑrtsɪ] *a*. **1**. 对艺术有一知半解的兴趣的。**2**. 过分装饰的,浮华的。

art·sy-craft·sy [ˌɑːtsiˈkrɑːftsi; ˏɑrtsɪˋkrɑftsɪ] *a*. 〔口〕**1**. (家具等)装饰浮华而不切实用的。**2**. 冒充懂艺术的,附庸风雅的。*an* ~ *chair* 华而不实的椅子。*an* ~ *person* 冒充懂艺术的人。

art·y [ˈɑːti; ˋɑrtɪ] *a*. 〔口〕冒充艺术品的;自命艺术家的。~***-and-crafty*** 〔口、谑〕华而不实的。

a·ru·gu·la [əˈruːgələ; əˋrugələ] *n*. 【植】芝麻菜。

Ar·um [ˈɛərəm; ˋɛrəm] *n*. 【植】白星海芋属。**arum lily** 【植】白星海芋。

a·run·di·na·ceous [əˌrʌndiˈneiʃəs; əˏrʌndɪˋneʃəs] *a*. 芦苇的,芦苇一样的。

a·rus·pex [əˈrʌspeks; əˋrʌspeks] *n*. (*pl*. ***-pi·ces*** [-pəsiːz; -pɪsiz]) 肠卜祭司〔古罗马从事以肠祭品卜吉凶的迷信活动的低级祭司〕。

Ar·vee [ɑːˈviː; ɑrˋvi] *n*. 游乐汽车。

Ar·vid [ˈɑːvid; ˋɑrvɪd] *n*. 阿维德〔男子名〕。

-ary *suf*. **1**. …的,有关…的: element*ary*, milit*ary*. **2**. …的人[物、场所]: advers*ary*, diction*ary*, gran*ary*.

Ar·y·an [ˈɛəriən; ˋɛrɪən] **I** *a*. **1**. 亚利安语系的〔或指印欧语系,或指印度波斯语系〕。**2**. 亚利安人种的。**II** *n*. **1**. 亚利安语。**3**. 亚利安人。

ar·yl [ˈæril; ˋærɪl] *n*. 【化】芳基。

ar·y·te·noid [ˌæriˈtiːnɔid, əˈritnɔid; ˏærɪˋtinɔɪd, əˋrɪtnɔɪd] **I** *a*. 【解】杓状的。**II** *n*. (咽喉的)杓状软骨或杓状肌。

as[1] [强 æz,弱 əz, z; æz, əz, z] **I** *ad*. (同…)一样…;同样〔在此是指 as... as... 结构中的第一个 as, 它在主句中为指示副词,第二个 as (在子句中)和第一个 as 相关联,故转为连接词(见 ***conj***. 各条)。第二个 as 引导的子句,可省略一部或全部,包括 as 本身〕。*It is* ~ *white* ~ *snow* (*is white*). 它白得像雪一样。*She is* ~ *wise* ~ (*she is*) *fair*. 她的聪明比得上她的美貌。*He is* ~ *clever* (~ *you*). 他(跟你)一样聪明。*I can do it* ~ *well* (~ *they*). (跟他们一样)这件事我也能做。*I have* ~ *many* [*much*]. 我也有这许多。*He did the work in two hours, but it took me* ~ *many days*. 他两小时做完这件工作,可是我要两天功夫才做完。**II** ***conj***. **1**. 〔此处指 as...as 结构中的第二个 as, 它与第一个 as 相关而表示比较〕同…(一样…)。*I am* ~ *tall* ~ *you*. 我和你一般高。*Mother loves her* ~ *dearly* ~ (*she loves*) *him*. 母亲对她和他都一样疼爱。*Mother loves her* ~ *dearly* ~ *he*. 母亲和他都同样疼爱她。**2**. 〔反面比较时现在常说作 not so... as 而少说 not as...as, 但在 n't 后仍常说 as... as〕不如…那样…。*Belgium is not so large* ~ *France*. 比利时没有法国那么大。*He doesn't work* ~ *hard* ~ *you*. 他工作没有你那样努力。**3**. 〔表示方式、程度、情况等〕如同;像;按照。*I work* ~ *others do*. 我跟别人一样工作。*Do* ~ (= *according* ~) *you are told*. 叫你怎样做就怎样做。*They will improve* ~ *they grow older*. 他们年纪大一些,进步也就快一些。*I remember it* ~ *it were but yesterday*. 我想起这件事就彷佛是昨天发生的事一样。*Two is to three* ~ (= *what*) *four is to six*. 二比三等于四比六。*Parks are to the city* ~ *lungs are to the body*. 公园对于都市正如肺脏对于身体一样。*China* ~ *she was fifty years ago*. 五十年前的中国。**4**. 〔as..., so ... 的结构,也表示同等程度的对比关系,但书面语色彩比较浓厚〕正如…一样。*As you like music, so I like poetry*. 正像你喜欢音乐一样,我喜欢诗歌。*As two is to three*, (*so*) *four is to six*. 四比六等于二比三。*As a man lives, so he dies*. 人有生也就有死。**5**. 〔时间〕当…时;一边…一边…。*He came up* ~ *I was speaking*. 我正在说话,他就来了。*I read the book* ~ *I went along*. 我边走边读。**6**. 〔原因〕因为〔语气比 because 或 for 轻〕;既然〔语气比 since 轻〕。*As I am ill, I won't go*. 我有病,不去了。**7**. 〔让步〕虽然,尽管〔词序倒装。语气比 though 强〕。*Successful* ~ *he is, he is not proud*. 他虽成功,却不骄傲。**8**. 〔结果、目的〕以致,以便。*He so arranged matters* ~ *to suit everyone*. 他把事情安排得人人满意。**III** ***prep***. **1**. 作为;以…身分。*language*, ~ *a means of intercourse* 作为交际工具的语言。*All hearts beat* ~ *one*. 大家一条心。*I have come here* ~ *a journalist*. 我是以记者身分到这里来的。**2**. 当作〔用在某些及物动词之后〕*I look upon him* ~ *a guest*. 我把他当作客人看待。*He treats me* ~ *a child*. 他把我当作小孩对待。**3**. 例如(= for instance)。*Some birds*, ~ *the parrot, can imitate human voice*. 有些鸟儿,如鹦鹉,能模仿人的声音。**IV** ***rel. pron***. **1**. 〔与 such, the same, as 连用〕。*such men* ~ *do you harm* 危害你的那些人们。*the same book* ~ *you have* 像你所有的同样书籍。~ *many children* ~ *came* 所有来的孩子们。**2**. 那是(由)…(知道)的。*He was a foreigner*, ~ *I knew from his accent*. 他是外国人,那是由他口音知道的。***and...*** ~ ***well*** 也。~ ***a general thing*** [***rule***] 通常,通例,概。~ ***above*** 如上。~ ***against*** 比[对]… (*The business done this year amounts to 50,000 dollars* ~ *against 30,000 dollars last year*. 今年交易总额为伍万元,而去年则为叁万元)。~ (*bright*) ~ ***any*** (*in the class*) (班级)中最(聪明)

的。~ **...** *as ever* 依旧。~ (*fast*) ~ ***possible*** [***one can***] 尽(快)。~ ***far*** ~ **1.** 〔限度〕尽…所…(*As far* ~ *I know* ... 尽我所知。*All right* ~ *far* ~ *it goes* 目前的状况还好)。**2.** 〔距离〕(一直)到。~ ***for*** 就…而论,至于,说到。~ ***from*** 由…日[契约生效日]起。~ ***good*** ~ 见 good 条。~ ***if*** 彷佛,恰像…一样(*As if you didn't know!* 别装蒜啦! *It isn't* ~ *if he were poor*. 他不见得穷)。~ ***is*** 〔美口〕原样,照原来样子。~ ***it is*** **1.** 〔在句尾时〕原样,照原来样子,照事实(*leave it* ~ *it is* 听其自然)。**2.** 原样的,现在的 (*the world* ~ *it is* 现在的世界)。**3.** 〔在句头时〕但事实上(*As it is, I cannot pay you*. (能付的话当然要付)但事实上我现在不能付给你)。~ ***it stands*** = as it is 1. 2. . ~ ***it was*** 其实是…。~ ***it were*** 可谓,好像。~ ***large*** ~ ***life*** 按实物大小。~ ***many*** (与…)同样多的,(与…)数量相同的。~ ***matters*** [***the case***] ***stand***(***s***) 在现状下。~ ***much*** 同量的;同样地(*I thought* ~ *much*. 我也同样想)。~ ***of*** (某月某日)的,当前的,现在的;到…时候为止的(*the U.S. Cabinet* ~ *of Sep. 1, 1964*. 一九六四年九月一日的美国内阁)。~ ***per*** 【商】照,按(~ *per advice* 照通知)。~ ***regards*** 至于,提到。~ ***soon*** ~ 见 soon 条。~ ***such*** 见 such 条。~ ***the world goes*** 照习惯说。~ ***things are*** 在现状下,照现况说。~ ***though*** = as if. ~ ***to*** = ~ for. ~ ***well*** (***as***) 见 well 条。~ ***who should say*** 〔古〕像要说…似的(*He smiled* ~ *who should say 'well done!'* 他像要说'做得好!'似的笑了)。~ ***yet*** 尚,还,至今还。***As you were!*** 〔口令〕复原! ***Be so kind*** [***good***] ~ ***to*** (*let me know*). 务必请(通知我)。***not so*** [~] (*white*) ~ (*snow*) 不及(雪白)。***so*** ~ ***to*** (*do*) (= *in order to*) 以便,为要…才…,为的是。**~-maintained** *a*. 〔美〕(按照国家标准局等所定度量衡制)规定的。**~-told-to** *a*. 〔美〕口述笔录式的。

as[2] [æs; æs] ***n***. (*pl*. ***as·ses*** [ˈæsiz; ˋæsɪz]) 阿斯〔**1.** 古罗马铜币。**2.** 古罗马重量单位,约 327.4 克〕。

as- *pref*. 〔用于 s 前〕 = ad-: *as*sert.

as·a·fet·i·da, as·a·foet·i·da [ˌæsəˈfetidə; ˏæsəˋfɛtɪdə] ***n***. 【植】阿魏〔伞形科植物〕;阿魏胶。

as·a·rum [ˈæsərəm; ˋæsərəm] ***n***. 【植】细辛。

as·bes·tic [æzˈbestik; æsˋbɛstɪk] ***a***. = asbestine (*a*.)

as·bes·tine [æzˈbestain; æsˋbɛstɪn] **I** ***a***. 石棉(状)的;不燃性的。**II** ***n***. 滑石棉。

as·bes·tos, as·bes·tus [æzˈbestɔs, -təs; æsˋbɛstəs, æz-] ***n***. 石棉。

as·bes·to·sis [ˌæzbesˈtəusis; ˏæzbɛsˋtosɪs] ***n***. 【医】石棉沉着病。

ASC = **1.** Air Service Command 〔美〕空军后勤司令部。**2.** Army Service Corps 〔英旧〕陆军后勤部队。**3.** altered state of consciousness 变态心理,变态意识。

ASCAP = American Society of Composers, Authors and Publishers 美国作曲家、作家与出版者协会。

as·ca·ri·a·sis [ˌæskəˈraiəsis; ˏæskəˋraɪəsɪs] ***n***. 【医】蛔虫病。

as·ca·rid [ˈæskərid; ˋæskərɪd] ***n***. 【动】蛔虫。

as·cend [əˈsend; əˋsɛnd] ***vi***. **1.** 上升,登高 (*opp*. descend)。**2.** 追溯。*The path* ~*s here*. 由此上坡。~ *to a height* 登高。~ *to a former century* 追溯到前一世纪。—***vt***. 攀登;登上。~ *the throne* 登上王位。

as·cend·ance, as·cend·ence [əˈsendəns; əˋsɛndəns] ***n***. = ascendancy.

as·cend·an·cy, as·cend·en·cy [əˈsendənsi; əˋsɛndənsɪ] ***n***. 优势;权势;主权。*have an* ~ *over* 优于,胜过。*get the* ~ 占上风,揽权。*attain the highest* ~ 鼎盛,全盛;登峰造极。

as·cend·ant, as·cend·ent [əˈsendənt; əˋsɛndənt] **I** ***a***. **1.** 向上的,上升的 (*opp*. descendant)。**2.** 占优势的;占支配地位的。**3.** 【天】向天顶上升的。**II** ***n***. **1.** 优势地位,支配地位。**2.** 祖先。**3.** 【卜】星位;(诞生时的)运星。*be in the* ~ 在优越地位上,有旭日初升之势,福星高照。*lineal* ~ 直系尊属。*the lord of* ~ 首座星。

as·cend·ing [əˈsendiŋ; əˋsɛndɪŋ] ***a***. **1.** 上升的;向上的。**2.** 【植】上向的;【解】上行的。*an* ~ *slope* 上坡。~ **inflorescence** 【植】上升花序。~ **powers** 【数】升幂。

As·cen·sion [əˈsenʃən; əˋsɛnʃən] ***n***. 阿森松〔南大西洋岛屿〕。

as·cen·sion [əˈsenʃən; əˋsɛnʃən] ***n***. **1.** 上升,升腾。**2.** 登位。**3.** 〔the A-〕(耶稣)升天。**A- Day** 耶稣升天节〔复活节后的第四十天〕。**~tide** ***n***. 从耶稣升天节至圣灵降临节间的十日。**-al** ***a***.

as·cen·sive [əˈsensiv; əˋsɛnsɪv] ***a***. **1.** 上升的。**2.** 【语法】强调的,加强语意的(= intensive)。

as·cent [əˈsent; əˋsɛnt] ***n***. **1.** (地位等的)上升,晋升。**2.** 登高,攀登。**3.** 追溯,上溯。**4.** 上坡;斜坡;坡度;阶梯。*the* ~ *of a mountain* 登山。*a rapid* [*gentle*] ~ 陡[缓]坡。***make an*** ~ ***of*** 登。

as·cer·tain [ˌæsəˈtein; ˏæsəˋten] ***vt***. **1.** 确定,查明,弄清。**2.** 〔罕〕确定,把…弄实在。~ *what really happened* 查明究竟发生了什么事。**-a·ble** ***a***. 可确定的;可查明的。**-ment** ***n***. 确定;查明;探知。

as·cet·ic [əˈsetik; əˋsɛtɪk] **I** ***n***. 禁欲主义者,苦行者。**II** ***a***. 苦行的,禁欲主义的。**-i·cal** ***a***. **-i·cal·ly** ***ad***.

as·cet·i·cism [əˈsetisizəm; əˋsɛtɪˏsɪzəm] ***n***. 苦行,禁欲主义。

as·cid·i·an [əˈsidiən; əˋsɪdɪən] ***n***. 【动】海鞘类动物。

as·cid·i·um [əˈsidiəm; əˋsɪdɪəm] ***n***. (*pl*. ***-cid·i·a*** [-ə; -ə]) 【植】瓶状体;瓶状叶。

as·ci·tes [əˈsaitiːz; əˋsaɪtiz] ***n***. 【医】腹水(肿)。

as·cle·pi·a·da·ceous [æsˌkliːpiəˈdeiʃəs; æsˏklipɪəˋdeʃəs] ***a***. 【植】(属于或类于)萝藦科的。

As·cle·pi·a·de·an [æsˌkliːpiəˈdiən; æsˏklipɪəˋdiən] **I** ***a***. 希腊诗人埃斯克里庇亚德斯 (Asclepiades) 散文诗格的。**II** ***n***. 上述诗格的诗。

As·cle·pi·us [æsˈkliːpiəs; æsˋklipɪəs] ***n***. 【希神】阿斯克勒庇俄斯〔医师的始祖〕。

as·co·carp [ˈæskəukɑːp; ˋæskokɑrp] ***n***. 【植】子囊果。**-ous** [-ˈkɑːpəs; -ˋkɑrpəs] ***a***.

as·co·go·ni·um [ˌæskəuˈgəuniəm; ˏæskoˋgonɪəm] ***n***. (*pl*. ***-ni·a*** [-ə; -ə]) 【植】产囊体。

as·co·my·ce·tes [ˌæskəumaiˈsiːtiːz; ˏæskomaɪˋsitiz] ***n***. *pl*. 【植】子囊菌。

a·scor·bate [əˈskɔːbeit; əˋskɔrbet] ***n***. 抗坏血酸盐。

as·cor·bic [əsˈkɔːbik; əsˋkɔrbɪk] ***a***. 治[防]坏血症的。~ **acid** 抗坏血酸[维生素 C]。

as·co·spore [ˈæskəuspɔː; ˋæskəˏspɔr] ***n***. 【植】子囊孢子。

As·cot [ˈæskət; ˋæskət] ***n***. **1.** 英国爱斯科赛马场;爱斯科赛马会。**2.** 〔a-〕爱斯科式领带。

as·crib·a·ble [əsˈkraibəbl; əsˋkraɪbəbl] ***a***. 可归于…的,起因于…的。*His failure is* ~ *to innocence*. 他的失败可归咎于无知。

as·cribe [əsˈkraib; əˋskraɪb] ***vt***. 把…归于,把…推诿到…上,…说是(某人)所… (*to*)。*He* ~*s his failure to fate*. 他把失败归咎于命运。*The alphabet is usually* ~*d to the Phoenicians*. 人们一般都说字母表是腓尼基人发明的。

as·crip·tion [əsˈkripʃən; əsˋkrɪpʃən] ***n***. **1.** 归与;归因;推诿。**2.** 【宗】(牧师在布道后所说"把荣耀归于上帝"等的)赞美词。

ASCU = Association of State Colleges and Universities (美国)州立学院及大学联合会。

as·cus [ˈæskəs; ˋæskəs] ***n***. (*pl*. ***as·ci*** [-sai; -saɪ]) 【植】子囊。

as·dic [ˈæzdik; ˋæzdɪk] ***n***. (英国早期的)潜艇探测器。

-ase *suf*. 【化】…酶: lact*ase*.

ASEAN = Association of Southeast Asian Nations 东南

亚国家联盟。

a·seis·mat·ic [ˌeisaiz'mætik; ˏesaɪsˋmætɪk] ***a***. 耐震的。

a·sep·sis [æ'sepsis; əˋsɛpsɪs] ***n***.【医】无菌(法);防腐(法)。

a·sep·tic [æ'septik; əˋsɛptɪk] **I** ***a***. **1.** 无菌的,防腐的。**2.** 无生气的,冷漠的;超然的,客观的。**3.** 使清洁的,起净化作用的。~ *surgery* 无菌手术。**II** ***n***. 防腐药。**-al·ly** ***ad***.

a·sex·u·al [æ'seksjuəl; eˋsɛkʃuəl] ***a***.【生】无性的;无性器官的。~ *reproduction* 无性生殖。**-ly** ***ad***.

a·sex·u·al·i·ty [æˌseksju'æliti; əˏsɛkʃuˋælətɪ] ***n***.【生】无性别,无性。

As·gard ['æsgɑːd; ˋæsgɑrd] ***n***. (北欧神话中的)天堂,仙境。

ash[1] [æʃ; æʃ] ***n***. **1.** 〔常 *pl*.〕灰。**2.** 〔*pl*.〕灰烬;废墟。**3.** 〔*pl*.〕骨灰,遗骨;〔诗〕遗骸。**4.** 灰色,苍白。**5.** 碳酸钠(= sodium carbonate)。*soda* ~ 纯咸。*the ~es of an ancient empire* 古帝国的废墟。***be reduced*** [***burnt***] ***to ~es*** 烧成灰烬,化为乌有。***bring back the ~es*** 〔英板球〕雪耻,转败为胜。***in dust and ~es***【宗】悲切忏悔。***lay... in ~es*** 使化为灰烬,烧光。***turn to dust and ~es***消失,(希望等)幻灭,化为尘埃。~**-bin** 垃圾桶,煤灰桶。~**cake** 焙制玉米饼。~ **can 1.** 〔美〕= ashbin (*into the* ~ *can* 丢脸)。**2.** 〔美口〕深水炸弹。~**-can** ***a***. (绘画等)如实地描写城市生活(阴暗面)的。~ **cart** 垃圾车。~ **fire** 灰火,余烬。~ **heap** 灰堆(*on the* ~ *heap* 被抛弃)。~ **man** 〔美〕除灰工人(= cinderman)。~**tray** 灰盘,烟灰缸。**A- Wednesday** 四旬节的第一天〔罗马天主教在这一天向忏悔者头上撒灰〕。

ash[2] [æʃ; æʃ] **I** ***n***. **1.**【植】梣,梣皮。**2.** 梣木。*a Chinese* ~ 梣,白蜡树。*a red* ~ 洋白蜡树。**II** ***a***. = ashen. ~ **key** 梣的翅果。

a·shamed [ə'ʃeimd; əˋʃemd] ***a***. 〔常用作表语〕羞耻,惭愧,害臊。***be*** ~ ***of*** 以为…是耻辱。***be*** ~ ***of oneself for*** 害羞,因…而害羞[惭愧]。***be*** ~ ***to*** (*tell*) 不好意思(说)。***feel*** ~ ***for sb***. 替某人感到羞愧。

A·shan·ti [ə'ʃænti; əˋʃæntɪ] ***n***. **1.** (*pl*. ~(***s***)) 非洲西部阿散蒂地区的人。**2.** 阿散蒂语。

ash·en[1] ['æʃn; ˋæʃən] ***a***. 灰的,灰色的。*turn* ~ 变苍白。

ash·en[2] ['æʃn; ˋæʃən] ***a***. 梣的,梣木的。

ash·er·y ['æʃəri; ˋæʃərɪ] ***n***. 钾咸厂;草咸制作场。

Ash·ke·naz·im [ˌæʃki'næzəm; ˏɑːʃkiˋnɑːzəm; ˏæʃkəˋnæzɪm, ˏɑrʃkɪˋnɑzɪm] ***n***. ***pl***. (*sing*. ***-naz***, ***-naz·i***) 北欧的犹太人〔区别于 sephardim (西班牙或葡萄牙的犹太人)〕。**-naz·ic** ***a***.

Ash·kha·bad [ˌɑːʃkɑ'bɑːd; ˋæʃkəbæd] ***n***. 阿什哈巴德〔土库曼城市〕。

ash·lar ['æʃlə; ˋæʃlɚ] ***n***. **1.**【建】方石,琢石。**2.**【建】墙面石板。

ash·lar·ing ['æʃləriŋ; ˋæʃlərɪŋ] ***n***. 砌[贴]方石墙面。

ash·ler ['æʃlə; ˋæʃlɚ] ***a***. = ashlar.

a·shore [ə'ʃɔː; əˋʃor] ***ad***. **1.** 上岸,上陆。**2.** 岸上,陆上。~ *and adrift* 陆上和海上。*be driven* ~ = *run* ~ 搁浅。*go* ~ 上岸,登陆。*life* ~ 陆上生活。

ash·ram ['æʃrəm; ˋæʃrəm] ***n***. **1.** 阿什拉姆〔印度教徒的一个团体隐居之地〕。**2.** 〔美〕嬉皮士群居村。

ash·y ['æʃi; ˋæʃɪ] ***a***. **1.** 灰的;覆盖着灰的。**2.** 灰色的,苍白的。*His face went* ~. 他脸色苍白。

A·sia ['eiʃə; ˋeʃə] ***n***. 亚洲。~ *Minor* 小亚细亚。

A·si·an ['eiʃən; ˋeʃən], **A·si·at·ic** [ˌeiʃi'ætik; ˏeʃɪˋætɪk] **I** ***a***. 亚洲的;亚洲人的。**II** ***n***. 亚洲人。★ 现多用 Asian, 如用 Asiatic 则带有贬意。

a·side [ə'said; əˋsaɪd] **I** ***ad***. **1.** 在旁边,在一边;到旁边,到一边。**2.**【剧】独(白),旁(白)。**3.** 撇开(…暂且不谈)。*draw the curtain* ~ 把幕布拉到一边。*It is* ~ *from the question*. 那是问题以外的事。*jesting* ~ 笑话不提(且说…)。~ ***from*** 〔美〕且别说,暂置不论;加之;除…外(*A- from a fright, he was uninjured*. 除了吓一跳以外,他没受伤)。***lay*** ~ 停止,抛弃,留着;打消;撇开(*lay the proposal* ~ *temporarily* 把建议暂时放在一边)。***put*** ~ 收拾起;暂搁;除外;停止,撇开(*Put your cares* ~. 请莫挂心。*put some money* ~ 储存一些钱)。***set*** ~ = put aside (*He set* ~ *that night to finish a paper*. 他留出一天晚上把论文写完)。***speak*** ~ 独语,暗暗说;【剧】(背朝着其他剧中人物而向观众)独白,旁白。***stand*** ~ 站开,让开路。***take*** [*draw*] (*a person*) ~ (*to speak to him*) 拉(某人)到一边(对他说)。***turn*** ~ 转向一边。**II** ***n***. **1.**【剧】旁白;独白。**2.** 离题的话。*a novelist's* ~ *to the reader* 作者致读者的话。

as·i·nine ['æsinain; ˋæsn̩ˏaɪn] ***a***. **1.** 驴的,驴子一样的。**2.** 愚蠢的,固执的。

as·i·nin·i·ty [ˌæsi'niniti; ˏæsəˋnɪnətɪ] ***n***. 愚蠢;蠢话,蠢事。

-asis *suf*. …病: elephantiasis 象皮病, psoriasis 牛皮癣。

ask [ɑːsk; æsk] ***vt***. **1.** 问,质问,询问。**2.** 求,请求,祈求。**3.** 需要。**4.** 讨(价)。**5.** 约,请,邀请。**6.** 〔古〕公布(结婚预告)。~ *the way* 问路。~ *the doctor to come* 请医生来。~ *sb. to a party* 邀人赴会。*He was ~ed out* (*to dinner*). 他被请去(吃饭)。*The matter ~s haste*. 事不宜迟。*The affair ~s secrecy*. 事要机密。"*This is the first time of ~ing*." "这是第一次宣读结婚预告"〔询问是否有人提出异议〕。—***vi***. 请求,问。~ (*sb*.) ***about*** 问某人…。~ ***after*** 问安,问候。~ ***again*** [***back***] 反问。~ ***for* 1.** 征求,请求,请(某人)给…,要(价) (~ *20 dollars for the book* 该书要价 20 元)。**2.** 来找 (*Did anybody* ~ *for me*? 有人来找没有?)。**3.** 要(~ *for money* 要钱)。~ ***for it*** 〔口〕= ~ ***for trouble*** 自找麻烦,自找苦吃。~ (*sb*.) ***in*** 叫(某人)进来。~ ***... of*** (*sb*.)向(某人)问[求] (*May I* ~ *a favour of you*? 我能不能请您行个方便?)。~ ***out*** 〔美〕辞职,引退。***be ~ed in church*** 请教堂预告结婚〔*cf*. banns〕。***if you*** ~ ***me*** 你若不见怪,不瞒你说,要说呢就是…。(*How do you like my hat*? 你喜欢我的帽子吗? *A little old-fashioned, if you* ~ *me*. 要说呢就是样子有点旧了)。

a·skance, a·skant [es'kæns, -t; əsˋkæns, -t] ***ad***. 横;斜;斜视。*The kids were eyeing him* ~. 孩子们斜眼看他。***look*** ~ ***at*** (因愤恨、嫉妒等而)斜楞着眼睛看,瞟。

as·kar·i ['ɑːskɑːri, ə'skɑːri; ˋæskərɪ, əˋskærɪ] ***n***. 非洲兵,非洲人警察〔尤指受雇用于殖民当局者〕。

ask·er ['ɑːskə; ˋæskɚ] ***n***. 请求者;发问者;乞丐。

a·skew [əs'kjuː; əˋskju] ***ad***. 斜,歪。*hang a picture* ~ 把图画挂歪。*look* ~ *at the dinner* 对饭菜不屑地一瞥。*wear one's hat* ~ 歪戴帽子。

ask·ing ['ɑːskiŋ; ˋæskɪŋ] ***n***. 问;请求。~ ***price*** (讨价还价的)要价。***for the*** ~ 只要索取,就免费供给 (*You may have it* [*It is yours*] *for the* ~. 承索即赠)。

ASL = American Sign Language 北美手势语。

a·slant [ə'slɑːnt; əˋslænt] ***ad***., ***prep***. **1.** 斜,倾。**2.** 斜跨。*walk with head* ~ 歪着头走路。***run*** ~ 和…抵触 (*run* ~ *laws and regulations* 与法令抵触)。

a·sleep [ə'sliːp; əˋslip] ***a***. 〔用作表语〕, ***ad***. **1.** 睡着,睡熟。**2.** 长眠,已死。**3.** 发呆,不活泼。**4.** (四肢)麻木,发麻。**5.** (陀螺)转得稳,(风帆鼓得)饱满不动。*The cat is* ~. 猫睡着了。*My arm is* ~. 我的胳膊发麻。~ ***at the switch*** 玩忽职守;坐失良机。

a·slope [ə'sləup; əˋslop] ***a***. 〔用作表语〕, ***ad***. 斜,倾斜。*lean* ~ *against the wall* 斜靠着墙。

ASM = air-to-surface missile 空对地导弹。

As·ma·ra [æz'mɑːrə; æzˋmɑrə] ***n***. 阿斯马拉〔埃塞俄比亚城市〕。

ASME = American Society of Mechanical Engineers 美国机械工程师学会。

As·mo·de·us [æs'məudjəs; æsˋmodjəs]【犹神】恶魔,魔王。★在密尔顿 (Milton) 的长诗《失乐园》(Paradise

A

Lost) iv. 168行中,须读作[æsməu'di:əs; æsmo`diəs]。
a·so·cial [ei'səuʃəl; e`soʃəl] *a*. 1. 不与人往来的,不合群的。2. (对别人利益)漠不关心的;自私的。
asp[1] [æsp; æsp] *n*. 小毒蛇,蝮蛇。
asp[2] [æsp; æsp] *n*., *a*. 〔诗〕= aspen.
ASP = American Selling Price 美国售价。
ASP [æsp; æsp] = Anglo-Saxon Protestant 英国新教徒。
ASPAC = Asian and Pacific Council 亚洲太平洋地区理事会;亚太理事会。
as·par·a·gine [ə'spærədʒi:n; ə`spærədʒin] *n*. 【生化】天冬酰胺。
as·par·a·gus [əs'pærəgəs; ə`spærəgəs] *n*. 【植】文竹,石刁柏,天门冬;龙须菜。
as·par·tame [əs'pɑ:teim; əs`pɑrtem] *n*. 阿斯巴特〔一种糖精〕。
as·par·tic [æs'pɑ:tik; æs`pɑrtɪk] *a*. ~ **acid** 【化】天冬氨酸。
ASPCA = American Society for the Prevention of Cruelty to Animals 美国防止虐待动物协会。
as·pect ['æspekt; `æspɛkt] *n*. 1. 样子,光景;容貌,神色。2. (房屋等的)方向,方位。3. 局势,形势,局面。4. (问题的)方面;见地。5. 【语法】体,态。*a beautiful* ~ 好景;美观。*a thing in its true* ~ 事物的真相。*The house has a southern* ~. 那间房子朝南。*the physical* ~ *of China* 中国的地势。*consider a question in all its* ~*s* 由各方面考虑问题。***assume* [*take on*] *a new* ~** 面目一新,呈新局面。~ **ratio** (电视影像的)纵横比;【空】展弦比。
asp·en ['æspən; `æspən] I *n*. 【植】白杨树;欧洲山杨。*the Chinese* ~ 响叶杨。*tremble like an* ~ *leaf* 飕飕飕地颤抖。II *a*. 1. 白杨的。2. (像白杨树叶)飕飕地颤抖的。
as·per ['æspə; `æspɚ] *n*. 阿斯皮尔〔土耳其和埃及从前的银币名,后来作为钱币的单位,等于1/120皮阿斯特〕。
as·per·ges [əs'pə:dʒi:z; ə`spɚdʒiz] *n*. 【天主】1. (作大弥撒前的)洒圣水仪式。2. 洒圣水仪式上唱的赞美诗。
As·per·gil·lin [ˌæspə'dʒilin; ˏæspə`dʒɪlɪn] *n*. 【药】曲霉素。
as·per·gil·lo·sis [ˌæspədʒi'ləusis; ˏæspədʒɪ`losɪs] *n*. 【医】曲霉病,曲菌病。
as·per·gil·lum [ˌæspə'dʒiləm; ˏæspɚ`dʒɪləm] *n*. (*pl*. *-gil·la* ['-dʒilə; -dʒɪlə]) (洒圣水仪式用的)洒水器〔如刷子、带孔容器〕。
as·per·gil·lus [ˌæspə'dʒiləs; ˏæspɚ`dʒɪləs] *n*. (*pl*. *-gilli* [-lai; -laɪ]) 【微】曲霉菌。
as·per·i·ty [æs'periti; æs`pɛrətɪ] *n*. 1. (表面)粗糙,(气候)严酷;(声音)刺耳。2. (性格)刻薄;(语言)粗暴。*speak with* ~ 粗暴地说。*the asperities of a winter campaign* 冬季作战的艰苦。
as·per·mous [æ'spə:məs; e`spɚməs] *a*. 【植】无种子的;【医】无精液的。*an* ~ *watermelon* 无子西瓜。
as·perse [əs'pə:s; əs`pɚs] *vt*. 1. 辱骂;诬蔑,中伤。2. 【天主】对…洒洗礼水;撒。~ *a fish with salt* 用盐撒在鱼上。~ *sb*.*'s character* [*honor*] 毁谤人格[名誉]。
as·per·sion [əs'pə:ʃən; əs`pɚʃən] *n*. 1. 诬蔑,中伤。2. 【天主】洒圣水。*cast* ~ *on* (*sb*.) 中伤(某人)。*baptize by* ~ 洒圣水洗礼。
as·per·so·ri·um [ˌæspə'sɔ:riəm; ˏæspə`sorɪəm] *n*. (*pl*. *-ri·a* [-ə; -ə], *-ri·ums* [-əmz; -əmz]) 1. 【宗】圣水盂。2. (洒圣水仪式用的)洒水器。
as·phalt ['æsfælt; `æsfælt] I *n*. 沥青,柏油。~ *concrete* 柏油混凝土。*an* ~ *pavement* 柏油路。II *vt*. 涂柏油,用柏油铺(路)。~ **cloud** 沥青云〔一种由反弹道导弹喷射出的沥青微粒,用以毁灭敌方导弹的隔热屏〕。~ **jungle** 沥青森林〔大城市或大城市中犯罪猖獗的某一区〕。
as·phal·tic [æs'fæltik; æs`fæltɪk] *a*. 柏油(质)的。
as·phal·tite ['æsfɔltait; æs`fɔltaɪt] *n*. 沥青岩。
as·phal·tum [æs'fæltəm; æs`fæltəm] *n*. = asphalt.
as·pho·del ['æsfədəl; `æsfəˏdɛl] *n*. 1. 【植】日光兰;水仙。2. 【希神】(乐园中的)常春花。
as·phyx·i·a [æs'fiksiə; æs`fɪksɪə] *n*. 【医】窒息。**as·phyx·i·al** *a*.
as·phyx·i·ant [æs'fiksiənt; æs`fɪksɪənt] I *a*. 窒息的;使气绝的;致假死的。II *n*. 窒息剂,绝气药;致窒息的环境或条件。
as·phyx·i·ate [æs'fiksieit; æs`fɪksɪˏet] *vt*. 使窒息。*an asphyxiating gas* 窒息性气体。
as·phyx·i·a·tion [æsˌfiksi'eiʃən; æsˏfɪksɪ`eʃən] *n*. 窒息。
as·phyx·i·a·tor [æs'fiksieitə; æs`fɪksɪˏetɚ] *n*. 1. 窒息剂。2. 动物窒息试验器。
as·phyx·y [æs'fiksi; æs`fɪksɪ] *n*. = asphyxia.
as·pic[1] ['æspik; `æspɪk] *n*. 〔诗〕= asp[1].
as·pic[2] ['æspik; `æspɪk] *n*. 肉冻。
as·pic[3] ['æspik; `æspɪk] *n*. 【植】熏衣草。
as·pi·dis·tra [ˌæspi'distrə; ˏæspɪ`dɪstrə] *n*. 【植】蜘蛛抱蛋。
as·pir·ant [əs'paiərənt; əs`paɪrənt] I *a*. 有志愿的,抱负不凡的,努力向上的。II *n*. 1. 有志者;(名誉、地位的)追求者。2. 候补者,考生。*an* ~ *after* [*for*, *to*] *honors* 追求名誉者。
as·pi·rate ['æspəreit; `æspəˏret] I *vt*. 1. 【语音】把…发成送气音。2. 【医】用吸管吸出。3. 吸入(空气等)。*aspirating dust into the lung* 把灰尘吸入肺里。II ['æspərit; `æspərɪt] *n*. 【语音】送气音,[h]音。III *a*. 【语音】送气音的,[h]音的(= aspirated)。
as·pi·rated ['æspəreitid; `æspəˏretɪd] *a*. 【语音】送气音的,[h]音的。
as·pi·ra·tion [ˌæspə'reiʃən; ˏæspə`reʃən] *n*. 1. 热望,切望,渴望;志愿,愿望,抱负 (*for*; *after*)。2. 【医】(从体腔中)吸出。3. 吸入。4. 【语音】发送气音,送气音。*She had* ~*s to be an actress*. 她想做女演员。
as·pi·ra·tor ['æspəreitə; `æspəˏretɚ] *n*. 1. 吸气器(= respirator)。2. 【医】吸引器。
as·pir·a·to·ry [ə'spairətəri; ə`spaɪrəˏtorɪ] *a*. 呼吸的,吸气的;适于呼吸或吸气的。
as·pire [əs'paiə; əs`paɪr] *vi*. 1. 热望,渴望;有志于,立志要。〔与介词 after, at, to, toward 连用或接不定式〕。2. 〔诗、古〕登,升;高耸。~ *after wealth* 追求金钱。~ *to be a hero* 渴望成为英雄。
as·pir·er [əs'paiərə; əs`paɪrɚ] *n*. 热望者,渴望者,追求者。
as·pi·rin ['æspərin; `æspərɪn] *n*. 阿司匹林〔退热药〕。
as·pir·ing [əs'paiəriŋ; əs`paɪrɪŋ] *a*. 1. 有大志的,抱负不凡的;热望的。2. 巍然高耸的。*an* ~ *writer* 胸怀大志的作家。*an* ~ *tower* 巍然屹立的塔。
a·squint [ə'skwint; ə`skwɪnt] *a*. 〔多作表语〕, *ad*. 横目,侧目,斜视〔一般指眼睛有生理缺陷所致〕。
ASROC = antisubmarine rocket 反潜(艇)火箭。
ass [æs; æs] *n*. 1. 驴子。2. 〔常 ɑ:s; ɑs〕傻子,笨蛋;老顽固。3. 〔美俚〕屁股;〔卑〕性交。*You silly* ~! 你这笨蛋! ***an* ~ *with two panniers*** 两臂各挽一女人招摇过市的男子。**~*es' bridge*** 笨人难过的桥〔命题"三角形两边相等,两底角亦相等"的别名〕,初学者难解的问题。***make an* ~ *of sb*.** 愚弄某人。***make an* ~ *of oneself*** 做傻事;出洋相。***not ... until the* ~ *ascends the ladder*** 万不能,决不能。***on one's* ~** 〔美俚〕处境恶劣;破产。***play the* ~** 作糊涂事,胡闹。~**-kisser** 〔美俚〕无耻已极的马屁精。
ass. = 1. assembly. 2. assistant. 3. association.
Assab ['æsəb; `æsəb] *n*. 阿萨布〔埃塞俄比亚港市〕。
as·sa·fet·i·da, as·sa·foet·ida [ˌæsə'fetidə; ˏæsə`fɛtɪdə] *n*. 阿魏;阿魏胶。

as·sa·gai, as·se·gai [ˈæsəgai; ˋæsə͵gaɪ] **I** ***n*****.** **1.** (南非人用的)标枪。**2.**【植】南非茱萸。**II** ***vt*****.** 用标枪刺。

as·sa·i [əˈsɑ:i; əˋsɑɪ] ***ad*****.**〔It.〕【乐】最,非常。*adagio* ~ 非常慢。*allegro* ~ 非常快。

as·sail [əˈseil; əˋsel] ***vt*****.** **1.** 攻击,袭击。**2.** (用言论)指责。**3.** 毅然应付(难局、工作等)。*Shouts ~ed our ears.* 呼叫声逼近了。~ *a task* 着手解决一项任务。***be ~ed by*** (*fears*) 被(恐怖)袭击。***be ~ed with*** (*questions*) 受到质问。**-able** ***a*****.** 可攻击的;有弱点的,有隙可乘的。

as·sail·ant [əˈseilənt; əˋselənt] **I** ***n*****.** 攻击者,加害者。**II** ***a*****.** 攻击的。

As·sam [ˈæsæm; æˋsæm] ***n*****.** 阿萨姆〔印度邦名〕。

As·sa·mese [ˌæsəˈmi:z, -ˈmi:s;͵æsəˋmiz, -ˋmis] **I** ***a*****.** (印度)阿萨姆邦的;阿萨姆人的;阿萨姆语的。**II** ***n*****.** **1.** (*pl*. ~) 阿萨姆人。**2.** 阿萨姆语。

as·sart [æˈsɑ:t; əˋsɑrt] **I** ***n*****.**【法】(灌丛地、林地的)开垦,开垦地。**II** ***vt*****.,** ***vi*****.**【法】开垦。

as·sas·sin [əˈsæsin; əˋsæsɪn] ***n*****.** 刺客,凶手。the Assassins【史】十字军东征时,暗杀基督教徒的穆斯林秘密团体成员。

as·sas·si·nate [əˈsæsineit; əˋsæsn̩͵et] ***vt*****.** **1.** 暗杀,行刺。**2.** 中伤,破坏(名誉等)。~ *sb.'s character* 进行人身攻击。

as·sas·si·na·tion [əˌsæsiˈneiʃən; ə͵sæsn̩ˋeʃən] ***n*****.** 暗杀。

as·sas·si·na·tor [əˈsæsineitə; əˋsæsn̩͵etɚ] ***n*****.** 凶手,刺客,暗杀犯。

as·sault [əˈsɔ:lt; əˋsɔlt] **I** ***n*****.** **1.** (动手或动口的)攻击。**2.**【军】猛袭,袭击,突击。**3.**【法】威胁;殴打。**4.**〔婉〕强奸。~ ***and battery***【法】口头威胁和动手殴打。~ ***at*** [***of***] ***arms*** **1.** 剑术比赛。**2.** 拼刺。***by*** ~ 用猛袭(攻克)。***make an*** ~ ***on*** 猛袭。**II** ***vt*****.** **1.** 攻击,袭击。**2.** 殴打;威胁。**3.**〔古〕非议。~ **boat** 登陆艇。~ **carrier** (可以发动空降突击或提供空中支援的)航空母舰。~ **troops** 突击队。**-a·ble** ***a*****.** 可攻击的,可袭击的。**-er** ***n*****.** 攻击者;殴打者。

as·say [əˈsei; əˋse] **I** ***n*****.** **1.** 化验;分析;鉴定,测定,验定。**2.** 被分析物,被化验物。**3.** 化验结果,化验报告。**4.**〔古〕企图,尝试。**5.**〔古〕(把食品给贵人以前预先)尝味。***do one's*** ~ 竭力,尽力。**II** ***vt*****.** **1.** 化验;试,试验。**2.** 企图。~ *one's strength* 检验自己的力量。~ *an alloy* 化验合金。—***vi*****.** 经验明含有。*The ore ~s high in silver.* 这种矿石验明含银量很高。~ **bar** (政府铸造来做为标准的)纯金[银]条。~ **master** 化验官。~ **ton** 化验吨〔29.166 克〕。

as·say·er [əˈseiə; əˋseɚ] ***n*****.** 试金者;化验者。

assd. = **1.** assessed. **2.** assigned. **3.** assured.

as·se·gai [ˈæsiˌgai; ˋæsə͵gaɪ] **I** ***n*****.** **1.** (南非部族人所用的)细木柄标枪。**2.**【植】南非茱萸。**II** ***vt*****.** 用标枪刺。

as·sem·blage [əˈsemblidʒ; əˋsɛmblɪdʒ] ***n*****.** **1.** 集合,会合,集会。**2.** 会众;集合物。**3.** (机器的)装配。**4.** 集合艺术,集合艺术品〔由布料、木料、金属、废品或其他东西的碎片组成〕。*an* ~ *of colours* 五彩缤纷。

as·sem·blag·ist [əˈsemblidʒist; əˋsɛmblɪdʒɪst] ***n*****.** 集合艺术家。

as·sem·ble [əˈsembl; əˋsɛmbl] ***vt*****.** **1.** 收集,集合 (*opp*. disperse)。**2.** 装配(机器等)。*an assembling plant* 装配厂。~ *information for a report* 为写报告收集资料。*The workers were ~d in the hall.* 工人们在会议厅集合开会。~ *a watch* 装配手表。—***vi*****.** 集合;聚集。**-r** ***n*****.** **1.** 装配工,做装配工作的人[机器]。**2.**【计】汇编程序。

as·sem·bly [əˈsembli; əˋsɛmblɪ] ***n*****.** **1.** 集合。**2.** 集会。**3.** 会众。**4.**〔A-〕立法会议,议院,(特指)下院〔美国州议会通常称作 General Assembly,有许多州将其下院称作 Assembly〕。**5.**【军】集合号,集合鼓;集合。**6.**【机】装配,装配车间;供装配的零件。**7.** (统计力学中的)系集。**General A-** **1.**〔美〕最高宗教裁判会议。**2.** 州议会。**3.** 联合国大会。***the National A-*** **1.**【法史】国民议会。**2.** 国民代表大会。~ **district**〔美〕可选一名州议会议员的选区。~ **hall** 会场;会馆。~ **line** 装配线,流水作业线。~ **plant** 装配厂。~ **program**【计】汇编程序,组合程序。~ **room** **1.** 会场;会议室;跳舞会场。**2.** (机械等的)装配室。

As·sem·bly·man [əˈsemblimən; əˋsɛmblɪmən] ***n*****.** **1.**〔美〕州议会议员。**2.** 装配工。

as·sent [əˈsent; əˋsɛnt] **I** ***n*****.** 同意,赞成 (*to*)。*the Imperial* [*Royal*] ~ (君主对议会议案的)批准。~ *and consent* (对预算案)赞成,通过。*by common* ~ 一致同意。*give one's* ~ *to* 同意,赞成。*with one* ~ 无异议,一致赞成。**II** ***vi*****.** 同意。~ *to* (*a proposal*) 赞同(提议)。

as·sen·ta·tion [ˌæsenˈteiʃən;͵æsɛnˋteʃən] ***n*****.** (特指盲从式的)同意,赞成;听从,附和。

as·sen·ti·ent [əˈsenʃiənt; əˋsɛnʃənt] **I** ***a*****.** 同意的,赞成的。**II** ***n*****.** 同意者,赞成者。

as·sen·tor [əˈsentə; əˋsɛntɚ] ***n*****.** 同意者;赞成者;附和者。

as·sert [əˈsə:t; əˋsɝt] ***vt*****.** **1.** 主张,硬说;断言,声明。**2.** 维护(权利),坚持。*They ~ed that the man was innocent.* 他们断言那人无罪。~ *one's rights* 维护自己权利。~ ***oneself*** 坚持自己的权利;表现自己 (*Justice will* ~ *itself.* 正义必将伸张;公道自在人心)。

as·ser·tion [əˈsə:ʃən; əˋsɝʃən] ***n*****.** **1.** 主张,断言,确言。**2.** 维护,坚持。***stand to one's*** ~ 坚持己见。

as·ser·tive [əˈsə:tiv; əˋsɝtɪv] ***a*****.** 断言的,肯定的;武断的。**-ly** ***ad*****.** **-ness** ***n*****.**

as·ser·tor [əˈsə:tə; əˋsɝtɚ] ***n*****.** 主张者;断言者;维护者。

as·sess [əˈses; əˋsɛs] ***vt*****.** **1.** 估定,评定(财产价值等)。**2.** 确定(税款、罚款、赔款的)数额。**3.** 征收,摊派(税款、会费等)。**4.** 评价(人物,工作等)。*His annual income was ~ed at ten thousand dollars.* 他的年收入估定为一万美元。~ *a tax on sb.'s property* 对某人的财产课税。~ *sb.'s efforts* 评价某人的工作。

as·sess·a·ble [əˈsesəbl; əˋsɛsəbl] ***a*****.** 可估定的,可估价的;可征税的,应抽税的。

as·sess·ment [əˈsesmənt; əˋsɛsmənt] ***n*****.** **1.** (价格的)评定,(税额的)估定,(损害额的)查定。**2.** 税额,摊派额。**3.**【商】应缴股款。**4.** (功过的)评价。*a standard of* ~ 课税标准。~ *of the work done* 计工。

as·ses·sor [əˈsesə; əˋsɛsɚ] ***n*****.** **1.** 财产估价人;估税员。**2.** 陪审法官;助理行政官。

ASSET = Association of Supervisory Staffs Executives and Technicians (英国)主管人员、行政官员及技术人员联合会。

as·set [ˈæset; ˋæset] ***n*****.** **1.** 资产;财产。**2.** 有用的资源,宝贵的人[物]。**3.**〔婉〕"星球大战"战备防御计划中全部武器的总称。*Good health is a great* ~. 健康就是财富。*He is a most valuable* ~ *to the firm.* 他是公司的宝贵人材。*~s and liabilities* 资产与负债。

as·sev·er·ate [əˈsevəreit; əˋsɛvə͵ret] ***vt*****.** 确言,断言,坚持说。*He ~d that he had seen a flying saucer.* 他坚持说,他看见了飞碟。

as·sev·er·a·tion [əˌsevəˈreiʃən; ə͵sɛvəˋreʃən] ***n*****.** 确言,断言。

as·sib·i·late [əˈsibileit; əˋsɪbl̩͵et] ***vt*****.**【语音】把…发成咝擦音,使齿音化。~ *the t of bastion* [ˈbæstʃən; ˋbæstʃən] 把 bastion 里的 t 发成咝擦音。

as·si·du·i·ty [ˌæsiˈdju(:)iti;͵æsəˋdjuətɪ] ***n*****.** **1.** 刻苦,勤勉。**2.**〔*pl*.〕(对人的)关心,照顾,殷勤。***with*** ~ 孜孜不倦,兢兢业业。

as·sid·u·ous [əˈsidjuəs; əˋsɪdʒuəs] ***a*****.** **1.** 刻苦的,勤勉的;百折不挠的。**2.** 殷勤的。*He is* ~ *in his studies.* 他学习勤奋。*He is* ~ *over his visitor.* 他对来访者很殷

勤。

ass·ify [ˈæsifai; ˋæsəˏfaɪ] ***vt*.** 愚弄。

as·sign [əˈsain; əˋsaɪn] **I *vt*. 1.** 分配,派给。**2.** 指定,选定,定。**3.** 把…归因于。**4.**【法】把(财产、权利等)转让,让与,过户给。*They* ~*ed me a small room*. 他们分给我一个小房间。*The rooms were* ~*ed to the workers*. 把房间分配给工人。*The teacher* ~*ed ten problems for today*. 老师今天指定十个问题。*The event is* ~*ed to various causes*. 这一事件被归因于各种原因。*detectives* ~*ed to the case* 负责侦破该案的刑警。~ *property to another* 把财产转让给别人。—***vi*.**【法】转让财产。**II *n*.**【法】受让人。*heirs and* ~*s* 继承人和受让人。**-a·ble *a*.**

as·sig·nat [ˌæsinˈjɑː; ˏæsɪnˋjɑ] ***n*.** 〔F.〕法国革命时发行的纸币。

as·sig·na·tion [ˌæsigˈneiʃən; ˏæsigˋneʃən] ***n*. 1.** 分配。**2.** (会场、时间的)指定,选定。**3.** 〔美〕约会,幽会,约定。**4.** 转让。**5.** 归因。

as·sign·ee [ˌæsiˈniː; ˏæsəˋni] ***n*.**【法】**1.** 受托者,代理人。**2.** 受让人 (*opp*. assignor)。

as·sign·ment [əˈsainmənt; əˋsaɪnmənt] ***n*. 1.** 分给,分配。**2.** 指定,委派。**3.** (理由等的)陈述;(错误等的)指出。**4.** (财产、权利的)转让,让与。**5.** 让与证书,委托证书。**6.** 〔美〕任命;任务,工作;(课外)作业。*give students* ~*s* 给学生留作业。*He left for his* ~ *in the Middle East*. 他去中东赴任。

as·sign·or [əsaiˈnɔː; əsaɪˋnɔr] ***n*. 1.** 分配者;委派者。**2.** (权利的)转让人,让与人 (*opp*. assignee)。

as·sim·i·late [əˈsimileit; əˋsɪmḷˏet] ***vt*. 1.** 同化。**2.** 使相似,使相同,使成一样。**3.** 将(甲)比作(乙) (*to*, *with*)。**4.** 消化,吸收。**5.** 使(语言等)融合。*The community* ~*d persons of many nationalities*. 这个社会同化了许多不同国籍的人。~ *life to a dream* 把人生比作梦。— ***vi*. 1.** 变得相似,变得相同。**2.** 被吸收,被同化。*Some foods* ~ *more readily than others* 有些食物比别的食物容易吸收。**3.**【语音】因同化而改变。**-able *a*.** 可同化的;可吸收的。

as·sim·i·la·tion [əˌsimiˈleʃən; əˏsɪmḷˋeʃən] ***n*. 1.** 吸收(作用)。**2.** 同化(作用)。*The p in cupboard has been lost by* ~ *to b*. cupboard 里的 p 由于和 b 同化而失去读音。

as·sim·i·la·tive, as·sim·i·la·to·ry [əˈsimilətiv, -təri; əˋsɪmḷˏetɪv, -torɪ] ***a*. 1.** 吸收的。**2.** 同化的。

as·sim·i·la·tor [əˈsimileitə; əˋsɪmḷˏetɚ] ***n*.** 吸收者;同化者。

as·sist [əˈsist; əˋsɪst] **I *vt*. 1.** (在某方面)帮助,援助,协助 (*in*, *with*)。**2.** 帮助某人做某事 (*in doing sth*; *to do sth*)。**3.** 搀扶(某人)上[下]车 (*in*) [*out of*]; 扶(某人)站起 (*to his foot*); 给(小孩)喂食 (*to*)。~ *an architect in project* 帮助设计师搞设计。*She* ~*ed him in correcting* [*to correct*] *the proof*. 她帮助他做改校样的工作。*I* ~*ed my son with homework*. 我帮助儿子做作业。~ *a child to food* 给小孩喂食。—***vi*. 1.** 援助,帮助 (*in*)。**2.** 出席,参加 (*in*, *at*)。~ *in a store* 在店里帮忙。~ *at a ceremony* 参加仪式。**II *n*. 1.** 援助,帮助;协助。**2.** 机器助手,辅助装置。*a financial* ~ 财政援助。**~ed memory** 辅助记忆。**~ed suicide** 辅助性自杀〔指借助他人而完成的自杀〕。

as·sis·tance [əˈsistəns; əˋsɪstəns] ***n*. 1.** 援助,帮助。**2.** 〔古〕出席;出席者。***come to sb.'s*** ~ 援助某人。***give*** [***render***] ~ (***to***) 给以援助。

as·sis·tant [əˈsistənt; əˋsɪstənt] **I *a*.** 帮助的,副的。*an* ~ *engineer* 副工程师。*an* ~ *manager* 协理,副理。*an* ~ *professor* 助理教授〔高于讲师,低于副教授 (associate professor)〕。**II *n*. 1.** 助手;帮手,助理。**2.** 助教。**3.** 店员,伙计。**4.** 辅助物;(染色的)辅助剂;起辅助作用的东西。*a shop* ~ 店员。*an* ~ *to memory* 帮助记忆的辅助物。**~ship** (大学)研究生奖学金〔该研究生同时任助教〕。

as·size [əˈsaiz; əˋsaɪz] ***n*. 1.** 〔常 *pl*.〕〔英〕巡回裁判(开庭期,开庭地)。**2.** 〔古〕(度量衡的)法定标准;(面包、啤酒的)法定价格。**3.** 条例,条令。***the Great A-***【神】最后审判(日)。

as·so·ci·a·bil·i·ty [əˌsəuʃjəˈbiliti; əˏsoʃɪəˋbɪlətɪ] ***n*. 1.** 可联合性。**2.** 可联想性。**3.**【医】交感性。**4.** 社交性。

as·so·ci·a·ble [əˈsəuʃjəbl; əˋsoʃɪəbḷ] ***a*. 1.** 可以联想的,联想得到的。**2.** 可联合的。**3.** 社交性的。**4.**【医】交感性的。

as·so·ci·ate [əˈsəuʃieit; əˋsoʃɪˏet] **I *vt*. 1.** 使联合 (*opp*. dissociate); 使加入[参加]。**2.** 由…联想到…,把…同…联系起来 (*with*)。*be* ~*d with sb. in an enterprise* 与某人联合从事一项企业。*It was impossible to* ~ *failure with him*. 想不到他会失败。— ***vi*.** 交往,结交。*Never* ~ *with bad companions*. 勿与恶友交往。~ ***oneself in*** 参加,加入。~ ***oneself with*** 赞同,支持;与…交往。**II** [-ʃiit; -ʃɪɪt] ***a*. 1.** 同伙的,同伴的。**2.** 准…,副的。**3.** 伴随的;有关的。— ***n*. 1.** 伙伴,朋友;同事,同人。**2.** 准会员,准社员,准校友。**3.** 联想观念,联想物。**4.** 相伴物。~ **degree** 〔美〕(大学上完两年的)肆业证书。~ **editor** 〔美〕副主笔。~ **judge** 陪审法官。~ **member** 准会员。~ **number**【数】联带数,相伴数。~ **professor** 〔美〕副教授〔低于正教授 (full professor),而高于助理教授 (assistant professor)〕。

as·so·ci·at·ed [əˈsəuʃieitid; əˋsoʃɪˏetɪd] ***a*. 1.** 联合的。**2.** 联想的。*an* ~ *university* 联合大学。***the A- Press*** (略作 A.P.)美国联合通讯社〔简称美联社〕。~ **mineral** 伴生矿物。

as·so·ci·a·tion [əˌsəusiˈeiʃən; əˏsosɪˋeʃən] ***n*. 1.** 联合;联系;联盟;合伙;交际,交往。**2.** 社团,协会;学会。**3.**【生】群落,社会。**4.** 联想。**5.**【化】缔合。**6.** 英式足球。*an* ~ *of banks and bankers* 银行公会。~ *of ideas* 联想。***in*** ~ ***with*** 与…联合。~ **book** [**copy**] 因与名人有关而受珍视的书〔如有作者本人签字、加注,或曾为名人所有等〕。~ **football** 英式足球(= soccer)。**-ism *n*.** 联想论;联想心理学。**-ist *n*. 1.** 联想论者。**2.** 协会会员。

as·so·ci·a·tive [əˈsəuʃjətiv; əˋsoʃɪˏetɪv] ***a*. 1.** 联合的,连带的。**2.** 联想的。**3.**【数】结合的。*an* ~ *responsibility* 连带的责任。

as·soil [əˈsɔil; əˋsɔɪl] ***vt*.** 〔古〕**1.** 赦免,释放。**2.** 补偿,赎。~ *sb. of* [*from*] *sin* 赦免某人的罪过。~ *one's fault* 赎罪。

as·so·nance [ˈæsənəns; ˋæsənəns] ***n*. 1.** 声音的相似,协音〔如: penitent, reticence〕。**2.** 只押母音的韵,半谐音〔如: late, make〕。

as·so·nant [ˈæsənənt; ˋæsənənt] **I *a*.** 协音的,半韵的。**II *n*.** 与另一个字合成半韵的字。

as·sort [əˈsɔːt; əˋsɔrt] ***vt*. 1.** 把…分级,把…分类。**2.** 配备;配齐(花色)。~ *apples for market* 把苹果分类出售。—***vi*. 1.** 相配,相称,调和。**2.** 相交,交际 (*with*)。*It ill* [*well*] ~*s with his character*. 这和他的性格不协调[很调和]。

as·sort·ed [əˈsɔːtid; əˋsɔrtɪd] ***a*. 1.** 配合的,相称的。**2.** 各色具备的,什锦的。~ *biscuits* 什锦饼干。*an ill-* ~ *pair* 不相称的配偶。*well-* ~ *goods* 各色俱全的货物。

as·sort·ment [əˈsɔːtmənt; əˋsɔrtmənt] ***n*. 1.** 分类,搭配。**2.** 种类,花色品种;一套[全套]物品。*an* ~ *of tools* 一套工具。

ASSR, A.S.S.R. = Autonomous Soviet Socialist Republic (前苏联的)苏维埃社会主义自治共和国。

asst. = assistant.

as·suage [əˈsweidʒ; əˋswedʒ] ***vt*. 1.** 缓和,减轻(痛苦)。**2.** 宽慰(人心);平息(怒气)。**3.** 满足(食欲),充(饥),解(渴)。~ *sorrow* 解忧。~ *thirst* 止渴。**-ment *n*.**

as·sua·sive [əˈsweisiv; əˋswesɪv] **I *a*.** 缓和的,使镇静

的,安慰的。**II** ***n*.** 缓和剂。

as·sum·a·ble [əˈsjuːməbl; əˋsjuməbl] ***a*.** **1.** 可假定的。**2.** 可采取的;可承担的。**3.** 可假装的。

as·sum·a·bly [əˈsjuːməbli; əˋsjuməblɪ] ***ad*.** 假想地,多半,大概;恐。

as·sume [əˈsjuːm; əˋsjum] ***vt*.** **1.** 执掌;接受;承担,担任。**2.** 假装,装作…的样子,采取(…态度)。**3.** 僭取,擅取,冒称。**4.** 假定,想像,设想;以…为先决条件。**5.** 表现为,呈。**6.** 穿…在身上。**7.** 承担(别人的)债务。**8.** 采用。~ *office* 就职,上任。~ *responsibility* 负责。~ *the reins of government* 执政,掌握政权。~ *the air of cheerfulness* 假装高兴。~ *a haughty mien* 采取傲然态度。~ *the offensive* 采取攻势。*The problem has ~d a new form*. 问题已经以一种新的方式出现。~ *the chair* 就议长席。*I ~ that you know*. 我以为你是知道的。~ *a new name* 用一个新名字。~ ***airs of*** 摆…的架子。***assuming that ...*** 假定…,若。

as·sumed [əˈsjuːmd; əˋsjumd] ***a*.** **1.** 假装的,装做…的,假的。**2.** 假定的;想像的。**3.** (债务)保付的,承付的。**4.** 僭越的。~ *ignorance* 假装不知道(的样子)。*an ~ name* 假名。*an ~ voice* 假装的声调,摹拟的声音。*hearing evidence in an ~ capacity* 以僭越的身份听取证词。~ **bonds**【商】保付证券〔由一公司发行、由另一公司保付的证券〕。

as·sum·ed·ly [əˈsjuːmidli; əˋsjumɪdlɪ] ***ad*.** 大概,也许。

as·sum·ing [əˈsjuːmiŋ; əˋsjumɪŋ] ***a*.** 僭越的,傲慢的。

as·sump·tion [əˈsʌmpʃən; əˋsʌmpʃən] ***n*.** **1.** 采取,承担。**2.** 假设,假定;臆说;想当然。**3.** 傲慢,僭越。**4.** 假装。**5.** 〔A-〕圣母升天(节)〔8月15日〕。**6.**【逻】小前提。*the ~ of an office* 就任。*the ~ of power* 掌权。*an air of ~* 傲慢的态度。***on the ~ that*** 假定。

as·sump·tive [əˈsʌmptiv; əˋsʌmptɪv] ***a*.** **1.** 假定的,假设的。**2.** 傲慢的,僭越的。**3.** 假装的。

as·sur·a·ble [əˈʃuərəbl; əˋʃurəbl] ***a*.** 可保证的。

as·sur·ance [əˈʃuərəns; əˋʃurəns] ***n*.** **1.** 保证,担保。**2.** 确信,自信;断言。**3.** 狂妄;厚脸皮,无耻。**4.** 〔英〕(人寿)保险。**5.**【法】财产转让(书)。*an easy ~ of manner* 悠然自信的态度。*an A- Co*. 保险公司。*give an ~ that ...* 保证…。*have* (*every*) *~ of* 有(一切)把握取得。*have the ~ to* (*do*) 厚着脸皮(做)…。*make ~ doubly* [*double*] *sure* 加倍小心。*with ~* 凭自信。

as·sure [əˈʃuə; əˋʃur] ***vt*.** **1.** 保证,担保,确告,郑重宣告。**2.** 使安心,让…放心,包。**3.** 使确信。**4.** 给…保险。*I ~ you of his honesty*. (那人)包你老实可靠。~ *one's life* 保人寿险。~ ***oneself of*** 弄清楚,查明(*I must ~ myself of the real situation*. 我必须查明真实情况)。***I ~ you that ...*** 包你…。

as·sured [əˈʃuəd; əˋʃurd] ***a*.** **1.** 有保证的,确实的。**2.** 自信的;狂妄的,胆大妄为的。**3.** 保着险的。*an ~ position* 有保证的职务。*His success is ~*. 他取得成功是无疑的。*You may rest ~ that ....* 对…你尽可放心。***be ~ of*** 确信,坚信。**the ~** 被保险人。**-ly** ***ad*.** **1.** 的确,无疑地。**2.** 自信;大胆。**-ness** ***n*.** **1.** 确实,确信。**2.** 狂妄。

as·sur·er, -or [əˈʃuərə; əˋʃurɚ] ***n*.** 保证者;〔英〕保险商。

as·sur·gent [əˈsəːdʒənt; əˋsɚdʒənt] ***a*.** **1.** 上升的。**2.**【植】倾斜向上的。**3.**【徽】由海中出来的。*a sea horse ~* 从海中出来的海马。

as·sur·ing [əˈʃuəriŋ; əˋʃurɪŋ] ***a*.** 确实的;使人放心的,使人有信心的。**-ly** ***ad*.** 一定,无疑地。

As·syr·i·a [əˈsiriə; əˋsɪrɪə] ***n*.** 亚西利亚〔亚洲西部古国,即亚述〕。

As·syr·i·an [əˈsiriən; əˋsɪrɪən] **I** ***a*.** 亚述的;亚述人[语]的。**II** ***n*.** 亚述人[语]。

As·syr·i·ol·o·gy [æˌsiriˈɔlədʒi; æˏsɪrɪˋɑlədʒɪ] ***n*.** 亚述研究。

A.S.T. = Atlantic Standard Time. 大西洋标准时间。

as·ta·cene, as·ta·cin [ˈæstəsiːn, -sin; ˋæstəsin, -sɪn] ***n*.**【生化】虾红素。

a·stat·ic [æˈstætik; æˋstætɪk] ***a*.** **1.**【物】无定向的。**2.** 不安定的。~ **galvanometer** 无定向电流计。~ **needle** 无定向(磁)针。

as·ta·tine [ˈæstətiːn; ˋæstəˏtin] ***n*.**【化】砹〔元素名,符号为 At〕。

as·ter [ˈæstə; ˋæstɚ] ***n*.** **1.**【植】紫苑;〔A-〕紫苑属。**2.**【动】星(状)体。*the China ~* 翠菊。

-aster *suf*. 〔蔑〕小,臭,丑等: poet*aster* 烂诗人。

aster- *comb. f*. 表示"星": *aster*oid.

as·ter·isk [ˈæstərisk; ˋæstəˏrɪsk] **I** ***n*.** **1.** 星号〔即 * 〕。**2.** 星状物。**II** ***vt*.** 给…注上星号。~ *a word that requires a footnote* 给一个需加注释的词打上星号。

as·ter·ism [ˈæstərizəm; ˋæstəˏrɪzəm] ***n*.** **1.**【印】三星标记〔即⁂〕。**2.**【天】星群。**3.**【矿】星状光彩,星芒。

a·stern [əsˈtəːn; əˋstɚn] ***ad*.** **1.**【海】在船[机]尾,向船[机]尾。**2.** 在后,向后。*ship next ~* 后续舰。~ ***of*** 在…的后面。***back ~*** 倒驶。***drop*** [***fall***] ***~*** 落在别船后头,被赶过。***Go ~!*** 后退! 〔口令〕。

a·ster·nal [əˈstəːnl; eˋstɚnl] ***a*.**【解,动】**1.** 不连胸骨的。**2.** 无胸骨的。

as·ter·oid [ˈæstərɔid; ˋæstəˏrɔɪd] **I** ***a*.** 星状的。**II** ***n*.** **1.**【天】(火星及木星轨道间的)小行星。**2.**【动】海星(= starfish)。**3.**【物】星状曲线。**-al** ***a*.**

as·the·ni·a [æsˈθiːnjə; æsˋθinɪə] ***n*.**【医】虚弱。

as·then·ic [æsˈθenik; æsˋθɛnɪk] ***a*.**【医】虚弱的。

as·the·no·pi·a [ˌæsθiˈnəupiə; ˏæsθɪˋnopɪə] ***n*.** 眼疲劳,视力衰弱。**-nop·ic** [-ˈnɔpik; -ˋnɔpɪk] ***a*.**

asth·ma [ˈæsmə; ˋæsmə] ***n*.**【医】气喘(病)。

asth·mat·ic [æsˈmætik; æsˋmætɪk] **I** ***a*.** 气喘的;患气喘病的。**II** ***n*.** 气喘患者。

as·thore [əsˈθɔː; əsˋθɔr] ***n*.** 〔Ir.〕〔呼唤用语〕= darling.

as·tig·mat·ic [ˌæstigˈmætik; ˏæstɪgˋmætɪk] **I** ***a*.** **1.** 散光的;【物】像散的。**2.** 矫正散光的。**3.** 不正视事实的。~ *eyes* 散光眼。~ *lenses* 散光眼镜。**II** ***n*.** 眼睛散光的人。~ **pencil**【物】散像光束。**-i·cal·ly** ***ad*.**

a·stig·ma·tism [æsˈtigmətizəm; əˋstɪgməˏtɪzəm] ***n*.** **1.** 散光,乱视。**2.**【物】散像性,散像现象。

a·stir [əsˈtəː; əˋstɚ] ***a*.** 〔多作表语〕, ***ad*.** **1.** 活动;哄动。**2.** 起床,行动。***be ~ with*** 因…而哄动(*The whole town was ~ with the news*. 因某消息而全城哄动)。***be early ~*** 早起。

ASTM, A. S. T. M. = American Society for Testing Materials 美国材料试验学会。

a·stom·a·tous [əˈstɔmətəs, -ˈstəumə-; əˋstɑmətəs, -ˋstomə-] ***a*.**【生】无口的,无呼吸孔的。

As·ton [ˈæstən; ˋæstən] ***n*.** 阿斯顿〔姓氏〕。

as·ton·ied [əsˈtɔnid; əˋstɑnɪd] ***a*.** 〔古〕大吃一惊的,惊奇的;困惑的。

as·ton·ish [əsˈtɔniʃ; əˋstɑnɪʃ] ***vt*.** 使吃惊,使惊讶。*be ~ed at* 对…感到惊讶。*be ~ed to see* 见到…感觉惊讶。

as·ton·ish·ing [əsˈtɔniʃiŋ; əˋstɑnɪʃɪŋ] ***a*.** 令人惊讶的。**-ly** ***ad*.**

as·ton·ish·ment [əsˈtɔniʃmənt; əˋstɑnɪʃmənt] ***n*.** **1.** 惊奇,惊讶。**2.** 令人惊讶的事物。***in*** [***with***] ***~*** 愕然,吃惊地(*stare in ~* 惊得目瞪口呆)。***to one's ~*** 令…惊讶的是(*To my ~, she were so politeless*. 使我惊讶的是,她竟这样没有礼貌)。

As·tor [ˈæstə, ˈæstɔː; ˋæstɚ, ˋæstɔr] ***n*.** 阿斯特〔姓氏〕。

as·tound [əsˈtaund; əsˋtaund] ***vt*.** 使…大吃一惊,使惊奇。

as·tound·ing [əsˈtaundiŋ; əˋstaundɪŋ] ***a*.** 可惊的;使人震惊的。**-ly** ***ad*.**

as·tra·chan [ˌæstrəˈkən; ˋæstrəkən] ***n*.** 俄国羔皮(= astrakhan)。

A

as·trad·dle [əsˈtrædl; əˋstrædl] **I** ***a.*** 〔多作表语〕, ***ad.*** 跨。*stand* ~ 两脚分开站着。**II** ***prep.*** 跨着。*sit* ~ *a horse* 跨在马上。

as·tra·gal [ˈæstrəgəl; ˋæstrəgḷ] ***n.*** **1.**【建】半圆饰。**2.**【解】距骨。

as·trag·a·lus [æsˈtrægələs; æsˋtrægələs] ***n.*** (*pl.* **-li** [-lai; -laɪ]) **1.**【解】距骨。**2.** 〔A-〕【植】黄芪属,黄蓍属。

As·tra·khan [ˌæstrəˈkæn; ˏæstrəˋkən] ***n.*** **1.** 阿斯特拉罕〔俄罗斯城市〕。**2.** 〔a-〕俄国羔皮;充羔皮;充羔皮织物。

as·tral [ˈæstrəl; ˋæstrəl] ***a.*** **1.** 星的;星状的;【生】星状体的。**2.** 星界的,星际的。~ **body** (迷信传说的)魂灵,魂魄。~ **hatch** (飞机上的)圆形天窗。~ **lamp** 无影灯〔一种没有投影的油灯〕。~ **spirits** (迷信传说的)星星上的鬼魂。

a·stray [əˈstrei; əˋstre] **I** ***ad.*** 迷路;堕落。*go* ~ 走错路;堕落,误入歧途。*lead* (*sb.*) ~ 误人;带坏,使人堕落,把人引入歧途。**II** ***a.*** 〔多作表语〕出正轨的,迷途的。*We are all* ~. 我们都迷路了。

as·trict [əsˈtrikt; əsˋtrɪkt] ***vt.*** **1.** 束缚,限制。**2.** (在道德和法律上)约束。**3.** 使收缩,使便秘。

as·tric·tion [əsˈtrikʃən; əsˋtrɪkʃən] ***n.*** **1.** 限制;收缩;束缚。**2.**【医】收敛(作用);便秘。

as·tric·tive [əˈstriktiv; əˋstrɪktɪv] **I** ***a.*** 收敛的。**II** ***n.***【药】收敛剂。

A·strid [ˈæstrid; ˋæstrɪd] ***n.*** 阿斯特丽德〔女子名〕。

a·stride [əsˈtraid; əˋstraɪd] **I** ***a.*** 〔多作表语〕, ***ad.*** 两脚分开,跨。***be*** ~ ***of a river*** (军队)跨河布阵。***sit*** ~ ***of a horse*** 骑(马)。**II** ***prep.*** **1.** 跨骑。**2.** 在两边。**3.** 占压倒性地位。*ride* ~ *a horse* 骑着马。*The city lay* ~ *the river.* 城市横跨河的两岸。*stand* ~ *the whole country* 统治全国。

as·tringe [əsˈtrindʒ; əˋstrɪndʒ] ***vt.*** **1.** 束缚,使收敛。**2.** 收缩,压缩。

as·trin·gen·cy [əsˈtrindʒənsi; əˋstrɪndʒənsɪ] ***n.*** **1.** 收敛性。**2.** 严肃性,严峻,严格。

as·trin·gent [əsˈtrindʒənt; əˋstrɪndʒənt] **I** ***a.*** **1.**【医】收敛的,止血的。**2.** 严厉的,严格的。~ *taste* 涩味。*an* ~ *style of writing* 犀利的文风。*Green persimmons are strongly* ~. 绿柿子非常涩。**II** ***n.***【药】收敛剂,止血药。**-ly** ***ad.***

as·tri·on·ics [ˌæstriˈɔniks; ˏæstrɪˋɑnɪks] ***n.*** 天文电子学。

astro- *comb. f.* 表示"外太空,宇宙,天体,天文,星": *astro*logy, *astro*metry.

as·tro·bi·ol·o·gy [ˌæstrəubaiˈɔlədʒi; ˏæstrobaɪˋɑlədʒɪ] ***n.*** 宇宙生物学。

as·tro·bleme [ˌæstrəuˈbliːm; ˏæstroˋblim] ***n.*** 陨石坑,太空疤痕。

as·tro·com·pass [ˈæstrəuˌkʌmpəs; ˋæstroˏkʌmpəs] ***n.*** 星象罗盘。

as·tro·cyte [ˈæstrəuˌsait; ˋæstroˏsaɪt] ***n.*** 星形(胶质)细胞。**-cyt·ic** [-ˈsitik; -ˋsɪtɪk] ***a.***

as·tro·dome [ˈæstrəudəum; ˋæstrəˏdom] ***n.***【空】(飞机机身顶部透明的半圆形)天文观测窗[室]。

as·tro·dy·nam·ics [ˌæstəudaiˈnæmiks; ˏæstrodaɪˋnæmɪks] ***n.*** 天文动力学,星际[宇宙]飞行力学。

as·tro·gate [ˈæstrəugeit; ˋæstrəˏget] ***vt.*** 驾驶(宇宙飞船);导引(火箭)在宇宙空间飞行。— ***vi.*** 作宇宙航行。**as·tro·gation** [ˌæstrəuˈgeiʃən; ˏæstrəˋgeʃən] ***n.*** 宇宙航行学,航天学。**as·tro·ga·tor** ***n.*** 宇宙航行者,宇航员。

as·tro·graph [ˈæstrəugrɑːf; ˋæstrəˏgræf] ***n.*** 天体照相仪,天文定位器。

as·troid [ˈæstrɔid; ˋæstrɔɪd] **I** ***a.*** 星状的,星形的。**II** ***n.***【数】星形线。

astrol. = **1.** astrologer. **2.** astrological. **3.** astrology.

as·tro·labe [ˈæstrəuleib; ˋæstroˏleb] ***n.***【天】(旧时天文学者用以测定天体位置的)星盘。

as·trol·o·ger [əsˈtrɔlədʒə; əˋstrɑlədʒə-] ***n.*** **1.** 星体研究者。**2.** 占星学家。

as·tro·log·ic, as·tro·log·i·cal [ˌæstrəuˈlɔdʒik(əl); ˏæstroˋlɑdʒɪk(əl)] ***a.*** 占星术的,占星学的。**-cal·ly** ***ad.***

as·trol·o·gy [əsˈtrɔlədʒi; əˋstrɑlədʒɪ] ***n.*** **1.** 占星术。**2.** 原始天文学。

as·tro·me·te·or·ol·o·gy [ˈæstrəuˌmiːtjəˈrɔlədʒi; ˏæstroˏmitɪəˋrɑlədʒɪ] ***n.*** 天体气象学。

as·trom·e·try [æsˈtrɔmitri; æsˋtrɑmɪtrɪ] ***n.*** 天体测量(学)。

astron. = **1.** astronomer. **2.** astronomical. **3.** astronomy.

as·tro·naut [ˈæstrəunɔːt; ˋæstrəˏnɔt] ***n.*** 宇(宙)航(行)员。**-ess** 女宇航员。

as·tro·nau·tic, -ti·cal [ˌæstrəuˈnɔːtik(əl); ˏæstrəˋnɔtɪk(əl)] ***a.*** 宇宙航行(员)的。**-tically** ***ad.***

as·tro·nau·tics [ˌæstrəuˈnɔːtiks; ˏæstrəˋnɔtɪks] ***n.*** 宇宙航行学。

as·tro·nav·i·ga·tion [ˌæstrəuˌnæviˈgeiʃən; ˏæstroˏnævɪˋgeʃən] ***n.*** 宇宙航行,天文导航。

as·tron·o·mer [əsˈtrɔnəmə; əˋstrɑnəmə-] ***n.*** 天文学家。**A- Royal** 格林尼治[爱丁堡]天文台台长。

as·tro·nom·ic [ˌæstrəuˈnɔmik; ˏæstrəˋnɑmɪk] ***a.*** = astronomical.

as·tro·nom·i·cal [ˌæstrəuˈnɔmikəl; ˏæstrəˋnɑmɪkḷ] ***a.*** **1.** 天文学(上)的。**2.** 〔口〕(数字等)庞大的。~ *figures* 〔美口〕庞大的数字,天文数字。~ **day** 天文日,平均太阳日。~ **observatory** 天文台。~ **time** 天文时。~ **unit** 天文单位〔地球至太阳间的平均距离〕。~ **year** 回归年。**-ly** ***ad.***

as·tron·o·my [əˈstrɔnəmi; əˋstrɑnəmɪ] ***n.*** 天文学。*gravitational* ~天体力学。*radio* ~射电天文学。

as·tro·pho·tog·ra·phy [ˌæstrəufəˈtɔgrəfi; ˏæstrəfoˋtɑgrəfɪ] ***n.*** 天体照相(术)。

as·tro·phys·ics [ˈæstrəuˈfiziks; ˋæstroˋfɪzɪks] ***n.*** ***pl.*** 〔用作单或复〕天体物理学。

as·tro·space [ˈæstrəuspeis; ˋæstrospes] ***n.*** 外太空,宇宙空间。

as·tro·sphere [ˈæstrəsfiə; ˋæstrəˏsfɪr] ***n.*** **1.**【生】中心球,细胞的摄引球。**2.**【地】地心圈,地核。

a·strut [əˈstrʌt; əˋstrʌt] ***a.*** 〔用作表语〕, ***ad.*** 大摇大摆,趾高气扬。

as·tu·cious [æsˈtuːʃəs, -ˈtjuː-; əˋstuʃəs, -ˋstju-] ***a.*** = astute.

as·tute [əsˈtjuːt; Am. əsˋtjuːt; əˋstjut, əsˋtut] ***a.*** 机敏的,伶俐的,狡猾的。**-ly** ***ad.*** **-ness** ***n.***

a·sty·lar [eiˈstailə; eˋstaɪlə-] ***a.***【建】无柱式的。

A·sun·ción [əˌsunsiˈəun; ˏɑsunˋsɪon] ***n.*** 亚松森〔巴拉圭首都〕。

a·sun·der [əˈsʌndə; əˋsʌndə-] ***a.*** 〔多作表语〕, ***ad.*** **1.** (分)开,(折)断,(扯)碎。**2.** 散,分离,隔离。*We are as wide* ~ *as the poles.* = We are whole worlds ~. 我们天南地北相隔极远。*break* ~折断。*come* ~ 离开,散开。*fall* ~崩散。*fly* ~逃散。*pull* ~拉开。*take* ~ 拆开,隔开。*tear* ~扯碎。

ASV = aircraft (或 air) to surface vessel (radar) 机载水面舰艇探知雷达,空对海搜索雷达。

ASW = **1.** antisatellite weapon 反卫星武器。**2.** antisubmarine warfare 反潜(艇)战。**3.** Association of scientific workers 科学工作协会。

As·wan [æˈswɑːn; ˋæswɑn] ***n.*** 阿斯旺〔埃及城市〕。**the** ~ **Dam** 阿斯旺大水坝。

a·swarm [əˈswɔːm; əˋswɔrm] ***a.*** 〔多作表语〕充满的,拥挤的,麇集的。*The square was* ~ *with people.* 广场上人山人海的。

a·sy·lee [əˋsaili:; əˋsaɪli] *n*. 政治流亡者〔尤指在美国政治避难者〕。

a·syl·lab·ic [ˌeisiˈlæbik; ˏæsəˋlæbɪk] *a*.【语音】非音节的,不成音节的。

a·sy·lum [əˈsailəm; əˋsaɪləm] *n*. **1.** (孤儿等的)收容所,养育院。**2.** 避难所。**3.**【国际法】庇护(权)。*a lunatic* ～精神病院。*a blind and dumb* ～ 盲哑院。*a foundling* [*an orphan*] ～ 孤儿院,育婴堂。*on* ～ *for lepers* 麻疯院。～ *for the aged* 养老院。*He sought* ～ *in the church*. 他到教堂去避难。*grant* ～ *to* 给予庇护。

a·sym·met·ric, a·sym·met·ri·cal [ˌæsiˈmetrik(əl); ˏæsɪˋmɛtrɪk(əl)] *a*. 不对称的。

a·sym·me·try [æˈsimitri; əˋsɪmɪtrɪ] *n*. 不对称(现象)。

a·symp·to·mat·ic [eiˌsimptəˈmætik; eˏsɪmptəˋmætɪk] *a*.【医】无症状的。

as·ymp·tote [ˈæsimptəut; ˋæsɪmˏtot] *n*.【数】渐近线。

a·syn·chro·nism [eiˈsiŋkrənizəm; əˋsɪŋkrənɪzəm] *n*. **1.** 时间不一致,非同时性。**2.**【电】异步。

a·syn·chro·nous [eiˈsiŋkrənəs; eˋsɪŋkrənəs] *a*. **1.** 时间不一致的,不同时的。**2.**【电】异步的。

a·syn·de·ton [æˈsinditən; əˋsɪndətən] *n*. **1.**【修】(并列复合句中)连接词的省略〔如: smile, shake hands, part〕。**2.**【图书馆学】目录中对照参考资料的省略。

a·syn·tac·tic [ˌæsinˈtæktik; ˏæsɪnˋtæktɪk] *a*.【语法】结构松散的,不合语法的。

AT, A.T. = **1.** Air Transport(ation). **2.**【电】ampere turn. **3.** antitank. **4.** Atlantic Time. **5.** alternative technology 替代技术。**6.** appropriate technology 适用技术。

at [强 æt, 弱 ət; 强 æt, 弱 ət] *prep*. **1.** 〔位置,地点、场合〕在,于,到;经由。～ *the foot* [*top*] *of the hill* 在山脚[顶]。*stand* ～ *the door* 站在门口。*live* ～ *Oxford* 住在牛津。*be* (*present*) ～ *the meeting* 出席会议。*be present* ～ *the funeral* [*wedding*] 参加葬仪[婚礼]。*arrive* ～ *one's destination* 到达目的地。*Smoke came out at the chimney*. 烟经过烟囱逸出。**2.** 〔时刻,年节、年龄〕在…。～ *five o'clock* 在 5 点。～ *noon* 在中午。～ *Christmas* 在圣诞节。～ (*the age of*) *forty* 年四十。**3.** 〔动作的一次〕～ *a bound* 一跳就。～ *a gallop* 飞奔;(骑马)奔驰。～ *a* [*one*] *sitting* 一口气。～ *a mouthful* 一口。**4.** 从事。～ *work* 做着,正在工作。～ *dinner* 正在吃饭。**5.** 〔表示性能〕在…方面。*be quick* [*slow*] ～ *learning* 记性好[坏]。**6.** 〔状态〕处于…中。～ *war* 在战争中。～ *will* 随意,任意。**7.** 〔动作的目标、方向〕向,对。*Up and* ～ *them, boys!* 弟兄们,向他们进攻吧! *aim* ～ *the target* 对准目标。*laugh* ～ *sb*. 嘲笑某人。**8.** 〔动作,感情的原因〕应,照,见…而,闻…而;一…(就)。*I did it* ～ *your request*. 照你请求的办了。*be surprised* ～ *the sight* 看见那光景就吓了一跳。**9.** 〔程度、比例、价格高低、距离等〕以、用、有。*sell* ～ *six dollars* 以六美元(价格)出售。*estimate a crowd* ～ *ten thousand* 估计群众有一万人。**10.** 从…。*The prisoners got good treatment* ～ *the hands of his captors*. 这些俘虏从捕获者那里受到良好的待遇。★(1) *at auction, at retail, at whole sale* 等的 *at* 系美式用法,英国则用 by. (2)美国俚语中常喜应用本可不用的 at. 例。*I want to know where it is* ～. ***and* ... ～ *that*** 而且;此外还,又 (*He lost an arm, and the right arm* ～ *that*. 他失去了一只手臂,而且又是一只右臂)。～ ***that*** 就照那样 (*I will take it* ～ *that*. 就照(你说)那样好了)。***be*** ～ 从事,做 (*What are you* ～ *now?* 你现在是做什么? *Be up and* ～ *it before sunrise*. 日出前起来做吧)。***where*** ... ～〔美俚〕身居何处 (*He doesn't know where he is* ～. 他不知道他自己的立场)〔英国英语不用 *at* 〕。

At =【化】astatine.

at- *pref*. 为词首 *ad-* 的同化形式,用在 t 字母前。

at. = **1.** airtight. **2.** atmosphere(s). **3.** atomic.

ATA = **1.** Air Transport Auxiliary 辅助空运。**2.** Air Transport Association (of America) (美国)空运协会。

at·a·bal [ˈætəbæl; ˋætəˏbæl] *n*. (摩尔人的)铜鼓,手鼓。

At·a·brine [ˈætəbrin; ˋætəbrɪn] *n*.【药】阿的平〔治疟药〕。

at·a·ghan [ˈætəgæn; ˋætəˏgæn] *n*. 土耳其剑〔穆斯林战士所用的一种长剑或弯刀〕。

at·a·man [ˈætəmən; ˋætəmən] *n*. (*pl*. ～*s*) (帝俄哥萨克军的)首领,长官。

at·a·mas·co lily [ˌætəˈmæskəuˈlili; ˏætəˋmæskoˋlɪlɪ] 孤挺花科葱莲属植物。

a·tap [ˈætæp; ˋætæp] *n*. **1.** (马来亚茅屋的)聂帕榈屋顶。**2.** 聂帕榈;聂帕果;聂帕果汁。

at·a·rac·tic, ata·ra·xic [ˌætəˈræktik, -ˈræksik; ˏætəˋræktɪk, -ˋræksɪk] **I** *n*. 镇静剂,安定药。**II** *a*. 镇静剂的,镇静作用的。

at·a·rax·i·a, at·a·rax·y [ˌætəˈræksiə, -si; ˏætəˋræksɪə, -sɪ] *n*. 不激动,不动心;心平气和。

a·taunt, a·taun·to [əˈtɔːnt, -əu; əˋtɔnt, -o] *ad*.【海】扯着所有风帆。***all*** ～万事齐备。

at·a·vism [ˈætəvizəm; ˋætəˏvɪzəm] *n*. **1.**【医】隔代遗传,返祖(现象),返祖性。**2.** 呈现返祖现象的人。**-vis·tic** [-ˈvistik; -ˋvɪstɪk] *a*.

a·tax·i·a [əˈtæksiə; əˋtæksɪə] *n*. **1.** 混乱,无秩序。**2.**【医】(肌肉的)运动失调,动作机能不协调。

a·tax·ic [əˈtæksik; əˋtæksɪk] **I** *a*. **1.** 混乱的,无秩序的。**2.** 运动失调的。**II.** *n*.【医】运动机能失调者。～ **deposit** 不成层矿床。

a·tax·y [əˈtæksi; əˋtæksɪ] *n*. = ataxia.

ATC = **1.** Air Training Corps〔英〕航空训练团。**2.** Air Training Command〔美〕空军训练部。**3.** Air Transport Command 空运勤务部。**4.** Air Traffic Control 空中交通管制。

ate [et, Am. eit; et, ɛt] eat 的过去式。

-ate[1] *suf*. 〔构成名词〕**1.** 官位,职位。consul*ate*. **2.**【化】…酸盐: sulf*ate*. **3.** 动作涉及的对象。leg*ate*, mand*ate*. **4.** 产品: condens*ate*. **5.** 团体: elector*ate*.

-ate[2] *suf*. 〔构成形容词〕**1.** 充满…的: foli*ate*. **2.** 有…特征的: collegi*ate*. **3.** 相当于以 -ed 结尾的过去分词。anim*ate* (= *animated*)。

-ate[3] *suf*. 〔构成动词〕**1.** 成为…: evapor*ate*. **2.** 使化合;处理: oxygen*ate*, vaccin*ate*. **3.** 原取自拉丁语的过去分词与其他词干的结合: actu*ate*, agit*ate*.

at·e·brin [ˈætəbrin; ˋætəbrɪn] *n*. = atabrine.

at·e·lec·ta·sis [ˌætiˈlektəsis; ˏætəˋlɛktəsɪs] *n*.【医】肺膨胀不全。

at·el·ier [ˈætəliei; ˋætlˏje] *n*. 〔F.〕 **1.** 工作室;画室。**2.** 制作室[车间]。

a tem·po [ɑːˈtempəu; ɑˋtɛmpo] 〔It.〕【乐】照原速。

ath·a·na·si·a [ˌæθəˈneizə; ˏæθəˋneʒɪə] *n*. 不死,不灭。

Ath·a·na·sian [ˌæθəˈneiʃən; ˏæθəˋneʒən] *a*. 阿他那修斯的〔Saint Athanasius 为希腊亚历山大城主教, 296? —373〕。～ **Creed** 阿他那修斯信条〔主张三位一体〕。

ath·an·a·sy [əˈθænəsi; əˋθænəsɪ] *n*. = athanasia.

Ath·a·pas·can, Ath·a·pas·kan [ˌæθəˈpæskən, -kæn; ˌæθəˈpæskən, -kæn] **I** *a*. 阿萨巴斯加人的〔包括纳瓦霍,阿帕斯部落在内的北美印第安人〕,阿萨巴斯加语族的。**II.** *n*. 阿萨巴斯加人[语]。

a·the·ism [ˈeiθiizəm; ˋeθɪˏɪzəm] *n*. 无神论 (*opp*. theism); 不信神。

a·the·ist [ˈeiθiist; ˋeθɪɪst] *n*. 无神论者;不信神的人。**a·the·is·tic, -ti·cal** [ˌeiθiˈistik, -tikəl; ˏeθɪˋɪstɪk, -tɪkəl] *a*.

A

ath·el·ing [ˈæθəliŋ; ˋæθəlɪŋ] *n*.（盎格鲁撒克逊的）太子，皇子，贵族，公子。

A·the·na, A·the·ne [əˈθiːnə, əˈθiːni(ː); əˋθinə, əˋθinɪ-(i)] *n*.【希神】雅典娜〔智慧、技术、学问、战争的女神〕。

Ath·e·nae·um, Ath·e·ne·um [ˌæθiˈniːəm; ˏæθəˋniəm] *n*. **1.** 雅典娜神殿〔古希腊文人学者集会处〕。**2.**〔a-〕古罗马法律[文艺]学校。**3.**〔a-〕文艺[科学]协会。**4.**〔a-〕图书馆，阅览室。

A·the·nai [ɑːˈθiːne; ɑˋθinɛ] *n*. Athens 的希腊名。

A·the·ni·an [əˈθiːnjən; əˋθinɪən] *a*.，*n*. 雅典的(人)。

Ath·ens [ˈæθinz; ˋæθənz] *n*. **1.** 雅典〔希腊首都〕。**2.**【史】雅典〔古希腊雅典城邦的首府〕。**3.**〔喻〕作为文学艺术中心的城市。

a·ther·man·cy [əˈθəːmənsi; əˋθɝmənsɪ] *n*.【物】不透辐射热(性)，不透红外线性质。**a·ther·mic** [-mik; -mɪk] *a*.

ath·er·o·ma [ˌæθiəˈrəumə; ˏæθəˋromə] *n*. (*pl*. ~*s*, *-ma·ta* [-mətə; -mətə])【医】**1.** 动脉粥样化。**2.** 粉瘤。**-tous** [-təs; -təs] *a*.

ath·er·o·scle·ro·sis [ˌæθərausklіəˈrəusis; ˏæθərosklə-ˋrosɪs] *n*.【医】动脉粥样硬化。**-scle·rot·ic** [-ˈrɔtik; -ˋrɑtɪk] *a*.

Ath·er·ton [ˈæθətən; ˋæθətən] *n*. 阿瑟顿〔姓氏〕。

a·thirst [əˈθəːst; əˋθɝst] *a*.〔仅作表语〕**1.**〔诗〕渴。**2.** 渴望。*be* ~ *for fame* 追求名誉。

ath·lete [ˈæθliːt; ˋæθlit] *n*. 运动员，体育家，强壮的人。~**'s foot**【医】脚气，脚癣。~**'s heart**【医】心脏肥大。

ath·let·ic [æθˈletik; æθˋlɛtɪk] *a*. **1.** 运动的，体育的。**2.** 有膂力的，强壮的，活跃的。*an* ~ *meet(ing)* 运动会。~ *sports* 体育运动。*the* ~ *type* 运动员体型。**-i·cal·ly** *ad*.

ath·let·i·cism [æθˈletisizəm; æθˋlɛtəsɪzəm] *n*. **1.** 运动练习；运动比赛迷。**2.** 运动员气质。

ath·let·ics [æθˈletiks; æθˋlɛtɪks] *n*. **1.**〔用作 *sing*. 或 *pl*.〕体育(运动)，竞技；〔英〕田径运动。**2.**〔用作 *sing*.〕体育(课)，运动法；健身术。

ath·o·dyd [ˈæθədid; ˋæθədɪd] *n*. 冲压式喷气发动机 (= aero-thermo-dynamic-duct)。

at-home [ətˈhəum; ətˋhom] *n*.（家庭）招待会。

a·thwart [əˈθwɔːt; əˋθwɔrt] **I** *ad*. **1.** 横穿过，横过，斜。**2.**【海】船侧朝风。**3.**〔罕〕逆，不顺，不便。*Everything goes* ~ (*with me*). 事事违愿。**II** *prep*. **1.** 横过。**2.** 逆，相反。**3.**【海】横越(航向)。***go*** ~ ***one's purpose*** 不如意，事与愿违。

-atic *suf*. …的：Asi*atic*, dram*atic*.

a·tilt [əˈtilt; əˋtɪlt] *ad*. **1.** 挺着枪，摆着冲刺姿势。**2.** 倾斜着。*run* [*ride*] ~ *at* [*against*] 向…挺枪冲过去。*Hold the bottle slightly* ~. 使瓶子微微倾斜。

-ation *suf*. **1.** 表示动作：alter*ation*. **2.** 表示状态：gratific*ation*. **3.** 表示结果：compil*ation*.

-ative *suf*. 表示关系、倾向、性质等：demonstr*ative*, inform*ative*, talk*ative*.

At·kins [ˈætkinz; ˋætkɪnz] *n*. 阿特金斯〔姓氏〕。

A.T.L. = Atlantic Transport Line 大西洋轮船运输公司。

Atl. = Atlantic.

At·lan·ta [ətˈlæntə; ætˋlæntə] *n*. 亚特兰大〔美国城市〕。

At·lan·te·an [ˌætlænˈtiən, ətˈlæntiən; ˏætlænˋtɪən, ət-ˋlæntɪən] *a*. **1.** 巨人阿特拉斯 (Atlas) 神的，强有力的。**2.** 阿特兰提斯洲[岛]的。

at·lan·tes [ətˈlæntiːz; ətˋlæntiz] *n*. *pl*.【建】男像柱。

At·lan·tic [ətˈlæntik; ətˋlæntɪk] **I** *a*. **1.** 大西洋的。**2.** 巨人阿特拉斯 (Atlas) 的。**II** *n*. 大西洋。*an* ~ *flight* 横越大西洋飞行。*an* ~ *liner* 大西洋航线定期船。~ *states* 美国大西洋沿岸各州。*the* ~ *Ocean* 大西洋。~ **Charter** 大西洋宪章。~ **city** 大西洋城〔美国新泽西州东南部城市〕。~ **Provinces**（加拿大）滨大西洋诸岛（指纽芬兰，新不伦瑞克，新斯科金和爱德华太子岛）。

At·lan·tis [ətˈlæntis, æt-; ətˋlæntɪs, æt-] 阿特兰提斯洲[岛]〔传说史前位于大西洋直布罗陀以西的一个洲或岛。古代著作家认为它是经地震而沉入大洋的〕。

At·las [ˈætləs; ˋætləs] *n*. **1.**【希神】阿特拉斯〔双肩掮天巨神〕；〔喻〕身负重担的人。**2.** 非洲阿特拉斯山。**3.**〔a-〕地图集，图表集。**4.**〔a-〕大张绘图纸。**5.**〔a-〕【解】寰椎。**6.**〔a-〕【建】男像柱。**7.** 大力神导弹〔美〕。~ **beetle** 印度大甲虫。~ **cedar** 小亚细亚雪松。~ **folio** 最大版本〔16×25 英寸〕。~ **moss** 东亚大蛾。~ **silk** 樗蚕丝。

ATM = automated-teller machine 自动柜员机。

at·man [ˈɑːtmən; ˋɑtmən] *n*.〔Sans.〕**1.** 灵魂，自我。**2.**〔A-〕宇宙的灵魂。

atmo- *comb*. *f*. 表示"气，蒸气"，*atmo*meter.

at·mol·y·sis [ætˈmɔlisis; ætˋmɑləsɪs] *n*.【化】微孔分气法。

at·mom·e·ter [ætˈmɔmitə; ætˋmɑmɪtɚ] *n*.（测定水的蒸发速度的）蒸发计，汽化计。

at·mos·phere [ˈætməsfiə; ˋætməsˏfɪr] *n*. **1.** 大气；大气层，气圈；空气。**2.** 四围情况，环境，气氛。**3.**（艺术品的）基调，风格。**4.** 气压。**5.**【化】雾。*a tense* ~ *at a meeting* 会场中的紧张空气。*a tiny inn full of* ~ 一个十分别致的小酒馆。*ion* ~ 离子雾。*electron* ~ 电子云。***clear the*** ~ 消除误会；缓和紧张空气。

at·mos·pher·ic [ˌætməsˈferik; ˏætməsˋfɛrɪk] *a*. **1.** 大气(中)的。**2.** 大气所致的。**3.** 空气的。**4.** 气压的。**5.** 有…气氛的。*high* (*low*) ~ *pressure* 高[低]气压。~ **depression** 低气压。~ **discharge**【电】天电放电。~ **disturbance**【无】天电干扰。**-i·cal** *a*. **-i·cal·ly** *ad*. 在大气影响下，气压上。

at·mos·pher·ics [ˈætməsˈferiks; ˏætməsˋfɛrɪks] *n*.【无】天电，天电扰乱；大气干扰。

at·mos·pher·i·um [ˌætməsˈferiəm; ˏætməsˋfɛrɪəm] *n*.（用以模拟大气现象的）大气馆。

ATO rocket = assisted takeoff rocket 助飞火箭。

at·oll [ˈætɔl; ˋætɑl] *n*.【地】环状珊瑚岛，环礁。~ **lake** 环礁湖。

at·om [ˈætəm; ˋætəm] *n*. **1.** 原子。**2.** 微粒；微量。*chemical* ~*s* 原子。*physical* ~*s* 分子。***have*** [***there is***] ***not an*** ~ ***of*** 一点也没有。***break to*** ~***s*** 粉碎 (*The vase was broken to* ~*s*. 花瓶敲得粉碎)。~**-blitz** *n*., *vt*. 用原子弹进行闪电空袭。~**-bomb** *n*., *vt*.（用）原子弹(轰炸)。~**-free** *a*. 无原子武器的。~ **gun** 回旋加速器。~ **mania** 原子弹狂。~ **probe** 原子探测器。~ **smasher** 核粒子加速器。~**-stricken** *a*. 受原子爆炸污染的。~**-tipped** *a*. 装有原子弹头的。

at·o·mar·i·um [ˌætəˈmaːriəm; ˏætəˋmarɪəm] *n*.（显示原子结构等的）原子馆。

a·tom·ic [əˈtɔmik; əˋtɑmɪk] *a*. **1.** 原子的。**2.** 极微的。**3.** 强大的。~ **age** 原子时代。~ **blackmail** 原子讹诈。~ **bomb** 原子弹。~ **cocktail**〔俚〕放射性治癌吞服剂。~ **energy**【化】原子能。~ **fission** 原子核裂变。~ **formula**【化】原子式，结构式。~ **group**【化】原子团。~ **intimidation** 原子恫吓。~ **model**【化】原子模型。~ **nucleus**【化】原子核。~ **number**【化】原子序数。~ **pile** 原子堆。~ **reaction** 原子反应。~ **reactor** 原子反应堆。~ **rocket** 原子火箭。~ **structure** 原子构造。~ **value**【化】原子价。~ **volume**【化】原子体积。~ **warhead** 核弹头。~ **weight**【化】原子量。~**-bearing** *a*. 携带原子弹的。~**-cosmic** *a*. 掌握原子能和空间宇宙技术的。~**-proof** *a*. 防原子的。~**-tipped** *a*. 装有原子弹头的。

a·tom·i·cal [əˈtɔmikəl; əˋtɑmɪkəl] *a*. = atomic. **-ly** *ad*.

at·o·mic·i·ty [ˌætəˈmisiti; ˏætəˋmɪsətɪ] *n*. **1.**【化】（气体分子中的）原子数。**2.** 原子价。

a·tom·ics [əˈtɔmiks; əˋtɑmɪks] *n*. 原子学，原子工艺学，

核工艺学。

at·om·ism [ˈætəmizəm; ˋætəmɪzəm] *n*. 原子说,原子论。

at·om·ist [ˈætəmist; ˋætəmɪst] *n*. 原子论者;原子学家。

at·om·is·tic [ˌætəˈmistik; ˏætəmˋɪstɪk] *a*. 原子的,原子论的;原子学家的。

at·om·i·za·tion [ˌætəmaiˈzeiʃən; ˏætəməˋzeʃən] *n*. 1. 原子化,化成微粒。2. 喷雾;雾化(法)。

at·om·ize [ˈætəmaiz; ˋætəmˏaɪz] *vt*. 1. 使化为原子,使成原子。2. 把…喷成雾,使雾化,使粉化。3.〔俚〕用原子弹轰炸。

at·omi·zer [ˈætəmaizə; ˋætəmˏaɪzɚ] *n*. (药品或香水的)喷雾器。

at·o·my[1] [ˈætəmi; ˋætəmɪ] *n*.〔古〕1. 原子;微粒;尘埃。2. 矮子。

at·o·my[2] [ˈætəmi; ˋætəmɪ] *n*.〔古〕1. 骸骨。2. 瘦人。

a·ton·a·ble [əˈtəunəbl; əˋtonəbl̩] *a*. (罪等)可赎回的;(过失等)可补偿的。

a·ton·al [eiˈtəunl; eˋtonl̩] *a*. 无调的,不成调的。**-ism** *n*. **-ist** *n*. **-ist·ic** *a*. **-ly** *ad*.

a·to·nal·i·ty [ˌeitəuˈnæliti; ˏetoˋnælətɪ] *n*.【乐】无调性,无调主义。

a·tone [əˈtəun; əˋton] *vi*. 补偿(过失),赎(罪)。—*vt*.〔古〕1. 偿。2.〔废〕和解,调解。~ **for** 偿,抵,赎(*Blood must* ~ *for blood* 以命抵命;血债要用血来还)。

a·tone·ment [əˈtəunmənt; əˋtonmənt] *n*. 补偿;赎罪。**make** ~ **for** 偿,赎(罪)。

a·ton·ic [æˈtɔnik; æˋtɑnɪk] I *a*. 1.【语音】(词或音节)非重读的。2.【语法】平音的。3.【医】(肌肉)缺乏张力的,弛缓的。II *n*. 1.【语音】无重读音的词[音节]。2.【语法】平音。

at·o·ny [ˈætəni; ˋætənɪ] *n*. 1. 无重读音;缺乏声调。2.【医】(肌肉)弛缓,张力缺乏。

a·top [əˈtɔp; əˋtɑp] *ad*., *prep*. 在(…)顶上。

-a·tor *suf*. …的人[物]: avi*ator*.

-a·to·ry *suf*. 表示"具有…特征的";"由…产生的": laud*atory*.

ATP = adenosine triphosphate【生化】三磷酸腺苷。

at·ra·bil·ious [ˌætrəˈbiljəs; ˏætrəˋbɪljəs] *a*. 1. 忧郁的,沉闷的。2. 乖张的;有疑心病的。**-ness** *n*.

a·trem·ble [əˈtrembl; əˋtrɛmbl̩] *ad*.〔诗〕发着抖,战慄着。

at·ri·cho·sis [ˌætriˈkəusis; ˏætrɪˋkosɪs] *n*.【医】(先天性)无毛症,毛发缺乏。

a·trip [əˈtrip; əˋtrɪp] *a*.〔用作表语〕1. 起锚。2. 扬帆。

a·tri·um [ˈɑːtriəm; ˋɑtrɪəm] *n*. (*pl*. **-tria** [-triə; -trɪə]) 1. (罗马建筑内部的)中庭。2.【建】门廊。3.【解】心房;(耳的)鼓室。4.【动】口前腔;气门室。

a·tro·cious [əˈtrəuʃəs; əˋtroʃəs] *a*. 1. 凶暴的,残忍的,万恶的。2.〔口〕糟透的。*an* ~ *pun* 恶毒的俏皮话。~ *weather* 恶劣的天气。**-ly** *ad*. **-ness** *n*.

a·troc·i·ty [əˈtrɔsiti; əˋtrɑsətɪ] *n*. 1. 凶恶,残忍;暴虐。2. 暴行。3.〔口〕令人不愉快的事物。*Her dress is an* ~. 她打扮得俗不可耐。

a·troph·ic [æˈtrɔfik; əˋtrɑfɪk] *a*. 萎缩(性)的,衰退的。

at·ro·phy [ˈætrəfi; ˋætrəfɪ] I *n*. 1.【医】萎缩症,虚脱。2.【生】衰退;退化,退缩。II *vt*., *vi*. (**-phied**; ~·**ing**) 1. (使)萎缩。2. (使)虚脱。*muscular* ~肌肉萎缩。

at·ro·pin(e) [ˈætrəpi(ː)n; ˋætrəˏpɪ(i)n] *n*.【化】颠茄碱阿托品。

at·ro·pism [ˈætrəpizəm; ˋætrəpɪzəm] *n*. 颠茄碱中毒,阿托品中毒。

ATS = 1. Air Training School 空军训练学校。2. American Technical Society 美国技术学会。3. American Television Society 美国电视学会。4. applications technology satellite 应用技术卫星。5. Army Transport Service 陆军水上运输部队〔美国〕。

att., **atty**. = attorney.

at·ta·bal, a·ta·bal [ˈætəˌbæl; ˋætəbæl] *n*. (摩尔人的)铜鼓或手鼓。

at·ta·boy [ˈætəbɔi; ˋætəbɔɪ] *int*.〔美〕顶好! 痛快痛快,好样的!〔That's the boy! 的转讹,表示赞赏〕。

at·tach [əˈtætʃ; əˋtætʃ] *vt*. 1. 附上,加上(条件等)。2. 贴上,系上,缚上。3. 使附属,使隶属。4. 使依恋,使执着。5. 逮捕;拘留;扣留;查封。6.【军】临时委派,指派。7. 签署。~ *a wire to a radio* 给收音机接线。*No blame is* ~*ed to his act*. 他的行为无可非议。*The tourist* ~*ed labels to all his bags*. 旅游者把他的行李都系上标签。~*a horse to a tree* 把马系到树上。*The hospital is* ~*ed to that university*. 这医院附属于那所大学。~ *part of sb.'s salary* 扣下某人部分薪金。~ **importance to** 把重点放在,重视。~ **oneself to** 1. 附着于,属于,加入(政党等)。2. 依恋。**be** ~**ed to** 1. 爱上,爱慕,依恋。2. 隶属于 (*She is deeply* ~*ed to him*. 她很爱慕他)。— *vi*. 附着,附属;相连;相伴 (*to*, *upon*)。*No blame* ~*es to him*. 他无可责备。**-a·ble** *a*.

at·ta·ché [əˈtæʃei, Am. ˌætəˈʃei; əˋtæʃe, ˏætəˋʃe] *n*. (大使,公使的)随员,专员;使馆职员。*a commercial* ~ 商务专员[参赞]。*a military* [*naval*] ~使馆陆[海]军武官。~ **case** (公文)手提皮箱。

at·tach·ment [əˈtætʃmənt; əˋtætʃmənt] *n*. 1. 附着,附着物;附属物,附件。2. 爱慕,依恋;依附 (*for*; *to*)。3.【法】逮捕;扣押(人,财产)。4. 扣押证。~*s to a sewing machine* 缝纫机的附件。*form a profound* ~ *for sb*. 对某人大为倾倒。~ **disorder**【精神】感情障碍。

at·tack [əˈtæk; əˋtæk] I *vt*. 1. 攻击 (*opp*. defend)。2. 非难,抨击。3. 着手,动手,投入。4. (疾病)侵袭。5.【化】腐蚀。*We will not* ~ *unless we are* ~*ed*; *if we are* ~*ed*, *we will certainly counter-* ~。人不犯我,我不犯人;人若犯我,我必犯人。~ *a task* 动手工作。~ *a problem* 着手解决问题。*Strong acids* ~ *metals*. 强酸对金属有腐蚀作用。**be** ~**ed with** (*a disease*) 害(病)。II *n*. 1. 攻击 (*opp*. defense), 袭击。2. 抨击。3.【空】迎角,冲角,攻角。4. 着手,动手。5. 发作,发病。6. (表演或竞赛中的)主动。*A- is the best defense*. 进攻是最好的防御。*an* ~ *formation* 攻击队形。*have an* ~ *of* 为…所侵袭;害,患(病)。*make an* ~ *on* 攻击。~ **ad** 攻击对手的竞选广告。~ **dog** 攻击犬(帮助警察或士兵执行任务或防范窃贼等)。**-er** *n*. 攻击者。

at·tain [əˈtein; əˋten] *vt*. 1. 达到,获得 (*opp*. miss);遂(愿)。2. 到达。~ *one's object* 达到目的。~ *one's end* 得遂所愿;如愿以偿。~ *the opposite shore* 到达彼岸。— *vi*. 达到,获得 (*to*)。~ *to man's estate* 达到成年。~ *to power* 得掌大权。**-a·ble** *a*. **-a·bil·i·ty**, **-a·ble·ness** *n*.

at·tain·der [əˈteində; əˋtendɚ] *n*. 1.【法】(对判处死刑者、逃犯)褫夺公权;剥夺财产。2.〔古〕耻辱。

at·tain·ment [əˈteinmənt; əˋtenmənt] *n*. 1. 达到,到达。2.〔*pl*.〕成就,造诣;学识,才能。*a man of varied* ~*s* 多才多艺的人。*a scholar of high* ~*s* 博学之士。~ **age** 学业成绩年龄 (= achievement age)。

at·taint [əˈteint; əˋtent] I *vt*. 1.【法】使被褫夺公权;使被剥夺财产。2. 污损(名誉);污辱。3.〔罕〕使感染。II *n*. 1. 公民权利(或财产)的剥夺。2.〔古〕污辱;污名。

at·tain·ture [əˈteintʃə; əˋtentʃɚ] *n*.〔废〕1. 民权剥夺,公权丧失。2. 玷辱,凌辱。

at·tar [ˈætə; ˋætɚ] *n*. 香精;玫瑰油。

at·tem·per [əˈtempə; əˋtɛmpɚ] *vt*. 1. 使缓和。2. 冲淡。3. 和匀;调和,调匀。4. 使适合。5. 调节(温度)。6.【冶】使回火。★现今各义通例均用 temper.

at·tempt [əˈtempt; əˋtɛmpt] I *vt*. 1. 试,企图。2. 窥伺,觊觎,意欲夺取;袭击。3.〔古〕诱惑。4.〔古〕企图杀害。~ *a difficult task* 想完成一件艰难工作。~ *a fortress* 欲夺取要塞。~ *too much* 不自量力地做;纵欲

过度。～ *sb.'s life* [*the life of sb.*] 想杀某人。**II** ***n.*** **1.** 企图,努力。**2.** 〔古〕攻击,袭击。**3.** 【法】未遂(罪)。*an ～ at an offence* 未遂罪。*a poor ～ at a smile* 强笑未成的笑脸。***in a vain ～*** 妄图。***make an ～ (at)*** 企图,尽力。***make an ～ on*** (*sb.'s life*; *a fortress*) 想结果(某人性命);欲夺取(要塞)。**-a·ble** ***a.*** 可以尝试的。

at·tend [əˈtend; əˋtɛnd] ***vt.*** **1.** 出席,到场,参加;上,到。**2.** 随侍,服侍;随行。**3.** 陪,伴,伴随。**4.** 看护,照料。**5.** 〔古〕注意。**6.** 〔古〕期待。～ *school* 上学。～ (*a course of*) *lectures* 听讲。*an ～ing physician* 主治医师。*The meeting was well ～ed.* 到会人数众多。～ *church* 上教堂(做礼拜)。*be ～ed by a doctor* 由医生照料。*be ～ed with difficulties* [*good results*] 遇到困难,收效良好。— ***vi.*** **1.** 注意,留意;倾听(*to*)。**2.** 照顾,办理(*to*)。**3.** 侍奉,服侍;陪,伴随(*on*, *upon*)。**4.** 出席。～ ***to*** (*one's work*; *health*) 照料(工作),注意(健康)。～ ***upon*** (*sb.*; *sb.'s wishes*) 侍奉(某人);听候(某人差遣)。

at·tend·ance [əˈtendəns; əˋtɛndəns] ***n.*** **1.** 出席,到场;参加(*at*)。**2.** 陪从,看护;照料。**3.** 出席者,参加者。**4.** 出勤率。*a large ～* 出席者[观众]不少。*medical ～* 医疗护理。***be in ～ on*** 服侍,随侍。***dance ～ on*** 奉承,献殷勤。～ **book** 签到簿。～ **area** (到公学上学的)就学地区。～ **officer** (检查学生出勤情况的)校纪检查官(= truant officer)。

at·tend·ant [əˈtendənt; əˋtɛndənt] **I** ***a.*** **1.** 随行的,跟随的(*on*, *upon*)。**2.** 出席的。**3.** 伴随的,附随的(*on*, *upon*)。～ *circumstances* 附带情况。～ *questions* 伴随而来的问题。～ *crowd* 在场群众。**II** ***n.*** **1.** 陪从,随员。**2.** 服务员;值班员。**3.** 出席人,参加人。**4.** 伴随物,附属品。

at·tent [əˈtent; əˋtɛnt] ***a.*** 〔古〕注意的,留意的。

at·ten·tat [ətɑːnˈtɑː; ətɑnˋtɑ] ***n.*** 〔F.〕谋刺(尤指未遂的政治上的谋杀)。

at·ten·tion [əˈtenʃən; əˋtɛnʃən] ***n.*** **1.** 注意,注目;留心,专心;注意力。**2.** 【军】立正。**3.** 〔*pl.*〕殷勤,厚待。**4.** 关照,礼貌。*He was all ～.* 他十分专心。～ *to a stranger* 对一个陌生人的礼貌。*A- please!* 请注意。*Your application will have ～.* 你的申请会得到考虑。***arrest*** [***attract***] ***sb.'s ～*** 惹起某人注意。***Attention!*** (略 'shun [ʃʌn; ʃʌn])立正!〔口令〕。***call away the ～*** 转移开注意。***call sb.'s ～ to*** 促使某人注意。***come to ～*** 【军】(采取)立正(姿势)。***devote one's ～ to*** 热中于,专心于。***fix one's ～ on*** 留意。***pay sb. ～s*** 殷勤招待某人。***pay one's ～s to*** **1.** 注意。**2.** (对女人)献殷勤。***stand at ～*** = come to ～. ***turn one's ～ to*** 注意。***with ～*** 注意,郑重。～**-getting** ***a.*** 引起注意的。～ **span** 一个人能集中注意力于某事的时间。**-al** ***a.***

at·ten·tive [əˈtentiv; əˋtɛntɪv] ***a.*** **1.** 注意的,留心的。**2.** 周到的,殷勤的。***be ～ to*** 注意;敬重;倾听(*be ～ to one's duty* 忠于职守)。**-ly** ***ad.*** **-ness** ***n.***

at·ten·u·ant [əˈtenjuənt; əˋtɛnjuənt] **I** ***a.*** 使变稀薄的。**II** ***n.*** 稀释剂。

at·ten·u·ate [əˈtenjueit; əˋtɛnjʊˏet] **I** ***vt.*** **1.** 使变稀薄,使淡,稀释。**2.** 弄细,弄薄。**3.** 使减弱。**4.** 使病毒毒性减弱。— ***vi.*** **1.** 变稀薄。**2.** 变细,变薄。**3.** 减弱,变弱;衰减,衰耗。**II** [əˈtenjuit; əˋtɛnjʊɪt] ***a.*** **1.** 稀薄的。**2.** 细的,薄的。**3.** 减弱的。**4.** 【植】渐尖的。

at·ten·u·a·tion [əˌtenjuˈeiʃən; əˏtɛnjʊˋeʃən] ***n.*** **1.** 变薄,变细。**2.** 减少,减弱。**3.** 稀释。**4.** 【物】衰减。

at·ten·u·a·tor [əˈtenjueitə; əˋtɛnjʊˏetɚ] ***n.*** 【物】衰减器。

at·test [əˈtest; əˋtɛst] ***vt.*** **1.** 证明,证实。**2.** 表明。**3.** 使发誓。**4.** 使服兵役。～ *the truth of a statement* 证明供词属实。*His works ～ his industry.* 他的工作表明他的勤奋。*an ～ed herd* 经过检疫证明无病的牲口。*The recruits were ～ed.* 新兵应征入伍。— ***vi.*** 证明,证实(*to*)。*The expert ～ed to the genuineness of the document.* 专家证明该文件系真品。

at·tes·ta·tion [ˌætesˈteiʃən; ˏætesˋteʃən] ***n.*** **1.** 证实,证明。**2.** 证据,证言;证明书。**3.** 宣誓。

at·tes·tor [əˈtestə; əˋtestɚ] ***n.*** 证人,证明者。

Att. Gen. = Attorney General.

At·tic [ˈætik; ˋætɪk] **I** ***a.*** **1.** 古希腊阿蒂卡(Attica)[雅典]的;雅典派的。**2.** 文雅的,古雅的。**II** ***n.*** **1.** 雅典人。**2.** 雅典城邦的希腊语。～ **faith** 坚定的信念。～ **order** 【建】角柱式。～ **salt** [**wit**] 文雅的机智,文雅的俏皮话。～ **taste** 雅兴。

at·tic [ˈætik; ˋætɪk] ***n.*** 屋顶室,楼顶间,顶楼。

At·ti·ca [ˈætikə; ˋætəkə] ***n.*** 阿蒂卡〔古希腊以雅典为统治中心的地区,在今希腊东南部〕。

at·ti·cism [ˈætisizəm; ˋætəsɪzəm] ***n.*** **1.** 雅典派[式]。**2.** 文雅的言辞[表现]。**3.** 对雅典的爱慕。

At·ti·la [ˈætilə; ˋætḷə] ***n.*** 阿提拉〔侵入罗马帝国的匈奴王(406?-453)〕。

at·tire [əˈtaiə; əˋtaɪr] **I** ***n.*** **1.** 服装,装束。**2.** (纹章上的)多叉鹿角。*the ～ of spring* 春(天的服)装。**II** ***vt.*** 打扮,装饰。*The girl was ～d in pink.* 这女孩一身粉红色打扮。

at·ti·tude [ˈætitjuːd; ˋætəˏtjud] ***n.*** **1.** 姿势,身段。**2.** 态度,看法。**3.** 【军】飞行姿态。**4.** 芭蕾舞的一个姿势。*the ～ of flight* 【空】飞行姿势。*the ～ of mind* 心情。*level ～* 【空】水平位置。***strike an ～*** 装腔作势,摆架子。***take*** [***assumed***] ***an ～ of*** 取…态度。

at·ti·tu·di·nize [ˌætiˈtjuːdinaiz; ˏætəˋtjudnˏaɪz] ***vi.*** **1.** 采取某种姿态。**2.** (在谈话、写作、行动中)装腔作势。

Att·lee [ˈætli; ˋætlɪ] ***n.*** 阿特利(艾德礼)〔姓氏〕。

attn. 〔美〕= attention.

atto- *comb. f.* 百亿亿分之一,微微微($=10^{-18}$)。

at·torn [əˈtəːn; əˋtɝn] ***vi.*** **1.** 〔古〕改换门庭(投靠新领主)。**2.** (佃户)承认新地主〔即同意在新地主门下继续当佃户〕。

at·tor·ney [əˈtəːni; əˋtɝnɪ] ***n.*** **1.** 〔美〕辩护律师;〔英古〕事务律师〔现在用 solicitor〕。**2.** 代理人;代言人。*a letter* [*power*, *warrant*] *of ～* 委任状。*an ～ at law* 〔美〕律师。*an ～ in fact* 代理人。*by ～* 凭代理人。*a circuit* [*district*] *～* 〔美〕地方检查官。～ **general** 首席检查官。**A- General** 〔美〕司法部长。**-ship** ***n.*** 代理人的身分[职务];代理,代言。

at·tract [əˈtrækt; əˋtrækt] ***vt.*** **1.** 吸引(*opp.* repel)。**2.** 引诱,诱惑。*A magnet ～s steel.* 磁石吸引钢铁。～ *a large audience* 吸引了很多观众,叫座。～ (*sb.'s*) *attention* 引(人)注意,惹眼。— ***vi.*** **1.** 有吸力。**2.** 引人注意。*It's a property of matter to ～.* 物质有引力。*be intended to ～* 旨在引人注目。**-or** ***n.*** 引人注意的人,有吸引力的人。**-a·ble** ***a.*** 可被吸引的。**-a·bil·i·ty** ***n.*** 吸引性。

at·tract·ant [æˈtræktənt; əˋtræktənt] ***n.*** 引诱物;【虫】引诱剂。

at·trac·tion [əˈtrækʃən; əˋtrækʃən] ***n.*** **1.** 引,吸引;【物】引力。**2.** 魅力。**3.** 引人注意的东西;有趣的东西,精彩节目。**4.** 【语法】形态同化。*the ～ of gravity* 重力。*magnetic ～* 磁力。*the chief ～ of the night* 今晚最精彩的节目。

at·trac·tive [əˈtræktiv; əˋtræktɪv] ***a.*** **1.** 有吸引力的。**2.** 引人注目的。**3.** 媚人的,俏的;标致的。**-ly** ***ad.*** **-ness** ***n.***

at·trib. = **1.** attribute. **2.** attributive(ly).

at·trib·ut·a·ble [əˈtribjutəbl; əˋtrɪbjutəbḷ] ***a.*** 可归因于…的,由…引起的(*to*)。*a disease ～ to alcoholism* 酒精中毒引起的疾病。

at·trib·ute [əˈtribju(ː)t; əˋtrɪbjut] **I** ***vt.*** **1.** 把(某事)归因于…。**2.** 认为…系某人所为。～ (*one's success*) *to* (*hard work*) 认为(成功)是(努力)的结果。***be ～d to*** 被认为是…所为(*The play is ～d to Shakespeare.* 这

剧本被认为是莎士比亚写的)。II [ˈætribjuːt; ˋætrə͵bjut] *n*. 1. 属性,特质。2. (人物、官职等的)标志,表征。3.【语法】属性形容词。*A scepter is the ~ of power*. 权杖是权力的标志。

at·tri·bu·tion [ˌætriˈbjuːʃən; ͵ætrəˋbjuʃən] *n*. 1. 归属,归因。2. 属性。3.〔古〕职权,权限。

at·trib·u·tive [əˈtribjutiv; əˋtrɪbjətɪv] I *a*. 1. 属性的,归属的。2.【语法】定语的,修饰语的。(*opp*. predicative). II *n*. 定语,修饰语。**-ly** *ad*.

at·trit [əˈtrit; əˋtrɪt] *vt*.〔美军俚〕1. 消耗。2. (以辱骂)降低(士气)。

at·trite [əˈtrait; əˋtraɪt] *vt*. (通过摩擦)使…消耗,磨损,削弱。

at·trit·ed [əˈtraitid; əˋtraɪtɪd] *a*. 磨损的,磨坏的。

at·tri·tion [əˈtriʃən; əˋtrɪʃən] *n*. 1. 摩擦。2. 磨损,磨灭;消耗。3. 缩员,缩减人员。4.【神】不彻底的忏悔。*a war of ~* 消耗战。

ATTU = Asian Table Tennis Union 亚洲乒乓球联盟,亚乒联盟。

at·tune [əˈtjuːn; əˋtjun] *vt*. 1. 调(音)。2. 使调和,使协调。*~ a violin to a piano* 使提琴与钢琴合调。

atty. = attorney.

Atty. Gen. = Attorney General〔英〕检查总长;〔美〕司法部长。

ATV = 1. Associated Television〔英〕联合电视公司。2. All-Terrain Vehicle 全地形交通工具。

a·twain [əˈtwein; əˋtwen] *ad*.〔古〕分为二。*cut ~* 切成两份。

a·tween [əˈtwiːn; əˋtwin] *prep*., *ad*.〔古〕在两者之间。

a·twit·ter [əˈtwitə; əˋtwɪtɚ] *a*. 〔用作表语〕〔俚〕高兴,兴奋。

at. wt. = atomic weight【化】原子量。

a·typ·ic, a·typ·i·cal [æˈtipik(əl); eˋtɪpək(l̩)] *a*. 非典型的;不规则的。

au [əu, F. o; o, F. o] *prep*. 〔F.〕= to the; at the; with the. ***au contraire*** [əu kɔŋˈtrer; o kɔŋˋtrɛr] 反之。***au courant*** [əu kurɑ̃; okuˋrɑ̃] 1. 熟悉,通晓(*with*)。2. 跟上时代。***au fait*** [əuˈfe; ͵oˋfɛ] 熟练,精通(*in*; *at*); 熟悉 (*with*) (*Put me au fait of*... 请教给我…)。***au fond*** [əuˈfɔ̃; ͵oˋfɔ̃] 根本上,实质上;彻底地。***au grand sérieux*** [ˌəuˈgrɑːŋ seirjˈəː; oˋgra seˋrjɚ] 极其认真地。***au lait*** [əu lei; oˋlɛ] 掺有牛奶的 (*café au lait* 牛奶咖啡)。***au naturel*** [əu natyrel; o natyˋrel] 1. 原样。2. 裸体。3. 供生吃的,略加烹调的。***au pied de la lettre*** [əu pjei d la ˈletr; o pje d la ˋlɛtr] 照字面意义。***au revoir*** [əu rəˈvwɑːr; o rəˋvwɑr] 再会。

Au =【化】aurum (= gold)。

A.U., AU = astronomical unit.

Au. = August.

au·bade [əuˈbɑːd; oˋbɑd] *n*. 〔F.〕晨歌;朝乐〔*cf*. serenade〕。

au·berge [əuˈbɛəʒ; oˋbɛrʒ] *n*. 〔F.〕旅馆。

au·ber·gine [ˌəubəˈʒiːn, ˌəubɛəˈʒiːn; ˋobɛr͵ʒin, ͵obɛrˋʒin] *n*. 1. 茄子。2. 紫红色。

Au·brey [ˈɔːbri; ˋɔbrɪ] *n*. 奥布里〔姓氏,男子名〕。

au·burn [ˈɔːbən; ˋɔbɚn] I *a*. 红褐色的。II *n*. 红褐色。

Au·bus·son [əubʌˈsəun; obyˋsɔn] *n*. 奥布松〔法国城市〕。*~* **rug** (奥布松出产的)精细的华丽地毯。

A.U.C. = ab urbe condita 从(罗马)城市建立以来。

Au·chin·leck [ˌɔːkinˈlek; ͵ɔkɪnˋlɛk] *n*. 奥金莱克〔姓氏〕。

Auck·land [ˈɔːklənd; ˋɔklənd] *n*. 奥克兰〔新西兰港市〕。

auc·tion [ˈɔːkʃən; ˋɔkʃən] I *n*. 1. 拍卖,标售。2. (桥牌)拍卖玩法 (= ~ bridge)。*a public ~* 拍卖。***a Dutch ~*** 喊价逐步减低的拍卖。***put up to*** [***at***] ~ 交付拍卖。***sell*** (*a thing*) ***by*** [〔美〕***at***] ~拍卖。II *vt*. 拍卖。

auc·tion·eer [ˌɔːkʃəˈniə; ͵ɔkʃənˋɪr] I *n*. 拍卖人。*a ~ hammer* 拍卖槌。II *vt*. 拍卖。

auc·to·ri·al [ɔːkˈtɔːriəl; ɔkˋtɔrɪəl] *a*. 著者的,作家的;作者(著)的。

au·cu·ba [ˈɔːkjubə; ˋɔkjəbə] *n*. 桃叶珊瑚属植物。

aud. = audit; auditor.

au·da·cious [ɔːˈdeiʃəs; ɔˋdeʃəs] *a*. 1. 大胆的。2. 厚颜无耻的;鲁莽的,蛮横无礼的。**-ly** *ad*. **-ness** *n*.

au·dac·i·ty [ɔːˈdæsiti; ɔˋdæsətɪ] *a*. 1. 大胆。2. 厚脸,无耻;无礼,鲁莽。***have the ~ to*** (*do*) 有脸(做)…,竟然敢(做)…,厚颜无耻地…。

Au·den [ˈɔːdn; ˋɔdn] *n*. 奥登〔姓氏〕。

au·di·bil·i·ty [ˌɔːdiˈbiliti; ͵ɔdəˋbɪlətɪ] *n*. 1. 听得见,可听性。2.【物】可闻度。

au·di·ble [ˈɔːdəbl; ˋɔdəbl̩] *a*. 听得见的。~ **frequency**【无】(成)声频(率)。**-ness** *n*. **au·di·bly** [ˈɔːdəbli; ˋɔdəblɪ] *ad*.

au·di·ence [ˈɔːdjəns; ˋɔdɪəns] *n*. 1. 听众;观众;读者。2. 谒见;接见。3. 倾听;听取。*a large* [*small*] ~ 大量[少数]观众。*a farewell ~* 告别谒见。***be given an ~*** 得到发言机会。***be received in ~*** 蒙召见,赐见。***give ~ to*** 听取;接见;召见。***grand*** (*sb*.) ***an ~*** 接见(某人),召见(某人)。***have ~ of*** 拜谒,拜会。***in general*** [***open***] ~ 当众,公然。***in sb.'s ~*** 当着某人面前,据某人所闻。~ **chamber** 接见室。~ **pictures**〔俚〕受观众欢迎的影片。~**-proof** *a*. (戏剧)肯定卖座的。

au·di·ent [ˈɔːdiənt; ˋɔdɪənt] *a*. 倾听的;注意的。

audi(o)- *comb*. *f*. 听:*audio*meter.

au·dile [ˈɔːdail; ˋɔdaɪl] I *a*. 听觉的;听得到的。II *n*.【心】对听觉印象特别敏感的人;听象型。

au·di·o [ˈɔːdiəu; ˋɔdɪ͵o] *a*.【无】听觉的,声音的,音频的;成音的。~**book** 有声读物,有声书籍。~ **frequency**【无】(成)声频(率)。

au·di·o·gram [ˈɔːdiəˌgræm; ˋɔdɪo͵græm] *n*. 听力敏度图。

au·di·ol·o·gy [ˌɔːdiˈɔlədʒi; ͵ɔdɪˋɑlədʒɪ] *n*. 听觉学,听觉病矫治学。**-o·log·i·cal** [ˌɔːdiəˈlɔdʒikl; ͵ɔdɪəˋlɑdʒɪkl̩] *a*. **-ol·o·gist** *n*. 听觉病矫治专家。

au·di·om·e·ter [ˌɔːdiˈɔmitə; ͵ɔdɪˋɑmətɚ] *n*. 听度计,听力计。

au·di·om·e·try [ˌɔːdiˈɔmitri; ͵ɔdɪˋɑmɪtrɪ] *n*.【物】测听术;听力测定。

au·di·on [ˈɔːdiən; ˋɔdɪən] *n*.【无】三极(真空)管。

au·di·o·phile [ˈɔːdiəfail; ˋɔdɪə͵faɪl] *n*. 高保真度录音(唱片)的爱好者;讲究音质者, hi-fi 迷。

au·di·o·tape [ˈɔːdiəuteip; ˋɔdɪo͵tep] *n*. 录音磁带。

au·di·o·typ·ing [ˌɔːdiəuˈtaipiŋ; ͵ɔdɪoˋtaɪpɪŋ] *n*. 录音打字。

au·di·o-vis·u·al [ˌɔːdiəuˈvizjuəl; ˋɔdɪoˋvɪʒuəl] *a*. 1. 视觉听觉的。2. 视听(教学法)的〔书本之外,借助电影,幻灯、录音、无线电等〕。~ **aids** 视听教具。

au·di·phone [ˈɔːdifəun; ˋɔdə͵fon] *n*. 助听器。

au·dit [ˈɔːdit; ˋɔdɪt] I *n*. 1. 会计检查,查账。2. (地主与佃户间的)决算。II *vt*., *vi*. 1. 检查,查(账)。2.〔美〕(大学生)旁听(课程)。*commissioners of ~* 会计检查官。

au·di·tion [ɔːˈdiʃən; ɔˋdɪʃən] I *n*. 1. 听,听觉。2. (招收演员时的)试听,声量检查。II *vt*. 试听(演员的发声)。— *vi*. (演员)试音。

au·di·tor [ˈɔːditə; ˋɔdɪtɚ] *n*. 1. 会计检查官,查账员,审计员。2. 听者。3.〔美〕旁听生。

au·di·to·ri·al [ˌɔːdiˈtɔːriəl; ͵ɔdəˋtorɪəl] *a*. 会计检查(官)的;审计的;审计员的。

au·di·to·ri·um [ˌɔːdiˈtɔːriəm; ͵ɔdəˋtorɪəm] *n*. (*pl*. ~*s*, *-ri·a* [-riə; -rɪə]) 1. 听众席,观众席。2.〔美〕讲堂,教室;会厅,大会堂,大礼堂。

au·di·to·ry [ˈɔːditəri; ˋɔdə͵torɪ] I *a*. 耳的,听觉的。II *n*. 1. 听众。2. 听众席。3. 礼堂,讲堂。~ **nerves** 听神

经。~ **meatus** 耳道。~ **localization** 声源定位。

au·di·tress [ˈɔːditris; ˋɔdɪtrɪs] ***n*.** **1.** 女查账员。**2.** 女听者〔*cf*. auditor〕。

Au·drey [ˈɔːdri; ˋɔdrɪ] ***n*.** 奥德丽〔女子名〕。

Au·du·bon [ˈɔːdəbɔn; ˋɔdəˏbɑn], **J.J.** 奥特朋〔1785-1851,美国鸟类学家〕。

Auf·klä·rung [G. ˈaufkleːruŋ; ˋaufˏklɛrʊŋ] ***n*.** 〔G.〕启蒙;(十八世纪的)启蒙思潮〔运动〕。

auf wie·der·se·hen [G. aufˈviːdərzeiən; aufˋvidɚˏzeən] 〔G.〕再会,再见。

Aug. = August.

Au·ge·an [ɔːˈdʒi(ː)ən; ɔˋdʒiən] ***a*.** 【希神】**1.** 奥吉亚斯王 (Augeas) 的。**2.** 极脏的。~ **stables** 奥吉亚斯王的牛厩〔相传养牛三千头,三十年未扫,后为 *Hercules* 用河水在一日内扫清〕,藏垢纳污的地方。

au·ger [ˈɔgə; ˋɔgɚ] **I** ***n*.** 螺(丝)钻,钻孔器;钻孔机。**II** ***vt*.** 钻(孔)。

aught[1] [ɔːt; ɔt] **I** ***n*.** 任何事物 (= anything)。(*He may starve*) ***for ~ I care*.** (他饿死也罢)我才不管呢。(*He may be rich*) ***for ~ I know*.** (他也许有钱)但我不大知道。**II** ***ad*.** 〔古〕一点也。***if ~ there be*** 〔古〕即使有也,就有也(极有限)。

aught[2] [ɔːt; ɔt] ***n*.** 〔俚〕零〔naught 的转讹〕;〔古〕无,乌有。

au·gite [ˈɔːdʒait; ˋɔdʒaɪt] ***n*.** 【矿】(普通)辉石。

aug·ment [ɔːgˈment; ɔgˋmɛnt] **I** ***vt*., *vi*.** **1.** (使)扩张,扩大;【军】扩编;(使)增大,增加。**2.** 【语法】(希腊文和梵文)(在…上)附加接头母音字母。**3.** 【乐】(在…上)增音。**4.** 【纹章】(在…上)加添新徽章。**II** [ˈɔːgmənt; ˋɔgmɛnt] ***n*.** **1.** 增大。**2.** 【语法】接头母音字母〔希腊文或梵文加在动词过去式字首的母音〕。

aug·men·ta·tion [ˌɔːgmenˈteiʃən; ˏɔgmɛnˋteʃən] ***n*.** **1.** 扩大,增加。**2.** 增加物。**3.** 【乐】增音。**4.** 【军】扩编。**5.** 【徽】名誉副徽。

aug·ment·a·tive [ɔːgˈmentətiv; ɔgˋmɛntətɪv] **I** ***a*.** **1.** 增大性的,增加的。**2.** 【语法】扩大〔增强〕词义的。**II** ***n*.** 【语法】增强语,扩张语〔指增强词义的词首、词尾或构词成分,如:*per*durable, eat *up*〕。

aug·ment·er [ɔːgˈmentə; ɔgˋmɛntɚ] ***n*.** 【机】助力器;增压器。

aug·ment·or [ɔːgˈmentə; ɔgˋmɛntɚ] ***n*.** **1.** = augmenter. **2.** (代替人在极危险环境中工作的)替身机器人。

au·gur [ˈɔːgə; ˋɔgɚ] **I** ***n*.** **1.** (古罗马的)卜占官;卜占师。**2.** 预言者。**II** ***vt*., *vi*.** **1.** 占卜;预卜,预言。**2.** 成为(…的)预兆,预示。*I ~ ill of his success*. 我看他的成功有问题。~ ***well*** [***ill***] 兆头好[不好]。

au·gu·ral [ˈɔːgjurəl; ˋɔgjʊrəl] ***a*.** **1.** 占卜的。**2.** 预言的;预兆性的。

au·gu·ry [ˈɔːgjuri; ˋɔgjərɪ] ***n*.** **1.** 占卜,占卜仪式。**2.** 征兆,预兆。*a happy* ~吉兆。

Au·gust [ˈɔːgəst; ˋɔgəst] ***n*.** **1.** 奥古斯特〔男子名〕。**2.** 八月。

au·gust [ɔːˈgʌst; ɔˋgʌst] ***a*.** **1.** 尊严的,威严的。**2.** 威风凛凛的;堂堂的,雄赳赳的。*your ~ father* 令尊。**-ly** ***ad*.** **-ness** ***n*.** 庄严,威严。

Au·gus·tan [ɔːˈgʌstən; ɔˋgʌstən] **I** ***a*.** **1.** 古罗马皇帝奥古斯都·凯撒的;奥古斯都时代的。**2.** 文艺全盛期的;古典的。**3.** 【英史】安妮女王时代的。**II** ***n*.** 奥古斯都时代的作家;文艺全盛时期的作家。~ **age** 文学的黄金时代。

Au·gus·tine [ɔːˈgʌstin; ɔˋgʌstɪn] ***n*.** **1.** 奥古斯廷〔姓氏〕。**2.** **Saint** ~奥古斯丁〔354-430,古罗马基督教神父〕。

Au·gus·tin·i·an [ˌɔːgəsˈtiniən; ˏɔgəˋstɪnɪən] ***n*.**, ***a*.** 奥古斯丁教义(的),奥古斯丁教团教士(的)。

Au·gus·tus [ɔːˈgʌstəs; ɔˋgʌstəs] ***n*.** **1.** 奥古斯塔斯〔男子名,爱称是 Gus, Gustus〕。**2.** 奥古斯都〔罗马帝国第一代皇帝 Octavianus Caesar 的尊称〕。

au jus [əuˈʒuː, əuˈdʒuːs; oˋʒy, oˋdʒus] 〔F.〕(肉)带原汁的。

auk [ɔːk; ɔk] ***n*.** 【动】海雀。

auk·let [ˈɔːklit; ˋɔklɪt] ***n*.** 小海雀。

auld [ɔːld; ɔld] ***a*.** 〔Scot.〕= old.

auld lang syne [ˈɔːld læŋˈsain; ˋɔld læŋˋsaɪn] (= old long since days gone by) 〔Scot.〕过去的日子,令人怀念的往日。

au·lic [ˈɔːlik; ˋɔlɪk] ***a*.** 宫廷的。**Aulic Council** 【史】**1.** 神圣罗马帝国枢密院。**2.** 旧德帝国的枢密院会议。

AUM = air-to-underwater missile 空对水下导弹。

Aum Shin·ri·kyo [ˈaumˈʃinrikjuː; ˋaumˋʃɪnrɪkju] ***n*.** 〔Jap.〕奥姆真理教〔日本一邪教团体,曾于 1995 年 3 月在东京地铁制造沙林毒气案,致使 12 人死亡,5,000 余人受伤〕。

a.u.n. = absque ulla nota (〔L.〕= unmarked) 无任何标记。

aunt [ɑːnt; ænt] ***n*.** **1.** 伯母,婶母;姨母,姑母;舅母。**2.** 阿姨,大妈〔对一般年长妇女的爱称〕。***Aunt Sally*** [ˈsæli] **1.** 掷棒击落女像口中所含烟斗的游戏。**2.** 〔英俚〕代人受过者;易遭批评的对象。**3.** 〔a- s-〕〔英俚〕任何无聊的娱乐节目。***My*** (***sainted***) ~! 嗳呀!啃! ***go and see one's*** ~〔俚〕去大便。

aunt·ie[1] [ˈɑːnti; ˋæntɪ] (*pl*. ~*s*) ***n*.** 伯母,阿姨〔aunt 的亲热称呼〕。

aunt·ie[2] [ˈɑːnti; ˋæntɪ] ***n*.** 〔口〕反导弹导弹。

aunt·y [ˈɑːnti; ˋɑntɪ] ***n*.** (*pl*. ***aunt·ies*** [-tiz; -tɪz]) = auntie[1].

au pair [əu pεə; o pɛr] 〔F.〕换工的。*She was an ~ girl who helped with the housework in return for room and board*. 她是换工的女孩,以帮助料理家务换取食宿。

au·ra [ˈɔːrə; ˋɔrə] ***n*.** (*pl*. ~***s***, ***-rae*** [-riː; -ri]) **1.** (人〔物〕的)气味;气氛,氛围。**2.** 【电】电风,辉光。**3.** 【医】(中风等的)先兆,预感。*a blue* ~ 蓝辉〔电子管中的辉光〕。*an ~ of culture* 文化气氛。

au·ral[1] [ˈɔːrəl; ˋɔrəl] ***a*.** **1.** 气味的,香味的;气氛的。**2.** 【电】电风的,辉光的。**3.** 【医】预兆的。

au·ral[2] [ˈɔːrəl; ˋɔrəl] ***a*.** 耳的,听觉的;听到的。

au·ra·min(e) [ˌɔːrəˈmiːn; ˏɔrəˋmin] ***n*.** 【化】金胺;(碱性)槐黄。

au·rar [ˈauraː; ˋaurɑ] ***n*.** ***pl*.** (*sing*. ***ey·rir*** [ˈeiriə; ˋeɪrɪr]) 奥拉〔冰岛货币单位,相当于 1/100 克朗〕。

au·re·ate [ˈɔːriit; ˋɔrɪɪt] ***a*.** **1.** 镀金的;金色的。**2.** 灿烂的。

au·re·li·an [ɔːˈriːljən; ɔˋrilɪən] **I** ***a*.** 蝶蛹的。**II** ***n*.** 鳞翅目昆虫研究专家;昆虫采集家。

Au·re·li·us [ɔːˈriːljəs; ɔˋrilɪəs] ***n*.** 奥里留斯〔121-180,罗马皇帝兼哲学家〕。

au·re·o·la [ɔːˈriələ; ɔˋrɪələ], **au·re·ole** [ˈɔːrəul; ˋɔrol] ***n*.** **1.** (神像画中头部或身体周围的)圆光,光环,光轮。**2.** (日、月等的)晕。

au·re·o·my·cin [ˌɔːriəuˈmaisin; ˏɔrɪəˋmaɪsɪn] ***n*.** 【药】金霉素 (chlortetracycline 的商标名)。

au re·voir [ˌəurəˈvwaːr; ˏorəˋvwɑr] 〔F.〕再见!

au·ric [ˈɔːrik; ˋɔrɪk] ***a*.** **1.** 金的;含金的。**2.** 【化】三价金的。

au·ri·cle [ˈɔːrikl; ˋɔrɪkl] ***n*.** **1.** 【解】外耳,耳廓。**2.** (心脏的)心房,心耳。**3.** 【解】耳形突;耳状骨。**4.** 【植】叶耳。

au·ric·u·la [əˈrikjulə; ɔˋrɪkjələ] ***n*.** (*pl*. ***-lae*** [-liː; -li], ~*s*) **1.** 【植】报春花。~ *primrose* 耳状报春花。**2.** = auricle.

au·ric·u·lar [ɔːˈrikjulə; ɔˋrɪkjəlɚ] **I** ***a*.** **1.** 耳的。**2.** 听觉的;耳语的。**3.** 耳状的。**4.** 【解】心耳的;耳廓的。~ *confession* 秘密忏悔。*an ~ finger* 小指。*an ~ tube* 【医】听诊器。**II** ***n*.** 〔*pl*.〕(鸟类的)耳羽。**-ly** ***ad*.** 用耳;用耳语。

au·ric·u·late [ɔːˈrikjulit; ɔˋrɪkjəlɪt] ***a.*** 有耳的;耳形的。
au·rif·er·ous [ɔːˈrifərəs; ɔˋrɪfərəs] ***a.*** 产金的;含金的。
au·ri·form [ˈɔːrifɔːm; ˋɔrɪˏfɔrm] ***a.*** 耳形的。
Au·ri·ga [ɔːˈraigə; ɔˋraɪgə] ***n.*** 【天】御夫座。
Au·rig·na·cian [ˌɔːrigˈneiʃən, -rigˈnei-; ˏɔrɪgˋneʃən, -rigˋne-] ***a.*** 奥里尼雅克期的〔指法国旧石器时代前期〕。
au·ris [ˈɔːris; ˋɔrɪs] ***n.*** 〔L.〕耳。~ ***externa*** 外耳。~ ***interna*** 内耳。~ ***media*** 中耳。
au·ris·cope [ˈɔːriskəup; ˋɔrɪˏskop] ***n.*** 耳镜。
au·rist [ˈɔːrist; ˋɔrɪst] ***n.*** 耳科医生,耳科学家。
au·rochs [ˈɔːrɔks; ˋɔrɑks] ***n.*** (*pl.* ~(*es*))【考古】西欧野牛。
au·ro·ra [ɔːˈrɔːrə; ɔˋrɔrə] ***n.*** **1.** 极光;曙光,晓光。**2.** 〔A-〕【罗神】曙光女神。~ **australis** [ɔːsˈtreilis; ɔsˋtrelɪs] 南极光。~ **borealis** [bɔːriˈeilis; ˏborɪˋelɪs] 北极光。~ **polaris** [pəuˈlɛəris; poˋlɛris] 极光。~ **yellow** 镉黄色。
au·ro·ral [ɔːˈrɔːrəl; ɔˋrorəl] ***a.*** **1.** 极光的;曙光的。**2.** 玫瑰红的。
au·rous [ˈɔːrəs; ˋɔrəs] ***a.*** **1.** 金的,含金的。**2.**【化】亚金的。
au·rum [ˈɔːrəm; ˋɔrəm] ***n.*** 〔L.〕【化】金。
AUS = Army of the United States 美国陆军。
Aus. = **1.** Australia. **2.** Austria. **3.** Austrian.
aus·cul·tate [ˈɔːskəlteit; ˋɔskəlˏtet] ***vt.***, ***vi.*** 【医】听诊。**-ta·tion** ***n.*** [ˌɔːskəlˈteiʃən; ˏɔskəlˋteʃən] 听诊。**-ta·tor** ***n.*** 听诊者;听诊器。
aus·pex [ˈɔːspeks; ˋɔspɛks] ***n.*** (*pl.* ***aus·pic·es*** [-pəsiːz; -pəsiz])(古代罗马的)鸟兽声迹占卜者。
aus·pi·cate [ˈɔːspikeit; ˋɔspəˏket] ***vt.*** 创始,开张,举行…开幕礼。— ***vi.*** 〔废〕占卜,预言。
aus·pice [ˈɔːspis; ˋɔspɪs] ***n.*** **1.** 前兆,吉兆。**2.** (根据鸟的飞行而进行的)占卜。**3.** 〔常 *pl.*〕保护,赞助;主办。***take ~s*** 卜吉凶。***under favourable ~s*** 吉利,顺遂。***under the ~s of*** 由…主办(主持);在…保护[赞助]下。
aus·pi·cial [ɔːsˈpiʃəl; ɔˋspɪʃəl] ***a.*** **1.** 预言的;占卜的。**2.** 吉兆的,幸运的。
aus·pi·cious [ɔːsˈpiʃəs; ɔˋspɪʃəs] ***a.*** **1.** 吉兆的,吉利的,吉祥的。**2.** 幸运的,顺利的。**-ly** ***ad.*** 吉祥如意地;幸而。**-ness** ***n.*** 吉兆,吉祥。
Aus·sie [ˈɔsi; ˋɔsɪ] ***n.*** 〔俚〕澳大利亚人[军人]。
Aus·ten [ˈɔstin; ˋɔstɪn] ***n.*** 奥斯汀〔姓氏〕。
aus·ten·ite [ˈɔːstənait; ˋɔstəˏnaɪt] ***n.*** 【冶】奥氏体〔钢的结构〕。~ **steel** 奥氏体钢。
Aus·ter [ˈɔːstə; ˋɔstɚ] 〔L.〕〔诗〕南风〔拟人化的说法〕。
aus·tere [ɔsˈtiə; ɔˋstɪr] ***a.*** **1.** 严格的,严厉的。**2.** 严肃的;自我克制的;苦行的。**3.** 朴素的;质朴的。**4.** 苦涩的。**-ly** ***ad.*** **-ness** ***n.***
aus·ter·i·ty [ɔsˈteriti; ɔˋstɛrətɪ] ***n.*** **1.** 严格;严肃。**2.** 简朴,朴素。**3.** 苦涩味。**4.** 〔常 *pl.*〕苦行。**5.** (经济的)紧缩。~ **program** 经济紧缩方案〔如减少消费,增加出口〕。
Aus·tin [ˈɔstin; ˋɔstɪn] ***n.*** 奥斯汀〔姓氏〕。
aus·tral [ˈɔːstrəl; ˋɔstrəl] ***a.*** **1.** 南方的;向南的,偏南的。**2.** 〔A-〕= Australian.
Aus·tral. = **1.** Australasia. **2.** Australia.
Aus·tral·a·si·a [ˌɔstrəˈleiʒjə; ˏɔstrəlˋeʒə] ***n.*** 澳大利西亚〔澳大利亚大陆、新西兰和新西兰附近各岛的总称,连南太平洋诸岛全部包括在内时,统称 Oceania〕。
Aus·tral·a·sian [ˌɔstrəˈleiʒjən; ˏɔstrəlˋeʒən] ***a.*** 澳大利西亚的。— ***n.*** 澳大利西亚人。
Aus·tral·ia [ɔsˈtreiljə; ɔˋstreljə] ***n.*** 澳大利亚〔大洋洲〕。
Aus·tral·ian [ɔsˈtreiljən; ɔsˋtreljən] **I** ***a.*** 澳大利亚的,澳大利亚人的。**II** ***n.*** 澳大利亚人。~ **ballot** (上有全部候选人名单的)圈选选票。
Aus·tra·loid [ˈɔːstrəlɔid; ˋɔstrəˏlɔɪd] **I** ***a.*** 澳大利亚土著居民的。**II** ***n.*** 澳大利亚土著居民。
Aus·tra·sia [ɔːsˈtreiʒə; ɔsˋtreʒə, -ʃə] 奥斯特拉西亚〔六至八世纪法兰克墨洛温王国的极东部,包括现在法国东北部,比利时和西德〕。
Aus·tri·a [ˈɔstriə; ˋɔstrɪə] ***n.*** 奥地利〔欧洲〕。
Aus·tri·a-Hun·ga·ry [ˈɔːstriəˈhʌŋgəri; ˋɔstrɪəˋhʌŋgərɪ] ***n.*** (第一次世界大战前的)奥匈帝国。
Aus·tri·an [ˈɔstriən; ˋɔstrɪən] **I** ***a.*** 奥地利的;奥地利人的。**II** ***n.*** 奥地利人。
Aus·tro- *comb. f.* = Austria. *Austro*-German 德奥的。
Aus·tro-As·i·at·ic [ˌɔːstrəuˌeiʒiˈætik; ˏɔstroˏeʒɪˋætɪk] **I** ***a.*** 奥亚语系的,东南亚语言的。**II** ***n.*** 流行于东南亚的语言〔包括越南语等〕。
aut- *pref.* 〔用于元音前〕= auto-.
au·ta·coid [ˈɔːtəkɔid; ˋɔtəˏkɔɪd] ***n.*** 【生】自体有效物质。
au·tar·chy [ˈɔːtɑːki; ˋɔtɑrkɪ] ***n.*** **1.** 绝对主权;专制。**2.** = autarky. **-chi·cal** ***a.*** **-chi·cal·ly** ***ad.***
au·tar·ky [ˈɔːtɑːki; ˋɔtɑrkɪ] ***n.*** 自给自足(政策)。
au·te·cious [ɔːˈtiːʃəs; ɔˋtiʃəs] ***a.*** 单主寄生的;(雌雄)异苞同株的;单寄主的。
aut·e·col·o·gy [ˌɔːtiˈkɔlədʒi; ˏɔtəˋkɑlədʒɪ] ***n.*** 【生】个体生态学。
au·teur [əuˈtəː; oˋtɚ] ***n.*** (*pl.* ~*s*)〔F.〕表现自我的电影导演,性格导演。**-ism** ***n.*** **1.** 在电影导演中表现的个人风格。**2.** 性格导演主持拍摄的影片。
auth. = **1.** authentic. **2.** author(ess). **3.** authorized.
au·then·tic [ɔːˈθentik; ɔˋθɛntɪk] ***a.*** **1.** 可信的;可靠的,确实的;有根据的。**2.** 真的,真正的。**3.**【法】认证了的,正式的。~ *news* 可靠消息。~ *signature* 真正手迹的签字。*an ~ deed* 手续完备的地契。
au·then·tic·ate [ɔːˈθentikeit; ɔˋθɛntɪˏket] ***vt.*** 为…出具证据,证实;鉴定;认证。*The document was ~d by a seal.* 此文件有印鉴为凭。
au·then·ti·ca·tion [ɔːˌθentiˈkeiʃən; ɔˏθɛntɪˋkeʃən] ***n.*** 确定,鉴定,证明;认证。**-ti·ca·tor** ***n.*** 确定者,认证者。
au·then·tic·i·ty [ˌɔːθenˈtisiti; ˏɔθənˋtɪsətɪ] ***n.*** 确实,确实性;真伪。
au·thor [ˈɔːθə; ˋɔθɚ] **I** ***n.*** **1.** 著者,作家。**2.** 著作物,作品。**3.** 创造者;发起人。*Scott is his favorite ~.* 他喜欢读司各脱(的作品)。*the ~ of mischief* 祸首;为非作歹者。***the A- of all being*** 造物主,上帝,神。**II** ***vt.*** 〔美〕**1.** 写,写作。**2.** 创造,创始。~ *a book* 写一本书。**3.** 【自】(在计算机上)制作(网页)。~ *a design* 设计一个图样。~ **catalog** (图书馆中)按作(译)者编排的图书目录。
au·thor·ess [ˈɔːθəris; ˋɔθɚɪs] ***n.*** 女作家〔通常仍用 author〕。
au·tho·ri·al [ɔːˈθɔːriəl; ɔˋθorɪəl] ***a.*** 著者的,作者的。
au·thor·ise [ˈɔːθəraiz; ˋɔθəˏraɪz] ***vt.*** = authorize.
au·tho·ri·tar·i·an [ɔːˌθɔriˈtɛəriən; əˏθɔrəˋtɛrɪən] **I** ***a.*** 权力主义的,命令[独裁]主义的。**II** ***n.*** 独裁主义者,命令主义者。**-ism** ***n.*** 命令主义。
au·thor·i·ta·tive [ɔːˈθɔritətiv; əˋθɔrəˏtetɪv] ***a.*** **1.** 有权威的,可靠的。**2.** 靠权力的;命令式的。**3.** 当局的,官方的。*an ~ opinion* 权威意见。*an ~ person* 权威人士。~ *information* 官方消息。**-ly** ***ad.*** **-ness** ***n.***
au·thor·i·ty [ɔːˈθɔriti; əˋθɔrətɪ] ***n.*** **1.** 权威,威信;权力,权柄;权限,职权,权能。**2.** 工程管理处[局,委员会等];〔*pl.*〕当局,官方。**3.** 根据,凭据。**4.** 权威者,泰斗,大家。**5.**【法】判决例,先例。**6.** 代理权。*an organ of ~* 权力机关。*the local authorities* 地方当局。*That is no ~.* 那不能做证据。*an academic ~* 学术权威。***the authorities concerned = the proper authorities*** 有关方面,当局。***by the ~ of*** 以…的权力;得…许可。***on good ~*** 由可靠方面,由确实根据。***on one's own ~*** 据一己之见,凭独断。***On whose ~?*** 得何人许可? ***those in ~*** 有权有势的人们,当权者。***with ~*** 凭威信,有权威。
au·thor·i·za·tion [ˌɔːθəraiˈzeiʃən; ˏɔθərəˋzeʃən] ***n.*** **1.**

A

授权,委任。2. 认可,核准。*without* ～ 擅自。

au·thor·ize [ˈɔːθəraiz; ˋɔθə͵raɪz] *vt*. 1. 授权,委托,委任。2. 批准,认可,允许。3. 正式承认,公认。*The city ~d a housing project*. 市政当局批准了盖房计划。*an expression ~d by custom* 约定俗成的用语。*be ~d to act for sb*. 被授权充当某人的代理人。**-iz·a·ble** *a*. 可授权的;可批准的;可认定的。

au·thor·ized [ˈɔːθəraizd; ˋɔθə͵raɪzd] *a*. 公认的,审定的,核准的。*an* ～ *agent* 指定的代理人。～ *capital* (公司被批准发放的)股额。*an* ～ *textbook* 审定的教科书。*an* ～ *translation* 经原著人认可的翻译。***Authorized Version*** 钦定圣经译本〔1611 年英王 James 一世核定发行的英译圣经,亦称 King James Version〕。

au·thor·ship [ˈɔːθəʃip; ˋɔθɚ͵ʃɪp] *n*. 1. 作者的身分[资格,职业]。2. 原作者。3. (谣言等的)来源。*a poem of unknown* ～ 作者不详的诗。

au·tism [ˈɔːtizəm; ˋɔtɪzəm] *n*.【心】孤独性;自我中心。**au·tis·tic** [-ˈtistik; -ˋtɪstɪk] *a*.

au·to [ˈɔːtəu; ˋɔto] I *n*. (*pl*. *~s*) 〔美口〕汽车。～ **boat** 汽艇。**~bus** 〔美〕公共汽车。～ **cade** 〔美〕汽车队,一长列汽车。～ **car** 〔古〕汽车。～ **court** 汽车旅馆。～ **parts** 汽车零件。～ **road** 汽车路。II *vi*. 坐汽车。

auto- *comb*. *f*. 1. 自,自己,自身: *auto*biography. 2. 自动: *auto*alarm. 3. 汽车: *auto*cade.

au·to·a·larm [ˈɔːtəuəˌlɑːm; ˋɔtoəˋlɑrm] *n*. 自动报警器。

au·to·bahn [ˈɔːtəubɑːn; ˋauto͵bɑn] *n*. (*pl*. *-en* [-ən; -ən]) 〔G.〕高速公路,汽车干路。

au·to·bike [ˈɔːtəubaik; ˋɔtə͵baɪk] *n*. 〔美口〕机器脚踏车。

au·to·bi·og·ra·pher [ˌɔːtəubaiˈɔgrəfə; ͵ɔtəbaɪˋɑgrəfɚ] *n*. 自传作者。

au·to·bi·o·graph·ic, au·to·bi·o·graph·i·cal [ˈɔtəuˌbaiəuˈgræfik(əl); ͵ɔtə͵baɪəˋgræfɪk(əl)] *a*. 自传(式)的。

au·to·bi·og·ra·phy [ˌɔːtəubaiˈɔgrəfi; ͵ɔtəbaɪˋɑgrəfɪ] *n*. 自传;自传文学。

au·to·boat [ˈɔːtəubəut; ˋɔtə͵bot] *n*. 汽艇。

au·to·bus [ˈɔːtəubʌs; ˋɔto͵bʌs] *n*. 〔美俚〕公共汽车。

au·to·cade [ˈɔːtəukeid; ˋɔto͵ked] *n*. 〔美〕(汽)车队(伍)。

au·to·car [ˈɔːtəukɑː; ˋɔtə͵kɑr] *n*. 汽车。

au·to·ca·tal·y·sis [ˌɔːtəukəˈtælisis; ͵ɔtokəˋtæləsɪs] *n*.【化】自动催化(作用)。

au·to·ceph·a·lous [ɔːtəuˈsefələs; ͵ɔtəˋsɛfələs] *a*. (教会等)独立的,自治的。

au·to·chang·er [ˈɔːtəuˌtʃeindʒə; ˋɔtə͵tʃendʒɚ] *n*. (电唱机的)自动换片器。

au·to·chrome [ˈɔːtəukrəum; ˋɔtə͵krom] *n*. 彩色照片;彩色底片。

au·toch·thon [ɔːˈtɔkθən; ɔˋtɑkθən] *n*. (*pl*. ～(*e*)*s* [-θəˌniːz; -θə͵niz]) 1. 土著,原居民。2. 土生土长的动植物。3.【地】原地岩。

au·toch·tho·nal [ɔːˈtɔkθənəl; ɔˋtɑkθənl], **au·toch·tho·nous** [ɔːˈtɔkθənəs; ɔˋtɑkθənəs] *a*. 1. 土生的,本地的。2.【地】原地(生成)的。

au·to·cide [ˈɔːtəusaid; ˋɔto͵saɪd] *n*. 自我毁灭;撞车自毁,用撞车方式自杀。

au·to·clave [ˈɔːtəukleiv; ˋɔtə͵klev] I *n*. 压热器,高压消毒锅,高压蒸锅。II *vt*. 用高压锅消毒[烹煮等]。～ **treatment** 压热法。

au·to·cod·er [ˌɔːtəuˈkəudə; ͵ɔtoˋkodɚ] *n*.【自】自动编码器。

au·to·co·her·er [ɔːtəukəˈhiərə; ͵ɔtokəˋhɪrɚ] *n*.【无】自动粉末检波器〔又作 autodetector〕。

au·to·coid [ˈɔːtəukɔid; ˋɔtə͵kɔɪd] *n*. 自体有效物质(指激素或抑素而言)。

au·to·col·li·ma·tion [ˌɔːtəuˌkɔləˈmeiʃən; ͵ɔto͵kɑləˋmeʃən] *n*.【物】自准直。

au·to·cor·re·la·tion [ˌɔːtəuˌkɔrəˈleiʃən; ͵ɔto͵kɑrəˋleʃən] *n*.【自】自相关。

au·toc·ra·cy [ɔːˈtɔkrəsi; ɔˋtɑkrəsɪ] *n*. 1. 独裁政治,专制政治。2. 独裁权。3. 独裁政府,专制国家。

au·to·crat [ˈɔːtəukræt; ˋɔtə͵kræt] *n*. 1. 独裁君主,专制君主;独裁者。2. 专横霸道的人。

au·to·crat·ic, au·to·crat·i·cal [ˌɔːtəuˈkrætik(əl); ͵ɔtəˋkrɪtɪk(əl)] *a*. 独裁的,专制的。**-i·cal·ly** *ad*.

au·to·crat·rix [ɔːˈtɔkrətriks; ɔˋtɑkrətrɪks] *n*. (旧俄的)专制女皇。

au·to·crit·i·cism [ˌɔːtəuˈkritisizəm; ͵ɔtəˋkrɪtəsɪzəm] *n*. 自我评定;自我反省,自我批评。

au·to·cy·cle [ˈɔːtəusaikl; ˋɔtə͵saɪkl] *n*. 机器脚踏车;摩托车。

au·to-da-fé [ˈɔːtəudɑːfei; ˋɔtodəˋfe] *n*. (*pl*. ***au·tos-*** [ˈɔːtəuz-; ˋɔtoz-]) 〔Sp.〕【宗】(中世纪宗教裁判所对异教徒的)死刑宣告[处决](特指火刑)。

au·to·di·dact [ˈɔːtəudiˌdækt; ͵ɔtodɪˋdækt] *n*. 自修者。

au·to·dom [ˈɔːtəudəm; ˋɔtodəm] *n*. 汽车制造与推销界。

au·to·drome [ˈɔːtəudrəum; ˋɔtodrom] *n*. 赛车跑道。

au·to·dyne [ˈɔːtəudain; ˋɔto͵daɪn] *a*., *n*. 1.【无】自拍(的),自差(的)。2. 自差接收机。

au·to·fin·ing [ˈɔːtəufainiŋ; ˋɔto͵faɪnɪŋ] *n*.【化】(石油)自动精炼,氢自供精炼。

au·tog·a·mous [ɔːˈtɔgəməs; ɔˋtɑgəməs] *a*.【植】自花受粉的;【动】自配的,自体受精的。

au·tog·a·my [ɔːˈtɔgəmi; ɔˋtɑgəmɪ] *n*.【动】自体受精;【植】自花受粉。

au·to·gen·e·sis [ˌɔːtəuˈdʒenisis; ͵ɔtoˋdʒɛnəsɪs] *n*.【生】自然发生。

au·tog·e·nous [ɔːˈtɔdʒinəs; ɔˋtɑdʒənəs] *a*. 1.【生】自生的;自体的。2. 气焊的。～ **soldering** 气焊法。～ **vaccine** 自体菌苗。

au·tog·e·ny [ɔːˈtɔdʒini; ɔˋtɑdʒɪnɪ] *n*.【生】自然发生;单性生殖。

au·to·gi·ro [ɔːtəuˈdʒaiərəu; ͵ɔtoˋdʒaɪro] *n*. = autogyro.

au·to·graft [ˈɔːtəugrɑːft; ˋɔto͵græft] *n*.【医】自体移植。

au·to·graph [ˈɔːtəugrɑːf; ˋɔtə͵græf] I *n*. 1. 亲笔,自署。2. 手稿。3. 真迹石版复制品。II *a*. 亲笔的,自署的。*an* ～ *album* 请人题字的纪念册。*an* ～ *fiend* 〔美俚〕爱用纪念册请人题字的人。III *vt*. 1. 亲笔写,自书,自署,署名。2. 用石版术复制。

au·to·graph·ic, au·to·graph·i·cal [ɔːtəuˈgræfik(əl); ɔtəˋgræfɪk(əl)] *n*. 1. 亲笔写成的。2. 亲笔签名的。3. 用石版复制的。

au·tog·ra·ph·o·me·ter [ˌɔːtəugrəˈfɔmitə; ͵ɔtogrəˋfɑmɪtɚ] *n*. 自动图示仪。

au·tog·ra·phy [ɔːˈtɔgrəfi; ɔˋtɑgrəfɪ] *n*. 1. 亲笔书写。2. 亲笔写的字。3.【印】石版复制术。

au·to·gra·vure [ˌɔːtəugræˈvjuə; ͵ɔtogrəˋvjʊr] *n*.【印】照相版雕刻法。

au·to·gy·ro [ˈɔːtəuˈdʒaiərəu; ͵ɔtoˋdʒaɪro] *n*. 自转旋翼飞机〔现已为直升机取代〕。

au·to·harp [ˈɔːtəuˌhɑːp; ˋɔto͵hɑrp] *n*. 自鸣筝〔一种古琴〕。

au·to·hyp·no·sis, au·to·hyp·no·tism [ˈɔːtəuhipnəusis, -nətizəm; ͵ɔtohɪpˋnosɪs, -nətɪzəm] *n*.【医】自我催眠。

au·to·im·mune [ˌɔːtəuiˈmjuːn; ͵ɔtoɪˋmjun] *a*. 自体免疫的。**au·to·im·mu·i·ty** [-niti; -nətɪ] *n*. 自我免疫性。

au·to·in·fec·tion [ˈɔːtəuinˈfekʃən; ͵ɔto·ɪnˋfɛkʃən] *n*.【医】自体感染。

au·to·in·oc·u·la·tion [ˈɔːtəuiˌnɔkjuˈleiʃən; ͵ɔtoɪn͵ɑkjʊˋleʃən] *n*.【医】自体接种。

au·to·in·tox·i·ca·tion [ˈɔːtəuinˌtɔksiˈkeiʃən; ˏɔtoɪnˏtɑksəˋkeʃən] *n*. 【医】自体中毒。

au·to·ist [ˈɔːtəuist; ˋɔtoɪst] *n*. 〔美口〕开汽车的人;乘车旅行的人。(= motorist)。

au·to·ki·net·ic [ˈɔːtəukaiˈnetik; ˏɔtəkaɪˋnɛtɪk] *a*. 自动运动的。

au·tol·o·gous [ɔːˈtɔləgəs; ɔˋtɑləgəs] *a*. 自体同源的,自体固有的。

au·tol·y·sate [ˌɔːtəuˈlaiseit, ɔːˈtɔliseit; ˏɔtəˋlaɪset, ɔˋtɑlɪset] *n*. 自溶产物。

au·to·ly·sin [ˌɔːtəuˈlaisin; ˏɔtəˋlaɪsɪn] *n*. 【生化】自溶素。

au·toly·sis [ɔːˈtɔlisis; ɔˋtɑləsɪs] *n*. 【生化】自溶,自体溶解。

au·to·lyze [ˈɔːtəlaiz; ˋɔtəˏlaɪz] *vt*., *vi*. (使)自溶,(使)自体分解。

au·to·man [ˈɔːtəumən; ˋɔtəˏmən] *n*. 汽车制造商(= automaker)。

au·to·mat [ˈɔːtəumæt; ˋɔtəˏmæt] *n*. 1. (食物的)自动售货机。2. 自动售货饮食店,自助食堂。3. 自动装置;自动开关。4. 自动枪[炮];自动照相机。

au·tom·a·ta [ɔːˈtɔmətə; ɔˋtɑmətə] *n*. automaton 的复数。

au·to·mate [ˈɔːtəmeit; ˋɔtəˏmet] *vt*. 1. 使(工厂、工序等)自动化。2. 使用自动化技术于(某方面)。*~d teaching* 自动控制教学,自动化教学。—*vi*. 自动化。*Many plants have begun to ~*. 许多工厂已开始实行自动化生产。~**d-teller machine** 自动柜员机,自动取款机。

au·to·mat·ic [ˌɔːtəˈmætik; ˏɔtəˋmætɪk] **I** *a*. 1. 自动的;机械的。2. 【生理】自动性的,无意识的。**II** *n*. 1. 自动机械;自动装置。2. 自动手枪。~ **cashier** 现金自动出纳机。~ **following** 自动跟踪 ~ **numbering machine** 自动号码机。~ **pilot** 【空】自动驾驶仪。~ **spotter** 【空】自动侦示机。~ **sprinkler** 自动灭火器;撒水装置。

au·to·ma·tic·i·ty [ˌɔːtəməˈtisiti; ɔˏtɑməˋtɪsətɪ] *n*. 1. 自动,自动性。2. 自动化程度。

au·to·ma·tion [ˌɔːtəˈmeiʃən; ˏɔtəˋmeʃən] *n*. 自动化,自动操作。

au·tom·a·tism [ɔːˈtɔmətizəm; ɔˋtɑməˏtɪzəm] *n*. 1. 自动,自动作用。2. 【生理】自动性;无意识行为。

au·tom·a·tize [ɔːˈtɔmətaiz; ɔˋtɑməˏtaɪz] *vt*. 1. 使自动化。2. 使用自动化技术于…。**-ti·za·tion** *n*.

au·to·mat·o·graph [ˌɔːtəuˈmætəgrɑːf; ˏɔtəˋmætəˏgræf] *n*. (人体无意识行动的)自动记录器(= autoscope)。

au·tom·a·ton [ɔːˈtɔmətən; ɔˋtɑməˏtɑn] *n*. (*pl*. *~s*, *-ta* [-tə; -tə]) 1. 自动物;自动玩具;自动开关;自动装置。2. 机械式工作的人。

au·to·mo·bile [ˈɔːtəməubiːl, Am. ˌɔːtəməuˈbiːl; ˋɔtəməˏbil, ˏɔtəˋmobɪl] **I** *n*. 〔主美〕汽车。**II** *vi*. 开汽车;坐汽车。**III** *a*. 自动的。*an ~ torpedo* 自动鱼雷。

au·to·mo·bil·ism [ˌɔːtəˈməubilizəm; ˏɔtəˋməˋbɪlɪzəm] *n*. 〔美〕汽车使用法[开法]。

au·to·mo·bil·ist [ˌɔːtəˈməubilist; ˏɔtəməbɪlɪst] *n*. 〔美〕开汽车的人。

au·to·mor·phic [ˌɔːtəuˈmɔːfik; ˏɔtəˋmɔrfɪk] *a*. 1. 【地】自形的。2. 【数】自守的,自同构的。

au·to·mo·tive [ˌɔːtəuˈməutiv; ˏɔtəˋmotɪv] *a*. 1. 自动的;自动机的。2. 汽车的。*the ~ industry* 汽车制造业。

au·to·nom·ic [ˌɔːtəuˈnɔmik; ˏɔtəˋnɑmɪk] *a*. 1. 自治的。2. 【解】自主的。3. 【植】自发的。

au·ton·o·mist [ɔːˈtɔnəmist; ɔˋtɑnəmɪst] *n*. 主张自治的人。

au·ton·o·mous [ɔːˈtɔnəməs; ɔˋtɑnəməs] *a*. 1. 自治的,自主的。2. 【植、生】自发的。*an ~ republic* 自治共和国。~ ***tariffs*** 国定税率,自主关税。

au·ton·o·my [ɔːˈtɔnəmi; ɔˋtɑnəmɪ] *n*. 1. 自治;自治权。2. 自治州;自治团体。3. 人身自由。4. 【哲】自律,意志自由。5. 【生】自发性。

au·to·nym [ˈɔːtəunim; ˋɔtənɪm] *n*. 1. 真名,本名[*opp*. pseudonym]。2. 署名作品,以真名发表的作品。

au·to·pen [ˈɔːtəupen; ˋɔtopɛn] *n*. 自动笔〔能模仿签名笔迹的装置。〕

au·to·phyte [ˈɔːtəufait; ˋɔtəˏfaɪt] *n*. 【植】自养植物。**-phyt·ic** [-ˈfitik; -ˋfɪtɪk] *a*. **-phyt·i·cal·ly** *ad*.

au·to·pi·a [ˈɔːtəupiə; ˋɔtopɪə] *n*. 汽车专用区。

au·to·pi·lot [ˈɔːtəupailət; ˋɔtoˏpaɪlət] *n*. 1. 【空】自动驾驶仪。2. [口]放任自流不顾后果。

au·to·plas·ty [ˈɔːtəuplæsti; ˋɔtəˏplæstɪ] *n*. 【医】自体移植[成形]术。

au·top·sy [ˈɔːtəpsi; ˋɔtɑpsɪ] *n*. 1. 尸体解剖[剖检]。2. (事后的)分析,检查。

au·top·tic, au·topt·i·cal [ɔːˈtɔptik(əl); ɔˋtɑptɪk(əl)] *a*. 以实地考察为根据的。*an ~ report* 实地考察报告。

au·to·ra·di·o·graph [ˈɔːtəuˈreidiəgrɑːf; ˏɔtəˋredɪəˏgræf] *n*. 自动射线照相。**-y** *n*. 自动射线照相术。

au·to·ro·ta·tion [ˌɔːtəurəuˈteiʃən; ˏɔtoroˋteʃən] *n*. 自动旋转;自转。

au·to·route [ˈɔːtəuruːt; ˋɔtoˏrut] *n*. (法语国家的)高速公路。

au·to·scope [ˈɔːtəuskəup; ˋɔtoskop] *n*. 1. 【医】自检器。2. 【机】点火检查示波器。

au·to·some [ˈɔːtəusəum; ˋɔtəˏsom] *n*. 常染色体。**-somal** [-ˈsəuməl; -ˋsoməl] *a*.

au·to·sta·bil·i·ty [ˌɔːtəustəˈbiliti; ˏɔtostəˋbɪlətɪ] *n*. 【物】固有安定性;自动稳定性;内在稳定性。

au·to·stra·da [ˌautəuˈstrɑːdɑː; ˏautoˋstrɑdɑ] *n*. (*pl*. ***-strade*** [ˌautəuˈstrɑːdei; ˏautoˋstrɑde]) 〔It.〕(汽车的)高速公路。

au·to·sug·ges·tion [ˈɔːtəusəˈdʒestʃən; ˏɔtosəˋdʒɛstʃən] *n*. 【心】自我暗示。

au·to·tel·ic [ˌɔːtəuˈtelik; ˏɔtoˋtɛlɪk] *a*. 自有其目的的;为其本身的。**-tel·ism** *n*. 艺术创作有其自身的目的。

au·to·tim·er [ˈɔːtəutaimə; ˋɔtotaɪmɚ] *n*. 自动定时器。

au·tot·o·mize [ɔːˈtɔtəmaiz; ɔˋtɑtəˏmaɪz] *vi*., *vt*. 【动】(使)自割;(使)自行分裂〔如螃蟹受到袭击时,自行把钳子卸掉〕。

au·tot·o·my [ɔːˈtɔtəmi; ɔˋtɑtəmɪ] *n*. 【动】自割,自截,自切。**-tom·ic** [ˌɔːtəuˈtɔmik; ˏɔtoˋtɑmɪk] *a*.

au·to·tox·e·mi·a, au·to·tox·ae·mi·a [ˌɔːtəutɔkˈsiːmiə; ˏɔtotɑkˋsimɪə] *n*. 自体中毒。

au·to·tox·in [ˌɔːtəuˈtɔksin; ˏɔtəˋtɑksɪn] *n*. 自体毒素。

au·to·trans·form·er [ˌɔːtəutrænsˈfɔːmə; ˏɔtotrænsˋfɔrmɚ] *n*. 【电】自耦变压器。

au·to·trans·fu·sion [ˌɔːtəutrænsˈfjuːʒən; ˏɔtotrænsˋfjuʒən] *n*. 自体输血法(将外科手术病人的血存储在贮器内,手术后输回其体内的一种输血法)。

au·to·troph [ˈɔːtəutrɔf; ˋɔtəˏtrɑf] *n*. 【生】自养生物。

au·to·troph·ic [ˌɔːtəuˈtrɔfik; ˏɔtəˋtrɑfɪk] *n*. 【生】自养的〔指植物通过光合作用,细菌通过化学合成作用自行制造食物〕。

au·to·truck [ˈɔːtəutrʌk; ˋɔtəˏtrʌk] *n*. 运货汽车,卡车(= motor truck)。

au·to·type [ˈɔːtəutaip; ˋɔtəˏtaɪp] **I** *n*. 1. 【印】单色印相法。2. 复印品,复制品。**II** *vt*. 用单色印相法复印;影印;复制。

au·to·work·er [ˈɔːtəuwəːkə; ˋɔtəˏwɝkɚ] *n*. 汽车厂工人。

au·tox·i·da·tion [ɔːˌtɔksiˈdeiʃən; ɔˏtɑksəˋdeʃən] *n*. 自动氧化。**-da·tive** [-tiv; tɪv] *a*.

au·tumn [ˈɔːtəm; ˋɔtəm] *n*. 1. 秋,秋季〔英国为八、九、十月;美国普通称 fall, 指九、十、十一月〕。2. 成熟期;凋落期;晚年。~ *harvesting* 秋收。***the ~ of life*** 中年。

au·tum·nal [ɔːˈtʌmnəl; ɔˋtʌmnḷ] *a*. 1. 秋的。2. 秋天

A

开花的,秋天结实的,秋熟的。3. 已过壮年的,中年的,近衰老的。~ **equinox** 秋分。~ **tints** (树叶的)秋色,红叶;霜叶。

au·tun·ite [ˈɔːtənait; ˋɔtənaɪt] *n*. 钙铀云母。

aux. = auxiliary.

au·xa·nom·e·ter [ˌɔːksəˈnɔmitə; ˏɔksəˋnɑmɪtɚ] *n*. 植物生长计〔用以测定植物生长速度〕。

aux·e·sis [ɔːgˈziːsis; ɔgˋzisɪs] *n*.【生】细胞增大性生长。**aux·et·ic** [-ˈzetik; -ˋzɛtɪk] *a*.

aux·il·ia·ry [ɔːgˈziljəri; ɔgˋzɪljərɪ] **I** *a*. 1. 辅助的。2. 补充的,备用的。3. 副的。~ *coins* 辅币。~ *troops* 援军。*an* ~ *vessel* 辅助舰。*an* ~ *verb*【语法】助动词。**II** *n*. 1. 辅助者。2. 辅助设备;辅助装置。3. 补助舰〔如油船,供应船〕。4. 〔*pl*.〕(外国来的)援军。5.【语法】助动词。6. 附属机构,附属团体。*This club has a women's* ~. 这个俱乐部有妇女的附属机构。

aux·i·mone [ˈɔːksiməun; ˋɔksəˏmon] *n*. 植物激长素。

aux·in [ˈɔːksin; ˋɔksɪn] *n*. (植物)生长素。

aux·o·chrome [ˈɔːksəkrəum; ˋɔksəˏkrom] *n*. 助色团〔用以使染料固着在织物上〕。

aux·o·troph [ˈɔːksətrɔf; ˋɔksəˏtrɑf] *n*.【生】营养缺陷型,营养缺陷体。

A.V. = Authorized Version.

av. = avenue; average; avoirdupois.

a.v., A/V = according to value.

a·vail [əˈveil; əˋvel] **I** *vi*. 〔多用否定结构〕有益于,有利于,有助于。*Nothing ~ed against the flood*. 什么都无助于防治这次洪水。*No words ~ed to pacify him*. 说什么都不能使他平静下来。— *vt*. 使对某人有利〔有益〕。*It ~ed him nothing*. 这对他毫无用处。~ **oneself of** (*an opportunity*) 利用时机,趁(机会)(*He ~ed himself of every opportunity*. 他利用了一切机会)。**II** *n*. 1. 效用〔现多用于成语中〕。2. 〔*pl*.〕〔古〕利益,收益。*a weapon of little* ~ 用处很少的武器。*the ~s of the sale* 销货收益。**be of** ~ 有用,有益(*Of what* ~ *is it*? 那有什么益处?) **be of no** (**little**) ~ 完全无用,全然无益;不怎样有用。**to little** ~ 不大有用。**to no** ~ = **without** ~ 无益,徒劳,无效。

a·vail·a·bil·i·ty [əˌveiləˈbiliti; əˏveləˋbɪlətɪ] *n*. 1. 有效,有益,可利用,可得到。2. 可得到的东西[人员]。3. (候选人的)当选可能性。*local availabilities* 可从当地获得的东西。*the* ~ *of a candidate* 候选人的当选可能性。

a·vail·a·ble [əˈveiləbl; əˋveləbl̩] *a*. 1. 有用的,可利用的。2. 可以得到的,可以买到的。3. 有效的。4. 有当选希望的;愿意参加竞选的。*He is not* ~ *for the job*. 他不适宜做这个工作。~ *water* 有效水分。*employ all* ~ *means* 用尽一切方法。*ticket* ~ *on day of issue only* 限当日通用[有效]的票子。*This book is not* ~ *here*. 这里没有这本书。*The doctor is* ~ *now*. 医生现在有空了。**-bly** *ad*. 有效地。**-ness** *n*. 有利,有效,效用,利用。

av·a·lanche [ˈævəlɑːnʃ; ˋævlˏæntʃ] **I** *n*. 1. 雪崩,崩落,崩坠。2. 蜂拥而来,纷至沓来;雪崩式打击。3.【物】离子雪崩。*with the momentum of an* ~ 以排山倒海之势。*an* ~ *of mail* 邮件的纷至沓来。*an* ~ *of blows* 劈头盖脸的打击。**II** *vi*. 雪崩;雪崩似地落下。**III** *vt*. 大量涌进(市场等)。

a·vant-cou·ri·er [ˈævɑ̃ːŋˈkuriə; ævɑ̃ˋkurɪɚ] *n*. 〔F.〕1. 先驱。2. 〔*pl*.〕前锋,先锋。

a·vant-garde [ˈævɑ̃ːŋˈgɑːrd; ɑvɑ̃ ˋgɑrd] **I** *n*. 〔F.〕1. 先锋,先驱。2. (艺术的)先锋派。**II** *a*. 1. 先锋的,先驱的。2. 先锋派的,标新立异的。~ *writers* 先锋派作家。**-ism** *n*. (文学艺术上的)先锋派主义。

av·a·rice [ˈævəris; ˋævərɪs] *n*. 贪心,贪婪。

av·a·ri·cious [ˌævəˈriʃəs; ˏævəˋrɪʃəs] *a*. 贪心的,贪婪的。~ *of wealth* 贪财。**-ly** *ad*. **-ness** *n*.

A·va·ru·a [ˌɑːvəˈruə; ˏɑvəˋruə] *n*. 阿瓦鲁阿〔库克群岛(新)首府〕。

a·vast [əˈvɑːst; əˋvæst] *int*.【海】停住! **A- heaving.** 停止曳绳!

av·a·tar [ˌævəˈtɑː; ˏævəˋtɑr] *n*. 1. (印度教中神的)下凡。2. 化身;体现,具体化。*the divinest* ~ *of common sense* 常识的最佳体现。

a·vaunt [əˈvɔːnt; əˋvɔnt] *int*. 〔古〕去! 走开!

AVC = 1. American Veterans Committee 美国退伍军人委员会。2. automatic volume control【无】自动音量控制。

avdp. = avoirdupois.

a·ve [ˈɑːvi; ˋɑvɪ] **I** *int*. 1. 欢迎! 2. 一路平安! 再会! **II** *n*. 1. 欢迎;一路平安。2. 〔A-〕= Ave Maria【天主】万福马利亚〔追念圣母马利亚的祈祷〕。~ **bell** 祈祷报时钟。

Ave. = Avenue.

A·ve·ling [ˈeivliŋ; ˋevlɪŋ] *n*. 埃夫林〔姓氏〕。

a·venge [əˈvendʒ; əˋvɛndʒ] *vt*. 为…报仇,替…雪耻;为…对…报复。~ *one's father* [*father's wrongs*] 报父仇。*I will* ~ *you*. 我一定为你复仇。*He ~d himself on his enemies*. 他对仇人实行报复。*She ~d her mother's death upon the Nazi soldier*. 她惩处了纳粹士兵以报杀母之仇。— *vi*. 报复,复仇。

a·veng·er [əˈvendʒə; əˋvɛndʒɚ] *n*. 报仇者。

av·ens [ˈævinz; ˋævɪnz] *n*.【植】水杨梅属植物。

a·ven·tu·rine [əˈventjurin; əˋvɛntʃərɪn] *n*. 1. 金星玻璃〔含有金色细粒的不透明玻璃,作装饰用〕。2.【矿】砂金石。

av·e·nue [ˈævinjuː; ˋævəˏnju] *n*. 1. 林荫路;道路;通路。2. 〔美〕(南北向)街道〔东西向者称 street〕。3. 〔喻〕手段,途径。*an* ~ *to success* 成功之道。*an* ~ *of escape* 逃路。

a·ver [əˈvəː; əˋvɝ] *vt*. 1. 宣告(某事)千真万确,断言(*that*)。2.【法】证明。*I* ~ *that I have spoken the truth*. 我断言,我说了真话。*as he ~s* 如他所说。

av·er·age [ˈævəridʒ; ˋævərɪdʒ] **I** *n*. 1. 平均,平均数。2. 一般水平,平均标准。3.【商】海损;海损费用;(给领航的)报酬。*arithmetical* [*geometrical*] ~【数】相加[相乘]平均数,算术[几何]平均数。*general* [*particular*] ~ 共同[单独]海损。*petty* [*accustomed*] *~s* (支付给领航、港口等的)小额[例行]酬劳费。**above** [**below**] **the** ~ 平常以上[以下]。**on an** [**the**] ~ 平均;一般说来。**take** [**strike**] **an** ~ 平均起来,折衷,扯平算。**up to the** ~ 合一般标准。**II** *a*. 1. 平均的。2. 普通的,一般的。3.【商】按海损估价的。*The* ~ *age of the boys here is ten*. 这些孩子的平均年龄是十岁。*students of* ~ *intelligence* 智力水平一般的学生。**III** *vt*. 1. 平均,均分。2. 平均是。*I* ~ *six hours work a day*. 我每天平均工作六小时。*If you* ~ *4 and 6, you get 5*. 4和6均分得5。— *vi*. 1. 平均。2. (为得到更有利的平均价格而)买进(或)卖出(更多的股票、货物等)。~ **down** [**up**] 以低于平均价格买进[以高于平均价格卖出]。~ **out** 1. 最终达到平衡。2. 达到平均数,平均为(*to*)(*The gain ~d out to 30 percent* 利润平均为百分之三十)。

a·ver·ment [əˈvəːmənt; əˋvɝmənt] *n*. 1. 断言,确定。2.【法】事实的陈述。

A·ver·nus [əˈvəːnəs; əˋvɝnəs] *n*. 1. 意大利一臭水湖〔在那不勒斯附近,传说湖边有一通道通往地狱〕。2. 地狱的入口,地狱。

a·verse [əˈvəːs; əˋvɝs] *a*. 1. 嫌恶的,反对的,不乐意的。2.【植】与茎方向相反的。**be** ~ **to** 〔后接名词、动名词或动词〕不喜欢,不爱,不愿意,讨厌。**-ness** *n*. 讨厌,嫌恶。

a·ver·sion [əˈvəːʃən; əˋvɝʒən] *n*. 1. 嫌恶,反感。2. 讨厌的人[东西]。3.【生】排斥。*one's pet* ~ 最厌恶的东西。**have an** ~ **to** [**for**] 讨厌,不爱,不喜欢。

a·vert [əˈvəːt; əˋvɝt] *vt*. **1.** 防止,避免。**2.** 避开,转移,把(脸、眼睛)转过去(*from*)。~ *one's glance from sth*. 避而不看某物。*He apologized to* ~ *trouble*. 他道歉以避免麻烦。

a·vert·i·ble [əˈvəːtəbl; əˋvɝtəbḷ] *a*. 可避开的,可防止的。

A·ver·tin [əˈvəːtin; əˋvɝtɪn] *n*. 阿佛丁〔一种口服麻醉剂的商标名,学名为 tribro-moethanol〕。

A·ves [ˈeiviːz; ˋeviz] *n*. 〔*pl*.〕〔L.〕【动】鸟纲。

A·ves·ta [əˈvestə; əˋvɝstə] *n*. 袄教经典。

A·ves·tan [əˈvestən; əˋvestən] **I** *a*. **1.** 袄教经典的。**2.** 用以写成袄教经典的印欧语;伊朗语。**II** *n*. 与古波斯语很接近的上述语言。

avg. = average.

av·gas [ˈævgæs; ˋæv ˏgæs] *n*. 航空汽油〔*av*iation *gas*oline 的缩略词〕。

a·vi·an [ˈeiviən; ˋevɪən] **I** *a*. 鸟类的;鸟纲的。**II** *n*. 鸟。

a·vi·a·rist [ˈeivjərist; ˋevɪərɪst] *n*. 飞禽饲养家;鸟类饲养家。

a·vi·ar·y [ˈeivjəri; ˋevɪˏɛrɪ] *n*. 鸟舍,飞禽饲养所。

a·vi·ate [ˈeivieit; ˋevɪˏet] *vi*. 飞行,驾驶飞机;航空。

a·vi·a·tion [ˌeiviˈeiʃən; ˏevɪˋeʃən] *n*. **1.** 飞行,航空。**2.** 飞行术,航空学。**3.** [集合词]飞机,军用飞机。**4.** 飞机制造业。~ **goggles** 航空眼镜。~ **ground** 飞机场。~ **meet** 飞行比赛会。~**'s spirit** 汽油。

a·vi·at·or [ˈeivieitə; ˋevɪˏetɚ] *n*. 飞行员,飞机师。*a civilian* ~民航飞机师。*a lady* ~〔美〕女飞行员。~ **glasses** 飞机师眼镜,金属框茶色镜片眼镜。~**'s ear** 〔口〕高空中耳炎。

a·vi·a·to·ri·al [ˌeiviəˈtɔːriəl; ˏevɪəˋtɔrɪəl] *a*. **1.** 航空的。**2.** 飞行员的。

a·vi·a·tress, a·vi·a·trix [ˈeivieitris, -triks; ˋevɪˋetrɪs, -trɪks] *n*. 女飞行员。

a·vi·cul·ture [ˈeivikʌltʃə; ˋevɪˏkʌltʃɚ] *n*. 养鸟;养鸟法,鸟类饲养。

av·id [ˈævid; ˋævɪd] *a*. **1.** 渴望的;贪婪的。**2.** 热心的。~ *for food* 渴望食物。*be* ~ *of* (*money*) 贪(财)。*an* ~ *reader of books* 热心的读者。

av·i·din [ˈævidin; ˋævədɪn] *n*. 【生化】抗生物素蛋白。

a·vid·i·ty [əˈviditi; əˋvɪdətɪ] *n*. **1.** 贪婪;饥渴;热望。**2.** 【化】亲合力,活动性。***with*** ~ 贪(*eat with* ~ 贪婪地吃)。

a·vi·e·tte [ˌeiviˈet; ˏevɪˋɛt] *n*. 小型滑翔机。

a·vi·fau·na [ˌeiviˈfɔːnə; ˏevɪˋfɔnə] *n*. (一地方或一国的)鸟类。

av·i·ga·tion [ˌæviˈgeiʃən; ˏævəˋgeʃən] *n*. 航空(术);空中导航。

av·i·ga·tor [ˈeivigeitə; ˋevɪgetɚ] *n*. 〔美〕飞机师;【空】领航员。

A·vi·gnon [əˈviːnjɔ̃ːŋ; aˏviˋnjɔ̃] *n*. 阿维尼翁〔法国城市〕。

a·vi·on [æˈvjɔ̃ːŋ; ˏaˋvjɔ̃] *n*. 〔F.〕军用飞机。~ ***de chasse*** [də fæs; də ʃas] 驱逐机。***par*** [pɑːr; par] ~ 航空邮寄。

a·vi·on·ics [ˌeiviˈɔniks; ˏevɪˋɑnɪks] *n*. 航空电子学;航空控制系统。

a·vir·u·lent [æˈvirjulənt; eˋvɪrjələnt] *a*. 无毒性的。

a·vi·so [əˈvaizəu; əˋvaɪzo] *n*. (*pl*. ~*s*) 〔Sp.〕**1.** 急件,急送公文。**2.** 通信艇。

a·vi·ta·min·o·sis [eiˌvaitəmiˈnəusis; eˏvaɪtəmɪnˋosɪs] *n*. 【医】维生素缺乏症。

AVM = Air Vice-Marshal.

avn. = aviation.

av·o·ca·do [ˌɑːvəˈkɑːdəu; ˏɑvəˋkɑdo] *n*. 【植】鳄梨,鳄梨树。

av·o·ca·tion [ˌævəuˈkeiʃən; ˏævəˋkeʃən] *n*. **1.** 副业,兼差。**2.** 〔罕〕正业,本职。**3.** 〔古〕消遣,娱乐。*He is a doctor by profession and a novelist by* ~. 他的职业是医生,副业是作家。

a·voc·a·to·ry [əˈvɔkətəri; əˋvɑkəˏtorɪ] *a*. 召回的,撤销的。*an* ~ *letter* 召回书。

av·o·cet [ˈævəuset; ˋævəˏsɛt] *n*. 【鸟】反嘴长脚鹬。

a·void [əˈvɔid; əˋvɔɪd] *vt*. **1.** 避,回避,避免,逃避;防止。**2.** 【法】使无效;撤销,废止。**3.** 〔废〕驱逐,逐出。~ *bad company* 避免和坏人来往。*I cannot* ~ *seeing him*. 我不能不会见他。~ *a purchase* 撤销一项购货。**-a·ble** [-əbl; -əbḷ] *a*.

a·void·ance [əˈvɔidəns; əˋvɔɪdəns] *n*. **1.** 回避,逃避。**2.** (牧师职位的)空缺。**3.** 【法】无效;废止。

avoir. = avoirdupois.

av·oir·du·pois [ˌævədəˈpɔiz; ˏævədəˋpɔɪz] *n*. **1.** 常衡〔16 ounces = 1 pound〕。**2.** 重量,体重。**3.** 〔美口〕肥胖。*5 lb*. ~ 常衡五磅。*a woman of much* ~ 异常肥胖的女人。~ **weight** 常衡。

a·vo·me·ter [əˈvɔmitə; əˋvɑmɪtɚ] *n*. 【电】安伏欧计,万用电表。

à vo·tre san·té [əˌvɔtr sɑːnˈtei; ɑˏvɔtrə sɑ̃ˋte] 〔F.〕〔祝酒词〕祝你健康! 为您的健康干杯!

a·vouch [əˈvautʃ; əˋvaʊtʃ] *vt*. **1.** 声音,断言。**2.** 保证,担保。**3.** 公开承认。— *vi*. 保证,担保(*for*);断言。**-ment** *n*. 声言;断言;保证。

a·vow [əˈvau; əˋvaʊ] *vt*. **1.** 声言,声明,承认。**2.** 【法】供认。~ *one's guilt* 认罪。~ *oneself* (*to be*) *in the wrong* 自认错误。~ ***oneself*** 自称为…(*He* ~*ed himself a patriot* 他自称是爱国者)。

a·vow·al [əˈvauəl; əˋvaʊəl] *n*. 声明,供认,承认。

a·vowed [əˈvaud; əˋvaʊd] *a*. 公然承认的,明言的。*an* ~ *work* 署名作品。*an* ~ *neutralist* 公开宣布中立的人。**-ly** *ad*.

a·vul·sion [əˈvʌlʃən; əˋvʌlʃən] *n*. **1.** 扯离,撕开。**2.** 【医】撕脱法,抽出术。**3.** 【法】河水改道后土地的转移〔指转入他人地产内〕。**4.** 撕裂开的部分。

a·vun·cu·lar [əˈvʌŋkjulə; əˋvʌŋkjələ] *a*. **1.** 叔伯的,似叔伯的。**2.** 〔废〕当铺的〔俚语当铺叫 uncle〕。

AW = **1.** Articles of War (美国)陆军法规。**2.** automatic weapon(s) 自动武器。**3.** actual weight 实际重量。**4.** aircraft warning 空袭警报。

aw [ɔː; ɔ] *int*. 哦! 噢! 〔表示抗议,厌恶,讨厌,怜悯等的感叹词〕。

a.w. = atomic weight.

a·wa [əˈwɑː, -ˈwɔː; əˋwɑ, -ˋwɔ] *ad*. 〔Scot.〕离开,远,那边(= away)。

AWACS, Awacs = airborne warning and control system 机载警报和控制系统。

a·wait [əˈweit; əˋwet] *vt*. 〔书〕等,等待;期待。~ *sb*. 等人。~ *a decision* 等待决定。*Awaiting the favor of your prompt attention*. 火速赐覆为盼〔信尾语〕。

a·wake [əˈweik; əˋwek] **I** *vt*. (***awoke*** [əˈwəuk; əˋwok], ***awaked***; ***awoke***, ***awaked***, ***awoken***) **1.** 唤起,叫醒,唤醒;提醒。**2.** 激起,激发,启发。~ *sb*. *from ignorance* 启人蒙昧。~ (*sb*.) ***to*** (*a sense of sin*) 激起(某人)(悔罪念头)。— *vi*. **1.** 醒。**2.** 觉醒,觉悟。奋起(*to*)。~ ***to a fact*** 开始发觉[领悟](某事)。~ ***to find*** …醒过来才知道[发现]。**II** *a*. 〔用作表语〕醒着,注意着,警戒着。*He tried to keep* ~. 他尽力醒着不睡。*He lay* ~. 他醒着躺在那里。*I was wide* ~. 我完全没有睡着。~ ***or asleep*** 无论醒着睡着。***be*** ~ ***to*** 不疏忽,深知。***be full*** ~ ***to*** 对…十分注意。***be wide*** ~ ***to*** 对…十分清醒。

a·wak·en [əˈweikən; əˋwekən] *vt*. 使觉醒,唤醒。*the* ~*ed people* 觉醒了的人民。~ *sb*.*'s sympathy* 唤起某人的同情心。— *vi*. 醒悟到,认识到(*to*)。~ *to the importance of* 认识到…的重要性。

A

a·wak·en·ing [əˈweikəniŋ; əˋwekənɪŋ] **I** ***n*. 1.** 醒,觉醒。**2.** 激励,启发。**II** ***a*.** 唤醒的;惊醒的。

a·ward [əˈwɔːd; əˋwɔrd] **I** ***vt*. 1.** 授与,给与;奖与。**2.** 断与,判归。~ *a prize to sb*. 授奖品给某人。~ *a damage of 1,000 dollars* 判定赔偿损失一千美元。**II** ***n*. 1.** 审判,裁定。**2.** 裁定书;裁定额。**3.** 奖品。

a·ware [əˈwɛə; əˋwɛr] ***a*.** 〔用作表语〕知道,晓得,发觉,觉得。***be*** ~ ***of*** (***that***) 知道,觉得。***become*** ~ ***of*** 发觉,注意到。***make sb*. ~ *that*** 提醒某人注意…。**-ness** ***n*.**

a·wash [əˈwɔʃ; əˋwɑʃ] ***a*., *ad*. 1.** (暗礁等)与水面齐平;被水覆盖着。**2.** 被波浪冲击[打湿]。**3.** 喝醉了的[地]。

a·way [əˈwei; əˋwe] **I** ***ad*. 1.** 离开。**2.** …去,…掉。**3.** 不在。**4.** 不断,继续,…下去。**5.** 到完,到底,完。**6.** 立刻。**7.**【棒球】退场 (= out)。**8.** 〔美〕远。★用于其他副词如 back, behind, down, off, up 等之前加强其义;常略作 'way, way. *go* ~去,走开。*run* ~逃掉。*work* ~做下去。*put* (*or lay*) ~收拾,放在一边。*fade* ~消失,褪色。~ *below the average* 远在平均以下,远在中等以下。~ (*to the*) *east* 远在东方。*turn* ~掉转身去。*He let the water boil* ~. 他听任水烧干。*Keep* ~ *from the fire*. 别靠近火。*give* ~放弃。*The sounds died* ~. 声音逐渐消逝了。***A-!*** 走开! ~ ***back*** 〔美口〕老早以前(~ *back in February* 早在二月里)。***A- with*** ...! 扫除掉,赶掉,拿开〔用于无动词的命令句或感叹句〕。***A- with him!*** 赶他出去! ***A- with it!*** 停止! 挪开! ***A- with you!*** 让开! 滚开! ***be*** ~ 不在,缺席;…去了 (*She is* ~ (*from home*) *today*. 她今天不在(家)。*He is* ~ *on journey* [*for the summer*]. 他旅行[避暑]去了)。***cannot*** ~ ***with*** 〔古〕不能忍耐[忍受]。***do*** ~ ***with*** 废除,干掉,杀死。***far and*** ~ …得多,最 (*far and* ~ *the best* 好得多)。***far*** ~ 很远,在很远地方。***Fire*** ~! 立刻开火! ***from*** ~ 〔美〕从远方。***make*** ~ ***with*** 废除 (*He made* ~ *with himself* 他自杀了)。***once and*** ~ 只一次,偶尔,间或。***out and*** ~ 远,甚,无比 (*out and* ~ *the best* 远为好;好得多)。***right*** [***straight***] ~ 马上,即刻。***Where*** ~? (船上所见物)是在什么方向[哪里]? **II** ***a*.** (运动)在对方场地上比赛的。

awe [ɔː; ɔ] **I** ***n*. 1.** 畏惧,敬畏。**2.** 〔古〕(使人敬畏的)威风。**3.** 怕。***be in*** ~ ***of*** 敬畏,怕。***be struck with*** ~ 懔然敬畏。***keep*** (*sb*.) ***in*** ~ 使(人)敬畏。***stand in*** ~ ***of*** 敬畏,怕。**II** ***vt*.** 使害怕,使敬畏。*be* ~*ed into obedience* [*silence*] 吓得乖乖服从[哑口无言]。

a·wear·y [əˈwiəri; əˋwɪrɪ] ***a*.** 〔诗〕 = weary.

a·weath·er [əˈweðə; əˋweðɚ] ***ad*.**【海】迎风,向风,向上风 (*opp*. alee)。***Helm*** ~! 迎风使舵!

a·weigh [əˈwei; əˋwe] ***a*.** 〔用作表语〕, ***ad*.**【海】(锚)快要离开水底,就要被拉上来。*with anchor* ~ 起锚。

awe·less [ˈɔːlis; ˋɔlɪs] ***a*. 1.** 〔古〕无威仪的,不会使人害怕的。**2.** 无畏惧的,大胆的。

awe·some [ˈɔːsəm; ˋɔsəm] ***a*. 1.** 可怕的;有威严的,使人敬畏的。**2.** 表示敬畏的。**3.** 〔俚〕极好的,棒极了的。*an* ~ *sight* 可怕的场面。*an* ~ *expression* 敬畏的表情。

awe-strick·en, awe-struck [ˈɔːstrikən, ˈɔːstrʌk; ˋɔ͵strɪkən, ˋɔ͵strʌk] ***a*.** 畏惧的,恐惧的,害怕的。

aw·ful [ˈɔːful; ˋɔful] **I** ***a*. 1.** 可怕的。**2.** 威风懔懔的,严肃的。**3.** [ˈɔːfl; ˋɔfl̩]〔口〕丑陋的,极坏的;厉害的;非常的,异常的;很大的。*die an* ~ *death* 死得可怕,死于非命。*an* ~ *miser* 极吝啬的人。**II** ***ad*.** 〔口〕非常,极其。*I'm* ~ *glad you came*. 你来了,我非常高兴。**-ize** ***vt*., *vi*.** 〔美〕(把…)往坏处想。

aw·ful·ly [ˈɔːfuli; ˋɔfulɪ] ***ad*. 1.** 令人畏惧地;令人敬畏地。**2.** 〔口〕糟糕地。**3.** [ˈɔːfli; ˋɔfl̩ɪ]〔口〕非常,很,了不得。~ *good* 好得了不得。*It is* ~ *good of you*. 您真好。*to behave* ~ 表现得很糟糕。

aw·ful·ness [ˈɔːfulnis; ˋɔfulnɪs] ***n*. 1.** 威严,庄严。**2.** [ˈɔːflnis; ˋɔfl̩nɪs]〔口〕不快,不愉快;丑态,卑鄙无耻,丢脸的行为。

a·while [əˈhwail; əˋhwaɪl] ***ad*.** 暂时,片刻。*After dinner sit* ~; *after supper walk a mile*. 午饭后歇一歇,晚饭后走一走。

a·whirl [əˈhwəːl; əˋhwɝl] **I** ***a*.** 〔用作表语〕旋转着。**II** ***ad*.** 旋转地。

awk·ward [ˈɔːkwəd; ˋɔkwɚd] ***a*. 1.** (机器等)有毛病的,难使用的,不称手的,(衣裳)不合身的。**2.** (质问,事情等)棘手的;为难的,麻烦的。**3.** 笨拙的,不灵活的,不雅观的;粗劣的。*be in* ~ *situation*, 处境困难。*He is* ~ *in his movements*. 他动作笨拙。*I felt* ~. 我觉得局促不安,真尴尬,真别扭。~ *customer* 难对付的家伙。*an* ~ *instrument* 不顺手的工具。~ *position* 狼狈处境。*an* ~ *remark* 不得体的话。~ **age** 将近成年的时期。~ **squad** 〔喻〕一群生手;训练不足的新兵班。**-ly** ***ad*.** **-ness** ***n*.**

awl [ɔːl; ɔl] ***n*.** (绱鞋用的)锥子。

AWL, A.W.L., a. w. l. = absent (or absence) with leave 请假离职。

aw·less = aweless.

awn [ɔːn; ɔn] ***n*.**【植】芒。**-ed** ***a*.** 有芒的。**-less** ***a*.** 无芒的。

awn·ing [ˈɔːniŋ; ˋɔnɪŋ] ***n*.** 布篷;船篷;凉篷;雨篷。

a·woke [əˈwəuk; əˋwok] awake 的过去式及过去分词。

AWOL, a. w. o. l. [ˈeiwɔːl; ˋewɔl] = absent without leave; absence without official leave 擅离职守,开小差。

AWOL·ism [ˈeiwɔːlizəm; ˋewɔ͵lɪzəm] ***n*.** 擅离职守的行为。

AWRE = Atomic Weapons Research Establishment 〔英〕原子武器研究所。

a·wry [əˈrai; əˋraɪ] **I** ***a*.** 〔常作表语〕 **II** ***ad*. 1.** 曲,歪,斜,拗,扭。**2.** 错误。***be*** ~ ***from*** 违反。***go*** ~ 失败,弄错。***look*** ~ 斜视,瞟。***run*** ~ = ***tread*** ~ = go ~. ***tread the shoe*** ~ **1.** 通奸。**2.** 失足。

AWS = Air Weather Service 〔美〕航空气象处。

axe, 〔美〕 **ax** [æks; æks] **I** ***n*.** (*pl*. ***ax·es*** [ˈæksiz; ˋæksɪz]) **1.** 斧。**2.** 战斧;(刽子手的)砍头斧。**3.** 〔美俚〕任何一种乐器。***get the*** ~ **1.** 被解雇,被开除(学籍)。**2.** (求爱等)被拒绝。**3.** 被杀头。***hang up one's*** ~ **1.** 放弃无益的计划。**2.** 洗手不干;退休。***have an*** ~ ***to grind*** 〔美〕别有企图,有私心。***lay the*** ~ ***to the root of*** 动手消灭…。***put the*** ~ ***in the helve*** 解谜,大刀阔斧解决难题。***send the*** ~ ***after the helve*** [***hatchet***] 吃了亏还要做,坚持做没有指望的事。***set the*** ~ ***to*** 动手砍倒[破坏]。***the*** ~ (经费的)大削减,彻底减少。**II** ***vt*. 1.** 用斧砍。**2.** 大刀阔斧地削减(经费等)。~ **man** 用斧(伐木)的人。~ **hammer** 斧槌。~ **stone** 斧形软玉石。

ax·es ***n*. 1.** [ˈæksiz; ˋæksɪz] ax(e) 的复数。**2.** [ˈæksiːz; ˋæksiz] axis 的复数。

ax·i·al [ˈæksiəl; ˋæksɪəl] ***a*. 1.** 轴的。**2.** 成轴的。**3.** 轴周围的,轴向的。~ **elements** 结晶常数。~ **pencil**【数】平面束。~ **root**【植】主根,直根。~ **symmetry**【数】轴对称。**-ly** ***ad*.** 在轴的方向,与轴平行地。

ax·il [ˈæksil; ˋæksɪl] ***n*.**【植】腋〔叶子,枝子同茎之间的角度〕。

ax·ile [ˈæksail, ˈæksil; ˋæksaɪl, ˋæksɪl] ***a*.**【植】轴的,轴上的。

ax·il·la [ækˈsilə; ækˋsɪlə] ***n*.** (*pl*. ~*s*, ***-lae*** [-liː; -li]) **1.**【解】胳肢窝,腋。**2.**【植】腋 (= axil)。

ax·il·la·ry [ækˈsiləri; ͵ækˋsɪlərɪ] **I** ***a*. 1.**【解】腋下的。**2.**【植】腋的,腋生的。**II** ***n*.** (鸟类的)腋羽。~ **bud** 腋芽。

axi·nite [ˈæksinait; ˋæksɪ͵naɪt] ***n*.**【矿】斧石。

ax·i·ol·o·gy [ˌæksiˈɔlədʒi; ͵æksɪˋɑlədʒɪ] ***n*.**【哲】价值论〔唯心主义的道德观、美学观、宗教观流派〕。**-log·i·cal** [-əlɔˈdʒikl; -əlɑˋdʒɪkl̩] ***a*.** **-log·i·cal·ly** ***ad*.**

ax·i·om [ˈæksiəm; ˋæksɪəm] *n*. 1. 自明之理。2.【逻,数】公理;原理,原则,通则。3. 格言。

ax·i·o·mat·ic, ax·i·o·mat·i·cal [ˌæksiəˈmætik(əl); ˏæksɪəˋmætɪk(əl)] *a*. 1. 公理的,自明的。2. 格言(多)的。**-i·cal·ly** *ad*. 照公理,公理上,自明地。**-ics** *n*. 公理体系[系统];公理学。

ax·i·on [ˈæksiən; ˋæksɪən] *n*.【原】轴子〔一种假想的粒子,中性,不旋转〕。

ax·is [ˈæksis; ˋæksɪs] *n*. (*pl*. **ax·es** [ˈæksiːz; ˋæksiz]) 1. 轴,轴线。2.【植】茎轴。3.【解】第二颈椎,第二脊骨。4.【政】轴心〔国家间的联盟,特指第二次大战中德义日等国的联盟〕。5.【化】晶轴,【物】光轴。*the* ~ *of the eye* 视轴。*the major* ~(椭圆的)长径,长轴。*the minor* ~(椭圆的)短径,短轴。***A- powers*** 轴心国。***the A-*** (第二次世界大战中的)德意日轴心。

ax·le [ˈæksl; ˋæksḷ] *n*. 心棒,轴,车轴。

ax·le·tree [ˈæksltriː; ˋæksḷˏtri] *n*. 1. 轮轴。2.【机】心棒。

Ax·min·ster [ˈæksminstə; ˋæksmɪnstɚ] *n*. (英国的一种以黄麻为底的)羊毛织花地毯。

ax·o·lotl [ˌæksəˈlɔtl; ˋæksəˏlɑtḷ] *n*.【动】(墨西哥)蝾螈。

ax·on [ˈæksɔn; ˋæksɑn] *n*.【动】(神经细胞的)轴索。~ **reflex** 轴突反射。

ax·o·no·me·try [ˌæksəˈnɔmitri; ˏæksəˋnɑmɪtrɪ] *n*. 1. 轴线测定;轴量法。2. 均角投影图法。

ax·seed [ˈækssiːd; ˋækˏsid] *n*. 多变小冠花。

ay[1], **aye** [ai; aɪ] **I** *int*. 是,行,赞成! *Aye*, ~, *sir*! 是,是,官长!〔海员对长官的回答〕。**II** *n*. 赞成票;赞成者。*the ayes and noes* 赞成票与反对票。*The ayes have it*. 赞成者占多数。

ay[2] [ei; e] *int*. 〔古、方〕唉! 呜呼!〔表惊愕,悔恨等〕。*Ay me*! 哀哉!

ay[3], **aye** [ei; e] *ad*. 〔诗、方〕常,永久。***for*** (***ever and***) ~ 永久,永远。

a·ya·tol·lah[ˌaijəˈtəulə;ˏaɪjəˋtolə] *n*. 阿亚图拉〔伊朗等国伊斯兰教什叶派领袖之尊号〕。

aye-aye [ˈaiai; ˋaɪˏaɪ] *n*.【动】指猴。

a·yin [ˈɑːjin; ˋajɪn] *n*. 希伯来语第十六个字母。

Ay·ma·ra [ˌaiməˈrɑː; ˏaɪməˋrɑ] *n*. 1. (*pl*. ~(*s*)) 艾马拉人〔南美的一支印第安人〕。2. 艾马拉语。**-n** *a*., *n*.

Ayr·shire [ˈɛəʃiə; ˋɛrʃɪr] *n*. 1. (苏格兰)额尔郡。2. 额尔郡乳牛。

a·yun·ta·mien·to [əˌjuntəˈmjentəu; əˏjuntəˋmjento] *n*. (*pl*. ~*s*) 〔Sp.〕(西班牙、南美的)市政府,市议会。

A-Z [ˌeitəˈzed; ˏetəˋzed] *n*. 〔英〕(附地名索引的)城市街道图。

a·zal·ea [əˈzeiljə; əˋzeljə] *n*.【植】杜鹃花。

a·zan [ɑːˈzɑːn; ɑˋzɑn] *n*. 伊斯兰教的祷告会〔由伊斯兰教寺院报祈祷时刻的人在尖塔上呼报召集,每日五次〕。

A·za·zel [əˈzeizl, ˈæzəzel; əˋzezl, ˋæzəzɛl] 亚撒色〔英国诗人密尔顿 (Milton) 所作《失乐园》中和撒旦一起反抗上帝的天使〕。

a·zed·a·rach [əˈzedəræk; əˋzɛdəˏræk] *n*. 1. 楝树。2. (苦)楝皮〔用以制泻药和呕吐剂〕。

a·ze·o·trope [eiˈziətrəup; eˋzɪətrop] *n*.【化】共沸混合物。**-trop·ic** [-trɔpik; -trɑpɪk] *a*.

Az·er·bai·jan [ˌæzəbaiˈdʒɑːn; ˏɑzɚbaɪˋdʒɑn] *n*. 阿塞拜疆。

A·zer·bai·ja·ni [ˌæzəbaiˈdʒɑːni; ɑzɚbaɪˋdʒɑnɪ] *n*. 1. (*pl*. ~(*s*)) 阿塞拜疆人。2. 阿塞拜疆语。

az·ide [ˈeizid; ˋæzaɪd] *n*.【化】叠氮化物。

A·zil·ian [əˈziljən; əˋzɪljən] *a*. 阿济尔期的〔指法国旧石器时代最后期与新石器时代之间的史前文化〕,阿济尔期文化的。

az·i·muth [ˈæziməθ; ˋæzəməθ] *n*. 1. 方位(角)。2.【天】地平经度。~ **angle** 方位角。~ **circle** 方位圈。~ **compass** 方位罗盘。~ **stabilizer**【空】纵舵机,方位稳定器。

az·i·muth·al [ˌæziˈmʌθəl; ˋæzəˏmʌθəl] *a*. 1. 方位角的。2.【天】(地)平经(度)的。

az·ine [ˈæziːn; ˋæzin] *n*.【化】连氮;吖嗪。

az·lon [ˈæzlɔn; ˋæzlɑn] *n*. 人造蛋白质纤维,再生蛋白质纤维。

az·o [ˈæzəu; ˋæzo] *a*.【化】偶氮的。~ **compound** 偶氮化合物。~ **dyes** 偶氮染料。

azo- *comb*. *f*. 表示"偶氮": *azo*benzene.

az·o·ben·zene [ˌæzəuˈbenziːn; ˏæzoˋbɛnzin] *n*.【化】偶氮苯。

a·zo·ic [əˈzəuik; əˋzo·ɪk] *a*. 1. 〔有时作 A-〕【地】无生物时代的。2. 无生命的。~ **era** 无生物时代。~ **group** 无生界。

az·ole [ˈæzəul; ˋæzol] *n*.【化】氮杂茂,唑。

az·on [ˈæzɔn; ˋæzɑn] *n*. 方向可变炸弹 (= ~ bomb)。

a·zon·al [eiˈzəunl; eˋzonḷ] *a*.【地】不分地带的。

a·zon·ic [æˈzɔnik; æˋzɑnɪk] *a*. 非局部地区的,非本地的。

A·zores [əˈzɔːz; əˋzɔrz] *n*. (大西洋北部的)亚速尔群岛。

az·ote [əˈzəut; əˋzot] *n*.【化】氮〔旧名〕。**a·zot·ic** [-tik; əˋzɑtɪk] *a*. (含)氮的。

az·o·te·mi·a [ˌæzəˈtiːmiə; ˏæzəˋtimɪə] *n*.【医】氮血(症)。

az·oth [ˈæzɔθ; ˋæzɑθ] *n*. 1. (炼金术的)水银。2. (传说为瑞士炼金家及医生巴拉塞尔斯所炼的)金丹[万灵药]。

az·o·tize [ˈæzətaiz; ˋæzəˏtaɪz] *vt*.【化】使氮化。

a·zo·to·bac·ter [əˈzəutəˌbæktə; əˋzotəˏbæktɚ] *n*.【微】(土壤中的)固氮(细)菌。

az·o·tom·e·ter [əˈzəutəmiːtə; əˋzotəˏmitɚ] *n*. 氮素计。

a·zo·to·my·cin [əˈzəutəˈmaisin; əˋzotəˋmaɪsɪn] *n*.【药】含氮霉素。

A·zov [ˈɑːzɔf; ˋɑzɑf] *n*. (黑海北面的)亚速海。*The Sea of* ~ 亚速海。

Az·ra·el [ˈæzreiəl; ˋæzrɪəl] *n*. (犹太教和穆斯林信仰中使灵魂离开躯体的)死神。

AZT = azidothymidine 叠氮胸苷〔一种抗艾滋病药〕。

Az·tec [ˈæztek; ˋæztɛk] **I** *n*. 1. 阿兹台克人〔墨西哥原始居民〕。2. 阿兹台克语。**II** *a*. 1. 阿兹台克人的。2. 阿兹台克语的。

az·ure [ˈæʒə; ˋæʒɚ] **I** *a*. 天蓝色的,淡青的,蔚蓝的;青天的。**II** *n*. 1. 天蓝色,浅蓝色。2. 〔诗〕苍天,青空。~ *eyes* 碧眼。**III** *vt*. 使成天蓝色。~ **stone** 琉璃;青金石,天青石。

az·u·rite [ˈæʒərait; ˋæʒəˏraɪt] *n*.【矿】石青,蓝铜矿。

az·y·gous [ˈæzəgəs; ˋæzɪgəs] *a*.【解】非双生的,单一的,不成对的。

az·ym(e) [ˈæzaim; ˋæzaɪm] *n*. 无酵母面包。

B

B, b [biː; bi] (*pl*. ***B's, b's*** [biːz; biz]) **1.** 英语字母表第二字母。**2.**【数】(顺序)第二,乙;第二已知数。**3.**【乐】B调,B音。**4.** B形物;[B] 表示铅笔芯软硬的符号。**5.**〔美〕[B](学业成绩)良好。**6.**〔B〕B级,第二流。**7.** B血型。*a B picture* 第二流影片。*a B student* 成绩乙等的学生。*B battery*【无】*B* 电池组。*B flat*【乐】降 *B* 调〔记号 B♭〕。*B major* [*minor*]【乐】B 大调[小调]。***not know B from bull's foot*** 见牛脚而不识 B 字;目不识丁;文盲〔英语字母 B 源于腓尼基象形文字"牛"。牛为偶蹄类,脚趾形似字母 B。见牛趾而不识 B 字,喻文盲极其无知,故有此说〕。

B., b. = **1.** bachelor. **2.**【乐】bass; basso. **3.** battery. **4.** bay. **5.** book. **6.** born. **7.** brother. **8.** Bible. **9.** Boston. **10.** British.

B.A., BA = Bachelor of Arts 文学士。

Ba =【化】元素钡 (barium 的符号)。

ba [bɑː; bɑ] ***n***.【埃神】魂灵〔被古埃及人描述成人头鸟身,死时飞离肉体,以后又要飞回,所以要保存尸体〕。

baa [bɑː; bɑ] **I** ***n***. 咩咩〔羊叫声〕。**II** ***vi***. (羊等)咩咩叫。~**-lamb** ***n***. 咩咩羊〔儿语羊的名称〕。

Ba·al [ˈbeiəl; ˋbeəl] ***n***. (*pl*. ~***s***, ***Ba·al·im*** [ˈbeiəlim; ˋbeəlɪm]) **1.** (古代腓尼基人等崇拜的)太阳神,山神,丰产之神。**2.** 邪神,神;偶像。**-ism** ***n***. 太阳神崇拜;偶像崇拜。

baas [bɑːs; bɑs] ***n***.〔南非〕老板;先生〔旧时黑人对白人的称呼〕。

baas·kaap [ˈbɑːskɑːp; ˋbɑskɑp] ***n***.〔S. Afr.〕(南非种族主义的)白人绝对统治方针。

Bab [bæb; bæb] ***n***. **1.** Barbara〔女子名〕的通称。**2.** 波斯巴比教祖的称号。

ba·ba au rhum [ˈbɑːbɑːəuˈrʌm; ˋbɑbɑoˋrʌm] ***n***.〔F.〕甜酒浸蛋糕。

ba·bas·su [ˌbɑːbɑːˈsuː; ˏbɑbɑˋsu] ***n***.【植】巴西棕榈 (= *Orbignya speciosa* 或 *Orbignya martiana*); 巴西棕榈油。

Bab·bitt [ˈbæbit; ˋbæbɪt] ***n***. 白璧特〔典型的粗俗实业家,得名于美国作家 Sinclair Lewis 的同名小说〕; 粗俗的市侩。

bab·bitt [ˈbæbit; ˋbæbɪt] **I** ***n***.【冶】**1.** 巴比特合金,巴氏合金,轴承合金〔锡、锑、铜合金〕。**2.** 巴氏合金轴承衬。**II** ***vt***. 给…浇巴氏合金。~ **metal** 巴氏[轴承]合金。

Bab·bitt·ry [ˈbæbitri; ˋbæbɪtrɪ] ***n***.〔常作 b-〕〔美〕庸俗的实业家性格,市侩作风;低级趣味。

-babble *comb. f*. "行话"、"术语"之意: bio*babble* 太空航行术语。

bab·ble [ˈbæbl; ˋbæbl̩] **I** ***vi***. **1.** (婴儿等)牙牙学语。**2.** 胡言乱语;喋喋不休,唠叨 (*about*). **3.** (流水)潺潺作声。— ***vt***. **1.** 喋喋不休地讲。**2.** (因多说话而)泄漏 (*out*). **II** ***n***. **1.** 牙牙学语声;听不清楚的话;胡话;空话。**2.** 潺潺(水声);【无】多路感应的复杂失真;(电话)串线杂音。

bab·bler [ˈbæblə; ˋbæbl̩ɚ] ***n***. **1.** 牙牙学语的婴儿。**2.** 胡言乱语[说话不清楚]的人;碎嘴子;(因多说话而)泄漏秘密的人。**3.**【鸟】莺类小鸟。

babe [beib; beb] ***n***. **1.**〔诗〕赤子,婴孩;孩子气的人,不知世故的人。**2.**〔美俚〕(美丽的)姑娘;宝贝〔对亲爱女人的称呼〕。~ ***in the wood***(***s***) 容易受骗的老好人。~ ***of love*** 非婚生子,私生子。~***s and sucklings*** 年轻小伙子们,娃娃们;太天真的人,没经验的人。

Ba·bel [ˈbeibəl; ˋbebl̩] ***n***. **1.**【圣】(古巴比伦人建筑未成的)通天塔〔见创世纪十一章〕。**2.** [b-]〔喻〕摩天楼;空想的计划。**3.** [b-] 喧哗,混乱声。*raise a* ~ *of criticism* 引起纷纷议论。**-ism** ***n***.〔有时作 b-〕(思想、语言等的)混乱。**-ize** ***vt***. 使(习俗、语言等)混杂。

Ba·bi [ˈbɑːbiː; ˋbɑbi] ***n***. (= Babism) 巴比教徒〔1844 年在波斯兴起〕。

ba·biche [bɑːˈbiːʃ; bɑˋbiʃ] ***n***.〔加拿大〕皮条,皮带。

Ba·bing·ton [ˈbæbiŋtən; ˋbæbɪŋtən] ***n***. 巴宾顿〔姓氏〕。

bab·i·ru·sa, bab·i·rou·sa [ˌbæbəˈruːsə; ˏbæbəˋrusə] ***n***.【动】马来野猪。

bab·ka [ˈbɑːbkə; ˋbɑbkə] ***n***. 老妈妈饼〔一种加有葡萄干的甜酒味发面糕〕。

ba·boo [ˈbɑːbuː; ˋbɑbu] ***n***. **1.**〔印尊称〕先生;印度绅士。**2.**〔蔑〕半英化印度人〔多指会写点英文的印度职员〕。~ **English** 矫揉造作不合习惯用法的英语。

ba·boon [bəˈbuːn; bæˋbun] ***n***.【动】狒狒。

ba·bou·che [bəˈbuːʃ; bəˋbuʃ] ***n***. 土耳其式拖鞋。

ba·bu [ˈbɑːbu; ˋbɑbʊ] = baboo.

ba·bul [bəˈbuːl; bəˋbul] ***n***. 巴布尔橡胶树;巴布尔橡胶树皮[树胶]。

ba·bush·ka [bəˈbuʃkə; bəˋbuʃkə] ***n***.〔美〕(只露面部的女用)三角头巾〔源出俄语,其本义为老太婆〕。

ba·by [ˈbeibi; ˋbebɪ] **I** ***n***. **1.** 婴儿,赤子,奶娃娃。**2.** 孩子气的人;幼小动物;小东西,一个集体[家庭]中最年幼的人。**3.**〔常作定语〕小型,微型。**4.**〔美俚〕姑娘;(美丽动人的)女人;爱人;(任何)人;(任何)物[东西];得意杰作。**5.**〔口〕容易的[讨厌的]差事[任务]。*a regular* ~ 十足的娃娃。*It's your* ~, *not mine*. 那是你的任务,不是我的。***carry*** [***hold***] ***the*** ~ **1.** 受束缚,不能自由行动。**2.** 担负讨厌的职务,做不愿意做的事;背包袱。**II** ***vt***. 把…当婴儿看待,对…娇生惯养。~ **act** 幼稚行为 (*plead the* ~ *act*〔美〕以幼稚无经验为口实)。~ **alps**〔美〕重量级拳击选手。~ **blue** 淡蓝色。~ **bond** 票面百元以下的债券。~ **book** 育婴指南。~ **boom** **1.** (尤指 1947—1961 年间美国的)生育高峰。**2.** 出生率激增。~ **boomer** 生育高产期出生的孩子。~**-bound** ***a***.〔美〕有孕的。~**break** 产假。~ **bust** 婴儿出生低潮。~ **bunting** 婴儿睡袋。~ **car** 童车;微型汽车。~ **carrier** 轻航空母舰。~ **carriage** [**buggy**]〔美〕童车。~**-face** 孩儿脸(的人)。~ **farm** 育婴院。~ **farmer** 代人育婴者。~ **firm**〔美〕托儿所。~ **grand** 小型卧式钢琴。~**-sitter** (论时计酬的)代人照看孩子的人。~**-hood** ***n***. 婴孩期;幼小时代,幼稚;〔集合词〕婴儿。~ **kisser**〔美俚〕为拉选票到处笼络人心的政治家。~ **moon** 喜庆月〔第一个小孩出生后给初当父母者带来无限快乐的那个月〕。

ba·by·ish [ˈbeibiiʃ; ˋbebɪɪʃ] ***a***. 婴孩一样的,孩子气的。

Bab·y·lon [ˈbæbilən; ˋbæbl̩ən] ***n***. **1.** 巴比伦〔古代巴比伦王国首都〕。**2.** 奢华淫靡的大都市。***the Modern*** ~ 现代巴比伦〔伦敦的别称〕。

Bab·y·lo·ni·a [ˌbæbiˈləunjə; ˏbæbl̩ˋonjə] ***n***. (古代)巴

比伦帝国。

Bab·y·lo·ni·an [ˌbæbiˈləunjən; ˏbæbl̀onjən] **I** *a*. **1.** 巴比伦的,巴比伦帝国的。**2.** 邪恶的;奢华堕落的。**II** *n*. 巴比伦人;迦勒底 (Chaldea) 人;占星家。

ba·by's breath [ˈbeibiz breθ; ˋbebɪz brɛθ]【植】**1.** 满天星,线形瞿麦,锥花丝石竹。**2.** 茜草科猎殃殃属植物。

ba·by-sit [ˈbeibiˌsit; ˋbebɪˏsɪt] *vi*. (*-sat*; *-sitting*) (临时代人)照管孩子,照看婴儿。

ba·by-watch [ˈbeibiˌwɔtʃ; ˋbebɪˏwɑtʃ] *vi*. = baby-sit.

BAC = **1.** British Agricultural Council 英国农业委员会。**2.** Boeing Airplane Company (美国)波音飞机公司。**3.** blood alcohol concentration 血液中酒精浓度。**4.** British Aircraft Corporation 英国飞机公司。

bac·ca [ˈbækə; ˋbækə] (*pl*. ***bac·cae*** [-ksiː; -ksi]) *n*. 浆果 (= berry)。

bac·ca·lau·re·ate [ˌbækəˈlɔːriit; ˏbækəˋlɔrɪɪt] *n*. **1.** 学士学位。**2.** 〔美〕(对大学毕业生的)训辞。

bac·ca·ra(t) [ˈbækərɑː; ˋbækərɑ] *n*. 〔F.〕【牌】比九点〔一种用三张牌拼凑九、十九、二十九点的玩牌法〕。

bac·cate [ˈbækeit; ˋbæket] *a*.【植】结浆果的;浆果状的。

bac·cha·nal [ˈbækənl; ˋbækənl] **I** *a*. **1.** 酒神的;酒神节的。**2.** 狂欢闹饮的,发酒疯的。**II** *n*. **1.** 酒神崇拜者;发酒疯的人,酒徒。**2.** 〔B-〕〔*pl*.〕酒神节。

Bac·cha·na·li·a [ˌbækəˈneiljə; ˏbækəˋneljə] *n*. **1.** 古罗马酒神节。**2.** 〔b-〕大酒宴;狂闹乱饮;狂饮的闹宴。

bac·cha·na·li·an [ˌbækəˈneiljən; ˏbækəˋneljən] *a*., *n*. = bacchanal.

bac·chant [ˈbækənt; ˋbækənt] **I** *n*. **1.** 酒神祭司。**2.** 信奉酒神的人。**3.** 爱酗酒胡闹的人。**II** *a*. = bacchanal (*a*.)。

bac·chan·te [bəˈkænt(i); bəˋkænt(ɪ)] *n*. **1.** 酒神女祭司。**2.** 信奉酒神的女人。**3.** 爱酗酒胡闹的女人。

Bac·chic [ˈbækik; ˋbækɪk] *a*. **1.** 酒神 Bacchus 的。**2.** 〔b-〕热闹的;狂欢乱闹的;闹宴的。

Bac·chus [ˈbækəs; ˋbækəs] *n*.【罗神】酒神 (=【希神】Dionysus)。***a son of*** ~ 大酒鬼。

bacci- *comb*. *f*. 表示"浆果"。

bac·cif·er·ous [bækˈsifərəs; bækˋsɪfərəs] *a*. 有浆果的,结浆果的。

bac·ci·form [ˈbæksifɔːm; ˋbæksəˏfɔrm] *a*. 浆果状的。

bac·civ·or·ous [bækˈsivərəs; bækˋsɪvərəs] *a*. 以浆果为食的。

bac·co [ˈbækəu; ˋbæko], **bac·cy** [ˈbæki; ˋbækɪ] *n*. (*pl*. ***-cies***) 〔英口〕烟草 (= tobacco)。

Bach [bɑːh; bɑh], **Johann Sebastian** 巴赫〔1685-1750, 德国作曲家〕。

bach [bætʃ; bætʃ] **I** *vi*. 〔美俚〕过独身[鳏夫]生活〔多用于短语 to bach it〕。**II** *n*. 独身男子,单身汉。

Bach(e) [beitʃ; betʃ] *n*. 贝奇〔姓氏〕。

bach·e·lor [ˈbætʃələ; ˋbætʃələ] *n*. **1.** 单身汉,独身男子;未交配的雄兽〔尤指海豹〕。**2.** 学士。**3.**【史】青年[下级]骑士[武士] (= bachelor at arms)。~ ***girl*** 自食其力的未婚独身女子。***B- of Arts*** 文学士〔略作 B.A. 或 A.B.〕。***B- of Science*** 理学士〔略作 B.S. 或 B.Sc.〕。~***'s buttons*** **1.** 花形似钮扣的植物〔矢车菊等〕。**2.** 杏仁小饼干。~***'s baby*** 私生子。~***'s hall*** 单身男子的住处。**-dom, -hood** 男子独身(身分),独身,独身时代。**-ism** (男子)独身,独身主义。**-ship 1.** (男子)独身。**2.** 学士学位。

bach·e·lor·ette [ˌbætʃələˈret; ˏbætʃələˋrɛt] *n*. 年轻未婚女子。

bacill- *comb*. *f*. 〔L.〕表示"小杆": *bacillin*.

bac·il·lar·y [bəˈsiləri, Am. ˈbæsileri; bəˋsɪlərɪ, bæslˏɛrɪ] *a*. 小杆的;杆状的;(杆状)细菌(性)的 (= bacilliform)。

ba·cil·li [bəˈsilai; bəˋsɪlaɪ] *n*. **bacillus** 的复数。

ba·cil·li·form [bəˈsilifɔːm; bəˋsɪlɪˏfɔrm] *a*. 杆状的;杆菌状的。

ba·cil·lin [bəˈsilin; bəˋsɪlɪn] *n*.【药】杆菌素。

ba·cil·lo·my·cin [bəˌsiləuˈmaisin; bəˏsɪloˋmaɪsɪn] *n*.【药】杆菌抗霉素。

ba·cil·los·po·rin [bəˌsiləuˈspɔːrin; bəˏsɪloˋspɔrɪn] *n*.【药】多黏菌素。

ba·cil·lus [bəˈsiləs; bəˋsɪləs] *n*. (*pl*. ***ba·cil·li*** [bəˈsilai; bəˋsɪlaɪ])【微】牙孢杆菌,杆菌;细菌,病菌。**Bacillus Cal·mette-Gué·rin** [kælˈmetgeiˈræn; kælˋmɛtgeˋræn]【药】卡介苗。~ **carrier** 杆菌载体。

ba·cil·y·sin [ˌbæsiˈlaisin; ˏbæsɪˋlaɪsɪn] *n*.【药】杆菌溶素。

bac·i·tra·cin [ˌbæsiˈtreisn; ˏbæsəˋtresɪn] *n*.【药】杆菌肽 (*bacillus subtillis*), 杆菌肽素,枯草杆菌抗生素。

back [bæk; bæk] **I** *n*. **1.** 背,背部;背脊;背面,反面;背后,后部,后面,里面。**2.** (指)甲;(刀)背;(手)背;(书)背;(椅子)靠背;(山)脊;(船的)龙骨;衬垫,底座。**3.** 体力;力气。**4.**【摔跤】仰面倒下。**5.**【剧】(舞台的)背景。**6.** 足球后卫。**7.**【语】舌根音[软口盖音]。**8.** (*pl*. ***-s***) 〔美〕假钞票。*at the* ~ *of a house*. 房屋背后。*the* ~ *of the mouth* 口腔深处。*full* ~ (足球的)后卫。*half* ~ 中卫。*lazy* ~ 椅子的靠背。***at sb.'s*** ~ 做某人的靠山。***at the*** ~ ***of*** 在…之后,在…背后 (*at the* ~ *of one's mind* 在心里,内心上;下意识)。~ ***and belly*** 背与腹;衣食;腹背(都)。~ ***and edge*** 尽力,拼命。~ ***to*** ~ (***with***) 背对背。***behind sb.'s*** ~ 在某人背后;背地里,暗中。***break one's*** ~ 折断脊背骨;负担过重,承受不住。***break the*** ~ ***of*** **1.** 毁坏;伤其要害。**2.** 克服某事最艰巨的部分;度过最困难的时刻。***cast sth. behind one's*** ~ 把某事置之脑后。***get off sb.'s*** ~ 停止对某人攻击[责难]。***get one's*** ~ ***up*** 发怒。***get*** [***put***, ***set***] ***sb.'s*** ~ ***up*** 〔口〕触怒某人,惹恼〔由猫怒弓背而来〕。***get the*** ~ ***of*** 绕至…的背后。***give*** [***make***] ***a*** ~ (游戏)弯背作马状供人跳过。***give the*** ~ ***to*** (转过身子)背向着,遗弃。***have*** [***with***] ***one's*** ~ ***to the wall*** 陷入绝境。***have sb. at one's*** ~ 以某人作靠山。***in*** ~ ***of*** 〔美口〕在…之后,在…的背面。***on one's*** ~ 仰向,朝天 (*lie on one's* ~ 仰卧。*fall on one's* ~ 仰面倒下;背,驮;逼近背后)。***on*** [***upon***] ***the*** ~ ***of*** 由…背后,紧靠…的后面,继续;此外,加之。***one's*** ~ ***is up*** (像猫发怒一样)耸着背 (*His* ~ *was up*. 他发怒了)。***put one's*** ~ ***into*** (*sth*.) 努力干(某事)。***see the*** ~ ***of*** 赶走,撵走;摆脱某人。***set one's*** ~ ***against the wall*** 以寡敌众,负隅顽抗。***show the*** ~ ***to*** 逃出,逃离。***slap sb. on the*** ~ 拍拍(某人)脊背〔表示赞成、鼓励〕。***the Backs*** 〔英口〕(Cambridge 大学的)校后校园。***the*** ~ ***of beyond*** 偏僻之地,遥远的地方。***to the*** ~ 到骨髓,完全。***turn the*** ~ 逃亡,败走。***turn the*** [***one's***] ~ ***on*** 不理睬;丢弃;逃出。

II *a*. **1.** 后部的,背部的;后面的 (*opp*. front); 内地的,偏僻的;〔美〕边远的,边陲的。**2.** (货物等)回程的;向后动的,逆的。**3.** (思想)落后的。**4.** 〔美〕未缴的,拖欠下的,未付的。**5.** (杂志等)过了期的。**6.**【语】舌根的。*a* ~ *street* 〔美〕背街。*a* ~ *door* 后门。~ *teeth* 大牙,槽牙。*a* ~ *settler* 边疆居民,边疆移住民。~ *cargo* 归程(载运的)货物。*a* ~ *current* 逆流。*a* ~ *salary* [*rent*] 欠薪[租]。*give a* ~ *answer* 回嘴;顶撞。***take a*** ~ ***seat*** 坐末位,坐下席;谦下。***take the*** ~ ***track*** 〔美〕回去,退去。

III *ad*. **1.** 向后,退,在后面,向背面,倒,回头,返,归,复;离开;隐匿。**2.** 压制着,勒,扣,阻碍。**3.** 以前,过去;从前。*answer* ~ 回嘴。*pay* ~ 付还。*send* ~ 送回。*What is the fare to London and* ~? 去伦敦来回要多少钱? *a few pages* ~ 两三页前。*for some time* ~ 前些时以来。*two years* ~ 二年前。

IV *vt*.【计】备份,把(文件等)备份(*up*)。*To* ~ *up files is tedious work*. 把文档备份是一项枯燥无味的工作。

B

B

B-! 回去! ~ ***and forth***〔美〕**1**. 来来去去。**2**. 翻来覆去。~ ***of***〔美口〕在…的后部,在…的背后。***be*** ~〔口〕回家;回来(*I'll be* ~ *in a minute*. 马上就回来)。***come*** ~ = **go** ~ 回,归。*go* ~ *from*[(*up*) *on*]抛弃,辜负;出卖(朋友)(*He went* ~ *on his friends*. 他背叛了朋友)。***go*** ~ ***from one's word*** 违约,食言。***keep*** ~! 不要过来! 不要前进! ***keep*** ~ (*sth*.) 阻止向前;忍住;勒住;扣下;隐匿[瞒](*keep* ~ *the truth* 隐瞒真相)。***look*** ~ 回顾。***talk*** ~ 回嘴,还嘴;反复重说。***there and*** ~ = **to and** ~ 往返;来回。

V *vt*. **1**. 裱(画);给…装背衬;装上(椅)背;作(风景等)的背景。**2**. 给…做后援,支持,资助;怂恿;下赌注于。**3**. 背书(支票等),落名(信后等)。**4**. 使后退,使折回。**5**. 乘,骑(马);〔口〕背,驮。**6**.〔美〕位于…的背后。~ *an automobile* 倒车,退车。~ *a picture* 裱画。~ *a check* 背书支票,在支票背面签字。— *vi*. 退后,倒退,逆行;(风向)反(时针)转。~ ***a sail***【海】转帆使船缓进。~ ***and fill***【海】(风向紊乱时)看风使舵因势前进;〔美〕逡巡,踌躇。~ ***down*** 放弃权利等,撤手;打退堂鼓,取消前言。~ ***off*** 退避;后退。~ ***on to***〔美〕背靠着。~ ***out*** (***of***) 缩手(放弃某事),取消;扭松,旋出;逃避(责任等)。~ ***the wrong horse***〔美口〕估计错;选错。~ ***up*** 支持,为…撑腰;堵塞,拦(水);【棒球】抢救后方;【计】把(文件等备份)。~**ache** 背痛,腰痛。~**-alley 1**. ***n***. 街后窄巷。**2**. ***a***. 陋巷的;穷困的。~**-bencher** 后座议员〔英国下院普通议员〕。~ **benches** 后座议员席。~ **bend** 桥形〔向后弯腰至头着地的杂技动作〕。~**bite 1**. ***vt***.〔口〕暗骂,背地里骂。**2**. ***vi***.〔口〕背后骂人。~**biter** 背地骂人的人。~ **blocks**〔澳〕偏僻的牧场;(都市中)贫民窟。~**board** 后板,背板;(篮球架上的)篮板;脊椎矫正板。~**-bone** 脊骨,脊椎;分水岭;主要山脉;主要成分;中枢;中坚,骨干;主力;刚毅,骨气;书脊(*the* ~*bone of a defence* 防御主力。*to the* ~*bone* 完完全全,纯粹,十足,彻头彻尾。*an Englishman to the* ~*bone* 道地的英国人)。~**boned *a***. 有脊骨的,有脊椎的;有骨气的。~**-breaking *a***. 极费力气的;累坏人的;极讨厌的。~**-burner *a***. 不重要的。~ **cap *n***.〔美俚〕揭别人阴私(*give sb. a* ~ *cap* 诽谤人,说人坏话)。~**-cap *vt***.〔美俚〕说…的坏话;毁谤。~ **channel**〔美〕秘密渠道,非正规途径。~**chat**〔口〕闲聊;回嘴;反唇相讥;(喜剧中)用俏皮话互相逗引[挖苦]。~**cloth**【剧】背景幕布;印花衬布。~**cross**【生】**1**. 回交,逆代杂交(的产物);回交种[品]。**2**. ***vt***., ***vi***. (使)回交,(使)逆代杂交。~**country**〔美〕穷乡僻壤,边远地区。~**date *vt***. **1**. 把发生的日期说成[写成]比实际的更早。**2**. 追溯至(过去某时)(~*-date the salary increase three months* 加薪自三个月前起算)。~**door *a***. 后门的,二门的;私下的,秘密的(~*door methods* 秘密[非法]途径,阴谋)。~**down**〔口〕原先要求[主张、态度、声明]的改变;让步;退却。~**drop**〔美〕背景;背景幕布。~ **end 1**. 核废料回收部分〔在核反应堆燃料循环中,将用过的燃料中有用的铀和钚从放射性核废料中分离出来〕。**2**. 后端。~**-field**〔美〕(足球场的)中圈。~**fill 1**. ***n***. (坑洞等的)回填土,回填料。**2**. ***vt***. 回填(坑洞等)。~**fire 1**. ***n***. (故意引燃以阻止野火蔓延的)迎火;逆火,回火〔内燃机因点火过早发生的不时爆发〕;(摩托车的)放气声。**2**. ***vi***. 发生回火;放迎火;发生意外;产生适得其反的恶果(*The plot* ~*fired*. 此阴谋招来了相反的结果)。~**formation**【语】逆构词;反成法〔如由 typewriter 逆构成 typewrite〕。~**ground *n***. **1**. 后景,背景;基本情况;(纺织品等的)底子;出身;经历。**2**. 隐蔽的[不引人注目的]地位;幕后。**3**. 衬托音乐,伴音;【无】干扰杂音(*students of workers'* ~*ground*. 工人出身的学生)。*in the* ~*ground* 背地下,背后;在幕后(活动)。~**grounder** 提供背景资料的记者招待会〔尤指政府为说明官方所采取的行动或方针政策而举行的非正式记者招待会〕。~**hand 1**. ***n***. 反向;【网球】反手拍;(书法)左斜体。**2**. ***vt***. 用反手击。**3**. ***a***., ***ad***. = ~-**handed**. ~**handed**. **1**. ***a***. 反手的;逆的;(书法)左斜体的;间接的,转弯抹角的,暧昧的,讽刺的;(绳子)反搓的(*a* ~*handed compliment* 挖苦的恭维话)。**2**. ***ad***. 反手地。~**hander 1**. 反手打,反拍;间接攻击;(反手倒给右座人的)第二杯酒。**2**.〔俚〕贿赂。~**house** 后屋,户外厕所。~**lash 1**. ***n***. 反击;后座;(政治方面)强烈的反响;(任何)对抗性的反应;【机】轮齿隙;齿隙游移;钓丝缠结。**2**. ***vi***. 发生后冲,产生对抗性的反应。~**lining**【建】背衬;【印】(加固书脊的)背衬料。~**list 1**. ***n***. 多年未绝版书书目;旧版书存货目录。**2**. ***vt***. 把…列入旧版书书目。~**log**〔美〕**1**. ***n***. (加置炉膛深处的)垫薪圆柴;〔口〕存货;储备金;应急预备用物;积压的工作;未交付的订货。**2**. ***vi***., ***vt***. 积压。~ **matter** (正文后的)附加资料。~**most *a***. 最后部的,顶后面的。~ **number** 过期杂志;落后于时代的人,老古董。~**-of-the-book *adj***.〔美〕(有关科技发展艺术和教育等)大众感兴趣的题材的。~**order**【商】留待将来交付的订货。~**-page *a***. (报纸的)最后几版的;没有多大新闻价值的。~**pedal *vi***. 倒踏脚踏板;(拳击)向后躲闪;变卦,收回意见[立场、主张]。~**plane**【计】(电脑的)底板。~ **resistance** 反向电阻。~**rest** (座椅等的)靠背。~**road** 便道;村间道路〔尤指未铺过的道路〕。~**room** 里屋;密室。~**room *a***. 在密室中(工作)的。~**room boy**〔英口〕幕后策划人,智囊。~**seat**〔口〕后座;低下的职位,无聊的工作(*won't take a* ~ *seat to anyone* 不愿屈居人下)。~**-seat driver**〔美口〕坐在后座乱指点司机的人;多管闲事的人;政治评论家。~**-seat driving**〔美〕管闲事;政治评论。~**set** 倒流;后退,倒退,挫折;(疾病的)复发;逆水,涡流。~**sheesh**, ~**shish** = baksheesh. ~**side 1**. 后部。**2**.〔常 *pl*.〕屁股。~**sight** 反视;【测】后视;照尺;【军】反觇;瞄准孔;表尺缺口。~ **slang** 倒读隐语〔如 pig 读作 gip〕。~**slap *vt***., ***vi***. 拍(某人的)背以示亲热。~**slapper**〔口〕(对人)过于推心置腹的人;热情太过的人。~**slide *vi***., ***n***. 倒退;退步;故态复萌;堕落;违背(宗旨等)。~ **slum** 贫民窟。~**space *vi***. (按打字机退格键)使倒退一格,倒格。~**spin** 反旋转。~**stage 1**. ***a***. 后台的,幕后的;关于戏剧界人物私生活的。**2**. ***ad***. 在后台;在幕后;私下,秘密地。~ **stairs**〔*pl*.〕**1**. 后楼梯。**2**. 密谋。~**stair(s) *a***. 见不得人的;肮脏的;暗地里的,秘密的(~ *stairs influence* 潜势力,有权势的后台)。~**stay**【机】后支条[撑条],背撑;【海】后支索,后索〔自桅至后舷侧的绳索〕。~**stitch 1**. ***n***. 扣针脚,倒缝。**2**. ***vt***., ***vi***. 倒缝。~**stop 1**. ***n***. 托架;后障;【机】棘爪;【棒球】挡球网;(击球手后的)接球手。**2**. ***vt***. 挡住;支持。~**-street *a***. 偷偷摸摸干的[做成的];秘密的,暗中的。~**stroke 1**. ***n***., ***vi***. 回击;反手击球;仰泳。**2**. ***vt***. 用反手击。~**swept *a***. 后掠(角)的。~**sword** 单刃剑;大砍刀;木剑。~ **talk** 回嘴还口;顶嘴,对吵。~**track *vi***. 走回头路;改变过去的意见[主张]。~**up 1**. ***n***. 后补物,替代物,备用物;支持;阻塞;【计】备份。**2**. ***a***. 后补的,副(手)的,替代的,备用的;支持性的;伴奏的(*a* ~*up pilot* 副领航员,助航员)。~ **vowel** (舌)后元音。~**wash** 回浪;逆流;反动;反响;余波。~**water 1**. ***n***. (被阻退回的)回水,回流;逆流;循环水,再用水;死水,滞水;〔喻〕停滞;文化落后的地方(*live in a* ~*water* 蛰居乡间)。**2**. ***vt***. 倒划,倒开船;〔美口〕放弃原来的立场;食言。~**woods**〔*pl*.〕〔美〕偏僻的森林地带;落后的边远地区。~**woodsman** 林区[边远区]居民;〔讽〕蛰居乡间的人;〔英〕不[很少]参加上议院活动的贵族。~**woodsy *a***.〔美〕乡下气的;粗野的。~**yard 1**. ***n***.〔美〕后院。**2**. ***a***. 本地的,私人的。~**yardism**〔美〕排外主义。

backed [bækt; bækt] ***a***. **1**. 有后援的,有支持的。**2**. 有后衬的;以…作背面的〔常用作带连字符的复合词词尾,意为有某种后援或后衬的:*well-*~ 后台硬的。*canvas-*~ 帆布背衬的〕。

back·er [ˈbækə; ˋbækɚ] ***n***. **1**. (期票的)背书人;主持人,后台老板,后援者;支持物。**2**. (打字机的)垫纸。**3**. (赛

马等的)赌客。～-up 支持者;指示轰炸目标的飞机。

back·gam·mon [bæk'gæmən, 'bækgæmən; ˏbæk-ˋgæmən, ˋbækˏgæmən] *n*. (二人各持十五子,掷骰行棋的)十五子棋。

back·ing ['bækiŋ; ˋbækɪŋ] *n*. 1. 后退,倒退,逆行。2. 支持物;支援;(一群)支持人。3. 衬垫物;(书的)背衬,衬里,照相底板。4.【建】隔板,衬板,底板;内墙。5. (法官等)对令状的签署批准。6.〔俚〕音乐伴奏。～ **light** (舞台)背景灯光;(汽车尾部)后退灯。

back·less ['bæklis; ˋbæklɪs] *a*. 无(靠)背的;无背部的。

back·ward[1], **back·wards** ['bækwəd, 'bækwədz; ˋbækwɚd, ˋbækwɚdz] *ad*. 向后,在后,在后方;倒,逆;回向原处。*lean* ～*s* 往后靠。*spell* ～*s* 倒拼;误解,曲解。～(*s*) ***and forward***(*s*) 忽前忽后;来回地。***go*** ～*s* 倒退,退步,堕落。***say*** ～*s* 倒说。

back·ward[2] ['bækwəd; ˋbækwɚd] *a*. 1. 向后方的,向后的。2. 倒的;反的,相反的。3. 落后的,晚的;迟缓的,慢的;进步慢的。4. 愚钝的;畏缩的,迟疑的,怕羞的。*a* ～ *child* 智力差(落于人后)的孩子。*The country is in a* ～ *state*. 那个国家是落后的。*Summer is* ～ *this year*. 今年夏天来得晚。***be*** ～ ***in*** (*preparations, duty*) (准备)迟缓;忽视(责任)。～ **blessing** 诅咒。～ **process** 相反的程序。**-ly** *ad*. **-ness** *n*. 落后,迟疑。

back·ward·a·tion [bækwə'deiʃən; ˏbækwɚˋdeʃən] *n*. 〔英〕(证券)交割延期(费)。

ba·con ['beikən; ˋbekən] *n*. 1. (用背或肋部肉加工的)熏猪肉,咸肉。2.〔美口〕报酬,利益,奖品。***bring home the*** ～ 1. 成功;得胜。2. 谋生。***save one's*** [*sb.'s*] ～ 使自己[某人]免于死亡[受害]。***sell one's*** ～ 卖身。

Ba·con ['beikən; ˋbekən] *n*. 1. 培根[姓氏]。2. **Francis** ～ 培根〔1561—1626,英国经验论哲学家〕。3. **Roger** ～ 培根〔1214—1294,英国自然科学、哲学家〕。

Ba·co·ni·an [bei'kəunjən; beˋkonɪən] I *a*. 培根的,培根派哲学的。II *n*. 培根派哲学家。～ **method** 归纳法。～ **theory** "培根写剧说"〔英国文学史研究中的一家之言,认为莎士比亚戏剧实际上全为培根所写〕。

ba·con·y ['beikəni; ˋbekənɪ] *n*. 咸猪肉一样的;脂肪质的,多油的。

bact. = 1. bacteriology. 2. bacteriological.

bac·te·re·mi·a [ˌbæktə'riːmiə; ˏbæktəˋrimɪə] *n*.【医】细菌血症。

bac·te·ri- *comb. f*. 表示"细菌(的)"。

bac·te·ri·a [bæk'tiəriə; bækˋtɪrɪə] *n*. *pl*. (*sing*. *bac·te·ri·um*) 1. 细菌。2.〔美俚〕拳击迷。*acid fast* ～ 抗酸细菌。～**-free** *a*. 无菌的。

bac·te·ri·al [bæk'tiəriəl; bækˋtɪrɪəl] *a*. 细菌的。～ **fertilizer** 细菌肥料。

bac·te·ri·cide [bæk'tiərisaid; bækˋtɪrəˏsaɪd] *n*. 杀菌剂。**-cid·al** *a*. 杀菌的。

bac·te·ri·o·chlo·ro·phyll [bækˌtiəriə'klɔ(:)rəfil; bækˏtɪrɪəˋklɔrəfɪl] *n*. 细菌叶绿素。

bac·te·ri·o·cin [bæk'tiəriəsin; bækˋtɪrɪəsɪn] *n*. = bacillin.

bac·te·ri·o·log·i·cal [bəkˌtiəriə'lɔdʒikəl; ˋbækˏtɪrɪəˋlɑdʒɪkl̩] *a*. 细菌学(上)的;使用细菌的。～ **warfare** 细菌战。～ **weapon** 细菌武器。

bac·te·ri·ol·o·gist [bækˌtiəri'ɔlədʒist; bækˏtɪrɪˋɑlədʒɪst] *n*. 细菌学家。

bac·te·ri·ol·o·gy [bækˌtiəri'ɔlədʒi; bækˏtɪrɪˋɑlədʒɪ] *n*. 细菌学。

bac·te·ri·ol·y·sin [bæktiəri'ɔlisin; bækˏtɪrɪˋɑləsɪn] *n*.【微】溶菌素。

bac·te·ri·ol·y·sis [bækˌtiəri'ɔləsis; ˋbækˏtɪrɪˋɑləsɪs] *n*.【微】溶菌(作用)。**-ri·o·lyt·ic** [-ˌtiəriə'litik; -ˏtɪrɪəˋlɪtɪk] *a*.

bac·te·ri·o·phage [bæk'tiəriəfeidʒ; bækˋtɪrɪəfedʒ] *n*.【生】噬菌体。

bac·te·ri·os·co·py [bækˌtiəri'ɔskəpi; bækˏtɪrɪˋɑskəpɪ] *n*. 细菌镜检法。

bac·te·ri·o·sta·sis, bac·te·ri·o·stat [bæktiəriə'steisis, -ə'stæt; bækˏtɪrɪəˋstesɪs, -əˋstæt] *n*.【生】抑菌作用。**-o·stat·ic** [-ə'stætik; -əˋstætɪk] *a*.

bac·te·ri·o·ther·a·py [bækˌtiəriəu'θerəpi; bækˏtɪrɪəˋθɛrəpɪ] *n*.【医】细菌疗法。

bac·te·ri·um [bæk'tiəriəm; bækˋtɪrɪəm] *n*. (*pl*. *bac·te·ri·a* [bæk'tiəriə; bækˋtɪrɪə]) 细菌〔单数不常用〕。

bac·te·rize ['bæktiraiz; ˋbæktəˏraɪz] *vt*. 使受细菌作用。**-ri·za·tion** *n*.

bac·te·roid ['bæktirɔid; ˋbæktəˏrɔɪd] I *n*. 假菌体,变形细菌。II *a*. 细菌状的。

bac·te·roid·al [ˌbæktə'rɔidl; ˏbæktəˋrɔɪdl̩] *a*. 细菌状的。

Bac·tri·a ['bæktriə; ˋbæktrɪə] *n*.【史】大夏〔即巴克特里亚王国,亚洲西部阿姆河与兴都库什山之间一古国〕。

Bac·tri·an ['bæktriən; ˋbæktrɪən] *n*., *a*. 大夏[巴克特里亚]人(的)。～ **camel** 双峰骆驼。

ba·cu·li·form [bæ'kjuːlifɔːm; bəˋkjuləfɔrm] *a*. 杆状的,直的。

bac·u·line ['bækjulain; ˋbækjʊlaɪn] *a*. 棍棒的;笞刑的。

bac·u·lum ['bækjələm; ˋbækjələm] *n*. (*pl*. ～*s*, *bac·u·la* ['bækjələ; ˋbækjələ]) (哺乳动物的)阴茎骨。

bad[1] [bæd; bæd] I *a*. (***worse*** [wəːs; wɝs]; ***worst*** [wəːst; wɝst]) 1. 坏的,恶的,歹的,不好的,不道德的。2. 不正确的,错误的。3. 不中用的;低劣的;拙劣的。4. 不利的;有害的。5. 腐败的;臭的。6. 痛的,病的,不舒服的。7. 使人不愉快的;懊恼的。8. 严重的,厉害的。9.【法】不成立的;空名的。*a* ～ *blunder* 大错。*a* ～ *conductor* 不良导体。*a* ～ *conscience* (做坏事后的)内疚。*a* ～ *guess* 猜错。*a* ～ *light* 不充足的亮度,不适当的见解。*a* ～ *year* 不景气的一年。～ *for the health* 损害健康的。～ *for the stomach* 伤胃的。～ *habits* 坏习惯。～ *pains* 剧痛。*Bad drivers cause* ～ *accidents*. 技术差的司机往往造成严重事故。*That's too* ～. 那太糟了;那太可惜了;那真过意不去。～ **actor**〔口〕坏人;难对付的动物;惯犯。～ ***blood*** 恨,恶感;敌对情绪。～ ***coin*** 劣币。～ ***check*** 空头支票。～ ***debts*** 倒账,收不回来的债。～ ***egg*** 坏蛋;〔俚〕混蛋,坏人。～ ***hat***〔俚〕混蛋,坏蛋,歹徒。～ ***language*** 骂人的话;下流话。～ ***law*** 错误的定律。～ ***lot*** (一个或一帮)坏家伙。～ ***news*** 凶报,恶耗;〔美俚〕困难;麻烦的事[人];期票。～ ***time*** 苦境。～ ***trip***〔美俚〕(吸毒者的)恶性迷幻〔引起痛苦、恐怖的幻觉等〕。～ ***woman*** 不正经的女人。***be*** [***be taken***] ～ 有病[生病](*be* ～ *with gout* 患痛风病)。***be*** ～ ***at*** 不善于,…不行(*be* ～ *at figures* 不擅长计算)。***be*** ～ ***for*** 对…有害,不适宜于(*Smoking is* ～ *for health*. 吸烟对身体有害)。***feel*** ～ 觉得不舒服;有病。***feel*** ～ ***about*** 为…感到懊悔,为…觉得遗憾(*feel* ～ *about an error* 为做错事感到懊悔)。***go*** ～ (食物)变坏,腐败。***have a*** ～ ***time*** (***of it***) 遭遇困难,倒楣,吃苦头。***in a*** ～ ***way***〔口〕情况很不好;不景气;(健康)可虑。***not*** (***so, half***) ～ 不坏;不错(*Not* (*so*) ～. 还不错,还好。*The boy is not half* ～. 这个男孩子还不错)。II *n*. 恶劣状态,恶;不幸,倒霉。***be in*** ～〔美口〕倒楣;失宠(*with*)(*He is in* ～ *with his father*. 他爸爸不喜欢他了)。(***go***) ***from*** ～ ***to worse*** 越来越坏;每况愈下,变本加厉。***go to the*** ～ 1. 变坏,堕落。2. 衰败;落魄,一筹莫展。3. 得病(*She wept at seeing her son go to the* ～. 她为儿子的堕落痛哭流涕)。***to the*** ～ 亏空,亏损,亏欠(*I am six pounds to the* ～. 我亏损了六镑)。***with a*** ～ ***grace*** 勉强地,风度不佳地(*He took his defeat with a* ～ *grace*. 他对自己的失败表现得不够有风度)。III *ad*.〔美口〕笨拙(*Do you need money that* ～? 你那么缺钱用吗?)。～ **blood** 恶感,仇恨。～ **conduct discharge** 品行不良勒令退伍。～ **debt** (无法收回的)坏

帐,呆账,倒账。～**land** 邪恶横行地区[赌风猖獗、盗匪横行的地区]。～**lands**〔*pl*.〕〔美〕荒原,荒瘠不毛地带。～**man** 偷牲口的贼;亡命徒;(美国早期西部)受雇用的带枪歹徒。～**mouth** *vt*. 诋毁,贬低;给…脸上抹黑;严厉批评。～**-neighbour policy** 恶邻政策,与邻国为敌的政策。～ **patch**〔英〕(一段)倒霉时光。～ **pay**〔美俚〕赖债的人。～ **scene**〔美俚〕不愉快的事。～ **shit**〔美俚〕臭屎,肮脏的东西。～**-tempered** *a*. 脾气坏的,易怒的,暴躁的。～ **trip** **1**.〔俚〕恐怖幻觉。**2**.〔口〕不愉快的经历。

bad² [bæd; bæd] *v*.〔古〕*bid* 的过去式。

Ba·da·ri·an [bɑːˈdɑːriən; bɑˋdɑrɪən] *a*. 巴达里期的〔指上埃及新石器时代文化,特点是开始驯养家畜,制作精美陶器和品种繁多的装饰品〕。

Ba·der [ˈbɑːdə; ˋbɑdɚ] *n*. 巴德〔姓氏〕。

bad·der·locks [ˈbædəˌlɔks; ˋbædɚˏlɑks] *n*.【植】翅菜。

bad·die [ˈbædi; ˋbædɪ] *n*.〔美口〕坏蛋〔尤指电影或小说中与主角为敌的恶人〕。

bad·dish [ˈbædiʃ; ˋbædɪʃ] *a*. 次的,不甚好的;相当坏的。

bade [beid, bæd; bed, bæd] **bid** 的过去式。

BADGE = Base Air Defense Ground Environment【美空军】基地防空地面警备系统。

badge [bædʒ; bædʒ] *n*. **1**. 徽章,像章,奖章。**2**. 标记;象征。*a* ～ *for rank* 军阶章[肩章,领章]。*a merit* ～ 奖章。*a school* ～ 校徽。*The pine is a* ～ *of constancy*. 松树是节操的象征。

badg·er¹ [ˈbædʒə; ˋbædʒɚ] *n*. **1**.【动】獾,穴熊;獾皮,獾毛。**2**.〔美〕〔B-〕威斯康星州人。*the B- State*〔美〕威斯康星州。～ **game**〔美口〕美人计。～**-legged** 两腿一长一短的。

badg·er² [ˈbædʒə; ˋbædʒɚ] *n*.〔方〕(卖食品的)小贩。

badg·er³ [ˈbædʒə; ˋbædʒɚ] *vt*. (一半开玩笑地)欺负,惹,撩;纠缠,使困恼;还(价)。*Stop badgering me*! 别再缠我了!

bad·i·nage [ˈbædinɑːʒ; ˋbædnɪdʒ] *n*., *vt*.〔F.〕打趣,开玩笑,嘲弄。

bad·ly [ˈbædli; ˋbædlɪ] *ad*. (***worse*** [wəːs; wɝs]; ***worst*** [wəːst; wɝst]) **1**. 坏,恶劣地。**2**. 笨,拙劣地;不正确地。**3**. 有害地。**4**.〔口〕严重地,厉害,非常。*He was* ～ *wounded*. 他受了重伤。*We need money* ～ *now*. 我们现在非常需要钱。***be*** ～ ***off*** 景况不好,没钱,困穷;(感到)缺少。★也作形容词用。***feel*** ～ 感到不舒服,有病。***feel*** ～ ***about*** 对…感到遗憾[懊恼](*I feel* ～ *about your leaving so soon*. 我对你这么早就走感到遗憾)。

bad·min·ton [ˈbædmintən; ˋbædmɪntən] *n*. **1**. 羽毛球。**2**. (英国的一种)葡萄酒苏打水。

bad·ness [ˈbædnis; ˋbædnɪs] *n*. 坏,恶劣,不良,不正;不吉;严重。

BAE = **1**. Bachelor of Arts in Education 教育学士。**2**. Bachelor of Art Education 艺术教育学士。**3**. Bachelor of Aeronautical Engineering 航空工程学士。**4**. Bachelor of Agricultural Engineering 农业工程学士。**5**. Bachelor of Architectural Engineering 建筑工程学士。

Bae·de·ker [ˈbeidikə; ˋbedəkɚ] *n*. (德国人 Karl ～ 于 19 世纪出版的)旅行指南;(一般的)导游手册。～ **raids** (1942 年)德军对英国一些历史名城的空袭。

baff [bæf; bæf] *n*., *vi*.【高尔夫球】刮地打(使球高飞)。

baf·fle [ˈbæfl; ˋbæfl̩] **I** *vt*. **1**. 使受挫折,挫败,破坏,阻碍(计划、努力等)。**2**. 使困惑;使人为难;使迷惑。**3**. 用隔音板隔(音)。**4**. 挡住(水流等)。*These questions* ～ *me*. 这些问题使我无法回答。～ *description* 难以形容。～ *enemy's plan* 挫败敌方计划。～ *inquiry* 问不出,追究不出。～ *one's pursuer* 使追赶者扑空。— *vi*. 折腾;徒作挣扎。**II** *n*. **1**. 迷惑。**2**. 缓冲板;折流板;挡板,隔板;障板;栅极;反射板。**3**. 遮护物;阻碍体;【军】迷彩。～**-board** (扬声器的)反射板;隔音板。～**gab**〔美口〕冗长难解的谈话[文章]。～ **painting**〔美〕船舶的保护色。

baf·fling [ˈbæfliŋ; ˋbæfl̩ɪŋ] *a*. 起阻碍作用的;使…为难的;不能理解的,原因不明的。*a* ～ *man* 难以理解的人。*a detective's most* ～ *case* 难侦破的案件。～ **wind** 方向无定的弱风。

baff·y [ˈbæfi; ˋbæfɪ] *n*. 木制短高尔夫球棒。

baft [bæft; bæft] *n*. 一种粗棉布。～ **ribbon** (全由经纱胶粘成的)胶纱带。

bag [bæg; bæg] **I** *n*. **1**. 袋,囊;枕套。**2**. 钱包;手提皮包;〔*pl*.〕财富。**3**. 猎囊;猎获物。**4**. 囊状物;【棒球】垒囊;(母牛、母羊等的)乳房;肿眼泡。**5**.〔美俚〕丑姑娘;妓女。**6**.〔*pl*.〕〔英俚〕大量,很多(*of*);裤子;肚子,内脏;〔美〕阴囊。**7**.〔俚〕啤酒壶。**8**.〔口〕专长,爱好。**9**.〔口〕情绪;境遇。**10**. 个人特有的生活方式[习惯]。**11**.〔美俚〕(一包)毒品。～ ***and baggage*** **1**. 全部所有物。**2**. 总的,整个地(*The equipment had disappeared* ～ *and baggage*. 那台设备全部失踪了)。～ ***of bones*** 瘦骨嶙峋的人[动物]。***a*** ～ ***of wind*** 夸夸其谈的人。～ ***worm***【动】袋虫。～***s of***〔俚〕许多。***bear the*** ～ 掌管银钱,握经济权。***empty the*** ～ 倒空袋子;〔口〕和盘托出;把话说完说尽。***get the*** ～〔口〕被解雇[辞退]。***give sb. the*** ～ 解雇[辞退]某人;给(求婚人)碰钉子。***give*** [***leave***] ***sb. the*** ～ ***to hold*** 困难时丢弃别人,使别人承担责任[背黑锅]。***green*** [***blue***] ～ (英国)律师用的公事包。***hold the*** ～〔美口〕分得最差的一份;独自一人承担本应与他人共同承担的全部责任。***in the*** ～〔俚〕已是囊中物;拿在手里,掌握着;十拿九稳的;〔俚〕喝醉了的。***in the bottom of the*** ～ 最后一手。***make a*** ～ ***of*** 捕获,消灭。***put sb. in a*** ～ 占某人上风,制胜某人。***set one's*** ～ ***for***〔美〕对…抱有野心;追逐某人[某物]。***the whole*** ～ ***of tricks*** 一切手段;一肚皮的诡计。**II** *vt*. **1**. (**-gg-**) 把…装进袋里,偷窃;私吞,吞没。**2**. 捕获;击落,杀。**3**. 使成袋状,使膨胀。**4**.〔口〕登上(山峰),登临。— *vi*. **1**. 膨胀[下垂]如囊。**2**. 怀孕。～ ***a title***〔美俚〕获得锦标。～ ***a win***〔美俚〕竞赛得胜。～***s*** **1**. …是我的:*Bags I that book*! 那本书是我的。*Bags I the corner*! (小孩玩抢位游戏时)这个角落是我的! **2**. 该让我…:*Bags I first drink*! 我先喝! ～**fox** 用袋装带到猎场放出使猎狗追逐的狐狸。～ **guy**〔美〕卖气球的。～ **job** (对间谍活动证据的)非法搜查。～ **lady** **1**. 无家可归的老妇。**2**. 携带行李露宿街头的女人。**3**. 女毒品贩子。～**-play** *n*. 巴结,拍马。～**wig** (18 世纪流行的)丝囊假发。

B. Ag. = Bachelor of Agriculture 农学士。

ba·gasse [bəˈgæs; bəˋgæs] *n*.〔F.〕蔗渣。

bag·a·telle [ˌbægəˈtel; ˏbægəˋtɛl] *n*.〔F.〕**1**. 琐事;小玩艺儿。**2**. 短小的乐曲,短钢琴曲。**3**. 九穴台球〔一种类似桌上高尔夫球的球戏〕。*To him money is a* ～. 金钱对他来说不算一回事。

Bag·dad, Bagh·dad [bægˈdæd; ˋbægdæd] *n*. 巴格达〔伊拉克首都〕。

ba·gel· [ˈbeigl; ˋbegl̩] *n*. 过水面包圈〔发面圈经滚开的水煮然后烤成〕。

bag·ful [ˈbægful; ˋbægfʊl] *n*. **1**. 满口袋,一袋。**2**. 相当多。

bag·gage [ˈbægidʒ; ˋbægɪdʒ] *n*. **1**.〔美〕(手提)行李〔英国叫 luggage〕;【军】军用行李;辎重。**2**. 精神包袱;多余的东西;过时货。**3**.〔口、旧〕荡妇,淫妇;妓女,〔现指〕轻佻的女人〔又叫 impudent ～〕。**excess** ～超重行李。*a large amount of* ～一大堆行李。*a piece of* ～一件行李。～ **allowance**〔美〕行李重量限度。～ **car**〔美〕行李车厢;【军】辎重车。～ **car(r)ousel** (机场的)转盘式行李传送带。～ **check**〔美〕行李票,行李上的牌子。～ **man**〔美〕行李房办事人员。～**master**〔美〕行李处处长;辎重队长。～**office** 行李房。～**-smasher**〔美俚〕(车站的)行李搬运员〔乱摔行李者之意〕。～ **stock**〔美〕搬运马戏团行李等的驮马。

bagged [bægd; bægd] *a*.〔俚〕**1**. 喝醉酒的;沉醉的。**2**. 松弛下垂的。

bag·ger [ˈbægə; ˋbægɚ] ***n*. 1.** 装袋人;装袋器。**2.**【棒球】…垒打。**3.** 泥斗,掘泥机。*two* [*three*] ~ 二[三]垒打。**4.**〔口〕(在峰顶留下背包证明本人已攀登上来的)山峰登临者。

bag·ging [ˈbægiŋ; ˋbægɪŋ] ***n*. 1.** 袋布,袋料。**2.** 装袋,装包。

bag·gy [ˈbægi; ˋbægɪ] ***a*.** (***-gi·er***; ***-gi·est***) 膨胀如袋的;宽大的,松弛下垂的。

Bagh·dad = Bagdad.

bag·man [ˈbægmən; ˋbægmən] ***n*.**〔英〕小贩,行商;〔美〕检信员;〔美俚〕舞弊者;行贿、赌博等的钱财收送经手人;诈骗钱财的小流氓。

bagn·io [ˈbɑːnjəu; ˋbænjo] ***n*.** (*pl*. ~*s*) **1.** (意大利、土耳其的)澡堂。**2.**〔古〕(土耳其等的)牢狱。**3.** 妓院。

bag·pipe(s) [ˈbægpaip(s); ˋbæg,paɪp(s)] ***n*. 1.** 风笛。**2.**【无】人为干扰发射机。

bag·pip·er [ˈbægpaipə; ˋbæg,paɪpɚ] ***n*.** 吹风笛的人。

ba·guet(te) [bæˈget; bæˋgɛt] ***n*. 1.** 狭长方形钻石[宝石]。**2.** 狭长方形。**3.**【建】小凸圆体花饰。

bah [bɑː; bɑ] **I *int*.** 呸!〔表示轻蔑、厌恶等〕。**II *vt*.** 嘲笑。

ba·ha·dur [bəˈhɑːdə; bəˋhɔdʊr] ***n*.**〔印〕阁下〔印度人加在姓名或官职前的尊称〕。

Ba·ha·i [bəˈhɑːiː; bəˋhɑ·ɪ] **I *n*.** (*pl*. ~*s*) **1.** 巴哈派教徒。**2.** = Bahaism. **II *a*.** 巴哈派教义的。

Ba·ha·ism [bəˈhɑːizəm; bəˋhɑ·ɪzm] ***n*.**【宗】巴哈派教义〔源出伊朗 19 世纪的一个穆斯林教派,主张四海之内皆兄弟、社会平等等〕。**Ba·ha·ist *n*., *a*.** 巴哈派信徒(的)。

Ba·ha·ma(s) [bəˈhɑːmə(z); bəˋhɑmə(z)] ***n*.** 巴哈马〔拉丁美洲〕。

Ba·ha·mi·an [bəˈhɑːmiən; bəˋhemɪən, -hɑ-] **I *a*.** 巴哈马群岛的。**II *n*.** 巴哈马群岛的本地居民。

Bah·rein, Bah·rain [bɑːˈrein; bɑˋraɪn] ***n*.** 巴林〔亚洲〕。

baht [bɑːt; bɑt] ***n*.** (*pl*. ~(*s*)) **1.** 铢〔泰国的货币名称〕。**2.** 铢的硬币。

Ba·hu·tu [bəhuːˈtuː; bəhuˋtu] ***n*.** (*pl*. ~(*s*)) **1.** 布隆迪和卢旺达农民。**2.** 班图语。

bai·gnoire [ˈbeinwɑː; ,bɛˋnwɑr] ***n*.** 〔F.〕(戏院中与厅座同一层的)大厅包厢。

Bai·kal [baiˈkɑːl; baɪˋkɑl] **Lake** 贝加尔湖。

bail[1] [beil; bel] **I *n*.**【法】保释金;保释人;保释。***accept*** [***allow***, ***take***] ~ 准许保释。***admit*** [***let***] (***sb*.**) ***to*** ~ 准许(某人)保释。***give*** ~ (被告)缴保释金。***give leg*** ~ (= take leg ~). go ~ for 做(某人)的保释人;〔喻〕保证,担保。I'll go ~ that ...〔口〕我肯定…。***jump*** ~ = skip ~. ***offer*** ~ = give ~. ***on*** ~, ***out on*** ~ 在保释中。***refuse*** ~ (法官)不准保释。***save*** [***forfeit***] ***one's*** ~ 保释后如期出庭[不出庭]。***skip*** ~ 保释中逃跑。***take*** ~ 允许保释。***take leg*** ~〔口、谑〕逃走;溜掉。**II *vt*. 1.**【法】准许保释;为…做保释人;救出。**2.** 帮助…摆脱困境。**3.** 将(财物)委托给…。~ ***out*** 保释(被告);委托(货物)。~ **bond** 保释保证书。~ **jumper** 从保释中逃亡的嫌疑犯。

bail[2] [beil; bel] **I *n*.** 戽斗[戽出船肚水用]。**II *vt*., *vi*.** 舀(水),从(船中)戽出水。~ *water out of a boat* = ~ *out a boat*. 戽出船肚里的水。~ ***out***〔俚〕(从飞机上)跳伞。

bail[3] [beil; bel] ***n*.**【板球】三柱门上的横木;【史】(欧洲中世纪)城堡的外围工事;城堡的内院;(马厩的)栅栏;【无】轨,排。

bail[4] [beil; bel] ***n*.** (篷帐的)半圆形支撑箍托;(桶、壶等的)半圆形拎环;(打字机上把纸张压在滚筒上的)夹紧箍。

bail·a·ble [ˈbeiləbl; ˋbeləbl] ***a*.**【法】可保释的。

bail·ee [beiˈliː; beˋli] ***n*.**【法】(财物的)受委托人。

bail·er [ˈbeilə; ˋbelɚ] ***n*. 1.** 戽水者;戽斗;泥浆泵。**2.**【板球】打中三柱门横木的球。

Bai·ley [ˈbeili; ˋbelɪ] ***n*.** 贝利〔姓氏,男子名〕。(***the***) ***Old*** ~ 伦敦中央刑事法院。~ **bridge**【军】活动便桥,军用轻便桥。

bai·ley [ˈbeili; ˋbelɪ] ***n*. 1.** 城郭,外栅。**2.** (欧洲中世纪)城堡外墙。

bai·lie [ˈbeili; ˋbelɪ] ***n*. 1.** [Scot.] 市高级行政官。**2.** [方] = bailiff.

bai·liff [ˈbeilif; ˋbelɪf] ***n*. 1.** 法警;执行官;监守者。**2.**〔英〕地主管家。**3.**【英史】镇长,低级地区行政官。*a water* ~ 取缔秘密打鱼的水上巡警。

bai·li·wick [ˈbeiliwik; ˋbelə,wɪk] ***n*. 1.** 执行官的职权范围[管辖区]。**2.**〔美〕个人活动[兴趣、职权]范围;最擅长的范围,专长。

bail·ment [ˈbeilmənt; ˋbelmənt] ***n*.**【法】(财物的)委托;保释。*a contract of* ~ 委托契约。

bail·or [ˈbeilə; ,belˋɔr] ***n*.**【法】(财物的)委托人。

bail·out [ˈbeilaut; ˋbel,aʊt] **I *n*.** 紧急跳伞。**II *a*.** 应付紧急状况的。

bails·man [ˈbeilzmən; ˋbelzmən] ***n*.** 保释人。

Bain [bein; ben] ***n*.** 贝恩〔姓氏〕。

bain·ite [ˈbeinait; ˋbenaɪt] ***n*.**【冶】贝菌体,贝氏体。

bain-ma·rie [bæn məˈriː; bæn məˋri] ***n*.** (*pl*. ***bains-ma·rie***) 隔水炖锅;水浴器。

Bai·ram [baiˈrɑːm; baɪˋrɑm] ***n*.** 拜兰节〔伊斯兰教节日,一年两次〕。

bairn [bɛən; bɛrn] ***n*.** 〔Scot.〕幼儿,小孩。

bait [beit; bet] **I *n*. 1.** 饵;引诱物;诱惑。**2.** (路上的)休息(或进食)。*cut* ~ *or fish* 要么撒手不干,要么耐心地干下去。*jump at the* ~ 轻易上当。*poison* ~ 毒饵。*rise to a* ~ (鱼)上钩;(人)上当。*swallow the* ~ 吞饵上钩;落进圈套。*a white* ~ 银鱼。**II *vt*. 1.** 把饵装到…上;引诱。**2.** (在路上)喂喂(马)。**3.** 使狗逗(熊等);欺负(人);作弄(人)。~ *a hook* 给钓钩装饵。— ***vi*.** (在路上)休息(或吃东西)。~ **advertizing**〔美口〕诱售广告〔在广告上刊登实际上并不出售的廉价商品,以招徕顾客至本店购买昂贵商品〕。**~-and-switch *a*.**〔美口〕诱售法的。

baize [beiz; bez] **I *n*.** 桌面呢。**II *vt*.** 用桌面呢做…的衬底;在…上铺桌面呢。

bake [beik; bek] **I *vt*. 1.** 烘,焙,烤,烧。**2.** 焙干,烧硬,烧固。~ *pottery in a kiln* 在窑内烧陶器。— ***vi*.** 烤面包[饼等];烤熟;烘干;(砖等)在焙干中。**II *n*.** 烘,焙,烤;烘烤的成品;[美]烧烤会餐。

Bak·er [ˈbeikə; ˋbekɚ] ***n*.** 贝克〔姓氏〕。

bak·er [ˈbeikə; ˋbekɚ] ***n*. 1.** 面包师傅。**2.**〔美〕轻便烤箱。~*'s dozen* 十三。~ *'s salt* 碳酸铵[制面包用]。~ *'s yeast* 面包酵母菌。**spell** ~〔美俚〕做难事。**~-kneed *a*.** 膝头内曲的,对鸡脚的。**~-legged *a*.** = ~-kneed.

bak·er·y [ˈbeikəri; ˋbekərɪ] ***n*.** 面包糕点饼干厂[铺]。

bake·house [ˈbeikhaus; ˋbekhaʊs] ***n*.** 面包厂;面包店。

ba·ke·lite [ˈbeikəlait; ˋbekəlaɪt] ***n*.**【商标】酚醛塑料[树脂],电木,胶木。~ **varnish** 胶木漆。

bake-shop [ˈbeikʃɔp; ˋbekʃɑp] ***n*.**〔美〕面包铺;面包烘房 (= bakery).

bak·ing [ˈbeikiŋ; ˋbekɪŋ] **I *n*.** 烘烤(面包等),焙烘。**II *a*.** 烘烤的,灼热的。~ *heat* 炎热。~ **powder** 发(酵)粉,焙粉[化学膨松剂]。~ **soda** 小苏打;碳酸氢钠。

bak·la·va [ˌbɑːkləˈvɑː; ,bɑkləˋvɑ] ***n*.** (希腊,土耳其的)果仁蜜馅点心。

bak·sheesh, bak·shish [ˈbækʃiːʃ; ˋbækʃiʃ] ***n*. 1.** (土耳其、埃及等地的)小费,酒钱,小账,赏金,**2.**〔美空军俚〕(不遇敌机时的)容易差事。

Ba·ku [bɑːˈkuː; baˋku] ***n*.** 巴库〔阿塞拜疆首都〕。

BAL = **1.** blood alcohol level 血液中酒精含量。**2.** basic assembly language【计】基本汇编语言。**3.** British Anti-Lewisite 英国抗路易斯毒气剂。

B

ba·laam [ˈbeilæm; ˋbeləm] *n*. 1. 〔B-〕【圣】遭驴子责备的先知。2. 不可靠的预言者[伙伴]。3. 〔英俚〕(报章杂志上的)补白备用资料;作废或不用的稿件。～ **box** 废稿箱。

Bal·a·kla·va, Bal·a·cla·va [ˌbæləˈklɑːvə; ˏbæləˋklɑvə] *n*. 1. 巴拉克拉瓦〔黑海一港口〕。2. 〔b-〕大绒帽。～ **helmet** 〔英〕大毡盔。

bal·a·lai·ka [ˌbæləˈlaikə; ˏbæləˋlaɪkə] *n*. 俄国巴拉拉伊卡琴〔三角琴〕。

bal·ance [ˈbæləns; ˋbæləns] **I** *n*. 1. 〔常作 a pair of ～s〕天平,秤。2. 平衡,均衡,对称;抵消;比较,对照,对比。3. (钟表的)平衡轮,摆轮。4. 平衡块,平衡力。5. 【商】收付平衡[差额];余额,找头,尾数。6. 〔B-〕【天】天平座,天平宫。7. (情绪的)稳定,镇静。8. (艺术作品中)布局和比例的协调。9. 〔美口〕〔the ～〕剩余部分。10. 【医】身心平衡治疗法。*You may keep the* ～. 尾数[找头等]你收下好了。*The* ～ *of the account is against me*. 两抵下来是我欠人。*a favorable* [*an unfavorable*] ～ *of trade* 顺[逆]差;贸易出[入]超。～ ***due*** 账簿中贷方超过借方的数。～ ***on hand*** 账簿中借方超过贷方的数。～ ***of accounts*** 对账。～ ***of clearing*** 汇划结算余额。～ ***of*** (***international***) ***payment*** 国际收支差额,国际收支。～ ***of power*** 力量对比;力量均势。～ ***of trade*** 贸易[输出入]差额。***be*** (***thrown***) ***off one's*** ～ 失去平衡;摔倒;张皇失措;烦恼。***be out of*** ～ 在不平衡状态下。***hang in the*** ～ = tremble in the ～. ***hold in*** ～ 悬置未决。***hold the*** ～ 掌握决定权;举足轻重。***in*** [***on***] ～ 总的来说。***in the*** ～ 犹豫未决,忐忑不安。***keep one's*** ～ 保持身体平衡;镇定。***lose one's*** ～ 身体失去平衡,摔倒;慌乱。***on*** (***the***) ～ 两抵,结果。***redress the*** ～ 公平处理[调整]。***strike a*** ～ 结账;衡量得失,作出结论。***throw sb. off his*** ～ 使(某人)失去身体平衡,使摔倒;扰乱,使(某人)狼狈不堪。***tremble in the*** ～ 处于紧要关头,吉凶未决。**II** *vt*. 1. (用天平等)秤。2. 使均等,使平衡。3. 比较,对照;权衡,斟酌。4. 和…相抵,两抵;抵消。5. 结算,清(账)。— *vi*. 1. 平衡,均等。2. 收支平衡。3. 踌躇;摇摆不定。4. (舞蹈)作摇摆动作。*a* ～*d criticism* 实事求是的批评。*a balancing plane* 【空】安定翼面;平衡翼。*a balancing test* 【空】平衡试验。～ *accounts* 使收支平衡;结账。～ *the book* 结清各账。～ *oneself* 保持身体平衡。～ *out* 【物】衡消。～ **account** 【商】差额账。～ **beam** 【体】平衡木。～ **bridge** 开启桥。～ **of nature** 自然界生态平衡。～ **of payments** 国际收支(表)。～ **of power** 1. 力量对比。2. (国际间的)均势。～ **of terror** (建立在核武器基础上的)恐怖均势。～ **of trade** 贸易差额。～ **sheet** 【商】资产负债表,资金平衡表。～ **wheel** 平衡轮,轮摆,均衡轮。

bal·ance·a·ble [ˈbælənsəbl; ˋbælənsəbl] *a*. 可秤的,可平均的,可使平衡的。

bal·anced [ˈbælənst; ˋbælənst] *a*. 1. 平衡的;稳定的。2. 和谐的;有条不紊的。～ **budget multiplier** 预算平衡率。～ **diet** (营养)均衡的食谱。～ **sentence** 【语法】平衡句〔由两个平行的从句构成〕。～ **yarn** 【纺】不卷缩纱线。

bal·anc·er [ˈbælənsə; ˋbælənsɚ] *n*. 1. 权衡者;平衡物。2. 走钢丝演员。3. (双翅类昆虫的)平衡器。

bal·as [ˈbæləs; ˋbæləs] *n*. 【矿】玫瑰红尖晶石,浅红晶石。

bal·a·ta [ˈbælətə; ˋbælətə] *n*. 1. (西印度)巴拉塔树。2. (能在热水中软化的)无弹性树胶(= ～ gum)。

Bal·bo·a [bælˈbəuə; bælˋboə] *n*. 1. V.N. de ～ 巴波亚(1475? —1517),西班牙探险家,西方太平洋发现人。2. 巴波亚〔巴拿马运河西端港口〕。3. 〔b-〕巴波亚〔巴拿马的一种硬币〕。

bal·brig·gan [bælˈbrigən; bælˋbrɪgən] **I** *n*. 1. 巴尔布里根棉织品〔爱尔兰织品名,用以做袜子、内衣等〕。2. 〔*pl*.〕巴尔布里根织品服装。**II** *a*. 巴尔布里根织品制的。

bal·co·nied [ˈbælkənid; ˋbælkənɪd] *a*. 有阳台的。

bal·co·ny [ˈbælkəni; ˋbælkənɪ] *n*. 1. 露台,阳台。2. (剧场二楼)楼座〔gallery 之下, dress circle 之上〕。3. 舰尾望台。

bald [bɔːld; bɔld] *a*. 1. 秃(头)的;【动】白头的。2. 无毛的;无叶的;无树的;无芒的。3. 无装饰的;单调的,枯燥的。4. 赤裸裸的,毫无掩饰的。*the* ～ *wheat* 裸麦。*the* ～ *eagle* 【动】(北美)白头海雕。*a* ～ *mountain* 童山,秃山。*a* ～ *lie* 睁着眼睛说瞎话。～ **coot** (= baldicoot). ～ **cypress** 【植】落羽杉。～ **face** 〔美俚〕劣等威士忌酒。～**-faced** *a*. (动物)脸上有白斑的;厚颜无耻的。～**head** 1. 秃头的人。2. 一种家鸽。～**headed** 1. *a*. 秃头的,秃顶的(*go* ～*headed for* [*at*, *into*] 冒险向…突进)。2. *ad*. 〔口〕鲁莽地。～**pate** 1. 秃头的人。2. 赤颈凫(= widgeon).

bal·da·chin, bal·da·quin [ˈbɔːldəkin; ˋbɔldəkɪn] *n*. 1. 锦缎。2. (祭坛或宝座上的)华盖。3. 【建】龛室。

bal·der·dash [ˈbɔːldədæʃ; ˋbɔldɚˏdæʃ] *n*. 1. 梦呓,胡言乱语,妄语。2. 〔废〕劣酒。

bal·d(i)·coot [ˈbɔːld(i)kuːt; ˋbɔld(ɪ)ˏkut] *n*. 1. 【鸟】骨顶鸟,大鹬。2. 秃子;和尚。

bald·ing [ˈbɔːldiŋ; ˋbɔldɪŋ] *a*. 〔口〕变秃的。*a* ～ *head* 头发日稀。

bald·ish [ˈbɔːldiʃ; ˋbɔldɪʃ] *a*. 快秃的,略秃的。

bald·ly [ˈbɔːldli; ˋbɔldlɪ] *ad*. 直言不讳地,坦率地。***put it*** ～ 直言不讳地写[讲];直截了当地说。

bald·ness [ˈbɔːldnis; ˋbɔldnɪs] *n*. 1. 秃,秃头。2. 毫无掩饰;露骨。

bal·dric [ˈbɔːldrik; ˋbɔldrɪk] *n*. (悬挂剑、号角等的)饰带,肩带;胸绶。

Bald·win [ˈbɔːldwin; ˋbɔldwɪn] *n*. 鲍德温〔姓氏〕。

bal·dy [ˈbɔːldi; ˋbɔldɪ] *n*. 〔美俚〕秃子。

bale[1] [beil; bel] **I** *n*. 1. 大包,大捆;多量。2. 〔*pl*.〕货物。3. 龟群。*a* ～ *of cotton* 一包棉花。*a* ～ *of hay* 一捆干草。**II** *vt*. 把…打包。*a baling press* 打包机。

bale[2] [beil; bel] *n*. 〔古、诗〕祸,灾害;不幸;痛苦;悲叹。

bale[3] [beil; bel] *vt*., *vi*. = bail[2].

ba·leen [bəˈliːn; bəˋlin] *n*. 【动】鲸须。

bale·fire [ˈbeilfaiə; ˋbelˏfaɪr] *n*. (户外的)大火堆,大篝火;焚尸火;烽火。

bale·ful [ˈbeilful; ˋbelfəl] *a*. 1. 有害的,破坏性的;恶毒的。2. 〔古〕悲惨的。

Bal·four [ˈbælfuə; ˋbælfʊr] *n*. 巴尔弗〔姓氏〕。

Ba·li [ˈbɑːli; ˋbɑlɪ] *n*. 巴厘(岛)〔印度尼西亚〕。

Ba·li·nese [ˌbɑːliˈniːz, ˌbæliˈniːz; ˏbɑləˋniz, ˏbælɪˋniz] **I** *a*. 巴厘(岛)的;巴厘人的;巴厘语的;巴厘文化的。**II** *n*. 1. (*pl*. ～) 巴厘人。2. 巴厘语。

balk, baulk [bɔːk; bɔk] **I** *n*. 1. 障碍,阻碍,妨碍。2. 失败;错误,过失,挫折。3. 田埂。4. 【体】波克〔运动员跑过起跳线以后又退回另跳〕;【棒球】(投球员的)假投;【台球】波克线与台边之间的部分。5. 【建】圆方料,梁木;【机】(多臂机的)摆动杆;【军】浮桥长梁;【矿】煤层中的岩石包裹体。*a* ～ *to traffic* 交通妨碍。*make a* ～ *of good ground* 失去好机会。**II** *vt*. 1. 使受挫折;阻碍。2. 〔古〕忽视;避免;逃避。— *vi*. 1. 突然停止,急止。2. (马等)逡巡不前;畏缩不前。***be*** ～***ed of*** (希望等)受挫折,为…所阻,打破。***do not*** ～ ***at*** 不惜,不避。***never*** ～ ***at*** 对…在所不惜。～ **back** 绒背呢。～**line** 1. 【体】波克线,田赛起点线,起跳线。2. 【台球】发球线;波克线〔与台边平行的四条井字线〕。

Bal·kan [ˈbɔːlkən; ˋbɔlkən] **I** *n*. 巴尔干(半岛)。***the*** ～***s*** 1. 巴尔干山脉。2. 巴尔干国家(= the ～ states). **II** *a*. 巴尔干半岛(山脉)的;巴尔干各国(人)的。～ **frame** (医治骨折的)吊架。**-ite** *n*. 巴尔干人。

Bal·kan·ize [ˈbɔːlkənaiz; ˋbɔlkənˏaɪz] *vt*. 使巴尔干化;使割据;使分裂成互相敌对的小国。**-za·tion** *n*. 巴尔干化。

balk·y [ˈbɔːki; ˋbɔkɪ] *a*. 〔美〕执拗的,顽劣的,不愿意干

的,逡巡不前的;(马)爱突然站住不走的。

Ball [bɔːl; bɔl] *n*. 鲍尔〔姓氏〕。

ball[1] [bɔːl; bɔl] **I** *n*. **1**. 球;球状物。**2**. 球戏,(特指)棒球;【棒球】坏球 (*opp*. strike)。**3**.【军】子弹,炮弹。**4**.(人体上的)圆形突出部分。**5**. 眼球。**6**.〔俚〕〔*pl*.〕睾丸;〔喻〕胡说。**7**.【兽医】丸剂,丸药。**8**.【烹】肉[鱼等]丸子;面(粉)团。**9**.【天】星球,天体;(特指)地球。**10**.〔the ~〕(企业等的)管理权。**11**.〔俚〕人,家伙。*a ~ of string* 一团绳子。*the earthly ~*地球。*The ~ is with you*. 该你发球了;轮到你了。*an advance ~* (录音机里的)滑动滚珠。*a spent ~* 死弹〔冲力已尽的子弹〕。***a ~ of fire*** 一团火;〔美〕精力奋发的学生[实干家];〔美俚〕特别快车。***a ~ of fortune*** 命途多舛的人。***~ of the eye*** 眼球。***~ of the foot*** [***thumb***] 拇趾[拇指]底部的肉球。***be on the ~*** 〔美俚〕精力奋发地干,熟习内情。***carry the ~*** 〔口〕负责。***catch*** [***take***] ***the ~ before the bound*** 抢接飞球;先发制人。***Get on the ~!*** 〔美俚〕灵敏一些! ***have nothing on the ~*** 〔美俚〕毫无本领。***have something*** [***a lot, much***] ***on the ~*** 〔美俚〕有点本事。***have the ~ at one's feet*** [***before one***] 机会就在眼前。***keep the ~ rolling*** [***up***] 不使(谈话)中断,不使(事业)中辍。***make a ~ of*** 把…弄糟。***no ~*** 【板球】犯规的球。***on the ~*** 机灵,灵敏。***play at ~*** 打球。***play ~*** 打球,开始赛球;开始活动;合作,共事;行事公道。***put*** [***leave***] ***the ~ in sb.'s court*** 把球踢到某人场地上〔逼他作出反应〕。***take up the ~*** 接下来讲;轮到,接替。***three golden*** [***brass***] ***~*** 三个金[铜]球〔当铺的标识〕。**II** *vt*. 使成球;把…抟成丸。— *vi*. 成球形。***be*** (***all***) ***~ed up*** 〔美俚〕混乱,着慌,不知所措,说不出话来。***~ and chain*** 〔美〕附有铁球的脚镣,束缚;〔喻〕妻,老婆。***~ and socket*** 球窝关节。~ **bearings** 滚珠轴承。~ **boy** (为打网球的人拾球的)球童。~ **carrier** (橄榄球)带球进攻的球员。~**cartridge** 实弹。~ **cock** 浮球活栓。~ **control** (篮球、足球比赛中拖延时间的)终场控球战术。~ **firing** 实弹射击。~**flower**【建】球心花饰,花球。~ **game 1**. 球类运动〔尤指棒球〕。**2**.〔美俚〕活动中心[领域]。**3**. 情况,形势。~ **lightning** 球状电闪,电火球。~ **park** 棒球[垒球]场。~**player** 棒球[垒球]手。~**pen**, ~**point pen** 圆珠笔。~**-proof** *a*. 避弹的。~**room** 舞厅。~ **turret** (战斗机枪手的)球形座位。~ **valve** (浮)球阀,球闸门,漂子门。

ball[2] [bɔːl; bɔl] **I** *n*. 跳舞会;〔俚〕狂欢会。*give a ~* 开跳舞会(招待宾客)。***have a ~*** 〔美俚〕狂欢作乐。***lead the ~*** 领导跳舞;开始行动。***open the ~*** 开始舞;领头做,取攻势。**II** *vi*.〔美俚〕狂欢,尽情作乐;与…发生性关系 (*with*)。~**room** 舞厅 (~*room dancing* 交际舞)。

bal·lad [ˈbæləd; ˋbæləd] *n*. **1**. 民谣,歌谣,小调。**2**.【乐】叙事曲。~ **metre**【韵】民谣调。~**monger** 民谣作者;民谣歌本叫卖人;〔蔑〕蹩脚诗人,打油诗作者。~ **stanza** 歌谣的诗节〔通常为 4 行,押 abcb 韵〕。

bal·lade [bæˈlɑːd; bæˋlɑd] *n*.〔F.〕**1**.【韵】三解韵格〔由八行句三节及四行跋词形成的法国诗体〕。**2**. 配乐民谣。**3**.【乐】(为钢琴等独奏谱写的)拟叙事乐曲。~ ***royal*** 各行由十音节形成的七[八]行诗体。

bal·lad·eer [bæləˈdiə; bæləˋdɪr] *n*. 民谣歌手;民谣作者。

bal·lad·rom·ic [ˌbæləˈdrɔmik; ˏbæləˋdrɑmɪk] *a*. (火箭、导弹的)准确飞向目标的。

bal·lad·ry [ˈbælədri; ˋbælədrɪ] *n*. **1**.〔集合词〕民谣。**2**. 民谣创作。

bal·last [ˈbæləst; ˋbæləst] **I** *n*. **1**. 镇重物,压载物,压舱物,底货(石、沙等);(轻气球的)沙囊。**2**.【铁路】道碴,道圆。**3**.【电】镇流电阻,镇流器。**4**. 使(性格)坚定的经验[道德等],稳定因素;〔喻〕沉着,稳定。***in ~***【海】只装底货;只装(沙、石等)压舱物。**II** *vt*. 在…上装压舱物[沙囊];为(铁路等)铺道碴;使稳定,使沉着。**-ing** *n*. **1**. 装底货,铺道碴。**2**. 压舱材料;道碴材料。

bal·le·ri·na [ˌbæləˈriːnə; ˏbæləˋrinə] *n*. (*pl*. ***bal·le·ri·ne*** [ˌbæləˈriːni; ˏbæləˋrinɪ])〔It.〕(芭蕾舞)女演员〔尤指女主角〕。

bal·let [ˈbælei, Am. bæˈlei; ˋbæle, bæˋle] *n*. **1**. 芭蕾舞,舞剧。**2**. 芭蕾舞剧团。**3**. 芭蕾舞音乐。~ **blan** (女演员穿白色裙的)白裙芭蕾。~ **dancer** 芭蕾舞女演员,舞剧演员。~**-skirt** 芭蕾舞裙。

bal·let·o·mane [bæˈletəmein; bəˋlɛtəˏmen] *n*. 芭蕾舞迷。

bal·let·o·ma·ni·a [bæˌletəˈmeinjə; bæˏlɛtəˋmenɪə] *n*. 芭蕾舞狂。

bal·lism [ˈbælizm; ˋbælɪzm] *n*.【医】颤搐 (= ballismus)。

bal·lis·mus [bæˈlizməs; bæˋlɪzməs] *n*.【医】舞蹈病,颤搐。

bal·lis·ta [bəˈlistə; bəˋlɪstə] *n*. (*pl*. ***bal·lis·tae*** [bəˈlistiː; bəˋlɪsti])〔L.〕(古代的)弩炮,投石器。

bal·lis·tic [bəˈlistik; bæˋlistɪk] *a*. 弹道(学)的;发射(技术)的。***go ~*** 〔口〕发怒,生气。~ **curve** 弹道曲线。~ **missile** 弹道导弹。~ **pendulum**【物】冲击摆。~ **rocket** 弹道火箭。~ **trajectory** (火箭的)放射弹道。

bal·lis·ti·cian [ˌbælisˈtiʃən; ˏbæləsˋtɪʃən] *n*. 弹道学家;发射体设计家。

bal·lis·tics [bəˈlistiks; bæˋlɪstɪks] *n*. **1**.【军】弹道学;(谋求最远飞行距离的)发射体设计学[技术]。**2**. (火器、弹药等的)发射特性。*rocket ~*火箭[导弹]弹道学。

bal·lis·tite [ˈbælistait; ˋbæləsˏtaɪt] *n*. 混合无烟火药〔原为商标名〕。

bal·lis·to·car·di·o·graph [bəˌlistəuˈkɑːdiəugrɑːf; bəˏlɪstoˋkɑrdɪogræf] *n*.【医】投影心搏计。

bal·lon d'es·sai [ˈbælɔːŋdeˈse; bɑˏlɔ dɛˋsɛ]〔F.〕试风向的小气球;〔喻〕(对舆论等的)试探。

bal·lo·net [ˌbæləˈnet; ˏbæləˋnɛt] *n*.〔F.〕**1**. 小气球。**2**. 小气囊,(飞船的)气室。

bal·loon [bəˈluːn; bəˋlun] **I** *n*. **1**. 轻气球,气球;气罐。**2**.【纺】气圈。**3**.【建】球饰。**4**.【化】球形大烧瓶。**5**. (漫画中人物的)讲话引线。*a captive ~*系留气球。*a dirigible ~* 可操纵气球,飞船。*an observation ~*(射弹)观测用气球。*a sounding ~* 探测气球。**II** *vi*. **1**. 用[坐]气球上升。**2**. 膨胀如气球。**3**. 激增。**4**.〔美〕(演员)忘记台词。— *vt*. 使充气,使膨胀如气球。*a ~ing eye*【纺】导纱钩。**III** *a*. **1**. 气球状的。**2**. (货物等)分量轻而体积大的。**3**. (分期付款)最后一笔大数目的。~ **angioplasty**【医】气囊血管成形术[清理术]。~ **barrage** 气球防空网。~ **construction** 轻捷型构造。~**fish** 河豚。~ **score** 〔美〕运动比赛的高分。~ **tire** 低压(汽车)轮胎;〔美俚〕(演员)下眼皮松弛。**-ing** 气球驾驶;气泡上升;【军】飞机拉飘;【商】股票上涨。**-ist** *n*. 气球驾驶人。

bal·lot [ˈbælət; ˋbælət] **I** *n*. **1**. 投票用纸,选票;投票用小球。**2**. 无记名投票。**3**. 投票;投票权。**4**. 投票总数。**5**. 抽签。**6**. 候选人名单。**7**.〔美〕决定总统候选人的选举。*take a secret ~* 举行无记名投票。*vote by ~* 投票表决。*elected by ~*投票选举。***cast a single ~*** 〔美〕造成一致通过的现象。**II** *vi*. **1**. 投票,投票表决 (*for*; *against*)。**2**. 拈阄,抽签。— *vt*. **1**. 通过投票[抽签]选出。**2**. 向…拉票。~**box** 投票箱。~**paper** 投票用纸。

bal·lot·age [ˈbælətidʒ; ˋbælətɪdʒ] *n*.〔F.〕决选投票〔对得票最多而又均未达到决定多数的几名候选人再次投票决选〕。

bal·lotte·ment [bəˈlɔtmənt; bəˋlɔtmənt] *n*.【医】**1**. 反击触诊。**2**. 按胎法。**3**. 摸腹壁检查浮肾法。

bal·lute [bəˈluːt; bəˋlut] *n*. (宇宙飞船的)减速气球,气球式降落伞。

bal·ly [ˈbæli; ˋbælɪ] *a*., *ad*.〔英俚〕讨厌,非常,极,究竟。★这是 bloody 的代用语,语气较委婉。*too ~ tired* 疲倦极了。*Whose ~ fault is that?* 究竟是谁不好?

bal·ly·hack [ˈbælihæk; ˋbælɪˏhæk] *n*.〔美俚〕毁灭,灭

B

亡,地狱。*go to* ～ 滚蛋！去他的！

bal·ly·hoo [ˈbælihuː; ˋbælɪˏhu] **I** *n*. 〔美俚〕**1.** 哗众取宠、大吹大擂的广告[文章,演说]。**2.** 喧闹,吵吵嚷嚷,宣传。*a* ～ *artist* 善于自吹的人。～ *in the street* 街头的喧闹声。**II** [bæliˈhuː; bælɪˋhu] *vi*. 大肆宣传。— *vt*. 为…大吹大擂。

bal·ly·rag [ˈbæliræg; ˋbælɪˏræg] *vt*., *vi*. (**-gg-**) 〔俚〕虐待,欺负,折磨,戏弄,骂。

balm [bɑːm; bɑm] **I** *n*. **1.** 香油,香脂,香膏。**2.** 芳香,香味。**3.** 止痛药,镇痛剂;〔喻〕安慰物。**4.**【植】滇荆芥,白壳杨。**II** *vt*. **1.** 在…上搽香油。**2.** 安抚,安慰。**3.** 止(痛)。～ **cricket** 蝉。

bal·ma·caan [ˌbælməˈkɑːn; ˏbælməˋkɑn] *n*. 粗呢套袖大衣。

Bal·mor·al [bælˈmɔrəl; bælˋmɔrəl] *n*. **1.** 巴莫拉尔宫〔英国 Victoria 女皇在苏格兰的离宫〕。**2.** 斜纹呢衬裙。**3.** 苏格兰厚呢无边便帽。**4.** 〔b-〕一种镶花边的靴子[鞋子]。

balm·y [ˈbɑːmi; ˋbɑmɪ] *a*. **1.** 芬芳的,有香气的;香脂味的。**2.** 止痛的,安慰的。**3.** (气候等)温和的。**4.** 〔俚〕笨的,愚鲁的;〔英〕轻狂的。

bal·ne·al [ˈbælniəl; ˋbælnɪəl] *a*. 关于洗澡的;关于浴室的。

bal·ne·ol·o·gy [ˌbæniˈɔlədʒi; ˏbænɪˋɑlədʒɪ] *n*.【医】浴疗学,矿泉疗养学。

bal·ne·o·ther·a·py [ˌbælniəˈθerəpi; ˏbælnɪoˋθerəpɪ] *n*.【医】浴疗法。

Ba·lo·ney Bou·le·vard [bəˈləuni ˈbuːlivɑː; bəˋlonɪ ˋbulɪvɑ] *n*. 美国纽约 Broadway 的别名。

ba·lo·ney [bəˈləuni; bəˋlonɪ] *n*. **1.** 〔口〕大香肠。**2.** = boloney. ～**dollar** 〔美口〕劣质金元。

bal·sa [ˈbɔːlsə; ˋbɔlsə] *n*. 〔Sp.〕**1.** 西印度轻木(*Ochroma lagopus*)。**2.** 轻木材。**3.** 救生筏。

bal·sam [ˈbɔːlsəm; ˋbɔlsəm] **I** *n*. **1.** 香液,香脂,香膏;枞胶。**2.** 镇痛剂;安慰物。**3.** 产香脂的植物。**4.**【植】香脂冷杉;凤仙花;凤仙花属植物。**5.** 〔美俚〕金钱。*the garden* ～ 凤仙花。**II** *vt*. 在…上搽香膏;安慰,止(痛)。～ **fir** 胶枞;胶冷杉。～ **pear** [**apple**] 苦瓜。

bal·sam·ic [bɔːlˈsæmik; bɔlˋsæmɪk] *a*. **1.** 香膏质的,香脂一样的。**2.** 止痛的;安慰的。

bal·sam·if·er·ous [ˌbɔːlsəˈmifərəs; ˏbɔlsəˋmɪfərəs] *a*. 产生香液[香脂]的。

bal·sam·ine [ˈbɔːsəmin; ˋbɔlsəmɪn] *n*.【植】凤仙花。

Bal·tic [ˈbɔːltik; ˋbɔltɪk] *a*. 波罗的海的。*the* ～ *Sea* 波罗的海。

Bal·ti·more [ˈbɔːltimɔː; ˋbɔltəˏmɔr] *n*. 巴尔的摩〔美国马里兰州一港口〕。

Bal·to-Sla·vic [ˈbɔːltəuˈslɑːvik, -ˈslæv-; ˋbɔltoˋslɑvɪk, -ˋslæv-] **I** *n*. 波罗的-斯拉夫语族。**II** *a*. 波罗的-斯拉夫语族的。

Ba·lu·chi [bəˈluːtʃiː; bəˋlutʃɪ] *n*. (*pl*. ～(*s*)) 俾路支人。

bal·un [ˈbælən; ˋbælʌn] *n*.【无】平衡—不平衡变换器。

bal·us·ter [ˈbæləstə; ˋbæləstɚ] *n*. **1.**【建】栏杆柱;〔*pl*.〕栏杆。**2.** 椅背支柱。

bal·us·trade [ˌbæləsˈtreid; ˏbæləsˋtred] *n*. 栏杆,扶栏,回栏,扶手。

Bal·zac [ˈbælzæk; ˋbælzæk], **Honoréde** 巴尔扎克〔1799—1850,法国小说家〕。**-ian** [bælˈzeiʃən; bælˋzeʃən] *a*. 巴尔扎克的,巴尔扎克文风的。

bam[1] [bæm; bæm] *vt*., *n*. (**-mm-**) 〔俚〕哄,诱骗。

bam[2] [bæm; bæm] *vt*. (**-mm-**) 〔美俚〕打,揍。

Ba·ma·ko [ˈbɑːməkəu; ˋbɑməko] *n*. 巴马科〔马里首都〕。

bam·bi·no [bæmˈbiːnəu; bæmˋbino] *n*. (*pl*. ～*s*, ***bam·bi·ni*** [bæmˈbiːniː; bæmˋbini]) [It.] **1.** 婴孩,幼儿。**2.** 幼年耶稣像。

bam·boo [bæmˈbuː; bæmˋbu] *n*. **1.** 竹。**2.** 竹竿,竹棍。～ *grove* [*thicket*] 竹林。～ *shoots* [*sprouts*] 竹笋。*a* ～ *chair* 兜子,竹轿。*a* ～ *ware* 精致竹器。*the sacred* ～ 南天竹。

bam·boo·zle [bæmˈbuːzl; bæmˋbuzl] *vt*. 〔俚〕**1.** 哄,骗,欺骗,愚弄。**2.** 迷惑,使困惑。～ (*sb*.) *into* (*doing*) 哄(某人)做…。～ (*sb*.) *out of* 骗取(某人的)…。— *vi*. 哄,骗。**-ment** *n*.

ban[1] [bæn; bæn] **I** *n*. **1.** 禁止,禁令。**2.** (社会上的)禁忌,(舆论上的)谴责。**3.**【宗】诅咒,逐出教门。*lift* [*remove*] *the* ～ 开禁,解禁。*place* [*put*] *under a* ～ 禁止。*under the* ～ 被禁止;被逐出教门;被放逐。**II** *vt*. (**-nn-**) **1.** 禁止,取缔(*opp*. allow). **2.** 把…逐出教门。— *vi*. 〔古〕诅咒。

ban[2] [bæn; bæn] *n*. **1.** 布告。**2.** (*pl*.) = banns. **3.**【史】(中世纪封建君主征召家臣从军的)召集令;被召集来的家臣。

ban[3] [bɑːn; bɑn] *n*. (*pl*. ***ba·ni*** [ˈbɑːni; ˋbɑnɪ]) 巴恩〔罗马尼亚货币名,等于 1/100 列伊〕。

Ban·a·gher [ˈbænəgə; ˈbænəgɚ] *n*. 巴纳格〔爱尔兰一地名〕。*beat* [*bang*] ～ 超过一切;极其,非常。

ba·nal [bəˈnɑːl; bəˋnɑl] *a*. 平庸的,陈腐的。

ba·nal·i·ty [bəˈnæliti; bəˋnælətɪ] *n*. 平庸,陈腐,陈词滥调。

ba·nal·ize [ˈbeinəlaiz; ˋbenḷˏaɪz] *vt*. 使陈腐,使庸俗。

ba·nan·a [bəˈnɑːnə; bəˋnænə] *n*. **1.**【植】香蕉;芭蕉树。**2.** 〔美俚〕喜剧演员。**3.** 〔美俚〕大鼻子。*a hand of* ～*s* 一串香蕉。～ **belt** 〔美俚〕(气候相对温暖的)避寒地带。～ **oil** **1.**【化】香蕉油,醋酸戊酯。**2.** 〔美俚〕圆滑,伪善。～ **republic** "香蕉国"[指只有单一经济作物的拉丁美洲小国]。～ **seat** (自行车)细长而后部翘起的车座。**-s** *a*. 〔美俚〕令人发疯的(*go bananas* 发疯,发狂)。

ba·naus·ic [bəˈnɔːsik; bəˋnɔsɪk] *a*. 仅以实用为目的的,实利的,机械的,通俗的。

Ban·bur·y cake [ˈbænbəri ˈkeik; ˋbænbərɪ ˋkek] *n*. (英国 Banbury 地方特产的)加料果馅饼。

banc [bæŋk; bæŋk], **ban·co** [ˈbæŋkəu; ˋbænko] *n*. 法官席。*in* ～ 全体法官列席,在大法庭上(*a hearing in* ～ 由大法庭审理)。

Ban·croft [ˈbænkrɔft; ˋbænkrɔft] *n*. 班克罗夫特〔姓氏〕。

band[1] [bænd; bænd] **I** *n*. **1.** 带,绳;带形物;箍;箍条;嵌条;镶边;锯条;〔*pl*.〕(法官等的)宽领带。**2.** 束缚,羁绊;义务;〔古〕缧绁,枷,镣,铐(等)。**3.**【建】带形装饰,带花;【生】横纹。**4.**【物】频带,波段;光带;【机】调带;【地】夹层;【无】波段。**5.** (装订)钉书线,缀线。*an iron* ～ 铁箍。*a legal* [*moral*] ～法律[道义]上的义务。*a rubber* ～ 橡皮筋,橡皮圈。**II** *vt*. **1.** 用带捆扎。**2.** 在…上加条饰[镶边]。**3.** [后接复数反身代词或用被动语态]团结,联合。*They are* ～*ed together closely*. 他们紧密团结。*We* ～ *ourselves closely against the invaders*. 我们紧密地团结起来抗击入侵者。— *vi*. 团结,联合(*with*). ～**-aid** *a*. 急忙拼凑的。～ **house** 〔美口〕监狱。～ **mill** 带锯制材厂。～**-pass filter** 选带滤波器。～ **saw** 带锯。～ **switching**【无】波段转换。～ **wheel**【机】带轮。

band[2] [bænd; bænd] *n*. **1.** 队,团,群;(盗贼等的)帮,伙。**2.** (吹奏)乐队。*a* ～ *of robbers* 一伙强盗。*a* ～ *of stray dogs* 一群野狗。*a dance* ～ 跳舞的伴奏乐队。*a military* [*marine*] ～ 陆军[海军]军乐队。*the B- of Hope* 〔英〕少年禁酒团。*beat the* ～ 〔美〕显眼,出众;猛烈地;非常(*It rained all day to beat the* ～. 大雨倾盆,终日不止。*Business fell off to beat the* ～. 生意一落千丈)。*when the* ～ *begins to play* 事态变严重时。～**master** 乐队指挥。～ **moll** 乐队女郎[和摇摆舞乐队演员鬼混的少女]。～ **razor** 装有单面刀刃卷带的安全剃刀。～**sman** 乐队队员。～**-stand** *n*. (户外的)音乐台。～**wagon** 〔美〕领头的乐队车;某一时期流行的思想[政

策](*jump* [*be*, *hop*, *climb*, *get*] *on* [*aboard*] *the* ~*wagon* 赶浪头)。

band·age [ˈbændidʒ; ˋbændɪdʒ] **I** ***n*.** 绷带,包带;带。*a triangular* ~三角形绷带。**II** ***vt*.** 包扎,用绷带缚上。—***vi*.** 给…上绷带。~ **roller** ***n*.**【军】看护兵。

Band-Aid, bandaid [ˈbænˌdeid; ˋbænˏded] ***n*.** 〔B-〕【商标】急救带〔一种急救包扎绷带〕;〔b-〕急救绷带。

ban·dan·(n)a [bænˈdænə; bænˋdænə] ***n*.** (印度)班丹纳花绸(大手帕,大头巾)。

ban·dar [ˈbʌndɑ:; ˋbandar] ***n*.**【动】印度狭鼻猴。~**-log** 胡说乱讲的人。

Ban·dar Abbas [bænˈdɑ: əˈbɑ:s; banˋdar əˋbas] 阿巴斯港〔伊朗港市〕。

Ban·dar Se·ri Be·ga·wan [bænˈdɑ: ˈsiəri: bəˈgɑ:wæn; bænˋdarˋsɪri bəˋgawæn] 斯里巴加湾港〔文莱首府〕。

b. & b. = **1.** bed and breakfast 铺床及早餐。**2.** bed and board 床铺及伙食,膳宿。

band·box [ˈbændbɔks; ˋbændˏbaks] ***n*.** **1.** (装衣帽等的)硬纸盒。**2.** [口]纸盒式小建筑。***look as if one had just come out of a*** ~ 衣着整洁。

B and E = breaking and entering (非法)破门而入。

ban·deau [ˈbændəu; ˋbænˋdo] ***n*.** (*pl*. ~***x*** [-z])〔F.〕**1.** (妇女用的)发带,头带;细带。**2.** 奶罩。

ban·de·ril·la [ˌbɑ:ndeˈri:ljɑ:; ˏbandeˋrilja] ***n*.** (西班牙斗牛的)短扎枪。

ban·de·ril·le·ro [ˌbɑ:nderi:ˈljerɔ:; ˏbanderilˋjero] ***n*.** 〔Sp.〕斗牛士,斗牛者。

ban·de·rol(e) [ˈbændərəul; ˋbændəˏrol] ***n*.** **1.** 小旗,旒旗,枪旗;葬旗;墓旗。**2.**【建】刻匾。**3.** (有铭文的)绶带。

ban·di·coot [ˈbændiku:t; ˋbændɪkut] ***n*.**【动】**1.** 印度大鼠。**2.** 澳大利亚袋狸。

ban·dit [ˈbændit; ˋbændɪt] ***n*.** (*pl*. ~***s***, ***-ti*** [bænˈditi(:); bænˋdɪtɪ]) **1.** 恶棍,暴徒;盗贼;土匪,匪。**2.** 〔英空军俚〕敌机。*a banditti* = *a set of* ~*s* 一队土匪。*mounted* ~*s* 马贼。*a* ~ *gang* 匪帮。**-ry** ***n*.** 盗匪活动(*commit banditry* 抢劫)。

B and O = Band and Orchestra 〔美〕乐队。

ban·dog [ˈbændɔg; ˋbænˏdɔg] ***n*.** (用铁链拴着的)看门狗,猛犬。

ban·do·leer, ban·do·lier [ˌbændəˈliə; ˏbændəˋlɪr] ***n*.**【军】子弹带。

ban·do·le·ro [ˌbændəˈliərrəu; ˏbændəˋlɪrro] ***n*.** 〔Sp.〕路劫强盗。

ban·do·line [ˈbændəli:n; ˋbændəˏlin] **I** ***n*.** 发油,头油。**II** ***vt*.**, ***vi*.** (给…)涂发油。

ban·dore [bænˈdɔ:, ˈbændɔ:; bænˋdor, ˋbændor] ***n*.** 班多拉琴〔略似吉他的古琴〕。

B and S = brandy and soda 掺苏打水的白兰地酒。

B and T 〔美俚〕熏肉番茄三明治(=B.T.)。

Ban·dung, Ban·doeng [ˈbɑ:nduŋ; ˋbanduŋ] ***n*.** 万隆(印度尼西亚城市)。

ban·dy[1] [ˈbændi; ˋbændɪ] **I** ***vt*.** **1.** 把(球)打来打去,丢来丢去;来回摆弄。**2.** 交换,互换,受授。**3.** 议论,谈论,传播。~ *blows with sb*. 与某人对打。~ *compliments with sb*. 互道寒暄,互相问候。~ *a rumour about* 散布谣言。~ ***words with*** 与(人)对吵[顶嘴]。**II** ***n*.** **1.** 〔废〕旧式网球。**2.** 曲棍球 (= hockey); 简化式曲棍球 (= shinny)。

ban·dy[2] [ˈbændi; ˋbændɪ] ***a*.** 膝向外曲的。~**-legged** ***a*.** 罗圈腿的。

ban·dy[3] [ˈbændi; ˋbændɪ] ***n*.** 印度马车,(特指)牛车。

bane [bein; ben] ***n*.** **1.** 巨毒。★此义现仅用于 ratsbane, henbane 等复合词。**2.** 毁灭者,害人精;祸害。**3.** 死,毁灭。

bane·ber·ry [ˈbeinberi; ˋbenˏberɪ] ***n*.** **1.** 类叶升麻属植物。**2.** 类叶升麻属植物的浆果。

bane·ful [ˈbeinful; ˋbenful] ***a*.** **1.** 有害的。**2.** 有毒的。**3.** 致死的,导致毁灭的。*a* ~ *superstition* 有害的迷信。~ *herbs* 毒草。

bang[1] [bæŋ; bæŋ] **I** ***vt*.** **1.** 咚地敲(鼓等);当地撞(钟等);轰地开(炮等);砰地关上(门等)。**2.** 粗手粗脚地摆弄。**3.** 〔俚〕痛打,重打。**4.** 〔俚〕胜过,超过。— ***vi*.** **1.** (钟等)当当响;(炮等)轰地放;(门等)砰地关上 (*to*). **2.** 砰砰作响。~ (***oneself***) ***against*** 砰地撞上,碰在…上。~ ***away at*** **1.** 专心致志地做 (*students* ~*ing away at their homework* 学生专心做功课)。**2.** 攻击,向…发动猛攻。~ ***in the arm*** 〔美〕打(吗啡等)麻醉针。~ (*sth.*) ***into sb***. [***sb.'s head***] 硬把(某事物)灌输进某人头脑。~ ***low*** 〔美〕(拳击)打腰带以下;犯规。~ ***off*** 轰然开炮;(织机)碰撞开车;立即。~ ***on*** 〔英口〕好,要得 (*That cap is exactly* ~ *on*. 那顶帽子正好)。~ ***out*** [***up***] 〔美口〕好! 好货色! ~ ***up*** **1.** 砰地摔上。**2.** 弄伤,弄坏。**II** ***n*.** **1.** 棒打,重打;冲击。**2.** 爆炸声;咚咚声,当当声,轰隆声,砰砰声。**3.** 〔美口〕猛冲,突然跃起。**4.** 热情,精力。**5.** 〔美俚〕刺激,快感;服用(麻醉品)。*a sonic* ~音速冲响。~ ***out of the buck*** 〔美俚〕投资的收益。***in a*** ~ 赶紧,急忙。***with a*** ~ **1.** 砰地一声,轰然。**2.** 剧烈而突然地。**3.** 成功地。**III** ***ad*.** **1.** 砰然,轰然。**2.** 蓦地,突然。**3.** 〔口〕正巧;全然。~ *in the middle* 正当中。*Bang went the gun*. 砰地响了一枪。*Bang went sixpence*. 六便士大洋完蛋了〔对吝啬鬼的讽刺〕。*go* ~ 砰地关上;咔嗒破裂。~**-bang** 战争影片。~ **zone** (飞机)声爆(影响所及)区。

bang[2] [bæŋ; bæŋ] **I** ***n*.** 前刘海(发式)。**II** ***vt*.** 把(前额头发)剪成刘海式(剪短)。~ **tail** 〔美俚〕比赛用的马。

bang[3] [bæŋ; bæŋ] = bhang.

ban·ga·lore [ˌbæŋgəˈlɔ:; ˏbæŋgəˋlor] ***n*.** 爆破筒 (= ~ torpedo).

bang·er [ˈbæŋə; ˋbæŋɚ] ***n*.** 〔英俚〕**1.** 香肠。**2.** 爆竹。**3.** 噪音大的破旧汽车,老爷车。

Bang·kok [bæŋˈkɔk; bæŋˋkak] ***n*.** 曼谷〔泰国首都〕。

Ban·gla·desh [ˌbɑ:ŋgləˈdeʃ; ˏbæŋgləˋdɛʃ] ***n*.** 孟加拉国〔亚洲〕。**-deshi** [-ˈdeʃi; -ˋdɛʃɪ] ***n*.** 孟加拉人。

ban·gle [ˈbæŋgl; ˋbæŋgl] ***n*.** 手镯;脚镯。

Ban·gui [bɑ:ŋˈgi:; baŋˋgi] ***n*.** 班吉〔中非共和国首都〕。

bang-up [ˈbæŋˈʌp; ˋbæŋˋʌp] ***a*.** 〔美俚〕上等的,顶好的。*a really* ~ *fur coat* 顶呱呱的一件皮大衣。

ban·gy [ˈbæŋgi; ˋbæŋgɪ] ***a*.** 〔美俚〕= bang-up.

ba·ni [ˈbɑ:ni; ˋbanɪ] ***n*.** *pl*. (*sing*. ***ban*** [bɑ:n; ban]) 巴尼〔罗马尼亚货币名〕。

ban·ian, ban·yan [ˈbæniən; ˋbænjən] ***n*.** **1.**【植】(印度)榕树。**2.** (印度人的)法兰绒宽衬衣。~ **day**【海】素餐日。

ban·ish [ˈbæniʃ; ˋbænɪʃ] ***vt*.** **1.** 把…充军,处…以流刑,流放,放逐。**2.** 消除,排除(恐惧等)。~ *sb*. *from* [*out of*] *the country* 把某人流放国外。~ (*sth.*) *from memory* 完全忘记。~ *care* 打消忧虑。

ban·ish·ment [ˈbæniʃmənt; ˋbænɪʃmənt] ***n*.** **1.** 充军,放逐,流刑,流放。**2.** 驱逐;排除。

ban·is·ter [ˈbænistə; ˋbænɪstɚ] ***n*.** **1.** 栏杆小柱。**2.** 〔*pl*.〕栏杆,楼梯扶手。

ban·jo [ˈbændʒəu; ˋbændʒo] ***n*.** (*pl*. ~(***e***)***s***) 班卓琴。**-ist** ***n*.** 班卓琴奏者。

Ban·jul [ˈbændʒu:l; ˋbændʒul] ***n*.** 班珠尔〔冈比亚(甘比亚)首都〕。

bank[1] [bæŋk; bæŋk] **I** ***n*.** **1.** 堤,堤防;岸,河畔。**2.** 埂,垄,堆。**3.** (海中水下的)沙洲,滩。**4.** 斜坡,边坡,坡度;转弯。【空】(飞机转弯时的)倾斜状态,倾斜。**5.**【矿】采煤工作面地区[通道],井口区;【撞球】(球台的)橡皮边。*the right* [*left*] ~(顺流方向的)右[左]岸。*a sand* ~ 沙洲。*the angle of* ~ (飞行中的)倾角。~ *of clouds* 云峰,云层。***from*** ~ ***to*** ~ (矿工)由下井到出井(的时间)。**II** ***vt*.** **1.** 在…旁筑堤;堆积;围;封(火)。**2.**【空】使倾斜;【撞球】使(球)碰边(入袋)。**3.** 使(公路、铁路转弯

处)外侧比内侧超高。～ *a fire* 封火。— ***vi*.** **1.** 形成堤;(云)拥积。**2.**【空】倾斜;倾斜着飞行;(汽车)倾斜着行驶。～ ***up*** 堵截(河流等);封(火);【冶】封炉;成堤状,(重叠)成层(*Clouds began to* ～ *up*. 云层开始重叠起来)。

bank[2][bæŋk; bæŋk] **I *n*.** **1.** 银行,金库。**2.** 庄家;庄家面前的赌本;赌场主。**3.** 库,贮藏所,贮备。*a blood* ～ 血库。*a savings* ～ 储蓄银行。***break the*** ～ 耗尽资源;(赌博)下庄,把庄上的钱全部赢来。***in*** ～ 存入银行;准备着,储蓄着。***safe as the*** ～ 十分安全。英格兰银行。**II *vt*.** **1.** 把(钱)存入银行。**2.** 资助,为…提供资金。— ***vi*.** **1.** 开银行。**2.** 在银行里存款;与银行往来(*with*)。**3.** (赌博)做庄家。～ ***on*** [***upon***]〔口〕信赖,依赖,指望,依靠。～ ***with*** 和(银行)有往来。～ **acceptance** 银行承兑[背书]支票。～ **account** 银行往来账,活期存款。～ **annuities** 英国统一公债。～ **balance** 银行存款余额。～ **bill**〔美〕钞票;〔英〕转账票据。～**book** 银行存折。～ **cable transfer** 银行电汇。～ **card** (赊账用的)银行信用卡。～ **clearing** 票据交换。～ **clerk**〔某〕银行雇员。～ **credit** 银行担保(书)。～ **demand *n*.** (国外汇兑的)银行即期支付。～ **deposit** 银行存款。～ **discount** 银行贴现。～ **draft** 银行汇票。**B- for International Settlement** 国际清算银行。～ **holiday**〔美〕(星期日以外的)银行假日;〔英〕(银行)公假日〔一年六次,即 Good Friday, Easter Monday, Whitmonday, 八月的第一个星期一, Christmas Day, Boxing Day〕。～ **manager** 银行分行经理。～ **money** 银行票据[本票,汇票等]。～ **night**〔美俚〕电影院举行观众抽奖的夜晚。～ **note** 纸币。～ **of circulation** [**issue**] 发钞银行。～ **paper** 钞票;(银行)承兑票据。～ **rags**〔美俚〕钞票。～**-rate** 银行贴现率,银行日息。～ **reserve** 银行准备金。～ **returns** 银行营业报告。～ **roll** **1.** ***n*.**〔Am.〕一卷钞票;货币储备;有效资金。**2.** ***vt*.**〔口〕为…提供资金,对…通融资金。～ **sneak** 银行贼。～ **year** 银行会计年度。**the Bank** = **the Bank of England** 英格兰银行。

bank[3][bæŋk; bæŋk] **I *n*.** **1.** 排,列,组,系列;【电】触排,线弧;组合。**2.**【乐】键座。**3.**〔美〕一排电梯。**4.** 桨手(座位);【法】法官席位。**5.** 报纸小标题。*transformer* ～*s* 变压器组。～***s of*** 成排[组]的。***in*** ～***s*** 成排[组]地。**II *vt*.** 把…排成一列。～ *the seats* 把座位摆成一排。

bank·a·ble [ˈbæŋkəbl; ˋbæŋkəbl̩] ***a*.** 银行肯保的,(证券等)银行可承兑的。

bank·er[1][ˈbæŋkə; ˋbæŋkɚ] ***n*.** **1.** 银行家;财东。**2.** (赌博)庄家;赌场账房。**3.** 一种(赌博性)纸牌戏。**4.**〔美口〕付账人。*Let me be your* ～. 我借钱给你。*a* ～*'s clearing house* 票据交换所。*Let him be the* ～ *this time*. 这回让他给钱好了。～**'s bill** 银行对外国银行开出的汇票。

bank·er[2][ˈbæŋkə; ˋbæŋkɚ] ***n*.** **1.** 堤防工人;〔英方〕挖沟工人。**2.** (纽芬兰近海的)捕鳕人[船]。**3.**【猎】跳过堤埂的猎马。

bank·er[3][ˈbæŋkə; ˋbæŋkɚ] ***n*.** (雕石像、砌砖等用的)造型台,工作台。

bank·ing[1][ˈbæŋkiŋ; ˋbæŋkɪŋ] ***n*.** **1.** 筑堤,堤防。**2.** (纽芬兰的)近海渔业。**3.**【空】横倾斜。

bank·ing[2][ˈbæŋkiŋ; ˋbæŋkɪŋ] ***n*.** 银行业;银行学;金融。～ **centre** 金融中心。～ **holiday** (周转不灵等时的)银行休业[搁浅]。～ **hours** 银行营业时间。～ **house** 银行。～ **power** 贷出能力。～ **reserve** = bank reserve.

bank·roll·er [ˈbæŋkrəulə; ˋbæŋkˏrolɚ] ***n*.** **1.** 提供资金者,资助者,财东。**2.**〔美俚〕红演员,红角,红播音员。

bank·rupt [ˈbæŋkrəpt; ˋbæŋkrʌpt] **I *n*.** **1.** 破产者,无力偿还债务者。**2.** 丧失(名誉、智力等)的人。*a moral* ～道德沦丧的人。**II *a*.** **1.** 破了产的;无支付力的,无力偿还债务的。**2.** (名誉)扫地的,(智力等)完全丧失的。**3.** 垮了的,枯竭的。*be declared* ～ 宣告破产。～ ***of*** [***in***] 完全丧失,完全缺乏(*be* ～ *in reputation* 声誉扫地)。***go*** ～ 破产。***play the*** ～ 破产;(用破产方式)骗钱;〔喻〕失信用。**III *vt*.** 使破产,使无力偿付。

bank·rupt·cy [ˈbæŋkrəptsi; ˋbæŋkrʌptsɪ] ***n*.** **1.** 破产,倒闭,倒账,无偿付能力。**2.** (勇气,智力等的)完全丧失(*of*; *in*)。***go into*** ～破产。～ **administrator**【法】破产管理人。

Banks [bæŋks; bæŋks] ***n*.** 班克斯〔姓名〕。

bank·si·a [ˈbæŋksiə; ˋbæŋksɪə] ***n*.**【植】山茂樫。

banks·man [ˈbæŋksmən; ˋbæŋksmən] ***n*.** (煤矿的)井外监工。

ban·lieue [bɑːnˈljə; bænˋlju] ***n*.**〔F.〕郊区;市郊住宅区。

ban·ner [ˈbænə; ˋbænɚ] **I *n*.** **1.** 旗,国旗,军旗,标帜,旗帜;横幅标语。**2.**〔美〕(报上横贯全页的)大字标题〔又称 ～ head 或 ～ line〕。**3.**〔中〕(内蒙古行政区划的)旗〔相当于县〕;【史】(满清军事组织的)旗。***carry the*** ～〔美俚〕(没有地方睡)在街上走一夜;流浪街头。***follow*** [***join***] ***the*** ～ ***of*** 投入…旗帜下。***under the*** ～ ***of*** 在…旗帜下。***unfurl one's*** ～ 使旗帜鲜明,表明主张。**II *a*.** **1.** 杰出的,第一流的,为首的。**2.**〔美〕突出地支持(某一政党)的。*a* ～ *year for crop* 丰年。*a* ～ *Democratic county* 一个突出支持民主党的县。～ **bearer** 旗手。～**-man** **1.** 旗手。**2.** (满清的)旗人。～ **screen** (吊在炉前的)防火隔屏。～ **state** 美国的主要州。

ban·ner·et(te) [ˌbænəˈret; ˏbænəˋrɛt] ***n*.** **1.** 小旗。**2.**【英史】小旗骑士〔能在自己的旗下率领部下上阵的骑士〕;小旗骑士爵位〔在 baron 之下〕。

ban·ner·ol(e) [ˈbænərəul; ˋbænəˏrol] ***n*.** = banderol(e).

ban·nis·ter [ˈbænistə; ˋbænɪstɚ] ***n*.** = banister.

ban·nock [ˈbænək; ˋbænək] ***n*.** (苏格兰的)燕麦[大麦]烤饼。

banns [bænz; bænz] ***n*.**〔*pl*.〕结婚预告〔于教堂中结婚前预告婚事〕。***ask*** [***call***, ***publish***, ***put up***] ***the*** ～ (在教堂中结婚前)预告婚事以防异议。***forbid the*** ～ 对别人婚事提出异议。***have one's*** ～ ***asked*** 请教堂公布结婚预告。

ban·quet [ˈbæŋkwit; ˋbæŋkwɪt] **I *n*.** (通常指正式的)宴会,请客;酒席。*give* [*hold*] *a* ～ 举行宴会。*a state* ～ 国宴。*a regular* ～ 豪华的酒席。**II *vt*.** 宴请,设宴招待。— ***vi*.** 饮宴,参加宴会;大吃大喝。

ban·quette [bæŋˈket; bæŋˋkɛt] ***n*.** **1.**【军】(战壕内的)射击踏垛。**2.** 弃土堆;填土;护坡道。**3.**〔美〕人行道。**4.** (公共马车等的)长凳。**5.**【建】窗口凳。

Ban·quo [ˈbæŋkwəu, ˈbæn-; ˋbæŋkwo, ˋbæn-] 班戈〔莎士比亚戏剧《麦克白》中的苏格兰勇将〕。

bans [bænz; bænz] ***n*.** = banns.

ban·shee, ban·shie [bænˈʃiː, ˈbænʃiː; bænˋʃi, ˋbænʃi] ***n*.** (英国古代民间传说中的)报丧女妖。

bant [bænt; bænt] ***vi*.**〔谑〕实行蔬食减胖法。

ban·tam [ˈbæntəm; ˋbæntəm] **I *n*.** **1.**〔B-〕【动】矮脚鸡。**2.** 矮小好斗的人;〔美俚〕不够征兵标准高度的矮子。**3.** 轻量级拳师。**4.**〔*pl*.〕(欧战时的)矮子大队。**II *a*.** **1.** 矮小好斗的。**2.** 小型的。～ **weight** ***n*.**【拳】最轻级〔体重 116(英),118(美)磅以下〕。

ban·ter [ˈbæntə; ˋbæntɚ] **I *n*.** **1.** (没有恶意的)开玩笑,逗乐。**2.**〔美方〕挑战。**II *vt*.** (没有恶意地)取笑;〔美方〕挑,逗。— ***vi*.** 开玩笑。**-ing** ***a*.** 开玩笑的。**-ly** ***ad*.**

Bant·ing·ism [ˈbæntiŋizəm; ˋbæntɪŋˏɪzm̩] ***n*.** 蔬食减胖疗法〔英国医生 W. Banting 所倡导〕。

bant·ling [ˈbæntliŋ; ˋbæntlɪŋ] ***n*.**〔蔑〕乳臭小儿。

Ban·tu [ˈbænˈtuː; ˋbænˋtu] ***n*.** (南非的)班图语;班图人。

ban·yan [ˈbæniən; ˋbænɪən] ***n*.** = banian.

ban·zai [ˈbɑːnˈzɑːi; ˋbɑnˋzɑɪ] **I *int*.**〔日〕万岁! 冲呀! **II *a*.** 拼死的,自杀式的。～ **attack** [**charge**] 敢死队的进攻[冲锋]。

ba·o·bab [ˈbeiəubæb; ˋbeoˏbæb] ***n*.**【植】猢狲面包树

〔非洲产，又名 monkey-bread tree，所产果实可供食用〕。

bap [bæp; bæp] *n*.〔Scot.〕小面包(卷儿)。

BAPS = British Association of Plastic Surgeons 英国整形外科医师协会。

bap·ti·si·a [bæpˈtiziə, -ˈtiʒə; bæpˋtɪzɪə, -ˋtɪʒə] *n*.【植】赝靛属植物。

bap·tism [ˈbæptizəm; ˋbæptɪzəm] *n*. **1.**【基督】洗礼，浸礼。**2.** 命名(式)。~ *of blood* 殉教。~ *of fire* **1.**（圣经中)圣灵的洗礼。**2.** 炮火的洗礼，初经战场；第一次战斗经验[严重经验]。*the clinic* ~ 病床洗礼，临终洗礼。

bap·tis·mal [bæpˈtizməl; bæpˋtɪzml] *a*. 洗礼的，浸礼的。*a* ~ *name* 洗礼名，教名。

Bap·tist [ˈbæptist; ˋbæptɪst] *n*. **1.**【基督】(主张全身浸水的)浸礼教徒。**2.** 圣徒约翰 (= St. John the ~)。**3.**〔b-〕施侵礼者。*the* ~ *Church* [*the* ~]（基督教新教)浸礼会。

bap·tis·t(e)r·y [ˈbæptist(ə)ri; ˋbæptɪst(ə)rɪ] *n*. **1.** 洗礼所，洗礼堂。**2.** 洗礼盘。

bap·tize, bap·tise [bæpˈtaiz; bæpˋtaɪz] *vt*. **1.**【基督】给…施行洗礼。**2.** 给…命名。**3.**（精神上)洗涤。使净化。— *vi*. 举行洗礼。

BAR = Browning automatic rifle 白朗宁自动步枪。

Bar [bɑː; bɑr] *n*. 巴尔〔南斯拉夫港市〕。

bar [bɑː; bɑr] **I** *n*. **1.** 棒，杆，条；棒状物。**2.** 横木，闩。**3.** 栅栏；关卡，城门。**4.** 障碍，妨碍 (*to*)。**5.**（河口的)沙洲。**6.**（法庭上的)围栏；法庭；刑事被告席；〔喻〕审判台；制裁；谴责；律师团；律师业；停止诉讼[权利要求]的申请。**7.**（酒吧等的)卖酒柜台；酒吧。**8.**（光、色等的)线，条。带。**9.**【乐】节线〔节间纵线〕；小节；【徽】盾的横线；【军】(领章上的)军阶线；【生】棒眼；【数】横；杆件；【物】巴〔压强单位〕。**10.**〔美〕蚊帐 (= mosquito ~)。*prison* ~*s* 监牢。*the color* ~ 对有色人种的歧视[差别待遇]。*a tie* ~ 连岛沙洲。***at the*** ~ 受到公开审问。***be a*** ~ ***to*** 成…的障碍。***be admitted to the B-***〔美〕= ***be called to*** [***before***] ***the B-*** 得到(法院所属)律师的资格。***be called within the*** ~ 被任命为皇室律师。***behind*** (***the***) ~***s*** 在监狱[禁闭室]中。***behind bolt and*** ~ 被关在监牢里。***cross the*** ~ 死，去世。***go to the*** ~ 当律师。***in*** ~ ***of***【法】为禁止，为防止；除…之外的。***let down the*** ~***s*** 撤除障碍。***play a few*** ~***s*** 奏几小节(曲子)。***practise at the B-*** 以律师为职业。***trial at*** ~【法】(全体法官)列席审判。***the*** ~ ***of conscience*** [***public opinion***] 良心[舆论]的制裁。***the*** ~ ***of the house*** 英下院的惩罚法庭。**II** *vt*. (*-rr-*) **1.** 闩，闩上。**2.** 阻挡，拦住，阻挠；防止，禁止；排斥；除去；【法】(用法律手段)阻止诉讼。**3.**〔俚〕反对，讨厌，不准。**4.** 在…上划线，在…上划出颜色线条，而色线配上 (*with*)。~ ***in*** 关在里面。~ ***out*** 关在外头；阻在外面。**III** ***prep***. 除，除…之外 (= barring)。~ *a few names* 除开四、五名。~ *none* 无例外。~ **bell**【体】杠铃。~**-chart** (统计用的)条线图。~ **code** (商品上示价的)条纹码。~ **fly**〔美〕酒徒，酒鬼。~ **girl** 常去酒吧间的妓女，酒吧女郎。~ **graph** = ~ **chart**. ~**hop** **1.** *n*.〔美俚〕酒吧女侍。**2.** *vi*. 一家又一家地逛酒店。~ **iron** 铁条，棒状铁。~ **keep(er)**〔美〕酒店主；酒吧服务员。~ **magnet** 磁棒，条形磁铁。~**maid** 酒吧女侍。~**man**〔英〕酒吧服务员。~**room** 酒吧间。~**tend** *vi*. 做酒店侍者。~**tender**〔Am.〕(= ~man)。

Ba·rab·bas [bəˈræbəs; bəˋræbəs] *n*.【圣】巴拉巴〔因耶稣替死而得释放的强盗〕。

bar·a·the·a [ˌbærəˈθiə; ˏbærəˋθiə] *n*. 巴拉瑟亚领带绸；巴拉瑟亚毛葛；巴拉瑟亚军服呢。

barb[1] [bɑːb; bɑb] **I** *n*. **1.** 倒钩，倒刺；毛刺，芒刺；〔喻〕刺耳之言。**2.**【动】(鸟毛的)羽枝；(鱼口边的)触须。**3.**（女修道士的)遮喉白布。**4.**〔美俚〕不加入学生会的大学生。**5.**【动】石首鱼。**II** *vt*. 在…上装倒钩；用刺耳之言伤(人)。**III** *a*. 具倒刺的；(话)带刺的。~ **words** 伤人之言。~**ed wire** 有刺铁丝。~**ed wire entanglement**【军】倒刺铁丝网。

barb[2] [bɑːb; bɑrb] *n*.（由非洲 Babary 输入西班牙的)巴巴利马；巴巴利鸽。

Bar·ba·dos [bɑːˈbeidəuz; bɑrˋbedoz] *n*. 巴巴多斯〔拉丁美洲〕。**Bar·ba·di·an** [bɑːˈbeidiən; bɑrˋbedɪən] *n*. 巴巴多斯人。

Bar·ba·ra [ˈbɑːbərə; ˋbɑrbərə] *n*. 芭芭拉〔女子名〕。

bar·bar·i·an [bɑːˈbeəriən; bɑrˋbɛrɪən] **I** *a*. 野蛮(人)的 (*opp*. civilized)。**II** *n*. **1.** 野蛮人，原始人。**2.** 无教养的人，粗汉。

bar·bar·ic [bɑːˈbærik; bɑrˋbærɪk] *a*. 未开化的，野蛮人一样的；粗俗的，煞风景的。

bar·ba·rism [ˈbɑːbərizəm; ˋbɑrbəˏrɪzəm] *n*. **1.** 野蛮(状况)，未开化；暴虐。**2.**（语文的)不纯粹，不规范；芜杂，芜杂的语句，鄙俗的语句。

bar·bar·i·ty [bɑːˈbæriti; bɑrˋbærətɪ] *n*. **1.** 野蛮行为，残忍，暴虐，凶猛，粗野。**2.**（语文的)不规范，芜杂。

bar·ba·ri·za·tion [ˌbɑːbəraiˈzeiʃən; ˏbɑrbəraɪˋzeʃən] *n*. **1.** 野蛮化。**2.**（语文等)不规范化。

bar·ba·rize [ˈbɑːbəraiz; ˋbɑrbəˏraɪz] *vt*., *vi*. **1.**（使)(人等)变野蛮。**2.**（使)(语文)变得不规范，变芜杂。

bar·ba·rous [ˈbɑːbərəs; ˋbɑrbərəs] *a*. **1.** 野蛮的，未开化的；粗野的；凶猛的，暴虐的，残忍的。**2.**（语言等)芜杂的，不纯粹的，不规范的；非希腊、拉丁语的；异国语的，无学识的，鄙俗的。**-ly** *ad*. **-ness** *n*.

Bar·ba·ry [ˈbɑːbəri; ˋbɑrbərɪ] *n*.（除埃及外)北非伊斯兰教国家的总称。~ **Coast** 北非海岸。~ **sheep** (北非)大角野绵羊。

bar·bas·co [bɑːˈbæskəu; bɑrˋbæsko] *n*. (*pl*. ~(*e*)*s*)【植】多花薯蓣 (*Dioscorea floribunda*).

bar·bate [ˈbɑːbeit; ˋbɑrbet] *a*.【动、植】有胡须[毛簇]的，有长绒毛的。

bar·be·cue [ˈbɑːbikjuː; ˋbɑrbɪˏkju] **I** *n*. **1.**（猪、牛等的)烧烤全牲。**2.**〔美〕(吃烧烤全牲的)野外大宴会。**3.** 野餐烤肉架。**4.** 咖啡豆干燥场。**II** *vt*. 全烧，全烤(猪、牛等)，红烧(肉块等)。

bar·bel [ˈbɑːbəl; ˋbɑrbl] *n*. **1.**（鱼类唇边的)触须。**2.** 有触须的鱼〔白鱼之类〕。**-led** *a*. 有触须的。

bar·bel·late [ˈbɑːbileit, bɑːˈbelit; ˋbɑrbɪlet, bɑrˋbelɪt] *a*.【植】有短硬毛的。

Bar·ber [ˈbɑːbə; ˋbɑrbɚ] *n*. 巴伯[姓氏]。

bar·ber [ˈbɑːbə; ˋbɑrbɚ] **I** *n*. **1.** 理发师〔多指为男子理发的人，为女子理发者多用 hair-dresser〕。**2.**〔美〕多嘴多舌的人。— *vt*. 为…理发剃须。**II** *vi*.〔美〕多嘴。*a* ~*'s shop* =〔美〕*a* ~ *shop* 理发店。~***'s itch*** [***rash***] 须疮。~***'s pole*** 理发店的红白条纹圆筒招牌。***do a*** ~〔美俚〕唠唠叨叨；话很多。~**shop** **1.** *n*. 理发店。**2.** *a*.〔美口〕(伤感歌曲等)男声重唱的。

bar·ber·ry [ˈbɑːbəri; ˋbɑrbərɪ] *n*.【植】伏牛花，伏牛花子。

bar·bet [ˈbɑːbit; ˋbɑrbɪt] *n*.【鸟】须䴕〔一种热带鸟〕。

bar·bette [bɑːˈbet; bɑrˋbɛt] *n*. **1.** 炮垛。**2.**（军舰的)露天炮塔，固定炮塔；炮架。

bar·bi·can [ˈbɑːbikən; ˋbɑrbɪkən] *n*. 外堡，碉楼。

bar·bi·cel [ˈbɑːbisel; ˋbɑrbɪsɛl] *n*.（鸟的)羽纤枝。

bar·bi·tal [ˈbɑːbitɔːl; ˋbɑrbəˏtɔl], **bar·bi·tone** [ˈbɑːbitəun; ˋbɑrbɪton] *n*. 巴比妥，安眠药〔二乙基丙二醯脲〕。

bar·bi·tu·rate [bɑːˈbitjərit; ˏbɑrbɪˋtjuret] *n*.【化】巴比妥酸盐。

bar·bi·tu·ric [ˌbɑːbiˈtjuərik; ˏbɑrbɪˋtjurɪk] *a*. ~ **acid**【化】巴比土酸。

bar·bo·la [bɑːˈbəulə; bɑrˋbolə] *n*. 黏附装饰〔用塑料糊把小花、果等黏附于小物件上〕(= ~ work)。

bar·bule [ˈbɑːbjuːl; ˋbɑrbjul] *n*.【动】**1.** 羽小枝。**2.** 小倒刺。

bar·ca·rol(le) [ˈbɑːkərəul; ˋbɑrkəˏrol] *n*.（意大利威

B

尼斯船工唱的)船歌。

Bar·ce·lo·na [ˌbɑːsiˈləunə; ˏbaslˋonə] ***n.*** 巴塞罗(隆)那〔西班牙港市〕。~ **chair** 钢架皮垫椅。

bar·chan [bɑːˈkɑːn, ˈbɑːkɑːn; barˋkan, ˋbarkan] ***n.*** 新月形沙丘。

Bar·clay [ˈbɑːkli; ˋbarklɪ] ***n.*** 巴克利〔姓氏,男子名〕。

B

bard[1] [bɑːd; bard] ***n.*** **1.** 吟游诗人,流浪乐人。**2.** (史诗等的)作者[吟诵者]。**3.** 〔古〕(抒情)诗人。**4.** 〔the B-〕= William Shakespeare. *a B- specialist* 〔美〕莎士比亚研究家。***the B- of Avon*** 莎士比亚的别称。

bard[2] [bɑːd; bard] ***n.*** (中世纪)马的铠甲。

bard·ic [ˈbɑːdik; ˋbardɪk] ***a.*** 吟游诗人的。

Bar·dol·a·ter [bɑːˈdɔlətə; barˋdalətɚ] ***n.*** 〔美〕莎士比亚崇拜者。

Bar·dol·a·try [bɑːˈdɔlətri; barˋdalətrɪ] ***n.*** 〔美〕莎士比亚崇拜。

bare[1] [bɛə; bɛr] **I** ***a.*** **1.** 裸的,裸体的;无遮蔽的,赤裸裸的。**2.** 空的,空虚的,无…的 (*of*). **3.** 仅有的,极少的,勉勉强强的;单,徒。**4.** 无装饰的,朴质的;坦率的;煞风景的。**5.** (织物)穿旧了的。~ *facts* 赤裸裸的事实,明摆着的事实。~ *feet* 赤脚。~ *hands* 徒手,空手。~ *sword* 出鞘的剑。*with one's* ~ *head* 不戴帽,光着头。*a* ~ *and barren land* 不毛之地。*a room* ~ *of furniture* 空无家具的屋子。*be* ~ *of credit* 缺乏信用。*a* ~ *contract* 【法】无条件契约。~ *necessities of life* 刚够维持生命的必需品。~ *possibility* 仅有的(一点点)可能性[希望]。*a* ~ *majority* 勉勉强强的过半数。***at the*** ~ ***thought*** [***idea***] 一想起…(就)。~ ***cloth*** 稀布;方眼布。~ ***livelihood*** 仅能糊口的生活。~ ***navy*** 〔美俚〕(海军)光是罐头的食品。***believe*** (*sth.*) ***on sb.'*** ~ ***word*** 光听某人的话就相信(某事)。***lay*** ~ 露出,暴露,揭发,戳穿;表白,说出。(***escape***) ***with*** ~ ***life*** 仅留性命(逃脱),仅以身免。**II** ***vt.*** **1.** 剥去,剥发;拔出(剑等)。**2.** 敞开,露出,暴露。~ *one's head* 脱帽。~ *one's heart* [*soul, thoughts*] 剖白[表明]心意。~ **back** ***a.***, ***ad.*** 无鞍(的);用滑马[裸马]。~**boat** ***a.*** (租船业务中)只租空船的。***n.*** 出租的空船(由客户负责配备人员、补给、保养等)。~**bones** 瘦人。~ **bones** 梗概。~**faced** 不戴面罩的;露骨的,无耻的 (~*faced falsehood* 信口雌黄)。~**foot(ed)** ***a.***, ***ad.*** 赤脚(的)。~**-handed** ***a.***, ***ad.*** 未戴手套(的);空手(的);赤手空拳(的)。~**headed** ***a.***, ***ad.*** 未戴帽子(的),无帽(的);光着头(的)。~**legged** ***a.*** 露着腿的。~**necked** ***a.*** 露着脖子的。~**sark** **1.** ***n.*** = berserker. **2.** ***ad.*** 不披挂甲胄地。

bare[2] [bɛə; bɛr] ***v.*** 〔古〕bear 的过去式。

ba·rège, ba·rege [bəˈreʒ; bəˋrɛʒ] ***n.*** 巴勒吉纱罗;巴勒吉披巾。

bare·ly [ˈbɛəli; ˋbɛrlɪ] ***ad.*** **1.** 仅,好容易才;几乎没有。**2.** 赤裸裸地,无遮蔽地。**3.** 公然地,露骨地。*He* ~ *escaped.* 他好容易才逃了出来。*There was* ~ *enough for all.* 就全体(人数)来说算是勉强够了。*He is* ~ *of age.* 他刚成年。

barf [bɑːf; barf] ***vi.***, ***vt.*** 〔美俚〕呕吐。

bar·gain [ˈbɑːgin; ˋbargɪn] **I** ***n.*** **1.** 契约,合同,协定,成交条件;交易,买卖。**2.** 便宜货,廉价品;(通过讨价还价)成交的商品。*A* ~*'s a* ~. 契约终是契约(成议不可妄毁)。*That's a* ~. 那已经决定了。*a bad* [*good*] ~ = *a losing* [*great*] ~买贵了[买得便宜]的东西。*a dead* ~ 买价极便宜的货物。***a*** ~ 便宜(*I got this a* ~. 买的便宜)。***beat a*** ~ 还价,讲价。***close*** [***conclude***] ***a*** ~ 定契约[合同]。***drive a*** ~ (不断)磋商,讲价。***drive a hard*** ~ 乱讲价[还价]。***in*** [***into***] ***the*** ~ 加之,而且(*He gave me 30 dollars into the* ~. 他另外又给了我三十元)。***make a*** ~ ***with*** 与…订约[约定]。***make the best of a bad*** ~ 善处逆境。***pick up*** ~***s*** (***at a sale***) 找便宜货。***sell sb. a*** ~ 戏弄,愚弄;使某人意外为难。***strike a*** ~ 进行交易,成交。**II** ***vi.*** 谈判,订约;约定;〔口〕讨价还价。— ***vt.*** **1.** 议(价);约定。**2.** 把…议价卖出;通过讲条件去掉…。**3.** 预料,预期。~ *a new wage increase* (通过谈判)达成增加工资的新协议。*I did not* ~ *for that.* 原来不是那样约定的,我料不到是那样的。~ ***away*** 廉价售出。~ ***for*** 期待;预计到。~ ***on*** 指望。***Dutch*** ~ 酒席上议定的生意。~ **basement** (地下室)廉价部。~**-basement** ***a.*** 便宜的,质量不佳的。~ **day** 廉价日。~ **counter** 〔美〕廉价柜台。~ **hunter** 到处找便宜货的人。~ **money** 定钱。~ **sale** 大廉价。

bar·gain·ee [ˌbɑːgiˈniː; ˏbargɪˋni] ***n.*** 买主。

bar·gain·er [ˈbɑːginə; ˋbargɪnɚ] ***n.*** 议价者,讨价还价者。

bar·gain·ing [ˈbɑːginiŋ; ˋbargɪnɪŋ] ***n.*** **1.** 讨价还价,议价。**2.** 交涉;契约。~ **policy** 互惠通商政策。~ **tariff** 互惠协定关税。~ **unit** 集体交涉时代表工人的工会。

bar·gain·or [ˈbɑːginə; ˋbargɪnɚ] ***n.*** 【法】卖主。

barge [bɑːdʒ; bardʒ] **I** ***n.*** **1.** 大平底船,驳船;〔美〕(有楼)游船,彩船。**2.** 游览汽车;(旅馆的)旅客接送车。**3.** 【美海军】司令[将官]专用汽艇;(国王的)御船;(Oxford 大学的)艇库。**4.** 〔俚〕争吵。**II** ***vt.*** 用驳船运,乘驳船去。— ***vi.*** **1.** 蹒跚前进 (*along*). **2.** 〔口〕闯入 (*in; into*). **3.** 〔口〕相撞 (*against*). ~ ***about*** 瞎跑瞎跳。~ ***around*** 〔美口〕闲荡,闲逛。~ ***in*** 闯入;〔美俚〕强行加入,干涉,管别人闲事。~ ***into*** **1.** 闯入。**2.** 撞上。~**board** 【建】挡风板。~ **couple** 【建】山墙上的椽;伸出山墙的椽。~ **course** 山墙沿瓦;山墙沿石板。~ **pole** 撑篙 (*I wouldn't touch it with a* ~ *pole.* 我很讨厌它;连碰也不想碰它)。

bar·gee, barge·man [bɑːˈdʒiː, ˈbɑːdʒmən; ˏbarˋdʒi, ˋbardʒmən] ***n.*** 〔英〕驳船[游船]船夫。***a lucky*** ~ 〔口〕幸运的家伙。

bar·ghest, bar·guest [ˈbɑːgest; ˋbargɛst] ***n.*** 〔Scot.〕〔北英〕(预告凶事的)犬形妖怪。

Bar·ham [ˈbærəm; ˋbærəm] ***n.*** 巴勒姆〔姓氏〕。

bar·i·at·rics [ˌbæriˈætriks; ˏbærɪˋætrɪks] ***n.*** 【医】肥胖症治疗学。

bar·ic[1] [ˈbærik; ˋbærɪk] ***a.*** 【化】钡的,含钡的。

bar·ic[2] [ˈbærik; ˋbærɪk] ***a.*** 气压(计)的。

ba·ril·la [bəˈrilə; bəˋrɪlə] ***n.*** 【化】苏打灰,海草灰苏打。

bar·ite [ˈbɛərait; ˋbɛraɪt] ***n.*** 【矿】重晶石。

bar·i·tone [ˈbæritəun; ˋbærəˏton] **I** ***n.*** 〔美〕【乐】**1.** (tenor 与 bass 之间的)男中音;男中音歌手。**2.** 萨克斯号。**3.** (歌剧中)供男中音唱的角色。**II** ***a.*** 男中音的。

bar·i·um [ˈbɛəriəm; ˋbɛrɪəm] ***n.*** 【化】钡。~ **chloride** 氯化钡。~ **hydroxide** 氢氧化钡。~ **peroxide** 过氧化钡。~ **sulfate** 硫酸钡。

bark[1] [bɑːk; bark] **I** ***vi.*** **1.** (狗等)吠,叫;(枪等)响。**2.** 咆哮,怒吼。**3.** 〔美口〕喀喀地咳嗽。— ***vt.*** **1.** 大声喊出,吼叫出。**2.** 大声叫卖。**II** ***n.*** **1.** 犬吠声。**2.** 枪声。**3.** 咳嗽声。*His* ~ *is worse than his bite.* 他嘴坏心不坏。~*ing irons* 〔美俚〕手枪。~ ***at*** 吠,咬。~ ***at the moon*** 白嚷,空嚷,徒劳。~ ***away*** [***back***] 喝走[叫回]。~ ***up the wrong tree*** 〔美口〕认错目标,弄错,看错。***Go*** ~ ***up another tree!*** 〔美口〕少管闲事,用不着你操心。

bark[2] [bɑːk; bark] **I** ***n.*** **1.** 茎皮,树皮;规那皮;鞣酸皮。**2.** 〔俚〕皮肤。**II** ***vt.*** **1.** 剥(树皮)。**2.** 用(树皮)盖(屋顶);用树皮鞣(革)。**3.** 擦破(膝盖等处的)皮。***between the*** ~ ***and the wood*** 双方无得失[损益]。***come*** [***go***] ***between the*** ~ ***and the tree*** 管闲事。***stick in*** [***to***] ***the*** ~ 〔美口〕不过分干预[接近]。***talk the*** ~ ***off a tree*** 〔美口〕大嚷。***tighter than the*** ~ ***on a tree*** 〔美口〕极吝啬的。***with the*** ~ ***on*** 〔美口〕粗鲁(*a man with the* ~ *on* 粗鲁的人)。~ **bed** 鞣皮的温床。~ **beetles** 一种棘胫小蠹科甲虫〔森林害虫之一〕。~ **borer** 蛀树皮虫。~ **bound** ***a.*** 被树皮紧箍因而生长受阻的。~ **pine** 白皮松。~ **stove** = ~**bed.**

bark[3], **barque** [bɑːk; bark] ***n.*** **1.** 三桅帆船。**2.** 〔诗〕帆

船,小船。

bark·an·tine, bar·ken·tine [ˈbɑːkəntiːn; ˋbarkən͵tin] *n*. = barquentine.

bark·er[1] [ˈbɑːkə; ˋbarkɚ] *n*. 1. 动辄就嚷嚷的人,愤怒咆哮的人。2. 吠叫的狗[狐]。3.〔美口〕(马戏场等门口的)叫客员;游览向导。4.〔俚〕大炮,手枪。*Great ~s are no biters*. 会叫的狗不会咬人。

bark·er[2] [ˈbɑːkə; ˋbarkɚ] *n*. 1. 剥树皮的人。2. 剥树皮机。

bark·er·y [ˈbɑːkəri; ˋbarkərɪ] *n*. 鞣皮场。

bark·ies [ˈbɑːkiz; ˋbarkɪz] *n*.〔美口〕= talkies.

Bar·kley [ˈbɑːkli; ˋbarklɪ] *n*. 巴克利〔姓氏〕。

bar·ley[1] [ˈbɑːli; ˋbarlɪ] *n*. 大麦。~**-break**, ~**-brake** (游戏)绕麦堆捉人。~**-bree** 麦芽酒;(特指)威士忌酒。~ **broth**〔Scot.〕烈性啤酒。~**corn** 1. 大麦粒。2. 古尺度名(=1/3 英寸)(*John Barleycorn* (拟人语)啤酒,威士忌)。~**-mow** 大麦堆。~ **sugar** 麦芽糖,麦精柠檬糖(= ~ candy). ~**-sugar** 1. *n*. 把他人手臂反扭到背后的动作。2. *vt*. 反扭(他人手臂)。~ **water** (病人饮用的)大麦茶。

bar·ley[2] [ˈbɑːli; ˋbarlɪ] *n*.〔Scot.〕(特指儿童游戏时喊的)停止,停战;停战谈判。*cry* ~ 喊停战。

bar·low (knife) [ˈbɑːləu; ˋbarlo] *n*. 单刃大刀。

barm [bɑːm; barm] *n*.〔英口〕(发酵时的)啤酒泡沫[酵母]〔现多用 yeast 或 leaven〕.

Bar·me·cide [ˈbɑːmisaid; ˋbarmə͵saɪd] **I** *n*. 允许给人好处而不兑现的人,口惠而实不至的人。**II** *a*. 口惠而实不至的,欺骗性的,虚伪的。~ **feast** 空想的利益,空头支票〔出自阿拉伯文学作品《一千零一夜》, Barmecide 用自称珍味而实系空杯空盘请客的酒席〕。

Bar·men [ˈbɑːmən; ˋbarmən] *n*. 巴门〔德国城市〕。

bar mitz·vah, bar miz·vah [bɑːˈmitsvə; barˋmɪtsvə] **I** *n*.〔也作 B- M-〕1. 犹太受戒龄少年〔犹太男孩年至十三岁即承担宗教义务〕。2.【犹】受戒仪式。**II** *vt*.【犹】使受戒。

barm·y [ˈbɑːmi; ˋbarmɪ] *a*. 1. (含)酵母的;发泡沫的。2.〔英俚〕轻狂的;傻头傻脑的。*go* ~ 发疯;发痴。

barn[1] [bɑːn; barn] *n*. 1. 仓,谷仓,库房。2.〔美〕厩,马房;牛房。3.〔蔑〕空空洞洞的房子。*a car* ~〔美〕电车车库。*between you and I and the* ~〔美口〕仅有你知我知的,保密的。~ **dance**〔美〕谷仓舞。~ **door** 1. 仓库大门。2.〔喻〕容易打中的目标。3.【无】挡光板(*as big as a* ~ *door*. 又大又宽。*not be able to hit a* ~ *door* 枪法不好)。~**-door fowl** 鸡。~**owl** 仓枭。~ **swallow** 家燕。~ **sash** 一种小窗框。~**yard** 1. *n*. 谷仓空场。2. *a*. 谷场近旁地区的;粗俗的。~**yard grass** [**millet**] 稗。~**-yard manure** 厩肥。

barn[2] [bɑːn; barn] *n*.【物】靶(恩)〔核反应截面单位 = 10^{-24} 厘米^2/核〕。

bar·na·cle [ˈbɑːnəkl; ˋbarnəkl] *n*. 1.【动】茗荷介,藤壶。2. 北极黑雁。3.〔口〕(对职位等)恋栈的人;瞎纠缠的人。

bar·na·cles [ˈbɑːnəklz; ˋbarnəklz] *n*.〔*pl*.〕1. (钉掌时制马用的)鼻钳。2.〔英方〕眼镜。

Bar·nard [ˈbɑːnəd; ˋbarnɚd] *n*. 巴纳德〔姓氏,男子名〕。

Barnes [bɑːnz; barnz] *n*. 巴恩斯〔姓氏〕。

Bar·net(t) [ˈbɑːnit; ˋbarnɪt] *n*. 巴尼特〔姓氏,男子名〕。

Bar·ney [ˈbɑːni; ˋbarnɪ] *n*. 巴尼〔男子名, Bernard 的昵称〕。

barn·storm [ˈbɑːnstɔːm; ˋbarn͵stɔrm] *vi*. 1. (竞选中)四出游说。2. (演员)到各地巡回演出。3. 飞行游览,作特技飞行表演。— *vt*. 在(某地)作巡回演出[飞行游览],到(某地)进行游说。**-er** *n*. 游说者;飞行游览者;作巡回演出者。

baro- *comb. f*. 重力,气压。

bar·o·dy·nam·ics [ˈbærəudaiˈnæmiks; ˋbærodaɪˋnæmɪks] *n*.【物】重结构力学,重(量)力学。

bar·o·gram [ˈbærəugræm; ˋbærə͵græm] *n*.【气】气压图,气压自计曲线。

bar·o·graph [ˈbærəugrɑːf; ˋbærə͵græf] *n*.【气】气压自记器;【空】自记高度计。

ba·rol·o·gy [bəˈrɔlədʒi; bəˋrɑlədʒɪ] *n*.【物】重力论。

ba·rom·e·ter [bəˈrɔmitə; bəˋrɑmətɚ] *n*. 1. 晴雨表,气压计。2.〔喻〕(舆论等的)标记。

bar·o·met·ric [͵bærəuˈmetrik; ͵bærəˋmɛtrɪk] *a*. 气压计(上)的,测定气压的。~ **gradient** 气压梯度。~ **pressure** (大)气压(力)。~ **maximum** [**minimum**] 最高[最低]气压。

ba·ro·met·ri·cal [͵bærəuˈmetrikəl; ͵bæroˋmɛtrɪkəl] *a*. = barometric. **-ly** *ad*. 用气压计。

ba·rom·e·try [bəˈrɔmitri; bəˋrɑmɪtrɪ] *n*. 气压测定法。

bar·on [ˈbærən; ˋbærən] *n*. 1. 男爵〔和姓并用时,英国男爵称 Lord X, 别国称 Baron X〕。2.【英史】贵族。3.〔美口〕富商,…大王。4.【法】有妇之夫(*opp*. feme). 5. (牛,羊的)脊肉。*an oil* ~煤油大王。~ *and feme*【法】夫妇。~ *of beef* (牛的)脊肉。**-age** 男爵阶级;贵族阶级;男爵勋位。**-ess** 男爵夫人;女男爵。★外国人称作 Baroness, 英国人称作 lady.

bar·on·et [ˈbærənit; ˋbærənɪt] *a*. 准男爵。**-cy** [-ci; -cɪ] *n*. 准男爵的身份[勋位]。

ba·rong [bəˈrɔŋ, -ˈrɔŋ; bəˋrɔŋ, -ˋrɑŋ] *n*. (菲律宾摩洛族人的)重鞘刀。

ba·ro·ni·al [bəˈrəuniəl; bəˋronɪəl] *a*. 1. 男爵的,像男爵的。2. 男爵领有的。3. 豪华的,堂皇的。

ba·ronne [bɑːˈrɔːn; barˋrɔn] *n*.〔F.〕男爵夫人。

bar·on·y [ˈbærəni; ˋbærənɪ] *n*. 1. 男爵领地。2. 男爵勋位。3.〔美〕…财阀,…王国。4.〔Scot.〕大庄园;〔爱尔兰〕郡的区划。

ba·roque [bəˈrəuk; bəˋrok] **I** *a*. 1. 怪异的;矫揉造作的。2.【建】巴罗克式的,建筑风格过分雕琢和怪诞的;【乐】在音乐上表现奇异风格的。**II** *n*. 1. 巴罗克建筑型式;巴罗克艺术风格。2. 新奇作品;奇怪的样式,怪异型。

bar·o·scope [ˈbærəskəup; ˋbærə͵skop] *n*. (一般的)验压器,气压计,大气浮力计。

bar·o·stat [ˈbærəstæt; ˋbærə͵stæt] *n*. 气压调节器,恒压器。

bar·o·ther·mo·graph [ˈbærəuˈθəːməgrɑːf; ͵bærəˋθɝmə͵græf] *n*. (自记)气压温度计;气压温度记录器。

ba·rouche [bəˈruːʃ; bəˋruʃ] *n*. 双马四轮大马车。

barque [bɑːk; bark] *n*. = bark[3].

bar·quen·tine [ˈbɑːkəntiːn; ˋbarkən͵tin] *n*. (只前桅有横帆的)三桅船。

bar·rack [ˈbærək; ˋbærək] **I** *n*. 1.〔常 *pl*.〕兵营,营盘,兵舍。2. 临时工房;简陋厂房[收容所等];〔美〕临时干草棚。*an army* ~*s* 一座兵营。**II** *vt*. 1. 使驻扎兵营内。2. 使住在棚屋内。— *vi*.〔澳〕1. 嘲弄。2. (观众)起哄,喝倒彩;声援,助威。~**-square** 兵营附近操练场。~**s bag** 战士行军袋,士兵背囊。

bar·ra·coon [͵bærəˈkuːn; ͵bærəˋkun] *n*. 奴隶[罪犯]集中场所。

bar·ra·cu·da [͵bærəˈkuːdə; ͵bærəˋkudə] *n*. (*pl*. ~(*s*))【动】魣鱼,梭鱼。

bar·rage [ˈbærɑːʒ, bæˈrɑːʒ; ˋbærɑʒ, bæˋrɪdʒ] *n*. 1.【军】掩护炮火,阻击火网;【无】阻塞,遮断;(菌丝体生长)阻隔现象。2.〔英〕[ˈbɑːridʒ; ˋbarɪdʒ] 拦河坝,堰。3.〔喻〕不断猛击,倾泻。*balloon* ~(防空)气球阻击网。*a box* ~缘边射击。*a creeping* ~诱导弹幕。*a protective* [*covering*] ~掩护弹幕。*a* ~ *of questions* 连珠炮一样的质问。~ **balloon** 阻塞气球。~ **fire** 弹幕射击。~ **jamming**【无】全波段干扰;阻塞干扰。~ **plan** 弹幕射击计划。

bar·ra·mun·da [ˈbærəˈmʌndə, ber-; ˋbærəˋmʌndə, bɛr-] *n*. (*pl*. ~(*s*)) 澳大利亚肺鱼(*Neoceratodus forsteri*).

B

B

bar·ra·mun·di [ˈbærəˈmʌndi; ˋbærəˋmʌndɪ] ***n***. (*pl*. ~, ~(*e*)*s*) 澳大利亚肺鱼(= barramunda)。

bar·ran·co, bar·ran·ca [bəˈræŋkəu, bəˈræŋkə; bəˋræŋko, bəˋræŋkə] ***n***. 〔Sp.〕绝壁,深(峡)谷;火山濑;羊尾沟。

Bar·ran·quil·la [ˌbɑːrɑːŋˈkiːljɑː; ˏbærənˋkiljə] ***n***. 巴兰基利亚〔哥伦比亚城市〕。

bar·ra·tor, bar·ra·ter [ˈbærətə; ˋbærətɚ] ***n***. **1**. 诉讼教唆者。**2**. 为非作歹的船员[船长]。**3**. 受贿的法官;卖官鬻爵者;(教会)出卖圣职者。

bar·ra·trous [ˈbærətrəs; ˋbærətrəs] ***a***. **1**. 教唆诉讼的。**2**. 有受贿罪的;出卖官职[圣职]的。**3**. 为非作歹的。

bar·ra·try [ˈbærətri; ˋbærətrɪ] ***n***. **1**.【法】诉讼教唆,无根据诉讼。**2**. 船长[船员]的不法行为。**3**. 法官的受贿罪。**4**. 官职[教会圣职]的买卖。

barred [bɑːd; bɑrd] ***a***. **1**. 被堵塞[阻碍]了的;上了闩的。**2**. 被禁止的。**3**. 划了线条的。~ **fabrics** 横条花布。

bar·rel [ˈbærəl; ˋbærəl] **I** ***n***. **1**. 桶,大琵琶桶。**2**. 装满的桶,桶装。**3**. 一琵琶桶(的分量)〔美国液量 = $31\frac{1}{2}$ gallons, 果蔬 = 105 dry quarts. 英国桶量有 36, 18 或 9 gallons 的,大小不一〕。**4**. 筒状物,枪筒,膛;【机】圆筒。**5**. (钟表的)发条匣;(照相机的)镜头筒;【火箭】燃烧室;火箭发动机。**6**. (牛、马的)身腔。**7**. 〔口〕许多。**8**. 〔美〕选举经费。*a* ~ *of monkeys* 许多猴子。~ *of the ear* 鼓室,中耳。~ *of fun* 〔美俚〕愉快的游玩。***have sb. over a*** ~ 〔美俚〕(在经济上)勒住[掐住]某人。**II** ***vt***. (***-rel***(***l***)**-**) 把…装桶。— ***vi***. 〔美俚〕高速行进。~ **bulk** ***n***. 五立方英尺容积。~**-chested** ***a***. 胸围特别宽阔的。~ **drain** 筒形排水渠。~ **goods** 〔美俚〕酒类。~ **house** 〔美俚〕低级酒馆;(美国南部)妓院;(早期)下流吵闹的爵士音乐。~ **house bum** 醉鬼。~ **organ** 手摇风琴。~ **roll**【空】(特技飞行中的)横滚;桶滚。~ **vault** 筒形穹窿。

bar·relled [ˈbærəld; ˋbærəld] ***a***. **1**. 桶装的。**2**. 有躯干的;有枪身的。*a double* ~ *gun* 双眼[双筒]枪。*a well* ~ *horse* 身躯发育壮美的马。

bar·ren [ˈbærən; ˋbærən] **I** ***a***. **1**. 不妊的,不会生育的,石女的。**2**. (植物)不结子的;不毛的,(土地)荒芜的。(*opp*. fertile). **3**. 无益的,无效的,(计划)无结果的;(思想等)贫乏的,无趣味的,无聊的。**4**. 空,缺,无(*of*)。*a* ~ *effort* 无效的努力。*be* ~ *of result* 无结果。**II** ***n***. 〔常 *pl*.〕不毛之地,荒地,芜原。**-ness** ***n***. 不妊;秕粒;不毛;无趣味。

bar·ren·wort [ˈbærənwəːt; ˋbærənˏwɝt] ***n***.【植】淫羊藿属;高山淫羊藿。

bar·re·ra [bɑːˈreirɑː; bɑˋrerɑ] ***n***. 〔Sp.〕**1**. 斗牛场栅栏。**2**. 〔*pl*.〕斗牛场第一排座位。

bar·ret [ˈbærit; ˋbærɪt] ***n***. 扁平便帽。

bar·re·try [ˈbærətri; ˋbærətrɪ] ***n***. = barratry.

Bar·rett [ˈbærət, ˈbærit; ˋbærət, ˋbærɪt] ***n***. 巴雷特〔姓氏,男子名〕。

bar·rette [bəˈret; bəˋret] ***n***. 发夹。

bar·ri·cade [ˌbæriˈkeid; ˏbærəˋked], **bar·ri·ca·do** [ˌbæriˈkeidəu; ˏbærɪˋkedo] **I** ***n***. **1**. 防寨,防栅;(阻断交通的)栅栏,路障,街垒,**2**. 防御,阻碍。**II** ***vt***. **1**. 在…筑防寨(设栅);在…设路障;用栅围住。**2**. 阻塞,遮住。*They* ~*d themselves in*. 他们设栅栏自卫。

Bar·rie [ˈbæri; ˋbærɪ] ***n***. 巴里〔姓氏,男子名〕。

bar·ri·er [ˈbæriə; ˋbærɪɚ] **I** ***n***. **1**. 栅,栅栏,隔栏,障壁,隔板,挡板;赛马的出发栅。**2**. 关口,(海关)关卡。**3**. 障碍;壁垒;界线。**4**. (扩伸到海洋中的)南极洲冰层。*a moisture* ~ 防湿层。*a potential* ~【物】势垒,位垒。*a* ~ *to progress* 进步的障碍。*set up a* ~ *between* 在…中间设置障碍。*the* ~*s of class* 阶级的壁垒。*the* ~ *physics* 边缘物理学。*the language* ~ 语言的隔阂。**II** ***vt***. 用栅围住。~ **bar** [**beach**] 滨外滩〔海浪造成的沙滩,常与海滩平行,中间为二者围成的湖〕。~ **crash**(为试验汽车防护性能而进行的)撞墙试验。~ **cream** 护肤霜. ~ **reef** 堡礁。

bar·ring [ˈbɑːriŋ; ˋbɑrɪŋ] ***prep***. 不包括,除,除…之外。*Barring accidents, I'll be there*. 若无意外我一定去。

bar·ri·o [ˈbɑːriəu; ˋbɑrɪo] ***n***. (*pl*. ~*s*) 〔Sp.〕**1**. (说西班牙语国家的)城市行政区。**2**. (拉丁美洲和菲律宾的)村庄,村镇,郊区。**3**. 美国城市(尤指西南部)说西班牙语居民的集居区。

bar·ris·ter [ˈbæristə; ˋbærɪstɚ] ***n***. **1**. 〔英〕(能出席高级法庭的)律师。**2**. 〔美〕法律顾问,律师。

bar·row[1] [ˈbærəu; ˋbæro] ***n***. **1**. 独轮车;〔英〕手推双轮车。**2**. 担架。**3**. (鲨鱼等的)鱼子。~**-boy** 〔英〕叫卖小贩。~**-man** 〔英〕叫卖菜贩。~ **pit** 路边开掘的沟渠;采石坑;手车运输的露天矿。

bar·row[2] [ˈbærəu; ˋbæro] ***n***. **1**. (史前人的)冢,古坟。**2**. (兽)穴。**3**. (现主要用于英国地名前)山。

bar·row[3] [ˈbærəu; ˋbæro] ***n***. 〔英方〕(阉过的)公猪。

bar·row[4] [ˈbærəu; ˋbæro] ***n***. 〔英〕无袖婴儿绒衣。

Bar·ry [ˈbæri; ˋbærɪ] ***n***. 巴里〔男子名〕。

Bar·ry·more [ˈbærimɔː; ˋbærɪmɔr] ***n***. 巴里莫尔〔姓氏〕。

Bart [bɑːt; bɑrt] ***n***. 巴特〔男子名, Bartholomew 的昵称〕。

bar·ter [ˈbɑːtə; ˋbɑrtɚ] **I** ***vt***. 以…物物交换,以(货)换(货)。~ *furs for powder* 用毛皮换火药。— ***vi***. 作易货贸易,作物物交换。~ *with natives* 与当地居民以货换货。~ ***away*** (因不善交易而)吃亏卖出;(因贪图物质利益而)出卖(名誉等)。**II** ***n***. **1**. 物物交换,换货,实物交易。**2**. 用以换货的交易品,互换品。**3**.【数】换算法。~ *system* 换货贸易制。*exchange and* ~ 以物易物。*expressed in* ~ *terms* 按实物交换比率来说。*on a* ~ *basis* 以易货方式。**-er** 进行易货贸易者。

Bar·thol·o·mew [bɑːˈθɔləmjuː; bɑrˋθɑləˏmju] ***n***. **1**. 巴塞洛缪〔男子名〕。**2**.【圣】基督十二使徒之一。~ **Fair** 〔英〕巴塞罗缪节大集市。**-tide** [-taid; -taɪd] ***n***. 巴塞罗缪节(8月24日)。

bar·ti·zan [ˌbɑːtiˈzæn; ˋbɑrtəzæn] ***n***.【建】小望楼,顶塔。

Bart·lett [ˈbɑːtlit; ˋbɑrtlɪt] ***n***. 巴特利特〔姓氏〕。

Bar·ton [ˈbɑːtn; ˋbɑrtn̩] ***n***. 巴顿〔姓氏〕。

bar·ton [ˈbɑːtn; ˋbɑrtn̩] ***n***. 〔英方〕**1**. (庄园中的)农场。**2**. 农家场院。

Bart's [bɑːts; bɑrts] ***n***. 伦敦 St. Bartholomew's Hospital (圣巴塞洛缪医院)的简称。

Bar·uch [ˈberək; ˋberək] ***n***. **1**.【基督】巴录,巴鲁〔先知耶利米的书记员〕。**2**. 巴鲁书〔上述人物的作品,新教教徒认为是伪经〕。**3**. 巴鲁克〔姓氏〕。

bar·y- *comb. f*. 重: *bary*tron.

bar·y·cen·tre, bar·y·cen·ter [ˈbærisentə; ˋbærɪsɛntɚ] ***n***.【物】重心,质(量中)心。

bar·ye [ˈbæri; ˋbæri] ***n***.【物】微巴(压力单位。1微巴 = 1达因/厘米^2)

bar·y·on [ˈbæriɔn; ˋbærɪɑn] ***n***.【核】重子。~ **number**【核】**1**. (原子)质量数。**2**. 重子数。

bar·y·sphere [ˈbærisfiə; ˋbærɪˏsfɪr] ***n***.【地】重圈,(地球)重核层,地核,地心圈。

ba·ry·ta [bəˈraitə; bəˋraɪtə] ***n***.【化】重土(氧化钡)。

ba·ry·te(s) [bəˈrait(iːz); bəˋraɪt(iz)] ***n***.【矿】重晶石。

bar·y·tone[1] [ˈbæritəun; ˋbærəˏton] ***n***. = baritone.

bar·y·tone[2] [ˈbæritəun; ˋbærəˏton] ***a***., ***n***.【希语法】最后音节无重音的(词)。

bar·y·tron [ˈbæritrɔn; ˋbærɪtrɑn] ***n***.【物】介子,重电子。

bas·al [ˈbeisl; ˋbesl̩] **I** ***a***. **1**. 基部的。**2**. 基础的,基本的。*the* ~ *parts of a column* 柱的底部。**II** ***n***.【地】基板。~ **area** 底面积;基域。~ **leaf**【植】基生叶。~ **metabolism** 基础代谢。~ **plane** 底(平)面,基面。

ba·salt [ˈbæsɔːlt; ˋbæsɔlt] ***n*.** **1.**【地】玄武岩。**2.** 一种黑色瓷器。

ba·salt·ic [bəˈsɔːltik; bəˋsɔltɪk] ***a*.** (含)玄武岩的,似玄武岩的。

bas·an, baz·an [ˈbæzən; ˋbæzən] ***n*.** 栎鞣羊皮革,书面羊皮。

bas·a·nite [ˈbæsənait; ˋbæsəˏnaɪt] ***n*.** **1.** 试金石。**2.**【地】碧玄岩。

bas bleu [ˈbɑːˈbləː; ˋbɑˋblɚ] ***n*.** 〔F.〕女学者,女才子;学者气派的女人。

B.A.Sc. = **1.** Bachelor of Applied Science 应用科学学士。**2.** Bachelor of Agricultural Science 农学士。

bas·cule [ˈbæskjuːl; ˋbæskjul] ***n*.**【建】(竖旋桥的)活动桁架。～ **bridge** 竖旋桥,升启桥。

base[1] [beis; bes] **I** ***n*.** **1.** 基底,基,根基,底座;底层,底子;(纪念碑等的)基址;(山)麓。**2.**【军】基地,根据地。**3.** 根据,基础。**4.**【化】碱;【纺】(染色)固色剂;媒染剂;【药】主剂。**5.**【数】底,底面,底边,基点,基线;基数。**6.**【体】起点,出发线;【棒球】垒;目标。**7.**【语】语根;词干。*an air* ～ 空军基地。*the economic* ～ 经济基础。*first* [*second, third*] ～【棒球】一[二、三]垒。*a* ～ *angle* 底角。*a bayonet* ～ 卡口灯座。*a code* ～ (信息论)编码基数。*a prisoner's* ～捉迷藏。～ *of operation* 作战根据地。***at the*** ～ ***of*** 在…之麓;在…的基部。***change one's*** ～〔口〕撤退。***get to first*** ～ 取得成功的。***off*** ～〔口〕**1.** 大错特错地。**2.** 冷不防地。**3.**〔美俚〕傲慢的。**II** ***vt*.** 把…的基础放在(…)上 (*on; upon*),以(…)作为…的根据[基地]。～ *one's arguments upon facts* 以事实作论辩根据。～ *one's hopes on* …把希望寄托在…上。～**band**【无】基(本频)带。～**board**【建】脚板;护壁板。～ **burner** 底燃火炉,自给暖炉。～ **course**【建】底层。～**-court** (城堡)外院;(农场)后院。～ **exchange** (海、空军)基地商店。～ **head**〔美俚〕吸食可卡因的吸毒者。～ **fertilizer** 基肥。～ **hospital**【军】后方医院。～ **level** 基面。～ **line** 基线;【网球】界限线。～**man**【棒球】守垒员。～ **map**【地】工作草图。～ **oil** 原油。～ **pair**【生化】碱基对。～ **paper** (造币)铜版币坯。～ **pay** 基本工资。～ **plate**【机】底板,支承板;【医】装假牙的底板。～ **price** 基价。～ **rate**〔英〕基本利率。～ **runner**【棒球】跑垒员。**-less** ***a*.** 无基础的,无根据的;无原由的。

base[2] [beis; bes] **I** ***a*.** **1.** 贱的,劣的;卑下的,低级的;卑鄙的。**2.** (子女)庶出的;私生的。**3.** (语言)不纯正的,粗俗的。**4.**【乐】低音的。**II** ***n*.**【乐】低音;低音部。～ **billon** 劣币。～**born** ***a*.** 出身低微的;私生的。～ **coin** 劣币;伪币。～ **court** (城堡)外院;(农庄)后院;〔英〕下级法院。～ **Latin** 拉丁俗语。～ **metals** 普通金币,贱金属(锡,铅等)。～**-minded** ***a*.** 品质卑劣的,下贱的,卑鄙的。**-ness** ***n*.** (品质等的)恶劣;下贱,卑鄙。

base·ball [ˈbeisbɔːl; ˋbesˋbɔl] ***n*.** **1.** 棒球。**2.** 棒球运动。*play* ～打棒球。*a* ～ *team* 棒球队。～ **classic**〔美〕棒球大比赛。～ **field** [**ground**] 棒球场。～ **fiend**〔美〕棒球迷。**-er, -ist** ***n*.** 〔美〕棒球员,棒球选手。

Ba·sel [ˈbɑːzəl; ˋbɑzəl] ***n*.** 巴塞尔〔瑞士城市〕。

base·ment [ˈbeismənt; ˋbesmənt] ***n*.** **1.** 建筑物的底部。**2.**【建】底层;地下室〔*cf*. cellar〕。～ **complex**【地】基地杂岩。～ **storey** 底层。

ba·sen·ji [bəˈsendʒi; bəˋsɛndʒɪ] ***n*.** 〔Ban.〕猴面犬。

ba·ses[1] [ˈbeisiz; ˋbesiz] base 的复数。

bas·es[2] [ˈbeisiːz; ˋbesɪz] basis 的复数。

bash [bæʃ; bæʃ] **I** ***vt*.** 〔英方、美俚〕猛击,痛击;打坏。— ***vi*.** 猛撞。**II** ***n*.** **1.** 猛击,痛打。**2.** 痛快的玩乐[消遣]。**3.**〔英方〕尝试。～ *sb. on the head* 猛击某人的头。*give him* ～*es and kicks* 对他拳打脚踢。***have a*** ～ ***at***〔英方〕试试看。***on the*** ～〔英方〕做娼妓。

Ba·sham [ˈbæʃəm; ˋbæʃəm] ***n*.** 巴沙姆〔姓氏〕。

ba·shaw [bəˈʃɔː; bəˋʃɔ] ***n*.** 〔古〕**1.** = pasha. **2.**〔口〕傲慢的官僚。

bash·ful [ˈbæʃful; ˋbæʃfəl] ***a*.** 害羞的,羞怯的,靦覥的。～ *manner* 忸怩。**-ly** ***ad*.** **-ness** ***n*.**

bas·ic [ˈbeisik; ˋbesɪk] **I** ***a*.** **1.** 基础的,基本的,根本的。**2.**【化】碱性的,碱式的。**3.**【矿】基性的,含少量硅酸的。**4.**【军】初步的;最下级的。～ *data* 基本数据。～ *industry* 基础工业。**II** ***n*.** 〔常 *pl*.〕**1.** 基础,基本。**2.** 基础训练。*work for the* ～*s* 为衣食住等操劳。～ **credit line**【美商】(准备银行的)贷款限额。～ **dye** 碱性染料。**B- English** 基本英语〔英国学者 C.K.Ogden 等人用 850 个英语基本词汇创制的一种国际辅助语〕。～ **private**〔美〕陆军三等兵。～ **process**【冶】碱性炼钢法。～ **slag** 碱性熔渣。**-ally** ***ad*.** 基本地

Basic = Basic English.

ba·sic·i·ty [bəˈsisiti; beˋsɪsətɪ] ***n*.**【化】碱度;碱性;【地】基性度。

ba·sid·io·my·cete [bəˌsidiəuˈmaisiːt; bəˏsɪdɪoˋmaɪsit] ***n*.**【植】担子菌。

ba·sid·i·o·spore [bəˈsidiːəuspɔː; bəˋsɪdioˏspor] ***n*.**【植】担子孢子。**-spor·ous** [-ˈspɔːrəs; -ˋsporəs] ***a*.**

ba·sid·i·um [bəˈsidiəm; bəˋsɪdɪəm] ***n*.** (*pl*. ***ba·sid·i·a*** [bəˈsidiə; bəˋsɪdɪə])【植】担子。**ba·sid·i·al** ***a*.**

ba·si·fi·ca·tion [beisifiˈkeiʃən; ˏbesəfɪˋkeʃən] ***n*.**【化】碱化;【地】基性岩化。

bas·i·fixed [ˈbeisifikst; ˋbesəˏfɪkst] ***a*.**【植】底着的。

ba·sif·uge [ˈbeisifjuːdʒ; ˋbesɪfjudʒ] ***n*.**【植】避碱植物,嫌碱植物。

bas·i·fy [ˈbeisifai; ˋbesɪˏfaɪ] ***vt*.**【化】使碱化。

Bas·il [ˈbæzl; ˋbæzl] ***n*.** 巴兹尔〔男子名〕。

bas·il [ˈbæzl; ˋbæzl] ***n*.**【植】罗勒;罗勒属植物。

bas·i·lar [ˈbæsilə; ˋbæsələ] ***a*.** **1.** 基底的,基础的。**2.** 脑壳底部的。**3.**【植】基部的;(花柱)基生的。

bas·i·lect [ˈbæsilekt; ˋbæsɪlɛkt] ***n*.** 下层社会的语言。

ba·sil·ic(al) [bəˈsilik(əl); bəˋsɪlɪk(əl)] ***a*.** **1.** 帝王的,皇家的。**2.** 王宫的;(古罗马)长方形大会堂[教堂]的。**3.**【解】主要的,重要的〔指静脉〕。～ **vein**【解】(上臂内侧的)大静脉;重要静脉。

ba·sil·i·ca [bəˈzilikə; bəˋzɪlɪkə] ***n*.** **1.** 王宫。**2.** (古罗马)长方形大会堂[教堂]。

ba·sil·i·con [bəˈzilikən; bəˋzɪlɪkən] ***n*.** 松脂蜡膏。

bas·i·lisk [ˈbæzilisk; ˋbæzɪˏlɪsk] ***n*.** **1.**【神】蛇怪〔传说出没于非洲沙漠,其目光或呼气均足以使人丧命〕。**2.**【动】(热带)蜥蜴。～ ***glance*** 使人见而遭殃的眼神。

ba·sin [ˈbeisn; ˋbesn] ***n*.** **1.** 脸盆;水盆。**2.** 满盆,(一)盆。**3.** 盆地,流域。**4.** 水坑,地塘;(港湾)深度;内湾,小湾;【船】船坞。**5.**【地】盘层,煤田。**6.**【解】骨盆,骨盆腔。～ *irrigation* 小块灌溉。*the Thames* ～ 泰晤士河流域。*a* ～ *of water* 一盆水。*a river* ～ 流域。*a setting* ～ 澄水池。～ **stand** 洗脸架。**-ful** ***n*.** 一满盆。

bas·i·net, bas·net [ˈbæsinit, ˈbæsnit; ˋbæsənɪt, ˋbæsnɪt] ***n*.** **1.** (中世纪欧洲的)露面钢盔。**2.** (盔下)衬帽。

ba·si·on [ˈbeisiən; ˋbesɪən] ***n*.** 颅底点。

ba·sip·e·tal [beiˈsipətl; beˋsɪpətl] ***a*.**【植】向基的。

ba·sis [ˈbeisis; ˋbesɪs] ***n*.** (*pl*. ***ba·ses*** [ˈbeisiːz; ˋbesiz]) **1.** 基础;基底;台座;【地】坡基。**2.** 根据,基准。**3.** 主要成份;主药。**4.**【数】基。*On a production* ～在大规模生产的基础上。*On what* ～? 凭什么条件(雇佣等)? *on the war* ～按战时体制。*the* ～ *of argument* 论据。*the* ～ *of assessment* 课税标准。***on the*** ～ ***of*** 以…为基础。

bask [bɑːsk; bæsk] ***vi*.** **1.** 晒太阳;取暖。**2.** 受宠,沐恩;〔喻〕感到舒适。— ***vt*.** 使(自身)受(暖),使(自身)受(太阳晒)。～ *oneself in a sunny place* 晒太阳。～ ***in sb.'s smile*** [***favor***] 得某人欢心[恩宠]。～ ***in the sunshine*** 晒太阳。～***ing shark*** 姥鲨。

Bas·ker [ˈbɑːskə; ˋbɑskɚ] ***n*.** 巴斯克〔姓氏〕。

bas·ket [ˈbɑːskit; ˋbæskɪt] **I** ***n*.** **1.** 篮,笼,篓,筐。**2.** 一篮[笼,篓,筐]。**3.**【空】(气球的)吊篮。**4.**【建】花篮状柱

头。5.（篮球运动的）篮；一次投篮得分。6. 一组问题。*a ~ of apples* 一篮苹果。*a ~ of clips* 赏心乐事，愉快。***be left in the ~*** 落选，卖剩。***make a ~***（篮球）投中一球。***sneeze into a ~*** 上断头台，被斩首。***the pick of the ~*** 精品。**II** *vt*. 把…装入篮内，把…丢入字纸篓里。~-**ball**【体】篮球。~ **carriage** 柳条车身的马车。~ **case** 四肢被截断的(病)人。~ **chair** 柳条椅。~ **clause**（文件等的）总括性条款。~ **cloth** 绣花(用)十字布。~ **dinner**〔美〕(大规模的)野餐。~ **fern**【植】绵马。~ **fish** 筐鱼 ~-**handle arch**【建】三心拱。~ **hilt**（刀剑的）篮状柄。~-**of-gold**【植】岩生庭荠。~ **star**【动】星鱼〔盘车类〕。~ **weave**【纺】方平组织。~ **work**（篮子等）编织品。~ **worm**【虫】结草虫。-**ful** *n*. 满篮，一篮。-**ry**（篮，篓，笼，筐等的）编织法；（篮子等）工艺品。

bas mitz·vah, bas miz·vah [bɑːsˈmitsvə; bɑsˋmɪtsvə] *n*. 1. 犹太受戒龄女孩。2.（犹太教）受戒仪式。

bas·net [ˈbæsnit; ˋbæsnɪt] *n*. = basinet.

ba·son [ˈbeisn; ˋbesn] *n*. = basin.

ba·so·phil·ic [ˈbeisəufilik; ˋbesəfɪlɪk], **ba·so·ph·i·lou** [beiˈsɔfiləs; beˋsɑfɪləs] *a*.（植物）适碱（性）的，喜碱（性）的。

Basque [bæsk, bɑːsk; bæsk, bɑsk] **I** *n*. 1. 巴斯克人〔西班牙比利牛斯山西部居民〕。2. 巴斯克语。3.〔b-〕巴斯克式妇女紧身衣，女人短裙。**II** *a*. 巴斯克地区的；巴斯克人的；巴斯克语的。

Bas·ra [ˈbæzrə; ˋbʌsrə] *n*. 巴士拉〔伊拉克港市〕。

bas-re·lief [ˈbæsriliːf; ˋbæsrɪˏlif] *n*. 半浮雕，浅浮雕。

bass[1] [beis; bes] **I** *n*.【乐】1. 男低音；低音奏唱者。2. 低音部。3. 低音乐器。**II** *a*. 低音的。~ **clarinet** 低音单簧管。~ **viol** 低音提琴（= violoncello）。

bass[2] [bæs; bæs] *n*.（*pl*. ~(*es*)）【鱼】欧洲鲈鱼。

bass[3] [bæs; bæs] *n*. 1.【植】椴树；椴属树木，美洲椴木。2. 椴树韧皮。3.〔*pl*.〕韧皮纤维制品〔如席子绳索等〕。

Bass [bæs; bæs] *n*. 巴斯(厂的)啤酒；一瓶巴斯啤酒。

bas·set[1] [ˈbæsit; ˋbæsɪt] *n*. 矮脚长耳猎狗。

bas·set[2] [ˈbæsit; ˋbæsɪt] **I** *n*.【矿、地】矿层露头。**II** *vi*.（矿脉）露出。~ **horn**（tenor 音的）木管箫。

Basse-Terre [bɑːˈsteə; bɑsˋtɛr] *n*. 巴斯特尔〔瓜德罗普岛(法)首府〕。

bas·si·net [ˌbæsiˈnet; ˏbæsəˋnɛt] *n*.（婴儿的）(柳条)摇篮，摇篮车。

bass·ist [ˈbeisist; ˋbesɪst] *n*. 倍大提琴演奏者，倍大提琴家。

bas·so [ˈbæsəu; ˋbæso] *n*.（*pl*. ~*s*, ***bas·si*** [ˈbæsi; ˋbæsi]）〔It.〕【乐】1. 低音(部)。2. 男低音，男低音歌手。~ **buffo** 歌剧中的低音滑稽歌手。~ **contante** 抒情低音。~ **profundo** 最低音；最低音歌手。

bas·soon [bəˈsuːn, bəˈzuːn; bəˋsun, bəˋzun] *n*.【乐】1. 巴松管，大管。2. 风琴上的低音簧。*a contra ~* 低音大管。-**ist** *n*. 巴松管吹奏者。

bas·so-ri·lie·vo [ˈbæsəuriˈliːvəu; ˋbæso·rɪˋlivo] *n*.〔It.〕= bas-relief.

bass·wood [ˈbæswud; ˋbæsˏwʊd] *n*.（美洲）椴树；椴木。

bast [bæst; bæst] *n*. 1.【植】韧皮部，韧皮(纤维)。2. 椴树的内皮。~ **fiber** 韧皮纤维。~ **fiber plants** 麻黄。~ **silk** 生丝。

bas·ta [ˈbɑːstɑː; ˋbɑstɑ] *int*.〔It.〕够了！罢了！足了！

bas·tard [ˈbæstəd; ˋbæstəd] **I** *n*. 1. 私生子。2.【动、植】杂种。3. 代用品，假冒品；劣货；粗劣的糖。4.〔俚〕坏蛋，讨厌鬼；〔俚〕家伙〔亲热的玩笑用语〕。**II** *a*. 1. 私生的。2. 杂种的；不纯粹的。3. 伪的，假的。4. 奇形怪状的，异常的。~ *charity* 伪善。~ **asbestos** 变种石棉。~ **file** 粗齿锉。~ **slip**【植】吸枝。~ **stucco** 混毛泥灰。~ **title**【印】简略标题。~ **wheat** 杂种小麦。~ **wing**（鸟类的）小翼羽。

bas·tard·ize [ˈbæstədaiz; ˋbæstəˏdaɪz] *vt*. 1. 判定〔证明〕…为私生。2. 使不纯，使品质变坏。3. 乱用，误用（言语等）。— *vi*. 变坏，变为不纯。-**i·za·tion** *n*.

bas·tard·ly [ˈbæstədli; ˋbæstədlɪ] *a*. 1. 私生的，出身低贱的；杂交的。2. 伪造的，赝制的。3. 卑鄙的。

bas·tard·y [ˈbæstədi; ˋbæstədɪ] *n*. 私生子身分；私生。

baste[1] [beist; best] *vt*. 用长针脚缝，疏缝，假缝。

baste[2] [beist; best] *vt*. 1.〔口〕痛打，狠揍。2. 痛骂，说…的闲话。3.〔美俚〕用枪打死，枪毙。

baste[3] [beist; best] *vt*. 在(烤肉、煎肉)上溜油[涂油]；撒上（粉等）。

Bas·til(l)e [bæsˈtiːl; bæsˋtil] *n*. 1. 巴士底监狱〔创建于 14 世纪的法国城堡和国家监狱，位于巴黎，1789 年法国大革命中被攻破〕。2.〔b-〕牢狱；〔古〕城砦；【建】堡塔。~ **Day** 巴士底日〔7 月 14 日，为法国国庆日，1789 年于该日攻破巴士底狱〕。

bas·ti·na·do [ˌbæstiˈneidəu; ˏbæstəˋnedo] **I** *n*. 1. 笞跖，打脚掌。2. 笞跖刑。3. 棍，杖。**II** *vt*. 打…的脚掌，对…处跖刑。

bast·ing[1] [ˈbeistiŋ; ˋbestɪŋ] *n*. 1. 疏缝，假缝。2.〔*pl*.〕绷线，假缝用线。

bast·ing[2] [ˈbeistiŋ; ˋbestɪŋ] *n*.（烤肉时的）涂油脂；涂在烤肉上的油脂。

bast·ing[3] [ˈbeistiŋ; ˋbestɪŋ] *n*. 一顿狠揍；一顿痛骂。

bas·ti·on [ˈbæstiən, Am. ˈbæsʃən; ˋbæstɪən, ˋbæsʃən] *n*. 1. 棱堡。2. 设防地区，阵地工事。3.〔喻〕堡垒。-**a·ry** *a*.

Ba·su·to [bəˈsuːtəu; bəˋsuto] *n*.（*pl*. ~*s*）巴苏陀人。

Ba·su·to·land [bəˈsuːtəulænd; bəˋsutoˏlænd] *n*. 巴苏陀兰〔莱索托的旧名〕。

BAT = Bachelor of Arts in Teaching 教学法学士。

bat[1] [bæt; bæt] **I** *n*. 1. 短棍；（棒球等的）球棒，（网球等的）球拍。2.（棒球等的）击球员；轮到击球。3. 砖块；（黏土等的）硬块。4.〔常 *pl*.〕棉卷，棉胎。5.〔口〕打击，猛击；（海上）导弹。6.〔英俚〕步调，速度。7.〔美俚〕喝闹酒，欢宴，狂欢。8.〔美俚〕一块钱。9.【矿】油页岩淀积。*a ~ breaker*【美棒球】击球凶猛的人。*behind the ~*（棒球）接球员的位置 *cross ~s with* 与…比赛（棒球）。*times at ~*（棒球）打数。***at ~***【棒球】就击球员位置；握紧打棒。~ ***hides***〔美俚〕（总称）钞票。***carry one's ~*** 1.【板球】没有犯规退场。2.〔口〕打赢，达到目的。***go full ~*** 急走，全速前进。***go off at a rare ~*** 飞快逃走。***go on a ~***〔美俚〕喝闹酒。***go to ~ for***〔美俚〕替…辩护；主张。***hot*** [***right***] ***off the ~***〔俚〕马上，立刻。***off one's own ~*** 凭自己努力，独力，独立。***on one's own ~***〔口〕独立，自力。***the side at ~***（棒球的）攻方。**II** *vt*.（-*tt*-）1. 用球棒[球拍]打(球)；打。2.〔俚〕突击；（为主义等）战斗。3. 详细讨论，反复考虑。— *vi*. 1. 用球棒[球拍]打球。2. 轮到击球。*Which side is batting now?* 现在是哪一方进攻？~ ***out*** 粗制滥造。~ ***round*** 1. 到处寻乐。2. 探讨，琢磨。

bat[2] [bæt; bæt] *n*. 1. 蝙蝠。2.〔俚〕妓女。***blind as a ~*** 瞎的；眼力不行的。***have ~s in the belfry*** 发痴；异想天开。~-**blind**, ~-**eyed** *a*. 眼力坏的，半瞎的；愚蠢的。~ **wing** 蝙蝠翼战斗机。

bat[3] [bɑːt, bæt; bɑt, bæt] *n*. 1.〔Ind.〕〔the ~〕（外国语中的）白话，口语。2.〔英口〕口语，成语，俗话。***sling the ~***〔军俚〕说外国话。

bat[4] [bæt; bæt] *vt*.（-*tt*-）〔方〕1. 眨(眼睛)。2. 拍(翅)。*a bird batting its wings* 鸟拍翅。***not ~ an eyelid*** [***eye***] 泰然不动。

Ba·ta [ˈbɑːtɑː; ˋbɑtɑ] *n*. 巴塔〔赤道几内亚港市〕。

Ba·ta·vi·a [bəˈteiviə; bəˋtevɪə] *n*. 巴达维亚〔1. 美国 New York 州西北部城市。2. 印尼首都和最大商港雅加达（Djakarta）之旧称〕。-**n** [-vjən; -vɪən] *a*. 巴达维亚的。

batch [bætʃ; bætʃ] *n*. 1.（面包等的）一炉。2. 一次投料量；一次生产量。3. 一宗，一批，一束，一组，一群。4.【计】成批(工作)。*the first ~ of goods* 第一批货物。

in ～*es* 分批;成批。～ **processing**【计】成批处理。

batch·y [ˈbætʃi; ˋbætʃɪ] ***a*.** 〔俚〕疯狂的,狂妄的。

bate[1] [beit; bet] ***vt*. 1.** 〔古〕减少;降低。**2.** 减轻,抑制,削弱。*not* ～ *a penny of it* 一文不减让。～ ***an ace*** 寸步不让。***with*** ～***d breath*** 屏息。— ***vi*.** 〔方〕减退;衰弱,变弱。

bate[2] [beit; bet] ***n*.** 〔英俚〕愤怒。*get in a* ～ 发怒,生气。

bate[3] [beit; bet] **I *n*.** (使皮革软化的)脱灰碱液。**II *vt*.** 把(皮革)浸入软化液,用脱灰碱液使(皮革)软化。

ba·teau [bæˈtəu; bæˋto] ***n*.** (*pl*. ～*x* [-z;-z]) **1.** (美国北部和加拿大的)平底河船。**2.** 搭浮桥的船。～ **bridge** 浮桥。

bate·ment-light [ˈbeitməntlait; ˋbetməntlaɪt] ***n*.**【建】跛窗。

Bates [beits; bets] ***n*.** 贝茨〔姓氏〕。

bat·fish [ˈbætfiʃ; ˋbætfɪʃ] ***n*.** (*pl*. ～, ～*es*) **1.** 蝙蝠鱼科的鱼。**2.** 鹞鲼 (*Aetobatus californicus*). **3.**【鱼】豹鲂鮄 (= flying gurnard).

bat·fowl [ˈbætfaul; ˋbætˏfaʊl] ***vi*.** 夜间点火捉巢中鸟。

bath [bɑːθ; bæθ] **I *n*.** (*pl*. **baths** [bɑːðz; bæðz]) **1.** 沐浴,洗澡。**2.** 浴缸;澡盆。**3.** 浴室,(公共)澡堂。**4.** 〔常 *pl*.〕(豪华的)大浴场;温泉浴场。**5.** 浸,泡;洗澡水;(泡酸菜的)卤水;染液。**6.**【化】浴;浴器,液盘,电镀槽,电解槽;【冶】炉底;平炉铁浆;【摄】定影液。*a cold* [*hot*] ～冷水[热水]浴。*a shower* ～淋浴。*a sand* ～ 砂浴。*a mud* ～ 泥浴。*a steam* [*vapor*] ～蒸气浴。*a succession* ～冷温交替浴。*a sun* ～ 日光浴。*a swimming* ～ 游泳浴池[附设室内游泳池]。*a Turkish* ～ 土耳其浴,蒸气浴。*a plating* ～电镀槽。*a public* ～ 公共浴场。*the Roman* ～*s* 古罗马公共浴场。～ ***of blood*** 浴血,大屠杀,血洗。***have*** [***take***] ***a*** ～ 入浴,洗澡。***take the*** ～*s* 洗温泉(治病)。**II *vt*.** 给(孩子等)洗澡。～ *a baby* 给孩子洗澡。— ***vi*.** 洗澡,入浴。～ **house** 浴室,澡堂;(海水浴场等的)换衣处。～ **mat** (浴室内的)防滑垫,揩脚垫。～**robe** 〔美〕浴衣(=〔英〕dressing gown). ～**-room** 浴室,沐浴间,洗澡间;盥洗室,〔书〕厕所。～**tub 1.** 澡盆,浴缸。**2.** 〔美空军俚〕(战斗机中枪手的)球形坐位;〔美俚〕摩托车的边车。～ **tub gin** 〔美俚〕私酿的杜松子酒。

Bath[1] [bɑːθ; bæθ] ***n*.** (英国的)巴斯勋位,巴斯勋章。***Order of the*** ～ 巴斯勋位[勋章]。

Bath[2] [bɑːθ; bæθ] 巴斯〔英国 Somerset 州首邑,以温泉著名〕。***go to*** ～! 滚蛋! 出去! ～ **brick** (研磨金属用的)巴斯研磨粉。～ **chair** (病人用的)车椅。～ **chap** 〔英〕(猪的)下颌肉。～ **stone** 巴斯石灰石〔建筑用〕。

bathe [beið; beð] **I *vt*. 1.** 把…浸泡在液体中 (*in*);给…洗澡。**2.** (光线、暖气等)充满于,笼罩,包覆(全身)。**3.** (浪)冲刷(岸等)。**4.** (用海绵等)洗,把…弄湿,润湿 (*in*, *with*). ～ *one's throat* (用水等)润喉。～ *a wound* 洗伤口。*a morning fog bathing the city* 笼罩城市的朝雾。*The Nile* ～*s Egypt*. 尼罗河灌溉埃及。～ (***oneself***) ***in*** (*water*; *the sun*) 泡在(水中);浸在(日光中)。— ***vi*. 1.** 洗澡。**2.** (在河、海等里)游泳。**3.** 沉浸,沐浴 (*in*). **II *n*.** 〔英〕(在河、海中的)游泳。***go for a*** ～ 去游泳。***have*** [***take***] ***a*** ～ 游泳,洗(海水)澡。**-a·ble *a*.** 可洗浴的,适于游泳的。

bath·er [ˈbeiðə; ˋbeðɚ] ***n*.** 游泳者,洗澡的人;浴疗者。

ba·thet·ic [bəˈθetik; bəˋθɛtɪk] ***a*. 1.**【修】顿降法的。**2.** 平凡的,陈腐的。**3.** 假作悲伤的,过分感伤的。

bath·i·nette [ˈbɑːθiˈnet; ˋbæθɪˋnɛt] ***n*.** 巴希奈小浴盆〔原为小儿浴盆商标名称;胶布制,轻便,可折叠〕;胶布小浴盆。

bath·ing [ˈbeiðiŋ; ˋbeðɪŋ] ***n*. 1.** 游泳;洗海[河、湖]水澡。**2.** (海滨等的)游泳条件。*He's fond of* ～. 他喜欢(在海、河、湖中)游泳。*The* ～ *here is safe*. 这里洗海水澡很安全。～ **beauty** (参加选美竞赛的)泳装美人。～ **cap** 女子游泳帽。～ **clothes** [**costume, dress, suit**] 游泳衣。～ **costume** 〔英〕游泳衣。～ **drawers** 游泳裤。～ **machine** (浴场)换衣马车〔曳入水中,以便游泳者更衣〕,～ **place** 海滨浴场,游泳场;浴疗场。～ **suit** 泳装。

batho- *comb*. *f*. = deep.

bath·o·chrome [ˈbæθəkrəum; ˋbæθəˏkrom] ***n*.**【化】向红团。

bath·o·lith [ˈbæθəliθ; ˋbæθəˏlɪθ], **bath·o·lite** [-lait; -laɪt] ***n*.**【地】岩基。

ba·thom·e·ter [bəˈθɔmitə; bəˋθɑmɪtɚ] ***n*.** = bathymeter.

bat·horse [ˈbæthɔːs; ˋbæthɔrs] ***n*.** (驮军官行李等的)驮马。

ba·thos [ˈbeiθɔs; ˋbeθɑs] ***n*. 1.**【修】顿降法〔由庄重突转庸俗之法〕;虎头蛇尾。**2.** 假悲哀;过分的感伤,感伤癖。**3.** 陈腐,平凡。

Bath·urst [ˈbæθə(ː)st; ˋbæθɚst] ***n*.** 巴瑟斯特〔Banjul 班珠尔的旧称〕。

bath·y·al [ˈbæθiəl; ˋbæθɪəl] ***a*.** 洋深的。

ba·thyb·ic [bæˈθibik; bæˋθɪbɪk] ***a*.** 深海性的。

ba·thym·e·ter [bæˈθimitə; bæˋθɪmɪtɚ] ***n*.** 水深测量器,测深仪。

bathy·met·ric [ˌbæθiˈmetrik; ˏbæθəˋmɛtrɪk] ***a*. 1.** 深测法的。**2.**【地】等深的。**3.** 关于深水生物分布的。

ba·thym·e·try [bæˈθimitri; bæˋθɪmətrɪ] ***n*. 1.** 海洋测深学[术]。**2.** 海洋生物分布学。

bath·y·scaph(e) [ˈbæθiskæf; ˋbæθəˏskef] ***n*.** 深海潜测艇,深海生物调查潜艇,深海潜艇。

bath·y·sphere [ˈbæθisfiə; ˋbæθɪˏsfɪr] ***n*.** 深海球形潜水器。

bath·y·ther·mo·graph [ˌbæθiˈθəːməgrɑːf; ˏbæθəˋθɝməˏgræf] ***n*.** 海水测温计,深海温度仪。

ba·tik [ˈbætik; ˋbætɪk] ***n*.** = battik.

bat·ing [ˈbeitiŋ; ˋbetɪŋ] ***prep*.** 〔古〕除…之外。***n*.**【化】(皮革的)软化。

ba·tiste [bæˈtiːst; bæˋtist] ***n*.** 细麻布,细棉布;麻纱。

bat·man [ˈbætmən; ˋbætmən] ***n*. 1.** 〔英〕(军官的)马夫;马弁;勤务兵。**2.** 〔美〕蝙蝠人。

bat-mon·ey [ˈbætmʌni; ˋbætmʌnɪ] ***n*.** 〔英〕(将校的)战地津贴。

ba·ton [ˈbætən; ˋbætn] **I *n*. 1.** (表示军阶、官阶的)官杖;司令杖。**2.** 警棍。**3.**【乐】指挥棒。**4.**【体】接力棍。*the* ～ *of a field marshal* 陆军元帅的官杖。*an orchestra under the* ～ *of* …某某人指挥的管弦乐队。***carry*** [***have***] ***a Marshal's*** ～ ***in one's knapsack*** 有将帅器量。***wield a good*** ～ 指挥灵活。**II *vt*.** 用短棒打。～ **charge** 警察的干涉。～ **gun** (发射硬橡胶子弹的)防暴枪。～ **round** 防暴子弹。～ **sinister**【徽】私生子的记号。**-ist *n*.** 指挥者。

bat·pay [ˈbætpei; ˋbætˏpe] ***n*.** 〔英军俚〕战时特别津贴。

Ba·tra·chi·a [bəˈtreikjə; bəˋtrekɪə] ***n*.** (*pl*. ***-ns***)【动】(无尾)两栖类;蛙类 (= Anura).

ba·tra·chi·an [bəˈtreikjən; bəˋtrekɪən] ***n*., *a*.** 两栖类(的),无尾类(的),蛙类(的)。

bats [bæts; bæts] ***a*.** 〔美口〕发狂的,发疯的。*He's gone* ～. 那家伙发疯了。

bats·man [ˈbætsmən; ˋbætsmən] ***n*.** (棒球等的)击球员。

bat·tal·ion [bəˈtæljən; bəˋtæljən] ***n*. 1.**【军】营,大队;营部。**2.** 〔*pl*.〕大军,部队;一大群人,一大批物品。～*s of bureaucrats* 一大群官僚。

Bat·tam·bang [ˈbætəm-bang; ˋbætəm-bang] ***n*.** 马德望〔柬埔寨城市〕。

bat·tel [ˈbætl; ˋbætl] ***n*. 1.** (牛津大学的)膳宿杂费(学期末结算清单)。**2.** 〔*pl*.〕(牛津大学的)学费〔包括膳宿杂费〕。

bat·ten[1] [ˈbætn; ˋbætn] **I *n*. 1.**【建】板条;挂瓦条,压缝条。**2.** 小方材,小圆材。**3.**【海】扣板,压条,条板。**4.** (舞台)装灯光的横木条。**5.** 万能曲线尺。～ *door* 条板门。

II *vt*. 装条板于;在…上钉扣板,把…用板条钉牢。~ ***down*** (*the hatches*)【海】(暴风雨或失火时)钉上扣板密闭舱口。

bat·ten² [ˈbætn; ˋbætn̩] *n*.【纺】筘(框)。

bat·ten³ [ˈbætn; ˋbætn] *vi*. 1. 饱餐,大吃 (*on*; *upon*). 2. 养肥自己,长胖 (*on*)〔尤指损人利己〕;肥私囊。~ *on the poor* 靠盘剥穷人养肥自己。— *vt*. 养肥(猪,羊等)。

B

bat·ter¹ [ˈbætə; ˋbætɚ] *n*.〔美〕(棒球等的)击球员。

bat·ter² [ˈbætə; ˋbætɚ] *n*.【烹】(做糕饼时用粉、牛奶等调成的)奶油面糊。

bat·ter³ [ˈbætə; ˋbætɚ] I *vt*. 1. 连续地猛打[捶,捣]。2. 炮击;攻击,乱轰。3. 打坏,敲碎,摧毁,捶薄;把…打得七凸八凹,打扁(帽子等)。4. 用坏(铅字等);磨损(家具等)。*badly ~ed and mauled* 碰得头破血流。~ *the door down* 把门撞垮。— *vi*. 1. 作连续猛打;乱打,炮轰 (*at*). 2.【建】(墙壁等的)内倾,倾斜。II *n*. (铅字的)磨损,毁损。*continue to ~ at the door* 不断地用力敲门。

bat·tered [ˈbætəd; ˋbætəd] *a*. 1. 打扁了的,打垮了的,敲碎了的。2. 用旧了的。3. (因生活困难等)憔悴的,消瘦的。***the ~ baby*** [***child***] ***syndrome*** 儿童被摧残造成的综合症。

bat·ter·ing [ˈbætəriŋ; ˋbætərɪŋ] *n*. 连续猛击。~ **artillery** 〔集合词〕攻城炮。~ **charge** 最大装(弹)药量。~ **ram** (古代的)破城槌,撞车;(铁匠的)大槌。~ **train** 攻城炮列。

bat·ter·y [ˈbætəri; ˋbætərɪ] *n*. 1. 炮兵连[营,中队];(军舰上的)炮组,炮列;炮台;炮(兵)阵(地);(炮的)待发射状态。2. (金属器具的)一套,一组;(问题等的)一连串。3.【法】欧打。4.【电】电池(组)。5.【纺】(自动织机的)纬管库。6.【棒球】投球员与接球员。7. (乐队的)一组打击乐器。8. 孵蛋箱组。*a ~ of questions* 一连串的质问。*a cooking ~* 一套烹调用具。*a local ~* 自给电池。*a solar ~* 太阳能电池。***change one's ~*** 变更攻击方向,换手攻击。***in ~*** 准备发射。***turn sb.'s ~ against*** [***upon***] ***himself*** 抓住对方理论反击对方,以子之矛攻子之盾。~ **charger** 电池充电器。~ **eliminator** 电池组代用器。**bat·ter·ied** *a*. (装配有)电池的。

bat·tik [ˈbætik; ˋbætɪk] *n*.【纺】1. 蜡染法,蜡防印花法。2. 蜡染花布。

bat·ting [ˈbætiŋ; ˋbætɪŋ] *n*. 1. (棒球等的)击球,击球法。2. 棉胎,棉絮,毛絮。~ **average** (棒球)击球平均得分数;〔口〕平均成功率;〔美〕能力。~ **eye** (棒球)击球的眼力。

bat·tle [ˈbætl; ˋbætl] I *n*. 1. 战,战斗(行动),交战,会战,战役,(一般)战争。2. 斗争,竞争;〔美〕竞赛。3. 胜利,成功。*a ~ of words* 论战。*the disposition for a ~* 战术的部署。*the ~ of life* 生存斗争。*The battle is not always to the strong*. 强者不一定常胜。*a naval ~* 海战。*a close ~* 近战,肉搏。*a decisive ~* 决战。*a general's ~* 战略和战术的较量,韬略战。*a soldier's ~* 勇气和力量的较量,兵力战。*a pitched ~ = a plain ~* 鏖战,酣战。*a sham ~*〔美〕模拟战,战斗演习。*a street ~* 巷战。***accept ~*** 应战,迎战。***be killed in ~*** 阵亡。***do ~ = fight a ~*** 挑战,开战,交战。***fall in ~*** 阵亡。***fight one's ~s over again*** 忆谈当年勇,反复叙述当年功绩[经历]。***gain a ~*** 打胜仗。***give ~ = do ~***. ***give the ~*** 认输,战败。***go into ~*** 投入战斗。***half the ~*** 成功[胜利]的一半 (*Youth is half the ~*. 年轻气锐就是一半成功)。***have the ~*** 战胜。***join ~*** 参战。***lose a ~*** 打败仗。***lose the ~*** 战败。***offer ~*** 挑战。***refuse ~*** 拒绝应战。II *vi*. 作战,战斗,斗争,奋斗 (*against*; *with*; *for*). ~ *with poverty* 与贫困作斗争。— *vt*.〔美〕与…作战,与…斗争。~ *the storm* 与暴风雨作斗争。~ **array** 战斗队形,阵容。~**-ax(e)** (中古的)战斧,大斧;〔美俚〕硕大凶悍的女人。~ **bill** 战门配置表。~ **bowler** 〔军口〕钢盔。~**bus** 〔美口〕流动竞选宣传车。~**-clad** *a*. 全副武装的。~ **cruiser** 战列巡洋舰。~ **cry** 1. (作战时的)呐喊,助攻声。2. 标语,(斗争)口号。~ **dress** 战地服装。~ **effectiveness** 战斗力。~ **fatigue** 战斗疲劳症。~**-field** 战场,战地。~ **formation** 战斗队形。~ **front** 战线。~**ground** 战场;论争的主题。~ **group** 战斗群。~ **line** 1. 战线,前线。2. (海军)作战队形。~ **painter** 军事题材画家。~ **piece** 战争画,战争记事。~**plane** 战斗机。~ **-ready** *a*. 作好战斗准备的。~ **royal** 1. (斗鸡)大战。2. 大混战,大论战。~**-scarred** *a*. 有战斗疤痕的;有战争痕迹的。~**ship** *n*. 战舰。~ **sky** 作战空域。~**-some** *a*. 爱争吵的,好口角的。~ **stations** 阵地,战斗岗位;紧急集结点。~ **trim** 战斗准备 ~ **wag(g)on** 〔俚〕战舰。~**-wise** *a*. 有战斗经验的;身经百战的。~**-worthy** *a*. (武器等)适合用于战斗的。~**-worthiness** 适合战斗的性能[状态]。

bat·tled [ˈbætld; ˋbætl̩d] *a*. 有城垛的,有雉堞的。

bat·tle·dore [ˈbætldɔː; ˋbætl̩ˏdɔr] I *n*. 1. 板羽球球板;板羽球游戏。2. (洗衣等用)杓状杵。***play ~ and shuttlecock*** 打板羽球。~ *the plan* 计划被推来推去。II *vt*. 把…扔来扔去。— *vi*. 互相间扔来扔去。

bat·tle·ment [ˈbætlmənt; ˋbætl̩mənt] *n*.〔常 *pl*.〕雉堞,城垛;有枪眼的防御墙。

bat·tue [bæˈtjuː; bæˋtu] *n*. 〔F.〕〔英〕1. (向猎人埋伏处)赶兽,追猎。2. 追猎队,追猎猎获品。3. 大量捕杀,滥杀。

bat·ty [ˈbæti; ˋbætɪ] *a*. 1. 蝙蝠(似)的。2.〔美俚〕愚蠢的,疯狂的;反常的。*go ~* 发疯。

bat·wing [ˈbætˌwiŋ; ˋbætwɪŋ] I *a*. 蝙蝠翼状的。II *n*. 蝙蝠翼战斗机。

bau·ble [ˈbɔːbl; ˋbɔbl̩] *n*. 1. 美观的便宜货,小玩意,骗钱货。2. 骗孩子的东西,玩具。3.【史】弄臣[丑角]的手杖。***A fool should never hold a ~ in his hand***. 不要自己出乖露丑。

baud [bɔːd; bɔd] *n*. 1. 波特〔发报速率单位〕。2. 计算机的秒速。

bau·de·kin, bal·da·chin [ˈbɔːdəkin, ˈbɔːldəkin; ˋbɔdəkɪn, ˋbɔldəkɪn] *n*. 1.【纺】宝大锦。2. 祭坛华盖;宝座华盖。3.【宗】祭坛上的华盖状大理石结构。

bau·drons [ˈbɔːdrənz; ˋbɔdrənz] *n*.〔Scot.〕猫〔不加冠词〕。

Bau·er [ˈbauə; ˋbaʊɚ] *n*. 鲍尔〔姓氏〕。

baulk [bɔːk, bɔːlk; bɔk, bɔlk] *n*., *v*. = balk.

Bau·mé [bauˈmei; boˋme] I *n*. 玻(美)度;玻美液体比重计。II *a*. 玻美标度的。~ **hydrometer** 玻美比[浮]重计,玻美表。~ **scale** 玻美比重标(度),玻氏比重计。

baux·ite [ˈbɔːksait; ˋbɔksaɪt] *n*.【矿】铝矾土,铝土矿。

Ba·var·i·a [bəˈveəriə; bəˋvɛrɪə] *n*. 巴伐利亚〔德国州名〕。**-n** 1. *a*. 巴伐利亚(人)的;巴伐利亚语的。2. *n*. 巴伐利亚人[语]。

bav·in [ˈbævin; ˋbævɪn] *n*. 柴,柴捆。~ *wood* 束材。

baw·bee [bɔːˈbiː; bɔˋbi] *n*.〔Scot.〕1. 半便士;小钱。2.〔口〕小事。

baw·cock [ˈbɔːkɔk; ˋbɔˏkɑk] *n*.〔古〕好人,好汉。

bawd [bɔːd; bɔd] *n*. 1. 鸨母,妓院女老板。2. 妓女。3. 淫猥语,猥亵语。

bawd·ry [ˈbɔːdri; ˋbɔdrɪ] *n*. 1.〔废〕开妓院;卖淫;私通,不贞。2.〔古〕猥亵的言语[行为]。

bawd·y [ˈbɔːdi; ˋbɔdɪ] I *a*. 淫猥的,猥亵的。II *n*. 淫猥的言辞。~ **house** 妓院。

bawl [bɔːl; bɔl] I *vi*. 1. 喊,叫,咆哮。2.〔口〕大哭。*She ~ed to me across the street*. 她在街对面大声叫我。— *vt*. 1. 大声喊出。2. 叫卖。3. 责骂。~ *one's wares in the street* 沿街叫卖。~ *one's dissatisfaction* 大嚷大叫地发泄不满。~ ***about*** 叫卖。~ ***and squall*** 怪喊怪叫。~ ***at*** [***against***] 叱责。~ ***out*** 喊叫;〔美〕大骂,痛责。II *n*. 叫喊(声);〔口〕大哭。

baw·ley [ˈbɔːli; ˋbɔlɪ] *n*.〔英方〕渔船。

Bax·ter [ˈbækstə; ˋbækstɚ] ***n*.** 巴克斯特〔姓氏〕。

bax·ter [ˈbækstə; ˋbækstɚ] ***n*.** 〔Scot.〕做面包的人。

bay[1] [bei; be] ***n*.** **1.** (比 gulf 小、比 cove 大的)湾,海湾。**2.** (山中的)凹地。**3.**【火箭】凹槽;盘,舱。**4.**【英军】战壕通路。*Hudson* ～ 哈德逊湾。*the* ～ *of Bengal* 孟加拉湾。**B- Area** (美国)圣弗朗西斯科湾地区。～ **salt** 粗盐。**B- State** 〔美〕= **Massachusetts** 州。**B- Stater** 〔美〕麻萨诸塞州人。

bay[2] [bei; be] **I** ***n*.** **1.** (猎犬等追捕猎物时的)吠声。**2.** 绝境,穷途末路(尤指走投无路时反噬的状态)。***be at*** ～ **1.** 走投无路;被包围,被遏制。**2.** 作困兽斗。***bring*** [***drive***] ***to*** ～ **1.** 穷追,使陷绝境。**2.** 迫使…作困兽斗。***come to*** ～ 陷入绝境;作困兽斗。***keep*** [***hold***, ***have***] ***at*** ～ **1.** 围住,使走投无路。**2.** 不使…接近,遏制 (*hold a stag at* ～ 围住一头鹿。*keep a danger at* ～ 竭力不使危险迫近)。***stand at*** ～ = be at ～. ***turn to*** ～ = come to ～. **II** ***vi*.** (猎犬追捕猎物时不断地)吠,叫,咆哮。— ***vt*.** **1.** 向…吠叫。**2.** 穷追;使陷入绝境。**3.** 阻止(敌人)不使前进。**4.** 用拉长的低沉声音说。～ *a defiance* 大声反抗。～ ***the moon*** (狂犬)吠月;无事空扰,空嚷,徒劳。

bay[3] [bei; be] ***n*.** **1.**【植】月桂树。**2.** 〔*pl*.〕桂冠;荣誉,名誉。～ **berry** 月桂果;杨梅属植物。～ **leaf** (食品中用以调味的)干月桂叶。～ **oil** 月桂油香精。～ **rum** 月桂(叶)油。～ **tree** 月桂树。

bay[4] [bei; be] ***n*.** **1.**【建】架间(跨度),格距;壁洞。**2.**【空】舱;【船】(军舰)中舱前部,船上救护室[病房]。**3.** 浮桥桥节。**4.** (谷仓)堆干草处。**5.** (停车场的)支线终点。**6.** 吊窗,凸窗。*a bomb* ～ 炸弹仓。*an engine* ～ 发动机舱。～ *of joists* 堆搁栅(托梁)的房间。*the sick* ～ 甲板上挤满病号士兵的地方。～**-line** (铁道的)专用支线。～ **window** (凸出墙外的)吊窗,凸窗;〔讽〕(胖子的)罗汉肚。

bay[5] [bei; be] **I** ***a*.** 赤褐色的,栗色的。**II** ***n*.** 栗色马,骝。*a* ～ *horse* 栗色马。

bay[6] [bei; be] **I** ***n*.** 堤防,河堤。**II** ***vt*.** 筑堤遏(水)。～ *water up* 筑堤堵水。

ba·ya·dère [ˌbeijəˈdɛə; ˏbajəˋdɛr] ***n*.** 〔F.〕**1.** (印度)寺院舞蹈女。**2.** 条花绸。

Bay·ard [ˈbeiɑːd; ˋbeɚd] ***n*.** 贝阿德〔姓氏〕。

bay·o·net [ˈbeiənit; ˋbeənɪt] **I** ***n*.** **1.** (枪上的)刺刀;〔喻〕武力。**2.** 〔*pl*.〕步兵。*by the* ～*s* 用武力。*2,000* ～*s* 步兵二千。***at the point of the*** ～ 用武力。***Charge*** ～***s***! 上刺刀。***Fix*** [***Unfix***] ～***s***! 〔号令〕上[下]刺刀! **II** ***vt*.** 刺杀,用刺刀刺;用武力迫使 (*into*). ～ *the enemy into submission* 用武力迫使敌人投降。～ **charge** 刺刀冲锋,白刃战。～ **drill** [**practice**] 劈刺训练。～ **fencing** 劈刺术。～ **holder** [**socket**] 卡口灯头。

bay·ou [ˈbaijuː; ˋbaɪju] ***n*.** (*pl*. ～***s***) **1.** (美国南部的)牛轭湖;长沼;(江,湖的)沼泽出入口。**2.** 河川的支流。**the B- State** = Mississippi 州。

bay·wood [ˈbeiˌwud; ˋbeˏwud] ***n*.** (墨西哥产的)桃花心木 (*Swietenia macrophylla*).

ba·za(a)r [bəˈzɑː; bəˋzɑr] ***n*.** **1.** (东方各国的)市场,集市。**2.** (英美等国的)廉价商店,百货店,小工艺品商店。**3.** 义卖展销。*a charity* ～ 义卖市场。*hold a* ～ *in aid of* …为支援…举行义卖。

ba·zoo [bəˈzuː; bəˋzu] ***n*.** 〔美俚〕**1.** 嘴。**2.** 鼻。**3.** 大话,吹牛,浮夸。

ba·zoo·ka [bəˈzuːkə; bəˋzukə] ***n*.** **1.** 火箭筒;反坦克火箭炮。**2.** (超高频)由平衡到不平衡的变换装置。～**-man** 火箭[筒,炮]手。

BB = Bachelor of Business 商学士。

BBA = Bachelor of Business Administration 工商管理学士。

BBC = British Broadcasting Corporation 英国广播公司。

BBE = Bachelor of Business Education 商务教育学士。

BB gun 汽枪。

bbl., **bbl** = barrel(s).

BC, **B.C.** = Before Christ 公元前。

B.C. = **1.** Bachelor of Chemistry. **2.** Bachelor of Commerce. **3.** British Council 英国文化委员会。

BCD = **1.** binary coded decimal.【计】二进制编码的十进制。**2.** bad conduct discharge 因品行不端而被勒令退伍。

BCE = **1.** Bachelor of Civil Engineering 土木工程学士。**2.** Bachelor of Chemical Engineering 化学工程学士。**3.** Before the Christian (或 Common) Era 公元前。

BCG = Bacillus Calmette-Guérin【药】卡介苗。

BCL = **1.** Bachelor of Canon Law 教会法规学士。**2.** Bachelor of Civil Law 民法学士。

B. Com. = Bachelor of Commerce 商学士。

B Complex 维生素 B 复合物,复合维生素 B。

BCS = **1.** British Computer Society 英国计算机学会。**2.** Bachelor of Commercial Science 商学士。**3.** Bachelor of Chemical Science 化学学士。

BCU = big close-up (电视中)演员的特写镜头。

BDA = **1.** British Dental Association 英国牙科协会。**2.** Bachelor of Domestic Arts 家政学士。**3.** Bachelor of Dramatic Art 戏剧艺术学士。

bdel·li·um [ˈdeliəm; ˋdɛlɪəm] ***n*.** **1.** 芳香树脂。**2.**【圣】宝石,珍珠,琥珀。

BDS = Bachelor of Dental Surgery 牙科学士。

BE = **1.** Bachelor of Engineering 工学士。**2.** Bachelor of Economics 经济学士。**3.** Bachelor of Education 教育学士。**4.** Bank of England (英国)英格兰银行。**5.** bill of exchange 汇票。

Bé = Baumé.

be [强 biː, 弱 bi; bi, bɪ] 〔陈述语气现在式〕(*I*) ***am***; (*you*) ***are***; 〔古〕(*thou*) ***art***; (*he*, *she*, *it*) ***is***; (*we*, *you*, *they*) ***are***. 〔陈述语气过去时〕(*I*) ***was***; (*you*) ***were***, 〔古〕(*thou*) ***wast*** or ***wert***; (*he*, *she*, *it*) ***was***; (*we*, *you*, *they*) ***were***. 假设语气现在式(通称、通数) ***be***; 假设语气过去式(通称、通数) ***were***, 但〔古〕(*thou*) ***wert***. 祈使语气 ***be***. 过去分词 ***been***. 现在分词 ***being***. 缩写:〔口〕***'m*** (= am), ***'s*** (= is), ***'re*** (= are); 〔口俚〕***ain't*** (= am 〔is, are〕 not) 〔〔俚〕***ben't*** (= be not)〕。***vi*.** **1.** 有…存在,生存。*Can such things be?* 会有这样的事吗? *There is no water in the vase.* 瓶里没有水。*There are seven of us.* 我们有七个人。*I think, therefore I am.* 我思故我在〔唯心主义哲学的一种说法〕。*Churchill is no more.* 邱吉尔已经不在人世。*To* ～, *or not to* ～: *that is the question.* 活还是死,是个要考虑的问题。**2.** 发生,产生,举行。*The accident was last week.* 事故是上周发生的。*When is the wedding to* ～? 婚礼何时举行? **3.** 在;逗留;到达,来到。*The book is on the desk.* 书在桌子上。*He is in London.* 他在伦敦。*Will you* ～ *here long?* 你在这里待得久吗? *Has anybody been here?* 有人来过吗? **4.** 听任(保持原状)。*Let it* ～. 随它去。*Let her* ～. 由她去,不要管她。**5.** 属于;伴随;降临〔用于祈使语气〕。*May good fortune* ～ *with you.* 祝你顺利。*Woe* ～ *to you!* 愿你倒霉〔诅咒语〕! **6.** 是…〔表示性质、状态等〕。*Iron is hard.* 铁是硬的。*I am a pupil.* 我是小学生。**7.** 是;值;等于〔表示时间、度量、价值等〕。*Today is Saturday.* 今天是星期六。*The station is two miles away.* 车站离这里两英里。*I am twenty* (*years old*). 我二十岁。*This book is five dollars.* 这本书价值五美元。*Twice four is eight.* 四乘二等于八。★以上 **6. 7.** 两项释义用于连接述语称为连系动词 (linking verb) 或系词 (copula). **8.** 做;成为,变成。〔多用命令语气或不定式〕*Be prudent.* 要谨慎小心。*Be a pupil before you become a teacher.* 先做学生,然后再做先生。*To* ～ *subjective means not to look at problems objectively.* 所谓主观性,就是不知道客观地看问题。*John wants to*

B

～ *a poet*. 约翰想成为诗人。— **v. aux. 1.** 〔be＋及物动词的过去分词构成被动语态〕。*We were awarded the first prize*. 我们获得了一等奖。*I was scolded by Father*. 我被父亲骂了。**2.** 〔be＋come, go 等不及物动词的过去分词构成完成时〕。*Spring is come*. 春天来了。*His health was broken*. 他的身体垮了。*I am finished*. 我完了。**3.** 〔be＋现在分词构成进行时〕。*I was walking in the park at the time*. 当时我正在公园里散步。*The ship is being built*. 船正在建造中。**4.** 〔be＋有 to 的不定式,表示约定、计划、职责、义务、愿望、可能、命运等〕。*He is to see me today*. 他今天要来看我。*The book is to come*. 书就会来的。*They are to ～ married in May*. 他们预定在五月结婚。*You are not to do that*. 你不该做那件事。*They knew that their love was to ～ eternal*. 他们深信彼此将永远相爱。*He was never to see his wife again*. 他此后就再没有和妻子见面了〔多用过去式〕。**5.** 〔were＋带 to 的不定式,表示虚拟的假定〕。*If I were to be* [*were I to be*] *here tomorrow* ... 假若我明天来这里的话…。～ ***at*** 从事于,做 (*What are you at*? 你在干什么?)。～ ***for* 1.** 到…去。**2.** 赞成,要 (*I am for New York*. 我到纽约去。*We are for just war*. 我们赞成正义的战争)。～ ***from* 1.** 从…来。**2.** 生在(某处) (*She is from London*. 她从伦敦来[她是伦敦人])。***Be gone***! 走开! 去! ***Be it so***! = ***So ～ it*** (= Let it ～ so). **1.** 就这样吧;这样也好;算啦,别管它了。**2.** 但愿如此;心诚所愿 (= amen!)。***Be it that*** 即使…,也得…。***Be seated*** 请坐。***be that as it may*** 即使如此,总得…。***have been*** 〔口〕来过 (*Has anyone been*? 有人来过没有?)。***have been*** (***and gone***) ***and*** 〔口〕干下了…〔与过去分词并用表示抗议、惊愕等〕(*And d'you know what she's been and gone and done*? 你知道她干了些什么吗? *Who has been and moved my paper*? 是谁动了我的文件? *You have been and bought a new pen*. 你买了一枝新笔啦)。***have been at*** [***in***, ***to***] 到过,去过 (*Have you ever been at* [*to*] *Taipei*? 你到过台北吗?)。***have been to*** 到(某处)去过了;去过,到过 (*I have been to New York*. 我到纽约去过了)。***if so ～*** 真是那样的话,如若是这样。(*Mrs. Smith*) ***that is*** [***that was***, ***that is to be***] 现在的[原来的,将来的]史密斯夫人。***the … to ～*** 未来的… (*the bride to ～*未来的新娘)。***There is*** [***was***, ***are*** 等] 有。

be- *pref*. **1.** be＋*vt*. 表示"到处"、"全体"等意义,如 *be*smear, *be*scorch. **2.** be＋*vt*. 表示"充分","过度"等意义,如 *be*deck. **3.** 使 *vi*. 变为 *vt*., 如 *be*moan. **4.** 使形容词、名词成为带有"使之"、"叫做"等意义的及物动词: *be*fool, *be*madam. **5.** 使名词成为带有"包围"、"看做"等意义的及物动词,如 *be*cloud, *be*friend. **6.** 变名词为以 **-ed** 结尾的形容词,常有轻蔑或取笑的含义,如 *be*spectacled. **7.** 加强语气,如 *be*labo(u)r.

BEA = British European Airways 英国欧洲航空公司(后已与 British Overseas Airways Corporation 英国海外航空公司合并,称 British Airways 英国航空公司)。

beach [biːtʃ; bitʃ] **I *n*. 1.** (湖、河、海的)滨,海滨。**2.** 海滩,沙滩。**3.** (水滨的)卵石,细砾。*take a walk along the ～* 沿海滨散步。***on the ～* 1.** 失业的;穷愁潦倒的。**2.** 【海】担任陆上职务。**II *vt*.** 使(船)冲上沙滩,使(船)靠岸;把(船)拖上海滩。～ *the landing craft* 使登陆艇靠岸。*The storm ～ed half the fleet*. 风暴使舰队的半数舰只搁浅。— ***vi*.** 船搁浅。**III *a*.** 在海滨使用[穿用]的。～ **ball** (在海滨和游泳池玩的)水皮球。～ **boy 1.** 海滨男侍者。**2.** 常在海滨游荡的纨绔子弟。～ **break** 近岸激浪。～ **buggy** 海滩汽车。～ **coat** 游泳衣上披的衣服,海滨服。～**comb** ***vi*.** 在海滨或码头上拣破烂或求乞为生。～**comber** ***n*.** 〔美〕**1.** 海滨巨浪。**2.** (太平洋各岛码头上的)白人乞丐[游民]。～ **flea** 沙蚤。～ **front** ***a*.** 海滩边的。***n*.** 海滩线,海滩地区。～ **grass** 海滨草。～**head** 【军】**1.** 滩头阵地。**2.** 滩头堡。～**-lamar** [ˈbiːtʃəˈmɑː; ˋbitʃləˋmɑr] 西南太平洋岛屿上流行的土腔英语。～**master** 登陆指挥官,陆战队指挥官。～ **music** 海滨音乐〔一种在黑人灵歌与强节奏哀怨曲基础上发展起来的美国流行音乐〕。～ **pea** 【植】海边香豌豆。～ **plum** 【植】海滨李。～**-rescue** 海滨浴场救生员。～ **ridge** 滩脊。～ **scape** 海滨风景。～ **umbrella** (海滩或花园用的)太阳伞。～ **volleyball**【体】沙滩排球。～ **wagon** (原名 station wagon)旅行汽车;客货两用汽车。～**wear** 海滩装。

beach·y [ˈbiːtʃi; ˋbitʃɪ] ***a*.** 〔废、罕〕有沙滩的,砂砾满地的。***Beachy Head*** 英国 Sussex 州高 565 英尺的海岬。

bea·con [ˈbiːkən; ˋbikən] **I *n*. 1.** (作为信号的)烽火,篝火。**2.** 信号所,望楼;灯塔,信标。**3.** 警标,界标。**4.** 【交】指向标;【物】标向波;〔喻〕警告,指南。*a home ～* 归航信标。*a nondirectional radio ～* 全向无线电信标。*a radar ～* 雷达指向标。*a tracking ～* 雷达应答器。～ **fire** 烽火,信号篝火。***Belisha ～*** (马路穿行道口的)黄色指示灯。～ **light** 信标灯(光)。～ **school** 灯塔学校〔下班后对公众开放,提供成人教育的公立学校〕。～ **station** 指向电台。**II *vi*.** 像灯塔般照耀。— ***vt*. 1.** 为…装设指向标;用灯引导。**2.** 照亮;〔喻〕警告,鼓励。

bead [biːd; bid] **I *n*. 1.** 有孔小珠,玻璃球;〔*pl*.〕(成串的)念珠,数珠。**2.** 露珠,滴;水泡。**3.** (枪的)照星,准星。**4.** 【建】珠缘,串珠线脚;【机】卷边,(轮)胎边,(车)轮(圆)缘。*a dielectric ～* 绝缘垫圈,电解质小球。*Baily's ～s* 【天】(全蚀时月边缘所显现的)粒状光。～ *tree* 苦楝树。～*s of perspiration* [*sweat*] 汗珠。～ *fabric* 轮胎布。***count*** [***bid***, ***tell***, ***say***] ***one's ～s*** 数念珠;(用念珠)祷告[念佛]。***draw*** [***get***] ***a ～ on*** 向…瞄准。***pray without*** (***one's***) ***～s*** 打错了算盘,算计错了。**II *vt*.** 用小珠装饰,把…连成一串。*a ～ed handbag* 饰有小珠的手提包。～*ed velvet* 提花丝绒。— ***vi*. 1.** 形成珠,起泡。**2.** 瞄准。*Sweat ～ed on his forehead* 他的头上冒出汗珠。～ **house** 收容所,救济院。～ **roll 1.** 名单,名册;目录。**2.** 一串念珠。～**-ruby** 加拿大舞鹤草。～ **-work** 串珠状细工;【建】珠状花边,串珠状缘饰。

bead·ing [biːdiŋ; ˋbidɪŋ] ***n*. 1.** (酒等的)起泡。**2.** 【建】串珠状缘饰;【纺】经纱起球;【电】玻璃熔接。

Bea·dle [ˈbiːdl; ˋbidl] ***n*.** 比德尔〔姓氏〕。

bea·dle [ˈbiːdl; ˋbidl] ***n*. 1.** 〔英〕教区事务员。**2.** (英国大学举行典礼时的)执权标领队者。**3.** (法院等处的)差役。**4.** 小官吏。

bea·dle·dom [ˈbiːdldəm; ˋbidldəm] ***n*.** 小官僚性格;小官僚作风;愚蠢的官僚主义。

beads·man [ˈbiːdzmən; ˋbidzmən] ***n*. 1.** 济贫院中的受济人。**2.** (受雇)为他人祈祷求福者。**3.** 〔苏格兰〕的官丐〔官准接收公共施舍的行乞者〕。

bead·y [ˈbiːdi; ˋbidɪ] ***a*. 1.** 珠子似的,饰有珠子的。**2.** 多泡沫的。～ *eyes* 亮晶晶的小眼睛。

bea·gle [ˈbiːgl; ˋbigl] ***n*. 1.** 猎兔、猎犬。**2.** 警察,密探。**3.** 〔俚〕自动搜索干扰(电)台。**4.** 执行官。**5.** 〔美俚〕香肠,红肠。**bea·gl·ing *n*.** 用小猎兔犬猎兔。

beak[1] [biːk; bik] ***n*. 1.** (猛禽等的)嘴,喙。**2.** 钩形鼻;〔美俚〕鼻子。**3.** 鸟嘴状物;(茶壶等的)壶嘴;(古代战舰舰首冲敌的)铁嘴;箫口。**4.** 【建】柱尖;壳尖;【地】喙形饰像。**5.** 圆口灯。**-ed *a*.** 有钩形嘴的;钩形的。**-y *a*. 1.** = beaked. **2.** 爱管闲事的。

beak[2] [biːk; bik] ***n*. 1.** 〔英俚〕治安法官。**2.** 〔学〕校长,先生。

beak·er [ˈbiːkə; ˋbikə] ***n*. 1.** 【化】烧杯。**2.** (有脚的)大酒杯;一大酒杯的量。*a ～ of gin* 一大杯杜松子酒。

bea·kie [ˈbiːki; ˋbikɪ] ***n*.** 〔美俚〕暗中监视工会会员的警察。

be-all [ˈbiːɔːl; ˋbiˏɔl] ***n*.** 重要的东西。***be-all and end-all* 1.** 主要原因;要素;一切的一切;整体;总体。**2.** 不可救药的人;无可补救的事。**3.** 极点,终极。

beam [biːm; bim] **I** ***n*.** **1.** 梁,栋梁,桁条;(船的)横梁。**2.** 船幅;(动物、人的)体幅。**3.** (秤)杆,杠杆,(织机的)卷轴,经轴;(鹿角的)主干;车辕;犁柄;锄把。**4.** (光线的)束,道,柱;【物】波束,射束。**5.** (笑容、表情等的)焕现。**6.**【无】有效播听范围。**7.**【空】信号电波,指向电波。*a ~ of light* 一束光线。*the common ~* 标准秤;准则。*~ and scales* 天平。*a ~ of delight* 高兴的表情,笑逐颜开。*an erector ~*【火箭】(发射时调整导弹位置的)千斤顶。*radio ~* 无线电领航信号。*a landing ~*【空】降落指示波。***abaft the ~*** = behind the ~【海】船横梁之后。***a ~ in one's eye*** 自己本身的大缺点〔与他人目中之刺相比,自己眼中有梁,源出《圣经》马太福音〕。***before the ~***【海】正横前。***broad in the ~***〔口〕臀部阔大。***fly the ~***【空】按指向电波飞行。***fly the wet ~***【空】顺着河流飞行。***kick [strike] the ~*** **1.** (秤一方)翘起;过轻,不足抗衡,无足轻重。**2.** 输,遭受失败。***off the ~*** 脱离航向,不顺利;不对头;做错。***on the ~*** **1.**【海】与龙骨垂直地,正横地。**2.** 在航向上;对头,做对。***on the port [larboard] ~***【海】左舷正横前。***on the starboard ~***【海】右舷正横前。***on the weather ~***【海】迎着正横风。***ride the ~ = fly the ~***. **II** ***vi*.** **1.** 辐射,发光,闪光。**2.** 微笑,眉开眼笑。— ***vt*.** **1.** 发射(光线、电波)。**2.** 向…放[播]送。**3.** (用雷达)探测。**4.** (用波束)导航(飞机等)。*~ the program at America* 向美国播送节目。*the sun ~ing overhead* 红日当头照。~ ***upon*** 看着…微笑。~ ***with joy*** 眉飞色舞,笑逐颜开。~ **antenna**【无】定向天线。~ **compass**, 长脚圆规,长径规。**~-ends** 〔*pl.*〕【海】船梁末端 (*on her ~-ends* 船身快要倾覆。*on one's [the] ~-ends* 濒临危境;计穷智尽;(经济)窘迫万分)。★亦可写作 *on the ~'s ends*. ~**cast** ***vt*.** 对…作定向无线电传真。~ **sea**【海】横波。~ **system**【无】定向制。~ **weapon** 死光武器,光束武器。**~-width**【无】射束宽度。~ **wind**【海】横风。

beam·ing [ˈbiːmiŋ; ˋbimɪŋ] ***a*.** **1.** 光闪闪的。**2.** 喜气洋溢的,眉飞色舞的。**-ly** ***ad*.**

beam·ish [ˈbiːmiʃ; ˋbimɪʃ] ***a*.** **1.** 放光的,放射的。**2.** 神采焕发的,愉快的。

beam·y [ˈbiːmi; ˋbimɪ] ***a*.** **1.** (船等)幅身广阔的。**2.** 〔诗〕(枪,矛等)梁一样的,粗大的。**3.** 〔罕〕光闪闪的;眉飞色舞的。**4.**【动】(雄鹿般)有叉角的。

bean [biːn; bin] **I** ***n*.** **1.** 豆;蚕豆;菜豆属植物。**2.** 豆形果实;结豆形果实的植物。**3.** 〔转义〕琐物;无价值的东西;〔*pl.*〕少量。**4.** 〔*pl.*〕〔俚〕申斥,惩罚。**5.** 〔*pl.*〕〔英俚〕钱;(特指)金币,硬币;〔美俚〕一块钱。**6.** 〔美俚〕头,脑袋。**7.** 〔英俚〕家伙,人。*asparagus ~* 豇豆,*small [red] ~* 红豆,小豆。*broad [garden] ~* 蚕豆。*French [kidney] ~* 菜豆、扁豆。*mung ~* 绿豆。*soy(a) ~* 大豆。*sword ~* 刀豆。*Egyptian ~* 莲子。*string ~* 豇豆。**II** ***vt*.** (投物)击…的头。***Every ~ has its black***. 各人有各人的缺点。***full of ~s*** **1.** 精力充沛,兴高采烈。**2.** 〔美俚〕完全错误的。***get ~s*** 〔俚〕被申斥,挨骂。***give (sb.) ~s*** 〔俚〕惩罚,申斥(某人)。***have too much ~s*** 精神旺盛。***haven't a ~*** 莫名一文。***know how many ~s make five*** 精明,会算计。***like ~s*** 猛烈地 (*run like ~s* 猛跑)。***not care a ~*** 毫不介意,不关心。***not know ~s*** 〔俚〕大傻瓜,什么也不懂。***old ~*** 〔英俚〕老兄〔熟人间的称呼〕! ***spill the ~s*** 〔美〕**1.** 不慎泄密,说漏嘴。**2.** 破坏计划。**3.** 陷入窘境。~**bag** (扔子游戏的)豆子袋;扔子游戏。~ **ball**【棒球】投向击球手头部的球〔犯规行为〕。~ **beetle** 瓢虫。~ **cake** 豆饼,豆渣。~ **counter** 〔美俚〕统计专家。~ **curd** 豆腐。~ **eater** 〔美〕波斯顿人的别名。~ **feast** ***n*.** 〔英〕东家请雇员的酒席;(一年一次的)村庄宴会;〔口〕愉快的宴会。**~-fed** ***a*.** 〔口〕精力充沛的,兴高采烈的。~ **head** ***n*.** 〔美〕蠢人,笨蛋。**~-noodle** ***n*.** 残粉,粉丝,粉条(*a ~-noodle mill* 粉坊)。**~-paste** ***n*.** 豆腐。~ **pod** ***n*.** 豆荚。~ **pole** **1.** 豆架。**2.** 瘦长的人。~ **rag** 〔美军俚〕(舰艇上的)用餐信号旗。~ **sheet** 〔美〕职工工作成绩表。~ **shooter** 儿童豆子枪〔玩具〕。~ **sprouts** 豆芽。~ **stalk** 豆茎。~ **town** 〔美〕波斯顿市的别名。**~-tree** 豆荚树〔如梓等会结荚的树木〕。~ **weevil**【虫】豆象象鼻;(学生戴在头顶的)小帽。

bean·e·ry [ˈbiːnəri; ˋbinərɪ] ***n*.** 〔美俚〕素饭馆,经济饭馆〔因供应烧豆为主菜而得名〕。~ **queen** 〔美口〕女招待。

bean·ie [ˈbiːni; ˋbinɪ] ***n*.** 〔口〕(有花饰或羽饰的)小圆女帽;童帽。

bean·o [ˈbiːnəu; ˋbino] ***n*.** (*pl.* ~***s***) 〔英俚〕 = bean-feast.

bean tote [ˈbiːn təut; ˋbin tot] 〔美〕立刻〔法语 *bientôt* 之讹〕。

bean·y[1] [ˈbiːni; ˋbinɪ] ***a*.** (***bean·i·er***; ***bean·i·est***) 〔口〕精神旺盛的;狂妄的。

bean·y[2] [ˈbiːni; ˋbinɪ] ***n*.** = beanie.

bear[1] [bɛə; bɛə] (***bore*** [bɔː; bor], 〔古〕***bare*** [bɛə; bɛr]; ***borne*** [bɔːn; born], ***born*** [bɔːn; born]) ***vt*.** **1.** 支,支持;背,负担,负载,负荷;承担(责任等)。**2.** 携带;运,运走〔除成语外,现多用 carry〕;引导。**3.** 具有(名声等),带有(特色等);(和…)有(关系,比率,比较等);佩有,佩戴(徽章等),载明,记有(日期),标有,刻有(记号);怀有(感情),抱(怨),含(恨),挟(嫌),记(仇)。**4.** 举止,处身;表现〔~ oneself〕。**5.** 堪,忍受,忍耐;容忍;经得起,耐得住〔主要用于否定句〕;适宜于;值得。**6.** 生(儿女),结(果实),产生。**7.** 挤压,推动,驱。**8.** 行使,掌握(支配权等)。**9.** 提供(证据等)。**10.** 保持(某种姿势等)。**11.** 散布,传播(流言等)。~ *a loss* 承担损失。~ *the weight of the roof* 承受屋顶的重量。~ *tales (gossip, news)* 搬是非,扯闲话。~ *a resemblance to it* 跟它相似。*a tree that ~s fruit* 一棵结果子的树。*His hands ~ the marks of toil*. 他手上有劳动标记[老茧]。*a ship ~ing the French colours* 挂着法国旗的船。*The letter ~s no date*. 这封信没注明日期。*We ~ him no grudge*. 我们对他无恶意。~ *testimony (witness) to* 证明…,担保…。~ *one's head high* 高高地昂起头。*I can't ~ being alone for long*. 我不堪长期孤独生活。*This cloth will ~ washing*. 这布经[耐]洗。*an expression that does not ~ translation* 无法翻译出来的语句。~ *a child* 生孩子〔现在一般是说 have a child. 此义多用 bear 的过去分词: She has borne two children 她生了两个孩子了〕。*He was born of poor parentage*. 他出身贫苦〔作"生育"解时用 borne, 作"出身"或"出生"解时用 born〕。— ***vi*.** **1.** 支,支持得住,经得起,受得住;忍耐。**2.** 靠;推,压迫(*on*; *upon*; *against*)。**3.** 位,坐落;朝向;倾向于(*to*)。**4.** 有关系[影响](*on*; *upon*)。**5.** 结果实。**6.** 开动,运动。*The discussion bore against the bill*. 讨论带有否决该法案的倾向。*The ice ~s*. 冰承受得住〔厚得能走人了〕。*We were borne backwards by the crowd*. 人群把我们挤到后面去了。~ *comparison with* 可与…相匹敌。*All these ~ upon him with cruching weight*. 这些问题使他的负担极其沉重。*The trees ~ well*. 这些树结的果实多。*The island ~s eastward*. 那个岛位于东面。*The ship ~s west*. 船向西开航。*Bear to the right*. 靠右边(走)。~ ***a hand*** 帮忙,帮助;参加(*in*). ~ ***a part in*** 分担,参加;在…中有一份。~ ***and forbear*** 一忍再忍。~ ***a rein upon a horse*** 用缰绳勒住马。~ ***arms*** **1.** 携带武器。**2.** 从军,参军。**3.** 武装反抗,对…作战(*against*). **4.** 饰有纹徽。~ ***away*** **1.** 夺走,抢去;(赢)得(奖品等)。**2.**【海】改变航行(驶向下风)。~ ***(away) the prize [bell]*** 得奖,得锦标,优胜。~ ***back*** **1.** 驱退(人群等)。**2.** 退。~ ***(sb.) company*** 和(某人)做伴。~ ***down*** **1.** 压倒,压服(对方)。**2.** 加紧干;全力以赴。~ ***down on [upon]*** **1.** 冲向,(船或人)向…逼近。**2.** 强调。**3.** 压迫,使承受负担。~ ***hard [heavily]*** 勉强忍受。~ ***in mind*** 记住,铭记不忘;注意。~ ***in with***【海】驶向陆地[他船]。~ ***no relation to*** 与

B

…无关系。～ ***off*** 1. 夺得,夺走(奖赏等)。2. 使避开(相撞)。3.【海】驶离(陆地等)。～ ***on*** [***upon***] 1. 压迫,使困苦(*The famine bore heavily* [*hard*] *on the farmers*. 灾荒使农民困苦不堪)。2. 靠,倚恃,压在…上。3. 瞄准,朝向。4. 与…有关系,对…有影响。～ ***oneself*** 举止,行为[与 *well*, *bravely*, *nobly* 等副词并用](*She ～s herself gracefully*. 她举止文雅。*He ～s himself bravely*. 他行为勇敢)。～ ***out*** 证明,证实(*The facts ～ me out*. 事实为我作了证明)。～ ***rule*** [***sway***] 统治,支配,掌权。～ ***the blame*** [***punishment***] 受责难[惩罚]。～ ***the test*** 经得起考验。～ ***up*** 1. 支持,拥护。2. 咬紧牙关坚持。3.【海】驶向下风。～ ***up for*** [***to***] 走向…;接近…方面。～ ***upon*** = ～ on. ～ ***with*** 宽恕,容忍。***borne away by*** (*anger*) 被(愤怒)驱使着。***borne in upon*** (*sb*.)(某人)确信,相信(*It was borne in upon me that* ..., 我相信…)。***born in the purple*** 生长王侯人家,出身显贵。

bear² [bɛə; bɛr] **I** ***n***. 1.【动】熊。2.【股】空头,卖方,看跌的人(*opp*. bull)。3.【机】打孔器;小型冲(孔)机。4. 粗暴的人,鲁莽汉。5.〔口〕有奇才的人,天才。*a ～ for physics* 物理学天才。*the black ～* 黑熊。*the brown ～* 罴。*the grizzly ～* 灰熊。*the polar ～* 北极熊。*～'s gall* 熊胆。***as cross as a ～*** 脾气极坏。***be a ～ for*** 1.(工作等)有干劲。2. 经得起,耐得住(*be a ～ for punishment* 经得起折磨,顽强)。***loaded for ～*** 作好准备;〔美俚〕准备打架。***play the ～ with***〔口〕糟蹋,搞坏。***Sell the skin before one has killed the ～***. 熊未到手先卖皮,过早乐观。***take a ～ by the tooth***. 作不必要的冒险。***the Great B-***【天】大熊座(= Ursa Mayor)。***the Little B-***【天】小熊座(= Ursa Minor)。**II** ***vt***.(以抛售等方法)使跌价。～ *the market by selling* 以抛售压低市价。～ **baiting** 逗熊游戏〔嗾狗去咬绑着的熊,16、17 世纪流行于英国,后被禁止〕。～ **berry** 1. 熊果。2. 熊莓;〔越橘,羊鼠李等植物的乡土名〕。～ **cat**〔美俚〕1. 勇猛的拳击选手;坚贞不屈的人,硬汉。2. 有权势者。3. 熊猫。4. 非常好用的器具。～ **garden** 1. 养熊场。2. 嘈杂喧闹的场所。～**hug** ***vt***. 紧抱住,像熊一样把…紧抱住。～ **leader** 1. 耍熊的人。2.〔谑〕带领学生旅行的人;家庭教师。～ **market** 跌风笼罩下的市场。～**-pit** 熊坑〔动物园中展出熊的场所,多为一凹坑〕。～**'s-breech**【植】老鼠簕属植物,茛苕。～**'s ear** 耳状报春花。～**'s foot**【植】斗篷草。～ **skin** 1. 熊皮;熊皮制品。2.(英国近卫兵的)黑皮高帽。3. 像熊皮的粗毛制品。**B- State** 熊州〔美国阿肯色州的别称〕。～**ward** 饲熊者。～ **wood**【植】药鼠李。

bear·a·ble [ˈbɛərəbl; ˋbɛrəbl] ***a***. 堪,忍受得住的,忍耐力强的;支持得住的,承受得起的。

beard [biəd; bɪrd] **I** ***n***. 1.(下巴上的)胡子。2.【虫】口鬃;【动】颌毛。3.(牡蛎等的)鳃。4.【植】芒。5.(箭、钓钩等的)倒钩;针钩。6.〔美俚〕广播错误;口齿不清的广播员;蓄胡须的人,"大胡子"〔尤指颓废派人物或大学生、教授等知识分子〕。*grow a ～* 生胡子。*He wears a ～*. 他(下巴上)留着胡子。*a heavy* [*light*] *～* 胡须浓[稀]。*a ～ hair* 刚毛。***in spite of sb.'s ～*** 违抗某人意志,蔑视某人。***laugh at sb.'s ～*** 愚弄(某人)。***laugh in one's ～*** 偷偷嘲笑。***meet*** [***run***] ***in one's ～*** 公然反对某人。***pluck*** [***take***] ***by the ～***. 毅然反对,大胆攻击。***seize sb.'s ～*** 侮辱某人。***speak in one's ～*** 喃喃地说。***to sb.'s ～*** 当面。**II** ***vt***. 1. 使有胡须[颌毛、芒刺]。2. 抓[捋]住…的胡子;拔…的胡子;〔喻〕公然反抗。～ ***a man*** [***the lion***] ***in his den*** 太岁头上动土,奋勇搏敌。***the Old-Man's Beard***【植】〔俚〕女萎。～ **tongue** 钓钟柳属植物;草本象牙红属植物。**-ed** ***a***. 有胡须的;有倒钩的;有颌毛的;【植】有芒刺的。**-less** ***a***. 无胡须的,年轻的,乳臭未干的;无倒钩的;无芒刺的。

Beard [biəd; bɪrd] ***n***. 比尔德〔姓氏〕。

Beards·ley [ˈbiədzli; ˋbɪrdzlɪ] ***n***. 比尔兹利〔姓氏〕。

bear·er [ˈbɛərə; ˋbɛrɚ] ***n***. 1.(票据、支票等的)持票人;送信人;搬运工人;抬棺人;轿夫;担架;运载工具。2.【机】托架;支座;垫块;承木。3. 有官职[身分]的人。4. 结子实的植物。5.【化】载体;【物】受力体。*a good* [*poor*] *～* 结实多[少]的植物,高[低]产作物。*a ～ of ill tidings* 报凶信的人。***payable to ～***【商】付持票人,见票即付。～ **battalion** [**company**]【军】担架大[中]队。～ **securities** [**cheque**] 不记名证券[票据]。

bear·ing [ˈbɛəriŋ; ˋbɛrɪŋ] ***n***. 1. 忍耐,忍受。2. 态度,举止,风采,姿态。3. 关系,影响,方面,联系(*on*; *upon*);意义。4.〔常 *pl*.〕方位,方位角,向位,(矿脉)走向,航向。5.【机】轴承,支座。6.〔常 *pl*.〕【纹】(盾上的)徽章,标记。7. 产子;结实;结实期。*I fail to see the ～ of that remark*. 我不明白该批评真意何在。*the ability to find one's ～s independently* 独立工作的能力。*a man of dignified ～* 举止庄重的人。*child ～* 生育。*consider the matter in all its ～s* 从各个方面考虑问题。*a ball ～* 滚珠轴承。*a plain ～* 滑动轴承。*The pilot radioed his ～*. 驾驶员用无线电定位。*directional ～* 定向探位。*a tree past ～* 已不会结果实的树。***be out of one's ～s = lose one's ～s***. ～ ***strength*** 抗压强。***beyond*** [***past***] ***all ～*** 忍无可忍。***bring sb. to his ～s*** 使(人)不致忘本,使(人)反省,使人清醒一些。***have a ～ on*** 关系到。***have no ～ on the question*** [***subject***] 和那个问题毫无关系。***in all its ～s*** 从各方面。***lose one's ～s*** 迷失方向;不知所措,惶惑。***take one's*** [***the***] ***～s*** 判明自己位置,观望形势。～ **bronze** [**metals**] 制造轴承的铜合金[金属]。～ **rein**【马术】支头短缰。～ **sword** 交由随从携带的长剑。

bear·ish [ˈbɛəriʃ; ˋbɛrɪʃ] ***a***. 1. 熊一样的;粗鲁的。2.【股】起跌风的,看跌的。**-ly** ***ad***. 粗鲁地,笨拙地。**-ness** ***n***. 粗鲁,笨拙。

beast [biːst; bist] ***n***. 1. 动物;(与鸟、鱼相对而说的)走兽〔普通说 animal〕;(与人相对而说的)畜牲。2. 牛马,家畜;〔英〕〔*pl*.～〕菜牛。3. 人面兽心的人,衣冠禽兽;凶残的人;举止粗鲁的人。4.〔俚、讽〕老顽固,坏蛋;〔学〕严格的老师。*You ～!* 你这畜牲。*Don't be a ～*. 别那么顽固。***a ～ of*** 恶劣;粗野(*Don't make a ～ of yourself*. 不要那副难看[馋]相。*It was a ～ of a day, bleak, cold, and rainy*. 冷风凄雨,天气恶劣)。～ ***of burden*** 役畜(牛、马等)。～ ***of prey*** 食肉兽,猛兽。～ ***of the chase*** 可猎兽。***the ～***(人的)兽性。***the B-***【基督教】反对基督的人。

beast·ie [ˈbiːsti; ˋbistɪ] ***n***.〔主苏格兰〕小动物。

beast·li·ness [ˈbiːstlinis; ˋbistlɪnɪs] ***n***. 1. 兽性;残忍,粗暴,凶恶;污秽;淫猥。2. 贪食;大醉;令人作呕的食物。

beast·ly [ˈbiːstli; ˋbistlɪ] **I** ***a***. 1. 野兽(一样)的。2. 肮脏的;卑鄙的;残忍的。3.〔英口〕恶劣的;讨厌的。*a ～ headache* 剧烈的头痛。～ *hours* 要命的[讨厌的]时刻〔如贪睡者指大清早等〕。～ *pleasures* [*appetites*] 兽欲。～ *weather* 恶劣的天气。**II** ***ad***.〔英口〕很,非常。*be ～ drunk* 烂醉。*It's ～ bad*. 糟透了。*It's ～ cold out*.(屋子)外面冷得很。

beat [biːt; bit] **I** ***vt***. (***beat***; ***beat·en*** [ˈbiːtn; ˋbitn̩],〔古〕***beat***) 1. 打,拍,敲,连打。2. 打败(敌人等);胜过,超过。3. 锤薄;锤平,敲平(金属)。4. 走出,踏出(道路);挤入,挤出。5. 在…中搜寻(猎物等)。6. 敲响,击(鼓),撞(钟);【乐】打(拍子)。7. 扑打(翅膀),鼓(翼)。8. 搅(蛋等起泡),捣(蒜、药等)。9. 烧过,逃过(约束等);缓和,减轻。10.〔俚〕使为难;使摸不着头脑;〔美俚〕欺骗。～ *a man black and blue* 把人打得青一块紫一块。*The long tramp ～ him*. 长途跋涉使他筋疲力尽。*You won't easily ～ that record*. 你恐怕不容易打破那个记录。*That ～s me*. 那就叫人哑口无言[认输]了。*That ～s everything I have heard*. 还没有听见过这样的怪事。*I ～ the truth out of him*. 我从他那里探出了真情。～ *swords into plowshares* 化剑为犁。*Princeton ～ Harvard at football*. 普林斯顿大学在橄榄球赛中

胜了哈佛大学。*You* ~ *me in French*. 你法语比我强。*It* ~*s me how he got the job*. 我不明白他怎么找到那个工作的。*If you want rest and change, you can't* ~ *a sea trip*. 你要想换个环境散散心,再没有比作一次航海旅行更好的了。~ *the woods for game* 在树林中搜寻猎物。*waves* ~*ing against the shore* 汹涛拍岸。— ***vi*. 1.** 连打,连敲(*at*). **2.**(风)吹,(浪)击,(雨)打(*against*),(日)晒,射(*on*; *upon*). **3.**(脉等)跳动,(心)悸动。**4.**(鼓)咚咚响。**5.**【海】迎风[逆流]斜驶,作锯齿形前进。**6.**(翅)扑打。**7.**(蛋等)打出泡沫。**8.** 在树林[灌木丛]搜索(*for*). **9.**〔口〕胜,赢。*This cream won't* ~. 这种奶油打不出泡沫。~ ***a charge*** 击鼓为号令冲锋。~ ***a path*** [***track***] 走成一条路。~ ***sb. all hollow*** [***all to sticks***]〔美俚〕使人大吃苦头。~ ***a retreat*** 匆忙撤退;打退堂鼓。~ ***about***【海】迎风斜驶。~ ***about for*** 搜索,找寻;设法(解决等)。~ ***about*** [***around***] ***the bush*** 拨打草丛搜索猎物;旁敲侧击的刺探人意。~ ***all*** [***anything, everything, creation, the band, the world***] **1.** 真是从来没有的怪事。**2.** 压倒一切;超过一切;极其,非常(*His impudence* ~*s everything*. 他的厚颜无耻简直令人难以置信。*It rained to* ~ *the band*. 大雨倾盆)。~ ***away*** **1.** 连打;打跑。**2.**【矿】凿开。~ ***back*** 击退。~ ***billy*** 猛烈地,拼命(跑等)。~ ***cock-fighting*** 瞎扯,胡说。~ ***down*** **1.** 打倒,推翻(制度、学说等);镇压。**2.** 使沮丧,使失望。**3.**〔口〕还(价),杀(价)。~ ***it***〔美俚〕**1.** 逃走,跑掉,匆匆走掉。**2.** 出去! 静一静! 别管他。~ ***off*** 击退,打退(进攻)。~ ***one's brains*** 绞脑汁。~ ***one's breast*** [***chest***] 捶胸悲叹。~ ***one's way*** **1.** 挤出。**2.**〔美俚〕无票乘车,(无票)混进。~ ***out*** **1.** 凿出,敲出;锤薄(金属等)。**2.** 弄明白,搞清楚(意义、真相等)。**3.** 击走,击退。**4.** 使筋疲力尽。~ ***sth. into sb.*** 向某人灌输(*I'll* ~ *some sense into him*. 我要教他懂点道理)。~ ***the air*** [***wind***] 徒劳,白费力气。~ ***the band***〔美俚〕迅猛地。~ ***the devil around the bush***〔口〕转弯抹角地说,旁敲侧击。~ ***the*** [***a***] ***drum*** 大肆宣传。~ ***the Dutch***〔美俚〕从来没有的怪事,叫人吃惊。~ ***the rap*** 逃脱刑事责任[处分]。~ ***time*** 打拍子(*to*). ~ ***to*** 打成…(~ *to death* 打死。~ *to a mummy* [*jelly*] 打得半死)。~ (*sb.*) ***to it***〔美〕瞒;占先,抢先一步。~ ***up*** **1.** 冷不防地,乘人不备(~ *up the quarters of* 突然访问)。**2.** 打鼓召集。**3.** 搅(蛋)。**4.**(帆船)迎风斜驶。**5.**〔美俚〕殴打,虐待,杀。~ ***up and down*** 上下奔走,左右奔逃。~ ***up for*** 为募集…而奔走。~ ***up on***〔美俚〕殴,打。**II *n*. 1.**(连续的)敲打;敲打声;鼓声;(时钟等的)滴答声。**2.**(心脏、脉搏等的)跳动,悸动。**3.**(巡警等的)巡逻区域;常去之地;一次巡逻任务;游猎区域。**4.**【乐】节拍,拍子;【物】拍,差拍;跳动;脉冲;〔诗〕(韵脚的)强音。**5.**(报馆发表新闻对同业的)占先,抢先;胜过他人[他物]的优点。**6.**〔美俚〕忘恩负义的人;骗子;食客。**7.**【计】取字时间。**8.**〔美口〕= beatnik. *I've never seen his* ~. 我从来没有见过胜过他的。~*s of fifth*【乐】五分之一拍。*cross* ~*s*【物】交叉跳动。*a dead* ~【物】无差拍;不摆。***on*** [***out of***] ***one's*** ~ [不]是…的专长[本行,专业];[不]在职权内;(钟表声的)[不]匀整。***off one's*** ~ **1.** 不再作做惯的事。**2.** 非本行;超出自己熟悉的领域。***off the*** ~ 不合拍子。***on the*** ~ **1.** 合拍子。**2.** 在巡逻中。***out of one's*** ~ = *off one's* ~. **III *a*. 1.**〔口〕疲乏的(= beaten). **2.** 颓废的;属于"垮掉的一代"的。***dead*** ~ 疲倦已极,筋疲力尽;惨败。~**-age** ***a***. 颓废派的。~**-beat** 一种利用雷达追踪导弹的系统。~(**-**)**box**〔口〕噪音匣子〔指便构成立体声收录机〕。~ **frequency**【物】拍频(率)。~ **generation**(美国)"堕落的一代"〔五十年代末美国青年中的一个颓废派,以蓄长发、堕落、奇装异服、酗酒、吸毒、玩世不恭等为特征〕。~**-out** ***a***. 疲倦不堪的。~**-up** ***a***.〔俚〕**1.** 衣衫褴褛的,破烂的,不体面的。**2.** 用坏了的;击碎了的。

beat·en [ˈbiːtn; ˋbitn̩] beat 的过去分词。***a*. 1.**(接连)被打击的。**2.** 打成的,(金属等)锤薄的,敲平的;(路等)踏平的,走出来的;〔喻〕陈腐的,平凡的。**3.** 打败了的;被打伤的;精疲力尽的;精神颓丧的。~ *gold* 金箔。*a* ~ *army* 败军。~ *work* 打制成的工艺品。***a*** ~ ***path*** [***track***] 走惯的路,常道,常轨,老路,惯例。***follow the*** ~ ***track*** 墨守成规,照例。***off the*** ~ ***track*** 不墨守成规,破例,越轨,别开生面。~**-up** ***a***. 破旧的,年久失修的。~ **zone**【军】落弹地带。

beat·er [ˈbiːtə; ˋbitɚ] ***n*. 1.** 打击者;帮助猎人从隐蔽处赶出野兽的助手。**2.** 杵,槌,锤,夯具;【造纸】打浆机,搅拌器;【纺】打手,翼子板;弹(棉)花器。*an egg* ~ 打蛋器。

be·a·tif·ic [ˌbiːəˈtifik; ˏbiəˋtɪfɪk] ***a*. 1.** 赐福的,使极乐的。**2.** 极乐的;有福的;天使般的。*a* ~ *smile* 恬淡的微笑。~ *vision*【天主】至福直观(天使等)。

be·at·i·fy [bi(ː)ˈætifai; bɪˋætəˏfaɪ] ***vt*. 1.** 赐福于,使极乐。**2.**【天主】为…行宣福礼〔宣布死者已升天堂的仪式〕。

beat·ing [ˈbiːtiŋ; ˋbitɪŋ] ***n*. 1.** 打,敲;搅打;笞打。**2.** 失败,溃败。**3.**(心脏的)跳动,脉搏;(翅的)拍打。**4.**【造纸】打浆;(把金属)打扁[锻伸],打制;【海】迎风斜驶。*deserve a* ~ 该打。*take* [*get*] *a* ~ 挨打,受打击,受谴责。*take the* ~吃败仗。~ **degree**【造纸】浆度。

be·at·i·tude [bi(ː)ˈætitjuːd; bɪˋætəˏtjud] ***n***. 至福;〔the Beatitudes〕【宗】耶稣登山训众所说的八种幸福。

Beatles [ˈbiːtlz; ˋbitlz] ***n***.(英国)披头士四人爵士乐队。**Beatlemania** 披头士热〔崇拜"披头士"乐队的狂热〕。

beat·nik [ˈbiːtnik; ˋbitnɪk] ***n***.(美国)"垮掉的一代"派的成员〔借用俄语 *sputnik* 一词的语尾造出的新字〕。

Be·a·trice [ˈbiətris; ˋbiətrɪs] ***n***. 比阿特丽斯〔女子名〕。

Be·a·trix [ˈbiətriks; ˋbiətrɪks] ***n***. 比阿特丽克斯〔女子名〕。

beau [bəu; bo] **I *n*.**(*pl*. ~**s**, ~**x** [-z; -z]) **1.** 纨袴子弟,花花公子。**2.** 爱人,情人;(妇女的)伴侣,向妇女献殷勤的男子。**II *vt*.** 为(妇女)做伴侣〔指社交活动〕。

beau [bəu; bo] ***a***.〔F.〕善,美。~ ***geste*** [ˈʒest; ˋʒɛst] **1.** 善行;大度,雅量。**2.** 漂亮话,故作大方,口惠而实不至的姿态。~ ***ideal*** 理想的极致,至美(*He is my* ~ *ideal of a soldier*. 他是我理想中最好的战士)。~ ***monde*** [mɔnd; mɑnd]〔旧〕社交界;上流社会。

beau·coup [bəuˈkuː; boˋku] ***a***.〔F.〕很多,大量。~ *jack*〔美俚〕充分。

Beaufort [ˈbəufət; ˋbofət] ***n***. 博福特〔蒲福〕(姓氏)。~ **scale**【气】蒲福风级〔将风力分为 0,1,2,3,4,5,6,7,8,9,10,11,12 级,称为 calm, light airs, slight breeze, gentle breeze, moderate breeze, fresh breeze, strong breeze, moderate gale, fresh gale, strong gale, whole gale, storm, hurricane 等,即无风、软风、轻风、微风、和风、清风、强风、疾风、大风、烈风、狂风、暴风、飓风〕。

Beaumé [bəuˈmei; boˋme] = Baumé.

Beau·mont [ˈbəumənt; ˋbomɑnt] ***n***. 博蒙特〔姓氏〕。

Beaune [bəun; bon] ***n***. 波恩红葡萄酒。

beaut [bjuːt; bjut] ***n***.〔美俚〕美人〔beauty 的略语,常作反语用〕。*His excuse was a* ~. 他的借口可真冠冕堂皇。

beau·te·ous [ˈbjuːtjəs; ˋbjutɪəs] ***a***.〔诗〕美,美丽的。**-ly *ad*. -ness *n*.**

beau·ti·cian [bjuːˈtiʃən; bjuˋtɪʃən] ***n*. 1.** 美容术专家,美容师。**2.** 美容用品制造者。

beau·ti·ful [ˈbjuːtəful, -ti-; ˋbjutəfəl, -tɪ-] ***a*. 1.** 美,美丽的,美好的;漂亮的,华丽的,优美的。**2.** 极好的。*a* ~ *girl* 美丽的少女。*a* ~ *speech* 精彩的演说。*a* ~ *character* 美好的人品。*have an eye for the* ~ 有审美眼光。*a* ~ *opportunity* 极好的机会,大好时机。*a* ~ *stratagem* 上策。*the true, the good, and the* ~ 真善美。~ **people** 漂亮人士〔或作 B- P-, 指上层社会时髦人物,缩写为 BP〕。**-ly *ad*. -ness *n*.**

B

beau·t·i·fy [ˈbjuːtifai; ˋbjutəˏfaɪ] *vt*. 使美丽,美化;修饰,装饰。— *vi*. 长美,变美。**-fi·ca·tion** *n*. 美化;装饰。**-ti·fi·er** *n*. 美化者;装饰者。

beau·ty [ˈbjuːti; ˋbjutɪ] *n*. **1.** 美,美丽,漂亮 (*opp*. ugliness); 美感。**2.** 〔the ~〕〔集合词〕美丽的人们; 〔a ~〕美人,佳人。**3.** 美好的东西[事物],美景,美貌〔俗语中常作反语用〕。**4.** 美点,妙处。**5.** 〔*pl*.〕名句集,佳句集。**6.**【原】美夸克〔衰变前可持续存在十万亿分之一秒左右的一种粒子〕。*She is ~ itself*. 她美透了。*That's the ~ of it*. 这就是它的妙处[优点]。*a society ~* 交际花。*the wits and ~ of the town* 城中的才子佳人。*Beauty is but skin-deep*. 美貌只是外表,人不可以貌相。*the beauties of nature* 大自然的美景。*She is a regular ~*. 她真是漂亮得吓人。*Well, you are a ~, you've lost me the game*. 好,你真能干,能干得输给我了〔反语〕。*Come along, my beauties!* (亲密地对人或动物,尤其是狗或马)来,来,一块儿来。~ **art** 美容术。~ **contest** 选美会。~ **culture** 美容术;美容业。~ **parlo(u)r**, ~ **salon**, ~ **shop** 美容院。~ **part** 最可取之处。~**-shopped** *a*. 〔美俚〕用美容术打扮起来的。~ **sleep** 前半夜的甜睡。~ **specialist** 美容技师。~ **spot 1.** 美人斑,美斑〔妇女面颊上化装的黑点〕。**2.** 痣;小瑕疵。**3.** 美景,名胜。~ **treatment** 美容,化妆。~ **wash** 化妆水。~ **water** 化妆香水。

beaux [bəuz; boz] beau 的复数。~ ***arts*** [bəuˈzɑːr; boˋzɑr] 美术。~***-esprits*** [ˈbəuzesˈpriː; ˋbozɛsˋpri] 〔F.〕*bel-esprit* 的复数。~ ***yeux*** [ˈbəuzˈjœ; ˋbozˋjɛ] 〔F.〕明眸,漂亮的眼睛;美貌;美人 (*We didn't hire you for your ~ yeux*. 我们不是因为你面孔漂亮才雇用你的)。

bea·ver[1] [ˈbiːvə; ˋbivɚ] *n*. **1.** 海狸,海獭。**2.** 海狸皮;獭皮帽;礼帽,高帽;獭皮手套。**3.**【纺】海狸呢;海狸绒布。**4.** 〔美俚〕(下巴上的)大胡子;蓄胡子的人。**5.** 工作勤恳的人。**6.** 〔俚〕干扰雷达的电台;轻[中]型飞机加油装置。**7.** 〔B-〕美国 Oregon 州人。*like a ~* 极勤奋,孜孜不倦。~ **board** 一种人造纤维板。~ **cloth** 海狸绒布。**B-State** 〔美〕Oregon 州的别名。

bea·ver[2] [ˈbiːvə; ˋbivɚ] *n*. (头盔遮防颜面下部的)护面甲;脸罩。

bea·ver[3] [ˈbiːvə; ˋbivɚ] *n*. 〔美俚〕胡须;留有漂亮胡须的人,美髯公。

Bea·ver·brook [ˈbiːvəbruk; ˋbivɚˏbrʊk] *n*. 比弗布鲁克〔姓氏〕。

bea·ver·ette [ˈbiːvəret; ˋbivərɛt] *n*. **1.** 獭皮一样的兔皮。**2.** 〔军俚〕轻装甲车。

bea·ver·teen [ˈbiːvətiːn; ˋbivɚtin] *n*. 仿海狸皮绒布。

be·bee·rine [biˈbiːriːn, -rin; bɪˋbirin, -rɪn] *n*.【药】贝比碱;卑比令碱。

be·bee·ru [biˈbiːruː; bɪˋbiru] *n*.【植】绿心树。

be-bop [ˈbiːbɔp; ˋbiˋbɑp] *n*. 〔美〕疯狂即兴爵士乐〔其特征为节奏疯狂急速〕。**-er** 疯狂即兴爵士乐演奏者。

be·call [biˈkɔːl; bɪˋkɔl] *vt*. 〔古、口〕骂。

be·calm [biˈkɑːm; bɪˋkɑm] *vt*. **1.**【海】(因风停)使(帆船)不能前进〔常用被动语态〕。**2.** 〔古〕使(海等)平静。*The ship was ~ed for three days*. 船因无风停航三天。

be·came [biˈkeim; bɪˋkem] become 的过去式。

be·cause [biˈkɔz, bəˈkɔz, biˈkəz; bɪˋkɔz, bəˋkɔz, bɪˋkəz] *conj*. 因为。*The boy was absent ~ he was ill*. 那个孩子因病缺席。*I love her all the more ~ she is poor*. 正因为她穷,我更爱她。*I respect him none the less ~ he is young*. 我并不因为他年轻而减少对他的尊重。~ **of** 因,因为,由于 (*The game was called off ~ of rain*. 比赛因雨停止)。★(1) ~ of 已往是用 ~ that (*conj*.)。(2) because 在口语中可代 that (*The reason I don't eat much is ~ [that] I've got indigestion*. 我吃得少是因为我消化不良)。(3)表示理由的从属连接词还有 since, as, 但其语气和主从关系不如 because 那样强和那样直接,至于 for 一词则语气更弱,关系更加间接。

bec·ca·fi·co [ˌbekəˈfiːkəu; ˏbɛkəˋfiko] *n*. (*pl*. ~*s*, ~*es*) (意大利人爱吃的)一种小鸟〔特指 garden warbler〕。

bé·ch·a·mel [ˌbeiʃəˈmel; ˏbeˏʃɑˋmɛl] *n*. 贝夏美调味酱〔一种由奶油、面粉等制成的白色调味品,得名于路易十四时代的御膳官贝夏美〕。

be·chance [biˈtʃɑːns, biˈtʃæns; bɪˋtʃɑns, bɪˋtʃæns] *vt*., *vi*. 〔罕〕发生;落到。

bêche-de-mer [ˌbeiʃdəˈmɛə; ˏbɛʃdəˋmɛr] *n*. (*pl*. ***bêches-de-mer***) 〔F.〕**1.** (中餐所吃的)海参。**2.** (太平洋西南的岛区本土人和白人所讲的)一种混杂着土语的英语 = beach-lamar.

Be·cher [ˈbiːtʃə; ˋbitʃɚ] *n*. 比彻〔姓氏〕。

be·chic [ˈbiːkik; ˋbikɪk] *a*.【医】治咳的。

Bech·u·a·na·land [ˌbetʃuˈɑːnəlænd; ˏbɛtʃʊˋɑnəˏlænd] *n*. 贝专纳 (Botswana 博茨瓦纳的旧称)〔非洲〕。

Beck [bek; bɛk] *n*. 贝克〔女子名, Rebecca 的昵称〕。

beck[1] [bek; bɛk] **I** *n*. 点头;招手〔以示召唤〕。***be at sb.'s ~ and call*** 惟…之命是从,听命于(某人)。***hang upon sb.'s ~*** 听从某人差遣[安排]。***have*** (*sb*.) ***at one's ~*** 随心所欲地使唤(某人),对(某人)颐指意使。**II** *vt*., *vi*. 〔古〕点头[摇头、打手势等]召唤,指使。

beck[2] [bek; bɛk] *n*. 〔英〕小河,急流,山溪,溪流。

beck·et [ˈbekit; ˋbɛkɪt] *n*.【海】环索,把手索,绳环。

Beck·et(t) [ˈbekit; ˋbɛkɪt] *n*. 贝克特〔姓氏〕。

beck·on [ˈbekən; ˋbɛkən] *vt*. **1.** 点头;招手,打手势;〔用头、手等动作〕指挥。**2.** 引诱,吸引。*He ~ed me to come nearer*. 他招手叫我走过去。*Lush grasslands ~ed the herdsman*. 肥沃的草地吸引了牧人。— *vi*. **1.** 表示召唤。**2.** 有诱惑力。*The mountains ~*. 青山诱人。*He ~ed to me to come nearer*. 他示意要我走过去。

Be·cky [ˈbeki; ˋbɛkɪ] *n*. 贝基〔女子名, Rebecca 的昵称〕。

be·cloud [biˈklaud; bɪˋklaʊd] *vt*. **1.** 遮暗,使黑暗;使模糊不清。**2.** 使混乱,使糊涂。*Angry words ~ed the issue*. 愤激的言辞使问题更加说不清了。

be·come [biˈkʌm; bɪˋkʌm] *vi*. (***became*** [biˈkeim; bɪˋkem]; ***become***) **1.** 变成,成为,转为,变得〔后接名词、形容词和分词等述语〕。*He has ~ a sailor*. 他成为一名水手。*It has ~ warmer*. 天暖和起来了。*At last the truth became known to us*. 我们终于知道了真相。**2.** 发生,产生。*It sometimes ~s that these accounts are misleading*. 这些说法有时会引起误解。— *vt*. 适宜,适合,适于;与…相称,与…相当。*Such words do not ~ a scholar*. 那样的话不像出自学者之口。*It would ill ~ you to praise yourself*. 你自夸自赞是很不得体的。*Your dress ~s you well*. 你的衣裳挺合身。~ **of** (人或事物的)情况,遭遇,结果,归属 (*What has ~ of him?* 他后来的情况怎样了?〔口〕他到哪里去了? *I don't know what will ~ of the children if their father dies*. 我不知道这些孩子在他们的父亲死后会发生什么情况)。

be·com·ing [biˈkʌmiŋ; bɪˋkʌmɪŋ] **I** *a*. 相合的,相称的;相当的,合适的。*a hairdo ~ to her* 适合她的发型。*~ conduct for a hero* 无愧于英雄称号的行为。**II** *n*. **1.** 适合,适应。**2.**【哲】生成;转化;变易;【心】生成,转成,转化。**3.** (礼仪等的)得体。***being and ~*** 存在和生成[发展的过程]。**-ly** *ad*. **-ness** *n*.

Bec·que·rel [ˌbekəˈrel; bɛkˋrɛl], **Henry** 昂利·贝克雷尔〔1852—1908,法国物理学家,1903 年诺贝尔奖金获得者〕。

bed [bed; bɛd] **I** *n*. **1.** 床,床铺;床位,铺;(动物的)窝;〔喻〕安乐窝,坟墓;床垫;睡眠;就宿。**2.** 婚姻,夫妇关系。**3.** 台,土台;苗床;圃,花坛;养殖场;河床;矿床;湖底,海底。**4.**【地】层,底;【火箭】试验台;基地;【机】底座;衬;机床床身;【建】地脚,地基;【铁路】路基;【印】版盘。**5.** 一层;(树叶等的)一堆。*He is too fond of his bed*. 他太贪睡了。*a single* [*double*] ～ 单[双]人床。*a feather* ～ 羽毛褥垫。*a cup of cocoa and then bed* 喝一杯可可再睡觉。*ten dollers for bed* 宿费十元。*a flower* ～ 花坛。*a* ～ *of clay* 黏土层。*an oyster* ～ 牡蛎养殖场。*reeds* ～ 苇地。～ *ways*【机】床身导轨。***be brought to*** ～ (*of a child*) 生(孩子),分娩,临盆,坐蓐,临产。***be contained to one's*** ～ 病倒床上,卧病。～ ***and board*** **1**. 膳宿;兼包伙食的宿舍。**2**. 夫妻关系,夫妻生活〔夫妻寝食与共〕。**3**.〔美〕家。～ ***of down*** [***roses***, ***flowers***] 安乐的生活,称心如意的处境;安乐窝。～ ***of dust*** 墓。～ ***of honour*** 阵亡将士墓。～***s of guns***【军】备炮过多的兵舰。～***-to-breakfast folks***〔美俚〕城市人〔一起来就吃的人们〕。***die in*** (***one's***) ～ 寿终正寝,病死,老死;善终。***get out of*** ～ 起床。***get out of*** ～ ***on the right*** [***wrong***] ***side*** 心情好(坏)。***go to*** ～ **1**. 睡,就寝;同床。**2**.〔卑〕不要吵了! **3**.【印】付印(*The paper went to* ～ *at three*. 报纸三点付印)。***go to*** ～ ***in one's boots*** 大醉。***have one's*** ～ 临产。***in*** ～ **1**. 睡着。**2**. 男女同床。***keep the*** ～ (因病)卧床。***keep to one's*** ～ 病倒床上,卧病。***lie in*** ～ 横躺在床上。***lie in*** [***on***] ***the*** ～ ***one has made*** 自作自受。***lie on a*** ～ ***of thorns*** 如坐针毡,坐卧不安。***make a*** [***the***] ～ 收拾床铺;铺床。***make one's*** ～〔口〕自作自受(*As you make your* ～, *so you must lie upon it*. 自食其果)。***make up a*** ～ 搭一临时床铺。(*one's*) ***narrow*** [***lowly***] ～ 坟墓。***put*** (*child*) ***to*** ～ **1**. 让(孩子等)睡觉。**2**.【美印】上版(备印);〔美俚〕(编辑)清稿(付排)。***put to*** ～ ***with a shove*** **1**. 把…葬掉。**2**.〔美俚〕把(醉汉)扶上床。***separate from*** ～ ***and board*** 夫妇分居〔但不离婚〕。***take to one's*** ～ (因病)睡倒,病倒床上。**II** ***vt***. (***-dd-***) **1**. 使睡;〔美〕为…提供住宿。**2**. 栽种;造苗林,移植(幼苗等)于苗床内(*out*). **3**. 安顿,给人铺床,给(牲畜)等铺垫草(*down*). **4**. 把…铺平;固定,嵌入。**5**. 把…分层。— ***vi***. **1**. 睡,就寝,住宿;同床,同居(*with*);睡下(*down*). **2**. (金属物置于他物上)搁稳,摆稳。**3**.【地】分层。*early to* ～ *and early to rise* 早睡早起。*bedding in earth*【植】假植。～ *it*〔美俚〕病倒。～ **well** 搁得稳(*The rail* ～*s well on the ballast*. 铁轨在道碴上搁得很稳)。～**-blocking** (年老贫穷的患者赖在医院中不走以便享受由福利金支付的住院生活待遇的)"赖病床"现象。～ **bug**〔美〕臭虫。～ **chair** 卧椅,躺椅。～**chamber**〔古〕卧室;英国王室的寝室(*groom of the* ～*chamber*〔英〕侍寝官〔王室卧房侍从的官职〕。*a lady of the* ～*-chamber*〔英〕宫女。*a lord of the* ～ *chamber*〔英〕侍从)。～ **clothes** ***n***. ***pl***. 寝具,铺盖[被、褥等]。～ **cover** 床单,垫单。～**fast** ***a***.〔美、英方〕卧床不起的,缠绵病榻的。～**fellow** **1**. 同床者;妻。**2**.〔喻〕伙伴;同事(*an awkward* ～*-fellow* 难同住的人;难共事的人,难接近的人,难打交道的人。*make strange* ～ *fellows*. 不择伙伴。*be* ～ *fellow to* 和…同床;和…非常要好)。～ **gown** (女)睡衣;〔Scot.〕女短衣。～**-in** 露宿示威。～ **jacket** 女睡衣短外套。～ **lamp** [**light**] 床头灯。～ **lift** 床靠〔病床的活动装置,可使病人坐起〕。～ **linen** 床用织品〔床单、枕套等〕。～ **load** 河床上被水流带来的沙石等。～ **maker** **1**. 制床工匠。**2**. (英牛津、剑桥大学)打扫寝室的工人。～ **moulding**【建】深凹饰。～ **pan** 夜壶,(病人在床上用的)便盆;(暖床用的)汤婆子。～**piece**, ～**plate**【机】底板,台板。～**post** 床柱(*between you and me and the* ～ *post* 暗地里,秘密〔莫对别人说〕。*in the twinkling of a* ～ *post* 转瞬间,立即,马上)。～**rail** 床栏。～**rock** **1**.【地】底岩,基岩;床岩。**2**. 根本原理[事实];根底,基础。**3**. 最低点,最少量(～*-rock price*〔美〕底价。*get down to* ～ *rock* 穷根究底;到了底;〔俚〕用得一文不剩)。～**roll** 铺盖。～**room** 寝室,卧室。～**room community** [**town**] 近郊居住区〔供在大城市工作的人居住〕。～**side** 床侧,枕边(*be* [*sit*, *watch*] *at the* ～*side of* (守)在床边〔多指守望病人〕。*good* ～*side manner* 医生对待病人的和蔼态度;〔讽〕逢迎周到)。～**sit**〔口〕**1**. ***vi***. 居住一间坐卧两用的房间。**2**. ***n***. = ～sitter. ～**sitter**〔英口〕坐卧两用的房间,寝室兼起居间。～**-sitting room** = ～sitter. ～**sore**【医】褥疮。～**space** (旅馆、医院、宿舍等的)床位(总数)。～**spread** 床单,垫单。～**spring** 弹簧床座;床座弹簧。～**stead** 床架,床凳。～**straw**【植】猪殃殃;砧草〔可编草垫〕((*Our*) *Lady's* ～ *straw*【植】蓬子菜)。～**table**【医】诊察台。～**tick** 褥布,褥套,垫褥套。～**time** 就寝时间。～**time story** 催眠故事;〔喻〕动听而不可信的解说。～**-wetting** 尿床,遗尿症。**-ward(s)** ***ad***. 上床,就寝。

be·dab·ble [biˈdæbl; bɪˋdæbl̩] ***vt***. 泼(水等),泼脏,溅湿。

be·dad [biˈdæd; bɪˋdæd] ***int***.〔爱〕= begad.

be·daub [biˈdɔːb; bɪˋdɔb] ***vt***. **1**. 涂,乱涂。**2**. 弄污;〔喻〕中伤,骂。**3**. 恶俗地装饰。

be·daz·zle [biˈdæzl; bɪˋdæzl] ***vt***. **1**. 使眼花,使眩惑。**2**. 使着魔。*be* ～*d by the lake and the green hills* 为湖光山色所迷。**-ment** ***n***. 眼花缭乱。

bed·der [ˈbedə; ˋbɛdɚ] ***n***. **1**. (英国大学学生宿舍中)收拾寝室的人。**2**. 苗圃[花坛]观赏植物。

bed·ding [ˈbediŋ; ˋbɛdɪŋ] ***n***. **1**. 寝具,床上用品。**2**. (家畜的)垫草。**3**. 基底;【建】基坑;【地】层里;【农】定植。～ **plane**【地】层面,顺层面。～ **plant** 花坛草花。

bed·do [ˈbed-dəu; ˋbɛd-do] ***n***. (日本人设计的)一种电子活动床。

bed·dy-bye [ˈbediˌbai; ˋbɛdɪˏbaɪ] ***n***. 床;上床[就寝]时间〔原为托儿所用语,现为幽默语〕。

Bede [biːd; bid] ***n***. 比德〔姓氏〕。

be·dead [biˈded; bɪˋdɛd] ***vt***.【医】使麻醉。

be·deck [biˈdek; bɪˋdɛk] ***vt***. 装饰。修饰(*with*).

bede·house [ˈbiːdˌhaus; ˋbidˏhaʊs] ***n***. 收容所,救济院(= beadhouse).

bedes·man [ˈbiːdzmən; ˋbidzmən] ***n***. (***pl***. ***-men*** [-mən; -mən]) **1**. 代人祈福者〔尤指被雇用代人祈福者〕。**2**. 收容所里的被收容者。**3**.〔Scot.〕乞丐(= beadsman).

be·dev·il [biˈdevl; bɪˋdɛvl̩] ***vt***. (***bedevil(l)ed***; ***bedevil(l)ing***) **1**. 魅(人),迷惑,骗。**2**. 虐待,折磨,纠缠。**3**. 使糊涂。*He is* ～*ed by his mistaken ideas*. 他被错误观念弄糊涂了。**-ment** ***n***. 着魔,迷惑;苦恼,懊恼。

be·dew [biˈdjuː; bɪˋdju] ***vt***. 沾湿,濡。*a pillow* ～*ed with tears* 泪水打湿的枕头。

Bed·ford [ˈbedfəd; ˋbɛdfɚd] ***n***. 贝德福德〔姓氏〕。

Bed·ford·shire [ˈbedfədʃiə; ˋbɛdfɚdˏʃɪr] ***n***. **1**. (英国)贝德福郡。**2**.〔儿〕= bed. ***go to*** ～〔儿〕上床困觉。

be·dight [biˈdait; bɪˋdaɪt] ***vt***. (～; ～, ～***ed***)〔古〕装饰。★常用过去分词。

be·dim [biˈdim; bɪˋdɪm] ***vt***. (***-mm-***) 使阴暗,使朦胧;使(思想等)模糊。

be·di·z·en [biˈdaizn; bɪˋdaɪzn̩] ***vt***. (俗里俗气地)装饰[打扮]。

bed·lam [ˈbedləm; ˋbɛdləm] ***n***. **1**. 疯人院,精神病院。**2**. 喧闹;吵闹的地方;疯狂状态。**3**.〔B-〕英国伦敦东南部圣母马利亚疯人院的俗称。*a* ～ *of laughter* 乱哄哄的一阵大笑。***Jack*** [***Tom***] ***o'Bedlam***〔古〕狂人。***like Bedlam***〔英〕吵闹的,混乱的;精神错乱的。

bed·lam·ite [ˈbedləmait; ˋbɛdləmˏaɪt] ***n***. 疯子,狂人;精神病院病人。

Bed·ou·in [ˈbeduin; ˋbɛdʊɪn] **I** ***n***. (***pl***. ～) **1**. 贝都因人〔沙漠地带从事游牧的阿拉伯人〕。**2**. 流浪者;游牧民。**II** ***a***. **1**. 贝都因人的;游牧的。**2**. 流浪的。

be·drab·bled [biˈdræbld; bɪˋdræbld] ***a***. 被雨泥弄脏的,拖泥带水的。

be·drag·gle [biˈdrægl; bɪˋdrægl̩] ***vt***. (在泥水中把衣服等)拖湿,拖脏。

B

bed·rid [ˈbedrid; ˋbɛdˏrɪd], **bed·rid·den** [ˈbedridn; ˋbɛdrɪdn] *a*. 卧病在床的,长期卧床不起的;不自由的。
Beds. = Bedfordshire.
BEE = Bachelor of Engineering 电机工程学士。
bee [biː; bi] *n*. 1. 蜂,蜜蜂;〔喻〕诗人;勤勉工作的人,忙忙碌碌的人。2. 〔美〕(邻里友人之间为互相帮忙、娱乐等举行的)聚会,游艺会。3. 古怪的念头,奇想。4. 〔英方〕蝇。***queen-right*** ～*s* 有王蜂群。*a queen* ～ 蜂王。*a working* [*worker*] ～ 工蜂。*a swarm* [*cluster*] *of* ～*s* 蜂群。*a sewing* ～ 缝纫会[妇女们一道做针线活的一种聚会]。*a spelling* ～ (小学生等的)拼字比赛会。***as busy as a*** ～ 颇忙碌。～ ***line*** = beeline. ***have a*** ～ ***in one's bonnet*** [***head***, ***brain***] 1. 苦思冥想;对某事入了迷;具有某种难以更改的想法。2. 胡思乱想;神经失常。***keep*** ～*s* 养蜂。***put the*** ～ ***on*** 〔口〕向…募捐[借钱]。***swarm like*** ～*s* 云集,群集。～**bird**【鸟】食蜂鸟。～**bread** 蜜蜂食料。～**eater** 食蜂鸟〔产于热带,羽毛极美丽〕。～**hive** 1. 蜂箱,蜂窝,蜂窠,蜂房。2. 嘈杂的场所,熙熙攘攘的地方。3. 蜂窠式发型。**Beehive State** 美国 Utah 州的别名。～ **house** 养蜂场。～**keeper** 养蜂人,养蜂家。～**line** 1. *n*. 捷径,最短距离,两点间的直线。2. *vi*. 走直线 (*in a* ～*line* 笔直,一直。*take* [*follow*, *make*, *strike*] *a* ～ *line* 一直走,对直走,走近路)。～ **martin** 〔美方〕 = kingbird. ～ **master** 养蜂家。～**'s knees** 〔俚〕极好的东西[人]。
Bee·be(e) [ˈbiːbi; ˋbibɪ] *n*. 毕比〔姓氏〕。
beech [biːtʃ; bitʃ] *n*. 【植】山毛榉,掬。
Bee·cham [ˈbiːtʃəm; ˋbitʃəm] *n*. 比彻姆〔姓氏〕。
beech·drops [ˈbiːtʃˌdrɔps; ˋbitʃˏdrɑps] *n*. 〔*pl*.〕【植】美国山毛榉寄生。
beech·en [ˈbiːtʃən; ˋbitʃən] *a*. 山毛榉的,掬科的。
Bee·cher [ˈbiːtʃə; ˋbitʃɚ] *n*. 比彻〔姓氏〕。
beech·mast [ˈbiːtʃmɑːst; ˋbitʃˏmɑst] *n*. (落在地上的)掬子。
beech·nut [ˈbiːtʃnʌt; ˋbitʃˏnʌt] *n*. 1. 掬子,山毛掬坚实。2. 〔俚〕地空通信系统。
beech·wood [ˈbiːtʃˈwud; ˋbitʃˏwud] *n*. 【植】山毛榉木。
beef [biːf; bif] I *n*. (*pl*. ***beeves*** [biːvz; bivz], ～*s*) 1. 牛肉;〔转义〕食用肉。2. 〔常用 *pl*.〕食用牛,菜牛。3. 〔口〕肌肉;体力,膂力,力量。4. 〔口〕肥瘦(程度),体重。5. 〔美口〕(*pl*. ～*s*) 不平,牢骚,诉苦;告发。*horse* ～ 马肉。*a wrestler with a great deal of* ～ 肌肉发达的摔跤选手。*The team was lacking in* ～. 该队体力不够。*I have my* ～ *about that*. 我对那件事很不满。***after the*** ～ 〔美口〕向警察局告发后。***ahead of the*** ～ 〔美口〕向警察局告发前。～ ***to the heels*** [***knees***] 肥胖太过。***dressed like Christmas*** ～ 〔英口〕穿得漂亮。***put on*** ～ 体重增加,长膘。***Put some*** ～ ***into it***! 〔英口〕加油干! II *vt*. 1. 使(菜牛等)长膘。2. 〔美俚〕加强,充实(*up*)。～ *up the army* 加强陆军。— *vi*. 〔美口〕1. 向警察局报告,告发。2. 发牢骚。III *a*. 1. 牛类的。2. 供食用的。～ **cake** 〔美俚〕男性的健美。～ **cattle** 菜牛。～ **eater** 1. 吃牛肉者。2. 身强力壮的人,大力士。3. 英王的卫兵;伦敦塔守卫人;〔讽〕饱食终日无所事事的人,饭桶;〔美俚〕英国人。～ **extract** 浓缩牛肉汁。～ **squad** 打手队,大力士队。**Beef State** 〔美〕德克萨斯州的别名。～ **steak** 牛肉块;牛排。～ **tea** 牛肉茶;二齿铁线子。～**-witted** *a*. 愚笨的,呆的。～**wood**【植】木麻黄。
beef·er [ˈbiːfə; ˋbifɚ] *n*. 1. 肉用牛,菜牛。2. 〔美口〕诉苦者,发牢骚者;告发者。
beef·y [ˈbiːfi; ˋbifɪ] *a*. 1. 牛似的,肌肉发达的;结实的,粗壮的。2. 愚钝的,戆。
Be·el·ze·bub [bi(ː)ˈelzibʌb; bɪˋɛlzɪˏbʌb] *n*. 1. 撒旦,魔王,恶魔,堕落的天使长。2. 〔南美〕猴子。***Call in*** ～ ***to cast out Satan***. 叫魔王赶撒旦;召鬼驱鬼。
been [biːn, bin; bin, bɪn] be 的过去分词。
beep [biːp; bip] I *n*. 1. (人造卫星等的)信号音。2. (汽车喇叭等的)嘟嘟声。3. 〔美俚〕小型警用汽车;吉普车。II *vt*. 1. 使(汽车喇叭等)嘟嘟响。2. 用嘟嘟声发出(警告等)。*drivers* ～*ed their horns* 嘟嘟鸣笛的驾驶员。*Impatient drivers* ～*ed their annoyance*. 等得不耐烦的驾驶员嘟嘟鸣笛表示不满。— *vi*. 1. 按喇叭。2. (汽车喇叭等)发嘟嘟声。**-er** *n*. 1. 给无人驾驶飞机发送信号的装置。2. 〔美俚〕无人驾驶飞机的遥控人员。
beer[1] [biə; bɪr] *n*. 啤酒,麦酒;(一般)发酵饮料。*black* [*dark*] ～ 黑啤酒。*ginger* ～ 姜汁啤酒。*nettle* ～ 荨麻啤酒。*draught* ～ = ～ *on draught* 生啤酒,桶装啤酒。*bock* [*duck*] ～ = *double* ～ 酒精含量高的啤酒。*a* ～ *place* 啤酒馆。***a small*** ～ 1. 酒精含量低的淡啤酒。2. 〔喻〕琐事,微不足道的东西。***in*** ～ 啤酒喝醉。～ ***and skittles*** 悠游的生活 (*Life is not all* ～ *and skittles*. 人生并不就是吃喝玩乐)。***think small*** ～ ***of*** 轻视,小视 (*think no small* ～ *of oneself* 妄自尊大,夜郎自大 *think no small* ～ *of* 珍视,重视)。～ **belly** 大肚子;肚子大的人。～ **garden** 屋外花园酒店。～ **house** 〔英〕啤酒铺。～ **mat** 啤酒杯垫子。～ **money** 〔英〕酒钱,小费。～ **parlour** 〔加拿大〕(有经营许可证的)啤酒店;(旅馆中的)啤酒酒吧。
beer[2] [biə; bɪr] *n*. 【纺】比尔〔英制经纱单位〕。
Beer·bohm [ˈbiəbəum; ˋbɪrbom] *n*. 比尔博姆〔姓氏〕。
beer·y [ˈbiəri; ˋbɪrɪ] *a*. (*-i·er*; *-i·est*) 1. 啤酒(一样)的。2. 喝啤酒喝醉了的;有点儿醉的。*a* ～ *breath* 满嘴啤酒味。
beest·ings, beast·ings, biest·ings [ˈbiːstiŋz; ˋbistɪŋz] *n*. 〔用作单数〕【畜】(哺乳动物、尤指母牛的)初乳。
bees·wax [ˈbiːzwæks; ˋbizˏwæks] I *n*. 蜜蜡,黄蜡。II *vt*. 涂蜜蜡于,给…上蜜蜡。
bees·wing [ˈbiːzwiŋ; ˋbizˏwɪŋ] *n*. 酒膜;陈年葡萄酒。
beet[1] [biːt; bit] *n*. 【植】萘菜,甜菜;〔*pl*.〕〔美〕亚麻捆 (= beetroot). ～**-faced** *a*. 鲜红的,红色的。～ **sugar** 甜菜糖。～**root** 甜菜根。
beet[2] [biːt; bit] *vt*. 〔英方〕1. 悔(过);改(过),抵(罪)。2. 修理,改进。3. 减轻;解(渴);充(饥);接济。4. 点着(火),使燃。
Bee·tho·ven [ˈbeit*h*əuvən; ˋbetovən], **Ludwig van** 贝多芬(1770—1827),德国大作曲家。**-i·an** *a*.
bee·tle[1] [ˈbiːtl; ˋbitl̩] I *n*. 1. 甲虫。2. 近视眼(的人);糊涂虫,笨虫[笨人]。～ ***blind*** = ***blind as a*** ～ 非常近视的。***deaf*** [***dumb***] ***as a*** ～ 全聋[哑]。II *vi*. 〔英〕(像甲虫一样)走来走去;匆匆忙忙地走,赶紧;瞎撞,乱撞。～ ***off*** 〔英俚〕急忙离开,赶。～**-crusher** 大靴子;大脚。
bee·tle[2] [ˈbiːtl; ˋbitl̩] I *n*. 大(木)槌;夯;杵;槌布机;搅打机。***between the*** ～ ***and the block*** 介于槌砧之间,上下交逼地,在危险中。II *vt*. 用大槌捶打[打进、打碎];用杵捣;捶(衣、布等)。
bee·tle[3] [ˈbiːtl; ˋbitl̩] I *a*. 突出的;愁眉苦脸的。II *vi*. (眉、毛、绝壁等)突出,伸出,俯临 (*over*). *a cliff that* ～*s over the sea* 俯临大海的悬崖。*The prospect of bankruptcy* ～*d over him*. 破产的前景威胁着他。*beetling walls* 绝壁。～**-browed** *a*. 额头突出的;眉毛浓厚的;眉头紧皱的;怒目而视的。～**-headed** *a*. 糊涂的,呆笨的。
beeves [biːvz; bivz] beef 的复数。
bee·zer [ˈbiːzə; ˋbizɚ] *n*. 〔美俚〕鼻子。
be·fall [biˈfɔːl; bɪˋfɔl] *vt*. (***befell*** [biˈfel; bɪˋfɛl]; ***befallen*** [biˈfɔːlən; bɪˋfɔlən]) 落到…的身上,降临于。*Evil befell him*. 灾祸落到他身上。— *vi*. 发生,降临。*What befell?* 发生什么事了?
be·fit [biˈfit; bɪˋfɪt] *vt*. (*-tt-*) 适合,适宜,与…相当,对…合式;为…的义务,对…为正常。*It ill* ～*s you to do so*. 你这样做是不适宜的。*His clothes* ～ *the occasion*. 他的服装适合那种场合。
be·fit·ting [biˈfitiŋ; bɪˋfɪtɪŋ] *a*. 相宜的,适当的,合适的 (*opp*. improper). ～ words 言词得体。**-ly** *ad*. 适当

地。

be·fog [bi'fɔg; bɪ`fɑg] *vt*. (-gg-) 1. 把…笼罩在云雾中。2. 使迷惑;使含糊;使神秘莫测。*Low-hanging black clouds beforgged the city*. 黑云压城。

be·fool [bi'fuːl; bɪ`ful] *vt*. 1. 愚弄,欺骗。2. 〔古〕骂…是傻瓜。

be·fore [bi'fɔː; bɪ`fɔr] I *ad*. 1. 在前,在前方,在前头,在前面。2. 在以前,从前,前此;较早。*run on* ~ 跑在前面。*look* ~ *and after* 瞻前顾后。*He is as happy as* ~. 他和从前一样幸福。*His garment buttoned* ~. 他的衣服前面扣上钮扣。*long* ~ 很久以前。*Begin at noon, not* ~. 正午开始,不要提前。II *prep*. 1. 在…以前;较…早[先]。*Lilacs come* ~ *the roses*. 紫丁香比蔷薇开得早。*the day* ~ *yesterday* 前天。*the night* ~ *last* 前晚。2. 在…的前面;当着…的面;向…;〔转义〕借…的力,被…推着;有…等待着,向…开放,供…使用。*put* [*lay*] *the matter* ~ *sb*. 在某人面前提出[汇报]这件事。*the question* ~ *us* 当前的问题。*man and wife* ~ *Heaven* 正式夫妇。*Pride goes* ~ *a fall*. 骄者必败。*The ship sailed* ~ *the wind*. 船顺风行驶。*The golden age is* ~ *us*. 黄金时代就在我们前面,前途无限美好。*Our services are* ~ *you*. 我们乐于为您服务。3. 先于,优于。*Ladies* ~ *gentlemen*. 女先男后。*A marquis is* ~ *a count*. 侯爵在伯爵之上。4. 与其…(不如),宁可…(也不)。*Death* ~ *dishonour*! 宁死不屈。*They would die* ~ *surrendering*. 他们宁死也不投降。III *conj*. 1. 〔表示时间关系〕比…早些,在…以前;还没有…(就);然后再,再;就;才。*They arrived* ~ *we expected*. 我们没有想到他们来得那么早。*I must finish my work* ~ *I go home*. 我必须把我的工作做完才回家。*It will not be long* ~ *Father returns*. 父亲不久就要回来。*Do it now* ~ *you forget*. 现在就做,免得忘记。*The sun had scarcely risen before the fog began to disappear*. 太阳刚一升起,雾气就开始消散。2. 〔表示选择关系〕与其…(不如);(宁愿);…也不。*He will die* ~ *he submit*. 他宁死不屈。***B- Christ*** 公元前 [B.C.]. ~ ***everything*** 先要,第一要。~ ***long*** 不久。~ ***now*** 从前。~ ***sb.'s very eyes*** 当某人面。~ ***one knows where one is*** 马上就,转瞬之间就,突然一下就。~ ***one's time*** 提前,过早;未出世[死]前。~ ***the mast*** 在桅前;做普通水手。~ ***the world*** 在全世界面前;公然,冒天下之大不讳。~ ***you can say knife*** [***Jack Robinson***] 一刹那,很快就。~**-mentioned** *a*. 上述的。~**-tax** *a*. 未抽税前的。

be·fore·hand [bi'fɔːhænd; bɪ`for͵hænd] *ad*. 1. 事先,预先。2. 赶先,超前,提前。*Please let me know* ~. 请事先通知我。*He is always* ~ *with his report*. 他总是提前交出报告。***be*** ~ ***with*** 1. 预先准备;先发制人。2. 太早,提早。***be*** ~ ***with the world*** 〔古〕手头有现款,手边宽裕。

be·fore·time [bi'fɔːtaim; bɪ`for͵taɪm] *ad*. 〔古〕以前,从前,往昔。

be·foul [bi'faul; bɪ`faʊl] *vt*. 1. 使污,弄脏。2. 说…的坏话,污蔑,中伤。~ ***one's own nest*** 说自家人坏话,家丑外扬。

be·friend [bi'frend; bɪ`frɛnd] *vt*. 友好对待,亲近;援助,帮助;照顾,扶助。**-er** *n*. 扶助者,恩人。

be·fud·dle [bi'fʌdl; bɪ`fʌdl] *vt*. 1. 使烂醉。2. 迷惑,蒙蔽。

beg [beg; bɛg] *vt*. (-gg-) 1. 乞求,请求;恳请。2. 讨(饭)。3. (议论等)回避(问题)。4. 请(原谅);请(允许)〔礼貌语〕。~ *one's bread*. 讨饭。— *vi*. 1. 乞求,恳请(*for*)。2. 讨饭,行乞。*a begging letter* 借钱信。*I* ~ *to be excused*. 请原谅。***Beg!*** 对(狗说)拜拜! 〔让狗举起前脚作乞讨状〕。~ ***for*** 乞,讨(~ *for mercy* 乞怜)。~ ***leave to*** (*do*) 很抱歉,对不起;〔商业信件用语〕敬启[复]者。(*I* ~ *leave to disagree* 恕不同意。*I* ~ *leave to say in reply* ... 敬复者。*I* ~ *leave to inform you that* ... 敬启者)。~ ***of*** (*sb*.), 求(人),请(人);奉恳,拜托(*I* ~ *of you not to run any risk*. 请你不要冒险。*I* ~ *a favour of you*. 我有一件事拜托您[求您])。~ ***off*** (用作不及物片语动词) 1. 对不能出席约会等表示歉意。2. 对不能出席约会等请求原谅后而不出席了(*He promised to come and help but has since* ~*ged off*. 他答应来帮忙,但已表示歉意不能来)。~ (*sb*.) ***off*** 辞退;谢绝;请求原谅(某人);(*He begged the servant off*. 他辞退了佣人)。~ ***sb.'s pardon*** 求饶,赔不是,道歉(*I* ~ *your pardon*. 1. 对不起〔抱歉语〕。2. (对不起)请再说一遍〔重读后部,用升调,亦可只说 ~ pardon〕。3. 非常遗憾〔提出异议前说的话〕。~ ***the question*** (故意回避论点时)以假定为论据的狡辩。~ ***to do*** = ~ ***leave to do***. ***B- your pudding*** [***pudden***] 〔英口〕= I beg your pardon. ***go begging*** 1. 去乞讨。2. 没有买主,无销路。

be·gad [bi'gæd; bɪ`gæd] *int* 〔口〕天哪! 的确! 一定! 完了! 糟糕! 〔by god 的委婉语〕。

be·gan [bi'gæn; bɪ`gæn] begin 的过去式。

be·get [bi'get; bɪ`gɛt] *vt*. (***be·got*** [bi'gɔt; bɪ`gɑt], 〔古〕 ***be·gat*** [bi'gæt; bɪ`gæt]; ***be·got·ten*** [bi'gɔtn; bɪ`gɑtn], ***be·got***) 1. (父亲)生(子女)。2. 产生,引起,招致。*Abraham begot Issac*. 亚伯拉罕生以撒。*Money* ~*s money*. 金钱生息。**Like** ~**s like**. 有其父必有其子。

be·get·ter [bi'getə; bɪ`gɛtɚ] *n*. 父。

beg·gar ['begə; `bɛgɚ] I *n*. 1. 乞丐,叫化子;穷人。2. 募捐者。3. 〔俚〕家伙〔对人的爱称、戏称〕。*a good* ~ 善于募捐;会讨东西。*Beggars must not be choosers*. 饥者难择食。*die a* ~ 穷死困死。*nice little* ~*s* 可爱的小家伙〔指幼儿、幼小动物说〕。*poor* ~! 可怜可怜! II *vt*. 1. 使做乞丐,使变穷。2. 使…无用,难以…。*Her beauty* ~*s description*. 她的美貌非笔墨所能形容。***I'll be*** ~***ed if*** ... 〔口〕决不会;如果…,让我变叫化子好了〔赌咒口吻〕。~**-my-neighbo(u)r** 1. *a*. (外交政策等)损人利益的。2. *n*. 【牌】乞食成霸〔一种纸牌戏,以一人吃尽所有人的纸牌为止〕。**-liness** *n*. 贫穷,卑贱;卑劣;贫弱。**-ly** *a*. 1. 乞丐似的,赤贫的;下贱的,卑劣的。2. 很少的,起码的(*a few beggarly dollars* 很少几元钱。*a beggarly amount of learning* 学识浅陋)。

beg·gar's-lice ['begəzˌlais; `bɛgɚz͵laɪs] *n*. (*pl*. ~) 1. 紫草科〔如:倒提壶属植物;郝吉利草属植物;鹤虱属植物〕。2. 上述植物之实(= beggar-lice)。

beg·gar's-ticks ['begəztiks; `bɛgɚz͵tɪks] *n*. (*pl*. ~) 1. 山马蝗属植物。2. 山马蝗属植物荚果的细裂片。3. 鬼针草属植物 (bur marigold); 鬼针草属植物的瘦果。4. = beggar's-lice (亦作 beggar-ticks).

beg·gar·weed ['begəwiːd; `bɛgɚ͵wid] *n*. 生长于荒地的多种三叶植物〔例如:篇蓄、兔丝子、金鸡菊等;尤指扭曲山马蝗〕。

beg·gar·y ['begəri; `bɛgərɪ] *n*. 1. 乞丐生活[处境],赤贫。2. 贫民窟。3. 〔总称〕乞丐。*be reduced to* ~ 变成赤穷,沦为乞丐。

be·gin [bi'gin; bɪ`gɪn] *vi*. (***be·gan*** [bi'gæn; bɪ`gæn]; ***be·gun*** [bi'gʌn; bɪ`gʌn]; ~***ning***) 1. 开始 (*opp*. end); 着手,动手。2. 始于,源于(*from*)。*School* ~*s on Monday*. 星期一开课。— *vt*. 1. 开始,创始;动手,着手。2. 创建。*It has begun to be done*. = *It has been begun*. 工作开始了。*He began* (*to speak*). 他开口了。*a book I began* (*to read*) 开始读的书。~ *a dynasty* 开创一个朝代。~ ***again*** 重做,从头另做。~ ***at*** 从…开始(~ *at the wrong end* 开错了头。~ *at page 10* 从第10页开始)。~ ***by*** (*doing* ...)从(做…)开始,先做…。~ ***on*** [***upon***] 着手,动手(*He has begun on a new book*. 他已开始读[写]另一本新书)。~ ***the world*** 开始为人[处世];开始独立生活。~ ***with*** 从…开始,先做(*A little caviar to begin with, madame*? 先吃一点鱼子

B

酱怎么样,女士?)。**not ~ to (do)**〔口〕决不会,完全不(*It does not ~ to meet the specifications*. 这完全不合规格。*I can't begin to tell you how grateful I am*. 我不知道怎样感激你才好)。**to ~ with** 首先,第一,第一个理由是;本来〔插入语〕(*To ~ with, he is too young*. 首先[第一],他太年轻了)。

be·gin·ner [biˈginə; bɪˋgɪnɚ] ***n*.** 1. 初学者,生手。2. 创立人,鼻祖。*a book for ~s* 初学者的入门书。*~ of the Impressionist school*. 印象派绘画的创始人。**~'s luck** 初学者的幸运,侥幸(*Making a grand slam the first time you play bridge is simply ~'s luck*. 你第一次打桥牌就打满贯,这纯粹是侥幸)。

be·gin·ning [biˈginiŋ; bɪˋgɪnɪŋ] ***n*.** 1. 初,当初;开始,端绪,发端;出发点。2. 本原,起源。3. 〔常 *pl*.〕早期阶段。4. 起头部分。*at the ~ of the month* 月初。*the ~ of a book* 书的开头部分。*the ~s of science* 科学的摇篮期。*rise from humble [modest] ~s* 出身微贱。*A misunderstanding was the ~ of their quarrel*. 他们的争吵起因于彼此误解。**at the (very) ~** 在当初;首先。**from ~ to end** 自始至终,始终;从头到尾。**In every ~ think of the end.** 凡事都要想到它的后果。**in the ~** 当初,起初。**make a ~** 开一个头,动手。**the ~ of the end** 事变的前兆,一叶落而知天下秋。

be·gird [biˈgəːd; bɪˋgɝd] ***vt*.** (***be·girt*** [biˈgəːt; bɪˋgɝt], ***begird·ed***) 1. 用带绕[束]。2. 围绕,包围。★常用过去分词 begirt. *a castle begirt with a moat* 有壕沟围绕着的城堡。

be·gone [biˈgɔn; bɪˋgɔn] **I** ***int*.** 出去! 去! 滚! **II** ***vi*.** 去,走开。*Tell her to ~*. 叫她走开。*order sb. to ~* 喝令某人走开。作★ ***vi*.** 时多用于此种句型。

Be·gon·ia [biˈgəunjə; bɪˋgonjə] ***n*.** 【植】秋海棠属;〔b-〕秋海棠。

be·got [biˈgɔt; bɪˋgɑt] beget 的过去式及过去分词。

be·got·ten [biˈgɔtn; bɪˋgɑtn̩] beget 的过去分词。*his only ~ son* 他的独生子。

be·grime [biˈgraim; bɪˋgraɪm] ***vt*.** (灰尘等)弄脏,沾污。***~d streets*** 灰尘遍地的街道。

be·grudge [biˈgrʌdʒ; bɪˋgrʌdʒ] ***vt*.** 1. 吝惜,舍不得给。2. 嫉妒。*She did not ~ the money spent on her children's education*. 她决不吝惜花在她子女身上的教育费。*No one ~s to help her*. 没有不乐意帮助她的。*She ~d her friend the award*. 她嫉妒她的朋友获奖。

be·guile [biˈgail; bɪˋgaɪl] ***vt*.** 1. 骗,欺诈;诱惑。2. 解(闷),消磨(时间);哄慰(孩子)。*~ sb. of [out of] sth*. 骗取某人的东西。*He ~d me into consenting*. 他甜言蜜语地使我答应了。*~ the long afternoon with a good book* 读一本好书消磨漫长的下午。*We ~d the children with fairy tales*. 我们讲童话故事哄孩子。**-ment** ***n*.**

be·guil·er [biˈgailə; bɪˋgaɪlɚ] ***n*.** 1. 欺骗者,骗子。2. 诱惑品;消遣的人;消遣品。

be·guil·ing [biˈgailiŋ; bɪˋgaɪlɪŋ] ***a*.** 消遣性的。**-ly** ***ad*.**

be·guine [biˈgiːn; bɪˋgin] ***n*.** 贝津舞〔西印度群岛的马提尼克岛和圣卢西亚岛上的一种土风舞,略似伦巴〕。

Beg·uine [ˈbegiːn; ˋbɛgin] ***n*.** 慈善修女〔12 世纪以来荷兰等国的一种半世俗女修道会的成员〕。

be·gum [ˈbiːgəm, ˈbeigəm; ˋbigəm, ˋbegəm] ***n*.** (印度穆斯林)贵妇,公主;(英国)英印混血贵妇;〔B-〕夫人〔对穆斯林贵妇等的尊称〕。

be·gun [biˈgʌn; bɪˋgʌn] begin 的过去分词。

be·half [biˈhɑːf; bɪˋhæf] ***n*.** 利益,维护,支持〔仅用于下列成语〕。**in ~ of** 为…,为…的利益〔现罕用〕。**in [on] sb.'s ~** 为,替,给,为了某人,代表某人(*He interceded in my ~*. 他给我说情。*She gave evidence on her own behalf*. 她为自己提出证据)。**in [on] this (that) ~** 关于这件[那件]事。**on ~ of** 1. 替、代表(*on ~ of my colleagues, I address you tonight*. 今晚我谨代表我的同事对诸位讲话)。2. 为…的利益(*He has returned safely from a mission on ~ of his country*. 他已经为国完成使命,安全归来)。

be·have [biˈheiv; bɪˋhev] ***vi*.** 1. 处身,行为,做人,举止,表现。2. (机器等)开动,运转。3. 行为得体,讲礼貌,守规矩。4. (对环境或刺激的)反应,反作用,显示特色。*He doesn't know how to ~*. 他不懂礼貌。*He ~d badly to me*. 他对我不好。*The ship ~s well*. 这条船走得不错。*Did the child ~?* 这孩子守规矩吗? *Do you notice how mysteriously the colors ~ here?* 你注意到这些色彩的情调在这里显得如何神秘吗? — ***vt*.** 〔用反身代词〕1. 使举止得当,使守规矩;表现。2. 使正常运转。*He ~d himself like a man*. 他做人有骨气。***B- yourself!*** (对孩子)安分点! 规矩点!

be·hav·iour, be·hav·ior [biˈheivjə; bɪˋhevjɚ] ***n*.** 1. 行为,品行;举止,态度,举动,表现,行动。2. (生物的)习性;(机器等的)特性,性能,状态;(药品等的)作用,功效。*gallant ~* 英雄行为。*a bad ~ at meals* 吃饭的难看相。*aerodynamic ~* 空气动力特性。**on [upon] one's good [best] ~** 1. 善自检点,谨慎,规矩。2. 在见习中,在试用期间(*The child was on his good ~*. 这孩子很规矩)。**put sb. on his best ~.** 劝告[警告]某人检点一些。**-al** ***a*.** 关于行为的(*behavioural science* 行为科学〔如社会学、人类学等〕)。~ **pattern**【社会学】行为模式。~ **therapy**【医】行为疗法〔一种心理疗法〕。**-ism** ***n*.** 【心】行为主义。**-ist** ***n*.** 【心】行为主义心理学家。

be·head [biˈhed; bɪˋhɛd] **I** ***vt*.** 把…斩首,砍…的头。**II** ***a*.** 被砍了头的;〔美俚〕被解雇的。~**ed river**【地】断头河,夺流河,被夺河。**-ing** ***n*.** 斩首;斩罪;【地】断头。

be·held [biˈheld; bɪˋhɛld] behold 的过去式及过去分词。

be·he·moth [biˈhiːməθ; bɪˋhiməθ] **I** ***n*.** 1. 【圣】巨兽。2. 〔美口〕庞然大物。**II** ***a*.** 巨大的。

be·hest [biˈhest; bɪˋhɛst] ***n*.** 〔书〕1. 命令,谕令,指示。2. 紧急指示。*the pope's ~* 教皇谕令。*act at sb.'s ~* 按某人指示办事。

be·hind [biˈhaind; bɪˋhaɪnd] **I** ***ad*.** 1. 在后,在后面,向后,已成过去。2. 背地,在幕后,在背后。3. 迟,过(期),落后。*lag ~* 落后。*My joy lies ~*. 我的欢乐已经消逝。*He came ten minutes ~*. 他迟到了十分钟。*glance [look] ~* 回头(看)。*The clock is more than five minutes ~*. 钟慢了不止五分。*Your watch runs ~*. 你的表慢了。*There is more ~*. 里头还有情况[内幕]。*The season is ~*. 季节拖迟了。**II** ***n*.** 〔口〕屁股。**III** ***prep*.** 1. 在…之后,向…后面;在…的那边。2. 在…的背后;作…的后盾;在…的里面,在…的幕后,操纵。3. 在…死后。4. 落后于;迟于;劣于。*get ~ a tree* 躲在树后。*He left ~ him a great reputation*. 流芳后世。*His house is a few yards ~ the church*. 他的家在教堂过去几步远。*an argument with experience ~ it* 经验之谈,有经验为证的论点。*He is ~ the plan*. 他是幕后策划人。*the person ~ the wheel of a car* 汽车驾驶人,司机。*His apprenticeship was ~ him*. 他的学徒期已满。*I am ~ my class in mathematics*. 我的数学比同班同学差。**be (far) ~** (非常)迟缓,落后;(很)坏(*Can spring be far ~?* 春天还会远吗?)。**be ~ in [with] (payments; work)** (支付)误期;(工作)落后,耽误。**~ the times** 落后,赶不上时代,不合时宜。**~ time** 误期,过期,过时,迟。**from ~** 从后。**get ~ = go ~** 追究…的根源[真相]。**leave ~** 留在后头;忘记(*He left his stick ~ him*. 他忘记拿手杖就走了)。**put ~ one** 拒绝考虑(某事)。~**hand** ***a*.** 〔只用作述语〕1. 落后,迟延;过期,误期。2. 入不敷出,困窘(*be [get] ~hand* 落后。*be ~hand in one's circumstances* 家境不好。*live ~hand* 入不敷出。*~hand with payments [work]* 支付误期[耽误工作])。~**-the-scene(s)** ***a*.** 幕后的(*a ~-the-scene(s) master [boss]* 后台老板)。

be·hold [biˈhəuld; bɪˋhold] **I** ***vt*.** (***be·held*** [biˈheld;

bi`held]; **be·held**)〔书〕观看,注视,观察。— *vi*. 看〔用于祈使语气〕。**II** *int*. 看哪! *lo and* ～嗨,你瞧! **-er** *n*. 观看者。

be·hold·en [bi'həuldən; bi`holdən] *a*. 蒙恩,见爱;铭感〔作述语用〕。*I am greatly* ～ *to you for your kindness*. 承蒙厚爱,十分感激。

be·hoof [bi'huːf; bi`huf] *n*.〔古〕利益〔仅用于词片语 for sb.'s ～等中〕。**for** [**in, on, to**] **sb.'s** ～ = *for* [*in, on, to*] *the* ～ *of sb*. 为了某人,为某人的利益(*The money was spent for his own* ～. 那笔钱是为他自己花的。*For whose* ～ *is this done?* 做这件事为了谁?)。

be·hove, be·hoove [bi'həuv, bi'huːv; bi`hov, bi`huv] *vt*. **1.** 对…来说是应该的,是…的义务。**2.** 对…来说是必要的〔主语均用 it〕。*It* ～*s everyone to do his duty*. 尽本分人人应该。— *vi*.〔古〕是责任,是义务〔主语用 it〕。*It* ～*s that I be silent*. 我应该沉默。*It* ～*s to write to her*. 应该写信给她。

Beh·ring ['beriŋ; `beriŋ] *n*. = Bering.

Behr·man ['bɛəmən; `bɛrmən] *n*. 贝尔曼〔姓氏〕。

beige [beiʒ; beʒ] **I** *n*. **1.** 原色哔叽;混色线呢。**2.** 米色。**II** *a*. 米色的。

be·in ['biːin; `biɪn] *n*. (在公园等公共场所举行的)狂欢会。

be·ing ['biːiŋ; `biɪŋ] be 的现在分词。**1.**〔用作独立片语中的系词〕*things* ～ *as they are*. 事情既然如此。*Dinner* ～ *over, they left the hall*. 他们吃完饭后离开了食堂。*B- a soldier, he has a strong sense of discipline*. 他是个士兵,有很强的纪律性。**2.**〔构成被动语态进行式〕…着。*These countries are* ～ *swept by an economic crisis*. 这些国家正在受着一场经济危机的冲击。**3.**〔由 be 的"存在","现存"等意义转来的分词,用作修饰语,修饰少数表示时间概念的名词〕。*for the time* ～ 暂时;一时;临时。*n*. **1.** 实在,存在。**2.** 生存,生命,人生,一生,人间。**3.** 物;生物,人;实在物。**4.** 本质,特质,本性。**5.**〔B-〕上帝,神;本体。*the aim of our* ～ 人生的目的。*actual* ～ 实在。*to the very depth of one's* ～ 灵魂深处。*a human* ～人,人间。*animate* [*inanimate*] ～生[无生]物。*the Supreme B-* 上帝。～ **as** [**that**]〔口〕既然;因为。～ **in itself**【哲】物自体。**call** [**bring**] **into** ～ 使产出,使形成。**come into** ～ 发生,诞生,成立(*The European Common Market came into* ～ *in 1958*. 欧洲共同体成立于 1958 年)。**in** ～ 现有的,现存的,存在的(*the fleet in* ～ 现有的舰队。*the record in* ～ 现存的记录)。**-less** *a*. 不存在的。

Bei·ra ['baiərə; `berə] *n*. 贝拉〔莫桑比克港市〕。

Bei·rut [bei'ruːt; be͵rut] *n*. 贝鲁特〔黎巴嫩首都〕。

be·jab·bers [bi'dʒæbəz; bi`dʒæbəz] **I** *int*. 啊呀呀! 真糟糕!〔表示惊奇、高兴、愤怒、烦恼等,是 by Jesus 的委婉说法〕。**II** *n*. 鬼东西,混账家伙。**beat** [**knock, scare**] **the** ～ **out of sb**. 狠狠揍某人一顿。

be·jew·el [bi'dʒuːəl; bi`dʒuəl] *vt*. (**-el**(**l**)-) 给…饰以珠宝,以宝石镶嵌。

Bel [bel; bɛl] *n*. 贝尔〔女子名, Arabella, Isabel, Isabella 等的爱称〕。

Bel. = Belgian; Belgium.

bel [bel; bɛl] *n*.【物】贝(尔)〔电平单位〕。

be·la·bour, be·la·bor [bi'leibə; bi`lebə] *vt*. **1.** 猛烈攻击;狠狠责备,痛骂。**2.** 啰啰嗦嗦地说明。**3.**〔古〕痛打。～ *an endless argument* 啰啰嗦嗦地议论不休。

be·lat·ed [bi'leitid; bi`letɪd] *a*. **1.** 落后了的,过了期的;过时的;已经迟了的;旧式的。**2.** 天已暗了的,(旅客等)天色已晚还在赶路的。～ **efforts** 为时已晚的努力。*a* ～ *view of world politics* 对世界政治的过时看法。～ *travelers* 天色已晚还在赶路的行旅。

be·laud [bi'lɔːd; bi`lɔd] *vt*. 褒扬;〔讽〕过分吹捧。

be·lay [bi'lei; bi`le] **I** *vt*. **1.**【海】把绳子作 S[8]形拴在(套索桩等上);停止。**2.** 把(绳)拴在身体[物体]上。**3.** (登山运动)把(人)系在绳端。— *vi*. **1.** 用绳系住。**2.**【海】停住〔用于命令句〕。**II** *n*. **1.** (登山时的)系绳处。**2.**【海】S 形挽椿。**Belay there!**〔海俚〕停止!

be·lay·ing pin [bi'leiiŋ pin; bi`leɪŋ pɪn] *n*.【船】缠索栓,套索桩,缆耳。

bel can·to [bel 'kɑːntəu; bɛl `kɑnto] *n*. [It.]【乐】美声唱法〔一种以发声洪亮圆润为特点的传统唱法〕。

belch [beltʃ; bɛltʃ] **I** *vi*. **1.** 打嗝,呃逆。**2.** 态度蛮横地发出(叱咤等)。**3.** (火山等)猛烈喷射,爆发。**4.**〔美俚〕发牢骚;〔罕〕讲,谈。— *vt*. **1.** (火山、大炮等)喷、冒(烟、火焰等)。**2.** 猛烈地发出。*an air shaft* ～*ing fire and smoke* 喷出烟火的烟囱。*Factories* ～ *forth clouds of smoke*. 工厂喷出团团烟雾。**II** *n*. **1.** 打嗝。**2.** 喷射,爆发(声)。**3.** 劣质啤酒。

bel·ch·er ['beltʃə; `bɛltʃɚ] *n*. **1.** (英国)蓝白花围巾〔常作～ handkerchief〕。**2.**〔美俚〕爱发牢骚的人;碎嘴子。

bel·dam(**e**) ['beldəm; `bɛldəm] *n*. 老太婆;泼妇,丑妇。

be·lea·guer [bi'liːgə; bi`ligɚ] *vt*. **1.** 围攻,围困,包围。**2.** 使烦恼。～ *a town* 围攻一座城市。～*ed with troubles* 诸事多烦恼。

bel·em·nite ['beləmnait; `bɛləm͵naɪt] *n*.【古生】箭石〔乌贼类化石〕。

bel es·prit [͵beles'priː; ͵bɛlɛs`pri] *n*. (*pl*. ***beaux esprits*** ['bəuzes'priː; `bozɛs`pri]) [F.] 才子。

Bel·fast [bel'fɑːst; bɛl`fɑst] *n*. 贝尔法斯特〔英国港市〕。

bel·fried ['belfrid; `bɛlfrɪd] *a*. 有钟楼的;有钟塔的。

bel·fry ['belfri; `bɛlfrɪ] *n*. **1.** (教堂等的)钟楼;钟塔;钟架。**2.**〔口〕头脑,脑筋。*a* ～ *full of curious notions* 满脑子古怪思想。**have bats in the** [**one's**] ～ 脑筋有点怪,有点神经失常。

Bel·gian ['beldʒən; `bɛldʒən] **I** *n*. 比利时人。**II** *a*. 比利时的;比利时人的。

Bel·gic ['beldʒik; `bɛldʒɪk] *a*. **1.** 古比利时族 (Belgae) 人的。**2.** 比利时(人)的。**3.** 古荷兰的。

Bel·gium ['beldʒəm; `bɛldʒɪəm] *n*. 比利时〔欧洲〕。

Bel·grade [bel'greid; `bɛlgred] *n*. 贝尔格莱德〔南斯拉夫首都〕。

Bel·gra·vi·a [bel'greivjə; bɛl`grevɪə] *n*. **1.** 贝尔格莱维亚区〔伦敦海德公园附近的高级住宅区〕。**2.** 典型的上层阶级;贵族。**3.** 中上阶层的人。

Bel·gra·vi·an [bel'greivjən; bɛl`grevɪən] **I** *a*. 贝尔格莱维亚区的;中上阶层的。**II** *n*. 高级住宅区居民;中上阶层分子。

Be·li·al ['biːljəl; `biljəl] *n*. **1.**【圣】恶魔,魔鬼〔出自《新约》〕**2.**【圣】邪恶〔出自《旧约》〕。*daughters of* ～ 不正经的女子。*sons* [*men*] *of* ～ 堕落者,浪子,无赖。

be·lie [bi'lai; bi`laɪ] *vt*. (～**d**; **-ly·ing**) **1.** 歪曲…的真相,伪装,使人误解。**2.** 证明…是假的;与…相背[相反、相左]。**3.** 辜负(希望等),违背(约言等)。**4.**〔美〕责备…虚假。*His clothes* ～ *his station*. 他的衣服掩饰了他的身分。*His acts* ～ *his words*. 他言行不一。*His trembling hands* ～*d his calm voice*. 他颤抖的双手戳穿了他平静的语调。*Summer* ～*s its name*. 今年夏天一点也不热。*The results* ～*d his father's expectations*. 后来的情形使他父亲的希望落空了。

be·lief [bi'liːf; bi`lif] *n*. **1.** 信,信任;相信 (*in*); 信仰,信心。**2.** 信念;意见。**3.**【基督新教】信条;教义;[the B-]使徒信条。*He has no great* ～ *in religion* 他不大相信宗教。*a man worthy of* ～ 可以信得过的人。*a person light of* ～ 轻信的人。*My* ～ *is that* …我相信,在我看来。**beyond** ～ 难以置信;非常,想像以外地。**in the** ～ **that** …相信…。**to the best of my** ～ 我相信,以我看来。

be·liev·a·ble [bi'liːvəbl; bi`livəbl̩] *a*. 可信(任)的。**-a·bil·i·ty, -ness** *n*. 可信任性。**-a·bly** *ad*.

be·lieve [bi'liːv; bi`liv] *vt*. **1.** 信,相信,确信。**2.** 想,以为,认为。*I* ～ *him*. = *I* ～ *what he says*. 我相信他

(的话)。*I* ～ *him to be honest*. 我认为他是诚实的。*I don't* ～ *I know him*. 我想我不认识他。*The fugitive is* ～*d to be headed for the border*. 逃犯被认为在向国境线逃窜。*I* ～ *so*. 我认为如此;我想是这样。— **vi**. **1**. 相信。**2**. 信任,信赖。**3**. 信奉,信仰(*in*)。*I* ～ *not*. 我认为不是这样。*Seeing is* ～*ing*. 百闻不如一见,眼见心服。*I* ～ *in you*. 我相信你,我对你有信心。～ *in Zoroastrianism* 信奉祆教。*I* ～ *in early rising*. 我相信早起是好的。*I don't* ～ *in marrying young*. 我不赞成早婚。～ ***it or not*** 〔美口〕信不信由你,我说的是真的。***B- me***. 真的,是真的呀。***make*** ～ 假装(*She make* ～ *not to hear me*. 她假装没有听到我的话)。***You'd better*** ～ 〔美口〕的确,无疑。

be·liev·er [bi'liːvə; bɪ`livɚ] ***n***. 相信的人;信仰者,信徒(*in*). *a* ～ *in Buddhism* 佛教信徒。

be·liev·ing [bi'liːviŋ; bɪ`livɪŋ] ***a***. 有信仰的,有信心的。**-ly *ad***.

be·like [bi'laik; bɪ`laɪk] ***ad***. 〔古〕或者,多半。

Be·lin·da [bi'lində; bə`lɪndə] ***n***. 比琳达〔女子名〕。

be·lit·tle [bi'litl; bɪ`lɪtl] ***vt***. 〔美〕**1**. (相形之下)使显得微小,缩小。**2**. 小视,轻视,贬损,贬低。*The bulk of the warehouse* ～*s the houses around it*. 货栈的庞大使周围的房屋显得矮小了。～ *oneself* 自卑。

Be·lize [be'liːz; bɛ`liz] ***n***. **1**. 伯利兹〔拉丁美洲〕。**2**. 伯利兹〔伯利兹原首府〕。

Bell [bel; bɛl] ***n***. **1**. 贝尔〔姓氏〕。**2**. **Alexander Graham** ～ 〔1847—1922,生于苏格兰的美国人,电话发明者〕。

bell[1] [bel; bɛl] **I *n***. **1**. 钟,铃;门铃;〔常 *pl*.〕【海】船钟;雾钟;轮班钟〔$4\frac{1}{2}$、$8\frac{1}{2}$、$12\frac{1}{2}$时各一击,其后每$\frac{1}{2}$时递增一击〕〔*cf*. *eight bells*〕。**2**. 钟声。**3**. (铁管的)承口;扩散管,漏斗;〔*pl*.〕喇叭裤;【建】圆屋顶;【动】(水母等的)伞膜;【植】钟状花冠。**4**. 〔美俚〕拳赛终了。*electric* ～*s* 电铃。*a hand* ～ 手摇铃。*a door* ～ 门铃。*answer the* ～ 听到铃声去开门。*There's the* ～. 有客来了。*marriage* ～*s* 婚钟。*passing* ～*s* 丧钟。*rise at the* ～ 鸣钟即起。*a set of* ～*s* 一组钟。(***as***) ***sound*** [***clear***] ***as a*** ～ 极健康[清楚]。***bear*** [***carry away***] ***the*** ～ **1**. 站在前头。**2**. 获胜,得奖品。～, ***book and candle*** 【宗】驱逐出教的威胁,教会的威权。***by*** ～ ***and book*** 凭着钟声和圣经起誓〔中世纪起誓用语〕。***gain the*** ～ 得胜。***hang all one's*** ～***s on one horse*** 把所有的财产遗留给独生子。***hang the*** ～ ***about the cat's neck***. 敢于冒险;敢于在危险中挺身而出。***lose the*** ～ 战败,败北。***ring a*** ～ 引起反应,使人想起某事(*That rings a* ～. 〔口〕那使人回想起某事来了)。***ring the*** ～ **1**. 敲钟,摇铃。**2**. 〔美俚〕使如愿以偿;使满意[欢迎,成功]。***ring the*** ～***s backward*** 报警,告急。***saved by the*** ～ (拳击手)因铃响宣告一个回合结束而免于被击倒;(人)因偶发事件而避开灾难。***That rings a*** ～. 那是一个提醒。***with*** ～***s on*** 〔口〕热切希望,很想,很喜爱。**II *vt***. **1**. 系铃于,给…装上铃。**2**. 使成铃状。**3**. 鸣钟[按铃]召(人)。**4**. 把…放在钟形罩内。～ *the man to come up* 鸣钟[按铃]叫人来。～ ***the cat*** 给猫系铃,想办难事。～ **bird** 钟声鸟。～ **-bottom trousers** 喇叭裤。～ **boy** 〔美〕**1**. 旅馆侍者。**2**. 随身电话装置,无线电话机。～ **buoy** 【海】(设在暗礁上的)打钟浮标。～ **button** 电铃的揿钮。～ **captain** 旅馆服务员领班。～ **flower** 【植】〔口〕风铃草(*Campanula*)(*the Chinese* ～ *flower* 桔梗)。～ **founder** 铸钟匠。～ **foundry** 铸钟厂。～ **glass** (钟形)玻璃罩。～ **hanger** (旧时的)装铃匠。～ **hop** 〔美口〕= bellboy。～ **jar** (钟状)玻璃罩。～ **lap** (赛跑比赛中)以钟声为信号的最后一圈。～**man** (教堂)打钟人;管警报钟的人;上街鸣钟向公众报事的人;更夫。～ **metal** 钟铜〔铜锡合金,即青铜〕。～**mouthed *a***. 钟口状的,钟口的。～**pull** 钟[门铃]的拉索;铃扣。～ **polisher** 〔美俚〕事情谈好还不回去的客人。～ **push** 电铃按钮。～ **ringer** 摇铃的人,敲钟的人,钟童。～ **ringing** 鸣钟;鸣钟法。～ **tent** 钟形帐篷。～ **tower** 钟楼。～ **wether** (做羊群领队的)系铃羊;前导。

bell[2] [bel; bɛl] **I *n***. (交尾期的)雄鹿鸣声。**II *vi***. (雄鹿)鸣,叫。

Bel·la ['belə; `bɛlə] ***n***. = Bel.

bel·la·don·na [ˌbelə'dɔnə; ˏbɛlə`dɑnə] ***n***. **1**. 【植】颠茄。**2**. 【药】颠茄制剂。～ **lily** 孤挺花。

bel·la·fi·gu·ra ['belɑːfiː'guːrɑː; `bɛlafi`gurɑ] ***n***. 〔It.〕良好的印象;优雅的风度。

Bel·la·my ['beləmi; `bɛləmɪ] ***n***. 贝拉米〔姓氏〕。

belle [bel; bɛl] ***n***. 〔F.〕美女,第一美人,…花。～ ***amie*** (美貌的)女朋友。***the*** ～ ***of society*** 交际花。***the*** ～ ***of the ball*** 舞会花魁〔第一美人〕。

belle époque, la [ˌbelei'pɔːk; bɛle`pɔk] 〔偶尔作 B- E-〕〔F.〕高雅风流年代〔指 1871 年普法战争结束至第一次世界大战前法国艺术大繁荣的时期〕。

Bel·ler·o·phon [bə'leərəfən; bə`lɛrəˏfɑn] ***n***. 【希神】柏勒洛丰〔骑着天马 Pegasus 杀死喷火怪物 Chimera 的科林斯勇士〕。**-tic *a***. (*Bellerophontic letter* 内容不利于送信者的信件)。

belles-let·tres [ˌbel'letr; ˏbɛl`lɛtr] ***n***. 〔*pl*.〕〔F.〕美文学;纯文学,纯文艺〔指诗歌、小说、戏剧等〕。

bel·let·rist ['bel'letrist; ˏbɛl`lɛtrɪst] ***n***. **1**. 美文学研究者。**2**. 纯文学作者。

bel·le·tris·tic ['belle'tristik; ˏbɛllɛ`trɪstɪk] ***a***. 有关美文学研究的;纯文学的。

bel·li·cose ['belikəus; `bɛləˏkos] ***a***. 好战的,爱打架的,好斗的。**-ly *ad***. **-ness *n***.

bel·li·cos·i·ty [ˌbeli'kɔsiti; ˏbɛlə`kɑsətɪ] ***n***. 好战,好斗(性)。

bel·lied ['belid; `bɛlɪd] ***a***. **1**. 有腹的;膨胀的,鼓起的;凸起的;张满的。**2**. …腹的〔用以构成复合词〕。*big-* [*pot-*] ～ 大腹便便的,大肚皮的;有孕的。*empty-* ～ 空着肚子的。*a* ～ *sail* 张满的风帆。

bel·lig·er·ence [bi'lidʒərəns, be'lidʒərəns; bə`lɪdʒərəns, bɛ`lɪdʒərəns] ***n***. **1**. 好战性。**2**. 交战,战争行为。

bel·lig·er·en·cy [bi'lidʒərənsi, be'lidʒərənsi; bə`lɪdʒərənsɪ, bɛ`lɪdʒərənsɪ] ***n***. **1**. (国与国等处于)交战中,交战状态。**2**. 好战性。

bel·lig·er·ent [bi'lidʒərənt, be'lidʒərənt; bə`lɪdʒərənt, bɛ`lɪdʒərənt] **I *a***. **1**. 交战中的;交战国的。**2**. 好战的,好斗的。～ *powers* 交战国。*a* ～ *tone* 挑衅的语调。**II *n***. 交战国;交战的一方。*the defeated* ～ 战败国;战败一方。

Bell·man ['belmən; `bɛlmən] ***n***. 贝尔曼〔姓氏〕。

Bel·loc ['belɔk; `bɛlɑk] ***n***. 贝洛克〔姓氏〕。

Bel·lo·na [bə'ləunə; bə`lonə] ***n***. **1**. 【罗神】女战神。**2**. (人格化的)战争。**3**. 身高体壮的美女,颀长的美女。

bel·low ['beləu; `bɛlo] **I *vi***. **1**. (公牛、象等)吼,大声叫。**2**. (人)怒吼,咆哮;(风)怒号;(海)呼啸;(大炮,雷)轰轰地响、轰鸣。～ *with rage* 怒吼。— ***vt***. 大声喊[发]出。*He* ～*ed his answer across the room*. 他从屋子那边大声地答复。～ ***off*** 大声驱赶;喝使哑口无言。～ ***out*** [***forth***] 大声咆哮(～ *out* [*forth*] *a laugh* 放声大笑)。**II *n***. **1**. (公牛等的)吼声。**2**. 咆哮;怒号。

Bel·low(s) ['beləu(z); `bɛlo(z)] ***n***. 贝洛(斯)〔姓氏〕。

bel·lows ['beləuz; `bɛloz] ***n***. 〔*sing*., *pl*.〕**1**. 手拉风箱,手用吹风器〔有两个把手的叫 a pair of ～,俗称皮老虎,固定的叫 (the) ～〕。**2**. (管风琴等的)风箱;【机】波纹管;(真空)膜盒;(照相机的)蛇腹。**3**. 〔俚〕肺。*a* ～ *pocket* 褶裥的口袋。～ *type gun* 风箱嘴油枪;风箱型喷射器。***have*** ～ ***to mend*** 〔俚〕(马等)喘气,发喘。～**-like *a***.

bel·lum ['beləm; `bɛləm] ***n***. (波斯湾的)小独木船。

bell·wort ['belˌwəːt; `bɛlˏwɝt] ***n***. **1**. 颚花属植物。**2**. 〔主英〕风铃草属植物。

bel·ly ['beli; `bɛlɪ] **I *n***. **1**. 肚子,腹,腹部(*opp*. back);胃;子宫。**2**. (物件的)凸部,凹部;前部,下部,内部。**3**.

胃口,食欲,贪心。**4.** 腹状物;腹状部;炉腰;(飞机、轮船等的)舱内部;【海】被风张满的帆;【机】桁腹;【建】隆腹形。*The ~ has no ears*. 肚子会饿不会听,衣食足而后礼义兴。*the ~ of a sail* 帆的鼓起部分。*a pot ~* 大肚子。***back and ~*** 背与腹;衣食。~ ***laugh*** 〔美口〕捧腹大笑;(戏剧中)叫人捧腹大笑的动作(等)。~ ***timber*** 食物。***full in the ~*** 〔口〕大肚子[怀孕]。***have fire in one's ~*** 肚里明亮,内心聪明。***lie on one's ~*** 匍匐。***make a god of one's ~*** 贪吃,嘴馋。**II** ***vt***. 使鼓起,使胀满;使胀。— ***vi***. **1.** 胀满,鼓起。**2.** 匍匐前进。~ ***in*** (飞机)以腹部触地降落。~ ***out*** (帆)迎风鼓起;(矿脉)突然增广。~**ache 1.** ***n***. 肚子痛,腹痛。**2.** ***vi***. 〔美俚〕哭诉,发牢骚,鸣不平。~**band** (马的)肚带。~**board** 冲浪运动中用的一种腹部贴卧的浮板。~**-bound** ***a***. (肠)秘结,便秘。~**button** 〔美俚〕脐。~**fat** 〔美俚〕浪费或多余的东西。~**flop** 〔口〕腹部击水的拙劣跳水动作;(滑雪时)肚子贴着雪橇的下滑。~ **god** 贪吃的人;考究饮食的人。~**hold** 机腹货舱。~**-land** ***vi***. 【空】以机腹着陆。~**-pinched** ***a***. 挨饿的。~ **tank** (用完就扔弃的)额外油筒。~**-up** ***a***. **1.** 死的。**2.** 破产的。~ **wash** 〔美口〕清凉饮料,冷饮品。~ **worm** 〔口〕蛔虫。~ **worship** 大吃大喝,暴饮暴食。**-ful** ***n***. 满腹,充分 (*of*).

Bel·mo·pan [ˈbelməpæn; ˋbɛlməpæn] ***n***. 贝尔莫潘〔伯利兹首都〕。

be·long [biˈlɔŋ; bəˋlɔŋ] ***vi***. **1.** 属,属(某人)所有,是(某人)的东西 (*to*); 应归入(某)部类 (*to, among, in, under, with*). **2.** 〔美口〕是…的会员[成员,附件] (*to*). **3.** 〔美口〕住,居住。**4.** 爱接近人,爱交际;适合于(某)环境。**5.** 〔俚〕拥有 (*to*). **6.** 〔Scot.〕应该〔后接不定式〕。*This book ~s to me*. 这本书是我的。*This book ~s in every home*. 这本书家家需要。*Poetry ~s with music*. 诗歌与音乐相近。*He ~s here*. 他是此地人。*Where do you ~ (to)?* 你是哪里人? *The lid ~s to this jar*. 盖子是这把壶上的。*Where did these things ~?* 这些东西原来放在哪里? *You don't ~ in this club*. 你不是这个俱乐部的成员。*She is smart and jolly, but she just doesn't ~*. 她爽直快活,就是有些孤僻。*We all ~*. 我们彼此合得来。*He doesn't ~*. 他人缘不好。*Your objection doesn't ~ to this discussion*. 你的反对意见和这场讨论没有关系。*Who ~s to this dictionary?* 〔俚〕这本字典是谁的? *They ~ to come at seven o'clock*. 他们应该在七点钟来。

be·long·ing [biˈlɔŋiŋ; bɪˋlɔŋɪŋ] ***n***. **1.** 〔常 *pl*.〕附属品,附件。**2.** 〔*pl*.〕所有物;财产;行李。**3.** 〔*pl*.〕〔口〕家属。**4.** 亲密关系。**-ness** ***n***. 有所归属;【心】相属关系。

Be·lo·rus·sia [ˌbjeləˈrʌʃə; ˏbjɛləˋrʌʃə] **I** ***n***. 白俄罗斯。**II** ***n***., ***a***. 白俄罗斯人(的),白俄罗斯(语)的。

be·lov·ed [biˈlʌvd, biˈlʌvid; bɪˋlʌvd, bɪˋlʌvɪd] **I** ***a***. **1.** [biˈlʌvd; bɪˋlʌvd] 被…爱的〔用作述语,与 *by*, *of* 连用〕。**2.** [biˈlʌvid; bɪˋlʌvɪd] 可爱的,亲爱的,被热爱的〔用作修饰语〕。*a ~ child* 爱儿。**II** ***n***. [biˈlʌvd; bɪˋlʌvd] 心爱的人,可爱的人。*My ~* 亲爱的 (= darling). the most ~ 最可爱的人。★本词作为古语 belove 的过去分词,现时只通用被动语态: She was ~ by [of] all who knew her. 凡是认识她的人都喜欢她。She is ~ of [by] John. 约翰喜欢她。

be·low [biˈləu; bəˋlo] **I** ***ad***. **1.** 在下面,向下;在下方。**2.** 在地上,在下界,在人世。**3.** 在地下,在地狱中。**4.** 在楼下;在甲板下,在舱面下,向船室〔*cf*. on deck〕;在下游。**5.** (在)下级。**6.** 在(书的)页末,在下文,列后。**7.** (动物)在下腹部;(舞台)台下。*B- there!* 喂,下面的人注意〔往下抛东西时叫人当心〕! *the vally ~* 下面的山谷。*see ~* 参见下文。*He was demoted to the class ~*. 他被降级。*the place ~* 地狱。*the court ~* 下级法院。**II** ***prep***. **1.** 在…之下。**2.** 低于;劣于。**3.** 在…的下游。**4.** 有失…的身分,无…的价值。**5.** (温度)零下的。*six ~* 零下六度。*next ~ a colonel* 上校之下。*sink ~ the horizon* 沉落到地平面以下。*sell ~ cost* 亏本出售。*~ the average* 平均水平以下。*an action ~ his notice* 不值得他注意的一件事。*It is ~ a lady to do such a thing*. 一位女士做这种事是有失身分的。*He is ~ her in intelligence*. 他知识比她差。**III** ***n***. 下面。*from ~* 从下面。~ ***the mark*** **1.** 在标准以下(的),劣等的。**2.** 身体不好。***down ~*** 地狱中;坟墓中;海底下。***go ~*** 【海】(由舱面)进舱内,下舱;下班。***here ~*** 在地上,在这个世界上。**-decks** ***adv***. 在船内。**-ground** ***a***. **1.** 地下的。**2.** 已经埋葬的。**-stairs** ***adv***., ***a***. 在楼下;在地下室。

belt [belt; bɛlt] **I** ***n***. **1.** 带,皮带;绶带;线条;带状物。**2.** 【机】传动带;【天】云状带;【军】子弹带;腰皮带;单层铁丝网;(战舰)吃水线以下的装甲带;(飞机)保险带。**3.** 〔美〕产区;地带,区域。**4.** 〔美〕环行电车[铁路]线。**5.** 〔美俚〕抽打;〔美俚〕快感,刺激。*a leather ~* 皮带。*a waist ~* 腰带。*a sword ~* 剑带。*the cotton ~* 产棉地带。*a green ~* (都市)绿化区。*the marine ~* 领海。*He caught me a ~ on the ear*. 他用皮带抽了一下我的耳朵。*the Great [little] Belt* (由北海通至波罗的海的)大[小]海峡。*the Black Belt* **1.** 美国南部黑土地带。**2.** 美国南方[城市]黑人多于白人的地区。***hit [strike] below the ~*** 【拳】击对手腰带下部犯规行为;【口】卑劣行为,玩卑鄙手段,暗箭伤人。***hold the ~*** (在拳击等比赛中)夺得锦标。***tighten [pull in] one's ~*** 〔讽〕勒紧肚带,饿着肚皮;含辛茹苦;紧缩开支。***under one's ~*** 〔俚〕**1.** 在肚皮里。**2.** 已有经验。**II** ***vt***. **1.** 在…上系带子。**2.** 用带扎上。**3.** 佩带(剑等)。**4.** 环绕。**5.** 用皮带抽打;〔口〕痛打。**6.** 〔口〕大声唱。**7.** 〔美〕环(状)剥(树皮)。**8.** 喝(酒) (*down*); 狂饮。*~ a sword on* 佩剑。— ***vi***. 急走,快速移动。*~ along the road* 顺路急进。~ ***the ball*** 【美棒球】打,连续打出稳球。~ ***out*** 【美拳】打倒。~ ***up*** 〔口〕〔命令〕住口! 别响! 〔口〕系上座位安全带。~ **bag** 腰包〔系在腰带上的钱包〕。~ **highway** 城市周围的环状公路。~ **line** (电车等的)环行路线。~ **man 1.** 机器修理工。**2.** (游泳池)救生员。

belt·ed [ˈbeltid; ˋbɛltɪd] ***a***. **1.** 束带的,佩绶带的。**2.** 有条纹的。**3.** 装甲的。*a ~ dress* 有绶带的服装。*a ~ cow* 花条母牛。~**-bias tyre** 带束斜交轮胎。

belt·ing [ˈbeltiŋ; ˋbɛltɪŋ] ***n***. **1.** 带料;带布。**2.** 〔集合词〕带,带类;【机】传动带(装置)。**3.** 〔口〕(用皮带等)抽打。*Give him a ~*. 用皮带抽他一顿!

be·lu·ga [bəˈluːgə; bəˋlugə] ***n***. (*pl*. *~(s)*) **1.** 欧洲鳇。**2.** 白鲸。

bel·ve·dere [ˈbelvidiə; ˋbɛlvəˋdɪr] ***n***. 〔It.〕**1.** 【建】望楼,了望塔;亭子。**2.** [the B-] 罗马梵蒂冈宫的绘画馆。

be·ly·ing [biˈlaiiŋ; bɪˋlaɪɪŋ] belie 的现在分词。

B.E.M. = British Empire Medal 不列颠帝国勋章。

be·ma [ˈbiːmə; ˋbimə], ***n***. (*pl*. ***bemata*** [ˈbiːmətə; ˋbimətə], *~s*) **1.** (教堂中高级教士的)高座。**2.** 讲坛。

be·mean [biˈmiːn; bɪˋmin] ***vt***. 〔~ oneself〕使变卑贱 (= demean).

be·mire [biˈmaiə; bɪˋmaɪr] ***vt***. **1.** 被泥弄脏,使沾上泥污。**2.** 使陷泥中。*The muddy road ~d the wagon*. 马车陷入了泥泞的道路。

be·moan [biˈməun; bɪˋmon] ***vt***. **1.** 悲叹,哀悼;惋惜。**2.** 对…不满。— ***vi***. 悲叹,哀悼。*~ one's fate* 悲叹自己的命运。

be·mock [biˈmɔk; bɪˋmɑk] ***vt***. 嘲弄,讥笑。

be·muse [biˈmjuːz; bɪˋmjuz] ***vt***. **1.** 使迷迷糊糊,使昏头昏脑;使发呆。**2.** 使着迷〔多用被动语态〕。*be ~d with drink* 喝酒喝得昏昏沉沉。

Ben [ben; bɛn] ***n***. 本〔男子名, Benjamin 的昵称〕。

ben[1] [ben; bɛn] ***n***. 〔Scot., Ir.〕…峰。***Ben-Nevis*** (英国最高的)尼维思峰。

ben[2] [ben; bɛn] **I** ***n***. 〔Scot.〕(相连二室的)内室。**II** ***a***., ***ad***. 在内部,在里面。*but and ~* 外室和内室。***be but***

B

and* ~ *with 与…有亲密关系。***far* ~** 在最里面一间；〔喻〕(和)…特别亲密(*with*).

ben·act·y·zine [bəˈnæktizi:n; bəˋnæktɪzin] ***n***.【药】苯乃静，胃复康〔治精神病的一种镇定剂〕。

be·name [biˈneim; bɪˋnem] ***vt***. (***-named***, ***-nempt*** [-ˈnempt; -ˋnɛmpt], ***-nempted*** [-ˈnemptid; -ˋnɛmptɪd]; ***-nam·ing***)〔古〕取名；叫做。

bench [bentʃ; bɛntʃ] **I *n***. **1**. 长凳，条凳。**2**. 船上的坐板；座，架，(木工、钳工等的)工作台；【矿】(煤矿的)台阶，(矿的)梯段；【地】阶地；【园艺】(温室中的)苗床；【机】拉丝机。**3**. (动物展览会的)陈列台；〔美〕畜犬展览会。**4**. 法院；法官席；列席法官；(英议院的)议席；(运动员的)特别席，选手席，队员席；场外的全体候补队员。**5**.【宗】主教。*a park* ~ 公园长凳。*an experimental* ~ 试验架。*a carpenter's* ~ 木工工作台。*front ~es* (英议会)政党领袖席，大臣席。*back ~es* (下院后座)一般议员席。*ministerial ~es* (议长右侧前方)政府部员席。*the Treasury* ~ 财政大臣席。*A weak* ~ *hurt their chances for championship*. 他们因后备运动员力量不足而妨碍了夺魁。***be raised to the* ~** 被任命为法官[主教]。**~ *and bar*** 法官和律师。***on the* ~ 1**. 做法官[主教]。**2**. (运动员)作为候补选手。***sit on the Penniless B-***. 一文不名，一贫如洗。***take a seat on the* ~** 当法官[主教]。***the free* ~** (英国法律上的)寡妇财产权。***the King's* [*Queen's*] *Bench*** 〔英〕高等法院。***the Upper Bench***【英史】皇家高等法院。**II *vt***. **1**. 在…安置凳子；使坐凳子上。**2**. 使坐席位；使坐名誉席。**3**. (把狗等)摆上台展览。**4**.【体】使(比赛员)退场，把(队员)调下来。**5**.【矿】从下面掘(煤层)。— ***vi***. **1**.【地】形成台地。**~board**【无】控制盘，台式配电器。**~ jockey** 喝对方倒采的运动员。**~ land** 滩池，沙洲。**~ lathe** 台式车床。**~-made *a***. 手工制的；定做的。**~man** 收音机[电视机]修理工。**~ mark 1**.【测】水准点。**2**. 标准；规范。**3**.【计】标准检查程序。**~ scientist** 实验(室)科学家。**~ show**〔美〕畜犬[家猫]展览会。**~ warmer** 候补席上的运动员。**~ warrant** 法院传票，逮捕证。**~ worker** 钳(床)工(人)。

bench·ed [bentʃt; bɛntʃt] ***a***.【美棒球】被调换下来的。

bench·er [ˈbentʃə; ˋbɛntʃɚ] ***n***. **1**. 坐凳子的人。**2**. 英国律师协会的主管委员。**3**. (小艇的)划手。**4**. 〔俚〕欢喜坐酒馆的人。

Bench·ley [ˈbentʃli; ˋbɛntʃlɪ] ***n***. 本奇利〔姓氏〕。

bend[1] [bend; bɛnd] **I *vt***. (***bent*** [bent; bɛnt], 〔古〕***~ed***; ***bent***, 〔古〕***~ed***) **1**. 弄弯，使弯曲，拗弯(棍子等)；屈(膝)；弯(弓)。**2**. 使屈服，压服。**3**. 热衷于，集中思想于。**4**. (耳、目等)转向；使(脚步等)改变方向。**5**.【海】系(绳索、帆等)。~ *a iron rod into a hoop* 把铁条弯成箍。~ *a crooked thing straight* 把弯曲的东西扳直。~ *the* (*one's*) *brows* 皱眉。*~ing strength* 抗弯强度。~ *one's knees* 屈膝(行礼)；跪。~ *the neck* 低头；屈服。~ *one's will* 使自己的意志屈从于他人。~ *sb. to one's will* 使别人屈从自己的意志。~ *one's eyes* [*gaze*] *on it* 把眼睛转向它。~ *one's way* [*steps*] *homeward* 往家里走。~ *one's energies to an end* 全力以赴地实现某个目的。~ *the cable* 把锚链系在锚环上。— ***vi***. **1**. 弯曲；转向；屈身。**2**. 服从，屈服。**3**. 倾注，集中力量于(*to*). *a bow that ~s easily* 一张易弯的弓。~ *down* 弯下身来。~ *to the east* [*left*] 向东(左)转。~ *toward the south* 向南转。*He will not* ~. 他断然不屈，不妥协。***be bent on*** 尽想，一心要(*He is bent on mischief*. 他尽想坏主意，他一心要捣蛋)。**~ *one's efforts for*** 致力，为…贡献力量。**~ *one's mind to* [*on*, *upon*]** 一心向，专心致志于。~ *oneself to* 竭力要，致力于。**~ *over* 1**. 弯腰，身子贴近，伏在…上(~ *over and pick up a thing* 弯下身子拾起一件东西。~ *over desk* 伏案工作)。**~ *over backward*(*s*)** (*to do sth.*)〔贬〕拼命(做某事)。**~ *to* 1**. 为…所屈；顺从(~ *to circumstances* 适应环境。~ *to fate* 屈服于命运)。**2**. 专心，用全力(~ *to the oars* 拼命划桨)。**II *n***. **1**. 曲，弯曲；弯曲部，曲处。**2**. 弯管，接头；可曲波导管。**3**. (心的)归向，倾向；屈服。**4**. [the ~s]〔口〕沉箱病，潜函病；〔美口〕航空病。**5**.【海】结索(法)；索结。**6**.〔*pl*.〕(木船的)外条板。**7**.【美军】特约酒馆。***above one's* ~**〔美〕为…力所不及的，是…办不了的。***Get a* ~ *on you*!**〔卑〕快点！加油！***go on the* [*a*] ~**〔美口〕狂欢，闹饮。***on the* ~** 用不法手段，用不正当的办法。***round the* ~**〔英口〕发狂，发昏。

bend[2] [bend; bɛnd] ***n***. **1**.【徽】(盾上自右上至左下的)右斜线。**2**.〔*pl*.〕(妇女)头带。**3**. 皮革的左[右]半张整皮。~ ***sinister***【徽】左斜线〔私生子的标志〕。

bend·ed [ˈbendid; ˋbɛndɪd] ***a***. **1**. 弯着的，弯曲的。**2**. 热心的。***on* [*upon*, *with*] ~ *knees*** 跪着；苦苦地。***with* ~ *bow***〔书〕拉满弓。

bend·er [ˈbendə; ˋbɛndɚ] ***n***. **1**. 弯曲者，弯曲物；【机】折弯机。**2**.〔英俚〕六便士银币；〔美俚〕狂饮；〔Scot.〕酒量大的人。**3**.【棒球】曲球；〔英方〕美妙的东西；〔美口〕两腿。*a* ~ *of a night* 美妙的一晚。

Ben·dix [ˈbendiks; ˋbɛndɪks] ***n***.〔美口〕洗濯器。

Ben·dy [ˈbendi; ˋbɛndɪ] ***n***.【植】秋葵

bene- *comb. f*. = well (*opp*. male-): *bene*diction, *bene*factor.

be·neath [biˈni:θ; bɪˋniθ] **I *prep***. **1**. 〔诗、古、书〕在…之下，低于；在…的(正)下方；在…脚下，在(或紧挨着)…的底下〔通常用 below, under〕。**2**. 不值得，不足取；有失…的身分，有损于(尊严等)，不称，不配；劣于，比…不如。*live* ~ *the same roof* 同住一屋。*the first drawer* ~ *the top one* 顶档以下的第一个抽屉。~ *attention* 不值得注意。~ *contempt* 不齿，极可鄙。*It would be* ~ *him to cheat*. 他去行骗未免有失身分。*marry* ~ *one* 和身分比自己低的人结婚。*be far* ~ (*sb*.) *in* (*attainments*) (造诣)远较(某人)为低。~ *one's breath* 低声。~ *one's dignity* 有损威严，不合身分。**II *ad***. **1**. 在下，在下面，在下方，在下位。**2**. 在地下。*The valley lay* ~. 山谷就在下面。*the heaven above and the earth* ~. 天上和地下。

Be·ne·di·ci·te [ˌbeniˈdaisiti; ˏbɛnəˋdɪsətɪ] **I *n***.【新教】万物颂(乐曲)；[b-] 饭前祷告。**II *int***. 天哪！我的天哪！

ben·e·dick [ˈbenidik; ˋbɛnəˏdɪk] ***n***. = benedict.

ben·e·dict [ˈbenidikt; ˋbɛnəˏdɪkt] ***n***. (放弃多年独身主义而结婚的)新郎〔出自莎士比亚的喜剧《无事烦恼》〕。

Ben·e·dict [ˈbenidikt; ˋbɛnəˏdɪkt] ***n***. 本尼迪克特〔姓氏，男子名〕。

Ben·e·dic·tine [ˌbeniˈdiktain; ˏbɛnəˋdɪktɪn] **I *a***. (五世纪意大利名僧)圣本尼迪克特(St. Benedict)的；本尼迪克特教团的。**II *n***. **1**. 本尼迪克特教团的僧侣。**2**. [b-] [ˌbeniˈdikti:n; ˏbɛnəˋdɪktin] (本尼迪克特教团僧侣所酿造的)法国费康(Fécamp)产的一种甜酒。

ben·e·dic·tion [ˌbeniˈdikʃən; ˏbɛnəˋdɪkʃən] ***n***. **1**.【基督】祝福，礼拜末尾的祝祷；(餐前餐后的)谢恩祷。**2**.【天主】(圣体)祝福式。**3**. 祈福，天恩。*give the* ~ 举行祝福式。**-al**, **-dic·tive**, **-dic·to·ry *a***. 祈福的，祝福的。

ben·e·fac·tion [ˌbeniˈfækʃən; ˏbɛnəˋfækʃən] ***n***. **1**. 慈善，慈善行为。**2**. 捐助，施舍；捐助物，捐款。*He is known for his many ~s*. 他以做了许多善事知名。*solicit ~s for earthquake victims* 为地震区灾民募捐。

ben·e·fac·tor [ˈbenifæktə; ˋbɛnəˏfæktɚ] ***n***. (*fem*. ***-tress*** [ˈbenifæktris; ˋbɛnəfæktris]) 恩人；保护人；捐助人。

be·nef·ic [biˈnefik; bəˋnɛfɪk] ***a***. 慈善的，行善的，仁慈的；仁爱的。

ben·e·fice [ˈbenifis; ˋbɛnəfɪs] **I *n***. **1**. 教士的有俸圣职；教区牧师享有的教产。**2**. 封地，采邑。**II *vt***. 使获得有俸圣职。

be·nef·i·cence [biˈnefisəns; bəˋnɛfəsns] ***n***. **1**. 慈善；善

行。2. 施舍物,捐款;救济品。*bestow many ~s* 捐赠许多救济品。

be·nef·i·cent [bi'nefisənt; bə`nɛfəsnt] *a*. 慈善的,行善的,仁慈的;仁爱的。*exert a ~ influence on* 施恩泽于。**-ly** *ad*.

ben·e·fi·cial [ˌbeni'fiʃəl; ˏbɛnə`fɪʃəl] *a*. 有利的,有益的,(*to*)(*opp*. injurious);【法】可享受利益的,有收入权益的。~ *birds* [*insects*] 益鸟[虫]。*a ~ association* 互助组合。**a ~ legacy** 一笔仅有收入权益的遗产〔可享受其收入,但无所有权和处理权〕。

ben·e·fi·ci·a·ry [ˌbeni'fiʃəri; ˏbɛnə`fɪʃərɪ] **I** *a*. (封建制度下)受封的;采邑的;臣服的。**II** *n*. 1. (遗嘱、保险等的)受益人;(退休金等的)领受人;〔美〕公费生;【邮】(国际汇兑的)收款人。2. 〔原义〕封臣。3. 受俸牧师。

ben·e·fit ['benifit; `bɛnəfɪt] **I** *n*. 1. 利益,好处;利润。2. 恩惠,恩泽;恩典,特典。3. (为赈灾等举行的)义演,义赛。4. 退休金;(依照社会保险付给的)津贴,救济金,抚恤金。5. 〔俚、反〕好机会,好差事。*a public ~* 公益。*for your special ~* 特为你(利益)打算。*a ~-match* 义赛。*a ~-night* 义演晚会。*medical* [*maternity*] *~s* 医疗[产妇]津贴。*I had no end of a ~ getting things straight*. 我那收拾东西的好差事没完没了。~ *of clergy* 牧师的特权;(结婚时)教会的证明。~ *society* [*club*] 共济会,互济会。***be of ~*** 有益,裨益。***for sb.'s ~ = for the ~ of*** 为…(利益)打算;〔反〕为惩戒…(*Was he doing that for my ~?* 他那样做是为我好吗? *He wasn't really angry, that was just an act for his girl friend's ~*. 他不是真生气,那是为了治治他那女朋友的)。***give* (*sb.*) *the ~ of the doubt*** 对(某人的过错等)作善意解释,(在证据不足的情况下)假定某人无辜,给(某人)"虽可疑但无罪"的处理。**II** *vt*. (*-t*(*t*)*-*) 对…有利,有益于…;使得利益。*a health program to ~ all mankind* 一项有益于全人类的卫生计划。— *vi*. 得益,受益(*by*; *from*)。*a person who has never ~ed from experience* 一个从不吸取经验教训的人。~ **society** 互济会,互助会。

Be·ne·lux ['benilʌks; `bɛnəlʌks] *n*. 比(利时)、荷(兰)卢(森堡)经济联盟。*the ~ countries* 比、荷、卢三国。

be·nempt [bi'nempt; bɪ`nɛmpt] 〔古〕 bename 的过去分词(= benempted)。

Be·nét [be'nei; bɛ`ne] *n*. 贝内〔姓氏〕。

be·nev·o·lence [bi'nevələns; bɪ`nɛvələns] *n*. 1. 仁爱,亲切;厚道,慈善。2. 善行,捐款;捐助。3. 【英史】(英国国王征收的)王税。

be·nev·o·lent [bi'nevələnt; bə`nɛvələnt] *a*. 1. 仁爱的,仁慈的。2. 乐善好施的,慈善的。3. 亲切的,善意的 *the ~ art* 仁术,医术。*her ~ smile* 她那亲切的微笑。**-ly** *ad*.

Ben·gal [beŋ'gɔːl; bɛŋ`gɔl] *n*. 1. 孟加拉〔亚洲〕。2. 孟加拉生丝(织品)。***Bay of ~*** 孟加拉湾。~ **light** [**fire**] 信号烟火。~ **stripes** 条花棉布。

Ben·ga·lee, Ben·ga·lese [beŋgə'liː, -z; ˏbɛŋgə`li, -z], **Ben·gal·i** [beŋ'gɔːli; bɛŋ`gɔlɪ] **I** *a*. 孟加拉的;孟加拉人的;孟加拉语的。**II** *n*. 〔*sing*., *pl*.〕 孟加拉人;孟加拉语。

ben·ga·line ['beŋgəliːn; `bɛŋgəˏlɪn] *n*. 【纺】罗缎。

Ben·ge [bendʒ; bɛndʒ] *n*. 本奇〔姓氏〕。

Ben·g(h)a·zi, Ben·g(h)a·si [beŋ'gɑːzi; bɛŋ`gɑzɪ] *n*. 班加西〔利比亚港市〕。

be·night·ed [bi'naitid; bɪ`naɪtɪd] *a*. 1. (旅客等)走到天黑的,赶路到黑的。2. 愚昧的,蒙昧的,无知的。*a ~ traveler* 赶路到天黑的旅客。~ *ages of barbarism and superstition* 野蛮迷信的蒙昧时代。

be·nign [bi'nain; bɪ`naɪn] *a*. 1. 仁慈的,宽厚的;亲切的;温和的。2. (气候等)温和的,良好的,有益于健康的。3. 吉祥的(*opp*. sinister)。4. 【医】良性的(*opp*. malignant)。~ *rule* 仁政。*a ~ climate* 温和的气候。*a ~ tumor* 良性瘤。**-ly** *ad*.

be·nig·nan·cy [bi'nignənsi; bɪ`nɪgnənsɪ] *n*. 1. 仁慈,亲切;(气候)温和。2. 【医】良性。

be·nig·nant [bi'nignənt; bɪ`nɪgnənt] *a*. 1. 仁慈的,亲切的;宽厚的。2. (气候)温和的;【医】良性的。

be·nig·ni·ty [bi'nigniti; bɪ`nɪgnətɪ] *n*. 1. 宽厚,亲切,仁慈。2. (气候)温和。3. 善行。*benignities born of selfless devotion* 由无私的献身精神产生的宽厚胸怀。

Be·nin [bə'nin; bə`nɪn] *n*. 贝宁〔非洲〕。

ben·i·son ['benizn; `bɛnɪzn] *n*. 〔古〕祝福(*opp*. malison);神恩。

Ben·ja·min ['bendʒəmin; `bɛndʒəmən] *n*. 1. 班杰明〔男子名,希伯来语源,意为"幸运儿"。爱称 Ben, Benjie, Bennie〕。2. 【圣】卞雅悯〔雅各的末子〕;〔喻〕老儿子,爱子,宠儿。3. 〔b-〕〔美俚〕男紧身大衣。~***'s mess*** (分东西时)特多的一份,头一份。

ben·ja·min = benzoin.

ben·(n)e ['beni; `bɛnɪ] *n*. 芝麻;芝麻籽,胡麻(= sesame)。

Ben·nett ['benit; `bɛnɪt] *n*. 贝内特〔姓氏,男子名,Benedict 的异体〕。

ben·nies ['beniz; `bɛnɪz] *n*. 〔美俚〕= Benny.

Ben·ny, Ben·nie ['beni; `bɛnɪ] *n*. 本尼〔男子名,Benjamin 的昵称〕。

ben·ny ['beni; `bɛnɪ] *n*. (*pl*. *-nies*) 〔美俚〕安非他明药片(= Benzendrine)。

Ben·son ['bensn; `bɛnsn] *n*. 本森〔姓氏〕。

bent[1] [bent; bɛnt] bend 的过去式及过去分词。**I** *a*. 1. 弯,弯曲的。2. 决心的;专心的。3. 〔口〕偷来的,有偷癖的。4. 〔口〕同性爱的。5. 〔美俚〕喝醉的。*be ~ double with age* 年老背驼。***be ~ on*** [***upon***] 决心要;专想,一心要(*be ~ on buying a new car* 决心要买一辆新车。*be ~ on mischief* [*gain*] 专想捉弄人[赚钱]。*be ~ over one's work* 专心工作)。**II** *n*. 1. 弯,曲,弯曲处。2. 倾向,嗜好,癖性,性格。3. 能力;耐力。4. 【机】弯头,曲轴;【建】桥脚;脚柱;框架结构。*square ~* (水管的)直角弯头。*a young man with a literary ~* 爱好文学的青年。*She has a natural ~ for painting* 她生性爱绘画。***follow one's ~*** 随心所好,凭爱好办事。***to the top of one's ~*** 尽量;尽力;尽情地。~**wing** 后掠机翼,后掠翼飞机。

bent[2] [bent; bɛnt] *n*. 1. 【植】小糠草;深山糠草;苇草;(同上草类的)枯茎,枯草。2. 〔Scot.〕(小糠草等繁生的)荒草地〔作为牧场、狩猎场等〕;荒野;沼泽地。

Ben·tham ['bentəm, 'benθəm; `bɛntəm, `bɛnθəm] *n*. 1. 本瑟姆(边沁)〔姓氏〕。2. **Jeremy ~** 杰·边沁〔1748—1832,英国法学家及哲学家〕。

Ben·tham·ism ['bentəmizəm; `bɛnθəmɪzm] *n*. 功利主义,多数幸福说〔边沁鼓吹的一种伦理学说〕。

Ben·tham·ite ['bentəmait; `bɛntəmˏaɪt] *n*. 功利主义者;边沁主义者。

ben·thic ['benθik; `bɛnθɪk], **ben·thal** ['benθəl; `bɛnθəl] *a*. 关于[发生于]水底[海底]的。

ben·thon ['benθɔn; `bɛnθɑn] *n*. 【生】生活于水底部分的生物。

ben·thos ['benθɔs; `bɛnθɑs] *n*. 1. (深海)海底,湖底。2. 海底生物,水底生物。

ben·tho·scope ['benθəskəup; `bɛnθəˏskop] *n*. (研究海底生物用的)球形深海潜水器。

Ben·ton ['bentən; `bɛntən] *n*. 本顿〔姓氏,男子名〕。

ben·ton·ite ['bentəˌnait; `bɛntənˏaɪt] *n*. 【矿】膨润土,皂土,膨土岩,班脱岩。

bent·wood ['bentˌwud; `bɛntˏwʊd] **I** *a*. 弯成木的〔指用弯成木做的家具〕。**II** *n*. (做家具用的)弯成木。*a ~ chair* 弯木椅。

be·numb [bi'nʌm; bɪ`nʌm] *vt*. 1. 使失去感觉,使麻木。2. 使麻痹,使瘫痪,使僵化。*be ~ed with* [*by*] *cold* 冻

麻木,冻僵。～ *the intellectual faculties* 失去智能,变呆。**-ed** *a*. 1. 失去感觉的,麻痹了的;冻僵的。2. 吓呆了的。

ben·zal·de·hyde [ben'zældiˌhaid; bɛn`zældəˏhaɪd] *n*. 【化】苯甲醛。

Ben·ze·drine ['benzidri(:)n; `bɛnzɪˏdrɪn] *n*. 【药】苯齐巨林〔amphetamine (安非他明,苯异丙胺)的商品名〕。

ben·zene ['benziːn, ben'ziːn; `bɛnzin, bɛn`zin] *n*. 【化】1. 苯。2. = benzine. *methyl* ～ 甲苯。*ethyl* ～ 乙苯。

ben·zi·dine ['benziˌdiːn; `bɛnzədin] *n*. 【化】联苯胺。

ben·zine ['benziːn; `bɛnzin], **ben·zin** ['benzin; `bɛnzɪn] *n*. 【化】挥发油;〔澳〕汽油。

benzo- *comb. f*. 【化】与苯有关的;安息香的。

ben·zo·ate ['benzəuˌeit; `bɛnzoɪt] *n*. 【化】苯(甲)酸盐〔酯〕。

ben·zo·caine ['benzəˌkein, -zəu-; `bɛnzəˏken, -zo-] *n*. 【化】苯坐卡因,对氨基苯酸乙酯。

ben·zo·ic [ben'zəuik; bɛn`zoɪk] *a*. 安息香的。～ **acid** 安息香酸,苯(甲)酸。

ben·zo·in ['benzəuin; `bɛnzoɪn] *n*. 【化】1. 苯偶姻;二苯乙醇酮。2. 安息香。

ben·zol ['benzɔl; `bɛnzol] *n*. 【化】1. = benzene. 2. (工业用)粗制苯。

ben·zol·ine ['benzəliːn; `bɛnzəˏlin] *n*. = benzine.

ben·zo·phe·none [ˌbenzəufi'nəun, -'fiːnəun; ˏbɛnzofi`non, -`finon] *n*. 【化】二苯甲酮,苯酮,苯酰苯。

ben·zo·py·rene [ˌbenzəu'pairiːn; ˏbɛnzo`paɪrin] *n*. 【化】苯并芘 (= benzpyrene)。

ben·zo·sul·fi·mide ['benzəu'sʌlfimaid; `bɛnzo`sʌlfɪmaɪd] *n*. 【化】糖精 (= saccharin)。

ben·zo·yl ['benzəuil; `bɛnzoɪl] *n*. 【化】苯(甲)酰;苯甲酰。

ben·zyl ['benzil; `bɛnzɪl] *n*. 【化】苄基,苯甲基。

Be·o·wulf ['beiəwulf; `beəˏwulf] *n*. 1.《贝奥伍尔夫》〔英国 8 世纪古代史诗〕。2. 贝奥伍尔夫〔上述史诗中的主人翁〕。

be·plas·ter [bi'plɑːstə; bɪ`plɑstɚ] *vt*. 在…上厚厚地涂;覆满,布满。～ *one's face with cosmetics* 把脸厚厚涂上一层脂粉,浓装艳抹。*a coat* ～*ed with medals* 挂满勋章的上衣。

be·pow·der [bi'paudə; bɪ`paudɚ] *vt*. 用粉撒上;在…上搽厚香粉。

beqt. = bequest.

be·queath [bi'kwiːð; bɪ`kwið] *vt*. 把…遗留给,把…传给(后代);【法】遗赠(动产)。～ *a large sum of money to one's daughter* 遗留一大笔钱给女儿。*a sword* ～*ed to the family by their forefathers* 祖传宝剑。**-ment, -al** *n*. 遗赠;遗产,遗物。**-er** 遗赠者。

be·quest [bi'kwest; bɪ`kwɛst] *n*. 1.【法】(动产)遗赠。2. 遗产,遗物;让与物。*He left* ～*s of money to all his friends*. 他给所有的朋友都遗赠了一些钱。

Be·rat [be'rɑːt; bɛ`rɑt] *n*. 培拉特〔阿尔巴尼亚城市〕。

be·rate [bɪ'reit; bɪ`ret] *vt*. 〔美〕责骂,训斥。

Ber·ber ['bəːbə; `bɝbɚ] **I** *n*. 1. (北非)柏柏尔人。2. 柏柏尔语。**II** *a*. 1. 柏柏尔人的。2. 柏柏尔语〔文化〕的。

Ber·ber·a ['bəːbərə; `bɝbərə] *n*. 伯贝拉〔索马里港市〕。

ber·ceuse [bεə'səːz; bɛr`sɝz] *n*. 〔F.〕【音】摇篮曲;音调柔和的乐曲。

be·reave [bi'riːv; bə`riv] *vt*. (～*d*, ***be·reft*** [bi'reft; bɪ`rɛft]; ***-reav·ing***) 1. 使丧失(家属等)〔过去式和过去分词一般用 ～d〕。2. 使失去(希望、理智等)〔过去式和过去分词一般用 bereft〕。*Illness* ～*d her of her son*. 她死了孩子。*a man bereft of sense* [*reason*] 疯子。*Indignation bereft him of speech*. 他愤怒得说不出话来。**-ment** *n*. (亲人等的)丧失,死别,丧亲之痛,居丧。

be·reaved [bi'riːvd; bə`rivd] *a*. 死了…的,丧…的;丧亡了家族的。*the* ～ 遗族,孤儿。*the* ～ *family* 遗族。***be*** ～ ***of*** (*one's husband*; *wife*) 丧(夫),丧(妻)。

be·reft [bi'reft; bɪ`rɛft] *a*. 被夺去,失去。*He is utterly* ～. 他全完了。***be*** ～ ***of*** (*hope*; *reason*) 失(望);失去(理智),发狂。

be·ret ['berei; `bɛre] *n*. 〔F.〕贝雷帽,荷叶帽,圆扁便帽;【英军】军帽。***the Green Berets*** 〔美〕特种部队〔戴绿色贝雷帽〕。

berg[1] [bəːg; bɝg] *n*. 大冰块,冰山〔iceberg 的缩略语〕。

berg[2] [bəːg; bɝg] *n*. 〔南非〕山。

ber·ga·mot ['bəːgəmɔt; `bɝgəˏmɑt] *n*. 1.【植】佛手柑;香柠檬。2. 佛手柑油,香柠檬油。3.【植】一种香梨。4. (意大利人 Bergamo 创制的)花毡。

Ber·gen ['bəːgən; `bɝgən] *n*. 卑尔根〔挪威港市〕。

Ber·ger ['bəːdʒə; `bɝdʒɚ] *n*. 伯杰〔姓氏〕。

ber·gère, ber·gere [bεə'ʒεə; bɛr`ʒɛr] *n*. 围手椅〔尤指 18 世纪法国式藤条椅子〕。

berg·mehl ['bəːgmeil; `bɝgmel] *n*. 矽藻土。

berg·schrund ['bεəgʃrund; `bɛrgʃrund] *n*. 〔G.〕【地】冰河上端的龟裂,悬岩与冰河间的罅隙。

Berg·son ['bəːgsən; `bɝgsn̩], **Henri** 柏格森〔1859—1941,法国哲学家〕。

Berg·so·ni·an [bəːg'səunjən; bɝg`sonɪən] **I** *a*. 柏格森(哲学)的。**II** *n*. 柏格森派。

Berg·son·ism ['bəːgsənizəm; `bɝgsnɪzəm] *n*. 柏格森哲学。

berg·y ['bəːgi; `bɝgɪ] *a*. 多冰山的,多大冰块的。

be·rhyme, be·rime [bi'raim; bɪ`raɪm] *vt*. 作诗颂扬;作诗讽刺。

ber·i·ber·i ['beri'beri; `bɛrɪ`bɛrɪ] *n*. 【医】脚气(病)。

Be·ring ['beriŋ; `bɛrɪŋ] *n*. 白令〔1680—1741,丹麦航海家〕。～ **Sea** 白令海。～ **Strait** 白令海峡。～ **time** 白令时间。

Berke·lei·an ['bɑːkli(:)ən; `bɝklɪən] **I** *n*. 【哲】贝克莱(主义)的。**II** *n*. 贝克莱主义者。**-ism** *n*. 贝克莱主义。

Berke·ley[1] [bɑːkli, 'bəːkli; `bɑrklɪ, `bɝklɪ] *n*. 1. 伯克利〔姓氏〕(贝克莱)。2. **George** ～ 贝克莱〔1685—1753,爱尔兰主教及哲学家〕。

Berke·ley[2] ['bəːkli; `bɝklɪ] *n*. 伯克利〔美国港市〕。

ber·ke·li·um ['bəːkliəm; bɝ`kɪlɪəm] *n*. 【化】锫〔人工放射性金属元素,略作 Bk〕。

Berks. = Berkshire.

Berk·shire ['bɑːkʃiə; `bɑrkʃɪr] *n*. 巴克夏〔英格兰南部郡名〕;巴克夏猪。

Ber·lin [bəː'lin; bɝ`lɪn] *n*. 柏林。～ **black** [**varnish**] 耐热漆。～ **blue** 柏林蓝,普鲁士蓝。～ **gloves** 毛线手套。～ **warehouse** 毛线商店。～ **wool** 细毛线。**-er** 柏林人,柏林居民。

ber·lin [bəː'lin; bɝ`lɪn] *n*. 1. 二人乘四轮轿式马车。2. 高级细绒线 (= Berlin wool)。

berm(e) [bəːm; bɝm] *n*. 【建】(城墙与外壕间的)狭道;〔美〕(马路两边的)边道,便道;小搁板。

Ber·mu·da(s) [bə(:)'mjuːdə(z); bɚ`mjudə(z)] *n*. 百慕大(百慕达)(群岛) (= the Bermuda Islands)〔大西洋西北部〕。～ **grass** 鸭茅。～ **Triangle** 百慕大神秘三角〔百慕大群岛、弗罗里达和波多黎各之间的三角形地区,许多船只、飞机均曾神秘地于该地区失踪〕。

Ber·na·dette [ˌbəːnə'det; ˏbɝnə`dɛt] *n*. 伯纳黛特〔女子名〕。

Ber·na·dine ['bəːnədiːn; `bɝnəˏdin] *n*. 伯纳丁〔女子名〕。

Ber·nal ['bəːnəl; `bɝnəl] *n*. 伯纳尔〔姓氏〕。

Ber·nard [bəː'nɑːd, 'bəːnəd; bɚ`nɑrd, `bɝnɚd] *n*. 1. 伯纳德〔姓氏〕。2. ['bəːnəd; `bɝnɚd] 伯纳德〔男子名〕。

Bern(e) [bəːn, bεən; bɝn, bɛrn] *n*. 伯尔尼〔瑞士首都〕。

Ber·nese [bəː'niːz; bɝ`niz] **I** *a*. (瑞士首都)伯尔尼的。**II** *n*. 〔*sing*., *pl*.〕伯尔尼人。

Ber·nice [ˈbəːnis, bəːˈniːs; ˋbɚnɪs, bɚˋnis] ***n*.** **1.** 伯尼斯〔姓氏〕。**2.** [ˈbəːnis; ˋbɚnɪs] 伯妮斯〔女子名〕。

Ber·nie [ˈbəːni; ˋbɚnɪ] ***n*.** 伯尼〔男子名, Bernard 的昵称〕。

Bern·stein [ˈbəːnstain; ˏbɛrnˋsten] ***n*.** 伯恩斯坦〔姓氏〕。

be(r)·ret·ta [biˈretə; bɪˋretə] ***n*.** 【天主】四角帽, 法冠 (= biretta)。

ber·ried [ˈberid; ˋbɛrɪd] ***a*.** **1.** 有浆果的。**2.** (虾等)有卵的。

ber·ry [ˈberi; ˋbɛrɪ] **I *n*.** **1.** 浆果〔如草莓等〕。**2.** (咖啡等的)子, 干种子, 干果仁。**3.** (鱼等的)子, 卵。**4.** 〔美俚〕一块钱〔*pl*.〕〔美俚〕钱, 上等东西。*lobsters and shrimps in* ~ 正在产子的龙虾和小虾。*barley berries* 大麦粒。*Coffee berries* 咖啡豆。*holy berries* 冬青果。*It's the berries*. 这个好极了。**II *vi*.** **1.** 结出浆果。**2.** 采集浆果。*go ~ing* 去采集浆果。*~ing shrubs* 结浆果的灌木。

ber·sa·glie·re [ˌbeəsɑːliˈɛəri(ː); ˏbɛrsəlˋjɛrɪ] ***n*.** (*pl*. ***-ri*** [-riː; -ri]) 〔It.〕【军】狙击兵。

ber·seem [bəˈsiːm; bəˋsim] ***n*.** 【植】埃及车轴草, 亚历山大车轴草。

ber·serk [bə(ː)ˈsəːk; ˋbɚˋsɚk] **I *n*.** = berserker. **II *a*.** 狂暴的。*with* ~ *fury* 狂怒。*go* ~ 变狂暴。

ber·serk·er [bə(ː)ˈsəːkə; ˋbɚˋsɚkɚ] ***n*.** (北欧传说中战前喜饮酒的)狂暴战士; 暴汉; 流寇。

Bert, Burt [bəːt; bɚt] ***n*.** 伯特〔男子名, Albert, Bertram, Herbert 的昵称〕。

berth [bəːθ; bɚθ] **I *n*.** **1.** (车、船等的)卧铺。**2.** 投锚处, 停泊地; 船台。**3.** (轮船上的)住舱; 住处。**4.** 〔英〕职位, 地位; 〔美〕队形, 球员位置。**5.** (船与沙滩等之间留出的)安全距离。*a foul* ~ (常易撞碰他船的)不好的停泊地。*plenty room for ten ~s* 可停 10 条船而绰绰有余。*The ship shifted its* ~. 船转移了停泊地。*find a snug* ~ 找个轻松愉快的工作。~ ***list*** 舱位分配表。***give a wide ~ to = keep a wide ~ of*** **1.** 远远离开…抛锚。**2.** 避开[躲开](某人)。***on the*** ~ 停泊待货的船。***take up a*** ~ 抛锚, 停泊。**II *vt*.** **1.** 使停泊, 开到抛锚处。**2.** 为…提供卧铺; (车库等)容纳。**3.** 使就职。~ *a plane in the hangar* 让一架飞机停进机库。— ***vi*.** **1.** 停泊。**2.** 占铺位。*The ship effortlessly ~ed*. 那条船顺利停泊。~ *beside one's father* 在父亲旁边的铺位就寝。

Ber·tha [ˈbəːθə; ˋbɚθə] ***n*.** 伯莎〔女子名〕。

ber·tha, berthe [ˈbəːθə, bəːθ; ˋbɚθə, bɚθ] ***n*.** (妇女服装上披肩状的)花边领。

berth·age [ˈbəːθidʒ; ˋbɚθɪdʒ] ***n*.** **1.** 停泊处, 泊位。**2.** 停泊税, 泊费。

Ber·tie [ˈbɑːti, ˈbəːti; ˋbɑrtɪ, ˋbɚtɪ] ***n*.** 伯蒂〔姓氏, Albert, Bertram, Bertha, Robbert 的昵称〕。

Ber·til·lon system [ˈbəːtilɔn; ˋbɚtɪlˏɑn] (通过指纹肤色等侦察犯罪的)柏提永氏人体测验法〔法国人类学者 A. ~(1853—1914)发明〕。

Ber·tram [ˈbəːtrəm; ˋbɚtrəm] ***n*.** 伯特伦〔男子名〕。

Ber·ty = Bertie.

Ber·yl [ˈberil; ˋbɛrɪl] ***n*.** 贝丽尔〔女子名〕。

ber·yl [ˈberil; ˋbɛrɪl] ***n*.** **1.** 【矿】绿柱石, 绿玉。**2.** 海绿色。

be·ryl·li·o·sis [bəˌriliˈəusis; bəˏrɪlɪˋosɪs] ***n*.** 【医】铍中毒。

be·ryl·li·um [bəˈriljəm; bəˋrɪlɪəm] ***n*.** 【化】铍〔别名 glucin(i)um〕。

Ber·ze·li·us [bəˈziːliəs; bɚˋzilɪəs] J. 伯泽列厄斯〔1779—1848, 瑞典化学家, 化学符号创制人〕。

B.E.S.A. = British Engineering Standards Association 〔旧〕英国工程标准协会。

be·seech [biˈsiːtʃ; bɪˋsitʃ] ***vt*.** (***be·sought*** [biˈsɔːt; bɪˋsɔt], ***~ed***; ***be·sought***, ***~ed***) 恳求, 哀求。~ (*sb*.) *for mercy* [*forgiveness*, *permission*] 求(人)怜悯[原谅、允许]。*They ~ed him to go at once*. 他们请他立即就去。~ *sb.'s help* 请求某人帮助。— ***vi*.** 恳求, 哀求。**-ing·ly *ad*.** 恳求地。

be·seem [biˈsiːm; bɪˋsim] ***vi*.** 〔书〕合式, 适当。*such a style as well ~s* 合适的文体。— ***vt*.** 〔书〕对…适当, 对…合式, 对…相称〔仅用于无人称句〕。*It ill ~s you to be ungrateful*. 你不像是忘恩负义的人。**-ing·ly *ad*.** 适当地, 适合地, 相称地。

be·set [biˈset; bɪˋsɛt] ***vt*.** (***be·set***; ***be·set·ting***) **1.** 包围, 围绕; 【海】被冰块包围。**2.** 扰, 攻, 袭; 缠扰, 为(病)所苦, **3.** 镶, 嵌。*His life is ~ with hardships*. 他的生活充满艰辛。*be ~ by enemies* 遭到敌人攻击。*a man ~ with a sense of guilt* 自知犯罪而内心不安的人。*be ~ by* (*innumerable*) *difficulties* 困难重重。*a dense forest that ~s the village* 围绕着村庄的密林。~ *a crown with pearls* 用珍珠镶嵌王冠。**-ting *a*.** **1.** 不断侵袭的 (*~ting sin* 易犯的恶习)。**2.** (念头等)缠绕人的。**-ment *n*.** **1.** (被)包围; (被)困扰; (被)围攻。**2.** 烦恼。

be·show [biˈʃəu; bɪˋʃo] ***n*.** 裸盖鱼 (= sablefish)。

be·shrew [biˈʃruː; bɪˋʃru] ***vt*.** 〔古〕咒。***B- me!*** 讨厌! 可恶! ***B- you!*** 该死! ***B- him*** [***it***]***!*** 讨厌的家伙[东西]! 该死! 可恶!

be·side [biˈsaid; bɪˋsaɪd] **I *prep*.** **1.** 在…旁边, 在…一侧, 在…附近。**2.** 和…相比, 比起…来; 比得上。**3.** 不中(目标), 不对(题), 与…无关。**4.** 除…之外。*the house ~ the river* 河边的房子。*B- Latin English is imperfect*. 比起拉丁语来, 英语是不严谨的。*musical achievement that can be ranked ~ masters* 堪与大师们相媲美的音乐成就。*His argument is ~ the subject in hand*. 他的议论离开了讨论的问题。*I have no treasure ~ this*. 我此外再没有钱了。***be ~ oneself*** 发狂, (乐极)忘形, 失常 (*He is ~ himself with rage*. 他愤怒得发狂)。~ ***the mark*** **1.** 未射中目标。**2.** 搞错, 离题, 不中肯 (= ~ ***the point*** [***question***])。**II *ad*.** 〔古〕= besides.

be·sides [biˈsaidz; bɪˋsaɪdz] **I *ad*.** 加之, 更, 又, 还有, 而且; 另外。*I am too tired to go,* (*and*) *~, it is late*. 我不去了, 太累啦, 而且时候又晚了。*They had a roof over their heads but not much ~*. 他们除了住房, 此外就没有什么财产。**II *prep*.** **1.** 在…之外(还有), …之余兼。**2.** 除…外(不再有)。*He speaks German ~ English*. 他懂英语而外还会说德语。*B- being a statesman, he was a painter*. 他是政治家, 又是画家。*There is no one here ~ Bill and me*. 这里只有比尔和我, 再没别人。

be·siege [biˈsiːdʒ; bɪˋsidʒ] ***vt*.** **1.** 围, 包围, 围困, 围攻。**2.** 拥挤在…周围。**3.** 对…不断提出(质问等)。*The vacationers besieged the travel offices* 度假者挤满了旅游社。~ *sb. with requests* 对某人提出一大堆要求。**-ment *n*.** (被)包围, (被)围攻; 攻城。

be·sieg·er [biˈsiːdʒə; bɪˋsidʒɚ] ***n*.** 围攻者; 攻城兵, 〔*pl*.〕围攻军。

be·slav·er [biˈsleivə; bɪˋslævɚ] ***vt*.** = beslobber.

be·slob·ber [biˈslɔbə; bɪˋslɑbɚ] ***vt*.** **1.** 流涎于, 用涎沾湿。**2.** 肉麻地吹捧。**3.** 乱吻。*The child ~ed his bib*. 这孩子的口水把围嘴都弄湿了。

be·smear [biˈsmiə; bɪˋsmɪr] ***vt*.** **1.** 涂搽, 涂抹, 涂满。**2.** 抹脏, 玷污; 中伤。*faces ~ed with pigments* 脸上涂得花花绿绿。~ *sb.'s reputation* 破坏某人的名誉。

be·smirch [biˈsməːtʃ; bɪˋsmɚtʃ] ***vt*.** **1.** 抹脏, 染污。**2.** 丑化, 糟塌(名誉等)。*Her soul was horribly ~ed*. 她的心灵已经变得肮脏不堪。

be·som [ˈbiːzəm; ˋbizəm] **I *n*.** **1.** 长把帚, 竹扫帚; 〔喻〕扫除(坏风气等)的手段。**2.** 【植】金雀花。**3.** 〔英方〕女流氓, 女二流子; 滥货。**II *vt*.** 扫除, 扫。

be·sot [biˈsɔt; bɪˋsɑt] ***vt*.** (***-tt-***) 使醉; 使糊涂; 使沉迷〔此

动词一般使用被动语态〕。*get ~ted* 吃醉酒。*a mind ~ted with fear* 害怕得六神无主。*He is ~ted by her youth and beauty*. 他被她的年轻美貌迷住了。**-tingly** *ad*.

be·sot·ted [bi'sɔtid; bɪ`sɑtɪd] *a*. 变糊涂的,昏迷的;沉迷…的。*be ~ about* [*with*] *sb*. 迷恋某人。**-ly** *ad*. **-ness** *n*.

be·sought [bi'sɔ:t; bɪ`sɔt] beseech 的过去式及过去分词。

be·span·gle [bi'spæŋgl; bɪ`spæŋgl] *vt*. **1.** 饰以闪闪发光的东西;饰以[包以]金[银]箔。**2.** 使灿烂发光。*the sky ~d with stars* 星光灿烂的天空。*poetry ~d with vivid imagery* 充满生动比喻的诗歌。

be·spat·ter [bi'spætə; bɪ`spætɚ] *vt*. **1.** 溅,溅污。**2.** 诽谤,辱骂,诋毁。*The truck ~ed my new suit with mud*. 卡车把我的新衣服溅一身泥。*be ~ed by malicious gossip* 遭到流言蜚语的攻击。

be·speak [bi'spi:k; bɪ`spik], *vt*. (**be·spoke** [bi'spəuk; bɪ`spok], 〔古〕 **be·spake** [bi'speik; bɪ`spek]; **be·spoken** [bi'spəukən; bɪ`spokən], **be·spoke**) **1.** 〔英〕预约,预定,定(货)。**2.** 预先请求。**3.** 表明,证明。**4.** 〔诗〕向…说。**5.** 〔废〕预示,暗示。

be·speck·le [bi'spekl; bɪ`spɛkl] *vt*. 使有斑点。

be·spec·ta·cled [bi'spektəkld; bɪ`spɛktək!d] *a*. 戴眼镜的。

be·spice [bi'spais; bɪ`spaɪs] *vt*. 用香料调(味),加香料于。

be·spoke [bi'spəuk; bɪ`spok] bespeak 的过去式及过去分词。**I** *a*. **1.** 〔英〕定做的;专做定货的 (*opp*. ready-made)。**2.** 已预定出去的。**3.** 〔方〕已订了婚的。*a ~ boot-maker* [*tailor*] 专接定货的靴匠[成衣匠]。*~ suits* 定做的衣服。*~ a seat in a theatre* 预定戏票。*~ a dress* 预定服装。*~ the reader's patience* 预先请读者耐心。*This ~s a kindly heart*. 这种行为显示了一颗善良的心。**II** *n*. **1.** (为募捐、赈灾等义演向演员)预约,要求。**2.** 〔英〕(借书)预约。**3.** 预定的货。

be·spo·ken [bi'spəukən; bɪ`spokən] bespeak 的过去分词。

be·spot [bi'spɔt; bɪ`spɑt] *vt*. 使有斑点。

be·spread [bi'spred; bɪ`sprɛd] *vt*. (**be·spread**; **be·spread**) 铺,覆盖,铺满。*a paddy field ~ with young rice plants* 一块铺满秧苗的稻田。*~ a table with fine linens* 给桌子铺上亚麻台布。

be·sprent [bi'sprent; bɪ`sprɛnt] *a*. 〔诗〕撒布,撒遍,洒满。*leaves ~ with raindrops* 洒满雨珠的树叶。

be·sprin·kle [bi'spriŋkl; bɪ`sprɪŋkl] *vt*. 洒,撒布。*grass ~d with dew* 洒满露珠的草。*~ one's food with salt* 在食物上撒盐。

Bess [bes; bɛs] *n*. 贝丝〔女子名, Elizabeth 的昵称〕。

Bes·se·mer ['besimə; `bɛsəmɚ] *n*. **1.** 贝西默〔姓氏〕。**2.** **Sir Henry ~** 贝西默爵士〔1813—1898,首创酸性转炉钢的英国人〕。~ **converter** 转炉。~ **process** 【冶】酸性转炉法。~ **steel** 酸性转炉钢。

Bes·sie ['besi; `bɛsɪ] *n*. 贝西〔女子名, Elizabeth 的昵称〕。

best [best; bɛst] **I** *a*. 〔good 和 well 的最高级〕(*opp*. worst)。**1.** 最好的。**2.** 最合适的。**3.** 最多的,大部分的。**4.** 〔口〕最厉害的,彻头彻尾的。*the ~ painter of our day* 当代最优秀的画家。*the ~ thing to do* 最好的办法。*She feels ~ in the morning*. 她早上精神最好。*the ~ man for the job* 最适合做那项工作的人。*the ~ part of a day* 大半天。*the ~ liar* 吹牛大家。**one's ~ boy** [**fellow**] 〔俚〕男朋友,情人。**one's ~ days** 全盛时代,得意时代。**one's ~ girl** 〔俚〕女朋友,情人。**put** [**set**] **one's ~ foot** [**leg**] **foremost** [**forward**] **1.** 〔英〕拼命走,赶快。**2.** 〔美〕逞能,自夸;拼命造成好印象。**II** *ad*. 〔well 的最高级〕最好,第一;〔口〕极,厉害地,大大地。*Everything goes ~ with me*. 我一切顺利。*~-suited* 最适合的。*~ known* 最有名的。*the ~ hated man* 最可恨的人。*the ~ abused book* 被批评得一无是处的书。**as ~** (**as**) **one can** [**may**] 尽可能,尽量。**had ~** 最好是;以…为最妙 (*You had ~ go with him*. 你最好是跟他去。*He had ~ have done so*. 他这样做了就最好了)。**III** *n*. **1.** 最佳,至上,最大努力。**2.** 最好的人;最好的事物[部分、衣服、结果、服装等]。*The ~ is the enemy of the good*. 至上乃致善之敌,标准过高反于成功不利。*Bad is the ~*. 决无好事。*the second ~* 次好。*The ~ of us can make mistakes*. 我们当中最好的人也会做错事。*the ~ of it* [*the joke*] 最好的地方,最精彩处[最好笑处]。*one's Sunday ~* 最漂亮的衣服,节日的服装。*That's the ~ I can do for you*. 我仅能帮你这么多忙了。**at** (**the**) **~** 至多,充其量也不过 (*You look a fool at the ~, and a knave at worst*. 你呀,说好呢不过像个傻瓜,说坏呢不过像个流氓。*We can not arrive before Friday at ~*. 我们在最好的情况下也得星期五到达)。**at one's** [**its**] **~** 最美时期;最得意处;全盛时代,发挥最高的技术水平,处于最佳健康[精神]状态(*He is at his ~ in short lyrics*. 他最擅长的是写抒情短诗。*at one's creative ~* 在创作能力最旺盛时期。*cherry-blossoms at their ~* 樱桃花盛开时节。*Beer is at its ~ when it is cool*. 冷啤酒味道最美)。**at the very ~** 〔强调语气〕= at best. ~ of all 首先,第一;最。do one's ~ 竭力,尽力。**do one's level ~** 〔俚、口〕竭尽个人最大可能,全力以赴。(**all**) **for the ~** **1.** 出于好意。**2.** 会[想]得到最好结果 (*Everything will turn out for the ~*. 一切到最后都会好的。*He did it all for the ~*. 他那样做全是好意。*Hope for the ~*. 切莫悲观。*It was at the time hard to realize how it could be all for the ~*. 当时很难想到怎么会有这么好的结果)。**get** (**have**) **the ~ of** 获胜;胜过 (*His arthritis gets the ~ of him from time to time*. 关节炎时常把他压倒)。**give sb. ~** 〔口〕向…屈服;向…认输 (*All right, I give you ~*. 算了,我认输)。**give it ~** 对(某事)罢念,想开。**have the ~ of it = get the ~ of it**. **make the ~ of** 尽量利用,善用,善处。**make the ~ of a bad job** [**business, bargain**] (处境不利时)尽量把损失减到最小,善处逆境。**make the ~ of one's way** 拼命快走。**make the ~ of things** 随遇而安。**none of the ~** 不甚好。**of the ~** 最好的;〔英口〕1 镑钞票 (*ten of the ~* 一镑钞票十张)。**to the ~ of one's** (*power*; *knowledge*) 竭力,不遗余力;竭尽(所能,所知)。**try one's ~** 尽全力。**with the ~** 不比任何人坏,不下于人。**IV** *vt*. 〔口〕 **1.** 超过,击败(某人)。**2.** 欺,骗,瞒。*He ~s me in the mathematics*. 他在数学方面超过我。~ **the pistol** 抢跑,枪未响即冲出起跑线。~ **bet** 〔美〕看来最可靠的办法,最适当的措施。~ **bib and tucker** 〔口〕漂亮衣服。~ **boy** 主要灯光助手。~ **buy** 买得最为合算的东西。~ **end** (羔羊等的)颈部肋条。~ **fellow** 〔口〕男朋友。~ **foot** 最吸引人的优点;拿手技术。~ **girl** 〔口〕女朋友。~ **man** 男傧相。~ **seller** 畅销货;畅销书;畅销书作者。**~-selling author** 畅销书作者。

be·star [bi'stɑ:; bɪ`stɑr] *vt*. 用星遮蔽,用星装饰。

be·stead[1] [bi'sted; bɪ`stɛd] *vt*. (**~ed**; **~ed**, ~) 帮助;援助;对…有所裨益,对…有用,有利于。

be·ste(a)d[2] [bi'sted; bɪ`stɛd] *a*. 〔古〕处境…的〔多与 ill, hard 等连用〕。**be ill** [**sore**] **~** 处境极难。**~ by** 被…困住。**~ with** 在…中。

bes·ti·al ['bestjəl; `bɛstɪəl] **I** *a*. **1.** 兽类的;畜牲一样的。**2.** 凶暴的;兽性的;兽欲的;下流的。*~ features* 狰狞面貌。*~ lust* 兽欲。*~ words* 下流言语,污言秽语。**II** *n*. 〔Scot.〕家畜;牛。**-ly** *ad*. 畜牲一样地,毫无人性地。

bes·ti·al·i·ty [ˌbesti'æliti; ˏbɛstɪ`ælətɪ] *n*. 兽性,兽心;兽行,兽欲;兽奸。

bes·tial·ize ['bestjəlaiz; `bɛstjəlaɪz] *vt*. 使兽化,使行同

禽兽。

bes·ti·ar·y [ˈbestjəri; ˋbestɪˏɛrɪ] ***n*.** 动物寓言(集)。

be·stir [biˈstəː; bɪˋstɝ] ***vt*.** (**-rr-**) 使发奋,使振作。~ ***oneself*** 发奋;活跃,努力(*You will fail unless you ~ yourself*. 你必须努力,否则就要失败)。

be·stow [biˈstəu; bɪˋsto] ***vt*.** **1.** 给与,授,赠,赐。**2.** 放置,安置,贮藏。**3.** 使用,用。**4.** 〔口〕给…提供住宿,让…留宿。~ *a benefit on sb*. 施恩于某人。~ *the trophy upon the winner* 把奖品赠给获胜者。*Time spent in study is well ~ed*. 把时间用于学习是值得的。~ *sb. for the night* 留某人过夜。*He ~ed his life on science*. 他一生钻研科学。

be·stow·al [biˈstəuəl; bɪˋstoəl] ***n*.** **1.** 赠与,授与;赠品。**2.** 贮藏。*the ~ of Medals of Honor* 授与荣誉勋章。*God's ~ upon man* 天赋,才能。

be·strew [biˈstruː; bɪˋstru] ***vt*.** (***~ed*; *~ed*, *~n*** [biˈstruːn; bɪˋstrun]) 撒布,撒满,散布在…。*grounds ~n* [*~ed*] *with pieces of paper* 撒满碎纸片的地面。~ *the path with flowers* 用花撒满道路。*Flowers ~ed the meadow*. 鲜花开满草原。

be·stride [biˈstraid; bɪˋstraɪd] ***vt*.** (***be·strode*** [biˈstrəud; bɪˋstrod], ***be·strid*** [biˈstrid; bɪˋstrɪd]; ***be-strid·den*** [biˈstridn; bɪˋstrɪdn], ***be·strid***) **1.** 骑,跨。**2.** 跨越,横跨于…上。**3.** 威慑,支配,高距于…之上。~ *a horse* [*bikes*] 骑马[自行车]。~ *a groove* 跨过沟。*a bridge bestriding the raging river* 横跨湍流的桥。

bet [bet; bɛt] **I *n*.** **1.** 赌,打赌。**2.** 赌金,赌品,赌注,被打赌的对象。**3.** 〔口〕意见。**4.** 适于做某事的人;适宜的手段[事物]。*a two-dollar ~* 两元钱的赌注。*That horse looks like a good ~*. 那匹马看来值得下注。*He is the poorest ~ for the job*. 他是最不适合于那种事的人了。*Your best ~ is to sell them now*. 你现在最好的办法就是把它们卖掉。*My ~ is that he won't come*. 我看他不会来了。*a heavy* [*paltry*] ~ 大[小]赌。***an even ~*** **1.** 互无输赢。**2.** 一对一的赌注,见一赔一。***lay sb. a bet*** 和某人打赌(*I will lay you a ~*. 我要和你打个赌)。***make*** [***place***] ***a ~ with sb.*** 和某人打赌。***take*** [***accept***] ***a ~*** 同意与人打赌[赌钱]。***win*** [***lose***] ***a ~ with*** [***against***] ***sb.*** 和某人打赌赌赢[输]。**II *vt*.** (***bet*, *bet·ted*** [ˈbetid; ˋbetɪd]) **1.** 用…打赌;与…打赌。**2.** 敢断定。*I will ~ ten dollars that he will fail*. 他必定失败,否则我愿输十元。~ *sb. on sth*. 与某人就某事打赌。~ *$ 30 on* [*upon*] *the horse race* 下赛马赌注 30 美元。~ *$ 10 against* [*on*] *his winning* 赌十美元断定他必输[必赢]。*I* [*I'll*] *~ he doesn't come*. 我敢断定他没有来。— ***vi*.** 赌,赌钱;下赌注;打赌。*Do you ever ~?* 你和人家打过赌吗? ~ ***money*** 〔美俚〕认为可靠。***~ one's boots*** [***bottom dollar*, *life*, *soul***] ***on*** **1.** 对…孤注一掷。**2.** 确信;可以断定(*You can ~ your boots no one's going to praise her*. 你可以相信绝对不会有人去赞扬她的)。***B- you*** 〔口〕当然,的确(*Bet you he meant it*. 他可不是说了玩的)。***I'll ~ my life*** 我敢用生命担保;当然,保管没错。***I ~ you*** 一定,必定(*I ~ you a shilling he has forgotten*. 他肯定忘掉了)。***You ~!*** 〔美俚〕当然,一定,必定,的确("*Is it in a safe place?*" "*You ~ it is*." "那东西放的地方保险吗?""当然保险啦")。***You ~?*** 〔口〕你敢肯定吗? 你有把握吗?

bet. = between.

be·ta [ˈbiːtə, ˈbeitə; ˋbitə, ˋbetə] ***n*.** **1.** 希腊字母第二字[B, β]。**2.** 第二位的东西。**3.** 【天】β 星〔星座中第二等最亮的星〕。~ **decay** 【原】β 衰变。~ **minus** 仅次于第二等。~ **particle** 【物】β 粒子,β 质子。~ **plus** 略高于第二等。~ **ray** 【化】β 射线。~ **test** 【心】不用文字及口答的一种智力测验。

be·ta·fite [ˈbiːtəfait; ˋbetəˏfaɪt] ***n*.** 铌钛铀矿。

be·ta·ine [ˈbiːtəiːn; ˋbitɪˏin] ***n*.** 【化】**1.** 甜菜碱,三甲胺乙内酯。**2.** 内酸盐,三甲(基)铵内酯。

be·take [biˈteik; bɪˋtek] ***vt*.** (***be·took*** [biˈtuk; bɪˋtʊk]; ***be·tak·en*** [biˈteikən; bɪˋtekən]) **1.** 〔书〕使用,诉诸于(*to*)。**2.** 〔古〕去,往,投身于,专心于,致力于(*to*)。★均用 ~ oneself 形式。~ *oneself to a debate* 加入一场争论。~ *oneself to one's heels* 一溜烟地逃走。~ *oneself to town* 进城去。

be·ta·tron [ˈbiːtətrɔn, ˈbei-; ˋbitəˏtrɑn, ˋbe-] ***n*.** 【物】电子回旋[感应]加速器。

be·tel [ˈbiːtəl; ˋbitl] ***n*.** 【植】蒟酱(= ~ pepper, 又名 piper ~)〔用其叶包槟榔嚼之〕。~ **nut** 槟榔果。~ **palm** 槟榔(树)。

bête noire [ˈbeitˈnwɑː; ˏbetˋnwɑr] 〔F.〕可怕的东西,极讨厌的东西[人]。

Beth [beθ; bɛθ] ***n*.** 贝丝〔女子名, Elizabeth 的昵称〕。

beth [beiθ, beθ; beθ, bɛθ] ***n*.** 希伯来语第二个字母。

beth·el [ˈbeθəl, beˈθel; ˋbɛθəl, bɛˋθɛl] ***n*.** **1.** 圣地,圣所。**2.** 〔美〕海员礼拜堂。**3.** 〔英讽〕反国教派教堂〔通常叫 little ~〕。

be·think [biˈθiŋk; bɪˋθɪŋk] ***vt*.** (***be·thought*** [biˈθɔːt; bɪˋθɔt]) **1.** 考虑,细想。**2.** 反省,提醒自己。**3.** 想起,忆起,想到 (*of*; *how*; *that*)。**4.** 决心。**5.** 〔古〕铭记。*I bethought myself a moment*. 我想了一下。~ *oneself of family obligations* 反省自己对家庭应负的责任。*She lives in the past now, ~ing herself of happier days*. 她现在整天回想过去,缅怀着往昔更美好的岁月。~ *oneself of learning Latin* 决心学拉丁文。— ***vi*.** 〔古〕考虑,细想,冥想。

Beth·le·hem [ˈbeθlihem; ˋbɛθlɪˏhɛm] ***n*.** **1.** 伯利恒〔巴勒斯坦地名,在耶路撒冷南方六英里之处,相传为耶稣降生地〕。**2.** 伯利恒〔美国一城市〕。

be·thought [biˈθɔːt; bɪˋθɔt] bethink 的过去式及过去分词。

Be·thune [ˈbiːtn, beˈθjuːn; ˋbitn̩, bɛˋθjun] ***n*.** 贝休恩(白求恩)〔姓氏〕。

be·tide [biˈtaid; bɪˋtaɪd] ***vi*.** 〔书〕(事故等)发生,(祸)起。*Whate'er* [*may*] *~, maintain your courage*. 无论有什么事发生,都不要惊慌失措。— ***vt*.** **1.** (灾难等)降临于〔多用于诅咒语〕。**2.** 预示,预兆。*Woe ~ the villain!* 愿那个恶棍遭殃! *These things ~ evil*. 这些事都是不祥之兆。

be·times [biˈtaimz; bɪˋtaɪmz] ***ad*.** 〔书〕**1.** 及时,准时,合时。**2.** 早。**3.** 即刻,不久以后。*He started ~ in the morning*. 他一大早就上路了。*He was up ~ doing his lessons*. 他及时做功课。*We hope to repay your visit ~*. 希望不久以后能对您回访。

bê·tise [beiˈtiːz; ˏbeˋtiz] ***n*.** 〔F.〕**1.** 愚钝,蠢笨。**2.** 愚行;蠢话,不合时宜的言行。**3.** 荒谬的事物,无价值的事物。

be·to·ken [biˈtəukən; bɪˋtokən] ***vt*.** **1.** 表示,表白。**2.** 预示,是…的预兆。*looks ~ing rage* 怒容。*a thunderclap that ~s foul weather* 预示着恶劣天气的雷声。

bét·on [ˈbetən, F. betɔ̃; ˋbetən, betɔ̃] ***n*.** 〔F.〕混凝土。~ **armée** 钢筋混凝土。

bet·o·ny [ˈbetəni; ˋbetənɪ] ***n*.** 【植】**1.** 水苏(属)。**2.** 石蚕(属)。

be·took [biˈtuk; bɪˋtʊk] betake 的过去式。

be·tray [biˈtrei; bɪˋtre] ***vt*.** **1.** 背叛,出卖,密告,陷害(朋友等)。**2.** 辜负。**3.** 诱惑;玩弄(女性)。**4.** 泄漏(秘密)。**5.** 不自觉地露出,暴露,表现。~ *one's country to the enemy* 卖国,做卖国贼。*He ~ed his friend's confidence*. 他辜负了朋友的信任。*She was ~ed into a snare*. 她被诱入陷阱。~ *a secret* 泄露秘密。*an unfeeling remark that ~s his lack of concern* 他那冷冷的话语表现出他的漠不关心。***Confusion ~s the guilty***. 慌张显出有罪,神色慌张必有鬼。

be·tray·al [biˈtreiəl; bɪˋtreəl] ***n*.** **1.** 背叛;背信;告密。**2.** 泄密;欺瞒。**3.** 引诱;玩弄(女性)。

B

B

be·tray·er [bi'treiə; bɪ`treə˞] ***n*. 1.** 卖国贼;叛徒;内奸;背信者;告密人。**2.** 欺骗者,诱惑者。

be·troth [bi'trəuð; bɪ`troð] ***vt*. 1.** 〔书〕(女子)同…订婚(*to*)〔多用被动语态〕。**2.** 〔古〕把(女儿)许配给…(*to*)。*become* [*be*] ~*ed to* (*sb*.) (已)和…订婚。~ *oneself to* 和…订婚。~ *one's daughter to sb*. 把女儿许配给某人。*The couple was* ~*ed with the family's approval*. 那对男女经家庭同意订了婚。

be·troth·al [bi'trəuðəl; bɪ`troðəl] ***n*.** 订婚(礼);婚约。*enter into* ~ 订婚。*a* ~ *party* 订婚宴。*break off a* ~ *with sb*. 同某人解除婚约。

be·trothed [bi'trəuðd; bɪ`troðd] **I *a*.** 订过婚的。**II *n*.** 未婚夫[妻]。*the* ~ *pair* 未婚夫妻。*He introduced us to his* ~. 他介绍我们同他的未婚妻见面。*the* ~ 已订婚的人,未婚夫[妻]。

Bets(e)y ['betsi; `bɛtsɪ] ***n*.** 贝齐〔女子名, Elizabeth 的昵称〕。

bet·ta ['betə; `bɛtə] ***n*.** 〔L.〕【鱼】搏鱼 (= fighting fish)。

bet·ter[1] ['betə; `bɛtə˞] **I *a*.** 〔good, well 的比较级〕(*opp*. worse) **1.** 较好的,更好的。**2.** 大半的,大部分的。**3.** 更合适的。**4.** 较有品德的。**5.** 健康状态较好的,(疾病)渐愈的。*He has seen* ~ *days*. 他曾经阔过一个时期。~ *people* 善良的人。*a* ~ *thing to do* 更合适的办法。*the* ~ *part of a lifetime* 大半生。*You'll feel* ~ *after a good sleep*. 你睡个好觉,精神就会好一些了。**II *ad*.** 〔well 的比较级〕**1.** 更,更加,更好地。**2.** 更多地,以上。*Do* ~ *another time*. 下次干好点。*I walked* ~ *than a mile to town*. 我步行一英里以上进城去。*He is* ~ *loved than ever*. 他更加受人爱了。***all the*** ~ 更好,更合适 (*I like her all the* ~ *for her simplicity*. 由于她单纯,我反而更喜欢她了)。***be*** ~ ***off*** 情况[处境]更好;更加富有。***be*** ~ ***than one's word*** 所做的超过所许诺的,比所许诺的更慷慨[做得更多,表现得更好]。***be the*** ~ ***for it*** 对…反而好,反而更好 (*Give the child no money, he'll be the* ~ *for it*. 不要给孩子钱,那样反而会对他有好处)。~ ***bet*** 〔美〕更好[聪明]的选择。***B- late than never***. 迟干胜于不干,亡羊补牢不算晚。***the*** ~ ***part of*** …的大部分 (*the* ~ *part of a month* 一个月的大部分时间,大半个月)。~ ***sort*** 长辈。~ ***than nothing*** 聊胜于无;不更坏就算运气。***for*** ~ (***or***) ***for worse*** 有福同享,有祸同当,祸福与共,同甘共苦,不论变好变歹〔出自祈祷书,举行结婚仪式时的用语〕(*They have taken each other for* ~ *or for worse*. 他们已结为夫妇,今后同甘共苦)。***for the*** ~ 转好 (*change for the* ~ (处境)改善;(病)转好;(职位)升迁)。***get*** ~(病)渐愈,快好。***get the*** ~ ***of*** 胜过,超出,占…的上风。***go*** (***sb***.) ~ 〔美俚〕胜过(某人),超过(某人),比(某人)体面。***had*** ~ 最好…,还是以…为好 (*You had* ~ *do so*. 你还是这样做好)。***know*** ~ 知道是不好[不对]的,很懂得,很明白(而不致于…) (*I know* ~. 没有的事,我不信。*She said she didn't cheat, but I knew* ~. 她说她没有欺骗人,但我深知不是那么一回事。*I know* ~ *than to quarrel*. 我傻也不会傻到就吵架的。*ought to know* ~ (*to do sth*.) 不该傻到去(做某事),不该这样傻)。***little*** ~ ***than*** 比…好不了多少。***no*** ~ ***than*** 并不比…好,简直就是;顶多不过是 (*He is no* ~ *than a shop-keeper*. 他顶多不过是一个店老板罢了)。***no*** ~ ***than he should be*** 行为不正,不规矩,不正派。***not*** ~ ***than*** 不比…更好;顶好也不过是。***one's*** ~ ***feelings*** 天良,优良的天性,高尚的感情。***one's*** ~ ***half*** 〔谑〕妻子[丈夫]。***one's*** ~ ***self*** 良心。***so much the*** ~ 这就更好[更妙、好极]了。***think*** ~ ***of* 1.** 另行考虑,改变对…的想法,经考虑后决定不做(某事)。**2.** 对…有较高评价。**III *n*. 1.** 较好的东西[事、条件、行为等]。**2.** (知识、能力、财产等)较优的人;〔*pl*.〕上级,上司;长上,长辈,前辈。*the* ~ *of two choices* 两个选择物中的较优者。*You'll soon get a* ~ *than Willy*. 很快就派一个比威利更高明的人给你。*Respect your* ~*s*. 尊敬你的长辈。*Do not ape your* ~*s*. 不要效颦。不要不自量力地模仿比你强的人。***for want of a*** ~ 因为没有更好的东西[人,办法等]。**IV *vt*. 1.** 改良,改善。**2.** 优于,胜过,超出。~ *one's previous record* 刷新本人过去的纪录。~ *oneself* 提高自己;改善个人处境。— ***vi*.** (情况等)有改善,变得有改进。~**-off *a*.** (经济)情况较好的。~**-to-do 1. *a*.** 较为富裕的。**2. *n*.** 〔*sing*., *pl*.〕较为富裕的人。

bet·ter[2] ['betə; `bɛtə˞] ***n*.** 打赌的人。

bet·ter·ment ['betəmənt; `bɛtə˞mənt] ***n*. 1.** 改良,改善,改正。**2.** (不动产的)增值。**3.** 〔常 *pl*.〕【法】(房屋等的)修缮,改建,扩建。

bet·ter·most ['betəməust; `bɛtə˞most] ***a*. 1.** 最好的,上等的。**2.** 大部分的。*the* ~ *part of the time* 这段时间的大部分。

bet·ting ['betiŋ; `bɛtɪŋ] ***n*.** 赌博,打赌。~**-book** 赌账。~**-shop 1.** 私营赛马赌券经营所。**2.** 政府许可开设的赌场。

bet·tor ['betə; `bɛtə˞] ***n*.** = better[2].

Bet·ty ['beti; `bɛtɪ] ***n*.** 贝蒂〔女子名, Elizabeth 的昵称〕。

bet·ty ['beti; `bɛtɪ] ***n*. 1.** 〔美〕长颈瓶。**2.** 〔俚〕(盗贼撬门用的)铁杆。**3.** 爱做家务的男子。**4.** 一种奶油果馅糕点。

be·tween [bi'twi:n; bə`twin] **I *prep*. 1.** 位于…之间;处在…之间;介于…间。**2.** 在…之间的时候。**3.** 来往于…之间。**4.** 比较;在…中任择其一。**5.** 为…所共有。**6.** 由…协力合作。**7.** 由于…作用的结果。**8.** 私下,暗中,私人之间。~ *three and four o'clock* 在三点到四点(钟)之间。*the sunshine* ~ *the leaves* 树叶间漏下的阳光。*with a cigarette* ~ *one's lips* 嘴上叼着香烟。*choose* ~ *the two* 二中择一。*They are* ~ *jobs*. 他们正在失业。*a color* ~ *pink and red* 介乎粉红与红之间的颜色。*a passageway* ~ *two rooms* 连接两个房间的过道。*I have no preference* ~ *the two wines*. 我对这两种酒没有偏爱。*He couldn't see the difference* ~ *good and bad*. 他不识好歹[不分善恶]。*B- two stools one falls to the ground*. 脚踏两边船,两不落实。*We'll keep this matter* ~ *the two of us*. 这件事将只有我们两人知道。*B- sewing, cleaning, and raising her children, she was kept busy*. 缝啦,洗啦,带孩子啦,弄得她从来不得松闲。*The children had one room* ~ *them*. 孩子们共住一间屋。*We did not have ten dollars* ~ *us*. 我们凑不出十块钱。*Divide these apples* ~ *you two* [*three*]. 你们俩[三]人分掉这些苹果吧。★严格地讲,本来二者之间是用 between, 三者以上之间是用 among, 但前者亦可代替后者使用,尤其是当有三方发生关系而每两方之间须分别考虑时。例如: *a treaty* ~ *three powers* 三国条约。*insert* ~ *the lines* 插入行间。*Have no quarrels* ~ *gentleman*. 君子自重。~ ***the cup and the lip*** 正要成功的时候,正在重要关头。~ ***ourselves*** = ~ *you and me and the gate-post* [*lamppost*] 你知我知,莫对人讲。~ ***two fires*** = ~ *the devil and the deep sea* 进退两难,进退维谷,左右为难。~ ***the lines*** 言外之意。~ ***whiles*** [***times***] 时时,偶尔。~ ***wind and water*** 【船】在吃水线间 (*be hit* ~ *wind and water* 被击中要害)。(***few and***) ***far*** ~ 很冷落,极少 (*In this part of Egypt houses are far* ~. 在埃及的这部分地区房屋极少,非常冷落。*visits that are far* ~ 相隔时间很长的访问)。**II *ad*.** 当中,中间。*two windows with a door* ~ 两扇窗户当中有一扇门。*We could not see the moon, for a cloud came* ~. 我们看不见月亮了,因为有云遮住。*the years* ~ 这中间的年月。***in*** ~ **1.** 在…期间;在中间;每隔… (*two houses and a yard in* ~ 两所房屋及夹在中间的院子。*I don't* *care if she's black, white or in ~*. 我不管她是黑皮肤、白皮肤,还是半黑半白)。2. 挡路 (*The dog got in ~*. 狗挡住了路)。~**-decks**【船】中舱。~**-maid**〔英〕(在侍女和烧饭女仆之间)两边打杂的女佣 = tweeny.

be·tween·brain [biˈtwiːnˌbrein; bəˋtwinˏbren] ***n.***【生】间脑 (= diencephalon)。

be·tween·times [biˈtwiːnˌtaimz; bɪˋtwinˏtaɪmz] ***ad.*** 有时;间或 (= betweenwhiles)。*a part-time teacher who studied law ~* 一个有时攻读法律的兼课教师。

be·twixt [biˈtwikst; bəˋtwɪkst] ***prep.***, ***ad.***〔古、诗、方〕= between. ~ ***and between*** 介于两者之间;模棱两可 (*The child of Anglo-Indian parents, he felt somehow ~ and between*. 作为一个英印混血儿,他在感情上似乎摇摆于两国之间)。***There is many a slip ~ the cup and the lip***〔见 slip 条〕。

Beu·lah [ˈbjuːlə; ˋbjulə] ***n.*** 1.【圣】以色列的别名。2. 安息地〔生命行程的终点,出自英国作家班扬的《天路历程》〕。3.〔英〕反国教派的礼拜堂。4. 比尤拉〔女子名〕。

BEV = black English vernacular 黑人英语。

Bev, BeV, bev = billion electron volts 十亿电子伏(特)。

Be·van [ˈbevən; ˋbɛvən] ***n.*** 贝文〔姓氏〕。

bev·a·tron [ˈbevətrɔn; ˋbɛvəˏtrɑn] ***n.***【物】高功率质子回旋加速器,高能质子同步稳相加速器。

bev·el [ˈbevəl; ˋbɛvəl] **I** ***n.*** 1. 斜角;倾斜,斜面;【数】斜截,斜削。2. 万能角尺,斜角规。3.【机】伞齿轮。**II** ***a.*** 斜的,倾斜的,斜角的;斜削的。**III** ***vt.*** 把…截成斜角形,斜切,斜截。— ***vi.*** 成斜角;倾斜,斜。~ **gear**【机】伞(形)齿轮。~ **square** 角度尺,斜角规。~ **wheel**【机】斜齿轮,歪角齿轮。

bev·er·age [ˈbevəridʒ; ˋbɛvərɪdʒ] ***n.*** 1. 饮料〔除水而外的饮料,如茶、酒、牛奶、汽水等〕。2.〔英方〕筵宴;餐费,酒费。*cooling ~s* 清凉饮料。~ **room**〔加〕(旅馆里的)酒吧。

Bev·er·idge [ˈbevəridʒ; ˋbɛvərɪdʒ] ***n.*** 贝弗里奇〔姓氏〕。

Bev·er·l(e)y [ˈbevəli; ˋbɛvəlɪ] ***n.*** 贝弗莉〔女子名〕。

Be·vin [ˈbevin; ˋbɛvɪn] ***n.*** 贝文〔姓氏〕。

bev·y [ˈbevi; ˋbɛvɪ] ***n.*** (鹌鹑等和妇女、姑娘等的)群。*a ~ of quails* 一群鹌鹑。*a ~ of young women* 一群年轻妇女。

BEW, B.E.W. = Board of Economic Warfare〔英旧〕经济作战局。

be·wail [biˈweil; bɪˋwel] ***vt.*** 悲叹,叹惜;哀悼;痛哭。~ *one's bad luck* 悲叹自己的命途多舛。— ***vi.*** 哀悼;悲叹 (*over, for*)。~ *over one's misfortune* 为自己的不幸而悲叹。~ *for sb.'s death* 哀悼某人的去世。

be·ware [biˈwɛə; bɪˋwɛr] ***vi.***, ***vt.*** 注意,当心,谨防。★这一动词无词尾变化,仅能用不定式或祈使语气或与助动词 must, should 等连用;其后接用 of (也有略去 of 的), lest, how, that, not 等。*I was told to ~ (of) pickpockets*. 人们告诉我要谨防扒手。*B- (of) fire*. 小心火烛,谨防引起火灾。*a man to ~ of* 一个要提防的人物。*B- lest you (should) fall [B- that you do not fall] into this mistake again*. 请注意不要再犯这种错误。

be·wil·der [biˈwildə; bɪˋwɪldɚ] ***vt.*** 1. 使为难,使着慌;使手足无措;使变糊涂。2.〔古〕使迷路。**-ing** ***a.*** 令人为难的,使人手足无措的,使人狼狈的。**-ingly** ***ad.*** **-ment** ***n.*** 1. 为难,狼狈,慌张;迷惑。2. 混乱(状态) (*be thrown into ~ment* 被弄得不知所措;被弄得迷惑不解。*We enter into a ~ment of smoke, noise and crowding people*. 我们进入了一个乌烟瘴气、吵吵闹闹和拥挤不堪的混乱环境中)。

be·witch [biˈwitʃ; bɪˋwɪtʃ] ***vt.*** 1. 迷,迷惑,蛊惑,(妖言)惑(众)。2. 令人心醉,(春色等)恼(人)。*He felt as if he had been ~ed by a fox*. 他觉得好像被一个狐狸精迷惑住了。*be ~ed by the glorious sunset* 被残阳如血的壮丽景色迷住了。

be·witch·ing [biˈwitʃiŋ; bɪˋwɪtʃɪŋ] ***a.*** 迷人的,妖媚的;蛊惑的。**-ly** ***ad.***

be·witch·ment [biˈwitʃmənt; bɪˋwɪtʃmənt] ***n.*** 迷惑,蛊惑;魔力,妖术。

be·wray [biˈrei; bɪˋre] ***vt.***〔古〕(无意之间)泄露;暴露(本性)。

bey [bei; be] ***n.*** 1. (土耳其帝国时代的)省督〔有时用作敬称,加在显贵人物的名后,已于 1934 年废止,如 *Ismet Bey* (伊斯迈特阁下)〕。2. 突尼斯 (Tunis) 本地统治者的称号。

bey·lic [ˈbeilik; ˋbelɪk] ***n.*** (土耳其帝国时代的)省督辖区,省。

be·yond [biˈjɔnd; bɪˋjɑnd] **I** ***prep.*** 1.〔场所〕在[向]…的那边;离…以外,远于。2.〔时间〕过了…,迟于。3.〔程度等〕超过…的范围,在…所不及处。4.〔能力等〕在…以上,胜过,优于。5. 除…以外〔多用于否定或疑问语气〕。*far ~ the sea* 远在大海那边。*B- those trees [green willows] you'll find his [my] house*. 在树林那边,你将找到他的家[绿柳深处是我家]。*a mile ~ the town* 离城一英里以外。*We saw peak ~ peak*. 我们眼前是重重山岭。~ *the horizon* 在地平线以外。~ *the tomb [grave]* 来世,死后。*I cannot go ~ a dollar*. 一元以上我就不买了。~ *possibility* 不可能。*injured ~ help* 受了无法医治的重伤。~ *endurance* 无法忍耐。*a skill ~ Raphael's* 拉斐尔〔意大利名画家〕之上的手法。*wise ~ all others* 比所有的人都聪明。*live ~ one's means* 生活支出超出收入,入不敷出。*B- this I know nothing*. 此外我全无所知。~ *the usual hour* 较迟于平常,过了平常时间。~ *the fixed time* 过了约定时间。~ ***all hope*** 完全绝望。~ ***all praise*** 夸奖不尽,好极。~ ***all question*** 毫无疑问,当然。~ ***all things*** 第一,首先。~ ***comparison [compare]*** 无与伦比,不可相提并论。~ ***comprehension*** 难于理解,难解。~ ***dispute*** 无争论余地,无疑。~ ***doubt*** 无可置疑,无疑。~ ***expectation*** 超出预想地,意外地。~ ***expression [description]*** 形容不出,非笔墨所能形容。~ ***measure*** 非常,极度,无可估量地。~ ***one [sb.]*** 某人能力所不及;某人所不能理解 (*The problem is ~ me [him]*. 这个问题不是我[他]能解决得了的)。~ ***one's depth*** 1. 在脚不着底的深处,深到要没顶的地方。2. 难以了解。~ ***one's [sb.'s] power*** 力所不及,怎样都不能 (*It is ~ my [his] power to give it to her*. 我[他]无法把这件东西给她)。~ ***the seas*** 在海外,在国外。***go ~ oneself*** 失度,忘形 (*He went ~ himself with joy*. 他欢喜得忘形了)。**II** ***ad.*** 1. 在[向]很远的那边,在[向]远处;更远地。2. 此外,以外。*as far as the house and ~* 直到那间房的远处。*What is ~?* 再往前还有什么东西? *He gave me nothing ~*. 他此外再没给我什么东西。***the life ~*** 来世,彼岸。***unable to see ~*** 囿于,看不穿。**III** ***n.*** 那边。***the back of ~***〔口〕远方,穷乡僻壤;天涯海角。***the (great) ~*** 死后的世界;未知的世界 (*go to the ~* 死,去到一个世界)。

Bey·routh [ˈbeiruːt; ˋberut] ***n.*** = Beirut.

bez·ant [ˈbezənt; ˋbɛznt] ***n.*** 1. 拜占庭币〔昔日拜占庭帝国的金币〕。2.【建】列圆饰;【徽】金黄小圆徽。

bez antler [ˈbezæntlə; ˋbɛzæntlɚ] ***n.*** (鹿角的)副枝,桠枝 (= bay antler)。

be·zazz [biˈzæz; bɪˋzæz] ***n.***〔俚〕1. 力,活力,生气,精神。2. 敏锐;风度;光彩;鉴别力;闪光 (= pizazz)。

bez·el [ˈbezəl; ˋbɛzl̩] ***n.*** 1. 凿刃的斜面。2. 宝石的斜面;(戒指)宝石座。3. (钟表等嵌玻璃的)沟缘。

be·zique [biˈziːk; bɪˋzik] ***n.***【牌】1. 比齐克牌戏〔64 张牌由二人或四人玩的一种纸牌戏,以赢墩数多寡计胜败〕。2. 凑四十分〔在比齐克牌戏中用两张牌(如黑桃皇后与方块贾克)配合作成 40 分的一种打法〕。

be·zoar [ˈbiːzɔː; ˋbizor] ***n.*** 1.【药】毛粪石,胃石,牛黄,马宝〔一种解毒剂〕。2.〔废〕解毒剂。

B

B

be·zugs schein [be'zugsʃaiin; bɛ`zugsʃaɪn] ***n***.〔G.〕购物证,日用品配给证。

bf, b.f. = **1.** boldface【印】黑体,粗体。**2.** bloody fool〔讽〕大傻瓜。**3.** board foot 板英尺。

B.F. = **1.** Bachelor of Finance 财政学学士。**2.** Bachelor of Forestry 森林学学士。

B/F, b.f. = brought forward【会计】结转。

BFRE【无】= before.

BFT = biofeedback training 生物反馈训练。

bg. = **1.** bag. **2.** bugler.

B-girl ['biːgəːl; `bigɚl] ***n***.〔美〕酒吧女郎。

bgs = bags.

bhak·ti ['bʌkti; `bʌktɪ] ***n***.【印度教】终身信奉一神,一神崇拜。

B'ham. = Birmingham.

bhang [bæŋ; bæŋ] ***n***. **1.** 印度大麻。**2.** 用印度大麻制成的麻醉药。

bhees·ty, bhees·tie ['biːsti; `bistɪ] ***n***. (*pl*. ***-ties***) 担水者〔印度为军队担水的人〕。

b.h.p., bhp = brake horsepower【机】制动马力。

Bhu·tan [buː'tɑːn; bu`tɑn] ***n***. 不丹〔亚洲〕。

Bhu·tan·ese [ˌbuːtə'niːz; ˏbutə`niz] **I *n***.〔*sing*., *pl*.〕不丹人;不丹语。**II *a***. 不丹的;不丹人的;不丹语的。

Bi【化】= bismuth.

bi [bai; baɪ] ***a***.〔美俚〕(在性欲上)对男女两性都感兴趣的。

bi- *pref*. **1.** 二,两,双,复。**2.**【化】二,重,双,联。**3.** (二)等分。**4.** 每…二次的,每二…一次的。

BIA = **1.** Brazilian International Airlines 巴西国际航空公司。**2.** Bachelor of Industrial Arts 工艺学士。**3.** Braille Institute of America 美国盲人学会。

Bi·a·fra [bai'ɑːfrə; bɪ`ɑfrə] ***n***. 比夫拉〔尼日利亚一地区〕。**-n *a***. 比夫拉的。

bia·ly [bi'ɑːli; bɪ`ɑlɪ] ***n***. (*pl*. ***bia·lys***) 葱花面筋薄饼卷 (= biali)。

bi·an·gu·lar [bai'æŋgjulə; baɪ`æŋgjəlɚ] ***a***. 有二角的,双角的。

bi·an·nu·al [bai'ænjuəl; baɪ`ænjuəl] ***a***. **1.** 一年二次的,半年一次的。**2.**〔废〕两年一次的。*a* ~ *meeting* 一年举行两次的会议。**-ly** [bai'ænjuəli; baɪ`ænjuəlɪ] ***ad***.

bi·an·nu·late [bai'ænjulit, -leit; baɪ`ænjəlɪt, -let] ***a***.【动】有双环的;有双色带的。

bi·as[1] ['baiəs; `baɪəs] **I *n***. **1.** 成见,先入之见,偏执,偏见 (*opp*. impartiality);倾向,嗜好;癖 (*towards*)。**2.** (衣服等上面缝的)斜线,斜痕;【无】偏,偏压;偏置。**3.**【体】使球斜进的偏力[偏重];(球的)歪圆形;不按直线前进的倾向;【电】偏压;【统】倾向统计值;【生】偏倚。*a racial* ~种族偏见。*a strong musical* ~ 对音乐的强烈爱好。*copper* ~【电】正偏压。*zinc* ~【电】负偏压。*cut on the* ~ 斜裁,斜切。***be free from*** ~ 丝毫不受偏见左右。***be under a*** ~ ***in favor of*** [***against***] 对…有偏爱[偏见]。***have a*** ~ ***to*** [***towards***] 对…有偏心。***without*** ~ ***and without favour*** 不偏不倚地,公公平平地。**II *a***. 斜的;【电】偏动的。~ *bands* 斜带。**III *ad***. 斜,偏。*cut material* ~ 斜切料,斜开料,斜裁。~**-ply tyre** 斜交薄布轮胎。

bias[2] ['baiəs; `baɪəs] ***vt***. (~***ed***, ~***ing***;〔英〕~***sed***, ~***sing***) **1.** 使有偏见,使偏重,使偏向一方。**2.**【电】加偏压于。*be bias(s)ed against* 对…抱有偏见。~ ... *into*【电】加偏压使进入…。*My ignorance ~ed me against my teacher*. 我由于无知而对老师抱有偏见。**-ed *a***. 有偏见的。

bi·ath·lete [bai'æθliːt; baɪ`æθlɪt] ***n***. 滑雪射击运动员。

bi·ath·lon [bai'æθlən, -lɔn; baɪ`æθlən, -lɑn] ***n***.【体】现代冬季两项〔包括滑雪和射击的冬季奥林匹克运动项目〕。

bi·aur·al [bai'ɔːrəl; baɪ`ɔrəl] ***a***. 有两耳的,用两耳的 (= binaural)。

bi·au·ric·u·late [ˌbaiɔː'rikjulit; ˏbaɪɔ`rɪkjəlɪt] ***a***.【解】有两耳的 (= biauricular)。

bi·ax·i·al [bai'æksiəl; baɪ`æksɪəl] ***a***.【光】二轴的。

Bib., bib., bibl. = Bible; Biblical.

bib [bib; bɪb] **I *n***. (小儿)围涎,围嘴;围腰的上部。~ ***and*** ~〔口〕衣服。***one's best*** ~ ***and tucker***〔口〕漂亮衣裳。**II *vi*., *vt***. (***-bb-***)〔古〕(经常地)喝(酒),慢慢地呷(烈酒)。~**-cock** 弯嘴龙头。**-ful *a*., *n***. 满涎布的(量) (*slobber a bibful*〔美口〕大谈特谈,唠叨不休)。

bi·bas·ic [bai'beisik; baɪ`besɪk] ***a***.【化】二元的;二盐基性的;二代的(指盐)。

bibb [bib; bɪb] ***n***. **1.** 弯管旋塞,龙头。**2.**【船】桅头用以支持棚木之旁木。

bib·ber ['bibə; `bɪbɚ] ***n***. 贪酒的人,酒鬼〔通例用于复合词: *a wine*- ~大酒鬼〕。

bi·be·lot ['bibləu; `bɪblo] ***n***.〔F.〕室内装饰品;床饰;小件古玩;小玩意儿。

bi-bi·va·lent [ˌbaibai'veilənt; ˏbaɪbaɪ`velənt] ***a***.【化】双二价的。

Bi·ble ['baibl; `baɪbl] ***n***. **1.**【基督、犹】〔the ~〕圣经。**2.** 经典。**3.**〔b-〕有权威的典籍;金科玉律。*The Mohammedan* ~ 伊斯兰教的圣经〔即古兰经, = the Koran〕。*The old sea captain regarded his Bowditch as his bible*. 老船长把他那本波迪奇航海手册奉为金科玉律。***Douai*** ~, ***Douay*** ~ 杜埃版《圣经》〔1582—1610年在多维地方由英国教士团将拉丁文《圣经》译为英语,并作修订,供天主教徒使用〕。***King James*** ~ 钦定《圣经》〔由英国国王詹姆士一世于1604年倡议,完成于1611年,是讲英语国家新教徒使用最广泛的英译本,又称 Authorized Version〕。***the Wicked*** [***Adulterous***] ~ 邪[秽]版《圣经》〔1631年版《圣经》,该版本将 Thou shalt not commit adultery 句中的 not 一词漏印,使"汝切勿通奸"一语变成"汝可通奸"〕。~ **belt**〔美〕美国南部和中西部正统主义派教徒多的几个州;〔转义〕教徒多的地方;〔讽〕伪君子多的地方。~ **Christians** 圣经主义派〔19世纪新教中的一派〕。~ **class** (主日学校的)读经班。~**-clerk** 读经生〔牛津大学二、三个学院中负有诵读圣经义务的公费生〕。~ **college** 培训宗教工作者的基督教大学。~ **drink** 祷告会;礼拜会。~ **oath** 吻《圣经》立的誓,庄严的誓言。~ **paper** 圣经纸〔用于印刷《圣经》等的一种极薄的纸〕。~ **pounder** [**puncher, ranter**]〔美口〕牧师,传道士。~ **punching**〔美俚〕讲经布道。~ **reader** 读经者〔挨门逐户向病人、穷人讲读《圣经》的人〕。~ **school** (进行宗教教育的)主日学校。~ **Society**《圣经》出版协会,《圣经》公会。~**-thump *vi***. 摆出一副传道士的架子。

Bib·li·cal ['biblikəl; `bɪblɪkəl] ***a***. 圣经的;合圣经宗旨的。*the* ~ *style* 圣经文体。~ *Stories* 圣经(上的)故事。

Bib·li·cist ['biblisist; `bɪblɪsɪst] ***n***. **1.** 拘泥于圣经的人;圣经主义者。**2.** 圣经通;圣经研究者。

bib·li·o- *comb*. *f*. 书籍的;圣经的。

bib·li·o·film ['bibliəufilm; `bɪblɪəˏfɪlm] ***n***. (图书摄影用的)显微胶卷。

bib·li·og. = bibliography [-phic, -phical, -pher].

bib·li·o·graph ['bibliəuˌgræf; `bɪblɪəˏgræf] ***vt***. **1.** (为书、文章)加书目提要,加书志,加书目。**2.** 作,的书目提要。

bib·li·og·ra·pher [ˌbibli'ɔgrəfə; ˏbɪblɪ`ɑgrəfɚ] ***n***. **1.** 书目编者;书目提要编者。**2.** 书志学家,目录学家,文献学家。

bib·li·o·graph·i·cal [ˌbibliəu'græfikəl; ˏbɪblɪə`græfɪkəl] ***a***. **1.** 书目的;书目提要的。**2.** 书志学的,文献学的。

bib·li·og·ra·phy [ˌbibli'ɔgrəfi; ˏbɪblɪ`ɑgrəfɪ] ***n***. **1.** 书目提要;书目,书志学,书志。**2.** 文献,文献学。

bib·li·o·klept [ˈbibliəuklept; ˋbɪblɪə͵klɛpt] ***n*.** 书贼,窃书人。

bib·li·ol·a·ter [ˌbibliˈɔlətə; ͵bɪblɪˋɑlətɚ] ***n*.** **1.** 书籍崇拜者。**2.** 圣经崇拜者。

bib·li·ol·a·trous [ˌbibliˈɔlətrəs; ͵bɪblɪˋɑlətrəs] ***a*.** **1.** 崇拜书籍的。**2.** 崇拜圣经的。

bib·li·ol·a·try [ˌbibliˈɔlətri; ͵bɪblɪˋɑlətrɪ] ***n*.** **1.** 书籍崇拜。**2.** 圣经崇拜。

bib·li·ol·o·gy [ˌbibliˈɔlədʒi; ͵bɪblɪˋɑlədʒɪ] ***n*.** **1.** 书志学;版本学;目录学。**2.** 〔常 B-〕圣经学。

bib·li·o·man·cy [ˈbibliəumænsi; ˋbɪblɪə͵mænsɪ] ***n*.** 圣经卦〔拿翻开圣经看到的句子占卜吉凶〕。

bib·li·o·ma·ni·a [ˌbibliəuˈmeinjə; ͵bɪblɪəˋmenɪə] ***n*.** 藏书癖;珍本书收集狂。

bib·li·o·ma·ni·ac [ˌbibliəuˈmeiniæk; ͵bɪblɪəˋmenɪæk] **I** ***a*.** 藏书癖的,书痴的。**II** ***n*.** 藏书家,书狂,书痴。

bib·li·op·e·gy [ˌbibliˈɔpidʒi; ͵bɪblɪˋɑpədʒɪ] ***n*.** 书籍装订术。

bib·li·o·phil(e) [ˈbibliəufail; ˋbɪblɪə͵faɪl], **bib·li·oph·ilist** [ˈbibliəufilist, -failist; ˋbɪblɪəfɪlɪst, -faɪlɪst] ***n*.** 爱书家,藏书癖者〔尤指玩赏版式设计、装帧、印刷者〕。

bib·li·o·ph·i·lism [ˌbibliˈɔfilizəm; ͵bɪblɪˋɑfəlɪzəm] ***n*.** (爱)书癖,藏书癖。

bib·li·o·pole [ˈbibliəupəul; ˋbɪblɪə͵pol] ***n*.** 书商,(特指)珍本书商。

bib·li·op·o·ly [ˌbibliˈɔpəli; ͵bɪblɪˋɑpəlɪ] ***n*.** 书籍买卖,珍本书买卖。

bib·li·o·the·ca [ˌbibliəuˈθiːkə; ͵bɪblɪəˋθikə] ***n*.** **1.** 〔集合词〕文库,藏书。**2.** 图书目录,(特指)书商售书目录。**3.** 〔B-〕〔废〕圣经。

bib·li·ot·ic [ˌbibliˈɔtic; ͵bɪblɪˋɑtɪc] ***a*.** 文献鉴定学的;笔迹鉴定学的。**-s** ***n*.** 文献鉴定学,笔迹鉴定学。

bib·u·lous [ˈbibjuləs; ˋbɪbjələs] ***a*.** 〔书〕**1.** 嗜酒的。**2.** 非常能吸水的,吸湿性强的。

bi·cam·er·al [baiˈkæmərəl; baɪˋkæmərəl] ***a*.** 有上、下院的,二立法机构的,两院制的。~ *system* 两院制。**-ism** ***n*.** 两院制主义者,主张两院制论者。

bi·cap·su·lar [baiˈkæpsələ, -sjulə; baɪˋkæpsəlɚ, -sjəlɚ] ***a*.** 【植】有双蒴果的。

bi·carb [baiˈkɑːb; baɪˋkɑrb] ***n*.** 〔美口〕= bicarbonate.

bi·car·bon·ate [baiˈkɑːbənit; baɪˋkɑrbənɪt] ***n*.** 【化】碳酸氢盐,重碳酸盐。~ *of soda* 碳酸氢钠,小苏打。

bice [bais; baɪs] ***n*.** **1.** 蓝色,绿色。**2.** 一种蓝色绘图颜料;绿色颜料。

bi·cen·te·nar·y [baisenˈtiːnəri; baɪsɛnˋtə͵nɛrɪ], **bi·cen·ten·ni·al** [baisenˈtenjəl; baɪsɛnˋtɛnɪəl] **I** ***a*.** **1.** 二百周年的,二百周年纪念的。**2.** 二百年间的,持续二百年的。**3.** 每二百年(一次)的。*a* ~ *exposition* 二百周年纪念展览会。*a* ~ *return of a comet* 彗星二百年一次的回归。**II** ***n*.** **1.** 二百周年(纪念)。**2.** 二百年间,持续二百年。**3.** 每二百年(一次)。*The town will have its* ~ *next year*. 该城的二百周年纪念日明年即将到来。

bi·ceph·a·lous [baiˈsefələs; baɪˋsɛfələs] ***a*.** 【生】(畸胎等)(有)二头的。

bi·ceps [ˈbaiseps; ˋbaɪsɛps] ***n*.** **1.** 【解】二头肌。**2.** 膂力。*brachial* ~ *muscle* 上臂二头肌。*femoral* ~ *muscle* 大腿[下股]二头肌。

bi·chlo·ride [ˌbaiˈklɔːraid, -rid; baɪˋkloraɪd, -rɪd] ***n*.** 【化】二氯化物。~ ***of mercury*** 二氯化汞,升汞。

bi·chro·mate [ˈbaiˈkrəumit, -meit; baɪˋkromɪt, -met] ***n*.** 【化】重铬酸盐。***a*** ~ ***cell*** 重铬酸盐电池。

bi·chrome [ˈbaikrəum; ˋbaɪkrom] ***a*.** 两色的。

bi·cip·i·tal [baiˈsipitəl; baɪˋsɪpɪtəl] ***a*.** **1.** 【生】(有)二头的。**2.** 【解】二头肌的。

bick·er[1] [ˈbikə; ˋbɪkɚ] **I** ***vi*.** **1.** 斗嘴,争吵。**2.** (雨等)哗啦哗啦地下;(溪水等)哗啦哗啦地流。**3.** (火焰、光等)一晃一晃地闪,闪烁。*They are forever* ~*ing and biting*. 他们常常拌嘴。*The raging stream* ~*ed down the valley*. 湍急的涧水哗啦哗啦地淌下山谷。*The afternoon sun* ~*ed through the leaves*. 午后的阳光闪烁于树叶之间。**II** ***n*.** **1.** 斗嘴,口角。**2.** (流水等)哗啦哗啦的声响;(雨的)淅淅沥沥声;(鸟的)啭鸣。**3.** (火焰等的)摇晃,闪烁。

bick·er[2] [ˈbikə; ˋbɪkɚ] ***n*.** 〔Scot.〕(盛酒等用的)木碗。

bi·col·or [ˈbaiˌkʌlə; ˋbaɪ͵kʌlɚ] ***a*.** 双色的 (= bicolored)。

bi·con·cave [baiˈkɔnkeiv; baɪˋkɑnkev] ***a*.** 两面凹的,双凹的。*a* ~ *lens* 双凹面透镜。

bi·con·vex [ˈbaiˈkɔnveks; baɪˋkɑnvɛks] ***a*.** 两面凸的,双凸的。

bi·corn [ˈbaikɔːn; ˋbaɪkɔrn] **I** ***a*.** **1.** 【动、植】有两角的,有两角状物的。**2.** 新月形的。*a* ~ *rhinoceros* 两角犀。**II** ***n*.** 有双角的帽子[动物] (= bicornuate)。

bi·cor·po·ral [baiˈkɔːpərəl, -prəl; baɪˋkɔrpərəl, -prəl] ***a*.** **1.** 有两体的,双身的。**2.** 【天】有两个主部的〔黄道十二宫的某些标志〕(= bicorporeal)。

bi·cron [ˈbaikrɔn; ˋbaɪkrɑn] ***n*.** 10^{-9} 米,毫微米〔一米的一千兆分之一,符号是 μμ〕。

bi·crural [baiˈkruərəl; baɪˋkrʊərəl] ***a*.** 双腿的。

bi·cul·tur·al [baiˈkʌltʃərəl; baɪˋkʌltʃərəl] ***a*.** 两种文化的;有关[包括]两种文化的。

bi·cus·pid [baiˈkʌspid; baɪˋkʌspɪd] **I** ***n*.** 【解】二尖齿,前臼齿。**II** ***a*.** 有二尖头的。~ **valve** 【解】二尖瓣。

bi·cy·cle [ˈbaisikl; ˋbaɪsɪkl̩] **I** ***n*.** **1.** 自行车,脚踏车〔又名 push-~,系对 motor-~ 而言〕。**2.** 〔美〕〔卡车驾驶员用语〕机器脚踏车。**3.** (学生作弊用的)夹带。*a lady's* ~ = *a* ~ *for ladies* 女用自行车,女车。*a racing* ~ 赛车,跑车。*a convertible* ~ 男女兼用型自行车。*a tandem* ~ 双座自行车。*ride* (*on*) *a* ~骑自行车。*go by* [*on a*] ~ 骑(自行)车去。*walk the* ~ 推着(自行)车。**II** ***vi*.** 骑自行车。~ *to the office* 骑(自行)车上班。

bi·cy·cler [ˈbaisiklə; ˋbaɪsɪklɚ], **bi·cy·clist** [ˈbaisiklist; ˋbaɪsɪklɪst] ***n*.** 骑自行车的(人)。*a professional* ~ 自行车运动员。

bi·cy·clic [baiˈsaiklik, -ˈsiklik; baɪˋsaɪklɪk, -ˋsɪklɪk] ***a*.** **1.** 双环的,形成双环的;两个轮子的;自行车的。**2.** 【植、化】二环的。

bid [bid; bɪd] **I** ***vt*.** (***bade*** [beid; bed], ***bid***, 〔古〕***bad*** [bæd; bæd]; ***bid·den*** [ˈbidn; ˋbɪdn], ***bid***) **1.** 〔书〕命令,嘱,吩咐〔过去式多用 bade〕。**2.** 〔书〕表示(欢迎),告(别),赠(言)祝〔过去式多用 bade〕。**3.** 出价,(拍卖时的)竞买,喊(价)〔过去式及过去分词多用 bid〕。**4.** 【古】邀,请;发表(结婚预告等),公告〔过去式多用 bade〕。**5.** 【牌】叫(牌)〔过去式和过去分词多用 bid〕。**6.** 〔美口〕接纳[吸收]…为会员[成员]。*Do as you are* ~ [*bidden*]. 请照吩咐去做。*Bid him go* [*to go*]. 叫他走开吧。~ *sb*. *good-night* 祝某人晚安。~ *farewell* 告别。~ *welcome* [*good-bye*] *to* 向…表示欢迎[告别]。~ *three spades* 叫牌打黑桃三。*a bidden guest* 邀来之客。— ***vi*.** **1.** 出价;〔美〕投标。**2.** 叫牌。**3.** 〔书〕嘱咐,吩咐。~ ***against each other*** 竞相出价。~ ***defiance to*** 见 defiance 条。~ ***fair to*** 有…的可能,有…的希望 (*This plan* ~*s fair to be a success*. 此项计划大有成功希望)。~ ***for*** **1.** 投标求包(工程)。**2.** 出价竞买(某物)。**3.** 争取得到(拥护等)。~ ***in*** 拍卖人故意抬高售价使(拍卖物)落入自手。~ ***off*** **1.** 使(拍卖物)卖出[标落他手]。**2.** 给以拍卖处分。~ ***on*** (*some project*) 承包(某工程等的)投标; ~ ***up*** (拍卖中)竞出高价,哄价,抬价。**II** ***n*.** **1.** 出价,喊价,投标。**2.** 【牌】叫牌;有资格叫牌的一手牌。**3.** 〔美俚〕邀请,提议。**4.** 努力,企图。***call for*** ~***s on*** 招标。***in a vain*** ~妄图。***make a*** [***one's***] ~ ***for*** **1.** 投标争取承包;(拍卖中)出价竞买。**2.** 企图得到(人望、恩宠等)。 ~***-proof*** ***a*.** 不易被外公司收购的。

B

b.i.d., **BID** = 〔L.〕*bis in die*【处方】一日两次（= twice a day）。

bi·dar·ka [baiˈdɑːkə; baɪˋdɑrkə], **bi·dar·kee** [baiˈdɑːki; baɪˋdɑrkɪ] ***n.*** （爱斯基摩人）用海豹皮做的皮舟。

bid·da·ble [ˈbidəbl; ˋbɪdəbl] ***a.*** **1.** 柔顺的，驯良的〔尤指孩子〕。**2.**【牌】有叫牌资格的。*a ~ suit at bridge* 桥牌中有叫牌资格的一手牌。

bid·den [ˈbidn; ˋbɪdn] bid 的过去分词。

bid·der [ˈbidə; ˋbɪdɚ] ***n.*** **1.** （拍卖中的）出价人，竞买人；投标人。**2.** 命令者，嘱咐者。**3.**【牌】叫牌人。**4.**〔美俚〕邀请。

bid·ding [ˈbidiŋ; ˋbɪdɪŋ] ***n.*** **1.** 出价，投标。**2.** 命令，吩咐。**3.** 邀请。**4.** 公告。**5.** 叫牌。***at one's*** [***sb.'s***] ~ 依嘱，遵命（*He seemed to have the whole world at his ~.* 他自以为全世界捏在他手里。*We went there at his ~.* 我们照他的吩咐去那里）。***do one's*** [***sb.'s***] ~ 照…的命令做，照…的话办。~ **block** 拍卖场。~ **prayer**〔英〕讲道前的祷告。

Bid·dle [ˈbidl; ˋbɪdl] ***n.*** 比德尔〔姓氏〕。

bid·dy[1] [ˈbidi; ˋbɪdɪ] ***n.*** 〔美，英方〕小鸡，鸡。

bid·dy[2] [ˈbidi; ˋbɪdɪ] ***n.*** 〔俚〕**1.** 大惊小怪〔小题大作〕的人。**2.** 神经质的老太婆；长舌妇。**3.** 女仆，女佣。**4.**〔俚〕女教师。

bide [baid; baɪd] ***vi.*** （~***d***, ***bode*** [bəud; bod], ***bade*** [beid, bæd; bed, bæd]; ~***d***,〔古〕***bid*** [bid; bɪd]）〔古、诗、方〕**1.** 持续。**2.** 等候，住，留。— ***vt.*** **1.** 忍耐，经受。**2.** 等待〔仅用于 ~ one's time 中〕。~ *a storm* 经受一场风暴。~ ***one's time*** 待机，等机会。

bi·dent [ˈbaidənt; ˋbaɪdənt] ***n.*** 两尖器，两叉矛。

bi·den·tate [baiˈdenteit; baɪˋdɛntet] ***a.***【生】有两齿的，两齿的；有两齿状的。

bi·det [ˈbiːdei; ˋbide] ***n.*** 〔F.〕**1.** 小马。**2.** （房内洗身用的）脚盆。

bi·di·a·lec·tal [baiˈdaiəˌlektəl; baɪˋdaɪəˏlɛktəl] ***a.***，***n.*** 能流利地说同一语言中两种方言的（人）。

bi·di·a·lec·tal·ism [baiˈdaiəlektəˌlizəm; baɪˋdaɪəlɛktəˏlɪzəm], **bi·di·a·lect·ism** [baiˈdaiəˌlektizəm; baɪˋdaɪəˏlɛktɪzəm] ***n.*** 对同一语言中两种方言的精通。

bi·don·ville [biːdɔ̃ˈviːl; bidɔ̃ˋvil] ***n.*** 〔F.〕（北非的）市郊贫民区。

bie·ber·ite [ˈbiːbərait; ˋbibəraɪt] ***n.***【矿】赤矾，钴矾。

bield [ˈbiːld; ˋbild] **I** ***n.*** 〔Scot.〕避难所，避雨处。**II** ***vt.*** 隐避，掩护，寄身。

Bie·lo·rus·sia = Byelorussia.

bien en·ten·du [bjæn ɔntɔnˈdjuː; bjæn ɑntɑnˋdju]〔F.〕那自然，不言而喻，必定。

bi·en·ni·al [baiˈeniəl; baɪˋɛnɪəl] **I** ***a.*** **1.** 二年一次的；持续两年的。**2.**【植】二年生的。**II** ***n.*** 二年生植物；二年一次的事物；两年一次的试验。**-ly** ***ad.*** 两年一次地；一连两年地。

bi·en·ni·um [baiˈeniəm; baɪˋɛnɪəm] ***n.*** （*pl.* ***bi·en·ni·a*** [baiˈenjə; baɪˋɛnjə]）〔L.〕二年间，两年的时期。

bien·ve·nue [bjæ̃nvəˈnjuː; ˏbjɛ̃vəˋny] ***n.*** 〔F.〕受欢迎（= welcome）。

bier[1] [biə; bɪr] ***n.*** **1.** 棺架，尸架。**2.** 棺材。

bier[2] [biə; bɪr] ***n.*** = beer[2].

biest·ings [ˈbiːstiŋz; ˋbistɪŋz] ***n.*** （牛产后的）初乳（= beestings）。

bi·fa·cial [baiˈfeiʃəl; baɪˋfeʃəl] ***a.*** **1.** （正反）两面一样的。**2.**【植】有两面的；（叶子等）正反两面不同的，异面的。~ *leaves* 异面叶。

bi·far·i·ous [baiˈfeəriəs; baɪˋfɛrɪəs] ***a.*** **1.**【植】二重的；相背的。**2.** 二纵列的。

bi·fer [ˈbaifə; ˋbaɪfɚ] ***n.*** 一年开花两次的植物。

biff [bif; bɪf] **I** ***n.*** 〔美俚〕梆地一打，啪地一击。**II** ***vt.*** （梆地）打，殴打。*give a ~ on the head* 对头上梆地一记。~***ing brawl***〔美口〕拳击比赛。

bif·fin [ˈbifin; ˋbɪfɪn] ***n.*** 〔英〕**1.** 深红色餐用苹果。**2.** 苹果饼。

bi·fid [ˈbaifid; ˋbaɪfɪd] ***a.***【天】二叉的，叉形的（慧星尾等）；【植】两裂的。

bi·fi·lar [baiˈfailə; baɪˋfaɪlɚ] **I** ***a.*** 双线的；涉及两条线的。**II** ***n.***【机】双线千分尺。**-ly** ***ad.***

bi·flag·el·late [baiˈflædʒilit, -ˌleit; baɪˋflædʒɪlɪt, -ˏlet] ***a.***【生】有两纤匐枝的，双鞭毛的。

bi·flex [ˈbaifleks; ˋbaɪflɛks] ***a.*** 有双处弯曲的。

bi·fo·cal [baiˈfəukəl; baɪˋfokl] **I** ***a.*** **1.**【物】双焦点的。**2.** （望远镜等）远近两用的。**3.** 有二重观点的。*a ~ view* 双重观点。**II** ***n.*** 〔*pl.*〕双光眼镜，远近视两用眼镜；双焦点透镜。

bi·fo·li·ate [baiˈfəuliit, baiˈfəulieit; baɪˋfolɪɪt, baɪˋfolɪet] ***a.***【植】有二叶的，双叶的。

bi·forked [ˈbaiˌfɔːkt; ˋbaɪˏfɔrkt] ***a.*** = bifurcate.

bi·form [ˈbaifɔːm; ˋbaɪˏfɔrm] ***a.*** 有两形的〔如人鱼等〕，两种形体结合成的；把不同两体的特征合在一起的。

Bif·rost [ˈbiːfrɔst; ˋbifrɑst] ***n.***【北欧神】从地上通向天宫的彩虹桥。

bi·fur·cate [ˈbaifəːkeit; ˋbaɪfɚˏket, baɪˋfɚkɪt] **I** ***a.***【植】成叉的，两叉的，分为二枝的。**II** ***vi.*** 成叉状；分叉。— ***vt.*** 使分叉。**-ly** ***ad.***

bi·fur·ca·tion [ˌbaifəːˈkeiʃən; ˏbaɪfɚˋkeʃən] ***n.*** **1.** 分枝，分叉。**2.** 分叉点，分枝点。

big [big; bɪg] **I** ***a.*** **1.** 大，巨大；大规模的；已长大的。**2.**〔口〕重要的，重大的；伟大的；出名的，极成功的，受欢迎的。**3.** 骄傲的，傲慢的，自大的。**4.** 怀着（孕），有（身子）；〔喻〕充满着…的，洋溢着…的（*with*）。**5.** 宽大的，宽宏大量的。**6.**〔口〕（风等）剧烈的。*a ~ house* 大房子。*a ~ enterprise* 大企业。*a ~ pay* 高薪。*art with a ~ A* 具有特种暗含意义的艺术；抽象的艺术。*the ~ man of the town* 城中名人。~ *words* 豪言壮语，大话。*He looks ~.* 他神气活现。*That's very ~ of you.* 你真宽宏大量。~ *with* (*young*, *child*) 怀孕，有喜。*a question ~ with the fate of the Empire* 有关帝国生死存亡的问题。*eyes ~ with tears* 满眼泪水。*a ~ storm* [*earthquake*] 剧烈的风暴〔地震〕。*a ~ piece of news* 重要新闻。***as ~ as life*** 和原物一样大。***be ~ on***〔口〕热衷；偏爱。***be*** [***get***, ***grow***] ***too ~ for one's boots*** [***breeches***, ***trousers***] 妄自尊大，目中无人。***go over ~***〔美口〕（演出等）大大成功；（演员等）大受欢迎。***make ~***〔美俚〕飞黄腾达。**II** ***ad.*** **1.**〔口〕非常大量。**2.**〔口〕自大，夸大。**3.** 宽宏大量地。**4.** 成功地。*talk ~* 吹牛。*eat ~* 食量大。*a ~ busy day* 忙得不可开交的一天。*pay ~* 付给高薪〔高报酬〕。**III** ***n.*** 大亨，巨子；大公司。**B~ Apple** **1.** 大地方（纽约市的别称）。**2.** 最重要部分；注意的中心；焦点。~ **bad (wolf)**〔美口〕市面萧条，不景气。~**-bang (theory)**【天】（宇宙起源的大爆炸（学说）；（改变事态进程的）轰动性事件。~ **beat** 摇摆音乐。~ **beef**〔美俚〕蠢汉。**B- Ben** 英国议会大厦上的大钟〔直径 2.8 米，重 13,500 公斤〕。**B- Bertha**〔美俚〕德国巨型加农炮；大型客机；【拳】拳击。**B- Board**〔美〕纽约证券交易所（行情牌）。~ **board**〔美〕热门股票。~ **box** 仓储式商店。~ **boy**〔美俚〕好家伙，好一个大汉；大人物；大型野炮；百元钞票；大学中特别突出的学生。~ **bozo** [ˈbəuzəu; ˋbozo]〔美俚〕著名拳击选手。~ **brother** 老大哥。〔B- B-〕专制国家〔组织〕（的领导）。~ **brute** = ~ bozo. ~ **bug**〔美俚〕要人，名人。~ **business** 大企业，大财阀。~ **butter-and-egg man**〔美俚〕骄傲俗气的乡下富翁，土财主。~ **cheese**〔美俚〕大人物；大亨；有权利的人，官老爷；粗鲁的男子。~ **coat**〔Scot.〕= overcoat. **B- Ditch**〔美俚〕**1.** 大洋。**2.**〔the B- D-〕大西洋；巴拿马运河。~ **dog** **1.** 看门狗；保镖。**2.**〔美俚〕大物。~ **dough**〔美俚〕巨款，大笔款子。~ **dress** 宽松式女服。~ **drink**〔美俚〕**1.** 大洋。**2.** 密西西比河。~ **enchi-**

lada 要人,要员;有影响[权势]的人。~ **end**【机】连杆头。~ **eye** 大眼鲷科鱼。~**-eyed** *a*. **1.** 大眼的。**2.** 惊讶的。**B- Five** 世界五强〔指第一次世界大战巴黎会议中的美、英、法、意、日,或指第二次大战后之中、美、英、法、苏〕。~ **friend**〔俚〕(己方的)轰炸机。~ **game**【猎】巨兽〔象、狮子等〕;(钓鱼)大鱼;〔俚〕(需冒危险获得的)特大奖赏[目标]。**B- Government** 实行高压统治的政府。~ **gun** = ~ bug. ~ **guy**〔美俚〕官吏;老板;暴徒头子;要人,名人,上帝。~ **hair** 大背头〔一种发型〕。~ **hand**〔美俚〕大喝彩。~ **head**〔美俚〕自大,自大的人;喝醉;(兽类)头部浮肿病。~ **headed** *a*. 自大的。~ **heart**(海一样)宽大的胸怀。~ **house**〔美俚〕州[联邦]监狱;村中首户;〔卑〕习艺所,济贫院。~ **idea**〔美〕计划,提议;意图,目的。**B- Inch**(二次大战中美国所筑)大输油管。~ **iron**〔口〕电脑主机硬件。~ **jeep**〔俚〕巨型轰炸机。~ **John**〔俚〕新兵。~**-leagued** *a*.〔美〕第一流的,头等的。~ **mouth**〔美俚〕多嘴多舌的人。~ **name**〔美俚〕名士。~**-name** *a*. 名人鼎鼎的。~ **noise**〔美俚〕轰动一时的事实[声明];名人,要人;重磅炸弹。~ **Navy**【政】大海军主义。~ **one**〔美俚〕**1.** 千元钞票。**2.** 大便。**3.**〔the ~〕重要节目。**B- pond** [**puddle**] 大西洋的别名。~ **shot**〔俚〕= ~ bug. ~ **stick**〔美〕**1.** 武力,实力,威吓,大棒政策。**2.**〔美口〕长梯,云梯。**3.**〔*pl.*〕大片森林带。~ **tent, Big Tent**"大帐篷"政策〔指包容各种不同政治和社会观点的政策〕;兼容并蓄的宽松政策。~**-ticket** *a*. 高价的。~ **time**〔口〕**1.**(杂技等的)大成功。**2.** 最高水准;最重要的位置。**3.** 欢乐愉快的时刻。~ **time** *a*. 有名的;有钱的;成功的。~ **toe** 脚拇趾。~ **tree**【植】巨杉。~ **wheel**〔美俚〕要人。~ **wig** = ~ bug. **-ness** *n*. 大,巨大,庞大,重大;夸大(*bigness scale* 粗测)。

big·a·lop·o·lis [ˌbigəˈlɔpəlis; ˏbɪgəˋlɑpɪs] *n*.〔美口〕大都市。

bi·gam·ic [baiˈgæmik, biˈgæmik; baɪˋgæmɪk, bɪˋgæmɪk] *a*. 重婚的。

big·a·mist [ˈbigəmist; ˋbaɪgəmɪst] *n*. 重婚者,犯重婚罪者。**-ic** *a*. **-ti·cal·ly** *ad*.

big·a·mous [ˈbigəməs; ˋbɪgəməs] *a*. 重婚的;犯重婚罪的。

big·a·my [ˈbigəmi; ˋbɪgemɪ] *n*. 重婚,重婚罪;【宗】违反教会诫律的婚姻。

big·ar·reau [ˌbigəˈrəu, ˈbigərəu; ˏbɪgəˋro, ˋbɪgəro] *n*.〔B-〕红白樱桃(= bigaroon)。

bi·gem·i·nal [baiˈdʒeminl; baɪˋdʒɛmɪnəl] *a*.【解】二联的,成双的,成对的。~ *pulse* 二联脉。

bi·gem·i·ny [baiˈdʒemini; baɪˋdʒɛmɪnɪ] *n*.【生理】重发状态,两两连发〔比如心脏的律动一跳是两下〕。

bi·gen·er [ˈbaidʒinə; ˋbaɪdʒənɚ] *n*.【生】属间杂种。

bi·ge·ner·ic [ˌbaidʒiˈnerik; ˏbaɪdʒəˋnɛrɪk] *a*.【生】属间杂种的。

big·foot [ˈbigfut; ˋbɪgfʊt] *n*. 大脚毛人(= sasquatch)。

bigg [big; bɪg] *n*.〔Scot.〕四棱大麦。

big·ge·ty [ˈbigiti; ˋbɪgɪtɪ] *a*.〔美〕傲慢的。

big·gie [ˈbigi; ˋbɪgɪ] *n*.〔口〕权贵,大亨,权要人物,名人,伟人,要人(= bigwig)。

big·gin [ˈbigin; ˋbɪgɪn] *n*. **1.**〔英方〕童帽。**2.** 睡帽。

big·ging, big·gin [ˈbigin; ˋbɪgɪn] *n*.〔英方〕大楼,建筑物。

big·gish [ˈbigiʃ; ˋbɪgɪʃ] *a*. 稍大的。

big·horn [ˈbighɔːn; ˋbɪgˏhɔrn] *n*. 巨角岩羊。

bight [bait; baɪt] I *n*. **1.**(海岸线或江岸等的)弯曲部;海湾。**2.**【海】绳耳,绳扣;一条松开的绳子中部。*the Great Australian B-* 澳大利亚大海湾。II *vt*. 把(绳子)结成扣;用绳扣缚住。

big·no·ni·a [bigˈnəuniə; bɪgˋnonɪə] *n*.【植】比格诺藤属植物。

big·ot [ˈbigət; ˋbɪgət] *n*. 顽固的迷信者,盲信者;执拗的人。**-ed** *a*. 顽固的,执迷不悟的,执拗的(*She is bigoted to* [*in*] *her opinion*. 她固执己见)。

big·ot·ry [ˈbigətri; ˋbɪgətrɪ] *n*. **1.** 固执,顽固,执拗;偏狭。**2.** 固执的行为。

Bi·har [biˈhɑː; bɪˋhɑr] **State** 比哈尔邦〔印度邦名〕。

bi·jou [ˈbiːʒuː; ˋbiʒu] I *n*. (*pl*. ***-joux*** [ˈbiːʒuːz; ˋbiʒuz]) 〔F.〕**1.** 宝石,珠宝;玉石装饰品。**2.** 小巧精致的物品。II *a*. (汽车、别墅等)小巧精致的。*a* ~ *villa* 小巧精致的别墅。

bi·jou·te·rie [biːˈʒuːtəri; bɪˋʒutərɪ] *n*.〔F.〕**1.** 宝石,珠宝。**2.** 小巧精致的装饰品。

bi·ju·gate [ˈbaidʒugeit, baiˈdʒuːgit; ˋbaɪdʒʊˏget, baɪˋdʒugɪt] *a*.【植】二对的,二对小叶的(= bijugous)。

bike[1] [baik; baɪk] I *n*.〔口〕**1.** = bicycle. **2.** 电动自行车。**3.** 摩托车。II *vi*. 骑自行车;骑摩托车。~ **grind**〔美〕自行车比赛。~ **way** 自行车道。**-r** *n*. 骑自行车的人。

bike[2] [baik; baɪk] *n*.〔Scot.〕**1.**(蚁、蜂等的)群体,大群,窝。**2.** 人群,群众。

Bi·ki·ni [biˈkiːni; bɪˋkinɪ] *n*. **1.** 比基尼岛〔1946 年美国原子弹实验地〕。**2.**〔b-〕(半裸体的)比基尼式女子游泳衣。

bi·la·bi·al [baiˈleibiəl; baɪˋlebɪəl] I *a*. **1.** 有两唇的,两唇的。**2.**【语音】唇音的,双唇音的(如 p, b, m 等)。II *n*.【语音】唇音。

bi·la·bi·ate [baiˈleibieit; baɪˋlebɪˏet] *a*.【植】二唇的,二唇形的。

bil·an·der [ˈbiləndə, ˈbailəndə; ˋbɪləndɚ, ˋbaɪləndɚ] *n*. 双桅小船。

bi·lat·er·al [baiˈlætərəl; baɪˋlætərəl] I *a*. **1.**【动、植】两侧[左右]对称的。**2.** 两侧的,两边的。**3.** 双方的,双边的。**4.** 双向(作用)的,双通的;对向的。**5.** 双系的。*the* ~ *symmetry of the organs* 器官左右对称。~ *affiliation* 双系亲属关系。~ *circuit* 双向电路。~ *switching* 双通开关。~ *treaty* 双边条约。II *n*. 双边会议;双边会谈。**-ism** *n*. **1.**(贸易)互惠主义。**2.**(动植物器官)的左右对称。

Bil·ba·o [bilˈbɑːəu; bɪlˋbɑo] *n*. 毕尔巴鄂〔西班牙港市〕。

bil·ber·ry [ˈbilbəri; ˋbɪlˏbɛrɪ] *n*.【植】欧洲越橘。

bil·bo[1] [ˈbilbəu; ˋbɪlbo] *n*. (*pl*. *~s*, *~es*)〔诗〕剑;(西班牙 Bilbo 地方产)比尔波剑;精工冶制的剑。

bil·bo[2] [ˈbilbəu; ˋbɪlbo] *n*. (*pl*. *~es*)〔常 *pl*.〕足枷式脚镣。

bil·bo·ism [ˈbilbəizəm; ˋbɪlbəɪzəm] *n*.〔美〕种族仇视;顽固,偏执。

bile [bail; baɪl] *n*. **1.**【生理】胆汁。**2.** 愤怒,生气,坏脾气,乖戾。*black* ~ 忧郁。***rouse*** [***stir***] ***sb.'s*** ~ 逗恼人,激怒人。~ **acid**【化】胆汁酸。~ **stone** *n*.【医】胆石。

bi·lec·tion [baiˈlekʃən; baɪˋlɛkʃən] *n*.【建】凸出嵌线(= bolection)。

bi·lev·el [baiˈlevl; baɪˋlɛvl] *n*. 两层平房〔第二层入口低于地面〕。

bilge [bildʒ; bɪldʒ] I *n*. **1.**(桶等的)中腹,鼓起部分。**2.**【海】船底弯曲部(尤指船底和船侧间的弯曲部)。**3.** 船底污水。**4.**〔口〕糊涂话,傻话;无聊文章。II *vi*. **1.**【海】船底开口;舱底漏水。**2.** 鼓胀,凸出。**3.**〔美俚〕考试不及格。— *vt*. 把(舱底)凿破,使(舱底)漏水。~ **keel** 舭龙骨。~ **pump** 舱底污水泵。~ **water**【海】舱水,舱底污水;〔俚〕废话。

bilg·y [ˈbildʒi; ˋbɪldʒɪ] *a*. 有船底污水臭味的。

bil·har·zi·a [bilˈhɑːziə; bɪlˋhɑrzɪə] *n*. 裂体吸虫,住血吸虫;住血吸虫病。

bil·har·zi·a·sis [ˌbilhɑːˈzaiəsis; ˏbɪlhɑrˋzaɪəsɪs] *n*. 裂体吸虫病,住血吸虫病。

bil·i·ar·y [ˈbiljəri; ˋbɪlɪˏɛrɪ] *a*. 胆汁的;输送胆汁的。*a* ~ *duct* 胆管。~ **calculus** 胆石。

bi·lin·e·ar [baiˈliniə; baɪˋlɪnɪr] *a*.【数】双线性的,双一

B

B

次性的。~ *coordinates* 双一次座标。

bi·lin·gual [baiˈliŋgwəl; baɪˋlɪŋgwəl] **I** ***a*.** **1.** 两国语言的。**2.** 能讲两国话的。**3.** 用两种语言书写[印刷]的。**II** ***n*.** 能讲两国话的人。**-ism** ***n*.** 使用[通]两种语言。**-ly** ***ad*.**

bi·lin·guist [baiˈliŋgwist; baɪˋlɪŋgwɪst] ***n*.** 通两国语言的人。

bil·ious [ˈbiljəs; ˋbɪljəs] ***a*.** **1.** 胆汁(质)的;胆汁病(引起)的。**2.** 易怒的,脾气大的。~ **complaint** 胆汁病。

bil·i·ru·bin [ˌbiliˈruːbin; ˏbɪləˋrubɪn] ***n*.**【生理】胆红素。

bi·lit·er·al [baiˈlitərəl; baɪˋlɪtərəl] ***a*.** **1.** 由两个字母构成的。**2.** 由两种字体构成的。*a* ~ *word* 两个字母构成的单词。

-bi·li·ty *comb. f.* 与 -ble, -able, -ible, -uble 相对应的构词成份: possi*bility*.

bil·i·ver·din [ˌbiliˈvəːdin; ˏbɪləˋvɝdɪn] ***n*.**【生理】胆绿素。

bilk [bilk; bɪlk] **I** ***vt*.** **1.** 逃避付钱给…,赖掉(账、债等)。**2.** 欺,骗,瞒。**3.** 挫败,使受挫。~ *a cabman* 蒙混坐车,白坐出租汽车。~ *his creditors* 赖账。~ *sb. out of his money* 骗取某人的钱。*She ~ed his efforts to discover her*. 她使他找寻她的努力落空。**II** ***n*.** **1.** 赖账,混骗。**2.** 骗子。**-er** ***n*.** 骗子;坐车不买票的人;赖账者。

Bill [bil; bɪl] ***n*.** 比尔〔男子名, William 的昵称〕。

bill[1] [bil; bɪl] **I** ***n*.** **1.** 账单;清单。**2.** 报单,贴条,招贴,告白,传单,广告;戏单,戏报。**3.**【商】证券;汇票,支票,票据;凭单。**4.**〔美〕纸币;〔美俚〕百元钞票。**5.** 议案,法案;【法】起诉书,诉状。*a time* ~ 时间表。*a grocery* ~ 食品店(收款)账单。*Post* [*Stick*] *no ~s*. 禁止招贴。*introduce* [*bring in*] *a* ~ 提出议案。*reject* [*throw out*] *a* ~ 否决议案。*a ten-dollar* ~ 一张十元钞票。~ *at* (*3 days'*) *sight* 见票后(三天)照付的汇票(等)。~ *for collection* 代收[托收]票据。~ *of clearance* 出港报表。~ *of costs*【法】讼费清单。~ *of credit* 取款凭单;付款通知书。~ *of debt* 期票。~ *of dishonour* 被拒付支票。~ *of entry* 入港报表,报税通知单。~ *of exchange* 汇票。~ *of fare* 菜单;戏单,剧目。~ *of health* (船员、船客)健康证书;检疫证。~ *of lading* 运货证书,提单,提货凭单〔略作 B/L〕。~ *of mortality* 死亡统计表。~ *of parcels* 发票。~ *of quantities*〔英〕建筑细则。*pay a* ~付账。**II** ***vt*.** **1.** 填报;填(表),把…列成表。**2.** 开账单给…。**3.** (以传单、广告等)宣布,贴海报。~ *goods* 开列商品清单[目录]。~ *passengers* 填报乘客名单。*The store will* ~ *me*. 百货店要给我送账单来了。*She is ~ed to lecture tonight*. 贴海报说她今晚演讲。***a B- of Oblivion*** 大赦令。~ ***of sale*** 卖据;【法】抵押证券。~ ***of sight*** (海关)临时起岸报单。~ ***of store*** (海岸)船上用品免税单;再输入免税单。~ ***payable*** [***receivable***] 应付[应取]票据。~ ***to bearer*** [***order***] 不记名[记名]票据。***fill the*** ~〔美口〕符合要求,解决问题。***find a true*** ~ (陪审团认为)诉状应予受理。***foot the*** ~〔口〕**1.** 负担费用,会钞。**2.** 承担责任。***head the*** ~ (演员)挂头牌,领衔主演。***ignore the*** ~ (陪审团认为)诉状不应受理。***kill the*** ~ 否决议案,阻止议案通过。***post*** (***up***) ***a*** ~ 贴标语(等)。***sell*** (*sb.*) ***a*** ~ ***of goods***〔美〕以花言巧语等骗得(某人)相信[同意]。**the B- of Rights** **1.**《权利法案》〔英国 1689 年颁布的确立君主立宪制的根本大法之一〕。**2.**《人权法案》〔美国宪法的第一次修正案, 1789 年通过〕。~ **board** **1.**〔美〕广告牌,揭示牌。**2.**【海】锚床。~ **book** 支票簿,解款[送金]簿。~ **broker** 证券经纪人。~ **discounter** 贴现业者。~ **fold** 单据夹,票夹,钱夹。~ **head** (印有招牌地址等的)空白单据[发票等]。~ **poster**, ~ **sticker** **1.** 贴广告(等)的人。**2.**〔美俚〕伪造票据者,伪造票据犯。~ **stamp** 印花税票。

bill[2] [bil; bɪl] **I** ***n*.** **1.** (水禽等细长而扁平的)嘴〔猛禽的钩状嘴通常叫 beak〕。**2.** 嘴状岬。**3.** 锚爪。**4.** 鹤嘴锄;钩镰;钩状戟。**II** ***vi*.** **1.** (鸽子似地)接嘴,亲嘴,接吻。**2.** 亲热,爱抚。~ ***and coo*** (鸽子)接嘴;〔喻〕(男女间)互相接吻,爱抚和喁喁情话。

bill[3] [bil; bɪl] ***n*.** **1.** (欧洲中世纪步兵用的)长柄矛。**2.** = billhook. ~**-hook** (剪枝等用的)钩镰,钩刀。

bill·a·bong [ˈbiləˌbɔŋ; ˋbɪləˏbɑŋ] ***n*.** **1.** 回水湖,回水池,死水潭。**2.** 只有在一定季节才涨水的干涸河床。

bill·bug [ˈbilˌbʌg; ˋbɪlˏbʌg] ***n*.**【虫】象岬。

bill·er [ˈbilə; ˋbɪlɚ] ***n*.** **1.** 开账单的人;开清单的人。**2.** 账单机。

bil·let[1] [ˈbilit; ˋbɪlɪt] **I** ***n*.** **1.**【军】分配令〔军事当局发给户主指示提供军人住宿地的命令〕。**2.** (兵士分住民家或公共建筑物时的)营舍。**3.**〔英〕职位,地位。**4.** 便条;短简。**5.**【海】船员宿舍。*a good* ~ 好差事。***Every bullet has its*** ~. 颗颗子弹有归宿;天命难违。**II** ***vt*.** 为…指定宿营地,为…分配宿舍 (*on*)。~ *soldiers on a village* 把士兵安顿在一个村子里宿营。*We arrange with the townspeople to* ~ *the students*. 我们和镇上人协商给学生提供宿舍。— ***vi*.** 住屯。*They ~ed in Youth Hotel*. 他们在青年饭店住下来。

bil·let[2] [ˈbilit; ˋbɪlɪt] ***n*.** **1.** 木柴块。**2.** (金属的)坯段;钢坯。**3.**【建】错齿饰。*steel* ~钢坯。*solid* ~ 整轧坯,实心坯。~ **wood** 圆材。

bill., billds = billiards.

bil·let-doux [bileiˈduː; bɪlɪˋdu] ***n*.** (*pl*. ***bil·lets-doux*** [ˈbileiˈduːz; ˋbɪleˋduz]) 〔F.〕情书;〔反〕不愿收到的信[催账信等]。

bill·fish [ˈbilfiʃ; ˋbɪlfɪʃ] ***n*.** (*pl*. ~, ~*es*) 长喙鱼〔有细长如鸟喙之颌的鱼,如针鱼〕,帆鱼,旗鱼,真旗鱼。

bil·liard [ˈbilijəd; ˋbɪljɚd] **I** ***a*.** 台球(用)的〔仅作修饰语〕。*a* ~ *cue* (台球)球棒。*a* ~ *marker* (台球)记分员。*a* ~ *room* 弹子房。*a* ~ *table* (台球)球桌,弹子台。**II** ***n*.**〔美口〕= carom ***n*.**

bil·liards [ˈbiljədz; ˋbɪljɚdz] ***n*.**〔*pl*.〕台球戏〔俗称"打弹子",常作单数用〕。*play* (*at*) ~ 打台球,打弹子。*have a game at* ~ 比赛台球,比赛打弹子。*B- isn't popular here*. 这里不流行玩台球。

Bil·lie [ˈbili; ˋbɪlɪ] ***n*.** **1.** 比莉〔女子名〕。**2.** = Billy.

Bil·li·ken [ˈbilikən; ˋbɪlɪkən] ***n*.**〔美〕福神(神像)。

bill·ing [ˈbiliŋ; ˋbɪlɪŋ] ***n*.** **1.** (节目单、剧院门口华盖等上的)演员表。**2.** (演员表上的)演员名次。

Bil·lings·gate [ˈbiliŋzgit; ˋbɪlɪŋzˏgɪt] ***n*.** **1.** (昔日的)伦敦鱼市场。**2.** [b-] 猥亵话,下流话,骂人话。

bil·lion [ˈbiljən; ˋbɪljən] ***n*., *a*.** **1.**〔法、美〕十亿(的)(= 10^9)。**2.**〔英、德〕万亿(的)(= 10^{12})。**3.** 无数(的)。*several ~s of people* 几十亿人。~ *electron-volts* 十亿电子伏。

bil·lion·aire [biljəˈnɛə; ˏbɪljənˋɛr] ***n*.** 亿万富翁。

bil·lionth [ˈbiljənθ; ˋbɪljənθ] **I** ***a*.** **1.** 第十亿(个)的〔美、法用法〕。**2.** 第一万亿(个)的〔英、德用法〕。**II** ***num*.** **1.** 第十亿,十亿分之一。**2.** 第一万亿,万亿分之一。

bil·lon [ˈbilən; ˋbɪlən] ***n*.** 金铜[银铜]铸币合金,金[银]与其他金属的合金。

bil·low [ˈbiləu; ˋbɪlo] **I** ***n*.** **1.** 巨浪;〔诗〕波涛;滚滚烟尘(等)。**2.**〔诗〕〔the ~s〕海。*angry ~s* 怒涛。*~s of flames* 烈焰翻滚。~ *cloud* 波状云。**II** ***vi*.** 起大浪,波涛汹涌;(烟尘)翻滚。*flags ~ing in the breeze*. 旗子飘扬。— ***vt*.** 使翻腾。

bil·low·y [ˈbiləui; ˋbɪloɪ] ***a*.** 巨浪的;巨浪似的;起巨浪的波涛汹涌的,波浪滔天的。*a rough*, ~ *sea* 翻江倒海卷巨浪。

Bil·ly, Billie [ˈbili; ˋbɪlɪ] ***n*.** 比利〔男子名, William 的昵称〕。

bil·ly[1] [ˈbili; ˋbɪlɪ] ***n*.** **1.** 警棍;棍棒。**2.**〔Scot.〕伙伴,朋友,弟兄。**3.**【英纺】粗纱机。~**boy**【英】独桅平底船。~ **club** 警棍,棍棒。~ **cock**〔英〕(宽边低顶的)毡帽。~**-goat** 公山羊。

B

bil·ly[2][ˈbili; ˋbɪlɪ] *n*.〔澳〕(野营烧水用的)洋铁罐,瓦罐。

billy-o(h) [ˈbiliəu; ˋbɪlɪo] *n*.〔英口〕极度〔仅与 like 连用〕。*like* ～ 猛烈地(*roar like* ～ 狂吼,咆哮如雷。*It rained like* ～. 大雨倾盆)。

bi·lo·bate [baiˈləubeit; baɪˋlobet] *a*.【植】二裂的,有二裂片的;有二叶的。

bi·lob·u·lar [baiˈlɔbjulə; baɪˋlɑbjʊlɚ] *a*.【植】具二室的。

bil·sted [ˈbilsted; ˋbɪlstɛd] *n*.【植】1. 胶皮糖香树。2. 胶皮糖香树木。3. 苏合香 (= sweet gum)。

bil·tong [ˈbiltɔŋ; ˋbɪl͵tɑŋ] *n*. (南非)干肉条。

bim [bim; bɪm] *n*.〔美俚〕女人〔尤指荡妇〕。

Bim·a·na [ˈbimənə; ˋbɪmənə] *n*.〔*pl*.〕【动】两手类。

bim·a·nous [ˈbimənəs, baiˈmeinəs; ˋbɪmənəs, baɪˋmenəs] *a*.【动】有两手的。

bi·man·u·al [baiˈmænjuəl; baɪˋmænjʊəl] *a*. 用两手的,须用两手的。*a machine designed for* ～ *operation* 须用双手操作的机器。**-ly** *ad*.

bim·bo [ˈbimbəu; ˋbɪmbo] *n*. 1. 柠檬汁葡萄酒。2.〔俚〕家伙;流氓。3.〔卑〕轻浮女子;邋遢女人;妓女。

bi·mes·ter [baiˈmestə; baɪˋmɛstɚ] *n*. 两个月(期间)。**-tri·al** [baiˈmestriəl; baɪˋmɛstrɪəl] *a*. 两月一次的;持续两月的。

bi·met·al [ˈbaiˈmetl; ˋbaɪˋmɛtḷ] I *a*. 1. 双金属的。2. 两本位制的;复本位制的 (= bimetallic)。～ *sheet* 双金属板。II *n*. 双金属物质,双金属片;复合钢材。

bi·me·tal·lic [ˌbaimiˈtælik; ͵baɪməˋtælɪk] *a*. 双金属的,(金银)两本位制的,复本位制的。～ *standard* 复本位制。

bi·met·al·lism [baiˈmetəlizəm; baɪˋmɛtḷ͵ɪzəm] *n*. (金银)两本位制;复本位制主义。

bi·met·al·list [baiˈmetəlist; baɪˋmɛtḷɪst] *n*. 复本位制主义者。

bi·mod·al [baiˈməudl; baɪˋmodḷ] *a*.【统】(分布曲线)双峰的。**-i·ty** *n*.

bi·mo·lec·u·lar [ˌbaiməˈlekjələ; ͵baɪməˋlɛkjəḷɚ] *n*.【化】双分子。

bi·month·ly [ˈbaiˈmʌnθli; baɪˋmʌnθlɪ] I *a*. 1. 两月一次的,隔月的。2. 每月两次的。II *ad*. 1. 隔月。2. 每月两次。III *n*. 1. 双月刊。2. 半月刊。

bi·morph [ˈbaimɔːf; ˋbaɪmɔrf] *n*.【电】双压电晶片。

bi·mor·phe·mic [ˈbaimɔːˈfiːmik; ˋbaɪmɔrˋfimɪk] *a*.【语】涉及双词素的,包含双词素的。

bi·mo·tored [baiˈməutəd; baɪˋmotɚd] *a*. 双发动机的 (= twin-engined)。

bin [bin; bɪn] I *n*. 1. (放五谷、煤炭等的)有盖大箱。2.〔英〕收采酒花的帆布袋。3. (地下室)葡萄酒贮藏库。4. 垃圾箱。5.〔口〕精神病院。6.〔英口〕裤子口袋。*a rubbish* [*dust*] ～ 垃圾箱。II *vt*. (**-nn-**) 把…装进贮藏库[大木箱]。

bin- *comb*. *f*.〔用于母音前〕= *bi-*: *bin*aural.

binac [ˈbainæk; ˋbaɪnæk] *n*. = *bin*ary *a*utomatic *c*omputer (二进制自动计算机).

bi·nal [ˈbainl; ˋbaɪnəl] *a*. 两倍的,两重的。

bi·na·ry [ˈbainəri; ˋbaɪnərɪ] I *a*. 二,双,复;【化】二元的;【数】二进制的。II *n*. 二,双,复;双体,复体;【天】双[联]星【数】二进制。～ **alloy**【冶】二元合金。～ **compound**【化】二元素化合物。～ **computer** 二进制计算机。～ **element**【无】双态元件。～ **measure**【乐】二拍子。～ **notation** 二进位符号,二进(位记数)法。～ **scale**【数】二进法。～ **star**【天】双[联]星。～ **system** 二进制;二元系;双星系。

bi·nate [ˈbaineit; ˋbaɪnet] *a*.【植】双生的,成对的。

bin·au·ral [binˈɔːrəl; bɪnˋɔrəl] *a*. 1. (用)双耳的。2. 立体声的。～ *broadcasting* 立体广播。*a* ～ *stethoscope* 双耳听诊器。

bind [baind; baɪnd] I *vt*. (**bound** [baund; baʊnd]; **bound**,〔古〕**bound·en** [ˈbaundən; ˋbaʊndən]) 1. 缚,捆,扎,绑;束;裹,卷 (*about*; *around*, *round*)。2. (用绷带)包扎 (*up*)。3. 定,缔结。4. 装订(书籍);给…镶边;收边。5. 使便秘。6. 支配,牵制;(义务等)束缚(人),使…受拘束,使…承担义务。7. (冰等)封住;(用水泥)黏固;使结合。8.〔英口〕使厌烦。～ *up a wound* (用绷带)包扎伤口。～ *a bargain* 定买卖契约。～ *a book in morocco* 用摩洛哥皮装订书。*This food* ～*s the bowel*. 这种食物引起便秘。*Please* ～ *the carpet before cleaning it*. 请在清洗地毯以前把边收一收。*I am bound to warn you*. 我应该警告你。*All are bound to obey the laws*. 人人有服从法律的义务。*Ice bound the soil*. 地面被冻实了。*a shirt that* ～*s me* 一件过紧的衬衫。*He was bound* (*as an*) *apprentice to a shoe-maker*. 他做了鞋店的学徒。*The movie* ～*s me*. 这场电影太无聊。— *vi*. 1. (门窗等)开关不灵便;(衣服等)紧身;(义务等)有约束力。2. 土、沙、雪等凝固,变硬;(车轮)黏牢不动。3.〔英口〕发牢骚。～ *about one's extraduties* 对做额外工作发牢骚。*Clay* ～*s to heat*. 黏土遇热变硬。*an obligation that* ～*s* 一项有约束力的义务。**be bound for** 船开往…。**be bound to do sth**. 有义务…,应该…,必须…,非…不可,决心要…。**be bound to sth**. 被束缚在…上。**be bound up with** 与…有密切联系;与…结合在一起。～ **oneself to** (**do sth**.) 发誓(做某事)。～ (**sb**.) **over to** (**do**) **sth**. 使具结,要…发誓 (*I bound him over to good behaviour*. 我要他发誓改过自新)。～ **up** 1. 包扎。2. 装订。II *n*. 1. 带子,索子;蔓,葛,藤。2.【乐】连线〔即⌒〕;【矿】(煤层间的)泥岩;〔英〕(鲑、毛皮等的)计数单位;【建】撑条,系杆。**in a** ～ 受很大压力,处于困境。**safe** [**S-**] ～ 见 safe 条。

bind. = binding.

bind·er[1][ˈbaində; ˋbaɪndɚ] *n*. 1. 缚者,绑者,包扎者;(书籍)装订工。2. 包扎物,包扎工具,绳索,带子;缀合物;绷带,(产妇用)腹带;(草捆的)扎结处。3.【农】割捆机(缝纫机)滚边器;【机】结合件;【建】接合料,系梁;连结石;【医】结合剂;【冶】黏合剂,胶合剂;胶合物;(书的)活页封面;装订机;【医】止泻药。4. 临时契约;购卖不动产的定金(收据)。5.〔英口〕感到厌烦的人;发牢骚的人。～ **board** 刨花板;纸板。

bin·der[2][ˈbində; ˋbɪndɚ] *n*.〔英〕(食物的)大量,多量。

bind·er·y [ˈbaindəri; ˋbaɪndərɪ] *n*.〔美〕书籍装订所。

bind·ing [ˈbaindiŋ; ˋbaɪndɪŋ] I *a*. 1. 缚[捆、绑]…的;黏合的;系连的,连结的。2. 有束缚力的,有拘束力的,附有义务的。3.〔口〕引起便秘的。4.〔英口〕发牢骚的。**be** ～ **on** 对…有约束力;使承担义务 (*The statement is unofficial and not* ～ *on either country*. 本声明系非官方性的,对两国均不具有约束力。*This regulation is* ～ *on everybody*. 本规则人人皆须遵守)。II *n*. 1. 捆绑,束缚;缀结,连接;黏合;【物】结合;键联。2. 滚条;绷带;(书籍的)装订,装帧;封面;边。3.【法】具结。4. 绑定。～ **agent** 黏合剂,接合剂。～ **energy**【物】结合能。～ **force** 结合[内聚]力。～ **joists**【建】梁;小梁。～ **musline** 书面布。～ **post**【物】接线柱。～ **screw**【电】接线螺钉;【机】紧固螺钉。

bin·dle [ˈbindl; ˋbɪndḷ] *n*.〔美俚〕流浪汉的小行李卷。～ **stiff** (带着一个小行李卷的)乞丐,流浪汉;流动工人。

bind·weed [ˈbaindwiːd; ˋbaɪnd͵wid] *n*.【植】旋花属植物;旋花。

bind·wood [ˈbaindwud; ˋbaɪnd͵wʊd] *n*.【植】常春藤。

bine [bain; baɪn] *n*. 1. (爬藤或攀生植物的)蔓,葛。2. 忽布[酒花]蔓。

bing [biŋ; bɪŋ] *n*.〔英方〕堆。*a* ～ *of potatoes* 一堆马铃薯。

binge [bindʒ; bɪndʒ] *n*.〔俚〕1. 欢闹;喝闹酒。2. 社交集会。

bin·gle[1][ˈbiŋgl; ˋbɪŋgḷ] I *n*.【棒球】稳打。II *vi*. 打出稳球。

bin·gle[2] [ˈbiŋgl; ˋbɪŋgl̩] *n*. 妇女剪的一种短发型。
bin·go [ˈbiŋgəu; ˋbɪŋgo] **I** *n*. **1**. 排五点〔一种赌博性游戏〕。**2**. 〔口〕白兰地酒。**II** *int*. 瞧!
bin·na·cle [ˈbinəkl; ˋbɪnəkl] *n*. 【海】罗经柜。
bin·o·cle [ˈbinɔkl; ˋbɪnəkl] *n*. 〔罕〕(双目)望远镜。
bi·nocs [bəˈnɔks; bəˋnɑks] *n*. 〔口〕 = binoculars.
bin·oc·u·lar [baiˈnɔkjulə, biˈn-; baɪˋnɑkjələ˞, bɪˋn-] **I** *a*. 双目的,双筒的。*a* ~ *telescope* [*microscope*] 双筒[目]望远镜[显微镜]。**II** *n*. 〔常 *pl*.〕双筒望远镜;双目显微镜。
bi·no·mi·al [baiˈnəumiəl; baɪˋnomɪəl] **I** *a*. **1**. 【数】二项(式)的。**2**. 【生】双名的,复名的。~ *theorem* 【数】二项式定理。~ *nomenclature* 【生】双名法。**II** *n*. **1**. 【数】二项式。**2**. 【生】二名法,双名法。
bi·nom·i·nal [baiˈnɔminl; baɪˋnɑmɪnl] *a*. = binomial. ~ *system* (以属名、种名命名动植物的)双名制。
bin·tu·rong [ˈbintjurɔŋ; ˋbɪntjʊrɑŋ] *n*. 【动】麝猫。
bi·nu·cle·ate [baiˈnuːkliːit; baɪˋnuklɪɪt] *a*. 二核的 (= binucleated, binuclear)。
bio- *comb*. *f*. = life, living things (生命,生物)。
bi·o[1] [ˈbaiəu; ˋbaɪo] *n*. = biography.
bi·o[2] [ˈbaiəu; ˋbaɪo] *n*. 个人经历,个人历史。
bi·o·a·cous·tics [ˌbaiəuəˈkuːstiks; ˏbaɪoəˋkustɪks] *n*. 〔用作单数〕【生】生物声学。
bi·o·as·say [ˌbaiəuˈæsei, -æˈsei; ˏbaɪoˋæse, -æˋse] **I** *n*. 【生】生物鉴定,生物测定。**II** *vt*. 对…作生物鉴定。
bi·o·as·tro·nau·tics [ˌbaiəuˌæstrəˈnɔːtiks; ˏbaɪoˏæstroˋnɔtɪks] *n*. 〔*pl*.〕宇宙航行生物学。
bi·o·belt [ˌbaiəuˈbelt; ˏbaɪoˋbɛlt] *n*. (太空航行员挂在腰间的)生理遥测器。
bi·o·cat·a·lyst [ˌbaiəuˈkætəlist; ˏbaɪoˋkætəlɪst] *n*. 生物触媒,生物催化剂。**-lyt·ic** *a*.
bi·oc·el·late [baiˈɔsəleit; baɪˋɑsəˏlet] *a*. 【生】有两只普通眼睛的,有两点眼状标记的。
bi·o·ce·nol·o·gy [ˌbaiəusiˈnɔlədʒi; ˏbaɪosɪˋnɑlədʒɪ] *n*. 生物群落学。
bi·o·ce·no·sis [ˌbaiəusiˈnəusis; ˏbaɪosɪˋnosɪs] *n*. 生物群落 (= biocoenosis, biocenose [-ˈsiːnəus; -ˋsinos])。
bi·o·ce·ram·ic [ˌbaiəusiˈræmik; ˏbaɪosɪˋræmɪk] *n*. (植入体内促使缺损骨质重新生长的)生物陶瓷。
bi·o·chem·i·cal [baiəuˈkemikl; ˏbaɪoˋkɛmɪkl] **I** *a*. 生物化学的。**II** *n*. 生物化学物质。**-ly** *ad*.
bi·o·chem·ics [ˈbaiəuˈkemiks; ˏbaɪoˋkɛmɪks], **bi·o·chemis·try** [ˈbaiəuˈkemistri; ˋbaɪoˋkɛmɪstrɪ] *n*. 生物化学,生理化学。
bi·o·chem·y [ˈbaiəukemi; ˋbaɪokɛmɪ] *n*. = biochemistry.
bi·o·cide [ˈbaiəsaid; ˋbaɪəˏsaɪd] *n*. 生物杀灭剂,杀虫剂。**-cid·al** *a*.
bi·o·clean [ˈbaiəukliːn; ˋbaɪoˏklin] *a*. 无菌的;十分清洁的。
bi·o·cli·ma·tol·o·gy [ˈbaiəuˌklaiməˈtɔlədʒi; ˋbaɪoˏklaɪməˋtɑlədʒɪ] *n*. 生物气候学。**bi·o·cli·mat·ic** [-klaiˈmætik; -klaɪˋmætɪk] *a*.
bi·o·crat [ˈbaiəukræt; ˋbaɪoˏkræt] *n*. 生物主义者〔代表生物科学界的科技人员〕。
bi·o·cy·ber·net·ics [ˈbaiəuˌsaibə(ː)ˈnetiks; ˋbaɪoˏsaɪbə˞ˋnɛtɪks] *n*. 生物控制论。
bi·o·de·grad·a·ble [ˌbaiəudiˈgredəbl; ˏbaɪodɪˋgredəbl̩] *a*. (废纸、饭屑等)可以进行分解和还原处理的〔和铅制品、塑料制品等相对而言〕。
bi·o·dy·nam·ics [ˌbaiəudaiˈnæmiks; ˏbaɪodaɪˋnæmɪks] *n*. 生物动力学。
bi·o·e·col·o·gy [ˌbaiəuiːˈkɔlədʒi; ˏbaɪoiˋkɑlədʒɪ] *n*. (生物)生态学。
bi·o·e·lec·tric·i·ty [ˌbaiəuiˈlektrisiti; ˏbaɪoɪˋlɛktrɪsətɪ] *n*. 生物电流。
bi·o·e·lec·tron·ics [ˌbaiəuilekˈtrɔniks; ˋbaɪoˏɪlɛkˋtrɑnɪks] *n*. **1**. 仿生电子学。**2**. 生物电子学。
bi·o·en·gi·neer·ing [ˌbaiəuˌendʒiˈniəriŋ; ˏbaɪoˏɛndʒəˋnɪrɪŋ] *n*. 生物工程学。
bi·o·eth·ics [ˈbaiəueθiks; ˋbaɪoɛθɪks] *n*. 生物伦理学〔探讨在器官移植、遗传工程、人工授精等科学研究中所涉及的伦理问题〕。
bi·o·feed·back [ˈbaiəuˌfiːdbæk; ˋbaɪoˏfidbæk] *n*. 机能反馈疗法〔利用机械医疗作用,使病人自动控制和调整正常机能的医疗技术〕。
bi·o·fla·vo·noid [baiəuˈfleivənɔid, -ˈflævə-; baɪoˋflevənɔɪd, -ˋflævə-] *n*. 生物黄酮类。
biog. = biography, biographical, biographer.
bi·o·gen·e·sis [ˈbaiəuˈdʒenisis; ˋbaɪoˋdʒɛnəsɪs] *n*. 【生】生源说。
bi·o·gen·ic [ˈbaiəuˈdʒenik; ˋbaɪoˋdʒɛnɪk] *a*. **1**. (发酵等)生物活动所产生的。**2**. (食物、水等)生物的生命活动所必需的。
bi·og·e·ny [baiˈɔdʒəni; baɪˋɑdʒənɪ] *n*. **1**. 生源说,生物续生说。**2**. 生物续生 (= biogenesis)。
bi·o·ge·o·chem·i·cal [ˌbaiəuˌdʒiəuˈkemikl; ˏbaɪoˏdʒɪoˋkɛmɪkl̩] **cycle** 生物地质化学循环,生物地理化学循环。
bi·o·ge·og·ra·phy [ˌbaiəudʒiˈɔgrəfi; ˏbaɪoˏdʒɪˋɑgrəfɪ] *n*. 生物地理学。
bi·o·glass [ˈbaiəuglɑːs; ˋbaɪoglæs] *n*. 【医】生物玻璃〔用于修复动物骨骼等的钙磷生物材料〕。
bi·o·graph [ˈbaiəugrɑːf; ˋbaɪəgræf] *n*. **1**. (初期的)电影放映机。**2**. 〔罕〕小传。
bi·og·ra·phee [baiˌɔgrəˈfiː; baɪˏɑgrəˋfi] *n*. 传记的主人公。
bi·og·ra·pher [baiˈɔgrəfə; baɪˋɑgrəfə˞] *n*. 传记作者。*sb.'s* ~ 为某人写传的人。
bi·o·graph·ic [ˌbaiəuˈgræfik; ˏbaɪəˋgræfɪk] *a*. = biographical.
bi·o·graph·i·cal [ˌbaiəuˈgræfikəl; ˏbaɪoˋgræfɪkl] *a*. 传记的,传记体的。~ *data* 传记材料。*a* ~ *dictionary* 人名辞典。*a* ~ *novel* 传记体小说。**-ly** *ad*. 成传记体;传记上。
bi·og·ra·ph·ize [baiˈɔgrəfaiz; baɪˋɑgrəˏfaɪz] *vt*. 为…作传记。
bi·og·ra·phy [baiˈɔgrəfi; baɪˋɑgrəfɪ] **I** *n*. **1**. 传,传记;(城市、团体等的)变迁史。**2**. 传记体;传记文学。*the* ~ *of Byron* 拜伦传。*the* ~ *of the town* [*village*] 镇[村]史。**II** *vt*. 为…写传记。
bi·o·herm [ˈbaiəuˌhəːm; ˋbaɪoˏhə˞m] *n*. **1**. 生物礁。**2**. 珊瑚礁 (= coral reef)。
biol. = biologist; biological; biology.
bi·o·log·ic [ˌbaiəˈlɔdʒik; ˏbaɪəˋlɑdʒɪk] *a*. = biological. **-s** *n*. 【药】生物制品。
bi·o·log·i·cal [baiəˈlɔdʒikəl; ˏbaɪəˋlɑdʒɪkl] **I** *a*. 生物学(上)的。*a* ~ *test* 生物学检验。**II** *n*. 【药】生物制品,生物制剂。~ **agent** 生物制剂。~ **clock** 【生】生物钟〔生物体内自动调节对时间的反应的一种机能〕。~ **control** 生物防治。~ **engineering** 生物工程;人工育种。~ **form** 生物小种;生物型。~ **races** 生物宗,生物族;生理宗。~ **sociology** 生物社会学。~ **strain** 【生】生物小种。~ **warfare** 细菌战;生物战。**-ly** *ad*. 生物学地,生物学上。
bi·ol·o·gist [baiˈɔlədʒist; baɪˋɑlədʒɪst] *n*. 生物学者。
bi·ol·o·gy [baiˈɔlədʒi; baɪˋɑlədʒɪ] *n*. **1**. 生物学。**2**. 生态学。**3**. 〔总称〕一个地区的生物。*the* ~ *of a worm* 一种虫子的生态学。*the* ~ *of Pennsylvania* 宾夕法尼亚州的生物。
bi·o·lu·mi·nes·cence [ˈbaiəuˌluːmiˈnesns; ˋbaɪoˏlumɪˋnɛsəns] *n*. 生物(性)发光。**-es·cent** *a*.
bi·ol·y·sis [baiˈɔlisis; baɪˋɑlɪsɪs] *n*. 【生】生物分解。**bi-**

o·lyt·ic [bai'ɔlitik; baɪ`ɑlɪtɪk] *a*.
bi·o·mass ['baiəumæs; `baɪo͵mæs] *n*. 【生态】生物量〔某一地域或单位面积内存在的生物的总量〕。
bi·o·ma·te·ri·al [͵baiəuməˈtiəriəl; ͵baɪomə`tɪrɪəl] *n*. 【医】(适用于修复术中与活组织接触的)生物材料。
bi·o·math·e·mat·ics [͵baiəu͵mæθiˈmætiks; ͵baɪo͵mæθə`mætɪks] *n*. 〔*pl*.〕生物数学。
bi·ome ['baiəum; `baɪom] *n*. 生物群落。
bi·o·me·chan·ics [͵baiəuməˈkæniks; ͵baɪomɪ`kænɪks] *n*. 〔*pl*.〕生命力学。**-me·chan·i·cal** *a*.
bi·o·med·i·cal ['baiəu'medikəl; `baɪo`mɛdɪkəl] *a*. 生物(学和)医学的。
bi·o·med·i·cine [͵baiəu'medisn; ͵baɪo`mɛdəsn] *n*. 生物药剂学。**-med·ic·al** *a*.
bi·o·me·te·or·ol·o·gy [͵baiəu͵miːtjəˈrɔlədʒi; ͵baɪo͵mitɪə`rɑlədʒɪ] *n*. 生物气象学,生物环境学。
bi·o·met·rics [͵baiəu'metriks; ͵baɪo`mɛtrɪks] *n*. 生物统计学,生物测定学。
bi·om·e·try [bai'ɔmitri; baɪ`ɑmətrɪ] *n*. **1.** 人寿测定(法)。**2.** = biometrics.
bi·o·mor·phi·sm [͵baiəu'mɔːfizm; ͵baɪo`mɔrfɪzm] *n*. (艺术上的)生物形态主义。
bi·on·ics [bai'ɔniks; baɪ`ɑnɪks] *n*. 仿生学。
bi·o·nom·ics [͵baiəu'nɔmiks; ͵baɪə`nɑmɪks], **bi·on·o·my** [bai'ɔnəmi; baɪ`ɑnəmɪ] *n*. (个体)生态学。
bi·on·o·my [bai'ɔnəmi; baɪ`ɑnəmɪ] *n*. **1.** 生理学。**2.** 生态学。
bi·o·phore ['baiəufɔː; `baɪə͵for] *n*. 【生】最小生活体,生源体。
bi·o·phys·ics [baiəu'fiziks; ͵baɪo`fɪzɪks] *n*. 〔*pl*.〕生物物理学。**-si·cist** [-zisist; -zɪsɪst] *n*. 生物物理学家。
bi·o·plasm ['baiəuplæzəm; `baɪo͵plæzm] *n*. 【生】活质,原生质。
bi·o·plast ['baiəuplæst; `baɪo͵plæst] *n*. 【生】活粒。
bi·o·poly·mer [͵baiəu'pɔlimə; ͵baɪo`pɑlɪmɚ] *n*. 生物(高分子)聚合物。
bi·op·sy [͵bai'ɔpsi; ͵baɪ`ɑpsɪ] *n*. 【医】活组织检查。
bi·o·re·search [͵baiəuri'səːtʃ; ͵baɪorɪ`sɝtʃ] *n*. 生物科学的研究。
bi·os ['baiɔs; `baɪɑs] *n*. **1.** 生物,生命。**2.** 【生化】酵母促生物。
bi·o·sat·el·lite [͵baiəu'sætlait; ͵baɪo`sætl̩aɪt] *n*. 生物实验卫星〔运载生物或人的人造卫星〕。
bi·o·sci·ence ['baiəu͵saiəns; `baɪo͵saɪəns] *n*. 外太空生物学。
bi·o·scope ['baiəskəup; `baɪə͵skop] *n*. **1.** (初期的)电影放映机。**2.** 〔主英〕电影院。
bi·os·co·py [bai'ɔskəpi; baɪ`ɑskəpɪ] *n*. 【医】生死检定法。
bi·o·sen·sor [͵baiəu'sensə; ͵baɪo`sɛnsɚ] *n*. 生物传感器。
bi·o·sphere ['baiəsfiə; `baɪə͵sfɪr] *n*. **1.** 生物圈,生命层,生物大气层。**2.** 生物界。
bi·o·stat·ics [͵baiəu'stætiks; ͵baɪo`stætɪks] *n*. 生物静力学。
bi·o·sta·tis·tics [͵baiəustə'tistiks; ͵baɪostə`tɪstɪks] *n*. 〔*pl*.〕生物统计学。**-ti·cal** *a*. **-ti·cian** *n*.
bi·o·stra·te·gic ['baiəustrə'tiːdʒik; `baɪostrə`tidʒɪk] *a*. 对动植物细菌病害用抗菌素疗法的。
bi·o·strat·e·gy ['baiəu'strætidʒi; `baɪo`strætɪdʒɪ] *n*. 【生】动植物细菌病害的抗菌素疗法。
bi·o·strome ['baiəu͵strəum; `baɪo͵strom] *n*. 生物层。
bi·o·syn·the·sis [͵baiəu'sinθisis; ͵baɪo`sɪnθəsɪs] *n*. 生物合成。**-thet·ic** *a*. **-thet·i·cal·ly** *ad*.
bi·o·sys·te·mat·ics [baiəu͵sisti'mætiks; baɪo͵sɪstə`mætɪks] *n*. 〔*pl*.〕生物分类学。**-mat·ic** *a*. **-mat·i·cal·ly** *ad*.
bi·o·ta [bai'əutə; baɪ`otə] *n*. 生物区;生物群。
bi·o·tech [͵baiəu'tek; ͵baɪo`tɛk] *n*. = biotechnology.
bi·o·tech·nol·o·gy [͵baiəutek'nɔlədʒi; ͵baɪotɛk`nɑlədʒɪ] *n*. 生物工艺学。
bi·o·te·lem·e·try [͵baiəuti'lemitri; ͵baɪotə`lɛmɪtrɪ] *n*. 生态遥测术〔宇宙飞船对地球〕。
bi·o·ther·a·py [͵baiəu'θerəpi; ͵baɪo`θɛrəpɪ] *n*. 生物制剂疗法。
bi·ot·ic [bai'ɔtik; baɪ`ɑtɪk] *a*. 生命的,生物的;生物引起的(= biotical)。
bi·o·tin ['baiətin; `baɪətɪn] *n*. 【生化】生物素,促生素,酵母生长素,维生素 H。
bi·o·tite ['baiətait; `baɪə͵taɪt] *n*. 【矿】黑云母。
bi·o·tope ['baiətəup; `baɪətop] *n*. 【生】群落生境;生活小区。
bi·o·tron ['baiəutrən; `baɪotrən] *n*. (密闭并可控制温度的)生物研究室。
bi·o·type ['baiətaip; `baɪətaɪp] *n*. 同型小种;生物型;生活型。**-typic** [-'tipik; -`tɪpɪk] *a*.
bi·o·ty·pol·o·gy [͵baiəutai'pɔlədʒi; ͵baɪotaɪ`pɑlədʒɪ] *n*. 体质类型学。
bi·pack ['baipæk; `baɪpæk] *n*. 【摄】二重胶片〔用于彩色摄影〕。
bi·pa·ri·e·tal [͵baipə'raiətl; ͵baɪpɚ`raɪət̩l] *a*. 左右颅顶骨的。
bip·a·rous ['bipərəs; `bɪpərəs] *a*. **1.** 【动】产双胞胎的。**2.** 【植】有二枝[二轴]的。
bi·par·ti·san [bai͵pɑːti'zæn; baɪ`pɑrtɪzn], **bi·par·ti·zan** [bai'pɑːtizən; baɪ`pɑrtɪzən] *a*. 两党的;代表两党的;获得两党支持的。*a* ~ *foreign policy* 获得两党支持的外交政策。**-ship** [美]两党合作。
bi·par·tite [bai'pɑːtait; baɪ`pɑrtaɪt] *a*. **1.** 由两部分构成的。**2.** 【法】一式两份的;(条约等)两方之间的。**3.** 【植】有二深裂的(叶子等)。**4.** 【数】除两次的。*a* ~ *contract* 一式两份的合同。*a* ~ *pact* 两国协定。~ *rule* 共同支配。*a* ~ *leaf* 二裂叶。
bi·par·ti·tion [͵baipɑː'tiʃən; ͵baɪpɑr`tɪʃən] *n*. 二分,双开,分为二。
bi·ped ['baiped; `baɪped] **I** *a*. 〔罕〕二足的。**II** *n*. 二足动物。*a feathered* ~鸟。
bi·ped·al ['bai͵pedl; `baɪpɛdl] *a*. 二足动物的;二足的。
bi·pet·al·ous [bai'petələs; baɪ`pɛtl̩əs] *a*. 有两花瓣的;二叶的。
bi·phen·yl [bai'fenl, -fiːnl; baɪ`fɛnl̩, -finl] *n*. 【化】联(二)苯;二苯基(= diphenyl)。
bi·pin·nate [bai'pineit; baɪ`pɪnet] *a*. 【植】(复叶)二回羽状的,两羽状的。
bi·plane ['baiplein; `baɪplen] *n*. 双翼(飞)机。
bi·pod ['baipɔd; `baɪpɑd] *n*. 两足支架〔如自动步枪的支架〕。
bi·po·lar [bai'pəulə; baɪ`polɚ] *a*. **1.** 【电】两极的,双极的。**2.** 有两种相反性质[见解]的。**3.** 关于或涉及地球两极地区的。**-i·ty** [͵baipəu'læriti; ͵baɪpo`lærətɪ] *n*.
bi·pro·pel·lant [͵baiprə'pelənt; ͵baɪprə`pɛlənt] *n*. 二元推进剂,二元燃料。
bi·quad·rate [bai'kwɔdrit, -reit; baɪ`kwɑdrɪt, -͵ret] *n*. 【数】四乘方,四次方,双二次方。
bi·quad·rat·ic [͵baikwɔ'drætik; ͵baɪkwɑd`rætɪk] **I** *a*. 【数】四次的,双二次的。**II** *n*. 【数】四次幂;四次方程式。
bi·quar·ter·ly [bai'kwɔːtəli; baɪ`kwɔrtɚlɪ] *a*. 每三个月二次的。
bi·ra·cial [bai'reiʃəl; baɪ`reʃəl] *a*. 含有两个种族的〔尤指黑人和白人〕,涉及两个种族的。
bi·ra·di·al [bai'reidiəl; baɪ`redɪəl] *a*. 【生】两辐对称的。
bi·ra·mous [bai'reiməs; baɪ`reməs] *a*. 二支的,两岔的。
birch [bəːtʃ; bɝtʃ] **I** *n*. **1.** 【植】桦,白桦;桦属。**2.** 桦木;

(处罚学童用的)桦枝,桦条〔又名～-rod〕。**3.** 桦皮船。*the black* ～ 西方桦。*the white* [*silver*, *Japanese*] ～ 白桦。**II** *vt*. 用桦条打。**III** *a*. 桦木的;桦木制的。

birch·en [ˈbəːtʃən; ˋbɝtʃən] *a*. 桦木的,桦木制的。～ *furniture* 桦木家具。

BIRD = International Bank for Reconstruction and Development (联合国)国际复兴开发银行。

bird [bəːd; bɝd] **I** *n*. **1.** 鸟,禽。**2.** 猎鸟〔供猎食的鸟,英国特指鹧鸪〕。**3.** 〔俚〕少女,姑娘;人,家伙,东西;〔讽〕非凡人物。**4.** 〔口〕飞机;〔美口〕火箭,导弹。**5.** 羽毛球。**6.** 〔the ～〕(蔑视、起哄时的)嘘嘘声;解雇。**7.** 〔美俚〕(代表军队的)鹰徽。**8.** 〔俚〕服徒刑,刑期。*The early* ～ *gets* [*catches*] *the worm*. 捷足先得,先下手为强。*Each* ～ *loves to hear himself sing*. 鸟都爱听自己唱,人都以为自己棒。*It's an ill* ～ *that fouls its own nest*. 弄脏自己窝巢的不是好鸟〔家丑不可外扬〕。*a game* ～ 供猎食的鸟,猎鸟。*a queer* ～ 怪人,奇人。*a gay* ～ 爽快的人。*a bonny* ～ 俏姑娘。*an early* ～ 早起者;早来的人。*an old* ～ 老练的人,城府很深的人;老混蛋。*my* ～ 可爱的孩子。*The* ～ *is* [*has*] *flown*. 对手[要捕捉的人,囚徒]逃走了。*A little* ～ *told me*. 有人告诉我了。***a*** ～ ***in*** [***the***] ***hand*** [***bush***] 现实[不现实]的利益,已经[尚未]到手的东西,有[无]把握的事情(*A* ～ *in the hand is worth two in the bush*. 双鸟在林不如一鸟在手,现得为上)。***a*** ～ ***of one's own brain*** 自己本身的想头。***a little*** ～ 〔口〕私下有人 (*A little* ～ *told me that* .... 听说…)。***Arabian*** ～ = ***of wonder*** 凤凰;长生鸟;唯一无二之物,稀世之珍。～ ***in one's bosom*** 良心;内心。～ ***of ill omen*** 凶鸟〔乌鸦、猫头鹰等〕;报凶讯的人。～ ***of Jove*** 鹰;鹫。～ ***of Juno*** 孔雀。～ ***of paradise*** 极乐鸟,凤鸟。～ ***of passage*** 渡鸟,候鸟;漂泊不定的人。～ ***of peace*** 鸽。～ ***of prey*** 猛禽(鹫、鹰、枭等)。～***s of a feather*** 同类的人;一丘之貉 (*Birds of a feather flock together*. 物以类聚)。***eat like a*** ～ 吃得很少。***for the*** ～***s*** 〔常作述语〕毫无意义;荒唐可笑(*Their opinions on art are for the* ～*s*. 他们对艺术的看法简直荒唐可笑)。***get a big*** ～; ***get the*** ～ 〔俚〕**1.** 被嘘嘘地奚落,被喝倒彩。**2.** 被解雇。***give*** (*sb*.) ***the*** ～ 〔俚〕**1.** 用嘘嘘声奚落;嘘,赶,撵。**2.** 解雇。***hear a*** ～ ***sing*** 私下听人说,得密报,密闻。***kill two*** ～***s with one stone*** 一举两得,一石两鸟,一箭双雕。***like a*** ～ 毫无困难;毫不犹豫 (*sing like a* ～ 唱得好。*work like a* ～ 干得麻俐)。***the*** ～***s and the bees*** (可对儿童解说的)有关两性关系的基本常识。***the secular*** ～ 不死鸟,凤凰。**II** *vi*. **1.** 捕鸟,打鸟。**2.** 在野外观察识别野鸟。～ **bath** (花园的)鸟(浴)池。～ **brain** 〔美俚〕轻浮无知的人;笨蛋。～ **cage** 鸟笼;鸟笼式房子〔牢房等〕;〔美俚〕女子宿舍;【航】鸟笼空域〔指机场周围处于空中交通管理下的天空〕。～ **call 1.** 哨子,鸟笛。**2.** 鸟叫声;类似鸟叫的声音;鸟求偶的叫声;模仿鸟叫的声音。～ **catcher** 捕鸟者,捕鸟器。～ **colonel** 〔美军俚〕陆军上校。～ **dog 1.** 捕鸟猎犬。**2.** 搜罗人才的人。**3.** 〔美俚〕兜揽生意的人,股票经纪人的囮子。**4.** 〔美军俚〕战斗机,歼击机。～**-dog** *vt*., *vi*. **1.** (猎犬)注视(鸟)。**2.** 搜索,网罗。～**-eyed** *a*. 目光锐利的。～**-fancier** 爱玩鸟的人;经营小鸟的商人。～ **farm** 【海】〔口〕航空母舰。～ **flu** 禽流感。～**-foot** *n*. 花或叶呈鸟足形的植物。～ **house** 鸟房,鸟舍,鸟馆。～**lime** 未黏鸟胶;陷捕物。～**man 1.** 飞行员;飞机乘客。**2.** 捕鸟者;鸟类学家,鸟类研究者。～**-minded** *a*. 〔美俚〕蠢,笨;轻浮的,不负责任的。～**-seed** 喂鸟的谷粒。～ **shot** 鸟枪子弹。～ **strike** 鸟撞击〔飞机和一群鸟相撞,可能造成失事〕。～ **watching** (作为一种爱好的)野鸟习性观察。～ **woman** 女飞行家。**-dom** 〔美俚〕美女世界。**-er** *n*. **1.** 捕鸟的人。**2.** 玩鸟的人。**3.** 野鸟研究家。

Bird [bəːd; bɝd] *n*. 伯德〔姓氏〕。

bird·ie [ˈbəːdi; ˋbɝdɪ] *n*. **1.** 小鸟〔爱称,多为儿语〕。**2.** 【无】(一万赫左右的差拍引起的)尖叫声。**3.** 【高尔夫球】得分少于标准分的一击。**4.** 〔美俚〕女性化的男子。***hear the*** ～***s sing*** 〔美俚〕被打昏过去。***Watch this*** ～***!*** 照这边,照相啦!

bird·ing [ˈbəːdiŋ; ˋbɝdɪŋ] *n*. **1.** 捕鸟,打鸟;玩鸟。**2.** 观察野鸟习性。～**-piece** 鸟枪。

bird's-eye [ˈbəːdzai; ˋbɝdzˏaɪ] **I** *a*. **1.** 俯视的,鸟瞰的;概观的。**2.** 鸟眼一样(有斑点)的;【纺】鸟眼花纹的。**II** *n*. **1.** 【植】一种有鲜艳小花的植物〔如粉报春等〕。**2.** 【纺】鸟眼花纹(织物)。**3.** (木材上的)鸟眼纹理。～ **diamond** 鸟眼花纹精纺毛织品。～**view** 鸟瞰图;概观 (*a* ～ *view of the city* 城市鸟瞰图。*a* ～ *view of ancient history* 古代史概观)。

bird's-foot [ˈbəːdzfut; ˋbɝdzfʊt] *n*. **1.** 叶或花似鸟足的植物〔尤指某些豆科植物〕;三叶草。**2.** 形似鸟足的动物,海盘车。～ **violet** 鸟足堇菜 (*Viola pedata*) 〔美国 Wisconsin 州的州花〕。

bird's-nest [ˈbəːdznest; ˋbɝdzˏnɛst] *n*. **1.** 鸟巢;燕窝。**2.** 【植】野参,野生胡萝卜。**3.** 内含水果、坚果等的菜肴。**4.** 【海】捕鲸船桅顶了望台。

bird's-nest·ing [ˈbəːdznestiŋ; ˋbɝdznɛstɪŋ] *n*. **1.** 摸鸟巢,掏鸟蛋。**2.** 〔讽〕马左右摆头癖。

bird·y [ˈbəːdi; ˋbɝdɪ] *a*. **1.** 似鸟的。**2.** 多鸟的。

bi·re·frin·gence [ˌbairiˈfrindʒins; ˏbaɪrɪˋfrɪndʒəns] *n*. 【物】双折射。**-gent** *a*.

bi·reme [ˈbairiːm; ˋbaɪrim] *n*. (古代的)对排桨海船。

bi·ret·ta [biˈretə; bəˋrɛtə] *n*. (天主教教士等戴的)四角帽,法冠。

Birk·beck [ˈbəːkbek; ˋbɝkbɛk] *n*. 伯克贝克〔姓氏〕。

birl [bəːl; bɝl] **I** *vt*., *vi*. **1.** 呼呼旋转。**2.** 踩着运转(浮木)。**3.** 〔口〕大把花钱;赌博。**II** *n*. 〔口〕**1.** 企图。**2.** 赌博。

birle, birl [bəːl; bɝl] *vt*. 〔主 Scot.〕注酒,劝酒。— *vi*. 〔主 Scot.〕痛饮,狂饮。

birl·ing [ˈbəːliŋ; ˋbɝlɪŋ] *n*. (伐木工人的)滚筏木游戏〔站在筏木上滚动筏木而保持身体平衡〕。

Bir·ming·ham [ˈbəːmiŋəm; ˋbɝmɪŋəm] *n*. **1.** 伯明翰〔英国城市〕。**2.** [ˈbəːmiŋhæm; ˋbɝmɪŋhæm] 伯明翰〔美国城市〕。

bi·ro [ˈbaiərəu; ˋbaɪro] *n*. (可以吸墨水的)圆珠笔。

bi·ro·ta·tion [bairəuˈteiʃən; ˏbaɪroˋteʃən] *n*. 【物】变异旋光。

birr [bəː; bɝ] **I** *n*. **1.** 冲力,动力;强调。**2.** 飕飕声,呼呼声。**II** *vi*. 作飕飕声;飕飕(声中)移动。

Bir·rell [ˈbirəl; ˋbɪrəl] *n*. 比勒尔〔姓氏〕。

birth [bəːθ; bɝθ] *n*. **1.** 出生,诞生;生产,分娩。**2.** 出身,家系;血统;门第,家世。**3.** 起源,开始。**4.** 〔古〕产物,产儿。*the date of one's* ～ 生日。*a still* [*difficult*] ～ 死[难]产。*five young at a* ～ 一胎产五仔。*a person of* ～ [*of no* ～] 出身高贵[卑微]的人。*of Grecian* ～ 希腊血统。*new* ～ 再生,更生,复活,新生。*B- is much, but breeding is more*. 教养比门第更重要。*kill the cases at* ～ 防微杜渐。*the* ～ *of Protestantism* 新教的起源。***by*** ～ **1.** 血统,出生于。**2.** 生来,天生是 (*She is French by* ～ *and British by marriage*. 她原是法国人,嫁给英国人就入英国籍了。*a musician by* ～ 天生的音乐家。*be a Parisian by* ～ 生在巴黎)。***give*** ～ ***to*** 生,产生,引起,使发生 (*give* ～ *to twin girls* 生下一对女双胞胎。*give* ～ *to a controversy* 引起一场争论。*This town gave* ～ *to many great men*. 该城出了很多伟人)。～ **control** 节(制生)育 (～*-control pill* 女用口服避孕药)。～**day** 生日,诞辰,成立纪念日 (*a* ～*day book* 生日登记簿。*keep* [*observe*] *a* ～ 过生日。*a* ～ *day gift* 生日礼品)。～**day honours** 在英国国王[女王]诞辰授与的勋爵。～**day suit 1.** 英国国王[女王]诞辰穿的礼服。**2.** 〔讽〕生来的衣裳,自己的皮肤,裸体。～ **mark 1.** 痣;黑斑胎记。**2.** 某人的特征。～ **pangs 1.**

(分娩时的)阵痛。**2.** 任何变化带来的困难或混乱。～ **parent** 生身父母。～ **pill** (口服)避孕丸。～ **place** 出生地,故乡;发祥地,发源地。～ **rate** 人口出生率。～**-right** **1.** 与生俱来的权利。**2.** 继承权〔尤指长子继承权〕(*sell one's* ～ *right for a mess of pottage* 一碗肉粥卖掉长子继承权,因小失大)。～**-stone** 诞生石〔迷信与诞生月星座有关系的宝石,常带身边可得幸福。如 2 月是 amethyst 紫水晶,4 月是 diamond 金刚石,6 月是 pearl 珍珠等〕。

birth·root [ˈbəːθˌruːt, -rut; ˋbɝθˏrut, -rʊt] ***n.*** 【植】延龄草属植物〔尤指直立延龄草〕。

birth·wort [ˈbəːθˌwəːt; ˋbɝθˏwɝt] ***n.*** 【植】马兜铃属植物。

BIS = Bank for International Settlements 国际清偿银行。

bis [bis; bɪs] **I** ***ad.*** 〔L.〕二度,二回,重,又;【乐】重叠,重复。*page 5* ～ 第 5 页的副页。**II** ***int.*** 再来一个! 再演〔唱〕一次!

B.I.S. = **1.** British Information Services 英国情报服务社。**2.** British Interplanetary Society 英国星际航行学会。

bis. = bissextile;【化】bismuth.

bis- *pref.* = bi-〔多用于 c 或 s 前,复杂的化学名词之前亦常用:*bis*sextile〕.

Bi·sa·yan [biˈsɑːjən; bɪˋsɑjən] ***n.***, ***a.*** **1.** (菲律宾)米沙鄢群岛(的)。**2.** 米沙鄢人(的)。**3.** 米沙鄢语(的)(= Visayan)。

Bis·cayne [bisˈkein, ˈbiskein; bɪsˋken, ˋbɪsken] ***n.*** 比斯坎湾〔美国〕(= ～ Bay)。

bis·cuit [ˈbiskit; ˋbɪskɪt] ***n.*** **1.** 饼干〔美国叫 cracker〕;〔美〕热松饼。**2.** 饼干色,淡褐色。**3.** 本色陶〔瓷〕器,素坯。*a ship's* ～ 硬面包。***take the*** ～〔英俚〕屈居末座。～ **hooks**〔美俚〕拳头,手。～ **shooter**〔美俚〕女招待。～ **ware** 本色陶器;充瓷器。

bise [biːz; biz] ***n.*** **1.** 北寒风〔瑞士、意大利及法国南部对农作物有害的干冷的北风或东北风〕。**2.**〔转义〕不幸,灾害。

bi·sect [baiˈsekt; baɪˋsɛkt] ***vt.*** **1.** 把…一分为二,二分,两分;平分;对开,对截;【数】二等分。**2.** 与…相交叉,横切。～ *a right angle* 将一个直角二等分。*the spot where the railroad tracks* ～ *the highway* 铁道与公路的交叉点。— ***vi.*** (道路等)分开,分叉。

bi·sec·tion [baiˈsekʃən; baɪˋsɛkʃən] ***n.*** **1.** 两断,两分,二等分,折半。**2.**【数】平分点,平分线。**3.** 平分的两部分之一。～ **theorem** 二等分定理,电路中分定理。**-al** ***a.***

bi·sec·tor, bisec·trix [baiˈsektə, baiˈsektriks; baɪˋsɛktɚ, baɪˋsɛktrɪks] ***n.*** **1.**【数】二等分线;平分面。**2.** 二等分物。

bi·ser·rate [baiˈsereit, -it; baɪˋsɛret, -ɪt] ***a.*** **1.**【植】重锯齿的。**2.**【动】具二锯齿的。

bi·sex·u·al [ˈbaiˈseksjuəl; ˋbaɪˋsɛksʃʊəl] **I** ***a.*** **1.** 两性的。**2.** 雌雄同体〔同株〕的。**3.**〔美俚〕(在性欲上)对男女两性都有兴趣的。**II** ***n.***【生】两性体。**-ism, -ity** ***n.*** 雌雄同体〔同株〕。

bish·op [ˈbiʃəp; ˋbɪʃəp] ***n.*** **1.** (基督教的)主教;(佛教的)住持。**2.** (国际象棋中的)象〔棋子为教士帽形〕。**3.** 香甜葡萄酒。～**'s lawn** 轧光细薄平布。～**'s length** 画布尺寸〔107×70 英寸〕。

bish·op·ric [ˈbiʃəprik; ˋbɪʃəprɪk] ***n.*** 主教(等)的职位〔管区〕。

bish·op's-cap [ˈbiʃəpsˌkæp; ˋbɪʃəpsˏkæp] ***n.*** 唢呐草属植物。

bisk [bisk; bɪsk] ***n.*** 海鲜禽汤〔贝禽类等煮成的浓羹〕。

Bis·ley [ˈbizli; ˋbɪzlɪ] ***n.*** (英国 Surrey 地方的)比兹利打靶场;比兹利打靶比赛会。

Bis·marck [ˈbizmɑːk; ˋbɪzmɑrk] ***n.*** **1. Ot·to von** ～ [ˈɔːtəufən; ˋɔtofən] 俾斯麦〔1815—1898,德国政治家,德意志帝国第一任首相〕。**2.** 俾斯麦群岛〔在太平洋西南部,新几内亚东北〕。

Bis·mil·lah [bisˈmilə; bɪsˋmɪlə] ***int.*** 以真主的名义!〔穆斯林誓语〕。

bis·muth [ˈbizməθ; ˋbɪzməθ] ***n.*** 【化】铋〔略作 Bi〕。～ **ocher** 铋华,赭铋矿。

bis·mu·thic [ˈbizməθik, bizˈmjuːθik; ˋbɪzməθɪk, bɪzˋmjuθɪk] ***a.*** 【化】含(五价)铋的。

bis·muth·ous [ˈbizməθəs; ˋbɪzməθəs] ***a.*** 【化】含(三价)铋的。

bi·son [ˈbaisn; ˋbaɪsn̩] ***n.*** (*pl.* ～)【动】(欧洲种和美洲种)野牛,犎牛。

Bis·pham [ˈbisfəm; ˋbɪsfəm] ***n.*** 比斯法姆〔姓氏〕。

bisque[1] [bisk; bɪsk] **I** ***n.*** **1.** (人像等的)本色陶器,素瓷。**2.** 黄褐色。**II** ***a.*** 黄褐色的。

bisque[2] [bisk; bɪsk] ***n.*** (网球等)比赛中让给弱方的 1 分。

bisque[3] [bisk; bɪsk] ***n.*** = bisk.

Bis·sau, Bis·são [biˈsau; bɪˋsaʊ] ***n.*** 比绍〔几内亚(比绍)首都〕。

bis·sex·tile [biˈsekstail; bɪˋsɛkstaɪl] **I** ***n.*** 【天】闰,闰年。**II** ***a.*** (有)闰年〔日〕的。*The years 1960 and 1964 were both* ～. 1960 和 1964 年都是闰年。

bi·sta·ble [baiˈsteibl; baɪˋstebl̩] ***n.***, ***a.*** 【物】双稳定(的),双稳态(的)。

bis·ter [ˈbistə; ˋbɪstɚ] ***n.*** 〔美〕= bistre.

bis·tort [ˈbistɔːt; ˋbɪstɔrt] ***n.*** 【植】拳参。

bis·tou·ry [ˈbisturi; ˋbɪstʊrɪ] ***n.*** (外科用的)柳叶刀。

bis·tre [ˈbistə; ˋbɪstɚ] **I** ***n.*** **1.** (由木煤烟中提出、多作底色用的)褐色颜料。**2.** 黄褐色。**II** ***a.*** 黄褐色的。

bis·tro [ˈbistrəu; ˋbɪstro] ***n.*** 〔口〕小咖啡馆;小酒馆;小夜总会。

bi·sul·cate [baiˈsʌlkeit; baɪˋsʌlket] ***a.*** **1.** 有两沟的。**2.**【动】偶蹄的;分趾蹄的。

bi·sul·phate, bi·sul·fate [baiˈsʌlfeit; baɪˋsʌlfet] ***n.*** 【化】酸式硫酸盐,硫酸氢盐。

bi·sul·phide, bi·sul·fide [baiˈsʌlfaid; baɪˋsʌlfaɪd] ***n.*** 【化】二硫化物。

bi·sul·phite, bi·sul·fite [baiˈsʌlfait; baɪˋsʌlfaɪt] ***n.*** 【化】亚硫酸氢盐;酸式亚硫酸盐。

bit[1] [bit; bɪt] ***n.*** **1.** 少许,一点儿,一些;(食物的)一口,少量食物。〔*pl.*〕吃剩的食物;小片。**2.**〔口〕一会儿,一转眼,短时间。**3.**〔英〕小银币,小铜币;〔美口〕十二分半。**4.** (戏里的)小角色;(电影、戏剧)一小段;(书)一小节。**5.**〔俚〕小姑娘,少女;女人 **6.**〔美〕表演,演奏;例行节目;〔转义〕老一套。**7.**【计】毕特〔二进位制信息单位〕;位,数位;环节。**8.**〔美俚〕刑期。*a* ～ *of chalk* 一点儿粉笔。*exchange* ～*s of gossip* 闲聊几句。*bite* [*tear*] *sth. into* ～*s* 咬〔撕〕碎。*wait a* ～ 等一下,等一会儿。*I was in India for a* ～. 我在印度作短期逗留。*six* ～*s* (美元)七角五分。*a twopenny* ～ 一枚两便士铜币。*make a supper from the* ～*s* 把上顿剩下的菜又当晚饭。***a*** ～ 有点儿〔作副词用〕(*I was a* ～ *impatient*. 我有点不耐烦了)。***a*** ～ ***and a sup*** 一点儿吃喝。***a*** ～ ***of*** 一点儿,少量的 (*a* ～ *of land* 一小块地。*Have a* ～ *of patience*. 请忍耐一下。*get a* ～ *of rest* 休息片刻)。***a*** ～ ***of a ...*** 有点儿…的味道,多少有些…(*a* ～ *of a girl* 有点儿像女孩子。*a* ～ *of a snob* 有点儿势利的味道。*I am a* ～ *of a reader myself*. 我自己好歹也是个读者)。***a*** ～ ***of all right***〔口〕无可挑剔的人〔物〕;美丽〔可爱〕的女人 ***a*** ～ ***of blood*** 纯血种(的马)。***a dainty*** ～ 一口好吃的东西。***a good*** ～〔俚〕相当长久。***a long*** [***short***] ～〔美俚〕一角五分〔一角〕钱。***a nice*** ～ ***of*** (*money*)〔俚〕很多(钱)。***at the*** ～〔Scot.〕适当其时。～ ***by*** ～ 一点一点地;渐次。～ ***of business***〔俚〕人;家伙。～ ***of stuff***〔俚〕(俗气的)女子。～***s and pieces*** 零星小玩意,杂物。***by*** ～***s*** = ～ ***by*** ～. ***do one's*** ～ 应尽一臂之力;尽自己本分。***every*** ～ 由任何一点

看;完全(*He is every ~ a scholar of him*. = *He is a scholar, every ~ of him*. 他是一个地道的学者)。**give (sb.) a ~ of one's mind** 直说;面责。**not a ~ (of it)** 一点没有,一点也不(*I don't mind a ~*. 毫无关系,我根本不放在心上。*O no, not a ~*. 啊不,没关系〔对别人向自己道歉的回答〕)。**pull to ~s** 1. 把…撕成碎片。2. 把…贬得一文不值。**quite a ~** 〔美俚〕相当多,相当。

B

bit[2] [bit; bɪt] **I** *n*. 1. 马衔,(马的)咬嘴,嚼子。2. 约束,抑制。3. (斧等的)刃口,(工具上的)切削刃;刀头,刀片;钻头;锥,凿子;钥匙齿。*jack ~* 岩心钻头。*finishing ~* (车工)光刀刀头。*a drill ~* 钻头(尖)。**draw ~** 勒马;勒着,减缓速度。**take [get] the ~ between [in] the [one's] teeth** (马)不服管;(人)不肯受约束,反抗。**take the ~s** (马张嘴)接受上嚼子。**II** *vt*. (**bit·ted** [ˈbitid; ˋbɪtɪd]; **bit·ting**) 1. 给(马)上嚼子;使(马)习惯于上嚼子。2. 约束,抑制,勒着。3. (钥匙)锉齿。

bit[3] [bit; bɪt] bite 的过去式及过去分词。

bi·tar·trate [baiˈtɑːtreit; baɪˋtɑrtret] *n*. 【化】酒石酸氢盐,酒石酸氢酯。

bitch [bitʃ; bɪtʃ] **I** *n*. 1. 母狗[母狼等]。2. 〔俚〕娼妇;淫妇;泼妇。3. 〔美俚〕【牌】黑桃女王。4. 牢骚;别扭事。*a ~ fox* 雌狐。*The test was a ~*. 那个测验真别扭。**make a ~ of** 〔口〕弄糟,弄坏。**son of a ~** 〔骂人语〕狗养的〔略作 s.o.b.〕。**II** *vi*. 〔美俚〕发牢骚,埋怨。— *vt*. 1. 弄糟,弄坏。2. 对…不满。3. 欺骗。~ **up** 〔俚〕弄糟,弄坏。~ **goddess** 发财,致富(*worship the ~ goddess* 追求金钱)。**-y** *a*.

bite [bait; baɪt] **I** *vt*. (**bit** [bit; bɪt]; **bit·ten** [ˈbitn; ˋbɪtn], **bit**) 1. 咬;咬住,咬掉(*off*);(蚊,蚤等)叮,螫,刺。2. (胡椒等)辣(鼻);(利器等)刺穿;(寒风等)刺痛;(霜等)把…冻伤。3. (酸等)腐蚀,侵蚀。4. (锚、齿轮等)吃住,咬住;紧抓住。5. 〔口〕欺骗;使恼怒;〔美俚〕偷。*A dog bit him on his arm*. 狗咬了他的手臂。*The file ~s the metal*. 锉刀锉得深。*Nitric acid ~s copper*. 硝酸能腐蚀铜。*The anchor ~s the ground*. 锚钩住海底。*an icy wind that ~s our face* 刺面的寒风。*She ~d me for a new coat*. 她骗我给她买件皮大衣。*I got bitten in a mail-order swindle*. 我在一场邮购骗局中上了当。*What's biting you?* 什么事让你这么生气?— *vi*. 1. 咬,咬着;喜欢咬人。2. 刺痛;辣;腐蚀。3. 刺穿。4. 固着,咬住,把住,紧抓住。5. (鱼)吞饵,上钩;受骗,上当。*This mustard does not ~ much*. 这种芥末不很辣。*The fish were biting well yesterday*. 昨天鱼上钩不少。*Does your parrot ~?* 你养的八哥啄人吗? *The dog may ~ at you*. 狗会咬你的。*The screw ~s*. 螺丝钉钉得牢。**be bitten with** 感染,被沾染上,害(疮等);迷上。~ **at** 1. 要咬…,向…咬去。2. 对…叫骂。~ **back** (咬住嘴唇)不说出来。~ **in [into]** 腐蚀;侵入。~ **off [away]** 1. 咬下,咬掉。2. 停止讲话。3. (广播中)截断(节目)。~ **off a big chunk** 〔美俚〕承担难事。~ **off more than one can chew** 贪多嚼不烂,担任自己不胜任的事。~ **off one's own head** 害人不到反害己。~ **one's lips** 压制着感情,忍怒;保持沉默。~ **one's nails** 咬指甲〔表示妒忌〕。~ **one's thumb at** 向…挑战,侮辱。~ **on granite** 做徒劳无益的事。~ **the bullet** 硬着头皮,咬紧牙关,死撑硬顶。~ **the dust [ground]** 倒在地上;阵亡,倒毙;败,一败涂地;〔美俚〕死,被杀,破产,失败。~ **the hand that feeds one** 恩将仇报,以怨报德。~ **the tongue [off]** 咬着舌头;保持沉默。**Once ~ [bitten], twice shy**. 一朝被蛇咬,十年怕草绳。**II** *n*. 1. 咬,叮,螫;紧咬;穿透力。2. 一小口(食物),少量(食物);〔口〕便餐。3. 咬伤,螫伤;冻伤;腐蚀;伤口;(伤口等的)疼痛,刺痛,苦痛。4. 辛辣,刺激性。5. 受骗,上当;(鱼)上钩。6. 【机】啮合。7. 【医】上下齿的啮合情况;(锯、锉等的)齿;切削刀头。8. 〔美口〕(捐税等一次次收取的)一笔。*I have not taken a ~ all day*. 我整天没有吃一点东西。*a screw with a good ~* 螺丝咬得紧。*give a ~ at the bone* 啃骨头。*a deep ~* 很深的伤口。*The air had a frosty ~*. 寒气袭人。*the ~ of the original* 原作的强烈风味。*whisky with a ~ in it* 辣嘴的威士忌酒。**(a) ~ and (a) sup** 饮食;便餐。**put the ~ on** 〔美俚〕向…借钱;向…敲竹杠。**take [make] two ~s at [of] a cherry** 1. 均分微不足道的东西;零敲碎打地搞,把(原可一气做完的)小事情分数次做。2. 踌躇;拘谨。

bit·er [ˈbaitə; ˋbaɪtɚ] *n*. 1. 辣嘴的东西,咬人的动物;上钩的鱼。2. 骗子。*That monkey is a ~*. 那只猴子咬人。**The ~ (is) bit [bitten]**. 骗人者反被人骗,害人反害己。**Great barkers are no ~s**. 会叫的狗不咬人。

bit·ing [ˈbaitiŋ; ˋbaɪtɪŋ] *a*. 1. 辛辣的,刺激性的;讽刺的。2. 锐利的,刺痛的;腐蚀性的。~ *cold* 刺骨的寒冷。*a ~ caricature* 辛辣的漫画。**-ly** *ad*.

BIT·NET [ˈbitnet; ˋbɪtnɛt] *n*. 【计】比特网。

bit·stock [ˈbitˌstɔk; ˋbɪtˏstɑk] *n*. 钻柄。

bitt [bit; bɪt] **I** *n*. 〔常 *pl*.〕【海】(系)缆柱。**II** *vt*. 把(缆)系在缆柱上。

bit·ten [ˈbitn; ˋbɪtn] bite 的过去分词。

bit·ter [ˈbitə; ˋbɪtɚ] **I** *a*. 1. (药等)苦。2. 严(寒),烈(风),厉害的;辛苦的,悲惨的。3. 怀恨的;抱怨的;讽刺的。~ *tincture* 苦味药酒。~ *tears* 辛酸的眼泪。*a ~ experience* 惨痛的经验。*a ~ winter* 严冬。~ *hatred* 刻骨仇恨。*have a ~ tongue* 刻薄嘴。~ *remarks* 刻薄话,恶毒的话。~ *discipline* 严格的训练。~ *enemy* 死敌,活冤家死对头。**be ~ against** 激烈反对。**to the ~ end** 坚持到底;拼命,直到死而后已(*fight to the ~ end* 血战到底)。**II** *n*. 1. 苦,苦味;苦味物。2. 〔常 *pl*.〕苦味药;苦味大补酒;(某些鸡尾酒的)配料;〔英〕苦啤酒。*the sweets and ~s of life* 人世间的悲欢。**get one's ~s** 〔美口〕遭天罚,报应。**III** *ad*. 非常,剧烈,厉害。*a ~ cold night* 酷寒的夜晚。**IV** *vt*. 把…弄苦,使变苦。*herbs employed to ~ vermouth* 用于给苦艾酒加苦味的药草。— *vi*. 变苦。~ **cup** 苦木杯。~ **end** 【海】1. 索端。2. 锚链末端。~**-ender** 〔美俚〕坚持不屈的人,顽抗到底的人。~**-enderism** 〔美俚〕顽抗主义。~ **lake** 盐湖。~ **nut** 心果山核桃。~ **root** 一种马齿苋。~ **rot** 植物炭疽病。~**-sweet** 1. *a*. 又苦又甜的;稍带苦笑的(*a ~-sweet memory* 甜蜜而又辛酸的回忆)。2. *n*. 又苦又甜的东西;【植】南蛇藤。~ **weed** 苦味植物〔如美洲豚草、堆心菊、珠蓍等〕。

bit·ter·ish [ˈbitəriʃ; ˋbɪtərɪʃ] *a*. 微苦的,带苦味的。

bit·ter·ly [ˈbitəli; ˋbɪtɚlɪ] *ad*. 1. 苦,惨痛地。2. 剧烈,酷,厉害地。*cry ~* 痛哭。

bit·tern[1] [ˈbitə(:)n; ˋbɪtɚn] *n*. 【鸟】麻鳽。

bit·tern[2] [ˈbitə(:)n; ˋbɪtɚn] *n*. 1. 盐卤,卤汁。2. (掺啤酒的)酒花汁。

bit·ter·ness [ˈbitənis; ˋbɪtɚnɪs] *n*. 1. 苦味。2. 苦难;悲哀。3. 酷烈。4. 讽刺。

bitts [bits; bɪts] *n*. 〔*pl*.〕【船】系柱。

bit·ty [ˈbiti; ˋbɪtɪ] *a*. 〔谑、儿〕小。

bit·u·lith·ic [ˌbitjuˈliθik; ˏbɪtjʊˋlɪθɪk] **I** *a*. 沥青混凝土的。**II** *n*. 沥青混凝土路。

bit·u·men [ˈbitjumin, Am. biˈtjuːmin; bɪˋtjumən, bɪˋtjumɪn] *n*. 1. 【矿】沥青,沥青质。2. 〔澳口〕柏油路。

bi·tu·mi·nite [biˈtjuːminait; bɪˋtjumɪnaɪt] *n*. 【矿】1. 烟煤,沥青煤。2. (芽胞)油页岩。

bi·tu·mi·nize [biˈtjuːminaiz; bɪˋtjuməˏnaɪz] *vt*. 1. 使成沥青。2. 使与沥青混合。

bi·tu·mi·nous [biˈtjuːminəs; bɪˋtjumənəs] *a*. 沥青的,含沥青的。~ *coal* 烟煤。~ *grout* 含沥青溶液,水沥青。

bi·u·nique [ˈbaiju(:)ˌniːk; ˋbaɪjʊˏnik] *a*. 【数】一对一的(关系)。

bi·u·ret [ˌbaijuˈret; ˏbaɪjʊˋrɛt] *n*. 【生化】缩二脲。

bi·va·lence [ˈbaiˌveiləns, ˈbivə-; ˋbaɪˋveləns, ˋbɪvə-]

n.【化】双化合价,双原子价,二价(= bivalency)。

bi·va·lent [ˈbaiˌveilənt; baɪˋvelənt] **I** *a*. **1.**【化】二价的。**2.**【生】二价染色体的。~ *chromosome* 二价染色体。**II** *n*.【生】二价染色体。

bi·valve [ˈbaivælv; ˋbaɪˏvælv] **I** *a*.【植】有两瓣的;【动】有双谷的。**II** *n*.【动】双壳贝;牡蛎。

bi·valved [ˈbaivælvd; ˋbaɪˏvælvd], **bi·val·vu·lar** [baiˈvælvjulə; baɪˋvælvjulɚ] *a*. = bivalve.

bi·vi·nyl [baiˈvainil; baɪˋvaɪnɪl] *n*.【化】丁(间)二烯。

biv·ou·ac [ˈbivuæk; ˋbɪvuæk] **I** *n*. 露营,野营;露营地。**II** *vi*. (*bivou·acked*; *biv·ou·ack·ing*) 露营,露宿。

bi·week·ly [baiˈwiːkli; baɪˋwiklɪ] **I** *a*. **1.** 二周一次的 **2.** 每二周的。**II** *ad*. **1.** 二周一次。**2.** 每周两次。**III** *n*. **1.** 双周刊。**2.** 半周刊。

bi·year·ly [baiˈjiəli; baɪˋjɪrlɪ] **I** *a*. **1.** 两年一次的。**2.** 一年两次的。**II** *ad*. **1.** 两年一次。**2.** 一年两次。

biz [biz; bɪz] *n*.〔俚〕= business. ~ **confab**〔美俚〕商量。

bi·zad [ˈbizæd; ˋbɪzæd] *n*.〔美俚〕商业管理科;商业管理科学生。

bi·zarre [biˈzɑː; bɪˋzɑr] *a*.〔F.〕希奇古怪的,不同寻常的。~ *clothing* 奇装异服。*The story has a certain ~ interest*. 这个故事听起来别有风味。

bi·zar·re·rie [biˈzɑːrəri; bɪzɑrəˋrɪ] *n*.〔F.〕希奇古怪,奇异;奇怪的东西。

Bi·zer·te [biˈzəːt; bɪˋzɝt], **Bi·zer·ta** [biˈzəːtə; bɪˋzɝtə] *n*. 比塞大〔突尼斯港市〕。

bi·zon·al [baiˈzəunl; baɪˋzonl̩] *a*. 两国共管区的,与两国共管区有关的。

BK =【化】berkelium.

BK. =【棒球】balks.

bk. = bank; bark; block; book.

bkg. = banking.

bkrpt. = bankrupt.

bkry. = bakery.

bkt. = basket.

BL = **1.** Bachelor of laws 法学士。**2.** Bachelor of letters (或 literature) 文学学士。**3.** British library 英国图书馆。**4.** British Legion 英国退伍军人协会。

B/L = bill of lading 提(货)单。

BLA = Bachelor of Liberal Arts 文(科)学士。

blaa [blɑː; blɑ] *int*., *n*. = blah.

blab [blæb; blæb] **I** *vt*. (*-bb-*) 泄漏(秘密等)。*She blabbed my confidences to everyone*. 她把我的隐私逢人便讲。— *vi*. 乱说乱讲。*Don't confide in him, because he ~s*. 不要对他推心置腹,他喜欢乱讲话。**II** *n*. **1.** 泄漏秘密者;喜欢乱说乱讲的人,搬弄是非者。**2.** 乱说乱讲。*These stories are false, just so much ~*. 那些故事都是假的,全是一派胡言。

blab·ber [ˈblæbə; ˋblæbɚ] *n*. 饶舌者,泄露秘密者。

blab·ber·mouth [ˈblæbəmauθ; ˋblæbɚˏmaʊθ] *n*.〔口〕碎嘴子。

Black [blæk; blæk] *n*. 布莱克〔姓氏〕。

black [blæk; blæk] **I** *a*. **1.** 黑,黑色的。**2.** 暗的;黑暗的。**3.** 皮肤黑的;黑种人的,有关黑人的。**4.** (教士等)穿黑衣的。**5.** 污染的,(手等)弄脏了的;丢脸的。**6.** 阴郁的,忧郁的;发着脾气的,怒冲冲的。**7.** (前途)暗淡的,有凶兆的,不吉利的;邪恶的。**8.** 黑市的,非法买卖的。**9.** (土地)被荒废的;(咖啡)不加糖的;(钢材等)未加工的。**10.**〔英〕被(罢工工人)抵制装卸的。**11.**〔美口〕纯粹的,完全的,极度的。~ *clouds* 黑云。*The street was ~ with people*. 街上黑压压的一片人群。*the ~ knight* 黑衣骑士。*a ~ night* 黑夜。*Things look ~*. 事态险恶,趋势恶劣。*be ~ with rage* 愤怒得脸色发紫。*give sb. a ~ look* 对人板面孔。*He is not so ~ as he is painted*. 他不像传说的那样坏。*a ~ heart* 黑心肠(的人)。*a ~ villian* 大坏蛋,恶棍。~ *areas of drought* 荒废的干旱地带。*half ~* 半加工的,半处理的。~ *in the face* 脸色发紫。*be beaten ~ and blue* 被打得青一块紫一块。~ *darkness* 漆黑一团。~ *day* 凶日。~ *despair* 大失所望。~ *diamond* 黑金刚石;〔*pl*.〕煤炭。~ *earth* 黑钙土。*B- English* 黑人英语。~ *flag* 海盗旗;(处决人犯时用的)死刑旗。~ *frost* 严霜。~ *gang*【海】火夫,输机人员。~ *ingratitude* 极端的忘恩负义。~ *words* 不吉利的话。~ ***art*** 魔术;妖术。~ ***dog*** 忧郁,不开心 (*be under the ~ dog* 绷着脸,皱着眉头)。~ ***eye*** 眼珠乌黑的眼;眼眶周围被打伤的紫斑;〔喻〕耻辱。***paint sb. ~*** 把某人描写成坏人。***say ~ in sb.'s eye*** 非难,谴责。

II *n*. **1.** 黑,黑色。**2.** 黑色染料,黑色颜料,黑色墨水。**3.** 黑人。**4.** 黑衣;丧服。**5.** 黑斑;污点;煤;(靶子等的)黑点。**6.** 黑马。~ ***or white*** 非此即彼的,不是黑就是白,走极端。***in the ~*** 出现黑字,赚钱 (*opp*. in the red)。***put the ~ on***〔卑〕输。***talk ~ into white = prove that ~ is white*** 认黑作白,指鹿为马,诡辩。

III *vt*. 把…弄黑;把(鞋等)搽黑;弄脏,染污。— *vi*. 变黑、成黑色。~ ***down*** 用柏油涂黑船具。~ ***out*** **1.** 用墨涂掉,抹杀;使停刊;封锁(新闻)。**2.**【剧】使舞台转暗;【空】(空袭时)熄灯;(战时)实行灯火管制。**3.** (飞机等急降时)眼睛发黑,头发昏;【无】干扰。~ ***and tan a***. **1.** 脊黑、头足茶褐色的〔指一种犬〕。**2.**〔常 B- and T-〕拥护〔实行〕黑人和白人在政治上按比例选举代表的。**3.** (夜总会等)黑人和白人都常去的。*n*. **4.** (脊黑,头足茶褐色的)猎犬。**5.** 黑人和白人都常去的夜总会。~ ***and white*** **1.** 白纸黑字;书写品;印刷品,黑白版钢笔画 (*have (something down) in ~ and white* 写下来,印下来)。**2.** 用墨水(在白纸上)写的;黑白的,未着色的,印刷的。**3.** 黑白电影。~**ball** **1.** *vt*. 投黑球(反对)。**2.** *vt*. 开除…的会籍,排斥。**3.** *n*. 黑球〔表示反对的投票〕。~ **beetle** 蟑螂,飞蠊。**B- Belt** (美国)黑人聚居地带;黑土带〔美国阿拉巴马及密西西比河沿岸棉花产区〕;(日本柔道协会标志)黑带。~**berry** **1.** *n*.【植】黑莓。(*plentiful as ~berries* 俯拾即是)。**2.** *vi*. 采黑莓(*go ~ berrying* 去采黑莓)。~**bird**〔英〕画眉;〔美〕燕八哥;〔澳〕(被诱卖异乡的)黑人。~**birding** (殖民主义者的)贩奴活动。~-**board** 黑板。~**board jungle** 黑板丛林〔秩序混乱、无法无天的市区学校〕;学校中混乱的状况。~ **body**【物】黑体〔指能全部吸收电磁辐射而毫无反应的一种理想物体〕。~ **book** **1.** 黑名单。**2.** 学生记过簿;黑皮书。**3.** 巫术书 (*be in sb.'s ~ book* 得罪了某人)。~ **bottle** 黑药(尤指三氯乙醛)。~ **bread** 黑面包。~-**browed** *a*. 愁眉苦脸的,阴郁的,凄凉的。~ **box**〔美俚〕**1.** 黑箱〔复杂电子仪器〕。**2.** 律师。**3.** (装在飞机上记录飞行情况等的)密封仪器。**4.**【自】未知框〔指内部特性未输出的框图等〕。**5.** 整体装拆自动电子元件。~ **bourse** 黑市。~ **cab** 出租汽车。~ **cap** **1.**【鸟】〔欧〕莺类;〔美〕白鹁鸟。**2.**【植】(美国)糙莓。**3.**〔英〕(宣判死刑时法官所戴的)黑色法官帽。~ **capitalism**〔美〕黑人资本主义〔黑人资本家拥有和经营私人企业〕。~**carpet**"黑地毯"〔指不友好的接待,和 red carpet 意思正相反〕。~ **cattle** (苏格兰及威尔士出产的)肉用牛。~-**coat** (贬)僧侣,牧师;〔英〕职员,领薪阶层。~**cock**【鸟】黑色公松鸡。~ **comedy** 黑色喜剧〔一种现代派剧作,其幽默源于荒唐、怪诞的场面〕。~ **coffee** (不加牛奶和糖的)浓咖啡。~ **crop** (对麦类而言的)豆类作物。~ **copper**【冶】粗铜。**B- Country** 黑乡〔英国中部煤铁产区〕。~ **damp** 矿井内的窒息性空气。~ **death** 黑死病。~ **dog**〔俚〕忧郁,沮丧。~ **draught** (泻叶与泻盐泡成的)泻药。~ **earth** 黑(钙)土。~ **economy** 黑色经济,地下经济。~ **eye** **1.** 乌黑的眼睛。**2.** (被打或被撞的)青肿眼眶。**3.** 沉重的打击。**4.** 丢脸的事。~-**eyed** *a*. 黑眼睛的;(被打得)眼圈发青的。~**face** **1.** 黑面羊;黑面兽。**2.** 装扮成黑人的演员。**3.**【印】粗黑体活字。~-**faced** *a*. **1.** 脸黑的;愁眉苦脸的,忧郁的。**2.**【印】粗黑体的。~**fellow** 澳洲本地人。~ **fin** 黑鳍笛鲷;黑鳍白鲑。~-fish 黑鱼类;巨头鲸;刚产卵后的鲑。~ fly 蚋。~foot 1.〔Scot.〕中人,媒人。2.〔B-〕美洲印第安人的一族。B- Forest 黑林〔德国西南部森林地带〕。Black Friday, ~ Friday 黑色星期五〔指经济领域内发生股票崩盘等巨大灾难的日子〕。~ game【鸟】(欧洲)松鸡。~ gang (船上的)伙夫。~ ginger 干生姜。~ gold 1. 石油。2. 橡胶。B- Hand 黑手党〔本世纪初纽约一个诈骗犯罪集团〕;秘密犯罪集团。~ head【鸟】黑头鸟;〔美〕黑头白胸鸭;【医】黑头面疱〔粉刺〕。~heart 1. 心形黑樱桃。2. (植物的)黑心病。~-hearted *a*. 黑心肠的,心毒的;罪大恶极的。~ hole 1.【天】黑洞〔假设存在于太空中的有巨大引力的洞穴,为天体坍陷所形成〕。2. 土牢;(军营中的)禁闭室。~ house 低矮无窗的小屋。~ humour 黑色幽默〔采用荒谬、怪诞、可怕场面的幽默文艺形式〕。~ ice 透明薄冰。~ ink〔美〕黑字,贷方。~-jack 1. *n*. (外涂柏油的革制)大酒杯;海盗旗;〔美〕(铅头)皮棍棒;【矿】方锌矿;【植】槲属;【牌】二十一点。2. *vt*.〔美〕拿铅头皮棍棒打。~ law 关于黑人的法律。~ lead【矿】石墨,笔铅。~lead *vt*. 在…上涂黑铅;用黑铅磨。~leg 1. 假赌徒,骗子;(破坏罢工的)工贼。2.【兽医】炭疽热;【植】黑脚病,甜菜蛇眼病。B- Legion 黑党〔美国一恐怖团体〕。~ letter【印】黑体字。~-letter *a*. 1. 黑体字的。2. 不吉利的,倒霉的(*a* ~ *letter day* 凶日,倒霉的日子)。~ light【物】不可见光。~-list 1. *n*. 黑名单。2. *vt*. 把…记入黑名单。~ lung 黑肺病。~ mail 1. *n*. 勒索,敲诈,讹诈;〔古英〕(盗匪征收的)保护费,免抢税(*nuclear* ~ 核讹诈)。2. *vt*. 勒索,敲诈,讹诈。~mailer 勒索者,敲诈钱财的人。b-man 1. = negro. 2.〔B- M-〕恶魔。B- Maria 1.〔口〕警察局的囚车。2.〔俚〕黑烟榴弹。~ mark 黑点〔学生品行不良的记载〕,污点。~ market 黑市。~market 1. *vi*. 做黑市交易。2. *vt*. 在黑市上卖。B- Mass 1. (天主教的)安魂弥撒。2. (异教徒的)恶魔崇拜。B- Monday 1. 复活节后的第一个礼拜一。2.〔学俚〕开学后的第一个礼拜一。~ money 黑钱〔没有报税的收入〕。B- Muslim (美国)黑人穆斯林运动的成员。~ nationalism 黑人民族主义。~out 1. *n*.【剧】舞台转暗;关灯;闭火;断电;(战时的)灯火管制;【空】(急降等时)眼睛发黑,突然发昏;暂时失去知觉;删除;(新闻)封锁;(广播等)停止。2. *a*. 防空袭的,灯火管制的(~ *curtains* 遮灯防空窗帘)。B- Panther (美国黑人)黑豹党的成员。~poll【鸟】黑头森莺。~ power (美国)黑人权力。~ pudding 血(香)肠。~ race 黑种人。B- Radio (心理战中)一方冒充另一方的电台广播。B- Rod 黑仗侍卫〔英国上院的侍卫〕。~ rot【植】黑斑病。~ rust【植】黑锈病。~ sand 黑砂〔含有砂金的砂〕。B- Sea 黑海。B- Shirt 黑衫党〔前意大利法西斯组织〕;希特勒警卫队;法西斯分子。~ sheep 害群之马;败家子;恶棍。~-smith 铁匠,锻工。~-snake 1. 黑蛇。2.〔美〕重皮鞭。~ stem rust【植】杆锈病。~strap 1. 混合酒。2.〔俚〕劣质葡萄酒。3. 糖渣。4.〔美俚〕咖啡。B- Stream 黑潮,日本海流。~ studies (美国)黑人文化研究。~ tea 红茶。~ terror 黑人拳击选手。~ thorn【植】黑刺李,〔美〕山楂属,〔爱〕用刺李木材做的手杖(*the* ~ *thorn winter* 刺李花开的冬天〔吹西北风的寒冷天气〕)。~ tie 1. (穿无燕尾礼服所戴的)黑蝴蝶领结。2. 晚会男礼服。~-tie *a*. (晚会)要求穿男礼服的。~top 1. *n*. 沥青路面。2. *vt*. 用沥青铺(路面)。~ vomit 1. 黄热病。2. 黄热病末期的呕吐物。B- Water〔美〕黑水州〔内布拉斯加州的别名〕。~ water fever 黑水热〔热带病〕。~ widow 1. (交媾后就吃掉雄性的)有毒黑蜘蛛。2. (美国)"黑寡妇"式夜间战斗机。~ wood 黑木相思树;黑檀。

black-a-moor [ˈblækəmuə; ˋblækəˏmʊr] *n*.〔蔑〕黑种人,黑色的人。

black·a·vised [ˈblækəvaist, ˈblækəvaizd; ˋblækəˏvaɪst, ˋblækəˏvaɪzd] *a*.〔古〕脸黑的,黑色的。

black·en [ˈblækən; ˋblækən] *vt*. 1. 使黑,使暗;中伤(名誉等),诽谤。— *vi*. 变黑,变暗。

black·en·ing [ˈblækəniŋ; ˋblækənɪŋ] *n*. 1. 变黑;上黑;致黑;【机】发黑处理;发黑度。2. 黑色涂料〔染料〕;炭粉〔铸造用〕。

Black·ett [ˈblækit; ˋblækɪt] *n*. 布莱基特〔姓氏〕。

black·guard [ˈblægɑːd; ˋblægɑrd] I *n*. 1. 下流人,流氓,恶棍。2. 满口脏话的人,爱骂人者。II *a*. 粗鄙的,下流的,嘴臭的。III *vt*. 用脏话骂(人)。*The pot is ~ing the kettle*.〔谚〕乌鸦笑猪黑,流氓骂恶棍。-ism *n*. 1. 粗鄙,下流,恶棍行为。2. 说脏话;乱骂人。-ly *a*. 粗鄙的,下流的;恶棍式的(*use* ~ *language* 口出不逊,使用下流语言)。

black·ing [ˈblækiŋ; ˋblækɪŋ] *n*. 黑色涂料;黑鞋油;炭粉。*put shoe* ~ *on* 给…上黑鞋油。

black·ish [ˈblækiʃ; ˋblækɪʃ] *a*. 稍黑的,带黑色的。

black·ly [ˈblækli; ˋblæklɪ] *ad*. 1. 黑;暗。2. 阴郁地,愤怒地。3. 阴险地,残忍地,邪恶地。*a plot* ~ *contrived to wreak vengeance* 一项阴险的复仇计划。

Black·more [ˈblækmɔː; ˋblækmɔr] *n*. 布莱克莫尔〔姓氏〕。

black·ness [ˈblæknis; ˋblæknɪs] *n*. 1. 黑,黑色。2. 阴郁。3. 阴险,凶恶。

Black·wood [ˈblækwud; ˋblækwʊd] *n*. 布莱克伍德〔姓氏〕。

black·y [ˈblæki; ˋblækɪ] *n*.〔蔑〕黑人;黑鸟;黑兽。

blad·der [ˈblædə; ˋblædɚ] *n*. 1.【解】膀胱;泡;囊。2. (球等的)胆,救生圈,气球;囊状物。3. 趾高气扬的人;吹牛的人。~nose【动】冠海豹(= hooded seal)。~-nut【植】省沽油属植物(的荚)。~ worm 囊尾蚴(= cysticercus)。~-wort *n*.【植】狸藻。

blad·der·y [ˈblædəri; ˋblædərɪ] *a*. 1. 膀胱状的,囊状的。2. 有气泡的。

blade [bleid; bled] *n*. 1. (壳、草等的)叶片,叶身,叶。2. 刀片;(安全)剃刀刀片(= razor ~);刀口,刃;刀,剑;击剑师,剑术家。3. 桨叶;(推进器的)翼;击球板;肩胛骨;【语音】舌的前部,舌面。4. 浮华少年;蛮横任性的人。*a single* ~ *of grass* 一片草叶,未吐穗。*a gay* ~ *from the nearly* 从邻区来的浮华子弟。*He is a good* ~. 他刀法〔剑术〕很高。*in the* ~ 正在长叶子,尚未吐穗。~bone【解】肩胛骨。~smith 刀剑匠。

blad·ed [ˈbleidid; ˋbledɪd] *a*. 有…叶片的;有…刀〔剑〕身的。

blae·ber·ry [ˈbleibəri; ˋblebərɪ] *n*.〔北英〕= bilberry.

Bla·go·vesh·chensk [ˌblɑːgəˈveʃtʃensk; ˏblɑgəˋveʃtʃɛnsk] *n*. 布拉戈维申斯克〔即海兰泡,俄罗斯城市〕。

blague [blɑːg; blɑg] *n*.〔F.〕吹牛;撒谎;愚弄,恶作剧。

blah [blɑː; blɑ] I *int*.〔美俚〕瞎说! 胡扯! 废话! II *n*. 浮夸的文章,胡扯,瞎谈。III *a*. 无聊的,枯燥无味的。*That's* ~.〔美〕那是骗人的,靠不住的呀。*What they say is* ~. 他们说的全是废话。

blain [blein; blen] *n*.【医】脓泡,水泡;【兽医】炭疽。

Blaine [blein; blen] *n*. 布莱恩〔姓氏,男子名〕。

Blair [bleə; blɛr] *n*. 布莱尔〔姓氏,男子名〕。

Blake [bleik; blek] *n*. 1. 布莱克〔姓氏〕。2. William ~ 布莱克〔1757—1827,英国漫画家,诗人〕。

blam·a·ble [ˈbleiməble; ˋbleməbḷ] *a*. 该责备的,有过失的。

blam·a·bly [ˈbleiməbli; ˋbleməblɪ] *ad*. 该责备地,有过失地。

blame [bleim; blem] I *n*. 1. 责怪,责备,非难,指责;挑剔;谴责。2. 过失,过错,罪,咎;责;责任。***bear*** [***take***] ***the*** ~ 负责,承担责任,背过。***in*** ~ ***of*** 责备… ***incur great*** ~ ***for*** 为…大受责备。***lay the*** ~ ***at the door of another*** 把责任推到别人头上。***lay*** [***cast***] ***the*** ~ ***on*** [***upon***] ***sb***. ***for*** 把…推在某人身上,使某人负…之责。***It is small*** ~ ***to sb***. ***that***! (发生了)…也不能多怪某人。II *vt*. 1. 责备,谴责,非难,挑剔。2. 把…归咎于,怪

在…头上(*on*; *upon*)。3.〔美俚〕〔诅咒语〕= damn. *B- it*!〔美俚〕该死! 去你的! *You ~ it on society*. 这是社会的责任。*be ~d for* …为(某事)受责备。*B- if I do* [*don't*] = *I'm ~d if I do* [*don't*]. 我决不…,死也不…〔一定要…,非得…不可〕。*B- my hide if I go*. 我决不去。***be to*** ~ 该负责,应受责(*I am to ~ for it*. 我该负责,是我不对)。

blamed [bleimd; blemd] **I** ***a***.〔美俚〕该死的,可恶的,混蛋的。(*I'm*) ~ *if* ...〔见 blame 条〕。*The ~ car won't start*. 这辆该死的车发动不起来。*I have a pain in every ~ joint*. 每一个讨厌的关节都有点儿痛。**II** ***ad***.〔美方〕非常,很。*The pistol looked so ~ dangerous*. 这支手枪看着挺危险。*It's ~ cold out tonight*. 今天晚上怪冷的。

blame·ful [ˈbleimfʊl; ˋblemfəl] ***a***. 该责备的;有过错的。**-ly** ***ad***.

blame·less [ˈbleimlis; ˋblemlɪs] ***a***. 无可责难的,无罪的,无过失的。*a ~ child* 没有过失的乖孩子。*lead a ~ life* 生活正派。**-ly** ***ad***. **-ness** ***n***.

blame·wor·thy [ˈbleimˌwəːði; ˋblemˏwɚðɪ] ***a***. 该责备的,有罪的,有过失的。*a ~ administration* 弊政。

blanch [blɑːntʃ; blæntʃ] ***vt***. 1.【化】漂白,使变白。2. 遮断日光使(植物)变苍白。3. 使(面色)变苍白;【烹】(用沸水)煮白;烫去(杏仁等的)皮。4. 在(金属)上镀锡,酸洗(金属)使变白。— ***vi***. 发白;变白;(面色)变苍白。~ ***over*** 粉饰。

Blanche [blɑːntʃ; blɑntʃ] ***n***. 布兰奇〔女子名〕。

blanc-mange [bləˈmɔnʒ; bləˋmɑnʒ] ***n***. 牛奶冻〔用牛奶、蛋、糖、玉米粉等做成的胶状甜食〕。

bland [blænd; blænd] ***a***. 1. (态度等)温和的,柔和的。2. 平淡无味的。3. (药等)刺激性少的,纯和的;(烟等)味醇的。4. 不动感情的,无动于衷的。**-ly** ***ad***. **-ness** ***n***.

blan·dish [ˈblændiʃ; ˋblændɪʃ] ***vt***., ***vi***. 谄媚,奉承,讨好。~ *sb. into* ...奉承某人使做某事。**-ment** ***n***.〔常 *pl*.〕奉承,讨好卖乖(*threats and ~ments* 又吓又哄)。

blank [blæŋk; blæŋk] **I** ***a***. 1. (表格等)空白的,(纸等)无字的;空着的;【商】(支票等)不记名的。2. (子弹等)空的,(精神等)空虚的;(努力等)无效果的;(年成等)饥荒的;无聊的,单调的;(诗等)没有韵的。3. 苍白的,失色的;发呆的,呆呆的,无表情的;漠然的。4. 无齿的,无槽的,无纹的。5. 完全的,纯粹的。*a ~ space* 空白,空处;空地。*a ~ map* 轮廓地图,白地图。*a ~ wall* 无修饰的墙,空墙。*a ~ existence* 空虚的生活。*a ~ mind* 心不在焉。~ *efforts* 白忙,空忙。*He looked perfectly ~*. 他完全呆了。*You ~ idiot*. 你这个大傻瓜。~ *stupidity* 愚蠢透顶。*a ~ refusal* 断然拒绝。**II** ***n***. 1. 空白;空白处,间隔;空地;白纸;〔美〕表格纸,空白表格〔英国叫 form〕。2. (精神上的)空虚;(个人生活中的)平淡时期,空签;【军】空弹;目标,靶心白点。3.【无】(阴极射线管的)底;熄灭脉冲。4.【机】胚(料),毛胚。5.〔古〕无韵诗。6.〔英〕(议案中用斜体字表示的)未决部分。7. (用横线"—"表示的)空白部分,某,某某。8.〔口、婉〕= damn〔用横线"—"作记号,读作~, ~y, ~ed, ~ety 等〕;省略号"—"的读注。*a telegraph ~*〔美〕电报空格纸。*I'm a ~ on the subject of Whiteman*. 我对惠特曼的作品没有作过研究。*B- him*〔it 等〕! 该死! *My mind became a complete ~*. 什么都忘了。*Mr*. — = *Mr*. Blank 某人。— — *Esq*. *of* — *Hall* = Blank Blank Esquire of Blank Hall 某宅某某先生。***draw*** (***a***) ~ 抽空签;〔口〕终于落空,失败。***in*** ~ 空白(待填)。**III** ***vt***. 1. 抹掉,使无效,作废,取消(*out*)。2.〔美口〕(比赛等)使(对方)不能得分。3. 使不能通行,封锁(*off*)。4.【机】冲切,下料。~ *out an entry* 抹去一笔账。~ *off a tunnel* 封锁隧道。— ***vi***. 1. 消失,湮灭。2. 失神。*The music ~ed out*. 乐声逐渐消失。*His mind ~ed out momentarily*. 他一时走神了。~ **application** 空白申请书。~ **book** 空白簿。~ **cartridge** [**firing**] 空弹〔空弹射击〕。~ **cheque** 1. 空白〔不记名〕支票。2. 无限制的权力,自由处理权(*give a ~ cheque to sb*. 给与某人无限制的可动用金额或权力)。~ **credit**【商】信用票据。~ **endorsement** (票据的)不记名背书。~ **form** 空白表格。~ **impossibilities** 完全不可能的事。~ **verse** 无韵诗。~ **wall** 1. 没有窗或门的墙。2. 障碍(*run into ~ wall* 遇到障碍)。

B

blan·ket [ˈblæŋkit; ˋblæŋkɪt] **I** ***n***. 1. 毛毯,绒被;毛毡状物,层,垫。2. (火箭)表面层;(反应堆)再生区;(空气动力的)阴影。*a thermal insulation ~* 绝热层。*sand ~* 砂盖层,过滤层。*a ~ of snow* 一层雪,白雪皑皑。*a ~ of smoke* 烟幕。***a wet*** ~ 扫兴的人,败兴的事[物]。***be born on the wrong side of the*** ~ 是私生儿。***split the*** ~〔美口〕离婚。***stretch the*** [***one's***] ~〔美口〕夸张。***throw a wet ~ on*** [***over***] 使扫兴,对…泼冷水,使锐气受挫折。***toss in a*** ~ 把…放在毯子上上下颠簸〔一种处罚〕。**II** ***a***.〔美〕一般的,总括的;无大差别的,(胜负等)不分上下的。**III** ***vt***. 1. 用毛毯包〔盖〕。2. 把(人)放在毯子上上下颠簸。3. 遮掩(丑事等)。4.【海】抢…的上风。5.〔美〕妨碍,干扰。6. (规则等)适用于。*the rates that ~ the whole region* (全区)通用运费。~ **agreement** 一揽子协议。~ **area** 1.【无】广播受干扰地区。2. 敷层面积。~ **bombing** 地毯式轰炸,成片轰炸。~ **drill**〔美俚〕午觉,歇晌;睡眠。~ **flower**【植】天人菊。~ **Indians** (用毯子裹身的)印第安人。~ **insurance** 总括保险。~ **policy** 总括保险单。~ **roll**【军】背袋,背包。~ **rules** 总则。

blan·ket·ing [ˈblæŋkitiŋ; ˋblæŋkɪtɪŋ] ***n***. 1.〔集合词〕毛毯类的东西(= blankets)。2. 把人置毛毯上上下颠簸的处罚。3.【电视】熄灭,匿影;【无】通讯受干扰。

blan·ket·y-blank, blank·y [ˈblæŋkitiˈblæŋk, ˈblæŋki; ˋblæŋkətɪˋblæŋk, ˋblæŋkɪ] ***a***., ***ad***. 该死〔诅咒语 damn, damned 的委婉说法〕。*the blankety-blank train* 该死的火车。*What the blankety-blank blue blazes went on*! 搞的什么鬼名堂!

blank·ly [ˈblæŋkli; ˋblæŋklɪ] ***ad***. 1. 无表情的,茫然,惘然。2. 完全地;斩钉截铁地。

blank·ness [ˈblæŋknis; ˋblæŋknɪs] ***n***. 1. 空白,空虚。2. 茫然;单调。

Blanqu·ism [ˈblɑːŋkizəm; ˋblɑŋkɪzəm] ***n***. 布朗基主义。

blare [bleə; blɛr] **I** ***vi***. 叫,吼,咆哮,怒号;(喇叭等)嘟嘟地大声响。*The trumpets ~d as the procession got under way*. 行列行进时,喇叭嘟嘟地响个不休。— ***vt***. 高声发出(或奏出);高声宣布。~ *out the threat of the war* 发出战争叫嚣。**II** ***n***. 1. (喇叭等的)响声;巨响;吼叫。2. (颜色等)耀眼的光泽。3. 大吹大擂。

blar·ney [ˈblɑːni; ˋblɑrnɪ] **I** ***n***. 奉承话;甜言蜜语。**II** ***vt***. 巧言引诱,甘言哄骗。— ***vi***. 说奉承话,拍马屁。**Blarney stone** 巧言石〔爱尔兰 Blarney 城上的石头,相传吻此石后即变得口齿伶俐〕。

bla·sé [ˈblɑːzei; ˋblɑze] ***a***.〔F.〕享乐过度而感到厌倦的,玩厌了的。

blas·pheme [blæsˈfiːm; blæsˋfim] ***vt***. 亵渎(神祇等),骂(天等);中伤,侮慢。— ***vi***. 骂天骂地;(语言)渎神。~**r** ***n***.

blas·phe·mous [ˈblæsfiməs; ˋblæsfɪməs] ***a***. 不敬的,骂神的,冒渎的;恶声的,侮慢的。

blas·phe·my [ˈblæsfimi; ˋblæsfɪmɪ] ***n***. 不敬,亵渎,骂神;咒骂。

blast [blɑːst; blɑst] **I** ***n***. 1. (风)一阵,(气流等的)一股;疾风,强风;【冶】鼓风,送风;喷气,喷焰。2. 管乐器声,汽笛声。3. 爆炸声;爆炸;爆破;冲击波;一次用的炸药。4. 毒气,瘟气;【农】稻瘟。5.【冶】鼓风机,喷砂器。6.【地】变晶。7.〔美口〕无线电广播;牢骚,怨言;〔美俚〕口头攻击;〔*pl*.〕〔美俚〕宣传文章。8.〔美俚〕热闹的聚会;闹宴;游艺会。*a ~ of wind* 一阵风。*wintry ~s* 寒风劲吹。*one ~ of siren* 汽笛一声长鸣。*a rocket ~*【火箭】

B

火舌。*H- bomb* ～ 氢弹爆炸。**at** [**in**] **full** ～ 1.（鼓风炉）开足，猛吹。2.〔口〕全速；竭尽全力；最强烈地。**at one** ～ 一口气，一直。**in** [**out of**] ～（鼓风炉或人）在工作〔在休息〕。**II** *vt*. 1. 使爆炸，爆破，炸掉；摧毁。2. 使枯萎，（霜等）冻死；摧残，损伤，毁坏。3.〔美俚〕骂倒，大肆攻击。4.〔美俚〕打，揍。～ *sb.'s reputation* 使某人声誉扫地。～ *sb.'s hope* 使某人的希望全成泡影。～ *the granite* 爆破花岗岩。～ *the evidence* 使该证据不能成立。— *vi*. 1. 发出尖响。2. 进行爆破。3. 吹牛，夸口。4.〔Scot.〕抽烟。5. 枯萎，衰亡。6.〔美俚〕广播；公开批评；发牢骚；射击。～ **away** 轰；【美体】拼命。**B- him** [**it**]！该死！活该！～ **off**（使）（火箭等）发火起飞。～ **out a homer**【美棒球】打出还垒球。**B- the time**！要命的时间〔表示时间紧迫〕！～ **furnace** *n*. 高炉，鼓风炉。～ **lamp** 风灯。～**-off**（火箭）发射。～ **pipe** 风管。

-blast *comb. f.*【生】胚；芽。

blast·ed [ˈblɑːstid; ˋblæstɪd] *a*. 1. 已枯萎的，被摧残掉的；被毁的。2.〔婉〕该死的，讨厌的。*The* ～ *pen never did work properly*. 这枝该死的笔总是出毛病。

blast·er [ˈblɑːstə; ˋblɑstɚ] *n*. 1. 爆破工人；爆裂药。2.〔美俚〕无线电广播员。

blas·te·ma [blæsˈtiːmə; blæsˋtimə] *n*. (*pl*. **blas·te·mata** [blæsˈtiːmətə; blæsˋtimətə])【生】胚芽，胚轴原，芽基。

blas·tie [ˈblɑːstiː, ˈblæstiː; ˋblɑsti, ˋblæsti] *n*.〔Scot.〕侏儒，矮子。

blasto- *comb. f.* "胚"，"芽"。

blas·to·coele, blas·to·cele [ˈblæstəusiːl; ˋblæstəˏsil] *n*.【生】囊胚腔；分裂腔。

blas·to·cyst [ˈblæstəusist; ˋblæstəsɪst] *n*.【生】囊胚（= blastula）。

blas·to·derm [ˈblæstəudəːm; ˋblæstədɚm] *n*.【生】胚盘，胚膜。

blas·to·disc, blas·to·disk [ˈblæstəudisk; ˋblæstodɪsk] *n*.【生】胚盘（= germinal disc）。

blas·to·gen·e·sis [ˌblæstəuˈdʒenisis; ˏblæstəˋdʒenəsɪs] *n*.【生】1. 芽生。2. 种质遗传。

blas·to·mere [ˈblæstəumiə; ˋblæstəˏmɪr] *n*.【生】胚节；分裂球；分沟细胞。

blas·to·my·cete [ˌblæstəumaiˈsiːt, -ˈmaisiːt; ˏblæstəmaɪˋsit, -ˋmaɪsit] *n*.【生】芽生菌。

blas·to·my·co·sis [blæstəumaiˈkəusis; ˏblæstomaɪˋkosɪs] *n*.【病】芽生菌病，酵母病。

blas·to·pore [ˈblæstəupɔː; ˋblæstəˏpor] *n*.【生】原口，胚孔。

blas·to·sphere [ˈblæstəuˈsfiə; ˋblæstəˏsfɪr] *n*.【生】囊胚（= blastula）。

blast-pipe [ˈblɑːstpaip; ˋblɑstpaɪp] *n*.【机】送风管，吹管。

blas·tu·la [ˈblæstjulə; ˋblæstʃulə] *n*. (*pl*. **-lae** [-liː; -li])【生】囊胚。

blat [blɑːt; blæt] *vi*.〔口〕（小牛小羊似地）叫；瞎说，胡说乱讲。— *vt*.〔口〕大声地说出，不谨慎地说出。

bla·tan·cy [ˈbleitənsi; ˋbletənsɪ] *n*. 1. 喧骚，吵闹。2. 炫耀。

bla·tant [ˈbleitənt; ˋbletnt] *a*. 1. 露骨的。2. 吼叫的，喧骚的。3. 炫耀的。～ *fraud* 无耻的欺诈。～ *radios* 吵吵闹闹的收音机。*the* ～ *colors of her dress* 她的服装过于艳丽。**-ly** *ad*. 悍然，嚣然。

blath·er [ˈblæðə; ˋblæðɚ] **I** *vi*. 胡说乱讲。— *vt*. 瞎扯（废话）。**II** *n*. 胡说，废话。～ **skite** *n*.〔口〕1. 胡说八道的人，吹牛大王。2. 无聊话，胡话。

blat·ter [ˈblætə; ˋblætɚ] *vi*.〔美方〕胡说；乱吹。

blat·tner·phone [ˈblætnəfəun; ˋblætnɚfon] *n*. 磁带录音机，钢丝录音机。

blau·bok [ˈblauˌbɔk; ˋblauˏbɑk] *n*. (*pl*. ～，～*s*)【动】蓝灰弯角羚。

blaw [blɔː; blɔ] *vt*., *vi*.〔英方，苏格兰〕吹。

blaze[1] [bleiz; blez] **I** *n*. 1. 火焰。2. 闪光，光明，光辉。3. 激发，爆发；（感情）昂扬。4.〔the ～s〕〔俚〕地狱。*the* ～ *of day* 光天化日。*the* ～ *of fame* 声名远扬。*the* ～ *of fury* 勃然大怒。*the* ～ *of publicity* 众所周知的事。**Go to** ～**s**！该死！活该！**in a** ～ 1. 四面着火，烧做一团。2. 激烈。**in a** ～ **of passion** 盛怒之下。**like** ～**s** 猛烈地。**Old Blazes**〔口〕恶魔。**What the** ～**s** (*am I to do*)？（我）到底〔究竟〕（该怎么办）？**II** *vi*. 1. 燃烧，冒火焰。2. 发（强）光，闪闪生辉。3. 激动，激昂。～ **away** [**off**] 1. 连连开枪。2. 猛干（*at*）。3. 扰攘不已。～ **out** 1. 燃烧；烧起来。2. 大怒。～ **up** 1. 燃烧起来。2. 暴怒。— *vt*. 1. 燃烧着…。2. 发出…光辉。3. 明显表示。

blaze[2] [bleiz; blez] *vt*.（大声）宣布；宣扬；传播。～ **about** [**abroad**] 传播，宣扬出去。

blaze[3] [bleiz; blez] **I** *n*. 1.（马等脸上的）白斑。2.（树皮上的）指路刻痕。**II** *vt*. 1. 在（树皮）上刻记号。2. 在树片上刻痕指示（道路等）。～ **the trail** 在树皮上刻路标；〔转义〕领先，开路。

blaz·er[1] [ˈbleizə; ˋblezɚ] *n*. 1. 燃烧物，发火焰物；大热天。2.（法兰绒的）运动上衣〔颜色鲜艳夺目〕。3. 大谎话。

blaz·er[2] [ˈbleizə; ˋblezɚ] *n*. 传播者；宣传者。

blaz·ing [ˈbleiziŋ; ˋblezɪŋ] *a*. 1. 炽烈燃烧的。2. 灿烂的；明显的，显著的。3.【猎】（猎物遗臭）浓烈的（*opp*. cold）。*the* ～ *sun* 大热天，烈日。*a* ～ *indiscretion* 过分轻率，太不慎重。～ **scent**【猎】（猎物）浓烈的遗臭。～ **seat** 防暴电击座〔功能和防暴电击枪有相似之处〕。～ **star** 1. 彗星；惹人注意的人物；趣味中心。2.【植】（北美产）蓟植物；矮百合。

bla·zon [ˈbleizn; ˋblezn] **I** *n*. 1. 徽，纹章；纹章解说，徽章法。2. 炫示，夸示；宣扬；表彰。*make a* ～ *of sb.'s error* 大肆宣扬某人的错误。**II** *vt*. 1. 画（纹章）；专门解释（徽章）；用徽章等装饰。2. 把…公开，宣扬，表彰（*forth*；*out*；*abroad*）。～ *the event abroad* 把这件事公之于众。

bla·zon·ry [ˈbleizənri; ˋbleznrɪ] *n*. 1. 纹章画法，纹章解说法；纹章。2. 装饰，美化。

bldg., blg. = building.

-ble *suf*. 可，能。★通例带有被动意义，相应的副词词尾是 -bly，名词词尾是 -bleness，-bility。

B.L.E. = Brotherhood of locomotive Engineers〔美〕火车司机兄弟会。

bleach [bliːtʃ; blitʃ] **I** *vt*. 漂白，漂；晒白；弄白。～*ed goods* 漂白布匹。— *vi*. 变白；脱色。**II** *n*. 漂白；漂白法；漂白剂；漂白度。**bleach·a·bil·i·ty** *n*. 可漂白程度〔性〕。**-able** *a*. 可漂白的。

bleach·er [ˈbliːtʃə; ˋblitʃɚ] *n*. 1. 漂白工人，漂白业者。2. 漂白器；漂白剂；漂白坯布。3.〔常 *pl*.〕〔美〕（棒球场等的）露天看台，廉价看台。

bleach·er·ite [ˈblitʃərait; ˋblɪtʃəˏraɪt] *n*.〔美〕露天看台的看客。

bleach·er·y [ˈbliːtʃəri; ˋblitʃərɪ] *n*. 漂白厂；漂白作坊。

bleach·ing [ˈbliːtʃiŋ; ˋblitʃɪŋ] **I** *n*. 漂白。**II** *a*. 漂白的。～ **fastness** 漂白坚牢度。～**-out** *a*. 褪色的。～**-powder** 漂白粉。～ **power** 漂白能力。

bleak[1] [bliːk; blik] *a*. 1. 风吹雨打的，无遮蔽的。2. 荒凉的，凄凉的，萧瑟的；阴冷的，寒冷的。3. 苍白的；暗淡的；惨淡的，悲哀的。*a* ～ *wind* 寒风，风萧萧。*a* ～ *prospect* 前途暗淡。*a* ～ *plain* 荒原。**-ly** *ad*. **-ness** *n*.

bleak[2] [bliːk; blik] *n*.【鱼】（淡水产）银鲤。

blear [bliə; blɪr] **I** *a*. 1.（眼睛）花的；湿的，烂的。2.〔诗〕朦胧的。*eyes* ～ *with tears* 泪眼模糊。**II** *vt*. 1. 使（眼）花〔湿、烂〕；使朦胧〔昏暗〕。2. 使误入歧途，蒙蔽。*a biting wind that* ～*ed the vision* 寒风吹得人眼睛发

花。III *n*. 视力模糊。~**-eyed** *a*. 烂眼的;朦胧眼的,目光不灵的;目光短浅的。

blear·y-eyed [ˈbliəriaid; ˋblɪrɪˏaɪd] *a*. 1. = blear-eyed. 2. 〔美口〕醉眼惺忪的。**-ness** *n*.

bleat [bliːt; blit] I *vi*. 1. (羊、小牛等)叫,咩咩地叫。2. 讲废话;哭诉。— *vt*. 1. 声音颤抖地讲。2. 以微弱的声音说。~ *out* 无力地[愚蠢地]说。II *n*. 1. (羊、小牛等的)叫声。2. 废话。3. 哭诉。*the ~ of distant horns* 远处号角的悲鸣。

bleb [bleb; blɛb] *n*. 1. 【医】起泡,水肿;泡疹。2. (水、玻璃等物中的)水泡,气泡。~ *ingot* 有泡钢锭。

bleed [bliːd; blid] I *vi*. (*bled* [bled; blɛd]) 1. 流血,出血,内出血;受伤,死,战死。2. 悲痛,同情(*for*)。3. 【植】(伤口)流液汁,伤流;(树脂)分泌出;(油液等)渗出;(印染等)渗色,渗开。4. 〔口〕掏腰包,被敲诈,被吸膏血。5. 【印】被印成出血版,被切边。~ *at* [*from*] *the nose* 流鼻血。~ *like a struck hog* 〔美口〕血流如注。*A nation ~s for its dead heroes*. 举国悼念为国死难的烈士。*fight and ~ for one's country* 为国流血,国殇,阵亡。*My heart ~s*. 忧思难忘,痛心极了。*All the colors bled when the dress was washed*. 这件衣服一洗,颜色都洇开了。— *vt*. 1. 使出血;【医】给…放血。2. 榨取…的液汁;放出(液、浆等);把…的水抽干。3. 【空】放(气);从…抽气减压。4. 〔口〕从…身上榨取钱财,敲…竹杠。5. 【印】把…印成出血版,切去(超出开本的边)。~ *a patient* 给病人放血。~ *one's family* 拼命向家里要钱花。*bled timber* 去脂材。~ (*sb.*) *white* (使)流尽鲜血;把…的血汗榨干;被榨干血汗。II *n*. 【印】出血版。III *a*. 【印】出血版的。

bleed·er [ˈbliːdə; ˋblidɚ] *n*. 1. 易出血的人,血友病患者。2. 放血人,静脉切开放血术医师。3. 泄水管,放水闸;【船】泄水孔;【机】放油开关;【电】分压器;分泄电阻,旁漏。4. 〔俚〕敲诈者;寄生者,食客;〔英蔑〕家伙。~ **cock** 放水龙头,旋塞。

bleed·ing [ˈbliːdiŋ; ˋblidɪŋ] I *n*. 1. 出血;放血;静脉切开术。2. 【植】伤流,泌脂。3. 〔美俚〕(车胎)放气,换油。4. 【纺】渗化,渗色,化开。5. (沥青路面的)泛油;(混凝土表面的)泛浆。*the ~ pressure of roots* 【植】根压。II *a*. 1. 流血的。2. 悲痛的。3. 渗色的。4. 〔卑、婉〕= bloody. ~ **heart** 1. 【植】荷包牡丹。2. 〔口〕软心肠的人;〔蔑〕自夸同情[关心]人的人。~**-off** *n*. 泄放,排出;除去,取消。

bleep [bliːp; blip] I *n*. 1. 哔哔〔汽车喇叭或自行车铃声〕。2. 嘟嘟〔电动警铃声〕。II *vi*. 发哔哔[嘟嘟]声。— *vt*. 1. 使发哔哔[嘟嘟]声。2. = blip.

bleep·er [ˈbliːpə; ˋblipɚ] *n*. 无线电呼唤机。

blem·ish [blemiʃ; ˋblɛmɪʃ] I *n*. 瑕疵,缺点,污点;不名誉。*a ~ on his record* 历史污点。*without* ~ 十分完美。II *vt*. 有损…的完美,损害…的名誉;玷污(*opp*. purify)。*The novel is ~ed by those long descriptions*. 那些冗长的描写使小说大为减色。

blench[1] [blentʃ; blɛntʃ] *vi*. 退缩,畏缩;退避。— *vt*. 无视,回避(事实)。

blench[2] [blentʃ; blɛntʃ] *vt*. 弄白,使苍白。— *vi*. 变白,变苍白。

blend [blend; blɛnd] I *vt*., *vi*. (~*ed*, *blent* [blent; blɛnt]) 混合,搀合,混杂,掺杂;融合调和。~ *the ingredients in a recipe* 按配方调料。*Sea and sky seemed to ~*. 海天一色。*The red sofa did not ~ with the purple wall*. 这种红色沙发和紫色墙壁不调和。~ *whisky* 调制威士忌酒。II *n*. 混合;混合种;混合色;合成语;混纺纱。*tea of our own* ~本店特有的配制茶。~ **word** 混成语,合成语〔如 brunch 由 breakfast 和 lunch 合成〕。

blende [blend; blɛnd] *n*. 1. 【矿】闪锌矿。2. (一般)硫化物。

blend·er [ˈblendə; ˋblɛndə] *n*. 1. 搅拌者,混合物。2. 搅拌器,拌和器,掺合机。

blend·ing [ˈblendiŋ; ˋblɛndɪŋ] *n*. 混合;融合;配料;折衷;【语】合成。~ **inheritance** 【生】融合遗传。

Blen·heim [ˈblenim; ˋblɛnɪm] *n*. 1. (spaniel 种)小猎犬〔头小,耳尖长〕。2. 〔英〕布雷尼单翼轰炸机。

blen·nor·rhea [ˌblenəˈriːə; ˏblɛnəˋriə] *n*. 【医】脓性卡他,脓性黏液溢。

blen·ny [ˈbleni; ˋblɛnɪ] *n*. 【鱼】鲇鱼,鳚鱼。

blent [blent; blɛnt] blend 的过去分词。

bleph·a·ri·tis [ˌblefəˈraitis; ˏblɛfəˋraɪtɪs] *n*. 【医】睑炎。

bles·bok [ˈblesbɔk; ˋblɛsˏbɑk] *n*. (南非)大羚羊。

bless [bles; blɛs] *vt*. (~*ed*, *blest* [blest; blɛst]) (*opp*. curse) 1. 赐惠于,赐福于,(上帝)保佑。2. 为…祈福,为…祝福。3. 感谢(上帝);赞美,颂扬(上帝)。4. 使神圣,净化(食物等)。5. 使幸福;使有幸得到。6. 〔反〕诅咒〔过去式和过去分词一般用 blest〕。7. 对…划十字〔为…祈福〕。*greatly ~ed in one's children* 大享儿女福气。*B- the name of the Lord*. 颂主之名〔基督教祈祷用语〕。*B- this house* 愿上帝给这一家赐福。*B- me* (*from all evils*)! 愿上帝保佑我(消灾去祸)! *I am ~ed with a good appetite*. 我幸而胃口好。*Well, I'm ~ed* [*blest*]! 奇怪! *I'm blest* [*Blest*] *if I do*. 我决不做。*I'm ~ed* [*blest*] *if I know*. 我一点儿也不知道;我要是知道,天诛地灭。**be ~ed** 受惠,幸好,有(*with*);〔反〕折(死),遭天报。**B- me**! = **God ~ me** [**you**, **him**, **her**, **them**]! = **B- the boy**! = **B- my soul**! = **Well, I'm blest**! 哎呀! 天呀! 完了! 啧啧! 谢天谢地! 〔表惊愕、愤怒、庆幸等,因人而异〕。~ **one's stars** 庆幸,运气好。~ **oneself** 自祝,庆幸;画十字祓除(*I ~ myself from such customers*. 不和这样一些顾客打交道真是谢天谢地)。**God ~ you**! 愿上帝保佑你! 谢天谢地,天呀!

bless·ed [ˈblesid; ˋblɛsɪd] I *a*. 1. 享福的,受惠的;有福的;【宗】死后已升天的;幸运的,令人愉快的。2. 神经的,清净的。3. 〔反〕遭殃的,受祸的,遭天罚的,该死的〔damned, cursed 的委婉说法〕。4. 用于加强语气(*every ~ cent* 每一分大洋)。*every ~ one* 每一个人,人人,大家。*not a ~ one* 一个也没有,谁都没有。*the whole ~ lot* 全部,统统。*the land of the ~* 天国。*B- are the pure in heart*. 清心的人有福了〔《圣经》马太福音中语〕。*the ~ assurance of a steady income* 有固定收入的可喜保障。*Those ~ bells*! 吵死人的鬼钟。*a ~ event* 〔美俚〕喜事,福气〔指生孩子,有时也指动物下崽〕。**of ~ memory** 前,先,已作古的(*my mother of ~ memory* 先母)。II *n*. 〔the ~〕有福者;【宗】死后已升天者。*the ~ in heaven* 天上诸圣。[*Isles*] *of the blest* 乐土。**the B- Trinity** 【基督】三位一体。**the B- Virgin** (基督教)圣母玛利亚。**-ly** *ad*. 幸福地,幸运地;幸喜地。**-ness** *n*. 幸福(*a state of single blessedness* 〔谑〕快乐的独身生活)。

bless·ing [ˈblesiŋ; ˋblɛsɪŋ] *n*. 1. 赐福;祝福。2. 【宗】饭前[饭后]祷告。3. 应允,纵容。4. 幸事。5. 〔婉〕责备。*an unappropriated ~* 〔谑〕未婚女子。*give the ~* (神父等)给教徒祝福。*ask* [*say*] *a ~* (教徒)饭前〔饭后〕祷告。*the ~ of liberty* 自由的幸福。*by the ~ of God* 蒙天佑助。*a proposed law with the ~ of the governor* 经州长同意而提出的一项法律。*He got quite a ~ from his superior*. 他被上级训了一顿。~ **in disguise** 祸中得福,变相的幸福〔历尽千辛万苦而得到幸福结局或宝贵经验等〕。**have the ~ of** 得到…同意。

blest [blest; blɛst] bless 的过去式及过去分词。*a*. 〔诗〕= blessed. *the Islands* [*Isles*] *of the ~* 乐土,极乐世界。

blet [blet; blɛt] I *n*. (水果熟透后的)腐烂。II *vi*. (**-tt-**) (水果熟透后)变腐烂。

bleth·er [ˈbleðə; ˋblɛðɚ] *v*., *n*. = blather.

blew [bluː; blu] blow 的过去式。

blew·it [ˈbluːit; ˋbluɪt] *n*. 【植】面口蘑〔蘑菇的一种〕。

B

Bligh [blai; blaɪ] ***n*.** 布莱〔姓氏〕。

blight [blait; blaɪt] **I *n*. 1.** (植物病理)枯萎病,火烧病;(对植物有大害的)阴冷天气〔土壤条件〕;虫害。**2.** (使士气崩溃,希望计划等落空的)破坏性因素;扼杀,打击。**3.** 黑影,阴影。**4.** 坏影响。*early* [*later*] ~ (植物的)早[晚]疫病。*bacterial* ~ *of rice* 稻田叶枯病。*urban* ~ 都市生活的恶劣影响。*Bankruptcy was the* ~ *of the family*. 破产毁了这一家。*His absence cast a* ~ *over the family*. 他的不在场使家庭笼罩上一层阴影。**II *vt*. 1.** 使(植物)有病,使枯萎。**2.** 妨害,挫折,摧残;损伤。*Frost ~ed the crops*. 霜冻使作物枯死。*Illness ~ed his hope*. 疾病摧毁了他的希望。*~ed being* 希望破灭的人〔尤指失恋的人〕。*~ed hopes* 希望化为泡影,失望。*~ed love* 失恋。— ***vi*.** (植物)生枯萎病。

blight·er [ˈblaitə; ˋblaɪtɚ] ***n*.** 〔俚〕**1.** 混蛋,讨厌东西。**2.** 家伙。

blight·y [ˈblaiti; ˋblaɪtɪ] ***n*.** 〔英军俚〕〔常 B-〕英国老家,英国本土。***a*** ~ (***one***) 需要送回英国本土治疗的伤〔第一次世界大战期间英军中的流行语〕。***get one's*** ~ (因负伤)送归本国。

bli·mey [ˈblaimi; ˋblaɪmɪ] ***int*.** 〔英口〕啊呀!

blimp [blimp; blɪmp] ***n*. 1.** 〔俚〕小型软式飞艇。**2.** 〔美俚〕可疑的(不正派的)女人。**3.** 电影摄影机上的隔音装置。**4.** 大胖子,大块头。***a Colonel B-*** (漫画中的)顽固保守分子。

blind¹ [blaind; blaɪnd] **I *a*. 1.** 盲,瞎,失明的;供盲人用的。**2.** 盲目的,轻率的,鲁莽的;胡来的;蛮干的;蒙昧的,愚昧的,无知的,无先见的。**3.** 无光的;隐蔽的,不显露的;匿名的。**4.** 堵死的;一端不通的。**5.** 未经眼见的;【空】单凭仪表操纵的。**6.** 无结果的;【植】不开花的。**7.** 难解的,不易识别的。**8.** 失去知觉的;〔俚〕喝醉了的。**9.** (书籍装订)不烫金的。*a* ~ *stupor* 完全昏迷。*a* ~ *passage in a book* 书中难懂的地方。*be* ~ *of* [*in*] *an eye* 一目失明。*He was* ~ *to all arguments*. 和他有理也讲不通。~ *tenacity* 死顽固。~ *chance* 纯出偶然。~ *obedience* 盲从。~ *faith* 迷信。~ *quotation* 未经核实的引文。*a* ~ *asylum* 盲人收容所。~ *education* 盲人教育。*a* ~ *ad* 匿名广告。***be*** ~ ***to*** 不明,不看(事实),对…是盲目的。***be*** ~ ***to the world*** 〔俚〕烂醉。***be*** ~ ***with*** 被…弄得眼花〔糊涂〕(*His mind was* ~ *with weeping*. 他哭糊涂了)。***go*** ~ 失明 (*I'm going* ~ *in one eye*. 我一只眼快失明了)。***go in*** ~ 〔美口〕猜测。***turn a*** [***one's***] ~ ***eye to*** 假装不见,熟视无睹。***with*** ~ ***fury*** 猛烈地。**II *ad*.** 〔口〕**1.** = blindly. **2.** 厉害地。***go it*** ~ **1.** 胡来,蛮干。**2.** 【空】单凭仪表操纵地。***be*** ~ ***drunk*** 〔俚〕烂醉。**III *vt*. 1.** 弄瞎,使失明;把…的眼睛弄花。**2.** 蒙蔽,欺瞒;使昏聩。**3.** 使隐蔽,使变暗,遮暗,使相形失色。**4.** 给(新路面)铺砂砾〔以填塞衔接处的空隙〕。*Her eyes were ~ed with the rain*. 雨水打得她的眼睛什么也看不见了。*The room was ~ed by the heavy curtains*. 厚窗帘把房间遮暗。*His resentment ~s his good sense*. 愤怒使他失去理智。*a radiance that ~s the sun* 使太阳黯然失色的强光。— ***vi*.** (驾驶员)瞎开车。**IV *n*. 1.** 遮目物;百叶窗;帘子,屏风;〔美〕(马的)眼罩。**2.** (猎人的)隐棚,埋伏地。**3.** 障眼物,挡箭牌,搪塞话,口实。**4.** 诱饵,囮子。**5.** 〔口〕痛饮,发酒疯。*Venetian* ~ 软百叶窗。***draw*** [***pull down***] ***the*** ~(*s*) (日常或家中有事故时)拉下百叶窗。~ **alley** 死胡同 (*a* ~ *alley occupation* 无出路的职业)。~ **baggage**【美铁路】铁闷子车(用作行李车、邮车等)。~ **bud** 叶芽,不开花结果的芽。~ **car**【铁路】行李车。~ **coal** 无烟煤。~ **date** 介绍会面〔由第三方介绍,为互不相识的男女安排的初次会见〕;介绍会面赴约者〔参加这种会见的任何一方〕。~ **ditch** 暗沟。~ **door** 假门〔作成门形的外壁〕。~ **fish**【动】盲鳉属鱼。~ **flying**【空】盲飞〔全凭仪表操纵的飞行〕。~ **god** 爱神,恋爱之神。~ **gut 1.** = cecum. **2.** 肠封闭;肠梗阻。~ **letter** 死信,姓名住址不明的信件。~ **man 1.** 瞎子,盲人。**2.** (邮局中的)辨字员。~ **nail** 暗钉。~ **pig** 〔美〕(实行禁酒法时的)秘密酒店。~ **radio** 〔美〕(邮局中的)辨字员。~ **reader** 〔美口〕(相对电视而言的)普通广播。~ **shell** 死弹,失效弹。~ **side** 未防备的一面;弱点 (*get sb. on his* ~ *side* 抓住某人弱点;攻其不备)。~ **spot** 盲点〔眼神经无光感处〕;个人不理解或不关心的方面;【无】静区〔收音不清楚的地方〕。~ **tiger** 〔美俚〕= ~ pig. ~ **trust** 绝对信任委托〔把管理钱财的事完全交给受托人代管,委托人完全不过问〕。~ **wall** 闷墙,无窗墙。~ **window** 假窗〔作成窗形的外壁〕。~ **worm**【动】蛇蜥蜴。~ **zone** 盲区〔雷达波探测不到的区域〕。

blind·age [ˈblaindidʒ; ˋblaɪndɪdʒ] ***n*.**【军】盲障,掩体。

blind·er [ˈblaində; ˋblaɪndɚ] ***n*. 1.** 眩眼的人〔物〕。**2.** 〔*pl*.〕〔美〕(马的)眼罩。**3.** 〔*pl*.〕障眼物。

blind·fold [ˈblaindfəuld; ˋblaɪnd͵fold] **I *vt*. 1.** 蒙住…的眼睛;弄昏〔弄花〕…的眼睛。**2.** 遮住…的视线。**3.** 蒙骗,迷惑。**II *a*.** 蒙住眼睛的,盲目的。**III *ad*.** 瞎来,胡乱地。*act* ~ 胡来,蛮干。**IV *n*.** 遮眼的蒙布;障眼物。

blind·ing [ˈblaindiŋ; ˋblaɪndɪŋ] **I *a*. 1.** 眩目的,晃眼的,使人眼花撩乱的。**2.** 使盲的;使人昏聩糊涂的。*a* ~ *day* 阳光刺眼的白天。~ *anger* 使人丧失理智的愤怒,狂怒。~ *tears* 泪眼模糊。**II *n*. 1.** (新铺路面的)填塞;(填塞路面的)细砂,细石子。**2.**【纺】失光。~ **tree** 土沉香。

blind·ly [ˈblaindli; ˋblaɪndlɪ] ***ad*. 1.** 盲目地。**2.** 没头没脑地;妄自,胡来地,乱来地,蛮干地。**3.** 一端不通地。*The passage ended* ~ *50 feet away*. 通道走下去五十英尺就不通了。

blind·man [ˈblaind*m*æn; ˋblaɪnd*m*æn] ***n*.** 〔现常分写为 blind man〕**1.** 盲人,瞎子。**2.** (邮局中的)辨字员。~**'s buff** 捉迷藏。~**'s holiday** 黄昏。

blind·ness [ˈblaind*n*is; ˋblaɪnd*n*ɪs] ***n*. 1.** 视觉缺失,失明。**2.** 愚昧,文盲。**3.** 昏聩胡涂;轻举妄动。*night* ~ 夜盲症。*taste* ~ 味盲,味觉失灵。

blin·i [bliˈniː; blɪˋni] ***n*.** 〔*pl*.〕(*sing*. ***blin*** [blin; blɪn])〔Russ.〕(中有鱼子酱和酸乳酪的)薄烤饼。

blink [bliŋk; blɪŋk] **I *vi*. 1.** 眨眼睛。**2.** (灯等)闪亮,闪烁。**3.** 眯着眼看 (*at*);惊愕地看 (*at*)。**4.** 无视,假装不见 (*at*)。*She ~ed to stop tears*. 她眨着眼止住眼泪。~ *at the harsh light* 眯着眼看那刺目的光。~ *at sb.'s sudden fury* 对某人的突然发脾气瞠目不知所措。~ *at the law* 无视法律。— ***vt*. 1.** 眨(眼);眨着眼挤掉(眼泪,眼中异物等)。**2.** 使闪烁。**3.** 无视,闭眼不看(事实等)。**4.** 用闪光信号表示。~ *one's eyes* 眨眼。~ *the light* 打灯光信号。*There is no ~ing the possibility of a scandal*. 不能无视发生丑闻的可能性。**II *n*. 1.** 眨眼睛;瞬间。**2.** 瞥见;一瞥。**3.** 闪光,灯光的明灭。**4.** 冰映光;水照云光。*the faithful* ~ *of the lighthouse* 灯塔定时的闪光。*not a* ~ *of light* 一点光亮也没有。***in a*** ~ **=** ***like a*** ~ 〔口〕立刻,马上。***on the*** ~ 〔俚〕(机器等)出毛病,需要修理;(人)不舒服。***without a*** ~ ***or qualm*** 不在乎,很镇静。

blink·ard [ˈbliŋkəd; ˋblɪŋkəd] ***n*.** 〔罕〕**1.** 老眨眼睛的人;眯缝着眼睛看的人。**2.** 不明事理的人,糊涂虫。

blink·er [ˈbliŋkə; ˋblɪŋkɚ] **I *n*. 1.** 眨眼睛的人;瞥视者;〔卑〕眼。**2.** 闪光信号灯;〔美〕(铁路栅口的)闪光警戒标。**3.** 〔*pl*.〕护目镜,防尘眼镜;(马的)眼罩。***be in*** ~***s*** 瞎,盲目,蒙住眼 (*run in* ~*s* 瞎跑)。**II *vt*. 1.** 给…上眼罩。**2.** 蒙蔽。

blink·ing [ˈbliŋkiŋ; ˋblɪŋkɪŋ] ***a*. 1.** 眨眼的;晃眼的。**2.** 〔英俚〕眼不忍见的,可恶的,该死的〔代 bloody 用的委婉语〕。*Stop that* ~ *noise*! 别那么吵死人了! *You* ~ *idiot*! 你这个大傻瓜。

blintz [blints; blɪnts] ***n*.** (卷有乳酪、果品等的)薄烤饼。

blip [blip; blɪp] **I *n*. 1.**【无】(显示器屏幕上的)尖头信号,标志,记号,(雷达的)可视信号。**2.** 疾而尖的音响。

3.(因抹音引起的)电视节目中的声音中断。4.〔美俚〕五分钱硬币。5.〔美俚〕(统计数字的)上下浮动。**II** *vi*.(*-pp-*)发信号。— *vt*. 在录像磁带上抹去(所录的音)。

Bliss [blis; blɪs] *n*. 布利斯〔姓氏〕。

bliss [blis; blɪs] *n*. 1. 无上幸福,至福。2. 天福;天堂;极乐。3. 狂喜;满足。*wedded* ~ 美满姻缘。*the road to eternal* ~ 通向天国之路。

bliss·ful [ˈblisful; ˋblɪsfʊl] *a*. 至福的,极乐的,有造化的。**-ly** *ad*. **-ness** *n*.

blis·ter [ˈblistə; ˋblɪstɚ] **I** *n*. 1. 水疱,水肿,火肿,疱(病)。2.(植物的)疱状突起。3.【医】起疱膏,发疱药。4.(钢,玻璃漆器等表面上的)气泡,砂眼。5.〔俚〕令人讨厌的人。6.【无】(雷达的)天线罩;【船】附加外壳;(军舰的)附雷隔堵;(飞机上的)固定舱座。**II** *vt*. 1. 使起水疱,把…烫出疱。2. 狠揍;痛斥;挖苦,责备,辱骂。— *vi*. 起疱,烫伤。~ **beetle**【动】斑蝥。~ **cloth** 泡泡呢。~ **copper** 粗铜。~ **gas** 糜烂性毒气。

blis·ter·ing [ˈblistəriŋ; ˋblɪstərɪŋ] *a*. 1. 使起疱的。2. 恶毒的;激烈的。3.〔口〕可恶的,该死的。*a* ~ *tongue* 刻薄嘴。*a* ~ *sun* 灼热的阳光。

blithe [blaið; blaɪð] *a*. 1. 欢乐的,愉快的(*opp*. joyless)。2. 活泼的,爽快的。3. 轻率的,冒失的;不注意的。**-ly** *ad*.

blith·er [ˈbliðə; ˋblɪðɚ] **I** *n*.〔美口〕废话,空谈。**II** *vi*. 瞎谈,噜噜苏苏地谈。

blith·er·ing [ˈbliðəriŋ; ˋblɪðərɪŋ] *a*.〔口〕1. 噜噜苏苏的,唠叨没完的。2. 绝顶的,无以复加的,头号的。*a* ~ *idiot* 大傻瓜。

blithe·some [blaiðsəm; ˋblaɪðsəm] *a*. 欢乐的,快活的,活泼的。

B.Lit(t)., **BLit(t)** = Bachelor of Literature 文学(学)士(= Bachelor of Letters)。

blitz [blits; blɪts] **I** *n*. 1.【军】闪电战,闪击战;大规模空袭。2.(疾病,宣传等的)闪电式行动,突然袭击,闪电攻势。**II** *a*. 闪电战的,闪电式的。**III** *vt*.〔口〕用闪电战攻击,用闪电战制服;对…进行猛烈空袭。

blitz·krieg [ˈblitsˌkriːg; ˋblɪtsˏkrig] *n*. = blitz.

bliz·zard [ˈblizəd; ˋblɪzɚd] *n*.〔美〕雪暴,暴风雪;〔俚〕大打击。

bloat [bləut; blot] **I** *vt*. 1. 熏制(鲱鱼等)。2. 使肿起,使胀。3. 使自负。— *vi*. 1. 肿起,胀。2. 自负,得意忘形。**II** *n*.〔美〕肿胀病人;(家畜的)气胀病;〔美俚〕醉鬼。

bloat·ed [ˈbləutid; ˋblotɪd] *a*. 1. 发胀的,肿起的,膨胀的;(因多食而)病态发胖的。2. 傲慢的,趾高气扬的。3.〔美俚〕喝醉的;(要求)过高的。

bloat·er [ˈbləutə; ˋblotɚ] *n*. 熏鲱,熏鱼。

blob [blɔb; blɑb] **I** *n*. 1.(墨水等的)一滴;(半流质物品的)一团;(颜料的)一抹;小斑点。2.(鱼)跳水声。3.【板球】零分。4.〔美俚〕错误。*on the* ~〔俚〕在口头上,用谈话方式。**II** *vt*.(墨水等)污染,弄脏。— *vi*. 1.(鱼)跳水。2.〔美俚〕弄错。

blob·ber-lipped [ˈblɔbəlipt; ˋblɑbɚˏlɪpt] *a*. 嘴唇厚而凸的。

bloc [blɔk; blɑk] *n*.〔F.〕1.(国家、团体等的)集团。2.〔美〕跨党派议员集团。*a position* "*outside* ~*s*" "超集团"立场。*the Axis* ~(第二次世界大战中的)轴心国集团。*the dollar* [*sterling*] ~ 美元〔英镑〕集团。*the farm* ~〔美〕农场主议员集团;农业区议员集团。

block [blɔk; blɑk] **I** *n*. 1. 片,块,大块;粗料,毛料;木料;石料;金属块;【建】块料,砌块;【地】地块。2. 俎,砧板,(切肉等的)墩,台;断头台;骑马台(等);【印】(插图)衬版,版垫;(印花)模板;剪裁样板;(装订)钢模;帽模,帽楦;【船】船台;煞车;【计】部件。3. 滑车,辘轳,滑轮组。4. 一组,一套,一批;黏贴的帐;大宗股票。5. 一排大建筑;〔英〕大楼,大厦;〔美〕街区〔四条街当中的地区〕街段,地段;区,区组。6.(铁路)区段,区截;(戏院)座位区;(政府分配移民等的)划区;〔澳〕〔the ~〕热闹街道,闹市,繁华的大马路。7.(橱窗陈列帽、假发等用的)木制假头;〔美口〕头;挂表;名誉不好的人;木头人,笨汉;铁石心肠的人。8. 障碍,阻碍;【无】停振;【医】阻滞;〔英〕(交通的)堵断;(对议案的)反对声明;【体】(合法)阻挡;【棒球】障碍球。9. 集团(= bloc)。*concrete* ~*s* 水泥板。*paving* ~*s* 铺路石板。*a* ~ *of stone* 石料。*building* ~ [~*s*]【建】砌块〔儿童玩的积木〕。*a hat* ~ 帽楦。*a single* [*double*] ~ 单〔复〕滑车。*traffic* ~ 交通堵塞。*a large* ~ *of tickets* 一大迭戏票。*He has a* ~ *when it comes to math*. 一碰上数学,他的脑子就木了。*an input* [*output*] ~【计】输入〔输出〕部件。*a swage* ~【机】型砧。*gauge* ~【机】块规。*screw* ~ 千斤顶。***as like as two*** ~***s*** 像极了的。***cut*** ~***s with a razor*** 剃刀砍木头,用非其当。***go*** [***be sent***, ***be brought***] ***to the*** ~(被送)上断头台;被提出拍卖。***in*** [***the***] ~ 成批,成套。***knock sb.'s*** ~ ***off*** 给某人吃苦头,痛揍某人。***on the*** ~ 拿出拍卖;〔澳〕逛闹市。***to do the*** ~ 散步,逛马路。**II** *vt*. 1. 妨碍,阻挠;堵塞,封锁;冻结(资金等);杜绝;〔英〕对(议案)事先作反对宣传。2. 把…放置台上;用木片等塞牢;使…成块状;用帽模打(帽样);给(书籍)烫金;(球类运动中合法)阻挡。3.【铁路】以区截制管理(行车)。4.【剧】排练(主要位置和动作)。5. 画出…的轮廓〔草图〕。~ *a hat* 打帽样。~*ed funds* 被冻结资金。*two-way* ~*ing positions* 两面阻击阵地。*a* ~*ing oscillator*【物】间歇振荡器。— *vi*. 1.【剧】排练。2.【体】(合法)阻挡。~ ***in*** 1. 画略图;设计。2. 堵塞。~ ***out*** 画略图;拟大纲,打草样。~ ***up*** 堵塞,隔断,封锁;停用。***Blocked***!〔揭示〕禁止通行! 此路不通! ~ **book** 木版书。~ **booking**(电影院对影片的)整批承包。~ **brush**【电】碳刷。~ **chain**(脚踏车等的)车链。~ **club**〔美〕互助委员会,地区居民保安联会。~ **cutter** 木版师。~ **diagram** 立体图,方块〔框〕图。~ **effect**【无】体效应。~ **head** 痴汉,木头人。~ **house**【军】防舍,圆木小屋;碉堡。~ **letter** 木版字,大型字体,大写印刷字体。~ **movement**【地】地块运动。~ **print**(木)版画。~ **printing** 木版印刷(版本);雕刻版印刷;木版印染法。~ **release**(欧洲国家企业界的)进修离职制。~ **ship** 沉没的障碍船舰。~ **signal**【交】闭塞信号。~ **stream** 岩流,泥石流。~ **structure**【地】块状结构。~ **style** 大写印刷字体;商业文书格式。~ **system**【铁路】闭塞制〔站与站间一次限行一车〕。~ **tin**(提炼过的)锡锭〔块〕。

block·ade [blɔˈkeid; blɑˋked] **I** *n*. 1. 封锁,堵塞。2. 实施封锁的武力〔部队〕。3.〔美〕(交通的)阻断。***enforce a*** ~ 实行封锁。***raise*** [***lift***] ***a*** ~ 解除封锁。***run the*** ~ 偷越封锁线。**II** *vt*. 封,堵塞,封锁,妨碍,阻止。*a* ~*d port* 被封锁的港口。*a* ~ *expedition* 执行封锁任务的远征军。~ **runner** 偷过封锁线者;偷过封锁线的船。

block·ad·er [blɔˈkeidə; blɑˋkedɚ] *n*. 封锁者,堵塞者;封港船,执行封锁任务的船。

block·age [ˈblɔkidʒ; ˋblɑkɪdʒ] *n*. 1. 封锁(状态)。2. 堵塞;障碍。3.【医】(心理)阻滞。*the* ~ *of the streets* 交通堵塞。*emotional* ~ 感情阻滞症。

block·bust·er [ˈblɔkˌbʌstə; ˋblɑkˏbʌstɚ] *n*.〔俚〕1. 高爆力巨型炸弹。2. 特别神通广大的人;风靡一时的事物〔尤指被大吹大擂以招徕观众、读者的消耗巨资拍摄的影片或小说等〕。3.(从事唆卖房屋)房地产掮客。

block·bust·ing [ˈblɔkˌbʌstiŋ; ˋblɑkˏbʌstɪŋ] *n*.(房地产掮客的)房屋唆卖生意。

block·ette [blɔˈket; blɑˋket] *n*.【自】数字组;子〔次〕字组;子群。

block·ish [ˈblɔkiʃ; ˋblɑkɪʃ] *a*. 1. 木头一样的。2. 愚钝的;顽固的。**-ly** *ad*. **-ness** *n*.

block·y [ˈblɔki; ˋblɑkɪ] *a*. 1. 块状结构的,短而粗的,结实的。2. 浓淡不匀的,斑驳的。

bloke [bləuk; blok] *n*. 1.〔俚〕家伙;〔伦敦隐语〕头子,首

领。2.〔海军俚〕〔the ～〕舰长。3. 醉鬼;笨蛋。*an old* ～ 老糊涂。

Blom [blɔm; blɑm] ***n.*** 布洛姆〔姓氏〕。

blond(e) [blɔnd; blɑnd] **I** ***a.*** **1.** (头发)亚麻色的,金色的。**2.** 美貌的;白肤金发碧眼的。**3.** (家具等)浅色的。*a ～ girl* 白肤金发碧眼的姑娘。**II** ***n.*** **1.** 白肤金发碧眼人〔指女性时拼作 blonde〕。**2.** = ～ lace. ～ **lace** 丝带,丝花边。

B

blood [blʌd; blʌd] **I** ***n.*** **1.** 血,血液;生命液。**2.** 血族,血统;种族;家族(关系);家世;门第;名门,门阀;〔the ～〕贵族血统。**3.** 生命,活力;元气。**4.** 流血,杀戮,杀人(罪),牺牲。**5.** 血气;气质,气性,脾气;热情;激怒;肉欲;兽欲。**6.**〔主英〕血气方刚的人;花花公子,纨袴子。**7.**〔集合词〕人员。**8.** (树木、果子等的)赤色汁液;〔美俚〕蕃茄酱。**9.** (马的)纯种。*the circulation of ～* 血液循环。*His ～ is up*. 他热情激昂[动怒,发火]。*They demand ～ for ～*. 他们要求以血还血。*avenge the ～ of one's father* 报杀父之仇。*be of mixed ～* 混血种。*a lady of ～* 贵妇人。*be related by ～* 有亲戚关系。*Blood is thicker than water*. 血比水浓;〔喻〕自己人总是自己人;近客不如远亲,疏不间亲。*My ～ be on your head*! 我若死其罪在你。*It made my ～ run cold*. 令人心惊胆寒,毛骨悚然。*We need fresh ～*. 我们需要新的人员。*the young ～s of Cambridge* 剑桥大学的少壮派。*a young ～* 血气方刚的少年。*a bit of ～* 纯种马。***bad ～*** 敌意;不和;仇恨;恶感(*make bad ～ between the brothers* 使兄弟之间不睦)。***～ and iron***【史】(德国宰相俾斯麦的)铁血政策;黩武政策。***～ in one's eyes***〔美〕期待必胜。***～ out of a stone*** (得到)冷酷人的同情。***～ transfusion*** 输血。***blue ～*** 贵族血统。***for the ～ of me*** 拼命,无论如何。***fresh ～*** (社团、家庭的)新成员;新手。***full*** [***whole***] ***～*** (同父母的)嫡亲关系。***get in the*** [***one's***] ***～*** 动人,迷人(*Golf is something that gets in the ～*. 高尔夫球是一项迷人的运动)。***get*** [***have***] ***one's ～ up*** (使)激动,(使)愤激。***half ～*** 异父[异母]关系。***ill ～*** = *bad ～*. ***in ～*** 生命力旺盛;欣欣向荣。***in cold ～*** **1.** 蓄意地(而非出于一时冲动地);残忍地。**2.** 冷静地。***in hot*** [***warm***] ***～*** 怒,愤激。***in sb.'s*** [***the***] ***～*** 遗传的,生来的。***man of ～*** 凶险的人,残忍成性的人;凶手。***make sb.'s ～ run cold*** 使人不寒而栗,毛骨悚然。***out for sb.'s ～*** 要某人的命。***out of ～*** 毫无生气。***penny ～***〔英俚〕(描写凶杀等惊险情节的)廉价小说[刊物]。***princes*** [***princesses***] ***of the ～*** 王子,亲王[公主]。***shed ～*** **1.** 流血[受伤或死]。**2.** 杀人。***spill ～*** 犯杀[伤]人罪。***spill the ～ of*** 杀死…。***sweat ～*** **1.** 没命地干,拼死拼活地干。**2.** 忧虑万分。***taste ～*** (猎狗等)尝鲜血味;〔喻〕初识真味。***to the last drop of one's ～*** 只要一息尚存。**II** ***vt.*** **1.** 使出血;抽…的血;〔古〕给…放血。**2.** 使(猎狗等)先尝(猎物的)鲜血味;使(新手等)先取得经验;使(新兵)初战。**3.** 用血染(皮革等);用血弄湿。～**-and-thunder** (小说、戏剧等)充满凶杀打斗等刺激性情节的。～ **bank** 血库。～ **bath** 血洗,大屠杀。～ **brother** 亲兄弟;结盟兄弟;〔美俚〕(同种族、宗教信仰等的)自家弟兄。～ **brotherhood** 兄弟[把兄弟]关系[情谊]。～ **cell** 血球。～ **corpuscle**【生理】血球。～ **count**【医】血球计数。～ **curdling** ***a.*** 令人心惊胆寒的;令人毛骨悚然的。～ **donor** 供血者,献血者。～ **feud** 家族之间的宿仇,族仇。～ **fin**【动】红鳍脂鲤。～ **fluke**【医】血吸虫,住血吸虫。～ **flux**【医】赤痢。～ **group**【医】血型。～ **grouping**【医】血型鉴定。～ **guiltiness** 杀人罪。～ **guilty** ***a.*** 杀过人的;犯杀人罪的。～ **heat** 血温〔摄氏 37 度,华氏 98.6 度〕。～ **horse** 纯种马。～**hound** **1.** (英国种)警犬。**2.** 侦探。～ **lefting**【医】抽血,放血;〔喻〕(战斗等的)流血。～ **line** 血统;世系。～ **lust** 杀戮欲。～**-mobile** 流动收血车。～ **money** **1.** 血腥钱;损人而得到的利益。**2.** 偿付被杀者亲属的钱。～ **plasma**【生理】血浆。～ **platelet**【生理】血小板。～ **poisoning**【医】败血症。～ **pressure** 血压。～ **pudding** 血肠。～ **purge** 血腥清洗。～**-red** ***a.*** **1.** 血红的。**2.** 血迹斑斑的,染满血的(*a ～-red sunset* 残阳如血)。～ **relation** 血族,骨肉。～**root** ***n.***【植】美洲血根草。～ **royal** 皇族。～ **serum**【生理】血清。～ **shed** ***n.*** 流血,虐杀(*revenge for ～ shed* 报仇)。～ **shot** 充血的(*see things ～ shot* 红了眼,杀气腾腾)。～ **sport** 流血娱乐,见红消遣〔狩猎、斗牛等〕。～**stain** 血迹。～**-stained** ***a.*** 血污的,血腥的,有血痕的;〔喻〕杀过人的。～**stock** 纯种马。～**stone**【矿】血玉髓;血滴石。～**stream**【生理】血流。～**sucker** 吸血动物;蛭;凶汉;吸血鬼,高利贷者,剥削者。～ **test** 验血。～ **thirstiness** 嗜血,杀人狂;残忍,凶恶。～**thirsty** ***a.*** 嗜血的,以血充饥的;残忍的,凶恶的。～ **transfusion** 输血(法)。～ **type** = ～ group. ～ **typing** = ～ grouping. ～ **vessel** 血管。～**worm** 鱼虫;(做钓饵的)蚯蚓[小红虫]。～**wort**【植】血红酸模。

blood·ed [ˈblʌdid; ˋblʌdɪd] ***a.*** **1.**〔作复合词用〕…血的。**2.**〔美〕(马、牛等)良种的,纯种的;(人)血统优良的,身世清白的。*warm-～ animals* 温血动物。*a cold-～ killer* 冷酷的杀人犯。

blood·i·ly [ˈblʌdili; ˋblʌdəlɪ] ***ad.*** 血淋淋地;残忍地,惨酷地,凶恶地。

blood·i·ness [ˈblʌdinis; ˋblʌdɪnɪs] ***n.*** 血污;残忍,残酷。

blood·less [ˈblʌdlis; ˋblʌdlɪs] ***a.*** **1.** 不流血的,无流血之惨的。**2.** 贫血的,无血色的,苍白的。**3.**〔喻〕无生气的,无精打彩的,冷淡的。**4.** 冷血的,冷酷的。*～ surgery* 无血手术。*a ～ face* 苍白的面容。*～ data* 无情的数据。

blood·y [ˈblʌdi; ˋblʌdɪ] **I** ***a.*** **1.** 血的;血一样的。**2.** 血糊糊的;血染的,血迹斑斑的。**3.** 嗜血的,好杀的。**4.** 血腥的,残忍的。**5.**〔口〕过分的,不合情理的。**6.**〔英俚〕= damned〔有时仅用以加强语气〕。*a ～ battle* 一场血战。*～ tissue* 血液组织。*a ～ king* 暴君。*not a ～ likely* 一点儿也不像。*It's a ～ shame*. 真是太丢脸了。*not a ～ one* 就是一个也没有。**II** ***ad.*** **1.**〔英口〕过分,太,不顾死活地。**2.** = damned. *be ～ drunk* 烂醉如泥。*It is ～ lucky*. 真是太走运了。★此词常略作 B-(d)y. **III** ***vt.*** 血污,血染。～ **mary** **1.** 番茄汁掺伏特加酒。**2.** [B- M-] 杀星玛丽〔英国女王 Maria (1516-1558)的绰号,因血腥迫害新教徒而得此名〕。～ **flux**【医】赤痢。～ **hand** **1.** 红手〔从男爵的纹章〕。**2.**〔英、古法〕侵犯他人猎区的证据。～**-minded** ***a.*** **1.** 残忍的,狠心的。**2.**〔英口〕故意不合作的;无理作对的。～ **murder** **1.** 血腥的谋杀。**2.**〔美俚〕一败涂地(*yell* [*scream*] *～ murder* 大喊救命)。～ **shirt** **1.** (被杀者的)血衣。**2.** 煽起复仇心理的手段(*wave the ～ shirt* 煽动复仇)。～ **work** 虐杀。

bloo·ey, bloo·ie [ˈbluːi; ˋblui] ***a.***〔美俚〕不灵的,不能使用的〔主要用于 go ～ (出毛病)〕。

bloom[1] [bluːm; blum] **I** ***n.*** **1.** 花〔特指观赏植物的花〕;开花(期);(花)盛开。**2.**〔*sing.*〕青春,风华正茂;最盛期。**3.** (面颊的)红润;(外观的)艳美[新鲜];(原棉的)光亮。**4.** (叶面、虫体等的)粉被,粉,霜;【化】起霜(作用)。**5.**【电视】刺眼的闪光。*the ～ of the cherry tree* 樱花。*The gardens are all in ～*. 鲜花满园,春色满园。*the ～ of Romanticism* 浪漫主义的鼎盛时期。*the ～ of the grape* 葡萄上的粉霜。***be out of ～*** 过了花期,花已落。***come into ～*** 开花。***in*** (***full***) ***～*** (花)盛开;充分发挥。***take the ～ off*** 使…失去美貌;使…显得不新鲜。***the ～ of youth*** 青春,年富力强。**II** ***vi.*** **1.** 开花;(花)盛开。**2.** 兴旺,繁盛。**3.** 进入青春时代。**4.** 发亮,闪烁生辉。*These plants ～ in spring*. 这些树春天开花。～ ***into*** 发育为,成长为。— ***vt.*** **1.** 使繁盛。**2.** 使开花。**3.** 使艳丽。**4.** 使模糊。*Industry ～s his talents*. 勤奋使他的才能发出光辉。*Their breath ～ed the frosty pane*. 他们的呼吸使冰冻的窗玻璃凝上一层雾气。

bloom[2] [bluːm; blum] **I** ***n.***【冶】大钢坯,钢锭;铁块,钢块,初轧坯。**II** ***vt.***【冶】把…轧成钢坯,初轧。

Bloom·er [ˈbluːmə; ˋblumɚ] ***n***. 布卢默〔姓氏〕。

bloom·er[1] [ˈbluːmə; ˋblumɚ] ***n***. **1.** 〔古〕布鲁姆女服〔纽约 *Bloomer* 夫人创始的一种有短裙和灯笼裤的女服〕；穿布鲁姆女服的妇女。**2.** 〔*pl*.〕女灯笼裤。～ **boy** 〔美俚〕伞兵。

bloom·er[2] [ˈbluːmə; ˋblumɚ] ***n***. **1.** 开花植物。**2.** 成年人，有作为的(年轻)人。**3.** 〔英俚〕大错误，大失策；失败。*a night* ～ 夜间开花的植物。*a late* ～ 大器晚成。

bloom·ery, bloom·a·ry [ˈbluːməri; ˋbluməri] ***n***. 【冶】土法〔木炭〕熟铁吹炼炉。

Bloom·field [ˈbluːmfiːld; ˈblumfild] ***n***. 布卢姆菲尔德〔姓氏〕。

bloom·ing [ˈbluːmiŋ; ˋblumɪŋ] **I** ***a***. **1.** 正开花的，(花)盛开的。**2.** 青春正盛的，妙龄的。**3.** 旺盛的。**4.** 〔英口〕异常的，无比的，十足的。～ *cheeks* 红润的双颊。～ *business* 生意兴隆。*a* ～ *fool* 十足的大傻瓜。**II** ***n***. 【物】敷霜，图像浮散，光学膜。

Blooms·bu·ry [ˈbluːmzbəri; ˋblumzbərɪ] ***n***. 布卢姆茨伯里区〔包含大英博物馆 (British Museum) 在内的伦敦地区名，从前是高级住宅区，今为学者、文人集中的文教区〕。

bloom·y [ˈbluːmi; ˋblumɪ] ***a***. **1.** 开花的，盛开的。**2.** 有粉衣的。

bloop [bluːp; blup] **I** ***n***. 【影】杂音；防杂音设备。**II** ***vi***. 发出杂音。— ***vt***. 消除…的杂音。

bloop·er [ˈbluːpə; ˋblupɚ] ***n***. 〔美俚〕**1.** (在广播中或电视上出的)差错〔洋相〕。**2.** 【棒球】仅仅击出内场的飞球。**3.** 【无】发出射频电流(对附近其他接收机起干扰作用的)接收机。

Bloor [bluː, bloə; blu, blɔr] ***n***. 布卢尔〔姓氏〕。

blos·som [ˈblɔsəm; ˋblɑsəm] **I** ***n***. **1.** 花〔特指果树花〕；群花。**2.** 开花时期；(发育的)初期。**3.** 兴旺时期。***in*** ～ 开着花。***in full*** ～ 盛开。**II** ***vi***. 开花；繁荣；兴旺，茂盛；发展成，长成 (*into*)。～ (*out*) *into a statesman* 〔讽〕(眼看着)变成政治家。***nip in the*** ～ 把…消灭于萌芽状态。

blot[1] [blɔt; blɑt] **I** ***n***. **1.** 墨污，墨渍，污点，污斑。**2.** 瑕疵；耻辱，污名。**3.** 〔古〕涂去，抹去。*a* ～ *on her past* [*her character*] 她历史[品格]上的污点。*drop an ink* ～ *on an envelope* 信封玷上了一块墨污。**II** ***vt***. (**-tt-**) **1.** 用(墨水等)弄脏，涂污。**2.** 涂去，抹掉(*out*)。**3.** 用吸墨纸吸干。**4.** 遮蔽(风景等)，遮暗，使昏暗。**5.** 玷污，损害(名誉等)。**6.** 〔美俚〕杀死；乱涂，乱写；〔诗〕擦掉。*The sun was* ～*ted by the moon*. 月亮遮暗了太阳，日蚀。～ *the wet pane* 擦干潮湿的窗玻璃。～*ting pad* 吸墨纸滚台。— ***vi***. **1.** (墨水)渗开；造成污渍。**2.** (纸等)玷上墨污；(吸墨纸)吸掉墨水。*This pen* ～*s*. 这枝笔漏墨水。*This paper* ～*s easily*. 这种纸容易吸水。～ ***one's copybook*** 损坏自己名誉。～ ***out*** **1.** 涂去(文字)。**2.** 遮掉(风景等)，遮暗。**3.** 〔美俚〕消灭，杀掉；毁掉。～**ting pad** 吸墨纸滚台。～**ting paper** 吸墨纸。

blot[2] [blɔt; blɑt] ***n***. **1.** (十五子棋中)易被吃掉的孤立棋子。**2.** 弱点。***hit a*** ～ 吃去弱子，突破弱点。

blotch [blɔtʃ; blɑtʃ] **I** ***n***. **1.** (皮肤上的)疱，疙瘩；(植物的)白斑，白斑病。**2.** (墨水等的)污点，斑污；印花色底。**II** ***vt***. 弄脏，涂污。

blotch·y [ˈblɔtʃi; ˋblɑtʃɪ] ***a***. (*-i·er*; *-i·est*) 有疱的；斑斑点点的；布满污痕的。

blot·ter [ˈblɔtə; ˋblɑtɚ] ***n***. **1.** 吸墨纸，吸墨用具。**2.** 弄脏东西的人；笔迹潦草的人。**3.** 【商】流水账；临时记录册；〔美〕(警察等的)事故登记簿，拘留记录簿。

blot·tesque [blɔˈtesk; blɑtˋɛsk] ***a***. (绘画)粗涂乱抹的。

blot·ting pa·per [ˈblɔtiŋ peipə; ˋblɑtɪŋ pepɚ] ***n***. 吸墨纸。

blot·to [ˈblɔtəu; ˋblɑto] ***a***. 〔俚〕泥醉的，烂醉的。

blouse [blauz; blauz] ***n***. **1.** 〔F.〕宽阔的罩衫；【美军】(作为日常军服穿的)短上衣。**2.** 女衬衫；〔法〕工装。

blous·on [ˈbluːsɔn; ˋblusɑn] ***a***. (衣裙)有长上衣式样的。

blow[1] [bləu; blo] ***vi***. (***blew*** [bluː; blu]; ***blown*** [bləun; blon]) **1.** (风)吹。**2.** (汽笛等)叫，鸣，响。**3.** 喘气；吹气；(鲸等)喷水；喷气。**4.** (轮胎等)爆炸；〔俚〕发怒；〔美口〕炫弄，夸口，吹牛。**5.** 〔俚〕走掉，逃掉。**6.** 【电】(熔丝等)熔断，熔解，熔化。**7.** (苍蝇)产卵。**8.** 〔美俚〕吸用麻醉品。～ *on one's hands* 以手指吹口哨。*It* ～*s*. 刮风了。*The whistle was* ～*ing*. 汽笛长鸣。*We heard the burgles* ～*ing*. 我们听见号角声响。*The old man was puffing and* ～*ing*. 这老人气喘吁吁。*He* ～*s too much*. 他好吹牛。～ *about one's medals* 炫弄自己的奖章。*The rear tire blew out*. 后胎炸了。— ***vt***. **1.** 吹，吹动，吹成，吹制，吹胀；吹着(火等)；使通气。**2.** 鸣(笛等)；吹奏(乐器等)。**3.** 使(马)喘气〔常用被动语态〕。**4.** 传播，发布，宣扬。**5.** 〔俚〕= damn, curse〔诅咒用语，此义过去分词用 ～ed〕。**6.** 挥霍，浪费(钱财)。**7.** 使(轮胎等)爆炸；使(保险丝)熔断；毁坏。**8.** (蝇等)下子于，产卵于。**9.** 〔俚〕使自负。**10.** 〔俚〕背叛。**11.** 【冶】吹炼。**12.** 〔美俚〕吸(毒)。*Try* ～*ing your nose*. 把鼻子擤一擤。～ *glass* 吹玻璃〔吹制玻璃器皿〕。～ *out one's cheeks* 鼓起腮帮子。～ *a tyre* 轮胎放炮。～ *a fuse* 烧断保险丝。～ *the rumor about* 传谣。～ *an egg* 吸蛋〔开小孔吸食〕。*The horse is badly blown*. 马骑得喘极了。*the trees blown down by the storm* 被风暴吹折的树。*He has* ～*n* (*in*) *the whole sum*. 他把全部款项都花完了。*I'm* ～*ed if I know*. 〔俚〕畜牲才知道，我知道不算人。*B- the cost*! 价钱真贵！～ *town* 离开城市。～ ***about*** [***away***] 吹散；传播。～ ***down*** **1.** 吹倒；吹落。**2.** (锅炉)喷出(蒸汽)。～ ***great guns*** (***and small arms***) 刮大风，(风)狂吹。～ ***high***, ～ ***low*** 在任何情况下，不管发生什么事。～ ***hot and cold*** 反覆无常，忽褒忽贬，无定见。～ ***in*** **1.** 鼓风入(熔铁炉)，(风)吹进来。**2.** 〔美口〕忽然来访。**3.** 〔美口〕乱花，浪费；花光(或几乎用光)。***B- it***! 混蛋！讨厌！～ ***itself out*** (风)停。***B- me down***! 〔美口〕真没料到！一惊；真不坏！～ ***off*** **1.** ***vi***. 刮掉，吹掉；喷出(蒸汽)；〔俚〕抱怨，诉苦；直言不讳。**2.** ***vt***. 放出(锅炉中的水、蒸汽等)；(以怒冲冲的谈话等)发泄(不满)〔又作 ～ off steam〕。～ ***one's bazoo*** [bəˈzuː; bəˋzu] 〔美口〕吹牛，夸口。～ ***one's lines*** 说错(台词)。～ ***one's nose*** 擤鼻子。～ ***one's own horn*** 〔美口〕自吹，自夸。～ ***one's own trumpet*** 自卖自夸，自赞，自大。～ ***out*** **1.** 停吹，停止鼓风。**2.** (吹)胀；吹破。**3.** (灯等)熄灭；把(灯等)吹灭。**4.** 〔美俚〕杀掉；(枪等)打穿(脑袋等)；(保险丝)烧断。～ ***out*** 〔美俚〕取消。～ ***over*** **1.** 经过，走过。**2.** (云)吹散，(风)已定；消灭。**3.** 被淡忘。～ ***sb***. ***to a dinner*** 〔美俚〕请某人吃饭。～ ***sb***. ***up*** 责备某人。～ ***the bellows*** [***the coals***, ***the fire***] 〔古〕挑唆，煽动。～ ***the show*** 〔美俚〕吹掉演出合同。～ ***up*** **1.** ***vi***. 炸，炸裂，被炸掉；〔俚〕失败，被揭穿；起(风)，来(风暴)，(暴风雨等)更加厉害；〔口〕发脾气(～ *up at sb*. *over sth*. 在某事上对某人发脾气)。**2.** ***vt***. 炸掉，炸破，爆破；吹胀；把(某人)捧上天，夸大；毁掉，弄糟；骂，责备；【摄】〔口〕放大(照相) (*A storm blew up*. 起风暴了。*The ship blew up*. 船爆炸了。～ *up a bridge* 把桥炸掉。*He blew himself up importantly*. 他趾高气扬，不可一世)。～ ***upon*** **1.** ***vt***. 害，使倒霉；使失信用；使乏味；告密，告发 (*His reputation is blown upon*. 他名誉扫地了)。**2.** ***n***. 吹风，一阵风；暴风，疾风；鼓风；擤鼻涕；吹奏(声)；大言不惭的人；(鲸的)喷水；(蝇的)产卵，蝇卵；〔口〕傲慢；(保险丝)熔断；【冶】吹炼 (*give the fire a* ～ 吹火。*clean the machinery with a* ～ 吹风打扫机器。*a few discordant* ～*s by bugler* 几声不协调的号声)。～**ball** (蒲公英等的)絮球。～**-by** ***n***. **1.** 漏气；漏液。**2.** (汽车的)废气燃烧器，尾气清理装置。～**-by-**～ ***a***. (讲述)极其详细的 (*a* ～*-by-*～ *account of a debate* 对一次论战的极详细叙述)。～**-cock** 放泄旋塞。～**-fish** **1.** 吹气的人〔物〕。**2.** 河豚；黄麻鲈。～**fly** 绿头大苍蝇。～**gun** 吹箭

B

B

筒。～**hard**〔美俚〕夸口大家,吹牛大家。～**hole**(鲸的)喷水孔;(铸件的)气泡。～**ing cat**〔美俚〕爵士乐师。～**-iron** 吹管。～**-job**【空】〔口〕喷气式飞机。～**-lamp** 喷灯。～**mobile** 一种放在滑雪屐上以螺旋桨推动的车辆。～**moulding**(玻璃器皿等的)吹气塑造法。～**-of-cotton**(棉花)吐絮。～**off** 1. 吹泄,喷出。2. 被吹掉之物。3.〔俚〕吹牛大家;〔俚〕绝顶,顶点。～**-off pipe**[**valve**](汽锅的)安全排汽[水]管[阀]。～**out** 喷出(口),爆发;【电】熔解;熄火,停炉;车胎的爆裂[裂口],沙丘的吹断;〔俚〕大宴会;大事件。～**pipe** 吹管,吹火筒;吹箭筒。～**torch** 喷灯;〔美俚〕喷气战斗机。～**tube** 玻璃吹制管。～**up** 1. 爆炸;崩殒;破裂。2.(脾气等的)发作。3.(照片等的)放大;放大了的照片等。**-er** ***n***. 1. 吹玻璃工人,吹者,吹的东西。2.【机】鼓风机,风箱;通风机;增压器;【空】螺旋桨。3.【动】鲸;河豚之类。4.〔美口〕夸口的人,吹牛家。

blow[2][bləu; blo] **I** ***vi***. (***blew***[blu:; blu]; ***blown***[bləun; blon])(花)开放。— ***vt***. 使开花;开(花)。**II** ***n***. 1. 花;开花(状态)。2. 绚丽多姿。*a rich, full ～ of color* 五彩缤纷。*in full* ～(花)盛开。

blow[3][bləu; blo] ***n***. 1. 打,打击,一击;殴打。2. 意外的灾害,横祸,不幸。3. 奇袭,猛攻。*a ～ to the head* 对头部的一击。*a ～ with the fist* 打来一拳。*a ～ to one's pride* 对自尊心的打击。***at a***(***single***)～[***at one*** ～]一击就…,一举,一下子。***at ～s*** 在殴打〔格斗〕。***come***[***fall***] ***to ～s*** 互相打起来;开战。***deal***[***give***] ***a ～ at*** 打击,给…一击。***exchange ～s*** 互殴,相打。***strike a ～ against*** 抵抗,抗击。***strike a ～ for*** 为…斗争;帮助,支持。***strike a ～ to*** 对…发起攻击,打击…。***without striking a ～*** 轻轻易易,坐享其成地,兵不血刃地。

blown[1][bləun; blon] **I** ***v***. blow[1]的过去分词。**II** ***a***. 1. 吹胀了的;胀起的;鼓起的。2.(马等)累得喘气的;疲劳极了的。3. 满是蝇卵的。4. 吹制的。5. 被炸毁的;坏了的;(食物等)走味的。～ *stomachs* 胀鼓鼓的肚子,大腹便便。*dispose of ～ canned goods* 对变质罐头食品的处理。～**-moulded** ***a***. 以吹气法塑造的。～**-up** ***a***. 1.(照片等)放大的。2.(因爆炸)损坏的。3.(气球等)膨胀的。4. 夸大的,吹牛的。

blown[2][bləun; blon] **I** ***v***. blow[2]的过去分词。**II** ***a***. 开了花的;(花)盛开的。

blow·y['bləui; `bloɪ] ***a***. (***-i·er***; ***-i·est***) 1. 刮风的,风大的。2. 风吹过的;被风吹来吹去的,容易被风吹起的。

blowzed, blowz·y[blauzd, 'blauzi; blaυzd, `blaυzɪ] ***a***. 1. 红脸的;相貌粗俗的。2. 邋遢的,头发蓬乱的(= blowsed, blowsy)。

bls. = bales; barrels.

BLS = 1. Bureau of Labour Statistics〔美〕劳工统计局。2. Bachelor of Liberal Studies 文(科)学士。3. Bachelor of Library Science 图书馆学学士。

blub[blʌb; blʌb] ***vi***. (**-bb-**)〔学俚〕哭。

blub·ber[1]['blʌbə; `blʌbɚ] **I** ***vt***. 1. 哭脏,哭肿(脸)。2. 哭诉,哭着说。～ *one's face* 哭肿(脏)脸。— ***vi***. 哇哇地哭;哭闹。**II** ***n***. 哭泣,哭闹。*in a* ～ 哭泣,哭闹。

blub·ber[2]['blʌbə; `blʌbɚ] ***a***. 肿大的;肥厚的,(嘴唇)厚嘟嘟的。*thick, ～ lips* 肥厚的嘴唇。

blub·ber[3]['blʌbə; `blʌbɚ] ***n***. 1. 鲸油,鲸脂;海兽脂。2. 多余的脂肪。

blub·ber·y['blʌbəri; `blʌbərɪ] ***a***. 1. 哭泣的。2. 脂肪多的,肥的;脂肪一样的。～ *lips* 厚嘴唇。

blu·cher['blu:tʃə, -kə; `blutʃɚ, -kɚ] ***n***. 〔*pl*.〕1. 布柳切半统靴〔因普鲁士元帅布柳切而得名〕。2.(鞋舌与鞋面是一块皮,鞋帮皮在鞋面皮之上的)浅腰皮鞋。

bludg·eon['blʌdʒən; `blʌdʒən] **I** ***n***. 大头棒。**II** ***vt***. 1. 用大头棒(不断地)打。2. 威胁,强迫。*The boss finally ～ed him into accepting responsibility*. 上司强迫他负起责任。*the ～ of satire* 讽刺性的抨击。

blue[blu:; blu] **I** ***a***. 1. 青,蓝,蓝色的,天蓝色的;(脸色)发灰[青]的,(皮毛等)青灰色的。2. 阴郁的,忧郁的,沮丧的,悲观的;(气候)阴凉的;(希望等)暗淡的,没精打采的。3. 穿蓝衣服的;以蓝色为标志的;〔美〕(南北战争中)联邦军的,北军的。4.〔英〕清教徒的,禁律严厉的。5.〔口〕(女子)有文艺趣味的,有学问的(女子)。6. 淫猥的,猥亵的,下流的;渎神的。～ *smoke* 青烟。*feel* ～ 不高兴。～ *from cold* 脸冻得发青。*look* ～ 愁眉不展;情绪不好;(形势)恶劣。*a ～ outlook* 悲观的见解。*Things look* ～. 事不称心,无希望。～ *talk* 下流言论。*The air was ～ with oaths*. 到处是不堪入耳的咒骂。***drink till all's*** ～ 大醉,烂醉,一醉方休。***in a ～ funk***〔俚〕非常恐怖。***like ～ murder*** 用全速力。***once in a ～ moon*** 机会极少地,千载难逢地。***till all is*** ～ 继续不断,长期地,彻底地,到最后。**II** ***n***. 1. 青色,蓝色;〔the b-〕碧空,苍天,青天;海,沧海。2. 蓝色颜料[染料](等);蓝布;穿蓝制服的人〔美〕(南北战争中的)联邦军,北军;(美国耶鲁(Yale)、英国剑桥、牛津大学的)大学色标,大学体育队选手〔尤指上述三大学〕。3. 英保守党员。4. 女学者。5.〔the ～s〕一种感伤的黑人民歌;布鲁斯舞(曲)〔爵士音乐及舞步的一种〕6.〔口〕〔the ～s〕忧郁,忧闷,不乐,沮丧。***dark*** ～ 暗青色(此色又指 Oxford 大学和 Harrow 公学及其体育代表队选手而言)。***in*** ～ 穿蓝衣。***in the*** ～ 在碧蓝的天空[海洋]里。***light*** ～ 淡青色〔此色又指 Combridge 大学和 Eton 公学及其体育代表队选手而言〕。***navy*** ～ 藏青,暗蓝。***the Blues*** 英国的近卫骑兵。***the men in*** ～ 警察;水兵;美国军队。***be in the ～s*** 没精打采;怏怏不乐,沮丧。***have the ～s*** = be in the ～s. ***out of the*** ～ 意外地,晴天霹雳,从天而降,突然。**III** ***vt***. 把…染成天青色[蓝色],给…上蓝;〔口〕浪费,滥花(金钱)。～ **alert** 空袭警报;台风警报。～ **baby** 有先天性心脏缺陷的婴儿。**Bluebeard** 青髯公〔法国民间故事中一个连杀六妻的恶人的别号〕;〔喻〕残酷的丈夫;乱娶妻妾的男子。～**bell**【植】圆叶风铃草(*the ～ bell of Scotland = harebell*)。～**-bellied Yankee**〔美〕地道的新英格兰人。～**belt**〔日〕蓝带〔授予受过三年训练的柔道家的带子〕。～**-berry**【植】乌饭树;乌饭树的紫黑浆果。～**bill**〔美方〕美洲蓝嘴鸟。**B- Bird** 女童露营团。～**bird**【鸟】(美国)蓝知更鸟。～**-black** ***a***. 深蓝色的。～**blood** 贵族,名门。～**-blooded** ***a***. 1. 出身贵族的,名门的。2.(马等)纯种的。～ **bonnet** 1.(苏格兰)蓝色便帽。2.【植】得克萨斯羽扇豆;(苏格兰)矢车菊。～ **book** 1.〔B- Book〕(英、美等国政府的)蓝皮书〔就某一专题发表的报告、外交文书等〕。2.〔美俚〕职工名册,名人录;(大学考试用)蓝皮拍纸簿。～**bottle** 1.【植】矢车菊。2.〔俚〕青蝇。3.〔俚〕蓝衣警察。～**-brick university**〔俚〕名牌大学(指牛津、剑桥等大学)。～ **chip** 热门的股票。～**-chip** ***a***., ***n***. 1. 热门的(股票);靠得住的(财产)。2. 第一流的;值钱的。～**coat** 蓝衣人〔水手、警察、美国南北战争中联邦军士兵等的别名〕(*a ～ coat boy* 慈善学校〔特指伦敦 B- School〕的学生;蓝衣侍者)。～**-collar** ***a***. 穿蓝领工装的;体力劳动的。**B- Cross** 1.〔美〕畜类保护协会。2. 医疗服务救济协会。3. 催嚏性毒气〔俗名〕。～**devils** 1. 忧郁;沮丧。2. 惊险的幻想。～**-eyed** ***a***. 1. 蓝眼的。2. 心爱的。3.〔美俚〕容易上当的。～**fish**【鱼】(美洲大西洋海岸产的)青鱼。～**-flag**〔美〕蓝鸢尾〔Tennessee 州州花〕。～ **funk** 1.〔美俚〕沮丧,为难。2. 难以抑制的恐惧。～ **gag** 下流话。～**gill**【鱼】翻车鱼。～**grass**〔美〕(盛产于肯塔基州中部的)蓝绿茎牧草。**B-Grass State**〔美〕肯塔基州〔别名〕。～ **grassers** 1. 肯塔基州人〔别名,又叫 ～ grass folks〕。2.〔美〕传统乡村音乐。～**heart**【植】鬼羽箭属。～ **helmet** 蓝盔军〔联合国武装部队〕的一员。～ **hens**〔美〕特拉华人〔别名〕。～**jack** 1. 硫酸铜。2. 栎属植物。～**jacket** 水兵。～ **jeans** 蓝色工装裤,牛仔裤。～ **jersey** 水兵,水手。～ **john**【矿】紫萤石。～ **laws**〔美〕1. 清教徒法规。2.〔美史〕星期日法规〔殖民地时代新英格兰禁止星期日跳舞、宴会等〕。～ **light(s)** 信号花火。～ **line**【体】(冰球场的)蓝线。～ **man**〔俚〕穿制服的警察。～ **mass**〔美〕= blue-pill. ～**nose** 1. 青鼻子的人。2. 清教徒,卫道士;〔B-〕〔加〕沿海各省〔尤指 Nova Scotia〕的居民〔船、马铃薯〕。～ **Monday** 四旬节 (Lent) 前的星期一;〔美〕不开心的星期一。～ **moon** 极长的一个时期。～ **movie** 色情电影。～ **murder** 恐怖的喊声。～**nose**〔俚〕拘谨的人。～**ointment**【医】水银药膏。～ **pig**〔美俚〕威士忌酒。～**-pencil** *vt*. 用蓝铅笔校订(原稿等);〔美俚〕否决,不批准。～ **pigeon**【海】测深锤。～**-pill** 1.【药】汞丸。2.〔美国〕子弹。～**-point**【贝】蓝点蛎。～**print** 1. *n*. 蓝色照相,蓝色版;蓝图,设计图;计划大纲;原本。2. *vt*. 为…制蓝图;晒(图);为…制订计划。～ **revolution** 1. (一些西方国家的所谓)"性解放"。2. 黄色读物的泛滥。～**-ribbon** *a*. 1. 第一流的。2. (陪审用)特选的。～**-ribbon jury** [**panel**]〔美俚〕(审理重大案件的)特选陪审团。～ **ruin** 低级杜松子酒。～**runner**【鱼】闪光鲹。～**stem** (北美西部作干草用的)蓝茎草。～**-sky** *a*. 1. (股票)不可靠的;财务不健全的。2. 纯理论性的。3. 不切实际的。～**-sky law**〔美〕无信用股票取缔法。～**stocking** 1. 女学者,女才子,女文学家。2. (冒充)学者气派的女性。～**stone**【矿】硫酸铜,胆矾;〔美〕(建筑或铺路用的)青石;黏土质砂岩。～ **streak** 1. 连续的事物。2. 极快的闪光,一闪即逝的东西。3. 连珠炮似的谈话(*talk a* ～ *streak* 讲话滔滔不绝。*like a* ～ *streak* 很快;极有成效地)。～**Sunday Law** 星期日禁止劳动法。～**throat** *n*.【动】蓝喉鸲。～ **water** 深海,沧海。～**weed**【植】蓝蓟。～ **white finish** (织物的)上蓝整理。～ **William**〔美俚〕五十元钞票。～ **wool** 高级有光羊毛。**-ness** *n*. 蓝色,青蓝。

blueing [ˈblu(:)iŋ; ˋbluɪŋ] *n*. = bluing.

blueish [ˈblu(:)iʃ; ˋbluɪʃ] *a*. = bluish.

blues·rock [ˈbluːzrɔk; ˋbluzrɑk] *n*. 布鲁斯摇摆乐〔以摇摆音乐为背景的一种黑人伤感音乐〕。

blu·et [ˈbluːit; ˋbluɪt] *n*.【植】茵草科青花植物之名;矢车菊等。

blue·y [ˈbluːi; ˋbluɪ] *a*. 带蓝色的。

bluff[1] [blʌf; blʌf] I *a*. 1. 绝壁的,壁立的,陡峭的。2. 直率的,爽快的,坦率的;粗率的 (*opp*. subtle)。3.【海】(船头等)前端平阔而垂直的。II *n*. 1. 峭壁,断崖。2. (船头等的)鼓起部分。*the B-* 高地。**-ly** *ad*. 率直地;粗率地。**-ness** *n*. 1. 陡壁。2. 朴直。

bluff[2] [blʌf; blʌf] I *vt*. 1.〔俚〕以假象欺骗;假装。2. (虚张声势地)恐吓,吓唬。3.【牌】(持弱牌时)下大注吓倒(对方)。～ *sb*. *into doing sth*. 欺骗某人使做某事。～ *sb*. *out of doing sth*. 吓倒某人使不敢做某事。～ *and deceive* 招摇撞骗。— *vi*. 虚张声势,装腔作势。II *n*. 1. 欺骗,吓唬。2. 虚张声势的人;吓唬人的人。*make a* ～ = *play a game of* ～ 采取恐吓手段。*call sb*.*'s* ～【牌】(顶住某人的下大注威吓)叫某人摊牌;揭露某人的外强中干 (*He always said he would quit, so we finally called his* ～. 他常以辞职相要挟,我们终于让他另谋高就)。*put on a good* ～ (*run a* ～ *on*) 虚张声势地恐吓,吓唬;蒙蔽,欺骗。

bluff·er [ˈblʌfə; ˋblʌfɚ] *n*. 1. 骗子,招摇撞骗的人。2. 虚张声势的人,吓唬人的人。

blu·ing [ˈbluːiŋ; ˋbluɪŋ] *n*.【化】上蓝剂,蓝色漂白剂〔用以防止白色织物洗染时变黄〕。

blu·ish [ˈblu(:)iʃ; ˋbluɪʃ] *a*. 带青色的,浅蓝色的。**-ness** *n*.

Blume [bluːm; blum] *n*. 布卢姆〔姓氏〕。

blun·der [ˈblʌndə; ˋblʌndɚ] I *n*. 大错,失策,疏忽。*commit a* ～ 犯大错。II *vi*. 1. 犯大错;出漏子。2. 跌跌撞撞地走[跑];慌张地走[跑] (*along*; *on*; *into*);摔,拌跤。*Without my glasses I* ～*ed into the wrong room*. 我因为没戴眼镜,跌跌撞撞地走错了房间。— *vt*. 1. 无意中说出,漏嘴说出。2. 弄糟,弄错,做错;办错。～ *the account* 算错账。～ ***against*** 碰着,撞着。～ ***away*** 错失(良机等)。～ ***into*** (*sense*) 无意中得(妙解)。～ ***on*** [***upon***] 无意中发现,碰见。～ ***out*** (*secret*) 不觉中泄漏出(秘密)。～ ***through*** (*one's lesson*) 胡乱做完(功课)。～ **head** 傻瓜。

blun·der·buss [ˈblʌndəbʌs; ˋblʌndɚˏbʌs] *n*. 1. 老式大口径短程霰弹枪。2. (因粗鲁、轻率而易做错事的)大笨蛋。

blun·der·er [ˈblʌndərə; ˋblʌndərɚ] *n*. 容易做错事的人;犯大错的人。

blun·der·ing [ˈblʌndəriŋ; ˋblʌndərɪŋ] *a*. 1. 浮躁的;粗笨的;粗卤的。2. 容易犯错误的;大错的。**-ly** *ad*.

blunge [blʌndʒ; blʌndʒ] *vt*. (烧窑时)将(胶泥)用水搅拌。～**r** 1. 拌胶泥工。2. 拌胶泥大桶;拌泥杵。

blunt [blʌnt; blʌnt] I *a*. 1. (刀等)钝,不快的,不锋利的,无锋刀的;(笔尖等)无尖锋的。2. (感觉等)迟钝的;愚钝的。3. 粗卤的,直率的,干脆的;呆板的。*short*, ～ *nose* 短小扁平的鼻子。～ *about the feeling of others* 对别人的感情很少理解〔觉察、体会等〕。***to be*** ～〔插入语〕老实说。4.〔美俚〕大麻烟卷。II *n*. 1. 短粗的针〔雪茄烟等〕。2. 钝器。3.〔俚〕现金,现钞。III *vt*. 1. 把…弄钝,使失锋刃。2. 使变愚钝;使受挫,减弱。*a knife* ～*ed from use* 用钝的刀。*imagination* ～*ed by wine* 想像力因喝酒而受损害。～ *the enemy's attack* 挫敌锋芒。**-ly** *ad*. (*to put it* ～〔插入语〕直截了当地说,(和你)直说吧)。**-ness** *n*.

blur [bləː; blɝ] I *n*. 1. 污点,污斑;污名。2. 暧昧不明,一片模糊,模糊不清的东西〔声音〕。～*s in one's life* 历史污点。*a book full of* ～*s* 满是污痕的书。*the foggy* ～ 雾气一片模糊。II *vt*. (-rr-) 1. 把…弄模糊。2. 污损,涂污,弄脏。— *vi*. 1. 沾染污迹。2. 变模糊。*Everything blurred as he ran*. 他奔跑的时候眼前一片模糊。～ ***out*** 1. 使变模糊。2. 抹掉,涂掉。

blurb [bləːb; blɝb] I *n*.〔美口〕1. 新书推荐广告〔多印在书的护封上〕。2. 大肆吹捧的广告。II *vt*. (通过护封简介)吹捧(作家);为…大做广告。**-ing** *n*.〔美口〕无线电广告。**-ist** *n*. 写护封书评者,吹捧者。

blurble [bləːbl; blɝbl] *vt*.〔美口〕大捧特捧,极力夸奖。

blurt [bləːt; blɝt] I *vt*. 突然说出,失口说出,漏出 (*out*)。*He* ～*s out all he hears*. 他漏嘴说出了他听到的一切。II *n*. 漏嘴说出的话。

blush [blʌʃ; blʌʃ] I *vi*. 1. 脸红,惭愧。2. 害臊,怕羞,忸怩 (*at*, *for*)。3. 呈现红色。～ *for sb*. 替某人脸红。～ *to the roots of one's hair* 脸红到发根,极度羞愧。*He did not* ～ *to* (*do*). 他厚颜无耻地(做)…。— *vt*. 1. 把…弄红。2. 因脸红而表露出(真实情感等)。～ *one's truth* 因脸红而表露出真情。II *n*. 脸红;红色;〔古〕一见,一瞥。***at*** [***on***] (***the***) ***first*** ～ 猛一见,骤然看来。～ ***at one's words*** 因失言而脸红。～ ***for*** [***with***] ***shame*** 羞愧得脸红。***put*** (***sb***.) ***to the*** ～ 使(某人)窘得脸红。***Spare my*** ～***es*** 别让我脸红了[不要过分夸赞我了]。**-er** *n*. 胭脂。～ **wine** 酡红葡萄酒〔色浅味淡〕。**-ful** *a*. (使人)脸红的。**-ingly** *ad*.

blus·ter [ˈblʌstə; ˋblʌstɚ] I *vi*. 1. (风等)狂吹;(浪等)汹涌。2. (人)咆哮,嚷。*A typhoon* ～*ed over the land*. 台风扫过大地。*He* ～*ed and swaggered like a conquering hero*. 他声势汹汹,不可一世。— *vt*. 1. 喝叱,恐吓。2. 怒冲冲地说 (*out*, *forth*)。*He* ～*ed his way through the crowd*. 他吆喝着挤出人群。～ *out* [*forth*] *threats* 大声威吓。～ ***about*** 叫嚣。～ ***at one's will*** 横行霸道。～ ***oneself into anger*** 勃然大怒。II *n*. 1. 狂风声,惊涛骇浪声,喧嚣声。2. 恫吓;大话。**-ous** [-əs; -əs], **-y** *a*. = blustering.

blus·ter·er [ˈblʌstərə; ˋblʌstərɚ] *n*. 咆哮的人,狂暴的人;吓唬人的人。

blus·ter·ing [ˈblʌstəriŋ; ˋblʌstərɪŋ] *a*. 1. 狂风大作的;(波涛)汹涌的。2. 恐吓的,狂暴的。**-ly** *ad*.

blvd = boulevard.

BM, B. M. = 1. Bachelor of Medicine 医学士。2. British Museum 不列颠博物馆(旧称大英博物馆)。3.

bowel movement〔口〕大便。4. Bachelor of Music 音乐学士。

BMA = British Medical Association 英国医学会。

BMD = ballistic missile defence 弹道导弹防御系统。

BMDS = ballistic missile defence system 防弹道导弹系统。

B

BME = 1. Bachelor of Mining Engineering 采矿工程学士。2. Bachelor of Mechanical Engineering 机械工程学士。3. Bachelor of Music Education 音乐教育学士。

BMEWS = ballistic missile early warning system 反弹道导弹预报系统,弹道导弹远程预警系统。

BMOC = big man on campus〔美学俚〕校内大人物。

BNS = 1. Bachelor of Nursing Science 护理学士。2. Bachelor of Natural Science 自然科学学士。3. Bachelor of Naval Science(s) 海军科学学士。

BO, B.O., b.o. = 1. back order 暂时无法满足的订货。2. body odo(u)r 体臭,狐臭。3. box office 戏院票房,戏院售票处。4. branch office 分支机构,分支办公室。

bo [bəu; bo] **I** *n*. 1.〔美口〕老兄,老弟,老朋友。2.〔美口〕浪子;流浪汉。3. 小伙子。**II** *int*. 表示惊讶。

bo·a [ˈbəuə; ˋboə] *n*. 1. 圆筒形皮毛〔羽毛〕围巾。2. 大蛇,蟒蛇。~ **constrictor** *n*. 王蛇,蟒蛇。

B.O.A. = British Olympic Association 英国奥林匹克委员会。

BOAC = British Overseas Airways Corporation 英国海外航空公司〔现已与 British European Airways 英国欧洲航空公司合并,称 British Airways 英国航空公司〕。

Bo·a·ner·ges [ˌbəuəˈnəːdʒiːz; ˏboəˋnɚdʒiz] *n*. 雷子〔耶稣赐与其门徒 James 及 John 的别号〕;〔用作 *sing*.〕嗓子大的传教师〔雄辩家〕。

boar [bɔː; bor] *n*. 1.(未阉的)公猪,公猪肉。2.〔又作 wild boar〕公野猪。

board [bɔːd; bord] **I** *n*. 1. 板〔通常指宽 4 英寸半以上厚 2 英寸半以下者〕,木板;纸板。2.(广告)牌;(棋)盘;〔口〕配电盘(等)。3.〔*pl*.〕【剧】舞台。4. 餐桌;食物;伙食;〔有时指〕膳宿。5. 会议桌;会议;全体委员;委员会;部,厅,局,管理处。6. 船的甲板;舷,舷侧;船内;车内。7.〔废〕边;海岸。*cloth* ~*s* (书籍的)布面精装。*a remote control* ~ 遥控盘,遥控台。*a* ~ *for checkers* 棋盘。*a piece of* ~ 一块板。*a groaning* ~ 盛宴,丰盛的饭菜。*a bulletin* ~ 布告牌。~ *and lodging* 膳宿。~ *of directors* 理事会,董事会。***above*** ~ 光明正大。~ ***and*** [***by, on***] ~ (船)并排。***B- of Education***〔英〕教育部〔现改名 the Ministry of Education〕; ~ ***of education*** (一般的)教育委员会;〔美〕(各州、县、市管理中小学的)教育管理委员会。~ ***of equalization***〔美〕税率调查委员会。***B- of Trade***〔英〕商业部;〔b- of t-〕〔美〕商会;芝加哥市农产品交易所。***by the*** ~ 在舷外,越过舷边,(由船上)向海中。***come on*** ~ 回船。***fall on*** ~ = run on ~. ***fall over*** ~ 从船上掉落水中。***free on*** ~【商】船上交货,离岸价格(略作 FOB 或 f.o.b.)。***go by the*** ~ (桅杆)折断落于船外;破产;(努力等)落空;(计划)成泡影,失败。***go on the*** ~***s*** 当演员。***have*** [***take***] ***...*** ***on*** ~ 载有,装有。***lay a ship on*** ~ 使船靠拢(他船)。***make short*** ~*s*【海】常常逆风斜进。***on*** ~ 1. 在船上,在船〔飞机〕中 (*on* ~ *the plane* 在飞机上);〔美〕在车上 (*go* [*get*] *on* ~乘船,乘车)。2.【棒球】〔口〕出垒。***on the*** ~*s* 登台,做演员。***on even*** ~ ***with*** 与…齐舷并进;在和…同条件下。***run on*** ~ (*of another ship*) 1. 撞着(别船)。2. 攻击。***sweep the*** ~ 赢得全部赌注,通吃;全胜。***tread the*** ~*s* = ***walk the*** ~*s* = go on the ~s. **II** *vt*. 1. 用板铺〔盖、围、堵〕上。2. 为…提供膳食〔包饭〕;使寄膳;〔美〕寄养(马)。3. 上(船),坐(船);〔美〕搭(车);乘(飞机)。4. 攻入(敌船等);强行靠近(敌船等)。~ *over a well* 用木板做井栏。*They* ~*ed him for $ 40 a week*. 他们按每周收费 40 美元给他包伙。*The pirate ship* ~*ed the clipper*. 海盗船强行靠近快艇。— *vi*. 1. 寄膳,搭伙,包饭。2.【海】逆风斜进。~ ***around***【美】轮餐〔教员轮流在学生家吃饭〕。~ ***at*** (*so much a week*) (每周)给膳费(若干)。~ ***in*** 在寄宿处寄膳。~ ***out*** 在外面寄膳。~ ***over*** 用木板铺上(围住)。~ ***up*** 用板钉上[围上] (~ *up the door* 把门用板钉上)。~ **chairman** 董事长。~ **foot** 板英尺〔木材计量单位,相当于厚一英寸、面积一平方英尺的木材〕。~ **game** 需用棋盘的游戏〔如 chess, checkers 等〕。~ **money** = ~ wages. ~**-out** *vt*. 使因病退伍。~ **room** (董事会等的)会议室。~**sailing** 风帆冲浪。~**-school** (英国的)公立小学校〔现在叫 county council school〕。~ **wages**〔*pl*.〕1.(给仆人等的)膳费折合的津贴;代作工资的膳宿。2. 仅够膳宿的工资。~**walk**〔美〕(海滨等的)木板(散步)路。

board·er [ˈbɔːdə; ˈbordɚ] *n*. 1. 寄膳者,寄宿生。2.(车船、飞机等的)乘客。3. 闯入敌船者,攻入敌船的队员。4.〔美〕寄养的马。*a day* ~ 寄膳不寄宿的人[学生]。~ **baby**〔美〕寄养婴儿或幼儿。

board·ing [ˈbɔːdiŋ; ˋbordɪŋ] *n*. 1. 围板,隔板,地板〔总称〕,木板;(由几块板拼成的)大木板。2. 寄膳,搭伙;寄膳宿。3. 上船[车、飞机]。4. 攻入[占领]敌船。*an uneventful* ~ 一次平安无事的乘船[车、飞机]旅行。~**-card** (班机等的)客货车。~ **house** (供膳的)寄宿处,公寓。~ **measure** 量木材的特用计量制。~**-out** 1. 在外寄膳。2.(孤儿的)寄养。~ **school** 寄宿学校〔*opp*. day school〕。

boar·fish [ˈbɔːfiʃ; ˋborˏfɪʃ] *n*. (*pl*. ~(*es*)) 豚鼻鱼。

boar·hound [ˈbɔːhaund; ˋborhaʊnd] *n*. 野猪猎犬。

boar·ish [ˈbɔːriʃ; ˋborɪʃ] *a*. 野猪一样的;卤莽的;凶猛的。

Bo·as [ˈbəuæz, ˈbəuəz; ˋboæs, ˋboəz] *n*. 博厄斯〔姓氏〕。

boast [bəust; bost] **I** *vi*. 夸,自夸;夸耀 (*of, about*)。*She* ~*ed of her family's wealth*. 她自夸家里有钱。*We must never brag and* ~. 我们决不可自吹自擂。— *vt*. 1. 夸,夸耀,夸口说。2. 以有…而自豪,有可以夸耀的…;自负有,自恃有。*The town* ~*s a fine park*. 该城以有一座漂亮的公园而自豪。*He* ~*s himself a genius*. 他自称是天才。~ ***of*** [***about***] 夸耀,自夸,吹嘘。~ ***oneself of*** 自夸,自负,自恃。***without*** ~***ing*** 并非夸口,不是自吹〔插入语〕(*Without* ~*ing, I may say* ... 并非夸口,我可以说…)。**II** *n*. 1. 夸,夸口,自负。2. 自负的事物,引为自傲的东西。*Talent is his* ~. 他自夸有才,他以才子自居。***great*** ~, ***small roast*** 夸夸其谈,所成无多;好大言者实行少。***make a*** ~ ***of*** 自夸,夸耀。

boast·er [ˈbəustə; ˋbostɚ] *n*. 自夸者,大言不惭的人。

boast·ful [ˈbəustful; ˋbostful] *a*. 夸口的,自负的,傲慢的。***be*** ~ ***of*** ...自夸是…,以…自夸。**-ly** *ad*. **-ness** *n*.

boat [bəut; bot] **I** *n*. 1. 小舟,小船,(小)艇,(大船所载)救生艇;帆船,渔船。2. 汽轮〔常指小汽轮〕;邮船,大轮船。3. 船形物,船行器皿;【化】舟皿;【宗】舟形香炉。*a motor* ~ 机帆船。*a sailing* ~ 帆船。*an open* ~ 无甲板船。*a rowing* ~ 划艇。*a sauce* ~ 船形佐料碟。~*'s length* 艇身 (*win by a* ~*'s length* 赛艇时领先一艇长的距离)。***burn one's*** ~***s*** 布背水之阵,破釜沉舟。***by*** ~ 乘船 (*go by* ~ 乘船去)。***fasten*** [***get out***] ***a*** ~ 系住船。***have an oar in every man's*** ~ 多管闲事,乱管闲事。***in one*** [***the same***] ~ 在同一状态下,处境相同;同舟共济,共患难。***man a*** ~ 为船配备船员。***miss the*** ~ 1. 失败;错过机会,坐失良机。2. 未能抓住(问题的)要点。***push the*** ~ ***out***〔口〕庆祝。***rock the*** ~ 捣乱。***ship's*** ~ 船上小艇;舰载救生艇。***take*** ~ 乘船,坐船。***take to the*** ~*s* 1. 乘船上小艇逃生。2. 仓猝放弃所进行的事业。**II** *vt*. 1. 用船装运。2. 把…装入船内。*They* ~*ed us across the bay*. 他们把我们用船运过〔摆渡过〕海湾。— *vi*. 1. 坐船去。2. 划船;乘船(游玩)。*We* ~*ed down the Thames*. 我们放舟直下泰晤士河。~ ***it*** 1. 坐船去;划船。2. 顺风驶。***B- the oars!*** 收桨! ~ **bill**【鸟】(南美)阔啄苍鹭。~**-billed heron**【鸟】舟嘴鹭。~

chocks 短艇架。~ **deck** 救生艇甲板。~ **drill**【海】救生演习。~ **fall** 短艇索。~ **fly** 船蝇。~ **hoist** 起艇机。~-**hook** 有钩的篙子。~**house** 船库,艇库〔水边停放游艇的处所〕。~ **line**【海】(由母船丢给小艇的)系索。~**load** *n*. 1. 一船货[旅客]。2. 载一船之量。~**man** 1. 船夫,船工;桨手。2. 出租[出售]游艇者,租船老板。~**manship** 划船术。~ **people**〔复〕(指越南等东南亚国家)乘船出逃的难民,船民。~ **race** 划船比赛。~ **train** (与船运衔接的)联运列车。-**ful** *n*. 一船所载的量。

boat·a·ble [ˈbəutəbl; ˋbotəbl̩] *a*. 1. 可用小船运输的。2. 可通航小船的。

boat·age [ˈbəutidʒ; ˋbotɪdʒ] *n*. 1. 小船运输。2. 小船运费。3. 救生艇[船载小艇]容量。

boat·el [bəuˈtel; boˋtɛl] *n*.〔美〕(附有停船设施的)汽艇游客旅馆。

boat·er [ˈbəutə; ˋbotɚ] *n*. 1. 乘小船的人,游艇乘客。2.〔英口〕硬壳平顶草帽〔19 世纪英国人夏季划船时所戴〕。

boat·ing [ˈbəutiŋ; ˋbotɪŋ] *n*. 划船;乘船(游玩)。*go* ~ 乘船〔尤指划船〕游玩。

boat·nik [ˈbəutnik; ˋbotnɪk] *n*.〔口〕水上人家,船户。

boat·swain, bo's'n, bo'sun, bosun [ˈbəusn,〔罕〕ˈbəutswein; ˋbosn̩, ˋbotswen] *n*. 1. (商船的)水手长。2. (军舰的)掌帆长;(掌帆缆的)准尉。~**'s chair** (绳系吊板的)高空作业台。~**'s mate** 掌帆长副手;副水手长。

bob[1] [bɔb; bɑb] I *n*. 1. (女人、小孩的)短发;束发;髻;卷毛,卷毛假发;(马等)截短的尾巴。2. 诗节落尾的叠句,歌曲的短叠句。II *vt*. (**-bb-**) 截短,剪短(发、尾等)。*They ~bed their hair to be in style*. 她们剪了赶时髦的短发式。*wear one's hair ~bed* 剪短发。~ **wig**〔英〕法官戴的假发。

bob[2] [bɔb; bɑb] *n*. 1.【物】摆锤,秤锤(等);耳珰;(钓丝的)浮子,漂。2. 一组钓钩;一串浮饵;一束叶子;一串花(葡萄等)。3. 急动;急牵;(点一点头)招呼;(快速一屈膝)行礼。4. 摆,摆动;跳舞;浮动,振动。5.〔俚〕步兵。6. = ~ sled. *a ~ of the head* 微微点一下头。*a plumb ~* (测量用)铅锤。II *vi*. (**-bb-**) 1. 上下跳动;急动,急牵。2. 行屈膝礼。3. 浮动;用浮漂钓 (*for*)。*The cork was ~bing on the water*. (钓丝的)浮子在水中上下跳动。— *vt*. 1. 轻敲;使敲(或撞)。2. 急速摆动。*~ the head* 头微微点一点。*~ a greeting*. 点头打招呼 (= *~ at sb*.)。~ **at** [**for**] (*apple*) 把(苹果)用线吊着用嘴去咬的游戏。~ **up** 急忙浮上;突然出现;突然站起 (*The question often ~s up*. 那个问题常被提起)。~ *up like a cork* 挽回颓势,东山再起;恢复元气 (*He ~s up like a cork*. 他虽然屡经挫折,总是能东山再起)。**dry** ~〔英〕板球组学生。**light** *~s*〔古〕轻装步兵。**wet** ~〔英〕划船组学生。

bob[3] [bɔb; bɑb] *n*. (*sing*., *pl*.)〔英口〕= shilling;〔美口〕= dollar.

bob[4] [bɔb; bɑb] *n*. 未断奶的小牛。

bob[5] [bɔb; bɑb] *n*.【动】(一群)沙蠋。

Bob, Bob·by [bɔb, ˈbɔbi; bɑb, ˋbɑbɪ] *n*. 鲍勃〔男子名, Robert 的昵称〕。*~'s your uncle*〔原英〕不要紧,没关系,放心好了,别着急 (*~'s your uncle when* ... 如果发生…的情况,请不必着急)。

Bob·a·dil [ˈbɔbədil; ˋbɑbədɪl] *n*. 好夸口的人,吹牛大家〔作家 Ben Johnson 的作品 *Every Man in His Humour* 中的人物〕。

bo·ba·tor·i·um [bɔdəˈtɔːriəm; bɑbəˋtorɪəm] *n*.〔美〕专剪短发型的理发店〔= bobber shop〕。

bobbed [bɔbd; bɑbd] *a*. 短毛的,短发的;截尾的。

bob·ber [ˈbɔbə; ˋbɑbɚ] *n*. 1. 晃动的人或物。2. 钓丝浮子。

bob·ber·y [ˈbɔbəri; ˋbɑbərɪ] I *n*.〔口〕吵闹,叫喊,骚动。*raise a ~* 大吵大闹。II *a*. 吵闹的。*a ~ pack* 一群吵闹的猎狗。

Bob·bie [ˈbɔbi; ˋbɑbɪ] *n*. 博比〔女子名, Roberta 的昵称〕。

bob·bin [ˈbɔbin; ˋbɑbɪn] *n*. 1. 木管,纱管,绕线筒;鼓轮。2. (拴在插梢绳末端的)小木球;(门扣上的)吊带把手。3.【纺】(纺纱机的)筒管,筒子;亚麻捆;【电】绕丝管,线圈架,点火线圈。*a ribbon ~* 色带盘。~ *oil* 锭子油。~ *and fly frame* 粗纺机。

bob·bi·net [ˌbɔbiˈnet, ˌbɑbəˈnet; ˏbɑbɪˋnɛt, ˏbɑbəˋnɛt] *n*.【纺】珠罗纱,六角网眼纱。

bob·bish [ˈbɔbiʃ; ˋbɑbɪʃ] *a*.〔俚〕高兴的,笑哈哈的,快活的,活泼的,精神抖擞的。

bob·ble [ˈbɔbl; ˋbɑbl] *vi*., *n*. 1. 反覆跳动;(篮球)在篮圈上跳动。2.〔英口〕水波荡漾;微波荡漾的小港湾。3. (球)漏踢,漏接;〔美俚〕失误。— *vt*.〔美俚〕失(球)。

Bob·by [ˈbɔbi; ˋbɑbɪ] *n*. 博比〔男子名, Robert 的昵称〕。

bob·by [ˈbɔbi; ˋbɑbɪ] *n*. 1.〔英俚〕警察。2. 初生之犊 (= ~ calf)。

bob·by-dazz·ler [ˈbɔbiˌdæzlə; ˋbɑbɪˏdæzlɚ] *n*.〔英方〕引人注目的东西;华而不实的东西。

bobby pin [ˈbɔbi pin; ˋbɑbɪ pɪn] *n*.〔美〕(短发型)发夹。

bob·by·socks, bob·by·sox [ˈbɔbisɔks; ˋbɑbɪˏsɑks] *n*.〔美口〕女孩短袜。

bob·by·sox·er, bob·by-sock·er [ˈbɔbisɔksə, ˈbɔbisɔkə; ˋbɑbɪˏsɑksɚ, ˋbɑbɪsɑkɚ] *n*.〔美口〕赶时髦的少女。

bob·cat [ˈbɔbkæt; ˋbɑbˏkæt] *n*.【动】美国山猫。

bo·bèche [bəuˈbeʃ; boˋbɛʃ] *n*.〔F.〕烛台托盘。

bob·o·link [ˈbɔbəliŋk; ˋbɑbl̩ˏɪŋk] *n*.【鸟】(北美洲的)食米鸟。

bob·sled, bob·sleigh [ˈbɔbsled, ˈbɔbslei; ˋbɑbˏslɛd, ˋbɑbˏsle] I *n*.〔美〕(滑雪和雪地运木材的)连橇。II *vi*. 乘双连雪橇。

bob·stay [ˈbɔbstei; ˋbɑbˏste] *n*.【海】船头斜桅支索。

bob·tail [ˈbɔbteil; ˋbɑbˏtel] I *n*. 1. 截短的尾;截短尾的动物〔犬、马等〕。2. 晚礼服。3.〔军俚〕罢免,革退。II *a*. 截尾的;截短了的。III *vt*. 截…的尾;截短。

bob·white [ˈbɔbˈhwait; ˋbɑbˋhwaɪt] *n*.【鸟】北美鹑。

BOC = British Oxygen Company 英国氧气公司。

bo·ca·sin [bɔˈkæsin; bɑˋkæsɪn] *n*. 一种细麻布。

Boc·cac·cio [bəuˈkaːtʃiəu; boˋkɑtʃɪˏo], **Gio·van·ni** [ˈdʒiːvaːni; ˋdʒiəvɑnɪ] 薄加丘〔1313-1375, 文艺复兴时期意大利作家,《十日谈》的作者〕。

boc·cie, boc·ce, boc·ci [ˈbɔtʃiː; ˋbɑtʃi] *n*. 木球。

Boche, boche [bɔʃ; bɑʃ] *n*.〔俚、蔑〕1. 德国人;德国兵。2. 暴民。3. 傻瓜。

bock [bɔk; bɑk] I *vi*. (Scot.)〔英方〕作呕,呕吐。II *n*. 烈性黑啤酒;一杯(黑)啤酒 (= ~ beer)。

BOD = biochemical oxygen demand 生化需氧量。

bod [bɔd; bɑd] *n*.〔英口〕人〔body 之略〕。~ **biz**〔美俚〕自我感觉训练 (= sensitivity training)。

bo·da·cious [bəuˈdeiʃəs; boˋdeʃəs] *a*.〔美俚〕胆大包天的〔由 bold 与 audacious 二词组合而成〕。

bode[1] [bəud; bod] *vt*., *vi*. 预示,预兆;〔古〕预报。*The news ~s evil days for him*. 这个消息对他是不祥之兆。*The beginning of that summer ~ed ill*. 夏季一开始就来势不善。~ **ill** [**well**] 主凶[吉]。

bode[2] [bəud; bod] bide 的过去式及过去分词。

bode[3] [bəud; bod]〔废〕bid 的过去式及过去分词。

bode·ful [ˈbəudful; ˋbodful] *a*. 预兆的;不祥的。

bo·de·ga [bəuˈdiːgə; boˋdigə] *n*. (Sp.) 1. 酒窖,酒库。2. 酒店;(特指西班牙籍美国人的)杂货店。

bode·ment [ˈbəudmənt; ˋbodmənt] *n*. 前兆,预兆,预示;凶兆,不祥之兆。

bo·dhi [ˈbəudi; ˋbodɪ] *n*.【佛】大彻大悟。

bo·dhi·sat [ˈbəudisæt; ˋbodɪsæt], **bo·dhi·satt·va** [bəudiˈsætvə; ˏbodɪˋsætvə] *n*.【佛】菩萨。

bod·ice [ˈbɔdis; ˋbɑdɪs] *n*. 1. (女人)紧身胸衣;女服的上部;妇女穿在衬衫外的背心。2. 鲸骨褡,乳褡。

bod·ied [ˈbɔdid; ˋbɑdɪd] *a*. 1. 有形体的,有躯体的。2.

B

具有…躯体[形体]的(用以构成复合词)。*strong-*~ 身体强壮的。*big-*~ 身体魁梧的。

bod·i·less [ˈbɔdilis; ˋbadɪlɪs] ***a.*** 无体的,无形的,脱离形体的。

bod·i·ly [ˈbɔdili; ˋbadlɪ] **I** ***a.*** **1.** 躯体的,身体的,肉体的。**2.** 有形的,具体的。~ *organs* 身体各器官。~ *defects* 身体缺陷。~ *punishment* 体罚。~ *and mental diseases* 肉体上和精神上的疾病。***in*** ~ ***fear*** 害怕危及身体。**II** ***ad.*** **1.** 肉体上。**2.** 有形体地。**3.** 亲身,自己。**4.** 一切,全部,悉,整体。*The audience rose* ~. 听众全体起立。~ **exercise** 体操。

bod·ing [ˈbəudiŋ; ˋbodɪŋ] **I** ***a.*** 凶兆的;预兆的。~ ***care*** 不祥的忧虑,不吉利的念头。**II** ***n.*** 凶兆;前兆,预兆。

bod·kin [ˈbɔdkin; badkɪn] ***n.*** **1.** 大针,粗针;锥子;串子。**2.** (束发)长别针。**3.**【印】活字铗。**4.**〔英口〕挤在两人当中的人。**5.**〔罕〕短剑。***sit*** ~ 挤坐两人当中。***ride*** ~ 夹在两骑当中。~**-work** (女服)金线衣边。

Bod·ley [ˈbɔdli; ˋbadlɪ] ***n.*** 博德利〔姓氏〕。

bod·y [ˈbɔdi; ˋbadɪ] **I** ***n.*** **1.** 身体,体躯,肉体;尸首;躯干,【林】立木。**2.** 本体,主体;主力;本文,正文;部分。**3.** (衣服的)上身部;女胸衣。**4.** 队,群,一团;团体,机关,机构。**5.**〔口〕人〔常用以构成复合词,如 anybody〕;(犯人、继承人等的)身份。**6.** 物体,(液)体;实质;(酒等的)密度,浓度。**7.** 车身;船身;【空】机身;(陶器等的)素胚;(乐器等的)共鸣部分;布身,布的厚薄软硬;【数】立体;【天】天体;【印】铅字身。*the human* ~ 人体。*cremate the* ~ 将尸体火化。*the* ~ *of a tree* 树的主干。*a regular* ~正多面体。*a solid* [*liquid*, *gaseous*] ~ 固[液,气]体。*the* ~ *of the population* 人口的主要成分。*a* ~ *of cavalry* 一队骑兵。*the* ~ *of the book* 本文。*the student* ~学生会。*a diplomatic* ~ 外交团。*a* ~ *of words* 一组单词。*a good sort of* ~好人。*an heir of the* ~ 直系继承人。*a* ~ *of facts* 一大堆事实。*heavenly bodies* 天体。*wine of good* [*full*] ~ 醇厚的葡萄酒。~ *corporate* 法人团体。~ ***and soul*** 整个,全心全意(*work night and day*, ~ *and soul* 日以继夜、全心全意地工作)。~ ***crash tactics*** (日本在第二次世界大战中以敢死飞机冲击军舰的)肉弹战术。~ ***of Christ*** 圣餐面包。~ ***politic*** 国家。***give*** ~ ***to*** 使…具体化,实现;使有形体。***heir of one's*** ~ 直系继承人。***in a*** ~ 全体,整个(*resign in a* ~ 总辞职)。***in*** ~ 亲身,自行。***in the*** ~ 生动;活着,神志清醒。***keep*** ~ ***and soul together*** 勉强维持生活,苟延残喘。***the main*** ~【军】主力部队。***the whole*** ~ 全身;全体。**II** ***vt.*** (***bod·ied***) **1.** 赋与…以形体。**2.** 使具体化,体现;实现;刻划;使呈现于心中(*forth*)。*Imaginations bodies forth the forms of things unknown* 想像力使未知事物的形象呈现于心中。~ **art** 人体艺术。~ **bag** 口袋〔带拉链的橡皮袋〕。~ **blow**【拳】向对手身体的打击。~ **builder** **1.** 车身制造者。**2.** 滋补品。**3.** 健身器械。**4.** 健身者。~**-centred** ***a.***【物】体心的。~ **check** **1.** ***n.*** (冰球赛等)用身体挡住对方。**2.** ***vt.*** 用身体阻挡。~ **burden** 人体负担(指身体所吸入的辐射或有毒物质)。~ **clock** 人体时钟,生理节奏。~ **colo(u)r** 不透明色。~ **corporate**【律】法人团体。~ **count** **1.** 敌尸计数。**2.** (死亡)人数统计。~ **double** 替身。~ **guard** 保镖,卫兵,警卫员。~ **heat** 体温。~ **jewelry** (直接戴在身体上而不是衣服上的)贴身首饰。~ **language** **1.** 身势语,体语。**2.** 身不由己的举动。~ **louse** 虱,虱子。~ **mechanics**〔用作单或复〕健美操。~ **mike**〔美俚〕贴身步话机。~ **odour** 人体的气味;体臭;汗臭。~ **paper**【造纸】铜版纸胚。~ **plan**【船】正面图。~ **shirt** 紧身衬衫〔背心〕。~ **shop** 车身制造〔修理〕工场。~ **snatcher** (为解剖等目的)盗尸的人;〔军俚〕担架兵。~ **stocking** 紧身衣(裤)。~**suit** 女式紧身连衫裤。~ **track** 调车场的车轨。~ **type**【印】用以排印正文的铅字。~ **wave** (从震心向各方辐射的)震波。~ **wood** 无枝桠材。~ **work** 车[机、船]身制造。

boehm·ite [ˈbeimait; ˋbemaɪt] ***n.***【矿】勃姆石;薄水铝矿。

Boe·o·tian [biˈəuʃjən; bɪˋoʃən] **I** ***a.*** 粗野的;愚钝的。**II** ***n.*** 粗野的人;愚钝的人。

Boer [bəuə; bor] **I** ***n.*** 布尔人〔南非荷兰人后裔〕。**II** ***a.*** 布尔人的。

boeuf bour·gui·gnon [bif buːgiːˈnjəun; bɪf bugiˋnjon]〔F.〕勃艮第牛肉丁〔牛肉丁加洋葱、蘑菇在红酒中煮沸〕。

boff [bɔf; baf] ***n.***〔俚〕**1.** 尽情的大笑,狂笑;引起大笑的情节。**2.** (戏剧、电影、歌曲等)空前成功的表演。

bof·fin [ˈbɔfin; ˋbafɪn] ***n.***〔英俚〕科学技术人员,科研工作者。

bof·fo [ˈbɔfəu; ˋbafo] **I** ***a.***〔俚〕受人欢迎的,很得人心的;非常成功的。**II** ***n.***〔俚〕尽情大笑。

bof·fo·la [bəˈfəulə; bəˋfolə] ***n.*** = boff 2.

Bo·fors [ˈbəufɔːz; ˋboforz] (**gun**) ***n.***【军】**1.** 博福斯式高射炮〔口径为 40 厘米的自动高射炮〕。**2.** 二弹连发高射炮。

bog [bɔg; bag] **I** ***n.*** **1.** 泥炭地,泥塘,沼泽。**2.** 潮湿地带,沼泽地带。**3.**〔常 *pl.*〕〔英口〕户外厕所。**II** ***vi.***, ***vt.*** (**-gg-**) (使)陷入沼泽,(使)沉入泥中(*down*)。~ ***down*** 阻碍;(使)陷入困境,(使)不能活动(*Things have ~ged down*. 事情已陷于停顿。*We were ~ged down by overwork*. 过分繁重的工作已经使我们陷入困境)。~ **bean** 睡菜(= buckbean)。~ **berry** 酸果蔓属植物。~ **brother**〔蔑〕爱尔兰人。~ **butter**【矿】沼油。~ **head** 藻煤,烟煤。~**-house**〔俚〕厕所。~ **iron** [**ore**] 沼铁,沼铁矿。~**-land**〔谑〕爱尔兰〔别名,因该地多沼泽〕。~ **oak** 泥炭中的黑橡。~ **wood** (泥炭地中的)埋木。

bo·gen·fah·ren [ˈbəugənfaːrən; ˋbogənfarən] ***n.***〔G.〕【滑雪】制动滑降。

bo·gey [ˈbəugi; ˋbogɪ] ***n.*** **1.** 妖怪,妖魔;可怕的人;可怕的东西;【军】可疑的飞机;〔美俚〕不明飞行物(= UFO)。**2.** 坦克负重轮;【高尔夫球】每穴击球分数;比赛的标准分数。~ **man** (讲出来吓唬孩子的)妖怪;可怕的东西。

bog·gle[1] [ˈbɔgl; ˋbagl̩] ***n.*** = bogle.

bog·gle[2] [ˈbɔgl; ˋbagl̩] **I** ***vi.*** **1.** (马等)惊跳。**2.** 犹豫,踌躇,退缩(*at*; *about*)。**3.** 装糊涂,搪塞(*at*)。**4.** 乱搞,胡乱地干。— ***vt.*** **1.** 搞坏(事情等)。**2.**〔英口〕使吃惊。**II** ***n.*** **1.** (马的)惊跳;吃惊。**2.** 犹豫;退缩。**3.** 搪塞。**4.** 胡乱干的工作。

bog·gy [ˈbɔgi; ˋbagɪ] ***a.*** **1.** 沼泽多的;沼泽状态的。**2.** 潮湿的。**-gi·ness** ***n.***

bo·gie [ˈbəugi; ˋbogɪ] ***n.*** **1.** = bogy. **2.**【铁路】转向架。**3.**〔美空军俚〕来路不明的飞机。**4.**〔英口〕(运石料等的)低座四轮卡车。

bo·gle [ˈbəugl; ˋbogl̩] ***n.*** 妖怪。

Bo·gor [ˈbəugɔː; ˋbogor] ***n.*** 茂物〔印度尼西亚城市〕。

Bo·go·ta [ˌbəugəˈtaː; ˏbogəˋta] ***n.*** 波哥大〔哥伦比亚首都〕。

bog·trot·ter [ˈbɔgtrɔtə; ˋbagtratɚ] ***n.*** **1.** 住在沼泽地带的人。**2.** = bog brother.

bo·gus [ˈbəugəs; ˋbogəs] **I** ***a.***〔美〕伪造的,假的。**II** ***n.*** 赝品,伪物。~ **certificate** 伪造的证件。~ **company** (骗人的)空头商行。~ **money** 伪币。~ **regime** 伪政权(组织)。

bo·gy(-man) [ˈbəugi(mæn); ˋbogɪ(mæn)] ***n.*** = bogey.

boh [bəu; bo] ***int.*** = bo.

Boh. = Bohemia; Bohemian.

bo·hea [bəuˈhiː; boˋhi] ***n.*** 武夷茶。

Bo·he·mi·a [bəuˈhiːmjə; boˋhimɪə] ***n.*** **1.** 波希米亚〔吉卜赛人最多的捷克斯洛伐克西部地区〕。**2.** 波希米亚式群落,放荡不羁的文化人〔主要指颓废派的文化人〕。

Bo·he·mi·an [bəuˈhiːmjən; boˋhimɪən] **I** ***a.*** **1.** 波希米

亚的;波希米亚语的。2. 流浪的,漂泊的。3. 放浪的,放荡不羁的,豪放的。II n. 1. 波希米亚人;波希米亚语。2. 流浪者;吉卜赛人。3. 放荡不羁的人〔尤指狂放的艺术家〕。-ism n. 放纵主义,放荡不羁;放荡生活。

Boho [bəu'həu; bo`ho] a. 波希米亚式的;颓废派文化人的,放荡不羁的。

Bohr [bɔr; bɔr], **Niels Henrik David** 玻耳〔1885-1962,丹麦物理学家,获 1922 年诺贝尔物理奖金〕。

boh·rium ['bəuəriəm; `boərɪəm] n.【化】铍〔第 107 号元素〕。

bo·hunk [bəu'hʌŋk; bo`hʌŋk] n.〔美俚〕外国劳工〔尤指从中欧移民来的工人〕。

boil[1] [bɔil; bɔɪl] I vi. 1. 沸腾,达到沸点,开,滚,煮滚;汽化。2. 激昂,奋激,鼎沸;汹涌。3. 被熬浓;可以压缩。*He ~s [is ~ing] with rage*. 他勃然大怒。*The sea ~ed in the storm*. 暴风雨中,大海波涛汹涌。~ ***down to*** (被)归结起来是…;(审判等到最后)表明 (*I suppose it all ~s down to this*. 我看归结起来可以这样说)。~ ***forth*** 口沫四溅地说。~ ***out*** 煮沸;试验。~ ***over*** 1. 沸溢。2. 发怒。~ ***up*** 煮滚,烧开。~***ing hot*** 沸腾;〔口〕酷热。***keep the pot ~ing*** 糊口,维持生活;维持市面。— vt. 1. 煮,使沸腾;使激动。2. 熬制(盐、糖等)。~ *eggs* 煮蛋。~ *the salt off the water* 熬盐。~ ***away*** 煮干。~ ***down*** 熬稠;煮干。~ ***sth. down to*** 把(文章等)压缩成;把(内容等)归结为。~ ***off*** 煮去,使脱胶,退浆。II n. 煮沸;沸腾。***be on [at] the ~*** 煮着,正在沸腾。***bring to the ~*** 使沸腾,烧滚。~ **off** n. 蒸发损耗。

boil[2] [bɔil; bɔɪl] n.【医】疡肿,脓肿;〔pl.〕疔,疖子。*a blind ~* 无脓[脓未出头的]疮。~ **smut** (玉米)黑粉病。

boiled [bɔild; bɔɪld] a. 1. 煮沸的,烧滚的。2. 〔美俚〕喝醉的。~ *eggs* 煮熟的蛋。*as an owl*〔美俚〕喝得烂醉的。~ **dinner**〔美〕配上蔬菜的煮肉。~ **linen** 脱胶亚麻布,精练亚麻布。~ **oil** 熟炼油〔尤指熟炼胡麻子油〕。~ **owl**〔美俚〕喝醉的人。~ **rag**〔美俚〕刚洗好的衬衫。~ **rice** 饭。~ **shirt**〔美俚〕硬胸衬衫;架子十足的家伙,不易亲近的人。~ **sweet**〔英〕硬糖果 (= hard candy)。

boil·er ['bɔilə; `bɔɪlɚ] n. 1. 煮器(壶、锅等);熬煮东西的人。2. 汽锅,锅炉;〔美俚〕酒类干馏器。3. 〔俚〕导弹。*a once through ~* 直流锅炉。***burst one's ~***〔美〕悲伤。~ **iron** 锅炉钢板。~ **maker** 1. 锅炉修理工。2. 〔口〕啤酒掺威士忌。~ **plate** (做锅炉用的)钢板;〔美〕做成纸型送来的新闻稿。~ **protector** 锅炉套。~ **room** 锅炉房;〔口〕(证券经纪人专靠电话买卖的)营业室。~ **scale** 锅垢。~ **suit**〔英〕外衣,罩衣;连衫裤工作服。

boil·ing ['bɔiliŋ; `bɔɪlɪŋ] I a. 1. 沸腾的;汹涌的。2. 激昂的。II ad. 非常,达到沸腾程度地。~ ***hot***〔口〕酷热 (*a ~ hot day* 要命的大热天)。***at the ~ point*** 大怒。III n. 1. 煮沸;沸腾,滚。2. 一次烹煮量[物]。3. 〔俚〕一群;全体。***the whole ~***〔俚〕全体。~**-point** 1.【物】沸点。2. 极度兴奋;激昂。~ **stone** 放在沸水里以阻止水涌出的小石。~ **water**〔美俚〕麻烦事,乱子。

Boi·se ['bɔisi; `bɔɪsɪ] n. 博伊西〔美国爱达荷州的首府〕。

bois·ter·ous ['bɔistərəs; `bɔɪstərəs] a. 1. 狂暴的,狂风暴雨的。2. 喧闹的,吵吵闹闹的,骚嚷的。*the ~ entertainment area* 喧闹的娱乐区。*a ~ wind* 狂风。**-ly** ad. **-ness** n.

boîte [bwɑt; bwɑt] n.〔F.〕小夜总会,宵夜酒店,小酒馆;酒楼。

bo·ko ['bəukəu; `boko] n.〔俚〕头,脑袋;鼻。

bo·koo ['bəuku:; `boku] a., ad.〔美口〕很多;非常〔法语 *beaucoup* 的别字〕。~ ***soused*** [sauzd; sauzd]〔美口〕大醉。

Bol. = Bolivia.

bo·la ['bəulə; `bolə] n. 套牛绳球〔长绳或皮条末端系有重球体物,作驱赶和套牛用〕(= bolas)。

bold [bəuld; bold] a. 1. 大胆的,果敢的。2. 不客气的,卤莽的,冒失的。3. 狂放的,富有想像力的,雄浑的;显眼的,突出的。4. 陡峭的,险峻的。5.【海】水深足够大船直接靠岸的。6.【印】用黑体铅字排的。*a ~ handwriting* 粗笔划的字,笔法雄浑。*a ~ mathematician* 思路开阔的数学家。~ *lines* 粗浅。*a ~ cliff* 悬崖绝壁。***in ~ relief*** 轮廓鲜明地浮出。***in ~ strokes*** (写字得)粗大。***make [be] (so) bold (as) to (do)*** 冒昧,敢,擅自,恕…无礼 (*I make ~ to give you my opinion*. 不揣冒昧贡献您一点意见)。***put a ~ face on*** (*the matter*) 对…假装不在乎。~ **face** 1. n.【印】黑体,粗体。2. vt. 把…印成黑体。~**-faced** a. 1. 厚颜无耻的,冒失的。2. 卤莽的。3.【印】黑体的,粗体的。**-ly** ad. 1. 大胆地;冒失地,卤莽地。2. 显然,醒目地,显著地。3. 粗,黑体。**-ness** n. 大胆,勇敢;冒失;厚脸皮;狂放,显著。

bole[1] [bəul; bol] n.【植】树干,干材。

bole[2] [bəul; bol] n. 1.【地】红玄武土,胶块土。2. 红褐色颜料。

bo·lec·tion [bəu'lekʃən; bo`lɛkʃən] n.【建】凸出嵌线。

bo·le·ro [bə'lɛərəu; bo`lɛro] n. (pl. ~s)〔Sp.〕1. 波莱罗舞(曲)。2. ['bɔlərəu; `bɔlero] (妇女)波莱罗短上衣。

bo·le·tus [bə'li:təs; bə`litəs] n.【植】牛肝菌属菌类。

Bol·eyn ['bulin; `bulɪn] n. 博林〔姓氏〕。

bo·lide ['bəulaid; `bolaɪd] n.【天】火流星,爆发流星,火球。

Bol·ing·broke ['bɔliŋbruk; `bɑlɪŋbrʊk] n. 博灵布鲁克〔姓氏〕。

Bol·i·var [bɔ'li:vɑ:, bɔ'libɑr; bə`livɑr, bə`lɪbɑr] n. 博利瓦〔姓氏〕。

Bo·liv·i·a [bə'liviə; bə`lɪvɪə] n. 玻利维亚〔拉丁美洲〕。

Bo·liv·i·an [bə'liviən; bə`lɪvɪən] I a. 1. 玻利维亚的。2. 玻利维亚人的。II n. 玻利维亚人。

boll [bəul; bol] n. (棉、亚麻等的)圆荚,珠蒴。~ **rot** 铃腐病。~ **stainer** 棉椿象,污棉虫。(**pink**) ~ **worm** (棉)红铃虫。

bol·lard ['bɔləd; `bɑlɚd] n. 1.【海】系缆柱,双系柱。2. 〔英〕(保护花坛等的)矮栏;(行人安全岛的)护柱。

bol·lix ['bɔliks; `bɑlɪks] I vt. 〔俚〕弄糟,做坏;笨手笨脚地弄坏〔常与 up 连用〕。*His interference ~ed up the whole deal*. 他的插手把全部事情都弄糟了。II n. 乱糟糟的一团。

bolo[1] ['bəuləu; `bolo] n. (菲律宾人用的)大砍刀。

bolo[2] ['bəuləu; `bolo] I n.〔美陆军俚〕枪法还不合格的士兵。II vi. 枪法还不够格。

Bo·lo·gna [bə'ləunjə; bə`lonjə] n. 1. 波洛尼亚〔意大利城市〕。2. 〔b-〕大红肠〔意大利波洛尼亚大香肠〕(= ~ sausage)。

bo·lo·graph ['bəuləgrɑ:f; `boləˌgræf] n.【物】1. 测辐射热仪。2. 测辐射热仪的记录。

bo·lom·e·ter [bəu'lɔmitə; bo`lɑmətɚ] n. = bolograph 1.

bo·lo·ney [bə'ləuni; bə`lonɪ] I n.〔美俚〕敷衍话;瞎扯。II int.〔美口〕瞎扯! 胡说!

Bol·she·vik ['bɔlʃəvik; `bɑlʃəvɪk] I n. (pl. ~s, ***Bolsheviki*** ['bɔlʃiviki; `bɑlʃɪvɪkɪ]) 布尔什维克。II a. 布尔什维克的,布尔什维主义的。

Bol·she·vism, bol·she·vism ['bɔlʃəvizəm; `bɑlʃəvɪzəm] n. 布尔什维主义。

Bol·she·vist, bol·she·vist ['bɔlʃəvist; `bɑlʃəvɪst] I n. 布尔什维主义者。II a. 布尔什维克的。

Bol·shie, Bol·shy ['bɔlʃi; `bɑlʃɪ] n., a.〔俚〕= Bolshevik.

bol·son ['bəulsən; `bolsən] n. 沙漠盆地,干湖地。

Bol·so·ver ['bɔlsəvə; `bɑlsəvɚ] n. 博尔索弗〔姓氏〕。

bol·ster ['bəulstə; `bolstɚ] I n. 1. 枕垫,长枕;枕状支持物〔枕梁、承板等〕。2.【机】软垫,垫木,枕;(车辆的)枕梁;【纺】(纺机的)锭管,锭脚;【建】承枕,托木;横撑。II vt. 1. (用支持物)支撑,垫。2. 援助,帮助;费力支持

(*up*);增强。*They* ~ *ed their morale by singing*. 他们用唱歌来鼓舞士气。

bolt[1][bəult; bolt] **I** ***n*.** **1.** 螺钉,螺栓。**2.** (门窗等的)插销;闩,锁簧。**3.** 箭,矢;弩箭;【军】枪机,枪栓。**4.** 电光,闪电。**5.** (水等的)喷射。**6.** (马等的)脱缰;跑掉,逃走,逃亡;缺课;〔美〕脱党,变节。**7.** (棉布等的)一匹;(纸等的)一卷。**8.** 短(木)材。*a* ~ *and nut* 螺栓与螺母。*He has shot his last* ~. 他已作出最后努力[弹尽矢绝]。*stud* ~柱[双头]螺栓。*anchor* ~ 地脚螺栓。*a thunder* ~ 雷电,霹雳。*a* ~ *of linen* 一匹亚麻布。***a*** ~ ***from the blue*** 晴天霹雳;祸从天降,意外事件。***A fool's*** ~ ***is soon shot*.** **1.** 蠢兵乱射箭,箭筒很快空;愚者易于智穷力竭。**2.** 愚者喜挥霍,很难存下钱。***do a*** ~〔俚〕逃出。***make a*** ~ ***of it*** = ***make one's*** ~〔俚〕逃走。***shoot one's*** ~ 竭尽最大努力,使出浑身解数,尽其所能。**II** ***vi*.** **1.** 射出,窜出,冲出,跳出,(马等的)脱缰;逃走,逃亡;〔美俚〕缺课。**2.**〔美〕拒绝支持本党政策[提名等],脱党,退出团体,变节。**3.** 狼吞虎咽。~ *off to catch the train* 飞跑去赶火车。~ *into* 窜入。— ***vt*.** **1.** 给(门窗等)上插销,闩(门);(用螺栓等)栓住。**2.** 发射(矢、石等)。**3.** 囫囵吞下,仓促咽下。**4.**〔美〕拒绝支持(本党的政策等);退出(党派、团体等)。**5.** 脱口说出 (*out*)。**6.** 把(纸等)卷成一卷。~ *a political party* 脱离某政党。~ *one's breakfast* 三口两口地吃完早饭。~ (***sb*.**) ***in*** 把(某人)关在屋内。~ (***sb*.**) ***out*** 把(某人)关在门外。**III** ***ad*.** 像箭似地,突然。~ ***upright*** 僵直,笔直 (*sit* ~ *upright* 坐得笔直,僵直地坐着)。~**-action** ***a*.** (步枪)有用手操作的枪机的。~ **boat** 适于在波涛汹涌的海上航行的船。~**-head** **1.** 螺栓头。**2.** 长颈烧瓶。**3.** (枪)机头。~**-hole** (动物的)避难穴;〔喻〕安全藏匿所,狡兔三窟。~**-on** ***a*.** (设计得)可上栓锁的。~**-rope**【海】(帆的)栓索,缝在帆边的粗绳。

bolt[2], **boult** [bəult; bolt] **I** ***n*.** 筛子。**II** ***vt*.** **1.** 筛。**2.** 淘汰;筛选。**3.**〔古〕细查。~ ***to the bran*** 筛到糠麸;精细查勘。~**ing cloth** 作筛眼用的麻布[纺织品]。

bolt·er[1][ˈbəultə; ˋboltɚ] ***n*.** **1.** (经常)脱缰的马。**2.** 跑开者;逃亡者,出走者。**3.**〔美〕脱党者,变节者,背叛者。

bolt·er[2][ˈbəultə; ˋboltɚ] ***n*.** **1.** 筛子;筛选机。**2.** 机筛工人。

bol·to·ni·a [bəulˈtəuniə, -jə; bolˋtonɪə, -jə] ***n*.**【植】波菊属植物。

bo·lus [ˈbəuləs; ˋboləs] ***n*.** **1.**【药】(给牛马服用的)大丸药。**2.** (嚼过的)食物团。

bomb [bɔm; bɑm] **I** ***n*.** **1.**【军】弹,炸弹。**2.**【地】火山弹〔火山喷出的球状熔岩〕。**3.**【医】(用于治疗的)放射源;高压弹〔高压气体容器〕;(储藏放射性物质的)铅容器〔如钴炮等〕。**4.** 惊人事件,(耸人听闻的)"炸弹"宣言;〔美俚〕(演出)大失败。**5.**〔美俚〕蛋;(足球)长传;(篮球)远投。**6.**〔the ~〕〔总称〕原子弹,原子武器;核武器。**7.**〔美俚〕加有麻醉毒品的香烟。*an aerosol* ~ 烟幕弹。*a flare* ~ 照明弹。*a depth* ~ 深水炸弹。*incendiary* ~ 燃烧弹。*a time* ~ 定时炸弹。*an atomic* ~ 原子弹。*a hydrogen* ~ [*H* ~] 氢弹。*a guided* [*controlled*] ~ 导弹。*a rocket* ~ 火箭导弹,弹道导弹。*a hung* ~ 挂弹〔发生故障未能投出的炸弹〕。**II** ***vt*.** **1.** 向…投炸弹,轰炸。**2.** 以巨大优势[比分等]压倒(对手)。— ***vi*.** **1.** 投弹。**2.**〔美俚〕惨败。~(***s***) ***away*** 投弹完毕。~ ***out*** **1.** 炸毁;被轰炸得由家里逃出。**2.**〔美俚〕惨败。~ ***up*** 给(飞机)装上炸弹。~ **bay** (轰炸机的)炸弹舱。~ **carrier** **1.** 轰炸机。**2.** 炸弹架。~ **cluster** 集束炸弹,集束燃烧弹。~ **damage**【军】轰炸效果。~**-disposal** 未爆弹处理。~**-dropping**【空】投弹。~**gas** 钢瓶[瓶装]气体。~**gear** 投弹器。~**-hatch**【空】(飞机上的)投弹门。~ **line** (空中地图上划开敌我阵地的)轰炸分界线。~**load** 载弹量。~**proof** **1.** ***a*.** 避弹的,防弹的。**2.** ***n*.**【军】防空洞,避弹房。**3.** ***vt*.** 使有防弹能力。~ **rack** (轰炸机上的)炸弹架。~**-release**【空】投弹器;投弹。~ **run** (自看到目标至投下炸弹之间的)轰炸航程。~**shell** **1.** 炸弹;炮弹。**2.** 爆炸性事件,突然轰动视听的事件[人物] (*a regular* ~*-shell* 大骚动,大惊吓)。~ **shelter** 防空洞。~ **sight**【空】轰炸瞄准器。~**site** 炸后遗迹[废墟]。~ **sniffer** 炸弹嗅探器。~ **thrower** 掷弹手;炸弹发射炮;掷弹筒。

bomb. = bombardment.

bom·bard[1] [ˈbɔmbɑːd; ˋbɑmbɑrd] ***n*.** 射石炮〔古时的臼炮〕。

bom·bard[2] [bɔmˈbɑːd; bɑmˋbɑrd] ***vt*.** **1.** 炮击;轰炸。**2.**【原】(以中子等)轰击;对…进行粒子辐射。**3.** 痛骂,攻击,痛斥,(连珠炮似地)质问。~ *a necleus* 轰击原子核。~ *sb*. *with questions* [*letters*] 像连珠炮似地对(某人)提出问题[信件像雪片一样地向(某人)飞来]。

bom·bar·dier [ˌbɔmbəˈdiə; ˏbɑmbɚˋdɪr] ***n*.** 炮击者;〔美〕轰炸员,投弹手;【史】炮手;〔英〕炮兵伍长。~ **beetle** 放屁虫〔一种受惊后即放出难闻气体的甲虫〕。

bom·bard·ment [bɔmˈbɑːdmənt; bɑmˋbɑrdmənt] ***n*.** **1.** 炮击;轰炸,轰击。**2.** 痛斥,连珠炮似的提问。

bom·bar·don [bɔmˈbɑːdn; ˋbɑmˋbɑrdən] ***n*.** **1.**【乐】低音大号。**2.**【乐】(风琴的)簧舌塞子。

bom·ba·sine [ˈbɔmbəziːn; ˏbɑmbəˋzin] = bombazine.

bom·bast [ˈbɔmbæst; ˋbɑmbæst] **I** ***n*.** 夸大其词的话[文章],豪言壮语。**II** ***a*.** 夸大的。

bom·bas·tic [bɔmˈbæstik; bɑmˋbæstɪk] ***a*.** 夸大的,夸张的,过甚其词的,夸夸其谈的。**-ti·cal** ***a*.** **-al·ly** ***ad*.**

bom·bax [ˈbɔmbæks; ˋbɑmbæks] ***a*.**【植】木棉科植物的。

Bom·bay [bɔmˈbei; bɑmˋbe] ***n*.** 孟买〔印度港口城市〕。~ **duck** 咸鱼。

bom·ba·zine [ˈbɔmbəziːn, ˈbɔmbəˌziːn; ˏbɑmbəˋzin, ˋbɑmbəˏzin] ***n*.** 邦巴辛毛葛,丝经毛纬,细斜纹。

bom·bé [bəumˈbei; bomˋbe] ***a*.**〔F.〕(家具)突起的,隆起的。*a* ~ *china cabinet* 圆肚瓷器柜。

bombe [bəumb; bomb] ***n*.**〔F.〕邦布冰果〔鸡蛋加糖等做成的冷冻点心〕。

bombed [bɔmd; bɑmd] ***a*.** **1.** 遭到轰炸[轰击]的。**2.**〔俚〕喝醉了酒的;吸毒麻醉了的。~**-out** ***a*.** **1.** 被炸毁的。**2.** 被炸得无家可归的。

bom·bee [bɔmˈiː; bɑmˋi] ***n*.** 被轰炸的人。

bomb·er [ˈbɔmə; ˋbɑmɚ] ***n*.** **1.** 投弹手。**2.**〔现今特指〕轰炸机。*a guided* ~ 导航[无人驾驶]轰炸机,可操纵飞航导弹。*a jet* ~ 喷气式轰炸机。*attack* [*dive*] ~ 攻击[俯冲]轰炸机。*heavy* [*light*] ~ 重[轻]型轰炸机。~ **escort** 掩护轰炸机的战斗机(群)。

bom·bi·nate [ˈbɔmbiˌneit; ˋbɑmbəˏnet] ***vi*.** (苍蝇似地)嗡鸣。**-nation** [ˌbɔmbiˈneiʃən; ˏbɑmbəˋneʃən] ***n*.**

bomb·ing [ˈbɔmiŋ; ˋbɑmɪŋ] ***n*.** 轰炸,投弹。~ **plane** 轰炸机。~ **run** 轰炸航程。~ **sight** 轰炸瞄准器。

bomb·let [ˈbɔmlit; ˋbɑmlɪt] ***n*.** 小型炸弹。

bom·by·cid [ˈbɔmbisid; ˋbɑmbɪsɪd] ***n*.**【动】蚕蛾。

bon [bɔ̃n, F. bɔ̃; bɑn, bɔ̃] ***a*.**〔F.〕= good. ~ ***ami*** [F. bɔ̃aˈmi; F. bɔ̃aˋmɪ] 男朋友;情人。~ ***jour*** [bɔ̃ˈʒuːr; bɔ̃ˋʒur] 您好! 早安! 日安! ~ ***mot*** [bɔ̃ˈmou; bɔ̃ˋmo] (*pl*. ***bons mots***) 警句,妙语,名言。~ ***sens*** [bɔ̃sɛ̃; bɔ̃sɛ̃] 良知。~ ***soir*** [bɔ̃swɑːr; bɔ̃swɑr] 晚安! ~ ***ton*** [bɔ̃ˈtɔ̃ːŋ; bɔ̃ˋtɔ̃ŋ] 优雅;礼让;时髦;上流社会。~ ***vivant*** [bɔ̃ˈviːvaŋ; bɔ̃ˋvivaŋ] (*pl*. ***bons vivants***) 考究饮食的人。~ ***voyage*** [bɔ̃vwajˈɑːʒ; bɔ̃vwajˋɑʒ]一路平安!

bo·na [ˈbəunə; ˋbonə] ***a*.**〔L.〕= good. ~ ***fide*** [ˈfaidi; ˋfaɪdɪ] 真正的,真实的,善意的,照实,真诚地,以诚意。~ ***fides*** [ˈfaidiːz; ˋfaɪdiz] 真实,诚意。

bo·nan·za [bəuˈnænzə; boˋnænzə] ***n*.** **1.**【地】富矿脉。**2.**〔口〕发财,走鸿运;富源,使人致富(走运)的东西。*a* ~ *business* 兴旺的事业。*a* ~ *year* 大丰年。*a* ~ *farm* 兴旺的大农场。***B- State*** ~ 美国 Montana 州的别名。***in*** ~ = ***strike a*** ~ **1.** 找到富矿脉。**2.** 大走鸿

运。

Bo·na·parte [ˈbəunəpaːt; ˋbonə͵part] ***n*.** 波拿巴〔法国科西嘉岛上的家族〕。**Napoleon** ～ 拿破仑·波拿巴〔1769—1821,法国皇帝〕。

Bo·na·part·ism [ˈbəunəpaːtizəm; ˋbonə͵partɪzm̩] ***n*.** 【法史】波拿巴主义。**-ist** ***n*.**【法史】波拿巴主义者。

bon·bon [ˈbɔnbɔn; ˋban͵ban] ***n*.** 〔F.〕糖果;夹心糖。

bon·bon·nière [F. bɔnbɔnjɛːə; bɔbɔˋnjɛr] ***n*.** 〔F.〕糖果店;糖果盒子。

bond[1] [bɔnd; band] **I** ***n*. 1.** 结合(物),结合力,黏合(剂),联结。**2.** 束缚,羁绊;〔*pl*.〕拘束;镣,铐。**3.** 契约,契约义务,盟约;同盟,联盟。**4.** 证券,公债,债券;借据;证券纸;(付款)保证书;保证人;【商】海关扣存(待完税)。**5.**【化】键;【电】耦合,固定;连结器,接头;【头】砌合;(砖等的)砌式;【铁路】轨条接线;【机】焊接。*the ～s of friendship* [*matrimony*] 友谊[婚姻]的纽带。*the ～ between nations* 国家间的同盟。*His word is as good as his ～.* 他的话是极可靠的[像契约一样可靠]。*My word is my ～.* 我是讲信用的。*a cross ～*【电】交叉扎线。*treasury ～s* 国库债券。*government ～s* 公债。*war ～* 国防公债。*brick ～* 砌砖法。*ionic ～*【化】离子键。*steel ～* 铁粉结合器。*rail ～* 导轨夹紧器。***break*** [***sever***] ***a*** ～ 废除[中断]契约。***break the ～ of*** (*convention*) 打破(成规)的束缚。***call a*** ～ 收兑(债券)。***consolidated*** ～ (英国发行的)统一公债。***enter into a*** ～ (***with***) (与…)订约。***give*** ～ ***for*** [***to do sth*.**] 为…作担保[担保做某事]。(***goods***) ***in*** ～ (货物被海关)扣存关栈以待完税。***in*** ～***s*** 被束缚着;被奴役;在拘留中。***take*** (***the goods***) ***out of*** ～ (完税后)提出被海关扣存的(货物)。**II** ***vt*. 1.** 以证券为(债务等)作保证抵押。**2.** 把(进口货)存入关栈以待完税。**3.**【建】砌合(砖);黏着(水泥等);【化】以化学键使结合在分子[结晶体]内。**4.** 使订契约。～**holder** 债券持有者。～**paper** 证券纸〔一种上等道林纸,用以印制证券、钞票、商业文书等〕。～ **servent** 奴隶;被奴役的人。～ **stone**【建】束石。**B- Street** 证券街〔伦敦最繁华的一条街,有很多高级商店〕。**-er** ***n*. 1.**【无】联接器,结合器。**2.** 发债券者。**3.** 将货物存入关栈者。**4.**【建】束石。**-ing** ***n*. 1.** 黏合工艺;搭接。**2.**【电】屏蔽接地;压焊。

bond[2] [bɔnd; band] **I** ***n*.** 〔废〕农奴;奴隶。**II** ***a*.** 被奴役的;奴隶的〔多用作复合词,如 ～ *maid* 女奴, ～(*s*) *man* 奴隶,农奴, ～ *woman* 女奴,等〕。

bond·age [ˈbɔndidʒ; ˋbandɪdʒ] ***n*. 1.** 奴隶处境,奴役,劳役。**2.** 束缚;监禁;屈从。**3.** (英国古代的)农奴租地法。*in ～ to* 被…奴役。*hold sb. in ～* 使某人被奴役[束缚、监禁]。

bond·ed [ˈbɔndid; ˋbandɪd] ***a*. 1.** 有债券作保证的;有抵押的,有担保的。**2.** (货物)存入[关栈]待完税的。**3.** (织物)多层黏合的;【化】化合的,结合的。～ **debt** 公债借款。～ **goods** [**merchandise**] 存关待完税货物。～ **store** =〔美〕～ **warehouse** (海关扣存待完税货物的)关栈。～ **whisky** 陈年威士忌酒。

bonds·man [ˈbɔndzmən; ˋbandzmən] ***n*. 1.** 奴隶,农奴(= bondman)。**2.**【法】保证人,保人。

bonds·wo·man [ˈbɔndzwumən; ˋbandzwumən] ***n*. 1.** 女奴(= bond-woman)。**2.**【法】女保证人。

bon·duc [bɔnˌdʌk; ˋban͵dʌk] ***n*.**【植】加拿大皂荚。

bone [bəun; bon] **I** ***n*. 1.** 骨(头);骨状物[象牙等];骨制品;(食用的)肉骨头。**2.** 〔*pl*.〕遗骸,尸体;骨骼;身体。**3.** 〔*pl*.〕〔口〕骰子;【乐】响板;(乐队)打拍员;(妇女)胸衣张骨。**4.**【矿】黑矸子。**5.** 〔美俚〕一块钱;用功的学生。**6.** 〔*pl*.〕〔口〕外科医生。**7.** 争端。*the pubic ～* 耻骨。*a ham ～* 火腿。*His ～s are massive.* 他骨骼粗大。*my old ～s* 我这把老骨头。*His ～s was laid in Westminster.* 他的遗骸安放在威斯敏斯特大教堂。***be upon the ～s of*** 攻击。～ ***in her teeth***【海】船头浪。～ ***of contention*** 争执的原因[题目],争端。～ ***of one's*** ～ (= *flesh of one's flesh*) 关系非常密切[亲密]的。～ ***top*** 〔美俚〕笨人。***bred in the*** ～ 生来的,改不了的。***carry a*** ～ ***in the mouth*** [***teeth***]【海】(船)破浪前进。***cast*** (***in***) ***a*** ～ ***between*** 使…之间起争端,离间。***cut to the*** ～ 根除;削减。***feel*** [***believe, know, think***] ***in one's*** ～***s*** 深知,深深感觉到,确信。***get into sb.'s*** ～***s*** 迷住。***have a*** ～ ***in one's throat*** [***leg***] 难于启齿[行动]。***have a*** ～ ***to pick with sb*.** 对某人有怨言,要与某人争论。***horse with plenty of*** ～ 骨骼[身段]良好的马。***in one's*** ～***s*** 天生的。***lay one's*** ～***s*** 死,埋葬。***make no*** ～***s of*** [***about, to*** (***do***)] 率直;对…毫不踌躇(*He makes no ～s about helping his wife with dishes.* 他毫不踌躇地帮助妻子洗碗碟)。***make old*** ～***s*** 〔用于否定句〕长寿(*I'm afraid he will never make old ～s.* 我看他活不长)。***No*** ～***s broken!*** 没有什么! 没事没事! ***point*** [***sing***] ***a*** ～ ***at sb*.** (澳洲土著居民)以符咒咒人遭灾[死、病等]。***roll the*** ～***s*** 吹牛、夸张;闲谈。***spare*** ～***s*** 不肯吃苦,懒。***the ten*** ～***s*** 十指。***to the*** ～ 彻骨,透骨,入骨;到极点,深,极端(*cut expenses to the ～* 把费用缩减到极限。*I'm tired to the ～.* 我累极了。*He worked his fingers to the ～.* 他拼命工作)。***without more*** ～***s*** 不再费力;立刻。**II** ***vt*. 1.** 去…的骨,剔掉…的骨。**2.** 用鲸骨撑大(妇女上衣等)。**3.** 施骨肥于。**4.** 〔俚〕盗,偷,抢去。**5.** 测量…的高度。～ *a turkey* 给火鸡剔骨。— ***vi*.** 〔美〕死用功,用苦功(*up*)。*She is boning up for her finals.* 她在拼命用功,准备大考。～ *up on Latin* 下苦功学拉丁语。～ **ash** 骨灰。～ **bed**【地】骨层。～ **bender** 〔美俚〕摔跤选手。～ **black** 骨炭〔一种漂白剂〕。～ **box** 〔美俚〕口,嘴。～ **china** 骨灰瓷〔一种含有骨灰的瓷器〕。～**-dry** ***a*. 1.** 十分干的,干透了的。**2.** 〔美俚〕绝对禁酒的。～ **dust** 骨粉。～ **eater** 〔美俚〕狗。～ **fish** 北梭鱼。～ **grace**【医】眼睑。～ **head** 〔美〕笨蛋,傻子;囚犯〔罪犯语〕= boner. ～ **idle,** ～**-lazy** ***a*.** 〔美俚〕懒透了的。～**less** ***a*. 1.** 无骨的。**2.** (文章等)无风骨的。～ **meal**【农】骨粉。～ **oil** 骨油。～ **orchard** 〔美俚〕墓地。～**-set 1.** ***vi*.** 接骨,正骨。**2.** ***n*.**【美植】贯叶泽兰,接骨草。～**-setter** 接骨者,正骨医生。～**setting** 接骨术。～**-shaker 1.** (早期)无橡皮轮胎的自行车。**2.** 〔俚〕破旧的车辆,颠散骨头的车。～ **top** 〔美俚〕笨人。～**-weary** ***a*.** 十分疲倦的。～**yard 1.** 〔美〕动物尸骨埋放地;废马屠杀场。**2.** 〔口〕墓地。**3.** 〔口〕废车、船存放地。

boned [bəund; bond] ***a*. 1.** 剔去骨头的。**2.** (女上衣等)撑上鲸骨的。**3.** 骨头…的〔用以组成复合词,如 *big-～* 骨头粗大的。*beautifully-～* 体型优美的等〕。**4.** 施过骨粉肥料的。～ *land* 施过骨粉肥料的土地。

bon·er [ˈbəunə; ˋbonɚ] ***n*.** 〔美俚〕(学生答卷里)可笑的错误;大错。

bon·fire [ˈbɔnˌfaiə; ˋban͵faɪr] ***n*.** 篝火,祝火,营火。***make a*** ～ ***of*** (*rubbish*) 烧掉(垃圾)。

bong [bɔŋ; baŋ] **I** ***n*.** (锣声)喤喤。**II** ***vi*.** 发喤喤声。

bon·go [ˈbɔŋgəu; ˋbaŋgo] ***n*.**【动】(非洲)大羚羊。

bon·ho·mie [ˈbɔnɔmiː; ˋbanami] ***n*.** 〔F.〕温和,和蔼;友好。**bon·ho·mous** [ˈbɔnɔməs; ˋbanaməs] ***a*.**

Bon·i·face [ˈbɔnifeis; ˋbanəfes] ***n*. 1.** 博尼费斯〔姓氏〕。**2.** 〔b-〕旅馆老板。

Bo·nin [ˈbəunin; ˋbonɪn] ***n*.** ～ **Islands** 小笠原群岛〔太平洋〕。

bon·i·ness [ˈbəuninis; ˋbonɪnɪs] ***n*.** 多骨,瘦骨嶙峋。

bon·ism [ˈbɔnizəm; ˋbanɪzm] ***n*.** (视现世为善,但尚未达到至善境地的)乐观主义,世善说(*opp*. malism)。

Bo·ni·ta [bəˈniːtə; bəˋnitə] ***n*.** 博妮塔〔女子名〕。

bo·ni·to [bəˈniːtəu; bəˋnito] ***n*.**【鱼】东方狐鲣。

bonk [ˈbɔŋk; ˋbaŋk] **I** ***vt*. 1.** 和…做爱。**2.** 敲打。— ***vi*.** 做爱。**II** ***n*.** 做爱。

bon·kers [ˈbɔŋkəz; ˋbaŋkɚz] ***a*.** 〔俚〕神经错乱的;疯狂的。

Bonn [bɔn; ban] 波昂〔德国城市〕。

B

bonne [bɔn; bɔn] **I** ***n.*** 〔F.〕女仆;保姆。**II** ***a.*** 好(= good)。～ ***amie*** [bɔn ˈæmi; bɔn ˋæmɪ] **1.** 亲密的女友。**2.** 爱人,情人。

bonne bouché [ˈbɔnˈbuːʃ; bɔnˋbuʃ] 〔F.〕(最后一口)美味;一小块好吃的东西〔糖果等〕。

bonne nuit [ˈbɔn ˈnwiː; ˋbɑn ˋnwi] 〔F.〕晚安。

Bon·ner [ˈbɔnə; ˋbɑnɚ] ***n.*** 邦纳〔姓氏〕。

bonnet [ˈbɔnit; ˋbɑnɪt] **I** ***n.*** **1.** (男用)无边苏格兰圆帽;(儿童或妇女戴的)有带户外软帽;(无边)矿工帽;(北美印地安人的)羽毛头饰。**2.** 帽状物;罩子;【机】阀帽,管帽,阀盖,烟囱帽;机罩;〔英〕汽车罩。**3.** 〔俚〕(赌场、拍卖场中的)囮子,合伙骗人者。～ ***laird*** 〔Scot.〕小地主。～ ***rouge*** [ˈbɔneˈruːʒ; ˋbɔneˋruʒ] 红帽子〔法国革命时革命派的标志〕;革命党员。***fill sb.'s*** ～ 取而代之;与人不相上下。***have a bee in one's*** ～ 发疯;心神不宁。***have a green*** ～ 生意失败。**II** ***vt.*** **1.** 给…戴帽子,给…加罩。**2.** 把(某人)帽子拉下遮掉眼睛。**3.** 〔俚〕合伙诱骗。— ***vi.*** 脱帽行礼。

Bon·nie [ˈbɔni; ˋbɑnɪ] ***n.*** 邦妮〔女子名〕。

bon·ny, bon·nie [ˈbɔni; ˋbɑnɪ] **I** ***a.*** 〔主 Scot.〕**1.** 美丽的。**2.** 健康的;强壮的;活泼的。**3.** 好的;(场所等)令人愉快的。**II** ***ad.*** 〔英方〕愉快;好。**III** ***n.*** 〔Scot.〕〔古〕美女。**bon·ni·ly** ***ad.***

bon·ny·clab·ber [ˈbɔniklæbə; ˋbɑnɪklæbɚ] ***n.*** 酸凝乳。

bon·sai [bɔnˈsai; bɑnˋsaɪ] ***n.*** 〔Jap.〕**1.** 盆景,盆栽植物。**2.** 盆景树木。

bon·spiel [ˈbɔnspiːl, -spəl; ˋbɑnspil, -spəl] ***n.*** 〔Scot.〕(两俱乐部或两城市之间举行的)冰上蹓石比赛。

bon·swar [bɔnˈswɑː; bɑnˋswɑr] ***int.*** 【美军】晚安〔法语的讹用〕。

bon·te·bok [ˈbɔntiˌbɔk; ˋbɑntɪˏbɑk] ***n.*** (*pl.* ～, ～*s*) 【动】南非羚羊。

bo·nus [ˈbəunəs; ˋbonəs] ***n.*** **1.** 奖金;额外津贴。**2.** 红利;额外股息。**3.** 退职金,退伍金;〔美〕出征奖金〔保险等〕。**4.** 〔口〕意外的礼物;(购货时另外给顾客的)奉送品。*Every purchaser of a pound of coffee received a box of cookies as a* ～. 每买一磅咖啡,奉送顾客一盒小甜饼。

bon·y [ˈbəuni; ˋbonɪ] ***a.*** **1.** 骨的,多骨的。**2.** 骨骼粗大的。**3.** 瘦的,憔悴的。*a* ～ *man* 骨骼粗大的人。～ *fingers* 瘦瘦的手指。

bonze [bɔnz; bɑnz] ***n.*** (中国、日本等的)和尚,僧。

bon·zer [ˈbɔnzə; ˋbɑnzɚ] ***a.*** 〔澳俚〕极好的,头等的。

boo[1] [buː; bu] **I** ***int.*** 呸〔表示厌恶、轻蔑等〕。***can't say*** ～ ***to a goose*** 非常胆小,怯懦。**II** ***vi.*** 发出"呸"的音。— ***vt.*** 对…发"呸"声(以示轻蔑等)。

boo[2] [buː; bu] ***n.*** 〔美俚〕大麻;粉蓝烟草。

boob [buːb; bub] **I** ***n.*** 〔美俚〕**1.** 笨蛋,蠢材。**2.** 大错误,大失策。**3.** 〔*pl.*〕(妇女的)乳房。**II** ***vi.*** 犯荒唐大错。～ **tube** **1.** 电视机;电视。**2.** 〔口〕(女人的)紧身胸衣。

boo-boo, boo·boo [ˈbuːbuː; ˋbubu] ***n.*** (*pl.* ～*s*) **1.** 〔俚〕愚蠢的错误;大错。**2.** 〔肌〕(皮肤的)微伤,擦伤,撞伤。

boo·by [ˈbuːbi; ˋbubɪ] ***n.*** **1.** 呆子,蠢材。**2.** 【鸟】鲣鸟。**3.** 得分最少的球队;演出最差的歌舞队。～ **hatch** **1.** 【海】(甲板上的)小舱口。**2.** 〔美俚〕精神病院。～ **mine** 〔军〕饵雷,诡雷。～ **prize** 末奖。～ **trap** **1.** "门顶陷阱"(置物于微开门上以惊打来人的恶作剧)。**2.** 【军】伪装地雷〔炸弹〕;陷阱,阴谋。～**-trap** ***vt.*** 在…设饵雷;在…设陷阱。

boo·by·ish [ˈbuːbiiʃ; ˋbubɪɪʃ] ***a.*** 呆,蠢。

boo·dle [ˈbuːdl; ˋbudl] ***n.*** **1.** 〔美俚〕大笔现款〔尤指政治上的贿赂〕。**2.** 不法利益;赃品;伪钞。**3.** 一群人,一套〔一堆〕东西。*the whole* (*kit and*) ～ 全部,全套。

boo·dler [ˈbuːdlə; ˋbudlɚ] ***n.*** 〔美俚〕受贿者,贪赃枉法的政界人士。

boog·a·loo [ˌbuːgəˈluː; ˏbugəˋlu] ***n.*** 波加洛舞〔一种两拍子节奏的摇摆舞〕。

boog·ie [ˈbu(ː)gi; ˋbʊgɪ] ***vi.*** (随着摇摆舞音乐节奏)摆动身体。～ **rock** 爵士摇摆乐。

boog·ie-woog·ie [ˈbu(ː)giˌwuːgi; ˋbʊgɪˋwʊgɪ] ***n.*** 低音连奏爵士乐〔爵士乐中的一种钢琴奏法〕。

booh [buː; bu] ***int.*** = boo.

boo·hoo [ˈbuːhuː; ˋbuhu] **I** ***vi.*** 哭闹。**II** ***n.*** [ˈbuːhuː; ˋbuhu] 哭闹,号哭。

book [buk; bʊk] **I** ***n.*** **1.** 书,书籍;著作;〔the B-〕基督教《圣经》。**2.** 〔常 *pl.*〕账簿;账册;名册。**3.** 卷,篇,册,本;(烟叶等的)一捆,包,把。**4.** (歌剧等的)歌词,脚本 **5.** 装订成册的车票〔支票等〕;(赛马赌博等的)赌注登记簿;电话号码簿。**6.** 〔美俚〕罪状的总和。**7.** 给人教益的东西;(从事某项工作的)全部知识〔经验〕;(历史等的)纪录。**8.** 〔the ～〕惯例,常规。～ *of time* 历史。～ *of reference* 参考书。*examine the* ～*s* 查账。*an account* ～ 账本。*an exercise* ～ 练习本。*The petrified tree was a* ～ *of nature.* 树木化石是大自然的历史记录。***a sealed*** ～ 天书;高深莫测的事。***according to an open*** ～ 人所共知的事物。***at one's*** ～***s*** 读书用功。***be written in the*** ～ ***of life*** 【宗】列入死后获救者名单。***bring*** (***sb.***) ***to*** ～ **1.** 诘问,盘问。**2.** 法办,判罪。***by*** (***the***) ～ **1.** 正式地;有根据地,正确地。**2.** 照章办事地;按照惯例。***close the*** ～***s*** **1.** 【会】结账,决算。**2.** 结束,终止。***come to the*** ～ 〔英口〕宣誓能做陪审员。***do*** [***get***] ***the*** ～ 〔美〕受最大处罚。***enter in the*** ～***s*** 把…记入账内。***hit the*** [***one's***] ～***s*** 〔美〕用功。***hold*** ～ 【剧】做提词人。***in one's*** ～ 根据自己的判断。***in sb.'s bad*** [***good***] ～***s*** 失〔得〕宠于某人,给某人留下不好〔良好〕的印象。***keep*** ～***s*** 上账,记账。***kiss the*** ～ 吻《圣经》宣誓。***know like a*** ～ 熟手,通晓。***like a*** ～ **1.** 一板一眼地,精确地。**2.** 正确地,彻底地。***make*** ～ **1.** 打赌;(赛马等)接受不同数目的赌注。**2.** 以接受打赌为业(*make* ～ *on it that* ... 就…打赌)。***off the*** ～***s*** 除名,退会。***on the*** ～***s*** 列名簿上,做会员。***one for the*** ～***s*** 〔口〕意外事,惊人事。***set*** ～***s*** 指定的备考书。***read sb. like a*** ～ 对某人的心思完全了解,看透某人。***shut the*** ～***s*** 停止交易〔来往〕。***speak like a*** [***by the***] ～ 确切地说话。***suit sb.'s*** ～ 适合某人目的,合某人意的;对某人方便的。***take a leaf out of another's*** ～ 仿效别人行动,学某人的样子,效颦。***take kindly to one's*** ～***s*** 好学。***the B- of B-s*** 《圣经》。***the devil's*** ～(***s***) 纸牌。***throw the*** ～ ***at*** 〔俚〕重罚,严罚。***without*** ～ **1.** 无根据,任意,随意(乱说等)。**2.** 默诵,默记。**II** ***vt.*** **1.** 登载,登记,记入,给…注册,给…挂号。**2.** 预定,定(戏位、车位等);托运(行李等)。**3.** (警察)记下(某人的)违法行为。**4.** 代理…接受(赛马等的)赌注。～ *one's order* 登记收到的订货单。～ *cinema seats* 预定电影票。— ***vi.*** **1.** 定坐位;定票。**2.** 〔主英〕(旅客在旅馆)登记姓名。***be*** ～***ed*** 〔俚〕被捉住,逃不脱(*I am* ～*ed* (*for it*). 我逃不脱了)。***be*** ～***ed for*** [***to***] 买有往…去的票子;非去不可,约好…,预定好…。***be*** ～***ed up*** 已经与人有约;(戏票等)已被预定一空;〔俚〕无丝毫闲空,太忙。～ ***in*** 〔主英〕登记住入(旅馆等)。～ ***through*** (*to London*) 买(到伦敦的)直达票。**III** ***a.*** **1.** 书籍的。**2.** 书本上的。**3.** 账面上的。*the* ～ *department downstairs* 楼下售书部。～ *knowledge* 书本知识。～ *profit* 账面利润。～ **account** 往来账户。～ **binder** 装订工人。～ **bindery** 装订厂。～ **binding** 装订,钉书。～**case** 书橱,书箱。～ **club** 读书会。～ **concern** 〔美〕出版社,发行所。～ **credit** 账面信用,赊销金额。～ **debt** 账面负债,赊购金额。～ **end** 书靠;书立,书挡。～**-end** ***n.*** 分两部分播放的电视广告。～ **hunter** 猎书者,珍本秘本书搜猎者。～ **jacket** (书的)护封。～**keeper** **1.** 簿记员,账房,管账人,记账人。**2.** 〔谑〕借书久借不还的人。～**-keeping** 簿记。～ **land** 【英史】特许保有地。～**-learned** ***a.*** 书上学到的,书本知识的;迷信书本的。～**learning** 书本知识;〔俚〕学问;正规教育,学校教育。～**let** 小册子。～ **lore** = ～ learning. ～ **louse** 【昆】

书虱。~ **lung**【动】书肺。~ **maker** 著作家;(以营利为本位的)编书人;(赛马等的)登记赌注者。~ **making** 1. 著作。2. 编辑。3. 赛马赌博登记簿。~**man** 1. 学者;文人。2. 书商。~**mark** 书签。~ **mobile** 流动书车;车上图书馆。~ **nonsense**〔美俚〕纸上谈兵。~ **page** 1. 书页。2. (报纸等的)书评专页。~**plate** 1. 书牌;(书面上的)贴头。2. 书页铅版。~ **post**〔英〕书籍邮件。~ **rack** 书架;(书籍)借阅架;书摊,书亭,书柜(台)。~ **rest** (置放摊开书本用的)阅书架。~ **review** 书评。~**seller** 书商。~**-selling** 售书。~**shelf** 书橱,书架。~**shop** 书店。~ **slide** 活动书架。~ **society** 读书会。~ **stack** 分层书架。~**stall** (旧)书摊;书亭;书店。~ **stand** 书柜台;书架;旧书摊。~**-store**〔美〕书店。~ **value** 1. 账面价值。2. 买卖净值。3. 股本净值。4. 单股价值。~**work** 理论研究,钻研书本;勤学。~**worm** 1. 蠹鱼,蛀书虫。2. 读书迷,书呆子。**-able** *a*.〔英〕可预购〔约、定〕的。

book·ie [ˈbuki; ˋbʊkɪ] *n*. 1.〔英口〕(赛马等的)赌注登记者。2.〔美口〕粗制滥造的作家。

book·ing [ˈbukiŋ; ˋbʊkɪŋ] *n*. 1. 记账;登记。2. (邀请讲演者、演出者等的)预约,演出契约。3. 挂号;(座位等的)预定。4. 售票。~ **agent** 1. 代订机票;戏票的人。2. (演员等的)经纪人。~ **clerk** 1. 售票员。2. 负责安排与登记旅客;货物;行李等的服务员。~ **hall**,〔美〕~ **office** 售票处。

book·ish [ˈbukiʃ; ˋbʊkɪʃ] *a*. 1. 书上的。2. 嗜书的,好读书的;博览群书的。3. 咬文嚼字的;学究气的,书本上的。*a* ~ *way of thinking* 书呆子的想法。

Bool·e·an [ˈbuːljən; ˋbuljən] **algebra** 布尔代数,逻辑代数。

boom[1] [buːm; bum] I *n*. 1. (雷、炮等的)隆隆声,轰轰声,(波浪的)澎湃声;(鼓等的)咚咚声;(蜂等的)嗡嗡声;(鹭鸶等的)鸣叫;有回响的声音。2. (市面的)忽然兴旺,景气,繁荣,勃兴;(候选人等的)突然大得人心[出名];(形势的)突然好转;(城市等的)急速发展;(物价等的)暴涨;(人口等的)激增。*the war* ~ 战争景气。*a building* ~ 建筑业的兴旺。II *vi*. 1. (雷等)隆隆响;(波浪声)澎湃;(鼓等)咚咚地响;(蜂声)嗡嗡;(鹭鸶等)鸣叫。2. (市面等)突然兴隆,繁荣;(物价等)暴涨;(人口等)激增;(城市等)急速发展;(形势等)突然好转;(候选人等)突然得人心[出名]。*Guns are ~ing*. 炮声隆隆。*Not far off the Pacific ~ed*. 不远处,太平洋的涛声轰鸣。— *vt*. 1. 用隆隆声发出。2. (用广告等)推广销路;捧(候选人等)。3. 使迅速发展,使兴旺。*He ~ed out the verse*. 他用低沉的声音朗读诗句。III *a*.〔美〕猛涨起来的,忽然发展[兴旺]起来的。~ *prices* 猛涨起来的物价。~**-and-bust** [**slump**] *n*. 经济繁荣与萧条的交替循环。~ **box** 噪音盒〔指便携式录放机〕。~ **carpet** (超音速飞机的)爆音(影响)区。~ **corridor** 超音速飞机限定航线,爆音走廊。~**er** 生育高峰期出生的人。~ **town** 新兴城市。

boom[2] [buːm; bum] I *n*. 1.【船】帆的下桁,帆邋,横杠,吊杆;悬[转、起重]臂。2. 横江铁索,(港口的)水栅,栅栏;水上航标;【林】筏堰。II *vt*. (以下桁)张开帆脚。— *vi*. (船)以最高速航行。~ *nets*【军】栅栏撒〔战时港口的水底铁丝网〕。*heavy* ~ 重吊杠。***lower the* ~ *on***〔口〕1. 禁止。2. 严惩。

boom·er [ˈbuːmə; ˋbumɚ] *n*. 1.〔美口〕走红运的人;讨人喜欢的东西。2.〔美俚〕(往来无定的)短工;赶往新兴地区安家者。3.〔澳〕雄性大袋鼠;(北美)山狸。**B- State** 美国俄克拉荷马州的别名。

boom·er·ang [ˈbuːməræŋ; ˋbuməræŋ] I *n*. 飞去来器〔澳大利亚土著居民扔出后能飞回的飞镖〕;〔喻〕自食其果的言行。II *vi*. 像飞镖似地返回;对自己的言行起反作用;害人反害己,自食其果。~ **baby** 成年后又回家与父母同住的子女。

boom·ing [ˈbuːmiŋ; ˋbumɪŋ] *a*. 1. 突然兴旺的。2. 大受欢迎的。3. 暴涨的;激增的。4. 发轰隆声的。

boom·let [ˈbuːmlit; ˋbumlɪt] *n*.〔美口〕小兴旺,小景气,暂时繁荣。

boom·ster [ˈbuːmstə; ˋbumstɚ] *n*.〔美俗〕造成兴旺的东西[人]。

boon[1] [buːn; bun] *n*. 1.〔古〕恳求。2. 赐物,赠物;恩惠,恩典;恩赐;福利;裨益,照顾。***ask a* ~ (*of sb*.)** 请求(某人)(*May I ask a* ~ *of you*? 我能请你帮个忙吗?)。***be* [*prove*] *a great* ~ *to* [*for*]** (成为)对…极可感谢的[有用的]东西(*The aid was a great* ~ *for the country*. 这项援助对该国有极大的好处)。

boon[2] [buːn; bun] *a*. 1. 愉快的,快活的。2.〔古诗〕(气候等)温和的;仁厚的。*a* ~ *companion* 酒友,好友。

boon·docks [ˈbuːndɔks; ˋbundɑks] *n*. *pl*.〔俚〕1. 孤立的森林;荒野。2. 偏僻的农村;边省;内地。

boon·dog·gle [ˈbuːndɔgl; ˋbundɑgl] I *n*.〔美俚〕1. (童子军的)皮绳;(皮或柳条制的)手工品。2. 无价值的琐事。II *vi*. (花钱费时间)做无价值的事〔尤指无价值的政府工程〕。

Boon(e) [buːn; bun] *n*. 布恩〔姓氏〕。

boop·er [ˈbuːpə; ˋbupɚ] *n*.〔美俚〕花腔舞剧歌手〔指常在歌词中穿插美妙音节的歌手〕。

boor [buə; bur] *n*. 农民;乡下人;粗俗的男子;〔B-〕= Boer.

boor·ish [ˈbuəriʃ; ˋbʊrɪʃ] *a*. 乡下气的,粗俗的,土俗的;粗鲁的。**-ly** *ad*. **-ness** *n*.

boost [buːst; bust] I *vt*. 1.〔美口〕(由下或由后)推,升,提。2.〔美俚〕吹捧(候选人等);支援;增加,提高;促进;煽起(买风)。3.【电】升(压);助(爆)。~ *the output of cotton* 提高棉花产量。~ *sb*. *into the wagon* 把某人推进马车。~ *one's hometown* 吹嘘自己的家乡。~ *prices* 提价。II *n*. 1. 升,后推。2. 帮助;促进。3. 提高,增加。4. 吹捧,宣传。5. 助推发动机,加速[助推]器。6.〔美俚〕(假扮顾客的)店铺扒手。*give sb*. *a* ~ *into the wagon* 把某人推进马车。*a* ~ *in price* 提价。

boost·er [ˈbuːstə; ˋbustɚ] *n*. 1.【电】升降压器;调压电阻;【机】升压机[泵];【导弹】助推器;多级火箭的第一级;【无】(电视等的)放大器;【原】增益棒;【军】助爆药;〔美〕辅助机车;【药】辅助药剂;转播站。2.〔美口〕援助者,后援者;煽动买风的人。3.〔美俚〕(假扮顾客行窃的)店铺扒手;足球运动员。*a negative* ~ 降压器;减压机。~ **dose** [**shot**]【药】促效剂,辅药。~ **station**【无】升压电台,(电视的)中继台。

boot[1] [buːt; but] I *n*. 1.〔美〕长筒靴。2.〔英〕(马车、汽车后部的)行李箱。3. 马脚绊;【史】靴状刑具,夹足刑具。4.【机】进料斗;接受器;【电】引出罩;(汽车等的)保护罩;〔空俚〕(飞机上)防结冰皮管。5.〔俚〕〔the ~〕解雇。6.〔美俚〕海军[海军陆战队]新兵。7.〔口〕愉快,开心。8.〔英〕〔*pl*. 作 *sing*. 用〕(旅馆)擦靴侍者。*high* ~*s*〔英〕长统靴。*elastic-side* ~*s* 长筒橡皮靴。*put on* [*off*] 穿[脱]靴。*a* ~*s*〔英〕旅馆的擦靴侍者〔兼管搬行李等〕。*laced* ~*s* 编带靴。*a* ~ *camp* 新兵宿舍。***be in sb*.'*s* ~*s*** 站在某人立场上,赞同某人。***bet your* ~*s*** 有把握,必然,一定(*You can bet your* ~*s I'll be there*. 我一定去)。***big for one's* ~*s*** 自大,自骄(*Don't get too big for your* ~*s*. 别太自大)。~ ***and saddle***〔美〕(骑兵)上马预备号。***die in one's* ~*s* = *die with one's* ~*s on*** 不是死在床上,暴死,死于非命,横死。***get the* ~**〔俚〕被解雇,被开除。***get* [*put*] *the* ~ *on the wrong leg*** 误释,错解。***give sb*. *a* ~** 使某人开心。***give sb*. *the* ~** 解雇某人。***go down in one's* ~*s***〔美口〕感到恐怖,害怕。***go to bed in one's* ~*s*** 烂醉如泥,酩酊大醉。***have one's heart in one's* ~*s*** 害怕;提心吊胆。***I'll eat my* ~*s if* ...** 我决不…;决无此事。***in seven league* ~*s*** 飞速,极快。***lick sb*.'*s* ~*s*** 向某人屈服,迁就;奉承某人。***lick the* ~*s off*** 使惨败(*He licked the* ~*s off me*. 他把我打得惨败)。***like old* ~*s***〔俚〕猛烈地,彻底地,可惊地(*It's raining like old* ~*s*. 大雨倾盆,正下大雨)。***move one's* ~*s***〔美口〕出发。***over shoes over* ~*s*** 将错

就错，一不做二不休。***put the ～ in*** 1. 猛踢。2. 采取决定性行动。***put the ～ on the wrong leg*** 错爱，错赏。***rise out of one's ～s*** 飞快地起床，从床上飞快跳起。***The ～ is on the other foot*** [***leg***]. 1. 责任在其他方面[人等]。2. 弄错人。3. 事实恰恰相反。***wipe one's ～s on sb***. 侮辱某人。***with one's heart*** [***voice***] ***in one's ～s*** 提心吊胆。**II** ***vt***. 1. 穿(靴)。2. 〔美〕用靴踢；踢出，赶出，轰走，〔俚〕解雇 (*out*)。—***vi***.【计】启动，引导装入程序 (*up*)。～ **black** 〔美〕以擦皮鞋为业者。～ **camp** 〔美〕(海军)新兵训练所。～**jack** 脱靴器。～ **lace** 靴带。～ **last** 靴型，靴楦，靴衬。～**leg** 1. ***vt***. 〔美俚〕偷卖[贩、酿、运](酒)。2. ***vi***. 违禁卖[贩、酿、运]酒。3. ***n***. 违禁的酒，私酒。4. ***a***. 违禁的，私酿的，私造的，私自贩运的。～**lick** ***vt***., ***vi***. 〔美俚〕巴结，奉承，拍马屁。～ **licker** 拍马者，奉承者。～ **maker** 制靴厂；靴匠。～ **stage**【植】抽穗期。～**strap** 1. ***n***. 拔靴带 (*pull* [*lift*, *raise*] *oneself up by one's* [*own*] ～ *straps* 凭自己的力量出人头地)。2. ***a***. 依靠自己力量的；自己做的 (*a* ～ *strap operation* 独立进行的一次手术)。～ **training** (美国海军的)新兵训练(期)。～ **tree** = boot last.

boot² [buːt; but] **I** ***n***. 〔古诗〕利益；救济，援助。***to ～*** 加之，而且 (*He is lame to* ～. 而且他又是跛子)。**II** ***vt***. 对…有利，对…有用。*It ～s* (*you*) *not to complain*. 怨天尤人(于你)毫无好处。*What ～s it to repeat how time is slipping underneath our feet*? 不断空喊光阴不待人又有何益?

boot·ed [ˈbuːtid; ˋbutɪd] ***a***. 1. 穿靴的。2. 〔美俚〕失了业的，已被解雇的。*be ～ and spurred* 穿了马靴，上了靴刺〔准备上马〕。

boot·ee [ˈbuːtiː; buti] ***n***. 1.【商】轻巧女鞋；小儿毛线鞋。2. 〔美俚〕被解雇的人。

Bo·ö·tes [bəuˈəutiːz; boˋotiz] ***n***.【天】牧夫座。

booth [buːð; buð] ***n***. 1. 小舍，棚，窝棚；货摊，摊子。2. 隔开的小间，(餐馆的)火车座。3. (选举)投票站。*a telephone ～* 电话间。*an announcer ～* 播音员室。*a public telephone ～* 公用电话亭。*a polling ～* (用帐篷等搭的)投票处。*a motion picture projection ～* 电影放映室。～ **man** ***n***. 〔美〕电影放映员。

Booth [buːð; buð] ***n***. 布斯〔姓氏〕。

boot·less [ˈbuːtlis; ˋbutlɪs] ***a***. 〔古〕无益的，无用的。**-ly** ***ad***. 无益，徒然，徒劳，白白地。**-ness** ***n***.

Boots [buːts; buts] ***n***. 布茨〔男子名〕。

boo·ty [ˈbuːti; ˋbutɪ] ***n***. 1. 缴获，战利品。2. 赃物，掠夺物。3. 奖品，赚头。*war ～* 战利品。***play ～*** 通同作弊，相互勾结，朋比为奸。

booze [buːz; buz] **I** ***vi***. 〔口〕1. 暴饮，痛饮，滥饮(酒) 2. 贪杯，经常饮酒。**II** ***n***. 1. 酒。2. 暴饮；酒宴。*go on the ～* 贪杯痛饮。*have a ～* 饮酒。*B- bourse* 〔美〕纽约 Brookly 区的别名。～ *fighter* 酒徒。***drive sb. to ～ or dope*** 使迷糊，使醉。***hit the ～*** 〔美俚〕饮酒。***on the ～*** 不停的喝酒，痛饮。～**-hoisting** 〔美俚〕喝酒。～**-up** 〔英俚〕狂欢作乐，纵酒狂欢。

booz·y [ˈbuːzi; ˋbuzɪ] ***a***. 大醉的；爱酒如命的。

bop [bɔp; bap] **I** ***n***. 〔美俚〕一击，一捆。**II** ***vt***. (用拳、棍棒等)打，打击。

bo·peep [bəuˈpiːp; boˋpip] ***n***. 躲猫〔一种躲在隐蔽处突然出现的逗小孩的游戏〕。***play ～*** 1. 玩躲猫游戏。2. (政客等)圆滑，耍花腔，躲躲闪闪。

Bo-Peep [bəuˈpiːp; boˋpip] ***n***. 〔英俚〕睡眠。

BOQ, B.O.Q.【美军】= Bachelor Officer's Quarters. 单身军官宿舍。

BOR = British Other Ranks 英国兵。

bor. = boron; borough.

bo·ra [ˈbɔːrə; ˋbɔrə] ***n***.【气】布拉风〔亚得里亚海北部干冷凶猛的东北风〕。

bo·rac·ic [bəˈræsik; bəˋræsɪk] ***a***. = boric. ～ **ointment** 硼酸药膏。

bo·ra·cite [ˈbɔːrəˌsait; ˋbɔrəˏsaɪt] ***n***.【矿】方硼石。

bor·age [ˈbɔridʒ; ˋbɔrɪdʒ] ***n***.【植】琉璃苣〔其药可作调味料〕。

bo·ral [ˈbɔːrəl; ˋbɔrəl] ***n***.【药】硼酒石酸铝〔用作收敛剂〕。

bo·rane [ˈbəurein; ˋboren] ***n***.【化】甲硼烷；甲硼烷衍生物。

bo·rate [ˈbɔːreit; ˋbɔret] **I** ***n***.【化】硼酸盐；硼酸酯。**II** ***vt***. 使与硼砂[硼酸]混合。

bo·rax¹ [ˈbɔːræks; ˋbɔræks] ***n***.【化】硼砂；月石。

bo·rax² [ˈbɔːræks; ˋboræks] ***n***. 〔俚〕好看的便宜货，〔特指〕式样繁多的便宜家具。

bo·ra·zon [ˈbɔːrəˌzɔn; ˋbɔrəˏzɑn] ***n***.【化】一氮化硼结晶体。

Bor·deaux [bɔːˈdəu; bɔrˋdo] ***n***. 1. 波尔多〔法国西南部商港〕。2. 波尔多白葡萄酒。～ **mixture** 波尔多液〔加硫酸铜于石灰乳中所成的一种农用杀霉菌剂和杀虫剂〕。

bor·del [ˈbɔːdl; ˋbɔrdl] ***n***. 〔古〕妓院。

bor·del·lo [bɔːˈdeləu; bɔrˋdelo] ***n***. 妓院。

bor·der [ˈbɔːdə; ˋbɔrdɚ] **I** ***n***. 1. 边，缘，边沿，框。2. 边界，国界，国境，边境；边地；领地。3. (女服的)滚边，布边；(印刷品等的)边饰。4. (庭园沿边或走道两旁的)花坛。*the ～ clashes* 边界冲突。*cross the ～* 越过国境线。*a ～ along the path* 沿路边的花坛。*the ～ of a lake* 湖畔。*the ～ army* 边防军。*the B- of B-s* 英格兰与苏格兰交界区。***on the ～ of*** 1. 将要，正要。2. 接近于，濒临于。***on the ～s*** 在边界上，接近交界边。***out of*** [***within***] ***～s*** 在国境[领地]外[内]。***over the ～*** 越过国境。**II** ***vi***. 1. 接界，邻接 (*on*, *upon*). 2. 近似，相近 (*on*, *upon*). *His conduct ～s upon madness*. 他的行为近乎疯狂。*The U.S. ～s on Canada*. 美国与加拿大接壤。— ***vt***. 1. 在(衣服等上)镶边[滚，加缘饰]。2. 与…接壤，邻接；接近。*a park ～ed by modern buildings* 为现代化建筑所环绕的公园。*the countries that ～ the Danube* 以多瑙河分界的国家。～ **land** 1. 国境地带，边境，边陲；边缘地带。2. 〔喻〕模糊不清的境界；梦境 (*lives on the ～ of society* 生活在社会的边缘地带。*the ～ between fantasy and reality* 幻想与现实之间的境地)。～ **line** 1. 国境线；分界线。2. 两可之间。～**line** ***a***. 1. 在国界[公界线]上的。2. 两可的，不明确的；语义暧昧的〔尤指近于下流的〕(*a ～line joke* 近于不雅的玩笑)。**-er** ***n***. 边境居民。**-ing** ***n***. 1. 立界标。2. 边，缘。**-ism** (英格兰与苏格兰)边境居民的特殊风习[语言]。

bor·de·reau [ˌbɔːdəˈrəu; ˏbɔrdəˋro] ***n***. (*pl*. ***-reaux*** [-ˈrəuz; -ˋroz]) 〔F.〕= invoice.

bor·dure [ˈbɔːdjuə; ˋbɔrdjʊr] ***n***.【纹】盾边。

bore¹ [bɔː; bɔr] **I** ***n***. 1. 膛；膛腔；孔，孔腔；眼，炮眼；枪膛，炮膛。2. 膛径，孔径，口径，内径。3. 钻[扩]孔器，锥，膛头。*basic ～*【机】基孔。～ *bit* 钻孔钻头。～ *size* 内径。**II** ***vt***. 1. 穿(孔)，钻(孔)，【机】膛(孔)；挖(洞)，在…上打眼，开凿(隧道等)。2. 挤入(人群)；【赛马】拨开(别的马)。～ *a plank* 在木板上钻孔。～ *a tunnel through the Alps* 凿一条穿过阿尔卑斯山的隧道。～ *an oil well 3,000 feet deep* 钻一眼3,000英尺深的油井。**II** ***vi***. 1. 打眼，钻孔；【机】膛孔；开凿，挖掘。2. 钻入，挤入 (*through*; *into*). *Certain types of steel don't ～ well*. 有些品种的钢材不容易打眼。～ *for oil* [*coal*] 钻探石油[煤炭]。～ ***from within*** 从内部破坏。～ ***one's way through*** (***the crowd***) 挤入(人群)。～**-hole** 钻孔，膛孔；炮眼井眼。～ **scope** 管道内孔探测镜；光学孔径仪。～**-sight** 1. 瞄准线，视轴。2. 炮膛觇视器，枪筒瞄准。

bore² [bɔː; bɔr] bear 的过去式。

bore³ [bɔː; bɔr] **I** ***n***. 使人讨厌的人[物]，讨厌的工作；打扰。*The play was a ～*. 这出戏没意思。*I'm afraid that I'm a ～ to you*. 我恐怕打扰您了。**II** ***vt***. 使厌烦，

烦扰,打扰(*with*)。*be ~d to death* 厌烦得要死。*Am I boring you?* 我打扰您了吧?*be ~d with the past* 对过去的事已不感兴趣。

bore[4][bɔː; bɔr] ***n.*** 高潮,怒潮;海啸。

bo·re·al [ˈbɔːriəl; ˋbɔriəl] ***a.*** **1.** 北(方)的;北风的。**2.** [B-]【希神】北风之神的。**3.** [B-](生长于)北半球北部山区的。

Bo·re·as [ˈbɔ(ː)riæs; ˋbɔriəs] ***n.***【希神】北风之神;〔诗〕北风;朔风。

bore·cole [ˈbɔːkəul; ˋbɔrkol] ***n.***【植】羽衣甘蓝。

bore·dom [ˈbɔːdəm; ˋbɔrdəm] ***n.*** **1.** 讨厌,无聊,无趣。**2.** 令人厌烦的事物。*in infinite* ~ 极其无趣。

bor·er [ˈbɔːrə; ˋborɚ] ***n.*** **1.** 穿孔者;镗工,钻工,打眼工。**2.** 钻孔器,钻头,钻机;凿岩机;錾;【机】镗床,镗孔刀具。**3.**【动】凿船虫,钻蛀虫。*a jig* ~ 座标镗床。*a collar* ~ 象鼻虫。*a maize* ~ 玉米螟。*a rice* ~ 稻螟虫。

bore·some [ˈbɔːsəm; ˋborsəm] ***a.*** 令人厌烦的,令人厌倦的;讨厌的;无聊的。

bo·ric [ˈbɔːrik; ˋborɪk] ***a.***【化】硼的,含硼的。~ **acid** 硼酸。

bo·ri·ckite [ˈbɔrikait; ˋbɑrɪkaɪt] ***n.***【矿】褐磷酸钙铁矿。

bo·ride [ˈbɔːraid; ˋboraɪd] ***n.***【化】硼化物。~ **cermet** 硼[金属]陶瓷。

bor·ing[1] [ˈbɔːriŋ; ˋborɪŋ] **I** ***n.*** **1.** 穿孔,钻孔;镗削;地质钻探。**2.**〔*pl.*〕镗屑,钻屑。**II** ***a.*** 镗(钻)孔的。~ **machine** 钻孔机,镗床。~ **sample** 岩心取样。

bor·ing[2] [ˈbɔːriŋ; ˋborɪŋ] ***a.*** 令人厌烦的,无聊的,无趣的。~ *people* 令人讨厌的人。

Bor·is [ˈbɔris; ˋbɑrɪs] ***n.*** 鲍里斯[男子名]。

born [bɔːn; bɔrn] 作"产,生"解的 bear[1] 的过去分词。***a.*** **1.** 出生的;出身于…的。**2.** 生来就…的,命中注定的。**3.** 天生的;有天才的。*one's first-* ~ *child* 第一个孩子。*a newly-* ~ *idea* 新产生的想法。*a Chicago-* ~ *New Yorker* 出生在芝加哥的纽约人。*He was* ~ *to be hanged.* 他命中注定要上绞架。*a* ~ *musician* 天生的音乐家。*a* ~ *fool* 生下来就是白痴。***be* ~ *again*** 再生,自新,更生。***be* ~ *of*** (*rich parents*) 出身于(有钱人家)。***be* ~ *to*** (*wealth*) 生来(有钱)。***be* ~ *with a silver spoon in one's mouth*** 生在富贵人家。~ ***and bred*** 在…生长大的;地地道道的,…本地的 (*a* ~ *and bred Parisienne* 地地道道的巴黎妇女)。~ ***of woman*** 同是娘养的。~ ***yesterday*** 天真的,乳臭未干的,无经验的。***in all one's* ~ *days*** 有生以来,一生中,生平 (*In all my* ~ *days I've never seen such a fool as you are.* 我有生以来还从没有见过你这样的傻子)。

borne [bɔːn; born] 不作"产,生"解的 bear[1] 的过去分词。★在作"产,生"解时只限于生育(子女等)一义,有以下两种情况:一是用于完成时,置于助动词 have 之后;一是用于被动语态,置于介词 by 之前。*She has* ~ *two children. Two children were* ~ *by her.* 她生了两个孩子。

borné [ˈbɔːnei; bɔrˋne] ***a.*** 〔F.〕心地狭窄的,小心眼儿的,偏狭的;局限的。

Bor·ne·o [ˈbɔːniəu; ˋbɔrnɪˏo] ***n.*** 婆罗洲〔Kalimantan 加里曼丹的旧称〕。

bor·ne·ol [ˈbɔːniɔl; ˋbɔrnɪɑl] ***n.***【化】龙脑;冰片。

born·ite [ˈbɔːnait; ˋbɔrnaɪt] ***n.***【矿】斑铜矿。

boro- *comb. f.* 硼: *boro*hide, *boro*n.

bo·ron [ˈbɔːrɔn; ˋborɑn] ***n.***【化】硼。~ **oxide** 二氧化硼。**-ic** ***a.*** **-ization** ***n.***【冶】渗硼。

bo·ro·sil·i·cate [ˌbɔːrəuˈsilikit; ˏborəˋsɪləkɪt] ***n.***【化】硼矽酸盐。~ *glass* 光学玻璃。*hard* ~ *glass* 耐火玻璃。

bor·ough [ˈbʌrə; ˋbɝo] ***n.*** **1.** 〔英〕(享有特权的)自治城市;有议员选举权的城市;〔美〕自治村镇;纽约市五个行政区之一。**2.** 〔古〕城,镇;〔美阿拉斯加〕县。***a close*** [***pocket***] ~ **1.** 为一人[一家]操纵的议员选区。**2.** 一人[一家,一集团]操纵的政治团体。***rotten*** ~【英史】朽镇〔虽已衰落但仍有选举权的市镇,1832 年被废止〕。~-**English** ***n.*** 〔英〕末子继承制〔英国某些地区的一种习俗,规定由末子[如无子嗣则由末弟]继承财产〕。

bor·row [ˈbɔrəu; ˋbɑro] **I** ***vt.*** **1.** 借,借用。**2.** 模仿,剽窃。**3.**【数】由上位借。*The neighbors* ~*ed my lawn mower.* 邻居们借用我的除草机。~ *a word from German* 借用一个德语词。~ (*money*) *from* [*of*] 由…处借(钱)。~ *1 from 4 in the number of 42 to add as 10 to 2* 在 42 这个数字中向 4 借 1 作 10 加给 2〔减法演算中的借位〕。~ ***money on*** ... 以…抵借,押借。— ***vi.*** **1.** 借钱,借用;【数】借位。**2.** 模仿,剽窃。**3.**【海】迎风[靠岸]航行。**4.**【高尔夫球】斟酌风向[斜度]打球。*Japanese has* ~*ed heavily from English.* 日语中借用了很多英语。~ ***trouble*** 喜作无益的忧虑,自找麻烦,自寻烦恼 (*It was her nature to* ~ *trouble.* 她生来喜欢自寻烦恼)。***in* ~*ed plumes*** 穿着别人的漂亮衣裳;借用他人声望。**II** ***n.*** **1.** 借,借用。**2.** 担保物,抵押。**3.**【英史】什一税。~ **pit** (筑堤取土挖成的)土坑。**-ed** ***a.*** 借来的 (*borrowed light* 反射来的光;内窗。*borrowed time* 奇迹般的获救,寿命的意外延长)。

Bor·row [ˈbɔrəu; ˋbɑro] ***n.*** 博罗[姓氏]。

bor·row·er [ˈbɔrəuə; ˋbɑroɚ] ***n.*** 借钱人,借用人;剽窃者。~*'s card* 借书证。

bor·row·ing [ˈbɔrəuiŋ; ˋbɑroɪŋ] ***n.*** 借,借用;借用的东西,借用的词[譬喻等];模仿其他民族的风俗。

borsch, borsht, borshtsh, bortsch [bɔːʃ, bɔːʃt, bɔːtʃ; bɔrʃ, bɔrʃt, bɔrtʃ] ***n.*** 俄国菜汤。

Bor·stal [ˈbɔːstl; ˋbɔrstəl] ***n.*** 〔英〕(青少年罪犯)教养院 (= ~ institution)。~ **boy**〔英〕教养院的青少年罪犯。

bort, bortz [bɔːt, bɔːts; bɔrt, bɔrts] ***n.*** (仅用于切削或研磨的)不纯金刚石,金刚石粒;金刚石粉。*short* ~ 劣等金刚石。

bor·zoi [ˈbɔːzɔi; ˋbɔrzɔi] ***n.*** (*pl.* ~*s*) 俄国大猎狗[猎狼狗]。

bos [bɔs; bɑs] ***n.***, ***vt.***, ***vi.*** 〔英俚〕做错,看差;猜错;弄糟。

Bo·san·quet [ˈbəuznkit; ˋbozənˏkɪt] ***n.*** 博桑基特[姓氏]。

bos·cage, bos·kage [ˈbɔskidʒ; ˋbɑskɪdʒ] ***n.*** 〔诗〕灌木丛;树丛。

bosch·bok; bosh·bok [ˈbɔʃbɔk; ˋbɑʃbɑk] ***n.*** (*pl.* ~, ~*s*)【动】林羚 (= bushbuck)。

Bosche [bɔʃ; bɑʃ] ***n.***, ***a.*** = Boche.

bosch·vark [ˈbɔʃvɑːk; ˋbɑʃvɑrk] ***n.***【动】非洲野猪。

bosh[1] [bɔʃ; bɑʃ] **I** ***n.*** 〔口〕胡说,空话,废话。**II** ***vt.*** 〔学俚〕愚弄,戏弄;欺负。**III** ***int.*** 胡说八道!瞎说!

bosh[2] [bɔʃ; bɑʃ] ***n.*** **1.** (鼓风)炉腹。**2.**【化】浴;锅;槽,桶。

bosk, bos·ket, bos·quet [bɔsk, ˈbɔskit; bɑsk, ˋbɑskɪt] ***n.*** 树丛;(园内)小树林。

bosk·y [ˈbɔski; ˋbɑskɪ] ***a.*** **1.** 矮树丛生的;林木荫蔽的,有丛林的。**2.** 〔英俚〕喝醉了的。

bo's'n [ˈbəusn; ˋbosn] ***n.***【海】= boatswain.

Bos·ni·a [ˈbɔzniə; ˋbɑzniə] ***n.*** 波斯尼亚〔南斯拉夫一地区〕。**-n 1.** ***a.*** 波斯尼亚(人)的。**2.** ***n.*** 波斯尼亚人。~ **and Herzegovina** 波斯尼亚—黑塞哥维那〔国名,简称"波黑"〕。

bos·om [ˈbuzəm; ˋbuzəm] **I** ***n.*** **1.** 胸;胸膛;心胸;胸怀,内心。**2.** 里面,内部,当中;亲密关系。**3.** (湖、海等的)宽阔的表面。**4.** (衣类的)胸部;〔美〕衬衫胸部。**5.** 〔*pl.*〕(女人的)乳房;〔古〕怀抱。*the wife of one's* ~ 〔古〕爱妻。*press sb. to one's* ~ 搂抱某人。*put a baby to the* ~ 给婴儿喂乳。*with panting* ~ 情绪激动。*in the* ~ *of the earth* 地球内部。*the tranquil* ~ *of the Seine* 塞纳河宁静的水面。***in Abraham's*** ~ 死,升天。***in the* ~ *of one's family*** 一家团聚;享天伦之乐。***keep in one's*** ~ 秘藏胸中。***speak one's*** ~ 倾吐衷曲。***take*** (***sb.***) ***to*** ~ **1.** 娶。**2.** 与…做心腹朋友。**3.** 重视。**II**

vt. 1. 搂抱。2. 怀有;把…秘藏心中;隐匿,把…藏起来。**Abraham's** ~ 天国。~ **chums**〔美俚〕虱。~ **friend** 心腹朋友,知交,密友。~ **secret** 重要秘密。~ **sin** 深藏心中的罪恶。

bos·omed [ˈbuzəmd, ˈbuːzəmd; ˋbuzəmd, ˋbuzəmd] *a*. 有(某种)胸部的〔用以构成复合词〕。*small-* ~ 胸部狭小的。

B

bos·om·y [ˈbuzəmi; ˋbuzəmɪ] *a*. 胸部隆起的,乳房丰满的。

bos·on [ˈbəusɔn; ˋbosɑn] *n*.【物】玻色子〔遵从玻色统计法的粒子〕。

Bos·po·rus, Bos·pho·rus [ˈbɔspərəs, ˈbɔsfərəs; ˋbɑspərəs, ˋbɑsfərəs] *n*. (黑海与马尔马拉海间的)博斯普鲁斯海峡。

bos·que [ˈbɔskei; ˋbɑske] *n*. 〔Sp.〕〔主美国西南部〕小林子,丛林。

bos·quet [ˈbɔskit; ˋbɑskɪt] *n*. 矮林,丛林(=bosket)。

BOSS=Bureau of State Security(南非的秘密情报组织)国家安全局。

boss[1] [bɔs; bɑs] **I** *n*. 1. 〔口〕头儿;老板;上司;经理;工头;工长。2. 〔美〕(政党)领袖,首领;伟人;支柱。*a political* ~ 政界大亨。*He is my* ~. 他是我的头儿。*His wife's the* ~ *in his family*. 他的妻子是一家之主。*a straw* ~ 工头助手。**II** *a*. 1. 〔口〕管事的,掌权的。2. 〔俚〕第一流的。~ *shoemaker* 第一流的鞋匠。**III** *vt*. 当…的首领;支配,统率,指挥,把…呼来喝去。~ *the house* 做一家之长。—*vi*. 1. 当头儿。2. 摆出上司架子。~ (*sb*.) ***about*** [***around***] 支配某人,把某人差来遣去。~ ***it*** 摆架子。~ ***the show*** 指挥,主持。~ **rule** 政党领袖对选民的操纵。~ **windjammer**〔美俚〕乐队领班。**-dom** *n*. 1. 政治领袖的势力范围。2. 政治领袖对政治的控制。

boss[2] [bɔs; bɑs] **I** *n*. 1. (动、植物身上的)结疤,瘤;突起部。2.【地】岩瘤;【建】浮凸饰;(盾中心的)浮雕。3.【机】轴套;套筒;轮毂。*a* ~ *on an animal's horn* 动物角上的瘤。*a* ~ *of granite* 一块突出的花岗岩。**II** *vt*. 1. 用凸饰装饰。2. 浮雕。

boss[3] [bɔs; bɑs] *n*., *v*. =bos。

boss[4] [bɔs; bɑs] *n*. 〔美〕1. 母牛,小牛。2. 牛〔对母牛和小牛的呼唤用语〕。

bossed [bɔst; bɑst] *a*. 有浮凸饰的,有结疤的。

bos(s)-eyed [ˈbɔsaid; ˋbɑsˏaɪd] *a*. 1. 〔俚〕独眼的;斜眼的;〔转义〕偏私的。

boss·ism [bɔsizəm; ˋbɑsɪzəm] *n*. 〔美俚〕头头控制〔首领对政党或政治机构的控制〕。

boss·y[1] [ˈbɔsi; ˋbɑsɪ] *a*. 有浮凸饰的;有结疤的。

boss·y[2] [ˈbɔsi; ˋbɑsɪ] *a*. 〔俚〕俏皮的,风流俊俏的。

boss·y[3] [ˈbɔsi; ˋbɔsɪ] *a*. 〔美俚〕霸道的,专横的。

boss·y[4] [ˈbɔsi; ˋbɑsɪ] *n*. 牛,牛宝宝〔对牛的一种爱称〕。

Bos·ton [ˈbɔstən; ˋbɔstn̩] *n*. 1. 波士顿〔美国城市〕。2. 〔b-〕波士顿纸牌戏〔四人用两副纸牌〕。3. 〔b-〕波士顿圆舞。~ **arm** 一种人造假手。~ **bag** 一种手提包。~ **rocker** 一种讲究的摇椅。~ **Tea Party**【美史】(1773 年波士顿居民抗议英国政府对殖民地进口茶叶征收苛税的)波士顿茶叶事件。**-i·an** *n*. 波士顿人。

bo·sun [ˈbəusn; ˋbosn̩] *n*. =boatswain。

Bos·well [ˈbɔzwəl; ˋbɑzwəl] *n*. 1. 博斯韦尔〔姓氏〕。2. **James** ~ 博斯韦尔〔1740—95,英国杰出的传记作家,著有 *Samuel Johnson* 传〕。

Bos·well·ian [bɔzˈweliən; bɑzˋwɛlɪən] *a*. 博斯韦尔(体)的。

Bos·well·ism [bɔzˈwelizəm; ˋbɑzwɛlɪzm] *n*. 博斯韦尔体〔写传记时巨细无遗地记述被作传者的言行〕。

bot [bɔt; bɑt] *n*. 1. 马蝇幼虫;马蝇。2. 〔the ~s〕马蝇寄生病。~**-fly** 马蝇。

bo·tan·ic [bəˈtænik; boˋtænɪk] *a*. 植物(学)的。*the United States B- Garden* 美国植物园。★本字仅用于植物园名称等。

bo·tan·i·cal [bəˈtænikəl; boˋtænɪkl] **I** *a*. 植物(学)的。~ **gardens** 植物园。~ **survey** 植物学调查。**II** *n*. 植物性药材。**-ly** *ad*. 植物学上。

bot·a·nist [ˈbɔtənist; ˋbɑtn̩ɪst] *n*. 植物学家,专门研究植物的人。

bot·a·nize, bot·a·nise [ˈbɔtənaiz; ˋbɑtənˏaɪz] *vi*. 1. 采集植物。2. 研究植物。—*vt*. 为研究植物品种而勘察(某地等)。

bot·a·ny [ˈbɔtəni; ˋbɑtnɪ] *n*. 1. 植物学。2. 〔总称〕一个地区的植物。3. 植物生态。4. 植物学书籍[论著]。*the* ~ *of Alaska* 阿拉斯加地区的植物生态。*the* ~ *of deciduous trees* 落叶树的生态。

Bot·a·ny [ˈbɔtəni; ˋbɑtn̩ɪ] *n*., *a*. 澳洲细羊毛(的)。~ (*wool*) 澳洲细羊毛。~ *yarn* 澳洲细毛线。

BOTB = British Overseas Trade Board 英国海外贸易局。

botch[1] [bɔtʃ; bɑtʃ] **I** *vt*., *vi*. 1. 粗拙地补缀。2. 笨手笨脚地弄坏。*He* ~*ed the job badly*. 他把活儿做得一塌糊涂。**II** *n*. 1. 拙劣的工作,笨活。2. 粗拙的补缀。*make a complete* ~ *of one's work* 把事情干得一团糟。

botch[2] [bɔtʃ; bɑtʃ] *n*. 〔英方〕疮,瘤。

botch·er [ˈbɔtʃə; ˋbɑtʃɚ] *n*. 1. 笨拙的工人[鞋匠等]。2. 拙劣的写作者。

botch·y [ˈbɔtʃi; ˋbɑtʃɪ] *a*. 工作拙劣的。**botch·i·ly** *ad*. **botch·i·ness** *n*.

bo·tel [bəuˈtel; boˋtɛl] = boatel.

both [bəuθ; boθ] **I** *a*. 两,双,双方,两面,二者。~ *times* 两次。~ *sides* 双方。~ *these books* 这两本书。~ (*the*) *brothers* 兄弟二人。~ *his hands* 两手。*B- girls are beautiful*. 两个姑娘都漂亮。*I don't want* ~ *books*. 我不是两本书都要〔只要其中一本〕。***have it*** ~ ***ways*** (在议论中)忽左忽右〔以自相矛盾的观点作为论据〕。***not*** ~ 一面,单独。**II** *pron*. 两者,二者,双方。*B- are dead*. 这两人都死了。~ *of them* 他们双方,两者都。*B- of the girls are beautiful*. 两个姑娘都漂亮。*They were scientists* ~. 双方都是科学家〔*both* 与 *they* 同格〕。*I don't know* ~. 我不是两个人都认识〔只认识其中之一〕。**III** *ad*. 皆,哪个都;并且,兼,又〔用在有 and 连接的二个以上词句前,与 neither...nor 正相反〕。*B- brother and sister are dead*. 哥哥和妹妹都死了。*It is* ~ *good and cheap*. 它又便宜又好,它价廉物美。*She can* ~ *sing and dance*. 她又会唱歌又会跳舞,她能歌善舞。~ *before the war and during the war* 无论在战前还是在战时。~ *Chaucer and Shakespeare and Milton* 无论是乔塞、莎士比亚还是弥尔顿。~ **hand·ed** *a*. 用两手的,两手都行的。

both·er [ˈbɔðə; ˋbɑðɚ] **I** *vt*. 1. 烦扰,打扰。2. 使迷惑,使糊涂,使伤脑筋。3. 〔口〕,=damn, confound〔表示厌烦等〕。*Don't* ~ *me with such trifles*. 不要用这些小事打扰我。*His baby sister* ~*ed him for candy*. 小妹妹缠着他要糖吃。*His inability to understand her* ~*ed him*. 他不能理解她,这使他大伤脑筋。*B- it*! [*B- you*!]讨厌! —*vi*. 烦恼;操心。*No one* ~*ed to visit him*. 没人想到去看他。~ *with trifles* 为小事烦恼[操心]。~ *with sb*. *about sth*. 为某事同某人发生纠纷。~ ***about*** 为…操心(*Don't* ~ *about getting dinner for me*. 别为我做饭麻烦了)。~ ***one's head*** [***brain***] ***about*** 为…伤脑筋。~ ***the record*** 〔美俚〕打破记录,创造新记录。***without*** ~***ing to reply*** 懒得回答。**II** *n*. 1. 麻烦,操心,累赘,烦扰;吵闹。2. 讨厌的人,麻烦的事物。*What is all this* ~ *about*? 这闹的是什么呀! *Doing the laundry every week is a terrible* ~. 每星期洗衣服麻烦死了。*Hey, don't go to any* ~. 嗨,别麻烦了。**III** *int*. 讨厌! *Oh*, ~! 真讨厌!

both·er·a·tion [ˌbɔðəˈreiʃən; ˏbɑðəˋreʃən] **I** *n*. 〔俚〕烦恼;麻烦。**II** *int*. 讨厌! *Oh*, ~! 真讨厌!

both·er·some [ˈbɔðəsəm; ˋbɑðəsəm] *a*. 讨厌的,麻烦的,累赘的,为难的。*How* ~ *it is to forget names*! 忘掉

人的名字真烦人！

Both·nia [ˈbɔθniə; ˋbɑθnɪə] ***n.*** 波士尼亚。***Gulf of*** ～ (瑞典芬兰间的)波士尼亚湾。

both·y, both·ie [ˈbɔθi; ˋbɑθɪ] ***n.*** 〔Scot.〕(农民等住的)茅屋；(独间)小屋，窝棚。

bo tree [ˈbəu triː; ˋbo tri] ***n.*** 菩提树。

bot·ry·oid(al) [ˌbɔtriˈɔid(əl); ˏbɑtrɪˋɔɪd(əl)] ***a.*** 一串葡萄状的。

bot·ry·o·my·co·sis [ˈbɔtriəumaiˈkəusis; ˏbɑtrɪomaɪˋkosɪs] ***n.*** 葡萄菌病。

bots [bɔts; bɑts] ***n.*** 蝇蛆病。

Bot·swa·na [bɔtˈswɑːnə; bɑtsˋwɑnə] ***n.*** 博茨瓦纳(波札那)〔非洲〕。

bott [bɔt; bɑt] ***n.*** = bot.

bot·tine [bɔˈtiːn; bəˋtin] ***n.*** 短筒女靴。

bot·tle[1] [ˈbɔtl; bɑtl] **I** ***n.*** **1.** 瓶；一瓶的量。**2.** 〔the ～〕奶瓶；(瓶装)牛奶。**3.** 〔the ～〕酒；饮酒。**4.** (装酒，油等的)皮囊。*a wine* ～ 酒瓶。*a* ～ *of wine* 一瓶酒。*a* ～ *messenger* (用作测定海流等试验的)海流瓶。*a three-* ～ *man* 酒量大的人。***be fond of the*** ～ 好酒贪杯。***bring up*** [***raise***] ***on the*** ～ 用奶瓶喂(婴儿)，用牛奶把(婴儿)哺育大。***crack a*** ～ 开瓶饮酒。***hit the*** ～ 〔俚〕饮酒过多，酗酒。***keep*** (***sb.***) ***from the*** ～ 不让(某人)喝酒。***keep to the*** ～ 爱喝酒，嗜酒。(***talk***) ***over a*** ～ 一面喝酒一面(谈话等)。***pass*** ～ 传杯轮饮。***take to the*** ～ 喝上酒，爱上酒。**II** ***vt.*** **1.** 把(酒等)装瓶；把(水果等)装罐贮藏。**2.** 忍着，含着(不平、怒气等)(*up*)。**3.** 〔英俚〕捕获(逃犯等)，使(逃犯、敌军等)陷入困境(*up*)。～ *grape juice* 把葡萄汁装瓶。～ *up one's temper* 克制住自己的脾气。***Bottle it!*** 〔美俚〕不要吵了！静一静！～ ***off*** 把…由桶中移装瓶内(～ *off a cask of wine* 把一桶酒分装进若干小瓶)。～ **up 1.** 把…封在瓶内；压住(感情)，隐匿(事实)。**2.** 封锁(交通等)；捕获(逃犯等)；使(逃犯等)陷入困境。*keep things* ～*ed up* 把事情瞒起来。*Traffic was* ～*ed up in the tunnel.* 隧道停止通行。～ **baby** 用奶瓶哺育的婴孩。～ **bank** 旧瓶回收站。～**brush 1.** 洗瓶刷。**2.** 【植】问荆，红千层属植物。～**chart**【海】(根据海流试验瓶画成的)漂瓶图，海流图。～**cap** 瓶盖。～**-fed** ***a.*** 人工喂养的，(婴儿)以牛奶哺育的。～**-feeding** (婴儿的)人工喂养。～**glass** (深绿色的)瓶料玻璃。～ **gourd**【植】葫芦。～ **green** 深绿色。～ **holder 1.** 瓶托，瓶架。**2.** 【拳】(拳击选手的)副手。**3.** 后援(人)。～**neck 1.** ***n.*** 瓶颈口；(交通易堵塞的)隘道，狭口；〔美〕(特指生产中的)妨碍进度的因素，薄弱环节。**2.** ***vt.*** 阻碍，限制。**3.** ***vi.*** 交通堵塞。**4.** ***a.*** (街道等)狭隘的。～**nose** 酒糟鼻，红鼻子。～ **opener** 开瓶起子，拔塞器。～ **party** 给人自带酒的宴会。～ **washer** 洗瓶工；杂役。**-d** ***a.*** **1.** 瓶装的。**2.** 〔俚〕醉醺醺的，喝醉了的(～*d gas* 瓶装煤气，瓶装液化石油气。～*d water* 瓶装纯净水)。

bot·tle[2] [ˈbɔtl; ˋbɑtl̩] ***n.*** 〔英方〕(干草等的)束，堆。***look for a needle in a*** ～ ***of hay*** 干草堆里找针，吃力不讨好，徒劳无益。

bot·tling [ˈbɔtliŋ; ˋbɑtl̩ɪŋ] ***n.*** 装瓶；灌注。*a* ～ *machine* 装瓶机。

bot·tom [ˈbɔtəm; ˋbɑtəm] ***n.*** **1.** 底，底部。**2.** 地基，基础；根底；底细，真相，原因，根源。**3.** (树的)根干；(山)麓；〔方，常 *pl.*〕河边低地，谷，洼地；(页的)下端；(餐桌，班级等的)末席，(名单的)末尾；〔英〕(港湾、街道等的)尽头，末端，(庭院等的)顶里面；【纺】(织物的)地，底子，底色。**4.** 水底，海底，湖底，河底。**5.** (吃水线以下的)船底(部)，舱底；货船，船舶。**6.** 臀部，屁股；〔*pl.*〕睡裤；(椅子的)椅垫。**7.** 精力，持久力，耐力。**8.** 〔*pl.*〕底部沉积物，残渣，脚子。**9.** 最低点；最坏的地步。**10.** 【棒】下半局。*the* ～ *of the stairs* 楼梯下段。*the* ～ *of a page* 一页纸的下端。*the* ～ *of a flatiron* 熨斗的底。*the* ～ *of the street* 街的尽头处。*foreign* ～*s* 外国船。*sit at the* ～ *of the table* 坐末席。*a horse of good* ～ 根底好的[有耐久力的]马。*Well, bless my fat* ～. 啊，我的天！***at*** (***the***) ～ 实际上，内心里；本质上(*a good man at* ～ 本质上是好人。*know at* ～ *that...* 心里明白…)。***at the*** ～ ***of fortune's wheel*** 时乖命舛，倒霉透顶。***be at the*** ～ ***of*** **1.** 在…深处。**2.** 是…的主动者〔主因〕，引起(*at the* ～ *of one's heart* 内心深处。*at the* ～ *of all these crimes* 引起这一切犯罪现象的原因是…)。～ ***up*** 倒置，反转。***Bottoms up!*** 〔美俚〕干杯！***from the*** ～ ***of one's*** [***the***] ***heat*** 发自内心深处，真心诚意。***from the*** ～ ***up*** 从一开始；彻底地。***get to the*** ～ ***of*** 走到…的尽头；彻底查明(问题等)。***go to the*** ～ 沉，沉没；深究，探究。***knock the*** ～ ***out of ...*** 证明…无价值，使…失去立足基础。***on her own*** ～ 【海】(商船、渔船等)无债，已付清应缴款项。***reach the*** ～ 达到水底。***scrape the*** ～ ***of the barrel*** 刮桶底；〔美俚〕使出最后一招。***send to the*** ～ 弄沉；打沉，击沉。***smell the*** ～ (***ground***) (船)擦泥缓行。***stand on one's own*** ～ 独立；自力更生。***swim to the*** ～ 〔谑〕下沉，沉下去。***to the*** ～ 到最底下，彻底(*drink the cup to the* ～ 饮干一杯。*search* (*sth.*) *to the* ～ 彻底探究，追根穷源)。***touch*** ～ **1.** (船)搁浅。**2.** (数值等)达到最低点。**3.** (研究等)接触根底，得到根据[结论]，理解。**II** ***a.*** **1.** 底部的；最下层的，最低的。**2.** 最后的；根本的。**3.** (鱼等)底栖的。*her* ～ *lip* 她的下嘴唇。～ *fish* 栖于水底的鱼。*the* ～ *book in the stack* 书架最下面一层的书。*the* ～ *floor* 最底一层。*the* ～ *cause* 根本原因。～ *dollar* 最后一块钱，所有的钱(*bet one's* ～ *dollar* 孤注一掷；保证，确信)。～ *prices* 底价，最低价格。～ *recessive* 【生】隐性基因纯合体。～ *rung* (社会阶梯的)底层。***come out*** ～ 考试成绩倒数第一名。**III** ***vt.*** **1.** 给…上底；给(椅子)装面。**2.** 给…打地基；给…打底；建立…的基础。**3.** 着(海等的)底，达到…的底。**4.** 测量(海底等)的深度；查明…的真相[原因]。～ *a chair* 给椅子装面。*arguments* ～*ed on facts* 言之有据，有事实作依据的论点。～ *sb's plan* 弄清某人的打算[计划]。～ *the sub* 使潜水艇沉下水底。— ***vi.*** **1.** 变得有基础，建立基础。**2.** 达到底，停于底部。*The submarine* ～*ed on the ocean floor.* 潜水艇停在洋底。～ **out** 降到最低点。～ **board** (短艇的)底板。～ **drawer** 〔英〕(妇女为结婚准备的)嫁衣。～ **fish** 水底鱼。～ **land** 〔美〕河边低地，洼地；河边野草。**-less** ***a.*** **1.** 无底的；深不可测的。**2.** 无限的。**3.** 深奥难解的。**4.** 无底板的(*a bottomless problem* 深奥的难题。*a bottomless abyss* 无底深渊)。～**-line** ***vt.*** 准确地报出…的最终结算额。**-most** ***a.*** 最下面的；最低的；最深的；最根本的。

Bot·tome [bəˈtəum; bəˋtom] ***n.*** 博托姆〔姓氏〕。

bot·tom·ry [ˈbɔtəmri; ˋbɑtəmrɪ] ***n.*** **1.** 以船作抵押的借款。**2.** 冒风险的放债。

bot·u·lin [ˈbɔtjulin; ˋbɑtʃəlɪn] ***n.*** 【生化】肉毒杆菌毒素。

bot·u·li·nus [ˌbɔtfəˈlainəs; ˏbɑtʃəˋlaɪnəs] ***n.*** 【生化】肉毒杆菌。

bot·u·lism [ˈbɔtjulizəm; ˋbɑtʃəˋlɪzəm] ***n.*** 【医】腊肠[腐肉]中毒；罐头食品中毒。

bou·clé, bou·cle [buːˈklei; buˋkle] ***n.*** 珠毛呢，仿羔皮呢。

bou·doir [ˈbuːdwɑː, buːˈdwɑː; ˋbudwɑr, buˋdwɑr] ***n.*** 〔F.〕闺房。

bouf·fant [buːˈfɑ̃ːŋ; buˋfɑ̃ŋ] ***a.*** 〔F.〕鼓起的；(裙)膨鼓的；(发)蓬松的。

bouffe [buːf; buf] ***n.*** 〔It.〕滑稽歌剧。

Bou·gain·vil·lae·a [ˌbuːgənˈviliə; ˏbugənˋvɪlɪə] ***n.*** 【植】九重葛属，叶子花属。

bough [bau; baʊ] ***n.*** **1.** 大枝，树枝。**2.** 〔古〕绞刑架。～**pot 1.** 大花瓶。**2.** 〔英方〕花束。**-ed** ***a.*** (树)长有大枝的。

bought [bɔːt; bɔt] buy 的过去式及过去分词。

bought·en [ˈbɔːtn; ˋbɔtn̩] *a*. 〔美方〕买来的 (*opp*. homemade)。
bou·gie [ˈbuːʒiː; ˋbudʒi] *n*. 1.【医】探条。2.【药】栓剂。3. 蜡烛。
bouil·la·baisse [ˌbuːljəˈbeis, ˌbuːjɑːˋbeis; ˏbuljəˋbes, ˏbujɑˋbes] *n*. 〔F.〕浓味炖鱼〔用两种以上的鱼加酒等烹调而成〕。
bouil·li [ˈbuːjiː; ˏbuˋji] *n*. 〔F.〕白煮肉;炖肉。
bouil·lon [ˈbuːjɔ̃ːŋ; ˋbujɑŋ] *n*. 〔F.〕1. 肉汁清汤〔用牛肉、鸡肉等作成〕。2.【兽医】蹄癌。3. (衣服的)膨褶。4. 一种细菌培养基。~ **cube** (切成方块的)浓缩肉汤冻。
boul. = boulevard。
bou·lan·ger·ite [buːˈlændʒərait; buˋlændʒəˏraɪt] *n*. 【矿】硫锑铅矿。
boul·der [ˈbəuldə; ˋboldɚ] *n*. 圆石,卵石;【地】冰砾,巨砾;漂砾。~ **clay**【地】泥砾;冰砾泥。**B- Dam** 顽石坝〔美国科罗拉多河上的大坝,高 221 米,坝顶长约 360 米〕。~ **setter** 砾石铺砌层。
Bou·le [ˈbuːliː; ˋbuli] *n*. 〔希〕1. (古希腊的)立法会议。2. (现代希腊的)议会〔尤指众议院〕。
bou·le·vard [ˈbuːlivaːd; ˋbuləˏvard] *n*. 1. 宽敞的步道,林荫路。2. 〔美〕大马路,干道,大街。
boule·var·dier [buːlvaːˈdje; ˏbulvarˋdjɛ] *n*. 〔F.〕巴黎林荫大道咖啡店的主顾;〔转义〕活跃于社交界的男子,花花公子。
boule·ver·se·ment [buːlveəsˈmɔn; bulversˋman] *n*. 〔F.〕颠倒;颠覆,推翻;混乱。
Bou·logne [buˈləun; buˋlon] *n*. 布伦〔法国北部一港口〕。
boult [bəult; bolt] *v*. = bolt[2]。
boul·ter [ˈbəultə; ˋboltɚ] *n*. 多钩粗钓丝。
bounce [bauns; baʊns] I *vi*. 1. (球等)跳起,弹起,反跳,弹回;(人)跳跃,跳起 (*up*),跳进 (*in*),跳出 (*out*),乱跳乱蹦 (*about*),急促地动。2. 夸口,吹牛,说大话;虚张声势。3. 〔俚〕(支票)退票,拒付。*The ball ~d off the wall*. 球从墙壁上反弹回来。~ *out of the room* 冲出屋外。~ *up and down on the seat* 在座位上前后颠簸。*His checks ~*. 他的支票被银行拒付。— *vt*. 1. 使弹回,使跳起;拍(球)。2. 〔口〕责骂。3. 〔英〕威胁,逼使;诈骗。4. 〔美俚〕赶出,撵走;解雇,辞退,开除,将…撤职。~ *a ball* 拍球。~ *sb. out of sth*. 骗走某人的东西。~ *sb. into* [*out of*] *doing sth*. 逼使某人做[不做]某事。~ ***a beauty*** 〔美、棒球〕打出好球。~ **back** 〔口〕很快挽回(颓势、败局),立即恢复(元气等)。II *n*. 1. 跳,弹,(球等的)弹回;〔口〕弹力;〔俚〕活力。2. 夸口,吹牛,自大;鲁莽。3. 猛击;【军】(在较高高度对敌机的)突然袭击。4. 〔美俚〕赶出,解雇。*rise with a ~* 猛地跳起。*contact ~* 【物】接点颤动。*This tennis ball has no more ~*. 这个网球已经失去弹力了。*get the* (*grand*) *~* 〔美俚〕被解雇[被辞退,撵走,斥退]。*give sb. the* (*grand*) *~* 解雇[辞退,撵走,斥退]某人。*There is ~ in this step*. 他步履轻捷[走路有精神]。III *ad*. 1. 猛跳。2. 猛然,突然,砰地。*come ~ into* [*gainst*] 与…砰地相撞。~-**back**【物】反冲,反射。~ **plate** 反跳板。
bounc·er [ˈbaunsə; ˋbaʊnsɚ] *n*. 1. (同类中特大的)巨人,巨物。2. 跳跃者。3. 大话,谎话;吹牛大家。4. 〔美俚〕戏院[旅馆]保镖。*That dog is a ~*. 那条狗长得特别大。
bounc·ing [ˈbaunsiŋ; ˋbaʊnsɪŋ] *a*. 1. 跳跃的。2. (人)强壮的,生气勃勃的,精神饱满的。3. 巨大的,异常的。4. 吹牛的。*a ~ sum* 一笔巨款。*a ~ lie* 大吹其牛。***a ~ baby*** 1. 活蹦乱跳的孩子。2. 〔军俚〕榴散地雷。
boun·cy [ˈbaunsi; ˋbaʊnsɪ] *a*. (*-ci·er*, *-ci·est*) 1. 生气勃勃的。2. 有弹力的。3. 自高自大的。
bound[1] [baund; baʊnd] I *n*. 〔*pl*.〕1. 界限,界线,限度。2. 边界,边境;边界线内的领土。3. 区域,领域,范围。*the ~s of space and time* 时空范围。*the farthest ~s of the ocean* 大洋最远的界限。***beyond the ~s of*** 越出…的范围以外,为…所不及。***break ~s*** 越轨;过度,逾限;【军】擅自进入军事禁区。***keep within ~s*** 使不过度;约束,守规;持中。***know no ~s*** 不知足,无厌,无限制。***out of ~s*** 1. 越界,越轨,越限。2. 禁止…入内 (*to*) (*The ball bounced out of ~s*. 球跳出界外。*The park is out of ~s to students*. 此公园不准学生入内)。***set*** [***put***] ***~s to*** 限制。***within*** (***the***) ***~s*** 在规定范围内,不越轨。II *vt*. 1. 限,限制。2. 形成…的界限[边界],以…为界,邻接。3. 指出…的范围[界限]。~ *one's desires by reason* 以理性约束欲望。*The United States is ~ed on the north by Canada*. 美国北与加拿大接壤。*The students were asked to ~ their country*. 学生被要求指出本国的国界。— *vi*. 〔古〕接界 (*with*)。
bound[2] [baund; baʊnd] I *n*. 跳,跳跃,跳起;弹跳;跃进。*a ~ forward* 向前跳跃。*hit a ball on the ~* 在球跳起来的时候击球。***at a*** [***with one***] ***~*** 一跃,一跳。***by leaps and ~s*** 连跑带跳地,飞快地(*advance by leaps and ~s* 进步飞跃)。II *vt*. 使跳跃,使弹起。— *vi*. 跳跃;跳起,弹起;跳开。~ *to one's feet* 一跃而起。*The ball ~ed against the wall*. 球从墙上反弹回来。~ ***into fame*** [***favor***] 一举成名[受欢迎]。~ ***on*** [***upon***] 猛扑(*The leopard ~ed on the prey*. 那只豹猛扑向猎物)。
bound[3] [baund; baʊnd] bind 的过去式及过去分词。*a*. 1. 绑着的,被束缚的。2. 负有义务的,有责任的,理应…的;受(合同、法律等)约束的。3. 装订的,有封面的。4. 被…封锁的;秘结的,便秘的。5. 必定的,肯定的。6. 〔美俚〕下了决心的,决心要…。7. 密切关联的;【化、物】结合的;黏合的,耦合的。*a ~ prisoner* 被绑缚着的犯人。*She is ~ to her family*. 她被家庭束缚住了。*man-~* 因人员不足不能开船的。*ice-~* 冰封的。*desk-~* 整日伏案工作的。*He is ~ by the terms of the contract*. 他受到合同条款的约束。*a book ~ in leather* 皮面精装书。~ *volume* 合订本。*It's ~ to happen*. 这件事必然要发生。*She is ~ to go*. 她决心要走。***be ~ up in*** 热中于,专心于,忙于(*~ up in one's work* 专心工作)。***be ~ up with*** 和…有密切关系。***I'll be ~*** 一定,保证,我可以担保。~ **charge**【物】束缚电荷。~ **medium**【化】黏合介质。~ **pocket** 暗口袋。~ **vector**【数】束缚矢量。~ **water**【化】结合[束缚]水。
bound[4] [baund; baʊnd] *a*. 〔作述语用〕1. 开往(某处)去的,要往(某处)去的。2. 〔古〕准备,打算。*Where are you ~* (*for*)? 你到哪里去? ***be ~ for*** 以…为目的地的 (*The train is ~ for Denver*. 列车开往丹佛)。
bound·a·ry [ˈbaundəri; ˋbaʊndərɪ] *n*. 边界,疆界,限界 (*between*);(球场)边线;界标;界限,范围,分野。*a ~ dispute* 边界纠纷。*the ~ between Canada and the United States* 美加国界。***boundaries on all sides*** 四方辐辏之所,四通八达。~ **condition**【数】边界条件。~ **effect**【物】边界效应。~ **layer**【物】边界层。~-**line** (边)界线。~ **rider** 〔澳〕牧场巡边工。~ **science** 边缘科学。
bound·ed [ˈbaundid; ˋbaʊndɪd] *a*. 1. 有界限的,有限制的。2. 【数】有界的。~ **function**【数】有界函数,囿函数。~ **set**【数】有界集,囿集。**-ness** *n*.
bound·en [ˈbaundən; ˋbaʊndən] bind 的古体过去分词。*a*. 1. 义不容辞的。2. 〔古〕受恩的。***be ~ to ... for ...*** 多亏…才,仗有…才(*I'm ~ to him for my success*. 我的成功多亏了他)。***one's ~ duty*** 义不容辞的责任,职责所在。
bound·er [ˈbaundə; ˋbaʊndɚ] *n*. 1. 〔英俚〕鲁莽[粗俗]的人。2. 【棒球】定界员。
bound·less [ˈbaundlis; ˋbaʊndlɪs] *a*. 无限的,无穷的,无边无际的。~ *ambition* 欲壑难填,无限大的野心。~ *energy* 无穷的精力。**-ly** *ad*. **-ness** *n*.
boun·te·ous [ˈbauntiəs; ˋbaʊntɪəs] *a*. 〔书〕1. 宽宏大量的,博爱的,慷慨的。2. 富裕的,丰富的,丰厚的。**-ly** *ad*.

-ness *n*.

boun·ti·ful [ˈbauntifʊl; ˋbaʊntəfəl] *a*. 1. 宽宏大量的, 慷慨的。2. 丰富的 (*of*). *a ~ giver* 慷慨解囊的人。*a ~ harvest* 丰收。**-ly** *ad*. **-ness** *n*.

boun·ty [ˈbaunti; ˋbaʊntɪ] *n*. 1. 慷慨, 仁爱, 博爱, 宽大; 恩惠。2. 赐物, 赠物; 赐金, 赠金。3. 赏金; 奖金 (*on*; *upon*; *for*). *She depends on his ~*. 她倚靠他的施舍生活。*There was a ~ on his head*. 悬赏买他的人头。*offer a ~ for dead wolves* 悬赏奖励打狼。***the ~ of nature*** 自然的恩赐。~ **hunter** 为获赏而追捕野兽[逃犯等]的人。~ **jumper** (美国南北战争时)领取入伍津帖后开小差的人, 壮丁油子。~ **land** (军功)赐地。~ **money** (军功)赏金。

bou·quet [ˈbu(ː)kei, buˈkei; buˋke, buˋke] *n*. 〔F.〕1. 花束; 一丛礼花, 一束烟火。2. 恭维话。3. [buˈkei, bʊˋke] (葡萄酒的)香, 芳香; (文艺作品的)特殊风格。*a ~ of roses* 一束玫瑰花。*~s and brickbats* 褒贬之词。***throw ~s at*** 赞美, 称赞。

Bour·bon [ˈbuəbən; ˋbʊrbən] *n*. 1.【法史】波旁皇室的一员。2. 〔美〕最顽固的保守分子; 极端保守的政治家。3. 〔b-〕波旁威士忌〔美国 Kentucky 洲 Bourbon 地方出产的烈性威士忌酒 = **b- whisky**〕。**-ism** *n*. 对波旁皇室的拥护; 保皇主义, 顽固的保守主义。

bour·don [ˈbuədən; ˋbʊrdn] I *n*. 1.【乐】(风琴的)最低音簧; 风笛的低音管。2. 嗡嗡的低音。3. 〔罕〕朝山香客的手杖。II *vi*. 发嗡嗡声。

bourg [buəg; bʊrg] *n*. 〔F.〕1. (中世纪筑有城堡的)村镇。2. 市镇。

bour·geois[1] [ˈbuəʒwɑː; bʊrˋʒwɑ] I (*pl*. ~) *n*. 1. 中产阶级的市民; 中世纪城镇的自由民。2. 业主, 店主, 商人。3. 有产者; (*pl*.)资产阶级。II *a*. 1. 资产阶级的, 中产阶级的。2. 商人根性的, 市侩的; 无教养的, 鄙俗的; 注意物质享受的。~ *taste* 庸俗趣味。

bour·geois[2] [bəːˈdʒɔis; bɚˋdʒɔɪs] *n*. 〔古〕【印】九点活字〔相当我国新五号铅字〕。

bour·geoi·sie [ˌbuəʒwɑːˈziː; ˏbʊrʒwɑˋzi] *n*. 商人阶级; 中产阶级, 资产阶级。

bour·geon [ˈbəːdʒən; ˋbɚdʒən] *vi*. = burgeon。

bourn(e)[1] [buən; bʊrn] *n*. 〔Scot.〕小河。

bourn(e)[2] [buən; bʊrn] *n*. 1. 〔古〕境界, 界限。2. 〔诗〕目的地; 目的。3. 领域。*the undiscover'd country from whose ~ no traveller returns* 那片渺渺茫茫的土地啊, 走向那里的旅客一去不复还〔莎士比亚剧本《哈姆雷特》中的诗句〕。

bour·rée [buːˈrei; buˋre] *n*. 1. 布列舞〔十七世纪法国的一种舞蹈〕。2. 布列舞曲。

bourse [buəs; bʊrs] *n*. 〔F.〕(证券)交易所; 〔B-〕巴黎证券交易所。

bouse[1] [buːz, bauz; buz, baʊz] *vi*., *n*. = booze。

bouse[2] [bauz; baʊz] *vt*., *vi*.【海】用辘轳吊(某物)。

bous·tro·phe·don [ˌbaustrəˈfiːdən; ˏbaustrəˋfidn̩] I *n*. 一行由右而左一行由左而右的写法。II *a*., *ad*. 右行左行交互书写的[地]。

bout [baut; baʊt] *n*. 1. (工作、闹饮等的)一阵, 一回, 一转, 一次, 一番。2. (耕地等的)一个来回; (赌赛等的)一场次较量, 一个回合。3. (绳的)一绕; 一缕; 一锄; 一犁; 一刈(等); (病的)发作(时期)。~ *of work* 干一阵工作。*a ~ of illness* 病发作一阵。*a drinking ~* 一次宴会。*a wrestling ~* 一场摔跤。*play a ~ or two* (赌博等)玩一两回。

bou·tique [bu(ː)ˈtiːk; buˋtik] *n*. 〔F.〕1. (妇女)时装用品小商店。2. 镶嵌珠宝[镀金]的日用品。3. 〔自备原料以满足订户特定需求的〕专酿优质酒小酒厂。~ **farm** (专营从国外引进作物等的)珍品农场。

bou·ton·nière [ˌbuːtɔˈnjeə; ˏbutn̩ˋjɛr] 〔F.〕钮孔花〔别在钮扣眼上的一束[朵]花〕。

bouts ri·més [ˈbuː ˈriːmei; buriˋme] 〔F.〕和韵; 和韵诗。

bou·zou·ki [buːˈzuːki; buˋzukɪ] *n*. 布素奇琴〔一种希腊弦乐器, 似曼陀林琴〕。

Bo·vey [ˈbuːvi; ˋbuvɪ] *n*. 博维〔姓氏〕。

bo·vid [ˈbəuvid; ˋbovɪd] I *a*. 牛科的。II *n*. 牛科动物。

bo·vine [ˈbəuvain; ˋbovaɪn] I *a*. 1. 牛科的; 牛的; 牛一样的。2. 鲁钝的。*a ~ temperament* 鲁钝的性格。*n*. 牛科动物。~ **pest** 牛瘟。~ **somatotropin**【生】牛生长素。~ **spongiform encephalopathy**【兽医】牛海绵状脑病〔俗称"疯牛病"〕。

bov·ril [ˈbɔvril; ˋbɑvrɪl] *n*. 〔英〕牛肉汁〔来源于商标名〕。

bov·ver [ˈbɔvə; ˋbɑvɚ] I *n*. 〔英俚〕(流氓等的)街头殴斗。II *vi*. 参加街头殴斗。~ **boot** 街斗靴〔一种装上平头钉和钢鞋尖的重靴, 用以踢击伤人〕。

bow[1] [bəu; bo] I *n*. 1. 弓; 石弩; 弓形物〔饰〕; 弓形弯曲; 弧。2.【乐】琴弓;【机】锯弓。3. 虹。4. 蝴蝶结, 蝴蝶结领带。5. 〔美〕眼镜框〔脚〕。6. 弓手。7. 凸肚窗。~ *compasses* 小圆规; 外卡钳。*tie a ribbon in a ~* 把缎带打一个蝴蝶结。~ *and arrow* 弓矢。*He is the best ~ in the country*. 他是国内最好的射手。***bend*** [***draw***, ***pull***] ***the*** [***a***] ***long ~*** 吹牛, 说大话。***draw a ~ at a venture*** 瞎开弓; 胡搞。~ ***have two*** [***many***] ***strings to one's ~*** 作好两[几]手准备。II *vt*. 1. 把…弯作弓形; 弯。2. 用弓拉奏。— *vi*. 1. 弯作弓形。2. 用弓拉琴。~-**backed** *a*. 驼背的, 弯腰屈背的。~ **compass(es)** 两脚规, 圆规; 外卡钳。~ **drill** 弓钻。~**fin** 弓鳍鱼。~-**front** *a*. 弓背形的, 凸形的(*a ~ front chest* 鸡胸) ~ **hand** 1. 持弓的手〔通常为左手〕。2. 拉琴弓的手〔通常为右手〕。~ **instrument** 弓弦乐器。~ **knot** 滑结, 活结。~-**leg** 〔常 *pl*.〕弓形腿, 罗圈腿。~**legged** *a*. 弓形腿的, 罗圈腿的。~ **man** 弓手。~ **pen** 两脚规。~ **saw** 弓锯。~ **shot** 箭的射程, 一箭之地〔约 200—400 英尺〕。~**string** 1. *n*. 弓弦; 绞索。2. *vt*. 给(弓)装弦, 绞死, 勒死。~ **tie** 蝴蝶结领带。~ **window**【建】凸肚窗, 弓形窗; 〔卑〕罗汉肚。**-ing** *n*. (弦乐器)弓法; (音乐家的)演奏技巧。

bow[2] [bau; baʊ] I *a*. 1. 点头, 鞠躬。2. 低头, 屈服。*with a low ~* 深深地鞠一躬。***a ~ and a scrape*** 打躬作揖。***make a ~ to*** 对…行礼。***make one's ~*** (讲完演说等)鞠躬而退出〔进入〕, 退场, 退席, 退出(社会生活等)。***take a ~*** (在鼓掌声中)点头答礼; 答谢。II *vi*. 1. 鞠躬, 打躬, 点头; (树等)弯屈。2. 屈服, 屈从 (*to*). ~ *to sb*. 向某人鞠躬〔点头招呼〕。~ *from the waist* 弯腰鞠躬。~ *one's thanks* 鞠躬致谢。~ *to sb.'s knowledge* 对某人的学识表示敬意。*The pines ~ed low*. 松树深深地弯曲着身子。— *vt*. 1. 弯(腰等); 低(头等); (点头)指示, 表示。2. 使屈从。3. 压弯 (*down*). ***be ~ed with*** (*age*; *care*) (年老)腰弯; (因操心而)意气消沉。~ ***and scrape*** 打躬作揖。~ ***before*** [***to***] ***the inevitable*** 屈服于(必然的)命运之前。~ ***down to*** 屈服于…之下; 给…行礼。~ ***out*** 〔美〕辞职; 退出, 退场。~ (*sb*.) ***in*** [***out***] 恭迎入内[恭送出门]。~ ***the knees to*** 对…行屈膝礼, 对…表示敬意, 崇拜, 信奉。~ ***the neck*** 屈服, 服从, 低头。~***ing acquaintance*** 点头之交。

bow[3] [bau; baʊ] *n*. 〔常 *pl*.〕1. 船首; 舰首; 机首。2. 前桨手。~***s on*** 船首向前; 勇往直前地。~***s under*** (船头)被淹没; 困难地(前进); 张皇失措地。***in ~s*** 1. 命令起桨开船。2. 准备靠岸[靠拢大船]。***on the ~*** 在船首方向〔船头前面左右 45 度弧内〕。~ **chaser** 舰首炮。~ **fast** 船首的铁链。~ **grace** (保护船首的)保险杠[垫]。~ **gun** 前枪, 前炮〔舰艇、坦克等前部的枪炮〕。~ **mar** 前桨手。~ **oar** 前桨; 前桨手。~ **spirit** 第一斜桅; 牙樯。~ **wave**【海】(头)激波, 船首波, 顶头波。

Bo·wa·ter [ˈbəuˌwɔːtə; ˋboˏwɔtɚ] *n*. 鲍沃特〔姓氏〕。

Bow bells [ˈbəuˈbelz; boˋbɛlz] 1. 伦敦市区。2. 道地的伦敦人〔源自伦敦 St. Mary-le-Bow 教堂的钟声所及处〕。***within the sound of Bow bells*** 在伦敦市区内。

bowd·ler·ize [ˈbaudləraiz; ˋbaʊdləraɪz] *vt*. 删去(书中)

B

B

不妥处〔尤指不适合青少年阅读处, 源出 Thomas Bowdler 1818 年出版莎士比亚作删节本〕; 删改。**-i·zation** *n*.

bowed [bəud; bod] *a*. 1. 弓一样弯曲的, 弓形的; 有弓的。2. (头等)低下的。*listen with a ~ head* 低头恭听。

bow·el [ˈbauəl; ˋbauəl] *n*. 1. 〔常 *pl*.〕(人)肠〔作修饰语或医学术语时用单数〕。2. 〔*pl*.〕内脏; 内部。3. 〔*pl*.〕同情心, 怜悯心。*the large* [*small*] *~s* 大[小]肠。*I have loose ~s*. 我泻肚了。*a ~ complaint* 肠道疾病。*The ~s move* [*are open*] 要大便。*move* [*loosen, relax*] *the ~s* 大便。*relieve the ~s* 通便, 大便, 小便。*bind the ~s* 止泻。*the ~s of the earth* 地球内部, 地壳深处。*The cabins were in the ~s of the ship* 客舱在船的内部。*have no ~s* 无情, 残忍, 不通情理。~ **movement** *n*. 1. 排便。2. 粪。

Bow·en [ˈbəuin; ˋboɪn] *n*. 鲍恩〔姓氏〕。

bow·er[1] [ˈbauə; ˋbauɚ] I *n*. 1. 亭子, 凉亭; 树荫处。2. 〔诗〕卧室, 闺房。3. 〔诗〕隐居处; 乡间茅舍, 村舍; 精舍。II *vt*. 荫蔽。~**-bird** 园丁鸟。~**-maid** 侍婢, 丫头。

bow·er[2] [ˈbauə; ˋbauɚ] *n*. 尤卡(euchre)牌戏中的王牌。*best ~* 百搭。*right ~* 王牌 jack。*left ~* 其它花色中的 jack。

bow·er[3] [ˈbauə; ˋbauɚ] *n*. 【船】大锚, 主锚, 船首锚。*the best* [*small*] *~* 右弦〔左弦〕主锚。

bow·er[4] [ˈbəuə; ˋbor] *n*. 用弓拉奏乐器的人。

bow·er·ed [ˈbauəd; ˋbauɚd] *a*. = bowery[1].

bow·ery[1] [ˈbauəri; ˋbauərɪ] *a*. 1. 有亭的, 凉亭似的。2. 有树荫的。*Trees made the meadow a ~ maze*. 树木使草原成了绿荫处处的迷宫。

bow·er·y[2] [ˈbauəri; ˋbauərɪ] I *n*. 1. 〔美〕(昔日南非、纽约等地的)荷兰移民农场。2. 〔the B-〕(纽约市小饭馆和流浪者多的)波威里街。II *a*. 俗丽的, 漂亮而不值钱的。

bow·ie [ˈbəui; ˋbo·ɪ] *n*. 〔美〕长猎刀 (= ~-knife). *Bowie State* 〔美〕Arkansas 州的别名。

bowl[1] [bəul; bol] *n*. 1. 钵, 碗; 一钵〔碗〕的量; 〔美〕盘, 盆。2. 〔诗〕饮器, 大杯; 〔喻〕烈酒; 欢宴, 狂饮。3. 碗状物; (天平秤等的)碗形等盘; 匙, 烟斗。4. 盆地; 〔美〕圆形竞技场。*a rice ~* 饭碗。*a sugar ~* 糖钵。*a ~ of soup* 一碗汤。*the flowing ~* 满杯的酒。***over the ~*** 在酒宴上; 一边喝酒一边(谈话等)。

bowl[2] [bəul; bol] I *n*. 1. (游戏用的)木球, 保龄球。2. 〔*pl*.〕滚木球戏, 九柱戏(ninepins), 〔美〕十柱戏(tenpins)。3. 【机】(离心机等的)转筒, 转子; 浮筒, 辊筒。*play* [*at*] *~s* 玩滚木球戏。*have a game of ~s* 玩一场滚木球戏。~ *mill* 【机】球磨机。*float ~* 浮筒。***at long ~s*** 远距离地(尤指军舰远程炮轰)。II *vt*. 1. 滚转(球、环、轮等); 使稳捷地行驶; (用车等)运送。2. (滚木球戏中)完成(规定的回数); 得到…分; 【板球】投(球); 打倒。*He ~s a good game*. 他的滚(木)球玩得好。~ *a 120 game* (滚木球戏)得 120 分。*~s 150* 得 150 分。— *vi*. 1. 转球, 投球; 玩滚(木)球。2. (像木球样)毂辘毂辘地滚走; (车等)稳捷地行驶。3. 【板球】投球给击球手。~ ***along*** 稳捷地走[行驶]。~ ***down*** 1. (滚木球戏等)用球击倒。2. 〔口〕打倒, 撞倒, 打败。~ ***off*** 【板球】打落。~ ***out*** 1. 【板球】击中三柱门[击落三柱门横木]。2. 〔俚〕戳穿(某人谎话)。3. = ~down. ~ ***over*** 1. (九柱戏中)击倒; 撞倒。2. 使狼狈, 使慌张(*He's ~ed over by a dashing horse*. 他被奔马撞倒。***~ed over by the evil news*** 噩耗传来, 不知所措)。

bowl·der [ˈbəuldə; ˋboldɚ] *n*. = boulder.

bowl·er[1] [ˈbəulə; ˋbolɚ] *n*. 1. 玩滚木球戏[九柱戏、十柱戏]者, 滚木球的人。2. 【板球】投球手。

bowl·er[2] [ˈbəulə; ˋbolɚ] I *n*. 〔英〕圆顶硬礼帽。~ *hat* 〔英〕圆顶硬礼帽。~**-hat** *vt*. 〔俚〕由(军队等处)退役, 退职。

Bowles [bəulz; bolz] *n*. 鲍尔斯〔姓氏〕。

bowl·ful [ˈbəulˌful; ˋbolˏful] *n*. 一满钵[碗、盘]。

bow·line [ˈbəulin; ˋbolɪn] *n*. 1. 【船】帆脚索。2. 单套结 (= ~ knot). ***on a ~*** 【海】趁风扬帆开行。***on an easy ~*** 【海】抢风满帆开行。

bowl·ing [ˈbəuliŋ; ˋbolɪŋ] *n*. 1. 滚木球, 玩滚木球戏; 玩九柱戏。2. (板球的)投球。~**-alley** 滚球场。~ **green** 木球草地, 草地滚球场。

Bow·man [ˈbəumən; ˋbomən] *n*. 鲍曼〔姓氏〕。

bow·pot [ˈbaupɔt; ˋbaupɑt] *n*. 1. 大花瓶。2. 花束。

bowse[1] [buːz, bauz; buz, bauz] *n*., *vi*. 〔古〕暴饮, 狂饮, 痛饮; 酒, 酒宴(= booze)。

bowse[2] [bauz; bauz] *vt*., *vi*. 【海】= bouse[2].

bows·er [ˈbauzə; ˋbauzɚ] *n*. 1. (机场等用的)加油车。2. 加油艇(= ~ boat)。

Bow·street [ˈbəustriːt; ˋboˏstrit] (伦敦中央违警罪法庭所在地的)玻街。**the ~ Court** 伦敦违警罪法庭。~ **officer** [**runner**] (19 世纪初期)伦敦违警罪管治科警官。

bow·wow [ˈbauˈwau; ˋbauˋwau] I *int*. (模仿狗叫的)汪汪! II [ˈbauwau; ˋbauwau] *n*. 1. 狗咬声。2. 〔儿〕汪汪狗(= *dog*)。— *vi*. 1. (狗)汪汪叫。2. 作狗叫声。***go to the ~s*** 〔美俚〕堕落; 毁灭。***the*** (***big***) ***~ style*** 武断语调〔笔调〕。~ **theory** 【语】拟声说。

bow·yer [ˈbəujə; ˋbojɚ] *n*. 1. 弓匠。2. 弓商。

box[1] [bɔks; bɑks] I *n*. 1. 箱, 柜, 匣, 盒; 罩壳; 钱柜; 〔美口〕保险箱; 邮箱, 信箱; 〔英〕礼盒; 礼物(旅行用)衣箱。2. 一箱, 一盒。3. (戏院等的)包厢; (饭店等的)分格座位; (马等的)格形厩; (法庭的)证人席; 陪审席; 被告席; 专席。4. 哨房, 岗亭, 信号所, 事务所; 〔英〕(猎人等的)小屋; 电话间; 〔美〕猎鸭小船。5. (马车等的)驭者座; (卡车的)车兜。6. (窗)框, 壁橱; 【机】轴承箱, 箱状部分; 箱状物。7. 【棒球】投手位; 打手位。〔俚〕(足球)禁区; (以线标出的)小区。8. 〔美〕(树上挖的)取液孔。9. (报纸上的)花边读物。10. 〔俚〕话匣子, 留声机; 电唱机; 电视机。11. 〔卑〕(女性的)外阴部; 〔俚〕弦乐器; 钢琴。*mail ~* 邮箱。*money ~* 钱匣。*a ~ of candy* 一盒糖果。*a press ~* 记者席。*witness ~* 证人席。*jury ~* 陪审员席。*a shooting ~* 狩猎小屋。*a call ~* 电话室。*a police ~* 岗亭。*black ~* (探测地下核试验的)黑箱。*key ~* 电键匣。*pull ~* (电线)分线盒。*a gear ~* 齿轮箱。*a fire-alarm ~* 火警报警器。*an eternity ~* 〔俚〕棺材。~ ***and needle*** 【航海】罗盘。***in a ~*** = ***in a bad*** [***tight***] ~ 处逆境, 为难, 困。***in the same ~*** 处于同一地位, 处于同样的困境。***in the wrong ~*** 搞错地方, 不得其所; 处于窘境。***out of*** [***beyond***] ***the ~*** 创造性地; 打破传统地。II *vt*. 1. 把…装盒[装箱], 给…装上罩壳; 包围。2. 把…做成箱形[盒形]。3. 分隔。4. 【海】使(船)顺风转向。5. 在树上挖孔采液汁。6. 【气】沿(风暴区)边缘作箱形飞行。7. 使挤在一处。~ *the glassware* 把玻璃器皿装箱。~ *a wheel hub* 给轮毂加罩壳。~ *a storm* 【气】在风暴区边沿作箱形飞行。*With no windows I felt ~ed in suffocating*. 由于没有窗户, 我觉得关在屋子里很闷气。~ ***a horse*** 把马系在格形厩栏里。~ ***about*** 【海】使(船)转向。~ ***in*** 1. = ~ up. 2. 【赛马】阻拦(他马)。~ ***off*** 1. 把…隔成小房。2. 使(船)微微调向。~ ***the compass*** 1. 依次列举罗盘的三十二方位。2. 屡变(议论、意见等)而终于采纳原议。~ ***up*** 1. 把…装箱。2. 把…困在狭小区域内, 使陷困境, 使挤在一处。3. 〔口〕弄乱; 弄错。~ **barrage** 【军】1. 边缘射击。2. 高射炮火网。~ **bed** 1. 四周围成箱形的床。2. 可以折成箱柜的床。~**board** (制盒、箱用的)硬纸板。~ **bridge** 【电】电阻箱电桥。~ **calf** (制靴的)小牛皮。~**car** 箱车; 〔美〕有盖货车; 〔*pl*.〕骰子的十二点〔在双骰赌中掷出者为输〕; 【物】矩形波串。~ **cloth** (做驭者大衣的)茶黄色厚呢, 缩绒厚呢。~ **coat** 驭者外套; 连披肩厚外套。~ **cotton** 标准样棉。~ **horn** 喇叭形天线。~**iron** 熨斗。~ **keeper** 包厢管理员。~ **kite** 箱形风筝〔测气象用〕。~ **lunch** 午餐盒餐。~ **number** 信箱号。~ **office** 售票室。~**-office** *a*. 卖座很好的; 受人欢迎的, 流行的。~**-office val-**

ue 票房价值。~ **oyster** 精选大蚝,礼蚝。~ **respirator** 箱形面具,防毒面具。~**score**【棒球】比赛纪录表。~ **seat** 1.(马车)驭者座。2.(剧院)包厢,(运动场)正面看台座。3.便于观看的地方。~ **spring** 弹簧床座。~ **stall** (厩的)分格栏。~**wagon**〔英〕有盖货车。~ **wrench** [**key, spanner**]【机】套筒扳手。

box[2] [bɔks; bɑks] **I** *n*. 一掌,一拳。*He gave the boy a ~ on his ear*. 他打了那个男孩一记耳光。**II** *vt*. 1. 用手打,用拳头打。2. 和…比拳。*~sb.'s ears* 打某人耳光。— *vi*. 打拳,从事拳击运动〔比赛〕。*He has ~ed since he was 16*. 他十六岁就参加拳击比赛了。~ ***it out*** 打(拳)到胜负分晓。

box[3] [bɔks; bɑks] *n*.【植】黄杨;黄杨木,(= ~wood)。

Box and Cox [ˈbɔks ənd ˈkɔks; ˋbɑks ənd ˋkɑks] **I** *n*. 1. 同室而难相见的人〔住同一房间,但因轮流外出工作而总是不在一起的两个人,出自 J. M. Morton 的笑剧〕。2. 轮流担任一事的人,交替保持一地位的人。*share a room in a ~ arrangement* 以两人轮流使用的安排方式同住一室。**II** *a*., *ad*. 轮流的〔地〕,相互交替的〔地〕。

box·ber·ry [ˈbɔksˌberi; ˋbɑksˏbɛrɪ] *n*.【植】1. 平铺白珠树;冬青油,冬绿油;白珠香料。2. 蔓虎刺;蔓虎刺果。

box·er[1] [ˈbɔksə; ˋbɑksɚ] *n*. 拳击家;拳师;参加拳击运动的人。***the Boxers***【史】义和团,义和拳。***the Boxer Indemnity***【史】庚子赔款。~ **shorts** (拳击运动服型)男短裤。

box·er[2] [ˈbɔksə; ˋbɑksɚ] *n*. 1. 制箱〔盒〕者。2. 装箱〔盒〕者。

box·haul [ˈbɔksˈhɔːl; ˋbɑksˋhɔl] *vt*.【海】使船顺风微转。

box·ing[1] [ˈbɔksiŋ; ˋbɑksɪŋ] *n*. 1. 装箱〔盒〕。2. 装箱〔盒〕木料。3. 窗箱,箱状罩壳。

box·ing[2] [ˈbɔksiŋ; ˋbɑksɪŋ] *n*. 拳击,拳术,打拳。~ **fiend** 〔美〕拳击迷。~ **glove** 拳击手套。~ **match** 拳击比赛。~ **ring** 拳击比赛场。~ **weights** 拳击体重等级。

Box·ing·day [ˈbɔksiŋdei; ˋbɑksɪŋde]〔英〕节礼日,圣诞礼馈赠日〔英国法定假日,是圣诞节的次日,如遇星期日则顺延一天,俗例于此日向雇员、邮递员等赠送礼品〕。

box·thorn [ˈbɔksˌθɔːn; ˋbɑksˏθɔrn] *n*.【植】宁夏枸杞(= matrimony vine)。

box·y [ˈbɔksi; ˋbɑksɪ] *a*. 似盒子状的,盒状的,四四方方的。**box·i·ness** *n*.

boy [bɔi; bɔɪ] **I** *n*. 1. 少年,童子,男孩;儿子。2. 孩子气的男子;活泼的男子,男子;青年;〔口〕小伙子;〔蔑〕家伙。3. 仆人,侍役,勤杂人员,服务员。4. 练习生;【海】见习水手。5.〔口〕情人,男朋友;〔美〕男学生。6.〔*pl*.〕〔美〕军人〔尤指战斗人员〕;〔*pl*.〕〔美俚〕外勤记者。*a nice old ~* 这家伙不错。*I have two ~s and a girl*. 我有二男一女。*the ~s overseas* 海外的大兵们。*college ~s* 男大学生。***a ~ in buttons*** 侍役。***a slip of a ~*** 瘦长小伙子。***my*** (***old***) ~ 我的儿子;喂〔招呼自己的儿子〕;喂,老兄〔招呼朋友〕;喂,小东西〔招呼自己的狗〕。***old ~*** 见 old 条。***one of the ~s***〔俚〕高等游民。***the ~***〔俚〕香槟酒。***the ~s*** 家中的男子。***the old ~*** = the devil. ***yellow ~s***〔俚〕金币。**II** *int*.〔美〕啾! 噢! 真的,当然了!〔表示惊奇、承认、不愉快等,也可说作 Oh, boy!〕。~ **friend** 要好的男朋友,爱人,未婚夫。~ **husband** [**lover**] 年轻的丈夫〔爱人〕。~**s gun** 坦克炮。~**'s play** 儿战。~ **scout** 1. 童子军(的一员)。2.〔美俚〕〔蔑〕极天真的男子;女子气的男子;乐于助人的人。**the B- Scouts** 童子军。~(-)**toy** *n*. 1. 年轻妓女。2. 男妓。

bo·yar(d) [bəuˈjɑː(d); boˋjɑr(d)] *n*. 1. 沙俄特权贵族,大贵族。2. 罗马尼亚旧时贵族。

boy·cott [ˈbɔikət; ˋbɔɪˏkɑt] **I** *vt*. 1. 联合抵制;抵制(货物等)。2. 一致与…绝交。~ *a nation* 对某国实行抵制。~ *a commercial product* 抵制某种商品。~ *sb*. 一致不与某人往来。**II** *n*. 联合抵制;联合拒绝购买[使用、经售等]。*a class ~* 罢课。*put sb*. [*shop, goods*] *under a ~* 对某人[商店、货物]实行联合抵制。

Boyd [bɔid; bɔɪd] *n*. 博伊德〔姓氏,男子名〕。

boy·hood [ˈbɔihud; ˋbɔɪhʊd] *n*. 1. 少年期,少年时代。2.〔集合词〕少年们,男孩们。*B- is a happy time of life*. 少年时代是人生的一个幸福阶段。*one's ~* 一个人的少年时代。

boy·ish [ˈbɔiiʃ; ˋbɔɪɪʃ] *a*. 少年的,(男)孩子气的;幼稚的。**-ly** *ad*. (男)孩子一样地。**-ness** *n*. (男)孩子气,幼稚。

Boyle[1] [bɔil; bɔɪl] *n*. 博伊尔〔姓氏〕。

Boyle[2] [bɔil; bɔɪl], **Robert** 波义耳〔(1627—1691),英国化学家、物理学家〕。~**'s law**【物】波义耳定律。

boy·sen·ber·ry [ˈbɔisnbəri; ˋbɔɪsnˌbɛrɪ] *n*.【美植】波森莓。

bo·zo [ˈbəuzəu; ˋbozo] *n*. (*pl*. ~*s*)〔美俚〕家伙,男人,大汉。~ **filter**【计】(能在因特网上删除掉尚未接收之无用信息的)傻瓜过滤器。

B.P., **BP** = 1. British Pharmacopoeia 英国药典。2. British Petroleum Company 英国石油公司。3. blood pressure 血压。4. British Patent 英国专利。5. Bachelor of Philosophy. 6. Bachelor of Pharmacy.

BP = 1. Beautiful People 风头人物。2. Black Panther 黑豹党员。

b.p. = boiling point 沸点。

B/P = 1. bill(s) payable 应付票据。2. bill of parcel 发票。3. blueprint. 4. board president 董事长。

BPE = 1. Bachelor of Physical Education 体育学士。2. Bachelor of Petroleum Engineering 石油工程学士。

B.Ph. = Bachelor of philosophy 哲学学士。

B.Pharm. = Bachelor of Pharmacy 药学士。

bpi = bits [bytes] per inch【自】每英寸位数。

Br = bromine.

B/R = 1. bill(s) receivable 应收票据。2. British Rail(ways) 英国铁路公司。

bra [brɑː; brɑ] *n*.〔口〕奶罩 = brassiere;〔口〕车头罩。**-less** *a*. 1. (女人)不戴奶罩的。2. 主张不戴奶罩的〔作为"妇女解放"的象征〕。

brab·ble [ˈbræbl; ˋbræbl̩] **I** *n*.〔古〕吵嘴,争执。**II** *vi*. 为小事争吵(*with*)。

brace [breis; bres] **I** *n*. 1. 支柱,支持物,撑柱;【机】撑臂,拉条;曲柄,把;【医】支架;〔*pl*.〕(牙齿)矫正器;【矿】支撑;竖坑口,井口。2.【印】大括弧;〔即{ }〕;【海】转帆索。3.〔*pl*.〕〔英〕(裤子)背带(=〔美〕suspenders);(弓手等的)护腕带。4.〔*sing*., *pl*.〕(猎获物等的)一双,一对。5.〔口〕(新兵等的)生硬的立正姿势。*a pair of ~s* 一副背带。*a ~ of grouse* 一对松鸡。*a pole ~* 电杆拉线。*a crank* [*hand*] *~* 手摇钻。~(***and***) ***bit*** 曲柄钻孔器,摇钻,弓钻。***in a ~ of shakes*** 马上,立刻。***splice the main ~***〔俚〕喝酒。***take a ~***〔美〕鼓起勇气,奋力。**II** *vt*. 1. 撑牢,支住。2. 给…装拉条;系紧;拉紧,张(弓),叉开(两腿)。3. 使(神经)紧张;激励,振作(精神);【海】以转帆索转(帆);【印】用大括弧括。4.〔美俚〕向…借钱;向…乞求, ~ ***oneself*** (***up***) = ~ ***one's energies*** 奋勇,鼓起精神,振作。~ **game** 欺诈的牌局。~ **jack** (舞台上放在背景后的)三角形支架。

brace·let [ˈbreislit; ˋbreslɪt] *n*. 1. 手镯,镯头。2.〔*pl*.〕〔谑〕手拷。

brac·er [ˈbreisə; ˋbresɚ] *n*. 1. 支持物;索,带。2. (射箭时佩戴的)薄臂套,腕甲。3.〔美俚〕兴奋剂,刺激品;刺激性饮料,清晨喝的酒。

bra·ce·ro [brəˈserəu; brəˋsɛro] *n*. (*pl*. ~*s*)〔Sp.〕墨西哥短工〔到美国去当临时工的墨西哥人,尤指季节性农业工人〕。

brach [brætʃ; brætʃ] *n*.〔古〕雌猎犬。

bra·chi·al [breikiəl; ˋbrekɪəl] *a*.【解】臂(状)的,臂状部分的。

bra·chi·ate [ˈbreikiit; ˋbrekɪɪt] **I** *a*.【植】交互对枝的,十字对生的。**II** *vi*. 双臂交互攀缘。**-a·tion** *n*.

bra·chi·o·pod [ˈbreikiəˌpɔd; ˋbrekɪəˏpɑd] *n*. 腕足类动

B

物。

bra·chi·um [ˈbreikiəm, ˈbrækiəm; brekɪəm, ˋbrækɪəm] *n*. (*pl*. *bra·chi·a* [ˈbreikiə; ˋbrekɪə]) **1**. 臂。**2**.【生】臂状部位。**3**.【动】肱;(上)臂;肘脉;前胫节。

brach·y·ce·phal·ic, brach·y·ce·pha·lous [ˌbrækiseˈfælik, ˌbrækiˈsefələs; ˏbrækɪsəˋfælɪk, ˏbrækɪˋsɛfələs] *a*. (人类)短头的,短头颅的。

brach·y·cra·ni·al [bræki ˈkreiniəl; brækɪˋkrenɪəl] *a*. (头指数在 81 以上的)宽颅的。(= brachycranic). **-crany** *n*.

brach·y·dac·tyl·ic [ˌbrækidækˈtilik; ˏbrækɪdækˋtɪlɪk] *a*.【解】短指[趾]的(= brachydactylous[-ləs; -ləs])。**-dac·ty·ly** *n*.

bra·chyl·o·gy [brəˈkilədʒi; brəˋkɪlədʒɪ] *n*. **1**.【语】省略法〔*He looked out* (*of*) *the window*〕. **2**. (语言的)简洁;简化的表达法。

bra·chyp·ter·ous [bræˈkiptərəs; bræˋkɪptərəs] *a*.【动】(鸟类)短翅的。

brach·y·u·ran [ˌbrækiˈjurən; ˏbrækɪˋjʊrən] **I** *a*.【动】十足甲壳类的(= brachyurous). **II** *n*. 十足甲壳类动物。

brac·ing [ˈbreisiŋ; ˋbresɪŋ] **I** *a*. 使拉紧的;振奋精神的;爽快的。~ *wire* [*cable*] 拉索。*a* ~ *breeze* 凉爽的清风。*the* ~ *mountain air* 山区的清新空气。**II** *n*. **1**.【建】拉条,联条;加强肘。**2**. 背带。**3**. 支柱,支撑物。**4**. 刺激。*radial* ~ 径向支撑。

brack·en [ˈbrækən; ˋbrækən] *n*.【英植】欧洲蕨。

brack·et [ˈbrækit; ˋbrækɪt] **I** *n*. **1**.【建】斗拱,托架,角撑架;【机】支架,悬臂,座;(墙上装的)煤气灯嘴[电灯座]。**2**. 〔*pl*.〕【印】括弧〔( ), [ ], { }〕。**3**.【数】(同一个括号内的)同类项。**4**. (按纳税额、收入、年龄等区分的)阶层,等级,类别。**5**.【军】(炮的)夹叉射击。*bearing* ~ 轴承座[架]。~ *crane* 悬臂式起重机。*high* [*low*, *middle*] *income* ~ 高[低、中等]收入阶层。*the 18 to 22 age* ~ 18—22 岁这一档。*the $ 20,000 income* ~ 年收入二万美元的阶层。*a different social* ~ 不同的社会阶层。*square* [*angle*] ~*s* 方括弧〔圆括弧普通称 *round* ~*s* 或 *parentheses*, 大括弧可简称 ~〕。**II** *vt*. **1**. 为…装托架。**2**. 用(方)括弧括,把…括在括号内;不予考虑。**3**. 把…分类。**4**.【军】夹叉射击(目标)。~ *into groups* 把…分成几类。*They* ~*ed discussion off for a moment*. 他们对问题暂停讨论。~ **up** 把…列为同类。~ **clock** 可搁设在托架上的小钟。~ **foot** (方形家具下端将两边相连的)托脚。~ **saw** 曲线锯。

brack·ish [ˈbrækiʃ; ˋbrækɪʃ] *a*. **1**. (水)略有盐味的,含盐的。**2**. 不好吃的,味道不好的;讨厌的。~ *tea* 味道不好的茶。

bract [brækt; brækt] *n*.【植】苞,托叶;苞片。~**-scale** 苞鳞。**-let** 小苞片。

brac·te·al [ˈbræktiəl; ˋbræktɪəl] *a*.【植】苞的,苞状的。

brac·te·ate [ˈbræktiit; ˋbræktɪɪt] *a*.【植】有苞的。

brad [bræd; bræd] *n*. 曲头钉,无头钉,角钉,土钉。~**-awl** 打眼钻,锥钻;(钻皮革等用的)小锥子。

brad·bury [ˈbrædbəri; ˋbrædbərɪ] *n*. 〔英俚〕〔常 B-〕一镑(或十先令)钞票。

Brad·bury [ˈbrædbəri; ˋbrædbərɪ] *n*. 布拉德伯里〔姓氏〕。

Brad·ford [ˈbrædfəd; ˋbrædfɚd] *n*. 布拉德福〔姓氏,男子名〕。

Brad·ley [ˈbrædli; ˋbrædlɪ] *n*. 布拉德利〔姓氏,男子名〕。

brad·y- *comb*. *f*. 表示"缓慢": *brady*cardia, *brady*pepsia.

brad·y·car·di·a [ˌbrædiˈkɑːdiə; ˏbrædɪˋkɑrdɪə] *n*.【医】心搏缓慢。

brad·y·pep·si·a [ˌbrædiˈpepsiə; ˏbrædɪˋpɛpsɪə] *n*.【医】消化徐缓。

brae [brei; bre] *n*. 〔Scot.〕急坡;斜堤;(沿河一带的)山坡。

brag [bræg; bræg] **I** *n*. 自夸,自大;自夸之物;自夸的人。***make*** ~ ***of*** 自夸(*He made* ~ *of his skill*. 他自夸技术高超)。**II** *vi*. (**-gg-**) 自大,自夸,吹嘘(*of*; *about*). *Many conceited people like to* ~. 许多骄傲的人都喜欢自吹自擂。— *vt*. 自夸,夸口说。*He bragged that he had won*. 他自夸打赢了。~ ***and boast*** 自吹自擂。***have the effrontery to*** ~ ***that*** 大言不惭地说。**III** *a*. 第一流的;极好的;〔罕〕活泼的。*a* ~ *crop* 丰收。*a* ~ *dancer* 第一流的舞蹈家,舞跳的极好的人。

Bragg [bræg; bræg] *n*. 布拉格〔姓氏〕。

brag·ga·do·ci·o [ˌbrægəˈdəutʃiəu; ˏbrægəˋdoʃɪˏo] *n*. **1**. 夸口,吹牛。**2**. 吹牛大家,自夸的人。

brag·gart [ˈbrægət; ˋbrægɚt] **I** *n*. 吹牛大家。**II** *a*. 吹牛的,自夸自大的。

Brah·ma [ˈbrɑːmə; ˋbrɑmə] *n*. 〔印度教〕婆罗吸摩,梵;梵天〔一切众生之父〕。

brah·ma [ˈbrɑːmə; ˋbrɑmə] *n*.【动】婆罗吸摩鸡,印度大种鸡。

Brah·man [ˈbrɑːmən; ˋbrɑmən] **Brah·man·ic** [brɑːˈmænik; brɑˋmænɪk], **Brah·man·ism** [ˈbrɑːmenizm; ˋbrɑmenˏɪzəm] = Brahmin, Brahminic, Brahminism.

Brah·min [ˈbrɑːmin; ˋbrɑmɪn] *n*. **1**. 婆罗门〔印度种姓(caste) 四等级中的最高等级,即僧侣〕。**2**. 〔美口〕名门贵族;文人雅士。

Brah·min·ee [ˌbrɑːmiˈniː; ˏbrɑmɪˋni] *n*. 女婆罗门。**b-(ox)** (印度的)圣牛。

Brah·min·ic, Brah·min·i·cal [brɑːˈminik, brɑːˈminikəl; brɑˋmɪnɪk, brɑˋmɪnɪkəl] *a*. 婆罗门的,婆罗门教的。

Brah·min·ism [brɑːˈminizm; brɑˋmɪnɪzəm] *n*. 婆罗门教。

Brah·min·ist [brɑːˈminist; brɑˋmɪnɪst] *n*. 婆罗门教徒。

Brah·mo·ism [ˈbrɑːməuizəm; ˋbrɑmoˏɪzəm] *n*. 新印度教。**-mo(ist)** *n*. 新印度教徒。

Brahms [brɑːmz; brɑmz], **Johannes** 勃拉姆斯〔1833—1897,德国作曲家〕。**-i·an** *a*. **1**. 勃拉姆斯(音乐作品)的。**2**. 爱好勃拉姆斯音乐的。

braid [breid; bred] **I** *n*. **1**. 缏子,条带,编带,编织物。**2**. 发辫。**3**. 束发带;(衣服上)穗带。*an elastic* ~ 松紧带。*a straw* ~ 草帽缏。*wear one's hair in* ~*s* 把头发编成辫子,打辫子。**II** *vt*. **1**. 编,把…打缏子。**2**. 用缏装饰。**3**. 把(头发)梳成辫子;给(衣服)镶穗带。~ *a rope* 编绳。~ *one's hair* 编头发辫。~*ed fabric* 编织物。~ ***St. Catharine's tresses*** 过处女生活,终生不嫁。

braid·er [ˈbreidə; ˋbredɚ] *n*. **1**. 打缏子的人,编织工。**2**. 编织机,编结机,编带机。

braid·ing [ˈbreidiŋ; ˋbredɪŋ] *n*. **1**. 辫线类。**2**. 辫线装饰。**3**. 编结。

brail [breil; brel] **I** *n*. **1**.【船】卷帆索;斜撑,斜杆。**2**. (捕鱼用的)抄网。**II** *vt*. **1**.【海】卷(帆),卷起(*up*). **2**. 用抄网拉(鱼)。~ *up the sail* 卷起帆。

braille [breil; brel] **I** *n*. (盲人用的)点字(法)〔法国人布雷尔(Louis Braille) 为盲人创制的凸点符号文字〕。**II** *vt*. 用盲文印[写]。

brain [brein; bren] **I** *n*. **1**. 脑,〔*pl*.〕脑髓;〔俚〕计算机;(导弹的)制导系统。**2**. 〔常 *pl*.〕智力,智能,智慧,脑力;头脑。**3**. 〔口〕聪明人;〔口〕〔*pl*.〕智囊,出谋划策者。★当作器官时用单数,当作物质时用复数。*be full of* ~*s*, *have good* [*plenty of*] ~*s* 聪明,好脑筋。*man of* ~*s* 聪明人。*have no* ~*s* 没头脑,笨。*have a lucid* ~ 思路清晰,头脑清醒。*the* ~ *of the conspiracy* 阴谋的策划者。*electron* ~ 〔俚〕电脑,电子计算机。***beat*** [***cudgel***, ***pound***, ***puzzle***, ***rack***] ***one's*** ~***s*** 绞脑汁,苦思。***beat one's*** ~***s out*** 拼命,竭力(*She beat her* ~*s out studying*. 她拼命用功)。***blow sb.'s*** ~***s out*** 使某人脑袋开

花。*coin one's* ～*s* 想方设法挣钱。*get* [*have*] (*sth*.) *on the* ～ 专心,全神贯注在(某事上)。*overtax one's* ～*s* 用脑过度。*pick* [*suck*] *sb*.'*s* ～*s* 采用〔窃取〕某人的主张〔想法,知识,研究成果等〕。*turn sb*.'*s* ～ 冲昏某人头脑,使自以为了不起。*water on the* ～ 脑水肿。**II** *vt*. 1. 打破〔碎〕…的脑袋。2. 打…的头部。～ **bleed** 1. 脑(血管)出血。2. 〔喻〕人才流失。～ **box** 〔日〕电子计算机,电脑。～ **case** 脑壳,头颅。～**child** 智力产儿〔指计划、主意、想法、作品等脑力劳动的成果〕。～ **damage** 【医】脑损伤。～ **death** 【医】脑死亡。～**-derby** 〔美〕学术竞争。～ **drain** 人才流失(国外)。～**-drain** 1. *vi*. 人才外流。2. *vt*. 使发生人才外流现象。～**-drainer** *n*. 外流人才。～**fag** 神经衰弱,用脑过度。～**fever** 【医】脑(膜)炎。～ **life** 【生】脑生命。～**man** 谋士,参谋,军师。～**-pan** 脑壳,头盖骨;〔美〕头。～**power** 1. 智力。2. 〔集合词〕智囊团,参谋团。～**sick** *a*. 神经错乱的,疯狂的。～**sludge** 脑渣〔指头脑中杂七杂八的无用信息〕。～**stealer** 剽窃者。～ **stem** 【解】脑干。～**storm** 1. 脑猝变,【医】脑猝病。2. 〔美俚〕灵机一动,突如其来的好思想[主意];(专家顾问对重大问题的)献策献计 (*a* ～*-storm specialist* 〔美俚〕理论家)。～**-teaser**, ～**-twister** 动脑筋游戏,(供消遣的)待解难题。～ **trust** 1. 〔美俚〕智囊团〔美国经济参谋本部的通称〕;(一般)专家顾问团。2. 〔英〕〔Brains Trust〕(广播电台中给听众解答问题的)答问员。～ **truster** 智囊团团员,顾问,参谋。**Brain virus** 脑病毒〔一种电脑病毒〕。～**wash** 1. *vt*. 对(人)实行洗脑,把某种思想强加于(人)。2. 通过宣传等说服。3. *n*. 洗脑,强行灌输思想。～ **wave** 1. 灵感,灵机,妙想。2. 【心】脑波。～**work** 脑力劳动。～**worker** 脑力劳动者。**-less** *a*. 没有头脑的,愚钝的,笨的。

brain·y [ˈbreini; ˋbrenɪ] *a*. 〔美口〕多智的,聪明的。

braise, braize [breiz; brez] *vt*. (用文火)炖,焖(肉)。

brake[1] [breik; brek] **I** *n*. 1. 制动器,制动装置,闸,煞车;〔喻〕妨碍(因素);(闸式)测功器。2. 麻梳,捶麻器;剥(柳条)皮器;榨汁机;揉面机。3. (碎土用的)大耙,唧筒柄。4. (金属板)压弯成形机。5. 〔英〕大型四轮游览马车。6. 〔古〕拷问架,行刑台。*a hydraulic* ～ 液压制动器,油煞车。*a hand* ～ 手闸。*an air* ～ 气闸。*a vacuum* ～ 真空闸。～ *block* 闸片,制动片。*press* ～ 弯板机,弯边机。*a flex* ～ 剥麻机。～ *horse-power* 制动马力,纯马力〔略作 ～**B. H. P.**〕. ～ *shoe* 闸瓦。*a shooting* ～ 〔俚〕电视车。*apply* [*put on*] *the* ～ 1. 关制动器,关闸。2. 使停止进行,使停顿。*ride the* ～ 半制动〔指煞车不踩到底〕。*take off the* ～ 开闸,松闸。**II** *vt*. 1. 关(闸),煞(车),制动。2. 剥(麻);用麻梳梳;用大耙碎(土);用揉面机揉(面);用榨汁机榨(汁)。～ *a car* 煞住车。— *vi*. (车)煞住,制动器起作用。*The car* ～*d to a stop*. 车煞住不走了。～ **band** 闸带。～ **block** 闸块。～ **drum** 制动鼓。～ **pedal** 煞车脚踏板。～**(s)man** 〔美〕司闸员,制动手。～ **van** 【铁路】缓急车,司闸车。

brake[2] [breik; brek] *n*. 【植】大羊齿,〔特指〕蕨。

brake[3] [breik; brek] *n*. 灌木丛,荆棘。

brake[4] [breik; brek] *v*. 〔古〕break 的过去式。

brake·age [ˈbreikidʒ; ˋbrekɪdʒ] *n*. 1. 煞车,制动器,制动装置。2. 制动作用,制动力。

brak·ie [ˈbreiki; ˋbrekɪ] *n*. 〔美俚〕司闸员,制动手(= brake(s)man)。

brak·y [ˈbreiki; ˋbrekɪ] *a*. 多蕨的;多荆棘的。

bram·ah [ˈbrɑːmə; ˋbrɑmə] *n*. (英国技师 Bramah 创制的)布拉马式机具。～ **lock** 布氏锁。～ **press** 布氏水压机。

bram·ble [ˈbræmbl; ˋbræmbḷ] *n*. 1. 荆棘。2. 【植】悬钩子;欧洲黑莓。

bram·bling [ˈbræmbliŋ; ˋbræmblɪŋ] *n*. 【鸟】花鸡。

bram·bly [ˈbræmbli; ˋbræmblɪ] *a*. 1. 多荆棘的;多刺的。2. 长满黑莓的。

Bra·min [ˈbrɑːmin; ˋbrɑmɪn] *n*. = Brahmin.

bran [bræn; bræn] *n*. 麸皮,糠。*shrimp* ～ 虾皮糠。～ **disease** 麸皮病〔马驹吃多麸皮生的一种软骨病〕。～**-pie** 摸彩盆〔盆中装糠,礼物藏于其中,让儿童摸取之〕。～**-tub** 摸彩桶〔类似于摸彩盆〕。

branch [brɑːntʃ; bræntʃ] **I** *n*. 1. (树)枝〔泛指大枝或小枝;bough 特指大枝,也指连花、果折下的枝;limb 指大枝;twig 指小枝〕。2. 支脉;支派;支管;支线;(家族的)支系;【语】(语系的)支,族。3. (学科)分科;部门,支部,分部,分行;分店。4. 〔美〕支流,小河,小川。5. 【电】分流;【计】转移。*the* ～*s of a deer's antelers* 鹿角的岔枝。～ *road* 岔道。*the various* ～*es of learning* 各门学科。*the executive* ～ *of the government* 政府的行政部门。*an overseas* ～ 海外分店。*the Germanic* ～ *of the Indo-European language family* 印欧语系的日耳曼语族。*a party* ～ 党支部。**root and** ～ 彻底的[地]。**II** *vi*. 1. (树)出枝,开叉。2. 分部,分门;分岔;分支。*The main road* ～*es off to the left*. 大道向左分出一条岔路。*Numerous lesser roads* ～*ed off from the main highway*. 从主要公路上分出无数小道。— *vt*. 1. 使分枝。2. 用枝、叶、花等图案装饰(织物)。～ *forth* (树)扩展枝叶;(商店等)扩展分支机构。～ *off* [*away*] (道路等)分叉,岔开。～ *out* 1. (树)发枝,长出枝条;(话等)横生枝节。2. (事业等)扩大规模。*His firm* ～*ed out to New York*. 他的公司把分支机构扩大到了纽约。～ **line** 支线。～ **litter** 枯枝层。～ **point** 【物】支化点;【计】转移点。～ **water** 1. 小溪的水。2. 水〔尤指普通自来水,用作威士忌配用水〕。

branched [brɑːntʃt; bræntʃt] *a*. 有枝的;分岔的。～ **chain** 【化】支(碳)链。

bran·chi·(o)- [ˈbræŋki(əu)-; ˋbræŋkɪ(o)-] *comb. f*. 鳃: branchia.

bran·chi·a [ˈbræŋkiə; ˋbræŋkɪə] *n*. (*pl*. *bran·chi·ae* [ˈbræŋkiiː; ˋbræŋkɪi]) (用复数)【鱼】鳃。

bran·chi·al, bran·chi·ate [ˈbræŋkiəl, ˈbræŋkieit; ˋbræŋkɪəl, ˋbræŋkɪɪt] *a*. 鳃的;鳃状的;有鳃的。～ *arch* 鳃弓。～ *cleft* 鳃孔。

branch·ing [ˈbrɑːntʃiŋ; ˋbræntʃɪŋ] **I** *n*. 1. 分支;分流;分科;支线;支流;支脉。2. 【物】分支放射;【化】支化(作用);【电】叉形接头,插销头;【计】转移。**II** *a*. 长枝的;分岔的。～ *program* 线路图。

bran·chi·o·pod [ˈbræŋkiəpɔd; ˋbræŋkɪə͵pɑd] *n*. 鳃足亚纲动物。

branch·y [ˈbrɑːntʃi; ˋbræntʃɪ] *a*. 枝多的,枝密的。*a* ～ *tree trunk* 桠叉多枝的树干。

brand [brænd; brænd] **I** *n*. 1. 燃烧着的木头;〔诗〕火炬;〔诗、古〕刀,剑。2. 烙铁;(古时打在罪犯等身上的)烙印;〔喻〕污名,耻辱。3. 【商】火印;牌子,牌号,商标;〔喻〕品种,品质。4. 【植】枯死病。*a* ～ *name* 商标名称。*the best* ～ *of coffee* 最上等的咖啡。～ *mark* 商标(符号)。*the* ～ *of villainy* 罪恶的烙印。***the burning*** 因悔过[经大难]得救的人〔出自《圣经》《撒迦利亚书》〕。***the*** ～ ***of Cain*** 杀人罪〔*cf*. *Cain*〕. ***the Jove's*** ～ 电光。***the Phoebus's*** ～ 一闪一闪的日光。**II** *vt*. 1. 在…上打火印[标记];鲸,在…身上刺字。2. 污辱,玷辱。3. 使铭记,使永志难忘。*be* ～*ed with infamy* 玷上污名。～ *the lesson on one's mind* 永远记住这个教训。～ *the scene in one's memory* 把这一景象铭刻在记忆中。～ *sb*. (*as*) *a heretic* 指某人为异教徒。～**ing iron** 烙铁,烙印。～**iron** 1. = ～ing iron. (烤肉的)铁丝网。2. (烘炉等里面的)薪架;(烤肉的)铁丝撒。

brand·er [ˈbrændə; ˋbrændɚ] *n*. 1. 打火印〔烙印〕的人。2. 〔Scot.〕烙器。

bran·died [ˈbrændid; ˋbrændɪd] *a*. 有白兰地酒味的。掺有白兰地酒的。

bran·dish [ˈbrændiʃ; ˋbrændɪʃ] **I** *vt*. 1. 挥,舞(刀、剑等)。2. 炫耀地挥舞(武器)。～ *one's sword* 挥剑,舞刀。**II** *n*. (刀、剑等的)挥舞。

B

brand·ling [ˈbrændliŋ; ˋbrændlɪŋ] *n*. (钓鱼时作饵用的)红纹蚯蚓。

bran(d)-new [ˈbræn(d)ˈnjuː; ˋbræn(d)ˋnju] *a*. 崭新的,新制的。*a* ~ *wallet* 崭新的皮夹子。*her* ~ *baby* 她刚生下的婴儿。

bran·dreth [ˈbrændriθ; ˋbrændrɪθ] *n*. 1. (堆干草等用的)三脚架。2. 井栏。

bran·dy [ˈbrændi; ˋbrændɪ] I *n*. 白兰地酒。*a* ~ 一杯白兰地酒。II *vt*. (*-died*) 1. 在…中加白兰地酒。2. 把…在白兰地酒中浸泡。~ **and soda** 搀汽水的白兰地酒。~ **and water** = ~-pawnee. ~ **ball** (带酒味的)白兰地糖果。~**-pawnee** *n*. 搀水白兰地酒。~ **sling** 白兰地冷饮〔以白兰地酒、水、糖、柠檬汁等制成〕。~**-snap** (带酒味的)白兰地姜饼。

branks [bræŋks; bræŋks] *n*. 1. 〔*pl*.〕口钳〔古代一种铁制的钳口刑具〕;〔英方〕马嚼子。2. 〔英方〕【医】腮腺炎。

bran·ner·ite [ˈbrænərait; ˋbrænəraɪt] *n*. 【矿】钛铀矿。

bran·ni·gan [ˈbrænigən; ˋbrænɪgən] *n*. 〔美俚〕1. 闹饮,喝酒乱闹。2. 放肆吵闹,大吵大闹。*go on a* ~ 闹饮一番;大吵大闹一番。

bran·ny [ˈbræni; ˋbrænɪ] *a*. (有)麸的,(有)糠的;似麸的,似糠的。

brant [brænt; brænt] *n*. = brent。

brash[1] [bræʃ; bræʃ] *n*. 1. 【医】胃灼热,反酸。2. 〔方〕(疾病的)发作。3. 〔英方〕骤雨,阵雨。

brash[2] [bræʃ; bræʃ] *n*. 1. (岩石等的)碎片;碎冰块;碎冰群。2. (修剪下的)碎树枝。~**y** *a*. 脆的,易脆的。

brash[3] [bræʃ; bræʃ] *a*. 〔口〕1. 好发脾气的,性情急躁的。2. 轻率的;莽撞的。3. 脆的,易破的。4. 活跃的。5. 傲慢的,无礼的。**-ly** *ad*. **-ness** *n*.

bra·sier [ˈbreizjə; ˋbreʒɚ] *n*. = brazier.

Bra·si·lia [brəˈziːljə; brəˋzijə] *n*. 巴西利亚〔巴西首都〕。

brass [brɑːs; bræs] I *n*. 1. 黄铜。2. 〔主 *pl*.〕黄铜制品;铜管乐器;〔*the* ~〕(乐队的)铜管乐器部;〔俚〕(刻有肖像、纹章等)黄铜纪念牌。3. 〔俚〕金钱〔尤指现金〕;好看而不值钱的东西;〔俚〕妓女。4. 〔口〕厚脸皮;〔美俚〕高级将领,高级官员。5. 【机】黄铜轴承衬;〔*pl*.〕(煤层内的)黄铁矿;空弹壳。*clean* [*do*] *the* ~*es* 把黄铜器皿擦亮。*medical* ~ 医学界的名流。*have the* ~ *to do* 厚着脸皮做(某事)。***as bold as*** ~ 老脸厚皮,厚颜无耻。***double in*** ~〔俚〕(在爵士乐队中)能演奏一种以上乐器的;多面手的。***pound*** ~ 〔俚〕按电键,发电报。II *a*. 1. 黄铜(制)的;含黄铜的。2. (天空系)黄铜色的。3. 声音洪亮的。4. 铜管乐器的。~ *rods* 黄铜棒。*the* ~ *band* 吹奏乐团,管乐团,军乐队。III *vt*. 1. 【冶】把…包铜。2. 〔口〕无耻地胡搞〔常作 ~it〕。3. 〔英〕付(款)。***be*** ~***ed off*** 〔英俚〕厌烦,满腹怨气,消沉。~ ***up*** 〔俚〕付(钱);付清。~**bound** *a*. 1. 包黄铜的。2. 顽固保守的。3. 不妥协的,不容变更的。4. 厚脸皮的 (*a* ~*bound idealist* 不妥协的理想主义者。*a set of* ~*bound regulations* 不容变更的一套规定)。~ **check** 〔美俚〕大财团暗中给报界人士的贿赂。~ **check sheets** 暗中接受财团贿赂的报纸。~ **farthing** 〔口〕铜钱,小钱;无价值的东西;极少的数量 (*not care a* ~ *farthing* 毫不在乎)。~ **foundry** 黄铜铸造厂。~ **hat** 〔俚〕高级将领;大官;大亨。~ **knuckles** (打架用的)指节铜套。~ **plate** (钉在门上或棺木上的)黄铜名牌。~ **pounder** 〔美俚〕电信技师。~ **rags** (水手、水兵等的)拖把,揩布 (*part* ~ *rags with someone* 〔海俚〕与人绝交,和人闹翻)。~ **ring** 1. 铜戒指。2. 得奖[发财]的机会。~ **section** 管弦乐队中的铜器乐队部分。~**smith** 黄铜匠。~ **tacks** 1. 黄铜平头钉。2. 〔俚〕具体事实,主要事实,要点;当务之急 (*get down to* ~ *tacks* 谈实质性问题;谈重要问题)。~**-visaged** *a*. 厚脸的。~**ware** 黄铜器皿。~ **winds** 铜器乐队(部)。

bras·sage [ˈbræsidʒ; ˋbræsɪdʒ] *n*. 铸币费。

bras·sard [bræˈsɑːd; ˋbræsɑrd] *n*. 1. 臂章。2. 臂铠。

bras·se·rie [ˈbræsəriː; ˌbræsˋri] *n*. (兼卖小吃的)啤酒店。

brass·ie [ˈbrɑːsi; ˋbræsɪ] *n*. 【高尔夫球】铜头球棒。

bras·sière [ˈbræsiə; brəˋzɪr] *n*. 〔F.〕奶罩。

brass·i·ly [ˈbrɑːsili; ˋbræsəlɪ] *ad*. 老脸厚皮地。

brass·i·ness [ˈbrɑːsinis; ˋbrɑsɪnɪs] *n*. 1. 黄铜质;黄铜色。2. 厚颜无耻。

brass·y [ˈbrɑːsi; ˋbræsɪ] I *a*. 1. 黄铜的;似黄铜的;(金属音)刺耳的。2. (趣味等)庸俗的;厚颜无耻的。3. 吵闹的。II *n*. 【高尔夫球】铜头球棒。

brat [bræt; bræt] *n*. 1. 〔蔑〕臭娃娃,小家伙〔尤指调皮捣乱的孩子〕。2. 美国大兵。

Bra·ti·sla·va [ˌbrætiˈslɑːve; ˋbrɑtɪˌslavə] *n*. 布拉迪斯拉发〔斯洛伐克首都〕。

Brat·tain [ˈbrætən; ˋbrætən] *n*. 布拉顿〔姓氏〕。

brat·tice, **brat·tic·ing** [ˈbrætis, ˈbrætisiŋ; ˋbrætɪs, brætɪsɪŋ] *n*. 1. (矿井通气用的)间壁,风幛。2. 【建】临时木建筑,(保护机械等的)围板;〔古〕(守城时的)临时胸墙。

brat·tle [ˈbrætl; ˋbrætl̩] I *n*. 〔Scot.〕咕隆声;(脚步的)呱哒声。II *vi*. 1. 咕咕隆隆地响。2. 呱哒呱哒地跑。

brat·wurst [ˈbrætwəːst; ˋbrætwɝst] *n*. 多味腊肠。

Braun [braun; braʊn] *n*. 布劳恩〔男子名〕。~ **tube**【物】布劳恩管,阴极射线管,示波管。

braun·ite [ˈbraunait; ˋbraʊnaɪt] *n*. 褐锰矿。

Braun·schwei·ger [ˈbraunʃwaigə; ˋbraʊnʃwaɪgɚ] *n*. 〔G.〕〔常 b-〕〔美〕五香肝肠。

bra·va [ˈbrɑːvɑː; ˋbrɑvɑ] *n*., *int*. 〔It.〕= bravo.

bra·va·do [brəˈvɑːdəu; brəˋvɑdo] *n*., *vi*. (*pl*. ~*s*, ~*es*)〔Sp.〕恐吓,虚张声势。*He flourished the weapon in an attempt at* ~. 他挥舞武器意在恐吓。

brave [breiv; brev] I *a*. 1. 勇敢的。2. 华丽的,漂亮的。3. 〔古〕极好的。*a* ~ *man* [*act*] 勇敢的人[行为]。*as* ~ *as lion* 狮子一样凶猛。*a girl decked out in a* ~ *dress* 浓妆艳抹的姑娘。*O* ~ *new world*, ...! 啊,多么好的新世界〔莎士比亚诗句〕! II *vt*. 1. 冒(风雨、危险等),拼,抵抗;不顾。2. 敢于做(某事),不把(强敌等)放在眼里,向…挑战。~ *misfortunes* [*difficulties*] 勇敢地面对不幸[困难]。~ *blizzards* 迎着暴风雪前进。*She* ~*ed the journey to New York*. 她毅然踏上去纽约的旅途。~ ***it out*** 拼着干下去。~ ***the wind and dew*** 风餐露宿。III *n*. 勇士;印第安人的战士。**-ness** *n*.

brave·ly [ˈbreivli; ˋbrevlɪ] *ad*. 1. 勇敢地,毅然。2. 漂亮地,华丽地。*fight* ~ *for a cause* 为事业英勇斗争。*a* ~ *decked house* 装饰华丽的房屋。

brav·er·y [ˈbreivəri; ˋbrevərɪ] *n*. 1. 勇敢,英勇,大胆,刚毅。2. 华丽,美装;盛装。*girls in Sunday* ~ 服装华丽的姑娘们。

bra·vis·si·mo [brɑːˈviːssiːmɔː; brɑˋvissimo] *int*. 好极了! 妙极了!

bra·vo[1] [ˈbrɑːˈvəu; ˋbrɑvo] I *n*. (*pl*. ~*s*, ~*es*) 1. 喝彩声,叫好声。2. 【讯】代表 b 字的讯号。II *int*. 好! 好啊! 妙啊! III *vt*. 向…喝采叫好。

bra·vo[2] [ˈbrɑːvəu; ˋbrɑvo] *n*. 刺客〔尤指被人雇佣的行刺者〕;歹徒;亡命之徒。

bra·vu·ra [brəˈvjuərə; brəˋvjurə] *n*. 〔It.〕1. 【乐】气势磅礴[雄壮华丽]的演奏[乐曲];要求演奏者毕竟其技的乐段。2. 壮举。

braw [brɔː; brɔ] *a*. 〔Scot.〕1. 衣着华丽的。2. 美好的;极好的。*a* ~ *new dress* 漂亮的新衣。*a* ~ *night* 美好的夜晚。

brawl [brɔːl; brɔl] I *vi*. 1. 吵闹,口角;互骂。2. (流水)哗哗地响。*the river* ~*ing by* 河水哗哗地流过。II *n*. 1. 吵闹,口角。2. 〔美俚〕闹宴;喧闹的舞会;乱哄哄的拳赛。*political* ~*s* 政治上的论战。*a* ~ *between husband and wife* 夫妇之间的争吵。**-er** *n*. 争吵者;喧闹者。**-ing** *n*., *a*. 争吵(的);喧闹(的)。**-y** *a*. 好争吵的;喧闹的。

brawn [brɔːn; brɔn] ***n*.** 1. 肌肉。2. 膂力,体力。3. 腌野猪肉;咸猪头。~ **drain** (劳动者、工人、运动员等的)体力外流。

brawn·y [ˈbrɔːni; ˋbrɔnɪ] ***a*.** 肌肉结实的,强壮的。**brawn·iness** ***n*.**

brax·y [ˈbræksi; ˋbræksɪ] **I** ***n*.** 1. 【兽医】羊炭疽。2. 患羊炭疽病的羊。**II** ***a*.** 患羊炭疽的。

bray[1] [brei; bre] **I** ***n*.** 1. 驴叫声。2. (喇叭)嘟嘟声。3. 喧哗,乱哄哄的抗议。**II** ***vi*.** 1. (驴)叫。2. (喇叭)嘟嘟响。3. 喧嚷;刺耳地喊。~ *at the top of one's voice* 尽着嗓门喊叫。— ***vt*.** 1. 嚷出,粗声粗气地说出。2. 乱哄哄地演奏。*The gramophone ~ed out its vulgar tune*. 留声机闹哄哄地唱着庸俗的小调。

bray[2] [brei; bre] ***vt*.** 1. 捣碎,研碎。2. 【印】薄涂(油墨等)。

Bray [brei; bre] ***n*.** 布雷〔姓氏〕。

bray·er [ˈbreiə; breɚ] ***n*.** 【印】(明)胶(墨)辊。

Braz. = Brazil(ian)。

braze[1] [breiz; brez] ***vt*.** 1. 用黄铜制造[镶饰,镀]。2. 〔古〕使坚如黄铜。3. 〔诗〕使成铜黄色。~ ***over*** 镀黄铜于。

braze[2] [breiz; brez] ***vt*.** 【机】(用锌铜合金)焊接,铜焊,硬焊。~*d joint* 【机】黄铜接头,硬钎焊接。

bra·zen [ˈbreizn; ˋbrezn̩] **I** ***a*.** 1. 黄铜制的;黄铜色的;(黄铜一样)坚硬的。2. (像破铜锣一样)声音响而刺耳的。3. 厚颜无耻的。*a ~ image of Buddha* 一尊铜佛。*a ~ liar* 厚颜无耻的说谎者。**II** ***vt*.** 厚着脸皮干(*out, through*). ~ ***it out*** [***through***] 厚着脸皮干下去[混下去](*He prefers to ~ it out rather admit defeat*. 他宁可厚着脸皮混下去,也不愿承认失败)。~ ***law of wages*** 【经】工资铁律(= iron law of wages). ~ **age** (希腊)黄铜时代,混战时代。~**-faced** ***a*.** 厚颜无耻的。**-ly** ***ad*.** 厚着脸皮,粗暴地,肆无忌惮地,悍然。

bra·zier[1] [ˈbreizjə; ˋbreʒɚ] ***n*.** 黄铜匠。**-y** ***n*.** 黄铜工艺制品厂;黄铜细工。

bra·zier[2] [ˈbreizjə; ˋbrezɪɚ] ***n*.** 1. (金属)火盆;焊炉。2. (烤肉)火锅。

Bra·zier [ˈbreiʒə; ˋbreʒɚ] ***n*.** 布雷热〔姓氏〕。

Bra·zil [brəˈzil; brəˋzɪl] ***n*.** 巴西〔拉丁美洲〕。~ **nut** 三角形巴西胡桃。~**wood** 【植】巴西苏木。

bra·zil [brəˈzil; brəˋzɪl] = Brazilwood.

Bra·zil·ian [brəˈziljən; brəˋzɪljən] **I** ***a*.** 巴西的;巴西人的。**II** ***n*.** 巴西人。

Braz·za·ville [ˈbræzəvil, ˌbrɑːzəˈviːl; ˋbræzəvɪl, brɑzəˋvɪl] ***n*.** 布拉扎维尔〔刚果首都〕。

BRCS = British Red Cross Society 英国红十字会。

BRE = Bachelor of Religious Education 宗教教育学士。

breach [briːtʃ; britʃ] **I** ***n*.** 1. (对法律、义务等的)破坏,违犯,违背,不履行;(对他人权利等的)侵害,侵犯。2. (友好关系的)破裂,绝交,不和。3. (城堡、防御线等的)破口,裂口,缺口;【军】突破,突破口。4. 【海】碎浪,冲击船[堤等]的波浪。5. 鲸跳〔鲸的跳出水面〕。6. 〔罕〕伤口。*a ~ of contract* 违约,违反合同。*a ~ of duty* 失职;不履行义务。~ *of trust* 背叛;辜负信任。~ *of prison* 越狱。*It caused a lifelong ~ with his father*. 这使得他们父子终身失和。***a clean*** ~【海】冲走甲板上物件的波浪。***a clear*** ~ 冲过甲板的波浪。~ ***of close*** 【法】非法侵入他人地界。~ ***of promise*** 毁约;【法】毁弃婚约。~ ***of the peace*** 【法】妨害治安(罪)。***heal the*** ~ 调停。***make a*** ~ ***in*** (*the wall*) 攻破(城墙);在(墙)上打开缺口。***slip one's*** ~ 死。***stand in*** [***throw oneself into***] ***the*** ~ 独当难局,首当其冲,独立承受攻击。**II** ***vt*.** 1. 攻破,突破,使有缺口。2. 违(约);不履行(义务);破坏(法律)。~ *the city wall* 攻破城墙。~ *an agreement* 违反协议。— ***vi*.** (鲸鱼)跳出水面。*a whale ~ing* 跳出水面的鲸鱼。

bread [bred; brɛd] ***n*.** 1. 面包。2. 食物,粮食;〔喻〕生计,生活必需品。3. 【基督】(圣餐式上的)一块[份]面包。4. 〔美俚〕钱。*a slice of ~* 一块面包。*black* [*brown*] ~ 黑面包。*the ~ of life* 活命粮。*one's daily ~* 每天的食物。***beg one's*** ~ 讨饭,行乞。~ ***buttered on both sides*** 两面涂黄油的面包;极幸福的境遇,安乐的生活。***break ~ with*** 1. 受…款待。2. 与…共用圣餐。***cast*** [***throw***] ***one's ~ upon the water***(***s***) 甘尽义务,施舍,行善。***eat the ~ of affliction*** [***idleness***] 受折磨,遭遇坎坷[坐食,游手好闲]。***in goog*** [***bad***] ~〔俚〕生活安乐[困苦]。***know*** (***on***) ***which side one's ~ is buttered*** 自知己利所在,善于为个人利益打算。***make*** [***earn***] ***one's ~*** 谋生。***out of ~*** 〔口〕无职业,失业。***quarrel with one's ~ and butter*** 自砸饭碗,与自己过不去。***ship's*** ~【海】硬饼干。***take the ~ out of sb.'s mouth*** 抢人饭碗。~ **and butter** 1. 涂黄油的面包。2. 必需的食物;生计。3. 主要的收入来源。~**-and-butter** ***a*.** 1. 有关生计的,日常生活的;提供最低(生活)需要的。2. 实利的,实用的。3. 主要的。4. 为所受款待表示谢意的。5. 〔主英〕孩子气的,不成熟的,年轻的(*a ~-and-butter account* 最低限度的经费。~*-and-butter products* 主要产品。~*-and-butter arguments* 讲求实际的议论。*a ~-and-butter letter* 给东道主的感谢信。*a ~-and-butter miss* 馋嘴的小姑娘,女学生;娇小姐。*a ~-and-butter item* 生活必需品)。~ **and cheese** 面包和干酪;家常食品,粗食,糊口的方法。~ **and circuses** 公共当局提供的饮食和娱乐。~ **and milk** 牛奶泡面包。~ **and salt** 面包和盐[待客的象征](**eat** [**share**] **sb.** ~ **and salt** 款待某人,待某人如贵宾)。~ **and scrape** 黄油涂得不足的面包。~ **and water** 面包和水,最简单的食物,粗粝之食。~ **and wine** 【基督教】圣餐。~**basket** 1. 面包篮;〔喻〕谷物产区。2. 〔俚〕胃,肚子。3. 〔美俚〕一种爆炸燃烧弹。(~*-basket land* 产粮区)。~**board** 1. 揉面板;切面包板。2. (手提式电子实验)线路板,模拟板,实验模型。~**box** 面包箱,糕点存放箱。~**crumb** 1. ***n*.** 〔常 *pl*.〕面包屑〔尤指专为烹调而揉碎者〕;面包心。2. ***vt*.** 把…裹上面包屑(煎、炸)。~ **fruit** 麦包果〔面包树的果实〕。~ **knife** 面包刀〔通常有波浪形或锯齿形刀锋〕。~ **line** [**queue**] 〔美〕排队领救济品的穷人队伍。~ **mold**【植】黑根霉。~ **riot** 饥饿〔缺粮〕骚动。~ **root** 【植】食用补骨脂(根)〔产于北美〕。~ **salesman** 〔美〕面包店的送货人。~**-stuffs** 〔*pl*.〕制面包的原料,面包粉;面包类。~ **ticket** 面包券,饭票。~ **tree** 面包树。~**winner** ***n*.** 1. 养家活口的人。2. 生计;职业;谋生的工具[手艺]。**-less** ***a*.** 无面包的,缺粮的;失去生计的。

breadth [bredθ; brɛdθ] ***n*.** 1. 宽度(*opp*. length, depth),幅,横幅,幅员;广度,宽广;(学识等的)广博。2. (布的)幅面;船幅。3. (性格、胸襟等的)宽宏大量,宽容;豪放,磊落。4. (绘画、作品等气势的)雄浑,恢弘。5. 【逻】外延。*This room is nine feet in ~*. 这个房间宽九英尺。*a ~ of cloth* 一幅布。~*s of grass* 辽阔的草地。~ *of mind* 心胸开阔。*a man of intellectual ~* 知识渊博的人。*There is too much ~ in his jokes* [*behaviour*]. 他的笑话[行为]太过火了。***by a hair's ~*** 差一点儿,险些,几乎。***in ~*** 幅宽,阔。***to a hair's ~*** 精确的。

breadth·ways, breadth·wise [ˈbredθweiz, ˈbredθwaiz; ˋbrɛdθˏwez, ˋbrɛdθˏwaɪz] ***ad*.** 横。*a course of bricks laid ~* 一排横着放的砖。

break [breik; brek] **I** ***vt*.** (***broke*** [brəuk; brok], 〔古〕***brake*** [breik; brek]; ***bro·ken*** [ˈbrəukən; ˋbrokən], 〔古〕***broke***) 1. 毁坏,弄坏,损坏,毁损。~ *a doll* 弄坏洋囡囡。~ *a sewing machine* 损坏缝纫机。2. 打破,碰破,撞破;打碎;折断;擦破;撕开。~ *a bottle* [*cup*] 打破瓶[杯]子。~ *a vase to pieces* 把花瓶打得粉碎。~ *an arm* 折断手臂。~ (*off*) *a branch* 折断树枝。~ *one's head* 撞破头。~ *the skin* 擦破皮肤。~ *cloth* [*paper*] 撕开布[纸]。3. 犯,违犯,破坏,违,违背;破除;通过法律

手续使(遗嘱)失效;取消,解除。~ *a promise* 违反诺言,食言。~ *the law* 违法,犯法。~ *a law* [*rule*] 触犯某项法律[规定]。~ *a contract* 违反合同。~ *off an engagement* 解除婚约。~ *a will* 取消遗嘱,使遗嘱失效。~ *the chains* 砸开锁链。**4.** 冲开(水面等),开垦(土地等),翻(土),梳(麻);打开(门等),挑开(水疱);破(门);闯入;冲破;越(狱),突(围),逃出,跳出;打开(局面等),开创(新路等)。~ *the door open* 冲开大门。~ *jail* [*prison*] 越狱。~ *ground* 破土(动工)。~ *fresh* ground 开辟新天地。*He broke the blister with a needle*. 他用针挑开水疱。~ *a siege* 突围,冲破围困。~ *a trail through the woods* 披荆斩棘在林中行进。~ *the water* (鱼)跳出水面。~ *surface* [*water*] (潜水艇)浮出水面。**5.** 使中止;打断;切断,截断,遮断;妨碍;打搅,搅乱;戒除;破除。~ *a journey* 中止旅程,中途下车。~ *an electric circuit* 切断电流。~ *the cigarette habit* 戒烟。~ *the tie* 打破不分胜负的局面。~ *the convention* 打破成规。~ *a strike* 使罢工停止。~ *sb.'s sleep* 打扰了某人的睡眠。~ *the silence with a cry* 以喊声打破寂静。*The railway communication is broken*. 铁路交通断绝了。**6.** 兑开(钞票);分开;拆开(整体),卸开(枪的)装弹和发射部。~ *a dollar bill into change* 把一元钞票兑成零钱。*The prism broke the light into all the colors of the rainbow*. 棱镜把阳光分解成虹的所有色彩。~ *a dining room set by buying a chair* 买走一把椅子使一套餐厅家具不再成套。**7.** 制服;驯(兽),使驯服;制止;阻止;破获(案件),破解(密码);解决,解开(难题等);削减,减弱;挫败,压倒。~ *a horse* 驯马。*The bushes will* ~ *his fall*. 灌木丛会减弱他摔下来的势头。~ *the case* 破获案件。~ *a cipher system* 破解开一套密码。*A stand of trees will* ~ *the wind*. 一排树会减弱风势。~ *a man of his bad habit* 制止某人的恶习。~ *the problem* 解决了问题。*He was broken by the threats*. 他被威胁压服了。~ *sb.'s spirit* 挫折某人的锐气。**8.** 暗示,泄漏,暴露(秘密等)。~ *secret plans to the enemy* 把秘密计划泄露给敌方。*He broke the good news to her at dinner*. 他吃饭时把好消息透露了给她。**9.** 使衰败;使破产;免(职),降(职);葬送(前途)。*He broke the bank at Monte Carlo*. 他在蒙特卡罗的豪赌使银行破产了。~ *one's career* 毁掉了前途。*He was broken from sergeant to private*. 他从军士降为列兵。**10.** 打破,超过(记录)。~ *all track records* 打破径赛项目的全部记录。~ *a speed record* 创造一项速度新记录。**11.** 驳倒,使(证据、辩辞等)不能成立。~ *down a witness* 驳倒伪证。~ *sb.'s alibi* 揭穿某人的辩词。**12.** 发动(宣传等)。**13.**【棒球】投(歪球),投(曲线球);【拳】制止(扭抱)。~ *a curve*【棒球】投出曲线球。**14.**【法】非法侵入。~ *a house* 非法侵入他人住宅。**15.** 使(股票等)猛跌价。— ***vi*.** **1.** 破裂,碎;损坏,发生故障;崩;断,折断;中断;受挫;挫折;(军队等)溃败;(疮)溃烂。*The glass broke*. 杯子打坏了。*A piece of china* ~*s easily*. 瓷器容易打碎。*The rope broke*. 绳子断了。*The TV set broke*. 电视机发生故障。*My heart will* ~. 我心要碎了。**2.** 闯入 (*into*); 逃出 (*from*; *out of*); 摆脱,离开。**3.** 突现,爆发,忽起;突变,【乐】变音;(霜、雾等)消散;(天)破晓,放晴。*The weather broke*. 天气变晴。*His face broke out into a smile*. 他变得笑逐颜开。*The day broke hot and sultry*. 天亮了,天气又热又闷。*Dawn began to* ~. 东方欲晓。*The storm broke*. 暴风雨突然来临。*The boy's voice has broken*. 这孩子发育变嗓音了。**4.** 破产,倒闭;(信用、名誉等)扫地;(健康等)垮掉,变弱,衰;(抵抗等)崩溃;(在压力等之下)屈服。*The bank broke*. 这家银行破产了。*His health broke after years of hardship*. 多年的困苦生活使他的身体垮了。**5.** (花)发芽,打苞,长(蕾)。**6.** (消息)传开,透露出。*The story broke in a morning paper*. 消息在一家晨报上透露出来了。**7.** (工作中)略事休息。~ ***for lunch*** 暂停下工作吃顿饭。**8.**【棒球】(球)曲行,(球)投歪。**9.**〔美〕(证券)行市暴跌;(潜艇等)突现于水面;〔美〕突进,猛冲 (*for*); (波浪)冲击 (*over*; *on*; *against*). **10.**【拳】(从扭抱中)放开,分开;〔裁判员命令扭抱中的双方〕分开! **11.** 发生,发展,进展。*For the team to succeed, everything has to* ~ *right*. 必须一切情况正常,该队才能打赢。~ ***a butterfly on the wheel*** 小题大作,杀鸡用牛刀。~ ***a lance with*** 与…交锋;与…争论。~ ***a leg*** 〔英俚〕演出成功 (*I hope you* ~ *a leg*. 我希望你演出成功)。~***away*** (*from*) **1.** 逃走,脱逃,脱身。**2.** (柄等)脱离,离开。**3.** 背弃,叛离。**4.** 戒除(积习),摆脱(陈规等)。**5.** (赛马时)抢先起步(~ *away from a habit* 戒除某项习惯。*The prisoner broke away from his guards*. 犯人趁看守不备逃跑了)。~ ***bounds*** 见 bound 条。~***bulk***【海】开始全部[部分]卸货。~ ***camp*** 拔营,起营。~***cover*** [***covert***] (猎物)跳[飞]出躲藏处[树丛]。~***down*** **1.** ***vt*.** 破坏,打破,击破,粉碎;击穿;压倒;把(化合物)分解,把(机器等)拆散,把(总帐等)分成细目 (*into*). **2.** ***vi*.** (机器)损坏,发生故障,(门等)坍陷;(计划)失败;(身体)变衰弱;(精神等)崩溃;(化合物)分解,(总帐等)细分,易于分成细目 (*into*); (发言等)突然中断;【物】衰[蜕]变。~ ***even*** 〔美口〕**1.** (球赛)不分胜负,打成和局。**2.** 得失相当,不赚不赔,扯平。~ ***formation*** 【军】打乱队形,离开编队。~***forth*** **1.** 喷出,涌出;爆发。**2.** 突然发出(欢呼、叫声等);开始滔滔不绝地讲(~ *forth in cheers* [*into singing*] 突然爆发出欢呼声[歌声])。~(***free***) ***from*** 脱离;突然离开。~***ground*** 动工,开工。【海】起锚(~ *ground for a new housing development* 新住宅建设破土动工)。~ ***hibernation*** 从冬眠中苏醒;【美】上演(一季的)开炮战。~ ***in*** **1.** 闯入;插嘴。**2.** 驯(马);训练(人)。**3.** 使物件[鞋]逐渐合用[脚]。**4.** (人)开始工作;(机器等)开始运转[活动]。~ *in a pony* 驯一匹小马。*The boss is* ~*ing in a new assistant*. 头儿正在训练一个新助手。*These shoes haven't been broken in*. 这鞋子还没有穿合脚。~ ***in on*** [***upon***] **1.** 突然袭击,突然出现,于…之前。**2.** 拦阻;打断,打扰(*The mob broke in on us*. 暴徒对我们突然袭击。~ *in on one's thought* 忽然想起)。~ ***into*** **1.** 闯进,侵入;拦(别人话头);侵占(别人时间等)。**2.** 突然…起来(~ *into a talk* 插嘴。~ *into tears* 哇地一声哭起来)。~ ***into*** [***to***] ***pieces*** 打碎。~ ***liberty*** 回船迟到〔水手上岸超出许可时间〕。~ ***loose*** **1.** 脱出,摆脱,挣脱开 (*from*). **2.** 迸发出来。~(***sb***. [***oneself***]) ***of a habit*** (自己)放弃某种习惯,(使某人)放弃某种习惯。~ ***off*** **1.** ***vt*.** 折取,掐,摘;把…折断;使脱落;打断,断绝,解除(婚约),使突然停止。**2.** ***vi*.** 折,裂,分;突然中止,中断;【军】突然改变航向;暂停工作,稍事休息(*He broke off a branch of the tree*. 他把一根树枝折断。*A branch of the tree broke off*. 一根树枝断了。~ *off the negotiation* 中断谈判。*Let's* ~ *off for a minute*. 我们来歇一会儿)。~ ***on the scene*** 突然出场。~ ***one's fast*** 停止绝食;〔古〕吃早餐〔早餐 breakfast 一词即源于此〕。~***one's mind to*** (***sb***.) 向(某人)表白心事,剖明心迹。~ ***open*** 砸开,打破;〔美〕现出,显出。~ ***out*** **1.** 起,发生;(战争等)突发,爆发。**2.** (囚犯等)逃脱,逃出。**3.** 忽然叫出[做出] (*into*). **4.** 倒空(容器);由(船舱)卸货。**5.**【海】起(锚)。**6.** 拖出,起出。**7.** 取出备用,使处于备用状态 (*An epidemic broke out*. 发生了传染病。~ *out the parachutes* 准备好降落伞。~ *out one's best wine* 拿出家藏的上品佳酿。~ *out a sled from the ice* 从冰中拖出雪橇。*He broke out into loud laughter*. 他忽然哈哈大笑起来)。~ (***the***) ***rank*** 【军】打乱队形。~ ***short*** 使突然终止,中断。~ ***step***【军】走乱步伐。~ ***the back*** [***neck***] ***of*** (*an undertaking*) 办完(某事)的极困难[重要]部分,大体做完(某事)。~ ***the ice*** 带个头;打破沉默,使气氛活跃。~ ***the ground*** **1.** 犁(地),翻(地)。**2.** 动工,着手。**3.**【军】挖战壕。~ ***through*** **1.** 挤过去;突破;打(洞等);(太阳

由云间)钻出。2. 犯(规),违(章)。~ *up* 1. *vt*. 弄破,打碎;拆散,拆开;剖割(兽体等);破坏;挖;垦(地);解散,驱散(人群等);终止,中断;分化;〔口〕使哄堂大笑;使苦恼。2. *vi*. (会)散,(队伍等)解散,(学校)放假;(家庭等)解体;(冰)溶,(雾等)消散;(身体)变衰弱,(士气)瓦解;细分为,分解为。~ *up the crowds* 驱散人群。(*school*) ~*s up for holidays* 学校放假。*They broke up into small groups*. 他们分散为各个小组。~ *up a friendship* 绝交。~ *up the audience* 使听众哄堂大笑。*The loss broke up the old man*. 这项损失使老人身心交瘁。~ *up an old ship* 拆掉旧船。*B- it up*! 住手[别吵了]! ~ ***upon*** 突然出现,显露。~ ***well*** 〔美〕(赛马等)起跑得好。~ ***wind*** 放屁。~ (***off***) ***with*** 与…断绝关系,与…绝交,与…决裂;破除(恶习等)(~ *with one's family* 与家庭决裂)。**II** ***n***. 1. 破,坏;损坏;裂,裂口,碎裂;折断(*a* ~ *in the window* 玻璃窗上的裂缝。*a* ~ *in the clouds* 云朵间的一线青天)。2. (天气的)突变;破晓,天亮(*a* ~ *in the weather* 天气骤变。~ *of day* 天亮)。3. 中止,停顿,断绝;(电视广播节目等的)暂停;休息(时间);决裂,绝交(*a* ~ *for the commercial* 广告节目。*a* ~ *with convention* 与陈规决裂。*a* ~ *in one's conversation* 谈话的暂停。*a lunch* ~午休。*a coffee* ~ 上下午的工间小休息,吃茶时间)。4.【台球】连得分数;(球的)反跳,屈折;【乐】急剧变调,换声点;短促停顿;【电】切断,中断,断线,断路(器);【矿】断裂,断层;【海】船楼端部;【建】断面;【印】(一行最末一词过长需转行接写的)断开处;连接符号"-"。【拳】(从扭抱中)分开。5. 逃走,跑出;(赛马等的)起跑;练马用马车,大型四轮马车(*a jail* ~越狱。*a* ~ *for freedom* (从囚禁中)逃跑)。6. 〔口〕闯进;猛冲,奔,突破;(飞机失速后的)突然下降;〔古〕爆发,激发(*The started deer made a* ~ *for the thicket*. 受惊的鹿奔向丛林)。7. 〔美俚〕错误,失策,失败;(市价等的)暴跌;语言无礼,举止不当(*a bad* ~ 失礼,失仪,失礼的举动)。8. 〔俚〕运气,命运;〔口〕机会;分歧点(*She's won too. What's a* ~! 她也赢了,真是好运气。*Give him a* ~. 给他一个改过的机会吧!)。9. 开垦地;(谷物的)春磨。***a lucky*** [***bad***, ***rotten***] ~ 好运气[倒楣]。***a*** ~ ***in one's life*** 一生中的转机[转折]。***an even*** ~〔美俚〕不相上下,(输赢)各半;均等的机会。~ ***for the hungry*** 〔美俚〕穷困时突如其来的好差使。~ ***the*** ~***s***【美体】碰到好运气,走运。***get a*** ~ 交好运,时来运转。***give*** (***sb***.) ***a*** ~ 给(某人)一个面子。***make a*** (***bad***) ~ 失礼,失仪,出丑。***make a*** ~ ***for*** 向…急跑。***make a*** ~ ***for home*** 1. 往家跑。2.【棒球】跑回本垒。***make a*** ~ ***of***【台球】连续得(分)。***without a*** ~ 连续地,不停顿地,不休息地。~**away** 1. 分离;【空】脱离队形;【美影】简易道具。2. ***a***. 脱党的,分离派的;【戏剧】(道具)简易的。~**bone** (**fever**)【美医】断骨热,登革热。~**-bulk** ***a***. 零件[小件]装运的。~ **dancer** 跳霹雳舞的人。~**-dancing** 霹雳舞。~**-even** ***a***. 得失相当的,不赚不赔的。~**-even point**【商】损益两平点。~**front** 1. ***a***. (橱柜等)中部凸出的。2. ***n***. 中凸橱柜。~**head** 船头破冰器。~**-in** 闯入;【军】突破;插入,挤入,嵌入;【机】试车,试运转。~ **lorry** 救险车。~**mark**【纺】(绸缎等的)灰点,疵点。~**-neck** ***a***. 极危险的(*at* ~*neck speed* 以危险的高速行驶)。~**out** 爆发;【军】突围;强行越狱;皮疹,皮炎。~ **over** (报刊上文章的)转页,转版。~**-point**【化】转效点;【电】断点,停止点。~**-point order**【自】返回指令。~**-promise** 违约者,食言者。~ **through**【军】突破(点);(科技等的)重大发现,重大进展;关键问题的解决;(物价等的)暴涨。~**up** 解散;瓦解,崩溃;分离,(夫妇)分居;分裂,脱离;停止,完结。~**up value** 破产企业的财产清理价值。~**water** 防波堤。~**wind**【英】幕;风障;防风林;挡风墙(篱)。**-able** 1. ***a***. 容易破碎的。2. ***n***. 〔常 *pl*.〕易破碎的东西。

break·age [ˈbreikidʒ; ˋbrekɪdʒ] ***n***. 1. 破坏,毁损;断裂;裂口,破损处;【电】断路,断线;【纺】断头率。2. 破损物;损耗量,破损量;【商】损耗补偿(款额);【海】(舱内装货后的)剩余空位。*There was a great deal of* ~ *in that shipment of glassware*. 那批玻璃器皿损坏了很多。~ **allowance**【商】破损折扣。

breakdown [ˈbreikdaun; ˋbrekˏdaun] **I** ***n***. 1. 崩溃,倒塌;破损,损耗;损伤;损坏,故障;失败,挫折;中断,停止。2.【空】下降;【电】击穿;【原】衰[蜕]变;【化】分解(作用),分析。3. (体力等的)衰弱,垮,衰退。4. 分类;分成细目,分类账。5. 〔美〕(黑人首创的)一种喧嚣、急促的集体舞。6. 〔*pl*.〕【机】粗轧板坯。*nervous* ~ 神经衰弱。*the* ~ *of communication* 交通中断。*the* ~ *current* 击穿电流。*a* ~ *in health* 身体垮下来。~ *of food during digestion* 食物在消化过程中分解。*a* ~ *of data* 数据的分类。**II** ***a***. 专门修理故障的。~ **gang** [**van**] (火车等出事故时的)抢修队[车]。~ **test** 耐久(力)试验,断裂试验,破坏试验,稳定性测验。~ **voltage** 击穿电压。

break·er[1] [ˈbreikə; ˋbrekɚ] ***n***. 1. 破坏者,破碎者;破碎装置,轧碎[石、煤]机;离解机;【纺】头道梳毛机。2.【海】(打在暗礁、海岸上的)碎浪花。3. 驯兽者。4.【电】断路器;汽车的拥胎带。5. (垦荒用的)锄;开拓者。*a* ~ *of idols* 捣毁偶像者。*a coal* ~碎煤机。*a horse* ~ 驯马师;驯马者。~***s ahead***!【海】注意暗礁! 危险! ~ **fabric** 轮胎布。~**-in** 训练牛、马的人。

break·er[2] [ˈbreikə; ˋbrekɚ] ***n***. (救生艇上的)淡水桶,小水桶。

break·fast [ˈbrekfəst; ˋbrɛkfəst] **I** ***n***. 早餐;早餐食物。*at* ~ 早餐时;正吃早餐。*a* ~ *of bacon and eggs* 一顿咸肉加鸡蛋的早餐。**II** ***vi***. 吃早餐。~ *on eggs* 以鸡蛋作早餐。— ***vt***. 为(某人)备早餐;请(某人)吃早餐。~ *sb*. *in the restaurant* 请某人进饭馆早餐。~ **food** 早餐食用的谷类食物。~**-in-bed folks** 〔美〕懒鬼。

break·ing [ˈbreikiŋ; ˋbrekɪŋ] ***n***. 1. 破坏;损伤;中断;折断;【电】断路。2. 驯兽,训练。3.【语音】音的分裂。4. 〔*pl*.〕亚麻下脚。~ **and entering**【法】破坏侵入。~ **down**【电】击穿;中断;冲淡(电池酸液)。~**-in** 1.【电】插入;滚动,碾平。2. (工具等的)用熟,使惯;试车,试运转。3. 开始生产[使用](*This car needs no* ~*-in*. 这部车子一使用就称心)。~ **point** 1. 断裂点,破损点;破损程度。2. 忍耐极限,自我抑制极限。~ **strength**【物】裂断强度。

bream[1] [briːm; brim] ***n***.【鱼】1. 鲤科的淡水鱼,鳊。2. 鲷科的海鱼;隆头鱼科的鱼。

bream[2] [briːm; brim] ***vt***.【海】(以加热和刮擦的方法)清扫(船底)。

breast [brest; brɛst] **I** ***n***. 1. 乳房;〔喻〕营养的来源。2. 胸;胸脯,胸膛;胸口;胸怀,心情。3. (山)腹;(衣服的)胸部。4. (扶栏、梁等的)下侧;(器物的)侧面;窗腰,窗下墙;炉胸;【矿】工作面;【船】中央系索。*bare one's* ~ 袒开胸部。*Joy filled his* ~. 他满心欢喜。***at the*** ~ 未断奶的(*a child at the* ~ 奶娃娃,吃奶的婴儿)。***give*** (*a child*) ***the*** ~ 给(婴儿)喂奶。***have a feeling heart in one's*** ~ 有同情心。***make a clean*** ~ ***of*** 完全说出(秘密等),坦白。***past the*** ~ 断了奶。**II** ***vt***. 1. 挺胸面对,挺胸承当;(运动员)以胸部触(线);挺进,逆…而进,冒着…前进;毅然对抗,慨然担起(难事等)。2. 吮吸(奶头);(鸟)用胸部护(小鸟)。3. 登,爬(山等)。*The sprinter* ~*ed*. 那个短跑运动员首先冲到终点。*The ship* ~*ed the waves*. 船破浪前进。~ *a hill* 爬山。*The coach* ~*ed a slight incline*. 马车上一个缓坡。~ ***it out*** 抵抗到底。~ ***the tape*** (赛跑时)冲到终点线(=〔美〕~ ***the yarn***)。~**-beating** 大声抗议,捶胸顿足。~**bone** 胸骨。~**-deep** ***a***. 深[高]及胸部的。~ **drill**【机】胸压手摇钻。~**-feed** ***vt***. 自己奶养(婴孩);给(婴儿)喂奶。~ **harness** 不戴颈环、只系胸带的马具。~**-high** ***a***. 高与胸齐的。~**hook**【海】尖蹼板;船首甲板撑材。~**-knot** 胸结。~**pin** 领带夹针;〔美〕胸口饰针。~**plate** 1. 胸甲;(使用胸压工具时佩挂的)胸垫。2. 胸前送[受]话器。3.

(龟的)腹甲。4. (马)鞅,胸带皮。5. (古时犹太教大祭司穿的)镶宝石法衣。~**-pump** (奶胀时用的)吸奶器。~**-rail** (船侧、窗前的)栏杆。~**-stroke**【体】俯泳〔蛙式、蝶式等〕。~ **summer**【建】横楣。~ **telephone** 挂胸(式)电话机。~ **transmitter** 胸前送话机。~**-wall** 胸壁,防浪墙,挡土墙。~**work**【军】胸墙;【船】前后两甲板的栏杆。**-ed** *a*. 贴…胸的(*a single* [*double*] *breasted coat* 钉有一[两]排纽扣的上衣)。

Breas·ted [ˈbrestid; ˋbrɛstɪd] *n*. 布雷斯特德〔姓氏〕。

breath [breθ; brɛθ] *n*. 1. 气息,呼吸。2. 呼吸力;生命。3. 一息,一气,一口气;微风;声息,微音;低语,喃喃;气味;香气(的漂动)。4. 一瞬间;休止,小歇。5. 迹象,表示。6.【语音】无声音,气音。7. 琐事,小事。8.〔美俚〕洋葱。*be short of* ~ 喘气,上气不接下气。*have foul* [*bad*] ~ 口臭。*a hard and jerky* ~ 急促的呼吸。*the* ~ *of spring* 春天的气息。*She stopped to regain her* ~. 她停下来换一口气。*Give him a little* ~. 让他歇会儿。*She got a* ~ *of the perfectly chill night air*. 她吸了一口清凉的夜气。*In a* ~ *the street was empty*. 转眼之间,大街上就空无一人了。*The* ~ *of slander never touched him*. 从来没有人对他造谣中伤。*There is not a* ~ *of air*. 一丝风也没有。*a* ~ *of wind* 一阵微风。*the* ~ *of roses* 玫瑰花的香味。***above one's*** ~ 大声,说出声。***at a*** ~ 一气,一口气。***below*** [***under***] ***one's*** ~ 小声,低声细语。~ ***of air*** 微风。~ ***of life*** [***the nostrils***] 生命,灵魂;生活的必需品(*Music is the* ~ *of life to him*. 音乐是他生活的必需品)。***catch one's*** ~ 歇一口气,休息一下。2. 别着呼吸,紧张起来。***draw a*** ~ 吸一口气(*draw a long* [*deep*] ~ 松一口气,放下心)。***fetch one's*** ~ 苏醒过来,活转来。***gather a*** ~ 透一口气。***get*** [***recover***] ***one's*** ~ (***again***) 恢复正常(呼吸)。***give up*** [***yield***] ***the*** ~ 死。***hold*** [***keep***] ***one's*** ~ 屏息。***in a*** ~ 1. 一瞬间,一刹那。2. 一口气,一举。***in one*** ~ 立刻;同时;一口气(*say yes and no in one* ~ 才说同意又说不同意)。***in the same*** ~ 同时(*She lost her temper and apologized in the same* ~. 她刚一发火又表示道歉)。***keep*** [***save***, ***spare***] ***one's*** ~ ***to cool one's porridge*** 不如沉默不言,何必白费口舌。***knock the*** ~ ***out of*** 使吓一跳。***lose one's*** ~ 透不过气来,呼吸困难。***not a*** ~ ***of*** 一点儿没有(*not a* ~ *of suspicion* 丝毫没有可疑的地方)。***out of*** ~ 大喘气,上气不接下气。***pant for*** ~ 喘。***put*** (***sb***.) ***out of*** ~ 弄死。***save one's*** ~ 不必多说,不作声,闭口不言。***spend*** [***waste***] ***one's*** ~ 徒费唇舌,说也无用,白说。***stop sb***.***'s*** ~ 闷死某人。***take*** ~ 歇一口气,歇一歇(*without taking* ~ 不歇地,一口气地。*take a deep* ~ 长长地吸一口气,深呼吸)。***take sb***.***'s*** ~ (***away***) 使大吃一惊〔美语常省去 *away*〕。***to the last*** ~ 至死(*fight to the last* ~ 战斗到最后一息)。***with bated*** ~ 屏息地,小声。***with one's bad*** ~ 心怀恶意。***with the last*** ~ 临终时;最后。~ **holding test**【医】屏息试验。~ **test** 呼吸(测醉)分析。~**-test** *vt*. 对…进行呼吸(测醉)分析。~ **sounds** 呼吸声。

breath·a·lyse [ˈbreθəlaiz; ˋbrɛθəˏlaɪz] *vt*. 对…的呼吸进行测醉试验。

breath·a·lys·er [ˈbreθəlaizə; ˋbrɛθəˏlaɪzɚ] *n*. (测醉用)呼吸试验器。

breathe [briːð; brið] *vi*. 1. 呼吸。2. 活着,生存;(肖像等)栩栩如生。3. 歇一口气,休息一下。4. (风等)微微吹动;(人)低语;(香气)飘溢;(酒)开瓶后接触空气。5. (内燃机)以空气维持燃烧。*Hardly a man* ~*s who has not loved a woman*. 没有产生过爱情的男子几乎是没有的。*I can* ~ *easier now*. 我现在可以松一口气了。— *vt*. 1. 呼吸。2. 使喘气,使疲劳;使(运动员)出力训练。3. 使歇口气,使休息。4. 发散(香气等);说出,吐露出(心意等),漏出(真相等);表现出(感情等)。5. 低声说[唱]出;【语】发(气息音)。6. 向…注入(新内容等),赋与…以(生气等)(*into*)。7. 喷(火);吐(血)。~ *fresh air* 呼吸一下新鲜空气。~ *a horse* 让马喘喘气,让马歇一歇。*He was so* ~*d that he could not walk*. 他累得走不动了。~ *a prayer* 小声祈祷。*The novel* ~*s despair*. 这部小说表现出绝望的情绪。*She* ~*d life into the party*. 她给舞会带来了生气。~ *blood* 吐血。*It's said that dragons* ~ *fire*. 据说龙能喷火。*She never* ~*d a word about it*. 她对这件事绝口不提。~ ***a vein*** 〔古〕切开血管放血。~ ***down one's neck*** 威吓,装着要追赶的样子。~ ***freely*** [***easy***, ***easily***, ***again***] (紧张之后)安下心,放下心。~ ***one's last*** (***breath***) 断气,死(*He* ~*d his last*. 他死了)。~ ***sober***〔美〕戒酒。~ ***upon*** 1. 对…哈气;使(玻璃等)失去光泽。2. 中伤。(***be***) ***still breathing*** 还活着。***not*** ~ ***a word*** [***syllable***] ***about*** [***of***] 对…严守秘密。~ **pack** (测试驾车人是否酒后开车的)测醉器械。**breath·a·ble, breathe·a·ble** *a*. **breathe·a·ble·ness** *n*.

breathed [breθt, briːðd; brɛθt, briðd] *a*. 1.【语】气息音的。2. 有…气息的〔用以构成复合词〕,*a long-*~ *speaker* 能一口气讲个不停的演说者。

breath·er [ˈbriːðə; ˋbriðɚ] *n*. 1. 呼吸者,生物。2. (使人大喘气的)激烈运动[费力的工作];〔美〕喘着气的拳击选手。3. 片刻的休息,使呼吸恢复正常的休息。4. 通气孔[管、筒];呼吸阀[瓶];(潜水服等的)送气装置;【电】(变压器用的)吸潮器。~ *pipe* 通气管。*have* [*take*] *a* ~ *after a heavy work* 干完重活后休息一下。*a heavy* ~ 鼻息重的人,气粗的人。*go for a* ~ 作一会儿体育锻练。

breath·ing [ˈbriːðiŋ; ˋbriðɪŋ] **I** *a*. 1. 呼吸的,活的。2. (画像等)栩栩如生的。**II** *n*. 1. 呼吸;通气,供氧。2. 空气的微微流动,微风;(香气的)飘溢。3. 愿望,向往;(意见的)发表,表示;发言。4.【语】气息音,气音符号。5. 歇息,休息。6.【化】放气;【电】(电压器的)受潮;(送话器电阻的)周期性小变化。~ *exercises* 呼吸运动。*It all happened in a* ~. 这都是一转瞬之间发生的。~**-capacity** 肺活量。~ **hole** 通气孔。~**-mask** 口罩。~ **pipe** 通气管。~**-place** 1. (歌唱、朗诵时的)停顿。2. 休息场所;空气清新的休养地。~**-space** 1. 休息时间[场所]。2. 喘息的机会,考虑问题的时间。3. 起码的活动余地或空间(*give the opponent no* ~*-space* 不给对手喘息的时间。*The bus was so crowded that there was hardly* ~*-space*. 公共汽车上挤得水泄不通)。

breath·less [ˈbreθlis; ˋbrɛθlɪs] *a*. 1. 气喘吁吁的;透不过气来的。2. (紧张得)屏住气息的;〔诗〕已死的,气绝的。3. 微风全无的,(空气等)静止的。*The blow left him* ~. 一拳打得他透不过气来。~ *listeners of the mystery story* 屏息静听神怪故事的听众。*a* ~ *summer day* 没有一丝风的夏日。***with*** ~ ***anxiety*** 提心吊胆地。***with*** ~ ***interest*** 屏住气,紧张着。**-ly** *ad*. **-ness** *n*.

breath·tak·ing [ˈbreθˌteikiŋ; ˋbrɛθˏtekɪŋ] *a*. 1. 使人吃惊的,惊人的。2. 令人透不过气来的。3. 惊险的。*a* ~ *car race* 惊险的汽车比赛。*his* ~ *ignorance* 他那惊人的无知。

breath·y [ˈbreθi; ˋbrɛθɪ] *a*. 大声呼气的,带有喘息声的。**breath·i·ly** *ad*. **breath·i·ness** *n*.

b. rec., **B. Rec.** = bills receivable.

brec·ci·a [ˈbretʃə; ˋbrɛtʃɪə] *n*.【地】(断层)角砾岩。

brec·ci·ate [ˈbreʃiˌeit; ˋbrɛtʃɪˏet] *vt*. 1.【地】(将岩石碎片)合成角砾岩。2. 将(岩石)击成碎片。**-a·tion** *n*.

bred [bred; brɛd] breed 的过去式及过去分词。

brede [briːd; brid] *n*. 〔古〕= braid.

bree [briː; bri] *n*. 〔Scot.〕清汤;肉汤。

breech [briːtʃ; britʃ] **I** *n*. 1. 屁股,臀部。2. (枪、炮的)后膛,尾部。3. 水平烟道;【机】滑车底部;【海】肘材。4.〔*pl*.〕= breeches. **II** *vt*. 1. 给…穿裤子。2. 给(枪,炮)装枪尾[炮尾]。3.〔古〕打(屁股)。~ **birth** = ~ delivery. ~**block** 枪闩,炮闩;(枪机柄的)螺体。~**bolt** 枪闩。

~**cloth**, ~**clout** 围腰布。~ **delivery**【产科】(臀位、横位等)异常分娩。~**-loader** 后膛枪，后膛炮。~ **loading** *a*. 后膛的，后装式的。~**-sight** 瞄准器。

breech·es [ˈbritʃiz; ˋbrɪtʃɪz] *n*. *pl*. 马裤；宫廷礼裤；〔口〕裤子；短裤。*wear the* ~〔英〕压制丈夫，女人当家。**B-Bible** 1560 年版英译圣经〔将《创世纪》中 apron 一词错作 breeches〕. ~ **buoy**【海】裤形救生圈。~ **part**【剧】(女子扮演的)男角。

breech·ing [ˈbritʃiŋ; ˋbrɪtʃɪŋ] *n*. **1**. (挽马用的)尻带。**2**. (阻止炮身发射时倒退的)驻退索。**3**. 烟道。

breed [briːd; brid] (*bred* [bred; brɛd]; *bred*) **I** *vi*. **1**. (动物)生产，生子，下崽，下蛋。**2**. 怀胎。**3**. 繁殖；育种。**4**. 产生，引起，滋生。*Many animals* ~ *in the spring*. 许多动物都在春天繁殖。*Bacteria will not* ~ *in alcohol*. 细菌不能在酒精内繁殖。~ *from a mare of good stock* 以一匹良种母马育种。*Militarism* ~*s in armies*. 军国主义造成穷兵黩武。— *vt*. **1**. 产(子)，下(崽)，下(蛋)。**2**. 孵(卵)；怀(胎)。**3**. 繁殖，饲养。**4**. 养育，抚养；教养，培育；训练。**5**. 产生，滋生，使发生，酿成，惹起，引起。**6**.【原】再生，增殖。*Every mother breeds not sons alike*. 母别子异，一个娘养的儿子一个样。~ *horse* 养马。*Stagnant water* ~*s mosquitoes*. 死水滋生蚊虫。*be bred to the law* 受法律教育。~ *several strains of corn together to produce a new variety* 用几个品系的玉米育新种。**bred and born** = **born and bred** 道地的，…本地的。~ **in and in** 同种繁殖；近亲结婚。~ **out** 在人工繁殖过程中消除(品种的特性)。~ **out and out** 异种繁殖。~ **of cat(s)** 〔俚〕种类 (*be a different* ~ *of cat from* ...和…是两回事)。~ **true to type** (杂种)形成定型〔生产同一特质的后代〕。~ **up** 养育；教育，养成。**ill** [**well**] **bred** 有[没有]教养。**what is bred in the bone** 遗传的特质，本性(*What is bred in the bone will come out in the flesh*. 本性难移，骨头里生的总要在肉里长)。**II** *n*. **1**.【遗传】品种。**2**. 种族，血统，家系。**3**. 种类，群，集团。*He belongs to that* ~ *of pups*. 〔美〕他是那一种人。*Scholars are a quiet* ~. 学者们大都沉默寡言。*fine* ~ 良种；高贵的血统。

breed·er [ˈbriːdə; ˋbridɚ] *n*. **1**. 繁殖的动[植]物；种畜。**2**. 饲养人；养育者；家畜繁殖家。**3**. 发起人；起因。**4**.【原】增殖(反应)堆。*slow* [*rapid*] ~*s* 繁殖慢[快]的动物。~ **reactor**【原】增殖反应堆。

breed·ing [ˈbriːdiŋ; ˋbridɪŋ] *n*. **1**. 孵化；饲养；繁育。**2**. 选种；育种。**3**. 繁殖，生育。**4**. 薰陶；养育，教养，礼貌。**5**.【原】增殖，再生。*a man of fine* ~ 有教养的人。*cross* [*out-and-out*] ~ 杂交繁育。*close* [*in-and-in*] ~ 近亲繁育。*mass* ~ 混合育种。*cattle* ~ 养牛业。~ **cocoon** 种茧。~ **ground** **1**. 饲养场。**2**. (产生、培养某种思想的)温床。~ **pond** 养鱼塘。~ **plumage** (鸟的)婚羽。~ **ratio** 增殖比。~ **season** 繁殖期。~ **station** 配种站。

breeks [briːks; briks] *n*. 〔*pl*.〕〔*Scot*.〕= breeches.

breen [briːn; brin] **I** *n*. 褐绿色。**II** *a*. 褐绿色的。

breeze[1] [briːz; briz] **I** *n*. **1**. 微风；柔风，和风。**2**.〔俚〕吵闹，小风波，小纷争。**3**.〔俚〕流言，谣言。**4**.〔美俚〕轻而易举的事情。*a faint* [*gentle*, *light*, *moderate*, *fresh*, *strong*] ~ 微[柔，轻，和，疾，烈]风。*The horse won in a* ~. 这匹马轻而易举地就跑赢了。**bat** [**shoot**] **the** ~〔口〕**1**. 闲谈，聊天。**2**. 吹牛，夸大。**in a** ~ 不费力地。**kick up a** ~ 惹乱子，引起风波。**II** *vi*. **1**. 刮微风。**2**.〔美〕轻快地急走；闯入，冲进。**3**. 逃走。~ *through the book* 不费力地很快读完了全书。*It* ~*d from the west all day*. 整天吹微微的西风。~ **in**〔美〕**1**. (比赛)轻易得胜。**2**. = ~ into. ~ **into** = ~ out. ~ **off**〔美俚〕住嘴；走开。~ **out**〔俚〕毫不在乎，漫不经心地行动，飘然出现。~ **up** 风渐渐大起来。— *vt*. 使全速飞跑。~ *a horse around the track* 策马沿跑道飞奔。~**way** (房屋与房屋之间的)有顶过道[走廊]。**-less** *a*. 无风的，平静的。

breeze[2] [briːz; briz] *n*. 〔英〕煤渣，煤屑；煤粉。~ *oven* 煤粉化铁炉。~ *blocks* (煤渣与水泥制的)煤渣砖。

breeze[3] [briːz; briz] *n*.【虫】虻，牛蝇〔又名~**-fly**〕。

breez·i·ly [ˈbriːzili; ˋbrizəlɪ] *ad*. **1**. 微风徐徐。**2**. 轻快地。**3**. 快活地。

breez·i·ness [ˈbriːzinis; ˋbrizɪnɪs] *n*. **1**. 微风的轻吹。**2**. 轻快，活泼。**3**. 快活。

breez·y [ˈbriːzi; ˋbrizɪ] *a*. **1**. 有微风的，通风良好的。**2**. 有生气的，活泼的，轻快的。**3**.〔美〕说说笑笑的；多嘴的，爱谈笑的；傲慢的。*a* ~ *slapstick*〔美〕妙透了的俏皮话。*talk in a* ~ *way* 谈笑风生。

breg·ma [ˈbregmə; ˋbrɛgmə] *n*. (*pl*. **breg·ma·ta** [-mətə; -mətə])【解】前囟。**-tic** [bregˈmætik; brɛgˋmætɪk] *a*.

brek·ker [ˈbrekə; ˋbrɛkɚ] *n*. 〔学生俚〕早餐。

Bre·men [ˈbreimən; ˋbrɛmən] *n*. 不来梅〔德国港市〕。

brems·strah·lung [ˈbremˌʃtrɑːluŋ; ˋbrɛmˏʃtrɑləŋ] *n*.【物】(原子弹)韧致辐射。

Bren [bren; brɛn] *n*. (捷克造)布朗式轻机关枪(= ~ gun, ~ machine gun). *a* ~ *carrier* 履带式小型装甲车。

Bren·da [ˈbrendə; ˋbrɛndə] *n*. 布伦达〔女子名〕。

Bren·nan [ˈbrenən; ˋbrɛnən] *n*. 布伦南〔姓氏〕。

Brent [brent; brɛnt] *n*. **1**. 布伦特〔姓氏，男子名〕。**2**. 〔b-〕【鸟】黑雁(= ~-goose)。

br'er [brəː; brɚ] *n*. 〔美方〕= brother.

bres·sum·mer [ˈbresəmə; ˋbrɛsəmɚ] *n*.【建】大木(= breast-summer)。

Brest [brest; brɛst] *n*. **1**. 布雷斯特〔法国港市〕。**2**. 布列斯特〔白俄罗斯城市〕。

breth·ren [ˈbreðrin; ˋbrɛðrən] *n*. *pl*. 〔古〕同党，同会，会友；同业；〔古〕同胞。

Bre·ton [bretən; ˋbrɛtn] *n*. (法国)布列塔尼地区的人；布列塔尼地区的语言。

Bret·ton Woods [ˈbretən wudz; ˋbrɛtən wudz] 布雷顿森林〔美国游览胜地〕。

breve [briːv; briv] *n*. **1**.【乐】二全音符(‖0‖)。**2**.【印】(母音上的)短音符号(˘)。**3**. (法律诉讼的)令状；(教皇的)训谕示；(国王的)敕令。

bre·vet [ˈbrevit; ˋbrɛvɪt] **I** *n*. 〔军〕(不提薪的)名誉晋级(令)，加衔(令)。**II** *vt*. 予以加衔，予以名誉晋升。**III** *a*. 名誉晋升的，加衔的。

bre·vet·cy [briˈvetsi; brɪˋvɛtsɪ] *n*. 名誉级，名誉衔〔提职不提薪〕。

brevi- *comb*. *f*. 短：*brevi*ostrate.

bre·vi·ar·y [ˈbriːvjəri; ˋbrivɪˏɛrɪ] *n*. **1**.【天主】每日祈祷；〔常 B-〕祈祷书。**2**. 节略。

bre·vier [brəˈviə; brəˋvɪr] *n*.【印】八点活字〔相当于六号铅字〕。

brev·i·ros·trate [ˌbreviˈrɔstreit; ˏbrɛvɚˋrɑstret] *a*.【动】短喙的。

brev·i·ty [ˈbreviti; ˋbrɛvətɪ] *n*. **1**. (语言等的)简洁；简短。**2**. (时间等的)短促，短暂。*B- is the soul of wit*. 言以简洁为贵，简洁是智慧的真谛。*the* ~ *of human life* 短促的人生，人生如寄。*send a telegram in its* ~ 打一份文字简洁的电报。

brew [bruː; bru] **I** *vt*. **1**. 酿造(啤酒等)；调(饮料)，泡(茶)。**2**. 酝酿，策划。*She* ~*ed a pot of soup from the leftovers*. 她用吃剩下的菜冲一盆汤。~ *mischief* 策划恶作剧。~ *trouble* 图谋捣乱。— *vi*. **1**. 酿酒；(水等)煮沸。**2**. (暴风雨等)即将来临，(脾气等)行将发作；(阴谋等)成熟，紧迫。*The tea* ~*s and we wait*. 茶泡上了，我们等一会儿。*There is something* ~*ing*. 眼看就要出什么乱子。*A storm is* ~*ing in the west*. 暴风雨就要从西边过来。**As you** ~, **so you must drink**. 自酿苦酒自家喝，自作自受。**II** *n*. **1**. 酿造；(一次)酿造量。**2**.

(酿造出的)饮料;热茶,热咖啡(等);混合饮料。3.(酒等的)品味。*a good strong* ~ 浓味佳酿。*the first* ~ *of tea* 刚泡的茶,头道茶。*a witches'* ~ 女巫调制的神秘药酒。

brew·age [ˈbruːidʒ; ˋbruɪdʒ] ***n.*** 1.(酒的)酿造;(饮料的)调制。2. 啤酒;饮料。3.(阴谋等的)策划;(暴风雨等的)酝酿。

brew·er [ˈbruːə; ˋbruɚ] ***n.*** 1. 酿(啤)酒人,酿(啤)酒商。2. 阴谋家。~**'s grain** (啤)酒糟。~**s' yeast** 1. 啤酒酵母。2.(啤酒酿成后的)酵母副产品。

Brew·er [ˈbru(ː)ə; ˋbru(u)ɚ] ***n.*** 布鲁尔〔男子名〕。

brew·er·y, brew·house [ˈbruəri, ˈbruːhaus; ˋbruərɪ, ˋbruˏhaus] ***n.*** 啤酒厂,酿酒厂。

brew·ing [ˈbruːiŋ; bruɪŋ] ***n.*** 1. 酿造(啤酒);一次酿造量;酿酒法。2. 混合,搀合。3.(阴谋等的)策划;(暴风雨等的)酝酿。

brew·is [ˈbruːis; ˋbruɪs] ***n.*** 〔方〕肉汁,肉汤;泡在肉汤[热奶]中的面包。

Brew·ster [ˈbruːstə; ˋbrustɚ] ***n.*** 布鲁斯特〔姓氏〕。

Bri·an [ˈbraiən; ˋbraɪən] ***n.*** 布赖恩〔姓氏,男子名〕。

bri·ar [ˈbraiə; ˋbraɪɚ] ***n.*** = brier[12].

Bri·a·re·us [braiˈɛəriəs; braɪˋɛrɪəs] ***n.*** 【希神】百手巨人。**Bri·are·an** [braiˈɛəriən; braɪˋɛriən] ***a.***

bri·ar·root [ˈbraiəˈruːt; ˋbraɪəˏrut] ***n.*** = brierroot.

bri·ar·wood [ˈbraiəwud; ˋbraɪɚˏwud] ***n.*** = brierwood.

brib·a·bil·i·ty [ˌbraibəˈbiliti; ˏbraɪbəˋbɪlətɪ] ***n.*** 受贿[被收买]的可能性;易受贿。

brib·a·ble [ˈbraibəbl; ˋbraɪbəbl̩] ***a.*** 能行贿的,可收买的,容易收买的。

bribe [braib; braɪb] **I** ***n.*** 1. 贿赂,私礼。2. 诱惑物。*take* [*offer*] *a* ~ 受[行]贿。*give* [*offer, handout*] ~*s to sb.* 向某人行贿。*The children were given candy as a* ~ *to be good.* 用糖果哄孩子们不要闹。**II** ***vt.*** 1. 用贿赂引诱;向…行贿,收买。2. 用贿赂影响。~ *sb. into silence* 用贿赂封住某人的嘴。—***vi.*** 行贿。

brib·ee [braiˈbiː; ˏbraɪbˋi] ***n.*** 行贿人。

brib·er [ˈbraibə; ˋbraɪbɚ] ***n.*** 行贿人。

brib·er·y [ˈbraibəri; ˋbraɪbərɪ] ***n.*** 1. 行贿,收买。2. 受贿。*commit* ~ 行[受]贿。

bric-à-brac [ˈbrikəbræk; ˋbrɪkəˏbræk] ***n.*** 〔F.〕(*sing*; *pl.*) 1. 古董,古玩,古物。2. 装饰品;小摆设。

Brice [brais; braɪs] ***n.*** 布赖斯〔姓氏,男子名〕。

brick [brik; brɪk] **I** ***n.*** 1. 砖;砖块。2. 砖形物;砖形面包;茶砖;方料,块料;积木(玩具);一砖的厚度。3.〔口〕好心人;好汉。*a fire* [*stone*] ~ 耐火砖。*a gold* ~ 金砖;坚固的东西。*bake* [*make, burn*] ~*s* 烧砖。*lay* ~*s* 砌砖。*one and a half* ~*s thick* 一砖半厚。*a Bath* [*Bristol*] ~ 砖形砂石[磨口]。*as dry as a* ~ 干得像砖头一样。*a regular* ~ 好汉,好人。*You've been a perfect* ~ *to me.* 你待我太好了。~ **by** ~ 一点一点。***drop a*** ~〔口〕出丑,出错,失言。***have a*** ~ ***in one's hat*** 有醉意。***hit the*** ~***s***〔美俚〕1. 走上街头。2. 罢工;巡察。3. 释放出狱。***like a*** ~〔口〕勇猛地,活泼地。***like a hundred*** [***thousand, a load, tons***] ***of*** ~***s***〔口〕勇敢地,猛烈地;以压倒优势。***make*** ~***s without straw*** 徒劳,做吃力不讨好的事情。**II** ***vt.*** 用砖砌;用砖镶填(*up*);用砖围砌(*in*);用砖铺筑,用砖建造。~ *up a disused entrance* 用砖堵死不再需要的入口。**III** ***a.*** 1. 用砖砌[铺]的。2. 砖似的。*a* ~ *pavement* 砖铺的人行道。*a* ~ *wall* 砖墙。~ **bat** 1. ***n.*** (扔人的)砖片,碎砖;贬责的话,严厉的批评。2. ***vt.*** 讽刺,攻击。~ **clay** 砖土,(制砖的)黏土。~ **dust** 砖粉,砖灰,砖屑。~ **field** 砖厂。~ **fielder**〔澳〕燥热的北风。~ **kiln** 砖窑,~ **layer** 砌砖工。~**laying** 砌砖;泥水业。~ **nogging**〔建〕木架砖壁。~**-on-edge** 侧(砌)砖。~**-on-end** 竖(砌)砖。~ **red** 红砖色。~**-red** ***a.*** 红砖色的。~ **tea** 砖茶。~ **work** 1. 砌砖工程,砖房。2. 砖圬工。~ **yard** 砖厂;售砖处。

brick·le [ˈbrikl; ˋbrɪkl] ***a.*** 〔方〕易碎的,脆的。**-ness** ***n.***

brick·y [ˈbriki; ˋbrɪkɪ] ***a.*** 砖的,砖一样的,砖色的。

bri·cole [ˈbrikəl; ˋbrɪkol] ***n.*** 1.〔古〕石弩。2.【台球】撞空;【网球】(碰壁)弹回;〔喻〕间接的一击。3.(拖炮用的)垫肩。

brid·al [ˈbraidl; ˋbraɪdl] **I** ***a.*** 1. 新人的,新娘的。2. 婚礼的。*a* ~ *suite* (旅馆等的)新婚夫妇房间。*a* ~ *couple* 新郎新娘。**II** ***n.*** 1. 婚礼,结婚仪式。2.〔古〕喜筵。~ **chamber** 新房,洞房。~ **veil** (新娘披的)面纱。~ **wreath**【植】笑靥花。

bride[1] [braid; braɪd] ***n.*** 1. 新娘;即将出嫁的女子。2.〔英俚〕十多岁的姑娘。*a* ~*-to-be* 未来的新娘。~ ***and groom on a raft***〔美俚〕鸡蛋烤面包片。***lead one's*** ~ ***to the altar*** 娶某女为妻〔指在教堂内结婚〕。~**-cake** ***n.*** 喜饼,礼饼。~**-price** (婚前男方给女方的)聘金,财礼。

bride[2] [braid; braɪd] ***n.*** 花边上连接花纹用的狭条;妇女宽边帽上的系带。

bride·groom [ˈbraidgrum; ˋbraɪdˏgrum] ***n.*** 新郎。

brides·maid [ˈbraidzmeid; ˋbraɪdzˏmed] ***n.*** 女傧相。

brides·man [ˈbraidzmən; ˋbraɪdzmən] ***n.*** 男傧相。

bride·well [ˈbraidwəl; ˋbraɪdwəl] ***n.*** 1.〔古〕监狱。2.〔美〕感化院。

bridge[1] [bridʒ; brɪdʒ] **I** ***n.*** 1. 桥,桥梁;【船】舰桥,船桥。2. 鼻梁;(假牙上的)齿桥;【乐】弦柱,弦马;【电】电桥;【机】天车,桥架;【台球】球棒架。3.(文艺作品的)过渡性章节,过场;穿插,插曲。*a* ~ *of boats* 船桥。*a bascule* ~ 活动桥。*a suspension* [*wire*] ~ 吊桥,悬索桥。*Wheatstone* ~【物】惠斯登电桥。*throw a* ~ *across* [*over*] *a river* 在河上架桥。~ ***of gold*** [***silver***] = ***golden*** [***silver***] ~ 退路,逃路,易于突破难关的办法。***burn one's*** ~***s*** (***behind one***) 布背水阵,破釜沉舟。***Don't cross the*** ~ ***until you come to it.*** 不要杞人忧天,不要预先自寻苦恼。***in*** ~【物】并联;跨接;加分路。**II** ***vt.*** 1. 在…之间架桥,搭桥于,用桥连接;【电】跨接。2.〔喻〕越过,跨过(*over*)。*The road* ~*s the river.* 在河上架桥把路连接起来。~ *over obstacles* 越过障碍。~**-board**【建】短梯基。~ **builder** ***n.*** 搭桥人;斡旋者,调解人。~ **crane** 桥式吊车。~ **head**【军】桥头堡。~ **host**【生】过渡寄生。~ **house** 桥旁小屋,【海】桥楼。~**-opening** 桥孔。~**-pier** 桥墩。~**-toll** 过桥费。~ **train**【军】架浮桥用具;架桥中队。~ **ward** 守桥人。~**-work** 桥梁工事;(假牙的)齿桥。

bridge[2] [bridʒ; brɪdʒ] ***n.*** 【牌】桥牌战,打桥牌。*auction* ~ 拍卖式桥牌。*contract* ~(打不到预定墩数要受罚的)合约式桥牌。

Bridg·es [ˈbridʒiz; ˋbrɪdʒɪz] ***n.*** 布里奇斯〔姓氏〕。

Bridg·et [ˈbridʒit; ˋbrɪdʒɪt] ***n.*** 布丽奇特〔女子名〕。

Bridge·town [ˈbridʒtaun; ˋbrɪdʒˏtaun] ***n.*** 布里奇敦(桥城)〔巴巴多斯首都〕。

Bridg·man [ˈbridʒmən; ˋbrɪdʒmən] ***n.*** 布里奇曼〔姓氏〕。

bridg·ing [ˈbridʒiŋ; ˋbrɪdʒɪŋ] ***n.*** 1. 造桥,架桥。2.【建】搁栅撑。

bri·dle [ˈbraidl; ˋbraɪdl] **I** ***n.*** 1. 笼头〔缰、辔、口衔的总称〕;拉手[缰绳]。2. 约束物;束缚,抑制;【机】束带,限动物;制动器;【海】系船索(链);【解】系带。***give the*** ~ ***to*** 放松缰绳;使…自由活动;放纵。***go well up to the*** ~ (马)听从骑者的驾驭,服从驾驭。***lay the*** ~ ***on the neck of*** 放松,放纵。***put*** [***set***] ***a*** ~ ***on*** 克制,抑制。**II** ***vt.*** 1. 给(马)套笼头[上辔头]。2. 抑制,约束。~ *one's passions* [*anger*] 克制欲望[愤怒]。—***vi.*** 仰头,昂首(表示傲慢、轻侮、愤怒)(*up*)。~ *up with anger* 气冲冲地昂起头。~ ***at*** 对…仰着头表示看不起。~ **bridge** 通马不通车的狭桥。~ **hand** 执缰绳的手[左手]。~**-joint** (木工)啮接。~ **path** [**road, way**] (不能通车的)马道。~ **rein** 马缰。~ **trail** 马踏成的路。~**-wise** ***a.*** 〔美〕(马)养乖了的,有训练的,听从骑者指挥的。

bri·doon [bri'du:n; brɪˋdun] ***n.*** (军马的)缰绳口衔,小勒缰。

Brie [bri:; bri] ***n.*** (法国布里产的)咸味白乳酪。

brief [bri:f; brif] **I** ***a.*** **1.** (时间)短暂的。**2.** (文体的)简洁的。**3.** (答复等)简短的。*a ~ stay in the country* 在该国小留数日。*a ~ life* 短暂的人生。*a ~ hope* 暂时的希望。*a ~ report* 简短的报告。*He is ~ of speech.* 他说话简单扼要。*a cold and ~ welcome* 寥寥几句冷淡的欢迎。*to be ~ with you* 简单地和你说吧。***to be ~*** 简单地说,一句话。**II** ***n.*** **1.** 概要,摘要;短文。**2.** 【法】诉讼事实摘要,诉讼事件;(律师的)辩护状。**3.** (攻击开始前给飞行员等的)指令,简短命令。**4.** (罗马教皇的)敕书。**5.** 〔*pl.*〕紧身裤,三角裤。**6.** 【剧】〔英〕免费入场券。**7.** 〔废〕信件。~ ***of title*** 【法】转让(财产等的)书面摘要。***have plenty of ~s*** (律师)承办的案件多。***hold a ~*** 当辩护律师。***hold a ~ for*** 为…辩护,主张…,为…大声疾呼。***in ~*** 简单地说,要言之。***make ~ of*** 把…很快办完。***take a ~*** (律师)接受诉讼案件。**III** ***vt.*** **1.** 节略,作…的摘要[提要]。**2.** 〔英〕向(律师)陈述诉讼事实摘要;委托…作辩护律师。**3.** 向…下达简令;对(飞行员等)作最后指示;对…事先作简要指点。*He ~ed his salesmen on the coming campaign.* 他就即将开展的推销运动向推销员作简短指示。~ **bag** 〔英〕= **~case.** 公文皮包。**-ing** ***n.*** **1.** 下达简令;情况简介[汇报]会。**2.** 简令;简要情况 (*a* (*news*) *~ing officer* 〔美〕新闻发布官。*a briefing chart* 任务简要讲解图。*a briefing room* 简令下达室)。

brief·less ['bri:flis; ˋbriflɪs] ***a.*** 无人委托诉讼的,无诉讼案件的。

brief·ly ['bri:fli; ˋbriflɪ] ***ad.*** 简短地,简单地,简略地。***to put it ~*** 简单地说。

brief·ness ['bri:fnis; ˋbrifnɪs] ***n.*** 简单,简略;简洁的风格。

bri·er[1], **bri·ar**[1] ['braiə; ˋbraɪɚ] ***n.*** 【植】多刺的木质茎植物(丛);野蔷薇(丛)。***~s and brambles*** 茂盛的刺丛。~ **grape** 刺葡萄。~ **rose** 【植】蔷薇莓。**-y** ***a.*** 荆棘丛生的,多刺的。

brier[2], **briar**[2] ['braiə; ˋbraɪr] ***n.*** **1.** 【植】石南。**2.** 欧石南根烟斗。~**root** 【植】欧石南根。~**wood** 欧石南木。

brig[1] [brig; brɪg] **I** ***n.*** **1.** 横帆双桅船。**2.** 〔美军俚〕舰上禁闭室;舰上警卫室。**3.** 〔美俚〕监狱;警察局。**II** ***vt.*** 监禁。

brig[2] [brig; brɪg] ***n.***, ***vt.*** 〔Scot.〕= bridge[1].

brig. = brigade; brigadier.

bri·gade [bri'geid; brɪˋged] **I** ***n.*** **1.** 【军】旅;大部队。**2.** (从事一定活动的)队,组。**II** ***vt.*** **1.** 【军】把…编成旅。**2.** 把…编成队[组]。*a fire ~* 消防队。*a rescue ~* 急救队。~**-major** 〔英〕副旅长。

brig·a·dier [ˌbrigə'diə; ˏbrɪgəˋdɪr] ***n.*** **1.** 旅长。**2.** 〔英〕陆军[海军陆战队]准将。**3.** 〔美〕= B- General. ***B-General*** 〔美〕陆军[空军、海军陆战队]准将,少将旅长。

brig·and ['brigənd; ˋbrɪgənd] ***n.*** 土匪,强盗。**-age, -ism** ***n.*** 抢劫;强盗行为。**-ish** ***a.*** 强盗般的。

brig·an·tine ['brigəntain; ˋbrɪgənˏtain] ***n.*** **1.** (前桅为横帆,主桅为纵帆的)纵横帆双桅船。**2.** = brig[1].

Brig· Gen. = Brigadier General 〔美〕陆军[空军、海军陆战队]准将。

Briggs [brigz; brɪgz] ***n.*** 布里格斯〔姓氏〕。

bright [brait; braɪt] **I** ***a.*** **1.** 光明的,明亮的;辉煌的,闪烁的;灿烂的;晴朗的。**2.** (水、酒等)透明的,晶莹的;(颜色)鲜艳的;(证据等)明白的;(声名)显赫的。**3.** 聪明的,伶俐的,乖巧的;细心的;机灵的。**4.** 活泼的;欣喜的,快活的;幸福的;有希望的。*~ coins* 亮闪闪的硬币。*a bright day* 大晴天。*~ passages of prose* 漂亮的文章,有文采。*a ~ wine* 晶莹的美酒。*the ~ water* 清可见底的水。*the ~ pageantry* 宫廷的富丽堂皇。*~ hope(s)* 光明的希望。*a ~ period* 辉煌的时期。*a ~ red dress* 鲜红的服装。*a ~ reputation* 声名显赫。*~ silk* 熟丝。*a ~ boy* 聪明的小伙子。*a ~ idea* 好主意,妙想。*the bird's ~ song* 欢快的鸟鸣。*a ~ and happy child* 活泼快乐的孩子。~ ***and early*** 大清早。~ ***in the eye*** 〔口〕微醉,带醉。~ ***side of things*** 事物的光明面(*look on* [*at*] *the ~ side of things* 对事物抱乐观态度)。**II** ***ad.*** = brightly. *The sun was shining ~.* 阳光灿烂。**III** ***n.*** **1.** 〔*pl.*〕(开行中的)车头灯 (*opp.* parking ~)。**2.** 烤得金黄的烟叶。**3.** 方尖画笔。**4.** 〔古〕光辉。~ **collar** 亮领阶层〔指从事电脑业等的专业人士,又称"智领"〕。~**-eyed** ***a.*** 眼睛清莹的。~ **field** 【物】明视场。~ **light districts,** ~ **lights** 〔口〕市区娱乐场所。~ **line** 【物】明线。~**work** (船、车等的)光亮的金属构件;【船】无漆木料构件。**-ly** ***ad.*** **-ness** ***n.***

Bright [brait; braɪt] ***n.*** 布赖特〔姓氏〕。**B-'s disease** 【医】肾炎〔总称〕。

bright·en ['braitn; ˋbraɪtn] ***vt.*** **1.** 使发光辉,使发亮,擦光,磨亮。**2.** 使活跃,使快活;使有希望;使聪明。*The new teacher ~ed the life of all his pupils.* 新来的老师使全体学生的生活变得活跃起来了。— ***vi.*** **1.** 闪耀,发亮,发光。**2.** (天)晴;(人)露喜色,快活起来。**3.** (前途)有希望。*His face ~ed.* 他喜形于色。*B- up!* 拿出精神来,别垂头丧气! **-ing** 【纺】增艳处理。

Brigh·ton ['braitn; ˋbraɪtn̩] ***n.*** 布赖顿〔英国城市〕。

Brig·id ['bridʒid; ˋbrɪdʒɪd] ***n.*** = Bridget.

Bri·gitte ['bridʒit; brɪˋʒit] ***n.*** 布丽奇特〔女子名,Bridget 的异体〕。

brill [bril; brɪl] ***n.*** (*pl.* ~, ~*s*) 【鱼】滑菱鲆鲆。

bril·liance ['briljəns; ˋbrɪljəns], **bril·lian·cy** ['briljənsi; ˋbrɪljənsɪ] ***n.*** **1.** 光彩,光辉,光泽。**2.** 【光】辉度,亮度。**3.** 漂亮;(名声)煊赫;文采;才气焕发,才华横溢。*the ~ of a fine diamond* 宝石的光辉。*the brilliancies of Congreve's wit* 康格里夫的出众才华。

bril·liant ['briljənt; ˋbrɪljənt] **I** ***a.*** **1.** 明亮的,辉煌的,灿烂的;漂亮的。**2.** 英明的;卓越的;极好的;(声名)显赫的;才气焕发的。**3.** 声音嘹亮的;(色彩)鲜明的。**4.** (武器等)智能化的。*a ~ star* 亮晶晶的星。*a ~ record* 辉煌的记录。*a ~ mind* 头脑敏锐的人,有才华的人。**II** ***n.*** **1.** (琢成多角形而呈现异彩的)宝石。**2.** 【印】$3\frac{1}{2}$ 点铅字。**-ly** ***ad.*** **-ness** ***n.***

bril·lian·tine [ˌbriljən'ti:n; ˋbrɪljənˏtin] ***n.*** **1.** 润发油。**2.** 【纺】亮光薄呢〔一种有光泽的棉毛交织品〕。

brim [brim; brɪm] **I** ***n.*** **1.** (杯、碗等容器的)缘,边;〔古〕水边,岸边。**2.** 帽边。*fill a glass to the ~* 把杯子倒满。*the ~ of a cup* 茶杯边。*the ~ of a hat* 帽子的翻边。***full to the ~*** 漫到边,满,溢。**II** ***vt.*** (**-mm-**) 把(容器)装满,注满,倒满。*~ the cup* 把茶杯倒满。— ***vi.*** 满,溢,漫出。*Tears ~med in her eyes.* 她的眼中充满了泪水。~ ***over with*** (精神等)饱满;(才华等)横溢;漫出,充满(*She is brimming over with health.* 她全身上下都焕发着健康的气息)。

brim·ful ['brim'ful; ˋbrɪmˋful] ***a.*** **1.** 漫到边的。**2.** 洋溢着…的。*her ~ eyes* 她那泪汪汪的眼睛。*a ~ cup* 满满的一杯(水、酒等)。*be ~ of hope and health* 充满了健康和希望。**-ness** ***n.***

brim·med [brimd; brɪmd] ***a.*** **1.** 满,漫到边的。**2.** 有(…)边的。*a broad-~ hat* 宽边帽。

brim·mer ['brimə; ˋbrɪmɚ] ***n.*** 满杯。

brim·stone ['brimstəun; ˋbrɪmˏston] ***n.*** **1.** 〔古〕硫黄石;【圣】地狱之火的燃料。**2.** 泼妇,悍妇。***Fire and ~*** 硫磺烈火〔《圣经》中讲的地狱之火,用以惩罚有罪者〕。~ **moth** 【动】黄蛾。

brim·ston·y ['brimstəuni; ˋbrɪmˏstonɪ] ***a.*** **1.** 硫黄质[色]的,有硫黄臭味的。**2.** 地狱般气氛的;恶魔的。

brin·ded ['brindid; ˋbrɪndɪd] ***a.*** 〔古〕= brindled.

brin·dle ['brindl; ˋbrɪndl̩] **I** ***n.*** **1.** 斑,斑纹。**2.** 斑皮动物;〔特指〕花狗。**II** ***a.*** = brindled.

B

brin·dled [ˈbrindld; ˋbrɪndḷd] ***a***. 斑驳的,有斑纹的,花的。

brine [brain; braɪn] **I** ***n***. **1**. 卤水;咸水,盐水;【化】盐溶液。**2**. 海水;海。**3**. 〔诗〕泪水。**II** ***vt***. 用盐水泡,用盐水处理。~ **pan** **1**. 盐田。**2**. 熬盐锅。~ **pit** 盐井。~ **shrimp** 盐水褐虾。

bring [briŋ; brɪŋ] (***brought*** [brɔːt; brɔt]; ***brought***) ***vt***. **1**. 拿来,带来,携来,取来;引来;使(人)来到;〔方〕陪,护送。**2**. 劝导,劝诱;迫使。**3**. 招致,导致;使处于某种状态。**4**. 生出,产生;(投资等)获得(利润)。**5**. 举出(论据等),提起(诉讼等),提出(议案等)。**6**. (货物等)能卖(多少钱),能换(多少东西)。*I have brought my umbrella with me*. 我带伞来了。*Her scream brought the police*. 她的叫声引来了警察。*I cannot* ~ *him to my point of view*. 我无法说服他同意我的观点。*I cannot* ~ *myself to do it*. 我实在不能干那件事。~ *the car to a stop* 使车子停下来。~ *sb*. *into the conversation* 使某人参加谈话。*The news brought him to his feet*. 这个消息使他惊得站了起来。*This car will* ~ *a good price*. 这汽车能卖大价钱。~ *an action for damages* 提出为所受损害要求赔偿的诉讼。~ ***about*** **1**. 造成;带来,引起。**2**. 【海】(使船)回转,掉头(~ *about a war* 引起战争。*What brought the quarrel about*? 争吵是怎么引起的? ~ *the ship about* 使船掉头)。~ ***along*** **1**. 带来。**2**. 指导,教导(*B- along your friend*. 请把你的朋友带来)。~ ***around*** [***round***] **1**. 说服,(某人)做某事(*to*). **2**. 〔口〕使恢复知觉[等]。**3**. 〔口〕把(某人)作为客人带来(*We can* ~ *him around to agreeing with the plan*. 我们可以说服他同意该项计划。*The new medicine brought him around*. 服用新药使他恢复了健康。*They brought around a new employee this morning*. 他们今天早晨请来了一位新雇员)。~ ***back*** **1**. 使回忆起。**2**. 使恢复。**3**. 送回,还回,拿回,带回(~ *sb*. *back to health* 使某人恢复健康)。~ ***close to*** 引近,领来。~ ***down*** **1**. 贬低;〔口〕煞(某人)威风,使受挫;把(人)毁掉;打倒。**2**. 使落下[跌落];射落,击落,打下;打伤,打死。**3**. 削减;降低。**4**. 致(祸),获(罪)。**5**. 放下,卸下(货物等)。**6**. 使浓缩。**7**. 把(记录)记到(某时)为止(~ *down the birds* 把鸟击落。~ *down the price* 降价)。~ ***down on oneself*** 招人恨[嫉妒、报复等]。~ ***down the house*** 博得满场喝采。~ ***forth*** **1**. 生,产生,产(子),结(实),开(花),出(芽)。**2**. 显现,提出,发表(~ *forth a son* 生儿子。~ *forth a proposal* 提出建议)。~ ***forward*** [***on***] **1**. 提出(计划等);提示;提前;公开;显出。**2**. 【会计】把(账目)结转(到次页)。**3**. 把…提前(*B- forward the prisoner*. 带犯人出庭! ~ *forward an opinion* 提出意见。~ *forward a meeting* 把会议召开日期提前)。~ (***sth***.) ***home*** (***to sb***.) **1**. 使(某人)清楚地认识到[痛切地感觉到了](某事)。**2**. 确凿证明(某人)犯(某罪)。~ ***home the bacon*** 〔口〕**1**. 成功;如愿以偿。**2**. 谋生。~ ***in*** **1**. 生产,产出;生(利);收获(农作物等);挣得(报酬等)。**2**. 带来,引入,传进。**3**. 提出(议案等);(陪审团)下(判决);【棒球】使跑回本垒(*His extra job doesn't* ~ *in much*. 他的兼职工作挣不了多少钱。)。~ ***sb***. ***in guilty*** [***not guilty***] 宣判某人有罪[无罪])。~ ***into effect*** 使生效;使起作用。~ ***into play*** 使活动,使发挥作用。~ ***off*** **1**. 办完,圆满完成。**2**. (从失事船只上)救出。~ ***on*** **1**. 惹起,引起(议论等),导致。**2**. 使发展;使出现。**3**. 提出;介绍;使(演员)与观众见面。**4**. 〔卑〕使(性欲)冲动。~ *on a crisis* 引起一场危机。*His words brought on a storm*. 他的话使全场哗然。~ ***out*** **1**. 公布,发表;说出;出版;上演。**2**. 显示出,揭示出,现出(颜色、性质等);显露(才华)。**3**. 使(女子)进入社交界(*Peril* ~*s out unsuspected qualities*. 危难使人显示出真实的品质。*She brought the fact out with shame*. 她羞愧地讲出了事实。~ *out a play* 上演一出戏。~ *out a book* 出版一本书)。~ ***over*** **1**. 把…带来;从外国运来;把…引渡。**2**. 把…拉入(某组织等);使改变意见[信仰等],把…争取过来。~ (***sb***.) ***through*** **1**. 帮助(某人)脱离险境[克服困难,突破障碍]。**2**. 救活(~ *a patient through* 救活病人)。~ ***to*** **1**. 使恢复知觉,使复苏。**2**. 【海】使停船。(~ *him to by artificial respiration* 以人工呼吸法使他恢复知觉)。~ ***to an end*** [***a close***, ***a stand***, ***a stop***] 使终止,使停止,结束。~ ***to bear*** **1**. 施加(压力等),使受(影响等)。**2**. 瞄准,把(枪、炮)向…对准。**3**. 集中(力量),竭尽(才智等)。**4**. 使成功,使(意见)被接受,完成,实现(~ *a gun to bear on the mark* 把大炮对准目标)。~ ***together*** 集合,召集(~ *together all kinds of talent* 把各种人才集合起来)。~ ***to light*** 暴露,公开,公布。~ ***to mind*** 想起,回想。~ ***to pass*** **1**. 使发生,引起。**2**. 做成,完成。~ ***under*** **1**. 压服,镇压。**2**. 抑制;把…置于(权力、支配等)之下。~ ***up*** **1**. 抚养,养育,教育,培养。**2**. 提出(问题等);派出(军队等),发出。**3**. 把(某人)带上法庭;准许(议员)发言;结转,滚入(计算)。**4**. 使(车辆等)突然停止;【海】抛锚;(船等)到终点。**5**. 呕吐(*a well brought-up young man* 一个有教养的青年。~ *up a new subject* 提出新问题。~ *up blood* 吐血。~ *up the car* 使车子猛然停住)。~ ***up the rear*** 殿后,压队,最后来。

bring·down [ˈbriŋdaun; ˋbrɪŋdaʊn] **I** ***n***. 〔美俚〕**1**. 使人灰心丧气[不满]的东西。**2**. 经常愁眉苦脸的人。**II** ***a***. **1**. 令人不满的;不能胜任的。**2**. 使人沮丧的;阴沉的。

bring·ing-up [ˈbriŋiŋˈʌp; ˋbrɪŋɪŋˋʌp] ***n***. **1**. (儿童的)养育,抚养。**2**. 教养。

brin·ja(u)l [ˈbrindʒɔːl; ˋbrɪndʒɔl] ***n***. 【植】茄子。

brink [briŋk; brɪŋk] ***n***. **1**. 边,界,涯,滨,岸。**2**. 〔喻〕濒临;(战争)边缘。*the* ~ *of a precipice* 悬崖边沿。*a* ~*-of-war policy* 战争边缘政策。*beyond the* ~ *of our endurance* 超出了我们忍耐的限度。***on the*** ~ ***of*** 即将要,濒临,在…的边缘(*be on the* ~ *of doing* 即将要做。*on the* ~ *of starvation* 快要饿死)。~(**s**)**man** 奉行战争边缘政策的人。

brink(s)·man·ship [ˈbriŋk(s)mənʃip; ˋbrɪŋk(s)mənʃɪp] ***n***. **1**. (战争)边缘政策。**2**. 玩弄(战争)边缘政策。

brin·y [ˈbraini; ˋbraɪnɪ] ***a***. **1**. 盐水的;咸的,腌的。**2**. 海水的。**3**. 〔诗〕泪水的。*a* ~ *taste* 咸味。***the*** ~ 〔俚〕海(水);大洋(*a dip in the* ~ 大海里的一滴水)。

brio [ˈbriːəu; ˋbrio] ***n***. 〔It.〕【乐】活泼;愉快;兴奋。*an elderly woman whose* ~ *astounds everyone* 一个活泼得使大家吃惊的上年纪的妇人。

bri·oche [ˈbri(ː)əuʃ; ˋbrɪoʃ] ***n***. 奶油鸡蛋小面包。

bri·o·lette [ˌbriəˈlet; ˏbriəˋlɛt] ***n***. 棱面金刚石;橄榄形宝石。

Bri·o·ni [briˈəuni; brɪˋonɪ] ***n***. 布里俄尼(群岛)〔原南斯拉夫〕。

bri·o·ny [ˈbraiəni; ˋbraɪənɪ] ***n***. 【植】泻根属植物(= bryony).

bri·quet(te) [briˈket; brɪˋkɛt] ***n***. 煤砖,煤球。

bri·sance [briˈzɑːns; brɪˋzɑns] ***n***. 炸药震力。**-sant** ***a***.

Bris·bane [ˈbrizbən; ˋbrɪzbən] ***n***. 布里斯班〔澳大利亚港市〕。

brise-bise [ˈbriːzˈbiːz; ˋbrizˋbiz] ***n***. 半截式窗帘。

brisk [brisk; brɪsk] **I** ***a***. **1**. 活泼的,轻快的,生气勃勃的(*opp*. languid). **2**. (天气)清新的;(生意)兴旺的。**3**. (酒等)嘶嘶冒泡的,味浓的。**4**. (语调等)刻薄的,尖酸的。*a* ~ *walk* 轻快的步调。*a* ~ *trade* 活跃的行情。*a* ~ *wind* 凉爽的风。~ *cider* 冒泡的苹果酒。**II** ***vt***. 使活泼;使活跃;使兴旺。***vi***. 活泼起来;兴旺起来(*up*). *Business* ~*ed up*. 生意兴旺起来了。**-ly** ***ad***. **-ness** ***n***.

bris·ket [ˈbriskit; ˋbrɪskɪt] ***n***. (兽的)胸,胸部;胸肉。

bris·ling, bris·tling [ˈbrisliŋ; ˋbrɪslɪŋ] ***n***. 【鱼】(北欧产)小鲱鱼。

bris·tle [ˈbrisl; ˋbrɪsḷ] **I** ***n***. **1**. (猪等的)鬃毛;(动、植物

的)短硬毛。2.(刷子等的)毛。3.(人的)胡须茬;鬃毛状物。*set up one's* ~*s* 勃然大怒,怒发冲冠。*set up sb.'s* ~*s* 激怒某人。**II** *vt*. 1. 使(毛发等)竖起;把…弄粗糙。2. 给(刷子等)安鬃毛。*The rooster* ~*d his crest*. 公鸡竖起了鸡冠。— *vi*. 1.(毛发等)倒竖。2. 发怒(*up*)。3.(树木等)密密地覆盖;(困难等)重重,充满(*with*)。*His hair* ~*d on his scalp with anger*. 他气得头发都竖起来了。*The hog* ~*d up* 公猪竖起了鬃毛。*The plain* ~*d with bayonet*. 平原上刀枪林立。~**tail**【虫】(双尾目和缨尾目中作鬃毛状的)无翼昆虫。**bris·tly** *a*. 1. 有硬毛的;硬毛般的。2.(毛发等)竖起的,直立的。3. 林立的,丛生的。4. 发怒的。

Bris·tol [ˈbristl; ˋbrɪstl] *n*. 1. 布里斯托尔〔英国港市〕。2.〔b-〕= B- board. ~ **alloy** 白铜。~ **board** [**paper**] (绘图等用)上等板纸。~ **cream** [**milk**] 芳醇的雪利酒。~ **diamond** [**stone, gem**]【矿】美晶石英。~ **fashion**【海】整洁的,有条不紊的。~ **glaze** 窑釉。

brit(t) [brit; brɪt] *n*. 1.【鱼】小鱼群,小鲱。2.(鲸鱼吃的)小浮游生物。

Brit. = Britailn; Britainnia; British.

Brit·ain [ˈbritən; ˋbrɪtən] *n*. 英国,不列颠〔英格兰、威尔斯和苏格兰的总称〕: *The United Kingdom of Great* ~ *and Northern Ireland* 大不列颠及北爱尔兰联合王国〔英国的正式名称〕。

Bri·tan·ni·a [briˈtænjə; brɪˋtænjə] *n*. 1.【史】布立吞里亚〔罗马人给不列颠岛起的名称〕。2.〔诗〕英国〔女性拟人名称〕。~ **metal, britania metal** 不列颠金〔锡、铜、锑的银白色合金〕。

Bri·tan·nic [briˈtænik; brɪˋtænɪk] *a*. 大不列颠的,英国的〔主要用于对国王的尊称: *His* [*Her*] ~ *Majesty* 英国国王[女王]陛下〕。

britch·es [ˈbritʃiz; ˋbrɪtʃɪz] *n*. *pl*.〔口〕裤子。***too big for one's*** ~〔口〕过分自信的;傲慢的。

Brit·(t)i·cism [ˈbritisizəm; ˋbrɪtəˏsɪzəm] *n*.〔美〕英国语法〔英国人特有的语言现象,如一些特有的词、习语、表达方式等,美国不用〕。

Brit·ish [ˈbritiʃ; ˋbrɪtɪʃ] **I** *a*. 1. 不列颠的,英国的。2. 不列颠人的,英国人的。3. 英联邦的。4. 古英语的;英国英语的。**II** *n*. 1.〔the B-〕〔集合词〕英国人;英联邦人。2. 英国英语;古英语。*the* ~ *Commonwealth of Nations* 英联邦。*the* ~ *Empire* 英帝国。*the* ~ *House of Lords* [*Commons*] 英国上[下]议院。*the* ~ *Isles* 英伦诸岛〔包括不列颠、爱尔兰和曼岛〕。~ **Academy** 英国科学院。~ **Association** 英国学术协会。~ **Council** 英国(对外)文化协会。~ **dollar**(香港、海峡殖民地通用的)英元。~ **English**(与美国英语等相区别的)英国英语。~ **lion** 英国国徽;英国国民。~ **meson**【物】介子。~ **Museum** 大英博物馆。~ **thermal unit**〔略 B.T.U., BTU 或 Btu〕英国热单位〔将一磅水升高摄氏一度的热量〕。~ **warn**(军用)厚呢短大衣。

British Columbia [ˈbritiʃ kəˈlʌmbiə; ˋbrɪtɪʃ kəˋlʌmbɪə] *n*. 不列颠哥伦比亚〔加拿大省名〕。

Brit·ish·er [ˈbritiʃə; ˋbrɪtɪʃɚ] *n*.〔美〕英国人。

Brit·ish·ism [ˈbritiʃizəm; ˋbrɪtɪʃɪzm̩] *n*. = Brit(t)icism.

Brit·on [ˈbritən; ˋbrɪtən] *n*. 1. 布立吞人〔古代不列颠南部凯尔特人的一支〕。2.(大)不列颠人,英国人。*a North* ~ 苏格兰人。

Brit·ta·ny [ˈbritəni; ˋbrɪtn̩ɪ] *n*. 布列塔尼〔法国西北部一地区〕。

brit·tle[1] [ˈbritl; ˋbrɪtl] *a*. 1. 易碎的,脆的;脆弱的;易损坏的。2. 虚幻的,靠不住的。3.(声音等)尖利的;容易生气的。4.(态度)冷淡的;利己的,专为自己打算的。*as* ~ *as glass* 像玻璃一样容易打碎。*a* ~ *fame* 浮名。*His promise turned out* ~. 他的诺言原来是靠不住的。*a* ~ *and selfish woman* 一个态度冷淡自私自利的女人。*a* ~ *personality* 容易生气的个性。**II** *vi*. 变脆。~ **hand** *a*.〔美〕(拳击选手)情况不妙的。**-ly, brittly** *ad*. **-ness** *n*. 脆弱,脆性,脆度。

brit·tle[2] [ˈbritl; ˋbrɪtl̩] *n*. 薄片脆糖。*peanut* ~ 薄片花生糖。

britz·ka, brits·ka [ˈbritskə; ˋbrɪtskə] *n*.(波兰的)四轮马车。

Br·no [ˈbəːnəu; ˋbɚno] *n*. 布尔诺〔捷克斯洛伐克城市〕。

bro. *n*. (*pl*. ~*s*) = brother.

broach [brəutʃ; brotʃ] **I** *n*. 1. 铁叉,烤肉叉。2. 尖塔,(塔上)尖阁。3.【机】三角锥;钻头;扩孔器;拉刀;(石工用的)宽凿。4.(女服)饰针。**II** *vt*. 1. 把(肉等)串在铁叉上。2.【建】粗刻;【机】拉削。3. 在(桶等)上开孔[打眼];向(矿藏等)里面开采[凿进];(用凿子)开(洞),把(眼子)弄大。4. 说出,提倡,提议;首次宣布。5.(风浪)使(船)横转。*a good time to* ~ *afresh the question* 重新提出问题的好时机。~ *a subject* 提出一个供讨论的题目。— *vi*. 1.(船因风向改变而)横转〔有倾覆危险〕;侧,横向。2.(鲸鱼、鱼雷等)冒出海面。

broach·er [ˈbrəutʃə; ˋbrotʃɚ] *n*. 1. 钻孔者;钻孔器;【机】扩孔器;拉刀。2. 倡议者,提倡者。

broad [brɔːd; brɔd] **I** *a*. 1. 广,广大;广袤,宽阔的,辽阔的;广泛的,普遍的;【纺】宽幅的。2. 气量大的,宽厚的,豁达的。3. 明朗的,明白的,显著的。4. 主要的,概括的,一般的。5. 露骨的,粗俗的,淫猥的,下流的。6. 地方音重的,口音重的;【语】(母音)成开音节的。~ *shoulders* 宽肩。*three feet* ~ 宽三英尺。~ *views* 开明的见解。*the* ~ *plains* 辽阔的原野。*a* ~ *daylight* 大白天。~ *accent* 十足的土腔。~ *humour* 下流的俏皮话。~ *words* 露骨的言词。*a* ~ *joke* 下流的笑话。*state one's views in* ~ *outline* 讲个概要,说个大意。*a* ~ *hint* 明白的暗示。**II** *n*. 1.〔英〕〔*pl*.〕河流的开阔部分,(由河流扩张成的)湖沼。2. 手[脚]掌的宽阔部分。3.〔英古〕金币;(摄影场的)地灯。4.〔美俚〕女人;娼妓。5.〔美俚〕〔*pl*.〕纸牌。*the* (*Norfolk*) *Broads*(英国东南部的)湖沼地带。***as*** ~ ***as it is long*** 宽长一样;半斤和八两,结果一样。~ ***place*** [***spot***] ***in the road***〔美〕小都市。~ ***on the beam***【海】垂直于船中横梁到船头方向的。~ ***rule*** 一般标准,常规,常例。~ ***Scotch*** 显著的苏格兰土腔。**III** *ad*. 1. 宽广地,充分地。2. 土腔十足地。~*awake* 十分清醒。*speak* ~土腔十足地说。~ **arrow** 1. 有倒刺镞的箭。2.(英国官方物品上的)箭头标记〔尤指印在囚衣上的标记〕。~ **ax(e)** 钺。~ **band** *n*.【无】宽带;宽波段。~ **bean** 蚕豆。~ **bill** 阔嘴鸭,野鸭。~-**blown** *a*.(花)满开的。~**brim** 1. 宽边帽。2.〔口〕Quaker 教徒。~-**brush** *a*. 粗线条的。**B- Church**(英国教会的)广教派。~**cloth** 1.【纺】(高级)绒面呢。2.〔美〕= poplin. ~-**goods** 阔幅绸缎。~ **gauge** 1. 宽轨距〔4 英尺 8 英寸半以上〕。2. 宽轨铁路;宽轨(铁路上的)火车。~-**gauge** *a*. 1.(铁路)宽轨距的。2.〔口〕气量大的。~ **hatchet** 阔斧。~ **jump**〔Am.〕跳远〔正式作 Long jump〕. ~-**leaf** 1. *n*. 宽叶烟草。2. *a*. 宽叶的。~-**leaved** *a*. 宽叶的。~**loom** *a*. 阔幅地毯[绸缎]的。~-**minded** *a*. 气量大的。~ **seal** 国玺;(政府的正式)印玺,公章。~**sheet**【印】单面[双面]印刷的大幅印张[印刷品]。~**side** 1. *n*.(水面以上的)舷侧;舷侧炮;偏舷(各炮)齐发;〔喻〕一连串的诽谤,排炮般的攻击;(建筑物的)侧面;宽面;= ~ sheet. 2. *ad*.(船、车等)侧向,露出侧面;齐射地;无目标地(*The truck hit the fence* ~*side*. 卡车侧着撞到篱笆上了)。3. *vi*.【海】(船)侧着前进;舷边排炮齐射。~-**spectrum** *a*.【物】宽谱的。~**sword** 大砍刀,腰刀;带腰刀的人。~**tail** 中亚大尾绵羊[羔羊];中亚大尾绵羊羔皮。~**way** *ad*. 横着,侧向着。~**wife**【美史】(以主人家的男奴为夫的)有夫女奴。~**wise**, ~**way(s)** *ad*. 横着,宽面朝前地。

Broad [brɔːd; brɔd] *n*. 布罗德〔姓氏〕。

broad·cast [ˈbrɔːdkɑːst; ˋbrɔdˏkæst] **I** *a*. 1. 撒播的;广泛散布的。2.【无】播音的,广播的。~ *rumors* 流传广

B

泛的谣言。*a* ~ *sower* 撒播机。*seed sown* ~撒播的种子。*a* ~ *program(me)* 广播节目。**II** ***n*.** **1.** (种子的)撒播。**2.** 无线电广播,播音;广播节目。~*band* 广播波段。~*relaying* 广播转播[中继]。*simultaneous* ~(各电台)联播。*today's* ~ *program* 今天的广播节目。**III** ***vt*.** (~,~**ed**) **1.**【无】广播。**2.** 散布,乱传(消息等)。**3.** 撒播(种子)。*The President will* ~ *his message on all stations tonight*. 总统今晚将向全国广播咨文。*She* ~(*ed*) *the gossip all over the town*. 她把这个流言传遍了全镇。— ***vi*.** **1.**【无】广播。**2.** 在广播节目上讲话[演出]。**3.** 散布消息[谣言等]。~ **on** 用…波长广播。

broad·cast·er [ˈbrɔːdˌkɑːstə; ˋbrɔdˏkæstɚ] ***n*.** **1.** 撒种机,撒播物。**2.**【无】广播者;广播电台;广播装置;广播协会。

broad·cast·ing [ˈbrɔːdˌkɑːstiŋ; ˋbrɔdˏkæstɪŋ] ***n*.** **1.** 广播,播音。**2.** 广播业。*chain* ~ 联播。*relayed* ~ 转播。*sound-sight* [*television*, *visual*] ~ 电视广播。*a* ~ *station* 广播电台。*a* ~ *studio* 播音室。*a career in* ~ 从事广播工作。*binaural* ~ 立体声广播。~ *transmitter* 广播发射机。

broad·en [ˈbrɔːdn; ˋbrɔdn̩] ***vt*.** 加宽,放阔,使扩大。*Reading and traveling* ~ *the mind*. 读书和旅行使人益智。— ***vi*.** 变宽,变阔。

broad·ly [ˈbrɔːdli; ˋbrɔdlɪ] ***ad*.** **1.** 广,宽。**2.** 明白;露骨。**3.** 粗鲁。**4.** 用土腔。~ ***speaking*** 总而言之,概括地说。

broad·ness [ˈbrɔːdnis; ˋbrɔdnɪs] ***n*.** **1.** 广阔,宽。**2.** 尺面,门面,幅。**3.** 明白。**4.** 粗鲁。

Broad·way [ˈbrɔːdwei; ˋbrɔdˏwe] **I** ***n*.** **1.** 百老汇大街〔美国纽约的繁华街道、剧院、夜总会等多设于此〕。**2.** 纽约的娱乐[戏剧]业。**II** ***a*.** **1.** 百老汇的。**2.** 纽约娱乐[戏剧]业的。**3.** 花哨的。*a* ~ *star* 纽约的戏剧明星。

Brob·ding·nag [ˈbrɔbdiŋnæg; ˋbrɑbdɪŋˏnæg] ***n*.** 大人国〔出自英国作家斯维夫特 (Swift) 所著《格列佛游记》〕。

Brob·ding·nag·i·an [ˌbrɔbdiŋˈnægiən; ˏbrobdɪŋˋnægɪən] **I** ***a*.** 大人国的,巨大的。**II** ***n*.** **1.** 大人国的居民。**2.** 巨人。

bro·cade [brəˈkeid; broˋked] **I** ***n*.** 锦缎,花缎;织锦。*gold* [*silver*] ~织金[银]锦缎。**II** ***vt*.** 在(织物上)织出花纹;把(花纹)织入织物。

bro·cad·ed [brəˈkeidid; brəˋkedɪd] ***a*.** **1.** 锦缎(一样)的。**2.** 穿着锦缎的,用锦缎装饰的。

broc·a·telle, broc·a·tel [ˌbrɔkəˈtel; ˏbrɑkəˋtɛl] ***n*.** **1.** 花缎;缎纹塔夫绸;凸花厚缎;织花被褥布。**2.** 彩色大理石。

broc·(c)o·li [ˈbrɔkəli; ˋbrɑkəli] ***n*.**【植】(仅茎可食用的)嫩茎硬花球,花椰菜,花茎甘蓝。

bro·ché [brəuˈʃei; broˋʃe] **I** ***a*.** 〔F.〕(织物)有提花图案的,有浮纹的。**II** ***n*.** 提花绸缎,浮纹织物,绒头花纹织物。~ *quilts* 提花床单布。

bro·chette [brəuˈʃet; broˋʃɛt] ***n*.** 烤肉小铁签子。

bro·chure [brəuˈʃjuə; broˋʃur] ***n*.** 假钉本,小册子。

brock [brɔk; brɔk] ***n*.** **1.**【动】獾。**2.**〔英方〕卑鄙的家伙,脏东西。

brock·et [ˈbrɔkit; ˋbrɑkɪt] ***n*.** 二岁雄鹿;〔南美〕短角小鹿。

bro·die [ˈbrəudi; ˋbrodɪ] ***n*.** 〔美俚〕〔有时作 B-〕**1.** 失败,失策,大错。**2.** (从桥上投水)自杀。*do a* ~(投水)自杀。

bro·gan [ˈbrəugən; ˋbrogən] ***n*.** = brogue[2].

brög·ger·ite [ˈbrɔːgərait; ˋbrɔgəˏraɪt] ***n*.**【矿】钍铀矿。

brogue[1] [brəug; brog] ***n*.** 土腔,〔特指〕爱尔兰土腔。

brogue[2] [brəug; brog] ***n*.** **1.** 生皮翻毛皮鞋。**2.** 低跟镂花牛皮鞋。

broi·der, broi·der·y [ˈbrɔidə, ˈbrɔidəri; ˋbrɔɪdɚ, ˋbrɔɪdərɪ] 〔诗〕= em-broider, embroidery.

broil[1] [brɔil; brɔɪl] **I** ***n*.** 吵闹,争辩;骚动。*a violent* ~ *over who was at fault* 在谁办错了事的问题上发生的激烈争吵。**II** ***vi*.** 大声争吵。**-er** ***n*.** 爱吵闹的人。

broil[2] [brɔil; brɔɪl] **I** ***vt*.** **1.** (用火)烤[焙,炙](肉等)。**2.** (太阳等)灼(人),(暑热等)蒸人;使直接受到灼热。~ *a steak* 烤牛排。*a* ~*ing sun* 赤日炎炎。— ***vi*.** **1.** 烤[焙、炙]肉。**2.** 被烤焦。**3.** (因恼怒、忧虑等)激动,焦燥不安。~ *with anger* 气得七窍生烟。**II** ***n*.** **1.** 烤,焙,炙;灼热。**2.** 被焙烤之物;烤肉。*a beef* ~ 一客烤牛肉。**-er** ***n*.** **1.** 烤肉师傅;烤肉器。**2.** (适合焙烤的)童子鸡。**3.** 〔口〕酷暑,大热天。

bro·kage [ˈbrəukidʒ; ˋbrokɪdʒ] ***n*.** = brokerage.

broke [brəuk; brok] break 的过去式;〔古〕break 的过去分词。**I** ***a*.** 〔口〕破了产的;〔俚〕分文不名的,一个钱也没有的〔仅用作述语〕。***be*** ~ ***to the wide*** [***world***] 〔口〕完全破产的,一个钱也没有的。***be clean*** [***dead***, ***flat***, ***stone***, ***stony***] ~〔口〕完全破产。***go*** ~ 〔俚〕破产。***go for*** ~ 〔俚〕竭力,全力以赴;耗尽全部财力。**II** ***n*.** 破纸;〔*pl*.〕(头部、腹部剪下的)劣等羊毛。

bro·ken [ˈbrəukən; ˋbrokən] break 的过去分词。***a*.** **1.** 破裂的,打碎了的,弄破了的;(腿、臂等)已骨折的。**2.** (地面等)起伏不平的;(天气)忽阴忽晴的。**3.** 灰了心的,已失望的,沮丧的,唉声叹气的;(身体)变衰弱的;【植】(花)染上碎斑病的。**4.** 破了产的,倒闭的;(家庭等)遭破坏的;(诺言等)被违背的。**5.** (语言等)拙劣的,不合标准[语法]的,乱七八糟的。**6.** (线条)虚线的,断续的;零碎的,七零八落的,拆散了的;被打断的。**7.** (马等)养驯了的,有训练的。**8.** (方向)不断改变的。**9.** 〔口〕降了级的。**10.**【印】不足一令(500 张)的。*a* ~ *vase* 打碎的花瓶。*a* ~ *leg* 打断的腿骨。*The fox ran in a* ~ *line*. 狐狸跑的时候不断地改变方向。~ *meat* 碎肉。*a* ~ *promise* 言而无信,违背诺言。*a* ~ *man* 心灰意懒的人。~ *health* 垮掉的身躯。*a well-* ~ *horse* 极驯服的马。*a* ~ *circle* 虚线圆。~ *sobs* 抽泣。*a few* ~ *words* 断断续续的几句话。~ *water* 波浪起伏的水面。~ *country* 起伏不平的田野。*a* ~ *firm* 一家破产的公司。*the* ~ *fortunes of his family* 家道中落。~ **bone** 〔美〕出事受伤的人。~ **clouds** 遮掉大半个天空的乌云。~ **colour** (绘画的)点描法;复色,配合色。~**-down** ***a*.** **1.** 毁坏了的,已被捣毁的。**2.** (健康)衰弱已极的;垮掉的。**3.** (企业等)败落了的;(人)毁掉的,堕落了的。**4.** (马)累得[衰弱得]不能动的;(机器等)临时出了故障的。~**-ends** (纱线的)断头。~ **English** 拙劣的英语;洋泾浜英语,不合语法[标准]的英语。~ **ground** **1.**【军】起伏不平的地面,崎岖地。**2.** 新开垦地。~ **heart** 失意,失恋。~**-hearted** ***a*.** **1.** 极度失望的,痛心的;心碎的。**2.** 失恋的,忧伤的。~ **home** 破裂的家庭〔夫妇分居或离婚所造成的〕。~ **line** **1.** 虚线。**2.**【数】折线。**3.** (马路上的)车道线。~ **lot**【商】零星股〔一百股以下〕。~ **lots** 〔美〕特价品。~ **money** 零钱。~ **numbers**【数】分数,余数,小数。~ **reed** 不可信赖的人[事物]。~ **sleep** 断断续续的睡眠,时醒时睡,不时被吵醒[打扰]的睡眠。~ **soldier** 残废的伤兵。~ **tea** 散茶,碎茶,茶叶末。~ **time** (因经常被打扰而变得)零零散散的工作时间。~ **weather** 阴晴不定的天气。~ **wind**【兽医】(马的)喘气病。~**-winded** ***a*.** (马)呼吸急促的,喘气的;呼吸器官有病的。~ **windows** 破窗理论〔指街头一扇打破的窗户会引发人们打碎更多窗户的现象,意指容忍破坏行为会导致更多违法行为〕。

bro·ker [ˈbrəukə; ˋbrokɚ] ***n*.** **1.** (股票等的)经纪人,掮客;(买卖的)中间人,代理人。**2.** 〔英〕旧货商人;当铺主;(经官方批准对债务人被扣押财物的)估价员[出售人]。**3.** 〔口〕婚姻介绍人。*a street* [*curbstone*] ~〔美〕场外经纪人。

broker·age [ˈbrəukəridʒ; ˋbrokərɪdʒ] ***n*.** **1.** 经纪业,掮客业。**2.** 佣金,回扣,经手费(= brokage)。

bro·king [ˈbrəukiŋ; ˋbrokɪŋ] **I** ***n*.** 经纪业。**II** ***a*.** 经纪(业)的;掮客(业)的,中间人的。

brol·ly [ˈbrɔli; ˋbrɑlɪ] ***n*.** **1.** 〔口〕洋伞。**2.** 〔英俚〕降落

伞。

bro·ma [ˈbrəumə; ˋbromə] *n*. 1. 去油可可粉。2. 去油可可(饮料)。3.【医】固体食物。

bro·mal [ˈbrəuməl; ˋbroməl] *n*.【化】溴醛;三溴乙醛。

bro·mate [ˈbrəumeit; ˋbromet] I *vt*. 使与溴化合,用溴处理。II *n*.【化】溴酸盐。

brome[1] [brəum; brom] *n*.【植】雀麦属植物 (= brome grass)。

brome[2] [bruːm; brum] *n*. 布罗姆〔姓氏〕。

bro·me·li·ad [brəuˈmiliˌæd; broˋmɪlɪˏæd] *n*.【植】凤梨科植物。

Brom·field [ˈbrəmfiːld; ˋbrɑmˏfild] *n*. 布罗姆菲尔德〔姓氏〕。

bro·mic [ˈbrəumik; ˋbromɪk] *a*. 溴的,含溴的;【化】五价溴的。~ *acid* 溴酸。

bro·mide [ˈbrəumaid; ˋbromaɪd] *n*. 1.【化】溴化物;溴化物乳剂。2.〔美俚〕平庸可厌的人,喜欢讲陈腔滥调的人;陈腔滥调。*silver* ~ 溴化银。~ **paper** 溴素纸;相片纸。

bro·mid·ic [brəuˈmidik; broˋmɪdɪk] *a*. 1. 平庸的,陈腐的;陈腔滥调的。2.(人)总是陈腔滥调的。

bro·mi·nate [ˈbrəumiˌneit; ˋbroməˏnet] *vt*.【化】溴化;溴化处理。**-nation** *n*.

bro·mine [ˈbrəumiːn; ˋbromin] *n*.【化】溴〔略作 Br.〕。

bro·mism [ˈbrəumizəm; ˋbromɪzm] *n*.【医】溴中毒。

bro·mize [ˈbrəumaiz; ˋbromaɪz] *vt*.【化】溴代;溴化(作用)。**-zation** *n*.

bro·mo·selt·zer [ˈbrəuməuˌseltsə; ˋbromoˏseltsɚ] *n*. 溴塞尔泽〔成药,一种治头痛的泡腾盐〕。

bro·my·rite [ˈbrəumirait; ˋbroməˏraɪt] *n*.【矿】溴银矿。

bronc [brɔŋk; brɑŋk] *n*. = bronc(h)o.

bron·chi [ˈbrɔŋkai; ˋbrɑŋkaɪ] *n*. bronchus 的复数。

bron·chi·al, bron·chic [ˈbrɔŋkiəl, ˈbrɔŋkik; ˋbrɑŋkɪəl, ˋbrɑŋkɪk] *a*.【解】支气管的。~ **tubes** 支气管。

bron·chi·ole [ˈbrɔŋkiˌəul; ˋbrɑŋkɪˏol] *n*.【解】细支气管。

bron·chi·tis [brɔŋˈkaitis; brɑnˋkaɪtɪs] *n*.【医】支气管炎。**-chi·tic** *a*.

bronch(o)- *comb. f*. 支气管: *broncho*scope.

bron·cho·cele [ˈbrɔŋkəusiːl; ˋbrɑŋkoˏsil] *n*.【医】支气管肥大;甲状腺肥大[囊状肿]。

bron·cho·pneu·mo·nia [ˈbrɔŋkəunjuːˈməunjə; ˋbrɑŋkonjuˋmonjə] *n*.【医】支气管肺炎。

bron·cho·scope [ˈbrɔŋkəskəup; ˋbrɑŋkəˏskop] *n*.【医】支气管窥镜。

bron·c(h)o [ˈbrɔŋkəu; ˋbrɑŋko] *n*. 1.〔美〕(北美西部平原的)半野生的马。2.〔Can.〕英国人〔尤指英国移民〕。

bron·c(h)o·buster [ˈbrɔŋkəuˌbʌstə; ˋbrɑŋkoˏbʌstɚ] *n*. 驯马师,(美国西部的)驯马牧童,牛仔。

bron·chus [ˈbrɔŋkəs; ˋbrɑŋkəs] *n*. (*pl*. **bron·chi** [ˈbrɔŋkai; ˋbrɑŋkaɪ])【解】支气管,细支气管。

Bron·të [ˈbrɔnti; ˋbrɑntɪ] *n*. 1. 布朗蒂〔姓氏〕。2. 英国小说家三姐妹〔**Anne** ~ (1820—1849),《阿格奈斯·格雷》的作者; **Charlotte** ~ (1816—1855),《简·爱》的作者;**Emily Jane** ~ (1818—1848),《呼啸山庄》的作者〕。

bron·tides [ˈbrɔntaidz; ˋbrɑntaɪdz] *n*.【地】(轻微地震引起的)短暂的震声。

bron·to·saur [ˈbrɔntəˌsɔː; ˋbrɑntəˏsɔr], **bron·to·saurus** [ˌbrɔntəˈsɔːrəs; ˏbrɑntəˋsɔrəs] *n*.【古生】雷龙。

Bronx [brɔŋks; brɑŋks] *n*. 1.〔the ~〕布朗克斯区〔美国纽约市一区名〕。2. 布朗克斯鸡尾酒。~ **cheer**〔美口〕(表示嘲笑厌恶等的)嘘嘘声。~ **vanilla**〔美〕大蒜。

bronze [brɔnz; brɑnz] I *n*. 1. 青铜,古铜。2. 青铜制品;青铜艺术品;(半身)铜像;〔古〕青铜币。3. 青铜色(颜料)。*gear* ~ 齿轮[磷]青铜。*gun* ~ 炮铜。~ *mica* 金云母。*a statue in* ~ 青铜像。~*s and ivories* 青铜和象牙艺术品。II *vt*. 1. 在…上镀青铜;上青铜色于。2. 使硬得像古铜。3.〔古〕使变冷酷。*The sun ~d his face*. 太阳把他的脸晒成古铜色。— *vi*. 变成青铜色;(皮肤)晒黑。III *a*. 青铜色的;青铜制的;青铜器的。**B-Age** 1. 青铜器时代。2.【希神】(人类的)青铜时代,战乱烽起的时代。~ **medal** 铜牌〔通常奖给比赛优胜的第三名〕。**B- Star Medal**【美军】铜星(奖)章(授与作战英勇者)。**-d** *a*. 镀青铜的;青铜色的;晒黑的。

bronz·ite [ˈbrɔnzait; ˋbrɑnzaɪt] *n*.【矿】古铜辉石。

bronz·y [ˈbrɔnzi; ˋbrɑnzɪ] *a*. 青铜一样的;青铜色的,黄褐色的。

brooch [brəutʃ; brotʃ] *n*. 饰针,胸针。

brood [bruːd; brud] I *n*. 1.(鸡雏等的)一窝;同窝幼雏;幼蜂;(昆虫等)一次产出的卵;(动物)一次下的崽。2.(动物的)种,属,群,种族;〔蔑〕(一家的)孩子们;同伙,同党,同胞;(事物的)一组。~ *box* (蜂的)育卵箱,子箱。*a ~ of chickens* 一窝鸡雏。*a ~ of modern paintings* 一组现代画。II *vt*. 1. 孵(蛋),孵出。2.(鸟、母鸡等)用翅膀护(幼雏、小鸡等)。3. 盘算,仔细考虑。*He ~ed the problem*. 他仔细考虑这个问题。— *vi*. 1. 孵卵,伏窝般地静坐。2. 焦急地考虑,郁闷地想(*over*; *on*). 3.(云、雾、忧愁等)低覆,笼罩(*over*; *on*). ~*ing twilight* 苍茫的暮色。*a ~ing hate* 日益郁结的仇恨。~ ***above*** [***over***] 1. 俯视。2. 笼罩(*The house on the hill ~ed above the village*. 山上的那间房子俯视着村庄。*Hate ~ed over the town*. 仇恨的情绪笼罩着全镇)。~ ***over*** [***on***] 焦急地考虑,郁闷地沉思(*~ on one's difficulties* 焦急地考虑所处的困境)。III *a*. 1. 传种用的,繁殖用的。2.(母鸡等)抱窝的;(昆虫等)产卵的。*a ~ mare* 传种母马。*a ~ hen* 抱窝的母鸡。~ **body**【生】繁殖体。~ **cell**【生】芽孢。~ **gemma**【生】芽孢体。

brooder [ˈbruːdə; ˋbrudɚ] *n*. 1. 育雏器,孵卵器;(育雏的)炕坊。2. 沉思的人。3. 育雏的人,炕坊师傅;孵卵的鸡〔鸟、动物〕。

brood·y [ˈbruːdi; ˋbrudɪ] *a*. 1. 要孵卵的,爱伏窝的;繁殖力强的。2. 郁郁不乐的,沉闷的。*a ~ hen* 爱伏窝的母鸡。

brook[1] [bruk; brʊk] *n*. 溪流,小河。**-like** *a*. 小溪般的。

brook[2] [bruk; brʊk] *vt*. 忍,耐,挨,容忍,忍受〔用于否定结构〕。*A great man cannot ~ a rival*. 两雄不并立,一山难容两虎。*It ~s no delay*. 事情不容延误[刻不容缓]。

Brook(e) [bruk; brʊk] *n*. 布鲁克〔姓氏〕。

brook·ite [ˈbrukait; ˋbrʊkaɪt] *n*.【矿】板钛矿。

brook·let [ˈbruklit; ˋbrʊklɪt] *n*. 细流,小溪。

brook·lime [ˈbruklaim; ˋbrʊklaɪm] *n*.【植】(玄参科的)婆婆纳。

Brook·lyn [ˈbruklin; ˋbrʊklɪn] *n*. 布鲁克林区〔美国纽约市的一区,在长岛西部〕。**-ese** 布鲁克林腔〔布鲁克林区的人特有的语言风格〕。

Brooks [bruks; brʊks] *n*. 布鲁克斯〔姓氏,男子名〕。

broom [bruːm; brum] I *n*. 1. 帚,扫帚。2.【无】自动搜索干扰振荡器。3.【植】金雀花,金雀花属植物。II *vt*. 扫除,用扫帚扫。***New ~s sweep clean***.【谚】新官上任三把火,新到职者办事热心认真。~**corn**【植】高粱〔可用来做扫帚〕。~**pine**【植】大王松。~**rape**【植】肉苁蓉。~**stick** 扫帚把 (*a witch on a ~stick* 乘扫帚柄飞行于空中的女巫〔一种民间传说〕。*a ~stick skirt*〔美〕帚花裙〔西南部印第安人穿的一种服装〕。*marry* [*jump*] *over a ~stick* [*broom staff*] 做露水夫妻,野合)。

broom·y [ˈbruːmi; ˋbrumɪ] *a*. 1. 扫帚的,帚状的。2. 金雀花的,金雀花多的。

Bros. = brothers: *Smith Bros. & Co*. 史密斯兄弟公司。

brose [brəuz; broz] *n*.〔英〕麦片粥。

broth [brɔ(ː)θ; brɔθ] *n*. (*pl*. **~s** [brɔ(ː)θs, brɔːðz; brɔθs, brɔðz]) 肉汁;肉汤;清汤;培养基。*chicken* ~ 鸡

B

汤。*a* ～ *of a boy*〔爱尔兰〕好汉,男子汉,好男儿。

broth·el [ˈbrɔθl; ˋbrɔθəl] ***n.*** 妓院,窑子。

broth·er [ˈbrʌðə; ˋbrʌðɚ] **I** ***n.*** (*pl.* ～*s*,〔古〕***brethren*** [ˈbreðrin; ˋbrɛðrɪn]) **1.** 兄弟,同胞。**2.**〔*pl.* 多用 brethren〕同事,同僚,同业,社友,同志,会友。**3.** 王兄〔帝王间相互的称呼〕。**4.**〔美国黑人用法〕黑人兄弟(= soul brother);〔泛指〕(任何)黑人。**5.**〔口〕老兄。**6.** (不准备接受圣职的)男修士,不出家的修士。*an elder* ～ 兄,哥哥。*a younger* ～ 弟弟。*one's bigger* [*little*] ～ 兄[弟]。*a whole* [*full*] ～ 同父母弟兄。*a half* ～ 异父[异母]弟兄。*the* ～*s Smith*, *the Smith* ～*s* 史密斯兄弟们。*Smith B-s* 史密斯兄弟公司[商店]。*professional brethren* (医生等的)同行。*a fraternity* ～ 会友。～*s in the trade* 同业。*a lay* ～ 不出家的修士。*All men are* ～*s*. 四海之内皆兄弟也。*a band of* ～*s* (利害关系相共的)一团体。*B-, can you spare a dime?* 老兄,能借给我一角钱吗? ～ ***of the brush*** 画工,油漆匠。***Brothers of the Coast*** (16—17 世纪加勒比海的)海盗。～ ***of quill*** (古代)著作家。～ ***of the whip*** 马车夫,驭者。**II** ***vt.*** 和…结成弟兄,对…以兄弟相待,视…如兄弟。**III** ***int.*** 真要命〔对别人厚脸皮的行为等表示厌恶、惊讶等〕! ～**-german** 同父母兄弟。～**-in-arms** 战友。～**-in-law** (*pl.* ～**s-in-law**) **1.** 姐夫,妹夫。**2.** 内兄,内弟。**3.** 大伯,小叔。**4.** 连襟〔广义用法〕。**B- Jonathan**〔英〕**1.** 美国政府,美国。**2.** (典型的)美国人〔此为旧日用语,现在叫 Uncle Sam〕. ～ **officer** 袍泽,军官同僚。～**-uterine** 同母异父兄弟。**-hood** ***n.*** **1.** 兄弟关系,手足之亲,同胞。**2.** 同事,会友,同业,同行。**3.** 社,会,协会,公会;团体;会友;〔美〕兄弟会〔美国工会名称、大指铁路工会〕。**4.** 四海一家,人类情谊(*universal* ～四海同胞。*international* ～ 国际亲善)。

broth·er·ly [ˈbrʌðəli; ˋbrʌðɚlɪ] **I** ***a.*** 弟兄的,亲弟兄似的,友情深厚的。～ *love* 手足之情。*in a most* ～ *manner* 态度极友善地。**II** ***ad.***〔古〕兄弟一样地;亲密地。**-li·ness** ***n.*** 弟兄之谊,友情,友爱,亲切。

brough·am [ˈbruːəm; ˋbrʊ(u)əm] ***n.*** **1.** 四轮轿式马车。**2.**〔废〕布鲁姆式汽车。

brought [brɔːt; brɔt] bring 的过去式及过去分词。

brou·ha·ha [bruːˈhɑːhɑː; ˋbruhɑhɑ] ***n.*** 〔F.〕**1.** 骚动,吵闹,暴动〔由较大事件引起的〕。**2.** 喧嚣,嘈杂,起哄〔由较小事件引起〕。

brow [brau; braʊ] ***n.*** **1.**〔常 *pl.*〕眉,眉毛。**2.** 额。**3.** 容貌;表情。**4.** 悬岩;岩顶,山顶,坡顶;陡坡。**5.**〔口〕智力水平。**6.**【海】跳板。*bend* [*knit*] *one's* ～*s* 蹙眉,皱眉头。*the heavy* ～*s* 浓眉。*raise one's* ～*s* 扬眉。*by the swent of one's* ～*s* 额头冒汗。*His* ～ *darkened*. 他沉下脸来。*She looked down over the* ～ *of the hill*. 她从山顶上望下去。～ **ache** 偏头痛。～ **tine** 眉叉[鹿角]。**-ed** ***a.*** 眉毛…的〔用以构成复合词〕(*dark-browed* 浓眉的)。

brow·a·gue [ˈbraueigjuː; ˋbraʊegiu] ***n.***【医】偏头痛,额部神经痛 (= brow ache)。

brow·beat [ˈbraubiːt; ˋbraʊˏbit] ***vt.*** (～; ～***en*** [ˈbraubiːtn; ˋbraʊbitn̩], ～)吓,威吓,威逼;对…扬眉怒目。*She* ～*ed him into agreeing*. 她威逼他同意自己的意见。

Brown [braun; braʊn] ***n.*** 布朗(姓氏)。～, ***Jones, and Robinson*** 张三李四,普通人 (= *Tom, Dick, and Harry*)。

brown [braun; braʊn] **I** ***a.*** **1.** 褐色的,棕色的。**2.** 阴郁的。**3.** 晒黑了的。～ *shoes* 棕色鞋。**II** ***n.*** **1.** 褐色,棕色,茶色。**2.** 褐色颜料[染料]。**3.** 黑皮肤的人。**4.**〔英俚〕铜币。**5.** [the ～]鸟群〔指飞行中黑鸦鸦一片的鸟群〕。*chestnut* ～栗色。*Spanish* ～ 羊肝色。***do*** ～ **1.** 把(面包)烤成褐色。**2.**〔卑〕欺骗,使…上当。***do it up*** ～ **1.**〔口〕彻底做好(某事),把(事情)干得漂亮,很好地完成。**2.** 把(面包)烘焦。***fire into the*** ～ **1.** 射击鸟群。**2.**〔喻〕向机群开炮[发射火箭]。***in a*** ～ ***study*** **1.** 沉思默想。**2.** 幻想,空想。**III** ***vt.*** **1.** 上褐色于,把…染成褐色。**2.** 烘焦。**3.** 晒黑。**4.** (向鸟群等)胡乱射击。～ *the onion* 把洋葱烘焦。— ***vi.*** **1.** 变成褐色。**2.** (皮肤)晒黑。～ ***off***〔美俚〕出大错。～ ***out***〔美〕使(灯光)暗淡〔为了防空或节约用电等〕。～**-bag** ***vt.***, ***vi.*** **1.** 自带牛皮纸袋(装饭食)。**2.** 自带牛皮纸袋(装一瓶酒去不售酒的饭店或俱乐部)。～ **bear**【动】棕熊。～ **belt** **1.** 褐带〔三段柔道家佩戴的标志〕。**2.** 褐带高手(指柔道家)。**B-Beret** **1.** 褐色贝雷帽。**2.** 美籍墨西哥人争取自身权利的组织。～ **betty** 苹果面包屑布丁〔亦作 B- Betty〕. ～ **Book** 褐皮书(英国每年发布的有关英国石油储存、开采和需求情况的报告)。～ **bread** 黑面包。～ **coal** 褐煤。～**ed-off** ***a.*** **1.** 厌烦透了的,感到无聊的。**2.** 不满的。～ **fat** 棕色脂肪〔冬眠动物体内的生热脂肪〕。～**field** 棕色地带〔指城市中拆除旧房后可盖新建筑物之空地〕。**B-George** 褐色大水缸。～ **haematite** [**iron ore**]【矿】褐铁矿。～ **goods** 褐色商品〔指收音机、电视机等电子产品,因其外壳多漆成茶褐色〕。～ **lace** 原色花边。～ **nose**〔美〕**1.** ***vt.*** 拍…的马屁。**2.** ***vi.*** 拍马屁,献媚。～**out** ***n.*** **1.** 灯火[部分]管制;节电。**2.** 灯光暗淡;电压不足。～ **paper** 褐色打包纸,牛皮纸。～ **polish**〔美〕黑白混血儿。**B- Power** "褐色权力"〔美籍墨西哥人提出的争取权利的口号〕。～ **rat**【动】褐鼠。～ **rice** 糙米。～ **shirt**〔常作 **B- S-**〕(纳粹德国)褐衫党党员,纳粹党党员。～ **stone** **1.** ***n.*** 褐色沙石,褐色沙石建筑物。**2.** ***a.*** 生活富裕的(～ *district*〔美〕高级住宅区)。～ **sugar** 红糖;【化】黄糖。～ **trout**【鱼】河鳟。～ **ware** 陶器。**-ish**, **-y** ***a.*** 带褐色的。**-ness** ***n.***

Brown(e) [braun; braʊn] ***n.*** 布朗〔姓氏〕。

brown·ie [ˈbrauni; ˋbraʊnɪ] ***n.*** **1.**〔Scot.〕棕仙〔传说中夜间来帮助农家做家务事的仙童〕。**2.** (8—11 岁的)幼年女童子军;〔美〕小孩子。**3.** 布朗尼照相机;〔俚〕轻便雷达装置。**4.**〔美俚〕(含大麻的)巧克力小方饼。

Brown·ing [ˈbrauniŋ; ˋbraʊnɪŋ] ***n.*** 布朗宁〔姓氏〕。～ **automatic rifle**〔美〕布朗宁自动步枪。～ **machine gun**〔美〕布朗宁机枪。

browse [brauz; braʊz] **I** ***n.*** **1.** (牲畜吃的)嫩草,嫩叶,嫩枝,嫩芽。**2.** (牲畜的)吃嫩枝[草等],放牧。*the cattle at* ～ 正在吃草的牛。**II** ***vt.*** **1.** (牲畜)吃(嫩枝,草等)。**2.** 放牧。**3.** 浏览(书刊),随便翻阅(书刊)。*a cow* ～*ing thistles* 正在吃蓟草的牛。*The deer are* ～*ing the hillside*. 鹿在吃山边的草。～ *cattle on twigs* 让牛吃嫩枝。*He is* ～*ing the shelves for something to read*. 他在书架上翻找可读的书。— ***vi.*** **1.** (牲畜)吃草;吃(*on*). **2.** 浏览,翻阅。～ *on shoots* (牲畜)吃嫩芽。～ *through the newspaper* 浏览一下报纸。～ *about* [*around, among*] *the second-hand bookshops*. 逛旧书店。～***ing by game*** (牧草地等的)兽害〔如野兔等的破坏牧草地〕。**browsing room** 图书浏览室。**-r**【计】(电脑的)浏览器。

Br. P. = British Patent 英国专利。

B. R. R. A. = British Rayon Research Association 英国人造丝研究会。

brt. for. = brought forward 结转,转下。

Bruce [bruːs; brus] ***n.*** 布鲁斯〔姓氏,男子名〕。

bru·cel·lo·sis [ˌbruːsəˈləusis; ˏbrusəˋlosɪs] ***n.***【医】布鲁士菌病,地中海热,马耳他热(= Malta fever).

bru·cine [ˈbruːsi(ː)n; ˋbrusɪ(i)n] ***n.*** 番木鳖碱;二甲马钱子碱。

Bru·in [ˈbru(ː)in; ˋbruɪn] ***n.*** **1.** 熊先生〔著名童话《列那狐的故事》中的拟人动物〕。**2.** [b-]熊〔尤指褐熊〕。

bruise [bruːz; bruz] **I** ***vt.*** **1.** 撞伤,打伤(人),使成瘀伤[暗伤];碰伤,擦伤(水果、植物等)。**2.**〔喻〕损害(感情)。**3.** 舂碎;捣烂,研碎。**4.** 在(木料、金属等)上造成凹痕。**5.**〔口〕使成残废;殴打,争斗。～ *apples* 碰伤苹果。*She* ～*d herself against the car*. 她碰到车子上撞伤了。～ *sb.'s feeling* 伤害了某人的感情。— ***vi.*** **1.** 撞伤,碰伤,擦伤;变青肿,产生瘀伤。**2.** (感情)受到损害。**3.**【猎】骑

马瞎冲乱跑。*Peaches* ~ *easily*. 桃子容易碰伤。*Her feelings* ~ *easily*. 她很容易动气。**II** ***n*.** **1.** (人体、水果、植物等因碰撞、跌压等造成的)伤痕,青肿,擦伤。**2.** (感情受到的)伤害。*cuts and* ~*s* 刀剑伤和跌打伤。

bruiser [ˈbruːzə; ˋbruzɚ] ***n*.** **1.** 爱斗殴的人。**2.** 职业拳击家。**3.** 〔美口〕彪形大汉。**4.** 捣碎机,压碎[扁]机。**5.** 骑马瞎冲的人。

bruit [bruːt; brut] **I** ***n*.** **1.** 【医】(心)杂音,(听诊器听出的)异常音。**2.** 〔古〕谣言,传闻。**3.** 〔古〕喧声,吵嚷。**II** ***vt*.** 〔古〕〔美〕传播,散布(谣言等)(*about*; *abroad*). *It is* ~*ed that* ... 谣传说…。*The report was* ~*ed through the village*. 消息传遍了全村。

Brum [bruːm; brum] ***n*.** 〔英口〕伯明罕(= Birmingham)〔英国城市〕。**-mie** 伯明罕人。

Bru·maire [bruːˈmɛə; bruˋmɛr] ***n*.** 〔F.〕雾月〔法兰西共和历的第二月,相当于公历10月22—23日至11月21—23日〕。

bru·mal [ˈbruːməl; ˋbruml] ***a*.** 〔古〕冬季的;冬天似的。

brum·by [ˈbrʌmbi; ˋbrʌmbɪ] ***n*.** 【澳俚】野马。

brume [bruːm; brum] ***n*.** 雾,霭。

Brum·ma·gem [ˈbrʌmədʒəm; ˋbrʌmədʒəm] **I** ***a*.** 〔口〕 **1.** (珠宝、钱币等)假的,冒充的。**2.** (装饰品等)花哨而便宜的。**II** ***n*.** 便宜货;假珠〔从擅长制造假珠宝等的城市 Birmingham 的转讹〕。

bru·mous [ˈbruːməs; ˋbruməs] ***a*.** 冬季的。

brunch [brʌntʃ; brʌntʃ] ***n*.** 〔俚〕(早点与午餐并作一顿吃的)晚早餐,早中饭〔**br**(eakfast) + (l)**unch**〕. ~ **coat** (女用)长围裙。

Bru·nei [ˈbruːnai; ˋbrʊˋnaɪ] ***n*.** **1.** 文莱〔亚洲〕。**2.** 文莱〔文莱首府〕。

bru·net [bruːˈnet; bruˋnɛt] **I** ***a*.** (白种人中男子)浅黑型的。**II** ***n*.** 浅黑型的男子。

bru·nette [bruːˈnet; bruˋnɛt] **I** ***a*.** (白种人中女子)浅黑型的。**II** ***n*.** 浅黑型的女子。

bru·ni·zem [ˈbruːniˌzem; ˋbrunɪˏzɛm] ***n*.** 黑(钙)土。

Bru·no [ˈbruːnəu; ˋbruno] ***n*.** **1.** 布鲁诺〔男子名〕。**2.** **Giordano** ~ 乔丹诺·布鲁诺〔1548? —1600, 意大利哲学家,为维护太阳中心说被宗教法庭烧死〕。

Bruns·wick [ˈbrʌnzwik; ˋbrʌnzwɪk] ***n*.** **1.** 不伦瑞克〔德国原中部州名,市名〕。**2.** 布伦斯威克〔澳、美、纽西兰地名〕。~ **black** 一种黑色清漆。~ **line** 汉诺威王室世系(= the House of Hanover)。

brunt [brʌnt; brʌnt] ***n*.** **1.** (来自攻击一方的)主要力量[冲势,压力]。**2.** 〔废〕袭击,突击,强攻。*His arm took the* ~ *of the blow*. 他的手臂承受了狠狠的一击。*She had to bear the* ~ *of the criticisms*. 她不得不承当批评的压力。*These exhausted men carried the* ~ *of the war*. 这些疲倦的士兵承受了战场上的主要压力。***bear the*** ~ 首当其冲,承担主要压力。

brush[1] [brʌʃ; brʌʃ] **I** ***n*.** **1.** 刷子,毛刷;刷状物;【电】电刷;刷形放电(= ~ discharge)。**2.** 画笔,毛笔;绘画风格,画法,画家。**3.** (作帜饰的)羽毛;(动物)粗大的尾巴;狐尾〔尤指作打猎纪念保存的狐尾〕。**4.** 【植】冠毛。**5.** (一)刷,擦,轻触,擦过。**6.** 〔美〕小冲突,遭遇战,激烈的小战斗。**7.** (骑马)疾驰。**8.** 〔美俚〕悍然拒绝。**9.** 〔澳、新西兰俚〕姑娘,年轻女人。*Give your hat another* ~. 再把你的帽子刷一刷[擦一擦]。*a paint* ~ 画笔。*a laundry* ~(洗衣)板刷。*a writing* ~毛笔。*get a* ~ *from* (*sth.*) 被(某物)擦了一下。*the* ~ *of Manet* 曼纳特的画风。*have a* ~ *with* ...和…发生小冲突。*a narrow* ~ *with death* 差点送命。***at a*** ~ 一举。***at a*** [***the***] ***first*** ~ **1.** 在最初的小冲突中。**2.** 最初,首先,一开头;立刻。***be tarred with the same*** ~ 一丘之貉,一路货色。***give sb. the*** [***a***] ~ 把某人打发掉,不理睬某人。***the*** ~ **1.** 画家。**2.** 画法,绘画风格。**II** ***vt*.** **1.** (用刷子)刷,擦,掸,拂;擦掉。**2.** 轻擦,轻触。~ *the dirt off his coat* 刷去衣服上的尘土。*His lips* ~*ed her ear*. 他用嘴唇轻轻地碰了一下她的耳朵。— ***vi*.** **1.** 擦过,掠过(*against*, *by*, *past*, *through*)。**2.** 飞跑,急奔。**3.** 刷牙;刷头发。*B- after meal*. 饭后刷牙。*He* ~*ed by without noticing me*. 他飞跑过去,没有注意到我。~ ***aside*** **1.** 刷去;扫除。**2.** 无视,不顾,漠视(*Our complaints were simply* ~*ed aside*. 我们的意见根本没有被理睬)。~ ***away*** **1.** 刷去,擦去。**2.** = ~ aside. ~ ***down*** 刷下来。~ ***off*** **1.** 刷去。**2.** 〔美俚〕不客气地拒绝,打发走;摒弃。**3.** 〔美俚〕跑脱,逃掉。**4.** 〔美俚〕走开〔常用于祈使句〕。~ ***over*** **1.** 轻轻上色。**2.** 用刷子刷;擦过。**3.** 〔美口〕浅耕。~ ***round*** 〔美俚〕活动一下(身体)。~ ***up*** (***on***) **1.** 刷光,擦亮;把…打扮整洁。**2.** 重新学习,重温,复习。**3.** 提高(技巧等);使完善(*I must* ~ *up on my French*. 我得把法语复习一下。~ *up one's acquaintance with another* 与人重温旧交)。~ ***up against*** 轻轻接触。~ **ability** (画家)运笔自如。~ **burn** 擦伤。~ **cut** 男子刷形发型。~ **discharge** 【电】刷形放电,电晕放电。~**-off** 〔美俚〕拒绝;打发走,断然解雇(免职),摒弃(*give sb. the* ~*-off* 把某人打发走,根本不睬某人)。~ **pencil** 画图笔。~**-stroke** **1.** 刷子[画笔等]的一挥。**2.** 绘画技巧。~**-up** **1.** 刷光,擦亮;打扮。**2.** 复习;学好,练好。**3.** 提高,改进,润色(*have a wash and* ~*-up* 梳洗打扮。*He gave his Spanish a* ~*-up*. 他温习了一下西班牙语)。~ **wheel** 【机】刷轮,刷车。~**work** **1.** 绘画。**2.** 画风。

brush[2] [brʌʃ; brʌʃ] ***n*.** **1.** 灌木丛,杂木林。**2.** 柴。**3.** 〔the ~〕〔美〕尚未开拓的土地;地广人稀的林区。~ **fire** 灌木丛的火灾〔有别于森林大火〕。~**-fire** ***a*.** 灌木林火式的,局部的,小规模的。~**fire war** ***n*.** 小规模[局部地区]的战争,灌木林火(式战争)。~**wood** **1.** 砍下的树枝。**2.** 密集的小树丛。

brushed [brʌʃt; brʌʃt] ***a*.** (织物)拉绒的。~ *fabrics* 拉绒织物。~ *goods* 拉绒针织品。

brush·ing [ˈbrʌʃiŋ; ˋbrʌʃɪŋ] **I** ***a*.** 飞跑过去的,一闪而过的。**II** ***n*.** **1.** 刷光,擦亮。**2.** 刷布;拉绒。**3.** 〔*pl*.〕扫[刷]拢来的东西。

brush·y [ˈbrʌʃi; ˋbrʌʃɪ] ***a*.** 矮林多的;毛刷一样的;毛厚的。

brusque, brusk [brusk; brusk] ***a*.** 粗暴的,无礼的,唐突的。*a* ~ *refusal* 粗暴的拒绝。**-ly** ***ad*.** **-ness** ***n*.**

brus·que·rie [ˌbruːskəˈriː; ˏbruskəˋri] ***n*.** 〔F.〕粗暴,无礼,唐突。

Brus·sels [ˈbrʌslz; ˋbrʌslz] ***n*.** 布鲁塞尔〔比利时首都〕。~ **carpet** 布鲁塞尔毛圈地毯。~ **lace** 布鲁塞尔枕结花边;机织花边。~ **sprouts** (可食用的)球芽甘蓝。

brut [bryt; brut] ***a*.** 〔F.〕(香槟酒)未加糖和香料的。

bru·tal [ˈbruːtl; ˋbrutl̩] ***a*.** **1.** 兽(一样)的,兽性的,肉欲的;残忍的;不讲理的,粗暴的。**2.** 〔俚〕讨厌的;(天气等)令人不愉快的。~ *nature* 兽性。~ *treatment* 野蛮拷打。~ *weather* 恶劣的气候。*a* ~ *brodie* 〔美〕严重错误。**-ly** ***ad*.**

bru·tal·ism [ˈbruːtəlizəm; ˋbrutəlɪzm̩] ***n*.** **1.** 兽行,残忍。**2.** 〔美〕野兽派艺术〔尤指建筑方面使用夸张和畸形以造成效果的艺术风格〕。**-ist** ***n*.**, ***a*.** 野兽派艺术家(的)。

bru·tal·i·ty [bruːˈtæliti; bruˋtælətɪ] ***n*.** 兽性;残忍;蛮横。

bru·tal·ize [ˈbruːtəlaiz; ˋbrutl̩ˏaɪz] ***vt*.** **1.** 把…弄成野兽一般;使变残忍。**2.** 把…当禽兽看待。*troops* ~*d by years of warfare* 因连年征战而变得野蛮了的士兵。*an accord not to* ~ *prisoners of war* 一项不得虐待战俘的协议。— ***vi*.** 变成野兽一样;变残忍,变凶猛。**-i·zation** ***n*.**

brute [bruːt; brut] **I** ***n*.** **1.** 动物,兽,畜生。**2.** 人面兽心的人,残暴的人。**3.** 〔the ~〕兽性,劣根性。**4.** 〔口〕可恶的东西[人]。*a* ~ *of a husband* 残横的丈夫。*heartless* ~ 没心肝的畜生。*the* ~ *in him* 他身上的兽性。

II *a*. 1. 畜生的,动物的。2. 粗暴的,残忍的,凶恶的;蛮横的。3. 无感觉的,无理性的,盲目的;无生物的。*the ~ creation* 兽类,畜生。*a ~ courage* 蛮勇,匹夫之勇。~ *force* [*violence*] 暴力。~ *matter* 非生物。~ *powers of nature* 盲目的自然力。*a ~ struggle* 〔美〕拳击比赛。**the ~s** 兽类,畜生。**-hood** *n*. 兽性的特点。

B

bru·ti·fy [ˈbruːtifai; ˋbrutə͵faɪ] *vt*., *vi*. = brutalize.

brut·ish [ˈbruːtiʃ; ˋbrutɪʃ] *a*. 1. 兽的,畜生般的。2. 粗暴的,残忍的;野蛮的,肉欲的。3. 粗鲁的,愚钝的。~ *appetite* 兽欲。**-ly** *ad*. **-ness** *n*.

bru·tum ful·men [ˈbruːtəm ˈfʌlmen; ˋbrutəm ˋfʌlmɛn] 〔L.〕吓唬,空口威胁,虚张声势。

Bry·an [ˈbraiən; ˋbraɪən] *n*. 布赖恩〔姓氏,男子名〕。

Bry·ant [ˈbraiənt; ˋbraɪənt] *n*. 布赖恩特〔姓氏〕。

Bryce [brais; braɪs] *n*. 布赖斯〔姓氏,男子名〕。

bry·ol·o·gy [braiˈɔlədʒi; braɪˋɑlədʒɪ] *n*. 苔藓植物学。

bry·o·ny [ˈbraiəni; ˋbraɪənɪ] *n*. 【植】泻根草;【药】泻根〔吐剂或泻剂〕。

bry·o·phyte [ˈbraiəˌfait; ˋbraɪə͵faɪt] *n*. 苔藓植物。**-phyt·ic** [-ˈfitik; -ˋfɪtɪk] *a*.

bry·o·zo·an [ˌbraiəˈzəuən; ͵braɪəˋzoən] *n*. 藓苔虫(= ectoproct).

Bryth·on [ˈbriθən; ˋbrɪθən] *n*. 1. 布立吞人〔从前居住在不列颠的凯尔特人〕。2. 讲布立吞语的人。

Bry·thon·ic [briˈθɔnik; brɪˋθɑnɪk] I *a*. 布立吞人的;布立吞语的。II *n*. (印欧语系的)布立吞语支。

BS, B.S. = 1. Bachelor of Science 理学士。2. balance sheet 资产负债表。3. British Standard 英国(工业)规格,英国(工业)标准。

b.s. = 1. balance sheet 资产负债表。2. bill of sale 卖契。

B/S = bill of sale 卖契。

BSA = 1. Birmingham Small Arms 〔英〕伯明翰轻武器公司。2. Boy Scouts of America 美国童子军。3. Bachelor of Science in Agriculture 农学士。4. bovine serum albumin 【生化】牛血清蛋白。

BSAA = Bachelor of Science in Applied Arts 应用文科学士。

BSAE = 1. Bachelor of Science in Architectural Engineering 建筑工程学士。2. Bachelor of Science in Aeronautical Engineering 航空工程学士。3. Bachelor of Science in Agricultural Engineering 农业工程学士。

BSB = Bachelor of Science in Business 商学士。

B.Sc., B Sc = Bachelor of Science 理学士。

B-school [ˈbiːˌskuːl; ˋbi͵skul] *n*. 〔口〕商业学校(= business school). **-er** 商业学校学生。

BSE = 1. Bachelor of Science in Engineering 工学士。2. Bachelor of Science in Education 教育学士。3. bovine spongiform encephalopathy "疯牛病"。

B.S.Ec., B.S.Econ. = Bachelor of Science in Economics 经济学士。

B.S.For. = Bachelor of Science in Forestry 林学士。

BSI = British Standards Institution 英国标准协会。

B-sta·tion [ˈbiːˈsteiʃən; ˋbiˋsteʃən] *n*. 船上的无线电台。

Btu, B.t.u. = British thermal unit(s) 英国热单位。

bu. = 1. bureau. 2. bushel(s).

bub [bʌb; bʌb] *n*. 〔美俚〕小兄弟,小伙子〔对部下,晚辈称呼用〕。

bu·bal(e) [ˈbjuːbəl; ˋbjubəl], **bu·ba·lis** [ˈbjuːbəlis; ˋbjubəlɪs] *n*. (北非)大羚羊。

bu·ba·line [ˈbjuːbəlain; ˋbjubəlaɪn] *a*. 1. 羚羊属的。2. 野牛的,野牛状的。

bub·ble [ˈbʌbl; ˋbʌbl] I *n*. 1. 泡,水泡;气泡;泡沫。2. 幻想,妄想,泡影;欺诈性的投机事业。3. 冒泡,起泡,沸腾(声)。4. 泡泡发型。5. 〔美俚〕防窃听密室。*soap ~s* 肥皂泡。*~s in glass* 玻璃中的气泡。*the Florida real-estate ~* 骗人的佛罗里达不动产投机公司。***blow ~s*** 1. 吹肥皂泡。2. 空谈,空想。~ ***and squeak*** 肉菜卷心菜〔有时加马铃薯等〕。***prick a ~*** 戳穿西洋镜,揭破真面目。***South Sea B-*** 【史】南海泡影〔十八世纪初英国一些人组织南海公司声称在南美进行开拓活动的大骗局〕。II *vt*. 1. 使冒泡。2. 滔滔不绝地讲(话)。3. 〔古〕骗,欺哄。*He ~d the good news*. 他不停嘴地报告好消息。— *vi*. 1. 起泡,冒泡;沸腾;沸沸地响;(泉等)涌。2. (水)潺潺地流;发噗噗声;(莺)啭;(人)咯咯地笑。3. 兴奋,欢闹。*The tea ~d in the pot*. 壶里的茶开了。*a bubbling stream* 潺潺流过的小溪。*The play ~d with songs and dances*. 这出戏载歌载舞,非常热闹。*Nationalism has been bubbling here*. 这里一直激荡着民族主义情绪。~ ***off*** 形成气泡溢出。~ ***out*** 勃突勃突地涌出。~ ***over*** 1. 冒泡漫出,煮沸溢出 (*over*). 2. 兴奋,欢闹。*She is bubbling over with enthusiasm*. 她情绪炽烈,激动不已。~ ***up*** 冒泡,发出气泡。~ ***with laughter*** [***wrath***] 哄堂大笑[怒气冲冲]。~ **bath** 1. (使浴水起泡的)芳香泡沫剂。2. (使用泡沫剂的)泡沫浴。~ **car** 微型汽车。~ **chamber**【原】泡沫室。~ **company** 为行骗而虚设的公司。~ **dance** 气球(虚掩的裸体)舞。~ **economy** 泡沫经济。~ **gum** 1. 可吹成泡泡的口香糖。2. 以青少年为主要对象的一种摇滚乐。~ **head** 〔美俚〕笨蛋。~**-top** 1. (车后部的)透明防弹窗;透明防弹罩。2. 圆顶透明伞。~ **wrap** 泡沫包装〔指用泡沫塑料做包装材料〕。

bub·bler [ˈbʌblə; ˋbʌblɚ] *n*. 1. 喷水式饮水口。2. 【化】起泡器,扩散器;水浴瓶。

bub·bly [ˈbʌbli; ˋbʌblɪ] I *a*. 泡多的;发泡的。II *n*. 〔英俚〕香槟酒。~**-jock** *n*. 〔Scot.〕雄火鸡。

bub·by[1] [ˈbʌbi; ˋbʌbɪ] *n*. 〔美〕= bub.

bub·by[2] *n*. 〔俚〕女性的胸脯,乳房,奶子。

bu·bo [ˈbjuːbəu; ˋbjubo] *n*. 【医】腹股沟腺炎。

bu·bonic [bjuːˈbɔnik; bjuˋbɑnɪk] *a*. 腹股沟腺炎性的。~ **plague** 淋巴腺鼠疫。

bu·bon·o·cele [bju(ː)ˈbɔnəsiːl; bjuˋbɑnə͵sil] *n*. 【医】腹股沟不全疝。

buc·cal [ˈbʌkəl; ˋbʌkl] *a*. 【解】口的;颊的。*the ~ cavity* 口腔。~ *division* 口部;颊部。

buc·ca·neer [ˌbʌkəˈniə; ͵bʌkəˋnɪr] I *n*. 1. 海盗。2. 无所顾忌的冒险家〔尤指在政治和商业方面〕。II *vi*. 1. 做海盗。2. 从事(政治、商业等的)冒险活动。**-ish** *a*. 海盗似的。

buc·ci·na·tor [ˈbʌksineitə; ˋbʌksɪ͵netɚ] *n*. 【解】颊肌。

bu·cen·taur [bjuˈsentɔː; bjuˋsentɔr] *n*. 1. (神话中的)半牛半人形怪物。2. 半牛半人形的船。

Bu·ceph·a·lus [bju(ː)ˈsefələs; bjuˋsɛfələs] *n*. 1. 亚历山大大帝的爱马。2. [b-]〔古〕马;悍马;〔谑〕乘用马。

Bu·cha·rest [ˈbjuːkərest; ˈbukəˋrest] *n*. 布加勒斯特〔罗马尼亚首都〕。

Buch·en·wald [ˈbukənwɔːld, G. ˈbuːhənvalt; ˋbukənwɔld, ˋbuhənvalt] *n*. 布痕瓦尔德〔德国市镇,1934—45年德国法西斯曾在此设立集中营,残酷屠杀爱国者和战俘〕。

buck[1] [bʌk; bʌk] I *n*. (*pl*. ~, ~*s*) 1. 雄鹿;公羊;公兔;雄鱼。2. 〔南非〕羚羊;〔美〕公羊毛。3. 纨袴子,花花公子;横冲直撞的年轻人。4. 〔美俚,蔑〕男黑人(= ~ nigger);男印第安人;最下级士兵。5. 【体】鞍马。6. 〔美,澳俚〕元。7. 【牌】做庄家的标记。*fifty ~s of candles* 值五十块钱的蜡烛。***cut the ~*** 1. 有效地[很快地]做。2. 干得漂亮。***in the ~*** 〔美俚〕手头有钱。***make a ~*** 挣钱,捞钞票。***Old ~!*** 老伙计,老朋友〔熟人之间称呼用〕。***pass the ~ to*** 把责任[工作]推给别人。II *vt*. 1. (马)拱背猛跳使(骑者)摔下 (*off*). 2. 〔美口〕(山羊等用头、角)抵,撞。3. 猛烈反抗,反对;突破(困难等)。4. (足球队员)带球冲入(敌阵)。~ *off the rider* 马猛跳使骑者摔下。*The plane ~ed a strong head wind*. 飞机顶着强风飞行。~*ing a trend* 反对某种倾向。~ *the* *question on to someone else* 把问题推给别人。— *vi*. 1. (马)猛然弓背跳起。2. (孤注一掷地)赌。3. 〔美〕传递;把(问题)推给(别人)。4. 〔美口〕(羊等)抵;撞过去,冲过去;(机器)颤动,(车等)颠簸,猛然开动。5. 〔美口〕抵抗;强烈反对 (*against*). *The pony* ～*ed*. 小马弓背跳起。～*against fate* 与命运抗争。～*against the suggestion* 反对该项建议。～*for vice-presidency* 拼命钻营副董事长的职位。～ **for** 〔俚〕(不择手段地)争取(升级、利益)等。～ **up** 1. 振作精神;鼓励。2. 打起精神来! 加油〔祈使语气〕! 3. 〔俚〕打扮。4. 匆忙。～ **up against** 〔美俚〕反抗;不甘沉默。**III** *a*. 1. 雄的;〔美俚〕男的。2. 〔美俚〕某一军衔等级中最低一级的。～**bean** 【植】睡菜。～ **fever** 〔美口〕1. (猎物接近时初猎者的)兴奋,紧张。2. (新鲜的)体验,(从未有过的)兴奋。～**horn** 鹿角。～**hound** 猎鹿用的小猎狗。～**jump** 1. *vi*. (马)弯背猛跳。2. *vt*. (马)弯背猛跳使(骑者)摔下。～**jumper** 劣马。～ **lunch** 〔俚〕男用盆餐。～ **passer** 推诿家〔专把责任推诿给他人的人〕。～ **private** 〔美俚〕大兵。～**saw** 木锯。～**shot** 鹿弹〔大粒散弹〕。～**skin** 1. 鹿皮。2. 〔*pl*.〕鹿皮裤;鹿皮衣。3. 〔美〕穿鹿皮色服装的人。～ **slip** 为推卸责任而写的便条。～**stick** 说大话的人,吹牛大王。～**-tooth** 獠牙,龅牙。～**thorn** 【植】鼠李。～**wheat** 荞麦;荞麦粉。**-er** 猛然跳起把人摔下的马。

buck[2] [bʌk; bʌk] *n*. (运货马车的)车身,车架;门框;〔美〕锯木架。～**-board** 弹簧板四轮马车。

buck[3] [bʌk; bʌk] *n*. 〔英〕捕鳝鱼的竹笼。

buck[4] [bʌk; bʌk] *ad*. 〔方〕完全。～ *naked* 全裸。

buck[5] [bʌk; bʌk] I *n*. 〔古、方〕1. 洗衣碱水;起泡肥皂水。2. 用碱水[肥皂水]浸洗过的衣服。**II** *vt*. 用碱水[肥皂水]浸[洗]衣服。～ **basket** 【古】洗衣筐。

buck. = buckram.

Buck [bʌk; bʌk] *n*. 巴克〔姓氏〕。

buck·a·roo [ˈbʌkəruː; ˋbʌkəˏru], **buck·ay·ro** [bəkˈɛərəu; bəkˋero] *n*. 〔美西部〕牧童,牛仔;驯野马者。

buck·een [ˌbʌkˈiːn; ˏbʌkˋin] *n*. 〔英、方〕(穷而高傲的)贵族青年。

buck·et [ˈbʌkit; ˋbʌkɪt] I *n*. 1. 水桶,提桶;吊桶。2. (唧筒的)活塞;(水车循环运转的)戽斗;(挖土机等的)铲斗,勺斗;(汽轮机等的)叶片。3. 一桶[勺斗],满桶[勺斗];大量。4. 〔俚〕交通工具〔尤指行驶缓慢的旧船,旧汽车等〕。5. 〔俚〕屁股。6. (篮球场的)篮下禁区。*a* ～ *of sand* 一勺斗黄沙。*shed* ～*s of tears* 泪如雨下。*skip* ～ 翻斗。*turbine* ～ 涡轮叶片。*flame* ～ 火焰反射器。***a drop in the*** ～ 沧海一粟,九牛一毛。***give sb. the*** ～ 〔俚〕解雇。***kick the*** ～ 〔俚〕死,翘辫子。**II** *vt*. 1. 用桶装,用桶运;〔美〕用桶打(水)。2. 〔英口〕催(马)猛奔。3. 〔美俚〕骗;利用(顾客的定钱、资金等)做投机生意。— *vi*. 〔口〕急奔;猛开车;猛划船。～ **brigade** 1. (救火时为传递水等排成的)一字长蛇阵,人墙。2. 应急突击队。～ **seat** (飞机等的)凹背座椅〔坐板可以翻起〕。～ **shop** 〔美俚〕小交易所;小酒馆。**-ful** *n*. 一满桶[勺斗];一桶[勺斗]的量 (*a bucketful of water* 一桶水)。

buck·eye [ˈbʌkai; ˋbʌkˏaɪ] I *n*. 1. (美国)橡树。2. 〔B-〕〔俚〕美国俄亥俄州的人。***the B- State*** 美国俄亥俄州〔别名〕。**II** *a*. (色彩等)奔放的,大胆的,花哨的。

Bucking·ham [ˈbʌkiŋəm; ˋbʌkɪŋəm] *n*. = Buckinghamshire. ***the*** ～ ***Palace*** (伦敦的)白金汉宫〔英国王宫〕。

Buck·ing·ham·shire [ˈbʌkiŋəmʃiə; ˋbʌkɪŋəmʃɪr] *n*. 白金汉郡〔英国郡名〕。

buck·ish [ˈbʌkiʃ; ˋbʌkɪʃ] *a*. 1. 爱时髦的,浮华的。2. 性急的,浮躁的;莽撞的。

buck·le [ˈbʌkl; ˋbʌkl̩] I *n*. 扣子,带扣;(衣,鞋等的)扣形装饰品。***hold*** [***bring***] ～ ***and thong together*** = 〔美〕 ***make*** ～ ***and tongue meet*** 使收支相抵,量入为出。**II** *vt*. 1. 用带扣扣住,把…扣紧,扣上(皮带等) (*on*, *up*);〔谑〕使…结婚。2. (加热或压力)使变弯曲,使翘棱;使起伏不平;使塌陷。3. 努力从事于。～ *a belt* 扣上带子。～ *on a sword* (用带扣)挂上佩剑。～ ***oneself to*** 专心从事于。— *vi*. 1. 扣住,扣紧。2. (由于受压、受热等)变弯曲,翘棱;弯成起伏不平;塌陷 (*up*). 3. 屈服,屈从,屈降。4. 专心做事。*His boot wouldn't* ～. 他的靴子扣不紧。*cornstalk* ～*ing in wind* 玉米秆被风吹得弯下来。*The supports* ～*d under the strain*. 支柱因为受力过重坍下来。～ *under press* 在压力下屈服。～ *up for safety* 把扣子扣紧以保安全。*He found it hard to* ～ *down*. 他很难专心做一样事情。～ ***on*** (***one's armour***) (用带扣)穿戴上(铠甲)。～ (***down***) ***to*** 倾全力于 (*She* ～*d down to housework*. 她埋头家务)。**-d** *a*. 1. (鞋等)有带扣的。2. 弯曲的,翘棱的。

Buck·le [ˈbʌkl; ˋbʌkl̩] *n*. 巴克尔〔姓氏〕。

buck·ler [ˈbʌklə; ˋbʌklɚ] I *n*. 1. 圆盾,孔盖板。2. 防御,防御物,庇护者。3. 【船】锚链孔盖。**II** *vt*. 1. (持圆盾)防卫。2. 防御,防护。

buck·mast [ˈbʌkmɑːst; ˋbʌkmæst] *n*. = beechmast.

buck·o [ˈbʌkəu; ˋbʌko] I *n*. 1. 〔海俚〕暴徒,恶霸,恶棍。2. 〔英方〕小伙子〔称呼语〕。**II** *a*. 1. 残忍的,虐待狂的。2. 粗鲁的,蛮横的。

buck·ra [ˈbʌkrə; ˋbʌkrə] I *a*. 〔贬〕白种人的,白佬儿的〔美国南部、西印度群岛及非洲黑人用语〕。*a* ～ *house* 白佬儿的房子。*a* ～ *manner* 白佬儿的气派。**II** *n*. 1. 白种人。2. 老板,先生。

buck·ram [ˈbʌkrəm; ˋbʌkrəm] I *n*. 1. 硬麻布,硬布。2. 〔古〕古板;拘泥;生硬。3. 色厉内荏,外强中干。*library* ～ 书面帆布。***men in*** ～ = ～ ***men***. **II** *a*. 1. 硬(麻)布制的。2. (态度)古板的;拘泥的;生硬的。3. 外强中干的,色厉内荏的。**III** *vt*. 1. (用硬麻布)衬硬。2. 〔古〕使变古板[拘泥]。3. 使摆出外强中干的架势。～ **men** 稻草人。

buck·shee [ˈbʌkʃiː; ˋbʌkʃi] I *n*. 1. 〔英,军俚〕额外津贴,额外供应品。2. 预料以外的赠与物。**II** *a*. 1. 额外获得的。2. 免费的。**III** *ad*. 免费地。

bu·col·ic [bju(ː)ˈkɔlik; bjuˋkɑlɪk] I *a*. 农家风味的;田园生活的;牧羊生活的,牧歌式的。*a simple* ～ *life* 简朴的田园生活。**II** *n*. 1. 〔常 *pl*.〕牧歌;田园诗。2. 〔古〕农民,乡下人。

bud[1] [bʌd; bʌd] I *n*. 1. 芽,萌芽,幼芽;蓓蕾,背朵;【动】芽体,芽状凸起。2. 未成熟的人[东西];〔喻〕少女,少年;〔美〕刚进社交界的姑娘。*a tactile* ～ 触觉芽。*a gustatory* ～ 味蕾。***in*** [***the***] ～ 含苞未放,发芽,尚在萌芽时期。***nip in the*** ～ 把…消灭在萌芽状态,防患于未然 (*nip a rebellion in the* ～ 把叛乱扑灭于萌芽状态)。**II** *vt*. 1. 使发芽。2. 【植】使芽接。— *vi*. 1. 发芽,萌芽;含苞待放。2. 开始发育[发展,成长]。3. 【植】芽接。4. 处于未成熟状态。～ ***off from*** 变成芽体从(母体)分离出来;〔喻〕从…分离出来,建立新组织。～ ***out*** 〔美俚〕打扮得漂漂亮亮。**-like** *a*. 芽似的,蓓蕾似的。

bud[2] [bʌd; bʌd] *n*. 〔口〕伙伴,兄弟〔buddy 的缩写〕。

Bu·da·pest [ˈbjuːdəˈpest; ˋbjudəˋpɛst] *n*. 布达佩斯〔匈牙利首都〕。

bud·ded [ˈbʌdid; ˋbʌdɪd] *a*. 发了芽的,有蓓蕾的,接了芽的。

Bud·dha [ˈbudə; ˋbudə] *n*. 佛陀〔佛教徒对释迦牟尼的尊称〕佛,如来佛。

Bud·dhism [ˈbudizəm; ˋbudɪzəm] *n*. 佛教;佛法。

Bud·dhist [ˈbudist; ˋbudɪst] I *n*. 佛教徒。*a* ～ *monk* 僧,和尚。*a layman* ～居士。**II** *a*. 佛陀的;佛法的;佛教徒的。

Bud·dhis·tic, Bud·dhis·ti·cal [buˈdistik(əl); buˋdɪstɪk(əl)] *a*. 佛陀的;佛法的,佛教(徒)的。

bud·ding [ˈbʌdiŋ; ˋbʌdɪŋ] I *a*. 1. 正发芽的,含苞待放的。2. 开始发育[发展]的。3. 初露头角的。*a* ～ *beauty* 妙龄女郎。*a* ～ *lawyer* 初露头角的律师。*a* ～ *scientist* 正在成长中的科学家。**II** *n*. 1. 发芽;含苞。2.

【植】芽接(法);(出)芽(繁)殖。

bud·dle [ˈbʌdl; ˋbʌdl] **I** ***n*.**【矿】洗矿槽,淘汰盘。**II** ***vt*.** 用洗矿槽[淘汰盘]洗(矿石)。

Bud·dle·ia [bʌdˈliːə; bʌdˋliə] ***n*.**【植】醉鱼草;醉鱼草属植物。

bud·dy [ˈbʌdi; ˋbʌdɪ] ***n*. 1.**〔美军口〕伙伴;弟兄〔尤指士兵间的称呼〕;好朋友;小朋友〔称呼用〕。**2.** 艾滋病患者之友〔指为艾滋病患者提供帮助和安慰的人〕。*a bosom* ~ 好朋友,密友。~-~ ***a*.**〔美俚〕亲热的。

B

Bud·dy [ˈbʌdi; ˋbʌdɪ] ***n*.** 巴迪〔男子名〕。

budge[1] [bʌdʒ; bʌdʒ] ***vt*.**〔通例用于否定句〕**1.** 微微一动,动。**2.** (立场等)动摇,让步。*The car won't* ~ *an inch*. 这辆车子一动也不动。*She wouldn't* ~ *on the issue*. 她在这个问题上不肯让步。— ***vt*. 1.** 推动。**2.** 使动摇,使让步。*The three of them couldn't* ~ *the rock*. 他们三个人都推不动那块石头。*Money can't* ~ *me*. 金钱不能使我改变立场。

budge[2] [bʌdʒ; bʌdʒ] ***n*. 1.** 羔皮。**2.** 革囊。**3.**〔美方〕酒。

budg·er·i·gar [ˈbʌdʒəriˌgɑː; ˋbʌdʒərɪˏgɑr] ***n*.**【动】虎皮鹦鹉。

budg·et [ˈbʌdʒit; ˋbʌdʒɪt] **I** ***n*. 1.** 预算,预算案。**2.** 经营费;生活费;(有限制的)供应,来源。**3.**〔古〕〔方〕小皮包;小皮包中的东西。**4.**〔喻〕(书信等的)一束,一捆;(要闻)汇编〔作报名用〕。*the Literary B-* 文艺汇编。*a* ~ *committee* 预算委员会。*the monthly* ~ *for a family of four* 一家四口的每月生活费。*His* ~ *of good will was running out*. 他的好心肠已经快没有了。~ *estimate* 概算。~ *statement* 预算书。~ *making* 编预算。***open*** [***introduce***] ***the*** ~ 向议会提出预算案。**II** ***vt*. 1.** 把…编入预算;按预算来安排(生活、工程等)。**2.** 安排,预定。~ *a new hospital* 把建立一座新医院列入预算。~ *manpower in a tight labor market* 在劳动力短缺的情况下安排人力。~ *one's time* 安排自己的时间。— ***vi*. 1.** 编预算。**2.** 作好安排。~ *for a vacation* 安排好时间去度假。~ *for the project* 为工程编制预算。~ **plan** 分期付款。~ **shoppers** 按照预算购物的顾客。**-ary** ***a*.** 预算上的。**-eer, -er** ***n*. 1.** 预算编制人。**2.** 受预算限制的人。

bud·let [ˈbʌdlit; ˋbʌdlɪt] ***n*.** 幼芽,小芽。

bue·nasno·ches [ˈbwenɑːsˈnɔːtʃes; ˋbwenɑsˋnɔtʃɛs]〔Sp.〕再见! 晚安!

Bue·nos Ai·res [ˈbwenəsˈaiəriz; ˋbwenəsˋɑɪres] ***n*.** 布宜诺斯艾利斯〔阿根廷首都〕。

bue·nosdi·as [ˈbwenɔːsˈdiːɑːs; ˋbwenɔsˋdiɑs]〔Sp.〕您好! 早安!

buff[1] [bʌf; bʌf] **I** ***n*. 1.** (水牛等淡黄色的)软皮;(擦镜头用的)麂皮;皮制军服;淡黄色印相纸。**2.** 淡黄色,柔皮色。**3.** (人)裸露的皮肤。**4.**〔美〕爱好者,迷;热心人。**5.**〔口〕野牛。**6.**【机】磨轮,抛光轮。*Civil War* ~*s* 爱好钻研美国南北战争史的人。*a trolley car* ~ 喜欢乘电车的人。***in*** ~ 赤身裸体。***strip to the*** ~ 使一丝不挂,把…的衣服剥得精光。**II** ***vt*. 1.** (用软皮等)擦亮,抛光,擦净。**2.** 把(皮革)弄软;把(皮革)染成纯黄色。*a* ~*ing machine* 抛光机。~ *shoes* 擦皮鞋。~ *a waxed floor* 把打蜡的地板擦亮。**III** ***a*. 1.** 软牛皮制的。**2.** 浅黄色的。~ **coat 1.** 麂皮制服。**2.** 穿麂皮制服的军人。

buff[2] [bʌf; bʌf] **I** ***vt*.** 减低…的力量,缓冲。**II** ***n*.**〔方〕打击。

buf·fa·lo [ˈbʌfələu; ˋbʌflˏo] **I** ***n*.** (*pl*. ~*es*, ~*s*,〔集合词〕~) **1.** 水牛;〔美〕野牛。**2.**〔军俚〕水陆两用坦克。**II** ***vt*.**〔美俚〕**1.** 威吓。**2.** 迷惑。*He was* ~*ed by the complexity of problem*. 他被复杂的问题弄得昏头昏脑。*He didn't let the older boys* ~ *him*. 他没有让大孩子们吓住。~ **bird** 香羽鸟。~ **chips**(做燃料用的)干牛粪。~ **cloth** 长绒大衣呢。**B- Indians** 平原地区印第安人。~ **range**〔美〕原野。

Buf·fa·lo [ˈbʌfələu; ˋbʌflˏo] ***n*.** 布法罗〔美国港市〕。

buff·er[1] [ˈbʌfə; ˋbʌfɚ] **I** ***n*. 1.**【机】缓冲器,缓冲垫;阻尼器,减震器;消声器。**2.**【化】缓冲,缓冲剂。**3.** 缓冲者;缓冲物;缓冲国(= ~ state)。**4.**【计】缓冲存储装置。*oil* ~【机】油压减震器。**II** ***vt*. 1.**【化】用缓冲剂处理。**2.** 缓和;缓冲;保护;使不利影响减少。~ *economy by raising interest rates* 以提高利率来保护经济。*The drug* ~*ed his pain*. 这剂药减轻了他的病痛。~ **computer** 缓冲型计算机。~ **solution**【化】缓冲溶液。~ **state** 缓冲国。~ **zone** 缓冲地带。

buff·er[2] [ˈbʌfə; ˋbʌfɚ] ***n*. 1.**【机】抛(光)盘,抛光轮,抛光棒。**2.** 抛光工人。

buff·er[3] [ˈbʌfə; ˋbʌfɚ] ***n*. 1.**〔英俚〕无能的人,老派人物。**2.** 家伙,人。**3.**【海】水手[掌帆]长副手。*He was a bit of* ~. 他有点低能。***an old*** ~ 老家伙,老糊涂,老朽。

buf·fet[1] [ˈbʌfit; bʌˋfɪt] **I** ***n*. 1.** 打击,殴打;一巴掌,一拳。**2.** (风、波浪等的)冲击;(命运等的)折磨,蹂躏。**3.**【空】抖振。*give* ~ *s to sb*. 殴打某人。*the* ~*s of the storm* 暴风雨的冲击。*recurrent* ~*s of fate* 命运多舛。**II** ***vt*. 1.** 用手打,用拳击,掴。**2.** (波浪等)冲击;(命运等)蹂躏,打击。**3.** (人与命运、波浪等)搏斗。*be* ~*ed by adversity* 处于逆境。*The wind* ~*ed the boats*. 风冲击着小船。*The ship* ~*ed her way through the waves*. 这艘船在浪涛中奋勇前行。— ***vi*. 1.** (用手)打,殴打。**2.** (与风浪等)搏斗,奋勇前进。

buf·fet[2] **I** ***n*. 1.** [ˈbʌfit; ˋbʌfɪt] 碗橱,餐具架。**2.** [ˈbufei; ˋbʊfe](车站,车内的)餐室;小吃店,快餐柜台,小卖部。**II** ***a*.** 快餐式的,自助式的〔无固定餐桌,就餐者自取食物〕。*cold* ~(菜单上的)冷肉。~ **car** (火车上的)餐车。~ **lunch** [**supper**] 简易午[晚]餐。~ **service** 快餐部。

buf·fle·head [ˈbʌflˌhed; ˋbʌflˏhɛd] ***n*.**【动】巨头鹊鸭。

buf·fo [ˈbufəu; ˋbufo] ***n*.** (*pl*. ***buf·fi*** [ˈbufiː; ˋbufi]) ***a*.**〔It.〕滑稽歌手(的),滑稽歌剧演员(的)。

buf·foon [bʌˈfuːn; bʌˋfun] **I** ***n*. 1.** 丑角;演滑稽戏的人。**2.** 言谈诙谐的人。*play the* ~ 当小丑。**II** ***vt*.** 丑化。— ***vi*.** 当小丑。**-ish** ***a*.** 滑稽的,小丑似的。

buf·foon·er·y [bʌˈfuːnəri; bʌˋfunərɪ] ***n*.** 滑稽(表演),插科打诨。

buf·fy [ˈbʌfi; ˋbʌfɪ] ***a*. 1.** 淡黄色的。**2.**〔俚〕喝醉了的。

Bu·ford [ˈbjuːfəd; ˋbjufəd] ***n*.** 比福德〔姓氏,男子名〕。

bu·fo·ten·ine [ˌbjuːfəˈteniːn; ˏbjufəˋtenin] ***n*.**【药】蟾蜍特宁,蟾毒色胺。

bug [bʌg; bʌg] **I** ***n*. 1.**〔英〕臭虫;〔美口〕虫,昆虫。**2.**〔口〕微生物,病菌。**3.** (机器、设计等的)小缺陷,瑕疵。**4.** 癖,狂,迷,热衷于(某事)者。**5.**【电】故障,损坏;干扰;〔俚〕雷达位置测定[指示]器;半自动发报键,电键。**6.** 窃听器;暗设报警器。**7.**〔古〕要人,名人。**8.** 星号。**9.** 小型汽车。*a lighting* ~〔美〕萤火虫。*an intestinal* ~ 肠菌。*a big* ~〔贬〕名人,要人。*The test flight was to discover the* ~*s in the new plane*. 试验飞行是要发现新飞机有何缺陷。*a sports car* ~ 赛车迷。*a* ~ *on education* 热衷于教育事业的人。~ ***under the chip***〔美〕秘密。***on*** ~ 给…迷上,热衷于…。***put a*** ~ ***in sb.'s ear*** 事先警告某人。**II** ***vt*.** (**-gg-**) **1.** 灭除(害虫)。**2.**〔美俚〕在,暗设报警器[窃听器];(通过窃听器)窃听。**3.**〔美俚〕烦恼,折磨,激怒。**4.** 使(眼珠)凸出。~ *the phone* 窃听电话。*Don't* ~ *me with petty details*. 不要讲那些琐碎的细节来烦我。— ***vi*. 1.** 捉臭虫。**2.** (眼珠)凸出。**3.**〔美俚〕离开;撤退。~ ***off***〔美俚〕滚开,匆匆走开。~ ***out* 1.**〔美俚〕逃窜;逃避。**2.** 眼珠暴突。**3.** 无趣地走开。~ ***up***〔美俚〕**1.** 激动起来。**2.** 被弄糊涂。~ **doctor**〔美俚〕(监狱等处的)精神病医师,心理学专家。~ **eaters**〔美〕内布拉斯加州人。~**-eyed** ***a*.**〔美〕眼球凸出的;惊得目瞪口呆的。~ **hole**【地】晶穴。~**-juice**〔美〕**1.** (劣等)酒,(低级)威士忌。**2.** 合成饮料,着色清凉饮料。~ **light** 小闪光灯;小灯塔。~ **out 1.**〔军俚〕匆

忙的撤退。2.〔俚〕擅离职守的人。~ **test**〔美俚〕智力测验;心理测验。

bug·a·boo [ˈbʌgəbuː; ˋbʌgəˏbu] *n*.〔美〕= bugbear.

bug·bane [ˈbʌgˌbein; ˋbʌgˏben] *n*.【植】升麻属植物。

bug·bear [ˈbʌgbɛə; ˋbʌgˏbɛr] *n*. 1. 吓人的东西,妖怪。2. 无端的惊恐。3. 令人头痛的事。

bug·eye [ˈbʌgai; ˋbʌgaɪ] *n*.〔美、海〕中型帆船。

bug·ger [ˈbʌgə; ˋbʌgɚ] **I** *n*. 1. 鸡奸者。2.〔卑〕坏蛋,坏家伙;坏东西。3. 家伙,小伙子〔多用于幽默、亲热的说法〕。*a cute little* ~ 一个聪敏伶俐的小家伙。**II** *vt*. 1. 鸡奸。2. 使疲乏不堪。3. 诅咒。— *vi*. 1. 搞鸡奸。2. 诅咒。~ ***about***〔英俚〕(人)追来追去。~ ***off***〔英俚〕走开,离开。~ ***up***〔俚〕搞坏,弄糟,搞乱 (~ *things up* 把事情搞糟)。**-y** *n*. 鸡奸。

bug·gy[1] [ˈbʌgi; ˋbʌgɪ] *a*. 1. 臭虫多的。2. 神经有毛病的;古怪的;淘气的。*a* ~ *old lady who continually mutters to herself* 一个不断自言自语的古怪老太婆。

bug·gy[2] [ˈbʌgi; ˋbʌgɪ] *n*. 1.〔英〕无盖二轮马车;〔美〕二轮[四轮]轻马车。2. 儿童车,婴儿手推车。3.(短途运送金属、矿石等的)短途运输车。4.〔美俚〕汽车〔尤指旧汽车〕。*a* ~ *bandit*〔美俚〕偷汽车的贼。~ ***days***〔美俚〕从前。

bug·house [ˈbʌghaus; ˋbʌgˏhaus] **I** *n*.〔美口〕精神病院,疯人院。**II** *a*. 1. 癫狂的,发疯的。2. 低能的。*a* ~ *fable* 荒唐无稽的故事[事情]。**B- Square** 疯人院广场〔美国纽约街头一广场,系一街头演说者聚集场所〕。

bug-hunt·er [ˈbʌghʌntə; ˋbʌgˏhʌntɚ] *n*.〔英俚,讽〕昆虫学家。**-ing** *n*. 昆虫采集。

bu·gle[1] [ˈbjuːgl; ˋbjugḷ] **I** *n*. 1. 军号,喇叭。2.〔古〕(狩猎时用的)号,角,笛。*blow* [*sound*] *a* ~吹号,鸣角。*a* ~ *call* 进军号,集合号。***like a*** ~ ***call*** 突然。**II** *vi*. 1. 吹号。2. 发出吼声。—*vt*. 1. 吹号集合。2. 吹号表示(冲锋、撤退等)。~ *reveille* 吹起床号。~**-horn** 号角;角笛;角杯。**-r** *n*. 号手;司号兵。

bu·gle[2] [ˈbjuːgl; ˋbjugḷ] **I** *n*.〔常 *pl*.〕(妇女装饰衣服的)玻璃[塑料]珠[小圆管]。**II** *a*.(衣服)有玻璃[塑料]珠装饰的。

bu·gle[3] [ˈbjuːgl; ˋbjugḷ] *n*.【植】夏枯草,筋骨草属植物,匍匐筋骨草。

bu·gle[4] [ˈbjuːgl; ˋbjugḷ] *n*.〔英俚〕鼻子。

bu·glet [ˈbjuːglit; ˋbjuglɪt] *n*.(汽车上的)小喇叭。

bu·gle·weed [ˈbjuːglˌwiːd; ˋbjugḷˏwid] *n*.【植】1. 夏枯草。2. 地笋属植物。

bu·gloss [ˈbjuːglɔs; ˋbjuglɑs] *n*.【植】牛舌草。

bug·o·lo·gy [bʌˈgɔlədʒi; bʌˈgɑlədʒɪ] *n*.〔口〕昆虫学。

bugs [bʌgz; bʌgz] *a*.〔美俚〕疯狂的。***go*** ~ 发疯。

bug·seed [ˈbʌgˌsiːd; ˋbʌgˏsid] *n*.【植】海索草叶虫实。

bug·shah [ˈbʌgʃə, -ʃɔː; ˋbʌgʃə, -ʃɔ] *n*. (*pl*. ~, ~*s*) 布格席〔叶门货币名,等于 1% 里亚尔〕。

buhl [buːl; bul], **buhlwork** [ˈbuːlwəːk; ˋbulˏwɝk] *n*. 1.(龟壳、金银等的)镶嵌装饰。2. 镶嵌工艺品。

buhr·stone [ˈbəːˌstəun; ˋbɝˏston] *n*. 1. 砂质多孔石灰岩。2. 细砂质磨石(= buhr). *a* ~ *mill* 石磨。

BUIC = backup interceptor control【军】后援截击机控制系统。

build [bild; bɪld] **I** *vt*. (***built*** [bilt; bɪlt],〔诗、古〕~***ed***; ***built***, ~***ed***) 1. 建,盖,建筑;建设,建造;筑,造。2. 建立,创立,确立,树立;培养。3. 抬高(身份),捧(演员);扩大 (*up*). ~ *a house* [*bridge*, *ship*] 盖房子[造桥,造船]。~ *a fire* 生火。~ *an empire* 创立帝国。~ *a fortune* 挣家私,治产。~ *a gun* 造大炮。~ *a pile of bricks into a factory* 用一堆砖头砌成厂房。*a novel built on four sections* 分成四部分的一部小说。~ *a new kind of morality* 建立一种新的道德风尚。~ *boys into men* 把少年培养成人。*He is very well built*. 他体魄健壮。*I am not built that way*.〔美〕我生来不是那样的人。*Don't* ~ *your future on dreams*. 不要把你的未来建立在空想上,不要好高骛远。— *vi*. 1. 被建造;从事营造业。2. 逐渐达到高峰;逐步扩大范围。~ *to a climax* 逐步发展到最高潮。*a line of people* ~*ing along the avenue* 沿着人行道越来人越多的队伍。~ ***down*** 衰减,降低。~ ***in*** 1. 加入,插进(用料);埋入,装入。2. 围以(房屋、围墙等)(~ *in bookcases between windows* 在窗户之间砌成嵌入式书架)。~ ***on*** [***upon***] 1. 把…建筑于。2. 依赖,靠,指望(*We* ~ *our hopes on our own efforts*. 我们把希望寄托在自己的努力上)。~ ***round*** 用建筑物包围。~ ***up*** 1.(用砖等)阻塞(门,窗等);把(空场)盖满(房子)。2. 建立,确立,树立(名誉,人格,产业等),组成机关等。3. 增进(健康),加强(体格),振兴,扩大,复兴。4.【军】集结(部队);聚集,积累。5. 赞扬,吹捧(~ *up a bank account* 开银行往来账。~ *up the body* 锻炼身体。~ *up a library* 建立一座图书馆。*a salesman* ~*ing up his product* 宣扬本企业产品的推销员。*clouds* ~*ing up on the horizon* 在天边愈积愈浓的云层)。**II** *n*. 1. 构造,造型。2. 骨格,体格,成形。3.〔俚〕优美的体型,肉体美。*The house was a modern* ~. 那座房子是现代式样。*He has a strong* ~. 他体格健壮。*She has some* ~. 她长得还不错。*of sturdy* ~ 体格健壮的。

build·er [ˈbildə; ˋbɪldɚ] *n*. 1. 建筑工人;经营建筑业者。2. 建设者;创建者。3.(增加洗涤剂清洁作用的)增洁剂;【化】组份;(计算机的)编码程序。*a master* ~ 营造大师。*a great empire* ~ 一个大帝国的创立者。~**'s knot**【海】卷结,8 字形套结。

build·ing [ˈbildiŋ; ˋbɪldɪŋ] *n*. 1. 建筑物,房屋,大楼,大厦。2. 制造;营造,建筑;组合,组装;建筑术。*a public* ~ 公共建筑物。*the art of* ~ 建筑术。*car* ~ 汽车制造。*fabricated* ~装配式建筑。~ **area** 建筑地积。~ **berth** [**slip**] 造船台。~ **block** 1.(儿童玩的)积木。2. 建筑砌块。~ **lease** 租地造屋权,造屋租地的年限。~ **line** 建筑界限,房基线。~ **machine** 轮胎装配床,配套机。~ **material** 建筑材料。~ **method** (制造汽油的)合成法。~ **paper** 防潮纸,油毛毡。~ **room** 装配间。~ **sheet** 建筑钢板。~ **society**〔英〕= ~ (**and loan**) **association**〔美〕住宅互助协会〔会员集股投资以帮助买房造房的互助组织〕。

build-up [ˈbildʌp; ˋbɪldˏʌp] *n*. 1. 组成,装配,组合,组装,安装。2. 上升,升高,增长,增强。3. 组成,结构,构造;(戏剧的)情节。4.【军】(战斗部队的)集合,集结;蓄积,积累,堆积(现象);结瘤,结垢。5. 捏造;吹嘘,宣传。6. 计算,作图。7. 形成,产生,出现。8. 用砖填塞(门窗)。9. 连续发生,连锁反应。10.(事前)准备。11. 鼓舞,鼓励。*the* ~ *of the nation's industry* 国家的工业建设。*They spent a lot of money on her* ~. 他们为给她做广告花掉不少钱。*the* ~ *of the salt deposit* 岩盐的蓄积过程。*a lengthy* ~ 长期的准备。

built [bilt; bɪlt] build 的过去式及过去分词。**I** *a*. 1. 建造成的,组合的,拼成的。2.〔俚〕体型美的。~ *like a castle* (马)体格健壮。*a* ~ *mast* (几根木料拼成的)组合桅。~ *frame* 拼装框架。*a slimly* ~ *girl* 身材苗条的姑娘。*She sure is* ~. 她的体型的确不错。**II** *n*.〔俚〕体型美,肉体美。

built-in [ˈbiltˈin; ˋbɪltˋɪn] **I** *a*. 1.(家具等)作为固定装置而建造的;固定的,不可分开的;嵌入的。2. 内在的;固有的。*a* ~ *bathtub* 固定浴盆。~ *cabinets* 固定壁橱。*a* ~ *trait of human nature* 人性的固有特征。**II** *n*. 嵌入式家具。

built-up [ˈbiltˈʌp; ˋbɪltˋʌp] *a*. 1. 组合的,拼成的,合成的。2. 围建的,建筑物多的。~ *gear* 组合齿轮。*This shoe has a* ~ *heel*. 这种鞋子的后跟是拼装式的。*a* ~ *city* 按计划建设成的城市。~ **area** 1. 盖满房屋的街区,房屋密集区。2. 组合面积。

Bu·jum·bu·ra [ˌbuːdʒəmˈburə; ˏbudʒəmˋbʊrə] *n*. 布琼布拉〔布隆迪(蒲隆地)首都〕。

B

Bu·kha·ra [buˈkɑːrɑ; buˋkɑrɑ] ***n***. 布哈拉〔乌兹别克城市〕。

bulb [bʌlb; bʌlb] **I** ***n***. **1**.【植】球根;鳞茎。**2**. 球状物;(寒暑表的)水银球;灯泡;烧瓶;真空管;测温包。**3**.【解】球;〔*pl*.〕扁桃腺。**4**. (照相机的)快门。**5**. (汽车的)圆顶车壳;【海】球形船首。*a lily* ~ 百合根。*an electric* ~ 电灯泡。*the* ~ *of a hair* 毛球,发根。*the* ~ *of the eye* 眼球。*the* ~ *of the spinal cord*【解】延髓。**II** ***vi***. **1**. 生球茎。**2**. 肿[涨]成球,形成球状。~ **up** (卷心菜等)打包,形成球状包。**-ed** ***a***. **1**. 有鳞[球]茎的。**2**. 鳞[球]茎形,圆形的。

bul·ba·ceous [bəlˈbeiʃəs; bəlˋbeʃəs] ***a***.【植】**1**. 鳞茎的;鳞茎状的;有鳞茎的。**2**. 由鳞茎生长的。

bul·bar [ˈbʌlbə; ˋbʌlbɑr] ***a***. **1**. 鳞茎的,球的。**2**.【解】延髓的。

bulb·if·er·ous [bʌlˈbifərəs; bʌlˋbɪfərəs] ***a***. 有球茎的,有鳞茎的。

bulb·i·form [ˈbʌlbifɔːm; ˋbʌlbɪˏfɔrm] ***a***. 球茎状的。

bul·bil, bul·bel [ˈbʌlbil, ˈbʌlbəl; ˋbʌlbɪl, ˋbʌlbəl] ***n***.【植】珠芽,零余子。

bul·bous [ˈbʌlbəs; ˋbʌlbəs] ***a***. 球茎状的,鳞茎状的;由球茎[鳞茎]长成的。*a* ~ *plant* 球茎[鳞茎]植物。

bul·bul [ˈbulbul; ˋbʊlbʊl] ***n***. **1**.【鸟】夜莺。**2**. 歌手,诗人。

Bul·gar [ˈbʌlgɑː; ˋbʌlgɑr] ***n***. = Bulgarian.

Bul·gar·i·a [bʌlˈgɛəriə; bʌlˋgɛrɪə] ***n***. 保加利亚〔欧洲〕。

Bul·gar·i·an [bʌlˈgɛəriən; bʌlˋgɛrɪən] **I** ***a***. 保加利亚的;保加利亚人的;保加利亚语的。**II** ***n***. 保加利亚人;保加利亚语。

bulge [bʌldʒ; bʌldʒ] **I** ***n***. **1**. 膨胀;肿胀。**2**. 凸出部分;(桶等的)鼓出部,(身体的)发胖部位。**3**. (体积、价格等的)暴涨。**4**.【海】(军舰外侧的)鱼雷防护线;(船的)底边。**5**. 〔美俚〕优越,优势。*a* ~ *in a wall* 墙面的不平部分。*a* ~ *in the rug* 地毯的鼓胀处。*the* ~ *keel* 船腹。*the* ~ *in profits* 利润的突然增长。***get*** [***have***] ***the*** ~ ***on*** 〔美俚〕胜过,赛过,占…的上风。***the Battle of the B-*** 第二次大战中德军的最后攻势。**II** ***vi***. **1**. 膨胀,鼓起,凸出;装满 (*with*). **2**. 上涨,急增。**3**. 船底破漏。*His stomach* ~*d after the dinner*. 他吃过饭以后,肚子都鼓起来了。*The box* ~*d with cookies*. 盒子里装满了甜饼。*bulging eyes* 凸眼。— ***vt***. 使膨胀,使鼓起,使凸出。*columns* ~*d a bit in the center* 中间被弄得有点鼓肚子的圆柱。

bulg·er [ˈbʌldʒə; ˋbʌldʒɚ] ***n***. **1**. 凸面高尔夫球棒。**2**. 〔美〕巨物。

bulg·y [ˈbʌldʒi; ˋbʌldʒɪ] ***a***. 膨胀的,凸出的。

bu·lim·i·a [bjuːˈlimjə; bjʊˋlɪmɪə], **bu·li·my** [ˈbjuːlimi; ˋbjulɪmɪ] ***n***. **1**.【医】易饥症,食欲过盛。**2**. 贪欲。

bulk [bʌlk; bʌlk] **I** ***n***. **1**. 体积,容积,大小。**2**. 巨大;庞然大物;大块;大批,大量。**3**. 货舱;船货;散装货物。**4**. 〔the ~〕,大半,大部分,大多数;主体。**5**.【物】胀量;松密度。**6**. 〔书〕身体;胖人,大块头;〔诗〕巨人,巨兽。*a ship of great* ~ 体积庞大的船。*The* ~ *of it!* 这东西真大! *The* ~ *of the debt was paid*. 大部分的债都还清了。*He lifted his huge* ~ *from the chair*. 他那庞大的身躯从椅子上站起来。~ *analysis*【化】总分析。~ *cargo* 散装货。***break*** ~ 下货,卸货。***by*** ~ 估堆,按堆(计算等)。***in*** ~ **1**. 不加包装,散装。**2**. 大批,大量(*load in* ~ 散装入船,散运。*sell in* ~ 原舱出售所装运的货,整批出售)。**II** ***vi***. **1**. 显得庞大;看上去重要。**2**. 增大,膨胀,胀大;堆积起来;形成大块;扩展;(重要性等)增加。**3**.(身体)发福。*The problem* ~*s large in his mind*. 这个问题在他心目中显得很重要。— ***vt***. **1**. 使膨胀;使增大。**2**. 堆积(鱼等)。**3**. 用眼力估计,毛估(重量、容量等)。~ ***large*** [***small***] ***in one's eyes*** [***minds***] 在某人眼[心目]中显得巨大[很小]。~ ***up*** **1**. 胀大。**2**. 形成大数目。~**-cheap** ***a***. 薄利多销的。~ **density** 松密度。~**-grade** (羊毛等的)大致等级。~ **head**【船】舱壁;【空】隔板;【矿】(坑内的)分壁;【建】挡土墙;堤岸;(通地下室的)盖板门。~ **modulus**【物】体积弹性率。~ **piling** 散(装容)积。~ **selection** 混合选择。

bulk·y [ˈbʌlki; ˋbʌlkɪ] ***a***. 庞大的,笨重的,体积大的。*a* ~ *book* 一本大厚书。*a* ~ *cargo* 体积庞大的货物。~ **yarn** 膨体纱。**bulk·i·ness** ***n***.

bull[1] [bul; bʊl] **I** ***n***. **1**. 公牛;雄象,雄鲸;雄性大动物。**2**. 躯体庞大的人,粗壮的人;〔美俚〕工头;农场监工;〔美俚〕火车头。**3**. 〔B-〕= John Bull;【天】金牛宫,金牛座。**4**. (股票投机中的)买方,多头 (*opp*. *bear*). **5**. 〔美俚〕警察;侦探。**6**. 瞎话,大话。**7**. 〔英俚〕(旧制)五先令银币。*an elephant* ~ 雄象。*He had a mother's soul in a body of* ~ 他身体粗壮而心地善良。***a china-shop*** ~ 动辄闯祸的粗人,瓷器店里的大象。~ ***in the ring*** (小孩子玩的)突围游戏。***like a*** ~ ***at a*** (***five-barred***) ***gate*** 狂怒地,猛烈地,凶猛地。***milk the*** ~ 做徒劳无功的事,想从公牛身上挤奶。***take the*** ~ ***by the horns*** 挺身面对危险,毅然处理难局;(斗牛士)敢抓公牛角。***throw*** [***shoot***] ***the*** ~ 吹牛,胡说八道。**II** ***a***. **1**. 雄的,公的;公牛一样的。**2**.【商】买方的,哄台证券价格的。~ *movement* (股票投机中)哄抬行情的活动,买方[多方]的策动。*a* ~ *head* [*neck*; *voice*] 公牛一样的头[颈,嗓音]。*a* ~ *whale* 公鲸。**III** ***vi***. **1**. 哄抬证券价格,做多头,做买方。**2**. 〔美俚〕排除困难前进,奋力前行。**3**. 〔美俚〕夸口,吹牛,自大,说空话。**4**. 〔俚〕配种,交尾。~ *through the crowd* 从人群中挤过去。— ***vt***. **1**. 哄抬(证券等的行情)。**2**. 强行通过(议案等),挤出(路等)。**3**.【海】(以船首)猛撞。~ *stocks* 哄抬股票行情。~ *a bill through congress* 在议会中强行通过一项议案。~ *one's way through the crowd* 从人群中挤出一条路。~ **baiting** 以狗逗牛戏〔现已废止〕。~ **bar**〔美口〕(汽车的)保险杠。~**bat**【动】蚊母鸟。~**boat** 牛皮浅水船。~ **calf** 小公牛;笨蛋。~**dog** **1**. 恶犬,斗犬,硬汉;〔学俚〕学监的随从;〔俚〕手枪,大炮;〔美〕晚报的第一版〔午前出版〕,晨报的第一版〔上半夜出版〕,〔美〕纸牌的老 K. **2**. ***a***. 勇猛的。**3**. ***vt***. 〔美西部〕抓住双角摔倒(小公牛)。~ **fiddle**. 〔美口〕低音提琴 (= **double bass**). ~**-fight** 斗牛。~**-fighter** 斗牛士。~**-finch** **1**.【鸟】红腹灰雀。**2**. (旁边有沟的)树篱。~**-frog** **1**.【动】牛蛙。**2**. 〔美俚〕声音低沉的电影演员。~**head** **1**.【鱼】大头鱼〔尤指杜父鱼、美洲鮰鱼〕。**2**. 小圆头。**3**. 〔美俚〕顽固的人,倔强的人。~**-hide** 厚灯芯布。~**horn** **1**. 手提式电子扩音机。**2**. 〔美俚〕大号(= tuba). ~ **market** 〔商〕上涨行情。~**necked** ***a***. 头颈粗短的。~**nose**【建】外圆角。~**pen** **1**. 牛栏。**2**. (候审犯人的)大拘留室。**3**. (棒球场内的)接替投手赛前练习室。**4**.【棒球】救援投手。~**ring** **1**. 斗牛场。**2**. 〔美俚〕(监狱里的)犯人散步场,监狱的围墙。**3**. 〔美〕圆形露天[室内]运动场。~ **roarer** **1**. 牛吼器〔以铜锣等系上木片扔出的一种玩具〕。**2**. 大嗓门的演说者。~**-session** 〔美俚〕自由讨论。~**'s-eye** **1**. 靶心;【军】(射击取得的)十环。**2**.【海】(舷侧)圆窗;单眼木制滑车。**3**. 圆天窗;【气】风暴眼。**4**. 牛眼灯,凸透镜。**5**. 圆形硬糖。**6**. 〔美〕大怀表 (*make* [*score*] *the* ~*'s-eye* 打中靶心;取得大成功)。~**shit** 〔英俚〕胡说,废话。~ **shot** 掺汤鸡尾酒〔用杜松子酒或伏特加酒和肉汤制成〕。~**-shooter** 〔美俚〕吹牛大家。~ **tewier** 虎斑猛犬〔英国种〕。~ **tongue** (耕棉田用的)牛舌形犁片。~ **trout** 〔英〕鳟鱼。~**whack** **1**. ***n***. 〔美〕牛鞭。**2**. ***vt***., ***vi***. 用牛鞭鞭打。~**whacker**〔美〕赶牛人。~ **wheel** (齿轮组中的)大齿轮,牛轮。~**whip** 长牛鞭。~**'s wool** 〔口〕劣质粗呢。~**work** 牛马活,苦活。

bull[2] [bul; bʊl] ***n***. (罗马教皇的)训谕,训令。

bull[3] [bʌl; bʌl] ***n***. 滑稽的矛盾,可笑的错误(= Irish ~). ***make an Irish*** ~ 说荒唐可笑的话。

bull(s). = bulletin(s).

bul·la [ˈbʌlə, ˈbulə; ˋbʌlə, ˋbʊlə] *n*. (*pl*. **bul·lae** [ˈbuli:; ˋbʊli])〔L.〕1. 垂饰,印玺。2.【医】水疱。3. 气门片。

bul·lace [ˈbulis; ˋbʊlɪs] *n*.【植】紫野生李;野生李树。

bul·late [ˈbʌleit; ˋbʊlɪt] *a*. 1.【动,植】有疱的。2. 水疱状的。3.【解】隆起的,肿胀的。

bull·doze [ˈbuldəuz; ˋbʊl͵doz] *vt*. 1.〔美俚〕威胁,恐吓。2. 用推土机推平,用压路机压平;排除(障碍)。～ *a building site* 用推土机把一处建筑工地推平。～ *trees from a building site* 用推土机把建筑工地上的树推平。

bull·doz·er [ˈbuldəuzə; ˋbʊl͵dozɚ] *n*. 1.〔美俚〕威吓者。2. 推土机,压路机。

bull·er [ˈbulə; ˋbʊlɚ] *n*.〔口〕代理人[讼师,学监]的助手。

bul·let [ˈbulit; ˋbʊlɪt] *n*. 1. 子弹,弹头,弹丸;【矿】取心弹,射孔弹。2. (钓丝上的)铅锤;插塞;锥形体;【印】着重号〔加在文字下面表示强调的黑点〕;〔*pl*.〕〔美俚〕豆〔尤指炒豆〕;钱,【牌】手中的 A 牌。*a stray* ～ 流弹。***bite the*** ～ 忍辱负重,忍气吞声。***Every*** ～ ***has its billet***. 每颗子弹都有归宿,命中注定无法逃。***ride a*** ～(在民意测验中支持率)飙升。～ **alloy** 子弹合金(含铅 94%,锑 6%)。～ **bait**〔美俚〕无战斗经验的新兵;炮灰。～-**drawer** 子弹钳。～-**head** 圆头;圆头人;〔俚〕傻瓜。～-**headed** *a*. 1. 似子弹头的,圆头的。2. 愚笨的,执拗的。～**proof** *a*. 1. 防弹的 (*a* ～*proof jacket* 防弹衣。*It's* ～*proof*.〔口〕我的话保险不错)。～ **train** (日本的)高速火车。

bul·le·tin [ˈbulitin; ˋbʊlətɪn] **I** *n*. 1. 告示;公告,公报;(学术团体等定期出版的)会刊。2. (关于要人的)病情公报。3. 新闻简报。**II** *vt*. 告示,揭示,用公报发表。～ **board** 公告牌;【计】(电脑网络上的)公告版。

bul·lion [ˈbuljən; ˋbʊljən] *n*. 1. (造币用的)金[银]块;条金[银]。2. 纯金,纯银。3. 条形金属。4. 粗金属锭;粗铅。5. 金[银]丝缨缝[花边]。*lead* ～ 铅锭。*copper* ～ 粗铜锭。*gold* ～ *standard* (货币的)金本位制。-**ism** *n*. 硬币主义。-**ist** *n*. 硬币论者。

bull·ish [ˈbuliʃ; ˋbʊlɪʃ] *a*. 1. 公牛一样的。2. 顽固的;愚蠢的。3.【商】股票行情看涨的;做多头的;〔喻〕乐观的。*a* ～ *market* 看涨的行情。-**ly** *ad*. -**ness** *n*.

bull·ock [ˈbulək; ˋbʊlək] **I** *n*. 1. (四岁以上的)小公牛。2. 阉牛。**II** *vi*. 像小公牛一样乱闯。～ ***one's ways*** 乱闯乱撞,横冲直撞。～**cart** 牛车。-**y** *a*. 小公牛似的。

bul·ly[1] [ˈbuli; ˋbʊlɪ] **I** *n*. 1. 暴徒;欺侮弱者的人;(学校中)以大欺小的学生;〔古〕打手。2. (足球等的)争球。3.〔古〕妓女的保镖,妓院的拉客者。4.〔古〕情人;好朋友;好家伙。***come the*** ～ ***over sb***. 对…盛气凌人。***play the*** ～ 欺侮人,以强凌弱。**II** *a*.〔美口〕1. 第一流的,顶好的。2. 快活的。3. 恶霸一样的,盛气凌人的。*feel* ～ 心情很好。**III** *int*. 好,妙(= bravo)。***B- for you***! 好极了,妙极了! **IV** *vi*. 盛气凌人,以强凌弱。— *vt*. 威吓;欺侮,欺负。～ ***sb***. ***into*** [***out of***] 恐吓某人使做[使停止做]某事 (～*sb*. *into working* 恐吓某人使他干活。*He bullied her into a car*. 他把她威逼进汽车)。～ **boy** 摆臭架子的恶棍;职业流氓。-**able** *a*. 可威吓的。

bul·ly[2] [ˈbuli; ˋbʊlɪ] *n*. 罐头牛肉(= ～ beef)。

bul·ly·rag [ˈbuliræg; ˋbʊlɪ͵ræg] *v*. = ballyrag.

bul·rush [ˈbulrʌʃ; ˋbʊl͵rʌʃ] *n*.【植】1. 藨草属植物。2.〔英〕宽叶香蒲;水烛。3. (《圣经》《旧约》中经常提及的)纸莎草。4. (美洲)灯心草。

bul·wark [ˈbulwə(:)k; ˋbʊlwɚk] **I** *n*. 1. 露天掩体;堡垒;寨,堡坞。2. 防波堤。3. 防御物,屏障,保障。4.〔*pl*.〕【船】舷墙。*The new dam was a* ～ *against future floods*. 新堤坝是抵御未来洪水的屏障。*the* ～*s of the State* 国之干城。**II** *vt*. 1. 用堡垒防护。2. 防御,保护。

Bul·wer [ˈbulwə; ˋbʊlwɚ] *n*. 布尔沃〔姓氏〕。

bum[1] [bʌm; bʌm] *n*.〔俚〕屁股。～-**sucker**〔英俚〕谄媚者,马屁精。

bum[2] [bʌm; bʌm] **I** *n*.〔美俚〕1. (无业)游民;懒鬼;酒鬼,酒徒。2. 寄食者;蹩脚运动员[工作者];(沉湎于体育运动、娱乐等而不顾家庭和前途的)玩角。3. 闹饮;放荡。*I called the umpire a* ～. 我认为裁判是个不中用的家伙。*ski* ～*s* 忘掉一切的滑雪迷。～***'s comforter*** 报纸。～***s on the plush*** 有钱的懒汉,富裕的玩角。～***'s rush*** 强制驱逐出境;粗暴打发走。***go on the*** ～ 过流浪生活。***on a*** ～〔俚〕正在闹饮。***on the*** ～〔美〕1. 过流浪生活。2. 游手好闲。3.〔口〕有毛病,失修 (*The oven is on the* ～ *again*. 炉子又有毛病了)。**II** *a*. 1. 质量低劣的,无价值的。2. 可怜的,不中用的。3. 瘦弱的,残废的。4. 假的,谬误的。～ *advice* 错误的劝告。*a* ～ *trip* 不愉快的旅行。*a* ～ *knee* 残废了的膝盖。*a* ～ *hunch*〔美俚〕错误的念头,错误的想像。*a* ～ *rap*〔美俚〕虚构的罪名。*a* ～ *steer*〔美俚〕假报告;有害的劝告,错误的情报。**III** *vi*. (-*mm*-)〔美口〕1. 流浪。2. 做懒汉闲吃,寄食。3. 闹饮。— *vt*. 乞讨,乞求。*He's always* ～*ming cigarettes from me*. 他经常向我讨烟抽。～**boat** 1. (向港内或岸边大船兜售杂货等的)小卖艇。2. 垃圾船。～(-)**bag**〔英〕腰带包。

bum·bail·iff [bʌmˈbeilif; bʌmˋbelɪf] *n*.〔英蔑〕(地方上的)小执行吏。

bum·ber·shoot [ˈbʌmbəʃu:t; ˋbʌmbɚʃut] *n*.〔美俚〕伞。

bum·ble[1] [ˈbʌmbl; ˋbʌmbl̩] *n*.〔英〕骄横的小官吏〔出自狄更斯小说《块肉余生记》(大卫·科波菲尔 中的一教区小吏)〕。-**dom** *n*. 妄自尊大,小官吏习性。-**bling** *a*. 官气十足的,妄自尊大的。

bum·ble[2] [ˈbʌmbl; ˋbʌmbl̩] *vi*. 1. 嗡嗡叫;营营响。2. 结结巴巴地讲话。3. 笨拙地[错乱地]行动;踉跄地前进。*He somehow* ～*d through two years of college*. 他胡乱地混过了两年大学生活。— *vt*. 弄糟,拙劣地做。-**bling** 1. *a*. 经常出差错的,不称职的。2. *n*. 无能,失职。

bum·ble·bee [ˈbʌmblbi:; ˋbʌmbl̩͵bi] *n*.【动】大黄蜂,土蜂,野蜂。

bum·ble·foot [ˈbʌmblfut; ˋbʌmbl̩͵fʊt] *n*.【兽医】(家畜因扭伤或细菌感染造成的)肿蹄。

bum·bo [ˈbʌmbəu; ˋbʌmbo] *n*. 香甜酒。

bumf [bʌmf; bʌmf] *n*. 1.〔英俚〕便纸,草纸。2.〔贬〕文件,公文。3. 撒纸赛跑。

bum·kin [ˈbʌmkin; ˋbʌmkɪn] *n*.〔贬〕乡下佬 (= bumpkin)。

bum·mer [ˈbʌmə; ˋbʌmɚ] *n*.〔美俚〕1. 懒汉,游手好闲的人。2. 失败;令人失望的事[人]。3. (吸毒后)严重不愉快的幻觉。～ **beat**〔美俚〕灾难性事件跟踪报道。

bump[1] [bʌmp; bʌmp] **I** *vi*. 1. 碰,撞,冲撞 (*against*; *into*)。2. (笨重车子在坏路上)嘎噔嘎噔地走,颠簸 (*along*)。～ *against a wall* 撞到墙上。*The old car* ～*ed along the road*. 那部老爷车在路上颠簸着行驶。—*vt*. 1. 撞,打肿,撞伤(头等);【赛船】追撞。2. 取消(旅行计划等);(依仗权势)排挤掉;解雇;否决。3. 哄抬(物价等)。4.〔美俚〕杀死,谋杀。*The cat* ～*ed the vase off the shelf*. 猫把花瓶从架上撞下来。*His car* ～*ed a truck*. 他的小汽车撞到了一辆货车上。*He* ～*ed the price of corn*. 他哄抬谷价。*The senator was* ～*ed by the voters*. 那位参议员被选民抛弃了。～ **into**〔口〕偶然碰见。～ **off** 1. 猛然推开,撞开。2.〔美俚〕干掉,杀死,谋杀。**II** *n*. 1. 碰撞,撞击,扑通一声。2. 肿;瘤;(骨相家所说的)头骨隆起;(骨相家认为因头骨隆起而显示的)才能;〔口〕能力。3.【赛船】撞声,追撞。4. (车的)颠簸;【空】突变的气流,(气流突变造成的)突降,簸动。5.〔美俚〕降职。*fall with a* ～ 扑通一声跌倒。～ ***on a log***〔美〕麻烦的同伴。***have no*** ～ ***of locality*** 记不牢地点,不熟习地理。**III** *ad*. 1. 突然地,猛烈地。2. 扑通一声。*come* ～ *on the floor* 扑通一声跌倒在地板上。

B

bump[2][bʌmp; bʌmp] **I** ***n*.** 鹭鸶的叫声。**II** ***vi*.** 作鹭鸶叫。

bump·er[1][ˈbʌmpə; ˋbʌmpɚ] ***n*.** **1.** 冲撞物;防撞器,缓冲器,减震器。**2.**(汽车后部的)保险杠。~ ***to*** ~(汽车)拥塞,挤撞(~ *to* ~ *traffic* 汽车一辆接一辆的交通挤拥)。~ **sticker**, ~ **strip** 汽车保险杠的招贴。

bump·er[2][ˈbʌmpə; ˋbʌmpɚ] **I** ***n*.** **1.**(干杯时的)满杯。**2.**〔俚〕丰收;(剧场等的)满场,满座。**3.**〔口〕同类中的特大者,巨物。~ ***book*** 内容空洞的大厚书。~ ***crowd***〔美〕满场观众。**II** ***a*.** 丰富的;丰收的。*a* ~ *audience* 满座。~ *crops* 大丰收。**III** ***vt*.** **1.** 把(酒杯)斟满。**2.** 撞(杯)。— ***vi*.** 干杯。

bump·ing-race [ˈbʌmpiŋreis; ˋbʌmpɪŋres] ***n*.** 追撞船赛。

bump·kin [ˈbʌm*p*kin; ˋbʌm*p*kɪn] ***n*.**〔贬〕粗人,乡下佬。**-ly** ***a*.**

bump·supper [ˈbʌm*p*ˈsʌpə; ˋbʌmpˋsʌpɚ] ***n*.** 追撞船赛祝捷晚餐会。

bump·tious [ˈbʌm*p*ʃəs; ˋbʌm*p*ʃəs] ***a*.**〔口〕傲慢的,狂妄的,唐突的。*be* ~ *over one's inferiors* 对下级态度傲慢。

bump·y [ˈbʌmpi; ˋbʌmpɪ] ***a*.** **1.**(路等)崎岖不平的。**2.**(车等)颠簸的。**3.**【空】气流变换不定的。*a* ~ *sidewalk* 崎岖不平的人行道。*have a* ~ *ride* 车子颠簸行驶。**-i·ly** ***ad*.**

bun[1][bʌn; bʌn] ***n*.** **1.** 葡萄干甜面包,小圆面包。**2.** 头;(小圆面包状的)圆髻。*She had her fair hair done up in a* ~. 她把自己漂亮的头发做成了个圆髻。***take the*** ~〔俚〕得头名;占第一位;获胜;登峰造极。~**-fight** 茶会。

bun[2][bʌn; bʌn] ***n*.**〔美俚〕**1.** 烂醉,酩酊大醉。**2.** 酒宴,闹饮。***have***[***get***] ***a*** ~ ***on***〔美俚〕喝醉。

bun[3][bʌn; bʌn] ***n*.** **1.**〔英方〕尾巴〔尤指兔尾〕。**2.**〔英〕(童话中的)兔先生,〔美〕(童话中的)松鼠先生。

Bu·na, bu·na [ˈbjuːnə; ˋbjunə] ***n*.**【化】(德国制)布纳(橡胶),丁(二烯)钠(聚)橡胶。~**-N** 丁腈橡胶。~**-S** 丁苯橡胶。

bunch [bʌntʃ; bʌntʃ] **I** ***n*.** **1.** 球,束,朵,串。**2.** 瘤;隆起,突起;【矿】小矿巢;【物】(电子)聚束。**3.**〔美俚〕一群,一帮;一团;牛群,马群;伙伴;一群好友。**4.** 亚麻纱小包〔每包 $1\frac{1}{2}$-12 绞〕;亚麻纱长度单位〔= 180,000 码〕。*a* ~ *of bananas* 一串香蕉。*a* ~ *of paper* 一束纸。*a* ~ *of cattle* 一群牛。*The whole* ~ *of thieves was arrested*. 一伙窃贼全部被捕。*an ore* ~ 矿巢,矿囊。~ ***of calico***〔美俚〕女人。~ ***of fives***〔俚〕拳头,手。***the best***[***pick***] ***of the*** ~ 精华,出类拔萃的人[物]。(*In our party he is the best of the* ~. 在我们这群人当中他是尖子。**II** ***vi*.** **1.** 捆成一束;穿成一串;(人)集拢。**2.** 起褶。**3.** 隆起。— ***vt*.** **1.** 使成束[串];集拢。**2.** 使起褶。~ *straw into sheaves* 把稻草打成把。~ **backed** ***a*.** 驼背的。~ **berry**【植】御缮橘。~ **flower**【植】墨花。~**-grass**(美国西部)簇生草,疏丛性牧草。~ **planting**【农艺】丛播,穴播。**-er** ***n*.**【无】(电子)聚束栅,群像器。

Bunch(e) [bʌntʃ; bʌntʃ] ***n*.** 本奇〔姓氏〕。

bunch·y [ˈbʌntʃi; ˋbʌntʃɪ] ***a*.** **1.** 成束的,成球的。**2.** 隆起的。*a round* ~ *face* 胖圆脸。~ **top**【植】簇顶病。~ **yarn** 竹节纱。

bun·co [ˈbʌŋkəu; ˋbʌŋko] **I** ***n*.**〔美俚〕(赌博中的)骗局。**II** ***vt*.** 骗,骗取。~ **game** 行骗的赌局。~ **man**, ~ **steerer**〔美俚〕骗子,(赌博的)囮子。

bun·combe [ˈbʌŋkəm; ˋbʌŋkəm] ***n*.**〔口〕讨好(选民)的演说;空话,废话。*talk*[*speak*] *for*[*to*] ~ 作讨好选民的演说。

Bund [bʌnd, G. bʌnt; bʌnd, G. bʌnt] ***n*.**(*pl*. ***Bünde*** [ˈbʌndə; ˋbʌndə])〔G.〕**1.**(政治上的)同盟,联盟。**2.**(美国三十年代的亲纳粹的)德美协会。**-ist** ***n*.**(美国三十年代的)亲纳粹派。

bund [bʌnd; bʌnd] ***n*.**(印度、日本、中国等的)堤岸,江[海]边大道;码头。

Bun·des·tag [ˈbundəstɑːk; ˋbʊndəsˏtɑk] ***n*.**(德国)联邦议院[下院]。

bun·dle [ˈbʌndl; ˋbʌndl] **I** ***n*.** **1.** 包袱,包裹。**2.** 包,捆,扎,束,卷,把,丛。**3.**【植】维管束;【生】(神经等的)纤维束。**4.**〔俚〕一大笔钱,一大堆(东西);(人等的)群,组。**5.**【纺】〔Ir.〕亚麻纱单位〔每 6000 码重 10 磅〕。*a* ~ *of clothes* 一包衣服。*a* ~ *of personal belongings* 行李卷。*a* ~ *of sticks* 一捆棍棒。*a* ~ *of rascals* 一群坏蛋。*a* ~ *of problems* 一大堆问题。***a*** ~ ***of nerves*** 动辄就紧张不安的神经过敏者。***make one's*** ~〔美俚〕挣一大笔钱。**II** ***vt*.** **1.** 包,捆,扎(*up*)。**2.** 把…乱七八糟地扔进[塞进](*in*, *into*);把…匆匆忙忙打发走。(*away*, *off*, *out*). **3.**〔美俚〕偷。**4.**【计】捆绑销售。*Microsoft is persuading PC makers to* ~ *its Internet browser software with every copy of Windows*. 微软公司正在说服个人电脑生产厂家把因特网浏览器软件和每个视窗版本捆绑销售。~ ***oneself up***(用…)把自己身体裹住,穿暖和些(~ *oneself up in blanket* 用毯子裹住身体)。~(***sb*.**) ***out***[***off***, ***away***] 把(某人)匆忙赶出,毫不留情地撵出。— ***vi*.** **1.** 急急忙忙收拾行李。**2.** 匆忙离去(*off*, *out*, *away*)。**3.** 和衣而睡。~ *clothes into a drawer* 把衣服乱七八糟塞进抽屉里。*They indignantly* ~*d out of the meeting*. 他们急匆匆地愤然离开会场。~ ***in*** 蜂拥而来。~ ***out***[***off***, ***away***] 仓皇离开。***B- out of this place***! 从这里走开! 快走开! ~ **handkerchiefs**〔英国〕深蓝格子手帕。

bung[1][bʌŋ; bʌŋ] **I** ***n*.** **1.**(桶口、瓶口等的)塞子。**2.** 桶口,桶孔。**3.** 家畜的盲肠[肛门]。**4.**〔俚〕撒谎,骗人的话。**II** ***vt*.** **1.**(用塞子)塞住(桶孔等)。**2.**〔俚〕扔(石子等)。**3.** 使膨胀。~ ***off***〔俚〕逃跑。~ ***up***〔美俚〕**1.** 打伤,把…打肿[打成青紫]。**2.** 使(鼻等)阻塞;塞满。**3.** 打破,撞破(*eyes* ~*ed up from fighting* 在斗殴中眼睛被打肿了。*My car was* ~*ed up from the accident*. 我的车子出事撞坏了)。**-hole** 桶孔,桶口。

bung[2][bʌŋ; bʌŋ] ***n*.**〔美俚〕**1.**(机器等的)故障,损坏。**2.** 破产。**3.** 死。***go*** ~〔美俚〕失败;破产;死(*Many firms went* ~ *in the panic*. 许多商号在这场经济恐慌中破产了)。

bun·ga·loid [ˈbʌŋgəlɔid; ˋbʌŋgəˏlɔɪd] ***a*.** 平房式的〔多带贬意〕。

bun·ga·low [ˈbʌŋgələu; ˋbʌŋgəˏlo] ***n*.** 有凉台的平房,平房。

bun·gee [ˈbʌndʒiː; ˋbʌndʒi] ***n*.** **1.** 橡皮筋,松紧绳,弹性束。**2.**【空】过度操纵防止器。~ **jumping**【体】绷极跳〔身拴橡皮绳从高处跳下的一种娱乐性体育运动〕。

bun·gle [ˈbʌŋgl; ˋbʌŋgl̩] **I** ***vt*.** **1.** 粗糙草率地修补;粗制滥造。**2.** 搞坏(事情等),做坏(工作等)。~ *the job* 工作搞得一塌糊涂。— ***vi*.** 拙劣地工作。*He is a fool who* ~*s consistently*. 他是一个总把活儿做得很糟的傻瓜。**II** ***n*.** 粗制滥造,笨拙。*make a* ~ *of* 把…搞得一塌糊涂。**-r** ***n*.** 手艺笨拙的人,把工作做坏的人。

bun·ion [ˈbʌnjən; ˋbʌnjən] ***n*.**【医】拇趾囊肿胀。

bunk[1][bʌŋk; bʌŋk] **I** ***n*.** **1.**(火车等椅床两用的)床铺,铺位,卧铺。**2.**〔口〕床,卧处。**3.** 牲口食槽;木材搬运车。**II** ***vi*.**〔口〕**1.** 睡(在床铺上),去睡。**2.** 与人同床睡(*with*). ~ *in the attic* 睡在阁楼上。*I* ~*ed with him*. 我和他同睡一张床。~ **bed** 双层床。~**mate** 住上下铺或邻铺的伙伴。

bunk[2][bʌŋk; bʌŋk] ***n*.**〔美俚〕**1.** 骗人的话,废话。**2.** 讨好选民的演说。

bunk[3][bʌŋk; bʌŋk] **I** ***vt*.**〔英俚〕从…缺席。~ *a history class* 上历史课时缺席。— ***vi*.** 逃走,避开。~ ***it***〔英俚〕逃掉,逃课。**II** ***n*.** 逃走〔仅用于 do a ~ 习语中〕。***do a*** ~ 逃走,走开。

bunk·er [ˈbʌŋkə; ˋbʌŋkɚ] **I** ***n.*** **1.** (兼充坐椅的)箱子,煤柜,(船上的)煤库;燃料仓;贮槽。**2.** (进料用的)漏斗,煤斗,料斗。**3.** 浅沟;障碍;【军】掩蔽壕,地堡;防护围墙;【高尔夫球】障碍洞。**4.** 〔美俚〕同房囚犯,同房间的人,战友。*a coal* ~ 煤箱,煤库。*a storage* ~ 贮藏箱,贮藏室。**II** ***vt.*** **1.** 把(煤等)堆入仓内。**2.** 【高尔夫球】把(球)打入洼洞内;〔喻〕使遇到障碍;使陷入困境。*a vessel full* ~*ed* 上满煤仓的船。~ **coal** 船用煤。~ **capacity** (船的)载煤力。~**-fatigue** 〔美俚〕**1.** 午睡。**2.** 病卧。

Bunk·er [ˈbʌŋkə; ˋbʌŋkɚ] ***n.*** 邦克〔姓氏〕。

bunk·house [ˈbʌŋkhaus; ˋbʌŋk͵haʊs] ***n.*** (建筑工等的)简易工棚;(矿工等的)简易住屋。

bun·ko [ˈbʌŋkəu; ˋbʌŋko] ***n.*** = bunco.

bun·kum [ˈbʌŋkəm; ˋbʌŋkəm] ***n.*** = buncombe.

bun·ny [ˈbʌni; ˋbʌnɪ] ***n.*** **1.** 〔口〕小兔子〔儿童对兔子的爱称〕。**2.** 〔美俚〕可爱的女郎。~ **(girl)** 衣着象征兔子的夜总会女招待。~ **hug** 一种美国交际舞。

Bun·sen [ˈbʌnsn; ˋbʌnsn̩], **R. W.** 本生,〔1811—1899,德国化学家〕。~ **burner** 本生灯〔一种煤气灯〕。

bunt[1] [bʌnt; bʌnt] **I** ***n.*** **1.** 抵,撞。**2.** 【棒球】短打;以短打打出的球。**II** ***vi.***, ***vt.*** **1.** (以头、角等)抵,撞。**2.** 【棒球】用短打打出(球)。~ *a curve* 用短打打出一个曲线球。

bunt[2] [bʌnt; bʌnt] **I** ***n.*** **1.** 【海】(帆等的)中央鼓起部分。**2.** (鱼网的)网身。**II** ***vi.*** (帆等)膨胀,鼓起。

bunt[3] [bʌnt; bʌnt] ***n.*** 【植】(小麦的)腥黑穗病;腥黑穗病病菌。

bun·ting[1] [ˈbʌntiŋ; ˋbʌntɪŋ] ***n.*** 【鸟】白颊鸟,黄胸鹀。

bun·ting[2] [ˈbʌntiŋ; ˋbʌntɪŋ] ***n.*** **1.** 旗布;幔幕。**2.** 信号旗;船旗;(节日装饰街、屋等的)彩旗〔美多用 *pl.* ~***s*** 〕. ~ **tosser** 〔军俚〕信号兵。

bunt·line [ˈbʌntlin, -ˌlain; ˋbʌntlɪn, -͵lain] ***n.*** 【海】帆脚索,篷缆。

bun·ya-bun·ya [ˈbʌnjəˌbʌnjə; ͵bʌnjəˋbʌnjə] ***n.*** 【植】披针叶南美杉。

Bun·yan [ˈbʌnjən; ˋbʌnjən] ***n.*** 巴尼安〔姓氏〕。**John** ~ 约翰·班扬〔1628—1688,英国著名宗教讽喻小说《天路历程》(Pilgrim's Progress) 的作者〕。

bun·yan [ˈbʌnjən; ˋbʌnjən] ***n.*** = bunion.

Bu. Ord. = Bureau of Ordnance【美】军器司。

bu·oy [bɔi; bɔɪ] **I** ***n.*** **1.** 浮标,浮子。**2.** 浮圈,救生圈。*an anchor* ~ 锚浮标。*a mooring* ~ 系船浮标。*a light* ~ 灯浮标。*a can* [*nun*] ~ 罐[锥]形浮标。**II** ***vt.*** **1.** 使浮起(*up*);〔喻〕支持,鼓励。**2.** 用浮标指示(礁、水道等)(*out*). *The life jacket* ~*ed her up until help arrived.* 救生衣使她浮在水上直到获救。*Hopes* ~*ed her up.* 希望在支撑着她。~ *a channel* 用浮标标出航道。—***vi.*** 浮,浮上。~ **boat** 拖住已捕获的鲸鱼的小船。

bu·oy·age [ˈbɔiidʒ; ˋbɔɪɪdʒ] ***n.*** **1.** 〔集合词〕浮标;浮标装置。**2.** (系船)浮标使用费。

buoy·ance [ˈbɔiəns; ˋbɔɪəns], **buoy·an·cy** [ˈbɔiənsi; ˋbɔɪənsɪ] ***n.*** **1.** 浮力;浮性。**2.** 活泼,轻快;开朗。**3.** 【商】涨风,上涨行情;(国家岁入的)增长趋势。*net* [*gross, reserve*] ~ 净[总,后备]浮力。*a* ~ *gauge* 浮力计。*the centre of* ~【物】浮力中心,浮心。

buoy·ant [ˈbɔiənt; ˋbɔiənt] ***a.*** **1.** 有浮力的,易浮的,会浮的。**2.** 轻快的;活泼的;开朗的;使人振奋的。**3.** (价格等)上涨的;(国家岁入等)趋向增长的。~ *matters* 浮体。~ *force* 浮力。*a* ~ *mine* 漂浮的水雷。~ *spirits* 活泼开朗。~ *steps* 轻快的步伐。~ *news for the depressed* 使意气消沉者振作起来的消息。

BUP = British United Press 英国合众社。

bup·leu·rum [bjuːˈplurəm; bjuˋplʊrəm] ***n.*** 【植】柴胡属。

bup·pie [ˈbʌpi; ˋbʌpɪ] *n.* 黑人雅皮士〔指地位上升的黑人专业人士〕。

bu·pres·tid [bjuːˈprestid; bjuˋprɛstɪd] ***n.*** 【动】吉丁虫科昆虫。

bur [bəː; bɝ] ***n.*** **1.** 栗刺,芒刺;草籽;带刺草屑。**2.** 【植】(栗、苍耳、牛蒡等)刺果植物;刺球状花序。**3.** 黏附物,钩着物;难以摆脱的人,吃闲饭的人,寄生虫(指人)。**4.** 【机】(铸件等的)毛口,毛头(= burr). ***a*** ~ ***in the throat*** 梗在喉咙里的东西,骨梗在喉。***stick like a*** ~ 如刺黏衣,难以摆脱。

bu·ran [buˈrɑːn; bʊˋrɑn] ***n.*** 【气】大风雪;风搅雪,布拉风。

Bur·bage [ˈbəːbidʒ; ˋbɝbɪdʒ] ***n.*** 伯比奇〔姓氏〕。

Bur·bank [ˈbəːbæŋk; ˋbɝbæŋk] ***n.*** 伯班克〔姓氏〕。

Bur·ber·ry [ˈbəːbəri; ˋbɝ͵bɛrɪ] ***n.*** 【商品名】柏帛丽大衣呢;柏帛丽防水布;柏帛丽雨衣。

bur·ble [ˈbəːbl; ˋbɝbl̩] **I** ***vi.*** **1.** (水等)发出潺潺声;【空】起气泡;产生涡流。**2.** 嘟嘟囔囔地说话;暗笑;暗暗地生气。*a burbling brook* 水声潺潺的溪流。**II** ***n.*** **1.** 空谈。**2.** 【空】气流分离;旋涡。~ **point**【空】临界角。**bur·bly** ***a.***

bur·bot [ˈbəːbət; ˋbɝbət] ***n.*** 【鱼】江鳕。

burd [bəːd; bɝd] ***n.*** 〔Scot.〕女士;少女,处女。

bur·den[1] [ˈbəːdn; ˋbɝdn] **I** ***n.*** **1.** 担子,驮子;负荷,装载量,载重吨数。**2.** 负担,包袱,重累。**3.** 责任,义务。*a beast of* ~ 驮兽。*a ship of* ~ 货船。*carry a* ~ *on one's back* 负重。*financial* ~ 财政上的负担。*the* ~ *of leadership* 领导者的重任。*a ship of a hundred tons* ~ 载重 100 吨的船。*Life has become a* ~ *to him.* 生活对他来说已经成了负担。*shoulder the* ~ *of responsibilities* 担起责任。***bear the*** ~ ***and heat of the day*** 吃苦耐劳;完成责任。***lay down life's*** ~ 〔婉〕死。(***the***) ~ ***of proof***【法】举证责任。**II** ***vt.*** **1.** 使负重担;使烦恼,劳累(*with*). **2.** 向(车、船等)上装货。~ *a horse with a load* 让马驮东西。~ *the people with heavy taxes* 使百姓承担沉重的赋税。*a ship heavily* ~*ed* 装满货的船。**-ed** ***a.*** **1.** 负荷的。**2.** 有负担的,负担沉重的。**3.** (两船相遇时)有义务让路的。

bur·den[2] [ˈbəːdn; ˋbɝdn̩] ***n.*** **1.** 歌曲末尾的迭句〔重唱句〕。**2.** 〔古〕(舞蹈的)伴唱。**3.** (诗歌、发言等的)重点,要点,主旨。*the* ~ *of argument* 论点的要旨。***like the*** ~ ***of a song*** 反反复复。

bur·den·some [ˈbəːdnsəm; ˋbɝdnsəm] ***a.*** **1.** 沉重的,难于负担的;累赘的;令人烦恼的。**2.** 〔美〕有输送能力的,(船)容积巨大的。*a* ~ *task* 一项艰巨的任务。**-ly** ***a.*** **-ness** ***n.***

bur·dock [ˈbəːdɔk; ˋbɝ͵dɑk] ***n.*** 【植】牛蒡,牛蒡属植物。

bu·reau [bjuəˈrəu; ˈbjuərəu; ˋbjʊro, ˋbɪʊro] ***n.*** (*pl.* ~***s***, ***bureaux*** [bjuəˈrəuz; ˋbjʊroz])〔英〕**1.** (有抽屉的)办公桌,写字台;〔美〕梳妆台,有镜衣柜。**2.** 〔美〕(政府机构的)局(=〔英〕office);司(=〔英〕department);处,办公署。**3.** 编辑部,事务所,社,室。*an employment* ~ 职业介绍所。*a travel* ~ 旅行社;旅行事务代办所。*an information* ~〔美〕讯问处,传达室。*Information B-* [*B- of Information*] 新闻处。*Tourist B-* 旅游事业管理局。***the B- of the Mint*** (美国财政部的)造币局。***the B- of the Budget*** 〔美〕预算局。***the B- of Customs*** 〔美〕关税局。~**-*scarf*** 〔美〕梳妆台罩布。

bu·reauc·ra·cy [bjuəˈrɔkrəsi; bjʊˋrɑkrəsɪ] ***n.*** **1.** 官僚主义;官僚政治,官僚机构。**2.** 〔集合词〕官僚。

bu·reau·crat [ˈbjuərəukræt; ˋbjʊrə͵kræt] ***n.*** **1.** 官僚主义者;官僚派头的人。**2.** 官僚,官吏。*the* ~*s* 官僚。**-ic, -ical** ***a.*** 官僚政治的,官僚主义的;官僚派头的。**-ism** 官僚主义;官僚派头。**-ist** ***n.*** 官僚主义者。

bu·reau·cra·tese [ˌbjuərəkrəˈtiːz; ͵bjʊrəkrætˋiz] ***n.*** 官僚语言,官腔;公文体。

bu·reau·cra·tize [bjuˈrɔkrətaiz; bjʊˋrɑkrətaɪz] ***vt.***, ***vi.*** (使)变为官僚主义;(使)官僚化。**-cra·ti·za·tion** [bjuˌrɔkrətaiˈzeiʃən; bju͵rɑkrətaɪˋzeʃən] ***n.***

B

bu·reaux [bjuə'rəuz; bjʊə`roz] ***n.*** bureau 的复数。

bu·ret(te) [bjuə'ret; bjʊə`rɛt] ***n.***【化】玻璃量管，滴定管。

burg [bəːg; bɝg] ***n.* 1.**【史】(中世纪的)城堡。**2.**〔英〕有权选举议员的城镇(= borough)。**3.**〔美口〕城市，城镇。

-burg, -burgh *comb. f.* 城，市。

bur·gage ['bəːgidʒ; `bɝgɪdʒ] ***n.*** (英国封建时代的)租地法，租地权

bur·gee ['bəːdʒiː; `bɝdʒi] ***n.*** (船的)燕尾旗；三角旗。

bur·geon ['bəːdʒən; `bɝdʒən] **I** ***n.*** 嫩芽，蓓蕾。**II** ***vi.* 1.** 发芽。**2.** (突然)发展，急速成长。*Willows have ~ed forth.* 柳树已经发芽。*The town ~ed into a city.* 这个集镇很快发展成一座城市。

bur·ger ['bəːgə; `bɝgɚ] ***n.*** 汉堡包，肉饼三明治(= hamburger)。

-burger *comb. f.* 构成类似汉堡包的各种肉类或肉类代用品的三明治：*fish ~* 鱼饼三明治；nut ~ 碎果仁饼三明治。

bur·gess ['bəːdʒis; `bɝdʒɪs] ***n.* 1.** (英国自治市的)市民，有市民权的居民。**2.**【史】(自治市或大学选出的)议员；【美史】美国独立前的马里兰州和维吉尼亚州议员。

Bur·gess ['bəːdʒiz; `bɝdʒɪz] ***n.*** 伯吉斯〔姓氏〕。

burgh [bəːg; bɝg] ***n.*** [Scot.] 自治市。

burgh·er ['bəːgə; `bɝgɚ] ***n.*** (自治市的)市民。

Burgh·ley ['bəːli; `bɝlɪ] ***n.*** 伯利〔姓氏〕。

bur·glar ['bəːglə; `bɝglɚ] ***n.*** (夜间闯入室内的)夜盗，夜间窃贼。***a belly ~*** 〔美俚〕伙食采购员，膳务员。***a cat ~*** (从屋顶潜入室内的)飞贼。**~ alarm** 防盗警报器。**-i·ous** ***a.*** 夜盗的，犯夜盗罪的(*a ~ious entry* 夜间入室盗窃)。

bur·glar·ize ['bəːgləraiz; `bɝglə͵raɪz] ***vi.*** 〔美〕夜间盗窃，做夜盗。— ***vt.*** 夜间潜入(某处)盗窃。*Thieves ~d the warehouse.* 盗贼夜晚潜入仓库作案。

bur·gla·ry ['bəːgləri; `bɝglərɪ] ***n.*** 盗窃；夜盗罪。*commit [a] ~* 夜间入室盗窃；犯夜盗罪。

bur·gle ['bəːgl; `bɝgḷ] ***vt., vi.*** 〔美口〕= burglarize.

bur·go·mas·ter ['bəːgəu mɑːstə; `bɝgə͵mæstɚ] ***n.*** (荷兰等国的)市长。**-ship** ***n.***

bur·go·net ['bəːgənet; `bɝgo͵nɛt] ***n.***【史】带面具的头盔。

bur·goo [bəː'guː; `bɝgu] ***n.* 1.** 〔海俚〕燕麦牛奶粥。**2.** 〔美方〕菜肉浓汤。

bur·grave ['bəːgreiv; `bɝgrev] ***n.***【史】**1.** (中世纪的)城防统帅。**2.** (世袭的)守城官。

Bur·gun·dy, bur·gun·dy ['bəːgəndi; `bɝgəndɪ] **I** ***n.* 1.** 勃艮第〔法国东南部一地区〕。**2.** 〔b-〕勃艮第(地区出产的红[白]葡萄酒；仿勃艮第葡萄酒。**3.** 〔b-〕暗红色。**II** ***a.*** 〔b-〕暗红色的。

bur·i·al ['beriəl; `bɛrɪəl] ***n.* 1.** 埋葬，葬礼。**2.** 埋葬地，墓地。*a ~ at sea [on shore]* 海葬[陆葬]。**~ case** 〔美〕棺材。**~ ground, ~ place** 埋葬地，墓地。**~ service** 葬礼，葬仪。

Bur·i·at ['buːriæt; `buriæt] ***n.*** 布利亚特人〔贝加尔湖畔的蒙古人〕，布利亚特语。

bur·ied ['berid; `bɛrɪd] bury 的过去式及过去分词。

bur·i·er ['beriə; `bɛrɪɚ] ***n.* 1.** 殡葬者。**2.** 殡具。

bu·rin ['bjuərin; `bjʊrɪn] ***n.* 1.** 金属雕刻刀，錾刀。**2.** 雕刻风格。**3.** (史前人用的)刀状打火器。**-ist** ***n.*** (铜版)雕刻家。

burke [bəːk; bɝk] ***vt.* 1.** 〔古〕勒死(某人)以出卖尸体(供解剖用)。**2.** 秘密镇压[取消，禁止]；扣压(议案等)。**3.** 暗中消灭(争端等)。*The proposal got ~d.* 提案被扣压了。*~ an issue* 暗中解决争端。

Burk(e) [bəːk; bɝk] ***n.*** 伯克〔姓氏，男子名〕。

burl [bəːl; bɝl] **I** ***n.* 1.** (线、布等的)线头，粒节，疵点。**2.** (树的)节疤，瘿。**II** ***vt.*** 消除(布上的)疵点，修(布)。

bur·lap ['bəːlæp; `bɝlæp] ***n.*** 〔美〕打包粗麻布；麻袋。

bur·lesque [bəː'lesk; bɚ`lɛsk] **I** ***a.* 1.** 滑稽的，诙谐的。**2.** 戏谑的，讽刺的。**II** ***n.* 1.** 打油诗，游戏笔墨；滑稽戏，笑剧；漫画。**2.** 〔美俚〕杂耍，脱衣舞。**III** ***vt.*** (以夸张的模仿手法)讥笑；使滑稽化。*~ old romances* 以夸张手法把古代传奇故事弄得滑稽可笑。**-r** ***n.*** 〔美〕滑稽戏演员。

bur·les·queen [͵bəːles'kwiːn; ͵bɝlɛs`kwin] ***n.*** 〔美俚〕滑稽戏女演员。

bur·let·ta [bəː'letə; bɚ`lɛtə] ***n.*** 小滑稽歌剧。

bur·ley, Bur·ley ['bəːli; `bɝlɪ] ***n.*** (产于美国肯塔基州及其附近诸州的)茫叶浅色烟草。

bur·ley·cue ['bəːlikjuː; `bɝlɪkju] ***n.*** 〔美俚〕= burlesque.

Bur·lin·game ['bəːlingeim; `bɝlɪŋ͵gem] ***n.*** 伯林盖姆〔姓氏〕。

bur·ly ['bəːli; `bɝlɪ] **I** ***a.* 1.** 魁伟的，结实的，健壮的，粗鲁的。**2.** 直率的，直截了当的。*a ~ oak* 高大的橡树。*a ~-set young man* 一个体格魁伟的青年。*a ~ way of speaking* 直截了当的讲话方式。**II** ***n.* 1.** 〔美俚〕身材魁伟的人。**2.** 〔美〕滑稽戏。**-i·ly** ***ad.*** **-i·ness** ***n.***

Bur·ma ['bəːmə; `bɝmə] ***n.*** 缅甸〔亚洲〕。

Bur·man ***n.*** (*pl.* ~*s*), ***a.*** = Burmese.

Bur·mese [bəː'miːz; bɚ`miz] **I** ***n.*** 〔*sing.*, *pl.*〕**1.** 缅甸人。**2.** 缅甸语。**II** ***a.*** 缅甸的；缅甸人的；缅甸语的。

burn[1] [bəːn; bɝn] (***burnt*** [bəːnt; bɝnt], **~*ed*; *burnt*, ~*ed***) **I** ***vt.* 1.** 烧；点(烛、灯等)。**2.** 烧焦，烧坏；烧伤，烫伤；烧死；〔美〕用电椅处死，电毙；对…处火刑。**3.** 烧制，焙烧(砖瓦等)；烧穿，烧通。**4.** 烙上(火印等)；使铭感。**5.** (用烙铁、硫酸等)炙，烙，烧灼。**6.**【化】使燃烧，使氧化，利用(铀等的)核能。**7.** 晒(黑等)；晒干。**8.** 使发烧；使(喉咙)辣得难受。**9.** 激怒，挑动。**10.** 消耗，浪费，挥霍。**11.** 〔美俚〕欺骗；出售(劣质或假的麻醉药品)。**12.** 〔美俚〕使(火箭发动机等)点火。*This furnace ~s gas.* 这个炉子烧的是煤气。*~ a torch* 点火把。*~ (sb.) alive* 把(某人)活活烧死。*~ clay to bricks* 把黏土烧成砖。*~ charcoal* 烧炭。*She ~ed the roast again.* 她又把肉烤焦了。*~ one's face in the sun* 晒黑脸孔。*~ a finger* 灼伤手指。*~ a hole in his sleeve* 衣袖上烧了一个洞。*heretics ~ed at the stake* 在火刑架上被烧死的异教徒。*~ one's money* 挥霍钱财。*~ one's energy* 浪费精力。— ***vi.* 1.** 燃烧，烧着；点着。**2.** 烧黑，烧焦，烧坏；烫痛；烫伤；晒黑。**3.** 发热，发光，发红；(因患病等)发热，发烫。**4.** (因吃辛辣食物等)辣得发烧。**5.** 激动，兴奋；〔美〕发火，发怒；渴望；(问题等)白热化。**6.**【化】氧化；热溶；【物】利用核能。**7.** 〔俚〕坐电椅(被处死)。**8.**【美俚】(火箭发动机等)点火。*a fireplace ~ing merrily* 炉火暖融融。*~ briskly* 火旺。*a light ~ing in the house* 屋内灯光明亮。*the ~ing sand* 发烫的沙子。*ears ~ing from cold* 耳朵冻得发痛。*Iodine ~s so.* 碘酒给人一种热辣辣的感觉。*~ing to tell the story* 急着要讲那个故事。*~ with jealousy* 妒火中烧。*the potatoes ~ed to a crisp* 白薯烧焦了。*She ~s easily.* 她的皮肤容易晒黑。*murderer sentenced to ~* 被判处上电椅的凶手。*~ with fever* (患病)发烧。***~ away* 1.** 烧完；烧落；烧去。**2.** 继续燃烧；(渐渐)消灭。***~ blue*** 烧得火光发青。***~ daylight*** 白昼点灯，徒劳无益。***~ down* 1.** 烧光，把…烧成平地。**2.** (蜡烛等)逐渐烧完；火力减弱(*The barn was ~ed down.* 谷仓被烧掉了)。***~ for*** 渴望，热中于。***~ into [in]* 1.** 烧进；(因氧化作用等)腐蚀。**2.** (在瓷器等上)烧上(装饰画等)，烙上；留下(深刻印象等)(*~ into memory* 深刻地留在记忆里)。***~ itself out [away]*** 烧完。***~ low*** 火头无气儿，火力弱。***~ off* 1.** 烧去；烫去(污点等)。**2.** 渐渐烧完(*The sun ~ed off the mist.* 太阳驱散雾霭)。***~ on*** 焚烧；焊接。***~ one's boats [bridges] (behind one)*** 破釜沉舟，自断退路。***~ one's finers*** 由于管闲事[鲁莽]而吃苦头。***~ oneself out*** (人等因过度劳累而)精疲力尽；(机器等因使用过度而)出故障；(爱情等因过于炽烈而)耗完。~

out 1. 烧起来;烧光;烧尽;烧坏,烧断。2.(精力等)耗尽;(炉子等因燃料耗完而)熄灭;(机器等因过度使用而)损坏。3. 放火把(野兽)赶出。4.(因房子起火)烧得逃了出来〔多用被动语态〕(*They are burnt out*. 他们因失火而逃了出来)。~ *the rats out* 用火把老鼠赶出来)。~ *the candle at both ends* 过分耗费精力。~ *the earth* [*wind*]〔美〕飞快地去,开足马力去;走马观花地旅行。~ *the midnight oil* 干到深夜,开夜车。~ *the water* 用灯光等诱捕(蛙等)。~ *together* 熔接,烧焊。~ *to the ground* 把…烧光,被烧成平地。~ *up* 1. 烧完,烧尽。2.(炉火等)烧了起来,旺起来。3. 使恼怒,激怒;〔美〕生气,发怒。4. 使变狂热,使热衷于(*The paper ~ed up in a minute*. 那张纸倾刻之间就烧掉了。*He was getting ~ed up about something*. 他在为某件事生气)。~ *up the cinders*〔美〕(赛跑时)拼命冲。*Burn you*! 该死的! *have money* [*time*] *to* ~〔美〕过分有钱[有时间]。*money ~s hole in one's pocket* 爱花钱;钱烧口袋漏,一有就不留。*One's* [*The*] *ears* ~. 有人说(自己)闲话,耳根发烧。*There you* ~! 1.(玩捉迷藏游戏快接近对方时喊叫)我可抓住你了! 2.(快解决问题时说)答案快找到了! **II** *n*. 1. 烧伤,火伤;灼伤,电击伤,辐射伤;烧焦;烧痕。2. 烧(制)。3. 怒火〔主要用于 slow ~词组中〕。4.〔美〕(森林等着火烧出来的)林间平地;烧山。5.〔口〕雪茄烟。6.〔美俚〕(宇宙飞行火箭发动机)在飞行中起动。7.〔*pl*.〕〔美俚〕短的连鬓胡子;鬓角。*a ~ on the hand* 手上的烧伤。*a ~ where fire ripped through the forest* 森林着火后烧出的林间平地。*first* [*second*, *third*] *degree* ~一度[二度,三度]烧伤。*slow* ~愈来愈上升的怒火。~ **artist**〔美俚〕出售假的或劣质毒品的人。~**-back** *n*.(焊接)烧结。~ **bag**(装着随时可烧毁的机密文件的)烧袋。~**-in** *n*. 烧上;黄化,预烧;【计】(对新生产的电脑的)试机。~**-off** *n*.(焊接)熔焊穿。~**-on** *n*. 焊上,焊补。~**-out** *n*. 1. 烧完,熄灭;(喷气发动机等的)歇火。2. 大火灾;烧毁,烧光。~**-up** 1.【物】燃耗。2. 耗尽。**-ed** *a*. 1. 烧焦的。2.〔美〕被处电刑的。

burn[2] [bəːn; bɚn] *n*. [Scot.] 小溪,小川,小河。

burn·a·ble [ˈbəːnəbl; ˋbɚnəbl̩] **I** *a*. 可燃烧的。**II** *n*. 可燃物〔尤指废料〕。

Burne-Jones [ˈbəːnˈdʒəunz; ˋbɚnˋdʒonz] *n*. 伯恩-琼斯〔姓氏〕。

burn·er [ˈbəːnə; ˋbɚnɚ] *n*. 1. 烧…人;气焊工,气割工。2. 燃烧物;炉子;灯;灯头,灯口;喷烧器,喷灯;喷嘴;燃烧室。3. 火药柱。*a charcoal* [*brick*] ~ 烧炭[砖]工人。*a gas* ~ 煤气灯。*an* U^{235} ~ 铀^{235}反应堆。*slow* ~缓燃剂。

bur·net [ˈbəːnit; ˋbɚnɪt] *n*.【植】(美洲)地榆。

Bur·nett [bə(:)ˈnet, ˈbəːnit; bɚˋnɛt, ˋbɚnɪt] *n*. 伯内特〔姓氏〕。

Bur·ney [ˈbəːni ˋbɚnɪ] *n*. 伯尼〔姓氏〕。

burn·ing [ˈbəːniŋ; ˋbɚnɪŋ] **I** *a*. 1. 燃烧的,像燃烧一样的;灼痛的;辛辣的。2. 猛烈的,强烈的;热烈的。3. 议论纷纷的;紧急的。4. 极恶劣的;明摆着的。*under a ~ sun* 酷日之下。*forests ~ with autumn tints* 满林秋叶红似火。*a ~ thirst* 渴得要命;急切希望。*a ~ love* 热恋。*a ~ taste* 辣味。*a ~ situation* 紧急事态。*in ~ need of* 亟需。*a ~ mistake* 明摆着的错误。*a ~ shame* 奇耻大辱。**II** *n*. 1. 燃烧。2. 烧制。3. 炎症。~ **glass** 凸透镜,火镜。~ **mountain** 火山。~ **oil** 燃油,灯油。~ **point** 燃(烧)点。

bur·nish [ˈbəːniʃ; ˋbɚnɪʃ] **I** *vt*. 1. 磨,打磨。2.【机】抛光,轧光;擦亮;使光滑。— *vi*.(金属等经擦、磨等而)发亮。*The stone ~s well*. 这种石头容易磨亮。**II** *n*. 光泽,光亮;光滑。*a high* ~ 很亮的光泽。**-er** *n*. 1. 把…磨亮的人,打磨工。2. 磨擦抛光辊,磨滑器,磨棒;(牙科用的)研磨器。**-ing** *n*. 磨擦抛光。

bur·noose, bur·nous [bəːˈnuːs; bɚˋnus], ***bur·nouse*** [bəːˈnuːz; bɚˋnuz] *n*.(阿拉伯人等穿的)带有包头巾的外衣。

Burns [bəːnz; bɚnz] *n*. 勃恩兹[彭斯]〔姓氏〕,**Robert** ~ 罗伯特·彭斯〔1759—1796,苏格兰诗人〕。

Burn·side [ˈbəːnsaid; ˋbɚnˏsaɪd] *n*. 彭希德〔姓氏〕。

burn·sides [ˈbəːnsaidz; ˋbɚnˏsaɪdz] *n*.〔*pl*.〕〔美口〕连鬓胡子。

burnt [bəːnt; bɚnt] burn 的过去式及过去分词。*a*. 1. 烧过的;烧伤的;烧制成的。2. 烧焦的;赭色的。3.(谷物)受病害的。*a ~ taste* 焦臭味。*taste* ~焦臭。~ *orange* 赭色的橘子。*A* [*The*] ~ ***child dreads the fire***. 烧伤过的孩子怕火,惊弓之鸟。~ **ochre** 烧赭土。~ **offering**【宗】烧祭,祭神的烧烤全牲。~ **plaster** 焦石膏。~ **sienna** 1. 富铁煅黄土。2. 深褐色;深褐色燃料。~ **umber** 烧赭土;赭色。

burp [bəːp; bɚp] *n*., *vi*.〔美俚〕打嗝。— *vt*.(用拍背或摩背的方法)使(婴儿)打嗝〔以排出胃中闷积的气体〕。~ **gun**〔美军俚〕手提机关枪[冲锋枪]。

burr[1] [bəː; bɚ] **I** *n*. 1.(发"r"音时小舌颤动的)粗喉音〔多为英格兰北部和苏格兰的地方音〕;粗浊的发音。2. 嘎嘎声,吓吓声。**II** *vt*. 用粗喉音说(话)。— *vi*. 用粗喉音说话,发音粗浊。

burr[2] [bəː; bɚ] *n*. 1.【机】垫圈;(冲孔机冲下的)金属小圆片。2.(月)晕,光圈。3.(木材的)瘤部木纹;【矿】坚硬石灰岩。

burr[3] [bəː; bɚ] *n*. 1.(铜版等的)粗刻纹,锯齿状刻纹。2.【机】毛口,毛头。3. 钻孔锥;(牙科用的)磨锥(= ~ drill)。4. = bur. ~**-breast**【纺】粗梳机。~**-wire** 锯齿钢丝。

burr[4] [bəː; bɚ] *n*. 粗磨(刀)石。

Burr [bəː; bɚ] *n*. 伯尔〔姓氏〕。

bur·ro [ˈburəu; ˋburo] *n*. 1. 美国西部小毛驴。2. 驴子。

Bur·rough(s) [ˈbʌrəu(z); ˋbɚoz] *n*. 1. 伯勒(斯)〔姓氏〕。2. **Edgar Rice** ~ 伯勒斯〔1875—1950,美国作家〕,系列小说集《泰山》(*Tarzan*)的作者。

bur·row [ˈbʌrəu; ˋbɚo] **I** *n*. 1.(狐、兔等的)穴,窟,地洞。2.(地下)躲藏处,避难所。**II** *vi*. 1. 掘穴,打洞。2. 穴居;钻入洞里,潜伏。3. 钻研,查阅(*into*). *Worms ~ into fruit*. 虫蛀水果。*a ~ing animal* 穴居动物。~ *into archives* 埋头查阅文件。— *vt*. 1. 打(地洞),掘(穴);掘成。2. 把(自己)藏入洞内,让(自己)躲藏起来。3. 埋藏。~ *a hole* 打地洞。~ *a path through the crowd* 从人群中钻出来。

burr·stone, bur·stone, buhr·stone [ˈbəːstəun; ˋbɚˏston] *n*. 磨石;臼石。

bur·ry [ˈbəːri; ˋbɚɪ] *a*. 1.【机】毛刺多的。2.【纺】(布)疵点多的。3.(讲话时)喉音重的。

bur·sa [ˈbəːsə; ˋbɚsə] *n*.(*pl*. ~*s*, ***bur·sae*** [ˈbəːsiː; ˋbɚsi]) 1.【解】囊;滑囊,黏液囊;翅囊。2.【植】交和伞。3.(中世纪的)大学宿舍。

bur·sar [ˈbəːsə; ˋbɚsɚ] *n*. 1.(英国大学等的)账房,会计[出纳]员。2.(中世纪)大学生;[Scot.] 大学生津贴[奖学金],领津贴大学生。

bur·sar·i·al [bəˈseriəl; bɚˋsɛrɪəl] *a*. 1.(大学等)管账的,会计的。2.(大学生)津贴的,奖学金的。

bur·sa·ry [ˈbəːsəri; ˋbɚsərɪ] *n*. 1.(大学或修道院的)财务处。2.〔英〕(大学)奖学金。

burse [bəːs; bɚs] *n*. 1. 钱包。2.(大学生的)奖学金(= bursary);奖学金基金。3.【天主】圣餐布箱。

bur·seed [ˈbəːˌsiːd; ˋbɚˏsid] *n*.【植】鹤虱属植物(= stickseed)。

bur·si·form [ˈbəːsiˌfɔːm; ˋbɚsəˏfɔrm] *a*.【解、动】囊状的;袋状的。

bur·si·tis [bəːˈsaitis; bɚˋsaɪtɪs] *n*.【医】黏液囊炎,滑囊炎。

burst [bəːst; bɚst] (~, ~*ed*) **I** *vi*. 1. 破裂,迸裂,爆炸;爆发出,喷出;(花蕾等)绽开,(洪水等)溃决;〔俚〕破产。2. 突然发作,忽然出现。3. 胀破;充满(*with*). *The*

B

shell ~ *overhead*. 炸弹在头上爆炸。*The buds are* ~*ing*. 花蕾正在绽开。*The door* ~ *open*. 门猛然打开。*Oil* ~ *to the surface*. 喷出地面的石油。~ *on the eye* 突然出现在眼前。*The applause* ~ *from the crowd*. 人群中爆发出掌声。*I am* ~*ing to tell him the news*. 我恨不得马上就告诉他那个消息。— *vt*. 1. 使破裂,使爆裂;打开,劈开,撞开;突破,冲破。2. 使充满,使胀破。~ *the baloon with a pin* 用针把气球戳破。*He became so excited that he almost* ~ *a blood vessel*. 他兴奋得几乎血管都要破裂了,他万分兴奋。~ *a door open* 把门撞开。~ *a conspiracy* 破获一起阴谋。~ *the restraints* 打破束缚。*banks* ~ *by flood* 被洪水冲破的堤防。**be ~ing to do** (**sth**.) 忍不住[急着]要做(某事)。~ **away** 1. 破裂,爆发。2. 〔诗〕急忙逃走。~ ***forth*** 忽然跳出;忽然出现;突然爆发;(血等)喷出(*A great epidemic* ~ *forth*. 突然发生了一场大瘟疫)。~ ***in*** 1. 扑进,闯进;打扰,侵入。2. 插嘴,打断(别人谈话)。3. 突然出现(*Sorry if we* ~ *in on you*. 突然来打扰您,非常抱歉)。~ ***into*** 1. 闯进。2. 突然发作,突然…起来(~ *into a room* 推进房内。~ *into fame* 忽然出名。~ *into flames* 忽然烧起来。~ *into laughter* [*tears*] 突然哈哈大笑[哇地一声哭起来]。~ *into bloom* 开花。~ *into speech* 急忙说起来)。~ ***one's sides*** (***with laughing***) 笑破肚皮。~ ***oneself*** (过劳)伤身。~ ***on the ear*** 忽然听见(*A sound* ~ *on* [*upon*] *their ears*. 一个声音突然传进他们耳中)。~ ***open*** 推开;忽然打开;(花)渐开,(板栗)裂开。~ ***out*** 1. 冒出;现出。2. 突然发作;突然发生;突然…起来。~ ***through*** 推开,拨开。~ ***up*** 1. 爆发。2. 失败,破产,垮台。3. 突然激动,勃然大怒。4. 使崩溃。~ ***upon*** [***on***] 突然出现;袭击(*A splendid view* ~ *upon us*. 我们的眼前突然呈现一片壮丽的景色。*The real situation* ~ *upon me*. 我突然认清了真实的形势)。~ ***with*** 装满,充满(*He is* ~*ing with health*. 他极其健康。*a bag* ~*ing with gold* 装满金子的口袋。*a heart ready to* ~ *with indignation* 容易动怒)。***go*** ~ 〔口〕失败,破产。**II** *n*. 1. 突然破裂,炸裂,爆炸。2. (油等的)喷出;(感情等的)爆发,(景物等的)突然出现。3. 突进,疾走;【军】(自动武器的)连发射击,扫射。4. 一口气,一阵,一下子。5. 【无】脉冲;正弦波群;〔口〕闹饮。*a* ~ *of tire* 轮胎爆裂。*a great* ~ *of light* 突然出现一大片亮光。*a* ~ *of passion* 激情的迸发。*a* ~ *of blood from the wound* 伤口喷血。*a* ~ *of mountain and plain* 突然展开的峰峦和平原的景色。*The car passed us with a* ~ *of speed*. 那辆车子突然加快速度超过我们。*a fine* ~ *of the countryside* 眼前突然呈现出一派秀丽的乡村景色。*a* ~ *in the dike* 堤防的缺口。*a* ~ *from the machine gun* 机枪的扫射。***at a*** [***one***] ~ 一阵;一口气;一举,一下(*go up a hill at a* ~ 一口气爬上山)。***go on the*** ~ 〔俚〕闹饮。***in sudden*** ~***s*** 一阵一阵[忽冷忽热]地工作(*work in sudden* ~*s* 冷一阵热一阵地做工作)。~**-up** 〔口〕垮台,破产。

burst·er [ˈbəːstə; ˋbɝstɚ] *n*. 1. = buster. 2. 进行爆破的人,爆破工,爆破兵;爆炸物。3. 炸药(= bursting charge)。

burst·ing [ˈbəːstiŋ; ˋbɝstɪŋ] *n*. 爆裂,爆炸,爆发;突然发生。~ **chamber** 爆炸室。~ **charge** 炸药。~ **layer** 爆破层;(防空洞上的)坚固覆盖层。~ **point** 爆发点;(情绪等的)忍耐极限(*His impatience was almost at its* ~ *point*. 他的不耐烦情绪几乎已经达到了顶点。*They habitually gorged to the* ~ *point on Sunday*. 他们每到星期天总要大吃大喝,直到快把肚子胀破)。~ **strength** 【物】破裂强度。

bur·then [ˈbəːðən; ˋbɝðən] *n*., *vt*. burden 的古体。

bur·ton [ˈbəːtn; ˋbɝtn̩] *n*. 【机】复滑车。***go*** [***knock***] ***for a*** ~ 〔俚〕无影无踪,消失,不再存在。

Bur·ton [ˈbəːtn; ˋbɝtn̩] *n*. 伯顿〔姓氏,男子名〕。

Bu·run·di [buˈrundi; buˋrundɪ] *n*. 布隆迪(蒲隆地)〔非洲〕。**-an** *n*. *a*. 布隆迪人(的)。

bur·weed [ˈbəːwiːd; ˋbɝwid] *n*. 【植】有刺壳果的植物〔如牛蒡、狼把草、欧龙牙草等〕。

bur·y [ˈberi; ˋbɛrɪ] *vt*. (**bur·ied**) 1. 埋葬,葬;为…举行葬礼。2. 埋藏,遮盖,掩蔽。3. 专心致志于,埋头于(*in*)。4. 忘却,从记忆中排除。5. 死去(家属)。6. 插入,刺入(*in*, *into*)。~ *treasure under the ground* 把宝物埋到地下。~ *sb*. *with military honors* 以军礼安葬某人。*She has buried two children*. 她已经死去两个孩子。~ *wrongs* 文过饰非。~ *one's face in one's hands* 以手遮面。*be buried in sloth* 懒散。~ *one's difference* 忘去(原有)争端。~ *oneself in the country* 隐退乡村。*be buried in oblivion* 被世人忘却。*be buried in thought* [*grief*] 沉思冥想[哀怨满腹]。~ *oneself in one's work* 埋头工作。***be buried alive*** 被活埋;隐居,退隐。~ ***one's head in the sand*** 把头埋进沙里,避眼不看现实。~ ***the hatchet*** [***tomahawk***] 埋起战斧,讲和,化除干戈。

Bur·y [ˈberi; ˋbɛrɪ] *n*. 布里〔姓氏〕。

bur·y·ing [ˈberiiŋ; ˋbɛrɪɪŋ] *n*. 埋,埋葬。*a* ~ *lot* 葬地。~ **ground**, ~ **place** 墓地,坟场。

bus [bʌs; bʌs] **I** *n*. (*pl*. ~**ses**, ~**es**) 1. 公共马车;公共汽车;客机。2. 〔口〕汽车,机器脚踏车;飞机。3. 【电】信息转移通路;悔流条,母线。4. 〔美俚〕(小餐馆等的)服务员(= ~ boy)。5. 〔美俚〕火箭[飞弹]的一级。6. 【计】(电脑的)总线。*a double-decker* ~ 双层公共汽车。*get a* ~ 乘公共汽车。***miss the*** ~ 1. 失掉机会。2. 事业失败。**II** *vi*. (**-s**(**s**)**-**) 〔美口〕1. 乘公共汽车。2. 充当餐馆服务员的下手[打杂工]。~ *for one's meal* 以充当饭馆打杂工换取饭费。*We bussed to New York*. 我们乘公共汽车去纽约。— *vt*. 用公共汽车接送学童〔为抵制学校的种族隔离政策而采取的一种措施〕。~ ***it*** 〔口〕乘公共汽车(~ *it from New York to Washington* 从纽约乘公共汽车去华盛顿)。~**-bar** 【电】汇流条,母线。~ **boy** 〔美俚〕餐馆服务员的下手,餐馆打杂工。~**-conductor** (公共汽车)售票员。~ **driver** 1. (公共汽车)驾驶员〔有时兼售票员〕。2. 〔俚〕轰炸机驾驶员。~ **girl** 〔美俚〕餐馆女打杂工,服务员的女下手。~**load** 公共汽车最大载客量。~**man** (公共汽车的)驾驶员[乘务员](*a* ~ *man's holiday* 照常工作的假日)。~ **nod** 【电】导(电)条。~ **queue** 等候公共汽车的长队。~**-shelter** (公共汽车)候车棚。~ **stop** 公共汽车站。~ **way** 公共汽车车道。

bus. = bushel; bushels; business.

bus·by [ˈbʌzbi; ˋbʌzbɪ] *n*. (英国陆军轻骑兵、近卫兵等戴的)熊皮鸟缨高顶帽。

bush[1] [buʃ; bʊʃ] **I** *n*. 1. 灌木;矮树丛;丛林。2. 〔the ~〕〔澳〕未开垦的丛林地。3. (从前酒店做招牌的)长春藤;〔古〕酒店。4. 〔俚〕蓬头;蓬发;蓬松的尾巴;【猎】狐尾,5. 〔*pl*.〕= ~ *league*. *trees and* ~*es* 高高矮矮的树木。*a clump of* ~*es* 一片灌木林。*Good wine needs no* ~. 酒好客自来(无需做广告)。***beat about*** [***around***] ***the*** ~ 旁敲侧击。***beat the*** ~***es*** 到处搜寻(*beat the* ~*es for engineers* 搜罗工程师)。***go*** ~ 〔澳俚〕1. (逃犯等)躲入丛林。2. (动物)变野(*a pack of dogs that have gone* ~ 一群变野了的狗)。***take to the*** ~ 逃入丛林地带;做强盗,当绿林好汉。**II** *vi*. 1. (毛发等)丛生。2. 形成灌木林。*His eyebrows* ~*ed together*. 他的眉毛浓密。— *vt*. 1. 用灌木围住,用灌木支持;在栽灌木。2. 〔美俚〕使筋疲力尽。*a frozen lake* ~*ed where the ice is not safe* 在上冻的湖面冰薄的地方栽上灌木〔作为危险标志〕。~ ***it*** 住入丛林地带。~**baby** 【动】猩〔非洲森林中的一种小猿,其声似婴儿啼哭〕。~ **buck** 南非羚羊。~ **cat** 【动】薮猫。~ **craft** 丛林中生活的技能。~**-fighter** 丛林游击兵。~**-fighting** 丛林战。~ **fire** 灌木林火(~*-fire war* 灌木林火式战争)。~ **hat** (澳大利亚军装的)

阔边帽。~**hammer** 1. 凿石锤。2. (使混凝土路面不致过滑的)气动凿毛机。~**hog** (南非)野猪。~**hook** (剪修灌木用的)长柄大镰刀。~ **jacket** 有腰带的棉布短上衣。~**land** 〔Can.〕原始森林区。~ **league** 1. (棒球等)次级竞赛联合会。2. 外行;次等。~**-league** *a*. 次级的,不成熟的,二流的。~**man** 1. 新垦地移民;〔澳〕林居人;乡下人。2. 〔B-〕(南非游牧民族)布希曼人。~**manship** = ~ craft. ~**master** (南非)大毒蛇。~ **parole** 〔美俚〕越狱。~ **pilot** 在无人区飞行的飞行员。~ **ranger** 丛林居民;〔澳〕土匪。~ **telegraph** 情报[谣言等]的迅速传播。~**veld** 丛林地带;南非草原。~ **warbler** 黄莺。~**whack** *vi*., *vt*. 1. 〔美〕开伐丛林。2. (利用丛林)伏击。~**whacker** 1. 〔美〕林中居民;开伐丛林的人。2. 【美史】(南北战争中的)游击兵。3. (砍伐丛林的)大镰刀。

bush[2] [buʃ; bʊʃ] **I** *n*. 【机】衬套,套管,套筒;轴衬,轴瓦。*insulating* ~ 绝缘套管。*brake* ~闸衬。**II** *vt*. 加(金属)衬套[轴衬]于。

Bush [buʃ; bʊʃ] *n*. 布什〔姓氏〕。

bushed[1] [buʃt; bʊʃt] *a*. 1. 〔澳口〕迷路在灌木林中的;不知所措的。2. 〔美口〕疲劳不堪的。*get* ~ *without a guide* 因没有向导在丛林中迷路。

bushed[2] [buʃt; bʊʃt] *a*. 【机】加有衬套的。

bush·el[1] [ˈbuʃl; ˋbʊʃl̩] *n*. 1. 蒲式耳〔谷物计量单位;美国 Winchester ~ = 35.238 升,英国 Imperial ~ = 36 升〕。2. 一蒲式耳的容器;容量相当于一蒲式耳的重量。3. 大量。~*s of gems* 大量珠宝。*a* ~ *of lies* 一大堆谎言。***hide one's light* [*candle*] *under a*** ~ 不露锋芒。***measure other people's corn by one's own*** ~ 拿自己的标准衡量别人,以己度人。~**basket** 一蒲式耳筐〔一筐式等于一蒲式耳〕。~ **iron** 碎铁。

bush·el[2] [ˈbuʃl; ˋbʊʃl̩] *vi*., *vt*. (*-ll-*) 〔美〕改[翻新]衣服。**-(l)er** *n*. 改制衣服的人;补衣工〔尤指成衣工助手〕。

Bu·shi·do [ˈbuːʃidəu; ˋbuʃɪ͵do] *n*. 〔Jap.〕武士道。

bush·ing [ˈbuʃiŋ; ˋbʊʃɪŋ] *n*. = bush[2].

bush·wa, bush·wah [ˈbuʃwɑː; ˋbʊʃwɑ] *n*. 〔美俚〕胡话,胡扯;空话,废话。

bush·y [ˈbuʃi; ˋbʊʃɪ] *a*. 1. 灌木似的。2. 灌木茂密的。3. (毛发等)浓密的。~ *eyebrows* 浓眉。~**-bearded** 胡须浓的。**-i·ly** *ad*. **-i·ness** *n*.

bus·i·ly [ˈbizili; ˋbɪzl̩ɪ] *ad*. 忙,繁忙,忙碌。*wag one's tongue* ~ 碎嘴,讲个不停。*study* ~ 忙着做功课。

bus·i·ness [ˈbiznis; ˋbɪznɪs] *n*. 1. 事务,业务;事,事业,行业,工作。2. 实业;商业,营业,买卖,交易;营业额,交易量;商情。3. 商店,企业,公司;事务所。4. 职责,本分;权利。5. 要事,要务;难事。6. 【剧】动作,表情。7. (会议等的)议程。~ *as usual* 照常营业。*follow the* ~ *of* 以…为业。*What line of* ~ *is he in*? 他是干什么的? *His* ~ *is poultry farming*. 他从事养鸡业。*hours of* ~[~ *hours*] 营业[办公]时间。*do good* [*a great*] ~ 生意好,赚钱[做大买卖]。*We shut up* ~ *at six*. 我们六点钟停止营业。*depression of* ~商情不景气。*domestic* [*foreign*] ~国内[对外]贸易。*open a* ~ 开店[开业]。*build* [*set*] *up a* ~开店,设商号。*His* ~ *is on the corner of Broadway and Elm street*. 他的商号设在百老汇和埃尔姆街拐角的地方。~ *centre* 商业中心。*What a* ~ *it is*! 实在麻烦! *an awkward* ~麻烦事。*What is your* ~ *here*? 有什么事? *It is none of your* ~. 不关你事,别管闲事。*I have* ~ *with him*. 我跟他有要紧的事要谈。*It's your* ~ *to wash the dishes now*. 现在该你洗碗碟了。***be doing good* ~ *with*** 和…关系不错。~ ***accounting unit*** 经济核算单位。***B- before pleasure***. 正事要紧。***the* ~ *end*** 〔俚〕(工具等)起作用的部分,使用[锐利]的一头 (*the* ~ *end of a scythe* 大镰刀的刀身。*the* ~ *end of a revolver* 手枪的枪身)。***B- is*** ~. 公事公办;生意是生意,交情归交情。***come* [*get*] *to*** ~ 动手做事;言归正传。***do sb.'s*** ~ = ***do the* ~ *for sb***. 〔口〕要某人的命(*That much will be enough to do his* ~. 那就足够要他的命了。*This will do the* ~ *for him*. 这会要他的命的)。***enter on* [*upon*]** ~ 开业。***Everybody's* ~ *is nobody's* ~.** 人人负责,结果无人负责。***get down to*** ~ 认真干起来。***get* [*give*] *the*** ~ 〔美俚〕(被)粗暴地对待;(被)作弄。***go about one's*** ~ 做自己的事;〔常作命令式〕(*Go about your* ~. 去你的,走开)。***go into*** ~ 入实业界做生意。***go out of*** ~ 停业;改行。***go to*** ~ 上班。***Good* ~!** 干得好! 妙极了! ***have no* ~ *to do* [*say*] *sth***. 没有做[说]某事的权利[道理]。(*You have no* ~ *coming into this house*. 你没有进这个屋子的权利。*The weather has no* ~ *to be so warm in winter*. 冬天的气候不该这样暖和)。***know one's*** ~ 精通本行。***like nobody's*** ~ 〔口〕特别地。***make* ~ *of*** 以…为业。***make a great* ~ *of it*** 觉得难办[棘手],甚觉麻烦。***make the* ~ *for*** 了结。***man of*** ~ 1. 实业家;事务家。2. 商业[法律]代理人(*He is a man of* ~. 他是一个实业家。*He is her man of* ~. 他是她的商业[法律]代理人)。***mean*** ~ (行动、话等)是当真的(*I mean* ~. 我是当真的,不是说笑。*By the fire in his eyes we know that he meant* ~. 从他愤怒的眼神中,我们看出他不是说着玩的)。***Mind your own* ~.** 不要管闲事。***monkey*** ~ 〔美俚〕胡闹;欺骗。***on*** ~ 因公,有事,有要事(*No admittance except on* ~. 非公莫入,闲人免进)。***out of*** ~ 破产,失业。***send sb. about his*** ~ 赶走某人;辞退[解聘]某人。***stick to one's*** ~ 专心做事。***talk*** ~ 说正经话,谈正经的。~ **card** 业务名片。~ **circle** 商界。~ **college** 商学院。~ **cycle** 经济危机周期;工商业循环。~ **English** 商业英语。~ **flying** (正常班次以外的)商务飞行。~**man** 实业家;商人。~ **office** 商业事务所。~ **school** 商业学校。~ **speak** 商业行话。~ **unionism** 工联主义。~**woman** 女实业家,女商人。**-like** *a*. 1. 事务式的;有条理的。2. 有效的,讲究实际的(*a* ~ *administration* 有效的经营。*He did his work in a* ~ *way*. 他踏踏实实地工作)。

busk [bʌsk; bʌsk] *n*. 1. (妇女紧身衣胸部的)鲸骨[铜片、木片等]架。2. 〔英方〕紧身衣。

busk·er [ˈbʌskə; ˋbʌskɚ] *n*. 街头音乐师;巡回[街头]艺人。

bus·kin [ˈbʌskin; ˋbʌskɪn] *n*. 1. (半)高统靴。2. (古代希腊、罗马悲剧演员穿的)厚底长编扣凉鞋。3. 悲剧。***put on the* ~*s*** 写[演]悲剧。

bus·kin·ed [ˈbʌskind; ˋbʌskɪnd] *a*. 1. 穿(半)长统靴的。2. 悲剧的;悲壮的,崇高的。*speak in a* ~ *language* 以悲壮激昂的语言讲话。

buss[1] [bʌs; bʌs] *n*. (用于捕鲱鱼的一种)双桅渔船。

buss[2] [bʌs; bʌs] *n*., *vt*., *vi*. 〔古、方〕接吻,吻。

bust[1] [bʌst; bʌst] *n*. 1. 半身像,胸像。2. (妇女的)胸部[胸围]。~ ***bodice*** (妇女的)紧身围腰。

bust[2] [bʌst; bʌst] **I** *n*. 〔俚〕1. 欢闹,闹饮。2. 失败;破产;经济萧条。3. 殴打。*a beer* ~ 吵吵闹闹地喝啤酒。*make* ~*s* 欢闹,闹饮。*give sb*. ~*s* 殴打某人。*He got a* ~ *on the nose*. 他鼻子上挨了一拳。**II** *vt*. 1. 〔口〕= burst. 2. 〔俚〕使破产[没落](*up*)。3. 〔口〕殴打。4. 驯服(野马等)。5. 【军】贬降(士兵等的)军阶。*The financial panic* ~*ed many firms*. 经济恐慌使许多家公司倒闭。*be* ~*ed from sergeant to private* 从士官降为士兵。— *vi*. 1. 爆裂;破裂。2. 破产;(力争成功紧张过度时的)失败,崩溃。~ ***a gut*** 〔美〕拼命努力。~ ***loose*** 〔美〕脱离,脱出,离开;破戒。~ ***up*** 拆散;解散;(夫妻)分居;(友谊)破裂。**III** *a*. 破产的;一文不名的。*be clean* [*dead*] ~(穷得)一文不名。*The company went* ~. 该公司破产了。~**-up** 1. (婚姻、友谊等的)破裂。2. 盛大的招待会;闹宴。

bust[3] [bʌst; bʌst] **I** *vt*. 〔美俚〕1. 逮捕。2. (警察)突然搜查。*be* ~*ed on a narcotic charge* 以吸毒罪被捕。**II** *n*. 1. 逮捕。2. 突击搜查。

bus·tard [ˈbʌstəd; ˋbʌstɚd] ***n.*** 〔鸟〕鸨。

bust·er [ˈbʌstə; ˋbʌstɚ] ***n.*** **1.** 〔美口〕破坏者,扑灭者;爆破者,爆破物;(巨型)炸弹。**2.** 〔美俚〕(同类中)特别巨大[漂亮]的东西,特别能干[漂亮]的人。**3.** 〔俚〕闹饮,纵酒闹饮的人。**4.** 〔美〕驯马人;(大洋洲)寒冷猛烈的西南风。**5.** 〔美俚〕健壮的孩子;〔常 B-〕老兄〔称呼语〕。**6.** 【机】钉头切断机;犁。*a tank* ~反坦克炮。*crime* ~*s* (侦破罪案的)侦探,探员。*B-, come here*. 老兄,到这边来。~**slab**【军】防弹墙。

bus·tle[1] [ˈbʌsl; ˋbʌsl] **I** ***vi.*** **1.** 喧闹。**2.** 忙乱,奔忙(*about; up*). ~ *about cooking breakfast* 忙着做早饭。~ *in* 匆匆忙忙地跑进来。*The office* ~*d with people and activity*. 办公室里人来人往,忙忙碌碌。—***vt.*** **1.** 催促,使忙乱。**2.** 使活跃。*He* ~*d her upstairs*. 他催着她跨上台阶。~ *the fire to make the kettle boil* 拨弄火使水壶快点烧开。~ ***up*** 赶快;急急忙忙(*Tell her to* ~ *up* 叫她快点儿)。**II** ***n.*** **1.** 奔走,奔忙,忙乱。**2.** 喧闹,熙攘。*be in a* ~忙乱;吵吵闹闹,乱哄哄。*the* ~ *of Christmas preparations* 乱哄哄地忙着准备过圣诞节。*the hustle and* ~ *in business quarters* 商业区一片闹哄哄的景象。*without hurry or* ~ 不慌不忙。**bus·tling** ***a.*** **bus·tling·ly** ***ad.***

bus·tle[2] [ˈbʌsl; ˋbʌsl] ***n.*** (妇女撑裙褶的)腰垫,裙撑。

bustop [ˈbʌstɔp; ˋbʌstɑp] ***n.*** (双层公共汽车的)车上层。

bus·y [ˈbizi; ˋbɪzɪ] **I** ***a.*** **1.** 忙,繁忙的;无闲空的(*opp.* unoccupied),〔美〕(电话)线没空,占线。**2.** 勤勉的(*opp.* indolent)孜孜不倦的,专心致志的。**3.** 爱管闲事的(*in*). **4.** 繁华的,热闹的。**5.** (花样)富丽的,繁杂的。*a* ~ *day* 忙碌的一天。*a* ~ *town* 热闹的城市。~ *idleness* 无事忙。*The place was* ~ *with passengers*. 那地方行人众多,非常热闹。*Line's* ~. (电话)占线! *get a* ~ *signal* 从(听筒中)听到占线的信号声。*be* ~ *in another's affair* 喜欢干涉别人的事。*a* ~ *floral wallpaper* 花纹图案复杂多变的糊壁纸。***a*** ~ ***bee*** 埋头工作者。***a*** ~ ***tongue*** 话多的人。***be*** ~ ***at*** [***about, over, with***] ***sth.*** (人等)忙于做某事(*be* ~ *at one's work* 忙着自己的工作)。***be*** ~ ***doing*** (***sth.***) 忙着干(某事)(*be* ~ *preparing for* 忙着为…作准备)。***get*** ~ 〔美口〕干起来,开始工作[奔走,活动]。**II** ***vt.*** (***bus·ied***) 使忙于,使奔走,使经营。*be busied with studies* 忙于研究工作。*She busied herself about the house*. 她忙于家务。*I have busied the gardener for the afternoon*. 我让园丁忙了一下午。~ ***oneself with*** [***at, in, doing*** (***sth.***)] 忙于,正在忙着做(某事)(*She busied herself imagining the worst possible*. 她不停地想着可能发生的最坏结果)。**III** ***n.*** 〔英俚〕侦探,包打听。~**body** 好事的人,爱管闲事的人。~ **signal** (电话的)占线信号。~**work**, ~**-work** 外加作业〔使学生不致空闲而故意外加的作业〕。**-ness** ***n.*** 忙碌;繁忙。

but[1] [强 bʌt; 弱 bət; 强 bʌt, 弱 bət] **I** ***conj.*** **1.** 但,但是,可是,然而,不过。*He is rich,* ~ (*he is*) *not happy*. 他有钱但是不幸福。*Lend me some novel,* ~ *an interesting one*. 借给我一本小说,不过得要有趣一点的。**2.** (不是…)而是,倒是,(非…)乃。*He is not a soldier* ~ *a sailor*. 他不是陆军而是海军。*It is not I* ~ *you who are to blame*. 该责备的是你而不是我。*Not that I love Caesar less,* ~ *that I love Rome more*. 不是我不爱凯撒,而是我更爱罗马。**3.** (虽…)仍,(尽管…)还是,还没有到…的地步。*No enemy is so ferocious* ~ [~ *that,* ~ *what*] *we can defeat it*. 不管敌人多么强大,我们都能打败他。*He is not such a fool* ~ *he knows it*. 他尽管笨,这个还是懂的;他还没有笨到连这个都不懂。*No one is so old* ~ *that he may learn*. 年纪再大也可以学习,活到老学到老。**4.** 除非…否则不;只有…(才能…)。*Nothing would satisfy him* ~ *I come along*. 只有我来他才会满意。*Who knows any man* ~ *he be his brother*? 除非是亲兄弟,否则谁了解谁? *It will go hard* ~ *I will get there*. 除非我到那里去,不然事情就难办了。**5.** 若非,要不是。*B- that I saw it, I could not have believed it*. 要不是我亲眼看见,我是不会相信的。*She would have fallen* ~ *that he caught her*. 要不是他抓住她,她就跌下去了。**6.** (不…则已,一…)就会…,总会…。*It never rains* ~ *it pours*. 天不下雨则已,一下就是暴雨倾盆;一倒霉就步步倒霉。*You cannot look into the index* ~ *you will find the word*. 你一查索引就会找到那个词。*There was never a new theory* ~ *some one objected to it*. 新理论一出现,总会有人反对。**7.** 只能,仅能,不得不。*I could not choose* ~ *speak the truth*. 我只能讲出事实真相。*They had no other choice* ~ [*to*] *surrender*. 他们别无选择,只能投降。*I can't help* ~ *feel sorry for him*. 我只能为他感到难过。*I can not* ~ *admire his courage*. 我不得不佩服他的勇敢。**8.** 〔用于否定词或疑问词之后,表示否定,相当于 that not〕. *Never fear* ~ *I'll go*. 不要担心我不走。*I don't know* ~ *it is all true*. 我可不能肯定这都不是真的。*Who knows* ~ *that everything will come out all right*? 谁能担保一切都不出差错呢? *There is no knowing* ~ *such an accident may happen*? 谁能说不会发生这种意外呢? *It was impossible* ~ *he should see it*. 他不可能没有看到它。*How is it possible* ~ *that we should be discontented*? 我们怎么会感到满意呢? 我们怎么能不感到不满呢? **9.** 〔用于 deny, doubt, question 等词的否定语气之后,无实义。仅仅相当于 that〕。*I do not doubt* ~ *that you are surprised*. 我敢断定你是感到吃惊了。*I do not deny* ~ *that it is difficult*. 我不否认这是件困难的事。*I don't question* ~ *you are correct*. 我不怀疑你是正确的。*I shouldn't wonder* ~ *she wants to be a singer*. 她想当歌手,我不应该感到惊讶。*There is no doubt* ~ (*that*) *he was murdered*. 毫无疑问,他是被谋杀的。**10.** 〔用于 odds, ten to one, a thousand to one 等述语之后,表示可能性,无实义,仅仅相当于 that〕。*It is odds* [*ten to one*] ~ *you lose*. 你十之八九要输。*It is a thousand to one* ~ *you'll succeed*. 你成功的机会只有千分之一,你几乎失败定了。**11.** 〔用于加强语气〕*Good heavens,* ~ *she's beautiful*! 天哪,她多漂亮呀! *Heavens,* ~ *it rains*! 啊呀,下大雨了! *Beg pardon,* ~ *haven't you met my sister on the way*? 对不起,您在路上碰见我妹妹了吗? **12.** 除(某人)以外,除了(某人)。见以下 ***prep.*** **2. II** ***rel. pro.*** 没有不…的〔相当于 who not, that not〕。*There is no rule* ~ *has exceptions*. 没有无例外的规律,任何规律都有例外。*Nobody* ~ *has his faults*. 人孰无过,没有人身上不存在缺点。**III** ***prep.*** **1.** 除了,除去,除…之外。*This letter is nothing* ~ *an insult*. 这封信完全是一种侮辱。*It's anything* ~ *modest*. 这绝不是谦虚。*owing nothing* ~ *his clothes* 除去身上的衣服,此外一无所有。*They live next door* ~ *one*. 他们的住处只有一户之隔。*He was the last* ~ *one to arrive*. 他是倒数第二个到的。*last* ~ *two* [*three*] 倒数第三[四]。**2.** 除(某人)以外,除了(某人)〔此种用法与用作 ***conj.*** 很难分清〕。*All are wrong* ~ *he* [*him*]. 除他以外,别人都错了。*No one* ~ *a fool would believe it*. 只有傻瓜才会相信它。*No one replied* ~ *me*. 除了我,没有别人回答。**3.** 只…,仅仅…〔引进名词子句〕。*Nothing would please her* ~ *that we go along*. 只有我们一道去,她才会高兴。*I ask nothing from you* ~ *that you should come to see me once in a while*. 我只要求你有时候来看看我。**IV** ***ad.*** **1.** 〔书〕不过,只,仅仅;只能,至少,好歹。**2.** 刚刚,才。**3.** 〔书〕然而,另一方面。*This took him* ~ *a few minutes*. 这仅仅花他几分钟时间。*She is* ~ *a child*. 她不过是一个孩子罢了。*I can* ~ *hear*. 我只能听听而已。*If I could* ~ *see him*! 我要是能见一见他就好了! *I can* ~ *try it*. 我好歹试试看。*He left* ~ *an hour ago*. 他一小时以前才离开。

It happened ~ *yesterday*. 这件事昨天刚发生。*B- I did go there*. 然而我确实是去过那里了。**V** ***vt***. 对(某人)讲"但是"(以示反对、拒绝等)。— ***vi***. (讲话时)总是"但是","但是"的。**VI** ***n***. **1**. (讲话时说的)"但是","不过"。**2**. 保留;反对;例外。*B- me no* ~*s*. 请你不要"但是,但是"的吧,请你别反对[拒绝、推诿]吧。〔前一个 but 是 ***vt***. 后一个 but 是 ***n***.〕. *Do as I tell you, no* ~ *about it*. 就照我说的办,不要有二话。***all*** ~ **1**. 几乎,差点〔but 作副词〕(*I all* ~ *fell into the well*. 我几乎跌下井去)。**2**. 除…而外的全部〔but 作介词〕(*He could find all* ~ *one of his books*. 他的书全能找到,只有一本除外)。~ ***definitely*** 〔美〕的确,不错。~ ***for*** 〔书〕**1**. 除…而外。**2**. 要不是,如果没有 (*B- for his footsteps, there was no other sound*. 除他的脚步声而外,再没有别的声音。*She would have fallen* ~ *for his sudden arm*. 要不是他一把抓住,她就摔倒了)。~ ***good*** 〔美俚〕完全,毫无疑问;狠狠地(*I chewed him out* ~ *good* — *it won't happen again*. 我把他狠狠地训斥了一番,这样的事不会再发生了)。~ ***then*** [***yet***] 但是,然而,可是,不过,另一方面(*She didn't want to go to Paris* — ~ *then she didn't want to be at home either*. 她不想去巴黎——但她也不想呆在家里)。~ ***what*** **1**. 〔= ~ those which〕(*There are no events* ~ *what have meaning*. 但凡发生事件,都必有其意义)。**2**. 〔= ~ that, 表示不肯定〕。(*I don't know* ~ *what I will go*. 我不知道我是不是去)。***not*** ~ = ***not*** ~ ***that*** = 〔方、口〕***not*** ~ ***what***... 虽不说不是,虽然(*I cannot do it; not* ~ *that a stronger might*. 我干不了这件事,虽然不能说比我强的人也干不了)。

but² [bʌt; bʌt] **I** ***ad***. 〔Scot.〕向外;向外室,向厨房。**II** ***n***. (苏格兰两间一套房屋的)外室,厨房。~ ***and ben with*** 与…亲密相处。(*apartments* ~ *and ben with each other* 外室相连的两套房间)。~ **-and-ben** **1**. ***n***. 两间一套的住所。**2**. ***ad***. 一前一后地,一来一往地。**3**. ***ad***. 在相对两端。

bu·ta·di·ene [ˌbjuːtəˈdaiiːn; ˌbjutəˋdaiin] ***n***. 【化】丁二烯。

bu·tane [ˈbjuːtein; ˋbjuten] ***n***. 【化】丁烷。

bu·ta·no·ic [ˌbjuːtəˈnəuik; ˌbjutəˋnoik] ***a***. 丁烷的。~ **acid** 【化】丁酸。

bu·ta·nol [ˈbjuːtənəl, -ˌnəul; ˋbjutənəl, -ˌnol] ***n***. 【化】丁醇(= butalalcohol)。

bu·ta·none [ˈbjuːtəˌnəun; ˋbjutəˌnon] ***n***. 【化】丁酮。

butch¹ [butʃ; butʃ] **I** ***n***. 〔俚〕**1**. 大老粗。**2**. 男人似的女子。**3**. 女性同性恋中充当男性的角色。**II** ***a***. **1**. (男子发型)平头的。**2**. 男人似的。~ **haircut** 〔美〕(男子发型的)平头。**2**. (女子发型的)短发。

butch² [butʃ; butʃ] ***vt***. 〔方〕**1**. 使崩溃,弄糟。**2**. 惨杀,屠杀。~ *a job* 弄坏事,做坏工作。

butch·er [ˈbutʃə; ˋbutʃɚ] **I** ***n***. **1**. 屠夫,屠户;屠杀者,刽子手;残酷的人。**2**. 〔口〕笨工拙匠。**3**. 〔美〕(在剧场、火车等处兜售糖果等杂物的)小贩。**4**. 〔美〕拳击选手;〔美俚,贬〕军医,外科医生;医生。**5**. 肉铺。*a pork* ~猪肉铺。*Hitler was as great a* ~ *as the world has seen*. 希特勒是有史以来最大的杀人狂。~***'s bill*** **1**. 屠户的账单。**2**. 阵亡者名单。**3**. 战费。**4**. 【植】假叶树。~***'s meat*** **1**. (猪、牛、羊等的)鲜肉;剁肉,斩碎的肉。**2**. 〔俚〕赊来的肉。~***'s wool*** 皮板毛。***the*** ~, ***the baker, the candlestick-maker*** 各行各业(的人),七十二行。**II** ***vt***. **1**. 屠宰;屠杀,虐杀;把…处死刑。**2**. 弄糟,做坏;(以粗暴的批评等)扼杀(作品等)。~ *hogs* 杀猪。~*the play beyond recognition* 把这个戏糟蹋得面目全非。~*a job* 做坏活儿。~**bird** 【鸟】百劳科的鸟,百劳。~ **knife** 屠刀。~ **shop** 肉店。**-ly** ***a***. 屠夫一样的;残忍的(*a* ~*ly act* 一桩残酷的行为。*a* ~*ly ruffian* 残忍的暴徒)。

butch·er·y [ˈbutʃəri; ˋbutʃəri] **I** ***n***. **1**. 大屠杀,惨杀。**2**. 屠场;肉店;屠宰业。**3**. 弄糟,做糟。**II** ***a***. 屠杀的;残忍的。***make a*** ~ ***of*** 粗手笨脚地弄糟。

bu·tene [ˈbjuːtiːn; ˋbjutin] ***n***. 【化】丁烯(= butylene)。

bu·te·o [ˈbjuːtiəˌəu; ˋbjutɪəˌo] ***n***. 【鸟】鵟属鸟。

but·le [ˈbʌtl; ˋbʌtl] ***vi***. 〔口〕当管事,做男管家。

but·ler [ˈbʌtlə; ˋbʌtlɚ] ***n***. **1**. 管事,男管家;(主管酒饭的)侍役长。**2**. 【史】(皇宫中的)司膳官,王室酒类管理官。~***'s pantry*** (厨房外餐厅后面的)配膳室。

But·ler [ˈbʌtlə; ˋbʌtlɚ] ***n***. 巴特勒〔姓氏〕。

butler·y [ˈbʌtləri; ˋbʌtləri] ***n***. = buttery.

butt¹ [bʌt; bʌt] ***n***. **1**. (钓竿、箭等的)粗端;(工具等的)柄,把,枪托;(树木等的)残端,根端;针脚;〔美俚〕屁股;〔美〕烟蒂;纸烟。**2**. 残片;残余部分。**3**. (制革的)厚皮,背皮;(铸件的)锭,坯。*a cigar* ~ 纸烟头;烟蒂。*a candle* ~ 蜡烛头。~ **buffer** 枪托缓冲器。~ **cut** 【林】根端材。~ **end** **1**. 枪托。**2**. 残部。**3**. 大头,粗端。

butt² [bʌt; bʌt] ***n***. **1**. 大酒桶。**2**. 桶〔英 = 108 加仑,美 = 129.7 加仑〕。**3**. 澳洲小包羊毛〔净毛重 112 磅〕。

butt³ [bʌt; bʌt] **I** ***n***. **1**. 〔常 *pl*.〕(练习箭术等的)靶子;射垛,箭靶垫;打靶场。**2**. 目的,目标;笑柄,(批评等的)对象。**3**. 【农】未犁的余地;〔古〕界限。**4**. 【建】铰链;【机】平接(合),对接。*make sb. the* ~ *of contempt* 使某人成为被轻蔑的对象。~ *of dirty jokes* 下流笑话的对象。~ ***and*** ~ 一头[端]接一头[端]。~***s and bounds*** 【法】地界,地积的宽窄长短。**II** ***vt***. 使邻接(*on, upon, against*);使两端对接;紧靠。~ *two strips of wallpaper* 把两张糊壁纸衔接起来。— ***vi***. 邻接,毗连。*The house* ~*s to a cemetery*. 这所房子和墓地相连。*The lot* ~*s on a croft*. 这块地和农场毗连。~**joint** 【木工】对接。~ **welding** 【机】对头焊接。

butt⁴ [bʌt; bʌt] **I** ***vt***. **1**. (用头、角等)抵触,顶撞,冲。**2**. 碰撞。*a couple of rams* ~*ing at each other* 两只正在用角互相抵触的羊。~ *a wall* 撞墙。~ *one's opponent heavily in the ribs* 猛撞对手的肋骨。— ***vi***. **1**. 抵触,顶撞 (*against; into*)。**2**. 伸出,突出 (*into; out*)。**3**. 〔口〕插手,干涉 (*in, into*)。~ *against a fense* 撞到篱笆上。~ *against* [*into*] *sb*. 撞到某人身上。~ *up against sb.'s policy* 与某人的方针相抵触。*a gallery* ~*ing out from the house* 从房屋伸出的走廊。**II** ***n***. **1**. 顶撞,冲撞,碰撞。**2**. (击剑中的)突刺。*give sb. a* ~ *in the stomach* 猛撞某人的腹部。**III** ***ad***. 用头撞;猛撞。~ ***in*** [***into***] 〔俚〕插手,插嘴(*Don't* ~ *into people's business*. 不要管闲事)。~ ***out*** 〔俚〕不干预;不多嘴(*Nobody asked your opinion so* ~ *out*. 没有人征求你的意见,请你别多嘴)。***come*** (***full***) ~ ***against*** 猛撞在…。

butte [bjuːt; bjut] ***n***. (美国西部平原上孤立的)小尖山;孤山;地垛。

but·ter [ˈbʌtə; ˋbʌtɚ] **I** ***n***. **1**. 黄油,白脱油。**2**. (植物)脂;脂状物,酱;像黄油的东西。**3**. 〔口〕奉承话,巴结话。**4**. 焊膏。*fresh* [*rancid*] ~ 新鲜[陈]黄油。*artificial* ~ 人造黄油。*spread bread with* ~ = *spread* ~ *on bread* 在面包上涂黄油。*apple* [*peanut*] ~苹果[花生]酱。*cocoa* ~ 可可脂。*antimony* ~【化】锑酪,三氯化锑。~ *of zinc* [*tin*]【化】氯化锌[锡]。*entice sb. with* ~ 用奉承话勾引某人。***B- to*** ~ ***is no relish***. 黄油加黄油不成美味;千篇一律的东西令人生厌。***lay on*** [***spread***] ~ 奉承,巴结。***look as if*** ~ ***would not melt in one's mouth*** 装出一副老实相,装得一本正经。**II** ***vt***. **1**. 在…上涂黄油[酱、黄油状物];用黄油煎[煮]食物。**2**. 〔口〕巴结,讨好(*up*). ~ ***one's bread on both sides*** 浪费,奢华。***Fine words*** ~ ***no parsnips***. 花言巧语是不顶用的。***have one's bread*** ~***ed for life*** 一辈子享福。***know which side one's bread is*** ~***ed*** (***on***) 对自己的利益很精明。~**-and-egger** = ~**-and-egg man** 〔美俚〕外表阔气的假大亨,假公子哥儿。~**-and-eggs** 【鱼】抑穿鱼。~**ball** 〔美口〕胖子;【动】巨头鹊鸭。~ **bean** 肾形豆;利马豆;棉豆。~**boat** (船形)黄油碟。~**bur** 【植】菊科蜂

斗叶属植物〔尤指紫蜂斗叶〕。~ **cooler** 黄油防融器〔内盛冷水储放黄油的器皿〕。~**-cup**【植】毛茛。~**fat** 乳脂(~ *fat content in milk* 牛奶中的乳脂含量)。~ **fingered** *a*. 手指柔弱的,拿不稳东西的;接到球容易掉落的;手笨的。~**fingers** 手指柔弱的人;不中用的人;拿不稳东西的人,容易失球的队员。~**fish**【鱼】酪鱼〔尤指鲳科鱼〕。~**milk** 提去奶油的牛奶,脱脂乳,酪乳,酪酱(*a* ~ *milk cow*〔美〕母牛)。~ **nut**【植】灰胡桃(树)。~**-scotch** 黄油硬糖。~ **weed**【植】加拿大莴苣(= horse-weed). ~**wort**【植】捕虫堇。**-ing** *n*. 1. 涂黄油。2. 巴结,奉承。3.【建】(用镘)抹灰浆。

but·ter·fly [ˈbʌtəflai; ˋbʌtə˴flaɪ] **I** *n*. 1. 蝴蝶;蝶式,蝶形。2.〔喻〕举止轻浮的人〔尤指轻浮的妇女〕;游手好闲的人。3.【机】蝶形阀;活动目标探测器;【雕】X 形支柱。4. (可收起放小的)折板桌。5.〔*pl*.〕(由紧张等情绪引起的)欲呕的感觉。*a social* ~ 轻浮的交际花。**II** *vt*. (*-flied*)【烹】(把鱼肉等)切开摊平。*a butterflied shrimp* [*steak*]. 切开摊平的烹虾[牛排]。***break a ~ on the wheel*** 杀鸡用牛刀,小题大作。***butterflies in the stomach*** 颤糖,害怕得发抖。~ **bomb** 蝶形炸弹。~ **chair** (金属架)蝶形帆布躺椅。~ **dive**【泳】蝶式[大字式]跳水。~ **effect** 蝴蝶效应〔指某处一个微小的运动力(如蝴蝶扇动翅膀等)可能在另一遥远处产生巨大效应(如刮起飓风)的理论〕。~ **fish**【鱼】蝴蝶鱼。~ **net** 捕虫网。~ **nut** 蝶形螺母。~ **stroke**【泳】蝶泳。~ **valve**【机】蝶形阀[活门]。

but·ter·in(e) [ˈbʌtəri(ː)n; ˋbʌtə˴rɪ(i)n] *n*. (动物质)人造黄油。

but·ter·is [ˈbʌtəris; ˋbʌtərɪs] *n*. (兽医等用的)削蹄刀。

but·ter·y[1] [ˈbʌtəri; ˋbʌtərɪ] *n*. 1. 饮食品库房;〔口〕配膳室;酒库。2. (牛津、剑桥等大学的)饮食服务处。~ **hatch** (食堂传递饮食品的)售货窗口。

but·ter·y[2] [ˈbʌtəri; ˋbʌtərɪ] *a*. 1. 黄油状的,涂有黄油的。2.〔口〕油滑的;谄媚的。

butt·in·sky, butt·in·ski [bʌˈtinski; bʌˋtɪnskɪ] *n*.〔美口〕爱管闲事的人。*Don't be a* ~。别管闲事。*Mr*. ~ 爱管闲事的先生,好事佬。

butt·leg·ger [ˈbʌtˌlegə; ˋbʌt˴lɛgɚ] *n*.〔美〕非法香烟贩子。

but·tock [ˈbʌtək; ˋbʌtək] **I** *n*. 1. 半边屁股。2.〔常 *pl*.〕臀部,屁股。3. 艄,船尾。4.【摔跤】背摔。**II** *vt*.【摔跤】背摔。~ **line**【船】船体纵剖线。

but·ton [ˈbʌtn; ˋbʌtn] **I** *n*. 1. 扣子;钮扣。2. 揿扣,电钮,按钮(开关);(浆的)插扣。3. 节,小球,(把手的)圆顶;(剑把上的)皮圆顶。4. 扣状物;【植】芽,苞;【冶】金属小珠;〔美〕领扣;袖扣;圆形小徽章。5.〔*pl*.〕〔英口〕(穿有金色排扣制服的)侍者,服务员;服务员制服;警察。6. 一点儿,少许;无价值的东西。7.〔*pl*.〕〔俚〕神经的健全。8.〔俚〕颏尖;钱。*a shell* ~ 贝壳钮扣。*fasten* [*unfasten, undo*] ~ 扣上[解开]钮扣。*war fought by pushing* ~*s* 按电钮的战争。*cobalt* ~ 钴粒。***a ~ short***〔英口〕脑子差点劲。***boy in ~s*** 穿制服的侍者[服务员]。***have a ~ [a few ~s] missing***〔俚〕神经失常。***have a soul above ~s*** 觉得自己不称职[不胜任]。***have all one's ~s***〔俚〕神经正常。***hold [catch, take] sb. by the ~*** 留人长谈,拖住人谈话。***not care a ~ (about)*** (对…)毫不介意。***not have all one's ~s***〔俚〕神经反常,失常。***not worth a ~*** 一文不值。***on the ~***〔美俚〕1. 击中下颌。2. 准确。3. 准时。***push [press, touch] the ~*** 1. 按(电铃等的)揿钮,按电钮。2. 拍快照。3.〔俚〕慌忙发动(某事)。***push [press] the panic ~***〔俚〕惊慌失措,因一时慌乱而铸成大错。**II** *vt*. 1. 钉钮扣于,用钮扣装饰。2. (用钮扣)扣住,扣紧(*up*)。~ *a glove* 给手套缝上钮扣。*He ~ed the top ~ of his shirt*. 他扣上衬衣的领扣。— *vi*. 1. 装有扣子。2. 扣上钮扣;扣得住。*These shoes ~ easily*. 这种鞋子容易扣紧。*This coat ~s, but that one zips*. 这件外衣用钮扣,那件外衣用拉链。~ *the banknote into a pocket* 把钞票装进口袋扣好。~ *up one's pockets* [*purse*] 拒绝给钱。~ ***up***〔俚〕1. 别讲话。2. 关闭(机器等)。3. 完全做好,完工;〔美军俚〕侥幸完成任务(*B- it up*. 静一静,别讲话。*Everything on the submarine was ~ed up*. 潜水艇上的机器都关闭了。*~ed up to the chin* 把外套[上衣等]的钮扣一直扣到下巴;穿直领西装。*The report is all ~ed up*. 报告全部写出来了)。***B- up your face [lips]!***〔美俚〕别讲了! 静下来! ~ **ball**〔美〕美国梧桐。~ **boot** 带扣长统靴。~**bush**【植】风霜树。~**down** 1. 活动衣领的。2. 圆通的;世故的;彬彬有礼的。3. (衣着等)守旧的。~ **ear** 前垂的狗耳。~**hold** *vt*.〔古〕硬留人长谈。~**holder** = ~ holer. ~**hole** 1. *n*. 钮扣眼,饰孔;钮扣眼上插的花。2. *vt*. 在…上开钮扣眼;抓住(某人的)钮扣;强留(客人)长谈。~**holer** 强留客人长谈的人。~ **hook** (皮鞋等上的)绊钩,钮扣钩。~ **man** (黑社会犯罪集团中的)爪牙。~**mold** 包钮。~ **-on** *a*. 用钮扣扣上去的。~ **stick** (擦亮金属钮扣时用以防止弄脏制服的)垫条。~**wood**〔美〕美国梧桐;使君子树。

but·tress [ˈbʌtris; ˋbʌtrɪs] **I** *n*. 1.【建】(前)扶垛,撑墙,扶壁;【矿】支壁。2. 支持物,支持人,后台老板。3. 扶壁状物;山的扶壁状凸出部;(植物根部的)根肿;(马蹄后根的角质)蹄突。*a flying* ~ 扶壁拱架。*the ~ of the home* 一家的台柱。*the ~ of public opinion* 舆论的支持。**II** *vt*. 1. 用扶壁支衬[支撑、加固]。2. 支持,鼓励(*up*). ~ *up an argument* 拥护某一论点。

but·ty [ˈbʌti; ˋbʌtɪ] *n*.〔英方〕1. 同事,伙伴。2. 监工,工头。3. 采煤承包人。

bu·tyl [ˈbjuːtil; ˋbjutɪl] *n*. 1.【化】丁基。2.【商标】丁基橡胶。~ **alcohol** 丁醇。~ **rubber** 异丁(烯)橡胶。

bu·tyl·ene [ˈbjuːtiliːn; ˋbjutɪlin] *n*.【化】丁烯。~ **glycol**【化】丁二醇。

Bu·tyn [ˈbjuːtin; ˋbjutɪn] *n*. 菩他卡因的商标名;〔b-〕【药】菩他卡因麻醉剂。

bu·ty·ra·ceous [ˌbjuːtəˈreiʃəs; ˏbjutəˋreʃəs] *a*. 油的,含油的;油性大的;油腻的。

bu·tyr·al·de·hyde [ˌbjuːtəˈrældiˌhaid; ˏbjutəˋældə˴haɪd] *n*.【化】丁醛。

bu·ty·rate [ˈbjuːtireit; ˋbjutə˴ret] *n*.【化】丁酸盐;丁酸脂。

bu·tyr·ic [bju(ː)ˈtirik; bjuˋtɪrɪk] *a*. 黄油的;酪酸的。~ *acid*【化】酪酸;丁酸。

bu·ty·rin [ˈbjuːtərin; ˋbjutərɪn] *n*.【化】三丁酸甘油脂。

bux·om [ˈbʌksəm; ˋbʌksəm] *a*. 1. (女性)丰满的,有健康美的。2. 活泼的。*a ~ blonde* 胸部丰满的金发女郎。**-ly** *ad*. **-ness** *n*.

buy [bai; baɪ] (***bought*** [bɔːt; bɔt]; ***bought***) **I** *vt*. 1. 买,购 (*opp*. sell)。2. 收买,雇用。3. (付出代价)赢得,获得。4.〔美俚〕采纳(他人意见);接受…的宣传。5. 具有…的购买力;同意,赞成。~ *sth. from* [*of*] *sb*. 从某人处购买某物。~ *sth. for sb*. 为某人购某物。~ *favour with flattery* 以谄媚获得恩宠。~ *a new centre* 请来一位(足球)中锋。~ *sb. to silence* 贿赂某人保持沉默。*The dollar ~s less today* 美元的购买力下降了。*Okay, I'll ~ that*. 好,赞成。*He bought the whole story*. 他相信了那套鬼话。~***-and-sell shop*** (纽约的)旧货店。~ ***a pig in a poke*** 不看清货色就买。~ ***for cash*** 用现金买。~ ***in*** 买进(股票);买回(自己送出拍卖的东西);大宗买进。~ ***into***〔俚〕(出钱)做股东[会员],买地位(~ *into the club* 花钱买了个俱乐部会员资格)。~ ***it***〔俚〕1. (解答不了谜语、问题等而)撒手,放手,放弃,认输(*I'll ~ it*. 我答不出,我想不出来)。2. 阵亡(*He bought it at Dunkirk*. 他在敦克尔克阵亡了)。~ ***off*** (用贿赂)收买;用钱疏通[保护,救](~ *off the police* 用钱疏通警察)。~ ***on credit*** 赊买。~ ***out*** 出钱使某人出让地位[产权等];买下…的全部产权。~ ***over*** (用贿赂)收买。~ ***time*** 设法延迟作出决定[采取

行动]。~ *up* **1**. 囤积;整批收购,卖尽。**2**. 购进(其他公司)(~*up all the goods* 购进全部货物)。— ***vi***. 买,购买,购物。**II** ***n***. **1**. 〔美〕购买。**2**. 买卖,交易。**3**. 〔俚〕便宜货,合算的买卖[交易等](*It's a real* ~ *at that price*. 这是一笔价钱合算的买卖)。~ **boat** 〔美〕(鱼行等的)买鱼船,收购船。~**-in** 〔美〕补偿购入〔证券交易中的一种程序〕。~**-out** 〔美〕全部买下(证券等);购空存货〔把某种商品的存货全部购入〕。**-able** ***a***. **1**. 可购买的。**2**. 可收买的。**-ing** ***n***. 购买(*buying power* 购买力)。

buy·er [ˈbaiə; ˋbaɪɚ] ***n***. **1**. 买方;买主。**2**. 采购员,货物代办人。~**s' market** 跌风笼罩下的市场。~**s' strike** 罢购,消费者的抵制行动。

buz·ka·shi [ˈbuːzˈkɑːʃiː; ˋbuzˋkɑʃi] ***n***. 抢羊比赛(阿富汗的民族体育运动)。

buzz [bʌz; bʌz] **I** ***vi***. **1**. (蜂等)嗡嗡地叫[飞](*about*; *over*; *in*; *out*);(机器等)发嗡嗡声,发蜂音,用蜂音器传呼。**2**. 喊喊喳喳地讲;(谣言等)传开。**3**. 〔俚〕跑来跑去(*about*);慌忙走开(*off*; *along*). **4**. 【空】低飞过原野[城市];(电话)发占线的信号声。*flies* ~*ing about* 嗡嗡乱飞的苍蝇。*The town was* ~*ing with the news*. 这个新闻传遍全城。*men* ~*ing about in a frantic activity* 跑来跑去忙得要命的人们。*B- off!* 快走开。— ***vt***. **1**. 使嗡嗡叫,使营营响。**2**. 喊喊喳喳地传播[散布](谣言等);异口同声地说。**3**. 〔口〕给…打电话;用蜂音器传呼;〔军俚〕(用信号)传送。**4**. 〔美军俚〕(飞机低飞)掠过,向…俯冲;飞近(另一飞机)进行骚扰。**5**. 猛扔(石头等)。**6**. 〔英方〕倒干(酒瓶),喝干(一瓶酒)。*The fly* ~*ed its wings*. 那只苍蝇振翅营营作响。~*a rumor* [*gossip*] 散布谣言[流言蜚语]。*He* ~*ed his secretary*. 他用蜂音器传呼秘书。*planes* ~*ing the crowd* 飞机低飞掠过人群。~ ***away*** 〔俚〕慌忙走开。~ ***off*** **1**. 搁断电话。**2**. 〔俚〕慌忙走开,溜掉。**II** ***n***. **1**. 营营声,嗡嗡声;【无】蜂音。**2**. 喊喊喳喳声,嘈杂声。**3**. 风声,流言,传闻;谣言。**4**. 蜂音器信号;〔俚〕电话;〔军俚〕电话兵。**5**. 〔美〕圆锯;〔口〕醉。*a* ~ *of conversation* 嗡嗡的谈话声。*My brain was in* ~. 我的脑袋嗡嗡响。*give sb. a* ~ 给某人打电话。***go with a*** ~ 进行得很成功,很顺利。**III** ***int***. (消息)早过时了! 老掉牙了! ~ **bomb** 〔军口〕"嗡嗡弹","V"型飞弹,喷气推进式炸弹。~**box** = ~ wag(g)on. ~**-saw** 〔美〕电动小圆锯。~ **session** 非正式的小型座谈会。~ **wag(g)on** 〔美俚〕汽车。~**wig** **1**. 假发;戴假发的人。**2**. 要人,伟人(*a political* ~*wig* 政界要人)。~ **word** (企业、政府、科技等方面的)流行词语[口号]。

buz·zard [ˈbʌzəd; ˋbʌzɚd] ***n***. **1**. 【动】鹈鹕,美国秃鹰。**2**. 营营发声的昆虫。**3**. 〔俚〕无耻之徒;贪婪的人;乖僻的人;老头儿,老糊涂。

buzz·er [ˈbʌzə; ˋbʌzɚ] ***n***. **1**. 营营发声的虫;(工厂的)汽笛;【无】蜂音器。**2**. 〔军俚〕信号兵,〔*pl*.〕信号部队。

BVDs = a pair of undershorts 短衬裤。

B.V.M. = Blessed Virgin Mary.

BW = **1**. bacteriological warfare 细菌战。**2**. biological warfare 生物战。

bwa·na [ˈbwɑːnə; ˋbwɑnə] ***n***. 〔常作 B-〕老爷;先生〔非洲部分地区对人的尊称,原为斯瓦希里语〕。

BX = Base Exchanger.

by [bai; baɪ] **I** ***prep***. **1**. 在侧,在旁;贴近,挨近,靠近,(方向)偏于。~ *the fire* 炉旁。~ *the seaside* 海边。*north* ~ *east* 北偏东。*a path* ~ *the river* 滨河路。**2**. 顺,经,沿,由;经过…旁边。*enter* ~ *the back door* 由后门进来。*She went right* ~ *him*. 她从他身边走过。*travel* ~ *land* [*water*] 走陆[水]路。~ *the nearest road* 抄近道,走近路。**3**. (交通,通讯等)坐,乘;以。~ *bus* [*train*] 乘公共汽车[火车]。*arrive* ~ *ship* 乘船到达。*tell sb. the news* ~ *letter* [*telegram*] 以书信[电报]将消息告知某人。*correspond* ~ *tape recorder* 以录音彼此通讯。**4**. 到,到…时为止,不晚于;到…已经。*He must be there* ~ *this time*. 他现在必定已经到那里了。*I usually finish work* ~ *five o'clock*. 我一般五点钟做完工作。~ *tomorrow* 到明天。**5**. 在(夜间、白天等)时间内。*walk* ~ *night* 夜行。*work* ~ *day* 白天工作。*lover's walk* ~ *moonlight* 恋人的月下散步。**6**. 被,由。(*written*) ~ *Byron* 拜伦(写的)著作。*Who is this poem* ~? 这首诗是谁写的? *My brother has one child* ~ *his first wife*. 我兄弟有一个前妻生的孩子。*be bitten* ~ *a dog* 被狗咬。**7**. 靠,用,通过,借助于〔表示方法、手段等〕。~ *this means* 通过这种方法。*earn one's living* ~ *writing* 靠写作为生。*learn* ~ *heart* 记牢,熟记,背熟。*take* ~ *force* 用武力夺取。*teach* ~ *example* 以身作则。*die* ~ *poison* [*madness*] 中毒[发疯]死去。**8**. 由于,因。*We meet* ~ *chance*. 我们偶然相遇。*I took his pen* ~ *mistake*. 我错拿了他的笔。**9**. 照,凭,据,按。*judge* ~ *appearance* 凭外表判断。*This is a bad movie* ~ *any standard*. 不管根据什么标准来看,这都是一部坏影片。*It's just five o'clock* ~ *my watch*. 我的表现在是五点。*sell* ~ *the yard* [*weight*] 按码[重量]卖。*work* ~ *the hour* [*day*] 按时[日]计工。*I'm paid* ~ *the week*. 我按周领薪。*live* ~ *faith* 遵照信仰生活。*He goes* ~ *the name of Nerville*. 他以尼维尔的名字进行活动。**10**. 逐一;连续。*one* ~ *one* 一个一个地。*drop* ~ *drop* 一滴一滴地。~ *degrees* 渐次。*little* ~ *little* 一点一点地。~ *twos and threes* 三三两两。**11**. 相差。*miss* ~ *a foot* 偏了一英尺左右。*miss the train* ~ *two minutes* 迟两分钟误了火车。*too many* ~ *one* 只多一个。*The production of foodstuff increased* ~ *50 percent*. 粮食产量增长50%。**12**. 在…方面是,就…来说是。*John* ~ *name* 名叫约翰。*They were peasants by occupation and Catholics* ~ *religion*. 他们的职业是务农,信仰上是天主教徒。*cousins* ~ *blood* 血统上是表弟兄。*a grocer* ~ *trade* 做杂货生意。~ *nature* 从本性上说。**13**. 对,比〔表示面积〕;对待,对于〔表示义务,态度等〕;用…去乘[除]。*3 ft*. ~ *5 ft*. 〔=3 ft. × 5 ft. = 3 ft. : 5ft.〕3 英尺宽 5 英尺长。*a room 10 feet* ~ *12 feet* 一间长 12 英尺宽 10 英尺的房间。*my duty* ~ *him* 我对他的义务。*do one's duty* ~ *one's friend* 尽朋友的责任。*He did well* ~ *his children*. 他对孩子很好。*Do as you would be done by*. 你想人怎样对你,你也要怎样对人。*Multiply* [*Divide*] *18* ~ *6*. 用 6 去乘[除]18。**14**. 在…部位〔表示动作所及处〕。*catch a dog* ~ *a tail* 抓住狗尾巴。*hold a horse* ~ *the nose* 牵住马鼻子。*The water pulled the ship down* ~ *the stern*. 水从船尾使船沉没。**15**. (客人等)来(串门,访问)。*Drop* ~ *my office this afternoon*. 下午到我办公室来谈谈。*She came* ~ *my house for a few minutes*. 她到我家坐了几分钟。**16**. 指,当,凭,对(天)赌咒[发誓]。*swear* ~ *all that is sacred* 凭着神圣发誓。*By god, I never observed it*. 老天爷在上,我绝没有注意过它。*By Heavens, I will have his heart's blood*. 上天作证,我一定要杀死他。**II** ***ad***. **1**. 在侧,在旁,在附近。**2**. (搁)在一边,(放)到旁边,(存)在一旁;收着。**3**. (由旁边)经过,过去。**4**. (岁月等)流过。**5**. 〔美口〕(请)来(访问,玩玩,谈谈等)〔与 call, come, stop 等连用〕。*No one was* ~. 没有人在旁边。*The school is close* ~. 学校就在近旁。*stand* [*sit*] ~ 站[坐]在一旁。*a store near* ~ 邻近的一家店铺。*pass* ~ 经过,走过,通过。*hurry* ~ 匆匆走过。*The car drove* ~. 汽车驶过。*The bird flew* ~. 鸟飞过。*Put your work* ~ *for a moment*. 把你的工作搁一搁。*These apples were put* ~ *for the winter*. 这些苹果储存起来冬天卖[吃]。*lay* ~ *enough money to retire* 储蓄足够的钱以便退休。*in days gone* ~ 往日。*Next time you're over this way, please come* ~. 下次路过这里,请来坐一坐。**III** ***a***. ★通例用作 by(e)-。**IV** ***n***. = bye. ~ ***and again*** 〔美〕时时,常常。

～ **and** ～ 不久以后,不一会儿(*The clouds will disappear* ～ *and* ～. 云很快就要散了)。～ **and large** 全盘,总的来说,一般地说,大体上。～ **far** 见 far 条。～ **half** 见 half 条。～ **oneself** [**itself**] 单独,独立;独自。～ **the** ～(**e**) 顺便说到。～ **the way** 见 way 条。～-**and**-～ *n*.(不远的)将来(*in the sweet* ～-*and*-～ 美好的未来)。～-**bidder** 抬价卖出者;拍卖者。～-**bidding** 抬价出卖;拍卖。～-**blow** 1. 偶然的[间接的]一击。2. 私生子。～-**channel** 支渠。～-**election** (英国国会的)补缺选举。～-**end** 1. 私意,私心。2. (诗歌等的)片断。～-**effect** 副作用。～-**lane** 小巷;僻巷;小路。～**law** 1. 附则,细则。2. (英国地方自治单位的)地方法。3. (协会、团体等的)会章,社章。～-**line** 1. *n*. (新闻杂志标题下的)作者署名;(铁路干线的)支线。2. 副业。3. *vt*. 在(新闻、杂志文章等的)下面署名(～-*line a magazine piece* 在一篇杂志文章下面署名)。～-**motive** 隐密的动机,暗中的打算。～-**mordant** 【化】辅助媒染剂。～**name** 1. 浑名,绰号;假名,伪名;别名。2. 姓,(古罗马人的)家名,第三名。～**pass** 1. *n*.【机】(煤气等的)旁(通)管;(为疏散交通而设的迂回的)旁路;小道,间道;【电】分路迂徊。2. *vt*. 为…加设旁路[旁通管];绕过,越过,超过;回避,忽视(～-*pass a congested city* 加设旁路疏散拥挤的城市交通。*bright sunshine* ～-*passing the thin curtains* 强烈的阳光透过薄窗帘。～-*pass congress* 绕过国会)。～-**passer** = passer-by. ～-**past** *a*. 过去的,以往的。～-**path** 小路,旁路,侧道,僻径。～-**place** 穷乡僻壤。～**play** 【剧】(主题以外)穿插戏;枝节故事。～-**plot** (小说、戏剧的)从属情节,次要情节。～-**product** 副产品。～**road** 小路,间道。～**stander** 旁观者,看热闹的,局外人(*a* ～*stander behavior* 局外人的态度)。～**street** 小街,背街。～-**talk** 闲话;杂谈。～-**time** 余暇,闲空,空闲。～**way** 小路,间道,侧道;〔喻〕次要方面;(研究等方面的)冷门(*highways and* ～*ways* 大路和小路;〔喻〕直接方面和间接方面,主要和次要方面。*a* ～*way of learning* 冷门学科)。～**word** 1. 俗话,谚语。2. 笑柄。3. 〔罕〕浑名,绰号;口头禅(*the old* ～*word of lookers-on seeing most of the game* 旁观者清的老话)。～**work** 副业,兼职,业余工作。～-**your-leave** 对不起〔因未获准许而作某事的道歉语〕。

by- *comb*. *f*. 1. 附随的,附属的;枝节的,第二义的,副的。2. 附近的,邻近的,旁边的,旁的;偏的。3. 秘密的,私,阴: *by*stander, *by*passer, *by*street, *by*path, *by*product.

bye [bai; baɪ] *n*. 1. 枝节,小事,附属事物。2.【板球】球越过打手及守门者时所得的分数。3.【体】(抽签)轮空的选手[队]。*by the* ～ [*by*] 顺便说到,就便提起(*By the* ～, *how do you spell your name*? 顺便问一句,您的名字怎样拼写?)。*drawa* ～ 抽签抽到轮空(不战而胜)。～ **team** (抽签轮空的)不战而胜队。

bye- *comb*. *f*. = by-.

bye-bye[1] [ˈbaibai; ˋbaɪˏbaɪ] **I** *n*. 〔儿〕瞌瞌;床。*go to* ～ 睡觉吧。**II** *ad*. 上床,睡觉。*go* ～ 去睡觉。

bye-bye[2] [ˈbaiˈbai; ˋbaɪˋbaɪ] *int*. 再会! 回头见!

Bye·lo·rus·sia [ˌbjeləˈrʌʃə; ˏbjeloˋrʌʃə] *n*. 白俄罗斯(= White Russia). **-n** *n*., *a*. 1. 白俄罗斯人(的)。2. 白俄罗斯语(的)。

bye-low [ˈbaiˌləu; ˋbaɪˏlo] *ad*., *int*. 〔儿〕嘘! 别响,静一静! 〔用于催眠曲和摇篮曲〕。

by·gone [ˈbaigɔ(:)n; ˋbaɪˏgɔn] **I** *a*. 〔书〕1. 过去的,已往的。2. 过时的,旧式的。*a* ～ *age* 昔日,往日。*in* ～ *years* 以往的年代。～ *days* 逝去的岁月。*revivals of* ～ *styles* 旧时式样[风格]的复活。**II** *n*. 过去的事;往事。*Let's not talk of* ～*s*. 我们不要谈旧事[翻老账]了。*let* ～*s be* ～*s* 过去的事就让它过去吧;忘掉过去的冤仇;捐弃前嫌;既往不究(*Let's let* ～*s be* ～*s and begin again*. 让我们忘却旧事重新开始)。

byn·oc·u·lar [baiˈnɔkjulə; baɪˋnɑkjʊlɚ] *n*. = binocular.

BYOB = Bring Your Own Bottles. 请自带酒。

Byrd [bəːd; bɝd] *n*. 伯德〔姓氏〕。

byre [baiə; baɪr] *n*. 〔英〕牛栏,牛棚。

Byrne(s) [bəːn(z); bɝn(z)] *n*. 伯恩(斯)〔姓氏〕。

byr·nie [ˈbəːni; ˋbɝnɪ] *n*. (甲胄)锁子甲,连环铠甲。

By·ron [ˈbaiərən; ˋbaɪrən] *n*. 拜伦〔姓氏〕。**George Noel Gordono** ～ 乔·拜伦〔1788—1824 英国诗人〕。

By·ron·ic [baiˈrɔnik; baɪˋrɑnɪk] *a*. 拜伦的;拜伦诗风的;慷慨悲歌式的。**By·ron·ism** 拜伦主义。**-ally** *ad*.

bys·si·no·sis [ˌbisiˈnəusis; ˏbɪsəˋnosɪs] *n*.【医】棉屑沉着病。

bys·sus [ˈbisəs; ˋbɪsəs] *n*. 1. 古代的亚麻纤维。2. (古埃及用以裹扎木乃伊的)亚麻布[棉、丝织物等]。3.【动】(贝类等的)丝足;【植】菌丝。

byte [bait; baɪt] *n*.【计】二进位组,信息组,字节,位组。

By·zan·tine [biˈzæntain; bɪˋzæntaɪn] **I** *a*. 1.【史】拜占廷的;东罗马帝国的。2.【建】拜占廷式的。3. 爱玩弄阴谋的,诡计多端的。**II** *n*. 1. 拜占廷人。2. 拜占廷式建筑,拜占廷风格的画家。～ **Church** 东正教。～ **Empire** 拜占廷帝国,东罗马帝国。

By·zan·tin·esque [biˌzæntiˈnesk; bɪˏzæntɪˋnɛsk] *a*.【建】拜占廷风格的。

By·zan·tin·ism [biˈzæntinizəm; bɪˋzæntɪnˏɪzəm] *n*. 1. (建筑、艺术等的)拜占廷风格。2. 拜占廷主义[精神]。

By·zan·ti·um [biˈzæntiəm; bɪˋzæntɪəm] *n*.【史】拜占廷〔古罗马城市,一度称为 Constantinople, 今名 Islanbul〕.

Bz. = benzene.

C

C, c [siː; si] (*pl*. **C's**, **c's** [siːz; siz]) 1. 英语字母表第三字母。2. C 形物。3.【乐】C 调,C 音;【数】第三个已知数;第三,丙。4. 〔美〕〔C〕(学业成绩)中。5. 〔C〕罗马数字 100。6. 〔C〕【化】元素碳 (carbon) 的符号。7. 〔C〕[电]库伦(coulomb)的符号。8. 〔C〕〔美俚〕可卡因 (cocaine)。*C major* [*minor*] C 大[小]调。*a C-spring* C 字形(承力)弹簧 (= Cee-spring)。CCCL = 350. C3[读作 ˈsiː θriː; ˈsi θri]丙等(的),体格劣等(的)。(*a C3 concert* 第三流音乐会)。*C and A Pocket* 〔美〕无业游民做在上衣里用来装多余粮食的口袋 (Chicago and Alton pocket)。*C and S*【美军】整洁而严肃的 (= clean and sober)。

C., **c.** = **1**. candle. **2**. capacity. **3**. Catholic. **4**. cathode. **5**. Celtic. **6**. cent(s). **7**. centigrade. **8**. 〔F.〕 *centime*. **9**. centimetre. **10**. century. **11**. chapter. **12**. Chancellor. **13**. 〔L.〕*circa*. **14**. copy; copyright. **15**. cost. **16**. cubic. **17**. Congress. **18**. Conservative. **19**. Corps. **20**. Court. **21**. city. **22**. cloudy. **23**. centre.

C/A = **1**. current account 往来账户,活期存款账户。**2**. capital account 资本账;股本账;公积账。**3**. cash account 现金账户。

CA = chlormadinone 氯地孕酮〔避孕药〕。

Ca【化】元素钙(calcium)的符号。

Caa·ba[ˈkɑːbə; ˋkɑbə] ***n***. (= Kaaba)(穆斯林参拜的)麦加的黑石;供有黑石的石造圣堂。

CAAC = General Administration of Civil Aviation of China 中国民用航空总局〔CAAC是前译名 Civil Aviation Administration of China 的缩写,现仍沿用〕。

CAB = **1**. Civil Aeronautics Board〔美〕民用航空局。**2**. Citizens' Advice Bureau (英国)市民咨询处。**3**. Civil Aeronautics Bulletin (美国)民航通报。

cab[1][kæb; kæb] **I** ***n***. **1**. 出租马车,出租汽车。**2**. (机车、卡车、拖拉机、起重机等的)司机室。*take a* ~坐马车[汽车]去。**II** ***vi***. (***cabbed***; ***cabbing***)〔俚〕〔常说作~ it〕坐出租马车[汽车]。*They cabbed to the theatre*. 他们坐出租汽车去剧场。~**driver** 出租汽车司机;赶马车的人。**-getter** 出租汽车的乘客。~**man** 出租马车驾驶人;出租汽车司机。~ **rank**〔英〕**1**. 等候出租的马车[汽车]行列。**2**. = ~stand. ~**stand** 出租马车[汽车]停车处。

cab[2][kæb; kæb] **I** ***vi***. (***cabbed***; ***cabbing***)〔英学俚〕抄夹带,作弊。**II** ***n***. 夹带;作弊。

cab[3][kæb; kæb] ***n***. 开普;古希伯来粮食等干物的量具名〔容量相当二夸脱〕。

ca·bal [kəˈbæl; kəˋbæl] **I** ***n***. **1**. (人数不多的)秘密组织;阴谋。**2**. 〔C-〕【英史】(查理二世时代)五大臣小组〔他们名字的开首字母:恰巧是 C, A, B, A, L 五个字母〕。**3**. (美术、文艺中的)派系。~ *system* 首字串联法〔把各词首字母连接成一词以记忆全文的方法〕。**II** ***vi***. (***-ll-***) 玩弄阴谋;结党(图谋)。

cab·a·la [kəˈbɑːlə, ˈkæbələ; kəˋbɑlə, ˋkæbələ] ***n***. **1**. (对《圣经》作神秘主义解释的)犹太神秘哲学。**2**. 神秘教义。

cab·a·lism [ˈkæbəlizəm; ˋkæbəlɪzəm] ***n***. **1**. 犹太神秘教义。**2**. (文字的)晦涩难解。

cab·a·list [ˈkæbəlist; ˋkæbəlɪst] ***n***. 犹太神秘哲学家;秘法家。

cab·a·lis·tic [ˌkæbəˈlistik; ˏkæbəˋlɪstɪk] ***a***. 犹太神秘哲学的;神秘的,玄妙的。

ca·bal·ler [kəˈbælə; kəˋbælɚ] ***n***. 阴谋家。

ca·bal·le·ro [ˌkæbəˈljɛərəu; ˏkæbəlˋjɛro] ***n***. 〔Sp.〕**1**. 绅士;骑士;骑马的人。**2**. (美国西南部)骑马者;妇女崇拜者。

ca·ba·ña [kəˈbɑːnə; kɑˋbɑnjɑ] ***n***. 〔Sp.〕小房间,私室;(海滨等处的)浴室。~ **set** (包括短袖上衣和短裤的)男士海滩装。

ca·bane [ˈkæbən; kəˋbæn] ***n***. 【空】翼柱,翼间架。

cab·a·ret [ˈkæbəret, ˈkæbərei; ˋkæbərɛt, ˋkæbəre] ***n***. **1**. (有舞蹈、音乐等表演的)餐馆。**2**. 餐馆里的歌舞表演(亦作 = show)。~ **tax** 娱乐税。

cab·bage[1][ˈkæbidʒ; ˋkæbɪdʒ] **I** ***n***. **1**. 【植】甘蓝,包心菜。**2**. 〔美俚〕劣等雪茄烟,粗烟。**3**. 〔美俚〕〔指纸币〕钱。**4**. 〔美俚〕少女。*Chinese* ~大白菜。~ *white* = ~ *butterfly* 白蝶。~ *rose* 洋蔷薇。**II** ***vi***. 长(菜)头,长成甘蓝状头。~**head**〔美〕笨蛋,呆子。~ **palm**【植】槟榔子。~**worm**【动】甘蓝虫。

cab·bage[2][ˈkæbidʒ; ˋkæbɪdʒ] **I** ***vt***. (裁缝)偷(布)。—***vi***. (裁缝)偷布,偷。**II** ***n***. 偷剪的布料;(裁剪剩下的)碎料;被偷的东西。

cabbie [ˈkæbi; ˋkæbɪ] ***n***. 〔口〕出租汽车司机。

cab·ba·la [ˈkæbələ; ˋkæbələ], **cab·ba·lism** [-lizəm; -lɪzəm] = cabala, cabalism.

cab·by, cab·bie [ˈkæbi; ˋkæbɪ] ***n***. 〔美口〕出租汽车司机(= cabman)。

Cab·ell [ˈkæbəl; ˋkæbl] ***n***. 卡贝尔〔姓氏〕。

ca·ber [ˈkeibə; ˋkebɚ] ***n***. (苏格兰等地投棒比臂力游戏中所用的)松木棒。*tossing the* ~投松木棒(比臂力)。

cab·e·zon [ˈkæbiˌzɔn; ˋkæbɪˏzɑn] ***n***. 【动】拟蝎鱼。

cab·in [ˈkæbin; ˋkæbɪn] **I** ***n***. **1**. 小屋,小室;〔英〕(铁路等的)信号室。**2**. 船室[舱],头[二]等客舱;【空】座舱;舰长室,长官室,军官室。**3**. 卧室;小房间,私室。**II** ***vt***. **1**. 把…关在小屋内;使受拘束。**2**. 隔开(房间)。—***vi***. 住在小屋内;寄住。~**boy** (船长室、舰长室、一二等客舱的)服务员。~ **class** 头等舱。~ **court** (公路旁为汽车游客服务的)家庭式小旅馆。~ **cruise** 带有住宿设备的汽艇。~ **de luxe** 贵宾室;特等舱。~**-officer** 有资格在军官餐室吃饭的军官。~**-passenger** 头二等船客。

Ca·bin·da [kəˈbində; kəˋbɪndə] ***n***. **1**. 喀丙达(卡宾达)〔非洲〕。**2**. 喀丙达(卡宾达)〔喀丙达(卡宾达)首府〕。

cab·ined [ˈkæbind; ˋkæbɪnd] ***a***. **1**. 狭窄的,被关进狭窄场所的。**2**. 有船室的。

cab·i·net [ˈkæbinit; ˋkæbənɪt] **I** ***n***. **1**. 〔常作 C-〕内阁;〔英〕内阁会议(室);〔美〕总统[州长、市长]顾问团。**2**. 小房间,私室,密议室。**3**. 陈列室;(矿物、生物、古钱币等)陈列品。**4**. 饰架,珍品橱,柜,箱,盒;【物】(机)箱。**5**. 【摄】六英寸片。*a card* ~卡片箱;(公用电话)收费箱。*a shadow* ~(在野党领袖虚拟的)影子内阁。**II** ***a***. **1**. 内阁的,秘密的。**2**. 小房间用的;小巧的,玲珑的。**3**. 细木工做的。**4**. (相片)六英寸的。~ **council** (内)阁(会)议。~ **crisis** 内阁(瓦解)危机。~ **edition** (书籍装帧的)中型版(式)。~**maker** **1**. 家具师,桌椅匠。**2**. 〔讽〕组阁者;新任内阁总理。~**making** **1**. 家具制造,家具业。**2**. 〔讽〕组阁。**Cabinet Minister** =〔美〕~ **member** [**officer**] 阁员。~ **organ** 竖立式小风琴。~ **photograph** 六英寸照片。~ **piano** (竖式)钢琴。~ **pudding** 干果布丁。~**work** 细木工家具;细木工。

cab·i·net·eer [ˌkæbiniˈtiə; ˏkæbənɪˋtɪr] ***n***. 〔美〕无能的[名气不好的]阁员。

Ca·ble [ˈkeibl; ˋkebl̩] ***n***. 凯布尔〔姓氏〕。

ca·ble [ˈkeibl; ˋkebl̩] **I** ***n***. **1**. 【船】锚链,锚索,(周长 10 英寸以上的)左捻三根三股索;粗索,巨缆;钢丝绳。**2**. 电缆;海底电线;海底电报;【空】张索;绞线;【电】多心导线,被覆线。**3**. 锚链〔= cable length 海上测距单位〕。**4**. 【纺】(针织)软轴。***by*** ~ 用海底电报。***cut*** [***slip***] ***one's*** [***the***] ~〔海俚〕死。**II** ***vt***. **1**. (用锚链,缆索等)系住。**2**. 给…打海底电报;通过海底电缆发(电报)。—***vi***. 打海底电报,用海底电线通讯。*a cabling machine* 搓绳机。~ ***up***(使)与…有线电视系统联网。***nothing to*** ~ ***home about***〔Aus.〕无足轻重,无用,不重要。~ **address** (地址姓名等的)海外电报挂号。~ **car** 缆车。~**cast** ***vt***. 用有线电视[公共天线]播放。~ **gram** 海底电报。~**-laid** ***a***. 【船】左捻三根三股的。~ **message** 海外电报。~ **length** 一锚链长〔185 米,即 1/10 浬〕。~ **modem**【电信】光缆调制解调器。~ **railway** 缆车道。~ **station** 海底电报局;海底电报,水线电报。~**-knitting** 绞花编结。~ **TV** **1**. 电缆[有线]电视。**2**. 公共天线。~**way** 索道。

ca·blese [keiˈbliːz; keblˋiz] ***n***. 电报用语〔如简省、缩写等〕。

ca·blet [ˈkeiblit; ˋkebl̩ɪt] ***n***. 【船】(周长小于 10 英寸的)左捻三根三股索。

ca·bling [ˈkeibliŋ; ˋkeblɪŋ] ***n***. 【建】**1**. 卷缆柱。**2**. 卷绳状雕饰。

ca·bob [kəˈbɔb; kəˋbɑb] ***n***. **1**. 叉烧肉片洋葱[西红柿]。**2**. 叉烧肉(= kebab, kabab, kebob)。

ca·bo·chon [ˌkæbəˈʃɔːŋ; ˏkaboˋʃɑŋ] ***n***. 〔F.〕(顶部磨成圆形并不加刻面的)圆顶平底宝石。***en*** ~ (宝石的)圆顶平底式。

ca·bom·ba [kəˈbɔmbə; kəˋbɑmbə] ***n***. 【植】水盾草属植物〔尤指鱼草 *Cabomb Caroliniana*〕。

ca·boo·dle [kəˈbuːdl; kəˋbudl̩] ***n***. 〔美口〕群,团;捆,堆。

the whole (*kit and*) ~ 全部,全体。

ca·boose [kəˈbuːs; kəˋbus] **n.** 1. (商船甲板上的)厨房。2. 〔美〕(货车后部车务员坐的)公务车。3. 小房间,狭窄的地方。

Cabot [ˈkæbət; ˋkæbət] **n.** 卡伯特〔姓氏〕。**John** ~约翰·卡伯特〔1450—1498?,意大利航海家,1497 年发现北美大陆〕。

cab·o·tage [ˈkæbətidʒ; ˋkæbətɪdʒ] **n.** 1. 沿(海)岸航行(权);沿(海)岸贸易。2. 【空】国内航空权。

ca·bret·ta [kəˈbretə; kəˋbrɛtə] **a.** 巴西绵羊皮革的;软羊皮革的。

ca·bril·la [kəˈbrilə, kəˈbriːjə; kəˋbrɪlə, kəˋbrɪjə] **n.** 【动】鲭科鱼。

C

cab·ri·ole [ˈkæbriəul; ˋkæbrɪˏol] **n.** (英国老式家具特有的)狮爪形弯腿。

cab·ri·o·let [kæbriəˈlei; ˏkæbrɪəˋle] **n.** 〔F.〕单马篷车;活顶小轿车。

cab·rit [ˈkæbrit; ˋkæbrɪt] **n.** 【动】美洲羚羊。

ca'can·ny [kɑːˈkæni, kɔː-; kɑˋkænɪ, kɔ-] **I vi.** 1. 〔Scot.〕(车辆)慢行。2. 〔英〕磨洋工,怠工。**II n.** 〔英〕怠工。

ca·ca·o [kəˈkɑːəu, kəˈkeiəu; kəˋkɑo, kəˋkeo] **n.** 【植】可可树;可可豆。

cac·ci·a·to·re [ˌkætʃiˈtɔːri; kɑtʃɑˋtore] **a.** (用橄榄油、番茄、洋葱等)在砂锅里焖煮的。*Chicken* ~罐焖鸡。

cach·a·lot [ˈkæʃəlɔt; ˋkæʃəˏlɑt] **n.** 【动】抹香鲸。

cache [kæʃ; kæʃ] **I n.** 1. (探险者等贮藏粮食、器材等的)暗窖,密藏处。2. 贮藏物。3.【计】高速缓冲内存。**II vt.** 1. 贮藏;密藏;窖藏。2.【计】把…储存到硬盘上。

ca·chec·tic [kəˈkektik; kəˋkɛktɪk] **a.** 【医】(由慢性病等造成的)恶病质的,极度瘦弱的。

cache·pot [ˈkæʃpɔt, -pəu; ˋkæʃˏpɑt, -po] **n.** 花盆,花瓶。

ca·chet [ˈkæʃei; ˋkæʃei] **n.** 〔F.〕 1. 药包,胶囊。2. (书信等的)封印;特征,标志。3. 纪念邮戳。4. (得自名人的)称赞。5. 威信;(高贵的)身分。***lettre de*** ~【法史】密令。

ca·chex·i·a, ca·chex·y [kəˈkeksiə, kəˈkeksi; kəˋkɛksɪə, kəˋkɛksɪ] **n.** 【医】(由慢性病等造成的)恶病(体)质;极度瘦弱。

cach·in·nate [ˈkækineit; ˋkækəˏnet] **vi.** 大笑,哄笑。

cach·in·na·tion [ˌkækiˈneiʃən; ˏkækəˋneʃən] **n.** 大笑,高声狂笑,哄笑。

cach·in·na·to·ry [kəˈkinətəri; kəˋkɪnəˏtɔrɪ] **a.** 大笑的,哄笑的。

cach·o·long [ˈkætʃəlɔŋ; ˋkæʃəˏlɑŋ] **n.** 【矿】美蛋白石。

ca·chou [kəˈʃuː, kæˈʃuː; kəˋʃu, kæˋʃu] **n.** 口香片(=catechu)。

ca·chu·cha [kəˈtʃuːtʃə; kəˋtʃutʃə] **n.** 〔Sp.〕(西班牙的)客曲洽舞[舞曲]。

ca·cique [kæˈsiːk; kəˋsik] **n.** 1. (西印度群岛、墨西哥、秘鲁等地的)印第安人酋长;(菲律宾等地的)大地主。2. 〔美〕地方政治首领。

ca·ciqu·ism [kəˈsiːkizəm; kəˋsikɪzəm] **n.** (由党魁等操纵的)腐败的地方政治。

cack [kæk; kæk] **n.** 〔美〕小儿用平底靴。

cack·le [ˈkækl; ˋkækl̩] **I n.** 1. (母鸡、鹅等的)咯咯叫声。2. 饶舌;〔美〕废话,空话。3. 尖声的笑。***cut the*** ~ 1. 〔俚〕使不说废话而抓住要点。2. (命令)住嘴,别响。**II vi.** 1. (鸡等下蛋后)咯咯地叫。2. 唠唠叨叨地讲。3. 咯咯地笑。—**vt.** 唠唠叨叨地讲出。

cack·ler [ˈkæklə; ˋkæklɚ] **n.** 1. 饶舌家,碎嘴子。2. 〔美俚〕戏剧演员,艺人。3. 〔*pl.*〕〔美俚〕鸡蛋。

caco- *comb. f.* 恶,丑。*caco*logy.

cac·o·dae·mon, cac·o·de·mon [ˌkækəˈdiːmən; ˏkækəˋdimən] **n.** 1. 恶鬼;恶人。2. 恶梦,梦魔。

cac·o·dyl [ˈkækədil; ˋkækəˏdɪl] **n.** 【化】卡可基;二甲胂基;四甲二胂。**-ic a.**

cac·o·e·py [ˈkækəuepi; ˋkækəˏɛpɪ] **n.** 发音不正。

cac·o·ë·thes [kækəuˈiːθiːz; kækoˋiθiz] **n.** 〔L.〕 1. 恶习,恶癖;(某种)狂癖。2. 【医】恶性殖疡。~ ***scribendi*** [skriˈbendai; skrɪˋbɛndaɪ]〔L.〕著作狂。

cac·o·gen·e·sis [ˌkækəˈdʒenisis; ˏkækəˋdʒɛnəsɪs] **n.** 【生】1. 构造异常。2. 畸形。

ca·cog·ra·pher [kæˈkɔgrəfə; kəˋkɑgrəfɚ] **n.** 1. 别字大王。2. 书法不好的人。

ca·cog·ra·phy [kæˈkɔgrəfi; kəˋkɑgrəfɪ] **n.** 1. 拼写错误,写别字。2. 拙劣的书法。**ca·cog·ra·phic(al) a.**

ca·col·o·gy [kæˈkɔlədʒi; kəˋkɑlədʒɪ] **n.** 1. 措词不当。2. 发音不正。

cac·o·mis·tle [ˈkækəˌmisl; ˋkækəˏmɪsl̩] **n.** 1. 【动】蓬尾浣熊。2. 蓬尾浣熊毛皮。

ca·coph·o·nous [kæˈkɔfənəs; kæˋkɑfənəs] **a.** 发音不和谐的,粗腔横调的。

ca·coph·o·ny [kæˈkɔfəni; kæˋkɑfənɪ] **n.** 1. 不愉快的音调;杂音。2. 【医】声音异常,口齿不清。3. 【药】噪音。

cac·ta·ceous [kækˈteiʃəs; kækˋteʃəs] **a.** 【植】仙人掌科植物的。

cac·tus [ˈkæktəs; ˋkæktəs] **n.** (*pl.* ~***es***, ***cac·ti*** [ˈkæktai; ˋkæktaɪ]) 1. 【植】仙人掌科植物。2. 〔美俚〕沙漠。

ca·cu·mi·nal [kəˈkjuːminl; kəˋkjumənl̩] **I a.** 【语音】卷舌的。**II n.** 卷舌音。

Cad [kæd; kæd] **n.** 〔美口〕卡迪拉克牌轿车。

cad [kæd; kæd] **n.** 1. 〔口〕下流人,粗鄙无礼的人。2. 〔英废〕车夫;仆人。

C.A.D., CAD = 1. cash against documents 押汇证。2. = computer-aided design 计算机辅助设计。

ca·das·tral [kəˈdæstrəl; kəˋdæstrəl] **a.** 地籍的,课税地的。*a* ~ *survey* 地籍测量。

cad·as·tra·tion [kædəsˈtreiʃən; ˏkædəsˋtreʃən] **n.** 地籍测量。

ca·das·tre, ca·das·ter [kəˈdæstə; kəˋdæstɚ] **n.** 地籍图。

ca·da·ver [kəˈdeivə, -ˈdæ-; kəˋdævɚ, -ˋdæ-] **n.** 1. (解剖用的)尸体。2. 〔美俚〕失败了的事业,破产事业。**-ic** [-rik; -rɪk] **a.**

ca·dav·er·ine [kəˈdævərin, -əˌriːn; kəˋdævərin, -əˏrin] **n.** 【生化】尸胺。

ca·dav·er·ous [kəˈdævərəs; kəˋdævərəs] **a.** 尸体一样的;灰白色的,形容枯槁的。

cad·dice [ˈkædis; ˋkædɪs] **n.** 毛翅目幼虫。~ **fly** 石蚕蛾。

cad·die [ˈkædi; ˋkædɪ] **I n.** 1. 【高尔夫球】(受雇做背球棒等杂事的)球童。2. 〔Scot.〕杂役。3. (运物用的)有轮手推车。**II vi.** 当球童。

cad·dis [ˈkædis; ˋkædɪs] = caddice.

cad·dish [ˈkædiʃ; ˋkædɪʃ] **a.** 下流的,粗鄙的。

Cad·do [ˈkædəu; ˋkædo] **n.** (*pl.* ~***es***, ~***s***, ~) 1. 卡多族〔美国一印第安部落名〕。2. 卡多人。3. 卡多语。

Cad·do·an [ˈkædəuən; ˋkædoəu] **I a.** (印第安人)卡多语系的。**II n.** 卡多语系。

cad·dy[1] [ˈkædi; ˋkædɪ] **n.** 1. 茶叶盒,茶叶罐。2. 柜,箱,(放唱片之类用的)盒。

cad·dy[2] [ˈkædi; ˋkædɪ] = caddie.

Cade [keid; ked] **n.** 凯德〔姓氏〕。

cade[1] [keid; ked] **a.** 作为爱畜驯养的。*a* ~ *lamb* 驯羊。

cade[2] [keid; ked] **n.** 【植】刺桧(*Juniperus oxycedrus*)。

ca·delle [kəˈdel; kəˋdɛl] **n.** 【动】大谷盗。

ca·dence [ˈkeidəns; ˋkedns] **I n.** 1. 音律;调子。2. 声音的抑扬。3. 节奏,拍子;(行军时的)步度。4. 【乐】乐章的结尾。5. 【电】步调信号。**II vt.** 使成节奏。**-d a.** 音调抑扬的。

ca·den·cy [ˈkeidənsi; ˋkedənsɪ] **n.** 1. = cadence. 2. 【纹】小辈分支家系。

ca·dent [ˈkeidnt; ˋkedənt] **a.** 1. 下降的。2. 有韵的,有节奏的,抑扬的。

ca·den·za [kəˈdenzə; kəˋdɛnzə] **n.** 〔It.〕【药】华彩乐

段；终止。

ca·det [kəˈdet; kəˋdɛt] *n*. **1**. 陆海军官学校的学员，英国通例叫 gentleman ～，美国 1902 年后正式叫 midshipman]；商船学校学生。**2**. 幼子，次子；弟弟。**3**. 〔C-〕(旧俄)立宪民主党党员。**4**. 〔纽西兰〕牧羊学徒；少年店员。**5**. 海蓝色，深蓝色。～ **corps**〔英〕学生军训队。**-ship** *n*. 军校学员的地位[级别，学习期限]。

ca·det [kəˈdet; kəˋdɛt] *n*. 〔F.〕弟〔附加姓名后与兄相区别 (*opp*. aîné)〕。

cadge [kædʒ; kædʒ] *vi*. **1**. 〔口〕行乞。**2**. 〔方〕做叫卖小贩。—*vt*. **1**. 〔口〕乞讨；敲诈，勒索(钱等)。**2**. 〔方〕叫卖(鱼、蛋等)。～ *a meal* 求食。

cadg·er [ˈkædʒə; ˋkædʒɚ] *n*. **1**. 乞丐；二流子；寄生虫。**2**. 叫卖小贩。

cadg·y [ˈkædʒi; ˋkædʒɪ] *a*. 〔Scot.〕**1**. 好色的；淫猥的；放荡的。**2**. 风流的；快活的。

ca·di [ˈkɑːdi, ˈkei-; ˋkɑdi, ˋke-] *n*. (*pl*. ～*s*)(穆斯林国家的)法官。

Cad·me·an [kædˈmiːən; kædˋmiən] *a*. 【希神】勇士卡德摩斯(Cadmus)的。～ **victory** 以巨大牺牲换得的胜利〔源出卡德摩斯种下龙牙，生成许多武士相互残杀殆尽的故事〕。

cad·mi·um [ˈkædmiəm; ˋkædmɪəm] *n*. 【化】镉。～ **spat** 菱镉矿。～ **yellow** 镉黄(颜料)。

Cadmus [ˈkædməs; ˋkædməs] *n*. 【希神】卡德摩斯〔曾杀一龙，种下龙牙，生成许多武士，相互残杀殆尽〕。

ca·dre [ˈkɑːdə, ˈkædri; ˋkɑdɚ, ˋkædrɪ] *n*. **1**. 骨干，干部。**2**. 骨骼，架子。～**man** 骨干。

ca·du·ce·us [kəˈdjuːsiəs; kəˋdjusɪəs] *n*. (*pl*. ***-ce·i*** [-siai; -sɪaɪ])(罗马神话中传信天使 Mercury 的)双蛇杖；(美国陆军军医部队的)双蛇杖标记。

ca·du·ci·ty [kəˈdjuːsiti; kəˋdjusətɪ] *n*. **1**. 暂时，无常；老衰；短命。**2**. 【植】早落[凋]性。

ca·du·cous [kəˈdjuːkəs; kəˋdjukəs] *a*. **1**. 易散的；易脱落的；易衰老的；短命的。**2**. 【植】早落的，早凋的；【动】脱落性的。

cae·cal, ce·cal [ˈsiːkəl; ˋsikəl] *a*. **1**. 一端密闭的，袋形的。**2**. 【解】盲孔的；盲肠的。

cae·cil·i·an [siːˈsiliən, -ˈsiljən; siˋsɪlɪən, -ˋsɪljən] *n*. 【动】蚓螈科(*Caeciliidae*)动物；蚓螈目〔无足目〕(*Gymnophionia*)。

cae·ci·tis [siːˈsaitis; siˋsaɪtɪs] *n*. 【医】盲肠炎。

cae·cum, ce·cum [ˈsiːkəm; ˋsikəm] *n*. (*pl*. ***-ca*** [-kə; -kə])【解】盲孔；盲肠；盲囊。

Caes. = Caesar.

Cae·sar [ˈsiːzə; ˋsizɚ] *n*. **1**. 【史】凯撒；罗马帝国。**2**. 暴君，独裁者。*Julius* ～朱利乌斯·凯撒〔公元前 100—44，罗马将军，皇帝，政治家，历史家〕。***Great*** ～! 啊呀！天哪！～ **salad** (用柠檬汁、橄榄油等调拌莴苣、大蒜、鳀鱼、油炸面包丁等而成的)凯撒色拉。

Cae·sar·e·an, Cae·sar·i·an [si(ː)ˈzeəriən; sɪˋzɛrɪən] **I** *a*. **1**. 凯撒的，(罗马)皇帝的。**2**. 独裁的，专制的。**II** *n*. 罗马皇帝[帝国]崇拜者；主张独裁主义的人。～ **birth** 【医】剖腹产。～ **operation** [**section**]【医】剖腹[宫]产(手术)〔因 Julius Caesar 是剖腹生的，故名〕。～ **salad** 凯撒色拉〔一种用长莴苣、大蒜、凤尾鱼、油泡面包片等拌成的色拉〕。

Cae·sar·ism [ˈsiːzərizəm; ˋsizərɪzəm] *n*. 独裁主义，专制政治，帝政。

Cae·si·ous [ˈsiːziəs; ˋsizɪəs] *a*. 青灰色的，苍白的。

cae·si·um, ce·si·um [ˈsiːziəm; ˋsizɪəm] *n*. 【化】铯。

caes·pi·tose [ˈsespitəus; ˋsɛspəˏtos] *a*. 【植】(藓苔等)簇生的，丛生的。

cae·su·ra [si(ː)ˈzjuərə; sɪˋʒurə] *n*. 〔诗〕行内[句中]休止；【乐】中间休止。**-l** *a*.

CAF, c.a.f. **1**. cost and freight. **2**. cost assurance and freight【商】到岸价格，成本加保险费及运费价格。

ca·fard [kəˈfɑː; kəˋfɑr] *n*. 〔F.〕苦闷；愁闷；忧郁；没精打采。

ca·fe [ˈkæfei, ˈkæfi; kəˋfe, kæˋfe] *n*. 〔英〕咖啡馆，(欧陆诸国的)餐馆；〔美〕酒馆；咖啡馆。～ *society*〔美〕经常上咖啡馆的人们。～ *chantant* [ˈʃɑːntɑːŋ; ʃɑ̃ˋtɑ̃] 有音乐等表演的咖啡馆。

ca·fé [kəˈfei; kəˋfe] *n*. 〔F.〕咖啡。～ ***au lait*** [əuˈlei; oˋle] 牛奶咖啡。～**curtain** 半截窗帘。～ ***filtre*** [filtr; fɪltr] 滴漏咖啡。～ ***noir*** [ˈnwɑːr; ˋnwɑr] (不加牛奶的)清咖啡。

caf·e·te·ri·a [ˌkæfiˈtiəriə; ˏkæfəˋtɪrɪə] *n*. 〔美〕(自取菜饭的)自助食堂。～ **plan**〔美〕"自助餐"式福利计划〔某些大公司实行的福利项目可由员工自由选择的办法〕。

caf·e·to·ri·um [ˌkæfiˈtɔːriəm; ˏkæfəˋtɔrɪəm] *n*. (学校等的)兼作食堂的礼堂。

caff [kæf; kæf] *n*. 〔美口〕小吃店。

caf·fe·ic [kəˈfiːik; kæˋfiɪk] *a*. (取自)咖啡的。～ **acid** 【化】咖啡酸。

caf·fe·ine [ˈkæfiːn; ˋkæfiɪn] *n*. 咖啡碱，咖啡因。

Caf·fre [ˈkæfə; ˋkæfɚ] *n*. = Kaf(f)ir.

caf·fy [ˈkæfi; ˋkæfɪ] *n*. 〔美俚〕咖啡；咖啡馆。

caf·tan [ˈkæftən, kæfˈtɑːn; ˋkæftən, kɑfˋtɑn] *n*. (中东的)束腰长袖长袍。

C.A.G. = Civil Air Guard〔美〕民用航空警卫队。

cage [keidʒ; kedʒ] **I** *n*. **1**. 笼；槛；监牢；战俘营。**2**. 电梯厢；(矿井内的)升降车。**3**. 外壳；(建筑物的)钢骨结构。**4**. 炮架，炮座。**5**. 【棒球】练球场；篮球的球篮；冰球的球门。*reinforcement* ～*s* 钢筋骨架。～ *gals*〔美俚〕女售票员。**II** *vt*. 把…关进笼内；把…关入槛中；把(冰球等)打入球门。～ *up* 把…收监。～ **antenna**【无】笼形天线。～**-work** 透孔织物[制品]。

cage·ling [ˈkeidʒliŋ; ˋkedʒlɪŋ] *n*. 笼鸟〔亦作 cagebird，指鹦鹉等〕。

cag·er [ˈkeidʒə; ˋkedʒɚ] *n*. 〔美俚〕篮球选手[运动员]。

cage·y [ˈkeidʒi; ˋkedʒɪ] *a*. 〔美口〕**1**. 狡猾的。**2**. 谨慎小心的；当心的。*a* ～ *reply* 谨慎的回答。

Ca·glia·ri [kæˈljɑːri, ˌkæliˈɑːri; kæˋljɑri, ˏkælɪˋɑrɪ] *n*. 卡利亚里〔意大利港市〕。

ca·gy [ˈkeidʒi; ˋkedʒi] *n*. = cagey. **-gi·ly** *ad*. **-gi·ness** *n*.

ca·hier [kɑːˈjei; kɑˋje] *n*. 〔F.〕**1**. 笔记本。**2**. 政策报告；程序报告。

ca·hoot(s) [kəˈhuːt(s); kəˋhut(s)] *n*. 〔美俚〕合伙，共同；共谋。*in* ～(*s*) 共同，共谋。*go* ～*s* = *go in* ～(*s*) 均分；分担。

CAI = computer-assisted [aided] instruction 用电子计算机辅助的教学。

cai·man [ˈkeimən; ˋkemən] *n*. = cayman.

Cain [kein; ken] *n*. **1**. 该隐〔《圣经》为亚当的长子。曾杀害其弟 Abel〕。**2**. 〔喻〕杀弟者；凶手；恶魔。～ ***and Abel*** [ˈeibl; ˋebl]〔美俚〕椅子和桌子。***raise*** ～〔俚〕引起骚乱；制造麻烦。

Cai·no·zo·ic [kainəˈzəuik, ˈkei-; ˏkaɪnəˋzoɪk, ˋke-] *a*. = Cenozoic.

ca·ique [kaiˈiːk; kɑˋik] *n*. **1**. (博斯普鲁斯海峡上的)划桨轻舟。**2**. (地中海东部的)小帆船。

caird [kɛəd; kɛrd] *n*. 〔Scot.〕**1**. 流动铜匠。**2**. 流浪汉。

cairn [kɛən; kɛrn] *n*. **1**. 石冢，累石堆；堆石标。**2**. (躯小，脚短的)㹴狗 (= ～ terrier)。

cairn·gorm [ˈkɛənˈgɔːm; ˋkɛrnˋgɔrm] *n*. 【矿】(苏格兰 Cairngorm 山出产的)烟水晶。

Cai·ro [ˈkaiərəu; ˋkaɪəro] *n*. 开罗〔埃及首都〕。

cais·son [ˈkeisən; ˋkesn] *n*. **1**. 弹药箱；弹药车；地雷箱。**2**. (打捞沉船用的)潜函，沉箱；充气浮筒；(船坞等的)铁浮门；蓄气装置。**3**. 【建】藻井。～ **disease**【医】潜函病，沉箱病。

cai·tiff [ˈkeitif; ˋketɪf] *a*.，*n*. 〔古、诗〕卑鄙的(人)。

caj·e·put [ˈkædʒipət; ˋkædʒəpət] *n*. = cajuput.

C

C

ca·jole [kəˈdʒəul; kəˋdʒol] ***vt***. 勾引,哄骗。~ (*sb*.) ***into*** [***out of***] ***doing sth***. 诱(人)做[停止做]某事。~ (*sth*.) ***out of*** [***from***] ***sb***. 花言巧语骗走某人的(某物)。**-ment** ***n***. 笼络,诱骗。**-r** ***n***. 骗子。

ca·jol·er·y [kəˈdʒəuləri; kəˋdʒolərɪ] ***n***. 笼络,诱骗。

Ca·jun, Ca·jan [ˈkeidʒən; ˋkedʒən] ***n***. **1**. 卡真人〔美国路易斯安那州的本地人,原系阿卡地亚法国移民后裔〕。**2**. 卡真方言。

caj·u·put [ˈkædʒəpət; ˋkædʒəpət] ***n***. 【植】白千层 (*Melaleuca leuca dendra*)。

cake [keik; kek] **I** ***n***. **1**. 饼,糕;〔古〕扁形小面包;〔Scot.〕燕麦饼;〔美〕烧饼。**2**. (肥皂等)饼状物,(衣服等上的)硬泥块。**3**. 〔美〕爱跟女同学厮混的男学生。**4**. 〔美俚〕妖娆女子。*a sponge* ~松软蛋糕。*a* ~ *of soap* 一块肥皂。*I wish my* ~*s were dough again*. 我要是还没有结婚就好了。***a piece of*** ~ 〔口〕容易事,快心事。~***s and ale*** 欢宴,狂喝闹饮;优游的岁月,世俗的享乐。***go off like hot*** ~***s*** 畅销;敏捷迅速地打发(处置等)。***Land of*** ~***s*** 苏格兰的别号。***One's*** ~ ***is dough***. 打算错误;计划失败(*My* ~ *is dough*. 〔美俚〕我(的计划)已经失败了)。***sell like hot*** ~ 畅销。***take the*** ~ 得一等奖;超人一等(*His arrogance takes the* ~. 他那份傲气可真不得了)。***You cannot eat your*** ~ ***and have it***. 不能两全;不能(两种利益)兼得。**II** ***vt***. **1**. 使成扁平的硬块,使固结;使烧结,使胶凝。**2**. 加块结物于…上。—***vi***. **1**. 块结,胶凝。**2**. 〔美俚〕跟女学生厮混。~**-eater** 〔美俚〕(醉生梦死过悠闲岁月的)浪子。~ **ink** 墨。~**-walk** (美国黑人的)步态舞;步态竞赛〔因当初是用蛋糕做奖品,故名〕。

cak·(e)y [ˈkeiki; ˋkekɪ] ***a***. 饼状的,凝固了的。

Cal. = **1**. California. **2**. large calorie(s)【物】大卡,千卡。

cal. = **1**. calendar. **2**. calibre. **3**. small calorie(s)【物】小卡。

Cal·a·bar [ˈkæləbɑː; ˋkæləbɑr] ***n***. 卡拉巴尔〔奈及利亚〕。~ *bean*【植】卡拉巴尔毒豆。

cal·a·bash [ˈkæləbæʃ; ˋkæləˏbæʃ] ***n***. 【植】葫芦。

cal·a·boose [ˈkæləbuːs; ˋkæləˏbus] ***n***. 〔美口〕监狱;拘留所。

ca·la·di·um [kəˈleidiəm; kəˋledɪəm] ***n***. 【植】杯芋 (*Caladium bicolor*)。

Cal·ais [ˈkælei, F. ˈkæli; ˋkæle, kæle] ***n***. 加来〔法国港市〕。

cal·a·man·co [ˌkæləˈmæŋkəu; ˏkæləˋmæŋko] ***n***. (*pl*. ~*es*, ~*s*)【纺】有光呢。

cal·a·man·der [ˌkæləˈmændə; ˏkæləˋmændɚ] ***n***. 【植】柿属 (*Diospyros*) 植物。

cal·a·ma·ry [ˈkæləməri; ˋkæləˏmɛrɪ] ***n***. 【动】枪鲗。

cal·a·mine [ˈkæləmain; ˋkæləˏmaɪn] ***n***. **1**. 【矿】异极矿;碳酸锌矿;菱锌矿。**2**. 【药】炉甘石。

cal·a·mint [ˈkæləˌmint; ˋkæləˏmɪnt] ***n***. 【植】塔花属植物〔尤指塔花 (*satureja calamintha*)〕。

cal·a·mite [ˈkæləmait; ˋkæləmaɪt] ***n***. 【古生】芦木。

ca·lam·i·tous [kəˈlæmitəs; kəˋlæmɪtəs] ***a***. 多灾多难的;悲惨的;不幸的。**-ly** ***ad***. **-ness** ***n***.

ca·lam·i·ty [kəˈlæmiti; kəˋlæmətɪ] ***n***. 灾难,灾害,困苦,不幸。~ **howler** 〔美俚〕凶事预言者。~ **issue** (选举时)对己党不利的灾难性问题。**C- Jane** 〔美〕(预示不祥的)杀星,凶星〔原为美国小说中边疆女英雄简·柏克的绰号,因为她枪法高明,一枪就能击毙对方〕。

cal·a·mon·din [ˌkæləˈmɔndin; ˏkæləˋmɑndɪn] ***n***. 【植】加拉蒙地亚桔 (*Citrus mitis*)。

cal·a·mus [ˈkæləməs; ˋkæləməs] ***n***. (*pl*. ***-mi*** [-mai; -maɪ]) **1**. 【植】菖蒲;芦苇;芦笛;芦管笔。**2**. [C-]【植】省藤属。**3**. 【鱼】鲷的一种。**4**. 【鸟】羽,羽根。

ca·lan·do [kəˈlændəu; kɑˋlɑndo] ***a***., ***ad***. 〔It.〕【乐】减少音量的[地];音量渐减和速度渐缓的[地]。

ca·lan·dri·a [kəˈlændriə; kəˋlændrɪə] ***n***. **1**. 【物】加热体,加热器。**2**. 【化】排管式。

ca·lash [kəˈlæʃ; kəˋlæʃ] ***n***. **1**. 双马四轮马车;车篷。**2**. (十八世纪女人的)皱纹丝头巾[女帽]。

cal·a·thus [ˈkæləθəs; ˋkæləθəs] ***n***. (*pl*. ***-thi*** [-θai; -θaɪ])古希腊水果篮(图案)〔象征丰产〕。

cal·a·ver·ite [ˌkæləˈvεərait; ˏkæləˋvεraɪt] ***n***. 【矿】碲金矿。

ca·lo [kɑːləu; kɑˋlo] ***n***. 卡洛语(生活在美国西南部的奇卡诺人青年讲的一种墨西哥西班牙语,其中有许多俚语和英语词)。

calc. = calculate.

calc- *comb*. *f*. 〔用于元音前〕石灰,钙: *calc*tufa.

cal·ca·ne·us [kælˈkeiniəs; kælˋkenɪəs] ***n***. (*pl*. ***-ne·i*** [-niai; -nɪaɪ]) **1**. 【解】跟骨。**2**. 空凹足。亦作 **cal·ca·neum**[-əm; -əm] (*pl*. ***-ne·a*** [-niə; -nɪə]). **cal·ca·ne·al** ***a***.

cal·car[1] [ˈkælkɑː; ˋkælkɑr] ***n***. (*pl*. ***cal·car·i·a*** [kælˈkεəriə; kælˋkεrɪə]) **1**. 【植】距管。**2**. 【动】距。**-ca·rate** [-kəreit, -rit; -kæret, -rɪt] ***a***.

cal·car[2] [ˈkælkɑː; ˋkælkɑr] ***n***. 【化】(熔化玻璃的)熔炉;煅烧炉。

cal·car·e·ous, cal·car·i·ous [kælˈkεəriəs; kælˋkεrɪəs] ***a***. 含钙的,石灰质的。

cal·ced·o·ny [kælˈsedəni; kælˋsεdənɪ] ***n***. 【矿】玉髓。

cal·ce·i·form [ˈkælsifɔːm; ˋkælsɪˏfɔrm] ***a***. 【植】拖鞋状的。

cal·ce·o·lar·i·a [ˌkælsiəˈlεəriə; ˏkælsɪəˋlεrɪə] ***n***. 【植】蒲包花属的植物;[C-]蒲包花属。

cal·ce·o·late [ˈkælsiəleit; ˋkælsɪəlet] ***a***. 【植】拖鞋状的〔如兰花瓣〕(= calceiform)。

calces [ˈkælsiːz; ˋkælsiz] ***n***. calx 的复数。

calci- *comb*. *f*. 〔用于辅音前〕石灰,钙: *calci*ferol.

cal·cic [ˈkælsik; ˋkælsɪk] ***a***. **1**. 含钙的。**2**. 石灰(质)的。

cal·ci·cole [ˈkælsikəul; ˋkælsəˏkol] ***n***. 【植】钙生植物。**-cic·o·lous** [kælˈsikələs; kælˋsɪkələs] ***a***.

cal·cif·er·ol [kælˈsifərəul; kælˋsɪfəˏrol] ***n***. 【生化】(麦角)钙化醇,骨化醇,维生素 D_2。

cal·cif·er·ous [kælˈsifərəs; kælˋsɪfərəs] ***a***. 含钙的。

cal·cif·ic [kælˈsifik; kælˋsɪfɪk] ***a***. 石灰质的,钙化的。

cal·ci·fi·ca·tion [ˌkælsifiˈkeiʃən; ˏkælsəfɪˋkeʃən] ***n***. **1**. 【医】石灰性变,钙化(作用)。**2**. 骨化部位。**3**. (意见、态度等的)硬化,僵化。

cal·ci·fuge [ˈkælsifjuːdʒ; ˋkælsəˏfjudʒ] ***n***. 【植】避钙植物,嫌钙植物。**-cif·u·gous** [kælˈsifjugəs; kælˋsɪfjʊgəs] ***a***.

cal·ci·fy [ˈkælsifai; ˋkælsəˏfaɪ] ***vt***., ***vi***. (***-fied***; ***-fying***) **1**. 【医】(使)钙化,(使)石灰质化。**2**. (使)硬化,(使)僵化。

cal·ci·mine [ˈkælsimain, -min; ˋkælsəˏmaɪn, -mɪn] **I** ***n***. 刷墙粉。**II** ***vt***. 刷墙粉于。

cal·ci·na·tion [ˌkælsiˈneiʃən; ˏkælsɪˋneʃən] ***n***. **1**. 【化】煅烧,焙烧;(石灰的)烧成。**2**. 【冶】氟化法;烧矿法;(铁矿的)整矿法。

cal·cine [ˈkælsain; ˋkælsaɪn] ***vt***., ***vi***. 煅烧;焙烧。~*d alum* 烧明矾,枯矾。~*d lime* 生石灰。~*d cocoon* 僵蚕茧。

cal·cite [ˈkælsait; ˋkælsaɪt] ***n***. 【矿】方解石。

cal·ci·tonin [ˌkælsiˈtəunin; ˏkælsɪˋtonɪn] ***n***. 【生化】降(血)钙素,甲状腺降钙素。

cal·ci·um [ˈkælsiəm; ˋkælsɪəm] ***n***. 【化】钙。~ **carbonate** 碳酸钙。~ **chloride** 氯化钙。~ **cyanamide** 氰氨化钙,石灰氮。~ **fluoride** 氟化钙,萤石。~ **hydroxide** 氢氧化钙。~ **light** 钙光;石灰光。~ **phosphate** 磷酸钙。~ **sulphate** 硫酸钙。~ **superphosphate** 过磷酸钙。

calc-sin·ter [ˈkælksintə; ˋkælksɪntɚ] ***n***. 【化】钙华,石灰华。

calc·spar [ˈkælkspɑː; ˋkælkspɑr] ***n***. 【矿】方解石(= calcite)。

calc·tu·fa [ˈkælktuːfə; ˋkælkˏtufə], **calc·tuff** [ˈkæltʌf; ˋkæltʌf] ***n.***【化】石灰华。

cal·cu·la·bil·i·ty [ˌkælkjuləˈbiliti; ˏkælkjələˋbɪlətɪ] ***n.*** **1.** 可计算性;可预见性。**2.** 可靠性,可依赖程度。

cal·cu·la·ble [ˈkælkjuləbl; ˋkælkjələbl̩] ***a.*** **1.** 能计算的;预想得到的。**2.** 可指望的,可依赖的。

cal·cu·la·graph [ˈkælkjuləgrɑːf; ˋkælkjələˏgrɑf] ***n.***【商标】(电话)记时器。

cal·cu·late [ˈkælkjuleit; ˋkælkjəˏlet] ***vt.*** **1.** 计算,核算。**2.** 预测,推测。**3.**〔多用被动语态〕计划,筹划;使充作;使适合 (*for*)。**4.**〔美口〕打算;想,以为;猜想。~ *an eclipse* 预测日(月)蚀。~ *the consequences of* 推测…的结果。***be ~d for*** 为了…(的目的),做成[制订]的。***be ~d to*** (*do*) 适于(做)…,计划(做)…。—***vi.*** **1.** 计算,考虑。**2.** 预料;指望 (*on*, *upon*)。**3.**〔美〕以为,认为。~ *on the fine weather tomorrow* 预料明天天晴。~ *on earning big money* 指望挣大钱。

cal·cu·lat·ed [ˈkælkjuleitid; ˋkælkjəˏletɪd] ***a.*** **1.** 有计划的,有意的,故意的。**2.** (预备)供…之用的,合于…之用的。**3.** 算清了的;被预测出的。*a ~ risk* 有意进行的冒险。

cal·cu·lat·ing [ˈkælkjuleitiŋ; ˋkælkjəˏletɪŋ] ***a.*** **1.** 计算(用)的;有打算的,不落空的。**2.** 精打细算的,慎重的,为自己打算的。~ *machine* 计算机。~ *scale* [*rule*] 计算尺。*a ~ man* 一个有心计的人。

cal·cu·la·tion [ˌkælkjuˈleiʃən; ˏkælkjəˋleʃən] ***n.*** **1.** 计算,计算法。**2.** 推定,预测。**3.** 深思熟虑,精打细算;慎重的计划;算计。*checking ~* 验算。*rough ~* 概算。*~ careful and meticulous* 精打细算。

cal·cu·la·tive [ˈkælkjulətiv; ˋkælkjəˏletɪv] ***a.*** **1.** (需要)计算的。**2.** 有打算的,不落空的。

cal·cu·la·tor [ˈkælkjuleitə; ˋkælkjəletɚ] ***n.*** **1.** 计算者。**2.** 计算机;计算机操纵者。**3.** (使计算方便的)一览表。**4.** 有打算的人,不落空的人;谋略家。*an electronic ~* 电子计算机。

cal·cu·lous [ˈkælkjuləs; ˋkælkjuləs] ***a.*** 石一样的;【医】结石(病)的。

cal·cu·lus [ˈkælkjuləs; ˋkælkjələs] ***n.*** (*pl.* *~es*, *-li* [-lai; -laɪ]) **1.**【医】结石,石;积石;牙垢。**2.**【数】运算,演算;微积分(学)。~ *of finite differences*【数】差分演算(法),差分学。~ *of variation* 变分法[学]。*differential* [*integral*] ~微[积]分(学)。*urinary ~*【医】尿结石。

Cal·cut·ta [kælˈkʌtə; kælˋkʌtə] ***n.*** 加尔各答〔印度港市〕。~ **hemp** 黄麻。~ **Tonnage Scale** 加尔各答运货吨数〔通常以 50 立方英尺或 20 英担为一吨〕。

cal·dar·ium [kælˈdɛəriəm; kælˋdɛrɪəm] ***n.*** (*pl.* ***-ri·a*** [-riə; -rɪə])〔L.〕(古罗马的)高温浴室。

Cal·der [ˈkɔːldə; ˋkɔldɚ] ***n.*** 考尔德〔姓氏〕。

cal·de·ra [kælˈdiərə; kælˋdɪrə] ***n.*** **1.**【地】破火山口。**2.** 大锅 (= caldron)。

cal·dron [ˈkɔːldrən; ˋkɔldrən] ***n.*** 釜,大锅 (= cauldron)。

Cald·well [ˈkɔːldwəl; ˋkɔldwəl] ***n.*** 考德威尔〔姓氏〕。

ca·lèche, ca·leche [kəˈleʃ; kəˋlɛʃ] ***n.*** = calash.

Cal·e·do·ni·a [ˌkæliˈdəunjə; ˏkælɪˋdonɪə] ***n.*** **1.**〔诗〕苏格兰。**2.** 卡列多尼亚〔女子名〕。

Cal·e·do·ni·an [ˌkæliˈdəuniən; ˏkælɪˋdonɪən] **I** ***a.*** **1.** 古代苏格兰的;〔诗〕苏格兰的;苏格兰人的。**2.**【地】加里东的。**II** ***n.*** 苏格兰人。

cal·e·fa·cient [ˌkæliˈfeiʃənt; ˏkæləˋfeʃənt] **I** ***a.***【医】使温暖的,发热的。**II** ***n.***【医】发暖剂。

cal·e·fac·tion [ˌkæliˈfækʃən; ˏkælɪˋfækʃən] ***n.*** **1.** 暖,发暖。**2.**【化】发暖作用。**3.** 热污染。

cal·e·fac·tive [ˌkæliˈfæktiv; ˏkælɪˋfæktɪv] ***a.*** 暖,热;温热性的。

cal·e·fac·to·ry [ˌkæliˈfæktəri; ˏkælɪˋfæktərɪ] **I** ***a.*** 温暖的;生热的。**II** ***n.*** (旧时常作起居室用的)修道院暖室。

cal·e·fy [ˈkælifai; ˋkælɪˏfaɪ] ***vt.***, ***vi.*** (***-fied***; ***-fy·ing***) (使)发暖,(使)变热,(使)发热。

cal·em·bour [ˈkæləmbuə; ˋkæləmbʊr] ***n.***〔F.〕俏皮话,双关妙语。

cal·en·dar [ˈkælində; ˋkæləndɚ] **I** ***n.*** **1.** 历,历法。**2.** 历书,日历,月历。**3.** 日程表;一览表;总目录;【法】案件日程表;〔美〕议会日程。*a perpetual ~* 万年历。*a wall ~* 挂历。*the lunatic* [*solar*] ~阴[阳]历。**II** ***vt.*** **1.** 把…记入日程表中;把…列入表中。**2.** 为(文件等)作分类索引。~ **art** 年历书。~ **clock** 日历钟。~ **day** (日)历日〔由午夜到午夜〕。~ **month** (日)历月。~ **watch** 日历表。~ **year** (日)历年〔scholastic year (学年), fiscal year (会计年度)等之对〕。

cal·en·der[1] [ˈkælində; ˋkæləndɚ] **I** ***n.*** **1.**【纺,造纸】轧光机;砑光机;压延机;轮压机。~ *printing* 辊筒印花。**2.**〔旧〕轧光机[压延机、轮压机]操作工。**II** ***vt.*** 用砑光机砑光;把…上轮压机。

cal·en·der[2] [ˈkælində; ˋkæləndɚ] ***n.*** (伊斯兰教国家的一种)游方教士。

cal·en·dry [ˈkælindri; ˋkæləndrɪ] ***n.*** 砑光机操作场。

cal·ends [ˈkælindz; ˋkæləndz] ***n.*** 〔*pl.*〕(古罗马历法的)朔日,初一。***at*** [***on***, ***till***] ***the Greek ~*** (或 **Calends**) 永远不会有[发生,实现等]的那一天。

ca·len·du·la [kəˈlendjulə; kəˋlɛndʒələ] ***n.***【植】**1.** 金盏花。**2.**〔C-〕金盏花属。

cal·en·ture [ˈkælintjuə; ˋkæləntʃʊr] ***n.*** **1.** (热带的)热病。**2.**【医】中暑。

ca·les·cence [kəˈlesns; kəˋlɛsn̩s] ***n.*** (逐渐)增热,(逐渐)增温。

ca·les·cent [kəˈlesnt; kəˋlɛsn̩t] ***a.*** 渐暖的;变热的。**ca·les·cence** ***n.***

calf[1] [kɑːf; kɑf] ***n.*** (*pl.* *calves* [kɑːvz; kɑvz]) **1.** 小牛,犊;(鲸、象等的)仔;犊皮。**2.**〔口〕傻头傻脑的青年人。**3.** 冰山崩落下来的漂流冰块。**4.** 大岛附近的小岛。~ ***round***〔美〕打转儿,彷徨,浪荡。***cast her ~*** (牛)流产。***golden ~*** (古以色列人崇拜的)金犊;〔喻〕黄金崇拜。***in*** [***with***] ~ 怀着孕的(牛)。***kill the fatted ~ for*** 盛宴接待[庆祝]。***slip the*** [***her***] ~ (牛)流产。~**bound** ***a.*** (书)用小牛皮装订的。~**dozer** 小型推土机。~ **love** 少年时代的恋爱。~**skin** 小牛皮。~**'s teeth** 乳齿。

calf[2] [kɑːf; kɑf] ***n.*** (*pl.* *calves* [kɑːvz; kɑvz]) 腓,腿肚子。~ **knee**【医】膝关节内翻。

Ca·li [ˈkɑːli; ˋkɑlɪ] ***n.***〔美〕= California.

Cal·i·ban [ˈkælibæn; ˋkælɪˏbæn] ***n.*** **1.** (莎士比亚戏剧《暴风雨》中的)半兽半人怪物。**2.**〔喻〕丑恶残忍的人。

cal·i·ber [ˈkælibə; ˋkæləbɚ] ***n.***〔美〕= calibre.

cal·i·brate [ˈkælibreit; ˋkæləˏbret] ***vt.*** **1.** 测定…的口径。**2.** 在(尺、秤等上)刻度,分度。**3.** 校准。**4.** 使标准化。

cal·i·bra·tion [ˌkæliˈbreiʃən; ˏkælɪˋbreʃən] ***n.*** **1.** 测定口径。**2.** 刻度,标度,划度数。**3.** 校准;标准化。

cal·i·bre [ˈkælibə; ˋkælɪbɚ] ***n.*** **1.** (枪;炮的)口径;(子弹、炮弹的)直径;炮口,枪口。**2.** 圆柱径。**3.** 能力,才干;器量;(价值的)等级,水准。**4.** 规,卡钳,测径器。**5.**【机】轧辊型缝。*a heavy* [*an intermediate*] ~大[中]口径。*a man of excellent ~* 才能出众的人。*books of this ~* 这一等级的书籍。

ca·li·ces [ˈkeilisiːz; ˋkælɪsiz] ***n.*** calix 的复数。

cal·i·che [kɑːˈliːtʃi; kɑˋlitʃɪ] ***n.*** **1.**【化】生硝;智利硝。**2.** (土壤的)钙质层。

cal·i·cle [ˈkælikl; ˋkælɪkl̩] ***n.***【生】杯状窝,杯状器官,小杯状体。

cal·i·co [ˈkælikəu; ˋkæləˏko] **I** ***n.*** (*pl.* *~s*, *~es*) **1.**〔英〕白布;〔美〕印花布。**2.** 花斑动物〔如花狗、斑马等〕。**3.**〔美俚〕女学生,女人。**II** ***a.***〔美〕杂色的,花的;印花布一样的。~ *horse* 花马。~ **paper** 印花纸。~ **printing**【纺】棉布印花。

C

cal·i·co·back [ˈkælikəuˌbæk; ˋkæləko͵bæk] *n*.【动】菜椿象 (harlequin bug)。

ca·lic·u·lar [kəˈlikjulə; kəˋlɪkjələ˞] *a*. 1.【生】杯状的。2.【植】副萼(性)的。

Calif. = California.

ca·lif [ˈkeilif, ˈkɑː-; ˋkelɪf, ˋkɑ-] *n*. = caliph.

Cal·i·for·nia [ˌkæliˈfɔːnjə; ͵kæləˋfɔrnjə] *n*. 加利福尼亚〔美国州名〕。～ **moccasins**〔美〕御寒厚袜。～ **pants**〔美〕条纹[格纹]羊毛裤。～ **poppy**【植】花菱草〔加州州花〕。～ **roll** 加利福尼亚馅卷〔一种加州寿司〕。

Cal·i·for·ni·an[ˌkæliˈfɔːnjən; ͵kæləˋfɔrnjən] *a*., *n*. 加利福尼亚州的[人]。

cal·i·for·ni·cate[ˌkælifɔːnikeit; ͵kælɪˋfɔnɪket] *vt*. 以都市化和工业化毁坏(州、风景区等的)自然景色;使加利福尼亚化。

cal·i·for·ni·um[ˈkæliˈfɔːniəm; ˋkæli ˋfɔrnɪəm] *n*.【化】锎。

ca·lig·i·nous[kəˈlidʒinəs; kəˋlɪdʒənəs] *a*.〔古〕黑暗的,幽暗的。

ca·lig·ra·phy[kəˈligrəfi; kəˋlɪgrəfɪ] *n*. = calligraphy.

cal·i·ol·o·gy[ˌkæliˈɔlədʒi; ͵kælɪˋɑlədʒɪ] *n*. 鸟巢学。

cal·i·pash[ˈkælipæʃ; ˋkælɪ͵pæʃ] *n*. 龟脊肉。

cal·i·pee[ˈkælipiː; ˋkælɪ͵pi] *n*. 龟肚肉。

cal·i·pers[ˈkælipəz; ˋkæləpəz] *n*. *pl*. = callipers.

cal·iph[ˈkælif, ˈkɑː-; ˋkelɪf, ˋkɑ-] *n*. 哈里发〔伊斯兰教国家政教合一的领袖的尊号〕。

cal·i·ph·ate [ˈkælifeit, ˈkɑː-; ˋkælɪ͵fet, ˋkɑ-] *n*. 哈里发的地位[政权,统治区]。

cal·i·sa·y·a [ˌkæləˈseijə; ͵kæləˋsejə] *n*.【植】黄金鸡纳树 (Cinchona calisaya)。～ *bark* 黄金鸡纳树皮。

cal·is·then·ic [ˌkælisˈθenik; ͵kælɪsˋθɛnɪk] *a*. = callisthenic. ～*s n*. = callisthenics.

calix [ˈkeiliks; ˋkelɪks] *n*. (*pl*. *-lices* [-lisiːz; -lɪsiz]) 1.【解】杯状窝,杯状器官;肾盂。2.【植】萼。

calk[1] [kɔːk; kɔk] I *n*.〔美〕(鞋底上防滑的)尖铁。II *vt*. 1. 加尖铁于。2. 用尖铁伤害。

calk[2] [kɔːk; kɔk] *vt*. = caulk.

calk[3] [kɔːk; kɔk] *vt*. 摹画复制,临,拓。

cal·kin [ˈkɔːkin; ˋkɔkɪn] *n*. = calk[1].

call [kɔːl; kɔl] I *vt*. 1. 大声念[说],喊,叫。2. 召唤,叫来,请来;召集,征召;号召;唤醒。3. 把…取名为,称呼,把…叫做。4. 以为,认为,看做。5. 命令;任命。6. 给…打电话。7. 要求,请求,催促;责备;【牌】要求(摊牌,出牌)。8.〔美〕【体】停止(比赛);判定。～ *sb*. *by name* 叫某人姓名。～ *a halt* 喝令停止。～ *a meeting* 召集会议。～ *a roll* 点名。～ *the roll*〔美〕点名。～ *sb*. *from sleep* 叫起某人。～ *the bill so much* 估计账款是这么多。*I* ～ *that mean*. 我以为那是小气的。*have nothing to* ～ *one's own* 什么也没有;一无所长。～*ed game*【棒球】评定胜负。*Call no man happy before he is dead*. 人未盖棺勿谓有福。—*vi*. 1. 高声念[说],呼喊,叫唤,鸣,啼。2. 到,访问,拜望。3. 鸣信号;命令,要求;打电话。4.【牌】叫牌;要求看牌。～ ***after*** 1. 追喊。2. 以…的名字命名。～ ***a spade a spade*** 是什么说什么,直言。～ ***at*** (*a house*; *a place*) 访问(某家);(车船)停靠(某地)。～ ***away*** 使转移开,排解(忧闷);叫走。～ ***back*** 1. 喊回,叫转来,召唤。2. 取消,收回(说错的话)。3. 回一个电话;再打一个电话来。～ ***down*** 1. 祈求,呼求(天恩)。2. 招惹(灾祸等)。3.〔美俚〕骂,申斥,谴责。～ ***for*** 1. 请求,要求,要,提倡,号召;招募。2. 去拿(物件);去接(某人)。3. (批注信封上)留交。4. 叫喊;(为喝彩等)喊出(演员等)(*This disease* ～*s for prompt treatment*. 这病必须急救)。～ ***forth*** 唤起,提起,用出,拿出(精神,勇气等)。～ ***heaven to witness*** 指天发誓。～ ***in*** 1. 回收(通货等)。2. 招,请,叫(医生等);叫进;引入,引起;调入。3. 来访(*Call in*, *or ring us up*. 你可以亲自来访,也可以打电话来)。4. 打电话到服务单位,请假。～ ***in question*** 疑,怀疑,对…表示异议;非难。～ ***in sick*** 打电话请病假。～ ***sign*** (电台,电视台等的)呼叫信号。～ ***slip*** (图书馆借书时填写的)借书单。～ ***into being*** [***existence***] 创造,产出,使成立。～ ***into play*** 使动作,使活动,使抒发。～ (*sb*.) ***names*** 咒骂,骂人。～ ***off*** 1. 叫开;转移开(注意力等)。2.〔口〕命令停止,宣告终止;丢手,放手;取消(婚约)。3.〔美〕点(名),列举(数字)。～ ***on*** [***upon***] 1. 访问。2. 指名要(某人)去干(某事);请求,要求;号召(*He* ～*ed upon me to make a speech*. 他请我演说)。～ ***out*** 1. 向…挑战。2. 动员;〔美口〕命令,号召(罢工);唤起。3. 大声叫喊。4. 诱出。5.〔美俚〕请…跳舞。～ ***over to*** 打电话给。～ ***sb.'s bluff***〔美〕接受挑战[请求]。～ ***the time*** 指挥事件的进行,领导行动。～ ***the tune*** [***shots***, ***turn***]〔美〕预定比赛结果;定调子;发号施令;操纵。～ ***things by their names*** 摆明(事实)说,明明白白地说。～ ***to account*** 1. 要求作出解释;要求认错;责备。2. 与…结账,向…送欠单。～ ***to arms*** 命令武装。～ ***to mind*** 想起。～ ***to order*** (议长)要求遵守秩序;〔美〕宣布开会。～ ***together*** 召集。～ ***up*** 1. 召唤,传,叫出来;召集,动员。2. 提起,提出。3. 打电话给;【讯】呼唤。4. 想出来,想起。***what one*** ～ ***s*** = ***what is*** ～***ed*** 所谓。II *n*. 1. 呼声,叫声,鸣声。2. 号声;角声。3. 叫喊;传唤;点名;招请,召集,号召。4. (电话)通话。5. 吸引力。6. 天职;命;必要,要求,义务。7. 访问,到来;停泊,停车。8. (旗、灯等的)信号。9. 请求,要求;【商】催收(股款等);(股票的)限价买进(*opp*. put);催付。10. (纸牌)叫牌,叫牌权,所叫的牌。*a* ～ *before the curtain* (闭幕后对演员)喝采要求谢幕。*a bugle* ～ 号声。*a telephone* ～(打)一次电话。*a messenger* ～(电话)传呼。*the* ～ *to battle* 战斗号召。*You have no* ～ *to interfere*. 用不着你来管闲事。*30 days after* ～见票后三十天照付。***at*** ～ 随叫随…,随要随…。***at sb.'s beck and*** ～ 随某人之意摆布;完全听命于某人。～ ***of nature*** 要上厕所,要解手。***close*** ～ 幸免,死里逃出,危险关头。***get the*** ～【美体】当选;被雇用。***have a*** ～ ***to*** 做…是天职。***have the*** ～ ***of the market*** 市面繁荣,供需旺盛。***house of*** ～ 客栈;酒馆。***make*** [***pay***] ***a*** ～ 访问,到。***money on*** ～ = call money. ***on*** ～〔美〕1. 随要随(付),承索即(寄)。2. 随时待命,时刻准备着。***place of*** ～ 停泊地,所到地。***receive a*** ～ 接待,接见。***return*** ～ 答拜,回访。***take a*** ～【剧】谢幕。***within*** ～ 声音到达之处,附近。～**-back** *n*.〔美俚〕1. 召回(暂时停雇职工)。2. 收回(待修产品)。3. 加班。4. 电话回话(服务)。～ **bell** 电铃。～**-bird** 媒鸟,囮子。～ **(-)blocking** 1.呼叫限制服务〔指电话局允许用户阻断某一电话号码打给用户的服务〕。2.(通话量超负荷造成的)电话系统堵塞。～**-board** (车站等地的)公告牌。～ **box** 1. 公共电话亭 (=〔美〕public telephone booth)。2. (由用户到邮局领邮件的)留局信箱。～**boy** (对出场演员的)呼喊员;【海】传令员;侍者。～**day** 报喜节〔法学院学生取得律师资格的日子〕;当日节目〔指听众用电话来提出的意见、问题或要求当日照办的广播或电视节目〕。～ **girl** (用电话召唤的)妓女。～ **house**〔美俚〕(妓女可应召外出的)妓院。～**-in** *n*.〔美〕电话点播节目。～ **loan**【商】活期贷款〔贷主有权随时要求归还〕。～ **money** 活期贷款的款子。～ **number** 图书馆(图书的)书架号码,索书号。～**-over** 点名 (= roll～)。～ **rate** 活期贷款利率。～ **signal**【无】呼号。～**-up** *n*. 征集令;征兵数,召集人数。

cal·la [ˈkælə; ˋkælə] *n*.【植】水芋;〔C-〕荷兰海芋属。

call·a·ble [ˈkɔːləbl; ˋkɔləbl̩] *a*. 可随时支取的〔尤指要求下即支付的(如贷款);要求下即兑付的(如公债)〕。

Call-A-Mart [ˈkɔːləmɑːt; ˋkɔləmɑrt] *n*. 电子计算机化的超级市场〔顾客可用电话订货〕。

cal·lan(t) [ˈkælən(t); ˋkɑlən(t)] *n*.〔Scot.〕少年。

Cal·la·o [kɑːˈjɑːəu; kɑˋjɑo] *n*. 卡亚俄〔秘鲁港市〕。

call·ee [kɔːˈliː; kɔˋli] *n*.〔美〕受访问者;被呼唤人;电话受

话人。

call·er[1] [ˈkɔːlə; ˋkɔlɚ] *n*. 呼唤者;招请者;召集者;访问者,来访者;打电话者。～ ID 来电者身份显示服务〔指电话商可让受话者知道打来电话者的身份〕。

cal·ler[2] [ˈkælə; ˋkælɚ] *a*. 〔Scot.〕 1. (鱼等)新鲜的。2. (天气等)凉爽的,舒适的。

cal·li·gram(me) [ˈkæligræm; ˋkælɪgræm] *n*. 画诗〔将诗文排列成与诗的主题有关的图画的一种诗〕。

cal·li·graph [ˈkæligrɑf; ˋkælɪgrəf] *vt*. 手书,手抄。

cal·lig·ra·pher, cal·lig·ra·phist [kəˈligrəfə, -fist; kəˋlɪgrəfɚ, -fɪst] *n*. 书法家,写字能手。

cal·li·gra·phy [kəˈligrəfi; kəˋlɪgrəfɪ] *n*. 善于书写(*opp*. cacography);书法;笔迹。

call·ing [ˈkɔːliŋ; ˋkɔlɪŋ] *n*. 1. 呼,唤,叫喊;点名。2. 招请,召集,号召;(神的)感召,天命;天职。3. 职业。4. 名称。5. 访问,到来;停靠(口岸)。6. 欲望;雌猫的叫春(期)。(*a carpenter*) **by one's** ～ 职业是(木匠)。～ **card** 〔美〕名片;〔美俚〕指纹。

Cal·li·o·pe [kəˈlaiəpi; kəˋlaɪəpɪ] *n*.【希神】卡拉培〔雄辩和叙事诗的女神,缪斯九神之首〕。

cal·lio·pe [kəˈlaiəpiː; kəˋlaɪəˏpi] *n*. 汽笛风琴。**-an** *a*.

cal·li·op·sis [ˌkæliˈɔpsis; ˏkælɪˋɑpsɪs] *n*.【植】金鸡菊属植物,金鸡菊,波斯菊(= coreopsis)。

cal·li·per [ˈkælipə; ˋkælɪpɚ] **I** *n*. 1. 〔*pl*.〕【机】卡钳,两脚规,测径器,测圆器(= ～ compasses)。2.【机】(阻力)制动片[夹]。3. (纸板等的)厚度。*inside* [*outside*] ～*s* 内[外]卡钳。*vernier* ～*s*【机】游标卡。**II** *vt*. 用卡钳测量。

cal·lis·then·ic [ˌkælisˈθenik; ˏkæləsˋθɛnɪk] *a*. 柔软体操的;健美体操的。～**s** *n*. 1. 〔作复数用〕(主指女子的)柔软体操(术)。2. 〔作单数用〕健美体操(术)。

Cal·lis·to [kəˈlistəu; kəˋlɪsto] *n*.【天】木卫四。

cal·li·thump [ˈkæliθʌmp; ˋkælɪθʌmp] *n*. 吵吵闹闹的游行〔以吹号角、敲铁锅及其他噪音乐器为主,以示嘲笑或敌意〕。

cal·li·thum·pi·an [kæliˈθʌmpiən; kælɪˋθʌmpɪən] *n*., *a*. 〔美俚〕吵吵闹闹的游行者(的)。

cal·lose [ˈkæləus; ˋkælos] *n*.【生】胼胝质。

cal·los·i·ty [kæˈlɔsiti; kæˋlɑsətɪ] *n*. 1. (皮肤)硬结;胼胝,老茧。2. 无情,无感觉,麻木。

cal·lous [ˈkæləs; ˋkæləs] **I** *a*. 1. 已硬结的,起老茧的。2. 无情的,硬心肠的;无感觉的(*to*)。**II** *vt*. 1. 使硬结。2. 使无感觉;使无情。**-ly** *ad*. **-ness** *n*.

cal·low [ˈkæləu; ˋkælo] **I** *a*. 1. 羽毛未生的;幼小的;未发育的;无经验的。2. 〔Ir.〕(草地)低湿的。**II** *n*. 〔Ir.〕低湿的牧场。

cal·lus [ˈkæləs; ˋkæləs] *n*. (*pl*. *-li* [-lai; -laɪ]) 1. 硬固部;硬瘤;【医】胼胝;骨痂;接骨质。2.【植】愈合组织,胼胝体;(禾本植物的)颖托。

calm [kɑːm; kɑm] **I** *a*. 1. (海洋、天气等)安静的,平静的。2. (人)平稳的;镇定的,沉着的。3. 〔俚〕恬不知耻的,若无其事的,脸皮厚的。**II** *n*. 1. 平静,镇定。2. 零级风,无风,风平浪静。*a* ～ *before the storm* 暴风雨来前的无风[平静]时期。**III** *vt*., *vi*. (使)平静下来,(使)镇定,(使)沉着,(使)从容。*Calm yourself*. 请别激动。～ **down** 平静下来(*The sea* ～*ed down*. 大海平静了下来)。～ **belt** 无风带。～ **day**【物】(地磁)平静日。**-ly** *ad*. **-ness** *n*.

cal·ma·tive [ˈkælmətiv, ˈkɑːm-; ˋkælmətɪv, ˋkɑm-] **I** *a*.【医】镇静的。**II** *n*.【医】镇静剂。

cal·o·mel [ˈkæləmel; ˋkæləml̩] *n*.【化】甘汞,氯化亚汞。

calori- *comb*. *f*. 热,热的:*calori*meter.

ca·lor·ic [kəˈlɔrik; kəˋlɔrɪk] **I** *n*. 热(量);【化】热质。**II** *a*. 热(量)的;热质的;蒸气推动的;卡(路里)的。**-al·ly** *ad*.

cal·o·ric·i·ty [ˌkæləˈrisiti; ˏkæləˋrɪsətɪ] *n*. 1.【医】食物的热量,生热力。2.【物】热值。

cal·o·ri·e [ˈkæləri; ˋkælərɪ] *n*. 1.【物】卡(路里)〔热量单位〕。2. 〔C-〕大卡,千卡。3. 产生一千卡热量的食物量。*large* [*great*] ～大卡,千卡。*small* ～小卡。

cal·o·ri·fa·cient [kəˌlɔriˈfeiʃənt; kəˏlɑrɪˋfeʃənt] *a*. (食物)(产)生热(量)的。

cal·o·rif·ic [ˌkæləˈrifik; ˏkæləˋrɪfɪk] *a*. 1. 发热的,生热的。2. 热(量)的。～ **power** 卡值,热值。

ca·lo·ri·fi·ca·tion [kəˌlɔrifiˈkeiʃən; kəˏlɑrɪfɪˋkeʃən] *n*. (动物体内)热的发生,生热;发热力。

cal·o·rif·ics [kæləˈrifiks; ˏkæləˋrɪfɪks] *n*. 1. 加热术。2.【物】热学。

cal·o·rif·i·er [kəˈlɔriˌfaiə; kəˋlɑrɪˏfaɪɚ] *n*. (液体的一种)加热装置。

cal·o·ri·fy [kəˈlɔrifai; kəˋlɑrəˏfaɪ] *vt*. 加热于。

cal·o·rim·e·ter [ˌkæləˈrimitə; ˏkæləˋrɪmətɚ] *n*. 热量计,卡计。

cal·o·rim·e·try [ˌkæləˈrimitri; ˏkæləˋrɪmɪtrɪ] *n*. 量热法,量热学。

cal·o·rize [ˈkæləraiz; ˋkæləraɪz] *vt*.【冶】热镀(铝),使铝渗入(某物)。

cal·or·stat [ˈkæləːstət ˈkælɔstət] *n*. 恒温器,恒温箱。

cal·o·ry [ˈkæləri; ˋkælərɪ] *n*. = calorie.

ca·lotte [kəˈlɔt; kəˋlɑt] *n*. 1. (无边)小帽。2. 帽状物。3.【动】纤毛帽;帽罩;(苔藓虫的)回缩盘。

cal·o·yer [ˈkælɔiə; ˋkælɔɪɚ] *n*. (东正教会的)修士。

cal·pac, cal·pack [ˈkælpæk; ˋkælpæk] *n*. (中近东的)羊皮帽,黑毡帽。

calque [kælk; kælk] *n*.【语】1. 仿造词〔如英语 masterpiece 是德语 meisterstück 的仿造词〕。2. 加倍;重复,反复;音节或词的重复。

Cal State [ˈkælsteit; ˋkælstet] 〔美俚〕加(利福尼亚)州(立)大学。

Caltech [ˈkæltek; ˋkæltɛk] *n*. 〔美俚〕加(利福尼亚)州理工学院。

CALTEX = California-Texas Petroleum Corporation (美国)加利福尼亚-得克萨斯石油公司(又译加德士石油公司)。

cal·trop, cal·trap [ˈkæltrəp; ˋkæltrəp] *n*. 1. 三角钉;【军】铁蒺藜。2.【植】蒺藜。**water** ～【植】菱。

cal·u·met [ˈkæljumet; ˋkæljuˏmɛt] *n*. (印第安人的)(长杆)旱烟袋;〔喻〕和平的象征。***smoke the*** ～ ***together*** 和睦相处。

ca·lum·ni·ate [kəˈlʌmnieit; kəˋlʌmnɪˏet] *vt*. 诽谤,诬蔑。

ca·lum·ni·a·tion [kəˌlʌmniˈeiʃən; kəˏlʌmnɪˋeʃən] *n*. 诽谤,诬蔑;【法】诬告。

ca·lum·ni·a·tor [kəˈlʌmnieitə; kəˋlʌmnɪetɚ] *n*. 诽谤者,诬蔑者;诬告者。

ca·lum·ni·a·to·ry, ca·lum·ni·ous [kəˈlʌmniətəri, -niəs; kəˋlʌmnɪəˏtorɪ, -nɪəs] *a*. 诽谤的,诬蔑的。

cal·um·ny [ˈkæləmni; ˋkæləmnɪ] *n*. 诽谤,诬蔑。

cal·u·tron [ˈkæljətrɔn; ˋkæljətrɑn] *n*.【物】电磁同位素分离器。

Cal·va·dos [ˈkælvəˌdəus, ˌkælvəˈdəus; ˋkælvəˏdos, ˏkælvəˋdos] *n*. 法国苹果白兰地。

cal·var·i·a [kælˈvɛəriə; kælˋvɛrɪə] *n*. = calvarium.

cal·var·i·um [kælˈveiriəm; kælˋverɪəm] *n*. (*pl*. *-var·i·a* [-ə; -ə])【解】颅顶,颅盖。**-i·al, -i·an** *a*.

cal·va·ry [ˈkælvəri; ˋkælvərɪ] *n*. 1. (十字架上的)耶稣受难像。2. 大磨难,苦恼。3. 〔C-〕耶稣受难处。

calve [kɑːv; kæv] *vi*. 1. (牛、鲸、鹿等)产(仔)。2. (冰河、冰块等)分离,崩解。—*vt*. 1. 生(小牛、小鹿等)。2. 使(冰块)崩解。

calved [kɑːvd; kævd] *a*. 有腿肚子的。

Cal·ver·ley [ˈkælvəli; ˋkælvəlɪ] *n*. 卡尔弗利〔姓氏〕。

Cal·vert [ˈkælvə(ː)t, ˈkɔːlvət; ˋkælvət, ˋkɔlvət] *n*. 卡

尔弗特〔姓氏〕。

calves [kɑːvz; kɑvz] calf 的复数。

Cal·vin [ˈkælvin; ˋkælvɪn] ***n*.** 卡尔文〔姓氏〕。**John** ～ 约翰·喀尔文〔1509—1564,法国宗教改革家〕。

Cal·vin·ism [ˈkælvinizəm; ˋkælvɪnɪzəm] ***n*.** 喀尔文教,喀尔文主义。

Cal·vin·ist [ˈkælvinist; ˋkælvɪnɪst] ***n*.** 喀尔文教徒。

Cal·vin·is·tic [kælviˈnistik; kælvɪˋnɪstɪk], **Cal·vin·is·ti·cal** [-kəl; -kəl] ***a*.** 喀尔文的,喀尔文教的。

cal·vi·ti·es [kælˈviʃiiːz; kælˋvɪʃɪiz] ***n*.** (*sing*., *pl*.)【医】秃头,脱发病。

C

calx [kælks; kælks] ***n*.** (*pl*. ***calces*** [ˈkælsiːz; ˋkælsiz]) 1. 金属灰[烧渣],矿灰。2.〔古〕生石灰。

ca·ly·ce·al [ˌkæliˈsiːəl; ˏkæliˋsiəl] ***a*.**【植】萼的,萼状的。

ca·ly·ces [ˈkeilisiːz, ˌkæ-; ˋkelɪsiz, ˋkæ-] ***n*.** calyx 的复数。

cal·y·ci·form [ˈkælisifɔːm; ˋkælɪsɪˏfɔrm] ***a*.**【植】萼状的。

ca·lyc·i·nal [kəˈlisinl; kəˋlɪsɪnəl], **cal·y·cine** [ˈkælisain; ˋkælɪsaɪn] ***a*.**【植】萼(一样)的。

cal·y·cle [ˈkælikl; ˋkælɪkl̩] ***n*.**【植】副萼。

ca·lyc·u·lus [kəˈlikjuləs; kəˋlɪkjələs] ***n*.** (*pl*. ***-li*** [-lai; -laɪ])【解】小萼;味蕾。

ca·lyp·so[1] [kəˈlipsəu; kəˋlɪpso] ***n*.**【植】匙唇兰。

ca·lyp·so[2] [kəˈlipsəu; kəˋlɪpso] ***n*.** (特里尼达等地居民临时编唱的一种)即兴小调。

ca·lyp·tra [kəˈliptrə; kəˋlɪptrə] ***n*.**【植】苔帽;根冠;冠状部。

ca·lyp·tro·gen [kəˈliptrədʒən; kəˋlɪptrədʒən] ***n*.**【植】根冠原。

ca·lyx [ˈkeiliks; ˋkelɪks] ***n*.** (*pl*. ～***es***, ***ca·ly·ces*** [ˈkeilisiːz; ˋkelɪsiz])【植】萼;【解】(肾)盂。

CAM = computer-aided manufacturing 计算机辅助制造,计算机辅助生产。

cam [kæm; kæm] ***n*.**【机】凸轮,偏心轮;靠模。～ **shaft** 凸轮轴。～**wood**【植】紫木。

Cam., **Camb.** = **Cambridge.**

cam. = camouflage.

Ca·ma·güey [ˌkɑːmɑːˈgwei; ˏkɑmɑˋgwe] ***n*.** 卡马圭〔古巴城市〕。

ca·ma·ra·de·rie [ˌkɑːməˈrɑːdəriː; ˏkɑməˋrɑdəri] ***n*.** 〔F.〕同僚间的感情;友谊;友爱。

ca·ma·ril·la [ˌkæməˈrilə; ˏkæməˋrɪlə] ***n*.** 〔Sp.〕1. 秘密顾问。2. 奸党。3. 秘密会议室。

cam·a·ron [ˈkæmərən; ˋkæmərən] ***n*.**【动】(淡水)大斑节虾。

cam·ass, **cam·as** [ˈkæməs; ˋkæməs] ***n*.**【植】卡马夏属(*Camassia*)植物。

Camb. = 1. Cambrian. 2. Cambridge. 3. Cambridgeshire.

cam·ber [ˈkæmbə; ˋkæmbɚ] **I** ***n*.** 1. 向上弯曲,翘曲;弯度;中凸形。2. 小船坞,筏渠。3.【空】(机翼的)弯曲,曲度弧。4.【船】梁拱,拱高。**II** ***vt*.** 把(道路、甲板等)造成弧形[上弯形]。—***vi*.** (梁、道路等)向上弯,翘起。～ **beam**【建】弓背梁。

cam·bist [ˈkæmbist; ˋkæmbɪst] ***n*.** 1. 各国度量衡及货币比值表[手册]。2. 汇兑商;汇兑行家。

cam·bi·um [ˈkæmbiəm; ˋkæmbɪəm] ***n*.**【植】形成层,新生层。

cam·blet [ˈkæmblet; ˋkæmblɛt] ***n*.** = camlet.

Cam·bo·di·a [kæmˈbəudiə; kæmˋbodɪə] ***n*.** 柬埔寨〔亚洲〕(= Kampuchea)。

Cam·bo·di·an [kæmˈbəudjən; kæmˋbodɪən] **I** ***a*.** 柬埔寨的;柬埔寨人的;柬埔寨语的。**II** ***n*.** 柬埔寨人;柬埔寨语(= kampuchean)。

cam·bo·gi·a [kæmˈbəudʒiə; kæmˋbodʒɪə] ***n*.**【化】藤黄。

Cam·bri·a [ˈkæmbriə; ˋkæmbrɪə] ***n*.**〔古〕= Wales.

Cam·bri·an [ˈkæmbriən; ˋkæmbrɪən] **I** ***a*.** 1.〔诗〕威尔士的。2.【地】寒武系[纪]的。**II** ***n*.** 1.〔诗〕威尔士人。2.【地】寒武纪。～ **system**【地】寒武系。

cam·bric [ˈkeimbrik; ˋkembrɪk] ***n*.** 1. 麻纱白葛布;麻纱手帕。2. 细漆布[电工材料]。～ **grass** 苎麻。～ **paper** 布纹纸。

Cam·bridge [ˈkeimbridʒ; ˋkembrɪdʒ] ***n*.** 1. 剑桥〔英国城市,剑桥大学所在地〕; 2. 坎布里奇〔美国麻萨诸塞州城市,哈佛大学所在地〕。

Cambs. = Cambridgeshire 剑桥郡〔英国〕。

Cam·den [ˈkæmdən; ˋkæmdən] ***n*.** 卡姆登〔姓氏〕。

came[1] [keim; kem] come 的过去式。

came[2] [keim; kem] ***n*.** (固定花格窗玻璃等用的)有槽铅条。

cam·el [ˈkæməl; ˋkæml̩] ***n*.** 1. 骆驼。2.【船】起重浮箱,打捞浮筒。*an Arabian* [*a Bactrian*] ～单峰[双峰]驼。***break the*** **～*'s back*** 受不了,忍无可忍。***swallow a*** ～ 默忍难于置信[容忍]的事。～**back** 驼背;驼峰。～**backed** ***a*.** 驼背的。～ **bird** 鸵鸟。～ **cade**〔美〕骆驼队。～ **corps**〔美俚〕步兵。～**'s hair** 骆驼毛,骆驼绒;粟鼠尾毛画笔。

cam·el·eer [ˌkæmiˈliə; ˏkæməˋlɪr] ***n*.** 赶骆驼的(人);骆驼骑兵。

ca·mel·li·a [kəˈmiːljə, kəˈmel-; kəˋmiljə, kəˋmɛl-] ***n*.**【植】山茶(花)。

ca·mel·o·pard [ˈkæmiləpɑːd, kəˈmeləpɑːd; ˋkæˋmɛləˏpɑrd, kəˋmɛləˏpɑrd] ***n*.** 1.〔罕〕【动】长颈鹿〔一般称 giraffe〕;〔C-〕【天】鹿豹座。2. [ˈkæmelepəd; ˋkæmɛlɛpəd]〔谑〕瘦长的女人。

Cam·e·lot [ˈkæmilɔt; ˋkæmələt] ***n*.** 卡米洛特〔传说中英国亚瑟王宫廷所在地〕;〔喻〕象征灿烂岁月或繁荣昌盛的地方。

cam·el·ry [ˈkæməlri; ˋkæməlrɪ] ***n*.** 1. 骆驼骑兵;骆驼队。2. 骆驼驮的货物。

cam·e·o [ˈkæmiəu; ˋkæmɪo] **I** ***n*.** 1. (玉石、贝壳上的)浮雕;有浮雕的玉石[贝壳等]。2.【影、剧】小品,片断。**II** ***a*.** 小型的,小规模的。～ **role** (衬托名星演员的)小配角。

cam·er·a [ˈkæmərə; ˋkæmərə] ***n*.** 1. (*pl*. ～***s***)【摄】照相机;电影摄影机;电视摄像机;暗箱;暗房。2. (*pl*. ***cam·er·ae*** [-əriː; -əri])【法】法官室。3. 罗马教廷的财政部。*load a* ～装胶卷到照相机内。*a sound* ～录音器。***in*** ～ 禁止旁听;秘密地。***on*** ～ 被电视机摄取;出现在电视上。～ **obscura** [əbsˈkjuərə; ɑbˋskjʊrə] 暗箱。～**cature**〔美〕电影动画。～ **gun**【军】(能自动拍摄空战射击情况的)照相枪。～ **lucida** [ˈluːsidə; ˋlusɪdə] 显像描绘器。～ **man** 照相师,(电影)摄影师;摄影记者。～ **plane** 摄影用飞机。～**-shy** ***a*.** 不愿照相的。～ **tube**【电视】析像管,阴极射线管。～ **work** 摄影技巧。

cam·er·al [ˈkæmərəl; ˋkæmərəl] ***a*.** 推事室的,咨询委员会的。

cam·er·a·lis·tic [ˌkæmərəˈlistik; ˏkæmərəˋlɪstɪk] **I** ***a*.** 1. 财政(上)的。2. 机关事务学的。**II** ***n*.** 〔*pl*.〕〔用作单数〕财政学。

Cam·er·on [ˈkæmərən; ˋkæmərən] ***n*.** 卡梅伦〔姓氏,男子名〕。

Cam·e·roon [ˈkæməruːn; kæməˋrun] ***n*.** 喀麦隆〔非洲〕。

cam·i·knick·ers [ˌkæmiˈnikəz; ˋkæməˋnɪkɚz] ***n*.** 〔*pl*.〕连裤女衬衣。

Ca·mil·(l)a [kəˈmilə; kəˋmɪlə] ***n*.** 卡米拉〔女子名〕。

cam·i·on [ˈkæmiən; ˋkæmɪən] ***n*.** 〔F.〕(军用)卡车。

cam·i·sade, **cam·i·sado** [ˌkæmiˈseid, ˌkæmiˈseidəu; ˏkæməˋsed, ˏkæməˋsedo] ***n*.**〔古〕【军】夜袭。

ca·mise [kəˈmiːs; kəˋmis] ***n*.** 宽大的衬衣[罩衣;袍子]。

cam·i·sole [ˈkæmisəul; ˋkæməˏsol] ***n*.** 1. 女人短袖衬

衣,贴身背心。2. 宽女外套,(绣花)化妆衣。3. 疯人紧身衣。

cam·let [ˈkæmlit; ˋkæmlɪt] *n*.【纺】羽纱。

ca·mo [ˈkæməu; ˋkæmo] *n*.【军】迷彩服;保护色。

cam·o·mile [ˈkæməmail; ˋkæmə͵maɪl] *n*.【植】春黄菊。

cam·ou·flage [ˈkæmuflɑːʒ; ˋkæmə͵flɑʒ] **I** *n*. 1.【军】伪装。2. 隐瞒,掩饰。3.〔喻〕幌子。*under* [*behind*] *the* ~ *of* 在…的掩盖[伪装]下。**II** *vt*. 使改头换面,伪装,掩饰;欺瞒。

ca·mou·flet [ˌkæmuˈflei; ͵kæməˋfle] *n*.〔F.〕1. (炸弹,地雷等的)地下爆炸。2. 地下爆炸的炸弹[地雷]。3. (地下爆炸造成的)弹坑。

cam·ou·fleur [ˈkæmufləː; ˋkæmə͵flɚ] *n*.〔F.〕伪装技术员。

Camp [kæmp; kæmp] *n*. 坎普〔姓氏〕。

camp [kæmp; kæmp] **I** *n*. 1. 野营,露营地;露营队,出征军;阵营,阵地,战场;军队生活。2. 露宿;帐幕,帐篷;〔美〕山中小房;(牧场中)作住处用的马车。3. 集团,阵营;〔美〕分会。4.〔美俚〕(原为同性恋圈子内行话)下流;庸俗;过分打扮[做作]。*a break* ~折叠帐篷。***be in the same*** [***enemy's***] ~ 是同志[敌人]。***go into*** ~ 布阵。***strike*** [***break up***] ~ 撤营。***the*** ~ ***eye***〔美〕守露营帐篷的。**II** *vt*. 1. 使扎营住宿。2. 临时安顿。—*vi*. 1. 露营;宿营;露宿。2. 住宿。~ ***out*** 露宿。~ **bed** 行军床。~ **car** 野营车。~ **chair** 折椅。~**craft** 野营术。**C-David** 戴维营〔美国总统别墅所在地〕。~ **fever** 露营病〔主指斑疹伤寒〕。~**fire** 营火;〔美〕营火会。~ **fire girl** 美国营火少女团团员。~ **follower** 1. 随营人员;营妓。2. 附和者,依附者。~ **ground** 野营地,野营布道会场。~**site** 营地。~ **stool** 折凳。**-er** *n*. 1. 露营者。2. =~car.

Cam·pa·gna [kæmˈpɑːnjə; kɑmˋpɑnjə] *n*. (*pl*. ***-pagne*** [-ˈpɑːnjei; -ˋpɑnje]) 1. (罗马四郊的)罗马平原。2.〔c-〕(一般的)平原。

cam·paign [kæmˈpein; kæmˋpen] *n*. 1. 战役。2. 竞选运动;运动,游说。3.【冶】开炉时间。*an advertising* ~ 大做广告。*a* ~ *against* [*for*] ... 反对[赞成]…的运动。***enter upon a*** ~ 走上征途;发动运动。***on*** ~ 从军,出征。**II** *vi*. 1. 从军,出征。2. 参加[从事](某一)运动。***go*** ~***ing*** 1. 从军。2. 参加(某一)运动。~ **club**〔美〕某候选人后援会。~ **emblem**〔美〕政党徽章。

cam·paign·er [kæmˈpeinə; kæmˋpenɚ] *n*. 1. 运动参加者,竞选者。2. 从军者。3. 老兵;老练的人。*an old* ~ 老兵;经验丰富的人,老手。

cam·pa·ni·le [ˌkæmpəˈniːli; ͵kæmpəˋnilɪ] *n*. (*pl*. ***-li*** [-liː; -li], ~*s*) (靠近教堂的)钟楼,钟塔。

cam·pa·nol·o·gy [ˌkæmpəˈnɔlədʒi; ͵kæmpəˋnɑlədʒɪ] *n*. 1. 鸣钟术。2. 铸钟术。

cam·pan·u·la [kəmˈpænjulə; kæmˋpænjulə] *n*. 1.【植】风铃草(属)。2.【动】铃状部[结构]。

cam·pan·u·late [kəmˈpænjuleit; kæmˋpænjulɪt] *a*.【植】钟形的,钟状的,铃状的。

Camp·bell [ˈkæmbl; ˋkæmbl] *n*. 坎贝尔〔姓氏〕。

camp·er [ˈkæmpə; ˋkæmpɚ] *n*. 1. 露营者。2. (可随车携带、折叠的)活动住房,野营帐篷。

cam·pe·si·no [ˌkɑːmpeˈsiːnə; ͵kɑmpeˋsinə] *n*. (*pl*. ***-nos*** [-nɔs; -nɑs])〔Sp.〕农民,农业工人。

cam·pes·tral [kæmˈpestrəl; kæmˋpestrəl] *a*.〔军〕野外的,乡村的。

cam·phene [ˈkæmfiːn; ˋkæmfin] *n*.【化】莰烯。

cam·phire [ˈkæmfaiə; ˋkæmfaɪr] *n*. 1.【植】散沫花。2. 散沫花染料。3. 棕色。

cam·phol [ˈkæmfɔl; ˋkæmfɔl] *n*.【药】龙脑,冰片。

cam·phor [ˈkæmfə; ˋkæmfɚ] *n*. 樟脑;【化】莰酮;〔美〕樟脑水。~ **ball** 樟脑丸。~ **glass** (樟脑脂状的)乳白(不透明)玻璃。~ **ice** 樟脑药膏。~ **tree**【植】樟树。~ **wood** 樟木。**-ism** 樟脑中毒。

cam·phor·ate [ˈkæmfəreit; ˋkæmfə͵ret] *vt*. 使与樟脑化合,在…中加入樟脑。**-d** *a*. 含樟脑的。

cam·phor·ic [kæmˈfɔrik; kæmˋfɔrɪk] *a*. (含)樟脑的;樟脑酸的。~ **acid** 樟脑酸。

camp·ing [ˈkæmpiŋ; ˋkæmpɪŋ] *n*. 野营,露营;帐篷生活,露营生活。

cam·pi·on [ˈkæmpjən, -piən; ˋkæmpjən, -pɪən] *n*.【植】剪秋罗属,狗筋蔓属植物。

cam·po [ˈkɑːmpəu; ˋkæmpo] *n*. (*pl*. ~*s*) 1. (巴西等地的)大草原。2.【植】坎普群落。

camp·o·ree [ˌkæmpəˈriː; ͵kæmpəˋri] *n*. 地区性童子军集会。

cam·po santo [ˈkæmpəu ˈsæntəu; ˋkɑmpo ˋsɑnto]〔It.〕坟地;(特指)公墓。

camp·shed [ˈkæmpʃed; ˋkæmp͵ʃɛd] *vt*. 堆土[石]堆并铺木板于(河岸)。

camp·shot [ˈkæmpʃɔt; ˋkæmpˋʃɑt] *n*. (堆土[石]堆并铺以木板的)护岸,河防。

cam·pus [ˈkæmpəs; ˋkæmpəs] *n*.〔美〕校园,学校范围内;大学。~ *activities* 校内活动。~ *cave*〔美〕学生消遣地。***off*** ~ 在校外。***on*** (***the***) ~ 在校内。

camp·y [ˈkæmpi; ˋkæmpɪ] *a*.〔美俚〕1. 同性恋爱的。2. 下流的;庸俗的;过分打扮的;矫揉做作的。

cam·py·lot·ro·pous [ˌkæmpiˈlɔtrəpəs; ͵kæmpɪˋlɑtrəpəs] *a*.【植】弯生胚珠的。

can(i)- *comb*. *f*. 表示"狗""犬": *can*ine.

can[1] [强 kæn, 弱 kən, kn; kæn, kən, kn] *v*. ***aux***. (***could*** [强 kud, 弱 kəd; kud, kəd]) 1.〔表示能力〕能,会。2.〔表示可能性〕(可)能,会得;(偶然,有时)会。3.〔口〕〔表示许可或请求〕可以…,行。4.〔表示轻微的命令语气,多与 not 连用〕(不)可以…,(不)能…。5.〔在疑问句中重读,表示惊异,不耐烦等〕怎么会,难道会;究竟。6.〔表示必须〕就得。7.〔与 see, hear, smell 等感觉动词连用,代替一般的现在式或过去式〕(看、听、嗅…)得到,(感觉)得出。*I* ~ *swim*. 我会游泳。*You* ~ *go*. 你可以去;去好了;去罢。*Curiosity* ~ *get you into trouble*. 好奇可能招引麻烦。*Do you think he* ~ *yet be living*? 你以为他还会活着吗? *How* ~ *you*? 你怎么能这样!你真做得出! *If you don't be quiet you* ~ *leave the room*. 你再不安静下来就得离开房间。*I* ~ *see her easily from here*. 我从这里很容易看到她。*I couldn't understand him*. 我听不懂他的话。***as ... as*** ~ ***be*** 很(*He is as happy as* ~ *be*. 他是很幸福的。他(幸福得)不能再幸福了)。~ ***but*** ... 只能…罢了(*I* ~ *but speak*. 我只能说说罢了)。~ ***not but*** ... 1. 不得不(= ***can not help***)。2. 不会不,不能不,必然(*I* ~ *not but speak that* ... = *cannot help speaking that* ... 我不得不说[认为]…。*One* ~ *not but be moved by his fate*. 人们不能不为他的命运所感动)。***cannot too*** 决不会…得太…,无论怎样…都不够(*You cannot be too modest*. 人越谦虚越好〔无论怎样谦虚都不为过〕。*We cannot praise him too much*. 我们无论怎样称赞他都不为过分)。~**-do** *a*. 有干劲的,勤奋的,热心的。

can[2] [kæn; kæn] **I** *n*. 1.〔美〕罐头,听头(=〔英〕tin);(装液体的)铁罐,玻璃罐(等);一罐(之量);茶杯。2.〔美俚〕保险箱。3.〔美俚〕监牢;警察局。4.〔美俚〕浴室;厕所;屁股。5.〔军俚〕驱逐舰;飞机;(深水)炸弹。6.〔俚〕〔*pl*.〕头戴听筒,耳机。6.〔美俚〕一盎司大麻麻醉药。~ ***moocher*** 破落到拣垃圾箱里罐头盒的浪子,不可救药的败家子。~ ***of corn***【美棒球】容易接的飞球。~ ***of worms*** 问题成堆的地方,老大难的工作;一团糟。***carry*** [***take***] ***the*** (***back***) ~ 负责任,受责备;代人受过。***in the*** ~ (影片等)编成,制成,现成(可用)。**II** *vt*. (***-nn-***) 1.〔美〕把…装成罐头。2.〔美俚〕解雇,辞退;抛弃;开除(学生);停用;停止。3.〔俚〕录音(在磁带上)。~ ***the ad lib***〔美剧俚〕请安静。~ ***the highbrow stuff***〔美俚〕停止夸口。~ ***the twit***〔美俚〕停止说话。~ **bank** 空罐集

C

中回收站。～**-box**【纺】条筒针梳机。～**carrier**〔美俚〕为某事负责任的人。～ **opener** 开罐头用具。

Can. = Canada; Canadian.

can. = canceled; canon; canto.

Ca·naan [ˈkeinən; ˋkenən] ***n*.** **1.** 迦南〔《圣经》中所说上帝赐给亚伯拉罕的地方,现在的巴勒斯坦西部〕。**2.** 〔喻〕希望之地;天国,乐土。

Ca·naan·ite [ˈkeinənait; ˋkenənˏaɪt] ***n*.** 迦南人[语]。

Can·a·da [ˈkænədə; ˋkænədə] ***n*.** 加拿大〔北美洲〕。

Ca·na·di·an [kəˈneidjən; kəˋnedɪən] **I** ***a*.** 加拿大的;加拿大人的。**II** ***n*.** 加拿大人。

Ca·na·di·an·ism [kəˈneidiənizəm; kəˋnedɪənzm] ***n*.** **1.** 加拿大习惯、特点、信仰。**2.** 加拿大英语特有的词或片语。

ca·naille [kəˈnɑːi; kəˋnaɪ] ***n*.** 〔F.〕〔集合词〕愚民,下层社会;乌合之众。

can·a·kin [ˈkænəkin; ˋkænəkɪn] ***n*.** = cannikin.

ca·nal [kəˈnæl; kəˋnæl] **I** ***n*.** **1.** 运河;沟渠,水道。**2.** 【建】沟;【解】管,道。**3.** 【天】火星表面的运河状细长沟纹。*the alimentary* ～消化管。*the Suez C-* 苏伊士运河。***the C- Zone*** 巴拿马运河区。**II** ***vt*.** (*-l*(*l*)*-*) 在…开运河;在…开沟,疏导。～ **boat** 运河船〔一种专门在运河中航行的大驳船〕。～ **rays**【物】极隧射线,阳极射线。

ca·nal·age [kəˈnælidʒ; kəˋnælɪdʒ] ***n*.** **1.** 开运河。**2.** 〔集合词〕运河,水道;运河运输。**3.** 运河通行税。

can·al·ic·u·late, can·al·ic·u·lated [ˌkænəˈlikjulit, -leitid; ˏkænəˋlɪkjulɪt, -letɪd] ***a*.** 【解、植】有小管的,有小沟的。

can·al·icu·lus [ˌkænəˈlikjuləs; ˏkænəˋlɪkjuləs] ***n*.** (*pl*. ***-li*** [-lai; -laɪ])【解】小管;小沟。

ca·nal·i·za·tion [ˌkænəlaiˈzeiʃən; kəˏnæləˋzeʃen] ***n*.** **1.** 开挖运河。**2.** 运河规划;渠道网;导管组织;堰闸法。**3.** 【医】穿通;造管术。**4.** (思想等的)开导。

ca·nal·ize [ˈkænəlaiz; kəˋnælaɪz] ***vt*.** **1.** 在…上开运河[沟];把(河道)改造成运河。**2.** 使(水)流向一定方向;〔喻〕把(思想等)导向某一途径。—***vi*.** 流入渠道。～*d development hypothesis*【生】限向发育说。

ca·nal·ler [kəˈnælə; kəˋnælɚ] ***n*.** 运河货船;运河船的船员。

can·a·pé [kænəˈpei; ˋkænəpɪ] ***n*.** 〔F.〕(上加鱼,肉,乳酪等的)开胃饼干[烤面包]。

ca·nard [kæˈnɑːd; kəˋnɑrd] ***n*.** 〔F.〕**1.** 谣言,误传。**2.** 【空】前置安定面飞机;前置安定面。**3.** 【烹】鸭。

ca·nar·i·ensis [kənɛəriˈensis; kənɛrɪˋɛnsɪs] ***n*.** 【植】金丝雀蔓草。

ca·nar·y [kəˈnɛəri; kəˋnɛrɪ] **I** ***n*.** **1.** 【鸟】金丝雀。**2.** (非洲)加那利群岛白葡萄酒〔又作 C- wine〕。**3.** 鲜黄色,嫩黄色。**4.** 〔美俚〕女歌手;女人;女学生。**5.** 〔美俚〕告密者。**6.** 〔*pl*.〕【美影】录音时刺耳的嘎嘎声。**II** ***a*.** **1.** 加那利群岛的。**2.** 鲜黄色的。～ **bird** 金丝雀;〔美俚〕罪犯。～**-bird flower**【植】金莲花。～ **creeper** 金丝雀蔓草。～ **grass**【植】虉草。～ **stone** 黄石髓。

Canary Islands [kəˈnɛəriˈailəndz; kəˋnɛrɪˋaɪləndz] ***n*.** 加那利群岛〔大西洋东北部〕。

ca·nas·ta [kəˈnæstə; kəˋnæstə] ***n*.** 加纳斯塔牌〔一种二至六人玩的纸牌游戏〕。

ca·nas·ter [kəˈnæstə; kəˋnæstɚ] ***n*.** **1.** 苇篮,蒲篮〔装烟叶用〕。**2.** (南美)板烟。

Can·ber·ra [ˈkænbərə; ˋkænbərə] ***n*.** 堪培拉(坎培拉)〔澳大利亚首都〕。

canc. = cancel, cancelled, cancellation.

can·can [ˈkɑ̃ŋkɑ̃ːŋ; ˋkænkæn] ***n*.** 〔F.〕(妇女跳的一种多踢足动作的)康康舞。

can·cel [ˈkænsəl; ˋkænsl] **I** ***vt*.** (*-ll-*, 〔美〕*-l-*) **1.** 划掉,略去,删去。**2.** 注销,盖销;取消,把…作废。**3.** 抵消,偿还。**4.** 撤消,解除。**5.** 【数】约去;消去(账目或方程式两边的相等部分)。*a cancelled cheque* 付讫的支票。～ *a contract* 取消合同。～ *each other* 互相抵消。*a cancelling stamp* 作废[注销]图章。—***vi*.** 相消,互相抵消 (*out*)。*The pros and cons* ～ *out*. 正反两种意见互相抵消。**II** ***n*.** **1.** 删略;取消;【数】(相)约,(相)消;盖销。**2.** 〔常 *pl*.〕轧票机,打孔铁 (*a pair of*) ～*s* 作废打孔器;轧票机。**-(l)er** ***n*.** **1.** 删略者,取消者。**2.** 【无】消除器,补偿设备。

can·cel·late, can·cel·la·ted [ˈkænsəleit, -tid; ˋkænsəˏlet, -tɪd] ***a*.** 【动】格子状的,网眼状的。

can·cel·la·tion [ˌkænsəˈleiʃən; ˏkænsəˋleʃən] ***n*.** **1.** 删除,勾消。**2.** 取消,撤消,注销;(邮票等的)盖销,盖销记号;废除;解除。**3.** 【数】(相)消,(相)约。

can·cel·lous [ˈkænsiləs; ˋkænsɪləs] ***a*.** **1.** 【解】网眼状的,多孔的;松质骨的。**2.** 【植】(某些叶子的)细密网状脉的 (= cancellate)。

can·cer [ˈkænsə; ˋkænsɚ] ***n*.** **1.** 【医】癌症;癌(瘤),肿瘤。**2.** 弊病;社会恶习。**3.** 〔the C-〕【天】巨蟹座;巨蟹宫。*gastric* ～胃癌。*lung* ～肺癌。***the Tropic of C-*** 夏至线,北回归线。～ **stick** 〔俚〕纸烟。**-d** ***a*.** 得了癌症的。

can·cer·o·gen·ic [ˈkænsərəuˈdʒenik; ˋkænsəroˋdʒɛnɪk] ***a*.** 产生癌的,致癌的。～ **substance**【医】致癌物质。

can·cer·ol·o·gy [ˌkænsəˈrɔlədʒi; ˏkænsəˋrɑlədʒɪ] ***n*.** 癌学。

can·cer·ous [ˈkænsərəs; ˋkænsərəs] ***a*.** **1.** 癌的,癌肿性的。**2.** 得了癌症的;不治的。

Can·cri [ˈkæŋkrai, -kri; ˋkæŋkraɪ, -krɪ] Cancer 的所有格。

can·croid [ˈkæŋkrɔid; ˋkæŋkrɔɪd] **I** ***a*.** **1.** 【医】癌肿状的。**2.** 蟹状的。**II** ***n*.** **1.** 角化癌;皮癌。**2.** 蟹状甲壳动物。

can·de·la [kænˈdiːlə; kænˋdilə] ***n*.** 【物】新烛光,坎(德拉)〔发光强度单位〕。

can·de·la·brum [ˌkændiˈlɑːbrəm; ˏkændəlˋɑbrəm] ***n*.** (*pl*. ***-bra*** [-brə; -brə], ～***s***) **1.** 枝状烛台,烛架。**2.** 【建】华柱。★也有以 candelabra 作单数,而以 candelabras 作复数的。

can·de·lil·la [ˈkændiˌlilə; ˋkændɪˏlɪlə] ***n*.** 【植】蜡大戟,蜡拖鞋花。

can·dent [ˈkændənt; ˋkændənt] ***a*.** 〔古〕白热的,炽烈的。

can·des·cence [kænˈdesns; kænˋdɛsns] ***n*.** 白热。

can·des·cent [kænˈdesnt; kænˋdɛsnt] ***a*.** 白热的。

C. & F. 【商】= cost and freight 成本加运费。

can·did [ˈkændid; ˋkændɪd] ***a*.** **1.** 正直的,耿直的,公正的。**2.** 率直的,坦白的,老实的,忠厚的。**3.** 真实的,传真的;非排演的;【摄】趁人不备时偷拍的。**4.** (光等)白色的。～ *camera* 趁人不备时快拍用的小照相机。～ *friend* 坦率的朋友。***to be*** ～ (*with you*) 老老实实讲,不瞒你说。**-ly** ***ad*.** **-ness** ***n*.**

can·di·da·cy [ˈkændidəsi; ˋkændɪdəsɪ] ***n*.** 候选(人)资格〔身分〕;提名候选。

can·di·date [ˈkændidit; ˋkændəˏdet] **I** ***n*.** **1.** 候选人;候补人 (*for*)。**2.** 学位应考人,投考生。**II** ***vi*.** [-deit; -det]〔美口〕提名候选。

can·di·da·ture [ˈkændiditʃə; ˋkændədətʃɚ] ***n*.** 〔英〕= candidacy.

can·died [ˈkændid; ˋkændɪd] **I** ***a*.** **1.** 糖渍的,蜜饯的。**2.** 冰糖一样坚硬的;亮晶晶的。**3.** 甜蜜的。*have a* ～ *tongue* 会讲甜言蜜语,嘴甜。**II** ***n*.** 【纺】浆斑。

Can·di·ot [ˈkændiɔt; ˋkændɪɑt] **I** ***a*.** 克里特岛(居民)的。**II** ***n*.** 克里特岛居民。

can·dle [ˈkændl; ˋkændl] **I** ***n*.** **1.** 蜡烛。**2.** 蜡烛状物。**3.** 【物】烛光〔光强度单位〕。*the international* ～国际标准烛光。*a lighted* ～夜会;宴会。***burn the*** ～ ***at both ends*** 浪费精力〔财产〕(等)。***cannot hold a*** ～ ***to*** 远不如,不能与…相比。***hide one's*** ～ ***under a bushel*** 不露

锋芒。*hold a ~ to another* 为别人尽力。*hold a ~ to the devil* 助纣为虐,为虎作伥,离开正道。*hold a ~ to the sun* 白费,徒劳。*not fit to hold a ~ to ... = can not hold a ~ to ...* 还不如,不能与…相比。*not worth the ~* 不上算,值不得,得不偿失。*sell by the ~ [by inch of ~]*(以蜡烛点完来决定成交的)拍卖。**II** *vt*. 用亮光检查(鸡蛋的)好坏。~ **berry 1.**【植】杨梅属植物;月桂果。**2.** = ~**nut**. ~ **bomb** 照明弹。~ **ends** 〔*pl*.〕蜡烛头;一点一点积蓄成的东西。~**fish** *n*. (*pl*. ~*es*)【动】太平洋烛鱼。~ **foot** 烛光英尺(= **foot-~**)。~ **holder** 烛台。~**light 1.** 烛光,灯火。**2.** 黄昏。~**nut**【植】石栗(树)。~**pin 1.** (一种游戏用的)烛形木柱。**2.** 〔*pl*.〕烛柱戏。~ **power**【物】烛光(*a burner of 50 ~ power* 五十支烛光的灯)。~**stick** 烛台。~**-wick** 烛芯;〔美〕织物上凸起的花纹。~**wood 1.**【植】蜡烛木。**2.** 有脂之树或灌木。**3.** (引火或作火炬用的)烛材。

Can·dle·mas [ˈkændlməs; ˋkændlməs] *n*.【宗】圣烛节(二月二日)。~ **Day** 〔Scot.〕春季结账日。

can·do(u)r [ˈkændə; ˋkændɚ] *n*. **1.** 公正,公平。**2.** 率直,坦率。**3.** 白色;光明。

CANDU, Candu = Canadian deuterium uranium (reactor)【核】加拿大重水铀反应堆。

C & R Sec = Courier and Runner Section【美军】传令组。

C & W, C-and-W = country and western〔美〕(用电吉他演奏的)仿西部乡土音乐。

can·dy [ˈkændi; ˋkændɪ] **I** *n*. **1.** 冰糖;水果糖,〔美〕蜜饯,糖果(=〔英〕sweets)。**2.** 〔美俚〕古柯碱;可卡因(= cocaine)。**3.** 砂糖,结晶冰糖。*He'd taken a ~ from a baby*.〔美口〕他是一个贪鄙的小人。*sugar ~* 冰糖(=〔美〕*rock ~*)。**II** *vt*. (*-died*; *-dy·ing*) **1.** 蜜饯,糖煮。**2.** 使结晶成冰糖〔块〕;把…煮成结晶。—*vi*. 结晶成糖。**III** *a*. 〔美俚〕(服饰)花哨的。~ **bar** 方糖块。~ **butcher** 〔美俚〕卖糖小贩。~ **floss** 〔英俚〕**1.** 棉花糖。**2.** 不切实际的主意〔计划〕。~ **pull** (备有糖果的青年人的)联欢会。~ **store** 〔美〕糖果店(=〔英〕sweet shop)。~**-stripe** (织物的)条纹图案,条子花。

can·dy·tuft [ˈkænditʌft; ˋkændɪˏtʌft] *n*.【植】屈曲花属植物;伞形屈曲花。

cane [kein; ken] **I** *n*. **1.** (藤、竹等的)茎,藤料,竹料。**2.** 甘蔗。**3.** 杖,手杖;笞杖;〔美〕棍棒,棒。*take up the ~* 拿起藤条(处罚学生)。**II** *vt*. **1.** 用棍打。**2.** 用藤做(椅背等)。~**-brake** 藤丛,竹丛。~ **chair** 藤椅。~ **gun** 手杖形手枪。~ **land** 甘蔗地。~ **rush** 〔美〕(校内)班级间的比赛。~ **sugar** 蔗糖。~ **work** 编藤细工。**-r** *n*. 藤椅编制工。

ca·nel·la [kəˈnelə; kəˋnɛlə] *n*. (做香料等用的)白桂皮。

ca·ne·pho·ros [keiˈniːfərəs, kəˈnef-; keˋnifərəs, kəˋnɛf-] *n*. (*pl*. *-roe* [-riː; -ri]) **1.** (古希腊)头顶盛有祭物篮子的少女。**2.**【建】(作建筑物装饰用的)顶篮童女雕塑(= canephor)。

ca·nes·cent [kəˈnesnt; kəˋnɛsnt] *a*. **1.** 变成白色或微灰色的。**2.**【植】(某些叶子)披灰白毛的。

can·ful [ˈkænfʊl; ˋkænfʊl] *n*. 一罐,满罐。

cang(ue) [kæŋ; kæŋ] *n*. 枷〔中国古时的一种刑具〕。

cani- *comb.f*. 表示"犬"(= can-)。

Ca·nic·u·la [kəˈnikjulə; kəˋnɪkjʊlə] *n*.【天】天狼星。

ca·nic·u·lar [kəˈnikjulə; kəˋnɪkjələ] *a*. **1.**【天】天狼星的;根据天狼星升起来度量的。**2.** 三伏天的,酷暑的。

ca·nine [ˈkeinain; ˋkenaɪn] **I** *a*. **1.** 犬的;似犬的。**2.** 犬属的。**3.** [ˈkænain; kəˋnaɪn]犬齿的。**II** *n*. **1.** 犬。**2.** 犬属动物。**3.** [ˈkænain; ˋkænaɪn]【解】犬齿。*a ~ laugh* 冷笑。*a ~ control officer* 搜捕无主野狗的公务员。~ **madness**【医】狂犬病。~ **species** 犬族。~ **tooth** 犬齿。

can·ing [ˈkeiniŋ; ˋkenɪŋ] *n*. **1.** 鞭打;笞刑。**2.** 藤料编制作业,编藤细工。*He wants a sound ~*. 得重重鞭他一顿才行。

Ca·nis [ˈkeinis; ˋkenɪs] *n*.【动】犬属。~ **Major** [**Minor**]【天】大[小]犬座。

can·is·ter [ˈkænistə; ˋkænɪstɚ] *n*. **1.** 罐,茶筒。**2.**【化】滤毒罐;【军】榴霰弹筒。**3.** 〔美俚〕挂表;手枪。~ **shot** 霰弹。

can·ker [ˈkæŋkə; ˋkæŋkɚ] **I** *n*. **1.**【医】痈溃疡;口疮。**2.**【兽医】口蹄疫;【植】黑腐病;(梨、茶等的)枝枯病;蛀孔。**3.**【虫】尺蠖;尺蠖类的害虫。**4.** 〔喻〕腐败;弊害;烦恼,苦恼。**II** *vt*., *vi*. **1.** (使)害痈病;(使)腐蚀,(使)(植物)生黑腐病;(使)殒烂。**2.** (使)受毒害。**3.** (使)苦恼。~ **worm**【虫】尺蠖;尺蠖类害虫。

can·ker·ous [ˈkæŋkərəs; ˋkæŋkərəs] *a*. **1.** 溃疡的,痈(似)的。**2.** 有腐蚀性的,引起溃烂的。

can·na [ˈkænə; ˋkænə] *n*.【植】美人蕉。〔C-〕美人蕉属。

can·na·bin [ˈkænəbin; ˋkænəbɪn] *n*.【化】大麻苷,大麻脂。

can·na·bis [ˈkænəbis; ˋkænəbɪs] *n*. **1.**【植】大麻。**2.** 大麻雌花顶部。

canned [kænd; kænd] **I** can[2] 的过去式及过去分词。**II** *a*. **1.** 〔美〕罐装的。**2.** 〔美俚〕酩酊大醉的。**3.** 〔美俚〕被解雇的;被囚禁的。**4.** 录音的。**5.** 〔美〕(新闻稿等)同时供几家报刊〔通讯社〕发出的;千篇一律的,刻板的。**6.** 〔美俚〕事先准备好的。~ **cow** 〔美俚〕炼乳。~ **editorials** 统一发出的社论。~ **goods** 〔美俚〕罐头(食品)。~ **heat** 〔美俚〕**1.** 小罐装的化学燃料〔多作野餐用〕。**2.** 烈酒。~ **music** 〔美俚〕唱片音乐。~ **speech** 〔美俚〕录音演说。

can·nel [ˈkænl; ˋkænl] *n*.【矿】烛煤(= ~-coal)。

can·nel·lo·ni [ˌkæniˈləuni; ˏkænɪˋlonɪ] *n*. 〔*pl*.〕〔集合词〕烤碎肉卷子。

can·ne·lure [ˈkænəljuə; ˋkænəljʊr] *n*. **1.** (唱片等的)槽。**2.**【军】弹壳槽线。

can·ner [ˈkænə; ˋkænɚ] *n*. **1.** 〔美〕罐头制造业者。**2.** (只能制狗食罐头用的)肉质低劣的动物。

can·ner·y [ˈkænəri; ˋkænərɪ] *n*. **1.** 〔美〕罐头工厂。**2.** 〔俚〕监狱。

Cannes [kæn; kæn] *n*. 戛纳〔法国港市〕。

can·ni·bal [ˈkænibəl; ˋkænəbl] **I** *n*. 食人者;吃同类的动物。**II** *a*. 吃人(肉)的;吃同类的。**-ism** *n*. **1.** 嗜食人肉的恶习;同类相残。**2.** 残忍。

can·ni·bal·is·tic [ˌkænibəˈlistik; ˏkænəblˋɪstɪk] *a*. **1.** 食人者的;同类相残的。**2.** 灭绝人性的,野蛮的。

can·ni·bal·ize [ˈkænibəlaiz; ˋkænəblˏaɪz] *vt*., *vi*. **1.** 吃(人);吃(同类)。**2.** 用拆下的零件修配(另一机器等),拆取(旧机器等的)零配件。**3.** 调拨(某一单位等的)人员充实另一单位。~ *a radio set from two old ones* 拆取两台旧收音机的零件修配一台新收音机。**-za·tion** *n*.

can·ni·kin [ˈkænikin; ˋkænəkɪn] *n*. 小罐;小酒杯[水杯];小木桶。

Can·ning [ˈkæniŋ; ˋkænɪŋ] *n*. 坎宁〔姓氏〕。

can·ning [ˈkæniŋ; ˋkænɪŋ] *n*. 〔美〕罐头制造业[法]。

can·nist·er [ˈkænistə; ˋkænɪstɚ] = canister.

Can·non [ˈkænən; ˋkænən] *n*. 坎农〔姓氏〕。

can·non [ˈkænən; ˋkænən] **I** *n*. (*pl*. ~*s*, 〔集合词〕~) **1.** 大炮;榴弹炮;【空】机关炮。**2.**【机】(二重)套轴。**3.**【动】(有蹄类的)管骨。**4.**【英台球】连撞二球。**5.** 〔美口〕连珠枪,手枪;扒手,小偷。**II** *vi*. **1.** 开炮,炮轰。**2.**【英台球】连撞二球,间接碰撞(*against*; *into*; *with*)。~ *off the red*【台球】连撞两个红球。—*vt*. **1.** 炮轰。**2.** 〔美俚〕对…偷窃。~ **ball 1.** *n*. 炮弹;快车;【网球】炮弹式发球;〔美俚〕犯人间秘密传递的消息。**2.** *vi*. (像炮弹般)疾飞。~**bit** 圆辔。~ **bone**【动】炮骨;马胫骨,管骨。~ **cracker** 大型鞭炮。~ **fodder 1.** 炮灰〔指兵士〕。**2.** 待磨的谷物。~**proof** *a*. 防炮弹的。~ **shot** 炮弹;射程,弹程。

can·non·ade [ˌkænəˈneid; ˏkænənˋed] **I** *n*. 连续炮击;

轰隆声。2.〔口〕口头攻击。II *vt*. 炮击。—*vi*, 炮击;轰隆轰隆地响。

can·non·eer [ˌkænəˈniə; ˏkænənˋɪr] *n*. 炮手,炮兵。

can·non·ry [ˈkænənri; ˋkænənrɪ] *n*. 1. 开炮,连续炮击。2.〔总称〕炮。

can·not [强 ˈkænɔt, 弱 ˈkænət; ˋkænɑt, ˋkænət] = can not.

can·nu·la [ˈkænjulə; ˋkænjʊlə] *n*. (*pl*. *-lae* [-liː; -li], ~)【医】套管,插管。

can·nu·lar [ˈkænjulə; ˋkænjʊlə˞] *a*. 管的,管状的,中空的 (= cannulate [-lit, -ˌleit; -lɪt, -ˏlet])。

can·ny [ˈkæni; ˋkænɪ] *a*. 1. 机警的,精明的,心细的;狡猾的。2.〔Scot.〕俭约的;安全的;安静的,稳定的,温和的;幸运的。3.〔英方〕悦目的,吸引人的。**-i·ly** *ad*. **-i·ness** *n*.

ca·noe [kəˈnuː; kəˋnu] I *n*. 独木舟;小划子;小游艇;皮舟。***paddle one's own*** ~ (靠自己力量)独力进行。II *vi*. 划[乘]独木舟。—*vt*. 用独木舟载运。

ca·noe·ing [kəˈnuːiŋ; kəˋnuɪŋ] *n*.〔美〕划独木舟。

ca·noe·ist [kəˈnuːist; kəˋnuɪst] *n*. 划独木舟的人。

can·on[1] [ˈkænən; ˋkænən] *n*. 1. 教规,宗规;圣典,经典;圣徒名单。2. 规则,规范,准则。3. 真作;真传经典;(基督教圣经的)正经。4.【乐】轮唱法,轮唱曲。5.【印】48 磅大活字。6.【天主教】弥撒的主要部分。~*s of taxation* 课税原则。~ **law** 教会法,寺院法。~ **sin** 死罪。

can·on[2] [ˈkænən; ˋkænən] *n*. 大教堂教士会成员;(天主教)教团团员。**-ess** [-is; -ɪs] *n*. 修女会会员;修女。

ca·ñon [ˈkænjən; ˋkænjən] *n*.〔Sp.〕= canyon.

ca·non·ic [kəˈnɔnik; kəˋnɑnɪk] *a*. 1. = canonical. 2.【乐】卡农的,轮唱曲的。

ca·non·i·cal[1] [kəˈnɔnikəl; kəˋnɑnɪkl] I *a*. 1. (合乎)宗规的,以寺院法为准则的;《圣经》正经的,真作的。2. 被认为正经的;规范的;典范的。3.【数】正则的,典型的。II *n*.〔*pl*.〕(布道时应穿的)法衣。~ **ensemble**【物】正则系综。~ **form**【数】(矩阵的)标准型。~ **hours** 1. (上午八点至下午三点的)祈祷时间,教堂婚礼时间。2. 合适的时间。~ **dress** 教士法衣。~**ly** *ad*.

ca·non·i·cal[2] [kəˈnɔnikəl; kəˋnɑnɪkl] *a*. 关于大教堂教士(会)的。

ca·non·i·cate [kəˈnɔnikeit, -kit; kəˋnɑnɪˏket, -kɪt] *n*. 大教堂教士会成员的职位(= canonry)。

can·on·ic·i·ty [ˌkænəˈnisiti; ˏkænənˋɪsətɪ] *n*. 1. 符合宗规。2. 可作为正典的资格。3. 合乎正规。

can·on·ist [ˈkænənist; ˋkænənɪst] *n*. 宗教[教会]法规学者。

can·on·ize, -ise [ˈkænənaiz; ˋkænənˏaɪz] *vt*. 1. 追认[尊崇](某死者)为圣徒。2. 承认…为正典[正经]。**-za·tion** [kænənaiˈzeiʃən; kænənaɪˋzeʃən] *n*.

can·on·ry [ˈkænənri; ˋkænənrɪ] *n*. 大教堂教士会成员的职位。

ca·noo·dle [kəˈnuːdl; kəˋnudl] *vi*.〔美俚〕1. 搂抱。2. 爱抚。—*vt*. 用爱抚[搂抱]来劝动(某人)。

can·o·pied [ˈkænəpid; ˋkænəpɪd] *a*. 有天篷的。

Ca·no·pus [kəˈnəupəs; kəˋnopəs] *n*.【天】老人星〔船底座 α〕。

can·o·py [ˈkænəpi; ˋkænəpɪ] I *n*. 1. 天篷;罗伞,华盖。2. 覆盖。3. (飞机的)座舱盖;(降落伞的)伞盖;【植】(树)冠;冠层。4. 天空。~ ***of heaven*** 穹苍。***under the*** ~〔美〕究竟,到底 (*Where under the* ~ *did you come from*? 你究竟是从哪儿来的?)。II *vt*. (*-pied*; *-pying*) 用天篷遮覆。

ca·no·rous [kəˈnɔːrəs; kəˋnorəs] *a*. 音调[音色]优美的;共鸣的。**-ly** *ad*. **-ness** *n*.

canst [强 kænst, 弱 kənst; kænst, kənst] *v*. *aux*.〔古〕= can[1]〔用于主语为 thou 时〕。

cant[1] [kænt; kænt] I *n*. 1. 行话;(盗贼的)黑话,隐语。2. (政党的)应时标语[口号];时髦话。3. 哀诉声。4. 伪善的口吻[言语]。~ *phrase* 时髦话;流行语;黑话。***in the*** ~ ***of the day*** 用时髦话来说。II *vi*. 1. 用伪善口吻解释;侈谈;〔罕〕哀诉,苦求。2. 讲时髦话,讲黑话。3.〔美俚〕瞎聊天。~**ing heraldry** 象征本人名字的徽章〔如 Shakespeare 用挥枪的鹰代表 shake spear〕。

cant[2] [kænt; kænt] I *n*. 1. (晶体、河岸等的)斜面;斜角。2. 有棱的木材;(船的)斜肋骨〔又作~ frame〕。3. 斜撞,斜推。4. 切角,斜切。II *vt*. 1. 使(船等)倾斜。2. 投掷(球等)。3. 把…的棱角切掉。4. 使(网等)倒转;突然改变…的方向。—*vi*. 1. 倾斜。2. 倒转。3. (船)改变方向。~ *over* 翻倒。~**hook** 滚木钩。**-ed** *a*. 有角的;倾斜的。

cant[3] [kænt; kænt] *a*.〔英方〕活泼有力的。

can't [kɑːnt, kænt; kɑnt, kænt] = cannot.

Cant. = Canterbury; Canticles; Cantonese.

Can·tab [ˈkæntæb; ˋkæntæb], **Can·ta·brig·i·an** [ˌkæntəˈbridʒiən; ˏkæntəˋbrɪdʒɪən] I *n*. 1. (英国)剑桥市人,剑桥大学学生[毕业生,校友]。2. (美国)麻萨诸塞州坎布里奇人,哈佛大学学生[毕业生,校友]。II *a*. 1. (英国)剑桥市的;(美国)坎布里奇市的。2. 剑桥大学的;哈佛大学的。

can·ta·bi·le [kænˈtɑːbili; kɑnˋtɑbɪle] I *a*., *ad*.〔It.〕【乐】像歌唱一样的[地];流畅的[地]。II *n*. 歌唱般的音乐。

can·ta·la [kænˈtɑːlə; kænˋtɑlə] *n*.【植】狭叶番麻 (= *Agave cantala*)。

can·ta·le·ver, can·ta·li·ver [ˌkæntəˈlevə, -liːvə; ˏkæntəˋlɛvə˞, -livə˞] *n*. = cantilever.

can·ta·loup(e) [ˈkæntəluːp; ˋkæntlˏop] *n*. 1.【植】(南欧)甜瓜,棱瓜。2.〔美俚〕棒球用球。

can·tan·ker·ous [kənˈtæŋkərəs; kænˋtæŋkərəs] *a*. 脾气坏的,爱吵闹的。**-ly** *ad*. **-ness** *n*.

can·tar, kan·tar [kɑːnˈtɑː; kɑnˋtɑ] *n*. 坎塔耳〔伊斯兰国家的一种重量单位,从 100 磅到 700 磅不等〕。

can·ta·ta [kænˈtɑːtə, kən-; kænˋtɑtə, kən-] *n*.〔It.〕【乐】清唱剧;大合唱。

can·ta·trice [ˈkæntətriːs, It. ˌkɑːntɑˈtriːtʃe; ˋkæntətris, ˏkɑntɑˋtrɪtʃe] *n*. (*pl*. ~*s* [-tris; -trɪs], It. *-trici* [-ˈtriːtʃi; -ˋtritʃɪ]) *n*.〔It.〕(歌剧中的)专业女歌唱家,女歌手。

can·teen [kænˈtiːn; kænˋtin] *n*. 1. (兵营等内部的)小卖部;小饭馆〔美国通常叫 Post Exchange (PX)〕;临时餐室。2. (军用)饭盒,水罐;炊具箱。3. (家用)餐具箱;小器皿箱。*a dry* [*wet*] ~不卖酒的[卖酒的]食品小卖部。*a public* ~公共小饭馆。

can·ter[1] [ˈkæntə; ˋkæntə˞] I *n*.【马术】普通跑步;慢跑。★马速共五种: walk, amble, trot, canter, gallop. *a preliminary* ~预备练习时的慢跑;〔喻〕预备动作。***win at*** [***in***] ***a*** ~ (马)轻易赛赢。II *vt*. 使(马)慢跑。—*vi*. (马)用普通慢跑前进 (*along*); 骑着马慢跑。

canter[2] [ˈkæntə; ˋkæntə˞] *n*. 1. 说黑话的人。2. 哀诉者。3. 伪善者。4. 流浪者。

Can·ter·bu·ry [ˈkæntəbəri; ˋkæntə˞ˏbɛrɪ] *n*. 1. 坎特伯雷〔英格兰东南部大城市〕。2.〔c-〕乐谱架。***The C-Tales*** (英国作家乔叟写的)《坎特伯雷故事集》。~ **bell**【植】风铃草,吊钟花。

can·thar·i·des [kænˈθæridiːz; kænˋθærɪˏdiz] *n*.〔*pl*.〕1. cantharis 的复数。2.〔作 *sing*. 用〕【药】斑蝥〔指其干燥制剂〕。

can·tha·ris [ˈkænθəris; ˋkænθərɪs] *n*. (*pl*. ***canthar·i·des*** [kænˈθæriˌdiːz; kænˋθærɪˏdiz])【动】斑蝥,花金龟 (= Spanish fly)。

can·thus [ˈkænθəs; ˋkænθəs] *n*. (*pl*. ***-thi*** [-θai; -θaɪ])【解】眼角,眦;【动】(昆虫眼的)刺突。

can·ti·cle [ˈkæntikl; ˋkæntɪkl] *n*. 1. (宗教)颂歌,赞歌。2. 咏歌,小歌曲。3.〔the Canticles〕(旧约圣经的)雅歌 (= The Song of Solomon)。

can·ti·le·na [ˌkænti'linə; ˏkæntə`lɪnə] *n*. 【乐】坎蒂列那〔优美动听的短歌〕。

can·ti·le·ver ['kæntiliːvə; `kæntḷivə] *n*. 1. (桥梁的)悬臂,肱梁;支架。2. 电缆吊线夹板;纸条盘。~ **bridge** 悬臂桥。~ **crane** 伸臂起重机。

can·til·late [ˌkæntə'leit; `kæntəˏlet] *vt*. (在犹太教礼拜仪式中)吟唱。

can·til·la·tion [ˌkæntə'leiʃən; ˏkæntə`leʃən] *n*. (犹太教礼拜仪式中的)吟唱。

can·ti·na [kæn'tiːnə; kæn`tinə] *n*. 1. 〔美方〕小酒馆,酒吧。2. 鞍头挂袋。

can·tle ['kæntl; `kæntl] *n*. 1. 鞍子的后弓〔后部翘起部份〕。2. 切下的一角;切头,残块。

cant·mould·ing ['kæntməuldiŋ; `kæntmoldɪŋ] *n*. 【建】斜状饰。

can·to ['kæntəu; `kænto] *n*. 1. (长诗的)篇章。2. 【乐】最高音部;歌,旋律。3. 〔美〕拳击的一局,比赛的一节。

Can·ton ['kæn'tɔn; `kæntɑn] *n*. (旧时欧美人所习称的)广州。~ **china** 广瓷。~ **crepe** 广绫〔做拷绸用〕;重双绉。~ **enamel** 广州搪瓷。~ **linen** 夏布。~ **River** (旧时欧美人所习惯的)珠江。

can·ton ['kæntɔn; `kæntən] **I** *n*. 1. (瑞士的)州。2. (法国的)市区,镇,村。3. ['kæntən; `kæntən] 【徽】(徽章或旗子的)右上角的小方块部分。**II** *vt*. [kæn'tɔn; kæn`tɑn] 1. 把…分成州[区、村] (*out*)。2. [kən'tuːn; kən`tun] 【军】使驻扎;分配营房给(部队等)。**-al** ['kæntənl; `kæntənḷ] *a*. 州的,县的。**-al·ism** *n*. 州郡行政制。

Can·ton·ese [ˌkæntə'niːz; ˏkæntən`iz] **I** *a*. 广州的。**II** *n*. 〔*pl*., *sing*.〕1. 广州人。2. 广州话。

can·ton·ment [kæn'tuːnmənt; kæn`tɑnmənt] *n*. 【军】〔常 *pl*.〕宿营地,(临时)兵营;冬营。

can·tor ['kæntɔː, -tə; `kæntɔr, -tɚ] *n*. (教会的)合唱指挥人,歌咏班领唱者。

can·to·ri·al [kæn'tɔːriəl; kæn`torɪəl] *a*. 歌咏班领唱人的,合唱指挥人的;教堂圣坛北边的。

can·trip ['kæntrip; `kæntrɪp] *n*. 〔主 Scot.〕1. (魔法的)符咒。2. 恶作剧。

Can·tuar. = Cantuaria(= Canterbury).

can·tus ['kæntəs; `kæntəs] *n*. (*pl*. ~)〔L.〕【乐】= canto. ~ **firmus** 【乐】定旋律。

cant·y ['kænti; `kæntɪ] *a*. 〔英方〕活泼的,快活的。

Ca·nuck [kə'nʌk; kə`nʌk] *n*. 1. 〔美口,常蔑〕法裔加拿大人[语]。2. 〔美俚〕加拿大人;加拿大种的马。

can·vas(s) ['kænvəs; `kænvəs] *n*. 1. 粗帆布。2. (一套)风帆。3. (一套)帐篷;天幕。4. (一块)油画布;(一幅)油画。5. 【美拳】拳击场的地板。*single* ~绣花十字布。***kiss the*** ~【美拳】被击倒。***under*** ~ 1. 挂着风帆。2. (军队支起帐篷)露营。~**back** 〔美〕(北美)灰背野鸭。~**boat** 帆布船。~**-duck** 粗帆布。~ **hotel** 〔美俚〕帐篷。~ **opera** 〔美俚〕马戏。~ **shoes** 〔*pl*.〕帆布鞋。~ **stretcher** 画布框。

can·vass ['kænvəs; `kænvəs] **I** *vt*. 1. 兜揽(生意);劝募,游说,运动(选票等)。2. 〔美〕详细检查,点(选票等)。3. (详细)讨论(问题等);详细考查[调查]。~ *a district* 在竞选区游说。~ *the votes cast* 〔美〕检点票数。—*vi*. 游说,运动,劝诱。~ *for* (*insurance*; *subscription*) 兜揽(保险等),劝募(捐款等)。~ *for votes* 活动竞选。**II** *n*. 1. (竞选)运动,活动;劝募。2. (详细)检查,检点;论究,讨论。

can·vass·er ['kænvəsə; `kænvəsɚ] *n*. 游说者,兜揽员,推销员;〔美〕检票员。

can·y ['keini; `kenɪ] *n*. 1. 藤(制)的。2. 多藤的。

can·yon ['kænjən; `kænjən] *n*. 峡(谷)。*the Grand C-* (美)科罗拉多大峡谷。

can·zo·ne [kæn'tsəuni; kæn`tsonɪ] *n*. (*pl*. **-ni** [-niː; -ni]) 1. 歌曲。2. 抒情诗;抒情歌曲(如牧歌)(= canzona [-nɑː; -nɑ])。

can·zo·net [kænzə'net; kænzə`nɛt] *n*. 【乐】(轻快优美的)短小歌曲,小歌。

caou·tchouc ['kautʃuk; `kaʊtʃuk] *n*. 【化】生橡胶;纯橡胶。

cap [kæp; kæp] **I** *n*. 1. 无边帽,便帽;制服帽;军帽;头巾。2. 鞘,(笔)套,盖,罩子;(鞋)尖。3. 【建】柱头;【矿】顶板岩石;【船】桅尖;【解】膝盖骨;【植】根冠;菌盖;【军】(枪弹等的)雷管,火帽。4. 【数】求交运算。5. 脱帽礼。6. 【猎】会费。7. 〔英〕(避孕用的)宫颈帽。8. 〔美俚〕一胶囊毒品[迷幻药等]。9. 〔美〕上限〔指中央政府为地方政府的财政预算规定的最高限额〕。*Where is your* ~? (对孩子说)脱帽行礼吧。*If the* ~ *fits, wear it*. 帽子合适就戴,批评合适就得接受。*a lamp* ~灯头。*the* ~ *of fools* 傻瓜大王。***bear the*** ~ ***and bells*** 成为众人取笑的对象。~ ***and bells*** (丑角戴的)系铃帽;小丑。~ ***and gown*** (大学校的)方帽长袍正式校服;学者。~ ***in hand*** 脱帽,谦恭地,恭敬地。~ ***of liberty*** 自由帽〔古罗马获得自由后的奴隶所戴的圆锥帽子〕;共和政体的标志。~ ***of maintenance*** 〔英〕(英王、贵族等的)冠冕。***fling*** [***throw***] ***one's*** ~ ***over the mill*** 不顾利害地干,冒身败名裂的危险。***fuddle one's*** ~ 酩酊大醉。***get one's*** ~ 〔英〕做选手。***pull*** ~***s*** 争吵,扭打。***put on one's considering*** [***thinking***] ~ 仔细考虑。***send the*** ~ ***round*** 传帽子(收集捐款等)。***set one's*** ~ ***at*** [美 ***for***] (女子向男子)挑逗,追求。***The*** ~ ***fits***. 评论[描写等]得正合适,言之中肯。**II** *vt*. (-*pp*-) 1. 给…戴帽。2. 〔Scot.〕授与给…以学位;使做选手。3. 在…上装雷管。4. 覆盖于…顶上,包覆于…顶端。5. 向…脱帽致意,向…行礼。6. 胜过,凌驾。7. (行诗令中)接引(诗句等)。8. 为…规定支出限额。—*vi*. 脱帽致意 (*to*)。*be capped for* 做…的选手。~ *an anecdote* 讲更有趣的话。~ ***the climax*** 走极端,过度,出乎意料。~ ***verses*** 行(诗句的)接尾令。***to*** ~ (***it***) ***all*** 最后又加上;超群出众。~ **gun** (用火药纸的)玩具手枪。~**-piece** 帽木。~ **product** 【数】卡积。

CAP = 1. Civil Air Patrol 〔美〕民间空中巡逻队。2. Common Agricultural Policy (欧洲经济共同体)共同农业政策。3. computer-aided production 计算机辅助生产。

cap. = capital; capitalize; capital (letter); captain; *caput* (= *chapter*)。

C.A.P. = chloro-aceto-phenone 【化】苯氯乙酮(毒药)。

ca·pa·bil·i·ty [ˌkeipə'biliti; ˏkepə`bɪlətɪ] *n*. 1. 能力,才能,本领。2. 性能;容量;功率,生产率。3. 〔*pl*.〕潜在能力。*first rate capabilities* 卓越的能力,过硬本领。*a man of great capabilities* 很有前途的人;可造之材。

ca·pa·ble ['keipəbl; `kepəbḷ] *a*. 有才能的,有手腕的,有技能的,有资格的 (*for*)。*a* ~ *teacher* 能干的教师。~ ***of*** 1. (事物)可以…的;能…的;易…的 (*of*)。2. (人)敢于…的,做得出…的;易于做出…的(*Hs is* ~ *of doing anything*. 他什么事都干得出。*This statement is* ~ *of various interpretations*. 对这一声明可以作各式各样的理解。*The cask is* ~ *of holding 8 gallons*. 这个桶能装八加仑)。**-ness** *n*. **ca·pa·bly** *ad*.

ca·pa·cious [kə'peiʃəs; kə`peʃəs] *a*. 1. 广阔的;容积大的。2. 气度宏大的。*a man of* ~ *mind* 心胸开阔的人。**-ness** *n*.

ca·pac·i·tance [kə'pæsitəns; kə`pæsətəns] *n*. 【电】电容;电容器。

ca·pac·i·tate [kə'pæsiteit; kə`pæsəˏtet] *vt*. 1. 使能够,赋与…以能力;使适合于 (*for*)。2. 授予…资格,使合格;使法律上有权利。3. 【生】使(精子)获得能育力〔突入卵子授胎的能力〕。**-ta·tion** [-teiʃən; -teʃən] *n*. 【生】(精子)能育力获得(过程)。

ca·pac·i·tive [kə'pæsitiv; kə`pæsətɪv] *a*. 【电】电容的。

ca·pac·i·tiv·i·ty [kəˌpæsi'tiviti; kəˏpæsɪ`tɪvətɪ] *n*.

【电】电容率〔米-千克-秒单位介电常数〕。

ca·pac·i·tor [kə'pæsitə; kə`pæsətɚ] ***n*.**【电】电容器(=condenser)。*a* ～ *microphone* 电容传声器[话筒,微音器]。

ca·pac·i·tron [kə'pæsitrɔn; kə`pæsɪtrɑn] ***n*.**【物】电容汞弧管;原子击破器。

ca·pac·i·ty [kə'pæsiti; kə`pæsətɪ] ***n*. 1.** 包容力,吸收力,收容力。**2.** 容积,容量;【电】电容,负载量。**3.** 能力,才干,本领;性能,机能。**4.** 地位,资格,身分。**5.**【法】法定资格,权力,权能。**6.** 生产额;(最大)产量[生产力]。*measures of* ～容积,容量。*a mind of great* ～度量大的人。*the crop* ～作物(最大)生产力〔单位面积产量〕。～ *crowd*〔美〕满座的观众。*be filled to* ～客满。～ *for heat* 热容量。～ *to action*【法】诉讼能力。*be in* ～法律上有资格。～ *tonnage* 载重量,吨位。～ *house*〔美〕客满的戏院。*in a civil* ～以市民身分。*in my individual* ～以我个人身分。*in one's* ～ *as* (*a critic*) 以(批评家)的立场[身分]。*to the utmost of one's* ～尽自己所能。

cap-a-pie*, *cap-à-pie [kæpə'piː; ˏkæpə`pi] ***ad*.**〔F.〕从头到脚,全身。*be armed* ～从头武装到脚,全副武装。

ca·par·i·son [kə'pærisn; kə`pærəsn] **I *n*. 1.** 华丽的马衣;装饰性的鞍辔。**2.** (武士的)盛装;服装;行头。**II *vt*.** 给(马)穿马衣;使…着盛装。

Cap·com ['kæpkɔːm; `kæpkɔm] ***n*.**〔美口〕(宇宙航行中心的)地面通讯主任。

cape[1] [keip; kep] ***n*.** 岬,崎,海角;〔C-〕好望角(=The Cape of Good Hope)。**C- boy** 黑白混血种的南非人。**C- cart** 有篷牛车。～ **chisel** 狭凿。**C- Cod** 科德角〔美国〕。**C- doctor** 好望角的东南风。**C- Horn** 合恩角(智利)。**C- Horn rainwater** 糖酒。**C- smoke** 南非产白兰地。

cape[2] [keip; kep] ***n*.** 披肩,短斗篷。

cap·e·lin ['kæpəlin; `kæpəlɪn] ***n*.** =caplin.

Ca·pel·la [kə'pelə; kə`pɛlə]【天】五车二(御夫座 α)。

ca·per[1] ['keipə; `kepɚ] **I *n*. 1.** 跳跃。**2.** 嬉戏。**3.**〔俚〕(盗贼的)持械抢劫。**II *vi*. 1.** 跳跃,雀跃。**2.** 嬉戏,开玩笑。***cut* ～*s* = *cut a* ～** 雀跃;嬉戏。

ca·per[2] ['keipə; `kepɚ] ***n*.**【植】续随子,驴蹄草;〔*pl*.〕续随子的花芽。

cap·er·cail·lie, cap·er·cail·zie [ˌkæpə'keilji, -'keilzi; ˏkæpɚ`keljɪ, -`kelzɪ] ***n*.**【鸟】雷鸟,松鸡。

cape·skin ['keipˌskin; `kepˏskɪn] ***n*.** 好望角羊皮〔一种精制羊皮革,常用来制手套〕。

Cape Town, Cape·town ['keiptaun; `kep`taʊn] 开普敦〔南非港市〕。

Cape Verde ['keip'vəːd; `kep`vɝd] ***n*.** 维德角(佛得角)〔非洲〕。**C- V- Islands** 维德(群)岛。

cap·ful ['kæpfʊl; `kæpfʊl] ***n*. 1.** 一帽子[瓶盖子](的数量);少许,少量。**2.** 一阵(轻风等)。*a* ～ *of wind* 轻风。*a* ～ *of detergent* 一瓶盖子清洁剂。*a* ～ *of beans* 一帽子豆子。

caph [kɑːf; kɑf] ***n*.** 希伯来文的第十一个字母,相当于拉丁字母 k(=kaph)。

ca·pi·as ['keipiæs; `kepɪəs] ***n*.**〔F.〕【法】拘票。

cap·il·la·ceous [ˌkæpi'leiʃəs; ˏkæpə`leʃəs] ***a*. 1.** 毛状细丝的,毛状纤维的。**2.** 发状的,线状的。

cap·il·lar·i·ty [ˌkæpi'læriti; ˏkæpl̩`ærətɪ] ***n*.**【物】毛细管状态;毛细管作用[现象]。

cap·il·lar·y [kə'piləri; kə`pɪlərɪ] **I *a*. 1.** 毛发状的,细长的。**2.** 毛细管作用[现象]的。**3.** 表面张力的。**II *n*.**【物】毛细管,微管。～ **action** 毛细管作用。～ **tube** 毛细管。

ca·pi·ta ['kæpitə; `kæpɪtə] ***n*.** caput 的复数。

cap·i·tal[1] ['kæpitəl; `kæpətl̩] **I *a*. 1.** 首位的,最重要的,主要的,基本的,根本的。**2.**〔口〕优秀的,上好的,第一流的。**3.** 大写(字母)的。**4.** 应处死刑的;致命的。**5.** 资本的。*C-!* 好极了! ～ *city* 首都。～ *construction* 基本建设。～ *crime* 死罪。～ *letter* 大写。～ *punishment* 死刑。～ *ship* 主力舰。**II *n*. 1.** 首都;首府。**2.** 大写(字母)。**3.** 资本;基金;股款,本钱;资源;资方,资产阶级。*circulating* [*floating*] ～流动资本。*financial* ～金融资本。*fixed* ～固定资本。*foreign* ～外资。*working* ～周转资本。*the relations between labour and* ～劳资关系。～*and interest* 本金和利息。***make* ～ (*out*) *of*** 利用,从中取利[捞一把]。～ **account** 资本账,股本账。～ **assets** 资本资产。～ **bonus** 红利,股息。～ **expenditure** 基本建设费用。～ **flight** 资金外逃。～ **goods** 资本货物。～**-intensive *a*.** 资本大量投资的。～ **levy** 资本课税。～ **stock** 股本。～ **structure** 资本构成。～ **sum** (给保险人的)最大保险金额。～ **transfer tax**〔英〕资本转移税〔政府对钱财从一人转移给另一人所收取的税,尤指对财产继承所收的税〕。

cap·i·tal[2] ['kæpitəl; `kæpətəl] ***n*.**【建】柱头。

cap·i·tal·ism ['kæpitəlizəm; `kæpətl̩ˏɪzəm] ***n*.** 资本主义(制度)。

cap·i·tal·ist ['kæpitəlist; `kæpətl̩ɪst] **I *n*.** 资本家;资本主义者;〔口〕财主。**II *a*. 1.** 有资本的。**2.** 资本主义的。*a* ～ *country* 资本主义国家。

cap·i·tal·is·tic [ˌkæpitə'listik; ˏkæpɪtl̩`ɪstɪk] ***a*. 1.** 在资本主义下存在[经营]的;有资本主义特征的。**2.** 赞成[推行]资本主义的。～*economy* 资本主义经济。**-ti·cal·ly *ad*.**

cap·i·tal·i·za·tion [kəˌpitəlai'zeiʃən; kəˏpɪtəlaɪ`zeʃən] ***n*. 1.** 资本化;〔美〕投资。**2.** (收入等的)资本估价。**3.** 作首都。**4.**〔美〕用大写。

cap·i·tal·ize [kə'pitəlaiz; `kæpətl̩ˏaɪz] ***vt*. 1.** 把…资本化,使成为资本,用…作资本,把…估价为资本;认可[决定]资本为…股。**2.**〔美〕对…投资,给…提供资本。**3.** 把(某一时期内的收益等)折合成当前价值。**4.** 把…定为首都。**5.**〔美〕用大写字母写[印]。—***vi*.** 利益(*on*; *upon*)。

cap·i·tal·ly ['kæpitəli; `kæpətl̩ɪ] ***ad*. 1.**〔口〕极好;妙。**2.** 按死刑(程序)办处。

cap·i·tate, cap·i·tated ['kæpiteit, -teitid; `kæpəˏtet, -tetɪd] ***a*.**【植】头状的,锤形的。

cap·i·ta·tion [ˌkæpi'teiʃən; ˏkæpə`teʃən] ***n*. 1.** 按人计算。**2.** 人头[人口]税。～ **fee** 按人均摊的用费。～ **grant** 按人计算的补助费。

Cap·i·tol ['kæpitəl; `kæpətl] ***n*. 1.** (古罗马的)丘比特(Jupiter)神殿。**2.**〔美〕国会大厦;〔c-〕州议会会堂。～ **Hill** 美国国会。

Cap·i·to·line ['kæpitəlain; `kæpətl̩ˏaɪn] **I *n*.** 罗马的卡彼托山〔罗马七丘之一〕。**II *a*.** 有关卡彼托山的;丘比特神殿的;古罗马神殿的。

ca·pit·u·lar [kə'pitjulə; kə`pɪtʃəlɚ] **I *a*.** 教士会的。**II *n*.** 牧师会会员。

ca·pit·u·lar·y [kə'pitjuləri; kə`pɪtʃəlɛrɪ] ***n*.** 教士会法规。

ca·pit·u·late [kə'pitjuleit; kə`pɪtʃəlet] ***vi*. 1.** (在一定条件下)投降。**2.** 停止抵抗。

ca·pit·u·la·tion [kəˌpitju'leiʃən; kəˏpɪtʃə`leʃən] ***n*. 1.** (有条件的)投降。**2.** 投降条约;〔*pl*.〕协定。**3.** (声明、协议等载明的)条款,条件[项目,概要,一览表]。***the C-s***【史】(给与住在本国的外国人的)治外法权条款。**-ism *n*.** 投降主义。**-ist *n*.** 投降主义者。

ca·pit·u·lum [kə'pitʃələm; kə`pɪtʃʊləm] ***n*.** (*pl*. **-la** [-lə; -lə]) **1.**【解、动】小头、头端、假头。**2.**【植】头状花序,头状体。

cap·las·to·me·ter [ˌkæpləs'tɔmitə; ˏkæpləs`tɑmɪtɚ] ***n*.**【物】黏度计。

cap·lin ['kæplin; `kæplɪn] ***n*.**【动】毛鳞鱼。

ca·po[1] ['keipəu; `kepo] ***n*.** (*pl*. ***-pos***)【乐】(吉他等的)品柱。

ca·po² [ˈkɑːpəu; ˋkɑpo] *n*. 〔美俚〕(黑手党等犯罪集团分支机构的)头目。~ **regime** (capo 之下的)副头目。

ca·pon [ˈkeipən; ˋkepən] *n*. 阉鸡。

ca·pon·ize, -ise [ˈkeipənaiz; ˋkepən͵aɪz] *vt*. 给(鸡)去势,阉(鸡)。

cap·o·ral [ˌkæpəˈrɑːl; ͵kæpəˋræl] *n*. 〔F.〕一种法国粗烟丝。

cap·o·ral [ˌkæpəˈrɑːl; ͵kæpəˋrɑl] *n*. 〔美方〕(美国西南部的)大牧场主。

ca·pot [kəˈpɔt; kəpɑt] **I** *n*. (两人对玩的皮克(piquet)牌戏中的)全胜〔40 点〕。**II** *vt*. 全胜(对方)。

ca·pote [kəˈpəut; kəˈpot] *n*. **1**. 连帽长外套;女式长袍;(斗牛士的)披肩。**2**. 系有带子的无边女帽。**3**. (可调整的)活动车篷。

cap·per [ˈkæpə; ˋkæpɚ] *n*. **1**. 制帽者。**2**. 〔美〕(拍卖商的)假买手,竟买囮子;引诱者,骗子的搭挡。**3**. (瓶罐等的)封口机,压盖机;封口[压盖]工人。**4**. 〔美俚〕结局,结尾;高潮。

cap·ping [ˈkæpiŋ; ˋkæpɪŋ] *n*. 〔美〕(拍卖时)使用假买手诱骗哄抬。

cap·re·o·late [ˈkæpriəleit, kəˈpriəlit; ˋkæprɪəlet, kəˋprɪəlɪt] *a*. 【植】有卷发的。

cap·ric [ˈkæprik; ˋkæprɪk] *a*. 公山羊的。~ **acid** 癸酸,羊蜡酸。

ca·pric·ci·o [kəˈpritʃiəu; kəˋprɪtʃɪ͵o] *n*. (*pl*. ~*s*) 〔It.〕**1**. 狂喜;怪想;异想天开。**2**. 【乐】随想曲,狂想曲。

ca·pric·ci·o·so [kəˌpriːtʃiːˈəuzəu; kə͵pritʃiˋozo] *a*., *ad*. 【乐】变化无常的[地],任意的[地],古怪的[地]。

ca·price [kəˈpriːs; kəˋpris] *n*. **1**. 反复无常,任性。**2**. 怪想,异想天开。**3**. 古怪[随意空想]的作品[乐曲]。

ca·pri·cious [kəˈpriʃəs; kəˋprɪʃəs] *a*. **1**. 反复无常的,任性的。**2**. 怪想的。**-ly** *ad*. **-ness** *n*.

Cap·ri·corn [ˈkæprikɔːn; ˋkæprɪkɔrn], **Cap·ri·cor·nus** [ˌkæpriˈkɔːnəs; ͵kæprɪˋkɔnəs] *n*. 【天】山羊座;摩羯宫。***the Tropic of*** ~ 冬至线,南回归线。

cap·ri·fi·ca·tion [ˌkæprifiˈkeiʃən; ͵kæprɪfɪˋkeʃən] *n*. (使用虫媒传送花粉的)无花果早熟法。

cap·ri·fig [ˈkæprifig; ˋkæprɪ͵fɪg] *n*. 【植】野生无花果。

cap·rine [ˈkæprain; ˋkæpraɪn] *a*. 公山羊(一样)的。

cap·ri·ole [ˈkæpriəul; ˋkæprɪol] *n*., *vi*. 【马术】跳跃,跃起〔扬蹄而不前进的动作〕。

ca·pri pants [ˈkɑːpri pænts; ˋkɑprɪ pænts]卡普里式[山羊式]紧身女裤。

ca·pris [kɑːˈpris; kəˋprɪz] *n*. *pl*. = capri pants.

ca·pro·ic [kəˈprəuik; kəˋproɪk] *a*. 山羊的。~ **acid** 【化】己酸,羊油酸。

cap·ro·lac·tam [ˌkæprəuˈlæktəm; ͵kæproˋlæktəm] *n*. 【化】己内酰胺。

ca·pron(e) [ˈkæprəun; ˋkæpron] *n*. 【化、纺】卡普隆〔聚己内酰胺纤维的商品名〕。

ca·pryl [ˈkæpril; ˋkæprɪl] *n*. 【化】**1**. 癸酰。**2**. (现多指)辛基;辛酰。

ca·pryl·ic [kəˈprilik; kəˋprɪlɪk] *a*. 【化】辛酸的。~ **acid** 【化】辛酸,羊脂酸。

caps. 【印】= capital letters.

cap·sa·i·cin [kæpˈseiəsin; kæpˋseəsɪn] *n*. 【化】辣椒素。

Cap·si·an [ˈkæpsiən; ˋkæpsɪən] *a*. 【考古】嘎普萨期的〔指北非旧石器时代文化〕。

Cap·si·cum [ˈkæpsikəm; ˋkæpsɪkəm] *n*. 【植】**1**. 辣椒属。**2**. 〔c-〕辣椒。

cap·sid [ˈkæpsid; ˋkæpsɪd] *n*. (病毒的)衣壳,壳体。**-al** *a*.

cap·size [kæpˈsaiz; kæpˋsaɪz] **I** *vt*., *vi*. (使)(船、车等)倾覆,(使)翻转。**II** *n*. 翻船,翻车。

cap·so·mere [ˈkæpsəmiə; ˋkæpsəmɪr] *n*. (组成病毒壳体的)壳粒,壳微体,子粒。

cap·stan [ˈkæpstən; ˋkæpstən] *n*. 起锚机,绞盘。~ **bar** 绞盘棒。

cap·stone [ˈkæpstəun; ˋkæp͵ston] *n*. **1**. 拱顶石;顶(层)石。**2**. 顶部;顶点。**3**. 海胆化石。

cap·su·lar [ˈkæpsjulə; ˋkæpsəlɚ] *a*. **1**. 【植】蒴果(状)的。**2**. 胶囊(状)的。**3**. 雷管的。

cap·su·late, cap·su·lated [ˈkæpsjuleit, -leitid; ˋkæpsə͵let, -letɪd] *a*. **1**. 【植】有蒴的。**2**. 胶囊包裹的。**3**. 装入雷管的。

cap·sule [ˈkæpsjuːl; ˋkæpsjul] **I** *n*. **1**. 【生理】荚膜,囊状物;【植】蒴,荚,种囊。**2**. 【化】(蒸发用的)小碟;小皿,小盒。**3**. 囊状器,帽状器,封瓶锡包,瓶帽;【药】胶囊。**4**. 【物】膜盒,传感器。**5**. 【宇】密闭舱。**6**. 提要。**II** *a*. **1**. 简略的。**2**. 小而结实的。*a* ~ *biography* 简历。*a* ~ *review* 简评,短评。**III** *vt*. **1**. 压缩,节略。**2**. 以瓶帽密封。

cap·sul·i·form [ˈkæpsjulifɔːm; ˋkæpsjʊlɪ͵fɔrm] *a*. 囊形的。

cap·sul·ize [ˈkæpsjulaiz; ˋkæpsjʊ͵laɪz] *vt*. **1**. 把…装于(胶)囊内,把…装于小容器内。**2**. 简明表达;压缩。

Capt. = Captain.

cap·tain [ˈkæptin; ˋkæptɪn] **I** *n*. **1**. 首领;领队者,指挥者;魁首,头子。**2**. 船长,舰长,机长。**3**. 〔英〕(陆军及海军陆战队)上尉〔空军上尉为 flight lieutenant〕;〔美〕(陆、空军及海军陆战队)上尉;〔英、美〕(海军)上校;舰长。**4**. (工厂等的)管理员,监督员。**5**. (球队的)队长;(学校班级的)级长,(小组的)组长。**6**. 名将,军事指挥家。**7**. 〔美〕消防队队长;政党的地方领导人。~ *of industry* 工业巨子,大企业家。*C- of the Fleet* 【英海军】舰队副官。***a copper*** ~ 冒充有地位的人。**II** *vt*. 统率,指挥,做…的首领。**-cy, -ship** *n*. **1**. 船长[上尉等]的地位[职权,辖区]。**2**. 主将之才,统率之才,统帅资格。

cap·tion [ˈkæpʃən; ˋkæpʃən] **I** *n*. **1**. 〔美〕标题,题目;【影】字幕;(插图的)说明;目录,节目。**2**. 【法】(法律文件等的)提要,标示。**3**. 〔英〕逮捕。**II** *vt*. 在(文件等)上加标题;在(图片等)上加说明;在(电影)上加字幕。

cap·tious [ˈkæpʃəs; ˋkæpʃəs] *a*. **1**. 吹毛求疵的;(评论等)恶意的。**2**. 强词夺理的,似是而非的,无理强辩的。~ *criticism* 恶意的批评。**-ly** *adv*.

cap·ti·vate [ˈkæptiveit; ˋkæptəvet] *vt*. **1**. (以某种感染力)吸住;迷惑住。**2**. 〔古〕逮捕;征服。

cap·ti·vat·ing [ˈkæptiveitiŋ; ˋkæptɪ͵vetɪŋ] *a*. 使人神魂颠倒的,有魅力的。

cap·ti·va·tion [ˌkæptiˈveiʃən; ͵kæptəˋveʃən] *n*. **1**. 迷惑,魅力。**2**. 〔古〕逮捕。

cap·ti·va·tor [ˈkæptiˌveitə; ˋkæptɪ͵vetɚ] *n*. 有吸引力的人[物]。

cap·tive [ˈkæptiv; ˋkæptɪv] **I** *a*. **1**. 被活捉到的;被监禁了的;被拴住的,被控制而无能独立行动的。**2**. 被迷住的。*a* ~ *bird* 笼中鸟。*a* ~ *shop* 职工商店,内部商店。*a* ~ *balloon* 系留气球。**II** *n*. 俘虏;被(爱情等)迷住的人。***take*** [***hold***, ***lead***] ~ 活捉,俘虏。

cap·tiv·i·ty [kæpˈtiviti; kæpˋtɪvətɪ] *n*. 囚禁;俘虏;束缚 (*opp*. freedom)。

cap·tor [ˈkæptə; ˋkæptɚ] *n*. **1**. 捕捉者,捕手;攻夺者;夺得者。**2**. 捕捉船。

cap·tress [ˈkæptris; ˋkæptrɪs] *n*. 女捕捉者,俘虏了(某人)的女人。

cap·ture [ˈkæptʃə; ˋkæptʃɚ] **I** *n*. **1**. 捕获,夺得;【原】俘获,掳掠,掠夺。**2**. 俘虏;捕获品,战利品。**II** *vt*. **1**. 俘获,捕获。**2**. 攻夺;取,夺取,夺得(奖品等);赢得,引起(注意等)。**3**. [转议]记录,接收,拍摄。~*d river* 被截断的河流。**-r** [ˈkæptʃərə; ˋkæptʃərɚ] *n*. 捕获者,俘获者。

cap·u·chin [ˈkæpjuʃin; ˋkæpjʊtʃɪn] *n*. **1**. 〔C-〕(天主教的)圣方济会托钵僧。**2**. 带风帽的女斗篷。**3**. 【动】(南美的)卷尾猴。~ **monkey** 戴帽猿。~ **pigeon** 有风帽状冠毛的鸽子。

ca·put [ˈkæpət; ˋkæpət] ***n.*** (*pl.* ***ca·pi·ta*** [ˈkæpitə; ˋkæpɪtə])【解】(骨等的)(瘤状)头。

ca·put mor·tu·um [ˈkæput ˈmɔːtjuəm; ˋkæput-ˋmɔtjuəm]〔L.〕**1.** 骷髅;头盖。**2.** (化石)废物,残渣。

cap·y·ba·ra [ˌkæpiˈbɑːrə; ˏkæpəˋbɑrə] ***n.***【动】水豚(*Hydrochoerus capybara.*)。

CAR = **1.** civil air regulations 民航条例。**2.** controlled avalanche rectifier 可控雪崩整流器。

car[1] [kɑː; kɑr] **I** ***n.*** **1.** 车辆;(小)汽车;电车。**2.** (火车)车厢;〔英〕运货马车;〔诗〕战车,凯旋门;(飞艇,电梯等的)吊舱。*a dining* ~(火车上的)餐车。*a freight* ~货车。***beat the*** ~〔美〕非常地,厉害地。**by** ~乘电车;乘汽车。*take a* ~乘(电)车。***the*** ~ ***of the sun***〔诗〕日轮,太阳。***the*** ~***s***〔美〕列车,火车。**II** ***vi.*** 坐汽车去。~ *it*〔美〕坐汽车旅行。~ **bed** 携带式婴儿小床。~**bra**〔口〕汽车车头罩。~ **catcher**〔美〕(火车)制动手。~ **coat** 短大衣。~ **fare**〔美〕(市内)电车费;火车费,票价。~ **hand**〔美〕铁路员工。~**hop**〔美〕**1.** ***n.*** (把饭菜递给汽车乘客的)路边餐馆服务员。**2.** ***vi.*** 充当路边餐馆服务员。~**jacking** 劫持汽车。~ **knock** [**whack**]〔美〕火车修理工人。~**load** 车辆荷载;一车皮货物;一车皮装载量。~**loading**〔常 *pl.*〕(以铁路货车计算的)货物运入[出]量。~ **lots**【美商】货车到站数。~**man** [ˈkɑːmən; ˋkɑmən] **1.** 赶马车的人。**2.** 电车[汽车等]的驾驶员,货车驾驶员。**3.** (车辆上货物的)搬运工人;火车检修工,车辆装造工。~ **park**〔英〕停车场。~**phone**, ~ **phone**(汽车上安装的)车载电话。~ **pool**〔美〕合伙使用汽车组织。~**port** (无门户的)敞开式汽车间。~**sick** ***a.*** 晕车的。~**sickness** 晕车。~**-top** ***vt.***, ***vi.***〔美〕装在汽车顶上运输。~ **topper** (可放在汽车顶上的)小汽艇。~ **wash** 汽车擦洗处。**-ful** ***n.*** 一车之量。**-less** ***a.*** 没有汽车的。

car[2] [kɑː; kɑr] ***a.***〔Scot.〕**1.** 惯用左手的。**2.** 不吉利的;不自然的。

car. = carat; carpentry.

ca·ra·bao [ˌkɑːrəˈbɑːəu; ˏkɑrəˋbɑo] ***n.*** (*pl.* ~*s*, ~)〔Phil.〕水牛。

car·a·bid [ˈkærəbid; ˋkærəbɪd] ***n.***【动】步行虫(= ground beetel)。

car·a·bin, car·a·bine [ˈkærəbin, ˈkærəbain; ˋkærəbɪn, ˋkærəbaɪn] ***n.*** 卡宾枪(= carbine)。

car·a·bi·neer, -nier [ˌkærəbiˈniə; ˏkærəbəˋnɪr] ***n.*** **1.** [the C-]〔英〕第六龙骑兵团。**2.** 卡宾枪手(= carbineer)。

car·a·cal [ˈkærəkæl; ˋkærəˏkæl] ***n.***【动】狞猫,山猫,山猫皮。

ca·ra·ca·ra [ˌkɑːrəˈkɑːrə; ˏkɑrəˋkɑrə] ***n.*** (南美等地的)一种长脚鹰。

Ca·ra·cas [kəˈrækəs; kəˋrɑkəs] ***n.*** 加拉加斯[委内瑞拉首都]。

car·a·col(e) [ˈkærəkəul; ˋkærəˏkol] **I** ***n.*** **1.**【马术】半旋转。**2.** 旋转跳跃的动作。**3.**【建】螺旋形楼梯,盘梯。**II** ***vi.*** (马)作半旋转动作;(骑马)作半旋转。

car·a·cul [ˈkærəkəl; ˋkærəkəl] ***n.***〔吉尔吉斯斯坦〕卡拉库尔[阿拉斯特罕]羔皮;仿羔皮。~ **cloth** 仿羔皮呢。

Ca·rad·oc [kəˈrædək; kəˋrædək] ***n.*** ~ **stage**【地】喀拉多克阶[晚奥陶世]。

ca·rafe [kəˈrɑːf; kəˋræf] ***n.*** (餐桌上的)玻璃水瓶,饮料瓶。

ca·ra·ga·na [ˌkærəˈgɑːnə; ˏkærəˋgɑnə] ***n.***【植】锦鸡儿(属)。

car·a·geen [ˈkærəˌgiːn; ˋkærəˏgin] ***n.***【植】**1.** 角叉菜。**2.** 多乳头杉海苔。

ca·ram·ba [kɑːˈrɑːmbɑː; kɑrˋrɑmbɑ] ***int.*** 啊![表示惊愕、恐怖的感叹词]。

ca·ram·bo·la [ˌkærəmˈbəulə; ˏkærəmˋbolə] ***n.***【植】杨桃,五敛子[产中国广东、东南亚及西印度群岛等地]。

car·a·mel [ˈkærəmel; ˋkærəml] ***n.*** **1.** (着色或加味用的)焦糖。**2.** (吃布丁用的)糖蜜;(果味)块糖。**3.** 淡褐色,酱色。

car·a·mel·ize [ˈkærəmelaiz, ˈkairmə-; ˋkærəmlˏaɪz, ˋkaɪmə-] ***vt.***, ***vi.*** (使…)变成焦糖。

ca·ran·gid [kəˈrændʒid; kəˋrændʒɪd] ***n.***【动】鲹科鱼。**-ran·goid** [-ˈræŋgɔid; -ˋræŋgɔɪd] ***a.***

car·a·pace [ˈkærəpeis; ˋkærəˏpes] ***n.***【动】甲壳;(龟等的)壳。

car·at [ˈkærət; ˋkærət] ***n.*** **1.** 克拉[宝石重量单位 = 200 毫克]。**2.** 开[黄金纯度单位,纯金为 24 开](= karat)。

car·a·van [ˈkærəvæn; ˋkærəˏvæn] **I** ***n.*** **1.** (沙漠地带的)商队;旅队;车马队。**2.**〔美〕移民列车;(马戏团的)搬运车;(吉卜赛人等的)有篷马车,大篷车。**3.**〔英〕活动住宅。**II** ***vi.*** (*-n(n)-*) 参加旅行队旅行。~ **park**, ~ **site** 活动房屋拖车停车场。**-eer** ***n.*** 乘有篷马车旅行者。**-ner** ***n.*** 乘有篷马车旅行者;〔英〕用汽车活动住屋住在野外者。

car·a·van·sa·ry, car·a·van·se·rai [ˌkærəˈvænsəri, -sərai; ˏkærəˋvænsərɪ, -səraɪ] ***n.*** **1.** (东方国家的)商队旅馆;大车客店。**2.**〔美〕旅馆。

car·a·vel [ˈkærəvel; ˋkærəˏvɛl] ***n.*** (16 世纪西班牙、葡萄牙人的)轻快帆船。

car·a·way [ˈkærəwei; ˋkærəˏwe] ***n.***【植】芷茴香,贳蒿。

carb- *comb. f.* = carbo-.

car·ba·mate [ˈkɑːbəmeit; ˋkɑrbəmet] ***n.***【化】氨基甲酸酯。

car·bam·ide [ˈkɑːbəmaid; ˋkɑrbəˏmaɪd] ***n.***【化】尿素,碳酰二胺。

car·ban·i·on [ˈkɑːbənaiən; ˋkɑrbənaɪən] ***n.***【化】碳酸根[基]离子,阴碳离子,负碳离子。

carbarn [ˈkɑːbɑːn; ˋkɑrbɑrn] ***n.***〔美〕(电车、公共汽车的)车库。

car·ba·ryl [ˈkɑːbəˌril; ˋkɑbəˏrɪl] ***n.*** 西维因,胺甲萘[一种杀虫剂,用于棉花、蔬菜、果树等作物防治害虫]。

car·baz·ole [ˈkɑːbəzəul; ˋkɑrbəˏzol] ***n.***【化】咔唑。

car·ba·zone [ˈkɑːbəzəun; ˋkɑrbəzon] ***n.***【药】卡巴肿。

car·ben·i·cil·lin [ˌkɑːbeniˈsilin; ˏkɑbɛnɪˋsɪlɪn] ***n.***【药】羧苄青霉素,卡比西林。

carb·he·mo·glo·bin [ˈkɑːbˌhiːməuˈgləubin; kɑrbˏhimoˋglobɪn] ***n.***【生化】碳酸血红蛋白。

car·bide [ˈkɑːbaid; ˋkɑrbaɪd] ***n.***【化】碳化物;碳化钙;电石[粗制 CaC_2]。

car·bine [ˈkɑːbain; ˋkɑrbaɪn] ***n.*** 马枪,卡宾枪。*a machine* ~冲锋枪,卡宾枪。

carbi·neer [ˌkɑːbiˈniə; ˏkɑrbəˋnɪr] ***n.*** 马枪手,卡宾枪手。

car·bi·nol [ˈkɑːbinɔl; ˋkɑrbəˏnol] ***n.***【化】甲醇。

car·bo- *comb. f.* 碳;羰: *carbo*hydrate.

car·bo·cy·clic [ˌkɑːbəˈsaiklik; ˏkɑrboˋsaɪklɪk] ***a.***【化】碳环型的。

car·bo·he·mo·glob·in [ˈkɑːbəuˌhiːməuˈgləubin; ˋkɑboˏhimoˋglobɪn] ***n.***【生化】碳酸血红蛋白(= carbhemoglobin)。

car·bo·hy·drate [ˈkɑːbəuˈhaidreit; ˋkɑrboˋhaɪdret] ***n.***【化】碳水化合物,醣类。

car·bo·lat·ed [ˈkɑːbəleitid; ˋkɑrbəˏletɪd] ***a.***【化】含酚盐(石炭酸盐)的。

car·bol·ic [kɑːˈbɔlik; kɑrˋbɑlɪk] ***a.***【化】**1.** 由炭和油中取得的。**2.** 煤焦油的。~ **acid** 石炭酸,苯酚。~ **oil** 酚油。~ **soap** 酚皂,石炭酸皂。

car·bo·lize [ˈkɑːbəlaiz; ˋkɑrbəˏlaɪz] ***vt.*** 用石炭酸洗[处理];用酚处理,使与酚化合。

car·bo·my·cin [ˌkɑːbəuˈmaisin; ˏkɑrboˋmaɪsɪn] ***n.***【药】碳霉素。

car·bon [ˈkɑːbən; ˋkɑrbən] ***n.*** **1.**【化】碳。**2.**【电】碳精棒[片、粉];碳精电极。**3.** (一张)复写纸。**4.** 复写的副本。*a* ~ *of a letter* 一封信的副本。~ **bisulfide** 二硫

化碳。～ **black** 松烟；炭黑。～ **brush** 碳精刷。～ **copy** 复写[打字]的副本；〔口〕极相像的人[物]。～**-copy** *vt*. 复制。～**-date** *vt*.【考古】用放射性碳素测定(年代)。～ **dating**【考古】碳 14 年代测定(法)。～ **dioxide** 二氧化碳，碳酐。(*frozen* ～ *dioxide* 干冰)。～ **filament** (灯泡用)碳丝。～ **monoxide** 一氧化碳。～ **paper** 复写纸。～ **spot** (硬币上的)碳斑，黑斑。～ **star**【天】碳星。

car·bo·na·ceous [ˌkɑːbəˈneiʃəs; ˏkarbəˋneʃəs] *a*.【化】碳的，碳质的，含碳的。

car·bo·na·do [kɑːbəˈneidəu; karbəˋnedo] **I** *n*. **1.** 黑金刚石。**2.** 烤肉片，烤鱼片。**II** *vt*. **1.** 烧，焙，烘，烤炙(肉片等)。**2.** 砍，在…上砍出深痕。

Car·bo·na·ri [ˌkɑːbəˈnɑːri; ˏkarboˋnarɪ] *n*. 〔*pl*.〕(*sing*. **-na·ro** [-ˈnɑːrəu; -ˋnaro])〔It.〕【史】烧炭党。

car·bon·ate [ˈkɑːbəneit; ˋkarbənɪt] **I** *vt*. **1.** 使与碳酸化合；给…充碳酸气。**2.** 使碳化，使化合成碳酸盐[脂]；把…烧成炭。**3.** 使活泼[活跃]。**II** *n*. [ˈkɑːbənit; ˋkarbənɪt] 碳酸盐[脂]；黑金刚石。**car·bon·a·tor** [ˈkɑːbəneitə; ˋkarbənetɚ] *n*. 碳酸化器。

car·bon·a·tion [kɑːbəˈneiʃən; karbəˋneʃən] *n*.【化】**1.** 碳酸饱和。**2.** 碳酸盐法。**3.** 碳化(作用)。

car·bon-date [ˈkɑːbən-ˈdeit; ˋkarbən-ˋdet] *vt*. 以含碳量测定(化石等的)年代。

car·bon·ic [kɑːˈbɔnik; karˋbanɪk] *a*.【化】(含)碳的，由碳得到的。～ **acid** 碳酸。

car·bon·if·er·ous [ˌkɑːbəˈnifərəs; ˏkarbəˋnɪfərəs] *a*. **1.**〔C-〕【地】石碳纪的。**2.** 含碳的。*C- Period* [*Strata*] 石碳纪[层]。

car·bon·ite [ˈkɑːbənait; ˋkarbənaɪt] *n*.【化】碳质炸药；硝酸甘油，硝酸钾；锯屑炸药。

car·bon·i·um [kɑːˈbəuniəm; karˋbonɪəm] *n*.【化】碳鎓，阳碳。

car·bon·i·za·tion [ˌkɑːbənaiˈzeiʃən; ˏkarbənɪˋzeʃən] *n*.【化】碳化(作用)。

car·bon·ize [ˈkɑːbənaiz; ˋkarbənˏaɪz] *vt*.【化】使碳化，使焦化；使与碳化合。

car·bon·ous [ˈkɑːbənəs; ˋkarbənəs] *a*. 含碳的；似碳的。

car·bon·yl [ˈkɑːbənil; ˋkarbənɪl] *n*.【化】羰基；碳酰。

car·bo·run·dum [ˌkɑːbəˈrʌndəm; ˏkarbəˋrʌndəm] *n*.【商标】金刚砂，碳化硅。～ **paper** (金刚)砂纸。

car·box·ide [kɑːˈbɔksaid; karˋbaksaɪd] *n*.【化】**1.** 羧基。**2.** 酮基。

carbox(y)- *comb*. *f*. 羧基。

car·box·yl [kɑːˈbɔksil; karˋbaksəl] *n*.【化】羧基。

car·box·yl·ase [kɑːˈbɔksileis; karˋbaksəles] *n*.【化】羧(基)酶，羧化酶。

car·box·yl·ate [kɑːˈbɔksileit; karˋbaksɪlet] **I** *n*.【化】羧化物，羧酸盐[酯]。**II** *vt*. 使羧化。**-yl·a·tion** *n*.

car·box·yl·ic [ˌkɑːbɔkˈsilik; ˏkarbakˋsɪlɪk] *a*. (含)羧基的。～ **acid** 羧酸。

car·boy [ˈkɑːbɔi; ˋkarbɔɪ] *n*. (用木箱或藤罩保护着、专装硫酸等腐蚀性液体的)大玻璃瓶，酸瓶，酸坛。

car·bun·cle [ˈkɑːbʌŋkl; ˋkarbʌŋkl] *n*. **1.**【矿】红玉，红宝石。**2.**【医】痈疔；面皮包，酒刺。**-d**, **-bun·cu·lar** [-ˈbʌŋkjulə; -ˋbʌŋkjulɚ] *a*.

car·bu·ret [ˈkɑːbjuret; ˋkarbərɛt] **I** *n*.【化】碳化物。**II** *vt*. (～(*t*)*ed*; ～(*t*)*ing*) **1.** 使与碳化合；给…增碳。**2.** 使(气体)与碳氢化合物混合。**3.** 汽化，使(汽油等)与空气混合。*carburetted hydrogen* 碳化氢，矿坑气。*carburetted spring* 碳酸泉。

car·bu·ret·ant [ˈkɑːbəˌreitnt; ˋkarbəˏrɛtn̩t] *n*.【化】碳化剂。

car·bu·ret·ter, car·bu·ret·or [ˈkɑːbjuretə; ˋkarbəretɚ] *n*. **1.**【机】汽化器，化油器。**2.**【化】增碳器。

car·bu·rize [ˈkɑːbjuraiz; ˋkarbjəraɪz] *vt*. **1.**【化】汽化；使汽油与空气混合。**2.**【冶】使渗碳。**-ri·za·tion** [ˌkɑːbjuraiˈzeiʃən; ˏkarbjuraɪˋzeʃən] *n*. 渗碳法[作用]。

car·bur·i·zer [ˈkɑːbjuraizə; karbjuraɪzɚ] *n*.【冶】渗碳器。

car·byl [ˈkɑːbil; ˋkarbɪl] *n*.【化】二价碳基。

car·byl·a·mine [ˌkɑːbiləˈmiːn; ˏkarbɪləˋmin] *n*.【化】胩；乙胩。

car·ca·jou [ˈkɑːkəˌdʒuː; ˋkarkəˏdʒu] *n*.【动】狼獾；狼獾毛皮。

car·ca·net [ˈkɑːkənet; ˋkarkəˏnɛt] *n*. (宝玉镶饰的)项圈，项链。

car·cass, car·case [ˈkɑːkəs; ˋkarkəs] *n*. **1.** (兽类的)尸体。**2.**〔蔑〕(人的)死尸；身躯。**3.** (家畜屠宰后的)躯体。**4.** (废屋、废船等的)骨架，遗骸。**5.** (车胎的)外胎身。*to save one's* ～ 为保全身体[性命]，怕送命[受伤]。～**-fabric** 轮胎织物。～ **flooring**【建】毛地板。～ **roofing**【建】毛屋顶。

carcin(o)- *comb*. *f*. 表示"肿瘤"，"癌"：*carcino*ma.

car·cin·o·gen [kɑːˈsinədʒən; karˋsɪnədʒən] *n*.【医】致癌物(质)，诱癌因素。

car·ci·no·ma [ˌkɑːsiˈnəumə; ˏkarsɪˋnomə] *n*. (*pl*. ～*s*, ～*ta* [-tə; -tə])【医】癌。～ **hepatis** 肝癌。～ **uteri** 子宫癌。～ **ventriculi** 胃癌。

car·ci·no·ma·to·sis [ˌkɑːsiˌnəuməˈtəusis; ˏkarsəˏnoməˋtosɪs] *n*.【医】癌扩散，癌转移，并发癌。

car·ci·no·tron [kɑːˈsinəutrən; karˋsɪnotran] *n*.【电】回波管。

card[1] [kɑːd; kard] **I** *n*. **1.** 纸牌；〔*pl*.〕纸牌机。**2.** 卡片(纸)；明信片；请柬；入场券；名片。**3.** 节目单；程序单；戏单；菜单；广告；个人启事[声明]。**4.** (磁石的)方位盘，罗盘面。**5.** 某种措施；手段；策略；办法；〔口〕(正合适的)事物。**6.**〔口〕别有风趣的人，怪人。**7.**〔美俚〕(吸毒者吸的)一服麻醉剂。**8.**【计】(装有电路元件的)电脑插件。*play* (*at*) ～*s* 打纸牌。*a New Year* ～ 贺年片。*a doubtful* ～ 不可靠的办法。*a sure* [*safe*] ～ 可靠的办法，安全的计划，万全之策。*a great* ～ 大名鼎鼎的人物。*a knowing* ～ 精明的家伙。*a leading* ～ 先例，榜样；有力的论点。*That's the* ～ *for it*. 那就最好；正是那个。***be at*** ～***s*** 在打牌。～***s and spades*** (过分自信时)大幅度让与弱方的有利条件。***count on one's*** ～ 指望着自己的机会[措施]。(***a***) ***drawing*** ～ 肯定叫座的人物[节目]。***have one's*** ～ ***up one's sleeve*** 成竹在胸。***have*** [***hold***] ***the*** ～***s in one's hand*** 有把握。***house*** [***castle***] ***of*** ～***s*** 厚纸制的房子[城堡]；空中楼阁，不可靠的计划。***in the*** ～***s*** 多半，可能。***lay*** [***place, put***] ***one's*** ～***s on the table*** 摊牌；公开[公布]计划。***make a*** ～ (牌戏)打成一墩。***leave one's*** ～ (***on***) (访人不遇)留名片而归。(***It is***) ***on the*** ～***s*** 多半，可能。***play one's best*** [***trump***] ～ 打出王牌，采取最好办法。***play one's*** ～***s well*** [***badly***] 手腕高明[不高明]，处理得好[不好]。***play one's last*** ～ 打出最后一张牌，采取最后手段。***put all*** ～***s on the table*** 把牌全亮出来，打开天窗说亮话。***send up one's*** ～ 递名片(给门房送进去)。***show one's*** ～***s*** 摊牌；公开自己计划。***shuffle the*** ～***s*** 洗牌；进行人事大调动；改变政策。***speak by the*** ～ 正确地说。***stack the*** ～***s*** 洗牌时作弊；暗中设立陷阱(进行欺骗)。***tell sb.'s fortune from*** ～***s*** 用纸牌给某人算命。***the*** (***proper***) ～ 正合适的东西[办法]。***The*** ～***s are in sb.'s hands***. 某人已操胜券[一定成功]。***throw up the*** ～***s*** 放弃计划，罢手；屈服。***turn down one corner of the*** ～ 把名片折一角(表示本人曾来访问)。**II** *vt*. **1.** 在…上附加卡片。**2.** 把…记入卡片内，把…制成卡片。**3.**〔美〕拟订(拳赛节目等)；把…列入时间表。**4.** 查验(某人)的身份证以证实其合法年龄〔通常用作拒绝某人进入夜总会等的一种手段〕。～**-carrying** *a*. **1.** 有党证的；(会员等)正式的。**2.** 道地的，货真价实的；典型的。～ **case** 卡片盒；名片盒。～ **catalog** 卡片目录。～ **index** 卡片式索引。～**man**〔美〕工会会员。～**phone** 磁卡电话。～**room** 桥牌室。～ **shark 1.** 玩纸牌老手。**2.** ＝ card sharp(er). ~**sharp(er)** 玩牌时经常作弊的人。~ **system** 信用卡记账法。~ **vote** 凭卡投票〔某些欧洲工会选举时,卡上记明所代表的工人数〕。

card[2][kɑːd; kɑrd] **I** ***n***.【纺】**1**. 梳理机,梳棉[毛、麻]机;(梳棉机)钢丝车。**2**. 纹板,花板。**3**. (梳牛马的)梳子。**II** ***vt***. **1**. (用梳棉机等)梳,刷。**2**. 使起绒毛。~**-cutter**【纺】纹板冲孔机。~**ing machine** 梳棉[毛,麻]机。

Card. = Cardinal.

car·da·mom, car·da·mum, car·da·mon [ˈkɑːdəməm, -mən; ˋkɑrdəməm, -mən] ***n***.【植】小豆蔻。

Car·dan, car·dan [ˈkɑːdən; ˋkɑrdən] ***n***.【机】万向节,万向接头(=~ joint)。~ **shaft** 万向轴。

card·board [ˈkɑːdbɔːd; ˋkɑrdbord] **I** ***n***. 硬纸板,卡(片)纸板,卡纸。*a sheet of* ~一张硬纸板。**II** ***a***. 纸板般的;有名无实的。*a* ~ *prime minister* 有名无实的总理。~ **city** 纸板城〔指大都市中无家可归者以纸板搭起栖身之所的集居区〕。

cardi- *comb. f.* = cardio-.

car·di·a [ˈkɑːdiə; ˋkɑrdɪə] ***n***.【解】贲门。

car·di·ac [ˈkɑːdiæk; ˋkɑrdɪˏæk] **I** ***a***.【医】**1**. 心脏(病)的。**2**. (胃的)贲门的。**II** ***n***. **1**. 心脏病患者。**2**. 强心剂。**3**. 健胃剂。~ **cycle** 心搏周期。~ **passion** 胃灼热[痛],心痛(= cardialgia)。~ **symptoms** 心脏病症状。

car·di·al·gi·a [kɑːdiˈældʒiə; kɑrdɪˋældʒɪə] ***n***.【医】胃灼痛,心痛。

Car·diff [ˈkɑːdif; ˋkɑrdɪf] ***n***. 加的夫〔英国港市〕。

car·di·gan [ˈkɑːdigən; ˋkɑrdɪgən] ***n***. (开襟)羊毛衫,羊毛背心,开襟绒线衫。

car·di·nal[1] [ˈkɑːdinəl; ˋkɑrdnəl] **I** ***a***. **1**. 主要的;基本的。**2**. 深红色的。**II** ***n***. **1**. 带头巾的女外套。**2**. 深红色。**3**. 〔常 *pl*.〕基数。**4**.【鸟】北美红雀(= ~-bird)。~ **flower**【植】红花半边莲。~ **number** [**numeral**]【数】基数,纯数。~ **points** (罗盘的)基本方位〔即东、南、西、北〕。

car·di·nal[2] [ˈkɑːdinəl; ˋkɑrdɪnəl] ***n***.【天主】枢机主教〔亦称红衣主教,为梵蒂冈教廷枢密院成员〕。**-ship** ***n***. = cardinalate.

car·di·nal·ate [ˈkɑːdinəleit; ˋkɑrdənəlet] ***n***. **1**. (天主教)枢机[红衣]主教的职位。**2**. 枢机[红衣]主教团。

car·di·nes [ˈkɑːdiniːz; ˋkɑrdɪniz] ***n***. cardo 的复数。

cardio- *comb. f.* 表示"心脏": *cardio*gram.

car·di·o·dyn·i·a [ˌkɑːdiəuˈdiniə; ˏkɑrdɪoˋdɪnɪə] ***n***.【医】心痛,胸痛。

car·di·o·gram [ˈkɑːdiəgræm; ˋkɑrdɪəˏgræm] ***n***.【医】心电图,心动描记曲线。

car·di·o·graph [ˈkɑːdiəgrɑːf; ˏkɑrdɪəˋgrɑf] ***n***.【医】心动描记器。

car·di·oid [ˈkɑːdiɔid; ˋkɑrdɪˏɔɪd] ***n***.【数】心脏线。

car·di·ol·o·gy [ˌkɑːdiˈɔlədʒi; ˏkɑrdɪˋɑlədʒɪ] ***n***.【医】心脏病学。**-ol·o·gist** ***n***. 心脏病学家。

car·di·om·e·ter [ˌkɑːdiˈɔmitə; ˏkɑrdɪˋɑmɪtɚ] ***n***.【医】心能测量器,心力计。

car·dio·res·pi·ra·to·ry [ˈkɑːdiəurisˈpaiərətəri; ˋkɑrdɪorɪsˋpaɪrətɔrɪ] ***a***. 心和肺的。

car·di·o·scope [ˈkɑːdiəskəup; ˋkɑrdɪəsˏkop] ***n***.【医】心脏镜。

car·di·o·ta·chom·e·ter [ˌkɑːdiəutəˈkɔmitə; ˏkɑrdɪotəˋkɑmɪtɚ] ***n***.【医】心动计数器,心率计。

car·di·o·ton·ic [ˌkɑːdiəuˈtɔnik; ˏkɑrdɪəˋtɑnɪk] **I** ***a***.【医】强心的。**II** ***n***. 强心剂。

car·di·o·vas·cu·lar [ˌkɑːdiəuˈvæskjulə; ˏkɑrdɪoˋvæskjulɚ] ***a***.【医】心血管性的。~ **system** 循环系统。

car·di·tis [kɑːˈdaitis; kɑrˋdaɪtɪs] ***n***.【医】心脏炎。*internal* ~心脏内膜炎。

car·do [ˈkɑːdəu; ˋkɑrdo] ***n***. (*pl*. ***car·di·nes*** [ˈkɑːdiniːz; ˋkɑrdɪniz])【动】轴节;阳(茎)基环。

car·doon [kɑːˈduːn; kɑrˋdun] ***n***.【植】刺菜蓟。

CARE = Cooperative for American Relief Everywhere 美国援外合作组织。

care [kɛə; kɛr] **I** ***n***. **1**. 忧烦,忧念;挂念,思念;心事,牵累。**2**. 关怀,爱护。**3**. 管理,监督,维护,照料,看护,抚养。**4**. 注意,留心,小心,当心;〔*pl*.〕需要小心的事。*free medical* ~免费[公费]医疗。*the* ~*s of state* 国事。*domestic* [*family*] ~*s* 家事。*worldly* ~*s* 人世间的操劳。*My first* ~ *was*... 我的第一件心事是…。***be free from*** ~***s*** 放心,安心,舒坦。***bestow*** [***give***] ***great*** ~ ***upon*** 对…煞费苦心。***C- killed the*** [***a***] ***cat***. 久虑伤身。~ ***committee***〔英〕贫民保护委员会。***care of***〔信封上用语,略作 c/o〕烦…转交(*Mr. A. c/o Mr. B.* 烦 B 先生转交 A 先生)。***have a*** ~ = take ~. ***in*** ~ ***of***〔美〕=~ of. ***in the*** ~ ***of*** = under the ~ of. ***take*** ~ 留心,当心(*Take* ~ *what you say*. 说话要慎重)。***take*** ~ ***of*** 照看,看管,〔美〕收拾,处理;清除。***take*** ~ ***of oneself*** 保重身体,注意健康。***take*** ~ ***to*** (*do so*) 采取办法,设法,竭力(这样做)。***take good*** ~ ***of*** 爱护。***under the*** ~ ***of*** 在…照看下,在…保护下,在…管教下(*leave under the* ~ *of* 委托…照料)。***with*** ~小心,注意,慎重(*Handle with* ~! 小心轻放〔货运包装用语〕)。**II** ***vi***. **1**. 挂念,思念,忧虑,愁(*for*, *about*)。**2**. 看管,照管,照应,看护,抚育,监督(*for*)。**3**. 关怀;关心(*for*);介意,计较,(不)管,(不)顾,(不)问(*for*, *about*)。**4**. 〔与 for 连用〕爱好;愿意,望,欲。~ *for her health* 挂念她的健康。*He* ~*s for music*. 他喜欢音乐。~ *for sb.'s education* 负责某人的教育。*Who* ~*s*? 管它呢? *a don't* ~ *condition*【计】自由选取条件。*That's more than I* ~ *for*. 那我可无所谓[关不关心]。—***vt***.〔方〕介意,计较;愿意(后接不定式)。*Nobody* ~*s what I do*. 没有人管我干什么。*I don't* ~ *a bit* [*a damn*, *a button*, *a fig*, *a straw*, *etc*.].〔口〕一点儿也不在乎。*I don't* ~ *if I go*.〔口〕去一去也好。*I should not* ~ *to be seen with him*. 我不喜欢让人家看见和他在一块儿。*Will he* ~ *to come with us*. 不晓得他愿不愿跟我们一块儿去。***for all I*** ~ **1**. 我不管,不关我事(*It may go to the devil for all I* ~. 无论如何我一概不管)。**2**. 也许,或者(*It may be true for all I* ~. 那也许是真的)。~ **label** (系在衣服或织物上的)清洗说明单。

ca·reen [kəˈriːn; kəˋrin] **I** ***vt***. **1**. 使(船)倾斜(以便修船底)。**2**. 在倾斜位置上修理(船)。**3**. 使倾斜。—***vi***. **1**. (船)倾斜;(车等)歪斜着行驶。**2**. 修理倾侧着的船。**II** ***n***. **1**. (船等的)倾斜。**2**.【船】倾(船)修(理)。***on the*** ~ 船身倾斜。

ca·reen·age [kəˈriːnidʒ; kəˋrinɪdʒ] ***n***. **1**.【船】倾船。**2**. 船底修理费,倾修费。**3**. 修船所。

ca·reer [kəˈriə; kəˋrɪr] **I** ***n***. **1**. 生涯;经历;履历;遭遇;(星球等的)轨迹。**2**. (外交官等的)职业;前途;成功,出头,发迹。**3**. 飞跑,全速。**4**. 〔古〕猛袭。*His* ~ *is run*. 他的一生[前途]完了。*a business* ~从事实业,在商界。*a political* ~从政。***in full*** ~ 用全速,极力飞跑。***in mid*** ~ 在中途。***make*** [***carve***] ***a*** ~ 追求名利,争取前途;向上爬。**II** ***a***. 〔美〕职业性质的。**III** ***vi***. 猛冲,飞跑(*about*)。

ca·reer·ism [kəˈriərizəm; kəˋrɪrɪzm] ***n***. 野心;追求名利。~ **man**〔美〕职业外交家,专业外交家。~ **woman** 职业妇女;〔美〕(事业上)成功的女人;有事业心(而轻结婚)的女人。

ca·reer·ist [kəˈriərist; kəˋrɪrɪst] ***n***. **1**. 专业人员。**2**. 投机分子,个人野心家。

care·free [ˈkɛəfriː; ˋkɛrˏfri] ***n***. 无忧无虑的,快活的。

care·ful [ˈkɛəfʊl; ˋkɛrful] ***a***. **1**. 注意的,小心谨慎的,周到的。**2**. 重视[关心]…的;细致的;精心的,严密的。**3**. 〔古〕忧虑的。*Be* ~! 小心点! *be* ~ *about* 注意,重视,关切;讲究。*be* ~ *for* 当心,挂虑,惦记。*be* ~ *of* 珍重,注意,留意。~ *painting* 精心的绘画。~ *reading*

精读,熟读。-ly *ad*. -ness *n*.

care·lad·en [ˈkɛəˌleidn; kɛrˏledn̩] *a*. 忧心忡忡的。

care·less [ˈkɛəlis; ˋkɛrlɪs] *a*. 1. 不注意的,粗心大意的;由粗心引起的。2. 漫不经心的,不介意的。3. 轻率的,粗鲁的,草率的;拙劣的。4. 〔古〕无忧无虑的。*a happy* ~ *youth* 快乐而轻率的青年。*a* ~ *life* 轻松随便的生活。*be* ~ *about* 不关心,不重视,不讲究,漠视。*be* ~ *of* 不放在心上,不关心。-ly *ad*. -ness *n*.

ca·ress [kəˈres; kəˋrɛs] I *n*. 爱抚[拥抱、接吻、抚弄等]。II *vt*. 1. 抚爱,抚摩;怜爱,宠爱。2. 奉承,哄骗。~ *the canvas* [*rosin*] 〔美俚〕【拳】被击倒。

ca·ress·ing [kəˈresiŋ; kəˋrɛsɪŋ] I *a*. 抚爱的,抚慰的。II *n*. 爱抚。-ly *ad*.

car·et [ˈkærət; ˋkærət] *n*. 脱字号,补注号(∨,∧)。

care·tak·er [ˈkɛəteikə; ˋkɛrˏtekɚ] *n*. 1. 看管者,管理人,看守(人);〔美〕看门的人,2. 暂时代理(职务)者。~ **cabinet** [**government**] (新内阁产生之前的)看守内阁[政府]。

care·worn [ˈkɛəwɔːn; ˋkɛrwɔrn] *a*. 操心的,焦虑的。

Car·ey [ˈkɛəri; ˋkɛrɪ] *n*. 凯里〔姓氏〕。

car·fax [ˈkɑːfæks; kɑrfæks] *n*. (四条或更多条马路的)交叉路口。

car·go [ˈkɑːgəu; ˋkɑrgo] *n*. (*pl*. ~*s*, ~*es*) 船货;负荷,荷重。*ship* [*discharge*] *the* ~装[卸]货。*a* ~ *boat*[*ship*, *vessel*] 货船。~ **capacity** 载货能力[量]。~**-liner** 【空】大型货(运飞)机。

Carib, Caribbee [ˈkærib, ˈkæribiː; ˋkærɪb, ˋkærɪbi] *n*. 1. 加勒比人。2. 加勒比语。

ca·ri·be [kəˈriːbei; kəˋribe] *n*. 【动】比拉鱼(= piranha)。

Car·ib·be·an [kæriˈbi(ː)ən; ˏkærəˋbiən] I *a*. 1. 加勒比人的。2. (拉丁美洲)加勒比海的。*the* ~ *Sea* 加勒比海。II *n*. 1. 〔the ~〕加勒比海(= the ~ Sea)。2. 加勒比人(= Carib)。

car·i·bou [ˈkæribuː; ˋkærəbu] *n*. (*pl*. ~, ~*s*) 【动】(北美)驯鹿。

car·i·ca·ture [ˌkærikəˈtjuə; ˋkærɪkətʃɚ] I *n*. 1. 漫画,讽刺画[文];漫画手法。2. 滑稽可笑的模仿,丑化(可笑)的相似物;丑化。*make a* ~ *of* 画…的漫画,把…画成漫画;使滑稽化。II *vt*. 用漫画表现[讽刺],把…画成漫画;使滑稽化。**-tur·a·ble** [-ˈtjuərəbl; -ˋtʃurəbl] *a*. 适于被讽刺的;具有被讽刺的形态的。**-tur·al** [-ˈtjuərəl; -ˋtʃurəl] *a*. 讽刺画[文]的,滑稽的。

car·i·ca·tur·ist [ˌkærikəˈtjuərist; ˏkærɪkəˋtʃurɪst] *n*. 漫画家。

car·ies [ˈkɛəriiːz; ˋkɛriz] *n*. 〔L.〕【医】1. 骨疡。2. 龋。~ *of the teeth* 蛀牙。

car·il·lon [kəˈriljən; kəˋrɪljən] I *n*. 1. 【乐】编钟;电子钟琴。2. 钟乐曲。3. (风琴的)钟乐音栓。II *vi*. (-*nn*-) 用编钟演奏乐曲,奏钟乐。

car·il·lon·neur [kəˌriljəˈnəː; ˏkærɪləˋnɝ] *n*. 〔F.〕钟琴演奏者。

Ca·ri·na [kəˈrainə; kəˋraɪnə] *n*. 〔L.〕【天】船底(星)座。

ca·ri·na [kəˈrainə; kəˋraɪnə] *n*. (*pl*. ~*s*, *-nae* [-niː; -ni]) 【生】1. 隆线,脊,突。2. 峰板。3. (珊瑚)脊板。-l *a*.

car·i·nate [ˈkærineit; ˋkærɪnet] *a*. 【动】有龙骨的;龙船状的,具有隆线的。

car·i·ole [ˈkæriəul; ˋkærɪol] *n*. = carriole.

car·i·ous [ˈkɛəriəs; ˋkɛrɪəs] *a*. 【医】患骨疡的;(齿)龋的;腐烂了的。*a* ~ *tooth* 虫牙,龋齿。

cark [kɑːk; kɑrk] I *vt*., *vi*. 〔古〕(使)烦恼,(使)焦虑。II *n*. 〔古〕痛苦,焦急。

cark·ing [ˈkɑːkiŋ; ˋkɑrkɪŋ] *a*. 忧虑的;烦躁的。~ *care*(*s*) 谋虑,操心。

Carl [kɑːl; kɑrl] *n*. 卡尔〔男子名,Karl 的异体〕。

carl(e) [kɑːl; kɑrl] *n*. 1. (普通的)人。2. 〔主 Scot.〕没有教养的人,粗野的人,家伙。

car·let [ˈkɑːlit; ˋkɑrlɪt] *n*. 〔美〕小车子;小汽车。

Car·ley [ˈkɑːli; ˋkɑrlɪ] *n*. (船上的)橡皮救生艇。(= ~ float)。

car·lin(e)[1] [ˈkɑːlin; kɑrlɪn] *n*. 〔Scot.〕1. 老太婆。2. 巫婆。

car·line[2], **car·ling** [ˈkɑːliŋ; ˋkɑrlɪŋ] *n*. 【船】短纵梁。

Car·lism [ˈkɑːlizəm; ˋkɑrlɪzəm] *n*. 【史】(拥护查理一世及其后裔继承王位)西班牙王室正统论。

Car·list [ˈkɑːlist; ˋkɑrlɪst] *n*. 1. 西班牙王室正统派成员。2. 法国王室正统派成员〔查理十世及波旁(Bourbon)王朝的支持者〕。

Car·los [ˈkɑːləs; ˋkɑrləs] *n*. 卡洛斯〔男子名,Charles 的异体〕。

Car·lo·vin·gi·an [ˌkɑːləuˈvindʒiən; ˏkɑrləˋvɪndʒɪən] *a*., *n*. = Carolingian.

Car·lo·witz [ˈkɑːləuwits; ˋkɑrloˏwɪts] *n*. (南斯拉夫)卡罗威次红葡萄酒。

Carl·ton [ˈkɑːltən; ˋkɑrltən] *n*. 卡尔顿(姓氏,男子名)。*the* ~ (*Club*) (英国保守党的)卡尔顿俱乐部。~ **table** (带有抽屉、小柜的)卡尔顿式写字台。

Car·lyle [kɑːˈlail, ˈkɑːlai; kɑrˋlaɪl, ˋkɑrlaɪ] *n*. 1. 卡莱尔〔姓氏,男子名〕。2. **Thomas** ~ 托马斯·卡莱尔〔1795—1881,英国作家,历史家,哲学家〕。**-ism** *n*. 卡莱尔的风格[信条]。

car·ma·gnole [ˈkɑːmənjəul; ˏkɑrməˋnjol] *n*. 〔F.〕1. (1789—1794 年法国革命派所着的、配以黑裤、红色小帽、三色腰带的)短上衣。2. (法国革命时代)伴唱革命歌曲的街头舞蹈(曲)。

Car·mel·ite [ˈkɑːmilait; ˋkɑrmlˏaɪt] *n*. 1. 【天主】(12 世纪创立于叙利亚卡迈尔山的)白袍修士,卡迈尔派男(女)修士。2. 〔c-〕法国平纹薄呢。

Car·men [ˈkɑːmen; ˋkɑrmen] *n*. 1. 卡门〔女子名〕。2. 法国作家梅里美同名短篇小说中的女主角。

car·min·a·tive [ˈkɑːminətiv; kɑrˋmɪnətɪv] I *a*. 【医】排除肠胃气胀[气体]的。II *n*. 【医】(医治肠胃气胀的)排气剂。

car·mine [ˈkɑːmain; ˋkɑrmaɪn] I *n*. 1. 洋红;胭脂红;卡红。2. 洋红色。II *a*. 洋红色的。

car·nage [ˈkɑːnidʒ; ˋkɑrnɪdʒ] *n*. 1. 大屠杀,残杀。2. 〔古〕(战场上)狼藉的尸体。

car·nal [ˈkɑːnl; ˋkɑrnl̩] *a*. 1. 肉体的;肉欲的,淫欲的。2. 世俗的,现世的,物质的。~ *ambition* 名利心,物质欲。~ *appetite* [*desire*, *lust*] 肉欲。~ *knowledge* 性经验;【法】性关系。~ *pleasures* 淫乐。**-ism** *n*. 肉欲(主义),好色。**-ize** *vt*. 使耽于淫欲。**-ly** *ad*.

car·nal·i·ty [kɑːˈnæliti; kɑrˋnælətɪ] *n*. 肉欲;淫荡,好色;(特指)性交。

car·nal·lite [ˈkɑːnəlait; ˋkɑrnl̩ˏaɪt] *n*. 【矿】光卤石;杂盐。

car·nas·si·al [kɑːˈnæsiəl; kɑrˋnæsɪəl] I *a*. 【动】食肉齿的。II *n*. 食肉齿,裂牙,裂齿。

car·na·tion [kɑːˈneiʃən; kɑrˋneʃən] I *n*. 1. 【植】麝香石竹〔美国俄亥俄州的州花〕。2. 淡红色,肉色;〔*pl*.〕【绘】肉色部。II *a*. 肉色的。III *vt*. 使带肉色。

car·nau·ba [kɑːˈnaubə; kɑrˋnaʊbə] *n*. 【植】巴西蜡棕(树)(*Copernicia cerifera*)。

Car·ne·gie [kɑːˈnegi; kɑrˋnɛgɪ] *n*. 卡内基〔姓氏〕。~ **Hall** 卡内基音乐堂〔美国纽约有名的演奏场所〕。~ **unit** (美国中学内)课程的学年及格分数。

car·nel·ian [kəˈniːljən; kɑrˋniljən] *n*. 【矿】光玉髓,肉红玉髓。

car·net [kɑːˈnɛ; kɑrˋnɛ] *n*. 〔F.〕1. 执照;(尤指欧洲边境地区通行所需的)海关文件,通行证。2. (公共汽车等的)车票本。3. 工作手册,笔记本。

car·ney, car·nie [ˈkɑːni; ˋkɑrnɪ] *vt*., *n*. = carny.

car·ni·fy [ˈkɑːnifai; ˋkɑrnəˏfaɪ] *vt.*, *vi.*【生】(使)变成肉质。

car·ni·tine [ˈkɑːnitiːn; ˋkɑrnɪˏtin] *n.*【生化】肉碱。

car·ni·val [ˈkɑːnivəl; ˋkɑrnəvl] *n.* **1.** 群众饮宴作乐〔尤指天主教国家在四旬斋前一周内之狂欢;通常有化装游行〕;嘉年华会,狂欢节。**2.** 庆祝,欢宴,狂欢。**3.** (巡回旅行的)杂技[杂耍]表演。**4.** 节目表演节目,〔美〕运动比赛,竞赛;博览会。~ **glass** 狂欢节彩色玻璃〔一种虹彩色调的压制玻璃〕。

Car·niv·o·ra [kɑːˈnivərə; kɑrˋnɪvərə] *n.* 〔L.〕〔*pl.*〕【动】食肉目;〔c-〕食肉动物。

car·ni·vore [ˈkɑːnivɔː; ˋkanəˏvor] *n.*【生】食肉动物;食虫植物。

car·niv·o·rous [kɑːˈnivərəs; kɑrˋnɪvərəs] *a.*【动】食肉(目)的。~ *animals* 肉食动物。~ *plants* 食虫植物。

car·no·tite [ˈkɑːnətait; ˋkɑrnəˏtaɪt] *n.*【矿】钒酸钾铀矿。

car·ny [ˈkɑːni; ˋkɑrni] **I** *n.* 〔俚〕**1.** 巡回游艺团。**2.** 巡回游艺团成员。**II** *vt.* (*-fied*; *-fy·ing*) (用甜言蜜语)哄骗。

car·ob [ˈkærəb; ˋkærəb] *n.*【植】蝗卵豆槐,角豆树。

ca·roche [kəˈrəutʃ, -ˈrəuʃ; kəˋrotʃ, -ˋroʃ] *n.* (十七世纪时隆重场合使用的)豪华马车;花车。

Car·ol [ˈkærəl; ˋkærəl] *n.* 卡罗尔〔姓氏,女子名,Caroline 的昵称〕。

car·ol [ˈkærəl; ˋkærəl] **I** *n.* 喜歌,颂歌;〔诗〕鸟的啼啭。*Christmas* ~*s* 圣诞颂歌。**II** *vi.*, *vt.* (〔英〕*-ll-*) **1.** 欢唱,唱颂歌(赞美)。**2.** 歌唱;啼啭。

Car·o·li·na [ˌkærəˈlainə; ˏkærəˋlaɪnə] *n.* (美国)卡罗来纳州。*the* ~*s* 南北卡罗来纳州(= North ~ and South ~)。~ **all-spice**【植】黑花腊梅。~ **nine** 〔美〕(骰子)对九。

car·ol(l)er [ˈkærələ; kærələ˞] *n.* 欢唱颂歌的人。

Car·o·line[1] [ˈkærəˌlain, -lin; ˋkærəˏlaɪn, -lɪn] *a.*【英史】英王查理 (Charles) 一世[二世]的。

Car·o·line[2] [ˈkærəlain; ˋkærəlaɪn] *n.* 卡罗兰〔女子名〕。

Caroline Islands [ˈkærəlain ˈailəndz; ˋkærəlaɪn ˋaɪləndz] 加罗林群岛〔西太平洋〕(= Carolines)。

Car·o·lin·gi·an [ˌkærəˈlindʒiən; ˏkærəˋlɪndʒɪən] **I** *a.* (公元 751 年成立的法兰克王国第二个王朝)加洛林王朝的。**II** *n.* 第二法兰克王朝的君主[人]。

Car·o·lin·i·an [kærəˈliniən; ˏkærəˋlɪnɪən] **1.** *a.*, *n.* 美国卡罗来纳州的(人)。**2.** = Caroline[1]。

car·om [ˈkærəm; ˋkærəm] *n.*, *vi.* = carrom.

car·o·tene [ˈkærətiːn; ˋkærətin] *n.*【生化】胡萝卜素;叶红素。

ca·rot·e·noid, ca·rot·i·noid [kəˈrɔtinɔid; kəˋrɑtɪnˏɔɪd] *n.*【生化】类胡萝卜素。

ca·rot·id [kəˈrɔtid; kəˋrɑtɪd] *n.*, *a.*【解】颈动脉(的)。

car·o·tin [ˈkærətin; ˋkærətɪn] *n.* = carotene.

ca·rous·al [kəˈrauzəl; kəˋrauzl] *n.* 欢乐喜闹的酒宴;闹饮。

ca·rouse [kəˈrauz; kəˋrauz] *n.*, *vi.* 聚饮;痛饮,大喝大闹。~ *it* 大喝,畅饮。

car·ou·sel [ˌkærəˈzel; ˏkærʊˋzɛl] *n.* **1.**【史】马上比枪;骑术比赛。**2.** (游艺场中的)旋转木马。**3.** 旋转式传送带。

carp[1] [kɑːp; kɑrp] *n.* (*pl.* ~, ~*s*)【动】鲤鱼;鲤科[属]鱼。*the black* ~青鱼。*the silver* ~白鲢。*the golden* ~ [*Prussian*] 鲫鱼。

carp[2] [kɑːp; kɑrp] *vi.* 挑剔,找错,吹毛求疵。~*ing criticism* 吹毛求疵的批评。~*ing tongue* 刻薄嘴。*make irresponsible and* ~*ing comments* 说风凉话。

carp. = carpenter; carpentry.

-carp *comb. f.* 表示"果实"。

carpal [ˈkɑːpl; ˋkɑrpl̩] *n.*, *a.*【解】腕关节(的)。~ *bone* 腕骨。

car·pa·le [kɑːˈpeiliː; kɑrˋpeli] *n.* (*pl.* *-li·a* [-ə; -ə]) = carpal.

Car·pa·thi·an Mountains [kɑːˈpeiθjən; kɑrˋpeθɪən] (中欧)喀尔巴阡山山脉(= the Carpathians)。

car·pe di·em [ˈkɑːpi ˈdaiem; ˋkɑrpɪ ˋdaɪɛm] 〔L.〕 **1.** 抓住时机(及时行乐)。**2.** 一种鼓吹及时行乐思想的抒情诗。

car·pel [ˈkɑːpel; ˋkɑrpl̩] *n.*【植】心皮;果爿。

Car·pen·ter [ˈkɑːpintə; ˋkɑrpɪntə˞] *n.* 卡彭特〔姓氏〕。

car·pen·ter [ˈkɑːpintə; ˋkɑrpəntə˞] **I** *n.* 木匠,木工(尤指粗木工);【海】船匠。*the* ~*'s son* 木匠之子〔耶稣〕。**II** *vt.* 以木工手艺造[修](家具、器物、房屋等)。~ *lieutenant*【海】海军船匠特务上尉。~**'s mate**【海】海军船匠。~**'s rule** 折尺。~**'s scene** 幕间节目〔以便换布景道具〕。~**'s shop** 木匠店。~ **'s square** 角尺,曲尺。

car·pen·try [ˈkɑːpintri; ˋkɑrpəntrɪ] *n.* **1.** 木匠业。**2.** 〔总称〕木工;木器。

carp·er [ˈkɑːpə; ˋkɑrpə˞] *n.* 吹毛求疵的人。

car·pet [ˈkɑːpit; ˋkɑrpɪt] **I** *n.* **1.** 地毯,桌毯;毛毯,绒毯。**2.**【建】磨耗层。**3.** 地毯状覆盖物。**4.** (装在飞机上的)雷达电子干扰仪。~ *of flowers* 繁花似锦。***on the*** ~ **1.** 在审议中,在研究中。**2.** (仆役,下级等)被叫去,被训斥 (*to have sb. on the* ~责备某人。*be called on the* ~ *for sth.* 为某事被召去受责备)。***red*** ~ 红地毯;〔喻〕隆重的接待[礼遇]。***roll out the red*** ~ ***for sb.*** 铺开红地毯接待某人。***shove sth. under the*** ~ 掩盖某事。**II** *vt.* **1.** 在…上铺绒毯[地毯(等)];把(花等)栽成地毯状。**2.** 〔英〕把(仆役等)叫来责斥。~**-area** 〔英〕室内面积。~**-bag** 毡制旅行提包。~**-bagger** 〔美〕(南北内战刚结束时,利用南部的未安定局面去谋利的)冒险家;不受欢迎的外来者[政客,候选人等]。~ **bed** (绒毯一样的)花坛。~ **blanket** 厚毛毯。~**bomb** *vt.* 对…实行地毯式轰炸。~ **bombing** (把全区炸平的)地毯式轰炸。~ **dance** (在地毯上跳的)即兴跳舞。~ **fire** 地毯轰炸造成的大火灾。~ **herb** 地皮草。~ **knight** 地毯骑士〔生活优裕的非战斗军人〕;吃喝玩乐的人。~ **rod** (扣住梯毯的)金属条。~ **snake** (澳洲)锦蛇,斑蛇。~ **sweeper** 扫毯器。~**weed**【植】粟米草。**-ing** *n.* 地毯料子[织品];〔集合词〕地毯,桌毯。**-less** *a.* 没有铺地毯的。

car·pi [ˈkɑːpai; ˋkɑrpaɪ] *n.* carpus 的复数。

carp·ing [ˈkɑːpiŋ; ˋkɑrpɪŋ] *a.* 吹毛求疵的;苛刻的;强词夺理的。**-ly** *ad.*

carpo- *comb. f.* 表示"果实": *carpo*logy.

car·po·go·ni·um [ˌkɑːpəˈgəuniəm; ˏkɑrpəˋgonɪəm] *n.* (*pl.* *-ni·a* [-ə; -ə])【植】果胞。

car·pol·o·gy [kɑːˈpɔlədʒi; kɑrˋpɑlədʒɪ] *n.*【植】果实(分类)学。

car·pool [ˈkɑːˌpuːl; ˋkɑˏpul] *vi.* 参加合伙用车;(根据合伙用车协议)轮流用个人的车运送。

car·poph·a·gous [kɑːˈpɔfəgəs; kɑrˋpɑfəgəs] *a.*【动】食果实的,以果实为生的。

car·po·phore [ˈkɑːpəfɔː; ˋkɑrpəfɔr] *n.*【植】**1.** 心皮柄;果瓣柄。**2.** 子实体。

car·po·phyl(l) [ˈkɑːpəfil; ˋkɑrpəfɪl] *n.*【植】大孢子叶。

car·port [ˈkɑːpɔːt; ˋkɑrport] *n.* 〔美〕简陋的汽车棚。

car·po·spore [ˈkɑːpəspɔː; ˋkɑrpəspor] *n.*【植】果孢子。

car·pus [ˈkɑːpəs; ˋkɑrpəs] *n.* (*pl.* *-pi* [-pai; -paɪ])【解】腕骨;腕;(马的)膝头;脉端;翅痣。

car·rack [ˈkærək; ˋkærək] *n.* 西班牙大帆船(= galleon)。

car·ra·g(h)een [ˈkærəgiːn; ˋkærəˏgin] *n.*【植】鹿角菜〔一种海藻〕。

car·re·four [ˌkærəˈfuə; ˏkærəˋfur] *n.* **1.** 十字路口。**2.** (位于道路交叉点上的)广场。

car·rel, car·rell [ˈkærəl; ˋkærəl] *n.* (图书馆在书库为个别读者提供的)特设小阅览室。

car·ri·age [ˈkæridʒ; ˋkærɪdʒ] *n.* **1.** 车;(四轮)马车;

〔英〕(铁路)客车车厢(=〔美〕car);【空】牵引车;(汽车的)座位。2. 运输,输送。3. 运费。4. 体态,步态;姿态;风度;〔古〕举止,行动。5. 炮架;【机】车架,台架,支架;(打字机等的)滑架,托架;(机床的)拖板,溜板;楼梯架。6.〔古〕经营;办理。7.(议案的)通过。*a close* [*an open*] ～有盖[无盖]马车。*a state* ～豪华的礼仪马车,花车。*a composite* ～混合客车。*a graceful* ～优美的姿势,优雅的态度。～ ***and pair*** [***four***] 双马[四马]马车。～ ***by land*** [***sea***] 陆路[水路]运输。***keep*** [***drive***] ***a*** ～ 自备马车。***start*** [***set up***] ***a*** ～ 开始备置自用马车。～ **clock** 正歪放置都会走动的钟。～ **drive** 1.(名胜公园内的)车道。2.(大住宅院内的)马车道。3. 汽车道。～ **folk** 〔俚〕有自备马车的人们。～**-forward** *ad*.〔英〕运费由收货人支付。～**-free** *ad*. 运费免付。～**-paid** *ad*. 运费已付。～ **porch** 停车廊。～ **trade** (自备马车的)上等顾客。～**way** 车行道(*a dual* ～*way* 复式车行道〔中央有分隔带〕)。

car·ri·age·ful [ˈkæridʒful; ˋkærɪdʒfʊl] *n*. 整整一(马)车的量。

Car·rie [ˈkæri; ˋkærɪ] *n*. 1. 卡里〔姓氏〕。2. 卡丽〔女子名,Caroline 的昵称〕。

car·rick [ˈkærik; ˋkærɪk] *n*. ～ **bend** 【船】(接两根绳子时所用的一种)单花大绳接结。～ **bitts** 【船】卷扬机柱,系缆桩。

car·ried [ˈkærid; ˋkærɪd] *a*. 1. 被携带的;被载运的。2.〔英方〕失神落魂的,精神恍惚的。

car·ri·er [ˈkæriə; ˋkærɪɚ] *n*. 1. 运送人,搬夫;负荷者;使役,〔美〕信差,邮递员;送报人;〔英〕运输行,运输业者。2. 传书鸽,信鸽。3.(车后的)货架;吊架;托架。4. 水管,引水沟。5. 运载工具;搬运机;移动滑车。6.【医】带菌者,病媒。7. 航空母舰。8.【电】载波;载流子;【拓】承载子;【化】载体,填料;导染剂。*a mail* [*letter*] ～邮递员。*a band* ～传送带。～ **aircraft** 1. 舰载机。2. 客机,货机,邮机。3. 母机。～ **bag** 〔美〕(购物用)拎包,提包(=〔美〕shopping bag)。～**-based**, ～**-borne** 舰载的。～**-gear** 过桥齿轮。～**-nation** 海运业国家。～ **pigeon** 信鸽。～ **plane** 舰载飞机。～**-rocket** *n*. 运载火箭。～ **ship** 航空母舰。～**'s note** 【商】提货证,提单。～ **wave** 【无】载波。

car·ri·ole [ˈkæriəul; ˋkærɪol] *n*. 1. 小单人马车;小篷车。2.(加拿大的)狗拉雪车。

car·ri·on [ˈkæriən; ˋkærɪən] **I** *n*. 腐尸;腐肉;腐臭之物。**II** *a*. 1. 腐尸的;腐肉的;腐臭的。2. 吃腐肉的。～ **crow** 【鸟】吃腐肉的乌鸦,黑兀鹰。

Car·rol(l) [ˈkærəl; ˋkærəl] *n*. 卡罗尔〔姓氏,男子或女子名〕。

car·rom [ˈkærəm; ˋkærəm] **I** *n*.〔美〕1.【台球】连中二球的一击(=cannon)。2. 撞击后弹回。**II** *vi*. 1.【台球】连中二球(=cannon)。2. 撞击后弹回。

car·ron·ade [ˌkærəˈneid; ˏkærəˋned] *n*.(旧时)大口径短炮。

car·rot [ˈkærət; ˋkærət] *n*. 1.【植】胡萝卜。2.〔*pl*.〕〔口〕红头发(的人)。3.〔喻〕空洞的政治许诺。*a policy of* (*the*) *stick and* (*the*) ～胡萝卜加大棒的政策,又打又拉的政策。***the donkey's*** ～ 梦想。～**-top** 〔美〕红发人。

car·rot·y [ˈkærəti; ˋkærətɪ] *a*. 1. 胡萝卜色的。2.〔俚〕(头发)红的;红发的。

car·rou·sel [ˌkæruˈzel; ˏkærʊˋzɛl] = carousel.

car·ry [ˈkæri; ˋkærɪ] **I** *vt*. (***-ried***; ***-ry·ing***) 1. 搬运,装运。2. 携带;佩带,怀有。3. 支持;掮,肩挑,担(重物);悬挂(旗、帆等)。4. 举动,处身,自处。5. 移转;传达,传送,传导。6. 领去,带去。7. 扩张,伸到。8. 使满意,使服气,使佩服。9. 推行,贯彻(自己主张);使(议案等)通过,使(候选人等)当选。10. 有,含有(意义);记得,不忘记;附带(权利、义务等);生(利息)。11. 占领,夺取,攻陷;获胜。12.【会计】转记;结转(次页);【数】进位;(由…)移来,移上一位。13.〔美〕登载,登出(消息等)。14.(把货物)摆在店里,卖;赊卖。～*a box on one's shoulder* 把箱子掮在肩头上走。～*a gun* 带着枪走。*C- arms*! 举枪! *The timber carries the whole weight of the roof*. 栋梁支撑屋顶全重。～ *an election* 竞选获胜。～ *conviction* (议论等)令人佩服。～ *one's point* 贯彻主张。*The motion is carried*. 这一提议业已通过。*be carried* [*away*; *out of oneself*; *to idleness*] 入迷,被迷住;发狂;变懒惰。*The sense these words* ～ *is*... 这几个字的含义是…。*We* ～ *a full line of canned goods*. 本店运销各种罐头。—*vi*. 1. 担任运送者。2.(声音等)能达到(多远),(枪等)能打到(多远)。3.(泥)黏附(鞋子等)。4. 保持某种姿势。5. 主张获得赞同,(议案等)获得通过。6. 被携带。7. 有感染力。*The trunks don't* ～ *easily*. 这些大箱子不便于携带。*This gun carries nearly a mile*. 这枪几乎能打一英里远。*These guns* ～ *true*. 打得准。～ ***a bone in the mouth*** [***teeth***] 【海】开足马力破浪前进。～ ***a flag*** 〔美俚〕无业游民改姓易名旅行。～ ***a safe*** 【美棒球】慢慢跑。～ ***a torch for*** 见 torch 条。～ ***a tune*** 准确地唱,一板一拍地唱。～ ***all*** [***everything***] ***before one*** [***it***] 获巨大成功,势如破竹,所向无敌。～ (*sb*.) ***along*** 使人佩服(*They were all carried along by his speech*. 他们都佩服他的话)。～ ***away*** 1. 带去,拿去,搬去;冲走;获得(印象)。2. 使冲昏头脑,使入迷,使神魂颠倒(*Music has carried him away*. 音乐使他陶醉)。～ ***back*** 拿回,带转来;使回想,使想起。～ ***down*** 搬下;取下;结转;滚入。～ ***forward*** 1. 结转,滚入,转入(下页,下期等)。2. 使进行;推进,扩张(业务);发扬(～ *the glorious tradition forward* 发扬光荣传统)。～ (*sb*.) ***high and dry*** 逗恼,戏弄(某人)。～ ***into effect*** [***execution***] 实施,实行。～ ***it*** 占优势;取胜。～ ***off*** 1. 得(奖);夺去;诱拐;(病)夺去人命。2. 坚持(～ *it off well* 若无其事,装作无事。*He was carried off by cholera*. 他患霍乱死了)。～ ***on*** 1. 继续;经营,处理;开展。2. 不得体[狂乱,幼稚]地行动。3. 与…有暧昧关系;与…调情(*with*)。～ ***one's life in one's hands*** 冒生命危险。～ ***one's liquor like a gentleman*** 慢慢地喝(酒)。～ ***oneself well*** [***gracefully***] 举止彬彬有礼[文雅]。～ ***out*** 1. 完成,成就,了结。2. 开展;贯彻,落实,实行,执行(*He hasn't the funds to* ～ *out his design*. 他没有落实他的计划的资本)。～ ***over*** 1. 贮存(货物等)供下季供应。2. 将(账目等)结转(次页);〔英〕(在交易所中)将…转期交割。3.(从以前的阶段、领域等)继续下去,遗留下来。4. 延期至…。～ ***the baby*** 〔口〕担负麻烦工作;担任不愿担任的工作。～ ***the can*** 〔英口〕单独承担全部风险[责任]。～ ***the day*** 取胜。～ ***the house*** 博得满堂喝彩。～ ***the war into the enemy's country*** [***camp***] 在辩论中进一步反攻,反驳;(战争中)反攻。～ ***the world before one*** 取得大成功。～ ***things*** (***off***) ***with a high hand*** 用高压手段[采取断然措施]处理事情。～ ***through*** 1. 坚持到底,支持到底。2. 贯彻,实行,完成(计划等)。～ (*sth*.) ***too far*** [***to extremes***] 过度[走极端]。～ ***true*** 奏效,恰到好处。～ ***weight*** (意见等)有力,有份量;(人物)有势力[地位];【赛马】(使优势马匹)负担较多重量。～ (*sth*., *sb*.) ***with one*** 1. 随身携带(某物,某人);在记忆中保留(某事,某人)。2. 说服(某人)。**II** *n*. 1.(枪的)射程。2.〔英〕二轮车。3.〔Scot.〕云的去向,云,空。4. 运载,携带,运载[携带]方法;〔美〕运输,水陆联运;(两条水道间)陆上运送。5.【军】举枪(或掮枪)的姿势;持剑礼;旗手持旗前进的姿势。6.【高尔夫球】(球的)距离。7.【数】移位,进位;进位数,进位指令。8.〔美俚〕需用救护车[担架]运送的病人。～ **all** 〔美〕单马拉轻便篷车;万用旅行提包;大型载客汽车;【矿】轮式铲运机。～**-cot** 〔英〕= car bed. ～ **on** 1. *n*.(飞机乘客的)随身行李。2. *a*.(飞机乘客的行李)可随身携带的。～**out** *a*.(饭馆等)饭菜供携出店外的,外卖的,送饮食上门的。～**-over** 余存部分;遗留物;余量;【商】滞销品;【会计】滚存,结转

C

(~*-over influence* 后效)。~ **topper** (可放在机车顶上载送的)车顶小艇。

car·ry·ing [ˈkæriiŋ; ˋkærɪɪŋ] **I** *a*. **1**. 装载的。**2**. 运送的,运输的。**II** *n*. **1**. 运送,运输。**2**.【纺】垫纱,给线。~ **capacity** 装载量,负荷载,输送力;【电】含储电量,荷电量。~ **charge 1**. 拥有财产所带来的费用〔如纳税〕。**2**. (分期付款购货的)附加价格。~ **over**【股】递延交易。~**s-on**〔俚〕轻薄行为,蠢举,丑态。~ **trade** 运输业。

car·sick [ˈkɑːsik; ˋkɑrˏsɪk] *a*. 晕车的。**-ness** *n*.

Car·son [ˈkɑːsn; ˋkɑrsn] *n*. 卡森〔姓氏,男子名〕。~ **City** 卡尔逊城〔美国内华达州首府〕。

C

cart [kɑːt; kɑrt] **I** *n*. **1**. (二轮运货)马车,大车;手推车。**2**. 一车之量。*a rubber-tired* ~胶轮大车。*a bullock* ~牛车。*be in the* ~〔俚〕为难,陷于困境,被打败。*put* [*set*] *the* ~ *before the horse* 前后倒置,本末颠倒。**II** *vt*. 用车装运。—*vi*. **1**. 赶运货马车。**2**.〔俚〕装运到过远的地方。~ *off* (强行)运走,拿走,带走(~ *yourself off*! 去你的!)。

cart·age [ˈkɑːtidʒ; ˋkɑrtɪdʒ] *n*. 马车运输;(马车)运费。

Car·ta·ge·na [ˌkɑːtəˈdʒiːnə, Sp. ˌkartaˈxeinɑ; ˏkɑrtəˋdʒinə, ˏkɑrtɑˋhenɑ] *n*. **1**. 卡塔赫纳〔哥伦比亚港市〕。**2**. 卡塔赫纳〔西班牙港市〕。

carte [kɑːt; kɑrt] *n*. (击剑手)手掌向上刺敌人右胸的姿势(=quart)。~ *and tierce* 剑术。

carte [kɑːt; kɑrt] *n*. **1**.〔F.〕菜单;价目表。**2**. 名片;〔罕〕纸牌。**3**.〔*pl*.〕纸牌戏。**4**.〔罕〕地图,海图。*à la* ~ 点菜。~ *blanche* [ˈkɑːtˈblɑ̃ːnʃ; ˋkɑrtˋblɑnʃ] 白纸;署名空白纸;全权委任。~ *de visite* [ˈkɑːtdəvi(ː)ˈziːt; ˋkɑrtdəvi(ɪ)ˋzit] 名片;(旧时作名片用的)小相片。

car·tel [kɑːˈtel; ˋkɑrtl̩] *n*. **1**. 俘虏交换协定。**2**. 决斗书,挑战书。**3**. 卡特尔,联合企业;政党间的联盟。**-ship** *n*. 俘虏交换船。

car·te·li·za·tion [ˌkɑːtəlaiˈzeiʃən; ˏkɑrtələˋzeʃən] *n*. 卡特尔化。

car·tel·ize [kɑːˈtelaiz; ˋkɑrtəˏlaɪz] *vt*., *vi*. (把…)组成卡特尔。

Car·ter [ˈkɑːtə; ˋkɑrtɚ] *n*. 卡特〔姓氏,男子名〕。

cart·er [ˈkɑːtə; ˋkɑrtɚ] *n*. 赶(运货)马车的人。

Car·te·sian [kɑːˈtiːzjən; kɑrˋtiʒən] **I** *a*. (法国哲学家)笛卡儿(Descartes)的;笛卡儿哲学的。**II** *n*. 笛卡儿哲学的信徒。~ **co-ordinates**【数】笛卡儿坐标。~ **devil** [**diver**]【物】浮沉子。~ **geometry** 解析几何。**-ism** *n*. 笛卡尔哲学[主义]。

cart·ful [ˈkɑːtful; ˋkɑrtful] *n*. (运货马车)一车的量。

Car·thage [ˈkɑːθidʒ; ˋkɑrθɪdʒ] *n*.【史】(北非)迦太基。

Car·tha·gin·i·an [ˌkɑːθəˈdʒiniən; ˏkɑrθəˋdʒɪnɪən] *a*., *n*. 迦太基(Carthage)的[人]。

Car·thu·sian [kɑːˈθjuːziən; kɑrˋθjuziən] **I** *n*. **1**. 卡尔特教团〔1084 年 St. Bruno 在法国 Chartreuse 山中成立的教团,提倡苦修冥想〕。**2**. (英国)卡尔特公学的学生[校友]〔该公学即 Charterhouse School,校址即原来的卡尔特教团修道院〕。**II** *a*. **1**. 卡尔特教团的。**2**. 卡尔特公学学生[教友]的。

car·ti·lage [ˈkɑːtilidʒ; ˋkɑrtl̩ɪdʒ] *n*.【解】软骨(组织)。

car·ti·lag·i·nous [ˌkɑːtiˈlædʒinəs; ˏkɑrtəˋlædʒənəs] *a*.【解】软骨(质)的。

cart·load [ˈkɑːtləud; ˋkɑrtˏlod] *n*. (运货马车)一车的装载量;〔口〕大量。*come down* (*on sb*.) *like a* ~ *of bricks* 大骂(某人),怒责。

car·to·gram [ˈkɑːtəgræm; ˋkɑrtəˏgræm] *n*. 统计图。

car·to·graph [ˈkɑːtəgrɑːf; ˋkɑrtəˏgræf] *n*. 地图,(特指)插图地图。

car·tog·ra·pher [kɑːˈtɔgrəfə; kɑrˋtɑgrəfɚ] *n*. 制图员。

car·to·graph·ic, -i·cal [ˌkɑːtəˈgræfik(əl); ˏkɑrtəˋgræfɪk(əl)] *a*. 制图的。

car·tog·ra·phy [kɑːˈtɔgrəfi; kɑrˋtɑgrəfɪ] *n*. 图法,制图学。

car·to·man·cy [ˈkɑːtəuˌmænsi; ˋkɑrtəˏmænsɪ] *n*. 纸牌占卜。

car·ton [ˈkɑːtən; ˋkɑrtn] *n*. **1**. 纸板,卡片纸;纸(板)匣;一纸匣的量[东西]。**2**. 靶心;正中靶心(的子弹)。

car·toon [kɑːˈtuːn; kɑrˋtun] **I** *n*. **1**. (壁画、织锦等的)草图,底图。**2**. (报刊上的)漫画;连环画。**3**.【影】动画(=animated ~s)。**II** *vt*., *vi*. **1**. (为…)画草图,(为…)画底样。**2**. (使)漫画化;(把…)画成漫画[动画]。**-ist** *n*. 底图画家;漫画家;动画画家。

car·touch(e) [kɑːˈtuːʃ; kɑrˋtuʃ] *n*. **1**.【建】(柱头、纪念碑等的)涡卷饰。**2**. (古埃及碑上王和神的名字周围一种椭圆形的)象形文字花框。**3**. 装饰镜板。**4**.〔废〕弹药筒。

car·tridge [ˈkɑːtridʒ; ˋkɑrtrɪdʒ] *n*. **1**.【军】弹药筒;子弹。**2**.【物】释热元件;【无】拾音器心座;(电唱机上的)针头。**3**.【机】夹头,卡盘;灯座;(圆珠笔上盛油墨的)笔芯。**4**.【摄】软片,胶卷。*a ball* ~实弹。*a blank* ~空弹。~ **bag** 弹药包。~ **belt** 子弹带,弹链。~ **box** (串在皮带上的)子弹盒。~ **case** 药筒;子弹壳。~ **chamber** 药室;弹膛。~ **clip** (机关枪等的)弹夹。~ **igniter**【火箭】爆管,导火管。~ **paper** 弹壳纸,火药纸;图画纸。~ **pouch** 弹药盒。

car·tu·lar·y [ˈkɑːtjuləri; ˋkɑrtʃuˏlərɪ] *n*. **1**. 契据[证书]集,契据登记簿。**2**. 契据登记员;契据[记录]保存处。

cart-wheel, cart wheel [ˈkɑːt*h*wiːl; ˋkɑrt*h*wil] *n*. **1**. 大型车轮。**2**.〔俚〕大银币;五先令银币,〔美俚〕一元银币。**3**.〔俚〕(四肢张开,像轮子转动似的)打虎跳;侧身筋斗。*turn* [*throw*] ~翻侧身筋斗。

Cart·wright [ˈkɑːt-rait; ˋkɑrtˏraɪt] *n*. 卡特赖特〔姓氏〕。

cart·wright [ˈkɑːt-rait; ˋkɑrtˏraɪt] *n*. 车匠。

car·un·cle [ˈkærəŋkl; ˋkærʌŋkl] *n*. **1**. (鸡的)肉冠,肉瘤。**2**.【解、医】肉阜,息肉。**3**.【植】脐阜,种阜。

car·va·crol [ˈkɑːvəkrɔl, -krəul; ˋkɑrvəkrɑl, -krol] *n*.【化】香芹酚。

carve [kɑːv; kɑrv] **I** *vt*. **1**. 切割,切开(盘中的肉)。**2**. 雕刻,刻;〔喻〕开拓(*out*)。~ *a figure out of stone* 用石头雕像。*an image* ~*d out of stone* 石像。—*vi*. **1**. 做雕刻工。**2**. 切开熟肉。~ *a niche* **1**. 挖出壁龛。**2**.【美体】创记录。~ *for oneself* 自由行动。~ (*stone*) *into* 把(石头)雕成。~ *out a career for oneself* 独立谋生,自己开辟前途。~ *out a victory*【美体】费九牛二虎之力获胜。~ (*a head*) *out of* 用…雕刻(头像)。~ *out one's* [*a*] *way* 开辟道路(~ *out a way through the enemy* 杀开一条血路)。~ *up* 切成几份,分切(肉等),瓜分,划分(遗产等)。~**-up**〔俚〕分得的一份(战利品等)。**II** *n*.〔美俚〕(作为食物、菜肴的)肉。

car·vel [ˈkɑːvəl; ˋkɑrvl̩] *n*. =caravel.

car·vel-built [ˈkɑːvəl-ˌbilt; ˋkɑrvəl-ˏbɪlt] *a*.【船】(船体木板)平镶的。

carv·en [ˈkɑːvən; ˋkɑrvən] *a*.〔古〕雕刻的。

Car·ver [ˈkɑːvə; ˋkɑrvɚ] *n*. 卡佛〔姓氏〕。

carv·er [ˈkɑːvə; ˋkɑrvɚ] *n*. **1**. 雕刻师,雕工,切肉人。**2**. 切肉刀;〔*pl*.〕切肉用具。*a* ~ *in wood* = *a wood* ~ 木刻家,木雕者。

carv·ing [ˈkɑːviŋ; ˋkɑrvɪŋ] *n*. **1**. 雕刻(术);雕刻物,雕刻品。**2**. 切肉。~ **fork** 切肉叉。~ **knife** 切肉刀。

Car·y [ˈkɛəri; ˋkɛrɪ] *n*. 卡里〔姓氏,男子名〕。

car·y·at·id [ˌkæriˈætid; ˏkærɪˋætɪd] *n*. (*pl*. ~*s*, ~*es* [-iːz; -iz])【建】女像柱。

cary(o)- *comb*. *f*. 核: *caryo*psis.

car·y·op·sis [ˌkæriˈɔpsis; ˏkærɪˋɑpsɪs] *n*. (*pl*. **-op·ses** [-siːz; -siz], **-op·si·des** [-sidiːz; -sɪdiz])【植】颖果。

car·zi·no·my·cin [ˈkɑːzinəuˈmaisin; ˋkɑrzɪnoˋmaɪsɪn] *n*.【药】癌霉素。

ca·sa·ba [kəˈsɑːbə; kəˋsɑbə] *n*. **1**.【植】(产于小亚细亚卡萨巴的)香瓜,甜瓜。**2**.〔美俚〕球。

Ca·sa·blan·ca [ˌkæsəˈblæŋkə; ˏkæsəˋblæŋkə] *n*. 卡萨布兰卡〔即 Dar el Beida 达尔贝达〕〔摩洛哥港市〕。

cas·al [ˈkeisəl; ˋkesl] *a*.【语法】(关于)格的。

ca·sa·va [kəˈsɑːvə; kəˋsɑvə] *n*. = cassava.

cas·bah [ˈkɑːzbɑː, ˈkæs-; ˋkɑzbɑ, ˋkæs-] *n*. 1.(北非)要塞,城堡。2. 北非城市;〔C-〕(阿尔及尔的)古旧闹市。

cas·ca·bel [ˈkæskəbel; ˋkæskə͵bɛl] *n*. 1.(由炮口装弹的炮的)尾座,尾钮。2.【动】响尾蛇;(响尾蛇的)响尾。3. 球形穿孔的铃。~ **plate**【军】尾座板。

cas·cade [kæsˈkeid; kæsˋked] I *n*. 1.(陡岩落下的)瀑布;【园艺】人工瀑布。2. 瀑布状物;波形花边。3.【物】级;级联,串联;【无】格,栅,格状物;【空】叶栅;【化】阶式蒸发器。II *vt*., *vi*. 1.〔罕〕(使)成瀑布落下。2.(使阶式地)串接,串联。

cas·car·a [kæsˈkɑːrə; kæsˋkɛrə] *n*.【植】药鼠李(= ~ buckthorn)。~ **sagrade** [sɑːˈgrɑːdə; sɑˋgrɑdə] 药鼠李皮〔可作缓泻剂〕。

cas·ca·ril·la [ˌkæskəˈrilə; ͵kæskəˋrɪlə] *n*. 1.【植】卡藜,苦香皮〔加斯加利刺(*Croton eluteria*)〕。2. 加斯加利刺的树皮〔用作兴奋剂,健胃剂〕。

CASE = computer-aided software engineering【计】计算机辅助软件工程。

case[1] [keis; kes] *n*. 1. 情况,状况;真相。2.(实)例,事例。3. 诉讼(事件),案件,判例;问题。4. 立场,主张;论据,论辩。5. 病症;病例;病人,患者。6.〔美口〕怪人;迷恋(的对象)。7.【语法】格。*a* ~ *of poverty* 穷苦的状况。*a* ~ *for conscience* 道义问题,良心问题。*a* ~ *for life and death* 生死问题。*a* ~ *in point* 恰当的实例,范例。*a* ~ *of smallpox* 天花病人。*a civil* [*criminal*] ~民事[刑事]诉讼。*a murder* ~杀人事件[案件]。*a leading* ~判(决)例。*That is not the* ~. 事实不是那样。*The plaintiff has no* ~. 原告无话可辩。*a gone* ~不可救药的人。*a hard* ~难症;难处的人,难缠的人;无赖,光棍。*a singular* ~奇例;怪人。***as is often the case*** 这是常有的事(*He was absent, as is often the* ~. 他没有来,这是常有的事)。***as the ~ may be*** 看情形,根据具体情况。***as the ~ stands*** 照现在的状况,事实上。***be in good*** [***evil***] ~ 幸福[不幸福],境况好[不好],身体好[不好]。~ ***by*** ~ 逐一,一件一件地;相机行事地,具体问题具体处理。***Circumstances alter ~s***. 随机应变。***drop a*** ~ 撤回诉讼。***give the ~ for*** [***against***] ***sb***. 作出对某人有利[不利]的判决。***in all ~s*** 一切,在一切情况下(*to proceed in all* ~*s from the interests of the people* 一切从人民的利益出发)。***in any*** ~ 无论如何,总之。***in*** ~ 1. 如果,若是,假如万一…,在…的时候〔用作连词〕(*In* ~ *it should rain, don't expect me*. 如果天下雨,我就不来了)。2. 以防,免得〔用作连词〕(*Take your umbrella, in* ~ *it rains*. 带伞去吧,以防下雨)。3. 作为准备;以防万一。〔用作副词〕(*It may rain, you'd better take your umbrella* (*just*) *in* ~. 天可能下雨,你最好带上伞以防万一)。***in ~ of*** 要是,如果,万一(*in* ~ *of war* 如果[万一]发生战争。*in* ~ *of need* 遇必要时,在紧急时)。***in nine ~s out of ten*** 十之八九,多半(*He will not come in nine* ~*s out of ten*. 他十之八九[多半]不会来了)。***in no*** ~ 决不。***in some ~s*** 有时候。***in the ~ of*** 就…说,至于…,论到,提到。***in this*** [***that***] ~ 既然是这[那]样,假若是这[那]。***just in*** ~ 以防万一;作为准备。***lay the*** ~ 陈述。***make out*** [***state***] ***one's*** ~ 摆明自己的理由。***put*** (***the***) ~ ***that***...〔古〕比如说,假定。***such*** [***that***] ***being the*** ~ 情况既然如此,因此。***There are ~s where***.... 有时候…。~ **book** 专题资料[案例]汇编。~ **history** 病历;个人历史。~ **law**【法】判例法〔以判例为根据的法律〕。~ **lawyer** 熟悉判例的律师。~ **load** 办案量;病例数。~ **note**〔美〕一元钞票。~-**sheet** *n*. 病史记录。~**study** *n*. 个案研究法(从一组个案研究得出总的结论和原则的社会学或教育学研究方法)。~ **work** (对申请户状况进行调查等的)社会福利工作;(社会学家进行的)个别情况调研。

case[2] [keis; kes] I *n*. 1. 箱,盒。2. 鞘,袋,套子,壳,罩,容器。3. 外侧,外板;框架。4.(一)组,一对,两个。5.〔美俚〕旅行箱。6.【印】活字(分格)盘。7.〔美口〕元,块。*a jewel* ~宝石盒。*a knife* ~刀鞘。*upper* [*lower*] ~【印】大写[小写]字盘;大写[小写]字母。*work at* ~排字。*a 5-* ~ *note* 一张五元钞票。II *vt*. 1. 把…装入箱内[袋内];把…插入鞘内;给…加框。2. 包,围(*with*; *up*; *over*)。3.〔美俚〕查看(地点),观察,窥探(尤指罪犯作案前的察看地点)。~ ***the joint***〔美俚〕(罪犯作案前的)现场窥探。~ **bay**【建】桁间。~ **bottle** (装箱)方瓶;有套瓶。~**harden** *vt*. 1.【冶】使(铁合金)表面硬化,淬火。2. 使厚颜无耻,使冷酷无情。~-**hardened** 1.【冶】表面硬化的。2.(思想等)已定型的;无情的。~ **knife** 带鞘小刀;餐刀。~ **shot** 霰弹。~ **worm** *n*.【虫】蛴螬。

ca·se·ase [ˈkeisieis; ˋkesɪes] *n*.【生化】酪蛋白酶。

ca·se·ate [ˈkeisieit; ˋkesɪ͵et] *vi*.【医】干酪性坏死。

ca·se·a·tion [ˌkeisiˈeiʃən; ͵kesɪˋeʃən] *n*. 1. 变成干酪,干酪化。2.【医】干酪状坏死。

ca·se·fy [ˈkeisiˌfai; ˋkesə͵faɪ] *vt*., *vi*.(使)变成酪状。

ca·se·in [ˈkeisiːin; ˋkesɪɪn] *n*.【化】酪朊,酪蛋白;酪素。

ca·se·in·o·gen [ˌkeisiˈinədʒən, keiˈsinə-; ͵kesɪˋɪnədʒən, keˋsɪnə-] *n*.【生化】酪素原,酪蛋白原。

case·mate [ˈkeismeit; ˋkesmet] *n*.【军】1.(堡墙上的)掩蔽部。2. 隐蔽炮台,暗炮台。3.【海】(军舰上的)炮塔。

Case·ment [ˈkeismənt; ˋkesmənt] *n*. 凯斯门特〔姓氏〕。

case·ment [ˈkeismənt; ˋkesmənt] *n*. 1.(可以开关的)窗框。2.〔诗〕窗;窗帘布。3.【建】窗扉,孔模。~ **cloth** 细棉布。~ **window** (普通的)玻璃窗。

ca·se·ose [ˈkeisiˌəus; ˋkesɪ͵os] *n*.【生化】酪脲。

ca·se·ous [ˈkeisiəs; ˋkesɪəs] *a*. 干酪(状)的。

ca·sern(e) [kəˈzəːn; kəˋzɜn] *n*.〔常 *pl*.〕(设防城镇中的)兵营。

cash[1] [kæʃ; kæʃ] I *n*. 现款,现金;〔口〕钱;小额支票。*a hard* ~硬币。*idle* ~〔口〕游资。***be in*** [***out of***] ~ 有[无]现款。***be short of*** ~ 现金不足,支付短少。~ ***and carry***【商】现金出售运输自理。~ ***down***【商】即期现款,即付(*sell for* ~ *down* 现卖)。~ ***in hand*** 现有金额(=〔美〕~ ***on hand***)。~ ***on delivery*** 货到收款〔略 **C.O.D.**〕;售价。***equal to*** ~〔口〕真正有价值[功劳]的。***keep the*** ~ 做现金出纳。***run out of*** ~ 现金短缺。II *vt*. 1. 把…兑换现款;为…付[收]现款(*for*)。2.【牌】先出(赢牌)。~ *a check* 把支票兑现。—*vi*. 赚钱。~ ***in***〔美俚〕1. 赚到钱,抓到赚钱的机会。2. 死。(*After her husband* ~*ed in, she lived with her sons*. 丈夫死后,她和儿子住在一起。) 3. 清算,决算,结束;断绝关系。4. 兑换成现金;变卖财产。5. 预先准备;乘机行事。~ ***in on***〔美口〕用…赚钱;利用(~ *in on one's ability to speak* 利用自己的口才)。~ ***in one's checks*** [***chips***] (赌毕)以筹码换现钱;〔俚〕死。~ **account** 现金账。~ **articles** 现金证券。~ **bar** 现卖饮料柜台〔与免费供应的 open bar 相对〕。~**book** 现金账(簿)。~**box** 钱箱[柜]。~**boy** (往来营业柜台与现金账台之间的)送款童子。~ **card**(可在自动提款机上提款的)现金卡。~ **carrier** 送款机。~ **cow** 摇钱树,可源源不断挤出现金的金牛。~ **credit** 暂欠货款。~ **crop**【农】商品作物。~ **customer**〔美〕买票入场的人。~ **dispenser** 自动提款机(= ~ machine)。~**less** *a*. 不用现钞的。~**less society** 不用现钞的信用卡社会。~ **payment** 付现。~ **price** 现款售价。~ **register** 现金收入记录机,现金出纳机。~ **sale** 现卖。

cash[2] [kæʃ; kæʃ] *n*.〔*sing*., *pl*.〕(印度和中国旧时的)铜钱,小铜币。

ca·shaw [kəˈʃɔː; kəˋʃɔ] *n*.【植】南瓜,倭瓜(= cushaw)。

cash·ew [kæˈʃuː; kæˋʃu] *n*.【植】(美洲热带的)槚如树(属);腰果(槚如树坚果或其果仁, = cashew nut)。

cash·ier[1] [kæˈʃiə; kæˋʃɪr] *n*. 出纳员;〔美〕(银行的)财务主任。~**'s order** [**cheque, check**] 银行本票。

ca·shier[2] [kəˈʃiə; kəˋʃɪr] *vt*. 1. 把…撤职;驱逐,革除。2.

废除,抛弃。

cash·mere [kæʃˈmiə; ˋkæʃmɪr] ***n***. 开士米〔喀什米尔产细羊毛;细羊毛绒线,织物,呢子〕,开士米围巾[羊毛衫,呢大衣]。~ **hair** 开士米山羊毛。~ **silk** 开士米毛葛。

cas·ing [ˈkeisiŋ; ˋkesɪŋ] ***n***. **1**. 装箱,装袋,入鞘。**2**.〔集合词〕包装箱[鞘、袋、筒、框等]。**3**.(窗等的)框子;围子;围墙。**4**.(做香肠用的)肠衣。**5**. 外(车)胎;套管;罩壳。

ca·si·no [kəˈsiːnəu; kəˋsino] ***n***. [It.] **1**.(可跳舞;赌博的)夜总会。**2**.(意大利的)小别墅,小住宅。**3**.(公园等处的)凉棚。**4**. 一种纸牌戏。~ **feet** 赌场脚病〔指长时间站着的赌徒易患的腿脚疼痛或肿胀疾病〕。

C

cask [kɑːsk; kæsk] ***n***. 桶;一桶。

cas·ket [ˈkɑːskit; ˋkæskɪt] ***n***. **1**. 珠宝盒[信件盒等]。**2**.(知识等的)宝库。**3**.〔美〕棺材;骨灰盒。

Cas·lon [ˈkæzlən; ˋkæzlən] ***n***. 卡斯隆[姓氏]。

Cas·pi·an [ˈkæspiən; ˋkæspɪən] ***a***. 里海(附近)的。~ **Sea** 里海。

casque [kæsk; kæsk] ***n***. **1**.〔主持〕盔。**2**.【植】盔瓣。

Cass [kæs; kæs] ***n***. 卡斯[姓氏]。

cas·sa·ba [kəˈsɑːbə; kəˋsɑbə] ***n***.【植】香瓜,甜瓜(=casaba)。

Cas·san·dra [kəˈsændrə; kəˋsændrə] ***n***. **1**. 卡姗德拉〔女子名,爱称 Cass〕。**2**. 卡姗德拉〔荷马史诗中 Troy 王 Priam 之女,能预知祸事〕。**3**. 不受人相信的凶事预言者。

cas·sa·tion [kæˈseiʃən; kæˋseʃən] ***n***.【法】(原判决的)撤销,废除。*the Court of C-* (法国、比利时等国的)最高上诉法院。

cas·sa·va [kəˈsɑːvə; kəˋsɑvə] ***n***. **1**.【植】木薯属 (Manihot) 植物。**2**. 木薯属植物的根[淀粉]〔可做面包和食用淀粉〕。

cas·se·role [ˈkæsərəul; ˋkæsəˏrol] ***n***. **1**.(有柄)砂锅,砂锅菜肴。**2**.【化】勺皿;瓷勺,柄皿。

cas·sette [kɑːˈset; kæˋset] **I** ***n***. **1**.(放珠宝或文件的)匣子;摄影胶卷暗匣;弹夹。**2**. 录音带盒。**3**.〔口〕盒式录音带。**II** ***vt***. 用盒式磁带[胶卷或录像磁带]录制。~ **tape recorder** 盒式录音机。~ **television** [**TV**] 盒式录像(电视机)。

Cas·sia [ˈkæsiə; ˋkæʃə] ***n***.【植】山扁豆属;〔c-〕低级肉桂。~ *bark* [*lignea*] 桂皮,肉桂。~ *oil* 肉桂油。

cas·si·mere [ˈkæsimiə; ˋkæsəˏmɪr] ***n***. 开士米细毛呢(=cashmere)。

Cas·si·o·pe·ia [ˌkæsiəˈpi(ː)ə; ˏkæsɪəˋpiə] ***n***.【天】仙后座(=~'s Chair)。

cas·si·o·pe·ium [ˌkæsiəˈpiːəm; ˏkæsɪəˋpiəm] ***n***.【化】镥(=lutecium)。

cas·sis [kæˈsiː; kæˋsi] ***n***. 黑醋栗酒[常掺入苦艾酒]。

cas·sit·er·ite [kəˈsitərait; kəˋsɪtəˏraɪt] ***n***.【矿】锡石。

cas·sock [ˈkæsək; ˋkæsək] ***n***. **1**.(教士穿的)黑袍法衣;军人长大衣;女外套。**2**.〔喻〕牧师,教士。

cas·sou·let [ˌkæsuˈlei; ˏkæsʊˋle] ***n***. 砂锅炖肉豆。

cas·so·war·y [ˈkæsəwɛəri; ˋkæsəˏwɛrɪ] ***n***.【动】食火鸡。

cast [kɑːst; kæst] **I** ***vt***. (***cast***; ***cast***) **1**. 投,扔,掷,抛。★此义动词通常用 throw, cast 只用于若干特殊句子。**2**. 丢弃,抛弃;脱掉(衣服);(蛇)脱(皮),(鸟)换(毛),(鹿)换(角);(树)落(叶);(马)脱落(掌铁)。**3**.(兽)早产,(果树)落(果)。**4**.【冶】浇铸,铸造;【印】把(纸型)浇成铅版。**5**. 计算;合计。**6**.【剧】分配(角色),选派(角色)。**7**.【法】使败诉。**8**. 解雇,辞退,赶走,撵走;淘汰(不及格学生)。**9**. 投射(影子、光线) (*on*);(眼光)钉住(某物)。**10**. 筑,挖造。**11**. 算(卦),占卜。**12**.【海】使改变航向。**13**. 使弯曲[翘起];扭弯。~ *anchor* 抛锚。~ *a net* 撒网。~ *seed* 撒种,播种。~ *a vote* 投票。~ *a dice* 掷骰子。~ *the lead*【海】锤测(水深)。~ *the blame on sb*. 加罪[嫁祸]于人。~ *a shoe* (马)掉了铁掌。~ *a spell on sb*. 迷惑人。~ *a stone at sb*. 拿石子打人;攻击[中伤]人。~ *a glance at* 把(眼光)钉住,用(眼光)一扫。~*a* (*new*) *light on* 给与(新的)解决线索[解释]。~*accounts* 计算。*be*.~ *in a different mould* 性质[气质]不同。*be* ~ *in a suit* 败诉。*be* ~ *in* [*for*] *damages* 被判决赔偿损失。*be* ~ *in heroic mould* 有英雄的性格。~ *a lot* 抽签。—***vi***. **1**. 抛出钓丝,垂钓。**2**.〔英方〕呕吐。**3**. 计算。**4**. 占卜,算卦;〔古〕预测;筹划。**5**.〔Scot.〕褪色。**6**.【猎】分头追寻。**7**.【海】改变航向。**8**. 浇铸成形。**9**. 产。*Timber* ~*s*. 木料会起翘。*Overheated metals may* ~ *badly*. 加热过甚的金属可能难浇铸成型。*The wheat* ~*s well*. 小麦年景好。~ ***about*** **1**. 设法,计划。**2**.【海】掉转航向。~ ***about for*** **1**. 找,寻觅;搜集;物色。**2**. 考虑,想(方法等)。**3**.(船)向…掉头。~ ***ashore*** (浪把船)抛到岸上。~ ***aside*** 抛弃,排除,废除(习惯等),消除(疑虑等)。~ ***away*** 抛弃;浪费;排斥;使(船只)破坏(*be* ~ *away* 漂流)。~ ***back*** 退回;恢复;追溯;回想。~(*sth*. [*sb*.]) ***behind*** 把…抛在脑后;疏远。~(*past deeds*) ***behind one's back*** (把往事)忘掉,置之脑后。~ (*sth*.) ***in sb.'s teeth*** 以(某事)当面责备某人。~ ***beyond the moon*** 任意推测。~ ***by*** 放弃;排除。~ ***down*** 推倒,打掉;打倒;放低,压低;使胆寒(*be* ~ *down* 丧胆,意气沮丧)。~ ***forth*** 抛出;逐出。~ (***in***) ***one's lot with*** 与…共命运。~ ***into the shade*** 使黯然失色;使向隅。~ ***loose*** 解开,放开;(自行)放开。~ ***off*** **1**. 丢弃,脱掉(衣服);抛弃,放弃。**2**.【纺】织完,收针。**3**.【海】放(船),解(缆)。**4**.【印】(据原稿)计划篇幅[版面]。~ ***on*** 急忙穿上(衣服);起针编织。~ ***oneself on*** [***upon***] 委身于,依赖,仰仗。~ ***out*** **1**. 扔出;逐出,赶出。**2**. 吐出,呕吐。**3**.〔Scot.〕吵闹,争吵。~ ***over***【纺】绕针。~ ***up*** **1**. 合计,计算。**2**. 责备。**3**. 呕吐,吐出。**4**. 打上,摔上;堆起(泥土)。**5**.〔Scot.〕突然出现;(云)密集;责备 (*to*)。**II** ***n***. **1**. 投;掷骰子;抛石子;撒网撒;垂钓;一掷,一举,试。**2**.【冶】浇铸,铸造;铸型,模子;铸成品。**3**.(目光)投射;瞥见;轻微的斜视[眼睛的一种缺陷]。**4**.(容貌、性质等的)特征;外观;倾向,型式;色调;种类。**5**. 计算。**6**. 角色分配,演员;演员表。**7**.【海】锤测。**8**.【印】版;纸版,铅版。**9**.(木板等的)反翘;(弓的)弹力。**10**. 脱落之物,(蛇的)蜕皮;(蚯蚓等翻到地面的)泥土(等)。*a bow's* ~一箭的射程。*a* ~ *of the net* 撒一次网,一网。*a good* ~(钓鱼或撒网的)好地方。*try another* ~再试一试。*a* ~ *in the eye* 轻微的斜视。*a woman of the old* ~旧式女人。*a man of noble* ~ 人品高尚的人。*an all star* ~名演员大会演。~*of features* 容貌。~ *of mind* 脾气。~ *of thought* 思想倾向。***the last*** ~ 最后一着;最后机会。~ **charge** (火箭发动机的)浇注火药柱。~ **iron** 铸铁。~ **steel** 铸钢。

Cas·ta·li·a [kæsˈteiliə; kæsˋtelɪə] ***n***.【希神】帕纳苏斯(*Parnassus*)山的神泉;诗的灵感的源泉。**Cas·ta·li·an** [kæsˈteiliən; kæsˋtelɪən] ***a***. 诗的灵感源泉的。

cas·ta·nets [ˌkæstəˈnets; ˏkæstəˋnets] ***n***.〔*pl*.〕【乐】响板〔套在大中指上舞蹈时合击发音〕。

cast·a·way [ˈkɑːstəwei; ˋkæstəˏwe] **I** ***n***. **1**. 遭难船;坐船遇难的人。**2**. 漂泊无依的人,流浪者,光棍。**II** ***a***. **1**. 遭了难的。**2**. 为世人所抛弃的;流浪的。

caste [kɑːst; kɑst] ***n***. **1**.(印度世袭的)种姓〔分婆罗门 (Brahman),刹帝利 (Kshatriya),吠舍 (Vaisya),首陀罗 (Sudra)四等〕;(世袭的)阶级;等级(制度)。**2**.(昆虫的)职别〔如工蜂等〕。~ *system* 种姓等级制度。*lose* ~ 失却社会地位,失去特权。

cas·tel·lan [ˈkæstələn; ˋkæstələn] ***n***.(古时的)城主,堡主,寨主。

cas·tel·la·ny [ˈkæstileini; ˋkæstəlenɪ] ***n***. **1**. 城主职位。**2**. 城堡领地。

cas·tel·lat·ed [ˈkæsteleitid; ˋkæstəˏletɪd] ***a***. **1**. 造成城形的,构造如城的。**2**. 有城的,多城的。

cas·tel·la·tion [ˌkæsteˈleiʃən; ˏkæstɛˋleʃən] ***n***. **1**. 城堡形建筑。**2**.【建】雉堞墙。

cast·er [ˈkɑːstə; ˋkæstɚ] *n*. 1. 投掷者。2. 赌博者。3. 铸工。4.〔印〕铸字机(= casting machine)。5. 计算者。6. 占卜者,算命先生。7. 分配角色的人。8. = castor[2].

cas·ti·gate [ˈkæstigeit; ˋkæstə͵get] *vt*. 1. 惩戒,严厉批评。2. 鞭责。3. 修订(文章等)。**-ga·tion** [ˌkæstiˈgeiʃən; ͵kæstɪˋgeʃən] *n*.

cas·ti·ga·tor [ˈkæstigeitə; ˋkæstə͵getɚ] *n*. 1. 惩戒者。2. 鞭责者。3. 修订者。

Cas·tile [kæsˈtiːl; kæsˋtil] *n*. 卡斯提尔〔古代西班牙中部北部地名〕。~ **soap** 橄榄油香皂。

Cas·til·i·an [kæsˈtiliən; kæsˋtɪlɪən] I *a*. 卡斯提尔(Castile) 的。II *n*. 1. 卡斯提尔人。2. 卡斯提尔语。3. 纯正的西班牙语。

cast·ing [ˈkɑːstiŋ; ˋkæstɪŋ] *n*. 1. 投,掷。2.【冶】铸造;铸件。3.【动】脱弃,脱落物〔如毛、皮等〕。4. 计算。5. 想法,手法。6.(木材等的)翘曲。7.【剧】配角。~ **vote**(赞成与反对同数时,主席所作的)决定性投票。

cast-i·ron [ˈkɑːstˈaiən; ˋkæstˋaɪɚn] *a*. 1. 铸铁制的。2. 硬的,无伸缩性的。3. 刚直的,不通融的。4. 强健的。*a ~ law* [*regulation*] 严厉的法律[规章]。*~ will* 坚强的意志。*a ~ stomach* 强健的胃。

cas·tle [ˈkɑːsl; ˋkɑsl] I *n*. 1. 城;(城堡形)建筑物。2. 船楼。3.(国际象棋中的)车。4.〔the C-〕都柏林城。5.(不受侵扰的)避居地。*the Windsor C-*(英国的)(英国国王居住的)温莎宫。*~ in the air* [*in Spain*] 空中楼阁,空想。II *vt*. 1. 把…置于城堡中;筑城堡防卫。2.(下国际象棋时)用车护(王)。~**-builder** 空想家。~ **nut**【机】开花螺帽。

cast·off [ˈkɑːstˈɔ(ː)f; ˋkæst͵ɔf] *a*. 被丢弃的,无用的,废弃的。~ *clothes* 不再穿的旧衣服。

Cas·tor [ˈkɑːstə; ˋkæstɚ] *n*.【天】北河二〔双子座 α 星〕。

cas·tor[1] [ˈkɑːstə; ˋkæstɚ] *n*. 1.【动】海狸。2. 海狸皮;海狸皮帽。3.〔俚〕帽。4.【药】海狸香。5. 一种大衣呢。

cas·tor[2] [ˈkɑːstə; ˋkɑstɚ] *n*. 1.(餐桌上的)调味瓶,调味瓶架子。2.(桌椅等的)脚轮。~ **sugar**(餐桌上用的)细白砂糖。

cas·tor[3] [ˈkɑːstə; ˋkɑstɚ] *n*.【海】(暴风雨时的)桅头电光。

cas·tor[4] [ˈkɑːstə; ˋkɑstɚ] *n*. 蓖麻(= ~-oil plant)。~**-bean**〔美〕蓖麻(子)。~**-oil** 蓖麻油(*a ~-oil artist* [*merchant*]〔美俚〕医生,郎中)。

cas·trate [kæsˈtreit; kæsˋtret] *vt*. 1. 割除(睾丸、卵巢),阉割;【植】去雄。2.〔喻〕删改,窜改(书籍)。

cas·tra·tion [kæsˈtreiʃən; kæsˋtreʃən] *n*. 阉割;【植】去雄;〔喻〕删改,窜改。

cas·tra·to [kɑːsˈtrɑːtəu; kɑsˋtrɑto] *n*. (*pl*. *-ti* [-iː; -i]) 阉歌手〔过去为使男孩歌手保持女高音或女低音的声调而把他阉割〕。

cas·u·al [ˈkæʒjuəl; ˋkæʒʊəl] I *a*. 1. 偶然的;碰巧的。2. 临时的,不定期的;即席的。3.〔俚〕荒唐的,漫不经心的。4. 随便的,非正式的。*a ~ visitor* 不速之客。*a ~ labourer* [*worker*] 临时工。*a ~ revenue* 临时收入。*the ~ poor*(需要临时救济的)无业游民。*a ~ remark* 临时想起的话,信口而出的话。*a ~ air* 满不在乎的态度。~ *clothes* 便服。~ *decisions* 草率的决定。*a very ~ sort of a man* 非常不尊重别人的人。II *n*. 1. 零工,散工(= ~ labourer)。2.〔英〕〔*pl*.〕(无业)游民;不定期接受救济金的人;衣着随便而花哨的年轻人。3.【军】暂编人员〔临时编在某一单位等候调配的军官士兵〕。4. 偶然来访者。~ **day** 便装日。~ **house**〔英〕济贫院。~ **restaurant**(不讲排场而专门创造一种轻松气氛的)休闲饭店。~ **ward**〔英〕(济贫院的)临时收容所。**-ness** *n*.

cas·u·al·ly [ˈkæʒjuəli; ˋkæʒʊəlɪ] *ad*. 偶然,不在意地;临时。*not to treat this ~* 不要等闲视之。

cas·u·al·ty [ˈkæʒjuəlti; ˋkæʒʊəltɪ] *n*. 1. 事故,横祸,灾难;损坏。2. 死伤(者),受伤者。3.〔*pl*.〕【军】伤亡(人数)。*heavy casualties* 巨大的伤亡[损失]。*the total casualties* 伤亡总数。~ *clearing station* 野战医院〔略 C.C.S.〕。~ **insurance** 灾害保险;火险。~ **ward** 战地临时收容室。

cas·u·a·ri·na [ˌkæsjuəˈriːnə; ͵kæʒuəˋrinə] *n*.【植】(大洋洲、西印度产)木麻黄。

cas·u·ist [ˈkæzjuist; ˋkæʒʊɪst] *n*. 独断论者;决疑者;诡辩家。

cas·u·is·tic(al) [ˌkæzjuˈistik(əl); ͵kæʒʊˋɪstɪk(əl)] *a*. 独断的;决疑的;诡辩的。

cas·u·ist·ry [ˈkæzjuistri; ˋkæʒʊɪstrɪ] *n*. 1. 决疑法;诡辩术。2. 用伦理学判断行为的是非。

ca·sus [ˈkɑːsus; ˋkesəs] *n*.〔L.〕事件;案例。~ ***bel·li*** [ˈbeliː; ˋbeli]〔L.〕开战的理由,宣战的原因[藉口]。~ ***foe·der·is*** [ˈfedəris; ˋfɛdərɪs] 条约中所涉及的事项。

CAT = 1. clear-air turbulence 晴空湍流(颠簸)。2. College of Advanced Technology.(英)工科大学,工学院。3. computerized axial tomography 计算机化轴向层面 X 射线摄影法。

cat[1] [kæt; kæt] I *n*. 1. 猫,(尤指)母猫〔公猫为 tomcat〕;猫科动物(= the Cats, the great Cats)〔狮、虎、豹等〕;〔英〕山猫(= lynx)。2. 脾气不好[爱骂人]的女人;爱抓人的孩子。3.(运煤等的)独桅艇。4.【海】起锚滑车。5.(无论如何摆放都用三脚站立的,有三对活动脚的)六脚器。6.(一种有九条皮带的)九尾鞭(= cat-o'-nine-tails)。7.〔英〕(一种击球游戏用的)橄榄状木球;(用棒击木球的)木球戏(= tipcat)。8.〔美俚〕(任何)人,男人;娼妓;流动工人;爵士音乐演奏者[爱好者]。9. 可惜,可怜;遗憾,抱歉。10.〔美俚〕"猫毒"〔一种与脱氧麻黄碱相似的毒品〕。*a barber's ~* 面有病容和饥色的人。***A ~ has nine lives***. 猫有九条命〔不易死亡〕。***a ~ in the pan***〔俚〕临阵脱逃者,叛徒。***A ~ may look at a king***. 猫也有权看看国王〔小人物也该有些权利〕。***a queer ~*** 怪人。***a sweel ~*** 好家伙。*as sick as a ~* 作恶心,不舒服;患重病。***bell the ~*** 为别人冒险,为公共的事冒险。***Care killed the ~***. 久患伤身。~***-and-mouse act***〔美俚〕绝食囚犯假释令。~***s and dogs*** 1.〔口〕大量。2.〔美俚〕不值钱的股票,不确实的有价证券;杂品。~***'s eye-brow*** [***meow***]〔美俚〕了不得的,极美的,极好的。~***'s pyjamas*** [***pajamas***]〔美俚〕(自以为)了不起的东西,不平常的东西。~***'s sleep*** 打盹。***Dog my ~s!***〔口〕畜牲!该死的! ***enough to make a ~ laugh*** [***speak***] 真可笑[漂亮],真蠢[好]。***fight like Kilkenny ~s*** 死斗,死拼。***lead a cat-and-dog life*** 过猫狗生活〔特指夫妇经常吵架的生活〕。***let the ~ out of the bag*** 使秘密泄漏,露马脚。***Let the old ~ die***.〔儿〕静等秋千自身慢慢停下来。***like a ~ on hot bricks*** [***tiles***] 焦躁不安,如热锅上的蚂蚁。***make a ~'s paw of sb***. 利用他人作为利己的工具。***no*** [***not***] ***room to swing a ~ in*** 地方窄狭。***not a ~'s chance*** 毫无机会。***rain ~s and dogs*** 大雨倾盆。***see which way the ~ will jump*** 观望形势(然后行动)。***shoot*** [***jerk***] ***the ~***(因饮酒过多而)呕吐。***tear a ~*** 妄语,傲语。***That ~ won't jump***.〔口〕那可不行,那一手行不通。***turn the ~ in the pan*** 变节,见利思迁。***wait*** [***watch***] ***for the ~ to jump*** 观望形势(然后行动)。***walk the ~ back*** 通过再现事件的全过程以了解真相。***When the ~'s away, the mice will play***. 猫儿不在,老鼠翻天。II *vt*. (-tt-) 1.【海】把(锚)吊放在锚架上。2.(用九尾鞭)鞭打。—*vi*. 1.〔口〕呕吐。2. 宿娼。~**-and-dog** *a*. 1. 不和谐的,爱争吵的。2.〔俚〕投机性的。~**-and-mouse** *a*. 折磨人的。~**bird**〔美〕猫声鸟(鸫属)(*~bird seat* 有权力的职位)。~ **block** 吊锚滑车。~**boat** 独桅艇。~ **burglar**〔俚〕(由屋顶潜入的)窃贼。~**call** 1. *n*.(会议或剧场内表示反对或喝倒彩的)嘘声。2. *vt*. 发嘘声反对,奚落。3. *vi*. 发出嘘声。~ **cracker**(石油)裂化催化器。~ **davit**【船】有档锚吊杆。~ **door** 猫门〔板壁等上供猫出入的小门〕。~**-eyed** *a*.

C

能在黑暗中辨别东西的。~ **fall**【船】吊锚索。~ **fish**【动】鲇;(美洲)鮰。~**gut** 肠线〔绷球拍等用〕;弦乐器。~**head** 锚架。~**hole**【船】锚链孔。~ **hook**【船】吊锚钩。~ **house**〔美俚〕妓院。~-**ice** 1. ***n***. (水面下降后与水面隔开的)乳白色薄冰。2. ***a***. 乳状的;发泡的;不规则的。~**lap**〔美俚〕(茶等)非浓缩的饮料。~-**let**〔美〕小猫,顽皮的姑娘。~ **nap** 打盹。~ **nip**【美植】假荆芥。~-**o'-nine'-tails** [ˈkætəˈnainteilz; ˋkætəˋnaɪntelz] 1. 九尾鞭。2.【植】香蒲。~**'s cradle** 编花框,翻绞绞〔小孩用绳子玩的游戏〕。~**'s -eye**【矿】猫眼石玻璃珠;(汽车等的)小型反光装置。~**'s-foot**【植】积雪草,连钱草。~-**shark** 鲨鱼。~-**silver**〔古〕云母。~ **skinner**〔美俚〕牵引车的司机。~-**sleep** 打盹(= cat nap)。~**'s paw** 1. 被人利用[愚弄]的人。2.【海】微风,猫掌风(*make a ~'s-paw of sb*. 拿某人当工具[傀儡])。~**'s stabber**〔美俚〕刺刀。~**'s-tail** ***n***.【植】问荆。~ **suit**(连衫)喇叭裤。~-**tackle**【海】起锚绞车。~**tail**【植】香蒲属植物。~**walk**〔美俚〕狭窄的人行道,桥上人行道;狭窄的通道。~**'s-whisker**【无】触须,晶须;〔*pl*.〕〔美俚〕(自以为)了不起的东西,引以自夸的东西,不平常的东西(= ~**'s pyjamas**)。~**walk** 狭窄人行道[通道]。

cat² [kæt; kæt] ***n***.〔军俚〕履带式拖拉机,任何有履带的车辆。

cat. = catalog(ue); catechism.

cat(a)- *comb. f*. 表示"在下";"相反";"完全";"关于": *cata*comb, *cata*genesis.

cat·a·bol·ic [ˌkætəˈbɔlik; ˏkætəˋbɑtɪk] ***a***.【生理】分解代谢的。-**al·ly** ***ad***.

ca·tab·o·lism [kəˈtæbəlizəm; kəˋtæbl̩ˏɪzəm] ***n***.【生理】分解代谢(*opp*. anabolism)。

ca·tab·o·lite [kəˈtæbəlait; kəˋtæbəˏlaɪt] ***n***.【生理】分解(代谢)产物。

ca·tab·o·lize [kəˈtæbəˌlaiz; kəˋtæbəˏlaɪz] ***vi***., ***vt***.【生理】(使)发生分解代谢。

cat·a·caus·tic [ˌkætəˈkɔːstik; ˏkætəˋkɔstɪk] **I** ***a***.【物】反射焦散曲线的。**II** ***n***.【物】反射焦散曲线。

cat·a·chre·sis [ˌkætəˈkriːsis; ˏkætəˋkrisɪs] ***n***. (*pl*. -*ses* [-siːz; -siz])【修】1. (在特定上下文中)语词的误用〔如 *the fruitful river in the eye*〕。2. (由于不了解语源、修辞手法生硬等导致的)比喻的乱用,引申错误〔如 blind mouth 的比喻〕。

cat·a·clas·tic [ˌkætəˈklæstik; ˏkætəˋklæstɪk] ***a***.【地】碎裂的。

cat·a·cli·nal [ˌkætəˈklainl; ˏkætəˋklaɪnəl] ***a***.【地】下倾型的。

cat·a·clysm [ˈkætəklizəm; ˋkætəˏklɪzəm] ***n***. 1. 特大洪水。2.【地】(地壳突然隆起而造成的)灾变;天翻地覆;(政治或社会的)大变动,大动乱。-**al**, -**mic** ***a***.

cat·a·comb [ˈkætəkəum; ˋkætəˏkom] ***n***. 1.〔常 *pl*.〕地下墓窟。2. 酒窖。

cat·ad·ro·mous [kæˈtædrəməs; kəˋtædrəməs] ***a***.【动】(鱼等)下海繁殖的;(为产卵而顺流)入河的,降河性的(*opp*. anadromous)。~ *fish* 降海[河]产卵鱼。

cat·a·falque [ˈkætəfælk; ˋkætəˏfælk] ***n***. 灵柩台;灵柩车。

Cat·a·lan [ˈkætələn; ˋkætlən] **I** ***a***. (西班牙)加泰罗尼亚(Catalonia) 地区的;加泰罗尼亚人[语]的。**II** ***n***. 加泰罗尼亚人[语]。

cat·a·lase [ˈkætəleis; ˋkætəles] ***n***.【生化】过氧化氢酶,接触酶。

cat·a·lec·tic [kætəˈlektik; ˏkætəˋlɛktɪk] ***a***.【韵】最后缺少一音节的,韵脚不完全的。

cat·a·lep·sy [ˈkætəlepsi; ˋkætəˏlɛpsɪ], **cat·a·lep·sis** [-ˈlepsis; -ˋlɛpsɪs] ***n***.【医】僵住(症状),强直性昏厥,僵强症。

cat·a·lep·tic [ˌkætəˈleptik; ˏkætəˋlɛptɪk] ***a***., ***n***. 僵住症的(患者)。

cat·a·lin [ˈkætəlin; ˋkætəlɪn] ***n***.【商标】铸塑酚醛塑料。

cat·a·lo [ˈkætələu; ˋkætəˏlo] ***n***. (*pl*. ~, ~*s*)〔美〕(家牛与野牛杂交生下的)杂种牛。

cat·a·log(ue) [ˈkætəlɔg; ˋkætl̩ˏɔg] **I** ***n***. 1. (图书或商品)目录,目录册。2.〔美〕(大学的)学校周年大事表,学校便览。★美语中多用 catalog, 但 2. 义则多用 catalogue. ~ *of articles for sale* 待售品目录。**II** ***vt***., ***vi***. 1. (为…)编目录,(把…)编目。2. (把…)按目录分类。~ **card** 目录卡。~ **drawer** 目录抽屉。~ ***raisonné*** [rezɔˈnei; rɛzɑˋne]〔F.〕附有说明的分类目录。~ **shopping** 目录购物〔顾客按商店送上门的商品目录勾出需购物品寄出后,由商店送货上门〕。

ca·ta·log(u)·er [ˈkætəlɔgə; ˋkætəˏlɔgɚ] ***n***. 编目者。

ca·tal·pa [kəˈtælpə; kəˋtælpə] ***n***.【植】梓;〔C-〕梓树属。

ca·tal·y·sis [kəˈtælisis; kəˋtæləsɪs] ***n***. (*pl*. -*ses* [-siːz; -siz])【化】接触反应,触媒作用,催化(作用)。~ **converter** 催化转化器〔汽车上的一种消除污染装置〕。

cat·a·lyst [ˈkætəlist; ˋkætl̩ɪst] ***n***.【化】触媒,催化剂,接触剂〔又作 catalytic agent〕;〔喻〕触发因素,〔口〕(善用热情、言语等打动他人的)有感染力的人。

cat·a·lyt·ic [ˌkætəˈlitik; ˏkætl̩ˈɪtɪk] ***a***.【化】催化(的)。-**i·cal·ly** ***ad***.

cat·a·lyze [ˈkætəlaiz; ˋkætl̩ˏaɪz] ***vt***.【化】催化。-**r** ***n***. 催化剂。

cat·a·ma·ran [ˌkætəməˈræn; ˏkætəməˋræn] ***n***. 1. 长筏,捆扎筏。2. 连筏船,双连小船。3.〔口〕泼妇,悍妇。

cat·a·me·ni·a [kætəˈmiːniə; ˏkætəˋminɪə] ***n***.〔*pl*.〕【医】月经。

cat·a·mite [ˈkætəmait; ˋkætəˏmaɪt] ***n***. 娈童。

cat·a·mount, cat·a·moun·tain [ˈkætəmaunt, ˌkætəˈmauntin; ˋkætəˏmaʊnt, ˏkætəˋmaʊntɪn] ***n***.【动】野猫,山猫;〔美〕美洲狮;猞猁狲;〔喻〕爱吵架的人。

Ca·ta·ni·a [kəˈteinjə; kəˋtenjə] ***n***. 卡塔尼亚〔意大利港市〕。

cat·a·pho·ra [ˈkætəfərə; ˋkætəfərə] ***n***.【语】后指〔与前指(anaphora)相对应意为所指物出现于代词之后〕。

cat·a·pho·re·sis [ˌkætəfəˈriːsis; ˏkætəfəˋrisɪs] ***n***.【物、化】阳离子电泳;电(粒)泳。

cat·a·phyll [ˈkætəˌfil; ˋkætəˏfɪl] ***n***.【植】低出叶,芽苞叶。

cata·plane [ˈkætəplein; ˋkætəplen] ***n***.【空】弹射(起飞)飞机。

cat·a·pla·si·a [ˌkætəˈpleiʒiə; ˏkætəˋpleʒɪə] ***n***. (*pl*. -*siae* [-ʒiiː, -ziiː; -ʒii, -zii])【生】退变。-**plas·tic** [-ˈplæstik; -ˋplæstɪk] ***a***.

cat·a·plasm [ˈkætəplæzəm; ˋkætəˏplæzəm] ***n***.【医】糊剂,泥罨[敷]剂。

cat·a·plex·y [ˈkætəˌpleksi; ˋkætəˏplɛksɪ] ***n***.【医】猝倒。

cata·pult [ˈkætəpʌlt; ˋkætəˏpʌlt] **I** ***n***. 1.【史】弩炮;石弩。2.〔英〕(儿童玩的)弹弓。3.【军】(导弹、飞机等的)弹射器;弹射座椅。**II** ***vt***. 1. 用弩炮[弹弓、弹射机]发射;用发射机射出(飞机)。2.〔美〕突然把…捧出名。—***vi***. (像被弹射似地)迅猛行动。~ **passage** 飞机弹射道。

cat·a·ract [ˈkætərækt; ˋkætəˏrækt] **I** ***n***. 1. 急瀑布,大瀑布;暴雨;奔流。2.【医】(白)内障。3.【机】(矿山唧筒的)水力制动机,节动机。**II** ***vt***., ***vi***. (使)像瀑布似地注流。

ca·tarrh [kəˈtɑː; kəˋtɑ] ***n***. 1.【医】卡他,(鼻)黏膜炎。2.〔英口〕感冒。*bronchial* ~支气管炎。-**al**, -**ous** ***a***.

cat·ar·rhine [ˈkætərain; ˋkætəraɪn] ***n***., ***a***.【动】狭鼻猿(的)。

ca·tas·ta·si [kəˈtæstəsis; kəˋtæstəsɪs] ***n***. (*pl*. -*ses* [-ˌsiːz; -ˏsiz]) 1. (古代戏剧中悲剧收场前或为全剧尾声作伏线的)高潮。2. (修辞中引出主旨的)开端叙述。

ca·tas·tro·phe [kəˈtæstrəfi; kəˋtæstrəfɪ] ***n***. 1. 大变动,突变,激变。2. 灾祸,事故;(人生的)灾难,大祸。3.【地】

灾变。4.【剧】(尤指悲剧的)结局。

cat·a·stroph·ic [ˌkætəˈstrɔfik; ˏkætəˋstrɑfɪk] *a*. 1. 大突变(灾难)的。2. 悲惨结局的。

ca·tas·tro·phism [kəˈtæstrəfizəm; kəˋtæstrəfɪzəm] *n*. 1.【地】灾变说。2. 大难难免论,劫数难逃论。**-phist** *n*., *a*. (信奉)灾变说的(人);(信奉)大难难免论的(人)。

cat·a·to·ni·a [ˌkætəˈtəuniə; ˏkætəˋtonɪə] *n*.【精】紧张症。**-ton·ic** [-ˈtɔnik; ˋtɑnɪk] *a*., *n*. 紧张症的(患者)。

Ca·taw·ba [kəˈtɔːbə; kəˋtɔbə] *n*. 1. (北美印第安 Sioux 族的)卡托巴部族人;卡托巴语。2. (美国东部产的)卡托巴葡萄;卡托巴白葡萄酒。

catch [kætʃ; kætʃ] **I** *vt*. (*caught* [kɔːt; kɔt]; *caught*) 1. 捕捉;逮着,捕获,拦截;用网捕(鸟等);迷惑住。2. 看到,看穿,看出,发觉。3. 听到,听清;领悟,了解,理会(意味)。4. 使进退两难,使害怕;(暴风雨等)袭击。5. 赶(得上)(火车等);追着。6. 钩住;挂住,绊住;(因说错话等而)突然中止(发言等);【机】挡住;(盆)承受(雨水),接住(球等);【棒球等】接住球(使击球员退出);打(中);碰着;(偶然)碰见。7. 感染,传染上,患(传染病等)。8. 着(火),烧。9. 惹得,引起(注意)。10. 遭受(处罚等)。11. 打(个盹),扫(一眼)。12. 〔美俚〕抽(烟)。~ *sb*. *by the arm* 抓住某人手臂。*be caught red-handed* 当场捉住。*A nail caught her dress*. 钉子挂住了她的衣服。~ *one's finger in a door* 门夹住指头。*The stone caught me on the nose*. 石头打中我的鼻子。*She caught him one in the eye*. 她在他的眼睛上打了一下。*The wind ~es a sail*. 风顶着船帆。*I caught* (*a*) *cold*. 伤了风,着了寒。*The flames caught the adjoining house*. 火延烧到隔壁。~ *one's breath* 忍住呼吸。*I did not ~ what you said*. 我没有听懂[清]你说什么。~ *the tune* 听出是什么曲调。*The dog ~es the scent*. 狗闻出臭迹。~ *a likeness* 画一个像。~ *a nap* 打个盹。~ *a glimpse of* 看一眼。—*vi*. 1. (想)捉住,(想)抓住 (*at*);(想)领悟 (*at*)。2. (门)被闩住,锁住;挂住,绊住,(手指)夹住,(脚)陷进 (*in*);〔英方〕(水)结冰;(声音等)闷住,塞住。3. 着火,发火。4. 传染;时兴,流行。5.【棒球】做接球员。6. 〔美口〕(庄稼)发芽。7. 〔英俚〕得人缘。*The match will not ~*. 火柴擦不着。*The kite caught in a tree*. 风筝被树挂住了。*The door lock ~es*. 这把门锁锁得牢。~ *for the entire game* (打棒球时)整场比赛都当接球手。*Will the disease ~*? 这病有传染性吗? *The lake ~es*. 〔英方〕湖面结薄冰了。***be caught in*** (*the rain*, *a trap*) 遇(雨);落入(陷阱,圈套)。***be caught over*** (指水面)结满了冰。~ ***a crab*** (划船时)一桨未划好[划得过深或未入水]。~ ***as*** ~ ***can*** 用尽一切办法,能抓到什么就抓到什么。~ ***at*** 抓住(东西);欢迎(意见等)(*He caught at the idea*. 他立即采纳了这个意见)。~ ***away*** 攫去,抢去。~ ***hold of*** 抓住,捉住;乘机抓住(对方的失言)。~ ***it*** 〔口〕挨骂,受责备,受罚 (*You will ~ it* (*hot*). 你会受(严厉)责备[处罚]的)。***Catch me*** (*at it*, *doing that*)! 〔口〕你看吧,我决不会干的。(*C- me ever telling him anything again*. 下次决不告诉他了)。~ ***off*** 睡着。~ ***on*** 〔口〕1. 投合人心,受欢迎(*The play caught on well*. 这场戏大受欢迎)。2. 理解,明白(*I don't ~ on*. 我不明白)。~ ***one's death*** (*of cold*) 因(重伤风)而死。~ ***out***【棒球】1. 接住球使击球员退出。2. 看破,看出,发觉 (*He was caught out*. 他的错误被发觉了)。~ ***sb***. ***at*** [***doing***]..., ~ ***sb***. ***napping*** 乘某人不注意。~ ***sb***. ***red-handed*** 当场捉住某人。~ ***the bird*** 睡午觉。~ ***the Speaker's eye*** (议会)获准发言。~ ***up*** 1. 追着,赶上,与…并驾齐驱 (*to*; *with*)。2. 扰乱(说话人)。3. 立即采纳(新意见、新词等)。4. 握住,吸住,把…卷入。5. 把…迅速拿[拾]起来。6. 指出差错 (*on*) (~ *sb*. *up on the details* 指出某人所说细节有出入)。**II** *n*. 1. 捕捉,把握;【棒球】接球,接球员;捕获数,渔获量。2. 利益;〔口〕希望得到的东西[人],动心的事物。3. (门的)拉手,把手,门扣,门钩。4. 陷阱,圈套,诡计;料不到的困难。5. (声息等的)梗塞,噎。6.【机】凸轮;制动器,掣子,轮档;抓爪;捕捉器;【化】(接)受器。7.【乐】滑稽轮唱歌曲;(歌曲的)片断。8. (庄稼的)茁壮。*a good ~* (*of fish*) 巨大的渔获量。*a great ~* 红人。*There is a ~ in his question*. 他的问话中有圈套。***by ~es*** 时而,常常,屡(停)屡(作),时(断)时(续) (*a diary written by ~es* 时断时续地写日记)。***no ~ = not much of a ~*** 买了上当的物品,不合算的东西。***the ~ of the season*** 社交季节中男女互相追逐。**III** *a*. 1. 引人注意的,有趣味的。2. 设有圈套的。*a ~ phrase* 妙语,警句。*a ~ question* 设有圈套的问题。~**all** 〔俚〕1. *n*. 垃圾箱;装零杂物品的东西,手提包;【化】截液器,分沫器;总受器。2. *a*. 包括诸色人等的,品种复杂的,包罗一切的。~**-as-~-can** 1. *n*. (各种抓法都可使用的)兰开夏式摔跤。2. *a*. 不择手段的;乱七八糟的;无计划的,胡搞的。~ **basin** 1. (阴沟等洞口的)滤污器。2. 贮水池。~**-colt** 〔美〕私生子。~ **crop**【农】间作;填闲作物。~ **cry** (旨在使人注意或争取支持的)呼号[口号]。~ **drain** 截水沟;承水渠。~ **fly**【植】捕蝇植物(如剪秋罗、麦瓶草)。~**-light** 反射光。~**line** 宣传性标语;【剧】滑稽插话,噱头。~**penny** *a*., *n*. 骗钱的(东西),花哨而不值钱的(东西)。~**-phrase** 警句,引人注意的话。~ **pit** = ~ **basin**. ~**pole**, ~**poll** 法警。~**-stitch** (裁缝的)Z形针迹。~**-up** (生产等停滞后的)加紧弥补。~**up** 〔美〕= ketchup. ~**weed**【植】猪殃殃。~**weight** *a*., *ad*. (参加比赛者)无体重限制的[地] (*a ~ weight wrestling match* 无体重限制的摔跤赛)。~**word** 1. 时髦语,流行语;标语,口号。2. (词典的)眉题[页上标示起迄的词]。3.【剧】(对话中引起对手接说的)提示语。4.【印】(印在上页右下角的下页首词)提示词。

Catch-22 [ˈkætʃ ˈtwentiˈtuː; ˋkætʃ ˋtwentɪˋtu] *n*. 第二十二条军规,不可逾越的障碍(美 J. Heller 小说的书名)。

catch-'em-a·live-o [ˈkætʃəməˈlaivəu; ˋkætʃəməlaɪvo] *n*. 捕蝇纸。

catch·er [ˈkætʃə; ˋkætʃɚ] *n*. 1. 捕捉者。2. 捕机;收集器;【化】(接)受器。3.【棒球】接球员。*a dust ~* 吸尘器。*a devil ~* 〔美俚〕牧师,教士。

catch·i·ly [ˈkætʃili; ˋkætʃɪlɪ] *ad*. 1. 有吸引力地,打动人地。2. 有欺骗性地,费解地。3. 时断时续地。

catch·i·ness [ˈkætʃinis; ˋkætʃɪnɪs] *n*. 1. 吸引性,动人之处。2. 迷惑性,费解之处。3. 断续性。

catch·ing [ˈkætʃiŋ; ˋkætʃɪŋ] *a*. 1. (疾病)传染性的。2. 动人的,迷人的,受欢迎的,有感染力的。

catch·ment [ˈkætʃmənt; ˋkætʃmənt] *n*. 1. 排水;集水。2. 贮水池。3. 流域。~**area**, ~**basin** 流域。

catch·y [ˈkætʃi; ˋkætʃɪ] *a*. 1. 投合时好的;动人的,迷人的。2. (曲调)易记的。3. (问题)费解的;易使人上当的,有圈套的。4. 断断续续的;反复不定的。

cate [keit; ket] *n*. 〔古〕美食;珍馐,美味;可口之物。

cat·e·chet·ic, cat·e·chet·i·cal [ˌkætiˈketik(əl); ˏkætəˋketɪk(l̩)] *a*. 1. 问答式(教学法)的。2.【宗】教义问答的。

cat·e·chin [ˈkætitʃin, -kin; ˋkætɪtʃɪn, -kɪn] *n*.【药】儿茶酸。

cat·e·chism [ˈkætikizəm; ˋkætəˏkɪzəm] *n*. 1. 问答教学法。2.【宗】教义问答集。3. (口试时的)盘问,提问。***put sb***. ***through a ~*** 详细盘问。

cat·e·chist [ˈkætikist; ˋkætəkɪst] *n*. 1. 问答式教学者。2. 传道师。

cat·e·chize [ˈkætikaiz; ˋkætəkaɪz] *vt*. 1. (常指宗教上)用问答法教授。2. 盘问。

cat·e·chol [ˈkætitʃəul; ˋkætəˏtʃol] *n*.【化】儿茶酚,焦儿茶酚,邻苯二酚(= pyrocatechol)。

C

cat·e·chu [ˈkætitʃuː; ˋkætəˏtʃu] ***n.***【药】儿茶。*Acacia* ～【植】儿茶。

cat·e·chu·men [ˌkætiˈkjuːmen; ˏkætəˋkjumən] ***n.*** **1.**【宗】新入教者;新信徒。**2.** 初学者,新来者。

cate·gor·e·mat·ic [ˈkætigɔriˈmætik; ˋkætɪgɑrɪˋmætɪk] ***a.***【逻】可单独使用的(*opp*. syncategorematic 必须与另一词结合使用的)。

cat·e·gor·i·cal [ˌkætiˈgɔrikəl; ˏkætɪˋgɔrɪkl] ***a.*** **1.**【哲】范畴的。**2.** 绝对的,无条件的。**3.** 明确的;直言的,断言的。～ **imperative**【伦】无上命令。～ **judg(e)ment** [**proposition**]【逻】直言判断[命题]。**-ly** ***ad.***

cat·e·go·rize [ˈkætigəraiz; ˋkætəgəˏraɪz] ***vt.*** 把…分门别类,把…分类。**-za·tion** [-ˈzeiʃən; -ˋzeʃən] ***n.***

cat·e·go·ry [ˈkætigəri; ˋkætəgorɪ] ***n.*** **1.** 类型,部门,种类,类别;类目。**2.**【哲、逻】范畴。**3.**〔*pl.*〕体重等级。*average* ～ *values*【数】各处理平均值。～ *of ships*【军】舰种。～ *of tax* 税目。～**killer**〔美〕(只专营某一类商品的)大型廉价零售店。～ **sales** (书籍)提类销售,按类发售。

ca·te·na [kəˈtiːnə; kəˋtinə] ***n.*** (*pl.* ***-nae*** [-niː; -ni])〔L.〕连锁,连续,链条。*a* ～ *of events* 一连串事故。

cat·e·nane [ˈkætnein; ˋkætnen] ***n.***【化】双环化合物。

ca·te·nar·i·an, cat·e·nar·y [ˌkætiˈnɛəriən, kəˈtinəri; ˏkætɪˋnɛrɪən, kəˋtinərɪ] ***n.***, ***a.*** **1.** 链(状的)。**2.**【数】悬链线(状的),垂曲线(的)。**3.** (电缆)吊线(的)。*a* ～ *bridge* 垂曲线桥。

cat·e·nate [ˈkætineit; ˋkætnˏet] ***vt.*** **1.** 链接;使连成一串。**2.**〔喻〕(滚瓜烂熟地)记住。

cat·e·na·tion [ˌkætiˈneiʃən; ˏkætɪˋneʃən] ***n.*** **1.** 链接;耦合。**2.** 熟记。

ca·ten·u·late [kəˈtenjulit, -leit; kəˋtenjəˏlɪt, -let] ***a.*** 链状的;链状排列的。

ca·ter[1] [ˈkeitə; ˋketə] ***vt.*** 为(宴会等)供应酒菜。～ *a party* 为酒会包办酒菜。—***vi.*** **1.** 供应伙食,给人包伙;包办宴席;筹办娱乐节目。**2.** 迎合,投合。～ *for* [*to*] *a banquet* 包办酒宴。～ *for* [*to*] *sb.'s enjoyments* 设法使某人高兴;为某人安排娱乐。

cater[2] [ˈkeitə; ˋketə] ***n.*** (骰子,纸牌的)四点。

cat·er·an [ˈkætərən; ˋkætərən] ***n.***〔Scot.〕苏格兰高地的强盗,绿林好汉,草莽英雄。

cat·er-cor·nered [ˈkætəˌkɔːnəd; ˋkætəˏkɔrnəd] **I** ***a.*** 对角线的。**II** ***ad.*** 成对角线地(= cater-corner)。

ca·ter-cous·in [ˈkeitəˌkʌzn; ˋketəˏkʌzn] ***n.***〔古〕密友,好友。

ca·ter·er [ˈkeitərə; ˋketərə] ***n.*** 包办伙食[宴席]的人;(娱乐节目等的)筹办者;逗人乐的人。

cat·er·pil·lar [ˈkætəpilə; ˋkætəˏpɪlə] ***n.*** **1.**【动】鳞翅目幼虫,蠋,毛虫。**2.**【机】链轨,履带;履带拖拉机(= ～ tractor)。**3.** 贪心汉。～ **track**[**tread**] (坦克车等的)履带。～ **grinder** 链式碎木机。～ **tractor**〔美〕履带拖拉机。

cat·er·waul [ˈkætəwɔːl; ˋkætəˏwɔl] **I** ***vi.*** (猫)叫春;(像叫春的猫一样)尖叫;〔蔑〕求爱,追求。**II** ***n.*** 猫的叫春声。

cat·form·ing [ˈkætˌfɔːmiŋ; ˋkætˏfɔrmɪŋ] ***n.***【化】催化重整。

cath- *pref.*〔用于送气音前〕= *cata-*,如:*catho*de.

Cath. = Catholic.

cath. = cathedral.

Catha·rine-wheel ***n.*** = Catherine-wheel.

ca·thar·sis [kəˈθɑːsis; kəˋθarsɪs] ***n.*** **1.**【医】导泻(法),通便(法);精神发泄。**2.**【哲】(通过对悲剧等艺术品的观赏而)感情净化。**3.** (精神分析学所说通过自觉或表达)优惧消解。

ca·thar·tic [kəˈθɑːtik; kəˋθartɪk] **I** ***n.***【医】泻药。**II** ***a.***【医】利泻的;洗涤(胃肠)的(= cathartical)。

Ca·thay [kæˈθei; kæˋθe] ***n.***〔古、诗〕中国。**-an** ***a.*** 中国(人)的。

ca·thect, ca·thec·ti·cize [kæˈθekt, -ˈθektəsaiz; kæˋθɛkt, -ˋθɛktəsˏaɪz] ***vt.*** (精神分析学所说)精神专注于(某人,某事或某种想法)。**-thec·tic** ***a.***

ca·the·dra [kəˈθiːdrə; kəˋθidrə] ***n.*** **1.** 主教座位。**2.** (教授的)讲坛,讲座。

ca·the·dral [kəˈθiːdrəl; kəˋθidrəl] **I** ***n.*** (英国教会等设有主教座位的)总教堂,大教堂(= ～ church);大圣堂,大会堂。**II** ***a.*** **1.** (像)大教堂的。**2.** 庄严的,权威的。～ **glass** 嵌花[马赛克]玻璃。

ca·thep·sin [kəˈθepsin; kəˋθɛpsɪn] ***n.***【生化】组织蛋白酶。

Cath·er [ˈkæðə; ˋkæðə] ***n.*** 卡瑟〔姓氏〕。

Cath·er·ine [ˈkæθərin; ˋkæθrɪn] ***n.*** 凯瑟琳(女子名)。～ **politician** 看风转舵的政治家。～ **wheel** **1.** 轮圈外缘装有倒钩的车轮。**2.**【建】轮形窗。**3.** 轮形图案。**4.** 轮转烟火。**5.** 侧身筋斗(*turn* ～*-wheels* 翻侧身筋斗)。

cath·e·ter [ˈkæθitə; ˋkæθɪtə] ***n.***【医】导(液)管。**-ize** ***vt.*** 在…插入导管。

ca·the·to·me·ter [ˌkæθiˈtɔmitə; ˏkæθɪˋtɑmɪtə] ***n.***【物】测高计,高差计。

ca·thex·is [kəˈθeksis; kəˋθɛksɪs] ***n.*** (精神分析学中所说的)精神专注〔指精神集中于某人,某事,某种想法或自己身上〕。

Cath·leen [ˈkæθliːn; ˋkæθlin] ***n.*** 凯瑟琳〔女子名, Catherine 的异体〕。

cath·ode [ˈkæθəud; ˋkæθod] ***n.***【电】阴极,负极。～ **leg** 阴极引线。～ **ray** **1.** (阴极发射出的)高速电子。**2.** 阴极射线。～**-ray gun** 电子枪。

Cath·o·lic [ˈkæθəlik; ˋkæθəlɪk] **I** ***a.*** **1.** 天主教的。**2.**〔c-〕统括一切的,普遍的;宽宏大量的。*Holy* ～ *Church* 圣公会。*Science is truly c-.* 科学是真正具有普遍性的。*His tastes are very c-.* 他的嗜好很广泛。**II** ***n.*** 旧教徒;(尤指)天主教徒;旧教信奉者〔指信奉宗教改革前的教会信条的人〕。**-i·cal·ly** ***ad.***

Ca·thol·i·cism [kəˈθɔlisizəm; kəˋθɑləˏsɪzəm] ***n.*** **1.** 天主教的信条[主张]。**2.**〔c-〕普遍性;宽宏大量。

cath·o·lic·i·ty [ˌkæθəˈlisiti; ˏkæθəˋlɪsətɪ] ***n.*** **1.** 普遍性;宽宏大量。**2.**〔C-〕= Catholicism.

ca·thol·i·cize [kəˈθɔlisaiz; kəˋθɑləˏsaɪz] ***vt.***, ***vi.*** **1.** (使)一般化,(使)普遍化。**2.**〔C-〕(使)变成天主教徒。

ca·thol·i·con [kəˈθɔlikən; kəˋθɑləkən] ***n.*** **1.** 万灵药。**2.**〔C-〕(希腊正教的)主教教堂。

cath·o·lyte [ˈkæθəlait; ˋkæθəlaɪt] ***n.***【化】阴极电解液。

cath·o·my·cin [ˌkæθəˈmaisin; ˏkæθəˋmaɪsɪn] ***n.***【药】新生霉素。

Cath·ryn [ˈkæθrin; ˋkæθrɪn] ***n.*** 凯瑟琳〔女子名, Catherine 的异体〕。

Cathy, Cathie [ˈkæθi; ˋkæθɪ] ***n.*** 凯茜〔女子名, Catherine 的昵称〕。

Cat·i·li·nar·i·an [ˌkætələˈnɛəriən; ˏkætəlɪˋnɛrɪən] **I** ***a.*** 从事阴谋[叛逆]活动的〔源出罗马进行阴谋活动的政治家 Catilina〕。**II** ***n.*** 参加阴谋活动的人;阴谋家。

cat·i·on [ˈkætaiən; ˋkætˏaɪən] ***n.***【化】阳离子,正离子(*opp*. anion)。

cat·ish [ˈkætiʃ; ˋkætɪʃ] ***a.***〔美俚〕美的;漂亮的。

cat·kin [ˈkætkin; ˋkætkɪn] ***n.***【植】葇荑花序;杨花;柳絮。

cat·like [ˈkætˌlaik; ˋkætˏlaɪk] ***a.*** 如猫的;无声的,偷偷的。

cat·ling [ˈkætliŋ; ˋkætlɪŋ] ***n.*** **1.** 小猫。**2.** (外科用)双刃小刀。**3.** 肠线;〔*pl.*〕弦乐器。

cat·mint [ˈkætmint; ˋkætˏmɪnt] ***n.***【植】猫薄荷。

cat·nip [ˈkætnip; ˋkætnɪp] ***n.***〔美〕= catmint.

C.A.T.O. = catapult-assisted take-off【空】弹射起飞。

Ca·to [ˈkeitəu; ˋketo] ***n.*** **1.** 加图〔人名〕。**2.** **Marcus Porcius** ～ 老加图〔234—149 B.C.,罗马政治家,将

军〕。3. **Marcus Porcius** ～ 小加图〔95—46 B.C.，罗马斯多噶派哲学家，政治家，为老加图之曾孙〕。

cat-o'-moun·tain [ˌkætəˈmauntn; ˏkætəˋmaʊntn̩] *n*. = catamountain.

cat-o'-nine-tails [ˌkætəˈnainˌteilz; ˏkætəˋnaɪnˏtelz] *n*. (*pl*. *-tails*) 九尾鞭。

ca·top·tric [kəˈtɔptrik; kəˋtɑptrɪk] *a*.【物】反射(镜)的。～ **system** 反射光组。

ca·top·trics [kəˈtɔptriks; kəˋtɑptrɪks] *n*. 〔*pl*.〕(动用单)【物】反射光学。

Cats·kill Mountains [ˈkætskil; ˋkætskɪl] 卡茨基尔山〔美国纽约州东部山脉〕(= the Catskills)。

cat·sup [ˈkætsəp; ˋkætsəp] *n*. 番茄酱[沙司](= ketchup)。

cat·(t)a·lo [ˈkætələu; ˋkætəˏlo] *n*. 〔美〕(野牛和家牛杂交生下的)杂种牛。

Cat·tell [kæˈtel; kəˋtɛl] *n*. 卡特尔〔姓氏〕。

cat·tery [ˈkætəri; ˋkætərɪ] *n*. **1**. 养猫场。**2**. 〔美俚〕妇女团体[公寓]，女生宿舍。

cat·ti·ly [ˈkætili; ˋkætɪlɪ] *ad*. **1**. 敏捷地。**2**. 狡猾地，恶毒地。**cat·ti·ness** *n*.

cat·tish [ˈkætiʃ; ˋkætɪʃ] *a*. 猫一般的；狡猾而阴险的，心怀不良的。

cat·tle [ˈkætl; ˋkætl̩] *n*. 〔*sing*., *pl*.〕**1**. 牛；家畜；〔俚〕马，牲口。**2**. 〔骂〕畜生。**3**. 〔美俚〕女学生。*beef* [*dairy*] ～肉[奶]牛。～ *breeding* 畜牧(业)。～ *for dual-purpose* 乳肉兼用牛。*C- low*. 牛叫。***kittle*** ～难以应付的人[事]。～**-lifter** 偷牛贼，偷家畜的贼。～**-lifting** 偷牛。～ **leader** 牛鼻环。～ **man** 〔英〕牧[养]牛人；〔美〕牧场主。～ **pen** 牛栏，牛圈，畜槛。～ **piece** (风景画家的)家畜画，牧牛图。～ **plague** 牛疫。～ **rustler** 〔美〕偷牛贼。～ **show** 家畜[畜牛]展览会。

cat·tle·ya [ˈkætliə, kætˈliə, -ˈleiə; ˋkætlɪə, kætˋlɪə, -ˋleə] *n*.【植】卡特来兰属植物。

cat·ty[1] [ˈkæti; ˋkætɪ] *n*. 斤〔中国过去使用的重量单位，等于0.5公斤或1.1023磅〕。

cat·ty[2] [ˈkæti; ˋkætɪ] *a*. = cattish.

CATV = **1**. Community antenna television 有线电视。**2**. cable TV.

Cau·ca·sia [kɔːˈkeiziə; kɔˋkeʒə] *n*. 高加索(高原)〔欧洲〕。

Cau·ca·sian [kɔːˈkeiziən; kɔˋkeʃən] **I** *a*. **1**. 高加索的；高加索人的，高加索语的。**2**.【人类】白种人的。**II** *n*. **1**. 高加索人；高加索语。**2**.【人类】白种人。

Cau·ca·soid [ˈkɔːkəsɔid; ˋkɔkəsˏɔɪd] **I** *a*. 高加索人种群的。**II** *n*. 高加索种群的人。

Cau·ca·sus [ˈkɔːkəsəs; ˋkɔkəsəs] *n*. **1**. 高加索山脉(= the ～ Mountains)。**2**. = Caucasia.

cau·cus [ˈkɔːkəs; ˋkɔkəs] **I** *n*. 〔美〕(政党等的)干部会议；秘密会议；核心小组；〔英〕(政党等)竞选指导委员会。**II** *vi*. 召开[参加]干部(秘密)会议；召开[参加]核心会议。

cau·dad [ˈkɔːdæd; ˋkɔdæd] *ad*.【解、动】向尾，向后；在后部。

cau·dal [ˈkɔːdl; ˋkɔdl̩] *a*.【解、动】尾的；尾部[侧]的，尾状的。～ *fin* 尾鳍。～ *appendage* 尾。

cau·date, cau·dat·ed [ˈkɔːdeit(id); ˋkɔdet(ɪd)] *a*.【动】有尾的。

cau·dil·lo [kɔːˈdiːljəu; kɔˋdiljo] *n*. 〔Sp.〕军事首脑；总指挥，(尤指游击队的)领导人。

cau·dle [ˈkɔːdl; ˋkɔdl̩] *n*. (病人食用的)粥汤〔粥中加入葡萄酒、番料、鸡蛋等〕。

caught [kɔːt; kɔt] catch 的过去式及过去分词。

caul [kɔːl; kɔl] *n*. **1**.【解】胎膜；大网膜。**2**. (旧时妇女的)发网，户内妇女头饰的后部。

caul- *comb*. *f*. = caulo-〔用于母音前〕。

caul·dron [ˈkɔːldrən; ˋkɔldrən] *n*. = caldron.

cau·les·cent [kɔːˈlesnt; kɔˋlɛsənt] *a*.【植】有茎的。

cau·li·flow·er [ˈkɔliflauə; ˋkɔləˏflauɚ] *n*. **1**.【植】花椰菜，菜花。**2**. 〔Scot.〕啤酒泡。**3**. 〔美俚〕(在拳击中打残废的)菜花耳(= ～ ear)。～ **code** 〔美俚〕拳赛规则。**C-Garden** 〔美〕= **Madison Square Garden** (纽约市的)麦迪逊广场花园。～ **vernacular** 〔美〕拳击用语[行话]。

cau·line [ˈkɔːlain; ˋkɔlɪn] *n*.【植】茎(上)的；茎上部的。

cau·lis [ˈkɔːlis; ˋkɔlɪs] *n*. (*pl*. *-les* [-liːz; -liz])【植】茎。

caulk [kɔːk; kɔk] *vt*. **1**. 用麻丝填塞(船缝)。**2**. 堵(缝)。**3**.【机】敛(钢板的)铆缝〔锤打铆好的钢板，使铆缝不致漏水、气〕。**-er** *n*. 填船缝工，敛铆缝工；堵缝的人；堵缝工具。**-ing** *n*. 堵缝；敛缝；挤缝，冲缝；砸边。

caulo- *comb*. *f*. 表示植物的"柄，茎"：*caulo*caline.

cau·lo·ca·line [ˌkɔːləuˈkeiliːn; ˏkɔloˋkelin] *n*.【植】成茎素。

caus. = causative.

caus·a·ble [ˈkɔːzəbl; ˋkɔzəbl̩] *a*. 可被引起的。**-a·bil·i·ty** *n*.

caus·al [ˈkɔːzəl; ˋkɔzəl] **I** *a*. **1**. (有)原因的；构成原因的；因果律的；【逻】表示原因的。**2**. 因果关系的。～ *relation* 因果关系。*a* ～ *force* 构成原因的力量。**II** *n*.【语法】表示原因的词[结构]。**-ly** *ad*.

cau·sal·gi·a [kɔːˈzældʒiə, -dʒi; kɔˋzældʒɪə, -dʒɪ] *n*.【医】灼痛。

cau·sal·i·ty [kɔːˈzæliti; kɔˋzælətɪ] *n*. **1**. 因果关系，因果性。**2**. 诱发性；原因作用。*the law of* ～因果律。

cau·sa si·ne qua non [ˈkɔːzə ˈsaini kwei ˈnɔn; ˋkɔzə ˋsaɪni kwe ˋnɑn] 〔L.〕不可缺少的原因[条件]，必要原因[条件]。

cau·sa·tion [kɔːˈzeiʃən; kɔˋzeʃən] *n*. **1**. 引起，惹起，导致。**2**. 因果关系。**3**. 原因作用，原因力。*the law of* ～ 因果律。

caus·a·tive [ˈkɔːzətiv; ˋkɔzətɪv] **I** *a*. **1**. 成为…的原因的，惹起…的。**2**.【语法】使役的。***be*** ～ ***of*** 为…的原因，引起…。～ **agent**【医】病原体。～ **value** 发展价值。～ **verb** 使役动词。**II** *n*.【语法】使役词，使役形式。

cause [kɔːz; kɔz] **I** *n*. **1**. 原因，起因；缘故，理由，根据，动机。**2**.【法】诉讼事由；诉讼案件；诉讼程序。**3**. 事业，事项，事件；(奋斗的)目标；问题。**4**. 主张，主义，目的，…运动。*the formal* ～形式原因。*the immanent* [*transient*] ～内[外]因。*the immediate* [*remote*] ～近[远]因。*the occasional* ～ 偶因，机缘。*a* ～ *for* (*complaint*) (抱怨)的原因[理由]。～ *and effect* 原因与结果，因果。～ *of* (*revolution*) (革命)事业。*the temperance* ～戒酒运动。***have*** ～ ***for*** (*joy*) 有理由(高兴)，当然(高兴)，应当(高兴)。***in the*** ～ ***of*** 为…(而工作等)。***make common*** ～ ***with*** 与…协力，与…合作，和…一致。***plead one's*** ～ 辩护，分辩。***show*** ～【法】提出理由，说明所以然。***the first*** ～【哲】第一推动力；【宗】造物主；上帝。***without*** (***due***) ～ 无缘无故。**II** *vt*. **1**. 成为…的原因，惹起，引起，使发生。**2**. 使遭受，给…带来，致使。～ *sb*.*'s ruin* 致使某人身败名裂。***be*** ～***d by*** 起因于，因…而起。～(*sb*.) ***to*** (*do*) 促使(人)(作)…。～(*sth*.) ***to be*** (*done*) 叫人(做)(某事、物)(*He* ～*d a house to be built*. 他叫人盖了一所房子)。

'cause [kɔːz; kɔz] *conj*. 〔口〕= because.

cause cé·lèb·re [kəuz seˈlebr; koz sɛˋlɛbr] (*pl*. ***causes cè·lèb·res*** [kəuz seˈlebr; koz sɛˋlɛbr]) 〔F.〕著名的[轰动一时的]讼案[论战]。

cause·less [ˈkɔːzlis; ˋkɔzlɪs] *a*. 无原因的；无理由的；偶然的。

caus·er [ˈkɔːzə; ˋkɔzɚ] *n*. 引起者；根由。

cau·se·rie [ˈkəuzəri(ː); ˋkozəri(ɪ)] *n*. 〔F.〕(*pl*. ～***s*** [-z; -z]) **1**. 漫谈，非正式讨论。**2**. (报章杂志上的)随笔，随感录。

cause·way, cau·sey [ˈkɔːzwei, -zei; ˋkɔzwe, -ze] **I** *n*.

C

1.（低湿地中的）堤道。2.（比马路高的）人行道。3. 公路。II *vt*. 在…上[穿过…]修建堤道[人行道,公路]。

caus·tic [ˈkɔːstik; ˋkɔstɪk] I *a*. 1.【化】腐蚀性的;苛性的。2. 讽刺的,刻薄的,挖苦的。3.【物】焦散的。～ *comments* 尖刻的评论。II *n*. 1. 刻薄;讽刺。2.【医】腐蚀剂。3.【物】焦散面;〔*pl*.〕焦散线。4.【化】苛性碱。*common* [*lunar*] ～【化】硝酸银。～ **curve**【物】焦散曲线。～ **potash**【化】苛性钾,氢氧化钾。～ **silver** 硝酸银。～ **soda**【化】苛性钠〔苏打〕,氢氧化钠,烧碱。～ **surface**【物】焦散面。**-al·ly** *ad*.

caus·tic·i·ty [kɔːsˈtisiti; kɔsˋtɪsətɪ] *n*. 腐蚀性;苛性度;（言语等的）刻薄,辛辣。

C

caus·tic·i·za·tion [ˌkɔːstisaiˈzeiʃən; ˏkɔstɪsaɪˋzeʃən] *n*.【化】苛化作用。

cau·ter·ant [ˈkɔːtərənt; ˋkɔtərənt] I *a*.（能）烧灼的。II *n*. 烙器,烙铁;有烧灼作用的物质。

cau·ter·i·za·tion [ˌkɔːtəraiˈzeiʃən; ˏkɔtəraɪˋzeʃən] *n*. 1.【医】烧灼,烙,腐蚀(作用)。2.（良心等的）麻木。

cau·ter·ize [ˈkɔːtəraiz; ˋkɔtəˏraɪz] *vt*. 1.【医】烙,烧灼;腐蚀。2. 使（良心等）麻木。

cau·ter·y [ˈkɔːtəri; ˋkɔtərɪ] *n*. 1.【医】烧灼(术),烙(术),腐蚀。2. 烧灼器,烙器。3. 烧灼剂,腐蚀剂。

cau·tion [ˈkɔːʃən; ˋkɔʃən] I *n*. 1. 小心,谨慎,慎重。2. 警惕;告诫,警告。3.〔Scot.〕【法】担保,保证。4.〔口〕须警惕的事[人];怪物,怪人。*Well, you're a* ～! 你这个要提防的家伙! 我可要留心你! *exercise* [*use*] ～ 小心,谨慎。*fling* ～ *to the winds* 不顾一切,莽撞从事。*for* ～*'s sake* 为慎重起见。*give* ～ *to* 警告,训诫。*take* ～ *against* 防备,提防,留心。*with* ～ 留心,慎重。II *vt*. 使小心,警告(*against, to do, not to do*);告诫。—*vi*. 告诫(*against*)。～ **money**〔英〕大学入学保证金;法学协会入会保证金。

cau·tion·a·ry [ˈkɔːʃənəri; ˋkɔʃənˏɛrɪ] *a*. 1. 警戒的,提醒注意的,告诫的。2.〔Scot.〕担保的,保证的。～ *advice* 忠告。～ *tales* 警诫性的故事。

cau·tious [ˈkɔːʃəs; ˋkɔʃəs] *a*. 谨慎的,小心的。*be* ～ *of* 留意,谨防。**-ly** *ad*. **-ness** *n*.

cav·al·cade [ˌkævəlˈkeid; ˏkævlˋked] *n*. 1. 骑兵队;车队;船队;一队人马。2. 游行队伍。

cav·a·lier [ˌkævəˈliə; ˏkævəˋlɪr] I *n*. 1. 骑士;（某种）勋章获得者。2. 骑士风度的男子,向妇女献殷勤的男子。3.〔美俚〕拳击选手。4.〔C-〕【英史】（查理一世时代的）保王党党员。II *a*. 1. 豪爽的,满不在乎的;勇敢的;傲慢的。2. 骑士风度的,向女子献殷勤的。3.〔C-〕（查理一世时代）保王党的。*He treated us in a* ～ *fashion*. 他待我们很不客气。III *vt*. 1. 护送(女人),(对女子)有骑士风度的。2. 态度傲慢。**-ly** *ad*.

ca·val·la [kəˈvælə; kəˋvælə] *n*. (*pl*. *-la*, *-las*)【动】1. 巨鲐,马鲛鱼(= cero)。2. 长面鲹(= crevalle)。★上列两种鱼。在英国亦称 horse mackerel.

cav·al·ry [ˈkævəlri; ˋkævlrɪ] *n*. 1.〔集合词〕(一队)骑兵;骑兵队。2.〔集合词〕骑者;马;〔废〕马术。3.【军】高度机动的地面部队。*heavy* [*light*] ～ 重[轻]骑兵。*a* ～ *orderly* 骑兵传令兵。～**man** 骑兵。～ **twill** 马裤呢。

ca·vate [ˈkeiveit; ˋkevet] *a*. 挖空岩石而成的;形成[像]山洞的。

cav·a·ti·na [ˌkævəˈtiːnə; ˏkævəˋtinə] *n*. (*pl*. *-ne* [-ni; -nɪ])〔It.〕【乐】短抒情曲;（歌剧中的）独唱短曲。

cave[1] [keiv; kev] I *n*. 1. 洞,穴,岩洞;〔方〕地窖。2.【英史】（从自由党分离出来的）分离派;脱党(者)。～ *period* 穴居时代。II *vt*. 1. 在…挖洞。2. 使陷下;使倒坍;使崩溃。3. 暗中破坏。—*vi*. 1. 陷下,倒坍。2. 投降,停止抵抗。～ (**back**) **over** 倒下,翻转。～ **in** 1.（地面）下陷,塌陷;（墙壁、帽子）凹进去,塌。2.〔口〕屈服,投降;〔美〕倒塌。～ **dweller**（史前的）穴居人;〔口〕（都市高层住宅的）大楼居民。～ **dwelling** [**house**] 窑洞。～**-in** 1.〔口〕陷落(处),塌方。2. 投降;失败,堕落。

ca·ve[2] [ˈkeivi; ˋkevɪ] *int*.〔英学俚〕小心〔老师来了〕! *keep* ～（学生干坏事时）把风。

ca·ve·at [ˈkeiviæt; ˋkevɪˏæt] *n*. 1.【法】中止诉讼的申请;〔美〕保护发明特许权的请求书;【商】停止支付的通知。2. 防止误解的说明。3. 要求停止某些行动的告诫,警告。*enter* [*put in*] *a* ～ 提出中止某事的申请。

ca·ve·at emp·tor [ˈkeiviæt ˈemptɔː; kevɪˏæt ˋɛmptɔr]〔L.〕【商】购者留心〔货物出门概不退换〕。

ca·ve ca·nem [ˈkɑːvei ˈkɑːnəm; ˋkɑve ˋkɑnəm]〔L.〕当心恶犬。

Cav·ell [ˈkævl, kəˈvel; kævḷ, kəˋvɛl] *n*. 卡维尔〔姓氏〕。

cave-man [ˈkeivmæn; ˋkevmæn] *n*. 1.（史前）穴居人;野蛮人。2.〔喻〕（感情,行为等）粗野的人（尤指对待妇女）。～ **stuff**〔美俚〕野蛮的求爱,强奸。

Cav·en·dish [ˈkævəndiʃ; ˋkævəndɪʃ] *n*. 卡文迪什〔姓氏〕。

cav·en·dish [ˈkævəndiʃ; ˋkævəndɪʃ] *n*.（压成块的）板烟。

cav·ern [ˈkævən; ˋkævən] I *n*. 大山洞,大洞穴。II *vt*. 1. 置…于山洞中。2. 挖空(*out*)。*The rock was* ～*ed out to make a tunnel*. 挖空岩石造隧道。**-ed** [-d; -d] *a*. 有洞穴的;洞窟状的;在洞穴中的。

cav·ern·ous [ˈkævənəs; ˋkævənəs] *a*. 1. 洞穴(状)的;（眼等）凹的;塌的。2. 多洞穴的。3. 瓮音的。4. 多孔的,海绵状的。～ **body** 海绵体。～ **roar**（狮子的）延音式吼声。

cave·(s)·son [ˈkævisən; ˋkævɪsən] *n*.（训练马时用的）鼻罩,鼻带[马具]。

ca·vet·to [kəˈvetəu; kəˋvɛto] *n*. (*pl*. *-vetti* [-veti; -vɛtɪ], *-vettos*)【建】截面为九十度弧的凹线脚。

ca·vi·ar(e) [ˈkæviɑː; ˋkævɪˏɑr] *n*. 1.（俄式）鱼子酱;美味。2.〔俚〕被检查员涂掉的句子。～ *to the general* 曲高和寡的事物。

cav·il [ˈkævil; ˋkævḷ] I *vi*. (*-ll-*) 挑剔,吹毛求疵(*at; about*)。—*vt*. 对…挑剔,对…吹毛求疵。II *n*. 无端指摘,吹毛求疵。**-(l)er** *n*. 吹毛求疵的人。

cav·i·ta·tion [ˌkæviˈteiʃən; ˏkævəˋteʃən] *n*. 1.【空】气穴现象;气涡现象。2.【物】成穴;空化,（超声波的）空穴作用;【医】成洞,成腔。～ **tunnel**【船】空泡式验筒。

cav·i·ty [ˈkæviti; ˋkævətɪ] *n*. 1.【解】穴,窝,盂,腔,空腔;【医】(空)洞。2.【物】模槽;气蚀区;空腔谐振器;【原】（反应堆中的）小室,暗盒。*the abdominal* [*mouth*] ～ 腹[口]腔。*the* ～ *in a tooth* 齿窝。～ **magnetron** 发电力巨大的磁控管。**vortex** ～ 涡流区。

ca·vo-ri·lie·vo [ˈkævəuriliˈeivəu; ˋkɑvorɪlɪˋevo] *n*. (*pl*. ～*s*)〔It.〕【美】凹浮雕,沉雕。

ca·vort [kəˈvɔːt; kəˋvɔrt] *vi*. 1.〔美口〕（马）跳跃,（骑者）骑马腾跃。2. 放荡的玩乐。

ca·vort·ings [kəˈvɔːtiŋz; kəˋvɔtɪŋz] *n*. 下流放荡的行为。

CAVU = ceiling and visibility unlimited【空】云高及可见度无限制。

ca·vy [ˈkeivi; ˋkevɪ] *n*.【动】天竺鼠,豚鼠。

caw [kɔː; kɔ] I *vi*.（乌鸦）哇哇地叫;（人）乌鸦似地叫(*out*)。II *n*. 乌鸦的叫声。

Cax·ton [ˈkækstən; ˋkækstən] *n*. 1. 卡克斯顿[姓氏]。2. **William** ～威廉·卡克斯顿〔1422? —1491,最初把印刷术传入英国的人〕。3.〔*pl*.〕卡克斯顿版本;卡克斯顿活字。

cay [kei; ke] *n*. 珊瑚礁;沙洲,小岛。

Cay·enne [keiˈen; keˋɛn] *n*. 卡宴〔圭亚那(法)首府〕。

cay·enne [keiˈen; kaɪˋɛn] *n*. 辣椒(粉)(= ～ pepper)。

cay·man [ˈkeimən; ˋkemən] *n*.【动】(中南美的)大鳄鱼。

Cay·man Is·lands [ˈkeimən ˈailəndz; ˋkemən ˋaɪləndz] *n*. 开曼群岛(英)〔拉丁美洲〕。

Ca·yu·ga [keiˈjuːgə, kai-; keˋjugə, kaɪ-] *n*. (*pl*. ～*s*,

～) 1. 卡育加人〔易洛魁印第安人的一个部族,居住于纽约州卡育加湖一带〕。2. 卡育加语。～ **Lake** 卡育加湖。

cay·use [kaiˈjuːs; kaɪˋjus] *n*. 1. 〔美西部〕印地安种小马,〔口〕马。2. 卡育斯人〔俄勒岗州东北部山区印第安人的一个部族〕。

cazic, ca·zique [kəˈziːk; kəˋzik] *n*. = cacique.

CB = 1. construction battalion 〔美军〕修建营。2. ～ chemical and biological 化学及生物的。

C.B. = 1. Cape Breton【地】布雷顿角。2. Chirurgiae Baccalaureus 外科学士。3. Companion of the Bath 〔英〕最低级巴斯爵士。4. = citizens band 〔美〕私人波段〔政府拨给私人无线电通讯使用的波段〕。

C.B., c.b., CB = confinement to barracks 〔美军〕禁止外出。

c.b. = centre of buoyancy【物】浮心。

Cb = 1.【化】(= columbium) 钶〔niobium 铌的旧名〕。2.【气】cumulonimbus 积雨云。

CBC = Canadian Broadcasting Corporation 加拿大广播公司。

CBD = cash before delivery【商】交货前付款。

C.B.E. = Commander (of the Order) of the British Empire 英帝国二等勋位爵士。

C.B.E.L., CBEL = Cambridge Bibliography of English Literature 〔英〕《剑桥(大学)英国文学书目》〔期刊名称〕。

C.B.er [ˈsiːbiːə; ˋsibiɚ] *n*. (政府拨给的)私人无线电通讯波段使用者。

CBI = 1. computer-based instruction 基于计算机的教学。2. Cumulative Book Index (美国)《累积图书索引》。3. Confederation of British Industry 英国工会联合会。

CBR = chemical, bacteriological, and radiological 化学的、细菌学的和放射学的。

CBS = Columbia Broadcasting System 〔美〕哥伦比亚广播公司。

CBU = cluster bomb unit 集束炸弹(装置)。

CBW = 1. chemical and biological warfare 化学生物战。2. Chemical and biological weapons 化学和生物武器。

C.C. = 1. compte courant([F.] = current account 往来账户,存款账户)。2. cashier's check 〔美〕(银行)本票。3. Circuit Court 巡回法庭。4. City Council(lor) 市议员。5. Civil Court 民事法庭。6. Common Councilman 〔美〕市政会成员,地方议会议员。7. County Council 〔英〕郡议会。8. County Court 〔英〕郡法院。9. Cricket Club 板球俱乐部。

cc. = chapters.

cc., c.c. = 1. carbon copy 复写本。2. cubic centimeter 立方厘米。3. centre to centre 中心间距,轴间距。

C.C.A. = 1. carrier controlled approach (system) (航空母舰)舰控飞机进场指挥(系统)。2. Circuit Court of Appeals 〔美〕巡回上诉法院。

C.C.C. = 1. Corpus Christi College (英国)基督圣体节学院。2. Civilian Conservation Corps (美国)地方资源养护队。3. Commodity Credit Corporation (美国农业部)商品信贷公司。

CCCO = Central Committee for Conscientious Objectors 非战主义者中央委员会。

CCD = 1. Charge-coupled device 电荷耦合器件。2. Confraternity of Christian Doctrine 基督教教义协会。

CCF = 1. Combined Cadet Force (英国)学生联合军训队。2. Cooperative Commonwealth Federation (加拿大)平民合作联盟。

C.C.P. = Court of Common Pleas 〔英〕高等民事法庭;〔美〕中级民事及刑事法庭。

C.Cr.P. = Code of Criminal Procedure 刑法典。

CCS = Combined Chiefs Staff 〔旧〕(英美)参谋长联席会议。

C.C.S. = Casualty Clearing Station 伤员后送站。

CCTV = closed-circuit television 闭路式电视,工业电视。

CCU = coronary care unit 冠心病护理小组。

CCUS = Chamber of Commerce of the U.S. 美国商会。

ccw = counterclockwise 反时针(方向)。

Cd = cadmium【化】镉。

cd. = cord 1. 绳,索。2. 木材堆的体积单位。

CD = 1. coastal defense 海岸防御,海防。2. civil defense 民防。3. certificate deposit 定期存款;证券存款。4. certificate of deposit 存款单。5. compact disc 激光唱片;【计】(信息容量极大的)光盘。6. current density 电流密度。

C / D, c / d = certificate of deposit 存款单,存据。

c.d. = 1. cash discount【商】付现折扣。2. cum dividend 附有红利,附股息。

CD player = compact disc player 激光唱机。

CD-E = CD-Erasible【计】可擦写光盘(技术)。

CD-I, CD-i = compact Disk-Interactive【计】互动式光盘。

Cdr., CDR = Commander.

CD-ROM = Compact disc read-only memory【计】(信息容量极大的)光盘只读存储器。

CDT = Central Daylight Time (美国)中部夏令时间。

CDTV = compact disk television 光碟电视〔该系统与录像机一般大小,可直接插入普通电视机〕。

CDV = compact video disk 影视光碟,激光[镭射]影碟。

Ce = cerium【化】元素铈的符号。

C.E. = 1. Chemical Engineer 化学工程师。2. Chief Engineer 总工程师;【海】轮机长;工兵主任。3. Church of England【宗】英国国教,圣公会。4. Civil Engineer 土木工程师。5. Council of Europe 欧洲理事会。

-ce *comb. f*. 构成抽象名词(= [L.]-tia): dilig*ence*, indig*ence*.

CEA = 1. Commodity Exchange Authority 〔美〕(农业部)农产品交易管理局。2. council of Economic Advisers 〔美〕(总统)经济顾问委员会。3. carcinoembryonic antigen 癌胚抗原。4. College English Association (美国)大学英语协会。

ce·a·no·thus [ˌsiːəˈnəuθəs; ˏsiəˋnoθəs] *n*.【植】(鼠李科的)美洲茶(属);美洲茶〔所含生物碱可作泻剂〕。

cease [siːs; sis] **I** *vi*. 停,终止,息。～ *from quarrelling* 停止吵闹。*The rain has* ～*d*. 雨停了。—*vt*. 停止,结束。～ *payment* 停止支付。*Cease fire*!【军】〔命令〕停火,停止射击。～ *out* 绝迹。～ *to be* (*sth*.) 不再是(某事物)。～ *to exist* 不再存在,死亡;灭亡。★ *cease* (*to do*; *doing*) 是书面语,现在普通说 *stop* (*doing*). **II** *n*. 终止,停止〔现在仅用于成语 without ～中。*without* ～ 不断地,不停地〕。～**-fire** 停战(*a* ～*-fire agreement* 停战协定)。

cease·less [ˈsiːslis; ˋsislɪs] *a*. 不停的,不绝的,无限的。**-ly** *ad*. 不断地。**-ness** *n*.

ceas·ing [ˈsiːsiŋ; ˋsisɪŋ] *n*. 终止,停止,间断。

Ce·bu [seˈbuː; sɛˋbu] *n*. 1. 宿务岛〔菲律宾〕。2. 宿务〔菲律宾港市〕。

CECF = Chinese Export Commodities Fair 中国出口商品交易会。

ce·cidi·um [seˈsidiəm; sɛˋsɪdɪəm] *n*.【动、植】瘿。

Ce·cil [ˈsesl, ˈsisl; ˋsɛsl̩, ˋsɪsl̩] *n*. 塞西尔〔姓氏,男子名〕。

Ce·cile [ˈses*i*l, ˈsesiːl; ˋsɛsɪl, ˋsesil] *n*. 塞西尔〔女子名,Cecilia 的异体〕。

Ce·cil·ia [siˈsiljə; sɪˋsɪljə] *n*. 塞西莉亚〔女子名〕。

Cec·i·ly [ˈsisili; ˋsɪsɪlɪ] *n*. 塞西莉〔女子名〕。

ce·ci·ty [ˈsiːsiti; ˋsisətɪ] *n*.〔古〕(精神上的)盲目。

ce·cro·pi·a moth [siˈkrəupiə mɔθ; sɪˋkropɪə mɑθ] *n*.【动】天蚕蛾(*Samia cecropia*)。

ce·cum [ˈsiːkəm; ˋsikəm] *n*. (*pl*. **-ca** [-kə; -kə]) 1.【解】盲肠;盲端。2.【动】单向腔孔(= caecum)。**ce·cal**

[ˈsiːkəl; ˋsikəl] *a*.

CED = 1. cohesive energy density 内聚能密度。2. Committee for Economic Development 〔美〕经济发展委员会。

ce·dar [ˈsiːdə; ˋsidɚ] *n*.【植】1. 雪松;雪松木,杉木杆。2. 香椿。~ **wood** 雪松属木料,杉木。

ce·darn [ˈsiːdən; ˋsidɚn] *a*.〔诗〕雪松(制)的,杉木(制)的。

cede [siːd; sid] *vt*. 让与,割让,放弃(权利、领土等)。~ *territory to* ...向…割让领土。~ *a point in debate* 在某一争论点上让步。**-er** *n*. 割让者,让步者。

ce·di [ˈsediː; ˋsɛdi] *n*. (*pl*. **-dis**) 塞地〔加纳货币单位〕。

ce·dil·la [siˈdilə; sɪˋdɪlə] *n*.【语】(法语某些词中字母 c 下的)勾形符号(¸)〔表示 a, o, u 前的 c 为 [s] 音: *façade*〕。

ce·drol [ˈsiːdrɔːl; ˋsidrɔl] *n*.【化】雪松醇,雪松脑〔亦称柏木脑〕。

ced·u·la [ˈsedʒulə; ˋsɛdʒələ] *n*. (西班牙语国家所颁发的)证明书,证件,执照。

cee [siː; si] **I** *n*. (英语字母)C, c. **II** *a*. C字形的。*a Cee spring*【机】(支持车身的)C形弹簧(= C spring)。

CEEB = College Entrance Examination Board (美国)大学入学考试委员会。

CEGB = Central Electricity Generating Board (英国)中央电力局。

cei·ba [ˈseibə, ˈsaibə; ˋsebɑ, ˋsaɪbə] *n*. 1.【植】吉贝〔木棉科植物〕;木棉树。2. 木棉花;木棉。

ceil [siːl; sil] *vt*. 1. 在…装天花板;在…装壁板。2. 在(木船)上装船底隔板。

ceil·ing [ˈsiːliŋ; ˋsilɪŋ] *n*. 1. 天花板,顶板,顶篷。2. (垫船底的)隔板,舱室垫板。3. (物价、工资等的)最高限度(*opp*. floor);【空】升限,上升限度;云幕高度,低层云与地面间的距离(= ~ height)。*hit the* ~ 〔美俚〕1. 发脾气;生气。2. (大学里)考试不及格。~ **capacity**【空】上升能力。~ **height**【空】升限。

ceil·o·me·ter [siːˈlɔmitə; sɪˋlɑmətɚ] *n*.【空】云高计;【气】云幕计。

cel. = celebrated.

cel [ˈsel; ˋsɛl] *n*.〔口〕蜂窝电话,移动电话,手机。

cel·a·don [ˈselədɔn; ˋsɛlədɑn] **I** *n*. 1. 灰绿色。2. 青瓷色。3. (中国产的)青瓷器。**II** *a*. 青瓷色的。

cel·an·dine [ˈseləndain; ˋsɛlənˏdaɪn] *n*.【植】白屈菜。

cel·an·ese [ˌseləˈniːz; ˏsɛləˋniz] *n*.【商标】纤烷丝〔一种人造丝〕。

-cele *comb*. *f*. 肿,曲张: varico*cele*.

celeb [siˈleb; sɪˋlɛb] *n*.〔美口〕名人;要人。

cel·e·brant [ˈselibrənt; ˋsɛləbrənt] *n*. 1. 司仪神父,主持弥撒的神父。2. 参加庆祝典礼的人。3. (某一事物或人的)赞赏者。

cel·e·brate [ˈselibreit; ˋsɛləˏbret] *vt*. 1. 举行(仪式);庆祝(胜利等)。2. 表扬,赞美,歌颂。3. 公布,发表。~ *a marriage* 举行婚礼。~ *one's birthday* 庆祝生日,做生日。*a man* ~*d in the headlines* 被报纸大加表扬的人。—*vi*. 1. 举行宗教仪式[庆典]。2. 〔口〕欢宴作乐。**-brat·er**, **-brat·or** *n*. 庆祝的人。

cel·e·brat·ed [ˈselibreitid; ˋsɛləbretɪd] *a*. 驰名的,有名的,大名鼎鼎的。

cele·bra·tion [ˌseliˈbreiʃən; ˏsɛləˋbreʃən] *n*. 1. 庆祝,庆祝会。2. (某些宗教性的)仪式;(尤指)圣餐礼(的举行)。3. 称赞,赞美。*in* ~ *of* 为庆祝…。*hold a* ~ 举行庆祝会。

ce·leb·ri·ty [siˈlebriti; səˋlɛbrətɪ] *n*. 1. 名声,扬名。2. 名人,知名之士。*of great* ~ 大名鼎鼎的。

ce·le·ri·ac [səˈleriæk; səˋlɛrɪˏæk] *n*.【植】块根芹(*Apium graveolens rapaceum*)。

ce·ler·i·ty [siˈleriti; səˋlɛrətɪ] *n*.〔书〕(行动的)迅速,神速;敏捷。

cel·er·y [ˈseləri; ˋsɛlərɪ] *n*.【植】芹菜。~ **cabbage** (中国)白菜。**wild** ~【药】独活。

ce·les·ta [siˈlestə; səˏlɛstə] *n*.【乐】钢片琴。

ce·leste [siˈlest; səˋlɛst] **I** *n*. 1. 天蓝色。2. (风琴的)音节栓。**II** *a*. 天蓝色的。

ce·les·tial [siˈlestjəl, siˈlestʃəl; səˋlɛstʃəl, sɪˋlɛstʃəl] **I** *a*. 1. 天的,天空的;天上的;天体的。2. 天国的;神圣的。3. 〔C-〕中国的,天朝的〔指封建时代的中国〕。4. 天体导航法的。*the C- City*【宗】天国。*the C- Empire* 天朝〔指封建时代的中国〕。**II** *n*. 1. 天人,神仙。2. 〔C-〕(指封建时代的)中国人,天朝之人。~ **body** 天体。~ **fire** 诗的灵感。~ **globe** 天球仪。~ **fix** 天体导航法测定船位。~ **latitude** [**longitude**] 黄纬[经]。~ **mechanics** 天体力学。**-ly** *ad*. **-ness** *n*.

cel·es·tine [ˈselistin, -tain, siˈlestin; ˋsɛlɪstɪn, -taɪn, sɪˋlɛstɪn] *n*. 天青石(= celestite)。

cel·es·tite [ˈselistait; ˋsɛlɪstaɪt] *n*.【矿】天青石。

Cel·ia [ˈsiːljə; ˋsiljə] *n*. 西莉亚〔女子名,Cecilia 的昵称〕。

ce·li·ac [ˈsiːliæk; ˋsilɪæk] **I** *a*.【解】腹的,腹腔的。**II** *n*. 腹腔病患者。

cel·i·ba·cy [ˈselibəsi; ˋsɛləbəsɪ] *n*. 1. 独身(生活)。2. 禁欲,贞洁。

cel·i·ba·tar·i·an [selibəˈtɛəriən; sɛlɪbəˋtɛrɪən] *n*., *a*. 独身主义者(的)。

cel·i·bate [ˈselibit; ˋsɛləbɪt] *n*., *a*. 独身者(的)。

cell [sel; sɛl] *n*. 1. 小室,单室;隔间,舱;〔诗〕茅舍;(单个的)蜂窝,蜂房。2. 〔诗〕墓穴,墓。3. (大修道院附属的)小修道院。4. 单人牢房。5.【生】细胞;【电】电池;元件;【建】(天花板的)方格板;隔板;【空】机翼构架;【原】晶格,晶胞;【计】单元,元件;【植】花粉囊;药室;(气球等的)气囊;【气】单体,环型。6. 基层组织,小组。7. 管,盒,槽。*a queen* [*royal*] ~王蜂的窝。*the phase* ~【统】相格。*a secondary* ~蓄电池。*a photosensitive* ~【无】光电管。*a rectifier* ~【无】整流片。*the narrow* ~ 墓。~-**block** (若干牢房组成的)监狱分区。~ **division** 细胞分裂。~ **fusion** 细胞融合。~ **lumina** 空胞。~ **membrane** [**wall**] 细胞膜[壁]。~ **nucleus** 细胞核;窝,凹处。~ **phone**, ~**phone** 蜂窝电话,移动电话,手机。

cel·la [ˈselə; ˋsɛlə] *n*.【建】(希腊神庙的内殿)神坛。

cel·lar [ˈselə; ˋsɛlɚ] **I** *n*. 1. 地窖,地下室;〔英〕(都市住宅的)地下煤窖。2. 地下酒窖;窖藏(葡萄)酒。3.【机】油盒。*a salt* ~盐瓶。~ *smaller* 〔美〕酒徒。~ *tenants*【美体】比赛中成绩最坏的一队。*the* ~〔口〕(竞赛组别中的)最低级位。*from* ~ *to rafter* 楼上楼下。*kees a good* [*small*] ~ 藏有大量[少量]的酒。**II** *vt*. 把…藏入地窖[酒窖]。

cel·lar·age [ˈseləridʒ; ˋsɛlərɪdʒ] *n*. 1. 〔总称〕地窖。2. 窖藏费。3. 地窖的容积。

cel·lar·er [ˈselərə; ˋsɛlərɚ] *n*. 1. 管窖人;酒窖管理员;(寺院等的)食品管理员。2. 酒商。

cel·lar·et(te) [ˌseləˈret; ˏsɛlɚˋɛt] *n*. (餐馆的)酒柜;酒橱。

cel·lar·way [ˈseləˌwei; ˋsɛlɚˏwe] *n*. 〔美〕地窖入口〔尤指梯口〕。

celled [seld; sɛld] *a*. 含有(某种或若干)细胞[小单位、小室等]的〔一般用作构词成分〕。*a single-* ~ *organism* 单细胞生物。

cel·list, **'cel·list** [ˈtʃelist; ˋtʃɛlɪst] *n*. 大提琴演奏者(= violoncellist)。

cel·lo, **'cel·lo** [ˈtʃeləu; ˋtʃɛlo] *n*. (*pl*. ~*s*) 1.【乐】大提琴(= violoncello)。2. 〔美俚〕嘎嗓子女演员。

cel·loi·din [siˈlɔidn; sɛˋlɔɪdn̩] *n*. (制作显微镜切片用的)火棉。

cel·lo·phane [ˈseləfein; ˋsɛləˏfen] *n*. 玻璃纸;胶膜,赛璐珞。

cel·lu·lar [ˈseljulə; ˋsɛljəlɚ] *a*. 1.【生】细胞的,细胞质[状]的。2.【建】区划[分格]式的;小室的。3. 多孔的;有

窝的。4. = ～ phone. ～ **phone** 蜂窝电话,移动电话,手机(= ～ telephone). ～ **rubber** 泡沫橡胶。～ **shirt** 网眼衬衫。～ **system** 1.【植】细胞组织。2.(犯人的)分隔监禁法。～ **tissue**【解】蜂窝状结缔组织。

cel·lu·lar·i·ty [ˌselju'læriti; ˏsɛljə`lærətɪ] ***n.***【生】细胞性,细胞结构。

cel·lu·lase ['seljuleis; `sɛljules] ***n.***【生化】纤维素酶。

cel·lu·late ['seljuleit; `sɛljʊlet] **I** ***a.*** = cellular. **II** ***vt.*** 使有细胞状组织。**-d** ***a.*** 细胞状的,蜂窝状的。

cel·lu·la·tion ['selju'leiʃən; `sɛljʊ`leʃən] ***n.*** 细胞组织;蜂窝状组织。

cel·lule ['selju:l; `sɛljul] ***n.*** 1.【医】小细胞,小房。2.【空】翼组。

cel·lu·lif·er·ous [ˌselju'lifərəs; ˏsɛljʊ`lɪfərəs] ***a.***【医】有小细胞的,产生小细胞的。

cel·lu·li·tis [ˌselju'laitis; ˏsɛljʊ`laɪtɪs] ***n.***【医】蜂窝织炎。

cel·lu·loid ['seljulɔid; `sɛljəˏlɔɪd] **I** ***n.*** 1.【化】赛璐珞(明胶);假象牙。2.〔美俚〕电影(胶片)。**II** ***a.*** 细胞状的。～ *fans*〔美俚〕影迷。

cel·lu·lose ['seljuləus; `sɛljəˏlos] **I** ***n.***【植】细胞膜质,纤维质;【化】纤维素。**II** ***vt.*** 用纤维素处理。～ **acetate** 醋酸纤维素。～ **plant** 纸浆厂。

cel·lu·los·ic [ˌselju'ləusik; ˏsɛljə`losɪk] **I** ***a.*** 纤维质的。**II** ***a.*** 纤维素质。

cel·lu·lous ['seljuləs; `sɛljələs] ***a.***〔罕〕有细胞的,充满细胞的。

ce·lom ['si:ləm; `siləm] ***n.*** 体腔(= coelom)。

Cel·o·tex ['seləˌteks; `sɛləˏtɛks] ***n.***〔美〕赛璐特克斯〔隔音板的商标名称〕。

Cels. = Celsius.

Cel·si·us ['selsiəs; `sɛlsɪəs] ***a.*** 摄氏的。～ **thermometer** 摄氏温度计。

Celt [kelt, Am. selt; kɛlt, sɛlt] ***n.***【史】凯尔特人。*the* ～*s* 凯尔特族。

celt [selt; sɛlt] ***n.***【考古】石凿,凿斧〔史前石制或金属工具〕。

Celt. = Celtic.

Cel·tic ['keltik, Am. `seltik; `kɛltɪk, `sɛltɪk] **I** ***a.*** 凯尔特人的,凯尔特族的;凯尔特语的。**II** ***n.*** 凯尔特语。***the*** ～ ***fringe*** 凯尔特系外缘人口〔指英国内的 Scots, Irish, Welsh 和 Cornish 人后裔〕。

cem. = cemetery.

cem·ba·lo ['tʃembələu; `tʃɛmbəˏlo] ***n.*** (*pl.* ***-li*** [-li:; -li], ***-los***)【乐】1. = harpsichord. 2. = dulcimer.

ce·ment [si'ment; sə`mɛnt] **I** ***n.*** 1. 水泥。2. 胶泥;胶合剂,接合剂,胶;【医】(牙科等用的)黏固粉。3.【解】(牙齿的)白垩质。～ *gland* 黏腺。*glass* ～玻璃胶。**II** ***vt.*** 1. 用水泥黏合,用水泥涂。2. 胶合,接合,溶接。3.【冶】对…作渗碳处理。4. 巩固,加强(友谊等),强化(关系等);把…结合在一起。～*ed steel* 渗碳钢。—***vi.*** 黏紧,黏牢。～**ing process**【冶】渗碳法。

ce·men·ta·tion [ˌsi:men'teiʃən; ˏsimən`teʃən] ***n.*** 1.【医】黏固(作用)。2. 接合;胶合,黏结。3.【化】胶结,硬化。4.【冶】渗碳(法),渗碳处理。

ce·ment·ite [si'mentait; sɪ`mɛntaɪt] ***n.***【冶】渗碳体,碳化铁体;西门体(结晶)。

ce·men·tum [si'mentəm; sə`mɛntəm] ***n.*** 1.【解】牙骨质。2. 黏固粉,水泥。

cem·e·ter·y ['semitri; `sɛməˏtɛrɪ] ***n.*** 墓地,公墓。

CEMF = counter electromotive force 反电动势。

cen. = centre; central; century.

cen·acle ['senəkl; `sɛnəkl] ***n.*** 1. 晚餐室;〔C-〕耶稣与门徒进最后晚餐的房间。2. 聚会室。3.(作家等的)结社,小组。

Cen. Am. = Central America 中美洲。

-cene *comb. f.* 表示"新","最近"。

ce·nes·the·sia [ˌsi:nis'θi:ʒə, -ʒiə, ˌsenis-; ˏsinɪs`θiʒə, -ʒɪə, ˏsɛnɪs-] ***n.***【心】普通感觉(= coenesthesia, cenesthesis)。

ceno-[1] *comb. f.* 表示"新","最近"。

ceno-[2] *comb. f.* 表示"共同"。

ce·no·bite ['si:nəubait; `sɛnəˏbaɪt] ***n.*** = coenobite.

ce·no·gen·e·sis [ˌsi:nə'dʒenisis, ˌsenəu-; ˏsinə`dʒɛnəsɪs, ˏsɛno-] ***n.***【生】新性发生;新生性变态。**-ge·net·ic** [-dʒi'netik; -dʒɪ`nɛtɪk] ***a.***

ce·no·phyte ['si:nəufait; `sinofaɪt] ***n.***【植】新生代植物。

ce·no·spe·cies ['si:nəspi∫i:z, 'senə-; `sinəspɪʃiz, `sɛnə-] ***n.***【生】群型种,杂交种。

cen·o·taph ['senətɑ:f; `sɛnəˏtæf] ***n.*** 衣冠冢;(葬于别处的死者)纪念碑。*the C-* (伦敦)第一次世界大战阵亡将士纪念碑。

ce·no·te [si'nəuti; sɪ`notɪ] ***n.***【地】(石灰岩溶蚀形成的)天然水井。

Ce·no·zo·ic [ˌsi:nə'zəuik; ˏsinə`zoɪk] ***n.***, ***a.***【地】新生代(的),新生界(的)。

cense [sens; sɛns] ***vt.*** 1.(向神)焚香。2. 用香熏。

cen·ser ['sensə; `sɛnsɚ] ***n.*** 香炉。

cen·sor ['sensə; `sɛnsɚ] **I** ***n.*** 1.(古罗马调查户口、检查社会风纪等的)监察官;(书刊等的)审查员,(信件等的)检查员。2.(牛津大学等的)学监。3. 有恶意的评论者。4.【心】抑制性潜意识。**II** ***vt.*** 1. 审查(书刊等);检查(信件等)。2. 删改。

cen·so·ri·al [sen'sɔ:riəl; sɛn`sorɪəl] ***a.*** 1. 监查官的;检查员的。2. 批判的,谴责性的。

cen·so·ri·ous [sen'sɔ:riəs; sɛn`sorɪəs] ***a.*** 检查员一样的;爱挑剔的,苛评的,吹毛求疵的,批判式的,谴责性的。**-ly** ***ad.*** **-ness** ***n.***

cen·sor·ship ['sensəʃip; `sɛnsɚˏʃɪp] ***n.*** 1. 审察员[检查员]的职权;古罗马监察官的职权。2. 检查(制度),审查(制度)。3.【心】潜意识中的抑制力。

cen·sur·a·ble ['senʃərəbl; `sɛnʃərəbḷ] ***a.*** 可批评的,该谴责的。**-bly** ***ad.***

cen·sure ['senʃə; `sɛnʃɚ] ***vt.***, ***n.*** 指责,批评;谴责(*opp.* praise)。～ *sb. for a fault* 谴责某人的错误。*a vote of* ～不信任决议[投票]。

cen·sus ['sensəs; `sɛnsəs] **I** ***n.*** 1. 人口[户口,国情]普查;【生】种群普查;调查。2.(调查获得的)统计数字。*take a* ～ (*of the population*) 举行(人口)普查。**II** ***vt.*** 调查(某地区等的)人口数字;统计…的数字。～ **paper** 人口调查表。～ **quadrat** 普查采样区〔一块划定的方形地区〕。～ **taker** (人口)普查员。

cent [sent; sɛnt] ***n.*** 1.〔美〕分〔货币单位〕;分币,零钱。2.(作单位的)百。*per* ～百分之…。～ *per* ～ 百分之百;毫无例外。***don't care a*** (***red***) ～ 毫不在乎。***put in one's two*** ～***s*** (***worth***) 发表意见;发言。

cent. = centigrade; centimetre; central; centum; century; centime.

CENTAG = Central Army Group (of NATO) (北约)中央军集团。

cent·age ['sentidʒ; `sɛntɪdʒ] ***n.***〔罕〕百分率。

cen·tal ['sentl; `sɛntl] ***n.*** 百磅〔称谷物用的重量单位,美国习惯说作 hundredweight〕。

cen·tare ['sentɑ:; `sɛntɛr] ***n.*** 平方米,平方公尺(= centiare)。

cen·taur ['sentɔ:; `sɛntɔr] ***n.*** 1.【希神】半人半马的怪物。2.(马术精妙的)名骑手。3.〔C-〕【天】半人马座。

cen·tau·re·a [sen'tɔ:riə; sɛn`tɔrɪə] ***n.***【植】矢车菊属(*Centaurea*)植物。

Cen·tau·rus [sen'tɔ:rəs; sɛn`tɔrəs] ***n.***【天】半人马(星)座。

cen·tau·ry ['sentɔ:ri; `sɛntɔrɪ] ***n.***【植】矢车菊。

cen·ta·vo [sen'tɑ:vəu; sɛn`tɑvo] ***n.*** 分,仙〔墨西哥、南美等国的小辅币名。= 1/100 peso〕。

C

cen·te·nar·i·an [ˌsentiˈnɛəriən; ˌsɛntəˋnɛriən] **I** ***n***. 百岁(以上)的老人。**II** ***a***. 百岁(以上)的;一百周年的。

cen·te·nar·y [senˈtiːnəri; sɛnˋtɛˏnɛrɪ] **I** ***a***. **1**. 一百年的,一世纪的。**2**. 一百周年纪念的。**II** ***n***. **1**. 百年间,一世纪。**2**. 一百周年纪念。

cen·ten·ni·al [senˈtenjəl, -niəl; sɛnˋtɛniəl, -nɪəl] **I** ***a***. **1**. (每)百年的;一百周年纪念的。**2**. 活了一百岁的,继续了百年之久的。**II** ***n***. 一百周年(纪念)。***the C- State*** 美国科罗拉多州的别称〔该州于 1876 年开国一百周年时加入合众国〕。

cen·ter [ˈsentə; ˋsɛntɚ] ***n***., ***vt***., ***vi***. 〔美〕= centre.

cen·ter·board [ˈsentəˌbɔːd; ˋsɛntɚˏbɔrd] ***n***.【船】滑动龙骨,活动防浪板,垂板龙骨。

cen·tered [ˈsentəd; ˋsɛntɚd] ***a***. **1**. 位于中心的。**2**. 以某一对象为(活动)中心的。*consumer-* ~以消费者为中心的。

cen·ter·fire [ˈsentəˌfaiə; ˋsɛntɚˏfaɪr] ***a***. 中心点火的。

cen·ter·ing [ˈsentəriŋ, ˈsentriŋ; ˋsɛntərɪŋ, ˋsɛntrɪŋ] ***n***. **1**. 定(中)心,定圆心,对中。**2**.【建】临时穹顶支架,拱膺架(装置)。

cen·tes·i·mal [senˈtesiməl; sɛnˋtɛsəml̩] ***a***. 百分之一的;【数】百分的,百进位的。

cen·tes·i·mo [senˈtesiˌməu; sɛnˋtɛsəˏmo] ***n***. (*pl*. ***-mos*** [-ˌməuz; -ˏmoz]; It. ***-mi*** [-ˈmiː; -ˋmi]) **1**. 分〔意大利货币单位,为 1/100 里拉〕;分〔乌拉圭货币单位,为 1/100 比索〕;分〔巴拿马货币单位,为 1/100 巴波亚〕;分〔智利货币单位,为 1/100 埃斯库多〕。**2**. 上述某些货币中的硬币。

centi- *comb*. *f*. 百;百分之一: *centi*meter.

cen·ti·are [ˈsentiɛə; ˋsɛntɪˏɛr] ***n***. 百分之一公亩,平方米。

cen·ti·bar [ˈsentibɑː; ˋsɛntɪbɚ] ***n***.【物】厘巴(= 1/100 bar)。

cen·ti·grade [ˈsentigreid; ˋsɛntəˏgred] ***a***. **1**. 百分度的。**2**. 摄氏温度计的。~ **thermometer** 摄氏温度计。

cen·ti·gram(me) [ˈsentigræm; ˋsɛntɪˏgræm] ***n***. 厘克(= 1/100 gram, 略作 cg.)。

cen·tile [ˈsentail, -til; ˋsɛntaɪl, -tɪl] ***n***. 百分位点(= percentile)。

cen·ti·li·tre, -ter [ˈsentiˌliːtə; ˋsɛntl̩ˏitɚ] ***n***. 厘升(= 1/100 litre, 略作 cl.)。

cen·til·lion [senˈtiljən; sɛnˋtɪljən] ***num***. **1**. 〔英、德〕100 万的 100 次乘方。**2**. 〔美、法〕1000 的 101 次乘方。

cen·time [ˈsɑːntiːm; ˋsɑntim] ***n***. 〔F.〕生丁(法国货币单位 = 1/100 franc)。

cen·ti·me·tre, -ter [ˈsentiˌmiːtə; ˋsɛntəˏmitɚ] ***n***. 厘米,公分(= 1/100 metre, 略作 cm.)。

cen·ti·me·tre-gram-sec·ond [ˈsentiˌmiːtəˈgræmˈsekənd; ˋsɛntəˏmitɚˋgræmˋsɛkənd] ***a***. 厘米克秒制的。

cen·ti·mil·li·me·tre, -ter [ˈsentiˈmiliˌmiːtə; ˋsɛntɪˋmɪlɪˏmitɚ] ***n***. 忽米(= 1/1,000 厘米,略作 cmm.)。

cen·ti·mo [ˈsentiməu; ˋsɛntəˏmo] ***n***. (*pl*. ~***s***) **1**. 分〔西班牙货币单位,为 1/100 比塞塔〕;分〔委内瑞拉货币单位,为 1/100 波利瓦〕;分〔哥斯达黎加货币单位,为 1/100科郎〕;分〔巴拉圭货币单位,为 1/100 瓜拉尼〕。**2**. 上述某些货币的硬币。

cen·ti·pede [ˈsentipiːd; ˋsɛntəˏpid] ***n***.【动】蜈蚣。

cen·ti·poise [ˈsentipɔiz; ˋsɛntɪpˏɔɪz] ***n***.【物】厘泊〔黏度单位〕(= 1/100 poise)。

cen·ti·sec·ond [ˈsentiˌsekənd; ˋsɛntɪˏsɛkənd] ***n***. 厘秒,百分之一秒。

cen·ti·stere [ˈsentistiə; ˋsɛntɪstɪr] ***n***. 百分之一立方米。

cent·ner [ˈsentnə; ˋsɛntnɚ] ***n***. 生奈尔〔德国、丹麦等 = 50 公斤;英国 = 100 磅;分析用微衡为 1 dram〕。*a metric* [*double*] ~一公担,100 公斤。

cen·to [ˈsentəu; ˋsɛnto] ***n***. (*pl*. ~***s***) **1**. (摘录别的作品拼成的)集锦诗;集锦曲。**2**. 拼接成的衣服,百纳衣;马鞍垫布。**3**. 拼凑而成的东西,大杂烩。

centr- *comb*. *f*. 中心: *centr*al.

cen·tra [ˈsentrə; ˋsɛntrə] ***n***. centrum 的复数。

cen·trad [ˈsentræd; ˋsɛntræd] **I** ***ad***.【解】中向。**II** ***n***.【数】百分之一弧度(= 1/100 radian)。

cen·tral [ˈsentrəl; ˋsɛntrəl] **I** ***a***. **1**. 中心的,中央的。**2**. 重要的,主要的。**3**. 中枢的;中枢神经系统的。**4**. (政治上)走中间道路的。**5**.【语】(中)央的。**II** ***n***. 〔美〕电话总局;接线员。*C- Executive Committee* 中央执行委员会。*C- Reserve Banks* 〔美〕中央准备银行。*C- Reserve Cities* 〔美〕中央准备市〔New York, Chicago, St. Louise 三市〕。~ **city** 特别市的中心城市。~ **figure** (绘画、戏剧等的)中心人物。~ **force** 向心力,辏力。~ **heating** (大厦的)中央供暖法,暖气。~ **staging** 观众围坐舞台四周的剧场。~ **station** 中央发电厂。~ **tendency**【统】集中趋势。~ **time** 〔美〕中部标准时间。~ **treasury** 中央金库。~ **vowel** (中)央母音。**-ly** ***ad***. **-ness** ***n***.

cen·tral·ism [ˈsentrəlizəm; ˋsɛntrəlˏɪzəm] ***n***. 中央集权制,集中制。

cen·tral·ist [ˈsentrəlist; ˋsɛntrəlɪst] **I** ***n***. 中央集权主义者。**II** ***a***. 中央集权的。

cen·tral·i·ty [senˈtræliti; sɛnˋtrælətɪ] ***n***. **1**. 中心性,中央状态。**2**. 中心地位。**3**. 向心性,归心性。

cen·tral·i·za·tion [ˌsentrəlaiˈzeiʃən; ˏsɛntrəlaɪˋzeʃən] ***n***. 中央集权;集于中心,集中(化)。

cen·tral·ize [ˈsentrəlaiz; ˋsɛntrəlˏaɪz] ***vt***. **1**. 把(权力)集中;使(国家等)实行中央集权制。**2**. 成为…的中心,把…集中起来。—***vi***. 形成中心,集中。

cen·tre, cen·ter [ˈsentə; ˋsɛntɚ] **I** ***n***. **1**. 中心;中心点;圆心;中央;中枢,核心;中心人物;根源,起源。**2**. 〔常 C-〕(政治上的)中间派。**3**. (足球等的)中锋;(军队、舞台等的)中央部分。**4**.【建】假框,拱架。**5**.【机】承轴;顶尖,顶针。**6**. 〔*pl*.〕中心距。*recruiting* ~*s* 征兵站。*cultural* ~*s* 文化馆。~ *field*【棒球】中外垒。~ *forward*【曲棍球等】中锋中卫。~ *of attraction* 引力中心;惹眼的东西,有名的东西;注意力的中心,(一个场所的)中心人物。~ *of gravity* 重心。~ *of motion* 动心。**II** ***vt***. **1**. 把…集中,使聚集于一点(*in*, *at*, *on*, *round*, *about*)。**2**. 把…置于中部。**3**. 定…的中心;矫正(透镜等的)中心。**4**. (足球等)传(球)给中锋。—***vi***. **1**. 居中。**2**. 有中心;做中锋。~**bit** **1**. (木匠用的)绳钻,转柄钻。**2**.【机】中心钻,打眼钻。~**board**【船】**1**. (船底中心的)垂直升降板。**2**. 装有升降板的小船。~**drill** = ~**bit**. ~**fielder**【棒球】中锋。~**fold** (报纸期刊的)中间折页〔常连成一大张多印彩色图片等〕。~ **forward** 〔足球〕中锋。~**piece**【建】中心装饰;放在(桌子等)中央的装饰。**-less** ***a***. 无中心的。**-most** ***a***. 在正中心的。

cen·tre·piece [ˈsentəpiːs; ˋsɛntəpis] ***n***. **1**. 占中心地位的人或物;最引人注目的东西。**2**. 在餐桌中摆放的花〔玻璃制品等〕。**3**. (政策、纲领等的)主要特点。

centri- *comb*. *f*. = centr-.

cen·tric, cen·tri·cal [ˈsentrik(əl); ˋsɛntrɪk(əl)] ***a***. **1**. 中心的;中央的;围绕着中心的。**2**. 神经中枢的。**-ly** ***ad***.

cen·tric·i·ty [senˈtrisiti; sɛnˋtrɪsətɪ] ***n***. 中心,归心性。

cen·trif·u·gal [senˈtrifjugəl; sɛnˋtrɪfjʊgl̩] **I** ***a***. **1**. 离心的(*opp*. centripetal);应用离心力的。**2**.【生】输出的,排泄的。**II** ***n***. 离心机。~**-box**【化纤】离心式纺丝罐。~ **blower** 离心吹风机。~ **effect** 离心作用。~ **force** 离心力。~ **inflorescence**【植】远心花序,上花先开。~ **machine** 离心机。~ **pump** 离心泵。~ **sugar** 分蜜糖。**-ly** ***ad***.

cen·trif·u·gal·ize [senˈtrifjugəlaiz; sɛnˋtrɪfjəgəlaɪz] ***vt***. 使受离心作用,离心分离。

cen·trif·u·ga·tion [senˌtrifjuˈgeiʃən, -əˈgei-; sɛnˏtrɪfjʊˋgeʃən, -əˋge-] ***n***. 离心(分离)。

cen·tri·fuge [ˈsentrifjuːdʒ; ˋsɛntrəfjudʒ] ***n***. 离心[分离]机;离心式脱水机。

cen·tring [ˈsentriŋ; ˋsɛntrɪŋ] *n*. = centering.

cen·tri·ole [ˈsentriəul; ˋsɛntrɪˏol] *n*. 【生】中心粒。

cen·trip·e·tal [senˈtripitl; sɛnˋtrɪpɪətl] *a*. **1**. 向心的(*opp*. centrifugal); 应用向心力的。**2**.【生】输入的。~ **force** 向心力。~ **inflorescence**【植】向心花序,下花先开。~ **pump** 向心泵。**-ly** *ad*.

cen·trist [ˈsentrist; ˋsɛntrɪst] *n*. 〔常 C-〕(议会中的)中间派[中立]议员;稳健派,温和派。

centro- *comb*. *f*. = centr-.

cen·tro·bar·ic [ˌsentrəˈbærik; ˏsɛntrəˋbærɪk] *a*. 与重心有关的。

cen·troid [ˈsentrɔid; sɛnˋtrɔɪd] *n*. [物]矩心;质心,质量中心(= centre of mass); 形心曲线;心迹线。

cen·tro·mere [ˈsentrəˌmiə; ˋsɛntrəˏmɪr] *n*. 【生】着丝点[粒]。**-mer·ic** [-ˈmerik, -ˈmiə-; -ˋmɛrɪk, -ˋmɪr-] *a*.

cen·tro·plasm [ˈsentrəplæzəm; ˋsɛntrəplæzəm] *n*. 【生】中心质。

cen·tro·plast [ˈsentrəplæst; ˋsɛntrəˏplæst] *n*. 【生】中心质体。

cen·tro·some [ˈsentrəsəum; ˋsɛntrəˏsom] *n*. 【生】中心小体。

cen·tro·sphere [ˈsentrəsfiə; ˋsɛntrəˏsfɪr] *n*. **1**.【地】地心圈,地核。**2**.【生】中心球;星状球。

cen·trum [ˈsentrəm; ˋsɛntrəm] *n*. (*pl*. ~*s*, *-tra* [-trə; -trə]) 中心;(地震的)震源;【解】椎体,中枢;【生】中心体。

cents-off *a*. 〔美,加拿大〕凭券减价几分钱推销的。

cen·tum [ˈsentəm; ˋsɛntəm] *n*. 〔L.〕百。*per* ~ = per cent.

cen·tu·ple [ˈsentjupl; ˋsɛntjupl] **I** *a*. 百倍的。**II** *n*. 百倍。**III** *vt*. 使增为百倍,用百乘。

cen·tu·pli·cate [senˈtjuːplikit; sɛnˋtjupləket] **I** *n*. 百倍。*in* ~ (印)一百份。**II** *a*. 百倍的。**III** [-keit; -ket] *vt*. 使增为一百倍。

cen·tu·ri·al [senˈtjuriəl, -ˈtur-; sɛnˋtjʊrɪəl, -ˋtʊr-] *a*. 百年的,一世纪的。

cen·tu·ri·on [senˈtjuəriən; sɛnˋtjʊrɪən] *n*. (古罗马军团的)百人队队长。

cen·tu·rium [senˈtjuriəm; sɛnˋtjʊrɪəm] *n*. 【化】钲〔现名 fermium 镄〕。

cen·tu·ry [ˈsentʃuri, -tʃəri; ˋsɛntʃərɪ, -tʃərɪ] *n*. **1**. 百年,一世纪。**2**. (古罗马)(军队的)百人队,(选举的)百人团。**3**. 百,百个;【板球】百分。**4**. 百镑(钞票);〔美俚〕百元(钞票);百码赛跑。*the twentieth* [*20th*] ~二十世纪(1901—2000 年)。*a* ~ *note* 〔美俚〕百元钞。*a* ~ *title* 〔美〕百码赛跑锦标。**centuries-old** *a*. 历史悠久的。~ **plant**【植】龙舌兰。

C.E.O., **c.e.o.** = Chief Executive Officer 总经理。

ceorl [ˈtʃeiˌɔːl; ˋtʃeˏɔrl] *n*. **1**.【英史】底层自由民。**2**. 〔古〕= churl.

cephal- *comb*. *f*. 〔用于母音前〕= cephalo-.

ceph·a·lad [ˈsefəˌlæd; ˋsɛfəˏlæd] *ad*. 【解、动】头向(*opp*. caudad)。

ceph·a·lal·gi·a [sefəˈlældʒjə; sɛfəˈlældʒjə] *n*. 【医】头痛。

ce·phal·ic [seˈfælik; səˋfælɪk] *a*. **1**. 头(部)的。**2**. 向着头部的;头附近的。

ceph·a·lin [ˈsefəlin; sɛfəlɪn] *n*. 【生化】脑磷脂。

ceph·a·li·za·tion [ˌsefəliˈzeiʃən; ˏsɛfəlɪˋzeʃən] *n*. **1**. 头部形成。**2**. 头向集中。

cephal(o)- *comb*. *f*. 〔用于子音前〕头: *cephalo*pod.

ceph·a·lo·chor·date [ˌsefələˈkɔːdeit; ˏsɛfələˋkɔrdet] **I** *n*. 【动】头索动物,无头动物。**II** *a*. 头索类的,属头索动物亚门的。

ceph·a·lom·e·ter [ˌsefəˈlɔmitə; ˏsɛfəˋlɑmətə] *n*. 头测量器,测颅器。**-lom·e·try** *n*. 测颅术,头测量法。

cepha·lo·pod [ˈsefələuˌpɔd; ˋsɛfələˏpɑd] *n*., *a*. 【动】头足动物〔乌贼等〕(的)。

ceph·a·lor·i·dine [sefəˈlɔːrədiːn; ˏsɛfəˋlɔrədin] *n*. 【药】先锋霉素 II,头孢类利定。

ceph·a·lo·spo·rin [ˌsefələuˈspɔːrin; ˋsɛfəloˋspɔrɪn] *n*. 【药】头孢霉菌素。

ceph·a·lo·thin [ˈsefələθin; ˋsɛfələθɪn] *n*. 【药】先锋霉素 I,头孢菌新素,噻孢霉素。

ceph·a·lo·tho·rax [ˌsefələuˈθɔːræks; ˏsɛfələˋθoræks] *n*. 【动】(甲壳类的)头胸部。

ceph·a·lous [ˈsefələs; ˋsɛfələs] *a*. 有头的。

-ceph·a·lous *comb*. *f*. 有头的: bi*cephalous*.

Ceph·e·id (variable) [ˈsefiid, ˈsiːfi-; ˋsɛfɪɪd, ˋsifɪ-]【天】造父变星。

Ce·pheus [ˈsiːfjuːs; ˋsifjus] *n*. 【天】仙王座。

-ceptor *comb*. *f*. 表示:"接受者,接受器"。

CEQ = Council on Environmental Quality (美国)改善环境质量委员会。

cer- *comb*. *f*. 〔用于母音前〕= cero-.

ce·ra·ceous [siˈreiʃəs; səˋreʃəs] *a*. 蜡状的;蜡质的。

ce·ram·al [siˈræməl; sɪˋræməl] *n*. 金属陶瓷,合金陶瓷(= cermet)。

ce·ram·ic [siˈræmik; səˋræmɪk] **I** *a*. 陶器的,陶瓷的,陶质的;制陶的。*the* ~ *industry* 陶瓷业,窑业。~ *manufactures* 陶器,瓷器。~ *fibre* 硅酸盐纤维,陶瓷纤维。**II** *n*. (一件)陶器。

ce·ram·ics [siˈræmiks; səˋræmɪks] *n*. **1**. 陶瓷学;陶瓷工艺,制陶术,窑业。**2**. 〔总称〕陶器。

ce·ram·ist [ˈserəmist; ˋsɛrəmɪst] *n*. 陶瓷工人[技师];窑业家。

ce·rar·gy·rite [siˈrɑːdʒirait; sɪˋrɑrdʒɪˏraɪt] *n*. 【矿】角银矿。

ce·ras·tes [siˈræstiːz; sɪˋræstiz] *n*. 【动】角蛇属毒蛇(尤指角蝰 (*Cerastes cornutus*))。

Ce·ras·ti·um [siˈræstiəm; sɪˋræstɪəm] *n*. 【植】寄奴花属;卷耳属。

ce·rate [ˈsiərit; ˋsɪret] *n*. 【药】蜡膏,蜡剂;【化】铈酸盐。

ce·rat·o·dus [siˈrætədəs, ˌserəˈtəudəs; sɪˋrætədəs, ˏsɛrəˋtodəs] *n*. **1**. 澳大利亚肺鱼属(*Ceratodus*)的鱼。**2**. 澳大利亚肺鱼(= barramunda)。

cer·a·toid [ˈserətɔid; ˋsɛrəˏtɔɪd] *a*. 角状的;角质的;有角的。

ce·rau·no·graph [səˈrɔːnəgrɑːf; səˋrɔnəgrɑf] *n*. 【气】雷电计。

Cer·ber·us [ˈsəːbərəs; ˋsɝbərəs] *n*. 【希神、罗神】冥府守门狗〔蛇尾三头,长年不眠〕。***a sop to*** ~ (收买看守、官员、敌对者等的)贿赂。

cer·ca·ri·a [səˈkeriə; səˋkɛrɪə] *n*. (*pl*. ***-ri·ae*** [-riiː; -rɪi]) 【动】摇尾幼虫,尾蚴。

cer·cis [ˈsəːsis; ˋsɝsɪs] *n*. 【植】紫荆。

cer·cus [ˈsəːkəs; ˋsɝkəs] *n*. (*pl*. ***cer·ci*** [-si; -sɪ]) 【动】尾发,尾铗,尾毛。

cere[1] [siə; sɪr] *n*. 【动】(鹦鹉、猛禽类等鸟喙底部的)蜡膜。

cere[2] [siə; sɪr] *vt*. **1**. 〔古〕用蜡布包裹(尸体)。**2**. 〔罕〕给…上蜡,涂蜡于。

ce·re·al [ˈsiəriəl; ˋsɪrɪəl] **I** *a*. 谷类的,谷类植物的,谷类制成的。**II** *n*. 〔常 *pl*.〕禾谷类,谷物;〔美〕(加过工的)谷类食物〔麦片粥等〕。*coarse* ~*s* 杂[粗]粮。~ **crops** 谷(类作)物。~**-leguminous crops** 豆类作物。

cer·e·bel·lum [ˌseriˈbeləm; ˏsɛrəˋbɛləm] *n*. (*pl*. ~*s*, *-la* [-lə; -lə]) 【解】小脑。

cer·e·bral [ˈseribrəl; ˋsɛrəbrəl] *a*. **1**. 大脑的,脑的。**2**. (文艺等)触动理智的;理智方面的;非感情方面的。~ **anaemia** 脑贫血。~ **haemorrhage** 脑溢血。~ **hyperaemia** 脑充血。~ **hemispheres** 大脑半球。

cer·e·bral·ism [ˈserəbrəlizəm; ˋsɛrəbrəlˏɪzm] *n*. **1**. 唯大脑机能论。**2**. 理智至上主义;抽象主义。

cer·e·brate [ˈseriˌbreit; ˋsɛrəˏbret] *vi*. 用脑;思索。

C

cer·e·bra·tion [ˌseriˈbreiʃən; ˏsɛrɪˋbreʃən] ***n.*** 大脑作用[机能];思想活动;思考。

cer·e·bri·tis [ˌseriˈbraitis; ˏsɛrəˋbraɪtɪs] ***n.***【医】大脑炎。

cerebro- *comb. f.*〔用于子音前〕脑〔母音前用 cerebr-〕。

cer·e·bro·ma·la·cia [ˌseribrəuməˈleisiə; ˏsɛrɪbroməˋlesɪə] ***n.***【医】脑软化。

cer·e·bro·scle·ro·sis [ˈseribrəuˏskliəˈrəusis; ˋsɛrɪbroˏsklɪˋrosɪs] ***n.***【医】脑硬化。

cer·e·bro·side [ˈseribrəusaid; ˋsɛrɪbrosaɪd] ***n.***【生化】脑苷脂类。

C

ce·re·bro·spi·nal [ˌseribrəuˈspainl; ˏsɛrəbroˋspaɪnl] ***a.***【解】脑脊髓的。*epidemic ~ meningitis* [*fever*] 流行性脑脊膜炎。

cer·e·brum [ˈseribrəm; ˋsɛrəbrəm] ***n.*** (*pl.* *~s, -bra* [-brə; -brə])【解】大脑;脑。

cere·cloth [ˈsiəkləθ; ˋsɪrˏklɔθ] ***n.*** (防水或包尸的)蜡布。

cer·e·ment [ˈsiəmənt; ˋsɪrmənt] ***n.*** **1.** 包裹木乃伊的蜡布。**2.**〔常 *pl.*〕尸衣。

cer·e·mo·ni·al [ˌseriˈməunjəl; ˏsɛrɪˋmonjəl] **I** ***a.*** 礼仪上的;讲究仪式的;正式的。~ **drill** 军仪教练。~ **usage** 礼仪上的惯例。**II** ***n.*** 仪式,礼仪;仪式书。~ **dress** 礼服。**-ism** ***n.*** 讲究仪式,拘泥形式,形式主义。**-ist** ***n.*** 墨守礼法的人,拘泥形式的人。**-ly** ***ad.*** 仪式上,礼仪上。

cer·e·mo·ni·ous [ˌseriˈməunjəs, -niəs; ˏsɛrəˋmonɪəs, -nɪəs] ***a.*** **1.** 礼仪的。**2.** 仪式郑重的,隆重的。**3.** (过分)讲究礼节的,客套的,古板的。*a ~ reception* 隆重的欢迎。**-ly** ***ad.*** **-ness** ***n.***

cer·e·mo·ny [ˈseriməni, Am. ˈseriˌməuni; ˋsɛrəˏmənɪ, ˋsɛrɪˏmonɪ] ***n.*** **1.** 典礼,仪式。**2.** 礼仪,礼节。**3.** 虚礼;客气。*a wedding ~*结婚仪式。*the Master of (the) Ceremonies* (英国皇室的)掌礼官;(正式集会的)司仪。***stand on*** [***upon***] ~ 墨守礼法,讲究仪式;讲客套,客气。***with*** ~ 正式,隆重。***without*** ~ 不拘礼节地,随便地。

Ce·res [ˈsiəriːz; ˋsɪriz] ***n.*** **1.**【罗神】谷(类女)神。**2.**【天】谷神星。

cer·e·sin(e) [ˈserisin; ˋsɛrɪsɪn] ***n.*** (纯)地蜡。

ce·re·us [ˈsiəriəs; ˋsɪrɪəs] ***n.***【植】仙影拳;〔C-〕仙影拳属。

ce·ri·a [ˈsiəriə; ˋsɪrɪə] ***n.***【化】二氧化铈。

ce·ric [ˈsiərik, ˈser-; ˋsɪrɪk, ˋsɛr-] ***a.***【化】高铈的,四价铈的。

cer·if, cer·iph [ˈserif; ˋsɛrɪf] ***n.***〔罕〕= serif.

ce·rif·er·ous [səˈrifərəs; səˋrɪfərəs] ***a.*** 产蜡的,生蜡的。

ce·rise [səˈriːz; səˋriz] ***n.***, ***a.***〔F.〕淡红[鲜红]色(的),樱桃色(的)。

ce·rite [ˈsiərait; ˋsɪraɪt] ***n.***【矿】铈硅石。

ce·ri·um [ˈsiəriəm; ˋsɪrɪəm] ***n.***【化】铈。

cer·met [ˈsəːmet; ˋsɝmɛt] ***n.*** = ceramal.

CERN =〔F.〕*Conseil Européen pour la Recherche Nucléaire* 欧洲原子核研究委员会〔现称 *Organisation Européene pour la Recherche Nucléaire* 欧洲原子核研究组织〕。

cer·nu·ous [ˈsəːnjuwəs; ˋsɝnjʊwəs] ***a.***【植】俯垂的。

cero- *comb. f.* 表示"蜡": *cero*plastic.

ce·ro [ˈsiərəu; ˋsɪro] ***n.*** (*pl.* ~, ~*s*)【动】巨鲐,马鲛鱼(*Scomberomorus cavalla*)。

ce·ro·graph [ˈsiːrəgrɑːf; ˋsɪrəˏgræf] ***n.*** = cerotype.

ce·rog·ra·phy [siˈrɔgrəfi; sɪˋrɑgrəfɪ] ***n.*** 蜡版雕刻术;蜡版印刷术;蜡画术[法]。

ce·ro·plas·tic [ˈsiərəuˈplæstik; ˋsɪroˋplæstɪk] ***a.*** 蜡塑的。~*s* 蜡塑术。

ce·rot·ic [siˈrɔtik; sɪˋrɑtɪk] ***a.*** 蜜蜡的,蜡脂的,出自蜜蜡的,出自蜡脂的。

ce·ro·type [ˈsiərəˌtaip; ˋsɪrəˏtaɪp] ***n.*** 蜡刻印版;蜡版印制品。

ce·rous [ˈsiərəs; ˋsɪrəs] ***a.***【化】三价铈的,(正)铈的。

cert. = certainly; certificate; certify.

cert [səːt; sɝt] ***n.***〔俚〕= certainty. *a dead* [*an absolute*] ~绝对确实的事物。***for a*** ~ 的确,确实。

cer·tain [ˈsəːtən; ˋsɝtən] **I** ***a.*** **1.** (数量、日期等)已确定的;(证据等)确凿的,无疑的;(知识、技术等)正确的,可靠的。**2.** 必然〔后接不定式〕;有把握,确信(*of, that*)〔只用作表语〕。**3.** 某,某一;某种,某些;相当的,一定程度的;(某种)不好意思说出来的〔只用作定语〕。*a ~ remedy for* 治…的一种特效药。*face ~ death* 面临无可避免的死亡。*a ~ Smith* 一个叫做史密斯的人。*a ~ unit* 某部队[单位]。*a lady of ~ age* 相当年龄的[四五十岁的]女人。*a woman in a ~ condition* 孕妇。*a woman of a ~ description* 行为不好的女人;娼妇。*There is a ~ charm about him.* 他有某种说不出的可爱处。*feel a ~ reluctance* 觉得有些讨嫌。*to a ~ degree* 到某种程度,多少。*I am ~ of success.* 我对成功有把握。*He is ~ to succeed.* 他一定成功。*be morally ~ that* 确有把握,决不致,包管。~ *evidence* 确实的证据。~ *illness* 某种病〔指性病〕。***for*** ~ 的确,一定(*I know for ~ ...* 我确实知道)。***make*** ~ [***of, that***] 把…弄明白,弄确实,保证(*make ~ when the guests leave* 弄清楚客人何时动身。*make ~ of the date of his arrival* 搞清楚他来的日期)。**II** ***pron.*** 某几个,某些。~ *of his relatives* 他的某些亲戚。

cer·tain·ly [ˈsəːtənli; ˋsɝtnlɪ] ***ad.*** **1.** 的确,无疑,一定,必定。**2.**〔口〕〔回答语〕当然,自然可以;不错,的确是那样,的确是的。*C-, you may take the keys.* 没问题,你当然可以把钥匙拿去。*It is ~ the case that ..., but....* (…)虽然很对,可是…。

cer·tain·ty [ˈsəːtənti; ˋsɝtntɪ] ***n.*** 确实(性);确定性;确实[定]的事,必然的事;确信,肯定。*the ~ of death* 死的必然性。*bet on a ~*十拿九稳地赌。***a dead*** ~ (竞赛时)必胜的马;十拿九稳,势所必然。***for*** [***to, of***] ***a*** ~ 的确,显然;毫无疑问。***moral*** ~ 靠得住,定准,一定。***with*** ~ 确信,的确。

Cert. Ed. = Certificate in Education 教育学证书。

cer·tes [ˈsəːtiz; ˋsɝtɪz] ***ad.***〔古〕的确,诚然,必然。

certif. = certificate(d)

cer·ti·fi·a·ble [ˈsəːtifaiəbl; ˋsɝtəˏfaɪəbl̩] ***a.*** 可证明的。**-bly** [-bli; -blɪ] ***ad.***

cer·tif·i·cate [səˈtifikit; sɚˋtɪfəkɪt] **I** ***n.*** **1.** 证明书;执照,凭照;(毕业)文凭。**2.** 证券,单据。**3.** 明证。*be married by ~*不依据宗教仪式结婚。*a health ~*健康证明书。*a leaving ~* 毕业[肄业;离职]证书。*a medical ~* 诊断书。*a gold ~*〔美〕金库券。*a ~ of birth* [*death*] 出生[死亡]证。*a ~ of deposit* 存款凭单。*a ~ of efficiency* 工作能力(优良)鉴定书。*a ~ of measurement*【美商】木材尺寸检查证。*a ~ of merit*【美军】奖状。*a ~ of shares* [*stock*] 记名股票。*a ~ of shipment*【英商】出口许可证。*a ~ of bravery* 勇敢品质的明证。**II** [səˈtifikeit; sɚˋtɪfɪket] ***vt.*** 发证明给…,批准;认可,鉴定。*a ~d teacher* 鉴定合格的教员,正式教员。

cer·ti·fi·ca·tion [ˌsəːtifiˈkeiʃən; ˏsɝtɪfɪˋkeʃən] ***n.*** **1.** 证明,鉴定,保证。**2.** 证明书的发给,执照的授与。**3.** 证明书。

cer·ti·fied [ˈsəːtifaid; ˋsɝtəˏfaɪd] ***a.*** **1.** 被证明了的,有保证的;鉴定的。**2.** 持有证明书的。*a ~ cheque*〔美〕保付支票。*a ~ public accountant*〔美〕(执有证书的)合格会计师。~ **mail** 只负责递送的邮件〔不保证赔偿〕。~ **milk** 消毒牛乳。

cer·ti·fi·er [ˈsəːtifaiə; ˋsɝtəˏfaɪɚ] ***n.*** 证明者。

cer·ti·fy [ˈsəːtifai; ˋsɝtəˏfaɪ] ***vt.*** (*-fied; -fy·ing*) **1.** (以保证书或许可证)证明。**2.**〔英〕证明…有精神病。**3.**〔美〕(银行)担保(支票)可付款。*I hereby ~ that ....* 兹证明…无误。—***vi.*** (以书面形式)证明(*to*);保证(*for*)。*I can ~ to her honesty.* 我可以证明她是诚实的。

cer·ti·o·ra·ri [ˌsəːtiəːˈrɛərai; ˏsɝʃɪəˋrɛrɪ] ***n.*** [L.][常作 writ of ～](上级法院向下级法院等发出的)诉讼文件[案卷]调取令(书)。

cer·ti·tude [ˈsəːtitjuːd; ˋsɝtəˏtjud] ***n.*** **1.** 确信;确定。**2.** 确实(性),必然性。

ce·ru·le·an [siˈruːljən; səˋruljən] ***n.***, ***a.*** 天蓝色(的)。

ce·ru·lo·plas·min [siˌruːləuplæzmin; sɪˏruloˋplæzmɪn] ***n.***【生化】血浆铜蓝蛋白。

ce·ru·men [siˈruːmen; səˋrumən] ***n.***【医】耳垢,耵聍。

ce·ruse [ˈsiəruːs; ˋsɪrus] ***n.*** **1.** 铅粉,铅白化妆品。**2.**【化】碳酸铅白。

ce·rus(s)·ite [ˈsiərəsait; ˋsɪrəˏsaɪt] ***n.***【矿】白铅矿。

Cer·van·tes [səːˈvæntiz; sɝˋvæntiz], **Miguel de ～** 塞万提斯[1547—1616,西班牙作家,《唐·吉诃德》的作者]。

cer·van·tite [səːˈvæntait; sɝˋvæntaɪt] ***n.***【矿】锑赭石,黄锑矿。

cer·vi·cal [ˈsəːvikəl; ˋsɝvɪkl̩] ***a.***【解】**1.** 颈(部)的。**2.** 子宫颈的。

cer·vi·ces [ˈsəːvisiːz, səˈvai-; ˋsɝvɪsiz, səˋvaɪ-] ***n.*** cervix 的复数。

cer·vi·ci·tis [ˌsəːviˈsaitis; ˏsɝvəˋsaɪtəs] ***n.***【医】子宫颈炎。

cer·vid [ˈsəːvid; ˋsɝvɪd] ***a.***【动】鹿科的。

cer·vine [ˈsəːvain; ˋsɝvaɪn] ***a.*** **1.** 鹿的;鹿一样的。**2.** 鹿毛色的;茶褐色的。

cer·vix [ˈsəːviks; ˋsɝvɪks] ***n.*** (*pl.* ***～es***, ***-vi·ces*** [-visiːz; -vɪsiz])【解】**1.** 颈;颈部。**2.** 子宫颈。

Ce·sar·e·an, -ri·an [si(ː)ˈzɛəriən; siˋzɛrɪən] ***a.*** = Caesarean.

ce·si·um [ˈsiːziəm; ˋsizɪəm] ***n.***【化】铯(= caesium)。～ **clock** 铯原子钟。

ces·pi·tose [ˈsespitəus; ˋsɛspɪtos] ***a.*** 簇生的,丛生的,密生的;(似)草皮的。

cess[1] [ses; sɛs] ***n.*** [Scot.]田赋;[Ir.]地方税[英国今用 rate]。

cess[2] [ses; sɛs] ***n.*** [Ir.]运气[只用于下一短语]。***Bad ～ to you!*** 你真该死!

ces·sa·tion [səˈseiʃən; sɛˋseʃən] ***n.*** 停止,休止。～ *of arms* [*hostilities*] 停战[停止敌对行动]。～ *of friendship* 绝交。

ces·ser [ˈsesə; ˋsɛsɝ] ***n.***【法】(期限、责任等的)中止,结束。

ces·sion [ˈseʃən; ˋsɛʃən] ***n.*** (领土的)割让,(权利等的)让与,转让。

ces·sion·ar·y [ˈseʃənəri; ˋsɛʃənˏɛrɪ] **I** ***a.*** 割让的,让与的;转让了财产的。**II** ***n.***【法】受让人。

cess·pit, cess·pool [ˈsespit, ˈsespuːl; ˋsɛsˏpɪt, ˋsɛspul] ***n.*** 污水坑;粪坑;[喻]污秽场所。*the ～ of iniquity* 罪恶的渊薮。

ces·ta [ˈsestə; ˋsɛstə] ***n.*** 回力球戏的手筐[捆在腕上,用来接球和扔球]。

c'est-à-dire [setəˈdiː; sɛtəˋdi] [F.]就是说;即是。

c'est la vie [seləˈviː; sɛləˋvi] [F.]这就是生活;生活就是这样的。

ces·tode [ˈsestəud; ˋsɛstod] **I** ***n.***【动、医】多节绦虫亚纲的动物,绦虫。**II** ***a.*** 绦虫的,多节绦虫亚纲的。

ces·toid [ˈsestɔid; ˋsɛstɔɪd] ***n.***, ***a.*** = cestode.

ces·tus[1] [ˈsestəs; ˋsɛstəs] ***n.*** (古罗马拳击用的)皮带手套。

ces·tus[2] [ˈsestəs; ˋsɛstəs] ***n.*** **1.** 带;【罗神】(爱神的)饰带。**2.**【动】带水母,带海蜇。

ce·su·ra [si(ː)ˈzjuərə; si(ɪ)ˋzjʊrə] ***n.*** = caesura.

ce·ta·cean [siˈteiʃjən; sɪˋteʃən] **I** ***n.*** 鲸类的动物[鲸、海豚等]。**II** ***a.*** 鲸类动物的。

ce·ta·ceous [siˈteiʃjəs; sɪˋteʃəs] ***a.*** 鲸类动物的。

ce·tane [ˈsiːtein; ˋsiten] ***n.***【化】十六烷,鲸蜡烷。～ **number**【化】十六烷值。

cet·e·ris pa·ri·bus [ˈsitəris ˈpæribəs; ˋsɛtərɪs ˋpærɪbəs] [L.](如)其他条件[情况]均同[均保持不变]。

ce·tol·o·gy [siːˈtɔlədʒi; səˋtɑlədʒɪ] ***n.*** 鲸类学。**-lo·gist** ***n.*** 鲸类学家。**-log·i·cal** [-ˈlɔdʒikl; -ˋlɑdʒɪkl̩] ***a.*** 鲸类学的。

Ce·tus [ˈsiːtəs; ˋsitəs] ***n.***【天】鲸鱼座。

Ce·u·ta [ˈsjuːtə; ˋsjutə] ***n.*** 休达[摩洛哥境内一港口,属西班牙]。

CEV = combat engineer(ing) vehicle【军】战地工程车。

ce·vi·tam·ic [ˌsiːvaiˈtæmik, -vi-; ˏsivaɪˋtæmɪk, -vɪ-] ***a.*** ～ **acid**【药】抗坏血酸,维生素 C。

Cey·lon [siˈlɔn; sɪˋlɑn] ***n.*** 锡兰[斯里兰卡(Sri Lanka)的旧称][亚洲]。～ **moss**【植】锡兰藻[一种红藻,可提取琼胶]。

Cey·lo·nese [ˌsiːləˈniːz; ˏsiləˋniz] **I** ***a.*** 锡兰(人)的。**II** ***n.*** [*sing.*, *pl.*]锡兰人。

C-4 [ˈsiː-fɔː(r); ˋsi-fɔ(r)] ***n.*** C-4 炸药[一种塑胶炸药,无色无味,极难被检测出来]。

C.F., c.f., C.&F. (= cost and freight)【商】离岸加运费价格,成本加运费价格。

C.F. = Chaplain to the Forces [英]随军牧师。

Cf = californium【化】锎。

c/f = carried forward【会计】转下页。

cf. = [L.] *confer*.

c.f. =【棒球】centre field.

CFC = chlorofluoro carbon 氟氯碳。

CFE = College of Further Education (英)进修学院。

C.F.I., c.f.i. = cost, freight, and insurance【商】到岸价格,成本加运费、保险费价格。

CFM = chlorofluoromethane 氟氯甲烷。

c.f.m. = cubic feet per minute 立方英尺/分。

c.f.s. = cubic feet per second 立方英尺/秒。

CG = **1.** centre of gravity【物】重心(有时用 cg)。**2.** Coast Guard 海岸警卫队。**3.** commanding general【军】(将军级)司令官。**4.** consul general 总领事。

cg. = centigram(me)(s).

C.G.H. = Cape of Good Hope【地】好望角。

cgm. = centigram.

CGS, C.G.S. = **1.** centimetre-gramme-second (system) 厘米、克、秒(制)[也可用 c.g.s. 或 cgs]。**2.** Chief of the General Staff 总参谋长。

CGT = [F.] *Confédération Générale du Travail* 法国总工会(= General Confederation of Labo(u)r)。

Ch. = Charles; China; Chinese; Church.

ch. = chapter; chief; [L.] *chirurgiae* (= of surgery); choice; church; chain.

C.H. = **1.** Captain of the Horse [英旧]骑兵上尉。**2.** clearing house 票据交换所;(技术)情报交流所。**3.** Court House 法院。**4.** Custom-House 海关。

c.h. = courthouse.

chab·a·zite [ˈtʃæbəzait; ˋtʃæbəzaɪt] ***n.***【矿】菱沸石。

Cha·blis [ˈʃæbliː; ˋʃæblɪ] ***n.*** (原产于法国沙百里的一种)无甜味白葡萄酒。

cha·b(o)uk [ˈtʃɑːbuk; ˋtʃɑbʊk] ***n.*** 东方某些国家施行(体刑用的)马鞭。

cha·cha [ˈtʃɑːtʃɑː; ˋtʃɑtʃɑ] **I** ***n.*** 恰恰舞[源出拉美的一种三拍子的、节拍急速的交际舞]。**II** ***vi.*** 跳恰恰舞(= cha-cha-cha)。

chac·ma [ˈtʃækmə; ˋtʃækmə] ***n.***【动】南非大狒狒,山都(= *Papio comatus*)。

cha·conne [ʃɑːˈkɔn; ʃæˋkɔn] ***n.*** 恰空舞(曲)。

cha·cun à son goût [ʃəˈken nə səun ˈguː; ʃəˋken nə son-ˋgu] [F.]各有所好。

Chad [tʃæd; tʃæd] ***n.*** 乍得(查德)[非洲]。**-i·an** [-iən; -ɪən] ***n.*** 乍德人。

Chad·band [ˈtʃædbænd; ˋtʃædbænd] ***n.*** 巧言令色的伪君子[原为英国作家 Dickens 所著小说 *Bleak House* 中的人物]。

chae·ta [ˈkiːtə; ˋkitə] ***n.*** (*pl.* ***-tae*** [-i; -ɪ])【动】(尤指某些毛虫身上的)体毛,毫毛,刚毛。

chae·tog·nath [ˈkiːtəgnæθ; ˋkitəgnəθ] ***n.*** *pl.*【动】毛颚动物门(*chaetognatha*)动物。

chae·to·pod [ˈkiːtəpɔd; ˋkitɑpəd] ***n.*** *pl.*【动】毛足纲(*Chaetopoda*)动物。

chafe [tʃeif; tʃef] **I** ***vt.*** **1.** 把(手、皮肤)擦热。**2.** 擦破;擦伤;擦痛。**3.** 惹怒,使急躁。~ *one's cold hands* 搓手取暖。—***vi.*** **1.** (动物在铁栏等上)擦身体 (*against*);(河)冲洗(崖岸等)(*against*)。**2.** (皮肤等)擦伤,擦痛。**3.** 发怒;着急,焦躁。~ ***at*** 生…的气。~ ***under*** (*teasing*) 因(受戏弄)而生气,发火。~ ***at the bit*** (马)焦躁;(人)(因延误而)不耐烦,想加快速度。**II** ***n.*** **1.** 摩擦;擦伤。**2.** 急躁,恼怒。**3.** (防止擦伤马的)马鞍环套皮。***in a*** ~ 愤然,发火。

chaf·er[1] [ˈtʃeifə; ˋtʃefɚ] ***n.*** 烧开水的器具;火炉。

chaf·er[2] [ˈtʃeifə; ˋtʃefɚ] ***n.***【虫】金龟子。

chaff[1] [tʃɑːf; tʃaf] ***n.*** **1.** 粗糠,禾壳。**2.** 切细的稻草[饲料],秣;麻杆碎屑;废物。**3.** 不值钱的假货。**4.** (干扰雷达的)金属碎箔。***be caught with*** ~ 受骗,上当。~ ***and dust*** 废物。***offer*** ~ ***for grain*** 挂羊头卖狗肉。~ **cutter** 去糠机;切草机。

chaff[2] [tʃɑːf; tʃaf] ***n.***, ***vt.***, ***vi.*** 戏弄,开玩笑〔多指无恶意的〕。

chaff·er[1] [ˈtʃɑːfə; ˋtʃafɚ] ***n.*** 戏弄者,恶作剧者。

chaf·fer[2] [ˈtʃæfə; ˋtʃæfɚ] **I** ***n.*** 讨论还价,讲价。**II** ***vi.*** **1.** 讨价还价。**2.** 〔英〕闲谈,聊天,交谈。—***vt.*** **1.** 为…讨价还价。**2.** 交换;以…作为交换物。

chaf·fer·er [ˈtʃæfərə; ˋtʃæfərɚ] ***n.*** 讲价者,讨价还价者。

chaf·finch [ˈtʃɑːfintʃ; ˋtʃæfɪntʃ] ***n.***【动】(欧洲)苍头燕雀。

chaff·y [ˈtʃɑːfi; ˋtʃafɪ] ***a.*** **1.** 禾壳状的,多糠的。**2.** 无用的,无价值的。

chaf·ing dish [ˈtʃeifiŋdiʃ; ˋtʃefɪŋdɪʃ] ***n.*** (在食桌上做菜或保持菜肴温度的)酒精炉盆,热水盆,火锅。

Cha·gas [ˈtʃɑːgɑːs; ˋtʃagas] ***n.*** 查格斯〔人名〕。~**'s disease**【医】南美锥虫病〔查格斯氏病〕。

cha·grin [ˈʃægrin, Am. ʃəˈgrin; ˋʃægrɪn, ʃəˋgrɪn] **I** ***n.*** 悔恨,懊恼;委屈。***to one's*** ~ 使人懊恼的是。**II** [ˈʃægrin, ʃəˈgriːn, Am. ʃəˈgrin; ˋʃægrɪn, ʃəˋgrin, ˏʃəˋgrɪn] ***vt.*** 使懊恼,使悔恨。***be*** [***feel***] ~***ed at*** [***by***] 因…而悔恨[懊恼]。

chain [tʃein; tʃen] **I** ***n.*** **1.** 链子,链条;项圈;表链。**2.** 连锁;连续,一系列,一连串;(山)脉。**3.** 〔常 *pl.*〕镣铐;羁绊,拘束。**4.**【化】链;【测】测链〔100 节全长 20 米或 66 英尺〕;【海】锚链;【纺】经线,【电】电路,回路,通路;信道,波道。**5.** (同属一家业主的)联号。*an endless* ~环链。*the home radar* ~飞机归航地面雷达链。*the camera* ~摄像系统。*a* ~ *of events* 一连串事件。*a* ~ *of mountains* 山系,山脉。*She owned a restaurant* ~. 她是几个饭馆的老板。~ *of command* 指挥系统。*A* [*The*] ~ *is not stronger than its weakest link*. 〔谚〕一环薄弱,全局不稳。***be in*** ~***s*** 被链条拴着;被拴在牢房内。~ ***and ball*** **1.** 〔美〕带铁球的脚镣。**2.** 束缚,拘束。**3.** 〔喻〕未婚妻,妻子。***in the*** ~***s***【海】站在舷侧测海水深度的链台上。**II** ***vt.*** **1.** 用链子拴住;束缚;连结。**2.**【测】用测链测量。~ *up a dog* 把狗拴起来。*be* ~*-ed to the desk* 拴在书桌上,被工作拴住(不能脱身)。~ **armo(u)r** = ~ mail. ~ **belt** 链带。~ **brake** 链韧闸,链煞车。~ **bridge** 铁链吊桥。~ **cable**【海】锚链;链索。~**-chew** ***vt.*** 一块接一块地大嚼(口香糖)。~**-cloth** (工业)滤布。~ **coupling**【铁路】链接;【机】链形联接器。~ **gang** 用链子拴成串的囚犯。~**-hop** ***vi.*** 频繁更换电视频道(以搜寻好看的节目)。~ **locker**【海】锚链舱。~ **mail** [**armour**] 锁子甲。~**man** [ˈtʃeinmən; ˋtʃenmən]【海】测链员。~ **mo(u)lding**【建】链条花边。~ **plate**【海】舷侧扣住支(桅)索的铁板。~ **pump** 链斗式水车。~**-react** ***vi.*** 发生连锁反应。~**-reaction**【原】连锁反应,链式反应。~ **riveting** 排钉,链式铆。~ **-rule**【数】连锁法。~ **shot** 链弹。~**-smoke** ***vi.***, ***vt.*** 一支接一支地吸(烟)。~**-smoker** (把将吸完烟头接在另一支烟上)连续抽烟的人。~**-stitch** ***vt.***, ***vi.***【纺】锁缝,用链状针脚缝。~ **stitch**【纺】链状针迹;链状线圈;绞花组织。~ **store** 〔美〕连锁店,联号〔同一公司下属的商店,英国叫 multiple shop〕。~(-)**surf** 频繁更换电视频道。~ **timber** (石匠的)系木。~ **wale**【海】拥桅索承扣板。~ **wheel** (自行车的)锁链轮,飞轮。~**-zap** = ~-hop. **-less** ***a.*** 无链的;无束缚的。**-let** ***n.*** 细链。

chair [tʃɛə; tʃɛr] **I** ***n.*** **1.** 椅子;〔古〕轿子(= sedan)。**2.** (大学的)讲座;大学教授的职位。**3.** 主席[议长、会长]的席位[职位];主席,议长,会长;〔美〕总统[州长]的职位;〔英〕市长职位。**4.**【铁路】(固定枕木的)轨座;【矿】罐座,垫板;【天】星座。**5.** 〔美俚〕电椅。**6.** 轻便单马车。**7.** 〔美〕证人席。*an easy* ~安乐椅。*a double* ~ 鸳鸯椅,双人椅。*a folding* ~折椅。*A Morris* ~大安乐椅。~ *of state* 王位。*sit in* [*on*] *a* ~ 坐在椅子上。★有扶手的椅子用 *in*,无扶手的椅子用 *on*。***address the*** ~ 向主席建议。***appeal to the*** ~ 请主席裁决。***be above*** [***below***] ***the C-*** 〔英〕(伦敦市参议会议员)有[无]市长资历。***Chair! Chair!*** 主席! 主席! 〔要求维持会场秩序〕。~***-borne troops*** 〔美谑〕美国陆军航空队的地勤人员。***escape the*** ~ 〔美俚〕得免死刑[免坐电椅]。***go to*** [***be sent to***, ***get***] ***the*** ~ 〔美俚〕被处死刑[坐电椅]。***in the*** ~ 担任会长[主席];处主席地位;〔俚〕(请客时)做东道。***leave the*** ~ 离开主席座位;散会。***sit on two*** ~***s*** 脚踏两头船。***take a*** ~ 入座,就座。***take the*** ~ 就任主席;主持会议;开会。**II** ***vt.*** **1.** 使就座,使入座。**2.** 使就职,使就位。**3.** 将(得胜者)用椅子抬着游行。~**-bed** 坐卧兼用床。~**borne** ***a.*** 〔美俚〕坐办公室的〔尤指不上前线的军官〕。~ **car** 〔美〕**1.** 没有活动坐椅的(铁路)客车。**2.** 设有特别单人坐椅的豪华客车。~ **lift** (山区游览用的)架空滑车。~**one**, ~**person** 主席,主任,主持人。~ **rail**【建】护墙板。~ **warmer** 〔美俚〕**1.** 长坐在旅馆门厅中休息的人〔不是付钱的住宿者〕。**2.** 懒鬼。

chair·man [ˈtʃɛəmən; ˋtʃɛrmən] **I** ***n.*** (*pl.* ***-men*** [-mən; -mən]) **1.** 议长,会长,主席,主任,委员长。★可男女兼用,称呼时可说作 Mr. Chairman 和 Madame Chairman. **2.** 〔古〕轿夫。**II** ***vt.*** 当(会议等)的主席[议长等]。**-ship** ***n.*** 议长[会长、主席、委员长]的地位[身分]。

chair·wom·an [ˈtʃɛəˌwumən; ˋtʃɛrˏwumən] ***n.*** (*pl.* ***-wom·en*** [-ˌwimin; -ˏwɪmɪn]) 女主席,女议长,女会长,女主任,女委员长。

chaise [ʃeiz; ʃez] ***n.*** 二轮轻便马车;四轮游览马车。

cha·la·za [kəˈleizə; kəˋlezə] ***n.*** (*pl.* ***-zae*** [-ziː; -zi], ***-zas***) **1.**【植】合点。**2.**【动】卵(黄系)带,(昆虫的)毛突。**-l** ***a.***

chal·can·thite [kælˈkænθait; kælˋkænθaɪt] ***n.***【化】胆矾,五水(合)硫酸铜,蓝矾。

chal·ced·o·ny [kælˈsedəni; kælˋsɛdnɪ] ***n.***【矿】玉髓。

chal·cid [ˈkælsid; ˋkælsɪd] ***n.***【动】寄生蜂(= fly)。

chalco- *comb. f.* 黄铜〔母音前用 chalc-〕。

chal·co·cite [ˈkælkəsait; ˋkælkəˏsaɪt] ***n.***【矿】辉铜矿。

chal·cog·ra·phy [kælˈkɔgrəfi; kælˋkɑgrəfɪ] ***n.*** 铜版雕刻(术)。

chal·coph·a·nite [kælˈkɔfənait; kælˋkɑfənaɪt] ***n.***【矿】黑锌锰矿。

chal·co·py·rite [ˌkælkəˈpaiərait; ˏkælkəˋpaɪraɪt] ***n.***【矿】黄铜矿。

Chal·da·ic [kælˈdeiik; kælˋdeɪk] ***n.*** = Chaldean.

Chal·de·an, Chal·dae·an [kælˈdi(ː)ən; kælˋdiən] **I** ***n.*** **1.** (古代巴比伦的)迦勒底人;古代巴比伦人。**2.** 占星者;预言者。**3.** 迦勒底人用的闪族语。**II** ***a.*** 迦勒底(人)

的;迦勒底语[文化]的。

Chal·dee [kæl'di:; kæl`di] *a.*, *n.* = Chaldean.

chal·dron ['tʃɔ:ldrən; `tʃɔldrən] *n.* 焦尔伦,查耳壮〔旧干量单位,英国为32至36蒲式耳,美国为2,500至2,900磅,用于称量煤、石灰等〕。

chal·et ['ʃælei; ʃæ`le] *n.* 1.(瑞士的)木造农舍,牧人小屋。2.(农舍式)木造别墅。3.(街道)公厕。

chal·ice ['tʃælis; `tʃælɪs] *n.* 1.(高脚)酒杯;【宗】圣餐杯。2.〔诗〕杯。3.【植】杯状花。

chalk [tʃɔ:k; tʃɔk] I *n.* 1. 白垩;粉笔。2. 用粉笔画的记号;〔英〕(比赛)得分纪录,记入借方的款项。3.〔美俚〕牛奶。*French* ~ = *tailor's* ~(裁缝划线用的)划粉。*coloured ~s* 彩色粉笔。**(as) *different as* ~ *from cheese* = (as) *like as* ~ *and* [to] *cheese*** 外貌相似实质不同,似是而非。***by a long* ~ = *by long ~s*** =〔英口〕***by ~s*** 相差很多,强得多,好得多。***come up to* (the) ~**〔美俚〕够标准,好;重行开始。***make sb. walk a* ~** 使人服从命令。***not know* ~ *from cheese*** 不辨黑白,不知好歹。***not to make* ~ *of one and cheese of the other*** 公平待遇,一视同仁,毫无偏袒。***stump one's* ~ = *walk one's* ~**〔俚〕走掉,逃走。***walk the* ~**〔俚〕笔直地走〔不醉的表现〕;严格遵守公共秩序;行为正派。II *vt.* 1. 用粉笔写[记下]。2. 用白垩粉擦;使苍白。3. 打…的图样。~ ***it up*** 公布,公告。~ ***on a barn door***〔美口〕大概算一算。~ ***out*** 1. 标出。2. 打样;设计。~ ***up*** 1. 用粉笔记下(分数、货账等);用粉笔写(在墙上等)。2. 把…归因于…(*to*)。3. 增多(利益等)。4.〔美〕提高(价格);赊出。5. 达到,得到。~ **bed**【地】白垩层。~ **board** (浅色)黑板。~ **line** 白粉笔线(*walk the* ~ *line* 保持直线;循规蹈距)。~ **mixture** 幼孩用止痢药。~**stone**【地】石灰岩;【医】痛风结石。~ **talk** (用粉笔在黑板上边作图、边作说明的)图示演说[讲课]。

chalk·y ['tʃɔ:ki; `tʃɔkɪ] *a.* 1. 白垩(质)的;富于白垩的;白垩色的。2. 无反响的;【摄】走了光的,模糊不清的。**chalk·i·ness** *n.*

chal·lah ['hɑ:lə; `hɑlə] *n.* (犹太人安息日和节日吃的)白面包卷(= hallah)。

chal·lenge ['tʃælindʒ; `tʃælɪndʒ] I *n.* 1. 挑战,挑战书,决斗书;(比赛等的)提议。2. 要求,需求,鞭策。3.(哨兵对行人的)盘问,(对飞机等的)信号盘问;口令。4. 质问;怀疑,驳斥;异议。5. 艰巨任务,难题。6.【法】(对陪审官等的)要求回避,表示反对,拒绝。7.【医】(用接触致病性传染物进行的)免疫性试验。*give* [*write*] *a* ~挑战。*accept* [*take*] *a* ~应战。***beyond* ~** 无可非议;无与伦比。***rise to the* ~** 应战;迎着困难上。***take a* ~ *lying down*** 在困难面前俯首贴耳。II *vt.* 1. 向…挑战。2. 要求,需要;引起。3.【军】向…发出盘问口令[信号]。4. 质问;怀疑,驳斥。5.【法】对(陪审官等)要求回避,宣布反对,拒绝。6.〔美〕不承认(投票人有投票资格)。~ *attention* 要求人们的注意。~ *sb.'s interest* 使某人发生兴趣。~ ***a result*** 质问表决结果,对之表示异议。~ (*sb.*) ***to*** (*a duel*; *a game*) 要求和(某人)(决斗;比赛)。—*vi.* 1. 提出挑战。2.【法】表示异议。3.(猎犬发现猎物时)吠叫。~ **cup** [**flag**] 优胜杯[旗]。**-leng·ing** *a.* 1. 挑战的。2. 引起争论[兴趣]的。

chal·leng·er ['tʃælindʒə; `tʃælɪndʒɚ] *n.* 1. 挑战人,要求决斗者。2. 提出异议者;质问者;驳斥者;【法】要求(陪审官等)回避者。3. 提出盘问者。

chal·lis, chal·lie ['ʃælis, 'ʃæli; `ʃælɪs, `ʃælɪ] *n.*【纺】印花毛[棉]薄织物。

chal·one ['kæləun; `kælon] *n.*【生化】抑素。

chal·u·meau ['ʃæljuˌməu; `ʃæljʊˏmo] *n.*【乐】1. 芦笛。2. 竖笛的最低音区。

cha·lutz [hɑ:'lu:ts; hɑ`luts] *n.* (*pl.* **-lutz·im** [-lu:'tsi:m; -lu`tsim]) 哈鲁茨〔以色列农业居民点中最早移入的犹太人拓荒者〕(= halutz)。

cha·lyb·e·ate [kə'libiit; kə`lɪbɪɪt] I *a.* (矿泉)含铁质的。II *n.* 含铁矿泉,铁剂。

cham [kæm; kæm] *n.*〔废〕= khan[1]. *the Great C-* 1. 鞑靼王,大可汗。2. 文坛权威〔特指 Samuel Johnson〕。

cha·made [ʃə'mɑ:d; ʃə`mɑd] *n.*〔F.〕〔古〕求和号[鼓],投降号[鼓];退却信号。

Cha·mae·le·on [kə'mi:ljən, -'mi:liən; kə`miljən, -milɪən] *n.*【天】蝘蜓(星)座(= Chameleon)。

cham·ae·phyte ['kæmiəfait; `kæmɪəfaɪt] *n.*【植】地上芽植物。

cham·ber ['tʃeimbə; `tʃembɚ] I *n.* 1.〔古、诗〕室,房间;寝室,卧室;〔*pl.*〕套房;〔*pl.*〕律师[法官]办公室。2. 会议室,会场;议会,议院;协会。3. 箱,暗箱;蜂箱。4.(枪的)弹膛,药室;螺管(动植物体的)窝,穴,腔;心室。5. 便壶,尿罐(= ~ pot)。6.【矿】矿车。*the upper* [*lower*] ~上[下]议院。*C- of Commerce* 商会。*C- of Deputies* (法、意、智利等的)下院。*C- of Peers* (旧时葡萄牙的)上院。*C- of Representatives* (比利时的)众议院。II *vt.* 1. 把…关在室内,禁闭。2.(枪上)装(子弹)。3. 使有房间。III *a.* 1. 秘密的。2.【乐】在小厅内表演的,小乐队演奏的。~ *concert* 室内音乐会。~ **council** 秘密会议。~ **counsel** 法律顾问;(律师的)私人意见,鉴定。~**maid** (旅馆的)女侍;〔美〕(一般)女仆;〔古〕侍女。~ **music** 室内音乐。~ **orchestra** 室内乐队。~ **pot** 尿罐,便壶。

cham·bered ['tʃeimbəd; `tʃembɚd] *a.* 有(…)房间的;处在房间[小室]里的。~ **corridor** 两旁边侧有房间的走廊。~ **rein**【矿】束状矿脉。

Cham·ber·lain ['tʃeimbəlin; `tʃembɚlɪn] *n.* 钱伯林,张伯伦〔姓氏〕。**(Arthur) Neville** ~ 张伯伦〔1869—1940,英国政治家,1937—1940年任首相〕。

cham·ber·lain ['tʃeimbəlin; `tʃembɚlɪn] *n.* 1.(国王的)侍从;(贵族的)管家。2.(村镇的)收款员,财务管理人;〔古〕(旅馆的)房间管理人。*the Grand C-* 侍从长。*the Lord C-* (*of the Household*) (英王的)宫内大臣;侍从长。*the Lord Great C-* (*of England*) 掌礼大臣。

Cham·bers ['tʃeimbəz; `tʃembɚz] *n.* 钱伯斯〔姓氏〕。

cham·bray ['ʃæmbrei; `ʃæmbre] *n.* 条格布。

cha·me·le·on [kə'mi:ljən; kə`miljən] *n.* 1.【动】石龙子,变色龙〔蜥蜴类〕。2. 反复无常的人。3.〔the C-〕【天】蝘蜓(星)座。~ **solution**【化】(过)锰酸钾溶液,变色液。

cha·me·le·on·ic [kəˌmi:li'ɔnik; kəˏmilɪ`ɑnɪk] *a.* 变色龙一样的;反复无常的。

cham·fer ['tʃæmfə; `tʃæmfɚ] I *n.* 1.【建】削角。2. 槽,凹线;〔美〕圆槽。3. 斜面,切角面,棱角。4.【机】圆角,倒角,倒棱,斜切。II *vt.* 1. 在…上雕槽[刻沟]。2. 去…的角,斜切。3.〔美〕(用圆凿)刳(木、石等),在…上挖圆槽。

cham·fron, cham·frain ['tʃæmfrən; `tʃæmfrən] *n.* 马头甲、马盔。

cham·ois ['ʃæmwɑ:; `ʃæmwɑ] *n.* (*pl.* ~ ['ʃæmwɑ:z; `ʃæmwɑz]) 1.【动】(南欧及西亚的)小羚羊。2. 羚羊皮,麂皮,油鞣革。

cham·o·mile ['kæməmail; `kæməˏmaɪl] *n.* = camomile.

Cha·mor·ro [tʃɑ:'mɔ:rəu; tʃɑ`mɔrro] *n.* 1.(*pl.* ~)夏莫洛人〔关岛和马里亚纳群岛本土人的一个部族〕。2. 夏莫洛人讲的印尼语。

cha·motte [ʃə'mɔt; ʃə`mɑt] *n.*【建】火泥。~ **brick** 耐火砖。

champ[1] [tʃæmp; tʃæmp] I *vt.* 1.(马)嚼(草料);格格地咬(马嚼子)。2. 捣烂。—*vi.* 1.(马)大声咀嚼。2.(人)(兴奋得)牙齿颤响;(怒得)咬牙切齿。3. 不耐烦,焦急。~ ***the bit*** (马)咬马嚼子;(人)(因拖延等而)焦急,不耐烦。II *n.* 嚼;嚼声。

champ[2] [tʃæmp; tʃæmp] *n.*〔美俚〕= champion.

cham·pac, cham·pak ['ʃæmpæk; `tʃæmpæk] *n.*【植】金香木。

cham·pagne [ʃæm'pein; ʃæm`pen] *n.* 1. 香槟酒。2. 微

C

黄色,极淡的黄绿色;香槟酒似的颜色。**3.**〔C-〕香槟省〔法国东北部一省〕。*still* ～无泡香槟酒。～ **cider** 苹果香槟酒;苹果汽酒。～ **cup** **1.** 香槟汽水。**2.** 大酒杯。～ **socialist**〔贬〕香槟酒社会主义者〔指生活豪华而口头上鼓吹社会主义的富翁〕。

cham·paign [ˈtʃæmpein; tʃæmˋpen] **I** ***n.*** 原野,平原。**II** ***a.*** (地势)平坦的。

cham·per·ty [ˈtʃæmpə(:)ti; ˋtʃæmpɚtɪ] ***n.***【法】(帮人诉讼胜诉后互分利益的)帮诉;帮诉罪。

cham·pi·gnon [tʃæmˈpinjən; tʃæmˋpɪnjən] ***n.***【植】香蕈,食用伞菌。

cham·pi·on [ˈtʃæmpjən; ˋtʃæmpɪən] **I** ***n.*** **1.** 战士;斗士;监督执行者;维护者,拥护者(*for*)。**2.** 锦标保持人,优胜者,冠军〔*cf.* runner-up〕;(博览会中的)特等奖得奖人[动物]。**3.** 倡导人,提倡者。*a national* ～全国冠军。～*flag* 优胜旗。～ *race* 锦标赛跑。*a* ～ *for* [*against*] *justice* 正义的维护者[反对者]。*King's* [*Queen's*] *C-*, *C- of England* (世袭的)英王加冕典礼护卫官。**II** ***a.*** 〔口〕头等的,优秀的;非常的。*a* ～ *idiot* 大傻瓜。*a* ～ *blunder* 大错。**III** ***vt.*** **1.** 维护,拥护,主张;为…而奋斗。**2.** 监督执行,主持。～ *a cause* 维护一项事业。**-less** ***a.*** 无冠军的。

cham·pi·on·ship [ˈtʃæmpjənʃip; ˋtʃæmpjənʃɪp] ***n.*** **1.** 拥护,支持;提倡;拥护者[支持者,提倡者]的身分。**2.** 锦标;优胜;冠军称号[地位]。**3.** 锦标赛(=～ series)。**4.** 保持冠军称号的时期。

champ·le·vé [ʃɑ:nliˈvei; ʃɑnlɪˋve] **I** ***a.*** 〔F.〕雕刻铜版的。**II** ***n.*** 雕刻铜版搪瓷器皿。

Chanc. = Chancellor; Chancery.

chance [tʃɑ:ns; tʃæns] **I** ***n.*** **1.** 偶然;运气,命运;偶然事件;意外事件(*opp.* necessity)。**2.** 机会,良机;幸运,侥幸;机缘。**3.**〔常 *pl.*〕概率,机率,或然率,可能性,或然性,把握,希望;形势。**4.**〔美〕危险,冒险;赌博;彩票。**5.**〔美俚〕大学校长。**6.**〔美俚〕时间;大量,许多。*a game of* ～ 碰运气的游戏;没有把握的行动;碰运气的(偶然的)事情。*If* ～ *will have me king*. 万一我做国王。*I will give you a* ～. 我姑且给你一个改过的机会〔下次不再宽恕了〕。*The* ～*s are against it*. 形势不利。*I stood there a pretty considerable* ～. 〔美〕我在那儿站了很久。*a smart* [*powerful*] ～ *of apples*〔美〕许许多多苹果。***a dog's*** ～ 极微小的一点儿机会。***a fat*** ～ 机会"多得很"〔反语〕。***an off*** ～ 万一的希望,很小的可能。***by any*** ～ 万一,碰巧。***by*** ～ 偶然,意外地(*by the merest* ～完完全全是偶然的,极意外地)。***by some*** ～ 不知道为什么。***even*** ～ 胜败各半,成败相等。***fighting*** ～ 虽有可能性但很难得到的机会。***have no*** ～ ***whatever*** 谈不上;没有任何希望。***leave things to*** ～ 听天由命,听其自然。***lose no*** ～ ***for*** 不放松,抓紧。***on the*** ～ ***of*** 指望,期待(*I came on the* ～ *of finding you*. 我来是想碰到你)。***on the off*** ～ 适值千载难逢的机会,侥幸。***run a*** ～ ***of failure***〔美〕有失败的危险。***stand a good*** [*fair*] ～ ***of*** 有相当把握,大有希望。***stand no*** ～ ***against*** 对…不操胜算[无把握]。***stand one's*** ～ 听天由命。***take a*** (***long***) ～ = ***take*** (***long***) ～ 冒险一试。***take one's*** [***the***] ～ 好歹试试看。***the main*** ～ 最有利的机会,绝好机会;赚钱机会(*have an eye to the main* ～ 追求个人利益,唯利是图,竭力钻营)。**II** ***a.*** 偶然的,意外的。*a* ～ *meeting* 邂逅。*a* ～ *child* 私生儿。**III** ***vi.*** 偶然发生,料不到会,偶然得到。*I* ～*d to meet him*. 偶然碰到了他。*He* ～*d to be present*. 他碰巧在场〔此义现在一般用 happen〕。—***vt.*** 冒…的险;〔口〕〔常作～ it〕试试看,碰碰看;〔美俚〕抓住(机会)。*I will* ～ *it*. 好歹试试看,碰碰运气看。***and*** ～ ***it***〔俚〕无论怎样,好歹。***as it may*** ～ 按当时形势。～ ***on*** [***upon***] 偶然发现,碰巧看见。～ ***one's arm***〔口〕冒险一试;抓牢机会。～ ***the consequence*** 成败由天。

chance·ful [ˈtʃɑ:nsful; ˋtʃænsful] ***a.*** **1.** 多变的;多事的。**2.**〔古〕取决于机会的;冒险的,危险的。

chan·cel [ˈtʃɑ:nsəl; ˋtʃænsəl] ***n.***【宗】(教堂中祭坛周围设有祭司及唱诗班席位的)高坛,圣坛。

chan·cel·ler·y [ˈtʃɑ:nsələri; ˋtʃænsələrɪ] ***n.*** **1.** 大臣[大法官、总理等]的职位。**2.** 大臣官邸,总理公署、官邸,大法官法庭。**3.** (大使馆或领事馆的)办事处;大使[领事]馆全体人员。

chan·cel·lor [ˈtʃɑ:nsələ; ˋtʃænsəlɚ] ***n.*** **1.**〔英〕(财政)大臣,司法官〔职位名〕。**2.**〔美〕平衡法院的首席法官;(大使馆等的)秘书长;〔英〕大学名誉校长,〔美〕大学校长。**3.**【史】(东罗马帝国的)掌玺官。**4.**【史】(旧时德、奥等国的)总理。*a* ～ *of a diocese* (英国教会)主教法律顾问。*the C- of the Exchequer*〔英〕财政大臣。*the Lord* (*High*) *C-* = *the C-* (*of England*)〔英〕大法官,阁员之一,议会开会期间兼任上院议长〕。**-ship** 大臣[大法官、总理]的职位[任期]。

chan·cel·lor·y = chancellery.

chance-med·ley [ˈtʃɑ:nsˈmedli; ˋtʃænsˋmɛdlɪ] ***n.*** **1.**【法】偶然杀人,过失[自卫]杀伤。**2.** 偶然(行动)。

chan·cer·y [ˈtʃɑ:nsəri ; ˋtʃænsərɪ] ***n.*** **1.**〔C-〕〔英〕大法院〔今为高等法院的一部〕。**2.**〔美〕平衡法院;平衡法院的法律[诉讼事务]。**3.** 档案处,记录处。**4.** 大臣[总理、大法官]的办事处。***a ward in*** ～ 受大法官监护的未成年人。***in*** ～ **1.** 在平衡法院[大法官法庭]诉讼中的。**2.**【拳】〔喻〕头被挟在对手腋下;进退两难。

chan·ci·ness [ˈtʃɑ:nsinis; ˋtʃænsɪnɪs] ***n.*** 不确定性,危险性。

chan·cre [ˈʃæŋkə; ˋʃæŋkɚ] ***n.***【医】(硬性)下疳。

chan·croid [ˈʃæŋkrɔid; ˋʃæŋkrɔɪd] ***n.***【医】软下疳(= soft chancre)。

chanc·y [ˈtʃɑ:nsi; ˋtʃænsɪ] ***a.*** **1.**〔口〕不确实的,危险的。**2.**〔Scot.〕幸运的〔常用于否定句〕。

chan·de·lier [ˌʃændiˈliə; ˏʃændlˋɪr] ***n.*** 枝形吊灯;【军】撑墙。

chan·delle [ʃɑ:nˈdel; ʃænˋdɛl] **I** ***n.***【空】急跃升。**II** ***vi.*** 作急跃升。

chan·dler [ˈtʃɑ:ndlə; ˋtʃændlɚ] ***n.*** **1.** 蜡烛制造人,蜡烛商。**2.** (杂货)零售商。

Chan·dler('s) [ˈtʃɑ:ndlə(z); ˋtʃandlə(z)] **wobble**【地】钱德勒颤动(造成经纬度变化的地球转动轴的极微位移)。

chan·dler·y [ˈtʃɑ:ndləri; ˋtʃændlərɪ] ***n.*** **1.** 蜡烛类;杂货类。**2.** 蜡烛店;杂货店。**3.** 蜡烛[杂货]仓库。

change [tʃeindʒ; tʃendʒ] **I** ***vt.*** **1.** 改变,变更,变换,变革。**2.** 交换;兑换;把(大票等)换成零钱;把(支票等)兑成现金。**3.** 换(车、衣服),更换。**4.**〔口〕使(味)变酸[坏]。～ *one's habits* [*way of thinking*] 改变习惯[想法]。～ *a horse* [*cars*] 换马[倒车]。～ *a fivepound note* 把一张五镑钞票兑换成零钱。～ *a fivepound note into gold* 把一张五镑钞票兑换成金币。—***vi.*** **1.** 变,改变,起变化。**2.** 换车,换衣服,改换办法[策略等]。*Where do we* ～? 我们在哪里换车? *It took me only five minutes to* ～. 我只用五分钟就换好了衣服。～ ***about*** 转换方向;变节;首尾互异,反覆无常。～ ***arms***【军】换(掮枪的)肩。～ ***at...*** 在(某处)换车。～ ***breath***〔美俚〕换换口味[换喝另一种酒]。～ ***colo(u)r*** 变脸色。～ ***down*** [***up***] (汽车)改成慢挡[快挡];开慢[快]。～ ***foot*** [***step***] 变方向;变态度;变步骤。～ ***for...*** 换车往(某处)。～ ***for the better*** [***worse***] 变好[坏]。～ ***... for...*** 以…换…(～ *the old shoes for the new ones* 以旧鞋换新鞋)。～ ***front***【军】改变攻击方向;〔喻〕转变论调。～ ***into*** **1.** 改穿(～ *into flannels* 换上法兰绒裤)。**2.** 变成(*Water* ～*s into steam*. 水变成汽)。～ ***one's note*** [***tune***]〔口〕(言谈中)改变口气[态度]。～ ***oneself*** 换衣裳。～ ***oneself into*** 变成…,化为。～ ***over*** (使)改变(目的,位置);改期。～ ***side*** 改变立场;脱党,变节。～ (***seats***) ***with*** (*sb.*) 与(人)换(座位)。**II** ***n.*** **1.** 变化;改

变,变换,变更;变动,变迁;改革;更迭。**2.** 交换,交替;换衣服;换车;换环境。**3.** 找头,零钱。**4.**【乐】转调,换调;钟声的变调。**5.**〔C-〕交易所(='Change, Exchange)。*a ~ of address* 住址的变更。*a ~ of cars* 换车。*a ~ of clothes* 换衣服。*a ~ of heart* 变心;改变主意。*the ~ of the moon* 月亮的(圆缺)变化;新月的出现。*a ~ of tide* 潮的交替;危机。*a changing bag* (换胶卷用的)暗袋。*I have no ~ about me.* 我没有零钱。*You need a ~.* 你应该改变改变环境。**be [go] on ~** 在交易所(做事)。**~ of air** 迁地(疗养)。**~ of life** (妇女的)更年期,绝经期,停经。**~ of pace** 换口味;变手法。**~ of voice** (青春期的)变嗓音。**for a ~** 为了改变一下,为了换换花样。**get no ~ out of** (*sb.*)〔俚〕从(某人)处得不到什么便宜;从(某人)探听不出什么。**give** (*sb.*)~ 给某人以报答;〔俚〕向某人报复,对某人予以还击。**give** (*sb.*) **no ~** 〔口〕不让某人知道;对某人秘而不宣。**put the ~ on [upon]** (*sb.*) 瞒,欺骗(某人)。**ring the ~s** 打钟打出(各种)调子;用种种言语[方式]说明;用种种方法试办。**small ~** 零钱。**take the ~ out of** (*sb.*)〔口〕报复,复仇。**Take your ~ out of that!** 〔还嘴、报复时语〕这就是回答! **~ gear [wheel]**【机】变速齿轮。**~over** *n.* **1.** 改变,转变;变更,转换。**2.** (电影换片时的)换机放映。**~room** 更衣室。**~-up** *n.*【垒球】(投球手每次投球的)变换手法。

change·a·bil·i·ty [ˌtʃeindʒəˈbiliti; ˏtʃendʒəˋbɪlətɪ] *n.* 易变,不安定;可变性。

change·a·ble [ˈtʃeindʒəbl; ˋtʃendʒəbl̩] *a.* 可变的,易变的,会变的;不确定的;无恒心的。**-ness** *n.* 易变,三心二意。

change·a·bly [ˈtʃeindʒəbli; ˋtʃendʒəblɪ] *ad.* 易变地;不安定地;会变似地。

change·ful [ˈtʃeindʒful; ˋtʃendʒfəl] *a.* 变化多的,易变的,不确定的。**~ gear**【机】变速齿轮。**-ly** *ad.*

change·less [ˈtʃeindʒlis; ˋtʃendʒlɪs] *a.* 不变的,确定的;单调的。**-ness** *n.*

change·ling [ˈtʃeindʒliŋ; ˋtʃendʒlɪŋ] *n.* **1.** (迷信说法中被仙女)偷换后留下的丑孩子,矮小丑陋的人[动物]。**2.**〔古〕低能儿。**3.**〔古〕见异思迁的人;不忠实的人,变节者。**4.** (集邮)颜色起化学变化的邮票。

chang·er [ˈtʃeindʒə; ˋtʃendʒɚ] *n.* 变更者;更换器;(电唱机)自动换片器。

chan·nel[1] [ˈtʃænl; ˋtʃænl̩] **I** *n.* **1.** 水路,水道,渠,沟;海峡;河床,河底。**2.** (柱等的)槽,凹缝;【机】槽铁,凹形铁。**3.**〔喻〕路线,手段;媒介,脉络,系统,途径。**4.**【无、电】波道;电路;信道;磁道;频道。*a talk ~* 通话线路。*a vision ~* 电视信道,视频信道。*the (English) C-* 英吉利海峡。*C- fever* 〔英〕怀乡病。*~ of command [communication]* 指挥[通讯]系统。*through a reliable ~* 通过可靠途径。**through the proper ~** 经由正当途径[手续]。**II** *vt.* (〔英〕**-ll-**) **1.** 在…开[形成]水道;在…上凿沟[凹缝]。**2.** 开(路),开辟(途径)。**3.** 为…开辟途径,引导。*~ one's interests* 对某人的兴趣加以引导。**—vi.** 形成水道[凹槽]。**~groping** 英国近海巡航。

chan·nel[2] [ˈtʃænl; ˋtʃænl̩] *n.* 〔常 *pl.*〕【海】突出舷侧承扣支索的铁板。

chan·nell·ed [ˈtʃænəld; ˋtʃænəld] *a.* 有沟(凹缝)的。**~ iron**【机】U 形铁。

chan·nel·ize [ˈtʃænəlaiz; ˋtʃænl̩ˏaɪz] *vt.* = channel *vt.* **-i·za·tion** *n.*

chan·son [ˈʃænsən; ˋʃænsən] *n.* 〔F.〕歌。***C- de Roland*** 《罗兰之歌》〔法国中世纪的民族史诗〕。

chant [tʃɑːnt; tʃɑnt] **I** *n.* **1.**【宗】颂歌,圣歌,赞美诗。**2.** 单调的歌;吟诵语调,单调的语调。**II** *vt.*, *vi.* **1.** 单调地唱,吟诵。**2.** 歌颂;颂扬,赞扬。**~ horses** 夸马(骗卖),登骗人广告。**~ the praises of** 极口称赞,颂扬。

chan·tage [ˈtʃɑːntidʒ; ˋtʃɑntɪdʒ] *n.* 〔F.〕勒索,讹诈。

chan·te·cler 见 chanticleer.

chant·er [ˈtʃɑːntə; ˋtʃɑntɚ] *n.* **1.** 歌唱者;领唱人。**2.** (风笛的)指管。**3.** 骗人的马贩子。**4.**【动】篱雀。

chan·te·relle [ˌtʃæntiˈrel, ˌtʃæn-; ˏʃæntɪˋrɛl, ˏtʃæn-] *n.* 【植】鸡油菌属(*Cantharellus*)植物〔尤指鸡油蕈〕(*Cantharellus cibarius*)。

chan·teuse [F. ʃɑ̃tøːz; ʃɑ̃toez] *n.* 女歌手〔尤指女民歌手〕。

chant·ey [ˈʃɑːnti; ˋʃɑntɪ] = chanty.

chan·ti·cleer, chan·te·cler [ˌtʃæntiˈkliə, -ˈklɛə; ˏtʃæntɪˋklɪr, -ˋklɛr] *n.* 雄鸡(先生)〔法国古代文学作品《列那狐的故事》中拟人化的雄鸡〕。

chan·tor [ˈtʃɑːntə; ˋtʃɑntɚ] *n.* = chanter.

chant·ress [ˈtʃɑːntris; ˋtʃɑntrɪs] *n.* 〔诗〕女歌手。

chan·try [ˈtʃɑːntri; ˋtʃantrɪ] *n.* **1.** (施主捐款建造的)歌祷堂;歌祷堂的捐建。**2.** 附属小礼拜堂。

chan·ty [ˈtʃɑːnti; ˋʃæntɪ] *n.* 水手起锚歌(= chantey)。

Cha·nu·kah [ˈkɑːnuˌkɑː; ˋkɑnʊˏkɑ] *n.* 犹太圣节(= Hanuka)。

cha·os [ˈkeiɔs; ˋkeɑs] *n.* **1.** 〔常 C-〕(天地未出现的)浑沌世界。**2.** 混乱。**3.** 〔古〕无底深渊。**~ theory** 混沌理论,混沌学。

cha·ot·ic [keiˈɔtik; keˋɑtɪk] *a.* 浑沌的;混乱的。**~ dynamics** 混沌动力学(= ~ theory)。**-i·cal·ly** *ad.*

chap[1] [tʃæp; tʃæp] *n.* **1.** 〔口〕家伙,小伙子。**2.** 〔英方〕买者,顾客。*a funny little ~* 有趣的小家伙。*my dear ~ = old ~* 老兄。

chap[2] [tʃæp; tʃæp] *n.* **1.** 〔*pl.*〕(动物的)颌;(人的)面颊。**2.** 猪头肉的颚颊部分。**lick one's ~s** 淌着口水等待(好菜),馋涎欲滴;(吃东西时)咂舌头。

chap[3] [tʃæp; tʃæp] **I** *n.* 〔常 *pl.*〕皲;皲裂(处),龟裂(处)。**II** *vt.*, *vi.* (**-pp-**) (使)(皮肤等)皲裂[发皲,龟裂,变粗糙]。

chap[4] [tʃæp; tʃæp] *n.* 〔Scot.〕(钟)报(时)。

chap. = chapel; chaplain; chapter.

cha·pa·ra·jos, -rehos [ˌʃæpəˈreiəus; ˏʃæpəˋreɪos] *n.* 〔美西部〕牧人皮套裤。

chap·ar·ral [tʃæpəˈræl; tʃæpəˋræl] *n.* 〔美西部〕小槲树(的丛林);(一般)树丛。

chap-book [ˈtʃæpˌbuk; ˋtʃæpˏbʊk] *n.* **1.** (旧时小贩沿街叫卖的)民间文艺(廉价)小册子[唱本]。**2.** 小书,小册子。

chape [tʃeip; tʃep] *n.* **1.** (剑鞘的)铜包头。**2.** (皮带上的)小圈。

cha·peau [ʃæˈpəu; ʃæˋpo] *n.* (*pl.* ~*s*, ***-peaux*** [-ˈpəuz; -ˋpoz]) 〔F.〕帽。*C- bas* [ˈbɑː; ˋbɑ]! 脱帽! *~ de poil* 海獭帽。~**-bras** 〔F.〕可折叠的三角帽。

chap·el [ˈtʃæpəl; ˋtʃæpl̩] *n.* **1.** 小教堂,附属教堂;〔英〕(国教分离派的)教堂;(学校、营房等的)附属礼拜堂[室];(在学校礼拜室中做的)礼拜。**2.** 印刷(厂工人)工会。**3.** 〔美俚〕殡仪馆。**a ~ of ease** 〔英〕(偏远教区的)小教堂。**father of the ~** 印刷厂工人工会主席。**hold a ~** 开印刷厂工会会议。**hold ~** (教皇等)参加礼拜。**keep a ~** 〔牛津、剑桥大学〕(按时)做礼拜。**keep one's ~s** 只按时做礼拜(此外不做)。**lose [miss] a ~** 没有去做礼拜。

cha·pelle ar·dente [ʃæˈpel ɑːˈdɑ̃ːnt; ʃæˋpɛl ɑrˋdɑ̃nt] 〔F.〕(名人死后点着蜡烛供人瞻仰的)停尸室。

chap·er·on(e) [ˈʃæpərəun; ˋʃæpəˏron] **I** *n.* (在交际场中监护少女的)年长女伴;保护人。**II** *vt.* 陪伴,伴随;护送(少女)。**-age** *n.* 陪伴,伴随(少女)。

chap·fall·en [ˈtʃæpˌfɔːlən; ˋtʃæpˏfɔlən] *a.* **1.** 下颌下垂的。**2.** 〔喻〕沮丧的,垂头丧气的。

chap·i·ter [ˈtʃæpitə; ˋtʃæpɪtɚ] *n.* 【建】柱头。

chap·lain [ˈtʃæplin; ˋtʃæplɪn] *n.* 随军[校内,院内]教士〔军队、学校、医院、监狱等中的教士,有时亦由非教士担任〕。**-cy, -ship** *n.* (随军等的)教士职位。

chap·let [ˈtʃæplit; ˋtʃæplɪt] *n.* **1.** 花冠;项圈。**2.** 念珠;

【建】串珠饰。3.（孔雀）冠毛；（昆虫）刺冠。**-ed** *a*. 戴着花冠的。

Chap·lin [ˈtʃæplin; ˋtʃæplɪn] *n*. 查普林，卓别林〔姓氏〕。

Chap·man [ˈtʃæpmən; ˋtʃæpmən] *n*. 查普曼〔姓氏〕。

chap·man [ˈtʃæpmən; ˋtʃæpmən] *n*. 叫卖小贩；行商。

chap·pie, chap·py[1] [ˈtʃæpi; ˋtʃæpɪ] *n*.〔口〕1. 花花公子。2. 家伙，小伙子。

chap·py[2] [ˈtʃæpi; ˋtʃæpɪ] *a*. 皲裂的。

chaps [tʃæps; ʃæps] *n*.〔*pl*.〕= chaparajos.

chap·ter [ˈtʃæptə; ˋtʃæptɚ] *n*. 1.（书籍、文章的）章，部分；（历史或人生的）一段经过。2.（大教堂）教士会；教士会集会，骑士团[修士团]的集会（会场）。3.〔美〕（俱乐部，协会，校友会等的）分会；〔美〕一次比赛。4.（钟表盘面上的）数字，符号。*a* ~ *of accidents* 一连串（不幸的）事故。*enough on that* ~ 这个问题就到此为止。*give* ~ *and verse for* 注明引证出处；指明确切依据。*read* (*sb*.) *a* ~ 教训（某人）。*to* [*till*] *the end of the* ~ 到最后；永远。~ **house** 教士会礼堂；〔美大学〕校友会会所。

char[1] [tʃɑː; tʃɑr] *n*., *vi*., *vt*. =〔美〕chare. ~**lady**, ~-**woman** 打杂女工。~**man** 勤杂工。

char[2] [tʃɑː; tʃɑr] I *n*. 木炭，炭；烧焦之物。II *vt*. 把…烧成炭；烧焦（木材表面）。—*vi*. 变焦黑。

char[3] [tʃɑː; tʃɑr] *n*.（*pl*. ~*s*）【鱼】红点鲑，白点鲑。

char[4] [tʃɑː; tʃɑr] *n*.〔英俚〕茶。

char-à-banc [ˈʃærəbæŋ; ˋʃærəˏbæŋ] *n*.（*pl*. ~*s* [-z; -z]）〔F.〕游览车。*a motor* ~ 游览汽车。

char·a·cin [ˈkærəsin; ˋkærəsɪn] *n*.【动】特色鱼（*Characinidae*）〔产于南美，中美和非洲〕。

char·ac·ter [ˈkæriktə; ˋkærɪktɚ] I *n*. 1. 性格，品格；特性，性状，特征；【生】形质。2. 身分，地位，资格。3. 名声，声望。4.（戏剧、小说中的）角色，人物。5. 人，〔口〕怪人，奇人。6. 字，字母；数字；（印刷）符号；电码组合；【计】字符。7. 品德证明书，鉴定，推荐书。8. 人物[性格]素描。*a man of* ~ 有个性[骨气]的人。*the national* ~ = *the* ~ *of a people* 国民性。*a generic* ~【生】属的特征，属性。*a leading* ~ 主角。*a bad* ~ 坏人，歹徒，恶棍。*He is quite a* ~. 他简直是一个怪人。*a Chinese* ~ 汉字。~ *portrayal* 性格描写。~ *sketch* 人物简评[素描]。*get a good* [*bad*] ~ 得好[坏]名。*give* (*sb*.) *a good* [*bad*] ~ 推奖[攻击]（某人）。*have an insight into* ~ 有知人之明。*in* ~（在）性格上；正合担任[扮演]；适当，相称。*in the* ~ *of* 以…的资格；扮演。*out of* ~ 不适当[适合]，不称（*go out of* ~ 越分妄为）。*take away sb.'s* ~ 夺人名誉。*take on* ~ 有特征[特色]。II *vt*. 1.〔诗、古〕写，画；刻。2. 表现…的特性；使具有特性。~ **actor** 性格演员。~ **assassination**（对知名人士等的）人格毁损。~ **book** 征信录，各界人士录。~ **building** 性格陶冶。**-less** *a*. 无特征的，平凡的。

char·ac·ter·is·tic [ˌkæriktəˈristik; ˏkærɪktəˋrɪstɪk] I *a*. 有特性的；表示…特性的，…特有的。*Japan's* ~ *art* 日本特有的艺术。II *n*. 特性，特征，性能，特色。*be* ~ *of* …所独有的特征，有…的特色。~ *of logarithm* 对数的首数。~ **curve** 特性曲线。~ **function** 示性函数。~ **radiation**【物】标志辐射。~ **species** 典型种。~ **test**【机】特性试验。**-cal·ly** *ad*.

char·ac·ter·i·za·tion [ˌkæriktəraiˈzeiʃən; ˏkærɪktəraɪˋzeʃən] *n*. 特性记述[表示、赋与]；性格描写；鉴定。

char·ac·ter·ize [ˈkæriktəraiz; ˋkærɪktəˏraɪz] *vt*. 1. 叙述[描写]…的特性；鉴定。2. 表示…的特性；以…为特性；使带有…的特征。*a style* ~*d by brevity* 具有简洁特色的文体。—*vi*.（文学作品中）塑造人物，描写性格。*be* ~*d by* 有…的（显著）特点，突出地表现为…。

char·ac·ter·y [ˈkæriktəri; ˋkærɪktərɪ] *n*.〔集合词〕符号，文字。

char·ac·to·nym [kəˈræktənim; kəˋræktənɪm] *n*. 说明某人特征的词[名称]。

char·ac·tron [ˈkærəktrɔn; ˋkærəktrɑn] *n*.【无】显像管；显示管，字码管。

cha·rade [ʃəˈrɑːd, Am. ʃəˈreid; ʃəˋrɑd, ʃəˋred] *n*. 1.（用诗、画、动作等构成的）哑剧字谜；哑剧字谜的谜底〔一个词或一句话〕。2.〔喻〕荒谬的借口，几乎不加掩饰的伪装。

char·bon [ˈʃɑːbɔ̃ːŋ; ˋʃɑrbɔ̃ŋ] *n*.〔F.〕【医】炭疽（脾脱疽）。

char·broil [ˈtʃɑːbrɔil; ˋtʃɑrbrɔɪl] *vt*. 用木炭火烤（肉）。

char·coal [ˈtʃɑːkəul; ˋtʃɑrˏkol] *n*. 1.（木）炭；【医】生物炭。2.（画用）炭笔。3. 木炭画。*activated* ~ 活性炭。*animal* ~ 骨炭，兽炭。~ **biscuit**（胃肠病吃的）炭饼干。~ **burner** 烧炭人；炭炉。~ **crayon** 炭笔。~ **drawing** 木炭画。~ **lily** 黑皮肤的少年。~ **rot**【植】黑腐病。

chard [tʃɑːd; tʃɑrd] *n*.【植】莙荙菜，牛皮菜（*Beta vulgaris cicla*）。

chare [tʃɛə; tʃɛr] I *n*. 1.〔美〕〔常 *pl*.〕（家庭中的）零碎工作，杂活，家务。2.〔口〕打杂女佣人，临时女帮工，计时女佣。II *vt*., *vi*. 1.（给…）打杂，（为…）做零活。2. 清扫，修理。~ *a leak* 检修屋漏。

charge [tʃɑːdʒ; tʃɑrdʒ] I *vt*. 1. 填；装（子弹）；充（电）；使饱和；使充满；堆积，装载。2. 命令；促；谕示，指令。3. 责备；告诫。4. 使承担（责任）。5. 把…归咎于（*to*, *on*, *upon*）；告发，在控告（*with*）。6. 要求收（费）；索（价）；课（税）。7. 为…支出；在（账）上记入…，记入…账内[名下]。8.【军】向…进击，袭击。~ *a pen*（钢笔）上墨水。*a charging machine* 装料机。*air* ~*d with moisture* 充满潮气的空气。~ *sb. with theft* 以窃盗罪控告某人，控告某人行窃。*I shall* ~ *you five dollars*. 我要你付五元。~ *a tax on* ... 对…征税。*I* ~*d him to see that all was right*. 托他妥为照料。—*vi*. 1. 收费，要价。2.【军】冲锋，向前冲。*He* ~*s high for it*. 他对之要高价。~ *and cheer* 一边冲锋一边呐喊。*C- bayonet*! 上刺刀！〔冲锋前的号令〕。~ *off*【会计】（在账簿中）注销（损失等），报损。~ *off* ... *to* 把…归于某一项[看作某事的一部分]。~ *oneself with* 负起…的责任，承担。~ *to sb.'s account* 记入某人账下（*C- these cigars to my account* [*against me*]. 这些雪茄烟请算在我账里）。~ (*sb*.) *with* 托付，使…负担；使负…的罪名，认为有…的嫌疑；使受…的责备。II *n*. 1. 负荷，装载物；（火器的）装填；充气；充电，电荷；（一定量的）炸药。2. 保护，监督，管理。3. 责任；义务，任务。4. 委托，委托物。5. 命令，指令。6. 控诉；告发；指责；嫌疑；罪状，罪过。7.〔常 *pl*.〕费用；捐税；代价；记账。8.【军】冲锋，进击；冲锋号；【足球】截住对方攻球，阻住对方前进；（猛兽的）袭击。9.〔美俚〕快感，刺激。10.【徽】（盾上）图形，图案。11.〔*pl*.〕〔美〕棒球队队员。12.〔口〕麻醉剂，毒品。*a bursting* ~ 炸药。*a rocket* ~ 火箭火药柱。*The books are under my* ~. 这些书归我保管。*a carrying* ~ 维修费。*a false* ~ 诬告。*a terminal* ~（给用户的）结算。*sound the* ~ 吹冲锋号。*at moderate* ~*s* 以公道的代价。*at one's own* ~ 自费。~ *for trouble* 手续费。~ *of sheer bone and muscle* 肉搏战。~*s forward* 运费等货到后由收货人自付。~ *of quarters* 营舍值班（士官）。~*s paid* 各费付讫。*free of* ~ 免费。*give in* ~ 寄存，委托（某物给某人）；交付（犯人给警察）。*have* ~ *of* 承受，承担。*in* ~ 主任[主管]（*the doctor in* ~ 主任医师）。*in* ~ *of* 主持，领导，管理[处理]…的，看管…的，受托…的（*the nurse in* ~ *of the child* 照管孩子的保姆）。*in full* ~ 负全责；猛然，突然。*in* [*under*] *the* ~ *of* 在…看护下的，交…照看的（*the child in the* ~ *of the nurse* 交保姆照看的孩子）。*lay to sb.'s* ~ 归罪于，指控（某人）。*make a* ~ *against* 责备；袭击；控告。*no* ~ *for admission* 免费入场。*on* (*a*) ~ *of* 以…罪控告。*on the* ~ *of* 因…的嫌疑。*put in* ~ *of* 委托。*return to the* ~ 再重新进攻；改变（意见等）。*take* ~ 掌管；〔俚〕（事物）控制不住，弄糟。*take* ~ *of* 担任，保管，看

守,看管,监督,负责。*take over* ~ *of* 承受,接办。*take personal* ~ 亲自处理[照管]。~ **account**【会计】赊销(户头)~ **conjugation**【物】电荷共轭。~ **nurse**〔英〕护士长。~**-a-plate**, ~ **plate** 赊货牌。~ **sheet**(警察局的)事故[案件]记录。

charge·a·ble [ˈtʃɑːdʒəbl; ˋtʃardʒəbl̩] *a*. 1.(税)应征收的。2.(罪)应指控的。3. 应由某人负担[应负责]的。4. 可充电的。**charge·a·bil·i·ty** *n*.

char·gé d'af·faires [ˈʃɑːʒei dæˈfɛə; ʃarˋʒe dæˋfɛr] (*pl*. ***chargés d'affaires*** [ˈʃɑːʒeiz dæˈfɛə; ˋʃarʒez dæˋfɛr])〔F.〕1. 代理大使,临时代办(正式说作 ***chargé d'affaires ad interim***)。2. 代办。

charg·er [ˈtʃɑːdʒə; ˋtʃardʒɚ] *n*. 1. 委托者,控诉者。2. 插弹夹;充电器,装料机。3. 突击者;【军】军官坐骑;战马。4.〔古〕大盘子。

char·i·ly [ˈtʃɛərili; ˋtʃɛrəlɪ] *ad*. 1. 小心地,谨慎地。2. 节俭地,吝啬地。

char·i·ness [ˈtʃɛərinis; ˋtʃɛrənɪs] *n*. 1. 小心,谨慎。2. 节俭,吝啬。

char·i·ot [ˈtʃæriət; ˋtʃærɪət] **I** *n*. 1.(古代双轮马拉)战车;(十八世纪的)四轮轻便马车;〔诗〕花车,凯旋车;长途马车。2.〔美俚〕汽车。3.【电】齿车;托架。**II** *vt*. 用马车[战车]运送。

char·i·ot·eer [ˌtʃæriəˈtiə; ˏtʃærɪəˋtɪr] *n*. 1. 马车[战车]驾驶者。2. [the C-]【天】驭夫座。

char·ism [ˈkærizəm; ˋkærɪzəm] *n*. = charisma.

cha·ris·ma [kəˈrizmə; kəˋrɪzmə] *n*. (*pl*. ***-ma·ta*** [-mətə; -mətə]) 1.【神】(迷信者所说的领袖人物的)超凡魅力,神授能力。2. 众望所归的作领导的特殊本领[品质]。**char·is·mat·ic** [ˌkærizˈmætik; ˏkærɪzˋmætɪk] *a*.

char·i·ta·ble [ˈtʃæritəbl; ˋtʃærətəbl̩] *a*. 仁爱的;慈善的;厚道的。**-ness** *n*.

char·i·ta·bly [ˈtʃæritəbli; ˋtʃærɪtəblɪ] *ad*. 仁爱地;慈善地。

char·i·tari·an [ˌtʃæriˈteiriən; ˏtʃærɪˋtɛrɪən] *n*.〔美〕慈善家。

char·i·ty [ˈtʃæriti; ˋtʃærətɪ] *n*. 1. 慈爱;仁爱,博爱,【宗】上帝之爱,(基督徒之间的)教友之爱。2.(对别人的)仁慈;宽大,宽容;慈悲心。3.〔常 *pl*.〕慈善(行为),施舍,捐助;抚恤金;慈善事业;慈善机关[团体];施诊所。*as cold as* ~ 极冷淡〔讽刺形式上的慈善〕。*be in* [*out of*] ~ *with* 爱[不爱]。~ *ball* [*concert*] 慈善募捐舞会[音乐会]。*C- begins at home*.〔谚〕仁慈先从亲属始〔常作拒绝捐款的借口〕。~ *hospital* 慈善医院,施诊所。*for* ~*'s sake* = *in* ~ = *out of* ~ 为慈善故,以仁爱精神。~ **boy** [**child**, **girl**] 孤儿院[慈善学校]中的男孩[孩子,女孩]。~ **school** 慈善学校。

cha·ri·va·ri [ˈʃɑːriˈvɑːri; ʃəˏrɪvəˋri] *n*. 1.(在新婚者屋前敲铁锅、铜罐等的)逗闹音乐;大嚷闹,嘈杂。2.〔C-〕《逗闹》杂志[法国一滑稽刊物]。*The London C-*〔英〕幽默刊物 *Punch* 杂志的别称。

char·la·tan [ˈʃɑːlətən; ˋʃarlətn̩] **I** *n*. 1. 骗子;假内行。2. 庸医。**II** *a*. 假充内行的,骗人的。**-ism**, **-ry** *n*. 吹牛;蒙混,欺骗。**-ish** *a*. 庸医般的,骗人的。

Charle·magne [ˈʃɑːləˈmein; ˋʃarləˏmen] *n*. 查理曼大帝〔742—814,世称 Charles the Great 或 Charles I,于768—814 为法兰克王,并于 800—814 为西罗马帝国皇帝〕。

Charles [tʃɑːlz; tʃarlz] *n*. 查尔斯〔姓氏,男子名〕。

Charles's Wain [ˈtʃɑːlziz ˈwein; ˋtʃarlzɪz ˋwen]〔英〕北斗七星。

Charles·ton [ˈtʃɑːlstən; ˋtʃarlstən] **I** *n*. 1. 查尔斯顿〔美国南卡罗来纳州港市〕。2. 查尔斯顿〔美国西弗吉尼亚州城市〕。3. 查尔斯顿舞〔本世纪二十年代开始流行〕。**II** *vi*. 跳查尔斯顿舞。

Char·ley, **Char·lie** [ˈtʃɑːli; ˋtʃarlɪ] *n*. 查利〔男子名〕。*c- horse*〔美口〕(因运动过度或受伤所致的)肌肉硬直。

Char·lie [ˈtʃɑːli; ˋtʃarlɪ] *n*. 1. = Charley. 2. 通讯中代表字母 C 的词。

char·lock [ˈtʃɑːlək; ˋtʃarlək] *n*.【植】田芥菜。

Char·lotte [ˈʃɑːlət; ˋʃarlət] *n*. 夏洛特〔女子名〕。

char·lotte [ˈʃɑːlət; ˋʃarlət] *n*.〔F.〕水果奶油布丁。

Char·lotte A·ma·lie [ˈtʃɑːlə əˈmɑːljə; ˋtʃarlə əˋmɑljə] 夏洛特阿马利亚〔美属维尔京群岛首府〕。

charm [tʃɑːm; tʃarm] **I** *n*. 1.(迷人的)魔力,诱惑力;〔常 *pl*.〕妩媚;妖媚,风骚,风韵,色相,2. 咒文;护符,符咒。3.(表链等的)小装饰品,小玩意儿。4.〔*pl*.〕〔美俚〕钱。*feminine* ~*s* 女性(特有)的妩媚。*act like a* ~ = *to a* ~ (药物等)效验如神;神妙地,十二万分地。**II** *vt*. 1. 迷(人),诱惑,夺(人)魂魄;使陶醉,使喜爱。2.〔古〕对…行魔法,用魔法保护[治疗];把(蛇等)养乖。*I shall be* ~*ed to see you tomorrow*. 我真希望明天能见到你。— *vi*. 1. 行魔法。2. 有魅力,令人陶醉。*Goodness* ~*s more than beauty*. 心地好胜过容貌好。***be*** ~***ed with*** 心醉于,给…迷住。***bear*** [***have***, ***lead***] ***a*** ~***ed life*** 有刀枪不入的能耐(*She bore a* ~*ed life, and prospered amid dangers and alarms*. 她似乎是刀枪不入的,经过种种危险还好好活了下来)。~ (*sb*.) ***asleep*** 用魔力催眠。~ ***away*** (*the fiend*) 用符咒驱除(恶魔)。~ (*a secret*) ***out of*** (*sb*.) 哄出(某人)的(秘密)来。**-ed** *a*. 着迷的;被施了魔法的;陶醉的;(蛇)养乖了的。

charm·er [ˈtʃɑːmə; ˋtʃarmɚ] *n*. 弄蛇人;魔术师;使人着魔的人[物];〔古、讽〕美女。

char·meuse [ʃɑːˈməːz; ʃarˋmɛz] *n*.【纺】软缎。~ **cotton** 棉缎。

charm·ing [ˈtʃɑːmiŋ; ˋtʃarmɪŋ] *a*. 迷人的,娇媚的,可爱的;有趣的。**-ly** *ad*.

char·nel [ˈtʃɑːnl; ˋtʃarnl̩] **I** *n*. 骨灰堂,藏骸所(= ~ house)。**II** *a*. 藏放尸骨场所的;死一样的。

Cha·ron [ˈkeərən; ˋkɛrən] *n*.【希神】(将亡魂渡到阴界去的)冥府渡神;〔讽〕摆渡的人。~***'s boat*** [***ferry***] 临终。

char·poy [ˈtʃɑːpɔi; ˋtʃarpɔɪ] *n*. (印度等地的)轻便床(= charpai)。

char·qui [ˈtʃɑːki; ˋtʃarkɪ] *n*. (秘鲁)干牛肉。

char·rette [ʃəˈret; ʃəˋrɛt] *n*. (一个团体请专家协助讨论的)问题研究会。

char·ring [ˈtʃɑːriŋ; ˋtʃarɪŋ] *n*. 烧焦,炭化(法),焦化(法)。

char·ry [ˈtʃɑːri; ˋtʃarɪ] *a*. 炭状的。

chart[1] [tʃɑːt; tʃart] **I** *n*. 1. 海图,航(线)图,航海图;地势图(= physical ~),(军用)地形图(= topographic ~)。2. 图,略图;图表;(物价、温度等的)曲线图,线标图。3.(仪器中用的)刻度记录纸。*a bathygraphic* ~海洋水深图。*a hydrographic* ~水道图。*a duty* ~工作时间[进度]表。*a flow* ~工艺流程图。*a record* ~自动记录带。*a toll rate* ~长途电话价目表。**II** *vt*. 1. 绘制…的海图[地图],把(航线等)绘入海图;〔喻〕指引(航向)。2. 用图表示[说明]。3. 制订…的计划。~ **house** [**room**](船上的)海图室。**-ist** *n*. 制图者。**-less** *a*. 1. 尚未绘入海图[地图]的。2. 无图可凭的。**-let** *n*.【海】小海图。

chart[2] [tʃɑːt; tʃart] *n*. 乐曲的改编;改编的乐曲。

char·ter [ˈtʃɑːtə; ˋtʃartɚ] **I** *n*. 1.(准许成立自治都市、工会等的)特许状;凭照,执照,(社团对成立分会等的)许可证。2. 特权,豁免权,专利权,(铁路等的)铺设权。3. 宪章。4. 契据,证书;【商】租船契约;租船合同(= ~ party)。5.(船只、飞机、公共汽车等的)租赁。*the C- of the U.N.* 联合国宪章。***a blank*** ~ 行动自由权,空白委任状。***the Great C-***(= Magna Charta)【英史】大宪章。***a time*** ~ 定期租船契约。**II** *vt*. 1. 给…发特许执照,特许(成立公司等)。2.(凭契约)租[包](船、车等);〔口〕雇(车等)。~ **member**〔美〕(公司等的)创立委员。~ **party** 租船契约[合同]。

char·tered [ˈtʃɑːtəd; ˋtʃartɚd] *a*. 1.(受)特许的。2.

(船等)租的。*a* ~ *bank* 特许银行。*a* ~ *ship* 租用的船。*a* ~ *libertine* 世所公认的浪子。~ **accountant** 〔英〕特许会计师〔略 C.A.〕。~ **cities** 特别市。

char·ter·er [ˈtʃɑːtərə; ˋtʃɑrtərə˞] *n*. (车、船等的)租用者。

Char·ter·house [ˈtʃɑːtəhaus; ˋtʃɑrtə˞ˏhaʊs] *n*. 1. 卡尔特修道院。2. 〔the ~〕卡尔特养老院〔1611 年在伦敦卡尔特修道院旧址上设立,故名〕。3. 卡尔特豪斯公立学校(=~ School)〔曾设立在卡尔特修道院旧址〕。

Chart·ism [ˈtʃɑːtizəm; ˋtʃɑrtɪzəm] *n*. 【英史】(1838—1848 年的)宪章运动;宪章主义。

Chart·ist [ˈtʃɑːtist; ˋtʃɑrtɪst] *n*. 宪章运动者;宪章主义者,宪章派。

C

char·tog·ra·pher [kɑːˈtɔgrəfə; kɑrˋtɑgrəfə˞] *n*. 制图家。

char·tog·ra·phy [kɑːˈtɔgrəfi; kɑrˋtɑgrəfɪ] *n*. 制图法;制图术(=cartography)。

char·treuse [ʃɑːˈtrəːz; ʃɑrˋtrɛz] *n*. 1. 〔C-〕(法国)沙特勒兹修道院。2. (沙特勒兹修道院所制)荨麻酒。3. 鲜嫩的黄绿色。

char·tu·lar·y [ˈkɑːtjuləri; ˋkɑrtʃʊˏlɛrɪ] *n*. =cartulary.

char·y [ˈtʃɛəri; ˋtʃɛrɪ] *a*. 1. 细心的,谨慎的。2. 谦恭的,腼腆的。3. 节俭的(*of*)。*be* ~ *of giving offense* 尽量避免伤人感情[得罪人]。*be* ~ *of strangers* 怯生,腼腆。*be* ~ *of one's praise* 不轻易称赞。

Cha·ryb·dis [kəˈribdis; kəˋrɪbdɪs] *n*. 1. 【希神】女妖。2. (Sicily 岛海面的)大旋涡。

Chase [tʃeis; tʃes] *n*. 蔡斯〔姓氏〕。

chase[1] [tʃeis; tʃes] I *vt*. 1. 追赶,追击;追随,追逐。2. 追寻,寻觅。3. 驱逐,驱除。4. 〔俚〕(男女间)竭力追求。5. 〔俚〕端递(食物),上(菜)。~ *fear from the mind* 驱除恐怖心。~ *a cat out of the garden* 把猫赶出花园去。*Please* ~ *the milk this way*. 请把牛奶递到这边来。—*vi*. 1. 追逐,追赶;跟踪(*after*)。2. 东奔西跑,匆忙地走。~ ***a wild goose*** 作徒劳的搜索[无益的举动]。~***all over*** = ~ ***around*** 在…到处奔走。~ ***around a stump*** 〔美〕讲废话浪费时间。~ ***away*** 赶走。~ ***off after*** 尾追。~ ***oneself*** 〔美〕走开,逃走。***C- yourself***! 〔美俚〕别打搅我,走开! II *n*. 1. 追赶,追击;追猎;追求。2. 〔the ~〕打猎。3. 〔英〕(私人的)猎场;狩猎地,(一定地区内的)狩猎权。4. 追求物;被追的野兽[人];被驱赶的船[车等]。5. 〔美俚〕紧张忙乱的活动。6. (网球的)一种击球法。***cut to the*** ~(说话)转入正题。***give*** ~ ***to*** 追踪;追击。***have*** [***hold***] ***in*** ~ 在追求[追赶、追击]中。***in*** ~ ***of*** 追赶,追踪;追求。***in full*** ~拼命追赶。***lead sb. a*** (***merry***) ~ 使追者困恼不堪;使追者追不着;(女性)对追求者设置种种困难。***lovers of the*** ~爱打猎的人。~ **gun** [**piece**] (追击时用的)舰首[尾]炮。~ **port** 船首[尾]炮门。

chase[2] [tʃeis; tʃes] *vt*. 在(金属上)雕花(作装饰);在(金属上)打出浮凸花样的装饰;刻镶(宝石);用螺纹梳刀刻(螺纹)。

chase[3] [tʃeis; tʃes] I *n*. 1. 沟;槽;(墙上的)水管槽,竖沟。2. (炮的)前身〔炮耳至炮口部分〕,炮身。3. 【印】(已排好的)活字版的框架。II *vt*. 在…上开槽。

chas·er[1] [ˈtʃeisə; ˋtʃesə˞] *n*. 1. 追赶者;追求者;追猎者,猎人。2. 【海】追击舰;追击炮;反击炮;【空】战斗机;歼击机。3. (越野)障碍赛跑参加者。4. 〔美俚〕酒后喝的少量清水[汽水等];咖啡后喝的酒。5. 〔英〕压台戏;观众退场时奏的进行曲。

chas·er[2] [ˈtʃeisə; ˋtʃesə˞] *n*. 1. 镂刻者,金属浮雕艺人。2. 【机】螺纹梳刀,梳刀盘。

chasm [ˈkæzəm; ˋkæzəm] *n*. 1. 【地】(地壳的)裂口;陷坑;裂罅,断层;峡谷。2. (感情等的)分歧,隔阂。*a* ~ *in time* 空白时间。*bridge over a* ~弥补隔阂。

chas·mal [ˈkæzəməl; ˋkæzml̩] *a*. 1. 【地】裂口的,断层的。2. (感情、意见等)分歧[隔阂]巨大的。

chas·mog·a·my [kæzˈmɔgəmi; kæzˋmɑgəmɪ] *n*. 【植】开花受精。

chas·my [ˈkæzmi; ˋkæzmɪ] *a*. 裂口多的,深壑多的;深壑般的。

chasse [ʃɑːs; ʃæs] *n*. 〔F.〕(喝咖啡或抽雪茄烟后喝的)小杯芳香浓烈甜酒,加味酒。

chas·sé [ˈʃæsei, F. ʃase; ʃæˋse, ʃase] I *n*. 〔F.〕(舞蹈的)快滑步,追步。II *vi*. 走[跳]快滑步。~ ***croisé*** [ˈkrwɑːzei; ˋkrwaze] 双重快滑步;〔喻〕无意义的来回移动。

chasse·pot [ʃəsˈpəu; ʃəsˋpo] *n*. 后膛快枪〔1866 年和 1874 年间法国军队使用〕。

Chas·sid·im [ˈhæsidim; ˋhæsdɪm] *n*. *pl*. (*sing*. ***Chassid*** [ˈhæsid; ˋhæsɪd]) 虔敬派信徒(= Hasidim)。**Chassid·ic** *a*. **Chas·sid·ism** *n*.

chas·sis [ˈʃæsi; ˋʃæsɪ] *n*. (*pl*. ~ [ˈʃæsiz; ˋʃæsɪz], ~*es* [ˈʃæsisiz; ˋʃæsɪsɪz]) 1. (马车、汽车车身的)底盘,底架,车台;炮座,炮底架;(收音机等的)机壳;【纺】轧液槽;【空】机架,机脚;机壳,机箱;(窗等的)框。2. 〔美俚〕(尤指女性的)体态,身段。*a* ~ *mount* 装框炮架。*a colour* ~彩色电视接收机机壳。

chaste [tʃeist; tʃest] *a*. 1. 贞节的,忠于配偶的;纯洁的,童贞的;高雅的。2. (文体等)简洁的,朴素的。3. 〔古〕未婚的。**-ly** *ad*. **-ness** *n*.

chas·ten [ˈtʃeisn; ˋtʃesn̩] *vt*. 1. 惩戒,责罚。2. 遏制,使…缓和。3. 磨炼(思想等);精练,推敲(文章等)。**-ed** *a*. (文章等)精练的;(思想等)有磨练的;变乖了的。**-er** *n*. 惩戒者;遏制者;推敲(文章)者。

chas·tis·a·ble [tʃæsˈtaizəbl; tʃæsˋtaɪzəbl̩] *a*. 该受责备的;应责备的,应惩戒的。

chas·tise [tʃæsˈtaiz; tʃæsˋtaɪz] *vt*. 1. 惩戒,惩罚,惩办。2. 〔美〕(比赛时)打败(对方)。3. 〔古〕纯化,净化。**-r** *n*. 惩戒者。

chas·tise·ment [ˈtʃæstizmənt, Am. tʃæsˈtaizmənt; tʃæsˋtaɪzmənt, ˋtʃæstɪzmənt] *n*. 惩罚,惩戒。

chas·ti·ty [ˈtʃæstiti; ˋtʃæstətɪ] *n*. 1. 贞节,贞操;童贞。2. (思想、感情的)纯洁;(文章的)简洁,朴素。

chas·u·ble [ˈtʃæzjubl; ˋtʃæzjubl̩] *n*. 【宗】(神父举行弥撒时穿的)无袖长袍。

chat[1] [tʃæt; tʃæt] I *n*. 1. 闲谈,聊天。2. 鸣禽。*have a* ~ *with* 与…闲谈,与…聊天(*with*)。II (**-tt-**) *vi*. 闲谈,聊天;(在电脑网络上)与网友聊天。~ **line** 聊天热线〔电话局提供的一种服务〕。~ **show**(电台或电视台的)现场采访节目。

chat[2] [tʃæt; tʃæt] *n*. = chit[1]

châ·teau [ˈʃɑːtəu; ˋʃæto] *n*. (*pl*. ~*s*, ***-teaux*** [-təuz; -toz]) 〔F.〕1. 城堡。2. 邸宅,公馆;大别墅。3. 大葡萄园。~ ***en Espagne*** 空中楼阁。**C- wine** 高级葡萄酒。

chat·e·lain [ˈʃætlein; ˋʃætl̩ˏen] *n*. 城堡的主人;城主,城守。

chat·e·laine [ˈʃætəlein; ˋʃætəlˏen] *n*. 1. 女城堡主人;大公馆的女主人。2. 〔新闻用语〕女主人。3. 女人腰带上的饰链。

Chat·ham [ˈtʃætəm; ˋtʃætəm] *n*. 查塔姆〔姓氏〕。

cha·toy·ant [ʃəˈtɔiənt; ʃəˋtɔɪənt] I *a*. 变色的,闪光的。~ *silk* 闪光丝。II *n*. 猫眼石,金绿宝石。**cha·toyance, cha·toyan·cy** *n*. 闪光。

chat·tel [ˈtʃætl; ˋtʃætl̩] *n*. 1. 【法】物,有体财产。2. 〔古〕奴隶。~ *personal* 动产。~ *real* 准不动产〔借地权等〕。*goods and* ~*s* 有体动产,家具杂物。

chat·ter [ˈtʃætə; ˋtʃætə˞] I *vi*. 1. 瞎谈,饶舌。2. (牙齿、机器等)振动,打颤;卡嗒地响。3. (鸟等)鸣,啁啾;(猴等)吱吱叫。—*vt*. 1. 瞎谈,喋喋不休地说。2. 使(牙齿)抖得卡嗒卡嗒地响。3. 〔英方〕撕碎。II *n*. 1. 饶舌,瞎谈。2. 卡嗒声。3. 啁啾。*monkey* ~ 〔口〕(电话)串话,交叉失真。

chat·ter·box [ˈtʃætəbɔks; ˋtʃætə˞ˏbɑks] *n*. 1. 唠叨多言的人。2. 〔军俚〕机关枪。

chat·ter·er [ˈtʃætərə; ˋtʃætərə˞] *n*. 1. 多言的人,嘴老是不停的人。2. 燕雀类小鸟。

Chat·ter·ton [ˈtʃætətn; ˋtʃætə˞tən] *n*. 查特顿〔姓氏〕。

chat·ty [ˈtʃæti; ˋtʃætɪ] *a*. 1. 爱唠叨的,爱闲聊的。2. 聊家常似的,亲切的。**-ti·ly** *ad*.

Chau·cer [ˈtʃɔːsə; ˋtʃɔsə˞] *n*. 1. 乔瑟(乔叟)〔姓氏〕。2. **Geoffrey** ~ 乔叟〔1340—1400,英国诗人,《坎特伯雷故事集》(*Canterbury Tales*)的作者〕。

Chau·ce·ri·an [tʃɔːˈsiəriən; tʃɔˋsɪrɪən] I *a*. 乔叟的;有关乔叟著作的。II *n*. 乔叟著作[生平]研究者。

chaud·froid [ˈʃəuˈfrwɑː; ˋʃoˋfrwɑ] *n*. 〔F.〕肉冻。

chauf·fer [ˈtʃɔːfə; ˋtʃɔfə˞] *n*. 小火炉,小炭盆,手炉。

chauf·feur [ˈʃəufə; ˋʃofə˞] I *n*. 1. (私人雇用的)汽车司机。2. 〔美俚〕飞机师。II *vi*. 做汽车司机。—*vt*. 1. 开(汽车等)。2. 开汽车运送。

chauf·feur·ette [ʃəufəˈret; ʃofəˋret] *n*. 〔美〕女(汽车)司机。

chauf·feuse [ʃəuˈfəːz; ʃoˋfəz] *n*. 女(汽车)司机。

chaul·mau·gra, chaul·moo·gra, chaul·mu·gra [tʃɔːlˈmuːgrə; tʃɔlˋmugrə] *n*. 【植】大风子。~ *oil* 大风子油。

chaunt [tʃɔːnt; tʃɔnt] I *n*. 〔古〕歌;赞美诗。II *vi*., *vt*. 单调地唱(赞美诗)。(=chant)。

chausses [ʃəus; ʃos] *n*. *pl*. 马裤〔尤指中古骑士的腿铠〕。

chaus·sure [ʃəuˈsjuə; ʃoˋsur] *n*. 〔F.〕鞋;履;靴;拖鞋。

Chau·tau·qua [ʃəˈtɔːkwə; ʃəˋtɔkwə] *n*. 1. (美国纽约州的)肖陶扩湖;肖陶扩村〔有名的夏令文娱活动中心〕。2. 〔c-〕〔美〕野外文化讲习会。

chau·vin·ism [ˈʃəuvinizəm; ˋʃovɪnˏɪzəm] *n*. 1. 沙文主义,大民族主义。2. 本性别第一主义,男[女]性至上主义。*great-nation* [*-power*] ~大国沙文主义。*dominant-nation* ~民族沙文主义。*male* [*female*] ~男子[女子]至上主义,大男[女]子主义。

chau·vin·ist [ˈʃəuvinist; ˋʃovɪnɪst] I *n*. 沙文主义者;男子[女子]至上主义者。II *a*. 沙文主义的;男[女]子至上主义的。

chau·vin·is·tic [ˌʃəuviˈnistik; ˏʃovɪˋnɪstɪk] *a*. 沙文主义的。

chaw [tʃɔː; tʃɔ] I *vt*., *vi*. 〔方、卑〕嚼,咀嚼。~ *up* 〔美〕(在比赛中)把…打得惨败,把…打成重伤。II *n*. 〔口〕所嚼物;一满嘴;(嚼烟草的)一口;〔美〕嚼烟草。~**-round** 〔美〕会话,谈话。

chay [tʃei, tʃai; tʃe, tʃaɪ] *n*. 【植】1. 伞形花耳草 (*Oldenlandia umbellata*)。2. 伞形花耳草植株。

cha·yo·te [tʃɑːˈjəuti; tʃɑˋjotɪ] *n*. 【植】佛手瓜 (*Sechium edule*)。

chaz·an, chaz·zan [ˈhɑːzn; ˋhɑzn̩] *n*. (犹太教堂的)合唱指挥,领唱者 (=hazan)。

Ch. Ch. =Christ Church (牛津大学)基督学院。

Ch. Clk. = Chief Clerk.

Ch. B. = 〔L.〕Chirurgiae Baccalaureus 外科学士。

CHD =coronary heart disease 冠心病。

Ch.D. =〔L.〕*Chirurgiae Doctor* 外科博士。

Ch. E. =Chemical Engineer 化学工程师。

cheap [tʃiːp; tʃip] *a*. 1. 廉价的,便宜的,贱 (*opp*. dear)。2. (钱)贬了值的;有折扣的。3. 粗劣的;恶俗的,低劣的,可鄙的;虚伪的。4. 〔俚〕身体虚弱的;垂头丧气的。5. (商店等)索价低的;〔英〕大减价的。*buy* ~ *and sell dear* 贱买贵卖。*dirt* ~ 〔俚〕极便宜的,便宜透顶的。***A*** ~ ***son of a bitch!*** 吝啬鬼。~***and cheerful*** 价廉而物美的。~ ***and nasty*** 价廉而质劣的。***feel*** ~ 〔俚〕1. 觉得身体不舒服。2. 扫兴,灰心,气馁;惭愧。***get things on the*** ~ 贪便宜。***hold*** (***sb.***) ~ 瞧不起,藐视,轻蔑。***make oneself too*** ~ 过份自卑,过份自轻〔动辄迁就别人〕。***on the*** ~ 便宜地,经济地。~ **car** (**ticket**) 减价电车(票)。~**-Jack**, ~ **-John** (走街串巷的)小贩,廉价商品兜销贩。~ **mit** 〔美俚〕小气鬼,吝啬鬼。~ **money** 利息低廉的借款;(为刺激经济而实行的)低利率货币制。~ **skate** 〔美俚〕吝啬鬼,小气鬼。~ **trip** [**tripper**] 廉价旅行[旅行者]。**-ly** *ad*. 便宜,廉价。**-ness** *n*. 廉价。

cheap·en [ˈtʃiːpən; ˋtʃipən] *vt*., *vi* 1. (使)减价,(使)跌价。2. (使)降低威信[地位]。3. (使)变低级[粗俗]。

Cheap·side [ˈtʃiːpˈsaid; ˋtʃipˋsaɪd] *n*. 切普赛德街〔伦敦中部东西向大街名,中古时为闹市〕。

cheat [tʃiːt; tʃit] I *vi*. 1. 哄骗,作弊。2. 〔俚〕(男女关系上)不忠实 (*on*)。*He never* ~*s to pass exam*. 他考试从不作弊。—*vt*. 1. 哄骗,欺骗,诈取。2. 消磨(时间),解(闷),消除(疲劳)。3. 逃脱(法网);用计挫败(对方)。*C- the devil!* 混蛋!〔水手骂人话〕。~ *the law by suicide* 以自杀逃避法律制裁。~ *at* (*cards*) (玩纸牌)作弊(骗钱)。~ *in* (*business*) (做生意)行骗。~ (*sb.*) *into* 诱骗(人)使…。~ (*sth.*) *of* [*out of*] (*sb.*) 骗(人)(东西)。~ *the journey* 消磨旅途的寂寞。II *n*. 1. 欺骗,欺诈。2. 骗子。3. 雀麦,稗草。4. 〔美俚〕(汽车上的)反光镜。5. 〔the ~〕〔卑〕绞刑架。*put a* ~ *upon* 使上当;欺骗。

cheat·ee [ˈtʃiːtiː; ˋtʃiti] *n*. 〔美〕易受骗的人。

cheat·er [ˈtʃiːtə; ˋtʃitə˞] *n*. 1. 骗子。2. 〔*pl*.〕〔美俚〕眼镜;女衬裤;赌博作弊物〔如作了记号的纸牌,骰子等〕。

cheat·ing [ˈtʃiːtiŋ; ˋtʃitɪŋ] *a*. 欺骗的。~ **stick** 〔美俚〕计算尺。

che·cha·ko [tʃiːˈtʃɑːkəu; tʃiˋtʃɑko] *n*. 〔Can.〕新来者,生手。

check [tʃek; tʃɛk] I *n*. 1. (象棋)将军(!),被将军的局面。2. (突然的)妨碍[制止,阻止];停顿,挫折;【猎】(猎狗闻不出嗅迹时的)站住;【语音】默止音。3. 制止,斥责;(军队等的)牵制,阻止,拦截,控制。4. 制止物[扣绳、制动机、塞子等];制止者。5. 〔美〕支票〔英国作 cheque;美国为表示郑重起见有时也用 cheque〕。6. 号牌,号码单,联单;对号,查对标记;核对,校对,验算,已核对的记号(√);〔美〕收据,发票,(餐馆)账单;〔美罕〕(赌钱用的)筹码。7. 棋盘格,方格图案;方格花布;小方块,小方格。8. (木料的)裂缝,罅缝;【建】幅裂;槽口。9. 〔美〕同意,允诺,答应。~ ***to bearer*** 见票即付的支票,无记名支票。~ ***to order*** 记名支票。~ ***variety*** 【植】对照品种。***draw a*** ~开发支票。***discover*** ~ (象棋中)移动一子露出棋路向对方将军。***hand*** [***pass***] ***in one's*** ~***s*** 1. 交还筹码给赌场主。2. 〔俚〕死;放弃。***hold*** [***keep***] ***in*** ~ 防止,阻止;制止。II *vt*. 1. 【象棋】将(对方的王棋)一军。2. 抑制,阻止,妨碍;击退。3. 在…上附加号牌,给…系上标签;(凭号牌)寄存,托运。4. 在…上记上查检记号,在…上打勾号〔√号〕;在…上加上双联号码;检查,检验,校对,核对,对照,比较。5. 使产生裂缝,在…上画[印]方格图案;【农】条插,方形栽植。6. 【棒球】牵制。*Small parcels* ~*ed here*. 本处寄存手提包裹。—*vi*. 1. 【猎】(猎狗)因嗅迹中断而站住。2. 〔美〕开发支票。3. 〔美〕(账目)相符。4. (油漆面等)干裂成小方块。5. 【象棋】将军。~ ***at*** 对…发火,气愤。~ ***in*** (在旅馆)登记,办理住宿手续;〔美俚〕死;〔美口〕签到;作笔记。~ ***into*** 〔美口〕去…上班。~ ***it*** 〔美〕吓唬;假装。~ ***off*** 查讫;记上查讫记号。~ (***up***) ***on*** 检查。~ ***out*** 〔美〕开支票(提款);(旅馆)付账后离开;合格,及格,辞职;〔美俚〕死。~ ***up*** 检查,核对,对照;〔美〕试验(工作的效率,精确程度等)。~ (***up***) ***with*** 与…相符合。III *int*. 1. 【象棋】将军! 2. 〔口〕行! 对! ~ **beam** 【空】验位电波。~**-book** 支票簿;存折。~ **cross** 验证杂交。~ **experiment** 对比[核对]试验。~ **formula** 验算公式。~ **in** *vi*. 〔美〕报到;(旅馆)登记。~**ing account** 〔美〕活期存款。~**ing-room** 衣帽间,衣帽寄放处。~**list** 〔美〕(核对用)清单;(特指选举人的)名单;调查表。~**mate** *vt*., *n*. (象棋)将军;困死〔通常说 mate 即可〕;打败,击破;(使)失败,(使受)挫折

(*play* ~*mate with* 使进退两难)。~ **nut** 螺钉帽。~**off** 〔美〕(工会)会费的催收。~**out** 1. 最后检查;(对新机器等的)使用练习。2. (购货时的)结账。3. (旅馆规定结账后必须离去的)离馆时限。~**-pawl** 【机】棘爪。~**plot** (试验地的)对照小区。~**-point** 公路检查站,关卡;【军】试射点。~**rein** 勒马缰绳。~**room** 〔美〕物品寄放处,衣帽间。~**row** 1. *n*. 方格谷物列;方格树列。2. *vt*. 把…种成方格形。~**stand** (超级市场的)验货收款台。~**taker** (戏院、车站等的)收票人。~**up** 〔美〕核对,对照,检验;(严格的)健康检查(*a* ~*up committee* 查账委员,查账委员会。*general* ~*up* 全身检查)。~ **valve** 【机】止回阀,单向活门。

C

checked [tʃekt; tʃɛkt] *a*. 1. 格子花的,棋盘花的。2. 【语音】受阻的,封闭的。~ **syllable** 受阻音节,闭音节。~ **vowel** 闭音节[封闭]母音。

check·er [ˈtʃekə; ˋtʃɛkɚ] *n*., *vt*. 〔美〕= chequer. ~**berry** 【植】平铺白珠树。~**board** 1. *n*. 〔美〕跳棋盘。2. *vt*. 在…上纵横交错地排列[分布]。~**work** 棋盘形结构;【建】甃。

check·ered [ˈtʃekəd; ˋtʃɛkɚd] *a*. = chequered; 〔美〕有波折的,有变化的;受挫折的。

Ched·dar [ˈtʃedə; ˋtʃɛdɚ] *n*. (原产英国 Cheddar 地方的)切达干酪(= ~ cheese)。

chedd·ite [ˈtʃedait, ˈʃed-; ˋtʃɛdaɪt, ˋʃɛd-] *n*. 谢德炸药〔最初在法国 Chedde 地方制造〕。

che·der [ˈkeidə; ˋkedɚ] *n*. 犹太儿童宗教学校(= heder)。

Che. E. = Chemical Engineer 化学工程师。

cheek [tʃiːk; tʃik] I *n*. 1. 脸,面颊。2. 〔口〕冒失行为[言语],无耻行为[言语];厚颜无耻。3. 〔*pl*.〕事物成对的两例;两侧成对的部件[器物];【机】滑车的外壳;颊板。4. (炸药的)面皮。*None of your* ~! 莫说了,没皮没脸的! 别吹牛! ~ ***by jowl with*** (和…)亲密地,(和…)紧靠着。***give*** ~ 说无耻话。***have plenty of*** ~ 老脸厚皮。***have the*** ~ ***to*** (*do*) 厚着脸皮(做)。***sour one's*** ~***s*** 哭丧着脸。***to one's own*** ~ 自己专用。***tongue in*** ~ 不老实,口是心非。***turn the other*** ~ 泰然容忍〔被人打一耳光后,再转过一面给人打〕。II *vt*. 厚着脸皮去,无耻地说。~ *it* 厚着脸皮干下去。~ ***up*** 无耻地回答。~**bone** 颧骨,颊骨。~**tooth** 臼齿。

cheek·y [ˈtʃiːki; ˋtʃikɪ] *a*. 〔口〕厚脸皮的,无耻的。**-i·ly** *ad*. **-i·ness** *n*.

cheep [tʃiːp; tʃip] I *vi*. (小鸟等)吱吱地叫。II *n*. 吱吱的叫声。*He didn't even* ~. 他一声不吭。

cheep·er [ˈtʃiːpə; ˋtʃipɚ] *n*. 吱吱叫的小鸟;毛娃娃。

cheer [tʃiə; tʃɪr] I *n*. 1. 欢呼,喝彩;鼓励。2. 心情。3. 兴致勃勃,愉快。4. 款待;丰盛的菜肴[食品],好菜。5. 〔古〕表情。*What* ~? 你好吧? *Be of good* ~! 加油! 鼓(起)劲儿(来)! *The fewer the better* ~. 人少些,吃得多些。*words of* ~ 鼓励话。~ *leader* 〔美〕啦啦队队长。*enjoy good* ~ 享受盛宴。*give three* ~*s for* 欢呼三声〔三呼 Hip, hip, hurrah!〕。***make good*** ~ 欢乐,笑笑闹闹;〔古〕欢宴。***with good*** ~ 高高兴兴地,乐意地。II *vt*. 1. 使振奋,使喜欢,使快慰,安慰。2. 对…欢呼;为…喝彩;(以欢呼声)鼓舞,奖励。~ *them* (*on*) *to victory* 声援他们取得胜利。*the cups that* ~ (*but not inebriate*) 使人提神而不醉的饮料〔指茶〕。—*vi*. 1. 欢喜,高兴,快活。2. 欢呼,喝彩。*C- up*! 鼓起劲儿来! 别灰心! ~ ***to the echo*** 欢声雷动。~ ***up at*** (*the news*) 听见(消息)兴奋起来。

cheer·ful [ˈtʃiəful; ˋtʃɪrfəl] *a*. 1. 高兴的,兴致勃勃的,欢乐的,快活的;爽快的。2. 使人愉快[振奋]的。3. 心甘情愿的。4. 〔反〕讨厌的,使人发愣的,可慨叹的。*a* ~ *room* 舒适的房屋。*a* ~ *worker* 兴致勃勃的工作者。*That's a* ~ *remark*. 〔反〕那真听不过去[听了使人发愣]。**-ly** *ad*. 高高兴兴地,兴致勃勃地。**-ness** *n*. 高兴,快活;愉快,爽快。

cheer·ing [ˈtʃiəriŋ; ˋtʃɪrɪŋ] *n*. 欢呼,喝彩;鼓励,安慰。

cheer·i·o(h), **cheer·o** [ˈtʃiəriˈəu, ˈtʃiərəu; ˋtʃɪrɪˏo, ˋtʃɪəˏro] I *int*. 〔英口〕珍重! 再会! 〔干杯贺语〕恭喜恭喜! II *n*. 告别话;祝酒词。

cheer·less [ˈtʃiəlis; ˋtʃɪrlɪs] *a*. 郁郁不乐的,沉闷的。

cheer·ly [ˈtʃiəli; ˋtʃɪrlɪ] I *a*. 〔古〕欢乐的,快活的。II *ad*. 【海】欣然,高高兴兴地。

cheers [tʃiəz; tʃɪrz] *int*. 祝你健康! 〔用于祝酒〕。

cheer·y [ˈtʃiəri; ˋtʃɪrɪ] *a*. 高兴的,快活的;愉快的,爽快的。**-i·ly** *ad*. **-i·ness** *n*.

cheese[1] [tʃiːz; tʃiz] *n*. 1. 干酪,乳酪;干酪状的东西。2. 〔美俚〕重要人物;上品,珍品。3. 【纺】筒子纱。4. 〔学俚〕微笑。*green* ~ 未熟干酪;绿皮干酪;(低级)乳清干酪。***bread and*** ~ 粗食;糊口之道。***chalk and*** ~ 形似而实非。***big*** [***small***] ~ 〔俚〕伟大[渺小]的人。***get the*** ~ 碰钉子,失望。***hard*** ~ 倒楣。***make*** ~***s*** 飘裙游戏〔女学生在旋转中突然弯下身子使裙子张大的游戏〕;(女人)弯腰行礼招呼。***Say*** '~'! (照相时叫对方)笑! ***That is*** [***quite***] ***the*** ~. 〔俚〕十分对头[得当]。~ **burger** 牛肉饼加乳酪。~**cake** 1. 干酪蛋糕。2. 〔美俚〕显示优美的女性体态[特别是大腿]的摄影。~**-cloth** 干酪包布〔一种粗棉布〕。~ **cutter** 大切刀;〔美俚〕自行车。~ **mite** 干酪虫。~**monger** 乳品(干酪、奶油等)商。~**paring** 1. *n*. 干酪的碎皮屑;吝啬;〔*pl*.〕无用的琐碎东西;私财。2. *a*. 吝啬的,小气的。~ **plate** 干酪盘子,中号盘子;大钮扣。~ **rennet** 酪条;【植】白花蓬子叶。~ **straws** 〔美 **sticks**〕〔*pl*.〕酥皮干。

cheese[2] [tʃiːz; tʃiz] *vt*. 〔俚〕停止。***Cheese it!*** 1. 停止吧! 〔美〕别吵! 静一点! 注意! 2. 逃呀! 走吧!

chees·y [ˈtʃiːzi; ˋtʃizɪ] *a*. 1. 干酪质[味]的。2. 〔俚〕俊俏的,时髦的,潇洒的。3. 〔美俚〕粗制滥造的,低级的;脸色苍白的,面黄肌瘦的;不愉快的。

chee·tah [ˈtʃiːtə; ˋtʃitə] *n*. 【动】(驯养后用以行猎的)猎豹;猎豹皮。

chef [ʃef; ʃɛf] *n*. 〔F.〕男厨师长;大师傅,厨师。~**'s salad** 【烹】大师傅沙拉〔足够吃饱一顿饭的一大盆什锦冷菜〕。

chef d'œuvre [ʃeiˈdəːvr; ʃeˋdœvr] *n*. (*pl*. ***chefs d'-***) 〔F.〕杰作。

cheir(o)- *comb*. *f*. = chiro-。

che·la[1] [ˈkiːlə; ˋkilə] *n*. (*pl*. ***-lae*** [-liː; -li]) (蟹、虾等的)螯;钳爪;倒钩骨。

che·la[2] [ˈtʃeilə; ˋtʃelɑ] *n*. 〔印度〕学徒,门徒;(学道的)徒弟。

che·late [ˈkiːleit; ˋkilet] I *a*. 【化】螯合的,螯形的。II *n*. 【化】螯合物。III *vt*. 【化】螯合,与(金属)结合成螯合物。—*vi*. 【化】生成螯合物。**-la·tion** *n*. 【化】螯合作用。

che·lic·er·a [kəˈlisərə; kəˋlɪsərə] *n*. (*pl*. ***-er·ae*** [-əri; -ərɪ]) 【动】螯角,螯肢,钩角。**-er·ate** [-əˌreit, -ərit; -əˏret, -ərɪt] *a*. 有螯角[肢]的。

che·lif·er·ous [kiˈlifərəs; kəˋlɪfərəs] *a*. 【动】具螯的,具钳爪的。

che·li·form [ˈkiːliˌfɔːm; ˋkiləˏfɔrm] *a*. 【动】螯形的,钳爪状的。

Chel·le·an [ˈʃeliən, ʃeˈliən; ˋʃɛlɪən, ʃɛˋlɪən] *a*. 【考古】(旧石器时代初期)莎楞文化的。

che·loid [ˈkiːlɔid; ˋkilɔɪd] *n*. 【医】瘢痕瘤;瘢痕疙瘩(= keloid)。

che·lo·ni·an [kiˈləuniən; kəˋlonɪən] *n*., *a*. 【动】龟鳖类(的);蠵鱼科(的);海龟(的)。

Chel·sea [ˈtʃelsi; ˋtʃɛlsɪ] *n*. (伦敦市)彻西区〔伦敦的文化区,作家、艺术家多居于此〕。~ *bun* [*pensioner*] 彻西残废军人休养院的残废军人。~ *Hospital* 彻西残废军人休养院。*dead as* ~ 人虽没死但已残废。*the Sage of* ~ 彻西区的圣人〔英国十九世纪作家 Thomas Carlyle 的别号〕。

chem. = chemical, chemist, chemistry.
chem- *comb. f.* 〔用于母音前〕= chemo-.
chemi- *comb. f.* 表示"化学": *chemi*sorb.
chem·ic [ˈkemik; ˋkɛmɪk] ***a*.** **1.** 〔古〕炼金术的。**2.** 化学的。
chem·i·cal [ˈkemikəl; ˋkɛmɪkl] **I** ***a*.** 化学的,化学作用的;应用化学的,用化学方法获得的。~ **castration** 药物阉割〔给强奸惯犯等注射化学药物以使其丧失性欲〕。~ **combination** 化合(作用)。~ **compounds** 化合物。~ **cotton** 漂白棉子绒。~ **formula** 化学式。~ **industry** 化学工业。~ **reaction** 化学反应。~ **warfare** 化学战。~ **weapon** 化学武器。~ **works** 制药厂。**II** ***n*.** 〔常 *pl*.〕化学制品;药品。*fine* ~*s* (用量微小的)精制化学品[药品]。*heavy* ~*s* (用量巨大的)农工业用化学品。**-ize** ***vt*.** 用化学药品处理。**-ly** ***ad*.**
chemico- *comb. f.* 〔用于子音前〕= chemi-.
chem·i·co·bi·o·lo·gy [ˌkemikəubaiˈɔlədʒi; ˏkɛmɪkobaɪˋɑlədʒɪ] ***n*.** 生物化学。
chem·i·co·physics [ˌkemikəuˈfiziks; ˏkɛmɪkoˋfɪzɪks] ***n*.** 物理化学,化学物理学。
chem·i·cul·ture [ˌkemiˈkʌltʃə; ˏkɛmɪˏkʌltʃɚ] ***n*.** 【农、植】水栽法。
Chemigum [ˈkemigʌm; ˋkɛmɪgʌm] ***n*.** 【商标】丁腈橡胶。
chem·i·loon [ʃemiˈluːn; ʃɛmɪˋlʊn] ***n*.** 〔美〕(女用)连裤内衣。
chem·i·lu·mi·nes·cence [ˌkemiˌluːmiˈnesns; ˏkɛməˏluməˋnɛsəns] ***n*.** 【化】化学发光,化合光。**-cent** ***a*.** 化学发光的。
che·min de fer [ʃəˌmæn də ˈfɛə; ʃəˋmændəˋfɛr] [F.] 十一点〔一种纸牌戏,法语原义为"铁路"〕。
che·mise [ʃiˈmiːz; ʃəˋmiz] ***n*.** **1.** (女人的)无袖衬衫。**2.** (堤的)护岸。
chem·i·sette [ˌʃemiːˈzet; ˏʃɛmɪˏzɛt] ***n*.** (女人的)胸衣,紧胸衬衣。
chem·ism [ˈkemizəm; ˋkɛmɪzəm] ***n*.** 化学作用[过程,机理]。
chem·i·sorb [ˈkemisɔːb, -ˌzɔːb; ˋkɛməˏsɔrb, -ˏzɔb] ***vt*.** 使用化学方法吸附。**-sorp·tion** ***n*.** 化学吸附。
chem·ist [ˈkemist; ˋkɛmɪst] ***n*.** **1.** 化学家;化学工作者。**2.** 〔英〕化学药品商,〔英〕药剂师。*a* ~*'s shop* 〔英〕药房。*a technical* ~药学士。
chem·is·try [ˈkemistri; ˋkɛmɪstrɪ] ***n*.** **1.** 化学。**2.** 物质的组成和化学性质;化学作用[现象]。**3.** 〔喻〕神秘的变化(过程)。*medical* ~ 药物学。*organic* [*inorganic*] ~ 有机[无机]化学。*the* ~ *of logic* 逻辑过程。
chem·i·type [ˈkemitaip; ˋkɛmɪˏtaɪp] ***n*.** 化学蚀刻凸版。
chemo- *comb. f.* "化学" = *chemo*ceptor.
chem·o [ˈkeməu; ˋkɛmo] ***n*.** 〔口〕化疗。
chem·o·au·to·troph·ic [ˌkeməuˌɔtəˈtrɔːfik, ˌkiməu-; ˏkɛmoˏɑtəˋtrɔfɪk, ˏkɪmo-] ***a*.** 化学自养的。**-i·cal·ly** ***ad*.** **-tot·ro·phy** [-ˈtɔtrəfi; -ˋtɑtrəfɪ] ***n*.** 化学自养。
chem·o·cep·tor [ˌkeməuˈseptə; ˏkɛməˋsɛptə] ***n*.** = chemoreceptor.
chem·o·ki·ne·sis [ˌkeməukiˈniːsis, -kai-, ˌkiːməu-; ˏkɛmokɪˋnisɪs, -kaɪ-, ˏkimo-] ***n*.** (生物的)化学运动性。
chem·o·mor·pho·sis [ˌkeməuˈmɔːfəsis; ˏkɛmoˋmɑrfəsɪs] ***n*.** 【生】化学诱变。
chem·o·pro·phy·lax·is [ˌkeməuˌprəufiˈlæksis; ˏkɛmoˏprofɪˋlæksɪs] ***n*.** 【医】(传染病的)化学预防。**-lac·tic** [-ˈlæktic; -ˋlæktɪc] ***a*.**
chem·o·re·cep·tor [ˌkeməuriˈseptə; ˏkɛmorɪˋsɛptɚ] ***n*.** 化学受体,化学感受器。**-tive** ***a*.**
chem·os·mo·sis [ˌkemɔsˈməusis; ˏkɛmɑsˋmosɪs] ***n*.** (*pl*. *-ses* [-siːz; -siz]) 化学渗透作用。**-mot·ic** [-ˈmɔtik; -ˋmɑtɪk] ***a*.**
chem·o·sphere [ˈkeməsfiə; ˋkɛməsfɪr] ***n*.** 【气】光化圈,臭氧层。
chem·o·ster·i·lant [ˌkeməuˈsterilənt, ˌkiːməu-; ˏkɛmoˋstɛrɪlənt, ˏkimo-] ***n*.** (灭虫的)化学绝育剂。
chem·o·sur·gery [ˌkeməuˈsədʒəri; ˏkɛmoˋsədʒərɪ] ***n*.** 化学外科;化学外科治疗。**-gi·cal** ***a*.**
chem·o·syn·the·sis [ˌkeməuˈsinθəsis; ˏkɛmoˋsɪnθəsɪs] ***n*.** 【化】化学合成。
chem·o·tac·tic [ˌkeməuˈtæktik; ˏkɛmoˋtæktɪk] ***a*.** 【生】趋化性的,趋药性的。
chem·o·tax·is [ˌkeməuˈtæksis; ˏkɛməˋtæksɪs] ***n*.** 【生】趋化性,趋药性。
chem·o·ther·a·peu·tant [ˈkeməuˌθerəˈpjuːtənt; ˏkɛmoˏθɛrəˋpjutənt] ***n*.** 化学治疗药。
chem·o·ther·a·py [ˌkeməuˈθerəpi; ˏkɛmoˋθɛrəpɪ] ***n*.** 【医】化学疗法(= chemotherapeutics)。**chem·o·thera·pist** ***n*.** 化学疗法专家。
chem·o·troph [ˌkeməuˈtrɔf; ˏkɛmoˋtrɑf] ***n*.** 【生】化能营养。**chem·o·troph·ic** ***a*.**
chem·o·troph·y [ˌkeməuˈtrɔfi; ˏkɛmoˋtrɑfɪ] ***n*.** = chemotroph.
chem·ot·ro·pism [ˈkemɔtrəpizm; ˋkɛmɑtrəpɪzm] ***n*.** 【医】向药性。**-trop·ic** [-ˈtrɔpik; -ˋtrɑpɪk] ***a*.**
chem·ur·gy [ˈkemədʒi; ˋkɛmɚdʒɪ] ***n*.** 农业化学。
che·nar [tʃiˈnɑː; tʃɪˋnɑr] ***n*.** = chinar.
che·nille [ʃəˈniːl; ʃəˋnil] ***n*.** **1.** 绳绒线,雪尼尔花线。**2.** 假绳绒线,毛虫状绒线(编织品)。
che·no·pod [ˈkiːnəpɔd, ˈkenə-; ˋkinəpɑd, ˋkɛnə-] ***n*.** 【植】藜科植物。
che·ong·sam, che·ong-sam [ˈtʃiːɑːŋˈsɑːm; ˋtʃiɑŋˋsɑm] ***n*.** 〔Chin.〕旗袍〔广东话"长衫"的音译〕。
Che·ops [ˈkiːɔps; ˋkiɑps] ***n*.** 基奥普斯〔公元前 3—4 世纪埃及第四王朝的法老,金字塔的建造者〕。
cheque [tʃek; tʃɛk] ***n*.** 【英商】支票。*a* ~ *for 100 dollars* 百元支票。*a blank* ~空白支票;〔喻〕自由行动的权力。*a crossed* ~划线支票。*a* ~ *drawer* [*holder*] 支票出票人[持票人]。*raise a* ~增改支票上金额。~**-book** 支票簿。
cheq·uer [ˈtʃekə; ˋtʃɛkɚ] **I** ***n*.** **1.** 〔英〕棋子;〔*pl*.〕西洋跳棋(= draughts)。**2.** 〔*pl*.〕棋盘图案,格子花;棋盘格子;【建】方格式排列的石块。**3.** 【植】花楸果。**II** ***vt*.** 使成格子花样;使(像光和影一样)交错;使变化多端〔常用被动语态〕。—***vi*.** 盛衰不定;(情绪等)变化多端。
cheq·uered [ˈtʃekəd; ˋtʃɛkɚd] ***a*.** 〔英〕**1.** 格子花样的;交错的。**2.** 变化多端的,盛衰无常的。~ *light and shade* 交错的光和影,光与影的交错。*a* ~ *fortune* [*career*] 波折重重的命运[一生]。
Cheq·uers [ˈtʃekəz; ˋtʃɛkɚz] ***n*.** (伦敦郊外)旧英国首相乡间别墅〔1917 年捐赠给国家〕。
cher·a·lite [ˈtʃerəlait; ˋtʃɛrəlaɪt] ***n*.** 【矿】富钍独居石。
Cher·bourg [ˈʃɛəbuəg; ˋʃɛrburg] ***n*.** 瑟堡〔法国港市〕。
cher·ish [ˈtʃeriʃ; ˋtʃɛrɪʃ] ***vt*.** **1.** 抚育。**2.** 爱护。**3.** 怀有,抱有(希望等)。~ *fond dreams of* 做…的美梦。~ *a grudge against* 对…怀恨。~ *justice* 坚持正义。~*ed desire* 夙愿。
cher·no·zem [ˈtʃɛənəzem; ˋtʃɛrnəzem] ***n*.** 【地】黑土,黑土地带。
Cher·o·kee [ˌtʃerəˈkiː; ˋtʃɛrəˏki] ***n*.** (*pl*. ~, ~***s***) (北美印第安人的)柴罗基部族。**c- rose** 【植】金樱子。
che·root [ʃəˈruːt; ʃəˋrut] ***n*.** 平头雪茄烟。
Cher·ry [ˈtʃeri; ˋtʃɛrɪ] ***n*.** 彻丽〔女子名〕。
cher·ry [ˈtʃeri; ˋtʃɛrɪ] **I** ***n*.** **1.** 樱桃;樱桃树。**2.** 樱桃色;樱桃酒。**3.** 〔美俚〕处女膜,处女状态,童贞。**II** ***a*.** **1.** 樱桃色的。**2.** 鲜红的。**3.** 有樱桃味的;樱桃木制的。**4.** 处女的。~ **bay** 月桂,桂树。~ **bomb** 球形红色烟火。~ **brandy** 樱桃白兰地。~ **coal** 软煤。~ **picker** 〔俚〕(修理电线等用的)车载升降台。~**-pick** ***vi*.** 挑选。~ **pie** **1.** 樱桃酱馅饼。**2.** 【植】香水草;柳叶菜(= heliotrope)。~ **red** 〔英俚〕街斗靴(= bovver boot)。~ **stone** **1.** 樱

C

桃核。2.(北美)小蛤蜊。~ **tree** 樱桃树。

cher·so·nese [ˈkəːsəniːz, -niːs; ˋkɚsə͵niz, -nis] *n*. 半岛。

chert [tʃəːt; tʃɚt] *n*.【矿】燧石,黑硅石。

cher·ub [ˈtʃerəb; ˋtʃɛrəb] *n*. 1.(*pl*. ***cher·u·bim*** [ˈtʃerəbim; ˋtʃerəbɪm],【圣】***-bin*** [-bin; -bɪn])(画上象征智慧与正义的)有翅的小天使。2.(*pl*. ~*s*)天真无邪的儿童;胖娃娃。

che·ru·bic [tʃəˈruːbik; tʃəˋrubɪk] *a*. 小天使似的;(面孔等)白胖可爱的。

cher·vil [ˈtʃəːvil; ˋtʃɚvɪl] *n*.【植】细叶芹属。

C

Chesh·ire [ˈtʃeʃə; ˋtʃɛʃɚ] *n*. 柴郡[英国郡名]。***grin like a ~ cat*** 露着牙齿嘻嘻笑。~ **cat** 动不动露着牙齿嘻嘻笑的人。~ **cheese** 英国饼状干酪。

Ches·nut(t) [ˈtʃesnʌt; ˋtʃɛsnʌt] *n*. 切斯纳特[姓氏]。

chess[1] [tʃes; tʃɛs] *n*. 国际象棋。*have a game of* ~ 下一盘象棋。*play (at)* ~下象棋。~**board** 棋盘。~**-man** 棋子。~**tournament** 象棋比赛。

chess[2] [tʃes; tʃɛs] *n*.(*pl*. ~*es*)架浮桥的木板。

chess[3] [tʃes; tʃɛs] *n*.【植】雀麦;稗草。

ches·sel [ˈtʃesəl; ˋtʃɛsl̩] *n*. 制干酪的模型。

chess·y·lite [ˈtʃesiilait; ˋtʃɛsə͵laɪt] *n*.【矿】蓝铜矿[石青]。

chest [tʃest; tʃɛst] *n*. 1. 箱,函,柜,匣。2. 银箱;金库,公款,资金。3. 胸部,胸腔;(特指)肺。*an ice* ~冰箱。*a medicine* ~药箱。~ *of drawers* 五屉柜。~ *trouble* 肺病。~ *voice* 胸声。*cold in the* ~咳伤风。***get sth. off one's*** ~ [口]吐出心里的话。***throw a*** ~ [俚]挺起胸部。~**note**【乐】最低音调,胸音。~ **protector**(绒布)护胸。~ **voice** 最低的歌声[话声]。

-chest·ed [ˈtʃestid; ˋtʃɛstɪd] *comb. f*. 胸部…的,有…胸的:*pigeon*-~【医】鸡胸的。*broad* [*flat*, *full*]-~ 胸部宽阔[扁平,挺出]的。

Ches·ter[1] [ˈtʃestə; ˋtʃɛstə] *n*. 切斯特[男子名]。

Ches·ter[2] [ˈtʃestə; ˋtʃɛstɚ] *n*. 柴郡[英国郡名](=Chestshire);柴郡的首府。~ **White** [美]切斯特种早熟白猪。

Ches·ter·field [ˈtʃestəfiːld; ˋtʃɛstɚfild] *n*. 切斯特菲尔德[姓氏]。

ches·ter·field [ˈtʃestəfiːld; ˋtʃɛstɚfild] *n*. 1. 睡椅,长靠椅。2. [Can.]沙发;(丝绒领的)单排扣大衣。

Ches·ter·ton [ˈtʃestətən; ˋtʃɛstətən] *n*. 切斯特顿[姓氏]。

chest·nut [ˈtʃesnʌt; ˋtʃɛsnət] I *n*. 1. 栗子,板栗[Spanish ~或 sweet ~的果实]。2. 栗树。3. 栗色,褐色。4. 栗毛马。5. 马前腿内侧胼胝。6. [美口]陈腐话,滥调。II *a*. 栗色的;栗毛的。*water* ~菱。(*Chinese*) *water* ~荸荠。***pull*** (***sb.'s***) ~***s out of the fire*** 为(某人)火中取栗,为解决别人困难而自己承担后果。

chest-on-chest [ˈtʃestənˈtʃest; ˋtʃɛstənˋtʃɛst] *n*. 叠式立柜[连在一起的两个柜,下面的那个比上面的大一些]。

chest·y [ˈtʃesti; ˋtʃɛstɪ] *a*. 1. [口]胸腔宽的;[英口]有(肺病等)胸腔病症状的;[俚](女人)胸部(乳房)突出的。2. [美]自负的,自命不凡的,骄傲的。

che·tah [ˈtʃiːtə; ˋtʃitə] *n*. =cheetah.

cheth [ket; kɛt] *n*. 希伯来文第八个字母(=het)。

che·val [ʃəˈvæl; ʃəˋvæl] *n*.(*pl*. ***-vaux*** [-ˈvəu; -ˋvo])[F.]马。~***-defrise*** [ʃəˈvældəˈfriːz; ʃəˋvældəˋfriz][F.] chevaux-de-frise 的单数形式。

che·va·let [ʃəˈvælei; ʃə͵vaˋlɛ] *n*. [F.]【乐】弦乐器。

che·val-glass [ʃəˈvælglɑːs; ʃəˋvælglɑs] *n*.(活动)穿衣镜。

Chev·a·lier [ʃəˈvæljei; ʃəˋvælje] *n*. 谢瓦利埃[姓氏]。

che·val·ier [ˌʃevəˈliə; ʃəˋvælɪr] *n*. 1. 骑士。2. 爵士,各级爵位[勋位]的成员。3. 法国贵族的见习军官,法国最下级贵族。4. 勇士,义士,侠客。~ ***d'industrie*** [dæŋdjuːsˈtriː; dæŋdjusˋtri] = ***a*** ~ ***of industry*** 骗子。

che·vaux-de-frise [ʃəˈvəudəˈfriːz; ʃəˋvodəˋfriz] *n*. *pl*. [F.]【军】(阻止骑兵进攻的)拒马,防栅,刺栏;(墙上的)防贼钉。

cheve·lure [ʃəvˈljuːə; ʃəvˋljʊr] *n*. [F.]头发(尤指假发)。

che·vet [ʃəˈvei; ʃəˋvɛ] *n*. [F.](教堂的)圆室,多角室。

Chev·i·ot [ˈtʃeviət; ˋtʃɛvɪət] *n*. 1.(英国)舍维绵羊。2. [c-]舍维呢。~ *Hills* 舍维山[英格兰与苏格兰之间的丘陵地带]。

chev·ron [ˈʃevrən; ˋʃɛvrən] *n*. 1.【徽】山形符号;【军】(下级军官的)山形袖章。2.【建】波浪饰。***in*** ~(盾状徽内的)虚线山形。***per*** ~(盾状徽内的)黑山形。

chev·ro·tain [ˈʃevrəutein; ˋʃɛvrə͵ten] *n*.【动】麝鹿,鼷鹿。

chev·y[1] [ˈʃeviː; ˋʃɛvɪ] *n*. [美口](美国)雪佛兰牌汽车。

chev·y[2] [ˈtʃevi; ˋtʃɛvɪ] I *n*. [口]追赶,追猎声;(游戏)捉俘虏。II *vt*. 1. 追赶,追捉。2. 使发窘,使困惑。—*vi*. 快跑,逃窜。

chew [tʃuː; tʃu] I *vt*. 咀嚼,嚼碎;嚼(烟)。—*vi*. 1. 咀嚼。2. 沉思,细想(*over*, *upon*)。3. [口]嚼烟。4. [美俚]吃;讲,谈话。***bite off more than one can*** ~ [美口]自不量力;过份自信。~ ***out*** [俚]严厉责备。~ ***the cud***(牛等)反刍,熟思,玩味(*of*)。~ ***the fat*** [***rag***] [美俚]闲谈,聊天。~ ***the scenery*** [美俚]做得过分(像做戏一样);发牢骚。~ ***upon*** [***over***] 沉思,细想。II *n*. 咀嚼;一口。

chewing-gum [ˈtʃu(ː)iŋ-gʌm; ˋtʃu(ʊ)ɪŋ-gʌm] *n*. 橡皮糖;口香糖。

chew·y [ˈtʃuːi; ˋtʃuɪ] *a*.(***chew·i·er***; ***chew·i·est***)耐嚼的。~ **candy** 橡皮糖,口香糖。**chew·i·ness** *n*.

Chey·enne [ʃaiˈen, -ˈæn; ʃaɪˋɛn, -ˋæn] *n*.(*pl*. ~*s*, ~)1. 晒延人[美国印第安人的一个部落的成员]。2. 晒延语。

chez [ʃei; ʃe] ***prep***. [F.]在,在家。

chg. = change; charge.

C.H.H. (= chain home high) [英]海岸高空远程警戒雷达网。

chi [kai, kiː; kaɪ, ki] *n*. 希腊语字母表第22字母(Χ, χ),相当于英语的 ch]。*a chi*[2] (= χ^2) *square test*【生】卡方测验。

Chi. = Chicago.

Chi·an [ˈkaiən; ˋkaɪən] I *a*.(希腊)凯奥斯岛(Chios)的。II *n*. 凯奥斯岛人。

Chi·an·ti [kiˈænti; kɪˋæntɪ] *n*.(意大利)基安蒂红葡萄酒。

chi·a·ro·scu·ro [kiˌɑːrəsˈkuərəu; kɪ͵ɑrəˋskjuro] *n*.(*pl*. ~*s*)[It.]【美】明暗对比法;浓淡的映衬;明暗对比画。

chi·as·ma [kaiˈæzmə; kaɪˋæzmə] *n*.(*pl*. ~*s*, ***-ma·ta*** [-mətə; -mətə])【生】染色体交叉点;【解】(视神经)交叉。**-l** *a*.

chi·as·ma·typ·y [kaiˈæzməˌtaipi; kaɪˋæzmə͵taɪpɪ] *n*.【生】染色体交叉。

chi·as·mus [kaiˈæzməs; kaɪˋæzməs] *n*.(*pl*. ***-mi*** [-mai; -maɪ])【修】交错配列法[例:*we live to die, but we die to live*]。***-as·tic*** [kaiˈæstik; kaɪˋæstɪk] *a*.

chiaus [tʃaus, tʃauʃ; tʃaʊs, tʃaʊʃ] *n*. [Turk.]使者;军曹。

Chi·ba [ˈtʃiːbə; ˋtʃibə] *n*. 千叶[日本城市]。

Chib·cha [ˈtʃibtʃə; ˋtʃɪbtʃə] *n*.(*pl*. ~*s*, ~)1. 切布查人[美洲印第安人一个部落的成员]。2. 已消亡的切布查语。

Chib·chan [ˈtʃibtʃən; ˋtʃɪbtʃən] *a*. 切布查语的。

chib·ol [ˈtʃibəl; ˋtʃɪbəl] *n*. [英方]带茎洋葱。

chi·bouk, chi·bouque [tʃiˈbuːk; tʃɪˋbuk] *n*.(土耳其的)(长杆)旱烟袋。

chic [ʃiːk, ʃik; ʃik, ʃɪk] I *n*. [F.] [口](美术上的)独创风格;别致,潇洒,时髦。II *a*. 别致的,潇洒的,漂亮的。

Chi·ca·go [ʃiˈkɑːgəu; ʃəˋkɑgo] ***n.*** 芝加哥〔美国城市〕。
chi·ca·lo·te [ˌtʃikəˈləuti; ˏtʃɪkɑˋlotɪ] ***n.***【植】阔果蓟罂粟(老鼠苏)(*Argemone platyceras*)。
chi·ca·na [ʃiˈkɑːnə; ʃɪˏkɑnə] ***n.***〔Sp.〕住在美国的墨西哥女人。
chi·cane [ʃiˈkein; ʃɪˋken] **I *n.* 1.** 卑鄙手法,诈骗;狡辩,诡辩。**2.**【英牌】(一手没有王牌的)牌。**II *vi.*** 施诡计;诈骗。—***vt.*** 诈骗。
chi·can·er·y [ʃiˈkeinəri; ʃɪˋkenərɪ] ***n.* 1.** 卑鄙手法,诈骗。**2.** 狡辩,诡辩。*use* ～玩卑鄙手段。
Chi·ca·no [tʃiˈkɑːnəu; tʃɪˋkɑno] ***n.***〔Sp.〕(*pl.* ～*s*) 墨西哥裔美国人;在美国的墨西哥男人。
chic·co·ry [ˈtʃikəri; ˋtʃɪkərɪ] ***n.*** = chicory.
chi·chi [ˈʃiːˈʃiː; ˋʃiʃi] ***a.* 1.** 装饰精致的,华美的。**2.** 装模作样的,小题大做的。**3.** 赶时髦的。
chick[1] [tʃik; tʃɪk] **I *n.*** 小鸡,小鸟;小宝宝;〔美俚〕少妇,年轻女人。**II *a.***〔美〕雅致的,潇洒的,漂亮的;小的。***the*** ～***s*** (家庭中的)孩子们。
chick[2] [tʃik; tʃɪk] ***n.***〔印〕竹帘子。
chick·a·bid·dy [ˈtʃikəbidi; ˋtʃɪkəˏbɪdɪ] ***n.***〔儿〕小鸡,鸡宝宝。
chick·a·ree [ˈtʃikəriː; ˋtʃɪkəˏri] ***n.***【动】(美洲)红松鼠。
Chick·a·saw [ˈtʃikəˌsɔː; ˋtʃɪkəˏsɔ] ***n.*** (*pl.* ～, ～*s*) **1.** 契卡索人[美国马斯科吉印第安人一个部落成员,过去住在密西西比州北部和田纳西州的部分地区,现在住在俄克拉荷马州]。**2.** 契卡索语。
chick·en[1] [ˈtʃikin; ˋtʃɪkɪn] ***n.*** (*pl.* ～, ～*s*) **1.** 鸡雏,小鸡;〔美口〕鸡。**2.** 鸡肉,童子鸡。**3.** 小海虾。**4.** 小儿,娃娃。**5.**〔美俚〕漂亮姑娘,年轻女人。**6.** 胆小鬼,懦夫。**7.**〔美俚〕军纪细节。**8.**〔口〕少年男妓;雏妓。*She is no* ～. 她不是小娃娃。*Don't be a* ～. 不要害怕。***count one's*** ～***s before they are hatched*** 蛋未孵出先数鸡,过早乐观。***like a*** ～ ***with its head off*** 发疯一样地。***play*** ～〔美俚〕互相挑战和威胁(以吓倒对方)。***That's your*** ～. 那是你自己的事(与人无关)。～**-and-egg *a.*** 难分先后的,难分因果关系的。～ **breast**【医】鸡胸。～**-breasted *a.*** 鸡胸的。～ **broth** 鸡汤。～ **cholera** 鸡瘟,家禽霍乱。～ **colonel**〔美军俚〕上校。～ **feed** 鸡食;〔美口〕小钱币[五分铜币等];一笔小数目的钱。～ **fixings**〔美〕炸童子鸡。～ **head**〔美俚〕笨蛋,蠢货。～**hearted**, ～**livered *a.*** 胆怯的,软弱的。～ **money**〔美俚〕海军军人退职金。～ **pox**【医】鸡痘,水痘。～ **roost**〔美俚〕戏院最上层座位。～ **yard** 鸡圈。
chick·en[2] [ˈtʃikin; ˋtʃɪkən] ***n.***〔印〕刺绣。
chick·en·y [ˈtʃikini; ˋtʃɪkənɪ] ***a.*** 胆小的。
chick·let(te) [ˈtʃiklit; ˋtʃɪklɪt] ***n.***〔美俚〕少女。
chick·ling [ˈtʃikliŋ; ˋtʃɪklɪŋ] ***n.* 1.** 小鸡。**2.**【植】野豌豆〔亦作 ～ vetch〕。
chick·pea [ˈtʃikpiː; ˋtʃɪkˏpi] ***n.***【植】鹰嘴豆。
chick·weed [ˈtʃikwiːd; ˋtʃɪkˏwid] ***n.***【植】繁缕。
chic·le [ˈtʃikl; ˋtʃɪkl̩] ***n.***〔美〕糖胶树胶[做橡皮糖用]。
chi·co [ˈtʃiːkəu; ˋtʃiko] ***n.*** (*pl.* ～*s*)【植】黑肉叶刺茎藜(= greasewood)。
chic·o·ry [ˈtʃikəri; ˋtʃɪkərɪ] ***n.***【植】菊苣[根可充作咖啡]。
chide [tʃaid; tʃaɪd] ***vt.*** (～*d*, ***chid*** [tʃid; tʃɪd]; ***chidden*** [ˈtʃidn; ˋtʃɪdn̩], ～*d*, ***chid***; ***chid·ing***) 呵叱,责骂;骂走,斥逐(*from*; *away*)。—***vi.* 1.** 责备,责骂。**2.**〔书〕(风、猎犬等)怒号,咆哮。
chief [tʃiːf; tʃif] **I *n.* 1.** 首领,领袖,酋长,族长。**2.**〔口〕主管人员,长官[部长、局长、科长等]。**3.** 重要部分。～ *of a section* 科长,组长。～ *pilot* 正驾驶员。～ *itch and rub*〔美俚〕头子。～ *of staff* 参谋长。*C- of the Royal Air Force* 英国空军大元帅。***in*** ～ 居领导地位的,最高的,长官的;主要,【法】直接(*the commander in* ～总司令。*for many reasons, and this one in* ～理由很多,但主要是这个理由)。**II *a.*** 首,长;主要的,第一的。*a* ～ *accountant* 会计主任,会计科科长。～ *attractions* 主要节目。～ *clerk*〔美〕= *a* ～ *secretary* 书记长,秘书长。～ *editor* 总编辑。*the C- Executive*〔美〕总统;州长;市长。～ *judge* [*justice*] 审判长。*the C- Justice of the Common Pleas*〔英〕民事高等法院院长。*the C- Justice of the King's Bench* 英国高等法院院长。*the C- Justice of the United States* 美国高等法院院长。*a* ～ *justiciar* 审判长;首席法官。*a* ～ *officer* [*mate*]【海】大副。*a* ～ *radio man*【美军】一等电讯兵。～ [～***est***] ***of all*** 尤其是,最重要的是。**-dom, -ship *n.*** 首领的地位[资格]。
chief·ly [ˈtʃiːfli; ˋtʃiflɪ] **I *ad.*** 第一,首先;主要。**II *a.*** 领袖(般)的。
chief·tain [ˈtʃiːftən; ˋtʃiftən] ***n.*** 首领;族长;酋长;(土匪等)头子,〔诗〕指挥官,队长。**-cy, -ship** chieftain 的身分,地位。
chiel [tʃiːl; tʃil] ***n.***〔Scot.〕小伙子,青年(= chield)。
chiff·chaff [ˈtʃiftʃæf; ˋtʃɪfˏtʃæf] ***n.***【动】嚣鹪。
chif·fon [ˈʃifən; ʃɪˋfɑn] **I *n.***〔F.〕**1.** 雪纺绸,薄绸。**2.**〔*pl.*〕女服花边。**II *a.*** 薄绸制成的;薄绸般透明[柔软]的。
chi·ffo·nier [ˌʃifəˈniə; ˏʃɪfəˋnɪr] ***n.*** 梳妆镜柜,小衣橱;碗碟柜。
chig·ger [ˈtʃigə; ˋtʃɪgɚ] ***n.* 1.** = chigoe. **2.**【动】恙螨。
chi·gnon [ˈʃiːnjɔːŋ; ˋʃinjɑŋ] ***n.*** 发髻。
chig·oe, chig·re [ˈtʃigəu; ˋtʃɪgo] ***n.***【动】沙蚤。
chik [tʃik; tʃɪk] ***n.*** = chick[2]。
chil·blain [ˈtʃilblein; ˋtʃɪlˏblen] ***n.***〔常 *pl.*〕【医】冻疮。*have* ～*s* 生冻疮。**-ed *a.*** 生冻疮的。
child [tʃaild; tʃaɪld] ***n.*** (*pl.* ***chil·dren*** [ˈtʃildrən; ˋtʃɪldrən]) **1.** 孩子,儿童,胎儿,婴儿。**2.** 孩子气的人,幼稚的人。**3.** 子孙;后裔;(空想等的)产物。**4.** 追随者,崇拜者,弟子。**5.** 某个时代的产物。*a forward* ～早熟[慧]儿。*a male* [*female*] ～男[女]孩。*a natural* ～私生子。*a spoilt* ～宠子,娇儿。*The* ～ *is father of* [*to*] *the man.* 从小看大。*Don't be a* ～! 不要孩子气! *fancy's children* 想像的产物,空想。～ ***of fortune*** 幸运儿。～ ***of nature*** 自然的宠儿;天真的人。～ ***of the devil*** 魔鬼之子,恶人。***as a*** ～在幼年时代。***drag up a*** ～〔口〕把孩子拉扯大。***from a*** ～ 自幼。***own a*** ～ 承认自己是孩子的父亲。***this*** ～〔美俚〕我,鄙人。***with*** ～ 怀孕。～ **abuse** 对儿童的虐待[尤指性虐待]。～**bearing** 生产,分娩。～**bed** 产褥,分娩。～**birth** 分娩,生产。～**bride** 年轻的新娘子;童养媳。～ **care**[**welfare**] 保育事业。～**hood** 幼年(时代)(*second* ～*hood* 第二幼年,老耄期)。～ **labour** 童工(劳动)。～**-placement agency**〔美〕有幼孩待人领养的机关。～**proof *a.*** 使儿童无法开启的,保护儿童安全的(指家用电器等)。～ **psychology** 儿童心理学。～**'s play** 儿戏;轻而易举的事情。**-like *a.*** 孩子似的;天真烂漫的,直率的,老实的。
Child(e) [tʃaild; tʃaɪld] ***n.*** 察尔德[姓氏]。
childe [tʃaild; tʃaɪld] ***n.***〔古〕贵胄,贵族青年[尤指骑士的候补者]。
child·ing [ˈtʃaildiŋ; ˋtʃaɪldɪŋ] ***a.* 1.**〔古〕怀孕的。**2.**【植】花旁生花的。
child·ish [ˈtʃaildiʃ; ˋtʃaɪldɪʃ] ***a.* 1.** 孩子似的,孩子气的;孩子的,幼年的。**2.** 幼稚的,傻里傻气的。**-ly *ad.* -ness *n.***
child·less [ˈtʃaildlis; ˋtʃaɪldlɪs] ***a.*** 无儿女的。
child·ly [ˈtʃaildli; ˋtʃaɪldlɪ] ***a.*, *ad.*** 孩子似的[地]。
chil·dren [ˈtʃildrən; ˋtʃɪldrən] child 的复数。～ ***of iniquity*** 歹人。～ ***of Israel*** 犹太人。～ ***of Izaak Walton*** 爱钓鱼的人们。～ **court** 少年法庭。**C-'s Day** 儿童节。
Chil·e [ˈtʃili; ˋtʃɪlɪ] ***n.*** 智利[拉丁美洲]。～ **pepper** 辣椒。～ **saltpetre** 智利硝。
chile con car·ne [ˈtʃili kɔn ˈkɑːni; ˋtʃɪlɪ kɑn ˋkɑrnɪ]〔Sp.〕辣椒肉末[墨西哥菜]。

Chil·ean, Chil·ian [ˈtʃiliən; ˋtʃɪlɪən] **I** ***n.*** 智利讲的西班牙语;智利人。**II** ***a.*** 智利(人)的;智利文化的。

chil·i [ˈtʃili; ˋtʃɪlɪ] ***n.*** = chilli. ~**-eater** ***n.*** 〔美俚〕墨西哥人。

chil·i·ad [ˈkiliæd; ˋkɪlɪˏæd] ***n.*** 一千;一千年。

chil·i·arch [ˈkiliɑːk; ˋkɪlɪˏɑrk] ***n.*** (古希腊)千夫长。

chill [tʃil; tʃɪl] **I** ***n.*** **1.** 冷,寒冷,发冷;冷却;冷冻;【冶】冷模,冷铸。**2.** 冷淡;薄情。**3.** 扫兴;沮丧,寒心。*a* ~ *in the air* 恶冷,透骨的冷。***cast a*** ~ ***over*** 使扫兴,泼冷水。***catch a*** ~ 受寒,发冷。~***s and fever*** 〔美方〕间歇热,疟疾,打摆子。***feel*** [***have***] ***a*** ~ 打冷颤,发冷。***take a*** ~ 受寒,发冷。***take the*** ~ ***off*** 热一热,烫一烫(酒等)。**II** ***a.*** **1.** 〔书〕冷,寒。**2.** 冷淡的,薄情的;隔膜的;冷酷的;扫兴的,使…寒心的。**III** ***vt.*** **1.** 使变冷;使感觉冷;冰冻(食物);冷却,冷藏。**2.** 使扫兴,使寒心。**3.** 【冶】冷铸,冷淬。**4.** 〔口〕把(酒等)温一下,热一下。—***vi.*** 冷却,变冷;发冷。**-ing·ly** ***ad.***

chilled [tʃild; tʃɪld] ***a.*** 已冷的,冷却了的;冷淬过的;(肉等)冷冻了的,经过冷藏的。~ *castings* 冷硬铸件。~ *meat* 冷藏肉。*a* ~ *shell* 硬铁弹。*a* ~ *projectile* 破甲弹。~ *to the bone* 冷彻骨髓。

chill·er [ˈtʃilə; ˋtʃɪlɚ] ***n.*** **1.** 惊险小说。**2.** (冰箱中的)冷冻格。**3.** 冷却装置。**4.** 冷冻工人。

chil·li [ˈtʃili; ˋtʃɪlɪ] ***n.*** (*pl.* ~*es*) **1.** 干辣椒。**2.** = chile con carne. ~ **sauce** 番茄辣酱。

chill·i·ness [ˈtʃilinis; ˋtʃɪlənɪs] ***n.*** 寒冷,严寒,恶冷;冷淡,疏远。

chill·y[1] [ˈtʃili; ˋtʃɪlɪ] **I** ***a.*** **1.** 寒冷的;怕冷的。**2.** 使人恐惧的。**3.** 冷淡的,疏远的。*a* ~ *story* 令人打冷战的故事。**II** ***ad.*** 〔罕〕冷,冷淡地。

chil·ly[2] [ˈtʃili; ˋtʃɪlɪ] = chilli.

chilo- *comb. f.* = lip, labial.

chi·lo·pod [ˈkailəpɔd; ˋkaɪləˏpɑd] ***n.*** 【动】唇脚类动物〔蜈蚣、蚰蜒等〕。

Chil·tern Hundreds [ˈtʃiltəːn ˈhʌndrədz; ˋtʃɪltɚn ˋhʌndrədz] 〔英〕切尔吞皇室领地〔在 Chiltern Hills 附近〕。*accept* [*apply for*] *the Chiltern Hundreds* 解除[请求解除]下院议员职务〔受任这个皇室领地的挂名主管人,等于辞去下院议员职务〕。

chi·mae·ra [kaiˈmiərə; kaɪˋmɪrə] ***n.*** = chimera.

chim·ar [ˈtʃimə; ˋtʃɪmɚ] ***n.*** = chimere.

chimb [tʃaim; tʃaɪm] ***n.*** = chime[2].

chime[1] [tʃaim; tʃaɪm] **I** ***n.*** **1.** (音调谐和的)一套钟;铁琴。**2.** 〔*pl.*〕合奏钟声,钟乐。**3.** 谐音,韵律;调和,一致。**4.** 单调。***fall into*** ~ ***with*** 与…调和,与…一致。***in*** ~ 调和,一致。***keep*** ~ ***with*** 和…步骤一致。**II** ***vt.*** **1.** 打(一套钟),奏(钟乐);敲钟报(时),打钟召集(人)。**2.** 机械地重复,单调啰嗦地说。— ***vi.*** **1.** (乐器、钟等)奏出和谐的音调。**2.** 合节奏;调和。~ ***in with*** 赞成,同意,附和,为…帮腔,与…一致[协调]。

chime[2] [tʃaim; tʃaɪm] ***n.*** **1.** (啤酒桶两端的)凸边。**2.** 【海】(甲板上的)沟。

chi·me·ra [kaiˈmiərə; kaɪˋmɪrə] ***n.*** **1.** 【希神】〔常 C-〕吐火女怪〔狮头,羊身,龙尾〕;怪物;【建】狮头羊身蛇尾装饰。**2.** 妄想,奇想。**3.** 【遗传】嵌合体,嫁接杂种。

chi·mere [tʃiˈmiə; tʃɪˋmɪr] ***n.*** (主教穿的)无袖罩袍。

chi·mer·i·cal [kaiˈmerikəl; kaɪˋmɪrɪkḷ] ***a.*** 空想的,妄想的;幻想的;梦一般的。**-ly** ***ad.***

chim·ney [ˈtʃimni; ˋtʃɪmnɪ] ***n.*** **1.** 烟囱;(煤油灯的)灯罩;烟囱状东西。**2.** (火山的)喷烟口;【地】冰川井柱状矿体;冰川竖井;【登山】(岩面可容一人攀登的)直立裂口。**3.** 〔美方〕壁炉。**4.** 〔美俚〕老抽烟的人。~ **cap** 烟囱帽。~ **corner** 壁炉边〔通常设有的座位〕(*the* ~*-corner law* 〔美〕习惯法)。~ **jack** 旋转式烟囱帽。~ **piece** 壁炉架 (= mantelpiece)。~ **pot** 烟囱顶管;高顶礼帽。~**-pot hat** 高顶礼帽。~ **rock** 柱状石。~ **shaft** (房顶上的)烟囱;(工厂等的)大烟囱。~ **stack** 丛烟囱;(工厂等的)大烟囱。~ **stalk** 〔英〕(工厂等的)大烟囱;屋顶烟囱。~ **swallow** 〔英〕(在烟囱上作巢的)燕子。~ **sweep(er)** 扫烟囱的人。~ **swift** 〔美〕= ~ **swallow.**

chimp [tʃimp; tʃɪmp] ***n.*** 〔口〕黑猩猩。

chim·pan·zee [ˌtʃimpənˈziː; tʃɪmpænˋzi] ***n.*** 【动】黑猩猩。

chin [tʃin; tʃɪn] **I** ***n.*** **1.** 颏,下巴。**2.** 〔美俚〕闲谈。**3.** 【体】(单杠)引体向上动作。***have a*** ~ 〔美〕聊天。***keep one's*** ~ ***up*** 〔口〕始终精神昂扬,不泄气,不灰心。***stick one's*** ~ ***out*** 暴露自己;自惹麻烦;甘冒风险。***take it on the*** ~ 〔俚〕吃败战,彻底失败;忍痛。***up to the*** ~ = ~***-deep***. ***wag one's*** ~ 唠叨。**II** ***vt.*** (*-nn-*) **1.** 〔口〕用下巴夹住(提琴等)。**2.** 〔~ oneself〕(单杠)引体向上使下巴高过横杠;— ***vi.*** 〔美俚〕说,讲,谈话,唠叨,聊天。~ **armor** 〔美俚〕连鬓胡子。~**bone** 颏骨。~ **buster** 〔美俚〕拳击选手。~**deep** ***a.*** 到下巴的,深深陷入的。~ **music** 〔美俚〕闲谈,空谈;口才;责骂。~ **turret** 机头[舰首]炮塔。~**-wag** ***n.***, ***vi.*** 〔美讽〕闲聊,闲谈。~**-wagger** 〔美〕碎嘴子。

Chin. = Chinese, China.

Chi·na [ˈtʃainə; ˋtʃaɪnə] ***n.*** 中国。***from*** ~ ***to Peru*** 到处。~ **aster** 【植】翠菊。~ **bark** = quinine. ~ **bean** 豇豆。~ **blue** 青瓷色。~ **cotton** 鸡脚棉。~ **crape** 广东绉纱。~ **cup** 茶碗。~ **grass** 【植】宁麻,线麻。~**-green** 【植】亮丝草,广东万年青。~ **ink** 墨。~**jute** 商麻,青麻。~**man** 〔旧、蔑〕中国佬。~ **orange** 橙。~ **rose** 月季花。~**-teasel** 【植】华川续断。~ **town** 唐人街,中国城。~ **tree** 【植】楝树,苦楝。~ **wood oil** 桐油。

chi·na [ˈtʃainə; ˋtʃaɪnə] ***n.*** 瓷器;瓷料,白瓷土,瓷质黏土。*a piece of* ~一件瓷器。~ **clay** 瓷土。~ **closet** 瓷器橱。~ **mania** 瓷器搜集热。~ **maniac** 瓷器搜集迷[人]。~ **plate** 〔英俚〕伙伴。~ **shop** 瓷器店。~ **stone** 做瓷器的石料。~**ware** 瓷器。~ **wedding** 瓷婚,结婚二十年纪念。

china·ber·ry [ˈtʃainəberi; ˋtʃaɪnəˏbɛrɪ] ***n.*** 【植】楝树。

chi·na·crin(e) [ˈkinəkriːn; ˋkɪnəˏkrin] ***n.*** 【药】阿的平。

Chinar [tʃiˈnɑː; tʃɪˋnɑ] ***n.*** 【植】悬铃木,法国梧桐。

chinch [tʃintʃ; tʃɪntʃ] ***n.*** **1.** 臭虫。**2.** 〔美〕麦椿象 (= ~ bug)。

chin·che·rin·chee [ˌtʃintʃəˈrintʃi; ˏtʃɪntʃəˋrɪntʃɪ] ***n.*** 【植】好望角虎眼万年青 (*Ornithogalum thyrsoides*)。

chin·chil·la [tʃinˈtʃilə; tʃɪnˋtʃɪlə] ***n.*** **1.** 【动】南美栗鼠(皮)。**2.** 栗鼠呢,珠皮呢。**3.** 银灰色。

chin·cough [ˈtʃinkɔf; ˋtʃɪnkˏɔf] ***n.*** 百日咳。

chine[1] [tʃain; tʃaɪn] **I** ***n.*** **1.** 脊骨;脊肉。**2.** 山脊,山岭。**3.** 【船】舭线。~ *boat* 一种快艇。**II** ***vt.*** 切出(脊肉),沿…脊梁切开。

chine[2] [tʃain; tʃaɪn] ***n.*** 〔英方〕狭而深的峡谷,幽谷。

chine[3] [tʃain; tʃaɪn] ***n.*** = chime[2].

Chi·nee [tʃaiˈniː; tʃaɪˋni] ***n.*** 〔俚〕中国人。

Chi·nese [ˈtʃaiˈniːz; tʃaɪˋniz] **I** ***a.*** 中国(人)的;中国(话)的。*the* ~ *Wall* 万里长城。**II** ***n.*** 〔*sing.*, *pl.*〕中国人;中国话,汉语。~ **copy** 惟妙惟肖的描摹[临写]。~ **indigo** 蓝靛。~ **ink** 墨。~ **lantern** 灯笼。~ **linen** 夏布。~ **puzzle** (九连环等)中国玩具;难解的问题。~ **red** 大红;朱红。~ **white** 白色颜料,氧化锌。~ **wood oil** 桐油。

chin·fest [ˈtʃinfest; ˋtʃɪnfɛst] ***n.*** 〔美俚〕茶话会;争论。

chi·ni·o·fon [kiˈniəfən; kɪnɪəfən] ***n.*** 【药】喹碘方,药特灵。

chink[1] [tʃiŋk; tʃɪŋk] **I** ***n.*** **1.** (金属)叮当声。**2.** 〔俚〕硬币,现款。**II** ***vi.***, ***vt.*** (使)叮当响。

chink[2] [tʃiŋk; tʃɪŋk] **I** ***n.*** 裂缝,裂口;漏洞,弱点。**II** ***vi.*** 破裂,开裂。—***vt.*** **1.** 使开裂。**2.** 〔美〕塞…的裂缝。

chinky [ˈtʃiŋki; ˋtʃɪŋkɪ] ***a.*** 有[多]裂缝的。

-chinned [tʃind; tʃɪnd] *comb. f.* 长着…下巴的〔构成复

合词]：*double*～ 双下巴的。

Chi·no- *comb. f.* =China. ～*-Japanese* 中日的。

chi·no [ˈtʃiːnəu, ˈʃiː-; ˋtʃino, ʃi-] ***n*. 1.** 丝光卡其布。**2.** [*pl.*]丝光卡其布男衬裤。

chin·oise·rie [ˌʃiːnwɑːz(ə)ˈriː; ˏʃinwɑz(ə)ˋri] ***n*.** (欧洲18世纪摹仿的)中国艺术风格；具有中国艺术风格的物品。

Chi·nook [tʃiˈnuːk; tʃɪˋnuk] ***n*.** (*pl.* ～, ～*s*) **1.** [美]切奴克族印第安人；切奴克族及其他印第安人语言和英语及法语的混合语。**2.** [常 c-] 俄勒冈州的温暖西南湿风，落矶山东边的暖燥风(=c- wind)。

Chi·nook·an [tʃiˈnuːkən; tʃɪˋnukən] **I** ***a*. 1.** 切奴克人的。**2.** 切奴克语的。**II** ***n*. 1.** (北美印第安人的)切奴克族。**2.** 切奴克语。

chin·qua·pin [ˈtʃiŋkəpin; ˋtʃɪŋkəpɪn] ***n*.** 【植】美国栗树，板栗。

chintz [tʃints; tʃɪnts] ***n*., *a*.** (*pl.* ～***es*** [-iz; -ɪz]) 擦光印花棉布(的)。

chintz·y [ˈtʃintsi; ˋtʃɪntsɪ] ***a*. 1.** 印花布的。**2.** [口]廉价的；低劣的；卑劣的；尖刻的；小气的；琐碎的。

chi·o·no·phil·ous [kiəˈnɔfiləs; kɪəˋnɑfɪləs] ***a*.** 【植】适雪的，喜雪的。

chi·o·no·pho·bous [ˌkiənəuˈfəubəs; ˏkɪənoˋfobəs] ***a*.** 【植】避雪的，嫌雪的。

chip[1] [tʃip; tʃɪp] **I** ***n*. 1.** 碎片，削片，薄片；碎屑；薄木片；无价值的东西。**2.** (陶器等的)缺损(处)。**3.** (赌博用)筹码；[*pl.*][英俚]钱。**4.** [*pl.*][口]炸马铃薯片。**5.** (作燃料的)干牛[马]粪。**6.** 集成电路唱片[块]。**7.** [口]小粒金刚石[水晶]。***a*** ～ ***of*** [***off***] ***the old block*** (脾气等)完全像父亲的儿子；一家的典型人物。(***as***) ***dry as a*** ～ 枯燥无味的。***buy*** ～***s*** 投资。***cash*** [***pass***] ***in one's*** ～***s*** 把筹码兑现；[俚]死。～ ***in porridge*** [***pottage***, ***broth***] 无关重要的东西，可有可无的东西。***do not care a*** ～ ***for*** 毫不介意。***have a*** ～ ***on one's shoulder*** [美俚]盛气凌人；好打架；好争吵。***have one's*** ～***s on*** 孤注一掷。***in the*** ～***s*** [美俚]有钱的。***let the*** ～***s fall where they may*** 不管后果如何。***when the*** ～***s are down*** [***get on the line***] 万不得已的时候，紧急时候。**II** ***vt*.** (*-pp-*) **1.** 切，削，凿，刻。**2.** 把…削成薄片；弄缺(刀口，瓷器等)。**3.** [口]戏弄；挖苦。**4.** (鸡雏等)啄碎(蛋壳)。—***vi*. 1.** 出现缺口。**2.** 碎裂，瓦解，破碎 (*off*)。～ ***at*** 对准…打，谩骂。～ ***in*** [口]插嘴，加入(打架等)；捐助；拿钱赌 (*They all chipped in to buy it.* 大家都要买了)。～ ***off*** 切下来，削下来。～**board** 废纸制成的纸板；刨花板。～**bonnet** [**hat**] 刨花帽。～ **card**【计】集成芯片卡[一种微型芯片，又称信息储存卡]。**chip·pings** (削下或凿下的)屑片。

chip[2] [tʃip; tʃɪp] **I** ***n*.** (摔跤时)用绊腿把对方摔倒的一种技巧。**II** ***vt*.** (*-pp-*) (用绊腿)摔倒(对方)。

Chip·e·wy·an [ˌtʃipiˈwaiən; ˏtʃɪpɪˋwaɪən] ***n*. 1.** 契帕瓦人[加拿大西北部阿撒巴斯卡印第安人的一个部族]。**2.** 契帕瓦语。

chip·muck, chip·munk [ˈtʃipmʌk, ˈtʃipmʌŋk; ˋtʃɪpmʌk, ˋtʃɪpmʌŋk] ***n*.** 【动】花栗鼠[北美产]。

Chip·pen·dale [ˈtʃipəndeil; ˋtʃɪpənˏdel] **I** ***n*.** (英国家具师切宾代尔设计的)切宾代尔样式(的家具)。**II** ***a*.** (家具)切宾代尔式的。

chip·per[1] [ˈtʃipə; ˋtʃɪpɚ] **I** ***a*.** [美口]活泼的；潇洒的，漂亮的；精力充沛的。**II** ***vt*., *vi*.** (使)鼓起精神，(使)高兴起来 (*up*)。

chip·per[2] [ˈtʃipə; ˋtʃɪpɚ] ***n*. 1.** 削片者。**2.** 削片机；錾刀，凿刀。

chip·per[3] [ˈtʃipə; ˋtʃɪpɚ] ***vi*.** (鸟)唧唧地叫，(人)喊喊喳喳地闲谈。

Chip·pe·wa, Chip·pe·way [ˈtʃipəwɑː, -wei; ˋtʃɪpəˏwɑ, -we] ***n*.** (北美印第安人)齐帕威部族[又叫 Ojibway, Ojibwa]。

chip·ping[1] [ˈtʃipiŋ; ˋtʃɪpɪŋ] ***n*.** [*pl.*](削、凿下的)碎屑，碎片，薄片；【机】切屑。

chip·ping[2] [ˈtʃipiŋ; ˋtʃɪpɪŋ] ***a*.** (雀，栗鼠等)唧唧叫的。

chip·py[1] [ˈtʃipi; ˋtʃɪpɪ] ***a*. 1.** 碎片的。**2.** [俚]枯燥无味的。**3.** (因饮酒过多而)心烧气躁的；易怒的。

chip·py[2] [ˈtʃipi; ˋtʃɪpɪ] ***n*. 1.** [美俚]行为不检的年轻荡妇；妓女。**2.** = chipmunk.

chirk [tʃəːk; tʃɝk] **I** ***a*.** [美]活泼的，高兴的。**II** ***vi*. 1.** 使快活[高兴]起来 (*up*)。**2.** (鸟，鼠等)唧唧地尖叫。—***vt*.** 使快活[高兴]起来。

chirm [tʃəːm; tʃɝm] **I** ***n*.** [方、罕]喃喃声；啾啾声；嗡嗡声；远处的喧噪声。**II** ***vi*.** [方、罕]作啾啾声；作嗡嗡声等。

chir(o)- *comb. f.* = hand: *chiro*graphy.

chi·rog·no·my [ˈkaiəˈrɔgnəmi; ˋkaɪˋrɑgnəmɪ] ***n*.** 手相术。

chi·ro·graph [ˈkaiərəgrɑːf; ˋkaɪrəˋgræf] ***n*.** 【法】亲笔字据；教皇的亲笔特许证书。

chi·rog·ra·phy [ˌkaiəˈrɔgrəfi; ˏkaɪˋrɑgrəfɪ] ***n*.** 笔迹；书法。

chirology [kaiˈrɔlədʒi; kaɪˋrɑlədʒɪ] ***n*.** 手语法；手的研究。

chiro·man·cer [ˈkaiərəmænsə; ˋkaɪrəmænsə] ***n*.** 手相家。

chi·ro·man·cy [ˈkaiərəmænsi; ˋkaɪrəˏmænsɪ] ***n*.** 手相术。

chi·rop·o·dist [kiˈrɔpədist; kɪˋrɑpədɪst] ***n*.** 【医】手足病医生[尤指足病医师]。

chi·rop·o·dy [kiˈrɔpədi; kɪˋrɑpədɪ] ***n*.** 【医】手足病治疗。

chi·ro·prac·tic [ˌkaiərəˈpræktik; ˏkaɪrəˋpræktɪk] ***n*.** 【医】**1.** (脊柱)按摩疗法。**2.** = chiropractor.

chi·ro·prac·tor [ˈkaiərəˌpræktə; ˋkaɪrəˏpræktɚ] ***n*.** 【医】(脊柱)按摩疗法医生。

chi·rop·ter [kaiˈrɔptə; kaɪˋrɑptɚ] ***n*.** 【动】蝙蝠。**-an** ***a*.**

Chi·rop·te·ra [kaiəˈrɔptərə; kaɪˋrɑptərə] ***n*.** [*pl.*] 【动】翼手目。**-n** ***a*.**

chirp [tʃəːp; tʃɝp] **I** ***n*.** (鸟的)啁啾声；(虫的)唧唧声；(无线电的)啁啾声信号。**II** ***vi*. 1.** (鸟等)啁啾地叫，(蟋蟀等)唧唧地叫。**2.** (人)喊喊喳喳地讲话。—***vt*.** 喊喊喳喳地讲出。

chir·py [ˈtʃəːpi; ˋtʃɝpɪ] ***a*.** 唧唧叫的；快活的，活泼的。

chirr [tʃəː; tʃɝ] **I** ***vi*.** (蟋蟀等)唧唧地叫。**II** ***n*.** 唧唧声。

chir·rup [ˈtʃirəp; ˋtʃɪrəp] **I** ***n*.** (颤动舌头哄婴孩或催马的)啧啧声；(鸟，虫等)不断发出的唧唧声。**II** ***vi*.** 发出啧啧声[哄婴孩或催马等]；唧唧地叫；[俚](在戏院中替自己人)喝彩。—***vt*.** 啧啧地说出。

chi·rur·geon [kaiəˈrəːdʒən; kaɪˋrɝdʒən] ***n*.** [古] = surgeon.

chis·el [ˈtʃizl; ˋtʃɪzl̩] **I** ***n*. 1.** 凿子，凿刀；錾子。**2.** [俚]诈骗。*a chipping* ～ 石錾子，平切錾。*a cold* ～錾子。*a pneumatic* ～气凿。***the*** ～ 雕刻刀具；雕刻术。**II** (*-ll-*) ***vt*. 1.** 凿，錾，镌，雕，刻。**2.** 凿成，錾成，镌成，雕琢 (*into*)；加工，润饰(文章)。**3.** [美俚]欺诈，骗取；不正当地处置。—***vi*. 1.** 凿，錾，镌，雕，刻。**2.** [美俚]骗，欺诈；弄手段，考试时作弊。**3.** 钻进(*in*)。～ ***in*** 干涉，钻空子。***full*** ～ [美俚]飞快地；猛冲。**-(l)ed** ***a*.** 凿过的，凿光的；轮廓清晰的(*chiselled features* [口](像雕成一样的)轮廓清晰的脸盘)。

chis·el·er [ˈtʃizlə; ˋtʃɪzlɚ] ***n*. 1.** 凿工。**2.** [美俚]骗子，行为不正的人。

chi-square [ˈkaiskwɛə; ˋkaɪskwɛr] ***n*.** 【统】χ^2检验法。

chit[1] [tʃit; tʃɪt] **I** ***n*.** 幼芽，嫩芽。**II** ***vi*.** (*-tt-*) [方]发芽。—***vt*.** [口]摘去…的芽。

chit[2] [tʃit; tʃɪt] ***n*.** 小孩；少女；黄毛丫头。

chit[3] [tʃit; tʃɪt] ***n*. 1.** 短信，字条。**2.** 收条，账单。**3.** (受雇

用者等的)保单,保证书。～-**book** 送文簿,签收簿。～-**system** 单据支付制度〔对现金支付而言〕。

chi·tal [ˈtʃiːtəl; ˋtʃitəl] *n*. (印度等地产的)白斑鹿。

chit·chat [ˈtʃittʃæt; ˋtʃɪt͵tʃæt] **I** *vi*. (-*tt*-) 闲谈,聊天。**II** *n*. 闲聊。

chi·tin[1] [ˈkaitin; ˋkaɪtɪn] *n*. 【动】(甲)壳质,明角质。

chi·tin[2] [ˈkaitin; ˋkaɪtɪn] *n*. 【生化】几丁质,壳多糖。

chi·tin·ous [ˈkaitinəs; ˋkaɪtɪnəs] *a*. 【生化】几丁质的,壳多糖的。

chit·lins, chit·lings [ˈtʃitlinz; ˋtʃɪtlɪnz] *n*. 〔*pl*.〕= chitterlings.

chi·ton [ˈkaitən; ˋkaɪtɑn] *n*. 〔古希腊〕长内衣。

chit·tack [ˈtʃitæk; ˋtʃɪtæk] *n*. 吉塔克〔印度重量单位,相当于一盎斯〕。

Chit·ta·gong [ˈtʃitəgɔŋ; ˋtʃɪtə͵gɔŋ] *n*. 吉大港〔孟加拉国港市〕。

chit·ter [ˈtʃitə; ˋtʃɪtɚ] *vi*. **1.** 〔美〕嘁嘁喳喳地闲聊。**2.** 〔Scot.〕〔方〕冷得发抖。

chit·ter·lings [ˈtʃitəliŋz; ˋtʃɪtɚlɪŋz] *n*. 〔*pl*.〕(猪等的)小肠(= chitlings)。

Chit·ty [ˈtʃiti; ˋtʃɪtɪ] *n*. 奇蒂〔姓氏〕。

chiv [ʃaiv; ʃaɪv] *n*. 〔美俚〕= chive[2].

chiv·al·ric [ˈʃivəlrik; ˋʃɪvl̩rɪk] *a*. 〔诗〕= chivalrous.

chiv·al·rous [ˈʃivəlrəs; ˋʃɪvl̩rəs] *n*. **1.** (像)骑士的;勇武的,豪侠的。**2.** 骑士时代的,骑士制度的。**3.** 敬重女人的。-**ly** *ad*. -**ness** *n*.

chiv·al·ry [ˈʃivəlri; ˋʃɪvl̩rɪ] *n*. **1.** 骑士制度。**2.** 骑士气概[精神(等)],豪侠。**3.** 骑士团。**4.** 妇女崇拜(者)。*laws of* ～骑士制度的条例。*the flower of* ～骑士(制度)的典范。

chive[1] [tʃaiv; tʃaɪv] *n*. 【植】细香葱。

chive[2] [tʃaiv; tʃaɪv] *n*. 〔美俚〕小刀。

chiv·(v)y [ˈtʃivi; ˋtʃɪvɪ] *n*., *vt*., *vi*. = chevy.

Ch.J. = Chief Justice 审判长,首席法官,法院院长。

C.H.L. (= chain home low) 〔英〕海岸低空飞机远程警戒雷达网。

chlam·y·date [ˈklæmideit; ˋklæmə͵det] *a*. 【动】有覆盖的。

chla·myd·o·spore [kləˈmidəspɔː; kləˋmɪdəspɔr] *n*. 【生】厚垣[壁,膜]孢子。

chla·mys [ˈkleiməs, ˈklæməs; ˋklemɪs, ˋklæməs] *n*. (*pl*. ～*es*, ***chlam·ydes*** [ˈklæmidiz; ˋklæmɪdɪz]) (古希腊人的)短外套。

chlor- *comb*. *f*. 〔用于母音前〕= chloro-.

chlo·ral [ˈklɔːrəl; ˋklɔrəl] *n*. 【化】氯醛,三氯乙醛;三氯乙二醇〔麻醉剂,又名 ～ hydrate 水合氯醛〕。-**ism** *n*. 三氯乙醛中毒症。

chlor·am·bu·cil [kləˈræmbjusil; klɑˋræmbjusɪl] *n*. 【药】苯丁酸氮芥,瘤可宁〔抗肿瘤药〕。

chlo·ra·mine [ˈklɔːrəmiːn; ˋklɔrə͵min] *n*. 【药】氯胺,氯阿明。

chlor·am·phen·i·col [ˌklɔːræmˈfenikɔːl, -kəul; ͵klɔræmˋfɛnəkol, -kol] *n*. 【药】氯霉素。

chlo·rate [ˈklɔːrit; ˋklɔrɪt] *n*. 【化】氯酸盐。

chlor·dan(e) [ˈklɔːdein; ˋklɔrden] *n*. 【化、农】氯丹,八氯化甲桥茚,1068〔剧毒杀虫剂〕。

chlor·di·az·e·pox·ide [ˌklɔːdaiˌeiziˈpɔksaid; ͵klɔrdaɪ-͵ezɪˋpɑksaɪd] *n*. 【药】利眠宁,甲氨二氮䓬〔安定药〕。

chlo·rel·la [klɔːˈrelə; kləˋrɛlə] *n*. 【植】小球藻。

chlo·ren·chy·ma [kləˈreŋkimə; kləˋrɛŋkɪmə] *n*. 【植】(含叶绿素的)绿色组织。

chlo·ric [ˈklɔːrik; ˋklɔrɪk] *a*. 【化】氯的,含五价氯的,从氯制得的。

chlo·ride [ˈklɔːraid; ˋklɔraɪd] *n*. 【化】氯化物,〔口〕漂白粉(= ～ of lime [soda, potash])。*sodium* ～氯化钠,食盐。

chlo·ri·dize [ˈklɔːridaiz; ˋklɔrɪd͵aɪz] *vt*. 【摄】用氯化物处理;在…上涂氯化银;使氯化。

chlo·ri·nate [ˈklɔːrineit; ˋklɔrɪ͵net] *vt*. 使氯化,给…加氯,用氯气处理。

chlo·rin·a·tion [ˌklɔːriˈneiʃən; ͵klɔrɪˋneʃən] *n*. 【化】氯化(作用),加氯(消毒)法。

chlo·rine [ˈklɔːriːn; ˋklɔrin] *n*. 【化】氯。～ *water* 氯水〔漂白液〕。

chlo·rite [ˈklɔːrait; ˋklɔraɪt] *n*. 【矿】绿泥石;【化】亚氯酸盐。

chlor·mad·i·none [kləˈmɑːdinəun; klɑˋmɑdɪnon] *n*. 【药】氯地孕酮〔避孕药〕(= ～ acetate)。

chloro- *comb*. *f*. 〔用于子音前〕**1.** 【动、植】绿。**2.** 【化】氯: *chloro*plast.

chlo·ro·ben·zene [ˌklɔːrəˈbenziːn; ͵klɔrəˋbɛnzin] *n*. 【化】氯苯。

chlo·ro·dyne [ˈklɔ(ː)rədain; ˋklorə͵daɪn] *n*. 【医】哥罗颠〔止痛麻醉剂〕。

chlor·o·form [ˈklɔ(ː)rəfɔːm; ˋklorə͵fɔrm] **I** *n*. 【化,医】三氯甲烷,氯仿。**II** *vt*. 用氯仿(麻醉);用氯仿杀死[处理]。-**ism** *n*. 氯仿中毒。-**ist** *n*. 管氯仿的人〔外科医生助手〕;爱用氯仿的医师。

chlo·ro·hy·drin(e) [ˌklɔːrəˈhaidrin; ͵klɔrəˋhaɪdrɪn] *n*. 【化】氯(乙)醇。

chlo·ro·my·ce·tin [ˌklɔ(ː)rəumaiˈsiːtin; ͵klorəmaɪˋsitin] *n*. 【药】氯霉素。

chlo·ro·phyl(l) [ˈklɔːrəfil; ˋklorə͵fɪl] *n*. 【植】叶绿素。

chlo·ro·phyl·lite [ˈklɔ(ː)rəfilait; ˋklɔ(ɑ)rəfɪ͵laɪt] *n*. 【矿】绿叶石。

chlo·ro·pic·rin [ˌklɔːrəˈpikrin; ͵klorəˋpɪkrɪn] *n*. 【化】氯化苦,三氯硝基甲烷(= nitrochloroform)。

chlo·ro·plast [ˈklɔ(ː)rəplæst; ˋklorə͵plæst] *n*. 【植】叶绿体。

chlo·ro·prene [ˈklɔ(ː)rəpriːn; ˋklorəprin] *n*. 【化】氯丁二烯。～ **rubber** 氯丁(二烯)橡胶。

chlo·ro·quine [ˌklɔ(ː)rəˈkwiːn; ͵klɔ(ɑ)rəˋkwin] *n*. 【药】氯奎。

chlo·ro·sis [kləˈrəusis; kləˋrosɪs] *n*. 【医】萎黄病;【植】缺绿病,褪绿,失绿。**chlo·rot·ic** [klɔːˈrɔtik; kləˋrɑtɪk] *a*.

chlo·rous [ˈklɔːrəs; ˋklɔrəs] *a*. 【化】与氯化合的,亚氯的,阴电性的。～ **acid** 亚氯酸。

chlor·phe·nir·a·mine [ˌklɔːfeniˈræmin; ͵klɔrfɛnɪˋræmɪn] *n*. 【药】氯苯吡胺,扑尔敏〔商品名称〕。

chlor·pic·rin [klɔːˈpikrin; klɔrˋpɪkrɪn] *n*. = chloropicrin.

chlor·prom·a·zine [klɔːˈprəuməzin; klɔrˋproməzɪn] *n*. 【药】氯普鲁马嗪〔商品名〕。

chlor·prop·a·mide [klɔːˈprəupəmaid; klɔrˋpropəmaɪd] *n*. 【药】氯磺丙脲〔降血糖药,治轻度糖尿病〕。

chlor·tet·ra·cy·cline [ˌklɔːˌtetrəˈsaiklin; klɔr͵tɛtrəˋsaɪklɪn] *n*. 【药】氯四环素,金霉素(= aureomycin)。

chm. = chairman; checkmate.

chmn. = chairman.

cho·a·na [ˈkəuənə; ˋkoənə] *n*. (*pl*. -***nae*** [-niː; -ni]) 【解】鼻后孔,内鼻孔。

Choate [tʃəut; tʃot] *n*. 乔特〔姓氏〕。

choc·ice [tʃɔkˈais; tʃɑkˋaɪs] *n*. 涂有巧克力的冰淇淋。

chock [tʃɔk; tʃɑk] **I** *n*. **1.** (防止滑动的)塞子,楔子;垫木;【机】塞块;(甲板、码头上的)角状柱;〔*pl*.〕【海】(大轮船上安置救生艇的)定盘,楔形木垫。**2.** 导缆钩,导缆器。**II** *vt*. 用楔子垫阻;把(救生艇)收置定盘上。～ ***up*** **1.** 用楔子垫稳。**2.** (用…)摆满,塞满(屋子)(*with*)。**III** *ad*. 紧,牢,稳;完全。*stand* ～ *still* 呆呆地站着。～-**a-block** *a*. 摆满,塞满(*with*)。～-**full** *a*. 塞满了的。

choc·o·late [ˈtʃɔkəlit; ˋtʃɑkəlɪt] **I** *n*. **1.** 巧克力(糖果)。**2.** 巧克力饮料。**3.** 巧克力色。*a bar* [*box*] *of* ～一块

[盒]巧克力。*a cup of* ～ 一杯巧克力茶。～ ***in cake*** [***powder***] 块状[粉状]巧克力。**II** ***a*. 1.** (含有)巧克力的。**2.** 巧克力色的。～ **cream** 奶油巧克力(糖)。～ **drop** 〔美〕〔贬〕黑种女孩。～ **soldier** 非战斗部队的军人。

choc·taw [ˈtʃɔktɔː; ˋtʃɑktə] ***n*.** (*pl*. ～, ～*s*) **1.**【溜冰】花式溜冰的一种。**2.**〔C-〕(印第安人的)巧克陶族;巧克陶语;难懂的语言[解释等]。

choice [tʃɔis; tʃɔɪs] **I** ***n*. 1.** 选择;挑选;选择力,选择权,选择的自由。**2.** 选择物,所爱好的物品;被选中的东西;入选者;精选品,精华。**3.** 供选择的种类。**4.** 审慎。**5.** 〔美〕移民的选定地。*the girl of one's* ～自己选中的女子,所喜爱的女孩。*Every man to his* ～. 各取所好。*There is no* ～ *between the two*. 二者半斤八两。*Which is your* ～? 你要哪一个? ***a great*** [***large***] ～ ***of*** 备有大量…以供选购。***a poor*** ～ 备货少(无从选择)。***at one's own*** ～ 随意,任意;自由选择地。***by*** ～ 出于自己的选择。***for*** ～ **1.** 出于自择。**2.** 要选(的话)就选…;特别,宁愿(要)。***have a*** [***the***] ～ (可以)选择。***have a wide*** [***large***] ～ ***of*** 有很多,…齐备。***have no*** (***particular***) ～ **1.** 哪个都好,并不特别喜欢哪一个。**2.** 无法选择。***have no*** ～ ***but to*** (*do*) 除…外别无他法,只好…。***have one's*** ～ 选择听便,可以挑选(*You have your* ～ *between the two*. 两者之中任拣一个)。***Hobson's*** ～ 就是这个要否听便[不许挑选]。***make*** ～ ***of*** 选择。***make*** [***take***] ***one's*** ～ 任意选取(*You may take your* ～ *for one dollar*. 每样一元听凭选择)。***of*** ～ 精选的,特别好的。***of one's*** ～ 自己选择[喜欢]的。***offer a*** ～ 听凭选择。***without*** ～ 不分好歹地,无选择地。**II** ***a*. 1.** 精选的,上等的,优良的;值得选用的。**2.** 爱选择的,挑七拣八的。**3.** 〔美〕宠爱的,爱惜的。***be*** ～ ***of*** 好挑剔(*be* ～ *of one's cloth* [*food*] 讲究衣着[饮食]的);〔美〕珍视(*It's my mother's trunk, and she is very* ～ *of it*. 这是我母亲的箱子,她很珍视它)。***be*** ～ ***over*** 珍爱,溺爱。～ ***bit of calico*** 〔美俚〕迷人的姑娘。～ ***goods*** 尖儿货,精选货品。**-ly** ***ad*.** 精选地,七挑八选地,认真地,严查地。**-ness** ***n*.** 精巧,优良,精选。

choir [ˈkwaiə; kwaɪr] **I** ***n*. 1.** (教堂的)唱诗队,唱诗班;唱诗队席位。**2.** 合唱团,舞蹈组,(天使、鸟、星等的)群,组;队。**II** ***vt*., *vi*.** 〔诗〕合唱,合奏。～ **boy** [**girl**] 唱诗班男[女]童。～ **organ** (教堂内)合唱伴奏风琴。～ **screen** 内坛围栏。

choke [tʃəuk; tʃok] **I** ***vt*. 1.** 使闭气,使闷死;使闷塞;扼(喉),绞死。**2.** 堵塞,填塞;【机】(为获得浓缩的燃料混合物而)阻塞…的气门。**3.** 阻止,妨止,扼止;干死(植物);减(火);压住,抑制(情感)。**4.**【棒球】握(球棒)中段。*Let go, you* ～ *me!* 放开呀,闷死我啦。—***vi*. 1.** 窒息,噎,哽。**2.** (管道等)塞住;说不出话来。**3.** 窘住;举止失措,行动失当。*The pipe* ～*s*. 管子塞住了。～ ***back*** 抑压住(感情),忍住(哭泣)。～ ***down*** 硬用力咽下;硬忍着(气),抑制住(感情、眼泪等)。～ ***in*** 〔美俚〕紧张得发呆[说不出话来]。～ ***off*** 把…闷死,绞死;使中止,使放弃(计划)。～ ***up*** 使闷死;枯死;〔口〕激动得说不出话来,紧张得发呆。～ ***up with*** 阻塞,填塞,塞满。**II** ***n*. 1.** 窒息;哽,噎;拥塞。**2.** (管的)闭塞部,节气门;【无】扼流圈[又作～ coil]。～**berry**【植】唐棣属(植物)。～**bore** 越近枪口越窄的枪筒。～**cherry** 〔美〕苦樱桃。～**damp** (煤坑、深井中的)碳酸气。～ **pear** 味涩的梨;难忍受的责备[事实]。～**-full** ***a*.** = chock-full.

chok·er [ˈtʃəukə; ˋtʃokɚ] ***n*. 1.** 使窒息的人,扼住喉咙的人;窒息物;难咽下的东西;〔俚〕使人哑口无言的事物,使人点头佩服的事物。**2.**【电】扼流线圈。**3.** 〔口〕很紧的项圈;硬高领;〔美俚〕阔领带;〔美俚〕= cheese. *a white* ～〔俚〕(教士夜礼服上的)宽大白颈巾;教士。*That's a* ～. 这倒使我没话可说了。

chok·ing [ˈtʃəukiŋ; ˋtʃokɪŋ] **I** ***a*. 1.** 窒息的,闷人的。**2.** 闭紧的;(声音)哽住的。**3.**【电】扼流(作用)的。*a* ～ *coil*【电】扼流线圈。**II** ***n*.** 闷气,闷住;拥塞,堵塞,塞住。

chok·y[1] [ˈtʃəuki; ˋtʃokɪ] ***a*.** 窒息的,闷人的。

chok·y[2] [ˈtʃəuki; ˋtʃokɪ] ***n*. 1.** 〔英俚〕拘留所,监狱。**2.** 〔印俚〕警察所;(征收过境税的)关卡。

chol(e)- *comb. f.* 胆汁:*chole*mia 胆血症。

cho·lane [ˈkəulein; ˋkolen] ***n*.**【化】胆(甾)烷。

cho·late [ˈkəuleit; ˋkolet] ***n*.** 胆酸盐[酯]。

chol·e·cyst [ˈkɔlisist, ˈkəuli-; ˋkɑləˏsɪst, ˋkolɪ-] ***n*.** 胆囊。

chol·e·cys·tec·to·my [ˌkɔlisisˈtektəmi, ˌkəuli-; ˏkɑləsɪsˋtɛktəmɪ, ˏkolɪ-] ***n*.** 胆囊切除术。

cho·le·cys·ti·tis [ˌkɔlisisˈtaitis; ˏkɑləsɪsˋtaɪtɪs] ***n*.**【医】胆囊炎。

chol·er [ˈkɔlə; ˋkɑlɚ] ***n*.** 〔诗、古〕脾气,怒气;胆汁(症)。

chol·er·a [ˈkɔlərə; ˋkɑlərə] ***n*.**【医】霍乱。*Asiatic* [*epidemic, malignant*] ～ 亚洲[传染性、恶性]霍乱。～ *morbus* 〔L.〕急性胃肠炎。*European* [*English, bilious, summer*] ～ 欧洲[非传染性,假性]霍乱。～**-belt** ***n*.** 预防霍乱症的肚围。

chol·er·a·ic [ˌkɔləˈreiik; ˏkɑləˋreɪk] ***a*.** 霍乱症的,霍乱性的;类似霍乱的。

chol·er·ic [ˈkɔlərik; ˋkɑlərɪk] ***a*.** 易怒的,躁急的;愤怒的,〔古〕胆汁质的。～ **temperament** 胆汁质。

chol·er·ine [ˈkɔlərain; ˋkɑlərɪn] ***n*.**【医】轻霍乱。

cho·le·sta·sis [ˌkɔliˈsteisis; ˏkɑlɪˋstesɪs] ***n*.**【医】胆汁郁积[阻塞]。

cho·les·ter·in(e) [kəˈlestərin; kəˋlɛstərɪn] ***n*.** = cholesterol.

cho·les·ter·ol [kəˈlestərəul, -rɔl; kəˋlɛstəˏrol, -ral] ***n*.**【生化】胆固醇,胆甾醇,异辛甾烯醇。

cho·lic [ˈkəulik; ˋkolɪk] ***a*.** ～ **acid**【生化】胆酸。

cho·line [ˈkəuliːn; ˋkolin] ***n*.**【生化】胆碱。

cho·lin·er·gic [ˌkəuliˈnəːdʒik, ˌkɔli-; ˏkolɪˋnɝdʒɪk, ˏkɑlɪ-] ***a*. 1.** 类胆碱(功)能的。**2.** 类胆碱(功)能药物的。

cho·lin·es·ter·ase [ˌkəuliˈnestəreis; ˏkolɪˋnɛstərˏes] ***n*.** 胆碱酯酶。

chol·la [ˈtʃəujə; ˋtʃoljɑ] ***n*.** 仙人掌属植物〔产于美国西南部及墨西哥〕。

cholo- *comb. f.* =〔用于母音前〕chol-.

chol·o·lith [ˈkɔləliθ; ˋkɑləˏlɪθ] ***n*.**【病】胆石。

chomp [tʃɔmp; tʃamp] **I** ***vt*., *vi*.** 〔方〕**1.** 吧哒吧哒地使劲咀嚼;格格地咬。**2.** 不断地咬。**II** ***n*.** 嚼;嚼声。**-er** ***n*.** 使劲咀嚼者。

Choms·ki·an [ˈtʃɔmskiən; ˋtʃamskɪən] ***a*.** (美国语言学家)乔姆斯基(Chomsky)语言理论的。

chon [tʃɔn; tʃan] ***n*.** (*pl*. ～) 分〔朝鲜辅币名称,为一元的 1/100〕。

chon·drin(e) [ˈkɔndrin; ˋkandrɪn] ***n*.**【化】软骨胶。

chon·dri·o·some [ˈkɔndriəsəum; ˋkandrɪəsˏom] ***n*.**【生】线粒体。

chon·drite [ˈkɔndrait; ˋkandraɪt] ***n*.**【地】球粒状陨石。**-drit·ic** [kɔnˈdritik; kanˋdrɪtɪk] ***a*.**

chondro- *comb. f.*【生】粒子:*chondro*ma.

chon·dro·cra·ni·um [ˌkɔndrəuˈkreinjəm; ˏkandroˋkrenjəm] ***n*.** (*pl*. ***-nia*** [-njə; -njə]) ***n*.**【解】软骨颅。

chon·dro·ma [kɔnˈdrəumə; kanˋdromə] ***n*.** (*pl*. ***-mas***, ***-ma·ta*** [-mətə; -mətə]) 软骨瘤。

chon·drule [ˈkɔndruːl; ˋkandrul] ***n*.** 陨石球粒。

choo-choo [ˈtʃuːtʃuː; ˋtʃuˏtʃu] **I** ***n*.** 〔儿〕火车头,火车头的噗噗声。**II** ***vi*.** 火车头发出噗噗声;坐火车旅行。

choose [tʃuːz; tʃuz] (***chose*** [tʃəuz; tʃoz]; ***cho·sen*** [ˈtʃəuzn; ˋtʃozn̩]; ***choos·ing***) ***vt*. 1.** 选,选择,挑选,拣,选定。**2.** 宁愿。**3.** 〔口〕欲,好,想,愿〔后接不定式〕。*There is nothing* [*little; not much*] *to* ～ *between them*. 全无[几乎没有;无多大]差别。—***vi*. 1.** 选择。**2.** 喜欢,看中。*She is deaf when she* ～*s*. 不合适她就不

C

听。(*How*) *can I* ~ *but weep*? 我哪能不哭? *if you* ~ (*to go*) 你若想(去)。***as you*** ~ 任便,听便。***cannot*** ~ ***but*** 不得不,只好。~ ***A before B*** 宁选A不选B,宁愿要A不要B。~ ***up*** (***sides***)〔口〕指定(运动)选手,分组(比赛)。***Let's*** ~ ***up to see*** … 看是选定…呢,究竟是让…呢。***pick and*** ~ 仔细挑选。

choos·er [ˈtʃuːzə; ˋtʃuzɚ] ***n***. 选择者;选举人;投票者。

choos·(e)y [ˈtʃuːzi; ˋtʃuzɪ] ***a***. 〔美口〕爱挑剔的,爱小题大作的。

chop[1] [tʃɔp; tʃɑp] **I** ***vt***. (**-*pp*-**) **1**. 切,砍(柴),伐,劈,断,剁(肉)。**2**. 切细,剁碎。**3**. 辟(路);开(路)前进。**4**.【网球】搓(球)。—***vi***. **1**. 切,砍,剁。**2**. 插嘴 (*in*)。**3**.【网球】搓球。~ ***about*** 乱砍(树木等);(风)突然转变方向,突变;迷,变心。~ ***at*** 打,砍。~ ***away*** 切掉,割去。~ ***down*** 斩掉,砍倒。~ ***fine*** 切细。~ ***in*** 多嘴,插嘴;切成。~ ***into*** 切成。~ ***off*** 切开,切断,切去。~ ***out*** (地层等)突然露出。~ ***up*** 切细;(地层等)突然露出;〔喻〕割断(历史等)。**II** ***n***. **1**. 砍,劈,剁,切断;(砍伐成的)裂缝。**2**. 排骨,(连骨的)一块肋肉。**3**. 随风翻变的波浪。~ **shop**〔美口〕被盗汽车拆卸店。

chop[2] [tʃɔp; tʃɑp] ***n***., ***pl***. **1**. 牙床,颚;腮;滑车的腭。**2**. (港湾、峡谷等的)入口。***lick one's*** ~***s*** 切盼,对…馋涎欲滴 (*over*)。~**-fallen** ***a***. = chapfallen.

chop[3] [tʃɔp; tʃɑp] ***n***. **1**. 公章,官印;出港证;登陆护照;旅行护照。**2**.〔口〕牌号,商标;品种,品质;等级。*the* ~ *of tea* [*silk*] 同一牌子的茶[生丝]。*the first* [*second*] ~〔口〕头[二]等,***no*** [***not much***] ~〔澳、新俚〕质量不佳。

chop[4] [tʃɔp; tʃɑp] **I** ***vi***. (**-*pp*-**) **1**. (风、浪)骤变,突变;**2**.〔英方〕(思想)动摇,波动,踌躇。~ ***back*** 急忙退回,急忙掉转方向。~ ***round*** 风突变。~ ***upon***〔俚〕突遇;袭来。—***vt***.〔古〕交换;辩论。~ ***logic*** 强词夺理地诡辩。~ ***words*** (相)骂。**II** ***n***. 骤变,突变。~ *and change* (*about*) 常常改变(方针、意见、职业),反复无常。

chop-chop [ˈtʃɔpˈtʃɔp; ˋtʃɑpˋtʃɑp] ***ad***., ***int***. 快快,赶快。

chop·fall·en [ˈtʃɔpˌfɔːlən; ˋtʃɑpˏfɔlən] = chapfallen.

chop·house [ˈtʃɔphaus; ˋtʃɑpˏhaʊs] **1**. 小饭馆,烤肉馆。**2**. (旧中国的)海关。

cho·pin(e) [tʃəuˈpiːn; ˋtʃoˋpin] ***n***. (十七世纪妇女穿的)厚底鞋。

chop·per [ˈtʃɔpə; ˋtʃɑpɚ] **I** ***n***. **1**. 切者,砍者,剁者;伐木人。**2**.〔美俚〕验票员。**3**. 斧子;屠刀,大砍刀;切碎机。**4**.【电】斩波器;断路器;遮光器,限制器。**5**.〔美俚〕机关枪;充当机关枪手的匪徒。**6**.【原】中子选择器。**7**.〔美俚〕直升机。**8**.〔*pl*.〕〔俚〕牙齿。**9**. 特别设计的摩托车。**II** ***vi***.〔美俚〕搭直升机。—***vt***.〔美俚〕用直升机运送。

chop·ping[1] [ˈtʃɔpiŋ; ˋtʃɑpɪŋ] ***n***. **1**. 砍,伐,剁。**2**. 树已伐尽的林中空地。*green* ~ 收青[庄稼未成熟时即收割]。~ **block** [**board**] 俎,砧板,肉礅。~ **knife** 菜刀。

chop·ping[2] [ˈtʃɔpiŋ; ˋtʃɑpɪŋ] ***a***. 波涛汹涌的。

chop·ping[3] [ˈtʃɔpiŋ; ˋtʃɑpɪŋ] ***n***.〔英口〕(儿童)身体强壮的。

chop·py[1] [ˈtʃɔpi; ˋtʃɑpɪ] ***a***. **1**. (风向、市场等)紊乱的,变动频繁的。**2**. 波浪滔滔的。

chop·py[2] [ˈtʃɔpi; ˋtʃɑpɪ] ***a***. **1**. 裂缝多的;断断续续的。**2**. 不匀称的;结构拙劣的。

chop·stick [ˈtʃɔpstik; ˋtʃɑpˏstɪk] ***n***.〔常 *pl*.〕(中国的)筷子。

chop-su·ey [ˈtʃɔpˈsuːi; ˋtʃɑpˋsuɪ] ***n***.〔美〕炒杂碎〔中国菜〕;中国菜馆。

cho·ra·gus [kəuˈreigəs, kə-; koˋregəs, kə-] ***n***. (*pl*. **-*gi*** [-dʒai; -dʒaɪ]) **1**. 古希腊戏剧中的歌队的队长。**2**. 合唱队,乐队领队。**cho·rag·ic** [-ˈrædʒik; -ˋrædʒɪk] ***a***.

cho·ral [ˈkɔːrəl; ˋkɔrəl] ***a***. 合唱队的,圣诗队的;合唱(曲)的。~ **service** 合唱礼拜。**-ly** ***ad***.

cho·ral(e) [kɔˈrɑːl; koˋrɑl] ***n***. (合唱的)赞美诗[歌];(唱赞美诗的)专业合唱团。

cho·ral·ist [ˈkɔːrəlist; ˋkorəlɪst] ***n***. 合唱队员;(教会)唱诗班成员,赞美诗歌手。

chord [kɔːd; kɔrd] **I** ***n***. **1**.〔诗〕(琴)弦;(心)弦;【乐】和弦,和(谐)音。**2**.【空】翼弦;【数】弦;【解】腱,带;【建】弦材,桁材。*the major* [*minor*] ~ 大[小]三和弦。*the spinal* ~ 脊髓。*the* ~ *organ* 和音(电子)风琴。*vocal* ~*s* 声带。***strike a responsive*** ~ 打动对方心弦。***touch the right*** ~ 触及心弦。**II** ***vt***. 上…的弦;调(弦)。—***vi***. **1**. 调和,和谐。**2**. 弹奏。

chor·da [ˈkɔːdə; ˋkɔrdə] (*pl*. **-*dae*** [-diː; -di]) ***n***.【解】索,带,腱。~ *dorsalis* 脊索。~ *tendinae* 腱索。

chor·dal [ˈkɔːdəl; ˋkɔrdəl] ***a***.【解】(脊)索的。

Chor·da·ta [kɔːˈdeitə; kɔrˋdetə] ***n***.【动】脊索动物类。

chor·date [ˈkɔːdeit; ˋkɔrdet] ***n***.【动】脊索动物类。

chordless [ˈkɔːdlis; ˋkɔrdlɪs] ***a***. 使用干电池的。*a* ~ *shaver* 干电剃刀。

chore [tʃɔː; tʃɔr] ***n***., ***vi***.〔美〕= chare. ~ ***around***〔美〕作短工。

cho·re·a [kɔˈriə; koˋriə] ***n***.【医】舞蹈病。

cho·reg·ra·phy [kəˈregrəfi; kəˋrɛgrəfɪ] ***n***. 舞蹈(尤指芭蕾舞)编写法,舞蹈设计;(芭蕾)舞蹈艺术,舞蹈表演。

chore·ic [kɔ(ː)ˈriːik; kɔ(ɑ)ˋriɪk] ***a***. 舞蹈病的。

cho·re·o·graph [ˈkɔ(ː)riəgrɑːf; ˋkɔ(ɑ)rɪəˏgrɑf] ***vt***. **1**. 为(芭蕾舞等)设计舞蹈动作。**2**. 设计,筹划。—***vi***. 从事舞蹈设计。**-er** ***n***. (芭蕾)舞蹈动作设计者。**-ic** ***a***. (有关)舞蹈艺术的。

cho·re·og·ra·phy [ˌkɔ(ː)riˈɔgrəfi; ˏkorɪˋɑgrəfɪ] ***n***.〔英〕= choregraphy.

chori- *comb*. *f*.〔用在母音前〕= chorio-.

chor·i·amb, **chor·i·am·bus** [ˈkɔ(ː)riæmb, -bəs; ˋkorɪˏæmb, -bəs] ***n***.【韵】扬抑抑扬格。**-bic** ***a***.

chor·ic [ˈkɔːrik; ˋkorɪk] ***a***. (古希腊剧)合唱曲的;合唱歌舞式的。

cho·rine [ˈkɔːriːn; ˋkorin] ***n***.〔美〕歌剧合唱队女歌唱[舞蹈]队员 (= ***chorus girl***)。

cho·ri·o·al·lan·to·is [kɔːriˌəuəˈlæntwis; kɔrɪˏoəˋlæntwɪs] ***n***. 绒(毛)膜尿囊。**-lan·toic** [-ˌælənˈtəuik; -ˏælənˋtoɪk] ***a***.

cho·ri·oid [ˈkɔːriˌɔid; ˋkɔrɪˏɔɪd] **I** ***a***.【解】似脉络膜的;似胎囊的。**II** ***n***.【解】脉络膜。

cho·ri·on [ˈkɔːriən; ˋkorɪən] ***n***. (*pl*. **-*ria*** [-riə; -rɪə])【解】绒(毛)膜;浆膜;(动)卵壳。

cho·ri·pet·al·ous [ˌkɔːriˈpetələs; ˏkorɪˋpetələs] ***n***.【植】离瓣的。

cho·rist [ˈkɔːrist; ˋkɔrɪst] ***n***. 合唱者,合唱歌手。

chor·is·ter [ˈkɔristə; ˋkɔrɪstɚ] ***n***. **1**. (教堂的)合唱者;少年合唱队队员。**2**. 唱诗班领唱者,[美]合唱队指挥员。*feathered* ~*s* 嘈杂啁啾的鸟群。

cho·ro·graph·ic [ˌkɔːrəˈgræfik; ˏkɔrəˋgræfɪk] ***a***. (地方性)地图绘制术的;地方地理学的。

cho·rog·ra·phy [kɔːˈrɔgrəfi; kɔˋrɑgrəfɪ] ***n***. **1**. 地方地理学;地方志,地方志编纂。**2**. 地方地图(绘制术)。

cho·roid [ˈkɔːrɔid; ˋkɔrɔɪd] **I** ***a***.【解】似脉络膜的;似胎囊的。**II** ***n***.【解】脉络膜;【生理】黑衣;【虫】黑基膜。

cho·rol·o·gy [kɔːˈrɔlədʒi; kɔˋrɑlədʒɪ] ***n***. 生物分布学,生物地理学,动植物分布论。

chor·tle [ˈtʃɔːtl; ˋtʃɔrtl] **I** ***n***. 哈哈大笑(声)。**II** ***vi***. **1**. 哈哈大笑。**2**. 高兴地唱歌。~ ***about*** [***over***]〔英俚〕对…表示高兴。

cho·rus [ˈkɔːrəs; ˋkorəs] **I** ***n***. **1**.【乐】合唱;合唱队;合唱歌(曲)。**2**.〔古希腊〕歌舞剧合唱的唱词;【英古剧】(宣读开场白和收场白的)剧情解说员。**3**. (歌的)叠句;合唱句,合唱。**4**. 歌舞团(表演)的歌舞。*join in a* ~ 参加合唱;唱合唱部分。*laugh* [*protest*] *in* ~ 齐声发笑[反对]。*meet with a* ~ *of protest* 遭到多数人的齐声反对。*in* ~ 合唱;异口同声地。**II** ***vt***. 合唱;齐诵;异口同

声地说。～ **girl** 歌剧合唱队女队员[配唱演员]。～ **master** 合唱队指挥。

chose[1] [tʃəuz; tʃoz] choose 的过去式。

chose[2] [ʃəuz; ʃoz] ***n.*** 【法】物,动产。*a* ～ *in action* 无形动产[可依法获得但尚未实际占有]。*a* ～ *in possession* 所有财产,所有物[已实际占有]。

chose ju·gée [ʃəuz ʒyˈʒei; ʃoz ʒyˋʒe] 〔F.〕无庸议论的事情,既定的事情。

cho·sen [ˈtʃəuzn; ˋtʃozn] **I** ***v.*** choose 的过去分词。**II** ***a.*** 拣过的;精选的,纯良的。*my* ～ *profession* 我所爱好的职业。*the* ～ *people* 【宗】上帝的选民[指犹太人]。

chott [ʃɔt; ʃɑt] ***n.*** 北非小盐湖盆地。

chou [ʃuː; ʃu] ***n.*** 〔F.〕**1.** (妇女衣帽上的)球结,花结,蝶结。**2.** 〔爱称〕= darling.

chough [tʃʌf; tʃʌf] ***n.*** 【鸟】红嘴乌鸦。

chouse [tʃaus; tʃaʊs] ***vt.***, ***n.*** 〔口〕骗,诈骗;欺骗。

chow [tʃau; tʃaʊ] ***n.*** **1.** 中国(黑鼻)狗。**2.** (中国的)州。**3.** 〔澳口〕中国人。**4.** 〔美军俚〕食品,军粮;吃饭。～ *mein* (中国)炒面。

chow-chow [ˈtʃauˈtʃau; ˋtʃaʊˏtʃaʊ] **I** ***n.*** **1.** 中国咸菜,腌菜;中国食品;杂碎,杂拌。**2.** 中国种的狗。**II** ***a.*** 杂,什锦的。～ **box** (日本的)漆制食盒。～ **shop** (中国的)杂货店。

chow·der [ˈtʃaudə; ˋtʃaʊdɚ] ***n.*** (纽芬兰、美国和新英格兰地区以鱼或蛤加洋葱、猪肉等做的)杂烩。～**head** 呆子,傻瓜。

CHQ = Corps Headquarters 军(司令)部。

Chr. = Christ; Christian; Christopher.

chre·ma·tis·tics [ˌkriːməˈtistiks; ˏkriməˋtɪstɪks] ***n.*** 理财学,货殖论;政治经济学。

chres·tom·a·thy [kresˈtɔməθi; krɛsˋtɑməθɪ] ***n.*** **1.** 有注解的文选;文章选读。**2.** (作家的)选集。

Chris[1] [kris; krɪs] ***n.*** 克里斯〔男子名, Christopher 的爱称〕。

Chris[2] [kris; krɪs] ***n.*** 克莉丝〔女子名, Christiana 或 Christine 的略称〕。

chrism [ˈkrizəm; ˋkrɪzəm] ***n.*** 【宗】圣油;圣油礼。

chrismal [ˈkrizməl; ˋkrɪzməl] ***a.*** 【宗】圣油的。

chris·ma·to·ry [ˈkrizmətəri; ˋkrɪzməˏtorɪ] **I** ***n.*** 【宗】圣油瓶。**II** ***a.*** 圣油的。

chris·om [ˈkrizəm; ˋkrɪzəm] ***n.*** **1.** = chrism. **2.** 〔废〕婴孩的洗礼衣。**3.** 不满月死亡的婴儿;〔古〕(天真无邪的)婴儿;幼儿(= ～ child)。

Christ [kraist; kraɪst] **I** ***n.*** **1.** 【基督】〔the ～〕救世主。**2.** 基督〔原为 Jesus 的称号,用作 Jesus the Christ,后来才变成 Jesus Christ 这一固有名词〕。***Before*** ～ 公元前〔略作 B. C.〕。*in* ～*'s name* 究竟〔强调语气〕(*What in* ～*'s name are you doing out there?* 你究竟是在那里干什么)。*to* ～ 真正,十分 (*I do hope to* ～ *he isn't going*. 他真的不去就好了)。**II** ***int.*** 〔俚〕哎呀! 岂有此理! 〔表惊愕、愤怒等〕。*Christ, it's cold*. 真冷呀! ～-**Church** ***n.*** (牛津大学的)基督学院。～-**cross** ***n.*** = crisscross.

Chris·ta·bel [ˈkristəbel; ˋkrɪstəbɛl] ***n.*** 克里斯塔贝尔〔女子名〕。

Christ·church [ˈkraist-tʃəːtʃ; ˋkraɪst-ˏtʃɝtʃ] ***n.*** 克赖斯特彻奇〔新西兰城市〕。

christ·cross [ˈkristkrɔs; ˋkrɪsˏkrɔs] ***n.*** 十字形的记号[签押]。～-**row** 字母表,字母系统。

chris·ten [ˈkrisən; ˋkrɪsn] ***vt.*** **1.** 【宗】为…施洗礼(使成基督教徒);施洗礼时命名。**2.** (举行仪式)命名(轮船等);给…取绰号。**3.** 隆重地首次启用(汽车、轮船等);〔口〕开始使用。*be* ～*ed John after one's father* (施洗礼时)照父名命名为约翰。-**ing** ***n.*** 施洗礼仪式;命名仪式。

Chris·ten·dom [ˈkrisəndəm; ˋkrɪsndəm] ***n.*** 基督教界;〔集合词〕基督教徒。***by my*** ～ 的确〔语调语势〕。

Christ·hood [ˈkraisthud; ˋkraɪsthʊd] ***n.*** 基督的品格[身分]。

Chris·tian[1] [ˈkristjən, -tʃən; ˋkrɪstjən, -tʃən] **I** ***n.*** **1.** 基督教徒;信徒。**2.** 〔口〕人类;文明人;正派人。**II** ***a.*** **1.** 基督(教)的;信基督教的。**2.** 〔口〕人(类)的;文明的;〔口〕正派的,高尚的。*a good* ～ *dinner* 丰盛的酒席。～ **era** 西历纪元。～ **faith** 基督教(信仰)。～ **name** 教名,洗礼名。

Chris·tian[2] [ˈkristjən; ˋkrɪstʃən] ***n.*** 克里斯琴〔男子名〕。

Chris·ti·an·a [ˌkristiˈɑːnə; ˏkrɪstɪˋænə] ***n.*** 克里斯蒂安娜〔女子名〕。

Chris·ti·a·ni·a [ˌkristiˈɑːniə; ˏkrɪstɪˋɑnɪə] ***n.*** **1.** 克里斯蒂安尼亚〔挪威首都旧名,现名 Oslo〕。**2.** 【滑雪】急转弯(= ～ turn)。

Chris·ti·an·ism [ˈkristʃənizəm; ˋkrɪstʃənɪzəm] ***n.*** = Christianity.

Chris·ti·an·i·ty [ˌkristiˈæniti; ˏkrɪstʃɪˋænətɪ] ***n.*** 基督教;基督教信仰;〔集合词〕基督教徒;基督徒精神。

Chris·tian·ise, -ize [ˈkristjənaiz; ˋkrɪstʃənˏaɪz] ***vt.***, ***vi.*** (使)成为基督教徒,(使)基督教化。

Chris·tie [ˈkristi; ˋkrɪstɪ] ***n.*** 克里斯蒂〔姓氏〕。

Chris·ti·na [krisˈtiːnə; krɪsˋtinə] ***n.*** 克丽丝汀娜〔女子名〕。

Chris·tine [ˈkristiːn, krisˈtiːn; ˋkrɪstin, krɪsˋtin] ***n.*** 克丽丝婷〔女子名〕。

Christ·less [ˈkraistlis; ˋkraɪstlɪs] ***a.*** 违反基督精神的,不信基督教的。

Christ·like, Christ·ly [ˈkraistlaik, -li; ˋkraɪstˏlaɪk, -lɪ] ***a.*** 具有基督精神[德性]的;像基督一样的。

Christ·mas [ˈkrisməs; ˋkrɪsməs] ***n.*** 圣诞节〔12 月 25 日。略写作 Xmas〕。～ **beetle** 【动】食根虫。～ **box** 圣诞节礼品;〔英口〕圣诞节给雇用人员的礼物或赏钱〔暗示明年继续雇用〕。～ **card** 圣诞贺片。～ **carol** 圣诞节颂歌。～ **Day** 圣诞节。～ **Eve** 圣诞节前夜[日]。～ **flower** 【植】一品红。～ **holidays** 圣诞节假期;(学校等)寒假。**C-Island** 圣诞岛〔一在爪哇南,一在太平洋〕。～ **log** = Yule log. ～ **rose** 【植】黑儿波。～ **stocking** 圣诞老人袜〔圣诞节前夕,孩子们睡觉前挂在床边,让圣诞老人把礼物塞在里面〕。～ **tree** 圣诞树。～ **waits** 圣诞节夜晚挨户唱歌的艺人。～**tide** 圣诞节节期〔12 月 24 日至 1 月 6 日〕。-**(s)y** ***a.*** 圣诞节似的,圣诞节情调的。

Chris·tol·o·gy [krisˈtɔlədʒi; krɪsˋtɑlədʒɪ] ***n.*** (研究耶稣基督的)基督学。

Chris·toph·a·ny [krisˈtɔfəni; krɪsˋtɑfənɪ] ***n.*** 【宗】基督再现。

Chris·to·pher [ˈkristəfə; ˋkrɪstəfɚ] ***n.*** 克里斯托弗〔男子名〕。

Christ's-thorn [ˈkraistsθɔːn; ˋkraɪstsˏθɔrn] ***n.*** 【植】滨枣。

Christy minstrels [ˈkristi ˈminstrəlz; ˋkrɪstɪ ˋmɪnstrəlz] 黑面歌手〔指涂黑面孔沿街唱黑人歌曲的卖艺人〕。

-chroic *comb. f.* (皮肤、植物等的)色。

chrom- *comb. f.* 色,色素;【化】铬(= chromo-)。

chro·ma [ˈkrəumə; ˋkromə] ***n.*** 色彩纯度;色品,色度。

chromat- *comb. f.* 〔用于母音前〕= chromato-。

chro·mate [ˈkrəumit; ˋkromet] ***n.*** 【化】铬酸盐。

chro·mat·ic [krəˈmætik; kroˋmætɪk] ***a.*** **1.** 色彩的;着色的,彩色的。**2.** 【生】染色质的。**3.** 【乐】半音(阶)的。～ *aberration* 【摄、电视】(镜头的)色(像)差,色散。～ *printing* 套色版;彩色印刷。～ *scale* 半音音阶。*a* ～ *semitone* 变化半音,花半音。～ *signs* 变音号。-**i·cal·ly** ***ad.*** **1.** 上色,套色。**2.** 成半音阶。

chro·ma·tic·i·ty [ˌkrəuməˈtisiti; ˏkroməˋtɪsətɪ] ***n.*** 染色性。

chro·mat·ics [krəˈmætiks; krəˋmætɪks] ***n.*** *pl.* (用作单)颜色学。

chro·ma·tid [ˈkrəumətid; ˋkromətɪd] ***n.*** 【生】染色单

C

体。

chro·ma·tin [ˈkrəumətin; ˋkromətɪn] *n*.【生】染色质,染色粒。

chro·ma·tism [ˈkrəumətizəm; ˋkromətɪzəm] *n*. **1**.【植】变色。**2**. 色散,色差。

chro·mat·ist [ˈkrəumətist; ˋkromətɪst] *n*. 颜色学家。

chromato- *comb*. *f*. 色;染色质:*chromato*graphy.

chro·mat·o·gram [krəuˈmætəgræm; kroˋmætəgræm] *n*.【化】色层(分离)谱,色彩谱。

chro·ma·to·graph [ˈkrəumətəgrɑːf; ˋkromətə͵græf] **I** *vt*. **1**. 用套色印刷复制。**2**. 用色层法分离(物质)。**II** *n*.〔古〕套色版。

C

chro·ma·tog·ra·phy [ˌkrəuməˈtɔgrəfi; ͵kroməˋtɑgrəfɪ] *n*.【化】层析,色层(分离)法。

chro·ma·tol·y·sis [ˌkrəuməˈtɔlisis; ͵kroməˋtɑləsɪs] *n*.【医】染色质消失[溶解]。**-mat·o·lyt·ic** [krəuˌmætəˈlitik; kro͵mætəˋlɪtɪk] *a*.

chro·mat·o·phore [ˈkrəumətəfɔː; ˋkromətə͵for] *n*.【生】色素细胞;(载)色体。

chro·mat·o·scope [ˈkrəumətəskəup; ˋkromətə͵skop] *n*.【天】闪烁反射望远镜;【医】彩光折射率计。

chro·ma·tron [ˈkrəumətrɔn; ˋkromətrɑn] *n*. 彩色电视显像管。

chro·ma·trope [ˈkrəumətrəup; ˋkromə͵trop] *n*. (成双的)旋转彩色幻灯片。

chro·ma·type [ˈkrəumətaip; ˋkromə͵taɪp] *n*. 铬盐相片,彩色相片;铬盐片照相法。

chrome [krəum; krom] **I** *n*.【化】**1**. 铬(= chromium)。**2**. 铬黄(= ~ yellow),黄色。**3**. 镀铬物件。~ **ocher** 铬华。~ **red** 铬铅红。~ **steel** 铬钢。**II** *vt*. 镀以铬;用镀铬化合物印染。

chro·mic [ˈkrəumik; ˋkromɪk] *a*.【化】铬的。~ **acid** 铬酸。

chro·mide [ˈkrəumaid; ˋkromaɪd] *n*.【动】丽鱼科鱼(= cichlid)。

chro·mi·nance [ˈkrəuminəns; ˋkromɪnəns] *n*.【无】**1**. 色品,色度。**2**. 彩色信号。

chro·mite [ˈkrəumait; ˋkromaɪt] *n*.【矿】铬铁(矿)。

chro·mi·um [ˈkrəumjəm; ˋkromɪəm] *n*.【化】铬。

chro·mize [ˈkrəumaiz; ˋkromaɪz] *vt*. 对(金属)作渗铬处理,铬化(金属)。**chro·miz·ing** *n*. 渗铬(处理),铬化(处理)。

chro·mo [ˈkrəuməu; ˋkromo] *n*. 彩色石印版。

chromo- *comb*. *f*. 色:*chromo*graph.

chro·mo·gen [ˈkrəumədʒən; ˋkromədʒən] *n*.【化】发色团,生色团;色(素)原,色母,产色细菌;【纺】铬精。

chro·mo·graph [ˈkrəuməgrɑːf; ˋkromə͵græf] **I** *n*. 胶版复制品。**II** *vt*. 用胶版复制器复制。

chro·mo·lith·o·graph [ˈkrəuməuˈliθəgrɑːf; ͵kromoˋlɪθə͵græf] *n*. 彩色石印图画。**-ic** *a*. 彩色石印术的。**-y** *n*. 彩色石印术。

chro·mo·mere [ˈkrəuməmiə; ˋkromə͵mɪr] *n*.【生】染色粒。**-meric** [-ˈmirik; -ˋmɪrɪk] *a*.

chro·mo·ne·ma [ˌkrəuməˈniːmə; ͵kroməˋnimə] *n*. (*pl*. *-ma·ta* [-tə; -tə])【生】染色线。**-mal** *a*.

chro·mo·phil [ˈkrəuməfil; ˋkroməfɪl] **I** *a*.【生】易染的。**II** *n*.【生】易染细胞;易染细胞部分。

chro·mo·phore [ˈkrəuməfɔː; ˋkromə͵fɔr] *n*.【生】载色体;发色团,生色团。**-phor·ic** [-ˈfɔːrik; -ˋfɔrɪk] *a*.

chro·mo·pho·to·graph [ˈkrəuməˈfəutəgrɑːf; ͵kroməˋfotə͵græf] *n*. 彩色照相。**-tog·ra·phy** *n*. 彩色照相术。

chro·mo·plast [ˈkrəuməplæst; ˋkromə͵plæst] *n*.【生】有色体。

chro·mo·pro·tein [ˌkrəuməˈprəutiːn; ͵kroməˋprotin] *n*.【生】色蛋白。

chro·mo·scope [ˈkrəuməskəup; ˋkromə͵skop] *n*.【电视】显色管。

chro·mo·some [ˈkrəuməsəum; ˋkromə͵som] *n*.【生】染色体。~ **complex**【生】染色体群。

chro·mo·sphere [ˈkrəuməsfiə; ˋkromə͵sfɪr] *n*.【天】(太阳的)色球层。

chro·mo·type [ˈkrəumətaip; ˋkromə͵taɪp] *n*. 彩色印刷术;彩色摄影。

chro·mo·xy·lo·graph [ˈkrəuməˈzailəgrɑf; ˋkroməˋzaɪləgræf] *n*. 套色[彩色]木版画。

chro·mous [ˈkrəuməs; ˋkroməs] *a*.【化】**1**. 亚铬的,二价铬的。**2**. 铬的。

chro·myl [ˈkrəumil; ˋkroməl] *n*.【化】**1**. 铬酰。**2**. 氧铬基。

Chron. = Chronicle.

chron., **chronol**. = chronology; chronological.

chron- *comb*. *f*. 表示"时间":*chron*ology.

chro·nax·ie, **chro·nax·y** [ˈkrəunæksi; ˋkronæksɪ] *n*.【医】时值。

chron·ic, **-i·cal** [ˈkrɔnik(l); ˋkrɑnɪk(l)] **I** *a*. **1**. 慢性的;长期的;积习成癖的。**2**.〔英俚〕剧烈的,(天气等)恶劣的。*a* ~ *disease* 慢性病,痼疾。*a* ~ *grumbler* 一年到头牢骚不停的人。*a* ~ *liar* 说谎成癖的人。**II** *n*. 慢性病人。**-i·cal·ly** *ad*. 慢性地,不断地。

chro·nic·ity [krəˈnisiti; krəˋnɪsətɪ] *n*. 慢性,长期性。

chron·i·cle [ˈkrɔnikl; ˋkrɑnɪkl] **I** *n*. **1**. 年代记,编年史;记录。**2**.〔C-〕《…新闻》〔报刊名〕。~ *history* [*play*] 年代史剧,纯史剧。*the Chronicles*【圣】《历王纪》。*The San Francisco* ~《旧金山新闻》〔报刊名〕。**II** *vt*. 把…载于编年史中,记录。

chron·i·cler [ˈkrɔniklə; ˋkrɑnɪklɚ] *n*. **1**. 年代记作者,编年史家。**2**. 记录者。

chro·nique scan·da·leuse [krɔːˈniːk skɑːŋdɑːˈləːz; krɔˋnik skɑŋdɑˋlɚz]〔F.〕丑闻录。

chrono- *comb*. *f*.〔用于子音字母前〕= chron-.

chron·o·bi·ol·o·gy [ˌkrɔnəubaiˈɔlədʒiː; ͵kronobaɪˋɑlədʒi] *n*.【生】时间生物学,生物钟学。**-gist** *n*.

chron·o·gram [ˈkrɔnəgræm; ˋkrɑnə͵græm] *n*. **1**. (用大写罗马数字之和表示的)纪年铭文。*LorD haVe MerCIe Vpon Vs* = 50 + 500 + 5 + 1,000 + 100 + 1 + 5 + 5 = 1666〔铭文意为"求主怜悯我们",其中嵌入 L. D. V. M. C. I. V. V. 等表示数字的大写罗马数字〕。**2**. 时间记录(图像)。

chron·o·graph [ˈkrɔnəgrɑːf; ˋkrɑnə͵græf] *n*. 计时器,录时器。

chron·o·lo·ger, **-gist** [krəˈnɔlədʒə, -dʒist; krəˋnɑlədʒɚ, -dʒɪst] *n*. 年代学者;年表编制者。

chron·o·log·i·c(al) [ˌkrɔnəˈlɔdʒik(əl); ͵krɑnəˋlɑdʒɪk(əl)] *a*. 年代学的,编年的,按照年月顺序的。**-ly** *ad*.

chro·nol·o·gize [krəˈnɔlədʒaiz; krəˋnɑlə͵dʒaɪz] *vt*. 把…按年排列,把…编年,给…作年表。

chro·nol·o·gy [krəˈnɔlədʒi; krəˋnɑlədʒɪ] *n*. **1**. 年代学。**2**. 年表。**3**. (资料等)按年代次序的排列。

chro·nom·e·ter [krəˈnɔmitə; krəˋnɑmətɚ] *n*. 精密计时表;航海时计,经线仪;天文钟;【乐】拍节机。

chron·o·met·ric, **-ri·cal** [ˌkrɔnəˈmetrik(əl); ͵krɑnəˋmetrɪk(əl)] *a*. (用)精密计时表[天文钟等](测定)的。

chro·nom·e·try [krəˈnɔmitri; krəˋnɑmətrɪ] *n*. 时刻测定;测时术,记时法。

chron·o·pher [ˈkrɔnəfə; ˋkrɑnəfɚ] *n*. 电气报时器。

chron·o·scope [ˈkrɔnəskəup; ˋkrɑnə͵skop] *n*. 瞬时计〔尤指炮弹等的速度测量器〕。

chrys- *comb*. *f*.〔用于母音字母前〕【化、矿】黄色的;金黄的,金的(= chryso)。

chrys·a·lid [ˈkrisəlid; ˋkrɪslɪd] **I** *a*.【动】蝶蛹的;〔喻〕准备期的。**II** *n*. = chrysalis.

chrys·a·lis [ˈkrisəlis; ˋkrɪslɪs] *n*. (*pl*. ~*es*, *chrysalides* [kriˈsælidiːz; krɪˋsælɪdiz]) **1**. 蝶蛹;蝶蛹茧。**2**.

〔喻〕过渡期,准备期;过渡期中的事物。

chrys·an·the·mum [kriˈsænθəməm; krɪsˋænθəməm] ***n.***【植】菊(花);〔C-〕菊属。~ *flower* 菊花。

chrys·a·ro·bin [ˌkrisəˈrəubin; ˏkrɪsəˋrobɪn] ***n.***【医】柯桠素。

chrys·el·e·phan·tine [ˌkriseliˈfæntain; ˏkrɪsɛlɪˋfæntɪn] ***a.*** 用金和象牙做成的。

chryso- *comb.f.*〔用于子音字母前〕= chrys-.

chrys·o·ber·yl [ˈkrisəberil; ˋkrɪsəˏbɛrɪl] ***n.***【矿】金绿宝石。

chry·so·lite [ˈkrisəlait; ˋkrɪslˏaɪt] ***n.***【矿】贵橄榄石。

chrys·o·prase [ˈkrisəpreiz; ˋkrɪsəˏprez] ***n.***【矿】绿玉髓。

chrys·o·tile [ˈkrisəˌtail; ˋkrɪsəˏtaɪl] ***n.***【矿】温石绵,织蛇纹石。

chs. = chapters.

chtho·ni·an [ˈθəuniən; ˋθonɪən] ***a.***【希神】冥府的;冥府鬼神的。

chthon·ic [ˈθɔnik; ˋθɑnɪk] ***a.*** 1. = chthonian. 2. 阴暗的;原始的,神秘的。

chub [tʃʌb; tʃʌb] ***n.*** (*pl.* ~*s*,〔集合词〕~)【鱼】雪鲦。

Chubb [tʃʌb; tʃʌb] ***n.*** (英国伦敦产的)丘伯锁(= Chubb lock)。

chub·by [ˈtʃʌbi; ˋtʃʌbɪ] ***a.*** 圆胖的,鼓鼓的,丰满的。**-ness *n.***

chuck[1] [tʃʌk; tʃʌk] **I *vt.*** 1.〔口〕抛出,扔出;逐出。2.〔美〕辞职,退职;放弃;丢弃。3. 呕出,吐出。4. 拍;抚摸。~ ***away*** 扔弃;浪费(金钱);失去(机会)。~ ***in*** 挑战。***Chuck it!***〔俚〕停下来! 别吵[闹]了! ~ ***one's weight about*** 摆架子,倨傲。~ ***out*** 赶出,撵出;〔口〕否决(议案)。~ ***over*** 驱逐。~ ***up*** 缩手,放弃,厌弃。~ ***up the sponge*** 认输。**II *n.*** 1. 抛出,扔弃;〔口〕放弃;辞退。2. 轻抚,爱抚。***give sb. the*** ~ 辞退[开除]某人。***get the*** ~ 被辞退[开除]。

chuck[2] [tʃʌk; tʃʌk] **I *n.***【机】(车床等的)卡盘,轧头;(罐头)封罐机。*independent* ~分动[四爪]卡盘。*scroll* ~ 三爪卡盘。**II *vt.***【机】用卡盘夹紧。

chuck[3] [tʃʌk; tʃʌk] **I *int.*, *n.*** 咕咕[呼鸡声],砸砸[呼马声];咯咯[母鸡叫声]。**II *vi.*** 咕咕[咯咯,嘟嘟]地叫;砸砸地赶马。

chuck[4] [tʃʌk; tʃʌk] ***int.*, *n.*** 亲爱的,宝贝,心肝〔对妻子、爱儿、小鸡等的爱称〕。

chuck[5] [tʃʌk; tʃʌk] ***n.*** 1. (牛等的)颈肉。2.〔美西部〕食品,粮食,伙食。~ **box** 食物匣。~ **wagon** (牧场等的)炊事车,伙食车。

chuck-a-luck [ˈtʃʌkəˌlʌk; ˋtʃʌkəˏlʌk] ***n.*** 掷骰赌博(= chuck-luck)。

chuck·er(-out) [ˈtʃʌkəˈraut; ˋtʃʌkɚˋaʊt] ***n.***〔英〕(戏院、旅馆等雇来撵走捣乱者的)护场员;护馆员。

chuck-far·thing [ˈtʃʌk-ˈfɑːðiŋ; ˋtʃʌk-ˋfɑrðɪŋ] ***n.*** (比赛用钱币投进小洞穴内的)投钱戏。***play (at)*** ~ ***with*** 孤注一掷,冒险一试。

chuck-full [ˈtʃʌk-ful; ˋtʃʌk-fʊl] ***a.*** (塞)满了的,挤得满满的(= chock-full)。

chuck·hole [ˈtʃʌkhəul; ˋtʃʌkˏhol] ***n.*** 人行道上的坑洼。

chuck·le [ˈtʃʌkl; ˋtʃʌkl] **I *n.*** 1. (母鸡的)咯咯声。2. 吃吃的笑,嘻嘻轻笑声。**II *vi.*** 1. (母鸡)咯咯地叫。2. 嗤的一笑,轻声地笑,暗笑。~ ***out*** 笑嘻嘻地说。~ ***over [at]*** 开心得笑嘻嘻,暗自得意。~ ***to oneself*** 独自发笑;暗中好笑[高兴]。~**head**〔口〕傻瓜,笨蛋。~**headed *a.***〔口〕愚蠢的,呆笨的。

chuck·wal·la [ˈtʃʌkˌwɑːlə; ˋtʃʌkwɑlə] ***n.***【动】叩壁蜥属蜥蜴〔产于墨西哥西北部和美国西南部〕。

chuck-will's·widow [ˌtʃʌkˌwilzˈwidəu; ˏtʃʌkˏwɪlzˋwɪdo] ***n.***【动】蚊母鸟。

chuck·y [ˈtʃʌki; ˋtʃʌkɪ] ***n.***〔英方〕鸡。

chud·dar [ˈtʃʌdə; ˋtʃʌdɚ] ***n.*** (印度毛料)披巾。

chuff[1] [tʃʌf; tʃʌf] ***n.*** 1. 乡下佬。2. 粗暴的人。3. 吝啬鬼。

chuff[2] [tʃʌf; tʃʌf] ***a.***〔英方〕1. 胖的,健壮的。2. 得意的,趾高气扬的。

chuff[3] [tʃʌf; tʃʌf] **I *n.*** (火车头排气的)噗噗声。**II *vi.*** (火车)噗噗地前进;(蒸气机等)噗噗地运转。*The train* ~*ed along.* 火车噗噗地前进。

chuffed [tʃʌft; tʃʌft] ***a.***〔英俚〕1. 高兴的,满意的。2. 不高兴的,不满意的。

chuff·y [ˈtʃʌfi; ˋtʃʌfɪ] ***a.***〔方〕矮胖的;肥胖的。

chug [tʃʌg; tʃʌg] **I *n.***〔美〕(发动机等短而钝的)嚓嘎声。**II *vi.*** (**-gg-**)(发动机等)嚓嘎嚓嘎地响;〔口〕(火车、汽船等)嚓嘎嚓嘎地前进。~-~〔口〕旧火车头,旧机车。

chug-a-lug [ˈtʃʌgəlʌg; ˋtʃʌgəlʌg] **I *ad.***〔美俚〕咕咚咕咚地喝完。**II *vt.*, *vi.*** (**-gg-**)〔美俚〕咕咚咕咚地喝完;痛饮,牛饮;狼吞虎咽。

chu·kar [tʃəˈkɑː; tʃəˋkɑr] ***n.***【鸟】欧石鸡(*Alectoris graeca*)〔原产于亚洲和欧洲〕。

chuk·ker [ˈtʃʌkə; ˋtʃʌkɚ] ***n.*** (马球戏)一局〔*7* 分 *30* 秒〕。

chum[1] [tʃʌm; tʃʌm] **I *n.***〔口〕(大学等的)同室朋友,同房间的人;密友;同事。*a great* ~ 极要好的朋友。*a new* ~〔大洋〕新来的移民。***get [make]*** ~***s with*** 和…成好朋友。***split*** ~***s*** 绝交。**II *vi.*** 同室居住;成为好朋友。~ ***up with***〔口〕与…成好朋友。

chum[2] [tʃʌm; tʃʌm] ***n.*** 鱼饵〔尤指切成小块作饵的鱼〕。

chum·mage [ˈtʃʌmidʒ; ˋtʃʌmɪdʒ] ***n.*** 1. 同室居住,同室交谊;合住。2.〔俚〕(监狱新来囚犯的)入伙钱。

chum·mer·y [ˈtʃʌməri; ˋtʃʌmərɪ] ***n.*** 同住一个房间的人。

chum·my[1] [ˈtʃʌmi; ˋtʃʌmɪ] **I *a.***〔口〕亲密的,有交情的。***be*** ~ ***with*** 与…交好[关系亲密]。**II *n.*** 1.〔俚〕好友,密友。2. 微型汽车。~ **flyabout**〔美〕私人用的小飞机。~ **roadster**〔美〕郊游用的小汽车。

chum·my[2] [ˈtʃʌmi; ˋtʃʌmɪ] ***n.***〔俚〕扫烟囱的小伙子。

chump [tʃʌmp; tʃʌmp] ***n.*** 1. 木片;木块。2. 大块肉片(= ~ chop)。3.〔俚〕头;〔口〕笨人,呆头傻脑的人。***(go) off one's*** ~〔英〕疯狂,发狂。***make a*** ~ ***out of*** 使…丢脸,侮辱。

chunk [tʃʌŋk; tʃʌŋk] ***n.*** 1. 大块。2. 大量,相当大的部分。3.〔美〕矮胖结实的人;结实的马。*a* ~ *of bread [meat]* 一大块面包[肉]。

chunk·y [ˈtʃʌŋki; ˋtʃʌŋkɪ] ***a.***〔美〕矮胖的,结实的。

chun·nel [ˈtʃʌnəl; ˋtʃʌnəl] ***n.*** 水底火车隧道。

Church [tʃəːtʃ; tʃɝtʃ] ***n.*** 丘奇〔姓氏〕。

church [tʃəːtʃ; tʃɝtʃ] **I *n.*** 1. 教堂,礼拜堂;〔C-〕教会;教派。2. 教徒团体;〔集合词〕基督教徒。3.〔the ~〕牧师[神父]职位,圣职。4.【宗】(教堂的)礼拜〔不用冠词 the〕。5. 教会的组织;教权。*C- of Humanity* 人道主义者,孔德主义者。*the* ~ *invisible* 天上的基督教徒们;天上教会。*the visible* ~ 地上的基督教徒们,地上教会,现世教会。*the Eastern C-* 东正教(会);希腊正教。*the Western C-* 西正教(会),罗马天主教会。*the established [state]* ~ 国教。*the C- of England [English C-, Anglican C-]* 英国国教,圣公会。*the High [Low] C-* (重礼仪的)高教[(不重礼仪的)低教]教会。***after*** ~ (在教堂)做礼拜之后,从教堂出来。***as poor as a*** ~ ***mouse*** 非常贫穷。***be at*** ~ = ***be in*** ~ 正(在教堂)做礼拜。***between*** ~***es*** 上次做礼拜与下次做礼拜相隔期间。***enter the C-*** = ***go into the*** ~ 做牧师,任圣职。***go to [attend]*** ~ 上教堂去做礼拜;〔口〕结婚。***talk*** ~ 讲有关宗教信仰的话〔枯燥无味的话〕;〔古〕讲行话。**II *vt.*** 1. 使(某人)去教堂接受宗教仪式。2. 为(妇女)做产后感恩礼拜。3. 按教会规章申斥[处罚]。~ **goer** (经常)上教堂去做礼拜的信徒。~**-going** 1. ***a.*** 经常上教堂去的。2. ***n.*** 上教堂去。~ **key** (开罐头用的)三角开刀。~**-man**〔古〕教士,牧师;〔英〕国教徒。~ **rate** (教区内

征收的)教堂维持费。**C- scot** 教区百姓供养教士的捐款。~ **service** 礼拜;祈祷书;说教。**C- session** 长老会。~ **text** 墓碑上的黑体字;【印】黑体字。~ **warden** 1. 教区委员,教会执事。2.〔英口〕陶制长烟斗。**~-woman** (英国国教的)女教徒。**~yard** 教堂庭院;(教堂的)墓地(*a ~yard cough*〔英〕衰竭无力的干咳。*a fat ~yard* 坟多的公墓)。**-ing** (妇女)安产感恩礼拜。**-ism** 墨守教会仪式;英国国教主义。**-ly** *a*. 1. 教会的,符合教会规章。2. 虔诚的。

Church·ill [ˈtʃəːtʃil; ˋtʃɝtʃɪl] *n*. 邱吉尔〔姓氏〕。**Sir Winston Leonard Spencer ~** 温斯顿·邱吉尔〔1874—1965,英国政治家,曾于1940—1945年,1951—1955年两次任首相〕。

church·y [ˈtʃəːtʃi; ˋtʃɝtʃɪ] *a*. 固守教会教条[礼仪]的,教会万能主义的。

churl [tʃəːl; tʃɝl] *n*. 1. 粗鄙的人;粪下人;吝啬鬼,守财奴;脾气坏的人,执拗的人。2.【英史】下层自由民。*put a ~ upon a gentleman* 好酒喝后喝劣酒。

churl·ish [ˈtʃəːliʃ; ˋtʃɝlɪʃ] *a*. 1. 乡下人的。2. 粗鄙的;脾气坏的。3. 吝啬的。4. (土地)难耕种的。**-ness** *n*.

churn [tʃəːn; tʃɝn] **I** *n*. (提制奶油用的)搅乳桶;〔英〕奶桶;【纺】黄化鼓;【机】摇转搅拌桶。~ *and burn* (股票的)频繁买进卖出,炒股。**II** *vt*. 1. (用搅乳桶)搅拌(牛奶等),制造(奶油等)。2. 用力搅拌(使起泡沫)。3.〔口〕频繁地买进卖出(股票)。—*vi*. 1. 用搅乳器搅拌。2. (浪等)猛烈冲洗海岸,(风)翻腾(波浪),(牛乳等)发泡。~ (*out*) 制造[做出]许多(粗制滥造的东西)。**~dasher**, **~staff** 搅乳装置,搅乳棒。**-ing** *n*. 搅乳,一次提制的奶油。

churr [tʃəː; tʃɝ] *vi*., *n*. (鹧鸪等)颤鸣(声)。

chut [tʃʌt; tʃʌt] *int*. 喳! 咄!〔焦急时的咂嘴声〕。

chute [ʃuːt; ʃut] **I** *n*. 1. 奔流,急流,瀑布;射水路。2. 斜槽;流槽;筏路;险陡滑道。3.〔口〕降落伞〔parachute 的缩写〕。*an air ~* 降落伞。*a flare ~* 照明伞。**II** *vt*., *vi*. (使)顺斜道滑行。~ *the ~s*〔口〕滑斜坡游戏。

chute-the-chute [ˈʃuːtðəʃuːt; ˋʃutðəˏʃut] *n*. 1. (儿童乐园的)惊险滑梯。2. 惊险情节。

chut·nee, chut·ney [ˈtʃʌtni; ˋtʃʌtnɪ] *n*. (印度式调味用)酸辣酱。

chutz·pah, chutz·pa [ˈhutspə; ˋhʊtspə] *n*.〔美口〕厚颜无耻;胆大妄为。

chyle [kail; kaɪl] *n*.【生】乳糜。

chyme [kaim; kaɪm] *n*.【生】乳糜汁,食糜。

chym·ist [ˈkimist; ˋkɪmɪst] *n*.〔古〕= chemist.

chy·mo·tryp·sin [ˌkaiməˈtripsin; ˏkaɪməˋtrɪpsɪn] *n*.【生化】胰凝乳蛋白酶,糜蛋白酶。

Ci = cirrus【动】触毛;【植】卷须。

CIAA = Central Intercollegiate Athletic Association (美国)大学间中央体育协会。

C.I. = 1. cast iron 铸铁,生铁。2. Channel Islands 海峡群岛。3. Colour Index【医】血色指数,比色指数。

CIA = Central Intelligence Agency〔美〕中央情报局。

Cia =〔Sp.〕Compania (= Company).

ciao [tʃəu; tʃo] *int*.〔It.〕〔见面问候语或告别语〕你好!再见!

ci·bo·ri·um [siˈbɔːriəm; sɪˋbɔrɪəm] *n*. (*pl*. ***-ria*** [-riə; -rɪə]) 1.〔古〕祭坛天盖。2.【天主】圣体盒。

Cic. = Cicero 西塞罗。

C.I.C. = 1. Counterintelligence Corps〔美〕反情报队。2. Combat Information Center 战斗情报中心。3. Commander in Chief 总司令。

ci·ca·da [siˈkeidə, siˈkɑːdə; sɪˋkedə, sɪˋkɑdə] *n*. (*pl*. ~*s*, ***-dae*** [-diː; -di])【动】蝉。

ci·ca·la [siˈkɑːlə; sɪˋkɑlə] *n*. (*pl*. ***-le*** [-le; -lɛ])〔It.〕= cicada.

cic·a·trice [ˈsikətris; ˋsɪkətrɪs] *n*. (*pl*. ~*s* [-siz; -sɪz]) 1. 痂,伤痕,疤痕。2.【植】叶痕,脱离痕。

ci·ca·tri·cle [ˈsikətrikl; ˋsɪkəˏtrɪkl] *n*.【生】(卵黄的)胚点;【植】叶痕,脱离痕。

cic·a·trix [ˈsikətriks; ˋsɪkətrɪks] *n*. (*pl*. ***cic·a·trices*** [sikəˈtraisiːz; sɪkəˋtraɪsiz]) = cicatrice.

cic·a·tri·za·tion [ˌsikətraiˈzeiʃən; ˏsɪkətrɪˋzeʃən] *n*. 长疤,生疤,愈合。

cic·a·trize [ˈsikətraiz; ˋsɪkəˏtraɪz] *vi*., *vt*. (使)长疤,(使)形成疤痕;(使)愈合。

Cic·e·ly [ˈsisili; ˋsɪsɪlɪ] *n*. 西塞莉〔女子名〕。

cic·e·ly [ˈsisili; ˋsɪsəlɪ] *n*.【植】欧洲汤药属植物,野胡萝卜属植物〔可供食用〕。

Ci·ce·ro [ˈsisərəu; ˋsɪsəˏro] *n*. 1. 西塞罗〔**Marcus Tullius** ~,公元前106—43年,古罗马政治家、雄辩家、著作家〕。2. 西塞罗市〔美国都市〕。

cic·e·ro·ne [ˌtʃitʃəˈrəuni, sisə-; ˏtʃɪtʃəˋronɪ, sɪsə-] *n*. (*pl*. ~*s*, ***-ni*** [-niː; -ni])〔It.〕(名胜古迹)讲解导游人。*do the ~* 担任讲解导游。

Cic·e·ro·ni·an [ˌsisəˈrəunjən, -niən; ˏsɪsəˋronjən, -nɪən] **I** *a*. 西塞罗式的,雄辩的;文字精炼优美的。**II** *n*. 西塞罗崇拜者[研究家]。

cich·lid [ˈsiklid; ˋsɪklɪd] **I** *n*.【动】丽鱼科(*Cichlidae*)鱼。**II** *a*. 丽鱼科的。

ci·cis·be·o [ˌtʃitʃizˈbeiəu; ˏtʃɪtʃɪzˋbeo] *n*. (*pl*. ***-bei*** [-biː; -bɪ])〔It.〕(17—18世纪时期)已婚贵妇的公开爱慕者,贵妇人的骑士护从。

C.I.D. = 1. Committee of Imperial Defence〔英〕帝国国防委员会。2. Criminal Investigation Department〔英〕刑事调查局。

Cid [sid; sɪd] *n*.〔Sp.〕首领。*The Cid* 1. 熙德〔十一世纪与摩尔人作战的西班牙英雄 Ruy Diaz 的称号〕。2.《熙德之歌》〔赞美熙德功绩的西班牙文学中最古老的史诗〕。

-cidal *suf*. 以-cide 作词尾的形容词形式。

-cide *suf*. 杀…者,杀[灭]…药。sui*cide*, insecti*cide*.

ci·der [ˈsaidə; ˋsaɪdɚ] *n*. 苹果汁,苹果酒。*sweet* [*hard*] ~未发酵的苹果汁[发过酵的苹果酒]。***All talk and no ~*** 空谈不已,结论全无;空谈而无实惠。***more ~ and less talk*** 内容丰富些,空话少些。***Smith C-*** 柳玉(品种)苹果。~ **brandy** 苹果白兰地酒。**~cup** 汽水酒。~ **drunk**〔美〕喝苹果酒的人;喝苹果酒喝醉了的。**~press** 苹果汁榨取器。

ci·de·vant [ˌsidəˈvɔːŋ; sidəˋvɑŋ] **I** *a*.〔F.〕在前的,以前的。*a ~ governor* 前任县长。**II** *n*. 过时的人[物];已失去权势的人。

cie =〔F.〕Compagnie (= company)。

Cien·fue·gos [sjenˈfwegɔːs; sjɛnˋfwɛgɔs] *n*. 西恩富戈斯〔古巴省名〕。

CIF, C.I.F., c.i.f. = cost, insurance, and freight 到岸价格,成本加保险费;运费价格。

C.I.F. & E. = cost, insurance, freight and exchange 到岸价格加汇费价格。

C.I.F. & I. = cost, insurance, freight and interest 到岸价格加利息价格。

cig〔美〕= cigarette.

ci·ga·la, ci·gale [siˈgɑːlə, -ˈgɑːl; sɪˋgɑlə, -ˋgɑl] *n*.【虫】蝉(= cicada)。

ci·gar [siˈgɑː; sɪˋgɑr] *n*. 雪茄烟,叶卷烟。*Have a ~?*〔美俚〕你好。~ **end** 雪茄烟的烟蒂。**~fish**【动】圆鲹。~ **holder** 雪茄烟烟嘴。**~shaped** *a*. 雪茄烟状的。

cig·a·ret(te) [ˌsigəˈret; ˏsɪgəˋrɛt] *n*. 香烟,卷烟,纸烟;烟卷状的催眠剂或其他药品。*a pack* [*tin*] *of ~s* 一包[听]香烟。~ **case** 香烟盒。~ **end** 烟头。~ **girl** (餐厅等地)卖香烟女子。~ **holder** 烟嘴。~ **paper** 卷烟纸。~ **store** 香烟店。

cig·a·ril·lo [ˌsigəˈriləu; ˏsɪgəˋrɪlo] *n*. (*pl*. ~*s*) 小雪茄;香烟。

C.I.G.S., CIGS = Chief of the Imperial General Staff

〔英〕帝国参谋总长。

cil·i·a [ˈsiliə; ˋsɪlɪə] *n*. (*sing*. *cil·i·um* [-əm; -əm]) 〔*pl*.〕【解】睫毛;【生】纤毛;(叶、翅等的)细毛。

cil·i·ar·y [ˈsiliəri; ˋsɪlɪərɪ] *a*. 眼睫毛的,睫状体的;纤毛的。~ **movement** (低级动物的)睫毛运动。

cil·i·ate [ˈsiliit; ˋsɪlɪɪt] **I** *n*. 【动】纤毛虫。**II** *a*. 有睫的,有纤毛的。

cil·i·at·ed [ˈsilieitid; ˋsɪlɪˏetɪd] *a*. 有睫毛的;有纤毛的。

cil·i·a·tion [ˌsiliˈeiʃən; ˏsɪlɪˋeʃən] *n*. 具有睫毛;〔总称〕睫毛;纤毛。

cil·ice [ˈsilis; ˋsɪlɪs] *n*. 粗毛布;粗毛布衣服。

cil·i·o·late [ˈsiliəlit, -leit; ˋsɪləˏlɪt, -let] *a*. 【植、动】具短纤毛的。

cil·i·um [ˈsiliəm; ˋsɪlɪəm] *n*. cilia 的单数。

cim·ba·lom, cym·ba·lom [ˈsimbələm; ˋsɪmbələm] *n*. 【乐】辛巴龙〔匈牙利民乐器〕。

ci·mex [ˈsaimeks; ˋsaɪmɛks] *n*. (*pl*. *cim·i·ces* [ˈsimisiːz; ˋsɪmɪsiz]) 【动】臭虫 (Cimex)。

Cim·me·ri·an [siˈmiəriən; səˋmɪrɪən] **I** *n*. 【希神】西米里族人〔荷马史诗中描写的,生活在阴暗潮湿国土上的西米里 (Cimmerii) 族〕。**II** *a*. 西米里族人的;黑暗的,阴惨的。~ *darkness* 一团漆黑。

C-in-C = commander in chief 总司令。

cinch [sintʃ; sɪntʃ] **I** *n*. 〔美〕**1**. (马鞍等的)肚带。**2**. 〔口〕紧握。**3**. 〔俚〕必定会发生的事。**4**. 〔口〕容易做的事,轻松的工作。*be a* ~…是确实的[有把握的,简单的]。**II** *vt*. **1**. 系(马的)肚带。**2**. 〔美俚〕确定,弄清楚,弄明白,确实掌握,确保。~ **notice** 〔美〕对成绩不良的警告。

cin·cho·na [sinˈkəunə; sɪnˋkonə] *n*. **1**. 〔C-〕【植】金鸡纳树属。**2**. 金鸡纳树,规那树;规那树皮;金鸡纳霜;奎宁。

cin·cho·nine [ˈsinkəuniːn; ˋsɪnkonin], **cin·choni·a** [siŋˈkəuniə; sɪŋˋkonɪə] *n*. 【药】去甲氧基奎宁碱,辛可宁,金鸡宁。

cin·cho·nism [ˈsinkənizəm; ˋsɪnkənɪzəm] *n*. 【医】奎宁中毒。

cin·cho·nize [ˈsinkənaiz; ˋsɪnkəˏnaɪz] *vt*. 【医】用奎宁处理,用辛可宁治疗。

Cin·cin·nat·i [ˌsinsiˈnæti; ˏsɪnsəˋnætɪ] *n*. 辛辛那提〔美国城市〕。

CINCLANT [ˈsiŋklənt; ˋsɪŋklənt] = Commander in Chief of the Atlantic Fleet 〔美〕大西洋舰队司令。

cinc·ture [ˈsiŋktʃə; ˋsɪŋktʃɚ] **I** *n*. **1**. 围绕;〔诗〕带。**2**. 【建】环带,边轮。**II** *vt*. **1**. 用带子缠绕。**2**. 给(柱头)加饰轮。

CINCUS = Commander-in-chief, United States Navy 美国海军总司令。

cin·der [ˈsində; ˋsɪndɚ] *n*. 煤渣;【冶】熔渣;煅渣;剥片;熔岩渣;火山渣;〔*pl*.〕灰烬。*burn to a* ~ 烧成灰烬。~ **burner** 〔美〕径赛运动员。~ **carnival** = 〔美〕~ **classics** 〔美〕(径赛)运动会。~ **path** 煤渣跑道。~ **sifter** 煤灰筛子;〔美〕沿铁路流浪的游民。~ **specialists** 〔美〕田径选手。~ **track** = ~ path. ~ **trials** 〔美〕径赛。

Cin·der·el·la [ˌsindəˈrelə; ˏsɪndəˋrɛlə] *n*. **1**. 灰姑娘〔童话中一美丽姑娘,被后母虐待,终日与煤渣为伴,故称灰姑娘〕。**2**. 美丽的贫苦姑娘;无名美女,前妻所生的姑娘。**3**. 打杂女仆。**4**. 价值被埋没的人[货品等];一举成名的人〔男人或女人〕。**5**. 以夜半 12 时为止的小跳舞会〔又叫 ~ dance〕。

cin·der·y [ˈsindəri; ˋsɪndərɪ] *a*. 煤渣的,煤灰多的。

cin·e [ˈsini; ˋsɪnɪ] *n*. 电影(院)。

cine- *comb*. *f*. = cinema.

cin·e·an·gi·o·gra·phy [ˈsiniˌændʒiˈɔgrəfi; ˋsɪnəˏændʒɪˋɑgrəfɪ] *n*. 血管活动摄影术。

cin·é·aste [ˈsiniæst; ˋsɪnɪˏæst] *n*. 〔F.〕**1**. 电影制片业人士。**2**. 影迷;电影鉴赏家。

cin·e·cam·er·a [ˈsiniˌkæmərə; ˋsɪnɪˋkæmərə] *n*. 电影摄影机。

cin·e·cism [ˈsinisizəm; ˋsɪnɪsɪzəm] 〔美〕电影批评,影评。

cin·e·col·o(u)r [ˈsiniˈkʌlə; ˋsɪnəˋkʌlɚ] *n*. 彩色电影。

cin·e·cult [ˈsinikʌlt; ˋsɪnəkʌlt] *n*. 电影热潮,电影崇拜。

cin·e·film [ˈsinifilm; ˋsɪnɪfɪlm] *n*. 电影胶片。

cin·e·kodak [ˈsiniˈkəudæk; ˋsɪnəˋkodæk] *n*. (柯达克)小型电影摄影机。

cin·e·ma [ˈsinimə; ˋsɪnəmə] *n*. **1**. 电影院。**2**. 电影,影片。**3**. 电影工业;电影制片术。*go to* ~ 看电影去。

cine·mact [ˈsinimækt; ˋsɪnəmækt] *vi*. 〔美〕做电影演员。

cin·e·mac·tor [ˌsiniˈmæktə; ˏsɪnəˋmæktə] *n*. 〔美俚〕电影演员。

cin·e·mac·tress [ˌsiniˈmæktris; ˏsɪnɪˋmæktrɪs] *n*. 〔美俚〕电影女演员。

cin·e·mad·dict [ˈsinimædikt; ˋsɪnəmædɪkt] *n*. 〔美俚〕影迷。

cin·e·ma-go·er [ˈsinimə-gəuə; ˋsɪnəməˏgoɚ] *n*. 常看电影的人;影迷。

cin·e·ma·nu·fac·ture [ˈsiniˌmænjuˈfæktʃə; ˋsɪnəˏmænjuˋfæktʃɚ] **I** *n*. 〔美〕影片摄制法。**II** *vt*., *vi* 摄制(影片)。

cin·e·ma·scope [ˈsiniməskəup; ˋsɪnəməˏskop] *n*. 〔有时作 C- S-〕【商标】立体声宽银幕电影。

cin·e·mas·ter [ˈsiniˈmɑːstə; ˋsɪnəˋmɑstɚ] *n*. 〔美〕电影明星。

cin·e·ma·theque [ˌsiniməˈtek; ˏsɪnəməˋtɛk] *n*. **1**. 影片贮藏库;影片图书馆。**2**. (放映文献片、非正规影片的)实验电影院。

cin·e·mat·ic [ˌsiniˈmætik; ˏsɪnɪˋmætɪk] *a*. 电影的。**-s** *n*. *pl*. 电影摄制(术)。

cin·e·ma·tize [ˈsinimətaiz; ˋsɪnɪməˏtaɪz] *vt*., *vi*. 〔英〕**1**. 把(小说、舞台剧等)拍摄成电影。**2**. 拍摄 (= cinematograph)。

cin·e·mat·o·graph [ˌsiniˈmætəgrɑːf; ˏsɪnəˋmætəˏgræf] **I** *n*. **1**. 电影摄影机;〔英〕电影放映机。**2**. 电影制片术。**3**. 电影(院)。**II** *vt*., *vi*. **1**. (把…)拍摄成电影。**2**. 摄制(影片)。**-ic** *a*.

cin·e·ma·tog·ra·pher [ˌsiniməˈtɔgrəfə; ˏsɪnɪməˋtɑgrəfə] *n*. 电影摄影师。

cin·e·mat·o·graph·ic [ˌsiniˌmætəˈgræfik; ˏsɪnəˏmætəˋgræfɪk] *a*. 电影摄影术的。**-i·cal·ly** *ad*.

cin·e·ma·tog·ra·phy [ˌsiniməˈtɔgrəfi; ˏsɪnəməˋtɑgrəfɪ] *n*. 电影摄影术。

cin·é·ma vér·i·té [ˈsiːneimə ˈveiriːˈtei; ˋsinemə ˋveriˋte] 〔F.〕实况记录影片。

cin·e·mi·cros·cop·y [ˈsinimaiˈkrɔskəpi; ˋsɪnəmaɪˋkrɑskəpɪ] *n*. 电影显微术。

cin·e·ole [ˈsiniəul; ˋsɪnɪol] *n*. 桉树脑 (= cucalyptol)。

cin·e·pan·o·ram·ic [ˈsiniˌpænəˈræmik; ˋsɪnəˏpænəˋræmɪk] *n*. 全景宽银幕电影。

cin·e·phile [ˈsinifail; ˋsɪnəfaɪl] *n*. 电影迷。

cin·e·plex [ˈsinipleks; ˋsɪnɪplɛks] *n*. 多厅影院〔附设各种娱乐和饮食场所〕。

cin·e·pro·jec·tor [ˈsiniprəˈdʒektə; ˋsɪnəprəˋdʒɛktɚ] *n*. 电影放映机。

cin·e·ram·a [ˌsinəˈrɑːmə; ˏsɪnəˋræmə] *n*. 宽银幕立体电影。

cin·e·rar·i·a [ˌsinəˈrɛəriə; ˏsɪnəˋrɛrɪə] *n*. **1**. 【植】爪叶菊。**2**. cinerarium 的复数。

cin·e·rar·i·um [ˌsinəˈrɛəriəm; ˏsɪnəˋrɛrɪəm] *n*. (*pl*. *cin·e·rar·i·a* [-riə; -rɪə]) 骨灰存放所。

cin·e·rar·y [ˈsinərəri; ˋsɪnəˏrɛrɪ] *a*. (存放)骨灰的;灰的。

cin·er·a·tor [ˈsinireitə; ˋsɪnəˏretɚ] *n*. 火葬场;(垃圾)焚化炉。

cin·e·ra·tion [ˌsinəˈreiʃən; ˏsɪnəˋreʃən] *n*. 【化】灰化;煅

灰法。

cin·e·re·cord [ˌsinəriˈkɔːd; ˏsɪnərɪˋkɔrd] *vi*. 拍摄记录电影。

cine·re·ous [siˈniəriəs; sɪˋnɪrɪəs] *a*. **1**. 已成灰的;灰一样的。**2**. (羽毛等)灰色的。

cin·er·in [ˈsinərin; ˋsɪnərɪn] *n*. 【化、农】丁烯除虫菊酯。

cin·e·the·o·dol·ite [ˌsinəθiˈɔdəlait; ˏsɪnəθɪˋɑdəlaɪt] *n*. 电影经纬仪。

Cin·ga·lese [ˌsiŋgəˈliːz; ˏsɪŋgəˋliz] *n*., *a*. (*pl*. ~) 锡兰岛人[语](的);(斯里兰卡)僧加罗人(的);僧加罗语(的) (= Sinhalese)。

C

cin·gu·late, cin·gu·lated [ˈsiŋgjəlit, -leit, -leitid; ˋsɪŋgjəlɪt, -ˏlet, -ˏletɪd] *a*. 【动】(昆虫腹部)有色带环绕的(亦作 cingulated)。

cin·gu·lum [ˈsiŋgjuləm; ˋsɪŋgjuləm] *n*. (*pl*. *-la* [-lə; -lə]) 【动】色带;系带。

cin·na·bar [ˈsinəbɑː; ˋsɪnəˏbɑr] **I** *n*. 【矿】朱砂,辰砂,银朱;【化】一硫化汞。**II** *a*. 朱红色的。~ **stick** 朱墨。

cin·nam·ic [siˈnæmik; sɪˋnæmɪk] *a*. **1**. 肉桂的;由肉桂提炼出来的。**2**. 肉桂酸的。

cin·na·mon [ˈsinəmən; ˋsɪnəmən] **I** *n*. **1**. 【植】樟属植物;樟属中几种树的芳香内皮,肉桂,桂皮;肉桂树。**2**. 肉桂色,黄棕色。**Chinese** ~ 肉桂。**II** *a*. 肉桂色的,黄棕色的。~**oil** 肉桂油。~**stone** 【矿】钙铝榴石。

cin·na·mon·ic [ˌsinəˈmɔnik; ˏsɪnəˋmɑnɪk] *a*. 肉桂的;由肉桂提炼出来的。

cinq(ue) [siŋk; sɪŋk] *n*. (骰子等的)五点;五。*Cinque Ports* 五港〔英国东南海岸的五个特别港 Dover, Sandwich, Hastings, Romney, Hythe〕。

cin·quain [siŋˈkein; sɪnˋken] *n*. 五行诗。

Cin·que·cen·tist [ˌtʃiŋkwiˈtʃentist; ˏtʃɪŋkwɪˋtʃɛntɪst] *n*. **1**. 十六世纪意大利的艺术家[诗人]。**2**. 十六世纪意大利文艺的研究者。

cin·que·cen·to [ˌtʃiŋkwiˈtʃentəu; ˏtʃɪŋkwɪˋtʃɛnto] *n*. 十六世纪意大利艺术。

cin·que·foil [ˈsiŋkfɔil; ˋsɪŋkˏfɔɪl] *n*. **1**. 【植】委陵菜属植物。**2**. 【建】五叶形[梅花形]装饰。

C.I.O. = Congress of Industrial Organizations 〔美〕产联〔产业工会联合会〕。

ci·on [ˈsaiən; ˋsaɪən] *n*. 【植】接穗(= scion)。

-cion *comb*. *f*. (= -tion): suspi*cion*.

Ci·pan·go [siˈpæŋgəu; sɪˋpæŋgo] *n*. 〔诗〕= Japan 日本国〔源出《马可波罗游记》〕。

ci·pher [ˈsaifə; ˋsaɪfɚ] **I** *n*. **1**. 零〔即 0〕。**2**. 数码,阿拉伯数字。**3**. 暗号,暗码,密码;密码索引(= ~ key)。**4**. (姓名首字母的)组合字,花押字。**5**. 【乐】(风琴出毛病时的)连响。**6**. 无价值的人[物]。*a mere* ~一无所长[毫无价值]的人。*a number of 5* ~*s* 五位数。~ *in algorism* 零;傀儡。*in* ~ 用密码。**II** *vt*., *vi*. **1**. 计算;〔美口〕算出。**2**. 用密码书写。~ *out* **1**. 〔美口〕想出,考虑出。**2**. 算出,解出。**3**. (风琴出毛病时)发出(鸣鸣的连响)。~ **code** [**telegram**] 数字密码[电报]。~ **device** 译码机。~ **key** 暗号索引[密码释译本]。~ **officer** 译电员。

cip·o·lin [ˈsipəlin; ˋsɪpəlɪn] *n*. (意大利的)白底绿花大理石。

cir., **circ**. = circa; circular.

cir = circumference.

cir·ca [ˈsəːkə; ˋsɝkə] ***prep***., ***ad***. 〔L.〕大约,前后〔用于年代前,通常略作 c., ca., cir., circ. 或 C.〕。*circ*. 1800 约 1800 年。

cir·ca·di·an [səˈkeidiən; sɝˋkedɪən] *a*. 【生】24 小时周期的;生理节奏的;日常生理律动性的〔指地球 24 小时转动一圈而产生于人的生活和生理的规律性反应,如新陈代谢,睡眠等〕。~ **rhythm** 生理节奏。**-ly** *ad*.

cir·can·ni·an [səˈkæniən; sɝˋkænɪən] *a*. 一年周期的,周年节奏的;每年活动或循环一次的。

Cir·ce [ˈsəːsi; ˋsɝsɪ] *n*. 【希神】女妖锡西〔荷马史诗《奥德赛》中把人变成猪的妖妇〕;妖媚的女人。

Cir·ce·an [səːˈsiːən; sɝˋsiən] *a*. 妖妇锡西的;有魅惑力的。

cir·ci·nate [ˈsəːsineit; ˋsɝsnˏet] *a*. 【植】拳卷的。

Cir·ci·nus [ˈsəːsinəs; ˋsɝsɪnəs] *n*. 【天】两脚规座。

Cir·cit·er [ˈsəːsitə; ˋsɝsɪtɚ] ***prep***., ***ad***. 〔L.〕= circa.

cir·cle [ˈsəːkl; ˋsɝkl] **I** *n*. **1**. 圆;圆周;圈;环;环状物。**2**. 圆形场地,马戏场;(铁路的)环行交叉口;(体育场的)圆形看台;(剧场的)楼厅。**3**. 周期,循环;(天体运行的)轨道;(体操的)环转运动;【逻】循环论法〔= vicious ~〕;(科学等的)完整体系,整体。**4**. 党派,圈子,集团,…界,(活动、势力、思想等的)范围。*the Arctic* [*Antarctic*] *C-* 北极[南极]圈。~ *of acquaintance* 交际圈。*the dress* ~(戏院的)花楼;月楼。*the upper* ~ 楼厅后座。*the upper* ~*s* 上层社会。*business* [*military*, *political*] ~*s* 实业[军、政]界。(*have*) ***a large*** ~ ***of friends*** 交游广阔。***a swing around*** [***round***] ***the*** ~ 发表政见的巡回旅行。***a vicious*** ~ **1**. 恶性循环。**2**. 【逻】循环论证。~ ***of illumination*** 【天】昼夜分界圈。~ ***of latitude*** [***longitude***] 【天】黄纬[黄经]圈。~ ***of vegetation*** 【生】群落环。***come full*** ~ 绕了一圈,兜了一个圈子。***full*** ~ (*thinking*) 充分的(考虑)。***go all round the*** ~ (话)婉转,兜圈子。***in a*** ~ 成圆形地,围着(…坐)(*argue in a* ~用循环论法论证)。***run round in*** ~***s*** 〔口〕忙得团团转。***square the*** ~ 求与圆面积相等的正方形;试图做不可能的事,妄想。**II** *vt*. 围,环绕;绕过。—*vi*. **1**. 盘旋,环行,兜圈子;旋转,回转。**2**. 流传。

cir·clet [ˈsəːklit; ˋsɝklɪt] *n*. **1**. 小圈,小环。**2**. (手镯等)环形饰物。

cir·cle·wise [ˈsəːklwaiz; ˋsɝklˏwaɪz] *ad*. 成圈状,成圆形。

cir·cling [ˈsəːkliŋ; ˋsɝklɪŋ] *n*. 【马术】环骑。

circs [səːks; sɝks] *n*. 〔*pl*.〕〔口〕= circumstances.

cir·cuit [ˈsəːkit; ˋsɝkɪt] **I** *n*. **1**. (某一范围的)周边一圈;巡回,周游;巡回路线[区域];迂路。**2**. 巡回审判(区);巡回律师会。**3**. 【电】电路,线路;回路,环道。**4**. 同行业联合组织;(戏院等的)轮演系统;轮回演出(节目)[上映(影片)]的戏院。**5**. 事物变化的顺序。*a postman's* ~邮递员的送信路线。*closed* [*open*] ~【电】通[断]路。*return* ~【电】回路。*integrated* ~集成电路。***be in*** ~ ***with*** 和…接成电路。***go the*** ~ ***of*** 绕…环行。***make a*** ~ 绕远路,迂回。***make the*** ~ ***of*** 绕…一圈。***ride the*** ~ (巡回法官)作巡回审判。**II** *vt*., *vi*. (绕…)环行。~ **attorney** 〔美〕地方检查官。~ **binding** 包边装订。~ **breaker** 【电】断路开关。~ **camera** 环转照相机。~ **closer** 【电】通路器。~ **court** 巡回法庭。~ **drive** [**clout**] 【棒球】本垒打。~ **judge** 巡回法官。~ **rider** 〔美〕(美以美教派的)巡回牧师。

cir·cu·i·tous [sə(ː)ˈkju(ː)itəs; sɝˋkjuɪtəs] *a*. **1**. 绕行的,迂回的。**2**. 间接的,迂远的。**-ly** *ad*. **-ness** *n*.

cir·cuit·ry [ˈsəːkitri; ˋsɝkɪtrɪ] *n*. 电路学;电路图;电路系统;电路。

cir·cu·i·ty [səˈkjuːiti; sɝˋkjuətɪ] *n*. 迂回;(说话等的)转弯抹角;间接手法。

cir·cu·lar [ˈsəːkjulə; ˋsɝkjələ] **I** *a*. **1**. 圆的,圆[环]形的。**2**. 循环的;巡回的。**3**. 通告的,环游的;供传阅的。**4**. 伙伴的,团体的。**5**. 【逻】循环论证的。*a* ~ *arc* [*cone*] 圆弧[锥]。*a* ~ *argument* 循环论证。~ *numbers* 循环数。*a* ~ *tour* 环游,周游。*a* ~ *letter* 传阅文件,通知。**II** *n*. **1**. 传阅文件;通报,通知;传单,报单。**2**. 无袖女外衣。~ ***file*** (尤指办公用的)废纸篓。~ **measure** 弧度法。~ **note** 旅行支票;(特指外交方面的)传阅文件。~ **saw** 圆锯。~ **stair** 环状楼梯。~ **ticket** 环程(车、船)票。**-ly** *ad*. 成圈状;循环地。

cir·cu·lar·i·ty [ˌsəːkjuˈlæriti; ˏsɝkjəˋlærətɪ] *n*. **1**. 圆,

圆形,圆状,环状。2.【化纤】充实度。

cir·cu·lar·ize [ˈsəːkjuləraiz; ˋsɝkjələˏraɪz] *vt*. 1. 对…发送通知;送…请传阅;传递;分发;向(多方面)征询意见[吁请支援]。2. (用通知等)公布。3. 把…弄成圆形。

cir·cu·late [ˈsəːkjuleit; ˋsɝkjəˏlet] *vt*. 1. 使(血液等)循环,使运行;使传观。2. 使流转;散播(谣言等)。3. 使(货币等)流通,使周转。*a* ～*d cheque* 流通支票。—*vi*. 1. 循环,运行。2. 流转;流行;传播。3. 流通,周转。4. 〔美〕巡回,各处访问。

cir·cu·lat·ing [ˈsəːkjuleitiŋ; ˋsɝkjʊletɪŋ] *a*. 流通的,循环的,运行的。～ **capital** 流动资本。～ **decimal** 循环小数。～ **door** 旋转门。～ **library** 流通图书馆。～ **medium** 通用货币;流通票据。～ **real capital** 动产,流动资产。

cir·cu·la·tion [ˌsəːkjuˈleiʃən; ˏsɝkjəˋleʃən] *n*. 1. 循环;运行。2. 传播;环流(量),流通(量)。3. (杂志等的)发行(额),销数,销路。4. 通货,货币;流通证券。5. 【空】环量,环流。*the* ～ *of the blood* 血液的循环。*have a good* [*bad*] ～血液循环良好[不好]。*the active* ～纸币的实际流通额。*the passive* ～纸币的准备额。*the* ～ *of a bank* 银行的纸币发行额。***be in*** ～ 传播中;流通中,通行着。***put in*** [***into***] ～ 传播;使(纸币等)流通,通用,使用。***withdraw ... from*** ～ 收回;停止发行。

cir·cu·la·tive [ˈsəːkjuleitiv; ˋsɝkjəˏletɪv] *a*. 1. 循环性的;促进循环的。2. (货币、报刊等)有流通性的。

cir·cu·la·tor [ˈsəːkjuleitə; ˋsɝkjəˏletɚ] *n*. 1. (谣言等的)传播者。2. 循环器。3.【数】循环小数。

cir·cu·la·to·ry [ˈsəːkjuleitəri; ˋsɝkjələˏtorɪ] *a*. (血液)循环的;循环上的。

CIRCUM = circumference.

cir·cum- *pref*. 周,围,环,诸方: *circum*aviation 环球飞行。

cir·cum·am·bi·ent [ˌsəːkəmˈæmbiənt; ˏsɝkəmˋæmbɪənt] *a*. 周围的,环绕的。**-ence**, **-en·cy** *n*. 环绕,围绕。

cir·cum·am·bu·late [ˌsəːkəmˈæmbjuleit; ˏsɝkəmˋæmbjəˏlet] *vt*., *vi*. 1. (绕…)运行,巡行,巡逻。2. 转弯抹角打探;绕着圈子说。**-tion** *n*. **-to·ry** *a*.

cir·cum·a·vi·ate [ˌsəːkəmˈeivieit; ˏsɝkəmˋevɪˏet] *vt*. 环绕(地球)飞行。**-tion** *n*. **-tor** *n*. 环球飞行员。

cir·cum·bend·i·bus [ˌsəːkəmˈbendibəs; ˏsɝkəmˋbɛndɪbəs] *n*. (说话,写文章等的)绕圈子;兜圈子的说法。

cir·cum·cen·tre, -ter [ˌsəːkəmˈsentə; ˏsɝkəmˋsɛntɚ] *n*. 【数】外心〔外接圆的中心〕。

cir·cum·cir·cle [ˌsəːkəmˈsəːkl; ˏsɝkəmˋsɝkl̩] *n*. 【数】外接圆。

cir·cum·cise [ˈsəːkəmsaiz; ˋsɝkəmˏsaɪz] *vt*. 1. 【宗】为…行割礼〔割除包皮,小阴唇,阴蒂〕。2. 【医】环切。3. 〔古〕使(心)净化,清除(罪孽)。

cir·cum·ci·sion [ˌsəːkəmˈsiʒən; ˏsɝkəmˋsɪʒən] *n*. 1. 【宗】割礼;【医】包皮环切(术);(精神)净化。2. 〔C-〕【宗】割礼节〔一月一日〕。3. 〔the ～〕〔总称〕犹太人。(心地)纯洁的人。

cir·cum·fer·ence [səˈkʌmfərəns; səˋkʌmfərəns] *n*. 四周,周围;圆周;圈线;周线。*ten miles in* ～周长十英里。

cir·cum·fer·en·tial [səˌkʌmfəˈrenʃəl; səˏkʌmfəˋrɛnʃəl] *a*. 1. 周围的,四周的。2. 委婉的。

cir·cum·flect [ˌsəːkəmˈflekt; ˋsɝkəmˏflɛkt] *vt*. 1. 把…弯成圆形;卷缠。2. 附加音调[长音]符号于。

cir·cum·flex [ˈsəːkəmfleks; ˋsɝkəmflɛks] **I** *n*. 【语】音调[长音]符号〔如 ∧ ⌒ ～〕 **II** *a*. 有音调[长音]符的;发长音的;曲折的。**III** *vt*. 附加音调[长音]符号于。

cir·cum·flu·ence [sə(ː)ˈkʌmfluəns; səˋkʌmflʊəns] *n*. 环流,回流。

cir·cum·flu·ent, cir·cum·flu·ous [sə(ː)ˈkʌmfluənt, -fluəs; səˋkʌmflʊənt, -flʊəs] *a*. 环[回]流的;缠绕的,围绕的。

cir·cum·fuse [ˌsəːkəmˈfjuːz; ˏsɝkəmˋfjuz] *vt*. 1. 使(光)向周围照射,在周围浇(水等);在周围散布。2. 缠绕,围绕。

cir·cum·fu·sion [ˌsəːkəmˈfjuːʒən; ˏsɝkəmˋfjuʒən] *n*. 周围灌注;散布;围绕。

cir·cum·gy·rate [ˌsəːkəmdʒaiəˈreit; ˏsɝkəmˋdʒaɪret] *vi*. 回转,旋转;周游。—*vt*. 使回转。

cir·cum·gy·ra·tion [ˌsəːkəmdʒaiəˈreiʃən; ˏsɝkəmdʒaɪˋreʃən] *n*. 1. 旋转。2. 〔谑〕翻筋斗。3. 周转,东挪西移。

cir·cum·ja·cent [ˌsəːkəmˈdʒeisnt; ˏsɝkəmˋdʒesn̩t] *a*. 周围的,邻接的,围绕着的。

cir·cum·lit·tor·al [ˌsəːkəmˈlitərəl; ˏsɝkəmˋlɪtərəl] *a*. 沿海的,临海岸的。

cir·cum·lo·cu·tion [ˌsəːkəmləˈkjuːʃən; ˏsɝkəmloˋkjuʃən] *n*. 1. 语言冗长,啰唆。2. 躲闪,遁辞;婉转曲折(的说法)。*C- Office* 拖拉衙门〔Dickens 小说 *Little Dorrit* 中办事拖拉的官僚机关〕。

cir·cum·loc·u·to·ry [ˌsəːkəmˈlɔkjutəri; ˏsɝkəmˋlɑkjəˏtorɪ] *a*. 1. 迂回的,委婉曲折的。2. 冗长的,啰唆的。

cir·cum·lu·nar [ˌsəːkəmˈluːnə; ˏsɝkəmˋlunɚ] *a*. 环月的,绕月的。

cir·cum·nav·i·gate [ˌsəːkəmˈnævigeit; ˏsɝkəmˋnævəˏget] *vt*. 环航(世界)。

cir·cum·nav·i·ga·tion [ˈsəːkəmˌnæviˈgeiʃən; ˋsɝkəmˏnævɪˋgeʃən] *n*. 环球航行。

cir·cum·nav·i·ga·tor [ˌsəːkəmˈnævigeitə; ˏsɝkəmˋnævɪˏgetɚ] *n*. 环球航行者。

cir·cum·nu·tate [ˌsəːkəmˈnjuːteit; ˏsɝkəmˋnjutet] *vi*. 【植】(茎、卷须等)回旋转头。

cir·cum·nu·ta·tion [ˌsəːkəmnjuˈteiʃən; ˏsɝkəmnjʊˋteʃən] *n*. 【植】回旋转头运动。

cir·cum·po·lar [ˌsəːkəmˈpəulə; ˏsɝkəmˋpolɚ] *a*. 1. 【地】极圈的,极地周围的。2. 【天】拱极的,围绕天极的。～ **stars** 周极星〔永远高于地平线〕。

cir·cum·ro·tate [ˌsəːkəmˈrəuteit; ˏsɝkəmˋrotet] *vi*. 旋转,循环。**-tation** *n*.

cir·cum·scis·sile [ˌsəːkəmˈsisəl; ˏsɝkəmˋsɪsəl] *a*. 【植】周裂的〔指果实〕。

cir·cum·scribe [ˈsəːkəmskraib, ˌsəːkəmˈskraib; ˋsɝkəmˋskraɪb, ˏsɝkəmˋskraɪb] *vt*. 1. 在…周围画线;为…立限界。2. 限定,限制。3. 【数】使外接,使外切。4. 为…下定义。～*d circle* 外接圆。～*d figure* 外接形。

cir·cum·scrip·tion [ˌsəːkəmˈskripʃən; ˏsɝkəmˋskrɪpʃən] *n*. 1. 限界,限制。2. 【数】外接。3. 界线;范围,区域。4. 〔古〕定义。5. (硬币周围的)齿刻,花边。

cir·cum·so·lar [ˌsəːkəmˈsəulə; ˏsɝkəmˋsolɚ] *a*. 围绕着太阳的,太阳周围的,绕日的。

cir·cum·spect [ˈsəːkəmspekt; ˋsɝkəmˏspɛkt] *a*. 慎重的,细心的,谨慎小心的,周到的,精密的。**-ly** *ad*. **-ness** *n*.

cir·cum·spec·tion [ˌsəːkəmˈspekʃən; ˏsɝkəmˋspɛkʃən] *n*. 慎重,周到。

cir·cum·stance [ˈsəːkəmstəns; ˋsɝkəmˏstæns] **I** *n*. 1. 〔常 *pl*.〕周围的)情况,情形,环境。2. 〔*pl*.〕(人的)境遇,境况。3. (事情的)详情,细节,本末,原委;(一桩)事故,事情,事实。4. 〔古〕形式,仪式;(仪式的)隆重。5. 命运,机会。*adverse* [*favourable*] ～*s* 逆[顺]境。*act according to* ～*s* 临机应变,因时制宜。*private* ～*s* 内幕,内情。*the whole* ～*s* 前后原委,始末根由。***a mere*** [***remote, poor***] ～ 〔美口〕无用的东西;不足道的人。***at no*** ～***s*** 在任何情况下都不…。***in bad*** [***needy, reduced***] ～***s*** 穷困。***in easy*** ～***s*** 生活安乐。***in good*** ～***s*** 顺遂。***in no*** ～***s*** = *under no* ～*s*. ***in straitened*** ～***s*** 困苦,穷困。***in the*** ～***s*** = *under the* ～*s*. ***not a*** ～ ***to*** 〔美口〕远不及,不能与…相比。***pomp and*** ～ 排场;装腔作势。***under all*** ～***s*** 无论如何。***under certain*** ～***s*** 在某

种情况下,看情形,有时。*under no* ～*s* 无论如何不,决不。*under the* ～*s* 在这种情形下,因为这种情形。*with* ～ 详细。*without* ～ 不讲虚套(仪式)地,直截地。*without omitting a single* ～ 毫无遗漏地。**II** *vt*. 把…置于某种情况下。

cir·cum·stanced [ˈsəːkəmstənst; ˋsɝkəmˏstænst] *a*. 在(某种)情形[情况]下。～ *as I am* 情形如此,所以我…。*differently* ～情形不同。*so* ～ *that* 事已如此(故)。*well* ～处境顺遂。

cir·cum·stan·tial [ˌsəːkəmˈstænʃəl; ˏsɝkəmˋstænʃəl] *a*. **1**. 按照情况(推测)的;看(当时)情形的。**2**. (故事等)详细的。**3**. 偶然的,不测的;不重要的。**4**. 礼节隆重的,仪节完备的。～ *report* 详尽报导。～*evidence*【法】间接证据,旁证。*of* ～ *importance* 次要的。**-ly** *ad*.

C

cir·cum·stan·ti·al·i·ty [ˈsəːkəmˌstænʃiˈæliti; ˏsɝkəmˏstænʃɪˋæləti] *n*. **1**. 情况详尽,富有细节。**2**. 〔*pl*.〕详情;具体细节。**3**. 偶然性。

cir·cum·stan·ti·ate [ˌsəːkəmˈstænʃieit; ˏsɝkəmˋstænʃɪˏet] *vt*. 证实(每一细节);(提供事实)详细说明,(提供证据)证明。

cir·cum·ter·res·tri·al [ˌsəːkəmtəˈrestriəl; ˏsɝkəmtəˋrɛstrɪəl] *a*. 围绕地球的。

cir·cum·val·late [ˌsəːkəmˈvæleit; ˏsɝkəmˋvælet] *vt*. 用城墙[壕沟、壁垒等]围住。

cir·cum·val·la·tion [ˌsəːkəmvəˈleiʃən; ˏsɝkəmvəˋleʃən] *n*. **1**. 被壁垒[城墙、壕沟等]围绕。**2**. 壁垒,城墙。

cir·cum·vent [ˌsəːkəmˈvent; ˏsɝkəmˋvɛnt] *vt*. **1**. 围绕,包围,围困。**2**. 用计超过[胜过、包围];(用欺骗手段)陷害。**3**. 用计防止;避免。

cir·cum·ven·tion [ˌsəːkəmˈvenʃən; ˏsɝkəmˋvɛnʃən] *n*. **1**. 包围,围困。**2**. 欺骗;计谋。**3**. 胜过;防止。

cir·cum·vo·lute [səːˈkʌmvəljuːt; sɝˋkʌmvəˏljut] *vt*. 围绕…旋转;卷绕,缠绕。

cir·cum·vo·lu·tion [ˌsəːkəmvəˈljuːʃən; ˏsɝkəmvəˋljuʃən] *n*. **1**. 卷缠,(围绕某物的)旋转,周转;涡线。**2**. 迂回运行。

cir·cum·volve [ˌsəːkəmˈvɔlv; ˏsɝkəmˋvɑlv] *vt*., *vi*. (绕…)旋转;缠绕。

cir·cus [ˈsəːkəs; ˋsɝkəs] *n*. **1**. (圆形的)马戏场;杂技场(古罗马的)圆形竞技场。**2**. 杂技团,马戏团;杂技[马戏]表演。**2**. 〔英〕圆形十字路口,圆形广场。**3**. 〔口〕乱哄哄的热闹场面;在作某种表演的一群人。**4**.【地】外轮山。**5**. 〔军俚〕游击队;飞行队;飞行表演。*pitch* [*put up*] *a* ～搭临时卖艺[马戏]场。*run a* ～演马戏,演出杂技。*travelling* ～流动杂技[马戏]团。**C- Maximus** 罗马的大竞技场。**Bread and** ～**es** 面包和竞技〔古罗马统治者有时为民众免费提供用以欺骗和麻醉他们的一种手段;〔泛指〕统治者的小恩小惠〕。

ci·ré [səˈrei; səˋre] **I** *a*. 涂蜡的。**II** *n*. 蜡光丝,蜡光草。

cirque [səːk; sɝk] *n*. **1**. 圆形场地;〔诗〕(天然)半圆形剧场。**2**.【地】冰斗,冰雪坑。**3**. 圆圈,环行物。

cir·rate [ˈsiəreit; ˋsɪret] *a*.【生】**1**. 有触毛的,有触须的。**2**. 有棘毛的。**3**. (腕足类)有腕丝的。**4**. (棘皮)有卷肢的。**5**. (甲壳类)有蔓足的。**6**. (昆虫)有细干卷的。**7**. (昆虫)有阴茎的。

cir·rho·sis [siˈrəusis; sɪˋrosɪs] *n*.【医】肝硬化;(任何器官的)慢性间质炎。

cir·ri [ˈsirai; ˋsɪraɪ] *n*. cirrus 的复数。

cirri- *comb*. *f*. = cirro.

cir·ri·ped, cir·ri·pede [ˈsiriped, -piːd; ˋsɪrɪˏpɛd, -pid] *n*.【动】蔓脚类动物。

cirro- *comb*. *f*. 触毛;卷须;卷云:*cirro*se.

cir·ro-cu·mu·lus [ˈsirəuˈkjuːmjuləs; ˏsɪrəˋkjumjʊləs] *n*.【气】卷积云,絮云。

cir·rose, cir·rous [siˈrəus, ˈsirəs; sɪˋros, ˋsɪrəs] *a*. **1**. (像)卷云的。**2**. 有[似]卷须的;有[似]触毛的。

cir·ro·stra·tus [ˈsirəuˈstreitəs; ˏsɪroˋstretəs] *n*.【气】卷层云。

cir·rus [ˈsirəs; ˋsɪrəs] *n*. (*pl*. *cir·ri* [ˈsirai; ˋsɪraɪ]) **1**.【植】卷须;孢子角。**2**.【动】粗纤毛,触毛;触须;(腕足类的)腕丝;(甲壳类的)蔓足;(虫类的)阴茎。**3**.【气】卷云。

cir·soid [ˈsəːsɔid; ˋsɝsɔɪd] *a*.【医】静脉怒张的,静脉肿胀的,静脉肿的。

CIS = Commonwealth of Independent States 独立国家联合体〔前苏联解体后成立〕。

cis- *comb*. *f*. **1**. 这一边 (*opp*. trans-, ultra-)。**2**. 以后 (*opp*. pre-)。**3**.【化】顺(式),顺向:*cis*atlantic.

cis·al·pine [sisˈælpain; sɪsˋælpaɪn] *a*. 阿尔卑斯山这边[南侧]的,意大利方面的〔有时指从欧洲北部等地说,也指阿尔卑斯山北侧〕。

cis·at·lan·tic [ˌsisətˈlæntik; ˏsɪsətˋlæntɪk] *a*. 大西洋这边的。

CISC = complex instruction set computing【计】复合指令集计算。

cis·co [ˈsiskəu; ˋsɪsko] *n*. (*pl*. ～*es*, ～*s*)【美动】加拿大雪鲦。

cis·lu·nar [sisˈluːnə; sɪsˋlunɚ] *a*.【天】位于地球与月球(轨道)之间的。

cis·mon·tane [sisˈmɔntein; sɪsˋmɑnten] *a*. **1**. (阿尔卑斯)山这边[北侧]的,非意大利方面的。**2**. = cisalpine. **3**. 在山这一边的。

cis·pa·dane [ˈsispədein; ˋsɪspəˏden] *a*. 在波河 (Po) 这边[南侧]的;在罗马这一方面的。

cis·soid [ˈsisɔid; ˋsɪsɔɪd] **I** *n*.【数】(尖点)蔓叶(曲)线。**II** *a*. 蔓叶线内的,凹边的〔指两条相交蔓叶线的夹角〕。

Cis·sy [ˈsisi; ˋsɪsɪ] *n*. 锡西〔女子名,Cecilia 的昵称〕。

cis·sy [ˈsisi; ˋsɪsɪ] *n*. 〔美俚〕没骨气的人,胆小鬼。

cist [sist; sɪst] *n*.【考古】石柜,石棺。

Cis·ter·ci·an [sisˈtəːʃjən; sɪsˋtɝʃən] *n*., *a*. (法国 Robert de Molesme 于 1098 年在 Cistercium 地方创建的)西斯特教团修士(的)。

cis·tern [ˈsistən; ˋsɪstɚn] *n*. **1**. (贮水用的)水缸[桶,箱,槽]。**2**. (天然的)水塘[池]。**3**. (餐桌上的)水瓶,洗手钵。**4**.【解】(贮分泌液的)池囊,淋巴间隙。

cis·ter·na [sisˈtəːnə; sɪsˋtɝnə] *n*. (*pl*. *-nae* [-niː; -ni])【解】池。**-l** *a*.

cis·tron [ˈsistrɔn; ˋsɪstrɑn] *n*.【生】顺反子,作用子。

cis·tus [ˈsistəs; ˋsɪstəs] *n*.【植】岩蔷薇属植物。

cit [sit; sɪt] *n*. **1**. 〔古〕市民〔蔑称〕。**2**. 〔美〕都市人,城里人,老百姓。**3**. 〔*pl*.〕〔美〕便服。

CIT = California Institute of Technology 〔美〕加利福尼亚理工学院。

cit. = citation; cited; citizen.

cit·a·ble [ˈsaitəbl; ˋsaɪtəbl] *a*. **1**. 可引用[引证]的。**2**. 可叫来(作证)的,可传呼来[传讯]的。

cit·a·del [ˈsitədəl; ˋsɪtədəl] *n*. **1**. (居高临下的)城寨,城堡,要塞。**2**. (军舰上的)炮廓。**3**. 〔喻〕根据地,大本营;避难所。

ci·ta·tion [saiˈteiʃən; saɪˋteʃən] *n*. **1**. 引证,引用,引文;例证;说到,列举。**2**.【法】传讯;传票;(对于法律先例等的)援引。**3**. 〔美〕(对杰出人物等的)表扬(证书),荣誉状,奖品;【军】嘉奖令。**-to·ry** *a*.

cite[1] [sait; saɪt] *vt*. **1**. 引用,引证;举(例),列举;说到。**2**.【法】传讯。**3**. 召集,发动。**4**. 〔美〕表扬;【军】传令嘉奖。

cite[2] [sait; saɪt] *n*. 〔口〕例证,引文(= citation)。

cith·a·ra [ˈsiθərə; ˋsɪθərə] *n*. 古希腊的三角竖琴;筝。

cith·er(n) [ˈsiθə(n); ˋsɪθɚ(n)] *n*.【乐】(十六、七世纪流行的吉他状)七弦琴。

cit·ied [ˈsitid; ˋsɪtɪd] *a*. **1**. 有城市的。**2**. 城市一样的。

cit·i·fied [ˈsitifaid; ˋsɪtɪˏfaɪd] *a*. 〔美,主蔑〕有城市(人)风的,城市化的。

cit·i·fy [ˈsitifai; ˋsɪtɪˏfaɪ] *vt*. 使城市化。

cit·i·zen [ˈsitizn; ˋsɪtəzn̩] *n*. **1**. 市民,城市居民。**2**. 〔美〕

(区别于军人而言的)平民,老百姓。**3.** 公民,国民。**4.** 居民,栖息者。*an American* ～美国公民。〔*cf*. a British subject〕。～ *of the world* 世界公民(指对全世界情况有兴趣的人,四海为家的人)。～**'s arrest** 公民扭送〔不成文法,公民发现罪犯,可扭送法院〕。～**s' band**【无】(专供私人无线电通信用的)民用波段。～**s' committee**〔美〕自警团。～**s' rally** 市民大会。**-hood** *n*. **1.** 公民[市民]身分;公民权。**2.** 国籍。**-ry**〔总称〕市民,公民;〔美〕(不同于军人的)平民。**-ship** *n*. **1.** 公民[市民]身分,公民的权利和义务。**2.** 国籍。**3.** 个人品德表现。

cit·i·zen·ess [ˈsitizənis; ˋsɪtəzənɪs] *n*. 〔罕〕女市民[公民]。

citr-〔用于母音前〕*comb*. *f*. 柠檬,柑橘(= citro-)。

citra- *comb*. *f*. = cis-.

cit·ral [ˈsitrəl; ˋsɪtrəl] *n*.【化】柠檬醛。

cit·rate [ˈsitreit; ˋsɪtret] *n*.【化】柠檬酸盐。

cit·re·ous [ˈsitriəs; ˋsɪtrɪəs] *a*. 柠檬色的,柠檬的。

cit·ric [ˈsitrik; ˋsɪtrɪk] *a*.【化】柠檬性的。～ **acid** 柠檬酸。

cit·ri·cul·ture [ˈsitriˌkʌltʃə; ˋsɪtrəˏkʌltʃɚ] *n*. 柑橘栽培。

cit·rin [ˈsitrin; ˋsɪtrɪn] *n*.【化】柠檬素,维生素 P.

cit·rine [ˈsitrin; ˋsɪtrɪn] **I** *a*. 柠檬的,柠檬色的。**II** *n*. **1.** 柠檬色。**2.**【矿】黄水晶。

cit·rin·in [ˈsitrini; ˋsɪtrɪnɪ] *n*.【化】橘霉素。

citro-〔用于子音前〕,*comb*. *f*. = citr-.

cit·ron [ˈsitrən; ˋsɪtrən] *n*.【植】**1.** 香橼,枸橼。**2.** 香橼皮蜜饯。**3.** 柠檬色。*the fingered* ～佛手柑。

cit·ron·el·la [ˌsitrəˈnelə; ˏsɪtrənˋɛlə] *n*.【植】香茅;香茅油。～ *circuit*〔常作 C- C-〕暑期剧团的巡回演出。

cit·ron·el·lal [ˌsitrəˈnelæl; ˏsɪtrəˋnɛləl] *n*.【化】香茅醛。

cit·rul·line [siˈtrʌliːn; sɪˋtrʌlin] *n*.【化】瓜胺酸。

Cit·rus [ˈsitrəs; ˋsɪtrəs] *n*. **1.**【植】柑橘属。**2.**〔c-〕柠檬,柑橘。～ *Metropolis*〔美〕柑橘市〔洛杉矶(Los Angeles)市的别号〕。

cit·tern [ˈsitən, ˈsɪtən] *n*. = cithern.

cit·y [ˈsiti; ˋsɪtɪ] *n*. **1.** 城市;市〔英国指设有大教堂的特许市;美国指大于 town 的重要城市〕;都市。**2.**〔the ～〕全市,全体市民。**3.**〔the C-〕伦敦商业中心区(= the C- of London)。**4.**【希史】城邦(= ～ state)。*be in the C-* 是实业家;在商业中心做事。*C- of a Hundred Towers* 百塔城〔意大利 Pavia 的别号〕。*C- of Brotherly Love* 友爱城〔〔美〕*Philadelphia* 市的别号〕。*C- of God* 天国。～ *of homes*〔美〕家乡城〔Philadelphia 的别号〕。*C- of Light* 灯城〔巴黎的别号〕。*C- of Masts* 桅城〔伦敦的别号〕。*C- of Prophet* 先知城〔阿拉伯 Medina 的别号〕。*C- of the dead* 墓地,公墓。*C- of the Seven Hills* 七山城〔罗马的别称〕。*C- of Victory* 胜利城〔埃及 Cairo 的别号〕。*the eternal* ～永恒之城〔指罗马〕。**C- article** (伦敦报纸上的)商业经济新闻。～ **assembly** 市议会。～ **billy**〔美〕在城市中长大的乡村音乐演唱者。～ **chicken** 串烤(小)牛肉(等)。**C- Company** 伦敦市商会。～ **convention**〔美〕(政党的)市代表会议。～ **council** 市参议会。～ **councillor** 市参议会议员。～ **dads**〔美俚〕市参议员。～ **editor**〔美〕(报馆的)本市栏编辑主任;〔英〕〔C-〕(报馆的)经济栏编辑。～ **employee** 市府公务员。～ **fathers**〔美俚〕市参议员(= ～ dads)。～ **hall** 市政厅。～ **item**【商】本市汇划汇票。**C- man**〔英〕实业家,资本家。～ **manager**〔美〕(市行政委员会任命的)市执政官。～ **office** 市政厅。～ **plan** 市街区划,都市计划。～ **room** 本市新闻版编辑(室)。～**scape** **1.** 城市风光画片。**2.** 市容,市景。～ **slicker**〔口〕(农民眼中的)城市滑头。～**-state** (古希腊的)城邦。～ **ward(s)** *ad*. 向都市。

Ciudad Tru·jil·lo [sjuːˈðɑːð truˈhijo; sjuˋðað trʊˋhɪjo] *n*. 特鲁希略城〔西印度多米尼加首都,使用过的新名,现又恢复旧称 Santo Domingo〕。

civ. = civic; civil; civilian。

civ·et [ˈsivit; ˋsɪvɪt] *n*. **1.**【动】香猫,麝猫。**2.**【化】麝猫香。～ **cat** 香猫(皮)。

civ·ic [ˈsivik; ˋsɪvɪk] *a*. **1.** 城市的。**2.** 市民的,公民的。～ **center** 市中心区。～ **crown** 槲叶环〔古罗马赠与救护市民者的荣冠〕。～ **life** 城市生活。～ **rights** [**duties**] 市民权,公民权[义务]。～**-minded** *a*. 关心社会福利的,有公德心的;有市[公]民意识的。～ **ethics**, ～ **virtues** 文明礼貌,公民道德。

civ·i·cism [ˈsivisizəm; ˋsɪvɪsɪzəm] *n*. **1.** 市政;市政至上主义。**2.** 公民道德,市民思想。

civ·ics [ˈsiviks; ˋsɪvɪks] *n*. 市政学,〔美〕公民学。

civ·ie [ˈsivi; ˋsɪvɪ] *n*. = civvy.

civ·ies [ˈsiviz; ˋsɪvɪz] *n*. 〔*pl*.〕〔军俚〕便装,便服;〔美〕便衣警探。

civ·il [ˈsivl; ˋsɪvl] *a*. **1.** 市民的,公民的;民用的;【法】民事的;根据民法的,法律规定的。**2.** 国内的,国民间的。**3.** 有礼貌的;文明的。**4.** 非军职的,文职的,文官的。**5.** 非圣职的,非宗教的。**6.** 历法规定的。*do the* ～ 行动郑重,为人诚恳。*keep a* ～ *tongue in one's head* 说话有礼貌。*say something* ～ 说恭维话,说应酬话。～ **action** 民事诉讼。～ **administration** 市政。～ **architecture** 民用建筑。～ **aviation** 民用航空。～ **bond** (地方)公债。～ **case** 民事案件。～ **clothes** 便装,便服〔与军服等相对〕。～ **code** 民法。～ **contract** (不依据宗教仪式的)民间契约,世俗约定〔如结婚等的〕。～ **day** 日历日;【海】常用日。～ **death** 褫夺公权;放逐;无期徒刑。**C- Defence** (主指防空的)民间防卫(组织)〔略 C.D.〕。～ **engineering** 建筑工程。～ **law** 民法;罗马法。～ **liberty** 公民自由;法律范围内的个人自由。～ **life** 社会生活,公民生活(*return to* ～ *life* 复员,退役)。～ **list**〔美〕文官薪级表;文官薪俸(总额);〔英〕〔C- L-〕皇室费。**Civil Lord** (英海军部的)文官委员。～ **marriage** 不举行宗教仪式的婚姻。～ **obligation** 公民义务。～ **occasion** 犯罪;过失;诱惑。～ **possession** 民法上的占有。～ **power** 统治权,政权。～ **procedure** [**proceedings**] 民事诉讼(程序)。～ **right** 公民权。～ **sanction** 民事上的制裁。～ **servant** (〔英〕**C- Servant**) 公务员,文职人员,文官。～ **service**〔英〕**C- Service** 全体公务员[文官];行政机构〔与军事机构相对〕。～ **state** (除军人、僧侣以外的)全体国民。～ **time** 民用时。～ **war** 内战(*the Civil War*〔英〕(1642～1649 年的)查理一世与议会的战争;〔美〕(1861—1865 年的)南北战争)。～ **year** 日历年。**-ly** *ad*.

ci·vil·ian [siˈviljən; səˋvɪljən] *n*. **1.** 市民。**2.** 平民;(军队中的)无军职人员。**3.** 文官。**4.** 民法学者,民法家;罗马法专家。～ **airman** [**aviator**] 民航飞行员。～ **clothes** 便装,便衣。

ci·vil·i·ty [siˈviliti; səˋvɪlətɪ] *n*. **1.** 礼貌;文明态度;〔*pl*.〕礼仪。**2.**〔古〕文明,文化。*vapid civilities* (陈腐的)虚礼。

civ·i·liz·a·ble, -lis·a·ble [ˈsivilaizəbl; ˋsɪvɪˏlaɪzəbl̩] *a*. 可开化的,可教化的。

civ·i·li·za·tion, -sa·tion [ˌsivilaiˈzeiʃən; ˏsɪvl̩əˋzeʃən] *n*. **1.** 文明,文化。**2.** 教育,教化,开化。**3.** 文明世界;文明利器;文明事物。

civ·i·lize, -lise [ˈsivilaiz; ˋsɪvl̩ˏaɪz] *vt*. 使文明;启发,教化,开化;教育。—*vi*. 变成文明(社会)。～ *away* 用文化教育革除(野蛮习性等)。

civ·i·lized, -lised [ˈsivilaizd; ˋsɪvl̩ˏaɪzd] *a*. **1.** 文明的,有礼貌的;有教养的。**2.** 已变成文明(社会)的。

civ·ism [ˈsivizəm, ˈsɪvɪzəm] *n*. 公民精神,公民[国民]道德。

Civ. Serv. = Civil Service. 文职人员;行政机构。

civ·vy [ˈsivi; ˋsɪvɪ] *n*. **1.**〔军俚〕平民;非军人。**2.**〔*pl*.〕便衣,便服。*C- Street*〔俚〕平民生活。

CJ, C.J. = Chief Justice 审判长,首席法官;法院院长。

C.J.C.S. = Chairman of the Joint Chiefs of Staff〔美〕参谋长联席会议主席。

CJD = Creutzfeldt-Jakob disease 克一雅二氏病(一种罕见,致命的海绵状病毒性脑病)。

ck. = cask; chalk; check; cook.

ckd = completely knocked down.

ckw = clockwise.

Cl = chlorine【化】氯。

cl. = centilitre; claim; class; classification; clause; clergyman; cloth.

clab·ber [ˈklæbə; ˋklæbɚ] **I** *n*. 凝结变酸的牛奶,酸牛奶;酸酪。**II** *vt*., *vi*. (使)(牛乳等)变酸而凝结。

clach·an [ˈklɑːkhən; ˋklɑkhən] *n*. [Scot.] 村庄;乡村客店;乡间教堂。

C

clack [klæk; klæk] **I** *vi*. **1**. 发毕剥声。**2**. [方]唠叨,刺刺不休地讲。**3**. (家禽)咯咯地叫。—*vt*. **1**. 使发毕剥声。**2**. 唠叨地说。**II** *n*. **1**. 毕剥声。**2**. 喋喋不休,饶舌,唠叨。**3**.【机】瓣(阀);【空】翼门止回阀。*Hold your ~!* 住嘴! 别作声! ~ **box**【空】翼门止回阀箱。~ **valve**【机】瓣阀。

clad [klæd; klæd] [古] clothe 的过去式及过去分词。**I** *a*. **1**. 穿衣的。**2**. 被覆盖的。**3**. 镀过(另一种)金属的;用金属包被的。*an iron-~ vessel* 装甲舰。**II** *vt*. (*clad*; *cladding*) 在(金属)外面包上另一种金属。**cladding** *n*.【物】镀;包层。

clad- *comb*. *f*. [用于母音前] = clado-.

cla·dis·tic [kləˈdistik; kləˋdɪstɪk] *a*. 基于遗传因素的。

clado- *comb*. *f*. 芽;枝: *clado*phyll.

cla·doc·er·an [kləˈdɔsərən; kləˋdɑsərən] *n*.【动】枝角。

clad·ode [ˈklædəud; ˋklædod] *n*. = cladophyll.

clad·o·phyll, clado·phyl·lon [ˈklædəfil, -filən; ˋklædəˏfɪl, -fɪlən] *n*.【植】叶状枝[茎]。

claim [kleim; klem] **I** *n*. **1**. (根据权利而提出的)要求,请求;认领,索取。**2**. (应得的)权利;(…的)资格。**3**. 主张,断言,声称,自称。**4**. 要求权;要求物;(矿区等的)申请购买地。*He has no ~ to scholarship*. 他不配称做学者。*I have many ~s on my time*. 我很忙。~**s agent** [美]专门代人向议会要求赔偿[救济]的代理人。~ **to order** 记名债权。**hold down a ~** 留住一地以便获得对土地的所有权。**jump a ~** [美]强占别人申请的购买地。**lay ~ to** 声称,要求(…是自己的);以…自任[自居],自以为是。**put in a ~ for = enter a ~ for** 提出(某项)要求;认领(某物)。**set up a ~ to** 声明对…的权利,提起对…的要求。**stake out [off] a ~** [美]立界标表明(土地等的)所有权;坚持要求(得到某物)。**II** *vt*. **1**. 要求(应得权利)。**2**. 主张,断言;声称,自称;要求承认。**3**. 理应获得,值得(重视等),需要(注意等),赢得。~ *a reward* 要求报酬。~ *a victory* 声称取得胜利。*This question ~s attention*. 这个问题需要注意。*His heroism ~s our admiration*. 他的勇敢行为应该得到我们的赞美。—*vi*. [罕]要求赔偿损失(*against*)。~ **jumper** [美]非法占取他人采矿权或土地所有权者。

claim·a·ble [ˈkleiməbl; ˋkleməbl̩] *a*. 可要求的;可认领的;可索取的。

claim·ant, claim·er [ˈkleimənt, ˈkleimə; ˋklemənt, ˋklemɚ] *n*. 提出要求者,索取者,申请者(*to*, *for*);【法】原告,债权人。

claims·man [ˈkeimzmən; ˋklemzmən] *n*. (*pl*. *-men*) (灾害保险的)调查员。

clair·au·di·ence [kleərˈɔːdjəns; klɛrˋɔdiəns] *n*. 透听,透听力,超人的听力。

clair·au·di·ent [kleərˈɔːdjənt; klɛrˋɔdiənt] **I** *a*. 有超人听力的。**II** *n*. 听力超人者,顺风耳。

Claire [kleə; klɛr] *n*. 克莱尔[女子名, Clara 的异体]。

clair·voy·ance [kleəˈvɔiəns; klɛrˋvɔɪəns] *n*. **1**. 超人的视力,透视力,千里眼。**2**. 洞察力。

clair·voy·ant [kleəˈvɔiənt; klɛrˋvɔɪənt] *a*., *n*. **1**. 视力超人的(人)。**2**. 明察秋毫的(人),有洞察力的(人)。

clam[1] [klæm; klæm] **I** *n*. (*pl*. ~, ~**s**) **1**.【动】蛤;蛤肉。**2**. [美口]沉默寡言的人,嘴紧的人。**3**. [美俚]银币,一元。*razor ~* 蛏。**as close as a ~** [美]一毛不拔的,守口如瓶的。**happy as a ~ (at high tide)** [美口]极幸福的。**II** *vi*. **1**. 捞蛤。**2**. [美俚]嘴紧,话少。~ **up** 嘴紧,死不开口。~**catchers** [美]新泽西州人的别号。~**-face** [美]胆小鬼。~ **trap** [美俚]嘴。**-like** *a*. 像蛤的;一言不发的。

clam[2] [klæm; klæm] *n*. [英]钳,夹子。

clam[3] [klæm; klæm] **I** *n*. [美俚](爵士音乐中)错误的音。**II** *vi*. 奏出[唱出]错音。

cla·mant [ˈkleimənt; ˋklemənt] *a*. [书] **1**. (孩子等)吵闹的,嚷的。**2**. 紧急的,迫切的,迫在眉睫的。

clam·a·to·ri·al [ˌklæməˈtɔːriəl; ˏklæməˋtɔrɪəl] *a*.【动】鹟科的。

clam·bake [ˈklæmbeik; ˋklæmˏbek] *n*. **1**. [美](海滨)吃蛤会,以吃蛤为主的海滨旅行。**2**. [美俚]即兴爵士音乐演奏会。**3**. [美俚]不精采的广播[电视]节目。

clam·ber [ˈklæmbə; ˋklæmbɚ] **I** *vt*., *vi*. 爬,攀登。~ *down the slope* 爬下陡坡。~ *to one's feet* 爬了起来。~ **up** 攀登,爬上。**II** *n*. 攀登。

clam·my [ˈklæmi; ˋklæmɪ] *a*. **1**. 滑腻的,黏糊糊的。**2**. (蛙身等)冰冷黏湿的。**3**. (态度)冷淡的。**-mi·ly** *ad*.

clam·or·ous [ˈklæmərəs; ˋklæmərəs] *a*. 吵闹的,扰嚷的。**-ly** *ad*. **-ness** *n*.

clam·o(u)r [ˈklæmə; ˋklæmɚ] **I** *n*. 吵闹,扰嚷;(表示抗议、支持等的)叫喊,(舆论的)鼎沸,哗然。**II** *vi*. 大嚷大叫,叫喊,吵闹,喧嚷。~ *for* 叫嚣;吵吵闹闹地要求。~ *against* 吵吵闹闹地反对。—*vt*. **1**. 用吵吵嚷嚷的方法迫使。**2**. 吵吵闹闹地发出[表示]。~ *down* 吵得使(演讲者等)说不下去[把演讲者轰下台]。~ (*sb*.) *into* [*out of*] *doing sth*. 吵吵闹闹迫使(某人)做[停止做]某事。

clamp[1] [klæmp; klæmp] **I** *n*. **1**. 钳,夹子。**2**.【机】压板,压铁;【建】夹板;【船】支梁板。**II** *vt*. (用夹钳等)夹紧,夹住;(用轮卡)锁住(违犯泊车规定的汽车)。~*ing bolt*【机】夹紧螺栓。~ *down* **1**. 箝制,压迫;取缔;勒紧。**2**. 强制执行(宵禁等)。~**down** *n*. 压制,取缔。~**-screw** 制动螺旋。

clamp[2] [klæmp; klæmp] **I** *n*. [英方](砖等的)堆。**II** *vt*. 把(砖等)堆高(*up*); 堆存。

clamp[3] [klæmp; klæmp] **I** *vi*. 叭哒叭哒地行走,脚步很重地走。**II** *n*. 重踏的脚步声。

clamp·er [ˈklæmpə; ˋklæmpɚ] *n*. **1**. [*pl*.] 夹子。**2**. 接线板。**3**. (防滑用)鞋底钉。

clam·shell [ˈklæmʃel; ˋklæmˏʃɛl] *n*. 蛤壳;蛤壳状挖泥器。

clan [klæn; klæn] *n*. **1**. 克兰[苏格兰高地人的氏族,部族]。**2**. 氏族,部族;[口]家族,一门。**3**.【生】导种集团,系。**4**. 党派,小集团。**5**.【美体】队。**-ship** *n*. **1**. 氏族[部族]制度。**2**. 氏族[部族]状态。**3**. 小集团精神。

clan·des·tine [klænˈdestin; klænˋdɛstɪn] *a*. 秘密的,暗中的,私下的。~ *dealings* 秘密交易。*a ~ marriage* 秘密结婚。~ *evolution* 不知不觉中的演化。**-ly** *ad*. **-ness** *n*.

clang [klæŋ; klæŋ] **I** *vt*. 使发铿锵[叮当]声。—*vi*. **1**. 发铿锵[叮当]声。**2**. (鹤等)鸣唳。**II** *n*. **1**. 铿锵(声),叮当(声)。**2**.【乐】音色,音质,音调。**3**. (鹤,雁等嘹亮而似乎有回声的)鸣唳。

clang·er [ˈklæŋə; ˋklæŋɚ] *n*. [英口]大错误;荒唐的错误。

clan·gor·ous [ˈklæŋgərəs; ˋklæŋgərəs] *a*. 叮叮当当响的,响亮的。**-ly** *ad*.

clan·go(u)r [ˈklæŋgə; ˋklæŋgɚ] **I** *n*. 铿锵声,叮当声。**II** *vi*. 铿锵地[叮当地]响。

clank [klæŋk; klæŋk] **I** *vt*., *vi*. (使)叮当地响。**II** *n*. 叮当(声);铿锵(声)。

clan·nish [ˈklæniʃ; ˋklænɪʃ] *a*. **1**. 克兰的,部族的。**2**.

宗派的,小集团的。**-ly** *ad*. **-ness** *n*.

clans·man [ˈklænzmən; ˋklænzmən] *n*. 同氏族[部落]的人。

clap[1] [klæp; klæp] **I** *vt*. (*-pp-*) **1**. 拍,轻拍;拍打;轻敲。**2**. 振(翼),拍(翅膀)。**3**. 拍地关上[碰上,装上]。**4**. 急促地放;急忙处理。~ *one's hands* 拍手(喝彩)。~ *spurs to a horse* 急急忙忙踢马飞跑。—*vi*. **1**. 拍手。**2**. 发出噼啪声[碰撞声]。~ ***by the heels*** 捉住;逮捕;投入监狱。~ ***eyes on*** 瞥见,(偶然)看见[常与 never 等否定词连用]。~ ***hold of*** 急忙捉住。~ (*sb*.) ***in prison*** [***gaol***] 猛地(把某人)关进牢房。~ ***on*** **1**. 急忙张(帆)。**2**. 征(税)。(*sb*.) ~ ***on the back*** 用手掌拍拍(某人的)脊背(以示打招呼、称赞)。~ ***up*** **1**. 赶忙处理[办理];赶忙决定[订定、讲妥](交易、契约等)。**2**. 赶着做(椅子、箱子等)。**II** *n*. **1**. 噼拍声;破裂声。**2**. 拍手(喝彩),鼓掌;轻拍。*a* ~ *of thunder* 雷鸣,霹雳。*give him a* ~给他鼓掌。***in a*** ~ 忽然,突然;迅速地。***in two*** ~***s of a lamb's tail*** 立即,赶快,急忙。~**ped-out** [俚]精疲力尽的;(器物因过分使用,长年无人照管等而)破烂不堪的。

clap[2] [klæp; klæp] *n*. [俚][the ~] 淋病。

clap·board [ˈklæpbɔːd; ˋklæp͵bord] *n*. [美]护墙板,隔板;[英]桶板;【影】(开拍前在镜头前敲响的)音影对号板。

Clap·ham [ˈklæpəm; ˋklæpəm] *n*. 克拉彭[姓氏]。

clap·net [ˈklæpnet; ˋklæpnɛt] *n*. (捕鸟)网。

clap·om·e·ter [klæˈpɔmitə; klæˋpɑmɪtɚ] *n*. 掌声测量计。

clap·per [ˈklæpə; ˋklæpɚ] *n*. **1**. 拍手者。**2**. 铃舌;钟舌,钟铎;拍板;(田间吓鸟雀的)鸣子;[俚]舌头。**3**. [常 *pl*.]响板。***like the*** ~***s*** [英俚]迅速地,很快地。

clap·trap [ˈklæptræp; ˋklæp͵træp] **I** *n*. 哗众取宠的言语[诡计]。**II** *a*. 博人喝彩的,哗众取宠的。

claque [klæk; klæk] *n*. [F.][集合词](戏院雇用的)鼓掌者,喝彩者,捧场者;随声附和的谄媚者。

claqueur [klæˈkəː; klæˋkɝ] *n*. [F.](受雇用的)喝彩者;随声附和者,谄媚者。

clar. =【印】中长黑体铅字 (=clarendon type)。

Clar·a [ˈklɛərə; ˋklɛrə] *n*. 克莱拉[女子名]。

clar·a·bel·la [klærəˈbelə; ͵klærəˋbɛlə] *n*.【乐】风琴的强音笛音栓。

Clare [klɛə; klɛr] *n*. 克莱尔[女子名,Clara 的异体]。

Clar·ence [ˈklærəns; ˋklærəns] *n*. 克拉伦斯[男子名]。

clar·ence [ˈklærəns; ˋklærəns] *n*. (旧时伦敦街上兜揽顾客的)四轮马车。

clar·en·don [ˈklærəndən; ˋklærəndən] *n*.【印】中长黑体铅字。**C- Press** 牛津大学出版部印刷所[原为 **Clarendon** 伯爵所创办]。

clar·et [ˈklærət; ˋklærət] **I** *n*. **1**. (法国波尔多产)红葡萄酒。**2**. [美俚]血。**3**. 紫红色。*tap sb.'s* ~把人打得鼻孔出血。**II** *a*. 紫红色的。~ **colo(u)r** 紫红色。~**-colo(u)red** *a*. 紫红色的。~ **cup** 客拉冽冰汽酒[红葡萄酒、白兰地、柠檬、苏打水、冰糖、香料等调成]。

clar·i·fi·ca·tion [klærifiˈkeiʃən; klærɪfɪˋkeʃən] *n*. **1**. 澄清(作用);澄清法;净化。**2**. 说明。

clar·i·fy [ˈklærifai; ˋklærə͵faɪ] *vt*. (*-fied*; *-fy·ing*) **1**. 澄清(液体等);【生】透化。**2**. 说明,讲清楚,阐明。**3**. 使(头脑等)变清楚。—*vi*. **1**. (液体等)澄清,净化。**2**. 变得清楚易懂。

clar·i·net [ˌklæriˈnet; ͵klærəˋnɛt] *n*.【乐】单簧管。

clar·i·net·(t)ist [ˌklæriˈnetist; ͵klærɪˋnɛtɪst] *n*. 单簧管演奏者。

clar·i·on [ˈklæriən; ˋklærɪən] **I** *n*. **1**. (中世纪一种声音嘹亮的)号角[喇叭]。**2**. [主诗]号角声,清脆嘹亮的音响。**II** *a*. 响亮清澈的。

clar·i·o·net [ˌklæriəˈnet; ͵klærɪəˋnɛt] *n*. = clarinet.

Cla·ris·sa [kləˈrisə; kləˋrɪsə] *n*. 克拉丽莎[女子名]。

clar·i·ty [ˈklæriti; ˋklærətɪ] *n*. 清澈;明了;明确。

clar·keite [ˈklɑːkait; ˋklɑkaɪt] *n*.【矿】水标铀矿。

Clark(e) [klɑːk; klɑrk] *n*. 克拉克[姓氏,男子名]。

Clar·ki·a [ˈklɑːkjə; ˋklɑkjə] *n*.【美植】山字草属。

cla·ro [ˈklɑːrəu; ˋklɑro] **I** *n*. [Sp.] 一种色淡味纯的雪茄烟。**II** *a*. (雪茄烟)色味俱淡的。

clar·y [ˈklɛəri; ˋklɛrɪ] *n*.【植】鼠尾草属;南欧丹参。

clash [klæʃ; klæʃ] **I** *n*. **1**. (金属撞击的)当当声,铿锵声,叮当声。**2**. (意见、利益等的)抵触,冲突;龃龉;不一致,不调和。**3**. [美]比赛。*the border* ~*es* 国界冲突。*avoid a* ~ *with* 避免和…冲突。**II** *vt*. **1**. 使当当[叮叮]地响。**2**. 使猛撞。—*vi*. **1**. (金属)碰撞作声,当当地响。**2**. 猛撞,冲突,抵触。**3**. [美]比赛;[口](色调等)不调和 (*with*)。~ ***into*** (*sb*.) 猛地撞上(某人)。

clasp [klɑːsp; klæsp] **I** *vt*. **1**. 扣住,钩住;扣紧。**2**. 紧紧抱住;握紧;(藤等用卷须)紧紧缠住。~ ***hands*** 紧紧握手;互相结合;结成联盟。~ ***one's hands*** 两手十指交叉[哀求、绝望等的表示]。—*vi*. **1**. 扣住,钩住;扣紧。**2**. 紧紧握手。*The hook won't* ~. 这钩子钩不紧。**II** *n*. **1**. 扣子,钩子;(挂徽章的)银质棒状扣;别针。**2**. 紧握;拥抱,搂抱;握手。~ **hook** 抱合钩,弯脚钩。~ **knife** (比一般铅笔刀大些的)折叠式刀。

clasp·er [ˈklɑːspə; ˋklɑspɚ] *n*. **1**. 扣,钩,扣紧物;(卷须等)缠绕物。**2**.【动】鳍脚;交合突,交尾器官。

class [klɑːs; klæs] **I** *n*. **1**. 阶级;社会等级。**2**. 学级;班级,年级,级,班;组;(有组织的)讲习班;[美]同年毕业班;【军】同年入伍士兵。**3**. (高低、优劣的)等级;类别。**4**. [英大学](荣誉考试)优等;[俚]高级,优秀;漂亮,优雅。**5**.【生】(分类学的)纲;【矿】晶族。**6**. (一节)课。*the working* ~工人阶级。*No* ~ *today*. 今天没课。*C- is over*. 下课。*boycott* ~*es* 罢课。*the first* [*second*] ~头[二]等。*high* [*low*] ~高[低]级。*There's a good deal of* ~ *about him*. 他有很多优点。*He is not* ~ *enough*. 他没有什么了不起。***at the top of one's*** ~ 出类拔萃;居首要位置。***be no*** ~ [俚]不足道;无价值。~ ***of the field*** [美]比赛的优胜候补人。***get a*** ~ = obtain a ~. ***in a*** ~ ***by itself*** 特好,出众。***in*** ~在上课中。***in the same*** ~ [美]同一类型的,同等的。***no*** ~ [俚]等外的,极坏的,蹩脚的[用作表语]。***not in the same*** ~ ***with*** 不能同…相比,无法和…相提并论,比不上…。***obtain a*** ~ = ***take a*** ~ 毕业考试得优等。***take a*** ~ ***at*** (*Oxford*) 在(牛津大学)进荣誉班。***take a*** ~ ***of*** (*beginners*) 担任(初级)班(的教师)。***take*** ~***es in*** (*history*) 听(历史)课,选修(历史)课程。***the*** ~***es*** 上层社会;知识阶级。***the*** ~***es and masses*** 各阶级和各阶层。**II** *vt*. 把…分类,把…分等[分级];给…定等级,把…分组。—*vi*. 属于…类[等、级、组]。~ **action**【法】集体诉讼。~ **baby** [美俚]同班生中最年轻者;同班生结为夫妻所生的子女。~**book** 教科书;[美]毕业纪念册。~ **champion** 优秀选手。~ **day** [美]毕业联欢会[常作 C- D-]。~ **fellow** 同班同学。~**-for-itself** 自为的阶级。~**-in-itself** 自在的阶级。~**list** 班级名簿;[英大学]考试成绩优等生名簿。~**man** (英大学)优等考试及格生 (*opp*. passman)。~**mate** 同班生,同班同学,级友。~ **meeting** 班会,级会。~ **noun** [**name**]【语法】类名词。~**room** 教室。~ **scrap** [美]大学各级对抗比赛。~ **section**【法】共同起诉(指由一名或数名原告代表多数有共同利益关系的人提起的诉讼)。~ **work** 课堂作业。**-able** *a*. 可分类[等级]的。**-less** *a*. 无阶级的。

class. = classic; classical; classification; classified.

clas·sic [ˈklæsik; ˋklæsɪk] **I** *a*. **1**. 最优秀的,(艺术作品等)第一流的;高尚的,优雅的;模范的,标准的。**2**. 古典(派)的;古希腊[古罗马]的;有名的,有历史渊源的。**3**. 传统的;不朽的;历史上值得纪念的;与古典名著[作家]有关的。**4**. 确实的,可靠的,典型的。*modern* ~ *writers* 第一流的当代作家。*a* ~ *example* 范例,典范。~ *style* 古典派风格;简练朴素的文体。~ *taste* 高尚的趣味。***become*** ~ 被公认为杰作,被列入经典著作中。**II**

n. 1. 文豪,大艺术家;古典[经典]作家;古典主义者。2. 〔*pl*.〕古典文学,古典语言〔特指希腊、拉丁语言〕。3. 〔*pl*.〕名著,名作,杰作。4. 〔美〕争夺锦标的大赛。5. 〔俚〕传统式样女服。6. 典范,楷模;典型事例;可靠的出典。***the* ~*s*** (古希腊、罗马的)古典文学。~ **city** 〔美〕波士顿 (Boston) 市的别号〔旧时美国知识分子大都集中在该地〕。~ **myth** 希腊[罗马]的神话。~ **races** (英国传统的)五大赛马。

clas·si·cal [ˈklæsikəl; ˋklæsɪkəl] *a*. 1. (文艺等)古典的,传统的,权威的;古典文学的;古典语文的;古希腊[古罗马]的;古典主义的,经典的。2. 人文科学的,文科的。3. = classic 1. ~ **education** 古典文教育。~ **music** 古典音乐。~ **school** 古典(经济)学派。~ **silk** 【纺】次优级生丝。**-ly** *ad*.

C

clas·si·cal·ism [ˈklæsikəlizəm; ˋklæsɪkl̩ˏɪzəm] *n*. 1. 古典主义。2. 古典文体[成语、风格]。3. 古典崇拜;拟古主义,古典模仿,古希腊、罗马美术的模仿。4. 古典文学研究;古典文学[知识]。

clas·si·cal·i·ty [ˌklæsiˈkæliti; ˏklæsəˋkælətɪ] *n*. 1. 卓绝;优美,优雅。2. 精通古典文学;古典文学知识。

clas·si·cism [ˈklæsisizəm; ˋklæsəˏsɪzəm] *n*. = classicalism.

clas·si·cist [ˈklæsisist; ˋklæsəsɪst] *n*. 古典主义者;古典学者;拟古派。

clas·si·cize [ˈklæsisaiz; ˋklæsəˏsaɪz] *vt*. 使古典化。— *vi*. 模仿古典。

clas·si·fi·a·ble [ˈklæsifaiəbl; ˋklæsəˏfaɪəbl̩] *a*. 可分类的,可分等级的。

clas·si·fi·ca·tion [ˌklæsifiˈkeiʃən; ˏklæsəfəˋkeʃən] *n*. 1. 选别;分等,分级;分选。2. 【动、植】分类(法)。〔分类级别为: phylum【动】及 division【植】门,class 纲,order 目,family 科,genus 属,species 种,variety 品种〕。3. 类别;等级;(文件的)保密级。*a* ~ *yard* (车站的)调车场。

clas·si·fi·ca·to·ry [ˌklæsifiˈkeitəri; ˋklæsəfɪkəˏtorɪ] *a*. 分类上的,类别的。

clas·si·fied [ˈklæsifaid; ˋklæsəˏfaɪd] *a*. 1. 分类[分级]的。2. 机密的,保密的。~ **ad(vertising)** (报刊上的)分类广告。~ **documents** 保密文件。

clas·si·fi·er [ˈklæsifaiə; ˋklæsɪfaɪr] *n*. 1. 分类者。2. 【矿】分级机。3. 【化】分粒器。4. (汉语等中的)量词。

clas·si·fy [ˈklæsifai; ˋklæsəˏfaɪ] *vt*. 1. 把…分类[分部;分等,分级]。2. 把…列为密件。

clas·sis [ˈklæsis; ˋklæsɪs] *n*. (*pl*. *-ses* [-siːz; -siz]) 【宗】地区教会委员会〔由一地区的教会代表组成的管理教会事务的机构〕;设有教会委员会的地区。

class·y [ˈklɑːsi; ˋklæsɪ] *a*. 〔俚〕上等的,优等的;〔美俚〕漂亮的,时髦的,美丽的。**-i·ly** *ad*. **-i·ness** *n*.

clas·tic [ˈklæstik; ˋklæstɪk] *a*. 【地】碎屑状的;【生】分裂的,分解的,可分离的。

clath·rate [ˈklæθreit; ˋklæθˏret] I *a*. 1. 【植】粗筛孔状的。2. 【化】笼形的。II *n*. 【化】笼形化合[包合]物。

clat·ter [ˈklætə; ˋklætɚ] I *n*. 〔只用 *sing*.〕1. (马蹄的)得得声,(金属物品碰撞的)铿锵声,(机器等运转的)卡嗒声。2. 喊喊喳喳的谈笑声。3. 喧嚷,骚动。II *vi*. 1. 得得[铿锵,卡嗒]地响。2. 喊喊喳喳地说笑。— *vt*. 使得得[铿锵、卡嗒]地响。~ ***along*** 得得地跑;骑马飞跑。~ ***down*** 哗啦啦地落下。**-er** *n*. 得得作响的东西;饶舌者。

clat·ter·ing·ly [ˈklætəriŋli; ˋklætərɪŋlɪ] *ad*. 1. 得得[铿锵、卡嗒]响地。2. 喋喋不休地,叽叽呱呱地。

Claud(e) [klɔːd; klɔd] *n*. 克劳德〔男子名〕。

Clau·di·a [ˈklɔːdjə; ˋklɔdɪə] *n*. 克劳迪雅〔女子名〕。

clau·di·ca·tion [ˌklɔːdiˈkeiʃən; ˏklɔdəˋkeʃən] *n*. 【医】跛,跛行。

claus·al [ˈklɔːzl; ˋklɔzl̩] *a*. 1. 【语法】子句的,从句的,分句的。2. 条款的。

clause [klɔːz; klɔz] *n*. 1. (章程、条约等的)条,项;条款。2. 【语法】子句,分句,主谓结构,从句。*memorandum* ~*s* 附加条款。*penal* ~*s* 罚则。*saving* ~*s* 附则,附言。*noun* ~名词从句。*principal* [*subordinate*] ~主要[从属]分句。

claus·tral [ˈklɔːstrəl; ˋklɔstrəl] *a*. 修道院的;隐遁的。

claus·tro·pho·bi·a [ˌklɔːstrəˈfəubjə; ˏklɔstrəˋfobɪə] *n*. 【心、医】幽闭[独居]恐怖症。

claus·tro·pho·bic [ˌklɔːstrəˈfəubik; ˏklɔstrəˋfobɪk] I *a*. 【心、医】幽闭恐怖症的。II *n*. 幽闭恐怖症患者。

cla·vate, cla·vat·ed [ˈkleiveit, -veitid; ˋklevet, -vetɪd] *a*. 【植】棒状的,纺锤状的,一端粗大的。

clave [kleiv; klev] cleave² 的过去式。

cla·ver [ˈkleivə; ˋklevɚ] *n*. 〔Scot.〕闲谈;闲话。

Clav·i·ceps [ˈklæviseps; ˋklævɪsɛps] *n*. 【微】麦角菌属。

clav·i·chord [ˈklævikɔːd; ˋklævəˏkɔrd] *n*. 翼琴〔钢琴的前身〕。

clav·i·cle [ˈklævikl; ˋklævəkl̩] *n*. 【解】锁骨;棍状体。

clav·i·corn [ˈklævikɔːn; ˋklævɪkɔrn] *a*. 【动】(昆虫)锤角组的。**-ate** [-ˈkɔːneit; -ˋkɔrnet] *a*.

cla·vic·u·lar [kləˈvikjulə; kləˋvɪkjulɚ] *a*. 【解】锁骨的。

clav·i·er [ˈklæviə; ˋklævɪr] *n*. 1. (钢琴等的)键盘;(练习用)无音键盘。2. [kləˈviə; kləˋvɪr] 键盘乐器。

clav·i·form [ˈklævifɔːm; ˋklævəˏfɔrm] *a*. 棒形的。

claw [klɔː; klɔ] I *n*. 1. (动物的)爪;(蟹等的)钳;爪形器具,钩。2. 〔贬〕(瘦得像爪子一样的)手;魔爪。~ ***thumpers*** 〔美〕马里兰州人。***cut*** [***clip, pare***] ***sb.'s*** ~***s*** 斩断魔爪;解除…的武装。***draw in one's*** ~***s*** 收敛气焰,抑制怒气;放弃强硬办法。***escape from the*** ~***s of sb***. 逃出某人的魔掌。***get one's*** ~***s into*** (*sb*.) 狠狠地揍人一顿;恶意中伤某人。***in sb.'s*** ~***s*** 在某人魔掌下。II *vt*. 1. 用爪子抓[挖,掘,撕]。2. 〔英方〕搔;用爪捕捉,用手探索。3. 〔美俚〕逮捕;(人)贪婪地抓住;搜刮(钱等)。— *vi*. 用爪子抓[挖、掘、撕]。~ ***back*** 〔英〕(政府用增税等办法)设法弥补。~ ***favour*** 献媚,拍马屁。~ ***hold of*** 抓紧。***C- me and I'll*** ~ ***thee***. 善来好往,一逗一诺,互相迎合。~ ***off*** [***away***] 1. 【海】把船头转朝上风。2. 退避,摆脱。3. 责骂。~**-back** 〔英〕1. 弥补。2. 欠缺,不利。~ **bar** 撬杆,撬杠。~ **hammer** 1. 羊角榔头,拔钉锤。2. 〔俚〕燕尾服〔又叫 ~-hammer coat〕。

clax·on [ˈklæksn ˋklæksn̩] *n*. 电气警笛;【机】电器喇叭 (= klaxon)。

Clay [klei; kle] *n*. 克莱〔男子名,Clayton 的昵称〕。

clay [klei; kle] *n*. 1. 黏土;泥土。2. (相对于灵魂而言的)人体,肉体;资质,天性。3. 陶制烟斗 (= ~-pipe)。4. 黏土状物。*potter's* ~陶土。*porcelain* ~瓷土。*a man of common* ~普通人,常人。***a yard of*** ~ 陶制长烟管。***as*** ~ ***in the hands of the potter*** 要捏成什么样就是什么样;听凭摆布。***dead and turned to*** ~ 死。***feet of*** ~ 泥足〔象征站不住脚的事物〕。***moisten*** [***soak, wet***] ***one's*** ~ 饮酒。~**-cold** *a*. 土一样冷的;死的。~ **court** 黏土网球场。~**-pigeon** (投掷空中练习射击的)鸽形土靶;〔美俚〕易被捉弄的人;容易的工作。~**-pipe** 陶制烟管。~**-slate** 【地】黏板岩。~**-stone** 【地】变朽黏土岩。**-ish** *a*. 黏土(多)的;黏土似的;泥质的。

clay·bank [ˈkleiˌbæŋk; ˋkleˏbæŋk] *a*. 棕黄色的。*a* ~ *horse* 棕黄马。

clay·ey [ˈkleii; ˋkleɪ] *a*. 黏土(多)的,黏土似的;泥质的 (= clayish)。

clay·more [ˈkleimɔː; ˋklemor] *n*. 剑;(十六世纪苏格兰高地部落的)双刃大砍刀。~ **mine** (爆炸时飞出金属颗粒的)霰粒爆炸装置。

Clay·ton [ˈkleitn; ˋkletn̩] *n*. 克莱顿〔姓氏,男子名〕。

clay·to·ni·a [kləˈtəuniə; kləˋtonɪə] *n*. 1. 【植】春美草。2. 〔C-〕春美草属。

CLC = Canadian Labour Congress 加拿大劳工大会。

-cle *comb*. *f*. = -cule.

clead·ing [ˈkliːdiŋ; ˋklidɪŋ] ***n***. **1.** 【机】(汽锅等的)保热套,套板;【矿】(隧道的)护尘板,衬板,覆板。**2.** 〔Scot.〕衣服。

clean [kliːn; klin] **I** ***a***. **1.** 清洁的,干净的;未染污的;(核武器等)无放射性尘埃的。**2.** (精神、品质等)纯洁的,(历史等)清白的;不淫猥的。**3.** (心地)正直的,光明正大的,不作弊的。**4.** 彻底的,完全的,十足的。**5.** 巧妙的,高明的;干净利落的。**6.** 有洁癖的,爱干净的;洗干净的。**7.** 没有用过的,新(鲜)的;无杂质的;无瑕疵的。**8.** 没有疾病的;〔俚〕没有麻醉毒瘾的。**9.** 光洁的;整齐的,(身材、四肢等)匀称的,好看的,端正的。**10.** 〔美俚〕分文没有的,两袖清风的;〔美俚〕不暗藏枪支[毒品等]的,(船舱等)已卸空的。**11.** (肉等)可供食用的;(鱼)非产期而宜食的。**12.** (田里)不生杂草的。*lose a ～ hundred dollars* 丢了整整一百元。*wine ～ to the taste* 爽口的葡萄酒。***as ～ as a pigsty*** 〔反〕像猪圈一样干净。***be ～ in one's person*** 爱干净,服装整洁。～ ***author*** 不作猥亵描写的作家。～ ***ball*** 好球。～ ***bill of health*** 健康证明书;船内安全报告;〔口〕人事保证。～ ***bill of lading*** 【海】无故障船货提单。***have ～ hands*** = ***keep the hands ～*** 廉洁清正,无可疵议。***keep it ～*** 〔俚〕不下流,守规矩。***keep oneself ～*** 保持身体清洁干净。***lead a ～ life*** 过清白日子。***make a ～ breast of*** 完全吐露,彻底坦白;剖白。***make a ～ sweep of*** 一扫,廓清。***show a ～ pair of heels*** 一溜烟逃走,溜掉。**II** ***ad***. **1.** 完全,十分,彻底地。**2.** 干净地,清洁地。**3.** 巧妙地,干净利落地。***be ～ bowled*** 〔俚〕被打得大败。***be hit ～ in the eye*** 正打中眼睛。～ ***full*** 使满帆;扯满所有风帆。～ ***gone*** 无影无踪。～ ***wrong*** 完全错误。***come ～*** 〔俚〕吐露真情,供认。***cut ～ through*** 洞穿。**III** ***vt***. **1.** 把,弄清楚,把…收拾干净,扫除;洗涤。**2.** 把…擦干净,擦亮,刷。**3.** 收清,搬空。**4.** 【化】纯化,净化;精炼,提纯。～ *field for sowing* 整地播种。～ *sb*. 〔美〕骗取(某人)所有的钱[财物]。—***vi***. **1.** 被弄干净。**2.** 打扫,扫除,做清洁工作。～ ***away*** [***off***] 擦去,清除。～ ***down*** 清扫(墙壁等);喝干;洗(马等)。～ ***house*** 整顿,清洗(组织)。～ ***one's plate*** 吃得盘底精光。～ ***out*** 扫除干净;〔俚〕(把钱)花完,输完。～ ***up*** 收拾干净,扫除清洗,肃清,扫荡;【机】改正,加工,圆正;〔俚〕赚厚利,发财。～ ***up on*** 〔美俚〕打垮。***have one's clothes ～ed*** 送衣服去干洗。～ **anchorage** 安全抛锚处。～ **bond** 无背书公债。～**-bred** ***a***. 纯血种的。～ **copy** 清整的原稿;誊清稿。～ **credit** 【商】无条件信用书。～ **cultivation** 【农】无覆盖播种。～ **culture** 【农】单播。～**-cut** ***a***. 样子好的,好看的,轮廓鲜明的;品种优良的;正确的,明确的。～ **fallow** 【农】绝对休闲。～ **fielding** (棒球等)无懈可击的防守。～ **fingered** ***a***. 廉洁的;(手)灵巧的。～ **fish** (非产期的)食用鱼。～**-handed** ***a***. 正直的,清白的。～**-limbed** ***a***. 手足匀称的,姿势好的。～**-living** ***a***. 生活作风正派的。～ **operation** 扫荡战。～**out** 清除。～ **page** 空白页。～ **proof** 【印】清样。～ **record** 清白履历。～ **room** 净室;绝对无尘室;无菌室。～ **shave** 〔美〕无可疵议的工作,美满完成的工作。～**-shaved** 剃净胡须的;干净利落的。～ **ship** 全无收获的捕鲸船。～**-skin** 〔Aus.〕不打烙印的放牧牲畜。～ **slate** 白纸(主义)〔不受义务、口约等所拘束〕;无疵可寻的履历。～ **shot** 高明的射手。～ **stroke** (打球等)干净利落的一击。～ **sweep** 〔美〕决定性胜利,大胜。～ **talk** 清谈。～ **timber** 无节疤的木料。～ **tongue** (不说脏话的)干净嘴(*keep a ～ tongue* 不说下流话)。～**up** ***n***. **1.** 〔口〕扫除,清扫运动;【化】提纯,净化,精炼,澄清。**2.** 〔美西部〕(金矿产地等定期的)清选。**3.** 〔俚〕赚头。

clean·er [ˈkliːnə; ˋklinɚ] ***n***. **1.** 清洁工人;(干洗)洗衣工人。**2.** 洗衣店(老板)。**3.** 除垢器。*a lower ～* 【纺】下绒辊。***take sb. to the ～s*** 〔俚〕把(某人)钱财骗光,使输光。

clean·ing [ˈkliːniŋ; ˋklinɪŋ] ***n***. **1.** 清洁法;扫除;清洗,洗涤;(种子的)清选。**2.** 〔常 *pl*.〕(牛、羊等的)胞衣。**3.** 【林】除伐。**4.** 〔*pl*.〕垃圾。**5.** 〔口〕(比赛等的)惨败,输光。**6.** 〔口〕巨额利润。*a general* [*thorough*] ～大扫除。***take a ～*** (球队等)惨败。～ **brush** 枪刷,除尘毛刷。～ **doctor** 【纺】刮浆刀。～ **rod** (枪口的)通条。

clean·li·ly [ˈklenlili; ˋklɛnlɪlɪ] ***ad***. 清洁,干净。

clean·li·ness [ˈklenlinis; ˋklɛnlɪnɪs] ***n***. 清洁。

clean·ly[1] [ˈklenli; ˋklɛnlɪ] ***a***. **1.** 爱清洁的;干净的,清洁的。**2.** 〔古〕纯洁的。

clean·ly[2] [ˈkliːnli; ˋklinlɪ] ***ad***. **1.** 干净地,清洁地。**2.** 清白地,纯洁地。**3.** 【古】完全,统统。

cleanse [klenz; klɛnz] ***vt***. **1.** 把…弄清洁,把…洗干净;消毒;澄清。**2.** 净化,使(思想等)变纯洁;【圣】治愈。～ ***one's bosom of perilous stuff*** 清心寡欲。

cleans·er [ˈklenzə; ˋklɛnzɚ] ***n***. **1.** 做清洁工作的人。**2.** 清洁剂[肥皂等],去污粉;擦亮粉。**3.** 滤水器,清洁器。

cleans·ing [ˈklenziŋ; ˋklɛnzɪŋ] **I** ***n***. **1.** 〔古〕清洁化,净化。**2.** 〔*pl*.〕垃圾;(牛羊等的)胞衣。**II** ***a***. 清洁用的,洗涤用的。

clear [kliə; klɪr] **I** ***a***. **1.** (水等)清澈的,透明的;(天气等)晴朗的,明净的,爽朗的;明亮的,皎洁的。**2.** 明白的,明了的,清楚的;显明的,容易分辨的。**3.** 无遮拦的,无障碍的;畅通的;开阔的,豁然的。**4.** 无疑的,的确的,确实的。**5.** (船)已卸净(货)的。**6.** 纯粹的,十足的;整整的;净得的。**7.** 无疵瑕的;(木材)无节疤的。**8.** 脱离的,还清(债务)的;清除了(障碍等)的;摆脱了(束缚等)的(*of*)。*Do I make myself ～?* 你明白我的意思吗? *He made it ～ that* …他说明…。*The train is ～ of the station*. 火车已离开车站了。*a ～ head* 清晰的头脑。～ *intellect* [*sight*] 明智。*a ～ outline* 鲜明的轮廓。*a ～ sky* 晴空。*a ～ space* 空地。*a ～ water* 开阔无阻的水面。*roads ～ of traffic* 没有人来往的路。*a ～ width* (布的)净阔,纯幅。*a ～ profit* 纯(收)益。*a ～ month* 整整一个月。*the ～ contrary* 恰恰相反。*a ～ majority* 绝对多数,过半数。*a ～ timber* 无节疤的木料。***All ～*** 无敌机,解除警报。(***as***) ～ ***as a bell*** 很清楚;很健全。(***as***) ～ ***as day*** 极明白,显而易见。***be ～ from*** (*suspicion*) 没有(嫌疑)。***be ～ of*** (*debt*; *worry*) 无(债、忧)。～ ***as mud*** 〔美〕不明显,很模糊,一塌糊涂。***get ～ away*** [***off***] 完全离开,逃掉。***get ～ of*** 脱离,离开,避掉。***get ～ out*** 完全脱离[离开]。***keep ～ of*** 避开,离着。***see one's way ～*** 前途无阻[顺畅]。**II** ***ad***. **1.** 显然地,清楚地。**2.** 离开,不接触。**3.** 一直。*hang ～* 挂开点,挂远点。*speak loud and ～*说话又响又清楚。*five miles ～*整整五英里。～ *on to the end* 一直到底。**III** ***vt***. **1.** 使变清澈,使无污垢。**2.** 把…弄明白,使清楚。**3.** 澄清,消除(嫌疑),宣布开释,辩明(无罪)。**4.** (议案等)通过(批准手续);批准,准许。**5.** 付清;抵消,结清;清讫。**6.** 扫除,除去;赶走,驱逐;打发掉。**7.** 开垦,砍伐,开拓。**8.** 穿过,超过,跳过,通过;突破(难关)。**9.** 为(船或船货等)结关[办好出港手续],(船)结关后离开(港口)。**10.** 【商】抛卖,贱卖,脱售;交换清算(票据);兑现(支票)。**11.** 【商】净赚,净得。～ *a fishing line* 解开钓丝。～ *an examination paper* 答完所有试题。～ *the air* 祛除郁暑;扫清疑惑[疑团]。～ (*the decks*) *for action* (收拾甲板)准备战斗。～ *the hurdle* 〔美〕克服障碍,走向成功。～ *a fence* 跳过栅栏。～ *a port* 出港。～ *the land* 驶离陆地。*My car only just ～ed the lorry*. 我的车险些儿没有避开卡车。—***vi***. **1.** 变清澈,变澄清;(天气)开晴。**2.** (船只等)办清出港手续,出港(*from*);〔俚〕离去;走出;逃掉。**3.** 【商】交换票据。**4.** (文件等)送审,报批。*great reduction in order to ～*出清存货大贱卖。*The sky is ～ing*. 天正转晴。～ ***away*** 扫除,收拾(餐具);排除,砍去;(雾等)消散。～ ***expenses*** 抵消开支。～ (*1,000 pounds*) ***from*** 因…赚得(一千镑)。～ ***...of*** 从…扫清…(*～ one's mind of doubt* 消除心中疑团。～ *the city of undesirables* 驱逐不良分子出市)。～ ***off*** 完成,做好,理清(工作等);清算,了清(债务等);卖掉;驱

逐,撵走;(雨)停,(云)散;〔俚〕走掉,逃掉。~ ***oneself of*** (***a charge***) 洗清(嫌疑),表白。~ ***out*** 1. 扫出;〔俚〕掏空腰包(钱袋);卖光,出清。2. 出港;〔俚〕离去。~ ***the land*** (船)离开陆地(以免触礁)。~ ***the way*** 作好准备。~ ***up*** 1. 整顿,理清。2. 解决,说明。3. (天气)转晴,变好。**IV** ***n***. 1.【机】间隙,余隙。2.【建】中空体内部的尺寸。3. = clearance. ***in the*** ~ 1. (两边之间的)内宽。2. 自由,无罪。3. 明码,不用暗号。4.〔美俚〕没有债务。~ **cole** (打底子的)油灰。~**-cut** ***a***. 轮廓鲜明的,清晰的。~**-eyed** ***a***. 目光锐利的,能判明是非的。~**-headed** ***a***. 头脑清楚的,聪明的。~**-sighted** ***a***. 英明的,聪明的,精明的。~**starch** ***vt***., ***vi***. 给(衣服等)上浆。~**story**【建】开窗假楼;〔美〕(火车车顶下面的)气窗 (= clerestory)。~ **way** (立体交叉,限制进入,保证畅通的)超高速公路。~ **wing**【动】透翅蛾 (*Aegeriidae*)。**-ly** ***ad***. **-ness** ***n***.

clear·age [ˈkliəridʒ; ˋklɪrɪdʒ] ***n***. 清除,清理,出清。

clear·ance [ˈkliərəns; ˋklɪrəns] ***n***. 1. 清除,扫除,除去;解除。2.【林】终伐;(伐去树木后的)林间空地。3. 出[入]港证;放行证;出入港手续(机场指挥塔发出的)起飞(或降落)许可。4.【机】(公差的)公隙;余隙,间隙;【建】净空〔如车辆通过隧道时两边所留空隙〕。5.【商】结算,清算;纯益;票据交换(额)。6. 参与机密工作的许可。*a ground* ~(飞机起落轮中心的)离地距离。***for*** ~ (足球)踢球门球。~ **fee** 出港手续费。~ **permit** 出港许可;出港证。~ **sale**〔英〕出清存货大贱卖。

clear·cole [ˈkliəkəul; ˋklɪrkol] **I** ***n***. (油漆墙壁等打底用的)细白垩胶,白铅胶。**II** ***vt***. 为…上细白垩[白铅]胶。

clear·ing [ˈkliəriŋ; ˋklɪrɪŋ] ***n***. 1. 清除,扫除,除去;清洁,纯化。2. 表白,雪冤,昭雪。3.【林】集材;(森林中的)开辟地,开垦地。4.【军】扫海。5.【商】清算;(银行间的)汇划结算;票据交换;〔*pl*.〕票据交换[汇划结算]额。~ **bank** 参加票据交换的银行。~ **hospital** 野战医院。~**-house** 1. 票据交换所。2. (技术)情报交流所。~ **items** 交换项目[物件]。~ **label** 出港证。~ **lamp** (电话)话终灯。~ **line** [**mark**] (航海图上的)避险标记。~ **sheet** 交换[结算]清单。~ **station**【军】医疗后送站,师救护所。

cleat [kliːt; klit] **I** ***n***. 1. (木器;鞋后跟等上的金属或木料的)楔形加固角;【空】加强[固]角片;【电】磁夹板。2.【船】系缆角[耳];羊角。**II** ***vt***. 用楔子加固;给…装楔子。

cleav·a·ble [ˈkliːvəbl; ˋklivəbl] ***a***. 1. 劈得开的;易劈的。2.【物,矿】可解理的。**-bil·i·ty** ***n***.

cleav·age [ˈkliːvidʒ; ˋklivɪdʒ] ***n***. 1. 劈开,劈裂;劈开处。2.【生】卵裂;分裂;【矿】解理,劈理。

cleave[1] [kliːv; kliv] ***vt***. (~***d***, ***clove*** [kləuv; klov], ***cleft*** [kleft; klɛft]; ~ ***d***, ***clo·ven*** [ˈkləuvn; ˋklovn], ***cleft***; ***cleav·ing***) 1. 劈,劈开。2. 把…分成若干小部分[小派别等]。3. (船)破(浪)前进;开(路)。—***vi***. 1. (木头等顺着纹路)被劈开,裂开。2. (船等)破浪前进;(鸟等)掠过空中。~ ***down*** 劈倒。~ ***in two*** 把…劈成两半。~ ***one's way through*** 排开…前进。

cleave[2] [kliːv; kliv] ***vi***. (~***d***, ***clave*** [kleiv; klev]; ~***d***; ***cleav·ing***) 1. 死守着,坚守;坚持;依恋 (*to*);紧密结合 (*together*)。2.〔古〕黏着,黏住 (*to*)。

cleav·er [ˈkliːvə; ˋklivɚ] ***n***. 1. 劈东西的人[器具];切肉大菜刀。2. (冰河或雪原的)岩脊。

cleav·ers [ˈkliːvəz; ˋklivɚz] ***n***. 〔*sing*., *pl*.〕1.【植】八重葎,猪殃殃。2.〔英方〕杂草(丛)。

cleek, cleik [kliːk; klik] ***n***. 1.〔主 Scot.〕铁钩;挂钩。2. 高尔夫球铁头球棒。

clef [klef; klɛf] ***n***.【乐】谱号。*F* [*G*] ~低[高]音谱号。

cleft[1] [kleft; klɛft] **I** cleave[1]的过去式和过去分词。**II** ***a***. 劈开的,裂开的;【植】尖裂的,半裂的。***in a*** ~ ***stick*** 进退两难。~**-grafting**【园艺】劈接(法)。~ **lip** 兔唇。~ **palate** 裂腭。~ **sentence**【语法】分裂句。

cleft[2] [kleft; klɛft] ***n***. 1. 裂缝,裂口,裂痕,V 字形凹刻。2. 裂片。

cleg [kleg; klɛg] ***n***.〔英〕虻,马蝇,牛蝇。

cleis·tog·a·mous [klaisˈtɔgəməs; klaɪsˋtɑgəməs], **cleis·to·gam·ic** [-təˈgæmik; -təˋgæmɪk] ***a***.【植】闭花受精的。

cleis·tog·a·my [klaisˈtɔgəmi; klaɪsˋtɑgəmɪ] ***n***.【植】闭花受精。

clem [klem; klɛm] ***vt***., ***vi***〔英方〕(使)挨饿,(使)受饥渴寒冷之苦。

Clem·a·tis [ˈklemətis; ˋklɛmətɪs] ***n***.【植】女萎属;〔c-〕女萎,铁线莲。

clem·en·cy [ˈklemənsi; ˋklɛmənsɪ] ***n***. 1. (气候等的)温和,温暖。2. 仁慈,宽厚。

Clem·ens [ˈklemənz; ˋklɛmənz] ***n***. 克莱门斯〔姓氏〕。**Samuel Langhorne** ~ 塞缪尔·克莱门斯〔美国小说家 **Mark Twain** 的真实姓名〕。

clem·ent [ˈklemənt; ˋklɛmənt] ***a***. 1. 仁慈的,宽厚的,宽大的。2. (气候)温和的,温暖的。

Clem·ent [ˈklemənt; ˋklɛmənt] ***n***. 克莱门特〔男子名〕。

clench [klentʃ; klɛntʃ] **I** ***vt***. 1. 握紧(拳头);咬紧(牙关)。2. (为加固目的)敲弯(钉头);敲紧,敲牢。3. 捏紧,抓牢。4. 解决,确定(论据等);决定(交易等)。~ *a bargain* 定契约。~ *one's teeth* [*jaws*] 咬紧牙关;下决心。—***vi***.〔通常用 clinch〕(铆钉等)钉牢;【拳】揪扭,扭住;(手)握紧;咬紧。**II** ***n***. 1. 敲弯的钉头。2. 钉牢;咬紧牙关;咬牙切齿。3.【拳】揪扭。

clench·er [ˈklentʃə; ˋklɛntʃɚ] ***n***. = clincher.

cle·o·me [kliˈəumi; klɪˋomɪ] ***n***.【植】醉蝶花,紫龙须;〔C-〕醉蝶花属,紫龙须属。

Cle·o·pa·tra [kliəˈpɑːtrə; ˏklɪəˋpetrə] ***n***. 1. 克娄巴特拉〔女子名〕。2. (古埃及)克娄巴特拉女王〔公元前 69—30〕;〔喻〕绝世美人。3.〔c-〕鲜蓝色。~***'s needle*** 古埃及方尖碑〔指现已被移置伦敦泰晤士河畔及纽约中央公园的两块〕。~***'s nose***〔喻〕历史发展中的偶然性因素,克娄巴特拉之鼻〔意谓她的容貌假如不美,就会使由此引起的一系列历史事件改观云云〕。

clepe [kliːp; klip] ***vt***. 1.〔废〕呼唤(人),对(人)说话。2.〔古〕呼名;命名。★过去分词通常使用已废弃的 yclept, ycleped.

clep·sy·dra [ˈklepsidrə; ˋklɛpsɪdrə] ***n***. (*pl*. ~***s***, ***-drae*** [-driː; -dri]) 漏壶,水漏,铜壶滴漏〔古代计时器〕。

clep·to·ma·ni·a [ˌkleptəˈmeinjə; ˏklɛptəˋmeniə] ***n***.【心、医】盗癖,偷窃癖 (= kleptmania)。

clere·sto·ry [ˈkliəstəri; ˋklɪˏstorɪ] ***n***. 1. 天窗;高侧窗;长廊,楼座。2. (火车车顶下面的)气窗 (= clearstory)。

cler·gy [ˈkləːdʒi; ˋklɝdʒɪ] ***n***. 1. 教士[牧师]职务;〔集合词〕教士,牧师。2.〔废〕学问。

cler·gy·man [ˈkləːdʒimən; ˋklɝdʒɪmən] ***n***. (*pl*. ***clergy·men***) 教士,牧师。~***'s sore throat***【医】(因说话过多所患的)慢性喉头炎。~***'s week*** [***fortnight***] 包括两个[三个]星期日的假期。

cler·gy·wom·an [ˈkləːdʒiˌwumən; ˋklɝdʒɪˏwʊmən] ***n***. (*pl*. ***cler·gy·wo·men*** [-ˌwimin; -ˏwɪmɪn]) 1. 女牧师,女教士。2.〔谑〕牧师太太,牧师小姐;牧师的女性家属。

cler·ic [ˈklerik; ˋklɛrɪk] **I** ***n***. 教士,牧师;教堂[宗教机构]中的工作人员。**II** ***a***.〔古〕= clerical **1**.

cler·i·cal [ˈklerikəl; ˋklɛrɪkəl] **I** ***a***. 1. 教士的,牧师的。2. 职员[办事员,事务员]的,办公室工作的。**II** ***n***. 1. 牧师,教士。2.〔贬〕(议会中主张扩张教士势力的)教士派议员。3.〔*pl*.〕牧师服,教士服。~ **error** 笔误。~ **force** 职员们,事务员们。~ **staff** (全体)职员,办事员。~ **type** 书写体。~ **work** 文书工作,事务,杂务。**-ism** ***n***. 教权主义;教士(不应有的)权力。**-ist** ***n***. 教权主义者。**-ly** ***ad***.

cler·i·sy [ˈklerisi; ˋklɛrɪsɪ] ***n***.〔旧〕知识阶层,(作为一个阶层的)受过相当教育的人们。

clerk [klɑːk, Am. kləːk; klɑk, klɝk] **I** ***n***. 1. (银行、公

司等的)事务员,办事员,职员,管理员;〔美〕(商店的)店员。2.【宗】教会文书,执事。3.(团体等的)秘书。4.〔古〕牧师,教士;识字的人,学者。*a town* ～市政府的公务员。*a bank* ～银行职员。*a correspondence* ～处理信件的秘书。*a* ～ *of the works* 监工。～ ***in holy orders*** 牧师,教士〔英国教会的正式用语〕。～ ***of St. Nicholas*** = ***St. Nicholas's*** ～ 盗贼,路劫。***C- of the Weather*** 风伯雨师;〔美谑〕气象台长。**II** ***vi.*** 担任事务员[职员];〔美〕做店员。

clerk·dom [ˈklɑːkdəm; ˋklɝkdəm] ***n.*** 职员的身分[职位]。

clerk·ly [ˈklɑːkli; ˋklɝklɪ] ***a.***, ***ad.*** 1.〔古〕教士(似)的[地]。2. 职员的[地]。3.〔古〕学者似的[地];善书写的[地]。～ **hand** 学者一样的笔迹。

clerk·ship [ˈklɑːkʃip; ˋklɝkʃɪp] ***n.*** 1. 职员的职位[身分];牧师的职位。2.〔古〕博学。3.(医科学生的)住院实习。

cleve·ite [ˈkliːvait; ˋklivaɪt] ***n.***【矿】钇铀矿。

Cleve·land [ˈkliːvlənd; ˋklivlənd] ***n.*** 1. 克利夫兰〔美国城市〕。2. 克利夫兰〔姓氏〕。

clev·er [ˈklevə; ˋklevɚ] ***a.*** 1. 灵巧的,能干的;聪明的;伶俐的,机敏的。2.〔美方〕性情温良的,和蔼可亲的。3.〔美方〕英俊的,神气的;壮健的;姿态美好的;风采优雅的。*He is* ～ *at cricket.* 他擅长板球。～ *fingers* 巧手,妙手。～ ***horse*** 善能跳越障碍物的马。～ ***dog***〔美俚〕聪明乖觉的人。**-ish** ***a.*** 有小聪明的,灵巧的。**-ly** 1. ***ad.*** 灵巧,能干;聪明;伶俐;机敏;〔方〕完全,全然。2. ***a.***〔美俚〕壮健,结实。**-ness** ***n.***

clev·is [ˈklevis; ˋklɛvɪs] ***n.***(连接拖车等用的)U字形铁扣,两齿叉形接头。

clew [kluː; klu] **I** ***n.*** 1. 线团,线球;(希腊神话中带人出迷宫的)引路线;(解决问题等的)线索,暗示。2.【海】帆耳〔横帆的下角及纵帆的后角〕;帆下角的铁圈。3.〔*pl.*〕吊床两头的绳子。***from*** ～ ***to earing*** 由(帆的)一角到另一角;从头到尾;完全地。***spread a large*** [***small***] ～ 多上[少上]风帆;大张[收缩]气势。**II** ***vt.*** 1. 把…绕成线球。2. 扯(帆)上桁。～ ***down*** (*a sail*)(张帆时)拉下风篷。～ ***up*** 1. 绕线球。2. 把帆下角扯到桁上;完成(工作)。

cli·ché [ˈkliːʃei, Am. kliːˈʃei; ˋkliʃe, kliˋʃe] **I** ***n.***〔F.〕【印】电铸版,(由纸型翻铸的)铅版;〔喻〕陈词滥调,老生常谈;(小说等)陈腐的题材[场面]。**II** ***a.*** 陈腐的。

click[1] [klik; klɪk] **I** ***vi.*** 1.(开枪扣扳机,关门上锁时)卡嗒一声响。2. 哇啦哇啦地说。3.【计】鼠击。*The pistol* ～*ed empty.* 手枪卡嗒一声射出子弹。*The door* ～*ed shut.* 门卡嗒一声关上。—***vt.*** 1. 使卡嗒响。2.(马)碰响(前后蹄铁掌)。3.【计】按击(鼠标)。～ *one's heels* (*together*)(兵士等敬礼时)卡地一声并拢双脚。～ *the door* 卡嗒一声关上门。**II** ***n.*** 1. 卡嗒声,的答声;啧啧声。2. 门闩,插锁;【机】棘爪,挡爪。3.【语音】(非洲霍屯督语,布须曼语等的)倒吸气音。4.【计】(鼠标的)点击。～**-beetle** 叩头虫。

click[2] [klik; klɪk] ***vi.*** 1. 正相吻合;一见如故;情投意合;(男女)一见倾心。2.〔美俚〕成功;做得好,达到目的;(演技)博得喝彩,大受欢迎;赌赢。

click·er [ˈklikə; ˋklɪkɚ] ***n.*** 1.【英印】排字工头。2. 制鞋工头。

click·e·ty·clack [ˈklikətiˈklæk; ˋklɪkətɪˋklæk] **I** ***n.*** 火车车轮的咔哒声。**II** ***vi.*** 发出车轮的咔哒声。

cli·ent [ˈklaiənt; ˋklaɪənt] ***n.*** 1. 诉讼[辩护]委托人;顾客,客人。2.〔古罗马〕(依附贵族的)门客;受保护者,依附他人者。3. 附庸国(=～ state)。～ **(-)server**【计】客户服务器。**-less** ***a.***(律师等)没有人委托的;(商店等)没有顾客的。

cli·ent·age [ˈklaiəntidʒ; ˋklaɪəntɪdʒ] ***n.*** 1. 委托关系;保护关系。2. = clientele.

cli·en·tele [ˌkliːɑ̃ːnˈteil; ˏklaɪənˋtɛl]〔集合词〕***n.*** 1. 诉讼委托人;顾客;(戏院的)常客。2. 被保护者;追随者。

cliff [klif; klɪf] ***n.***(海岸等的)峭壁,断崖,绝壁,悬岩。*walls of a* ～断崖侧面。～ **dweller**〔俚〕1. 住公寓大厦的人。2. 美国西南史前印第安悬岩洞人。～**-hanger** (连载的)惊险小说;惊险[紧张]的事件[比赛]。～**-hanging** ***a.*** 扣人心弦的。～ **swallow** 崖燕。

Clif·ford [ˈklifəd; ˋklɪfɚd] ***n.*** 克利福德〔姓氏,男子名〕。

cliffs·man [ˈklifsmən; ˋklɪfsmən] ***n.*** 惯于攀登险崖的人。

cliff·y [ˈklifi; ˋklɪfɪ] ***a.*** 有峭壁陡岩的,险峻的。

cli·mac·ter·ic [klaiˈmæktərik; klaɪˋmæktərɪk] **I** ***n.*** (女性的)更年期,绝经期;(果实的)完熟期;(据信人的命运每七年一次的)关口,转折点。***the grand*** ～ 大关〔据信为63岁〕。**II** ***a.*** = **climac·teri·cal** [klaiməkˈterikl; klaɪməkˋtɛrɪkl̩] 更年期的;危机的;关口上的。

cli·mac·tic [klaiˈmæktik; klaɪˋmæktɪk] ***a.*** 极点的,顶点的,高潮的。**-al·ly** ***ad.***

cli·mate [ˈklaimit; ˋklaɪmɪt] ***n.*** 1. 气候;水土,风土;地带。2.(社会思想等的)趋势,倾向,风气,思潮。*continental* [*marine*] ～大陆性[海洋性]气候。

cli·mat·ic [klaiˈmætik; klaɪˋmætɪk] ***a.*** 1. 气候的,水土的,风土的。2. 一般趋势的,风气的。～ **year**〔美〕气候年〔10月1日——次年9月30日〕。**-al·ly** ***ad.***

cli·ma·tol·o·gy [ˌklaiməˈtɔlədʒi; ˏklaɪməˋtɑlədʒɪ] ***n.*** 气候学,风土学。**-log·ic** ***a.***

cli·ma·tron [ˈklaimətrən; ˋklaɪmətrən] ***n.***(大型不分隔的)人工气候室。

cli·max [ˈklaimæks; ˋklaɪmæks] **I** ***n.*** 1.【修】渐强(而达顶点的)修辞法。2. 顶点,最高峰,极点;(事件的)高潮。3.【生】顶极(群落),演替顶极。***come to a*** ～ 达到顶点,达到高潮。**II** ***vi.***, ***vt.***(使)达到顶点[高潮]。～ **forest stage**【林】最后森林阶段。

climb [klaim; klaɪm] **I** ***vi.*** 1. 攀登,爬上;(太阳等)徐徐上升;(飞机)爬高;(植物)攀缘向上。2. 向上爬,钻营。3.(物价)上涨;(数目)渐增。—***vt.*** 1. 爬,攀登,爬上。2.(植物)依附…攀缘向上。3. 使(飞机)爬高。～ (*up*) *a mountain* [*tree*] 爬山[树]。*The sun has* ～*ed the sky.* 太阳已经高照。～ ***aboard***〔美〕上车。～ ***down*** 爬下来;(从高位)退下来;断念,放弃(要求);让步,屈服。～ ***into the square***〔美〕爬上拳击台开始比赛。～ ***into*** [***out of***] ***one's overalls*** 匆忙穿上[脱下]工作服。～ ***on the band wagon***〔美〕加入轰轰烈烈的运动;和群众共同行动。～ **over** (*a wall*) 翻过(墙壁)。～ ***the rigging*** 发脾气。～ ***through the ropes***〔美〕= ～ into the square. ～ ***to power*** 爬到掌权地位,掌权。～ ***up*** 攀登,冒险爬。**II** ***n.*** 1. 攀登;【空】爬高。2. 需要攀登的地方,山坡。～**-down** ***n.*** 1. 向下爬。2.〔口〕(议论等的)让步;退让,屈服;(声明的)爬回。～**-out**【空】急速爬升。

climb·a·ble [ˈklaiməbl; ˋklaɪməbl̩] ***a.*** 可攀登的,爬得上去的。

climb·er [ˈklaimə; ˋklaɪmə] ***n.*** 1. 爬山者。2.【植】攀缘植物;【动】〔*pl.*〕攀禽类〔啄木鸟等〕。3.〔喻〕野心家,向上爬的人。4.(登山靴上的)助爬钉。

climb·ing [ˈklaimiŋ; ˋklaɪmɪŋ] **I** ***a.*** 攀缘而上的;上升的。**II** ***n.*** 攀登;【空】爬升。～ **angle**【空】上升角。～ **fern**【植】蟹草属。～ **fish** [**perch**]【动】攀木鱼。～**iron** ***n.*** 攀树器;〔*pl.*〕(登山鞋上的)助爬钉。～ **plant**【植】攀缘植物。～ **power**【空】上升力。～ **turn**【空】上升盘旋。

clime [klaim; klaɪm] ***n.***〔诗〕地区;气候,风土。

cli·mo·graph [ˈklaiməgræf; ˋklaɪməˏgræf] ***n.*** 气象图。

cli·nan·dri·um [kliˈnændriəm; klɪˋnændrɪəm] ***n.*** (*pl.* **-dri·a** [-ə; -ə])【植】某些兰科植物的药床。

clinch [klintʃ; klɪntʃ] ***n.***, ***vt.***, ***vi.*** 1. = clench. 2.〔美俚〕热烈拥抱。

clinch·er [ˈklintʃə; ˋklɪntʃɚ] ***n.*** 1. 敲弯钉尖的用具;紧钳,夹子。2.〔口〕定论,无可置辩的议论。3.(汽车的)钳

C

入[紧钳]式轮胎。*That's a* ～.那就叫我没话可说了。～**-built** *a*. =clinker-built。

cline [klain; klaɪn] *n*.【生】(物种演变曲线中的)倾斜。**-nal** *a*.

cling [kliŋ; klɪŋ] *vi*. (*clung* [klʌŋ; klʌŋ]) 1. 黏住;缠住,绕住;抱住 (*to*)。2. 沿(岸)前进,贴着(墙)走 (*to*)。3. 依恋(朋友等);依靠,依附;赖住,守牢(家庭);抱定(希望);坚信,坚持,墨守 (*to*)。～ ***like grim death to*** 死抱住…不放。～ ***to the last hope*** 抱定最后希望,决不灰心。～ ***to the peak*** 【美棒球】保持联赛中的最高地位。～**ing garments** 紧身衣。～**ing vine**〔美俚〕惯于依靠男人的妇女。

cling·fish [ˈkliŋˌfiʃ; ˋklɪŋ,fɪʃ] *n*. (*pl*. ～, ～*es*)【动】腹印鱼目 (*Xenopterygii*) 的鱼。

cling·stone [ˈkliŋstəun; ˋklɪŋ,ston] *n*. (果肉与核分离不开的)黏核桃。

cling·y [ˈkliŋi; ˋklɪŋɪ] *a*.〔罕〕黏住的,紧贴的。

clin·ic [ˈklinik; ˋklɪnɪk] *n*. 1. 临床讲授;临床实习课。2. 诊所;门诊部。3. 特殊病例分析;会诊。

clin·i·cal [ˈklinikəl; ˋklɪnɪkəl] *a*. 1. 临床(讲授)的;病房(用)的;诊所的。2. (态度等)冷静的,慎重的。～ **lectures** 临床讲义。～ **medicine** 临床医学。～ **thermometer** 体温表。**-ly** *ad*.

cli·ni·cian [kliˈniʃən; klɪˋnɪʃən] *n*. 临床医师,门诊医师[心理学家]。

cli·nique [kliˈniːk; klɪˋnik] *n*.〔F.〕临床讲义。

clink[1] [kliŋk; klɪŋk] I *vi*., *vt*. 1. (使)叮当地响。2.〔诗〕(使)押韵。3.〔英方〕痛打。～ *one's money in one's pocket* 使钱在口袋里叮当叮当地响。～ *glasses* (干杯时)叮当碰杯。～ ***down*** [***off***]〔英方〕急忙走开。II *n*. 1. 叮当声。2.〔Scot.〕〔俚〕硬币,现金。3.〔方〕瞬间。4.〔俚〕猛击;搬弄是非。5. 音韵。6.【冶】裂缝。

clink[2] [kliŋk; klɪŋk] *n*.〔英口〕监狱。***be in*** ～ 在坐牢。

clink·er[1] [ˈkliŋkə; ˋklɪŋkə] I *n*. 1. 炼砖,缸砖,硬砖。2.【冶】渣块,烧结块,铁渣;煤渣。3.〔美俚〕饼干。4.〔*pl*.〕〔美俚〕硬币;现金;系囚犯的铁链。5.〔俚〕大错;大失败。6.【拳】猛击。～*-free cement* 无熟料水泥。II *vt*., *vi*. (使)矿石[煤等](在燃烧中)结成硬块,炼渣。

clink·er[2] [ˈkliŋkə; ˋklɪŋkɚ] *n*.〔英俚〕上等品,极好的东西。*a regular* ～ 上等品;妙人。

clink·er-built [ˈkliŋkəˌbilt; ˋklɪŋkɚ,bɪlt] *a*.【船】重叠搭造的,鳞状搭造的〔指木船言,铁船用 lap-jointed〕。

clink·ing [ˈkliŋkiŋ; ˋklɪŋkɪŋ] I *a*. 1. 叮当叮当响的。2.〔英俚〕无比的,无上的,极好的。II *ad*.〔英俚〕很,极。*a* ～ *fine day* 天气极好的日子。

clink·stone [ˈkliŋkˌstəun; ˋklɪŋk,ston] *n*.【矿】响岩。

cli·nom·e·ter [klaiˈnɔmitə; klaɪˋnɑmətɚ] *n*.【机】倾斜仪,测角器;磁倾计。*a gyroscopic* ～【空】陀螺式倾斜仪。

clin·quant [ˈkliŋkənt; ˋklɪŋkənt] I *a*.〔古〕金光闪闪的,银光闪闪的;闪亮的。II *n*.〔古〕镀金叶子;(金属)箔,仿金箔。

Clin·ton [ˈklintən; ˋklɪntən] *n*. 克林顿〔姓氏,男子名〕。

clin·to·ni·a [klinˈtəuniə; klɪnˋtonɪə] *n*.【植】七筋菇;〔C-〕七筋菇属。

Cli·o [ˈklaiəu; ˋklaɪo] *n*. 1. 克莱奥〔女子名〕(Gr. = famous)。2.【希神】主管历史,史诗的女神。3.〔美〕(每年授与广播、电视广告节目中最佳制作或表演等的)克莱奥女神奖。

clip[1] [klip; klɪp] I *vt*. (***clipped*** [-t; -t]; ***clipped***, ***clipt*** [klipt; klɪpt]; ～**·ping**) 1. 剪去,剪短,修剪;剪取;轧(车票等);〔美〕剪辑(报纸等)。2. 删削;削减。3. (拼法,发音等)省略,缩略,说漏(语音)。4.〔美俚〕殴打,痛打。5.〔俚〕诈骗(钱财)。～ *sheep* 剪羊毛。～ *one's hair close* 把头发剪短。—*vi*. 1. 剪下,剪短;剪辑。2.〔口〕急走,飞跑,快速动作。～ ***and keep*** (剪下后保存起来)剪贴。～ ***sb.'s wings*** 剪掉翅膀,使某人活跃不起来,使无能为力。～ ***one's words*** 发音不明,使语尾变浊。***clipped words*** 缩略词〔例如 bus (< omnibus), ad (< advertisement)〕。II *n*. 1. 剪短,修剪;〔*pl*.〕剪刀,指甲刀。2. 一剪,(一季或一次的)剪毛量。3.〔美俚〕痛打;鞭子的一抽。4.〔口〕快速动作,进度,速度。5.〔美口〕一次,一度。***a*** ～ ***on the ear*** 一个耳光。(*a week*) ***at a*** ～ 连续(一星期)。***at one*** ～ 一次。***go at a good*** ～ 飞快地去。～ **joint**〔美俚〕索价高昂的咖啡馆[夜总会等];专敲顾客竹杠的场所。～ **sheet** (为剪贴方便而)单面排印的新闻[通告等]。

clip[2] [klip; klɪp] I *n*. 1. 夹子,钳子;纸夹,钢夹;曲别针;可别在衣服上的装饰物。2.【军】(机关枪的)弹夹。3.【无】接线柱。*a diamond* ～一枚钻石别针。II *vt*., *vi*. (*-pp-*) 1. 握紧;夹牢;紧紧围住;〔古〕拥抱。2. (美式足球中)在(对方球员)身后冲撞[下绊]。～**board** 有夹纸装置的书写板;【计】文件夹式计算机,文件夹式电脑。～**-fed** *a*. (子弹)自动上膛的。～**-on** *a*. 用夹子夹上去的。

clip·per [ˈklipə; ˋklɪpɚ] *n*. 1. 剪取人;削取人;〔*pl*.〕大剪刀,剪子。2. 快速大帆船;快速大飞艇;快马。3.【无】削波器,限幅器。4.〔俚〕上等品,上好的东西;第一流人物。*a nail-* ～*s* 指甲剪[刀]。*the barber's* ～*s* 理发推子。

clip·pie [ˈklipi; ˋklɪpɪ] *n*.〔口〕(电车等的)女售票员。

clip·ping [ˈklipiŋ; ˋklɪpɪŋ] I *n*. 剪断,剪裁;剪取物;〔美〕(报纸等的)剪辑(=〔英〕cutting);剪报;(报纸的)杂讯栏;〔*pl*.〕零头衣料。*the hair* ～*s* 剪下的头发。～ *bureau*〔美〕报纸、杂志资料供应社、剪报服务社。II *a*. 1. 剪的。2.〔口〕快速的。3.〔俚〕头等的,极好的;恰好的。*Come in* ～ *time*. 来得恰好。

clipt [klipt; klɪpt] clip 的过去式和过去分词。

clique [kliːk; klik] I *n*. 派系,集团,帮会;〔美俚〕棒球队。*an academical* ～学术小系派。II *vi*.〔口〕结党。

cliquey [ˈkliːki; ˋklikɪ] *a*. =cliquy.

cli·quish [ˈkliːkiʃ; ˋklikɪʃ] *a*. 有派系成见的,党同伐异的;小集团的。**-ly** *ad*. **-ness** *n*.

cli·quism [ˈkliːkizəm; ˋklikɪzm̩] *n*. 派系心,派系成见,宗派主义,小集团倾向。

cli·quy [ˈkliːki; ˋklikɪ] *a*. 有派系成见的;党同伐异的;小集团主义的。

clis·tog·a·my [klaisˈtɔgəmi; klaɪsˋtɑgəmɪ] *n*. = cleistogamy.

cli·tel·lum [klaiˈteləm; klaɪˋtɛləm] *n*. (*pl*. ***-la*** [-lə; -lə])【动】(蚯蚓等的)环带[生殖带]。

cli·to·ris [ˈklaitəris; ˋklaɪtərɪs] *n*.【解】阴核,阴蒂。

Clive [klaiv; klaɪv] *n*. 克莱夫〔姓氏,男子名〕。

clk. = clerk; clock.

clo·a·ca [kləuˈeikə; kloˋekə] *n*. (*pl*. ***-cae*** [-kiː; -ki])〔L.〕1. 下水道,阴沟,暗渠;厕所。2.【鸟】泄殖腔。

cloak [kləuk; klok] I *n*. 1. 斗篷;大氅〔有时也指有袖子的〕,外套。2. 覆盖物。3. 托辞,口实,借口;幌子,伪装。***under a*** ～ ***of*** (*snow*) 被(雪)盖着。***under the*** ～ ***of*** 1. 借口,借名,假装 (*under the* ～ *of charity* 假装慈善)。2. 在…的掩护下,趁着(*under the* ～ *of night* 趁黑)。II *vt*. 1. 给…披斗篷;给…穿外套。2. 盖,覆,遮掩,包庇。～**-and-dagger** *a*. 1. 间谍的,特务的,阴谋活动的。2. (作品、作家等描写间谍等)惊险性的。～**-and-suiter** 1. 服装店;(特指)现成服装店。2.〔美〕犹太人。

cloak-room [ˈkləukru(ː)m; ˋklok,rum] *n*. 1. (戏院等的)寄物处,衣帽间;〔美〕议员休息室;(车站的)随身物品寄存处。2.〔英,婉〕厕所。

clob·ber [ˈklɔbə; ˋklɑbɚ] *vt*.〔美俚〕1. 连续打击;打破。2. 彻底打垮。

clo·chard [klɔˈʃɑː; ˋkloʃɚd] *n*.〔F.〕流浪者,流浪乞丐。

cloche [kləuʃ; kloʃ] *n*.〔F.〕1. (圆顶狭边的)钟形女帽。2. (防植物霜害的)玻璃罩。

clock[1] [klɔk; klɑk] I *n*. 1. 钟;挂钟,座钟,上下班计时计。2.〔俚〕记秒表,卡马表;〔美俚〕〔*pl*.〕驾驶仪表,速度表,里程计。3.〔英俚〕(人的)面孔。4.〔the C-〕【天】时

钟座〔星座名〕。5.【自】(电子计算机的)时钟脉冲(器)。*a Dutch* ～(报时发杜鹃鸣声的)杜鹃钟(= cuckoo-～)。*an eight-day* ～八日上一次发条的钟。*a musical* ～八音钟。*the face of a* ～钟的字码盘。*What of the* ～?〔古谑〕= *What o'clock is it*? 现在是几点钟? *wind up the* ～上(钟的)发条。***around the*** ～ = ***round the*** ～. ～ ***calm*** 海面平静如镜。***fight the*** ～ 抢时间。***like a*** ～ 钟表似地,准确地,按部就班地。***put*** [***set***, ***turn***] ***back the*** ～ 把钟拨慢,倒拨;〔喻〕阻碍进步;复古;开倒车;隐瞒年龄;扭转历史车轮。***race the*** ～ 争分夺秒。***regulate*** [***set***] ***a*** ～ ***by*** …根据…对钟。***round the*** ～ = ***the*** ～ ***round*** 昼夜不停,连续一整天。***set ahead a*** ～ 把钟拨快。***when one's*** ～ ***strikes*** 临终。***work against the*** ～ 抢时间做完。**II** ***vt***. **1.** 为(比赛等)计时;(运动员等)用…时间跑[游]完。**2.** (用机械)记录(速度、距离、次数等)。～ *a swimmer* (用跑表)记录游泳选手的成绩。～ *five minutes for the whole distance* 用5分钟跑[游]完全程。—***vi***. (在自动计时器上)记下考勤。～ ***in*** [***out***] = ～ ***on*** [***off***] (用钟铃装置自动)鸣报开始[终止]时间;(职工用自动记录时钟)记录上班[下班]时间。～ ***in*** (*an hour*) ***at*** (*the work*) 花(一小时)在(工作上)。～**-hour** 60分钟一节课。～**maker** (制造、修理时钟的)钟匠。～**radio** 定时(开动及停止)收音机。～**watch** 报时表,自鸣钟。～**watcher** 混工作的人〔老是看钟点盼望下班〕。**-er** ***n***. (比赛等的)计时员;交通量计算员。

clock[2] [klɔk; klɑk] **I** ***n***. 袜子跟部[侧面下方]的织绣花纹。**II** ***vt***. 织[绣]上袜跟部[侧下方]花纹。

clock·ing [ˈklɔkiŋ; ˋklɑkɪŋ] ***a***. 〔英方〕(母鸡)伏窝孵卵的。

clock·like [ˈklɔkˌlaik; ˋklɑkˏlaɪk] ***a***. 准确如时钟的;时钟般有规律的。

clock·wise [ˈklɔkwaiz; ˋklɑkˏwaɪz] ***a***., ***ad***. 顺时针方向转动的[地],正转的[地]。

clock·work [ˈklɔkwəːk; ˋklɑkˏwɝk] ***n***. 钟表机构,发条装置。***like*** ～ 有规律地;精确地;准确无误地。***with*** ～ ***precision*** 简直像机械一样精确地。～ **feed** 发条。～ **toys** 有发条装置的玩具。

clod [klɔd; klɑd] **I** ***n***. **1.** (土)块,泥块。**2.** 〔the ～〕泥土;〔喻〕(相对于灵魂而言的)肉体。**3.** 牛肩肉。**4.**【矿】煤层顶底板页岩。**5.** 老粗,乡下人;呆子,傻瓜。**6.** 〔英俚〕〔*pl*.〕铜币。*a* ～ *of earth* 一块土。*break* (*up*) *the* ～*s* 耕地。*this corporeal* ～ 肉体。**II** ***vt***., ***vi***. (***-dd-***) (向…)掷土块。

clod·dish [ˈklɔdiʃ; ˋklɑdɪʃ] ***a***. **1.** 土块一样的。**2.** 土头土脑的,粗鲁的;呆笨的,笨拙的。

clod·dy [ˈklɔdi; ˋklɑdɪ] ***a***. **1.** 土块多的,土块一样的。**2.** 不值钱的。**3.** 矮而结实的。

clod·hop·per [ˈklɔdˌhɔpə; ˋklɑdˏhɑpɚ] ***n***. **1.** 〔贬〕乡下佬。**2.** 笨人,粗人。**3.** 〔*pl*.〕大土鞋〔一种笨重的大鞋子〕。

clod·hop·ping [ˈklɔdˌhɔpiŋ; ˋklɑdˏhɑpɪŋ] ***a***. 粗鲁的,乡下佬似的。

clod·pate, clod·pole, clod·poll [ˈklɔdpeit, -pəul; ˋklɑdpet, -pol] ***n***. 笨人,呆子。

clo·fi·brate [kləuˈfaibreit; kloˋfaɪbret] ***n***.【药】祛脂乙酯,安妥明。

clog [klɔg; klɑg] **I** ***n***. **1.** 阻碍,阻塞;制动器;(系在兽脚上限制其行动的)坠子;枷。**2.** 木底鞋;木屐;木屐舞。**II** ***vt***. (***-gg-***) **1.** 阻碍,妨碍。**2.** 塞满,填满(管子、道路等)。—***vi***. **1.** (油垢等)腻住,黏住;凝成一块。**2.** (容易)阻塞;(心胸)闷塞。**3.** 跳木屐舞。～**-dance** 木屐舞〔用鞋底的木块踏出响亮的拍子〕。

clog·gy [ˈklɔgi; ˋklɑgɪ] ***a***. **1.** 易黏牢的;黏糊糊的。**2.** 妨碍的,易阻塞的。

cloi·son·né [klwɑːˈzɔnei; ˏklɔɪzəˋne] **I** ***a***. 〔F.〕景泰蓝(制)的。**II** ***n***. 景泰蓝(= ～ enamel)。

clois·ter [ˈklɔistə; ˋklɔɪstɚ] **I** ***n***. **1.** 修道院,修道院生活,隐居地。**2.** (修道院、学校等地的)回廊,走廊。***the*** ～ 修道院生活,隐居。**II** ***vt***. **1.** 把…关在修道院里,使出家,使与尘世隔绝。**2.** 在…设回廊。**-ed** ***a***. **1.** 住在修道院中的,隐居的。**2.** 有走廊的。

clois·tral [ˈklɔistrəl; ˋklɔɪstrəl] ***a***. **1.** (关入)修道院的;修道院式的。**2.** 隐居的,遁世的;静寂的。

cloke [kləuk; klok] ***n***. 〔古〕= cloak.

clomb [kləum; klom] climb 的过去式和过去分词的古体。

clom·i·phene [ˈklɔməfiːn; ˋklɑməfin] ***n***.【药】克罗密芬〔一种助孕剂〕(= ～ citrate)。

clomp [klɔmp; klɑmp] ***vi***. 以刺耳的脚步声行走;顿着脚走。

clone [kləun; klon] **I** ***n***. **1.**【生】无性(繁殖)系,克隆;无性(繁殖)系个体,克隆体。**2.** 复制品;(几乎)一模一样的人。**3.** (不动脑筋)机械行事的人;机器人。**II** ***vt***.【生】无性繁殖;〔喻〕复制。*The* ～*d sheep is named Dolly*. 这只克隆羊取名为"多莉"。

clon·al [ˈkləunl; ˋklonl] ***a***.【生】无性系的。

clon·ic [ˈklɔnik; ˋklɑnɪk] ***a***.【医】阵挛(性)的。

clonk [klɔŋk; klɑŋk] **I** ***n***. 〔口〕**1.** 沉闷的金属声;沉重的一击。**2.** 〔俚〕笨蛋。**II** ***vt***., ***vi***. 发出沉闷金属声移动[撞击](= clunk)。

clo·nus [ˈkləunəs; ˋklonəs] ***n***.【医】阵挛(性)。

cloop [kluːp; klup] **I** ***n***. 砰〔拔瓶塞声〕。**II** ***vi***. 发出砰声。

clop [klɔp; klɑp] **I** ***n***. (兽蹄声似的)得得响。**II** ***vi***. (***-pp-***) 作得得响,发出脚步声[蹄声]。

clo·qué [kləuˈkei; kloˋke] ***n***. 泡泡纱(状织物)。

close[1] [kləuz; kloz] **I** ***vt***. **1.** 关(窗等),闭(眼等);盖(盖子等);锁闭,封闭,塞,隔绝。★对 door, box, drawer 等,口语较常用 shut。**2.** 完结;结束;停闭。**3.** 讲好(价钱等),商定(交易等);结清(帐目等)。**4.**【电】接通(电流);使靠拢,使接近;【海】靠近,逼近(其他船只等);【军】使(队伍)靠紧。*His eyes are* ～*d*. 他死了。*My mouth is* ～*d*. 无话可说。*That chapter is* ～*d*. 话已完结,问题已有结果。～ *a hole* 填穴。～ *a speech* 结束演说。～ *a bargain* 订约,讲好买卖,成交。～ *a discussion* (主席)宣布讨论终结。—***vi***. **1.** (门等)关上;闭合;(烟斗)塞住。**2.** 完结,结束,散会。**3.** 接近,挨近,靠近,(船)靠岸。**4.** 接战,格斗,扭打。**5.** 集合。**6.** 同意,与…一致(*on*, *upon*, *with*) ～ ***about*** [***around***, ***round***] 包围,围住,逼近…周围。～ ***sb.'s eye*** 打肿(某人的)眼睛。～ ***accounts*** 结算,清账。～ ***an account*** (清帐后)停止信用交易,停止赊购。～ ***down*** 〔美〕关掉,封闭;停止,(电台)停播。～ ***down on*** 限制,禁止;抓牢,逼迫。～ ***in*** **1.** 围拢,迫近。**2.** (白天)渐短。～ ***it up*** 靠拢(*You people* ～ *it up now*! 大家靠拢一点!)。～ ***off*** 结(账);隔离;封锁;阻塞。～ ***on*** [***upon***] 围拢,围上来;隐没;协议,同意。～ ***one's career*** [***life***, ***days***] 死。～ ***one's parent's eyes*** 给父母送终。～ ***one's purse to*** 不出钱给…。～ ***out*** 〔美〕处理(物品),抛售;〔美〕停闭(业务)。～ ***over*** 封盖;淹没。～ ***the door on*** 停止讨论…,对…关门。～ ***the door upon*** 堵塞…的门路,不给与…机会。～ ***the rank*** [***files***] **1.** 使队伍排紧,使密集。**2.** (政党等)巩固阵营,加强团结。～ ***together*** 密集。～ ***up*** **1.** 密集,靠紧。**2.** (伤)愈合。**3.** 密闭,阻塞;〔美〕结束。～ ***upon*** (手、指)握紧(某物);(箱子)关着;(夜)渐深,(眼向着某物)渐闭;死。～ ***upon*** (***the world***) 死。～ ***with*** **1.** 突击,与…肉搏。**2.** 谈妥;与…达成协议;同意,答应。***have*** [***with***] ***one's eyes*** ～***d*** 看不见;不肯看;不管,不理会。**II** ***n***. **1.** 完结,终结,终。**2.**【乐】终止(法);结尾复纵线(∥)。**3.** 肉搏(战),白刃战。**4.** (私人的)围地,围场;围墙内;学校场院。**5.** 〔英方〕(大街通到场院的)小路。***bring to a*** ～ 结束,弄完。～ ***of the year*** 年底。***come*** [***draw***] ***to a*** ～ 将完,临终。～**-down** ***n***. **1.** (工厂等的)关闭,停歇,封闭。**2.** (夜幕)降临。**3.** (电台)停止播音。

C

close[2][kləus; klos] **I** ***a*****.** **1.** 关闭着的,密闭的。**2.** 窄狭的,局促的;严密的;紧密的;严丝合缝的,吻合的。**3.** 闷气的,闷热的。**4.** 有限制的,限定的。**5.** 不公开的,秘密的。**6.** 吝啬的,小气的。**7.** 近的,紧贴的,接近的;亲密的。**8.** 密集的,稠密的。**9.** 绵密的,精密的,详细的。**10.** 危急的,千钧一发的。**11.** 差不多相等的;〔美〕(选举上)势均力敌的。**12.**【语音】闭塞音的。**13.** 禁猎的。**14.** 沉默的,嘴紧的。**15.** (钱等)难弄到的。*a ~ lid* 严密的盖子。*a hot ~ day* 闷热的日子。*Money is ~.* 钱紧。*a ~ corporation* (股票不对外公开的)内股公司。*a ~ crop* 接近根部地割剪。*a ~ combat* 肉搏战。*a ~ district* 〔美〕竞选激烈的选举区。*a ~ election* 〔美〕势均力敌的选举战。*a ~ game* 势均力敌的比赛。*a ~ friend* 亲密的朋友。*a ~ order* [*formation*]【军】密集队形。*a ~ copy* 准确的复写[复制品]。*a ~ investigation* 细查。*a ~ translation* 忠实的[准确的]翻译。*a ~ port* 闸港。*a ~ season* [〔美〕*a closed season*] 禁猎期。**II** ***ad*****.** **1.** 精密地,细密地,紧密地。**2.** 秘密地。**3.** 接近,密接;亲密地。***a ~ call*** [***thing***] 千钧一发的情况;侥幸的脱险。***a ~ shave*** **1.** 剃光头发。**2.** (差点打中的)危险的子弹,侥幸的脱险(= *a ~ shot*)。*~ about a matter* 对一件事情严守秘密。***be ~ to*** 接近;不离。***be ~ with one's money*** 用钱吝啬。***~ at hand*** 就在眼前;紧迫。***~ by*** 近,旁边。(***a***) ***~ call*** [***thing***] 〔口〕千钧一发;十分危险的情况。***~ cut*** 〔美〕近路,问道,捷径。***~ on*** (***upon***) 大概,差不多;紧接着。***~ quarters*** 狭窄拥挤处;肉搏战(*come to ~ quarters* 接战)。***~ to*** 接近于;在附近。***cut ...~*** 接近根部割剪。***fit ~*** 吻合。***live ~*** 俭约地过日子。***in ~ proximity to*** 逼近,贴近;近似。***keep ~*** 隐匿着。***keep*** (***sth.***) ***~*** 把(东西)收藏着。***lie ~*** 隐藏着。***press sb. ~*** 紧逼某人。***run sb. ~*** (赛跑)几乎赶上,紧紧跟住。***stand*** [***sit***] ***~*** 站[坐]拢。~ **breeding** 近亲繁殖。~ **buyer** 专买便宜货的人。~**-cropped**, ~**-cut** ***a*****.** (头发等)剪短的。~**-fisted** ***a*****.** 吝啬的,小气的。~**-fitting** ***a*****.** 紧身的,贴身的。~**-grained** ***a*****.** 木理细密的;有条不紊的。~**-hauled** ***a*****.**【海】迎风开的,抢风开的。~**-in** ***a*****.** **1.** 近战的。**2.** 接近(市)中心的。~**-knit** ***a*****.** **1.** 紧紧结合在一起的。**2.** (论据等)严谨的。~**-lipped**, ~**-mouthed** ***a*****.** 嘴紧的。~ **planting** 密植。~ **shot** (电影等的)近景。~ **stool** 马桶(箱)。~**-up**【影】特写;〔美俚〕精密观察;详细检查;详图;用扩音器播送出来的声音。**-ly** ***ad*****.**

closed [kləuzd; klozd] ***a*****.** **1.** 关闭着的,封闭着的;密闭着的;保密的。**2.**〔美〕准备好了的;定了契约的。**3.**【语音】闭音节的。***with ~ door*** 禁止旁听。~ **association**【植】郁闭群丛。~ **book** 未知之事,不可理解的事情。~ **bundle**【生】有限维管束。~ **caption**, **close-circuit caption** (供聋子和听力困难的人收看电视节目的)闭路字幕。~ **circuit**【无】闭路式(电视)。~**-circuit** ***a*****.** 闭路式的。~**-door** ***a*****.** 绝密的,不公开的。~**doorism** 关门主义。~**-end** ***a*****.** 资本额固定的。~ **loop**【无】闭合回路。~ **pipe** 一端封闭的管子。~ **port** 不开放海港。~ **primary** 仅由一个政党的成员参加的预选。~ **rule** (议会禁止对某一议案再提修正案的)议决规定。~ **sea** 领海(*opp.* open sea 公海)。~ **season** 禁猎或禁渔季节。

close·ness [ˈkləusnis; ˋklosnɪs] ***n*****.** **1.** 密闭,紧密;狭窄;闭塞;闷热。**2.** 接近。**3.** 严密;精密。**4.** 亲密。**5.** 吝啬。

clos·er [ˈkləuzə; ˋklozɚ] ***n*****.** **1.** 关闭者;闭塞器。**2.**【建】镶墙边的砖石。*a king* [*queen*] ~【建】去角[纵剖]砖。

clos·et [ˈklɔzit; ˋklɑzɪt] **I** ***n*****.** **1.** 内室,小间;议事室,密室。**2.**〔美〕壁橱;碗橱;衣橱。**3.** 盥洗室,厕所;抽水马桶(= water ~)。~ *consultation* 秘密会议。***of the ~*** 理论的,不切实际的。**II** ***vt*****.** 把…关进小室;把…引入内室密谈。***be ~ed with*** 与…密谈。**III** ***a*****.** **1.** 隐蔽的,暗藏的,不公开的。**2.** 闭门造车的,空谈的。~ *racist* 隐蔽的种族主义者。~ *homosexual* [*queen*, *queer*] 隐蔽的搞同性爱者。~ ***play*** [***drama***] 仅供阅读的剧本,不适宜上演的戏剧。~ ***strategist*** 纸上谈兵的战略家。

clos·ing [ˈkləuziŋ; ˋklozɪŋ] **I** ***n*****.** **1.** 封闭,停闭;封闭口;【植】郁闭。**2.** 终结,结尾;完工。**3.** (交易等的)谈妥;结账;地产成交会。**II** ***a*****.** 结尾的,末了的;闭会的。*a ~ account* 决算。*a ~ address* 闭会词。*a ~ hour* 停止营业的时间;临终时刻。*the ~ date* 决算日。*the ~ day* 截止日期。*the ~ time* 截止时间;停止时间。~ **costs** 地产成交价。~ **quotations** 收盘市价。

clos·trid·i·um [klɔsˈtridiəm; klɑsˋtrɪdɪəm] ***n*****.** (***pl*****.** ***-trid·i·a*** [-ə; -ə]) 【生】梭菌(属)。**-trid·i·al** ***a*****.**

clo·sure [ˈkləuʒə; ˋkloʒɚ] **I** ***n*****.** **1.** 关闭,停业;截止;末尾,结束;〔英议会〕终止辩论(=〔美〕cloture)。**2.** 闭塞物;【建】隔板;围墙;填塞砖;【空】节气门;【数】闭包;【机】锁合;【电】闭合;【地】闭合度。**II** ***vt*****.** 使结束,使停止辩论。

clot [klɔt; klɑt] **I** ***n*****.** **1.** 泥团;(血等的)凝块。**2.** (人、动物等的)聚集,群集。**3.**〔俚〕呆子,笨蛋。**II** ***vi*****.**, ***vt*****.** (***-tt-***) (使)凝结;(使)群集,(使)拥塞。*clotted cream* 凝结成块的奶油。*clotted hair* 结成一团的头发。**clotted** ***a*****.** **1.** 凝结的,(头发等)结成一团的;拥塞的。**2.**〔英口〕纯粹的(*clotted nonsense* 纯粹一派胡言)。

cloth [klɔ(:)θ; klɔθ] ***n*****.** (***pl*****.** ~***s*** [klɔ(:)θs; klɔ(ɑ)θs]〔用于 kinds of ~之意〕, [klɔːðz; klɔðz]〔用于 pieces of ~〔之意〕) **1.** 织物,布类,毛织品,呢绒;(一块)布;衣料;(白)桌布;擦布,揩布。**2.** (职业)制服,(特指)黑色教士服;〔the ~〕牧师,教士。**3.**【海】帆。**4.**【剧】布景画布。*American ~* 彩色防水布,人造革。*Italian ~* 意大利棉毛呢;黑色直贡呢。*long ~* 漂白细棉布。~ *merchant* 呢绒布匹商。***all ~ made***【海】满帆,鼓着风。***bound in ~*** 布面装钉的。***carry much ~***【海】张大风帆。~ ***of gold*** [***silver***] 金[银]线绵。~ ***of state*** [***estate***] 宝座背上的饰布。***cut from the same ~*** 一路货色,一丘之貉。***cut one's coat according to one's ~*** 量入为出,量布裁衣。***draw the ~*** (饭后)收拾餐桌。***have*** [***shake***] ***a ~ in the wind***〔口〕有点醉意;〔转〕穿破烂衣服。***lay the ~*** 在餐桌上铺桌布放餐具预备开饭。***made out of whole ~*** 凭空捏造。***out of the whole ~***〔美〕彻头彻尾(瞎说,谎言等)。***remove the ~*** (饭后)收拾餐桌。***renounce the ~*** (修士等)还俗。~**back** 布面装订的书。~**binding** (书的)布面装钉,布封面。~**-bound** ***a*****.** 布面装订的。~**-cap** ***a*****.**〔英〕布帽的〔指工人及劳动者〕。~**-eared** ***a*****.** 重听的,听觉不灵的。~ **ears** 重听,听觉迟钝。~ **measure** 布尺。~ **yard** **1.** 布码尺(3 英尺)。**2.** 长箭(3 英尺)。

clothe [kləuð; kloð] ***vt*****.** (***clothed***,〔古〕***clad*** [klæd; klæd]; ***clothed***, ***clad***; ***cloth·ing***) **1.** 给…穿衣,给…衣服,把衣服穿(在身上);使披上,覆盖上。**2.** (用语言)表现(思想等)。**3.** 使蒙受(耻辱)(*with*; *in*)。**4.** 赋与…以(权力、特性等)。~ *one's family* 使全家人有衣服穿。*fields ~d with trees* 树木蔽野。*be ~ with shame* 受辱,蒙耻。*be ~d* [*clad*] *in rags* 穿着破烂衣裳。*trees ~d in fresh leaves* [*with verdure*] 长满了嫩叶的树木。—***vi*****.** 穿衣服。

clothes [kləuðz; kloðz] ***n*****.** **1.** 衣服。**2.**〔集合词〕被褥。**3.** (送去洗的)衬衣被单等。*Fine ~ make the man.* 马靠鞍装人靠衣裳。***in long ~*** 在襁褓中的;幼稚的。~**bag**, ~**-basket** 盛放待洗[已洗净]衣物的袋[篮]。~**brush** 衣刷。~**horse** 晒衣架;爱穿时髦服装的人(特指女人)。~**line** 晒衣绳;〔美俚〕爱搬弄是非的人。~**man**〔俚〕旧衣商。~ **moth** (蛀蚀衣服等的)蠹虫。~ **peg**,〔美〕~**pin** (晒衣用的)衣夹。~ **pole** [**prop**] 晒衣绳支架。~**press** 衣橱。~ **tree** 柱式衣架,衣帽架。~ **wringer** 衣服绞干器。

cloth·ier [ˈkləuðiə; ˋkloðjɚ] ***n*****.** **1.** 呢绒布匹商;服装商;织造业者。**2.** 织布工,裁缝。

cloth·ing [ˈkləuðiŋ; ˋkloðɪŋ] ***n*****.** **1.**〔集合词〕衣服,衣类;被服。**2.**【海】帆装。~ **hair**【动】披毛〔披覆动物全身的

毛]。

Clo·tho [ˈkləuθəu; ˋkloθo] *n*.【希神】(命运三女神中)纺生命之线的女神,命运之神。

clot·ty [ˈklɔti; ˋklɑtɪ] *a*. 易凝固的;多团块的。

clo·ture [ˈkləutʃə; ˋklotʃɚ] **I** *n*. (美议会)辩论终结;限期结束辩论。**II** *vt*. 结束对(问题等的)辩论。

clou [kluː; klu] *n*. 〔F.〕最令人感兴趣之点;最吸引人的东西[节目,部分];中心思想。

cloud [klaud; klaʊd] **I** *n*. **1**. 云。**2**. 云状尘埃、烟(等);(鸟、虫、飞机等的)大群,大队。**3**. (水晶等的)雾斑,(镜子等上的)云斑。**4**. (显出疑惑、不满、悲哀等的)阴郁脸色;遮暗物,阴影。**5**. (编结的质地轻柔的)女围巾。**6**. (名誉等的)污点。*a* ～ *of steam* 雾气。*a* ～ *of dust* 一团尘雾。*a* ～ *of birds* (像云一样的)一大群鸟。*a* ～ *of arrows* 一阵稠密的乱箭。***a*** ～ ***of words*** 暧昧话。***be lost in a*** ～ 烟消云散。***be lost in the*** ～ 隐入云中。***blow a*** ～ 〔俚〕抽烟,吞云吐雾。***cast a*** ～ (***up***) ***on*** 在…上投下一层暗影。***Every*** ～ ***has a silver lining***. 乌云朵朵衬白底,黑夜漫漫有尽头;任何困难情况都有可盼的希望。***drop from the*** ～ 从天而降。(*lose oneself*) ***in the*** ～***s*** **1**. 在云层中;[喻]虚无飘渺。**2**. (人)空想,呆想,茫然;(事情)不落实,不现实。***kick the*** ～***s*** 〔俚〕被绞死。***on a*** ～〔俚〕满心欢喜,兴高采烈。***under a*** ～ 不得意,失宠,受嫌疑,遭白眼,处困境。***under*** ～ ***of night*** 趁黑。***wait till the*** ～***s roll by*** 等乌云散开,等时机到来。**II** *vt*. **1**. 使乌云密布,使变黑暗。**2**. 在(心)上投下苦恼的[忧愁的]暗影,使心情黯然。**3**. 破坏(名誉),损伤(友谊)。*face* ～*ed with anger* 因为生气而面色阴沉。—*vi*. **1**. 云层密布,变黑暗;(镜面等)布满云斑。**2**. (心)变忧郁,变黯然(*over*, *up*);(脸色)阴沉下来。～**berry**【植】野生黄莓。～**-built** *a*. 云一样的,空想的。～**burst** 倾盆大雨,暴雨。～**-capped** *a*. 白云笼罩着的,高耸云霄的。～ **castle** 空中楼阁,空想,幻梦。～**-compeller** 云神;〔谑〕吞云吐雾的人,抽烟人。～ **drift** 浮云,飞云。～ **chamber**【物】云室。～**-hopping**【空】云中飞行,穿云飞行。～**-kissing** *a*. 高耸云霄的。～**land** 云界,云景;幻境,仙境(=～-cuckoo)。～ **line** 幸福感,兴高采烈。～ **nine** 〔俚〕狂喜,幸福状态(*to be on* ～ *nine* 感到无比幸福)。～ **point** 浊点。～ **rack** 断云层,浮云。～**scape** 云景,云的景致;云的图画。～ **seeding** (人工降雨的)云的催化。～ **stone** 陨石。～**world** = ～land. **-less** *a*. 无云的,晴朗的。**-let** *n*. 微云,朵云,片云。

cloud·ed [ˈklaudid; ˋklaʊdɪd] *a*. **1**. 阴云密布的,阴暗的;有暗影的。**2**. (人)糊涂的。**3**. 愁容满面的。**4**. 有云状花纹的。*a* ～ *tiger* 云纹老虎。

cloud·i·ly [ˈklaudili; ˋklaʊdɪlɪ] *ad*. 云雾迷漫;黯然;朦胧。

cloud·ing [ˈklaudiŋ; ˋklaʊdɪŋ] **1**. (染色面的)云状花纹,闷光,无光泽。**2**.【无】(图像)模糊,云斑。

cloud·i·ness [ˈklaudinis; ˋklaʊdɪnɪs] *n*. 朦胧;阴暗;【化】混浊性,(混)浊度。

cloud·y [ˈklaudi; ˋklaʊdɪ] **I** *a*. **1**. 阴天的,阴云密布的。**2**. 云(状)的。**3**. 朦胧的。**4**. 愁容满面的。**5**. 受人怀疑[蔑视]的。**6**. (水晶等)带云雾纹的;(酒等)混浊的。**II** *n*. 多云天。

clough [klʌf; klʌf] *n*. 〔英方〕深谷;峡谷。

clout [klaut; klaʊt] **I** *n*. **1**. 〔古、方〕补丁;破布,碎布;布片;抹布,揩布。**2**. 婴儿的衣服。**3**. (射箭的)靶心;(箭的)命中。**4**. (鞋底的)角铁[铁片];鞋底大头钉(=～-nail);(防止磨损的)铁掌。**5**. 〔口〕(用指关节往头上的)一击,一敲;【美拳】打击;【棒球】击球。**6**. 〔美口〕势力,影响力;权势。*a* ～ *king* 击球大王。*In the* ～! 命中! **II** *vt*. **1**. 〔古、方〕(用布片等)补;用破布盖上;用布擦。**2**. 给(鞋跟等)加上铁掌;给(鞋底)钉大头钉。**3**. 〔口〕(用手)猛击,击打,敲打。～ **nail** 鞋底大头钉。～**-shoe** 穿粗布鞋的人,农民。～ **shooting** 远距离射击。**-ed** *a*. 打了补钉[铁掌]的。

clove[1] [kləuv; klov] cleave[1]的过去式。

clove[2] [kləuv; klov] *n*.【植】丁香。～ **hitch**【海】丁香结,酒瓶结。

clove[3] [kləuv; klov] *n*.【植】小鳞茎,珠芽。

clove[4] [kləuv; klov] *n*. 〔美〕溪谷,壑,峡;山路。

clo·ven [ˈkləuvn; ˋklovən] **I** *v*. cleave[1]的过去分词。**II** *a*. **1**. 劈开的,裂开的。**2**.【动】分趾的,偶蹄的。***show the*** ～ ***hoof*** [***foot***] 现原形,露马脚〔旧时以为魔鬼的脚像牛羊那样是偶蹄的〕。～**-hoofed** *a*. **1**. 偶蹄的。**2**. 恶魔的。

clo·ver [ˈkləuvə; ˋklovɚ] *n*.【植】三叶草,车轴草。*bur* ～苜蓿。*Dutch* ～白三叶草。*sweet* ～草木樨。*white* [*yellow*] *sweet* ～白花[黄花]草木樨。***in*** (***the***) ～ 养尊处优;富裕;飞黄腾达。***pigs in*** (***the***) ～暴发户。

clo·ver·leaf [ˈkləuvəliːf; ˋklovɚ,lif] **I** *n*. (*pl*. **-leaves**) 苜蓿叶形立交路口〔公路交叉点的一种天桥设计,便于四面车子畅通无阻〕。**II** *a*. (公路口等)苜蓿叶形的,立体交叉的。

Clow [kləu; klo] *n*. 克洛〔姓氏〕。

clown [klaun; klaʊn] **I** *n*. **1**. (马戏团、喜剧等中的)小丑,丑角。**2**. 乡下佬;笨拙粗鲁的人。**3**. 经常闹笑话的人;好说笑话的人;逗人笑乐的人;可笑的人。**4**. 〔美俚〕村镇警察;小气鬼,守财奴。**II** *vi*. 扮小丑;闹笑话;说笑话,逗趣。

clown·er·y [ˈklaunəri; ˋklaʊnərɪ] *n*. 滑稽;可笑;粗鲁;笨拙。

clown·ish [ˈklauniʃ; ˋklaʊnɪʃ] *a*. 滑稽的;粗鲁的;笨拙的。

cloy [klɔi; klɔɪ] *vt*. **1**. 使过饱,使吃腻(美味等)。**2**. (因享乐等过度而)使(人)腻烦(*with*)。～ *the appetite by eating too much food* 因吃油腻过多而倒了胃口。*be* ～*ed with pleasure* 享乐过度而玩腻了。—*vi*. 过饱,倒胃口,吃腻;玩腻。

cloze [kləuz; kloz] *a*.【教】补漏测验法的。～ **procedure**【教】补漏测验法〔语文教学中,教师在选读一段文字时,有计划地缺漏一些单字,看学生能否补足,以便测验学生的语文能力〕。

C.L.R. = Central London Railway 〔英〕伦敦中央铁道。

CLT = Computer Language Translator 计算机语言翻译程序。

CLU = Chartered Life Underwriter 特许人寿保险人。

club [klʌb; klʌb] **I** *n*. **1**. 棍棒;(马球等的)球棒;【生】锤节,(昆虫触角中的)棒,棒状构造[器官]。**2**. 俱乐部,夜总会,会,社,(俱乐部等的)会所。**3**. (纸牌的)梅花;〔*pl*.〕一组梅花牌。*an Alpine* ～ 登山俱乐部。*a compaign* ～ 〔美〕竞选俱乐部。*Indian* ～*s* (体操用)健身棒。***be on the*** ～得到互助会的金钱支援。***Christmas*** ～ 圣诞礼品储金〔每月储蓄一个固定数目,到十二月份付还〕。**II** *vt*. **1**. 用棍棒打;把(枪等)当棍棒用;使形成棒状物,把(头发等)束集成棍棒状。**2**. 凑集(款项等),贡献(意见等)。**3**. 〔主英〕使乱成一团。～ *a dog to death* 用棍子打死一只狗。～ *a rifle* 倒拿着枪(当棍子用)。—*vi*. **1**. 组成俱乐部,联合(*together*, *with*)。**2**. 共摊费用。**III** *a*. **1**. 俱乐部的。**2**. 客饭性质的〔不自行点菜〕。～**foot** 畸形足。～**footed** *a*. 畸形足的。～ **hair** 杵状毛。～**hand** 畸形手。～**haul** *vt*.【海】弃锚抢风把(船)掉转方向〔避往下风海岸〕。～**house** 俱乐部会所,运动员更衣室。～**land** (伦敦 St. James's 宫附近俱乐部集中的)俱乐部区。～ **law** 暴力政治。～**man** 俱乐部会员;〔美〕交际家;〔英〕拿棍棒的人。～ **moss**【植】石松。～**room** 俱乐部礼堂[聚会厅]。～ **root**【植】根肿病。～ **sandwich** 〔美〕鸡肉夹心烤面包。～ **steak** 小牛排。～**woman** 俱乐部女会员;爱往俱乐部交际的女人。

club·(b)a·ble [ˈklʌbəbl; ˋklʌbəbḷ] *a*. 合乎俱乐部会员资格的,爱交际的,善于交际的。

club·bed [klʌbd; klʌbd] *n*. 棒状的〔指畸形的手、植物、果实等〕。

C

club·by [ˈklʌbi; ˋklʌbɪ] *a*. 〔口〕 **1**. 亲切近人的,热忱对人的。**2**. (某些俱乐部)会员资格限制很严的,排他的。

cluck[1] [klʌk; klʌk] **I** *vi*. **1**. (母鸡)咯咯地叫。**2**. (谈话中)发出吸气声。**II** *n*. **1**. 咯咯地叫声。**2**. (言谈中的)吸气声,啧啧的赞叹声。

cluck[2] [klʌk; klʌk] *n*. 〔俚〕傻瓜,糊涂虫。

clue [kluː; klu] **I** *n*. (调查、研究等的)线索;迹象;(故事的)关键情节;〔罕〕= clew. *give a* ～提供线索。**II** *vt*. 为…提供线索;提示。

clum·ber [ˈklʌmbə; ˋklʌmbɚ] *n*. 〔或 C-〕矮脚长耳猎犬。

clump [klʌmp; klʌmp] **I** *n*. **1**. 丛,薮;树丛;密集的大群人[建筑物]。**2**. 沉重的脚步声;加厚(皮)鞋底;根基。**3**. (土、细菌等的)凝集硬块;一团,一块。～*s of Frenchmen* 一大群法国人。**II** *vt*. **1**. 把…栽成一丛;使成群;使结块[结团]。**2**. 给(靴子)加厚鞋底。—*vi*. **1**. 用沉重的脚步行走。**2**. 丛生;【生】群生;成群;结块[团]。～ **block** 【海】强厚滑车。～ **foot** 畸形足 (= clubfoot)。～ **sole** 特厚鞋底。

clump·y [ˈklʌmpi; ˋklʌmpɪ] *a*. 凝块的;多树丛的;笨重的。

clum·si·ly [ˈklʌmzili; ˋklʌmzɪlɪ] *ad*. 笨拙,粗陋;粗俗。

clum·sy [ˈklʌmzi; ˋklʌmzɪ] *a*. **1**. (手脚)笨拙的。**2**. 愚笨的,不圆滑的。**3**. 制作粗陋的;(文体等)臃肿的。**clum·si·ness** *n*.

clunch [klʌntʃ; klʌntʃ] *n*. 【地】硬化黏土,耐火黏土;硬质白垩。

clung [klʌŋ; klʌŋ] cling 的过去式及过去分词。

clunk [klʌŋk; klʌŋk] *n*. = clonk.

clunk·er [ˈklʌŋkə; ˋklʌŋkɚ] *n*. 〔俚〕年久失修的机器〔尤指噪音很大的破旧汽车〕。

clu·pe·id [ˈkluːpiːid; ˋklupiɪd] **I** *n*. 【动】鲱科鱼。**II** *a*. 鲱科的。

clu·pe·oid [ˈklʌpiɔid; ˋklʌpɪˏɔɪd] **I** *a*. 【动】青鱼科鱼的,青鱼科状鱼的。**II** *n*. 青鱼科鱼。

clus·ter [ˈklʌstə; ˋklʌstɚ] **I** *n*. **1**. 丛集;丛;(葡萄等的)串,挂;(花)团;(秧)蔸;组。**2**. (蜂、人等的)丛,群,群集。**3**. 【物】聚集,组件;【化】类族,基;(原子)团;【天】星团。**4**. 【美军】(表示又一个同等勋章的)金属片。**5**. 【语音】音丛,音群,义丛,词组。**6**. 集中建筑群〔在一大片土地上集中兴建住宅,以提供较大的公共休息场所〕。*in a* ～成串的;成团[群]的。**II** *vi*., *vt*. (使)成群;(使)群集。～*ed column* 【建】簇柱。～ **bomb** 榴霰弹,子母弹。～ **bomb unit** 集束炸弹。～ **college** (文科大学中模仿牛津、剑桥的)独立学院,专科学院。～ **headache** (每日或每两三天几次发作并在停顿数月后再度复发的)集束性头痛。～ **point** 【数】聚点。

clutch[1] [klʌtʃ; klʌtʃ] **I** *vt*., *vi*. 抓,抓住;攫住;握紧。～ *at a straw* (危急时)捞稻草;急不暇择;急来抱佛脚。～ *the gunny* 〔美〕不及格。**II** *n*. **1**. (一把)抓住;〔常 *pl*.〕掌握,(抓牢不放的)手,魔掌,毒手。**2**. 【海】有叉支柱;〔*pl*.〕(鹰等的)爪;【机】离合器(踏板)。**3**. (女用)没有提梁的手提包〔由于需用手抓住〕。**4**. 〔美口〕(体育比赛中的)紧要关头。*be in sb.'s* ～*es* 在某人掌握之下。*full* [*get*] *into the* ～*es of* 遭…毒手,被…抓牢。*get out of the* ～*es of* 逃脱…魔掌。*in the* ～*es* 在紧急关头。*within* ～ 在抓得到的地方,在伸手可及之处。～ **coupling** 【机】离合联轴节。～ **pedal** 【汽车】离合器踏板。

clutch[2] [klʌtʃ; klʌtʃ] *n*. 一次孵的蛋;一窝雏;一捆(书等);一组(人等)。*a whole* ～ *of chorus girls* 整整一队女子合唱团团员。

clut·ter [ˈklʌtə; ˋklʌtɚ] **I** *n*. **1**. 〔方〕喧嚣。②混乱,(房屋等)拥挤杂乱的一团。**II** *vt*. 〔英方,美〕弄乱,搅乱;乱七八糟地堆满 (*up*, *with*)。—*vi*. 〔方〕喧闹,吵吵闹闹地跑 (*along*)。

CLUW = Coalition of Labor Union Women (美国)工会妇女联盟。

Clyde [klaid; klaɪd] *n*. 克莱德〔姓氏,男子名〕。

Clydes·dale [ˈklaidzdeil; ˋklaɪdzˏdel] *n*., *a*. 强健的拖车马(的)〔源出苏格兰 Clyde 地方所产名马〕。

clyp·e·ate [ˈklipieit; ˋklɪpɪˏet] *a*. 【生】**1**. 盾形的。**2**. 有唇基的,有盾状甲片的(= clypeated)。

clyp·e·us [ˈklipiəs; ˋklɪpɪəs] *n*. (*pl*. *clyp·e·i* [ˈklipiai; ˋklɪpɪaɪ]) (古代的)圆盾;(昆虫的)盾部,额板,唇基。

clys·ter [ˈklistə; ˋklɪstɚ] **I** *n*. 〔罕〕【医】灌肠(剂),灌肠法。**II** *vt*. 给…灌肠。

Cm =【化】curium 锔。

cm. = centimetre(s).

C.M., c.m. = **1**. common metre〔诗〕普通韵律。**2**. corresponding member(学会、协会的)通讯会员。**3**. Church Missionary 教会传教士。**4**. Court-Martial 军事法庭。**5**. circular mil 圆密耳(直径为密耳数的金属丝面积单位)。**6**. centre of mass 质量中心。

CM = Command Module 指挥舱,指令舱。

C.M.A. = Circulation Managers' Association〔美〕发行经理协会。

C.M.B. = coastal motorboat 沿海摩托艇。

CMEA, C.M.E.A. = Council for Mutual Economic Assistance [Aid]经济互助委员会〔简称"经互会"〕。

cml. = chemical; commercial.

cmm. = centimillimetre(s).

C'mon [kmɔn; kmɑn] *int*. 来吧(= Come on)!

CMP = cytidine monophosphate【化】磷酸胞苷,胞苷酸。

cmpd = compound【化】化合物;化合。

C.M.S. = **1**. centre-of-mass system【物】质心系统。**2**. Church Missionary Society 教会传教士协会。

C.M.T.C. = Citizens' Military Training Camps〔美〕国民军事训练营。

CNC = nomputer numerical control 计算机数字控制。

CND = Campaign for Nuclear Disarmament 核裁军运动。

CNN = Cable News Net (美国)有线电视新闻网。

CNO = Chief of Naval Operations〔美〕海军作战部部长。

C-note [ˈsiːnəut; ˋsinot] *n*. 〔美俚〕百元钞票。

C.O. = **1**. cash order 现金票据;现金订货单。**2**. Colonial Office〔英旧〕殖民部。**3**. Commanding Officer 指挥官。

Co = **1**. cobalt【化】钴。**2**. concentration 浓度;浓缩;【矿】富集,选矿。

Co., **co.** = **1**. company. **2**. county.

C.O., **CO** = **1**. Colonial Office〔英〕殖民部。**2**. commanding officer 指挥官。**3**. conscientious objector (为了道德或宗教上的原因)拒服兵役者。

c/o, **c.o.** = **1**. care of 由…转交。**2**. carried over (簿记用语)转入。

co- *pref*. **1**. 与,共同,共通,相互:*co*heir. **2**. 辅,陪;【数、天】余,补(= complement):*co*sine. **3**. 副:*co*-flyer。

co·ac·er·vate [kəuˈæsəveit; koˋæsəvet] *n*. 【化】凝聚层。

co·ac·er·va·tion [kəuˌæsəˈveiʃən; koˏæsəˋveʃən] *n*. 凝聚。

coach [kəutʃ; kotʃ] **I** *n*. **1**. 轿式马车;(四马拉)公共马车,驿车。**2**. 【铁路】客车(=〔美〕day ～);〔美〕卧车。**3**. (四门)轿式汽车;(长途)公共汽车。**4**. 私人教师,家庭教师;辅导员;【体】教练。**5**. 【海】(军舰顶层后甲板下面的)舰长专舱。**6**. 【美,棒球】= coacher。**7**. 汽车拉的活动房屋。**8**. 客机二等舱。*a slow* ～ 动作[头脑]迟钝的人,落后分子。*drive a* ～*-and-four through a new law* [*an Act of Parliament*] 明目张胆地钻新法案的漏洞,设法使新法案无效。**II** *vt*. **1**. 用马车运送。**2**. 教,指导,辅导;教练,训练(应考生、运动员等)。—*vi*. **1**. 坐马车旅行。**2**. 准备应考。**3**. 受训练[辅导]。**4**. 作指导[辅导,教练]。～**-built** *a*. (汽车车身)木制的。～**-and-four**

[**-six**] 四[六]马拉大马车。~ **box** (马车)驾驶人座位。~ **dog** 看车狗。~ **fellow** (同拉一车的)马伴儿;伴侣,伙伴。~ **house** 马车房。~**man** 1. 马车夫。2. (钓鱼用的)假蝇钩。~**whip** 1. 马鞭。2. 马鞭蛇。~**work** 汽车车身的设计、制造和装配。

coach·ee[1] [ˈkəutʃi; ˋkotʃɪ] ***n.*** (马车)车夫。

coach·ee[2] [kəuˈtʃiː; ˏkoˋtʃi] ***n.*** 受指导[训练]的人。

coach·er [ˈkəutʃə; ˋkotʃɚ] ***n.*** 1. 辅导员;教练。2. 〔美〕(公共)马车。3. 【棒球】跑垒及击球指挥员。

co·act [kəuˈækt; koˋækt] ***vi.*** 协作,协力。

co·ac·tion[1] [kəuˈækʃən; koˋækʃən] ***n.*** 强制;强迫。**-ac·tive** ***a.***

co·ac·tion[2] [kəuˈækʃən; koˋækʃən] ***n.*** 1. 协力。2. 【生态】相互作用。

co·ac·ti·va·ted [kəuˈæktiveitid; koˋæktɪˏvetɪd] ***a.*** 【化】共激活的。

co·ac·ti·va·tor [kəuˈæktiveitə; koˋæktɪˏvetɚ] ***n.*** 【化】共激活剂,共活化剂。

coad. = coadjutor.

co·ad·ja·cent [ˌkəuəˈdʒeisnt; ˏkoəˋdʒesn̩t] ***a.*** 互相邻接的,毗邻的;(思想)接近的。

co·ad·ju·tant [kəuˈædʒutənt; koˋædʒətənt] **I** ***a.*** 相助的,互补的,互助的。**II** ***n.*** 协力者,合作者,帮手。

co·ad·ju·tor [kəuˈædʒutə; koˋædʒətɚ] ***n.*** 助手;【宗】副主教。

co·ad·u·nate [kəuˈædjunit; koˋædʒunɪt] ***a.*** 1. 连结的,接合的。2. 【植】叶茎连生的。

co·a·gent [kəuˈeidʒənt; koˋedʒənt] ***n.*** 帮手,伙伴;合作[协助]因素。

co·ag·u·la·ble [kəuˈægjuːləbl; koˋægjələbl̩] ***a.*** 能凝结的。**-bil·i·ty** ***n.*** 可凝结性。

co·ag·u·lant [kəuˈægjulənt; koˋægjələnt] ***n.*** 【化】凝结剂。

co·ag·u·lase [kəuˈægjuːleis; koˋægjəˏles] ***n.*** 【生化】凝固酶。

co·ag·u·late [kəuˈægjuleit; koˋægjəˏlet] **I** ***vt.***, ***vi.*** (使)凝结;(使)成一体。**II** ***a.*** 凝结的。

co·ag·u·la·tion [kəuˌægjuˈleiʃən; koˏægjəˋleʃən] ***n.*** 凝固(作用);凝结物。

co·ag·u·la·tive [kəuˈægjuˌleitiv; koˋægjəˏletɪv] ***a.*** (引起)凝结的。

co·ag·u·la·tor [kəuˈægjuˌleitə; koˋægjəˏletɚ] ***n.*** 【化】凝结器[剂]。

co·ag·u·lum [kəuˈægjuləm; koˋægjələm] ***n.*** (*pl.* **-la** [-lə; -lə]) 凝结物;凝(结)块。

coal [kəul; kol] **I** ***n.*** 1. 煤,煤块,煤堆。2. 〔*pl.*〕〔美〕(一堆)烧红的煤。3. 〔常 *pl.*〕〔英〕(几块)供燃烧的煤。4. 木炭。*broken* ~碎煤。*brown* ~褐煤。*craw* [*crow*] ~劣煤。*hard* ~〔美〕无烟煤,硬煤。*small* ~煤屑。*soft* ~〔美〕烟煤。*white* ~(发电用的)水力。*a live* ~ 通红的火炭。***a cold ~ to blow at*** 无成功希望的工作。***blow hot ~s*** 暴怒。***blow the ~s*** 嗾使,唆使,挑唆,煽动。***call*** [***haul***] ***over the ~s*** 申斥,谴责。***carry*** [***bear***] ~***s*** 做低三下四的工作;甘受屈辱 (*Gregory, on my word, we'll not carry ~s.* 格列高里,我们绝对不能忍辱受屈呀)。***carry*** [***send***] ~***s to Newcastle*** 多余的举动,徒劳无益[Newcastle 是产煤地]。***heap*** [***cast, gather***] ~***s of fire on sb.'s head*** 使某人痛苦[惭愧]难当。***stir*** ~挑拨(是非)。***take in*** ~上煤(到船内)。***take*** [***rake, drag***] ***over the*** ~***s*** = *call over the ~s*. **II** ***vt.***, ***vi.*** 1. (给…)上煤,(给…)加煤。2. (把…)烧成炭。~ **bed** 煤层。~**-black** ***a.*** 漆黑。~ **box** 煤箱;〔军俚〕发黑烟的炸弹。~ **breaker** = ~ cracker. ~ **bunker** 煤舱。~ **capacity** 载煤量。~ **cellar** 地下煤库。~ **cracker** 碎煤机。~ **cutter** 采[截]煤机。~ **cutting** 采[截]煤。~ **drop** 卸煤机。~ **dust** 煤粉。~ **endurance** 续航力。~ **face** 采煤工作面。~ **factor** 煤商。~ **field** 煤田,产煤区。~**fish** 【鱼】黑鳕,军曹鱼。~ **gas** 煤气。~ **hatch** (船的)上煤口。~**-heaver** 上[卸]煤工人;运煤工人。~**hole** (地下)煤库;地下煤库通到街上的洞穴。~**ing station** 装煤港[站]。~**master** 煤矿主。~ **measures** 【地】煤系。~ **mine** 煤矿。~ **miner** 煤矿工人。~**mouse** = ~tit. ~ **oil** 石油,原油;煤油。~ **pit** 煤矿坑,竖井;〔美〕炭窑。~**sack** 装煤麻袋;【天】煤袋〔银河中靠近南十字座的黑洞〕。~ **plant** 煤中所含的树木化石 ~ **screen** 煤筛。~ **scuttle** 煤篓;(舷侧)上煤口。~ **seam** 煤层。~ **series** 【地】煤系。**C- State** 〔美〕煤州〔Pennsylvania 州的别名〕。~ **tar** 煤焦油。~**tit** 【鸟】四十雀。~ **vase** = ~ scuttle. ~**-whipper** 卸煤工人;卸煤机。

coal·er [ˈkəulə; ˋkolɚ] ***n.*** 1. 煤船;煤车;运煤铁路。2. 〔*pl.*〕〔美〕运煤铁路股票;煤炭搬运工人;煤商。

co·a·lesce [ˌkəuəˈles; ˏkoəˋlɛs] ***vi.*** 1. (断骨等)接合;(创口等)愈合,合口。2. 结合;(政党等)合并,联合;合作。

co·a·les·cence [ˌkəuəˈlesns; ˏkoəˋlɛsns] ***n.*** 接合;结合;合并,联合;愈合;【化】聚结。**-les·cent** ***a.***

coal·i·fi·ca·tion [ˌkəulifiˈkeiʃən; ˏkolɪfɪˋkeʃən] ***n.*** 【矿】煤化(作用)。

coal·ing [ˈkəuliŋ; ˋkolɪŋ] ***n.*** 装煤,上煤。~ **base**, ~-**place**, ~ **station** 供煤港;(供)煤站。

Coal·ite [ˈkəulait; ˋkolaɪt] ***n.*** 【商标】固来特煤〔一种无烟燃料〕。

co·a·li·tion [ˌkəuəˈliʃən; ˏkoəˋlɪʃən] ***n.*** 结合,合并;(政党等的)联合,联盟。~ **cabinet** [**ministry**] 联合内阁。~ **government** 联合政府。

co·a·li·tion·ist [ˌkəuəˈliʃənist; ˏkoəˋlɪʃənɪst] ***n.*** 1. (政治上主张)联合论者。2. 参加联盟者。

coal·y [ˈkəuli; ˋkolɪ] ***a.*** 多煤的;煤质的;煤(状)的;墨黑的。

coam·ing [ˈkəumiŋ; ˋkomɪŋ] ***n.*** 〔*pl.*〕挡水围栏;井栏;【船】舱口栏板[围板]。

Co·an·chor [ˈkəuˈæŋkə; ˋkoˋæŋkə] **I** ***vt.***, ***vi.*** 联合主持(电台或电视节目)。**II** ***n.*** (广播节目的)联合主持人。

co·apt [kəuˈæpt; koˋæpt] ***vt.*** 使(骨头等)接合,接(骨),使接牢。

co·ap·ta·tion [ˌkəuæpˈteiʃən; ˏkoæpˋteʃən] ***n.*** 接合;【医】接骨术。

co·arc·tate [kəuˈɑːkteit; koˋɑrktet] ***a.*** 【生】1. 狭缩的,缩窄的。2. (某些虫蛹的)密闭于最后一层蛹皮内的。**-ta·tion** ***n.***

coarse [kɔːs; kɔrs] ***a.*** 1. 粗糙的,粗劣的,粗制滥造的,下等的。2. 粗鄙的,粗俗的,粗暴的,下流的;猥亵的,(言语等)鄙俗的。~ *fare* 粗食。~ *fish* 杂鱼。~ **counts** 【纺】(纱的)粗支(数),低支(数)。~**-fibred** ***a.*** 粗纤维的;〔喻〕粗鲁的。~ **fish** 〔英〕(除鲑鱼以外的)淡水鱼。~**-grained** ***a.*** 1. 粗粒的;木理粗糙的。2. 粗鲁不文的。**-ly** ***ad.*** **-ness** ***n.***

coars·en [ˈkɔːsn; ˋkɔrsn] ***vt.***, ***vi.*** (使)变粗糙。

coast [kəust; kost] **I** ***n.*** 1. 海岸;海滨。2. 〔美〕(雪橇等的)滑下,下坡;【空】滑翔,惯性飞行。3. 〔古〕边疆。4. (吸毒者等过瘾后的)飘然状态。***Clear the ~!*** 〔俚〕躲开! 让开! ***off the ~*** 在海面上。***on the ~*** 在岸上,沿岸。***skirt the ~*** 沿海岸航行;谨慎行事。***the C-*** 〔美〕太平洋沿岸,太平洋沿岸各州。***The ~ is clear.*** 〔走私黑话〕道路通畅,无问题,时机正好! **II** ***vi.*** 1. 沿岸航行[旅行]。2. (由坡上)滑(行)下(去),溜下。3. (人)一帆风顺。4. (吸毒者等)飘飘然。~ ***home*** 〔美〕轻易得胜。~ ***in*** 〔美〕轻易夺得锦标。~ **artillery** 海岸炮(兵)。~ **defence ship** 海防舰。~ **guard** 水上警察;〔英〕海岸警备队;〔C- G-〕〔美〕海岸救难[缉私]警备队(队员)。~**-guard(s) man** 沿岸警备队队员。~**land** 沿海地带。~**line**海岸线。~ **pilot** 〔美〕(政府出版的)沿岸航海指南。~ **waiter** 海关沿岸检查员。~**ward** ***ad.***, ***a.*** ~-

wards *ad*. 朝着[向着]海岸。～wise 1. *a*. 近海(岸)的,沿岸的。2. *ad*. 顺着海岸,沿岸;靠近海岸。

coast·al [ˈkəustl; ˋkostl] I *a*. 沿海的,临海的;沿岸的。II *n*. 〔英〕海防飞机。**C- Command** 空军海防总队。**C-Eastern** 〔美〕美国东部大西洋沿岸使用的美国英语。～ **plain** 滨海平原。～ **waiter** 〔英〕= coast waiter.

coast·er [ˈkaustə; ˋkostə] *n*. 1. 沿岸贸易[航行]者;沿岸贸易船[航船];沿海居民。2. (餐桌上放酒瓶的带轮)银盆;(杯盘等的)垫子。3. (儿童的)滑板,橇;滑翔机;滑行者;【军】惯性滑翔飞弹。4. (自行车)前叉放脚处。～ **brake** (自行车的)倒轮闸,脚煞车。

coast·ing [ˈkəustiŋ; ˋkostɪŋ] *n*. 1. 沿岸航行,沿岸贸易;(雪橇等的)滑降游戏;海岸线。2. 【机】惰转;惰行。～ **flight** 【空】惯性飞行;滑翔飞行。～ **lead** 【海】(120—360英尺水深的)滨海测锤。

coat [kəut; kot] I *n*. 1. 上衣,外衣,外套。★厚大衣叫 over*coat*, 〔英〕 great*coat*. 2. (女人、孩童的)短大衣。3. 锁子甲。4. (动物的)毛皮,被覆;(植物的)表皮。5. (漆等的)涂层;【解】外膜,膜。6. 〔*pl*.〕〔古〕裙子。*first* (*floating*; *setting*) ～(漆等的)头(二、三)道。～*s of the stomach* 胃膜。～ *of mail* 锁子甲。***black*** ～ 牧师,教士。***change one's*** ～ 变节;改变立场。～ ***and skirt*** (上衣下裙相配的)西式女套装。～ ***of arms*** 战袍;(代表某一个人,家族,团体等的)盾形纹章。***dust*** [***smoke***] ***sb.'s*** ～ (***for him***) 殴打某人。***in*** ～ ***and skirt*** (妇女)穿着出门的衣服。***lace sb.'s*** ～ 鞭打某人。***pick a hole in sb.'s*** ～ 找人短处[错儿]。***take off one's*** ～ 脱掉上衣(预备打架或使劲干)。***The*** ～ ***fits***. 衣服合身;说[想]对了。***trail one's*** ～ 故意地找碴子争吵,挑衅。***turn one's*** ～ 变节;改变立场。***wear the king's*** [***queen's***] ～ 〔英〕服兵役,当兵。II *vt*. 1. 给…穿上上衣[外套]。2. 包上,涂上,盖上。*be* ～*ed with* 用…包上[涂上、蒙上]。～*ed paper* 铜板纸。上浆纸。*a* ～*ed tape* 涂粉磁带。***My tongue is*** ～***ed***. 长舌苔了。～ **armo(u)r** 铠甲上穿的外衣;纹章,家徽。～ **card** (纸牌中)有人像的牌,花牌。～ **hanger** 衣架。～ **holder** 给(争斗者,竞技人等)拿上衣的人,旁观者。～ **rack** 衣帽架。～ **room** 衣帽间。

coat·tail [ˈkautteil; ˋkotˏtel] *n*. 1. 男上衣后摆;男子燕尾服的尾;〔*pl*.〕女子长外衣的下摆。2. 〔*pl*.〕〔美口〕(可提携声望较差的候选人的)政治威信,政治影响。***ride on sb.'s*** ～***s*** 依靠别人的声望荣升(指政治方面),附骥尾。***trail sb.'s*** ～***s*** 向(某人)挑衅,招惹(某人)。

coat·ee [ˈkəuti:, kəuˈti:; ˋkoti, koˋti] *n*. 紧身短上衣。

co·a·ti [kəuˈɑ:ti; koˋɑtɪ] *n*. 【动】(美洲产)长吻浣熊(= ～-mundi, ～-mondi)。

co·au·thor [kəuˈɔ:θə; koˋɔθə] *n*. 合著者,合作者,共同研究者。

coat·ing [ˈkəutiŋ; ˋkotɪŋ] *n*. 1. 被覆,表皮,涂层;包覆物;(食品上的)面衣,糖衣;涂料。2. 上衣料;细呢,花呢。

coax [kəuks; koks] I *vt*. 1. 用好话劝诱;哄。2. 巧妙地[用心地]处理,轻轻地弄好。～ *sb. to do* [*into doing*] 哄某人去做…。～ *a fire to burn* 轻轻把火拨燃。—*vi*. 哄骗。～ *and plead* 又哄又劝。～ ***round*** (用好话)搪塞,哄骗。II *n*. 〔俚〕 1. 油嘴滑舌的人。2. 花言巧语。3. 同轴电缆(= coaxial cable)。**-ing** *n*., *a*. 哄骗(的)。

co·ax·al, co·ax·i·al [kəuˈæksəl, -iəl; koˋæksəl, -ɪəl] *a*. 【数】同轴的,共轴的。～ **cable** 同轴电缆。

cob[1] [kɔb; kɑb] *n*. 1. (面包等的)小圆块;〔常 *pl*.〕(煤、石头、矿石等的)圆块,一小堆。2. 〔美〕玉米的穗轴(= corn cob)。3. 雄天鹅(= ～-swan)。4. 结实的短脚马。5. 〔英口〕蜘蛛。6. 大榛子,欧洲榛(= cobnut)。7. 〔英方〕要人。～ **coal** 圆煤块。～ **house** 土墙房子。～**-loaf** 圆面包。

cob[2] [kɔb; kɑb] *n*. (搀有干草的)抹墙泥。

cob[3] [kɔb; kɑb] *vt*. (*-bb-*) 1. 打碎,捣碎。2. (用偏物)打(臀部)。

co·bal·a·min [kəuˈbɔləmin; koˋbɑləmɪn] *n*. 【生化】钴胺素,维生素 B_{12}。

co·balt [kəˈbɔ:lt, ˈkəubɔ:lt; kəˋbɔlt, ˋkobɔlt] *n*. 1. 【化】钴。2. 钴类颜料。3. 深蓝色。～ **blue** 钴蓝,深蓝。～ **bomb** 钴弹。～ **green** 钴绿。～ **yellow** 钴黄。

co·bal·tic [kəuˈbɔ:ltik; kəˋbɔltɪk] *a*. 【化】(三价)钴的,含钴的。

co·balt·ite co·balt·ine [kəuˈbɔ:ltait, -in; koˋbɔltaɪt, -ɪn] *n*. 【矿】辉砷钴矿。

co·bal·tous [kəuˈbɔ:ltəs; koˋbɔltəs] *a*. 【化】(亚)钴的;二价钴的。～ **sulphate** 硫酸钴。

cob·ber [ˈkɔbə; ˋkɑbə] *n*. 〔澳俚〕(男)朋友,伙伴。

cob·bies [ˈkɔbiz; ˋkɑbɪz] *n*. 〔*pl*.〕一种镶有楔形后跟的女式平底鞋〔又名 wedgies〕。

cob·ble[1] [ˈkɔbl; ˋkɑbl] I *n*. 1. 鹅卵石;【地】中砾。2. 〔*pl*.〕卵石路;〔*pl*.〕圆煤块。II *vt*. 在…铺鹅卵石。

cob·ble[2] [ˈkɔbl; ˋkɑbl] I *vt*. 1. 修补(鞋)。2. 马虎地修补 (*up*)。3. 粗制滥造 (*up*)。II *n*. 〔俚〕粗制滥造的物品。

cob·bler [ˈkɔblə; ˋkɑblə] *n*. 1. 补鞋匠,皮匠。★现通用 shoemaker. 2. 手艺笨拙的工匠。3. 〔美〕果馅饼。4. 冰杜松子酒柠檬水。5. 〔*pl*.〕〔英〕愚蠢而不诚恳的话;胡说。～**'s wax** 鞋线蜡。

cob·bler·y [ˈkɔbləri; ˋkɑblərɪ] *n*. 〔美〕补鞋店。

cob·ble·stone [ˈkɔblstəun; ˋkɑblˏston] *n*. 圆石,鹅卵石。

cob·bly [ˈkɔbli; ˋkɑblɪ] *a*. 用大鹅卵石铺的;崎岖的。

cob·by [ˈkɔbi; ˋkɑbɪ] *a*. 1. 像结实的矮脚马似的。2. 〔英方〕活跃的;执拗的。

Cob·den [ˈkɔbden; ˋkɑbdən] *n*. 1. 科布登〔姓氏〕。2. **Richard** ～李查·科布登〔1804—1865 英国工业家,商人,经济学家,政治家〕。**-ism** *n*. 科布登主义,自由贸易主义。**-ite** *n*. 科布登主义[自由贸易主义]信徒。

co·bel·lig·er·ent [ˌkəubiˈlidʒərənt; ˏkobəˋlɪdʒərənt] *n*. 共同参战国[参战者];友邦。

Cob·ham [ˈkɔbəm; ˋkɑbəm] *n*. 科伯姆〔姓氏〕。

co·bi·a [ˈkəubiə; ˋkobɪə] *n*. 【动】军曹鱼 (*Rachycentron canadus*)。

co·ble, cob·ble [ˈkəubl; ˋkobl] *n*. 1. (英国东北部的)一种小渔船。2. (苏格兰的)一种平底渔船。

cob·nut [ˈkɔbnʌt; ˋkɑbˏnʌt] *n*. 1. 大榛子,欧洲榛。2. 碰榛子游戏〔以线端所击榛子互相碰击的游戏〕。

COBOL [ˈkəubɔl; ˋkobɑl] *n*. 【计】通用商业(程序)语言〔*co*mmon *b*usiness *o*riented *l*anguage〕。

co·bra[1] [ˈkəubrə; ˋkobrə] *n*. 【动】眼镜蛇,毒帽蛇。

co·bra[2] [ˈkəubrə; ˋkobrə] *n*. 〔澳〕头;头盖骨。

cob·web [ˈkɔbweb; ˋkɑbˏwɛb] I *n*. 1. 蜘蛛网,蛛丝。2. 蛛网状的薄织物(纱帕等)。3. (蛛网一样)易破的东西。4. 〔*pl*.〕薄弱的推论;混乱的思想;混乱,陈腐,暧昧。～*s of the law* 陈腐的法律。***blow*** [***clear***] ***away the*** ～***s from one's brain*** 使头脑清醒一下。***have a*** ～ ***in the throat*** 口渴。II *vt*. (*-bb-*) 使布满蛛网。～ **throat** 〔美〕没有喝酒;想喝酒。

cob·webbed [ˈkɔbwebd; ˋkɑbwɛbd] *a*. 1. 布满蛛网的;蛛网状的。2. 〔美〕头脑混乱的。

cob·web·by [ˈkɔbwebi; ˋkɑbˏwɛbɪ] *a*. 1. 蛛网似的,布满蛛网的。2. 长久不用的;黏满了灰尘的。

co·ca [ˈkəukə; ˋkokə] *n*. 【植】古柯〔南美药用植物〕;古柯叶;古柯叶制剂。

co·ca-co·la, Co·ca-Co·la [ˈkəukəˈkəulə; ˋkokəˋkolə] *n*. 〔美〕可口可乐〔一种饮料,商标名〕。

co·caine [kəˈkein; koˋken] *n*. 【药】可卡因,古柯碱。

co·cain·ism [kəˈkeinizəm; koˋkenɪzəm] *n*. 【医】古柯碱瘾;古柯碱中毒。

co·cain·ize [kəˈkeinaiz; koˋkenaɪz] *vt*. 用古柯碱麻醉。**-cain·iza·tion** *n*.

co·car·box·y·lase [ˈkəukɑ:ˈbɔksileis; ˋkokɑrˋbɑksɪles]

n.【生化】辅羧酶,羧化辅酶。

cocc-, cocci- *comb*. *f*. 小球状体,浆果:*cocci*diosis.

coc·ci [ˈkɔksai; ˋkɑksaɪ] *n*. coccus 的复数。

coc·cid [ˈkɔksid; ˋkɑksɪd] *n*.【动】介壳虫。

coc·cid·i·oi·do·my·co·sis [kɔkˌsidiˌɔidəumaiˈkəusis; kɑkˏsɪdɪˏɔɪdomaɪˋkosɪs] *n*. (牲畜的)球孢子虫病。

coc·cid·i·o·sis [kɔkˌsidiˈəusis; kɑkˏsɪdɪˋosɪs] *n*.【医】(人体)球虫病。

coc·cif·er·ous [kɔkˈsifərəs; kɑkˋsɪfərəs] *a*.【植】结浆果的,有浆果的。

cocco- *comb*. *f*. = cocc-.

coc·co·lith [ˈkɔkəliθ; ˋkɑkəlɪθ] *n*.【植】颗石藻。

coc·cus [ˈkɔkəs; ˋkɑkəs] *n*. (*pl*. *cocci*) 1.【微】球菌。2.【植】(果实的)分果爿。

coc·cyg·eal [kɔkˈsidʒiəl; kɑkˋsɪdʒɪəl] *a*.【解】尾骨的。

coc·cyx [ˈkɔksiks; ˋkɑksɪks] *n*. (*pl*. *coc·cy·ges* [kɔkˈsaidʒiːz; kɑkˋsaɪdʒiz], ~*es*)【解】尾骨。

Co·cha·bam·ba [Sp. ˌkotʃaˈbambə; ˏkotʃaˋbambə] *n*. 科恰班巴〔玻利维亚城市〕。

co·chair [kəuˈtʃɛə; koˋtʃɛə] *vt*. 担任…的联合主席。

Co·chair·man [kəuˈtʃɛəmən; koˋtʃɛrmən] *n*. 1. 联合主席,两主席之一。2. 副主席。

Co·chin, co·chin [ˈkəutʃin; ˋkotʃɪn]【动】(越南的)交趾鸡。

Cochin-China [ˈkɔtʃinˈtʃainə; ˋkotʃɪnˋtʃaɪnə] *n*. 1.【史】交趾支那。2. 〔cochin-china〕交趾支那鸡。

coch·i·neal [ˈkɔtʃiniːl; ˏkɑtʃəˋnil] *n*. 1.【动】胭脂虫。2. (由胭脂虫制成的)虫红,洋红(颜料)。

coch·le·a [ˈkɔkliə; ˋkɑklɪə] *n*. (*pl*. *-ae* [-iː; -i], ~*s*)【解】(耳)蜗;【植】卷荚。

coch·le·ate, coch·le·ated [ˈkɔkliit, -eit, -eitid; ˋkɑklɪɪt, -et, -etɪd] *a*.【动】螺旋状。

cock[1] [kɔk; kɑk] **I** *n*. 1. 雄鸡,公鸡。2. 雄禽。★有时与其他动物名连用;表示雄性。3. 雄螯虾[蟹、鲑]。4. 野鹬〔= wood ~〕。5. 首领,领袖;架子十足的人。6. 塞子;【机】(水管等的)龙头,开关,旋塞;(活)栓;节气门。7. (枪的)击铁,扳机,系机;击铁待发位置,准备击发(状态)。8. 风标,风信鸡;(日晷、天平等的)指针。9. (帽的)卷边;(鼻子的)上翘;(眼梢的)翘起;(帽子等)歪戴,歪着。*a threeway* ~三通旋塞。*turn the* ~开龙头。***at* [*on*] *full* [*half*]** ~ 把击铁扳上[拨上一半],处于全[半]击发状态;充分准备[准备未周]。~ ***of the loft* [*dunghill*]** 小霸主,土皇帝,地头蛇,自命不凡的头子。~ ***of the north***【鸟】花鸡。~ ***of the school*** 学生领袖;(校中)最横行霸道的学生。~ ***of the walk*** 〔美〕有威望的头领。~ ***of the wood***【鸟】(北美产的)一种啄木鸟。***go off at half-cock*** 操之过急。***live like fighting* ~*s*** (像斗鸡一样)吃得好,过阔气日子。***Old* ~!** 〔昵称〕老兄。***red* ~** 纵火引起的火灾。***set* (*the*) ~ *on* (*the*) *hoop*** 纵饮,放纵。***That* ~ *won't fight*.** 那一手行不通,那种话说不过去。**II** *vt*. 1. 扳上(枪的)扳机。2. 使朝上,使翘起,耸起(耳朵);(把帽檐翘起)歪戴(帽子)。— *vi*. 1. (狗)翘尾巴,翘起,竖起。2. 扳上扳机(准备击发)。3. 趾高气扬(地走)。~ ***a snoot* (*at*)** 不屑一顾,轻视。~***ed and primed*** 装上弹药和扳起扳机;作好(战斗)准备。~***ed hat*** 卷边帽;(海军军人等的)三角帽;三柱球戏。~ ***one's eye at*** 〔俚〕向上一瞟;使眼色。~ ***one's nose*** 抬起鼻子〔轻蔑的表情〕。~ ***up*** 耸起,竖起,翘起;〔学俚〕打板子。~**-and-hen** *a*. 适用于两性的。~**boat** (附设于大船上的)小艇。~ **chafer**【虫】金龟子。~**crow(ing)** 黎明,清晨。~**-eyed** *a*. 斗鸡眼的;〔俚〕歪在一边的;愚蠢的;可笑的;狂乱的,喝醉的。~**fighting** 1. *n*. 斗鸡(戏)(*This beats* ~*fighting*. 这有趣极了)。2. *a*. 爱斗鸡的。~**horse** 1. *n*. (骑在上面可前后摇动的)玩具木马。2. *ad*. 得意地;趾高气扬地。~**pit** 斗鸡场;战场;(戏院的)正厅;(军舰内的)伤兵室。【空】(飞机上的)座舱;船尾座位(*the* ~*pit of Europe* 比利时的别号)。~**roach**【虫】蟑螂,油虫。~ **robin** 雄知更鸟;(知更鸟一样)灵巧的矮子。~**shy**, ~**shot** 掷棒打靶游戏;掷棒戏的靶子,投掷一次。~ **sparrow** 公麻雀,矮小强悍的人。~**-spur**(鸡的)距;【植】稗属植物;【虫】跳蝼蛄。~ **strut** 〔美〕骄傲自大的步态。~**sure** *a*. 确信(*of*; *about*);(事情)一定会发生;一定…(*to do*);独断的,太自信的(*of*)。~**swain** 〔古〕= coxswain. ~**tail** 1. *n*. 鸡尾酒;(正菜前用蟹肉,牡蛎肉或水果等做成的)开胃小吃,尾巴切短的马;非纯种的赛马;出身低微的人。2. *a*. 鸡尾酒的(*a* ~ *party* 鸡尾酒会。*the* ~ *hour* 〔美〕喝鸡尾酒时间,指下午五时左右);(女服)在半正式场合穿的。~**tail belt** (经常出席酒会的)上流人士住宅区。~**tailed** *a*. 切短了尾巴的。~**up** 1. *a*. 尖儿向上翘起的。2. *n*.【印】(篇首的)特高大写字母;附在字母右肩上的字,〔大写字等〕上角字[码];〔俚〕一团糟,混乱。

cock[2] [kɔk; kɑk] **I** *n*. (圆锥状)干草堆;粪堆。**II** *vt*. 把(干草等)堆成圆锥状小堆。

cock·ade [kɔˈkeid; kɑkˋed] *n*. 1. 帽章,帽上的花结。2. 〔C-〕〔美〕马里兰(Maryland)州的别号。

cock-a-doo·dle-doo [ˈkɔkəduːdlˈduː; ˋkɑkəˏdudlˋdu] *n*. (*pl*. ~*s*) 1. (雄鸡的)喔喔叫声,鸡鸣。2. 〔儿〕大公鸡。

cock-a-hoop [ˈkɔkəˈhuːp; ˏkɑkəˋhup] *a*., *ad*. 得意洋洋的[地];骄傲的[地]。**-ness** *n*.

Cock·aigne, Cock·ayne [kɔˈkein; kɑˋken] *n*. 1. (幻想中的)安乐乡。2. 伦敦的别号〔= the land of C-〕。

cock-a-leek·ie [ˈkɔkəˈliːki; ˋkɑkəˋlikɪ] *n*. 韭菜鸡肉汤(= cockyleeky)。

cock·a·lo·rum [ˌkɔkəˈlɔːrəm; ˏkɑkəˋlorəm] *n*. 1. 小公鸡;自负不凡的小人物。2. 蛙跳游戏(= high ~)。3. 大话,吹牛。

cock·a·ma·mie [ˈkɔkəˌmeimiː; ˋkɑkəˏmemi] *a*. 〔美俚〕愚蠢的;荒唐可笑的;质量极差的,劣等的〔表示很不赞许的一般用语〕。

cock-and-bull [ˈkɔkənˈbul; ˋkɑkənˋbʊl] **I** *n*. 荒唐话,无稽之谈。**II** *a*. 荒唐无稽的。

cock·a·teel, cock·a·tiel [ˌkɔkəˈtiːl; ˏkɑkəˋtil] *n*.【动】澳大利亚玄凤〔一种鹦鹉〕(*Nymphicus hollandicus*)。

cock·a·too [ˌkɔkəˈtuː; ˏkɑkəˋtu] *n*. 1.【动】白鹦。2. 〔澳俚〕小农。3. 〔俚〕(替盗贼)把风者。*a rose* ~【鸟】红鹦鹉。

cock·a·trice [ˈkɔkətrais; ˋkɑkətrɪs] *n*. 1. (传说中的)鸡身蛇尾怪;(传说人被它看上一眼即死的)毒蛇。2. 妖妇;极恶毒的人。

Cocke [kəuk; kok] *n*. 科克〔姓氏〕。

cocked [kɔkt; kɑkt] *a*. 1. 翘起的,竖起的。2. (枪)处于准备击发状态的。~ *hat* 三角帽,两端尖的帽子。***knock* (*the plan*) *into a* ~ *hat*** 使(计划等)完全失败。***make a* ~ *hat of sb*.** 把某人打得一蹶不振。

Cock·er [ˈkɔkə; ˋkɑkɚ] *n*. 科克尔〔姓氏〕。**Edward** ~ 爱德华·科克尔〔1631—1675,英国有名的数学教师。著有《算术大全》(*The Complete Arithmetician*)〕。***according to* ~** 精确的;精确地说。

cock·er[1] [ˈkɔkə; ˋkɑkɚ] *vt*. 娇养,溺爱,放纵(*up*)。

cock·er[2] [ˈkɔkə; ˋkɑkɚ] *n*. 一种矮脚长耳猎犬(= ~ spaniel)。

cock·er[3] [ˈkɔkə; ˋkɑkɚ] *n*. 斗鸡迷。

cock·er·el [ˈkɔkərəl; ˋkɑkərəl] *n*. (未满一岁的)小公鸡;血气方刚的青年。

cock·i·ly [ˈkɔkili; ˋkɑkɪlɪ] *ad*. 〔俚〕趾高气扬地,自高自大地。

cock·i·ness [ˈkɔkinis; ˋkɑkɪnɪs] *n*. 自大;过于自信;趾高气扬。

cock·le[1] [ˈkɔkl; ˋkɑkl] *n*. 1.【贝】乌蛤;海扇壳。2. (浅底)小船。~***s of the heart*** 内心深处,心底的感情(*delight* [*warm*] *the* ~*s of the heart* 令人深深满意[深感温暖]。~**boat** 轻舟。~ **hat** (朝香者)以海扇壳装饰的帽子。~**-stairs** 螺旋楼梯。

C

cock·le[2][ˈkɔkl; ˋkakl̩] ***n***. 【植】麦仙翁。

cock·le[3][ˈkɔkl; ˋkakl̩] **I** ***n***. (纸张等的)皱折，褶。**II** ***vt***., ***vi***. (使)皱折。

cock·le[4][ˈkɔkl, ˋkakl̩] ***n***. 火炉。

cock·le·bur[ˈkɔklbəː; ˋkakl̩ˏbɝ] ***n***. 【植】苍耳属(*Xanthium*)。

cock·le·shell[ˈkɔklˌʃel; ˋkakl̩ˏʃɛl] ***n***. **1.** 海扇[乌蛤]壳。**2.** 这类贝壳的通称。**3.** 小艇。

cock·loft[ˈkɔklɔft; ˋkakˏlɔft] ***n***. (小)顶楼，阁楼，顶层。

cock·ney[ˈkɔkni; ˋkaknɪ] **I** ***n***. **1.** 〔亦作 C-〕伦敦佬〔尤指伦敦东区的人〕；伦敦话，伦敦口音〔含轻蔑意〕。**2.** 〔主美〕柔弱的都市人。**3.** 装模作样的女人。**4.** 〔罕〕被宠坏的孩子。**II** ***a***. 〔贬〕**1.** 伦敦佬的，伦敦佬气派的。**2.** 伦敦腔的。～ **accent** 伦敦口音。**-dom** **1.** 〔集合词〕伦敦佬；伦敦佬的脾性。**2.** 伦敦佬居住区，伦敦人居民区的社会。**-fy** ***vt***. 使有伦敦佬的派头[腔调]。**-ish** ***a***. 伦敦佬派头的；带点伦敦腔的。**-ism** 伦敦佬派头，伦敦口音[语调]。**-ize** ***vt***., ***vi***. (使)有伦敦佬派头；用伦敦语调说话。

C

cocks·comb[ˈkɔkskəum; ˋkaksˏkom] ***n***. **1.** 鸡冠。**2.** 【植】鸡冠花。**3.** 小丑的帽子(= coxcomb)。

cocks·foot[ˈkɔksfut; ˋkaksˏfʊt] ***n***. 【植】鸭茅。

cock·sy[ˈkɔksi; ˋkaksɪ] ***a***. 骄傲自大的，趾高气扬的(= coxy)。

cock·y[ˈkɔki; ˋkakɪ] ***a***. 〔口〕骄傲的，自大的；过分自信的；趾高气扬的。*be* ～(*at success*) (因为成功而)翘尾巴。

cock·y-leek·y, cock·y-leek·ie[ˈkɔkiˈliːki; ˋkakɪˋlikɪ] ***n***. 〔Scot.〕韭菜鸡肉汤。

cock·y·ol·(l)y bird[ˌkɔkiˈɔli bəːd; ˏkakɪˋalɪˏbɝd] 〔儿〕鸟儿〔对小鸟的爱称〕。

co·co[ˈkəukəu; ˋkoko] **I** ***n***. (*pl*. ～**s** [-z; -z]) **1.** 【植】椰子树 (= coconut tree [palm], ～-palm)；椰子。**2.** 〔美俚〕(人的)脑袋。**II** ***a***. 椰子壳纤维制的。

co·coa[ˈkəukəu; ˋkoko] ***n***. **1.** 可可粉，可可(茶)。**2.** 可可树。**3.** 深褐色。～ **bean** 可可豆。～ **butter** 可可脂，药用，化妆用)。～**mat** 椰子树片编织物；(置于门口的)席垫。～ **nibs** 可可豆的子叶。～ **powder** 一种褐色火药。

co·co(a)·nut[ˈkəukənʌt; ˋkokənət] ***n***. **1.** 椰子(果)。**2.** 〔俚〕头，脑袋。***That accounts for the milk in the*** ～. 〔谑〕啊，原来是这样。～ **butter** = ～ oil. ～ **matting** 椰毛编织的垫子，棕垫。～ **milk** [**water**] 椰子汁。～ **oil** 椰子油〔可食用或制肥皂用〕。～ **palm** [**tree**] 椰子树。

COCOM = Coordinating Committee (Controlling East-West Trade) 东西方贸易统筹委员会(亦称巴黎统筹委员会)。

co·con·scious[kəuˈkɔnʃəs; koˋkanʃəs] ***a***. **1.** 意识到同样事物的。**2.** 并(存)意识的。**-ness** ***n***. 【心】并(存)意识。

co·con·spir·a·tor[ˈkəukənˈspirətə; ˋkokənˋspɪrətɚ] ***n***. 共谋者。

co·coon[kəˈkuːn; kəˋkun] **I** ***n***. **1.** (蚕)茧；(昆虫的)卵袋；(蚯蚓等的)土房；(蜘蛛等的)子囊。**2.** 茧状物；(军用物品等的)塑料披盖，防护喷层。**II** ***vt***. **1.** 作茧包藏，把…包在茧内。**2.** 以茧状物[喷层]包(军用品等)。～ *the patient in blanket* 把病人裹在毯子里。—***vi***. 作茧，成茧状。～ **shells** 出壳茧。～ **strippings** 茧皮。

co·coon·e·ry[kəˈkuːnəri; kəˋkunərɪ] ***n***. 养蚕场，蚕室。

co·cotte[1][kəˈkɔt; kəˋkat] ***n***. 〔F.〕妓女〔尤指(巴黎的)高等娼妓〕；淫妇，作风不正派的女人。

co·cotte[2][kəˈkɔt; kəˋkat] ***n***. 砂锅〔饭馆中用来蒸煮原汁菜肴之用〕。

co·co·zel·le[ˌkəukəˈzeli, -ˈzel; ˏkokəˋzɛlɪ, -ˋzɛl] ***n***. 可可绿皮南瓜〔西葫芦之类〕。

co·crys·tal·li·za·tion[ˈkəuˌkristəlaiˈzeiʃən; ˋkoˏkrɪstəlaɪˋzeʃən] ***n***. 【物】共结晶。

co·cur·ric·u·lum[ˌkəukəˈrikjuləm; ˏkokəˋrɪkjʊləm] ***n***. (*pl*. **-la** [-lə; -lə]) 辅助课程。

cod[1][kɔd; kad] ***n***. (*pl*. ～, ～**s**) 【鱼】鳕(= ～fish)。*the Bank* ～纽芬兰鳕。～**-liver** 鳕肝。～**-liver oil** 鱼肝油。

cod[2][kɔd; kad] ***n***. **1.** 〔方〕荚，壳，蒴(= pod)；〔古〕袋，阴囊。**2.** 〔Scot.〕枕头，靠垫。

cod[3][kɔd; kad] ***vt***., ***vi***. 〔俚〕哄骗，愚弄。

cod[4][kɔd; kad] ***a***. 〔英方〕滑稽的，讽刺的。

COD, C.O.D. = **1.** cash on delivery 货到付款。**2.** collect on delivery 货到收款。**3.** *Concise Oxford Dictionary* 〔英〕《简明牛津词典》。

co·da[ˈkəudə; ˋkodə] ***n***. 〔It.〕**1.** 【乐】结尾。**2.** (小说、戏剧等的)结局部分。

cod·ding[ˈkɔdiŋ; ˋkadɪŋ] ***n***. 捕鳕，捕鳕业。

cod·dle[ˈkɔdl; ˋkadl] **I** ***vt***. **1.** 娇养，溺爱；过分细心地照料。**2.** 用文火煮，嫩煮(鸡蛋等)。～ ***oneself*** 对自己过分娇养。**II** ***n***. 〔口〕娇生惯养的人，身体虚弱的人。

code[kəud; kod] **I** ***n***. **1.** 法典；法规。**2.** 规则，准则；(社会、阶级等的)惯例，习俗，制度。**3.** (电)码，代码，密码，暗码；代号，略号，暗号。**4.** 【生】遗传(密)码。*the civil* [*criminal*] ～民[刑]法典。*the moral* ～道德准则。～ *of signals* 信号密码(本)。～ *of the school* 校规。～ ***and conventions*** 规章制度。***C- Napoléon***[ˈkɔːd nəpəuleiˈɔːŋ; ˋkɔd nəpoleˋɔŋ] 拿破仑法典。***C- of Hammurabi*** (古代巴比伦的)汉穆拉比法典。～ ***of honour*** 社会礼法；决斗惯例。～ ***of written law*** 成文法典。***the International Code*** 国际电码。***the Morse*** ～ 摩尔斯电码。**II** ***vt***. **1.** 把…编成法典[法规]。**2.** 把…译成[编成]电码；编(码)；译(码)。～ **address** 电报挂号。～ **book** 电码本，密码本。～**breaker** 密码译电员。～ **flag** 信号旗。～ **machine** 译码机。～**-message** 密码电信。～ **name** 代号。～**switching** 【计】编号系统转换。～ **translator** 译码机。**-r** ***n***. 【自】编码装置；【讯】记发器。

co·dec·li·na·tion[ˌkəudekliˈneiʃən; ˏkodɛklɪˋneʃən] ***n***. 【天】极距(= polar distance)，赤纬的余角。

co·de·fend·ant[ˈkəudiˈfendənt; ˏkodɪˋfɛndənt] ***n***. 【法】共同被告，株连被告。

co·de·in(e)[ˈkəudiːin; ˋkodɪˏɪn] ***n***. 【药】可待因。

co·dep·o·si·tion[ˈkəuˌdepəˈziʃən; ˋkoˏdɛpəˋzɪʃən] ***n***. 【化、物】共淀积。

co·det·ta[kəuˈdetə; koˋdɛta] ***n***. 〔It.〕【乐】小结尾。

co·dex[ˈkəudeks; ˋkodɛks] ***n***. (*pl*. ***co·di·ces***[ˈkəudisiːz, ˈkɔdisiːz; ˋkodɪsiz, ˋkadɪsiz]) 〔L.〕**1.** (圣经等古籍的)抄本。**2.** 〔古〕法典。**3.** 【医】处方书，药典。

cod·fish[ˈkɔdfiʃ; ˋkadˏfɪʃ] ***n***. 【动】鳕，大头鱼。～ *aristocracy* 〔美〕捕鳕致富的人，暴发户。

codg·er[ˈkɔdʒə; ˋkadʒɚ] ***n***. 〔口〕怪人，有怪癖的老头子；家伙；〔英方〕吝啬鬼。

cod·i·cil[ˈkɔdisil; ˋkadəˏsɪl] ***n***. **1.** 【法】遗嘱的附录。**2.** 附注；备考，附录。

cod·i·cil·la·ry[ˌkɔdiˈsiləri; ˏkadɪˋsɪlərɪ] ***a***. 附注的；备考的。

cod·i·fi·ca·tion[ˌkɔdifiˈkeiʃən; ˏkadɪfɪˋkeʃən] ***n***. 法规汇编。

cod·i·fy[ˈkɔdifai, ˈkəud-; ˋkadəˏfaɪ, ˋkodə-] ***vt***. (**-fied**; **-fy·ing**) **1.** 把…编成法典。**2.** 编纂，整理。

cod·ing[ˈkəudiŋ; ˋkodɪŋ] ***n***. 编码；译成电码。

cod·lin, cod·ling[1][ˈkɔdlin, -liŋ; ˋkadlɪn, -lɪŋ] ***n***. (做菜用的)尖头苹果；未成熟的小苹果。

cod·ling[2][ˈkɔdliŋ; ˋkadlɪŋ] ***n***. 幼鳕。

co·don[ˈkəudən; ˋkodən] ***n***. 【生】(遗传)密码子。

cod·piece[ˈkɔdˌpiːs; ˋkadˏpis] ***n***. 十五、十六世纪男子短裤前面所悬的袋状物。

cods·wal·lop[ˈkɔdzˌwɔləp; ˋkadzˏwaləp] ***n***. 〔英俚〕胡说八道，愚蠢而没有价值的话[文章]。

Co·dy[ˈkəudi; ˋkodɪ] ***n***. 科迪[姓氏]。

co·ed[ˈkəuˈed; ˋkoˋɛd] **I** ***n***. 〔美口〕(男女同校的)女生〔co-education 的略语〕。**II** ***a***. 男女同校的，(男女同校)

女学生的。**co·ed·i·sm** *n*.〔口〕男女同校制度。
co·e·di·tion [ˌkəuiˈdiʃən; ˏkoɪˋdɪʃən] *n*.(在不同国家用不同文字同时出版的同一部著作的)联合出版版本;合作出版版本。
co·ed·na [kəuˈednə; koˋɛdnə] *n*.〔美〕女大学生。
co·ed·u·cate [kəuˈedjukeit; koˋɛdjuˏket] *vt*., *vi*. **1**.(使…)实行[受]男女同校教育。**2**.〔美口〕(使)和异性交际。
co·ed·u·ca·tion [ˈkəuˌedju(ː)ˈkeiʃən; ˏkoɛdʒəˋkeʃən] *n*. 男女同校;〔美口〕与异性交际。**-al** *a*., **-al·ly** *ad*.
coef., **coeff**. = coefficient.
co·ef·fi·cient [kəuiˈfiʃənt; koəˋfɪʃənt] **I** *a*. 共同作用的。**II** *n*. **1**. 共同作用;协同因素。**2**.【数,物】系数,率;程度。~ *of absorption* 吸收率[系数]。~ *of expansion* 膨胀系数。~ *of displacement* 排水量[系数]。
coe·la·canth [ˈsiːləˌkænθ; ˋsiləˏkænθ] *n*.【古生】空棘鱼(化石)。
coe·len·ter·ate [siˈlentəreit; sɪˋlɛntəˏret] *n*., *a*.【动】腔肠动物(的)。
coe·len·ter·on [siˈlentərən; sɪˋlɛntəˏrɑn] *n*. (*pl*. *-tera* [-rə; -rə])【动】体肠腔。
c(o)e·li·ac [ˈsiːliæk; ˋsilɪˏæk] *a*.【生理】腹的,下腹的,腹腔的。
coe·lom, **coe·lome** [ˈsiːləm, ˈsiːləum; ˋsiləm, ˋsilom] *n*. (*pl*. *coe·lo·ma·ta* [siˈləumətə; sɪˋlomətə], ~*s*)【动】体腔。
coe·lo·stat [ˈsiːləˌstæt; ˋsiləˏstæt] *n*.【天】定天镜。
co·emp·tion [kəuˈempʃən; koˋɛmpʃən] *n*. **1**. 囤积,搜购。**2**.【罗马法】买卖婚姻。
coen-, **coeno-** *comb*.*f*. 共同: *coeno*cyte.
coe·nen·chy·ma [siˈlenkimə; sɪˋlɛnkɪmə] *n*. (*pl*. *-ta* [-tə; -tə])【动】共质轴;共骨骼。
coe·nes·the·sia [ˌsiːnisˈθiːzjə; ˏsinɪsˋθizjə] *n*.【心】一般感觉(= coenesthesis)。
coe·no·bite [ˈsiːnəubait; ˋsɛnəˏbaɪt] *n*. 修道院住院修士。
coe·no·bit·ism [ˈsiːnəubaitizəm; ˋsinəˏbaɪtɪzəm] *n*. 修道院制。
coe·no·cyte [ˈsiːnəusait; ˋsinoˏsaɪt] *n*.【生】多核细胞,多核体;合胞体。
coe·no·gen·e·sis [ˌsiːnəuˈdʒenisis; ˏsinoˋdʒɛnɪsɪs] *n*.【生】后生变态。
coe·no·sarc [ˈsiːnəuˌsɑːk; ˋsinoˏsɑrk] *n*.【生】共体,共肉。
coe·no·zy·gote [ˌsiːnəuˈzaigəut; ˏsinoˋzaɪgot] *n*.【生】多核合子。
coe·nu·rus [siˈnjurəs; sɪˋnjurəs] *n*. (*pl*. *-ri* [-ai; -aɪ])【动】共尾幼虫。
co·en·zyme [kəuˈenzaim; koˋɛnzaɪm] *n*.【生化】辅酶。
co·e·qual [kəuˈiːkwəl; koˋikwəl] *a*., *n*. (地位、能力等)互相平等的(人),同权的(人),同身分的(人)。**-ly** *ad*.
co·e·qual·i·ty [ˌkəui(ː)ˈkwɔliti; ˏkoˑiˋkwɑlətɪ] *n*. 互相平等,同等,同权。
co·erce [kəuˈəːs; koˋɝs] *vt*. 强制,强迫,胁迫;压制。~ *sb*. *into* (*doing*) 强迫某人(做)。
co·er·ci·ble [kəuˈəːsibl; koˋɝsəbl̩] *a*. **1**. 可强迫的。**2**. 可压凝的;可压缩成液态的。
co·er·cion [kəuˈəːʃən; koˋɝʃən] *n*. 强迫;胁迫;高压政治[统治]。~ *and bribery* 威胁利诱。*No* ~! 反对强制[高压统治]。
co·er·cion·a·ry [kəuˈəːʃənəri; koˋɝʃənərɪ] *a*. = coercive.
co·er·cion·ist [kəuˈəːʃənist; koˏɝʃənɪst] *n*. 高压统治论者,强制主义者。
co·er·cive [kəuˈəːsiv; koˋɝsɪv] *a*. 强制的,强迫的,胁迫的,高压的。~ **force**【物】矫顽[磁]力。**-ly** *ad*.
coes·ite [ˈkəusait; ˋkosaɪt] *n*.【矿】柯石英。
co·es·sen·tial [ˌkəuiˈsenʃəl; ˏkoəˋsɛnʃəl] *a*. 同素的,同体的,同质的。
co·e·ta·ne·ous [ˌkəuiˈteiniəs; ˏkoɪˋtenɪəs] *a*. = coeval.
co·e·ter·nal [ˌkəuiˈtəːnl; ˏkoˑiˋtɝnl̩] *a*. 同样永存的,永远共存的。
co·e·val [kəuˈiːvəl; koˋivəl] **I** *a*. 同时代[年代、时期、年龄]的(*with*)。**II** *n*. 同时代的人,同年代的人[东西]。
co·e·val·i·ty [ˌkəuiːˈvæliti; ˏkoiˋvælətɪ] *n*. 同时代,同时期;同年龄。
co·ex·ec·u·tor [ˌkəuigˈzekjutə; ˏkoˑɪgˋzɛkjətɚ] *n*. (*fem*. *-trix* [-triks; -triks])【法】(遗嘱的)共同执行人,共同受托人。
co·ex·is·tence [ˈkəuigˈzistəns; ˋkoɪgˋzɪstəns] *n*. 共存,共处。*peaceful* ~和平共处。
co·ex·ist [kəuigˈzist; ˋkoˑɪgˋzɪst] *vi*. (在同地)同时存在,同在,共存(*with*)。~ *with* … *peacefully* 与…和平共处。
co·ex·ist·ent [ˌkəuigˈzistənt; ˏkoˑɪgˋzɪstənt] *a*. 同在的,共存的,同时代的。
Co·ex·tend [ˈkəuiksˈtend; ˏkoˑɪksˋtɛnd] *vi*., *vt*. (在时、空方面)(使)共同扩张。
co·ex·ten·sive [ˈkəuikstensiv; ˋkoˑɪkstɛnsɪv] *a*. 同广阔的,同久远的,(时空)共同扩张的。**-sion** *n*.
co·fac·tor [kəuˈfæktə; koˋfæktɚ] *n*. **1**.【数】余因子。**2**.【生】辅(助)因素。
C. of C. = Chamber of Commerce.
C. of. E. = Church of England.
cof·fee [ˈkɔfi; ˋkɔfɪ] *n*. 咖啡(树、豆、粉或色)。*a cup of* ~一杯咖啡。*black* ~(不加牛奶的)咖啡。*white* ~牛奶咖啡。~*-and*〔美口〕一杯咖啡和少许糕点等。~ **bar**〔英〕咖啡馆。~ **bean**, ~**berry** 咖啡豆。~ **break** (上班时的)喝咖啡休息〔一般在上午十时和下午三时〕。~ **cake** 早餐点心〔以面粉、奶油、蛋、糖等制成〕。~ **cooler** 偷懒耍滑的人。~ **cup** 咖啡杯。~ **extract** 咖啡精。~ **grinder** **1**. 咖啡磨。**2**.〔美俚〕飞机引擎。~ **grounds** 咖啡渣。~ **hour** 正式会议后的自由聚谈〔多有咖啡招待〕。~**house** 咖啡馆。~ **maker** 煮咖啡的壶。~ **lightener** 掺在咖啡里的人造牛奶。~ **mill** 咖啡豆的磨具;〔美军俚〕机关枪。~ **palace** = ~house. ~ **pot** 咖啡壶;〔美俚〕小餐馆。~ **room** 咖啡室[店]。~ **shop** 咖啡店;(一般的)小餐馆。~ **stall**, ~ **stand** (街头)咖啡摊。~ **table** 咖啡桌〔放在沙发前的小桌或茶几〕。~**-table book** 陈设在咖啡小桌上的书(多为精装大开本画册)。~ **tavern** (不卖酒的)小餐馆。~ **tree** 咖啡树。~ **whitener** = ~ lightener.
cof·fer [ˈkɔfə; ˋkɔfɚ] **I** *n*. **1**. 贵重品箱;保险箱,银柜。**2**.〔*pl*.〕资产,财源;国库,金库。**3**. 围堰;潜水箱;沉箱;浮船坞;【船】隔离舱,【建】天花板的镶板,藻井。*the* ~*s of the state* 国库。**II** *vt*. **1**. 把…装入箱内,把…放存金库内,贮藏。**2**.【建】用镶板装饰。~ **dam** *n*. 围堰;沉箱;隔离舱。**-ing** *n*. 格子天花板。
Cof·fey [ˈkɔfi; ˋkɑfɪ] *n*. 科菲〔姓氏〕。
Cof·fin [ˈkɔfin; ˋkɑfɪn] *n*. 科芬〔姓氏〕。
cof·fin [ˈkɔfin; ˋkɔfɪn] **I** *n*. **1**. 棺材。**2**. (马的)蹄槽。**3**.【印】木框。**4**. (不适于航海的)破旧的船(= ~-ship)。**5**. (运送放射性物质的)重屏蔽容器。*drive a nail into sb.'s* ~ 促人早死。*in one's* ~ 已死,已葬。**II** *vt*. 把…入殓,收殓;收藏(书籍等)。~ **boat**〔美〕猎野鸭的小船。~ **bone** 蹄骨。~ **joint** 蹄关节。~ **nail**〔美俚〕香烟,烟卷儿。~ **plate** 棺盖上的金属名牌〔记生死年月日〕。~ **varnish**〔美〕烈酒。
cof·fin·ite [ˈkɔfinait; ˋkɑfinaɪt] *n*.【矿】水硅铀矿。
cof·fle [ˈkɔfl; ˋkɑfl̩] *n*. (连锁着的)一长列奴隶[兽类]。
co·flyer [kəuˈflaiə; koˋflaɪr] *n*. 副飞行员。
co·found·er [kəuˈfaundə; koˋfaundɚ] *n*. 共同创立者。

C

C of S = chief of staff 参谋长。

co·func·tion [kəu'fʌnkʃən; ko'fʌnkʃən] *n*.【数】余函数。

cog[1] [kɔg; kɑg] **I** *n*.【机】(齿轮的)钝齿,嵌齿【建】雄榫,凸榫。*have a* ~ *loose* (脑子等)有些不正常,有点毛病。*hunting* ~*s*【机】追逐齿;〔口〕处于从属地位但不可缺少的人[物]。*slip a* ~ (意外地)失算;失错,疏漏。**II** *vt*., *vi*. (*-gg-*) (在…上)装齿轮,(在…上)楔榫。~ **wheel** 嵌齿轮。

cog[2] [kɔg; kɑg] *vt*. (*-gg-*) (用假骰子)欺骗;行贿。~ *a die* [*the dice*] 用骗人手段掷骰子。

cog[3] [kɔg; kɑg] *n*. 小船;附属于大船的供应船。

cog. = cognate; cognate with.

co·gen·cy ['kəudʒənsi; 'kodʒənsɪ] *n*. **1**. 说服力;(理论等的)中肯;恳切。**2**. 〔*pl*.〕有说服力的说法。

co·gent ['kəudʒənt; 'kodʒənt] *a*. 有说服力的,使人信服的;无法反驳的。**-ly** *ad*.

cogged[1] [kɔgd; kɑgd] *a*. 有齿轮的。

cogged[2] [kɔgd; kɑgd] *a*. 有弊的,骗人的。

Cog·ge·shall ['kɔgzɔːl; 'kɑgzɔl] *n*. 科格索尔〔姓氏〕。

cog·ging ['kɔgiŋ; 'kɑgɪŋ] *n*.【建】接头;〔集合词〕榫。

cog·i·ta·ble ['kɔdʒitəbl; 'kɑdʒətəbl̩] *a*. 可以思考的,可以想像的。

cog·i·tate ['kɔdʒiteit; 'kɑdʒə,tet] *vi*., *vt*. 慎重思考,考虑;【哲】思维。

cog·i·ta·tion [ˌkɔdʒi'teiʃən; ˌkɑdʒɪ'teʃən] *n*. 思考,考虑,思考力;〔常 *pl*.〕思想;计划,设计。

cog·i·ta·tive ['kɔdʒitətiv; 'kɑdʒə,tetɪv] *a*. 深思熟虑的,有思考力的。

cog·i·ta·tor ['kɔdʒiteitə; 'kɑdʒə,tetə] *n*. 深思熟虑的人。

co·gi·to er·go sum ['kɔdʒiˌtəu'əːgəu'sʌm; 'kɑdʒɪ,to-'ɜgo'sʌm] 〔L.〕我思故我在〔笛卡儿语〕。

cogn. = cognate.

co·gnac ['kəunjæk, 'kɔn-; 'konjæk, 'kɑn-] *n*. (法国)柯纳克(Cognac) 产的白兰地酒;〔口〕(品质优良的)白兰地酒。

cog·nate ['kɔgneit; 'kɑgnet] **I** *a*. **1**. 同族的;【法】女系亲戚的,母族的。**2**. 同类的,同性质的,同种的(*with*)。**3**.【语言】同源的;同语根的;同语族的。**II** *n*. **1**.【法】亲族;外戚。**2**. 同源物;同性物。**3**.【语言】同源[根]词。~ **languages** 同语族语言。~ **object** [**accusative**]【语法】同义受辞〔例:tell a tale 中的 tale〕。

cog·na·tion [kɔg'neiʃən; kɑg'neʃən] *n*. **1**. 同族;亲戚;外戚,女系亲戚。**2**.【语言】同语族;同词源。

cog·ni·tion [kɔg'niʃən; kɑg'nɪʃən] *n*. 认识;认识力;(在认识过程中形成的)知识。**-al** *a*.

cog·ni·tive ['kɔgnitiv; 'kɑgnətɪv] *a*. 认识的,有认识力的。~ *powers* 认识力。~ **dissonance**【心】内心冲突。~ **science** (以人脑智能活动为研究对象的)认知科学。

cog·ni·za·ble ['kɔgnizəbl, 'kɔn-; 'kɑgnəzəbl, 'kɑn-] *a*. **1**. 可认识的。**2**.【法】可受理的,审判权限内的。**-bly** *ad*.

cog·ni·zance ['kɔgnizəns; 'kɑgnəzəns] *n*. **1**. 认识;承认;认识范围。**2**. 管辖(权),监督(权);【法】审理,审判权。**3**. 纹章图案;标记,记号。*beyond* [*out of*] *one's* ~ 认识不到的;不受…管辖的。*come to one's* ~ 知道。*have* ~ *of* 认识到;注意到;有审判权。*lack of* ~ 认识不足。*take* ~ *of* 认识;受理审判。*take no* ~ *of* 对…置之不理。*within one's* ~ 可以认识到的;在…管辖以内。

cog·ni·zant ['kɔgnizənt; 'kɑgnɪzənt] *a*. **1**. 认识,知道。**2**. 有管辖权的,有审判权的。*be* ~ *of* 认识到,知道。

cog·nize [kɔg'naiz; 'kɑg,naɪz] *vt*. 知道,认识。

cog·no·men [kɔg'nəumen; kɑg'nomən] *n*. (*pl*. ~*s*, ***cog·no·min·a*** [kɔg'nɔminə; kɑg'nɑmɪnə]) 姓;(古罗马人的)家名,第三名〔例:Caius Julius Caesar 的 Caesar〕;别名;绰号。

co·gno·scen·te [ˌkɔnjəu'ʃenti; ˌkɑnjo'ʃɛntə] *n*. (*pl*. *-ti* [-tiː;-ti]) 〔It.〕(美术品的)鉴定家。

cog·nos·ci·ble [kɔg'nɔsibl; kɑg'nɑsəbl̩] *a*. 可以认识得到的;可以打听明白的,可知的。

cog·no·vit [kɔg'nəuvit; kɑg'novɪt] *n*.【法】(承认原告诉讼理由为正当的)被告承认书,具结。

Co·gon [kə'gəun; kə'gon] *n*.【植】白茅属〔尤指白茅,茅针(*Imperata cylindrica*)〕。

co·hab·it [kəu'hæbit; ko'hæbɪt] *vi*. (男女)同居(*with*);〔旧〕共同生活。

co·hab·i·tant [kəu'hæbitənt; ko'hæbətənt] *n*. 同居者。

co·hab·i·ta·tion [ˌkəuhæbi'teiʃən; ˌkohæbə'teʃən] *n*. 同居,同住,同国。

Co·han [kəu'hæn; ko'hæn] *n*. 科汉〔姓氏〕。

co·heir ['kəu'ɛə; 'ko'ɛr] *n*. 共同继承人。

co·heir·ess ['kəu'ɛəris; 'ko'ɛrɪs] *n*. 女性共同继承人。

Co·hen ['kəuin; 'koɪn] *n*. 科恩〔姓氏〕。

co·here [kəu'hiə; ko'hɪr] *vi*. **1**. (互相)挤紧,黏合,凝聚。**2**. 一致(*with*),团结。**3**. (理论等)前后一贯,有条理,紧密。

co·her·ence, co·her·en·cy [kəu'hiərəns, -si; ko-'hɪrəns, -sɪ] *n*. **1**. 紧密的结合,凝聚。**2**. 统一,首尾一贯;一致性。**3**.【物】同调;【光】相干性,相参性;【化】内聚力;内聚现象。

co·her·ent [kəu'hiərənt; ko'hɪrənt] *a*. **1**. 紧密地结合着的;凝聚性的。**2**. (话等)有条理的,首尾一贯的;一致的。**3**.【光】相干的,相参的。

co·her·er [kəu'hiərə; ko'hɪrə] *n*. **1**. 密聚[凝聚]者。**2**.【电】金屑[粉末]检波器。

co·he·sion [kəu'hiːʒən; ko'hiʒən] *n*. **1**. (各部的)结合;【物】(分子的)凝聚,内聚,内聚力,内聚性;〔喻〕结合力,团结。**2**.【植】连着。*It undermines* ~ *and creates dissension*. 这件事会破坏团结,制造纠纷。

co·he·sive [kəu'hiːsiv; ko'hisɪv] *a*. 有黏着力的,有附着力的;凝聚性的;内聚性的,有结合力的。~ **force** 凝聚力,内聚力,黏合力。**-ly** *ad*. **-ness** *n*.

co·ho ['kəuhəu; 'koho] *n*. (*pl*. ~, ~*s*)【动】银大马哈鱼〔原产北太平洋,现大量引进美国北部淡水湖(河)〕(= coho salmon)。

co·ho·bate ['kəuhəubeit; 'kohobet] *vt*. 再[多次]蒸馏。

co·hort ['kəuhɔːt; 'kohɔrt] *n*. **1**. (古罗马的)步兵大队(300—600 人)。**2**. 〔常 *pl*.〕军队;一群,队(*of*)。**3**.【生】区,股。**4**. 助手;同伴;共犯,同谋者;追随者。

co·hosh ['kəuhɔʃ, kə'hɔʃ; 'kohɑʃ, kə'hɑʃ] *n*.【植】**1**. 毛茛科植物〔如升麻、类叶升麻〕。**2**. 唐松草叶葳岩仙(*Caulophyllum thalictroides*)。

C.O.I. = Central Office of Information 〔英〕中央新闻署。

coif [kɔif; kɔɪf] **I** *n*. **1**. 一种紧包在头上的小帽;【史】(盔下戴的)衬帽。**2**. (高级律师 sergeant-at-law 戴的)白帽;高级律师的地位[身份]。**3**. [kwɑːf; kwɑf] = coiffure (*n*.) **II** *vt*. 使戴布帽[白帽]。

coif·feur [kwɑː'fəː; kwɑ'fɜ] *n*. 〔F.〕理发师。

coif·fure [kwɑː'fjuə; kwɑ'fjur] **I** *n*. 〔F.〕理发;发型,发式;发饰。**II** *vt*. 把(头发)做成某种发式。

coign(e) [kɔin; kɔɪn] *n*.【建】外角;隅;隅石;楔。~ *of vantage* 有利地位。

coil[1] [kɔil; kɔɪl] **I** *vt*., *vi*. 卷,盘绕,(把…)盘[卷]成一圈(*up*)。**II** *n*. **1**. (一)卷,(一)盘,(一)圈。**2**. 螺旋管,蛇管。**3**.【电】线圈,绕组。~ **paper** 筒纸,卷纸。~ **spring** 螺形弹簧。

coil[2] [kɔil; kɔɪl] *n*. 〔古〕混乱;纠纷。(*shuffle off*) *this mortal* ~ (摆脱)人世的纷扰。

COIN = counterinsurgency.

coin [kɔin; kɔɪn] **I** *n*. **1**. 硬币;〔俚〕金钱。**2**. 〔古〕=

coign. *a base* ～劣币。*a false* ～ 伪币;赝品。*a silver* ～银币。*a small* ～小钱。*a subsidiary* ～辅币。**pay** (*sb*.) (**back**) **in his own** ～ 以其人之道还治其人之身。**ring a** ～ 敲响硬币检查真假。**II** *vt*., *vi*. 铸造(货币);制造,新创(新语等);靠…赚钱。～ **money** 〔俚〕大发其财,发横财;情况好。～ **one's brains** 动脑筋挣钱。～ **certificate** 〔美〕(政府发行的)兑换券。～ **telephone** 投币式公用电话。～**ing rate** (贵金属)铸造比率。

coin·age [ˈkɔinidʒ; ˋkɔɪnɪdʒ] *n*. **1**. 造币;铸币;(某国某时代的)货币(全部);货币制度;造币费。**2**. 创制品;新造语词。*the* ～ *of new words* 新词的创造。*the* ～ *of fancy* [*one's brain*] 空想[头脑]的产物。

co·in·cide [ˌkəuinˈsaid;ˏkoɪnˋsaɪd] *vi*. 与…一致,相合,符合,相符,相巧合(*with*)。*My opinion* ～*s with his*. 我的意见跟他巧合。*These two triangles* ～. 这两个三角形相互重合。*These two lines* ～ *with each other*. 这两条线彼此相合。

co·in·ci·dence [kəuˈinsidəns; koˋɪnsədəns] *n*. 一致(性),符合;巧合,暗合;【数】重合,叠合(素);同时发生[存在]。**a mere** ～ 偶合,巧合。

co·in·ci·dent [kəuˈinsidənt; koˋɪnsədənt] **I** *a*. (与…)一致[符合]的,(与…)暗合[巧合]的;同时发生的。～ *indicator* 【经】(与经济状况直接相关的)相关指数[指示物]。**II** *n*.【经】= ～ indicator. **-ly** *ad*.

co·in·ci·den·tal [kəuˌinsiˈdentl; koˏɪnsɪˋdɛntl̩] *a*. 符合的,暗合的,巧合的。**-ly** *ad*.

coin·er [ˈkɔinə; ˋkɔɪnɚ] *n*. 造币者;伪币制造者;(新词等的)创造者。

co·in·stan·ta·ne·ous [ˌkəuinstænˈteinjəs; ˏkoɪnstənˋteniəs] *a*. 同时(发生的)。

co·in·sti·tu·tion·al [kəuˌinstiˈtjuːʃənəl; koˏɪnstɪˋtjuʃənəl] *a*. (中学等)男女分班的。

co·in·sur·ance [kəuinˈʃuərəns; ˏkoɪnˋʃurəns] *n*. 共同担保[保险]。

co·in·sure [kəuinˈʃuə; koɪnˋʃur] *vt*., *vi*. **1**. (保险业的)联保。**2**. (保险业的)分保。

coir [ˈkɔiə; kɔɪr] *n*. 椰子皮壳纤维[制品]。～ **rope** 棕绳。

cois·trel, cois·tril [ˈkɔistrəl; ˋkɔɪstrəl] *n*. 〔古〕**1**. (骑士的)马僮;跟班。**2**. 恶棍,无赖,流氓。

co·i·tal [ˈkəuitl; ˋkoɪtl̩] *a*. 交媾的。

co·i·tion, coi·tus [kəuˈiʃən, ˈkəuitəs; koˋɪʃən, ˋkoɪtəs] *n*. (特指人类的)交媾,交合。

Coke [kəuk, kuk; kok, kuk] *n*. 科克〔姓氏〕。

coke[1] [kəuk; kok] **I** *n*. 焦(炭)。*mineral* ～天然焦。*a* ～ *oven* 炼焦炉。**II** *vt*. 把…炼制成焦炭。—*vi*. 炼焦;成焦炭。

coke[2] [kəuk, kok] *n*. **1**. 〔俚〕= cocaine. **2**. 〔美口〕可口可乐(= coca-cola)。**go and eat** ～ 别作打扰别人的事[少管闲事]。

co·ker·nut [ˈkəukənʌt; ˋkokɚˏnʌt] *n*. = cocoanut.

COL = **1**. computer-oriented language【计】面向计算机的语言。**2**. cost of living 生活费用。

col [kɔl; kɑl] *n*. **1**. (峰与峰之间的)山口,坳口。**2**.【气】鞍状等压线,气压谷。

col. = collector; college; colony; colour; column.

Col. = Colonel; Colorado; Colossian; Columbia.

col-[1] [用在 l 字母前] = com-.

col-[2] = colo-.

COLA = Cost of Living adjustment 〔美〕生活费用调节(指因生活费用上涨而给予的社会福利津贴)。

co·la[1] [ˈkəulə; ˋkolə] *n*. **1**.【植】(非洲)可乐树。**2**. 可乐〔可乐树子制成的饮料〕。

co·la[2] [ˈkəulə; ˋkolə] *n*. colon[2]的复数。

co·la·hol·ic [ˌkəuləˈhɔlik; ˏkoləˋhɑlɪk] *n*. 〔美俚〕喝可口可乐过度的人。

col·an·der [ˈkʌləndə; ˋkʌləndɚ] *n*. (洗菜等用的)滤器,漏勺。

co·lat·i·tude [kəuˈlætitjuːd; koˋlætəˏtjud] *n*.【天】余纬(度)。

col·can·non [kəlˈkænən, kɔl-; kəlˋkænən, kɑl-] *n*. (爱尔兰式)土豆炖白菜泥。

col·chi·cin(e), col·chi·ci·a [ˈkɔltʃisi(ː)n, kɔlˈkiʃiə; ˋkɑltʃəsin, kɑlˋkɪʃɪə] *n*.【化】秋水仙碱,秋水仙素。

col·chi·cum [ˈkɔltʃikəm; ˋkɑltʃɪkəm] *n*.【植】秋水仙;秋水仙制剂。

Col·clough [ˈkəukli, ˈkɔlklʌf; ˋkoklɪ, ˋkɑlklʌf] *n*. 科尔克拉夫〔姓氏〕。

col·co·thar [ˈkɔlkəθə; ˋkɑlkəθɚ] *n*.【化】铁丹〔由硫酸亚铁烧成的褐红色铁氧化物〕。

cold [kəuld; kold] **I** *a*. **1**. 冷,寒,冻;冰凉的。**2**. 冷静的,冷淡的,无情的,冷酷的;无趣味的;沉闷的;令人打冷颤的;扫兴的;【美】有冷感的,冷色的。**3**. (谜语)难猜中的(*opp*. hot)。**4**. (猎物嗅迹)已变淡的。**5**. (土壤)黏湿的;(肥料)腐熟缓慢的。**6**. 〔俚〕已死亡的。*He has to quit* ～. 他不得不完全放弃。*be* ～ *in manner* 态度冷淡。～ *as all get out* 〔美〕冷极。**get** [**have**] **sb**. ～〔口〕任意摆布(某人)。**give** [**show**] **the** ～ **shoulder to** 冷待,对…冷淡。**have** ～ **feet** 〔军俚〕意气沮丧,吓破了胆子。**in** ～ **blood** 无动于衷地,冷酷地,若无其事地(*kill in* ～ *blood* 杀人不眨眼)。**leave sb**. ～ 对人冷酷无情;未说动某人。**make sb**.**'s blood run** ～ 使某人不寒而栗。**pour** [**throw**] ～ **water on** (对他人计划等)泼冷水,扫…的兴。**turn the** ～ **shoulder on** 冷待,对…冷淡。**II** *n*. **1**. 寒冷;冰点下。**2**. 感冒,着凉,伤风。*fifteen degrees of* ～冰点下 15 度。**be left out in the** ～ 被…冷遇[摈弃]。**catch** [**take**] ～ 着凉,伤风。～ **in the head** 鼻炎,淌清鼻涕,鼻塞。**come in from the** ～ 不再被忽视;摆脱孤立。～ **on the lungs** 伤风咳嗽。**Feed a** ～ **and starve a fever**. 伤风要吃,发热要饿。**have a** ～ 伤风。～**blooded** *a*. 冷血的;杂种的(马等);怕冷的;冷酷的,冷淡的。～ **cash** 现款。～ **chisel** 冷錾。～**coil** 冷却用蛇管。～ **colours** 冷色〔灰、蓝、绿等〕。～ **comfort** 敷衍人的安慰。～ **counsel** [**news**] 不愿听的忠告[通知]。～ **cream** 冷霜〔化妆品〕。～ **cuts** 什锦冷盘。～ **dark matter**【天】冷黑体。～ **deck** 〔美俚〕作弊用的牌。～**-drawn** *a*. (金属丝等)冷抽的;(油等)冷提的。**C- Duck** 〔美〕冷鸭酒〔杂酒〕。～ **feet** 冰冷的脚;〔美俚〕害怕,胆小。～ **fusion**【物】冷(核)聚变。～ **game** 〔美〕胜败分明的比赛。～ **hardening** 加工硬化。～ **hardiness** 耐[抗]寒力。～**hearted** *a*. 冷酷的。～**-livered** *a*. 冷淡的。～ **meat** 冷的熟肉;经济菜;〔美俚〕死尸。～**-meat party** 〔美俚〕守夜;丧事。～ **peace** 冷和平〔敌对势力之间勉强维持的脆弱和平局面〕。～ **pig** 〔俚〕**1**. 零售退回的商品。**2**. 退回的空瓶等。**3**. 尸体。～**-proof** *a*. 御寒的。～ **purse** 无钱;贫穷。～**resistance** 抗[耐]寒性。～ **room** 冷藏室。～ **scent**【猎】(已走远了的野兽留下的)轻微的气味。～ **seeds** 瓜子。～ **sheets** 贞操。～**short** *a*. (金属)冷脆的。～ **shoulder** 冷冻烤羊排;藐视,冷眼对待。～**shoulder** *vt*. 疏远。～ **shudder** 〔美俚〕没钱的同伴,被人讨厌的人。～ **snap** 乍冷,骤冷。～ **sore** 唇疱疹,嘴边疱疹。～ **steel** 利器[刀剑等]。～ **storage** 冷藏;冷藏库;〔俚〕牢监。～ **turkey** 无准备,即席;突然,莽撞;〔美俚〕定价出售。～ **war** 冷战。**C- Warrior** 冷战政治家。～**-water** *a*. 没有水暖系统的。～ **wave 1**. 寒流。**2**. 冷烫(头发)。～ **weld** 冷焊。～**-work** *vt*. 冷加工(金属)。**-ly** *ad*. **-ness** *n*.

coldish [ˈkəuldiʃ; ˋkoldɪʃ] *a*. 微冷的。

Cole [kəul; kol] *n*. 科尔〔姓氏〕。

cole [kəul; kol] *n*. 蔬菜〔芸薹等,特指油菜〕。

co·lec·to·my [kəˈlektəmi; kəˋlɛktəmɪ] *n*.【医】结肠切除术。

Cole·man [ˈkəulmən; ˋkolmən] *n*. 科尔曼〔姓氏〕。

cole·man·ite [ˈkəulmənait; ˋkolməˏnaɪt] *n*.【矿】硬硼

C

钙石,硬硼酸钙石,硼炭石。

co·le·op·ter [ˌkɔliˈɔptə; ˌkɑlɪˋɑptɚ] *n*. 1.【动】独角虫。2. 环翼飞机,直升飞机。

Co·le·op·ter·a [ˌkɔliˈɔptərə; ˌkɑlɪˋɑptərə] *n*. 〔*pl*.〕【动】甲虫类,鞘翅目。

co·le·op·ter·on [ˌkəuliˈɔptəˌrɔn, kɔli-; ˌkolɪˋɑptəˌrɑn, kɑlɪ-] *n*. (*pl*. **-ter·a** [-ə; -ə])【动】鞘翅目昆虫(= coleopteran)。

col·e·op·ter·ous [ˌkɔliˈɔptərəs; ˌkɑlɪˋɑptərəs] *a*.【动】甲虫类的,鞘翅目的。

co·le·op·tile [ˌkəuliˈɔptl, -ˌkɔli-; ˌkolɪˋɑptl̩, -ˌkɑlɪ-] *n*.【植】胚芽鞘。

C

co·le·o·rhi·za [ˌkəuliəˈraizə; ˌkolɪəˋraɪzə] *n*. (*pl*. **-zae** [-ziː; -zi])【植】胚根鞘。

Co·le·ridge [ˈkəulridʒ; ˋkolrɪdʒ] *n*. 1. 利尔里奇〔姓氏〕。2. **Samuel Taylor** ~ 萨·柯尔律治〔1772—1834,英国诗人〕。

cole·seed [ˈkəulsiːd; ˋkolˌsid] *n*.【植】油菜(籽)。

cole·slaw [ˈkəulslɔː; ˋkolˌslɔ] *n*. 凉拌卷心菜(= cold-slaw)。

co·le·us [ˈkəuliəs; ˋkolɪəs] *n*.【植】锦紫苏。

cole·wort [ˈkəulwəːt; ˋkolˌwɝt] *n*.【植】海甘蓝,油菜(等)。

C.O.L.I. = cost of living index 生活费指数。

col·ic [ˈkɔlik; ˋkɑlɪk] **I** *n*.【医】(腹)绞痛;疝痛。**II** *a*.【医】(腹)绞痛的;疝痛的。

col·ic·in [ˈkɔlisin; ˋkɑlɪsɪn] *n*.【生化】大肠杆菌素。

col·ick·y [ˈkɔliki; ˋkɑlɪkɪ] *a*. (腹)绞痛的。

col·ic·root [ˈkɔlikˌruːt; ˋkɑlɪkˌrut] *n*. 1.【植】被粉肺筋草(*Aletris farinosa*)。2. 任何可治腹痛等的植物〔如块根马利筋〕。

col·ic·weed [ˈkɔlikˌwiːd; ˋkɑlɪkˌwid] *n*. 加拿大荷包牡丹(= squirrel corn)。

co·li·form [ˈkəuliˌfɔːm, ˈkɔli-; ˋkoləˌfɔrm, ˋkɑlɪ-] *a*. 筛状的;筛骨的。

Co·lin [ˈkɔlin; ˋkɑlɪn] *n*. 科林〔男子名, Nicholas 的昵称〕。

col·in [ˈkɔlin; ˋkɑlɪn] *n*.【动】鹑。

-coline = -colous.

col·i·se·um [ˌkɔliˈsiəm; ˌkɑləˋsɪəm] *n*. 1. 〔C-〕= Colosseum. 2. 戏院;音乐厅;体育场。

co·li·tis [kəuˈlaitis; koˋlaɪtɪs] *n*.【医】结肠炎。*acute* ~急性结肠炎。

col·khoz [kɔlˈkəuz; kɑlˋkoz] (前苏联的)集体农庄(= kolkhoz)。

coll. = collateral; colleague; collection; collector; college; colloquial; 〔L.〕collyrium【药】洗眼剂;栓剂。

col·lab·o·rate [kəˈlæbəreit; kəˋlæbəˌret] *vi*. 1. 合作,共同研究;(国家间的)协调,提携。2. 与敌合作,通敌;勾结(*with*)。

col·lab·o·ra·tion [kəˌlæbəˈreiʃən; kəˌlæbəˋreʃən] *n*. 1. 合作,合著,共同研究。2. 与敌合作,通敌,勾结。*in* ~ *with* 1. 与…合作[合著、合编]。2. 与…勾结。**-ism** 鼓吹与敌人合作;通敌。**-ist** *n*. 通敌分子,卖国贼。

col·lab·o·ra·tor [kəˈlæbəreitə; kəˋlæbəˌretɚ] *n*. 1. 合作者,共同研究者。2. 与敌合作分子,通敌分子,卖国贼。

col·lage [kɔˈlɑːʒ; kəˋlɑʒ] *n*. 1. (用火柴商标、车票、纸牌等拼贴而成的)拼贴(画)。2. 抽象派拼贴画。3. (互不相干物件的)大杂烩。

col·la·gen [ˈkɔləˌdʒən; ˋkɑləˌdʒən] *n*.【生化】(骨)胶原,成胶质。**-ic** *a*.

col·lap·sar [kəˈlæpsɑː; kəˋlæpsɑr] *n*.【天】崩塌(恒)星,黑洞(= black hole)。

col·lapse [kəˈlæps; kəˋlæps] **I** *vi*. 1. (屋顶等)倒塌,塌下;(政府等)崩溃,瓦解。2. (价格等)暴跌;(计划等)失败;(身体、健康等)衰退,消沉,颓丧;(用具等)折叠,压扁;压缩。—*vt*. 1. 使倒塌;使崩溃,使衰弱。2. 折叠。**II** *n*. 1. 倒塌,崩溃,衰弱。2. (价格等的)暴跌。3.【医】虚脱;萎陷。

col·lap·sar [kəˈlæpsɑː; kəˋlæpsɑr] *n*. 塌陷星,太空黑洞。

col·laps·i·ble, col·laps·a·ble [kəˈlæpsəbl; kəˋlæpsəbl̩] *a*. (椅子等)可折叠的,可压扁[压缩]的。*a* ~ *chair* 折椅。~ **tube** 收缩管,软管。

col·lar [ˈkɔlə; ˋkɑlɚ] **I** *n*. 1. 衣领;硬领;项圈;护肩,(牲口的)轭。2. 环状物;【机】端箍,轴环;【建】柱环;系梁,底梁;【植】根颈。3. (猪肉等的)肉卷。4. (一杯啤酒表面的)泡沫。5.【橄榄球】紧抱。6. 〔美俚〕逮捕。*against the* ~ (马上坡时)轭具勒紧肩膀;冒着困难,下死力(干等),千辛万苦。*be hot under the* ~〔俚〕发怒;奋激。*be in* [*out of*] ~ (马套上[卸下]轭具)听候[解除]役使;〔俚〕有[无]工作,担任[失去]职务。*in the* ~ 受压制[束缚]。~ *of SS* [*esses*] SS 连锁形颈章。*fill one's* ~〔口〕尽本分,尽职。*keep sb. up to the* ~ 把人当牛马使唤。*seize take* (*sb.*) *by the* ~ 抓住领口。*slip the* ~ 避开困难;挣脱,逃脱。*wear sb.'s* ~〔口〕听人差遣。**II** *vt*. 1. 扭住领口;上衣领;使戴项圈。2. 〔口〕捕,捉;取,窃取;拉用,扯用;(不断谈话)留住不放。3.【橄榄球】抱住。4. 做(肉)卷。*Who's* ~*ed my pen*? 谁拿走了我的钢笔? ~ **beam**【建】系梁。~**bone**【解】锁骨。~ **button** [**stud**] (把硬[软]领扣在无领衬衫上用的)领扣。**C- day** 〔英〕颈饰日;〔谑〕绞刑日。~ **gall** 马颈上的擦伤。~ **harness** 颈部的马具。~ **work** 吃力的工作;【冶】冷作。

col·lard [ˈkɔləd; ˋkɑlɚd] *n*.【植】(菜叶不包卷起来的)散叶甘蓝。

col·lared [ˈkɔləd; ˋkɑlɚd] *a*. 有领的,戴着领圈的;(肉)成卷的。

col·lar·et(te) [ˌkɔləˈret; ˌkɑləˋrɛt] *n*. 女用围巾,女用领巾。

col·lat. = collateral; collaterally.

col·late [kɔˈleit; kɑˋlet] *vt*. 1. 核对,对照,校对;(装钉)整理,检查。2.【宗】授与牧师职。

col·lat·er·al [kɔˈlætərəl; kəˋlætərəl] **I** *a*. 1. 侧面的;旁边的;旁系的;间接的;副的;附属的,附带的;附加的,追加的。2. 平行的,并列的。**II** *n*. 1. 旁系亲属。2. 〔美〕附属担保物〔*cf*.〔英〕security〕;附带事项,附属部分。3.【解】侧突。~ **damage**〔婉〕间接损害,附带损害〔指战时造成的平民伤亡和非军设施的损失〕。~ **evidence** 旁证,间接证据。~ **issue** 附带诉讼。~ **office** 兼职。~ **relatives** 旁系亲属。~ **security** 附属担保物。~ **surety** 副保证人。**-ly** *ad*.

col·la·tion [kɔˈleiʃən; kɑˋleʃən] *n*. 1. 核对,校对,校勘;整理。(页码的)检查。2. 牧师职的委任。3. 小吃,零食,茶点;(端日的)夜点。

col·la·tor [kɔˈleitə; kɑˋletɚ] *n*. 核对者,校对者;整理人;牧师职授任者。

col·league [ˈkɔliːg; ˋkɑlig] *n*. 同事,同行。

col·lect[1] [kəˈlekt; kəˋlɛkt] **I** *vt*. 1. 收集,收藏;召集;征收(税等),募(捐),领取(信件等)。2. 集中,整理(思想);镇定;鼓起(勇气);把牢(缰绳)。3. 〔古〕推测。~ *a horse* 将马把牢。—*vi*. 聚集;堆积;募捐(*for*);〔美〕收账,收款。~ *on delivery*〔美〕= cash on delivery. ~ *oneself* 平心静气,镇定一下。**II** *a*., *ad*. 由接收者付款的[地]。*to telephone* ~打一个由受话者付款的电话。~**ing agent** 收款代理人。

col·lect[2] [ˈkɔlekt; ˋkɑlɛkt] *n*.【宗】短祷。

col·lect·a·ble, col·lect·i·ble [kəˈlektəbl; kəˋlɛktəbl̩] *a*. 可收集的,可收取的;可代收的。

col·lec·ta·ne·a [ˌkɔlekˈtɑːnjə; ˌkɑlɛkˋtenɪə] *n*. 〔L.〕〔*pl*.〕总集,文集,杂录;杂集。

col·lect·ed [kəˈlektid; kəˋlɛktɪd] *a*. 1. 收集成的。2. 泰然自若的,镇定的。~ *papers* 论文集。~ *works* 全集。**-ly** *ad*. 泰然,冷静地。**-ness** *n*. 镇定。

col·lec·tion [kə'lekʃən; kə`lɛkʃən] ***n*.** **1.** 收集,采集;集团,收集品,珍藏;(收藏丰富的)美术馆。**2.** 征收,收款;征税;捐款;募捐。**3.** 〔*pl*.〕(牛津大学等各学院的)学期考试。***make*** [***take up***] ***a*** ~ ***for*** 为…募捐。

col·lec·tive [kə'lektiv; kə`lɛktɪv] **I** ***a*.** 集合的;聚合性的;共同的,集体的,集团的。~ *wishes of the people* 人民的共同愿望。**II** ***n*.**【语法】集合名词;【统】集体。~ **action** 集体行动。~ **agreement** [**bargaining**] (劳资间的)集体协定[合同]。~ **behaviour** 集体行为。~ **effort** 集体的力量,协力。~ **farm** = kolkhoz. ~ **farming** 集体农业。~ **fire** 集合射击。~ **fruit**【植】聚合果〔桑子等〕。~ **goods** 集体财产,公共设施〔公园、道路等〕。~ **intervention** 共同干涉。~ **note** 连名通知。~ **noun**【语法】集合名词。~ **ownership** 集体所有(制)。~ **species**【植】综合种。**-ly** ***ad*.**

col·lec·tiv·ism [kə'lektivizəm; kə`lɛktɪv͵ɪzəm] ***n*.** 集体主义。

col·lec·tiv·ist [kə'lektivist; kə`lɛktɪvɪst] ***n*., *a*.** 集体主义者(的)。

col·lec·tiv·i·ty [ˌkɔlek'tiviti;͵kɑlɛk`tɪvətɪ] ***n*.** 全体,总体;集体,集团;集体主义,集体精神;集体状态。

col·lec·tiv·ize [kə'lektivaiz; kə`lɛktɪ͵vaɪz] ***vt*.** 使成为共同的,使集体化。

col·lec·tor [kə'lektə; kə`lɛktɚ] ***n*.** **1.** 收集家;采集者;收集器。**2.** 收税员;收款员;募捐人;〔美〕(海关的)征收员;收票员。**3.**【电】集电器,集电极;集流器[环];整流子;换向器;【机】集合器;集尘器;【计】编辑机。**-ship** ***n*.** **1.** 收税员[收款员等]的职权。**2.** (古董等的)收集,收藏。

col·leen ['kɔli:n; `kɑlin] ***n*.** 〔Ir.〕少女,(金发碧眼的)姑娘;〔美〕爱尔兰姑娘。~ *bawn* [bɔ:n; bɔn] 漂亮的姑娘。

col·lege ['kɔlidʒ; `kɑlɪdʒ] ***n*.** **1.** (综合大学中的)学院。**2.** 〔美〕分科[单科]大学;高等(专科)学校;〔英〕大学预科专门学校。**3.** (以上各学校的)校舍;院;(牛津、剑桥等大学的自治组织)宿舍。**4.** (英国的)私立中等学校〔亦称"公学"〕;(法国的)私立高等学院。**5.** 团体,学会。**6.**【宗】长老会,红衣主教团。**7.** 〔俚〕监牢,感化院;(老弱残废人的)收容所。*C- of Arms* = *Herald's C-* 徽章院。*C- of Cardinals* = *Sacred C-* (梵蒂冈教廷的)枢密院。*C- of Justice* 苏格兰高等法院。~ *of the apostles* (十二)使徒团。*C- of Surgeons* 外科医学会。~**-bred** ***a*.** 受过大学教育的。~ **cap** 大学帽。~ **forest** 实验林。~ **ice** 〔美〕= sundae. ~ **living** 大学牧师的薪水。~ **man** 高等学校毕业生。~ **pudding** 一人一份的葡萄干布丁。~ **woman** 女大学生,高等学校毕业女生。

col·leg·er ['kɔlidʒə; `kɑlɪdʒɚ] ***n*.** **1.** 〔英〕伊顿 (Eton) 公学的公费生。**2.** 〔美〕大学生。

col·le·gi·al [kə'li:dʒiəl; kə`lidʒɪəl] ***a*.** = collegiate.

col·le·gi·al·i·ty [kəˌli:dʒi'æliti; kə͵lidʒɪ`ælətɪ] ***n*.** **1.** 共同掌权。**2.**【天主】教皇与主教分权的原则。

col·le·gi·an [kə'li:dʒiən; kə`lidʒɪən] ***n*.** **1.** 高等学校[专科学校等]的学生[毕业生]。**2.** 某些团体[集体]的成员。**3.** 〔古、俚〕监狱中同房间的人。

col·le·gi·ate [kə'li:dʒiit; kə`lidʒɪɪt] **I** ***a*.** **1.** 学院的,大学的,高等学校(学生)的;大学程度的。**2.** (某些)集体组织的。**3.** 〔美俚〕愉快的,有趣的。**II** ***n*.** 学院[高等学校,大学]学生。~ *church* 置有牧师会的大教堂;〔Scot.〕由几个牧师共同管理的教堂;〔美〕协同教会〔教堂〕。~ *education* 大学教育。

col·le·gi·um [kə'li:dʒiəm; kə`lidʒɪəm] ***n*.** **1.** 学院。**2.** 长老会。

col·lem·bo·lan [kə'lembəulən; kə`lɛmbolən] ***n*.**【动】弹尾目昆虫(= springtail)。

col·len·chy·ma [kə'leŋkimə; kə`lɛŋkɪmə] ***n*.**【植】厚角组织。

col·let ['kɔlit; `kɑlɪt] ***n*.** **1.** (戒指上的)宝石座。**2.**【机】有缝夹头,套爪;(钟表中的)油丝固着环。

col·lide [kə'laid; kə`laɪd] ***vi*.** (车等)碰撞 (*with*);(意志等)冲突,抵触 (*with*)。**-r** ***n*.**【物】(高速粒子)对撞机。

col·lie ['kɔli; `kɑlɪ] ***n*.** 柯利狗〔苏格兰牧羊长毛狗〕。

Col·lier ['kɔliə; `kɑlɪɚ] ***n*.** 科利尔〔姓氏〕。

col·li·er ['kɔliə; `kɑlɪɚ] ***n*.** **1.** 〔英〕(煤矿的)矿工。**2.** 煤船;煤船船员[水手]。**3.** 〔废〕煤商。

col·lier·y ['kɔljəri; `kɑljərɪ] ***n*.** (包括建筑、设备在内的)煤矿。

col·lie·shang·ie ['kɔliʃæŋi; `kɑlɪʃæŋɪ] ***n*.** 〔Scot.〕争吵。

col·li·gate ['kɔligeit; `kɑlɪ͵get] ***vt*.** **1.** 把…绑扎在一起。**2.** 总括(事实),综合。

col·li·mate ['kɔlimeit; `kɑlɪmet] ***vt*.** **1.** 瞄准,校准,使准直。**2.** 使成平行。*a ~d light beam* 平行光束。

col·li·ma·tion [ˌkɔli'meiʃən;͵kɑlɪ`meʃən] ***n*.** 校准,瞄准;【物】准直。

col·li·ma·tor ['kɔlimeitə; `kɑlɪ͵metɚ] ***n*.**【物】准直仪,准直管,平行光管。

col·lin·e·ar [kɔ'linjə; kə`lɪnɪɚ] ***a*.**【数】共线的。

Col·lins[1] ['kɔlinz; `kɑlɪnz] ***n*.** 柯林斯〔姓氏〕。

Col·lins[2] ['kɔlinz; `kɑlɪnz] ***n*.** 〔亦作 c-〕果汁水酒〔鸡尾酒的一种〕。

Col·lins[3] ['kɔlinz; `kɑlɪnz] ***n*.** 〔英口〕(访客走后寄来的)感谢信。

col·lin·si·a [kə'linziə, -siə; kə`lɪnzɪə, -sɪə] ***n*.**【植】寇林希草属的草。

col·li·sion [kə'liʒən; kə`lɪʒən] ***n*.** 碰撞;冲突,抵触,(政党等的)倾轧。***come into*** ~ ***with*** 和…相撞[冲突,抵触]。***in*** ~ ***with*** 和…相撞[冲突]。~**mat**【海】防漏垫。

col·lo·cate ['kɔləkeit; `kɑlo͵ket] ***vt*.** 把…并置,并列;排列,配置。~ *books on a shelf* 把书排列在书架上。

col·lo·ca·tion [ˌkɔlə'keiʃən;͵kɑlə`keʃən] ***n*.** **1.** 并列,并置;排列,配置,安排,布置。**2.**【语法】连语(法),(习惯上的)搭配(关系)。

col·loc·u·tor ['kɔləkju:tə; `kɑləkjutɚ] ***n*.** 谈话的对手,对话者。

col·lo·di·on, col·o·di·um [kə'ləudjən, -diəm; kə`lodɪən, -dɪəm] ***n*.**【化】珂珞酊,火棉胶,胶棉。**-ize** ***vt*.** 用胶棉处理。~ **silk** 胶丝。

col·logue [kə'ləug; kə`log] ***vi*.** 密谈;〔方〕密谋 (*with*)。

col·loid ['kɔlɔid; `kɑlɔɪd] ***a*., *n*.** 胶质(的),胶体(的),胶态(的)。~ **chemistry** 胶体化学。

col·loi·dal [kə'lɔidl; kə`lɔɪdl] ***a*.** 胶质的,胶态的。

col·lop ['kɔləp; `kɑləp] ***n*.** **1.** 〔英方〕薄肉片;小薄片。**2.** 〔古〕(肥胖动物或人的)皮肤的皱褶。

col·loq. = colloquial(ism); colloquially.

col·lo·qui·al [kə'ləukwiəl; kə`lokwɪəl] ***a*.** 口语的;通俗语的,会话上的。**-ism** ***n*.** 口语(体)。**-ly** ***ad*.** 用口语。

col·lo·quist ['kɔləukwist; `kɑlokwɪst] ***n*.** (正式会谈的)会谈者;对谈者。

col·lo·qui·um [kə'ləukwiəm; kə`lokwɪəm] ***n*.** (*pl*. ***-qui·a*** [-ə; -ə], ~***s***) 学术讨论会。

col·lo·quy ['kɔləkwi; `kɑləkwɪ] ***n*.** **1.** (正式的)会谈;讨论;对谈,会话;(美议会)自由讨论。**2.** 对话体著作。

col·lo·sol ['kɔləusɔl; `kɑlə͵sɑl] ***n*.**【化】溶胶。

col·lo·type ['kɔləutaip; `kɑlə͵taɪp] ***n*.**【印】珂罗版(印刷品,印刷术)。

col·lude [kə'lju:d; kə`lud] ***vi*.** 共谋。~ ***with*** 勾结。

collun. = collunarium.

col·lu·nar·i·um [ˌkɔlju'nεəriəm;͵kɑljə`nɛrɪəm] ***n*.** (*pl*. ***-nar·i·a*** [-'nεəriə; -`nɛrɪə])【医】点鼻剂。

col·lu·sion [kə'lju:ʒən; kə`luʒən] ***n*.** 共谋;互相勾结。*the parties in* ~ 参加共谋的几方面(人)。***in*** ~ ***with*** 与…串通[勾结]。

col·lu·sive [kə'lju:siv; kə`ljusɪv] ***a*.** 共谋的。

col·lu·to·ri·um [ˌkɔlə'tɔriəm;͵kɑlə`torɪəm] (*pl*. ***-to-***

C

ri·a[-tɔriə; -tɔrɪə]) = collutory.
col·lu·to·ry [ˈkɔlətəri; ˋkɑlə͵torɪ] ***n.*** 漱口剂;漱口药。
col·lu·vi·al [kəˈluːviəl; kəˋluvɪəl] ***a.*** 【地】崩积的。
col·lu·vi·um [kəˈluːviəm; kəˋluvɪəm] ***n.*** (*pl.* ***-vi·a*** [-ə; -ə], ~***s***)【地】崩积层。
col·ly[1] [ˈkɔli; ˋkɑlɪ] ***n.*** = collie.
col·ly[2] [ˈkɔli; ˋkɑlɪ] **I** ***n.*** 煤灰,锅灰。**II** ***vt.*** 〔英方〕(被煤灰等)弄黑,弄脏。
col·lyr·i·um [kɔˈliriəm; kəˋlɪrɪəm] ***n.*** (*pl.* ***-ia*** [-iə; -ɪə])【医】洗眼剂;眼药(水)。
col·ly·wob·bles [ˈkɔli͵wɔblz; ˋkɑlɪ͵wɑblz] ***n.*** 〔*pl.*〕〔口、谑〕肚子痛,肚子响,肚子不舒服。

C

Col·man [ˈkəulmən; ˋkolmən] ***n.*** 科尔曼〔姓氏〕。
Col·ney Hatch [ˈkəuni ˈhætʃ; ˋkonɪ ˋhætʃ] (伦敦的)一所疯人院。
Colo. = Colorado.
col·o·bus [ˈkɔləbəs; ˋkɑləbəs] ***n.*** 【动】疣猴。
co-lo·cate [ˈkəul*əu*ˈkeit, Am. kəuˈləukeit; ˋkoloˋket, koˋloket] ***vt.***, ***vi.*** (两个以上部队等的)共同驻扎一地,共处在一地。**-ca·tion** ***n.***
col·o·cynth [ˈkɔləsinθ; ˋkɑləsɪnθ] ***n.*** 【植】药西瓜〔干果可作导泄药〕。
Co·logne [kəˈləun; kəˋlon] ***n.*** **1.** 科隆〔德国城市〕。**2.** 〔c-〕科隆香水,花露水(= ~ water)。
Co·lom·bi·a [kəˈlɔmbiə; kəˋlʌmbɪə] ***n.*** 哥伦比亚〔拉丁美洲〕。
Co·lom·bi·an [kəˈlɔmbiən; kəˋlʌmbɪən] **I** ***a.*** 哥伦比亚(人)的。**II** ***n.*** 哥伦比亚人。
Co·lom·bo [kəˈlʌmbəu; kəˋlʌmbo] ***n.*** **1.** 科伦坡〔斯里兰卡首都〕。**2.** 【天】月面第四象限的壁平原。
Co·lón [kɔˈlɔn; kɑˋlɑn] ***n.*** 科隆〔巴拿马港市〕。
co·lon[1] [ˈkəulən; ˋkolən] ***n.*** 冒号(:)。
co·lon[2] [ˈkəulən; ˋkolən] ***n.*** (*pl.* ~***s***, ***co·la*** [-lə; -lə])【解】结肠,大肠。
co·lon[3] [kəuˈləun; koˋlon] ***n.*** 科朗〔哥斯达黎加和萨尔瓦多的货币单位〕。
co·lon[4] [kəˈləun; kəˋlon] ***n.*** 〔F.〕殖民者〔尤指种植园主〕。
colo·nel [ˈkəːnl; ˋkɝnl] ***n.*** 〔美〕陆军〔空军、海军陆战队〕上校,〔英〕陆军〔海军陆战队〕上校〔空军上校叫 group captain〕。*a lieutenant* ~〔美〕陆军〔空军〕中校,〔英〕陆军中校〔空军中校叫 wing commander〕。~ *commandant* 〔英〕旅长。~*-in-chief* 〔英〕名誉团长(皇族)。**-cy**, **-ship** ***n.*** 陆〔空〕军上校的职位,团长的职位。
co·lo·ni·al [kəˈləunjəl; kəˋlonɪəl] **I** ***a.*** **1.** 殖民(地)的;殖民地化的。**2.** 〔常 C-〕〔美〕英领殖民地时代的,美国初期的;从前的,旧时的。**3.** 【生】群体的,集群的。**II** ***n.*** 殖民地居民;〔*pl.*〕〔英〕殖民地股票。*old* ~ *days* (独立前美国)英领殖民地时代。*the C- Bureau* [*Secretary*] 殖民局[大臣]。~ **architecture** (美国初期)殖民时代建筑式样。~ **militia** 屯田兵。**C- Office** 〔英〕殖民部。
co·lo·ni·al·ism [kəˈləunjəlizəm; kəˋlonɪəl͵ɪzəm] ***n.*** **1.** 殖民主义,殖民政策。**2.** 殖民地特征。**3.** 〔美〕守旧主义。
co·lon·ic [kəˈlɔnik; kəˋlɑnɪk] ***a.*** 结肠的。
col·o·nist [ˈkɔlənist; ˋkɑlənɪst] ***n.*** **1.** 殖民者,移住民;殖民地居民。**2.** 【生】外来动[植]物。*summer* ~*s* 避暑客。
co·lo·ni·tis [͵kɔləˈnaitis; ͵kɑləˋnaɪtɪs] ***n.*** 【医】结肠炎。
col·o·ni·za·tion [͵kɔlənaiˈzeiʃən; ͵kɑlənaɪˋzeʃən] ***n.*** 殖民;殖民地化,拓殖;【生】移植。
col·o·nize [ˈkɔlənaiz; ˋkɑlə͵naɪz] ***vt.*** **1.** 在(某处)开拓殖民地。**2.** 向(殖民地)移民。**3.** 〔美〕把选民非法移入(某地区)〔以扩充政党势力〕。**4.** 〔美〕(为政治目的)打入,混入(某部门等)。**5.** 【生】移植[植物]。—***vi.*** **1.** 开拓殖民地。**2.** 移居于殖民地;移植植物。
col·o·ni·zer [ˈkɔlənaizə; ˋkɑlə͵naɪzɚ] ***n.*** 殖民地开拓者,殖民者。
col·on·nade [͵kɔləˈneid; ͵kɑləˋned] ***n.*** **1.** 【建】柱廊,列柱。**2.** 成列的街树,行道树。*the method of* ~ *foundation* 【建】(桥梁工程中的)管柱钻孔法。
col·o·ny [ˈkɔləni; ˋkɑlənɪ] ***n.*** **1.** 殖民地;【希史】殖民城市;【罗史】征服区驻防地。**2.** 殖民[移民]团。**3.** 侨居地,侨民区;〔集合词〕侨民。**4.** (外交家等的)聚居地。**5.** 【动】(鸟、蚁、蜜蜂等的)集团,群;【生】群体,集群;【地】(异系统内的)化石群。**6.** (有特殊作用的)居住区〔如失业救济,收容难民等〕。*a leper* ~ 淋疯病人隔离区。~ *formation* 群居生活。*morale of the* ~(蜂)群势。*size of* ~*s* 群势的大小。***the Colonies*** (英国在美国最初设立的)东部十三州。
col·o·phon [ˈkɔləfən; ˋkɑlə͵fən] ***n.*** **1.** (印有著者、发行者及出版日期等的书籍的)末页,底页,版权页。**2.** (书籍的)扉页。**3.** 出版社的商标[徽章]。*from title page to* ~(全书)从头到尾。
col·o·pho·ny [kəˈlɔfəni; kəˋlɑfənɪ] ***n.*** 松香,松脂,树脂(= resin)。
col·o·quin·ti·da [͵kɔləˈkwintidə; ͵kɑləˋkwɪntɪdə] ***n.*** = colocynth.
col·or [ˈkʌlə; ˋkʌlɚ] 〔美〕=〔英〕colour。
color- = colour-.
col·or·a·ble [ˈkʌlərəbl; ˋkʌlərəbl] ***a.*** = colourable.
Col·o·rad·o [͵kɔləˈrɑːdəu; ͵kɑləˋrado] ***n.*** **1.** 科罗拉多〔美国州名〕。**2.** 〔the ~〕科罗拉多河〔北美洲〕。~ **beetle** 马铃薯甲虫。
col·o·ram·a [͵kʌləˈrɑːmə; ͵kʌləˋramə] ***n.*** 【物】彩色光。~ **lighting** 色光照明。
col·or·ant [ˈkʌlərənt; ˋkʌlərənt] ***n.*** 色料,颜料,染料。
col·or·a·tion [kʌləˈreiʃən; ͵kʌləˋreʃən] ***n.*** **1.** 染色(法),着色(法)。**2.** (天然)色,色彩。**3.** 【乐】赋色。*protective* ~保护色。
col·o·ra·tu·ra [͵kɔlərəˈtuərə; ͵kʌlərəˋtjurə] ***n.*** 〔It.〕【乐】**1.** 花腔。**2.** 花腔女高音(歌手)(= ~ soprano)。
col·or·cast [ˈkʌlə͵kɑːst, -͵kæst; ˋkʌlɚ͵kæst, -͵kæst] **I** ***n.*** 彩色电视广播。**II** ***vt.***, ***vi.*** (~, ~***ed***; ~, ~***ed***) 用彩色电视广播。
col·or·i·fic [͵kɔləˈrifik; ͵kʌləˋrɪfɪk] ***a.*** **1.** 能产生颜色的,能传色的。**2.** 色彩的;着了色的。**3.** (文体等)华丽的。
col·or·im·e·ter [͵kʌləˈrimitə; ͵kʌləˋrɪmətɚ] ***n.*** 色度计,比色计。**-metry** [͵kʌləˈrimitri; ͵kʌləˋrɪmətrɪ] ***n.*** 比色法。**-met·ric** ***a.***
co·los·sal [kəˈlɔsl; kəˋlɑsl] ***a.*** **1.** 巨像(似)的;巨大的,庞大的。**2.** 〔口〕异常的,非常的。*a* ~ *scheme* 宏伟的计划。***by a*** ~ ***accident*** 由于异常事故。***in one's*** ~ ***ignorance*** 因为丝毫不知道。
Col·os·se·um [͵kɔləˈsiəm; ͵kɑləˋsɪəm] ***n.*** **1.** 罗马椭圆形竞技场。**2.** 〔c-〕公共娱乐场。
Col·os·sian [kəˈlɔʃən; kəˋlɑʃən] ***n.*** (小亚细亚古城)歌罗西 (Colossae) 人[基督教徒]。
col·os·sus [kəˈlɔsəs; kəˋlɑsəs] ***n.*** (*pl.* ***-si*** [-sai; -saɪ]; ~***es*** [-iz; -ɪz]) **1.** 巨像;巨人,巨物。**2.** 〔C-〕(Rhodes 港入口处)阿波罗 (Apollo) 神青铜巨像〔约 36 米〕。**3.** 巨大的势力。
co·los·to·my [kəˈlɔstəmi; kəˋlɑstəmɪ] ***n.*** 【医】结肠造口术。
co·los·trum [kəˈlɔstrəm; kəˋlɑstrəm] ***n.*** (产妇的)初乳。
co·lot·o·my [kəˈlɔtəmi; kəˋlɑtəmɪ] ***n.*** 【医】结肠切开术,人工肛门造成术。
col·our, **col·or** [ˈkʌlə; ˋkʌlɚ] **I** ***n.*** **1.** 颜色,色彩;色调;着色;色素,颜料,染料;〔*pl.*〕图画颜料。**2.** 脸色,血色;(有色人种的)肤色。**3.** (声音、文章等的)格调,情调,风格;【乐】音色。**4.** 个性,特色;外观;口实;〔*pl.*〕立场,观点。**5.** 〔常 *pl.*〕军旗,团旗,军舰旗;船旗;优胜旗;【美海军】对军舰旗的敬礼。**6.** 〔*pl.*〕(作为某种标志的)彩色装饰[衣饰],徽记,绶带。7.〔美口〕精彩,生动,有声有色。8.〔美〕(矿砂中)贵金属微粒[量]。9.【印】油墨用量。*fundamental [primary, simple]* ~*s* 原色〔一般指红、蓝、黄〕。*secondary* ~*s* (二原色混合成的)等和色。*oil [water]* ~*s* 油画[水彩画]颜料。*fading [fugitive]* ~*s* 易褪的颜色。*fast* ~ *s* 经久不变的颜色。*contrast* ~反衬色。*He has very little* ~. 他脸色不好。*Her* ~ *came and went as she listened*. 她一面听一面脸色忽红忽白。*a high* ~良好的血色。*true [false]* ~*s* 真[假]面目。*The program lacks* ~.〔美口〕节目欠精彩。*local* ~地方色彩。*a person of* ~ 非白种人,(特指)黑人。*some* ~ *of truth* 若干真实味。*call to the* ~*s* 征兵,召服军役[入伍]。***change*** ~***s*** (激动得)变脸色。***come off with flying*** ~***s*** 旌旗飘扬地凯旋;大告成功;获得重大胜利。***come out in their true*** ~***s*** 暴露本来面目。***desert one's*** ~***s*** 变节;逃走。***gain [gather]*** ~ 血色变好。***get [win] one's*** ~***s***〔英〕当选为(运动)选手。***give sb. his*** ~ 选某人为选手。***give a false*** ~ ***to*** 把…描画得[渲染得]像真的一样,歪曲。***give*** ~ ***to*** 使(话说得)像真的一样,使…动听[生色],渲染;润饰。***haul down one's*** ~***s*** 投降。***hang out false*** ~***s*** 带着假面具,挂羊头卖狗肉,假表态。***have a high*** ~面色红润。***in one's true*** ~***s*** 露原形,发挥本性。***join the*** ~***s*** 入伍。***(the) King's [Queen's]*** ~ 英国军队的团旗。***lay on the*** ~***s (too thickly)*** 渲染太过;夸大。***lose*** ~ 脸色变青,失色;退色。***lower one's*** ~***s*** 降低要求;退让;放弃权利[主张];投降。***nail one's*** ~***s to the mast*** 高竖旗帜,坚决主张。***off*** ~ (瓷器等)色泽不佳;音色不好;〔俚〕脸色不好,没有精神;〔美俚〕低级趣味的。***paint in bright [dark]*** ~***s*** 画得鲜艳[晦暗];赞扬[贬损]。***put false*** ~***s upon*** 歪曲,故意曲解。***sail under false*** ~***s*** (船)挂着别国的国旗航行;打着骗人招牌,凭伪善、欺骗过日子。***salute the*** ~***s*** 对军旗敬礼。***see [not see] the*** ~ ***of sb.'s money*** 接受[不接受]某人款项。***see things in their true*** ~***s*** 看清事物真相。***serve (with) the*** ~***s*** 服兵役,当兵。***show one's*** ~***s*** 打出鲜明旗帜,说出自己意见[计划],现出本来面目。***show one's true*** ~***s*** 露出真面目,露马脚。***stick to one's*** ~***s*** 严守原则;坚持自己的立场。***strike one's*** ~***s*** 放下旗帜(投降)。***take one's*** ~ ***from*** 仿效,模仿。***under*** ~ ***of*** 在某种幌子下。***with*** ~***s flying and band playing*** 大张旗鼓,得意扬扬。***with the*** ~***s*** 当着兵;现役。***without*** ~ 不加渲染;无特色。**II** ***vt***. 1. 给…着色,给…上色;染。2. 渲染,粉饰,使带上色彩,歪曲。3. 使具有特征。*an account* ~*ed by prejudice* 带有成见色彩的报道。—***vi***. 1. 获得颜色。2. (水果因熟)变黄[红等];脸红 (*up*). ~ *up to the temples* (脸)红到发根。~ **bar** 对有色人种的歧视[隔离]。~ **bearer** 旗手。~**-blind** ***a***. 1. 不辨颜色的,色盲的。2. 无种族歧视的。~ **blindness** 色盲。~ **box** 颜料盒。~ **cast** ***v***., ***n***. 彩色电视广播。~ **caster** 讲评精彩的广播员。~ **chest** 信号旗箱。~**-code**, ~**-key** ***vt***. 对(电线、管道等)作上色彩标记。~ **combination** 配色。~**distinction** 种族歧视。~ **film** 彩色胶片[影片]。~ **filter**【摄】彩色滤光片。~ **guard** 护旗队。~ **line** = ~ bar. ~**man** 颜料商;染色师。~ **painter** 突出着色的抽象派画家。~ **photography** 彩色摄影。~**plate**【印】彩色版;套色彩印图片。~ **printing** 套色版,彩印。~ **response** 色谱敏感性。~ **question** 人种问题。~ **sergeant** 护旗中士。~ **stuff**〔美口〕生动的记事文。~ **television** 彩色电视。~ **telly**〔英俚〕彩色电视。~ **transparency** 彩色幻灯片。~ **wash** 彩色涂料;刷色。~ **way**【纺】配色,色组。

col·our·a·ble [ˈkʌlərəbl; ˋkʌlərəbl] ***a***. 1. 可着色的。2. 经过渲染的。3. 貌似有理的;表面上的,虚伪的。~ *imitation* 外观好看的仿制品。~ *sorrow* 假悲伤。**-bly** ***ad***.

col·our·ant [ˈkʌlərənt; ˋkʌlərənt] ***n***. 颜料,染料。

col·our·a·tion [ˌkʌləˈreiʃən; ˏkʌləˋreʃən] ***n***. = coloration.

col·oured [ˈkʌləd; ˋkʌlɚd] **I** ***a***. 1. 有彩色的,着了色的,染过的。2. 有色(人种)的,皮肤黑的;〔美〕黑种人的。3. 虚饰的,花哨的,似是而非的。*a* ~ *person* 非白人;黑人。~ **stone** (钻石之外各种色彩的)宝石。**II** ***n***.〔the ~〕有色人种的人〔尤指黑人〕;混血种人。

co·lour·ful [ˈkʌləful; ˋkʌlɚfəl] ***a***. 富于色彩的,花哨的;华美的;精彩的;丰富多彩的;有趣的;生动活泼的。**-ly** ***ad***. **-ness** ***n***.

col·our·ing [ˈkʌləriŋ; ˋkʌlərɪŋ] ***n***. 1. 着色(法),彩色颜料,染料。2. (脸上的)血色。3. 外观;外貌,伪装。4. 渲染;特色;(某种)倾向,色彩。~ *matter* 色素,染料。

col·our·ist [ˈkʌlərist; ˋkʌlərɪst] ***n***. 1. 着色者,善用彩色的人[配色师,画家]。2. 笔墨生动的作家。

col·our·less [ˈkʌləlis; ˋkʌlɚlɪs] ***a***. 1. 无色的;苍白的;退了色的。2. 不精彩的,无特色的。3. 中立的,公平的,无偏袒的;(新闻报道等)无倾向[色彩]的。**-ly** ***ad***. **-ness** ***n***.

col·our·y [ˈkʌləri; ˋkʌlərɪ] ***a***. 多色的,多彩的;【商】(货物)色泽优良的。

-colous *suf*. 住在[生在]…的。

col·pi·tis [kəulˈpaitis; kolˋpaɪtɪs] ***n***.【医】阴道炎。

col·por·tage [ˈkɔlˌpɔːtidʒ; ˋkɑlˏportɪdʒ] ***n***. 宗教书刊贩卖。

col·por·teur [ˈkɔlpɔːtə; ˋkɑlˏportɚ] ***n***.〔F.〕书贩;(尤指)贩卖圣经等宗教书籍的小贩。

Col.-Sergt, Col.-Sgt = Colour-Sergeant 掌旗军士;〔英〕(海军陆战队)上士。

Colt [kəult; kolt] ***n***. 柯尔特式自动手枪(= ~revolver)。

colt [kəult; kolt] **I** ***n***. 1. 幼小的公马[骆驼];顽皮小伙子;不懂事的男孩子。2. 没有经验的新手;【体】生手。3.【海】笞绳,绳鞭。**II** ***vt***.【海】用绳鞭抽打。~**'s tail**【气】凹凸云,卷云。~**'s teeth** 轻薄,放荡。

col·ter [ˈkəultə; ˋkoltɚ] ***n***. 前小犁,犁刀,犁头(=〔美〕coulter)。

colt·ish [ˈkəultiʃ; ˋkoltɪʃ] ***a***. 小马似的;没有经验的;轻浮的。

colts·foot [ˈkəultsfut; ˋkoltsˏfʊt] ***n***.【植】款冬。

col·u·brid [ˈkɔlubrid; ˋkɑljəbrɪd] ***n***. 黄颔蛇。

col·u·brine [ˈkɔljubrain; ˋkɑljʊˏbraɪn] ***a***. 1. 蛇(似)的。2. 无毒蛇的。~ *nature* 蛇似的性格。

co·lu·go [kəˈluːgəu; kəˋlugo] ***n***.【动】猫猴〔东南亚树居的一种哺乳动物〕(= flying lemur)。

Col·um [ˈkɔləm; ˋkɑləm] ***n***. 科勒姆〔姓氏〕。

Co·lum·ba [kəˈlʌmbə; kəˋlʌmbə] ***n***.【天】天鸽座。

col·um·ba·ri·um [ˌkɔləmˈbeəriəm; ˏkɑləmˋbɛrɪəm] ***n***. (*pl*. **-ria** [-riə; -rɪə]) 1. (古罗马的)鸽棚[房]。2. (一格一格的)骨灰匣壁龛,骨灰安置所。

col·um·bar·y [ˈkɔləmbəri; ˋkɑləmˏbɛrɪ] ***n***. 鸽棚;鸽房。

Co·lum·bi·a [kəˈlʌmbiə; kəˋlʌmbɪə] ***n***. 1. 哥伦比亚〔美国 Carolina 州的首府〕,(纽约的)哥伦比亚大学。2.〔诗〕美洲,美国〔意为 Columbus 发现之地〕。3. 哥伦比亚杂交羊〔Lincoln 种和 Rambouillet 种的杂交,体格特大〕。***the District of*** ~ 哥伦比亚特区〔美国首都华盛顿所在的行政区域,略作 D.C.〕。~ **University** 哥伦比亚大学。

Co·lum·bi·an [kəˈlʌmbiən; kəˋlʌmbɪən] **I** ***a***. 1. 哥伦比亚的。2.〔诗〕美国的。3. 哥伦布 (Columbus) 的。**II** ***n***.【印】一种活字。

col·um·bine[1] [ˈkɔləmbain; ˋkɑləmˏbaɪn] ***a***. 鸽的,鸽似的;鸽色的。~ *innocence* 鸽子一样纯洁无邪的。

col·um·bine[2] [ˈkɔləmbain; ˋkɑləmˏbaɪn] ***n***.【植】美洲耧斗菜。

co·lum·bite [kəˈlʌmbait; kəˋlʌmbaɪt] ***n***.【矿】铌铁矿。

co·lum·bi·um [kəˈlʌmbiəm; kəˋlʌmbɪəm] ***n***.〔废〕【化】铌〔现名 niobium〕。

C

Co·lum·bus [kəˈlʌmbəs; kəˋlʌmbəs] ***n*.** **1.** 哥伦布〔地名,美国 Ohio 州首府〕。**2.** **Christopher** ～ 哥伦布〔1446? —1506,据传于 1492 年发现北美洲〕。～ ***Day*** 〔美〕哥伦布节〔10 月 12 日,= Discovery Day〕。

co·lu·mel·la [ˌkɔljuˈmelə; ˏkɑljuˋmɛlə] ***n*.** (*pl*. ***-lae*** [-liː; -li]) **1.** 【生】小柱;【动】(爬虫的)中耳小骨;(螺的)轴柱,壳轴。**2.** 【植】蒴轴,果轴。

col·u·mel·li·form [ˌkɔljuˈmelifɔːm; ˏkɑljəˋmɛləˏfɔrm] ***a*.** 小柱形的。

col·umn [ˈkɔləm; ˋkɑləm] ***n*.** **1.** 【建】圆柱;圆柱状物〔如烟柱〕。**2.** 【军】纵队 (*opp*. line);队;(舰队的)纵阵,纵列,舰列。**3.** (报纸的)栏;【数】(纵)行;【印】栏;【化】塔。**4.** 【植】雌雄合体的柱状花蕊。**5.** 〔美〕(党派、候选人的)全体支持者。**6.** (报纸上的)专栏(文章)。*the* ～ *of the nose* 鼻梁。*spinal* ～ 脊柱,脊梁。*advertisement* [*literary*] ～广告[文学]栏。～ *of fours* 四路纵队。～ *of mercury* [*water*] 水银[水]柱。～*s of smoke* 烟柱。*in* ～ *of sections* [*platoons*, *companies*] 【军】按分队[小队,中队]编队。***in our*** [***these***] ～***s*** 〔报纸编者用语〕在本栏内,在本报上。**-ed** ***a*.** 图柱(状)的,有图柱的。

co·lum·nar [kəˈlʌmnə; kəˋlʌmnɚ] ***a*.** **1.** 圆柱的,柱状的,圆筒形的。**2.** (报纸等)专栏的。

co·lum·ni·a·tion [kəˌlʌmniˈeiʃən; kəˏlʌmnɪˋeʃən] ***n*.** **1.** 【建】列柱,列柱法。**2.** (页的)分栏。

co·lum·ni·form [kəˈlʌmnifɔːm; kəˋlʌmnɪˏfɔrm] ***a*.** (圆)柱状的。

col·um·nist [ˈkɔləmnist; ˋkɑləmnɪst] ***n*.** 〔美〕(报纸的)专栏作家。

co·lure [kəˈljuə; koˋljʊr] ***n*.** 【天】分至圈,两至圈,分至经线,四季线。*the equinoctial* ～ 二分圈,昼夜平分圈。*the solstitial* ～二至圈。

Col·vin [ˈkɔlvin; ˋkɑlvɪn] ***n*.** 科尔文〔姓氏〕。

col·za [ˈkɔlzə; ˋkɑlzə] ***n*.** 菜籽(油)。～ **oil** 菜(籽)油。

COM = **1.** Computer-Output Microfilm 计算机输出缩微胶卷。**2.** Computer-Output Microfilmer 计算机输出缩微摄影机。

Com. = Commander; Commission(er); Committee; Commodore.

com. = comedy; comic; comma; commander; commentary; commerce; commercial; commission; committee; commodore; common(ly); communication.

com- *pref*. 与,共,总共,全,等〔在 b, p, m 前用 com-;在 l 前改用 col-;在 r 前改用 cor-;在母音及 h, gn 前改用 co-;在其他场合下改用 con-〕。

co·ma[1] [ˈkəumə; ˋkomə] ***n*.** (*pl*. ～***s***) **1.** 【医】昏迷(状态)。**2.** 怠惰;麻木。

co·ma[2] [ˈkəumə; ˋkomə] ***n*.** (*pl*. ***-mae*** [-miː; -mi]) **1.** 【植】种毛,种缨;序缨,树冠。**2.** 【天】(彗星的)彗发。**3.** 【物】(透镜的)彗形像差。

co·make [ˈkəumeik; ˋkomek] ***vt*.** (***-made***; ***-mak·ing***) (担保)联署;共同签字(= cosign)。**-r** ***n*.** (担保)联署者;共同签字者。

co·man·age·ment [ˈkəuˈmænidʒmənt; ˋkoˋmænɪdʒmənt] ***n*.** 共同经营;共同管理(指工人参与企业管理)。

Co·man·che [kə*u*ˈmæntʃiː; koˋmæntʃi] ***n*.** (北美印第安人的)科曼奇族(语)。

co·mate[1] [ˈkəumeit; koˋmet] ***a*.** 【植】有种发的,有芒刺的;毛状的。

co·mate[2] [kə*u*ˈmeit; koˋmet] ***n*.** 伙伴。

co·ma·tose [ˈkəumətəus; ˋkoməˏtos] ***a*.** **1.** 【医】昏迷的。**2.** 怠惰的;麻木的。

co·mat·u·la, co·mat·u·lid [kəuˈmætʃuːlə, -lid; koˋmætʃulə, -lɪd] ***n*.** (*pl*. ***-lae*** [-liː; -li]) 【动】毛头星(= feather star)。

comb[1] [kəum; kom] **I** ***n*.** **1.** 梳,篦,梳机;【纺】精梳机;【空】排管。**2.** 鸡冠;鸡冠形物[山顶、浪头等]。**3.** 蜂房;【动】栉。**4.** 刻螺纹的某些器具。***cut the*** ～ ***of*** 挫其锐气,杀傲慢气焰,使屈辱。***go through*** [***over***] ***with a fine*** ～ 详细检查[研究]。**II** ***vt*.** 刷(毛),梳(发);(到处)搜寻,搜遍。—***vi*.** (波浪)涌起浪花。～ ***sb.'s hair the wrong way*** 使人发怒。～**-out** ***n*.** **1.** 清除。**2.** 彻底搜查。**3.** 搜罗。**4.** 梳理头发。

comb[2] [kuːm; kum] ***n*.** = combe.

com·bat [ˈkɔmbət; ˋkɑmbæt] **I** ***n*.** **1.** 格斗,搏斗;战斗。**2.** 论战。**3.** 〔美〕竞赛,比赛。*a single* ～(一对一的)格斗。*air* ～空战。**II** ***vi*.** (***-t***(***t***)***-***) 打,战斗;(和…)斗争(*with*; *against*);(为…)奋斗(*for*)。—***vt*.** 反对(不良现象等);防止。～ *forest fires* 防止林火。～ **car** 战车。～ **crew** 战斗人员。～ **fatigue** 战斗疲劳症。～ **gains** 战绩。～ **gasolines** 军用级汽油。～ **orders** 战斗命令。～**-plane** 〔美〕战斗机。～**-ready** ***a*.** 作好战斗准备的。～**-unit** 战斗部队。～**-worthy** ***a*.** 有战斗力的。

com·bat·ant [ˈkɔmbətənt; ˋkɑmbətənt] **I** ***a*.** (参加)战斗的;好斗的。**II** ***n*.** **1.** 斗士;战士;战斗部队,战斗员(*opp*. noncombatant)。**2.** 【美体】队员;【徽】二兽相斗式。～ **branch** (陆军)战斗部队。～ **nation** 交战国。

com·bat·ive [ˈkɔmbətiv; ˋkəmbætɪv] ***a*.** 好战的,斗志旺盛的。**-ly** ***ad*.** **-ness** ***n*.**

combe [kuːm; kum] ***n*.** 〔英〕(三面皆山或深入海中的)峡谷。

comb·er [ˈkəumə; ˋkomɚ] ***n*.** **1.** 梳者;精梳机,梳棉机。**2.** 卷浪,碎浪。

com·bi·na·tion [ˌkɔmbiˈneiʃən; ˏkɑmbəˋneʃən] ***n*.** **1.** 结合,合并,混合,联合,配合,组合。**2.** 合作;共谋,同谋;同党。**3.** 〔*pl*.〕〔英〕连裤衬衣。**4.** 【化】化合(物);【矿】聚形;〔*pl*.〕【数】组合;【语法】组合词。**5.** 附有旁座的摩托车。**6.** 暗码锁(的暗码)。*a crystal* ～合晶。*a missile-cruiser* ～配备有导弹的巡洋舰。***in*** ～ ***with*** 和…共同[结合、协同、协力、共谋]。～ **car** 〔美〕(头二三等的)混合客车。～ **cracking** 【化】(液相和汽相)联合裂化。～ **gas** 富(含石油气的)天然气。～ **lock** 暗码锁。～ **room** (剑桥大学的)特别研究员餐后休息室。～ **salad** 〔美俚〕垃圾。～ **vessel** 客货(混合)船。

com·bi·na·tive [ˈkɔmbinətiv; ˋkɑmbəˏnetɪv] ***a*.** 结合(性)的,集成的。

com·bine[1] [kəmˈbain; kəmˋbaɪn] ***vt*.** **1.** 使结合,合并。**2.** 兼备,兼有(各种性质等)。**3.** 使化合。*be* ～*d in* 化合成。*be* ～*d with* 与…结合着,与…分不开。～ *A with B* 使甲乙相结合[化合];兼备甲乙。～*d accounts* 总账。～*d card* 联合梳麻机。～*d efforts* 合作,协力。～*d operations* 【军】(海陆空军的)联合作战。～*d parlour and sitting room* 客房。—***vi*.** **1.** 联合,合并,合作,配合,协力。**2.** 化合。～ *with* 与…联合,与…化合。**combining stress** 复应力。**combining form** 【语法】构词成分。**combining power** 【化】化合力。

com·bine[2] [ˈkɔmbain, kəmˈbain; ˋkɑmbaɪn, kəmˋbaɪn] **I** ***n*.** 〔美口〕**1.** (政治上的)联合。**2.** 联合企业[工厂],综合工厂。**3.** 联合收割机(= ～harvester)。**4.** 〔美口〕组合艺术。**II** ***vt*.** 用联合收割机收割(庄稼)。～ **harvester** 联合收割机。

comb·ing [ˈkəumiŋ; ˋkomɪŋ] ***n*.** 【纺】**1.** 精梳。**2.** 〔*pl*.〕各级精梳毛;精梳落棉;短亚麻秸。～ **machine** 精梳机。

com·bo [ˈkɔmbəu; ˋkɑmbo] ***n*.** **1.** = combination. **2.** 〔口〕小爵士乐队。**3.** 〔澳俚〕与土著女子结婚的白人。

com·bus·ti·bil·i·ty [kəmˌbʌstəˈbiliti; kəmˏbʌstəˋbɪlətɪ] ***n*.** 燃烧力,可燃性。

com·bus·ti·ble [kəmˈbʌstəbl; kəmˋbʌstəbl] **I** ***a*.** **1.** 易燃的,燃烧性的。**2.** 易怒的。**II** ***n*.** 〔常 *pl*.〕燃料,可燃物。*a high-strung* ～ *nature* 一碰就发火的性格。

com·bus·tion [kəmˈbʌstʃən; kəmˋbʌstʃən] ***n*.** **1.** 燃烧,发火,点火。**2.** (有机体内营养料的)氧化。**3.** 骚动。**spontaneous** ～自燃。～ **bomb** 燃烧弹。～ **engine** 内燃机。

com·bus·tor [kəmˈbʌstə; kəmˋbʌstɚ] ***n.***【机】燃烧室。

comb·y [ˈkəumi; ˋkomɪ] ***a.*** 蜂窝似的,蜂房状的。

comd. = command.

comdg. = commanding.

comdr. = commander.

comdt. = commandant.

come [kʌm; kʌm] **I** ***vi.*** (***came*** [keim; kem]; ***come***) **1.** 来,过来;去,上,赴。*He came* (*to my house*) *last night*. 他昨晚(到我家里)来过。*Come nearer* (*to me*). 再过来一点。*Come* (*and*) *see me* . = *Come to see me*. 来(我家)玩呀。〔俚语尤其美国俚语中常略去 and 或 to〕。*I will* ～ (*to see you*) *soon*. 我过几天去(看你)。*Let'em all* ～! 让他们都来吧! *Light* ～, *light go*. 来得容易去得快。*Will you* ～ *with me to London*? 你愿意和我一道去伦敦吗? **2.** (时间、季节等)到来。*Spring has* ～. 春天到了。*The time will* ～ *when....* …的时候快到了。*in the years to* ～在今后的几年里。*in time(s) to* ～(在)将来。*the world to* ～ 来世。(*It will be*) *two years* ～ *Christmas* (= *when Christmas* ～*s*). 到圣诞节就两年了〔例句中的 come 是假设语气现在式〕。**3.** (事情)发生,落到…身上 (*to*). *whatever* ～*s to me* 我无论发生什么事(都…)。**4.** 来源于 (*of*),得自 (*from*)。*Dispute came of a trifling*. 争论是由一件小事引起的。*His money* ～*s from* …他的钱是从…那里得到的。**5.** 生自,出身于,是在…生长大的 (*of*; *from*)。～ *of a poor family* 出身贫苦。*I* ～ *from Shanghai*. 我是在上海生长大的,我是上海人。**6.** 想起,想出,想得;出现于。*A good plan came to me*. 我想起一个好办法。*It* ～*s on page 10*. 那在第十页上。*A knock came to my door*. 有人敲门了。**7.** 日渐成熟。*The wheat began to* ～. 小麦发芽了。**8.** 达到,伸展到。*The road* ～*s to the station*. 此路一直通到车站。**9.** 做成。*The butter will not* ～. (怎样搅拌)奶油(始终)搅不出来。**10.** 有,装,存。*This shirt* ～*s to three sizes*. 这种衬衫有三种尺寸。*The lemonade* ～*s in a can*. 柠檬水是罐装的。**11.** 变…了,…起来,开始…,以至于,终于是〔接不定式或形容词型表语〕。*Things will* ～ *right*. 一切会顺利进行的。*I have* ～ *to like him*. 我对他喜欢起来了。～ *into sb.'s favour* 为某人所器重。～ *to grief* 失败。～ *to harm* 受伤,受害。～ *apart* 分开了。**12.** 〔与 how 连用〕(怎么)会的。*How* ～ *you to hear of it*? 你怎么知道的? **13.** 需要(某种)代价(才能买到、实现、得到等)。*Good service* ～*s high*. 服务好,收费高。**14.** 生活过得(如何)。*How is she coming these weeks*? 她这几个星期(过得)怎么样? **15.** 合计成;归结为。*Your bill* ～*s to 5 dollars*. 尊账共计五元。*What you say* ～*s to this*. 你所说的总括来就是这样。**16.** 装作[冒充]…的样子。～ *the swell* [*great man*] 装阔,装做了不起的样子。**17.** 〔命令法〕喂! 嗜! 唉唉! *C-, tell me all about it*. 喂! 全告诉我吧。*C-, don't flatter me*. 嗜! 不要乱捧我。**18.** 〔美俚〕达到肉体刺激的顶点。—***vt.*** **1.** 〔口〕搞,做。**2.** 〔口〕假装。**3.** 达到(某一年龄)。***Come***! 〔美〕请进来 (= Come in!)。～ ***about*** **1.** 发生 (*How did all this* ～ *about*? 这一切是如何发生的?)。**2.** 发生;(风等)变向;【海】抢风调向。～ ***across*** **1.** (穿过…)来到。**2.** (偶然)遇见(某人),无意中发现(～ *across one's friend in* [*on*] *the street* 街上遇见朋友)。**3.** 〔美俚〕还(债);尽(义务)。**4.** 难理解,不可信。**5.** 招认。～ ***after*** 相继;跟着…来,续来;探寻,找;来取。～ ***again*** 〔美俚〕请再说一遍。～ ***along*** **1.** 一道来。**2.** 进步;同意,赞成。**3.** 〔祈使语气〕请过来,快一点儿! ～ ***and get it*** 〔美口〕(饭预备好了)请过来吃。～ ***and go*** 来来去去,忽(来)忽(去);变化无定(*Her colour came and went*. 她的脸色一忽儿红一忽儿白)。～ ***around*** = ～ round. ～ ***at*** **1.** 袭击,向…打来。**2.** 赶上,得到;达到(～ *at a true knowledge of* 得知…的真相。*Just let me* ～ *at you*! 让我跟你比一下;来,我跟你比! *First-class men are hard to* ～ *at*. 第一流人物难得)。～ ***away*** **1.** 脱掉。**2.** (一同)离开(某地)★ Go away 则是叫人"走开"。～ ***back*** **1.** 回来;想起来;〔口〕复原,恢复,复苏。**2.** 〔美俚〕还嘴。～ ***before*** **1.** 先来,优于。**2.** 被交付(审判等),被提出。～ ***between*** 介入…之间;离间。～ ***by*** **1.** 〔by 介词〕到手,获得。**2.** 〔by 副词〕通过附近;〔美俚〕拜访,看望。～ ***clean*** 〔美俚〕**1.** 坦白承认,说出实话,和盘托出。**2.** 修完课程。～ ***down*** **1.** 降,落,下来;走向台口;(物价)下跌;(树)被砍倒,(屋)被毁。**2.** (俚)大学毕业。**3.** 传,传下来 (*from*)。**4.** 败落,没落;〔美口〕病了起来 (*with*)。**5.** 〔口〕(慷慨)解囊,拿出钱(常加 *with*) (*He came down when I was hard up*. 我困难时他照顾过我)。～ ***down on*** [***upon***] **1.** 袭击;反对;责骂,骂。**2.** 向…索取(钱财) (*for*)。**3.** 严厉追究。～ ***down out of the tree*** 〔美〕拿出精神来;留神点;好好地干。～ ***down with*** **1.** 害病;病倒。**2.** 〔口〕出(钱),付。～ ***for*** 来取(物);来迎接(人)。～ ***forth*** 出来;涌现;提出,公布。～ ***forward*** **1.** 出来,出现;出头;(候选人)出来候选,应(众望)而起,自告奋勇,挺身而出。**2.** 增长。～ ***home*** **1.** 回家。**2.** 【海】锚脱掉。**3.** 说得正对;刺中(…心病),打动人心,影响深远 (*to sb., sb.'s heart, etc.*)。～ ***in*** **1.** 进入,进来,入场 (*Come in*! 请进来! 请过来!)。**2.** 当选,就任;上台,当权;(党派)组阁,取得政权。**3.** 到达。**4.** 流行起来;兴起。**5.** 到时候;到成熟期。**6.** 有用(起来)(～ *in useful* 有用,中用)。**7.** (现款)收进,到手,(比赛中)获得…名。**8.** 起作用,有效,(幽默话的)有意义(*Where do I* ～ *in*? 我的作用在哪儿呢? 我的好处在哪儿呢? *Where does the joke* ～ *in*? 什么地方好笑[意义在那里]?)。**9.** 干涉,妨碍。**10.** 〔美俚〕(母牛)下仔。～ ***in for*** 来取;接受,领取(份儿);受到(处分等)。～ ***in on*** [***upon***] 打动…,留在某人心里。～ ***in through the cabin window*** 〔美〕靠亲戚关系发迹,走后门。～ ***into*** **1.** 归入,进入;开始 (～ *into notice* 使人注目,引起注意。～ *into sight* 被人看见,出现,靠近。～ *into use* 开始应用。～ *into the world* 出生,出世)。**2.** 缔结,订立,赞成,加入;支持。**3.** 得到,继承。～ ***into one's own*** **1.** 收回自己的正当权利,恢复地位。**2.** 被人认识。～ ***it over*** 胜过;欺骗。～ ***it strong*** 〔口〕使劲[坚决]干;干得过分;夸大(*He* ～*s it too strong*. 他干得过分了)。～ ***near*** **1.** 不劣于,不亚于,及得上。**2.** 几乎,差一点就…。～ ***of*** **1.** 由于,是…的结果(～ *of drinking* 是喝酒所致)。**2.** 生自,出身,是在…生长大的。～ ***of age*** 成年。～ ***off*** **1.** (人)走了;(扣子、齿、发)脱落,(油漆)剥落。**2.** 成为(胜利者等)(～ *off victorious* (战争)胜利。～ *off a gainer* [*loser*] (做生意等)赚钱[蚀本])。**3.** (计划等)实现,实行 (*When does the ceremony* ～ *off*? 仪式什么时候举行?)。**4.** (预言)应验。**5.** (事业)完成,结果(～ *off well* [*badly*] 成功[失败],顺利[不顺利]。*They came off with flying colours*. 他们凯旋而归。*Everything came off satisfactory*. 结果事事如意)。**6.** 离开,〔祈使语气〕停止;别那么说啦! (～ *off your high horse* 〔美〕别那样骄傲,不要那样自大,不要那样固执。～ *off your perch* 〔美〕不要那样神气,放下你的臭架子)。**7.** 〔美口〕孵出。～ ***off with*** 发表(言论),讲出,宣布。～ ***on*** **1.** 〔on 介词〕= ～ upon. **2.** 〔on 副词〕(演员)出台,进步;进行(很好),发展(*The crops are* ～*ing on nicely*. 庄稼长得很好)。**3.** (冬、夜)等来临,接近;(敌人)袭来,攻来;(雨)下起来(*It came on to rain*. 下起雨来了)。**4.** (暴风雨等)起,发作;(病、苦痛等)加深,加重;(人物)给人突出印象,取得扎实的效果。**5.** (问题)提交讨论;(事件)被提出来。**6.** 〔祈使语气〕跟我来! 〔挑斗〕来吧! 快点来! (*He is coming on*. 他(一天天)好起来了。*A trial* ～*s on*. 要开审了)。～ ***on in*** 〔美〕= ～ on. ～ ***out*** **1.** 出来;(花)开出。**2.** (书等)出版,发行。**3.** (秘密等)现出,露出。**4.** (新玩意儿)初次出现;初次登台,初进社交界;参加 (*for*)。**5.** 【数】解答出来。**6.** 罢工,罢业。**7.** 〔美〕结果是;考取(第…名)(*The play* ～*s out well on the* *stage*. 这个剧本演出效果不错。*You* ~ *out well in that photo*. 你那张相片照得很好。*Nothing came out of all this talk*. 谈来谈去,结果全无。*The truth* ~*s out*. 真相大白,水落石出)。**8.** 消失。~ ***out against*** 出头反对,反抗。~ ***out of*** 出自,生自;(冲破…)出来。***Come out of that***! 走开!〔美俚〕去你的! 滚蛋! ~ ***out with*** **1.** 发表,公布;讲出;泄露(秘密)(~ *out with an advertisement* 登出广告)。**2.** 展出,供应。**3.** 跟…同行。~ ***over*** **1.** 〔over 介词〕(动)密布(天空);(变化)发生在…;(感情)抓住(人)。**2.** 〔over 副词〕从远方来,渡过来,传来;(从敌方)过来,投奔过来;变挂,变节;〔口〕欺骗;顺便来访。~ ***right*** 无事。~ ***pass*** 通过。~ ***round*** **1.** 来,转到。**2.** (生气的人)消除怒气;(病后)复原;苏醒。**3.** (风向等)改变;改变意见。**4.** 让步,同意。**5.** 笼络,诱骗(*You can't* ~ *round me with such yarns*. 你别想用这套花言巧语来哄骗我)。~ ***through*** **1.** 成功,胜利;脱险。**2.** (消息)传出;(电话)接通;通用,通行。**3.** 〔美〕改变信仰,变节;欺骗。**4.** 终结,完成。**5.** 招认,坦白。**6.** 支付;捐献。~ ***to*** **1.** 〔to 介词〕总计为,达到;结果是,终于(*Has it* ~ *to this*? 弄到这个地步了吗? 弄成这个样子了吗?)。**2.** 〔to 副词〕苏醒,复原;把船朝着风头,逆风;停泊。~ ***to a point*** 渐渐变尖。~ ***to think of it*** 〔口〕这样一想,那么。~ ***to bat*** 遇到难题,需要对付困难〔考验等〕。~ ***to no good*** 弄不好,结果不好。~ ***to oneself*** 〔***one's senses***〕苏醒;醒悟;复原。~ ***to pass*** 发生,兴起,遭遇。~ ***to stay*** 〔美〕木已成舟,(事)成定局,变成永久性的东西。~ ***to the point*** 恰当,得要领。~ ***to the same thing*** 殊途同归。~ ***to the scratch*** 采取断然处置,采取行动。~ ***to time*** 〔美〕服从命令;满足要求。~ ***together*** 会合。~ ***together again*** 和好如初。~ ***under*** **1.** 编入,归入…类〔项目〕。**2.** 受…的(影响),被…支配。~ ***unstuck*** 碰到困难;垮台,失败。~ ***up*** **1.** 来,走近。**2.** 上升,发芽;抬头。**3.** (暴风雨等)起,发作。**4.** 上京,晋京。**5.** 〔英〕搬进(学校)宿舍。**6.** 流行起来。**7.** 被提出。~ ***up against*** 遇到(困难),遭到(反对);与…矛盾。~ ***upon*** **1.** 碰到,碰见;忽然想到;突袭。**2.** 要求(~ *upon sb. for sth*. 向某人要求某物)。**3.** (人)成为…的累赘〔负担〕;(工作)落到(…头上)(*The disabled men* ~ *upon the town*. 残废人得到地方照顾)。~ ***up to*** 到达;及得上,不亚于;不负(期待),适合(标准等)。~ ***up with*** **1.** 赶上。**2.** 补充;提供,提出。**3.** (向人)报仇。~ ***what may*** 〔***will***〕= ~ ***weal or woe*** 无论发生什么事情,怎样都,反正都。***for months to*** ~ 此后数月。***How*** ~ ? 〔口〕为什么? ***How*** ~***s it that ...***? 怎么会…了呢? ***the to-come*** 〔俚〕未来,将来〔作名词用〕。

II ***int***. 〔表示鼓励、责备、不耐烦等〕注意! 得啦! 别忙! ~**-and-go** **1.** ***n***. 往来,来回,交通;收缩膨胀。**2.** ***a***. 近似的,大致的;易变的。~**-at-able** ***a***. 〔口〕易接近,易见面;不远;容易到手的。~**back** 〔口〕**1.** (声望等的)恢复;重整旗鼓,转好。**2.** 〔俚〕巧妙的反驳〔回答〕;〔美俚〕还嘴(*have a* ~*back like a cork* 随即恢复〔振作起来〕。*stage a* ~*back* 卷土重来;复辟)。**3.** 〔美俚〕不满〔抱怨〕的理由(*He was well treated and had no* ~. 他得到很好的待遇,没有什么可抱怨的了)。~ **down** 败落,落魄,没落;退步;(飞机的)下降。~**-hither** **1.** ***a***. 〔美俚〕诱惑人的,迷人的。**2.** ***n***. 诱惑,挑逗。**3.** 〔对家畜呼叫声〕来来! ~**-on** **1.** ***n***. 引诱;诱惑物;受骗者。**2.** ***a***. 有诱惑力的。~**-outer** 〔美〕脱党〔退会〕分子;急进分子。

co·me·di·an [kəˈmiːdiən; kə`midɪən] ***n***. **1.** 喜剧演员;滑稽人物。**2.** 〔罕〕喜剧作家。

co·me·dic [kəˈmiːdik, -ˈmedik; kə`midɪk, -`mɛdɪk] ***a***. (关于)喜剧的。

co·me·di·enne [kəˌmediˈen; kəˏmɪdɪ`ɛn] ***n***. 〔F.〕喜剧女演员;滑稽妇女。

co·me·di·et·ta [kəˌmediˈetə; kəˏmɪdɪ`ɛtə] ***n***. 小喜剧。

com·e·dist [ˈkɔmidist; `kɑmədɪst] ***n***. 喜剧作家。

com·e·do [ˈkɔmidəu; `kɑmɪˏdo] ***n***. (*pl*. ***com·e·dones*** [ˌkɔmiˈdəuniːz; ˏkɑmɪ`doniz], ~***s***)【医】(黑头)粉刺。

com·e·dy [ˈkɔmidi; `kɑmədɪ] ***n***. 喜剧;喜剧场面,喜剧事件;喜剧性。*a light* ~轻松喜剧。*a low* ~滑稽戏。*a musical* ~音乐喜剧。~ ***of manners*** (英国十七世纪末的)风俗喜剧。***cut the*** ~ 〔俚〕不再开玩笑。~ **relief** 【影】穿插在紧张场面中的轻松镜头。

come·li·ness [ˈkʌmlinis; `kʌmlɪnɪs] ***n***. **1.** 清秀,美丽。**2.** 〔古〕合宜,适当。

come·ly [ˈkʌmli; `kʌmlɪ] ***a***. **1.** 好看的,清秀的,美丽的。**2.** 〔古〕适当的,合宜的;满意的。

com·er [ˈkʌmə; `kʌmɚ] ***n***. **1.** 来的人,前来(申请…)的人。**2.** 〔美口〕有(成功)希望的人〔事〕。*a chance* ~偶然的来客,不速之客。*the first* ~先来者。***all*** ~***s*** 全体来人(申请人、应征者、中途加入者等)(*open to all* ~*s* 随意加入,欢迎加入)。

co·mes·ti·ble [kəˈmestibl; kə`mɛstəbl̩] **I** ***a***. 可以吃的。**II** ***n***. 〔常 *pl*.〕食粮,食物。

com·et [ˈkɔmit; `kɑmɪt] ***n***. 【天】彗星;【空】彗星机。~ **finder** 〔**seeker**〕观测彗星用的一种望远镜,寻彗镜。~ **wine** (彗星出现年酿造的)葡萄酒,醇美的葡萄酒。

com·et·ar·y, co·met·ic [ˈkɔmitəri, kɔˈmetik; `kɑmɪtərɪ, kɑ`mɛtɪk] ***a***. 彗星(状)的。

co·meth·er [kəuˈmeðə; ko`mɛðɚ] ***n***. 〔英爱、方〕**1.** 事情,事件;情况。**2.** 友谊,友好关系。***put the*** ~ ***on*** 劝说,劝诱。

come·up·pance [kʌmˈʌpəns; kʌm`ʌpəns] ***n***. 〔美口〕报应;应得的惩罚。

com·fit [ˈkʌmfit; `kʌmfɪt] ***n***. (球状)糖果;蜜饯,糖衣果仁。~ **cocoons** 僵蚕茧。

com·fort [ˈkʌmfət; `kʌmfɚt] **I** ***n***. **1.** 安慰。**2.** 安慰的东西,慰劳品;安慰者。**3.** 舒适,愉快。**4.** 〔常 *pl*.〕(现代化)生活舒适用品〔设备〕。**5.** 〔美〕鸭绒被。**6.** 〔古〕【法】援助。*cold* ~聊胜于无的安慰。*creature* 〔*bodily*〕~*s* 物质上的舒适(指衣、食等)。*What* ~? 〔古〕你好吗? ***be cold*** ~ 不很畅快。***be of*** (***good***) ~ 畅快。***gifts of*** ~ ***and thanks*** 慰问品。***give*** ~ ***to*** 安慰。***live in*** ~ 生活舒适。***take*** ~ ***in*** 以…自慰。**II** ***vt***. 安慰;使(痛苦等)缓和,使安乐;〔古〕援助,帮助。~**bag** 慰问袋。~**station** 〔**room**〕〔美〕公厕。~ **stop** 〔美〕长途汽车中途的休息停车。~ **woman**(二战时期日本军队中的)慰安妇,军妓。**-less** ***a***. 无安慰的,不舒服的;孤单的,孤寂的。

com·fort·a·ble [ˈkʌmfətəbl; `kʌmfɚtəbl̩] **I** ***a***. 愉快的,安乐的,舒适的;令人感到安慰的。**II** ***n***. 绒线围巾;〔美〕鸭绒被。**-ness** ***n***.

com·fort·a·bly [ˈkʌmfətəbli; `kʌmfɚtəblɪ] ***ad***. 愉快,安乐,称心如意地。

com·for·ter [ˈkʌmfətə; `kʌmfɚtɚ] ***n***. **1.** 慰问者。**2.** 〔the C-〕【宗】圣灵。**3.** 〔英〕毛围巾。**4.** 〔美〕鸭绒被。**5.** 〔英〕(哄小孩的)橡皮奶头。

com·fort·ing [ˈkʌmfətiŋ; `kʌmfɚtɪŋ] ***a***. 安慰的;令人鼓舞的。**-ly** ***ad***.

com·frey [ˈkʌmfri; `kʌmfrɪ] ***n***. 【植】**1.** 紫草科植物。**2.** = daisy.

com·fy [ˈkʌmfi; `kʌmfɪ] ***a***. (*-fi·er*; *-fi·est*) 〔口〕= comfortable.

com·ic [ˈkɔmik; `kɑmɪk] **I** ***a***. **1.** 喜剧的。**2.** 滑稽的,好笑的。**3.** 连环图画的。**II** ***n***. 〔美〕**1.** 滑稽品;滑稽新闻。**2.** 连环漫画。**3.** 〔英俚〕(杂技团的)丑角,滑稽演员。***the*** ~ 人间喜剧〔文学、人生等滑稽有趣的一面〕。~ **book** 〔美〕连环漫画杂志。~ **opera** 喜歌剧。~ **paper** 报纸的连环图画版。~ **relief** = comedy relief. ~ **strip** 连环漫画。

com·i·cal [ˈkɔmikəl; `kɑmɪkəl] ***a***. 滑稽的,好笑的,有趣的;喜剧性的;〔方、俚〕奇妙的。**-ly** ***ad***.

com·i·cal·i·ty [ˌkɔmiˈkæliti; ˏkɑmɪ`kælətɪ] ***n***. 诙谐,滑稽;滑稽的人〔物〕。

C

Com-in-Ch = Com-in-Chf = Commander-in-chief.

com·ing [ˈkʌmiŋ; ˋkʌmɪŋ] **I** *a*. **1.** 就要来的,正在来的,来(年),次(日),下(月、周)。**2.** 有前途的,正在崛起的,蒸蒸日上的,(人)新进的。**II** *n*. 进来;到达;〔美方〕发芽;〔*pl*.〕萌芽。*C-, Sir*! (本人)马上就来! *She is ~ nineteen*. 她快要满十九岁了。*the ~ week* 下星期。*~ up* 〔美口〕立正! 预备! *~ out*【商】新发行的股票(*bargain for the* "*C- Out*" 新股买卖)。*have it ~* (奖、惩等)是应得的。*have sb. ~ and going* 使无路可逃,使进退维谷。*the ~ thing* 〔美口〕就要变得时髦[有重要性]的东西。*~ in* **1.** 进入,开始。**2.** 〔常作 comings in〕收入。**~-of-age** *n*. (*pl*. ~s-of-age) 成年;成熟。**~-on** *a*. 顺从的。

com·int, COMINT [ˈkɔmint; ˋkɑmɪnt] *n*. 通信情报(系统)。

Com·in·tern [ˈkɔmintəːn; ˋkɑmɪnˏtɝn] *n*. 第三国际(= Komintern) 〔1919—1943〕。

co·mique [ˈkɔmik; kəˋmik] *n*. 〔F.〕丑角;滑稽歌手;滑稽歌曲。

co·mi·ti·a [kəˈmiʃiə; kəˋmɪʃɪə] *n*. 〔*sing*., *pl*.〕(古罗马的)公众议事集会,公民会议。

comitus gentium [ˈkɔmitəs ˈdʒentiəm; ˋkɑmɪtəs ˋdʒɛntɪəm] 〔L.〕国际礼让。

com·i·ty [ˈkɔmiti; ˋkɑmətɪ] *n*. 礼貌,礼让。*the ~ of nations* 国际礼让〔指互相尊重对方法律、风俗等〕。

coml. = commercial.

comm. = commentary; commander; commerce; commission; committee; commonwealth.

com·ma [ˈkɔmə; ˋkɑmə] *n*. **1.** 逗号(,)。**2.**【乐】小音程,差音程。*inverted ~s* = quotationmarks. *~* **bacillus**【生】弧杆菌。

com·mand [kəˈmɑːnd; kəˋmænd] **I** *vt*. **1.** 命令,指令;指挥,统率(军队等)。**2.** 左右,支配,控制,管理,掌握。**3.** 自由使用。**4.** 博得,得到(同情等)。**5.** (某一地点)远望,俯瞰,俯视。*You ought to ~ us*. 请随意指派我们吧。*~ the sea* [*air*] 掌握制海[空]权。*~ one's temper* 压制愤怒。*~ a good price* 能以高价卖出。*~ a ready sale* 获得畅销。*~ a view of* 眺望,俯瞰,展望。—*vi*. 指挥,命令。*Who ~s here*? 谁在这里指挥? 这里的指挥人是谁? *~ oneself* 克己,自制。*~ the services of* 可自由使用。*Yours to ~* 敬请赐示〔信末的客套话〕。**II** *n*. **1.** 命令,号令;指挥,统率;指挥权;支配权;【自】指令,信号。**2.** 部属;管区。**3.** 控制力,自由运用[操纵]力。**4.** 司令部,指挥部;统帅地位。**5.** 眺望,俯瞰,展望。*at ~* 得自由使用;支配自如。*at* [*by*] *sb.'s ~* 照某人嘱咐,听某人支配。*~ of the air* [*sea*] 制空[海]权。*get ~ of* 控制…(的要地)。*have a good ~ of* (*English*) 能自由应用(英语)。*have at one's ~* 得自由使用[能充分掌握]。*in ~ of* 指挥(着)。*lose ~ of oneself* 失却自制力。*take ~ of* 担任指挥。*under ~ of* 在…指挥下,由…所统率。*~* **car** 〔美〕指挥车。*~* **code**【计】指令码,操作码。*~* **module**【宇】(宇宙飞船上的)指挥[指令]舱。*~* **night** 〔英〕举行御前演出的晚场。*~* **performance** 〔英〕奉命进行的演出,御前演出。*~* **post**【军】(战地)指挥部[所]。**-ism** *n*. 命令主义。**-ist** *a*. 命令主义的。

com·man·dant [ˌkɔmənˈdænt; ˏkɑmənˋdænt] *n*. **1.** 司令官;指挥官;防区[要塞]司令官。**2.** 〔美〕(陆军军官学校的)校长。

com·man·deer [ˌkɔmənˈdiə; ˏkɑmənˋdɪr] *vt*. **1.** 征用;强征(壮丁等);征发(粮食等)。**2.** 〔口〕强取,强占。

com·mand·er [kəˈmɑːndə; kəˋmændɚ] *n*. **1.** 指挥者;【军】指挥官,司令官。**2.**【海军】中校,副舰长。**3.** 木槌。*the supreme ~* 最高统帅。*the C- of the Faithful* 大教长〔Sultan 或 Caliph 的称号〕。*the ~ of the point* 侦察组组长。

com·mand·er in chief [kəˈmɑːndərinˈtʃiːf; kɑˋmændərɪnˋtʃif] *n*. (*pl*. *~s in chief*) 总司令;(海军的)舰队司令。

com·mand·er·y [kəˈmɑːndəri; kəˋmændərɪ] *n*. **1.** 〔古〕骑士团管领地。**2.** 〔美〕社团[秘密结社等]的分团。

com·mand·ing [kəˈmɑːndiŋ; kəˋmændɪŋ] *a*. **1.** 指挥的。**2.** 威风凛凛的,外表庄严的。**3.** 占有险要地位的,(高处等)居高临下的。

com·mand·ment [kəˈmɑːndmənt; kəˋmændmənt] *n*.【宗】戒律;戒条,训条。*the Ten C-s*【圣】十诫;〔俚〕十指。*taboos and ~* 清规戒律。

com·man·do [kəˈmɑːndəu; kəˋmændo] *n*. (*pl*. ~*s*, ~*es*) **1.**【史】(南非布尔战争时代的)义勇队。**2.** 突击队(队员)。*~-Glider Corps* 〔美〕滑翔登陆部队。*~* **vessel** 登陆艇。

com·meas·ure [kəˈmeʒə; kəˋmɛʒɚ] *vt*. 使等量,使成比例。**-ura·ble** *a*. 可成比例的。

comme il faut [kɔmiːlˈfəu; kɔmilˋfo] 〔F.〕〔只作表语用〕得当;得体;合乎礼仪。

com·mem·o·ra·ble [kəˈmemərəbl; kəˋmɛmərəbl̩] *a*. 可纪念的,值得纪念的。

com·mem·o·rate [kəˈmeməreit; kəˋmɛməˏret] *vt*. 纪念,庆祝;(某物)成为…的纪念。

com·mem·o·ra·tion [kəˈmeməˈreiʃən; kəˋmɛməˋreʃən] *n*. **1.** 纪念(物);纪念节日,庆祝会。**2.** 〔C-〕牛津大学校庆。*in ~ of* 为纪念…,纪念…的。

com·mem·o·ra·tive, com·mem·o·ra·to·ry [kəˈmemərətiv, -təri; kəˋmɛmərətɪv, -torɪ] *a*. 纪念(性)的。

com·mence [kəˈmens; kəˋmɛns] *vt*., *vi*. **1.** 开始。**2.** 〔英〕获得(M.A. 等的)学位。*~ on* 着手。*~ with* 从…开始。

com·mence·ment [kəˈmensmənt; kəˋmɛnsmənt] *n*. **1.** 开始,发端。**2.** 〔the ~〕学位授予典礼,毕业典礼;〔美〕授奖典礼日(=〔英〕speech-day)。

com·mend [kəˈmend; kəˋmɛnd] *vt*. **1.** 交托,委托,委任。**2.** 褒奖,称赞。**3.** 推荐,推举。*~ sth. to sb.'s care* 委托某人照管某物。*~ him to the directory* 向董事会推荐某人。*~ itself* [*oneself*] *to* (*sb*.) 给(某人)留下好印象,中(某人)的意。*C- me to* 〔古〕**1.** 请代我向…致意。**2.** 〔口〕我还是比较喜欢[比为…比较好];〔常作反语用〕(*C- me to a decayed country parson for a dull dog*. 说到糊涂虫,那就要数老朽的乡下牧师了)。

com·mend·a·ble [kəˈmendəbl; kəˋmɛndəbl̩] *a*. 值得赞美[推荐]的,很好的。**-ably** *ad*. **-ness** *n*.

com·men·dam [kəˈmendæm; kəˋmɛndæm] *n*. **1.** (在正式牧师出缺时代理其职务时所享受的)薪俸代领权。**2.** 代领的薪俸。

com·men·da·tion [ˌkɔmenˈdeiʃən; ˏkɑmənˋdeʃən] *n*. **1.** 称赞,赞美。**2.** 推荐。**3.** 奖品。**4.** 〔旧〕赞词,祝词,问候。

com·mend·a·to·ry [kəˈmendətəri; kəˋmɛndəˏtorɪ] *a*. **1.** 称赞的,表扬的。**2.** 推荐的。

com·men·sal [kəˈmensəl; kəˋmɛnsəl] **I** *a*. **1.** 同桌的,共餐的。**2.**【生】共生的,共栖的。**II** *n*. **1.** 共食者。**2.**【生】共生体,共栖体。**-ism, -ity** [ˌkɔmenˈsæliti; ˏkɑmənˋsælətɪ] *n*.【生】共生,共栖。

com·men·su·ra·bil·i·ty [kəˌmenʃərəˈbiliti; kəˏmɛnʃərəˋbɪlətɪ] *n*. **1.**【数】公度性,通约性。**2.** 同单位;相应,相称。

com·men·su·ra·ble [kəˈmenʃərəbl; kəˋmɛnʃərəbl̩] *a*. **1.** 有公度的;有等数[等量]的,同单位的;能通约的(*with*)。**2.** 相应的,匀称的;成比例的;相称的(*to*)。*~* **number** [**quantity**]【数】可通约数[量]。

com·men·su·rate [kəˈmenʃərit; kəˋmɛnʃərɪt] *a*. **1.** 同量的,同大的;同单位的(*with*)。**2.** 相称的,相应的,相当的(*to*; *with*);能通约的。

com·men·su·ra·tion [kəˌmenʃəˈreiʃən; kəˏmɛnʃə-

ˋreʃən] *n*. 1. 公度,通约。2. 相称,相应。

com·ment [ˈkɔment; ˋkament] **I** *n*. 1. 注解,说明。2. 评语;评论,批评,闲话,流言。*Her strange behavior caused a good deal of* ~. 她的反常行为引起了不少闲话。**II** *vi*. 注释,评论,提意见(*upon, on*)。~ *on* [*upon*] *a text* [*a current topic*] 对原文[一个当前问题]作评论。***No*** ~. 无可奉告[对新闻记者等提问时的惯用语]。***without*** ~ 不必多说。

com·men·tar·y [ˈkɔməntəri; ˋkamən,tɛrɪ] *n*. 1. 注释,评注。2. (编者的)按语;评论,批评。3. [常 *pl*.]纪事。*the Commentaries of Caesar* 凯撒的《高卢战记》。***a running*** ~ (书)逐句[逐段]的评注;(时事等的)系统评述;【无】(运动等的)实况广播[报导]。

com·men·tate [ˈkɔmənˌteit; ˋkamən,tet] *vt*. 1. 给(文章等)作注解,释义,评注。2. 连续地口头评述(比赛等)。—*vi*. 作评论员[注释者]。

com·men·ta·tor [ˈkɔmenteitə; ˋkamən,tetɚ] *n*. 1. 注解者,注释者。2. (电台的)时事评论员,实况广播报导员。3. 主持[解释]宗教仪式的非教士。

com·men·ter [ˈkɔmentə; ˋkamɛntɚ] *n*. 批评家;注解者。

com·merce [ˈkɔmə(ː)s; ˋkamɝs] *n*. 1. 商业;商务,贸易。2. 社交;(思想的)交流;交际,应酬。3. [古]性交。*a chamber of* ~商会。*the world's* ~国际贸易。*have no* ~ *with* 跟…无来往[交往]。*the intellectual* ~ *between scholars* 学者间的智慧交流。

com·mer·cial [kəˈməːʃəl; kəˋmɝʃəl] **I** *a*. 1. 贸易的,商业上的;营业性的。2. [美](能)大量生产的;营利(性质)的;面向市场的;[美](广播)广告性质的。3. [美]中等的[指商品肉的等级]。**II** *n*. [英口]跑生意的,旅行兜销员(=~ traveller);[美]商业广告广播[节目]。~ **agency** 商业征信所。~ **agent** 贸易事务官;商务官;代理商。~ **analysis**【化】商品分析。~ **articles** 商品;(报上的)商业新闻。~ **attaché** (大使馆)商务参赞。~ **availability**【化】工业效用。~ **chestnut** [美]商业文件中的陈词滥调。~ **company** 贸易公司。~ **credit bureau** = ~ **inquiry office** 商业征信所。~ **firm** [**concern**] 商店,贸易公司。~ **museum** 商品陈列馆。~ **operation** 商业行为,交易。~ **paper** 商业票据。~ **par** 商业平价。~ **room** (旅馆中租给行商的)客商室。~ **run**【化】工业过程,工业方法。~ **size**【化】工业规模。~ **sulphuric acid** 工业用硫酸。~ **treaty** 通商条约。~ **unit** 工业设备;工商业单位。~ **usage** 商业习惯。~ **value** 交换价值。~ **weight** 正量。原量。**-ese** [-ʃəˈliːz; -ʃəˋliz] *n*., *a*. (函件上的)商业用语(的)。**-ism** *n*. 商业主义,商业精神,商业习惯;商业文体[用语]。**-ist** *n*. 商业家,商业主义者,营利主义者。**-ize** *vt*. 使商业化,使商品化;使成营业性质;使供应市场(**commercialized vice** 公娼制度)。**-ly** *ad*.

com·mie [ˈkɔmi; ˋkamɪ] *n*., *a*. [口,常 C-] = Communist.

com·mi·nate [ˈkɔmineit; ˋkamə,net] *vt*. (以上天的惩罚来)威吓。

com·mi·na·tion [ˌkɔmiˈneiʃən; ,kamɪˋneʃən] *n*. 威吓;【宗】以蒙受神谴进行威吓。***the*** ~ ***service*** (英国教)大齐忏悔。**-to·ry** *a*.

com·min·gle [kəˈmiŋgl; kəˋmɪŋgḷ] *vt*., *vi*. 混合;掺合。

com·mi·nute [ˈkɔminjuːt; ˋkamə,njut] *vt*. 把(矿物等)粉碎;研细;把(土地等)细分,分割。

com·mi·nu·tion [ˌkɔmiˈnjuːʃən; ,kaməˋnjuʃən] *n*. 1. 粉碎,研细。2. 磨损。3.【医】粉碎性骨折(= comminuted fracture).

com·mis·er·a·ble [kəˈmizərəbl; kəˋmɪzərəbḷ] *a*. 可怜悯的。

com·mis·er·ate [kəˈmizəreit; kəˋmɪzə,ret] *vt*. 怜悯;同情,哀悼。

com·mis·er·a·tion [kəˌmizəˈreiʃən; kə,mɪzəˋreʃən] *n*. 怜悯,同情;[*pl*.]悼词。

com·mis·er·a·tive [kəˈmizəreitiv; kəˋmɪzə,retɪv] *a*. 有怜悯[同情]心的;哀悼的。**-ly** *ad*.

com·mis·sar·i·al [ˌkɔmiˈsɛəriəl; ,kaməˋsɛrɪəl] *a*. 1. 代表的,委员的。2.【宗】代理主教的。3.【军】兵站部的。

com·mis·sar·i·at [ˌkɔmiˈsɛəriət; ,kaməˋsɛrɪət] *n*.【军】兵站部,军粮经理部;给养,军粮。

com·mis·sar·y [ˈkɔmisəri; ˋkamə,sɛrɪ] *n*. 1. 代表,委员;【宗】代理主教。2.【军】粮秣员,兵站负责人员(= commissar);[美](军队、矿山等的)日用物资供销店;【影】(制片厂等的)内部食堂。~ **general** 兵站总监。~ **line** 补给线。

com·mis·sion [kəˈmiʃən; kəˋmɪʃən] **I** *n*. 1. 命令,训令;委任,委托;任务;职权。2. 委员,委员会。3. (陆海军军官的)任命。4.【商】代办,经纪;手续费,佣金。5.【法】作为,犯(罪)。*the C- of Overseas Chinese Affairs* 华侨事务委员会。~*agency* 代办业,经纪业。~ *agent* 代办人,代办商。~ *broker* 经纪人,掮客。~ *of inquiry* 调查委员会。~ *of the peace* [英]治安裁判权;治安陪审团。~ *sale* = *sale on* ~ 代售,寄售,经销。~ *weaver* 代加工织造厂。*sin of* ~违法罪。***get one's*** ~ 被任命为军官。***go beyond one's*** ~ 越权。***go out of*** ~ 退役;衰老死亡。***in*** ~ 1. 现役的,服役中的。2. 被委任的,带有任务的。3. 委员代办的(*put a ship in* ~ 征船;把军舰编入现役队)。***on*** ~ 受委托(*sell on* ~托销);收取佣金。***on the*** ~ 担任治安陪审员。***out of*** ~ 退役,非现役;搁置不加使用中,(武器等)已损坏(*put a ship out of* ~ 放回征用船;把军舰编入预备役)。**II** *vt*. 1. 给与…以职权,委任;任命。2. 委托。3. 把(军舰)编入现役。4. (军官)被委任指挥(舰只)。~*ed officer* (少尉以上的)军官。~*ed ship* 现役舰。

com·mis·sion·aire [kəˌmiʃəˈnɛə; kə,mɪʃəˋnɛr] *n*. [英] 1. (穿制服的)门警。2. (伦敦退役军人转业的)雇工协会会员。

com·mis·sion·er [kəˈmiʃənə; kəˋmɪʃənɚ] *n*. 1. (官厅委任的)专员委员;特派员。2. (税务等的)督察(官)。3. (某些地方或机构的)长官。~ *of banking* [美]银行督察(官)。~ *of education* [美]教育局长。

com·mis·su·ral [ˌkɔmiˈsjuərəl; kəˋmɪʃərəl] *a*. 接缝的,连合的。

com·mis·sure [ˈkɔmisjuə; ˋkamɪ,ʃʊr] *n*. 1. 接缝处,缝口。2.【植】(心皮的)接着面;【解】连合。3. (昆虫的)神经接索。

com·mit [kəˈmit; kəˋmɪt] *vt*. 1. 犯(罪等);干(坏事等),做(某事)。2. 托;委;委任;(把议案等)交付委员会。3.【法】提(审);判处;收(监);下(牢)。4. 使承担义务,使作保证;【军】使投入战斗。5. 损坏(名誉等),累及。6. 说明自己立场[身分等]。~ *an infringement* 违犯规则。~ *a crime* 犯罪。~ *sin* 犯(宗教、道德上的)罪过。~ *robbery* 抢劫。~ *suicide* 自杀。~ *outrages* 蛮干,横行。~ *sb. to prison* 监禁某人。*be in no way* ~*ted to* 决不偏袒。~ ***one's soul to God*** [***God's mercy***] 逝世,寿终正寝。~ ***oneself to*** 委身于,专心致志于。~ ***to memory*** 记住。~ ***to oblivion*** 置之脑后。~ ***to sb.'s care*** 委托某人。~ ***to paper*** [***writing***] 写上,记下。~ ***to the earth*** 埋葬。~ ***to the water*** [***flame***] 投入水中[烧掉];水[火]葬。***feel oneself committed*** 觉得有损自己名誉,觉得自己受到牵连[受义务束缚]。

com·mit·ment [kəˈmitmənt; kəˋmɪtmənt] *n*. 1. (某种)作为;犯罪。2. 委任,委托;(对委员的)托付。3. 许诺,诺言;(受)约束;(承担)义务;债务。4. 拘留,关押。5. 信仰;赞助。6. 投入(战斗)。7.【股】买卖(契约)。

com·mit·tal [kəˈmitl; kəˋmɪtḷ] *n*. = commitment.

com·mit·tee [kəˈmiti; kəˋmɪtɪ] *n*. 1. 委员会;[集合词](全体)委员。2. [ˌkɔmiˈtiː; ,kamɪˋtɪ]【法】受托人,财产代管人,保护人,(白痴等的)监护人。***in*** ~ 由委员会审

议中。~ ***English*** 公文英语。***C- of One*** 一人委员会〔被授与全权、行使一个委员会职权的个人〕。***C- of Supply*** 〔英〕预算委员会。***C- of the whole*** (***House***) 议院全体委员会。***C- of Ways and Means*** 岁入调查委员会。~-**man** 委员。~**woman** 女委员。

com·mix [kɔ'miks; kə`mɪks] ***vt***., ***vi***. 〔古、诗〕混合。**-ture** ***n***. 混合(物)。

commn. = commission.

com·mode [kə'məud; kə`mod] ***n***. **1**. 五斗柜。**2**. 洗脸台。**3**. 便桶(= night-~)。

com·mo·di·ous [kə'məudiəs; kə`modɪəs] ***a***. **1**. 宽敞的。**2**. 方便的,便利的。**-ly** ***ad***. **-ness** ***n***.

com·mod·i·ty [kə'mɔditi; kə`madətɪ] ***n***. **1**. 〔常 *pl*.〕日用品;商品;农〔矿〕产品;有用物品。**2**. 〔旧〕便利;利益。*prices of commodities* 物价。*staple commodities* 主要商品。~ **money** 商品货币。

com·mo·dore ['kɔmədɔː; `kamə͵dɔr] ***n***. **1**. 海军准将。**2**. 〔英〕分舰队司令官。**3**. 〔用作客气的称呼〕前任舰长〔船长〕;游艇俱乐部会长;领港长。**4**. 商船队的向导船。*an air* ~〔英〕空军准将。

com·mon ['kɔmən; `kamən] **I** ***a***. **1**. 共通的,共同的,共有的。**2**. 公众的;公共的。**3**. 普通的,通常的,寻常的,平常的。**4**. 平凡的,通俗的;粗俗的,低劣的。**5**. 【数】共通的,公约的;【语法】通性的;通格的。***be*** ~ ***to*** 共通。***by*** ~ ***consent*** 全场一致,无异议,按公意。~ ***as dirt*** 最平凡的。~ ***or garden*** 普普通通的。~ ***run of*** 最普通的。**II** ***n***. **1**. 公(有)地。**2**. (牧场等的)共〔公〕用权(= right of ~)。**3**. 〔*pl*. 作 *sing*. 用〕见 *commons* 词条。***above*** [***beyond***] ***the*** ~ = out of the ~. ***in*** ~ (*with*) 共通,共同,(与…)同样(*charges borne in* ~共同负担的费用)。***keep*** [***be in***] ~***s*** (在大学等)聚餐。***the*** (***House of***) ***C-*** 〔英〕下院,众议院。***out of*** (***the***) ~ 异常的,非凡的。~ **beam** 标准天平;标准。~ **cardinal vein** 总主静脉。~ **carrier** 【法】运输业者,运输公司,转运行。~ **cold** 感冒。~ **council** 市会;村会。~ **crier** 广告员,报告员。~ **denominator** 公分母;共同特色。~ **doings** 常食,粗食。~ **factor** 【数】公约数。~ **gender** 【语法】通性。~ **good** 公益。~ **honesty** 常有的诚实。~ **jury** 小陪审团。~ **knowledge** 常识。~ **language** 共同语言。~ **law** 习惯法,不成文法律。~-**law** ***a***. 根据习惯法;按习惯法同居的;(子女等)由同居男女所生的。(~-*law marriage* 【法】非正式结婚,同居。*a* ~-*law wife* 同居的配偶)。~ **manners** 粗鲁。~ **market** 【经】共同市场(组织)。**C- Market** 欧洲共同市场〔即"欧洲经济共同体"〕。~**measure** 【数】公约数;【乐】= ~ time. ~ **nuisance** 妨害治安。**C- Pleas** 〔英〕高等民事法院;〔美〕民事法院。~ **right** 公民权。~ **room** (牛津大学)特别研究员的餐后休息室;(学校的)教员公用室。~ **salt** 食盐。~ **saying** 俗话,谚语。~ **school** 〔美〕公立小学校。~ **scold** 爱吵架的女人。~ **sense** 通情达理,常情。~-**sense** ***a***. 有常识的;明白的,一望而知的。~ **stock** 【经】普通股。~ **talk** 传闻。~ **time** 【乐】普通拍子。~ **touch** 平易近人的特征。~ **welfare** 公共福利。~ **trust fund** 托拉斯联合基金。~ **woman** 私娼。~ **year** 【天】平年〔相对于闰年而言〕。**-ly** ***ad***.

com·mon·a·ble ['kɔmənəbl; `kamənəbl̩] ***a***. **1**. 准许在公地上放牧的。**2**. (土地)共有的,公用的,共同的。

com·mon·age ['kɔmənidʒ; `kamənɪdʒ] ***n***. **1**. (牧场的)共用权。**2**. 共有地;公地。**3**. 〔集合词〕平民,老百姓。

com·mon·al·i·ty ['kɔmə'næliti; `kamə`nælətɪ] ***n***. **1**. 民众,老百姓。**2**. 共同性;共通性。

com·mon·al·ty ['kɔmənəlti; `kamənəltɪ] ***n***. **1**. 平民,老百姓,民众。**2**. 〔集合词〕法人,团体。**3**. 〔罕〕平凡的事物。*the* ~ *of mankind* 人类社会。

com·mon·ar·ea ['kɔmən͵ɛəriə; `kamən͵ɛrɪə] ***n***. 公用面积。~ **charge** 〔美〕(房租以外的)公用面积租金。

com·mon·er ['kɔmənə; `kamənɚ] ***n***. **1**. 平民。**2**. (牛津大学等的)自费生;普通学生〔不是 fellow (特别研究员)。scholar (官费生)或 exhibitioner (领助学金的学生)的学生〕。**3**. 有共有权的人。**4**. 〔罕〕英国下院议员。*the First C-* 〔英〕(现指)枢密院议长;(原指)下院议长。

com·mon·place ['kɔmənpleis; `kamən͵ples] **I** ***a***. 平凡的;陈腐的。**II** ***n***. **1**. 平常话;口头弹,常套话。**2**. 常事,平常物品。**3**. 备忘录(= ~ book)。**III** ***vt***. **1**. 把…记入备忘录。**2**. 由备忘录中摘出。~ **book** 备忘录;笔〔札〕记本。**-r** ***n***. 作笔记者。

com·mons ['kɔmənz; `kamənz] ***n***. 〔*pl*. 常用作单数〕**1**. 平民,民众。**2**. 众议院(议员)。**3**. 公共餐桌,公共食堂;〔牛津、剑桥大学〕份食;(一般)食物。**4**. 公地。*a* ~ *of bread and butter* 一份黄油面包。*short* ~质量不好的份食。***be*** (***put***) ***on short*** ~ 吃不饱,被减食。

Com·mons ['kɔmənz; `kamənz] ***n***. 康芒斯〔姓氏〕。

com·mon·sen·si·ble, com·mon·sen·si·cal [͵kɔmən'sensibl, -sikəl; ͵kamən`sensɪbl̩, -sɪkəl] ***a***. 通情达理的,符合常情的。

com·mon·weal ['kɔmənwiːl; `kamən͵wil] ***n***. **1**. 公益。**2**. 〔古〕国家;共和国;全体公民。

com·mon·wealth ['kɔmənwelθ; `kamən͵wɛlθ] ***n***. **1**. 公民(社会);团体。**2**. 国家;(尤指)共和国;联邦。**3**. 〔美〕州〔只用于 Massachusetts, Pennsylvania, Virginia 及 Kentucky 州〕。***the British C- of Nations*** = the British Empire. ***the C-*** 【英史】(1649—1956 年的)共和政体。~ **Day** 〔英〕联邦日(5 月 24 日为英国维多利亚女王诞辰;加拿大以 5 月 24 日前的最后一个星期一为联邦日)。~ **preference** 〔英〕英联邦特惠制。

com·mo·tion[kə'məuʃən; kə`moʃən] ***n***. 骚扰,骚动,暴动。*be in* ~在动荡中。

com·move [kə'muːv; kə`muv] ***vt***. 使激动,搅乱。

commr. = commander; commissioner; commoner.

com·mu·nal ['kɔmjunl; `kamjʊnl̩] ***a***. **1**. 自治体的,村社的,巴黎公社的;〔印〕部落的。**2**. 群居的;社会的,公共的。**3**. 对立宗教〔种族〕间的。~ **marriage** 共婚,杂婚,群婚。~ **politics** 社会政治学。~ **socialism** 地方自治社会主义。**-ism** ***n***. 地方自治主义。**-ist** ***n***. **1**. 地方自治主义者。**2**. (1871 年的)巴黎公社参加者。

com·mu·nal·ize ['kɔmjunəlaiz; `kamjʊnl̩͵aɪz] ***vt***. 把…收归地方团体所有。**com·mu·nal·i·za·tion** [-'lai'zeiʃən; -`laɪ`zeʃən] ***n***.

Com·mu·nard ['kɔmjunaːd; `kamjʊnard] ***n***. 〔F.〕巴黎公社社员;巴黎公社支持者。***the Wall of the*** ~***s*** 巴黎公社社员墙〔1871 年一批巴黎公社社员曾在此墙下英勇牺牲〕。

com·mune[1] [kə'mjuːn; kə`mjun] **I** ***vi***. **1**. (亲密地)商量,交谈,谈心 (*with*)。**2**. 〔美〕接受圣餐。~ *with oneself* [*one's own heart*] 沉思,内省。**II** ['kɔm-; `kam-] ***n***. 亲密的会谈;沉思。

com·mune[2] ['kɔmjuːn; `kamjun] ***n***. **1**. 法、义、比利时等国最小行政区划的市区、村镇自治体。**2**. 〔美〕(嬉皮士等的)群居组织。***the Paris C-*** 巴黎公社。

com·mu·ni·ca·ble [kə'mjuːnikəbl; kə`mjunɪkəbl] ***a***. 可以传达〔传授〕的;(疾病)可传染的;〔古〕爱说话的。**-ness** ***n***. **-bly** ***ad***.

com·mu·ni·cant [kə'mjuːnikənt; kə`mjunɪkənt] **I** ***n***. **1**. 圣餐接受者。**2**. (消息等的)传达者。**II** ***a***. **1**. 通信息的;相通的,相交往的 (*with*)。**2**. 接受圣餐的。

com·mu·ni·cate [kə'mjuːnikeit; kə`mjunə͵ket] ***vt***. **1**. 传达;传授。**2**. 【宗】授与(圣餐)。**3**. 传染(疾病)。—***vi***. **1**. 通信,交通 (*with*)。**2**. 相通 (*with*)。**3**. 【宗】接受圣餐。**4**. 传,移 (*to*). ~ *by telegram* 用电报通信。*This room* ~*s with another room*. 这间屋子和另外一间屋子相通。

com·mu·ni·ca·tion [kə͵mjuːni'keiʃən; kə͵mjunə`keʃən] ***n***. **1**. 通讯,通知;交换;信息;书信,口信,通报。**2**. 传达,传授;传播;传染。**3**. 交通,交通机关;联系,连络

C

(设备)。4.【宗】接受圣餐。*a means of* ~交通工具。~ *equipment* 通讯设备。**cut off** ~ 切断连络[通讯]。***have no*** ~ ***with*** 与…无联系[不通信息]。***in*** ~ ***with*** 与…连络[通信息]。***privileged*** ~【法】1. 法律准许不外泄的内情。2. 法律准许作为证词而提供的内情〔不构成诽谤罪等〕。~ **cord** (火车中的)报警索。~**s carrier** 〔美〕信息递送者。~ **gap** 信息沟,通讯隔阂〔不同年龄、阶层等的人们因缺乏互通信息而产生的隔阂〕。~ [~s] **theory** 信息论,传播理论。~ **trench**【军】交通壕。~ **zone**【军】后勤区。

com·mu·ni·ca·tive [kəˈmjuːnikətiv; kəˋmjunɪketɪv] ***a***. 1. 爱传话的;爱说话的,藏不住话的。2. 通讯联络的。

com·mu·ni·ca·tor [kəˈmjuːnikeitə; kəˋmjunəˏketɚ] ***n***. 1. 通信员,传达者。2. 发信机;报知器;通话装置。***agitate the*** ~ 〔口〕拨动某种传递信息设备铃〔如使用通话装置等〕。

com·mun·ion [kəˈmjuːnjən; kəˋmjunjən] ***n***. 1. 共享,共有;共同参与。2. 亲密交谈;(思想、感情的)交流。3. 同信仰的人[团体,教派]。4. 〔C-〕【宗】圣餐式;圣餐拜受 = (Holy C-)。***be of the same*** ~ 是同派教友。***hold*** ~ ***with*** 与…有(思想上)交往。***hold*** ~ ***with oneself*** 沉思,内省。***in*** ~ ***with*** 与…有连络,有共同利害关系。~ **cup** 圣餐杯。**C- Service** 圣餐礼。**-ist** ***n***. 领圣餐者。

com·muni·qué [kəˈmjuːnikei; kəˋmjunəke] ***n***. 〔F.〕公报,官报。

com·mu·nism [ˈkɔmjunizəm; ˋkɑmjʊˏnɪzəm] ***n***. 共产主义。

com·mu·nist [ˈkɔmjunist; ˋkɑmjʊˏnɪst] **I** ***n***. 共产主义者,共产党员。**II** ***a***. 共产主义(者)的;共产党(员)的。

com·mu·nis·tic [kɔmjuˈnistik; ˏkɑmjʊˋnɪstɪk] ***a***. 共产主义(者)的。**-cal·ly** ***ad***.

com·mu·ni·tar·i·an [kəˌmjuːniˈtɛəriən; kəˏmjunɪˋtɛrɪən] ***a***., ***n***. 公有制社会的(成员);鼓吹公有制社会的(人)。

com·mu·ni·ty [kəˈmjuːniti; kəˋmjunətɪ] ***n***. 1. 村社;社会,集体;乡镇,村落;【生】群落,群社。2. 共有,共用;共同体,共同组织;联营(机构)。3. 共(通)性;一致(性);类似性。*the European Atomic* ~欧洲原子能联营。*the European Coal and Steel* ~欧洲煤钢联营。~ *of interests* 利害相通。~ *of property* 财产的共有。*the Jewish* ~犹太人社会〔一个地区全部犹太人的〕。~ **antenna** 共用天线。~ **antenna television** 共用天线电视。~ **centre** 〔美〕公共礼堂。~ **chest** 〔美〕共同(募捐来的)基金;公共资金。~ **singing** 团体合唱。~ **welfare department** 〔美〕社会福利部。

com·mut·a·ble [kəˈmjuːtəbl; kəˋmjutəbḷ] ***a***. 可以交[互]换的;可以折换[抵偿]的。*offences not* ~ *by fine* 不能用罚款折换刑罚的罪行。

com·mu·tate [ˈkɔmjuteit; ˋkɑmjʊˏtet] ***vt***. 【电】使(电流)换向;变换(交流电)为直流电。

com·mu·ta·tion [ˌkɔmju(ː)ˈteiʃən; ˏkɑmjʊˋteʃən] ***n***. 1. 换算,交换,变换。2. 减刑;抵偿;抵偿金;划拨。3.【电】整流,换向。4. 〔美〕使用长期票(在两地间)经常来往。~**ticket** 〔美〕长期来往车票,月(季)票〔英国作 season ticket〕。

com·mut·a·tive [kəˈmjuːtətiv; kəˋmjutətɪv] ***a***. 相互的,交互的,(可)交[互]换的。~ **law** 互换律。~ **field**【数】域(体)。

com·mu·ta·tor [ˈkɔmjuteitə; ˋkɑmjʊˏtetɚ] ***n***. 1.【电】换向器,整流器。2. 整流子。3. 交换机,交换台。4.【数】换位子。~ **circuit**【计】环形计数器。~ **rectifier**【电】换向整流器。

com·mute [kəˈmjuːt; kəˋmjut] **I** ***vt***. 1. 交换,变换;互换,兑换;划拨,换算。2. 减免(刑罚)。3. 抵偿,折算(*into*; *for*)。4.【电】变向,整流。~ *stone into gold* 点石成金。~ *foreign currency to domestic* 兑换外币为本国货币。~ *imprisonment into a fine* 以罚款代监禁。—***vi***. 1. 交换。2. 用钱折算(*into*; *for*)。3. 划拨。4.【数】对易。5. 〔美〕使用长期票经常旅行[来往],通勤来往(*between*)。**II** ***n***. 通勤来往;通勤来往的途程[距离]。

com·mut·er [kəˈmjuːtə; kəˋmjutɚ] ***n***. 1. 交换者。2. 〔美〕使用长期票经常来往者,使用月票上下班者,长期票通勤旅客。3.【电】= commutator. ~ **belt** [~ **land**, ~**dom**, ~**ville**] (在市内上班的)郊区通勤人员居住者。~ **time** 上下班时间。

Com·my [ˈkɔmi; ˋkɑmɪ] ***n***. = commie.

COMNAVFE, Comnavfe [kɑmˈnævfi; kɑmˋnævfɪ] = Commander, United States Naval Forces, Far East 美国驻远东海军司令。

Com·o·ro [ˈkɔmərəu; ˋkɑməro] **Islands** ***n***. 科摩罗群岛〔非洲〕。

Com·oros [ˈkɔmərəus; ˋkɑməros] ***n***. 科摩罗〔非洲〕。

co·mose [ˈkəuməus; ˋkomos] ***a***.【植】具有丛毛的;多毛的。

comp[1] [kɔmp; kɑmp] ***n***. 〔美〕恭维话;招待券。

comp[2] [kɔmp; kɑmp] ***n***. 〔口〕排字(工人)。

comp[3] [kɔmp; kɑmp] ***vi***. 进行(不规则的)爵士乐自由伴奏〔accompany 的缩略〕。

comp. = comparative; compare; compiler; composer; composition; compositor; compound; comprising.

com·pact[1] [ˈkɔmpækt; ˋkɑmpækt] ***n***. 契约,协议,条约。***by*** ~ 照契约。***enter into a*** ~ 订契约,订合同。

com·pact[2] [kəmˈpækt; kəmˋpækt] **I** ***a***. 1. 挤满的,密集的;紧密的;(物质)致密的;(体格)结实的。2. 简洁的,(文体等)紧凑的;【拓】紧列的。3. 〔诗〕由…组成的(*of*)。**II** ***vt***. 1. 把…弄紧密,把…弄结实,压实。2. 使(文体)简洁,简化。3. 使紧凑地组合成,由…组成。—***vi***. 变紧密,变结实。**III** [ˈkɔm-; ˋkɑm-] ***n***. 随身携带的粉盒;小型汽车。~ **video disk** 激光[镭射]影碟。**-ly** ***ad***. **-ness** ***n***.

com·pac·tion [kəmˈpækʃən; kəmˋpækʃən] ***n***. 紧密;致密;压缩。

com·pa·dre [kəmˈpɑːdrei; kəmˋpɑdre] ***n***. 〔美〕知友,至交;伙伴。

com·pa·ges [kəmˈpeidʒiːz; kəmˋpedʒiz] ***n***. 〔*pl*.〕骨架,结构。

com·pag·i·nate [kəmˈpædʒineit; kəmˋpædʒɪˏnet] ***vt***. 使牢固结合。

com·pa·ñe·ro [ˌkəmˈpəˈnjerəu; ˏkəmpəˋnjɛro] ***n***. 〔Sp.〕同伙,伙伴。

com·pan·ion[1] [kəmˈpænjən; kəmˋpænjən] **I** ***n***. 1. 伙伴,伴侣;朋友。2. (一对中的)一方。3. 最下级勋爵。4. 〔书籍杂志名〕指南,必读,必携,手册, 5. 〔*pl*.〕伴生种,伴(细)胞;【天】伴星(= ~ *star*)。6. 雇来照料病人[老人]的人。*a boon* ~酒友。~ *for life* 终身侣伴[配偶]。*a Teachers' C- to* ... 教师用…(参考书)。~ *volume* 姐妹篇。***a ladie's*** ~ 女人手提包。~ ***at*** [***in***] ***arms*** 战友。*C- of the Bath* 第三级[最下级]巴斯勋爵。***make a*** ~ ***of*** 与…作伴,与…为友。**II** ***vt***. (与…)同行;(跟…)搭伴儿去。~ **crops**【农】混间作物。~ **lode**【矿】副矿脉。**-ship** 伙伴关系;交往,友谊;〔英〕排字的伙伴。

com·pan·ion[2] [kəmˈpænjən; kəmˋpænjən] ***n***. 1.【船】升降口。2. = ~ hatch [head]. 3. = ~ladder [~way]. ~**hatch** [**head**]【船】升降口盖[罩]。~ **ladder** [~**way**] 1.【船】升降口扶梯。2.【空】坐舱走道。

com·pan·ion·a·ble [kəmˈpænjənəbl; kəmˋpænjənəbḷ] ***a***. 1. 可交往的。2. 爱与人作伴的;人缘好的。

com·pan·ion·ate [kəmˈpænjənit; kəmˋpænjənɪt] ***a***. 〔美〕伙伴的;友好的。~ **marriage** 试婚;同居。

com·pa·ny [ˈkʌmpəni; ˋkʌmpənɪ] ***n***. 1. 交际,交往;作伴;伴侣;朋友;来客。2. (社交)集会,聚会。3. 一队,一行;(演员的)一班。4. 行会;公司,商号,商社;合伙者。5.【军】连,中队;【海】全体船员。6. 消防队。*love one's* *own* ～爱独自一人(生活,行事等)。*Two's* ～, *three's none*. 二人成一对,三人不顺遂。*a theatrical* ～剧团。*a strolling* ～流动剧团。*a City C-* 伦敦的商业[同业]公会。*a limited liability* ～[英]有限公司〔略 Co., Ltd.〕。... *and Co*. ... 公司;…之流,…一伙,…等。*Hitler and Co*. 希特勒之流。*bear* [*keep*] *sb*. ～陪伴某人。*be good* [*bad*] ～是个能[不能]相处得很好的伙伴。***fall into*** ～ ***with*** 和…交往[作伴]。***find*** (*sb*.) ***poor*** ～ 觉得(某人)不是个能相处的人。***for*** ～ 陪著。***get*** [***receive***] ***one's*** ～ 升为连长[上尉]。***give*** (***him***) ***one's*** ～ 陪他。***go into*** ～ 到大伙中。***have*** ～ 有客。***in sb.'s*** ～ 与某人一道[同席]。***in*** ～ 在大伙中,在人面前(假装做…)。***in*** ～ ***with*** 和…一道。***keep*** ～ ***with*** 和…常来往;同…结伴。***keep good*** [***bad***] ～ 与好人[坏人]来往。***keep to one's own*** ～ 独自一人。***know sb. by his*** ～ 观友见其人。***like sb.'s*** [***one's own***] ～ 爱和某人在一起[独自一人]。***part*** ～ ***with*** 与…告别[有分歧;绝交]。***present*** ～ ***excepted*** 在场者[在座者]除外。***see a great deal of*** ～ 交际广。～ **commander** 连长。～ **manners** 在客人面前的虚礼,客套。～ **officers** 【军】尉级军官。～ **union** 〔美〕公司(的御用)工会。

compar. = comparative; comparison.

com·pa·ra·ble [ˈkɔmpərəbl; ˋkɑmpərəbl̩] ***a***. **1**. 可相比的 (*with*); 敌得上…的 (*to*)。**2**. 类似的。**-bly *ad***.

com·par·a·tist [kəmˈpærətist; kəmˋpærətɪst] ***n***. 比较语言学[文学]研究者。

com·par·a·tive [kəmˈpærətiv; kəmˋpærətɪv] **I *a***. **1**. 比较(上)的。**2**. 相当的,还可以的。**3**.【语法】比较级的。**4**.〔婉〕(广告等)比较性的,攻击竞争者的。**II *n***. **1**. 可匹敌者;可比拟物。**2**.〔the ～〕【语法】比较级。*in* ～ *comfort* 相当舒适地。*with* ～ *ease* 比较容易地。～ **adjective** 比较级形容词。～ **advertising** 比较式广告。～ **method** 比较(研究)法。**-ly *ad***. (～*ly speaking* 比较地说来〔插入语〕)。**-tiv·ist** = comparatist.

com·pa·ra·tor [ˈkɔmpəreitə; ˋkɑmpəˏretɚ] ***n***.【机】比测器,比较仪,比长仪;【化】比色计;比…器;【无】比较器;比较电路。～ **block** 【生】比色匣。

com·pare [kəmˈpɛə; kəmˋpɛr] **I *vt***. **1**. 比较,对照 (*with*); 参照。**2**. 把…比作为 (*to*)。**3**.【语法】把(形容词、副词)变成比较级[最高级]。—***vi***. 相比,匹敌 (*with*)。(***as***) ～***d with*** 和…比起来。***be*** ～***d to*** 好比 (*Life is* ～*d to voyage*. 人生好比航海)。～ ***notes*** 对笔记;交换意见。**II *n***. 比较。***beyond*** [***past***, ***without***] ～ 无与伦比的,不可及的。

com·par·i·son [kəmˈpærisn; kəmˋpærəsn] ***n***. **1**. 比较,对照;类似。**2**.【语法】比较法;【修】比喻。*There is no* ～ *between the two*. 两者无法相比。***bear*** [***stand***] ～ ***with*** 不亚于,比得上。***beyond*** ～ 天壤之别;不可相比。***by*** ～ 比较起来。***Comparisons are odious*** [***odorous***]. 不怕不识货,只怕货比货;不和人家比,不显自己臭。***in*** ～ ***with*** 和…比起来。***without*** ～ 无与伦比。

com·part [kəmˈpɑːt; kəmˋpɑrt] ***vt***. 区划;隔开,分割。

com·part·ment [kəmˈpɑːtmənt; kəmˋpɑrtmənt] ***n***. **1**. 间隔,区划;(小)室,隔室;舱,隔水舱;(火车的)分格车室;【林】林班。**2**. (英国议院在政府规定期限内讨论的)特殊协议事项。*a smoking* ～(舟车中的)吸菸室。*a control* ～【火箭】操纵舱。～ *under regeneration*【林】更新地。*be* [*live*] *in water-tight* ～和别人完全隔绝。～ **ceiling** 格子天花板。～ **roofing** 分区划的屋顶。**-al *a***.

com·part·men·tal·ize [kəmˌpɑːtˈmentəlaiz; ˏkəmpɑrtˋmɛntl̩aɪz] ***vt***. 把…分成各自独立的几部分,把…分成区;把…分门别类。**-i·za·tion *n***.

com·pass [ˈkʌmpəs; ˋkʌmpəs] **I *n***. **1**. 周围;界限,区域范围;【乐】音域。**2**. 罗盘,罗针仪,指南针。**3**.〔*pl*.〕两脚规,圆规。**4**. 迂回的路径。*a radio* ～ *station* 无线电定向台。***beyond sb.'s*** ～某人力所不及。***beyond the*** ～ ***of*** 越出…范围以外。***fetch*** [***go***] ***a*** ～ 迂回,绕道。***in small*** ～ 紧凑,简洁,在小范围内。***keep*** (***one's desires***) ***within*** ～ 克制着(欲望),不作妄想。***speak within*** ～ 谨慎小心地说。***within sb.'s*** ～ 某人力所能及。***within the*** ～ ***of a lifetime*** 在人的一生中。**II *vt***.〔古〕围绕;沿着…划一圆圈,沿…绕行一圈。**2**. 达成,完成(目的)。**3**. 图谋,计划。**4**. 了解,领悟。～ *the death of* ... 图谋杀害…。～ *one's object* 达到目的。～ **card** 罗盘的盘面。～ **plane** 凹刨,刳刨。～ **plant** 指向植物。～ **saw** 截圆锯。～ **timber** 弯料。～ **window**【建】半圆形凸窗。

com·pas·sion [kəmˈpæʃən; kəmˋpæʃən] ***n***. 怜悯,同情。***have*** [***take***] ～ ***on*** 怜悯,同情。***fling oneself on*** [***upon***] ***sb.'s*** ～ 乞求某人怜悯。

com·pas·sion·ate [kəmˈpæʃənit; kəmˋpæʃənet] **I *a***. **1**. 富于同情心的。**2**. (津贴等)特赐的。～ *allowance* 特别津贴。～ *leave* 特准的休假。**II** [-ʃəneit; -ʃənet] ***vt***. 怜悯,体恤,同情。**-ly *ad***.

com·pat·i·bil·i·ty [kəmˌpætiˈbiliti; kəmˏpætəˋbɪlətɪ] ***n***. 适合,适应;兼容(性);一致(性),协调(性)。

com·pat·i·ble [kəmˈpætəbl; kəmˋpætəbl] ***a***. **1**. 协调的,相容的,可两立的,不矛盾的 (*with*)。**2**.【计】兼容的。～ **colour** 黑白电视机亦可收看的彩色电视节目。～ **colour TV system** 兼容制彩色电视,兼容彩色电视制式。

com·pat·ri·ot [kəmˈpætriət; kəmˋpetrɪət] **I *n***. 同国人,同胞。**II *a***. 同国的。**-ic *a***.

com·peer [kɔmˈpiə; kəmˋpɪr] ***n***. (等级、能力等)同等的人,同辈;伙伴。

com·pel [kəmˈpel; kəmˋpɛl] ***vt***. 强迫;协迫;使不得不;迫使(服从、沉默等)。～ *sb. to one's will* 逼人服从自己。～ *tears from one's audience* 使观众掉泪。*a compelling argument* 使对方无话可说的论据。*a compelling smile* 迷人的微笑。*a compelling gaze* 咄咄逼人的凝视。***be compelled to*** (***do***) 不得不(做)。**com·pel·la·ble *a***. 可强迫的。**com·pel·la·bly *ad***.

com·pel·la·tion [ˌkɔmpəˈleiʃən; ˏkɑmpəˋleʃən] ***n***. **1**. 称呼;呼唤(对方的名字或称谓)。**2**. 头衔;姓名。

com·pend [ˈkɔmpend; ˋkɑmpɛnd] ***n***. = compendium.

com·pen·di·ous [kəmˈpendiəs; kəmˋpɛndɪəs] ***a***. 简明扼要的;简略的。**-ly *ad***. **-ness *n***.

com·pen·di·um [kəmˈpendiəm; kəmˋpɛndɪəm] ***n***. (*pl*. ～*s*, *-di·a* [-diə; -dɪə]) 梗概,概论;摘要,概略;纲领;总目录。

com·pen·sa·ble [kəmˈpensəbl; kəmˋpɛnsəbl] ***a***. 有权要求补偿[赔偿]的;应予以补偿[赔偿]的;可补偿[赔偿]的。

com·pen·sate [ˈkɔmpenseit; ˋkɑmpənˏset] ***vt***. **1**. 赔偿,补偿。**2**. 酬劳,〔美〕给…付工钱,给…报酬。**3**.【经】(调整金币成色以)稳定(货币的)购买力。**4**.【物】补偿…的变差;【机】补整。—***vi***. 补偿;赔偿 (*for*)。～ (*sb*.) *for loss* [*services*] 赔偿某人损失[付予酬劳]。*compensating gear*【机】差动齿轮。

com·pen·sa·tion [ˌkɔmpenˈseiʃən; ˏkɑmpənˋseʃən] ***n***. **1**. 赔偿;补偿(金);报酬 (*for*);〔美〕薪水,工资 (*for*);【机】补整;【船】补强。～ *for damage* 损害赔偿。～ *for removal* 退职金,遣散费。～ **balance** 补整平衡。～ **method** 补偿法,对消法。～ **pendulum**【物】补偿摆。***in*** ～ ***for*** 以作…的赔偿[报酬]。

com·pen·sa·tive, **com·pen·sa·to·ry** [kəmˈpensətiv, -təri; kəmˋpɛnsətɪv, -tərɪ] ***a***. 赔偿的,补偿的;报酬的;补充的。

com·pen·sa·tor [ˈkɔmpenseitə; ˋkɑmpənˏsetɚ] ***n***. **1**. 赔偿者。**2**.【机】补偿器;胀缩件;补偿棱镜;【电】调相机。

compère [ˈkɔmpɛə; ˋkɑmpɛr] **I *n***.〔F.〕(演出等的)节目主持人,报幕员。**II *vt***. 主持(演出节目)。

com·pete [kəmˈpiːt; kəmˋpit] ***vi***. **1**. 竞争 (*with*; *in*); 比得上,及得上;匹敌。**2**. 比赛。*There is no book that can* ～ *with this*. 没有一本书抵得上这本的。～ *in a* race 参加赛跑。～ ***with*** [***against***] (*others*) ***for*** (*a prize*) 和(人们)争夺(奖赏)。～ ***with*** (*sb.*) ***in*** 和(某人)竞争。

com·pe·tence, com·pe·ten·cy [ˈkɔmpitəns, -si; ˋkɑmpətəns, -sɪ] ***n*. 1.** 资格,能力(*for*; *to do*);反应能力,胜任(性);相当的资产[财力];(对于某种语言的)运用能力。**2.**【法】权能,权限。**3.**【生】(细菌的)遗传变化力,耐药力。*acquire a* ～得到相当的财产。*challenge the* ～对权限提出疑问。*exceed one's* ～越权。*have* ～ *over* 对…具有管辖权。

C

com·pe·tent [ˈkɔmpitənt; ˋkɑmpətənt] ***a*. 1.** 适任的,称职的,有能力的,有资格的。**2.** 有职权的;正当的;合法的;有管辖权的。**3.** 充足的,相当的。**4.**【生】(对抗生素等)有适应力的,有耐药性的;有抵抗力的。*It is perfectly* ～ *for me to refuse.* 我拒绝是十分正当的。*It is* ～ *to Parliament to prohibit it.* 议会有禁止它的权力。～ *income* 相当的收入。*the* ～ *authorities* 主管当局。*the* ～ *minister* 主管部长。**-ly *ad*.**

com·pe·ti·tion [ˌkɔmpiˈtiʃən; ˏkɑmpəˋtɪʃən] ***n*. 1.** 竞争。**2.** 比赛,竞赛。**3.**【生】生存竞争。*a boxing* ～拳击比赛。～*in arms* 军备竞赛。***be*** [***stand***] ***in*** ～ ***with*** (*sb.*) ***for*** 为…和(某人)竞争。***put*** (*sb.*) ***in*** [***into***] ～ ***with* ...**使(某人)与(另一人)竞争。

com·pet·i·tive [kəmˈpetitiv; kəmˋpɛtətɪv] ***a*.** 竞争的,竞赛的。～ *bidding system* 招标制。～ *examination* 竞争考试。～ *exhibition* 竞赛(展览)会。～ **shading**【植】(植株间的)互相荫蔽。**-ly *ad*.**

com·pet·i·tor [kəmˈpetitə; kəmˋpɛtətɚ] ***n*.** 竞争者;敌手。

com·pet·i·to·ry [kəmˈpetitəri; kəmˋpɛtəˏtorɪ] ***a*.** = competitive.

com·pet·i·tress, com·pet·i·trix [kəmˈpetitris, -triks; kəmˋpɛtətrɪs, -trɪks] ***n*.** 女竞争者;女对手。

com·pil·a·tion [ˌkɔmpiˈleiʃən; ˏkɑmpɪˋleʃən] ***n*.** 汇集,编辑(物);汇编。

com·pil·a·to·ry [kəmˈpailətəri; kəmˋpaɪləˏtorɪ] ***a*.** 汇集的,编辑的。

com·pile [kəmˈpail; kəmˋpaɪl] ***vt*.** 汇集,编辑,编制;搜集(资料)。～ *a dictionary* 编词典。～ *a budget* 编预算。

com·pil·er [kəmˈpailə; kəmˋpaɪlɚ] ***n*. 1.** 汇集者,编辑(人)。**2.**【计】自动编码器;自动编码[编译]程序。

compl. = complement.

com·pla·cence, com·pla·cen·cy [kəmˈpleisns, -si; kəmˋplesn̩s, -sɪ] ***n*.** 满足,(特指)骄傲自满,自得。

com·pla·cent [kəmˈpleisnt; kəmˋplesn̩t] ***a*.** 满足的,(特指)自满的,得意的,自得的。*We must not become* ～ *over any success.* 我们决不能一见成绩就自满。**-ly *ad*.**

com·plain [kəmˈplein; kəmˋplen] ***vi*. 1.** (对某事)诉苦,抱怨,叫屈;发牢骚。**2.** (病人)自诉有…病痛(*of*)。**3.** 向某人(*to*)申诉,控诉(*of*, *about*)。**4.**〔诗〕呻吟,呜咽,哀号。*He* ～*ed to the manager about the service.* 他抱怨服务员态度不好。～ *of a stomach-ache* (病人)自诉有胃痛病。～ *to the city authorities of a public nuisance* 向市政当局控诉公害。—***vt*.** 抱怨,控制〔与 that 子句连用〕。*They* ～*ed that the price of books had increased.* 他们抱怨说书籍价格提高了。

com·plain·ant [kəmˈpleinənt; kəmˋplenənt] ***n*. 1.** 诉苦者,抱怨者。**2.** 控诉者;原告。

com·plaint [kəmˈpleint; kəmˋplent] ***n*. 1.** 不平,牢骚,委屈,意见,怨言。**2.** 不平的来由,痛苦根源。**3.** 控诉;申诉;〔美〕(民事诉讼中原告一方的)指控。**4.** 疾病;病痛;【医】主诉。*a bowel* ～肠炎。***make*** [***lodge*, *lay***] ***a*** ～ ***against*** 控告。～ **department** 顾客意见接纳处。

com·plai·sance [kəmˈpleizəns; kəmˋplezn̩s] ***n*.** 殷勤,恳切,亲切(行为);讨好(行为)。

com·plai·sant [kəmˈpleizənt; kəmˋplezn̩t] ***a*.** 殷勤的;恳切的;讨好的。**-ly *ad*.**

com·pla·nate [ˈkɔmplənit; ˋkɑmplənɪt] ***a*.** 平坦的;平面的。

com·pla·na·tion [ˌkɔmpləˈneiʃən; ˏkɑmpləˋneʃən] ***n*. 1.** 平面化。**2.**【数】曲面求积法。

com·plect [kəmˈplekt; kəmˋplɛkt] ***vt*.** 〔古〕交缠,交织。

com·plect·ed [kəmˈplektid; kəmˋplɛktɪd] ***a*.** 〔美方,口〕面色…的,肤色…的〔常用以构成复合词〕。*a light*-～ *boy* 肤色白的少年。

com·ple·ment [ˈkɔmplimənt; ˋkɑmpləmənt] ***n*. 1.** 补足(物);补全;互补(成分),补充。**2.** (必需的)定量,全量;整套,整组;【海】(船员的)定额;【军】编制人数,定额装备。**3.**【语法】补(足)语;【数】余角,余弧,余数;余集;【计】补数,补码;反码;【乐】补足音程;【生】补体[免疫];组[细胞]。*The regiment had its* ～ *of men.* 这个团的兵员已足额。～ *of nine's* 十进制反码。～ *of one's* 二进制反码。～ *of ten's* 十进制补码。～ *of two's* 二进制补码。～ *of an angle* 余角。—[ˈkɔmpliment; ˋkɑmpləˏmɛnt] ***vt*.** 补充,补足。～ *each other* 互为补充。

com·ple·men·tal, com·ple·men·ta·ry [ˌkɔmpliˈmentl, -təri; ˏkɑmpləˋmɛntl̩, -tərɪ] ***a*.** 补充的;补足的;互补的;【生】互配(力)的。～ **colour** 余色,补色。～ **event**【统】相补[互补]事件。～ **factor** 互补因子。～ **interval**【乐】补足音程。～ **minor**【数】余子式。

com·ple·men·tar·i·ty [ˌkɔmplimenˈtæriti; ˏkɑmpləmɛnˋtærətɪ] ***n*.** 互补(性);互关性;【物】并协性;【生】(核苷酸的)互配能力。

com·plete [kəmˈpliːt; kəmˋplit] **I *a*. 1.** 完全的;圆满的,全面的,全能的。**2.** 完成的,结束的。**3.**〔古〕老练的。*a* ～ *ass* 大傻瓜。～ *works* (作品的)全集。*a* ～ *set* 全套。*a* ～ *success* [*failure*] 大成功[失败]。*This month is now* ～. 本月到此结束。*The task is* ～. 任务完成了。*a* ～ *divorce*【法】离婚。*a* ～ *angler* 钓鱼名手。**II *vt*.** 完成,使完满,使完工,完结;配齐,凑满。～ *a task* 完工。～ *sb.'s happiness* 使某人快乐到极点。～ *the whole course* 修毕全部课程。***To*** ～ (***the sum of***) ***one's misery*.** 不幸之上再加不幸,祸不单行。**-ly *ad*. -ness *n*.**

com·ple·tion [kəmˈpliːʃən; kəmˋpliʃən] ***n*. 1.** 成就,完成,实现;【数】求全法。**2.** 期满;毕业。*bring* [*be brought*] *to* ～使完成[完工]。～ *of a course* 修毕课程,毕业。～ *of a term* 满期,结束。

com·plex [ˈkɔmpleks; kəmˋplɛks] **I *a*. 1.** 复杂的,错综的。**2.** 合成的,综合的;【化】络合的。**3.**【语法】复合的;含有从属子句的。**II *n*. 1.** 复杂;合成物。**2.** 联合企业。**3.**【化】络合物,复合物,综合体;【生】染色体组;【数】复数;线丛;【语法】复合句;【心】意结,情结,变态[复合]心理。*an iron and steel* ～钢铁联合企业。*the inferiority* ～自卑情结〔一种由自卑感引起的复杂心理状态〕。*the superiority* ～自高情结〔由自我优越感引起的一种复杂心理〕。～ *of circles*【数】圆丛。～ *of external conditions* 外界条件总体。～ **builder**【化】螯合剂。～ **ion**【化】络离子。～ **plane** 复数平面。～ **sentence**【语法】复合句。

com·plex·ion [kəmˈplekʃən; kəmˋplɛkʃən] ***n*. 1.** 面色,气色,肤色。**2.** (天)色,情况,形势,局面;【物】配容。**3.**〔古〕(人的)天性,气质。*give a fair* ～装得美丽漂亮。*put a false* ～ *on a remark* (故意)歪曲某一句话。*put another* ～ *on* 改变…的局面。*the* ～ *of the war* 战局。**-al, -ed *a*.**〔常用以构成复合词〕面[肤]色…的,天性…的(*fair*-[*dark*-] ～*ed* 面[肤]色白[黑]的)。**-less *a*.** (面色等)苍白的。

com·plex·i·ty [kəmˈpleksiti; kəmˋplɛksɪtɪ] ***n*. 1.** 复杂性,复合状态。**2.** 复合物;复杂的事物[情况]。

com·pli·a·ble [kəmˈplaiəbl; kəmˋplaɪəbl̩] ***a*.** = compliant.

com·pli·ance, com·pli·an·cy [kəmˈplaiəns, -si; kəm-

ˋplaɪəns, -sɪ] **n.** **1.** 应允,答应(要求等)。**2.** 和蔼,温和;顺从,服从;盲从;【物】柔量;【数】顺性。*feigning* ~ 阳奉阴违,假装同意。***in*** ~ ***with*** (*your wishes*) 遵照(您的愿望)。

com·pli·ant [kəmˈplaiənt; kəmˋplaɪənt] **a.** 应允的;服从的;温顺的。

com·pli·ca·cy [ˈkɔmplikəsi; ˋkɑmpləkəsɪ] **n.** **1.** 复杂性,错综性;混乱状态。**2.** 错综复杂的事物[情况]。

com·pli·cate [ˈkɔmplikeit; ˋkɑmpləˏket] **I** **vt.** 把…弄复杂,使错综,使混乱。*That would* ~ *matters.* 那会使事情弄得更麻烦的。*be* ~*ed in* 卷入…(的麻烦中)。—**vi.** 变复杂。**II** **a.** **1.** 复杂的,麻烦的。**2.** (昆虫的翅)纵折的。

com·pli·cat·ed [ˈkɔmplikeitid; ˋkɑmpləˏketɪd] **a.** 复杂的,错杂的,混乱的,麻烦的。**-ly** **ad.** **-ness** **n.**

com·pli·ca·tion [ˌkɔmpliˈkeiʃən; ˏkɑmpləˋkeʃən] **n.** **1.** 错杂,混染;纠纷。**2.** 【医】并发症。**3.** 【心】混化,复化;精神错乱。*to cause* ~节外生枝。

com·plice [ˈkɔmplis; ˋkɑmplɪs] **n.** 〔古〕同谋者,纵犯。

com·plic·i·ty [kəmˈplisiti; kəmˋplɪsətɪ] **n.** 共谋;共犯,牵连 (*in*)。

com·pli·er [kəmˈplaiə; kəmˋplaɪə] **n.** 依从者,听从者。

com·pli·ment [ˈkɔmplimənt; ˋkɑmpləmənt] **I** **n.** **1.** 恭维话,赞辞;敬意,礼仪。**2.** 〔*pl.*〕道贺,贺词,问候。**3.** 〔古、美〕礼物,慰劳品。*He did me the* ~ *of listening.* 他郑重其事地[很客气地]倾听了我的话。*Your presence is a great* ~. 承蒙光临,不胜荣幸。*a doubtful* [*left-handed*] ~挖苦[恶意]的恭维话。***Give*** [***Present***] ***my*** ~***s to*** 请向…致意[问候]。***make*** [***pay, present***] ***one's*** ~***s*** 问好,问候。***make*** [***pay***] ***a*** ~ ***to*** 恭维,夸奖,颂扬;问候,表示敬意。***return the*** ~ 答礼,还礼;报复。***send one's*** ~***s*** 致意,致候。***the*** ~***s of the season*** 恭贺佳节[贺年等]。***with the*** ~***s of*** (*the author*) = ***with*** (*the author's*) ~***s*** (著者)敬赠。**II** **vt.** **1.** 向…问候[致敬]。**2.** 恭维,夸奖;祝贺。**3.** 赠呈。—**vi.** 说恭维话。~ ***away*** 说好话解决。~ (*sb.*) ***into*** (*compliance*) 用恭维话使(某人)应允。~ (*sb.*) ***on*** (*his courage*) 夸奖(某人勇敢)。~ (*sb.*) ***out of*** (*his money*) 恭维(某人)以骗取(钱财)。~ (*sb.*) ***with*** (*a book*) 赠(书)给(某人)。

com·pli·men·ta·ry [ˌkɔmpliˈmentəri; ˏkɑmpləˋmɛntərɪ] **a.** **1.** 问候的,祝贺的,致敬的;称赞的。**2.** 会说恭维话的,善于辞令的。**3.** 免费赠送的。*He is too* ~. 他太客气[会说恭维话]。~ **address** 贺辞。~ **ticket** 招待券,优待券。

com·plin(e) [ˈkɔmplin; ˋkɑmplɪn] **n.** 【宗】晚祷。

com·plot [ˈkɔmplɔt; ˋkɑmplɑt] **I** **n.** 共谋,密谋。**II** [kəmˈplɔt; kəmˋplɑt] **vt., vi.** 〔古〕共谋。

complt. = complainant.

com·ply [kəmˈplai; kəmˋplaɪ] **vi.** 应允,答应,依从,同意;遵照。*to* ~ *with sb.'s request* 答应某人要求。~ *with the rules* 遵守规则行事。~ ***with a formality*** 履行手续。

com·po[1] [ˈkɔmpəu; ˋkɑmpo] **n.** **1.** 混合(物);组合(物);混合涂料,灰沙,人造象牙。**2.** (船员的)部分工资,预付的部分工资。~ **rations** 大包综合配给口粮〔供若干天食用的〕。

com·po[2] [ˈkɔmpəu; ˋkɔmpo] **n.** 〔澳俚〕工伤赔偿金。

com·po·nent [kəmˈpəunənt; kəmˋponənt] **I** **a.** 构成的,组成的,合成的,成分的。~ *motion* 【物】分运动。~ *part* 组成部分。**II** **n.** 部分,成分;【物】分力,分向量;【自】元件,组件,部件。~ *of force* 【物】分力。~ (*star*) 【天】子星。~*s of cost* (各种)生产费用。

com·port [kəmˈpɔːt; kəmˋpɔrt] **vt.** 〔书面语〕处身,持己,表现;举动,行为 (*oneself*)。~ *oneself with dignity* 举止庄重。*He* ~*ed himself as if he had already been elected.* 他表现出好像他已经当选了似的。—**vi.** 与…一致,相称,相适应。*His remark simply does not* ~ *with his known attitude.* 他的发言同他一贯的态度极不相称。

com·pose [kəmˈpəuz; kəmˋpoz] **vt.** **1.** 组成,构成。**2.** 创作(诗歌,乐曲等);撰写;为(歌词等)谱曲;构(图),设计。**3.** 【印】排(字)。**4.** 使安定[平静,镇定]。**5.** 正(容);整顿;安顿(死尸)。**6.** 调停(纷争等)。~ *a poem* 作诗。~ *a novel* 写小说。~ *a dispute* 调解纷争。~ *one's features* 使面色[态度]平静下来。~ *one's thoughts for action* 打定主意[考虑好办法]准备行动。~ *one's mind* 平心静气,安心。—**vi.** **1.** 创作,作曲。**2.** 排字。***be*** ~***d of*** 由…组成。~ ***oneself*** 使自己镇定[安心]下来 (*to sleep* 等)。

com·posed [kəmˈpəuzd; kəmˋpozd] **a.** 镇静的,沉着的,从容自若的。**-ly** [-zidli; -zɪdlɪ] **ad.** **-ness** [-zidnis; -zɪdnɪs] **n.**

com·pos·er [kəmˈpəuzə; kəmˋpozɚ] **n.** **1.** 作曲家;作者。**2.** 调停人,和解人。**3.** 设计者,制图者。

com·pos·ing [kəmˈpəuziŋ; kəmˋpozɪŋ] **I** **a.** 起镇静作用的,镇静的。**II** **n.** 【印】排字。~ **frame** 排字架。~ **medicine** 镇静剂。~ **machine** 排字机。~ **room** 【印】排字车间。~ **stick** 排字盘。

com·pos·ite [ˈkɔmpəzit, -zait; kəmˋpɑzɪt, -zaɪt] **I** **a.** **1.** 并合的,复合的,混成的,合成的,集成的。**2.** 【建】混合式的;【船】铁骨木壳的。**3.** 【植】菊科的。**II** **n.** **1.** 合成物;混合蜡烛,混合客车,综合照片;混合式(建筑物)。**2.** 【植】菊科植物。~ **candle** 混合蜡烛。~ **carriage** 混合客车。~ **forest** 中林。~ **number** 【数】合成数,非素数。~ **photograph** (由几张底片合印成的)综合照片。~ **ship** 铁骨木皮船。~ **system** 金银本位并用制;【电】报话复合制。

com·po·si·tion [ˌkɔmpəˈziʃən; ˏkɑmpəˋzɪʃən] **n.** **1.** 作文(法),作诗(法),作曲(法);作品,文章;乐曲;文体,措辞。**2.** 编制;结构,构造,组成,组织;成分;合成物。**3.** 素质,性格。**4.** 构图,配合,布置。**5.** 妥协,和解(条件);(私下了结的)和解费,(议定的)偿付额。**6.** 【印】排字。**7.** 【逻】综合法,合成推理;【语法】复合法;【社】结合体。*Latin prose* ~*s* 拉丁散文作品。*a stone* ~石刻品。*He has not a spark of generosity in his* ~. 他(性格中)一点肚量也没有。*a* ~ *of 5sh. in the pound* 每镑照赔五先令。~ *for violin* 提琴曲。~ *of a picture* 绘画构图。~ *of air* 空气成分。***make a*** ~ ***with*** (*sb.'s creditors*) 和(各债权人)议定偿还办法。~ **billiard-ball** 【台球】人造象牙球。~ **book** 〔美〕作文簿。~ **cloth** 防水帆布。

com·po·si·tion·a·lism [kəmpəˈziʃənəlizəm; kɑmpəˋzɪʃənəlɪzəm] **n.** 【文艺】构成派。

com·po·si·tive [kəmˈpɔzitiv; kəmˋpɑzətɪv] **a.** 合成的,综合的。

com·pos·i·tor [kəmˈpɔzitə; kəmˋpɑzɪtɚ] **n.** 【印】排字工人。

compos mentis [ˈkɔmpɔs ˈmentis; ˋkɑmpəs ˋmɛntɪs] 〔L.〕【法】精神健全[正常]的。

com·pos·si·ble [kɔmˈpɔsəbl; kəmˋpɑsəbl̩] **a.** 可共存的;并行不悖的。*The two theories vary, but they are* ~. 这两种理论虽然各有千秋,但它们是并行不悖的。

com·post [ˈkɔmpɔst; ˋkɑmpost] **I** **n.** **1.** 混合物,合成物。**2.** 【农】混合肥料,堆肥;混合涂料,灰泥。**II** **vt.** 【农】使成混合肥料[堆肥];给…施堆肥。

com·po·sure [kəmˈpəuʒə; kəmˋpoʒɚ] **n.** 镇静,沉着。***keep*** [***lose***] ***one's*** ~ 沉住[沉不住]气。***with great*** ~ 泰然自若,极镇静。

com·po·ta·tion [ˌkɔmpəˈteiʃən; ˏkɑmpəˋteʃən] **n.** 〔书〕共饮,会饮,聚饮。

com·po·ta·tor [ˈkɔmpəteitə; ˋkɑmpəˏtetɚ] **n.** 酒伴,共饮者,会饮者。

com·pote [ˈkɔmpəut; ˋkɑmpot] **n.** **1.** 水果糖浆〔如糖水樱桃等〕;〔美〕(饭后的)一碟甜食。**2.** (高脚)果碟。

C

com·pound[1] [kəmˈpaund; kəmˋpaund] **I** *vt*. **1.** 使混合,调合,配合;【语】复合,合成。**2.** (通过互相让步等)解决(纠纷);用钱了结(债务等);一次清算;部分偿还。**3.** 【电】复绕[复激、复卷]。~ *a medicine* 配药。~ *a felony* 【法】用钱抵赎罪罚。—*vi*. 和解,谈妥,和平了结。~ **with** (*sb*.) 与(某人)和解[和平了结]。**II** [ˈkɔmpaund; ˋkɑmpaund] *a*. 混合的,复合的;合成的,复式的。**III** *n*. 混合物,合成品;【化】化合物;【语】复合词。*cutting* ~润削剂。*filling* ~填料。*sealing* ~封口胶。~ **animal** 【动】群栖动物。~ **addition** [**subtraction**] 复名数加[减]算。~ **discount** 【商】复贴现。~ **engine** 【机】复合机。~ **eye** 【动】复眼。~ **flower** 【植】聚合花。~ **fracture** 【医】哆开[开放]骨折,有创骨折。~ **glass** 多层玻璃。~ **motor** 复激电动机。~ **number** 【数】复名数。~ **sentence** 【语法】并列句。~ **statement** 【计】复合语句。~ **word** 复合词。

compound[2] [ˈkɔmpaund; ˋkɑmpaund] *n*. **1.** (印度等地工厂、住宅的)圈占地区(南非等地用围墙等围起的)矿工居住区。**2.** 圈有围墙[篱笆]等的场地〔临时战俘营收容所等〕;(同族聚居的)村寨。

com·pra·dor(e) [ˌkɔmprəˈdɔː; ˏkɑmprəˋdɔr] *n*. (旧时中国的)买办。

com·preg [ˈkɔmpreg; ˋkɑmprɛg] *n*. (渗)胶合(缩)木材。

com·pre·hend [ˌkɔmpriˈhend; ˏkɑmprɪˋhɛnd] *vt*. **1.** 了解,领悟。**2.** 包含,包括。

com·pre·hen·si·bil·i·ty [ˈkɔmpriˌhensəˈbiliti; ˋkɑmprɪˏhɛnsəˋbɪlətɪ] *n*. 能理解,易了解。

com·pre·hen·si·ble [ˌkɔmpriˈhensəbl; ˏkɑmprɪˋhɛnsəbl̩] *a*. 能理解的。

com·pre·hen·sion [ˌkɔmpriˈhenʃən; ˏkɑmprɪˋhɛnʃən] *n*. **1.** 理解,理解力。**2.** 包含,包括,含蓄;概括公理;【逻】内包;【修】推知法;【宗】包容政策。*a term of wide* ~意义广泛的术语[名词]。***be above*** [***pass, be beyond***] ~ 难理解,不可解。

com·pre·hen·sive [ˌkɔmpriˈhensiv; ˏkɑmprɪˋhɛnsɪv] *a*. **1.** 广泛的,全面的,完整的,包含多的,综合的。**2.** 有理解力的,悟性好的。*a* ~ *knowledge* 渊博的知识。*a* ~ *mind* 宽大的心胸。*a* ~ *account* [*description*] 全面的说明[记载]。*a* ~ *survey* 全面调查。~ *faculty* 理解力。*a* ~ *English-Chinese dictionary* 综合英汉词典。*be* ~ *of* 包含…。~ *utilization* 综合利用。**-ly** *ad*. **-ness** *n*.

com·pre·hen·siv·ist [ˌkɔmprihensivist; ˏkɑmprɪˋhɛnsɪvɪst] *n*. **1.** 知识广博论者;反对专业化的人。**2.** 〔英〕主张中学教育综合化的人。

com·press [kəmˈpres; kəmˋprɛs] **I** *vt*. 压缩,浓缩;使(文章等)变简练。—*vi*. 经受压缩。**II** [ˈkɔmpres; ˋkɑmprɛs] *n*. **1.** 【医】压布,敷布;罨,敷。**2.** (棉花等的)打包机。*hot* ~热敷布;热敷法。*ice* ~冰罨。

com·pressed [kəmˈprest; kəmˋprɛst] *a*. **1.** 压缩过的;(文字)简练的。**2.** 【植】(左右)扁平的;【动】侧扁的,宽度大于长度的。~ *air* 压缩空气。~ *wallboard* 压扁壁板。

com·pres·si·bil·i·ty [kəmˌpresiˈbiliti; kəmˏprɛsəˋbɪlətɪ] *n*. 压缩性;压缩系数;压缩率。

com·pres·si·ble [kəmˈpresəbl; kəmˋprɛsəbl̩] *a*. 可压紧的,可压缩的。

com·pres·sion [kəmˈpreʃən; kəmˋprɛʃən] *n*. **1.** 压缩;压紧;浓缩,紧缩。**2.** 加压;压抑。**3.** (表现的)简练。**4.** 应压试验。~ *of ideas* 思想的概括。~ *of the earth* 地球椭[扁]率。~ **joint** 压力接合;承压缝,挤压节理。~ **member** 抗压构件。~ **pump** 压气泵。~ **test** 耐压试验。

com·pres·sive [kəmˈpresiv; kəmˋprɛsɪv] *a*. 有压力的,压缩的,压榨的。~ **strength** 抗压强度。**-ly** *ad*. **-ness** *n*.

com·pres·sor [kəmˈpresə; kəmˋprɛsɚ] *n*. **1.** 压缩物。**2.** 压缩器,压气机,压榨器。**3.** 【解】收缩肌,压肌。

com·pris·al, com·priz·al [kəmˈpraizəl; kəmˋpraɪzl̩] *n*. **1.** 包含,包蓄。**2.** 梗概,大要。

com·prise, com·prize [kəmˈpraiz; kəmˋpraɪz] *vt*. 包含,包括;由…组成[合成]。*The house* ~*s nine bedrooms*. 这栋房子有九间卧室。*the chapters that* ~ *the first part of the book* 构成该书第一部的几章。—*vi*. 由…构成(*of*)。*funds comprising of subscriptions* 由捐款构成的基金。

com·pro·mise [ˈkɔmprəmaiz; ˋkɑmprəˏmaɪz] **I** *n*. **1.** 妥协,调和,和解,互让了结,私下了结(*between*)。**2.** 妥协方案,折衷方案,调和契约;中间物,折衷物。**3.** (名誉等的)损害;连累;危及。~ ***between a fish and a snake*** 非鱼非蛇的中间生物。~ ***of principles*** 原则上的让步。***make*** ~ ***with*** 和…妥协。**II** *vt*. **1.** 对…妥协,和解,互让了结,私下了结。**2.** 连累,危及。**3.** 损伤(名誉等),放弃(原则等);泄露(秘密等)。*be* ~*d by* 被…所危害[连累]。~ *oneself* 做出有失体面[有损自己名誉]的事情。~ (*one's own*) *reputation* 损坏(自己)名誉。—*vi*. 妥协,和解,让步。~ *with* (*sb*.) *on* (*a point*) (在某点上)和(某人)和解[妥协]。

com·pro·vin·cial [ˌkɔmprəˈvinʃəl; ˏkɑmprəˋvɪnʃəl] *a*. 同一省区的;同一管区的。

comp·to·graph [ˈkɔmtəgrɑːf; ˋkɑmtəˏgræf] *n*. 自动计算器。

comp·tom·e·ter [kɔmpˈtɔmitə; kɑmpˋtɑmɪtɚ] *n*. 【商标】业务用计算机。

Comp·ton [ˈkɔmptən; ˋkɑmptən] *n*. **1.** 康普顿(姓氏)。**2.** **A.H.** ~ 康普顿〔1892—1962,美国物理学家〕。

comp·trol·ler [kənˈtrəulə; kənˋtrolɚ] *n*. 审计员[官],主计员。

com·pul·sion [kəmˈpʌlʃən; kəmˋpʌlʃən] *n*. **1.** 强迫,强制。**2.** 打动人的力量。**3.** 【心】难抗拒的冲动。***by*** ~ 强迫地。***on*** [***upon, under***] ~ 被迫,不得不。***take part under*** ~ 胁从;被迫参与。

com·pul·sive [kəmˈpʌlsiv; kəmˋpʌlsɪv] *a*. 强迫的,有强迫力的;在强迫下发生[造成]的,不由自主的。**-ly** *ad*. **-ness** *n*.

com·pul·so·ri·ly [kəmˈpʌlsərili; kəmˋpʌlsərɪlɪ] *ad*. 强迫,强制。

com·pul·so·ry [kəmˈpʌlsəri; kəmˋpʌlsərɪ] *a*. 强迫的,强制的;义务的;必修的。~ **contribution** 勒捐,派捐。~ **education** 强迫教育,义务教育。~ **execution** 强迫执行。~ **measures** 强迫手段。~ **service** 征兵,义务兵役。~ **subjects** 必修科目。

com·punc·tion [kəmˈpʌŋkʃən; kəmˋpʌŋkʃən] *n*. 良心的责备,后悔,懊悔,悔恨。***without*** (***the slightest***) ~ 毫不在乎,无动于衷。

com·punc·tious [kəmˈpʌŋkʃəs; kəmˋpʌŋkʃəs] *a*. (使)内疚的,惭愧的,(使)后悔的。**-ly** *ad*.

com·pur·ga·tion [ˌkɔmpəːˈgeiʃən; ˏkɑmpɚˋgeʃən] *n*. 〔古〕【法】根据证人宣誓证实宣布被告无罪。

com·pur·ga·tor [ˈkɔmpəːˌgeitə; ˋkɑmpɚˏgetɚ] *n*. 被告无罪证实人。

com·put·a·ble [kəmˈpjuːtəbl; kəmˋpjutəbl̩] *a*. 能计算的,能算出的。

com·pu·ta·tion [ˌkɔmpju(ː)ˈteiʃən; ˏkɑmpjəˋteʃən] *n*. **1.** 计算,估算。**2.** 计算法。**3.** 计算结果,得数。

com·pu·ta·tion·al [ˌkɔmpju(ː)ˈteiʃənəl; ˏkɑmpjəˋteʃənl̩] *a*. 计算的。~ **linguistics** 【语言】(用)计算机(进行研究的)语言学。

com·pute [kəmˈpjuːt; kəmˋpjut] **I** *vt*., *vi*. 计算,估计;算定。~ *tare* 估计皮重。*computing centre* 计算中心。~ (*one's loss*) ***at*** ... (损失)估计为…。~ ***from*** 由…起算。**II** *n*. 计算,估计。***beyond*** ~ 不可计量。

com·put·er [kəmˈpjuːtə; kəmˋpjutɚ] *n*. **1.** 计算者。**2.** (电子)计算机;计量器。*an electronic* ~电子计算机。

～ **graphics** 电子计算机制图。～ **language** 电子计算机语言。～**like** *a*. 计算机般的。～**-on-a-chip** 微型电子计算机。**-ism** 电子计算机主义〔认为电子计算机万能等〕。**-er·ite, -nik** 计算机专家;计算机工作者。～ **speak** 电脑行话。～ **virus** 电脑病毒(破坏电脑之程式,又称 soft bomb)。

com·put·er·ize [kəmˈpjuːtəˌraiz; kəmˋpjutəˏraɪz] *vt.*, *vi.* **1.** (给…)装备电子计算机;(使)电子计算机化。**2.** 用电子计算机计算[操纵、操作、编排等]。**-za·tion** *n.*

Comr. = Commissioner.

com·rade [ˈkɔmrid; ˋkɑmrɪd] *n.* 同志;伙伴,同事;战友。～ *in arms* 战友。**-ship** *n.* 伙伴关系,友谊(关系)。(～*ship in arms* 战斗友谊)。

COMSAT =〔美〕Communication Satellite Corporation 通信卫星公司。

com·sat [ˈkɔmsæt; ˋkɑmˏsæt] *n.* 通信卫星。

Com·so·mol [ˈkɔmsəmɔl; ˋkɑmsəˏmɑl] *n.* = Komsomol.

Com·stock [ˈkʌmstɔk, ˈkɔmstɔk; ˋkʌmstɑk, ˋkɑmstɑk] *n.* 康斯托克〔姓氏〕。

Com·stock·er·y [ˈkɔmstɔkəri; ˋkʌmˏstɑkərɪ] *n.* 对妨害风化的文化艺术的干涉。

COMSUBRON = Commander, Submarine Squadron〔美〕潜艇分遣队司令。

Comte [kɔ̃ːnt, kɔːnt; kɔ̃nt, kɔnt], **Auguste** 孔德〔1798—1857,法国实证主义哲学家〕。

Com·ti·an [ˈkɔ̃ːntiən; ˋkɔntɪən] *a.* 【哲】(孔德的)实证主义(学派)的。

Comt·ism [ˈkɔ̃ːntizəm; ˋkɔntɪzəm] *n.* 【哲】(孔德的)实证主义[哲学]。

Comt·ist [ˈkɔ̃ːntist; ˋkɔntɪst] *n.* 【哲】实证主义者。

Com.Ver. = Common Version (Bible) (基督教《圣经》的)普通译本。

Co·mus [ˈkəuməs; ˋkoməs] *n.* 【希、罗神】宴会欢乐之神。

Com Z = Communication Zone【美军】兵站区。

con [kɔn; kɑn] ***prep.*** 〔It.〕【乐】以,用。～ ***amore*** [əˈmɔːri; əˋmɔrɪ] 亲切地,热烈地,真诚地。～ ***brio*** [ˈbriːəu; ˋbrio] 活泼地,精神勃勃地。～ ***espressione*** [ˈespresˈsjɔːnei; ˋɛsprɛsˋsjone] 有表现力地,富于表情地。～ ***fuoco*** [ˈfwɔːko; ˋfwɔko] 充满热情。～ ***gracia*** [ˈgrɑːtʃiə; ˋgrɑtʃɪə] 愉快地。

con[1] [kɔn; kɑn] *vt.* (**-nn-**) 精读,研读,研究;熟读;默记(*over*)。

con[2] [kɔn; kɑn] **I** *vt.*, *vi.* (**-nn-**)【海】指挥(操舵);指挥(船的)航路。*a ～ning tower* (军舰的)司令塔。**II** *n.* 指挥操舵;指挥操舵者的位置。

con[3] [kɔn; kɑn] **I** *n.* 反对(论点);反对票,反对者。***the pros and ～s*** 赞成者和反对者;赞成票数与反对票数;正面理由和反面理由。**II** *ad.* 反对。**III** *prep.* 反对。*forces pro and ～ the act* 赞成和反对法案的两支力量。

con[4] [kɔn; kɑn] **I** *vt.* (**-nn-**)〔美俚〕欺骗,欺诈。**II** *a.* 欺诈的,骗取信任的。*a ～ game* 骗局。*a ～ man* 骗子。

con[5] [kɔn; kɑn] *n.* 〔美俚〕囚犯(= convict);肺病(= consumption);电车售票员(= conductor)。

con- *pref.* = com-.

con. = concerto; conclusion; conics; connection; consigned; consignment; *contra* ([L.] = against); consolidate(d); contra.

Con. = Consul.

CONAC = Continental Air Command〔美〕本土空军司令部。

CONAD = Continental Air Defense Command〔美〕本土防空司令部。

Co·na·kry [ˈkɔnəkri; ˋkɑnɑˋkrɪ] *n.* 科纳克里〔几内亚首都〕。

Co·nan [ˈkəunən, ˈkɔnən; ˋkonən, ˋkɑnən] *n.* 科南〔男子名〕。

Co·nant [ˈkɔnənt; ˋkonənt] *n.* 科南特〔姓氏〕。

co·na·tion [kə*u*ˈneiʃən; koˋneʃən] *n.* 【心】努力,企求,欲求。

con·a·tive [ˈkɔnətiv, ˈkəunə-; ˋkɑnətɪv, konə-] *a.* **1.** 【心】努力企求的,欲求的。**2.** 【语法】增强性的,(动词)表示努力企求的,意动的。～ **verb**【语法】意欲动词。

co·na·tus [kə*u*ˈneitəs; koˋnetəs] *n.* (*pl.* ～) **1.** 努力;企图;尽力。**2.** 【生】(动植物的)自然企求力,自然倾向。

conc. = concentration; concerning.

con·cat·e·nate [kɔnˈkætineit; kɑnˋkætnet] **I** *vt.* 使(成串地)连结[衔接]起来。**II** *a.* 连锁状的。

con·cat·e·na·tion [kənˌkætiˈneiʃən; kənkætṇˋeʃən] *n.* 连锁;连结成串,连续。

con·cave [ˈkɔnˈkeiv, ˈkɔnkeiv; kɑnˋkev, ˋkɑnkev] **I** *a.* 凹的,凹面的 (*opp.* convex)。**II** *n.* 凹,凹线,凹面(物)。***the*** (***spherical***) ～〔诗〕苍穹。**III** *vt.* 把…弄成凹(面)。～ **lens** 凹透镜。～ **mirror** 凹面镜。～ **tile** 牝瓦。**-ly** *ad.* **-ness** *n.*

con·cav·i·ty [kɔnˈkæviti; kɑnˋkævətɪ] *n.* 凹状;凹性;凹度;凹处,凹面;成凹形。

con·ca·vo-con·cave [kɔnˈkeivə*u*ˈkɔnkeiv; kɑnˋkevokɑnˋkev] *a.* 两面凹进的,双凹的。

con·ca·vo-con·vex [kɔnˈkeivə*u*ˈkɔnveks; kɑnˋkevoˋkɑnˋvɛks] *a.* 一面凹一面凸的,凹凸的。

con·ceal [kənˈsiːl; kənˋsil] *vt.* 隐藏,隐蔽,隐匿。～ ***from*** (*sb.*) 对(人)隐蔽 (*I ～ nothing from you.* 我对你一切公开)。～ ***oneself*** 躲起来,躲藏,潜伏,埋伏。

con·ceal·ment [kənˈsiːlmənt; kənˋsilmənt] *n.* **1.** 隐匿,隐蔽;潜伏。**2.** 埋伏处,躲避处。***remain in*** ～ 隐藏着,躲着。

con·cede [kənˈsiːd; kənˋsid] *vt.* **1.** (勉强)承认。**2.** 让与,放弃赢得…的希望。**3.** 〔俚〕【体】失(局)。～ *a point in* (*argument*) 在(争论)中退让一步。～ *a game* 输一局。～ *that* (*the statement is true*) 勉强承认(陈述是真实的)。—*vi.* 让步。～ *to* (*sb.*) 对(某人)让步。

con·ced·ed·ly [kənˈsiːdidli; kənˋsidɪdlɪ] *ad.* 〔美〕明白地,众所承认地。

con·ceit [kənˈsiːt; kənˋsit] **I** *n.* **1.** 自负,自大,自满。**2.** 奇想,幻想;(作品的)做作,(比喻的)牵强附会,(构思的)奇巧。**3.** 意见,想法;私见,独断。**4.** 不切实用的花哨物品。**5.** 〔古〕理解力。**6.** 〔英方〕喜欢,中意。***be full of*** ～ 十分自负。***be out of*** ～ ***with*** 厌倦,嫌弃,厌弃。***in one's own*** ～ 自以为;自夸 (*He is wise in his own* ～. 他自以为聪明)。***lose*** ～ ***of oneself*** 失去自信。***put*** (*sb.*) ***out of*** ～ ***with*** (*sth.*) 使(某人)厌弃。***take the*** ～ ***out of*** (*sb.*) 打消(某人的)傲气[自信];挫折,折磨(某人)。**II** *vt.* **1.** 〔方〕想像。**2.** 〔英方〕喜欢,中意于。**3.** 〔古〕理解。

con·ceit·ed [kənˈsiːtid; kənˋsitɪd] *a.* **1.** 自负的,自夸的,逞能的。**2.** 狂想的,奇想的。**3.** 花哨的。**4.** 〔旧〕聪明的,机智的。*He is ～ and short-sighted.* 他自高自大,目光短浅。*a well ～ play* 构想巧妙的戏剧。***be*** ～ ***about*** 自负,自夸。**-ly** *ad.* **-ness** *n.*

con·ceiv·a·ble [kənˈsiːvəbl; kənˋsivəbḷ] *a.* 可以想到的,可以想像的,可能的。*by every ～ means* 千方百计,用一切手段。*It is ～ that ...?* 难道是…的吗? **-bil·i·ty** [-ˈbiliti; -ˋbɪlɪtɪ] *n.* **-ness** *n.*

con·ceiv·a·bly [kənˈsiːvəbli; kənˋsivəblɪ] *ad.* 想得到地,想像上。

con·ceive [kənˈsiːv; kənˋsiv] *vt.* **1.** 怀(胎)。**2.** 想到(计划等);想像;以为;想出;怀(恨等),蓄(意),抱有(思想);〔旧〕理解。**3.** 〔常用被动语态〕表达,陈述。～ *a child* 怀胎。～ *a hatred* 怀恨。*a badly ～d petition* 词不达意的请愿书。*a badly ～d scheme* 拙劣的计划。～ *prejudices* 抱偏见。～ *an aversion to* 对…抱反感。—*vi.* **1.** 怀孕。**2.** 想像,设想 (*of*)。～ *of* (*a plan*) 想出(计

C

划)。

con·cel·e·brate [kɔn'selibreit; kɑn`sɛlıbret] ***vt.*** 共同做(弥撒)〔由两个或更多的司祭牧师一起进行祷告〕。**-bra·tion *n.***

con·cent [kən'sent; kən`sɛnt] ***n.*** 〔古〕**1.** (音乐的)谐调,和谐。**2.** 协调;一致。

con·cen·ter [kɔn'sentə; kɑn`sɛntɚ] ***vi.***, ***vt*** 〔美〕= concentre.

con·cen·trate ['kɔnsentreit; `kɑnsn͵tret] **I** ***vt.*** **1.** 集中;使…集中于一点。**2.**【化】提浓,浓缩,凝缩;【冶】汰选。~ *fire* 集中火力(射击)。—***vi.*** 专心,凝(神);倾全力。~ *in class* 专心听讲。~ ***one's attention on*** [***upon***] 把注意力集中在。~ ***on*** [***upon***] 集中在;专心于。**II** ***n.*** 浓缩物;【畜】精料;【矿】精砂。

con·cen·trat·ed ['kɔnsentreitid; `kɑnsn͵tretıd] ***a.*** **1.** 集中了的;浓缩了的;汰选出来的。**2.** 聚精会神的。~ *fire* 集中射击,集中火力。~ *food* [*feed*] 浓缩食品[饲料]。~ *study* 悉心研究,专心学习。

con·cen·tra·tion [͵kɔnsen'treiʃən; ͵kɑnsn`treʃən] ***n.*** **1.** 集中。**2.**【化】提浓,蒸浓,浓缩;浓度;稠密度;【矿】汰选,选矿,富化。**3.** 集中注意,专心。*multi-stage ore* ~ 多段选矿法。*with deep* ~专心。~ **camp** (俘虏等的)集中营。~ **cell** 浓差电池。~ **ring**【军】集索圈。

con·cen·tra·tive ['kɔnsentreitiv; `kɑnsn͵tretıv] ***a.*** **1.** 集中(性)的。**2.** 一心一意的,专心的。

con·cen·tra·tor ['kɔnsentreitə; `kɑnsɛn͵tretɚ] ***n.*** **1.** 集中者;浓缩器;【冶】选矿厂,选矿机;【电】集线器。**2.** (特定课题的)钻研者。

con·cen·tre, con·cen·ter [kɔn'sentə; kɑn`sɛntɚ] ***vi.***, ***vt.*** (使)聚集于同一中心;(使)集中;(使)会聚。

con·cen·tric [kɔn'sentrik; kən`sɛntrık] ***a.*** 同心的,同轴的(*with*);集中的,会聚的。***be*** ~ ***with*** 与…同心。~ **circles**【数】同心圆。~ **fire** 集中火力。**-al·ly *ad.*** **-i·ty *n.***

Con·cep·ción [kən͵sepsi'əun; ͵kɔnsɛp`sjon] ***n.*** 康塞普西翁[智利城市]。

con·cept ['kɔnsept; `kɑnsɛpt] ***n.*** **1.**【哲】概念。**2.** 观念,思想,意思,心意。*the* ~ *of operations* 作战方针,作战思想。★ concept 指具体的概念, conception 则着重指概念的形成。

con·cep·ta·cle [kən'septəkl; kən`sɛptəkl] ***n.***【植】(某些藻类的)生殖窠。

con·cep·tion [kən'sepʃən; kən`sɛpʃən] ***n.*** **1.** 妊娠,受孕;胚胎,胎儿;起源,发端。**2.** 概念作用;概念;印象。**3.** 设想,构想;见解,看法。*a clear* [*vague*] ~清楚的[模糊的]概念。*a clever* ~聪明的想法。*a poetic* ~诗的构想。*his* ~ *of himself* 他对他自己的看法。*have too rigid a* ~ *of* 对…的看法太刻板。*the materialistic* ~ *of history* 唯物史观。*the idealist* ~ *of history* 唯心史观。*the* ~ *of the United Nations* 联合国的创立。***form a*** ~ ***of*** 对…抱有一种想法。***have no*** ~ ***of*** 完全不知[不懂]。

con·cep·tion·al [kən'sepʃənəl; kən`sɛpʃənəl] ***a.*** 概念的。

con·cep·tive [kən'septiv; kən`sɛptıv] ***a.*** **1.** 概念(上)的;设想上的。**2.** 〔罕〕会受孕的。

con·cep·tu·al [kən'septʃuəl; kən`sɛptʃuəl] ***a.*** 概念的。~ *knowledge* (抽象的)概念知识(*cf.* perceptual knowledge 感性知识)。~ **art** (表达概念而不是形像的)概念艺术。**-ism *n.***【哲】(介乎唯名论与实在论之间的)概念论。**-ist *n.*** 概念论者。

con·cep·tu·al·ize [kən'septjuəlaiz; kən`sɛptʃuəl͵aız] ***vt.*** 使形成概念,使产生想法;使概念化。**-za·tion *n.***

con·cern [kən'sə:n; kən`sɝn] **I** ***vt.*** **1.** 关系到;影响,涉及(某人的)利害。**2.** 〔用被动语态〕干与,干涉,参加,从事(*in*)。**3.** 使关心(*with*),担心,挂念,忧虑(*for*, *about*, *over*)〔参看 ~*ed*〕。*It doesn't* ~ *me*. = *I am not* ~*ed with it*. 那件事和我没关系[我不知情]。*I am* ~*ed to tell you of it*. 我打算把那件事告诉你。*I am much* ~*ed to hear that* ... 我听见…后十分着急。*be* ~ *ed about* 关心;挂念,顾虑。*Don't* ~ *yourself about his opinion*. 不要管他的意见。*be* ~ *ed in* 和…有关系,牵涉到。*be* ~*ed with* 干与,参与;关怀。~ *oneself about* 关心,挂念。~ *oneself with* [*in*] 从事,参与,干与,干涉。*My honour is* ~*ed*. 有关我的名誉。***as*** ~***s*** 关于。***so far as I am*** ~***ed*** 就我个人来说。**II** ***n.*** **1.** 关系;利害关系。**2.** 关心,挂念,担心。**3.** 商行,公司;财团;康采恩;事业,业务;〔*pl.*〕事件,事情。**4.** 〔口〕(泛指)事物,家伙〔指有缺点的人〕。*It is no* ~ *of mine*. 与我无关。*a flourishing* ~兴盛的事业[商号]。*a going* ~开着的商店。*a rickety old* ~年久失修的老建筑。*a petty* ~细事。*a selfish* ~自私的家伙。*everyday* ~*s* 日常事务。*worldly* ~*s* 世事。*I can manage my own* ~*s*. 自己的事总可以解决。*feel* ~ *about* 担心,挂念。*have a* ~ *in* 和…有利害关系。*have no* ~ *for* 毫不关心;完全不怕。*have no* ~ *with* 和…毫无关系。*matter of the utmost* ~(关系)重大的事件。*of* ~ 关系重大的;有关系的。*with* ~ 忧虑着,惦记着。*He inquired with* (*grow*) ~. 他殷切询问。*without* ~不关心;不怕。

con·cerned [kən'sə:nd; kən`sɝnd] ***a.*** **1.** 担心的,忧虑的。**2.** 关心政治的,关心社会的。**3.** 〔常用于名词之后〕有关(方面);被牵连的。*the authorities* ~有关当局。*the parties* ~关系人,当事人。*I'm not* ~. 于我无关。*Everyone* ~ *in the murder case has been identified*. 与凶杀案有牵连的人都已查明。***be much*** ~ ***about*** 十分挂念。***with a*** ~ ***air*** 用关心的态度。**-ly** [kən'sə:nidli; kən`sɝnıdlı] ***ad.***

con·cern·ing [kən'sə:niŋ; kən`sɝnıŋ] ***prep.*** 关于,论及,就…说。~ *the matter* 提到那件事。

con·cern·ment [kən'sə:nmənt; kən`sɝnmənt] ***n.*** **1.** 关系;参与;重要。**2.** 悬念,挂念。**3.** 关系事项,事务。(*a matter*) *of* ~ 关系重大的(事情)。***of general*** ~ 一般的。***of vital*** ~关系非常重大的。

con·cert ['kɔnsət; `kɑnsɚt] **I** ***n.*** **1.** 音乐会,演奏会,合奏(曲);【乐】协奏曲。**2.** 一致,协力,和谐。***in*** ~ 异口同音地,同声;齐。***in*** ~ ***with*** 和…相呼应[合作](*act in* ~ *with* 和…一致行动。*proceed in* ~ *with* 和…采取一致步骤)。**II** [kən'sə:t; kən`sɝt] ***vt.*** 协商;合订(计划)。—***vi.*** 协同工作(*with*)。~ **grand** 演奏会用大钢琴。~ **hall** [**room**] 音乐堂[厅]。~ **master**, ~ **meister**【乐】音乐指挥;首席小提琴演奏者。~ **needles** (留声机)唱针。~ **pitch**【乐】合奏调,较高音调;较高效能。

con·cert·ed [kən'sə:tid; kən`sɝtıd] ***a.*** 商定的,协商好的;预定的;协力一致的;【乐】合拍调的。*a* ~ *plan of operations* 协商好的作战计划。*take* ~ *action* 取一致行动。

con·cer·ti·na [͵kɔnsə'ti:nə; ͵kɑnsɚ`tinə] ***n.*** **1.** 六角手风琴。**2.**【军】(可移动)蛇腹式铁丝网。~ **movement** 折叠[蛇腹]式构造。~ **table** 折叠桌。

con·cer·ti·no [͵kɔntʃeə'ti:nəu; ͵kɑntʃɚ`tino] ***n.***【乐】**1.** 小协奏曲〔通常只有一个乐章〕。**2.** 主奏组〔协奏曲中的一组独奏乐器〕。

con·cert·ize ['kɔnsətaiz; `kɑnsɚ͵taız] ***vi.*** 独唱[独奏]表演〔在音乐会上独唱或独奏,尤指巡回演出时〕。

con·cer·to [kən'tʃə:təu; kən`tʃɛrto] ***n.*** 〔It.〕【乐】协奏曲。

con·ces·sion [kən'seʃən; kən`sɛʃən] ***n.*** **1.** 让步;迁就;让与。**2.** (政府的)核准,许可,特许;特许权。**3.** 租借地,租界。**4.** 〔美〕(商店等在公园、球场等公共场所的)场地特许使用(权);特许使用的场地。*an oil* ~石油开采权。***make a*** ~ ***to*** 对…让步。

con·ces·sion·aire [kən͵seʃə'nɛə; kən͵sɛʃə`nɛr] ***n.*** 受让人;特许权获得者(= concessioner)。

con·ces·sion·ar·y [kən'seʃənəri; kən`sɛʃən,ɛrɪ] **I** ***a.*** 让与的;让步的;让渡特权的。**II** ***n.*** 受让人;特许权获得者。

con·ces·sive [kən'sesiv; kən`sɛsɪv] ***a.*** 让与的;让步的。~ **clause**【语法】让步子句。

conch [kɔŋk, kɔntʃ; kɑŋk, kɑntʃ] ***n.*** (*pl.* ~*s* [-ks; -ks], ~*es* [-tʃiz; -tʃɪz]) **1.**【希神】海神特里顿(Triton)的响螺;【动】风螺,海螺;海螺壳。**2.**【建】半圆形穹顶。**3.**【解】外耳;耳壳;(鼻)甲。**4.**〔俚〕西印度巴哈马(Bahama)岛人。

con·cha ['kɔŋkə; `kɑŋkə] ***n.*** (*pl.* **-chae** [-ki:; -ki]) **1.**【解】外耳,耳壳;(鼻)甲。**2.**【建】半圆形穹顶。

con·chie ['kɔntʃi; `kɑntʃɪ] ***n.*** = conchy.

con·chif·er·ous [kɔŋ'kifərəs; kɑŋ`kɪfərəs] ***a.*** 有贝壳的;【地】生贝壳的。

con·choid ['kɔŋkɔid; `kɑŋkɔɪd] ***n.***【数】蚌线,螺旋线;螺线管;【矿、地】贝壳状断面。

con·choi·dal [kɔŋ'kɔidl; kɑŋ`kɔɪdl] ***a.*** 贝壳状的;【数】蚌线的。

con·chol·o·gist [kɔŋ'kɔlədʒist; kɑŋ`kɑlədʒɪst] ***n.*** 贝壳学者,贝类学者。

con·chol·o·gy [kɔŋ'kɔlədʒi; kɑŋ`kɑlədʒɪ] ***n.*** 贝壳学,贝类学。

con·chy ['kɔntʃi; `kɑntʃɪ] ***n.***〔英俚〕由于信仰的驱使而抵制者[拒绝服兵役者](= conscientious objector)。

con·ci·erge [kɔ:nsi'ɛəʒ; ,kɑnsɪ`ɛrʒ] ***n.***〔F.〕**1.** 门房,门警。**2.**(公寓等的)管理员。**3.**(大旅馆中能说几种外语的)接待员。

con·cil·i·ar [kən'siliə; kən`sɪlɪɚ] ***a.*** 议(事)会的,来自[通过]议(事)会的。

con·cil·i·ate [kən'silieit; kən`sɪlɪ,et] ***vt.*** **1.** 安抚,抚慰,劝慰;说服(反对者)。**2.** 赢得(支持,好感)。**3.** 调停,调解。

con·cil·i·a·tion [kən,sili'eiʃən; kən,sɪlɪ`eʃən] ***n.*** **1.** 安抚,劝慰;说服。**2.** 调停,调解;妥协。**3.** 迎合;获得。***Court of*** ~【法】调解法庭。***The C- Act***〔英〕(工潮的)调停法。**-ism** ***n.*** 调和主义。**-ist** ***n.*** 调和主义者。

con·cil·i·a·tive, con·cil·i·a·to·ry [kən'siliətiv, -liətəri; kən`sɪlɪ,etɪv, -lɪə,torɪ] ***a.*** 安抚的,说服的,和解的;调解的。

con·cil·i·a·tor [kən'silieitə; kən`sɪlɪ,etɚ] ***n.*** 安抚者,说服者;调停者,和解者。

con·cin·ni·ty [kən'siniti; kən`sɪnətɪ] ***n.***(文章等的)妥贴,和谐,优雅,优美。

con·cise [kən'sais; kən`saɪs] ***a.*** 简洁的,简明扼要的。*Talks and articles should all be ~ and to the point.* 讲话和写文章都应该简明扼要。**-ly** ***ad.*** **-ness** ***n.***

con·ci·sion [kən'siʒən; kən`sɪʒən] ***n.*** **1.** 简洁,简明。**2.**〔废〕切断;切分;切除。

con·clave ['kɔnkleiv; `kɑnklev] ***n.*** **1.** 秘密会议。**2.**【天主】教皇选举密议室;教皇选举会议;(教廷内的)红衣[枢机]主教团。***be in ~ with*** 和…密议中。***sit in ~*** (*with*) (与)密议。

con·clude [kən'klu:d; kən`klud] ***vt.*** **1.** 结束,终止,使完毕。**2.** 议定,缔结(条约等)。**3.** 推断,断定。**4.**〔美〕(最后)决定。~ *a speech* 终止演说。~ *peace* 缔结和约。~ *a treaty* 订立条约。*From what you say I ~ that ...* 从你的话中我断定…。—***vi.*** **1.** 结束,终止。**2.** 断定,决定,达成协议。***to be ~d*** (连载的文章)下期[次]登完。***to ~*** 最后(一句话)。

con·clu·sion [kən'klu:ʒən; kən`kluʒən] ***n.*** **1.** 终结,结局,最后结果。**2.** 结论;决定,断定。**3.** 缔结;商定,议定。***at the ~ of*** 当…完结时。***bring to a ~*** 使结束;谈定(买卖等)。***come to a ~*** 结束,告一段落;得到一个结论。***come to the ~ that ...*** 所得结论是…,断定。***draw the ~*** 得出结论,推断。***foregone ~*** 可预断的[免不了的]结果。***in ~*** 最后,总之。***leap*** [***jump***] ***to a ~*** 贸然断定,过早下结论。***try ~s with*** 和…决最后胜负,争(最后)优劣。**-al** ***a.*** **-al·ly** ***ad.***

con·clu·sive [kən'klu:siv; kən`klusɪv] ***a.*** 决定的,结论性的,确定性的;最后的,无争论余地的。*a ~ answer* 断然的回答。~ **evidence** [**proof**] 确证,真凭实据,结论性的证据。~ **presumption**【法】(不容反驳的)决定性推断。**-ly** ***ad.***

con·coct [kən'kɔkt; kɑn`kɑkt] ***vt.*** **1.** 调制,泡制(汤、饮料、肥皂等)。**2.** 捏造,编造,虚构。**3.** 图谋,策划,计划。~ *a new dish* 配制新菜。~ *a story* 虚构事实。~ *a plot* 图谋不轨。

con·coc·tion [kən'kɔkʃən; kɑn`kɑkʃən] ***n.*** **1.** 调制;调合[混合]品。**2.** 捏造。**3.** 策划,图谋。*meat ~s* 串荤〔荤素混合菜,杂烩〕。

con·coc·tive [kən'kɔktiv; kən`kɑktɪv] ***a.*** 调制的;捏造的;图谋的。

con·col·o(u)r·ous [kən'kʌlərəs; kɑn`kʌlərəs] ***a.*** 同色的,单色的。

con·com·i·tance, con·com·i·tan·cy [kən'kɔmitəns, -tənsi; kən`kɑmɪtəns, -tənsɪ] ***n.*** **1.** 相伴,并在;共存。**2.**【宗】(圣餐中)耶稣的血肉并在。

con·com·i·tant [kən'kɔmitənt; kən`kɑmɪtənt] **I** ***a.*** 相伴的,并在的,伴生的,附随的。**II** ***n.***〔常 *pl.*〕相伴物,附随物。**-ly** ***ad.***

con·cord ['kɔŋkɔ:d; `kɑnkɔrd] ***n.*** **1.** 协和,一致;(国际间的)和谐。**2.**(国际间的)协定,协约。**3.**【乐】谐音,协和音;【语法】(数、性、格、人称等的)一致。***Book of ~***【宗】信仰忏悔录。***in ~*** 协和,和谐;一致。

con·cord·ance [kən'kɔ:dəns; kɑn`kɔrdns] ***n.*** **1.**(著作、作家的)词汇索引(*to*)。**2.** 协和,调和,一致;【统】和谐性。**3.**【地】整合,整一。***be in ~*** 一致,协和。***in ~ with*** 依照。

con·cord·ant [kən'kɔ:dənt; kɑn`kɔrdnt] ***a.*** 协和的,一致的(*with*);【乐】协和音的;【地】整合的。~ **twin** 相似孪生。**-ly** ***ad.***

con·cor·dat [kɔn'kɔ:dæt; kɑn`kɔrdæt] ***n.*** **1.** 协定。**2.**【宗史】(罗马教皇与各君主[政府]间的)宗教事务协约。**3.**(宗派间的)协议。**-da·to·ry** ***a.***

Con·corde ['kɔnkɔ:d; `kɑnkɔrd] ***n.***(英法合作制造的)协和式超音速客机。

Con·cor·di·a [kɔŋ'kɔ:diə; kɑn`kɔrdɪə] ***n.***【罗神】协和女神。

con·course ['kɔŋkɔ:s; `kɑŋkɔs] ***n.*** **1.** 集合;辐辏;合流,总汇;群集。**2.**〔美〕(公园中的)中央广场,(车站内的)中央大厅。**3.** 车道,马路,林荫路。

con·cres·cence [kən'kresns; kɑn`krɛsəns] ***n.*** **1.**【生】接合,结合,会合;合生。**2.** 增生,增殖。

con·crete ['kɔnkri:t; `kɑnkrit] **I** ***a.*** **1.** 具体的,有形的;实在的,实际的。**2.** 固结成的,混凝土制的。**3.** 图案诗歌的(参阅 ~ poetry)。*a ~ fact* 具体事实。*a ~ vessel* 混凝土船。***in the ~*** 具体地,实际上。**II** ***n.*** 具体物;凝结物;混凝土;【逻】具体名词;【文学】具体诗歌。*a ~-mixer* 混凝土搅拌器[机]。*mushy* [*poured*] ~注入的混凝土。*reinforced* [*armoured*] ~钢筋混凝土。**III** ***vt.***, ***vi.*** **1.** [kən'kri:t; kɑn`krit] (使)固结,(使)凝固;(使)结合。**2.** ['kɔnkri:t; `kɔnkrit] 用混凝土修筑;(在…上)浇注混凝土。~ **noun**【语法】具体名词。~ **number**【数】名数。~ **poetry**【文学】(用形象的字母、单词、符号等而不是用传统的文句来表达的)图案诗歌。**-ly** ***ad.***

con·cre·tion [kən'kri:ʃən; kɑn`kriʃən] ***n.*** **1.** 凝结,固结;具体化。**2.** 固结物;连生体;【医】结石;凝结物;硬块;【地】结核,凝岩。**-ary** ***a.*** 凝固的,已凝结的;【地】结核性的(构造),由凝岩形成的。

con·cret·ism [kən'kri:tizəm; kən`kritɪzəm] ***n.***【文艺】具体主义〔具体诗歌的理论和实践〕。

con·cre·tive [kən'kri:tiv; kɑn`kritɪv] ***a.*** 凝结性的,有

凝固力的;【医】结石的;凝结(物)的。

con·cre·tize [ˈkɔnkri(ː)taiz; ˋkɑnkrɪˏtaɪz] ***vt.***, ***vi.*** (使)具体化;(使)凝固。~ *abstractions* 使抽象概念具体化。

con·cu·bi·nage [kənˈkjuːbinidʒ; kɑnˋkjubənɪdʒ] ***n.*** **1.** 非法同居。**2.** 蓄妾,妾的地位。

con·cu·bi·nar·y [kənˈkjuːbiˌnəri; kɑnˋkjubəˏnɛrɪ] ***a.*** (作)妾的;妾生的。

con·cu·bine [ˈkɔŋkjubain; ˋkɑŋkjuˏbaɪn] ***n.*** 妾;姘妇。

con·cu·pis·cence [kənˈkjuːpisəns; kɑnˋkjupəsns] ***n.*** **1.** 性欲。**2.**【宗】贪欲,世俗欲念。

C

con·cu·pis·cent [kənˈkjuːpisnt; kənˋkjupɪsnt] ***a.*** **1.** 好色的,色欲旺盛的。**2.** 多欲的,贪婪的。

con·cu·pis·ci·ble [kənˈkjuːpisəbl; kənˋkjupɪsəbl̩] ***a.*** 由性欲引起的。

con·cur [kənˈkəː; kənˋkɝ] ***vi.*** (*-rr-*) **1.** 同时发生,并发;合作,共同作用 (*with*)。**2.** 同意,一致 (*with*)。*Everything ~red to make him happy*. 每一件事都凑在一起使他快活[幸福]。*They all ~red in giving him the prize*. 他们一致同意给他奖赏。

con·cur·rence [kənˈkʌrəns; kənˋkɝrəns] ***n.*** **1.** 同时发生,并发。**2.** 同意,一致;合作,联合。**3.**【数】(数线的)交点。**4.**【法】(权利的)共有,权利等同。

con·cur·rent [kənˈkʌrənt; kənˋkɝənt] **I** ***a.*** **1.** 同时发生的,并发的,并存的,共存的;合作的。**2.** (意见)一致的。**3.**【动】趋合的;【数】共点的;【机】并流的。**4.** (权力等)由两个负责当局共同行使的,有相等裁定权的。~ *insurance* (*policy*) (对于一投保物的)共同保险(合同)。~ *post* 兼职。~ *sentence* (适用于多个被告的)共同判决。**II** ***n.*** **1.** 并发事件;共存[共有]物;并在原因。**2.** 竞争者。**3.**【数】共点。**-ly** ***ad.*** (*hold a post concurrently* 兼任)。

con·cuss [kənˈkʌs; kənˋkʌs] ***vt.*** **1.** 猛烈撞击(使成脑震荡);使震动,使震伤。**2.** 〔Scot.〕胁迫,恐吓。

con·cus·sion [kənˈkʌʃən; kənˋkʌʃən] ***n.*** **1.** 震动,冲击,撞击,冲激。**2.**【医】(脑)震荡。**3.** 〔Scot.〕威胁,胁迫。a ~ *of the brain* 脑震荡。~ **fuse** 触发信管。~ **grenades** 触发手榴弹。

con·cus·sive [kənˈkʌsiv; kənˋkʌsɪv] ***a.*** 震荡的,有激动[冲击]力的,震动性的。

cond. = condenser; conditional; conductivity; conductor.

con·demn [kənˈdem; kənˋdɛm] ***vt.*** **1.** 定(某人)罪,判(某人)罪,宣告(死刑等)。**2.** 责备,谴责。**3.** 宣告(患者)无法治疗。**4.** 宣告…完全无用;决定废弃,报废。**5.** 宣告没收(船舶、私货等)。*His looks ~ him*. 他的模样显得是有罪的。*be ~ed to death* 被宣布(死刑)。~ (*sth.*) *as unfit for* 宣告(某物)不适于…。

con·dem·na·ble [kənˈdemnəbl; kənˋdɛmnəbl̩] ***a.*** **1.** 该定罪的。**2.** 该谴责的。**3.** 该废弃的。

con·dem·na·tion [ˌkɔndemˈneiʃən; ˏkɑndɛmˋneʃən] ***n.*** **1.** 定罪,宣告有罪。**2.** 谴责,非难。**3.** 定罪理由。**4.** 报废。**5.** 征用,(宣告)没收。*conditional* ~缓刑。~ **factor** 报废率。

con·dem·na·to·ry [kənˈdemnətəri; kənˋdɛmnətərɪ] ***a.*** 处罚的,宣告有罪的;谴责的。

con·demned [kənˈdemd; kənˋdɛmd] ***a.*** **1.** 已被定罪的,已被定罪者使用的。**2.** 被认为不当的;受谴责的。**3.** 被认为不适用的。~ **cell** [**ward**] 死刑犯监房。

con·den·sa·bil·i·ty [kənˌdensəˈbiliti; kənˏdɛnsəˋbɪlətɪ] ***n.*** 可凝结性,可冷凝性,可压缩性。

con·den·sa·ble [kənˈdensəbl; kənˋdɛnsəbl̩] ***a.*** 可凝结的;可压缩的;可缩短的。

con·den·sate [kənˈdenseit; kənˋdɛnset] **I** ***n.*** 浓缩物;【化】冷凝物[液]。**II** ***a.*** 浓缩的,冷凝的,凝结的。

con·den·sa·tion [kɔndenˈseiʃən; ˏkɑndɛnˋseʃən] ***n.*** **1.** 浓缩;【物】冷凝(作用),凝聚(作用);压缩;缩合;凝块。**2.** (著作等的)压缩;压缩后的形式,节本。~ **point**【物】凝点。~ **trail**【空】凝结尾〔喷射机经过后肉眼可见的白带状水气凝结物〕。~ **wave**【物】凝聚波。

con·den·sa·tor [kənˈdenseitə; kɑnˋdɛnˏsetɚ] ***n.*** = condenser.

con·dense [kənˈdens; kənˋdɛns] ***vt.*** **1.** 压缩;使浓缩;聚集(光线);加强(电力)。**2.**【物、化】冷凝,使凝结。**3.** (著作等的)缩短,压缩。~*d film* 缩合膜。~*d milk* 炼乳。~*d spark* 高电炉火花。*condensing lens* 聚光透镜。~ *vapour into rain* 使水气凝结成雨。~ *an essay* 压缩一篇文章。—***vi.*** **1.** 浓缩,凝结。**2.** (气体)变成液体[固体]。

con·dens·er [kənˈdensə; kənˋdɛnsɚ] ***n.*** 冷凝器;凝汽器;电容器;聚光器;【纺】集棉器;搓条机。~ **leg** (**pipe**) 冷凝器气压管。~ **paper** 绝缘纸。~ **pipe** 冷凝管。

con·den·ser·y, **con·den·sar·y** [kənˈdensəri; kənˋdɛnsərɪ] ***n.*** 〔美口〕炼乳厂。

con·den·si·ble [kənˈdensəbl; kənˋdɛnsəbl̩] ***a.*** = condensable.

con·de·scend [kɔndiˈsend; kɑndɪˋsɛnd] ***vi.*** **1.** 谦虚地做,俯就,屈尊。**2.** 堕落到做(下流事情)。**3.** 抱着优越感施惠于人,以恩赐[高高在上]态度对待别人。~ *to accept a bribe* 堕落[不要脸]到接受贿赂。*She does not ~ to such little things*. 她不屑理睬那种小事。~ **upon** 〔Scot.〕不厌其烦地细说。**-ing** ***a.*** 屈尊的;抱恩赐态度的。**-ing·ly** ***ad.***

con·de·scend·ence [ˌkɔndiˈsendəns; ˏkɑndɪˋsɛndəns] ***n.*** **1.** = condescension. **2.** 〔Scot.〕详细列举[细述]。

con·de·scen·sion [ˌkɔndiˈsenʃən; ˏkɑndɪˋsɛnʃən] ***n.*** 屈尊;恩赐[高高在上]态度。

con·dign [kənˈdain; kənˋdaɪn] ***a.*** 相当的,应得的,适当的。~ *punishment* [*vengeance*] 应得的处罚[报复]。

con·di·ment [ˈkɔndimənt; ˋkɑndəmənt] ***n.*** 佐料,调味品。**-al** [-ˈmentəl; -ˋmɛntəl] ***a.***

con·di·tion [kənˈdiʃən; kənˋdɪʃən] **I** ***n.*** **1.** 状态,状况,情形;品质。**2.** 〔*pl.*〕外界状况,周围情形。**3.** 地位,身分。**4.** 条件;【语法】条件子句。**5.**【纺】含潮量;(套毛)含脂含杂量。**6.** 健康状态;〔口〕病痛。**7.** 〔美〕补考及格才能随班附读的规定条件;补考学科。*the ~ of affairs* 事态。*a man of ~* [*humble ~*] 有身分的[身分低的]人。*the ~s of peace* 媾和条件。***be in a certain*** [***an interesting***] ~ 在怀孕。***be in*** [***out of***] ~ (人)健康[不健康],身体好[不好];(物)保存良好[不好];合用[不合用];耐[不耐]…,堪[不堪]…。***change one's*** ~ 〔口〕结婚。***in*** [***under***] ***favourable*** [***difficult***] ~*s* 在顺利[困难]景况[条件]下。***in good*** [***bad***, ***poor***] ~ 情况良好[不好];健康[不健康];(物件)无[有]破损;(食品)新鲜[不新鲜]。***make ~s*** 规定条件。***make it a ~ that*** 以…为条件。***make no*** ~ 毫无条件。***on*** ~ (***that***) 在…的条件下。***on this*** ~ 在这一条件下。***on no*** ~ 在任何条件下都不…。***under existing ~s*** [***the present ~***] 就现况说。**II** ***vt.*** **1.** 决定;规定,作为…的条件,限定;制约。**2.** 改善;增进(牛、马等的)健康;调节(室内空气)。**3.** 使适应,使习惯于(环境)。**4.** 〔美〕(若要升级)必须补考…。**5.**【心、生】使发生条件反射。**6.**【商】检验(生丝,棉纱等)。*to ~ public opinion* 煽动舆论。*She ~ed her leaving upon the weather*. 她动身与否,视天气而定。*Diligence ~s success*. 勤奋为成功的条件。*the things that ~ happiness* 决定幸福的事物。***be ~ed by*** 以…为转移[条件],受…所制约。***the ~ed***【哲】受制约物;【逻】(条件推论的)后项。

con·di·tion·al [kənˈdiʃənl; kənˋdɪʃənl̩] **I** ***a.*** **1.** 带有条件的,有限制的;视…而定的。**2.**【语法】条件的,假设的。**3.** 引起条件反射的。**II** ***n.***【语法】条件子句,条件词。***be ~ on*** [***upon***] 在…条件下,以…为条件,取决于。~ **condemnation** 缓刑。~ **contract** 有条件契约,暂行契约。~ **reflex**【心】条件反射。~ **sale** 搭卖(法)。**-ity** ***n.***

受限制性,有条件性,制约性;条件限制。**-ly** *ad*.

con·di·tioned [kən'diʃənd; kən`dɪʃənd] *a*. **1**. 有条件的,有限制的。**2**. 〔美〕暂准入学[升级]的。**3**. 情形…的,适合…的。**4**. 有…调节的。**5**. 习惯于…的(*to*)。*the* ~ *air* (*of a theater*)(戏院中的)有调节的空气。*a* ~ *reflex* [*response*]【心】条件反射[反应]。*become* ~ *to the rough weather* 已适应恶劣气候。

con·di·tion·er [kən'diʃənə; kən`dɪʃənə] *n*. **1**.【机】调节器;(冷、暖)空气调节装置。**2**. (硬水)软化剂。**3**.【体】教练员。**4**. (商品)检查员。*soil* ~土壤改良剂。

con·di·tion·ing [kən'diʃəniŋ; kən`dɪʃənɪŋ] *n*. **1**. (商品的)检验。**2**. (空气、湿度等)调节。**3**.【冶】整修。**4**.【心】条件作用。*a silk* ~ *house* 生丝检验所。*air* ~空气调节。~ **oven** 烘箱。

con·do ['kəndəu; `kɑndo] *n*. (多层公寓中有独立所有权的)一套公寓房间,一个住宅单元〔condominium 的缩略词〕。

con·do·la·to·ry [kən'dəulətəri; kən`dolə͵torɪ] *a*. 吊唁的,慰问的。

con·dole [kən'dəul; kən`dol] *vi*. 吊慰,表示悼念;慰问。*He* ~*d with me on* [*upon*] *the death of my father*. 我父亲死了,他向我表示吊唁。—*vt*. 〔古〕哀悼。**-ment** *n*. = condolence.

con·do·lence [kən'dəuləns; kən`doləns] *n*. 吊唁,吊慰;悼词;追悼。*express one's* ~ *to* 向…表示吊唁。*a letter of* ~吊唁信。

con do·lo·re [kɔ:n dɔ:'lɔ:re; ͵kɑndo`lore]〔It.〕【乐】悲哀地。

con·dom ['kəndəm; `kɑndəm] *n*. 保险套,男用避孕套。

con·do·min·i·um [ˌkəndə'miniəm; ͵kɑndə`mɪnɪəm] *n*. **1**. 共管(地),共同统治(地);共同所有权。**2**. (多层公寓中有独立所有权的)一套公寓房间,一个住宅单元。

Con·don ['kəndən; `kɑndən] *n*. 康登〔姓氏〕。

con·do·na·tion [kəndəu'neiʃən; ͵kɑndo`neʃən] *n*. 赦免,宽恕(特指对配偶有通奸行为的宽容)。

con·done [kən'dəun; kən`don] *vt*. **1**. 宽恕,宽容(配偶的通奸行为)。**2**. 用(行动、事实)抵消(罪行),赎罪。

con·dor ['kəndɔ:, 'kəndə; `kɑndor, `kɑndə] *n*. **1**.【动】(南美)秃鹰,神鹰。**2**. [kən'dɔr; kɑn`dɔr]〔Sp.〕(智利等国的)秃鹰金币。

con·dot·tie·re [ˌkəndɔ'tjεrə; ͵kondo`tjεrə] *n*. 〔It.〕(*pl*. ***-ri*** [-ri:; -ri])(14—16 世纪的)雇佣兵队长;(军事)冒险家,投机分子。

con·duce [kən'dju:s; kən`djus] *vi*. 导致;有助于,有益于。*Rest* ~*s to health*. 休息有助健康。

con·duc·i·ble [kən'dju:səbl; kən`djusəbl̩] *a*. = conducive.

con·du·cive [kən'dju:siv; kən`djusɪv] *a*. 导致…的;有助于…的;助长…的。*be* ~ *to* (*health*) 增进(健康)。

con·duct ['kəndəkt; `kɑndʌkt] *n*. **1**. 行为,举动;操行,品格。**2**. 指导;带领;护送。**3**. 处理,管理,经营;指挥。**4**. (戏剧等的)处理法,进展,情节,趣向;方法,做法。**5**. 〔英〕伊顿(Eton)公学礼拜堂的牧师。*a testimonial of good* ~操行优良证明。*a safe* ~(战时)护照,通行证。~ *of the background* 背景处理法。***under the*** ~ ***of*** 在…指导[管理]下。—[kən'dʌkt; kən`dʌkt] *vt*. **1**. 〔~ oneself〕行动,表现,为人。**2**. 指导;带领;护送;陪伴(游客等)。**3**. 处理,管理,经营,办(事);指挥。**4**. 传导,传(热、电等)。~ *a business* 经营生意。~ *an orchestra* 指挥管弦乐队。~ *a campaign* 指挥作战。~ *oneself nobly* 为人高尚。—*vi*. **1**. 引导,带领;指导;指挥乐队演奏。**2**. 传导。**3**. (道路)通向(*to*)。*He* ~*ed well*. 他对乐队演奏指挥得法。*A metal* ~*s well*. 金属是良导体。*a* ~*ing-wire* 导线。~ (*sb*.) ***into*** [***to***] 引导(某人)…。~ (*sb*.) ***over*** (*a place*) 引导[陪伴](某人)参观(某处)。~ **sheet**【军】操行[奖惩]记录。

con·duct·ance [kən'dʌktəns; kən`dʌktəns] *n*.【电】电导;电导系数;传导(性)。

con·duct·i·bil·i·ty [kənˌdʌkti'biliti; kən͵dʌktə`bɪlətɪ] *n*. 传导性[力]。

con·duct·i·ble [kən'dʌktəbl; kən`dʌktəbl̩] *a*. 可传导的。

con·duc·tion [kən'dʌkʃən; kən`dʌkʃən] *n*. (用管对流体的)引流;【物】传导,导电;【生理】神经脉冲的传导。

con·duc·tive [kən'dʌktiv; kən`dʌktɪv] *a*. 传导(性)的,有传导力的。

con·duc·tiv·i·ty [ˌkəndʌk'tiviti; ͵kɑndʌk`tɪvətɪ] *n*.【物】传导性[力],传导率;导电率[性,系数]。~ **water** 校准电导水。

con·duc·tom·e·ter [ˌkəndʌk'təmitə; ͵kɑndʌk`tɑmɪtə] *n*.【物】热导计,电导计。

con·duc·tor [kən'dʌktə; kən`dʌktə] *n*. **1**. 指导者,向导者;护送者;处理人,管理人;指挥人;【乐】指挥。**2**. (电车、公共汽车上的)售票员;【美铁路】(列车)乘务长(=〔英〕guard);列车员;【英军】下士。**3**.【物】导体;导管,导线;【数】前导子;【建】竖承雷;避雷针(= lightning-~)。*a good* [*bad*, *poor*, *non-*] ~ 良[不良、非]导体。**-to·ri·al** [-'tɔ:riəl; -`torɪəl] *a*.

con·duc·tress [kən'dʌktris; kən`dʌktrɪs] *n*. conductor 的女性。

con·duit ['kəndit; `kɑndɪt] *n*. 导管(=~ pipe);水管,水道,沟渠,暗渠;【电】导线管,管道(电缆)。~ **system** (电车的)地下电线[管道]系统;(电灯的)暗线装置[系统]。

con·du·pli·cate [kən'dju:plikit; kɑn`djupləkɪt] *a*.【植】(叶)对折的。

con·dy ['kəndi; `kɑndɪ]【商标】过锰酸钾液(= Condy's fluid 一种消毒剂)。

con·dyle ['kəndil; `kɑndəl] *n*.【解】髁;(关节处)骨顶部,骨阜,髁状突起。**external** ~外髁。**femoral** ~股骨外髁。~ **femoral** 股骨上髁。

con·dy·loid ['kəndilɔid; `kɑndɪlɔɪd] *a*. 髁(状)的。

con·dy·lo·ma [ˌkəndi'ləumə; ͵kɑndə`lomə] *n*. (*pl*. ***-ma·ta*** [-mətə; -mətə])【医】湿疣。

cone [kəun; kon] **I** *n*. **1**. 圆锥,锥形物;锥面;锥体。**2**. 火山锥,圆锥形火山;锥状地区。**3**.【植】球果,球花。**4**. 风暴信号。**5**.【动】芋螺(= cone shell)。~ *of rays*【光】光锥。*an ice cream* ~蛋卷冰淇淋。*a parasitic* ~寄生火山锥。**II** *vt*. **1**. 使成锥形;把…卷于锥状体上。**2**. 〔用被动语态〕(探照灯)集中探照(敌机)。—*vi*. (松树等)结球果。~**-buoy** 锥形浮标。~ **gear** 锥轮联动机。~ **pulley** 锥形轮。

cone·flow·er ['kəunflauə; `kon͵flaʊə] *n*.【植】金光菊(属)。

Con·el·rad ['kənəlræd; `kɑnəl͵ræd] *n*.【无】电磁波辐射控制(= control of electromagnetic radiation)。

cone·nose ['kəunnəuz; `kon͵noz] *n*.【动】锥鼻虫(*Conorhinus sanguisuga*)〔见于美国南部和美洲热带地区〕。

Con·es·to·ga (**wagon**) [ˌkənis'təugə; ͵kɑnɪs`togə] *n*. 〔美〕康内斯托加式宽轮大篷马车〔拓荒者在草原地带使用〕。

co·ney ['kəuni; `konɪ] *n*. = cony.

conf. = confer; confessor; conference.

con·fab ['kənfæb; `kɑnfæb] *n*., *vi*. 〔口〕= confabulation, confabulate.

con·fab·u·late [kən'fæbjuleit; kən`fæbjʊ͵let] *vi*. **1**. 谈论,谈笑,闲谈,谈心(*with*)。**2**.【心】(在记忆的缺失处)插入虚构情节。**-la·tion** [-'leiʃən; -`leʃən] *n*. **-fab·u·la·to·ry** [-'fæbjulətəri; -`fæbjulətərɪ] *a*.

con·fab·u·la·tor [kən'fæbjuleitə; kən`fæbjuletə] *n*. 谈笑者,闲谈者。

con·far·re·a·tion [kənˌfæri'eiʃən; kən͵færɪ`eʃən] *n*.【史】献糕式婚礼〔古罗马最隆重的结婚仪式,由大司祭主持,向朱庇特献奉斯佩尔特小麦糕〕。

C

con·fect [ˈkɔnfekt; ˋkɑnfɛkt] **I** ***n*.** 糖果。**II** [kənˈfekt; kənˋfɛkt] ***vt*.** 制造;调制;泡制。

con·fec·tion [kənˈfekʃən; kənˋfɛkʃən] **I** ***n*.** **1.** (糖果等的)制造,调制;糖果蜜饯[点心];【医】糖果剂。**2.** 精巧的制品;妇女时装用品。**II** ***vt*.** 〔古〕调制。

con·fec·tion·ar·y [kənˈfekʃənəri; kənˋfɛkʃən,ɛrɪ] **I** ***a*.** 糖果点心(业、商)的。**II** ***n*.** 〔总称〕糖果点心(店)。

con·fec·tion·er [kənˈfekʃənə; kənˋfɛkʃənɚ] ***n*.** 糖果(点心)制造人[商],糖果点心店。

con·fec·tion·er·y [kənˈfekʃənəri; kənˋfɛkʃən,ɛrɪ] ***n*.** **1.** 糖果点心类〔糖果,蜜饯,糕点等总称〕。**2.** 糖果点心铺。**3.** 糖果点心制造(法、业)。

C

Confed. = Confederate, Confederacy.

con·fed·er·a·cy [kənˈfedərəsi; kənˋfɛdərəsɪ] ***n*.** **1.** 同盟,联盟,联邦。**2.** 共谋;秘密结社;帮派。*the C-* 【美史】(南北战争时的)南部同盟,南部邦联〔正式名称为 the Confederate States of America〕。

con·fed·er·al [kənˈfedərəl, -ˈfedrəl; kənˋfɛdərəl, -ˋfɛdrəl] ***a*.** 同盟的,联盟的,邦联的。

con·fed·er·ate [kənˈfedəreit; kənˋfɛdəret] **I** ***vt*., *vi*.** (使)结成同盟,(使)联合;(使)成帮派[秘密结社](*with*)。~ ***oneself with*** 与…结盟;联盟,结成一帮。**II** ***n*.** **1.** 同盟者;〔口〕联合者;联盟成员。**2.** 共谋者,同伙。**3.** 〔the C-〕【美史】(南北战争时)南部同盟的支持者,南部邦联的支持者。***play*** ~ ***to*** 策应。**III** [kənˈfedərit; kənˋfɛdərɪt] ***a*.** 同盟的,联合的;〔C-〕【美史】(参加)南部同盟的,南北邦联的。

con·fed·er·a·tion [kən,fedəˈreiʃən; kən,fɛdəˋreʃən] ***n*.** **1.** 同盟,联盟;(特指)邦联。**2.** 〔the C-〕【美史】(1781—1789 年)十三州邦联;【史】加拿大联盟〔指英属加拿大四省联盟,于 1867 年获得自治领地位〕。

con·fed·er·a·tive [kənˈfedərətiv; kənˋfɛdə,retɪv] ***a*.** 同盟[联盟,邦联]的。

con·fer [kənˈfəː; kənˋfɝ] ***vt*.** 授与,颁与(称号、学位等)。~*a medal* [*title*] *on* [*upon*] *sb*. 授与某人以勋章[称号]。—***vi*.** 商议,协商,谈判。~ *with sb*. *on* [*about*] *sth*. 与某人协商[商议]某事。

con·fer [kənˈfəː; kənˋfɝ] 〔L.〕 ***vt*.** 〔祈使语气〕比较,对照,参看〔略作 cf.〕。

con·fer·ee [,kɔnfəˈriː; ,kɑnfəˋri] ***n*.** **1.** 会议的参加者[出席者],参加商谈者。**2.** 被授(学位、称号)者。

con·fer·ence [ˈkɔnfərəns; ˋkɑnfərəns] ***n*.** **1.** 协商,谈判,商议;讨论会,协商会;会议。**2.** (学位等的)授与。**3.** 〔美〕(宗教,学术,运动团体的)联合会。*a press* [*news*] ~记者招待会。*be in* ~会议中。*call* [*convene*, *convoke*] *a* ~召集会议。*call together* (*the members of a society*) *to a* ~召集(会员)开会。*have a* ~ *with* 和…协商[谈判]。*hold a* ~开会。~ **call** 电话会议。

con·fer·ment [kənˈfəːmənt; kənˋfɝmənt] ***n*.** (学位等的)授与。

con·fer·ree [,kɔnfəˈriː; ,kɑnfəˋri] = conferee.

con·fer·rer [kənˈfəːrə; kənˋfɝɚ] ***n*.** 授与人。

con·fer·va [kənˈfəːvə; kənˋfɝvə] ***n*.** (*pl*. **-vae** [-viː; -vi], ~***s***) 【植】水绵属植物。**-l *a*.**

con·fer·void [kənˈfəːvɔid; kənˋfɝvɔɪd] 【植】**I** ***a*.** 水绵状的。**II** ***n*.** 水绵。

con·fess [kənˈfes; kənˋfɛs] ***vt*.** **1.** 自白,承认,供认。**2.** 表白(信仰);忏悔,向上帝[神父等]忏悔(罪恶)。**3.** (教士)听取(教徒)忏悔。**4.** 证明。~ *oneself to be in the wrong* 承认错误。~ *oneself* (*to be*) *guilty* 承认有罪。~ *a crime* 坦白罪行。~ *allegiance to* ... 表明忠诚于… *The priest* ~*ed the young man*. 神父听取那个青年的忏悔。—***vi*.** **1.** 供认,承认。**2.** 忏悔。**3.** (神父)听取忏悔。~ *before a priest* 在神父面前忏悔。~ *to a weakness for smoking* 承认有爱吸烟的缺点。~ ***and avoid*** 【法】承认所控事实但同时举出其他事实抗辩,主张所控罪名在法律上不能成立。***I*** ~ (***that***) ... 〔口〕得承认,这实在是。*to* ~ ***the truth*** 说实话。

con·fessed [kənˈfest; kənˋfɛst] ***a*.** **1.** 众所公认的,已有定论的,明白的。**2.** 已认罪的,已自首的。**3.** 【宗】已向神父忏悔(而得到赦免)的。**4.** 被公开信仰的。*a* ~ *and unconquerable difficulty* 众所公认的无法克服的困难。*a* ~ *fact* 明白的事实。***stand*** ~ ***as*** 被揭露为,被认为是。

con·fess·ed·ly [kənˈfesidli; kənˋfɛsɪdlɪ] ***ad*.** 已公开承认;明白无疑地,众所公认地。

con·fes·sion [kənˈfeʃən; kənˋfɛʃən] ***n*.** **1.** 自白;承认,坦白;(对神父所作的)忏悔。**2.** 【法】自白书,口供。**3.** 【宗】(惠督教会具有某种特殊教规的)殉教者坟墓[祭坛]。**4.** 信仰的宣告[声明];教规;教派。~ ***of faith*** 信仰声明〔获准入教前所作〕。***make an*** ~ 交代。**-sion·al, -sion·ary** **1.** ***a*.** 自白的;忏悔的。**2.** ***n*.** 听取忏悔室。

con·fes·sor [kənˈfesə; kənˋfɛsɚ] ***n*.** **1.** 坦白者,自白者;忏悔者。**2.** (遭遇宗教迫害时)声明自己信仰的人。**3.** 听忏悔的牧师[神父]。

con·fet·ti [kənˈfeti(ː); kənˋfɛtɪ] ***n*.** *pl*. 〔作单数用〕**1.** 糖果。**2.** (婚礼中投掷的)五彩碎纸。

con·fi·dant [,kɔnfiˈdænt; ,kɑnfəˋdænt] ***n*.** 〔F.〕(可以秘密托付的)心腹朋友。

con·fi·dante [,kɔnfiˈdænt; ,kɑnfəˋdænt] ***n*.** 〔F.〕知心女友。

con·fide [kənˈfaid; kənˋfaɪd] ***vt*.** **1.** 吐露(秘密)。**2.** 信托,交托,委托。~ *a secret to* (*sb*.) 对(某人)吐露秘密。~ *a task to* (*sb*.) 对(某人)托付任务。—***vi*.** **1.** (对知己)吐露秘密 (*in*)。**2.** 信任,信赖 (*in*)。~ *in one's friend* 向朋友谈个人心事。

con·fi·dence [ˈkɔnfidəns; ˋkɑnfədəns] **I** ***n*.** **1.** 信任,信赖。**2.** 自信,确信;自恃。**3.** (偷偷吐露的)秘密,心事。**4.** (多指怀恶意的)胆量;厚脸,无耻。*exchange* ~*s* 互谈心事。*forfeit* ~丧失信用。~ *game* 〔美〕= ~ trick 〔英〕骗局。~ *in oneself* 自信 (= self-~)。~ *man* 〔美〕骗子。***enjoy*** [***have***] (*sb*.'*s*) ~受到某人的信赖。***give*** ~ ***to*** = ***have*** ~ ***in*** 信任,信赖。***have the*** ~ ***to*** (*deny it*) 胆敢,无耻(否认)。***in*** ~ 秘密地,偷偷地,暗中。***in the*** ~ ***of*** 受…信任;参与…的机密。***make*** ~***s*** [***a*** ~] ***to*** (***sb*.**) = ***take*** (***sb*.**) ***into one's*** ~ 对(某人)吐露秘密,把(某人)当做心腹朋友。***misplace one's*** ~ 误信(某人),信任不可靠的人。***place*** [***put***, ***repose***, ***show***] ~ ***in*** 信任,信赖。***want of*** ~ ***in the Cabinet*** [***Ministry***] 〔英〕对内阁不信任。***with*** (***great***) ~ 很有把握地,满怀信心地。**II** ***a*.** 骗得信任的,欺诈的。*a* ~ *tricker* 骗子。~ **belt** 【自】置信带。~ **game** 〔美〕骗局。~ **man** 〔美〕骗子。~ **trick**〔英〕= ~ game.

con·fi·dent [ˈkɔnfidənt; ˋkɑnfədənt] **I** ***a*.** **1.** 确信,深信;自信 (*in*; *of*; *that*)。**2.** 有自信的;沉着的。**3.** 大胆的,过分自信的;厚颜无耻的。*a* ~ *manner* [*smile*] 充满信心的态度[微笑]。*a* ~ *attack* 大胆的攻击。*a very* ~, *uppish young man* 极其冒失逞能的小伙子。*be* ~ *of* (*success*) 对(成功)满怀信心。*I am* ~ *that* 我深信。**II** ***n*.** 知己,心腹朋友。**-ly *ad*.**

con·fi·den·tial [kɔnfiˈdenʃəl; kɑnfəˋdɛnʃəl] ***a*.** **1.** 极信任的,心腹的。**2.** 秘密的,机密的。**3.** (语气等)亲密的。*Confidential* (此系)密件[信封用语]。*Strictly* ~绝密。*a* ~ *clerk* 极受信任的职员。*a* ~ *creditor* 优先债权人。*a* ~ *inquiry* 秘密调查[打听]。*a* ~ *opinion* 心里话。*a* ~ *document* 密件,保密文献。~ *papers* 机密文件。~ *communication* 密告;(不对外公开的)秘密通知。~ *price list* (内部的)秘密价目单。**-ly *ad*. -ness *n*.**

con·fid·ing [kənˈfaidiŋ; kənˋfaɪdɪŋ] ***a*.** 信任的;轻信的,相信不疑的。*a* ~ *nature* 不疑人[轻信]的性格。*a* ~ *wife* 十分信任丈夫的妻子。

con·fig·u·ra·tion [kən,figjuˈreiʃən; kən,fɪgjəˋreʃən] ***n*.** **1.** 结构;构造;圆形,外形。**2.** 组合,布置;配置。**3.**

地形;【天】(行星等的)相对位置,方位;【化】(分子中原子的)组态,排列;【物】位形;组态。

con·fig·u·ra·tion·ism [kənˌfigəˈreiʃəˌnizm; kənˏfɪgəˋreʃəˏnɪzm] *n*. 形态心理学;格式心理学 (= Gestalt psychology)。

con·figure [kənˈfigə; kənˋfɪgɚ] *vt*. 使成形。

con·fine [kənˈfain; kənˋfaɪn] **I** *vt*. **1.** 限制 (*to*; *within*);【物】约束,吸持。**2.** 幽禁;监禁;使闭居,蛰居。—*vi*. 〔罕〕接界,邻接 (*with*)。***be ~d*** 闭居;坐月子,分娩。***expect to be ~d*** (***on a date***) 预期在(某日)分娩。***be ~d to barracks*** (士兵)被禁止外出。***be ~d to one's bed*** 卧病床上 (*He is ~d to his bed with a cold*. 他因为伤风病倒了)。~ ***oneself to*** 在…闭门不出;以…为限。**II** [ˈkɔnfain; ˋkɑnfaɪn] *n*. **1.** 〔常 *pl*.〕境界,界限,国界,疆界;边界,边境。**2.** 限度;范围。***between the ~s of*** …之间的界线。***on the ~s of*** 濒于,差一点儿就 (*on the ~s of the indecent* 再进一步就流于猥亵了)。***the ~s of a town*** 城区,市区。***within the ~s of*** 在…范围内。

con·fined [kənˈfaind; kənˋfaɪnd] *a*. **1.** 有限的,狭窄的。**2.** 被禁闭着的。**3.** 产期内的。**4.** 受约束的。~ *water* 受压水,有压水。

con·fine·ment [kənˈfainmənt; kənˋfaɪnmənt] *n*. **1.** 限制,界限,拘束;(电磁)吸持。**2.** 幽禁,监禁;拘留;【物】密封,密闭。**3.** 闭居,退隐。**4.** 产期,分娩期。*major* [*minor*] ~重[轻]监禁。*solitary* ~单独监禁。*a difficult* ~难产。

con·firm [kənˈfəːm; kənˋfɝm] *vt*. **1.** 使更坚固[坚定,坚强]。**2.** (进一步)证实[确定]。**3.**【法】使有效,确认,批准,认可。**4.**【宗】给…行按手礼[坚信礼]。**5.** 坚持认为 (*that*)。~ *a treaty* 批准条约。~ *sb*. *in his belief* 使某人信仰更坚定。*It wants yet to be ~ed*. 还待确证。~ *an order* (卖主)确证已收到订单。~ *a plane reservation* (乘客)向航空公司确认所订机票不作变动。**-able** *a*. 可确定的;能证实的;可批准的。

con·fir·mand [ˌkɔnfəˈmænd, ˈkɔnfəˌmænd; ˏkɑnfɚˋmænd, ˋkɑnfəˏmænd] *n*.【宗】请受坚信礼[按手礼]者。

con·fir·ma·tion [ˌkɔnfəˈmeiʃən; ˏkɑnfɚˋmeʃən] *n*. **1.** (进一步)确定[确立、证实]。**2.** 确认,认可,批准。**3.**【宗】按手礼;坚信礼。***in ~ of*** 以(便)证实…。

con·firm·a·tive [kənˈfəːmətiv; kənˋfɝmətɪv], **con·firm·a·to·ry** [-təri; -tɔrɪ] *a*. 确证的,确定的;批准的;【宗】坚信礼的。

con·firmed [kənˈfəːmd; kənˋfɝmd] *a*. **1.** 坚定的;确定[证实]了的。**2.** 根深蒂固的;难治的,慢性的。*a ~ disease* 老毛病。*a ~ fool* 无可救药的傻瓜。*a ~ habit* 积习。*a ~ invalid* 痼疾病人。

con·fis·ca·ble [kənˈfiskəbl; kənˋfɪskəbl̩] *a*. 可没收[充公]的。

con·fis·cate [ˈkɔnfiskeit; ˋkɑnfɪˏsket] *vt*. 没收,把…充公;征用。**-ca·tion** [-ˈkeiʃən; -ˋkeʃən] *n*.

con·fis·ca·tor [ˈkɔnfiskeitə; ˋkɑnfɪsketɚ] *n*. 没收者。

con·fis·ca·to·ry [kənˈfiskətəri; kənˋfɪskəˏtorɪ] *a*. 没收的,充公的。

con·fit·e·or [kɔnˈfitiɔː; kənˋfɪtɪɔr] *n*.【宗】忏悔祈祷(文)。

con·fi·ture [ˈkɔnfitʃuə; ˋkɑnfɪˋtʃʊr] *n*. 糖果,蜜饯,糖渍。

con·fla·grant [kənˈfleigrənt; kənˋflegrənt] *a*. 燃烧的,炽燃的。

con·fla·gra·tion [ˌkɔnfləˈgreiʃən; ˏkɑnfləˋgreʃən] *n*. 大火(灾);战火。

con·fla·tion [kənˈfleiʃən; kənˋfleʃən] *n*. 熔合;合成,(两种不同版本、异文的)合刊本。

con·flict [ˈkɔnflikt; ˋkɑnflɪkt] **I** *n*. **1.** 争斗;纠纷,倾轧。**2.** 冲突,矛盾,抵触。**3.** 〔美俚〕竞赛,比赛。*a ~ of opinions* [*views*] 意见的冲突。*a ~ of laws* 法律条文的相抵触。*undergo an inner* ~思想上产生矛盾。***come into ~ with*** 和…冲突。***in ~ with*** 和…冲突[矛盾]。**II** [kənˈflikt; kənˋflɪkt] *vi*. **1.** 争斗,倾轧 (*with*)。**2.** 冲突,抵触,矛盾 (*with*)。

con·flict·ing [kənˈfliktiŋ; kənˋflɪktɪŋ] *a*. 互相斗争的,互不相容的;相冲突的,矛盾的。~ *emotions* 矛盾情绪。~ *purposes* 互相冲突的目的。

con·flu·ence [ˈkɔnfluəns; ˋkɑnflʊəns] *n*. **1.** 合流;汇流(处);汇合而成的河流。**2.** 会合,群集;汇聚(的人群)。

con·flu·ent [ˈkɔnfluənt; ˋkɑnflʊənt] **I** *a*. **1.** 合流的;汇合的;【植】会合的。**2.**【医】融合性的。**II** *n*. 汇流;支流。

con·flux [ˈkɔnflʌks; ˋkɑnflʌks] *n*. = confluence.

con·fo·cal [kɔnˈfəukl; kɑnˋfokl̩] *a*.【数】共焦(点)的。

con·form [kənˈfɔːm; kənˋfɔrm] *vt*. 使一致[符合];使顺应,依照(习惯);使遵照 (*to*)。~ *one's habits to those of the local inhabitants* 使自己的习惯与当地居民相一致。—*vi*. **1.** 一致;遵照;依据 (*to*, *with*)。**2.**【宗】遵奉国教。~ *to customs* [*rules*] 遵守习惯[规则]。~ (***oneself***) ***to*** 遵照;顺应;遵守。**-a·bil·i·ty** *n*. 适合,一致,顺应,相似;顺从;【地】(地层的)整合性。**-able** *a*. 相似;一致,适合,依照 (*to*; *with*);遵从 (*to*);【地】整合的。**-ably** *ad*.

con·for·mal [kənˈfɔːml; kɑnˋfɔrml̩] *a*. **1.**【数】共形的,保形的,保角的。**2.** (地图等)形状完全如实[相似]的。

con·form·ance [kənˈfɔːməns; kənˋfɔrməns] *n*. 相似,相符,一致。

con·for·ma·tion [ˌkɔnfɔːˈmeiʃən; ˏkɑnfɔrˋmeʃən] *n*. **1.** 适应,相应,符合,一致。**2.** 构形;形态;结构,组成。**-tion·al** *a*. **-al·ly** *ad*.

con·form·ist [kənˈfɔːmist; kənˋfɔrmɪst] *n*. **1.** (法律、习惯等的)遵守者。**2.** 〔常 C-〕英国国教徒。

con·form·i·ty [kənˈfɔːmiti; kənˋfɔrmətɪ] *n*. **1.** 相似,符合;适合,一致。**2.** 遵从,顺从;【英史】遵奉国教。**3.**【地】整合。***in ~ to*** [***with***] 和…相适应,和…一致[符合];遵照。

con·found [kənˈfaund; kɑnˋfaʊnd] *vt*. **1.** 混淆,使混同[混杂],使混乱。**2.** 使惊慌失措,使狼狈;使羞愧。**3.** 反驳;挫败(计划、希望等)。**4.** [ˈkɔnˈfaund; ˋkɑnˋfaʊnd] 〔口〕〔比 damn 轻的骂语〕让…死掉,可恶,活该。***be ~ed at*** [***by***] ***the sight of*** 看见…大惊失色。***be ~ed with*** . . . 和…混淆了。~ *right and wrong* 混淆是非。~ *the means with the end* 把手段与目的相混淆,颠倒本末。***C- you*** [***him***]! 这个[那个]家伙! 混蛋,去你[他]的! ***C- it***! 讨厌,该死的!

con·found·ed [kənˈfaundid; kənˋfaʊndɪd] *a*. **1.** 混乱的,狼狈的。**2.** [ˈkɔnˈfaundid; ˋkɑnˋfaʊndɪd] 〔口〕讨厌的,无理的,非常的。*I've been kept waiting a ~ long time*. 叫我傻等多时。*a ~ idiot* 十足的大傻瓜。**-ly** *ad*. 〔口〕非常,极度,特别。

con·fra·ter·ni·ty [ˌkɔnfrəˈtəːniti; ˏkɑnfrəˋtɝnətɪ] *n*. (宗教、互助、慈善性质的)团体;协会,公会。

con frère [ˈkɔnfreə; ˋkɑnfrɛr] *n*. 〔F.〕同事;同仁,同行;(同一结社的)会员,社员。

con·front [kənˈfrʌnt; kənˋfrʌnt] *vt*. **1.** 面对;在…的正对面;勇敢正视;对付(危险等)。**2.** (困难等)横阻在…的面前。**3.** 使面临;使对质,使对证。**4.** 对照,使对比。***be ~ed with*** [***by***] (*a difficulty*) 碰到(困难)。~ (*the accused*) *with* (*his accuser*) 使(被告)和(原告)对质。*the hardships ~ing the miners* 矿工们面临的艰苦环境。

con·fron·ta·tion [ˌkɔnfrʌnˈteiʃən; ˏkɑnfrʌnˋteʃən] *n*. 面对;遭遇;对峙;对抗;对质。**-ist** *n*. 主张在国际关系中持对抗态度的人,对抗[对峙]主义者。

con·fu·cian [kənˈfjuːʃən; kənˋfjuʃən] **I** *a*. 孔子的;儒家的。**II** *n*. 孔门弟子[门徒];儒家。**-ism** *n*. 孔子学说,儒教,儒家(学说)。

C

Con·fu·cius [kən'fjuːʃəs; kən`fjuʃəs] *n*. 孔子。

con·fuse [kən'fjuːz; kən`fjuz] *vt*. **1.** 使混乱,弄乱;混淆;弄错。**2.** 使慌乱,使困窘,使狼狈;使糊涂〔常用被动语态〕。~ *accounts* 搞乱账目。~ *dates* 弄错日期。~ *liberty with license* 混淆自由和放纵。*be* [*become, get*] ~*d with one's blunder* 因做错事而发慌[窘],不知所措。

con·fus·ed [kən'fjuːzd; kən`fjuzd] *a*. 混乱的;慌乱的,狼狈的。**-ly** *ad*. **-ness** *n*.

con·fu·sion [kən'fjuːʒən; kən`fjuʒən] *n*. **1.** 混乱,紊乱,混同,混淆。**2.** 慌乱;狼狈。**3.** 〔骂〕混账,该死。**4.** 〔古〕毁灭。*be thrown into* ~陷入慌张失措[混乱]中。*chaotic* ~大混乱。*covered with* ~慌慌张张。*drink* ~ *to* (*the enemy*) 为(敌人)完蛋干杯。*in* ~ 狼狈;慌乱,胡乱。*in the* ~ *of the moment* 趁着混乱。*C-*! 该死。*C- on* [*upon*] ... ! …该死! ~ ***worse confounded*** 更加混乱,一团糟。

con·fu·ta·tion [ˌkɔnfjuː'teiʃən;ˏkɑnfjʊ`teʃən] *n*. 驳倒;反证。

con·fute [kən'fjuːt; kən`fjut] *vt*. **1.** 驳倒。**2.** 〔旧〕糟蹋。

cong. = congregation; congress(ional).

con·ga ['kɔŋgə; `kɑŋgə] **I** *n*. 〔美〕康茄舞(曲)。**II** *vi*. 跳康茄舞。

con·gé ['kɔ̃ːnʒei; `kɑnʒe] *n*. 〔F.〕**1.** (突然的)撤职。**2.** 辞行,告别,行告别礼(= congee[1])。**3.** 离去的许可。**4.** 【建】四分之一弧凹形边饰,拇指圆饰。~ ***d'élire*** (国王颁发的)主教选举许可令。***get*** [***receive***] ***one's*** ~ 被免职。***give sb. his*** ~ 免某人职。***pour prendre*** ~ (= to take leave) 辞行〔略作 P.P.C.,辞行时写在名片下端〕。***take one's*** ~ 告别。

con·geal [kən'dʒiːl; kən`dʒil] *vi*., *vt*. (使)冻结,(使)凝结。*Fear* ~*ed my blood*. 吓得我血液都凝结起来了。**-able** *a*. 可冻结的,可凝结的。**-er** *n*. 冷冻机,冷却器,冷藏箱。**-ment** *n*. 冻结,凝结。

con·gee[1] ['kɔndʒiː; `kɑndʒi] *n*., *vi*. 〔古〕辞行,告别;行告别礼[鞠躬]。

con·gee[2] ['kɔndʒiː; `kɑndʒi] *n*. 粥,稀饭。

con·ge·la·tion [ˌkɔndʒi'leiʃən;ˏkɑndʒə`leʃən] *n*. **1.** 冻结(物),凝结(物)。**2.** 冻伤,冻疮。

con·ge·ner ['kɔndʒinə; `kɑndʒɪnɚ] *n*. **1.** 同属的动植物。**2.** 同一种类的人[东西]。

con·ge·ner·ic [kɔndʒi'nerik; kɑndʒɪ`nɛrɪk] *a*. 同源[种、属、类]的。

con·gen·ial [kən'dʒiːnjəl; kən`dʒinjəl] *a*. **1.** 同性质的,性格相似的,意气相投的,思想感情相同的 (*with*; *to*)。**2.** 适意的,合适的 (*to*)。~ *spirits* 意气相投的人物。*a* ~ *work* 合意的工作。*be* ~ *to* 对…意趣相合的。*in* ~ *society* 与意气相投的人们在一起。

con·ge·ni·al·i·ty [kənˌdʒiːni'æliti; kənˏdʒinɪ`ælətɪ] *n*. 思想感情相同,趣味相同,意气相投;适意,合适。

con·gen·i·tal [kən'dʒenitl; kən`dʒɛnətl] *a*. 生来的,天赋的,先天的。~ *deformity* 先天的残疾人。**-ly** *ad*.

con·ger, **con·ger·eel** ['kɔŋgə, -gə'riːl; `kɑŋgɚ, -gə`ril] *n*. 【动】海鳗。

con·ge·ries [kən'dʒiəriːz; kɑn`dʒɪriz] *n*. 〔*sing*., *pl*.〕团集,聚集(体);堆积,堆。

con·gest [kən'dʒest; kən`dʒɛst] *vt*., *vi*. **1.** (使)充血。**2.** 充满、拥塞。*a* ~*ed district* 人口稠密[拥挤]的地方。*The cold* ~*ed his sinuses*. 他因受凉堵了鼻子。

con·ges·tion [kən'dʒestʃən; kən`dʒɛstʃən] *n*. **1.** 【医】充血。**2.** (交通的)拥挤;(货物的)充斥;(人口)过剩,稠密。*traffic* ~交通拥塞。~ *of the brain* 脑充血。

con·ges·tive [kən'dʒestiv; kən`dʒɛstɪv] *a*. 【医】充血的,充血性的。~ *symptoms* 充血性症状。

con·gi·us ['kɔndʒiəs; `kɑndʒɪəs] *n*. (*pl*. ***-gi·i*** [-ai; -aɪ]) **1.** 【史】康吉斯〔古罗马液量单位,略小于七品脱〕。**2.** 【药】一加仑。

con·glo·bate ['kɔŋgləubeit; kɑn`globet] **I** *vt*., *vi*. (使)变成球,(使)形成球状。**II** *a*. 成球(状)的。

con·glo·ba·tion [ˌkɔŋgləu'beiʃən;ˏkɑnglo`beʃən] *n*. 球形,球形体。

con·glom·er·ate [kən'glɔmərit; kən`glɑmərɪt] **I** *a*. **1.** 成球(状)的;结成团块的。**2.** 由不同种类的各部分组成的,混杂会聚在一处的。**3.** 【地】砾岩(性)的。**II** *n*. **1.** 团集物。**2.** 集团;联合大企业,多种经营大公司,多业公司。**3.** 【地】砾岩。**III** [kən'glɔməreit; kən`glɑməˏret] *vt*., *vi*. (使)结聚成一团。

con·glom·er·a·tion [kənˌglɔmə'reiʃən; kənˏglɑmə`reʃən] *n*. **1.** 结聚作用;结聚。**2.** 团块;堆集。**3.** 集团。

con·glom·er·a·tor [kən'glɔməreitə; kən`glɑməˏretɚ] *n*. 联合大企业[多业公司]的组成者[主持人]。

con·glu·ti·nant [kən'gluːtinənt; kən`glutɪnənt] *a*. **1.** 黏合的;愈合的;收口的。**2.** 【医】促使(伤口)愈合的,加速(伤口)收口的。

con·glu·ti·nate [kən'gluːtineit; kən`glutəˏnet] **I** *vt*., *vi*. (使)黏合,(使)黏在一块;【医】(使)愈合。**II** *a*. 黏合的;【医】愈合的。

con·glu·ti·na·tion [kənˌgluːti'neiʃən; kənˏglutɪ`neʃən] *n*. 黏合,黏着;【医】愈合。

Con·go ['kɔŋgəu; `kɑŋgo] *n*. 〔the ~〕**1.** 刚果〔非洲〕。**2.** 刚果河〔即扎伊尔河〕〔非洲〕。~ **dye**, ~ **colour** 一种偶氮染料。~ **eel** [**snake**] 【动】蛇状两栖鲵。~ **paper** 一种化学试纸〔遇酸变蓝色,遇碱变红色〕。~ **red** 刚果红〔一种染料〕。

Con·go·lese [ˌkɔŋgə'liːz;ˏkɑŋgo`liz] **I** *a*. 刚果(人)的;刚果语的。**II** *n*. 刚果人;刚果语。

con·go(u) ['kɔŋgəu; `kɑŋgu] *n*. (中国的)工夫红茶。

con·grat·u·lant [kən'grætjulənt; kən`grætʃələnt] **I** *a*. 祝贺的。**II** *n*. 祝贺者。

con·grat·u·late [kən'grætjuleit; kən`grætʃəˏlet] *vt*. 祝贺,向…致祝词。*I* ~ *you on your success* [*birthday*]. 我祝贺你的成功[生日]。*I* ~ *myself on* [*upon*] *my narrow escape*. 我庆幸自己死里逃生。

con·grat·u·la·tion [kənˌgrætju'leiʃən; kənˏgrætʃə`leʃən] *n*. 祝贺;〔*pl*.〕祝词,贺辞。*a matter for* ~值得庆贺的事情。*offer one's* ~*s* 致祝词,道贺。*Congratulations*! 恭喜恭喜!

con·grat·u·la·tor [kən'grætjuleitə; kən`grætʃəˏletɚ] *n*. 祝贺者。

con·grat·u·la·to·ry [kən'grætjulətəri; kən`grætʃələˏtorɪ] *a*. 祝贺的。*a* ~ *address* 祝词。*a* ~ *telegram* 贺电。

con·gre·gant ['kɔŋgrigənt; `kɑŋgrəgənt] *n*. (会众中的)召集人。

con·gre·gate ['kɔŋgrigeit; `kɑŋgrɪˏget] **I** *vt*., *vi*. (使)聚集,集合。**II** *a*. 聚集的;集团的。

con·gre·ga·tion [ˌkɔŋgri'geiʃən;ˏkɑŋgrɪ`geʃən] *n*. **1.** 集合;(特指宗教的)集会;会众,听众。**2.** 〔the C-〕【犹史】以色列人(全体);犹太民族(= C- of the Lord.)。**3.** (牛津大学的)教职员全体会议。**4.** 〔美〕(殖民时代的)教区,行政区,农庄,农垦地。**5.** (遵守共同教规的)天主教结社;(由几个修道院结合起来的)修士团分团;(教廷中协助教皇处理各种事务的)十一个常设委员会之一;(处理某种特殊问题的)主教会议。

Con·gre·ga·tion·al [ˌkɔŋgri'geiʃənəl;ˏkɑŋgrɪ`geʃənl] *a*. **1.** 【宗】公理会的。**2.** 〔c-〕集会的;(教堂、教会)会众的。**-ism** *n*. **1.** 【宗】公理会。**2.** 〔C-〕地方教会自治主义。**-ist** **1.** *n*. 公理会教友。**2.** *a*. 公理会的。

con·gress **I** ['kɔŋgres; `kɑŋgrəs] *n*. **1.** (代表)大会。**2.** 国会;国会会期;〔C-〕美国国会。**3.** 集会,交际;社交。**4.** 协会。**5.** 群。*a medical* ~医学会议。***in C-*** 〔美〕在国会开会期间。**II** [kən'gres; kən`grɛs] *vi*. 开会,集合。~ **boot** [**gaiter**, **shoe**] 〔美〕两侧有松紧布的半统靴。~ **folk**〔单复同〕〔俚〕国会议员。~ **man** 〔美〕(男性)国会议

员,(特指)众议院议员。～**person** 国会议员〔妇权运动者用语〕。～**woman**〔美〕国会女议员。

con·gres·sion·al [kənˈgreʃənəl; kənˋgrɛʃənəl] ***a*.** 会议的;委员会的;〔C-〕〔美〕国会的。**C- district**〔美〕(由州议会划分的选举众议员的)国会选区。**C- Record**〔美〕国会议事录。

Con·gress·ite [ˈkɔŋgresait; ˋkɑŋgrɪˏsaɪt] ***n*.** 印度国大党党员。

Con·greve [ˈkɔŋgriːv; ˋkɑŋgriv] ***n*.** 康格里夫〔姓氏〕。

con·gru·ence, con·gru·en·cy [ˈkɔŋgruəns(i); ˋkɑŋgruəns(ɪ)] ***n*.** **1.** 适合,和谐,【语法】一致。**2.**【数】叠合,相合,全等;同余(式)(线)汇。～ **field**【数】同余域。～ **lines** 线汇。

con·gru·ent [ˈkɔŋgruənt; ˋkɑŋgruənt] ***a*.** **1.** 适合的,相合的,一致的。**2.**【数】全等的,叠合的,同余的。～ **points** 叠合点。

con·gru·ity [kɔŋˈgru(:)iti; kənˋgruətɪ] ***n*.** **1.** 适合,一致,调和。**2.**【数】全等。*a* ～ *of ideas* 思想一致。

con·gru·ous [ˈkɔŋgruəs; ˋkɑŋgruəs] ***a*.** **1.** 一致的,适合[协调]的,符合的 (*with*; *to*)。**2.**【数】全等的。

con·ic [ˈkɔnik; ˋkɑnɪk] **I** ***n*.** 圆锥(形);圆锥[二次]曲线。〔*pl*.〕锥线法[论]。**II** ***a*.** 圆锥(形)的。～ **pendulum** 锥动摆。～ **projection** 锥顶射影。～ **section** 圆锥截面;圆锥[二次]曲线。～ **spring** 锥形弹簧。

con·i·cal [ˈkɔnikəl; ˋkɑnɪkəl] ***a*.** 圆锥(体、形)的。**-ly** ***ad*.** 成圆锥形。

co·nic·i·ty [kəuˈnisiti; koˋnɪsətɪ] ***n*.**【物】锥削度。

con·i·coid [ˈkɔnikɔid; ˋkɑnəkɔɪd] ***n*.**【数】二次曲面,(特指)双曲面。

co·nid·i·al [kəuˈnidiəl; koˋnɪdɪəl] ***a*.**【植】**1.** 无性芽胞(状)的。**2.** 产生无性芽胞的 (= conidian)。

co·nid·i·o·phore [kəuˈnidiəfɔː; koˋnɪdɪəfɔr] ***n*.**【植】分生孢子柄[梗]。

co·nid·io·spore [kəuˈnidiəspɔː; koˋnɪdɪəspɔr] ***n*.**【微】分生孢子。

co·nid·i·um [kəuˈnidiəm; koˋnɪdɪəm] ***n*.** (*pl*. ***-nidia*** [-ˈnidiə; -ˋnɪdiə])【植】分生孢子。

co·ni·fer [ˈkəunifə; ˋkonəfɚ] ***n*.**【植】针叶树。

co·ni·f·er·ae [kəuˈniferiː; koˋnɪfɛri] ***n*.** 〔*pl*.〕【植】松柏科。

co·nif·er·ous [kəuˈnifərəs; koˋnɪfərəs] ***a*.** 结毬果的,松柏科的。

co·ni·form [ˈkəunifɔːm; ˋkonɪˏfɔrm] ***a*.** 圆锥形的。

co·ni·ine [ˈkəuniiːn, -in; ˋkonɪin, -ɪn] ***n*.**【化】毒芹碱 (= conine)。

co·ni·ol·o·gy [ˌkəuniˈɔlədʒi; ˏkonɪˋɑlədʒɪ] ***n*.**【气】微尘学 (= koniology)。

Co·ni·o·se·li·num [ˌkəuniəusiˈlainəm; ˏkonɪosɪˋlaɪnəm] ***n*.**【植】川芎属。

co·ni·um [ˈkəuniəm; ˋkonɪəm] ***n*.** 毒芹属植物〔如芹叶钩吻 (*Conium maculatum*)〕。

conj. = **1.** conjugation. **2.** conjunction; conjunctive.

con·jec·tur·a·ble [kənˈdʒektʃərəbl; kənˋdʒɛktʃərəbḷ] ***a*.** 可推测[猜想]到的。

con·jec·tur·al [kənˈdʒektʃərəl; kənˋdʒɛktʃərəl] ***a*.** 推测的,猜想的。**-ly** ***ad*.**

con·jec·ture [kənˈdʒektʃə; kənˋdʒɛktʃɚ] **I** ***n*.** 推测,猜想;辨读;设想。～ *of the most vague and shadowy description* 瞎猜,捕风捉影的推测。***form*** [***make***] ～***s upon*** 推想。***found a*** ～ ***on*** 根据…推测。***hazard*** [***venture***] ***a*** ～ 猜猜看,估估看。**II** ***vt*., *vi*.** 推测,猜想,估量;辨读,设想。

con·jee [ˈkɔndʒiː; ˋkɑndʒɪ] ***n*.** = congee[2].

con·join [kənˈdʒɔin; kənˋdʒɔɪn] ***vt*., *vi*.** (使)结合,(使)连接;(使)联合。

con·joined [kənˈdʒɔind; kənˋdʒɔɪnd] ***a*.** 结合的;联在一起的;【徽】重叠的,相连的。

con·joint [ˈkɔndʒɔint; kənˋdʒɔɪnt] **I** ***a*.** 相连的,黏合的,结合的;连带的,共同的。～ *action* 共同动作。**II** ***n*.** 〔*pl*.〕夫妇。**-ly** ***ad*.**

con·ju·gal [ˈkɔndʒugəl; ˋkɑndʒʊgḷ] ***a*.** 婚姻上的,夫妇(间)的。～ *affection* 夫妇爱。～ *laws* 婚姻法。～ *understanding* 婚约。**-i·ty** [-ˈgæliti; -ˋgælətɪ] ***n*.** **-ly** ***ad*.**

con·ju·gant [ˈkɔndʒəgənt; ˋkɑndʒəgənt] ***n*.**【生】接合体。

con·ju·gate [ˈkɔndʒugit; ˋkɑndʒəˏget] **I** ***a*.** 成对的;结合的;【语法】同源[根]的;【数、物、化】共轭的,缀合的;【生】配合的;【植】对生的。～ *angles* 共轭角。*a* ～ *point* 共轭点。**II** [-geit; -get] ***vt*.** **1.** 使结合,使配合。**2.**【语法】列举(动词)变化,变位。—***vi*.** **1.** 结合;(动物)交尾;【生】配合。**2.**【语法】(动词)变化。～***d protein***【化】拼合蛋白。

con·ju·ga·tion [ˌkɔndʒuˈgeiʃən; ˏkɑndʒəˋgeʃən] ***n*.** **1.** 结合(作用),配合。**2.**【语法】动词的变化[变位]。**3.**【化】共轭,拼合;【生】(雌雄配子等的)接合(作用),配合。*strong* [*weak*] ～【语法】强[弱]变化,不规则[规则]变化。

con·junct [kənˈdʒʌŋkt; kənˋdʒʌŋkt] ***a*.** 连接的,结合的;联合的。**-ly** ***ad*.**

con·junc·tion [kənˈdʒʌŋkʃən; kənˋdʒʌŋkʃən] ***n*.** **1.** 连合,结合,连接;联合;联系。**2.** (事件的)同时发生。**3.**【语法】连(接)词。**4.**【天】(行星等的)会合,(月的)朔;【数】契合,合取;【计】逻辑乘法,逻辑乘积。*coordinate* [*subordinate*] ～*s* 并列[从属]连词。***in*** ～ ***with*** 与…共同,与…协力,联络着;连带着。**-al** ***a*.**

con·junc·ti·va [ˌkɔndʒʌŋkˈtaivə; ˏkɑndʒʌŋkˋtaɪvə] ***n*.** 〔L.〕(*pl*. ～***s***, ***-vae*** [-viː;-vi])【解】(眼球的)结膜。

con·junc·tive [kənˈdʒʌŋktiv; kənˋdʒʌŋktɪv] **I** ***a*.** **1.** 连结(着)的;【数】契合的,合取的;【语法】(有)连接(作)用的。**2.**【计】逻辑乘法的。**II** ***n*.**【语法】连词。～ **mood**【语法】连接语态。～ **symbiosis**【生】合体共生。**-ly** ***ad*.**

con·junc·ti·vi·tis [kənˌdʒʌŋktiˈvaitis; kənˏdʒʌŋktəˋvaɪtɪs] ***n*.**【医】结膜炎。

con·junc·ture [kənˈdʒʌŋktʃə; kənˋdʒʌŋktʃɚ] ***n*.** **1.** 局面,场合,地步;(某种)机缘;紧要关头,非常时候。**2.** 结合;连接。***at*** [***in***] ***this*** ～ 在这(危急)时候。

con·ju·ra·tion [ˌkɔndʒuəˈreiʃən; ˏkɑndʒuəˋreʃən] ***n*.** **1.** 祈求;恳求。**2.** 魔法;咒语。**3.**【法】犯罪图谋[合谋]。

con·jure [ˈkʌndʒə; ˋkʌndʒɚ] ***vt*.** **1.** 使用魔术变出。**2.** [kənˈdʒuə; kənˋdʒʊə] 祈求。**3.** 想像出 (*up*)。*I* ～ *you by all that is holy to desist*. 务祈作罢。～ *an egg out of an empty cup* 从空杯里变出一枚鸡蛋。—***vi*.** 施魔法;变戏法。～ ***away*** 念咒驱逐[消除]。～ ***down*** 召来(魔鬼)。～ ***out*** 念咒语使出现;变戏法变出。～ ***up*** 念咒召来;(凭想像)作出,使现出,想像出。

con·jur·er, con·jur·or [ˈkʌndʒərə; ˋkʌndʒərɚ] ***n*.** **1.** 咒法家,邪术家;魔术师。**2.**〔口〕极聪明厉害的人。*He is no* ～. 他不大行。***without being a*** ～ 虽不怎样精明。

con·jur·y [ˈkʌndʒəri; ˋkʌndʒərɪ] ***n*.** 咒法,邪术;魔术。

conk[1] [kɔŋk; kɑŋk] **I** ***n*.** 〔俚〕鼻子;〔美俚〕头,脑袋;头上的一击。**II** ***vi*.** 〔口〕(机械等)坏掉,出毛病;疲劳已极,累透 (*out*);昏厥;死亡。—***vt*.** 〔美俚〕打…的脑袋,敲…的头。～ ***out***〔美口〕突然停止,发生故障。～ **out** ***n*.** 发生故障。

conk[2] [kɔŋk; kɑŋk] **I** ***vt*.** 把(非洲人卷紧的头发)弄成波浪形或弄直。**II** ***n*.** 把卷紧的头发展平[成波浪形]的发式。

conk·er [ˈkɔŋkə; ˋkɑŋkɚ] ***n*.** **1.**【植】七叶树。**2.** 〔*pl*.〕〔动词用单数〕打栗子〔一种儿童游戏,双方各执一串七叶树栗,以打碎对方的一串为胜〕。

conk·y [ˈkɔŋki; ˋkɑŋkɪ] ***a*., *n*.** 〔俚〕鼻子大的(人)。

con·man·ship [ˈkɔmənʃip; ˋkɑmənʃɪp] ***n*.** 骗术,骗子手

法。

con mo·to [kɔn ˈməutəu; kɔn ˋmoto] *n*. 〔It.〕【乐】速度加快。

conn [kɔn; kɑn] **I** *vt*. (驶)船,掌握(船的)驾驶。**II** *n*. 驶船(指挥)。

Conn. = Connecticut.

con·nate [ˈkɔneit; ˋkɑnet] *a*. **1**. 生来的;先天的;【生】原生的;合生的。**2**. 同源[族]的;同性质的。*a ~ deposit* 原生沉积。*a ~ disease* 先天性疾病。

con·nat·u·ral [kəˈnætʃərəl; kəˋnætʃərəl] *a*. **1**. 生来的,固有的(*to*)。**2**. 同性质的,同种[族]的。

con·nect [kəˈnekt; kəˋnɛkt] *vt*. **1**. 连接,接合,连接。**2**. 使有联系,为…接通电话。**3**. 联想。*two towns ~ed by a railway* 由铁路连接的两个市镇。*The telephone operator ~ed us*. 话务员给我们接通了电话。—*vi*. 连通,连接,衔接,连续(*with*)。*This pipe ~s with a smaller one*. 这管子和一个较小的管子连通着。***be ~ed with*** 与…有关[联]系。***be well-~ed*** 有有钱有势的亲戚[朋友]〔主要指亲戚,也可扩大到指某种后台〕。**~ (up) with** 和…有关系。★ ~ up 是美语。**~ *oneself with*** 和…联系。***You are ~ed***. (电话)接通了〔话务员用语〕。**~ time**【计】联通时间。

con·nect·ed [kəˈnektid; kəˋnɛktɪd] *a*. 有联络的,联系着的;连续[贯]的。~ *ideas* 连贯的思想。*a ~ plan* 通盘计划。**-ly** *ad*. **-ness** *n*.

Con·nect·i·cut [kəˈnetikət; kəˋnɛtɪkət] *n*. 康涅狄格〔美国州名〕。

con·nect·ing [kəˈnektiŋ; kəˋnɛktɪŋ] *a*. 连接着的;起连接作用的。**~ trenches**【军】交通壕。**~ tube** 导管。

con·nec·tion [kəˈnekʃən; kəˋnɛkʃən] *n*. 〔美〕= connexion.

con·nec·tive [kəˈnektiv; kəˋnɛktɪv] **I** *a*. 连接的。**II** *n*. **1**. 连接物。**2**.【语法】连接语,连词。**3**.【植】药隔;【动】连索。**~ fibre [tissue]**【解】结缔纤维[组织]。**-ly** *ad*.

con·nec·tor [kəˈnektə; kəˋnɛktɚ] *n*. **1**. 连合者;连结者。**2**. 连接物。**3**.【电】连接器,接头,插塞,插头,连接管。

con·nex·ion [kəˈnekʃən; kəˋnɛkʃən] *n*. **1**. 连接;关系;联系;【电】合闸。**2**. 联络;交情,交际;男女关系。**3**. 团体;教派,宗派。**4**. 〔总称〕主顾,顾客;有贸易关系的商号[人物]。**5**. (前后)关系;连贯(性);联想。**6**. 亲戚;社会关系〔多指有权有势的〕。**7**. 交通手段;联运船[车]。**8**. (电报、电话)通讯线。**9**. 性交。**10**. 〔美俚〕毒品贩子。*There is no ~ between them*. 他们无关系。*You are in ~*. (电话)接通了。*hot water ~s* 热水管。*outside ~*(电话)外线。*criminal ~*通奸。*break off a ~*断绝关系。***enter into a ~ with*** 与…发生关系[打交道]。***form useful ~s*** 构成有帮助的社会关系。***have a ~ with*** 和…有关系,通着,勾搭着。***have ~ with*** 和…发生关系,和…勾搭上。***in ~ with*** 和(车、船等)联络着;与(人)共同,与…有关系[联络]。***in this ~*** 就此而论,关于这一点。***make ~s at*** (火车、轮船等)在…衔接[联络、转搭]。***miss one's ~*** (搭火车等)迟到而未搭上。***sever ~*** 脱离关系;分手。***take up one's ~s*** 〔美俚〕离开学校。**~ *ticket*** (车、船)联运票。**~-peg** 临时接通电流的插头。

Con·nie [ˈkɔni; ˋkɑnɪ] *n*. 康妮〔女子名,Constance 的昵称〕。

con·ning tower [ˈkɔniŋ ˈtauə; ˋkɑnɪŋ ˋtauɚ] *n*. (军舰的)司令塔;(潜艇的)指挥塔〔亦用作出入口〕。

con·nip·tion [kəˈnipʃən; kəˋnɪpʃən] *n*. 〔美口〕歇斯底里发作;大发脾气,激怒 (= ~ fit)。***throw a ~*** 大发雷霆。

con·niv·ance, con·niv·an·cy [kəˈnaivəns(i); kəˋnaɪvəns(ɪ)] *n*. 默许,放任,纵容;【法】(不当的对罪行的)默许 (*at*; *in*)。

con·nive [kəˈnaiv; kəˋnaɪv] *vi*. **1**. 假装不见;默许,纵容,放任 (*at*)。**2**. 共谋,成立默契,私通 (*with*)。**3**.【生】逐渐集中一处,靠合。

con·niv·ent [kəˈnaivənt; kəˋnaɪvənt] *a*.【生】会接的,靠合的,逐渐集中的。

con·nois·seur [ˌkɔniˈsəː; ˏkɑnəˋsɝ] *n*. (美术品的)鉴定家,行家,内行,权威 (*in*; *of*)。~ *in wine* 葡萄酒鉴定家。*play the ~* 充内行。**-ship** 鉴赏能力;行家地位[资格]。

Con·nor(s) [ˈkɔnə(z); ˋkɑnɚ(z)] *n*. 康纳(斯)〔姓氏〕。

con·no·ta·tion [ˌkɔnəuˈteiʃən; ˏkɑnəˋteʃən] *n*. **1**. 言外之意,含蓄;(词的)涵义。**2**.【逻】内涵,内包。

con·no·ta·tive [ˈkɔnəuteitiv, kəˈnəutətiv; ˋkɑnəˏtetɪv, kəˋnotətɪv] *a*. **1**. 含蓄的;有涵义的。**2**.【逻】内包的,包涵的。**-ly** *ad*.

con·note [kɔˈnəut; kəˋnot] *vt*. **1**. 暗示,指点。**2**. 含蓄,包含;意味;【逻】内涵,包摄 (*opp*. denote)。**3**. 〔俚〕意思就是。

con·nu·bi·al [kəˈnjuːbjəl; kəˋnjubjəl] *a*. 婚姻的,结婚的;夫妇的;配偶的。~ *love* 夫妇爱。**-ly** *ad*. 婚姻上,作为夫妇来说(*not connubially inclined* 不想结婚)。

con·nu·bi·al·i·ty [kəˌnjuːbiˈæliti; kəˏnjubɪˋælətɪ] *n*. 夫妇关系;结婚(状态);结婚风俗。

co·no·dont [ˈkəunədɔnt, ˈkɔnə-; ˋkonədɑnt, ˋkɑnə-] *n*.【古生】牙形虫。

co·noid [ˈkəunɔid; ˋkonɔɪd] **I** *n*. 圆锥体[形];【数】劈锥曲面。**II** *a*. 圆锥形[体]的。**-al** *a*.

co·no·scope [ˈkəunəskəup; ˋkonəskop] *n*.【物】锥光偏振仪。

con·quer [ˈkɔŋkə; ˋkɔŋkɚ] *vt*. **1**. 征服;攻克;打败(敌人)。**2**. 克服(困难等),改正(恶习等);抑制(情欲等)。**3**. 〔古、诗〕赢得(名誉,某人的感情等)。~ *the enemy* 征服敌人。~ *bad habits* 克服不良习惯。~ *passions* 压制情欲。*the ~ed* 被征服者,败者。—*vi*. 得胜。***stoop to ~*** 忍辱取胜;降低身分以达到目的。***To ~ or to die***. 非胜即死,不成功便成仁。

con·quer·a·ble [ˈkɔnkərəbl; ˋkɑnkərəbḷ] *a*. 可征服的;能赢得的;能克服的。

con·quer·or [ˈkɔŋkərə; ˋkɑŋkərɚ] *n*. **1**. 征服者,胜利者。**2**. 〔废〕决胜败的争斗。***play the ~*** 〔口〕(游戏中同分数者)举行决赛。***William the C-***【英史】征服者威廉第一〔1066 年征服英国的 Normandy 公爵 William〕。

con·quest [ˈkɔŋkwest; ˋkɑŋkwɛst] *n*. **1**. 征服;获得(物);赢得(物);征服地,占领地。**2**. 感情上被征服的人;受笼络[诱惑]的人。***for the ~ of*** 为要征服…。***make a ~ of*** 征服;赢得…的感情。***the C-***【英史】1066 年威廉的征服英国。

con·qui·an [ˈkɔŋkiən; ˋkɑŋkɪən] *n*. 碰对牌戏 (= cooncan)。

con·quis·ta·dor [kɔnˈkwistədɔː; kɑnˋkwɪstəˏdɔr] *n*. (*pl*. ~*s*, ~*es*) 〔Sp.〕征服者〔指 16 世纪征服秘鲁、墨西哥等地的西班牙人〕。

Con·rad [ˈkɔnræd; ˋkɑnræd] *n*. 康拉德〔姓氏,男子名〕。

Con·rail [ˈkɔnˌreil; ˋkɑnˏrel] *n*. 〔美〕联合铁路公司,联铁(美国一家接受联邦资助的私营公司,主要经营东北部的铁路)。

cons. = consecrated; 〔L.〕【处方】conserva (= conserve 请保存); consigned; consignment; consolidated; consonant; constable; constitution; construction; consul.

con·san·guin·e·ous [ˌkɔnsæŋˈgwiniəs; ˏkɑnsæŋˋgwɪnɪəs] *a*. 血亲的,近亲的,同血统的。*a ~ marriage* 血亲婚姻,近亲婚姻。

con·san·guin·i·ty [ˌkɔnsæŋˈgwiniti; ˏkɑnsæŋˋgwɪnətɪ] *n*. **1**. 血族,血缘,血亲,亲族。**2**. 密切关系。*a collateral ~*旁系亲族。*a lineal ~*直系亲族。

con·science [ˈkɔnʃəns; ˋkɑnʃəns] *n*. 良心。*a bad [guilty] ~* 做贼心虚,深感内疚。*a good [clear] ~* 问心无愧,安然自得。*a matter of ~*良心问题。*liberty of*

～信仰自由。**for ～(') sake** 为了良心关系[问心无愧],请凭良心(做某事)。**have sth. on one's ～** 觉得内疚,感到心中难受。**have the ～ to (do)** 竟厚着面皮(做某事)。**in (all) ～**〔口〕真的,当然。**My ～!** 哎呀,哼,嗯,呸〔表示惊讶、反驳、疑心等〕。**sleep on a calm ～** 安心睡眠。**upon my ～** 凭良心说,的确,一定。～ **money** (为求良心安逸而拿出的)悔罪金。～**-smitten** *a*. 受良心责备的。～**-stricken** [ˈkɔnʃəns-ˌstrikən; ˋkɑnʃəns-ˏstrɪkən] *a*. 内疚的,悔恨的;良心不安的。**-less** *a*. 没良心的,没有道德心的。

con·sci·en·tious [ˌkɔnʃiˈenʃəs; ˏkɑnʃɪˋɛnʃəs] *a*. **1.** 认真(负责)的,真心实意的。**2.** 有[凭]良心的,诚实的,正大光明的,耿直的。**3.** 严正的;谨慎的。**be far from ～** 很不认真。～ **objector** 真心实意拒绝参加罪恶战争(等)的人。**-ly** *ad*. **-ness** *n*.

con·scion·a·ble [ˈkɔnʃnəbl; ˋkɑnʃənəbl] *a*. 〔古〕凭良心办理的,正直的,正当的。

con·scious [ˈkɔnʃəs; ˋkɑnʃəs] *a*. **1.** 有意识的,有知觉的;神志清醒的。**2.** 自觉的,自己知道的,明明知道的(*of*; *that*);有意的,故意的。**3.** (痛苦、感情、冷气等)感觉得到的;意识到的。**4.** = self-conscious. **5.** 有…意识的〔常用以构成复合词〕。*Man is a ～ being*. 人是有意识的生物。*He became ～*. 他清醒[苏醒]了。*a hardly ～ movement* 不自觉[自然而然]的动作。*be* [*become*] *～ of* 意识到。*be ～ of one's own blame* 自知理亏。*be too ～* 极腼腆。*the ～ simper* 忸怩的强笑。*with a ～ air* 故作谦虚地。*with ～ superiority* 带着故作高人一等的神气。**-ly** *ad*.

con·scious·ness [ˈkɔnʃəsnis; ˋkɑnʃəsnɪs] *n*. 意识;知觉;觉悟(性);自觉。**lose** [**recover**] **one's ～** 失去[恢复]知觉,不省人事[苏醒过来]。～**-expanding** *a*. 迷幻的,使人感到飘飘然的。

con·scribe [kənˈskraib; kənˋskraɪb] *vt*. 征募,招募;征用。

con·script [ˈkɔnskript; ˋkɑnskrɪpt] **I** *a*. 被征入伍的。**II** *n*. 应征新兵。— [kənˈskript; kənˋskrɪpt] *vt*. = conscribe. ～ **fathers** (古罗马,中世纪意大利的)元老院议员;〔谑〕立法议会议员。

con·scrip·tee [ˌkɔnskripˈtiː; ˏkɑnskrɪpˋti] *n*. 〔美口〕被征入伍者。

con·scrip·tion [kənˈskripʃən; kənˋskrɪpʃən] *n*. 征兵;征集,征发,征用。～ *of wealth* (对不服兵役者所征)兵役税;【经】资本课税。～ **age** 适役年龄。～ **system** 征兵制度。

con. sec. = conic sections.

con·se·crate [ˈkɔnsikreit; ˋkɑnsɪˏkret] *vt*. **1.** 奉献,献祭。**2.** 把…奉为神圣,尊崇。**3.** (用宗教仪式)授予…以某种职位。*a ～d ground* 圣地。*a life ～d to science* 献身科学的一生。

con·se·cra·tion [ˌkɔnsiˈkreiʃən; ˏkɑnsɪˋkreʃən] *n*. **1.** 献祭;奉献。**2.** 神圣化。**3.** 授(圣)职。**4.** 献身。

con·se·cra·to·ry [ˈkɔnsikreitəri; ˋkɑnsɪkrəˏtorɪ] *a*. 使神圣化的,授(圣)职的,奉献的。

con·se·cu·tion [ˌkɔnsiˈkjuːʃən; ˏkɑnsɪˋkjuʃən] *n*. **1.** 连贯;(逻辑)顺序,推理顺序[步骤];前后关连。**2.** 【语法】(词序,语法变化等的)连贯,一致。

con·sec·u·tive [kənˈsekjutiv; kənˋsɛkjətɪv] *a*. **1.** 连续的,串联的,依次相续的;连贯的。**2.** 【语法】表示结果的。*It rained four ～ days*. 连续下了四天雨。～ *account of the accident* 事件的顺序叙述。～ *days* 连续几天。～ **clause**【语法】(表示结果的)副词子句。～ **fifths**【乐】连续五度。～ **numbers**【数】相邻数。**-ly** *ad*. **-ness** *n*.

con·se·nes·cence, con·se·nes·cen·cy [ˌkɔnsiˈnesns, -si; ˏkɑnsɪˋnesəns, -sɪ] *n*. 衰老。

con·sen·su·al [kənˈsenʃuəl; kənˋsenʃuəl] *a*. **1.** 【法】在双方同意下成立的。**2.** 【生理】交感反应的。**3.** 【心】(指本能活动)意识作用激发的,交感的。～ **sex**(得到女方认可的而非强暴或性骚扰的)认同的性行为。

con·sen·sus [kənˈsensəs; kənˋsensəs] *n*. **1.** (意见等的)一致,合意。**2.** 【生理】交感。*The ～ of opinion is that ....* 一致的意见是…。～ **gentium** 〔L.〕民意,公论。

con·sent [kənˈsent; kənˋsent] **I** *vi*. 同意,赞成,应允,答应(*to*; *to do*; *that*)。～ *to a proposal* 赞同提案。～ *to give a lecture* 答应演讲。**II** *n*. 同意,赞同,赞成,答应。*Silence gives ～*. 不说话就是答应。**age of ～**【法】承诺年龄〔尤指少女法律上达到可以自主的年龄〕。**give** [**refuse**] **one's ～** 答应[拒绝]。**with one ～ = by common ～** 异口同声,全体一致。**with the ～ of** 得…的同意。

con·sen·ta·ne·ous [ˌkɔnsenˈteiniəs; ˏkɑnsɛnˋtenɪəs] *a*. **1.** 同意的;一致的。**2.** 合意的;适合的(*to*; *with*)。

con·sent·er [kənˈsentə; kənˋsentɚ] *n*. 同意者,答应者,赞同者。

con·sen·tient [kənˈsenʃənt; kənˋsenʃənt] *a*. 同意的,赞同的;一致的。

con·se·quence [ˈkɔnsikwəns; ˋkɑnsəkwɛns] *n*. **1.** 结果,成果,影响,后果;【数】后承;【逻】结论。**2.** 重要(性);重大意义。**answer for the ～s** 对后果负责。**face the ～s of one's action** 自食其果。**in ～** 因此,结果。**in ～ of** …的结果,因为…的原故,由于。**of ～** 有势力的;重要的(*a man of ～* 有势力的人物。*a matter of no ～* 没有什么重要性的事)。**take the ～s** 自食其果,承担责任(*He must take the ～s of his own deeds*. 他得自食其果)。**take upon oneself the ～s** 自己承担后果。

con·se·quent [ˈkɔnsikwənt; ˋkɑnsəkwent] **I** *a*. **1.** 继起的,因…而起的(*on*; *upon*);(逻辑上)必然的,当然的。**2.** 【地】顺向的。**II** *n*. (当然的)结果;【逻】后件;结论;【数】后项;【语法】(条件结构中的)结果子句。～ **divide** 顺向分水岭。～ **drainage** 顺向水系。～ **pole**【物】庶极。**-ly** *ad*.

con·se·quen·tial [ˌkɔnsiˈkwenʃəl; ˏkɑnsəˋkwɛnʃəl] *a*. **1.** 随之而起的,后果的;继起的;必然的。**2.** 有重要性的。**3.** 以重要人物自居的,傲慢的。～ **damages**【法】间接损害。**-ly** *ad*. **-ness** *n*.

con·ser·van·cy [kənˈsəːvənsi; kənˋsɝvənsɪ] *n*. **1.** (天然资源的)管理,保管,保护,保存;水土保持;资源保护区。**2.** (河、港等的)管理局[委员会];〔集合词〕管理员。*build water ～ projects* 兴修水利。*a water ～ project* 水利工程。*the Thames C-* 泰晤士河管理委员会。

con·ser·va·tion [ˌkɔnsə(ː)ˈveiʃən; ˏkɑnsɚˋveʃən] *n*. **1.** 保存,维持(健康),保守;保护;保护森林[河道](等)。**2.** 【物】守恒,不灭。～ *of energy* [*mass*] 能量[质量]守恒。～ *of heredity* 遗传性的保守性。～ *of water and soil* 水土保持。～ *of wildlife* 野生动物保护。～ **plant** 废料再生工厂;废料利用工厂。**-al** *a*.

con·ser·va·tion·ist [ˌkɔnsəˈveiʃənist; ˏkɑnsɚˋveʃənɪst] *n*. 自然资源保护论者。

con·serv·a·tism [kənˈsəːvətizəm; kənˋsɝvətɪzəm] *n*. **1.** 保守主义,守旧(性)。**2.** 〔C-〕〔英〕保守党(的主张[政策])。

con·serv·a·tive [kənˈsəːvətiv; kənˋsɝvətɪv] **I** *a*. **1.** 保守的,守旧的;有保存力的。**2.** 〔C-〕保守党的(*opp*. Liberal, Radical)。**3.** 稳健的;(估计等)谨慎的。**II** *n*. **1.** 保守主义者;〔C-〕保守党员;稳健派。**2.** 防腐剂;保护料。～ *grazing* 适度放牧。*C- party* (英国的)保守党。**-ly** *ad*. **-ness** *n*.

con·ser·va·toire [kənˈsəːvətwɑː; kənˏsɝvəˋtwɑr] *n*. 〔F.〕音乐[艺术]学校[学院]。

con·ser·va·tor [ˈkɔnsə(ː)veitə; ˋkɑnsɚˏvetɚ] *n*. **1.** 保存者,保护者;管理人;〔英〕(河、港、森林等的)管理委员。**2.** [kənˈ-; kənˋ-]〔美〕(疯子等的)监护人;(银行的)监督。

con·ser·va·to·ry [kənˈsəːvətri; kənˋsɝvəˏtorɪ] **I** *a*. **1.** (有)保存(力)的。**2.** 保管人的。**II** *n*. **1.** (植物的)暖房,

温室。2. 音乐[艺术、戏剧]学院。3. 防腐剂。

con·serve [kən'səːv; kən`sɝv] **I** *vt*. 1. 保存。2. 糖渍。3.【物,化】使守恒。**II** *n*.〔常 *pl*.〕糖食,蜜饯;果酱;【医】糖剂。

con·sid·er [kən'sidə; kən`sɪdɚ] *vt*. 1. 考虑,细想;估量,斟酌;留意,研究。2. 尊重;体谅;给(赏钱[小费])。3. 以为,认为〔后接 that 引导的子句〕。4. 把(某人、某事)看作…,认为(某人、某事)如何〔后接 as ..., of ..., (to be) ... 等〕。~ *a matter well before deciding* 慎重考虑后再决定。~ *her ill health* 照顾她体弱。~ *the servants* 给仆役赏钱。~ *reform as revolution* 认为改革是一场革命。~ *sb*. (*to be*) *a fool* 拿人当傻瓜。—*vi*. 考虑,细想。*Let me* ~ *a moment*. 让我想一想。

C

con·sid·er·a·ble [kən'sidərəbl; kən`sɪdərəbl] **I** *a*. 1. 该注意的,应考虑的,不可忽视的,重要的。2. 相当(大、多)的,不少的;很多的,大量的,巨额的。***by*** ~〔美口〕不少,大大。~ ***of***〔美口〕大量。**II** *ad*.〔美口〕= **-a·bly** *ad*. **-ness** *n*.

con·sid·er·ate [kən'sidərit; kən`sɪdərɪt] *a*. 1. 对…关心爱护的,体谅(人)的,照顾到…的(*of*)。2.〔古〕经过斟酌的,细心的,慎重的。**-ly** *ad*. **-ness** *n*.

con·sid·er·a·tion [kənˌsidə'reiʃən; kənˏsɪdə`reʃən] *n*. 1. 考虑,考察;讨论,商量。2. 照顾,关心;体谅,体恤。3. 报酬,补偿。4. 尊敬,敬意。5. 原因,理由;须考虑到的事实[问题];理由。6.〔罕〕重要性。*a man of* ~要人。*That's a* ~. 那是一个值得考虑的问题。***after due*** ~ 经相当考虑后。***be of no*** ~ 并不紧要,没有什么问题。***for a*** ~ 为求报酬,为求补偿(*He sold it for a* ~. 为了换取一点补偿,他把它低价卖掉了)。***for the*** ~ ***of*** 作为…的参考。***give adequate*** ~ ***to*** 适当照顾。***in*** ~ ***of*** 考虑到,因,由于;以作…的谢礼,酬劳。***leave out of*** ~ 置之度外,不以…为意。***not on any*** ~ 决不。(***be***) ***of*** ~ 值得考虑[重要]的。***on no*** ~ 决不(*On no* ~ *could I consent*. 我决不能同意)。***out of*** ~ ***for your feelings*** 看你面上,由于照顾你的情绪。***take into*** ~ 估量到,斟酌。***show*** [***have***] ~ ***for*** (*sb*.'*s position*) 考虑[照顾]到(某人处境)。***taking one*** ~ ***with another*** 对各方面进行考虑。***the first*** ~ 第一要件,最重要的事。***under*** ~ 考虑中,研究中。***under no*** ~ 决不。***without due*** ~ (不假思索)贸然,轻率。

con·sid·ered [kən'sidəd; kən`sɪdɚd] *a*. 考虑过的;被尊重的。

con·sid·er·ing [kən'sidəriŋ; kən`sɪdərɪŋ] **I** *prep*. 就…而论,照…说来,与…比起来,以…看起来。*C- her age, she looks young*. 照年龄说来,她显得年轻。~ (*that*) *she is a woman* 因为她是一个妇女,所以…。*That is not so bad*, ~ (*the circumstances*). 照(实情)说,那还算不错;从多方面说来,还过得去。**II** *ad*.〔口〕细想起来,认真说,委实。*The boy does well*, ~. 认真说,那个小孩干得是不错的。

con·sign [kən'sain; kən`saɪn] *vt*. 1. 委托,托付;【商】托运。2. 托卖,寄售,寄存,存(款)。3. 用作,当作(*to*)。~ *a task to somebody* 把一项任务交付给某人。*We beg to* ~ *the following per S.S. 'London'*. 请由"伦敦"号轮船运交下列各物。~ *money in a bank* 把款子存在银行里。~ *a letter to the post* 付邮。*be* ~*ed to misery* 陷入可悲境地。~ *sth. to oblivion* 把某事置之脑后;忘却。

con·sig·na·tion [ˌkɔnsai'neiʃən; ˏkɑnsɪg`neʃən] *n*. 交付,委托;寄存。***to the*** ~ ***of*** 运交[寄交、转交]…处。

con·sign·ee [ˌkɔnsai'niː; ˏkɑnsaɪ`ni] *n*. 收存人,受托人;收货人,承销人。

con·sign·er, con·sign·or [kən'sainə; kən`saɪnɚ (和 consignee 相对应时作) ˌkɔnsai'nɔː; ˏkɑnsaɪ`nɔr] *n*. 交付者,委托者;发货人,托运人,托销的货主。

con·sign·ment [kən'sainmənt; kən`saɪnmənt] *n*. 1. 交付,委托。2. 寄售,托卖 (=~ sale),托卖货。*a new* ~ *of summer suit* 新到夏服。~ *goods* 托卖品。~ *invoice* 发货单。~ *note* 发货通知书。~ *out* 寄销品。~-*sheet* 收货清单。***on*** ~ 寄售,以寄售方式处理。

con·sil·i·ence [kən'siliəns; kən`sɪlɪəns] *n*. 符合,一致。

con·sist [kən'sist; kən`sɪst] *vi*. 1. 由…组成 (*of*)。2. 存在于 (*in*)。3. (与…)一致,适合;并存,并立 (*with*)。4.〔古〕生存;共存。*The book* ~*s of eight chapters*. 那书共有八章。*Happiness* ~*s in contentment*. 幸福在乎知足。*Health does not* ~ *with intemperance*. 健康与纵欲[无节制]不能相容。

con·sis·tence, con·sis·ten·cy [kən'sistəns, -si; kən`sɪstəns, -sɪ] *n*. 1. 无矛盾,相容(性);始终一贯;稳定(性);(言行)一致,(色调)调和。2. 坚强,坚定,坚固,结实;坚实度。3. 浓度,稠度;黏度。

con·sist·ent [kən'sistənt; kən`sɪstənt] *a*. 1. 一致的,协调的,相容的,不矛盾的 (*with*); 首尾一贯的。2. 言行一致的;坚定的,有操守的。3. 坚实的,密实的,稠的,浓厚的。*a policy* ~ *with public good* 符合公众利益的政策。*the firm and* ~ *policy* 坚定不移的方针。*He is not* ~ *in his statement*. 他的陈述前后不符。**-ly** *ad*.

con·sis·tom·e·ter [kən'sistəmitə; kən`sɪstəmɪtɚ] *n*.【物】稠度计。

con·sis·to·ri·al [ˌkɔnsis'tɔːriəl; ˏkɑnsɪs`torɪəl] *a*. 1. 宗教法庭的。2.【天主】教庭议会上院的。

con·sis·to·ry [kən'sistəri; kən`sɪstərɪ] *n*. 1. 宗教会议,宗教法庭;【天主】(教庭的)参议院;【英国教】主教法庭,(长老派的)长老法庭。2. 集会,协议会,参议会。

con·so·ci·ate [kən'səuʃieit; kən`soʃɪˏet] *vt*., *vi*. (使)结合[结成一伙],(使)联合 (*with*)。

con·so·ci·a·tion [kənˌsəusi'eiʃən; kənˏsosɪ`eʃən] *n*. 1. 联合,组合。2.【宗】宗教法庭。3.【生】单优种社会,小社会群。

consol. = consolidated.

con·sol·a·ble [kən'səuləbl; kən`soləbl] *a*. 可安慰的。

con·so·la·tion [ˌkɔnsə'leiʃən; ˏkɑnsə`leʃən] *n*. 1. 安慰,慰藉,安抚,抚恤。2. 安慰物,抚恤金。~ **money** 抚恤金;(辞退被雇用者时给的)慰藉金。~ **prize** (给落选人的)安慰奖,副奖。~ **race** [**match, game**] (特为竞赛失败者举行的)安慰赛。

con·sol·a·to·ry [kən'sɔlətəri; kən`sɑləˏtorɪ] *a*. 安慰的。*a* ~ *letter* 慰问信。~ *words* 安慰话。

con·sole[1] [kən'səul; kən`sol] *vt*. 安慰,慰问。

con·sole[2] ['kɔnsəul; `kɑnsol] *n*.【建】1. 悬臂(梁),突梁,肘托,(涡卷形)托石;角(撑)架。2. (用落地支架靠墙安设的)涡形支腿桌案 (=~-table)。3.【机、空】(计算机等的)控制台,操纵台;仪表板[台];键盘台;(管风琴的)演奏台。4. (收音机、电视机的)落地式支座。

con·sol·i·date [kən'sɔlideit; kən`sɑləˏdet] *vt*. 1. 使坚固,巩固;加固,强化。2. 合并,统一;整顿,整理(公债、土地、公司等)。3.【医】变实,愈合。—*vi*. 结成一体,变巩固。

con·sol·i·dat·ed [kən'sɔlideitid; kən`sɑlɪdetɪd] *a*. 加固的;整理过的,统一的。~ **annuities**〔英〕统一公债〔简称 consols〕。~ **school**〔美〕合并的公立小学〔常指农村小学〕。~ **ticket office**〔美〕(各路火车)联合售票处。

con·sol·i·da·tion [kənˌsɔli'deiʃən; kənˏsɑlə`deʃən] *n*. 1. 巩固,强化,加强;凝固;固结,压实,渗压。2.【经】统一,合并,调整(期)。3.【医】变实,愈合;【植】着生。*Party* ~整党。*training and* ~整训。~ **line** 渗压曲线。

con·sols [kən'sɔlz; kən`sɑlz] *n*.〔*pl*.〕(英国)统一公债。

con·so·lute ['kɔnsəljuːt; `kɑnsəljut] *a*.【化】共溶质(会与另一种液体完全混溶的液体)的,混溶质的。

con·som·mé [kən'sɔmei; kɑn`same] *n*.〔F.〕【烹】清炖肉[鸡]汤。

con·so·nance ['kɔnsənəns; `kɑnsənəns] *n*. 1.【乐】谐和音;【物】共鸣。2. 和谐,调和,一致。***in*** ~ ***with*** 和…一致[调和、共鸣]。

con·so·nan·cy [ˈkɔnsənənsi; ˋkɑnsənənsɪ] ***n*.** **1.** 协和,协调,一致。**2.**【乐】谐和音。

con·so·nant [ˈkɔnsənənt; ˋkɑnsənənt] **I** ***a*.** (和…)一致的,调和的 (*with*; *to*);【乐】谐和(音)的;【语音】元音的。**II** ***n*.**【语音】元音(符号);谐和音。**-al** [-ˈnæntl; -ˋnæntl] ***a*.**

con·sort I [ˈkɔnsɔːt; ˋkɑnsɔrt] ***n*.** **1.** 配偶(特指在位君主的夫或妻)。**2.** 伙伴,会员。**3.** 僚舰,僚艇。**4.** 合作,协力,协同。**5.** 一组乐师;一组同类乐器。*a prince* [*king*] ~女王的丈夫。*a queen* ~王后。***in*** ~ ***with sb*.** 和某人共同[协力]。**II** [kənˈsɔːt; kənˋsɔrt] ***vt*.** 〔~ oneself〕使结合,使陪伴。—***vi*.** 一致,调和,相称 (*with*)。*His practice does not* ~ *with his preaching*. 他言行不一。

con·sor·ti·um [kənˈsɔːtjəm; kənˋsɔrʃɪəm] ***n*.** **1.** (国际)财团;(国际性)金融协议;组合,共同体。**2.**【法】配偶的地位和权利。**3.** 〔美〕(小型大学集中人力、物力办学的)大学联盟协定。

con·spe·cif·ic [ˌkɔnspiˈsifik; ˏkɑnspɪˋsɪfɪk] **I** ***a*.**【生】同种的。**II** ***n*.** 同种。

con·spec·tus [kənˈspektəs; kənˋspɛktəs] ***n*.** 梗概,大要,大纲,纲要,一览(表)。

con·spic·u·ous [kənˈspikjuəs; kənˋspɪkjʊəs] ***a*.** **1.** 显著的,显眼的。**2.** (服装等)过分花哨的;令人注目的,触目的;明显的;著名的,特出的,出众的。*be* ~ *by its absence* 因为(某人)缺席反而引人注意。~ *error* 显著的错误。***cut a*** ~ ***figure*** 放异彩,令人注目。***make oneself*** ~ (标新立异)惹人注目。~ **consumption** 摆阔性消费〔出于炫耀财产而花钱购物等,并非出于需要〕。**-ly** ***ad*.** **-ness** ***n*.**

con·spir·a·cy [kənˈspirəsi; kənˋspɪrəsɪ] ***n*.** **1.** 共谋。**2.** 阴谋,反叛 (*against*)。*form a* ~ *against* 秘密策划进行反对[破坏、杀害等]。*take part in a* ~参与阴谋。*get scent* [*wind*] *of a* ~发觉阴谋。~ ***of silence*** 保守秘密的约定。***in*** ~共谋,搞派系活动。

con·spir·a·tor [kənˈspirətə; kənˋspɪrətɚ] ***n*.** 共谋者,阴谋家,谋反者。

con·spir·a·tress [kənˈspirətris; kənˋspɪrətrɪs] ***n*.** 女共谋者,女阴谋家。

con·spir·a·to·ri·al [kənˌspirəˈtɔːriəl; kənˏspɪrəˋtɔrɪəl] ***a*.** **1.** 阴谋的,阴谋者的;阴险的。**2.** (爱)搞阴谋的。**3.** 共谋的。**-ly** ***ad*.**

con·spire [kənˈspaiə; kənˋspaɪr] ***vi*.** **1.** (结党)密谋,同谋,搞阴谋。**2.** 协力;巧合;共同促成。~ *against the state* 图谋卖国。*All things* ~*d to make him happy*. 事事巧合使他心满意足。*All things* ~ *against me*. 事事凑合起来跟我作对。~ ***with*** 勾结。—***vt*.** 〔罕〕共谋,图谋。

con·spi·ri·to [kɔnˈspiritəu; kɑnˋspɪrəto] ***n*.** 〔It.〕【乐】热烈地,精神饱满地。

con·spue [kənˈspjuː; kənˋspju] ***vt*.** 叫嚷着表示憎恶;要求驱逐[废除](人物,政策等);唾弃。

Const. = Constantine; Constantinople.

const. = **1.** constable. **2.** constant. **3.** constitution. **4.** construction.

Con·sta·ble [ˈkʌnstəbl, ˈkɔnstəbl; ˋkɑnstə bl̩, ˋkʌnstəbl] ***n*.** 康斯特布尔[姓氏]。

con·sta·ble [ˈkʌnstəbl; ˋkʌnstəbl] ***n*.** **1.** 〔英〕警察,警官。**2.**【史】(中世纪的)王室[贵族]总管;王室[贵族]城堡的主管。*Chief C-* 〔英〕警察厅长。*a special* ~(非常时期的)临时民警。***outrun*** [***overrun***] ***the*** ~ 负债。***the C- of France*** (法国王朝时代的)元帅。***the Lord High C- of England*** (英国中古的)保安长官,(现指举行仪式时临时任命的)侍从武官长。

con·stab·u·lar·y [kənˈstæbjuləri; kənˋstæbjəlɛrɪ] **I** ***n*.** **1.** 警区。**2.** (全体)警察。**3.** (负责治安的)保安部队。**II** ***a*.** 警察的,治安的。

Con·stance [ˈkɔnstəns; ˋkɑnstəns] ***n*.** 康斯坦斯〔女子名〕。

con·stan·cy [ˈkɔnstənsi; ˋkɑnstənsɪ] ***n*.** **1.** 恒定不变,定型性,恒久(性)。**2.** 恒心;不屈不挠,坚忍不拔;坚贞;忠实。

con·stant [ˈkɔnstənt; ˋkɑnstənt] **I** ***a*.** **1.** 恒定不变的,固定的,稳定的,恒久的;继续不断的。**2.** 不屈不挠的,坚韧的。**3.** 忠实的,有节操的。*be* ~ *in love* 忠贞不渝的爱情。*two days of* ~ *rain* 两天接连下雨。~ *to one's duty* 忠于职守。~ *wind* 恒风。**II** ***n*.**【数、物】常数,恒量;恒定(值);(常)系数,率;【语法】(转换语法用语)定项。*the circular* ~圆周率。~ **current** 直流电。~ **error** 常在误差。~**-level ballon** (搜集大气层资料的)定高气球。~ **temperature** 恒温。**-ly** ***ad*.**

Con·stan·ta, Con·stan·tsa [kənˈstɑːntə, -tsə; kənˋstɑntsɑ, -tsə] ***n*.** 康斯坦察〔罗马尼亚港市〕。

con·stant·an [ˈkɔnstəntæn; ˋkɑnstəntæn] ***n*.**【冶】(温度系数接近恒定不变的)康铜。

Con·stan·tine[1] [ˈkɔnstəntain; ˋkɑnstənˏtaɪn] ***n*.** **1.** 康斯坦丁〔男子名〕。**2.** ~ **the Great** 康士坦丁大帝,罗马皇帝(288? —337)〔全名是 *Favius Valerius Aurelius Constantinus*〕。

Con·stan·tine[2] [ˈkɔnstəntain; ˋkɑnstənˏtaɪn] ***n*.** 君士坦丁〔阿尔及利亚城市〕。

Con·stan·ti·no·ple [ˌkɔnstæntiˈnəupl; ˏkɑnstæntəˋnopl] ***n*.** 君士坦丁堡〔Istanbul 伊斯坦布尔的旧称〕〔土耳其港市〕。

con·stel·late [ˈkɔnstəleit; ˋkɑnstəˏlet] ***vt*.** **1.** 形成星座;使群集。**2.** 用星群样的饰物装饰。*the* ~*d sky* 群星灿烂的天空。—***vi*.** **1.** 形成星座。**2.** 群集。

con·stel·la·tion [ˌkɔnstəˈleiʃən; ˏkɑnstəˋleʃən] ***n*.** **1.** 星座;星群;(占星术中认为与某人命运有关的)星宿;(杰出人物等的)灿如明星的集团。**2.** 型。**3.** (组织上的)配合。**4.**【心】(思想感情)丛。**5.**【语法】并列关系。**6.** 〔C-〕美国 C-69 型星座式远程客机。

con·ster·nate [ˈkɔnstə(ː)neit; ˋkɑnstɚˏnet] ***vt*.** 使惊愕〔常用被动语态〕。

con·ster·na·tion [ˌkɔnstə(ː)ˈneiʃən; ˏkɑnstɚˋneʃən] ***n*.** 惊愕,恐怖,惊惶失措。***throw*** (*sb*.) ***into*** ~ 使(某人)大吃一惊,使愕然。***to one's*** ~ 极其可惊的是。***with*** ~ 愕然。

con·sti·pate [ˈkɔnstipeit; ˋkɑnstəˏpet] ***vt*.** **1.** 使迟滞,使闭塞。**2.**【医】使便秘。*be* ~*d* 便秘;〔俚〕吝啬。

con·sti·pa·tion [ˌkɔnstiˈpeiʃən; ˏkɑnstəˋpeʃən] ***n*.**【医】便秘。

con·stit·u·en·cy [kənˈstitjuənsi; kənˋstɪtʃʊənsɪ] ***n*.** **1.** (议员所代表的)选民(全体);选(举)区。**2.** 〔集合词〕顾客;(期刊的)订户,赞助者。***nurse a*** ~ 笼络一批选民。

con·stit·u·ent [kənˈstitjuənt; kənˋstɪtʃʊənt] **I** ***a*.** **1.** 构成的,组织的,成分的。**2.** 有选举权的,有提名权的,有宪法制定[修改]权的。~ **parts of water** 水的成分。~ **power** 宪法制定[修改]权。**II** ***n*.** **1.** 要素,成分,组分。**2.** 构成者,制定者,设立者。**3.** 选民。**4.** (指定代理者的)委托人,当事者本人。**5.**【语言】(结构)成分,组成成分。**C- Assembly**【法史】国民议会。~ **assembly** 宪法制定[修改]会议。~ **body** 选民团。~ **corporation**【经】子公司。~ **republics** 构成联邦的各共和国。~ **structure**【语法】(转换语法用语)成分结构。

con·sti·tute [ˈkɔnstitjuːt; ˋkɑnstəˏtjut] ***vt*.** **1.** 构成,组成,成为…的本质。**2.** 制定,设立。**3.** 委托…为(代表),指定,任命。**4.** 引起(某种状态等);等于。*Seven days* ~ *a week*. 七天为[构成]一星期。*What* ~*s virtue*? 美德的本质是什么? *I am not so* ~*d that* ... 我不是…性格的人。*be* ~*d representative of* ...当选为…的代表。~ *d authorities* 当局。*He* ~*d himself as their judge*. 他自命为他们的裁定人。

con·sti·tu·tion [ˌkɔnstiˈtjuːʃən; ˏkɑnstəˋtjuʃən] ***n*.** **1.** 构成,构造,结构;组织;成分。**2.** 体格,体质,素质。**3.** 制

C

定,设立;任命。**4.**【政】宪法;政体;法规;章程;【法】制度组织。*a republican* ～共和政体。*a written* ～成文宪法。*a draft* ～宪法草案。*a nervous* ～神经质。***by*** ～天性,体质上。***have a good*** [***poor***] ～ 体格好[差]。***suit*** [***agree with***] ***sb.'s*** ～ 适合某人体质[性格]。***undermine sb.'s*** ～ (***by***...) (因…)伤害身体。

con·sti·tu·tion·al [ˌkɔnstiˈtjuːʃənl; ˏkɑnstəˋtjuʃənl] **I** *a*. **1.** 生来的,固有的;体质上的。**2.** 宪法(上规定)的;立宪的,拥护宪法的;法制的。**3.** 有益健康的,保健的。**4.** 组织的,构成的。**II** *n*. 保健运动[散步]。*a* ～ *disease* [*disorder*] 体质病。*a* ～ *convention* 〔美〕制宪[修宪]代表会议。*a* ～ *government* 立宪政体[政治]。*a* ～ *formula*【化】结构式。～ *infirmity* 生来的虚弱。～ *law* 宪法。～ *walk* 保健散步。*take a* ～散步。*the C- assembly* 制宪会议。**-ism** *n*. 立宪制度,立宪主义,宪政;宪法论,拥护宪政,护宪论。**-ist** *n*. 宪法学者;立宪主义者,护宪论者,拥护宪政者。

con·sti·tu·tion·al·i·ty [ˌkɔnstiˌtjuːʃəˈnæliti; ˏkɑnstəˏtjuʃəˋnælətɪ] *n*. 立宪(性),合法性。

con·sti·tu·tion·al·ly [ˌkɔnstiˈtjuːʃənəli; ˏkɑnstəˋtjuʃənəlɪ] *ad*. **1.** 本质地;体质上。**2.** 宪法上,按照宪法。

con·sti·tu·tive [ˈkɔnstitjuːtiv; ˋkɑnstəˏtjutɪv] *a*. **1.** 构成的,组织的;要素的,本质的。**2.** 有制定权的。***be*** ～ ***of*** 由…构成。

con·sti·tu·tor [ˈkɔnstitjuːtə; ˋkɑnstəˏtjutɚ] *n*. 构成者,组织者;制定者。

con·strain [kənˈstrein; kənˋstren] *vt*. **1.** 强迫,强制(*to*)。**2.** 束缚,约束;使紧张,紧压,使不舒服[不自由]。**3.** 把…关进,监禁。*be* ～*ed to* (*do*) 不得不;被迫。～ *oneself* 勉强,自制。～*ing force* 抑制力;【物】约束力。*feel* ～*ed* 觉得不自如[受压迫,不舒服]。

con·strain·ed [kənˈstreind; kənˋstrend] *a*. 被强迫的;受压制的;不自然的,勉强的。*a* ～ *manner* 不自然的[局促的]样子。*a* ～ *smile* (勉强做作的)苦笑。**-ly** [-ˈstreini*d*li; -ˋstreni*d*lɪ] *ad*.

con·straint [kənˈstreint; kənˋstrent] *n*. **1.** 强迫,拘束。**2.** 约束,压抑,拘泥。**3.** 强制力。**4.** 紧张感[状态]。*by* ～ 勉强,强迫。*feel* ～觉得局促不安,感受压迫。*show* ～显得局促。*under* [*in*] ～ 被迫,不得不;被束缚着。

con·strict [kənˈstrikt; kənˋstrɪkt] *vt*. **1.** 压缩,使收缩。**2.** 妨害,阻碍。*a* ～*ed outlook* 狭窄的眼界。—*vi*. 收缩。

con·stric·tion [kənˈstrikʃən; kənˋstrɪkʃən] *n*. **1.** 压缩,收缩;狭窄,缩窄。**2.** (胸部等的)压迫感,憋闷感。**3.** 压束物,阻塞物。**4.** 被压束部分;缩颈。

con·stric·tive [kənˈstriktiv; kənˋstrɪktɪv] *a*. 收缩(性)的;压缩的,紧缩的。

con·stric·tor [kənˈstriktə; kənˋstrɪktɚ] *n*. **1.** 压缩物,收缩物;压缩器;收缩器;【火箭】收敛〔尾部收缩〕式燃烧室。**2.**【解】括约肌 (= ～ muscle)。**3.**【动】大蟒 (= boa-～)。

con·stringe [kənˈstrindʒ; kənˋstrɪndʒ] *vt*. 压缩,使紧缩。

con·strin·gen·cy [kənˈstrindʒənsi; kənˋstrɪndʒənsɪ] *n*. 收缩(性),收敛,压缩。

con·strin·gent [kənˈstrindʒənt; kənˋstrɪndʒənt] *a*. 使收缩的,收敛性的。

con·stru·a·ble [kənˈstruːəbl; kənˋstruəbl] *a*. **1.** (句子等)能理解的,能作语法分析的。**2.** 可解释为…的 (*as*)。

con·struct I [kənˈstrʌkt; kənˋstrʌkt] *vt*. **1.** 构成,建造,建筑,铺设,架设;【数】作(图);【语法】造(句),作(文)。**2.** 构想,创立。**3.** 解释。～ *a bridge* 造桥。～ *a theory* 创立学说。**II** [ˈkɔnstrʌkt; ˋkɑnstrʌkt] *n*. **1.** 结构(物)。**2.** 思维产物;构想;【心】构成概念。**3.**【语法】结构(体),结构成分。

con·struc·tion [kənˈstrʌkʃən; kənˋstrʌkʃən] *n*. **1.** 建筑,结构,构造,架设,铺设;建设;设计;工程;建筑法,构造法,建筑物;【剧】搭置,布景,结构,编排。**2.** (法律等的)解释;推定。**3.**【语法】结构(体);句法结构;构词法;【数】作图。*capital* ～基本建设。*the order of* ～施工程序。*a sandwich* ～层状结构。***bear a*** ～ 可作某一解释;可解释为。***put a false*** ～ ***on*** 故意曲解。***put a good*** [***bad***] ～ ***upon*** 善[恶]意解释。***under*** [***in course of***] ～ 建筑中,建造中。～**-way** 临时铁路,毛路。～ ***engine*** 工程机车。～ ***gang*** 〔美〕铁路土方工人队。～ ***gauge*** 【工】建筑界限。～ ***labourer*** 〔美〕铁路土方工人。～ ***problem***【数】作图题。～ ***train*** 建设材料运输列车。～ ***work*** 建设工程。**-al** *a*.

con·struc·tion·ism [kənˈstrʌkʃənizəm; kənˋstrʌkʃənɪzəm] *n*.【数】构造论;【美学】构成主义,构成派。

con·struc·tion·ist [kənˈstrʌkʃənist; kənˋstrʌkʃənɪst] *n*. **1.** (法律条文等的)解释者。**2.** 〔美〕构成派书家。*a strict* [*liberal*] ～(对法律条文等)作严格[自由]解释者。

con·struc·tive [kənˈstrʌktiv; kənˋstrʌktɪv] *a*. **1.** 构成的,建设(性)的;积极的。**2.**【法】推定的;解释(性)的。**3.**【数】作图的;【物】相长的。～ *criticism* 建设性的批评。*a* ～ *faculty* 组织力,建设力。～ **crime**【法】推定罪行。～ **fraud**【法】推定欺诈〔虽非恶意诈骗但已通过其不实之言行而使他人或公共利益受到侵害之行为〕。～ **total loss** (水险)准海损。**-ly** *ad*. **-ness** *n*.

con·struc·tiv·ism [kənˈstrʌktivizəm; kənˋstrʌktɪvɪzəm] *n*.【美学】结构主义。

con·struc·tor [kənˈstrʌktə; kənˋstrʌktɚ] *n*. **1.** 建造者,建设者。**2.**【海军】造船技师。

con·strue [kənˈstruː; kənˋstru] **I** *vt*. **1.** 分析(语法);(逐字)翻译,(特指)口译。**2.** 解释,给…下注解;推论。**3.** 结合,连用;使与…联系 (*with*)。"*Depend*" *is* ～*d with* "*on*". *Depend* 与 *on* 连用。—*vi*. 解释;能解释;能分析。*The sentence does not* ～. 那一句不能分析。**II** [ˈkɔnstruː; ˋkɑnstru] *n*. **1.**【语法】语法分析;分析练习句。**2.** 解释。**3.** 直译。

con·sub·stan·tial [ˌkɔnsəbˈstænʃəl; ˏkɑnsəbˋstænʃəl] **I** *a*. **1.** 同质的,同体的。**2.**【神】三位一体的。*The Son is* ～ *with the Father*. 圣子与圣父同体。**-ly** *ad*. **-ism** *n*. **II** [-ʃəlizm; -ʃəlɪzm] *n*.【神】圣体共在论。**-ist** [-ʃəlist; -ʃəlɪst] *n*. 圣体共在论者。

con·sub·stan·ti·al·i·ty [ˌkɔnsəbstænʃiˈæliti; ˏkɑnsəbstænʃɪˋælətɪ] *n*.【神】同体,同质,同性。～ *of the three Persons of the Trinity* (把上帝、耶稣、圣灵当作一身同体看的)三位一体。

con·sub·stan·ti·ate [ˌkɔnsəbˈstænʃieit; ˏkɑnsəbˋstænʃɪˏet] *vt*. 使同体[同质,同性]。—*vi*. 变成同体;【宗】鼓吹圣体共在论。

con·sub·stan·ti·a·tion [ˈkɔnsəbˌstænʃiˈeiʃən; ˏkɑnsəbˏstænʃɪˋeʃən] *n*.【宗】圣餐中面包和酒与耶稣的血肉同在(论)。

con·sue·tude [ˈkɔnswitjuːd; ˋkɑnswɪˏtjud] *n*. (有法律效力的)习惯,惯例。

con·sue·tu·di·nar·y [ˌkɔnswiˈtjuːdinəri; ˏkɑnswɪˋtjudnˏɛrɪ] **I** *a*. 习惯(上)的;习惯法的。*a* ～ *law* 习惯法,不成文法。**II** *n*. 习惯法,不成文法;(教堂的)惯例书,宗仪书。

con·sul [ˈkɔnsəl; ˋkɑnsəl] *n*. **1.** 领事。**2.**【罗马史】执政官。**3.**【法史】执政。*an acting* ～ 代理领事。*a* ～*-general* 总领事。*an honorary* ～名誉领事。*a vice* ～副领事。*the Chinese* ～ *at* ... 中国驻…领事。**-ship** *n*. 领事职位,领事任期。

con·su·lage [ˈkɔnsjulidʒ; ˋkɑnsjəlɪdʒ] *n*. 领事签证手续费。

con·su·lar [ˈkɔnsjulə; ˋkɑnsjəlɚ] *a*. **1.** 领事的。**2.**【史】执政官的。*a* ～ *agent* 代理领事。*a* ～ *attaché* 领事随员。*a* ～ *invoice* 领事签证。

con·su·late [ˈkɔnsjulit; ˋkɑnsjəlɪt] *n*. **1.** 领事职位;领事

任期。**2.** 领事馆。**3.**〔C-〕【法史】执政府时代。**4.**(古罗马)执政官职位。~ *general* 总领事馆。

con·sult [kən'sʌlt; kən`sʌlt] ***vi.*** 商量,协商,商议(*with*);【医】会诊。~ *with a friend about* [*on*] *a matter* 和朋友商量一件事。—***vt.*** **1.** 请教,咨询;与…商量。**2.** 查考,查阅(参考书);看(表)。**3.** 上(医生处去)就诊,请…鉴定。**4.** 考虑,顾及;谋(便利),图(利益)。~ *a dictionary* 查词典。~ *a doctor* 找医生诊治。~ *a mirror* [*watch*] 照镜子[看表]。~ *one's own interests* 考虑到自己的利益。~ *sb.'s pleasure* 观察[考虑]某人高兴不高兴。~ *the meeting* 征求与会者意见。~ ***one's pillow*** 通夜思索。

con·sult·an·cy [kən'sʌltənsi; kən`sʌltənsɪ] ***n.*** **1.** 顾问工作;顾问职位。**2.** 咨询服务公司。**3.** = consultation.

con·sult·ant [kən'sʌltənt; kən`sʌltənt] ***n.*** **1.** 求教者,(与人)商议者,征求意见者,查阅者。**2.** (受人咨询的)顾问;会诊医生,(顾问)医生。

con·sul·ta·tion [ˌkɔnsəl'teiʃən; ˏkɑnsəl`teʃən] ***n.*** **1.** 商量,协商,评议;(专家的)会议,协商会,审议会。**2.**【医】会诊;(律师的)鉴定。**3.** 参考,查阅。

con·sult·a·tive [kən'sʌltətiv; kən`sʌltətɪv] ***a.*** 商议的,协商的;咨询的,顾问的,咨询机关。*a* ~ *committee* 顾问委员会。

con·sult·er [kən'sʌltə; kən`sʌltɚ] ***n.*** 与人商量者;向人咨询者;查阅者。

con·sult·ing [kən'sʌltiŋ; kən`sʌltɪŋ] ***a.*** 咨询的,顾问的。*a* ~ *engineer* 顾问工程师。*a* ~ *physician* 会诊医生。~**-room** 诊室。

con·sul·tor [kən'sʌltə; kɑn`sʌltɚ] ***n.*** 顾问;(天主教会主教的)顾问神父。

con·sum·a·ble [kən'sjuːməbl; kən`suməbl] **I** ***a.*** 可消费的,可消耗的,能用尽的。*a* ~ *ledger* 消费[耗]品总账。**II** ***n.***〔*pl.*〕消费[耗]品。

con·sume [kən'sjuːm; kən`sjum] ***vt.*** **1.** 消费,消耗,用掉;浪费。**2.** 毁灭,消灭。**3.** 吃光,喝光。**4.** 烧光。*a half* ~*d cigar* 吸剩半根的雪茄烟。*be* ~*d by a fire* 烧掉。—***vi.*** **1.** 消费掉,用掉,用完。**2.** 烧光;消尽,消灭。**3.** 消磨。**4.** 枯萎;衰萎,憔悴。*The flowers* ~*d away*. 花枯萎了。***be*** ~***d with*** (*envy, fever, ambition*) (因嫉妒,热病,野心)而憔悴[心疲力竭]。~ ***away with*** (*grief*) (因抑郁)而逐渐憔悴[死去]。

con·sum·ed·ly [kən'sjuːmidli; kən`sumɪdlɪ] ***ad.*** 过分地,极端地。

con·sum·er [kən'sjuːmə; kən`sumɚ] ***n.*** **1.**【经】消费者,用户。**2.** 用电设备。**3.**【生】消费有机体。*a small* ~【电】普通用户。~*s' cooperative society* 消费合作社。~**-city** 消费城市。~**('s) credit** 分期付款销售(法);给予分期付款购买者的信贷。~**s' goods** 消费品。~ **strike** (消费者的)罢购。

con·sum·er·ism [kən'sjuːmərizəm; kən`sjumərɪzəm] ***n.*** **1.** 保护用户[消费者]利益主义。**2.**【经】消费主义〔认为社会消费力愈大对整个经济愈有利〕。**3.** (商品和劳务的)消费,销售。**con·sum·er·ist** [-rist; -rɪst] ***n.*** 用户第一主义者;主张消费主义经济理论的人。

con·sum·mate I ['kɔnsʌmeit; `kɑnsəˏmet] ***vt.*** 使圆满;作成,完成;使(幸福等)达到顶点。~ *a marriage* 成婚,完婚。*His happiness was* ~*d when he heard the good news*. 他听到喜讯后快乐到极点。**II** [kən'sʌmit; kən`sʌmɪt] ***a.*** 无上的,至上的,完全的,圆满的;无比的。~ *happiness* 无上的幸福。*a* ~ *ass* 大傻瓜。**-ly** ***ad.***

con·sum·ma·tion [ˌkɔnsʌ'meiʃən; ˏkɑnsə`meʃən] ***n.*** **1.** 圆满,完备;成就,完成;顶点,极端;终结,终极。**2.** 成婚。*Death is the* ~ *of life*. 死是生命的终结。

con·sum·ma·tor ['kɔnsʌmeitə; `kɑnsʌmetɚ] ***n.*** 圆满完成者;(某方面的)专家,能手。

con·sump·tion [kən'sʌmpʃən; kən`sʌmpʃən] ***n.*** **1.** 消费(量);消尽,消耗,灭绝。**2.**【医】结核病;痨病,肺痨(= pulmonary ~)。*The speech was meant for foreign* [*home*] ~. 那篇讲话是让国外[本国]人听的。~ *goods* 消费品。~ *of the bowels* 肠结核。~ *tax* [*duty*] 消费税。

con·sump·tive [kən'sʌmptiv; kən`sʌmptɪv] **I** ***a.*** **1.** 消费的;消耗性的。**2.** 痨[结核]病的。~ *warfare* 消耗战。**II** ***n.*** (肺)结核病患者。

cont. = **1.** containing. **2.** contents. **3.** continent. **4.** continue. **5.** contract.

con·ta·bes·cence [ˌkɔntə'besns; ˏkɑntə`besn̩s] ***n.*** 萎缩;衰萎;【植】雄蕊萎缩。

con·tact ['kɔntækt; `kɑntækt] **I** ***n.*** **1.** 接触;联系;交涉。**2.**〔美〕(有势力的)熟人;门路。**3.**【数】相切;【电】接触;触头;触点;【无】通讯;【军】(飞机和地上部队的)联络。**4.** 曾与传染病接触者;【医】传染病带菌嫌疑人。*a man of many* ~*s* 交际广[门路多]的人。*an auxiliary* ~联锁触头。*first* ~【天】初亏。*fourth* [*last*] ~【天】复圆。*a radar* ~雷达搜获目标。***be in*** ~ ***with*** 和…接触着,和(某人)接近。***break*** ~断开电路。***brought ... into*** ~ ***with ...*** 使…和…接触。***come in*** (*to*) ~ ***with*** 和…接触[冲突];碰见。***make*** ~ 接通电路。***make useful*** ~***s with ...*** 和…进行有用[利]的来往。**II** [kən'tækt; kən`tækt] ***vt.*** **1.** 使接触。**2.**【无】与…通讯;与…通话。**3.**〔美口〕与…交际,接近(某人)。~ *a station in America* 和美国一电台通话[接触]。—***vi.*** 接触,联系。★ contact 作动词,多用于商业上或极亲密的朋友之间。**III** ***a.*** **1.** 保持接触的,有关系的;由接触引起的。**2.**【空】可看见地面景物的。**IV** ***ad.***【空】以目力观察(飞行)。**V** [kən'tækt; kən`tækt] ***int.*** 开动〔让飞机发动的信号〕。~ **action** 接触作用。~ **agent** 1.【化】触媒。2.【军】卫生联络员。~ **breaker**【电】接触断路器。~ **flying** [**flight**] 目视飞行(*opp*. blind flying)。~ **lens** (装在眼睑内的)隐形镜片。~ **light** (机场)跑道灯。~ **maker**【电】电流开关装置。~ **man** (厂商雇用的)交际员,跑街。~ **mine** 触发水雷。~ **twin**【矿】接合双晶。

con·tac·tee [ˌkɔntæk'tiː; ˏkɑntæk`ti] ***n.*** 被接触者(尤指被所谓不明飞行物上的外星球人接触过的人)。

con·tac·tor ['kɔntæktə; `kɑntæktɚ] ***n.***【电】接触器,开关。

con·ta·di·na [ˌkɔntə'diːnə; ˏkɑntə`dinə] ***n.***〔It.〕(*pl.* **-ne** [-nei; -ne]) 农妇。

con·ta·di·no [ˌkəuntə'diːnɔ; ˏkɑntə`dino] ***n.***〔It.〕(*pl.* **-ni** [-niː; -ni]) 农夫。

con·ta·gion [kən'teidʒən; kən`tedʒən] ***n.*** **1.** (接触)传染;传染病;(传染性的)病原体,病毒,病菌。**2.** (思想,风气等)传播,蔓延,流行。**3.** (传播中的)不良影响,歪风邪气。

con·ta·gi·os·i·ty [kənˌtædʒi'ɔsiti; kənˏtædʒɪ`ɑsətɪ] ***n.*** 接触传染率。

con·ta·gious [kən'teidʒəs; kən`tedʒəs] ***a.*** **1.** 传染病的;传染性的;会蔓延的,有感染力的。**2.** 为对付传染病用的。*a* ~ *disease* 传染病。*a* ~ *ward* 传染病病房。**-ly** ***ad.*** **-ness** ***n.***

con·ta·gi·um [kən'teidʒiəm; kən`tedʒɪəm] ***n.*** (*pl.* ***-gia*** [-dʒiə; -dʒɪə])【医】接触传染病原体[病菌,病毒]。

con·tain [kən'tein; kən`ten] ***vt.*** **1.** 含有,包含;能容纳。**2.** 相当于,等于。**3.** 克制,忍耐。**4.**【数】除尽,整除;(边)夹(角),包围(图形)。**5.**【军】牵制,箝制,拦截,包围;遏制。*This box* ~*s soap*. 这只箱子装着肥皂。*I cannot* ~ *my urine*. 小便急得憋不住了。*15* ~*s 3 and 5*. 15 能用 3 和 5 除尽。*4 is* ~*ed in 12 three times*. 12 是 4 的 3 倍。~*ing force*【军】牵制部队。*be* ~*ed between* [*within*] 被包容[夹在]…之间[之中]。—***vi.*** 自制。*She could* ~ *no longer*. 她再也克制不住自己。~ ***oneself*** 克制自己,忍耐(*I could not* ~ *myself for joy*. 我喜欢得忍耐不住)。**-ment**【军】牵制(*the policy of containment* 遏制政策)。

con·tain·er [kən'teinə; kən`tenɚ] ***n*.** **1.** 容器,箱,匣。**2.** 集装箱。~**ship** 集装箱船。~ **shipping** 集装箱运输。**-i·za·tion** ***n*.** (运输)集装箱化。**-ize** ***vt*.** 使用集装箱运输;使集装箱化。

con·tam·i·nant [kən'tæminænt; kən`tæmənənt] ***n*.** 沾染物(质),(使清洁空气等污染的)污染物。

con·tam·i·nate [kən'tæmineit; kən`tæmə͵net] **I** ***vt*.** **1.** 沾染,弄污,弄脏,污染;使受放射性物质影响而无法使用。**2.** 损害,毒害。*a ~d area* 撤毒区。(放射性粒子等的)污染地区。*~d blood* 污血。*~ a laboratory* 使实验室受到放射性物质的影响而无法使用。**II** ***a*.** 〔古〕污染的。

C

con·tam·i·na·tion [kən͵tæmi'neiʃən; kən͵tæmə`neʃən] ***n*.** 污染;污秽,污物;(语言的)交感,感染错合;(文章,故事等的)混合,拼凑。*ideological* ~精神污染。

con·tam·i·na·tive [kən'tæminətiv; kən`tæmɪ͵netɪv] ***a*.** (使)污染的;弄脏了的。

con·tan·go [kən'tæŋgəu; kən`tæŋgo] ***n*.** (*pl*. *~es*) (伦敦股票交易所)交易延期费,延期日息。*a ~ day* 交割限期日。

contd. = continued.

conte [kɔ̃nt; kɔ̃nt] ***n*.** 〔F.〕(极短的、多为情节奇特的)短篇小说,小故事。

con·te ['kəuntei; `konte] ***n*.** 〔It.〕伯爵。

con·temn [kən'tem; kən`tɛm] ***vt*.** 轻蔑,藐视。

contemp. = contemporary.

con·tem·plate ['kɔntempleit; `kɑntəm͵plet] ***vt*.** **1.** 熟视,注视,细心观察。**2.** 熟思,细想,仔细考虑。**3.** 期待,预期;企图,打算。*I'm ~ visiting France*. 我打算上法国去游览。—***vi*.** 沉思,冥想。

con·tem·pla·tion [͵kɔntem'pleiʃən; ͵kɑntəm`pleʃən] ***n*.** **1.** 注视,凝视;静观。**2.** 仔细考虑;沉思,默想,冥想。**3.** 打算,企图,计划;期待,预期。**4.** 【宗】默祷;感知神之存在。**under** [**in**] ~ 计划中的 (*a new building under* ~计划兴建的新楼)。**be lost in** ~ 想得出神。**have** (*sth*.) **in** ~ 企图,筹划。

con·tem·pla·tive ['kɔntempleitiv; `kɑntəm͵pletɪv] ***a*.** **1.** 熟思的;爱默想的,冥想的。**2.** 【宗】默祷的。**be** ~ **of** 注视,细想,仔细考虑。

con·tem·pla·tor ['kɔntempleitə; `kɑntəm͵pletɚ] ***n*.** 冥想者,沉思者,深思熟虑的人。

con·tem·po·ra·ne·i·ty [kən͵tempərə'ni:iti; kən͵tɛmpərə`niətɪ] ***n*.** 同时代(性),同时期(性),同时发生性。

con·tem·po·ra·ne·ous [kən͵tempə'reinjəs; kən͵tɛmpə`renjəs] ***a*.** 同时期的,同时代的;同时发生的。**be** ~ **with** 与…同时代[同时期,同时发生]。**-ly** ***ad*.** **-ness** ***n*.**

con·tem·po·ra·ry [kən'tempərəri; kən`tɛmpə͵rɛrɪ] **I** ***a*.** **1.** 当代的,现代的。**2.** 同年龄的;同时代的。*be ~ with* 和…同时代。*~ literature* 当代文学。*~ opinion* 时论。**II** ***n*.** **1.** 同时代的人,同代者;同年龄的人,同年者。**2.** 同时代的报刊,报刊同业。*our contemporaries* 同时代的人们,当代人物。*our* ~我们同代的报刊,报刊同业。

con·tem·po·rize [kən'tempə͵raiz; kən`tɛmpə͵raɪz] ***vt*.,** ***vi*.** **1.** (使)成同时代。**2.** (使)合乎时代。**3.** (使)同时发生。*This writer has a power of contemporizing himself with the bygone times*. 这位作家能把古代写得栩栩如生。

con·tempt [kən'tem*p*t; kən`tɛm*p*t] ***n*.** **1.** 轻蔑,藐视。**2.** 耻辱,屈辱。**3.** 不管,不顾。*bring into* ~ 污辱。*bring upon oneself the ~ of* 自讨…屈辱。*~ of court* 藐视法庭[法官]罪。*feel ~ for* 对…发生轻蔑心理。*have a ~ for* 对…有轻蔑感。*live in* ~在屈辱中生活。*show ~ for sth*. 对某事表示轻视。*have* [*hold*] ... *in* ~蔑视,看不起,轻视。**fall into** ~ 受辱,丢脸。**in** ~ **of** 看不起,蔑视。

con·tempt·i·ble [kən'tem*p*təbl; kən`tɛm*p*təbl] ***a*.** 可鄙的,可轻视的,下贱的;不值一谈的。**con·tempt·i·bil·i·ty** [-'biliti; -`bɪlətɪ] ***n*.** **-i·bly** ***ad*.** **-ness** ***n*.**

con·temp·tu·ous [kən'tem*p*tjuəs; kən`tɛm*p*tʃʊəs] ***a*.** (表示)轻蔑的;傲慢不恭的。*be ~ of* 瞧不起。*~ air* 傲慢态度。**-ness** ***n*.**

con·tend [kən'tend; kən`tɛnd] ***vi*.** **1.** 争夺,竞争;斗争,战斗。**2.** 争论,争辩。*~ against one's fate* 和自己的命运奋斗。*~ with difficulties* [*an opponent*] 和困难[对手]斗争。*~ with each other for hegemony* 互相争霸。*~ with sb. about a matter* 与某人争辩某事。—***vt*.** (坚决)主张 (*that*)。*It is ~ed that* ... 人们坚持认为…。~ **for** 争取。**have much to** ~ **with** 有不少困难待克服。

con·tent[1] ['kɔntent; `kɑntɛnt] ***n*.** **1.** 容积,容量,含量,【数】容度;收容量。**2.**【哲】内容 (*opp*. form);要旨,真意。**3.** 〔*pl*.〕内容,内含物;(一本书的)目次。*a table of ~s* 目录。*the unity of ~ and form* 内容和形式的统一。*linear ~(s)* 长,长度。*solid* [*cubical*] *~(s)* 容积,体积。*superficial ~(s)* 面积。*a ~ word* 实义词。

con·tent[2] [kən'tent; kən`tɛnt] **I** ***vt*.** 使满意,使满足。*~ oneself with* 自满于,甘于。*Nothing can ~s her*. 她永无厌足之时。**II** ***n*.** **1.** 满足,自得。**2.** 〔*pl*.〕(英国上院)(投)赞成票(者)。**to one's heart's** ~ 尽情,尽量。**III** ***a*.** 〔只作表语用〕**1.** 满足,甘心。**2.** 喜欢,满意;赞成〔英国上院不说 yes, no 用说~, not ~, 下院则说 ay, no〕。**be** ~ **with** 以…为满足。**cry** ~ **with** 满足于。**live** [**die**] ~ 心满意足地过日子[死去]。

con·tent·ed [kən'tentid; kən`tɛntɪd] ***a*.** 满足的,满意的;甘心的。*He is ~ with his lot*. 感到满足。*a superior hard to be* ~难于使之感到满意的上司。*a ~ look* 满意的表情。**be** ~ **to do** 乐意地[甘心情愿地]做…。**-ly** ***ad*.** **-ness** ***n*.**

con·ten·tion [kən'tenʃən; kən`tɛnʃən] ***n*.** **1.** 斗争,竞争,争论。**2.** (争论中的)论点,主张。

con·ten·tious [kən'tenʃəs; kən`tɛnʃəs] ***a*.** **1.** 好争吵的,爱议论的。**2.** 引起争论的,有争论的。*be of a ~ disposition* 好争辩的性格。*~ case* 抗争事件,诉讼事件。*~* ***clause in a treaty*** 条约中有争议的条款。**-ly** ***ad*.**

con·tent·ment [kən'tentmənt; kən`tɛntmənt] ***n*.** **1.** 满意,知足。**2.** 〔古〕令人满意(的事物)。

con·ter·mi·nal [kɔn'tə:minl; kɑn`tɝmɪnəl] ***a*.** = conterminous.

con·ter·mi·nous [kɔn'tə:minəs; kɑn`tɝmənəs] ***a*.** **1.** 具有共同边界的,邻接的。**2.** (时、空意义等)同广度的。**3.** 处于同一范围以内的;美国本部内的〔指阿拉斯加和夏威夷以外的美国国土〕。

con·test **I** ['kɔntest; `kɑntɛst] ***n*.** **1.** 竞争,争论。**2.** 竞赛,比赛。*a musical* ~音乐比赛会。*an oratorical* ~辩论会。*the ~ of strength* 力量的较量。**II** [kən'test; kən`tɛst] ***vt*.** **1.** 争夺(胜败,土地等)。**2.** 争议,辩驳,争论。*~ a prize* 争夺奖赏。*~ an election* 竞选。*~ed election* 竞选;〔美〕有异议的选举。*~ed passage* (文中)有争论的段落[文句]。—***vi*.** 争夺;竞争;争论 (*against*, *with*)。*~ with* [*against*] (*an adversary*) 和(敌方)竞争。

con·test·ant [kən'testənt; kən`tɛstənt] ***n*.** **1.** 〔主美〕竞争者;争论者;竞赛参加者,选手。**2.** (对选举结果)有异议者。

con·tes·ta·tion [͵kɔntes'teiʃən; ͵kɑntɛs`teʃən] ***n*.** 争论,论战;论点;争讼。**in** ~ 争执中的。

con·test·ee [͵kɔntes'ti:; ͵kɑntɛs`ti] ***n*.** 竞争者;竞赛者;〔美〕有争议的候选人。

con·text ['kɔntekst; `kɑntɛkst] ***n*.** **1.** 上下文;文章的前后关系[脉络]。**2.** (事情等的)关节,范围,场合,处境,条件;来龙去脉。*tell the meaning of a word from its* ~

从一个字的上文下推知其字义。***in one*** ～ 在一定场合,在某一范围内。***in the*** ～ ***of*** 在…情况下。***in this*** ～ 关于这一点,在这种场合下。***outside the*** ～ ***of*** 在…之外。

con·tex·tu·al [kən'tekstjuəl; kɑn`tɛkstjʊəl] ***a.*** (按照)上下文的,由(文章)前后关系来看的。*a* ～ *quotation* 原文引用。**-ly** ***ad.***

con·tex·ture [kən'tekstʃə; kən`tɛkstʃɚ] ***n.*** 组织,构造,结构,交织(物);上下文。

con·ti·gu·i·ty [ˌkɔnti'gjuːiti; ˏkɑntə`gjuətɪ] ***n.*** **1.** 接触,接近,邻接。**2.** 〔罕〕连续(物)。

con·tig·u·ous [kən'tigjuəs; kən`tɪgjʊəs] ***a.*** 连接,接近,邻接 (*to*)。*The bridge is* ～ *to the house.* 桥屋相邻。*a* ～ *angles* 【数】邻角,接角。**-ly** ***ad.*** **-ness** ***n.***

con·ti·nence, con·ti·nen·cy ['kɔntinəns(i); `kɑntənəns(ɪ)] ***n.*** **1.** 克己,自制;禁欲,节欲。**2.** 克制力。

con·ti·nent[1] ['kɔntinənt; `kɑntənənt] ***a.*** **1.** 自制的。**2.** 节欲的,贞洁的;禁欲的。

con·ti·nent[2] ['kɔntinənt; `kɑntɪnənt] ***n.*** **1.** 大陆;陆地。**2.** 〔the C-〕欧洲大陆;〔美〕北美洲大陆。

con·ti·nen·tal [ˌkɔnti'nentl; ˏkɑntə`nɛntl] **I** ***a.*** **1.** 大陆的;大陆性的。**2.** 〔C-〕欧洲大陆的,〔C-〕〔美〕(独立战争时)美洲殖民地的。**II** ***n.*** **1.** 欧洲大陆人。**2.** 〔美〕(独立战争中的)美国兵[纸币]。**3.** 〔C-〕〔美俚〕(起源于英国的)欧洲大陆发式。***do not care a*** ～ 〔美俚〕毫无关系。***not worth a*** ～ 〔美俚〕毫无价值。～ **bill** 汇到欧洲大陆的票据〔汇到英国的叫做 a sterling bill〕。～ **breakfast** 包括面包与热饮料的早餐。～ **climate** 大陆性气候。～ **code** 大陆电码〔即莫尔斯电码〕。～ **currency** 欧陆的通货。**C- Divide** (北美)洛矶山脉分水岭。～ **drift** 大陆飘移。～ **facies** 陆相。～ **island** 陆边岛。～ **seating** 不留中间过道的剧场座位。～ **shelf** 【地】陆棚,陆裙,大陆架。～ **slope** 【地】大陆坡。～ **Sunday** 〔常作 C- S-〕娱乐星期日(与英美人星期日作礼拜和休息习俗不同,故名)。**con·ti·nen·tal·i·za·tion** [ˌkɔntiˌnentəlai'zeiʃən; kɑntɪˏnɛntəlaɪ`zeʃən] ***n.*** **1.** 欧洲大陆化。**2.** 【地】大陆成形。

con·tin·gence [kən'tindʒəns; kən`tɪndʒəns] ***n.*** **1.** 接触。**2.** = contingency.

con·tin·gen·cy [kən'tindʒənsi; kən`tɪndʒənsɪ] ***n.*** **1.** 偶然[可能](性)。**2.** (意外)事故;意外事件,临时[可能]事件。**3.** 临时费。*future contingencies* 以后的偶然[可能]事件。***in case of*** ～ = ***in the supposed*** ～ 在万一[可能]的情况下。***not by any possible*** ～ 未必…可能。***provide against contingencies*** 以备万一。～ **fund** 应急费用。～ **reserve** 应急费用储备金。～ **table** 【统】列联表。

con·tin·gent [kən'tindʒənt; kən`tɪndʒənt] **I** ***a.*** **1.** 可能的;偶然的 (*to*); 临时的;附随的。**2.** 因情况而异的,视条件而定的 (*upon*)。**3.** 应急(用)的。～ *fund* 应急费。*Such risks are* ～ *to the trade.* 这种危险对于那种生意是可能有的。**II** ***n.*** **1.** 偶然[可能]事件。**2.** 部分,份额;【军】小分队,分遣队[舰队];代表团。*a crack* ～精锐部队。*reduce ... down to token* ～*s* 把…裁减到象征性的限额。～ **on** [**upon**] 视…而定 (*fee* [*remuneration*] ～ *on success* 成功才给的报酬)。**-ly** ***ad.*** 偶然,意外;看情况;相应地。

con·tin·u·al [kən'tinjuəl; kən`tɪnjʊəl] ***a.*** 不断的,连续的;频繁的。～ *bouts of toothache* 一阵接一阵的牙痛。**-ly** ***ad.***

con·tin·u·ance [kən'tinjuəns; kən`tɪnjʊəns] ***n.*** **1.** 持续;继续,连续。**2.** 继续期间;继续部分,(小说等的)续篇;【法】诉讼延期。*a* ～ *of* [*in*] *prosperity* 长时期的繁荣。*of long* ～长期不断的。

con·tin·u·ant [kən'tinjuənt; kən`tɪnjʊənt] **I** ***a.*** 【语音】连续音的。**II** ***n.*** 连续音〔可拖长发音的 f. v. s. r 等辅音〕;【数】牎夹行列式。

con·tin·u·ate [kən'tinjueit; kən`tɪnjʊet] ***a.*** 〔废〕**1.** 继续的。**2.** 连续的;持久的。

con·tin·u·a·tion [kənˌtinju'eiʃən; kənˏtɪnjʊ`eʃən] ***n.*** **1.** 继续,连续;持续。**2.** 延续,续篇;(线路等的)延长。**3.** 【乐】延留音。**4.** 〔*pl.*〕连接短裤的帮腿,〔俚〕裤子,袜子。*C- follows.* 待续。～ **day** 〔英〕(交易所)交割限期日。～ **school** (成人业余)补习学校;(加拿大边区的)简易中学。

con·tin·u·a·tive [kən'tinjuətiv; kən`tɪnjʊˏetɪv] ***a.*** 连续的;继续的;【语法】接续的。

con·tin·u·a·tor [kən'tinjuˌeitə; kən`tɪnjʊˏetɚ] ***n.*** 〔L.〕继续者,续作者。

con·tin·ue [kən'tinju(ː); kən`tɪnjʊ] ***vi.*** **1.** 连续,继续;延伸。**2.** 仍旧,依旧,留。*The rain* ～*d all day.* 雨终日不停。*The door* ～*d to bang all night.* 这门砰当砰当地响了一晚上。*He* ～*d at his post.* 他留任原职。～ *at school* 留校。～ *in command.* 继续担任指挥。～ *on page 20.* 下接 20 页。—***vt.*** 接续,继续;使留任;延续,延长;【法】使(诉讼)延期。*To be* ～*d.* 待续。～ *a boy at school* 使孩子继续求学。～**d bond** 延期偿付公债。～**d fraction** 连分数。～**d story** (报刊上的)连载小说[故事]。

con·tin·u·ing [kən'tinjuiŋ; kən`tɪnjʊɪŋ] ***a.*** 继续的,连续的,持续的。～ **education** 进修教育。～ **partner** 继续合伙人。

con·ti·nu·i·ty [ˌkɔnti'njuːiti; ˏkɑntə`nuətɪ] ***n.*** **1.** 连续(性),继续;连结,连合,连锁。**2.** 【影】剪辑;分镜头电影剧本;(详细分段的)广播[电视]剧本;广播节目[电视]的情节说明;连环画的故事梗概说明。～ **girl** 〔口〕(影片的)剪辑员。～ **writer** 分镜头电影剧本作者。

con·tin·u·o [kən'tinjuəu; kən`tɪnjʊo] ***n.*** (*pl.* ～*s*) 【乐】(西欧室内音乐中)键盘乐器的低音部;连续的低音伴奏,通奏低音。

con·tin·u·ous [kən'tinjuəs; kən`tɪnjʊəs] ***a.*** **1.** 连续的,继续的,无间断的。**2.** 【植】无节的。*a* ～ *current* 恒(向电)流。～ *fire* 连续射击。～ *rain* 连绵不断的雨。*a* ～ *train of thoughts* 一连串的思想。*a* ～ *wave* (*radar*) 等幅波(雷达)。**-ly** ***ad.***

con·tin·u·um [kən'tinjuəm; kən`tɪnjʊəm] ***n.*** (*pl.* **-ua** [-uə; -jʊə]) 【哲】连续(统一体);【数】连续统,闭联[连续]集;【物】连续区。*space-time* ～时空连续。

contl. = Continental.

cont·line ['kɔntlain; `kɑntlaɪn] ***n.*** (绳子的股与股之间;并排放的桶与桶之间的)空隙。

Cont O 【美军】= Contact Officer.

con·to ['kɔntəu; `kɑnto] ***n.*** (*pl.* ～*s*) 康多〔货币计算名称,在葡萄牙等于 1000 埃斯库多,在巴西等于 1000 克鲁赛罗〕。

con·tort [kən'tɔːt; kən`tɔrt] ***vt.*** 扭,扭歪,拧弯;曲解(文义等)。～ *one's features* 扭歪着脸〔如由于疼痛、忧愁〕。

con·tor·tion [kən'tɔːʃən; kən`tɔrʃən] ***n.*** 扭弯,扭歪;曲解;【医】捩转,转位,脱节。**-ist** ***n.*** **1.** 柔软杂技演员。**2.** (语义的)曲解者。

con·tour ['kɔntuə; `kɑntʊɚ] **I** ***n.*** **1.** 外形,轮廓;周线,轮廓线。**2.** 等高线,恒值线;【电视】等场强线(= ～-line)。**3.** 概略,大要;形势。**4.** 【电】回路。*the irregular* ～ *of the coast* 曲折的海岸线。*the* ～*s of things* 情势。**II** ***a.*** **1.** 与轮廓相合的。**2.** (表示[循着])等高线的。**III** ***vt.*** **1.** 描画…的轮廓;画…的等高[等值]线。**2.** 顺等高线(作业)〔如开沟,筑路等〕。～ **chasing** 【空】低空飞行。～ **map** 等高线(地)图,曲线地图。～ **planting** 等高造林。～ **plowing** 等高耕作。

contr. = **1.** contract(ed). **2.** contraction. **3.** contractor. **4.** contrary. **5.** control.

con·tra ['kɔntrə; `kɑntrə] **I** ***n.*** **1.** 反对(意见),反对票。**2.** 【会计】对方〔尤指贷方〕。*pros and* ～*s* 赞成与反对。**II** ***ad.*** 反对地。**III** ***prep.*** 对于。～ *credit* [*debit*] 对于

贷方[借方]。

contra- *pref*. 反,逆,抗,对应。

con·tra·band [ˈkɔntrəbænd; ˋkɑntrə͵bænd] **I** *n*. **1.** 非法买卖[运输];走私。**2.** (战时)禁运品(=～ of war);走私品,私货。**3.** 【美史】南北战争时私逃投奔[被秘密送往]北军的黑人。**II** *a*. 禁运的,非法的。**-ist** *n*. 买卖走私品者;走私者。

con·tra·bass [ˈkɔntrəˈbeis; ˋkɑntrə͵bes] **I** *n*. 【乐】倍低音乐器[提琴等]。**II** *a*. 倍低音的,最低音的。

con·tra·bas·soon [ˌkɔntrəbəˈsuːn; ͵kɑntrəbæˋsun] *n*. 【乐】低音大管[巴松管]。

C

con·tra·cept [ˈkɔntrəsept; ˋkɑntrəsɛpt] *vt*. 使避孕。

con·tra·cep·tion [ˌkɔntrəˈsepʃən; ͵kɑntrəˋsɛpʃən] *n*. 避孕(法)。

con·tra·cep·tive [ˌkɔntrəˈseptiv; ͵kɑntrəˋsɛptɪv] **I** *a*. 避孕(用)的。**II** *n*. 避孕药物[用品]。

con·tra·clock·wise [ˌkɔntrəˈklɔkwaiz; ͵kɑntrəˋklɑk-͵waɪz] *a*., *ad*. 反时针方向的[地]。

con·tract[1] [ˈkɔntrækt; ˋkɑntrækt] **I** *n*. **1.** 契约,合同。**2.** 婚约。**3.** 承包(合约)。**4.** 【法】契约法。**5.** 【牌戏】定约,合约桥牌。**6.** 〔主英方〕月(季)票。**7.** 〔美〕工作,事情。**8.** 〔美俚〕小恩小惠,贿赂。*It's a bit of a* ～. 〔美〕这是相当难的工作。*a bare* ～ 无条件契约。*a simple* [*parole*] ～暂约。*a verbal* [*oral*] ～口头约定。*be built by* ～包工建造。*draw up a* ～拟定合同。～ *drawing* 承包施工图。～ *system* 承包制。～ *work* 包工。***make*** [***enter into***] ***a*** ～ ***with*** 与…订约。***put out to*** ～ 包出去,给人承包。**II** [kənˈtrækt; kənˋtrækt] *vt*. **1.** 订(约),立(合同);约定。**2.** 订婚〔通例用被动语态〕,把…许配给 (*to*)。**3.** 结交(朋友等)。**4.** 招,患(病),染(恶习)。**5.** 负债。～*ed a bad cold* 得了重伤风。*be* ～*ed to* 是…的未婚夫[妻]。～ *an alliance* (*with*) 结盟。～ *a marriage with* 与…订婚。～ *friendship with* 与…交朋友。～ ***oneself out of*** 订立契约免除…,照契约不必…。—*vi*. 订约;订婚;承包。～*ing parties* 订约双方当事人。*High Contracting Parties* [*powers*] 缔约国。～ *for labour and material* 包工包料。～ **bridge** 合约桥牌。～ **miner** 按工计酬的矿工。

con·tract[2] [kənˈtrækt; kənˋtrækt] *vt*., *vi*. **1.** 收缩,紧缩;(使)皱起。**2.** (使)缩短;(使)缩小。**3.** 【语法】缩略,缩约。～ *one's brows* 皱拢眉头。～*ing muscles* 收缩肌。

con·tract·ed [kənˈtræktid; kənˋtræktɪd] *a*. **1.** 收缩了的,缩小的;缩略的;(心胸,思想等)狭小的;贫困的。**2.** 订过(婚)约的。**-ly** *ad*. **-ness** *n*.

con·tract·i·ble [kənˈtræktəbl; kənˋtræktəbḷ] *a*. 会缩的,可缩的。

con·trac·tile [kənˈtræktail; kənˋtræktḷ] *a*. 会缩的,有收缩性的。～ *force* 收缩力。

con·trac·til·i·ty [ˌkɔntrækˈtiliti; ͵kɑntrækˋtɪlətɪ] *n*. 收缩性;收缩力。

con·trac·tion [kənˈtrækʃən; kənˋtrækʃən] *n*. **1.** 缩短,收缩;【医】挛缩。**2.** (开支等)缩减;收敛,狭窄;缩度。**3.** 【语法】缩略〔如将 never 略成 ne'er, do not 略成 don't 等〕;略体,缩写〔如 department 缩为 dep't〕。**4.** 得病;习染;招致;(负债等的)陷入。

con·trac·tive [kənˈtræktiv; kənˋtræktɪv] *a*. 收缩(性)的。

con·trac·tor[1] [kənˈtræktə; kənˋtræktɚ] *n*. 立约人,承包人。

con·trac·tor[2] [kənˈtræktə; kənˋtræktɚ] *n*. 【解】收缩肌。

con·trac·tu·al [kənˈtræktjuəl; kənˋtræktʃuəl] *a*. 契约上(规定)的。**-ly** *ad*.

con·trac·ture [kənˈtræktʃə; kənˋtræktʃɚ] *n*. 【医】挛缩。

con·tra·dance [ˈkɔntrədɑːns; ˋkɑntrə͵dæns] *n*. = contredanse.

con·tra·dict [kɔntrəˈdikt; ͵kɑntrəˋdɪkt] *vt*. **1.** 反驳,反对,抗辩;否认。**2.** 与…矛盾,与…抵触。～ *the rumour* 辟谣。～ *oneself* 自相矛盾。—*vi*. 反驳。**-able** *a*. 可反驳的。**-or** *n*. 反驳者;相矛盾的人;抵触者。

con·tra·dic·tion [ˌkɔntrəˈdikʃən; ͵kɑntrəˋdɪkʃən] *n*. **1.** 反驳,抗辩;否定,否认。**2.** 矛盾,抵触,相反。*a* ～ *in terms* 语词矛盾〔如 *a square circle* 一个正方的圆形〕。

con·tra·dic·tious [ˌkɔntrəˈdikʃəs; ͵kɑntrəˋdɪkʃəs] *a*. **1.** 相抵触[矛盾]的。**2.** 爱争辩的。**-ly** *ad*. **-ness** *n*.

con·tra·dic·to·ri·ly [ˌkɔntrəˈdiktərili; kɑntrə-ˋdɪktərɪlɪ] *ad*. 反驳;相反,矛盾。

con·tra·dic·to·ry [ˌkɔntrəˈdiktəri; ͵kɑntrəˋdɪktərɪ] **I** *a*. **1.** 反驳的,反对的,抗辩的。**2.** 矛盾的,相反的。**II** *n*. 对立的一方,矛盾的一方;【逻】正反对(命题)。

con·tra·dis·tinc·tion [ˌkɔntrədisˈtiŋkʃən; ͵kɑntrədɪ-ˋstɪŋkʃən] *n*. 对照的区别,对比的区别,对比。***in*** ～ ***to*** [***from***] 与…对比;与…截然不同。

con·tra·dis·tin·guish [ˌkɔntrədisˈtiŋgwiʃ; ͵kɑntrədɪ-ˋstɪŋgwɪʃ] *vt*. 通过比较来区别,通过对照来区别,对比。

con·tra·fac·tu·al [ˌkɔntrəˈfæktjuəl; ͵kɑntrəˋfæktʃʊəl] *a*. 违反事实的。*a* ～ *conditional* 违反事实的假设。

con·trail [ˈkɔntreil; ˋkɑntrel] *n*. 【空】(飞机、导弹等航迹中云状的)凝结尾流[迹],凝迹;逆增[转换]轨迹。

con·tra·in·di·cate [ˌkɔntrəˈindikeit; ͵kɑntrəˋɪndə-͵ket] *vt*. 【医】禁忌(某种疗法等)。

con·tra·in·di·ca·tion [ˌkɔntrəˌindiˈkeiʃən; ͵kɑntrə-͵ɪndɪˋkeʃən] *n*. 【医】(表明不宜采用某种疗法的)禁忌征象。**-dic·a·tive** *a*.

con·tra·lat·er·al [ˌkɔntrəˈlætərəl; ͵kɑntrəˋlætərəl] *a*. 【解】对侧的。

con·tral·to [kənˈtræltəu; kənˋtrælto] **I** *n*. (*pl*. ～**s**, **-ti** [-tiː; -ti]) 【乐】女低音;女低音歌手[角色]。**II** *a*. 女低音的。

con·tra-mis·sile [ˈkɔntrəˈmisail; ˋkɑntrəˋmɪsaɪl] *n*. 反导弹导弹。

con·tra·pose [ˈkɔntrəpəuz; ˋkɑntrə͵poz] *vt*. **1.** 以…针对着;使对照 (*to*)。**2.** 【逻】换(命题)的质位。

con·tra·po·si·tion [ˌkɔntrəpəˈziʃən; ͵kɑntrəpəˋzɪʃən] *n*. **1.** 对置;对照;对位。**2.** 【逻】换质换位法〔例:若"A 是 B",则可推演为"非 B 就非 A"〕。***in*** ～ ***to*** [***with***] 跟,位置相反。

con·tra·pos·i·tive [ˌkɔntrəˈpɔzətiv; ͵kɑntrəˋpɑzətɪv] *a*. 对照的;针对的。

con·tra·prop [ˈkɔntrəprɔp; ˋkɑntrəprɑp] *n*. 【空】同轴成相对方向旋转的推进器。

con·trap·tion [kənˈtræpʃən; kənˋtræpʃən] *n*. 〔口〕新设计,新发明;〔蔑〕样子古怪的新发明(物品)。

con·tra·pun·tal [ˌkɔntrəˈpʌntl; ͵kɑntrəˋpʌntḷ] *a*. 【乐】对位(法)的。

con·tra·pun·tist [ˈkɔntrəpʌntist; ͵kɑntrəˋpʌntɪst] *n*. 【乐】擅长对位法的作曲家。

con·trar·i·ant [kənˈtreəriənt; kənˋtrɛrɪənt] *a*. 反对的,对立的,敌对的。

con·tra·ri·e·ty [ˌkɔntrəˈraiəti; ͵kɑntrəˋraɪətɪ] *n*. **1.** 反对,矛盾,矛盾性。**2.** 〔*pl*.〕相反物;矛盾物;对立面。

con·tra·ri·ly [ˈkɔntrərili; ˋkɑntrɛrəlɪ] *ad*. **1.** 反之,相反地,反对地,逆。**2.** [kənˈtreərili; kənˋtrɛrɪlɪ] 〔口〕故意闹别扭。

con·tra·ri·ness [ˈkɔntrərinis; ˋkɑntrərɪnɪs] *n*. **1.** 对立,相反,反对。**2.** 〔口〕乖张,别扭。

con·trar·i·ous [kənˈtreəriəs; kənˋtrɛrɪəs] *a*. 〔罕〕相反的〔尤指别扭的,乖张的〕。

con·tra·ri·wise [ˈkɔntrəriwaiz; ˋkɑntrɛrɪ͵waɪz] *ad*. 反之,相反地,反对地。

con·tra·ry [ˈkɔntrəri; ˋkɑntrɛrɪ] **I** *a*. **1.** 反对的,相反的;格格不入的,矛盾的,对抗的。**2.** 〔口〕 [kənˈtreəri; kənˋtrɛrɪ] 乖张的,别扭的,执拗的。**3.** 【植】直角的。*He* *looked the ~ way*. 他把脸转了过去。*be ~ to expectations* 出乎意外。~ *child* 不听话的孩子。~ *wind* 逆风。**II** *ad*. 反对地,相反地。~ **to** 跟…相反[相违背](~ *to his expectation* 跟他的预料相反。*act ~ to nature* 违反自然[常情])。**III** *n*. **1.** 反对;矛盾。**2.** 〔*pl*.〕对立物;【逻】反对令题[名词]。*Quite the ~*. 正相反。*He is neither tall nor the ~*. 他不高不矮。**by contraries** 正反对地,相反地,出乎预料地(*Dreams go by contraries*. 梦是相反的〔旧时一种圆梦的说法〕。*interpret by contraries* 相反地解释)。**on the ~** 反之,正相反。**to the ~** 反对地,和这相反的(*a rumour to the ~* 完全相反的谣言。*There is no evidence to the ~*. 没有反证。*Unless I hear to the ~*. 除非我听说不是那样。*I know nothing to the ~*. 我不知道有和这相反的情况)。

con·trast [ˈkɔntræst; ˋkɑntræst] **I** *n*. **1.** 对照,对比;(对照中的)差异。**2.** 对立面,对照物;【摄】反差。**3.** 【修】对照法。*What a ~ between them!* 他们之间真是大不相同! ~ *colours* 反衬色。**for the sake of ~** 为了对比[反衬]。**gain by ~** 对比之下显出优点。**in ~ with** 和…成对比;和…大不相同。**present [form] a striking ~ to** 和…成显著的对比。**II** [kənˈtræst; kənˋtræst] *vt*. 使对照,使对比。*C- birds with fishes*. 拿鸟和鱼对比。—*vi*. (和…)形成对照;(和…)成很好的对照(*with*)。~ **finely with ...** 和…对比起来更加鲜明。

con·trast·y [kənˈtræsti; kənˋtræstɪ] *a*. (尤指照相负片)调子硬的,明暗对比强的,反差强的。

con·trate [ˈkɔntreit; ˋkɑntret] *a*. 【机】横齿的。

con·tra·test [ˈkɔntrətest; ˋkɑntrətɛst] *a*. 对比试验的。

con·tra·val·la·tion [ˌkɔntrəvæˈleiʃən; ˏkɑntrəvəˋleʃən] *n*. 【军】(防止被围者突围的)对垒(工事)。

con·tra·vene [ˌkɔntrəˈviːn; ˏkɑntrəˋvin] *vt*. **1.** 违反,违背,犯(法等)。**2.** 否定,反驳,推翻(论据等)。**3.** 背叛(主义),抵触,与…不相容。

con·tra·ven·tion [ˌkɔntrəˈvenʃən; ˏkɑntrəˋvɛnʃən] *n*. **1.** 违反,违背。**2.** 〔Scot.〕【法】违警罪。**3.** 否定,反驳。**in ~ of** (*the law*) 违(法)。

con·tre·coup [ˈkɔntrəˌkuː, ˈkəun-; ˋkɑntrəˏku, ˋkon-] *n*. 【医】对侧反激伤〔如头部正面受冲击,后脑勺撞在墙上而伤在后脑部〕。

con·tre·danse [ˈkɔntrədɑːns; ˋkɑntrəˏdɑns] *n*. **1.** 对列舞〔一种农村舞〕。**2.** 对列舞曲。

con·tre·temps [ˈkɔ̃ːntrətɑ̃ːŋ; ˋkɔ̃trətɑ̃ŋ] *n*. 〔F.〕 **1.** 令人窘困的(意外)事故;意料不到的困难[阻碍]。**2.** 【乐】节调,约调,切分法。

contrib. = contributor.

con·trib·ute [kənˈtribju(ː)t; kənˋtrɪbjʊt] *vt*. **1.** 捐赠(款项)。**2.** 投稿(给杂志等)。**3.** 贡献出。*Everybody ~s his ideas and his strength*. 人人想办法,个个出力量。~ (*money*) *to* 捐(款)给。~ (*an article*) *to* (*a magazine*) 投寄(一篇论文)给(某杂志)。—*vi*. **1.** 出力,作出贡献。**2.** 捐款,捐献。**3.** 投稿。~ *to* [*towards*] 捐助,帮助,贡献,出力;给…投稿。*contributing factors* 促成因素。*contributing editor* 特约编辑[撰稿人]。

con·tri·bu·tion [ˌkɔntriˈbjuːʃən; ˏkɑntrəˋbjuʃən] *n*. **1.** 贡献,赠送;捐赠,捐助。**2.** 投稿,来稿。**3.** 捐款,献金;献品,补助品。**4.** 【军】(向占领地人民征收的)军税;【法】分担(额)。**lay under ~** 强制派捐,勒派军税。**make a ~ to [towards]** 捐赠;贡献给。

con·trib·u·tive [kənˈtribjutiv; kənˋtrɪbjʊtɪv] *a*. **1.** 捐赠的;贡献的,出资[分担]的。**2.** 有帮助的,增进…的。

con·trib·u·tor [kənˈtribju(ː)tə; kənˋtrɪbj(ʊ)tɚ] *n*. **1.** 贡献者。**2.** 捐助者,赠送者。**3.** 投稿人。

con·trib·u·to·ry [kənˈtribjutəri; kənˋtrɪbjʊtorɪ] *a*. **1.** 捐助的;参加力量的;有贡献的。**2.** 有助于(*to*)。*various ~ factors* 各种起配合[促进]作用的因素。~ *negligence* 【法】(车祸等中)受伤一方本身的粗心。

con·trite [ˈkɔntrait; ˋkɑntraɪt] *a*. **1.** 悔罪的,悔悟的,悔恨的。**2.** 表示悔罪[忏悔]而作出的。**-ly** *ad*. **-ness** *n*.

con·tri·tion [kənˈtriʃən; kənˋtrɪʃən] *n*. 悔罪,悔悟,悔恨。

con·triv·a·ble [kənˈtraivəbl; kənˋtraɪvəbl̩] *a*. 可设计的;可发明的;可设法做到的。

con·triv·ance [kənˈtraivəns; kənˋtraɪvəns] *n*. **1.** 发明,设计(方案),计划。**2.** 发明[设计]的才能;机巧,巧思。**3.** 奇巧的制作物,新发明,装置,设备。**4.** 计策,奸计,诡计。**5.** 人为的修饰,巧饰。*an automatic ~* 自动装置。

con·trive [kənˈtraiv; kənˋtraɪv] *vt*. **1.** 发明,创制,设计。**2.** 图谋;企图。**3.** 设法做到。**4.** 挖空心思(而弄巧成拙);周到反而弄得(不利等)。~ *a new kind of tape recorder* 设计出一种新型录音机。~ *a robber* 企图抢劫。~ *to do it well* 设法做好这件事。*He ~d to make a mess of the whole thing*. 他挖空心思反而把事情全盘弄糟了。*He ~d to persuade me*. 他千方百计想说服我。*He ~d to get himself disliked*. 他费了许多苦心反而弄得大家都讨厌他了。—*vi*. **1.** 妥为料理;设法[巧妙]应付(*to do*)〔尤指治家,料理家务〕。**2.** 设计,图谋。*I can ~ without meat*. 我没有肉也能凑合(吃这顿饭)。**cut and ~** 妥善地安排[应付]。

con·trived [kənˈtraivd; kənˋtraɪvd] *a*. 使用机巧的;人为的;非天然的。

con·triv·er [kənˈtraivə; kənˋtraɪvɚ] *n*. **1.** 发明者,设计者,创制者;筹谋者。**2.** 善于安排[应付]的人;善于持家的人。

con·trol [kənˈtrəul; kənˋtrol] **I** *n*. **1.** 支配,管理,管制,统制,控制;监督。**2.** 抑制(力);压制,节制,拘束;【农】防治。**3.** 检查;核对;(试验中的)对照(处理)。**4.** (记录等的)留底;底本;存根。**5.** 【空】驾驶;〔*pl*.〕操纵装置。**6.** (飞机的)修理站;(车赛等的)慢行地区;(同上地区内车身等的)检查站。**7.** 【棒球】制球能力。*remote [distance] ~* 远距离操纵,遥控。*homing ~* 【火箭】导引;自导。*traffic ~* 交通管制。*wage ~* 工资管理。*price ~* 物价控制。*birth ~* 生育控制,节(制生)育。*automatic ~* 自动控制(装置)。~ *of light* 灯火管制。**beyond ~** 无法控制。**in ~ (of)** 由…控制(住),管理。**get out of ~** 失掉控制(能力),控制不住。**get under ~** 抑制,治理(水患),防止(火灾)(*The fire was got under ~*. 火已压下去了)。**have ~ of [over] oneself** 控制[克制]自己。**have no ~ over** 不能控制,无控制力。**keep under ~** 抑制,控制,统制。**lose ~ of** 失却对…的控制力,控制不住。**out of ~** 失去控制。**under the ~ of** 受管制[管理、支配],在…管辖下的。**without ~** 不受管制地,无拘束地。**II** *vt*. **1.** 管理,统制;节制,抑制,控制;监督;防治。**2.** 核对,核实,对照;检查。~ *oneself* 自制。~ **board** 仪表板。~ **chart** (工厂中的产品质量)控制图。~ **company** 【经】控股公司。~ **dam** 节流闸。~ **experiment** 受控[对照]实验。~ **figures** (计划中的)控制数字。~ **lever [stick]** 【空】操纵杆。~ **line** 【林】防火线。~ **room** (潜艇的)调度室,操纵室。~ **stick** (飞机的)操纵杆。~ **top** 【军】桅楼指挥所。~ **tower** 【空】机场中的起落指挥塔。

con·trol·la·ble [kənˈtrəuləbl; kənˋtroləbl̩] *a*. 可支配[管理]的;可抑制[控制]的,可操纵的。

con·trol·ler [kənˈtrəulə; kənˋtrolɚ] *n*. **1.** 管理人,主管人。**2.** (会计的)主计人,检查员;【英】(特指宫廷、海军等的)出纳官〔常作 comptroller〕。**3.** (电车的)驾驶器;【机】控制器;操纵器;【电】整流器;【船】(锚链的)制链器。~ **general** 主计长。

con·tro·ver·sial [ˌkɔntrəˈvəːʃəl; ˏkɑntrəˋvɝʃəl] *a*. **1.** (有)争论的,被争论的。**2.** 好争论的。*a ~ issue* 有争论的问题。**-ism** *n*. 争论癖。**-ist** *n*. 争论者,有异议者。

con·tro·ver·sy [ˈkɔntrəvəːsi; ˋkɑntrəˏvɝsɪ] *n*. (尤指纸上的)争论,辩论,论战(*with*; *about*; *between*)。*a barren ~* 无结果[无益]的争论。*be in a ~ with sb.*

C

和某人争论中。***beyond*** [***without***] ～ 无争论余地。***enter into a*** ～ ***with*** 和…论争。

con·tro·vert [ˈkɔntrəvəːt; ˋkɑntrə͵vɝt] ***vt.*** 争论;辩驳,反驳,攻击。—***vi.*** 参加争论。**-er**, **-ist** ***n.*** 争论者;辩驳者。

con·tro·vert·i·ble [ˈkɔntrəvəːtəbl; ͵kɑntrəˋvɝtəbl̩] ***a.*** 可争论的;可辩驳的。

con·tu·ma·cious [ˌkɔntju(ː)ˈmeiʃəs; ͵kɑntjʊˋmeʃəs] ***a.*** **1.** 抗拒的,拒不服从的,顽抗的。**2.**【法】违抗法院命令的,蓄意藐视法庭的。

con·tu·ma·cy [ˈkɔntjuməsi; ˋkɑntjʊməsɪ] ***n.*** **1.** 抗拒,顽抗,不服从。**2.**【法】违抗法院命令,蓄意藐视法庭。

con·tu·me·li·ous [ˌkɔntju(ː)ˈmiːljəs; ͵kɑntjʊˋmiliəs] ***a.*** 傲慢无礼的,轻侮的。

con·tume·ly [ˈkɔntju(ː)mli; ˋkɑntjʊmlɪ] ***n.*** 傲慢无礼;轻侮,侮辱。

con·tuse [kənˈtjuːz; kənˋtjuz] ***vt.*** 打伤,挫伤,撞伤,(尤指)使受暗伤,使受内伤。

con·tu·sion [kənˈtjuːʒən; kənˋtjuʒən] ***n.*** 殴打;伤害;受(内)伤;【医】打伤,挫伤。

co·nun·drum [kəˈnʌndrəm; kəˋnʌndrəm] ***n.*** (字)谜,谜语;难解的问题。

con·ur·ba·tion [ˌkɔnəˈbeiʃən; ͵kɑnəˋbeʃən] ***n.*** (由中心大城市及卫星城镇构成的)集合城市。

CONUS = Continental United States 美国大陆。

con·va·lesce [ˌkɔnvəˈles; ͵kɑnvəˋlɛs] ***vi.*** (病后逐渐)复元,恢复,康复。

con·va·les·cence [ˌkɔnvəˈlesns; ͵kɑnvəˋlɛsn̩s] ***n.*** **1.** 康复,恢复。**2.** 康复期的,恢复期的。

con·va·les·cent [ˌkɔnvəˈlesnt; ͵kɑnvəˋlɛsn̩t] **I** ***a.*** **1.** 病后渐愈的。**2.** 康复期的。*become* ～逐渐复元。**II** ***n.*** 康复期病人。*a* ～ *hospital* 疗养院,休养所。

con·vect [kənˈvekt; kənˋvɛkt] ***vi.*** 对流传热。—***vt.*** 使(热空气)对流循环;借对流传(热)。

con·vec·tion [kənˈvekʃən; kənˋvɛkʃən] ***n.*** **1.** 传送。**2.**【物】运流,环流;【气】对流,上升气流。～ **current** 对流;【电】运流。～ **light** 集中光束。

con·vec·tive [kənˈvektiv; kənˋvɛktɪv] ***a.*** **1.** 有传送力[运输力]的,传送性的。**2.**【物】对流的。

con·vec·tor [kənˈvektə; kənˋvɛktɚ] ***n.*** 对流式热空气循环加热器。

con·ven·a·ble [kənˈviːnəbl; kənˋvinəbl̩] ***a.*** 可召集的,可召唤的。

con·ve·nance [ˈkɔ̃ːŋvinɑ̃ːns; ˋkɑnvə͵nɑns] ***n.*** 〔F.〕习俗,惯例;〔*pl.*〕仪式,礼仪。

con·vene [kənˈviːn; kənˋvin] ***vt.*** 召集。—***vi.*** 聚集,集合。

con·ven·ience [kənˈviːnjəns; kənˋvinjəns] ***n.*** **1.** 便利,方便(机会)。**2.**〔*pl.*〕(生活上的)便利设备。**3.**〔英〕厕所。**4.**〔古〕公共马车。*a marriage of* ～有某种谋利目的的婚姻。*await sb.'s* ～等某人方便时。*a* ～ *outlet*【电】万能插头。***as a matter of*** ～ 为了方便。***at one's*** (***own***) ～顺便;得便时,方便的时候。***at your earliest*** ～ 务请从速,有便即请。***for*** ～(') ***sake*** 为了便利起见。***for the*** ～ ***of*** 为…的方便起见。***make a*** ～ ***of*** (*sb.*)〔口〕利用(某人)(*He is simply making a* ～ *of me.* 他不过是利用我罢了)。***suit sb.'s*** ～ 对某人便利(*if it suits your* ～若对你方便)。***suit*** [***consult***] ***one's own*** ～ 只图一己方便。～ **food** 方便(速食)食品〔指罐头食物,方便(速食)面条等〕。

con·ven·ient [kənˈviːnjənt; kənˋvinjənt] ***a.*** **1.** 便利的,合宜的。**2.**〔英方,美〕附近的,不远的。*if it is* ～ *to you* 若你方便。*place* ～ *for bathing* 适宜游泳的地方。**-ly** ***ad.***

con·vent [ˈkɔnvənt; ˋkɑnvent] ***n.*** 修(道)女团;女修道院。***go into a*** ～ 去做修女。

con·ven·ti·cle [kənˈventikl; kənˋventɪkl̩] ***n.*** **1.** 集会;【宗】秘密集会。**2.**【英史】集会(场所);〔蔑〕独立教派的小教堂;(苏格兰长老派的)野祷(场所)。

con·ven·tion [kənˈvenʃən; kənˋvɛnʃən] ***n.*** **1.** 集会,会议;【英史】(1660,1688 年的)(非由英王召集的)非常议会;〔美〕(政党等的)全国代表大会,〔集合词〕(出席的)代表们。**2.** (国际间的)公约,协定。**3.** (社会)习俗,惯例,常规;【牌】(玩牌者公认的)规定〔出牌或叫牌法〕。*stage* ～*s* 舞台惯例[程式]。*break away from* ～打破常规[习俗]。***the National C-*** **1.**【法史】国民议会〔1792—1795〕。**2.**【英史】宪章党员大会。**3.**〔美〕(政党决定总统候选人的)全国代表大会。～ **money** (两国以上协定发行的)同本位货币。

con·ven·tion·al [kənˈvenʃənl; kənˋvɛnʃənl̩] ***a.*** **1.** 因袭的,传统的。**2.** 习用的;平常的,常规的;形式上的。**3.** 约定的,协定的;会议的。*a* ～ *ceremonial* 常礼,惯例。*a* ～ *greeting* 常规的问候。～ *morality* 相沿成习的道德。*the* ～ 相沿成习的事物,传统。～ *neutrality* 约定中立,义务中立。*the* ～ *wisdom* 公众的一般看法,群众意见,公众态度。*a* ～ *phrase* 常套语。～ **duties** 协定关税。～ **tariffs** 协定税率。～ **war** [**weapon**] (不使用核武器的)常规战争[武器]。～ **wisdom** 公众意见;普遍的看法。**-ism** ***n.*** 依从俗例;因袭主义;惯例,习惯做法,常规旧套;陈言套语;【数】约定论。**-ist** ***n.*** 拘泥习俗[遵守惯例]的人。**-ly** ***ad.***

con·ven·tion·al·i·ty [kənˌvenʃəˈnæliti; kən͵vɛnʃəˋnælətɪ] ***n.*** **1.** 因袭(性)。**2.** 传统;常套;惯例,习俗。

con·ven·tion·al·ize [kənˈvenʃənəlaiz; kənˋvɛnʃənl̩͵aɪz] ***vt.*** 使照惯例,使习俗化,使按传统形式。～*d flowers* (照传统形式画成的)定型的花。

con·ven·tion·eer [kənˌvenʃəˈniə; kən͵vɛnʃəˋnɪɚ] ***n.*** 到会者;〔美〕(代表大会的)出席代表。

con·ven·tu·al [kənˈventjuəl; kənˋvɛntʃʊəl] **I** ***a.*** **1.** 女修道院(似)的。**2.**〔C-〕圣芳济会修士(团)的。**II** ***n.*** 修(道)女;〔C-〕圣芳济会修士。

con·verge [kənˈvəːdʒ; kənˋvɝdʒ] ***vi.*** **1.** 会聚,集中(于一点或一处);辐辏。**2.**【物、数】收敛。*converging fire* 集中射击。—***vt.*** 使聚合[集中]于一点,使辐辏(*on*; *upon*)。**-r** ***n.*** 〔美口〕擅长精细推理的人。

con·ver·gence, **con·ver·gen·cy** [kənˈvəːdʒəns, -dʒənsi; kənˋvɝdʒəns, -dʒənsɪ] ***n.*** **1.** 聚合,会聚,辐辏,汇合。**2.** 集合点;【数、物】收敛;【生】趋同(现象)。

con·ver·gent [kənˈvəːdʒənt; kənˋvɝdʒənt] **I** ***a.*** **1.** 渐集一点的,会聚性的;包围集中的。**2.**【数】收敛的。**II** ***n.*** 【数】收敛子;渐近分数。～ **evolution** 趋同进化。～ **lens** 会聚透镜。～ **pencil**【物】会聚光线锥。～ **series**【数】收敛级数。

con·verg·er [kənˈvəːdʒə; kənˋvɝdʒɚ] ***n.*** 【心】长于逻辑推理的人。

con·vers·a·ble [kənˈvəːsəbl; kənˋvɝsəbl̩] ***a.*** 健谈的;谈得来的,适于闲聊的。

con·ver·sance, **con·ver·san·cy** [kənˈvəːsəns, ˈkɔnvə-, -si; kənˋvɝsəns, ˋkɑnvɚ-, -sɪ] ***n.*** **1.** 亲近,接近。**2.** 熟悉,通晓,精通。

con·ver·sant [kənˈvəːsənt; kənˋvɝsənt] ***a.*** **1.** 亲近的,有交情的。**2.** 精通…的,熟悉…的。**3.** 有关的 (*in*; *about*; *with*)。***be*** ～ ***with*** 精通;和…有交情。

con·ver·sa·tion [ˌkɔnvəˈseiʃən; ͵kɑnvɚˋseʃən] ***n.*** **1.** 会话,谈话;会谈 (*on*; *about*);(人与计算机的)人机对话。**2.** 接交,交往,交际。**3.** 交媾,性交。～ *goes on* [*stagnates*, *languishes*, *stops*, *revives*] 会谈正在进行[不畅,冷落,停止,重新活跃]。*drop* [*break off*, *interrupt*, *close*, *resume*] ～停止[中止,打断,结束,又开始]谈话。*a topic of* ～话题。*criminal* ～通奸。***enter into*** ～ ***with*** 和…谈起来。***hold*** [***have***] ***a*** ～ ***with*** 和…交谈。～ **piece** **1.** 一种有情节的人物画。**2.** 可作话题的东西,题材。～ **pit** 谈话间(指客厅等内供谈话用的专设场所)。

con·ver·sa·tion·al [ˌkɔnvəˈseiʃənl; ˌkɑnvəˋseʃənḷ] *a.* 1. 会话的,谈话的。2. 健谈的,善应酬的。

con·ver·sa·tion(·al)·ist [ˌkɔnvəˈseiʃən(əl)ist; ˌkɑnvəˋseʃənɪst] *n.* 1. 谈话者。2. 健谈者,会应酬的人。

con·ver·sa·zi·o·ne [ˌkɔnvəˌsætsiˈəuni; ˌkɑnvəˌsɑtsɪˋonɪ] *n.* (*pl.* ~*s*, 〔It.〕 ***-ni*** [-niː; -nɪ]) 〔It.〕(学术性)座谈会。

con·verse[1] [ˈkɔnvəːs; kənˋvɝs] *vi.*, *n.* 1. 〔书〕谈话(*with*; *on*; *upon*); (人与计算机)谈话。2. 〔古〕交际;接交;交往;性交。

con·verse[2] [kənˈvəːs; ˋkɑnvɝs] **I** *n.* 【逻】倒转命题,逆命题;逆叙(= ~ statement)。【数】逆,反。**II** *a.* 倒转的,逆(转)的。~ **proposition** 【逻】逆命题。~ **statement** 逆叙〔把 if I were you 说作 if you were I 等〕。**-ly** *ad.*

con·ver·sion [kənˈvəʃən; kənˋvɝʃən] *n.* 1. 变换,转化,转换;换算,换位。2. (意见、信仰等的)改变〔特指改信基督教〕;(车身,设备等的)改装,改造。3. 【法】变更;强占;【数】换算法;【逻】换位(法);【心】(心理冲突转化为生理病态的)变形表现,变形发泄;【军】改换装备;改装;【商】兑换;更换(字据等)。4. 【橄榄球】触地得分,(篮球)罚球得分。~ **parity** 兑换平价。~ **pig** 炼钢生铁。~ **table** 换算表。~ **unit** 【化】反应设备。

con·vert [kənˈvəːt; kənˋvɝt] **I** *vt.* 1. 变换,转换,转化;更改,改造,改装。2. 使改变信仰[意见、立场],使弃恶从善;使转变;使回心转意。3. 【法】强占。4. 【逻】转换,换位;【商】兑换,更换。5. 【橄榄球】使触地得分。~ *sugar into alcohol* 把糖变为酒精。~ *notes into gold* 把纸币兑换为黄金。~*ed goods* 加工织物。*be* [*get*] ~*ed* 悔改。~ (*sb.*) *to* 使(某人)改信(某教,尤指改信基督教)。~*ed cruiser* 改装巡洋舰。~*ed timber* 锯制材。**II** [ˈkɔnvəːt; ˋkɑnvɝt] *n.* 改宗者,皈依者,改变信仰者。*make a* ~ *of sb.* 使某人转变[改变]信仰。

con·vert·er [kənˈvəːtə; kənˋvɝtɚ] *n.* 1. 使转变[改变信仰]的人。2. 改装者,改装品。3. 【冶】炼钢炉,吹风转炉;【电,无】换流器,变压器;变频器;【自】变换器;密码翻译[编制]机。~ **pig** 转炉(用)生铁。

con·vert·i·bil·i·ty [kənˌvəːtəˈbiliti; kənˌvɝtəˋbɪlətɪ] *n.* 可改变,可变换;可兑换,可转化性,可转变性。

con·vert·i·ble [kənˈvəːtəbl; kənˋvɝtəbḷ] **I** *a.* 1. 可转换的;可转变的;可改装的;可兑换的。2. (汽车)车篷可折起[取掉]的。**II** *n.* 1. 可改变的事物。2. 敞篷车〔有活动折篷的汽车〕。~ **husbandry** 【农】轮作。~ **note** [**paper**] 可兑换纸币[证券]。~ **terms** 同义语,可代换用语。**-bly** *ad.*

con·vert·i·plane [kənˈvəːtiplein; kənˋvɝtəplen] *n.* 【空】垂直起落换向式飞机,平直两用飞机。

con·vert·ite [ˈkɔnvəˌtait; ˋkɑnvəˌtaɪt] *n.* 〔古〕= convert.

con·vex [ˈkɔnˈveks; ˋkɑnˋvɛks] **I** *a.* 中凸的,凸圆的,凸面的。**II** *n.* 凸状,凸面,凸圆体。~ *glasses* 远视眼镜,老花眼镜。~ **lens** 凸透镜。~ **mirror** 凸面镜。**-ly** *ad.*

con·vex·i·ty [kɔnˈveksiti; kɑnˋvɛksətɪ] *n.* 凸度;凸状;凸面(体)。

con·vex·o-con·cave [kɔnˈveksəuˈkɔnkeiv; kənˋvɛkso-ˋkɑnkev] *a.* 一面凸一面凹的,凸凹(形)的。

con·vex·o-con·vex [kɔnˈveksəuˈkɔnveks; kənˋvɛkso-ˋkɑnˋvɛks] *a.* 双凸面的。

con·vex·o-plane [kɔnˈveksəuˈplein; kənˋvɛksoˋplen] *a.* 一面凸一面平的,凸平形的。

con·vey [kənˈvei; kənˋve] *vt.* 1. 输送;搬运,转运,运输。2. 传达,传递;传导;传播;通知,通报;表达(意义)。3. 【法】让与,转让(财产等)。4. 〔古〕偷。5. 〔废〕秘密带走。~ *goods in a lorry* 用卡车运货。*Words fail to* ~ *our grateful feelings.* 我们的感激之情非言语所能表达。*Please* ~ *to him my best wishes.* 请向他转达我最良好的祝愿。**-able** *a.*

con·vey·ance [kənˈveiəns; kənˋveəns] *n.* 1. 运输;输送。2. 运输用具(车船等),输送带,搬运器。3. 【法】(不动产的)让与;让与证据,卖据。~ *by land* [*water*] 陆路[水路]运输。*means of* ~交通[运输]工具。*a push-plate* ~无限连锁式传送工具(运煤用)。

con·vey·anc·er [kənˈveiənsə; kənˋveənsɚ] *n.* 1. 运输者;传达者。2. 【法】不动产让与(证书)经办人。

con·vey·anc·ing [kənˈveiənsiŋ; kənˋveənsɪŋ] *n.* (律师的)财产转让业务;让与证书制作(业);不动产让与手续。

con·vey·er, con·vey·or [kənˈveiə; kənˋveɚ] *n.* 1. 运送者,传达者;传送器,运送机。2. 让与人。*a* ~ *belt* 传送带。*a green* ~轮饲牧场。*a coal* ~送煤机。

con·vict **I** [kənˈvikt; kənˋvɪkt] *vt.* 1. 证明…有罪,宣告…有罪,定…的罪。2. 使知罪,使认罪。*be* ~*ed of arson* 被判决为纵火犯。~ (*sb.*) *of* (*murder*) 判决(某人)有(杀人)罪。*a person* ~*ed of sin* 自知有罪的人。~*ed prisoner* 已定罪人。**II** [ˈkɔnvikt; ˋkɑnvɪkt] *n.* 1. 罪犯。2. (长期服刑的)囚犯。3. 〔美俚〕马戏团的斑马。*ex-* ~ 有前科的罪犯,惯犯。~ **goods** 服劳役囚犯生产的物品。~ **prison** 徒刑监狱。~ **system** 徒刑制度;流刑制度。

con·vic·tion [kənˈvikʃən; kənˋvɪkʃən] *n.* 1. 有罪判决,定罪。2. 确信,坚信。3. 服罪,【神】悔罪。***be open to*** ~ 能够[愿意]接受正当理由,愿意服理。***carry*** ~ (话,论点等)令人信服。***in the full*** ~ ***that*** 充分信服…。***listen with*** ~ (虚心)倾听。***under*** ~ 【宗】悔悟中。

con·vic·tive [kənˈviktiv; kənˋvɪktɪv] *a.* 有说服力的,定罪的。**-ly** *ad.*

con·vince [kənˈvins; kənˋvɪns] *vt.* 1. 使确信,说服,使承认。2. 使悔悟;使认错[罪]。~ *people by sound arguments* 以理服人。***be*** ~***d of*** [***that***] 确信,深知。***be fully*** ~***d*** 充分相信。~ (*sb.*) ***of*** [***that***] 使(人)承认[信服]。~ ***oneself of*** 充分弄明白。

con·vin·ci·ble [kənˈvinsəbl; kənˋvɪnsəbḷ] *a.* 可说服的,可使信服的。*a* ~ *person* 知情达理的人。

con·vinc·ing [kənˈvinsiŋ; kənˋvɪnsɪŋ] *a.* 使人信服的,有说服力的,令人心悦诚服的。*a* ~ *argument* 有说服力的论点。**-ly** *ad.* **-ness** *n.*

con·viv·i·al [kənˈviviəl; kənˋvɪvɪəl] *a.* 1. 宴会的,欢宴的;欢乐的,快活的。2. 爱(和人)吃喝玩乐的。*a* ~ *meeting* [*gathering*] 联欢会,欢乐的宴会。**-ist** *n.* 爱吃喝玩乐的人。**-ly** *ad.*

con·viv·i·al·i·ty [kənˌviviˈæliti; kənˌvɪvɪˋælətɪ] *n.* 1. 宴乐;欢宴。2. 爱(和人)吃喝玩乐的性格。

con·vo·ca·tion [ˌkɔnvəˈkeiʃən; ˌkɑnvəˋkeʃən] *n.* 1. (会议的)召集;集会。2. 〔美〕(圣公会)主教区会议[管区];(牛津大学等的)评议会;(加拿大某些大学的)学位授与典礼。*to address a* ~寄发开会通知。

con·voke [kənˈvəuk; kənˋvok] *vt.* 召集(会议等),召集…开会。~ *Parliament* 召开国会。

con·vo·lute [ˈkɔnvəljuːt; ˋkɑnvəˌlut] **I** *a.* 1. 【动、植】包卷形的,回旋状的。2. 【医】迂曲的,蟠曲的。3. 迂回的,盘旋形的。**II** *n.* 包旋体。**III** *vt.*, *vi.* 盘旋,包卷。**-d** *a.* = 1. convolute. 2. 复杂的,难解的(~ *convoluted horns* 回旋状的(羊)角。~ *arguments* 绕弯子的论证,难解的论点。★作形容词用时,多用 convoluted 而不常用 convolute)。

con·vo·lu·tion [ˌkɔnvəˈljuːʃən; ˌkɑnvəˋluʃən] *n.* 1. 回旋,卷旋,盘旋;旋圈,卷褶;涡流。2. 【动,植】包卷,旋绕;【解】回转(部);脑回;【数】褶[卷]积;褶合式;【统】结合式。

con·volve [kənˈvɔlv; kənˋvɑlv] *vi.*, *vt.* 卷绕,缠绕。

con·vol·vu·lus [kənˈvɔlvjuləs; kənˋvɑlvjələs] *n.* (*pl.* ***-li*** [-lai; -laɪ], ~***es***) 【植】旋花属植物〔如旋花,牵牛花等〕。

con·voy **I** [ˈkɔnvɔi; ˋkɑnvɔɪ] *n.* 1. (战时的)护航队。2.

C

被护送者。3. 护送。*a ~ of transport ships* 有护航的运输船队。*under* ~在护航[护送]下。*under the ~ of troops* 在军队护送下。II [kən'vɔi; kən`vɔɪ] *vt*. 护航,护送;〔古〕引导(宾客等);伴送。*a merchant ship ~ed by a destroyer*. 由驱逐舰护航的一艘商船。

con·vulse [kən'vʌls; kən`vʌls] *vt*. 1. 使(地等)震动;震撼[震动](全国等)。2. 〔常用被动语态〕使痉挛;使大笑不止。*be ~d* 惊厥;(小儿)惊风。~ ***sb. with laughter*** 令人捧腹,使人绝倒。***be ~d with laughter*** 捧腹大笑。

con·vul·sion [kən'vʌlʃən; kən`vʌlʃən] *n*. 1. 震动,激动;动乱;【地】激变,灾变。2. 【医】〔常 *pl*.〕惊厥;搐搦;惊风。3. 〔*pl*.〕捧腹大笑。~ ***of the whole kingdom*** 〔英〕全国鼎沸。***have ~s*** 惊厥。***throw into ~s*** 使惊厥;使捧腹大笑。

C

con·vul·sion·a·ry [kən'vʌlʃənəri; kən`vʌlʃənərɪ] I *a*. 1. 剧烈震动的;灾变性的;激动(性)的。2. 惊厥的。II *n*. 惊厥者。

con·vul·sive [kən'vʌlsiv; kən`vʌlsɪv] *a*. 痉挛性的;惊厥的;骤发的;震动性的。*a ~ effort* 拼死努力。~ *laughter* 捧腹大笑。~ *rage* 震怒。**-ly** *ad*. **-ness** *n*.

co·ny, co·ney ['kəuni; `konɪ] *n*. 1. 兔;兔皮。2. (在《圣经》中提到的)蹄兔。3. 【动】狗鱼。4. 笨伯;受骗者。~-**catcher** 骗子。

coo[1] [ku:; ku] I *vi*., *vt*. (鸽等)咕咕地叫;低声软语地谈(情话),温柔亲切地说。~ *one's words* 轻轻地说话。***bill and*** ~亲热地抚爱[亲吻]。II *n*. 鸽叫声。

coo[2] [ku:; ku] *int*. (伦敦话)哦! 呀! 〔表示惊异〕。

cooch [ku:tʃ; kutʃ] *n*. 〔美俚〕(色情的)扭肚舞。~ *dancer* 扭肚舞舞女。

coo·coo ['ku:ku; `kuku] *a*. 〔俚〕狂乱的;愚蠢的,傻的(= cuckoo)。

coo·ee, coo·ey ['ku:i:; `kuɪ] I *n*., *int*. 喂! 〔澳洲本地人的招呼声〕。II *vi*. 叫一声喂!

coo·er ['ku(:)ə; `kuɚ] *n*. 鸽,语言柔和而可爱的人,甜言蜜语的人。

cook [kuk; kʊk] I *vt*. 1. 烹调,煮,烧(食物)。2. 〔口〕虚报,窜改(账目等),捏造(报告等)。3. 〔美俚〕损坏,破坏。4. 〔英俚〕(热得)使发昏,使筋疲力竭。5. 〔俚〕给…上电刑。~ *food* 做饭。*be ~ed alive in the tropics* 在热带地方热得像活活被火烤似的。~ *accounts* 伪造账目。—*vi*. 1. (食物)在煮[烧]着。2. 做饭,做菜;当厨师。3. 〔美口〕发生。*What's ~ing at the station?* 车站上出了什么事? *The dinner is ~ing*. 晚餐正在做。~ ***off*** (火药包、炮弹等因过热而)走火。~ ***sb.'s goose*** 〔俚〕破坏某人的计划,使某人彻底失败[完蛋]。~ ***up*** 捏造;炮制;〔美〕计划,图谋(~ *up a report* 捏造报告)。~ ***well*** 容易煮(*Eggs ~ well*. 鸡蛋容易煮熟)。***sb.'s goose is ~ed*** 某人的计划[前途,名誉等]已完蛋。II *n*. 1. 厨子;厨娘。2. (工业、技术上的)煮制过程。***a cold*** ~ 〔俚〕做殡仪馆生意的人。***Too many ~s spoil the broth***. 厨子多了煮坏汤。~**book** 〔美〕1. 烹调全书,食谱(大全)。2. 详细说明书。~-**chill** *n*. (食物的)先煮熟后速冻。~**house** 厨房;船内厨房;露天厨房。~**house yarns** 忽然流传起来的谣言。~-**in** 烹饪讲座。~ **off** 烹饪比赛。~**out** 野餐郊游。~**room** = ~house. ~**shop** 菜馆;饭店。~**stove** 〔美〕烹调用火[电]炉。~**top** 1. 炉灶口。2. (山等的)平顶。

Cook(e) [kuk; kʊk] *n*. 库克〔姓氏〕。

cooked [kukt; kʊkt] *a*. 1. 煮得…的。2. (报告等)捏造的。3. 〔俚〕(热得)要死的。4. (跑得人)筋疲力尽的。5. 〔俚〕喝醉了的。6. 【影】(胶片)露光过久的。

cook·er ['kukə; `kʊkɚ] *n*. 1. 炊具,蒸煮器。2. 〔口〕菜果(适于做菜的果类)。3. 虚报账目的人;造谣者,说谎者。*a gas* ~煤气灶。*a pressure* ~高压锅。

cook·er·y ['kukəri; `kʊkərɪ] *n*. 1. 烹调术。2. 〔美〕厨房。~-**book** 〔英〕= cookbook.

cook·ie ['kuki; `kʊkɪ] *n*. 1. 〔Scot.〕甜面包;〔美〕(家常)小甜饼;饼干。2. 〔俚〕厨娘;厨师助手。3. 〔口〕(对心爱的人的称呼)亲爱的。4. 〔俚〕精明能干的家伙;吸引人的年轻妇女。5. 〔*pl*.〕〔俚〕吃到肚里的食物。*a tough* ~ 硬汉子。*shoot one's cookies* 〔美俚〕呕吐。

cook·ing ['kukiŋ; `kʊkɪŋ] I *a*. 烹调用的(水果、锅、炉等)。II *n*. 烹调(法)。~ **top** 立柜式四眼煤气(或电)灶。

Cook Islands *n*. 库克群岛〔南太平洋〕。

cook·up ['kukʌp; `kʊkʌp] *n*. 临时拼凑的东西;杜撰物。

cook·y ['kuki; `kʊkɪ] *n*. = cookie.

cool [ku:l; kul] I *a*. 1. 凉,凉爽。2. 沉着的,冷静的,慎重的。3. 冷淡的,薄情的;不动感情的,冷酷的。4. 〔口〕(价格)不夸大的;实价的;(数额)不打折扣的,整整。5. 【猎】(动物臭迹)淡薄的,些微的,一点点的。6. (颜色)素净的,冷色的〔指以蓝、绿光谱段为基调的〕。7. 〔美俚〕极好的,绝妙的,"酷"。8. 轻描淡写的,不作充分说明的。9. 冷藏着的;有冷藏设施的。10. 厚脸皮的,无礼的。11. (音乐、绘画等)超然冷漠的,强调理性的。12. 未被放射性污染的。*a ~ customer* [*card*, *fish*, *hand*] (不动感情,不怕羞的)厚皮脸〔指男人〕。*a ~ head* 头脑冷静(的人)。*a ~ matting* 凉爽的席子。*a ~ thousand pounds* 整整一千镑。*a real ~ comic* 一个十分出色的喜剧演员。~ *chamber* 冷藏室。~ *cheek* 厚脸皮。~ *frock* 单薄的外衣。~ *tankard* 冷饮。~ ***as a cucumber*** 冷静沉着。***get*** ~ 冷了;凉了。***keep*** ~ 冷(藏)着;乘凉;沉住气。***Keep*** ~! 别慌。***leave sb.*** ~ 不能引起某人兴趣。***play it*** ~ 〔美俚〕压住感情,冷静处理[对待]。***remain*** ~ 保持冷静,很沉着。II *vt*. 1. 使冷却,冷一冷,冰一冰(酒)。2. 使消除放射性,使减少放射性。3. 使镇定,使冷静,止(怒)。—*vi*. 1. 凉了,冷了;变冷却。2. (怒气)平息;变冷静,沉着。~ ***down*** 冷起来,凉了;冷却;冷静下来。~ ***it*** 〔俚〕沉着;轻松冷静地[从容不迫地]做。~ ***off*** 〔口〕沉着,变冷静,平静下来。~ ***one's coppers*** 喝解醉饮料。~ ***one's heels*** 久等。III *n*. 1. 冷气;凉爽的空气;凉快的地方[时间、东西等]。2. 平静,冷静,镇定。3. 〔美〕一种较保守的爵士音乐。*in the ~ (of the evening)* (晚)凉时候。~-**hunter** 〔美〕新潮追求者,求"酷"族。**-ly** *ad*. **-ness** *n*.

cool·ant ['ku:lənt; `kulənt] *n*. 【机】冷却剂;(减热的)润滑剂。

cool·er ['ku:lə; `kulɚ] *n*. 1. 冷却器;冰箱。2. 冷却剂;冷饮,清凉饮料。3. 〔美俚〕监狱;单人监房;〔军俚〕兵营仓库。***put in the*** ~ 〔口〕搁置起来,撂到一边。

cool-head·ed ['ku:l'hedid; `kul`hɛdɪd] *a*. 头脑冷静的,沉着的。

coo·li·bah ['ku:libə; `kulɪbə] *n*. 澳洲橡胶树。

Coo·lidge ['ku:lidʒ; `kulɪdʒ] *n*. 1. 柯立芝〔姓氏〕。2. **Calvin**~ 卡尔文·柯立芝〔1872—1933,美国第三十任总统,任期为1923—1929〕。

coo·lie, coo·ly ['ku:li; `kulɪ] *n*. 苦力(特指东方的廉价劳动力)。

cool·ing ['ku:liŋ; `kulɪŋ] *n*., *a*. 冷却(的)。~ **cup** 冷却杯。~ **down** 【体】准备活动。~ **drink** 冷饮。~ **fins** 【机】散热片。~ **room** 冷却室。~-**off** *a*. 可使头脑冷静的,缓和情绪的(~-***off period*** 发生劳资纠纷时的缓和期〔在此期间不罢工,先行协商〕)。

cool·ish ['ku:liʃ; `kulɪʃ] *a*. 微冷的;觉得冷的,有冷意的。

cool·ly[1] ['ku:lli; `kullɪ] *ad*. 冷,沉着,冷静;冷淡;厚着脸皮。

cool·ly[2] ['ku:li; `kulɪ] *n*. = coulee.

coolth [ku:lθ; kulθ] *n*. 〔谑〕= coolness.

coom [ku:m; kum] *n*. 煤灰,煤烟;〔Scot.〕煤;〔方〕锯屑。

coomb(e) [ku:m, kəum; kum, kom] *n*. 深谷,小山沟;(三面皆山的)无川峡谷;海边小溪崖。

coon [ku:n; kun] *n*. 1. 【美动】浣熊(= racoon)。2. 〔口〕猾头,机灵鬼。3. 〔美俚〕黑人〔对黑人的蔑称〕。*an old* ~老奸巨猾的人。***a ~'s age*** 很长一段时日,好多年。~ ***skinners*** 〔美〕乡下佬。***go the whole*** ~ 〔美〕彻底干。

(*a*) *gone* ～ 没希望的人,不可救药的家伙。*hunt* [*skin*] *the same old* ～〔美俚〕老是干同一工作。*tree the* ～〔美口〕追究问题的原因;穷追。～ **cat**【动】蓬尾浣熊(= cacomistle)。～**skin** *n*., *a*. 浣熊皮(制的)。～ **songs** (美国南部感伤的)黑人歌曲。

coon·can [ˈkuːnkæn; ˋkunˏkæn] *n*. 碰对牌戏〔一种用两副纸牌玩的牌戏〕。

coon·tie [ˈkuːnti; ˋkuntɪ] *n*.【植】全绿叶泽米。

coon·y [ˈkuːni; ˋkunɪ] *a*. (浣熊一样)狡猾的,机灵的。

coop [kuːp; kup] **I** *n*. (养鸡兔等的)笼[栏,小舍];〔英〕捕鱼笼;牢狱。*fly the* ～〔美俚〕逃走。**II** *vt*. **1**. 把(家禽)关进笼子[棚]。**2**. 把…关起来 (*in*; *up*)。—*vi*.〔美俚〕(值夜班警察)在警车内打瞌睡。

co-op [ˈkəuɔp; ˋkoɑp]〔口〕= co-operative store [society].

co-op. = cooperative.

Coop·er [ˈkuːpə; ˋkupɚ] *n*. 库珀〔姓氏〕。

coop·er [ˈkuːpə; ˋkupɚ] **I** *n*. **1**. 桶匠。**2**. (装桶贩卖的)酒商。**3**. (由葡萄酒和烈啤酒合成的)混合黑啤酒。**4**. (北海上的)小贩船。*dry* [*wet*] ～ 干品用[液体用]桶类制造者。*white* ～ (普通)桶匠。**II** *vt*. **1**. 修理(桶类)。**2**. 把…装入桶内。**3**.〔口〕修饰外表 (*up*)。—*vi*. 做桶匠。

coop·er·age [ˈkuːpəridʒ; ˋkupərɪdʒ] *n*. 木桶业;桶匠工作;桶匠工钱;桶铺。

co·op·er·ant [kəuˈɔpərənt; koˋɑpərənt] *a*. 合作的。

co-op·er·ate [kəuˈɔpəreit; koˋɑpəˏret] *vi*. 合作;协作;互助。～ *with* (*sb*.) *for* (*a purpose*) 为(某目的)和(某人)合作。～ *with* (*sb*.) *in* (*a work*) 和(某人)合作(某事)。

co·op·er·a·tion [kəuˌɔpəˈreiʃən; koˏɑpəˋreʃən] *n*. 合作;协作;互助。*a consumers'* [*consumptive*] ～消费合作。*a producers'* [*productive*] ～生产合作。*in* ～ *with* 和…合作[协作,共同]。

co·op·er·a·tive [kəuˈɔpərətiv; koˋɑpəˏretɪv] **I** *a*. **1**. 合作的,协作的,共同的。**2**. 合作社的。**3**.〔美〕(大学文科)有关[包含]各种实习活动的。*a* ～ *society* 合作社。*a* ～ *store* 合作商店。**II** *n*. 合作社。**-ly** *ad*. **-ness** *n*.

co·op·er·a·tor [kəuˈɔpəreitə; koˋɑpəretɚ] *n*. 合作[协作]者;合作社社员。

coop·er·y [ˈkuːpəri; ˋkupərɪ] *n*. 箍桶活;桶店;桶器。

co·opt [kəuˈɔpt; koˋɑpt] *vt*. **1**. (原有成员)增选(新成员)。**2**. 选用,任命。**3**. 吸取,罗致。**-ion**, **-a·tion** *n*. **-a·tive** *a*.

co·or·di·nal [kəuˈɔːdinl; koˋɔrdn̩əl] *a*.【植、动】同目[属]的。

co·or·di·nate [kəuˈɔːdinit; koˋɔrdnɪt] **I** *a*. **1**. 同等的,同位的;协调的,配合的;【语法】对等的。**2**.【数】坐标的。**3**. (图书、资料编目)交叉索引查阅法的。**II** *n*. **1**. 同等者,同等物;同位。**2**.〔*pl*.〕【数】坐标;(图书、资料编目的)交叉索引。**III** [kəuˈɔːdineit; koˋɔrdnˏet] *vt*. 使成同等;使成同位;使配合;使(各部分)动作协调,调整。～ *with each other* 互助策应[配合]。～ **bond** [**link**]【化】配位键。～ **clause**【语法】对等子句。～ **valence**【化】配位价。～ **paper** 坐标纸。～ **system** 坐标系。

co·or·di·na·tion [kəuˌɔːdiˈneiʃən; koˏɔrdnˋeʃən] *n*. 同等,同位,对等;同等关系;调整;配合;协作,协调;【生理】(器官等的)共同调济,协调(一致);【物,化】配位;【语法】并列(关系)。*the close* ～ *between two partners* 两个合伙人之间的紧密配合。

co·or·di·na·tive [kəuˈɔːdinətiv; koˋɔrdnˏetɪv] *a*. (使)同等的,同位的;协调的;配合的;整合的;【语法】对等的。

co·or·di·na·tor [kəuˈɔːdineitə; koˋɔrdəˏnetɚ] *n*. **1**. 同等的人;同等物;配合者[物];整合物;【生理】共同调济器(官)。**2**. 协调人。**3**.【语法】对等连接词。

coot [kuːt; kut] *n*. **1**.【鸟】水鸭,大鹬;〔美〕黑鸭。**2**.〔俚、方,美〕笨人,傻瓜。(*as*) *bald as a* ～ 头发光秃。(*as*) *stupid as a* ～ 笨拙。

coot·ie [ˈkuːti; ˋkutɪ] *n*.〔美军俚〕虱子。

co-own·er [kəuˈəunə; koˋonɚ] *n*.【法】共有人。

Cop. = **1**. Copenhagen. **2**. Copernican. **3**. Coptic.

cop[1] [kɔp; kɑp] *n*. **1**. 纺锤状线团,管纱;纡子。**2**.〔英方〕(山)顶;(鸟)冠毛。

cop[2] [kɔp; kɑp] *n*.〔俚〕警察。*a plain clothes* ～便衣警察。～ **shop**〔口〕警察局;派出所。

cop[3] [kɔp; kɑp] **I** (*-pp-*) *vt*.〔俚〕**1**. 捕捉,逮捕(犯人)。**2**. 取胜,赢得。**3**. 偷。～ *a plea* 自首,招认(希望减轻刑罚)。～ *big*〔美俚〕胜利,赢得;巧中。～ *hours*〔美俚〕优胜,获胜。～ *it*〔学俚〕挨骂,遭罚;被杀死。～ *out*〔美俚〕**1**. 自首(并告发同犯)。**2**. 反悔,失言,躲赖;逃避(义务);放弃,妥协;退出;离开。～ *the curtain*【美剧】谢幕。**II** *n*.〔俚〕抓获,捕捉。*a fair* ～ 不小的胜利。*no* ～, *not much* ～ 没有什么价值[用处]。～**-out** *n*. **1**. 逃路。**2**. 躲避。**3**. 逃跑者。

co·pa·cet·ic [ˌkəupəˈsetik; ˏkopəˋsetɪk] *a*.〔美俚〕极好的;令人十分满意的;完全正确的。

co·pai·ba, **co·pai·va** [kəuˈpaibə, -və; koˋpaɪbə, -və] *n*.【医】苦配巴香脂;苦配巴香胶。

co·pal [ˈkəupəl; ˋkopəl] *n*. 硬树脂;柯巴脂。

co·palm [ˈkəuˌpɑːm; ˋkoˏpɑm] *n*. **1**.【植】香枫。**2**. 香枫脂膏。

co·par·ce·nar·y [ˌkəuˈpɑːsinəri; koˋpɑrsn̩ˏɛrɪ] **I** *n*.【法】共同继承(的土地);共同所有(的土地)。**II** *a*. 共同所有[继承]的。

co·parce·ner [ˈkəuˈpɑːsinə; koˋpɑrsn̩ɚ] *n*. (土地的)共同继承人。

co·part·ner [ˈkəuˈpɑːtnə; koˋpɑrtnɚ] *n*. 合作者;(有平等权利的)合伙人。**-ship** *n*. 合作;损益分担;合伙人(身份)。

co·pa·set·ic [ˌkəupəˈsetik; kopəˋsetɪk] *a*. = copacetic.

cope[1] [kəup; kop] *vi*. **1**. 竞争,抗衡,对抗 (*with*)。**2**. 对付,应付;克服,善处(困难等) (*with*)。**3**.【古】接触 (*with*)。*He was scarcely able to* ～ *with the situation*. 他几乎不知道如何去应付这个局面。—*vt*. **1**.〔英口〕应付。**2**.〔废〕遇见,接触。

cope[2] [kəup; kop] **I** *n*. **1**. (教士等举行宗教仪式等时穿的)斗篷式长袍,罩袍;(剑桥大学神学博士举行仪式时穿的)肩衣。**2**. 笼罩物;夜幕;苍穹。**3**. 铸钟模型顶部;【建】顶盖,墙帽。*under the* ～ *of night* 在夜幕的遮盖下。～ *in steel beam*【建】削梁。*under the* ～ *of heaven* 普天之下。**II** *vt*. **1**. 给…穿上教士罩袍。**2**. 加盖于,覆盖,给…砌上顶盖[墙帽]。**3**.【铸】修型。*walls* ～*d with broken bits of china* 顶部覆盖有碎瓷片的墙。—*vi*. 突出如墙帽 (*over*)。

co·peck [ˈkəupek; ˋkopɛk] *n*. 戈比〔旧俄及前苏联货币,值1/100卢布〕;〔美俚〕一元银币。

Co·pen·hag·en [ˌkəupənˈheigən; ˏkopənˋhegən] *n*. 哥本哈根〔丹麦首都〕。**-i·an** *n*. 哥本哈根人。

co·pe·pod [ˈkəupiˌpɔd; ˋkopəˏpɑd] *n*.【动】桡脚亚纲的动物。

Co·pep·o·da [kəuˈpepədə; koˋpepədə] *n*.〔*pl*.〕【动】桡脚亚纲。

cop·er[1] [ˈkəupə; ˋkopɚ] *n*.〔英方〕马贩子。

cop·er[2] [ˈkəupə; ˋkopɚ] *n*. (北海的)烟酒贩卖船。

Co·per·ni·can [kəuˈpəːnikən; koˋpɝnɪkən] *a*. 哥白尼(学说)的。～ **theory** 太阳中心说,地动说。

Co·per·ni·cus [kəuˈpəːnikəs; koˋpɝnɪkəs], **Nicolaus** 哥白尼〔1473—1543,波兰天文学家〕。

co·pe·set·ic [ˌkəupəˈsetik; ˏkopəˋsetɪk] *a*. = copacetic.

cope·stone [ˈkəupstəun; ˋkopˏston] *n*. **1**. 墙帽,盖顶石。**2**. 盖面活;收尾工作,尾活。*put the* ～ *on sb.'s embarrassment* 使人在窘迫时更加窘迫。

cop·i·er [ˈkɔpiə; ˋkɑpɪɚ] *n*. **1**. 誊写[复写]员;抄录者。

C

2. 仿效者；剽窃者。3. 誊写笔；复印机。

co·pi·lot [ˈkəupailət; koˋpaɪlət] *n.* 【空】副驾驶员；自动驾驶仪。

cop·ing [ˈkəupiŋ; ˋkopɪŋ] *n.* (墙等的)顶盖。～ **saw** 钢丝锯。～**-stone** *n.* = copestone.

co·pi·ous [ˈkəupjəs; ˋkopiəs] *a.* 1. 丰富的；大量的。2. 冗长的。*a* ～ *harvest* 丰收。～ *material* 丰富的材料。～ *notes* 详注。*a* ～ *speaker* 多言者。*a* ～ *style* 冗长的文体。～ *tears* 大量的眼泪。*a* ～ *vocabulary* 丰富的词汇。*a* ～ *writer* 多产作家。**-ly** *ad.* **-ness** *n.*

co·pla·nar [kəuˈpleinə; koˋplenɚ] *a.* 【数】共面的。

Cop·land [ˈkɔplənd, ˈkəuplənd; ˋkaplənd, ˋkoplənd] *n.* 科普兰〔姓氏〕。

co·pol·y·mer [kəuˈpɔlimə; koˋpaləmɚ] *n.* 【化】共聚物。

co·pol·y·mer·ize [kəuˈpɔliməraiz; koˋpaləmərˏaɪz] *vt.*, *vi.* 【化】(使)异分子聚合。

co·pol·y·mer·i·za·tion [kəuˌpɔliməraiˈzeiʃən; koˏpaləməraɪˋzeʃən] *n.* 【化】共聚合(作用)。

cop·per[1] [ˈkɔpə; ˋkapɚ] **I** *n.* 1. 铜；紫铜。2. 铜币，铜钱，〔*pl.*〕零钱。3. 铜器；铜罐，铜壶，铜锅；铜管；铜制品。4. (紫)铜色。5. 〔*pl.*〕〔俚〕喉咙。～ *nitrate* 硝酸铜。*a few* ～*s* 几枚铜币。***cool*** [***clear***] ***one's*** ～ 喝点解酒饮料润润喉(见 cool 条)。***have hot*** ～***s***〔俚〕喝大量酒后觉得喉咙干燥发烧。**II** *a.* 1. 铜(制)的。2. (紫)铜色的。～ *pipe* 铜管。～ *plate* [*sheet*] 铜板。—*vt.* 用铜板[铜皮]盖[包]。～ **beech**【植】铜红山毛榉。～ **bit** 铜焊夹。～**bottom** *vt.* 用铜板包(船底等)。～**-bottomed** *a.* 铜板包底的(船)；航海经久的，结实的。～ **captain**〔英〕假船长，冒充的大人物。～ **facing** 镀铜。～**-head**【动】铜斑蛇；〔C-〕【美史】南北战争时同情南方的北方人。～**hearted** *a.*〔美〕说谎的，靠不住的。～ **Indian** (北美)印第安人。～**nose** (红鼻子)酒鬼。～**plate** 1. *n.* 铜板；铜版(印刷)(*write like* ～ *plate* 写得非常工整)。2. *a.* 用铜板雕刻的；用铜版印刷的；(印刷似地)美丽的(字体)。～**skin** *n.* = redskin. ～**smith** 铜匠；铜器制造人。**C- State**〔美〕威斯康星(**Wisconsin**)州的别号。～**sulphate** [**vitriol**] 胆矾，硫酸铜。～ **sulphide** 硫化铜。～**top**〔俚〕红毛人。～ **wire** 铜丝。～**-worm** 蛀船虫；衣裳蛀虫；癣虫。**-ish** [ˈkɔpəriʃ; ˋkapərɪʃ] *a.* 有点像[含]铜的。**-ize** [ˈkɔpəraiz; ˋkapərˏaɪz] *vt.* 镀铜于…；用铜处理。

cop·per[2] [ˈkɔpə; ˋkapɚ] *n.*〔英俚〕警察。

cop·per·as [ˈkɔpərəs; ˋkapərəs] *n.* 【化】(水)绿矾；皂矾，呈天然结晶状态的硫酸亚铁。

Cop·per·belt [ˈkɔpəbelt; ˋkapəˏbɛlt] *n.* 铜带省〔赞比亚省名〕。

Cop·per·field [ˈkɔpəfiːld; ˋkapəˏfild] *n.* 科波菲尔〔姓氏〕。

cop·per·y [ˈkɔpəri; ˋkapərɪ] *a.* 含铜的；铜一样的；铜制的，铜质的；(紫)铜色的。

cop·pice [ˈkɔpis; ˋkapɪs] *n.*〔英〕矮林，小树林，灌木林；萌生林，杂木林 (= ～-wood)。

copr. = copyright.

cop·ra [ˈkɔprə; ˋkaprə] *n.* 椰肉干〔可榨油〕。

co·precipitate [ˌkəupriˈsipiteit; ˏkoprɪˋsɪpɪˏtet] *vt.*, *vi.* (使)一同沉淀。

co-pres·i·dent [ˈkəuˈprezidənt; ˋkoˋprɛzɪdənt] *n.* (和他人一起担任相同职务的)行政长官之一。

copr(o)- *comb. f.* 粪：*copro*lite.

cop·ro·dae·um [ˌkɔprəˈdiːəm; ˏkaprəˋdiəm] *n.* 【动】粪道。

cop·ro·lite [ˈkɔprəlait; ˋkaprəˏlaɪt] *n.* 【地】粪化石。

cop·rol·o·gy [kɔˈprɔlədʒi; kapˋralədʒɪ] *n.* 1. 【医】粪便学。2. 污物，猥亵文字[图画]。**-log·i·cal** *a.*

co·p·roph·a·gous [kɔˈprɔfəgəs; kapˋrafəgəs] *a.* 【动】(甲虫等)吃粪的。

cop·ro·phil·i·a [ˌkɔprəˈfiliə; ˏkaprəˋfɪlɪə] *n.* 【心医】嗜粪癖。

copse [kɔps; kaps] *n.* = coppice.

copse·wood [ˈkɔpswud; ˋkapsˏwʊd] *n.* 1. = copse. 2. (杂木林下的)矮树丛。

Copt [kɔpt; kapt] *n.* 1. 哥普特人〔古埃及原住民的后裔〕；埃及本地人。2. 【宗】哥普特教会〔埃及的基督教派〕。

cop·ter [ˈkɔptə; ˋkaptɚ] *n.*〔美〕helicopter (直升飞机)的缩略词。

Cop·tic [ˈkɔptik; ˋkaptɪk] **I** *a.* 1. 哥普特人[语]的。2. 【宗】哥普特教会的。**II** *n.* 哥普特语[人]。

cop·tis [ˈkɔptis; ˋkaptɪs] *n.* 【植】黄连；〔C-〕黄连属。

cop·u·la [ˈkɔpjulə; ˋkapjələ] *n.* (*pl.* ～*s*, *-lae* [-liː; -li]) 1. 【逻，语法】系词〔be, seem, appear 等〕。2. 【解】联桁，结合肌。3. 【法】交媾；【生】交合。4. 介体，介沟。**-r** *a.* 连系(动词)的。

cop·u·late [ˈkɔpjuleit; ˋkapjəˏlet] **I** *vi.* 1. 性交，交配，交尾。2. 结合；连接，连系。**II** *a.* 连接的，配合的。

cop·u·la·tion [ˌkɔpjuˈleiʃən; ˏkapjəˋleʃən] *n.* 1. 性交，交配，交尾。2. 接合，结合，连系。

cop·u·la·tive [ˈkɔpjulətiv; ˋkapjəˏletɪv] **I** *a.* 1. 结合的。2. 交配的。3. 【语法】系词的。**II** *n.* 【语法】连词，系词〔*and* 等〕。

cop·u·la·to·ry [ˈkɔpjulətəri; ˋkapjələˏtorɪ] *a.* 连接的；交配的。

cop·y [ˈkɔpi; ˋkapɪ] **I** *n.* 1. 抄本，缮本，誊本，摹本，复制品，【影】拷贝；【法】副本 (*opp.* script)。2. (书的)一部，一册，(报纸的)一份。3.〔不用不定冠词及 *pl.*〕(印刷的)原稿；新闻材料。4.〔罕〕范本，习字贴 (= copybook)；〔英口〕(学校的)作文(习题)。*duplicate copies* 正副两本。*a clean* [*fair*] ～ 誊清的稿子[文件]；清样。*a foul* [*rough*] ～底稿，草稿。*make a rough* ～ *of* 起草。～ *of verses* 短诗；习作诗。***hold*** ～ 做校对员的助手。***keep a*** ～ ***of*** 留副本。***make good*** ～ 成为(报纸等的)好材料。***paint*** [***write***] ***from a*** ～ 临画[临帖]。***take a*** ～ 复写。**II** *vt.*, *vi.* 1. 抄，誊，临(帖)，模写，复写。2. 模仿，仿效。3.〔英学俚〕抄袭(别人试卷)。～ *a great man* 模仿伟人。～ *into a notebook* 做笔记。～ *fair* 誊清。～ *out a document* 全文抄下一份文件。～ *from* (*the*) *life* 写生。～**book** 习字帖；〔美〕复写簿 (*blot one's* ～ *book* 做了损害自己名誉的事情。～*books maxims* [*morality*] 陈腐浅薄的格言[教训])。～ **boy**〔美〕(递送原稿、印样等的)送稿生。～**cat** 1. *n.* 盲目模仿者。2. *vt.* 盲目模仿。～ **chief**〔美〕(报馆的)编辑主任，主编。～**cutter** (剪贴新闻稿的)报馆排版工人。～ **desk** (报馆内马蹄形的)编辑桌；〔转义〕编辑部。～ **editor**〔美〕报馆编辑。～**graph** 油印机；油印图。～**-hold** *n.*, *a.* 【英法】誊本保有权；登录不动产保有权。～**-holder** 1. 【英法】誊本保有权者。2. 校对助手。3. (打字机的)原稿压。～**money** 稿费；版税。～**reader**〔美〕(报馆、出版社的)编辑。～**right** 1. *n.* 版权，著作权 (～*right reserved* 版权所有)。2. *a.* 版权的，著作权的。3. *vt.* 为(书等)取得版权(～*righted* 版权所有。～*right a book* 为一本书取得版权)。～**writer** 撰稿人〔尤指写广告文字者〕。

cop·y·ing [ˈkɔpiiŋ; ˋkapɪɪŋ] *n.*, *a.* 复写(的)，誊写(的)。～ **ink** 复写墨(水)。～ **paper** 复写纸。～ **pencil** 字迹很难擦去的铅笔。～ **press** 拷贝机。～ **ribbon** (打字机的)墨带，色带。

cop·y·ist [ˈkɔpiist; ˋkapɪɪst] *n.* 誊写者，抄写员；模仿者；剽窃者。

coq au vin [kɔk əu ˈvæn; kak o ˋvæn]〔F.〕酒烹嫩炸鸡。

coque [kɔk; kak] *n.* 装饰女帽的小丝带圈[羽毛圈]。

coque·li·cot [ˈkəuklikəu; ˋkoklɪko] *n.* 1. 【植】虞美人草。2. 鲜艳的橙红色。

co·quet [kəuˈket; ko`kɛt] **I** ***vi*.** **1.** (女子)卖弄风情,卖俏;闹着玩儿〔指轻佻无诚意的调情〕。**2.** 玩弄;轻浮对待,玩忽。~ ***with*** (*a man*) 玩弄(男子)。~ ***with*** (*one's duty*) 玩忽(职守)。**II** ***n*.** = coquette.

co·quet·ry [ˈkəukitri; `kokɪtrɪ] ***n*.** **1.** (女子的)卖弄风情,卖俏,撒娇。**2.** 娇态,媚态,妖娆。**3.** 玩弄。

co·quette [kəuˈket; ko`kɛt] **I** ***n*.** **1.** (轻佻的)卖弄风情的女子。**2.** 蜂鸟。**II** *vi*. = coquet.

co·quet·tish [kəuˈketiʃ; ko`kɛtɪʃ] ***a*.** 卖弄风情的,卖俏的;轻佻的;妖娆的。**-ly** ***ad*.** **-ness** ***n*.**

co·quille [kəuˈkiːl, F. kɔkij; ko`kil, kokɪj] ***n*.** 〔F.〕 **1.** 用贝壳(状容器)盛的菜。**2.** 贝壳状容器。

co·qui·na [kəˈkiːnə; ko`kinə] ***n*.** 【矿】(可供筑路用的)(介)壳灰岩,贝壳岩。

co·qui·to (palm) [kəuˈkiːtəu; ko`kito] ***n*.** 【植】智利棕榈〔树液和壳果可供食用〕。

Cor. = **1.** Corinthians. **2.** Coroner.

cor. = corner; cornet; corrected; correction; correlative; correspondent; corresponding.

cor- *pref*. = com-.

Cor·a [ˈkɔːrə; `korə] ***n*.** 科拉〔女子名〕。

cor·a·ci·i·form [ˌkɔːriˈsaiəfɔːm; ˌkorɪ`saɪəform] ***a*.** 【动】佛法僧目的〔鱼狗,犀鸟等鸟〕。

cor·a·cle [ˈkɔrəkl; `kɔrəkl] ***n*.** (用柳条扎成骨架并覆以防水布的)柳条艇。

coraco- *comb. f*. 表示"喙突";"喙"。

cor·a·coid [kɔːrəkɔid, ˈkɔr-; `kɑrəˌkɔɪd, `kɑr-] **I** ***a*.** 【解】喙骨的。**II** ***n*.** 【解】喙骨;喙突。

cor·al [ˈkɔrəl; `kɑrəl] **I** ***n*.** **1.** 珊瑚;珊瑚虫;珊瑚工艺品,珊瑚玩具。**2.** 珊瑚色。**3.** 龙虾卵。**II** ***a*.** 珊瑚的;珊瑚色的。~ *island* 珊瑚岛。~ **polyp** 珊瑚虫。~ **rag** 珊瑚石灰岩。~ **reef** 珊瑚礁。**C- Sea** (大洋洲东北的)珊瑚海。

cor·al·bells [ˈkɔːrəlˌbelz; `korəlˌbɛlz] ***n*.** (*pl*. ~) 【植】珊瑚钟(*Heuchera sanguinea*)。

cor·al·ber·ry [ˈkɔːrəlˌberi; `korəlˌbɛrɪ] ***n*.** 【植】小花雪果(*Symphoricarpos orbiculatus*.)。

coralli- *comb. f*. 表示"珊瑚";"珊瑚形状"。

cor·al·line [ˈkɔrəlain; `kɑrəlaɪn] **I** ***a*.** 珊瑚的;珊瑚状的;珊瑚色的;生产珊瑚的。**II** ***n*.** 【动】珊瑚(虫);珊瑚状动物,蓟苔虫;珊瑚状构造;【植】珊瑚藻。~ **crag** 山灰岩。~ **ware** 珊瑚色陶器。

cor·al·lite [ˈkɔrəlait; `kɑrəˌlaɪt] ***n*.** 【地】**1.** 珊瑚单体;珊瑚石。**2.** 珊瑚色大理石。

cor·al·loid [ˈkɔrəlɔid; `kɑrəˌlɔɪd] ***a*.** 珊瑚状的。

Cor·al·root [ˈkɔːrəlruːt, -rut; `korəlrut, -rʊt] ***n*.** 【植】珊瑚兰属(*Corallorhiza*)。

co·ram [ˈkɔːrəm; `korəm] ***prep*.** 〔L.〕在…的面前。~ **judice** [-ˈdʒuːdisi; -`dʒudɪsɪ] 在法官面前。~ **populo** [-ˈpɔpjuləu; -`pɑpjʊlo] 在民众面前,公然。

Co·ran [kɔ(ː)ˈrɑːn; ko`rɑn] ***n*.** = Koran.

cor an·glais [ˈkɔːˈɔŋglei; `kɔr`ɑŋgle] ***n*.** 〔F.〕 = English horn.

co·ran·to [kəˈræntəu; kə`rænto] ***n*.** 库兰特舞;库兰特舞曲(= courante **1.**)。

cor·beil [ˈkɔːbel; `kɔrbɛl] ***n*.** 【建】花篮饰;【筑城】小堡篮。

cor·bel [ˈkɔːbəl; `kɔrbḷ] **I** ***n*.** 【建】翅托。**II** ***vt*.** 用翅托支承,给…砌上翅托。—***vi*.** 砌翅托。~ **arch** 突拱。~ **course** 突腰线。~ **piece** 挑出块。~**-steps** 挑出踏步,马头墙。~ **table** 挑檐。

cor·bic·u·la [kɔːˈbikjulə; kɔr`bɪkjələ] ***n*.** 【动】蚬。

cor·bie [ˈkɔːbi; `kɔrbɪ] ***n*.** 〔Scot.〕大鸦。~ **steps** = corbel-steps.

cor·cho·rus [ˈkɔːkəurʌs; `kɔrkorʌs] ***n*.** 【植】黄麻。

cord [kɔːd; kɔrd] **I** ***n*.** **1.** 绳子,索子;弦;【电】软线,塞绳。**2.** 〔常 *pl*.〕束缚。**3.** 【纺】灯芯绒;布上凸起的楞条;棱凸纹;〔*pl*.〕〔口〕灯芯绒裤。**4.** 【解】索状组织,韧带,神经。**5.** 层积〔柴薪体积单位,合 8×4×4 立方英尺〕。*the spinal* ~脊髓。*the vocal* ~*s* 声带。~ *of discipline* 纪律的束缚。***the silver*** ~ 生命。**II** ***vt*.** 用索子捆〔绑、扎〕;堆积(柴薪)。~ **adjuster** 【电】磁葫芦。

cord·age [ˈkɔːdidʒ; `kɔrdɪdʒ] ***n*.** **1.** 绳索,(船的)索具。**2.** (柴薪的)层积数量。

cor·date [ˈkɔːdeit; `kɔrdet] ***a*.** 【植】心脏形的。

cord·ed [ˈkɔːdid; `kɔrdɪd] ***a*.** **1.** 用绳索捆扎的。**2.** (柴草)按层积堆积的。**3.** 绳制的。**4.** 起棱纹的。**5.** (肌肉)紧张的。

cor·delle [kɔːˈdel; kɔr`dɛl] **I** ***n*.** 〔美〕纤绳。**II** ***vt*.** 用纤拉(船)。

cor·dial [ˈkɔːdjəl; `kɔrdʒəl] **I** ***a*.** **1.** 亲切的,恳挚的,热诚的。**2.** 提神的,强心的。*a* ~ *smile* 由心里发出的微笑。*a* ~ *welcome* 热诚的欢迎。*a* ~ *meeting* 一次亲切的会见。~ *medicine* 强心剂,补药。**II** ***n*.** **1.** 爽心之物。**2.** 【医】补药,强心药,兴奋剂。**3.** 甘露酒,浸果酒。**-ly** *ad*. 诚心诚意地;恳挚地(~*ly yours* = yours ~ly 〔美〕谨上〔信尾语〕)。**-ness** ***n*.**

cor·di·al·i·ty [ˌkɔːdiˈæliti; ˌkɔrdɪ`ælətɪ] ***n*.** 诚实;恳挚,热诚。*hate* [*love*] *with great* ~痛恨[深爱]。

cor·di·er·ite [ˈkɔːdiərait; `kɔrdɪəraɪt] ***n*.** 【矿】堇青石。

cord·i·form [ˈkɔːdifɔːm; `kɔrdəˌfɔrm] ***a*.** 心脏形的。

cor·dil·le·ra [kɔːdiˈljeərə; ˌkɔrdɪl`jɛrə] ***n*.** 〔Sp.〕山脉。**-ran** ***a*.**

cord·ing [ˈkɔːdiŋ; `kɔrdɪŋ] ***n*.** **1.** 绳索。**2.** 棱纹[楞条]织物〔如灯芯绒〕;【纺】吊综工作。

cord·ite [ˈkɔːdait; `kɔrdaɪt] ***n*.** 无烟线状火药,硝棉甘油石油脂火药。

cord·less [ˈkɔːdlis; `kɔrdlɪs] ***a*.** **1.** 无绳的。**2.** 不用电线的;可用电池供电的。*a* ~ *electric shaver* 干电池剃刀。~ **phone** 无绳电话。

Cór·do·ba [ˈkɔːdəuvə; `kɔrdəvə] ***n*.** **1.** 科尔多瓦〔阿根廷城市〕。**2.** 科尔多瓦〔西班牙城市〕。

cor·do·ba [ˈkɔːdəbə; `kɔrdəbə] ***n*.** 科多瓦〔尼加拉瓜货币单位〕。

cor·don [ˈkɔːdən; `kɔrdṇ] **I** ***n*.** **1.** 【筑城】(堡垒外壕的)壁顶冠石;【建】带饰。**2.** 【军】哨兵线;警戒线,封锁线;防疫隔离线。**3.** 饰带,绶章;衣带。**4.** 【园艺】单干形。*a sanitary* ~防疫线。~ *of police* (警察站成一线形成的)警戒线。*post* [*place*, *draw*] *a* ~布设警戒线。~ ***bleu*** [kɔːdɔ̃blǝː; kɔr`dɔ̃`blœ] **1.** (法国 Bourbon 王朝时最高勋位的)蓝绶章。**2.** 名流;〔谑〕第一流厨师。~ ***sanitaire*** [kɔːrˈduŋsɑːniteər; kɔr`duŋsɑnɪtɛr] 〔F.〕 **1.** 防疫线。**2.** (国家之间的)封锁线。**II** ***vt*.** 布设警戒线,封锁交通。

cor·do·va [ˈkɔːdəvə; `kɔrdəvə] = cordoba.

Cor·do·van [ˈkɔːdəvən; `kɔrdəvən] **I** ***a*.** (西班牙)科尔多瓦城的。**II** ***n*.** **1.** 科尔多瓦人。**2.** 〔c-〕科尔多瓦皮革。

cor·du·roy [ˈkɔːdərɔi; `kɔrdərɔɪ] **I** ***n*.** **1.** 灯芯绒;〔*pl*.〕灯芯绒的衣服[裤子]。**2.** 〔美〕铺木路(= ~ road)。**II** ***a*.** **1.** 用灯芯绒做的。**2.** (路)用木头铺成的。**III** ***vt*.** 〔美〕铺筑木路于;用木排修(路)。

cord·wain·er [ˈkɔːdweinə; `kɔrdwenɚ] ***n*.** **1.** 〔古〕科尔多瓦皮制造工人。**2.** 鞋匠。

cord·wood [ˈkɔːdwud; `kɔrdˌwʊd] ***n*.** (堆成 128 立方英尺出售的)层积柴堆。

CORE = Congress of Racial Equality 〔美〕争取种族平等大会。

core [kɔː, kɔə; kɔ, kɔr] **I** ***n*.** **1.** 果心。**2.** (事物、问题等的)中心,核心;精髓。**3.** (地球的)地核;【地】岩心;【铸】型心;【建】衬心;【电】(线)心,心线;(计算机的)磁心;(原子反应堆的)堆芯,活性区;(燃料元件)芯体。**4.** (羊内脏中的)种瘤。**5.** 〔美〕(各专业学生共修的)基础课。***throw away the apple because of the*** ~ 因噎废食。***to the*** ~ 到心,彻底(*rotten to the* ~ 透心腐烂;坏入骨髓,糟糕透

C

顶。*English to the* ～道地的英国人)。**II** *vt*. 挖去…的果心。～ **city** (大都市的)中心城市。～**loss**【电】铁心损失。～ **memory** [**storage**] (计算机的)磁心贮存器。～ **tube** (插入大堆物质抽取样品的)取样器。～ **wall** 隔水墙。

Co·re·a(n) [kəˈriən; koˋrɪən] *a*., *n*. = Korea(n).

co·re·la·tion [ˌkəuriˈleiʃən; ˏkorɪˋleʃən] *n*. 〔英〕= correlation.

co-re·li·gion·ist [ˈkəuriˈlidʒənist; ˋkorɪˋlɪdʒənɪst] *n*. 同宗教〔教派〕的人。

cor·e·op·sis [ˌkɔriˈɔpsis; ˏkɔrɪˋɑpsɪs] *n*. **1.**【植】金鸡菊属植物;〔C-〕金鸡菊属。**2.** 波斯菊。

cor·er [ˈkɔːrə; ˋkorɚ] *n*. (水果的)去心器;岩心钻取器。

co·re·spond·ent [ˈkəurisˌpɔndənt; ˏko·rɪˋspɑndənt] *n*.【法】(离婚诉讼中的)共同被告〔指私通者双方〕。

corf [kɔːf; kɔrf] *n*. 〔英〕**1.** 运煤〔矿〕小车;煤炭篓。**2.** 鱼笼。

cor·gi [ˈkɔːgi; ˋkɔrgɪ] *n*. **1.** (威尔斯产脚短身长的)狗。**2.** 〔俚〕微型汽车。

cor·i·a·ceous [ˌkɔriˈeiʃəs; ˏkorɪˋeʃəs] *a*. 皮革制的;皮革一样(牢)的。

cor·i·an·der [ˌkɔriˈændə; ˏkorɪˋændɚ] *n*. **1.**【植】芫荽,胡荽,香菜;芫荽〔胡荽〕子。**2.** 〔卑〕钱。

Cor·inth [ˈkɔrinθ; ˋkɑrɪnθ] *n*. 科〔考〕林斯〔希腊南部港口城市,《新约》中译本作哥林多〕。

Co·rin·thi·an [kəˈrinθiən; kəˋrɪnθɪən] **I** *a*. **1.** 科林斯(人)的;【建】(古希腊)科林斯(式)的〔尤指带有叶形饰钟状柱顶的建筑〕。**2.** 古雅的。**3.** 奢侈的;〔古〕放荡的。**II** *n*. **1.** 科林斯人〔《新约》旧译作哥林多人〕。**2.** 耽于奢华生活的人;富有的享乐者;富有的业余运动爱好者〔尤指游艇运动爱好者〕。～ **order**【建】科林多柱型。

Cor·in·to [kəuˈrintəu; koˋrɪnto] *n*. 科林托〔尼加拉瓜港市〕。

Cor·i·o·lis force [ˌkɔːriˈəulis; ˏkɔrɪˋolɪs] 地球自转偏向力〔得名于法国数学家科里奥利〕。

co·ri·um [ˈkɔːriəm; ˋkorɪəm] *n*. (*pl*. **-ria** [-riə; -rɪə]) **1.**【解】真皮。**2.** 革片;(古罗马的)皮铠。

Cork [kɔːk; kɔrk] *n*. 科克〔爱尔兰共和国港市〕。

cork [kɔːk; kɔrk] **I** *n*. **1.** 软木;木栓;软木塞,塞子;(钓鱼用)软木浮子。**2.**【植】外皮。**3.** 〔美俚〕落第。*burnt* ～(演员化妆用的)软木炭。～ *jacket* 软木救生衣。～ *oak* 栓皮槠。**like a** ～ 精神活泼地;马上恢复元气。**II** *vt*. **1.** 用软木塞塞紧。**2.** 抑制,制止,压制(感情)〔常与 *up* 连用〕。**3.** (滑稽歌剧化妆中)用软木炭把脸涂(黑)。**III** *a*. 用软木制的。～ **cambium**【植】木栓形成层。～ **oak**, ～ **tree**【植】栓皮槠。～ **opera** 〔美俚〕演员把脸涂黑的滑稽歌剧。

cork·age [ˈkɔːkidʒ; ˋkɔrkɪdʒ] *n*. 拔去塞子,塞上塞子;(在餐馆中喝自备的酒所付的)开塞费。

corked [kɔːkt; kɔrkt] *a*. 塞着塞子的;软木底的,软木后跟的(鞋子等);有软木塞气味的(酒等);〔美俚〕喝醉了的。

cork·er [ˈkɔːkə; ˋkɔrkɚ] *n*. **1.** 塞瓶工人;塞瓶机[器]。**2.** 〔美俚〕定论,定局。**3.** 大谎话。**4.** 杰出的、惊人的人[物]。*That show was a* ～! 那场演出真好[十分动人]! ***play the*** ～ 举动过火(叫人看不顺眼)。

cork·ing [ˈkɔːkiŋ; ˋkɔrkɪŋ] **I** *a*. 〔美俚〕极好的。**II** *ad*. 极,非常。***have a*** ～ ***time*** 过[玩]得非常愉快。

cork·screw [ˈkɔːkskruː; ˋkɔrkskru] **I** *n*. (拔瓶塞的)螺丝锥;【空】螺旋飞行。**II** *a*. 螺旋形的。～ *cloth* 螺旋斜纹呢。～ *curl* 螺状卷发。～ *dive*【空】螺旋降落。**III** *vt*., *vi*. 蜿蜒前进[移动];扭成螺旋;〔俚〕探听(消息)。～ ***a secret out*** (*of sb*.) 把(某人的)秘密探听出来。

cork·wood [ˈkɔːkwud; ˋkɔrkwʊd] *n*. 轻木。

cork·y [ˈkɔːki; ˋkɔrkɪ] *a*. **1.** 软木塞一样的;干缩的。**2.** 软木塞气味的。**2.** 〔口〕没有分量的,轻佻的;活泼的。**3.** 〔口〕喝醉了的。

corm [kɔːm; kɔrm] *n*.【植】球茎;群居体。

cor·mel [ˈkɔːməl; ˋkɔrməl] *n*.【植】新生小球茎。

cormo- *comb*. *f*. 表示"茎","根","干"。

cor·mo·rant [ˈkɔːmərənt; ˋkɔrmərənt] **I** *n*. **1.**【动】鸬鹚,鹈鹕,水老鸦。**2.** 贪吃的(人),贪婪的人。**II** *a*. 水老鸦似的;食欲大的。

corn[1] [kɔːn; kɔrn] **I** *n*. **1.** 谷粒;(胡椒等的)子;谷类,谷物。**2.** 一个地区的主要谷类;〔美〕玉米;〔Scot.〕〔爱〕燕麦;〔英〕小麦。**3.** 〔美俚〕威士忌酒;零钱;平凡的音乐〔戏剧〕;陈腐的艺术。*a sheaf of* ～一捆谷子。*Chinese* ～ 谷子,粟,小米。*gather* ～拾谷子。*grow* [*raise*] ～种谷物。*house* ～ 把谷类堆入谷仓里。*Indian* ～ = *Turkey* ～玉米。～ *in the ear* 带总苞的玉米棒子。*waxy* ～糯玉米。*pop* ～〔美〕爆玉米;爆玉米花。***acknowledge*** [***admit***, ***confess***] ***the*** ～ 认罪,认输。***be worth*** [***earn***] ～〔口〕仅够工本。～ ***and horn go together*** 谷贱肉亦贱。***eat one's*** ～ ***in the blade*** 钱未到手先花销,寅吃卯粮。***measure another's*** ～ ***by one's own bushel*** 按自己尺度去衡量别人;以己律人。***up*** ～, ***down horn*** 谷贵(牛)肉贱。**II** *vt*. **1.** 制成细粒。**2.** 播种玉米;用玉米喂(牛)。**3.** 用盐腌,用盐水泡。**4.** 〔俚〕使醉。—*vi*. (谷穗)成熟,结子。～ **ball 1.** *n*. 爆玉米花糖;〔俚〕乡下人。**2.** *a*. 陈腔滥调的;多愁善感的。～ **beef** 咸牛肉。**C- Belt 1.** 美国中部主要产玉米地带。**2.** ～ **belt** 玉米主要产区。～ **binder** 玉米收割机。～ **borer** 玉米螟虫。～ **brash** 粗钙质砂岩。～ **bread** 玉米面包。～ **chandler** 粮食零售商。～ **cob 1.** 棒子芯,玉米穗轴。**2.** 棒子芯烟斗。～ **cockle**【植】麦仙翁;瞿麦。～ **colour** 淡黄色。～ **cracker** 〔美蔑〕美国南方的穷苦白人。～ **crake** 秧鸡。～ **dodger** 〔美〕玉米饼,玉米团子。～ **earthwarm** 棉铃虫。～**-exchange** 谷物交易所。～**-factor** 谷物商(=〔美〕grain broker)。～**-fed 1.** *a*. 〔英〕喂粮食的;〔美〕精神饱满的;健壮的;天真的(音乐家)。**2.** *n*. 健康的人。～**field** 稻田;麦田;玉米田。～ **flag**【植】水仙菖蒲。～ **flakes** 玉米渣儿。～ **flour** 玉米面。～ **flower**【植】矢车菊。～**land** 适于种谷物的土地。**C- Law** 〔英史〕谷物法。～**loft** 谷仓。～**-meal** 玉米粉。～ **mill 1.** 〔英〕面粉机。**2.** 〔美〕玉米面粉机。～ **picker** 玉米收割机。～ **pone** 玉米饼。～ **salad**【植】野苣。～ **silk**【植】玉米花丝。～ **smut** 玉米黑粉病。～ **snow** (早春的)粒雪。～ **syrup** 玉米糖浆。～**stalk** 麦秸,玉米秆(等);高个子(人);〔C-〕澳洲土生白人。～ **starch** 玉米淀粉。～ **whisky** 玉米威士忌酒。

corn[2] [kɔːn; kɔrn] *n*.【医】(脚趾上的)鸡眼,钉胼。***tread*** [***trample***] ***on sb.'s*** ～***s*** 揭人疮疤,伤某人的感情。

Corn. = **1.** Cornish. **2.** Cornwall.

corn·cake [ˈkɔːnˌkeik; ˋkɔrnˏkek] *n*. 〔美〕玉米饼 (= Johnnycake)。

corn·crib [ˈkɔːnˌkrib; ˋkɔrnˏkrɪb] *n*. 〔美〕玉米透风仓,玉米囤。

corn·dog [ˈkɔːnˌdɔːg; ˋkɔnˏdɔg] *n*. 〔美〕(蘸玉米面糊食用的)玉米热狗。

cor·ne·a [ˈkɔːniə; ˋkɔrnɪə] *n*.【解】角膜。～ *transplant*【医】角膜移植。**-l** *a*.

corned [kɔːnd; kɔrnd] *a*. 弄成细粒的;盐腌的;〔英俚〕醉了的。～ *beef* 罐头咸牛肉。

cor·nel [ˈkɔːnəl; ˋkɔrnəl] *n*.【植】山茱萸(的果实)。

Cor·nel·ia [kɔːˈniːljə; kɔrˋniljə] *n*. 科妮莉亚〔女子名〕。

cor·nel·ian [kɔːˈniːljən; kɔrˋniljən] *n*.【矿】光〔肉红〕玉髓。

Cor·nel·ius [kɔːˈniːljəs; kɔrˋneljəs] *n*. 科尼利厄斯〔男子名〕。

Cor·nell [kɔːˈnel; kɔrˋnɛl] *n*. 科内尔〔姓氏〕。

cor·ne·ous [ˈkɔːniəs; ˋkɔrnɪəs] *a*. 角(质)的;角状的。

cor·ner [ˈkɔːnə; ˋkɔrnɚ] **I** *n*. **1.** (桌等的)角,棱,隅。**2.** 天涯海角,僻远地方;偏僻处,角落。**3.** (街道)拐角,壁角;【数】隅角;边缘。**4.** 困境,绝境。**5.**【商】囤积居奇;

【棒球】(本垒的)棱角〔投球员方面〕;(足球)踢角球。*meet a friend at the corner of a street* 在马路拐角地方遇见一位朋友。*a tight* ～困境。*from every* ～ *of the earth* 由世界各地。***around the*** ～ =〔英〕*round the* ～. **cut ～s**〔美〕抄近路;节约(*cut* ～*s on production costs* 节约生产费用)。***cut off a*** ～ 抄近路。***do in a*** ～ 秘密干。***drive into a*** ～ 把…逼入死地,追究。***establish*** [***make***] ***a*** ～ ***in*** (*wheat*) 垄断[囤积](小麦)。***four*** ～***s*** 四隅;十字路口(*the four* ～*s of the earth* 世界各处。*within the four* ～*s of a document* 文件的范围)。***keep a*** ～ 保住一角,占据一角。***on the*** ～〔口〕失业。***put*** [***stand***] (*a child*) ***in the*** ～ (罚小孩)立壁角。***out of the*** ～ ***of one's eyes*** 斜着眼睛偷(看)。***rough*** ～***s*** 粗鲁。***round the*** ～〔英〕在拐角处;在附近。***the C-***〔俚〕伦敦 Tattersall's 马市场和赛马场。***turn the*** ～ 拐过街角;(疾病等)有转机;脱险。**II** ***vt.*** **1.** 使有棱[角];收在[放在]角内;角相接;转角,拐弯。**2.** (把)逼入绝境,紧逼,使无路可走。**3.** 垄断,囤积居奇。～ *the market* 垄断市场。—***vi.*** **1.** 位于(拐)角上 (*on*)。**2.** 形成一个角。**3.** 垄断,囤积 (*in*)。**III** ***a.*** **1.** 在拐角处的;适于拐角地方的。**2.** (美式足球)翼卫的。～**back** ***n.*** (美式足球)翼卫。～**boy**〔英〕游民,光棍。～**man** 翼卫队员;囤积居奇的人。～**stone** 隅石;(奠基礼的)基石;基础,柱石。～**wise**, ～**ways** ***ad.*** 斜,斜交成角地。**-ed** ***a.*** 有…角的。

cor·ner·er [ˈkɔːnərə; ˋkɔrnərə˞] ***n.*** 【商】垄断者,囤积居奇者。

cor·net [ˈkɔːnit; ˋkɔrnɪt] ***n.*** **1.** 【乐】(有音栓的)短号〔又名～-*àpistons*〕;(风琴的)音栓。**2.** (修女团团员的)大白帽。**3.** 【英史】骑兵旗手;海军信号旗。**4.** 三角纸袋;〔英〕(圆锥形)蛋卷冰淇淋。

cor·net-à-pis·tons [kɔːˈnetɑpistənz; ˋkɔrˋnɪtəˋpɪstnz] ***n.*** (*pl.* ***cor·nets-à-pis·tons*** [-nˈetsə-; -nˋɛtsə-]) 【乐】短号(=cornet)。

cor·net·(t)ist [ˈkɔːnitist; ˋkɔrˋnɛtɪst] ***n.*** 短号吹奏者。

corn·ey [ˈkɔːni; ˋkɔrnɪ] ***a.*** 〔俚〕= corny 4.

corn·husk·er [ˈkɔːnkʌskə; ˋkɔrn͵hʌskə˞] ***n.*** 玉米穗剥皮人(机)。*C- State*〔美〕内布拉斯加州的别号。

corn·husk·ing [ˈkɔːnˌkʌskiŋ; ˋkɔrn͵hʌskɪŋ] ***n.*** 〔美〕**1.** 剥玉米。**2.** 剥玉米会〔玉米收下后亲友邻里大家来帮着剥玉米,一般还有舞会等余兴〕。

cor·nice [ˈkɔːnis; ˋkɔrnɪs] ***n.*** 【建】上楣(柱);【登山】雪檐。～ *boarding* 花檐板。

cor·niche [ˈkɔːniʃ; ˋkɔrnɪʃ] ***n.*** 悬崖盘旋道路。

Cor·nish [ˈkɔːniʃ; ˋkɔrnɪʃ] ***a.*** 〔英〕康瓦尔 (Cornwall) 郡的。～**man** 康瓦尔郡人。

cor·no·pe·an [kəˈnəupjən; kəˋnopjən] ***n.*** 【乐】= cornet.

cor·nu [ˈkɔːnjuː, -nuː; ˋkɔrnju, -nu] ***n.*** (*pl.* ***-nu·a*** [-njuə; -njuə]) 【解】角状突起,角状物;【医】钉胼,鸡眼。**-al** [-əl; -əl] ***a.***

cor·nu·co·pi·a [ˌkɔːnjuˈkəupjə; ͵kɔrnəˋkopɪə] ***n.*** **1.** 【神话】丰饶角。**2.** 丰产的象征;丰富,丰饶;圆锥形糖果容器,糖果角。

cor·nu·co·pi·an [ˌkɔːnjuˈkəupjən; ͵kɔrnjəˋkopjən] ***a.*** 丰产的,丰饶的。

cor·nut·ed [kɔːˈnjuːtid; kɔrˋnjutɪd] ***a.*** 有角的。

cor·nu·to [kɔːˈnuːtɔː; kɔrˋnuto] ***n.*** 〔It.〕(*pl.* ***-ti*** [-tiː; -ti]) 奸妇的丈夫(=cuckold)。

Corn·wal·lis [kɔːnˈwɔlis; kɔrnˋwɑlɪs] ***n.*** 康沃利斯〔姓氏〕。

corn·y[1] [ˈkɔːni; ˋkɔrnɪ] ***a.*** **1.** 谷类的;谷类丰富的。**2.** 〔英方〕酒醉的。**3.** 〔美俚〕(爵士音乐)伤感的 (*opp.* hot)。**4.** 〔美俚〕陈腐的,枯燥的;天真的,朴素的;粗野的。

corn·y[2] [ˈkɔːni; ˋkɔrnɪ] ***a.*** 有鸡眼的。

coroll. = corollary.

co·rol·la [kəˈrɔlə; kəˋrɑlə] ***n.*** 【植】花冠。

cor·ol·la·ceous [ˌkɔrəˈleiʃəs; ͵kɑrəˋleʃəs] ***a.*** 花冠(状)的。

cor·ol·lar·y [kəˈrɔləri; ˋkɔrə͵lɛrɪ] ***n.*** 【逻、数】系;系定理;推论;必然的结果。

Co·ro·na [ˈkɔrənə; ˋkɑrənə] ***n.*** 科罗娜〔女子名〕。

co·ro·na [kəˈrəunə; kəˋronə] ***n.*** (*pl.* ***-nae*** [-niː; -ni]) **1.** (古罗马授与立功战士的)花冠。**2.** 【植】小冠,副冠;【解】(齿等的)冠;【动】(海胆的)谷;(轮虫的)轮盘;【建】花檐底板;(教堂的)圆形烛架。**3.** 【天】(全蚀时的)日冕;【电】电晕放电。**4.** 花冠牌雪茄烟。*C- Australis* [*Borealis*]【天】南[北]冕座。

cor·o·nach [ˈkɔrənək, ; ˋkɔrənək] ***n.*** 〔Scot., Ind.〕葬歌,挽歌,哀乐。

co·ro·na·graph [kəˈrəunəˌgræf; kəˋronə͵græf] ***n.*** 【天】日冕仪。

co·ro·nal [ˈkɔrənl; ˋkɔrənl] **I** ***n.*** 冠;花冠;冠状物;【解】冠状合缝。**II** [kəˈrəunl; ˈkəˋronl] ***a.*** 冠的;花冠的;【解】头颅的;冠状合缝的;【天】日冕的;【语音】舌尖的。

cor·o·nar·y [ˈkɔrənəri; ˋkɔrə͵nɛrɪ] ***a.*** 冠的,花冠的;冠状的。*the* ～ *arteries* [*veins*] (心脏的)冠状动脉[静脉]。～ *thrombosis* 【医】冠状动脉血栓形成。

cor·o·nate [ˈkɔrəneit; ˋkɑrə͵net] **I** ***vt.*** 给…加冕。**II** [ˈkɔrənit; ˋkɑrə͵nɪt] ***a.*** **1.** 【动】冠端的。**2.** 【植】有副花冠的。

cor·o·na·tion [ˌkɔrəˈneiʃən; ͵kɑrəˋneʃən] ***n.*** 加冕礼,即位典礼。

cor·o·ner [ˈkɔrənə; ˋkɔrənə˞] ***n.*** **1.** 验尸官。**2.** (从前英国的)王室私产管理官。*Coroner's Court* 验尸法庭。～*'s inquest* 验尸。

cor·o·net [ˈkɔrənit; ˋkɔrənɪt] ***n.*** **1.** (贵族、王族的)宝冠;(女用)冠状头饰;【诗】花冠。**2.** 【建】华丽的三角墙;【兽医】蹄冠。**-ed** ***a.*** 戴冠的;贵族的,高贵的。

cor·o·noid [ˈkɔrənɔid; ˋkɑrənɔɪd] ***a.*** 【解】鸟喙状的。

co·ro·zo [kəˈrəuzəu; kəˋrozo] ***n.*** 【植】(南美)象牙棕榈。～**nut** 象牙棕榈果。

corp. = **1.** corporal. **2.** corporation.

cor·po·ra [ˈkɔːpərə; ˋkɔrpərə] ***n.*** corpus 的复数。

cor·po·ral[1] [ˈkɔːpərəl; ˋkɔrpərəl] **I** ***a.*** 肉体的,身体上的;〔罕〕个人的,人身的;【动】躯干的。**II** ***n.*** 圣餐布。～ *defects* 身体上的缺点。～ *oath* 〔古〕用手接触圣餐布、圣经(等)所行的宣誓。～ *punishment* 体罚,体刑〔主指笞刑〕。

cor·po·ral[2] [ˈkɔːpərəl; ˋkɔrpərəl] ***n.*** **1.** 【军】下士,班长。**2.** 〔美〕牧牛头子。**3.** [C-]〔美〕单段式地对地导[飞]弹。*a lance* ～代班长。～*'s bull* 〔美〕香烟头,烟蒂。～*'s guard* (班长带领的)少数卫兵;少数随员;少数人的会集(等)。*the Little C-* 矮小的下士〔拿波仑第一的绰号〕。

cor·po·ral·i·ty [kɔːpəˈræliti; kɔrpəˋrælətɪ] ***n.*** **1.** 具体性;肉体;物质。**2.** 〔美〕体格;身体。**3.** 〔*pl.*〕肉欲。

cor·po·rate [ˈkɔːpərit; ˋkɔrpərɪt] ***a.*** **1.** 〔古〕团结的。**2.** 法人的,团体的。**3.** 共同的,全体的。**4.** (大)公司的。**5.** 总体国家的。*a* ～ *body* = *a body* ～法人团体。～ *responsibility* 共同责任。*a* ～ *town* 自治城市。***in one's*** ～ ***capacity*** 以法人身份。～ **culture** 企业文化。～ **image** 公司形象,公司给人的印象。～ **spying** 商业间谍活动。

cor·po·ra·tion [ˌkɔːpəˈreiʃən; ͵kɔrpəˋreʃən] ***n.*** **1.** 团体;协会,公会;法人;(市)自治体。**2.** 〔美〕(股份有限)公司 (= jointstock ～)。**3.** 〔口〕(凸出的)大肚子。*a closed* ～股权不能外让的公司。*a trading* ～贸易公司。*the municipal* ～ = *the C-* 市自治体,市政府。*develop a* ～肚子肥大凸出。～ **aggregate** 集合法人,社团法人。～ **cork** (水管、煤气管的)总开关。～ **farm** 〔美〕规模巨大的农场。～ **law** 〔美〕公司法。～ **lawyer** [**attorney**]〔美〕公司法律顾问。～ **police** 〔美〕(公司等的)自备警察。～ **sole** 单独法人,单一法人。

cor·po·rat·ist [ˈkɔːpərətist; ˋkɔrpərətɪst] ***a.*** 社团主义

的，各阶级合作性质的。**-ism** ***n.***

cor·po·ra·tive [ˈkɔːpəreitiv, -rə-; ˋkɔrpə,retɪv, -rə-] ***a.*** 法人(团体)的，团体的，全体的。～ **state** 总体国家〔指法西斯统治时期的意大利〕。

cor·po·ra·tor [ˈkɔːpəreitə; ˋkɔrpə,retə] ***n.*** **1.** (一个团体的)成员，发起人。**2.** 公司的股东〔尤指最初的创办人〕。**3.** 市政机关职员。

cor·po·re·al [kɔːˈpɔːriəl; kɔrˋpɔrɪəl] ***a.*** 肉体的；物质的(*opp.* spiritual)；【法】有形的。～ *property* [*movables*] 有形财产[动产]。**-ly** ***ad.*** 肉体上；物质上。

cor·po·re·al·i·ty [kɔːˌpɔːriˈæliti; kɔr,pɔrɪˋælətɪ] ***n.*** 肉体的存在；有形[有体]状态；肉身；〔谑〕身体。

cor·po·re·i·ty [ˌkɔːpəˈriːiti; ,kɔrpəˋriɪtɪ] ***n.*** 形体的存在；物质性；〔谑〕身体；体格。

cor·po·sant [ˈkɔːpəzænt; ˋkɔrpə,zænt] ***n.*** 桅顶电光〔一种雷电发生时在高塔等尖顶上出现的放电现象〕(= St. Elmo's fire)。

corps [kɔː, 〔*pl.*〕 kɔːz; kɔr, 〔*pl.*〕 kɔrz] ***n.*** (*sing.*, *pl.*) **1.** 【军】军(团)。**2.** 【军】特殊兵种的部队[单位]；特殊部队。**3.** 某种工作者的全体，团体。**4.** (德国大学的)校友会。*a* ～ *commander* 军长，军团司令。*an army* ～军团。*the Army Ordnance C-* 陆军军械部。*the Army Service C-* 辎重部队，陆军兵站部。*the marine* ～海军陆战队。～ *area*. 军管区。～ *d'armée* [ˈdɑːmei; ˋdɑme] 〔F.〕军团。～ *de ballet* [dəˈbælei; dəˋbæle] 〔F.〕舞剧团。～ *d'élite* [dəˈlit; dəˋlɪt] 〔F.〕精选出来的骨干[拔尖]人物。～ *diplomatique* [diplomæˈtiːk; dɪplo,mæˋtik] 〔F.〕外交(使)团(= diplomatic ～)。～ *dramatique* [drəməˈtiːk; drəməˋtik] 剧团。～ *troops* 军直属部队。～ *volant* [volɑːŋ; volɑŋ] 游击队。

corpse [kɔːps; kɔrps] **I** ***n.*** **1.** 尸体。**2.** 行尸走肉；没有活动力的人。**II** ***vt.*** 〔俚〕杀死。～ **candle** [**light**] 预兆死亡的鬼火。

corps·man [ˈkɔːzmən; ˋkɔrzmən] ***n.*** (*pl.* ***-men*** [-mən; -mən]) 战斗部队医务员(= aidman)。

cor·pu·lence, cor·pu·len·cy [ˈkɔːpjuləns, -si; ˋkɔrpjələns, -sɪ] ***n.*** 肥胖。

cor·pu·lent [ˈkɔːpjulənt; ˋkɔrpjələnt] ***a.*** 肥胖的。**-ly** ***ad.***

cor·pus [ˈkɔːpəs; ˋkɔrpəs] ***n.*** (*pl.* ***-po·ra*** [-pərə; -pərə]) **1.** 躯体，身体；〔主谑〕尸体。**2.** (法典等的)集成，全集。**3.** (事物的)主体；【法】主体(财产)，基金；本钱，资本。**4.** 【解】(脂肪)体；【植】原体。**5.** 【语】资料。～ *adiposum* 脂肪体。～ *callosum* 胼胝体。～ *delicti* [diˈliktai; dɪˋlɪktaɪ] 【法】犯罪事实；(谋杀案中的)被杀尸体。～ *juris* [ˈdʒuəris; ˋdʒuərɪs] 法令大全。～ *luteum* 【解】黄体；【医】黄体激素，妊娠激素。～ *striatum* 【解】纹状体。

cor·pus·cle, cor·pus·cule [ˈkɔːpʌsl, kɔːˈpʌskjuːl; ˋkɔrpʌsl, kɔrˋpʌskjul] ***n.*** 小体，细胞；【物】微粒，粒子。*blood* ～*s* 血细胞，血球。*bone* ～*s* 骨小体，骨细胞。*red* [*white*] ～*s* 红[白]血球；红[白]细胞。

cor·pus·cu·lar [kɔːˈpʌskjulə; kɔrˋpʌskjələ] ***a.*** 【物】微粒子的。

corr. = **1.** correction. **2.** correlative. **3.** correspond (-ence; -ent; -ing). **4.** corrupt(ion).

cor·rade [kəˈreid; kəˋred] ***vt.***, ***vi.*** 【地】(流水、冰川等的)磨蚀，侵蚀。**-ra·sion** [-ˈreiʒən; -ˋreʒən] ***n.*** **-ra·sive**[-siv; -sɪv] ***a.***

cor·ral [kəˈrɑːl; kəˋræl] **I** ***n.*** 〔美〕畜栏，畜槛；(捕象等用的)栅栏；(用车辆等拦成的)应急防御车阵，车栅。**II** ***vt.*** 〔美〕关在槛内，养在槛内；(把车辆)排成围栅；〔口〕围捕；〔美口〕捕获，获得，取得。

cor·rect [kəˈrekt; kəˋrekt] **I** ***a.*** 正确的；恰当的，合适的；(品行等)端正的。*a* ～ *account* 正确的说明。*a* ～ *young man* 品行端正的青年。*the* ～ *card* 〔俚〕(运动会等的)节目单，次序表；礼仪，规章。*the* ～ *thing* 〔俚〕正事，应该的事。**II** ***vt.*** 改正，更正，修正，订正；调整，补正(机件等)；校正(印件等)；矫正，制止(恶劣倾向等)，使中和，解(毒)；惩罚，训斥。～ *the proof sheets* 改正校样。～ *a child for disobedience* 训斥不听话的孩子。*I stand* ～*ed*. 我承认错误，接受改正。**-ly** ***ad.*** **-ness** ***n.***

cor·rec·tion [kəˈrekʃən; kəˋrɛkʃən] ***n.*** 修正，改正；校正；矫正；〔古〕惩罚；勘误表，补正。*a copy disfigured by numerous* ～*s* 修改得一塌糊涂的文稿。*first* ～ *of proofs* (校样的)初校，头校。*a free air* ～海平校正数。*Gregorian* ～*s* 【天】格列高里改正历，阳历。*a steering* ～【火箭】控制信号，稳定信号。**under** [**subject to**] ～ 容有错误，尚待订正(*I speak under* ～. 我说的不一定都对)。**-al** ***a.***

cor·rect·i·tude [kəˈrektitjuːd; kəˋrɛktə,tjud] ***n.*** 正确(性)；(品行的)端正。

cor·rec·tive [kəˈrektiv; kəˋrɛktɪv] **I** ***a.*** 纠正的，改正的；矫正的，惩治的；【药】矫味[中和]的。**II** ***n.*** 改善办法[措施]；矫正物；补救办法；矫味[中和]剂[药]。

cor·rec·tor [kəˈrektə; kəˋrɛktə] ***n.*** 修正者，校正者，校对(员)，矫正者，惩治者；【医】矫味剂，中和剂。*a* ～ *of the press* 〔英〕校对员(= proof-reader)。

correl. = correlative(ly).

cor·re·late [ˈkorileit; ˋkɔrə,let] **I** ***n.*** 互相关联，相互关系；相关物。**II** ***vi.*** 和…相关(*with*; *to*)。—***vt.*** 把…同某事结合起来；使互相关联。*Her research results* ～ *with his*. 她的研究成果和他的研究成功相关联。*The diameter and the circumference of a circle* ～. 圆的直径与圆周互相关联。～ *facts* 使事实互相关联。～ *geography with other studies* 把地理学同其他学科联系起来。**III** ***a.*** 关联的，相关的。

cor·re·la·tion [ˌkoriˈleiʃən; ,kɔrəˋleʃən] ***n.*** 相互关系，相关(性)；对比；交互作用；【数】对射，异射。～ *index* 关联指数。～ *mineral* 对比矿物。

cor·rel·a·tive [koˈrelətiv; kəˋrɛlətɪv] **I** ***a.*** 有相互关系的，相关的(with; to)。**II** ***n.*** 有相互关系的人[物]，互相依赖的人[物]，伙伴；【语法】关联词，相关联词〔例 both ... and; such ... as 等〕。～ **conjunction** 【语法】关系连词。～ **figures** 对射图形。～ **terms** 【心】相关名词。**-ly** ***ad.*** 相关地。

cor·rel·a·tiv·i·ty [kəˌreləˈtiviti; kə,rɛləˋtɪvətɪ] ***n.*** 相互关系，相关(关系)。

cor·re·spond [ˌkorisˈpond; ,kɔrəˋspɑnd] ***vi.*** **1.** 相当(于)，【数】对应；与…一致，符合(*to*; *with*)。**2.** 通信(*with*)。*The broad lines on the map* ～ *to roads*. 图上粗线表示[相当于]道路。*His words* ～ *with his action*. 他言行一致。*We* ～ *regularly*. 我们经常通信。

cor·re·spon·dence [ˌkorisˈpondəns; ,kɔrəˋspɑndəns] ***n.*** **1.** 通信；信件。**2.** 符合，一致；相当；对应。**3.** 【文艺】通感。～ *column* (报上的)读者来信栏。～ *course* 〔美〕函授课程。～ *department* 文书科。～ *school* 函授学校。***bring ... into*** ～ ***with*** 使…与(…)一致起来；使某人与另一人通信。***drop*** [***let drop***] ***one's*** ～ ***with*** 停止和…通信。***enter into*** ～ ***with*** 开始与…通信。***keep up*** ～ 保持通信。

cor·re·spon·den·cy [ˌkorisˈpondənsi; ,kɔrɪsˋpɑndənsɪ] ***n.*** **1.** 符合，一致。**2.** 相当，类似。

cor·re·spond·ent [ˌkorisˈpondənt; ,kɔrəˋspɑndənt] ***n.*** 通信者；通讯员；【商】外地客户，外地代理店。*a bad* ～ 不爱写信的人。*a good* ～爱写信的人。*our London* ～ 本社伦敦通讯员。*a special* ～(报馆的)特派记者。*a war* ～随军记者。**-ly** ***ad.***

cor·re·spond·ing [ˌkorisˈpondiŋ; ,kɔrəˋspɑndɪŋ] ***a.*** **1.** 相当的，对应的，符合…的(*to*; *with*)。**2.** 通信的。～ *angles* 【数】同位角。～ *member* 〔英〕通信会员；〔美〕(无表决权的)准会员。～ *period of last year* 去年中的同一时期。

cor·re·spon·sive [ˌkɔriˈspɔnsiv; ˏkɔrəˋspɑnsɪv] *a*. 〔古〕= corresponding.

cor·ri·da [kɔːˈriːðɑː; korˋriðɑ] *n*. 〔Sp.〕斗牛。

cor·ri·dor [ˈkɔridɔː; ˋkɔrədɔr] *n*. 【建】走廊;通路;【筑城】覆道。～ *carriage* 〔英〕有走廊的客车。～ *train* 通廊列车。～*s of power* (复数)"权力走廊"(指暗中左右决策的权力中心)。

cor·rie [ˈkɔri; ˋkɔrɪ] *n*. 〔Scot.〕(圆形)山凹;冰坑,冰斗。

cor·ri·gen·dum [ˌkɔriˈdʒendəm; ˏkɔrɪˋdʒendəm] *n*. (*pl*. **-da** [-də; -də]) 应改正的错误;〔*pl*.〕勘误表。

cor·ri·gent [ˈkɔridʒənt; ˋkɔrɪdʒənt] *n*. 【药】矫味[中和]药。

cor·ri·gi·ble [ˈkɔridʒəbl; ˋkɔrədʒəbl̩] *a*. 可改正的;易矫正的。

cor·ri·val [kəˈraivəl; kəˋraɪvəl] *n*. 〔罕〕竞争者。

Corr. Mem. = corresponding member (学、协会的)通讯会员。

cor·rob·o·rant [kəˈrɔbərənt; kəˋrɑbərənt] *a*., *n*. 【医】滋补(性)的;补药;确定的(事实)。

cor·rob·o·rate [kəˈrɔbəreit; kəˋrɑbəˏret] *vt*. **1**. 使(信仰等)坚定,使巩固;使加强。**2**. 确定,证实。

cor·rob·o·ra·tion [kəˌrɔbəˈreiʃən; kəˏrɑbəˋreʃən] *n*. 加强,坚固,坚定;确定,证实。*in* ～ *of sb.'s argument* 为了证实某人的论据。

cor·rob·o·ra·tive, cor·rob·o·ra·tory [kəˈrɔbərətiv, -rətəri; kəˋrɑbəˏretɪv, -rətərɪ] **I** *a*. **1**. 确定的,证实的。**2**. 滋补的。**II** *n*. 强状剂,滋补剂。

cor·rob·o·ra·tor [kəˈrɔbəreitə; kəˋrɑbəˏretɚ] *n*. 证实者。

cor·rob·o·ree [kəˈrɔbəri; kəˋrɑbərɪ] *n*. (澳洲原住民的)庆祝跳舞会[舞歌];狂欢宴会[集会];大集会。

cor·rode [kəˈrəud; kəˋrod] *vt*. 腐蚀,侵蚀;渐渐消灭。— *vi*. 腐蚀。

cor·ro·den·tia [kɔrəuˈdenʃiə; koroˋdenʃɪə] *n*. 〔*pl*.〕【动】啮虫目。

cor·rod·i·ble [kəˈrəudəbl; kəˋrodəbl̩] *a*. 可腐蚀的;可侵蚀的。

cor·ro·sion [kəˈrəuʒən; kəˋroʒən] *n*. 腐蚀,侵蚀;【植】溶蚀。～ *preventive* 防腐剂。

cor·ro·sive [kəˈrəusiv; kəˋrosɪv] **I** *a*. 腐蚀(性)的,侵蚀性的。**II** *n*. 腐蚀物,腐蚀剂。～ *action* 腐蚀作用。～ *sublimate* 【化】氯化汞,升汞 **-ly** *ad*.

cor·ru·gate I [ˈkɔrugeit; ˋkɔrəˏget] *vt*., *vi*. (使)成波状;〔古〕使起皱纹;皱缩成波状。**II** [-git; -gɪt] *a*. 起皱的,波状的,有沟纹的。～*d bar* 竹节钢筋[条]。～*d glass* 波纹玻璃。

cor·ru·ga·tion [ˌkɔruˈgeiʃən; ˏkɔrəˋgeʃən] *n*. 起皱;皱纹,皱折;波曲度;波纹度;(铁皮等的)波状;沟纹;沟畦。

cor·ru·ga·tor [ˈkɔrugeitə; ˋkɔrəˏgetɚ] *n*. 波纹[瓦楞]板轧制机;波纹纸制造工[机];【解】皱眉肌。

cor·rupt [kəˈrʌpt; kəˋrʌpt] **I** *a*. **1**. 腐败的,腐烂的,污浊的;道德败坏的,堕落的,品行坏的;贪污的(官吏等)。**2**. (文献等)错误百出的,不可靠的。～ *air* 污浊的空气。～ *morals* 坏风气。～ *officials* 贪污的官吏。～ *practices* 舞弊,行贿。～ *language* 传讹语。**II** *vt*., *vi*. 使腐败,使颓废;使堕落;行贿收买;败坏(风俗等),抄错,印错,转述错(文献,原词等);腐败,恶化。**-ly** *ad*. **-ness** *n*.

cor·rupt·i·ble [kəˈrʌptəbl; kəˋrʌptəbl̩] *a*. 易腐败的;易堕落的;易贿赂[收买]的;易传讹[讹误]的。**-bil·i·ty** *n*. **-bly** *ad*.

cor·rup·tion [kəˈrʌpʃən; kəˋrʌpʃən] *n*. **1**. 腐败,堕落,败坏;恶化;贪污,舞弊,贿赂。**2**. (文献等的)讹误;【语】传讹。**3**. 〔美〕脓。～ *in language* 语言的传讹。

cor·rup·tion·ist [kəˈrʌpʃənist; kəˋrʌpʃənɪst] *n*. 贪污腐化分子,行贿受贿分子。

cor·rup·tive [kəˈrʌptiv; kəˋrʌptɪv] *a*. 使腐败[堕落]的;腐败性的;败坏的。

cor·sage [kɔːˈsɑːʒ; korˋsɑʒ] *n*. (女服的)胸部,腰身;胸衣;〔美〕女服腰部或肩部的装饰花束。

cor·sair [ˈkɔːseə; ˋkorsɛr] *n*. **1**. 私掠船。**2**. 海盗,海盗船。

corse [kɔːs; kors] *n*. 〔诗〕= corpse.

Corse [F. kɔrs; kors] *n*. = Corsica.

Cor. Sec. = Corresponding Secretary (学会、协会的)干事,文书,公文秘书。

cor·se·let, cors·let [ˈkɔːslit; ˋkorslɪt] *n*. 胸甲,体甲;胸衣;(昆虫的)前胸(部),(鱼的)胸甲。

cor·set [ˈkɔːsit; ˋkorsɪt] *n*. (常 *pl*.)女服胸衣;【医】胸衣。*a* ～ *cover* 罩在胸衣外面的背心。**-ed** *a*. 带有胸衣的,穿着胸衣的。

cor·se·tiere [ˌkɔːsiˈtiə, -tjə; ˏkorsɪˋtɪr, -tjə] *n*. **1**. 女服胸衣裁缝。**2**. 女服胸衣商。

cor·set·ry [ˈkɔːsitri; ˋkorsɪtrɪ] *n*. 女服胸衣类缝制业,胸衣类销售(商店)。

Cor·si·ca [ˈkɔːsikə; ˋkorsɪkə] *n*. 科西嘉(岛)〔法国〕。

Cor·si·can [ˈkɔːsikən; ˋkorsɪkən] *a*., *n*. 科西嘉岛的(居民)。*the* ～"科西嘉人"〔拿破仑第一的绰号〕。

cor·tège [kɔːˈteiʒ; korˋteʒ] *n*. 〔F.〕**1**. (葬礼等)行列,仪仗。**2**. 扈从人员。

Cor·tes [ˈkɔːtes, -tez; ˋkortɪz, -tɛz] *n*. 〔*pl*.〕(西班牙、葡萄牙的)议会,国会。

cor·tex [ˈkɔːteks; ˋkortɛks] *n*. (*pl*. ***-ti·ces*** [-tisiːz; -tɪsiz]) 外皮;【解】皮质,皮层;【药】(药用植物的)皮。

cor·ti·cal [ˈkɔːtikəl; ˋkortɪkəl] *a*. 外皮的;皮质的,皮层的。

cor·ti·cate, cor·ti·cat·ed [ˈkɔːtikeit, -kit, -keitid; ˋkortɪket, -kɪt, -ketɪd] *a*. 有外皮的,有皮层的。

cor·ti·coid [ˈkɔːtikɔid; ˋkortɪkɔɪd] *n*. = corticosteroid.

cor·ti·co·ste·roid [ˌkɔːtikəuˈstiərɔid; ˏkortəkoˋstɪərɔɪd] *n*. 【生化】(肾上腺)皮质激素类,皮质甾(类),皮质类固醇。

cor·ti·cos·ter·one [ˌkɔːtiˈkɔstərəun; ˏkortəˋkɑstəron] *n*. 【生化】(肾上腺)皮质甾[固]酮。

cor·ti·co·tro·phin [ˌkɔːtikəuˈtrəufin; ˏkortəkoˋtrofin] *n*. 【生化】促肾上腺皮质激素(= corticotropin)。

cor·tin [ˈkɔːtin; ˋkortɪn] *n*. 【生化】(肾上腺)皮质激素。

cor·ti·sol [ˈkɔːtiˌsəul; ˋkortɪˏsol] *n*. 【生化】皮质醇;【药】氢可的松。

cor·ti·sone [ˈkɔːtiˌsəun, -zəun; ˋkortɪˏson, -zon] *n*. 【生化】(肾上腺)皮质酮[素];【药】可的松。

co·run·dum [kəˈrʌndəm; kəˋrʌndəm] *n*. 【矿】刚石,刚玉;【机】金钢砂(磨料);金刚砂磨轮。

cor·us·cate [ˈkɔrəskeit; ˋkɔrəsˏket] *vi*. 闪烁;(才气)焕发。

cor·us·ca·tion [ˌkɔrəsˈkeiʃən; ˏkɔrəˋskeʃən] *n*. 闪光;焕发。

cor·vée [ˈkɔːvei; korˋve] *n*. **1**. (封建社会的)徭役。**2**. (强派的)劳役。

corves [kɔːvz; korvz] *n*. corf 的复数。

cor·vet(te) [kɔːˈvet; korˋvet] *n*. (旧时木造帆装的)海防舰;轻巡洋舰;(现代的)小型护卫舰。

cor·vi·na [kɔːˈviːnə; korˋvinə] *n*. 【动】**1**. 无鳔石首鱼。**2**. 细须石首鱼和犬牙石首鱼属(= corbina)。

cor·vine [ˈkɔːvain; ˋkorvaɪn] *a*. 乌鸦(似)的。

Cor·vus [ˈkɔːvəs; ˋkorvəs] *n*. 【天】乌鸦座。

Cor·y·bant [ˈkɔriˌbænt; ˋkɔrəˏbænt] *n*. (*pl*. ～*s*, ～*es* [-tiːz; -tiz]) **1**. 【希神】母神 (Cybele) 的狂欢乱舞的随从;供奉母神的阉割过的祭司。**2**. 〔c-〕喝酒狂欢的人。

Cor·y·ban·tic [ˌkɔriˈbæntik; ˏkɔrɪˋbæntɪk] *a*. (有关) Corybant 的;疯狂的,狂欢乱舞的。

co·ryd·a·lis [kəˈridlis; kəˋrɪdlɪs] *n*. 【植】紫堇(属)。

cor·ymb [ˈkɔrimb; ˋkɔrɪmb] *n*. 【植】伞房花序。

cor·ym·bose [kəˈrimbəus, kɔrimˈbəus; kəˋrɪmbos, kɔrɪmˋbos] *a*. 【植】伞房状的。

C

cor·y·phae·us [ˌkɔriˈfiːəs; ˏkɔrəˋfiəs] *n*. (*pl*. **-phaei** [-ˈfiːai; -ˋfiaɪ]) 1.(古希腊合唱队的)领唱歌手。2.(派系、运动等的)领导人,领袖。

cor·y·phée [ˈkɔrifei; ˏkɔrəˋfe] *n*. 芭蕾舞(仅次于主要演员的)重要演员。

co·ry·za [kəˈraizə; kəˋraɪzə] *n*.【医】鼻炎,鼻感冒[伤风]。

cos [kɔs; kɑs] *n*.【植】科斯(岛产的)长叶莴苣。

C.O.S., COS = cash on shipment 装货付款。

Co·sa Nos·tra [ˈkəusə ˈnəustrə; ˋkosə ˋnostrə] "科萨·诺斯特拉"〔美国黑手党犯罪集团的秘密代号,1962 年始被揭露,意为"我们自己的事"〕。

C

co·saque [kɔːˈzaːk; kɑˋzɑk] *n*. = cracker (bonbon).

cose [kəuz; koz] *vi*., *n*. = coze.

cosec. = cosecant.

co·se·cant [ˈkəuˈsiːkənt; ˋkoˋsikənt] *n*.【数】余割。

co·seis·mal, co·seis·mic [kəuˈsaizməl, -mik; koˋsaɪzməl, -mɪk] *a*.【地】同震的〔同时受地震影响的〕。*a* ~ *area* 同震区。

co·sey [ˈkəuzi; ˋkozɪ] *a*., *n*. = cosy, cozy.

cosh [kɔʃ; kɑʃ] **I** *n*.〔英俚〕(金属心、外包橡皮的)棍子;警棍。**II** *vt*. 用棍子打。

cosh·er[1] [ˈkɔʃə; ˋkɑʃɚ] *vt*. 1. 给好吃东西。2. 溺爱,娇养。—*vi*. 享受盛宴款待。

cosh·er[2] [ˈkɔʃə; ˋkɑʃɚ] *n*.〔口〕开怀畅谈。

cosh·er[3] [ˈkəuʃə; ˋkoʃɚ] *v*. = kosher.

cosign [ˈkəuˈsain; ˋkoˋsaɪn] *vt*., *vi*. 1. 担保联署。2. 联署,共同签字。**-er** *n*.

co·sig·na·to·ry [ˈkəuˈsignətəri; koˋsɪgnəˏtorɪ] **I** *a*. 联署的,连名的。**II** *n*. 联署人[国]。

co·si·gner [ˈkəusainə; ˋkosaɪnɚ] *n*. 联署人。

co·si·ly [ˈkəuzili; ˋkozɪlɪ] *ad*. 舒适地,适意地。

co·sine [ˈkəusain; ˋkosaɪn] *n*.【数】余弦。

co·si·ness [ˈkəuzinis; ˋkozɪnɪs] *n*. 舒适,安乐;适意。

cosm- *comb. f*.〔用于母音前〕= cosmo-.

cos·met·ic [kɔzˈmetik; kɑzˋmɛtɪk] **I** *n*.〔常 *pl*.〕化妆品;美发油,发蜡;美容术。**II** *a*. 1. 化妆用的;美发用的。2. 装点门面的;表面的。*a* ~ *urge*〔美〕化妆品广告。~ **surgery** 美容手术。**-ti·cian** [-ˈtiʃən; -ˋtɪʃən] *n*. 制造[出售,使用]化妆品者。

cos·met·i·cize [kɔzˈmetəsaiz; kɑzˋmɛtəˏsaɪz] *vt*. 用化妆品打扮;粉饰,为…涂脂抹粉。

cos·me·tol·o·gy [ˌkɔzməˈtɔlədʒi; ˏkɑzməˋtɑlədʒɪ] *n*.〔美〕美容术;美容业。

cos·mic [ˈkɔzmik; ˋkɑzmɪk] *a*. 1. 宇宙的;宇宙论的。2. 有秩序的,有条不紊的。3. 广大无边的。~ **dust** 宇宙尘。~ **fog** [**clouds**] 星云。~ **inventory** 宇宙万物。~ **philosophy** 宇宙(演化)哲学。~ **rays** 宇宙(射)线。~ **string**【物】(大爆炸后形成的)宇宙带〔指能量的带状浓密集结〕。~ **year**【天文】宇宙年。**-cal·ly** *ad*.

cos·mi·cal [ˈkɔzmikəl; ˋkɑzmɪkəl] *a*. = cosmic.

cos·mism [ˈkɔzmizəm; ˋkɑzmɪzəm] *n*.【哲】宇宙(演化)论。

cosmo- *comb. f*.〔用于子音前〕= cosmos: *cosmodrome*.

cos·mo·dom [ˈkɔzməudəm; ˋkɑzmodəm] *n*. 太空站。

cos·mo·drome [ˈkɔzməudrəum; ˋkɑzməˏdrom] *n*.(苏联的)人造卫星及宇宙飞船发射场;太空站的降落部分。

cos·mog·o·ny [kɔzˈmɔgəni; kɑzˋmɑgənɪ] *n*. 1. 宇宙的发生[起源,演化]。2. 星原学,天体演化学,宇宙(演化)论。

cos·mo·grad [ˈkɔzməugrəd; kɑzˋmogrɑd] *n*. 太空城。

cos·mog·ra·pher [kɔzˈmɔgrəfə; kɑzˋmɑgrəfɚ] *n*. 宇宙志学者。

cos·mo·graph·ic [ˌkɔzməˈgræfik; ˏkɑzməˋgræfɪk] *a*. 宇宙志的。

cos·mog·ra·phy [kɔzˈmɔgrəfi; kɑzˋmɑgrəfɪ] *n*. 宇宙志。

Cos·mo·line [ˈkɔzməˌliːn; ˋkɑzməˏlin] **I** *n*. "柯斯莫林"重油〔商标名,尤指武器等的防锈润滑油〕;〔c-〕(柯斯莫林)防腐润滑油。**II** *vt*.〔c-〕涂以(柯斯莫林)防腐润滑油。

cos·mol·og·i·cal [ˌkɔzməˈlɔdʒikəl; ˏkɑzməˋlɑdʒɪkəl] *a*. 宇宙论的。

cos·mol·o·gist [kɔzˈmɔlədʒist; kɑzˋmɑlədʒɪst] *n*. 宇宙论者。

cos·mol·o·gy [kɔzˈmɔlədʒi; kɑzˋmɑlədʒɪ] *n*. 宇宙论。

cos·mo·naut [ˈkɔzməunɔːt; ˋkɑzməˏnɔt] *n*. 宇航员,太空人。

cos·mo·naut·ic [ˌkɔzməuˈnɔːtik; ˏkɑzmoˋnɔtɪk] *a*. 太空(宇宙)航行的,宇宙飞行的,航天的。

cos·mo·nau·tics [ˌkɔzməˈnɔːtiks; ˏkɑzməˋnɔtɪks] *n*. 宇(宙)航(行)学,航天学。

cos·mo·nette [ˌkɔzməˈnet; ˏkɑzməˋnɛt] *n*. 女宇航员。

cos·mo·plas·tic [ˌkɔzməˈplæstik; ˏkɑzməˋplæstɪk] *a*. 宇宙形成的。

cos·mop·o·lis [kɔzˈmɔpəlis; kɑzˋmɑpəlɪs] *n*. 国际[世界]都市〔指居民中有许多不同国籍的人〕。

cos·mo·pol·i·tan [ˌkɔzməˈpɔlitən; ˏkɑzməˋpɑlətn̩] **I** *n*. 世界主义者。**II** *a*. 1. 世界主义的。2. 全世界的。3. 世界性的;全世界各地都有的。*a* ~ *population* 世界各地的人都有的居民。*a* ~ *city* 国际都市。**-ism** *n*. 世界主义。**-ize** *vt*., *vi*.(使)世界主义化。

cos·mop·o·lite [kɔzˈmɔpəlait; kɑzˋmɑpəˏlaɪt] *n*., *a*. 1. = cosmopolitan. 2.【生】世界种,遍生种。

cos·mo·ra·ma [ˌkɔzməˈrɑːmə; ˏkɑzməˋrɑmə] *n*. 世界各地景色图片。

cos·mos [ˈkɔzmɔs; ˋkɑzməs] *n*. 1. 宇宙。2. 完整的体系。3. 秩序,和谐 (*opp*. chaos)。4.【植】大波斯菊(属);秋英(属)。~ *fibre* 破麻布再生纤维。

cos·mo·tron [ˈkɔzməˌtrɔn; ˋkɑzməˏtrɑn] *n*.【原】宇宙线级回旋加速器,(高能)同步稳相加速器,质子同步加速器。

COSPAR = Committee On Space Research (国际科学协会理事会)空间(太空)研究委员会。

co·spon·sor [ˌkəuˈspɔnsə; ˏkoˋspɑnsɚ] **I** *n*. 联合发起[主办]人之一。**II** *vt*. 作…的联合发起[主办]人。**-ship** *n*.

Cos·sack [ˈkɔsæk; ˋkɑsæk] **I** *n*. 哥萨克人;哥萨克骑兵;哥萨克式服装;〔美〕(用以镇压工人的)骑警。**II** *a*. 哥萨克的,哥萨克人的。

cos·set [ˈkɔsit; ˋkɑsɪt] **I** *n*. 亲手饲养大的小羊;亲手饲养的禽兽;宠儿。**II** *vt*. 宠养;宠爱。

cost [kɔst; kɔst] **I** *n*. 1. 费用;代价,价格;成本。2. 牺牲;损害,损失。3.〔*pl*.〕讼费。*living* ~*s* 生活费用,物价。*first* [*prime*, *initial*] ~ 生产成本。***at all ~s = at any ~*** 无论如何,不惜任何牺牲。***at ~*** 照成本。***at sb.'s ~*** 某人出钱;损及某人。***at the ~ of*** 以…为牺牲,舍…而。~ ***and freight*** 成本加运费〔略作 C. & F.〕。~ ***of living*** 生活费(用)。~ ***of living index*** 物价指数。~ ***of operation*** 管理费用。***count the ~*** 估计费用;先盘算盘算。***free of ~*** 免费,(奉)送。***to sb.'s ~*** 归某人负担,算作某人损失;叫某人受累;某人吃亏后才 (*as I know to my* ~我吃亏后才知道。*I knew it to my* ~. 这个我(因吃过苦头)是见而有戒了。*He found to his ~ that motoring is dangerous*. 他(吃过苦头后才)知道开汽车是危险的)。**II** *vt*. (**cost**; **cost**) 1. 值,要价(若干);花费,需要。2. 使花费,使损失,牺牲。3. 估定(…的)成本。—*vi*. 花费,付代价。*It ~s five dollars*. 值五元,要价五元。*It ~ me much labour*. 费了我不少劳力[麻烦]。*His ambition ~ him his life*. 他的野心断送了自己一条命。~ (*sb*.) ***dear***(***ly***) 代价极大,费用极高;闯大祸,吃大亏(*If you attempt it, it will ~ you dear*. 你试试看,一定要吃大亏的)。~ ***what it***

may 不惜任何代价,无论代价多少;无论如何。~ **accounts** 成本账(户)。~ **accounting** 成本会计。~**-effective** ***a.*** 节省成本的。~**-free** 免费的,奉送的。~ **keeper** 成本会计师。~ **price** 成本(价格)。~**-push** 成本增加(趋势)。~ **taking** 成本计算。~ **sheet** 成本单。

cos·ta [ˈkɔstə; ˋkastə] ***n.*** (*pl.* ***-tae*** [-tiː; -ti])【解】肋骨;【虫】前缘脉;【植】缘;中脉,主脉。

cos·tal [ˈkɔstl; ˋkastl] ***a.***【解】肋骨的;前缘脉的。~ *fold* 膜垂;前缘褶。

co-star [kəuˈstɑː; ˋkoˋstar] **I** ***vt.***, ***vi.***【影】(使)共同主演[充任并立主角]。**II** ***n.*** 合演主角,并立主角。

cos·tard [ˈkʌstəd; ˋkastəd] ***n.*** 英国大苹果(树);〔古、谑〕头。

Cos·ta Ri·ca [ˈkɔstə ˈriːkə; ˋkastə ˋrikə] 哥斯达黎加(哥斯达黎加)〔拉丁美洲〕。

cos·tate [ˈkɔsteit; ˋkastet] ***a.***【解】有肋骨的;有中脉的。

cost-book [ˈkɔstbuk; ˋkastbuk] ***n.*** 成本账。

cos·tean, cos·teen [ˈkɔstiːn; ˋkastin] ***vi.***【矿】井探,掘井勘探,水力冲刷勘探。

Cos·tel·lo [kɔsˈteləu; kasˋtelo] ***n.*** 科斯特洛〔姓氏〕。

cos·ter, cos·ter·mon·ger [ˈkɔstə, -mʌŋgə; ˋkastə, -ˋmʌŋgə] ***n.*** 〔英〕(水果、鱼类的)叫卖小贩。

cos·tive [ˈkɔstiv; ˋkastɪv] ***a.*** **1.** 便秘的。**2.** 吝啬的。**3.** 〔美〕昂贵的。

cost·li·ness [ˈkɔstlinis; ˋkastlɪnɪs] ***n.*** 高价,昂贵;奢华。

cost·ly [ˈkɔstli; ˋkɔstlɪ] ***a.*** 昂贵的,费用大的;奢华的,浪费的。*a ~ victory* 代价高的胜利。

cost·mar·y [ˈkɔstmɛəri; ˋkastˏmerɪ] ***n.***【植】艾菊。

costo- *comb. f.* 肋骨:*costo*tomy.

cos·tot·o·my [kɔsˈtɔtəmi; kasˋtatəmɪ] ***n.*** 肋骨切除术。

cost-plus [ˈkɔːstˈplʌs; ˋkɔstˋplʌs] ***a.*** (定货合同中)成本加利润(价格)的。

cos·trel [ˈkɔstrəl; ˋkastrəl] ***n.*** 〔古,方〕背挎水瓶,腰挎水瓶。

cos·tume [ˈkɔstjuːm, -ˈtjuːm; ˋkastjum, -ˋtjum] **I** ***n.*** **1.** 服装,装束;衣服。**2.** 女服;女装。**3.** 服装式样;化装用服装;戏装。*a bathing-~* 游泳衣。**II** [kɔsˈtjuːm; kasˋtjum] ***vt.*** 为…提供服装。~ **ball** 化装跳舞会。~ **designer**【剧、影】服装设计员。~ **piece** [**play**] 古装戏。

cos·tum·er, cos·tu·mi·er [kɔsˈtjuːmə, -miə; kasˋtjumə, -mɪə] ***n.*** 〔美〕**1.** 服装[戏装]供应[缝制,出售或出租]商。**2.** 衣帽架。

co·sy [ˈkəuzi; ˋkozɪ] **I** ***a.*** (***-si·er***; ***-si·est***) **1.** 舒适的,舒服的,安乐的。**2.** 畅快的;投合的;亲切友好的。**3.** 自满的,自得的。*a ~ job* 容易的工作。**II** ***n.*** **1.** 有遮盖的双人座位。**2.** 保暖罩〔例:tea-~ 茶壶暖罩〕。**II** ***vt.*** 〔口〕使放心,保证;哄骗 (along)。—***vi.*** 〔美口〕~ ***up to*** 巴结,奉承,讨好,表示好感。

cot. = cotangent.

cot[1] [kɔt; kat] ***n.*** **1.** 〔诗〕= cottage; 小屋。**2.** (羊)槛,(鸽)舍。**3.** 套子,罩子。

cot[2] [kɔt; kat] ***n.*** **1.** 帆布床;(船上的)吊床,吊铺。**2.** 小儿卧床,儿科病床。~ **death**【医】(原因不明的)婴孩猝死(症)。

co·tan·gent [ˈkəuˈtændʒənt; ˋkoˋtændʒənt] ***n.***【数】余切。

COTAR = correlation tracking and range 相关跟踪测距系统。

cote [kəut; kot] ***n.*** (家畜、家禽的)槛,栏。

co·teau [kəuˈtəu; koˋto] ***n.*** 〔F.〕(*pl.* ***-teaux*** [-z; -z])〔美、加拿大〕高地,高原。

co·tem·po·ra·neo·us, co·tem·po·rar·y [kəutempəˈreinjəs, -rəri; koˏtɛmpəˋreniəs, -rərɪ] = contemporaneous, contemporary.

co·ten·ant [ˈkəuˈtenənt; koˋtɛnənt] ***n.*** 共同租户〔租地人,租屋人〕;共同佃户。

co·te·rie [ˈkəutəri; ˋkotərɪ] ***n.*** 同人俱乐部;小集团,小圈子。

co·ter·mi·nous [kəuˈtəːminəs; koˋtɝmənəs] ***a.*** = conterminous.

co·thur·n(us) [kəuˈθəːn(əs); koˋθɝn(əs)] ***n.*** (*pl.* ***-ni*** [-nai; -naɪ]) (古希腊罗马)悲剧角色厚底高统靴;〔诗〕〔the ~〕悲剧(风格)。

co·tid·al [kəuˈtaidl; koˋtaɪdl] ***a.*** 等潮(时)的,同潮的。~ *lines on a map* 地图上的等潮(时)线。

co·til·l(i)on [kəˈtiljən, kəu-; koˋtɪljən, ko-] ***n.*** **1.** 一种不断更换舞伴、热闹的交际舞;这种舞曲。**2.** (为初进社交界的少女开的)正式舞会。

co·to·ne·as·ter [kəˌtəuniˈæstə; kəˏtoniˋæstə] ***n.***【植】栒子灌木。

Co·to·nou [ˌkəutəˈnuː; ˏkotəˋnu] ***n.*** 科托努〔达荷美港市〕。

cot·quean [ˈkɔtˌkwiːn; ˋkatkwin] ***n.*** 〔古〕**1.** 泼妇。**2.** 做家务的男子。

Cots·wold [ˈkɔtswəuld; ˋkatswold] ***n.*** (英国)柯茨窝尔山;柯次窝尔羊。*the ~ lion* 〔谑〕羊。

cot·ta [ˈkɔtə; ˋkatə] ***n.*** **1.** 短袖或无袖白色短法衣;外衣,束腰外衣。**2.** 极粗劣的毯子。

cot·tage [ˈkɔtidʒ; ˋkatɪdʒ] ***n.*** **1.** 〔英〕乡下房子,农舍;小房子。**2.** 〔美〕(农舍式的)别墅;(郊外的)新式住宅;(大院内的)单幢住宅;〔澳〕平房。**3.** 竖式小钢琴 (= ~ piano)。~ **cheese** 〔美〕用酸牛奶做的软干酪。~ **hospital** (无住院医生的)诊疗所,(乡下)小医院;医院分院。~ **industry** 家庭手工业。~ **loaf** 大小两个叠合的面包。~ **piano** 竖式小钢琴。~ **pudding** 〔美〕乡下布丁。

cot·tag·er [ˈkɔtidʒə; ˋkatɪdʒə] ***n.*** 住乡下房子的人,〔英〕农场雇工;〔美〕(避暑地等的)别墅客,度假客。

cot·tar, cot·ter[1] [ˈkɔtə; ˋkatə] ***n.*** 住屋狭小的人,贫农;〔Scot.〕农场雇工。

cot·ter[2], **cot·ter·el** [ˈkɔtə, -rəl; ˋkatə, -rəl] ***n.***【机】栓,销;开尾销(= ~ pin)。

cot·ti·er [ˈkɔtiə; ˋkatɪə] ***n.*** 〔英〕(住在农村小舍里的)小[贫]农;〔爱〕(投标定租的)佃农。

Cotton [ˈkɔtn; ˋkatn] ***n.*** 科顿〔姓氏〕。

cot·ton [ˈkɔtn; ˋkatn] **I** ***n.***【植】草棉;棉,棉花;棉线;棉布,棉织品;〔美口〕脱脂棉。*upland* [*sea-island*] ~陆地[海岛]棉。*tree* ~木棉。*ginned* ~皮棉。*unginned* ~籽棉。*raw* ~原棉。*dead* ~废棉。**II** ***vi.*** 一致,赞同(*with*);接近,亲近(*to*; *with*);(对提案等)抱好感,欢迎。~ ***to*** [***with***] 发生好感,喜欢起…来。~ ***on to*** 〔俚〕明白,了解。~ ***up*** 〔口〕接近,亲近(*to*)。—***vt.*** 娇养,娇宠。**C- Belt** 〔美〕(东南部)产棉地带[区域]。~ **cake** 棉籽饼。~ **gin** 轧棉机。~ **grass**【植】牛胡子草(属)。~ **gum** 紫树(属)。~ **holiday** 〔美〕(因生产过剩)暂时停种棉花。~ **lord** 棉花大王;纱业大王。~ **manies** [-ˈmeiniː; -ˋmeiniː]〔美〕田纳西州人〔别号〕。~ **meal** 棉籽饼。~ **mill** 纱厂。~ **oil** 棉子油。~ **picker** 采棉机。~ **piece goods** 棉布类(商品)。~ **plant** 棉株,草棉。~ **powder** 火棉炸药。~ **press** 榨棉机。~ **print** 印花棉布。~ **seed** 棉子。~ **shirting** 细棉布。**C- State** 〔美〕阿拉巴马州的别号。~ **stainer** 棉椿象。~ **tail**【动】美洲白尾灰兔。~ **thread** 棉线。~ **textile** [**tissue**] 棉织品。~ **tree** 木棉(树)。~ **waste** (揩擦机械用的)纱头。~ **weed**【植】母子草,鼠曲草。~ **wood** 加拿大杨;三角叶杨。~ **wool** 原棉;棉絮;脱脂棉。~ **yarn** 棉纱。

cot·ton·oc·ra·cy [ˌkɔtənˈɔkrəsi; ˏkatənˋakrəsɪ] ***n.*** 〔口〕棉纱业暴发户[集团];〔美〕(南北战争前南部的)棉花种植场主。

Cot·ton·op·o·lis [ˌkɔtənˈɔpəlis; ˏkatənˋapəlɪs] ***n.*** 〔谑〕棉都〔英国 Manchester 的别号〕。

cot·ton·pick·ing [ˈkɔtənpikiŋ; ˋkatənˋpɪkɪŋ] ***a.*** 〔美俚〕糟透的,该死的,可恨的。

cot·ton·y [ˈkɔtni; ˋkatnɪ] ***a.*** **1.** 棉花状的;柔软的。**2.** 有绒毛的。**3.** 棉质的,粗劣的。

C

cot·y·le·don [ˌkɔtiˈliːdən; ˌkɑtlˋidn̩] *n*.【植，解】绒毛叶，子叶。**-don·ous, -don·al** *a*.

cot·y·loid [ˈkɔtilɔid; ˋkɑtɪlɔɪd] *a*.【解】髋臼状的，杯状的。

couch[1] [kautʃ; kaʊtʃ] **I** *n*. **1.** 〔诗〕床，卧榻。**2.** 躺椅，长沙发椅〔背部比沙发低〕。**3.** 休息处；(兽)窝，窟，巢穴。**4.**【绘】底子。**5.**【酿造】麦芽床。*a studio* ～坐卧两用沙发。**II** *vt*. **1.** 横躺着(身体)，使横卧〔常用被动〕。**2.** 挺着(枪)。**3.** 表述，暗含(真意)，暗示(要求等)。**4.**【医】除去白内障。*be ～ed on a bed of flowers* 生活奢华。～ *one's refusal in polite terms* 婉言拒绝。—*vi*. **1.** 躺，睡。**2.** 蹲着，弯着身子(作要跳的姿势)；埋伏。**3.** (树叶等)堆积〔发酵，沤肥〕。～ ***out by the tube*** 成天泡在电视机(或录像机)前。～ **potato** 成天看电视的人。

couch[2] [kautʃ; kaʊtʃ] **I** *n*.【植】= ～ grass. **II** *vt*. 铲除麦斛。～ **grass** 麦斛，匍匐冰草，茅根。

couch·ant [ˈkautʃənt; ˋkaʊtʃənt] *a*.【徽】昂首蹲着的(兽)，昂首伏卧状的。

cou·che [ˈkuːʃei; ˋkuʃe] *a*. 〔F.〕【徽】微微前倾的。

cou·chee [ˈkuːʃei; ˋkuʃə] *n*. **1.** 重伤兵。**2.** 晚上的接见。

cou·chette [kuːˈʃet; kuˋʃɛt] *n*. 〔F.〕【铁道】(客车上的)卧铺分隔间；卧铺铺位。

cou·gar [ˈkuːgə; ˋkugɚ] *n*.【动】美洲狮。

cough [kɔf; kɔf] **I** *n*. **1.** 咳，咳嗽。**2.** 咳嗽声，咳嗽病。**3.** (机关枪等的)连续发射声。**II** *vi*. **1.** 咳嗽。**2.** (引擎等)发噗噗声。—*vt*. 咳；咳出 (*out*; *up*)；咳哑(声音)。～ ***down*** (听众)用咳嗽声轰演讲者。～ ***oneself hoarse*** 咳嗽得嗓子嘶哑。～ ***out*** [***up***] 咳出；〔美俚〕(被迫)说出；付出，交出(～ *up one's dough* 说出[吐出]藏金)。～ ***up one's cookies*** 〔美俚〕呕吐。～ **drop** 咳嗽糖。～ **lozenge** 咳嗽片。～ **mixture** 止咳药水。～ **syrup** 止咳糖浆。

could [强 kud, 弱 kəd; kʊd, kəd] ***auxil***. *v*. (can 的过去式) **1.** 〔特殊用例〕打算，要，想。*I ～ laugh for joy*. 我高兴得想笑。*Really I ～ not think of it*. 真的那是我不愿意考虑的。*I couldn't think of allowing it*. 我没有允许的意思。★could 与感觉动词连用时，表示"要，想"，与一般动词连用而表示"能够"时，为避免与"要，想"混淆起见，通例不说 could 而改说 was [were] able to, 若所指行动须经过努力或会遇到困难，则通例不说 could 而改说 managed to, succeeded in -ing. 例：I *could* do it = I *was able to* do it. He *could* reach the top of the mountain. = He *managed to* reach [*succeeded in reaching*] the top of the mountain. **2.** 〔用于假设语气的条件句〕*if I ～* 〔现在〕假定可能的话(但事实上不可能)。*if I ～ have done so* 〔过去〕假定做到了(但事实上没有做到)。**3.** 〔用于虚拟语气的结论句〕*I ～ if I would*. 〔现在〕假定我要做就可以做到〔但事实上不打算做〕。*I ～ have done it*. 〔过去〕假定我本来是可以做到的〔但未做〕。

could·n't [ˈkudnt; ˋkʊdn̩t] = could not.

couldst [kudst; kʊdst] 〔古、诗〕could 的单数第二人称。

cou·lee [ˈkuːli; ˋkulɪ] *n*. **1.** 〔美〕斜壁峡谷；低地；(时干时流的)深山沟(山溪)。**2.**【地】熔岩流；(熔岩)岩席。

cou·leur de rose [ˈkuːlə(ː) dəˈrəuz; ˋkulɚ dəˋroz] 〔F.〕玫瑰色；粉红色；乐观(情绪)；美好的前景。

cou·lisse [kuːˈliːs; kuˋlis] *n*. **1.**【机】滑槽；滑板；滑动片；游标。**2.**【剧】侧面布景；〔*pl*.〕二片侧面布景之间的空间；〔*pl*.〕后台。**3.**【建】穿堂门厅。*the gossip of the ～s* 后台传闻，剧坛消息。*experienced in the ～s of* 熟悉…的内幕。

cou·loir [ˈkuːlwɑː; kuˋlwɑr] *n*. 〔F.〕 **1.** 峡谷。**2.** 挖泥机，浚泥机。**3.** 通道；管道。

cou·lomb [ˈkuːlɔm; ˋkuˋlɑm] *n*.【电】库仑。

cou·lom·e·ter [kuːˈlɔmitə; kuˋlɑmɪtɚ] *n*.【电】电量计，库仑计。

coul·ter [ˈkəultə; ˋkoltɚ] *n*. = colter.

cou·ma·rin(e) [ˈkuːmərin; ˋkumərɪn]【化】香豆素，氧杂萘邻酮。

cou·ma·rone [ˈkuːməˌrəun; ˋkumərοn] *n*.【化】香豆酮，氧茚，苯并呋喃。

coun·cil [ˈkaunsil; ˋkaʊnsɪl] *n*. **1.** 议事[行政，参议，立法]机构；委员会；理事会；公会。**2.**【宗】宗教[教法]会议；〔美〕地方工会代表会议。**3.** 计议，协商，讨论；〔美〕忠告，劝告。*a cabinet ～* (内)阁(会)议。*a municipal* [*city*] ～市政参议会。*a common ～*〔美〕市[镇]参议会。*a county ～*〔英〕州(议)会。*the World Peace C-* 世界和平理事会。*the United Nations Security C-* 联合国安理会。*the C-*〔英〕= *the Privy C-* 枢密院。*C- of Defence* 国防会议。*C- of State* (法国等的)参议院，国务会议。～ *of war* (战地的)军事会议；〔喻〕行动方针的商讨；(英美以外的)军事参议院。～ *of Europe* 欧洲会议。～ **board** 会议桌；(正在进行的)会议。～ **chamber** 会议室。～ **house** 会堂，议场；〔Scot.〕市政厅；州[市]营住宅。～**man** 议事机构的成员；〔美〕市[镇、村]会议员〔英国通常用 councillor〕。～ **manic** 〔美〕市[镇、村]议员的。～ **school** 〔英〕(市政议会主办的)公立小学校。

coun·cil·(l)or [ˈkaunsilə; ˋkaʊnslɚ] *n*. (市会、镇会等的)参议员；委员；顾问，参赞。*a county ～*〔英〕州议员。*a Privy C-* 枢密顾问官〔略 P. C., 用在名字之后〕。**-ship** 参议员[顾问等]的职位。

coun·sel [ˈkaunsəl; ˋkaʊnsl̩] **I** *n*. **1.** 商议；劝导，忠告。**2.** 〔古〕深思熟虑，审慎。**3.** 意图，目的，计划。**4.** 法律顾问，辩护人。*Deliberate in ～, prompt in action*. 熟思断行。*He takes ～ of his heart, but not of his head*. 他感情用事而不理智。*the King's* [*Queen's*] *C-* 王室法律顾问。***adopt a ～ of despair*** 采取自暴自弃[不顾一切]的态度。～ ***for the Crown*** 〔英〕检查官。***follow sb.'s ～*** ***close*** 牢记某人忠告。***give ～*** 提出忠告[建议]。***keep one's own ～*** 不暴露自己意图。***take ～*** (***with***) 与…商量。***take*** [***hold***] ～ ***together*** 协商。***take ～ with oneself*** 好好考虑考虑。***take sb. into one's ～*** 和某人商量。**II** *vt*. 忠告，劝告。—*vi*. 互相商议；提出劝告[建议]；接受劝告[建议]。

coun·sel·(l)or [ˈkaunsələ; ˋkaʊnsl̩ɚ] *n*. **1.** 顾问，参事；参赞，辅导员；〔美，爱〕法律顾问，律师(= ～-at-law)。**2.** (儿童夏令营等中的)领队[教导员]。

count[1] [kaunt; kaʊnt] **I** *vt*. **1.** 计数，计算，列举，清点。**2.** 算进，计进；包括。**3.** 认为，相信为；算为。～ *heads* [*noses*] 数人数。*I ～ that he will come*. 〔美俚〕我想他会来的。—*vi*. **1.** 计数，计算。**2.**【乐】打拍子。**3.** 被算入…数内；有价值，重要，值得考虑。**4.** 指望，期待，依赖 (*on*; *upon*)。*That does not ～*. 那不作数；不算问题。*See that everything ～s*. 事事都不可疏忽；要事事都办妥贴。*Every vote ～s*. (选举时)每一张票都值得重视。***be ～ed on one's fingers*** 屈指可数。～ ***sb. among one's friend*** 把某人看做朋友。～ ***against sb.*** 认为…对某人不利。～ ***... as*** [***for***] 以为，当作是(～ *sb. as dead* 当他是死了)。～ ***down*** (9, 8, 7, ... 0 地)倒数；(火箭发射时)倒数秒数。～ ***for little*** [***nothing***] 无足轻重，不足取。～ ***for much*** 非常重要。～ ***in*** 算入，归入…中计算。～ ***kin*** (***with***) (与…)是近亲；〔Scot.〕(与)比血统[门第]。～ ***off*** (点算后)分出，挑出；〔口令〕报数。～ ***on*** [***upon***] 指望；依赖。～ ***on one's fingers*** 屈指计算。～ ***out*** **1.** 一面数一面取出，点数；一面数一面分开；除开，忽视。**2.** 〔美〕(开票时)少算一部分票数(使某候选人落选)〔常用被动式〕。**3.**【拳】(对被打倒者数完十下后)宣告失败。～ ***out the House*** 〔英下院〕(议长)(因不足法定人数)宣告延会。～ ***out a measure*** [***a member***] 〔英〕(议长因不足法定人数)宣布停止讨论某议案[某议员发言]。～ ***... over*** 重算；数完。～ ***the house*** 清点出席人数。～ (***the***) ***ties*** 〔美〕沿着铁路徒步旅行。～ ***up to*** 数到，数完，总计。**II** *n*. **1.** 计算；数(目)；〔古〕总数，总计；顾虑，考虑。**2.** 价值，评价。**3.**【法】起诉理由，罪

状。**4.**【纺】支〔每克纱的米数〕;〔美〕论件出售的东西,(英下院)由于法定人数不足的延会;【拳】(给被击倒者再起来比赛的宽延时间)数十秒。***his ~ of years*** 他的年龄。***keep*** [***lose***] ~ (***of***) 无错漏地数下去[因点错而数不下去](*There were so many that he couldn't keep ~ of them*. 太多了,他无法数清他们)。***on all ~s*** 从所有方面说;【法】就所有诉讼理由[罪状]说。***out of ~*** 数不完的,无数的。***set no ~ on*** 看不起,轻视,眼中没有。***take ~ of*** 清点;重视。***take*** [***make***] ***no ~ of*** 眼中没有,轻视。***take the ~*** 【拳】(裁判员对被击倒者)数十下。**-able** **1.** ***a.*** 可数[计算]的。**2.**【语法】***n.*** 可数名词。

count[2] [kaunt; kaʊnt] ***n.*** (英国以外的)伯爵〔英国叫 earl〕。

count·down [ˈkauntˌdaun; ˋkaʊntˏdaʊn] ***n.*** **1.** (火箭、核弹等准备发射、爆炸时的)时间计算(阶段);(火箭、核弹发射、爆炸前)计时系统。**2.** (雷达的)回答脉冲比;(电视的)脉冲分频[脱漏]。**3.** 读数,示度;计数损失[漏失]。

coun·te·nance [ˈkauntinəns; ˋkaʊntənəns] **I** ***n.*** **1.** 容貌,相貌;脸色,气色;面目。**2.** 奖励;鼓励;纵容;支持,赞助。**3.** 镇定。*a sad* [*jovial*] ~悲苦[欢快]的面容。*a man with an expressive* ~脸上富于表情的人。*catch some familiar* ~认出是相识。***find no ~ in*** 不受欢迎,得不到…的支持。***for*** (***a***) ***~*** 为了面子。***get out of ~*** = ***lose ~***. ***give*** [***lend***] ***~ to*** (暗暗)嘉奖,支持,默认。***give ~ to*** 赞成。***give oneself ~*** 沉住气。***have the ~ of*** 得到…的援助。***in the light of sb.'s ~*** 由于某人帮助。***keep*** (***sb.***) ***in ~*** 留人面子,不抓破某人面子;不叫人为难。***keep one's ~*** 泰然自若,不露声色;忍住不笑。***lose ~*** 失色,慌张起来。***put*** (***sb.***) ***out of ~*** 使狼狈,使丢脸。***stare*** (***sb.***) ***out of ~*** 盯着看,使人不好意思起来。***with a good ~*** 十分沉着。**II** ***vt.*** 暗暗奖励,嘉奖;支持,赞助,鼓动;纵容,默认。

count·er[1] [ˈkauntə; ˋkaʊntɚ] ***n.*** **1.** 计算者;计算器;计数器。**2.** 筹码,号码;伪币;劣币;〔蔑〕钱;棋子;凑数的人,玩具似的人。**3.** 柜台,账台;〔英〕(旧时)债务人监狱。*~s for gambling* 赌博用筹码。*a girl behind the* ~女店员。***pay over the ~*** 在(进门处)账柜上交款。***sit*** [***serve***] ***behind a ~*** 当店员;做商人。***under the ~*** 私下(交易)。

coun·ter[2] [ˈkauntə; ˋkaʊntɚ] **I** ***n.*** **1.** 反对物,反面。**2.** (鞋底的)后跟。**3.** 马的前胸部;船尾突出部。**4.**【乐】反对次中音。**5.**【拳】回击,迎击;【溜冰】逆转。**6.** 铅字笔划间的凹处。**II** ***a.*** 相反的,反对的;一对中之一,副的。*a ~ list* 副名单。**III** ***ad.*** 相反地,反对地;逆向地。***act*** [***run***, ***go***] ***~ to*** 违反,与…相反。***hunt*** [***go***, ***run***] ***~*** 向相反方向追猎。**IV** ***vt.*** **1.** 对抗;反击,反抗,反对;针对。**2.** (象棋)下针锋相对的一着。**3.** 换鞋跟;打后掌。—***vi.*** 进行反击;还击 (*against*)。

counter- *comb. f.* 反对,反,逆,防;对应,补,副:*counter*agent。

coun·ter·ac·cu·sa·tion [ˌkauntəˌækjuˈzeiʃən; ˏkaʊntɚˏækjuˋzeʃən] ***n.*** 反控。

coun·ter·act [ˌkauntəˈrækt; ˏkaʊntɚˋækt] ***vt.*** 对…采取直接反对行动;抵抗,抵制,阻碍,打破(计划);消减,抵消,解(毒),中和。~ *a man's influence* 削弱某人的影响。

coun·ter·ac·tion [ˌkauntəˈrækʃən; ˏkaʊntɚˋækʃən] ***n.*** 反对行动;反作用,反动,对抗(作用);中和,抵消。

coun·ter·ac·tive [ˌkauntəˈræktiv; ˏkaʊntɚˋæktɪv] **I** ***a.*** 反对的,抵抗的,反作用的;中和性的,起抵消作用的。**II** ***n.*** 中和剂;中和力。

coun·ter·a·gent [ˌkauntəˈreidʒənt; ˋkaʊntɚˏedʒənt] ***n.*** 对抗力[者,物];中和力,反抗力,反对动作;反作用[中和]剂。

coun·ter-ap·proach [ˈkauntərəprəutʃ; ˋkaʊntərəˏprotʃ] ***n.*** 〔常 *pl.*〕筑城对壕(作业);(守军的)反抗行动。

coun·ter·at·tack [ˈkauntərəˌtæk; ˋkaʊntərɚˏtæk] ***vt.***, ***vi.***, ***n.*** 反攻,反击。

coun·ter·at·trac·tion [ˈkauntərəˌtrækʃən; ˏkaʊntərəˋtrækʃən] ***n.*** 反[对抗]引力;对抗物。

coun·ter·bal·ance [ˌkauntəˈbæləns; ˏkaʊntɚˋbæləns] **I** ***vt.*** 使平均,使平衡;补充,弥补;抵消(…的作用)。**II** [ˈkauntəbæl-; ˋkaʊntɚˏbæl-] ***n.*** 抗衡,等衡,平衡量;平衡力;【机】平衡锤。

coun·ter·blast [ˈkauntəblɑːst; ˋkaʊntɚˏblæst] ***n.*** **1.** 对抗气流,逆风。**2.** 强硬的抗议,猛烈的反驳。

coun·ter·blow [ˈkauntəˌbləu; ˋkaʊntɚˏblo] ***n.*** 反击。*deliver a ~ against the aggressor* 对侵略者予以反击。

C

coun·ter·buff [ˈkauntəbʌf; ˋkaʊntɚˏbʌf] ***n.***, ***vt.*** 反击;击退;挫败。

coun·ter-cei·ling [ˈkauntəˌsiːliŋ; ˋkaʊntɚˏsilɪŋ] ***n.*** 【建】(隔音,隔热)吊平顶。

coun·ter·change [ˌkauntəˈtʃeindʒ; ˏkaʊntɚˋtʃendʒ] ***n.***, ***vt.***, ***vi.*** 交换,交替,掉换;(起)交互作用;(使)交错,(使成)棋盘花[杂色]。

coun·ter·charge [ˈkauntətʃɑːdʒ; ˋkaʊntɚˏtʃardʒ] ***n.***, ***vt.*** 反攻;【法】反诉,反告。

coun·ter·check [ˈkauntətʃek; ˋkaʊntɚˏtʃɛk] **I** ***n.*** 阻挡,对抗;制止;核对,复查;〔古〕反驳,回嘴。*the quarrelsome* ~对骂。**II** ***vt.*** 制止,防止;核对,复查。

coun·ter·claim [ˈkauntəkleim; ˏkaʊntɚˋklem] ***n.***, ***vi.***, ***vt.*** (提出)反要求;反诉。

coun·ter·clock·wise [ˌkauntəˈklɔkwaiz; ˏkaʊntɚˋklɑkˏwaɪz] ***a.***, ***ad.*** 反时针方向的(地)。

coun·ter·cul·ture [ˈkauntəkʌltʃə; ˋkaʊntɚkʌltʃɚ] ***n.*** 反传统[主流]文化〔六十年代以来在美国青少年中盛行的一种思潮言行〕。

coun·ter·cur·rent [ˈkauntəˌkʌrənt; ˋkaʊntɚˏkʌrənt] ***n.*** 逆流,对流,反流;【电】逆[反向]电流。

coun·ter·deed [ˈkauntədiːd; ˋkaʊntɚˏdid] ***n.*** 【法】反对证书〔声明前一文件无效的文件,大都为密件〕。

coun·ter·dem·on·stra·tion [ˈkauntəˌdemənsˈtreiʃən; ˋkaʊntɚˏdɛmənˋstreʃən] ***n.*** 反示威〔指反对某一示威的反示威〕。

coun·ter·de·vice [ˈkauntəˌdivais; ˋkaʊntɚˏdɪvaɪs] ***n.*** **1.** 对抗装置。**2.**【军】反导[飞]弹装置。

coun·ter·drain [ˈkauntədrein; ˋkaʊntɚˏdren] ***n.*** (堤底的)副渠,漏水渠,副阴沟。

coun·ter·drive [ˈkauntədraiv; ˋkaʊntɚˏdraɪv] ***n.*** 【军】反攻,反袭击。

coun·ter·drug [ˈkauntədrʌg; ˋkaʊntədrʌg] ***n.*** 戒瘾药。

coun·ter·es·pi·on·age [ˈkauntəˌrespiəˈnɑːʒ; ˏkaʊntɚˋɛspɪənɪdʒ] ***n.*** 反间谍行动。

coun·ter-ev·i·dence [ˈkauntəˈrevidəns; ˋkaʊntɚˋɛvədns] ***n.*** 反证。

coun·ter·feit [ˈkauntəfit; ˋkaʊntɚfɪt] **I** ***a.*** 仿造的,假冒的;虚伪的,假的。*a ~ note* 伪钞。~ *sickness* 假病。**II** ***n.*** 伪物,伪品,仿造品;伪币;伪作;肖像,画像;〔古〕骗子。**III** ***vt.***, ***vi.*** **1.** 作伪;伪造(货币、文件等)。**2.** 假冒,伪;仿造,仿效,摹仿。~ *death* 装死。

coun·ter-fire [ˈkauntəfaiə; ˋkaʊntɚfaɪr] ***n.*** 【林】迎火,逆火。

coun·ter·flow [ˈkauntəfləu; ˋkaʊntɚˏflo] ***n.*** 逆流。

coun·ter·foil [ˈkauntəfɔil; ˋkaʊntɚˏfɔɪl] ***n.*** 存根,票根。

coun·ter·force [ˈkauntəˌfɔːs; ˋkaʊntɚˏfors] ***n.*** 反击力〔尤指用战略空军和导[飞]弹核武器在战争一开始就摧毁敌方核攻击力量〕。

coun·ter·fort [ˈkauntəfɔːt; ˋkaʊntɚˏfort] ***n.*** 【建】护墙,扶壁;后扶垛,拱柱;【地】山的支脉。

coun·ter·glow [ˈkauntəgləu; ˋkaʊntɚˏglo] ***n.*** 【天】对日

照。

coun·ter-guard [ˈkauntəgɑːd; ˋkaʊntə͵gɑrd] *n*. 筑城堡障,垒障。

coun·ter·in·sur·gen·cy [ˌkauntərinˈsəːdʒənsi; ͵kaʊntərɪnˋsɝdʒənsɪ] *n*. 反暴动(行动),反骚动(行动),反叛乱(行动)。

coun·ter·in·tel·li·gence [ˈkauntərinˌtelidʒəns; ͵kaʊntərɪnˋtɛlədʒəns] *n*. 【军】对敌[反]情报活动;反情报部队[机构](= C- Corps)。

coun·ter-ir·ri·tant [ˌkauntəˈiritənt; ͵kaʊntəˋɪrətənt] *n*. 【医】对抗刺激剂,诱导剂。

coun·ter·ir·ritate [ˌkauntəˈiriteit; ͵kaʊntəˋɪrə͵tet] *vt*. 对抗刺激〔指施加刺激以抵消附近的炎症〕;对…施用对抗刺激剂。

coun·ter·jum·per [ˈkauntədʒʌmpə; ˋkaʊntə͵dʒʌmpə] *n*. 〔口、蔑〕商店售货员,站柜台的。

coun·ter·light [ˈkauntəlait; ˋkaʊntə͵laɪt] *n*. 面对面的窗子;逆光。

count·er·man [ˈkauntəˌmæn, -mən; ˋkaʊntə͵mæn, -mən] *n*. (*pl*. **-men** [-ˌmen, -mən; -͵mɛn, -mən]) (自助餐馆等)柜台服务员。

coun·ter·mand [ˌkauntəˈmɑːnd; ͵kaʊntəˋmænd] *vt*., *n*. [ˈkauntəmɑːnd; ˋkaʊntə͵mænd] **1**. (下反对命令)取消(前一命令);撤回,召回,调回。**2**. 改变定货,取消(定货)。

coun·ter·march [ˈkauntəmɑːtʃ; ˋkaʊntə͵mɑrtʃ] **I** *n*. 【军】反向行进;后退,倒退。**II** *vi*., *vt*. [ˌkauntəˈmɑːtʃ; ͵kaʊntəˋmɑrtʃ] (使)向反对方向行进。

coun·ter·mark [ˈkauntəmɑːk; ˋkaʊntə͵mɑrk] **I** *n*. **1**. (金首饰等上的)戳记,刻印。**2**. (货物等上的)副标记,附加记号。**3**. 【兽医】(隐瞒马匹年龄而作的)人造齿瘢。**II** *vt*. 刻印记;加副号。

coun·ter·meas·ure [ˈkauntəmeʒə; ˋkaʊntə͵mɛʒə] *n*. 对案,对策,对抗[报复]手段;【无】干扰。

coun·ter·mine [ˈkauntəmain; ˋkaʊntə͵maɪn] **I** *n*. 【军】(对敌军所挖地道的)对抗地道;(反炸敌人水雷的)反水雷;对抗计划[谋略]。**II** *vt*. 用反地道防御;用对抗计策挫败[破坏]。

coun·ter·move [ˈkauntəmuːv; ˋkaʊntə͵muv] *n*. 对抗行动;对抗手段,报复手段[行动]。

coun·ter·mure [ˈkauntəmjuə; ˋkaʊntəmjʊr] *n*. 筑城副壁。

coun·ter·of·fen·sive [ˈkauntərəˌfensiv, ˌkauntərəˈfensiv; ˋkaʊntərə͵fɛnsɪv, ͵kaʊntərəˋfɛnsɪv] *n*. 反攻,反击。

coun·ter·of·fer [ˈkauntəˌɔːfə; ˋkaʊntə͵ɔfə] *n*. 还价,反建议。

coun·ter·pane [ˈkauntəpein; ˋkaʊntə͵pen] *n*. 床罩。

coun·ter·part [ˈkauntəpɑːt; ˋkaʊntə͵pɑrt] *n*. **1**. 【法】(正副两份中的)一份,(尤指)副本;极相似的人[物],一对中之一个,骑缝图章的一半。**2**. 相对物;变体,变型。**3**. 【乐】对应部。*It has no* ~ *in the world*. 举世无双。

coun·ter·plea [ˈkauntəpliː; ˋkaʊntə͵pli] *n*. 【法】附带抗辩。

coun·ter·plot [ˈkauntəplɔt; ˋkaʊntə͵plɑt] **I** *n*. 对抗策略。**II** *vt*., *vi*. 用对抗策略对付。

coun·ter·point [ˈkauntəpɔint; ˋkaʊntə͵pɔɪnt] **I** *n*. **1**. 【乐】对位法,对位音;旋律配合法;重复旋律法。**2**. 对偶;对比;对照(法)。**II** *vt*. 用对照法衬托。

coun·ter·poise [ˈkauntəpɔiz; ˋkaʊntə͵pɔɪz] **I** *vt*. (使)均衡[平衡];补偿,抵补。**II** *n*. 平衡,均衡,平衡力,衡重体,秤锤,砝码;【无】平衡网络,地网。**be in** ~ 保持平衡〔均衡〕。

coun·ter·pro·duc·tive [ˈkauntəprəˌdʌktiv; ˋkaʊntəprə͵dʌktɪv] *a*. 起反作用的。

coun·ter·pro·ram·ming [ˌkauntəˈprəugræmiŋ; ͵kaʊntəˋpro͵græmɪŋ] *n*. 竞争[对抗]性节目编排。

coun·ter·pro·po·sal [ˈkauntəprəˌpəuzl; ˋkaʊntəprə͵pozl] *n*. 反建议,反提案。

coun·ter·ref·or·ma·tion [kauntəˌrefəˈmeiʃən; ͵kaʊntə͵rɛfəˋmeʃən] *n*. 反改革。

coun·ter·rev·o·lu·tion [ˈkauntərevəˈljuːʃən; ͵kaʊntə͵rɛvəˋluʃən] *n*. 反革命。**-ary** *n*., *a*. 反革命分子(的)。**-ist** *n*. 反革命(分子)。

coun·ter·scarp [ˈkauntəskɑːp; ˋkaʊntə͵skɑrp] *n*. (堡垒壕沟的)外削壁。

coun·ter·sea [ˈkauntəsiː; ˋkaʊntə͵si] *n*. 逆浪,逆行海流。

coun·ter·shaft [ˈkauntəʃɑːft; ˋkaʊntə͵ʃæft] *n*. 【机】副轴,对轴,平行轴,逆转轴;天轴。

coun·ter·sign [ˈkauntəsain; ˋkaʊntə͵saɪn] **I** *n*. **1**. 【军】(对哨兵盘问时)回答口令;呼应暗号;【海】应讯信号。**2**. 副签,副署;【商】会签。**II** *vt*. 副署,连署;同意,承认。

coun·ter·sig·na·ture [ˌkauntəˈsignitʃə; ͵kaʊntəˋsɪgnətʃə] *n*. 副署,连署。

coun·ter·sink [ˈkauntəsiŋk; ˋkaʊntə͵sɪŋk] **I** *vt*. (**-sunk** [-sʌŋk; -sʌŋk]) 打孔装埋(螺钉头),打埋头孔。**II** *n*. 埋头钻;埋头孔,暗钉眼。

coun·ter·spy [ˈkauntəspai; ˋkaʊntə͵spaɪ] *n*. 反间谍。

coun·ter·stroke [ˈkauntəstrəuk; ˋkaʊntə͵strok] *n*. 反击;还击,回击;【医】反击损伤。

coun·ter·ten·or [ˈkauntəˈtenə; ˋkaʊntəˋtɛnə] *n*. 【乐】上次中音〔男声最高音部〕;上次中音歌手。

coun·ter·trade [ˈkauntəˌtreid; ˋkaʊtə͵tred] *n*. 对应贸易,以货易货贸易。

coun·ter·type [ˈkauntəˌtaip; ˋkaʊntə͵taɪp] *n*. **1**. 相反典型。**2**. 对等型;相似型。

coun·ter·vail [ˈkauntəveil; ͵kaʊntəˋvel] *vt*., *vi*. **1**. 对抗,抵敌;与…势均力敌。**2**. 补偿;抵消。

coun·ter·view [ˈkauntəvjuː; ˋkaʊntə͵vju] *n*. **1**. 反对意见。**2**. 对质。

coun·ter·weigh [ˌkauntəˈwei; ͵kaʊntəˋwe] *vt*. 使平衡;抵消。

coun·ter·weight [ˈkauntəweit; ˋkaʊntə͵wet] **I** *n*. 平衡重量;砝码;抗衡。**II** *vt*. = counterweigh.

coun·ter·word [ˈkauntəwəːd; ˋkaʊntə͵wɝd] *n*. 转用词,代用词〔例: swell 意为 first-rate 等〕。

coun·ter·work [ˌkauntəˈwəːk; ͵kaʊntəˋwɝk] **I** *vt*., *vi*. 对抗行动;阻碍;破坏。**II** *n*. [ˈkauntəwəːk; ˋkaʊntə͵wɝk]对抗;【军】对垒。

count·ess [ˈkauntis; ˋkaʊntɪs] *n*. **1**. 伯爵夫人〔英国指 earl 的妻子,欧洲大陆指 count 的妻子〕。**2**. 女伯爵。

count·ing [ˈkauntiŋ; ˋkaʊntɪŋ] *n*. 计算。~ *house* 〔英〕= ~ *room* 〔美〕账房;会计室;事务室。~ *overseer* [*witness*] (投票的)唱票监察人。

count·less [ˈkauntlis; ˋkaʊntlɪs] *a*. 无数的,数不尽的。

count·out [ˈkauntˈaut; ˋkaʊntˋaʊt] *n*. (英下院)不满法定人数(40 人)的休会;【拳】(对被击倒者宽限的)十秒,数十下;〔美〕被故意少报票数而落选的候选人。

coun·tri·fied [ˈkʌntrifaid; ˋkʌntrɪ͵faɪd] *a*. 土里土气的;粗鲁的。

coun·tri·fy [ˈkʌntrifai; ˋkʌntrɪfaɪ] *vt*. 使土头土脑,使成乡下派头;使粗鲁。

coun·try [ˈkʌntri; ˋkʌntrɪ] **I** *n*. **1**. 国家;国土;(全)国民,民众。**2**. 本国,祖国;家乡,故乡。**3**. 乡下,农村;土地,地方,地区;领域,范围。**4**. (代表群众的)陪审(团)。**5**. 【矿】围岩(= ~ rock)。**6**. 【海】(船内的)室,间;士官室(= the officer ~)。**7**. 【板球】外野。*a developing* ~ 发展中的国家。*a beautiful* ~ 美丽的地区。*town and* ~ 城乡。*a flat* ~ 平原地区。*a hill* ~ 丘陵地带。**II** *a*. **1**. 地方的,乡村的;粗鲁的。**2**. 祖国的;故乡的,家乡的。**3**. 【美乐】乡村音乐的。*across* ~ (不走正路)横断田野,越野的(赛跑等)。~ *cousin* 乡下亲戚,(衣

C

着朴素态度恳直的)乡下人。~ *gentleman* 乡下地主。~ *note* 地方(银行发行的)钞票。~ *party* (代表农村利益的)农民党。***go*** (***out***) ***into the*** ~ 下乡〔美国说 ***go up*** (***the***) ~〕。***go*** [***appeal***] ***to the*** ~ 〔英〕解散议会(进行普选)。***in the*** ~ 在乡下;【板球】远离三柱门。***live in the*** ~ 住在乡下〔美国说 ***live up*** ~ 〕。***put*** [***throw***] ***oneself upon the*** ~ 要求陪审团审判。~ **and western**〔缩 **C&W**〕 ***a***.【美乐】西部乡村音乐的。~-**born** ***a***. 生在乡下的。~-**bred** ***a***. 在乡下长大的。~ **damage**【商】因风雨或处置失当所造成的损失。~-**dance** (英国的)土风舞,乡村舞。~ **folk** 乡下人;同国人,同胞。~ **house** (乡绅贵族等的)庄宅(*opp*. town house);庄园式地主住宅;〔美〕别墅。~ **jake**〔美〕乡下人。~**man** 乡下人;某地[国]的人;同国人,同胞,同乡(*fellow* ~ *man* 同胞)。~ **mile** 很远的距离。~ **music** (尤指美国南部)乡村音乐。~ **party**【英史】在野派。~**people** 乡下佬。~ **road** 1. (旧时英国的)农村公路。2. 乡间道路。~ **rocky**【美乐】西部乡村摇摆音乐。~ **seat** = ~ house. ~**side** 乡下,农村;地方;地方居民。~**wide** ***a***. 全国(性)的。~**woman** 乡下妇女;女同胞,女同乡。

coun·ty [ˈkaunti; ˋkauntɪ] ***n***. **1**. 〔英〕郡〔与专有名词连用时用 shire. 例: Yorkshire = the ~ of York〕。**2**. 〔英〕郡中世家,郡中社交频繁的阶层;全郡居民。**3**. 〔美〕县。***the home counties***〔英〕伦敦附近六郡。~ **alderman** 郡参议员。~ **borough** 市。~ **commissioner**〔英〕郡治安法官,〔美〕县长。~ **corporate**〔英〕自治市,特别市。~ **council** 郡议会。~ **council school**〔英〕郡立小学校。~ **court**〔英〕郡法院,〔美〕县法院;县监察委员会。~-**court** ***vt***.〔英口〕向郡法院控告。~ **family**〔英〕郡中世家。~ **farm** [**house**]〔美〕县济贫农场,县贫民收容所。~ **hall** 郡议事厅;〔the C- H-〕(特指)伦敦郡议事厅。~ **seat**〔美〕县城。~ **sessions** 郡治安法官执行的四季裁判。~ **society** 郡中上层社会(集团)。~ **town**〔英〕郡城;〔美〕县城。

coup [kuː; ku] ***n***. 〔F.〕**1**. 突然的一击。**2**. 突然而敏捷的行动;大成功。**3**. (军事)政变。*at one* ~ 一举,一气。***make*** [***pull off***] ***a great*** ~ 大大成功。~ ***de foudre*** [ˈkuː dəˈfuːdrə; ˋku dəˋfudrə]〔F.〕雷击;晴天霹雳;一见钟情。~ ***de grâce*** [ˈkuːdəˈgrɑːs; ˋkudəˋgrɑs]〔F.〕(使其少受痛苦而)一下打死;一举消灭;致命一击。~ ***de main*** [ˈkuːdəˈmɛ̃ːŋ; ˋkudəˋmɛ̃ŋ]〔F.〕【军】奇袭。~ ***de maître*** [kuːdəˈmetrə; kudəˋmɛtrə]〔F.〕巧妙的手段。~ ***d'état*** [ˈkuːdeiˈtɑː; ˋkudeˋtɑ]〔F.〕(武装)政变。~ ***de théâtre*** [ˈkuːdateiˈɑːtr; ˋkudateˋɑrtr]〔F.〕(富有效果的)戏剧(性)手法。~ ***d'œil*** [ˈkuːˈdəːi; ˋkuˋdɜɪ]〔F.〕一瞥,概观;【军】能迅速看清局势的眼力。

cou·pé [ˈkuːpei; ˋkupe] ***n***. 〔F.〕双座四轮轿式马车;轿式小汽车;〔英〕(客车末端的)分隔车厢。

coup·ist [ˈkuːist; ˋkuɪst] ***n***. 企图(军事)政变者;支持(军事)政变者。

cou·ple [ˈkʌpl; ˋkʌpl] **I** ***n***. **1**. 一对,一双。**2**. 配偶,夫妇,未婚夫妻,一对舞伴。**3**. 〔口〕交媾;【物】力偶;电偶;【天】联星。**4**. 〔口〕(少数)几个,两三个。*an old* ~老两口儿。*a married* ~夫妇。*a pack of 20* ~二十对的一群猎犬。*a thermo-electric* ~温差电偶。*a* ~ *of days* 二三日,数日。***go*** [***hunt***, ***run***] ***in*** ~***s*** 总是成双成对;协力。**II** ***vt***. **1**. (两支)拴在一起,配合,连接。**2**. 使结婚;(使)交配。**3**. 由…联想到(…);把…同联系起来。~ *two railroad coaches* 把两节铁路车厢连接起来。—***vi***. 拥抱,搂抱;交尾;结婚;结合,配合。

cou·pler [ˈkʌplə; ˋkʌplɚ] ***n***. **1**. 连结者,配合者。**2**. 联结器;【无】耦合器;【铁路】车钩;【摄】发色剂;【乐】(风琴上连结两组键盘的)联奏器。

cou·plet [ˈkʌplit; ˋkʌplɪt] ***n***. 两行诗〔两行构成一节的诗体〕;对句;〔*pl*.〕对联。*the heroic* ~ 英雄史诗式两行诗。

cou·pling [ˈkʌpliŋ; ˋkʌplɪŋ] ***n***. 联结;交尾;【机】管箍;联结器;轴接;(火车的)车钩,【电】耦合。

cou·pon [ˈkuːpɔn, ˈkuːpɔ̃ːŋ; ˋkupɑn, ˋkupɔ̃ŋ] ***n***. **1**. 【商】(附在证券上的)息票;(火车等使用一次剪下一张的)票,通票。**2**. 【商】赠券;(连在广告上的)预约券,优待券。**3**. 配给票。**4**. 〔英俚〕(政党领袖提出的)候选人名单。**5**. 【技术】试样,试件,试棒,试片,切片。*a food* [*oil*] ~ 粮[油]票。~ *system* 附送赠品的商品推销法。~ *ticket* (使用一次剪下一张的)多次入场票。*cum* ~ =~ *on* 带有息票的(公债票等)。*ex* ~ =~ *off* 不带息票的。

cour·age [ˈkʌridʒ; ˋkɝɪdʒ] ***n***. 勇气,胆量;精神;〔美俚〕钱。*Dutch* ~〔俚〕酒后之勇,虚勇。*moral* ~ 精神之勇,坚信不移之勇。*physical* ~ 不怕身体危险的勇气,刚勇。*stoic* ~坚忍不拔的精神。***have the*** ~ ***of one's convictions*** [***opinions***] 勇于坚持自己的主张[信仰]。***lose*** ~ 丧气,丧胆。***take*** [***muster up***, ***pluck up***, ***screw up***] ~ 鼓起勇气。***take one's*** ~ ***in both hands*** 勇敢地干,敢作敢为。

cou·ra·geous [kəˈreidʒəs; kəˋredʒəs] ***a***. 勇敢的,英勇的。-**ly** ***ad***. -**ness** ***n***.

cou·rant [kuˈrænt; kʊˋrænt] **I** ***n***. 报(纸)〔现仅作报名用〕。**II** ***a***. 【徽】步行状的。

cou·rante, cou·rant [kuːˈrɑːnt; kuˋrɑnt] ***n***. **1**. 库兰特舞。**2**. 库兰特舞曲。**3**. 〔英方〕乱跑。

cou·reur de bois [kuːˈrəː dəˈbwɑː; kuˋrɝdəˋbwɑ] (*pl*. ***cou·reurs de bois***) (早期在加拿大边界流窜的)法国非法毛皮贩子;非法猎取毛皮者。

cour·gette [kuːəˈʒet; kuəˋʒɛt] ***n***. 〔F.〕绿皮南瓜汁〔一种冷饮〕。

cour·i·er [ˈkuriə; ˋkʊrɪr] ***n***. **1**. 信使,急件递送人。**2**. (欧洲的)伴游服务员。**3**. 〔C-〕(用作报刊名)信使报。*the Liverpool C-* 利物浦信使报。

cour·lan [ˈkulən; ˋkʊlən] ***n***. 【动】(美洲热带的)哭鸟,长嘴鸟。

course [kɔːs; kors] **I** ***n***. **1**. 进程,经过,过程,趋势;经过期间。**2**. 进路;水路;路程;路线;航线;【火箭】导引。**3**. 行进方向;航向;走向,(矿)脉;(行动的)方针,方法;程序;举动;行动;〔*pl*.〕〔古〕品行,行为。**4**. 行列,层次。**5**. 学科,课程,教程;【医】疗程。**6**. 经历,生涯。**7**. 赛跑场;跑道;跑马场。**8**. (用狗)追猎。**9**. (比赛的)一场,一回合;一道菜;【建】一层(砖等),一排;【船】下桁大横帆。**10**. 〔*pl*.〕月经。**11**. 〔又写作 'course〕〔俚,美〕= of ~. *a dog* ~ = *a pursuit* ~【空】追踪飞行。*a pre-computed* ~【火箭】程序控制导引;自动导航。*a collision* ~【空】迎面航向;拦截方向。*What* ~ *do you advise?* 你说怎么办好呢? *the science* [*literature*] ~(大学的)理[文]科。*the preparatory* ~预科。*a dinner of five* ~*s* 五道菜的一餐饭。*a* ~ *of lectures* 连续讲演,讲座。*a degree in* ~〔美〕(经过)正式(课程而获得的)学位。(***as***) ***a matter of*** ~ (作为)当然的事情。***adopt a middle*** ~ 采取稳健办法。***be on her*** [***its***] ~ (船)航向不变。***by*** ~ ***of*** 照…的常例。~ **bond** = ~ ***of headers***【建】丁砖层。~ ***crabbing***〔美俚〕讨好老师,取得老师的欢心。~ ***of events*** 事件的经过。~ ***of exchange*** (外汇)兑换率[行情表]。~ ***of things*** 事态,趋势。~ ***of treatments***【医】疗程。***follow a middle*** ~ 采取稳健办法。***follow*** [***persue***] ***her*** ~ 照一定航线航行。***hold*** [***keep on***] ***one's*** ~ 不变方向;抱定宗旨。***in*** ~ **1**. 〔美〕按正规课程(得到的)。**2**. 〔俚〕= of ~. **3**. 〔古〕= ***in due*** ~. ***in*** ~ ***of*** 在…中(*The house is in* ~ *of construction*. 房子正在建造中)。***in due*** ~ 及时;顺次,依次序。***in full*** ~〔口〕快;用全速。***in mid*** ~ 在半路,中途。***in short*** ~〔口〕立即,马上。***in the*** ~ ***of*** 在…之中(*in the* ~ *of today* 在今天以内。*in the* ~ *of things* 在事情顺利发展中,在正常情况下)。***in the ordinary*** ~ ***of events*** 按正常趋势。***lay the*** ~ 砌砖。***of*** ~当然。***run***

C

its [*their*] ～ (疾病、岁月等自然而然地)经过,进展。*shape one's* ～ 决定路线;制定方针。*stay the* ～ 坚持到底,始终不渝。*take a* ～【海】采一定航路。*take one's own* ～ 按自己办法,走自己的道路。*take to evil* ～*s* 开始放荡。*walk over the* ～【赛马】(因无劲敌)从容得胜。**II** *vt*. 追,赶,猎,跑马,越过,跑过,横断(原野)。—*vi*. (用猎狗)追猎;(马、孩子等的)快跑;(血液)循环;(眼泪)不住地淌;(云等)乱飞;决定航线[方针]。~**dinner** (丰盛的)正式晚餐。~**ware**【计】教学软件。

cours·er[1] [ˈkɔːsə; ˋkɔrsɚ] *n*. **1**. 快跑者,行进者[人或物]。**2**. 追猎者。**3**. 猎狗。

cours·er[2] [ˈkɔːsə; ˋkɔrsɚ] *n*. 〔诗〕骏马,军马。

cours·er[3] [ˈkɔːsə; ˋkɔrsɚ] *n*.【动】(亚洲和非洲产的)快跑走禽。

cours·ing [ˈkɔːsiŋ; ˋkɔrsɪŋ] *n*. **1**. (使用猎狗)追猎。**2**. 快跑,追赶;运行,奔驰。

court [kɔːt; kort] **I** *n*. **1**. 法院,法庭;法官。**2**. 宫廷,朝廷;朝臣;朝见,谒见;御前会议;(公司等的)委员会;董事会;委员,董事。**3**. 院子,天井;场子,网球场;(展览会中的)馆。**4**. 奉承,讨好;(尤指男人向女人)求爱,求婚。**5**. 短巷,短街。*a law* ～法庭。*the district* ～地方法院。*a summary* ～即决法院。*the Crown C-* 〔英〕刑事法院。*the High C- of Parliament* 英国议会。*a grass* [*hard*] ～草地[硬地]网球场。*appear in* ～出庭。*at* ～在宫中,在朝廷上。*be presented at* ～ 在宫中受接见。*C- of Admiralty*【英史】海军法庭。*C- of Appeal* 上诉法院。*C- of Claims* 〔美〕(华盛顿)行政法院。*C- of Conscience* [*Requests*] (少额)债权法院;〔喻〕良心。～ *of inquiry* 咨询会议。～ *of justice* [*judicature*] = ～ *of law* 法院,法庭。*C- of St. James's* 英国宫廷。*go to* ～ 觐见。*hold a* ～ (*C-*) 开庭,开审;举行(觐见礼)。*in* ～ 在法庭上。*laugh out of* ～ 置之一笑,一笑了之。*order the* ～ *to be cleared* 命令旁听人退庭。*out of* ～ 在法庭外;无审判价值的,无诉讼权利的;无足轻重的,不值一顾的(议论等)。*pay* [*make*] *one's* ～ *to* 奉承,献殷勤,(向女人)求爱,求婚。*present at* ～ 陪…入宫谒见,做谒见陪客。*put out of* ～ 不顾,蔑视。*put oneself out of* ～ 做出[讲出]让人瞧不起的事情[话]。*settle* (*a case*) *out of* ～ (在法院外)私下和解。*take* (*a matter*) *into* ～ 弄到上法庭,提出诉讼。**II** *vt*., *vi*. 献殷勤;(向女人)求爱,求婚;寻求;博(人喝彩等),招惹(祸事等),诱(人) (*into*; *to*; *from*);〔英俚〕向法院控诉。～ **card** 〔英〕有人头的纸牌〔King, Queen, Jack〕。～ **circular** 宫廷公报。～ **day** 开庭日,审判日;(朝廷中的)典礼日。～ **dress** 朝服,大礼服。～ **fool** 朝廷中的弄臣。～ **guide** 〔英〕名绅录。～ **house** 法院;〔美〕县政府。～ **lady** 朝廷中女官,宫女。～ **martial** 军事法庭;〔俚〕交军事法庭。～ **mourning** 宫丧,废朝。～ **plaster** (往时英国宫女贴在脸上增进美感的宫膏,转为)橡皮膏;〔俚〕死缠不休的求婚者。～ **roll** (租佃)地册,地籍登记簿。～ **room** 审判室。～**ship** (男向女)求爱,求婚;求爱期间;【动】求偶(现象)。～**yard** 庭院,院子。

cour·te·ous [ˈkəːtjəs; ˋkɝtɪəs] *a*. 有礼貌的;殷勤的,周到的 (*opp*. rude)。**-ly** *ad*. **-ness** *n*.

cour·te·san, cour·te·zan [ˌkɔːtiˈzæn; ˋkortəzn̩] *n*. 高等妓女;原指王公显贵的情妇。

cour·te·sy [ˈkəːtisi, ˈkɔːtisi; ˋkɝtəsɪ, ˋkɝtsɪ] *n*. 礼貌,殷勤周到;亲切;好意;〔古〕行礼,请安。*be granted the* ～ [*courtesies*] *of the port* 〔美〕准予在海关免除检查。*by* ～ 按惯例,礼貌上;〔美〕情面上。*by* [*through*] ～ *of* 〔美〕由于…好意,蒙…特许。～ *of the port*【海】外国军舰入港时相互访问的礼节。～ **light** (汽车车门打开后即自动开灯的)车箱灯。～ **title** (非法律规定的)礼貌上的尊称。

court·i·er [ˈkɔːtjə; ˋkortɪɚ] *n*. **1**. 朝臣。**2**. 谄媚者;受宠遇者。

court·li·ness [ˈkɔːtlinis; ˋkortlɪnɪs] *n*. 礼让,殷勤,周到。

court·ly [ˈkɔːtli; ˋkortlɪ] *a*. 朝廷的;有礼貌的,殷勤的;周到的。

cous·cous [ˈkuːskuːs, kuːsˈkuːs; ˋkuskus, kusˋkus] *n*.【烹】(北非的)粉蒸羊肉;粉蒸鸡。

cous·in [ˈkʌzn; ˋkʌzn] *n*. **1**. 堂[表]兄弟,堂[表]姊妹;亲戚,远亲。**2**. 卿〔国王对贵族或别国元首的敬称〕。**3**. 朋友,伙伴。**4**. 同族者,同类者,同辈。**5**. 〔美俚〕容易受骗的人;无意中使对方占便宜的人。*first* [*full*, *own*] ～*s* (第一代)嫡堂[表]兄[弟、姊、妹]。*first* ～*s once removed* =〔俚〕*second* ～*s* (第二代)隔房堂[表]兄[弟、姊、妹]。*call* ～*s* (*with*) 认(某人)是亲戚;称兄道弟,建立亲密关系。*C- Anne* 〔美俚〕威尔斯人矿工的妻子。*C- Jack* 〔美俚〕到美国来谋生的威尔斯人矿工。～ *Jacky* [*Jan*] 〔英俚〕康瓦尔 (Cornwall) 人的绰号。*C- Johnathan* 美国人的绰号。～**-german** = *first* ～. ～**-hood**, ～ **ship** 堂[表]兄弟[姊妹]关系;亲戚关系。**-ly** *a*. 堂[表]兄弟[姐妹]关系(一样)的;亲戚似的。

cous·in·ry [ˈkʌzənri; ˋkʌzənrɪ] *n*. 〔集合词〕表兄弟姊妹们,堂兄弟姊妹们;亲戚们。

coûte que coûte [ˈkuːt kəˈkuːt; ˋku tkəˋkut]〔F.〕无论代价如何,不惜任何牺牲。

couth [kuːθ; kuθ] *a*. **1**. 〔谑〕文雅的;有教养的;文明的。**2**. 〔古〕人所共知的;熟悉的。

couth·ie [ˈkuːθi; ˋkuθɪ] *a*. 〔Scot.〕**1**. 友好的,和善的。**2**. 舒适的。

cou·ture [F. kuˈtyːr; kuˋtur] *n*. 妇女时装业;妇女时装。

coutu·rier [F. kutyrˈje; kuˋturɪɚ] *n*. (*fem*. **-rière** [-riˈɛə; -ˋrjɛr]) 〔F.〕妇女时装设计师;时装店主。

cou·vade [kuːˈvɑːd; kuˋvɑd] *n*. 父代母育风俗[某些原始部族的风俗,婴儿出生后,父亲代替母亲卧床]。

co·va·lence [kəuˈveiləns; koˋveləns] *n*.【化】共[协]价。～ **electron** 共价电子。**-va·lent** *a*.

co·var·i·ance [kəuˈveəriəns; koˋverɪəns] *n*.【统】协方差,协变性;共离散。

co·var·i·ant [kəuˈveəriənt; koˋverɪənt] *a*., *n*.【统】协变的[式]。

cove[1] [kəuv; kov] **I** *n*. **1**. (河)湾;小海湾,峻岨的海角[山凹]。**2**.【建】穹窿,拱。**3**. 凹圆线。**II** *vi*., *vt*. (使)成拱形;(使)内凹。

cove[2] [kəuv; kov] *n*. 〔英俚〕家伙;〔澳俚〕老板(特指牧场经理)。*a rum* ～可笑的家伙。

cov·en [ˈkʌvən, ˈkəuvən; ˋkʌvən, ˋkovən] *n*. (女巫)大聚会;集会。

cov·e·nant [ˈkʌvinənt; ˋkʌvɪnənt] **I** *n*. **1**. 协议,协定;协议书,协定条款。**2**.【宗】誓约;(上帝对信徒的)圣约。**3**. 〔the C-〕国联盟约;【史】(1638 年苏格兰长老会反对主教派教会的)国民契约 (= the National C-);(1643 年英格兰和苏格兰议会协议保护长老会的)严肃盟约 (= the Solemn League and C-)。**4**.【法】契约(条款);违约诉讼。**II** *vi*., *vt*. (订)协定,缔结盟约 (*with*; *for*; *to do*; *that*)。～ **marriage** 契约婚姻〔指婚前男女双方就财产、家庭义务等先订立契约〕。

cov·e·nan·tee [ˌkʌvinænˈtiː; ˏkʌvɪnænˋti] *n*. 契约受益方。

cov·e·nant·er [ˈkʌvinəntə; ˋkʌvɪnəntɚ] *n*. 协定的,结盟者;〔C-〕【史】国民契约及严肃同盟的结盟者。

Cov·ent Garden [ˈkɔvənt gɑːdn; ˋkɑvənt gɑrdn] 考文特花园〔**1**. 伦敦中部一个蔬菜花卉市场。**2**. = the Covent Garden Theatre 伦敦中心戏院〕。

cov·en·trate, cov·en·trize [ˈkɔvəntreit, -traiz; ˋkɑvəntret, -traɪz] *vt*. 集中轰炸摧毁〔来自 Coventry, 英国城市名,1940 年几乎全部被纳粹空军炸毁〕。

Cov·en·try [ˈkɔvəntri; ˋkɑvəntrɪ] *n*. 考文垂〔英国城市〕。*send sb. to* ～ 逐出社交圈子,抵制,与…绝交。

cov·er [ˈkʌvə; ˋkʌvɚ] **I** *vt*. **1**. 覆盖,遮蔽,包裹;戴帽子;包庇,隐蔽,掩盖;灭迹,(用纸)表(墙)。**2**. 孵(小鸡);(种马)交配。**3**. (炮火等)控制;对准射击;【军】掩护。**4**.

涉及,包括,包含;网罗;适用。5. 通过,走过(若干里);讲完(几课),看完(几节)。6. 足敷,足以抵补[补偿];(用保险办法)保护;出大牌压倒(对方)。7.【商】补进(预先卖出的商品)。8.【宗】恕宥。9.〔美〕采访(新闻、报导会议情形等)。10. 掩没。11.(与雌的)交配。~ *the table* 铺桌布和摆餐具(准备开饭)。*Pray be ~ed*. 请戴好帽子。*The troops ~ed the country*. 军队遍布国内。~ *the landing* [*retreat*] *of an army* 掩护军队登陆[退却]。*His studies ~ed a wide field*. 他的研究涉及广大范围。*The rules ~ all cases*. 那规则普遍适用。*He once ~ed a mile in three minutes*. 他有一次在三分钟内跑了一英里。*My income barely ~s my expenses*. 我的收入刚刚够用。***be ~ed with*** 盖满,覆满(灰尘等),落满(苍蝇等),充满(恐慌、羞耻等)。~ ***in*** 用屋顶遮盖;用土填洞等。~ ***into the Treasury***〔美〕解交国库。~ ***oneself with*** 蒙受,获得(*He ~ed himself with glory*. 享受荣誉)。~ ***over*** 遮遍,完全封蔽。~ ***shorts*** [***short sales***](交易所)补进空头股数。~ ***up*** 1. 蒙盖;隐蔽。2. 包庇(某人);为某人打掩护。—*vi*. 1. 展延。2. 代替(*for*)。3.(拳击中)掩护脸部。**II** *n*. 1. 覆盖物,盖子,套子,罩子,(书的)封面,壳子;(车辆的)外胎。2. 隐蔽,遮蔽;假托,借口,假装。3. 掩护物〔森林、凹地等〕;(禽兽)隐藏处。4.(一份)餐具。5.【商】担保,保证金。6.【板球】后卫场所;【网球】防守范围;【乒乓】触球。*a dinner of 50 ~s* 供五十个人食用的一次正餐。*C-s were laid for five*. 预备了五份饭菜。***be under*** ~ 是秘密的,在隐蔽处。***break*** ~ 由隐蔽处跳出[飞出]。***draw a*** ~ 把(猎物)由树丛中赶出。***from*** ~ ***to*** ~ 从头到尾〔指书籍〕。***provide*** ~ ***for*** 给…打掩护。***take*** ~【军】利用[凭]掩护物;隐蔽。***under separate*** ~ 另函包寄。***under*** (***the***) ~ ***of*** 躲在…之下;在…掩护下;趁着(夜色等);借…为口实。***under*** ~ ***to*** 附在…信中。***under the same*** ~ 在同一包[封]中,附在信中。~ **charge**(饭店)附加费,服务费。~ **crop** 护田[肥田]的农作物,覆盖作物。~ **girl** 封面女郎。~**lid** = ~let. ~ **note** 暂保单,保险证明。~ **point**【板球】后卫。~**-up** [ˈkʌvərʌp; ˋkʌvərʌp] *n*. 掩盖手段[手法]。

cov·er·age [ˈkʌvəridʒ; ˋkʌvərɪdʒ] *n*. 范围,规模,总额;〔美〕保险额;保证金,现金准备;〔美〕(新闻)报导(范围);【植】优势度。~ *diagram*【空】搜索范围。

cov·er·all [ˈkʌvəˌrɔːl; ˋkʌvəˏɔl] *n*.〔通常为 *pl*.〕连衣裤工作服。

Cov·er·dale [ˈkʌvədeil; ˋkʌvəˏdel] *n*. 科弗代尔〔姓氏〕。

cov·ered [ˈkʌvəd; ˋkʌvəd] *a*. 隐蔽着的,掩藏着的;有屋顶的;有盖的;戴着帽子的;〔复合词〕盖满…的〔如:moss-~〕。*a ~ position* 隐蔽阵地。*a ~ wagon*〔美〕有篷马车;汽车拉着走的活动房子。~ **smut**【农】坚黑穗病。~ **way**【军】覆道,暗道;【建】廊道。

cov·er·ing [ˈkʌvəriŋ; ˋkʌvərɪŋ] *n*. 被覆,外被;外封;房顶;上覆物,掩护;【商】了结,补进。~ *fire* 掩护射击。~ *for* (*chair, hand* ...)(椅、手…)套。~ *letter*(寄送物件等作为说明的)附信。~ *note*【火灾保险】承保通知单。~ *party*【军】掩护队。~ *price*(一切计算在内的)总价。

cov·er·let [ˈkʌvəlit; ˋkʌvəlɪt] *n*. 1. 床单,桌布(等)。2. 盖子,罩子。

cov·ert [ˈkʌvət; ˋkʌvət] **I** *a*. 隐蔽的,偷偷摸摸的,隐密的;【法】有丈夫(保护)的。*a feme* ~【法】有夫之妇。~ *cloth* 细纹薄呢。**II** [ˈkʌvə, ˈkʌvət; ˋkʌvə, ˋkʌvət] *n*. 掩蔽物;隐伏处〔树丛等〕;〔*pl*.〕【动】覆羽。***break*** ~ = break cover. ***draw a*** ~ = draw a cover. **-ly** *ad*.

cov·er·ture [ˈkʌvətjuə; ˋkʌvətʃə] *n*. 1. 被覆;保护;掩护物,隐伏处。2.【法】有丈夫之妇的身份。***under*** ~有丈夫。

cov·et [ˈkʌvit; ˋkʌvɪt] *vt*., *vi*. 妄想(别人东西),贪求。*All ~ all lose*. 贪多无所得。**-a·ble** *a*. 可垂涎的,可羡慕的。

cov·et·ous [ˈkʌvitəs; ˋkʌvətəs] *a*. 贪婪的。***be ~ of*** 渴望,贪求。**-ly** *ad*. **-ness** *n*.

cov·ey [ˈkʌvi; ˋkʌvɪ] *n*.(鹌鹑、鹧鸪等的)一群,一窝;〔谑〕(人的)一群,一伙;(东西的)一套,一批。

cov·in [ˈkʌvin; ˋkʌvɪn] *n*. 1. 变节;背信;欺诈;阴谋集团,诈骗集团。2.【法】共谋暗算他人。

cov·ing [ˈkəuviŋ; ˋkovɪŋ] *n*.(河等的)湾,弯处;【建】弧形饰;穹窿;拱;凹圆线。

cow[1] [kau; kaʊ] *n*.(*pl*. ~s,〔古、方〕*kine* [kain; kaɪn]) 1. 母牛,乳牛(*opp*. bull);(象、犀、鲸等的)母兽。2.〔美、方〕〔*pl*.〕= cattle. 3.〔美俚〕牛奶,奶油;牛肉;〔俚〕粗壮邋遢的女人;〔卑〕儿女多的妇女;老妓。***give 'em Brown's*** ~〔美〕(马戏团)缩短表演。***salt the*** ~ ***to catch the calf***〔美口〕用间接手段达到目的。***till the ~s come home*** 长久,永远。~ **age**【植】发痒黧豆(= ~hage)。~**bane**【植】毒芹。~**bell**(牛的)颈铃;【植】白玉草。~**berry**【植】牙疙疸,越橘。~**bind**【植】白泻根;异株泻根。~**bird**【鸟】(北美产)燕八哥。~**boy** 牧童;〔美、加拿大〕骑马牧童;〔美俚〕违章驾驶的汽车司机;〔美俚〕西部风味的夹心面包。~**boy boot**〔美〕牛仔靴。~**boy hat**〔美〕牛仔帽。~**boy suit**(儿童)牛仔装。~**catcher**〔美〕(车头前面的)排障器;(电车的)救助网;〔美俚〕无线电广播要目前后的广告。~ **chips**〔美〕(燃料)粪干。~ **college**〔美俚〕农学院;规模小的乡村大学。~**-herb**【植】面篮菜。~**fish**【动】海牛;角鱼;海豚。~ **grass**【植】紫云英。~**gun**〔海俚〕海军重炮。~**hage** = ~age. ~**hand**〔美方〕= ~boy. ~**heel** 牛蹄冻;炖(牛)蹄筋。~**herd** 牧牛者。~**-hide** 1. *n*. 牛皮;〔美〕牛皮鞭。2. *vt*. 用牛皮鞭抽打。~**-house** 牛棚。~**lick**〔美〕(牛舐过似的)一绺梳不平的乱发。~ **lily**【植】萍蓬草属。~**man**〔英〕放牛者;〔美〕牧牛业者;牧场主人。~ **parsnip**【植】欧洲防风,欧洲防风根;白芷属植物。~**pea**〔美〕藜豆〔饲料〕;豇豆。~**poke**〔美俚〕= ~boy. ~**-pony**〔美〕(牧牛者骑的)矮种马。~**pox** 牛痘。~**puncher**〔美口〕= ~-boy. ~***'s breakfast***〔美俚〕草帽。~**shed** 牛舍,牛棚。~**shot**【板球】弯身用力斜打。~**skin** 牛皮;〔美〕牛皮鞭。~**slip**【植】黄花九轮草,立金花。~**'stail**, ~ **tail** 散开的绳头。~ **to cover**〔美〕= butter. ~**tree**(南美产)乳树。~ **with the iron tail**〔美俚〕牛奶掺水用唧筒;【植】黄花九轮草,西洋樱草;〔美〕猿猴草的一种。

cow[2] [kau; kaʊ] *vt*. 吓(倒),恐吓。***be ~ed*** 被吓退[吓倒]。

Cow·ard [ˈkauəd; ˋkaʊəd] *n*. 考厄德〔姓氏〕。

cow·ard [ˈkauəd; ˋkaʊəd] **I** *n*. 懦夫,胆小鬼;【赛马】胆小的马。**II** *a*.〔诗〕怯懦的;【徽】夹着尾巴的。*a greyhound ~* 夹着尾巴的猎犬。

cow·ard·ice, cow·ard·li·ness [ˈkauədis, -linis; ˋkaʊədɪs, -lɪnɪs] *n*. 怯懦,懦弱,胆小。

cow·ard·ly [ˈkauədli; ˋkaʊədlɪ] *a*., *ad*. 怯懦的〔地〕。

cow·er [ˈkauə; ˋkaʊə] *vi*. 畏缩,退缩。

Cowes [kauz; kaʊz] *n*. 考斯〔英格兰 Isle of Wight 的港口,著名海滨浴场及快艇竞赛场〕。

cow·ish [ˈkauiʃ; ˋkaʊɪʃ] *a*. 牛一样的;笨拙的;怯懦的。

cowl [kaul; kaʊl] *n*. 1.(修道士的)头罩,带头罩的僧衣;兜帽;苏格兰睡帽。2. 烟囱罩;(风筒上的)通风帽。***take the*** ~出家当修士。

cowled [kauld; kaʊld] *a*. 1. 带有头罩的。2.【动、植】僧帽状的。

Cow·ley [ˈkauli; ˋkaʊlɪ] *n*. 考利〔姓氏〕。

cowl·ing [ˈkauliŋ; ˋkaʊlɪŋ] *n*.【机】罩,外壳,盖,帽。

cowl·staff [ˈkaulˌstɑːf, -ˌstæf, ˈkəul-; ˋkaʊlˏstɑf, -ˏstæf, ˋkol-] *n*.〔古〕扁担。

co-work·er [kəuˈwəːkə; koˋwɜkə] *n*. 共同工作者,合作者,帮手,同事。

Cow·per [ˈkaupə, ˈkuːpə; ˋkaupə, ˋkupə] *n*. 考珀〔姓氏〕。

C

C

cow·rie, cow·ry [ˈkauri; ˋkaʊrɪ] *n*.【贝】玛瑙贝。
cox [kɔks; kɑks] I *n*.〔口〕(赛艇的)舵手,艇长。II *vt*., *vi*. 做舵手[艇长]。
cox·a [ˈkɔksə; ˋkɑksə] *n*. (*pl*. *cox·ae* [ˈkɔksiː; ˋkɑksi]) 1.【解】髋。2.【虫】基节。
cox·al [ˈkɔksəl; ˋkɑksəl] *a*. 基节的;髋骨的。～ *gland* [*joint*] 腰腺(节)。～ *process* 基节突。
cox·al·gi·a [kɔkˈsældʒiə, -dʒə; kɑkˋsældʒɪə, -dʒə] *n*.【医】1. 髋痛。2. 髋关节结核。**-al·gic** *a*.
cox·comb [ˈkɔkskəum; ˋkɑksˏkom] *n*. 1. 纨袴子。2.【史】(中世纪丑角的)鸡冠帽。3.【植】鸡冠花。
cox·comb·i·cal [kɔksˈkəumikəl; kɑksˋkɑmɪkəl] *a*. 纨袴气的,虚浮的,浮夸的。
cox·comb·ry [ˈkɔkskəumri; ˋkɑksˏkomrɪ] *n*. 虚浮,浮夸;爱打扮;纨袴子弟。
cox·swain [ˈkɔkswein, ˈkɔksn; ˋkɑksˏwen, ˋkɑksn̩] I *n*. (赛艇的)艇长,舵手[略 cox];(舰船的)艇手。～ *of the plow*〔美〕新水兵。～*'s box* 舵手座位。II *vt*. 充当(赛艇的)艇长。
cox·y [ˈkɔksi; ˋkɑksɪ] *a*.〔学俚〕= cocky.
Coy [kɔi; kɔɪ] *n*. 科伊〔姓氏,男子名〕。
Coy = company.
coy [kɔi; kɔɪ] *a*. 1. 腼腆的,羞怯的;对…感到害羞 (*of*, *about*)。2. 献媚的,卖弄风情的。3.〔古〕隐蔽的,偏僻的(地方)。*be* ～ *of speech* 怕羞说不出话来。～ *tricks* 卖弄风情。**-ly** *ad*. **-ness** *n*.
coy·ote [ˈkɔiəut, kɔiˈəuti; kaɪˋot, kaɪˋotɪ] *n*. (*pl*. ～*s*, 〔集合词〕～)【动】(美国西部大草原中的)草原狼,郊狼;〔喻〕歹人,恶棍。
coy·pu [ˈkɔipuː; ˋkɔɪpu] *n*. (*pl*. ～*s*, 〔集合词〕～)【动】(南美)海狸鼠〔毛皮称 nutria, 颇名贵〕。
coz [kʌz; kʌz] *n*.〔口〕= cousin.
coze [kəuz; koz] I *vi*. 聊天,谈心。II *n*. 亲热的谈话[茶话]。
coz·en [ˈkʌzn; ˋkʌzn̩] *vt*. 1. 骗走某人的某物 (*out of sth*.)。2. 诱哄某人做某事 (*into doing sth*.)。—*vi*. 招摇撞骗。**-age** *n*. 欺骗;招摇撞骗。
co·zi·ly [ˈkəuzili; ˋkozɪlɪ] *ad*. = cosily.
co·zi·ness [ˈkəuzinis; ˋkozɪnɪs] *n*. = cosiness.
co·zy [ˈkəuzi; ˋkozɪ] *a*. = cosy.
CP = 1. Communist Party 共产党。2. Command Post【军】指挥所。3. Common Pleas〔美〕中级法院。
C.P. = 1. chemically pure 化学纯的。2. Common Pleas〔美〕(某些州的)民事法院。3. Court of Probate〔美〕遗嘱(检验)。4. current paper 最新文献。
cp. = 1. compare. 2. centipoise.
c.p. = candlepower.
CPA, CPAL = 1. Canadian Pacific Airlines 加拿大太平洋航空公司。2. Cathay Pacific Airways (香港)国泰航空公司。3. Catholic Press Association 天主教新闻协会。
C.P.A. = Certified Public Accountant.〔美〕(特许)会计师。
CPC = Communist Party of China 中国共产党。
CPI = Consumer Price Index 消费者价格指数。
Cpl, cpl. = Corporal 下士。
cpm = counts per minute 计数/分。
cpn. = coupon【会计】息票,利息券;(食品、布匹等的)配给券。
CPPCC = Chinese People's Political Consultative Conference 中国人民政治协商会议。
CPR = 1. Canadian Pacific Railway 加拿大太平洋铁路。2. cardiopulmonary resuscitation 心肺复苏术。
cps = 1. counts per second 计数/秒。2. cycles per second 周/秒。
CPSU(B) = Communist Party of the Soviet Union (Bolsheviks) 联共(布)
CPU = Central Processing Unit【自】中央处理机。
CQ = 1. call to quarters〔公告等的广播开始信号;业余无线电爱好者相互通讯前的信号〕。2. charge of quarters【军】内务值班;内务值班军士。
CQD = Come quick, danger〔遇难求救信号〕。
CQT = College Qualification Test 大学合格考试。
Cr = Chromium.
cr. = 1. credit; creditor. 2. crown(s).
C.R., CR = Costa Rica.
crab[1] [kræb; kræb] I *n*. 1. 蟹;蟹肉;〔C-〕【天】巨蟹座,巨蟹宫。2.【虫】阴虱。3.〔*pl*.〕(骰子)双幺。4.〔口〕不利,失败;【机】起重绞车。5.〔空俚〕侧飞;偏差,偏出。*a case of* ～*s* 失败,不利的下场。*catch a* ～(划船)插桨入水过深;〔俚〕一桨没划好,划坏。～ *fleet*〔美俚〕蟹舰队〔学生练习舰队〕。*turn out* [*come off*] ～*s* 终于失败。II *vt*. 1. 用爪抓。2. 使侧航;使斜行。—*vi*. 捕蟹;〔美口〕缩手,摆脱;侧航,偏飞。～ *out of*〔美口〕摆脱。～ *the wind*【美空】横飞。～ **apple**【植】山楂。～ **louse**【虫】阴虱。～**sidle** *vi*. 侧航;横行。～ **winch** 起重机。
crab[2] [kræb; kræb] *vt*. 1.〔美口〕苛责,挑剔,贬损;〔美俚〕干涉。2. 使人扫兴;使变乖戾。—*vi*. 抱怨;发牢骚 (*about*)。～ *sb.'s act*〔美俚〕干涉人,扫人兴。
crab[3] [kræb; kræb] *n*.【植】沙果;沙果树(= ～ apple, ～ tree)。
Crabb(e) [kræb; kræb] *n*. 克拉布〔姓氏〕。
crab·bed [ˈkræbid; ˋkræbɪd] *a*. 1. 乖张的;刻薄的;执拗的。2. 晦涩的(文章等);难辨认的(字迹等)。3. 又酸又涩的。
crab·ber[1] [ˈkræbə; ˋkræbɚ] *n*. 捕蟹人;捕蟹小船。
crab·ber[2] [ˈkræbə; ˋkræbɚ] *n*. 专爱挑剔[吹毛求疵]的人;爱发牢骚的人。
crab·bing [ˈkræbiŋ; ˋkræbɪŋ] *n*. 捕蟹;【纺】(染色)煮呢。*a* ～ *machine* 煮呢机。
crab·by[1] [ˈkræbi; ˋkræbɪ] *a*. 蟹似的;蟹多的。
crab·by[2] [ˈkræbi; ˋkræbɪ] *a*. 乖张的,别扭的,执拗的。
crab·fest [ˈkræbfest; ˋkræbˏfɛst] *n*.〔美〕牢骚(话),诉苦(话)。
crab·like [ˈkræblaik; ˋkræblaɪk] *a*., *ad*. 蟹似的(地)。
crab·stick [ˈkræbˌstik; ˋkræbˏstɪk] *n*. 1. 沙果树木棍棒。2.〔古〕脾气坏的人。
Crab·town [ˈkræbtaun; ˋkræbˏtaʊn] *n*.〔美〕(美国海军学校所在地) Annapolis 的别号。
crack [kræk; kræk] I *vt*. 1. 使破裂;敲破,敲碎,砸碎(陶器等);嗑(瓜子等);【化】裂化(石油等)。2. 把(枪打得、鞭子抽得)噼啪噼啪(等)地响。3. 打开(酒瓶)喝。4. 弄伤,损坏(信用等);弄哑(嗓子);使发狂。5. 说(笑话)。6.〔口〕解决;辨认(暗号);破(案)。7.〔美俚〕兑开(钞票)。8.〔口〕闯入。9. 撬开(门)。10. 微启窗户。11. 刻苦攻读。12.【计】非法侵入(他人电脑系统)。—*vi*. 1. 破裂;断掉;(地面等)坼裂;皲裂;缩裂;〔美〕破晓 (= day ～s)。2. 发坼裂[爆裂]声,(手枪、鞭子等)噼啪噼啪地响。3. (嗓子)发哑;(发育期)变嗓子。4. 损坏;(精神)受打击。5.〔Scot., 北英〕谈,谈话;〔俚〕说笑话;讥讽。6.【计】非法侵入他人电脑系统。*This is a hard nut to* ～。这是一个难解决的问题。～ *sunflower seeds* 嗑瓜子。～ *a book*〔美俚〕读书,用功。～ *a bottle with* 和…开瓶酒喝。～ *a crib*〔口〕溜门撬锁(偷窃)。～ *a mark* [*record*]【美军】打破纪录,创新纪录。～ *a prospect*〔美俚〕推销成功。～ *a smile*〔俚〕微笑。～ *back*〔美俚〕回嘴。～ *down*〔美俚〕敏捷地做;拼命做。～ *down on*〔美俚〕对…采取严厉措施,对…进行制裁。～ *on* 满帆前进;〔俚〕开足马力前进,飞快前进;继续前进。～ *out laughing* 发笑。～ *the lingo*〔美俚〕讲本行行话。～ *the party*〔美俚〕不请自来赴会。～ *up* 1. 夸奖;吹捧某人(～ *oneself up* 自夸,自大)。2. (人、身体等)疲惫不堪,有气无力;〔美俚〕(飞机)坠毁,撞毁;引起(哄堂)大笑;忍不住大笑;笑痛肚子。～ *wise*〔美〕讲俏皮话,打哈哈。*get*

~ing〔俚〕开动,动工;动手,开始做。**II** *n*. **1**. 裂缝,裂纹,皲裂,龟裂;【化】裂化。**2**. 破裂声,爆裂声,(手枪、鞭子等的)噼啪声;打击声,打击。**3**. 疵瑕,缺点;精神错乱。**4**. (发育期)换嗓,变声。**5**.〔口〕第一流人物;名马;(竞技的)名手;优良的船。**6**.〔古、俚〕自大,自夸;〔Scot., 北英〕闲谈;〔*pl*.〕奇闻。**7**.〔美俚〕警句,俏皮话,挖苦话。**8**.〔口〕一会儿,片刻。**9**.〔俚〕溜门撬锁。*Open the window a* ~. 把窗子开一条缝。*the* ~ *of a whip* 鞭声。*the* ~ *of thunder* 雷鸣。*a* ~ *on the head* 头上的一击。*There is a* ~ *in your head*. 你有点疯啦。(*at*) ~ ***of day*** 〔英方,美〕(在)黎明,天亮时。~ ***of doom*** 世界末日的霹雳信号(*till the* ~ *of doom* 到世界毁灭时,到最后)。***in a*** ~ 即刻,立刻。**III** *a*.〔口〕最好的,第一流的;出名的,当当的。*a* ~ *hand* 妙手,能手。*a* ~ *performer* 名演员。*a* ~ *player* (竞赛等的)能手。*a* ~ *regiment* 精锐团。~ *troops* 精锐部队。*a* ~ *team* 名队。**IV** *ad*. 噼啪地,啪的一声,尖锐地。*The pistol went off* ~. 手枪啪的一声打了出去。~**brain** 精神错乱的人。~**brained** *a*. 精神错乱的。~**down**〔美俚〕制裁;猛击。~**head** 染上强效可卡因毒瘾的人。~**jaw** *a*.〔口〕难发音的;拗口的。

crack·a·jack [ˈkrækədʒæk; ˋkrækə͵dʒæk] *n*.〔美〕= crackerjack.

cracked [krækt; krækt] *a*. **1**. 弄破了的,弄裂了的。**2**. 嗓子弄哑了的,声音起了变化的。**3**.〔口〕疯了的,精神失常的。~ *ice* 碎冰;〔美俚〕钻石。*a* ~ *reputation* 坏名。*be* ~ 声音发哑;发疯。~ *wheat* (碎)麦片。

crack·er [ˈkrækə; ˋkrækɚ] *n*. **1**. 爆竹;鞭炮。**2**.〔美〕脆饼;〔美〕饼干(=〔英〕biscuit)。**3**.〔学俚〕谎话。**4**.〔*pl*.〕胡桃夹,破碎器;〔谑〕牙齿。**5**.〔C-〕〔美南部〕贫穷的白种人。**6**.〔俚〕全速力。**7**. 破门撬锁者。**8**. 说大话的人。**9**. (石油)裂化设备。***the C-State***〔美〕乔治亚洲的别名。***go a*** ~ 开足马力;压扁。

crack·er·jack [ˈkrækədʒæk; ˋkrækə͵dʒæk] **I** *n*. **1**.〔美〕玉米花核桃饼。**2**.〔美俚〕专家,能手,杰出人物。**II** *a*.〔美俚〕熟练的,第一流的。

crack·ers [ˈkrækəz; ˋkrækɚz] *a*.〔俚〕发疯,发狂〔常用作表语〕。***drive sb***. ~ 使某人发狂。***go*** ~ ***about sth***. 给…迷住;热中于。

crack·ing [ˈkrækiŋ; ˋkrækɪŋ] *a*. 分裂的,分解的;〔美俚〕极快的,猛烈的。~ *distillation*【化】裂解蒸馏(法)。~ *salt* 响盐。***get*** ~ (*on*)〔俚〕忙起来;发奋,努力。

crack·le [ˈkrækl; ˋkrækl] **I** *n*. 噼啪声,爆裂声;(碎瓷上的)裂纹;【医】尖锐的肺泡音。**II** *vi*. 噼噼啪啪地响,生气勃勃,兴奋不安(等)。

crack·le·ware [ˈkræklˌwɛə; ˋkrækl͵wɛr] *n*. 碎纹陶瓷。

crack·ling [ˈkrækliŋ; ˋkræklɪŋ] *n*. 噼噼啪啪的响声;(饼干等的)松脆;(烧猪的)脆皮;〔主美〕猪油渣。

crack·ly [ˈkrækli; ˋkræklɪ] *a*. 噼噼啪啪响的;松脆的。

crack·nel [ˈkræknəl, ˈkræknəl] *n*. 脆饼;〔*pl*.〕〔英方,美〕脆煎(猪)肉饼;〔*pl*.〕猪油渣。

crack·pot [ˈkrækpɔt; ˋkræk͵pɑt] *n*., *a*.〔美俚〕疯子,怪人;想入非非的,不切实际的。*Joe's* ~ *scheme* 空想的计划。

cracks·man [ˈkræksmən; ˋkræksmən] *n*.〔俚〕强盗。

crack·up [ˈkrækʌp; ˋkræk͵ʌp] *n*. (车辆的)相撞;(飞机的)坠毁;〔口〕(体力或精神的)崩溃。

crack·y [ˈkræki; ˋkrækɪ] *a*. (*-i·er*; *-i·est*) 多裂缝的,易破的;〔口〕疯狂的。

Cra·cow [ˈkrækəu; ˋkræko] *n*. 克拉科夫〔波兰城市〕。

-cra·cy [krəsi; krəsɪ] *suf*. 统治(权);统治阶级。

cra·dle [ˈkreidl; ˋkredl] **I** *n*. **1**. 摇篮。**2**. 婴儿时代;(文化等的)发源地。**3**. (雕铜版用的)凿刀。**4**.【农】(附在大镰刀上,使割下的谷物整齐排列的)配禾架;(船厂的)船架,活动滑台;(砌拱洞等的)支架;(电话的)听筒架;【医】(骨折)护架,接骨台;【矿】淘汰机;炮鞍;(支持有反座力的炮身的)摇架。**5**.〔美俚〕无盖货车。*the* ~ *of an art* 一种艺术的发祥地。*a launching* ~【火箭】发射台。***from the*** ~ 自幼。***from the*** ~ ***to the grave*** 从生到死,一生中。***in the*** ~ 在初期,在幼年时代。***rob the*** ~ 选比自己小得多的人做情人[配偶]。***stifle in the*** ~ 把…掐死在摇篮里,防患于未然。***the*** ~ ***of the deep*** 海。***watch over the*** ~ 看着长大。**II** *vt*. **1**. 放在摇篮内,摇摇篮催眠(小孩);抚养。**2**. 刈割;用架支住;淘洗(矿沙)~**land** 发祥地。~**song** 摇篮曲。

cra·dling [ˈkreidliŋ; ˋkredlɪŋ] *n*. 选矿,淘汰,抚育,育成;【建】弧顶架。

craft [krɑːft; kræft] *n*. **1**.〔古〕技巧,手腕;鬼聪明,诡计。**2**. 技术,技能,手艺;手工业;工艺;(需要特殊技能的)专业,行业;同业,同行;同业工会。**3**.〔单复同形〕船舶;飞机,飞船。**4**.〔美〕竞赛中的同组伙伴。*a hydrofoil* ~ 水翼船。***art***(*s*) ***and*** ~(*s*) 艺术和手工艺,美术工艺。***by*** ~ 用诡计[手腕]。***with*** ~ 有技巧地,巧妙地。~ ***brother*** 同行。~ ***guild*** 技艺[手工艺]行会。~ ***union*** 职业工会。***the*** ~ ***of the wood*** = ***the woodcraft***. ***the gentle*** ~ 钓鱼术;钓鱼伙伴。

-craft *comb. f*. 术,法;行业。

craft·i·ly [ˈkrɑːftili; ˋkræftɪlɪ] *ad*. 狡猾地,诡计多端地。

craft·i·ness [ˈkrɑːftinis; ˋkræftɪnɪs] *n*. 狡猾,诡计多端。

crafts·man [ˈkrɑːftsmən; ˋkræftsmən] *n*. 手艺人,工匠,名匠。**-ship** *n*. (工匠的)技术,技艺。

craft·y [ˈkrɑːfti; ˋkræftɪ] *a*. 狡猾的,诡诈的;〔古〕巧妙的,灵巧的,能干的。

crag[1] [kræg; kræg] *n*. 岩崖,巉崖;岩石碎块。~ ***and tail*** 一边有巉岩另一边有缓坡的地层,鼻尾丘。

crag[2] [kræg; kræg] *n*.〔Scot.〕脖子;喉咙;(鸡等的)嗉子。

crag·ged [ˈkrægid; ˋkrægɪd] *a*. = craggy. **-ness** *n*.

crag·gy [ˈkrægi; ˋkrægɪ] *a*. 多岩石的,嵯峨的,崎岖的。**-giness** *n*.

crags·man [ˈkrægzmən; ˋkrægzmən] *n*. 爬岩崖名手。

Craig [kreig; kreg] *n*. 克雷格〔姓氏,男子名〕。

Craig·a·von [kreigˈævən; kregˋævən] *n*. 克雷加文〔姓氏〕。

Crai·gie [ˈkrægi; ˋkregɪ] *n*. 克雷吉〔姓氏〕。

Craik [kreik; krek] *n*. 克雷克〔姓氏〕。

crake [kreik; krek] **I** *n*.【鸟】秧鸡,秧鸡的叫声。**II** *vi*. (秧鸡等)叫。

Cram [kræm; kræm] *n*. 克拉姆〔姓氏〕。

cram [kræm; kræm] **I** *vt*. (***crammed***, ***cram·ming***) 塞入,填入;喂饱,填饱(鸭子等);塞满(屋子等),填鸭式地教,死记(*up*)。*a bus crammed with passengers* 挤满乘客的一辆公共汽车。~ *papers into a drawer* 把文件塞入抽屉。—*vi*. 狼吞虎咽地吃;吃得太饱;填鸭式地死用功;考试前临时抱佛脚[死背硬记]。~ *up on mathematics* 仓促准备应付数学考试。~ (*sth*.) ***down sb.'s throat*** 填饱;反复地对人说(某事)。***to sit up late*** ~-***ming*** 开夜车准备功课。~ ***oneself*** 塞满肚皮;吃饱。**II** *n*. 填塞;填鸭式用功;考试前临时硬记;超额拥挤;〔俚〕压碎;〔俚〕瞒骗。~ **school** 强化训练学校〔多指为考生提供强化课程的补习学校〕。

cram·be [ˈkræmˌbiː; ˋkræm͵bi] *n*.【植】海甘蓝〔一种地中海油料作物〕(*Crambe abyssinica*)。

cram·bo [ˈkræmbəu; ˋkræmbo] *n*. **1**. 对韵游戏。**2**. 拙劣的诗词[韵文]。

cram·mer [ˈkræmə; ˋkræmɚ] *n*. 填塞者;赶教应考者的补习老师,填鸭式用功[死背硬记]的学生;〔俚〕谎话。

cram·ming [ˈkræmiŋ; ˋkræmɪŋ] *n*. 填鸭式[死背硬记]的学习[教法]。

cram·oi·sy, **cram·oi·sie** [ˈkræmˌɔizi; ˋkræm͵ɔɪzɪ] **I** *a*.〔古〕深红色的。**II** *n*.〔古〕红布。

cramp[1] [kræmp; kræmp] **I** *n*. **1**. 夹子;扣钉;爬钉(= ~ iron)。**2**. (制靴)弓状木。**3**. 束缚,约束。**II** *a*. **1**. 难懂的,难读的,难认的。**2**. 受拘束的;狭窄的。*a* ~ *word*

难认的字。*a* ～ *corner* 狭窄的角落。**III** *vt*. 用夹子夹紧;用扒钉接牢;拘束,束缚(自由等);禁闭(up)。～ *sb.'s style* 〔美俚〕拘束某人使不能充分发挥才能。

cramp[2] [kræmp; kræmp] **I** *n*. 【医】(痛性)痉挛;〔*pl*.〕〔美口〕(经期)腹痛。**II** *vt*. 使痉挛,使抽筋;〔美俚〕使扫兴。*writer's* ～书写痉挛。

cramp·fish [ˈkræmpfiʃ; ˋkræmp͵fɪʃ] *n*. 【动】电鳐。

cram·pon [ˈkræmpən; ˋkræmpən] *n*. **1**. 〔常 *pl*.〕(起重,搬冰块等用的)钩铁;(登山)鞋底尖钉。**2**. 【植】攀缘根,气根。

cran [kræn; kræn] *n*. 〔Scot.〕鲱斗〔计量鲱鱼用单位,= 37½ 加仑〕。

C

cran·age [kreinidʒ; ˋkrenɪdʒ] *n*. 起重机的使用(费)。

cran·ber·ry [ˈkrænbəri; ˋkræn͵bɛrɪ] *n*. 【植】酸果蔓(属);大酸果蔓。～ **bush** [**tree**] 【植】三裂叶荚蒾。～ **glass** 带青紫色的透明红玻璃。

cran·dall [ˈkrændəl; ˋkrændəl] *n*. (石工)小锤。

Crane [krein; kren] *n*. 克兰〔姓氏〕。

crane [krein; kren] **I** *n*. **1**. 鹤;〔口〕苍鹭,鹭鸶,鹳;〔C-〕【天】天鹤座。**2**. 起重机,吊车,摄影升降机;虹吸器;(机车的)上水管;(炉边挂铁壶的)吊钩。*a sacred* ～丹顶鹤。*a whiteheaded* ～锅鹤。*a white-naped* ～灰鹤。*a floating* ～水上起重机。*a gantry* [*gauntry*] ～龙门起重机。*a slewing* ～旋臂起重机。*a universal* ～万能起重[装卸]机。**II** *vt*. 伸(颈);用起重机搬移。—*vi*. 伸着脖子(看)(*out*; *over*; *down*);踌躇(*at*)。～ **fly** 【动】大蚊,蚊姥;〔美〕盲蜘蛛。～**'s-bill** 【植】老鹳草(属),天竺葵;【医】钳子。

cra·ni·al [ˈkreinjəl; ˋkrenɪəl] *a*. 颅的;颅侧的。

cra·ni·ate [ˈkreiniit; ˋkrenɪɪt] **I** *a*. **1**. 有颅骨的;有头骨的。**2**. 有头动物的,颅骨动物的。**II** *n*. 有头动物,颅骨动物。

cra·ni·o- *comb. f*. 颅骨,头:*cranio*logy.

cra·ni·ol·o·gist [ˌkreiniˈɔlədʒist; ͵krenɪˋɑlədʒɪst] *n*. 颅学者。

cra·ni·ol·o·gy [ˌkreiniˈɔlədʒi; ͵krenɪˋɑlədʒɪ] *n*. 颅骨学。

cra·ni·om·e·ter [ˌkreiniˈɔmitə; ͵krenɪˋɑmətɚ] *n*. 颅测量器。

cra·ni·om·e·try [ˌkreiniˈɔmitri; ͵krenɪˋɑmətrɪ] *n*. 颅测量法。

cra·ni·o·sa·cral [ˌkreiniəuˈsækrəl, -ˈseikrəl; ͵krenɪoˋsækrəl, -ˋsekrəl] *a*. **1**. 颅骶的。**2**. 副交感神经的(= parasympathetic)。

cra·ni·ot·o·my [ˈkreiniˈɔtəmi; ͵krenɪˋɑtəmɪ] *n*. (*pl*. **-mies**)【医】颅骨切开术;穿颅术。

cra·ni·um [ˈkreinjəm; ˋkreniəm] *n*. (*pl*. **-ni·a** [-niə; -nɪə])【解】颅,头颅(= brain case)。

crank[1] [kræŋk; kræŋk] **I** *n*. **1**. 【机】曲柄;(刑具)旋盘。**2**. (言语或思想的)奇特的转折;狂想,幻想;〔美俚〕想法古怪的人;〔口〕脾气乖戾的人。**3**. 〔古〕弯曲,曲折。～ *axle* 曲柄轴。**II** *vi*. 转动曲柄;弯曲而行;(转动电影摄影机的曲柄)拍摄;〔英俚〕注射毒品。—*vt*. 弯成曲柄状;装上曲柄,用曲柄连结;转动曲柄开动(引擎)(*up*);(转动电影摄影机的曲柄)摄影;〔英俚〕注射(毒品)。～ **out** 制作,制成。～ **up** 开动;加快;作好准备。～ **axle** 曲柄轴。～ **case** 曲柄轴箱。～**pin** 【机】曲柄销,拐轴销。～ **shaft** 【机】曲轴,机轴。

crank[2] [kræŋk; kræŋk] *a*. (建筑物等)松松垮垮的,摇晃不稳的;(船)易翻的,像要翻似的;〔英方〕不健康的,虚弱的。

crank[3] [kræŋk; kræŋk] *a*. 〔美、英方〕**1**. 活泼的,精神好的。**2**. 骄傲的,逞能的。

cran·kle [ˈkræŋkl; ˋkræŋkl̩] *vt*., *vi*., *n*. 弯曲;扭弯;(弄成)曲曲弯弯。

crank·ous [ˈkræŋkəs; ˋkræŋkəs] *a*. 〔Scot.〕胡思乱想的;急躁的,易怒的。

crank·y [ˈkræŋki; ˋkræŋkɪ] *a*. (**-i·er**; **-i·est**) **1**. 胡思乱想的;疯狂的;古怪的,易发脾气的。**2**. (多)弯曲的。**3**. 易翻倒的,动摇不稳的;虚弱的。**be** ～ **on** 〔俚〕全神贯注在…,热中于,被…迷住。

cran·nied [ˈkrænid; ˋkrænɪd] *a*. 有[多]裂缝的。

cran·ny [ˈkræni; ˋkrænɪ] *n*. 裂缝,隙缝。*search every* ～到处寻找。

Cran·ston [ˈkrænstən; ˋkrænstən] *n*. 克兰斯敦〔美国城市〕。

crap[1] [kræp; kræp] **I** *n*. 掷双骰子〔一种赌博〕;(掷输的)一掷。**II** *v*. (**-pp-**)〔仅用于〕～ **out** **1**. 〔俚〕放弃计划(等)。**2**. 〔俚〕休息;打盹。**3**. (赌博)掷输。

crap[2] [kræp; kræp] **I** *n*. **1**. 〔卑〕大便,粪便。**2**. 费话,胡话。**3**. 夸张,吹牛;谎话。**4**. 垃圾,废料,破烂东西。**II** *vi*. (**-pp-**) **1**. 〔卑〕拉屎。**2**. 〔美俚〕胡搞。*He used to* ～ *around like that*. 他老做那样的傻事。

crape [kreip; krep] **I** *n*. **1**. (丧服用的)黑纱,(帽子等上面的)黑丧章。**2**. 绉纱,绉绸(= crêpe)。**II** *vt*. **1**. 使绉。**2**. 用黑纱覆盖。**3**. 使穿戴黑纱。～ **hanger** 忧郁悲观的人;〔俚〕扫兴的人。～ **myrtle** 【植】百日红,紫薇属。

craped [kreipt; krept] *a*. 戴黑纱[丧章]的;绉的。

crap·pie [ˈkræpi; ˋkræpɪ] *n*. 〔美〕【动】克勒皮鱼,日鲈。

craps [kræps; kræps] *n*. 〔用作 *sing*.〕〔美〕掷双骰子〔一种赌博〕。*shoot* ～ 掷双骰子。

crap·shoot·er [ˈkræpˌʃuːtə; ˋkræp͵ʃutɚ] *n*. 掷双骰子赌徒。

crap·u·lence [ˈkræpjuləns; ˋkræpjuləns] *n*. 暴饮暴食(致病,酗酒);无节制;纵欲。

crap·u·lent, crap·u·lous [ˈkræpjulənt, -ləs; ˋkræpjulənt, -ləs] *a*. 无节制(而致病)的,吃得[喝得]过多的;大醉的,中酒毒的。

crap·y [ˈkreipi; ˋkrepɪ] *a*. **1**. 绉纱状的。**2**. 戴黑纱[丧章]的。**3**. 弯弯曲曲的,波状的。

crash[1] [kræʃ; kræʃ] **I** *vi*. **1**. 砰的碎掉,粉碎,哗啦一声坏掉;哗啦啦地倒塌(*down*, *through*);(雷、炮)隆隆地响(*out*);(轰隆一声)碰到,撞在(*into*; *against*)。**2**. (计划等)失败,破产;(飞机)坠毁,(飞机师)摔死;(汽车)碰撞,撞坏。**3**. 〔美俚〕(从服用麻醉品迷幻状态中)恢复常态,醒过来。**4**. 〔美俚〕躺下睡觉,住宿。—*vt*. **1**. 撞击(使发大声)。**2**. 使粉碎,打碎;使(飞机)坠毁;击落(敌机);使(汽车)碰撞。**3**. 〔美俚〕擅自闯入。**4**. 〔美俚〕轰动一时地取得(…地位)。～ *the headlines* 成了轰动一时的头条新闻。～ *in* [*on*]〔俚〕闯入,擅自进入。～ *the gate* 〔美俚〕擅自闯进(招待会等),无票进入(戏院等)。**II** *n*. **1**. (坍塌等时的)猛烈声音,轰隆声;【剧】轰隆声发声装置。**2**. (碰得)粉碎,毁坏;撞击;(飞机的)坠毁。**3**. 失败,破产;崩溃,瓦解。*a sweeping* ～(经济等的)总崩溃。～ *dive* (潜艇)急速潜入水中。*with a* ～轰隆[哗啦]一声。**III** *ad*. 〔口〕= *with a* ～. *A stone came* ～ *through the window*. 一块石头哗啦一声打破窗子飞了进来。～ **barrier** 〔英〕(置于快速公路中线的)防撞栏。～**-helmet** (摩托运动员等戴的)防护头盔。～ **land** *vt*., *vi*. (使)强行着陆。～ **pad** 〔美俚〕临时住宿处,栖身处。～ **program** 应急计划。～**worthy** *a*. 防[耐]碰撞的。

crash[2] [kræʃ; kræʃ] *n*. 粗(麻)布。

crash·ee [ˈkræʃiː; ˋkræʃi] *n*. 〔美〕破产的资本家。

crash·er [ˈkræʃə; ˋkræʃɚ] *n*. 发猛烈声音的东西,痛击,猛撞;〔美俚〕擅自闯入者(= gate-crasher)。

crash·ing [ˈkræʃiŋ; ˋkræʃɪŋ] *a*. 〔口〕完全的;彻底的。*a* ～ *bore* 讨厌已极的人。

cra·sis [ˈkreisis; ˋkresɪs] *n*. (*pl*. **-ses** [-siːz; -siz]) **1**. (体质成分的)配合;体质,气质。**2**. 【语】(二母音的)融合,异词母音结合〔如拉丁语中 coopia 融合为 copia〕。

crass [kræs; kræs] *a*. **1**. 〔书〕非常的,彻底的;〔古〕粗厚的(麻布等)。**2**. 愚钝的。**-ly** *ad*.

cras·si·tude [ˈkræsitjuːd; ˋkræsə͵tjud] *n*. 粗糙,粗厚;愚钝。

-crat *suf*. (某种统治形式,统治集团的)支持者;参与者: aristo*crat*, auto*crat*, demo*crat*.

cratch [krætʃ; krætʃ] *n*. 〔英方〕饲料箱,饲料架。

crate [kreit; kret] **I** *n*. **1**. 竹篾[柳条]篮[篓、筐];条板箱;一箱(60×30×30cm)的量。**2**. 〔俚〕旧飞机;旧汽车;牢监。**II** *vt*. 〔美〕(用篮筐或板条箱)装起来,装箱。

cra·ter [ˈkreitə; ˋkretɚ] **I** *n*. **1**. 火山口。**2**. 〔C-〕【天】巨爵座;(月球上的)环形山。**3**. (炸成的)弹坑;陨石坑;陷口。**II** *vt*., *vi*. (使)成坑状。~**-kin**, ~**-let** 小火山口。~ **wall** 火山口壁。**-ed** *a*. 形成火山口的。

cra·ter·i·form [ˈkreitərifɔːm; ˋkretɚɪfɔrm] *a*. 火山口状的,漏斗状的。

craunch [ˈkrɔːntʃ, krɑːntʃ; ˋkrɔntʃ, krɑntʃ] *vt*., *vi*., *n*. 嘎扎嘎扎地咀嚼[碾压,踏过](= crunch)。

cra·vat [krəˈvæt; krəˋvæt] *n*. (旧式)领带;〔古〕(男用)围巾;三角绷带;(女用)领饰。*a hempen* ~ 〔古〕绞索。

crave [kreiv; krev] *vt*. **1**. 切望,热望,渴望。**2**. 恳求,恳请,乞求。**3**. (情形)要求,需要。—*vi*. 热望,渴望,恳求〔同 for, after 连用〕。

cra·ven [ˈkreivən; ˋkrevən] **I** *n*. 懦夫。**II** *a*. 怯懦的,畏缩的,胆小的。*cry* ~ 叫饶,投降。**-ly** *ad*.

crav·en·ette [kreivənˈet, kræv-; krevənˋɛt, kræv-] *n*. 【商标】(伦敦)克来文雨衣(料)。

crav·ing [ˈkreiviŋ; ˋkrevɪŋ] *n*. 渴望,热望;恳请,恳求。*have a* ~ *for* 渴求。

craw [krɔː; krɔ] *n*. **1**. 【鸟】嗉子。**2**. 【动】胃。**3**. 〔美俚〕喉咙。~*thumper* 〔美〕马里兰 (Mariland) 州人(的绰号)。

craw·dad [ˈkrɔːdæd; ˋkrɔˏdæd] *n*. 〔美俚〕= crawfish.

craw·fish [ˈkrɔːfiʃ; ˋkrɔˏfɪʃ] **I** *n*. **1**. 【动】淡水小龙虾,蝲蛄(= crayfish)。**2**. 〔美口〕后退者,变节者,叛徒。~*land* 〔美〕低湿的地方。**II** *vi*. 〔美口〕**1**. 捕小龙虾(作为消遣)。**2**. (像蝲蛄一样)向后退,退缩;撒手;变节。

crawl[1] [krɔːl; krɔl] **I** *vi*. **1**. 爬;爬行;(车辆、病人等)慢吞吞地行进;(时间)慢慢过去;偷偷地溜走;爬来爬去。**2**. 巴结。**3**. (皮肤)发痒。**4**. (虫)成群地蠕动 (*with*)。**5**. 用自由式游;〔美俚〕跳舞。**6**. (地毯等)移动皱缩(不平)。**7**. 〔英俚〕(出租汽车)往来兜生意。**8**. 〔美俚〕食言;悔约。~ *home on one's eyebrows* 〔口〕累得精疲力尽地慢慢走回家。**II** *n*. 爬行,徐行;〔美俚〕跳舞;自由式游泳。*a pub* ~〔俚〕一连走几家酒店喝串门酒。*go at a* ~ 慢吞吞地走;(出租汽车等)往来兜生意。*go for a* ~去散散步。*the* ~ 爬泳,自由式游泳 (= ~-stroke)。~**-way** (为运输火箭或宇宙飞船而修建的)慢速道。

crawl[2] [krɔːl; krɔl] *n*. (圈养鱼类的)鱼围;〔罕〕= kraal.

crawl·er [ˈkrɔːlə; ˋkrɔlɚ] *n*. **1**. 爬行者,爬行动物,爬虫。**2**. 〔美口〕蛇及蜻蜓等的幼虫;虱子。**3**. 拍马屁的人;懒汉。**4**. 〔英口〕(沿街兜生意的)出租汽车。**5**. 〔主 *pl*.〕〔英〕(婴孩的)爬服,罩衣。**6**. 履带式牵引车。

crawl·y [ˈkrɔːli; ˋkrɔlɪ] *a*. (*-i·er*; *-i·est*) 〔口〕痒痒的,麻辣辣的;毛骨悚然的。

cray·fish [ˈkreifiʃ; ˋkreˏfɪʃ] *n*. = crawfish **1**.

cray·on [ˈkreiən; ˋkreən] **I** *n*. 颜色(铅)笔,色粉笔,蜡笔;色粉[蜡笔]画;(弧光灯的)碳精棒。*in* ~(*s*) 用色粉[蜡笔]画的。**II** *vt*. 用色粉[蜡笔]画;勾轮廓;拟计划。

craze [kreiz; krez] **I** *vt*. **1**. 使发狂[通常用被动语态]。**2**. 使(陶器)现裂纹。—*vi*. 发狂;(陶器)出现裂纹。*be ~d about* 热中于。**II** *n*. **1**. 疯狂;狂妄;狂热,热中,大流行。**2**. (陶器的)裂纹;裂痕。*be the* ~ 大流行。~ *for* (*gold*) (发财)狂。

crazed [kreizd; krezd] *a*. **1**. 疯狂的,狂热的。**2**. 有裂纹的。

cra·zy [ˈkreizi; ˋkrezɪ] *a*. **1**. 摇晃不稳的,破烂的(船、房子等);〔古〕(身体)虚弱的。**2**. 疯狂的;狂妄的;怪诞的、古怪的;〔口〕对…极度热心[迷恋] (*about*)。**3**. 〔美俚〕极好的,极妙的;令人惊异的。*Are you* ~? 你疯了吗? *be* ~ *for* 渴望,痴想。*be* ~ *with* (*pain*) (痛苦)得发狂。~ *as a bedbug* 〔美〕发疯的;荒唐的。*like* ~ 发狂似地,激昂地。~ **act** 〔美〕滑稽戏。~ **bone** 〔美〕= funny bone. ~ **cat** 〔美〕笨蛋,傻瓜。~ (**patch**) **work** 碎料拼活(工艺)。~ **quilt** 〔美〕碎料缝成的褥子。~ **pavement** [walk] 碎石铺道。

cra·zy·weed [ˈkreiziˌwiːd; ˋkrezɪˏwid] *n*. 【植】疯草,黄芪属植物和棘豆属植物 (= locoweed)。

creak [kriːk; ˋkrik] **I** *n*. 吱吱嘎嘎声,辗轧声。*with a* ~ 吱嘎一声(开门)。**II** *vi*. 吱吱嘎嘎地响。

creak·y [ˈkriːki; ˋkrikɪ] *a*. (*-i·er*; *-i·est*) (容易)吱吱嘎嘎响的。

cream [kriːm; krim] **I** *n*. **1**. 奶油,乳皮;奶油色,淡黄色;液面皮。**2**. 〔the ~〕精华;真髓;妙处。**3**. 奶油色的马。**4**. 奶油糕点[冰淇淋等];(化妆用)雪花膏,香脂;【化】乳剂。~ *cake* 奶油蛋糕。~ *de goo* [-dəˈguː; -dəˋgu] 〔美俚〕牛奶烤面包。~ *ice* 〔英〕= *ice* ~. ~ *laid paper* 嫩黄色平行罗纹纸。~ *of lime* 石灰乳。~ *of tartar* 酒石酸氢钾。~ *of the crop* 〔口〕精华,精选物。~ *of the society* 社会名流。~ *puff* 奶油气鼓饼;可爱的人;〔美俚〕懦夫;无骨气的男子;〔美俚〕外观特好的旧汽车。~ *separator* 奶油分离器。*get the* ~ *of* 取其精华。**II** *vt*. **1**. 提取奶油,取乳皮。**2**. 抽取精华,拔粹。**3**. 【烹】搅成奶油状;加奶油(在菜,茶里)。**4**. 搽雪花膏。**5**. 〔俚〕痛打,打伤。—*vi*. **1**. 结乳皮,成奶油状。**2**. 起泡沫。~**-colo(u)red** *a*. 奶油色的;淡黄色的。~**ware** 奶油色陶器。

cream·cups [ˈkriːmkʌps; ˋkrimˏkʌps] *n*. 【植】美国平蕊罂粟 (*platystemon californicus*)。

cream·er [ˈkriːmə; ˋkrimɚ] *n*. **1**. 撇取乳皮的盆[人]。**2**. 奶油分离器。**3**. 〔美〕(餐桌上的)奶油瓶。

cream·er·y [ˈkriːməri; ˋkrimərɪ] *n*. 奶油干酪厂;(兼卖茶的)奶品商店。

cream·y [ˈkriːmi; ˋkrimɪ] *a*. 奶油状的;含奶油的;奶油色的;浓厚的,浓艳的。

crease[1] [kriːs; kris] **I** *n*. **1**. (衣等的)摺痕,摺缝;皱褶。**2**. 【地】古冰川流迹。**3**. 【板球】投手[打手]界线。**II** *vt*., *vi*. **1**. 使有摺缝,变皱。**2**. 〔美口〕(被流弹)擦伤。

crease[2] [kriːs; kris] *n*. = creese.

creas·er [ˈkriːsə; ˋkrisɚ] *n*. 压摺缝的器具。

cre·a·sote [ˈkriːəsəut; ˋkriəˏsot] *n*. = creosote.

creas·y [ˈkriːsi; ˋkrisɪ] *a*. 摺缝多的,有摺痕的,变皱了的。

cre·ate [kri(ː)ˈeit; krɪ(ɪ)ˋet] *vt*. **1**. 创造;创作;产生,引起。**2**. 创设,设立;建设(国家等)。**3**. 封爵,把…封为(贵族)。~ *peers* 册封贵族。*be ~d* (*a*) *baron* 被封为男爵。—*vi*. **1**. (进行)创作。**2**. 〔俚〕大叫大喊;发牢骚。*be quick to imitate but powerless to* ~善于模仿拙于创作。*You need not* ~ *about it*. 你不必大惊小怪。~ *about nothing* 无事自扰。

cre·a·tin(e) [ˈkriːətin; ˋkriəˏtɪn] *n*. 【生化】肌酸,肌肉素。

cre·at·i·nine [kriːˈætiˌniːn, -nin; kriˋætɪˏnin, -nɪn] *n*. 【生化】肌酸酐。

cre·a·tion [kri(ː)ˈeiʃən; krɪˋeʃən] *n*. **1**. 创造,创作;发生。**2**. 创造物;天地万物,宇宙。**3**. 创设;建设。**4**. (爵位等的)封授。**5**. 创造性演出,新型服装。**6**. 〔美口〕(作感叹词用)哎呀,天哪。*since the* ~从开天辟地以来。*the whole* ~ 万物;宇宙,全世界。*That beats* [*licks*, *whips*] (*all*) ~. 〔美口〕那倒是惊人极了;那打破一切纪录了。*C-! How he looked*. 哎呀! 他那个面孔。*the latest Paris ~s* 最新巴黎式样(服装)。~ *of genius* 天才作品。~ *of new species* 新种的发生。*in all* ~ 〔美口〕究竟,到底。*like all* ~ 〔美口〕拼命,猛烈,严重。

cre·a·tion·ism [kri(ː)ˈeiʃənizəm; krɪˋeʃənɪzəm] *n*. 【生】神造论,特别创造说。

cre·a·tive [kri(ː)ˈeitiv; krɪˋetɪv] *a*. 有创造力的,创造

的;造成的。*be* ~ *of* 能产生…的。~ *power* 创造力;创作力。~ *talent* 创作的才能。

cre·a·tiv·i·ty [ˌkri:ei'tiviti; ˏkrieˋtɪvətɪ] *n.* 创造力;艺术创新。

cre·a·tor [kri(:)'eitə; krɪˋetɚ] *n.* 1. 创造者;创作家;创设者;发生原因;新衣设计人;新演技创造人,新型演员。2.【宗】〔the C-〕造物主,上帝。

cre·a·tress [kri(:)'eitris; krɪˋetrɪs] *n.* 女创造者;女创办人;女创作家。

crea·ture ['kri:tʃə; ˋkritʃɚ] *n.* 1. 创造物;生物,(特指)动物;〔美〕牛马,家畜。2. (某人)一手提拔的人;(他人的)工具;奴才,走狗。3. 〔怜爱、轻蔑〕人,家伙,东西。*good* ~*s* 衣服饮食。*dumb* ~*s* 牲畜。*fellow* ~*s* 和我们同样的人,同胞。*a pretty* ~美丽的女人。*Poor* ~! 可怜的家伙! *that* ~ *there* 那家伙。*What a* ~! 好家伙! ~ ***of circumstances*** 环境的奴隶[产物]。~ ***of the age*** 时代的产物。~***s of the dictators*** 独裁者的走狗。***the*** ~ ['kri:tə, 'kreitə; ˋkritɚ, ˋkretɚ]〔谑〕烈酒,(特指爱尔兰产的)威士忌酒〔常照爱尔兰音拼作 crater, crat(h)ur 等〕。~ **comforts** = good ~s.

crèche [kreiʃ; krɛʃ] *n.* 1. (日托)托儿所。2. 育婴堂,孤儿院。3.【宗】马槽中初生耶稣画像。

cre·dal ['kri:dl; ˋkridl̩] *a.* 信条的,教义的,纲领的。

cre·dat Ju·dae·us (*A·pel·la*) ['kri:dæt dju'di:əs(ə'pelə); ˋkridæt djuˋdiəs(əˋpɛlə)]〔L.〕只有犹太的迷信者(阿佩拉)相信〔我可不信〕。

cre·dence ['kri:dəns; ˋkridəns] *n.* 1. 信用;信任;凭证。2.【宗】祭器台,供桌;(中世纪欧洲的)餐具柜,餐桌旁的伺服用桌。*a letter of* ~介绍信,(大使等的)国书。*find* ~受到信任。***give*** [***refuse***] ~ ***to*** 相信[不信]。

cre·den·da [kri'dendə; krɪˋdɛndə] *n.* 〔*pl.*〕(*sing.* **-den·dum** [-dəm; -dəm]) 信条;教条。

cre·dent ['kri:dnt; ˋkridn̩t] *a.* 1. 〔罕〕相信的,有信仰的。2. 〔废〕可信的。

cre·den·tial [kri'denʃəl; krɪˋdɛnʃəl] I *a.* 〔罕〕信任的。II *n.* 凭证,证件;〔*pl.*〕国书。*present one's* ~*s* 呈递国书。~*s committee* 资格审查委员会。**-ism** 文凭主义,资格主义〔特指使用人员中过分重视学历〕。

cred·i·bil·i·ty [ˌkredi'biliti; ˏkrɛdəˋbɪlətɪ] *n.* 可靠性,确实性。*It rests on the* ~ *of* .... 那要看…的是否可靠了。*an account lacking in* ~靠不住的话。~ **gap** 信用差距〔指政府官员等言论与事实的不符〕;(两类人之间的)缺乏信任;(言行等的)不相符合;可信性的不足。

cred·i·ble ['kredəbl, -ibl; ˋkrɛdəbl̩, -ɪbl̩] *a.* 可信的,可靠的。*It is hardly* ~ *that*. 想不到。

cred·i·bly ['kredəbli, -ibli; ˋkrɛdəblɪ, -ɪblɪ] *ad.* 确实,由可靠方面。*I am* ~ *informed that* 由可靠方面听说。

cred·it ['kredit; ˋkrɛdɪt] I *n.* 1. 信用,信任。2. 名誉,名望,声望。3. 赞扬,称许;光荣,功劳,勋绩,荣誉。4. 信贷;赊销;贷款;存款;债权。5.【会计】贷方(金额)〔略 Cr.〕(*opp.* debit)。6. 〔美〕(某科目)学分及格证;〔俚〕优等。7.【商】活支汇信,信用状(= letter of ~)。8.【美无】广告。*a man of* ~德高望重的人。*an open* ~(无担保)信用贷款;无条件活支汇信。***be a*** ~ ***to*** 是…的光荣[功劳]。***be bare of*** ~ 名誉不好,没有信用;没有名气。***be to sb.'s*** ~ 是某人的光荣[功劳]。***deserve no*** ~ 不足信,可疑。***do*** ~ ***to sb.*** = do sb. ~ 使某人大为光荣,增加某人的身价;证明某人具有某种才能或品质。***gain*** [***lose***] ~ 得[失]信任。***get*** ~ ***for*** 因…出名。***get the*** ~ ***of*** 得到…的名誉[光荣](*The wrong man got the* ~ *of it*. 给别人抢了功)。***give*** (***a person***) ~ ***for*** 把…贷给(某人),把…记入(某人)付方;把…归功于(某人),认为是…的功劳;认为当然有(某种性质等)(*I gave you* ~ *for more sense*. 我以为你还要聪明一些(那晓得这样笨)。*I did not give you* ~ *for such skill*. 我没想到你有这个本事)。***give*** ~ ***to*** 相信。***have*** ~ ***at*** 有存款在;在…有势力[信誉]。***have*** ~ ***for*** = *get* ~ *for*. ***have*** ~ ***with*** 对…有信用。***have the*** ~ ***of*** = *get the* ~ *of*. ***lose*** ~ ***with sb.*** 失去某人的信任。***on*** ~ 赊(*deal on* ~ 信用交易,赊账买卖)。***open*** ~ ***with*** 和…开始信用交易。***place*** [***put***] ~ ***in*** 相信。***reflect*** ~ ***on*** 使…光荣,成为…的光荣。***take*** ~ ***for*** = *get* ~ *for*. ***take*** ~ ***to oneself*** 把功劳归自己。***to sb.'s*** ~ 在某人贷方,值得嘉奖[表扬],是…的光荣。II *vt.* 信用,信任;【会计】记入贷方;归(功于某人);〔美〕发及格证给(学生)。*He is* ~*ed with the invention*. 这个发明是他的功劳。~ (***sb.***) ***with*** (*an amount*; *a quality*) 把(某数)记入(某人)账户的贷方,记入为(某人)存款;相信(某人)具有(某性质)。~ (*an amount*; *success*) ***to*** (*sb.*) 把(某数)记入(某人)账户的贷方;把(成功)归(某人)。~ **bureau** (商业)征信所。~ **hour**【教育】学分。~ **line** 1. (出版物、展出物等上标注的)作者名,来件人姓名(等)。2. (= ~ limit) 贷款限额,信用限额。~ **man** 信用调查员。~ **sales** 赊销。~ **worthy** *a.* (资产殷实)可给予〔扩大〕信贷的。

cred·it·a·ble ['kreditəbl; ˋkrɛdɪtəbl̩] *a.* 声誉好的,可钦佩的;可信任的;可称许[赞扬]的;可信用[给予信贷]的。**-bil·ity** [-'biliti; -ˋbɪlətɪ] *n.*

cred·it·a·bly ['kreditəbli; ˋkrɛdɪtəblɪ] *ad.* 美满地,有信誉地;值得称许地;不愧,有体面,很好地。

cred·i·tor ['kreditə; ˋkrɛdɪtɚ] *n.* 债权人(*opp.* *debtor*);【会计】贷方〔略 Cr.〕。~ *nation* 债权国。~*'s sale*〔美〕破产者所有股票的拍卖。

cre·do ['kri:dəu; ˋkrido] *n.*【宗】教义;信条。

cre·du·li·ty [kri'dju:liti; krəˋdulətɪ] *n.* 轻信。

cred·u·lous ['kredjuləs; ˋkrɛdʒələs] *a.* 轻信的,易受骗的。**-ly** *ad.* **-ness** *n.*

Cree [kri:; kri] *n.* 北美印第安人的克里族;克里语。

creed [kri:d; krid] *n.* 1.【宗】教义,信条。2. 主义,纲领,宗派。

Creek [kri:k; krik] *n.* 克里克人〔以马斯科吉部族为主的美国一印第安大部族,原住美国乔治亚州和阿拉巴马州,现住俄克拉荷马州〕;克里克语。

creek [kri:k; krik] *n.* 1. (河、湖的)小湾;小港。2. 〔美〕小川,支流,溪河;山间小平地。3. 〔废〕弯曲狭窄的通路。***up the*** ~〔俚〕困难起来;处于困难中。

creek·y ['kri:ki; ˋkrikɪ] *a.* 多小湾的;曲折的。

creel [kri:l; kril] *n.* 1. (捕)鱼篮;捕虾篮。2.【纺】经轴架,筒子架。*coup the* ~*s*〔Scot.〕弄乱,变杂乱。

CREEP = Committee for the Reelection of the President (美国)支持总统连任委员会。

creep [kri:p; krip] I *vi.* (***crept*** [krept; krɛpt]; ***crept***) 1. 爬行;(蔓、根等)蔓延。2. 偷偷前进,(病人,老者)衰弱迟缓地前进(*in*; *into*; *up* 等);蠕动;【铁路】潜动;【纺】蠕变,潜伸。3. 〔喻〕讨好[巴结]。4. (文章等)单调,生涩。5. (身上)发痒;毛骨悚然,发抖。6.【海】用探海钩探海底。*Age* ~*s upon us*. 我们不知不觉地就老了。~ ***away*** 偷偷离开。~ ***in*** 悄悄混进。~ ***into sb.'s favour*** 逐步巴结而取得某人的好感。~ ***on*** (时间)悄悄地过去。~ ***out*** 偷偷出去。~ ***over*** (*sth.*) (蔓等)爬上;〔喻〕偷偷逼近(进行袭击)。***make sb.'s flesh*** ~ = *make sb.* ~ *all over* 令人不寒而栗,令人毛骨悚然。II *n.* 1. 爬行,匍匐;徐行;蠕动,【纺】蠕变,潜伸。2. 〔*pl.*〕虫爬似的感觉,毛骨悚然的感觉。3. (动物)爬穿的洞;(铁路路基下的)拱洞。4.【地】潜动,蠕动。***give*** (***sb.***) ***the*** ~*s* 使毛骨悚然。~ **hole** (动物)躲藏的洞穴;遁辞,借口。~ **joint**〔美口〕流窜赌场;(盗骗顾主财物的)妓院;下流暗娼。~ **rate** 蠕变率。~ **ratio** 蠕流比。

creep·age ['kri:pidʒ; ˋkripɪdʒ] *n.* 缓慢移动;蠕动;渗水;【纺】蠕变;【电】漏电。

creep·er ['kri:pə; ˋkripɚ] *n.* 1. 爬行物;蠕虫;爬虫;卑躬屈节[巴结讨好]的人。2. 攀缘植物;匍匐枝;啄木鸟。3.【机】螺旋[定速]输送器。4. 打捞钩,探海钩。5.

〔*pl*.〕〔美〕(绑在脚下防滑用的)铁钉板。**6**.〔*pl*.〕【建】藤蔓浮雕。**7**. 滚球。**8**.【机】上螺丝器。**9**. (用于在汽车下面工作的)躺人小车。**10**. (大卡车的)爬坡排挡 (= ~ gear)。**11**. (婴儿的)爬行服。**12**. (斯里兰卡的)种茶学生。

creep·ie-peep·ie [ˈkriːpiˈpiːpi; ˋkripɪˋpipɪ] *n*. 携带式电视摄像机。

creep·ing [ˈkriːpiŋ; ˋkripɪŋ] *a*. **1**. 爬行的;蠕动的;蠕变的;遍地蔓延的。**2**. 迟缓的,悄悄的。**3**. 巴结奉承的。**4**. 痒痒的;毛骨悚然的。~ *discharge*【电】蠕缓[潜流,沿面]放电。~ *Jesus*〔英俚〕怕迫害而躲藏的人,胆小鬼。~ *motion* 蠕动。~ *things* 爬虫类。

creep·mouse [ˈkriːpmaus; ˋkripmaʊs] *n*. 爬行的老鼠;老鼠爬行般的刺痒。

creep·y [ˈkriːpi; ˋkripɪ] *a*. 慢慢爬行的;痒痒的;毛骨悚然的;〔英学〕讨好老师的。**~-crawly** *a*. (动物,虫类)爬行的;毛骨悚然的。

creese [kriːs; kris] *n*. (马来人的)波刃短剑 (= cris, kris)。

creesh [kriːʃ; kriʃ] *n*., *vt*.〔Scot.〕油脂,润滑脂;涂油,搽油。

cre·mains [krəˈmeinz; krəˋmenz] *n*. *pl*. (尸体火化后的)骨灰。

cre·mate [kriˈmeit; ˋkrɪmet] *vt*. 烧成灰;火葬。

cre·ma·tion [kriˈmeiʃən; krɪˋmeʃən] *n*. 烧化,火葬;(垃圾)焚化(法)。**-ist** *n*. 火葬论者。

cre·ma·tor [kriˈmeitə; krɪˋmetɚ] *n*. 火葬者,焚尸人;焚尸炉;垃圾焚化炉。**-to·ri·al** [-ˈtɔriəl; -ˋtɔrɪəl] *a*.

cre·ma·to·ri·um [ˌkreməˈtɔːriəm; ˏkriməˋtɔrɪəm] (*pl*. *~s*, *-ria* [-riə; -rɪə]) *n*. 火葬场,垃圾焚化场。

cre·ma·to·ry [ˈkremətəri; ˋkrɛməˏtorɪ] **I** *n*. = crematorium. **II** *a*. 火葬的。

crème [kreim; krɛm] *n*.〔F.〕= cream 奶油状溶液。~ ***de cacao*** 可可酒。~ ***de la*** ~ [-dəlɑː-; -dəlɑ-] 尖子;头等人物;精华。~ ***de menthe*** [-dəˈmɑ̃ːnt; -dəˋmɑ̃nt] 薄荷酒。

Cre·mer [ˈkriːmə; ˋkrimɚ] *n*. 克里默〔姓氏〕。

Cre·mo·na, c- [kriˈməunə; krɪˋmonə] *n*. (意大利)克里莫纳提琴。

cre·nate(d) [ˈkriːneit(id); ˋkrinet(ɪd)] *a*.【植】圆(形锯)齿状的,钝齿状的。

cre·na·tion [kriˈneiʃən; krɪˋneʃən] *n*. 圆齿状,钝齿状;(红细胞的)皱缩。

cren·a·ture [ˈkrenətʃə; ˋkrɛnətʃɚ] *n*. (叶边的)圆齿,钝齿。

cren·el, cre·nelle [ˈkrenəl, kriˈnel; ˋkrɛnl̩, krɪˋnɛl] *n*. **1**. 雉堞(上的枪眼);〔*pl*.〕城垛。**2**. = crenature.

cren·el·ate,〔英〕**cren·el·late** [ˈkrenileit; ˋkrɛnɪˏlet] *vt*. 造雉堞,开枪眼。*~d moulding*【建】圆齿状花边[线脚]。

cren·el(l)a·tion [ˌkreniˈleiʃən; ˏkrɛnl̩ˋeʃən] *n*. 筑雉堞;开枪眼(工作);圆齿状突出。

cren·el·et [ˈkrenilit; ˋkrɛnlɪt] *n*. 小雉堞。

creno- *comb*. *f*. 泉水。

cren·u·late [ˈkrenjuːlit, -ˈleit; ˋkrɛnjəlɪt, -ˋlet] *a*. 具小扇的;细圆齿状的;具细圆齿的 (= crenulated)。

cren·u·la·tion [krenjuːˈleiʃən; krɛnjuˋleʃən] *n*. 小钝锯齿(状)。

cre·o·dont [ˈkriəˌdɔnt; ˋkrɪəˏdɑnt] *n*.【古生】肉齿亚目,古肉食亚目。

Cre·ole [ˈkriːəul; ˋkriol] **I** *n*. **1**. 克利奥尔人〔西印度及南美各地的西班牙、法国移民的后裔〕(= ~ white)。**2**.〔c-〕黑白混血种;西印度、南美等处生长的黑人 (= ~ negro)。**3**.〔美〕路易斯安那州的法国移民的后裔;路易斯安那州的法国土话。**II** *a*. 克利奥尔人(特有)的。~ **State** 美国路易斯安那州〔别号〕。

cre·o·sol [ˈkriəˌsəul, -ˌsɔːl; ˋkrɪəˏsol, -ˏsɔl] *n*.【化】木焦油酚,甲氧甲酚。

cre·o·sote [ˈkriəsəut; ˋkrɪəˏsot] *n*.【化】杂酚油,烟油。【商】石炭酸 (= carbolic acid)。~ ***oil*** 杂酚油。

cre·owls [ˈkriːəuls; ˋkriols] *n*.〔美〕路易斯安那州人〔别号〕。

crepe, *crêpe* [kreip; krep] *n*.〔F.〕**1**. 绉绸[纱]。**2**. 黑纱丧章。**3**. 油煎薄饼。~ *de Chine* [ˈkreipdəˈʃiːn; ˋkrepdəˋʃin]【纺】双绉。~ *hanger* 忧郁悲观的人;扫人兴的人。~ *paper* 绉纸。~ *rubber* 绉纹薄橡皮板。

crêpes su·zette [ˌkreipsuˈzet; ˏkrepsʊˋzɛt] *n*. 白兰地油煎饼。

crep·i·tant [ˈkrepitənt; ˋkrɛpətənt] *a*. **1**. 噼啪响的。**2**.【医】捻发音的,捻发音的。

crep·i·tate [ˈkrepiteit; ˋkrɛpəˏtet] *vi*. **1**. (火里的盐等)噼啪响,作碎裂声。**2**. (肺炎病人等的肺)发呻轧音。

crep·i·ta·tion [ˌkrepiˈteiʃən; ˏkrɛpɪˋteʃən] *n*. 噼啪声,爆裂声;裂声;【医】呻轧音,捻发音。

cré·pon [ˈkrepɔːŋ; ˋkrepɑŋ] *n*.〔F.〕重绉纹织物。

crept [krept; krɛpt] creep 的过去式及过去分词。

cre·pus·cu·lar [kriˈpʌskjulə; krɪˋpʌskjəlɚ] *a*. **1**. 朦胧的,微明的,半明半暗的;拂晓的;黄昏的;薄暮的。**2**. 在黄昏时候活动的(动物)。**3**. 曙光时代的,半开化的,蒙昧的。~ ***ray*** 曙光;朦胧的微光。

cre·pus·cule [kriˈpʌskjuːl; krɪˋpʌskjul] *n*. 黄昏,薄暮。曙光 (= crepuscle)。

cres., cresc. = crescendo.

cres·cen·do [kriˈʃendəu; krəˋʃɛndo] **I** *ad*.〔It.〕【乐】渐强;(感情、动作)逐渐加强。**II** *n*. 渐强音[音节];声音渐强;(向高潮)进展。

cres·cent [ˈkreznt, ˈkresnt; ˋkrɛznt, ˋkrɛsnt] **I** *n*. **1**. 新月,娥眉月。**2**. 新月状物[街巷等];(旧土耳其帝国的)新月旗,土耳其帝国,土耳其军,伊斯兰教(新月形记号)。**3**.〔美〕月牙形面包 (= ~ bun [roll])。***the Cross and the C-*** 基督教和伊斯兰教。**II** *a*. 新月(形)的,月牙形的;〔诗〕(新月一般)渐渐增大的,逐渐变圆的。**C- citizen**〔美〕新奥尔良市民。**C- City**〔美〕新奥尔良市〔别号〕。

cres·cent·ade [kresnˈteid; krɛsntˋed] *n*. 新月军,伊斯兰教军。

cres·cive [ˈkresiv; ˋkrɛsɪv] *a*.〔罕〕增长的,增加的。

cre·sol [ˈkriːsɔl; ˋkrisol] *n*.【化】甲酚〔防腐等用〕。

cress [kres; krɛs] *n*.【植】水芹。

cres·set [ˈkresit; ˋkrɛsɪt] *n*. 号灯,标灯,篝灯;油盏。

crest [krest; krɛst] **I** *n*. **1**. 鸡冠;冠毛。**2**. 羽毛饰,(盔上的)饰毛,翎毛,顶饰;〔诗〕盔。**3**. (山)脊,山顶;(浪)峰,浪头。**4**. (动物的)颈脊;(马等的)鬣;【徽】(楯形上部的)饰章;【建】脊饰;【解】头上隆起,骨节,脊突。~ *voltmeter*【电】巅值伏特计。~ *table*【建】墙帽。~ *tile* 屋脊瓦。***erect*** [*elevate*] ***one's*** ~〔古〕得意洋洋。***on the*** ~ ***of the wave*** 在波浪顶上;得意已极。***one's*** ~ ***falls*** 垂头丧气。**II** *vt*. **1**. 加上顶饰。**2**. 用作顶饰。**3**. 到达…的顶部。—*vi*. **1**. 形成冠毛状顶部;(波浪)山涌。**2**. 到达顶部。*~**ed note-paper*** 顶上印有标章的信纸。**~-fallen** *a*. 垂头丧气的。

crest·ing [ˈkrestiŋ; ˋkrɛstɪŋ] *n*.【建】屋[墙]脊饰。

cre·syl·ic [kriˈsilik; krɪˋsɪlɪk] *a*.【化】甲酚的;杂酚油的;从甲酚[杂酚油]中提取的。

cre·ta [ˈkriːtə; ˋkritə] *n*.【化】**1**. 白垩。**2**. 漂白土。

cre·ta·ceous [kriˈteiʃəs; krɪˋteʃəs] **I** *a*. 白垩(质)的。~ *period* [*system*]【地】白垩纪[系]。**II** *n*.〔C-〕【地】白垩纪[系]。

Cre·tan [ˈkriːtən; ˋkritən] *a*., *n*. 克里特岛的(人)。

Crete [kriːt; krit] *n*. 克里特(岛)〔希腊〕。

cre·tic [ˈkriːtik; ˋkritɪk] *n*.【韵】扬抑扬音步。

cret·in [ˈkretin, ˈkriːtin; ˋkrɛtɪn, ˋkritɪn] *n*.【医】呆小病患者,愚侏病患者,克汀病患者。**-ism** *n*.【医】(阿尔卑斯山地常有的)呆小病,愚侏病。**-ous** *a*.

cre·tonne [kreˈtɔn; krɪˋtɑn] *n*.〔F.〕大花窗布;印花装

饰布。

cre·val·le [kri'væli; krɪ`vælɪ] ***n***.【动】长面鱼参(*Caranx hippos*)。

cre·vasse [kri'væs; krə`væs] ***n***.〔F.〕(冰河等的)裂隙;裂口。

crev·ice ['krevis; `krɛvɪs] ***n***.罅隙,裂缝。～ *plant* 石隙植物。

crew[1] [kru:; kru] ***n***.(全体)乘务员,(中下级)船员,水手;【体】划艇队员;〔蔑〕同伴;组,班,队,群;〔美〕同事们,工友们;〔俚〕(青少年结成的)帮派。*officers and* ～高级和低级全体船员。*a train* ～列车乘务员。*air* [*ground*] ～*s* 空勤[地勤]人员。*the whole* ～ *of Jingoes* 主战派全班人马。～ **cut** (发式)平头。～**-man** 〔美〕(飞机、轮船等的)乘务员;(军队的)部队人员。

crew[2] [kru:; kru]【军】crow 的过去式。

crew·el ['kruil; `kruəl] ***n***. **1**. 刺绣用的细绒线。**2**. =～**work** 绒线刺绣。

crib [krib; krɪb] **I** ***n***. **1**. 秣槽;牛槛,牛舍。**2**. (有围栏的)儿童床;〔俚〕摇篮。**3**. 框;【建】叠木框架,脚手架。**4**. 木头小屋;小房间,狭小的地方。**5**.〔俚〕偷窃,剽窃(*from*)。**6**. (学生用的)本国文与外国文对照本,注解书。**7**. (盗贼隐语)人家,店家,仓库,保险柜(等行窃对象)。**8**.〔俚〕= cribbage. **9**.〔美俚〕酒吧,赌场,妓院(等)。**10**.〔英〕(工人带到工地吃的)盒饭。*crack a* ～闯入行窃地点。**II** ***vt***. **1**. 关进(狭小的地方);拘束。**2**.〔俚〕偷;剽窃,抄袭。**3**. 搁秣槽(在牛栏等里)。—***vi***. **1**. 剽窃,抄袭。**2**. (学生考试时)作弊,作挟带;用注释本。**3**. (马等)咬秣槽。～ **crime**〔美俚〕对老人进行的行凶抢劫。～ **death**【医】婴儿猝死综合症。

crib·bage ['kribidʒ; `krɪbɪdʒ] ***n***.【牌】每人发牌 6 张,先凑足 121 分或 61 分者为赢牌的玩法。

crib·ber ['kribə; `krɪbɚ] ***n***. **1**. 剽窃者,作弊者。**2**. (缚住马颈以防马咬秣槽的)皮带。**3**. 有咬秣槽淌口水习癖的马。**4**. 支撑物。

crib·bing ['kribiŋ; `krɪbɪŋ] ***n***. 剽窃[抄袭]行为;(学生的)作弊,作挟带; =crib-biting.

crib·bit·ing ['kribiŋ; `krɪbɪŋ] ***n***. (马)咬住秣槽喘气的习癖。

crib·ble ['kribl; `krɪbl̩] **I** ***n***. 粗筛;粗粉。**II** ***vt***. (用粗筛子)筛。

crib·el·lum [kri'beləm; krɪ`bɛləm] ***n***. (*pl*. **-la** [-lə; -lə])【动】(蜘蛛等的)纺绩突起。

crib·ri·form ['kribrifɔ:m; `krɪbrɪˏfɔrm] ***a***. 筛状的。

crib·work ['kribwə:k; `krɪbˏwɝk] ***n***.【建】叠木框架。

cri·ce·tid [krai'si:tid, -'set-; kraɪ`sitɪd, -`set-] ***n***.【动】啮齿科动物〔包括美洲鼠在内〕;仓鼠。

Crich·ton ['kraitn; `kraɪtən] ***n***. 克赖顿〔姓氏〕。

Crick [krik; krɪk] ***n***. 克里克〔姓氏〕。

crick [krik; krɪk] **I** ***n***.【医】(颈、脊、腰等的)肌肉[关节]痉挛。**II** ***vt***. (颈等)引起痉挛。

crick·et[1] ['krikit; `krɪkɪt] ***n***.【虫】蟋蟀。***as merry as a*** ～ 极快活的。

crick·et[2] ['krikit; `krɪkɪt] **I** ***n***.【体】板球〔双方各 11 人玩的球戏,英国最为流行〕;光明正大,公正的行为[态度]。**II** ***a***.〔口〕公正的。*It's not* ～.〔俚〕这个不公正。*play* ～ 打板球;光明正大地做。

crick·et[3] ['krikit; `krɪkɪt] ***n***.〔美〕矮木凳;垫脚凳。

crick·et[4] ['krikit; `krɪkɪt] ***n***. 斜沟小屋顶。

crick·et·er ['krikitə; `krɪkɪtɚ] ***n***. 板球运动员。

cri·coid ['kraikɔid; `kraɪkɔɪd] ***a***.【解】环状的。

cri de cœur [F. kri də kœ:r; krɪ də kœr] 衷心的呼喊;强烈抗议;满腹牢骚。

cri du chat [ˌkri:du'ʃɑ:; ˏkridʊ`ʃɑ]【医】猫鸣综合症。

cri·er ['kraiə; `kraɪɚ] ***n***. **1**. 喊叫者,哭喊者,哭娃娃。**2**. (乡下)传布公告的(= town ～)。**3**. 大声宣扬做广告的。**4**. (法院的)传唤者,法警。**5**. 叫卖小贩。

cri·key ['kraiki; `kraɪkɪ] ***int***.〔俚〕嗳呀!唷!〔又作 By ～!〕。

crim. con. = criminal conversation.

crime [kraim; kraɪm] **I** ***n***. 犯罪;罪恶;〔俚〕坏事;〔口〕蠢事。**II** ***vt***. 指控犯罪;判定犯罪;处罚军事犯。*a capital* ～死刑罪。*commit a* ～犯罪。*collude with ... as partners in* ～与…狼狈为奸[进行犯罪活动]。～ *sheet*【军】处罚记录。～*s against the state* 国事犯。***put*** [***throw***] ***a*** ～ ***upon sb***. 把罪推在某人身上。

Cri·me·a [krai'miə; kraɪ`mɪə] ***n***. 克里米亚(半岛);克里木(半岛)〔前苏联〕。*the* ～ *Conference* (1945 年英美苏联的)克里米亚会议〔= Yalta Conference〕。**-an** ***a***.

crim·i·nal ['kriminl; `krɪmənl̩] **I** ***a***. 犯罪的;刑事上的;〔口〕恶劣的,蛮不讲理的。**II** ***n***. 罪犯,犯人。*a habitual* ～惯犯。*a war* ～战犯。～ **abortion** 堕胎罪。～ **act** 犯罪行为。～ **action** 刑事诉讼(= ～ suit)。～ **assault** 强奸。～ **attempt** 犯罪未遂。～ **conversation** [**connexion**] 通奸。～ **jurisprudence** 刑法学。～ **law** 刑法。～ **offence** 刑事罪。～ **operation** 堕胎罪。～ **psychology** 犯罪心理学。～ **suit** 刑事诉讼。**-ist** ***n***. 刑事学家,罪犯学家。

crim·i·nal·is·tics [ˌkriminə'listiks; ˏkrɪmənl̩ɪstɪks] ***n***. *pl*. 犯罪侦察学,刑事学。

crim·i·nal·i·ty [ˌkrimi'næliti; ˏkrɪmə`nælətɪ] ***n***. 犯罪(行为),罪行,罪恶。

crim·i·nal·ly ['kriminəli; `krɪmɪnəlɪ] ***ad***. 刑法上;犯罪。*proceed against sb*. ～对某人提起刑事诉讼。

crim·i·nate ['krimineit; `krɪməˏnet] ***vt***. **1**. 控告…有罪。**2**. 证明…有罪;定罪。**3**. 责备。～ *oneself* 说出对自己不利的事情;泄露[证明]自己有罪。

crim·i·na·tion [ˌkrimi'neiʃən; ˏkrɪmɪ`neʃən] ***n***. 控告;定罪;责备。～***s and recriminations*** 互相告发〔指责对方犯罪〕。

crim·i·na·tive, crim·i·na·to·ry ['kriminətiv, 'krimineitəri; `krɪməˏnətɪv, `krɪmənəˏtɔrɪ] ***a***. 控告的,举罪告发的;责难的。

crim·i·ne, crim·i·ny ['krimini; `krɪmɪnɪ] ***int***.〔俚〕嗳呀!〔惊叹声〕。

crim·i·no·log·i·cal [ˌkriminə'lɔdʒikəl; ˏkrɪmənə`lɑdʒɪkəl] ***a***. 犯罪学(上)的。

crim·i·nol·o·gy [ˌkrimi'nɔlədʒi; ˏkrɪmə`nɑlədʒɪ] ***n***. 犯罪学,刑事学。

crim·i·nous ['kriminəs; `krɪmənəs] ***a***. 犯罪的。*a* ～ *clerk* 犯罪僧,破戒僧。

crim·mer ['krimə; `krɪmɚ] ***n***. 克里默羔皮(= krimmer)。

crimp[1] [krimp; krɪmp] **I** ***vt***. **1**. 卷(头发)。**2**. 使有折缝,使发皱。**3**. (在鱼肉等上)划裂痕(使挛缩)。**4**. (把鞋革等)做成鞋形。**5**. 轧在一起,叠在一起。**6**. 妨碍,阻碍。**II** ***n***.〔常 *pl*.〕〔美〕卷发;卷缩机;抑制物,障碍。***put a*** ～ ***in***(***to***)〔美俚〕妨[阻]碍。

crimp[2] [krimp; krɪmp] **I** ***n***. 兵贩子,人贩子。**II** ***vt***. 诱骗…(当兵等)。

crimp·ing·iron ['krimpiŋaiən; `krɪmpɪŋaɪən] ***n***. 卷发器,烫发铗。

crim·ple ['krimpl; `krɪmpl̩] **I** ***n***. 皱折,折缝。**II** ***vt***., ***vi***. (使)皱,(使)缩,(使)卷缩。

crimp·y ['krimpi; `krɪmpɪ] ***a***. (**-i·er**; **-i·est**) **1**. 皱缩[卷缩]的。**2**.〔美俚〕冷得要命的。

crim·son ['krimzn; `krɪmzn̩] **I** ***n***. 深红,鸡冠红,绯红;深红色颜料。**II** ***a***. **1**. 深红的。**2**.〔喻〕流血的,血腥的。**III** ***vt***., ***vi***. 染成[变成]深红色;(脸)变通红。**C- Beauty** 艳红品种苹果。～ **lake** 洋红〔图画颜料〕。～ **pool**〔美俚〕亏空。～ **satin** 牙兰缎。

cri·nal ['krainl; `kraɪnl̩] ***a***. 毛发的。

cringe [krindʒ; krɪndʒ] ***n***., ***vi***. 畏缩;卑躬曲膝,战战兢兢。

crin·gle ['kriŋgl; `krɪŋgl̩] ***n***.【船】索眼;索圈。

cri·nite [ˈkrainait; ˋkraɪnaɪt] *a*. 毛发状的;【动】有发状尾的;【植】有长毛的,长毛的。

crin·kle [ˈkriŋkl; ˋkrɪŋkl] **I** *n*. **1**. 皱纹,折痕;条子泡泡纱。**2**.【植】绉叶病。**3**. 沙拉沙拉声。**II** *vt*. 使皱。—*vi*. **1**. 起皱,卷缩。**2**. 沙拉沙拉地作声。~*d paper* 皱纸。

crin·kle·root [ˈkriŋkl,ruːt, -ˈrut; ˋkrɪŋkl,rut, -ˋrut] *n*.【植】二叶石芥花 (*Dentaria diphylla*)。

crin·kly [ˈkriŋkli; ˋkrɪŋklɪ] *a*. (衣料等)起皱的,皱折多的;波状的;(毛发等)卷曲的;沙拉沙拉响的。~ *curve* 怪曲线。

crin·kum-cran·kum [ˈkriŋkəmˈkræŋkəm; ˋkrɪŋkəm-ˋkræŋkəm] **I** *n*.〔口〕弯曲;弯弯曲曲的东西。**II** *a*. 弯弯曲曲的,错综复杂的。

cri·noid [ˈkrainɔid, ˈkrin-; ˋkraɪnɔɪd, ˋkrɪn-] **I** *a*. 海百合类的。**II** *n*. 海百合。

Cri·noi·de·a [kraiˈnɔidiə; kraɪˋnɔɪdɪə] *n*.〔*pl*.〕【动】海百合纲。

crin·o·line [ˈkrinəliːn; ˋkrɪnlɪn] *n*. **1**. 做裙衬的硬毛布[马鬃布];裙子的衬架;有硬毛布衬(架)的裙子。**2**. (军舰的)水雷防御网。

cri·num [ˈkrainəm; ˋkraɪnəm] *n*.【植】文殊兰。

cri·o·llo [kriːˈəuləu; kriˋolo] **I** *n*. (*fem*. *cri·o·lia*) **1**. 西班牙裔拉美人;西班牙、拉美混血儿。**2**. 拉美繁殖的家畜。**II** *a*. 西班牙裔拉美人的;西班牙、拉美混血儿的。

cri·o·sphinx [ˈkraiəsfiŋks; ˋkraɪə,sfɪŋks] *n*. 狮身羊头像。

crip·ple [ˈkripl; ˋkrɪpl] **I** *n*. **1**. 跛子,瘸子,瘫子,残废(人)。**2**.〔美方〕杂木丛生的沼地。**3**. 脚凳;脚手架;〔美俚〕破汽车。*be a* ~ *for life* 成终生残疾。**II** *vt*. 使成瘫子[跛子],使残废;削弱;使失去战斗力。—*vi*.〔Scot.〕一瘸一瘸地走 (along)。*be financially* ~*d* 财政拮据。~*d soldier* 残废士兵。**-dom**, **-hood** *n*. 残废;无能。

Cripps [krips; krɪps] *n*. 克里普斯[姓氏]。

cris [kriːs; krɪs] *n*. = creese.

cri·sis [ˈkraisis; ˋkraɪsɪs] (*pl*. *-ses* [-siːz; -siz]) *n*. **1**. 危急关头,紧要关头;(政治、经济上的)危机,危局;恐慌;激变。**2**.【医】转变期,骤退;临界;危象。**3**.【剧、影】危急情节,转折点。*a cabinet* ~内阁危机。*a financial* ~金融恐慌,财政危机。*economic* ~经济危机。*political* ~政治危机。~ **of confidence** 信任危机。~ **of conscience** 精神危机,信仰危机。***bring to a*** ~ 使紧迫[危急]。***face a*** ~ 面临危局。~ **centre** 个人疑难咨询中心。

crisp [krisp; krɪsp] **I** *a*. **1**. 卷缩的;起皱的;有微波的。**2**. 脆的,易碎的。**3**. 有脆声的(纸)。**4**. 新鲜的,爽快的,有力的,有劲儿的(文章等);干脆的,够味的(说法等)。*the* ~ *air* 清新的空气。*a* ~ *manner* [*utterance*] 干脆的态度[语调]。*eat* ~吃着松脆。**II** *vt*. **1**. 弄卷(头发);使起皱;使生小波浪。**2**. 烘脆(面包等);(寒冷使地面)冻硬。—*vi*. **1**. 卷曲,起皱;起小浪。**2**. 变脆;(地面等)冻硬。**III** *n*. 脆(性);〔俚〕钞票;〔*pl*.〕〔英〕油炸马铃薯片。(*be burned*) *to a* ~(烧)脆(焦)。**-ly** *ad*. **-ness** *n*.

cris·pate [ˈkrispeit; ˋkrɪspet] *a*. 卷缩起皱的,卷曲的;【动、植】卷缩状的,皱成波状的,有皱缘的。

crisp·er [ˈkrispə; ˋkrɪspɚ] *n*. (电冰箱中的)新鲜蔬菜储藏格。

cris·pin [ˈkrispin; ˋkrɪspɪn] *n*. 鞋匠;〔美〕鞋匠工会会员。**St. C~** (罗马神话中的)鞋匠之神。

crisp·ing·iron [ˈkrispiŋaiən; ˋkrɪspɪŋ,aɪən] *n*. 卷发器,卷发铗,烫发剪。

crisp·y [ˈkrispi; ˋkrɪspɪ] *a*. 卷曲的;脆的,松脆的,易碎的;爽快的,干脆的。

criss·cross [ˈkriskrɔs; ˋkrɪs,krɔs] **I** *n*. **1**. 十字押,十字号[图案];十字交叉形式。**2**. 龃龉,抵触;混乱。**3**.〔古〕字母 (= christ-cross)。**4**.〔美〕= *tick-tack-toe*. **II** *a*., *ad*. **1**. 十字形的[地];交叉的[着]。**2**. 龃龉;脾气大,别扭。*a* ~ *pattern* 十字形花样。~ *traffic* 纵横交叉的交通。**go** ~ **with** 跟…作对。**III** *vt*. 划十字押;做成十字形;使交叉。~**-row** *n*. 字母。**-ing** *n*. 交叉回交。

cris·sum [ˈkrisəm; ˋkrɪsəm] *n*. (*pl*. *-sa* [-ə; -ə])【解】**1**. 肛周。**2**. 围肛羽。**cris·sal** *a*.

cris·ta [ˈkristə; ˋkrɪstə] *n*. (*pl*. *-tae* [-tiː; -ti])【解、动】脊;卵鞘脊。

cris·tate [ˈkristeit; ˋkrɪstet] *a*. 鸡冠状的;有冠毛的。

crit. = critical; criticism; criticized.

cri·te·ria [kraiˈtiəriə; kraɪˋtɪrɪə] *n*. criterion 的复数。

cri·te·ri·on [kraiˈtiəriən; kraɪˋtɪrɪən] *n*. (*pl*. *-ria*) (评判等的)标准,准则。

crith [kriθ; krɪθ] *n*. 克瑞[气体重量单位,摄氏 0 度、气压 760 毫米下 1 公升氢的重量, =00896 克]。

crit·ic [ˈkritik; ˋkrɪtɪk] *n*. **1**. 批评家,评论家;鉴定家。**2**. 吹毛求疵的人。**3**.〔废〕= critique. *a dramatic* [*literary*] ~戏剧[文学]评论家。

crit·i·cal [ˈkritikəl; ˋkrɪtɪkl] *a*. **1**. 批判的,批评的;(在某方面)有鉴定力的 (*in*)。**2**. 吹毛求疵的;爱挑剔别人的 (*of*, *about*)。**3**. 危机的,危急的;决定性的,重大的;急需的(物资等);【医】危象的;极期的。**4**.【数,物】临界的;中肯的;足够发生连锁反应的。*I am nothing, if not* ~. 只有这张刻薄的嘴,是我的长处。*be* ~ *about* 爱挑剔。~ **acumen** 明察秋毫的敏锐。~ **age** (妇女的)绝经期。~ **angle** 临界角。~ **condition** (病的)危险状态;临界状态。~ **days** (病的)危险期。~ **evidence** 决定性证据。~ **length** (纤维的)致断长度。~ **moment** 危机;紧要关头,关键时刻。~ **path** (**analysis**) 统筹方法,关键路线法,主要矛盾线路法。~ **point**【物】临界点,驻点。~ **radius** 中肯半径。~ **region**【统】判域。~ **situation** 严重的局势[形势]。~ **temperature**【物】临界温度。~ **writer** 评论家。**-ly** *ad*.

crit·ic·as·ter [ˈkritikæstə; ˋkrɪtɪk,æstɚ] *n*. 低劣的批评家。

crit·i·cise [ˈkritisaiz; ˋkrɪtə,saɪz] *vt*., *vi*. = criticize.

crit·i·cism [ˈkritisizəm; ˋkrɪtə,sɪzəm] *n*. **1**. 批评,批判,评论;非难。**2**. 鉴定,审定,考证,校勘;鉴定法。**3**.【哲】批判主义[哲学]。**4**. 评论文章;文艺批评理论。*the higher* [*lower*, *textual*] ~义理方面的[文字上的]校勘。*self-* ~自我批评。***be beyond*** [***above***] ~ 无可批评。***be beneath*** ~ 无批评价值。***open to*** ~ 待批评的。

crit·i·cize [ˈkritisaiz; ˋkrɪtə,saɪz] *vt*., *vi*. 批评,批判;鉴定;校勘;非议,非难,挑剔。

crit·i·co- *comb*. *f*. 批评的。

cri·tique [kriˈtiːk; krɪˋtik] *n*. 批评,批判,评论;鉴定,审定;校勘;检阅;批评法;鉴定法。

crit·ter, **crit·tur** [ˈkritə; ˋkrɪtɚ] *n*.〔方〕动物等 (= creature)。

CRM = **1**. counter-radar measures 反雷达措施。**2**. counter-radar missile 反雷达导[飞]弹。**3**. counting rate metre 计数率测量计,计数表。

CRMP = Corps of Royal Military Police (英国)皇家宪兵队。

c. r. o. = cathode-ray oscilloscope.【无】阴极射线示波器。

croak [krəuk; krok] **I** *n*. **1**. (鸦、蛙等的)哇哇的鸣声;嘎声。**2**. 怨言,牢骚。**3**. 不吉利的话。***give a*** ~ ***of a taugh*** 发出一声干笑;哑然失笑。**II** *vi*. **1**. 哇哇地叫;发嘎声。**2**. 喊冤,抱怨;发牢骚。**3**. 预报不吉;哭丧着说。**4**.〔美俚〕死,断气。—*vt*. **1**. 用阴抑的语声叙述(不吉的事情等)。**2**.〔美俚〕杀死。

croak·er [ˈkrəukə; ˋkrokɚ] *n*. **1**. 哇哇叫的东西。**2**. 喊冤者,抱怨者。**3**. 预报凶事者;悲观者。**4**.〔俚〕尸首。**5**. (北美产)叫鱼。**6**.〔美俚〕医生。*yellow* ~黄(花)鱼。

croak·y [ˈkrəuki; ˋkrokɪ] *a*. **1**. 哇哇叫的。**2**. 嘎声的。

C

3. 阴抑不吉的(声音等)。

Cro·at [ˈkrəuət; ˋkroæt] ***n.*** 克罗地亚人[语]。

Cro·a·tia [krə*u*ˈeiʃjə; kroˋeʃə] ***n.*** 克罗地亚(国名)。

Cro·a·tian [krəuˈeiʃən; kroˋeʃən] ***a.*** 克罗地亚的。

croc [krɔk; krɑk] ***n.*** 〔口〕= crocodile.

cro·ce·ate [ˈkrəusieit; ˋkrosɪˏet] ***a.*** 藏红花(色)的。

cro·ce·in [ˈkrəusiin; ˋkrosɪɪn] ***n.*** 【化】藏(红)花精。

cro·chet [ˈkrəuʃei; ˋkrɑtʃɪt] **I** ***n.*** **1.** 钩针编织(品)。**2.** 【动】趾钩。*the fillet* [*single*] ~方格[简单]编织法。~ *hook* 编花边等的钩针。**II** ***vt.***, ***vi.*** 用钩针织。

cro·cid·o·lite [krəˈsidəlait; kroˋsɪdəˏlaɪt] ***n.*** 【矿】青石绵。

crock[1] [krɔk; krɑk] ***n.*** **1.** (瓦)罐,(瓦)缸;碎瓦片;〔英方〕三足铁釜。**2.** 〔俚〕荒唐的话[行为];不老实的话;胡说;自相矛盾的话。

crock[2] [krɔk; krɑk] **I** ***n.*** 废马,老马;〔Scot.〕老母羊;无用的人,病弱残废人;(学校等中)不(能)运动的人;废物。**II** ***vt.*** 〔俚〕使无用,使成残废,弄成废物。—***vi.*** 变衰竭;破损。~ *sb. up* 使人无法工作。~ ***up*** 〔美俚〕(飞机)坠毁,跌碎;(人体)变衰弱。

crock[3] [krɔk; krɑk] **I** ***n.*** **1.** 〔方〕(炊具等的)烟垢,煤炱。**2.** (色布上)掉下的有色物质。**II** ***vt.*** 用烟垢弄脏。—***vi.*** (布)掉色。~**-meter** 耐摩擦度测定器。

crocked [krɔkt; krɑkt] ***a.*** 〔俚〕喝醉了的。

crock·er·y [ˈkrɔkəri; ˋkrɑkərɪ] ***n.*** 〔集合词〕陶器,瓦器。

crock·et [ˈkrɔkit; ˋkrɑkɪt] ***n.*** 【建】卷叶饰。

Crock·ett [ˈkrɔkit; ˋkrɑkɪt] ***n.*** 克罗基特〔姓氏〕。

croc·o·dile [ˈkrɔkədail; ˋkrɑkəˏdaɪl] ***n.*** **1.** 鳄鱼。**2.** 假装慈悲的人,伪善者。**3.** 〔英俚〕双列女学生队;(汽车等的)长蛇阵。~ **bird** (非洲)鳄鸟。~ **tears** 假慈悲〔据说鳄鱼一面吃一面哭它所吃的动物〕。

croc·o·dil·i·an [ˌkrɔkəˈdiliən; ˏkrɑkəˋdɪlɪən] **I** ***a.*** 鳄鱼(一样)的。**II** ***n.*** 鳄鱼(类动物)。

cro·co·i·site [ˈkrə*u*kəuzait; ˋkrokoˏzaɪt] ***n.*** = crocoite.

cro·co·ite [ˈkrəukəuait; ˋkrokoaɪt] ***n.*** 【地】铬铅矿。

cro·cus[1] [ˈkrəukəs; ˋkrokəs] ***n.*** (*pl.* ~***es***, ***cro·ci*** [-sai; -saɪ]) **1.** 【植】藏红花(属);英国报春花。**2.** 藏红花色,橘黄色。**3.** 紫红(氧化)铁粉〔一种研磨料〕。

cro·cus[2] [ˈkrəukəs; ˋkrokəs] ***n.*** 〔美俚〕庸医。

Croe·sus [ˈkriːsəs; ˋkrisəs] ***n.*** 克利萨斯〔公元前六世纪 **Lydia** 王,以富有著称〕;大富豪。

Croft [krɔft; krɔft] ***n.*** 克罗夫特〔姓氏〕。

croft [krɔft; krɔft] ***n.*** 〔英〕(住宅附近的)园地,小农场,小牧草地。**-er** ***n.*** (苏格兰西部)小农场佃农。

Crofts [krɔfts; krɑfts] ***n.*** 克罗夫茨〔姓氏〕。

crois·sant [krəˈsɑːnt; krəˋsɑnt] ***n.*** 新月形小面包。

Cro·ker [ˈkrəukə; ˋkrokɚ] ***n.*** 克罗克〔姓氏〕。

Cro-Mag·non [krəuˈmænjɔ̃ːŋ; kroˋmænjəŋ] ***n.***, ***a.*** 克罗马尼翁人(的)〔欧洲史前人种〕。

crom·lech [ˈkrɔmlek; ˋkrɑmlɛk] ***n.*** 【考古】**1.** = dolmen. **2.** (史前)环列巨石柱群。

Cromp·ton [ˈkrʌm*p*tən; ˋkrɑm*p*tən] ***n.*** **1.** 克朗普顿〔姓氏〕。**2.** **Samuel** ~萨穆尔·克伦顿〔1753—1827,英国纺纱机发明人〕。

Crom·well [ˈkrɔmwəl; ˋkrɑmwəl] ***n.*** **1.** 克伦威尔〔姓氏〕。**2.** **Oliver** ~奥利弗·克伦威尔〔1599—1658,英国将军,政治家〕。

crone [krəun; kron] ***n.*** 皱皮老太婆;老母羊。

Cro·nin [ˈkrəunin; ˋkronɪn] ***n.*** 克罗宁〔姓氏〕。

cro·ny [ˈkrəuni; ˋkronɪ] ***n.*** 密友,好友,老友。

crook [kruk; krʊk] **I** ***n.*** **1.** (河道等的)弯曲(部)。**2.** 钩;壶钩;锅钩;曲把拐杖。**3.** 诡计,狡计。**4.** 〔俚〕骗子,盗贼,恶棍,坏蛋。**5.** 【乐】弯曲管,调管。***a*** ~ ***in one's lot*** 〔Scot.〕不幸,灾难,波折。***by hook or by*** ~ 千方百计地,不择手段地。***have a*** ~ ***in one's back*** [***nose***, ***character***] 驼背[鹰钩鼻,性情别扭]。***on the*** ~ 用不正当手段。**II** ***a.*** **1.** = crooked. **2.** 不正当的,骗人的,歹徒的。**III** ***vt.*** **1.** 弄曲,弄弯,弄成钩状。**2.** 用钩钩;钩取;〔美俚〕偷。—***vi.*** 弯曲。~ ***the elbow*** [***the little finger***] 〔俚〕喝酒。~**back** ***n.*** 驼背。~**backed** ***a.*** 弓腰驼背的。

crooked [ˈkrukid; ˋkrʊkɪd] ***a.*** **1.** 弯曲的;歪扭的。**2.** 不正常的;诈欺的;〔俚〕用不正当手段得来的。**3.** [krukt; krʊkt] 有钩状柄的。~ ***as dog's hind leg*** 〔美俚〕极不老实的。~ **money** 不义之财。~ **stick** (牧羊者的)曲把手棍;顽固分子,顽梗的人。**-ly** ***ad.*** **-ness** ***n.***

Crookes [kruks; krʊks] ***n.*** **1.** 克鲁克斯〔姓氏〕。**2.** **Sir William** ~克鲁克斯〔1832—1919,英国化学、物理学家〕。~ **rays** 克鲁克斯射线,阴极射线。~ **tube** 克鲁克斯(真空)管。~ **vacuum** 克鲁克斯真空。

crook·neck [ˈkruknek; ˋkrʊknɛk] ***n.*** 〔美〕长颈南瓜。

croon [kruːn; krun] **I** ***vi.*** 低声歌唱,低吟,哼(歌曲)。—***vt.*** **1.** 低唱[哼]。**2.** 低声哼着安慰(小儿等)。~ *a child to sleep* 低声哼着使小孩睡觉。**II** ***n.*** 低唱[哼],低吟;单调的哼歌曲声;低声哼的感伤性流行歌曲。

croon·er [ˈkruːnə; ˋkrunɚ] ***n.*** 〔美〕低声哼唱感伤性流行歌曲的歌手。

crop [krɔp; krɑp] **I** ***n.*** **1.** 农作物,庄稼;收获;收成;〔the ~s〕一季的收获量,产量。**2.** (同一时期出现的人物等)一批,一群,大量。**3.** 剪短;短发。**4.** 猎鞭;鞭柄。**5.** 〔鸟〕嗉囊。**6.** (家畜的)耳印。**7.** (树等的)顶,梢,尖儿;【建】叶尖;【矿】露头。*an abundant* [*a bumper*] ~丰收。*a bad* [*poor*] ~歉收。*a rice* ~水稻作物。*industrial* ~*s* 经济作物。*row* ~*s* 中耕作物。*standing* [*growing*] ~*s* 植株,青苗。*a catch* ~填闲作物。*the black* ~豆类作物。*the green* ~菜类作物;牧草类作物。*the white* ~谷类作物。*this year's* ~ *of students* 今年毕业的一批学生。*a* ~ *of troubles* 麻烦一大堆。*a close* ~剪短发。*a* ~ *of* (*disputes*; *questions*) 一大批(争论、问题)。*a* ~ *of pimples* 一大批[一大片]粉刺[疙瘩]。~ *and root* 全部。~ *capacity* 谷物单位面积产量。~ *rotation* 轮作(法),轮种。~ *succession* 轮作顺序。~ *tree* 林木。~ *yield* 茬地作物的产量。***in*** [***under***] ~ 种着作物,在耕种。***out of*** ~ 未种作物,未耕种。***the*** ~***-mowing season*** 收割季节。**II** [***cropped***, ***cropt***] ***vt.*** **1.** 修剪,剪(树枝,头发等);割去(动物耳朵的)一角(作标记),剪掉(书上的)多余白边;(马)啃去(草尖等)。**2.** 收割,收获。**3.** 种植,栽培,播种。—***vi.*** **1.** 生产;发生,发芽。**2.** (性质等)突然出现,(问题等)突然发生,(矿床等)露出(*out*; *forth*; *up*)。**3.** (羊、鸟等)吃去嫩芽。*All sorts of unexpected difficulties* ~*ped up*. 种种想像不到的困难都发生了。*cropping system* 耕作制度。~ **circle** 作物怪圈〔指 1990 年出现于英国的作物呈环形倒状的一种神秘现象〕。~**-dust** ***vi.***, ***vt.*** 撒药飞行。~**-duster** 撒药飞机。~**-eared** ***a.*** 割耳的;【英史】剪短头发露出耳朵的,短发的。~**-over** 〔西印度群岛〕甘蔗收割后的狂欢庆祝。

crop·per [ˈkrɔpə; ˋkrɑpɚ] ***n.*** **1.** 种植者;(以收成一部分作佃租的)佃农。**2.** 刈割者;修剪者;(布等的)剪头机,刈毛机。**3.** 作物,庄稼。**4.** 〔口〕倒转坠下,栽跟斗;大失败。**5.** 【动】大嗉[球胸]鸽。*a heavy* [*light*] ~丰[歉]收。***come*** [***fall***, ***get***] ***a*** ~ 〔口〕(从马上等)摔下来;垮台;大失败。

crop·pie [ˈkrɔpi; ˋkrɑpɪ] ***n.*** (*pl.* ~*s*, ~) 【动】北美日鲈 (= crappie)。

crop·py [ˈkrɔpi; ˋkrɑpɪ] ***n.*** 头发剪成平头的人;(1798 年爱尔兰同情法国革命的)光头派;清教徒。

cropt [krɔpt; krɑpt] ***v.*** 〔罕〕crop 的过去时和过去分词。

cro·quet [ˈkrəukei, -ki; kroˋke, -kɪ] ***n.*** 【体】(户外)槌球。

cro·quette [krəuˈket; kroˋkɛt] ***n.*** 〔F.〕炸丸子,炸肉饼。

cro·quis [ˈkrəukiː; ˋkroki] ***n.*** (*pl.* ~ [-ki, -kiːz; -kɪ, -kiz]) 草图〔尤指妇女时装草图〕。

crore [krɔː; krɔr] ***n.*** 〔印〕一千万(卢比)。

cro·sier [ˈkrəuʒə; ˋkroʒɚ] ***n*.** **1.** 【宗】牧杖〔主教职标〕。**2.** 【植】(蕨等嫩叶的)卷头。

cross[1] [krɔs; krɔs] **I** ***n*.** **1.** 十字架;〔the C-〕耶稣受刑的十字架。**2.** 〔the C-〕基督教(教义,国家)。**3.** 不幸,苦难;挫折,折磨,考验。**4.** 十字〔+,×,†,✢,T 等〕;十字形(物);十字装饰;十字形花押;十字勋章;十字杖;十字路;【天】南[北]十字星座。**5.** (字母 T 等的)横线。**6.** 杂种,杂交;混合物,中间物。**7.** 〔俚〕欺诈,骗局;(拳斗等)骗人的比赛。**8.** 〔俚〕钱。**9.** 【机】十字管,四通;【电】交扰;【测】直角器。*the Buddhist* ～卍字。*a double* ～双杂交。*an off-*～天然杂交。*a* ～ *between a horse and a donkey* 马与驴的杂交种。*a* ～ *between a breakfast and lunch* 早午餐合并的上午饭。*bear one's* ～*es* 忍受苦难。～ *and pile* 〔古〕钱的正反面;事物的两方面;(卜卦的)运气。～ *of St. Andrew* ×形十字,斜十字。～ *of St. Anthony* 丁字十字。～ *of St. George* (英格兰的)白底红色正十字。～ *of St. Patrick* (爱尔兰的)白底红色 T 形十字。***in*** ～ = ***per*** ～. ***make one's*** ～ (文盲)画十字花押。***on the*** ～ 斜着;〔俚〕不老实地,为非作歹地(生活等)。***go on the*** ～ 走坏路,入邪道。***per*** ～ 照十字形;交叉地。***take*** (***up***) ***one's*** ～ 忍受苦难。***take*** (***up***) ***the*** ～【史】接受十字章,加入十字军;(教徒)为信仰受难。***the True C-*** 钉死耶稣的十字架。**II** ***a*.** **1.** 横斜的,交叉的。**2.** 反对的,相冲突的;逆向的;不吉的,不幸的。**3.** 〔口〕暴躁的,易怒的,脾气不好的。**4.** 相互的,交替的。**5.** 杂种的。**6.** 〔俚〕不正当的;用非法手段(得来)的。*a result* ～ *to a purpose* 与目的相反的结果。***be as*** ～ ***as two sticks*** [***as a bear with a sore head***]〔俚〕非常不高兴,非常恼火。***run*** ～ ***to*** 与…相反,逆着。**III** ***vt*.** **1.** 使交叉;使相交;搭着放,横放;画横线,画线。**2.** 渡(河),横越,翻(山)越(岭),穿过;使穿过;〔口〕跨上(马);擦过,错过;妨碍。**3.** (用手)画十字。**4.** 打叉叉[画线]勾销,划掉。**5.** 使杂交。—***vi*.** **1.** 交叉。**2.** 越过,横断,穿过,渡过。**3.** 相交;错过[双方的信件]。**4.** 杂交,成杂种。***be*** ～***ed in*** 对…失望。***be*** ～***ed in love*** 失恋。～ ***a cheque*** 把支票画上平行线。～ ***a horse*** 跨上马。～ ***each other on the road*** 在路途上互相错过。～ ***keys***【徽】交叉钥匙。～ ***mallets***〔美〕打马球。～ ***off accounts*** 销账。～ ***one's arms*** 抱着手臂。～ ***oneself*** 在自己身上画十字。～ ***one's fingers*** (把中指与食指交叉搭住)期待好运;希望减轻罪过。～ ***sb.'s hand with silver*** 悄悄给以贿赂。～ ***one's legs*** 交叉着腿(坐)。～ ***one's mind*** 想起。～ ***one's lips*** 说出来。～ ***sb.'s path*** 碰见,遇见;遮拦,阻碍。～ ***one's t's*** 不遗忘画 t 字的一横;一笔一划[一举一动]都不草率。～ ***out*** [***off***] 划掉,取消,注销。～ ***over*** 横越,穿过;〔美〕死;【生】(染色体的)交杂。～ ***swords with*** 与…斗剑,与…交战,与…争论[论战]。～ ***the cudgels*** 不参与(争斗等)。～ ***the dope***〔美〕(比赛结果)和预料相反。～ ***the line*** (船等)越过赤道。～ ***the path of*** 碰到,遇着;拦阻。～ **action**〔法〕反诉。～**arm** 电线杆上的横木。～**bar** 闩,横木;横臂;十字管,四通;【橄榄球】决胜柱的横木。～**beam** 大梁,横桁。～**-bearer** 十字杖捧持者;为耶稣忍苦受难的人;支持炉格的横杠。～**bedded** ***a*.**【地】交错层的。～**belt** 斜挂在肩上的子弹带[武装带]。～**-bench** **1.** ***a*.** 中立的。**2.** ***n*.** 中立议员席。～**-bencher** 中立议员;中立人士。～**-bias** 一种倾向[偏见]掩盖着的另一种倾向[偏见]。～**bill**【鸟】交喙鸟。～**birth**【医】横产。～**bones**〔*pl*.〕交叉的大腿骨[通常画在骷髅下,象征死亡]。～**bow** 石弓,弩。～**bred** ***n*., *a*.** 杂交(的),杂种(的)。～**-breed** **1.** ***n*.** 杂交;杂种。**2.** ***vt*., *vi*.** (*p*., *p.p*. ～**-bred**) (使)杂交。～**bun** (耶稣蒙难节用的)蒙难节圣糕〔也叫 hot cross bun〕。～**busing** ***n*.** (美)(学校为平衡黑白学童比例)互用校车接送另一区的儿童。～**-buttock** ***n*., *vt*.**【摔跤】拦腰抱摔;冷不防的投掷[打]。～**-check** ***n*., *vt*.** 反复核对;多方查证。～**-counter**【拳】反击。～**-cloth** (妇女)扎头带。～**-country** ***a*.** 越野的;横越(全国)的。～**cousins** 姑表或舅表兄弟姐妹。～**-coupling** **1.** ***n*.** 相互作用;交叉耦合(干扰)。**2.** ***a*.**【空】交感的。～**current** 逆流;相反思潮[意见,倾向]。～**cut** **1.** ***n*.** 横切;直路,捷径;【矿】横巷,石门;【建】横锯。**2.** ***a*.** 横切的,斜切的;横锯的;纹路交叉的(锉子)。**3.** ***vt*.** 横断。～**debt** 互相抵消的债务;冲账。～**-disciplinary** ***a*.** 两种以上学科的,多学科的。～**-dress** ***vi*.** 穿着异性服装〔女扮男装或男扮女装〕。～**-examination**【法】反复讯问,盘问。～**-examine** ***vt*.**【法】反复讯问,盘问。～**eye** 内斜视[眼]。～**-eyed** ***a*.** 内斜视(眼)的;〔美俚〕喝醉了的。～**-fertilization** 异花[异体]受精。～**-fertilize** ***vt*., *vi*.** (使)异花[异体]受精。～**-file** ***vi*.**〔美〕在初选中申请备案作为两个以上政党的候选人。～**-garnet** T 字蝶铰。～**-grained** ***a*.** (木料)纹理不规则的,扭丝的;(性子)拗的,倔强的,脾气大的。～ **hairs** (光学仪器等上的)十字(丝)准线。～**hatch** ***vt*.** (钢笔画等)画上横直交叉平行线的阴影。～**head** ***n*.**【机】T 字头;(报纸等的)小标题 (= cross-heading)。～**-index** ***vt*., *vi*.** 编制[附有]相互参照的索引[注释]。～**jack** 后桅下桁上挂的大横帆。～**-legged** ***a*.** 交叉着腿的。～**let** (徽章的)小十字形。～**light** 交叉光线;不同的看法[意见]。～**-link** 交叉[横向]耦合;(聚合物的)交联(键)。～**over**【铁路】岔道,转线路,【生】(杂色体的)交杂,交换;交换型;〔英〕(交搭胸前的)女围巾。～**patch** 脾气坏的人;淘气的孩子。～**piece** 腕木,横木;横档儿;(剑的)小锷。～**-ply** (轮胎的)交叉帘布。～**-pollination**【植】异花授[受]粉。～**-purposes** 相反的目的[意志,计划];〔*pl*.〕(一种滑稽游戏)答非所问(*be at* ～*-purposes* 矛盾,龃龉;互相误解)。～**-question** ***vt*., *n*.** 盘问;反复讯问 (～*-question and crooked answers* 答非所问,答非所问游戏)。～ **rate** 第三国外汇牌价。～ **ratio** 交比,非调和比,重比。～**-refer** ***vi*., *vt*.** 相互参照。～**-reference** 相互参照(条目),互见条目。～**road** 横路;交叉道路;〔*pl*.〕(英国旧时埋藏自杀者的)十字路口;〔美〕大路交会处所[多成为居民点],村镇中的闹市;活动、聚会中心地点。～ **section** (有代表性的)横截面,剖面;抽样,样品;【原】有效截面。～**-sterility** 杂交不育。～**-stitch** 十字缝,十字形针迹。～ **talk** (电话)串话,串线;斗嘴,争论,口角;对口相声。～**tie**〔美〕【铁路】枕木。～**-town** ***a*.** 横贯全城镇的,穿城的。～ **trade** 买空卖空。～ **traffic** 设红绿灯的交叉路口。～**-train**【体】多项目交叉训练。～**trees**〔*pl*.〕【船】桅顶横桁;撑持桅楼的横档。～**-under**【物,电】穿接;交叉,交叠。～**walk** 人行横道;斑马线。～**way** 十字路口;活动、聚会的中心地点。～**ways**, ～ **wind** 逆风。～**wise** ***ad*.** 斜横;成十字状,交叉;相反地;别扭地,恶意地。～**word** (**puzzle**) 纵横字谜。～**yard**【海】横桁。

Cross(e) [krɔs; krɑs] ***n*.** 克罗斯〔姓氏〕。

crosse [krɔs; krɔs] ***n*.** (加拿大 lacrosse 球戏用来抛球和捕球的)有网曲棒。

crossed [krɔst; krɔst] ***a*.** 十字的,装成十字的;交叉的;划线的(支票);注销的,划十字勾销掉的;受到阻碍的(爱情、野心等)。～ **cheque** 划线支票。

cros·sette [krɔˈset; krɔˋsɛt] ***n*.**【建】(钉于门窗下缘一角的)门耳,窗耳。

cross·ing [ˈkrɔsiŋ; ˋkrɔsɪŋ] ***n*.** **1.** 交叉,相交;横切,横断;横越,横渡。**2.** 交叉点;十字街口;人行横道;(河的)渡口,(铁路的)闸口,平交道。**3.** 〔古〕阻碍,挫折。**4.** 划十字;划线。**5.**【生】杂交。**6.** (横加)阻挠。*have a good* [*rough*] ～风平浪静[风浪险恶]的渡航。*a grade* ～〔美〕= *a level* ～〔英〕平面交叉。*a street* [*footway*] ～人行横道。*zebra* ～ 斑马线。

cross·ing-o·ver [ˈkrɔːsiŋˈəuvə; ˋkrɔsɪŋˋovɚ] ***n*.**【生】交换。

cross·ite [ˈkrɔːsait; ˋkrɔˏsaɪt] ***n*.**【地】青铝闪石。

cross·ly [ˈkrɔsli; ˋkrɔslɪ] ***ad*.** 横,斜;发着脾气,别扭地,拗着。

cross·ness [ˈkrɔsnis; ˋkrɔsnɪs] ***n*.** 情绪坏,别扭。

C

cros·sop·te·ryg·i·an [krəˌsɔptəˈridʒiən; krəˏsɑptəˋrɪdʒɪən] *n*.【动】总鳍组鱼。

cross·ruff [ˈkrɔːsˌrʌf; ˋkrɔsˏrʌf] *n*.【牌】惠斯特纸牌戏的一种玩法。

crotch [krɔtʃ; krɑtʃ] *n*. 1. (人的)胯。2. 叉状物;(树等的)丫叉;【海】叉柱;〔美〕(路等的)岔口。

crotch·et [ˈkrɔtʃit; ˋkrɑtʃɪt] *n*. 1. 小钩;叉架,叉柱;【筑城】钩形路;【解、植】枝叉,丫叉。2. 怪想,奇想;怪癖。3.【乐】四分音符。

crotch·et·eer [krɔtʃiˈtiə; krɑtʃəˋtɪr] *n*. 奇想家,奇癖家,怪人。

C

crotch·e·ty [ˈkrɔtʃiti; ˋkrɑtʃətɪ] *a*. 有怪想的,有怪癖的。

cro·ton [ˈkrəutən; ˋkrotn̩] *n*.【植】巴豆(属)。~ **bug** 小蟑螂。~ **oil** 巴豆油。

crouch [krautʃ; krautʃ] **I** *vi*., *vt*. 蹲下;蜷着,缩着;弯腰低头 (*to*)。**II** *n*. 蹲;【滑雪】屈膝姿势。***be ~ing in a corner*** 缩在角落里。***~ing start***【体】蹲下起跑法。

croup [kruːp; krup] *n*.【医】假膜性喉炎,格鲁布,哮吼。

croup(e) [kruːp; krup] *n*. (马等的)臀部;〔谑〕(人的)屁股。

croup·er [ˈkruːpə; ˋkrupɚ] *n*. = crupper.

crou·pi·er [ˈkruːpiə; ˋkrupɪɚ] *n*. 1. (赌场上的)管钱人。2. (公共宴会的)副主持人。

croup·ous, croup·y [ˈkruːpəs, -pi; ˋkrupəs, -pɪ] *a*.【医】格鲁布性(的)。

Crouse [kraus; kraus] *n*. 克劳斯〔姓氏〕。

crouse [kruːs; krus] *a*. 〔英方〕活泼的;大胆的;生气勃勃的。

croû·ton [ˈkruːtɔn; kruˋtɑn] *n*. 〔F.〕油炸面包丁。

crow[1] [krəu; kro] *n*. 1. 鸦〔包含 raven, rook, jackdaw, chough, 英国特指 carrion crow〕。2. = ~ bar. 3.〔C-〕【天】乌鸦座。***as the ~ flies = in a ~ line*** 笔直。***eat (boiled) ~*** 〔美口〕忍辱,屈服。***have a ~ to pick [pluck, pull] with (sb.)*** 有一件非与(某人)争论不可的事,非得跟某人讲个明白不可。***white ~*** 珍奇的东西,珍品;南非产秃鹰。~**bar** 铁挺,铁橇;起货钩;【物】急剧短路,断裂。~**berry**【植】岩高兰(属);〔美〕红莓苔子。~**foot** 1. (*pl*. *-foots*)【植】毛茛(属);玉柏;牛角花;臭荠状车前;老鹳草(属)。2. (*pl*. *-feet*)【军】铁蒺藜,拦路钩;【摄】防滑三角架。3. (*pl*. *-feet*)【海】吊索。~**-quill** 乌鸦的羽毛(管),鸦羽笔;(作图用)细笔尖。~**bill**, ~**'s-bill**【医】鸦嘴钳。**Crow Jim**〔美俚〕黑人对白人的歧视。~**'s-foot** (*pl*. *-feet*) 1. (眼外角的)鱼尾(皱)。2.【军】= caltrop. 3.【空】(控制气球,飞船的)拉索钢缆。~**'s-nest** 桅楼守望台。~**step** 屋侧山形墙头的墙级。~**toe**【植】百脉根。~ **vetch**【植】草藤,广布野豌豆。

crow[2] [krəu; kro] **I** *n*. 鸡叫声;儿童欢闹声。**II** *vi*. (~*ed*, *crew*; ~*ed*) 1. (雄鸡)叫,鸣,报晓。2. (儿童)欢叫。3. 欢呼;欢笑,得意洋洋。~ ***over one's enemy [victory]*** 向敌人呼喊示威[欢呼胜利]。

crowd[1] [kraud; kraud] **I** *n*. 1. 人群;拥挤。2. 〔the ~〕民众,群众,大众,老百姓。3. (物的)大量,许多。4. 〔美口〕一伙,伙伴;〔美罕〕家伙,东西;〔美〕一群;〔军俚〕部队。*~s [a ~] of people* 一大群人。*He belongs to a fast ~*. 他是一个放荡鬼。*He's a bad ~*. 他是一个坏东西。*a ~ of (books)* 许许多多的(书)。~ *psychology* 群众心理。***far from the madding ~*** 远离扰攘的公众。***follow [go with] the ~*** 随大流。***in ~s*** 成群,大群地。***might [would] pass in a ~*** 〔俚〕不会十分坏;可以过得去。**II** *vt*. 1. 挤;排挤。2. 塞满,挤满。3. 〔美俚〕逼迫;勒索。~ *a child out of his way* 将小孩挤开。~ *sb. for money* 催某人付款。—*vi*. 群聚,拥挤 (*about*; *round*; *in*; *to*);(大群人)挤进 (*into*)。*a ~ing pen* 〔美〕给牲畜烧烙印的小围场。***be ~ed with*** 被…挤满;满是…。***come ~ing in*** 一拥而入。~ ***about*** 围住,包围。~ ***on [in, upon]*** 蜂拥而来,逼拢来。~ ***out*** 挤出,推开,排挤,驱逐。~ ***(on) sail***【海】扯满所有风帆。~ ***the mourners*** 〔美俚〕急躁地行动;操之过急。~ ***up*** 推上,挤上。~ ***upon one's mind*** (百感)交集,涌上心头。

crowd[2] [kraud; kraud] *n*. = crwth.

crowd·ed [ˈkraudid; ˋkraudɪd] *a*. 拥挤的,挤满人的,客满的;充满(东西)的;多事的;【植】郁闭的。*a ~ career* 丰富的经历。*a ~ hour* 事情安排得紧紧的时间。*a ~ week* 忙忙碌碌的一周。~ *solitude* 在人群中感到的孤独。

crown [kraun; kraun] **I** *n*. 1. (胜利的)花冠;荣誉;〔美俚〕锦标。2. 王冠,冕;王位;君权;〔the C-〕国王,君主。3. 王冠印记[图案]。4. 印有王冠的硬币;〔旧〕五先令英国硬币;克朗〔某些国家的货币单位名称〕。5. (一切东西的)顶部;头顶,(特指)圆形的顶部;帽顶;峰顶;绝顶,极致,至上。6.【解】齿冠;【海】锚冠;【建】冠顶;【植】冠;根茎;副花冠(= corona);【动】冠状部。7. 一种纸张尺寸〔15×20 英寸;〔美〕15×19 英寸〕。8. 晕,光环,光轮,圆光。9.【机】隆起;凸面。10. 冕牌玻璃。*an officer of the ~* (国王任命的)官吏。*pleas of the ~*【英法】公诉。~ *and anchor* (在印有王冠、铁锚等的盘子上用骰子玩的)掷冕锚游戏。~ *of one's labors* 工作中的最终成就。~ *of the head* 头顶。~ *of the year* 秋收季节。~ *of thorns*【植】虎刺;棘冕,荆冠;痛苦。**II** *vt*. 1. 为…加冕;使戴王冠;使登极,立…为君主;(跳棋)加冕使成为王棋。2. 加在顶上;戴;装饰…的顶,作…的冠饰;【齿】装金帽,镶齿冠。3. 授予荣誉,表扬,酬劳。4. 作…的最后点缀,完成,成就。5.〔美俚〕打脑门顶。6.【农】打顶尖。7. 镶上齿冠。*a high [low] ~ed hat* 高顶[低顶]帽子。*be ~ed with success* 最后得到成功,以成功结束。~ *a tooth* 镶齿罩[冠]。*~ed heads* 国王与王后。***to ~ all*** 在一切之上,更…的是。~ **bud** 根茎芽。~ **cap** 铁皮瓶盖。**C- Colony** 英国直辖殖民地。~ **density** 郁闭度。**C- Derby** 英国 Derby 制陶器〔印有王冠商标〕。~ **forest**〔英〕王室林。~ **gear** = ~ **wheel**. ~ **glass** 冕牌玻璃。~ **imperial** 皇冠;【植】壮丽贝母。~ **jewels**〔英〕加冕礼用珠宝类。~ **land**〔英〕王室领地;(自治领的)公有土地。~ **law**〔英〕刑法。~ **lawyer**〔英〕王室律师;刑事律师。~ **layer** 树冠层。~ **lens** 冕牌玻璃透镜;消色差凸透镜。**C- Office** 1. 英国高等法院的刁惯法事务处理部。2. 大法官厅的国玺部。~ **piece** (旧制)旧五先令硬币。~**piece** 顶部,冠饰;马笼头顶部。~ **prince** 皇太子。~ **princess** 皇太子妃。~ **saw** 筒形锯。~ **vetch**【植】多变小冠花。~ **wheel**【机】冕状轮〔差动器侧面伞形齿轮〕。~ **witness**【英法】(刑事案件的)原告证人。~ **work**【筑城】冠状工事;【齿科】(镶装)假齿冠[罩]。

crown·er [ˈkraunə; ˋkraunɚ] *n*. 1. 授冠者;授予荣誉者。2. 最后完成者。3. 倒栽葱;(因而)跌伤头顶。4.〔英方〕验尸官 (coroner)。

crown·ing [ˈkrauniŋ; ˋkraunɪŋ] **I** *a*. 无上的;无比的;登峰造极的;顶部的。~ *glory* 无上光荣。**II** *n*. 1. 加冕。2. 圆满完成;终结;登峰造极。

croy·don [ˈkrɔidn; ˋkrɔɪdn̩] *n*. 轻快二轮单马车。

croze [krəuz; kroz] *n*. 1. (木桶的)栓槽;桶顶槽。2. 凿槽具。

cro·zier [ˈkrəuʒə; ˋkroʒɚ] *n*. = crosier.

c. r. s. = cold-rolled steel 冷轧钢。

CRT = cathode-ray tube 阴极射线管。

cru·ces [ˈkruːsiːz; ˋkrusiz] *n*. crux 的复数。

cru·ci·al [ˈkruːʃjəl, ˈkruːʃəl; ˋkruʃəl, ˋkruʃɪəl] *a*. 1. 严酷的;极为困难的。2. 极紧要的;决定性的。3.【医】十字形的。*the ~ moment* 关键时刻,重要关头。*a ~ incision* 十字切开。

cru·cian [ˈkruːʃən; ˋkruʃən] *n*.【动】鲫鱼。~ *carp* 欧洲鲫。

cru·ci·ate [ˈkruːʃiit; ˋkruʃɪɪt] *a*.【植、动】十字形的;交叉的。

cru·ci·ble [ˈkruːsibl; ˋkrusəbl] *n*. **1.** 坩埚;熔罐。**2.** 很严酷的考验。 *in the ~ of* 处于…的残酷考验中。

cru·ci·fer [ˈkruːsifə; ˋkrusəfɚ] *n*. **1.** 十字花科的植物。**2.**【宗】捧持十字架者。

Cru·cif·e·rae [kruːˈsifəriː; kruˋsɪfə͵ri] *n*.〔*pl*.〕【植】十字花科。

cru·cif·er·ous [kruːˈsifərəs; kruˋsɪfərəs] *a*. **1.**【植】十字花科的;有十字形花的。**2.**【宗】捧持十字架的。

cru·ci·fix [ˈkruːsifiks; ˋkrusə͵fɪks] *n*. (十字架状)耶稣受难像;(象征基督教信仰的)十字架。

cru·ci·fix·ion [ˈkrusifikʃən; ͵krusəˋfɪkʃən] *n*. **1.** 被钉死在十字架。**2.**〔the C-〕耶稣被钉死在十字架上的画。**3.** 苦痛的考验;受难;极大的痛苦。

cru·ci·form [ˈkruːsifɔːm; ˋkrusə͵fɔrm] *a*. 十字形的,十字架状的。

cru·ci·fy [ˈkruːsifai; ˋkrusə͵faɪ] *vt*. *-fied* **1.** 钉[绑]在十字架上;处以钉在十字架的死刑。**2.** 迫害,虐待,折磨。**3.** 抑制,压灭〔情欲等〕。

crud [krʌd; krʌd] **I** *n*. **1.**〔俚〕沉渣。**2.** 可鄙的人或物。**3.**〔美〕怪病。**4.**〔方〕= curd. **II** *vi*., *vt*. (使)凝结(成块)。

crude [kruːd; krud] **I** *a*. **1.** 天然的,未加工的。**2.** 粗(制)的,低级的;未熟的,生的;生硬的;粗糙的,粗杂的,粗鲁的。**3.** 赤裸裸的;未加修饰的(现实情况等)。**4.**【统】未整理的。**5.**【语法】无词尾变化的。**II** *n*. 原[生]材料,天然物质;原油。~ *materials* 原料。~ (*mineral*) *oil* = ~ *petroleum* 原油。~ *rubber* 生橡胶。~ *manners* 粗鲁的态度。*a* ~ *method* 粗暴的方法。*the* ~ *birth rate* 总出生率。*a* ~ *fact* 赤裸裸的事实,事实真相。**-ly** *ad*. **-ness** *n*.

cru·di·ty [ˈkruːditi; ˋkrudətɪ] *n*. 生,未熟;生硬;芜杂,粗杂;未成熟物,未成品;粗鲁的行为[言语]。

cru·el [ˈkruːəl; ˋkruəl] **I** *a*. **1.** 残忍的,残酷的。**2.** 令人痛苦的,无情的;严酷的,铁面无私的。**II** *ad*.〔口〕极度,非常。*It hurt me something* ~. 痛极了。**-ly** *ad*. **-ness** *n*.

cru·el·ty [ˈkruəlti, -il-; ˋkrʊrltɪ, -ɪl-] *n*. **1.** 残酷,冷酷,刻毒。**2.**〔*pl*.〕残酷行为,横蛮行为。**3.**【法】(残酷)虐待。~ **man**〔口〕(英国)全国防止虐待儿童协会官员;皇家防止虐待动物协会官员。

cru·et [ˈkru(ː)it; ˋkrʊɪt] *n*. **1.** (餐桌上的)调味瓶(瓶架)。**2.**【宗】祭坛用瓶。~ **stand** 调味瓶架。

cruise [kruːz; kruz] **I** *n*. **1.** (军舰等)巡逻,巡航。**2.**〔口〕游览,旅行,周游。**II** *vi*. **1.** 巡逻,巡航,游弋。**2.**〔口〕游览,漫游。**3.** (营业汽车)在街上慢行兜揽生意。**4.**〔美〕森林勘查,估测。**5.** (在公共场所)勾搭异性(舞伴等)。—*vt*. (在公共场所)勾搭(异性舞伴等)。~ **missile** 巡航导弹。**cruising radius**【海】续航距离。**cruising taxi** 在街上兜揽搭客的出租汽车。

cruis·er [ˈkruːzə; ˋkruzɚ] *n*. **1.** 巡洋舰。**2.** 游艇(= cabin ~)。**3.** 巡航飞机;远程导[飞]弹。**4.**〔美〕漫游者;(警察)巡逻汽车;揽客汽车。**5.**〔拳口〕= ~weight. **6.**〔美〕森林勘查者(穿的长统靴)。**7.**〔俚〕(在街上来回走动勾搭嫖客的)娼妓。*an armoured* ~ 装甲巡洋舰。*an auxiliary* ~ 补助巡洋舰[武装商船]。*a battle* ~ 巡洋战舰。*a converted* ~ 改装[伪装]巡洋舰。*a protected* ~ (有装甲甲板的)装甲巡洋舰。~**weight**〔拳口〕轻重量级拳击家〔161 磅至 176 磅〕。

crul·ler [ˈkrʌlə; ˋkrʌlɚ] *n*.〔美〕油炸麻花;〔方〕煎饼,油炸面包圈。

crumb [krʌm; krʌm] **I** *n*. **1.**〔常 *pl*.〕(面包的)碎屑;碎片;团粒。**2.** 面包心(*opp*. crust)。**3.** 些少,少许。**4.**〔美俚〕可鄙的人物。*pick up a few ~s of information* 稍微打听一下。~ *brush* (餐桌用)面包屑刷子。~ *of comfort* 些许的安慰。*to a* ~ 精细地;仔细周到地。**II** *vt*. 捏碎,弄碎;【烹】裹上面包屑(用油煎),加面包屑使(汤)变浓;〔美口〕扫去(餐桌上的)面包屑。~**cloth** (铺在餐桌下地毯上的)面包屑承接布。~ **structure** 团粒[屑粒状]结构。

crum·ble [ˈkrʌmbl; ˋkrʌmbl̩] *vt*. 弄碎,粉碎。—*vi*. 破碎;崩溃,溃散;灭亡,消灭。~ *to* [*into*] *dust* 化为尘土。

crum·bly [ˈkrʌmbli; ˋkrʌmblɪ] *a*. 易碎的,脆弱的。

crumb·y [ˈkrʌmi; ˋkrʌmɪ] *a*. **1.** 尽是面包屑的;裹了面包屑的;柔软的(面包)。**2.**〔美俚〕肮脏,可厌,劣等,低廉,可鄙的;虱子多的。

crum·mie, crum·my[1] [ˈkrʌmi; ˋkrʌmɪ] *n*.〔英方〕曲角牛;牛。

crum·my [ˈkrʌmi; ˋkrʌmɪ] *a*. **1.**〔英俚〕丰满的,健美的(女人);娇媚的,可爱的。**2.** 有钱的。**3.**〔英俚〕尽是虱子的,肮脏的;低廉的,劣等的。

crump [krʌmp; krʌmp] **I** *vi*. **1.** 嘎扎嘎扎作声。**2.** (炸弹)猛然爆炸。—*vt*. **1.** 嘎扎嘎扎地嚼。**2.**〔俚〕猛打(板球)。**3.**〔军俚〕用巨弹猛轰。**II** *n*. **1.** 嘎扎嘎扎的咀嚼声。**2.** 猛打。**3.**〔军俚〕猛轰;(炮弹)爆裂声;爆裂弹。

crum·pet [ˈkrʌmpit; ˋkrʌmpɪt] *n*. **1.**〔英〕松脆热煎饼。**2.**〔俚〕娇媚(的女性)。**3.**〔俚〕头。*be barmy* [*balmy*] *on the* ~ = *be off one's* ~ 疯狂的;神经不正常的。

crum·ple [ˈkrʌmpl; ˋkrʌmpl̩] *vt*., *vi*. 揉皱;击溃;变皱,折坏;崩溃。~ ... *into a ball* 揉成一团。~ *up* 揉皱;压倒;垮台,崩溃。

crum·pled [ˈkrʌmpld; ˋkrʌmpl̩d] *a*. 变皱了的;别扭的(牛角等)。

crum·ply [ˈkrʌmpli; ˋkrʌmplɪ] *a*. 易皱的;易弄皱的。~ *paper* 皱纹纸。

crunch [krʌntʃ; krʌntʃ] **I** *vi*., *vt*. 嘎扎嘎扎地咀嚼(饼干等);(车轮、皮靴等)嘎喳嘎喳地(在砂砾路上)碾过[踏过](*through*)。*The dog was ~ing a bone*. 狗正在啃骨头。**II** *n*. **1.** 咬碎,咬,嚼;〔方〕碎屑;嘎扎嘎扎的响声。**2.**〔美俚〕摊牌(时刻),紧要[决定性]关头;困境;(经济等)紧缩状态。

crunch·y [ˈkrʌntʃi; ˋkrʌntʃɪ] *a*. (咀嚼时)嘎吱作响的。**-i·ness** *n*.

cru·or [ˈkruːɔː; ˋkruɔr] *n*. 凝血,血块。

crup·per [ˈkrʌpə; ˋkrʌpɚ] **I** *n*. (勒在马的臀部上的)后秋;马屁股;〔俚、谑〕(人的)屁股。**II** *vt*. 上屁秋。

cru·ral [ˈkruərəl; ˋkrʊrəl] *a*.【解】股的,腿的;腕钩的。

crus [krʌs; krʌs] (*pl*. *cru·ra* [ˈkruərə; ˋkrʊrɚ]) *n*.【解】下腿(由膝至踝的部分);腕钩。

cru·sade [kruːˈseid; kruˋsed] **I** *n*.【史】十字军;(宗教性的)圣战;讨伐;改革运动;肃清运动,扑灭运动。~ *against Fascism* 肃清法西斯运动。~ *in favour of birth control* 节制生育运动。**II** *v*. 发动十字军,加入十字军;讨伐,从事改革[肃清]运动。

cru·sad·er [kruːˈseidə; kruˋsedɚ] *n*. 十字军从军骑士;十字军战士;参加讨伐者;改革运动参与者。

cruse [kruːz; kruz] *n*.〔古〕瓦罐,坛子。*a widow's* ~ 寡妇的坛子〔喻取之不竭的资源〕。

crush [krʌʃ; krʌʃ] **I** *vt*. **1.** 压碎;压扁,压坏(帽子等);捣碎,弄碎;挤榨。**2.** 压倒,压服,扑灭(疫病等);打倒;击溃(敌人等);扼杀;(使受)挫折。**3.** 喝(酒等)。**4.**〔口〕压皱,揉皱(衣服等)。—*vi*. **1.** (被)压扁,压坏,压烂。**2.** (人群)挤进,蜂拥而来,向前推进(*into*; *through*)。**3.** 变皱。~ *a beetle with the foot* 用脚踩烂一只甲虫。*be ~ed to pieces* 压成碎片。~ *down* 镇压,压服;碾碎。~ *out* 扑灭,歼灭;榨取,榨出,挤出;〔美俚〕越狱。~ *up* 粉碎,碾碎;揉成一团;挤过来。**II** *n*. **1.** 压烂,压碎,碾碎,粉碎。**2.** 拥挤;〔口〕扰嚷的集会;〔军俚〕部队。**3.**〔澳〕(给牲畜打火印设置的)漏斗状围栏。**4.** (榨出的)鲜果汁。**5.**〔美俚〕(特指女子对男性的)迷恋。*have* [*get*] *a* ~ *on* 迷恋。~ **barrier** (公共场所拦阻人群挤入的钢制)栏栅。~ **hat** 可折摺而不致损坏的帽子(= opera hat)。~**-proof** *a*. 防碰撞的。~ **room** (戏院等的)休息处。

C

crush·er [ˈkrʌʃə; ˋkrʌʃɚ] ***n*.** 1. 压碎者,压碎器[机]。2. 〔口〕猛烈的一击;压服人的议论,使人哑然失色的事实。3. 〔俚〕警察。

crush·ing [ˈkrʌʃiŋ; ˋkrʌʃɪŋ] ***a*.** 压倒的,决定性的。*a* ~ *defeat* 大溃败。*a* ~ *sorrow* 肝肠欲碎的忧愁。*a* ~ *retort* 使人闭口无言的反驳,斩钉截铁的回答。

Cru·soe [ˈkruːsəu; ˋkruso] ***n*.** 1. 鲁宾逊·克鲁索〔英国作家笛福 (Defoe) 所作小说《鲁宾逊飘流记》的主人翁〕。2. 像鲁宾逊一样飘流到荒岛上的人,孤独的人。

crust [krʌst; krʌst] **I** ***n*.** 1. 面包皮 (*opp*. crumb);干面包片;生活口粮,糊口之资。2. 外皮,壳;〔美〕雪壳;【地】地壳;【动】甲壳;【医】痂;(酒等的)浮渣;水垢。3. (事物的)皮相,外表,表面。4. 〔美俚〕老面皮,厚颜无耻,没礼貌;(人的)脑壳。~ *movement* 地壳移动。***earn one's*** ~ 挣钱糊口。***have a*** ~ 〔美俚〕脸皮太厚;太大胆,太鲁莽,太冒失。***the upper*** ~ 〔古、俚〕上层社会。**II** ***vt*., *vi*.** 用外皮覆盖;结成硬皮;生痂儿。*The snow has* ~*ed over*. 雪在地上结成冰壳。~**-hunt** ***vi*.** 〔美〕在硬雪上猎麋鹿(等)。

Crus·ta·ce·a [krʌsˈteiʃjə; krʌsˋteʃjə] ***n*.** 〔*pl*.〕【动】甲壳纲。

crus·ta·ce·an [krʌsˈteiʃjən; krʌsˋteʃən] ***a*., *n*.** 甲壳类的(动物)。

cru·sta·ce·ous [krʌsˈteiʃjəs; krʌsˋteʃəs] ***a*.** 外皮的;硬皮的;(甲)壳(质)的;【动】甲壳类的;有甲壳[硬壳]的;【植】坚脆的;(地衣)覆生的。

crus·tal [ˈkrʌstl; ˋkrʌstl] ***a*.** 外壳的〔尤指地球外壳〕。

crust·ed [ˈkrʌstid; ˋkrʌstɪd] ***a*.** 外面结成硬皮的,有壳的;长了酒垢的,古色古香的;陈腐的;顽梗的。~ *habit* 陋习。~ *tories* 顽固的守旧分子。

crust·i·ly [ˈkrʌstili; ˋkrʌstəlɪ] ***ad*.** 执拗地,顽固地,态度顽梗地。

crust·i·ness [ˈkrʌstinis; ˋkrʌstɪnɪs] ***n*.** 执拗,顽固,倔强。

crust·y [ˈkrʌsti; ˋkrʌstɪ] ***a*.** 壳一样的;有(硬)壳的,(面包)皮硬的 (*opp*. crumby);执拗的,顽固的;态度恶劣的,脾气乖戾的。

crutch [krʌtʃ; krʌtʃ] **I** ***n*.** 1. 拐杖,(跛子腋下的)T字杖。2. 支柱,叉柱;〔喻〕支持;依靠(物)。3. 【船】船尾肘木,叉木;桨架。4. 〔古〕(人的)胯部。*the* ~ *of one's declining years* 老来依靠。***from cradle to*** ~ 从小到老。**II** ***vt*.** 用拐杖[支柱等]支住。

crutched [krʌtʃt; krʌtʃt] ***a*.** 1. 挂着T字杖[拐杖]的;用支柱撑着的。2. [ˈkrʌtʃid; ˋkrʌtʃɪd] 带[挂]着十字架的。

crux [krʌks; krʌks] ***n*.** (*pl*. ~*es* [-iz; -ɪz], ***cru·ces*** [ˈkruːsiːz; ˋkrusiz]) 1. 【徽】十字(架)形。2. 要点;症结;难题,难点;难解的谜。3. 〔C-〕【天】南十字座。~ *ansata* T字形十字。~ *play* 悬疑剧。

cru·zei·ro [kruːˈzeirəu; kruˋzero] ***n*.** (*pl*. ~*s*) 克鲁塞罗〔巴西货币单位,等于一百 centavos〕。

crwth [kruːθ; kruθ] ***n*.** 1. 克楼得〔凯尔特古乐器〕。2. 〔英方〕小提琴(= crowd[2])。

cry [krai; kraɪ] **I** ***vi*.** 1. 叫,喊;(禽兽)啼,鸣,嗥,(犬)吠。2. 哭泣,号哭。— ***vt*.** 1. 叫,喊,大声叫喊,大声说。2. 呼报,呼告,叫卖。3. 〔古〕乞求。4. 〔美俚〕诉委屈,发牢骚,哭诉。5. 哭出;以哭泣促使。~ *the news all over the town* 遍街大声报导消息。~ *one's wares* 叫卖货物。~ *against* 对…大声反对。~ ***back*** 〔Scot.〕叫回来,【猎】(狗)跑回来,折回来;(动物等)重现祖先的性状,反祖遗传。~ ***bitter tears*** 痛哭流涕。~ ***down*** 轰下,轰走(演讲者等),贬损,侮蔑,责骂。~ ***for*** 乞求,请求;要求,哭着要;迫切需要 (~ *for the moon* 空想,妄想)。~ ***for company*** 陪哭。~ ***halves*** 要求平分。~ ***from*** [***on***] ***the house-top***(***s***) 公开宣称,扬言。~ ***halt*** 命令停止。~ ***hands off*** 叫(竞争者)放手,警告退避。~ ***in company*** 陪哭。~ ***on the God*** 求神。~ ***off*** (***from***) 撤回,取消(前约等);(从交易等上)撤手;宣布退出。~ ***oneself to sleep*** (婴儿)哭到睡着。~ ***one's eyes out*** 把眼都要哭瞎了;长时间大哭。~ ***one's heart out*** 极伤心地痛哭。~ ***out*** 大叫,对…大声反对 (*against*);喊着要求 (*for*)。~ ***out before one is hurt*** 〔喻〕牢骚发得太早。~ ***over*** 叹息(不幸等)。~ ***over spilt milk*** 作无益的后悔[谴责]。~ ***quarter*** 乞命,求免一死。~ ***quits*** 见 quits 条。~ ***shame upon*** 责备,非难,大骂。~ ***stinking fish*** 叫卖臭鱼;暴露自己的丑事。~ ***to*** [***unto***] 向…求援,求…保护;苦求。~ ***up*** 夸奖,褒扬。~ ***up wine and sell vinegar*** 挂羊头卖狗肉。~ ***wolf*** 作虚假的警报;谎报军情。**II** ***n*.** 1. 叫喊;呼声;叫声;哭声;吠声;号哭。2. 喝彩,呐喊;大声宣扬;呼吁;叫卖声。3. 哭诉,哀求。4. 谣传,舆论;运动,风尚。5. (政党的)口号,标语。6. 一群猎狗(的呼叫声)。***a far*** ~ 远距离;悬殊很大的东西。***all*** ~ ***and no wool*** = ***more*** ~ ***than wool***. ***all the*** ~ 大流行;最新式样。***be within*** ~ ***of*** …声听得见的地方[距离]。~ ***against*** 反对…的呼声,…的反对运动。~ ***for*** 要求…的呼声,…的要求运动。***follow in the*** ~ 随声附和。***give a*** ~ 大喊一声。***have a good*** ~ 尽情痛哭。***in full*** ~ 猎狗一齐追赶着,在拚命追赶中;一齐。***more*** ~ ***than wool*** = ***much*** [***a great***] ~ ***and little wool*** 雷声大雨点小;力气花得不少,结果甚微。***out of all*** ~ 过分,过度。***out of*** ~ 在叫声不能听到的地方;〔喻〕力量够不着的地方。~ **baby** 爱哭[诉]的人。

cry·ing [ˈkraiiŋ; ˋkraɪɪŋ] ***a*.** 叫喊的,嚎哭的;突出的,显著的,厉害的;紧急的。*a* ~ *evil* 突出的[急应矫正的]弊病。*a* ~ *need* 迫切需要。*a* ~ *shame* 奇耻大辱。

cryo- *comb*. *f*. 低温,冷,冰,霜。

cry·o·bi·ol·o·gy [ˈkraiəubaiˈɔlədʒi; ˏkraɪobaɪˋɑlədʒɪ] ***n*.** 低温生物学〔尤指研究低温对生物影响的学科〕。**-biol·o·gist** ***n*.**

cry·o·chem·is·try [ˈkraiəuˈkemistri; ˋkraɪoˋkɛmɪstrɪ] ***n*.** 低温[深冷]化学。

cry·o·e·lec·tron·ics [ˌkraiəuiˌlekˈtrɔniks; ˏkraɪoɪˏlɛkˋtrɑnɪks] ***n*.** 低温电子学。

cry·o·gen [ˈkraiəudʒən; ˋkraɪədʒən] ***n*.** 【化】致冷剂,冷冻剂;低温[冷却]粉碎。

cry·o·gen·ic [ˌkraiəuˈdʒenik; ˏkraɪoˋdʒɛnɪk] ***a*.** 低温学的;低温实验法的。

cry·o·gen·ics [ˌkraiəuˈdʒeniks; ˏkraɪəˋdʒɛnɪks] ***n*.** 低温(物理)学;低温实验法。

cry·og·e·ny [kraiˈɔdʒini; kraɪˋɑdʒɪnɪ] ***n*.** 低温物理学冷却法。

cry·o·hy·drate [ˌkraiəˈhaiˌdreit; ˏkraɪəˋhaɪˏdret] ***n*.** 冰盐;低(共)熔冰盐结晶;饱凝分晶体。

cry·o·lite [ˈkraiəulait; ˋkraɪəˏlaɪt] ***n*.** 【矿】冰晶石。

cry·om·e·ter [kraiˈɔmitə; kraɪˋɑmətɚ] ***n*.** 低温计,深冷[低温]温度计。

cry·on·ics [kraiˈɔniks; kraɪˋɑnɪks] ***n*.** 【医】人体冷冻学。

cry·o·phil·ic [ˌkraiəuˈfilik; ˏkraɪoˋfɪlɪk] ***a*.** 【生】好冷性的,嗜寒的,喜低温的,低温下繁茂的。

cry·oph·o·rus [kraiˈɔfərəs; kraɪˋɑfərəs] ***n*.** 【物】凝冰器〔显示水因自身蒸发而结冰的仪器〕。

cry·o·phyte [ˈkraiəufait; ˋkraɪoˏfaɪt] ***n*.** 【植】冰雪植物。

cry·o·probe [ˈkraiəuˌprəub; ˋkraɪoˏprob] ***n*.** 【医】冰冻探子,冷冻器,冷刀。

cry·o·pump [ˈkraiəupʌmp; ˋkraɪoˏpʌmp] ***n*.** 【机】低温泵。

cry·o·scope [ˈkraiəuskəup; ˋkraɪoˏskop] ***n*.** 【物】冰点测定器。

cry·os·co·py [kraiˈɔskəpi; kraɪˋɑskəpɪ] ***n*.** 冰点测定学;冰点降低测定法。

cry·o·stat [ˈkraiəuˌstæt; ˋkraɪoˏstæt] ***n*.** 低温恒温器;致冷器,低温箱。

cry·o·sur·ger·y [ˌkraiəuˈsəːdʒəri; ˏkraɪoˋsɝdʒərɪ] ***n*.**

冷冻手术;冷冻破坏法。**-sur·gi·cal** *a*.

cry·o·ther·a·py [ˌkraiəuˈθerəpi; ˏkraɪoˋθerəpɪ] *n*. 【医】冷(冻)疗法。

cry·o·tron [ˈkraiəutrɔn; ˋkraɪotrɑn] *n*. 冷子管,低温管,冷持元件。

crypt [kript; krɪpt] *n*. **1**. 地窖,地穴;(特指)教堂地下室〔常作墓穴用〕。**2**.【解】滤胞腺,腺窝,小囊,隐窝。

crypt- (接元音) = crypto- (接辅音)。

crypt·a·nal·y·sis [ˌkriptəˈnælisis; ˏkrɪptəˋnæləsɪs] *n*. 密码分析,密码分析学。**-lyst** [-ˈtænəlist; -ˋtænəlɪst] *n*. **-lyt·ic** [-ˈtænəˌlitik; -tænəˏlɪtɪk] *a*.

cryp·tic, cryp·ti·cal [ˈkriptik, -kəl; ˋkrɪptɪk, -kəl] *a*. **1**. 隐藏的,秘密的;神秘的;难解的。**2**.【动】(适于)隐藏的。~ *colouring*【动】保护色。*a* ~ *remark* 有言外之意的话。~ *species*【生】同形种。

cryp·to [ˈkriptəu; ˋkrɪpto] *n*. (政党、社团等的)秘密成员,秘密支持者。

crypto- *comb. f*. 隐藏,隐蔽,潜藏;秘密。

cryp·to·clas·tic [ˌkriptəuˈklæstik; ˏkrɪptoˋklæstɪk] *a*. 【矿】隐屑质的。

cryp·to·com·mer·cial·ism [ˈkriptəukəˈməːʃəlizəm; ˋkrɪptokəˋmɝʃəlɪzəm] *n*. 勾心斗角的商业竞争。

cryp·to·crys·tal·line [ˈkriptəuˈkristlin; ˋkrɪptoˋkrɪstlɪn] *a*. 【矿】潜晶(质)的,隐晶(质)的。

cryp·to·gam [ˈkriptəugæm; ˋkrɪptəˏgæm] *n*. 【植】隐花植物 (*opp*. phanerogam)。

cryp·to·ga·mi·an, cryp·to·gam·ic, cryp·togamous [ˌkriptəuˈgeimiən, -ˈgæmik, kripˈtɔgəməs; ˏkrɪptoˋgemɪən, -ˋgæmɪk, krɪpˋtɑgəməs] *a*. 隐花(植物)的。

cryp·to·gen·ic [ˌkriptəuˈdʒenik; ˏkrɪptəˋdʒenɪk] *a*. 【医】隐原性的,隐发性的,病原不明的。

cryp·to·gram [ˈkriptəugræm; ˋkrɪptəˏgræm] *n*. 密码(文件);暗号。

cryp·to·graph [ˈkriptəugrɑːf; ˋkrɪptəˏgræf] I *n*. 密码;密码打字机;暗码记录法。II *vt*. 译成密码。

cryp·tog·ra·pher [kripˈtɔgrəfə; krɪpˋtɑgrəfɚ] *n*. 密码员(包括译电员;编码员);暗号使用者。

cryp·tog·ra·phy [kripˈtɔgrəfi; krɪpˋtɑgrəfɪ] *n*. 密码学,密码翻译术;密写术。

cryp·tol·o·gy [kripˈtɔlədʒi; krɪpˋtɑlədʒɪ] *n*. **1**. 隐语。**2**. 密码学[术]。

cryp·to·me·ri·a [ˌkriptəuˈmiəriə; ˏkrɪptəˋmɪrɪə] *n*. 【植】柳杉属(植物)。

cryp·to·nym [ˈkriptəunim; ˋkrɪptənɪm] *n*. 匿名,假名。

cryp·to·pine [ˈkriptəupiːn; ˋkrɪptopin] *n*. 隐品碱。

cryp·to·sex·u·al [ˈkriptəuˈseksjuəl; ˋkrɪptoˋsɛkʃʊəl] *a*. 难辨性别的。

cryp·to·xan·thin, cryp·to·xan·thol [kriptəuˈzænθin, -təˈzænθəul; krɪptoˋzænθɪn, -ˋtəˋzænθol] *n*. 隐黄质。

cryst. = crystalline; crystallized.

crys·tal [ˈkristl; ˋkrɪstl] I *n*. **1**. 结晶,(结)晶体;晶粒;水晶(= rock ~);石英。**2**.【无】晶体。**3**. 结晶玻璃;雕玻璃;〔美〕水晶玻璃。**4**.〔诗〕水晶一样的东西〔冰、水、泪、眼睛等〕。**5**.〔俚〕神秘的征兆;预言,占卜。**6**.〔美俚〕厕所。*eyes as clear as* ~*s* 一双眼睛明如秋水。*a necklace of* ~*s* 水晶珠项链。*the* ~*s of sugar* 糖的结晶体。II *a*. **1**. 水晶(制)的。**2**. 水晶一般的;透明的,清澈的。**3**.【无】晶体的,运用晶体检波器的。~ *water* 晶莹的水。~ *ball* (占卜者用的)水晶球。~**-ball** *vt*., *vi*. (用水晶球)占卜。~**-clear** *a*. 像水晶一样透明的,清澈的,明白的。~ **detector** 晶体检波器。~ **diode** [**triode**] 晶体二极管[三极管]。~ **receiver** [**set**] 矿石[晶体]收音机。~ **gazer** (用水晶球)占卜的人,预言者。~ **wedding** 晶婚〔结婚 15 周年〕。

crys·tal·lif·er·ous [ˌkristəˈlifərəs; ˏkrɪstəˋlɪfərəs] *a*. 生结晶体的,含结晶体的。

crys·tal·line [ˈkristəlain; ˋkrɪstˏl̩ɪn] I *a*. 水晶的,由水晶做成的;结晶的,【化、矿】结晶质的;透明的。II *n*. 结晶质,结晶体,晶态;(眼球)水晶体。~ **lens** [**humour**] (眼球的)水晶体。~ **nucleus** 雏晶。

crys·tal·lite [ˈkristəˌlait; ˋkrɪstəˏlaɪt] *n*. 【矿】**1**. 雏晶,微晶;细晶体,晶粒(子)。**2**. 雏晶岩。**-lit·ic** [-ˈlitik; -ˋlɪtɪk] *a*.

crys·tal·liz·a·ble [ˈkristəlaizəbl; ˋkrɪstəˏlaɪzəbl̩] *a*. 可结晶的。

crys·tal·li·za·tion [ˌkristəlaiˈzeiʃən; ˏkrɪstəlaɪˋzeʃən] *n*. 晶化,结晶(作用,过程);结晶体;具体化,明朗化。

crys·tal·lize [ˈkristəlaiz; ˋkrɪstlˏaɪz] *vt*. **1**. 使结晶。**2**. 使(计划、思想等)明确化,具体化。**3**. 使蘸糖,使包上一层糖。—*vi*. **1**. 晶化,结晶。**2**. 明确化,具体化。~*d sugar* 冰糖。~*d fruit* 蘸糖水果。~*d ginger* 糖姜。

crys·tal·log·ra·phy [ˌkristəˈlɔgrəfi; ˏkrɪstl̩ˋɑgrəfɪ] *n*. 结晶学。

crys·tal·loid [ˈkristəlɔid; ˋkrɪstlˏɔɪd] I *a*. 似晶的;结晶状的;透明的。II *n*.【化】(类)晶体;(似)晶质;【植】假结晶,假晶体。

crys·tal·lon [ˈkristələn; ˋkrɪstəˏlɑn] *n*.【化】籽晶。

CS = **1**. chief of staff 参谋长。**2**. civil service〔总称〕文职人员;(军队以外的全部)行政机构。

cs. = case(s).

C. S. = **1**. capital stock【商】股本。**2**. Chemical Society〔美〕化学学会。**3**. Court of Session〔英〕苏格兰最高民事法庭。

Cs =【化】c(a)esium.

C / S, c / s = cases; cycles per second.

C × S = count × strength 品质指标。

C. S. A. = **1**. Confederate States Army【美史】南部联军。**2**. Confederate States of America【美史】美国南部邦联。

C. S. B.〔美〕= Central Statistical Board.

C. S. C. = Conspicuous Service Cross〔英〕特等功勋十字章。

CSC = Civil Service Commission 文官委员会。

CSCE = Conference on Security and Cooperation in Europe 欧洲安全和合作会议(简称欧安会)。

CSE = Certificate of Secondary Education (英国)中等教育证书。

c / sec = cycles per second 周/秒。

C Sig O = Chief Signal Officer 通信主任。

CSM = *Christian Science Monitor*〔美〕《基督教科学箴言报》。

Csn =【军】caisson.

C. S. N. = Confederate States Navy【美史】南部联邦海军。

C. S. O. = Chief Signal Officer 通信主任。

CST = **1**. Central Standard Time〔美〕中部地区标准时间。**2**. convulsive shock therapy 抽搐休克疗法。

CT = **1**. cell therapy 细胞疗法。**2**. Central Time. **3**. Certificated Teacher 合格教师。**4**. code telegram(s) 电码电报。**5**. computerized tomography 计算机化 X 线体层照像术。

Ct =【化】celtium.

Ct. = Connecticut; Count; Court.

ct. = carat; cent; certificate; count; county; court.

c. t. =【电】current transformer.

C. T. C. = Cyclists' Touring Club〔英〕自行车旅行俱乐部。

CTD = circling the drain〔俚〕【医】快要断气的。

CTI = computer telephony integration 计算机[电脑]电话组合。

cten- (接元音), **cteno-** (接辅音) *comb. f*. 有栉状部分的。

cte·noid [ˈtiːnɔid; ˋtinɔɪd] I *a*.【动】栉状的;有栉齿状边缘的;栉齿鳞科的。II *n*. 栉鳞鱼。

cte·noph·o·ran [tiˈnɔfərən; tɪˋnɑfərən] ***a.*** 【动】栉水母的;栉水母纵带的。**II *n.*** 栉水母类动物,栉水母门(ctenophora)。

cten·o·phore [ˈtenəˌfɔː, ˈtiːnə-; ˋtɛnəˏfɔr, ˋtinə-] ***n.*** 【动】栉水母门动物。

CTOL = conventional takeoff and landing (飞机的)常规起落;常规起落飞机。

CTP = 【化】Cytidine triphosphate 三磷酸胞苷,胞苷三磷酸。

ctr. = center.

cts. = centimes; cents; certificates.

ct / sec = counts per second 计数/秒。

CTT = capital transfer tax 〔英〕资本转移税。

CTU = centigrade thermal unit.

CTV = Color Television 彩色电视。

C-type virus [ˈsiːˈtaip; ˋsiˋtaɪp] = type C virus C类肿瘤病毒。

Cu = 【化】cuprum.

C. U. = **1.** Cambridge University. **2.** Columbia University (美国)哥伦比亚大学。**3.** Consumers Union (美国)消费者联合会。**4.** Cornell University (美国)康奈尔大学。

cu. = 【天】cumulus (clouds).

cu., cub = cubic.

cub [kʌb; kʌb] **I *n.*** **1.** 仔兽;幼狐;〔美〕小熊;(狼、虎等的)仔。**2.** 〔谑、蔑〕小捣乱,野孩子〔指男孩〕,不懂事的小伙子[小姑娘]〔常叫 an unlicked ～〕;〔美〕生手记者 (= ～ reporter);生手,没经验的人;幼年童子军 (= wolf ～)。**II *a.*** 没经验的。**III *vi.*** **1.** (野兽)生仔。**2.** 捉幼狐[幼兽]。

Cu·ba [ˈkjuːbə; ˋkjubə] ***n.*** 古巴〔拉丁美洲〕。

cu·bage, cu·ba·ture [ˈkjuːbidʒ, ˈkjuːbətʃə; ˋkjubɪdʒ, ˋkjubətʃɚ] ***n.*** 求容积[体积]法;容积,体积。

Cu·ban [ˈkjuːbən; ˋkjubən] ***a., n.*** 古巴的[人]。

cu·ba·ture [ˈkjuːbətʃə; ˋkjubətʃɚ] ***n.*** **1.** 求容积法,求体积法。**2.** 容积,体积。

cub·bing [ˈkʌbiŋ; ˋkʌbɪŋ] ***n.*** 【猎】捉幼兽〔幼狐等〕。

cub·bish [ˈkʌbiʃ; ˋkʌbɪʃ] ***a.*** **1.** 幼兽一样的;笨拙的。**2.** 粗野的,没规矩的。

cub·by [ˈkʌbi; ˋkʌbɪ] ***n.*** 整齐的场所[小房间];狭窄的房间;小柜,(鸽舍式)小书架,分类架;〔军俚〕小壕沟(等)。～**hole** = cubby.

cube[1] [kjuːb; kjub] **I *n.*** **1.** 立方体[形],正六面体。**2.** 立方,三次幂,三乘;〔*pl.*〕〔美俚〕骰子。**3.** 立体闪光灯 (= flashcube)。*magic* ～ 魔方[积木式玩具]。**II *vt.*** **1.** 三乘;求体积;使成立方体;铺方石。**2.** (把马铃薯等)切成(小)方块;切成丁。～ **farm** 办公农场〔指由多个小间隔成的办公室〕。～ **powder** 方形火药。～ **root** 【数】立方根。～ **sugar** 方糖。

cu·be[2] [ˈkjuːbei, ˈkuː-; ˋkjube, ˋku-] ***n.*** 【植】尼古矛果 (*Lonchocarpus nicou*)。

cu·beb [ˈkjuːbeb; ˋkjubɛb] ***n.*** 【植】荜澄茄;〔美〕荜澄茄卷烟〔旧时用来治伤风鼻炎〕。

cub·hood [ˈkʌbhud; ˋkʌbhʊd] ***n.*** (兽类的)幼兽期,幼稚期;〔喻〕(事物的)初期。

cubi- *comb. f.* 表示"立方体","立方":*cubi*form.

cu·bic [ˈkjuːbik; ˋkjubɪk] **I *a.*** **1.** 立方体[形]的,正六面体的。**2.** 【数】三次的,立方的。**II *n.*** 【数】三次曲线;三次方程式;三次多项式;三次函数。～ **content** 体积,容积。～ **density** 假比重。～ **displacement** 【船】排水量[吨位]。～ **measure** 容量。～ **saltpetre** 智利硝石。～ **sugar** 方糖。～ **system** 【物】立方晶系。

cu·bi·cal [ˈkjuːbikəl; ˋkjubɪkəl] ***a.*** **1.** 立方(体)的。**2.** 【数】三次方的。**3.** 体积的,容积的。

cu·bi·cle [ˈkjuːbikl; ˋkjubɪkl] ***n.*** 寝室,(特指学校宿舍中分隔开的)小卧室;小室;(设在书架旁的)库内阅览席,单人阅览室;室;部分;段;(游泳池的)更衣室。

cu·bic·u·lum [kjuˈbikjuləm; kjʊˋbɪkjʊləm] ***n.*** (*pl.* ***-u·la*** [-lə; -lə]) **1.** (地下墓窟的)停柩室;殡葬室。**2.** 小卧室;小室。

cu·bi·form [ˈkjuːbifɔːm; ˋkjubɪˏfɔrm] ***a.*** 立方形的。

cub·ism [ˈkjuːbizəm; ˋkjubɪzəm] ***n.*** 〔美〕(艺术上的)立体派。

cub·ist [ˈkjuːbist; ˋkjubɪst] ***n.*** **1.** 立体派艺术家。**2.** 玩魔方的人,魔方专家。

cu·bit [ˈkjuːbit; ˋkjubɪt] ***n.*** 【史】腕尺〔约 18 至 22 英寸〕。

cu·bi·tal [ˈkjuːbitl; ˋkjubɪtl] ***a.*** 【解】肘的;前膊的;尺骨的。～ *vein* 肘脉。

cu·bi·tus [ˈkjuːbitəs; ˋkjubɪtəs] ***n.*** 【解】肘;肘骨,尺骨;前臂。

cu·boid [ˈkjuːbɔid; ˋkjubɔɪd] **I *a.*** **1.** 立方形的;骰子形的。**2.** 【解】骰骨的。**II *n.*** **1.** 【解】骰骨。**2.** 长方体,矩形体。～ *bone* (*of the foot*) (足的)骰骨。**-boi·dal** [kju(ː)ˈbɔidəl; kju(ʊ)ˋbɔɪdəl] ***a.***

cu·chi·fri·to [ˌkuːtʃiːˈfriːtəu; ˏkutʃiˋfrito] ***n.*** 【烹】油炸猪肉丁。

cuck·ing stool [ˈkʌkiŋ stuːl; ˋkʌkɪŋ stul] ***n.*** (旧时把行为不端的妇女绑在上面示众的)惩椅。

cuck·old [ˈkʌkəld; ˋkʌkl̩d] **I *n.*** 〔谑〕乌龟〔奸妇的本夫〕。**II *vt.*** 使戴绿头巾,使做乌龟;与…的妻子私通。

cuck·old·ry [ˈkʌkəldri; ˋkʌkl̩drɪ] ***n.*** **1.** (与有夫之妇的)私通,通奸。**2.** 做乌龟,戴绿头巾。

cuck·oo [ˈkukuː; ˋkʊku] **I *n.*** **1.** 【鸟】郭公鸟,杜鹃,布谷鸟。**2.** 杜鹃的啼声。**3.** 傻子;〔俚〕人,家伙。**II *a.*** 〔美俚〕疯狂的,傻,笨。*the* ～ *in the nest* 夺取[破坏]他人骨肉之爱(父母对儿女之爱)的人,破坏他人家庭感情的人。～ **clock** (报时似杜鹃鸣声的)杜鹃钟。～ **flower** 【植】布谷鸟剪秋罗 (= ragged robin)。～ **pint** 【植】斑叶阿若母。

cu·cm. = cubic centimeter(s).

cu·cu·li·form [kjuˈkjuːləˌfɔːm, ˌkə-; kjʊˋkjuləˏfɔrm, ˏkə-] ***a.*** (似)杜鹃的;杜鹃鸟目的。

cu·cul·late(d) [ˈkjuːkəleit(id); ˋkjukəˏlet(ɪd)] ***a.*** 戴僧(状)帽的;【植】兜[勺]状的。

cu·cum·ber [ˈkjuːkəmbə; ˋkjukʌmbɚ] ***n.*** 【植】黄瓜;〔美〕锐叶木兰。(*a*) *sea* ～ 海参。(*as*) ***cool as a*** ～ **1.** (令人感到爽快地)冰凉的。**2.** 极冷静地,沉着地。～ **tree** 【植】(美洲)渐尖木兰。

cu·cur·bit [kju(ː)ˈkəːbit; kjʊˋkɝbɪt] ***n.*** 【植】葫芦;【化】(葫芦形)蒸馏瓶。

cu·cur·bi·ta·ceous [kju(ː)ˌkəːbiˈteiʃəs; kjʊˏkɝbɪˋteʃəs] ***a.*** 【植】葫芦科的。

cud [kʌd; kʌd] ***n.*** **1.** 反刍的食物。**2.** 瘤胃〔反刍兽类的第一胃〕。**3.** 〔俚〕嚼烟;口香糖。***chew the*** ～ **1.** (牛等)反刍。**2.** 细想,反省。～**-chewer** 反刍动物〔牛、羊等〕。

cud·bear [ˈkʌdbɛə; ˋkʌdbɛr] ***n.*** 石芯地衣;苔色素〔紫色染料〕。

cud·dle [ˈkʌdl; ˋkʌdl̩] **I *vt.*** 拥抱,搂抱,怀抱。**—*vi.*** 紧贴着身子睡,抱着睡 (*together*);蜷着身子(睡) (*up*)。**II *n.*** 搂抱,拥抱。*have a bit of a* ～ 紧紧拥抱。～**some *a.*** 引人拥抱(似)的;可爱的。

cud·dly [ˈkʌdli; ˋkʌdlɪ] ***a.*** **1.** 引人拥抱的,可爱的。**2.** 喜欢拥抱的。

cud·dy[1] [ˈkʌdi; ˋkʌdɪ] ***n.*** **1.** 〔Scot.〕驴子 (= ～ ass);傻瓜。**2.** 三脚铁梯,三脚杠杆。**3.** 【动】军曹鱼,绿鳕。

cud·dy[2] [ˈkʌdi; ˋkʌdɪ] ***n.*** (从前船上兼做客厅的)餐厅;(小船的)厨房,餐具室;(船头、船尾的)小室;(渔船的)渔网台。

cudg·el [ˈkʌdʒəl; ˋkʌdʒəl] **I *n.*** (粗短的)棍棒;〔美俚〕(棒球)棒。***take up the*** ～***s for*** 拿棍防卫;毅然为…辩护[辩论]。**II *vt.*** (〔英〕***-ll-***)用棍棒打。～ ***one's brains*** 绞脑汁,伤脑筋。～ **play** 斗棍;棍术比赛。

cud·weed [ˈkʌdwiːd; ˋkʌdˏwid] ***n.*** 【植】鼠曲草(属)。

Cud·worth [ˈkʌdwəːθ; ˋkʌdwɝθ] ***n.*** 卡德沃斯〔姓氏〕。

cue[1][kjuː; kju] **I** ***n*. 1.**【剧】(暗示对方接言的)尾白,提示。2. 暗示,指示,线索,暗号。**3.** 情绪,心情。**4.** (必需扮演的)角色;必需做的事。**5.** 刺激。**II** ***vt*. 1.** 给…暗示[出主意]。**2.** 把…插入演出。~ *sb. on his lines* 给某人提示台词。~ *in a violin section* 插进一段小提琴演奏的曲调。***be in*** ~ ***for*** 想…,有意要…。***be in good*** ~ 心情好。***be not in the (right)*** ~ ***for*** 不想,无意。***drop a*** ~〔俚〕进棺材,死亡。***give (sb.) the*** ~ 暗示给人,递点子。***miss a*** ~ 搞错;〔口〕抓不着要点,领会错误。***take one's*** ~ ***from*** 得到某人的指点[暗示]。

cue[2][kjuː; kju] ***n*. 1.**【撞球】球杆。**2.** 发辫(= queue);尾,尾状物。**3.** (买票等的)排队。***stand in*** ~ 排队(站着)。~ **ace**〔美〕台[撞]球选手。

Cuen·ca [ˈkweŋkɑː; ˋkwɛŋkɑ] ***n*. 1.** 昆卡〔厄瓜多尔城市〕。**2.** 昆卡〔西班牙城市〕。

cue·ist [ˈkjuːist; ˋkjuɪst] ***n*.**〔口〕台[撞]球家,打弹子的名手。

cues·ta [ˈkwestə; ˋkwɛstə] ***n*.**【地】鬣丘,单面山。

cuff[1][kʌf; kʌf] ***n*. 1.** 袖口;(套袜的)罗口;〔美〕裤脚的卷摺。**2.**〔*pl.*〕手铐。~ *cover* 袖套。~ *links* [〔美〕*buttons*]袖扣。***off the*** ~〔美俚〕马上,(未作预先准备)当场;即兴地;非正式地。***on the*** ~〔美俚〕**1.** 赊。**2.** 免费。***shoot one's*** ~***s*** (在上衣袖口下)露出一截衬衫袖口〔意味着服装整齐〕。

cuff[2][kʌf; kʌf] ***n*., *vt*., *vi*.** (用拳头或手掌)打,殴打。***be at*** ~***s*** 打架。~***s and kicks*** 拳打脚踢。***fall*** [***go***] ***to*** ~ 打起架来。***give sb. a*** ~ 给某人一巴掌。

cu. ft. = cubic foot [feet] 立方英尺。

cui bo·no [ˈkwiːˈbɔnəu; ˋkwiˋbono]〔L.〕什么人得益?〔转义〕有什么益处[目的]? 为了谁?

cui·rass [kwiˈræs; kwɪˋræs] **I** ***n*. 1.** 妇女胸衣。**2.** 胸甲,【动】保护(骨)板,鳞甲;(军舰的)装甲。**II** ***vt*.** 给…披上胸甲。**-ed** [-t; -t] ***a*.** 穿着胸甲的;(军舰等)装甲的。

cui·ras·sier [kwirəˈsiə; ˏkwɪrəˋsɪr] ***n*.**【史】(法国的)胸甲骑兵。

cui·sine [kwi(ː)ˈziːn; kwɪˋzin] ***n*. 1.** 厨房;烹调法,烹饪。**2.** 菜肴。

cuisse, cuish [kwis, kwiʃ; kwɪs, kwɪʃ] ***n*.** 腿甲。

culch [kʌltʃ; kʌltʃ] ***n*. 1.** (铺垫牡蛎养殖场水底的)贝壳屑,砂砾。**2.** 牡蛎卵。**3.**〔方〕垃圾,碎屑,废物。

cul-de-sac [ˌkuldəˈsæk; ˋkuldəˋsæk] ***n*.**〔F.〕**1.** 死巷,死胡同。**2.**【军】(三面被围的)绝境;困境;绝路。**3.**【解】盲管,盲肠。

-cule *comb. f.* 小:animal*cule*; poetic*ule*.

cu·let [ˈkjuːlit; ˋkjulɪt] ***n*.** (打磨成首饰的)钻石的底面。

cu·lex [ˈkjuːleks; ˋkjulɛks] ***n*.** (*pl.* ***-li·ces*** [-lisiːz; -lɪsiz])【动】(普通)家蚊。

cu·lic·id [kjuːˈlisid; kjuˋlɪsɪd] **I** ***a*.**【动】蚊科的。**II** ***n*.** 蚊子。

cu·li·nar·y [ˈkʌlinəri; ˋkʌlɪnərɪ] ***a*.** 厨房的,烹饪的,烹调用的。~ *arts* 烹饪术。

cull[1][kʌl; kʌl] **I** ***vt*.**〔书〕**1.** 采,摘(花);拣,选拔。**2.** 拣出,剔出。**II** ***n*.** 拣出的东西;拣剩的东西;(不合格的)等外品;(社会中的)败类。

cull[2][kʌl; kʌl] ***n*.**〔俚〕= cully.

cul·len·der [ˈkʌlində; ˋkʌlɪndɚ] ***n*.** = colander.

cul·let [ˈkʌlit; ˋkʌlɪt] ***n*.** (供回炉的)碎玻璃。

cul·lion [ˈkʌljən; ˋkʌljən] ***n*.**〔废〕卑下可鄙的人。

cul·lis [ˈkʌlis; ˋkʌlɪs] ***n*.**【建】承溜;沟。

cul·ly [ˈkʌli; ˋkʌlɪ] **I** ***n*. 1.**〔英俚〕呆子,傻瓜。**2.**〔俚〕伙伴,家伙。**II** ***vt*.** 欺骗。

culm[1][kʌlm; kʌlm] **I** ***n*.**【植】(竹、芦、草等空心的)茎,杆。**II** ***vi*.** 长成(空心)茎秆。

culm[2][kʌlm; kʌlm] ***n*. 1.** 低级无烟煤。**2.** 碎煤,灰煤。**3.**〔C-〕【地】碳质页岩。

cul·mif·er·ous [kʌlˈmifərəs; kʌlˋmɪfərəs] ***a*. 1.**【地】含有碳质页岩的。**2.**【植】生成空心茎杆的。

cul·mi·nant [ˈkʌlminənt; ˋkʌlmənənt] ***a*. 1.** 达到顶点的,绝顶的。**2.**【天】子午线上的,中天的。

cul·mi·nate [ˈkʌlmineit; ˋkʌlməˏnet] ***vi*. 1.** 到绝顶,达于极点,达最高潮;【天】到中天[最高度]。**2.** 告终(*in*)。—***vt*. 1.** 使达到顶点。**2.** 使告终。~ ***in*** ...(…到极点)终至成为,(结果)竟成(*Animal life* ~*s in man.* 动物发达到顶点而成为人)。

cul·mi·na·tion [ˌkʌlmiˈneiʃən; ˏkʌlməˋneʃən] ***n*. 1.** 顶点,极点,极度。**2.** 最高潮;极盛期,绝顶;成就,完成。**3.**【天】中天。

cu·lottes [kju(ː)ˈlɔts; kjuˋlɑts] ***n*.**〔*pl.*〕(女用)裙裤。

cul·pa [ˈkulpə, ˈkʌl-; ˋkʌlpə, ˋkʌl-] ***n*.**〔L.〕**1.** 过失;犯罪。**2.**【法】疏忽;过失。

cul·pa·bil·i·ty [ˌkʌlpəˈbiliti; ˏkʌlpəˋbɪlətɪ] ***n*.** 该罚,有罪。

cul·pa·ble [ˈkʌlpəbl; ˋkʌlpəbl̩] ***a*.** 该责备的,应受罚的;有罪的,有过失的。~ *negligence* 应受惩罚的疏忽[失职]。*hold (sb.)* ~ 认为(某人)有罪[应受惩罚,谴责]。

cul·pa·bly [ˈkʌlpəbli; ˋkʌlpəblɪ] ***ad*.** 该罚地,该责备地;有罪地。

cul·prit [ˈkʌlprit; ˋkʌlprɪt] ***n*. 1.** 犯人,罪犯。**2.**【英法】刑事被告,未决犯,嫌疑犯。

Cul·ross [ˈkʌlrɔs; ˋkʌlrɑs] ***n*.** 卡尔罗斯[姓氏]。

cult [kʌlt; kʌlt] ***n*. 1.** (宗教)崇拜;祭礼,祭仪,礼拜;信仰;邪教,异教,会道门。**2.** 狂热崇拜,迷信(对象)。**3.** 巫术疗法,祈祷疗法。**4.**〔集合词〕崇拜[歌颂]者;(狂热的)信徒。*the personality* ~ 个人崇拜。***the*** ~ ***of*** ...…崇拜,…的流行[风尚],…热(*the* ~ *of the individual* 个人崇拜。*the* ~ *of nature* [*beauty*] 自然[美]的歌颂[崇拜]。*the* ~ *of the eye-glass* 单眼镜的大流行。*the* ~ *of the jumping cat* 观望主义)。~**-figure** 崇拜对象。

cultch [kʌltʃ; kʌltʃ] ***n*.** = culch.

cul·ti·gen [ˈkʌltidʒen; ˋkʌltədʒən] ***n*.**【植】栽培种。

cul·ti·va·ble [ˈkʌltivəbl; ˋkʌltəvəbl̩] ***a*. 1.** 可耕种的,可栽培的。**2.** 可培养的;可教化的。

cul·ti·var [ˈkʌltiˌvɑː, -ˌvə; ˋkʌltəˏvɑr, -ˏvə] ***n*.**【植】栽培变种。

cul·ti·vate [ˈkʌltiveit; ˋkʌltəˏvet] ***vt*. 1.** 耕作,耕种;开垦;〔美〕中耕,培土,养(鱼等);栽培。**2.** 教化,培养,养成;修习,磨炼。**3.** 谋求;追求;发展,培养(友谊、感情等);细心照料。~ *a moustache* 留胡子。~ *the acquaintance of* 设法与…交往,谋求与…结识。

cul·ti·vat·ed [ˈkʌltiveitid; ˋkʌltəˏvetɪd] ***a*. 1.** 在耕种[栽培]中的。**2.** 有修养[教养]的,文雅的。~ *land* 耕地。~ *plants* 栽培植物。~ *silk* 桑[家]蚕丝。~ *taste* 高雅的趣味。

cul·ti·va·tion [ˌkʌltiˈveiʃən; ˏkʌltəˋveʃən] ***n*. 1.** 耕种,耕作;中耕;开垦;造林;栽培;(细菌等的)培养;(鱼等的)养殖。**2.** 教养,研究,修养;优雅,高尚。*intensive* [*extensive*] ~ 集约[粗放]耕作。***bring*** (*waste land*) ***under*** ~ 开垦(荒地)。***land under*** ~ 耕地。

cul·ti·va·tor [ˈkʌltiveitə; ˋkʌltəˏvetɚ] ***n*. 1.** 耕种者;栽培者。**2.** 教养者;修习者。**3.** 中耕机。*a multi-purpose* ~ 多用途耕作机。

cul·trate, cul·trated [ˈkʌltreit, -id; ˋkʌltret, -ɪd] ***a*.** 小刀状的,锐利的。

cul·tur·al [ˈkʌltʃərəl; ˋkʌltʃərəl] ***a*. 1.** 耕作的,开垦的,栽培[培养]的。**2.** 教养的,修习的。**3.** 文化的。~ *control* 耕作防除。~ *exchange* 文化交流。**-ly** ***ad*.** (*a culturally advanced country* 高度文明的国家)。

cul·tu·ra·ti [ˌkəltʃəˈrɑːti; ˏkəltʃəˋrɑtɪ] ***n*.**〔*pl.*〕有文化的阶层;有文化的人们;文化人。

cul·ture [ˈkʌltʃə; ˋkʌltʃɚ] **I** ***n*. 1.** 教养;修养;磨炼。**2.** 文化,(精神)文明。**3.** 人工培养,养殖;培养菌,培养组织。**4.** 耕作;栽培;造林。*a man of* ~ 有教养的人,文

C

化人。～ *of mind and body* 身心修养。*intellectual* [*moral*, *physical*] ～ 智[德、体]育。～ *of cotton* 棉花栽培。*silk* ～ 养蚕。**II** *vt*. 使有教养。～ **gap** 文化沟〔两种文化间的差异〕。～ **fluid** [**tube**] 培养液[管]。～ **medium** 培养基。～ **pan** 种植钵,营养钵。～ **pearl** 人工培养的珍珠。～ **shock** 文化冲击〔在陌生的文化环境中不知所措等〕。～**-vulture**〔美俚〕文化秃鹰〔对文化艺术有高度或过分兴趣的人〕。

cul·tured [ˈkʌltʃəd; ˋkʌltʃɚd] *a*. 1. 有教养的,有修养的,高尚的。2. 耕作了的;所种植的。3. (人工)培养[栽培,养殖]的。*the* ～ *minds* 有(文化)教养的人们。

C

cul·tur·ist [ˈkʌltʃərist; ˋkʌltʃərɪst] *n*. 1. 栽培者;培养者;养殖者。2. 文化主义者。

cul·tur·ol·o·gy [ˌkʌltʃərəˈlɔdʒikəl; ˏkʌltʃərəˋlɑdʒɪkəl] *n*. 〔美〕文化学〔研究文化现象〕。

Cul·tus [ˈkʌltəs; ˋkʌltəs] *n*. 〔L.〕 = cult.

cul·ver [ˈkʌlvə; ˋkʌlvɚ] *n*. 〔英方〕鸽;野鸽。

cul·ver·in [ˈkʌlvərin; ˋkʌlvərɪn] *n*. 1. (中世纪)火枪。2. (15—16世纪的)长炮,重炮。

cul·vert [ˈkʌlvət; ˋkʌlvɚt] *n*. 暗渠,阴沟;【电】电缆管道;涵洞。

cum [kʌm; kʌm] *prep*. 〔L.〕 1. = with. 2. 附属,联合〔用于固有名词间〕;兼。*Stow-cum-Quy*, Stow 与 Quy 的联合教区。*a dwelling-cum-workshop* 兼作住宅的工厂,住宅兼工厂。～ ***call*** 附催缴款项通知单。～ ***coupon*** 附有息单。～ ***dividend*** 附有红利 (*opp*. ex div.)。～ ***grano*** (***salis***) 〔L.〕 [ˈgreinəu (ˈseilis); ˋgreno (ˋselɪs)] 有保留地,打个折扣(听等)(*Take things* ～ *grano salis*. 〔口〕事事应加斟酌。*Take what he says* ～ *grano salis*. 〔口〕他讲的话要打个折扣听)。～ ***laude*** 〔L.〕 [ˈlɔːdiː; ˋlɔdi] 受到赞许,优等〔以优等成绩毕业〕。～ ***new*** 附有新股。

cum. = cumulative.

cum·ber [ˈkʌmbə; ˋkʌmbɚ] **I** *vt*. 拖累,妨害,阻碍;阻塞(地方)。**II** *n*. 妨碍(物)。

Cum·ber·land [ˈkʌmbələnd; ˋkʌmbɚlənd] *n*. 1. 〔英〕坎伯兰郡〔英格兰一郡名〕。2. 坎伯兰〔姓氏〕。

cum·ber·some [ˈkʌmbəsəm; ˋkʌmbɚsəm] *a*. 1. 麻烦的;讨厌的。2. 繁重的;笨重的,累赘的。**-ly** *ad*. **-ness** *n*.

cum·brance [ˈkʌmbrəns; ˋkʌmbrəns] *n*. 麻烦[讨厌]的负担。

Cum·bri·an [ˈkʌmbriən; ˋkʌmbrɪən] **I** *a*. (英国古代)坎伯兰 (Cumbria) 王国的;(现代)坎伯兰(郡)的。**II** *n*. 坎伯兰人。

cum·brous [ˈkʌmbrəs; ˋkʌmbrəs] *a*. = cumbersome.

cum d. = cum dividend【会计】附有红利,附股息。

cum·in [ˈkʌmin; ˋkʌmɪn] *n*.【植】枯茗,欧莳萝,小茴香,小茴香子。

cum·mer, kim·mer [ˈkʌmə, ˈkimə; ˋkʌmɚ, ˋkɪmɚ] *n*. 〔Scot.〕 1. 教母。2. 女伴,女友。3. 女人;姑娘。

cum·mer·bund [ˈkʌməbʌnd; ˋkʌmɚˏbʌnd] *n*. (印度人的)腰围,腰带;徽带,绶带。

cum·min [ˈkʌmin; ˋkʌmɪn] *n*. = cumin.

Cum·ming(s) [ˈkʌmiŋ(z); ˋkʌmɪŋ(z)] *n*. 卡明(斯)〔姓氏〕。

cum·quat [ˈkʌmkwɔt; ˋkʌmkwɑt] *n*. = kumquat.

cu·mu·late [ˈkjuːmjulit; ˋkjumjəˏlet] **I** *a*. 堆积的,累积的。**II** [-leit; -let] *vt*. 堆积,积累,蓄积。

cu·mu·la·tion [ˌkjuːmjuˈleiʃən; ˏkjumjəˋleʃən] *n*. 堆积;积累;累积法;蓄积;重叠。

cu·mu·la·tive [ˈkjuːmjulətiv; ˋkjumjəˏletɪv] *a*. 1. 累积的,蓄积的;渐增的;累加的,附加的。2.【法】(证据等与同一事实)相重的;(判刑等)加重的。～ **dividend** 累加红利。～ **evidence**【法】累积证据,复证。～ **medicine** 少量常服的缓效药。～ **offence** 累犯。～ **preference shares** 累积优先股,累积红利先取股。～ **time** 总[累积]时间。～ **volume** 总[累积]体积。

cu·mu·li [ˈkjuːmjulai; ˋkjumjəlaɪ] *n*. cumulus 的复数。

cu·mu·li·form [ˈkjuːmjuliˌfɔːm; ˋkjumjələˏfɔrm] *a*.【气】有积云状的。

cumulo- *comb. f*. 表示"积云":*cumulo*cirrus.

cu·mu·lo·cir·rus [ˈkjuːmjuləuˋsirəs; ˏkjumjəloˋsɪrəs] *n*.【气】叠卷云,积卷云。

cu·mu·lo·nim·bus [ˈkjuːmjuləuˈnimbəs; ˏkjumjəloˋnɪmbəs] *n*.【气】积雨云。

cu·mu·lo·stra·tus [ˈkjuːmjuləuˈstreitəs; ˏkjumjəloˋstretəs] *n*.【气】层积云。

cu·mu·lous [ˈkjuːmjuləs; ˋkjumjələs] *a*.【气】积云状的,由积云形成的。

cu·mu·lus [ˈkjuːmjuləs; ˋkjumjələs] *n*. (*pl*. **-li** [-lai; -laɪ]) 1. 堆,堆积物。2.【气】积云。

cunc·ta·tion [kəŋkˈteiʃən; kʌŋkˋteʃən] *n*. 〔罕〕耽搁,迟延。**-ta·tive** [ˈkʌŋkteitiv, -tətiv; ˋkʌŋktetɪv, -tətɪv] *a*.

cu·ne·al, cu·ne·atic [ˈkjuːniəl, -niːætik; ˋkjunɪəl, -nɪætɪk] *a*. 楔的,楔形的。

cu·ne·ate [ˈkjuːniit, -eit; ˋkjunɪɪt, -et] *a*. (叶等)楔形的。

cu·ne·i·form [ˈkjuːniifɔːm; ˋkjunɪəˏfɔrm] **I** *a*. 楔形的;楔形文字的;楔状骨的。**II** *n*. 1. 楔形文字[文献]。2.【解】楔状骨。

cu·nette [kjuˈnet; kjuˋnet] *n*. 壕底(排水)渠。

cun·ning [ˈkʌniŋ; ˋkʌnɪŋ] **I** *a*. 1. 狡猾的,诡诈的。2. 巧妙的,灵巧的;老练的;精巧的。3. 〔美口〕(孩子等)伶俐的,可爱的。*a* ～ *baby* 可爱的婴儿。**II** *n*. 狡猾;诡诈;机巧,巧妙。*have a great deal of* ～ 很狡猾。**-ly** *ad*. **-ness** *n*.

Cun·nin·gham [ˈkʌniŋəm; ˋkʌnɪŋhæm] *n*. 坎宁安〔姓氏〕。

cunt [kʌnt; kʌnt] *n*. 〔俚〕 1. 女性阴部。2. 〔贬〕人,女人。

CUP = 1. Cambridge University Press (英国)剑桥大学出版社。2. Columbia University Press (美国)哥伦比亚大学出版社。

cup [kʌp; kʌp] **I** *n*. 1. (有柄的)茶杯;(有脚)(酒)杯;奖杯,优胜杯;圣餐杯。2. 一杯(约 1/2 pint)。3. 酒;(圣餐礼的)葡萄酒,饮酒。4. 〔喻〕命运;人生经验。5. 杯状物;【植】萼;【解】杯状窝,骨臼;【勺球】球洞;【火箭】罩帽,喷注室。6.【医】干吸杯,火罐。7. 杯状凹地,盆地。8. (酒、糖、冰等配成的)冷饮。9.【数】求并运算。*One's* [*The*] ～ *of happiness* [*misery*] *is full*. 幸福[不幸]极了,快乐[悲苦]极了。*One's* ～ *of happiness runs over* [*overflows*]. 太幸福了。*a* ～ *of wine* 一杯酒。*a queen* ～【养蜂】王台。***a*** ～ ***of cold water*** 象征性的施舍。***a*** ～ ***too low*** 无精打采,意气消沉。***be*** ～ ***and can*** 好友。***between the*** ～ ***and the lip*** 差不多要成功[到手]之时;眼看要成功但尚未最后定夺时。***bitter*** ～ 艰苦的经历。～ ***and ball*** 杯球〔一种玩具〕。～***-and-ball joint***【解】球窝关节。～ ***and saucer*** 一套茶杯和碟子。***drain*** [***drink up***] ***the*** ～ ***of humiliation*** 忍受耻辱。***drain the*** ～ ***of life to the bottom*** [***dregs***] 备尝辛酸;享尽快乐。***have had*** (***got***) ***a*** ～ ***too much*** 〔俚〕喝醉了。***in one's*** ～***s*** 在酒醉的时候,醉醺醺地。***kiss the*** ～ 呷,饮;饮酒。***sb.'s*** ～ ***of tea*** 〔口〕 1. (某人)喜爱之物;(对某人)适宜的事物。2. 命运。3. 颇堪怀疑的东西。***the*** ～***s that cheer but not inebriate*** 茶。***win the*** ～ 优胜。***withhold the*** ～ 不喝圣餐葡萄酒尽吃面包。**II** *vt*. 1. 把…弄成杯形(凹形)。2. 把…置于杯内。3.【医】给…拔火罐,用吸杯吸。4.【高尔夫球】用打棒打(地面)作发球势。—*vi*. 1. 成杯形(凹形)。2.【医】使用吸杯。～**-bearer** (宫廷筵席上的)上酒人;侍臣。～ **event**【体】锦标赛。～ **final**【体】决赛。～ **holder** 奖杯保持者。～ **product**

【拓】上积。～ **seaming** 包缝缝合。～ **tie** 优胜杯决赛。～**-tied** *a*.〔英〕参加优胜杯比赛的。

cup·board [ˈkʌbəd; ˋkʌbɚd] *n*. 食橱,碗柜;〔英〕小橱。*cry* ～〔口〕喊饿,想吃东西。～ *love* 有所意图的亲热表示。*skeleton in the* ～ 家丑。

cup·cake [ˈkʌpkeik; ˋkʌpˏkek] *n*. **1.** 杯形蛋糕。**2.**〔美俚〕女人模样的家伙;讨厌的人。

cu·pel [ˈkjuːpəl; ˋkjupɛl] **I** *n*.【冶】(鉴定贵金属用的)烤钵,灰皿,灰吹盘。**II** *vt*.(〔英〕*-ll-*)用烤钵鉴定,用灰皿提炼。～ **furnace** 灰吹炉。

cu·pel·la·tion [ˌkjuːpəˈleiʃən; ˏkjupəˋleʃən] *n*.【冶】烤钵鉴定法;烤钵冶金法。

cup·fer·ron [ˈkʌpfəˌrɔn, ˈkuːp-; ˋkʌpfəˏrɑn, ˋkup-] *n*.【化、冶】铜铁灵,铜铁试剂。

cup·ful [ˈkʌpful; ˋkʌpˏfʊl] *n*. 一满杯,一杯之量〔约 1/2 pint〕。

Cu·pid [ˈkjuːpid; ˋkjupɪd] *n*. **1.**【罗神】丘比特〔爱神,其形象为一背生双翼、手持弓箭的美童〕。**2.**〔c-〕美童,美少年。～*'s bow* 爱神的弓;弓形嘴唇。

cu·pid·i·ty [kju(ː)ˈpiditi; kjuˋpɪdətɪ] *n*. 贪欲,贪婪。

cu·po·la [ˈkjuːpələ; ˋkjupələ] *n*. **1.** 圆顶;圆顶篷;圆顶阁。**2.**【冶】化铁[冲天]炉。**3.**【军】旋转炮塔。**4.**【解】钟形感器。*a blast* ～化铁炉。

cup·pa [ˈkʌpə; ˋkʌpə] *n*.〔英口〕一杯茶。*What about a* ～? 想喝杯茶吗?

cup·ping [ˈkʌpiŋ; ˋkʌpɪŋ] *n*. **1.**【医】杯吸术。**2.**(木材的)翘曲。～ **axe**【林】采脂斧。～ **glass**【医】吸杯,火罐。

cup·py [ˈkʌpi; ˋkʌpɪ] *a*. **1.** 杯形的;凹的。**2.**(地面上)窟窿多的。

cu·pre·ous [ˈkjuːpriəs; ˋkjuprɪəs] *a*. 含铜的;似铜的,铜色的。

cu·pri- *comb*. *f*. 表示"铜";"二价铜":*cupri*ferous.

cu·pric [ˈkjuːprik; ˋkjuprɪk] *a*.【化】(正;二价)铜的;含铜的。～ **chloride** 氯化铜。～ **oxide** 氧化铜。～ **sulphate** 硫酸铜。

cu·prif·er·ous [kju(ː)ˈprifərəs; kjuˋprɪfərəs] *a*. 含铜的,产铜的。

cu·prite [ˈkjuːprait; ˋkjupraɪt] *n*.【矿】赤铜矿。

cu·pro- *comb*. *f*. 表示"铜","一价铜":*cupro*nickel.

cu·pro·nick·el [ˈkjuːprəuˈnikl; ˏkjuproˋnɪkl̩] *n*. 铜镍合金,白铜。

cu·prous [ˈkjuːprəs; ˋkjuprəs] *a*.【化】亚[一价]铜的;= cupreous. ～ **oxide** 氧化亚铜。

cu·prum [ˈkjuːprəm; ˋkjuprəm] *n*.【化】铜。

cu·pu·late [ˈkjuːpjuleit; ˋkjupjulet] *a*. **1.** 杯状的,壳斗状的。**2.** 有壳斗的。

cu·pule [ˈkjuːpjuːl; ˋkjupjul̩] *n*. 杯形器,杯状凹,杯状托;【动】(杯状)吸盘;【植】杯状体,壳斗。

cur [kəː; kɝ] *n*. **1.** 野狗,杂种狗。**2.** 卑劣可鄙的人。

cur. = currency; current.

cur·a·bil·i·ty [ˌkjuərəˈbiliti; ˏkjʊrəˋbɪlətɪ] *n*. **1.**(病的)治愈可能性。**2.**(水果等的)可保存性能。

cur·a·ble [ˈkjuərəbl; ˋkjʊrəbl̩] *a*. **1.** 可医治的,医得好的。**2.**(水果等)能贮存的。

Cu·ra·çao, cu·ra·ço·a [kjuərəˈsəu, -ˈsəuə; ˏkjʊrəˋso, -ˋsoə] *n*. **1.**(委内瑞拉西北的)库拉索岛。**2.**〔c-〕陈皮酒。

cu·ra·cy [ˈkjuərəsi; ˋkjʊrəsɪ] *n*. 副牧师的身份[职位]。

cu·ra·re, cu·ra·ri [kjuˈrɑːri; kjuˋrɑrɪ] *n*. **1.**(南美印第安人用以涂箭头的)箭毒。**2.**【植】马钱子,可提取箭毒的植物。

cu·ra·rine [ˈkjuərərain; ˋkjʊrəraɪn] *n*.【化】箭毒碱。

cu·ra·rize [kjuˈrɑːraiz, ˈkjuːrəˌraiz; kjuˋrɑraɪz, ˋkjurəˏraɪz] *vt*. **1.**【医】对…施用箭毒。**2.** 用箭毒使瘫痪。**-za·tion** [kjuˌrɑːriˈzeiʃən, ˈkjuːrəri-; kjuˏrɑrɪˋzeʃən, ˋkjurərɪ-] *n*.

cu·ras·sow [ˈkjuərəsəu; ˋkjʊrəˏso] *n*.【动】(中、南美的)凤冠鸟。

cu·rate [ˈkjuərit; ˋkjʊrɪt] *n*. **1.**〔英〕副牧师;教区牧师。**2.**〔谑〕拨火棍。(*good in parts*, *like*) *the* ～*'s egg*〔英谑〕好坏混杂(之物)。

cur·a·tive [ˈkjuərətiv; ˋkjʊrətɪv] **I** *a*. 治疗的;有疗效的。**II** *n*. 医药,药品;治疗物[法]。

cu·ra·tor [kjuəˈreitə; kjuˋretɚ] *n*. **1.**(博物馆、图书馆等的)馆长;保管员。**2.**(幼年继承人等的)监护人。**3.**〔英〕(大学)学监;校董会中的财务保管员。～**ship** *n*. 馆长[学监等]的职位[身份]。**-to·ri·al** [-ˈtɔːriəl; -ˋtɔrɪəl] *a*.

curb [kəːb; kɝb] **I** *n*. **1.** 勒马绳,马衔索。**2.** 限制,抑制,拘束;制止。**3.**(生于后足使马成瘸脚的)硬瘤。**4.**(人行道的)镶边;井栏;【建】缘饰。**5.**〔美〕(证券的)场外市场〔又作 ～ market (=〔英〕kerb market)〕;场外经纪人。～ *for fire place* 壁炉槛。*on the* ～〔美〕(交易所开市前)在街头,在场外。*put* [*place*] *a* ～ *on* [*upon*] 限制,抑制。**II** *vt*. **1.** 给(马)扣上马衔。**2.** 制止,束缚。**3.** 用石块镶…的边;在…处设井栏。～ *one's desires* 抑制欲望。～ **bit** 马嚼子。～ **exchange**, ～ **market** (股票的)场外交易。～ **roof**【建】复斜屋顶。～ **service** (给来往乘客坐在车上吃的)饮食供应业务。～**-side** 街头。～**stone** **1.** *n*. 镶边石,栏石(=〔英〕kerbstone);〔*pl*.〕〔美俚〕烟头,烟屁股。**2.** *a*. 场外(证券)交易的 (*a* ～*stone broker* [*operator*]〔美〕场外经纪人;非内行的 (*a* ～ *stone critic* 门外汉批评家))。

curb·ing [ˈkəːbiŋ; ˋkɝbɪŋ] *n*. **1.** 做路边石的材料。**2.** = curb.

curch [kəːtʃ; kɝtʃ] *n*.〔Scot.〕妇女头巾。

cur·cu·li·o [kəːˈkjuːliəu; kɝˋkjulɪo] *n*.【动】象鼻虫。

cur·cu·ma [ˈkəːkjumə; ˋkɝkjumə] *n*.【植】〔C-〕姜黄属;姜黄(～ **longa**)。～ **paper** 姜黄纸。

curd [kəːd; kɝd] **I** *n*. 凝乳;凝乳状物[食品]。*bean* ～(*s*) 豆腐。～*s and whey* 凝乳,奶酪。**II** *vt*., *vi*.(使)成凝乳状。～ **soap** 乳白肥皂。

cur·dle [ˈkəːdl; ˋkɝdl] *vt*. **1.** 使凝结,使凝固。**2.** 使(牛奶等)凝结变质,使变坏。—*vi*. **1.** 凝结,凝固。**2.**(牛奶等)变质,变坏。～ *the* [*sb*.*'s*] *blood* (*with horror*) = *make sb*.*'s blood* ～ 使极度恐怖。

curd·y [ˈkəːdi; ˋkɝdɪ] *a*. 凝乳状的,凝结的。

cure[1] [kjuə; kjʊr] **I** *n*. **1.** 治愈,痊愈;医治,治疗 (*of*);(对社会问题等的)处治,对策。**2.** 药,治疗用剂 (*for*);疗法。**3.** 疗养;疗程;矿泉疗养地。**4.** 补救(办法),矫正法 (*for*)。**5.** 牧师的职位[职责]。**6.**〔美俚〕离婚〔医治家庭病的良药之意〕。**7.**(橡胶的)硫化;干固,固化。**8.**(鱼等用腌、熏、晒、烤等的)加工保藏(法)。*the best* ～ *for a cough* 止咳良药。*a good* ～ *for lying* 治谎良策。*a* ～ *for unemployment* 失业问题的对策。**II** *vt*. **1.** 治愈,治疗,医治。**2.** 救治,矫正,扫除(恶习等)。**3.**(用腌,熏等法)保藏(鱼肉等),加工。**4.** 硫化(橡胶)。*be* ～*d of* (*a disease*)(病)治好了。～ *drunkenness* 矫正[改掉]酒癖。～ *mental worry* 消除精神烦恼。～ *oneself of* 自行矫正,自己改正(恶习等)。—*vi*. **1.** 医病;治愈。**2.**(谷草等)晒干;(鱼等用腌熏等法)进行加工。**3.**(橡胶)受硫化。*The hay is curing in the sun*. 谷草正在太阳下晒干。

cure[2] [kjuə; kjʊr] *n*.〔俚〕怪人,奇人。

cu·ré [kjuəˈrei; kjuˋre] *n*.〔F.〕教区牧师。

cure-all [ˈkjuərɔːl; ˋkjʊrˏɔl] *n*.〔美〕万应良药。

cure·less [ˈkjuəlis; ˋkjʊrlɪs] *a*. **1.** 病入膏肓的,无法医治的。**2.** 已难补救的,难以矫正的。

cur·er [ˈkjuərə; ˋkjʊrɚ] *n*. **1.** 熏腊食品制造人。**2.** 治疗者;治疗器。**3.**(加工食品等的)烘焙机。*fish* ～ 腌鱼商。

cu·ret·tage [kjuəˈretidʒ; kjʊrˋrɛtɪdʒ] *n*.【医】刮除术〔尤指刮子宫〕。

cu·ret(te) [kjuˈret; kjuˋrɛt] **I** *n*.【医】刮匙;刮器。**II**

vt.【医】用刮器刮(宫)。

cur·few [ˈkəːfjuː; ˋkɚfju] *n*. **1**. (中世纪通知已到规定熄灯时间的)晚钟(声);晚钟时刻。**2**. (戒严时期的)宵禁(时间);熄灯令。*impose* [*lift*] a ~ 实行[撤消]宵禁。

cu·ri·a [ˈkjuəriə; ˋkjʊrɪə] *n*. (*pl*. **-ri·ae** [-riiː; -rɪˏi]) **1**. (古罗马行政区划的)族区;族区礼拜堂;元老院。**2**. [the C-]【史】罗马教廷(= the C- Romana)。**3**. [英]封建时代的法庭。**-l** *a*.

Cu·rie [ˈkjuəri; ˋkjʊri] *n*. **1**. 居里[姓氏]。**2**. **Marie** ~ 居里夫人[1867—1934,著名女物理学家]。**3**. **Pierre** ~ 皮埃尔·居里[1859—1906,法国物理学家,与居里夫人共同发现镭]。

C

cu·rie [ˈkjuəri; ˋkjʊri] *n*.【物】居里[放射性强度单位]。

cu·ri·o [ˈkjuəriəu; ˋkjʊrɪˏo] *n*. 古董,骨董,(珍奇)古玩。

cu·ri·o·sa [ˌkjuəriˈəusə, -zə; ˏkjʊrɪˋosɚ, -zə] *n*. [*pl*.] **1**. 珍品。**2**. 色情书籍。

cu·ri·os·i·ty [ˌkjuəriˈɔsiti; ˏkjʊrɪˋɑsətɪ] *n*. **1**. 好奇心;爱打听的癖好。**2**. 引起好奇心的事物;珍品,古董;奇人。**3**. 奇特性。~ *shop* 古玩铺。***from*** ~ = ***out of*** ~ 在好奇心驱使下。***in open*** ~ 公然出头过问与己无关的事。

cu·ri·o·so [ˌkjuəriˈəusəu; ˏkjʊrɪˋoso] *n*. [It.] (*pl*. **-si** [-sai; -saɪ], ~**s**) 美术品爱好家,古董搜集家。

cu·ri·ous [ˈkjuəriəs; ˋkjʊrɪəs] *a*. **1**. 好奇心旺盛的;好事的,爱看热闹的。**2**. 稀奇的,古怪的,奇妙的。**3**. (书等)猥亵的,趣味低级的。**4**. [古]非常细致的,精细的。*He is very* ~. 他是好管闲事的(人)。*a* ~ *inquiry* 寻根问底。***be*** ~ ***about*** (***sth***.) 对(某事物)感到好奇。***be*** ~ ***to say*** 说来真稀奇。**-ly** *ad*. 好奇地;奇妙地;[加强语气]怪,很,非常(*a curiously bad accent* 怪重的土腔)。**-ness** *n*.

cu·rite [ˈkjuərait; ˋkjʊraɪt] *n*.【矿】板铅铀矿。

cu·ri·um [ˈkjuəriəm; ˋkjʊrɪəm] *n*.【化】锔。

curl [kəːl; kɚl] **I** *vt*. **1**. 使卷曲,使成螺旋状;弄卷(毛、发),捻(髭);(狗等)蜷着(身子);使(水等)起波纹。**2**. 用卷毛装饰。—*vi*. **1**. 卷曲,卷缩;(烟等)缭绕,袅袅上升;(蔓等)绕缠;(球、路等)弯曲。**2**. [Scot.] 冰上作溜石饼游戏。**3**. [美口]得到极好成绩。~ ***one's lip*** (轻蔑地,厌恶地)歪歪嘴,翘翘上唇。~ ***up*** **1**. 卷缩;卷起。**2**. [口]衰弱,无精神;蜷着一团。**3**. [俚](使)崩溃,垮台;打倒,驳倒,说服(~ *oneself up* 把身体蜷作一团,蜷着睡)。***make sb.'s hair*** ~ [口]使战栗,吓坏。**II** *n*. **1**. 卷发,卷毛;卷曲物。**2**. 蜷缩,盘曲;涡流。**3**. (植物的)卷叶病。**4**.【机】旋度。~ *of the lip* (轻蔑的)歪嘴,抿嘴。~ *of wave* 波浪的翻滚。***go out of*** ~ [口]无精打采,精疲力尽。***keep the hair in*** ~ 卷着头发。**-er** *n*. **1**. 卷曲者;卷曲物。**2**. 作冰上溜石饼游戏者。

cur·lew [ˈkəːluː; ˋkɚlu] *n*. (*pl*. ~, ~**s**)【鸟】杓鹬(属);麻鹬。

curl·i·cue, curl·y·cue [ˈkəːlikjuː; ˋkɚlɪˏkju] **I** *n*. **1**. 卷曲装饰;(字的)花体。**2**. 花式溜冰法。***cut a*** ~ (在冰、雪等上)作花式滑行。**II** *vt*. 以花体装饰。—*vi*. 形成花体。

curl·i·ness [ˈkəːlinis; ˋkɚlɪnɪs] *n*. 卷缩,卷曲;旋涡。

curl·ing [ˈkəːliŋ; ˋkɚlɪŋ] *n*. **1**. 卷缩,卷曲。**2**. (苏格兰)冰上溜石饼游戏。~ **irons** [**tongs**] 卷发夹。~ **stone** (玩冰上溜石饼游戏用的)石饼。

curl-pa·per [ˈkəːlpeipə; ˋkɚlˏpepɚ] *n*. 卷发纸。

curl·y [ˈkəːli; ˋkɚlɪ] *a*. **1**. 卷缩的;有卷毛的。**2**. 蜷作一团的;翘翘的。**3**. 旋涡形的。**4**. (植物)有卷叶病的。~ **dwarf**【植】卷叶病,萎缩病。~ **grains** 皱状纹理。~ **top**【植】曲顶病。

curl·y·cue [ˈkəːlikjuː; ˋkɚlɪˏkju] *n*. = curlicue.

curl·y·locks [ˈkəːliləks; ˋkɚlɪˏlɑks] *n*. [*pl*.] [美]头发卷曲的人。

curl·y-pate [ˈkəːlipeit; ˋkɚlɪˏpet] *n*. [口]头发卷曲的人。

Curme [kəːm; kɚm] *n*. 柯姆[姓氏]。

cur·mudg·eon [kəˈmʌdʒən; kɚˋmʌdʒən] *n*. **1**. 脾气坏的人。**2**. [古]讨厌的吝啬鬼。**-ly** *a*.

curn [kəːn; kɚn] *n*. [Scot.] **1**. 谷物,谷类。**2**. 少量。

curr [kəː; kɚ] *vi*. (鸽子;猫等)发出低微的咕咕声;低语。

cur·rach, cur·ragh[1] [ˈkʌrə; ˋkʌrə] *n*. [Scot., Ir.] = coracle.

cur·ragh[2] [ˈkʌrə; ˋkʌrə] *n*. 沼泽地。

cur·ra·jong, cur·re·jong, cur·ri·jong [ˈkəːrədʒɔŋ, -dʒɔːŋ; ˋkɚrəˏdʒɑŋ, -ˏdʒɔŋ] *n*.【植】异叶瓶木(= kurrajong)。

cur·rant [ˈkʌrənt; ˋkɚənt] *n*. **1**. 无核小粒葡萄干。**2**.【植】茶藨子,穗状醋栗[= garden ~]。*black* ~**s** 茶藨子。*red* [*white*] ~**s** 红[白]茶藨子。

cur·ren·cy [ˈkʌrənsi; ˋkɚənsɪ] *n*. **1**. 通货。**2**. 通用,流通,流传,传播。**3**. 市价,行情。**4**. 流通时间。*fractional* ~ 辅币。*paper* ~ 纸币。*metallic* ~ 硬币。***gain*** ~ ***with*** 流行开,流通开,得到…信任。***give*** ~ ***to*** 散播(谣言等)。***in common*** ~ 一般通用。***lose*** ~ ***with*** 停止流通[使用];失却…的信任。~ **notes** 流通券。~ **system** 币制。

cur·rent [ˈkʌrənt; ˋkɚənt] **I** *a*. **1**. 通用的,流行的。**2**. 现在的,现时的,当时的。**3**. 流畅的;草写的。*the* ~ *price* 市价。~ *news* 时事。~ *expenditure* 经常费。~ *expenses* 日常费用。*the* ~ *issue* [*number*] (杂志的)本期。*the* ~ *week* 本星期。*the* ~ *year* 今年。*the 10th* ~ [*curt*.] 本月十日。~ *account* 往来存款账;【法】交互计算。~ *English* 现代通行英语,日常英语。~ *handwriting* 草书。~ *money* 通行货币。~ *rate* 现价,成交价。~ *thoughts* 现时代思潮。***pass*** [***run, go***] ~ 通用,流行。**II** *n*. **1**. 水流;气流;电流。**2**. 思潮,潮流;趋势,倾向。**3**. 进行,过程。*a cold* ~ 寒流。*the Japan* ~ 日本海流,黑潮。*the great* ~ *of events* 天下大势。*a density* 密着(海)流。*an alternating* [*a direct*] ~【电】交[直]流电。~ *of air* 气流。~ ***of time*** [***the times***] 时势,时代潮流 (*go* [*swim*] *with* [*against*] *the* ~ *of the times* 顺应[违反]时势)。~ **breaker**【电】断流器。~ **density** 电流密度、扩散流密度。~ **feed** 电流馈接。~ **gauge** [**meter**] 电流表;流速计,流量计。~ **transformer** 变流器。

cur·rent·ly [ˈkʌrəntli; ˋkɚəntlɪ] *ad*. **1**. 通常,一般;现在。**2**. 容易;流畅。

Cur·rer [ˈkʌrə; ˋkɚə] *n*. 柯勒[姓氏]。

cur·ri·cle [ˈkʌrikl; ˋkɚɪkl] *n*. 双马二轮小马车。

cur·ric·u·la [kəˈrikjulə; kəˋrɪkjələ] *n*. curriculum 的复数。

cur·ric·u·lar [kəˈrikjulə; kəˋrɪkjələ] *a*. 课程的,功课的。

cur·ric·u·lum [kəˈrikjuləm; kəˋrɪkjələm] *n*. (*pl*. ~**s**, **-la** [-lə; -lə]) **1**. (一个学校,专业,或学科的)全部课程。**2**. (取得毕业资格等的)必修课程。~ ***vitae*** [ˈvaitiː; ˋvaɪti] [L.] (简短的)履历。~ **schedule** 课程表。

cur·rie [ˈkʌri; ˋkɚɪ] *n*. = curry[1].

cur·ried [ˈkʌrid; ˋkɚɪd] *a*. **1**. (菜)用咖喱烧的。**2**. (马等)梳刷过的。**3**. (皮革)鞣制过的。~ *rice with beef* 咖喱牛肉饭。

cur·ri·er [ˈkʌriə; ˋkɚɪɚ] *n*. **1**. 制革工,鞣皮匠。**2**. 梳马工人。

cur·ri·er·y [ˈkʌriəri; ˋkɚɪərɪ] *n*. **1**. 鞣皮业;制革业。**2**. 鞣皮工场;制革厂。

cur·rish [ˈkəːriʃ; ˋkɚɪʃ] *a*. **1**. 恶狗似的;爱吵闹的,脾气坏的。**2**. 卑劣的,下贱的。**-ly** *ad*. **-ness** *n*.

Cur·ry [ˈkʌri; ˋkɚɪ] *n*. 柯里[姓氏]。

cur·ry[1] [ˈkʌri; ˋkɚɪ] **I** *n*.【烹】咖喱(粉);咖喱饭菜。~ *and rice* 咖喱炒饭。*a chicken* ~ 咖喱鸡。**II** *vt*. 在…中加咖喱粉调味。*curried rice* 咖喱饭。~ **paste** 咖喱酱。~ **powder** 咖喱粉。

cur·ry² [ˈkʌri; ˋkɝɪ] *vt*. **1.** 制(革),鞣(皮)。**2.** 用马栉梳(马毛等)。**3.** 打(人),鞭笞。~ ***below the knee*** 〔美〕过分讨好,巴结。~ ***favour with*** (*sb.*) 巴结,讨好(某人),拍(某人)马屁。~**comb** **1.** *n*. 马栉。**2.** *vt*. 用马栉梳。

curse [kəːs; kɝs] **I** *vt*. (~*d*, ***curst*** [kəːst; kɝst]; ~*d*, ***curst***) **1.** 咒,诅咒 (*opp*. bless);咒骂;恶骂。**2.** 咒逐,把(某人)逐出教门。**3.** 使遭天罚;使受灾祸;使苦恼,使困苦〔多用被动语态〕。*C- it*! 混账! *C- you* [*your folly*]! 笨蛋! ***be ~d with*** 受到某种灾祸;被…所苦;生(疮等)。—*vi*. 诅咒,咒骂。~ ***and swear*** 咒骂。**II** *n*. **1.** 诅咒,恶骂,咒语。**2.** 咒逐,逐出教门。**3.** 祟,天罚;祸害,灾祸;灾害的原因,祸因。**4.** 〔俚〕〔the ~〕月经(期间)。***call down a*** ~ (***up***) ***on*** = ***lay sb. under a*** ~ 诅咒(某人遭受灾祸)。***Curses come home to roost***. 诅咒他人,反而应验到自己身上[害人反害己]。~ ***of drink*** 饮酒之害。~ ***of Scotland*** 【牌】方块九点。***C- upon it***! 混账! ***not care*** [***give***] ***a*** ~ (***for***) 丝毫不顾;不以为意,怎么都好。***not worth a*** ~ 毫无价值。***under a*** ~ 被诅咒,受某种灾害。

curs·ed [ˈkəːsid; ˋkɝsɪd] *a*. **1.** 被诅咒的。**2.** 该罚的;该咒的,可恶的;〔口〕讨厌的。**3.** [ˈkʌsid; ˋkʌsɪd] 〔古〕性子拗的,脾气坏的。**-ly** *ad*. **-ness** *n*.

cur·sive [ˈkəːsiv; ˋkɝsɪv] **I** *a*. (字迹)草写的,手写体的。**II** *n*. 草书;手写原稿。~ *characters* 草字。*a* ~ *hand* [*handwriting*] 草书,行书。**-ly** *ad*. **-ness** *n*.

cur·sor [ˈkəːsə; ˋkɝsɚ] *n*. **1.** (计算尺的)游标。**2.** 【计】(电脑显示屏上的)光标〔有三角形、长方形、十字形等多种形状〕。

cur·so·ri·al [kəːˈsɔːriəl; kɝˋsorɪəl] *a*. 【动】走禽类的;疾走的。~ *insects* 只走不飞的昆虫。~ *birds* 走禽兽。

cur·so·ry [ˈkəːsəri; ˋkɝsərɪ] *a*. 匆促的,仓卒的;草率的;粗率的,(知识等)浅薄的。**-ri·ly** *ad*. **-ri·ness** *n*.

curst [kəːst; kɝst] curse 的过去式及过去分词。

curt [kəːt; kɝt] *a*. 简短的;简略的;草率的,粗率的,敷衍了事的。*a* ~ *answer* 草率无礼的回答。*a* ~ *refusal* 不客气的拒绝。**-ly** *ad*. **-ness** *n*.

cur·tail [kəːˈteil; kɝˋtel] *vt*. **1.** 缩短,省略(讲话、节目等)。**2.** 削减,节减(经费等)。**3.** 褫夺,剥夺(特权、官衔等)。~ *him of his title* 取消他的官衔。~*ed words* 缩略词〔例: bus, phone 等〕。*have one's pay* ~*ed* 被减薪。**-ment** *n*.

cur·tain [ˈkəːtən; ˋkɝtən] **I** *n*. **1.** 帘幕;窗帘,帘子。**2.** (舞台的)幕;启[落]幕。**3.** 幕状物;(两棱堡间的)中堤幕墙;【建】隔壁,间壁。**4.** 〔*pl*.〕〔美俚〕死;终结。*The* ~ *rose on the war*. 战争揭幕[开始]了。~ *of smoke* 烟幕。***behind the*** ~ 在幕后,秘密。***call an actor before the*** ~ 要求演员到幕前来(谢幕);叫幕。***C-***! 听众注意! ***draw a*** ~ ***on*** [***over***] 拉(窗)帘遮住(窗子等);(把话头)截止,停讲(不谈下文)。***draw the*** ~ 拉幕〔开幕或闭幕〕。***draw the*** ~***s*** 拉上所有窗帘。***drop*** [***raise***] ***the*** ~ 闭[开]幕,停[开]演。***lift the*** ~ ***on*** 开始,扯开幕布使看;公布;明说。***ring down the*** ~ 响铃闭幕;使结束;使终止(事件)。***take a*** ~ (演员到幕前)谢幕。***work up the*** ~ (戏剧)在收场时作出兴奋激昂的表演。**II** *vt*. 在…挂帘子;用幕[帘子]隔开[遮住] (*off*);遮蔽,隐藏。~ **call** (要求演员到幕前来的)叫幕声。~ **fall** 闭幕;(事件的)结尾,大团圆。~ **fire** 【军】弹幕,掩护射击。~ **lecture** (妻子对丈夫说的)帐中私话,对丈夫的训斥。~ **line** 全剧[一幕]的最后一行台词。~ **raiser** 开幕戏;(球赛等的)开幕戏;(大事发生前的)小事。~ **ring** 窗帘圈。~ **rod** 窗帘棍。~ **speech** (剧作者、演出人等)剧中在幕前的致词。~ **time** 开幕时间。~**-up** (表演开始时的)幕启。

cur·tal [ˈkəːtl; ˋkɝtl] **I** *a*. 〔废〕切短的;削减的。**II** *n*. 〔废〕**1.** 剪短尾的马。**2.** 切短物,截短物。~ **ax** 短弯刀 (= cutlass)。

cur·ta·na [kəːˈteinə, kəːˈtɑːnə; kɝˋtenə, kɝˋtɑnə] *n*. 无尖刀,慈悲剑〔英王加冕式上表示仁慈的器物〕。

cur·tate [ˈkəːteit; ˋkɝtet] *a*. 削短的,缩短的,缩减的。

cur·te·sy [ˈkəːtisi; ˋkɝtəsɪ] *n*. 【法】鳏夫产权。

cur·ti·lage [ˈkəːtilidʒ; ˋkɝtlɪdʒ] *n*. 【法】庭园,宅地。

Cur·tis(s) [ˈkəːtis; ˋkɝtɪs] *n*. 柯蒂斯〔姓氏〕。

curt·sey, curt·sy [ˈkəːtsi; ˋkɝtsɪ] **I** *n*. (女子的)屈膝礼。***make*** [***bob***, ***drop***] ***a*** ~ 请个安,行屈膝礼。**II** *vi*. 行屈膝礼 (*to*)。

cu·rule [ˈkjuəru(ː)l; ˋkjʊrʊl] *a*. 〔古罗马〕有权坐公共集会显要席的;(官职)显要的。~ *chair* [*set*] 显要席;高位,显职。~ *office* 显要官位。

cur·va·ceous [kəːˈveiʃəs; kɝˋveʃəs] *a*. 〔口〕(女性)有曲线美的;(身段)苗条的。

cur·va·ture [ˈkəːvətʃə; ˋkɝvətʃɚ] *n*. **1.** 弯曲(部分)。**2.** 【数】曲率,曲度。

curve [kəːv; kɝv] **I** *n*. **1.** 曲线;弯曲;弯曲物。**2.** 曲线规 (= French ~);【机】曲线板;【棒球】曲线球;【统】曲线图。**3.** 诈欺;〔美〕使对方难应付的策略。**4.** 〔*pl*.〕(圆)括号。~ *of beauty* 曲线美。**II** *vt*. 弄弯;使弯曲。—*vi*. 成弯曲状;(依)曲线行进;呈曲线美。~ **ball** (乒乓球的)弧圈球;〔喻〕狡猾手段。~ **fitting** 【统】曲线求律法,曲线拟合。

cur·vet [kəːˈvet; ˋkɝvet] *n*. (*-tt-*) *vi*. 【马术】腾跃;〔古〕嬉戏,跳跃。*cut* [*make*] *a* ~ 腾跃,跳跃。

cur·vi·lin·e·al, cur·vi·lin·e·ar [ˌkəːviˈliniəl, ˌkəːviˈliniə; ˏkɝvəˋlɪnɪəl, ˏkɝvəˋlɪnɪɚ] *a*. 曲线的。*a* ~ *tracery* 【建】曲线花样窗格。

curv·y [ˈkəːvi; ˋkɝvɪ] *a*. (***curv·i·er***; ***curv·i·est***) **1.** 弯曲的。**2.** 〔口〕体态丰满的,有曲线美的。*a* ~ *road* 弯曲的道路。

Cus·co [ˈkuːskəu; ˋkusko] *n*. = Cuzco.

cus·cus [ˈkʌskʌs; ˋkʌskʌs] *n*. 【动】袋貂属 (*Phalanger*)。

cu·sec [ˈkjuːsek; ˋkjusɛk] *n*. 秒立方英尺〔灌溉流量单位,每秒一立方英尺, cubic feet per second 之略〕。

cush [kʌʃ; kʌʃ] *n*. 〔美俚〕钱;薪水;收入〔尤指利润、贿赂〕。

cush·at [ˈkʌʃət; ˋkʌʃət] *n*. 〔英方〕(欧洲)斑鸠。

cu·shaw [kəˈʃɔː; kəˋʃɔ] *n*. 【植】南瓜,倭瓜 (*Cucurbita moschata*)。

cush·i·ly [ˈkuʃili; ˋkʊʃɪlɪ] *ad*. 轻松地,舒适地。

Cush·ing [ˈkuʃiŋ; ˋkʊʃɪŋ] *n*. 库欣〔姓氏〕。

cush·ion [ˈkuʃən; ˋkʊʃən] **I** *n*. **1.** 软垫,椅垫,靠垫。**2.** 【机】缓冲垫层,汽垫,胶垫,缓冲器;【植】叶枕。**3.** (撞球台面四边的)橡皮衬垫。**4.** (猪等的)后腿肉。**5.** (衬裙子的)腰垫。**6.** 假发。**7.** 针扎,针插(= pin-~)。**8.** (马的)蹄叉。**9.** 【棒球】〔俚〕= base. **10.** 〔*pl*.〕〔美〕安慰,慰藉,安慰物;安乐,奢侈。**11.** 〔俚〕积贮,存款。**II** *vt*. **1.** 把…摆在坐垫[桌垫]上;给…安上垫子,用软垫垫上。给…装上汽垫。**2.** 【撞球】使(球)碰触台边衬垫〔先碰触后击中另一球或先击中一球后碰触衬垫后再击中另一球〕。**3.** 使(反抗,冲击等)变缓和;掩饰(丑闻等)。*a* ~*ed voice* 柔软的声音。~*ing effect* 缓冲作用。~ **capital** 【建】罗曼式[带枕]柱头。~ **craft** 气垫汽车;气垫船。~ **tyre** (填满碎橡皮的)半实心轮胎。

cush·ion·y [ˈkuʃəni; ˋkʊʃənɪ] *a*. **1.** 垫子似的;柔软的。**2.** = cushy.

Cush·it·ic [kʌˈʃitik, kuʃ-; kʌˋʃɪtɪk, kʊʃ-] **I** *a*. (东非的)库什特语族的。**II** *n*. 库什特语族。

cush·y [ˈkuʃi; ˋkʊʃɪ] *a*. **1.** 〔俚〕容易的,(工作)轻松的,舒适的。**2.** 〔军俚〕(伤等)轻的,不要紧的。*all very* ~ 〔口〕非常愉快。

cusk [kʌsk; kʌsk] *n*. (*pl*. ~*s*, 〔集合词〕~)【动】卡斯克鳕,单鳍鳕。

cusp [kʌsp; kʌsp] *n*. **1.** (齿、叶等的)尖端,尖头。**2.** 【天】月角;【建】尖角;【数】(二曲线的)尖点,歧点,会切点;(曲线等的)波峰。**-ed** [kʌspt; kʌspt] *a*. 有尖的

(*~ed arch*【建】尖拱)。

cus·pate [ˈkʌspit, -ˌpeit; ˋkʌspɪt, -ˏpet] *a*. 尖的,(叶子等)有尖端的(= cuspated, cusped)。

cus·pid [ˈkʌspid; ˋkʌspɪd] *n*. (人的)犬齿。

cus·pi·dal [ˈkʌspidl; ˋkʌspɪdl] *a*. 尖的,有尖端的。

cus·pi·date, cus·pi·dat·ed [ˈkʌspideit, -id; ˋkʌspɪˏdet, -ɪd] *a*. 尖的;(叶子等)有尖端的。*a ~ tooth* 犬齿。

cus·pi·da·tion [ˌkʌspiˈdeiʃən; ˏkʌspɪˋdeʃən] *n*.【建】尖形饰,饰以尖头[尖顶]。

cus·pi·dor(e) [ˈkʌspidɔː; ˋkʌspəˏdɔr] *n*.〔美〕痰盂。

C

cuss [kʌs; kʌs] **I** *n*. **1**.〔口〕粗话,诅咒。**2**.〔美口〕古怪可憎的东西〔指人或动物〕。*a queer ~* 怪家伙。***not care a ~*** 毫不介意。***not worth a tinker's ~*** 一文不值。**II** *vt*., *vi*.〔口〕= curse.

cuss·ed [ˈkʌsid; ˋkʌsɪd] *a*.〔美口〕**1**. = cursed. **2**. 别扭的,性子拗的。**-ly** *ad*.〔口〕别扭地,拗着。

cuss·ed·ness [ˈkʌsidnis; ˋkʌsɪdnɪs] *n*.〔美口〕乖戾;(事情)别扭;不如意。

cus·tard [ˈkʌstəd; ˋkʌstɚd] *n*. 乳蛋糕,蛋羹。~ **apple**【植】番荔枝,释迦果。~ **glass** 乳黄色(不透明)玻璃。~ **pudding** 乳蛋布丁。

Cus·ter [ˈkʌstə; ˋkʌstɚ] *n*. 卡斯特〔姓氏〕。

cus·to·des [kʌsˈtəudiːz; kʌsˋtodiz] custos 的复数。

cus·to·di·al [kʌsˈtəudjəl; kʌsˋtodɪəl] **I** *a*. 看管的,管理的,保管的;看守的。*a ~ engineer*〔美〕房屋看管人。*a ~ officer* 物资保管员;〔美〕狱吏。**II** *n*.【宗】圣物保藏器。

cus·to·di·an [kʌsˈtəudjən; kʌsˋtodɪən] *n*. 看管人,管理人;保管人。**-ship** *n*. 看守人[保管人]的职位[责任]。

cus·to·dy [ˈkʌstədi; ˋkʌstədɪ] *n*. **1**. 保管,管理;保护,监护,看守。**2**. 拘留,监禁,收容。***be in the ~ of*** 托…保管,受…监视;受…保护。***have the ~ of*** 保管;保护。***in ~*** 被监禁,被拘留着。***in the ~ of*** 在…监护下。***keep (sb.) in ~*** 拘留(某人)。***take sb. into ~*** 逮捕,拘留(某人)。

cus·tom [ˈkʌstəm; ˋkʌstəm] **I** *n*. **1**. 习惯,风俗;惯例,常规;【法】习惯法。**2**. 经常光顾;〔集合词〕顾客,主顾。**3**. 〔the ~s〕海关;〔*pl*.〕关税。**4**.【史】经常赋役。*as his ~ then was* 照他当时的习惯。*social ~s* 社会风俗。***have plenty of ~*** (商店等)经常主顾多。***have sb.'s ~*** 受某人照顾。***present* [*give*] *one's ~ to ...*** 经常光顾,成为…的经常主顾。**II** *a*.〔美〕(衣服等)定做的,定制的。**~-built** *a*. 定制的。~ **cloth** [**suit**]〔美〕定做的(讲究的)衣服。**~s detention** 海关扣留。**~(s)-house** [**office**] 海关(*a ~(s) house broker* 代客报关服务行)。**~-made** = ~-built. **~tailor 1**. *n*.〔美〕承接定做衣服的裁缝。**2**. *vt*. 定制,定做。**~s clearance** 出口结关。**~s duty** [**due**] 关税。**~s entry** 进口报关。**~s shed** [**warehouse**] 海关仓库,关栈。**~s tariff** 关税率。**~-tailor** *vt*. 分别对待,分别计划;按各种规格改制[设计、建造]。

cus·tom·a·ble [ˈkʌstəməbl; ˋkʌstəməbl̩] *a*.〔主美〕可征收关税的。

cus·tom·a·ri·ly [ˈkʌstəmərili; ˋkʌstəmərɪlɪ] *ad*. 照例,通常,素来,习惯上。

cus·tom·a·ry [ˈkʌstəməri; ˋkʌstəmˏɛrɪ] **I** *a*. 通常的,向来的;照惯例的。*a ~ law* 习惯法。**II** *n*.〔*pl*.〕风俗志,习俗志。

cus·tom·er [ˈkʌstəmə; ˋkʌstəmɚ] *n*. **1**. (经常的)顾客,主顾,客户,买主。**2**.〔口〕(打交道的)人,家伙;〔*pl*.〕〔美口〕观众,听众。*a queer ~* 怪人,好笑的家伙。*a tough ~* 粗暴的[难对付的]家伙。

cus·tom·ize [ˈkʌstəmaiz; ˋkʌstəmˏaɪz] *vt*. 定制,定做;按规格改制。

cus·tos [ˈkʌstɔs; ˋkʌstɑs] *n*.〔L.〕(*pl*. ***cus·to·des*** [kʌsˈtəudiːz; kʌsˋtodiz])〔L.〕保管人;看守人。~ ***rotulorum*** [rɔtjuˈlɔːrəm; rɔtjuˋlɔrəm]〔英〕(兼管文件的)郡法院首席法官。

cus·tu·mal [ˈkʌstjuməl; ˋkʌstjʊməl] *n*. (某一城市的)习俗志。

cut [kʌt; kʌt] **I** *vt*. (*cut*; *cut·ting*) **1**. 切,割,截,斩,砍(树),剪(发等);切断,割下;采伐;剪下;修剪,刈。*I have ~ my finger*. 我切伤了指头。*I had my hair ~ at the barber's*. 我在理发店理了发了。**2**. 削减(物价等),节减(费用);删节(文章等)。*~ prices* 降价。*~ an article* 删节一篇文章。**3**. 开辟,开凿,挖掘;(船)破(浪)前进;(鸟)掠(空)而飞。*The ship ~ her way through the waves*. 船破浪前进。**4**. 雕,刻,琢磨(宝石等)。*~ a figure in stone* 雕刻石像。**5**. 剪裁,裁(衣)。*The jacket was cut too long*. 这件短上衣裁剪得太长。**6**.〔口〕停止,断绝(关系);〔口〕缺(课),怠(课),停(课);〔口〕假装没看见,不睬,不理。*~ school* 逃学。*He ~ me in the street*. 他在街上假装没看见我。**7**.【数】(线)切,交,相交。*One line ~s another at right angles*. 两线相交成直角。**8**.〔口〕显出。*He ~s a poor figure*. 他显得可怜,他显得寒酸。**9**. (用鞭子)抽打;使像刀切一样疼痛;使极为痛心;(风等)刺骨,透彻心肺。*The cold wind ~s me to the bone*. 寒风刺骨。*~ to the heart* 使深深地感到痛心。**10**. 溶解,搀,混合。*~ resin with alcohol* 用酒精溶解树脂。**11**. 生,长,出(牙齿)。**12**. 阉割,骟(马)。**13**. (球)斜打,削(球);【牌】切(牌)〔把另一人洗好的一叠牌从上面随便拿一叠部分换在下面〕;【影】停止拍摄;剪辑(胶片)。**14**. 录音于(磁带等上)。—*vi*. **1**. 切;(锐利)能切,(被)切,(被)割断,(被)剪裁。*This knife ~s well*. 这把小刀很快。**2**. 切开,切进(*through*)。**3**. (牙齿)长出。**4**. 横切,横穿过,直穿过,走近路(*across*)。**5**.〔口〕急忙走开,跑开;跑;〔命令〕去! 滚! *I ~ after him with all speed*. 我拼命赶他。*I must ~*. 我要跑了。*C- (it)!* 滚! **6**. 像刀割似地使人感到疼痛。*The wind ~s*. 风如刀割。**7**. (画色)过浓。**8**.〔俚〕缺课。**9**.〔美〕尽投一[二]人的票。**10**.【牌】切牌;削球。~ ***a fat hog***〔美俚〕虚摆架子,虚张声势。~ ***a joke*** 说笑,打诨。~ ***a loss*** 趁损失不大而及早丢手,相机撤手,知难而退。~ ***a melon***〔美俚〕分配[分得]巨大利益。~ ***a swath***〔美俚〕成名,有名起来。~ ***a ticket***〔美俚〕全给一个候选人投票。~ ***a tooth*** 长牙齿;长见识。~ ***about*** 乱跑。~ ***across*** 抄近路穿过,对直穿过。~ ***adrift*** 分别,永远走掉。~ ***and carve*** 切开,分割。***C- and come again*** (请)尽量吃。~ ***and run***〔口〕连忙逃走。~ ***at*** 猛打,痛打;〔口〕使(精神上)受重大打击;打断(希望等);砍,斩。~ ***away* 1**. 匆匆跑掉,逃走。**2**. 切开,剪去,切去;连砍,乱砍。~ ***back* 1**. 回叙往事;(影片中为强调前面某一镜头而)再次映出;倒叙。**2**. 中止(合同等)。**3**.【化】稀释。**4**. 缩减。**5**. 修剪(树枝等)。**6**. (足球)急退。~ ***both ways*** 抱骑墙态度。~ ***(sb.) dead*** 见到(某人)假装不认识,不理睬(某人)。~ ***down*** 砍倒;削减,缩减;减价,减低;使失色,夺去…活动力,(疾病)使(人)躺倒。~ ***fine*** 只能得到极少的利益。~ ***in* 1**. 突然插入。**2**. (汽车)超车。**3**. 抢去别人的舞伴。**4**. 在电话里窃听。**5**. 把…剁入。**6**.【电】接通。~ ***into*** 插入话头;多嘴,干涉;打断(话头)突然加入。~ ***it***〔命令式〕停止! 别响! ~ ***it (too) fat***〔俚〕做得过分,做得过火。~ ***it fine*** 尽量节约(时间、用费等)。~ ***it out***〔俚〕停止! 别响! ~ ***it quick*** 快去,快逃! ~ ***loose* 1**. 割断绳索[铁链],放下,放开,断绝(关系),摆脱(束缚)。**2**. 逃;随意去做,自由行动。**3**. 开始攻击;开始活动。**4**.〔美俚〕痛痛快快讲,痛饮。~ ***lots*** 抽签。~ ***no ice***〔俚〕毫无效果,不起作用;无关紧要。~ ***off* 1**. 切开,切断,割掉,削除,伐除;截止;截断(退路等),断绝(关系等)。**2**. 妨害;使(人)闭口无言。**3**. (病等)把(人)弄死(*be ~ off in one's prime* 盛年夭折)。~ ***off with a shilling*** (只给一先令)实际断绝继承关系。~ ***on*** 急速前进。~ ***on the right side***〔美俚〕赚到钱。~ ***one's coat according to one's cloth*** 量入为出,量体裁衣。~ ***one's stick*** 逃。~ ***out* 1**. 割掉;除去,删

去;剪下;开辟。**2.** 裁制(衣服)。**3.** 使适合(*be* ~ *out for the job* 天性适合那个工作)。**4.** 筹划,设计,准备,预备。**5.** 遮断(*from*)。**6.** 取而代之,抢先一着,胜过;夺取,捕获(敌船)。**7.** 〔美俚〕停止(~ *it* [*that*] *out* 停止!别响!)。~ ***over*** 【林】主伐。~ ***prices*** [〔美〕***rates***](为竞争而)减价。~ ***round*** 〔美〕卖弄,夸示,故意做给人看。~ ***short*** **1.** 打断(讲话);使停止。**2.** 缩减;缩短,从简(*to* ~ *the matter short* 简单地说,总之。*C- it short!* 〔口〕讲得简单点!别说了! *I* ~ *him short*. 不让他讲下去)。~ ***the buck*** 〔美俚〕满足要求。~ ***the comedy*** 〔美俚〕别开无聊的玩笑,别演戏吧! ~ ***the gun*** 制止发动机[马达]。~ ***the*** (***Gordian***) ***knot*** 快刀斩乱麻似地处理(难事)。~ ***the mustard*** 〔美俚〕满足要求。~ ***the record*** 【体】打破纪录。~ ***the rough stuff*** 〔美俚〕矫正粗鲁的行为。~ ***to pieces*** 切碎,粉碎(敌军);严厉批评(新书)。~ ***to the bone*** (把价钱等)减到不能再减。~ ***under*** 〔美〕落价卖,亏本卖。~ ***up*** **1.** 割裂;弄伤;歼灭(敌军)。**2.** 酷评,痛骂,使心痛。**3.** 连根拔除,根绝;【林】带伐。**4.** 〔美〕引起(骚动)。**5.** 卖弄,耍花招。**6.** 杀,宰;可宰;可裁。**7.** 留下遗产(*This ox will* ~ *up well*. 这头牛壮得可以宰杀了。*He* ~ *up fat* [*very well*]. 他留下不少财产)。~ ***up rough*** [***savage***, ***crusty***, ***stiff***, ***ugly***, ***nasty***] 忿怒,发脾气,横暴起来。

II ***a*.** **1.** 切过的,切下的,修过的,剪过的,剪下的;【植】尖裂的。**2.** 刻好的,雕好了的;磨过的;加过工的。**3.** 削减了的,缩小了的。**4.** (牲畜等)阉过的;〔俚〕喝醉了的。~ *flowers* 瓶花。~ *glass* 雕花玻璃。~ *horse* 骟过的马。~ *plane* 剖面。~ *alchy* [ˈælki; ˋælkɪ] 〔美俚〕酒。***at*** ~ ***rate*** 〔美〕打折扣(卖等)。~ ***out for*** 〔口〕适于,合适。***finely*** ~ ***features*** 端正秀丽的容貌。

III ***n*.** **1.** 刀伤,切口,伤口;一切,一击,一刀[剑、鞭等]。**2.** 隧道;坑;运河,沟渠;挖土,挖方。**3.** 一片,一块,切片;〔美〕肉片;〔口〕分得的份儿;(一张唱片内的)一首歌曲;【影】剪辑;书面[镜头]的突然转变;〔美〕被排挤掉的候选人。**4.** (印刷用的)铜板,木板(等);版面,木刻画;插画,插图。**5.** 【牌】(牌洗好后)切牌;切牌人;(球戏)斜打,削球。**6.** 近路,捷径(= *short* ~)。**7.** 剪裁(法),做法;制作,加工;样式,类型。**8.** 无情的攻击,尖锐的讽刺;不理睬,不打招呼。**9.** 削减,削除;删节;减价;〔美〕折扣,减低(租金等)。**10.** (学生的)旷课,缺课,逃学。**11.** 黄麻支数长度单位(〔英〕=300 码)。***a*** ~ ***above*** [***below***] 〔口〕高[低]一等,胜[次]于。(*This was*) ***a*** ~ ***at*** (*me*)(这是)对(我)的攻击。***a*** ~ ***off the nut*** 〔谑〕菜食,素食。~ ***of one's face*** 相貌。~ ***of one's jib*** 外表,仪表。~ ***of timber*** 木材的采伐量。~ ***of wool*** 剪毛量。***draw*** ~***s*** 抽签。***give*** (*one*) ***the*** ~ ***direct*** (故意)不理睬(人)。***have*** [***take***] ***a*** ~ 吃(一片肉的)简单的饭食。***the most unkindest*** ~ ***of all*** 无情到极点的作风[举动]。~**-and-come-again** ***n*.** (肉等的)尽量吃;丰富,丰饶。~**-and-dry** [**-dried**] ***a*.** **1.** 早已准备好的。**2.** 呆板的。~ **and thrust** 劈刺;肉搏;激战;激烈争吵。~**-and-thrust** ***a*.**, ***n*.** 劈刺两用的(剑)。~**-and-try** ***a*.** 试验性的。~**-away** ***a*.**, ***n*.** 下摆裁成圆角的(上衣)(特指常礼服)。~**-back** (电影等)倒叙;【园艺】剪枝;修剪过的果树;〔美〕削减生产,减产;(冲浪运动中的)冲浪急转;回冲浪峰。~ **bank** 陡岸。~**-grass** 【植】李氏禾(属)。~**-in** **1.** ***n*.** 【影】插入字幕;【印】(插图等的)插入,排入;【火箭】接通,开动。**2.** ***a*.** 插入的。~ **number** 【影】镜头号码。~**off** **1.** 〔美〕近路,捷径。**2.** 【机】停车(装置);【火箭】切断,停止工作。**3.** 〔美〕运河。~**out** **1.** 挖去,剪去;(幼儿书的)剪纸;(卡通片中用的)剪纸画;嵌花;(著作等的)删去部分。**2.** 【电】断流器,保险装置;(内燃机的)排气阀。~ **over** **1.** 〔美〕树木砍光了的原野(*a* ~ *over forest* 主伐林)。**2.** 【讯】接入。~**purse** 扒手。~**-rate** ***a*.** 减价的,便宜的;次等的。~**throat** **1.** ***n*.** 凶手;〔Scot.〕角灯;〔美〕(涩味)红葡萄。**2.** ***a*.** 杀人的,凶恶的,残忍的;剧烈的;【牌】三人玩的。~**-up** **1.** 打击,酷评,痛骂。**2.** 〔美俚〕爱打诨的人,爱诙谐的人。~**water** **1.** 【海】船头破浪处;桥墩的分水角。**2.** 黑色楸水鸟。~**-work** 挖花花边〔桌布等〕。~**worm** 【虫】夜盗虫,鳞翅目幼虫。

cut·a·bil·i·ty [ˌkʌtəˈbiliti; ˏkʌtəˋbɪlətɪ] ***n*.** **1.** 可割,可分割。**2.** 净肉〔屠宰后牲畜躯体上可供出售的瘦肉的分量〕。

cu·ta·ne·ous [kju(:)ˈteinjəs; kjuˋteniəs] ***a*.** 皮肤(上)的;影响皮肤的。

cutch [kʌtʃ; kʌtʃ] ***n*.** 【植】儿茶(= catechu)。

cut·cher·ry, cut·chery [kʌˈtʃeri; kʌˋtʃɛrɪ] ***n*.** 〔印度〕行政机关;法院;种植园事务所。

cute [kjuːt; kjut] **I** ***a*.** 〔美口〕**1.** 聪明的,伶俐的;逗人爱的。**2.** 做作的。~ ***as a bug's ear*** 〔美口〕非常可爱的[美丽的]。**II** ***n*.** 〔美俚〕25 分(硬币)。**-ly** ***ad*.** **-ness** ***n*.**

cu·tey [ˈkjuːti; ˋkjutɪ] ***n*.** **1.** 〔口〕灵巧的美人儿〔尤指少妇〕。**2.** 〔俚〕(安插在敌方内部的)内线;巧妙的策略[手腕]。

Cuth·bert [ˈkʌθbət; ˋkʌθbɚt] ***n*.** **1.** 卡斯伯特〔姓氏,男子名〕。**2.** 〔c-〕〔英俚〕(借口公务)逃避兵役的人。

cu·ti·cle [ˈkjuːtikl; ˋkjutɪkl] ***n*.** 【解】表皮,护膜;【生】角质层;角皮,小皮;(液面的)薄膜。**-u·lar** [-ˈtikjulə; -ˋtɪkjʊlɚ] ***a*.**

cut·ie [ˈkjuːti; ˋkjutɪ] ***n*.** **1.** = cutey. **2.** 机智灵巧的运动员。**3.** 欺骗行为。***a*** ~ ***pie*** **1.** 灵巧可爱的人;情人。**2.** 携带式辐射能测定仪。

cu·tin [ˈkjuːtin; ˋkjutɪn] ***n*.** 【植】角质,蜡状质。

cu·tin·i·za·tion [ˌkjuːtiniˈzeiʃən; ˏkjutɪnɪˋzeʃən] ***n*.** 【植】角化(作用)。**cu·tin·i·ze** [-aiz; -aɪz] ***vt*.**, ***vi*.** (使)角化。

cu·tis [ˈkjuːtis; ˋkjutɪs] ***n*.** (*pl*. ~***es***, ***cu·tes*** [ˈkjuːtiz; ˋkjutɪz]) 〔L.〕【解】真皮,下皮肤;【植】表皮。~ **plate** 生皮层,皮节。

cut·las(s) [ˈkʌtləs; ˋkʌtləs] ***n*.** (从前水手用以肉搏的)短剑[刀],弯刀。

cut·ler [ˈkʌtlə; ˋkʌtlɚ] ***n*.** 刀匠;卖刀人;磨刀人;刀具商,刀具制造人。

cut·ler·y [ˈkʌtləri; ˋkʌtlərɪ] ***n*.** 刀具;餐刀;刀剑制造[修理、贩卖]业者。

cut·let [ˈkʌtlit; ˋkʌtlɪt] ***n*.** (炸)肉片,(炸)肉排。

cut·or [ˈkjuːtə; ˋkjutɚ] ***n*.** 〔美俚〕检察官。

cut·ter [ˈkʌtə; ˋkʌtɚ] ***n*.** **1.** 切者;裁衣人;【影】剪辑员。**2.** 切刀,切断机;刻纹[录音]头,利齿,门牙,前牙。**3.** 〔美〕(单马)小橇;〔美俚〕检察官。**4.** 【海军】小汽艇;独桅前后帆快船。**5.** 砌面砖。**6.** 〔美〕老牛。*a life* ~ 救生艇。

cut·ting [ˈkʌtiŋ; ˋkʌtɪŋ] **I** ***n*.** **1.** 切断,切下;切片;【园艺】扦插,插条;〔英〕剪裁,(报纸等的)剪辑;(宝石等的)加工,琢磨,开凿。**2.** 大贱卖;剧烈的竞争。**3.** 【林】采伐;【畜】剪毛。**4.** (马的)互踢。**5.** 【机】切削。~ ***into the womb*** 剖腹产术。**II** ***a*.** **1.** 切得动的,锐利的。**2.** 像刀割似的;刺骨的。**3.** 讽刺的,尖酸刻薄的。**4.** (目光)炯炯的,敏锐的。**5.** 〔俚〕卖得贱的。~ *wind* 刺骨的寒风。~ *retort* 尖锐的反驳。~ *trade* 薄利多销。~ **continuity** 【影】剪辑用脚本。~ **edge** 前沿,尖端。~ **paper dolls** 〔美口〕被打得头昏眼花,眩晕。~ **tool** 切削工具。**-ly** ***ad*.**

cut·tle·bone [ˈkʌtlbəun; ˋkʌtḷˏbon] ***n*.** 乌贼骨,墨鱼骨,海螵蛸。

cut·tle·fish [ˈkʌtlfiʃ; ˋkʌtlˏfɪʃ] ***n*.** 【动】乌贼,墨鱼。~ **tactics** (驱逐舰等的)烟幕战术。

cut·ty [ˈkʌti; ˋkʌtɪ] **I** ***a*.** 〔Scot.〕**1.** 切短的。**2.** 性急的。**II** ***n*.** **1.** 短匙;(陶制的)短柄烟斗;短胖的女人。**2.** 〔口〕品行坏的女人;〔谑〕脾气大的女人。**3.** 兔子;气枪。~ *stool* 矮凳;〔古〕〔Scot.〕(给奸妇坐的)忏悔椅。

cu·vette [kjuːˈvet; kjuˋvɛt] ***n*.** (度谱术和光度术使用的)小玻璃管;透明小容器;小池,电池。

Cu·vier [ˈkjuːviei; ˋkjuvɪˏe] ***n*.** **1.** 居维叶(姓氏)。**2.**

Georges ～ 格·居维叶〔1769—1832,法国自然科学家,比较解剖学的创始者〕。

cuz [kəz;kəz] *conj*.〔口〕因为(=because)。

Cuz·co [ˈkuːskəu; ˋkusko] *n*. 库斯科〔秘鲁城市〕。

cv. = convertible.

c. v. = coefficient of variation【纺】变异系数,变差系数。

C. V. = Common Version (基督教《圣经》的)通行本。

CW, cw, c-w = **1.** continuous wave 等幅波;连续波。**2.** cosine wave 余弦波。**3.** clockwise 顺时针(方向)。

CWA = Civil Works Administration〔美〕土木工程署。

CWAR = continuous wave acquisition radar 等幅波搜索雷达。

C

cwm [kuːm; kum] *n*.【地】圆形峪(= cirque)。

c. w. o. = cash with order【商】定购即付,定货付款。

C. W. O. = Chief Warrant Officer〔美〕(陆军或空军)一级准尉。

CWS = Chemical Warfare Service〔美〕化学兵,化学勤务。

cwt. = hundredweight (=〔L.〕*centum* + *weight*)。

cy. = copy; currency.

-cy *suf*. 表示"状态","性质","职权","地位":**1.** 加于词尾为 -t 或 -n 的名词后:bankrupt*cy*, captain*cy*. **2.** 使动词变成名词:occupan*cy* (< occupy), vacan*cy* (< vacate). **3.** 使词尾为 -ant, -ent, -te, -tic 等的形容词变成名词:ascendan*cy* (< ascend*ant*), expedien*cy* (< expedi*ent*), adequa*cy* (< adequa*te*), luna*cy* (< luna*tic*).

cyan- *comb. f*. (接元音或 h-) = cyano-.

cy·an·am·ide [saiˈænəmaid;ˏsaɪəˋnæmaɪd] *n*.【化】**1.** 氰(化)胺,氨基氰。**2.** 氨腈 (RNHCN)。

cy·a·nate [ˈsaiəneit; ˋsaɪəˏnet] *n*.【化】氰酸盐。

cy·an·ic [saiˈænik; saɪˋænɪk] *a*. **1.**【化】氰的,含氰的。**2.** 青蓝色的。～ **acid** 氰酸。

cy·a·nide [ˈsaiənaid; ˋsaɪəˏnaɪd], **cy·a·nid** [-nid; -nɪd] **I** *n*.【化】氰化物。～ *process* 氰化(物)法〔用氰化物从矿物中提取贵金属的方法〕。**II** *vt*. 用氰化法处理。

cy·a·nine [ˈsaiənain; ˋsaɪəˏnin] *n*. 花青(染料)。

cy·a·nite [ˈsaiənait; ˋsaɪəˏnaɪt] *n*.【矿】蓝晶石。

cyano- *comb. f*. **1.** 表示"氰","氰化物"。**2.** 表示"青","深蓝"。

cy·a·no·co·bal·a·min [ˌsaiənəukəˈbɔləmin;ˏsaɪənokoˋbæləmɪn] *n*.【生化】维生素 B_{12}。

cy·an·o·gen [saiˈænədʒin; saɪˋænədʒən] *n*.【化】氰〔即乙二腈 ethane dinitrile〕。

cy·a·no·ge·net·ic, cy·a·no·gen·ic [ˌsaiənəudʒiˈnetik, ˈsaiənəuˈdʒenik;ˏsaɪənodʒɪˋnɛtɪk, ˏsaɪənoˋdʒɛnɪk] *a*. 能产生氰化物的。

cy·a·no·hy·drin [ˌsaiənəuˈhaidrin;ˏsaɪənoˋdrɪn] *n*.【化】借醇腈,氰醇。

cy·a·nom·e·ter [ˌsaiəˈnɔmitə;ˏsaɪəˋnɑmɪtɚ] *n*. (测量天空、海洋蓝度的)蓝度表。

Cy·a·no·phy·ce·ae [ˈsaiənəuˈfaisei:; ˋsaɪənoˋfaɪsɛi] *n*.【植】蓝藻网。**-phy·cean** *n*., *a*. 蓝藻(的)。

cy·a·no·sis [ˌsaiəˈnəusis;ˏsaɪəˋnosɪs] *n*.【医】青紫,发绀。

cy·a·not·ic [ˌsaiəˈnɔtik;ˏsaɪəˋnɑtɪk] *a*.【医】发绀的,青紫的。

cy·an·o·type [saiˈænətaip; saɪˋænəˏtaɪp] *n*. 蓝晒[氰印]相片(法);晒蓝图。

cy·a·nu·rate [ˌsaiəˈnjuːreit, -it;ˏsaɪəˋnjuret, -ɪt] *n*.【化】三聚氰酸脂,三聚氰酸盐。

cy·a·nu·ric [ˌsaiəˈnjuərik;ˏsaɪəˋnurɪk] *a*. ～ **acid**【化】氰尿酸,三聚氰酸。

Cyb·e·le [ˈsibili; ˋsɪblɪ] *n*.【希神】母神〔小亚细亚神话中女神,作为自然之母的象征〕。

cy·ber [ˈsaibə;ˋsaɪbə] *a*. 电脑(网络)的。～(-)**café** 网络咖啡馆,网吧。～**punk** 黑客电脑高手。～**space** 网络空间,虚拟现实。～**speak** 网络用语。～**surf** 网上冲浪,网上漫游。

cy·ber·cul·ture [ˈsaibəˌkʌltʃə; ˋsaɪbəˏkʌltʃɚ] *n*. 电脑文化〔指社会文化在电子计算机影响下的状态〕。**-tural** *a*.

cy·ber·ia [ˈsaibəriə;ˋsaɪbərɪə] *n*.【计】网络世界。

cy·ber·ize [ˈsaibəraiz;ˋsaɪbəraɪz] *vt*. 使联网。

cy·ber·nate [ˈsaibəneit; ˋsaɪbəˏnet] *vt*. 以电子计算机和自动化控制,使电子计算机化和自动化。

cy·ber·na·tion [ˌsaibəˈneiʃən;ˏsaɪbəˋneʃən] *n*. 电子计算机和自动化控制。

cy·ber·naut [ˈsaibənaut;ˋsaɪbənot] *n*. 网络用户,网民。

cy·ber·net·ic [ˌsaibəːˈnetik;ˏsaɪbɚˋnɛtɪk] *a*. 控制论的。

cy·ber·net·i·cist [ˌsaibəːˈnetisist;ˏsaɪbɚˋnɛtɪsɪst] *n*. 控制论学者,自动化专家。

cy·ber·net·ics [ˈsaibəːˈnetiks;ˏsaɪbɚˋnɛtɪks] *n*. 控制论。

cy·borg [ˈsaibɔːg; ˋsaɪbɔrg] *n*. **1.** (在太空)靠机械装置维持生命的人。**2.** 受控机体〔部分机能被各种电子装置控制或代替了的人或其他生物体〕。

cyb·o·tac·tic [ˌsibəˈtæktik;ˏsɪbəˋtæktɪk] *a*.【化】群聚的。

cyc., cyclo. = cyclopaedia; cyclopaedic.

cy·cad [ˈsaikæd; ˋsaɪkæd] *n*. 铁树目裸子植物。

cy·cas [ˈsaikəs; ˋsaɪkəs] *n*.【植】铁树,苏铁。

cycl- *comb. f*. (循)环;回旋[转];环(状,合,化);圆〔辅音前用 cyclo-〕。

cy·cla·mate [ˈsaikləmeit, ˈsiklə-; ˋsaɪkləˏmet, ˋsɪklə-] *n*.【化】环己胺磺酸盐。

cyc·la·men [ˈsikləmən; ˋsɪkləmən] *n*.【植】仙客来。

cy·cle [ˈsaikl; ˋsaɪkl] **I** *n*. **1.** 循环,周期,一转。**2.** 周时,周年,年纪。**3.** (诗、故事等的)始末。**4.** 自行车,三轮车,摩托车。**5.**【电】周波;【数】环;【拓】闭链;【地】旋回;【植】(从枯凋到再生的)一轮回;天体运转的轨道。*the business* ～ 商业盛衰的周期性。*the life* ～【生】生命周期,生活史。*the Arthurian* ～《亚瑟王记》。*the Calippic* ～ 七十六年周期。*the Trojan* ～《特洛伊战争史诗集》。**II** *vi*. **1.** 轮转,循环。**2.** 骑自行车[三轮车等]。—*vt*. 使循环,使轮转。～**car** (机动)三轮车[四轮车]。**-ry** (出售或修理自行车的)自行车铺。

cy·cler [ˈsaiklə; ˋsaɪklɚ] *n*. **1.**【空】周期计。**2.**〔主美〕= cyclist.

cy·cler·y [ˈsaikləri; ˋsaɪklərɪ] *n*. (兼营出售和维修业务的)自行车行。

cy·clic, cy·cli·cal [ˈsaiklik, -likəl; ˋsaɪklɪk, -lɪkəl] *a*. **1.** 周期的;轮转的,循环的。**2.**【化】环状的;【植】轮列的,轮卷的。**3.** 组诗的;故事始末的。～ **flower** 轮生花。～ **number**【数】完全数。～ **poets** (歌咏特洛伊战争等故事的)史诗诗人。

cy·clist [ˈsaiklist; ˋsaɪklɪst] *n*.〔英〕骑自行车[摩托车]的人。

cy·cli·za·tion [ˌsaikliˈzeiʃən;ˏsaɪklɪˋzeʃən] *n*.【化】环合,环的形成。

cy·cli·zine [ˈsaikliˌziːn; ˋsaɪklɪˏzin] *n*.【药】环嗪,马内嗪〔一种抗组胺药〕。

cy·clo [ˈsiːkləu, ˈsaikləu; ˋsiklo, ˋsaɪklo] *n*. (出租载客的)三轮摩托车 (= ～taxi)。～**-pousse** [ˌsiːkləuˈpuːs;ˏsikloˋpus] (载客的)脚踏三轮车,摩托三轮车。

cyclo- *comb. f*. = cycl-.

cy·clo·bu·tane [ˈsaikləuˈbjuːtein; ˋsaɪkloˋbjuten] *n*.【化】环丁烷。

cy·clo·cross [ˌsaikləuˈkrɔs;ˏsaɪkloˋkrɑs] *n*.【体】摩托车越野赛。

cy·clo·graph [ˈsaikləugrɑːf; ˋsaɪkləˏgræf] *n*. **1.** 圆弧规。**2.**【摄】轮转全景照相机。**3.** 金属硬度测定仪。

cy·clo·hex·ane [ˌsaikləuˈheksein;ˏsaɪkloˋhɛksen] *n*.【化】环己烷。

cy·clo·hex·i·mide [ˌsaikləuˈheksimaid; ˏsaɪkloˋhɛksɪmaɪd] *n*. 【微】放线(菌)酮,环己酰亚胺。

cy·cloid [ˈsaiklɔid; ˋsaɪklɔɪd] **I** *n*. **1.** 【数】摆线,旋轮[圆滚]线。**2.** 【动】圆鳞鱼。**3.** 循环精神病。**II** *a*. **1.** 圈状的,圆形的。**2.** (有)圆鳞的。**3.** 易患循环精神病的。

cy·cloi·dal [saiˈklɔidl; saɪˋklɔɪdl] *a*. **1.** 摆线的。**2.** (鱼鳞)圆形的。

cy·clom·e·ter [saiˈklɔmitə; saɪˋklɑmətə] *n*. **1.** 回转计,转数表。**2.** 里程表。**3.** 圆弧测定器。

cy·clom·e·try [saiˈklɔmitri; saɪˋklɑmətrɪ] *n*. 【数】测圆法。

cy·clone [ˈsaikləun; ˋsaɪklon] *n*. **1.** 【气】气旋;旋风。**2.** 旋风器,吸尘器。**3.** 【化】环酮,四芳基茂酮。~ *cellar* [*pit*] 〔美〕(草原地带的)旋风避难穴;逃避处。~ *wind* 气旋风。**cy·clon·ic** *a*.

cy·clo·nite [ˈsaikləunait; ˋsaɪkloˏnaɪt] *n*. 【化】旋风〔黑索今〕炸药,六素精,三次甲基三硝基胺。

cy·clo·o·le·fin [ˌsaikləuˈəuləfin; ˏsaɪkloˋoləfɪn] *n*. 【化】环烯。

cy·clo·p(a)e·di·a [ˌsaikləuˈpiːdjə; ˏsaɪkləˋpidiə] *n*. 百科全书。

cy·clo·p(a)e·dic [ˌsaikləuˈpiːdik; ˏsaɪkləˋpidɪk] *a*. 百科全书的;渊博的,广泛的。

cy·clo·par·af·fin [ˌsaikləuˈpærəfin; ˏsaɪkloˋpærəfɪn] *n*. 【化】环烷(属)烃,环烷。

Cy·clo·pe·an, Cy·clo·pi·an, Cy·clop·ic [saiˈkləupjən, ˌsaiˈklɔpik; ˏsaɪkləˋpjən, ˏsaɪˋklɑpɪk] *a*. **1.** 【希神】独眼巨人的。**2.** 〔c-〕巨大的;【建】巨石堆积的。

cy·clo·pen·tane [ˌsaikləuˈpentein; ˏsaɪkloˋpenten] *n*. 【化】环戊烷。

cy·clo·ple·gi·a [ˌsaikləuˈpliːdʒiə; ˏsaɪkləˋplidʒɪə] *n*. 【医】睫状肌麻痹。**-ple·gic** [-dʒik; -dʒɪk] *a*.

cy·clo·pro·pane [ˌsaikləuˈprəupein; ˏsaɪkləˋpropen] *n*. 【药】环丙烷〔麻醉剂〕。

Cy·clops [ˈsaiklɔps; ˋsaɪklɑps] *n*. (*pl*. ***Cy·clo·pes*** [saiˈkləupiːz; saɪˋklopiz], *~es*) 【希神】独眼巨人;〔喻〕独眼人。

cy·clo·ra·ma [ˌsaikləuˈrɑːmə; ˏsaɪkləˋrɑmə] *n*. **1.** 环形画景。**2.** 【剧】半圆形透视背景。**-ram·ic** *a*.

cy·clo·sis [saiˈkləusis; saɪˋklosɪs] *n*. 【生】(细胞中的)胞质环流。

cy·clos·to·mate [saiˈklɔstəmeit; saɪˋklɑstəmɪt] *a*. 【动】**1.** 有圆口的。**2.** 圆口动物的 (= cyclostomatous)。

cy·clo·stome [ˈsaikləustəum; ˋsaɪkləˏstom] *n*. 【动】圆口类(亚纲)。

cy·clo·style [ˈsaikləustail; ˋsaɪkləˏstaɪl] *n*. **1.** 滚齿轮铁笔复写器。**2.** 围柱式建筑物。

cy·clo·thyme [ˈsaikləuθaim; ˋsaɪkloˏθaɪm] *n*. 【医】(躁郁)循环性精神病患者。

cy·clo·thy·mi·a [ˌsaikləuˈθaimiə; ˏsaɪkləˋθaɪmɪə] *n*. 【医】(躁郁)循环性气质。**-thy·mic** *a*., *n*.

cy·clo·tron [ˈsaiklətrɔn; ˋsaɪkləˏtrɑn] *n*. 【物】回旋加速器。~ **resonance** 回旋共振。

cy·der [ˈsaidə; ˋsaɪdə] *n*. 〔英〕= cider.

cyg·net [ˈsignit; ˋsɪgnɪt] *n*. 小天鹅。

Cyg·nus [ˈsignəs; ˋsɪgnəs] *n*. **1.** 【鸟】天鹅属。**2.** 〔the ~〕【天】天鹅座。

cyl. = cylinder; cylindrical.

cyl·in·der [ˈsilində; ˋsɪlɪndə] *n*. **1.** 圆筒;机筒;烘筒;量筒;(印刷机等的)滚筒。**2.** 【数】柱(面),柱体。**3.** 【机】汽缸;【化】(装氧气等的)钢筒,钢瓶。**4.** (左轮手枪的)旋转弹膛。**5.** 【考古】(巴比伦和亚述的)圆筒形石印(= ~ seal);(雕有阿拉伯人楔形文字的)圆柱形陶器。(***work***) ***on all*** *~s* 〔口〕尽全部力量(大干)。~ **ga(u)ge** 缸径规,圆筒内径测量器。~ **head** [**cap**] 汽缸盖。~ **mirror** 柱面镜。~ **machine** 圆网(造纸)机。~ **press** 〔美〕= ~ **printing machine** 轮转[滚筒]印刷机。

cy·lin·dri·cal [siˈlindrikəl; sɪˋlɪndrɪkəl] *a*. 圆柱体的,圆柱形的,长圆形的。**-cal·i·ty** [-ˈkæliti; -ˋkælətɪ] *n*.

cyl·in·droid [ˈsilindrɔid; ˋsɪlɪnˏdrɔɪd] *n*., *a*. 【数】**1.** 圆柱性面(的),拟圆柱面(的)。**2.** 椭圆柱(的)。

cy·lix [ˈsailiks, ˈsiliks; ˋsaɪlɪks, ˋsɪlɪks] *n*. (*pl*. ***cyl·i·ces*** [ˈsilisiːz; ˋsɪlɪsiz]) (古希腊)高脚双柄宽口浅酒杯 (= kylix)。

cy·ma [ˈsaimə; ˋsaɪmə] *n*. (*pl*. *~s*, ***-mae*** [-miː; -mi]) **1.** 【建】反曲线;波状花边[线脚]。**2.** 【植】= cyme.

cy·mar [siˈmɑː; sɪˋmɑr] *n*. (宽大无袖的)女便袍,女衬袍。

cy·ma·ti·um [siˈmeiʃiəm; sɪˋmeʃɪəm] *n*. (*pl*. ***-tia*** [-ʃiə; -ʃɪə]) 【建】反曲线状;波状(拱顶)花边。

cym·bal [ˈsimbəl; ˋsɪmbl̩] *n*. 〔常 *pl*.〕【乐】铙钹,钗(钹)。**-ist** *n*. 击钹者。

cym·bid·i·um [simˈbidiəm; sɪmˋbɪdɪəm] *n*. 【植】兰属植物。

cym·bi·form [ˈsimbifɔːm; ˋsɪmbəfɔrm] *a*. 【解】【植】船形的,舟状的。

cyme [saim; saɪm] *n*. 【植】聚伞花序。

cy·mene [ˈsaimiːn; ˋsaɪmin] *n*. 【化】伞花烃,百里香素;甲基[异丙基]苯。

cymo- *comb*. *f*. 表示"波":*cymo*scope.

cy·mo·gene [ˈsaiməudʒiːn; ˋsaɪmoˏdʒin] *n*. 【化】粗丁烷,近纯丁烷。

cy·mo·graph [ˈsaiməugrɑːf; ˋsaɪməˏgræf] *n*. = kymograph.

cy·moid [ˈsaimɔid; ˋsaɪmɔɪd] *a*. 【植】聚伞状的,聚伞花序状的。

cy·mom·e·ter [saiˈmɔmitə; saɪˋmɑmətə] *n*. 【电】波长计,自记波频计。

cy·mo·phane [ˈsaiməufein; ˋsaɪmoˏfen] *n*. 猫眼石,金绿宝石。

cy·mo·scope [ˈsaiməuskəup; ˋsaɪməˏskop] *n*. 【无】检波器,振荡指示器。

cy·mose, cy·mous [ˈsaiməus, ˈsaiməs; ˋsaɪmos, ˋsaɪməs] *a*. 【植】有聚伞花的;聚伞状的。

Cym·ric [ˈkimrik, ˈsimrik; ˋkɪmrɪk, ˋsɪmrɪk] *a*. = Welsh.

Cym·ry [ˈkimri, ˈsimri; ˋkɪmrɪ, ˋsɪmrɪ] *n*. 威尔士族。

Cyn·ic [ˈsinik; ˋsɪnɪk] **I** *n*. **1.** (古希腊)犬儒学派的门徒。**2.** 〔c-〕好挖苦人的人,好嘲笑的人;玩世不恭的人,愤世嫉俗的人。**II** *a*. **1.** 犬儒学派的。**2.** 〔c-〕= cynical.

cyn·i·cal [ˈsinikəl; ˋsɪnɪkəl] *a*. 爱嘲笑人的,冷嘲热讽的,讥诮的;玩世不恭的,愤世嫉俗的。***be ~ about*** (*sincerity*) 不相信(人的诚实)。**-ly** *ad*. **-ness** *n*.

cyn·i·cism [ˈsinisizəm; ˋsɪnəsɪzəm] *n*. **1.** 〔C-〕(古希腊的)犬儒哲学,犬儒主义。**2.** 讥诮(癖),冷笑(癖);玩世不恭,愤世嫉俗。

cyno- *comb*. *f*. 犬:*cyno*phobia.

cy·no·ceph·a·lus [ˌsainəuˈsefələs; ˏsɪnoˋsefələs] *n*. **1.** 【动】犬面狒狒。**2.** 【神话】狗头人身的人(像)。

cy·no·pho·bi·a [ˌsainəuˈfəubiə; ˏsɪnoˋfobɪə] *n*. 【医】恐犬病。

cy·no·sure [ˈsinəzjuə, ˈsain-; ˋsɪnəˏzjʊr, ˋsaɪn-] *n*. **1.** 〔C-〕【天】小熊座 (Little Bear 的别名),北极星。**2.** 指针,目标;众目之的,众望所归,赞美的目标。***the ~ of all eyes*** [***of the world***] 人人注意的目标。

Cyn·thi·a [ˈsinθiə; ˋsɪnθɪə] *n*. **1.** 辛西雅〔女子名〕。**2.** 〔诗〕月亮〔拟人化的说法〕。**3.** 【希神】辛西雅(即 Artemis 或 Diana,月亮和狩猎女神)。

cy·pher [ˈsaifə; ˋsaɪfə] *n*., *v*. = cipher. **~punk** 解密高手。

cy-pres [ˈsiːˈprei; ˋsiˋpre] **I** *n*. 【法】力求近似(原则)〔指对于遗嘱等文件的解释有困难时,力求使解释接近立遗嘱者的愿望,尤其适用于公益捐款等方面〕。**II** *a*., *ad*. 【法】力求近似的[地]。

cy·press [ˈsaipris, -prəs; ˋsaɪprɪs, -prəs] ***n*. 1.**【植】柏(属);扁柏,丝柏;丝柏木料。**2.** 丝柏枝〔哀悼标记〕;致哀黑纱。~ **vine**【植】茑萝。

Cyp·ri·an [ˈsipriən; ˋsɪprɪən] **I *a*. 1.** 塞浦路斯[人,语]的。**2.** 关于爱神阿芙罗狄蒂 (Aphrodite) 的;色情的;淫荡的。**II *n*. 1.** 塞浦路斯人[语]。**2.** 爱神阿芙罗狄蒂的崇拜者;淫荡的人,娼妓。

cy·prin·o·dont [siˈprinədɔnt, siˈprainə-; sɪˋprɪnə-ˏdɑnt, sɪˋpraɪnə-] ***n*.**【动】鳉科鱼。

cyp·ri·noid [ˈsiprinɔid; ˋsɪprəˏnɔɪd] **I *a*.**【动】鲤科的。**II *n*.** 鲤科鱼 (= cyprinid [-nid; -nɪd])。

Cyp·ri·ot, Cyp·ri·ote [ˈsipriɔt, -əut; ˋsɪprɪət, -ot] **I *a*.** 塞浦路斯岛的;塞浦路斯人[语]的。**II *n*.** 塞浦路斯人[语]。

cyp·ri·pe·di·um [ˌsipriˈpiːdiəm; ˏsɪprɪˋpidɪəm] ***n*.** (*pl*. ~***s***, ***-di·a*** [-ə; -ə])【植】**1.** 杓兰(属)。**2.** 兜兰(属)(*Paphiopedilum*)。

Cy·prus [ˈsaiprəs; ˋsaɪprəs] ***n*.** 塞浦路斯〔亚洲〕。

cyp·se·la [ˈsipsələ; ˋsɪpsələ] ***n*.** (*pl*. ***-lae*** [-ˌliː; -ˏli])【植】连萼瘦果。

Cy·re·na·ic [ˌsaiəriˈneiik; ˏsaɪrəˋne·ɪk] **I *a*. 1.** (北非古城)昔勒尼的。**2.** 昔勒尼学派的。**II *n*. 1.** 昔勒尼人。**2.** 昔勒尼学派的信徒。**-i·cism** [-isizəm; -ɪsɪzəm] ***n*.** 昔勒尼学派〔古希腊一种鼓吹享乐为人生唯一目的的学派〕。

Cy·ril [ˈsiril; ˋsɪrəl] ***n*.** 西里尔〔男子名〕。

cy·ril·lic [siˈrilik; sɪˋrɪlɪk] ***a*.** 西里尔 (Cyril) 字母的。~ **alphabet** 西里尔字母〔九世纪时传教士西里尔发明的字母,系现代俄语等字母的本源〕。

cyrto- *comb*. *f*. 弯曲,弓状:*cyrto*meter.

cyr·tom·e·ter [səːˈtɔmitə; sɝˋtɑmətɚ] ***n*. 1.** 圆量尺,测曲面器。**2.** 测胸围器,测头颅器。

Cy·rus [ˈsaiərəs; ˋsaɪrəs] ***n*.** 赛勒斯〔男子名〕。

cyst [sist; sɪst] ***n*. 1.**【生】胞,囊;包囊;膀胱。**2.**【医】囊肿。**3.**【植】孢囊,胚囊。*the urinary* ~ 膀胱。**-ic *a*.**

cyst-〔接元音〕, **cysti-**〔接辅音〕*comb*. *f*. = cysto-: *cyst*eine, *cysti*cercus.

cys·tec·to·my [sisˈtektəmi; sɪsˋtɛktəmɪ] ***n*.**【医】囊切;(胆囊,膀胱)切除(术)。

cys·te·ine [ˈsistiiːin; ˋsɪstɪin] ***n*.**【生化】半胱胺酸。

cyst·ic [ˈsistik; ˋsɪstɪk] ***a*. 1.** 膀胱的;胆囊的。**2.** 胞的,囊的。**3.** 胞状的,囊状的;有胞的,有囊的。

cys·ti·cer·coid [ˌsistiˈsəːkɔid; ˏsɪstɪˋsɝkɔɪd] ***n*.**【动】拟囊尾幼虫。

cys·ti·cer·co·sis [ˌsistisəˈkəusis; ˏsɪstɪsɝˋkosɪs] ***n*.** (*pl*. ***-co·ses*** [-ˈkəusiːz; -ˋkosiz])【医】囊尾幼虫病。

cys·ti·cer·cus [sistiˈsəːkəs; ˏsɪstɪˋsɝkəs] ***n*.** (*pl*. ***-ci*** [-sai; -saɪ])【动】囊尾幼虫。

cys·ti·form [ˈsistifɔːm; ˋsɪstɪˏfɔrm] ***a*.** 胞状的,囊状的。

cys·tin(e) [ˈsistiːn; ˋsɪstin] ***n*.**【生化】胱胺酸。

cys·ti·tis [sisˈtaitis; sɪsˋtaɪtɪs] ***n*.**【医】膀胱炎。

cysto- *comb*. *f*. 表示"胞","囊","膀胱":*cysto*cele.

cys·to·carp [ˈsistəkɑːp; ˋsɪstəˏkɑrp] ***n*.**【植】囊果。

cys·to·cele [ˈsistəsiːl; ˋsɪstəˏsil] ***n*.**【医】膀胱突出(症)。

Cy·sto·flag·el·la·ta [ˈsistəuˌflædʒəˈleitə; ˏsɪsto-ˏflædʒəˋletə] ***n*.** 〔*pl*.〕【动】胞状鞭毛虫类。

cys·toid [ˈsistɔid; ˋsɪstɔɪd] **I *a*.** 胞囊状的,囊肿一样的。**II *n*.**【医】类囊肿,假囊肿。

cys·to·lith [ˈsistəliθ; ˋsɪstəlɪθ] ***n*. 1.**【医】胆石;膀胱结石。**2.**【植】钟乳体。

cys·to·scope [ˈsistəskəup; ˋsɪstəˏskop] ***n*.**【医】膀胱镜。

cys·tos·to·my [sisˈtɔstəmi; sɪsˋtɑstəmɪ] ***n*.**【医】膀胱造口(导尿)术。

cys·tot·o·my [sisˈtɔtəmi; sɪsˋtɑtəmɪ] ***n*.**【医】膀胱切开术,膀胱结石[肿疡]截除术。

cyt- *comb*. *f*. = cyto-.

cy·tase [ˈsaiteis; ˋsaɪtes] ***n*.**【生化】细胞溶(解)酶。

-cyte *suf*. 细胞,球:leuco*cyte*.

Cyth·er·e·a [ˌsiθəˈri(ː)ə; ˏsɪθəˋri(ɪ)ə] ***n*.**【希神】爱神〔阿芙罗狄蒂 (Aphrodite) 的别称〕。

Cyth·er·e·an [ˌsiθəˈriːən; ˏsɪθəˋriən] **I *a*.**【希神】爱神的,阿芙罗狄蒂的。**II *n*.** 爱神崇拜者。

cyt·i·dine [ˈsaitədin; ˋsaɪtədɪn] ***n*.**【生化】胞苷。

cyt·i·dyl·ic [ˌsitiˈdilik; ˏsɪtɪˈdɪlɪk] ***a*.** ~ **acid**【生化】胞苷酸。

cyto- *comb*. *f*. 细胞(质):*cyto*logy.

cy·to·chem·is·try [ˈsaitəuˌkemistri; ˏsaɪtoˋkɛməstrɪ] ***n*.** 细胞化学。

cy·to·chrome [ˈsaitəuˌkrəum; ˋsaɪtəˏkrom] ***n*.**【生】细胞色素。

cy·to·gen·e·sis [ˌsaitəuˈdʒenisis; ˏsaɪtəˋdʒɛnəsɪs] ***n*.**【生】细胞发生,细胞生成。

cy·to·ge·net·ics [ˌsaitəudʒiˈnetiks; ˏsaɪtodʒəˋnɛtɪks] ***n*.** 细胞遗传学。**-net·ic, -neti·cal *a*. -neti·cal·ly *ad*. -net·i·cist *n*.**

cy·tog·e·nous [saiˈtɔdʒinəs; saɪˋtɑdʒɪnəs] ***a*.**【生】细胞发生的,细胞生成的。

cy·to·ki·ne·sis [ˈsaitəukaiˈniːsis; ˋsaɪtokaɪˋnisɪs] ***n*.**【生】细胞质分裂,减数分裂(= cytodieresis)。

cy·to·kin·in [ˌsaitəuˈkinin; ˏsaɪtoˋkɪnɪn] ***n*.**【生】细胞激动素。

cy·tol·o·gist [saiˈtɔlədʒist; saɪˋtɑlədʒɪst] ***n*.** 细胞学者。

cy·tol·o·gy [saiˈtɔlədʒi; saɪˋtɑlədʒɪ] ***n*.** 细胞学。

cy·tol·y·sin [saiˈtɔlisin; saɪˋtɑləsɪn] ***n*.**【生】溶细胞素。

cy·tol·y·sis [saiˈtɔlisis; saɪˋtɑləsɪs] ***n*.**【生】细胞溶解。**cy·to·lyt·ic** [ˌsaitəˈlitik; ˏsaɪtəˋlɪtɪk] ***a*.**

cy·to·mem·brane [ˌsaitəuˈmembrein; ˏsaɪtoˋmɛmbren] ***n*.**【生】细胞膜。

cy·to·plasm [ˈsaitəuplæzəm; ˋsaɪtəˏplæzəm] ***n*.**【生】(细)胞质。

cy·to·plast [ˈsaitəuˌplæst; ˋsaɪtoˏplæst] ***n*.**【生】= cytoplasm. **-ic *a*.**

cy·to·sine [ˈsaitəsiːn; ˋsaɪtəsin] ***n*.**【生化】胞(核)嘧啶,胞嘧。

cy·to·tax·on·o·my [ˌsaitəutækˈsɔnəmi; ˏsaɪtotæk-ˋsɑnəmɪ] ***n*.** 细胞分类学。

cy·to·troph·o·blast [ˌsaitəuˈtrɔfəblæst; ˏsaɪto-ˋtrɑfəblæst] ***n*.**【生】细胞滋养层。**-ic *a*.**

cy·to·sol [ˈsaitəusɔl; ˋsaɪtosɑl] ***n*.**【生】细胞溶质。

cyt·u·la [ˈsitjulə; ˋsɪtjulə] ***n*.**【生】合子;受精卵。

C. Z. = Canal Zone (Panama) (巴拿马)运河区。

czar [zɑː; zaɪ] ***n*.** = Tsar.

czar·das [ˈtʃɑːdæʃ, -dɔʃ; ˋtʃardæʃ, -dɑʃ] ***n*.** (匈牙利)恰尔达什舞(曲)。

Czech, Czekh [tʃek; tʃɛk] **I *n*.** 捷克人[语]。**II *a*.** 捷克的,捷克人[语]的。

Czech·ic, Czech·ish [ˈtʃekik, ˈtʃekiʃ; ˋtʃɛkɪk, ˋtʃɛkɪʃ] ***a*.** 捷克的,捷克人[语]的。

Czech·o·slo·vak [ˈtʃekəuˈsləuvæk; ˏtʃɛkoˋslovæk] **I *n*.** 捷克斯洛伐克人。**II *a*.** 捷克斯洛伐克(人)的。

Czech·o·slo·vak·i·a [ˈtʃekəusləuˈvækiə; ˏtʃɛkəslo-ˋvækɪə] ***n*.** 捷克斯洛伐克〔欧洲〕。

Czech·o·slo·vak·i·an [ˈtʃekəusləuˈvækiən; ˋtʃɛkoslo-ˋvækɪən] = Czechoslovak.

D

D, d [diː; di] (*pl*. *D's*, *d's* [diːz; diz]) **1.** 英语字母表第四字母。**2.**【乐】D 音, D 调。**3.**【数】第四个已知数。**4.** 第四。**5.** (学业成绩)劣或勉强及格。**6.** D 字形物。*D flat*【乐】降 D 调。*D major* [*minor*]【乐】D 大调[小调]。*D sharp*【乐】升 D 调。*a D student* 劣等生。*a D slide valve* D 形滑阀。

D [diː; di] **1.**【化】= deuterium 元素氘的符号。**2.** (罗马数字)500. *CD* = 400. *DC* = 600. $\bar{D}$ = 500,000〔有时 = 5,000〕.

D. = **1.** December. **2.** Democrat; Democratic. **3.** Doctor. **4.** Don. **5.** Duchess. **6.** Duke. **7.** Dutch.

d. = **1.** date. **2.** daughter. **3.** day(s). **4.** dead. **5.** degree. **6.** dele; delete. **7.**〔L.〕*denarius*; *denarii* (旧)便士 (= penny; pence). **8.** deputy. **9.** deserted; deserter. **10.** diameter. **11.** died. **12.** dime. **13.** director. **14.** dividend. **15.** dollar. **16.** dorsal. **17.** dose. **18.** dyne.

'd [d; d]〔口〕**1.** = had: *I'd* ... = I had .... **2.** = did: *Where'd* ... = Where did .... **3.** = should (或 would): *He'd* ... = He should (或 would). **4.** = -ed: *foster'd*.

d' [d; d]〔口〕**1.** = do: *How d'you* ... = How do you ... **2.** = did.

da [dɑː; dɑ] ***n.***〔口〕= dad.

D.A., DA = District Attorney〔美〕地方检察官。

D. A. = delayed action (bomb) 定时(炸弹); direct action; documents against [for] acceptance.

D / A, d / a **1.** = days after acceptance. **2.** = deposit account. **3.** digital-to-analog【计】数(字)-模(拟)。

d. a. = duck's ass〔美俚〕鸭屁股男发型。

dab[1] [dæb; dæb] **I** ***vt.*** **1.** 轻敲, 轻拍; 轻抚 (*sth*.)。**2.**〔美俚〕在…上摁指纹印。*a plaster to be wetted and ~bed on* 润湿后轻轻敷上的膏药。*~ one's forehead with a handkerchief* 用手帕轻拍脑门(揩汗)。—***vi.*** 轻拍, 轻敷; 涂擦 (*on*, *at*); (鸟)啄。**II** ***n.*** **1.** 轻打, 轻拍; 轻抚。**2.** 涂擦。**3.** 啄。**4.** 指纹印。**5.** 少量, 些许; 一小块。*a ~ of butter* 一小块奶油。*a ~ of powder* 一刷子白粉。

dab[2] [dæb; dæb] ***n.*** 小鲽; 比目鱼。

dab[3] [dæb; dæb] ***n.***〔口〕名手, 能手 (*at*)。*a ~ at tennis* 网球能手。

DAB, D. A. B. = **1.** *Dictionary of American Biography*. **2.** digital audio broadcasting (使用卫星进行的)数字式广播。

dab·ber [ˈdæbə; ˋdæbɚ] ***n.*** **1.** 轻拍的人[物]。**2.** (木版印刷的)涂墨擦。**3.** (打纸型的)硬毛刷。

dab·ble [ˈdæbl; ˋdæbl] ***vt.*** **1.** 弄湿, 溅湿。**2.** 蘸, 浸, 沾。*be ~d with mud* (被)溅满泥浆。—***vi.*** **1.** 玩水。**2.** 浅尝, 涉猎, 涉足。*~ in literature* 涉猎文学。*~ in [with] stocks* 经营一部分股票。*~ with the text* 窜改原文。

dab·bler [ˈdæblə; ˋdæblɚ] ***n.*** **1.** 玩水者。**2.** 浅尝者, 涉猎者; (业余)爱好者。*~ in [at] wood engraving* 业余木刻者。

dab·chick [ˈdæbtʃik; ˋdæbˏtʃɪk] ***n.***【鸟】鸊鷉。

dab·ster [ˈdæbstə; ˋdæbstɚ] ***n.*** **1.**〔英方〕能手, 老手。**2.**〔口〕业余爱好者。

da ca·po [dɑːˈkɑːpəu; dɑˋkɑpo]〔It.〕【乐】从头(重复一遍)。〔略作 D. C.〕。

Dac·ca [ˈdækə; ˋdækə] ***n.*** 达卡〔孟加拉国首都〕。

dace [deis; des] ***n.*** (*pl*. *~s*,〔集合词〕~)【鱼】(鲤科)鲦鱼。

dach·a, ***datch·a*** [ˈdɑːtʃə; ˋdɑtʃə] ***n.***〔Russ.〕别墅, 乡间邸宅。

dachs·hund [ˈdækshund; ˋdɑkshʊnd] ***n.*** 达克斯狗〔体长脚短, 常用于猎獾、狐等〕。

da·coit [dəˈkɔit; dəˋkɔɪt] ***n.*** (印度、缅甸的)土匪, 强盗。**-coit·y** [-i; -ɪ] ***n.*** 土匪的抢劫。

Da·cron [ˈdeikrɔn, ˈdækrɔn; ˋdekrɑn, ˋdækrɑn] ***n.*** **1.**【商标】达克纶。**2.**〔d-〕聚酯纤维; 达克纶; 涤纶织物〔俗名的确良〕。

dacry(o)- *comb*. *f*. 泪: *dacryo*cyst 泪囊。

dac·tyl [ˈdæktil; ˋdæktɪl] ***n.*** **1.**【韵】扬抑抑格, 长短短格〔如: take her up tenderly〕。**2.**【动】指, 趾。

dac·tyl·ic [dækˈtilik; dækˋtɪlɪk] ***a.***, ***n.*** 扬抑抑〔长短短〕格的(句子)。

dactyl(o)- *comb*. *f*. 指, 趾: *dactylo*gram.

dac·tyl·o·gram [dækˈtiləgræm; dækˋtɪləˏgræm] ***n.*** 指纹。

dac·ty·log·ra·phy [ˌdæktiˈlɔgrəfi; ˏdæktɪˋlɑgrəfɪ] ***n.*** 指纹学, 指纹法, 指纹术。

dac·tyl·ol·o·gy [ˌdæktiˈlɔlədʒi; ˏdæktɪˋlɑlədʒɪ] ***n.*** (聋哑人的)指语术。

dac·ty·los·co·py [ˌdæktiˈlɔskəpi; ˏdæktəˋlɑskəpɪ] ***n.*** 指纹鉴定法。

dad[1] [dæd; dæd] ***n.***〔口〕爹爹, 爸爸。

dad[2] [dæd; dæd] ***int.***〔美口〕神。*~-blasted* [*-blamed*] 讨厌, 可恶。

Da·da = Dadaism.

dad·a [ˈdædə; ˋdædə] ***n.***〔儿〕= dad[1].

Da·da·ism [ˈdɑːdəizəm; ˋdɑdəɪzəm] ***n.*** 达达派〔1916—1922 年间兴起的一种西方文艺流派, 其特征为运用怪诞的象征手法以表达潜意识的东西, 运用虚无主义的讽刺手法等〕。

Da·da·ist [ˈdɑːdəist; ˋdɑdəɪst] ***n.*** 达达派艺术家。

dad·dy [ˈdædi; ˋdædɪ] ***n.*** **1.**〔口〕= dad[1]. **2.**〔俚〕爱在少女身上花钱的老色迷(= sugar ~)。

dad·dy-long·legs [ˈdædiˈlɔŋlegz; ˋdædɪˋlɔŋlɛgz] ***n.*** **1.** 大蚊子。**2.** 长脚蜘蛛。

da·do [ˈdeidəu; ˋdedo] ***n.*** (*pl*. *~s*, *~es*) **1.**【建】(柱墩的)墩身; 护壁板, 墙裙。**2.** (木工的)开榫槽。

DAE, D. A. E. = *Dictionary of American English* 《美国英语词典》。

dae·dal [ˈdiːdl; ˋdidl̩] ***a.***〔诗〕巧妙的; 错综复杂的; 千变万化的。*the ~ hand of nature* 大自然的鬼斧神工。

Dae·da·le·an, Dae·da·li·an [diˈdeiljən; dɪˋdeljən] ***a.*** **1.** 代达罗斯 (Daedalus) 的。**2.**〔d-〕错综复杂的; 巧妙的。

Dae·da·lus [ˈdiːdələs; ˋdidl̩əs] ***n.***【希神】代达罗斯〔建造 Crete 迷宫的名匠〕。

D

dae·mon [ˈdiːmən; ˋdimən] ***n***. (*pl*. ~***s***, ~***es*** [-iːz; -ˏiz]) = demon.
daff[1] [dæf; dæf] ***vi***.〔Scot.〕演丑角;举止滑稽。
daff[2] [dæf; dæf] ***vt***.〔废〕**1.** 推开。**2.** 丢开。~ ... ***aside*** 摆脱。
daf·fa·down·dil·ly [ˌdæfədaunˈdili; ˏdæfədaʊnˋdɪlɪ] ***n***.〔诗〕= daffodil.
daf·fo·dil, daf·fo·dil·ly [ˈdæfədil, -i; ˋdæfədɪl, -ɪ] ***n***. **1.**【植】水仙。**2.** 鲜黄色。
daff·y [ˈdæfi; ˋdæfɪ] ***a***.〔美口〕**1.** 疯狂的,愚笨的。**2.** 轻浮的。
daft [dɑːft; dɑft] ***a***. **1.** 愚蠢的。**2.** 疯狂的。**3.**〔Scot.〕玩闹的。***go*** ~ 发狂;发痴。
dag. = decagram(me).
dag·ga [ˈdægə; ˋdægə] ***n***. **1.** 大麻。**2.** 大麻干叶子(= marijuana)。
dag·ger [ˈdægə; ˋdægɚ] **I** ***n***. **1.** 短剑,匕首。**2.**【印】剑号〔即 †〕。**3.**〔*pl*.〕敌意。*a double* ~ 双剑号〔即 ‡〕。***at*** ~***s drawn*** 势不两立,互相仇视,剑拔弩张。***look*** ~***s at*** 瞪着眼看,怒视。***speak*** ~***s to*** (*sb*.) 说刻毒话,恶言伤人。**II** ***vt***. **1.** 用剑刺。**2.** 用剑号标明。
dag·gle [ˈdægl; ˋdægl] ***vt***., ***vi***. **1.** 拖脏(衣服等)。**2.** 溅湿,弄脏。**3.** 拖着(衣服)走。*clothes ~d by the splash of passing vehicles* 过路的车辆把衣服溅脏。
dag·lock [ˈdægˌlɔk; ˋdægˏlɔk] ***n***. (羊犬等的)凝污卷毛。
da·go [ˈdeigəu; ˋdego] ***n***. (*pl*. ~***s***, ~***es***)〔常 D-〕〔美蔑〕意大利或西班牙血统的人。~ **red**〔美〕(意大利人酿的和喝的)低级红葡萄酒。
da·go·ba [ˈdɑːgəbə; ˋdɑgəbə] ***n***. (印度的)舍利子塔。
Da·gon [ˈdeigɔn; ˋdegɑn] ***n***. (古代腓力斯人和腓尼基人的)半人半鱼的神。
da·guerre·o·type [dəˈgerəutaip, -rətaip; dəˋgɛrəˏtaɪp, -rətaɪp] ***n***. (从前的)银板照相(法)。
dah[1] [dɑː; dɑ] ***n***. 无线电或电报电码中的一长划。
dah[2] [dɑː; dɑ] ***n***. (缅甸人的)大刀。
da·ha·bee·yah, da·ha·bi·ah, da·ha·be·ah, da·ha·bi·yeh [dɑːhəˈbiːjə, -ˈbiːə, -ˈbiːə, -ˈbiːje; dɑhəˋbijə, -ˋbiə, -ˋbiə, -ˋbijɛ] ***n***.〔Ar.〕尼罗河中的舫式渡船。
dah·li·a [ˈdeiljə; ˋdæljə] ***n***. **1.**【植】大丽花。**2.** 浓紫色。*a blue* ~ 不会有的东西。
Da·ho·man [dəˈhəumən; dəˋhomən] **I** ***n***. 达荷美人。**II** ***a***. 达荷美人的;达荷美的。
Da·ho·mey [dəˈhəumi; dəˋhomɪ] ***n***. (西非)达荷美。
da·hoon [dəˈhuːn; dəˋhun] ***n***. 达宏冬青。
Dail Eir·eann [ˈdail ˈɛərən; ˋdɔɪl ˋɛrən] 爱尔兰的众议院。
dai·ly [ˈdeili; ˋdelɪ] **I** ***a***. 逐日的,每日的。**II** ***n***. **1.** 日报(= ~(news)paper)。**2.**〔英口〕不住宿的仆人;白天做家务的女佣(= ~ girl)。~ *bread* 每日食粮,生计。~ *capacity* 每日产量。~ *interest* 日息。**III** ***ad***. 每日,逐日,天天。~ **double** 两场连赌法〔赛马或赛狗赌博中对连续两场比赛的结果统押一注的赌法〕;〔喻〕同时在两个不同的领域取得成功。~ **dozen** 每天的体育健身活动。
dai·mon [ˈdaimɔn; ˋdaɪmɑn] ***n***. = demon.
dain·ti·ly [ˈdeintili; ˋdentɪlɪ] ***ad***. **1.** 优雅,好看。**2.** 好吃,爽口。**3.** 讲究,考究。*be ~ dressed* 衣着雅致。*fare ~* 吃得好。
dain·ti·ness [ˈdeintinis; ˋdentɪnɪs] ***n***. **1.** 优雅,美丽。**2.** 美味。**3.** 讲究,考究。
dain·ty [ˈdeinti; ˋdentɪ] **I** ***a***. **1.** 优美的,好看的,雅致的。**2.** 好吃的,爽口的。**3.** 讲究的,有洁癖的。*a ~ lass* 美极了的姑娘。~ *bits* 美味。*a ~ feeder* 考究吃的人。*born with a ~ tooth* 生来嘴馋。**II** ***n***. 美味,可口之物。
dai·qui·ri [ˈdaikəri; ˋdaɪkərɪ] ***n***. 台克利酒,鸡尾酒。
dair·y [ˈdɛəri; ˋdɛrɪ] ***n***. **1.** (制)酪场,牛奶棚;牛奶场。**2.** 牛奶店。**3.** 奶品制造业。~ **cattle**〔集合词〕奶牛。~ **farm** 奶场。~ **farmer** 奶农。~ **maid** 奶场女工。~**man** 奶场场主;挤奶工人;奶品商。~ **products** 奶产品。~ **stock** 奶牛。**-ing** 奶品制造业。
da·is [ˈdeiis; ˋdeɪs] ***n***. **1.** (为贵宾或演说者设置的)上座;讲坛。**2.** (大厅一端的)台,高台〔用以放置高桌、宝座等〕。**3.** (露天的)平台。**4.**〔古〕(宝座上的)华盖。
Dai·sy [ˈdeizi; ˋdezɪ] ***n***. 戴西〔女子名〕。
dai·sy [ˈdeizi; ˋdezɪ] **I** ***n***. **1.**〔英〕雏菊,延命菊。**2.**〔美〕牛眼菊(= oxeye ~)。**3.**〔美俚〕上品,逸品;〔美〕卓越人物。**4.** 去骨肩胛肉熏制的火腿(= ~ ham)。***turn*** (***up***) ***one's toes to the daisies***〔俚〕死。***under the daisies***〔俚〕葬在地下。**II** ***a***.〔美俚〕极好的;可爱的。~ **chain** **1.** (给女学生戴的)雏菊花环。**2.**〔俚〕搞同性恋爱的集团。**3.**【计】菊链,(电脑的)串行〔系列〕连接。~ **cutter**〔俚〕**1.** 跑时举足极低的马。**2.**【板球等】(贴近地面的)滚球。**3.**【军】榴霰弹。~ **ham** 去骨熏腿。
Dak·ar [ˈdækə; dɑˋkɑr] ***n***. 达喀尔(达卡)〔塞内加尔首都〕。
da·koit [dəˈkɔit; dəˋkɔɪt] ***n***. = dacoit.
Da·ko·ta [dəˈkəutə; dəˋkotə] **I** ***n***. **1.** 达科他人〔北美印第安人〕。**2.** 达科他语。**3.** 达科他〔美国过去一地区名,现分为南、北达科他州〕。**II** ***a***. **1.** 达科他人的。**2.** 达科他语的。**3.** (南、北)达科他(州)的。**the** ~**s** 南、北达科他。
dal [ˈdɑːl; ˋdɑl] ***n***. = dhal.
dal. = decalitre.
Da·la·dier [dɑlɑˈdjei; dalaˋdje] ***n***. ***the*** ~ ***line*** 达拉第防线〔在法国、比利时、卢森堡之间,是马奇诺防线 (Maginot line) 的延长部分,由当时法国总理(1938—1940)兼国防部长 Edouard Daladier (1884—1970)负责筑成〕。
Da·lai La·ma [ˈdælai ˈlɑːmə; dəˋlaɪ ˋlɑmə] ***n***. 达赖喇嘛。
Dale [deil; del] ***n***. 戴尔〔姓氏,男子名,女子名〕。
dale [deil; del] ***n***.〔诗、方〕谷,山谷。***o'er hill and*** ~ 翻山越岭。
dales·man [ˈdeilzmən; ˋdelzmən] ***n***. (英国北部的)山谷居民。
da·leth, da·ledh [ˈdɑːlet, ˈdɑːləd; ˋdɑlet, ˋdɑləd] ***n***. 希伯来字母表中的第四个字母。
Dal·las[1] [ˈdæləs; ˋdæləs] ***n***. 达拉斯〔姓氏,男子名〕。
Dal·las[2] [ˈdæləs; ˋdæləs] ***n***. 达拉斯〔美国城市〕。
dal·li·ance [ˈdæliəns; ˋdælɪəns] ***n***. **1.** 调戏;调情,调笑;嬉戏。**2.** 浪费时间,混日子。
dal·ly [ˈdæli; ˋdælɪ] ***vi***. **1.** 调戏;调情,嬉戏;戏弄(*with*)。**2.** 闲荡;延误(时机等)(*over*)。—***vt***. 浪费(时间)。~ ***away*** 混日子;延误。~ ***with danger*** 瞎冒险。~ **money** 感情伤害赔偿金〔指玩弄对方的非婚同居者一方付给受害一方的赔偿〕。
Dal·ma·tia [dælˈmeiʃjə; dælˋmeʃɪə] ***n***. 达尔马提亚〔前南斯拉夫一地区〕。
Dal·ma·ti·an [dælˈmeiʃiən; dælˋmeʃɪən] **I** ***a***. 前南斯拉夫达尔马提亚地方的。**II** ***n***. **1.** 达尔马提亚人。**2.** 达尔马提亚狗〔白毛,有黑斑或褐斑〕。
dal·mat·ic [dælˈmætik; dælˋmætɪk] ***n***. **1.** (主教等的)法衣。**2.** (英国国王的)加冕服。
dal se·gno [dæl ˈseinjəu; dɑl ˋsenjo] [It.]【乐】反复记号〔从 $ 记号处开始重复一遍,略号 D. S.〕。
Dal·ton [ˈdɔːltən; ˋdɔltn̩] ***n***. **1.** 多尔顿〔姓氏,男子名〕。**2.** **John** ~道尔顿〔1766—1844,英国化学、物理学家,原子学说首倡人,红绿色盲的发现者〕。
dal·ton [ˈdɔːltən; ˋdɔltən] ***n***. 道尔顿(分子量单位)。
dal·ton·ism [ˈdɔːltənizəm; ˋdɔltn̩ɪzm̩] ***n***.【医】色盲;(特指)先天性红绿色盲。
Da·ly [ˈdeili; ˋdelɪ] ***n***. 戴利〔姓氏〕。
dam[1] [dæm; dæm] **I** ***n***. **1.** 水闸,坝,堰。**2.** 坝中的水。**3.**【矿】坑道堰。**4.** (牙科用的)橡皮障。**5.**〔喻〕障碍。*a regulating* ~ 拦洪坝。*a fascine* ~ 草坝。*a hy-*

draulic ～ 现代水闸。*a storage* ～ 蓄水坝。*weir* ～ 量水堰。**II** *vt*. **1.** 筑水闸堵住。**2.** 阻塞,遮断。**3.** 抑制。～ *up inflation* 抑制通货膨胀。～ *back one's tears* 忍住眼泪。

dam[2] [dæm; dæm] *n*. **1.** 母兽。**2.** 〔古、蔑〕母亲。

dam·age [ˈdæmidʒ; ˋdæmɪdʒ] **I** *n*. **1.** 损害,损伤;〔口〕伤害,毁坏。**2.** 〔口〕费用,代价。**3.** 〔*pl*.〕【法】赔偿损失;赔偿金。*What's the* ～? 〔口〕要花多少钱? *a claim for* ～*s* 赔偿损失的要求。*costs and* ～*s* 讼费和损害费。*I will stand the* ～. 我来掏腰包好啦。**do** [*cause*, *inflict*] ～ **to** 损害。**sustain great** ～ 受到重大损害。**II** *vt*. 损坏(房屋等),损伤;毁坏(名誉等)。～ *one's reputation* 毁坏名誉。—*vi*. 被损害。**-a·ble** *a*. 易受损害的。

dam·an [ˈdæmən; dæˋmən] *n*. 非洲蹄兔,蹄兔(= hyrax)。

dam·ar [ˈdæmə; ˋdæmə˞] *n*. **1.** 澳洲松脂。**2.** 达马脂〔用以制油漆〕。

Dam·a·scene [ˈdæməsiːn; ˋdæmə͵sin] **I** *a*. 大马士革的。**II** *n*. **1.** 大马士革人。**2.** 〔d-〕西洋李子。**3.** 〔d-〕(钢铁等烧后现出的)波状花纹。**4.** 〔d-〕镶嵌;金银线镶嵌工艺。**III** *vt*. 〔d-〕(在金属上)用金银线镶嵌;使现波状花纹。

Da·mas·cus [dəˈmæskəs; dəˋmæskəs] *n*. 大马士革〔叙利亚首都〕。～ *steel* = damask steel.

dam·ask [ˈdæməsk; ˋdæməsk] **I** *n*. **1.** 缎子,花缎,锦缎;花布。**2.** (呈现波状花纹的)大马士革钢(= ～ steel)。**3.** 淡红色。**II** *a*. **1.** 淡红色的。**2.** 缎子的。**3.** 大马士革钢的。～ *rose* 淡红色玫瑰。**III** *vt*. 使织出花纹;使呈淡红色。

dam·as·keen [ˌdæməsˈkiːn; ͵dæməˋskin] *vt*. = damascene.

dame [deim; dem] *n*. **1.** 〔古、诗〕贵妇人;〔古〕(私塾的)女教师;〔古〕主妇。**2.** 太太,夫人;〔美口〕妇女;少女。**3.** 〔英〕(knight 或 baronet 的)夫人。**4.** (英国 Eton 公学的)舍监〔现在是男人〕。*an old* ～ 〔谑〕老太婆。

dam·mar, dam·mer [ˈdæmə; ˋdæmə˞] *n*. **1.** 澳洲松脂。**2.** 达马(树)脂。

dam·mit [ˈdæmit; ˋdæmɪt] = damn it.

damn [dæm; dæm] **I** *vt*. **1.** 指责,攻击。**2.** 毁坏,糟踏。**3.** 咒骂,诅咒;〔古〕使堕地狱。**4.** 讨厌! 该死! 什么话! 〔常讳作 D— 或 d—n〕。*I'll be* [*I am*] ～*ed if it is so* [*if I do*]. 我决不会有这样的事[我决不做这种事]。*D-me, but I'll do it*. 我一定要干,我死也要干。*God* ～ *you*! = *Be* ～*ed to you*! = *D- you*! 混帐! *Oh d—*! 讨厌! *D-* [*God* ～](*it*)! 该死! 糟了! *D- the rain*! 讨厌的雨! **II** *vi*. 咒骂。～ **all** 完全没有。**do** [*know*] ～ **all** 简直什么都不干[知道]。～ **with faint praise** 用冷淡的称赞反对[贬责]。**III** *n*. **1.** 诅咒。**2.** 些微。**not care** [*give*] **a** ～ 毫不在乎。**not worth a** ～ 毫无价值。**Who gives a** ～? 谁管呢? **IV** *ad*. 〔俚〕= damned.

dam·na·ble [ˈdæmnəbl; ˋdæmnəbl] *a*. **1.** 该罚的,该死的。**2.** 〔俚〕讨厌的。～ *weather* 讨厌的天气。

dam·na·bly [ˈdæmnəbli; ˋdæmnəblɪ] *ad*. **1.** 该罚地,该死地。**2.** 讨厌地。*It is* ～ *hot*. 热得要命。

dam·na·tion [dæmˈneiʃən; dæmˋneʃən] **I** *n*. **1.** 指责。**2.** 该死,该下地狱。**3.** 诅咒,痛骂。**4.** 毁坏,破灭。**II** *int*. 糟了! 完了! 该死! *curse a person to* ～ 咒骂某人不得好死。

dam·na·to·ry [ˈdæmnətəri; ˋdæmnə͵torɪ] *a*. **1.** 该咒的,该罚的,该死的。**2.** 指责的。～ *evidence* 不利的证据;铁证。

damned [dæmd; dæmd] **I** *a*. **1.** 该死的;该咒的,该罚的。**2.** 讨厌的。**3.** 〔俚〕要命的,非常的。*a* ～ *lie* 弥天大谎。*You* ～! 该死! 混蛋! **II** *ad*. 非常,极,要命地。*It was so* ～ *hot*. 热死了。**do** [*try*] **one's** ～**est** [*damndest*] 拼命干。

dam·ni·fi·ca·tion [ˌdæmnifiˈkeiʃən; ͵dæmnəfɪˋkeʃən] *n*. 【法】损伤,损害。

dam·ni·fy [ˈdæmnifai; ˋdæmnəfaɪ] *vt*. 【法】损害,损伤。

damn·ing [ˈdæmiŋ; ˋdæmɪŋ] **I** *n*. 咒诅。**II** *a*. **1.** 该死的。**2.** 身败名裂的;逃避不了的。～ *evidence* 逃避不了的罪证。

Dam·o·cles [ˈdæməkliːz; ˋdæmə͵kliz] *n*. 达摩克里斯〔Syracuse 国王 Dionysius 的廷臣〕。**the sword of** ～ 即将临头的危险〔Damocles 常说帝王多福, Dionysius 乃以一发悬剑,命他坐其下,以示帝王多危〕。**-cle·an** [-ˈkliːən; -ˋkliən] *a*.

dam·oi·selle, dam·o·sel, dam·o·zel [ˌdæməˈzel; ͵dæməˋzɛl] *n*. 〔古、诗〕小姐。

Da·mon and Pyth·i·as [ˈdeimən ənd ˈpiθiæs; ˋdemən ənd ˋpɪθɪəs] 生死朋友,莫逆。

damp [dæmp; dæmp] **I** *n*. **1.** 湿气,潮湿。**2.** (矿井里的)有毒气体。**3.** 消沉,沮丧。**cast** [*throw*, *strike*] **a** ～ **over** [*into*] 给…泼冷水,使沮丧。**II** *a*. **1.** 有湿气的,潮湿的。**2.** 消沉的,沮丧的。～ **squib** 〔俚〕湿爆竹;〔喻〕完全的失败;无效的东西,没用的东西;引不起注意[同情]的事情。**III** *vt*. **1.** 弄湿,濡湿,打湿。**2.** 给…泼冷水,使沮丧。**3.** 抑止,阻抑。**4.** 【电】阻尼,使减幅,使衰减。**5.** (用灰等)封(火)(*down*)。**6.** 【乐】制止弦的振动。—*vi*. **1.** 变湿。**2.** (振幅)衰减。～ **down** (用灰把火)封上。～ **off** (植物因霉病而)枯萎。～**ing coil** 阻尼线圈。**damping-off** 【植】枯萎病。～ **proof** *a*. 防湿的,耐湿性的。**-ly** *ad*.

damp·en [ˈdæmpən; ˋdæmpən] *vt*. **1.** 使潮湿。**2.** 抑制;减少;减轻。～ *a sponge* 把海绵弄湿。～ *sb.'s spirits* 打击某人的情绪。—*vi*. 变潮湿。

damp·er [ˈdæmpə; ˋdæmpə˞] *n*. **1.** 使人扫兴的人[事]。**2.** 【乐】(钢琴的)制音器。**3.** 【电】阻尼器;减震器。**4.** (火炉等的)风门,节气闸。**5.** 〔美俚〕现金记录机。**6.** 〔澳〕(在篝火上烤的)硬烧饼。*an air* ～ 气压制动器。*an acoustical* ～ 消声器。～ *pedal* 制音踏板。**cast a** ～ **on** 使…扫兴。

Dam·pier [ˈdæmpjə; ˋdæmpɪə˞] *n*. 丹皮尔〔姓氏〕。

damp·ing [ˈdæmpiŋ; ˋdæmpɪŋ] *n*. 【物】阻尼,减幅,衰减。～ *resistance* 阻尼电阻。

damp·ish [ˈdæmpiʃ; ˋdæmpɪʃ] *a*. 湿渍渍的,潮湿的。

damp·ness [ˈdæmpnis; ˋdæmpnɪs] *n*. 潮湿,润湿;湿度。

dam·sel [ˈdæmzəl; ˋdæmzl̩] *n*. 〔古、诗〕闺女,小姐。

dam·son [ˈdæmzən; ˋdæmzn̩] *n*. **1.** 西洋李子。**2.** (暗)紫色。～ *cheese* 蜜李〔一种甜食〕。

Dan[1] [dæn; dæn] *n*. 丹〔男子名 Daniel(l) 的昵称〕。

Dan[2] [dæn; dæn] *n*. 〔古诗〕= Master; Sir.

Dan[3] [dæn; dæn] *n*. 【圣】**1.** 雅各的第五子。**2.** 在巴勒斯坦北部定居的一族,其后裔即为以色列族。

Dan[4] [dɑːn; dɑn] *n*. 〔Jap.〕段〔表示棋手等技术水平的级别〕。

Dan. = Daniel; Danish.

Da·na [ˈdeinə, ˈdænə; ˋdenə, ˋdænə] *n*. 戴纳〔姓氏,男子名,女子名〕。

Dan·a·ë [ˈdæneiiː; ˋdænei] *n*. 【希神】达那厄〔Argos 王之女,天神宙斯化作金雨与她相会,后生子 Perseus〕。

Da Nang [ˈdɑːˈnɑːŋ; ˋdɑˋnɑŋ] 岘港〔越南港市〕。

dance [dɑːns; dæns] **I** *vi*. **1.** 跳舞,舞蹈,舞。**2.** 跳跃,(影子等)摇晃,(水波)荡漾。—*vt*. **1.** 使跳舞;跳(狐步等)舞。**2.** 舞弄(孩子)。～ **after** 抑…鼻息,听从…指挥,百依百顺地服从(某人)。～ **attendance upon** [*on*] (*sb*.) 侍奉(某人)。～ **away** [*off*] 继续不断地跳舞;错过,失去;跳掉(～ *one's chance away* (因跳舞)失去机会。～ *one's sense off* 跳得忘形)。～ **on** [*upon*] **air** [*a rope*] 被吊死。～ **oneself into** (*a room*; *sb.'s favour*) 舞进(房间)里;舞得(某人宠爱)。～ **to another tune** 改变意见[态度、行动等]。～ **to sb.'s pipe** [*tune*] 跟着某人笛子跳舞,唯某人马首是瞻。～ **upon**

D

nothing 被吊死。~ *with the wolf* 与狼共舞〔和危险人物相过从〕。**II** ***n*.** **1.** 跳舞,舞蹈。**2.** 舞曲。**3.** 舞会。*a social* ~ 交际舞。*a stage* ~ 舞台舞。*~s and delight* 极愉快的跳舞(= delightful ~)。~ *of joy* 〔美〕五月一日的野外土风舞。***give a*** ~ 举行跳舞会。***lead*** **(*sb*.)** ***a pretty*** **[*jolly*]** ~ 拖昏[拖疲](某人)。***lead the*** ~ 领头跳;提倡。

danc·er [ˈdɑːnsə; ˋdænsɚ] ***n*.** 舞女;舞蹈家。*a taxi* ~ (舞厅里的)舞女。*merry ~s* 〔Scot.〕北极光。

danc·ery [ˈdɑːnsəri; ˋdænsərɪ] ***n*.** 跳舞厅。

dan·cette [dɑːnˈset; dænˋsɛt] ***n*.**【建】曲摺饰(= chevron molding)。

danc·ing [ˈdɑːnsiŋ; ˋdænsɪŋ] ***n*.** 跳舞,舞蹈(法)。~ *girl* 舞女。~ *hall* 〔美〕舞厅。~ *master* [*mistress*] 舞蹈教师[女教师]。~ *party* 舞会。~ *saloon* 〔英〕跳舞场。~ *steps*【建】(螺旋形)均衡梯级〔梯级的一端略窄于另一端,也称为 balanced steps〕。

D

dan·de·li·on [ˈdændilaiən; ˋdændɪˏlaɪən] ***n*.**【植】蒲公英。

D and D, D & D = 〔美俚〕**1.** drunk and disorderly (警察用语)酒醉后扰乱治安的。**2.** deaf and dumb 又聋又哑的;〔喻〕装聋作哑的(尤指因为怕报复而对坏事不加告发)。

dan·der [ˈdændə; ˋdændɚ] ***n*.** **1.** 头垢,头皮屑。**2.**〔口〕怒气。*get one's* ~ *up* 发怒。

dan·di·a·cal [dænˈdaiəkəl; dænˋdaɪəkəl] ***a*.** 纨绔子弟(dandy)似的,打扮漂亮的。*a* ~ *pose* 吊儿郎当的样子。

Dan·die Din·mont (terrier) [ˈdændi ˈdinmənt; ˋdændɪ-ˋdɪnmɑnt] 矮鬃犬〔脚短身长的垂耳小犬, Dandie Dinmont 系 Scott 的小说中的人物,他养了两只这种小犬,故名〕。

dan·di·fy [ˈdændifai; ˋdændɪˏfaɪ] ***vt*.** 使像花花公子;使打扮得花哨[时髦]。*dandified ways* 纨绔子弟的行为。

dan·dle [ˈdændl; ˋdændl̩] ***vt*.** **1.** (上下颠动着)舞弄(孩子)。**2.** 宠爱,娇养。

dan·driff, dan·druff [ˈdændrif, -drəf; ˋdændrɪf, -drəf] ***n*.** 头垢,头皮屑。**-y** ***a*.** 头垢多的。

dan·dy[1] [ˈdændi; ˋdændɪ] **I** ***n*.** **1.** 纨绔子弟,花花公子,服装时髦的人。**2.**〔口〕最好的东西,上品。**3.**【英海】(船尾装有一桅的)快艇。*a* ~ *of a boy* 〔美口〕漂亮的少年。**II** ***a*.** **1.** 时髦的,服装华丽的。**2.** 花花公子的。**3.**〔美口〕最好的,第一流的。~ **brush** 鲸须马刷。~ **cart** 〔英〕(送奶人用的)弹簧货车。~ **fever**【医】登革热(= dengue)。~ **roll** 造币业中做水印的滚筒。

dan·dy[2] [ˈdændi; ˋdændɪ] ***n*.** = ~ fever.

dan·dy·ish [ˈdændiiʃ; ˋdændɪɪʃ] ***a*.** 花花公子似的,时髦的。

dan·dy·ism [ˈdændiizəm; ˋdændɪɪzm̩] ***n*.** **1.** 华丽,时髦。**2.** 花花公子的派头[行为]。

Dane[1] [dein; den] ***n*.** 戴恩〔姓氏〕。

Dane[2] [dein; den] ***n*.** 丹麦人。*the* ~ 丹麦民族。*a Great* ~ 丹麦种大狗。

Dane·geld [ˈdeinˌgeld; ˋdenˏgɛld] ***n*.** 抗丹税〔盎格鲁-萨克逊时代为反丹麦入侵而征收的一种税,后作为土地税沿袭征收〕。

dang [dæŋ; dæŋ] ***v*., *n*.** 〔俚〕= damn.

dan·ger [ˈdeindʒə; ˋdendʒɚ] ***n*.** **1.** 危险。**2.** 危险物,威胁。**3.**〔废〕权力,势力范围。*The signal is at* ~.【铁路】(前面)有危险信号。*a* ~ *to peace* 对和平的威胁。*You stand within his* ~, *do you not*? 你的生命捏在他手里呀。***be in*** ~ ***of*** 有…危险。***in*** ~ 在危险中,垂危。***run the*** ~ ***of*** 冒…的危险。***out of*** ~ 脱离危险。~ **money** 从事危险工作的额外报酬,风险补贴。~ **signal** 危险信号。~ **space** (子弹)危险界;(高射炮的)爆炸圈。~ **zone** 危险地带[区域]。

dan·ger·ous [ˈdeindʒərəs; ˋdendʒərəs] ***a*.** 危险的。*a most* ~ *dog* 恶狗。*look* ~ 表现凶狠(不可接近)。**-ly** ***ad*.** 危险。**-ness** ***n*.**

dan·gle [ˈdæŋgl; ˋdæŋgl̩] ***vi*.** **1.** (晃来晃去地)吊着;悬挂着。**2.** 尾随,追逐(女人)(*about*; *after*; *round*)。—***vt*.** 使(晃来晃去地)吊着挂;吊着晃来晃去地引诱。*He ~d a bone in front of the dog*. 他晃动骨头逗狗。**dangling participle**【语】独立分词〔如 After marrying him, her trouble began 中的 marrying〕。

dan·gler [ˈdæŋglə; ˋdæŋglɚ] ***n*.** **1.** 吊着晃来晃去的东西。**2.** 追逐女人的男人。

Dan·iel [ˈdænjəl; ˋdænjəl] ***n*.** **1.** 丹尼尔〔姓氏,男子名〕。**2.** (旧约圣经)《但以理书》。**3.** 有名法官。

da·ni·o [ˈdæniˌəu; ˋdænɪˏo] ***n*.** (*pl*. *~s*) 鲤科鱼。

Dan·ish [ˈdeiniʃ; ˋdenɪʃ] **I** ***a*.** 丹麦的;丹麦人的;丹麦语的。**II** ***n*.** 丹麦语。

Dan·ite [ˈdænait; ˋdænaɪt] **I** ***a*.** 达恩希伯来族的。**II** ***n*.** **1.** 达恩希伯来族人。**2.** 达恩分子〔摩门教的秘密组织的成员〕。

dank [dæŋk; dæŋk] **I** ***a*.** **1.** 潮湿的。**2.** (杂草等)繁茂的。**II** ***n*.** **1.** 潮湿。**2.** 沼泽地,低湿地。

danse du ventre [dɑːns djuː ˈvɑːntrə; ˋdɑ̃s dju ˋvɑntrə] 〔F.〕肚皮舞。

danse ma·ca·bre [dɑːns məˈkɑːbr; ˋdɑ̃sˏməˋkɑbrə] 〔F.〕死的舞蹈;死亡的象征(尤指中世纪绘画中出现的象征死亡的骷髅带领人们走向坟墓的舞蹈)。

dan·seur [dɑːŋˈsəːr; dɑ̃ˋsœr] ***n*.** 芭蕾舞男演员。~ *noble* 芭蕾舞男演员。

dan·seuse [dɑːnˈsəːz; dɑnˋsɜz] ***n*.** (*pl*. *~s* [-səːz; -sɜz]) 〔F.〕芭蕾舞女演员。

Dan·te [ˈdænti; ˋdæntɪ], **Alighieri** 但丁〔1265—1321,意大利诗人,《神曲》(*Divine Comedy*) 作者〕。

Dan·te·an [dænˈtiːən; dænˋtɪən] **I** ***n*.** 但丁研究者;以但丁作模范的人,崇拜但丁的人。**II** ***a*.** 但丁的;但丁式的。

Dan·tesque [dænˈtesk; dænˋtɛsk] ***a*.** 但丁式的。

Dan·ube [ˈdænjuːb; ˋdænjub] ***n*.** 多瑙河〔欧洲〕。

Danu·bi·an [dænˈjuːbiən; dænˋjubɪən] ***a*.** 多瑙河的。

Dan·zig [ˈdæntsig; ˋdæntsɪg] ***n*.** 但泽〔波兰港口,波兰语叫 Gdansk〕。

DAP = Draw-a-Person【心】画人测验(为一种心理测验方法,根据接受治疗者所画人像分析其个性特征等)。

dap [dæp; dæp] **I** ***vi*.** (***dapped***; ***dup·ping***) **1.** 将钓饵轻轻放在水面上钓鱼;垂钓。**2.** (球)弹跳;(石片在水面上)漂掠。**3.** (鸟)轻捷地潜入(水中)。**4.** (在木材上)切出槽口。**II** ***n*.** **1.** (球的)弹跳。**2.** (木材衔接处的)槽口。

Daph·ne [ˈdæfni; ˋdæfnɪ] ***n*.** **1.** 达芙妮〔女子名〕。**2.**【希神】为躲避 Apollo 的追逐而变作月桂树的女神。**3.** 〔d-〕【植】瑞香。

dap·per [ˈdæpə; ˋdæpɚ] ***a*.** **1.** 短小精悍的,小巧玲珑的。**2.** 整洁的。*be* ~ *in dress* 衣冠楚楚。*be* ~ *in appearance* 风度翩翩。

dap·per·ling [ˈdæpəliŋ; ˋdæpɚlɪŋ] ***n*.** 短小精悍的人。

dap·ple [ˈdæpl; ˋdæpl̩] **I** ***n*.** **1.** 斑纹。**2.** 花斑马(等)。**II** ***a*.** 有斑纹的,花斑的。**III** ***vt*., *vi*.** (使)起斑纹。*a ~d deer* 梅花鹿。*a ~d shade* 斑斑点点的树荫。**~-grey** ***a*., *n*.** 灰色而有深色斑点的(马)。

D. A. R. = Daughters of the American Revolution 美国革命女儿会。

darb [dɑːb; dɑrb] ***n*.** 〔美俚〕出众的人;高级的东西。

dar·by [ˈdɑːbi; ˋdɑrbɪ] ***n*.** **1.** (瓦工用的)双耳抹子。**2.** 〔俚〕钱。**3.** 〔*pl*.〕〔俚〕手铐。

Dar·by and Joan [ˈdɑːbi ənd ˈdʒəun; ˋdɑrbɪ ənd ˋdʒon] 白头偕老的夫妇。

Dard [dɑːd; dɑrd] ***n*.** 达尔德语族〔阿富汗东北部、巴基斯坦西部和克什米尔居民讲的印欧语〕(= Dardle)。

Dar·da·nelles [dɑːdəˈnelz; dɑrdn̩ˋɛlz] ***n*.** 达达尼尔海峡。

dare [dɛə; dɛr] **I** ***vi*.** (*~d* [dɛəd; dɛrd], 〔古〕***durst***

[dəːst; dɝst]; ～d) *v. aux.*〔在陈述句中,用作主要动词,接带 to 的不定式;在疑问、否定、条件句中,用作助动词,其后接不带 to 的不定式。〕敢,胆敢。*He ～ not fight.* 他不敢打。*D- he do it?* 他敢做那件事吗? *He won't ～ (to) deny it.* 他未必敢否认那件事。*He ～s to insult me.* 他竟敢侮辱我。*Don't you ～ to touch me.* 你敢碰我?! — *vt.* 1. 冒险;敢于承担。2. 挑逗[激](某人做某事) ～ *all dangers* 冒种种危险。*I ～ damnation.* 我不怕刀山火海。*He ～d me to jump.* 他挑唆我跳。*I will do it if I am ～d to.* 如果有人激我,我一定做。***I ～ say*** 我想,我看(大概) (*I ～ say you are mistaken.* 我认为你错了)。***I ～ swear.*** 我确信,一定。II *n.*〔口〕1. 胆量,勇气。2. 挑逗。

dare·dev·il [ˈdɛəˌdevl; ˋdɛrˏdɛvl] *a., n.* 胆大的(人),冒失的;冒失鬼。**-il·try,**〔英〕**-il·ry** *n.* 鲁莽,冒失。

Dar el Bei·da [ˈdaːr el baiˈdaː; ˋdar ɛl baɪˋda] 达尔贝达〔即 Casablanca 卡萨布兰卡〕〔摩洛哥港市〕。

daren't [dɛənt; dɛrnt] = dare not.

dare·say [ˈdɛəsei; ˋdɛrse] *v.* = dare say.

Dar es Sa·laam [ˈdaːr es səˈlaːm; ˋdar ɛs səˋlam] 达来(斯)撒拉(姆)(达累斯萨拉姆)〔坦尚(桑)尼亚首都〕。

dar·ing [ˈdɛəriŋ; ˋdɛrɪŋ] I *a.* 1. 胆大的,勇敢的。2. 意气风发的。*Never before have they been so inspired, and so ～ as at present.* 从来也没有看见他们像现在这样精神振奋,意气风发。II *n.* 大胆,勇敢。**-ly** *ad.* **-ness** *n.*

Da·ri·us [dəˈraiəs; dəˋraɪəs] *n.* **Hystaspis** 大流士一世(558?—486 B. C.),古代波斯王,在位期间 521—486 B. C.,世称 ～ the Great.

Dar·jee·ling [daːˈdʒiːliŋ; darˋdʒilɪŋ] *n.* (印度)大吉岭茶。

dark [daːk; dark] I *a.* 1. 暗,暗黑的;微暗的,阴沉的。2. 浅黑的,(皮肤)带黑色的;深,浓(色)。3. 秘密的,隐秘的。4. 难解的;(句法等)含糊的。5. 阴郁的;希望暗淡的。6. 愚昧的,蒙昧无知的。7. 狠毒的,(计划等)阴险的。8. 郁郁不乐的。9. (戏院等)已熄灯关门的。10.【语音】浊。11. (咖啡)掺了少量牛奶[奶油]的。*look on the ～ side of things* 看事物的黑暗面,悲观。*keep a thing ～* 保守某事的秘密。*in a ～ temper [humour]* 不高兴。***keep ～*** 隐瞒;隐藏。II *n.* 1. 暗黑;暗处;暗色。2. 愚昧,无知。3. 隐晦,隐秘。4. 夜,傍晚。5.〔美〕阴影;浓(淡)。***at ～*** 黄昏时候。***in the ～*** 1. 在暗处。2. 秘密,暗中(*plot in the ～* 暗中策划)。3. 不知(*be in the ～ about it* 完全不知道那个。*leave one in the ～* 不给某人知道)。～**-adapt** *vt.* 使(瞳孔)适应黑暗。～ **ages** (中世纪的)黑暗时代。～ **blue** 深蓝色。～ **comedy** 黑色幽默,黑色喜剧 (*cf.* black 条)。～ **day** 1. 密云[浓雾]笼罩下的日子;不吉利的日子,倒霉时候。2.〔*pl.*〕失意时代,不得意的时候;(冬季)夜长昼短的日子。～ **deeds** 坏事。～ **horse**【赛马】实力未明的马;(竞赛等的)预想不到的劲敌;'黑马'。～ **lantern** 有遮光装置的提灯。～ **lantern caucus**〔美〕秘密会议。～ **l** 浊音 l〔辅音前或语尾的 l: silk, tall. 元音前的 l 叫清音 l: look, clear〕。～ **light** 不可见光。～ **matter**【天】暗物质,黑体〔据称宇宙的 90% 都是由此种不发光的物质组成的〕。～ **plan** 秘密计划。～ **repair**【生】暗修复(不用光线,借助特殊的酶修复受损或断裂的 DNA 分子链)。～ **room**【摄】暗室。～ **secret** 谁也不知道的秘密。

dark·en [ˈdaːkən; ˋdarkən] *vt.* 1. 使暗,遮暗。2. 弄模糊。3. 使愁闷。4. 弄污。5. 弄瞎。— *vi.* 1. 变黑暗,阴。2. 变瞎。～ ***counsel*** 使乱上加乱,使更加纠纷。～ ***sb.'s door*** 访人(*Don't ～ my door again.* 下次不要再到我家来了)。

dark·ey [ˈdaːki; ˋdarkɪ] *n.*〔蔑〕= darky.

dark·ish [ˈdaːkiʃ; ˋdarkɪʃ] *a.* 微黑的;浅黑的;阴暗的。

dar·kle [ˈdaːkl; ˋdarkl] *vi.* 1. 变黑;变暗;阴沉下来。2. 板起面孔。3. 躲进暗处。

dark·ling [ˈdaːkliŋ; ˋdarklɪŋ]〔古〕I *a.* 1. 在黑暗中的。2. 朦胧的。II *ad.* 在黑暗中。

dark·ly [ˈdaːkli; ˋdarklɪ] *ad.* 1. 暗;黑。2. 朦胧,模糊。3. 秘密,暗中。4. 恶,毒。*seeing a ship but ～ against the horizon* 隐约看见天边一只船。*The storm clouds gathered ～.* 阴云密集。*glancing ～ at his opponent* 恶狠狠地看着敌人。

dark·ness [ˈdaːknis; ˋdarknɪs] *n.* 1. 黑暗,阴暗。2. 秘密。3. 盲目。4. 蒙昧,无知。5. 黑心,阴险。6. 含糊。***the velvet ～*** 乌黑。*Egyptian ～* 漆黑。***cast sb. into the outer ～*** 赶走,解雇。***deeds of ～*** 坏事,罪恶。***the Prince of ～*** 魔王,恶魔。

dark·some [ˈdaːksəm; ˋdarksəm] *a.* 1.〔诗〕微暗的;带黑色的,阴暗的,阴郁的。2.〔古〕晦涩难解的。

dark·y, darkie [ˈdaːki; ˋdarkɪ] *n.*〔美蔑〕黑人。

dar·ling [ˈdaːliŋ; ˋdarlɪŋ] I *n.* 1. 爱人,情人。2. 宠儿;宠物。*My ～!* 亲爱的〔夫妻间的称呼〕;宝宝〔父母对儿女的称呼〕。***the ～ of fortune*** 幸运儿。II *a.* 心爱的;中意的;宝贵的。

darn[1] [daːn; darn] *vt., n.* 1. 缝补,补缀。2. 补丁。

darn[2] [daːn; darn] *vt., n.*〔主美〕= damn. *D- it!* 讨厌! *He could not see a ～ without his glasses.* 他不戴眼镜就什么也看不清楚了。

darned [daːnd; darnd] *a.*〔美〕= damned.

dar·nel [ˈdaːnl; ˋdarnl] *n.*【植】毒麦。

darn·ing [ˈdaːniŋ; ˋdarnɪŋ] *n.* 缝补;缝补物。～ **ball [egg]** (衬着缝补衣物用的)缝补球。～ **last** 缝补台。～ **needle** 缝补针;〔美方〕蜻蜓。

Darn·ley [ˈdaːnli; ˋdarnlɪ] *n.* 达恩利〔姓氏〕。

Dar·row [ˈdærəu; ˋdæro] *n.* 达罗〔姓氏〕。

Dar(r)yl [ˈdæril; ˋdærɪl] *n.* 达里尔〔男子名〕。

dar·shan [ˈdəːʃən, ˈdaː-; ˋdɝʃən, ˋdar-] *n.* (能见伟人一面而)有德;沾光,增禄;得福〔印度教徒的迷信〕。

dart [daːt; dart] I *n.* 1. 标枪,短矛;镖。2.〔*pl.*〕掷标枪。3. 突进。4. (虫的)螫,刺。5. (缝纫)暗针,暗线;捏褶。6. 飞快的一瞥;飞快的移动。7. 突然的刺痛。II *vt., vi.* 1. 投掷(标枪等);发射,放射。2. 急冲;突进。

dart·er [ˈdaːtə; ˋdartɚ] *n.* 1. 掷标枪的人;突进者。2.【鸟】鹈类。3.【鱼】飞鱼。

dar·tle [ˈdaːtl; ˋdartl] *vt., vi.* 连续发射;不断突进;不断伸缩。*an adder's dartling tongue* 蝰蛇的不断伸缩的舌头。

Dart·moor [ˈdaːtmuə; ˋdartmʊr] *n.* 1. (英国 Devon 郡的)达特姆尔高原。2. 达特姆尔监狱。3. 达特姆尔羊(毛粗而长)。

Dart·mouth [ˈdaːtməθ; ˋdartməθ] *n.* 1. (英国 Devonshire 的)达特茅斯港口。2. 达特茅斯皇家海军学校。

Dar·von [ˈdaːvɔːn; ˋdarvɔn] *n.* 达而丰〔一种止痛药的商标〕。

Dar·win[1] [ˈdaːwin; ˋdarwɪn] *n.* 达尔文〔澳大利亚港市〕。

Dar·win[2] [ˈdaːwin; ˋdarwɪn] *n.* 1. 达尔文〔姓氏,男子名〕。**Charles** ～ 达尔文〔1809—1882,英国博物学家,进化论创始人〕。2. 月面第三象限的壁平原。

Dar·win·i·an [daːˈwiniən; darˋwɪnɪən] I *a.* 达尔文的。II *n.* 达尔文派(的人)。～ **Theory** 达尔文的进化论。

Dar·win·ism [ˈdaːwinizəm; ˋdarwɪnˏɪzəm] *n.* 达尔文主义,进化论。**-win·ist** *n.* 进化论者。

DASH = drone antisubmarine helicopter 无线电遥控反潜艇攻击机。

dash [dæʃ; dæʃ] I *vt.* 1. 猛冲,猛撞;猛掷。2. 撞破,碰碎,打碎,掼碎。3. 浇,洒,泼(水等);溅。4. 乱涂。5. 匆忙完成 (*down; off*)。6. (少量)搀,混和。7. 使(计划等)失败;使失望。8. 使沮丧,使狼狈。9.〔英〕= damn. ～ *a mirror to pieces* 把镜子摔得粉碎。～ *water in [over] a person's face* 泼水到脸上。*D- it!* 可恶! 讨厌! *I'll be ～ed if = I'll be damned if.* — *vi.* 1. 猛冲,猛进。2. 猛击。3. 炫耀衣着。～ ***against [upon]***

与…碰撞,撞在…上。～ ***down*** 猛掷,猛掼。～ ***forward*** 突进,猛冲。～ ***in*** 跳进。～ ***off*** **1.** 飞出;急忙离开。**2.** 一气写成[写完](文章等)。～ ***out*** **1.** 删去,涂掉。**2.** 跳出,跑开。～ ***to pieces*** 粉碎。～ ***up*** 冲上前;跑来。**II** ***n*.** **1.** 猛冲,猛进;冲锋,突击。**2.** 碰撞。**3.** (浪、雨等)打击声。**4.** (少量的)搀和;少量的搀和物。**5.** 锐气,闯劲。**6.** 笔触,笔势。**7.** 炫耀,虚饰;外观,门面。**8.** 挫折,打击。**9.** 【印】长划,破折号。**10.** (莫尔斯电码的)长划〔与 dot 相对〕。**11.** 【体】短跑。**12.** = ～ board. *a* ～ *of brandy* 少许白兰地。*red with a* ～ *of purple* 有点发紫的红色。*a hundred-meter* ～ 百米赛跑。*a swung* ～ 代字号〔即～,又叫 tilde〕。***a*** ～ ***to one's hopes*** 希望落空。***at a*** ～ 一气,一举。***cut a*** ～ 大出风头;铺张门面,打扮漂亮。***have both skill and*** ～ 既有技巧,又有干劲。***make a*** ～ ***for*** 向…猛冲。～ **board** **1.** (马车的)遮泥板。**2.** 【海】防波板。**3.** (墙的)遮雨板。**4.** (汽车的)仪表盘。～ **light** 仪表板灯。～ **plate** 【机】缓冲板。～ **pot** 缓冲器,减震器,阻尼延迟器。

D

da·sheen [ˌdæˈʃiːn; ˏdæˋʃin] ***n*.** 【植】芋头(= taro)。

dash·er [ˈdæʃə; ˋdæʃɚ] ***n*.** **1.** 猛冲者。**2.** (奶油)搅拌器。**3.** 〔美〕遮泥板;遮水板。**4.** 〔口〕有干劲的人。

dash·ing [ˈdæʃiŋ; ˋdæʃɪŋ] ***a*.** **1.** 勇敢的,有锐气[干劲]的。**2.** 浮华的,打扮漂亮的。**-ly** ***ad*.**

dash·y [ˈdæʃi; ˋdæʃɪ] ***a*.** 外表好看的,浮华的;漂亮的,时髦的。

das·sie [ˈdɑːsiː; ˋdɑsi] ***n*.** 蹄兔科动物。

das·tard [ˈdæstəd; ˋdæstɚd] **I** ***n*.** 懦夫〔尤指干了坏事而不承当责任的人〕。**II** ***a*.** 怯懦的,畏缩的。**-ly** ***a*.** (*a* ～*ly act* 卑劣的行为)。

das·yure [ˈdæsijuːə; ˋdæsɪjuə] ***n*.** 【动】袋猫。

DAT = digital audio tape 数字式录音磁带。

da·ta [ˈdeitə; ˋdetə] ***n*.** **1.** 资料,材料〔此词系 datum 的复数。但 datum 罕用,一般即以 data 作为集合词,在口语中往往用单数动词;如系指一件资料,则说作 this ～〕。**2.** 〔美〕(观察所得的)事实,知识。*a* ～ *book* 参考资料书。*gather* ～ *on* ...收集…的资料[数据]。*The* ～ *is not enough to be convincing*. 资料不足,尚难令人信服。～ **bank** 资料库,数据库。～ **link** 【计】数据自动传送装置,数据传输器。～ **logger** 【计】数据记录器。～ **highway** 信息(高速)公路〔由电脑网络组成〕。～ **logging** 【自】数据记录。～ **mining** 【计】数据挖掘。～ **phone** 【讯】数据送话机。～ **processing** 【自】数据处理。～ **processor** 数据处理机;处理数据的人。～ **set** 【计】**1.** 数据集。**2.** 数传机。～ **warehouse** 【计】数据仓库。

dat·a·ble [ˈdeitəbl; ˋdetəbḷ] ***a*.** 可推定[测定]日期[年代]的。

da·tal·ler [ˈdeitələ; ˋdetəlɚ] ***n*.** = daytal(l)er.

da·ta·ma·tion [ˌdeitəˈmeiʃən; ˏdetəˋmeʃən] ***n*.** **1.** 【计】自动数据处理。**2.** (生产、出售、提供数据处理设备的)数据处理业。

da·ta·ry [ˈdeitəri; ˋdetərɪ] ***n*.** 【天主】**1.** (罗马教廷)教廷官员资格与圣俸审查官署。**2.** 掌管此官署的红衣主教。

datch·a [ˈdɑːtʃə; ˋdɑtʃə] ***n*.** = dacha.

date[1] [deit; det] **I** ***n*.** **1.** 日期。**2.** 时期;时代,年代。**3.** 〔美口〕(和异性的)约会;〔美俚〕约会的对象。**4.** 〔口〕同日;本日。*make a* ～ 定一个(会面的)日期。*She is his* ～. 她跟他有约会。***at an early*** ～ 日内。***bear*** ～ …载有(某某)年月日。***break*** [***cut***] ***the*** ～ 不遵守约会。***down to*** ～ = to ～. ***of early*** ～ 初期的,古代的。***out of*** ～ 过时的,陈腐的,旧式的。***to*** ～ 到今天,至今,到现在。***under*** ～ (***of***) (*Jan*. 5) 于(一月五号)。***up to*** ～ **1.** 直到现在(的),直到最近(的)。**2.** 最新式的,时兴的。***without*** ～ 〔美〕无期。**II** ***vt*.** **1.** 给…注明日期。**2.** 断定(事物的)年代。**3.** 〔美口〕和…约会。*a bill* ～*d the 7th of May* 五月七日的支票。— ***vi*.** **1.** 记有日子。**2.** 起,始(*from*)。**3.** 进行约会。～ **back to** 回溯至,(年代)远在。～ **bait** 〔美俚〕勾引男子与自己约会的女子。～ **book** **1.** (记载约会日期等的)记事册。**2.** 台历。～ **line** **1.** 【天】日界线〔东经或西经 180 度的子午线〕。**2.** = ～line. ～**line** **1.** ***n*.** 日期;〔口〕电讯电头。**2.** ***vt*.** 注明电讯发稿日期和地点,写上电讯电头。～**mark** 日戳。～ **slip** (图书馆)借书卡。～ **stamp** 邮戳。**-less** ***a*.** **1.** 无日期的,年代不明的。**2.** 太古的。**3.** 〔美俚〕没有异性伴侣的。**4.** 经住时间考验的。**5.** 无限期的。

date[2] [deit; det] ***n*.** **1.** 海枣属。**2.** 海枣。*a Chinese* ～ 枣,中国枣。～ **palm** 枣椰树。

Da·tel, da·tel [deiˈtel, ˈdeitel; deˋtɛl, ˋdetɛl] ***n*.** (英国的)数据用户电报(为用户提供的一种用计算机高速传输数据的业务)。

dat·er [ˈdeitə; ˋdetɚ] ***n*.** 日期戳子。

dat·ing [ˈdeitiŋ; ˋdetɪŋ] ***n*.** **1.** 记日期。**2.** 【商】(支付的)延期日期。**3.** 〔美〕幽会。～ **machine** [**perforator**] 日期戳子。～ **nail** 【铁路】(钉在枕木上的)日期钉。～ **parlor** (尤指男女学生的)幽会。

da·tive [ˈdeitiv; ˋdetɪv] **I** ***n*.** 【语法】与格。**II** ***a*.** **1.** 【语法】与格的。**2.** 【法】(物品等)可随意赠与他人的;(官员等)可免职的。

da·to, dat·to [ˈdɑːtəu; ˋdɑto] ***n*.** (*pl*. ～*s*) (菲律宾)摩洛部族酋长。

da·tum [ˈdeitəm; ˋdetəm] ***n*.** (*pl*. ***da·ta*** [ˈdeitə; ˋdetə]) [L.] **1.** 〔常 *pl*.〕数据,资料。**2.** 论据,作为论据的事实。**3.** 【数】已知数。**4.** 【测】基点,基线,基面。～ **level** 基准水平面。～ **line** 基准线。～ **mark** 【测】基(准)点。～ **plane** 【测】基(准)面。

da·tu·ra [dəˈtjuərə; dəˋtjʊrə] ***n*.** 【植】蔓陀罗。

daub [dɔːb; dɔb] **I** ***n*.** **1.** 涂抹。**2.** 涂料。**3.** 拙劣的画。**II** ***vt*., *vi*.** **1.** 涂,涂抹(*with*)。**2.** 弄脏;乱涂(颜料)。**3.** 胡画(拙劣的画)。～ *a wall with mud* 用泥巴抹墙。*a poor picture carelessly* ～*ed over* 草率画成的蹩脚画。

daub·er [ˈdɔːbə; ˋdɔbɚ] ***n*.** **1.** 涂抹者;涂抹工具。**2.** 拙劣的画匠。**3.** 泥水匠。**4.** 〔美俚〕精神,勇气。*Just keep your* ～ *up and your mouth shut*. 打起精神,闭住嘴。

daub·ster [ˈdɔːbstə; ˋdɔbstɚ] ***n*.** 拙劣的画家。

daub·y [ˈdɔːbi; ˋdɔbɪ] ***a*.** **1.** 黏性的。**2.** 潦草的,乱画的。

daugh·ter [ˈdɔːtə; ˋdɔtɚ] **I** ***n*.** **1.** 女儿(*opp*. son)。**2.** (某地的)妇女。**3.** 【生】子体,子代。**4.** 【原】子核;产物。～ *of revolution* 革命女儿。～ ***of Eve*** 女人。～ ***of Momus*** 受嘲弄的人,滑稽的人。**II** ***a*.** **1.** 女儿(般)的。**2.** 【生】第一代的。～ **cell** (经细胞分裂而新形成的)子细胞。～ **element** 【化】子元素。～**hood** **1.** 女儿的身份;女儿时代。**2.** 〔集合词〕女儿们。～**-in-law** (*pl*. ～***s-in-law*** [ˈdɔːtəzinlɔː; ˋdɔtɚzɪnˏlɔ]) 儿媳妇;继女。**-ly** ***a*.** 女儿(似)的。

daunt [dɔːnt; dɔnt] ***vt*.** **1.** 吓,恐吓。**2.** 使畏缩,使胆怯,使气馁。*No difficulties in the world can* ～ *us*. 世界上任何困难都吓不倒我们。*He was* ～*ed by the amount of work still to be done*. 他被那百废待举的形势弄得灰心丧气。**-less** ***a*.** 不屈不挠的,大胆的,大无畏的。

dau·phin [ˈdɔːfin; ˋdɔfɪn] ***n*.** 法国皇太子〔1349 年至 1830 年的称呼〕。**-e** [ˈdɔːfi(ː)n; ˋdɔfɪn], **-ess** [-nis; -nɪs] ***n*.** 法国皇太子妃。

daut [dɔːt, dɔt; dɑt, dɔt] ***vt*.** 〔Scot.〕爱抚;宠爱。

Dav·en·port [ˈdævnpɔːt; ˋdævənˏpɔrt] ***n*.** 达文波特〔姓氏〕。

dav·en·port [ˈdævənpɔːt; ˋdævənˏpɔrt] ***n*.** **1.** 〔英〕(有盖)书桌。**2.** 〔美〕(坐卧两用)长沙发。

Da·vid [ˈdeivid; ˋdevɪd] ***n*.** **1.** 大卫〔《圣经》古以色列国王〕。**2.** 戴维〔姓氏,男子名〕。～ ***and Jonathan*** 同生共死的朋友。

Da·vid·son [ˈdeividsn; ˋdevɪdsn] ***n*.** 戴维森〔姓氏〕。

da Vin·ci [dəˈvintʃi; dəˋvɪntʃɪ], ***Leonar·do*** 达芬奇〔1452—1519,意大利的画家、雕刻家、建筑家、工程师〕。

Da·vis [ˈdeivis; ˋdevɪs] ***n*.** 戴维斯〔姓氏,男子名〕。~ **cup** 戴维斯杯〔美国人 D. F. Davis 捐献给国际网球比赛的银杯〕。~ **tournament** 戴维斯杯锦标赛。

Da·vis·son [ˈdeivisn; ˋdevɪsn̩] ***n*.** 戴维森〔姓氏〕。

dav·it [ˈdævit; ˋdævɪt] ***n*. 1.** (轮船上的)吊艇柱,吊艇架。**2.** (放锚和起锚用的)吊柱,吊杆。

Da·vy [ˈdeivi; ˋdevɪ] ***n*.** 戴维〔男子名, David 的昵称〕。~ **Jone's** 〔海俚〕海魔(*go* [*be sent*] *to* ~ *Jone's locker* 淹死,葬身海底)。~ **lamp** (初期的)矿灯。

da·vy [ˈdeivi; ˋdevɪ] ***n*.** 〔俚〕= affidavit. ***take one's*** ~ 宣誓,发誓。

daw[1] [dɔː; dɔ] ***n*.** 【鸟】= jackdaw.

daw[2] [dɔː; dɔ] ***vi*.** 〔Scot.〕破晓,黎明。

daw·dle [ˈdɔːdl; ˋdɔdl] ***vt*., *vi*.** 混日子,偷赖,磨蹭。~ ***away one's time*** 混日子。**-r** 游手好闲的人,懒人。

dawk [dɔːk; dɔk] ***n*.** (政治、外交主张)介乎鸽派 (dove) 和鹰派 (hawk) 之间的中间派,非鹰非鸽派。

dawn [dɔːn; dɔn] **I *n*. 1.** 黎明,拂晓;曙光。**2.** 开端,发端,端绪,萌芽。**3.** 醒悟。*before the* ~ *of history* 有史以前。***at*** ~ 拂晓,天一亮。***from*** ~ ***till dusk*** 从早到晚。**II *vi*. 1.** 破晓,东方发白,露曙光。**2.** 开始出现,渐露端倪。**3.** 渐渐明白,渐悟 (*on*, *upon*)。*It* [*Day*, *Morning*] ~*s*. 天亮了,东方发白了。*This fact has just* ~*ed upon me*. 这件事我现在才明白了。~*ing consciousness* 开始醒悟。

dawn·ing [ˈdɔːniŋ; ˋdɔnɪŋ] ***n*. 1.** 黎明,拂晓。**2.** 东方。**3.** 开端,端绪。**4.** 曙光。*the* ~ *of a new era* 新时代的曙光。

Daw·son [ˈdɔːsn; ˋdɔsn] ***n*.** 道森〔姓氏〕。

dawt [dɔːt, dɑt; dɑt, dɔt] ***vt*.** 爱抚;宠爱(= daut)。

Day [dei; de] ***n*.** 戴〔姓氏〕。

day [dei; de] ***n*. 1.** 日,一日。**2.** 节日;规定的日期,约定的日子。**3.** 昼,白昼,白天;日光。**4.** 〔常 *pl*.〕时代;全盛时代。**5.** 寿命,生平。**6.** (某日的)战斗;胜负,胜利。*May 1st International Labour D-* 五一国际劳动节。*the National D-* 国庆节。*in a* ~ *or two* 过一二日,一两天内。*a creature of a* ~ 短命的生物。*before* ~ 天亮前。*His* ~ *is done*. 他的得意时代已经过去了。*Every dog has his* ~. 每人一生中总有得意的日子。*The* ~ *is doubtful*. 胜负难料。*The* ~ *is ours*! 胜利是我们的。*How goes the* ~? 战况如何? ***all*** ~ (***long***) 终日,一天到晚。***at that*** ~ 那时候。***better*** ~***s*** 黄金时代(*have seen better* ~*s* 曾过过好日子)。***between two*** ~***s*** 通夜,终夜。***by*** ~ 白天,在白天。***by the*** ~ 计日,论日(工作等)。(*We will*) ***call it a*** ~ 〔俚〕今天就这样算了,结束了。***carry the*** ~ 得胜;胜利完成。~ ***about*** 隔日。~ ***after*** ~ = ~ ***by*** ~ 成天,天天,每天。~ ***and night*** 日日夜夜,昼夜。~ ***in*** (***and***) ~ ***out*** 日日夜夜,一天又一天。~ ***of grace*** 到期票据的宽限日〔通常为缓期三天〕。~ ***of obligation*** 须停止工作去做礼拜的日子。~ ***to*** ~ ***money*** 暂时的借款。***during the*** ~ = by ~. ***end one's*** ~***s*** 死。***every other*** ~ 每隔一天。***for*** ~***s on end*** 接连数日。***from*** ~ ***to*** ~ 日日,日复一日,一天一天。***from this*** ~ ***forth*** 从今天以后。***give the time of*** ~ 问候,致意。***have one's*** ~ 转运,走运,有得意的时候。***if a*** ~ 至少(*He is fifty*, *if a* ~. = *He is fifty*, *if he is a* ~ *old*. 他至少五十岁)。***in a*** ~ 一日,一朝一夕。***in broad*** ~ 在大白天。***in*** ~***s gone by*** = ***in*** ~***s of old*** [***yore***] 在从前,已往。***in*** ~***s to come*** 将来,后世。***in one's*** ~ 年轻时候;在旺盛的时候。***in our*** ~***s*** 如今,目下。***in those*** ~***s*** 当时,那时候。***keep one's*** ~ 守约。***man of other*** ~***s*** 古人。***man of the*** ~ 当代名人。***name the*** ~ (女子)决定(结婚等的)日期。***night and*** ~ 不分昼夜,始终。***of the*** ~ 当时的;现在的(问题等)。***one*** ~ (过去或将来的)某一天。***one of these*** (***fine***) ~***s*** 日内,不日。***one*** ~ ***before*** [***after***] ***the fair*** 过早[迟],太早[迟]。***one's*** ~ ***has gone*** 大势已去。***pass the time of*** ~ 问候,致意。***some*** ~ 有一天,某一天。***the*** ~ ***after tomorrow*** 后天。***the*** ~ ***before yesterday*** 前天。★上两条美语常省去 the. ***the*** ~ ***of*** ~***s*** 重大的日子。***The*** ~ ***will come when*** .... 终归有一天将会…。***the other*** ~ 前几天。***these*** ~***s*** 现在,今天。***this*** ~ ***week*** [***year***] 上星期[去年]的今日;下星期[明年]的今日。***till this*** ~ 到今天。***to a*** ~ 恰恰,正巧(*It is now five years to a* ~. 正好五年)。***to this*** ~ 直到今天。***up to this*** ~ 到今天。***win*** [***lose***] ***the*** ~ 打胜[败]。***without*** ~ 无期,不定期。~**bill** (戏剧等的)海报,广告招贴。~ **bed** 兼作沙发用卧铺。~ **blindness** 昼盲症。~ **boarder** 走读生。~**book 1.**【商】日记账,流水簿。**2.**【海】航海日记。~**break** 黎明,拂晓。~**-by-**~ ***a*.** 每日的 (*a* ~*-by-*~ *account* 每日汇报)。~ **clock** 每日上一次的钟。~ **coach** 普通客车。~**dream** 幻想,空想,白日梦。~**dreamer** 空想家。~**-flower** 鸭跖草属花。~**fly**【虫】蜉蝣。~ **hospital** 只看门诊的医院。~ **labo(u)r** 日工,零工。~ **labo(u)rer** 做零工的工人。~ **letter** 〔美〕(比一般电报缓慢的)日间电报。~**long *a*.** 终日的,整天整日的;(*ad*.) 终日,一日到头。~**man 1.** 按日计工的人。**2.** 做日班的人。~ **nursery** 日间托儿所。~**-off** 休息日。~**-release** 〔英〕职工脱产进修制度。~ **return** 〔英〕(火车或长途汽车)当日来回票。~**room** (学校等的)休息室;(军营等的)娱乐室。~**-sailer *n*.** 〔主英〕短途游览帆船。~ **school** 日校;走读学校。~**spring 1.** 〔诗〕黎明,拂晓。**2.** 开端。~**star 1.** 晨星。**2.** 〔诗〕太阳。~ **tal(l)er** 按日雇用的短工。~**-time** 日间,白天。~**-to-**~ ***a*.** 日常的。~ **trader** 当日买卖投机者。~**work *n*. 1.** 白天的工作。**2.** 按日或按小时计酬的工作。

Day·ak, Dy·ak [ˈdaiæk; ˋdaɪæk] ***n*. 1.** 达雅克人〔婆罗洲内地的本土人〕。**2.** 达雅克语。

Day-Glo [ˈdeiˈgləu; ˋdeˋglo] **I *n*.** "狄格洛"加色剂〔一种颜料,染料的加色剂的商标名〕。**II *a*.** "狄格洛"加色剂的;"狄格洛"加色剂状的。

day·light [ˈdeilait; ˋdeˏlaɪt] ***n*. 1.** 日光;白昼,白天;清早,黎明。**2.** 公开,发表。**3.** (竞赛中船与船间等的)间隔。**4.** 〔*pl*.〕〔俚〕眼睛;视力;智力;活动力。***at*** ~ 黎明,拂晓,天一亮。***beat*** [***frighten***, ***scare***] ***the*** (***living***) ~***s out of sb*.** 痛打,威吓。***burn*** ~ 白费精力,做无益的事。~ ***lamp*** 日光灯。~ ***saving*** 日光节约。~***-saving time*** 夏令时,夏季时间。***in broad*** ~ 在大白天,在光天化日之下。***let*** ~ ***into*** 〔俚〕开孔;刺死。***No*** ~! (主人对客人)斟满〔指酒与酒杯边缘之间没有间隔〕。***see*** ~ 〔俚〕**1.** 了解。**2.** 有(完成、解决的)希望。

daze [deiz; dez] **I *vt*. 1.** 使眼花,耀眼。**2.** 使迷乱,使茫然。**II *n*.** 迷乱,茫然。

daz·zle [ˈdæzl; ˋdæzl] **I *vt*. 1.** 使眼花,耀眼,使眼花缭乱。**2.** 使茫然。— ***vi*.** 闪,耀;晃眼。**II *n*. 1.** 眩惑,炫耀。**2.** 使人眼花缭乱的事物。~ **lamps** [**lights**] (汽车的)强光前灯。~ **paint** (涂在船身上的)掩护色。

daz·zling [ˈdæzliŋ; ˋdæzlɪŋ] ***a*.** 晃眼睛的,灿烂的。*a* ~ *advertisement* 五光十色的广告。

db. 【物】= decibel(s) 分贝(电平、音强单位)。

D. B. = double bottom 双层底;daybook 日记账;〔美〕= disciplinary barracks 军人监狱;〔美口〕= drop-by 礼节性顺访;社交性亮相。

D-B = Daimler-Benz (德国)戴姆勒-奔驰汽车公司。

DBA = **1.** Doctor of Business Administration 工商管理学博士。**2.** dihydrodimethyl-benzopyranbutyric acid 【生化】二氢—二甲基—苯并吡喃—丁酸。**3.** doing business as 以…公司名义营业。

D. B. H. = diameter breast high【林】树干直径。

DBS = direct broadcasting by satellite 卫星直播。

DBST = Double British Summer Time 英国双重夏令时(比格林尼治时间提早 2 小时,比夏令时间提早 1 小时)。

dbt. = debit 借方。

DC, D. C. = **1.** direct current 直流电：*a DC generator* 直流发电机。**2.** District of Columbia 哥伦比亚特区〔美国首都华盛顿所在的行政区域〕：Washington, *D. C.* 美国首都华盛顿。**3.**〔It.〕*da capo* (= repeat from the beginning). **4.** Deputy Consul 副领事。**5.** District Court〔美〕地方初审法院。

DCC = digital compact cassette 数字式高密录音带〔激光卡带〕。

D. Ch. E. = Doctor of Chemical Engineering 化学工程学博士。

D. C. L., DCL = Doctor of Civil Law 民法学博士。

D. C. M. = **1.** Distinguished Conduct Medal〔英〕(陆军)特等军功章。**2.** District Court-Martial 地方军事法庭。

DC of S = Deputy Chief of Staff 副参谋长。

D. D. = **1.** Doctor of Divinity 神学博士。**2.** double deck 双层甲板的。

D

d. d. = *dono dedit*〔L.〕作为礼物赠送。

D / D = demand(ed) draft 即期汇票。

D/D, D/d, d. d. = days after date 期后日数(票据)。

d / d = delivered 已交付，已交货。

d—d [diːd, dæmd; did, dæmd] = damned〔口〕该死的。

D-Day [ˈdiːdei; ˋdi-de] ***n*.** **1.** (第二次世界大战中盟军在西欧发起反攻的)反攻日。**2.** (一般的)攻击发起日。**3.** 十进日〔英国将货币与度量衡改为十进制的日子〕。

DDD = dichloro-diphenyl-dichloroethane【化】二氯二苯二氯乙烷；滴滴滴〔一种杀虫剂〕。

DDS = **1.** Doctor of Dental Surgery〔美〕牙科博士。**2.** Doctor of Dental Science 牙科学博士。

DDT = dichloro-diphenyl-trichloroethane【化】二氯二苯三氯乙烷，滴滴涕〔一种杀虫剂〕。

DDVP = dimethyl dichloroving phosphate 敌敌畏(商品名，一种杀虫剂)。

DE = destroyer escort 护航驱逐舰。

de[1] [diː; di] ***prep*.**〔L.〕= down from, from, off. ***de fac·to*** [-ˈfæktəu; -ˋfækto] 事实上(的)。***de fide*** [-ˈfaidi; -ˋfaɪdɪ] 该作信条遵守的。***de in·te·gro*** [-ˈintigrəu; -ˋɪntɪgro] 重行，另行，再。***de jure*** [ˈdʒuəri; ˋdʒuərɪ] 根据权利的，(王等)正当的，法律上的，法律上的。***de no·vo*** [-ˈnəuvəu; -ˋnovo] 从头，再。***de pro·fun·dis*** [ˈdiːprəuˈfʌndis; ˋdiproˋfʌndɪs] 从深处，从心底里；从(悲哀、绝望等的)深渊中发出来的叫声。

de[2] [də; də] ***prep*.**〔F.〕= of; from. ***de haut en bas*** [dəoːtɑ̃ba; dəotɑ̃ba] 傲慢地，侮蔑地，不客气地。***de luxe*** [-ˈluks; -ˋlʊks] 豪华的，上等的，特制的，精装(版本等)(*train de luxe* 花车)。***de nou·veau*** [F. də nuvo; də nʊvo] 从新，另，再。***de règle*** [F. də rɛgl; də rɛgl] 习惯的；适当的。***de ri·gueur*** [riˈgəː, F. rigœːr; rɪˋgɝ, rɪgœr] 不可缺少的，礼仪上必要的。***de trop*** [-ˈtrəu, F. -tro; -ˋtro, -tro] 多余的，不受欢迎的，碍事的。★ **1.** 母音前的 de 常作 d'：*coup d'état*. **2.** 贵族出身者的名前常加用 de：*Guy de Maupassant*; *d' Alembert*.

de- *pref*. **1.** 表示"离开"，"除去"：*de*pilate, *de*rail. **2.** 表示"向下"：*de*press, *de*cline. **3.** 表示"完全"：*de*funct. **4.** 表示"相反"，"解除"：*de*frost, *de*code.

Dea. = Deacon.

dea·con [ˈdiːkən; ˋdikən] **I *n*.** **1.**【宗】(新教，长老会等的)执事；(英国教会，罗马教会的)副主祭，(希腊教会的)助祭。**2.**〔Scot.〕工会会长。**3.**〔美〕初生小牛(皮)。**II *vt*.** **1.** 把(水果等)包装成全像一级品。**2.** 搀混，蒙混。**3.** 屠宰幼畜。**-ess *n*.** 女执事；慈善妇女会会员。**～-hood, -ry, -ship *n*.** 执事的职位。

de·ac·ti·vate [diːˈæktiveit; dɪˋæktɪˏvet] ***vt*.** **1.** 解散(军队)，使复员；使(军队)处于非战斗状态。**2.** 使失去活力[作用]。**3.** 取下(炮弹等的)雷管使成死弹。**4.**【化】使不活化，去除活化。

dead [ded; dɛd] **I *a*.** **1.** 死的；无生命的，无生物的。**2.** 无感觉的。**3.** (炭等)已熄灭的；无生气的，呆滞的，停顿的；冷落的，不景气的；(土地)贫瘠的；不生产的，(货物等)积压着的；(饮料)走了味的。**4.** 静寂的，死一样的；无声响的，发音钝浊的；无光泽的，(色调等)阴沉沉的。**5.** 已废的，不通行的，已成空文的。**6.** 无凸凹的，平滑的。**7.** 完全的，全然；必然的，确实的。**8.**〔美〕被矫正过来的，改邪归正的。**9.**〔美口〕精疲力竭的。*Aren't you ～?* 你是不是太疲劳了？*She is ～.* 她死了。～ *sleep* 酣睡。～ *law* 已废的法律。*a ～ certainty* 绝对确实。*a ～ failure* 完全失败。***be ～ and done for*** 死定了。***be ～ to ...*** 对…无感觉。***be shot ～*** 被枪打死。***be stone ～*** 死定，全无气息。***come to a ～ stop [stand]*** 完全停止[停顿]下来。～ ***above the ears***〔美俚〕笨的，蠢的，傻的。～ ***act***【美剧】不受欢迎的一幕。～ ***and alive***〔口〕郁郁不乐，烦闷；无聊，无趣味。～ ***and gone*** 死去。～ ***as a dodo***〔美俚〕已废的，老朽的，消灭了的。～ ***as mutton [as a doornail, as a herring, as a salmon]*** 死透，死定；完蛋；不活泼。～ ***to shame*** 无廉耻；不知耻。～ ***to the world***〔美俚〕对世事不闻不问；熟睡；烂醉。***fall ～*** 死；(风)平息。***in a ～ line*** 一直线。***in ～ earnest*** 十分认真，真心实意。***more than half ～*** 快死的。***on a ～ level*** 真正的水平。***over sb.'s ～ body*** 不顾别人的激烈反对，硬要。**II *ad*.** 全然，完全，十足。～ ***asleep*** 熟睡。～ ***straight*** 一直，对直。～ ***ahead*** 直接向前。***be ～ against*** (*a plan*) 坚决反对(某项计划)。***be ～ sure*** 确信，包管。***cut*** (*a person*) ～ 假装不认识(某人)似地走过。**III *n*.** **1.** 死者。**2.** (死一样的)寂静。**3.** 极寒时候。*Let the ～ bury their ～.* 既往不咎。***at [in the] ～ of night*** 在深夜。***in the ～ of winter*** 在隆冬。***rise [raise] from the ～*** (使)复活。***the quick and the ～*** 生者和死者。～**-alive,** ～**-and-alive *a*.** 郁郁不乐的，无精神的；烦闷的；单调的。～ **angle**【军】死角。～**beat *n*.**〔美俚〕无经济收入的人；赖债不还的人；游手好闲者。～**beat *a*.**〔俚〕精疲力尽的。～**beat 1. *a*.** 非周期的；差拍的；不摆的。**2. *n*.** 不摆；无差拍；〔美俚〕赖账的人。～ **beer** 走了气的啤酒。～ **block** (货车等的)缓冲板。～ **calm** 全然无风，极平静。～**-cat bounce** "死猫"式反弹〔指股票市场上的低价股出现欺骗性的临时回升〕。～ **center**【机】(冲程的)死点；(车床的)死顶尖。～**-colour** 底色。～ **description** 缺乏生气的描写。～ **duck**〔美俚〕无价值的人[物]，注定要失败的人。～ **end 1.** (铁路等)终点；尽头；死胡同。**2.** 僵局，绝境(*The discussion reached a ～ end.* 讨论陷入僵局)。～**end *a*.** 行不通的；没出路的。～**eye 1. *n*.** 神枪手，三眼滑轮。**2. *a*.** 精确的。～**fall 1.** 陷阱。**2.**〔美〕枯死而倒下的林木。**3.**〔美〕下等酒店，赌场。～ **fingers** (冻)僵了的手指。～ **fire** 桅顶电光。～ **floor** 无反响的地板。～ **forms** 形式，虚礼。～ **freight** (包船位装货不满时应付的)空舱运费。～**-from-the-neck-up**〔俚〕笨的，愚钝的。～ **ground 1.**【军】(火力不能达到的)死角。**2.**【电】完全接地。～ **hand 1.** 永远管业。**2.** 过去对现今的影响。～**head 1. *n*.** 木浮标；免票的人；光吃饭不干事的人；跑空趟的车子。**2. *vt*.** 优待某人免票看戏[搭车]；使火车放空车。**3. *vi*.** 免票看戏[搭车]；放空车。～ **heat** 不分胜负的赛跑。～ **horse 1.** 预付的工资。**2.** 旧债。**3.** 无益的话题，徒劳的事物。～ **hours** 深更半夜。～ **house** 停尸所，太平间。～ **language** 死语[拉丁语等]。～ **leaves** 枯叶。～ **letter 1.** (无法投递的)死信。**2.** (法律上)已废的规定，空文。～ **lift 1.** (不用滑车)凭气力往上拉。**2.**〔古〕需全力以赴的难事。～**-light**【海】舷窗盖。～**line 1.** (囚犯逾越即格杀勿论的)死线。**2.** 截止时间。**3.** (新闻)原稿截止时间。～ **load 1.** 静荷重，自重；底载。**2.**【电】固定负载。～ **loan** 呆账，倒账。～**lock 1.** 停顿，停滞。**2.** 僵局。**3.** 没有弹簧的锁(*break the ～lock* 打开僵局。*come to a ～lock* 陷于僵局)。～**locked**【美体】实力相等的，得分相同的，不分胜负的。～**matter** 无机物。～**melting** 静熔。～

men [marines]〔俚〕空酒瓶。~ **men's shoes** 死后遗留下来的财产[地位]。~ **office** 丧礼，葬礼。~**pan** 1. *n*. 没有表情的脸，一点也不笑的丑角，毫无表情的喜剧演员。2. *a*., *ad*. 没有表情的(地)，不带感情色彩的(地)。~ **pigeon**〔美俚〕注定要完蛋的人。~ **point** = ~ center. ~ **pull** = ~ lift. ~ **reckoning**【海】(根据仪器推算而不是根据天文观察的)船位推测法。~ **river** 平静得好像没有流动的河流。~ **room** 静室，消声室。**D- Sea** 死海。~ **season** 停滞季节，淡季。~ **set** 1. 猎犬指示猎物所在的不动姿势。2. (为得到某物而做的)坚决的努力。3. 坚决的攻击[反对](*make a ~ set at sb*. 断然反对某人)。~ **shot** 百发百中的人，神枪手；命中弹。~ **soil** 不毛之地。~ **soldier**〔美俚〕空酒瓶。~ **spot**〔美〕无线电收音困难的地区。~ **stand** 完全的静止。~ **star** 灾星；克星。~ **stick landing**【美空】停止发动机降落。~ **stock** 1. 呆滞商品[资金]。2. 农具，农业机械 (*opp*. livestock)。~ **sure**〔美〕绝对可靠[确实]的。~ **surface** 无光泽的表面。~ **time** 停滞期。~ **wall** 无窗户的墙壁。~ **water** 1. 死水，静水。2. 船驶过所成的旋涡。3. 炮火达不到的水面。~ **weight** 1. 重负，重担。2. 净重。3.【船】总载重量。4.【铁路】(车身的)自重。5. 按重量收费的货物。~**weight ton** 长吨，载重吨(= 2,240 磅)。~-**weight tonnage** (商船的)载重容量。~ **wind** 逆风。~-**wood** 1. 枯枝；沉木。2. 卖不掉的货，陈货。3. 没用的东西，没用的人。4.〔美俚〕优势(*have [get] the ~ wood on sb*. 占某人上风)。

dead·en [ˈdedn; ˋdɛdn] *vt*. 1. 缓和，使弱，使钝；使消失，使(酒等)走味。2. 使无声音；使不发光；使失知觉。— *vi*. 死灭；减弱，变钝；变哑；走味。

dead·en·ing [ˈdedəniŋ; ˋdɛdənɪŋ] *n*. 1. 隔音材料。2. 去光泽的涂料。

dead·li·ness [ˈdedlinis; ˋdɛdlɪnɪs] *n*. 致命伤。

dead·ly [ˈdedli; ˋdɛdlɪ] I *a*. 1. 要命的，致命的，(伤等)致死的。2. (脸色等)死人似的。3. 极其有害的。4. 不共戴天的(仇敌等)。5.〔口〕非常的，极。***be perfectly*** ~〔口〕太厉害，真受不了。***be insidious and*** ~ 阴险毒辣。***in*** ~ ***haste*** 飞快。***the seven*** ~ ***sins*** 七项可遭天罚的大罪〔指骄、贪、欲、怒、馋、妒、懒〕。II *ad*. 1. 死了一样地。2.〔口〕极，非常。~ **nightshade**【植】颠茄 (= belladonna)。~ **sins**【宗】(应受天罚的)大罪。~ **weapon** 凶器。

dead·ness [ˈdednis; ˋdɛdnɪs] *n*. 1. 死；死的状态。2. 无生气，无感觉。3. (酒等的)走味。

de·aer·ate [diˈeiəreit; dɪˋɛret] *vt*. 使除去空气；使除去气体；使除去氧气。

deaf [def; dɛf] *a*. 1. 聋。2. 不听的；不理的，装聋的。***be*** ~ *to advice* 不听劝告。~-*and-dumb alphabet* (聋哑人用的)手语字母 (= manual alphabet)。~ ***as an adder [a post, a door, a door-post]*** 全聋。***None so*** ~ ***as those that won't hear***. 最聋者莫过于不听劝说的人。***the*** ~ 聋子。***turn a*** ~ ***ear to*** 充耳不闻，不听，完全不理。**-ness** *n*. 聋；不听。

deaf·en [ˈdefn; ˋdɛfən] *vt*. 1. 使聋；使听不见。2. 震聋。3. (用更大的声音)淹没(声音)。4.【建】使(墙等)不漏音。

deaf·en·ing [ˈdefniŋ; ˋdɛfənɪŋ] I *a*. 震耳欲聋的，吵聋耳朵的。II *n*. 防音[隔音]装置[材料]。

deal[1] [diːl; dil] (***dealt*** [delt; dɛlt]) I *vt*. 1. 分派，分配(*out*; *round*)。2. 分，发(牌)。3. 分给；授，赐，给与，使受(打击)。~ *determined counter-blows to the interventionists* 给干涉者以坚决的回击。~ *a blow at sb*. 打人。— *vi*. 1. 做买卖，交易。2. 处理；应付，对付。3. 从事，参与。4. (和…)来往，交际，打交道。5. 发牌。~ *honourably* 光明正大地行事。~ (*fairly*) ***by [with] sb***. (秉公)待人，(秉公)发落某人。~ ***in*** 买卖(货物)；办理；经营，参与。~ ***with*** 办理，处理；对待；与…交涉，与…交往；与…交易(*He is hard to ~ with*. 他很难对付)。II *n*. 1. 发牌(者)；所发的牌；一圈，一场。2.〔口〕交易，买卖；〔美〕密约，(秘密)协定。3.〔美〕(尤指经济上的)政策。***a raw*** ~〔口〕不公平的待遇[处理]。***a square [fair]*** ~〔口〕公平待遇[处理]。***a big*** ~〔美口〕要人；重要的事。***Big*** ~！妙极了！〔假装赞叹的讽刺语〕。***do a*** ~ ***with*** 与…交易；与…妥协；与…说合。***Good*** ~！〔美俚〕好极了！***It's a good*** ~.〔口〕我同意你提的条件。***make a big*** ~ ***out of*** 对…极为重视；就…小题大做。***the New D-***〔美〕(1933 年罗斯福实行的)新政(策)。

deal[2] [diːl; dil] *n*. 量，数额；〔口〕大量。*a vast* ~ 非常(多)。***a*** ~ = ***a great [good]*** ~ 很多。***by a great*** ~ 远远(*He is cleverer than you by a great ~*. 他远比你聪明)。

deal[3] [diːl; dil] I *n*. (松等的)木板；木材，木料。II *a*. 松木的。

de·a·late [diːˈeileit; diˋelet] *a*.【动】脱翅的。**-la·tion** [-ˈleiʃən; -ˋleʃən] *n*.

deal·er [ˈdiːlə; ˋdilɚ] *n*. 1. 商人，…商。2. 发牌人，庄家。3. 以某种方式待人的人。*a* ~ *in grocery* 杂货商。*a wholesale [retail]* ~ 批发[零售]商。~ *aids [helps]* 推销员；广告(等)。*a fair [plain]* ~ 行为正直的人。*a double-* ~ 表里不一的人。

deal·er·ship [ˈdiːləʃip; ˋdilɚʃɪp] *n*. 商品经销特许权；商品特许经销商。

deal·ing [ˈdiːliŋ; ˋdilɪŋ] *n*. 1. 待遇；处置。2. (对人的)行为，举动。3. [*pl*.] 生意，交易；交际。4. 纸牌的分发。*have ~s with* 和…有关系；和…有交往。

dealt [delt; dɛlt] deal[1]的过去式及过去分词。

de·am·bu·la·to·ry [diːˈæmbjulətəri; diˋæmbjʊlətərɪ] *a*., *n*. = ambulatory.

de·am·i·nase [diːˈæmineis; dɪˋæmɪnes] *n*.【生化】脱氨(基)，去胺酶。

de·am·i·nate [diːˈæmineit; dɪˋæməˏnet] *vt*. 脱去氨，去胺基；去掉氨(胺)基。**-na·tion** [-ˈneiʃən; -ˋneʃən] *n*.

de·am·i·nize [diːˈæminaiz; dɪˋæməˏnaɪz] *vt*. = deaminate. **-za·tion** [-ˈzeiʃən; -ˋzeʃən] *n*.

Dean [diːn; din] *n*. 迪安〔姓氏，男子名〕。

dean[1] [diːn; din] *n*. 1.【宗】副主教；地方主教。2. (大学的)院长，系主任；(美大学)辅导主任；(牛津大学的)学监。3. (一个团体中的)老前辈 (= doyen)。*the* ~ *of the diplomatic corps* 外交团团长。

dean[2] [diːn; din] *n*.〔英〕(树林繁茂的)深谷。

Deane [diːn; din] *n*. 迪恩〔姓氏，男子名〕。

dean·er·y [ˈdiːnəri; ˋdinərɪ] *n*. 地方主教[院长、系主任、学监等]的职位[宅邸]。

dear[1] [diə; dɪr] I *a*. 1. 亲爱的，心爱的，可爱的，敬爱的。2. 贵重的，宝贵的 (*to*)。3. 昂贵的，高价的。4. 热切的。*D- Sir* = *My* ~ *Sir* 先生，老兄〔亲切的招呼用语，有时含有奚落之意，在一般书信中作抬头称呼用语〕。★ D- Mr. ... 在英国是形式上的称呼，在美国是亲爱的称呼。My D- Mr. ... 在英国是亲爱的称呼，在美国是形式上的称呼。*one's ~est wish* 真诚的愿望。*a* ~ *year* 物价昂贵的年份。★ dear 与 high, cheap 与 low 的不同用法：The price of this book is high [low]. = This book is dear [cheap]. ***for*** ~ ***life*** 拼命(*run for ~ life* 拼命跑)。***hold (sb.)*** ~ 重视，宠爱，觉得可爱。II *n*. 爱人；可爱的人[东西]，宠物。*There's a* ~. (做得好)真是好孩子；= *That's a* ~. 好孩子。*What ~s they are*! 多可爱！ *My* ~ [~*est*] 亲爱的，您，老兄。III *ad*. 贵。*sell* ~ 贵卖。*That will cost him* ~. 他那样做会吃苦头的[要付出很大代价的]。IV *int*. (表示惊愕、怜悯等)哎呀！ 唷！ *D-*, ~！= *D- me*! = *Oh*, ~！唷！哎呀！嗳呀妈呀！天哪！ *Oh*, ~, *no*! 呀，没有什么，呀，不行！ **D- John letter** 女子给男子的断情书。

dear[2] [diə; dɪr] *a*.〔古〕严厉的，厉害的。

dear·ie [ˈdiəri; ˋdɪrɪ] *n*. = deary.

D

dear·ly [ˈdiəli; ˋdɪrlɪ] *ad*. 深深地(爱等);昂贵。*a ~ bought victory* 付出巨大牺牲得到的胜利。

dear·ness [ˈdiənis; ˋdɪrnɪs] *n*. 1. 高价。2. 贵重。3. 亲爱。~ *allowance* 物价津贴。

dearth [dəːθ; dɝθ] *n*. 1. 缺乏。2. 饥荒。*a ~ of food* 粮食缺乏。***in time of*** ~ 饥荒时候。

deary [ˈdiəri; ˋdɪrɪ] *n*. 〔口〕亲爱的,宝贝儿〔用作表示亲爱的称呼,有时也含有讽刺或幽默的意思〕。

deasil [ˈdiːzəl; ˋdizəl] *ad*. 顺时针方向地。

death [deθ; dɛθ] *n*. 1. 死,死亡。2. 死状,死法;惨死;死因。3. 褫夺公权。4. 死刑。5. 绝灭,消灭。6. 谋杀;惨案。7. 〔古〕瘟疫;黑死病(= black ~)。8. 〔D-〕死神;杀气。*as pale as* ~ 死人一样苍白。*die a hero's* ~ 壮烈牺牲。*black* ~ 黑死病。*civil* ~ 褫夺公权。*the* ~ *of one's hope* 希望的破灭。*D- was in the air*. 杀气冲天。***as sure as*** ~ 必定,的确。***be at ~'s door*** 将死。***be ~ on*** 〔俚〕1. 善于,是…的能手。2. 极爱。3. 极恨,极反对(*He's ~ on curves*. 他善于投转弯的球。*He is ~ on brandy*. 他极爱喝白兰地。*The publisher is ~ on sloppily typed manuscripts*. 出版商极反对打字不清的原稿)。***be in at the*** ~ 1. (猎狗)看到猎获物已死。2. 看到事情的结果。***be the ~ of*** 〔口〕成为…致死的原因,要了…的命;逼得…苦死;把人笑死〔指笑话〕。***be worse than*** ~ 坏极了。**D-!** 要死啦! 糟糕! 不得了啦! ***hang*** [***hold***] ***on like grim*** ~ 死不放手。***put to*** ~ 处死刑,杀死(=〔古〕do to ~)。***to*** ~ 到极点,已极,…死了(*tired to* ~ 疲倦死了)。***to the*** ~ 至死,到底(*fight to the* ~ 战斗到底)。~ **adder** (澳洲)一种毒蛇。~ **agony** 临终时痛苦。~**bed** 1. *n*. 死亡时的卧床;临终(时)。2. *a*. 临终时做的(*~bed will* 遗嘱。*~bed confession* 临时的坦白)。~ **bell** 丧钟。~ **benefit** 死亡保险金。~ **blow** 致命打击。~ **camp** (尤指第二次世界大战期间的)死亡集中营。~ **cell** 死囚牢房。~ **certificate** 死亡证书。~ **chair** 电椅。~ **chamber** 1. 死了人的房间。2. (罪犯)行刑室。~ **cup** 鬼笔鹅膏〔一种有毒的蘑菇〕。~ **dust** 放射尘。~ **duty**【英法】遗产税。~ **feud** 不共戴天之仇。~ **grant** (英)(支付给死者家属或遗嘱执行人的丧葬)补助金。~ **house** 死囚行刑前的监房。~ **knell** 丧钟。~ **penalty** 死刑。~ **point**【生】致死温度,死亡温度。~ **rate** 死亡率。~ **rattle** 临终时痰声。~ **ray** 死光。~ **roll** 死亡表册。~ **row** 死囚室。~ **sand**【军】(含有放射能的)摧命沙。~ **toll** 死亡人数。**D-Valley** 死谷〔美国 California 州东部不长树木的干燥盆地〕。~ **warrant**【法】死刑执行令;致命的打击。~**'s-head** [ˈdeθshed; ˋdɛθsˏhɛd] (象征死的)骷髅;骷髅画,骷髅像。~**'s-head moth**【虫】骷髅蛾。~ **trap** 1. 不安全的建筑物。2. 死的陷阱。~**watch** 1. 临终病人的看护;守夜。2. 死囚看守人。3.【虫】蛀木器的小甲虫。~ **wound** 致命伤。

death·ful [ˈdeθful; ˋdɛθfʊl] *a*. 1. 死一样的。2. 致命的;杀人的。

death·less [ˈdeθlis; ˋdɛθlɪs] *a*. 不死的,不朽的,永恒的,不灭的。

death·ly [ˈdeθli; ˋdɛθlɪ] I *ad*. 1. 死一样地。2. 非常,十分。II *a*. 死一样的;致死的,致命的;〔诗〕死的。

deb [deb; dɛb] *n*. = debenture; 〔口〕débutante.

de·ba·cle, *dé·bâ·cle* [deiˈbaːkl; deˋbakl] *n*. 〔F.〕1. (冰河的)溃裂,解冻;(河水的)奔溢,泛滥。2.【地】山崩。3. 溃散;瓦解,崩溃,毁灭。4. 突然地大混乱;(政府等)大崩溃。

de·bag [diːˈbæg; diˋbæg] *vt*. 〔英口〕剥下裤子(取闹、惩罚)。

de·bar [diˈbaː; dɪˋbar] *vt*. 阻止,防止,禁止;排除。~ (*sb*.) ***from*** 使…不,阻止(~ *a person from a place* 禁止某人进某处。~ *a person from doing something* 禁止某人做某事)。**-ment** *n*.

de·bark [diˈbaːk; dɪˋbark] *vt*., *vi*. = disembark.

de·bar·ka·tion [ˌdiːbaːˈkeiʃən; ˏdibarˋkeʃən] *n*. 上岸,登陆。

de·bar·rass [diːˈbærəs; diˋbærəs] *vt*. 解除疑难,使摆脱(累赘等)。

de·base [diˈbeis; dɪˋbes] *vt*. 贬损(品格等),降低(品质);(使货币)贬值。~ *the value of the dollar* 使美元贬值。~ *oneself for money* 为金钱而卑躬屈膝。**-ment** (品质的)降低,贬质;贬值;变坏,堕落。

de·based [diˈbeist; dɪˋbest] *a*. 1. 下贱的;品质恶劣的。2.【徽】反形的。

de·bat·a·ble [diˈbeitəbl; dɪˋbetəbl̩] *a*. 1. 可争辩的。2. 成问题的。3. (土地)有争执的。*a* ~ *ground* [*land*] 争执不决的边境。

de·bate [diˈbeit; dɪˋbet] I *n*. 讨论,争论,辩论。***the ~s*** (议会的)讨论报告。***hold ~ with oneself*** 独自考虑[盘算]。II *vt*., *vi*. 1. 辩论;讨论。2. 细想,盘算。3. 〔古〕争(胜负等),争执。~ ***upon*** [***on***] (*a question*) 讨论(问题)。~ ***with oneself*** 盘算。~ ***the victory*** 争取胜利。**-bating society** 讨论会,辩论会。

de·bat·er [diːˈbeitə; dɪˋbetɚ] *n*. 讨论者;辩论者。

de·bauch [diˈbɔːtʃ; dɪˋbɔtʃ] I *vt*. 使堕落;诱奸(妇女);败坏,伤害(风俗),使(趣味)低下。— *vi*. 放荡,淫逸。II *n*. 放荡,淫逸,沉湎酒色;暴饮暴食。

deb·au·chee [debɔːˈtʃiː, -ˈʃiː; ˏdɛbɔˋtʃi, -ˋʃi] *n*. 荡子。

de·bauch·er·y [diˈbɔːtʃəri; dɪˋbɔtʃərɪ] *n*. 1. 放荡。2. 诱惑,诱奸。3. 〔*pl*.〕大吃大喝的宴会。

de·ben·ture [diˈbentʃə; dɪˋbɛntʃɚ] *n*. 1. (公司)债券。2. (海关)退税凭单。~ **stock** 〔英〕公司债券。

de·bil·i·tate [diˈbiliteit; dɪˋbɪləˏtet] *vt*. 使虚弱,使衰弱。

de·bil·i·ty [diˈbiliti; dɪˋbɪlətɪ] *n*. 虚弱,衰弱。

deb·it [ˈdebit; ˋdɛbɪt] I *n*. 1. (账簿的)借方。2. 增入(栏)(*opp*. credit)。~ ***side***【会计】增入栏,借方。II *vt*. 把…记入增入栏。~ *one with* $ 100 = ~ $ 100 *against* [*to*] *sb*. 记入某人增入栏内 100 元。

de·blai [ˈdeiblei; ˋdeble] *n*. 〔F.〕(筑城)壕沟掘出土。

deb·o·nair [ˌdebəˈneə; ˏdɛbəˋnɛr] *a*. 〔古〕殷勤的;温雅的;快活的。

de·boost [diːˈbuːst; diˋbust] *vi*. (导弹、宇宙飞船等)减速。

Deb·o·ra(h) [ˈdebərə; ˋdɛbərə] *n*. 黛博拉〔女子名〕。

de·bouch [diˈbautʃ; dɪˋbuʃ] I *vi*. (河水等)流出;(军队)进入(开阔地)。II *n*. = débouché. **-ment** 河口;【军】前进(地点)。

dé·bou·ché [ˌdeibuːˈʃei; debuˋʃe] *n*. 〔F.〕1.【军】(通向开阔地的)进路;出口。2. (商品的)销路。

De·bre·cen [ˈdebretsen; ˋdɛbretsɛn] *n*. 德布勒森〔匈牙利城市〕。

dé·bride·ment [F. ˌdebridˈmɑ̃; ˏdɛbrɪdˋmɑ̃] *n*.【医】(外科)清创术。

de·brief [diˈbriːf; dɪˋbrif] *vt*. 1. 听取(飞行员、使者等的)报告执行任务情况;(飞行员等)报告(执行任务情况)。2. 指令(离职人员等)保守机密。~ *one's mission* 述职。— *vi*. (飞行员等)汇报执行任务情况。**-ing** *n*.

deb·ris [ˈdebriː, ˈdeib-; dəˋbri, ˋdeb-] *n*. 〔*sing*., *pl*.〕1. (破坏物的)碎片,破片。2.【地】岩屑。3. (登山中遇到的崩落的)冰块堆。

dé·brouil·lard [F. debrujaːr, -ard; debrujar, -ard] *n*., *a*. 〔F.〕机灵的(人),有办法的(人),足智多谋的(人)。

Debs [debz; dɛbz] *n*. 德布斯〔姓氏〕。

debt [det; dɛt] *n*. 1. 借款,欠款,债务,债。2. 情义,恩,恩义。3.【宗】罪孽。*a floating* ~ 暂借款,短期负债。*a national* ~ 国债。*contract* [*incur*] *a* ~ 借债。***be deep in*** ~ 一身是债。***be in*** ~ (***to***) 借着…的钱,受着…的恩惠。***be in sb.'s*** ~ 欠某人的债;受某人恩惠。***be out of*** ~ 不欠债。~ ***of gratitude*** 恩情。~ ***of honour***

因打赌或赌博而欠下的债务。～ ***of* [*to*] *nature*** 死(*pay one's* ～ *to nature* 死,归土)。***fall in*** ～ = *get into* ～ = *run into* ～. ***get out of*** ～ 还债。***keep out of*** ～ 不借债。***out of*** ～, ***out of danger***〔俚〕无债一身轻。***pay off a*** ～ 清欠。***run into*** ～ 借债,负债。

debt·ee [deˈtiː; dɛˋti] ***n*.** 债权人。

debt·or [ˈdetə; ˋdɛtɚ] ***n*.** **1.** 债务人。**2.** 借方。**3.** 受恩人。～ ***and creditor*** 借方和贷方。

de·bug [diːˈbʌg; diˋbʌg] ***vt*.** (***-bugged***; ***-bug·ging***) **1.** 驱除(某处的)害虫。**2.** 排除(飞机等的)故障;(自动化装置中)移去(程序等中的)错误。**3.**【无】调整,调谐。**4.** 寻出并拆除…内的窃听器。**5.** (用电子仪器)使(窃听器)失效。**de·bug·ger** 拆除窃听器专家。

de·bunk [diːˈbʌŋk; diˋbʌŋk] ***vt*.**〔美口〕**1.** 暴露,揭穿真面目。**2.** 说…的坏话。

de·bunk·er [diːˈbʌŋkə; diˋbʌŋkɚ] ***n*.**〔美俚〕暴露者,揭穿真面目者。

de·bus [diːˈbʌs; dəˋbʌs] ***vt*.**, ***vi*.** 上下公共汽车。

dé·but [ˈdeibuː; ˋdebju] ***n*.**〔F.〕**1.** 初次登台。**2.** 初次参加社交活动。*make one's* ～ **1.** 初次登台。**2.** 初次参加社交活动。

dé·bu·tant [debju(ː)ˈtɑ̃ːŋ; dɛbjuˋtɑnt] ***n*.** (*fem*. ***-tante*** [-ˈtɑ̃ːnt; -ˋtɑ̃ːnt])〔F.〕**1.** 初次登台的演员。**2.** 初次参加社交活动的人。

Dec. = December.

dec. = deceased; decimeter; declaration; declension; declination; decrease.

dec(a)- *comb*. *f*. 表示"十":*deca*gon, *deca*meter.

dec·ad·al [ˈdekədəl; ˋdɛkədəl] ***a*.** 十的;十年间的。

dec·ade [ˈdekeid; ˋdɛked] ***n*.** **1.** 十,十个一组。**2.** 十年,十年间。***for*** ～***s on end*** 数十年如一日。

dec·a·dence, dec·a·den·cy [ˈdekədəns(i); ˋdɛkədəns(ɪ)] ***n*.** 衰退,退步,堕落;(文学等的)颓废。

dec·a·dent [ˈdekədənt; ˋdɛkədənt] **I** ***a*.** **1.** 堕落的;颓废的。**2.** 文艺颓废期的,颓废派的。～ *wave*【物】减幅波。**II** ***n*.** 颓废派艺术家[文人]。

de·caf [ˈdiːkæf; ˋdikæf] ***n*.** 脱(去)咖啡因(的)咖啡。

de·caf·fein·ate [diːˈkæfəneit; diˋkæfənet], **de·caf·fein·ize** [diːˈkæfinaiz; diˋkæfənaɪz] ***vt*.** 除去…中的咖啡碱。

dec·a·gon [ˈdekəgən; ˋdɛkə͵gɑn] ***n*.**【数】十角形,十边形。

de·cag·o·nal [diˈkægənl; dɛkə͵gɑnl] ***a*.** 十角形的。

dec·a·gram, dec·a·gramme [ˈdekəgræm; ˋdɛkə͵græm] ***n*.** 十克。

dec·a·he·dral [dekəˈhedrəl; dɛkəˋhɛdrəl] ***a*.**【数】有十面的,十面体的。

dec·a·he·dron [dekəˈhedrən; dɛkəˋhɛdrən] ***n*.** (*pl*. ～***s*** [-z; -z], ***-dra*** [-drə; -drə]) 十面体。

de·cal [ˈdikæl; dɪˋkæl], **de·cal·co·ma·ni·a** [diˌkælkəˈmeinjə; dɪ͵kælkəˋmenjə] ***n*.** **1.** 移画印花法〔把绘在特殊纸上的图案移印到瓷器、玻璃等上的方法〕。**2.** 移画印花法所用的图画[图案]。

de·cal·ci·fy [diːˈkælsifai; diˋkælsə͵faɪ] ***vt*.** (***-fied***; ***-fy·ing***) 使(骨头)脱钙。

de·ca·les·cence [ˌdikəˈlesns; ͵dɪkəˋlɛsns] ***n*.** 钢条吸热。***-les·cent a*.**

dec·a·li·ter, dec·a·li·tre [ˈdekəˌliːtə; ˋdɛkə͵litə] ***n*.** 十升。

dec·a·log(ue) [ˈdekəlɔg; ˋdɛkə͵lɔg] ***n*.**【宗】十诫(= the ten commandments)。

De·cam·er·on [diˈkæmərən, deˈkæm-; dɪˋkæmərən, dɛˋkæm-] ***n*.** **1.**《十日谈》〔意大利 14 世纪作家 Boccaccio 的名著〕。**2.**〔d-〕《十日谈》式的故事,语涉色情的故事。

Dec·a·mer·on·ic [diˌkæmərˈɔnik; dɪ͵kæmərˋɑnɪk] ***a*.** (文学作品等)《十日谈》式的。

dec·a·me·ter, dec·a·me·tre [ˈdekəmiːtə; ˋdɛkə͵mitə] ***n*.** 十公尺。

dec·a·me·tric [ˌdekəˈmiːtrik; ͵dɛkəˋmitrɪk] ***a*.** **1.** 十公尺的。**2.**【无】波长为十公尺的,高频无线电波的。

de·camp [diˈkæmp; dɪˈkæmp] ***vi*.** **1.** 撤营。**2.** 逃走,逃亡。***-ment n*.**

de·can [ˈdiːkæn; ˋdikæn] ***vt*.**【核物理】去除…的保护性外壳。

de·ca·nal [diˈkeinl; dɛˋkənl] ***a*.** 副主教[院长、学监等](管辖)的。

dec·ane [ˈdekein; ˋdɛken] ***n*.**【化】癸烷。

de·cant [diˈkænt; dɪˈkænt] ***vt*.** **1.** 轻轻倒出(液体);滗。**2.** (把液体从一容器)移注(另一容器)。**3.** 卸(货),下(客)。*to* ～ *passengers at an ideal site for lunch* 让乘客在理想的地点下车用餐。

de·can·ta·tion [ˌdiːkænˈteiʃən; ͵dikænˋteʃən] ***n*.** **1.** 移注。**2.** 滗。**3.**【化】倾析。

de·cant·er [diˈkæntə; dɪˋkæntɚ] ***n*.** **1.** 有玻璃塞子的圆酒瓶。**2.** 滗析器。

de·cap·i·tate [diˈkæpiteit; dɪˋkæpə͵tet] ***vt*.** **1.** 把…斩首。**2.**〔美俚〕(因政治原因而)解雇,免…的职。

de·cap·i·ta·tion [diˌkæpiˈteiʃən; dɪ͵kæpɪˋteʃən] ***n*.** **1.** 斩首。**2.** 解雇。

de·cap·i·ta·tor [diˈkæpiteitə; dɪˋkæpə͵tetɚ] ***n*.** **1.** 刽子手。**2.** 解雇者。

dec·a·pod [ˈdekəpɔd; ˋdɛkə͵pɑd] **I** ***a*.** 有十足的,有十臂的。**II** ***n*.** **1.**【动】十足类〔蟹、虾等〕。**2.**【动】十腕类〔乌贼等〕。

de·car·bon·ate [diˈkɑːbəneit; diˋkɑrbənet] ***vt*.** (***-at·ed***; ***-at·ing***) 除去碳素,除碳。

de·car·bon·ize [diːˈkɑːbənaiz; diˋkɑrbə͵naɪz] ***vt*.**【化】使脱碳。

de·car·box·y·la·tion [ˌdikɑːˌbɔksiˈleiʃən; ͵dɪkɑr͵bɑksɪˋleʃən] ***n*.** **1.**【化】脱羧基。**2.**【医】脱羧(作用)。***-box·y·late vt*.**, ***vi*.**

dec·are [ˈdekεə; ˋdɛkɛr] ***n*.** 十公亩。

dec·a·stere [ˈdekəstə; ˋdɛkə͵stɪr] ***n*.** 十立方米(= 10 m^3)。

dec·a·style [ˈdekəstail; ˋdɛkə͵staɪl] **I** ***a*.**【建】十柱式的。**II** ***n*.** 十柱式柱廊。

de·ca·sua·lize [diːˈkæʒjuəlaiz; diˋkæʒjuə͵laɪz] ***vt*.** 使无临时工人。

dec·a·syl·lab·ic [ˌdekəsiˈlæbik; ͵dɛkəsɪˋlæbɪk] ***n*.**, ***a*.** 十音节(的)。

dec·a·syl·la·ble [ˈdekəsiləbl; ˋdɛkə͵sɪləbl] ***n*.** 十音节的一行诗。

de·cath·lon [diˈkæθlɔn; dɪˋkæθlɑn] ***n*.** 十项运动〔指百米、四百米、跳远、铅球、跳高、一百一十米跳栏、铁饼、撑杆跳、标枪、一千五百米,总分最高者为优胜者〕。

de·cau·ville [dəˈkɔːvil; dəˋkɑvɪl] ***a*.** 轻便铁路的。～ *railway* 轻便铁路。

de·cay [diˈkei; dɪˋke] **I** ***vi*.** **1.** 朽,腐烂。**2.** 衰减,衰退。**3.** 凋谢,枯。— ***vt*.** 使朽坏;使衰退。**II** ***n*.** **1.** 衰微,衰退。**2.** 朽,腐烂。**3.**【无】衰变。*tooth* ～ 蛀牙。***be far gone in*** ～ 衰弱过甚,凋落不堪。***go to*** ～ = ***fall into*** ～ 腐朽,凋谢,衰微。

de·cayed [diˈkeid; dɪˋked] ***a*.** 已朽的,腐烂了的;衰退了的。*a* ～ *tooth* 龋齿,蛀牙。

decd. = deceased.

de·cease [diˈsiːs; dɪˋsis] ***n*.**, ***vi*.** 死,死亡。

de·ceased [diˈsiːst; dɪˋsist] ***a*.** 已死的。*the* ～ *father* 先父。*the* ～ *wife* 亡妻。*the* ～ 死者,已故者。

de·ce·dent [diˈsiːdənt; dɪˋsidnt] ***n*.**【美、法】死者。

de·ceit [diˈsiːt; dɪˋsit] ***n*.** 欺骗,欺诈;诡计。*a man of* ～ 奸诈的人。

de·ceit·ful [diˈsiːtful; dɪˋsitfəl] ***a*.** 欺诈的,虚假的,骗人的;不诚实的。***-ly ad*.**

de·ceiv·a·ble [di'siːvəbl; dɪ'sivəbl] *a*. 容易受骗的。

de·ceive [di'siːv; dɪ'siv] *vt*. 1. 欺,瞒。2. 使弄错,使失望。~ *oneself* 骗自己;误解,想错。~ *sb.'s hopes* 辜负某人的希望。— *vi*. 欺诈,欺骗。

de·ceiv·er [di'siːvə; dɪ'sivɚ] *n*. 欺骗者。

de·cel·er·ate [diː'seləreit; dɪ'sɛləret] *vt*., *vi*. 降低速度。

de·cel·er·on [di'selərɔn; dɪ'sɛlərɑn] *n*. (飞机的)减速副翼〔副翼和减速板的组合〕。

De·cem·ber [di'sembə; dɪ'sɛmbɚ] *n*. 十二月。

De·cem·brist [di'sembrist; dɪ'sɛmbrɪst] *n*. (俄国)十二月党人。

de·cem·vir [di'semvə(ː); dɪ'sɛmvɚ] *n*. (*pl*. ~*s*; *-viri* [-vərai; -vəraɪ]) 1. (古罗马)十大执政官之一。2. 十人团的一人。

de·cem·vi·rate [di'semvirit; dɪ'sɛmvərɪt] *n*. 十大执政官的职位[任期];十头政治。

D

de·cen·cy ['diːsnsi; 'disnsɪ] *n*. 1. 正派,庄重,端庄。2. 〔*pl*.〕礼仪,礼节;面子。3. 〔古〕合宜,适当。4. 〔*pl*.〕过体面的生活所需要的东西。*public* ~ 风俗。***D- forbids***. 君子自重不可小便(等)。***for*** ***~'s sake*** 为了面子。

de·cen·na·ry [di'senəri; dɪ'sɛnərɪ] *n*., *a*. 十年间(的)。

de·cen·ni·ad [di'seniæd; dɪ'sɛnɪæd] *n*. 十年间。

de·cen·ni·al [di'senjəl; dɪ'sɛnjəl] I *a*. 1. 十年间的。2. 每十年发生一次的。II *n*. 〔美〕十周年,十周年纪念。**-ly** *ad*.

de·cen·ni·um [di'seniəm; dɪ'sɛnɪəm] *n*. (*pl*. ~*s*, *-nia* [-niə; -nɪə]) 十年间。

de·cent ['diːsnt; 'disnt] *a*. 1. 正派的,庄重的。2. (服装等)相称的,合宜的。3. 〔口〕像样的,相当好的,过得去的。4. 〔学俚〕宽宏的,不严格的。5. 〔口〕穿好了衣服的。*a very ~ fellow* 老好人。*live in ~ conditions* 生活相当好。*quite a ~ house* 很不错的一所住宅。*a ~ fortune* 相当多的财产。*Are you ~?* 〔口〕您穿好衣服了吗? ***get ~ marks*** (学生)得分相当多。**-ly** *ad*.

de·cen·tral·ize [diː'sentrəlaiz; di'sɛntrəl,aɪz] *vt*. 1. 分散(行政权)。2. 疏散(工厂、人口等)。*a ~d state* 实施地方分权的国家。**-li·za·tion** [-lai'zeiʃən; -laɪ'zeʃən] *n*.

de·cep·tion [di'sepʃən; dɪ'sɛpʃən] *n*. 1. 瞒骗,欺诈。2. 受骗。3. 骗局;骗人的东西。

de·cep·tive [di'septiv; dɪ'sɛptɪv] *a*. 骗人的,靠不住的,虚伪的。*Appearances are ~*. 不可貌相。**-ly** *ad*. **-ness** *n*.

de·cern [di'səːn; dɪ'sɝn] *vt*. 1. 辨别,分辨。2. 辨认;弄清。3. 【苏格兰法】判决。

de·chris·tian·ize [diː'kristjənaiz; di'krɪstjən,aɪz] *vt*. 使非基督教化。

deci- *pref*. 十分之一: *deci*gram.

dec·i·are ['desieə; 'dɛsɪɛr] *n*. 十分之一公亩(= 10m²)。

dec·i·bel ['desibel; 'dɛsə,bɛl] *n*. 【物】分贝〔音量单位〕。

de·cid·a·ble [di'saidəbl; dɪ'saɪdəbl] *a*. 可决定的,可判定的。

de·cide [di'said; dɪ'saɪd] *vt*. 1. 决定,决心。2. 使下决心,使决断;使解决。3. 裁决,判决。— *vi*. 1. 决定,决心,选定。2. 判决。*That ~s me*. 那使我下了决心。~ ***against*** 决心不…,决定不采取;决定反对;判决(某人)败诉。~ ***between*** 于…中抉择其一,判断。~ ***for*** [***in favour of***] 决定;判定(某人)胜诉。~ ***on*** [***upon***] (*a course of action*) 决心,决定(采取某种行动)。

de·cid·ed [di'saidid; dɪ'saɪdɪd] *a*. 1. 明白的,明确的,无疑的。2. 决定的;断然的,果断的。*a ~ success* 明显的成功。**-ly** *ad*. **-ness** *n*.

de·cid·er [di'saidə; dɪ'saɪdɚ] *n*. 1. 决定者。2. 【体】决赛。

de·cid·u·a [di'sidʒuə; dɪ'sɪdʒʊə] *n*. 【胚胎】蜕膜。**-u·al** *a*.

de·cid·u·ous [di'sidjuəs; dɪ'sɪdʒʊəs] *a*. 1. 【动、植】(在某个生长期或季节)脱落的。2. 每年落叶的。3. 非永久的,暂时的。~ *teeth* 乳齿。*a ~ tree* 落叶树。

dec·i·gram, dec·i·gramme ['desigræm; 'dɛsə,græm] *n*. 分克(=1/10克)。

dec·ile ['desil; 'dɛsəl] *n*. (10分中的)一分,一成。

dec·i·li·ter, dec·i·li·tre ['desi,liːtə; 'dɛsə,litɚ] *n*. 分升(=1/10升)。

de·cil·lion [di'siljən; dɪ'sɪljən] *n*. 1. 〔美、法〕1000的11次乘方〔在1后加33个零所得的数〕。2. 〔英、德〕100万的10次乘方〔在1后加60个零所得的数〕。

dec·i·mal ['desiməl; 'dɛsəml] I *a*. 十数的,以十作基础的,十进的;小数的。~ *carry* 十进制进位。~ *classification* (图书等的)十进制分类(法)〔用三位数字表示图书的主要分类,用小数点后的数字表示次要分类〕。~ *coinage* 十进币制。~ *currency* 十进制通货,小通货。~ *fraction* 小数。~ *notation* 十进记数法。~ *numeration* 十进法。*a ~ point* 小数点。*the ~ system* 十进制;十进法。II *n*. 1. 小数。2. 〔*pl*.〕十进算术。*a circulating* [*recurring*, *repeating*] ~ 循环小数。*to three places of ~s* 到小数第三位。

dec·i·mal·ism ['desiməlizəm; 'dɛsəməlɪzəm] *n*. 十进法[制]。

dec·i·mal·i·za·tion [,desiməlai'zeiʃən; ,dɛsəməlaɪ'zeʃən] *n*. 十进法化,采用十进制。

dec·i·mal·ize ['desiməlaiz; 'dɛsəml,aɪz] *vt*. 1. 使成为十进制。2. 使变为小数。~ *the currency* 使货币成为十进制。

dec·i·mal·ly ['desiməli; 'dɛsəməlɪ] *ad*. 1. 用十进法。2. 用小数,用小数形式。

dec·i·mate ['desimeit; 'dɛsə,met] *vt*. 1. 从十个…中抽一。2. 抽杀[罚]…的十分之一人。3. (传染病等)使死去多人。4. 【史】向…征收(十一税)。*Famine ~d the population*. 饥饿使人口大批死亡。**-ma·tion** [-meiʃən; -meʃən] *n*.

dec·i·me·tre, dec·i·me·ter ['desi,miːtə; 'dɛsə,mitɚ] *n*. 分米(=1/10米)。

de·ci·pher [di'saifə; dɪ'saɪfɚ] I *vt*. 1. 译解(密码等)。2. 解释(古代文学)。3. 辨认,辨读(潦草字迹)。II *n*. 密电(或密信)的译文。**-able** *a*. 译得出的,辨认得出的。**-ment** *n*. 1. 译解,解释,辨认。2. 译文。

de·ci·sion [di'siʒən; dɪ'sɪʒən] *n*. 1. 决定。2. 判决。3. 决议。4. 决心;决断。5. 【美拳】(根据分数而不是根据击倒对方做出的)裁判。*a man of ~* 有决断力的人,果断的人。***come to a ~*** 做出法定。~ ***by majority*** 取决于多数。***give a ~ for*** [***against***] 判决对…有利[不利]。***with ~*** 断然。~ ***table*** (列出对付某问题各项可选择办法的)决策表。

de·ci·sive [di'saisiv; dɪ'saɪsɪv] *a*. 1. 决定性的。2. 决然的,断然的;果断的;明确的。*a ~ battle* 决战。*a ~ evidence* 确证。~ *measures* 断然的措施。***be ~ of*** 对…具有决定性。**-ly** *ad*. **-ness** *n*.

dec·i·stere ['desi,stiə; 'dɛsə,stɪr] *n*. 十分之一立方米。

de·civ·i·lize [di'sivilaiz; dɪ'sɪvɪl,aɪz] *vt*. 使陷入野蛮状态。*the decivilizing effect of the wars* 战争的使人陷入野蛮状态的作用。

deck [dek; dɛk] I *n*. 1. 甲板,舱板;覆盖物。2. 【建】平屋顶;桥面;【铁路】客车车顶。3. 〔俚〕地面,地。4. 〔主美〕(纸牌的)一组。5. (报纸的)副标题。6. 〔美口〕装海洛因等毒品的袋子。7. 录音座。8. (打了孔的)卡片组。*fly close to the ~* 低空飞行。*clear the ~s* (*for action*) (战舰)准备战斗[动作]。~ *passenger* (没有船舱铺位的)甲板船客。***hit the ~*** 〔俚〕1. 起床。2. 倒在地上。3. 准备行动。***on ~*** 1. 到舱面上,在甲板上。2. 准备好。3. (打棒球)依次等着,下一个轮到。***sweep the ~s*** (海浪)漫过甲板。II *vt*. 1. 给(船)铺甲板。2. 装饰,修饰 (*with*)。*a double ~ed bridge* 铁路公路两用桥。~

beam【建】上承梁。~ bridge 上承桥,跨线桥。~ chair 帆布睡椅。~ hand 甲板水手,普通水手。~ house 舱面船室。~ load 放在甲板上的露天货物。~ log (船上的)守望记事簿。~ passage 甲板舱位〔最廉价的舱位〕,统舱。~ plate 铁甲板。~-tube 上甲板鱼雷发射管。~ watchman 停泊值班水手。

Deck·er [ˈdekə; ˋdɛkɚ] *n*. 德克〔姓氏〕。

deck·er [ˈdekə; ˋdɛkɚ] *n*. 1. 装饰者。2. 〔口〕甲板水手;甲板船客。3. 有(多少)层的东西,有(多少)层甲板的船。4. (造纸用的)脱水机。*a two-* ~ 两层军舰。*a double-* ~ 双层公共汽车[电车]。

deck·le [ˈdekl; ˋdɛkl̩] *n*. 1. (造纸的模子四边的)稳纸框。2. 毛边。~ *edge* 纸的毛边。

de·claim [diˈkleim; dɪˋklem] *vt*., *vi*. 1. 巧辩;雄辩。2. (口若悬河地)演说。3. 朗诵,朗读。4. (用激动的语气)攻击。~ ***against*** 抗议,攻击。**-er** *n*.

dec·la·ma·tion [ˌdekləˈmeiʃən; ˏdɛkləˋmeʃən] *n*. 1. 雄辩,雄辩法。2. (口若悬河的)演说。3. 朗读,背诵。**-clam·a·to·ry** [-ˈklæmətəri; -ˋklæməˏtorɪ] *a*. 1. 适于朗诵的。2. 慷慨激昂的,口若悬河的。

de·clar·a·ble [diˈklærəbl, -ˈkler-; dɪˋklærəbl̩, -ˋklɛr-] *a*. 可申报(交税)的,须报关纳税的。

de·cla·ra·tion [ˌdekləˈreiʃən; ˏdɛkləˋreʃən] *n*. 1. 宣言,布告;公告,声明。2. 【法】(原告的)申诉;(证人的)陈述,口供。3. (纳税品在海关的)申报。4. 【牌】摊牌;叫牌。~ *of intention* 【法】(外国人归化某国的)意志的表示。~ *of the poll* 选举结果公告。~ *of war* 宣战公告。***the D- of Independence*** (美国)独立宣言〔1776年7月4日〕。***the D- of Rights*** (1689年规定英国宪法基本原则的)民权宣言。

de·clar·a·tive, de·clar·a·to·ry [diˈklærətiv, -təri; dɪˋklærətɪv, -torɪ] *a*. 1. 宣言的,布告的。2. 呈诉的;陈述的,叙述的。*a* ~ *sentence* 【语法】陈述句。

de·clare [diˈkleə; dɪˋklɛr] *vt*. 1. 声称(*that*);声称[宣布]某人是,宣布。2. 公布;发表;披露。3. 声明;断言(*that*)。4. 【法】招,供述,陈述。5. 申报(纳税品)。6. 【牌】摊牌;宣布(某种牌)是王牌。~ *a state of emergency* [*peace*]宣布紧急状态[和平]。~ *sb. winner* 宣布某人获胜。*Anything to* ~? 有东西要报税吗? — *vi*. 表明态度(*for*, *against*)。~ ***against*** 声明反对。~ ***for*** [***in favour of***]声明赞成。~ ***off*** 宣布…作废[作罢];宣布退出,毁约。~ ***oneself*** 发表意见,表明态度,宣布自己身分(*They openly* ~ *themselves as atheists*. 他们公开宣布自己是无神论者)。~ ***war on*** [***upon***]对…宣战。..., ***I*** ~! 的确是…的。***Well, I*** ~! 怪了!

de·clared [diˈkleəd; dɪˋklɛrd] *a*. 公开宣称的。*a* ~ *atheist* 自命的无神论者。*a* ~ *value* (进口货在海关纳税的)申报价格。

de·clar·ed·ly [diˈkleəridli; dɪˋklɛrɪdlɪ] *ad*. 公然。

de·class [diːˈklɑːs; diˋklæs] *vt*. 使某人失去社会地位,使某人降低社会地位。

dé·clas·sé [deiˈklæsei, Am. ˌdeiklɑːˈsei; deˋklæˋse, ˏdeklɑˋse] I *a*. (*fem*. ***-sée*** [-sei; -se])〔F.〕丧失了(社会)地位的。II *n*. 落伍者,落魄者。

de·clas·si·fy [diˈklæsifai; dɪˋklæsəfaɪ] *vt*. (***-fied***; ***-fy·ing***)(文件报告等)不再作机密论,降低机密等级并公开化。**-fi·ca·tion** [ˈdiˌklæsifiˈkeiʃən; ˋdɪˏklæsəfɪˋkeʃən] *n*.

de·clen·sion [diˈklenʃən; dɪˋklɛnʃən] *n*. 1. 【语法】(名词、代词、形容词的)变格,词形变化。2. 倾斜,偏差。3. 堕落;衰微,衰退。4. 婉言谢绝。*the* ~ *of virtue* 道德败坏。*his* ~ *of the nomination* 婉言谢绝被提名。**-al** [-əl; -əl] *a*.

de·clin·a·ble [diˈklainəbl; dɪˋklaɪnəbl̩] *a*. 【语法】可以变化词尾的,可以变格的。

dec·li·na·tion [ˌdekliˈneiʃən; ˏdɛkləˋneʃən] *n*. 1. 下倾,倾斜。2. 衰微。3. 谢绝,拒绝。4. 【天】赤纬。5. 【物】偏角,偏差,磁偏角。**-al** *a*. 下倾的,偏差的;赤纬的。

dec·li·na·tor [ˈdeklineitə; ˋdɛkləˌnetɚ] *n*. 偏差仪;测斜仪;赤纬计。

de·cline [diˈklain; dɪˋklaɪn] I *vi*. 1. 下倾,下降;跌落;歪斜;(树枝等)下垂,(头)低下。2. 衰落,衰老。3. 堕落,退步;落魄。4. 接近终了;近尾声。5. 进行词形变化。6. 谢绝,拒绝。*The birth rate in our country has been declining for several years*. 我国人口的出生率几年来一直在下降。*Prices begin to* ~. 物价开始下降。*the rotten and declining system* 腐朽没落的制度。*She invited me to dinner but I* ~*d on account of urgent business*. 她请我吃饭,但我因有急事谢绝了。— *vt*. 1. 谢绝,拒绝。2. 使下倾,使下降,使歪斜,使(头)低垂。3. 【语法】变化(名词、代名词、形容词的)词尾。*She* ~*d her head in despair*. 她垂头丧气。*He never* ~*s to do what his mother asks him to do*. 母亲叫他做什么,他从来不拒绝。~ *an invitation* 谢绝邀请。~ ***... with thanks*** 婉言谢绝。II *n*. 1. 倾斜。2. 衰退,减退。3. (物价的)下落。4. 衰弱(病),(特指)肺病。5. 斜坡,下坡。*in the* ~ *of his life* 在他的晚年。***fall*** [***go***] ***into a*** ~ 衰弱;患肺病。***on the*** ~ 没落;在低落中,在下坡路上;在衰退中。

dec·li·nom·e·ter [ˌdekliˈnɔmitə; ˏdɛkləˋnɑmɪtɚ] *n*. 偏角计,测斜仪。

de·cliv·i·tous [diˈklivitəs; dɪˋklɪvətəs] *a*. 向下倾斜的,下坡的。

de·cliv·i·ty [diˈkliviti; dɪˋklɪvətɪ] *n*. 1. 倾斜,下斜。2. 倾斜面,斜坡。

de·cli·vous [diˈklaivəs; dɪˋklaɪvəs] *a*. 向下的,倾斜的,下坡的。

de·clutch [ˌdiːˈklʌtʃ; diˋklʌtʃ] *vi*. 脱开(汽车上的)离合器。— *vt*. (脱开离合器)使停止运转。

de·co [ˈdekəu; ˋdɛko] *n*. 〔口〕= decoration.

de·co·coon [ˈdiːkəˈkuːn; ˋdikəˋkun] *vt*. (装配或使用前)除去(设备等的)外包皮。

de·coct [diˈkɔkt; dɪˋkɑkt] *vt*. 煎,熬,煮。

de·coc·tion [diˈkɔkʃən; dɪˋkɑkʃən] *n*. 1. 煎,煮。2. 煎汁;煎好的药;煮成的东西。

de·code [ˌdiːˈkəud; diˋkod] *vt*. 译码;解码;译出指令。

de·cod·er [diːˈkəudə; diˋkodɚ] *n*. 译电员;译码机;解码器;判读器。

de·col·late [diˈkɔleit; dɪˋkɑlet] *vt*. 1. 斩(首);杀(头)。2. 拆散(电子计算机的多层复印副本)。

de·col·la·tion [ˌdiːkəˈleiʃən; ˏdikəˋleʃən] *n*. 1. 斩首。2. 【医】(难产胎儿的)头截断术。3. (电子计算机多层复印副本的)拆散。

dé·col·le·tage [deiˌkɔliˈtɑːʒ; ˏdekɑlˋtɑʒ] *n*. 〔F.〕1. 袒胸露肩衣服的低领。2. 袒胸露肩衣服。

dé·colle·té [deiˈkɔltei; ˏdekɑlˋte] *a*. 〔F.〕袒胸露肩的;穿袒胸露肩衣服的。*a robe* ~ 露胸女人夜礼服。

de·col·o·ni·za·tion [diːˌkɔlənaiˈzeiʃən; diˏkɑlənaɪˋzeʃən], **de·co·lo·ni·al·i·za·tion** [diːkəˌləuniəliˈzeiʃən; dikəˏlonɪəlɪˋzeʃən] *n*. 非殖民主义化。

de·col·o·nize [diːˈkɔlənaiz; diˋkɑləˏnaɪz] *vt*. 使非殖民主义化。

de·col·o(u)r [diːˈkʌlə; diˋkʌlɚ] *vt*. 使脱色,漂白。

de·col·o(u)r·ant [diːˈkʌlərənt; diˋkʌlərənt] I *a*. 脱色的;漂白的。II *n*. 漂白剂,脱色剂。

de·col·o(u)r·a·tion [diːkʌləˈreiʃən; ˏdikʌləˋreʃən] *n*. 脱色,退色;漂白。

de·col·o(u)r·ize [diˈkʌləraiz; dɪˋkʌləˏraɪz] *vt*. 使脱色,漂白。**-za·tion** [-ˈzeiʃən; -ˋzeʃən] *n*.

de·com·pen·sa·tion [diːˌkɔmpənˈseiʃən; diˏkɔmpɛnˋseʃən] *n*. 【医】(心脏)代偿失调,心力衰竭。

de·com·pose [ˌdiːkəmˈpəuz; ˏdikəmˋpoz] *vt*., *vi*. 1. (使)分解,分析,(使)还原。2. (使)腐烂;衰变。~*d dung* 腐熟厩肥。**-pos·a·ble** *n*. 可分解[分析]的。~r

D

【微】分解体。

de·com·po·site [ˌdiːˈkɔmpəzit; ˏdikɑmpəzɪt] **I** *a*. **1**. 再混合的,与混合物混合的。**2**.【植】重复状的,数回复生的。**II** *n*. **1**. 再混合物。**2**. 二重合成语〔newspaperman 等〕。

de·com·po·si·tion [ˌdiːkɔmpəˈziʃən; ˏdikɑmpəˋzɪʃən] *n*. **1**. 分解,分析,溶解,还原(作用)。**2**. 腐朽,解体。

de·com·pound [ˌdiːkəmˈpaund; ˏdikəmˋpaʊnd] *vt*. **1**. 再混合,使与混合物混合。**2**. 分解。**3**. 使腐败。**4**.【生化】多回分裂。**5**.【植】多回复出。— [diːˈkɔmpaund; diˋkɑmpaʊnd] *a*., *n*. = decomposite.

de·com·press [ˌdiːkəmˈpres; ˏdikəmˋprɛs] *vt*. 使减压,使降压。— *vi*. (过度紧张之后)放松,松弛。**-or** *n*. 减压装置。**-pres·sion** *n*.

de·con·cen·trate [diˈkɔnsəntreit; dɪˋkɑnsənˏtret] *vt*. 使[权力]分散。**-tra·tion** [-ˈtreiʃən; -ˋtreʃən] *n*.

de·con·gest·ant [ˌdikənˈdʒestənt; ˏdɪkənˋdʒɛstənt] *n*. 减充血剂。

de·con·se·crate [diːˈkɔnsikreit; diˋkɑnsɪˏkret] *vt*. 把(教堂等)改供俗用。

de·con·tam·i·nate [ˈdiːkənˈtæmineit; ˏdikənˋtæməˏnet] *vt*. **1**. 纯化,净化,去污,弄清洁。**2**. 清除毒气;消除(放射性)污染。**3**. 对(文件等)作删密处理,删除(将公开发表的文件的)保密部分。**-na·tion** [-ˈneiʃən; -ˋneʃən] *n*.

de·con·trol [ˌdiːkənˈtrəul; ˏdikənˋtrol] *vt*., *n*. (*-ll-*) 解除管理[管制]。

déc·or [ˈdeikɔː; deɪkɔr] *n*. 〔F.〕 **1**. 舞台装置,电影布景。**2**. 装饰(品);布置。

dec·o·rate [ˈdekəreit; ˋdɛkəˏret] *vt*. **1**. 修饰,装饰,布置。**2**. 把(勋章)授给(某人)。~ *a house for May Day* 装饰房子过五一节。~ *sb*. *with a medal* 授与某人勋章。~**d architecture [style]** 盛饰[尖拱式]建筑。

dec·o·ra·tion [ˌdekəˈreiʃən; ˏdɛkəˋreʃən] *n*. **1**. 装饰,装璜。**2**. 〔*pl*.〕装饰品。**3**. 勋章。**D- Day**〔美〕先烈纪念日〔在美国大多数州,将5月最后一个星期一定为法定纪念日,纪念在所有战争中阵亡的将士〕。

dec·o·ra·tive [ˈdekərətiv; ˋdɛkəˏrətɪv] *a*. 装饰的。~ **art** 装饰美术。~ **procelain** 彩瓷。**-ly** *ad*. **-ness** *n*.

dec·o·ra·tor [ˈdekəreitə; ˋdɛkəretɚ] **I** *n*. 室内装饰师[油漆匠等];【剧】制景人员。**II** *a*. 适于室内装饰的。

dec·o·rous [ˈdekərəs; ˋdɛkərəs] *a*. 有礼貌的,端庄的,正派的,谦恭的。**-ly** *ad*. **-ness** *n*.

de·cor·ti·cate [diˈkɔːtikeit; dɪˋkɔrtəˏket] *vt*. 使脱皮[脱壳等]。~*d rice* 脱壳大米。

de·co·rum [diˈkɔːrəm; dɪˋkorəm] *n*. **1**. 礼貌;端庄,正派。**2**. 〔*pl*.〕礼节,礼仪。*behave with* ~ 行为得体。*lose one's* ~ 失礼。

de·cou·page, dé·cou·page [ˌdeikuːˈpɑːʒ; ˏdekuˋpɑʒ] *n*. **1**. 剪贴工艺。**2**. 剪画,剪影。

de·coy [diˈkɔi; dɪˋkɔɪ] **I** *n*. **1**. 引诱物,囮子。**2**. 诱捕鸟兽的场所,圈套。**3**. 诱骗者,诱人入圈套的东西。~ *bird* 囮子。~ *duck* 做囮子的野鸭;囮子。*a police* ~ 警察的密探。**II** *vt*. 引诱。~ *enemy troops into a place* 把敌军诱到某地。

de·crease [ˈdiːkriːs; ˋdikris] *n*. **1**. 减少,减小,减退。**2**. 减少额,减小量。*a* ~ *in production* 生产减少。*Cases of this nature are on the* ~. 这类案件正在减少。— [diːˈkriːs; dɪˋkris] *vt*., *vi*. 减,减少,减退;(温度表等)下降。~ *the number to* ... 把数目减少到…。~ *in size* 尺寸减小。

de·creas·ing·ly [diːˈkriːsiŋli; dɪˋkrisɪŋlɪ] *ad*. 渐减地。

de·cree [diˈkriː; dɪˋkri] **I** *n*. **1**. 法令,命令,公告。**2**. 天命,天意。**3**.【法】判决。**4**. (教会的)教令。~ ***nisi*** [ˈnaisai; ˋnaɪsaɪ]【英法】离婚判决书〔六星期内无异议即生效〕。**II** *vt*. 颁布(法令);判决;(命运)注定。— *vi*. 发布命令。

dec·re·ment [ˈdekrimənt; ˋdɛkrəmənt] *n*. **1**. 消耗,递减,减缩。**2**. 减少率,减缩量;减幅。**3**. 减缩率。

de·crem·e·ter [diˈkremitə; dɪˋkrɛmɪtɚ] *n*.【无】减缩量计,衰减计,减幅计。

de·crep·it [diˈkrepit; dɪˋkrɛpɪt] *a*. 衰老的,老弱的;老朽的。*a* ~ *stove* 破旧的火炉。*be* ~ *with old age* 年老体衰。

de·crep·i·tate [diˈkrepiteit; dɪˋkrɛpəˏtet] *vt*. 毕里剥落地烧(盐等),烧爆。— *vi*. 烧得毕里剥落响,爆裂。**-ta·tion** [-ˈteiʃən; -ˋteʃən] *n*.

de·crep·i·tude [diˈkrepitjuːd; dɪˋkrɛpɪˏtjud] *n*. 衰老,老朽。

de·cre·scen·do [ˈdiːkriˈʃendəu, ˈdei-; ˏdikrəˋʃɛndo, ˏde-] **I** *a*., *ad*. 〔It.〕【乐】渐弱。**II** *n*. 渐弱音,渐弱音演唱的片段。

de·cres·cent [diˈkresnt; dɪˋkrɛsnt] *a*. **1**. 渐小的,渐少的。**2**. 下弦的(月)。

de·cre·tal [diˈkriːtl; dɪˋkritl] **I** *a*. 法令的。**II** *n*. **1**. 法令。**2**. 罗马教皇的教令;〔*pl*.〕教令集。

de·cre·tive [diˈkriːtiv; dɪˋkritɪv] *a*. 命令的,法令的。

dec·re·to·ry [ˈdekritəri; ˋdɛkrəˏtorɪ] *a*. **1**. 根据命令解决的。**2**. 有法令性质的,有法令效力的。

de·cri·al [diˈkraiəl; dɪˋkraɪəl] *n*. 诽谤,诋毁。

de·crus·ta·tion [ˌdiːkrʌsˈteiʃən; ˏdikrʌsˋteʃən] *n*. 脱皮,脱壳。

de·cry [diˈkrai; dɪˋkraɪ] *vt*. **1**. 谴责。**2**. 诋毁。**3**. 大声反对。**4**. (公告钱币等的)贬值。

de·crypt [diˈkriːpt; dɪˋkrɪpt] *vt*. 解…的密码[暗号]。

de·cub·i·tus [diˈkjuːbitəs; dɪˋkjubətəs] *n*. **1**.【医】褥疮(= bedsore)。**2**. 卧姿,卧床。

de·cum·bence, de·cum·ben·cy [diˈkʌmbəns(i); dɪˋkʌmbəns(ɪ)] *n*. 俯伏,匍匐。

de·cum·bent [diˈkʌmbənt; dɪˋkʌmbənt] *a*. **1**. 爬卧地上的,俯伏性的。**2**. (植物的茎)匍匐地上而枝端向上的。

dec·u·ple [ˈdekjupl; ˋdɛkjupl] **I** *a*. **1**. 十倍的。**2**. 以十计的。**II** *n*. 十倍。**III** *vt*. 使成十倍,将…乘以十。

de·cu·ri·on [diˈkjuriən; dɪˋkjurɪən] *n*.【罗马史】**1**. 十人长,什长。**2**. 市或殖民地元老院的元老。

dec·ur·rent [diˈkʌrənt; dɪˋkɝənt] *a*.【植】(叶)向下生长的,下延的。

de·curved [diˈkəːvd; dɪˋkɝvd] *a*.【动】下曲的,向下弯的。~ ***bill*** 向下弯的鸟嘴。

dec·u·ry [ˈdekjuri; ˋdɛkjərɪ] *n*.【罗马史】**1**. 十人团体。**2**. (审判官的)十人小组。

de·cus·sate [diˈkʌseit; dɪˋkʌset] **I** *vt*., *vi*. 交叉成×形,交叉成十字形,交错。**II** [-sit; -sɪt] *a*. 交叉着的,×形的;【植】交互对生的。

de·cus·sa·tion [ˌdiːkʌˈseiʃən; ˏdikʌˋseʃən] *n*. 十字交叉,×形交叉。

de·dal [ˈdiːdəl; ˋdidəl] *a*. = daedal.

de·da·li·an [diːˈdeiljən; dɪˋdeljən] *n*. = daedalian.

de·dans [dəˈdɑ̃; dəˋdɑ̃] *n*. 〔F.〕 **1**. 网球场发球线背后的看台。**2**. 〔the ~〕网球赛观众。

ded·i·cate [ˈdedikeit; ˋdɛdəˏket] *vt*. **1**. 献给,奉献,供奉,献上 (*sth*. *to*)。**2**. [用反身代词]献身,委身。**3**. (把精力、时间等)专门用于某事 (*to*)。**4**. (在自己著作前)题献(给某人)。*The ancient Greeks ~d many shrines to Aphrodite*. 古代希腊人为女神阿芙罗狄蒂造了许多神庙。~ *a memorial* 献纪念品。~ *one's life to* ... 毕生致力于。~ *oneself to* 献身于,致力于。

ded·i·ca·tee [ˌdedikəˈtiː; ˏdɛdəkəˋti] *n*. 被题献者。

ded·i·ca·tion [ˌdediˈkeiʃən; ˏdɛdəˋkeʃən] *n*. **1**. 奉献。**2**. 忘我精神,献身。**3**. 题献;题辞,献辞。

ded·i·ca·tor [ˈdedikeitə; ˋdɛdəˏketɚ] *n*. 奉献者;题献者;献身者。

ded·i·ca·to·ry [ˈdedikətəri; ˋdɛdəkəˏtorɪ] *a*. 奉献的;题献的。

de·duce [di'dju:s; dɪˋdjus] **vt.** **1.** 推论,推断,演绎(*from*)。**2.** 追溯根源。

de·duc·i·ble [di'dju:səbl; dɪˋdjusəbl] **a.** 可推断的。

de·duct [di'dʌkt; dɪˋdʌkt] **vt.** **1.** 扣除,除去。**2.** (演绎地)推论。~ *10% from the cost* 由费用中扣去一成。

de·duc·tion [di'dʌkʃən; dɪˋdʌkʃən] **n.** **1.** 扣除,折扣。**2.** 扣除额,折扣额。**3.** 推论,推定;【逻】演绎法(*opp.* induction)。

de·duc·tive [di'dʌktiv; dɪˋdʌktɪv] **a.** 推论的,推断的;演绎的。~ *method* 演绎法。~ *reasoning* 演绎推理。**-ly** **ad.**

dee[1] [di:; di] **n.** D 字;(兜住马鞍的)D字形铁环;D形物。

dee[2], **deed** [di:, di:d; di, did] **a.** = damned.

deed[1] [di:d; did] **I** **n.** **1.** 行为,行动;实行;事实。**2.** 事迹,功迹。**3.** 【法】证书,契约。*a title* ~ 地契。*a trust* ~ 财产信托证书〔常用以进行抵押〕。~ ***of arms*** 战功。***in*** ~ ***and not in name*** 有实无名,不是名义上而是实际上。***in*** ~ ***as well as in name*** 有名有实。***in name, but not in*** ~ 有名无实。***in word and*** (***in***) ~ 言行俱…。***in*** (***very***) ~ 实际上,真的。**II** **vt.** 〔美〕立契转让(财产)。

deed[2] [di:d; did] **ad.** 〔口〕= indeed.

dee·jay ['di:'dʒei; ˋdiˋdʒe] **n.** = DJ.

deem [di:m; dim] **vt.**, **vi.** 〔古〕想,以为,认为;相信。*I* ~ *it proper to refuse.* 我想以拒绝为好。~ *highly* [*meanly*] *of* 尊重[轻视]。

de-em·pha·sis [di:'emfəsis; diˋɛmfəsɪs] **n.** **1.** 降低重要性。**2.** 不强调;去加重,减加重。

de-em·pha·size [di:'emfəsaiz; diˋɛmfəˏsaɪz] **vt.** 降低…重要性;不再加以强调。

deem·ster ['di:mstə; ˋdimstɚ] **n.** (英属 Man 岛的)法官。

deep [di:p; dip] **I** **a.** **1.** 深的;深处的;…深的,有深度的。**2.** 深远的;深奥的,奥妙的;深谋远虑的。**3.** 深陷…中;埋头…中,热中于(*in*)。**4.** 重大的,深刻的。**5.** (同情等)强烈的,痛切的,深厚的。**6.** 心计深的,奸滑的。**7.** (颜色)浓厚的。**8.** (声音等)深沉的。*The lot is 100 feet* ~. 地基进深 100 英尺。*soldiers four rows* ~ 排成四排的军队。~ *breathing* 深呼吸。~ *disgrace* 奇耻大辱。~ *drinker* 酒量大的人。~ *fat* 炼得火辣的油。~ *gaming* 滥赌。~ *gratitude* 重谢,铭感。~ *oil* 深层油,埋藏很深的石油。~ *one* 〔俚〕心计深的家伙,阴险的家伙。~ *red* 深红。~ *road* 泥泞的道路。~ *sigh* 长叹。~ *sleep* 熟睡。~ *thinker* 哲学家。~ ***in*** 沉湎(冥想等)中,埋头(书本等)中,专心致力于;深陷(债务等)中;深入…中(~ *in debt* 遍身是债。~ *in a subject* 造诣深)。***go off*** [***go off at, go in at***] ***the*** ~ ***end*** 〔美俚〕**1.** 跳入深水。**2.** 冒险从事一项事业。**3.** 发脾气,变兴奋。***in*** ~ ***waters*** (因债务等)愁困不堪;潦倒困顿。**II** **n.** **1.** 〔诗〕〔the ~〕海,大洋。**2.** 〔常 *pl.*〕(海、河的)深度,深处,深渊。**3.** 正当中。*wonders of the* ~ 海的奇迹。*in the* ~ *of winter* 在隆冬。**III** **ad.** 深;迟。*drink* ~ 狂饮。*talk* ~ *into the night* 谈到深夜。***Still*** [***Smooth***] ***water runs*** ~. 水深河静;深谋者寡言。***the*** ~ ***six*** **1.** 〔美海军俚〕海葬。**2.** 〔美俚〕完全拒绝(*give his plans the* ~ *six* 完全拒绝他的计划)。~**-browed** **a.** 眉宇间智慧焕发的。~**-chested** **1.** 胸膛厚的。**2.** 发自肺腑的。~**-drawn** **a.** (叹息、呼吸等)深长的。~**-dyed** **a.** **1.** 染得浓艳的。**2.** 深染恶习的,坏透的(*a* ~*-dyed villain* 大坏蛋)。~ **end** **1.** (游泳池的)深端。**2.** 困境。~**-felt** **a.** 深深感觉到的,深刻的。~**-freeze** **1.** **n.** 冷藏箱,电冷箱(= ~-freezer);冷藏;停止活动。**2.** **vt.** 冷藏,冷冻。~**freezer** 电冷箱。~**-going** **a.** 深入的,深刻的。~ **green** 环境保护激进份子。~**laid** **a.** 秘密策划的,深谋远虑的。~**-mouthed** **a.** 声音沉重、洪大的(猎犬)。~ **pockets** 雄厚的财力(指诉讼的一方财大气粗)。~**-read** **a.** 深通的,精通的。~**rooted** **a.** 根深蒂固的。~**-sea** **a.** 深海的(~*-sea fishing* 远洋渔业)。~**-seated** **a.** 根深蒂固的,由来已久的,顽固的(~*-seated disease* 老毛病,慢性病)。~**set** **a.** (眼睛等)深陷的。~ **space** (太阳系以外的)深太空,远太空。~ **strike** 【军】(对敌人后方的)纵深攻击。~ **structure** (转换生成语法所讲的)深层结构。~**-think** 〔美俚〕〔常作定语〕(不切实际的)迂腐想法。~ **throat** 〔美,加拿大〕政府中犯罪活动的告密者。~**-water** **a.** 深水的,深海的;靠近海洋的。

deep·en ['di:pən; ˋdipən] **vt.** 加深;加重;加浓;使(音调等)深沉。— **vi.** 变深;变深沉;变浓。

dee·pie ['di:pi; ˋdipɪ] **n.** 〔口〕立体电影。

deep·ly ['di:pli; ˋdiplɪ] **ad.** **1.** 深深地。**2.** 深刻地。**3.** (颜色)浓,深。**4.** (声音)低沉。**5.** 巧妙。***be*** ~ ***versed in*** 精通,深通。~ ***committed*** 深陷(某事中)无法自拔。***feel*** ~ ***for*** 痛感。

deer [diə; dɪr] **n.** 〔*sing.*, *pl.*〕鹿。*a river* ~ 獐。*small* ~ 〔集合词〕无足轻重的动物[东西]。~ *forest* 猎鹿的旷地。~ *lick* (鹿常去舐食的)含盐的泉水或湿地。~ *mouse* 鼷鼠。~ *park* 猎鹿场。~ *shot* 猎鹿用的子弹。***run like a*** ~ 飞跑。***stalk*** ~ (偷偷逼近)猎鹿。~**hound** 猎鹿的狗。~ **lick** 含盐的泉水[沼泽地](鹿常去舐食盐分,故名)。~ **neck** 鹿颈(指瘦长的马颈)。~**-skin** 鹿皮。~**stalker** 猎鹿的人;旧式猎帽。

de·es·ca·late [di:'eskəleit; diˋɛskəˏlet] **vi.**, **vt.** 逐步降(级);缩小(冲突范围),降低(战争等的)等级。**-la·tion** [-'leiʃən; -ˋleʃən] **n.**

def. = defective; defendant; defense; deferred; defined; definite; definition.

def [def; dɛf] **a.** 〔俚〕优秀的,杰出的;好极了的。

de·face [di'feis; dɪˋfes] **vt.** **1.** 损伤…的外观。**2.** 涂销,盖销(邮票等)。**3.** 毁伤,磨灭(碑文等)。~ *a wall by writing on it* 墙上题字有损观瞻。**-ment** **n.** 毁损,磨灭;涂销。

de·fal·cate ['di:fælkeit; diˋfælket] **vi.** 挪用[盗用、侵吞]公款,亏空。

de·fal·ca·tion [ˌdi:fæl'keiʃən; ˏdifælˋkeʃən] **n.** **1.** 盗用公款。**2.** 亏空额。

de·fal·ca·tor ['di:fælkeitə; diˋfælˏketɚ] **n.** 盗用公款者。

def·a·ma·tion [ˌdefə'meiʃən; ˏdɛfəˋmeʃən] **n.** 毁谤。~ *of character* 毁谤人格。

de·fam·a·to·ry [di'fæmətəri; dɪˋfæməˏtorɪ] **a.** 毁谤的。~ **writer** 以中伤别人为能事的作者。

de·fame [di'feim; dɪˋfem] **vt.** 毁谤,中伤,破坏…的名誉;丑化。

de·fat ['di:'fæt; ˋdiˋfæt] **vt.** (**-tt-**) 使脱去脂肪。

de·fault [di'fɔ:lt; dɪˋfɔlt] **I** **n.** **1.** 不履行;违约;拖欠。**2.** 【法】不履行债务;缺席。**3.** 欠缺,缺乏。*judgment by* ~ 缺席裁判。*make* ~ 缺席。*suffer a* ~ 受缺席裁判。***be in*** ~ 不履行(契约)。***in*** ~ ***of*** 因无…,若缺少…时,若没有…时(*He was silent in* ~ *of any excuse.* 他无可推诿,哑口无言)。**II** **vi.**, **vt.** **1.** 拖欠(欠款等),不履行。**2.** (使)不到案;(比赛)不出(场),不参加到底。**3.** 缺席裁判(某人),因不出场而输掉(比赛)。~*ing subscriber* (电话)欠费用户。

de·fault·er [di'fɔ:ltə; dɪˋfɔltɚ] **n.** **1.** 不履行者;拖欠者;缺席者。**2.** 亏空(公款)者。**3.** 〔英〕违犯军规者。~ **sheet** 【军】违犯军规登记表〔*cf.* conduct sheet〕。

de·fea·sance [di'fi:zəns; dɪˋfizəns] **n.** **1.** (契约的)作废,废止,废除。**2.** 使契约作废的条款。

de·fea·si·ble [di'fi:zəbl; dɪˋfizəbl] **a.** 可作废的。

de·feat [di'fi:t; dɪˋfit] **I** **vt.** **1.** 打破,摧毁(计划等)。**2.** 打败(敌人);使受挫折。**3.** 【法】宣告无效,作废,废除。*be* ~*ed* 被打败。*be* ~*ed in one's design* 计划被打破。**II** **n.** **1.** 战胜,击败。**2.** 战败,失败;挫折。**3.** 【法】废除。***bring*** ~ ***upon oneself*** 招致失败。***suffer a*** ~ (战斗、比赛中)失败。**-ism** **n.** 失败主义(的态度、行为),失败情

D

绪。**-ist** ***n*.** 失败主义者。

de·fea·ture [diˈfiːtʃə; dɪˋfitʃɚ] ***vt*., *n*.** 损坏外貌。

def·e·cate [ˈdefikeit; ˋdɛfə͵ket] ***vt*.** 澄清,提净,滤净。— ***vi*. 1.** 澄清。**2.** 通便。**-ca·tor** ***n*.** 澄清器,滤清器。**-ca·tion** [-ˈkeiʃən; -ˋkeʃən] ***n*.**

de·fect[1] [diˈfekt; dɪˋfɛkt] ***n*. 1.** 缺陷,缺点,弱点;短处。**2.** 不足,缺乏。*have some ~ in eyesight* 目力不佳。*have the ~s of one's qualities* 美中不足之处。***in ~ of*** 若无…时;因无。

de·fect[2] [diˈfekt; dɪˋfɛkt] ***vi*.** 叛变;逃走。*He ~ed to the West*. 他叛逃到西方。

de·fec·tion [diˈfekʃən; dɪˋfɛkʃən] ***n*. 1.** 缺点。**2.** 缺乏,丧失。**3.** 叛党,脱党,叛教,变节。**4.** 不履行义务;不尽职。*a sudden ~ of courage* 突然失去勇气。*~ from a party* 脱党。

de·fec·tive [diˈfektiv; dɪˋfɛktɪv] **I *a*. 1.** 有缺陷[缺点]的,有瑕疵的,不完全的(*in*)。**2.**【语法】变化不全的。**3.** 智力低于正常的。**II *n*. 1.** 身心有缺陷的人。**2.** 变化不全的词。~ ***verb***【语法】不完全变化动词(*may*, *must*, *can* 等)。~ **virus** 缺陷病毒。**-ly** ***ad*. -ness** ***n*.**

de·fence [diˈfens; dɪˋfɛns] ***n*. 1.** 防御,防备。**2.** 保卫,保护;辩护。**3.** 防卫物;〔*pl*.〕【军】防御工事,堡垒。**4.** 护身术。**5.**【法】(被告的)抗辩,答辩;被告一方(包括被告及其辩护律师)。**6.**【体】守方。*legal ~* 正当防卫。*line of ~*【军】防线。*national ~* 国防。*The best ~ is offence*. 最好的防御是进攻,先下手为强。*counsel for the ~* (刑事被告的)辩护人。*a ~ against an attack* 防御(敌人的)进攻。~ ***in depth*** 纵深防御。***in ~ of*** 以防卫,为保护…,为…辩护。***put oneself in the state of ~*** 摆开防御姿势。***the D- of the Realm Act***〔英〕国防条例〔略 DORA,1914 年 8 月的法令,规定政府在战争期间有广泛的权力〕。***the science* [*art*] *of ~*** 护身术[拳术、剑术等]。

de·fence·less [diˈfenslis; dɪˋfɛnslɪs] ***a*.** 无防御的,无防备的;不设防的;无可辩护的。**-ly** ***ad*. -ness** ***n*.**

de·fend [diˈfend; dɪˋfɛnd] ***vt*. 1.** 保卫(国家等);防御,防守,保护…使免于(*from*, *against*)。**2.** 为(某观点)辩护,作(某人)的辩护律师,为…进行辩护,抗辩。**3.**〔罕〕禁止。~ ***against* [*from*]** 保卫,抵抗;否认。~ ***oneself*** 自卫;自行辩护,答辩。***God ~!*** 断断没有(这种事)。

de·fend·ant [diˈfendənt; dɪˋfɛndənt] ***n*., *a*.**【法】被告(人)(的)(*opp*. plaintiff)。*the ~ company* 被告方面。

de·fend·er [diˈfendə; dɪˋfɛndɚ] ***n*. 1.** 防御者,保卫者,辩护人。**2.**【体】锦标保持者。***D- of the Faith*** 护教者〔英国君主的称号,最初由教皇利奥十世授给亨利八世〕。

de·fen·es·tra·tion [diːfeniˈstreiʃən; di͵fɛnəˋstreʃən] ***n*.** 扔出窗外,掷出窗外。

de·fense [diˈfens; dɪˋfɛns] ***n*.**〔美〕= defence.

de·fen·si·ble [diˈfensəbl; dɪˋfɛnsəbl̩] ***a*.** 能防御的;能辩护的。**-bly** ***ad*. -bil·i·ty** [-ˈbiliti; -ˋbɪlətɪ] ***n*.**

de·fen·sive [diˈfensiv; dɪˋfɛnsɪv] **I *a*. 1.** 防卫的,防御的;守势的。**2.** 辩护的。*assume a ~ attitude* 采取守势。*a ~ alliance* 防守同盟。*a ~ warfare* 防御战。*~ works* 防御工事。**II *n*. 1.** 守势。**2.** 辩护。***assume the ~*** 采取守势。***be* [*stand*, *act*] *on the ~*** 取防守姿态,在防御立场上。~ **medicine** 防御性医疗。**-ly** ***ad*. -ness** ***n*.**

de·fen·so·ry [diˈfensəri; dɪˋfɛnsərɪ] ***a*.** = defensive.

de·fer[1] [diˈfəː; dɪˋfɝ] ***vt*. (-rr-) 1.** 拖延,迁延,展缓;扣存。**2.**【军】使延期入伍。*His military service was ~red*. 他被允许缓期服役。*~red annuity* 扣存退休费。*~red pay*〔英〕(兵士死亡或离队时发还的)扣存薪饷。*~red shares*〔英〕红利扣存股,红利后取股。*~red telegram* (收费较廉的)慢(发)电(报)。— ***vi*.** 迁延;因循。

de·fer[2] [diˈfəː; dɪˋfɝ] ***vi*. (-rr-)** 服从,听从,遵从(*to*)。*We all ~ to him in these matters*. 在这类事情上我们都听从他。— ***vt*.** 把(某事)交由(某人)决定(*to*)。*We ~ questions of this kind to him*. 我们把这类问题交给他决定。

def·er·ence [ˈdefərəns; ˋdɛfərəns] ***n*. 1.** 服从;依从,敬服。**2.** 敬意,尊敬。*blind ~* 盲从。***in ~ to*** (*your wishes*) 遵从,听从(您的意愿)。***pay* [*show*] *~ to*** 对…表示敬意。***treat with ~*** 谦逊地对待。***with all due ~ to you*** 尊意虽好,但是…〔表示不同意时的客气讲话〕。

def·er·ent[1] [ˈdefərənt; ˋdɛfərənt] ***a*.** 传送的,输送的。*a ~ duct*【解】输送管,输精管。

def·er·ent[2] [ˈdefərənt; ˋdɛfərənt] ***a*.** = deferential.

def·er·en·tial [͵defəˈrenʃəl; ͵dɛfəˋrɛnʃəl] ***a*.** 表示敬意的,谦让的,谦逊的,恭敬的。

de·fer·ment [diˈfəːmənt; dɪˋfɝmənt] ***n*.** 拖迟,延期,展期。

de·fer·ra·ble, de·fer·a·ble [diˈfəːrəbl; dɪˋfɝrəbl̩] **I *a*.** 能延期的;能缓役的。**II *n*.**〔美〕有缓役资格者。

de·fer·ves·cence [͵diːfəˈvesns, ͵defə-; ͵difəˋvɛsn̩s, ͵dɛfə-] ***n*.**【医】退烧,退热期。

de·fi·ance [diˈfaiəns; dɪˋfaɪəns] ***n*. 1.** 挑衅,挑战。**2.** 反抗;蔑视。***be at open ~ with*** 公然反抗。***bid ~ to ...*** = ***set ... at ~*** 反抗;蔑视,藐视。***in ~ of*** 无视,不顾,不管。

de·fi·ant [diˈfaiənt; dɪˋfaɪənt] ***a*. 1.** 挑战的;反抗的。**2.** 大胆的。**3.** 无礼的,目中无人的。***be ~ of*** 蔑视。**-ly** ***ad*. -ness** ***n*.**

de·fib·ril·late [diˈfibrileit, -ˈfaibri-; dɪˋfɪbrəlet, -ˋfaɪbrə-] ***vt*.** 用电流停止心脏纤维性颤动。**-ril·la·tion** ***n*. -ril·la·tor** ***n*.**

de·fi·cien·cy [diˈfiʃənsi; dɪˋfɪʃənsɪ] ***n*. 1.** 缺乏,不足,短缺。**2.** 缺陷。**3.** 不足额;亏空。*a ~ of food* 食物不足。*~ disease* 亏损病,维生素(等)缺乏病。***make good* [*up for*] *a ~*** 补足亏空。

de·fi·cient [diˈfiʃənt; dɪˋfɪʃənt] **I *a*. 1.** 不足的,缺乏的。**2.** 不完全的,有缺陷的。**3.** 痴呆的。**II *n*.** 有缺陷的人[东西]。***be ~ in*** 欠缺。***be mentally ~*** 精神上有缺陷。

def·i·cit [ˈdefisit; ˋdɛfəsɪt] ***n*.** 不敷,亏空(额),赤字;欠缺。*cover the ~* 弥补亏欠。*What? Another ~!* 咳!又亏了! *~ financing* 赤字财政〔政府为刺激生产和消费而大量增加开支的做法〕。*~ spending* 赤字开支〔政府通过借债而不是通过税收来支付开支〕。

de·fi·er [diˈfaiə; dɪˋfaɪɚ] ***n*.** 挑战者;反抗者;蔑视者。

def·i·lade [͵defiˈleid; ͵dɛfəˋled] **I *vt*.**【军】根据地势部署军队。**II *n*.**【军】遮蔽(物),掩护(物)。

de·file[1] [diˈfail; dɪˋfaɪl] ***vt*. 1.** 弄脏,污损。**2.** 损坏(名誉等)。**3.** 亵渎,玷污。*They that touch pitch will be ~d*. 近墨者黑。

de·file[2] [diˈfail; dɪˋfaɪl] **I *vi*.** 排成纵列[单列]前进。**II** [ˈdiːfail; ˋdifaɪl] ***n*. 1.** 隘路,狭路,峡谷。**2.** 纵列行进。

de·fin·a·ble [diˈfainəbl; dɪˋfaɪnəbl̩] ***a*.** 可限定的,有界限的;能下定义的。

de·fine [diˈfain; dɪˋfaɪn] ***vt*. 1.** 为…立界限,限定,规定。**2.** (弄)明确。**3.** 为…下定义,定界说。*be well ~d* 划分明白。*~ one's meaning* [*position*] 明确自己心意[立场]。*ill- ~d duties* 权限不明的任务。*a well- ~d word* [*figure*] 意义明确的文字[轮廓分明的图像]。***the defining moment*** 决定性时刻。

de·fin·i·en·dum [͵difiniˈendəm; ͵dɪfɪnɪˋɛndəm] (*pl*. ***de·fin·i·en·da*** [-ə; -ə]) ***n*.** 被下了定义的词。

de·fin·i·ens [diˈfiniˌenz; dɪˋfɪnɪ͵ɛnz] (*pl*. ***de·fin·i·en·tia*** [diˌfiniˈenʃə; dɪ͵fɪnɪˋɛnʃə]) ***n*.** 定义。

def·i·nite [ˈdefinit; ˋdɛfənɪt] ***a*. 1.** 明确的;确定的。**2.** 一定的。**3.**【植】(雄蕊等)有一定数目的。*be more ~ in your statements* 请说得更明白点。*a ~ answer* 明确的答复。*a ~ article* 定冠词〔即 the〕。**-ness** ***n*.**

def·i·nite·ly [ˈdefinitli; ˋdɛfənɪtlɪ] ***ad*. 1.** 明确。**2.**

〔口〕的确，一定。3.〔有否定词时〕决，绝对。*Will you go?* — *D-*. 你去吗？一定去。*I will not do it*, ~. 我绝对不干。

def·i·ni·tion [ˌdefiˈniʃən; ˏdɛfəˋnɪʃən] *n*. 1. 限定。2. 定义，界说。3. 明确。4.（透镜的）明晰度。5.（收音机的）清晰度。6.（印花）轮廓。

de·fin·i·tive [diˈfinitiv; dɪˋfɪnɪtɪv] *a*. 1. 限定的，明确的。2. 确定的，决定（性）的，最后的。~ *host*【生】定局［最后］宿主。~ *organs*【生】定形器官。~ *sentence* 最后判决。**-ly** *ad*. **-ness** *n*.

de·fin·i·tude [deˈfinitjuːd; dɛˋfɪnɪtjud] *n*. 明确，精确。

def·la·grate [ˈdefləgreit; ˋdɛfləˏgret] *vt*., *vi*.（使）突然燃烧，（使）爆燃。**def·la·gra·tion** [ˌdefləˈgreiʃən; ˏdɛfləˋgreʃən] *n*. 爆燃（作用）；焚烧。**-gra·tor** *n*.【电】突燃器，爆燃器。

de·flate [diˈfleit; dɪˋflet] *vt*. 1. 抽去（空气等）。2. 降低…的重要性，使泄气。3. 收缩，紧缩（通货）。**de·fla·tion** *n*. 1. 抽气；（汽球的）放气。2. 通货收缩。3.【地】风蚀，吹蚀。

de·fla·tion·a·ry [diˈfleiʃənəri; dɪˋfleʃənərɪ] *a*. 通货收缩的。

de·flect [diˈflekt; dɪˋflɛkt] *vt*. 使偏斜，使转向，使弯曲。— *vi*. 偏移，偏转，偏离。~ *a stream from its original course* 使河流改道。**de·flec·tion** *n*.〔美〕= deflexion. **-tor** [diˈflektə; dɪˋflɛktɚ] *n*. 偏导装置，转向装置，折转板，导流片，导风板；【海】偏针仪。

de·flex·ion [diˈflekʃən; dɪˋflɛkʃən] *n*. 1. 歪斜，偏斜。2.【物】偏转（度）；偏差。3.【工】挠曲；挠度。4.【军】（枪弹的）偏差。~ *shooting*（把飞机的移动计算在内而把炮火射到飞机前面的）修正瞄准射击。

de·flo·rate [diːˈflɔːrit; dɪˋflorɪt] *a*.【植】过了开花期的。

de·flo·ra·tion [ˌdiːflɔːˈreiʃən, def-; ˏdɛfləˋreʃən, dɛf-] *n*. 1. 摘花，采花。2. 摘录书中精彩部分，拔萃。3. 奸污处女，破坏贞操。

de·flow·er [diːˈflauə; dɪˋflauɚ] *vt*. 1. 摘花，采花。2. 抽取…的精华。3. 奸污（处女），破坏（处女贞操）；蹂躏。

De·foe [diˈfəu, dəˈfəu; dɪˋfo, dəˋfo] *n*. 1. 迪福〔姓氏〕。2. **Daniel** ~迪福〔1659？—1731，英国小说家，《鲁宾逊飘流记》（*Robinson Crusoe*）的作者〕。

de·fog [diːˈfɔg; diˋfɑg] *vt*.（**-gg-**）扫（雾）。**de·fog·ger** [diːˈfɔgə; diˋfɑgɚ] *n*. 扫雾器。

de·fo·li·ant [diˈfəuliənt; dɪˋfolɪənt] *n*. 脱叶剂，落叶剂。

de·fo·li·ate [diˈfəulieit; dɪˋfolɪˏet] **I** *vt*., *vi*.【植】（使）落叶。**II** *a*.【罕】落了叶的。**-li·a·tion** [diˌfəuliˈeiʃən; dɪˏfolɪˋeʃən] *n*. 落叶；叶子的脱落。

de·force [diˈfɔːs; dɪˋfors] *vt*.【法】1. 霸占，强占。2. 不让人享有合法权益。**-ment** *n*.

de·for·ciant [diˈfɔːʃənt; dɪˋforʃənt] *n*.【法】强占者，霸占者。

De For·est [dəˈfɔrist; dɪˋfɔrɪst] *n*. 1. 德福雷斯特〔姓氏〕。2. **Lee** ~德福来斯特〔1873—1961，改进收音机、有声电影及电视机的美国发明家〕。

de·for·est [diˈfɔrist; dɪˋfɔrɪst] *vt*. 砍伐森林；去掉树木。**-a·tion** [-ˈteiʃən; -ˋteʃən] *n*.

de·form [diˈfɔːm; dɪˋfɔrm] *vt*. 1. 使变丑，毁伤…的形体，使成畸形。2.【物】使变形。— *vi*. 变形。**-a·tion** [-ˈmeiʃən; -ˋmeʃən] *n*. 1.（形体的）损伤；改丑（*opp*. reformation）。2. 畸形。3.【物】变形。**-ed** *a*. 变了形的；丑陋的；畸形的。

de·form·i·ty [diˈfɔːmiti; dɪˋfɔrmətɪ] *n*. 1. 畸形，残废，残疾；丑陋。2.（制度等的）缺陷。3. 畸形的人［东西］。

de·frag(·ment) [diˈfræg(mənt); dɪˋfræg(mənt)] *vt*.【计】去除…的文件碎片（使硬盘上的储存物逐一归位）。

de·fraud [diˈfrɔːd; dɪˋfrɔd] *vt*. 骗取，诈取；欺骗。***be*** **~*-ed of*** (*one's estate*) 被骗去（财产）。~ ***a person of something*** 骗去某人的东西。***with intent to*** ~【法】蓄意诈骗。

de·fraud·er [diˈfrɔːdə; dɪˋfrɔdɚ] *n*. 诈骗者。

de·fray [diˈfrei; dɪˋfre] *vt*. 支付，支给。*The expenses are* ~*ed by the company*. 费用由公司支付。**-al, -ment** *n*. 支付，支出。

de·frock [diːˈfrɔk; diˋfrɑk] *vt*. 剥夺…的牧师资格（或职务），免去…的圣职（= unfrock）。

de·frost [di(ː)ˈfrɔ(ː)st; diˋfrɔst] *vt*. 使溶解，使解冻，去冰霜。— *vi*. 解冻。

de·frost·er [di(ː)ˈfrɔ(ː)stə; diˋfrɔstɚ] *n*.（飞机等的）熔冰机；除霜器。

deft [deft; dɛft] *a*. 灵巧的，巧妙的，熟练的（*opp*. awkward）。*She is a* ~ *hand with a needle*. 她针线做得好。**-ly** *ad*. **-ness** *n*.

de·funct [diˈfʌŋkt; dɪˋfʌŋkt] *a*. 1. 死了的；（公司）倒闭了的，已不存在的。2. 已废止的，已失效的。*the* ~ 故人，死者。

de·fuse, de·fuze [diːˈfjuːz; diˋfjuz] *vt*. 1. 拆除…的雷管；使失去导火线。2. 使变为无害。~**r** *n*.（危险局面的）调解人。

de·fy [diˈfai; dɪˋfaɪ] *vt*.（***-fied***；***-fy·ing***）1. 挑，激。2. 蔑视，藐视，不顾，公然反抗。3. 使不能，使落空。~*ing laws human and divine* 无法无天。~ *death to defend* 誓死保卫。*I* ~ *you to do that*. 我看你敢不敢那么干。*They* ~ *all comparison*. 没有能和他们比较的。~ *description* 难以形容。*The door defies all attempts to open it*. 门怎么也弄不开。

deg. = degree.

dé·ga·gé [F. deigɑːˈʒe; degɑˋʒe] *a*.〔F.〕潇洒的，不拘束的。

de·gas [diːˈgæs; diˋgæs] *vt*. 排气；排除煤气。

de·gauss [ˈdiːˈgaus; diˋgaus] *vt*. 使消磁；消除（船只的）磁场〔以防磁性水雷〕。~*ing cable*（防磁性水雷的）消磁电缆。

de·gen·er·a·cy [diˈdʒenərəsi; dɪˋdʒɛnərəsɪ] *n*. 1. 退步，退化；衰退。2. 堕落，颓废。

de·gen·er·ate [diˈdʒenəreit; dɪˋdʒɛnəret] **I** *vi*. 1. 腐化，堕落，颓废。2. 衰败；【生】退化（*to*）；【生理】变质。*Liberty often* ~*s into lawlessness*. 自由常常变质为无法无天。**II** [diˈdʒenərit; dɪˋdʒɛnərɪt] *a*., *n*. 1. 腐化的，堕落的，颓废的（人）；退化的（动物）。2. 蜕化变质的（分子）；变了质的（东西）；变态性欲的（人）。

de·gen·er·a·tion [diˌdʒenəˈreiʃən; dɪˏdʒɛnəˋreʃən] *n*. 1. 退步；恶化。2. 颓废，堕落。3.【生理】变性，变质。4.【生】简并，退化（病）。5.【物】退化，简并化。

de·gen·er·a·tive [diˈdʒenərətiv; dɪˋdʒɛnəˏretɪv] *a*. 变坏的；退化的；变性的；堕落的。

de·glu·ti·nate [diˈgluːtineit; dɪˋglutɪˏnet] *vt*. 从…中提取麦麸。**-na·tion** [-ˈneiʃən; -ˋneʃən] *n*.

de·glu·ti·tion [ˌdiːgluːˈtiʃən; ˏdigluˋtɪʃən] *n*. 咽，吞，咽下，吞咽能力。

deg·ra·da·tion [ˌdegrəˈdeiʃən; ˏdɛgrəˋdeʃən] *n*. 1. 降级；免职。2. 退化；堕落。3.【地】（地表的）剥蚀。4.【化】降解，递降分解（作用）。5.【物】（能的）退降。*advancement and* ~ 升级和降级。

de·grade [diˈgreid; dɪˋgred] *vt*. 1. 降格，降级。2. 撤职，免职。3. 降低品格［身价、价值（等）］；使堕落；使受屈辱。4.【化】降解。5.【生】使退化。6.【地】使剥蚀。— *vi*. 1. 降低；堕落。2.【生】退化。3.（剑桥大学）把名誉学位考试延期一年。**de·grad·ed** *a*. 被降了级的；被免了职的；堕落了的；贬低了的；退化了的。**de·grad·ing** *a*. 堕落的，可耻的，卑鄙的。

de·grease [diːˈgriːz; diˋgriz] *vt*. 去除…的油污；【化】使脱脂。

de·gree [diˈgriː; dɪˋgri] *n*. 1. 程度；等级。2. 阶层，地位。3. 学位，学术。4. 度，度数。5.【数】次；幂。6.【乐】阶，度，音程。7.【语法】（形容词和副词的）级。8.【法】亲等。*He was tired to such a* ~ *that he fainted*. 他疲乏得

D

昏了过去。*people of every* ～ 各阶层的人们。*a man of high* ～ 地位高的人们。*give* [*take*] *a* ～ 授与[取得]学位。*the prohibited* ～*s* (*of marriage*) 禁止结婚的亲等〔一、二、三等亲〕。*third* ～〔美〕(警察的)严厉的拷问。**by** ～**s** 渐次,渐渐,逐渐。**by slow** ～**s** 慢慢,一点儿一点儿地。～ **of frost** 零下(*10* ～*s of frost* 零下10度)。**in a** ～ 有一点儿。**in its** ～ 各有(所长等)(*Each is useful in its* ～. 各有不同程度的用处)。**in some** ～ 多少。**to a certain** ～ 相当。**to a** ～ 非常;〔美〕有点。**to the last** ～ 极端,再…没有了。～**-day** 度－日〔气温较标准每降低 1°时,一日内暖房所需燃料单位〕。

de·gres·sion [diˈgreʃən; dɪˋgrɛʃən] **n**. 1. 下降。2. (税率的)递减。**-sive a**.

de·gust [diˈgʌst; dɪˋgʌst] **vt**., **vi**. 〔罕〕尝味〔尤指品尝〕。**-gusta·tion** [ˌdiːgəsˈteiʃən; ˏdigəsˋteʃən] **n**.

de gus·ti·bus non dis·pu·tan·dum (***est***) [diˈgʌstibəs nɔn ˌdispjuːˈtændəm; dɪˋgʌstɪbəs nɑnˏdɪspjuˋtændəm] 〔L.〕各有所好,无可计较。

D. E. H. = diameter at height of the eye. 【林】目高(树干)直径。

de·hisce [diˈhis; dɪˋhɪs] **vi**. 1. 张嘴,开口。2. 【植】(种皮、豆荚等的)裂开。**-his·cence** [diˈhisns; dɪˋhɪsns] **n**. 【植】裂开,张开。**-cent** [-ˈhisnt; -ˋhɪsn̩t] **a**. 【植】裂开性的。

de·horn [diˈhɔːn; dɪˋhɔrn] **vt**. 1. 〔美〕除去(牛等的)角。2. 〔军俚〕除去(炸弹的)雷管。

de·hor·ta·tion [ˌdiːhɔːˈteiʃən; ˏdihɔrˋteʃən] **n**. 劝阻,劝戒。**-ta·tive** [diːˈhɔːtətiv; dɪˋhɔrtətɪv] **a**. 劝戒的。

de·hu·man·ize [diːˈhjuːmənaiz; dɪˋhjumənaɪz] **vt**. 使失人性;把(人)看成(动)物;使(艺术作品等)失去个性。

de·hu·mid·i·fy [ˌdiːhjuːˈmidifai; ˏdihjuˋmɪdəfaɪ] **vt**. 使除去湿气[水分]。**-i·fi·ca·tion** [ˈdiːhju(ː)ˌmidifiˈkeiʃən; ˋdihjuˏmɪdɪfɪˋkeʃən] **n**. **-fi·er** [-hju(ː)ˈmidifaiə; -hjuˋmɪdɪfaɪə] **n**.

de·hy·drate [diːˈhaidreit; dɪˋhaɪdret] **vt**., **vi**. (使)脱水。～*d eggs* 蛋粉。～*d vegetables* 脱水蔬菜。

de·hy·dro·canned [diːˌhaidrəˈkænd; diˏhaɪdrəˋkænd] **a**. 脱水装罐头的。

de·hy·dro·freez·ing [diːˈhaidrəuˈfriːziŋ; dɪˋhaɪdroˋfrizɪŋ] **n**. 脱水冷冻。

de·hy·dro·gen·ase [diːˈhaidrədʒəˌneis, ˌdiːhaiˈdrɔdʒəˌneis; dɪˋhaɪdrədʒəˏnes, ˏdihaɪˋdrɑdʒəˏnes] **n**. 脱氢酶。

de·hy·dro·gen·ate, de·hy·dro·gen·ize [diːˈhaidrəudʒəneit, -naiz; dɪˋhaɪdrodʒənet, -naɪz] **vt**. 脱氢;去氢。**-gen·a·tion** [diːˌhaidrəudʒəˈneiʃən; diˏhaɪdrodʒəˋneʃən] **n**.

de·hyp·no·tize [ˈdiːˈhipnətaiz; dɪˋhɪpnəˏtaɪz] **vt**. 使解除催眠状态,使解除催眠术。

de·ice [diːˈais; dɪˋaɪs] **vt**. 除去…上的冰,防止…结冰。**de·icer** [-ə; -ə] **n**. (机翼上的)除冰装置。

de·i·cide [ˈdiːisaid; ˋdiəˏsaɪd] **n**. 杀神(者)。

deic·tic [ˈdaiktik; ˋdaɪktɪk] **a**. 直接指出的;直接证明的;【逻】直证的;【语法】指示的。

de·i·fi·ca·tion [ˌdiːifiˈkeiʃən; ˏdiəfəˋkeʃən] **n**. 1. 祀为神,奉作神圣。2. 神化,神格化。3. 神的化身。

de·i·form [ˈdiːifɔːm; ˋdiəˏfɔrm] **a**. 神一样的;神性的。

de·i·fy [ˈdiːifai; ˋdiəˏfaɪ] **vt**. (***-fied***; ***-fy·ing***) 把…祀奉为神,奉…为神圣。～ *prudence* 慎重第一。

deign [dein; den] **vi**. 1. 俯准,垂顾。2. 降低身分;屈尊。～ *to visit* 光临。*He doesn't* ～ *to acknowledge his old friends*. 他连老朋友也不理了。— **vt**. 惠准,赐予。*He* ～*ed no reply*. 他不予答复。

de·i gra·ti·a [ˌdiːai ˈgreiʃiei; ˋdiaɪ ˋgreʃɪə] 〔L.〕凭上帝的恩典。

deil [diːl; dil] **n**. 〔Scot.〕1. 恶魔。2. 歹徒。

de·i·on·i·za·tion [diːˌaiənaiˈzeiʃən; diˏaɪənaɪˋzeʃən] **n**. 去离子化。

de·i·on·ize [diːˈaiəˌnaiz; dɪˋaɪəˏnaɪz] **vt**. 【物】除去…的离子。

de·ism [ˈdiːizəm; ˋdiɪzəm] **n**. 自然神论[17、18 世纪的学说,说上帝创造世界及其自然规律,但此后不再参与其事]。

de·ist [ˈdiːist; ˋdiɪst] **n**. 自然神论者。**-tic** [diːˈistik; dɪˋɪstɪk] **a**.

de·i·ty [ˈdiːiti; ˋdiətɪ] **n**. 1. 神;神性;神的身分。2. 〔the D-〕上帝,造物主。*a society in which money is the only* ～ 金钱万能的社会。

dé·jà vu [ˈdeiʒɑːˈvjuː; ˏdeʒɑ ˋvju] 〔F.〕【心】记忆幻觉;【医】似曾相识症。

de·ject [diˈdʒekt; dɪˋdʒɛkt] **vt**. 使沮丧,使寒心,使气馁。*be* ～*ed* 垂头丧气。

de·jec·ta [diˈdʒektə; dɪˋdʒɛktə] **n**. 〔*pl*.〕排泄物,粪便。

de·ject·ed [diˈdʒektid; dɪˋdʒɛktɪd] **a**. 垂头丧气的,郁郁不乐的。**-ly ad**. **-ness n**.

de·jec·tion [diˈdʒekʃən; dɪˋdʒɛkʃən] **n**. 1. 沮丧,气馁,灰心,失意。2. 【医】排泄(物);粪便。

dé·jeu·ner [ˈdeiʒənei; ˋdeʒəˏne] **n**. 〔F.〕早餐;午餐。

deka- *pref*. = deca-.

Dek·ker [ˈdekə; ˋdɛkɚ] **n**. 德克〔姓氏〕。

dek·ko [ˈdekəu; ˋdɛko] **n**. 〔俚〕看一眼,看一看。*Let's have a* ～. 给我们看一看。

Del. = Delaware. **del**. = delegate; delete; *delineavit* (〔L.〕 = he [she] drew it) 此画为某某所画;〔美〕deliver.

de·laine [dəˈlein; dəˋlen] **n**. 1. 细毛料,棉毛混纺布料。2. 一种羊毛[用以作精纺毛纱]。

de·la·foss·ite [ˌdeləˈfɔsait; ˏdɛləˋfɑsaɪt] **n**. 【地】铜铁矿。

de·lam·i·nate [diːˈlæmiˌneit; dɪˋlæməˏnet] **vt**., **vi**. (使)分层。

de·lam·i·na·tion [diːˈlæmiˈneiʃən; diˏlæməˋneʃən] **n**. 分层[尤指胚胎的分层]。

De·land [ˈdiːlənd; dɪˋlænd] **n**. 迪兰〔姓氏〕。

de·late [diˈleit; dɪˋlet] **vt**. 1. 控告,告发。2. 〔古〕宣扬,公布。**-la·tion n**. 告发,控告。

Del·a·ware [ˈdeləweə; ˋdɛləˏwɛr] **n**. 1. 特拉华〔美国州名〕。2. 〔美〕特拉华河。3. (*pl*. ～, ～*s*) 居住在特拉华河流域的一种印第安人。

de·lay [diˈlei; dɪˋle] **I vt**. 延迟,拖延,耽搁。*We'll* ～ *the party for two week*. 我们要把会期延迟两周。*The train was* ～*ed by heavy snow*. 火车因大雪误点了。— **vi**. 耽搁,耽误,迟误。*It's getting late; don't* ～. 时间已晚,别再耽误了。**II n**. 延迟,拖延,耽搁,耽误。*No more* ～*s, comrades*. 同志们,再迟不行了。**admit of on** ～ 不能耽搁。**without** ～ 赶快,立刻,马上。～**-line** 延迟线。**-er n**. 延迟器;缓燃剂。

de·layed-action [diˈleidˈækʃən; dɪˋledˋækʃən] **I a**. (雷管、炸弹等)延期爆炸的,定时的。**II n**. 延迟动作[作用]。

del cred·e·re [delˈkredəri; dɛlˋkrɛdərɪ] 〔It.〕(掮客对)买主支付能力的保证。

de·le [ˈdiːli(ː); ˋdilɪ] **I vt**. 〔L.〕【印】(校对用语)删去〔略 d.〕。**II n**. 删去号。

de·lec·ta·ble [diˈlektəbl; dɪˋlɛktəbl̩] **a**. 1. 使人愉快的。2. 美味的。**-ness n**. **-bly ad**.

de·lec·ta·tion [ˌdiːlekˈteiʃən; ˏdilɛkˋteʃən] **n**. 1. 愉快。2. 娱乐,享受。

de·lec·tus [diˈlektəs; dɪˋlɛktəs] **n**. (学习用)拉丁[希腊]文选。

del·e·ga·cy [ˈdeligəsi; ˋdɛləgəsɪ] **n**. 1. 选出代表,被选为代表。2. 代表权。3. 代表团。

del·e·gate [ˈdeligeit; ˋdɛləget] **I n**. 1. 委员,代表,特派员。2. 〔美〕(Virginia, West Virginia, Maryland 等州

的)众议院议员。3.(众议院中准州地区的)代表〔无投票权〕。~s *without power to vote* 列席代表。*a walking* ~ (工会的)交涉代表。II *vt*. 1. 派…做代表。2. 委任,委托。~ *authority to sb*. 授权某人。

del·e·ga·tion [ˌdeliˈgeiʃən;ˏdɛləˋgeʃən] *n*. 1.(代表的)委派,派遣。2. 代表团。3.〔美〕(某)州议员团。*a* ~ *bringing gifts and thanks* 慰问团。

de·lete [diˈliːt; dɪˋlit] *vt*. 删去。*His name was* ~*d from the list*. 他的名字从名单上删去了。

del·e·te·ri·ous [ˌdeliˈtiəriəs;ˏdɛləˋtɪrɪəs] *a*. (对身心)有害的,有毒的。**-ly** *ad*. **-ness** *n*.

de·le·tion [diˈliːʃən; dɪˋliʃən] *n*. 1. 删除。2. 删除部分。3.(遗传学上染色体的)缺失。

delf, delft [delf, delft; dɛlf, dɛlft] *n*. 荷兰德尔夫特出产的陶器。~**ware** 荷兰蓝白彩釉陶器。

Del·hi [ˈdeli; ˋdɛlɪ] *n*. 德里〔印度城市〕。~ **belly** 〔俚〕德里腹泻(旅行者去印度得的腹泻)。

del·i [ˈdeli; ˋdɛlɪ] *n*. (*pl*. *del·is*)〔美口〕熟食店(= delicatessen)。

Del·ia [ˈdiːljə; ˋdiljə] *n*. 迪莉娅〔女子名〕。

de·lib·er·ate [diˈlibəreit; dɪˋlɪbəret] I *vt*. 1. 考虑。2. 商议。~ *the question* 考虑那个问题。*They are deliberating what to do*. 他们正在商议该做什么。— *vi*. 思考(*on, over*);与某人(*with*)协商,讨论某事(*over, upon, on*)。*I* ~*d with him on his future plans of study*. 我和他商讨关于他将来学习的计划。~ *on* [*over*] *a question* 思考问题。II [diˈlibərit; dɪˋlɪbərɪt] *a*. 1. 深思熟虑的,盘算周到的。2. 故意的,蓄意的。3. 审慎的,慎重的;沉着的,从容的。*a* ~ *aim* 从容不迫的瞄准。*a* ~ *decision* 慎重的决定。*a* ~ *murder* 蓄意谋杀。**-ly** *ad*. **-ness** *n*.

de·lib·er·a·tion [diˌlibəˈreiʃən; dɪˏlɪbəˋreʃən] *n*. 1. 深思熟虑。2. 协商,评议。3. 故意。4. 慎重,细心;沉着。***after long*** ~ 经过深思熟虑后。***be taken into*** ~ 被审议。***under*** ~ 在考虑中;在审议中。***with*** ~ 慎重。

de·lib·er·a·tive [diˈlibəreitiv; dɪˋlɪbəretɪv] *a*. 1. 考虑过的,慎重的。2. 协商的,评议的。*a* ~ *body* [*assembly*] 协商机关[会议]。*have a* ~ *voice* 有协商发言权。*a* ~ *speech* 提案审查报告。~ **poll** 议后民意测验〔在专家向被测者作讲解和讨论之前和之后分别进行的民意调查〕。

del·i·ca·cy [ˈdelikəsi; ˋdɛləkəsɪ] *n*. 1. 优美;精巧,精致。2. 柔弱,脆弱。3. 敏感;审慎,周到,体贴。4. 微妙;棘手。5. 美味,好菜。6. 正派,一本正经。7.【语言学】(语言范畴中各亚类的)细微差别。*a* ~ *of constitution* 虚弱的体质。*the* ~ *of one's sense of right and wrong* 敏锐的正义感。*diplomatic negotiations of great* ~ 极微妙的[极伤脑筋的]外交谈判。*the delicacies of the season* 应时好菜。***feel a*** ~ ***about*** 对…伤脑筋。***fake*** ~ 假正经,一本正经。

del·i·cate [ˈdelikit; ˋdɛləkət] *a*. 1. 巧妙的,优美的,优雅的。2. 柔弱的;脆弱的。3. 精巧的,精致的;(仪器)灵敏的。4. 美味的,鲜美的。5. 敏感的;周到的。6. 需要审慎的,微妙的,伤脑筋的。7. 有洁癖的,爱挑剔的。*a* ~ *touch* 巧妙的笔锋,精致的手艺。~ *colours* 淡色,柔和的颜色。*a* ~ *balance* 准确的天平。~ *food* 美味。*a* ~ *operation* 困难的手术。*a* ~ *hint* 微妙的暗示。***be in*** ~ ***health*** 身体虚弱。***be in the*** ~ ***condition*** 〔美俚〕有喜,怀孕。***have a*** ~ ***ear for music*** 对音乐有鉴赏力。**-ly** *ad*. **-ness** *n*.

del·i·ca·tes·sen [ˌdelikəˈtesn;ˏdɛləkəˋtɛsn] *n*. 〔*pl*.〕〔美〕1. 现成食品,熟食。2.〔用作单数〕熟食店,现成食品店。

de·li·cious [diˈliʃəs; dɪˋlɪʃəs] I *a*. 1. 美味的,好吃的,可口的。2. 美妙的,爽快的;极有趣的。II *n*. 〔D-〕〔美〕"美味"苹果〔一种冬季的红苹果〕。**-ly** *ad*. **-ness** *n*.

de·lict [ˈdiːlikt, diˈlikt; ˋdilɪkt, dɪˋlɪkt] *n*. 不法行为,违警罪。***in flagrant*** ~ 在作案时。

de·light [diˈlait; dɪˋlaɪt] I *n*. 1. 欢喜,高兴,愉快。2. 爱好的事物;嗜好。*The dance was a* ~ *to see*. 这个舞蹈看着愉快。*scorn* ~*s and live laborious days* 唾弃欢乐,刻苦度日。***take*** ~ ***in*** 喜欢;嗜好。***to one's*** ~ 说来真使某人高兴。***with*** ~ 欣然。II *vt*. 使欢喜,使高兴,使快乐。*I shall be* ~*ed to come*. 我一定来。— *vi*. 欢喜,快乐。*They* ~ *in travels*. 他们喜欢旅行。***be*** ~***ed with*** 喜欢,中意,合意。~ ***in music*** 喜欢音乐。~ ***to hono(u)r*** 衷心尊敬[称赞]。

de·light·ed [diˈlaitid; dɪˋlaɪtɪd] *a*. 喜欢的,高兴的。*a* ~ *look* 喜气洋洋。**-ly** *ad*.

de·light·ful [diˈlaitful; dɪˋlaɪtfəl] *a*. 1. 极快乐的,极愉快的。2. 可爱的,讨人欢喜的。**-ly** *ad*. 大喜,欣然。**-ness** *n*.

de·light·some [diˈlaitsəm; dɪˋlaɪtsəm] *a*. 〔古、诗〕= delightful.

De·li·lah [diˈlailə; dɪˋlaɪlə] 1.(《圣经》中)迪莱勒〔力士 Samson 的情妇,她把 Samson 出卖给腓力斯人〕。2. 妖妇。

de·lim·it [diːˈlimit; dɪˋlɪmɪt], **de·lim·i·tate** [di(ː)ˈlimiteit; dɪˋlɪmɪtet] *vt*. 为…定界,划界。**de·lim·i·ta·tion** [diˌlimiˈteiʃən; dɪˏlɪmɪˋteʃən] *n*. 定界,划界;区划。**de·lim·it·er** *n*. 定义符,定界符〔表示一个数据单位开始或终结的字符,如磁带上的这类字母〕。

de·lin·e·ate [diˈlinieit; dɪˋlɪnɪˏet] *vt*. 1. 描…的外形,画…的轮廓,勾画。2. 叙述,描写。

de·lin·e·a·tion [diˌliniˈeiʃən; dɪˏlɪnɪˋeʃən] *n*. 1. 描写,描画。2. 轮廓,图形,略图;线条写生画。3. 叙述。

de·lin·e·a·tor [diˈlinieitə; dɪˋlɪnɪˏetɚ] *n*. 1. 描写者,描画者,制图者。2. 叙述者。3. 图型。4. 描画器。5.(夜间公路上标示拐弯处的)一排照明灯。

de·lin·quen·cy [diˈliŋkwənsi; dɪˋlɪŋkwənsɪ] *n*. 1. 懈怠,失职,怠工。2. 过失,失职罪;罪过;【法】(青少年的)不法行为,罪行。3. 拖欠的债务[税款]。*juvenile* ~ 少年犯罪。

de·lin·quent [diˈliŋkwənt; dɪˋlɪŋkwənt] I *a*. 1. 不尽责的,怠工的。2.〔美〕拖欠(税款)的。3. 有过失的,有罪的。II *n*. 1. 懈怠者。2. 过失者;违犯者。3. 少年罪犯。

del·i·quesce [ˌdeliˈkwes;ˏdɛləˋkwɛs] *vi*. 1. 融解,溶化。2.【化】潮解。3.【植】(叶脉的)扩散;(蘑菇等因成熟、衰老)变软而液化。

del·i·ques·cence [ˌdeliˈkwesns;ˏdɛləˋkwɛsns] *n*. 1. 溶解。2.【化】潮解(性)。3.【植】(叶脉的)扩散;(蘑菇等的)液化。

del·i·ques·cent [ˌdeliˈkwesnt;ˏdɛləˋkwɛsnt] *a*. 1. 溶解的,溶化的。2.【化】潮解性的。3.【植】扩散的,液化的。

de·lir [diˈliə; dɪˋlɪr] *vi*. 神志昏迷;说胡话;产生幻觉。

del·i·ra·tion [ˌdeliˈreiʃən;ˏdɛləˋreʃən] *n*. 〔罕〕谵妄,精神错乱。

de·lir·i·ous [diˈliriəs; dɪˋlɪrɪəs] *a*. 1. 谵妄的,精神错乱的,语无伦次的。2. 极兴奋的,发狂的。~ *with joy* 狂喜。

de·lir·i·um [diˈliriəm; dɪˋlɪrɪəm] *n*. (*pl*. ~*s*, **-ri·a** [-riə; -rɪə]) 1. 精神错乱,谵妄。2. 极度兴奋,发狂。*lapse into* ~ 陷入谵妄状态,说起胡话来。~ ***tremens*** [ˈtriːmenz; ˋtrimənz]【医】(醉后的)酒狂,震颤性谵妄。

del·i·tes·cence [ˌdeliˈtesns;ˏdɛlɪˋtɛsəns] *n*. 1.(传染病等的)潜伏期,潜伏状态。2.(炎症等的)突然消退。**-cent** *a*.

de·liv·er [diˈlivə; dɪˋlɪvɚ] *vt*. 1. 救,救出,解放出(*from*)。2. 引渡,移交,交付(*up; over; to; into*)。3. 递送,投递,送(信等);传达,传(话等)。4. 发表(意见)。5. 加,给与(打击等);抛,投球。6. 射出,喷出。7. 陈说,讲述,吐露。8. 使分娩,助产。~ *sb*. *from danger* 从危险中救出某人。*The oil well* ~*s 500 tons a day*. 这口油井每天喷油500吨。*a well* ~*ed sermon* 天

花乱坠的说教。**be ～ed of** 生(孩子);作(诗);说(俏皮话)。**～ a gaol [jail]** 把囚犯提交法院。**～ battle** 开始攻击。**～ oneself of** (*an opinion*) 发表(意见)。**～ *oneself to*** (*the police*) (向警察)自首。**～ *oneself well*** 讲得不错。**～ *the goods*** 交货;履行诺言;〔美〕不负所望。

de·liv·er·ance [di'livərəns; dɪ'lɪvərəns] ***n*.** **1.** 救援,救助;释放。**2.** 陈述;(意见的)发表。**3.** (正式)意见;判决。

de·liv·ered [di'livəd; dɪ'lɪvəd] ***a*.** 【商】在…交货的;包括运费在内的。**～** *at station* 车站交货。**～** *price* 包括运费在内的价格。

de·liv·er·er [di'livərə; dɪ'lɪvərə] ***n*.** **1.** 救助者。**2.** 引渡人,交付者。**3.** 递送人。**4.** 〔罕〕陈述者。

de·liv·er·y [di'livəri; dɪ'lɪvərɪ] ***n*.** **1.** 引渡,交付;【商】交货;【法】正式让渡。**2.** 运送;投递;传送。**3.** 分娩。**4.** 陈述,讲演;口才。**5.** 【棒球】投球。**6.** 救助;释放。*the means of* ～ 发射工具。*an express* ～ 快信,快件。*the two o'clock* ～ 两点钟投递的邮件。*aerial* ～ 空投。*easy* [*difficult*] ～ 顺[难]产。*a good* [*poor*] ～ 能说会道[笨嘴拙舌]。～ *book* 交货簿,送货簿。～ *of canal* 渠道输水量。～ *port* 输出港。～ ***on arrival*** 货到交付。～ ***on term*** 定期交付。***take*** ～ ***of*** 收到送货(*The balance will be paid on taking* ～ *of the machine*. 收到机器就付还差额)。～ **book** 交货簿。～ **order** 出栈凭单。～ **port** 输出港。～ **receipt** 送货回条。～ **room** **1.** 医院的分娩室,产房。**2.** 出纳台,图书馆的借书处。

dell [del; dɛl] ***n*.** (有树林环抱的)小山谷。

Del·lin·ger ['delindʒə; 'dɛləndʒə] ***n*.** 德林杰〔姓氏〕。

Del·mar·va ['delmɑːvə; 'dɛlmɑrvə] ***n*.** 美国 Delaware, Maryland, Virginia 三州的总称。

de·lo·cal·ize [diː'ləukəlaiz; di'lokl,aɪz] ***vt*.** **1.** 使离开原位。**2.** 使不受局部地方限制;消除地方性。**3.** 【物】使(电子)移位。～ *an industry* 使工业不偏重于一方。～ *sb.'s accent* 使无地方口音。

de·louse ['diː'laus; di'laʊs] ***vt*.** 灭虱。

Del·phi ['delfai; 'dɛlfaɪ] ***n*.** 特尔斐〔古希腊城市,因有阿波罗神殿而出名〕。

Del·phi·an, Del·phic ['delfiən, 'delfik; 'dɛlfɪən, 'dɛlfɪk] ***a*.** **1.** (希腊)特尔斐的;阿波罗神殿的。**2.** 神示的;神秘的,玄妙的;模棱两可的。

del·phi·nine ['delfiniːn, -nin; 'dɛlfənin, -nɪn] ***n*.** 【化】翠雀宁。

del·phin·i·um [del'finiəm; dɛl'fɪnɪəm] ***n*.** 飞燕草,翠雀属植物。

Del·phi·nus [del'fainəs; dɛl'faɪnəs] ***n*.** 海豚(星)座。

del·ta ['deltə; 'dɛltə] ***n*.** **1.** 希腊语字母表第四字母〔Δ, δ〕。**2.** (河流的)三角洲;三角形物。**3.** 〔D-〕通讯中用以代替 d 的词。～ *metal* δ 齐, δ 合金。*the* ～ *of the Nile* 尼罗河三角洲。～ **rays** 【物】δ 射线。～ **wave** 【生】三角波〔显示熟睡状态的脑电波〕。

del·ta·ic [del'teiik; dɛl'teɪk] ***a*.** (有)三角洲的;三角形的。

del·ti·ol·o·gist [ˌdelti'ɔlədʒist; ˌdɛltɪ'ɑlədʒɪst] ***n*.** 图画明信片收藏家。

del·toid ['deltɔid; 'dɛltɔɪd] **I *a*.** 三角形的;三角肌的。**II *n*.** 【解】三角肌 (= ～ muscle)。

de·lude [di'luːd; dɪ'lud] ***vt*.** 欺骗,哄骗。～ *oneself* 自欺;误解。

del·uge ['deljuːdʒ; 'dɛljudʒ] **I *n*.** **1.** 大洪水;泛滥。**2.** 倾盆大雨。**3.** 洪水般的涌来。*a* ～ *of rain* 大雨。*a* ～ *of tears* 泉涌似的泪。*a* ～ *of fire* 火海。***After me the D-!*** (身)后(之)事于我何干。***the D-*** 【圣】诺亚 (Noah) 时的洪水。**II *vt*.** 泛滥,涌集。*be ～d with applications* 申请书雪片似地飞来。

de·lu·sion [di'luːʒən; dɪ'luʒən] ***n*.** **1.** 欺骗,迷惑。**2.** 幻想;【心】妄想。**3.** 误解,谬见,误会。*have a* ～ *that* 幻想。***labour under a*** ～ 因妄想而苦恼;误解。***be under no*** ～ ***as to*** 对…所见不差,对…没有误解。

de·lu·sion·al [di'luːʒənl; dɪ'luʒənl] ***a*.** 幻想的,妄想性的。

de·lu·sive [di'ljuːsiv; dɪ'ljusɪv] ***a*.** 欺骗的,虚妄的,不可靠的。**-ly *ad*.** **-ness *n*.**

de luxe [di'lʌks, di'luks; dɪ'lʌks, dɪ'lʊks] ***a*.** 豪华的,奢侈的,高级的。*a* ～ *edition* 精装本。

delve [delv; dɛlv] **I *vt*., *vi*.** 〔古、方〕**1.** 掘,挖。**2.** 探究,钻研。**II *n*.** 穴,凹,坑。～ *into books* 钻研书本。～ *into the past* 调查过去的情况。

dem [dem; dɛm] ***v*.** 〔卑〕= damn.

Dem. = Democrat(ic).

de·mag·net·ize ['diː'mægnitaiz; di'mægnə,taɪz] ***vt*.** 除去…的磁性,给…退磁。**-mag·net·i·za·tion** [-ˌmægnitai'zeiʃən; -ˌmægnətaɪ'zeʃən] ***n*.** 退磁。

dem·a·gog·ic, -i·cal [ˌdemə'gɔgik(əl); ˌdɛmə'gɑdʒɪk(əl)] ***a*.** 煽动(性)的,造谣生事的,蛊惑的。**-gog·ism,** 〔美〕**-gog·uer·y *n*.** 煽动主义,煽动行为,造谣生事。

dem·a·gogue, dem·a·gog ['deməgɔg; 'dɛmə,gɔg] ***n*.** **1.** 煽动者,蛊惑人心者,造谣生事的人。**2.** (古代的)民众领袖。

dem·a·gog·y ['deməgɔgi; 'dɛmə,godʒɪ] ***n*.** 煽动的行为,蛊惑的性质。

de·man [di'mæn; dɪ'mæn] ***vt*., *vi*.** **1.** 裁减(…的)人员。**2.** (使)变得无男子气。

de·mand [di'mɑːnd; dɪ'mænd] **I *vt*.** **1.** 要求,请求;需要。**2.** 询问,盘问,追究。**3.** 【法】召唤。～ *an interview* 要求会面。*The work ～s care*. 那项工作需要细心。～ *sb.'s name* 询问姓名。～ (*sth*.) *of* [*from*] (*sb*.) 向(某人)要求(某物)。*She ～ed that we let her in*. 她要我们让她进来。— ***vi*.** 要求,查问。★后面子句中的动词,美国人多用假设语气现在式,即第三人称单数现在时不加 -s, 如: She ～s that he *assume* the responsibility. (她要求他承担责任。)英国人则用 *should assume*. **II *n*.** **1.** 要求,请求。**2.** 需要;销路。*I have a* ～ *to make of him*. 我对他有一个要求。*supply and* ～ 供给和需要。～ *for a commodity* 商品的需要[销路]。*There are many ～s on my purse*. 我有许多事情要花钱去办。***be in*** ～ 有需要,销路好。***on*** ～ 请求即(*a bill payable on* ～ 见票即付的票据)。***present one's ～s*** 提出要求。～ **bill** [**draft, note**] 见票即付的票据,即期票据。～ **deposit** 活期存款。～ **inflation,** ～**-pull** 【经】需求膨胀。**-er *n*.** 要求者。,

de·mand·a·ble [di'mɑːndəbl; dɪ'mændəbl] ***a*.** 可要求的。

de·mand·ant [di'mɑːndənt; dɪ'mændənt] ***n*.** **1.** 要求者。**2.** 询问者。**3.** 【法】原告。

de·mand·er [di'mɑːndə; dɪ'mændə] ***n*.** 要求者,请求者。

de·man·toid [di'mæntɔid; dɪ'mæntɔɪd] ***n*.** 翠榴石,钙铁榴石。

de·mar·cate [di'mɑːkeit; dɪ'mɑrket] ***vt*.** **1.** 划界,定界线。**2.** 区别,分开。

de·mar·ca·tion [ˌdiːmɑː'keiʃən; ˌdimɑr'keʃən] ***n*.** **1.** 边界,分界。**2.** 划界,没界限。**3.** 区分,划分。*a line of* ～ *between* …之间的界线。*draw a clear line of* ～ 划清界线。

dé·marche ['deimɑːʃ; de'mɑrʃ] ***n*.** 〔F.〕**1.** (外交用语)手段,步骤,措施,反措施。**2.** (口头的或书面的)表示。**3.** 行动的方针。

de·mark [di'mɑːk; dɪ'mɑrk] ***vt*.** = demarcate.

de·ma·te·ri·al·ize ['diːmə'tiəriəlaiz; 'dimə'tɪrɪəl,aɪz] ***vt*., *vi*.** (使)非物质化,(使)失去物质的性质。

deme [diːm; dim] ***n*.** **1.** 【希腊史】(古 Attica 的)市区。**2.** 【生】同类群。

de·mean[1] [di'miːn; dɪ'min] ***vt*.** 〔古〕〔～ oneself〕行动,表现,举动。～ *oneself well* [*ill*] 行为好[不好]。

de·mean[2] [di'miːn; dɪ'min] ***vt*.** 〔通例 ～ oneself〕降低(身

分),损坏(人品)。to ~ *oneself by taking a bribe* 因受贿而贬低自己。

de·mean·or, de·mean·our [di'mi:nə; dɪ`minɚ] ***n***. 态度,行为,举动,品格,品行。*assume a haughty* ~ 采取高傲的态度。

de·ment [di'ment; dɪ`mɛnt] ***vt***. 〔罕〕使发狂。

de·ment·ed [di'mentid; dɪ`mɛntɪd] ***a***. 疯狂的,发狂的。*be* [*become*] ~ 发狂。*drive* (*sb*.) ~ 〔口〕(忧愁等)使(人)发狂。

dé·men·ti [dei'mɑ̃:nti:; demɑ̃`ti] ***n***. 〔F.〕(外交上)正式否认,正式辟谣。

de·men·ti·a [di'menʃiə; dɪ`mɛnʃɪə] ***n***. 【医】痴呆。*epileptic* ~ 癫痫性痴呆。~ *praecox* ['pri:kɔks; `prikɑks]【医】早发性痴呆,精神分裂症。

de·mer·it [di:'merit; di`mɛrɪt] ***n***. **1**. 缺点,短处;过失。**2**. (学校的)记过。*the merits and* ~*s* 优点缺点;功过。*He already has three* ~*s on his record*. 他已记过三次。

dem·e·rol ['demərɔl; `dɛmərɔl] ***n***. 【商标】德美罗〔止痛药〕。

de·mesne [di'mein; dɪ`men] ***n***. **1**. (土地的)占有;地主的不出租的地产。**2**. (领主的)领地,庄园周围的土地。**3**. 范围,领域。*hold estates in* ~ 有许多地产。*a Royal* ~ 〔英〕御地。*a State* ~ 国有地。

De·me·ter [di'mi:tə; dɪ`mitɚ] ***n***. 【希神】德墨特尔〔主管生产、社会治安等的女神〕。

de·mi ['di:mai; `dimaɪ] ***n***. demos 的复数。

demi- *pref*. 表示"半"、"部分"、"略小": *demi*god, *demi*tasse.

dem·i·god ['demigɔd; `dɛmə,gɑd] ***n***. 半神半人;神与人所生的后代;神一样的人。

dem·i·john ['demidʒɔn; `dɛmə,dʒɑn] ***n***. (用柳条编壳保护着的)小颈大瓶。

de·mil·i·ta·rize ['di:'militəraiz; di`mɪlətə,raɪz] ***vt***. 解除武装,废除军备,解除军事管制。**-rized** ***a***. 非武装的。~*d zone* 非军事区。

dem·i·lune ['demilu:n; `dɛmɪ,lun] ***n***. **1**. 半月,新月。**2**. 半月形堡垒。

dem·i·min·i ['demi'mini; `dɛmɪ`mɪnɪ] **I** ***a***. 超超短的。**II** ***n***. 超超短裙。

dem·i·mon·daine [,demimɔn'dein; ,dɛmɪmɑn`den] ***n***. 〔F.〕妓女;交际花。

dem·i·monde ['demi'mɔ̃:nd; `dɛmɪ`mɑnd] ***n***. 〔F.〕**1**. 〔集合词〕名声不好的女人。**2**. 妓女。**3**. 娼妓界。**4**. 形迹可疑的一群人。

de-min·ing [di'mainiŋ; dɪ`maɪnɪŋ] ***n***. 【军】排雷。

de·mi-pen·sion [demi'pɑ:nsjɔ:n; dɛmi`pɑnsjɔn] 〔F.〕(旅馆、宿舍等处的)半寄膳(除住宿外,供应早餐和午餐)。

dem·i·re·lief [,demiri'li:f; ,dɛmɪrɪ`lif] ***n***. 半浮雕。

dem·i·rep ['demirep; `dɛmɪ,rɛp] ***n***. 名声不好的妇女,不正派的妇女。

de·mise [di'maiz; dɪ`maɪz] **I** ***n***. **1**. 【法】(不动产的)转让;遗赠。**2**. 让位。**3**. 崩,薨;〔口〕逝世,死。*the* ~ *of the Crown* 王位的继承。**II** ***vt***. **1**. 转让,遗赠。**2**. 逊(位),让(位)。~ *the Crown* 让位。**de·mis·a·ble** ***a***.

dem·i·sem·i·qua·ver ['demisemi,kweivə; `dɛmɪ`sɛmə,kwevɚ] ***n***. 【乐】三十二分音符。

de·mis·sion [di'miʃən; dɪ`mɪʃən] ***n***. **1**. 放弃(职务,权力);辞职。**2**. 免职,撤职。

de·mit [di'mit; dɪ`mɪt] ***vt***. (**-tt-**) **1**. 辞(职),放弃。**2**. 〔古〕罢免。— ***vi***. 辞职。

dem·i·tasse ['demitɑ:s; `dɛmə,tæs] ***n***. 小咖啡杯;一小杯咖啡。

dem·i·tint ['demitint; `dɛmɪ,tɪnt] ***n***. (介乎浅色与深色之间的)晕色。

dem·i·urge ['demiə:dʒ; `dɛmɪ,ɝdʒ] ***n***. (*pl*. ***-ur·gi*** [-dʒai; -dʒaɪ]) **1**. 〔D-〕(柏拉图哲学里所说的)造物主。**2**. (古希腊城邦的)行政官。

dem·i·ur·gic, dem·i·ur·gi·cal [,di:mi'ə:dʒik(əl); ,dimɪ`ɝdʒɪk(əl)] ***a***. 造物主的;创造世界的。

dem·i·volt ['demivəult; `dɛmɪ,volt] ***n***. (骑马时马前足抬起的)半腾空。

Dem·o ['deməu; `dɛmo] ***n***. (*pl*. ***-os***) 〔美〕民主党员。

dem·o ['deməu; `dɛmo] ***n***. 〔美口〕**1**. 示威。**2**. 示威者。**3**. (新歌手等用以试探听众反应的)示范唱片,试播唱片。**4**. (游行示威时播放示威内容的)示威唱片。

de·mob [di:'mɔb; di`mɑb] 〔英口〕**I** ***n***. **1**. = demobilization. **2**. 复员军人。**II** ***vt***. = demobilize.

de·mo·bi·li·za·tion ['di:,məubilai'zeiʃən; ,dimobl̩ə`zeʃən] ***n***. 复员;遣散。~ *order* 复员令。

de·mo·bi·lize [di:'məubilaiz; di`mobl̩,aɪz] ***vt***. 【军】复员;遣散。*a* ~*d soldier* 复员军人。

de·moc·ra·cy [di'mɔkrəsi; dɪ`mɑkrəsɪ] ***n***. **1**. 民主政治;民主政体,民主制度;民主主义;民主精神。**2**. 民主国家。**3**. 〔D-〕〔美〕民主党。**4**. 〔the ~〕平民,老百姓。

dem·o·crat ['deməkræt; `dɛmə,kræt] ***n***. **1**. 民主主义者。**2**. 〔D-〕〔美〕民主党党员。~ **wagon** 〔美〕(农场用的)二马轻便马车。

dem·o·crat·ic [,demə'krætik; ,dɛmə`krætɪk] ***a***. **1**. 民主政体的,民主主义的;民主作风的。**2**. 民众的;平等的。**3**. 〔D-〕〔美〕民主党的。~ *centralism* 民主集中制。~ *parties and groups* 民主党派。*the D- Party* (美国的)民主党。~ *personnel* 民主人士。

de·moc·ra·tism [di'mɔkrətizəm; dɪ`mɑkrətɪzəm] ***n***. 民主主义;民主制;民主原则。

de·moc·ra·tize [di'mɔkrətaiz; də`mɑkrə,taɪz] ***vt***., ***vi***. (使)民主化。**de·moc·ra·ti·za·tion** [di,mɔkrətai'zeiʃən; də,mɑkrətaɪ`zeʃən] ***n***.

De·moc·ri·tus [di'mɔkritəs; dɪ`mɑkrɪtəs] ***n***. 德谟克利特(460? —370? B. C.)古希腊哲学家。**-te·an** [-ti:ən; -tiən] ***a***.

dé·mo·dé [F. deimə'dei; dəmo`de] ***a***. 〔F.〕过时的,已不时兴的,老式的。

de·mod·ed [di:'məudid; di`modɪd] ***a***. 过时的,老式的。

de·mod·u·late [di:'mɔdju:,leit; di`mɑdʒə,let] ***vt***. 【无】解调;检波。

de·mod·u·la·tion [di:,mɔdju'leiʃən; di,mɑdʒə`leʃən] ***n***. 【无】解调,反调制;检波。

De·mo·gor·gon ['di:məu'gɔ:gən; ,dimə`gɔrgən] ***n***. (古代神话中的)魔王。

de·mo·graph·ic [di:mə'græfik; ,dimə`græfɪk] ***a***. 人口统计(学)的。

de·mog·ra·phy [di'mɔgrəfi; dɪ`mɑgrəfɪ] ***n***. 人口统计学。

de·moi·selle [demwɑ:'zel; ,dɛmwɑ`zɛl] ***n***. 〔F.〕**1**. (未婚)少妇,少女。**2**. 【鸟】蓑羽鹤。**3**. 【虫】豆娘〔一种蜻蜓〕。**4**. 【地】菌状石。**5**. 【动】一种在珊瑚礁里栖息的热带鱼。

de·mol·ish [di'mɔliʃ; dɪ`mɑlɪʃ] ***vt***. **1**. 拆毁(建筑物等),毁坏,破坏(组织等),推翻(计划、制度等)。**2**. 〔俚〕吃光。*The automobile was* ~*ed in a collision with the train*. 汽车与火车相撞而被毁坏。*They simply* ~*ed that turkey*. 他们把那只火鸡一下子吃光了。

dem·o·li·tion [,demə'liʃən; ,dɛmə`lɪʃən] ***n***. **1**. 爆破,破坏。**2**. 〔*pl*.〕废墟。**3**. 〔*pl*.〕爆破的炸药。~ **bomb** 爆破炸弹。~ **Derby** 撞车比赛〔参加者驾车互撞,直至最后有一辆仍可驶行者获冠军〕。

de·mon ['di:mən; `dimən] ***n***. **1**. 鬼,恶魔。**2**. 恶棍。**3**. 精力过人的人。**4**. (古希腊的)守护神。*the little* ~ (*of a child*) 调皮娃娃。*a regular* ~ 坏家伙。*He is a* ~ *for work*. 他做起工作来真是精力过人。*the* ~ *of a bulldog* 凶猛的斗犬。

de·mon·e·tize [di:'mʌnitaiz; di`mʌnə,taɪz] ***vt***. **1**. 使

(货币)失去标准价值。2. 停止用(金银)做货币本位。**-mon·e·tiza·tion** [-ˌmʌnitaiˈzeiʃən; -ˏmʌnətaɪˋzeʃən] *n*.

de·mo·ni·ac [diˈməuniæk; dɪˋmonɪˏæk] **I** *a*. 1. 着魔的。2. 恶魔的。3. 恶魔似的,凶恶的,疯狂的。**II** *n*. 着魔的人。

de·mo·ni·a·cal [ˌdi:məˈnaiəkəl; ˏdiməˋnaɪəkəl] *a*. = demoniac. ~ *possession* 着魔,凶神附体。

de·mon·ic [di:ˈmɔnik; diˋmɑnɪk] *a*. 1. 有魔力的,神通广大的,超人的。2. = demoniac.

de·mon·ism [ˈdi:mənizəm; ˋdimənˏɪzəm] *n*. 对魔鬼的信仰。**de·mon·ist** *n*. 魔鬼信仰者。

de·mon·ize [ˈdi:mənaiz; ˋdimənˏaɪz] *vt*. 使成鬼;使着魔。

de·mon·o- *comb*. *f*. = demon.

de·mon·oc·ra·cy [di:məˈnɔkrəsi; ˏdimənˋɑkrəsɪ] *n*. 魔鬼的统治[支配]。

D

de·mon·ol·a·try [ˌdi:məˈnɔlətri; ˏdimənˋɑlətrɪ] *n*. 崇拜魔鬼。

de·mon·ol·o·gy [ˌdi:məˈnɔlədʒi; ˏdimənˋɑlədʒɪ] *n*. 1. 对魔鬼的研究;对魔鬼的信仰。2. 〔美俚〕仇敌名单。

de·mo·nop·o·lize [ˌdi:məˈnɔpəlaiz; ˏdiməˋnɑpəˏlaɪz] *vt*. 解除专卖权。

dem·on·stra·ble [ˈdemənstrəbl; ˋdɛmənstrəbl] *a*. 可表明的;可论证的。**-bil·i·ty** [ˌdemənstrəˈbiliti; ˏdɛmənstrəˋbɪlətɪ] *n*. 论证可能性。**-bly** *ad*. 可证明地,确然,了然。

dem·on·strate [ˈdemənstreit; ˋdɛmənˏstret] *vt*. 1. 表明,表示(感情)。2. 论证,证明。3. (用实例、实验)说明,示范,表演。~ *one's anger by slamming a door* 把门砰地关上表示愤怒。~ *a philosophical principle* 论证一次哲学原理。~ *how to cook with a pressure cooker* 当众表演如何使用高压力锅。— *vi*. 1. 举行示威运动。2. 【军】示威,佯动。

dem·on·stra·tion [ˌdemənstˈreiʃən; ˏdɛmənstˋreʃən] *n*. 1. 表明,表示。2. 论证,证明。3. 实物示教,示范;实物说明。4. 示威(运动);示威游行。5. 【军】示威行动,佯动。*give a* ~ *of love* 表示爱情。*to* ~ 决定地,断然,明确地。**-al** *a*. 示威(运动)的。**-ist** *n*. 参加示威运动者。

de·mon·stra·tive [diˈmɔnstrətiv; dɪˋmɑnstrətɪv] **I** *a*. 1. 论证的,证明的。2. 【语法】指示的。3. 感情外露的,易动感情的。**II** *n*. 【语法】指示词。*a* ~ *person* 易动感情的人。*a* ~ *pronoun* 指示代词。**-ly** *ad*. **-ness** *n*.

dem·on·stra·tor [ˈdemənstreitə; ˋdɛmənˏstretɚ] *n*. 1. 证明者;示范者;实验示教者;实物说明者。2. 示威者。3. 用来向顾客作示范表演的产品。

de·mor·al·ize [diˈmɔrəlaiz; dɪˋmɑrəlˏaɪz] *vt*. 1. 败坏风纪[道德],伤风败俗。2. 挫折锐气;【军】使士气沮丧。3. 使陷入混乱。**-za·tion** [-ˈzeiʃən; -ˋzeʃən] *n*. 道德败坏,风纪败坏;士气沮丧。

de mor·tu·is nil ni·si bo·num [di:ˈmɔ:tʃu:is nil ˈnaisai ˈbəunəm; diˋmɔrtʃuɪs nɪl ˋnaɪsaɪ ˋbonəm] 〔L.〕对于死者唯有称美。

de·mos [ˈdi:mɔs; ˋdimɑs] *n*. (*pl*. ***de·mi*** [ˈdi:mai; ˋdimaɪ]) 1. (古希腊的)平民。2. (一般的)人民,民众。

De·mos·the·nes [diˈmɔsθəni:z; dɪˋmɑsθəˏniz] *n*. 德摩斯梯尼〔公元前 384—322,古希腊的政治家、雄辩家〕。

Dem·os·then·ic [ˌdemɔsˈθenik; ˏdɛməsˋθɛnɪk] *a*. 雄辩的。

de·mote [diˈməut; dɪˋmot] *vt*. 〔美〕使降级 (*opp*. promote)。

de·moth·ball [di:ˈmɔ:θbɔl; diˋmɔθˏbɔl] *vt*. 重新使用(已转入后备役保存起来的船舶、飞机、大炮等)。

de·mot·ic [di(:)ˈmɔtik; dɪˋmɑtɪk] **I** *a*. 1. 民众的;通俗的。2. (古埃及经过简化的)通俗文字的。**II** *n*. 1. (古埃及经过简化的)通俗文字。2. 〔D-〕现代希腊日常用语 (*opp*. Katharevusa)。

de·mo·tion [diˈməuʃən; dɪˋmoʃən] *n*. 降级。

de·mount [di:ˈmaunt; diˋmaʊnt] *vt*. 卸除。*to* ~ *a motor* 卸除马达。**-able** *a*.

de·mul·cent [diˈmʌlsnt; dɪˋmʌlsn̩t] **I** *a*. 【医】缓和的,止痛的。**II** *n*. 缓和药;润药。

de·mul·si·fy [diˈmʌlsifai; dɪˋmʌlsəˏfaɪ] *vt*. 【化】反乳化。**-si·fi·ca·tion** [-sifiˈkeiʃən; -səfəˋkeʃən] *n*. 反乳化作用。

de·mur [diˈmə:; dɪˋmɝ] **I** *vi*. (**-rr-**) 1. 表示异议,反对 (*to*; *at*)。2. (因怀疑或反对而)迟疑。3. 【法】抗辩。**II** *n*. 异议,反对。*No* ~ . 没有异议。*without* ~ 无异议。

de·mure [diˈmjuə; dɪˋmjʊr] *a*. 1. 娴静的,拘谨的,庄重的。2. 假装正经的。*a quiet and* ~ *woman* 文雅端庄的妇女。**-ly** *ad*. **-ness** *n*.

de·mur·ra·ble [diˈmə:rəbl; dɪˋmɝəbl̩] *a*. 可抗辩的,可提出异议的。

de·mur·rage [diˈmʌridʒ; dɪˋmɝɪdʒ] *n*. 1. 【商】(轮船、货车因未能如期装卸、运行而)逾期;逾期费。2. (英格兰银行的)金银块兑换费。

de·mur·rer [diˈmʌrə; dɪˋmɝɚ] *n*. 1. 【法】异议,抗辩。2. [diˈmə:rə; dɪˋmɝɚ] 抗辩者。*enter* [*put in*] *a* ~ 提出异议,反对。

de·my [diˈmai; dɪˋmaɪ] *n*. 1. 〔英〕22.5×17.5 英寸开(的纸);〔美〕21×16 英寸开(的纸)。2. (英国牛津大学 Magdalen College 的)半津贴生。

de·my·e·lin·ate [di:ˈmaiəlineit; diˋmaɪəlɪˏnet] *vt*. 【医】脱髓鞘。**-na·tion** [-ˌmaiəliˈneiʃən; -ˏmaɪələˋneʃən] *n*.

de·my·thol·o·gize [ˌdi:miˈθɔlədʒaiz; ˏdimɪˋθɑləˏdʒaɪz] *vt*. 去掉(《圣经》等中的)神话色彩(以便于理解和领受)。

Den. = Denmark.

den [den; dɛn] **I** *n*. 1. 兽穴,窝。2. 匪窟,贼窝。3. 小而脏的屋子。4. 小而舒适的书斋。5. 〔Scot.〕溪谷。6. (幼年童子军的)小组,小队。**II** *vi*. 1. 穴居。2. 入洞,进窝(冬眠)。— *vt*. 把…赶入洞中。

de·nar·i·us [diˈnɛriəs; dɪˋnɛrɪəs] *n*. (*pl*. ***-ri·i*** [-riai; -rɪaɪ]) 第纳里〔古罗马银币,英国旧便士 (penny, pence) 以该词首字母 d 为缩略号〕。

de·na·ry [ˈdi:nəri; ˋdɛnərɪ] *a*. 十的,十进的,十倍的。~ *scale* 十进法。

de·na·tion·al·ize [di:ˈnæʃənəlaiz; diˋnæʃənlaɪz] *vt*. 1. 使(国家)失去国家地位[特点]。2. 使(人)失去国籍[公民权]。3. 使(企业)非国有化,变成私营。**-za·tion** [ˈdi:ˌnæʃənəlaiˈzeiʃən; ˋdiˏnæʃənələˋzeʃən] *n*.

de·nat·u·ral·ize [di:ˈnætʃrəlaiz; diˋnætʃrəlaɪz] *vt*. 1. 使不自然;使改变本性。2. 剥夺国民[市民]权利,开除…的国籍。**-za·tion** [-ˈzeiʃən; -ˋzeʃən] *n*.

de·na·tur·ant [di:ˈneitʃərənt; diˋnetʃərənt] *n*. 变性剂。

de·na·ture [di:ˈneitʃə; diˋnetʃɚ] *vt*. 1. 使变性。2. 使(酒精)不能饮用。3. 使(蛋白质)变质。4. 使(核燃料)中毒〔加入不裂变物质使裂变物质不适于制造原子弹〕。~*d alcohol* 变性酒精。~*d protein* 变性蛋白质。

de·na·zi·fy [di:ˈnɑ:tsifai; diˋnɑtsəˏfaɪ] (***-fied***; ***-fying***) *vt*. 消除…的纳粹影响;清除…的纳粹分子,使非纳粹化。

dendr(i)- *comb*. *f*. 〔用于子音前〕= dendro-.

den·dri·form [ˈdendrifɔ:m; ˋdɛndrəˏfɔrm] *a*. 树木状的。

den·drite [ˈdendrait; ˋdɛndraɪt] *n*. 1. 【矿】松树石,树石。2. 【化】枝状晶体。3. 【解】(神经的)枝状突起;树突。

den·drit·ic, den·drit·i·cal [denˈdritik(əl); dɛnˋdrɪtɪk(əl)] *a*. 枝状的。

dendr(o)- *comb*. *f*. 树木〔母音前用 dendr-〕。

den·dro·cli·ma·tol·o·gy [ˈdendrəuˌklaiməˈtɔlədʒi; ˋdɛndroˏklaɪməˋtɑlədʒɪ] *n*. 年轮气候学。

endroi·d(al) [den'drɔid(əl); `dɛndrɔɪd(əl)] *a*. 树状的;分枝状的。

en·dro·lite ['dendrəulait; `dɛndrə͵laɪt] *n*. 树木化石,化石植物。

en·drol·o·gy [den'drɔlədʒi; dɛn`drɑlədʒɪ] *n*. 树木学。

en·drom·e·ter [den'drɔmitə; dɛn`drɑmɪtɚ] *n*. 测树器。

en·dron ['dendrɔn; `dɛndrɑn] *n*. 【解】= dendrite.

ene[1] [diːn; din] *n*. (树木繁茂的)幽谷。

ene[2] [diːn; din] *n*. (海滨的)沙地;沙丘。

en·eb ['deneb; `dɛnɛb] 【天】天津四〔天鹅座 α〕。

. Eng. = Doctor of Engineering 工程学博士。

en·e·ga·tion [ˌdeni'geiʃən; ͵dɛnə`geʃən] *n*. 否认;拒绝。

en·gue ['deŋgi; `dɛŋgɪ] *n*. 【医】登革热〔蚊子传染的热带病,症状为关节痛、发烧、出疹子〕。~ **fever** 【医】登革热。

e·ni·a·ble [di'naiəbl; dɪ`naɪəbl̩] *a*. 可否认的,可反对的;可拒绝的。

e·ni·al [di'naiəl; dɪ`naɪəl] *n*. 1. 否认,否定。2. 拒绝承认,拒绝相信,拒绝接受。3. 克制 (= self-~)。*general* [*specific*] ~ 全部[部分]否认。*make a* ~ *of* 否定,否认。*take no* ~ 不许否认,不许说不,硬要。

e·nic·o·tin·ize [diː'nikətinaiz; dɪ`nɪkətɪn͵aɪz] *vt*. (从烟草中)除去尼古丁。**-za·tion** [-ˌnikətinai'zeiʃən; -͵nɪkətɪnaɪ`zeʃən] *n*.

e·ni·er[1] [di'naiə; dɪ`naɪɚ] *n*. 否认者;拒绝者。

e·nier[2] ['diniei; də`nɪr] *n*. 1. 法国古银币名。2. 纤度,紥〔生丝纤度单位,长 450 米重 0.05 克时为 1 denier〕。~**-meter** 纤度计。

en·i·grate ['denigreit; `dɛnə͵gret] *vt*. 1. 涂黑。2. 污蔑,诽谤。**-gra·tion** [ˌdeni'greiʃən; ͵dɛnə`greʃən] *n*. **-grat·or** *n*. 诽谤者。**-grato·ry** [-grətəri; -grətorɪ] *a*.

en·im ['denim; `dɛnɪm] *n*. 1. 斜纹粗棉布。2. 〔*pl*.〕(蓝色斜纹粗棉布制成的)工作服,工装裤。

en·imed ['denimd; `dɛnɪmd] *a*. 穿粗斜棉布衣服的。

en·ise [də'niːz, də'niz] *n*. 丹妮斯〔女子名〕。

e·ni·trate [diː'naitreit; di`naɪtret] *vt*. 从…除去硝酸盐,使脱硝。

e·ni·tra·tion [diːnai'treiʃən; dinaɪ`treʃən] *n*. 脱硝。

e·ni·tri·fy [diː'naitrifai; di`naɪtrə͵faɪ] *vt*. (**-fied**; **-fy·ing**) 1. 去掉…的氮气。2. 使脱去硝酸盐。~*ing bacteria* 反硝化细菌;脱氮细菌。

en·i·zen ['denizn; `dɛnəzn] **I** *n*. 1. 居民。2. (享有某些或全部公民权的)外籍居民,归化者。3. 外来语;外来动植物。4. 暂住某处的人;常去某处的人。*winged* ~*s of the forest* 森林中的鸟类。**II** *vt*. 给与…以市民权;准许…归化;移植。

en·mark ['denmaːk; `dɛnmɑrk] *n*. 丹麦〔欧洲〕。

en·(n)is ['denis; `dɛnɪs] *n*. 丹尼斯〔姓氏,男子名〕。

e·nom·i·nate [di'nɔmineit; dɪ`nɑmə͵net] *vt*. 为…命名,给…取名,把…叫做,把…称做。

e·nom·i·na·tion [diˌnɔmi'neiʃən; dɪ͵nɑmə`neʃən] *n*. 1. 命名;名目,名称。2. (度量衡等的)单位;票面金额。3. 种类;教派,宗派;派别。*plants falling under different* ~*s* 种种植物。*money of small* ~*s* 小钱,零钱。*What* ~? 什么票面的钱币? *all sects and* ~*s* 各党各派。**-al** [-nl; -nl̩] *a*. 名称上的;宗派的,教派的。

e·nom·i·na·tion·al·ism [diˌnɔmi'neiʃənəlizəm; dɪ͵nɑmə`neʃənl͵ɪzəm] *n*. 1. 宗派原则。2. 宗派制度。3. 宗派主义。4. 分成宗派。

e·nom·i·na·tive [di'nɔminətiv; dɪ`nɑmə͵netɪv] *a*. 1. 有名称的;可命名的。2. 【语法】出自名词[形容词]的。"*To eye*" *is a* ~ *verb*. To eye (目视)是来自名词的动词。

e·nom·i·na·tor [di'nɔmineitə; dɪ`nɑmə͵netɚ] *n*. 1. 命名者。2. 【数】分母。3. (爱好、见解等的)标准。4. 共同特性。*a* [*the least*] *common* ~ 公[最小公]分母。*manufacturers catering to a low* ~ *of public taste* 力求迎合大众低水平爱好的制造商。*Only a single* ~ *do they share*. 他们只有一种共同的特点。

de·not·a·ble [di'nəutəbl; dɪ`notəbl̩] *a*. 可表示[指示]的。

de·no·ta·tion [ˌdiːnəu'teiʃən; ͵dino`teʃən] *n*. 1. 指示,表示。2. 名称;符号。3. (字面)意义〔*cf*. connotation〕。4. 【逻】外延。5. 命名。

de·no·ta·tive [di'nəutətiv; dɪ`notətɪv] *a*. 1. 指示…的,表示的 (*of*)。2. 【逻】外延的 (*opp*. connotative)。**-ly** *ad*.

de·note [di'nəut; dɪ`not] *vt*. 1. 指示,表示;意味着。2. 【逻】概述,概指 (*opp*. connote)。*Dark clouds* ~ *rain*. 黑云表示有雨。**-ment** 指示,表示,表示方法。

dé·noue·ment [dei'nuːmɑ̃ːŋ; de`numɑ̃] *n*. 〔F.〕(小说等的)大团圆,收场;结局。

de·nounce [di'nauns; dɪ`naʊns] *vt*. 1. 指责,谴责;声讨,斥责。2. 〔古〕恐吓,扬言要(报仇等)。3. 告发,揭发。4. 通告废除(条约等)。~ *a man as a traitor* 指责某人是叛徒。~ *a person to the police* 向警察告发某人。~ *vengeance against* 扬言要向…报仇。**-ment** *n*. = denunciation.

dense [dens; dɛns] *a*. 1. 密集的,(物质等)密度大的,(人口等)稠密的。2. (烟、雾等)浓密的,浓厚的。3. 愚钝的。4. 【摄影】(页片)高密度的。*a* ~ *forest* 密林。*a* ~ *metal* 密度大的金属。*a* ~ *fog* 浓雾。*a man with a* ~ *brain* 头脑愚昧的人。*My* ~ *lady, can't you follow*? 哎呀,我的傻太太,你真的听不懂吗? **-ly** *ad*. **-ness** *n*.

den·si·fy ['densifai; `dɛnsə͵faɪ] *vt*. (**-fied**; **-fy·ing**) 使增加密度。**-fi·ca·tion** [-fi'keiʃən; -fə`keʃən] *n*.

den·sim·e·ter [den'simitə; dɛn`sɪmətɚ] *n*. 比重计,密度计。

den·si·tom·e·ter [ˌdensi'tɔmitə; ͵dɛnsə`tɑmətɚ] *n*. 1. = densimeter. 2. (测量底片的)显影密度计。

den·si·tom·e·try [ˌdensi'tɔmitri; ͵dɛnsə`tɑmətrɪ] *n*. 测密度术;测光密度术;显微测密术。

den·si·ty ['densiti; `dɛnsətɪ] *n*. 1. 稠密;浓厚。2. 【物】浓度;密度;比重。3. 愚钝,昏庸。*traffic* ~ 交通量。*the* ~ *of population* 人口密度。~ **recorder** 自记比重计,比重记录器。

den·som·e·ter [den'sɔmitə; dɛn`sɑmɪtɚ] *n*. 1. (纸张的)透气度测定计。2. = densimeter.

Dent [dent; dɛnt] *n*. 登特〔姓氏〕。

dent[1] [dent; dɛnt] **I** *n*. 1. 凹,凹痕,压痕。2. 〔英方〕打,击。3. 削减。4. 进展。***make a*** ~ 使注意;开始有进步[有进展](*The doctor told him to stop smoking, but it didn't make a* ~. 医生让他停止抽烟,但没有引起注意。*I haven't even made a* ~ *in this job*. 我这工作没有取得进展)。**II** *vt*. 1. 敲凹,使凹下。2. 削减。— *vi*. 凹进。

dent[2] [dent; dɛnt] *n*. (齿轮等的)齿;【纺】竹筘齿格。

dent- (接元音) = denti-.

dent. = dental; dentist; dentistry.

dent·al ['dentl; `dɛntl̩] **I** *a*. 1. 牙齿的;牙科(用)的。2. 【语音】齿音的。**II** *n*. 1. 【语言】齿音;齿音字[d, t, n 等]。2. 〔谑〕牙医。*a* ~ *parlor* 〔美〕牙医诊室。~ *paste* 牙膏。*a* ~ *surgeon* 牙医生。~ *surgery* 牙科,口腔外科。**-ize** *vt*. 使齿音化。**-gi·a** [den'tældʒiə; dɛn`tældʒɪə] *n*. 齿痛。

den·ta·li·um [den'teiliəm; dɛn`telɪəm] *n*. (*pl*. ***-li·a*** [-lə; -lə]) 角贝属动物。

den·tate ['denteit; `dɛntet] *a*. 1. 有牙齿的。2. 【植】(叶子)锯齿状的。

den·ta·tion [den'teiʃən; dɛn`teʃən] *n*. 齿状(构造)。

denti- (接辅音) *comb. f*. 齿牙; *denti*form.

den·ti·care ['dentikeə; `dɛntɪkɛr] *n*. (加拿大等国实行

D

的)儿童牙齿免费保健计划。

den·ti·cle [ˈdentikl; ˋdɛntɪkl̩] *n*. **1**. 小牙,细齿状突起。**2**.【建】齿饰。**-tic·u·lar** [denˈtikjulə; dɛnˋtɪkjələ˞] *a*. 细齿状的。**-tic·u·late** [denˈtikjulit; dɛnˋtɪkjəlɪt] *a*. 有细齿的,锯齿状的。**-tic·u·la·tion** [denˌtikjuˈleiʃən; dɛnˏtɪkjəˋleʃən] *n*. 细齿状(突起),〔常 *pl*.〕一副细齿。

den·ti·form [ˈdentifɔːm; ˋdɛntɪˏfɔrm] *a*. 齿形的。

den·ti·frice [ˈdentifris; ˋdɛntəˏfrɪs] *n*. 牙粉;牙膏。

den·tig·er·ous [denˈtidʒərəs; dɛnˋtɪdʒərəs] *a*. 生齿的,有牙齿的。

den·til [ˈdentil; ˋdɛntɪl] *n*.【建】(屋檐下的)齿饰。

den·ti·la·bi·al [ˌdentiˈleibiəl; ˏdɛntɪˋlebɪəl] *a*., *n*. = labiodental.

den·ti·lated [ˈdentileitid; ˋdɛntɪletɪd] *a*. 形成齿状的。

den·ti·lin·gual [ˌdentiˈliŋgwəl; ˏdɛntɪˋlɪŋgwəl] *a*.【语音】齿舌音〔[θ], [ð] 等子音〕的。

den·tin, den·tine [ˈdentin, -tiːn; ˋdɛntɪn, -tin] *n*. (牙齿的牙釉下的)牙质。

den·tist [ˈdentist; ˋdɛntɪst] *n*. 牙科医生。

den·tist·ry [ˈdentistri; ˋdɛntɪstrɪ] *n*. 牙科医术;牙医业。

den·ti·tion [denˈtiʃən; dɛnˋtɪʃən] *n*. **1**. 出牙齿,长牙齿。**2**. 牙列,齿列。**3**. 〔集合词〕(一口)牙齿。

dento- *comb. f.* = denti-.

den·toid [ˈdentɔid; ˋdɛntɔɪd] *a*. 牙齿状的。

Den·ton [ˈdentən; ˋdɛntən] *n*. 登顿〔男子名〕。

den·to·sur·gi·cal [ˌdentəuˈsəːdʒikl; ˏdɛntoˋsɝdʒəkəl] *a*. 牙外科的。

den·ture [ˈdentʃə; ˋdɛntʃə˞] *n*. **1**. 一副牙齿。**2**. 一副假牙。*a full* [*partial*] ~ 全副[一部份]假牙。

de·nu·cle·ar·ize [diːˈnjuːkliəraiz, -ˈnjuː-; diˋnuklɪəˏraɪz, -ˋnu-] *vt*. 使非核武器化。**-za·tion** [-ˌnjuːkliəraiˈzeiʃən; -ˏnjuklɪəraɪˋzeʃən] *n*.

de·nu·cle·ate [diːˈnjuːklieit; diˋnjuklɪˏet] *vt*. 除去(原子、分子、动物细胞等的)核,使去核。**-cle·a·tion** [-ˌnjuːkliˈeiʃən; -ˏnjuklɪˋeʃən] *n*. 去核(作用)。

de·nu·da·tion [ˌdiːnjuːˈdeiʃən; ˏdinjuˋdeʃən] *n*. **1**. 剥裸;除光,裸露。**2**.【地】剥蚀。**3**.【林】滥伐。

de·nude [diˈnjuːd; dɪˋnjud] *vt*. **1**. 除光,剥裸。**2**. 剥去;剥夺。**3**.【地】剥蚀。**4**.【化】溶蚀;去垢。*Most trees are ~d of their leaves in winter*. 许多树木冬季都要落叶。

de·nu·mer·a·ble [diˈnuːmərəbl, -ˈnjuː-; dɪˋnjumərəbl̩, -ˋnju-] *a*. 可数的。

de·nun·ci·ate [diˈnʌnsieit, -ʃieit; dɪˋnʌnsɪˏet, -ʃɪˏet] *vt*. = denounce.

de·nun·ci·a·tion [diˌnʌnsiˈeiʃən; dɪˏnʌnsɪˋeʃən] *n*. **1**. 指责,弹劾。**2**. 控诉,告发,揭发。**3**. 警告,恐吓。**4**. 声讨檄文。**5**. 废约通告。

de·nun·ci·a·tor [diˈnʌnsieitə; dɪˋnʌnʃɪˏetə˞] *n*. 指责者;告发者;恐吓者。

de·nun·ci·a·to·ry [diˈnʌnsiətəri; dɪˋnʌnsɪəˏtorɪ] *a*. 指责的;恐吓的。

Den·ver [ˈdenvə; ˋdɛnvə˞] *n*. 丹佛〔美国城市〕。**-ite** [-vərait; -vəˏraɪt] *n*. 丹佛人。

de·ny [diˈnai; dɪˋnaɪ] *vt*. (***-nied***; ***-ny·ing***) **1**. 否定,否认;不承认。**2**. 拒绝(要求等),不给与。**3**. 不接受,推卸;摒弃。**4**. 谢绝(宾客)。*He denied the charges against him*. 他否认他有嫌疑。*There is no ~ing the fact*. 事实无可否认。~ *one's signature* 否认是自己的署名。*This night before the cock crows, you shall ~ me three times*. 今夜鸡叫以前,你要三次不认我。*I was denied this*. = *This was denied* (*to*) *me*. 这个我未曾得到。*I was denied satisfaction*. 我未曾满足。*Peace was denied him*. 他心境不安。~ ***oneself*** **1**. 自制,克己。**2**. 放弃(*He must ~ himself many of the comforts of life*. 他必须放弃自己生活上的许多享受)。~ ***oneself to*** 不会见客人等(*She denied herself to all callers*. 她不会见任何来客)。~ ***sb. to*** (*callers*) 使某人不会见客人(*I told the door-keeper to ~ me to all callers*. 我关照传达室不接见任何客人)。— *vi*. 否定,拒绝。

de·ob·stru·ent [diˈɔbstruːənt; diˋɑbstruənt] *n*., *a*.【药】便通剂(的)。

de·oc·cu·py [diˈɔkjupai; dɪˋɑkjəpaɪ] *vt*. (***-pied***; ***-py·ing***) 解除对…的占领。

de·o·dar [ˈdiəudɑː; ˋdiəˏdɑr] *n*.【植】喜马拉雅杉。~ *ceder* 雪松。

de·o·dor·ant [diːˈəudərənt; diˋodərənt] **I** *a*. 除臭的。**II** *n*. 防臭剂,除臭药。

de·o·dor·ize [diːˈəudəraiz; diˋodəˏraɪz] *vt*. 除去…的臭味,防止…的臭味。**-ri·za·tion** [diˌəudəraiˈzeiʃən; dɪˏodəraɪˋzeʃən] *n*. 防臭,脱臭(作用)。**-iz·er** [-zə; -zə˞] *n*. 除[防]臭剂;防臭喷雾器。

de·on·tol·o·gy [diːɔnˈtɔlədʒi; diɑnˋtɑlədʒɪ] *n*.【伦】义务论,道义学。

de-or·bit [diː-ˈɔːbit; di-ˋɔrbɪt] **I** *vt*. 使脱轨。**II** *n*. 脱轨。

De·o vo·len·te [ˈdiːəu vəuˈlenti; ˋdio voˋlɛntɪ] 〔L.〕若承天意;若无阻碍〔略 D. V.〕。

de·ox·i·di·za·tion, de·ox·i·da·tion [diːˌɔksidaiˈzeiʃən, -ˈdeiʃən; diˏɑksədaɪˋzeʃən, -ˋdeʃən] *n*. 脱氧;还原。

de·ox·i·dize, de·ox·i·date [diːˈɔksidaiz, -deit; diˋɑksəˏdaɪz, -ˏdet] *vt*.【化】使去氧;使还原。

de·ox·i·di·zer [diːˈɔksidaizə; diˋɑksəˏdaɪzə˞] *n*. 脱氧剂;还原剂。

de·ox·y·gen·ate [diːˈɔksidʒineit; diˋɑksədʒəˏnet] *vt*. = deoxidize.

de·ox·y·ri·bo·nu·cle·ic [diːˈɔksiˌraibəunjuːˈkliːik; diˋɑksəˏraɪbonjuˋkliɪk] *a*. ~ **acid**【生化】脱氧核糖核酸(DNA)。

de·ox·y·ri·bo·nu·cle·o·tide [diːˈɔksiˌraibəunjuːˈkliətaid; diˋɑksəˏraɪbonjuˋkliətaɪd] *n*.【生化】脱氧核(糖核)苷酸〔DNA 的组成成分之一〕。

de·ox·y·ri·bose [diːɔksiˈraibəus; diˏɑksɪˋraɪbos] *n*.【生化】脱氧核糖。

dep. = department; departs; departure; deponent; deposed;【银行】deposit; depot; deputy.

de·part [diˈpɑːt; dɪˋpɑrt] *vi*., *vt*. **1**. 〔古、诗〕离开。**2**. (火车等)开行(*opp*. arrive)。**3**. 不合(情理等)(*from*)。**4**. 死亡,消失。~ *at 5:30* 五点半开〔略作 *dep*. 5:30 a. m.〕。~ *from* (*this*) *life* 去世,死。~ *this life* 去世。~ ***for*** (*London*) 去(伦敦)。~ ***from*** 不合(习惯等);背离;违反(~ *from one's word* 违约)。~ ***hence*** 由这儿去。

de·part·ed [diˈpɑːtid; dɪˋpɑrtɪd] *a*. **1**. 已往的,过去的。**2**. 已去世的。*the* ~ 死者,故人。

de·part·ment [diˈpɑːtmənt; dɪˋpɑrtmənt] *n*. **1**. 部门;〔美〕部(=〔英〕ministry);〔英〕局,课,科;车间。**2**. (法国等的)省,县。**3**.【军】军(管)区。**4**. (学校、学术机构的)系;学部。**5**. 知识范围;活动范围。**6**. (期刊或广播节目的)专栏。*the physics* [*literature*] ~ 物理学[文学]部。*D- of the Interior* 〔美〕内政部。*the State D-* 〔美〕国务院。*the accountant's* ~ 会计科。*the Statistics D-* 〔英〕统计局。*the Hawaiian D-* 〔美〕夏威夷军区。~ *store* 百货商店,百货公司。*D- of Trusteeship Council* (联合国)托管理事会。

de·part·men·tal [ˌdiːpɑːtˈmentl; dɪˏpɑrtˋmɛntl] *a*. 部门[科、系、局等]的。**-ism** *n*. 分散主义;本位主义。**-ize** [-aiz; -ˏaɪz] *vt*. 把…分成部门。**-ly** *ad*.

de·par·ture [diˈpɑːtʃə; dɪˋpɑrtʃə˞] *n*. **1**. 起程,出发;(火车的)开行。**2**. 背离,违反(*from*);偏差。**3**.【测】东西距离,横距。**4**. 〔古〕逝世。**5**.【海】航迹推算起点。~ ***and arrival*** 开出和到达。~ ***from the truth*** 失真,伪。***new*** ~ 新政策,新方案。***take one's*** ~ 出发,起身。~ **hall** (飞机场的)候机室。~ **platform** 发车月台。

de·pas·ture [diːˈpɑːstʃə; dɪˋpæstʃə˞] *vt*., *vi*. **1**. (使)吃

草;放牧。2.(把)(某地)作放牧[牧草]基地。**-pas·tur·age** [-ˈpɑːstʃəridʒ; -ˋpɑstʃərɪdʒ] ***n.*** 放牧(权)。

de·pau·per·ate [diːˈpɔːpəreit; dɪˋpɔpəˏret] **I** ***vt.*** **1.** 使贫穷。**2.** 使衰落;使萎缩。**II** ***a.*** **1.** 贫穷的。**2.** 发育不全的,萎缩的。**-a·tion** [-ˌpɔːpəˈreiʃən; -ˏpɔpəˋreʃən] ***n.*** **1.** 贫穷。**2.** 衰落。**3.**【植】萎缩,变质。

de·pau·per·ize [ˈdiːˈpɔːpəraiz; ˋdiˋpɔpəraɪz] ***vt.*** **1.**〔美〕使贫穷。**2.**〔英〕使脱离贫穷。

de·pend [diˈpend; dɪˋpɛnd] ***vi.*** **1.** 取决于,因…而定,靠,凭(*on*; *upon*)。**2.** 依赖,依靠;信任(*on*; *upon*)。**3.**(树枝等)下垂,悬挂(*from*)。**4.**〔古〕(案件等)悬而不决。**5.**【语法】从属。*Success ~s on* [*upon*] *your own exertions*. 成功全靠自己努力。*You can ~ on him*. 你信任他好了。*~ on depth to avoid breakthrough*【军】以纵深配备防止突破。***a man to be ~ed on*** 可靠的人。***~ on*** [***upon***] ***... for*** 要看…,靠…供给…,赖…做…(*He ~s on his pen for his living*. 他靠写作吃饭)。***D- upon it!*** 靠得住! 的确的! 你看好啦! 你相信好啦(*D- upon it, you will succeed*. 你准能成功)。***That ~s.*** = ***It all ~s.*** 那要看情况了,不能一概而论,要看时间与地点而定(*Sometimes I support him, and sometimes he supports me; that ~s*. 有时我支持他,有时他支持我,这要看情况而定)。

de·pend·a·ble [diˈpendəbl; dɪˋpɛndəbl] ***a.*** 可靠的,可信任的。**-bly** ***ad.*** **-bil·i·ty** [-ˌpendəˈbiliti; -ˏpɛndəˋbɪlətɪ] ***n.*** 可靠性,可信任程度。**-ness** ***n.*** 可靠,可信任。

de·pend·ant [diˈpendənt; dɪˋpɛndənt] ***n.***, ***a.*** = dependent. *family ~s* 供养的直系亲属。

de·pend·ence [diˈpendəns; dɪˋpɛndəns] ***n.*** **1.** 依赖,依靠。**2.** 依靠之物,靠山。**3.** 信任,信赖。**4.** 从属;隶属。**5.**【物】依存(关系)。**6.**【法】未决。

de·pend·en·cy [diˈpendənsi; dɪˋpɛndənsɪ] ***n.*** **1.** 依存,从属。**2.** 从属物。**3.** 属国,属地,保护地。~**culture** 依赖性文化〔指公众已习惯于依赖国家各种补助之社会环境和风气〕。~**ratio** 总人口与劳动人口之比例。

de·pend·ent [diˈpendənt; dɪˋpɛndənt] **I** ***a.*** **1.** 依靠的,依赖的。**2.** 从属的,隶属的,【语法】从属的。**3.** 由…决定的。**4.** 下垂的,悬吊的。*be ~ on* [*upon*] 依靠,取决于。**II** ***n.*** **1.** 受赡养者,靠人生活的人。**2.** 扈从,侍从。**3.** 依存[从属]物。*~ clause*【语法】从属子句[从句,分句]。*a ~ domain* 领地。*He listed four ~s on his income-tax form*. 他在所得税表格上填写了四个受赡养人。

de·perm [diːˈpəːm; diˋpɝm] ***vt.*** 减少[消除](船体周围)的磁性。

de·per·son·al·ize [diːˈpəːsənəˌlaiz; diˋpɝsənəlˏaɪz] ***vt.*** **1.** 使…失去个性;对…作客观处理。**2.** 使失去自我感。**-per·son·ali·za·tion** [-ˌpəːsənəlaiˈzeiʃən; -ˏpɝsənəlaɪˋzeʃən] ***n.***

De·pew [diˈpjuː; dɪˋpju] ***n.*** 迪皮尤〔姓氏〕。

de·phased [diːˈfeizd; diˋfezd] ***a.***【无】有相位差的;相位移后的。

de·phleg·mate [diːˈflegmeit; diˋflɛgˏmet] ***vt.***【化】除去…的过量水分;使分馏,使分凝。**-ma·tion** [ˌdiːflegˈmeiʃən; ˏdiflɛgˋmeʃən] ***n.*** 分馏;分凝。**-tor** ***n.*** 分馏塔;分凝器。

de·phos·phor·ize [diːˈfɔsfəraiz; diˋfɑsfəˏraɪz] ***vt.*** 使脱去磷酸。

de·pict [diˈpikt; dɪˋpɪkt] ***vt.*** **1.** 画,刻画。**2.** 描写;叙述。**de·pic·tion** [-ˈpikʃən; -ˋpɪkʃən] ***n.*** 描写,叙述。**de·pic·tive** [-ˈpiktiv; -ˋpɪktɪv] ***a.*** 描写的。**-ture** [-ˈpiktʃə; -ˋpɪktʃɚ] ***vt.*** = depict.

dep·i·late [ˈdepileit; ˋdɛpəˏlet] ***vt.*** 使脱毛,除去…的毛。**-la·tion** [ˌdepiˈleiʃən; ˏdɛpəˋleʃən] ***n.*** 脱毛。**-to·ry** [diˈpilətəri; dɪˋpɪləˏtorɪ] ***a.***, ***n.*** **1.** 有除毛力的。**2.**【医】脱毛剂。

de·plane [diːˈplein; diˋplen] ***vi.*** 下飞机。

de·plen·ish [diˈpleniʃ; dɪˋplɛnɪʃ] ***vt.*** 弄空(*opp*. replenish)。*a ~ed house* (没有家具的)空荡荡的房子。*a ~ed purse* 囊空如洗。

de·plete [diˈpliːt; dɪˋplit] ***vt.*** **1.** 减少,损耗。**2.** 弄空,耗尽,用尽。**3.**【医】减液,放血。*~ one's strength* 竭尽全力。*a lake recklessly ~d* 乱捕鱼(使鱼源枯竭)的湖。

de·ple·tion [diˈpliːʃən; dɪˋpliʃən] ***n.*** **1.** 损耗。**2.** 弄空;耗尽。**3.**【医】减液;放血;(缺液引起的)衰竭(状态)。

de·ple·tive [diˈpliːtiv; dɪˋplitɪv] ***a.*** **1.** 引起枯竭的,有耗尽作用的。**2.** 减液的;放血的。

de·ple·to·ry [diˈpliːtəri; dɪˋplitərɪ] ***a.*** = depletive.

de·plor·a·ble [diˈplɔːrəbl; dɪˋplorəbl̩] ***a.*** 可叹的,悲惨的。***in ~ order*** 极杂乱。**-ness** ***n.*** **-bly** ***ad.*** **-bil·i·ty** [diˌplɔːrəˈbiliti; dɪˏplorəˋbɪlətɪ] ***n.***

de·plore [diˈplɔː; dɪˋplor] ***vt.*** **1.** 悲悼,痛惜。**2.** 悔恨。*~ the death of one's friend* 哀悼朋友的逝世。**-plor·ing·ly** ***ad.***

de·ploy [diˈplɔi; dɪˋplɔɪ] ***vt.***, ***vi.*** **1.**【军】展开,散开,疏散开。**2.** 部署。**3.**(使)张开。*~ a battalion* 使队伍散开。*The army ~ed to the right*. 部队向右方展开。**-ment** ***n.*** 部署(*rational deployment of labour power* 合理安排劳动力)。

de·plume [diːˈpluːm; diˋplum] ***vt.*** **1.** 拔去…的羽毛。**2.** 夺去,剥夺(荣誉、财产等)。

de·po·lar·ize [diːˈpəuləraiz; diˋpoləˏraɪz] ***vt.*** **1.**【物】减极,去极,退极化。**2.** 消除(偏见等);使丧失(信心等)。**-zer** [-zə; -zɚ] ***n.*** 退极化剂。**-za·tion** [ˈdiːˌpəuləraiˈzeiʃən; ˋdiˏpolərаɪzeʃən] ***n.***

de·po·lit·i·cize [ˌdiːpəˈlitisaiz; ˏdipəˋlɪtɪˏsaɪz], **de·po·lit·i·cal·ize** [ˌdiːpəˈlitikəlaiz; ˏdipəˋlɪtɪkəˏlaɪz] ***vt.*** 使非政治化。

de·pone [diˈpəun; dɪˋpon] ***vt.***, ***vi.***〔古〕发誓证明。

de·po·nent [diˈpəunənt; dɪˋponənt] **I** ***a.***【拉丁语语法】异态的,词形被动词义自动的。**II** ***n.*** **1.** 异态(词形被动词义自动的)动词,异相动词。**2.**【法】宣誓作证者。

de·pop·u·late [diːˈpɔpjuleit; diˋpɑpjəˏlet] **I** ***vt.***(战争,疫病等)消灭[减少](某地的)人口。— ***vi.***〔罕〕人口减少。**II** ***a.***〔古〕人口减少的。**-la·tion** [-ˌpɔpjuˈleiʃən; -ˏpɑpjəˋleʃən] ***n.***

de·port [diˈpɔːt; dɪˋport] ***vt.*** **1.**〔~ oneself〕行动,举动。**2.** 运输,输送。**3.** 把…驱逐出境。*~ oneself well* [*ill*] 行为好[坏]。*~ dangerous aliens* 把危险的外国人驱逐出境。**-ta·tion** [ˌdiːpɔːˈteiʃən; ˏdiporˋteʃən] ***n.*** 驱逐出境。**-tee** [ˌdiːpɔːˈtiː; ˏdiporˋti] ***n.*** 被驱逐出境者。

de·port·ment [diˈpɔːtmənt; dɪˋportmənt] ***n.*** 行为,品行;举止,态度。

de·pos·al [diˈpəuzəl; dɪˋpozəl] ***n.*** 罢免,免职;废位。

de·pose [diˈpəuz; dɪˋpoz] ***vt.*** **1.** 把…免职,废黜(国王等)。**2.**【法】宣誓证明(*that*)。**3.** 放置。*~ sb. from office* 免去某人的职务。*~ sth. on the table* 把某物放在桌上。— ***vi.*** 宣誓作证。*~ to a fact* 宣誓证明某事。**-a·ble** ***a.*** 可废除的,可罢免的。

de·pos·it [diˈpɔzit; dɪˋpɑzɪt] **I** ***vt.*** **1.** 放置,安置。**2.** 使淤积,使沉淀。**3.** 储蓄。**4.** 付保证金。**5.** 寄存,委托保管。**6.**(把硬币)放入(自动售货机,公用电话机)。*~ money in the bank* 把钱存入银行。*~ sth. with sb.* 把某物委托某人保管。— ***vi.*** **1.** 淤积,沉淀;附着。**2.** 存贮;寄存。**II** ***n.*** **1.** 淤积[沉积]物;【矿】矿藏,矿床。**2.** 储蓄,存款。**3.** 保证金,押金。**4.** 寄存,寄存品。**5.** 寄存处,仓库。*oil ~s* 石油埋藏量。*current* [*fixed*] *~* 活期[定期]存款。*money on ~* 存款。*have* [*place*] *money on ~* 有存款[攒、存钱]。***~ at bank*** 银行存款。***~ at call*** 活期存款。***~ in security*** 保证金,押金。***~ in trust*** 信托存款。~ **account** 存款账户。

de·pos·i·ta·ry [diˈpɔzitəri; dɪˋpɑzəˏtɛrɪ] ***n.*** **1.** 受托人,保管人。**2.** 保管所,贮藏所,仓库。

dep·o·si·tion [ˌdepəˈziʃən; ˏdɛpəˋzɪʃən] ***n.*** **1.** 免职,罢

免;废位。2. 淤积[沉积](物,作用)。3. 耶稣从十字架上放下(的画、雕刻)。4. 寄存,委托;委托物。5.【法】口供,证言;口供书。

de·pos·i·tor [diˈpɔzitə; dɪˋpɑzɪtɚ] *n*. 1. 存放人;存款人。2. 沉淀器。

de·pos·i·to·ry [diˈpɔzitəri; dɪˋpɑzəˏtorɪ] *n*. 1. 寄存处,存放处,贮藏所,仓库。2. 受托人,保管人。*a ~ of learning* 知识的宝库。~ *library* 〔美〕指定免费接受政府出版物的图书馆。

dep·ot [ˈdepəu, Am. ˈdiː-; ˋdipo, ˋdɛ-] *n*. 1. 〔英〕贮藏所,仓库。2. 〔美〕火车站;航空站。3.【军】兵站,补给站。4. 〔英〕团司令部;新兵训练站;俘虏收容所。~ *ship* 供应舰,修配舰。

de·prave [diˈpreiv; dɪˋprev] *vt*. 1. 使堕落,使腐化。2. 弄坏,败坏。**-d** *a*. 堕落的,腐败的。**-va·tion** [ˌdeprəˈveiʃən; ˏdɛprəˋveʃən] *n*. 颓废,堕落。

de·prav·i·ty [diˈpræviti; dɪˋprævətɪ] *n*. 1. 堕落;腐败;邪恶。2. 〔*pl*.〕恶劣行为,腐化堕落的行为。

dep·re·cate [ˈdeprikeit; ˋdɛprəˏket] *vt*. 1. 不赞成,反对(战争等)。2. 祈免,求免(灾殃等)。3. 贬低。~ *sb.'s anger* 求某人息怒。**-ca·tion** [ˌdepriˈkeiʃən; ˏdɛprəˋkeʃən] *n*. 1. 不赞成,反对。2. 求免,求情。**-ca·to·ry** [ˈdeprikətəri; ˋdɛprəkəˏtorɪ] *a*. 1. 反对的。2. 求情的,道歉的。*a ~ letter* 反驳的信。

de·pre·ci·ate [diˈpriːʃieit; dɪˋpriʃɪˏet] *vt*. 1. 使减值,使贬值;使跌价。2. 贬低,轻视。— *vi*. 减价,贬值。**-at·ing·ly** [-ˈpriːʃieitiŋli; -ˋpriʃɪˏetɪŋlɪ] *ad*. 轻视地,贬低地(*speak depreciatingly of* 贬损,讥笑)。

de·pre·ci·a·tion [diˌpriːʃiˈeiʃən; dɪˏpriʃɪˋeʃən] *n*. 1. 减价,贬值。2. 折旧;【机】损耗。3. 藐视,轻视。~ *in price* 减价。*a ~ of currency* 通货贬值。~ *funds* 折旧费。

de·pre·ci·a·tive, de·pre·ci·a·to·ry [diˈpriːʃjətiv, -ətəri; dɪˋpriʃɪˏetɪv, -əˏtorɪ] *a*. 1. 价值低落的,减价的,贬值的。2. 蔑视的,贬低的。

dep·re·date [ˈdeprideit; ˋdɛprɪˏdet] *vt*., *vi*. 掠夺,劫掠(*sth*., *on sth*.)。**-da·tion** [ˌdepriˈdeiʃən; ˏdɛprɪˋdeʃən] *n*. 劫掠;〔*pl*.〕劫余残迹。

de·press [diˈpres; dɪˋprɛs] *vt*. 1. 压下,压低(声调等),放低(*opp*. raise)。2. 使沮丧,使消沉,抑制。3. 使萧条,使跌价。4. 使衰弱。

de·press·ant [diˈpresənt; dɪˋprɛsnt] **I** *a*. 1.【医】有镇静作用的。2. 使消沉的。3. 引起萧条的。**II** *n*. 镇静剂。

de·pressed [diˈprest; dɪˋprɛst] *a*. 1. 被压下的,被压低了的。2. 中间凹下的。3. 抑郁的,消沉的。4. 萧条的。5.【动、植】扁平的〔横向扁者叫 depressed, 纵向扁者叫 compressed〕。*feel ~* 闷闷不乐。*The market is ~*. 市况萧条。~ *area* 〔英〕不景气地区。~ *classes* 最下层人民。~ *roadway* 低陷的道路。

de·press·i·ble [diˈpresibl; dɪˋprɛsəbl̩] *a*. 可压低的。

de·press·ing [diˈpresiŋ; dɪˋprɛsɪŋ] *a*. 抑压的;郁闷的。**-ly** *ad*.

de·pres·sion [diˈpreʃən; dɪˋprɛʃən] *n*. 1. 压低,降低,陷落。2. 凹洼;洼地,沉降地。2. 不景气,萧条,不振。3. 沮丧,消沉。4. 低气压。5.【天】地平线以下星体的角度距离;【测】俯角。6.【病】机能降低,抑郁症。*atmospheric ~* 低(气)压。*nervous ~* 神经衰弱。*suffer from* [*be affected with*] *~* 患神经衰弱症。

de·pres·sive [diˈpresiv; dɪˋprɛsɪv] *a*. 1. 抑压的,压下的。2. 郁闷的,消沉的。

de·pres·so·mo·tor [diˈpresəuˌməutə; dɪˋprɛsoˏmotɚ] **I** *a*. 抑制运动功能的。**II** *n*. 运动抑制剂。

de·pres·sor [diˈpresə; dɪˋprɛsɚ] *n*. 1. 抑压者。2.【化】抑制剂。3. (血压)降压剂。4.【解】下牵肌。5.【医】压舌板,压低器。~ *nerve* 降压神经。*a tongue ~* 压舌板。

de·priv·a·ble [diˈpraivəbl; dɪˋpraɪvəbl] *a*. 可剥夺的。

de·priv·al [diˈpraivəl; dɪˋpraɪvəl] *n*. 剥夺,褫夺。

dep·ri·va·tion [ˌdepriˈveiʃən; ˏdɛprɪˋveʃən] *n*. 1. 剥夺;(圣职等的)褫夺,免职;废止。2. 丧失(氧气、维生素等)。

de·prive [diˈpraiv; dɪˋpraɪv] *vt*. 1. 剥夺,使(*sb*.)不能享受(*of*)。2. 免职(特指圣职)。~ (*sb*.) *of* ... 使(人)失去(*An accident ~d him of his sight*. 意外的事故使他失明)。*be ~d of* 失却(*I was ~d of education at ten*. 我十岁时就失学了)。

de pro·fun·dis [ˌdiː prəuˈfʌndis, ˌdei-; ˏdi proˋfʌndɪs, ˏde-] 1. 悲惘以极的。2. [D- P-]《圣经》第一百三十诗篇〔篇首语是此二词,故以之代篇名〕;哀悼经。

dep·side [ˈdepsaid, -sid; ˋdɛpsaɪd, -sɪd] *n*.【化】缩酚酸。

dept. = 1. department. 2. deponent. 3. deputy.

depth [depθ; dɛpθ] *n*. 1. 深;深度。2. (色泽的)浓度;(声音的)低沉;(感情等的)深厚,深沉,深刻。3. 进深。4. 〔常 *pl*.〕深处;深渊,深海,海。5. 正中,当中。6. 深奥,奥妙。***beyond*** [***out of***] ***one's ~*** 在深不着底的地方;不能理解,力所不及。~ ***bomb*** [***charge***] 深水炸弹。~ ***of shade*** 色度。***from the ~ of the mind*** 诚心,真心,从心底里。***in ~*** 广泛,彻底,详细。***in the ~ of*** 在正中;在深处。***keep within one's ~*** 在(某人)可能限度内蹚水;做(某人)力所能及的事情。***to the ~s of one's heart*** 内心深处。***with a great ~ of feeling*** 深深同情。

dep·u·rate [ˈdepjureit; ˋdɛpjəˏret] *vt*. 除去…的杂质,净化,提纯。**-ra·tion** [ˌdepjuˈreiʃən; ˏdɛpjəˋreʃən] *n*. 净化(作用)。**-ra·tive** [ˈdepjurətiv, diˈpjuər-; ˋdɛpjəˏretɪv, dɪˋpjʊr-] *a*., *n*. 净化的;净化剂。**-ra·tor** [ˈdepjureitə; ˋdɛpjəˏretɚ] *n*. 净化器;净化剂。

dep·u·ta·tion [ˌdepju(ː)ˈteiʃən; ˏdɛpjəˋteʃən] *n*. 1. 代理,代表;代表团。2. 派代表,委派。*a ~ to the conference* 参加会议的代表团。

de·pute [diˈpjuːt; dɪˋpjut] *vt*. 使…做代理,派为代理;委托代理。

dep·u·tize [ˈdepjutaiz; ˋdɛpjəˏtaɪz] *vt*. 〔美〕委任…为代表。— *vi*. 〔口〕做代理人(*for*)。

dep·u·ty [ˈdepjuti; ˋdɛpjətɪ] **I** *n*. 1. 代理,代表。2. [D-](法、意等的)下院议员。3. 〔英〕(客栈的)管理员。**II** *a*. 代理的,副的。*a ~ to the city council* 市议会代表。*by ~* 由别人代理[代表]。***the Chamber of Deputies*** (法国等的)国民会议,下院。~ **chairman** 副主席,代理主席。~ **director** 副主任。~ **mayor** 副市长。**D- Speaker** 副议长,代理议长。

De Quin·cey [də ˈkwinsi; dɪ ˋkwɪnsɪ] *n*. 德昆西〔姓氏〕。

der. = derivation; derivative; derived.

de·rac·i·nate [diˈræsineit; dɪˋræsəˏnet] *vt*. 1. 根除,灭绝。2. 隔绝,隔离。

de·raign [diˈrein; dɪˋren] *vt*.【法】(当事人)以决斗来解决(争端)。

de·rail [diˈreil; dɪˋrel] *vt*. 使(火车等)出轨。— *vi*. 出轨。*be* [*get*] *~ed* 出轨。**-ment** *n*. 出轨。

de·rail·leur [diˈreilə; dɪˋrelə] *n*. 1. (自行车的)换挡装置。2. 有换挡装置的自行车。

de·range [diˈreindʒ; dɪˋrendʒ] *vt*. 1. 扰乱(秩序),打乱(计划)。2. 使精神错乱,使发狂。*be ~d* 发疯。**-ment** *n*. 1. 扰乱;混乱。2. (精神)狂乱,错乱〔较 insanity 轻〕。

de·rate [diːˈreit; dɪˋret] *vt*., *vi*. 减税,免税。

de·ra·tion [ˈdiːˈræʃən; ˋdiˋreʃən] *vt*. 取消(粮食等的)定额分配。

de·ray [diˈrei; dɪˋre] *n*. 〔废〕混乱〔尤指狂乱无度的饮闹〕。

Der·by[1] [ˈdɑːbi, Am. ˈdəːbi; ˋdarbɪ; ˋdɝbɪ] *n*. 1. (英国 Epsom Downs 的)德比赛马。2. 大赛马;大竞赛。3. [d-] [ˈdəːbi; ˋdɝbɪ]〔美〕常礼帽,圆顶礼帽(= ~ hat)。

Der·by[2] [ˈdɑːbi, Am. ˈdəːbi; ˋdarbɪ, ˋdɝbɪ] *n*. 德比(英国 Derbyshire 的首府)。~ **china** 德比瓷器〔一种精致的彩色瓷器〕。

der·by·lite [ˈdəːbilait; ˋdɝbɪˏlaɪt] *n*.【矿】锑钛铁矿。

de·reg·is·ter [diˈredʒistə; dɪˋrɛdʒɪstɚ] *vt*. 撤销…的登记。

de·re·ism [diˈriːizm; dɪˋriɪzm] *n*.【心】内闭性〔对外部世界不感兴趣,背离正常的逻辑思维〕。**-is·tic** *a*.

De·rek [ˈderik; ˋdɛrɪk] *n*. 德里克〔男子名〕。

der·e·lict [ˈderilikt; ˋdɛrəˏlɪkt] **I** *a*. **1**. 被抛弃了的,(船的)无主的。**2**.〔美〕玩忽职守的。**II** *n*. **1**.【法】遗弃物,无主物,(特指)漂流船。**2**. 海水减退后露出的新陆地。**3**. 被(社会所)唾弃的人,无家可归的人,无固定职业的人。**4**.〔美〕玩忽职守的人。

der·e·lic·tion [ˌderiˈlikʃən; ˏdɛrəˋlɪkʃən] *n*. **1**. 遗弃,放弃。**2**. 玩忽职守,懈怠(*of*)。**3**. 海水退后露出的新陆地。~ ***of duty*** 玩忽职守。

de·req·ui·si·tion [diːˌrekwiˈziʃən; diˏrɛkwəˋzɪʃən]〔英〕**I** *vt*. 取消对…的征用,把(征用的土地、财产等)归还原主。**II** *n*. 撤消征用,归还征用财产。

de·re·strict [ˈdiːrisˈtrikt; ˋdirɪsˋtrɪkt] *vt*. 取消对…的限制。

de·ride [diˈraid; dɪˋraɪd] *vt*. 嘲笑,愚弄,嘲笑。~ *a person's ignorance* 嘲笑某人无知。

de·rid·er [diˈraidə; dɪˋraɪdɚ] *n*. 愚弄者,嘲笑者。

de·rid·ing·ly [diˈraidiŋli; dɪˋraɪdɪŋlɪ] *ad*. 嘲弄似地,愚弄地,嘲笑地。

de ri·gueur [də riːˈgəː; də riˋgœːr]〔F.〕**1**. 礼节上所必需的;合乎礼数的。**2**. 时髦的,追求新奇的。

de·ris·i·ble [diˈrizibl; dɪˋrɪzəbl] *a*. 该当嘲笑的。

de·ri·sion [diˈriʒən; dɪˋrɪʒən] *n*. **1**. 嘲笑。**2**. 被嘲笑的人[事物];笑柄。***be in*** ~ 被嘲笑。***be the*** ~ ***of*** ... 是…的笑柄,被…嘲笑。***bring*** ... ***into*** ~ 使成笑柄,使受嘲笑。***hold*** [***have***] ***a person in*** ~ 嘲弄[愚弄]某人。***in*** ~ ***of*** 嘲弄。

de·ri·sive, de·ri·so·ry [diˈraisiv, -səri; dɪˋraɪsɪv, -sərɪ] *a*. **1**. 嘲弄的,愚弄的。**2**. 可笑的,值得嘲笑的。**-ly** *ad*.

de·riv·a·ble [diˈraivəbl; dɪˋraɪvəbl] *a*. 可引申出来的,可诱导出来的;可推论出来的。

der·i·va·tion [deriˈveiʃən; ˏdɛrəˋveʃən] *n*. **1**. 引出,导出。**2**. 出处,由来,起源。**3**.【语】词源;派生。**4**. 衍生;生物。

de·riv·a·tive [diˈrivətɪv; dɪˋrɪvətɪv] **I** *a*. 导出的;派生的。**II** *n*. **1**. 派生物。**2**.【语】派生词。**3**.【化】衍生物。**4**.【医】诱导法[剂]。**5**.【数】导数,纪数,微商。**-ly** *ad*.

de·rive [diˈraiv; dɪˋraɪv] *vt*. **1**. 得到,导出(*from*)。**2**. 追寻起源。**3**. 推论,推究(*from*)。— *vi*. 由来;派生出来。***be*** ~***d from*** 由…而来[生出]。~ ***itself from*** 由…而来。~***d fossils*** 转生化石。~***d protein***【生化】衍生朊。

derm [dəːm; dɝm] *n*. = derma.

-derm *suf*. 表示"皮","皮层"。

der·ma[1] [ˈdəːmə; ˋdɝmə] *n*.【解】真皮;皮肤。

der·ma[2] [ˈdəːmə; ˋdɝmə] *n*. 面包馅烤肉。

der·mal [ˈdəːməl; ˋdɝməl] *a*. 真皮的,皮肤的。

der·mat- *comb. f*. = dermato-.

der·ma·ti·tis [ˌdəːməˈtaitis; ˏdɝməˋtaɪtɪs] *n*. 皮肤炎,皮炎。

der·ma·to- *comb. f*. 皮(肤)的。

der·mat·o·gen [dəˈmætədʒən; dəˋmætədʒən] *n*.【植】表皮原。

der·ma·tog·ra·phy [ˌdəːməˈtɔgrəfi; ˏdɝməˋtɑgrəfɪ] *n*. 皮肤解剖记录。

der·ma·toid [ˈdəːmətɔid; ˋdɝməˏtɔɪd] *a*. 像皮肤的。

der·ma·tol·o·gist [ˌdəːməˈtɔlədʒist; ˏdɝməˋtɑlədʒɪst] *n*. 皮肤学者,皮肤科医生。

der·ma·tol·o·gy [ˌdəːməˈtɔlədʒi; ˏdɝməˋtɑlədʒɪ] *n*. 皮肤(病)学。**-log·i·cal** [-ˈlɔdʒikəl; -ˋlɑdʒɪkəl] *a*.

der·ma·tome [ˈdəːmətəum; ˋdɝmətom] *n*. **1**.【解】生皮节。**2**. 皮刀,植皮刀。

der·ma·to·neu·ri·tis [ˌdəːmətənjuˈraitis; ˏdɝmətənjəˋraɪtɪs] *n*. 神经性皮炎,皮肤神经炎。

der·ma·top·a·thy [ˌdəːməˈtɔpəθi; ˏdɝməˋtɑpəθɪ] *n*. 皮肤病。

der·ma·to·phyte [ˈdəːmətəufait, dəˈmætə-; ˋdɝmətəˏfaɪt, dəˋmætə-] *n*. 皮肤真菌,皮癣霉菌。

der·ma·to·plas·ty [ˈdəːmətəuplæsti; ˋdɝmatoˏplæstɪ] *n*. 皮成形术,植皮术。**-tic** [-ˈplæstik; -ˋplæstɪk] *a*.

der·ma·to·sis [ˌdəːməˈtəusis; ˏdɝməˋtosɪs] *n*. 皮肤病。

der·mic [ˈdəːmik; ˋdɝmɪk] *a*. = dermal.

der·mis [ˈdəːmis; ˋdɝmɪs] *n*.【解】= derma.

der·mo- *comb. f*. = dermato-.

der·moid [ˈdəːmɔid; ˋdɝmɔɪd] *a*. **1**. 皮样囊肿的。**2**. 皮状的。

der·mop·ter·an [dəˈmɔptərən; dəˋmɑptərən] *n*. 皮翼目动物〔包括猫猴〕。

der·mo·trop·ic [ˌdəːməˈtrɔpik; ˏdɝməˋtrɑpɪk] *a*. 亲皮肤的;趋向皮肤的。

dern [dəːn; dɝn] *v*.〔美卑〕= darn[2].

der·ni·er [ˈdəːniə, F. derˈnjei; ˋdɝnɪɚ, dɛrˋnjɛ] *a*.〔F.〕最后的。~ ***ressort*** [reˈsɔːr; rəˋsɔr] 最后手段。

der·nier cri [dəːˈnjei ˈkriː; dɛrˏnje ˋkri]〔F.〕(服装等)最新样式;极品。

der·o·gate [ˈderəgeit; ˋdɛrəˏget] *vi*., *vt*. **1**. 毁损,减损。**2**. 贬损,贬低。*He ~d from his ancestors*. 他毁坏了祖祖辈辈的名声。~ *from rights* 丧失权利。**-ga·tion** [ˌderəˈgeiʃən; ˏdɛrəˋgeʃən] *n*. **1**. 毁损,减损(权力,地位等)。**2**. (法律等的)部分废除。**3**. 贬低自己,失去地位。

de·rog·a·to·ry [diˈrɔgətəri; dɪˋrɑgəˏtorɪ] *a*. 减损…的,毁损(名誉)的;有伤品格的。~ *from authority* 有损权威的。~ *to one's dignity* 降低品格的。"*Politician*" *is used in a* ~ *sense*. "政客"是贬义用法。

der·rick [ˈderik; ˋdɛrɪk] *n*. **1**.【机】动臂起重机,塔式起重机,起货桅。**2**. 油井架,钻(井高)塔;(飞机的)起飞塔。**3**.〔美俚〕小偷。~**-car** 起重机车。

der·ri·ère [ˌderiˈɛə; ˏdɛrɪˋɛr] *n*. 臀部。

der·ring-do [ˈderiŋˈduː; ˋdɛrɪŋˋdu] *n*.〔古〕蛮勇;大胆行为。

der·rin·ger [ˈderindʒə; ˋdɛrɪndʒɚ] *n*. 大口径短筒手枪。

der·ris [ˈderis; ˋdɛrɪs] *n*. 鱼藤属〔植物〕。

der·vish [ˈdəːviʃ; ˋdɝvɪʃ] *n*. 伊斯兰教苦修教士。

de·sal·i·na·tion [diːˌsæliˈneiʃən; diˏsæləˋneʃən], **de·sal·i·ni·za·tion** [diːˌseilinaiˈzeiʃən; diˏselənaɪˋzeʃən] *n*. 脱盐(作用),减少盐分。**-nate, -nize** *vt*. 脱盐化。

de·salt [diːˈsɔːlt; diˋsɔlt] *vt*. 除去…的盐分。**-er** *n*. 脱盐设备。

de·scale [ˈdiːˈskeil; diˋskel] *vt*. 除去…的锅垢。

des·cant[1] [ˈdeskænt; ˋdɛskænt] **I** *n*. **1**.〔诗〕歌曲,曲调。**2**.【乐】童高音。**II** *vi*. 唱歌。

des·cant[2] [disˈkænt; dɛsˋkænt] **I** *n*. 详谈,评论。**II** *vi*. 详谈,评论(*on*; *upon*)。~ *on the wonders of nature* 畅谈大自然的奇迹。

Des·cartes [deiˈkɑːt, dekart; deˋkɑrt, dekart], **René** ~笛卡儿〔1596—1650,法国哲学家,数学家〕。

de·scend [diˈsend; dɪˋsɛnd] *vi*. **1**. 下来,下降。**2**. 下斜,下倾。**3**. (财产等)传给,传下,遗传。**4**. 系出,是…的后裔(*from*)。**5**. 转而说到,涉及(细节等)。**6**. 降低身分去做。**7**. 突然袭击,突然访问。**8**.【天】移向南方,移向地平线。~ *from a hill* 由山上下来。~ *to particulars* [*details*] 转而谈到细节。*He never ~s to such meanness*. 他决不干那种卑鄙事。— *vt*. 下,降。~ ***from*** = ***be*** ~***ed from*** 是…的后裔。~ ***on*** [***upon***] 袭击;突然访问。

de·scend·a·ble [diˈsendəbl; dɪˋsɛndəbl] *a*. = descendible.

D

de·scend·ant [di'sendənt; dɪ`sɛndənt] **I** *n*. **1.** 子孙,后代(*opp*. ancestor)。**2.** 弟子,门生。**3.** 从某一来源派生的东西;派生物。**II** *a*. = descendent.

de·scend·ent [di'sendənt; dɪ`sɛndənt] *a*. **1.** 祖传的,遗传的。**2.** 下降的,下行的。**3.** 派生的。

de·scend·i·ble [di'sendibl; dɪ`sɛndəbl̩] *a*. **1.** 能遗传[遗赠]的。**2.** 能走下[降下]的。

de·scend·ing [di'sendiŋ; dɪ`sɛndɪŋ] *a*. 下降的,下行的;递降的。*a* ~ *letter* 下垂字母〔g, p, y 等〕。~ *powers* 【数】降幂。*a* ~ *scale* 【乐】下行音阶。

de·scen·sion [di'senʃən; dɪ`sɛnʃən] *n*. 降下,降落。

de·scent [di'sent; dɪ`sɛnt] *n*. **1.** 下降,降下。**2.** 下坡,倾斜。**3.** 家世,门第,血统。**4.** 【法】继承,世袭。**5.** 一代;〔古〕子孙,后裔。**6.** 突然袭击。**7.** 屈尊,降格。*be of France* ~ 祖籍是法国。***be of good*** ~ 出身好。~ ***of man*** 人类由来。***make a*** ~ ***upon*** 袭击,侵入。

de·school [di:'sku:l; di`skul] *vt*. 废除…的传统学校,使没有传统式的学校。

de·school·er [di:'sku:lə; di`skulə] *n*. 提倡废除传统学校的人。

des·cloi·site, des·cloi·zite [dei'klɔizait; de`klɔɪ͵zaɪt] *n*. 【矿】钒铅锌矿。

de·scrib·a·ble [dis'kraibəbl; dɪs`kraɪbəbl̩] *a*. 能描写的。

de·scribe [dis'kraib; dɪs`kraɪb] *vt*. **1.** 记述,叙述,描写,形容;评述。**2.** 制(图),画(图形),作图。**3.** (行星等)周转,运行。*the falling star describing a long curve in the sky* 在夜空中划下一道长长弧线的流星。~ ***sb. as*** 把某人评为,叫某人做。

de·scrib·er [dis'kraibə; dɪs`kraɪbɚ] *n*. 叙述者,描写者;制图人。

de·scri·er [dis'kraiə; dɪs`kraɪɚ] *n*. 发现者。

de·scrip·tion [dis'kripʃən; dɪs`krɪpʃən] *n*. **1.** 记述,叙述,描写;记载。**2.** 叙事文;(物品)说明书;相貌说明书。**3.** 种类。**4.** 作图;绘制。*a man answering* (*to*) *that* ~ 和相貌说明书符合的人。*pencils of every* ~ 各种铅笔。*persons of that* ~ 那一类人。*a speech of the poorest* ~ 内容平淡到极点的演说。*beyond* ~ 难以形容。*give* [*make*] *a* ~ *of* 叙述…的样子;说明。*the* ~ *of a circle* 画圆圈。

de·scrip·tive [dis'kriptiv; dɪ`skrɪptɪv] *a*. 记述的,叙述的;说明的。*a* ~ *catalogue* 带有说明的目录。*a* ~ *writing* 叙事文。*the* ~ *geometry* 画法几何(学)。~ ***of*** 描写…的,记述…的,说明…的。**-ly** *ad*.

de·scrip·tor [dis'kriptə; dɪs`krɪptɚ] *n*. 【自】(数据处理中表示某一项目的)主字码。

de·scry [dis'krai; dɪ`skraɪ] *vt*. **1.** 远远地看出[看到]。**2.** (由调查等)发现。

des·e·crate ['desikreit; `dɛsɪ͵kret] *vt*. 把(神物)供俗用;亵渎,玷污。**-cra·tion** [͵desi'kreiʃən; ͵dɛsɪ`kreʃən] *n*. 亵渎神圣。

de·seg·re·gate [di:'segri͵geit; di`sɛgrəget] *vt*., *vi*. 废除种族隔离。**-ga·tion** [di:segri'geiʃən; dɪ͵sɛgrə`geʃən] *n*.

de·se·lect [͵di:si'lekt; ͵disə`lɛkt] *vt*. 中途淘汰(培训的选手)。

de·sen·si·tize [͵di:'sensitaiz; di`sɛnsə͵taɪz] *vt*. **1.** 【摄】使减少感光度。**2.** 【医】使减少敏感性。**3.** 使感觉迟钝。**-tiz·er** ['di:'sensitaizə; `di`sɛnsə͵taɪzɚ] *n*. 减感剂,脱敏剂。

De·seret ['dezərit; `dɛzərɪt] *n*. 〔美〕犹他州的别名。

des·ert[1] ['dezət; `dɛzɚt] **I** *a*. 荒芜的,不毛的;沙漠的;无人的。*a* ~ *island* 荒岛。**II** *n*. **1.** 沙漠;荒漠。**2.** 〔喻〕荒凉的境地;枯燥无味的学科;历史上的荒芜时代(等)。*the Gobi D-* 戈壁滩。**Desert Storm** "沙漠风暴"〔指1990年以美国为首的38国联军对入侵科威特的伊拉克进行的军事打击〕。

de·sert[2] [di'zə:t; dɪ`zɝt] *vt*. **1.** 丢开,抛弃。**2.** 擅离(职守)。~ *one's colours* (兵)开小差;叛变。*His presence of mind* ~*ed him*. 他失去镇静。— *vi*. 逃亡,逃走(*from*);开小差。*He* ~*ed to the enemy*. 他投敌去了。

de·sert[3] [di'zə:t; dɪ`zɝt] *n*. **1.** 功过;该受奖赏[处罚]的品质[行动]。**2.** 应得的报酬,应得的奖赏[处罚]。**3.** 功劳,美德。*get* [*meet with*] *one's* ~*s* 受相当奖赏[处罚]。*The honour is above my* ~. 荣誉过当。

de·sert·ed [di'zə:tid; dɪ`zɝtɪd] *a*. 无人居住的,荒废了的;被抛弃了的。*a* ~ *village* 荒村。

de·sert·er [di'zə:tə; dɪ`zɝtə] *n*. 遗弃者;脱党者;逃亡者,逃兵。

de·ser·tion [di'zə:ʃən; dɪ`zɝʃən] *n*. **1.** 遗弃,抛弃。**2.** 脱党;逃走。**3.** 荒废。

de·serve [di'zə:v; dɪ`zɝv] *vt*. 应受,该得,值得,当。~ *attention* [*sympathy*] 值得注意[同情]。*He* ~*s his fate*. 他命该如此。— *vi*. 应受赏[罚]。~ *to be rewarded* [*punished*] 该奖[罚]。~ ***ill*** [***well***] ***of*** 有罪[功]于(*He has* ~*d well of his country*. 他有功于国家)。

de·serv·ed [di'zə:vd; dɪ`zɝvd] *a*. 该奖[罚]的,理所当然的。**-ly** *ad*.

de·serv·ing [di'zə:viŋ; dɪ`zɝvɪŋ] **I** *a*. **1.** 该受奖[罚]的。**2.** 有功劳的。**3.** 值得…的 (*of*)。**4.** 值得帮助的。*be* ~ *of death* 该死。(*a crime*) ~ *of death* 该处死刑的(罪)。*the* ~ *poor* 值得帮助的穷人。**II** *n*. 赏罚,功过。**-ly** *ad*.

de·sex [di:'seks; di`sɛks] *vt*. **1.** 使无性欲。**2.** 使失去性特征。**3.** 使失去性能力。

de·sex·u·al·ize [di:'seksjuəlaiz; di`sɛkʃuəl͵aɪz] *vt*. (= desex). **-za·tion** [di:͵seksjuəlai'zeiʃən; di͵sɛksjuəlaɪ`zeʃən] *n*.

des·ha·bille [deiza:bi:'jei; ͵dezɑ`bi`je] *n*. 〔F.〕= dishabille.

des·ic·cant ['desikənt; `dɛsəkənt] **I** *a*. 干燥用的,去水分的,去湿气的。**II** *n*. 干燥剂。

des·ic·cate ['desikeit; `dɛsə͵ket] *vt*. **1.** 干燥,弄干,晒干(等);使脱水。**2.** 用干燥法保存(食物)。**3.** 使(生命力等)枯竭。~*d milk* 奶粉。*desiccating agent* 干燥剂。*a* ~*d woman* 干瘦的妇女。— *vi*. 变干。**-ca·tion** [͵desi'keiʃən; ͵dɛsə`keʃən] *n*. 干燥,干化。**-ca·tive** [de'sikətiv; də`sɛkətɪv] *a*., *n*. = desiccant. **-ca·tor** [-tə; -tɚ] *n*. **1.** (鱼等的)干货制造者。**2.** 干燥器,吸湿器。

de·sid·er·a·ta [di͵zidə'reitə; dɪ͵zɪdə`retə] *n*. desideratum 的复数。

de·sid·er·ate [di'zidəreit; dɪ`sɪdə͵ret] *vt*. 迫切需要,渴望得到。~ *an impossibility* 希求不可能的事情。**-a·tion** [di͵zidə'reiʃən; dɪ͵zɪdə`reʃən] *n*.

de·sid·er·a·tive [di'zidərətiv; dɪ`sɪdə͵etɪv] **I** *a*. 【语法】希求的。**II** *n*. (动词的)希求[愿望]语气;愿望动词。

de·sid·er·a·tum [di͵zidə'reitəm; dɪ͵sɪdə`retəm] *n*. (*pl*. ***-ta*** [-tə; -tə]) 〔L.〕急需品,需要物。

de·sign [di'zain; dɪ`zaɪn] **I** *vt*. **1.** 计划,企图,立意要…。**2.** 指定,预定;留给,留着。**3.** 设计,草拟,拟定,筹划;起草,画草图,打(图)样。~ *an attack* 计划进攻。~ *one's son for* [*to be*] *a soldier* 立意要儿子做军人。~ *a room for one's library* 指定一间屋子做某人书房。— *vi*. 计划;打样,打图样 (*for*)。**II** *n*. **1.** 计划;企图;目的,意图,野心,阴谋。**2.** (小说等的)提纲,结构,构想,情节。**3.** 设计,图案,图样。***by*** ~ ***and not by accident*** 是故意不是偶然。***have a*** ~ ***on*** 对…有野心,企图。***have*** ~***s upon*** [***against***] ***sb.'s life*** 拟加害某人。~ ***paper*** 制图纸。

de·sign·a·ble[1] [di'zainəbl; dɪ`zaɪnəbl̩] *a*. 能设计[计划]的,可企图的。

des·ig·na·ble[2] ['dezignəbl; `dɛzɪgnəbl̩] *a*. 能指定的。

es·ig·nate [ˈdezigneit; ˋdɛzɪgˏnet] I *vt*. 1. 指出,指明。2. 指出…的名字;把…叫做(*as*)。3. 指定,选定,任命某人任某职(*to*; *for*)。II [-nit; -nɪt] *a*. 指定而尚未上任的;选出而尚未上任的〔用在名词后〕。*a captain* ~ 指定而尚未上任的船长。**-tive**, **-tory** *a*.

es·ig·nat·ed [ˈdezigneitid; ˋdɛzɪgˏnetɪd] *a*. 指定的,派定的。

les·ig·na·tion [ˌdezigˈneiʃən; ˏdɛzɪgˋneʃən] *n*. 1. 指出,指明。2. 任命,选派。3. 名称,称呼;【军】番号。

es·ig·na·tor [ˈdezigneitə; ˋdɛzɪgˏnetɚ] *n*. 1. 指定者。2. 〔古罗马〕定席次的官。

le·signed [diˈzaind; dɪˋzaɪnd] *a*. 设计好的;故意的,有计划的。**-ly** *ad*. 特意,故意,有计划地。

les·ig·nee [ˌdezigˈniː, des-; ˏdɛzɪgˋni, dɛs-] *n*. 被指名人。

le·sign·er [diˈzainə; dɪˋzaɪnɚ] I *n*. 1. 设计师,打样师,制图员。2. 阴谋者。II *a*. 署名设计的,名牌的。~ *water* 名牌矿泉水。~ *food* 名牌食品。

le·sign·ing [diˈzainiŋ; dɪˋzaɪnɪŋ] I *a*. 1. 狡猾的,有野心[阴谋]的。2. 计划性的,有远见的。II *n*. 设计(工作)。

le·sir·a·ble [diˈzaiərəbl; dɪˋzaɪrəbl] I *a*. 1. 理想的,希望到手的。2. 称心的,令人满意的。II *n*. 称心如意的人[东西]。**-ness** *n*. **-bil·i·ty** [diˌzaiərəˈbiliti; dɪˏzaɪrəˋbɪlətɪ] *n*. **-a·bly** *ad*.

le·sire [diˈzaiə; dɪˋzaɪr] I *vt*. 1. 想要,渴望,希望(做某事)。2. 要求某事(*sth*.);要求做到(*that*);要求[请求]某人做某事。*He* ~*s to see you*. 他想要见见你。*We* ~ *to have a good result*. 我们希望有个好结果。*I* ~ *an immediate answer of yours*. 我请您立即回信。*They* ~ *that you will come at once*. 他们要求你马上来。*He* ~*d me to wait*. 他要我等着。*Please* ~ *him to come in*. 去请他进来。— *vi*. 愿望,期望。***leave much*** [***nothing***] ***to be*** ~***d*** 缺点不少[一点也没有]。II *n*. 1. 愿望,欲望。2. 要求。3. 食欲,情欲。4. 想望的东西。***at one's*** ~ 照某人希望。~ ***for fame*** 虚荣心。***get one's*** ~ 得到所希望的东西。

de·sir·ous [diˈzaiərəs; dɪˋzaɪrəs] *a*. 〔用作述语〕要,想,欲(*to do*; *that*)。***be*** ~ ***of*** 想得到,想(*Everybody is* ~ *of success* [*to succeed*]. 每人都想获得成功)。

de·sist [diˈzist; dɪˋzɪst] *vi*. 停止,休想,断念。*You had better* ~. 你最好打消念头吧。~ *from talking* [*a scheme*] 停止谈话[一项计划]。

de·size [diːˈsaiz; diˋsaɪz] *vt*. 【纺】除去…的浆液。

desk [desk; dɛsk] I *n*. 1. 书桌,办公桌。2. 值勤台。3. 〔美〕讲道坛。4. 〔the ~〕文书工作。5. (报馆的)编辑部。6. 乐谱架。7. (一机构中专门负责某方面事务的)部,司,组。8. (乐队里演奏者的)席位,席次。*He is at his* ~. 他在用功[办公]呢。*a roll-top* ~有活动盖板的办公桌。*an inquiry* ~ 询问处。*the city* ~ (报馆的)社会部。~ *lamp* 台灯。~ *work* [*job*] 文书工作,办公室工作。*a first-* ~ *violinist* 第一提琴手。*sit at the* ~ 写着字;办着公。II *a*. 书桌上用的。III *vt*. 派某人做办公室工作。~ **bound** *a*. 埋头事务的,书呆子气的;内勤的;后勤的(*chair-borne commandos and* ~ *bound doughboys* 支前民兵和后勤步兵)。~ **man** (*pl*. ~-**men**) 1. 新闻助理编辑。2. 坐办公桌的人。~**organizer** 【计】案头电脑办公用具〔由 PC 软件和多功能板组合而成,可协助处理日常文秘事务〕。~ **room** [**space**] (在别人办公室内租借的)办公地位。~ **pad** 1. (附有吸水纸的)书桌盖。2. 便条,便笺。~ **set** 一套文具。~ **study** 纸上谈兵,桌上研究〔指未经过实地的或实验室的试验〕。~**-top** 1. *n*. 台式电脑。2. *a*. (电脑)台式的。

D. ès L. [F.] = *Ducteur ès Lettres* (= Doctor of Letters) 文学博士。

des·man [ˈdesmən; ˋdɛsˏmən] *n*. (*pl*. ~*s*) 食虫水栖鼹鼠。

des·mid [ˈdezmid; ˋdɛzmɪd] *n*. 绿藻门植物(亦作 desmidian)。

desm(o)- *comb*. *f*. 表示"结合的";"带状的";"丝状的": *desmo*bacteria.

des·mo·bac·ter·i·a [desməbækˈtiəriə; dɛsməbækˋtɪrɪə] *n*. 【医】丝状细菌属。

des·mo·en·zyme [ˌdezməˈenzaim; ˏdɛzməˋɛnzaɪm] *n*. 【生化】不溶性酶;固定酶。

des·moid [ˈdesmɔid; ˋdɛsmɔɪd] *a*. 1. 似韧带的。2. (肿瘤)纤维样的,纤维性的。

Des Moines [diˈmɔinz; dɪˋmɔɪnz] *n*. 得梅因〔美国衣阿华 Iowa 州的首府〕。

des·mo·lase [ˈdesməleis; ˋdɛsməˏles] *n*. 【生化】碳链酶。

des·mol·y·sis [dezˈmɔlisis; dɛzˋmɑləsɪs] *n*. (*pl*. *-ses* [-siːz; -siz])【化】碳链分解作用;解链作用。

Des·mond [ˈdezmənd; ˋdɛzmənd] *n*. 德斯蒙德〔男子名〕。

des·mo·some [ˈdezməsəum; ˋdɛzməsom] *n*. 【生】桥粒。

des·o·late I [ˈdesəlit; ˋdɛsəlɪt] *a*. 1. 荒无人烟的,荒凉的;荒废的。2. 孤独的;凄凉的。II [ˈdesəleit; ˋdɛsəlˏet] *vt*. 1. 使荒无人烟,使荒芜。2. 使凄凉,使孤单。**-ly** *ad*. **-ness** *n*.

des·o·la·tion [ˌdesəˈleiʃən; ˏdɛsl̩ˋeʃən] *n*. 1. 荒芜,荒凉。2. 寂寥,孤独;凄凉。3. 荒地,废墟。

de·sorb [diˈsɔːb; dɪˋsɔrb] *vt*. 【化】使解除吸附,使放出。**-sorp·tion** [-ˈsɔːpʃən; -ˋsɔrpʃən] *n*. 解吸(作用)。

de·soxy- *comb*. *f*. 脱氧(= deoxy-)。

des·ox·y·date [diˈsɔksideit; dɪˋsɑksəˏdet] *vt*. 【化】使脱氧。

de·spair [disˈpeə; dɪsˋpɛr] I *n*. 1. 绝望,失望。2. 令人绝望的原因〔指人或事〕。3. 望尘莫及的人[事物]。*Defeat after defeat filled us with* ~. 接二连三的失败,使我们感到绝望。*She gave up the attempt in* ~. 她失望地放弃尝试。*He is my* ~. 他是无可救药的了[他是我万万赶不上的]。*He is his mother's* ~. 他使他妈绝望了。***abandon oneself*** [***give oneself up***] ***to*** ~ 只会悲观失望。***be driven to*** ~ 遭到失望。***in*** ~ 绝望地。***out of*** ~ 出于绝望而…。***the*** ~ ***of*** 使某人失望;使某人感到望尘莫及。***yield*** [***give way***] ***to*** ~ 打断念头,深自绝望。II *vi*. 绝望,失望。~ *of success* 失却成功希望。*His life is* ~*ed of*. 他的一生完了。

de·spair·ing [disˈpeəriŋ; dɪsˋpɛrɪŋ] *a*. 感到绝望的,表示失望的。*a* ~ *look* 绝望的样子。**-ly** *ad*.

des·patch [disˈpætʃ; dɪsˋpætʃ] *n*., *v*. = dispatch.

des·per·a·do [ˌdespəˈrɑːdəu, -ˈrei-; ˏdɛspəˋrɑdo, -ˋre-] *n*. (*pl*. ~*s*, ~*es*) 无赖;〔美〕暴徒〔尤指美国西部的土匪〕;亡命徒。

des·per·ate [ˈdespərit; ˋdɛspərɪt] *a*. 1. 不顾死活的,拼命的。2. 悲观失望的,穷途末路的,无可救药的。3. 猛烈的,厉害的。4. 极想得到的。*D- diseases require* ~ *remedies*. 绝症需猛药。*a* ~ *remedy* 非常手段,最后手段。~ *weather* 恶劣的天气。*a* ~ *fool* 大傻瓜。***be*** ~ ***for*** (*a cup of tea*) 极想(喝一杯茶)。**-ly** *ad*. 绝望地;拼命;〔口〕非常,极。**-ness** *n*. 拼命;绝望。

des·per·a·tion [ˌdespəˈreiʃən; ˏdɛspəˋreʃən] *n*. 拼命,不顾死活;绝望。***be driven to*** ~ 不得不拼命。***drive*** (***a person***) ***to*** ~ 使拼命;〔口〕使大发脾气。***in*** ~ 拼死,无可奈何地。

des·pi·ca·ble [ˈdespikəbl; ˋdɛspɪkəbl̩] *a*. 恶劣的,卑鄙的,可鄙的。**-bly** *ad*.

de·spise [disˈpaiz; dɪsˋpaɪz] *vt*. 轻视,藐视,看不起。*Strategically we should* ~ *all our enemies*. 在战略上我们要藐视一切敌人。**-spis·ing·ly** *ad*.

de·spite [disˈpait; dɪsˋpaɪt] I *n*. 〔古〕1. 恨,怨恨,憎恨。2. 恶意。3. 轻蔑;侮辱。II *prep*. 不管,不顾,任凭。(*in*) ~ ***of*** ...不管,任凭,不把…当事儿。***die of*** ~ 抱恨而死,冤死。***in one's own*** ~ 〔古〕无可奈何地。

de·spite·ful [disˈpaitfəl; dɪsˋpaɪtfəl] *a*. 〔古〕=

D

spiteful.

de·spit·e·ous [disˈpitiəs; dɪsˋpɪtɪəs] ***a.*** 〔古〕怀恨的;恶意的。

de·spoil [disˈpɔil; dɪsˋpɔɪl] ***vt.*** 剥夺;掠夺。～ *sb. of his right* 剥夺某人权利。**-ment** ***n.***

de·spo·li·a·tion [disˌpəuliˈeiʃən; dɪsˌpolɪˋeʃən] ***n.*** 掠夺,强夺,遭受掠夺。

de·spond [disˈpɔnd; dɪsˋpɑnd] **I** ***vi.*** 灰心,消沉。**II** ***n.*** 〔古〕沮丧,失望。**-ence, -cy** ***n.*** 灰心,消沉。

de·spond·ent [disˈpɔndənt; dɪsˋpɑndənt] ***a.*** 垂头丧气的,心灰意懒的。

de·spond·ing·ly [disˈpɔndiŋli; dɪsˋpɑndɪŋlɪ] ***ad.*** 垂头丧气地,心灰意懒地。

des·pot [ˈdespɔt; ˋdɛspət] ***n.*** 专制君主;暴君。*a local* ～ = *a* ～ 地方恶霸。**-pot·ic** [desˈpɔtik; dɪˋspɑtɪk] ***a.*** 专制的,专横的,暴虐的。**-pot·i·cal·ly** ***ad.***

des·pot·ism [ˈdespətizəm; ˋdɛspətɪzəm] ***n.*** **1.** 专制;专制政治。**2.** 暴政,苛政。**3.** 专制国家,专制政府。

de·spu·mate [ˈdespjumeit; ˋdɛspjʊˌmet] ***vt.*** **1.** 除去浮沫。**2.** 当作浮沫扔掉。**-tion** [ˌdespjuˈmeiʃən; ˌdɛspjʊˋmeʃən] ***n.***

des·qua·mate [ˈdeskwəmeit; ˋdɛskwəˌmet] ***vi.*** 【病】脱屑,脱皮。**-ma·tion** [ˌdeskwəˈmeiʃən; ˌdɛskwəˋmeʃən] ***n.***

des·sert [diˈzəːt; dɪˋzɝt] ***n.*** **1.** 餐后食品〔点心、水果等〕。**2.** 〔英〕甜食后的新鲜水果。*a* ～ *service* 一套餐后食品用具。～ **spoon** 点心匙。～ **wine** 强烈的葡萄酒。

de·sta·bi·lize [ˈdiːˈsteibilaiz; ˋdiˋstebɪˌlaɪz] ***vt.*** 使打破平衡;使不稳定。

de·stain [diːˈstein; diˋsten] ***vt.*** 使标本脱色(以便用显微镜观察)。

de·ster·i·lize [diːˈsterilaiz; diˋstɛrəˌlaɪz] ***vt.*** 〔美〕**1.** 解封(黄金)〔解封库存黄金,存入中央银行,以扩大信贷和货币发行〕。**2.** 恢复使用(长期闲置的物资)。

de Stijl [də stail; də staɪl] ***n.*** (荷兰)德斯太尔抽象画派。

des·ti·na·tion [ˌdestiˈneiʃən; ˌdɛstəˋneʃən] ***n.*** **1.** 〔罕〕指定,预定,注定。**2.** 目的地,指定地。**3.** 目的,目标。*We are at last at our* ～. 我们终于到达目的地。*the port of* ～ 目的港。

des·tine [ˈdestin; ˋdɛstɪn] ***vt.*** 〔常用被动语态〕**1.** 命定,注定。**2.** 派定,指定,预定。*My letter was* ～*d never to reach him.* 我的信注定是交不到他手里了。*a building* ～*d for that purpose* 指定作那一目的用的建筑物。

des·ti·ny [ˈdestini; ˋdɛstənɪ] ***n.*** **1.** 命运,天数,定数。**2.** 〔the Destinies〕命运的三女神〔the three Fates〕。*a master of one's own* ～ 掌握自己命运的人。

des·ti·tute [ˈdestitjuːt; ˋdɛstəˌtjut] ***a.*** **1.** 缺乏…的,无…的(*of*)。**2.** 贫穷的。*The people are* ～. 民不聊生。***be*** ～ ***of*** (*morality*) 无(道德)的。***be left*** ～ 贫穷下去。～ ***and homeless*** 流离失所。***the*** ～ 穷人。

des·ti·tu·tion [ˌdestiˈtjuːʃən; ˌdɛstəˋtjuʃən] ***n.*** **1.** 缺乏。**2.** 贫穷,穷困。

des·tri·er [ˈdestriə, desˈtriə; ˋdɛstrɪɚ, dɛsˋtrɪr] ***n.*** 〔古〕军马,战马。

de·stroy [disˈtrɔi; dɪsˋtrɔɪ] ***vt.*** **1.** 毁坏,破坏;摧残。**2.** 肃清,消灭,歼灭(敌人),扑灭(害虫等),驱除。**3.** 打破〔希望、计划〕,使失败。*be* ～*ed by fire* 被火烧毁。～ ***itself*** 自灭。～ ***oneself*** 自杀。

de·stroy·er [disˈtrɔiə; dɪsˋtrɔɪɚ] ***n.*** **1.** 破坏者;扑灭者,驱除者。**2.** 驱逐舰。～ *escort* 护航驱逐舰。

de·struct [disˈtrʌkt; dɪsˋtrʌkt] **I** ***vi.*** (中途失灵的导[飞]弹、火箭等)自毁(以防落入敌方手中)。**II** ***n.*** 自毁〔此词系从 destruction 逆生而成〕。

de·struct·i·ble [disˈtrʌktəbl; dɪsˋtrʌktəbl̩] ***a.*** 能毁坏的,易破坏的。**-bil·i·ty** [diˌstrʌktiˈbiliti; dɪˌstrʌktəˋbɪlətɪ] ***n.*** 破坏性,破坏力。

de·struc·tion [disˈtrʌkʃən; dɪsˋtrʌkʃən] ***n.*** **1.** 破坏;亡;消灭,扑灭,驱除。**2.** 毁灭的原因;破坏手段。*Ov confidence was his* ～. 自负是他垮台的原因。**-ist** 破坏分子;破坏主义者。

de·struc·tive [disˈtrʌktiv; dɪsˋtrʌktɪv] ***a.*** 破坏性的;害的。***be*** ～ ***of*** 对…有破坏作用。***be*** ～ ***to*** 有害…的 ～ **bird** 害鸟。～ **distillation** 干馏。～ **interferen** 【物】相消干涉。～ **range** (炸弹等的)破坏半径。**-ly** ***a*** **-ness** ***n.***

de·struc·tor [disˈtrʌktə; dɪsˋtrʌktɚ] ***n.*** **1.** 〔英〕垃圾化炉。**2.** 破坏器;爆破装置。

de·suda·tion [desjuˈdeiʃən; dɛsjʊˋdeʃən] ***n.*** 【医】大量汗。

des·ue·tude [diˈsjuːitjuːd; ˋdɛswɪˌtjud] ***n.*** 废止,废除 *fall* [*pass*] *into* ～ (习惯、风俗等)不时兴,衰废。

de·sul·phur·ize [diːˈsʌlfəraiz; diˋsʌlfəˌraɪz] ***vt.*** 使硫。**-za·tion** [-ˌsʌlfəraiˈzeiʃən; -ˌsʌlfəraɪˋzeʃən] ***n.*** 硫。

des·ul·to·ry [ˈdesəltəri; ˋdɛslˌtɔrɪ] ***a.*** **1.** 散漫的,杂的。**2.** 不连贯的,无条理的。**3.** 离奇的,古怪的。*a conversation* 漫谈。*a* ～ *remark* 离题的话。*a* ～ *r search* 漫无边际的研究。*a* ～ *walk* 漫步。*a* ～ *pr ject* [*thought*] 离奇的设想。**-i·ly** ***ad.*** **-i·ness** ***n.***

de·su·per·heat·er [diˌsjupəˈhiːtə; dɪˌsjʊpəˋhitɚ] ***n.*** 热蒸气降温器。

det. = **1.** detach. **2.** detachment. **3.** detail. detector.

Det. = detective.

DET = diethyltryptamine 二乙色胺〔一种迷幻药〕。

de·tach [diˈtætʃ; dɪˋtætʃ] ***vt.*** **1.** 分开,分离,拆开 (*opp* attach)。**2.** 派遣(军队等)。***be*** ～***ed from*** 脱离。**-a·b** ***a.*** 可分离的;可派遣的。**-ly** ***ad.*** **-ness** ***n.***

de·tached [diˈtætʃt; dɪˋtætʃt] ***a.*** **1.** 分离的,孤立的。分遣的;派遣的。**3.** 公平的;超然的。*a* ～ *house* 独立住宅。*a* ～ *palace* 离宫。*a* ～ *force* 分遣队,别动队 ～ *duty* 【军】临时任务。*a* ～ *mind* 超然的见解。***in*** ～ ***way*** 客观地。***take a*** ～ ***view*** 抱客观[公平]态度。

de·tach·ment [diˈtætʃmənt; dɪˋtætʃmənt] ***n.*** **1.** 脱离分离。**2.** 超然,超脱,不偏不倚。**3.** 派遣;分遣队,支队。

de·tail [ˈdiːteil, diˈteil; ˋditel, dɪˋtel] **I** ***n.*** **1.** 〔*pl.*〕细;详情。**2.** 细目;琐事,小事。**3.** 【军】支队;〔英〕行动令。**4.** 详图,明细图。**5.** 零件,元件。*a matter of* ～ 事。***beat*** [***defeat***] ***in*** ～ 【军】各个击破。～ ***by*** ～ 一。***go*** [***enter***] ***into*** ～(***s***) 详述,逐一细说。***in*** ～ 细。**II** ***vt.*** **1.** 详述,详记。**2.** 【军】特派,选派 (*for*; *do*)。～ *particulars of an event* 详述某事的细节。～ *man for sentry duty* 派人站岗。— ***vi.*** 画详图。 **man** 制药厂的推销员。

de·tailed [ˈdiːteild; dɪˋteld] ***a.*** **1.** 详细的,明细的。**2.** 综复杂的,千头万绪的。*a* ～ *account* 详细的叙述。～ *problem* 一个错综复杂的问题。

de·tain [diˈtein; dɪˋten] ***vt.*** **1.** 留住,阻住。**2.** 扣留;留。*He was* ～*ed by business.* 他因有事而留下了。 *sb. as a suspect* 把某人当做嫌疑犯而加以拘留。**-er** ***n*** **1.** 阻留者。**2.** 【法】(财产的)非法占有;拘留,扣押;继拘留指令。

de·tain·ee [ˌdiːteiˈniː; dɪˌteˋni] ***n.*** 被拘留者(多指政犯等)。

de·tas·sel [diːˈtæsl; diˋtæsl] ***vt.*** (～(***l***)***ed***; ～(***l***)***ing***) 掉(玉蜀黍的)穗状雄花(以杂交)。

de·tect [diˈtekt; dɪˋtɛkt] ***vt.*** **1.** 发觉,发现,看破。**2** 【化】检定;【无】检波。*be* ～*ed in* (*doing*) …做(坏等)被发觉。～ *a flaw in an argument* 发现论点中有破绽。**-a·ble, -i·ble** ***a.*** 能发觉的;能检查出来的。

de·tec·ta·phone [diˈtektəfəun; dɪˋtɛktəˌfon] ***n.*** (窃听电话的)窃听器,侦听器。

de·tec·tion [diˈtekʃən; dɪˋtɛkʃən] ***n.*** **1.** 探知;发现,发

觉;败露。2.【化】检定,检查;【讯】检波。

de·tec·tive [di'tektiv; dɪ`tɛktɪv] **I** *a*. 侦查(用)的。*a* ~ *agency* 秘密侦探所。*a* ~ *police* 侦探,密探。*a* ~ *story* 侦探小说。**II** *n*. 侦探,密探。

de·tec·tor [di'tektə; dɪ`tɛktɚ] *n*. 1. 发觉者。2. 侦查器。3.【化】检定器。4.【电】检电器。5.【讯】检波器,指示器。*a crystal* [*tube*] ~ 晶体[真空管]检波器。

de·tent [di'tent; dɪ`tɛnt] *n*. 1.【机】(棘)爪,掣子;扳手。2. (钟表机件的)擒纵装置。

dé·tente [dei'tɑ̃:nt; de`tɑ̃nt] *n*. [F.] (国际关系等的)缓和。

de·ten·tion [di'tenʃən; dɪ`tɛnʃən] *n*. 1. 阻止;阻留。2. 扣留,拘留,监禁。3. (罚学生的)课后留校。4. (非法)占有。~ *barracks* [*camp*] (俘虏等的)临时收容所。~ *home* 青少年罪犯的拘留所。~ *hospital* (传染病的)隔离病院。*under* ~ 拘留中,扣留中。

dé·te·nu [deitə'nu:; detə`nu] *n*. [F.] (*fem*. ***détenue***) 被扣留者。

de·ter [di'tə:; dɪ`tɝ] *vt*. (**-rr-**) 防止,阻止,制止,使不敢,使踌躇。*paint sth. to* ~ *rust* 涂…防锈。~(*sb.*) ***from*** 制止(人)…。

de·terge [di'tə:dʒ; dɪ`tɝdʒ] *vt*. 洗净(伤口等)。

de·ter·gen·cy, de·ter·gence [di'tə:dʒənsi, -dʒəns; dɪ`tɝdʒənsɪ, -dʒəns] *n*. 脱垢力,去垢性。

de·ter·gent [di'tə:dʒənt; dɪ`tɝdʒənt] **I** *a*. 有洗净力的。**II** *n*. 洗净剂;除垢剂,去污剂。*synthetic* ~ 合成洗涤剂。

de·te·ri·o·rate [di'tiəriəreit; dɪ`tɪrɪə͵ret] *vt*., *vi*. 1. 弄坏,使恶化。2. 败坏(风俗);降低(品质等)。3. 堕落。~ *one's health* 弄坏身体。~ *relations with other countries* 恶化同其他国家的关系。

de·te·ri·o·ra·tion [di͵tiəriə'reiʃən; dɪ͵tɪrɪə`reʃən] *n*. 1. 恶化;变质;退化。2. 堕落,颓废。3. 凋萎;衰败。**-tive** *a*.

de·ter·ment [di'tə:mənt; dɪ`tɝmənt] *n*. 1. 制止,威慑。2. 制止物,威慑物。

de·ter·mi·na·ble [di'tə:minəbl; dɪ`tɝmɪnəbl̩] *a*. 1. 可决定[确定]的。2. 可终止的。

de·ter·mi·na·cy [di'tə:minəsi; dɪ`tɝmɪnəsɪ] *n*. 1. 确定性。2. 坚定性。

de·ter·mi·nant [di'tə:minənt; dɪ`tɝmənənt] **I** *a*. 决定性的,限定性的。**II** *n*. 1. 决定因素。2.【逻】限定词。3.【数】行列式。4.【生】决定体,遗传因素。

de·ter·mi·nate **I** [di'tə:minit; dɪ`tɝmənɪt] *a*. 1. 确定的,一定的,决定的。2. 毅然决然的。3.【植】(花序)有限的。4.【数】有定值的,有定数的。*a* ~ *variation* 定向变异。*a* ~ *reply* 毅然决然的回答。**II** [di'tə:mineit; dɪ`tɝmə͵net] *vt*. [罕] 1. 确定,确保。2. 认明。**-ly** *ad*. 明确地;断然。**-ness** *n*.

de·ter·mi·na·tion [di͵tə:mi'neiʃən; dɪ͵tɝmə`neʃən] *n*. 1. 决心,决意。2. 决定,确定。3. 倾向。4.【法】判决;(权利的)消失,终止。5.【物】测定,鉴定。6.【逻】规定,限定。7.【医】(血的)涌集。

de·ter·mi·na·tive [di'tə:minətiv; dɪ`tɝmə͵netɪv] **I** *a*. 决定的;指定的;限定的。**II** *n*. 1. 决定因素。2.【语法】限定词。

de·ter·mi·na·tor [di'tə:mi͵neitə; dɪ`tɝmə͵netɚ] *n*. 1. 决定因素。2.【语】限定词。

de·ter·mine [di'tə:min; dɪ`tɝmɪn] *vt*. 1. 决心,决意。2. 使下决心[多用被动结构]。3. 决定;断定,推定,确定;限定,规定。4.【法】了结,使终结。5. 限制。6.【物】测定。*They ~d to do this at any cost*. 他们不惜任何牺牲来作此事。*I'm ~d to learn French*. 我决心学习法语。*The news ~d her against further delay*. 这消息使她下决心不再拖延。*to* ~ *what metals are present in the ore* 测定矿石中有什么金属存在。*A hill ~d my view*. 一座山挡住我的视线。— *vi*. 1. 决心;决定。2.【法】终结,终止。

de·ter·mined [di'tə:mind; dɪ`tɝmɪnd] *a*. 坚决的;毅然的;确定的。*a* ~ *character* 果断的性格。*in a* ~ *manner* 决然。**-ly** *ad*. **-ness** *n*.

dé·ter·min·er [di'tə:minə; dɪ`tɝmɪnɚ] *n*. 1. 决定因素。2.【语法】限定词[如 the, a, an 等]。

de·ter·min·ism [di'tə:minizəm; dɪ`tɝmɪnɪzəm] *n*.【哲】决定论。**-min·ist** [-minist; -mɪnɪst] *n*. 决定论者。**-min·is·tic** [di͵tə:mi'nistik; dɪ͵tɝmɪ`nɪstɪk] *a*. 决定论的。

de·ter·rence [di'terəns; dɪ`tɛrəns] *n*. 1. 制止,威慑。2. 制止物,威慑力量;制止因素,威慑因素(指保持庞大军力以遏制敌方不敢发动战争)。

de·ter·rent [di'terənt; dɪ`tɝənt] **I** *a*. 制止的,威慑的。**II** *n*. 阻碍物,制止物;威慑物。~ *policy* 威慑政策。~ *power* 威慑力量。

de·ter·sive [di'tə:siv; dɪ`tɝsɪv] **I** *a*. 有清洁效力的。**II** *n*. 洗净剂,清洁剂。

de·test [di'test; dɪ`tɛst] *vt*. 嫌恶,憎恶,嫌。~ *evil* 嫉恶如仇。**-a·ble** *a*. 极可恶[讨嫌]的。**-a·bly** *ad*.

de·tes·ta·tion [di:tes'teiʃən; ͵ditɛs`teʃən] *n*. 1. 憎恶,嫌恶,讨厌。2. 极讨厌的东西。***be in*** ~ 被厌恶。***hold*** [***have***] ***in*** ~ 嫌恶,讨厌。***regard with great*** ~ 非常讨厌。

de·throne [di'θrəun; dɪ`θron] *vt*. 1. 废黜,废立。2. 撵走,推翻。**-ment** *n*. 废立,废位。

det·i·nue ['detinju:; `dɛtɪ͵nju] *n*.【法】对他人动产的非法扣留;收回被非法占有动产的诉讼。

det·o·nate ['detəuneit; `dɛto͵net] *vt*., *vi*. 1. (使)爆炸,(使)爆发。2. 触发(一连串事件)。*detonating agent* 起爆剂。*detonating cap* 雷管。*detonating fuse* 导爆索;起爆信管。*detonating powder* 起爆(火)药。

det·o·na·tion [͵detəu'neiʃən; ͵dɛto`neʃən] *n*. 1. 爆炸,爆发。2. 爆炸声。**-na·tor** *n*. 1. 发爆剂;雷管;发爆管,起爆剂。2.【铁路】(浓雾时作信号用的)爆鸣器。

de·tour, dé·tour ['deituə; `ditʊr] **I** *n*. 1. 弯路,迂路。2. 迂回,曲折。*make a* ~ 迂回。**II** *vt*., *vi*. 迂回,(使)绕道。

de·tox·i·cate [di:'tɔksikeit; di`tɑksə͵ket] *vt*. = detoxify.

de·tox·i·fy [di:'tɔksi͵fai; di`tɑksə͵faɪ] *vt*. 除去…的毒物,使解毒。**-fi·ca·tion** [-͵tɔksifi'keiʃən; -͵tɑksəfə`keʃən] *n*.

de·tract [di'trækt; dɪ`trækt] *vt*., *vi*. 1. 降低,减损(价值,名誉等)。2. 诬蔑,损坏,伤害。3. 转移(注意)。~ ***from*** 损伤,损坏(*That does not* ~ *from his merit*. 那无损于他的功绩)。**-tion** *n*. **-tive** *a*. **-tor** *n*. 诬蔑者。

de·train [di:'trein; di`tren] *vi*. [英]下火车。— *vt*. 使(军队等)下车。**-ment** *n*.

de·trib·a·lize [di:'traibəlaiz; di`traɪbl̩͵aɪz] *vi*., *vt*. (使)脱离部落,使消除部落习惯。**-za·tion** [di:'traibəlai'zeiʃən; di͵traɪbəlaɪ`zeʃən] *n*.

det·ri·ment ['detrimənt; `dɛtrəmənt] *n*. 1. 损害,伤害。2. 有害物。***to the*** ~ ***of*** 有损于,不利于。***without*** ~ ***to*** 不损害[损伤],无损于。

det·ri·men·tal [͵detri'mentl; ͵dɛtrə`mɛntl] **I** *a*. 有害的,不利的 (*to*)。**II** *n*. 1. [俚]不受欢迎的求婚者。2. 有害的人[物]。**-ly** *ad*.

de·tri·tion [di'triʃən; dɪ`trɪʃən] *n*. 耗损,磨损。

de·tri·tus [di'traitəs; dɪ`traɪtəs] *n*. 1.【地】碎岩;碎屑。2. 碎石堆。

de trop [də'trəu; də`tro] [F.] 多余的;无用的。*A topcoat was* ~ *with the thermometer standing at 72 degrees*. 温度 72 度时,大衣是多余的。

de·trude [di'tru:d; dɪ`trud] *vt*. 1. 推下,推落。2. 推走,推出。**-tru·sion** *n*.

de·trun·cate [di:'trʌŋkeit; dɪ`trʌŋket] *vt*. 削去,切去

(…的一部分)。

de·tu·mes·cence [ˌdiːtu(ː)ˈmesns, -tjuː-; ˏdituˋmɛsns, -tju-] *n*.【医】消肿。**-cent** *a*.

deuce[1] [djuːs; djus] **I** *n*. **1.** (纸牌的)两点。**2.**【网球】(终局前的)平分。**3.**〔美〕二元券[纸币]。**II** *vt*.【网球】扯平。

deuce[2] [djuːs; djus] *n*.〔口〕**1.** 不幸,遭殃,倒楣。**2.** 魔鬼。**3.**〔美〕胆小鬼。**4.**〔用作感叹词〕讨厌! 哼! ★相当于 devil,表示厌恶、忿怒、惊奇、强意否定等。*The ~ is in it if I cannot*. 我要不能那就见鬼了。*The ~ he isn't*. 他不是那才见鬼啦。*The (very) ~ is in them*! 他们真的见了鬼啦! *The ~ it is*! 奇怪,见鬼! *The ~ you are*! 你这样还了得(岂有此理)! ***a ~ of a***... 非常(讨厌的、愉快的)(*a ~ of a lovely day* 愉快的一天)。(***the***) ~ ***a bit*** 完全不,一点儿不,毫不((*The*) ~ *a bit I care*. 毫不在乎)。(***the***) ~ ***a man*** 一个人也没有。(***the***) ~ ***a one*** 没有一个[一种等]。***D- knows***! 天晓得! ***D- take it***! 见鬼! 该死! 糟了! ***go to the*** ~ 灭亡(*Go to the* ~! 滚! 去见你的鬼去!)。***like the*** ~ 猛然。***play the*** ~ ***with*** 把…弄得一团糟。***The*** ~! 见鬼! 糟了! ***the*** ~ 究竟(*Who* [*What*] *the* ~ *is that*? 那究竟是谁[什么东西]? *Why* [*Where*] *the* ~ ...? …究竟为了什么[在哪儿]?)。***the*** ~ ***and all*** 好好歹歹全都;全没一个好的。***the*** ~ ***of a*** = *a* ~ *of a*. ***the*** ~ ***to pay*** 此后困难,后患(*There will be the* ~ *to pay*. 后果可怕,后患堪虞)。~**-ace** **1.** (骰子的)丁丁[两点和一点]。**2.** 倒楣。

deuced [djuːst, ˈdjuːsit; ˋdjusɪd, ˋdjusɪd] *a*., *ad*.〔口〕过度,非常;很,极,异常。~ *bad* 极坏。*a* ~ *fine girl* 非常美丽的姑娘。*in a* ~ *hurry* 急急忙忙。**-ly** *ad*.

De·us [ˈdeius, ˈdiəs; ˋdeus, ˋdɪəs]〔L.〕上帝。

de·us ex ma·chi·na [ˈdiːəs eks ˈmeikinei; ˋdiəs ɛks-ˋmækɪne]〔L.〕**1.** (古希腊、罗马戏剧中)用舞台机关送出来参与剧情进展的神仙。**2.** (小说等中)突然出现以解围的人物。**3.** 在紧要关头突然出现而扭转局面的人。

Deut. = Deuteronomy.

deu·ter·ag·o·nist [ˌduːtəˈrægənist, ˈdjuːt-; ˏdutə-ˋrægənɪst, ˋdjut-] *n*. **1.** (古希腊戏剧中)演二流角色的演员。**2.** 给别人当配角的人。

deu·ter·an·ope [ˈdjuːtərəˌnəup, ˈduːt-; ˋdjutərəˏnop, ˋdut-] *n*. 绿色盲患者。

deu·ter·an·o·pi·a [ˌdjuːtərəˈnəupiə, duːt-; ˏdjutərə-ˋnopɪə, dut-] *n*. 绿色盲,第二型色盲。

deu·ter·at·ed [ˈdjuːtəreitid, ˈduːt-; ˋdjutəˏretɪd, ˋdut-] *a*. 氘化了的,氘水合物的,重水合物的。

deu·ter·ide [ˈdjuːtəraid, ˈduːt-; ˋdjutəˏraɪd, ˋdut-] *n*. 重氢化合物。

deu·te·ri·um [djuːˈtiəriəm; djuˋtɪrɪəm] *n*.【化】氘,重氢。~ *oxide* 重水。

deu·ter·o- *comb. f*. 表示"第二","再": *deutero*plasm.

deu·ter·o·ca·non·i·cal [ˌdjuːtəˌrəukəˈnɔnikl, ˌduːt-; ˏdjutəˏrokəˋnɑnɪkl, ˏdut-] *a*.【圣】圣典别集的。

deu·ter·og·a·my [ˌdjuːtəˈrɔgəmi; ˏdjutəˋrɑgəmɪ] *n*. 再婚。**-mist** 再婚者。

deu·ter·o·gen·e·sis [ˌdjuːtərəuˈdʒenisis; ˏdjutə-o-ˋdʒɛnɪsɪs] *n*.〔L.〕【生】后期发生。

deu·ter·on [ˈdjuːtərɔn; ˋdjutəˏrɑn] *n*.【化】氘核。

Deu·ter·on·o·mist [djuːtəˈrɔnəmist; ˏdjutəˋrɑnəmɪst] *n*. 圣经旧约申命记的作者[编者]。

Deu·ter·on·o·my [ˌdjuːtəˈrɔnəmi; ˏdjutəˋrɑnəmɪ] *n*.《申命记》〔旧约圣经中的一卷〕。

deu·ter·op·a·thy [ˌdjuːtəˈrɔpəθi; ˏdjutəˋrɑpəθɪ] *n*.【医】继发病。

deu·to- *comb. f*. = deutero-.

deu·ton [ˈdjuːtɔn; ˋdjutɑn] *n*.〔美〕= deuteron.

deu·to·plasm [ˈdjuːtəplæzəm; ˋdjutəplæzəm] *n*.【生】滋养质,副浆,卵黄质。

deutsch [ˈdɔitʃ; ˋdɔɪtʃ] *a*.〔G.〕德国的。

deut·sche mark [ˈdɔitʃəˌmɑːk; ˋdɔɪtʃəˏmɑrk]〔G.〕马克〔德国货币名称,缩写为 DM〕。

Deut·sches Reich [ˈdɔitʃəs ˈraiç; ˋdɔɪtʃəs ˋraɪç]〔G.〕德意志帝国〔第二次世界大战前德国的正式国名〕。

Deutsch·land [ˈdɔitʃlənd; ˋdɔɪtʃˏlənd] *n*.〔G.〕德国,德意志。

deut·zi·a [ˈdjuːtsjə; ˋdjutsɪə] *n*.【植】溲疏属植物。

Dev. = Devonshire.

de·va [ˈdeivə; ˋdevə] *n*. (印度神话的)神,善灵。

de·val·u·ate, de·val·ue [diːˈvæljueit, -ljuː; dɪˋvælju-ˏet, -lju] *vt*. 使降低价值;【经】使币(货)贬值。

de·val·u·a·tion [ˌdiːvæljuˈeiʃən; ˏdivæljuˋeʃən] *n*.【经】(货币)贬值。**-ist** *n*.【经】主张货币贬值者。

De·va·na·ga·ri [ˌdeivəˈnɑːgəri; ˏdevəˋnɑgəri] *n*. 天城文书〔梵文等所由派生的文字〕。

dev·as·tate [ˈdevəsteit; ˋdɛvəsˏtet] *vt*. 蹂躏,破坏;使荒废。*a devastating blow* 毁灭性的打击。**-ta·tion** [ˌdevəsˈteiʃən; ˏdɛvəsˋteʃən] *n*. 蹂躏;荒废;〔*pl*.〕劫后余迹。**-ta·tor** [ˈdevəsteitə; ˋdɛvəsˏtetɚ] *n*. 蹂躏者,劫掠者。

dev·el [ˈdevl; ˋdɛvəl] **I** *n*.〔Scot.〕沉重打击;令人发晕的一击。**II** *vt*.〔Scot.〕给…以沉重的一击。

de·vel·op(e) [diˈveləp; dɪˋvɛləp] *vt*. **1.** 使发达,使发展;使发生;使进化。**2.** 开发,开展,扩大。**3.**【摄】使显影。**4.**【军、数】展开。**5.** 使显出,产生,研制,发现(新事实)。**6.**〔美〕揭露,暴露。~ *industry and agriculture simultaneously* 工业与农业同时并举。~ *a mine* 开矿。*a motor that* ~*s 100 horse-power* 一百匹马力的发动机。— *vi*. **1.** 发育;发生,进化。**2.** 发展,发达(*from*);发达成(*into*)。**3.** (剧情等)展开;(局面)进展;(像)显现出来。**4.**〔美〕(新事实等)发现,出现。*a developing country* 发展中的国家。~**ing paper**【摄】显像纸。

de·vel·op·er [diˈveləpə; dɪˋvɛləpɚ] *n*. **1.** 开发者。**2.**【摄】显影剂,显像剂。

de·vel·op·ment [diˈveləpmənt; dɪˋvɛləpˏmənt] *n*. **1.** 发展,发达;进化。**2.** 展开;扩充;开发。**3.** 发达物,新事物,发展阶段。**4.**【生】发育(史);【军,数】展开;【摄】显影,显像;【乐】展开(部);研制,研制成果。~ *area*〔英〕新开发地区。~ *of heat* 放热,生热。

de·vel·op·men·tal [diˌveləpˈmentəl; dɪˏvɛləpˋmɛntəl] *a*. **1.** 发展的,开发的。**2.** 促使成长的,发育上的;进化的。~ *diseases* 发育病。*a long-range* ~ *program* 长期发展规划。

de·verb·a·tive [diˈvəːbətiv; dɪˋvɝbətɪv] **I** *a*. 从动词派生的。**II** *n*. 动词派生词。

de·vest [diˈvest; dɪˋvɛst] *vt*. = divest.

de·vi·ant [ˈdiːviənt; ˋdivɪənt] **I** *a*. 离经叛道的,偏离正道的。**II** *n*. 行为不轨的人。**-vi·an·cy, -vi·ance** *n*.

de·vi·ate [ˈdiːvieit; ˋdivɪˏet] **I** *vi*. 越(轨),脱离(常轨);违背;误入歧途(*from*)。— *vt*. 使脱离常轨。**II** *a*. 脱离常轨的。**III** *n*. 脱离常轨的人。

de·vi·a·tion [ˌdiːviˈeiʃən; ˏdivɪˋeʃən] *n*. **1.** 脱离,越轨,背离(*from*)。**2.** 偏向,偏差。**3.** (统计上的)误差。**4.**【海】(故意)偏航。**5.**【数】偏差数。*the* ~ *of the magnetic needle* 磁针的偏差。**-ism** *n*. (政治上的)脱离正道。**-ist** *n*. 脱离正道者,异端分子。

de·vice [diˈvais; dɪˋvaɪs] *n*. **1.** 设计,计划;方法,手段。**2.**〔*pl*.〕意志,欲望。**3.** 谋略,策略,诡计。**4.** 器具,器械,设备,装置。**5.** 图案,图样;花样;纹章;标记,商标;(纹章上的)题铭。*a safety* ~ 安全设备。*a pressure* ~ 压力计。*a homing* ~ 自动寻的[导引]装置。***leave sb. to his own*** ~***s*** 让某人自行其是。

dev·il [ˈdevl; ˋdɛvl] **I** *n*. **1.** 魔鬼,恶魔;〔the D-〕魔王。**2.** 人面兽心的人,恶棍。**3.** 冒失鬼。**4.** 精力绝伦的人。**5.** 可怜的家伙。**6.** 猛兽。**7.** …鬼,…狂者。**8.** 斗志,好胜心。**9.** 难事;难操纵的东西。**10.** (律师等的)代笔者;

(印刷厂等的)学徒;见习护士;助手。11.【烹】辣子肉。12.【机】切碎机。13.〔口〕飞沙走石的风暴,尘卷风。14.〔口〕〔the ~〕表示"究竟","决不"等惊叹语气〔与 who, how, why, where, what 等连用〕。*a poor* ~ 可怜的家伙。*a printer's* ~ 印刷所学徒。*He has lost his job, poor* ~. 他失业了,这个可怜的家伙。*Who the* ~ *is he*? 他究竟是谁? *The* ~ *I will*. 我决不干。*work like the* ~ 拚命工作。***a*** ~ ***of a …*** 异常的,吓人的;麻烦的,讨厌的,愉快的(等)。***and the*** ~ ***knows what*** 其他种种。***be a*** ~ ***for …*** 是…狂(*He is a* ~ *for gambling*. 他是赌棍)。***between the*** ~ ***and the deep sea*** 进退两难。***blue*** ~***s*** 意气消沉。~ ***a bit*** 毫不。~ ***a one*** 无一个。***D- take it***! 糟了! 该死! ***give the*** ~ ***his due*** 平心而论,公平对待。***go to the*** ~ 1. 败落,落魄。2.〔生气时用语〕滚开(*Go to the* ~! 去见你的鬼去! 滚!)。3. 惨败,落空。***have the*** ~***'s*** (***own***) ***luck*** (坏人)得意一时。***like the*** ~ 猛烈,拼命。***Needs must when the*** ~ ***drives***. 情势所迫,只好如此。***paint the*** ~ ***blacker than he is*** 诽过其实。***play the*** ~ ***with*** 损害,糟踏;使为难。***raise the*** ~ 1. 起哄,作乱。2. 引起麻烦。3. 弄得非常热闹。***say the*** ~***'s paternoster*** 嘟哝不满,发牢骚。***Talk of the*** ~ ***and he will appear***. 谈鬼鬼到,说起某人某人就到。***the*** ~ ***among the tailors*** 〔英〕吵闹;一种烟火。***the*** ~ ***and all*** 一切坏事。***the*** ~ (***of it***) 难点。***the*** ~***'s own luck*** 〔俚〕极好[坏]的运气。***the*** ~***'s own time*** 非常痛苦的经验。***The*** ~ ***take the hindmost***. 让逃得最慢的人被魔鬼抓去吧〔意为不管别人,只顾自己逃命等〕。***the*** ~ ***to pay*** 此后困难,后患。***whip the*** ~ ***round the stump*** [***post***] 推卸责任。**II** ***vt***. (〔英〕***-ll-***) 1. 用辣子烤(肉等)。2. (用切碎机)切碎。3. 〔美口〕虐待,折磨,纠缠。— ***vi***. (替作家、律师等)做助手(*for*)。~**-box** 〔口〕电子计算机。~ **dog** 〔美俚〕水兵,海军陆战队队员。~**dodger** 牧师,教士。~**dom** 1. 魔鬼的统治。2. 魔鬼所在地区。3. 〔集合词〕魔鬼。~**-fish**【动】鸢魟;灰色鲸;鮟鱇;琵琶鱼,章鱼,乌贼。~ **horse** 螳螂。~**-may-care** 不顾一切的;嬉闹的,满不在乎的,随遇而安的。~ **'s advocate** 吹毛求疵的人,故意唱反调的人。~**'s bedpost**【牌】梅花四点。~**'s bones** 骰子。~**'s books** 纸牌。~**'s darning needle** 〔美俚〕蜻蜓。~**'s dozen** 十三。~**'s food cake** 巧克力蛋糕。~**'s tattoo** 用手指或脚在桌上或床上得得得的敲击。

Devil's Triangle 魔鬼三角地(亦称 Bermuda Triangle 百慕大三角地)。

dev·il·ish [ˈdevliʃ; ˋdɛvlɪʃ] **I** ***a***. 1. 魔鬼似的;可怕的,穷凶极恶的。2. 〔口〕异常的,非常的。**II** ***ad***. 〔口〕非常,极。**-ly** ***ad***.

dev·il·ism [ˈdevlizəm; ˋdɛvlˌɪzəm] ***n***. 1. 魔鬼似的品性,魔鬼似的行为。2. 魔鬼崇拜。

dev·il·kin [ˈdevəlkin; ˋdɛvəlkɪn] ***n***. 小魔鬼;小精灵。

dev·il·ment [ˈdevlmənt; ˋdɛvlmənt] ***n***. 1. 鬼脾气;鬼举动。2. 怪事,怪现象。3. 恶作剧。

dev·il·ry [ˈdevlri; ˋdɛvlrɪ] ***n***. 1. 恶劣行为。2. 魔法,妖术。3. 恶作剧;胡作非为。4. 妖怪学。5. 魔界。

dev·il·try [ˈdevltri; ˋdɛvltrɪ] ***n***. = devilry.

de·vi·ous [ˈdiːvjəs; ˋdivjəs] ***a***. 1. 远离大路的,偏僻的。2. 误入歧途的;无一定路线的。3. 不正当的;狡猾的,诡计多端的。4. 迂回的,曲折的。*Let's take the* ~ *route home to avoid the crowds in the main roads*. 为了避免大街上的拥挤,我们还是绕道回家去吧。**-ly** ***ad***. **-ness** ***n***.

de·vis·a·ble [diˈvaizəbl; dɪˋvaɪzəbl̩] ***a***. 1. 能想出[发明、设计]的。2.【法】能遗让的。

de·vis·al [diˈvaizl; dɪˋvaɪzəl] ***n***. 设计,计划;图谋。

de·vise [diˈvaiz; dɪˋvaɪz] **I** ***vt***. 1. 设计,制定,创造,发明。2. 图谋;策划。3.【法】遗让(财产)。*They* ~*d a plan to escape from prison*. 他们设计越狱。**II** ***n***. 1. 遗让,遗赠(财产)。2. 遗赠财产的遗嘱(或其中的条款)。3. 遗赠的财产。**de·vi·see** [diˈvaiˈziː; dɪˋvaɪˋzi] ***n***.【法】被遗赠者,受遗让者。**-vis·er** ***n***. 1. 设计者,发明者。2. 图谋者。3.【法】= devisor.

dev·i·sor [ˌdeviˈzɔː, divaiˈzɔː; dɪˋvaɪzɔ, dɪˋvaɪzɚ] ***n***.【法】遗赠者。

de·vi·tal·ize [diːˈvaitəlaiz; diˋvaɪtlˏaɪz] ***vt***. 1. 使失去生命,使失去生命力。2. 使伤元气,使衰弱。**-za·tion** [diːˌvaitəlaiˈzeiʃən; diˏvaɪtəlaɪˋzeʃən] ***n***.

de·vi·ta·min·ize [diːˈvitəminaiz; diˋvɪtəmɪˏnaɪz] ***vt***. (烹调或去皮壳时)使(食物)失去维生素。

de·vit·ri·fy [diːˈvitrifai; diˋvɪtrəˏfaɪ] ***vt***. 使失去玻璃光泽;使玻璃不透明。

de·vo·cal·ize [diːˈvəukəlaiz, ˈdiːvəu-; diˋvokəlaɪz, ˋdi-ˋvo-] ***vt***.【语音】使(浊音)变成清音。

de·voice [diˈvɔis; dɪˋvɔɪs] ***vt***. = devocalize.

de·void [diˈvɔid; dɪˋvɔɪd] ***a***. 无一的,缺…的(*of*)。*a book* ~ *of content* 一本毫无内容的书。*be* ~ *of common sense* 缺乏常识。~ *of vegetation* 草木不生的。

de·voir [dəˈvwɑː, ˈdevwɑː; dəˋvwɑr, ˋdɛvwɑr] ***n***. 1. 本分,义务。2. [*pl*.] 敬意;问候。***do one's*** ~ 尽本分。***pay*** [***tender***] ***one's*** ~***s to*** 表示敬意,问候…,对…致敬。

de·vo·lute [ˈdiːvəljuːt; ˋdivəljut] ***vt***. 〔罕〕= devolve.

de·vo·lu·tion [ˌdiːvəˈljuːʃən; ˏdɛvəˋluʃən] ***n***. 1. (责任、权利、财产等的)转移。2. (议会对所属委员会的)授权代理。3. (中央对地方的)权力下放。4.【生】退化。

de·volve [diˈvɔlv; dɪˋvɑlv] ***vt***. 转移,移交。~ *a work on somebody else* 将工作交代给别人。— ***vi***. 1. 移归,授与。2. 流[滚]向下(向前)。*the work that* ~*s upon sb*. 移归某人负责的工作。*streams devolving from the mountains* 从山上流下的河流。

Dev·on [ˈdevn; ˋdɛvən̩] ***n***. 德文郡〔英国郡名〕(= ~-shire)。

De·vo·ni·an [deˈvəuniən; dəˋvonɪən] **I** ***a***. 1. (英国)德文郡的。2.【地】泥盆纪的。**II** ***n***. 1. 德文郡人。2.【地】泥盆纪。

Dev·on·shire [ˈdevnʃiə; ˋdɛvənˏʃɪr] ***n***. (英国)德文郡。

de·vote [diˈvəut; dɪˋvot] ***vt***. 1. 献(身),专心致力于,贡献。2. 把…专用于(*to*)。3. 听任。*He* ~*d his life to art*. 他终生献身艺术。*I don't think we should* ~ *any more time to this question*. 我认为我们在这个问题上不应当花费更多的时间了。~ *one's country to evil fate* 听任国家遭受厄运的摆布。~ ***one's energy to*** 用全力。~ ***oneself to*** (*study*; *amusement*) 致力于,专心从事(研究);一味贪玩。

de·vot·ed [diˈvəutid; dɪˋvotɪd] ***a***. 1. 献身…的,埋头…的,热中…的(*to*)。2. 深爱(*to*);忠实的。3. 注定要遭殃的。*a* ~ *wife* 忠实的妻子。**-ly** ***ad***. 一心;忠实。**-ness** ***n***.

dev·o·tee [ˌdevəuˈtiː; ˏdɛvəˋti] ***n***. 1. 热爱者。2. 皈依者(*of*)。*a* ~ *of the ballet* 芭蕾舞爱好者。

de·vo·tion [diˈvəuʃən; dɪˋvoʃən] ***n***. 1. 信仰,信心;〔*pl*.〕祈祷。2. 献身;热诚,忠诚;专心,热心(*to*)。3. 充作,派用,利用。*He works with greater* ~. 他工作更安心了。*be at one's* ~*s* 正在祈祷。*the* ~ *of a mother for her child* 母亲对儿女的热爱。*the* ~ *of one's time to scientific advancement* 把个人的时间用于科学的发展。**-al** ***a***. 虔诚的;祈祷的。***n***. 简短的礼拜。

de·vour [diˈvauə; dɪˋvaur] ***vt***. 1. 狼吞虎咽地吃,拼命吃;吞没,吃光;舐光。2. 吞灭,毁灭。3. 贪读;凝视;倾听。4. 使(好奇心、忧虑等)被吸引住,…到极点。*He is* ~*ing novel after novel*. 他一味贪看小说。~ *the way* 〔诗〕(马等)兼程急进。*I am* ~*ed with anxiety*. 我忧愁极了。*He* ~*ed every word*. 他一字不漏地倾听着。

de·vour·ing·ly [diˈvauəriŋli; dɪˋvaurɪŋlɪ] ***ad***. 贪婪地,贪;吞灭似地。

de·vout [diˈvaut; dɪˋvaʊt] ***a***. 热诚的;虔诚的。**-ly** ***ad***.

-ness *n*.

dew [djuː; dju] **I** *n*. **1**. 露;露水一样的东西(泪等)。**2**. 爽快,清新,轻快。~-*lit eyes* 〔诗〕挂着泪珠的双眼。*the ~ of youth* 青春的朝气。*the timely ~ of sleep* 甜睡。**II** *vt*. 喷湿,(露水等)弄湿。— *vi*. 结露水。*It ~s*. 结露水。~**berry**【植】悬钩子。~ **cell** 露管〔测定露点的仪器〕。~**claw** (狗等脚上不与地面接触的)无机能趾;悬蹄。~**drop** 露,露珠。~**fall** 结露,起露;黄昏(结露的)时刻。~**lap** (牛等颈部)垂皮,垂肉。~ **point**【物】露点。~ **pond** 露池〔山区高地用以蓄水的浅池〕。~ **ret** *vt*. 把(麻等)放在雨露下浸湿。~ **worm** (作鱼饵用的)蚯蚓。

de·wan [diˈwɑːn; dɪˋwɑn] *n*. 〔印〕财政部长;邦政府的首席部长。

Dew·ar [ˈdjuːə; ˋdjuəː] *n*. 迪尤尔〔姓氏〕。

Dew·ar ves·sel [ˈdjuːə ˈvesəl; ˋdjuəː ˋvesəl] *n*. 保温真空瓶〔又作 **Dewar**, **Dewar flask**. 苏格兰物理学家 Sir James Dewar 发明〕。

de·wa·ter [diːˈwɔːtə; diˋwɔtəː] *vt*. 使脱水,使浓缩。

de·wax [diːˈwæks; diˋwæks] *vt*.【化】使脱蜡。

Dew·ey [ˈdju(ː)i; ˋdju(ʊ)ɪ] *n*. 杜威〔姓氏〕。

dew·i·ly [ˈdjuːili; ˋdjuəlɪ] *ad*. **1**. 带露水地;露水般地。**2**. 纯洁地,清新地。

de·windt·ite [dəˈwintait; dəˋwɪntaɪt] *n*.【矿】磷铅铀矿。

dew·i·ness [ˈdjuːinis; ˋdjuɪnɪs] *n*. 露水大;湿润。

DEW line = Distant Early Warning line【军】远程早发警报线。

DEW radar = Distant Early Warning radar【军】远程早发警报雷达。

DEWS = Distant Early Warning System【军】远程早发警报系统。

dew·y [ˈdjuːi; ˋdjuɪ] *a*. **1**. 露大的,带露水的;似露的。**2**. (眼睛)泪汪汪的,舒服的(睡眠等)。**3**. 纯洁的,清新的。~ *tears* 晶莹的泪滴。*a ~ maiden* 纯洁直率的姑娘。

dex·i·o·trop·ic [ˌdeksiəˈtrɔpik; ˏdɛksɪəˋtrɑpɪk] *a*. (如软体动物的螺形外壳等)向右的,右旋的。

Dex·e·drine [ˈdeksidriːn, -drin; ˋdɛksədrin, -drɪn] *n*.【药】右旋苯异丙胺〔dextroamphetamine 的商标名,用作中枢神经兴奋剂〕。

Dex·ter [ˈdekstə; ˋdɛkstəː] *n*. 德克斯特〔男子名〕。

dex·ter [ˈdekstə; ˋdɛkstəː] *a*. **1**. 右边的,右手的。**2**. (因面向右边或出现在右边而)预兆吉利的。**3**.【纹】(盾徽)右边的 (*opp*. sinister)。

dex·ter·i·ty [deksˈteriti; dɛksˋtɛrətɪ] *n*. **1**. (手)灵巧,熟练,巧妙。**2**. (头脑)敏捷、机敏。**3**. 用惯右手。

dex·ter·ous [ˈdekstərəs; ˋdɛkstərəs] *a*. **1**. 灵巧的,巧妙的,手快的,手巧的。**2**. 敏捷的,机敏的。**3**. 右手灵便的。-**ly** *ad*. -**ness** *n*.

dex·tral [ˈdekstrəl; ˋdɛkstrəl] *a*. **1**. 在右(边)的,向右(边)的。**2**. 用右手的。**3**. (软体动物的螺形外壳等)右旋的,右卷的 (*opp*. sinistral)。-**i·ty** [deksˈtræliti; dɛksˋtrælətɪ] *n*. -**ly** *ad*.

dex·tran [ˈdekstrən; ˋdɛkstrən] *n*.【化】葡聚糖。

dex·trin [ˈdekstrin; ˋdɛkstrɪn] *n*.【化】糊精。

dex·tro [ˈdekstrəu; ˋdɛkstro] *a*.【化】**1**. 右旋的,顺时针向的。**2**. (某些水晶)使光的偏振右旋的。

dextro- *comb. f*. 表示"向右的","右旋的":*dextro*rotatory.

dex·tro·am·phet·a·mine [ˌdekstrəuæmˈfetəˌmiːn; ˏdɛkstroæmˋfɛtəmin] *n*. 右旋苯异丙胺,右旋安非他命〔中枢神经兴奋药〕。

dex·tro·glu·cose [ˌdekstrəuˈgluːkəus; ˏdɛkstroˋglukos] *n*. 葡萄糖;右旋糖。

dex·tro·gy·rate [ˈdekstrəuˈdʒairit; ˋdɛkstroˋdʒaɪret] *a*. **1**. 右旋的,顺时针向的。**2**. (某些水晶)使光的偏振右旋的。

dex·trone [ˈdekstrən; ˋdɛkstrən] *n*. = dextran(e).

dex·tro·ro·ta·tion [ˌdekstrəurəuˈteiʃən; ˏdɛkstrəroˋteʃən] *n*. 右旋,顺时针方向旋转。

dex·tro·ro·ta·to·ry [ˌdekstrəuˈrəutəˌtəri; ˏdɛkstrəˋrotəˏtɔrɪ] *a*. **1**. 右旋的,顺时针方向的。**2**. (某些水晶)使光的偏振右旋的。

dex·trorse [ˈdekstrɔːs; ˋdɛkstrɔrs] *a*.【植】右旋的,右旋向上的。~ *vine* 右旋葡萄藤。

dex·trose [ˈdekstrəus; ˋdɛkstros] *n*.【化】右旋糖,葡萄糖。

dex·trous [ˈdekstrəs; ˋdɛkstrəs] *a*. = dexterous.

dey [dei; de] *n*. 总督;帕夏〔土耳其人建立的奥斯曼帝国在北非的官员〕。

D. F. = **1**. Dean of the Faculty (大学的)系主任。**2**. direction finding 测向。**3**. Doctor of Forestry 林学博士。

D / F = direction finding. **d / f** = day of fire (每)日弹药基数。

DFA = Doctor of Fine Arts 美术博士。

D. F. C. = Distinguished Flying Cross〔英〕优异飞行十字勋章。

D. F. E. = directional frictional effect 方向性摩擦效应。

D. F. M. = Distinguished Flying Medal〔美〕优异飞行勋章。

dft. = defendant; draft.

D. G. = **1**. *Dei gratia* (= by the grace of God)【宗】蒙上帝保佑。**2**. *Deo gratias* (= thanks to God) 感谢上帝。**3**. Director-general 总裁。**4**. Dragoon Guards〔英〕龙骑兵禁卫团。

dg. = decigram(me)(s)。

d. h. 1. *das heisst* 〔G. = that is to say〕. **2**. deadhead.

DH = **1**. designated hitter〔棒球〕指定击球手。**2**. Doctor of Humanities 古典文学博士。

dhal [dɑːl; dɑl] *n*. (印度的)木豆。

dhar·ma [ˈdɑːmə; ˋdɑrmɑ] *n*. **1**. 〔印〕【佛】宇宙法规(包括自然法规和道德法规)。**2**. 遵守法规。**3**. 〔D-〕达摩。

dhar·na [ˈdɑːnə; ˋdɑnə] *n*. 〔印〕绝食伸冤〔印度会流行过的一种消极抗议方式,受冤毒的人坐在当事人家门口,长坐绝食而致于死〕。

DHL = Doctor of Hebrew Letters (或 Literature) 希伯来文学博士。

dho·bi(e) [ˈdəubi; ˋdobɪ] *n*. 〔印〕洗衣工人。~ **itch** 腹股沟癣〔据说是送到外面洗的衣服传染的〕。

dho·ti, dhoo·ti [ˈdəuti, ˈduːti; ˋdotɪ, ˋdutɪ] *n*. 〔印〕(男子的)围腰布。

dhow [dau; daʊ] *n*. (阿拉伯沿海的)独桅帆船。

D. H. Q. =〔美〕Division Headquarters 师部。

DHSS = Department of Health and Social Services (英国)卫生和社会事务部。

dhur·na [ˈdəːnə; ˋdəːnə] *n*. = dharna.

dhur·rie [ˈdʌri; ˋdəːri] *n*. 〔印〕厚棉布;厚棉布地毯。

di-[1] *pref*. = dis-[1].

di-[2] *pref*. 二,双,二重,二倍:*di*archy.

di-[3], **dia-** *pref*. 〔后接子音时用 dia-, 接母音时用 di-〕。**1**. 表示"通过","横过":*dia*phragm, *dia*gonal. **2**. 表示"分离":*dia*gnose, *dia*critical.

di(a). = diameter.

di·a·base [ˈdaiəbeis; ˋdaɪəˏbes] *n*.【矿】辉绿岩。

di·a·be·tes [ˌdaiəˈbiːtiːz, -tiːs; ˏdaɪəˋbitɪz, -tis] *n*.【医】**1**. 糖尿病〔~ mellitus〕。**2**. 尿崩症〔又作 ~ insipidus〕。

di·a·bet·ic [ˌdaiəˈbetik, -ˈbiːtik; ˏdaɪəˋbɛtɪk, -ˋbitɪk] **I** *a*. (患)糖尿病的。**II** *n*. 糖尿病病人。

di·a·ble·rie, di·ab·le·ry [diˈɑːbləri, diˈæbləri; dɪˋɑblərɪ, dɪˋæblərɪ] *n*. **1**. 魔法,妖术。**2**. 妖怪传说。**3**. 妖魔世界。

di·a·bol·ic, -i·cal [daiəˈbɔlik, -ikəl; daɪəˋbɑlɪk, -ɪkl] *a*. **1**. 〔通例 diabolic〕恶魔(一样)的。**2**. 〔通例 diabolical〕凶暴的,穷凶极恶的。~ *arts* 魔术。

di·ab·o·lism [daiˈæbəlizəm; daɪˋæbəˏlɪzəm] *n*. **1**. 魔

术,妖术。2. 相信魔鬼,崇拜魔鬼。3. 魔鬼行径,恶行。

di·ab·o·lize, di·ab·o·lise [daiˈæbəlaiz; daɪˋæbəˏlaɪz] *vt*. 1. 使成恶魔。2. 把…描绘成恶魔。

di·ab·o·lo [diˈɑːbələu; dɪˋæbəˏlo] *n*. 空竹〔*cf*. the devil on two sticks〕。

di·a·chron·ic [ˌdaiəˈkrɔnik; ˏdaɪəˋkrɑnɪk] *a*.【语】历时的语言学的〔指语言系统在历史过程中的变化而言〕。~ **linguistics**【语】历时语言学。**-cal·ly** *ad*.

di·ach·ron·y [daiˈækrəni; daɪˋækrənɪ] *n*.【语】历时语言学。

di·ach·y·lon, di·ach·y·lum [daiˈækilən, -əm; daɪˋækəlɑn, -əm] *n*.【医】铅硬膏。

di·ac·id [daiˈæsid; daɪˋæsɪd] **I** *a*.【化】1. 二酸的。2. 二价酸的。**II** *n*. 二酸。

di·ac·o·nal [daiˈækənl; daɪˋækənl̩] *a*. deacon 的。

di·ac·o·nate [daiˈækənit; daɪˋækənɪt] *n*. 1. 副主祭[执事]的职位[任期]。2. 副主祭团;执事团。

di·a·cous·tic [ˌdaiəˈkuːstik; ˏdaɪəˋkustɪk] *a*. 折声的。**-tics** *n*. 折声学。

di·a·crit·ic [ˌdaiəˈkritik; ˏdaɪəˋkrɪtɪk] **I** *a*. 1. = diacritical. 2.【医】= diagnostic. **II** *n*. = diacritical mark.

di·a·crit·i·cal [daiəˈkritikəl; daɪəˋkrɪtɪkəl] *a*. 区分的,区别的。~ **marks** [**points, signs**] 区别音符〔如 ā, ă, ä 所标的 ¯, ˘, ¨ 等〕。

di·ac·tin·ic [ˌdaiækˈtinik; ˏdaɪækˋtɪnɪk] *a*.【物】有化学线透射性能的,能透光化线的。

di·ac·tin·ism [daiˈæktinizəm; daɪˋæktənɪzəm] *n*. 透光化线性能。

di·ad[1] [ˈdaiæd; ˋdaɪæd] *n*. 1. 二;一双。2.【数】并矢(量)。3.【化】二价元素;二价基。4.【生】二分体;二分细胞。

di·ad[2] [ˈdaiæd; ˋdaɪæd] *a*.【物】二重(对称)的。~ *axis* 二重轴。

di·a·del·phous [ˌdaiəˈdelfəs; ˏdaɪəˋdɛlfəs] *a*.【植】1. (雄蕊的)二体排列的。2. 二体雄蕊的。

di·a·dem [ˈdaiədem; ˋdaɪəˏdɛm] **I** *n*. 1. 王冠,冕〔尤指东方君主的头带〕。2. 王权,王位。**II** *vt*. 用王冠装饰;授以王冠。

di·ad·ro·mous [daiˈædrəməs; daɪˋædrəməs] *a*. 1.【植】(叶子)扇形脉序的。2.【动】(鱼等的)洄游于海水和淡水中的。

di·aer·e·sis [daiˈiərisis; daɪˋɛrəsɪs] *n*. (*pl*. *-ses* [-siːz; -siz]) 1. 二连续母音的音节区分。2. (表示二连续母音须分别发音的)区分音符〔如 coöperate 中的 ¨; cooperate, zoology 等常用词常有省去¨的倾向; naïve 等外来语则仍沿用〕。

diag. = diagonal; diagram.

di·a·gen·e·sis [ˌdaiəˈdʒenisis; ˏdaɪəˋdʒɛnɪsɪs] *n*.【地】成岩作用,岩化作用。

di·a·ge·o·tro·pism [ˌdaiədʒiˈɔtrəpizm; ˏdaɪədʒɪˋɑtrəpɪzm̩] *n*. (植物枝、茎的)横向地性。**-trop·ic** [-ˌdʒiəˈtrɔpik; -ˏdʒɪəˋtrɑpɪk] *a*.

di·a·glyph [ˈdaiəglif; ˋdaɪəglɪf] *n*. 凹雕 (= intaglio)。

di·ag·nose [ˈdaiəgnəuz; ˋdaɪəgnoz] *vt*. 1.【医】诊断(疾病)。2. 判断(问题)。*The doctor ~d her illness as diabetes mellitus*. 医生诊断她患糖尿病。*The teacher ~d the boy's reading difficulties*. 老师找出那孩子阅读上困难的原因。

di·ag·no·sis [ˌdaiəgˈnəusis; ˏdaɪəgˋnosɪs] *n*. (*pl*. *-ses* [-siːz; -siz]) 1. 诊断。2.【生】(分类学上的)特征简述。3. 调查分析,判断。*mistake in* ~ 误诊。*form a correct* ~ *on* [*upon*] *a disease* 确诊。

di·ag·nos·tic [ˌdaiəgˈnɔstik; ˏdaɪəgˋnɑstɪk] **I** *a*. 1. 诊断的。2. 特征的。**II** *n*. 1. 征候,特征。2. 〔*pl*.〕诊断法,诊断学。**-ti·cally** *ad*. 诊断上,按照诊断。

di·ag·nos·ti·cian [ˌdaiəgnɔsˈtiʃən; ˏdaɪəgnɑsˋtɪʃən] *n*. 诊断者,诊断专家。

di·ag·o·nal [daiˈægənl; daɪˋægənl̩] **I** *a*. 1. 对角线的。2. 斜的;斜纹的。**II** *n*. 1.【数】对角线,对顶线。2. 斜纹布。~ **matrix**【数】对角(矩)阵。**-ly** *ad*. 斜,斜对。

di·a·gram [ˈdaiəgræm; ˋdaɪəˏgræm] **I** *n*. 图,图形,图解;【数】作图。*a* ~ *of an engine* 发动机设计图。**II** *vt*. (*-gram(m)ed*; *-gram·(m)ing*) 用图表示,图解。

di·a·gram·mat·ic, -i·cal [ˌdaiəgrəˈmætikəl; ˏdaɪəgrəˋmætɪkəl] *a*. 图解的,图式的;概略的。**-i·cal·ly** *ad*.

di·a·gram·matize [ˌdaiəˈgræmətaiz; ˏdaɪəˋgræməˏtaɪz] *vt*. 把…作成表,用图表示。

di·a·graph [ˈdaiəgrɑːf; ˋdaɪəˏgræf] *n*. 分度画线仪;分度尺;绘图器;放大绘图器。

di·a·ki·ne·sis [ˈdaiəkaiˈniːsis; ˋdaɪəkaɪˋnisɪs] *n*.【生】(生殖细胞分裂的)终变期〔指母染色体和父染色体在核中配对的时期〕。

di·al [ˈdaiəl; ˋdaɪəl] **I** *n*. 1. 日晷 (= sun-~)。2. (钟表等的)针盘;(仪表等的)标度盘;(电话的)拨号盘。3. 矿用罗盘;航海罗盘。4. 〔俚〕脸(盆)。*a radio* ~ 收音机刻度盘。**II** *vt*., *vi*. (*~(l)ed*; *~(l)ing*) 拨(电话号码),打(自动电话);用矿用罗盘测量。~ *a radio* 转动收音机的旋钮选收。~**-a-bus** [亦作 ~**-a-ride**] *n*. 〔美口〕电话传呼出租汽车业务。~ **indicator** 千分表。~ **plate** (针盘的)标度板。~ **telephone** 自动电话机。

dial. = 1. dialect. 2. dialectic.

Di·al-A-, di·al-a- [ˈdaiələ; ˋdaɪələ] (美)表示"拨号": *Dial-A-Meal* 拨号送饭菜上门服务; *Dial-A-Porn* (收费昂贵的)色情电话热线; *dial-a-ride* 电话叫车服务。

di·a·lect [ˈdaiəlekt; ˋdaɪəlɛkt] *n*. 1. 方言,地方话。2.【语】语支。3. (某人的)谈吐,语调。4. (某职业的)专业用语。*the Lancashire* ~ 兰开夏的方言。*English is an Indo-European* ~. 英语是印欧语的一支。*the lawyer's* ~ 律师用语。~ **atlas** 方言分布图。**di·a·lec·tal** *a*.

di·a·lec·tic [ˌdaiəˈlektik; ˏdaɪəˋlɛktɪk] **I** *a*. 1. 辩证(法)的。2. 方言的。**II** *n*. 1.【哲】辩证法。2. 〔常 *pl*.〕(以问答方式进行的)论证;雄辩术。*D- studies how opposites can become identical*. 辩证法研究对立物是怎样变统一的。*materialistic* ~ 唯物辩证法。

di·a·lec·ti·cal [ˌdaiəˈlektikəl; ˏdaɪəˋlɛktɪkl] *a*. 1. 辩证(法)的。2. 方言的。~ *materialism* 辩证唯物论。*the ~-materialist theory of knowledge* 辩证唯物论的认识论。**-ly** *ad*.

di·a·lec·ti·cian [ˌdaiəlekˈtiʃən; ˏdaɪəlɛkˋtɪʃən] *n*. 1. 辩证家;逻辑学家。2. 方言学家。

di·a·lec·tics [ˌdaiəˈlektiks; ˏdaɪəˋlɛktɪks] *n*. 辩证法。*materialist* ~ 唯物辩证法。

di·a·lec·tol·o·gy [ˌdaiəlekˈtɔlədʒi; ˏdaɪəlɛkˋtɑlədʒɪ] *n*. 方言学。**-logist** 方言学家。

di·al·lage [ˈdaiəlidʒ; ˋdaɪəlɪdʒ] *n*. 异剥石。

di·al·ling [ˈdaiəliŋ; ˋdaɪəlɪŋ] *n*. 1. 日晷制作;以日晷测时。2. (自动电话)拨号。~ *system* (电话机的)自动式。~ *tone* (自动电话的)拨号音,表轨声。

di·a·log(ue) [ˈdaiəlɔg; ˋdaɪəlɔg] **I** *n*. 1. 问答,对语。2. 问答题,对话体。3. (小说中的)对白。*in* ~ 用对话体,照问答题。**II** *vi*. 对话。— *vt*. 用对话表达。**-log·ic** *a*. 对话(体)的,问答题的。~ **box**【计】对话框。**-al·o·gism** [-ˈælədʒizəm; -ˋælədʒɪzəm] *n*. 对话式讨论法。

dial·o·gist [daiˈælədʒist; daɪˋælədʒɪst] *n*. 问答者,对话者;对话体作者。

dial(-)pad, dial·pad [ˈdaiəlpæd; ˋdaɪəlpæd] *n*. 按钮式拨号簿〔指按钮式电话机使用的组合数字或字母〕。

di·a·lyse [ˈdaiəlaiz; ˋdaɪəˋlaɪz] *vt*.【化】渗析,透析。

di·a·lys·er [ˈdaiəlaizə; ˋdaɪəlaɪzɚ] *n*. 透析器,渗析器;渗析膜。

di·al·y·sis [daiˈælisis; daɪˋæləsɪs] *n*. (*pl*. *-ses* [-siːz; -siz]) 1. 分离,分解。2.【化】渗析,透析。

D

di·a·lyt·ic [ˌdaiəˈlitik; ˏdaɪəˋlɪtɪk] *a*. 【化】有分离力的,透析的,渗析的。

di·a·lyze [ˈdaiəlaiz; ˋdaɪəˏlaɪz] *vt*. 〔美〕= dialyse.

diam. = diameter.

di·a·mag·net·ic [ˌdaiəmægˈnetik; ˏdaɪəmægˋnɛtɪk] **I** *a*. 【物】抗磁性的。**II** *n*. 抗磁性体。**-ally** *ad*.

di·a·mag·net·ism [ˌdaiəˈmægnitizəm; ˏdaɪəˋmægnəˏtɪzəm] *n*. 【物】**1**. 抗磁性。**2**. 抗磁力;抗磁现象。**3**. 抗磁学。

di·a·man·té [ˌdiəˈmɑːnˈtei, -ˈmɑːntei; ˏdɪəˋmɑnˋte, -ˋmɑnte] **I** *a*. 嵌以钻石的;饰以闪光珠宝的。~ *sandals* 嵌着钻石的拖鞋。**II** *n*. 珠光宝气的装饰品。

di·a·man·tif·er·ous [ˌdaiəmænˈtifərəs; ˏdaɪəmænˋtɪfərəs] *a*. = diamondiferous.

di·am·e·ter [daiˈæmitə; daɪˋæmətɚ] *n*. **1**. 直径。**2**. (显微镜等的)放大倍数。*a lens magnifying 2,000 ~s* 能放大二千倍的透镜。

di·am·e·tral [daiˈæmitrəl; daɪˋæmətrəl] *a*. 直径的。

di·a·met·ric, di·a·met·ri·cal [ˌdaiəˈmetrik(əl); ˏdaɪəˋmɛtrɪk(əl)] *a*. **1**. 直径的。**2**. 正好相反的。*They are in diametrical opposition to each other*. 他们彼此针锋相对。**-cal·ly** *ad*.

di·am·ine [daiˈæmiːn, ˈdaiəˌmiːn; daɪˋæmin, ˋdaɪəˏmin] *n*. **1**. 二胺化合物。**2**. 肼,联氨。**3**. 二(元)胺;双胺染料。

di·a·mond [ˈdaiəmənd; ˋdaɪəmənd] **I** *n*. **1**. 金刚钻,金刚石,钻石。**2**. 菱形;菱饰;(纸牌的)方块。**3**. 【棒球】内野;棒球场。**4**. 【印】钻石体活字〔$4\frac{1}{2}$点〕。**5**. (切玻璃用的)钻刀。**6**. 〔D-〕〔美〕Delaware 州的别名。**7**. 〔*pl*.〕〔美俚〕煤。**II** *a*. **1**. 钻石(一样)的;钻石制成的,镶有钻石的。**2**. 菱形的。~ *in the rough* = *rough* ~ **1**. 天然金刚石。**2**. 言行粗鲁而心地善良的人。**3**. 〔美俚〕初露光芒的设想。*black ~s* 黑金刚石;煤。*a small* ~ 一副方块同花牌中最小的牌。~ ***cut*** ~ 以强制强,硬碰硬,棋逢对手。~ ***of the first water*** 最好的钻石;第一流人物。~**back** *a*. 菱纹背的。~ **drill** 金刚锥。~ **field** 钻石产地。~ **jubilee** [**anniversary**] 60(或 75)周年纪念。~**-point** *a*. 有钻石尖的;用有钻石尖的工具制作的。~ **point 1**. 钻石刻刀。**2**. 【交】铁轨菱形交叉处。~ **snake** 菱纹蛇。~ **spar** 刚石,钢玉。**D- State** 美国 Delaware 州的别名。~ **wedding** 钻石婚,结婚 60(或 75)周年纪念。~**-wise** *ad*. 成菱形。

di·a·mon·dif·er·ous [ˌdaiəmənˈdifərəs; ˏdaɪəmənˋdɪfərəs] *a*. 产钻石的。

Di·an·(n)a [daiˈænə; daɪˋænə] *n*. 黛安娜〔女子名〕。

Di·an·a [daiˈænə; daɪˋænə] *n*. **1**. 【罗神】戴安娜(月亮和狩猎的女神)。**2**. 〔诗〕月。**3**. 女猎人;善骑的女人;女独身主义者。

di·an·drous [daiˈændrəs; daɪˋændrəs] *a*. 【植】具有两雄蕊的。

di·a·no·et·ic [ˌdaiənəuˈetik; ˏdaɪənoˋɛtɪk] *a*. 逻辑推理的,从逻辑推理出发的;非直觉的。

di·an·thus [daiˈænθəs; daɪˋænθəs] *n*. 石竹属植物〔如麝香石竹(康乃馨),美国石竹等〕。

di·a·pa·son [ˌdaiəˈpeisn, -ˈpeizn; ˏdaɪəˋpesn, -ˋpezn] *n*. **1**. 和声;旋律。**2**. 全声域;全音域。**3**. 有管风琴的主要音栓。**4**. 音叉。**5**. 领域;范围。

di·a·pause [ˈdaiəˌpɔːz; ˋdaɪəˏpɔz] *n*. 【生】滞育〔指某些昆虫的发育停滞〕。

di·a·pe·de·sis [ˌdaiəpiˈdiːsis; ˏdaɪəpɪˋdisɪs] *n*. 【医】血细胞渗出。

di·a·per [ˈdaiəpə; ˋdaɪəpɚ] **I** *n*. **1**. 菱形花样;织成的菱形花纹。**2**. 【建】菱形格子。**3**. 菱纹麻布;手巾。**4**. (婴儿)尿布。**II** *vt*. **1**. 用尿布衬上。**2**. 用菱形花纹装饰。~ *cover* 衬尿布的橡皮布。

di·aph·a·nous [daiˈæfənəs; daɪˋæfənəs] *a*. **1**. 半透明的。**2**. 朦胧的,飘渺的;模糊不清的。~ *cloth* 半透明的布料。

di·a·phone [ˈdaiəfəun; ˋdaɪəˏfon] *n*. 【语】类音〔如 half, 读 [hæf; hæf] 或 [hɑːf; hɑf]〕。

di·a·pho·re·sis [ˌdaiəfəˈriːsis; ˏdaɪəfəˋrisɪs] *n*. (大量)发汗,出汗。

di·a·pho·ret·ic [ˌdaiəfəˈretik; ˏdaɪəfəˋrɛtɪk] *a*., *n*. 发汗的;发汗剂。

di·a·phragm [ˈdaiəfræm; ˋdaɪəˏfræm] *n*. **1**. 隔膜,膜。**2**. 【物】光圈,光阑。**3**. 【机】隔板。**4**. 【解】横隔膜,膈。**5**. (电话机等的)振动膜。**6**. (避孕用)子宫帽。**-mat·ic** [ˌdaiəfrægˈmætik; ˏdaɪəfrægˋmætɪk] *a*. 膈的,膈膜的。

di·aph·y·sis [daiˈæfisis; daɪˋæfəsɪs] *n*. (*pl*. **-ses** [-siːz; -ˏsiz])【解】骨干〔指长骨的中间部分〕。

dia·pos·i·tive [ˌdaiəˈpɔzitiv; ˏdaɪəˋpɑzətɪv] *n*. 透明的照相正片(如幻灯片)。

di·ar·chi·al [daiˈɑːkiəl; daɪˋɑkɪəl] *a*. 二人执政的,两头政治的。

di·arch·y [ˈdaiɑːki; ˋdaɪɑrkɪ] *n*. 两头政治。

di·ar·i·al [daiˈɛəriəl; daɪˋɛrɪəl] *a*. 日记的;日记体的。

di·a·rist [ˈdaiərist; ˋdaɪərɪst] *n*. 记日记的人。

di·a·ris·tic [ˌdaiəˈristik; ˏdaɪəˋrɪstɪk] *a*. 日记体的。

di·a·rize, di·a·rise [ˈdaiəraiz; ˋdaɪəˏraɪz] *vi*. 记日记。— *vt*. 把…记入日记。

di·ar·rh(o)e·a [ˌdaiəˈriə; ˏdaɪəˋriə] *n*. 【医】腹泻。*have* ~ 下痢,泻肚子。**-rh(o)e·al** [-əl; -əl], **-rh(o)e·ic** [ˌdaiəˈriːik; ˏdaɪəˋriɪk], **-rh(o)et·ic** [ˌdaiəˈretik; ˏdaɪəˋrɛtɪk] *a*.

di·ar·thro·sis [ˌdaiɑːˈθrəusis; ˏdaɪɑrˋθrosɪs] *n*. (*pl*. **-ses** [-siːz; -siz])【解】动关节。

di·a·ry [ˈdaiəri; ˋdaɪərɪ] *n*. 日记,日志;日记簿。*a pocket* ~ 袖珍日记。*keep a* ~ 记日记。

Di·as·po·ra [daiˈæspərə; daɪˋæspərə] *n*. **1**. 犹太人的分散;分散各地的犹太人;犹太人散居的地方。**2**. 〔d-〕(同一起源的人民的)分散,散居。

di·a·spore [ˈdaiəˌspɔː; ˋdaɪəˏspɔr] *n*. 【矿】水铝石。

di·a·stase [ˈdaiəsteis; ˋdaɪəˏstes] *n*. 【生化】淀粉(糖化)酶。**-sta·tic** [ˌdaiəˈstætik; ˏdaɪəˋstætɪk] *a*.

di·as·ta·sis [daiˈæstəsis; daɪˋæstəsɪs] *n*. 【医】**1**. (骨骼等的)脱离,分离。**2**. 心舒张后期。

di·a·stem [ˈdaiəˌstem; ˋdaɪəˏstɛm] *n*. 【地】(沉积物沉积的)小间断。

di·a·ste·ma [ˌdaiəˈstiːmə; ˏdaɪəˋstimə] *n*. (*pl*. **-ste·ma·ta** [-tə; -tə])【齿】间隙,齿隙。**-mat·ic** [-stiˈmætik; -stɪˋmætɪk] *a*.

di·as·ter [daiˈæstə; daɪˋæstɚ] *n*. 【生】(有丝分裂的)双星体,双星期。**-tral** *a*.

di·as·to·le [daiˈæstəli; daɪˋæstəli] *n*. **1**. 【生理】(心)舒张;心舒张期。**2**. 【诗】音节延长。**-tolic** [ˌdaiəˈstɔlik; ˏdaɪəˋstɑlɪk] *a*.

di·as·tro·phism [daiˈæstrəfizəm; daɪˋæstrəˏfɪzəm] *n*. 地壳的变动;(一般的)变形,变动。

di·a·tes·sa·ron [ˌdaiəˈtesərən; ˏdaɪəˋtɛsəˏrɑn] *n*. (由四福音书改编成的)一览福音书。

di·a·ther·mal [ˌdaiəˈθəːməl; ˏdaɪəˋθɝməl] *a*. 【物】透热(辐射)的。

di·a·ther·man·cy [ˌdaiəˈθəːmənsi; ˏdaɪəˋθɝmənsɪ] *n*. 【物】透热性。

di·a·ther·ma·nous [ˌdaiəˈθəːmənəs; ˏdaɪəˋθɝmənəs] *a*. 【物】透热的。

di·a·ther·mia [ˌdaiəˈθəːmiə; ˏdaɪəˋθɝmɪə] *n*. 【医】透热疗法。

di·a·ther·mic [ˌdaiəˈθəːmik; ˏdaɪəˋθɝmɪk] *a*. **1**. 有关透热(疗)法的。**2**. 透热的。

di·a·ther·mize [ˌdaiəˈθəːmaiz; ˏdaɪəˋθɝmaɪz] *vt*. 施透热法。

di·a·therm·y, di·a·ther·mi·a [ˈdaiəθəːmi, ˌdaiəˈθəːmiə; ˋdaɪəθɝmɪ, ˋdaɪəˋθɝmɪə] *n*. 透热(疗)法。

di·ath·e·sis [daiˈæθisis; daɪˋæθɪsɪs] ***n.*** 【医】(易患某种疾病的)素质,体质。*tuberculous* ~ 易患结核病的体质。**-a·thet·ic** [ˌdaiəˈθetik; ˏdaɪəˋθɛtɪk] ***a.***

di·a·tom [ˈdaiətəm; ˋdaɪətəm] ***n.*** 【植】硅藻,矽藻。

di·a·to·ma·ceous [ˌdaiətəˈmeiʃəs; ˏdaɪətəˋmeʃəs] ***a.*** (含)硅[矽]藻的。~ *earth* 硅[矽]藻土。

di·a·tom·ic [ˌdaiəˈtɔmik; ˏdaɪəˋtɑmɪk] ***a.*** 【化】双原子的。~ *acid* 二价酸。

di·at·om·ite [daiˈætəmait; daɪˋætəˏmaɪt] ***n.*** 硅藻土,矽藻土。

di·a·ton·ic [ˌdaiəˈtɔnik; ˏdaɪəˋtɑnɪk] ***a.*** 【乐】全音阶的。*the* ~ *scale* 全音阶,自然音阶。

di·a·tribe [ˈdaiətraib; ˋdaɪəˏtraɪb] ***n.*** 恶骂;酷评。

di·at·ro·pism [daiˈætrəpizəm; daɪˋætrəpɪzəm] ***n.*** 【植】斜屈性。**-pic** [ˌdaiəˈtrɔpik; ˏdaɪəˋtrɑpɪk] ***a.***

di·a·ze·pam [ˌdaiəˈzepem; ˏdaɪəˋzɛpɛm] ***n.*** 【药】苯甲二氮䓬〔一种镇静安眠药〕。

di·a·zin(e) [ˈdaiəziːn, daiˈæzin; ˋdaɪəzin, daɪˋæzɪn] ***n.*** 【化】二嗪,二氮(杂)苯。~ *colours* 二嗪染料。

di·az·i·non [daiˈæzinɔn; daɪˋæzɪnɑn] ***n.*** 二嗪农(农药)。

di·a·zo [daiˈæzəu; daɪˋæzo] ***a.*** 【化】重氮基的。~ **colours** 重氮染料。

di·az·o·am·i·no [daiˌæzəuəˈmiːnəu, daiˌeizəu-; daɪˏæzoəˋmino, daɪˏezo-] ***a.*** 【化】重氮氨基的。

di·a·zo·ni·um [ˌdaiəˈzəuniəm; ˏdaɪəˋzonɪəm] ***a.*** 重氮(化)的。

di·az·o·tize [daiˈæzətaiz; daɪˋæzəˏtaɪz] ***vt.*** 【化】使形成重氮化合物,使重氮化。**-za·tion** [-ˌæzətaiˈzeiʃən; -ˏæzətaɪˋzeʃən] ***n.*** 重氮化(作用)。

dib[1] [dib; dɪb] ***n.*** **1.** (羊等的)关节骨,羊拐子;〔*pl.*〕把关节骨当球玩的儿戏。**2.** (打牌用的)骨制筹码。**3.** 〔*pl.*〕〔美〕要求,权利,保留权。**4.** 〔俚〕(小额的)钱。***have*** ~***s on*** 对…有权利,对…有要求(*I have* ~*s on that piece of cake*. 我要吃那块蛋糕)。

dib[2] [dib; dɪb] ***vi.*** (***dib·bed***, ***dib·bing***) = dap.

Di·bai [diˈbai; dɪˋbaɪ] ***n.*** = Dubai.

di·bas·ic [daiˈbeisik; daɪˋbesɪk] ***a.*** 【化】二碱价的,二元的;二代的。~ *acid* 二元酸。~ *ester* 二价酸酯。~ *salt* 二代盐。

dib·ber [ˈdibə; ˋdɪbɚ] ***n.*** = dibble.

dib·ble[1] [ˈdibl; ˋdɪbl] **I** ***vt.*** **1.** 用小锹在(地)上掘穴。**2.** 穴植,点播。— ***vi.*** 使用点播器;点播。**II** ***n.*** 掘穴具,点播器。~ *in potatoes* 穴播马铃薯。

dib·ble[2] [ˈdibl; ˋdɪbl] ***vi.*** **1.** = dib. **2.** = dable.

dib·buk, dyb·buk [ˈdibək; ˋdɪbək] ***n.*** (犹太民间传说)阴魂附体。

di·bran·chi·ate [daiˈbræŋkiːit; daɪˋbræŋkɪɪt] ***a.*** 【动】二鳃目的,属于二鳃目的。

di·car·box·yl·ic [daiˌkaːbɔkˈsilik; daɪˏkarbɑkˋsɪlɪk] ***a.*** 【化】二羧基的。~ *acid* 二羧酸。

di·cast [ˈdikæst, ˈdaikæst; ˋdɪkæst, ˋdaɪkæst] ***n.*** (古雅典法庭的)审理官。

DICBM = detection (of) intercontinental ballistic missile (system) 洲际弹道导弹的探测(系统)。

dice[1] [dais; daɪs] **I** ***n.*** 〔本为 die[2]的复数;但在口语中亦可作单数用。其复数形为 ~(s)〕**1.** 骰子;掷骰子。**2.** 小方块。*cut potatoes into* ~ 把马铃薯切成丁。***play at*** ~ 掷骰子。***no*** ~ 〔俚〕反对,拒绝;失败(*As for the rest, no* ~. 其余各人全都失败[落空]了)。**II** ***vt.*** **1.** 把…切成骰子形[小方块],把…切成丁。**2.** 掷骰子赌…。— ***vi.*** 掷骰子。~ ***away*** 赌输。

dice[2] [dais; daɪs] **I** ***n.*** 〔美俚〕(赛车名次的)激烈争夺。**II** ***vi.*** (赛车)争夺名次。

di·cen·tra [daiˈsentrə; daɪˋsɛntrə] ***n.*** 荷包牡丹属植物〔如:荷包牡丹和兜状荷包牡丹〕。

di·ceph·a·lous [daiˈsefələs; daɪˋsɛfələs] ***a.*** (某些怪胎的)有双头的。

dic·er [ˈdaisə; ˋdaɪsɚ] ***n.*** **1.** 掷骰子的人,赌钱人,赌徒。**2.** (食物)切丁机。**3.** 〔俚〕帽子(尤指圆顶礼帽)。

dic·ey [ˈdaisi; ˋdaɪsɪ] ***a.*** 〔主英口〕危险的,冒险的;不确实的。

dich- = dicho-.

di·cha·si·um [daiˈkeiziəm, -ʒiː-; daɪˋkezɪəm, -ʒɪ-] ***n.*** (*pl.* ***-si·a*** [-ə; -ə])【植】二歧聚伞花序,二歧式。

di·chlo·ride, di·chlo·rid [daiˈklɔːraid, -rid; daɪˋklɔraɪd, -rɪd] ***n.*** 【化】二氯化物。

di·chlo·ro·di·phen·yl·tri·chlor·o·eth·ane [daiˈklɔːrəu daiˌfenil traiˌklɔːrəuˈeθein; daɪˏkloro daɪˏfɛnɪl traɪˏkloroˋɛθen]【化】滴滴涕,二氯二苯三氯乙烷。DDT。

dicho- *comb. f.* 二分,分为二:*dicho*tomy.

di·chog·a·my [daiˈkɔgəmi; daɪˋkɑgəmɪ] ***n.*** 【植】(为防止自花授粉而)雌雄[蕊]异熟。**-a·mous, -cho·gam·ic** [ˌdaikəˈgæmik; ˏdaɪkəˋgæmɪk] ***a.***

di·chon·dra [daiˈkɔndrə; daɪˋkɑndrə] ***n.*** 旋花科葵苔属植物。

di·chot·o·mic [ˌdikəˈtɔmik; ˏdɪkəˋtɑmɪk] ***a.*** = dichotomous.

di·chot·o·mize [daiˈkɔtəmaiz; daɪˋkɑtəˏmaɪz] ***vt.***, ***vi.*** 二分,对分,叉分;(把…)分成两叉。~ *the animal world into vertebrate and invertebrate* 把动物界分为脊椎动物和无脊椎动物。

di·chot·o·mous [daiˈkɔtəməs; daɪˋkɑtəməs] ***a.*** **1.** 两分的。**2.** 对生的;二歧的;二叉的。~ *branching* 叉状分枝。**-ly** ***ad.***

di·chot·o·my [daiˈkɔtəmi; daɪˋkɑtəmɪ] ***n.*** **1.** 二等分。**2.** 【天】弦月,半月。**3.** 【植】对生;二歧式;二叉分枝式。**4.** 【逻】二分法。*a* ~ *into the good and the evil* 善与恶的一分为二。

di·chro·ic, di·chro·it·ic [daiˈkrəuik, -itik; daɪˋkroɪk, -ɪtɪk] ***a.*** 有二色的。~ *crystal* 有二色的水晶。

di·chro·ism [ˈdaikrəuizəm; ˋdaɪkroˏɪzəm] ***n.*** **1.** 【物】二向色性。**2.** 【物】二色性。

di·chro·mate [daiˈkrəumeit; daɪˋkromet] ***a.*** 【化】重铬酸盐。

di·chro·mat·ic [ˌdaikrəˈmætik; ˏdaɪkroˋmætɪk] ***a.*** **1.** 现二色的,二色性的。**2.** 【生】二色变异的。**3.** 【医】二色性色盲的。

di·chro·ma·tism [daiˈkrəumətizəm; daɪˋkromәˏtɪzəm] ***n.*** **1.** 【物】二色(性)。**2.** 【生】二色变异。**3.** 【医】(红、蓝、绿三色中只能辨别二色的)二色性色盲。

di·chro·mic [daiˈkrəumik; daɪˋkromɪk] ***a.*** 重铬的。~ *acid* 重铬酸。

di·chro·scope, di·chro·o·scope [ˈdaikrəˌskəup, daiˈkrəuəˌskəup; ˋdaɪkrəˏskop, daɪˋkroəˏskop] 二(向)色镜。

dic·ing [ˈdaisiŋ; ˋdaɪsɪŋ] ***n.*** **1.** 掷骰子。**2.** (皮面的)菱形花纹。*a* ~ *house* 赌场。

dick [dik; dɪk] ***n.*** **1.** 〔口〕家伙。**2.** 〔俚〕皮围裙。**3.** 〔俚〕誓言,声明。**4.** 〔美俚〕侦探。**5.** 标准。*take one's* ~ 发誓。***up to*** ~ 合乎标准。

Dick·ens [ˈdikinz; ˋdɪkɪnz] ***n.*** **1.** 迪肯斯〔姓氏〕。**2.** **Charles** ~ 狄更斯〔1812—1870,英国小说家〕。

dick·ens [ˈdikinz; ˋdɪkɪnz] ***n.*** **1.** = devil, deuce. **2.** 困难。*What the* ~ *is it*? 究竟是什么? *The* ~! 哎呀! 糟了! 混账。***as the*** ~ 真是,实在是(*He is noble as the* ~. 他真高尚)。

Dick·en·son [ˈdikinsn; ˋdɪkɪnsn] ***n.*** 迪肯森〔姓氏〕。

dick·er[1] [ˈdikə; ˋdɪkɚ] ***n.*** 【商】十;〔特指〕十张皮革。

dick·er[2] [ˈdikə; ˋdɪkɚ] **I** ***n.*** 〔美〕**1.** 小生意;物物交换;讨价还价。**2.** 【美政】谈判,交涉。**II** ***vi.*** 做小生意,用物换物;讨价还价。

dick·ey[1] [ˈdiki; ˋdɪkɪ] ***n.*** 〔俚〕**1.** (公)驴。**2.** 小鸟(=

~-bird)。3. (只有前胸的)假衬衫,小孩围嘴。4. (马车的)车夫座位;(随员坐的)马车后座。

dick·ey² [ˈdiki; ˋdɪkɪ] *a*. 〔俚〕(脚)站不稳的,软弱的;靠不住的;可怜的。*It's all ~ with him*. 他完全靠不住了[无希望了]。*The table was in a ~ state*. 桌子不行了。

dick·eybird [ˈdikibəːd; ˋdɪkɪˏbɝd] *n*. 〔儿〕小鸟。

di·cli·nous [daiˈklainəs; daɪˋklaɪnəs] *a*. 【植】雌雄异花的,单性的。**-nism** [ˈdaiklainizəm; ˋdaɪklaɪnɪzəm], **-ny** [-ni; -nɪ] *n*.

di·cot [ˈdaikɔt; ˋdaɪkɑt] *n*. 双子叶植物(= dicotyledon)。

di·cot·y·le·don [daiˌkɔtiˈliːdən; ˏdaɪkɑtlˋidn] *n*. 双子叶植物。**-ous** *a*.

di·cou·ma·rin, di·cou·ma·rol [daiˈkuːmərin, daiˈkuːmərəl; daɪˋkumərɪn, daɪˋkumərɑl] *n*. 双香豆素〔用作抗凝血药〕。

D

di·crot·ic [daiˈkrɔtik; daɪˋkrɑtɪk] *a*. 【医】重脉的,二重脉搏的。**-ism** *n*. 重脉。

dict. = dictation; dictator; dictionary.

dic·ta [ˈdiktə; ˋdɪktə] *n*. dictum 的复数。

Dic·ta·belt [ˈdiktəbelt; ˋdɪktəbɛlt] *n*. 〔亦作 d-〕(口述录音机或录音电话机上使用的)口述录音带,电话录音带。

dic·ta·phone [ˈdiktəfəun; ˋdɪktəˏfon] *n*. 【商标】录音机。

dic·tate [dikˈteit; ˋdɪktet] **I** *vt*. 1. (将信稿等内容向某人)口授,(口述文句等叫人)听写 (*sth. to*)。2. 命令,支配。~ *some letters to a secretary* 口述几封信叫秘书笔录下来。*The teacher ~d the phrase to the class*. 老师让全班同学听写这个短语。~ *peace terms to a conquered enemy* 向被征服的敌人提出和谈条件。— *vi*. 1. 口述,听写。2. 命令,支配,摆布。*I will not be ~d to*. 我不愿受人指挥。**II** [ˈdikteit; ˋdɪktet] *n*. 〔常 *pl*.〕命令,指挥,指令,意旨。*the ~s of fancy* 时兴的趋向。*the ~s of conscience* 良心的驱使。

dic·ta·tion [dikˈteiʃən; dɪkˋteʃən] *n*. 1. 默写,听写;口授。2. 命令,指令,指挥。

dic·ta·tor [dikˈteitə; dɪkˋtetɚ] *n*. 1. 发号施令者,(特指)独裁者;专政者。2. 口授者。3. 〔古罗马〕执政官。

dic·ta·to·ri·al [ˌdiktəˈtɔːriəl; ˏdɪktəˋtorɪəl] *a*. 执政者的;专政的,独裁的;傲然的,唯我独尊的。**-ly** *ad*. **-ness** *n*.

dic·ta·tor·ship [dikˈteitəʃip; dɪkˋtetɚˏʃɪp] *n*. 1. 执政者的职位[任期]。2. 专政,独裁。3. 独裁权。

dic·ta·to·ry [ˈdiktətəri; ˋdɪktəˏtorɪ] *a*. = dictatorial.

dic·ta·tress [dikˈteitris; dɪkˋtetrɪs] *n*. 女独裁者。

dic·tion [ˈdikʃən; ˋdɪkʃən] *n*. 1. 用语的选择;措辞,用字。2. 〔美〕(讲话、唱歌的)发音法,朗诵法。*good* [*faulty*] ~ 确切的[错误的]说法。*bad* [*poor*] ~ 不妥当的措辞。*a Latin* ~ 拉丁用语。

dic·tion·a·ry [ˈdikʃənəri; ˋdɪkʃənˏɛrɪ] *n*. 字典,词典;【自】代码字典。*consult a* ~ 查阅词典。*a walking* [*living*] ~ 活字典,知识渊博的人。*a ~ of English* 英语词典。~ **catalog(ue)** (图书馆按字母顺序编排的)词书体书目。~ **English** [**style**] 古板的英语[体裁]。

Dic·to·graph [ˈdiktəgrɑːf; ˋdɪktəgræf] *n*. 【商标】窃听器;电话录音器;室内传话器。

dic·tum [ˈdiktəm; ˋdɪktəm] *n*. (*pl*. ~*s*, *-ta* [-tə; -tə]) 1. 断言,断定。2. 名言,格言。3. 【法】法官的意见。

dic·ty [ˈdikti; ˋdɪktɪ] *a*. 〔美俚〕1. 高级的,上等的。2. 傲慢的;势利的。

di·cu·ma·rol [daiˈkuːmərəl; daɪˋkumərəl] *n*. 【化】血液凝固防止剂。

di·cy·an [daiˈsaiən; daɪˋsaɪən] *n*. 【化】1. 氰。2. 二氰(基)。

did [did; dɪd] do 的过去式。

di·dact [ˈdaidækt; ˋdaɪdækt] *n*. 说教者。

di·dac·tic [diˈdæktik, daiˈd-; dɪˋdæktɪk, daɪˋd-] *a*. 教导的;启发人的;说教的。*a ~ manner* 启发人的态度。**-ti·cal·ly** *ad*. 在教导上;启发式地。**-tic·ism** *n*. 教导法;教师的品质;启发。

di·dac·tics [diˈdæktiks, dai-; dɪˋdæktɪks, daɪ-] *n*. 教授法,教学法。

di·dap·per [ˈdaidæpə; ˋdaɪdæpɚ] *n*. = dabchick.

did·dle [ˈdidl; ˋdɪdl] *vt*. 〔口〕1. 骗(钱等)。2. 浪费(时间)。3. 快速摇动。— *vi*. 前后移动,前后摇摆。

Di·de·rot [ˈdiːdərəu; ˋdidəˏro] *n*. 1. 狄特罗〔姓氏〕。2. **Denis** ~ 〔1713—1784,法国哲学家,百科全书编者〕。

did·n't [ˈdidnt; ˋdɪdnt] = did not.

di·do [ˈdaidəu; ˋdaɪdo] *n*. (*pl*. ~*es*, ~*s*) 〔美口〕〔常 *pl*.〕胡闹,开玩笑。*cut* (*up*) ~*s* 乱开玩笑。

Di·do [ˈdaidəu; ˋdaɪdo] *n*. 传说中迦太基 (Carthage) 的建国者和女王。

didst [didst; dɪdst] 〔古、诗〕(thou 后用的) did.

di·dy [ˈdaidi; ˋdaɪdɪ] *n*. 〔口〕尿布。

di·dym·i·um [daiˈdimiəm; daɪˋdɪmɪəm] *n*. 镨钕混合物。

did·y·mous [ˈdidiməs; ˋdɪdəməs] *a*. 【植、动】双生的,孪生的。

di·dyn·a·mous [daiˈdinəməs; daɪˋdɪnəməs] *a*. 【植】二强雄蕊的。

die¹ [dai; daɪ] *vi*. (*died*; *dy·ing*) 1. 死。2. 灭亡,消灭;熄灭;枯死,凋落。3. 漠然不受影响,感觉不到 (*to*)。4. 泄气。5. 〔口〕渴望,盼望[参看 dying]。6. 【棒球】出局。7. 〔美口〕好得要死,妙极了。*I thought I should have ~d*. 要命要命〔大笑后口吻〕。*The secret ~d with him*. 秘密跟他同时埋葬了〔至死未曾吐露秘密〕。*My heart ~d within me*. 我疲倦死了。~ **a beggar** 穷困潦倒而死。~ **a dog's death** 死得可鄙。~ **a glorious death** 死得光荣,壮烈牺牲。~ **a martyr** 杀身成仁,殉道,殉教。~ **an unnatural** [**untimely**] **death** 死于非命;暴卒。~ **at one's post** 殉职。~ **away** (风、声音等)渐息,渐弱;渐渐凋落,枯萎。~ **back** 【植】顶枯;枯萎(根未死)。~ **by violence** 凶死。~ **daily** 虽生犹死;遭受精神的痛苦。~ **down** = ~ away. ~ **for one's country** 殉国,为国牺牲。~ **from** (*a wound*) 因伤致死。~ **game** 奋战而死,至死不屈。~ **hard** 壮烈牺牲;难断气;难绝灭。~ **in harness** 至死不倦,积劳而死,殉职。~ **in one's bed** = ~ **a natural death** 寿终正寝,老死,好死。~ **in one's shoes** [**boots**] 1. 横死;被绞死。2. 至死犹劳累不倦。~ **in the last ditch** 奋斗到死。~ **of** 因…而死。~ **of age** 老死。~ **of hunger** 饿死。~ **off** 一个一个死去;顺次枯死。~ **old** [**young**] 寿终[(夭)折]。~ **on the air** (钟声等)渐渐消失。~ **on the vine** (计划等)失败,中途夭折。~ **out** 消灭,死绝。~ **standing by** 【美剧】演出无人喝彩。~ **the death** 毙命;受死刑。~ **to self** 舍己,无我。~ **to shame** 死不要脸,恬不知耻。~ **unto sin** 不受罪恶的摆布。**It is to die**. 〔美口〕好得要死! 棒极了! **Never say** ~! 不要气馁! 不要悲观! ~-**in** *n*. (以死亡相威胁的)死亡抗议,死亡示威。~-**up** *n*. 1. (因天灾等而造成的)牲畜的大批死亡。2. 大批死亡的牲畜。

die² [dai; daɪ] *n*. (*pl*. *dice* [dais; daɪs]) 1. 骰子;骰子状物;一粒骰子。2. (*pl*. *dies* [daiz; daɪz]) 钢型,硬模;冲模;螺丝模;拉丝模。3. 【建】(柱墩的)墩身。~ *casting* 模铸。**straight** [**level**, **true**] **as a** ~ 笔直的,平坦的;决无错误的。**The** ~ **is cast**. 事已决定,事已至此,无可翻悔。**upon a** [**the**] ~ 在危急存亡关头,有关…的存亡。~-**cast** *a*. 以印模铸造的。~ **maker** 雕刻印模者。

die-away [ˈdaiəwei; ˋdaɪəˏwe] *a*. 没精神的,颓丧的,忧郁的。*a ~ look* 无精打采的样子。

die·back [ˈdaiˌbæk; ˋdaɪˏbæk] *n*. 【植】顶枯病,顶死。

dieb. alt. = 〔拉〕diebus alternis (处方用语)每隔一日 (= every other day).

dieb. secund. = 〔拉〕diebus secundis (处方用语)每两日 (= every second day).

dieb. tert. = 〔拉〕diebus tertius (处方用语)每三日 (= every third day).

di·e·cious [daiˈiːʃəs; daɪˋiʃəs] ***a***. = dioecious.

dief·fen·bach·i·a [ˌdiːfnˈbækiə; ˏdifn̩ˋbækɪə] ***n***. 花叶万年青属植物。

die-hard [ˈdaihɑːd; ˋdaɪhɑrd] **I** ***n***. **1.** 拼死抵抗的人,顽强的人。**2.**【政】顽固[保守]分子,死顽固。**II** ***a***. 极右派的,死硬派的。

diel·drin [ˈdiːldrin; ˋdildrɪn] ***n***.【化】狄氏剂,氧桥氯甲桥萘〔一种长效杀虫剂〕。

di·e·lec·tric, di·e·lec·tri·cal [ˌdaiiˈlektrik(əl); ˏdaɪəˋlɛktrɪk(əl)] **I** ***a***. 非传导性的,绝缘的,介电的。**II** ***n***. 电介质,电介体,绝缘体。~ **constant** 介电常数,介电恒量,电容率。

Dien Bien Phu [ˈdjen ˈbjen ˈfuː; ˋdjɛn ˋbjɛn ˋfu] 奠边府〔越南城镇〕。

di·en·ceph·a·lon [ˌdaienˈsefələn; ˏdaɪɛnˋsɛfəˏlɑn] ***n***.【解】间脑。**-ce·phal·ic** [-siˈfælik; -sɪˋfælɪk] ***a***.

di·er·e·sis [daiˈiərəsis; daɪˋɛrəsɪs] ***n***. (*pl*. ***-ses*** [-siːz; -siz]) = diaeresis.

Di·es [ˈdaiiːz; ˋdaɪiz] ***n***. (*sing*., *pl*.) 〔L.〕日。~ ***I·rae*** [ˈaiəriː; ˋaɪəri] **1.** 最后审判日。**2.** 由~ Irae 开头的拉丁文赞美诗。***dies non*** [ˈnɔn; ˋnɑn] **1.** 停审日,休庭日。**2.** (须扣除不算的)假日。

Die·sel [ˈdiːzəl; ˋdizəl] ***n***. **1.** [d-] = ~ engine [motor] 柴油机,内燃机。~ *oil* 柴油。**2. R.** ~ 狄赛尔(1858—1913),德国柴油机发明者。

die·sel·ize [ˈdiːzəlaiz; ˋdizl̩ˏaɪz] ***vt***. 用柴油发动机装备(轮船)。

die·sink·er [ˈdaisiŋkə; ˋdaɪsɪŋkɚ] ***n***. 制模工。

di·e·sis [ˈdaiəsis; ˋdaɪəsɪs] ***n***. (*pl*. ***-ses*** [-ˌsiːz; -ˏsiz]) 双剑号(‡) (= double dagger).

die·stock [ˈdaiˌstɔk; ˋdaɪˏstɑk] ***n***. (切削螺纹用的)板牙扳手,板牙架,螺丝绞板。

di·es·trum, di·es·trus [daiˈestrəm, -trəs; daɪˋɛstrəm, -trəs] ***n***.【生】间(动)情期。**-trous** [-trəs; -trəs] ***a***.

di·et[1] [ˈdaiət; ˋdaɪət] **I** ***n***. **1.** 饮食,食物;规定的饮食。**2.** 日常看[听]的东西,日常做的事情。*a subsistence* ~ 维持健康所必需的最少食量。*a vegetable* [*meat*] ~ 素[肉]食。**II** ***vt***. 给与(病人)规定的饮食。~ *oneself on vegetables* 吃素。— ***vi***. 吃规定的饮食,忌嘴,忌口。~ **pill** 〔美口〕减肥丸。**-er** (旨在减肥的)节食者,吃规定饮食的人。

di·et[2] [ˈdaiət; ˋdaɪət] ***n***. 〔常 D-〕(丹麦、日本等的)议会,国会。

di·et·a·ry [ˈdaiətəri; ˋdaɪətərɪ] **I** ***a***. 饮食的;规定食物的。**II** ***n***. 规定的食物;规定的食量;食谱。*a* ~ *cure* 食物疗法。

di·e·tet·ic, die·tet·i·cal [ˌdaiəˈtetik(əl); ˏdaɪəˋtɛtɪk(əl)] ***a***. 饮食的,营养的;(特指限制糖分的)特定饮食的。**-ly** ***ad***. **-tet·ics** ***n***. 饮食学,营养学。**-ti·tion, -ti·cian** [ˌdaiəˈtiʃən; ˏdaɪəˋtɪʃən] ***n***. 饮食学家,营养学家。

di·eth·yl [daiˈeθil; daɪˋɛθəl] ***n***.【化】二乙基的。~ **ether**【化】二乙醚。~ **ketone**【化】二乙酮,戊酮。

di·eth·yl·stil·b(o)es·trol [daiˌeθilstilˈbestrəul; daɪˏɛθɪlstɪlˋbɛstrol] ***n***.【药】己烯雌酚〔雌性激素的代用品〕。

Dieu et mon droit [ˈdjɔ ei məun ˈdrɔit; ˋdjɔ e monˋdrɔɪt] 〔F.〕上有天帝,我有权利〔英王的座右铭〕。

dif- *pref*. = dis-[1].

diff. = difference; different; differential.

dif·fer [ˈdifə; ˋdɪfɚ] ***vi***. **1.** 不同,不一样,不一致,有差别。**2.** 意见不同[不合]。~ *in opinion* 意见不同。*I beg to* ~. 很抱歉,我不赞成。***agree to*** ~ 求同存异;彼此保留不同意见。~ ***from*** **1.** 和…不同,和…不一致。**2.** 和…意见不同(~ *from each other* 互异)。~ ***with*** 和…意见不同。

dif·fer·ence [ˈdifrəns; ˋdɪfərəns] **I** ***n***. **1.** 差异,差别。**2.** 不和,争论。**3.**【数】差,差额。**4.**【逻】特殊性。*There is no* ~ *between them*. 两者毫无差别。*the* ~ *of jetsam from flotsam* 弃货不同于浮货。*What* ~ *can it make*? 不是一样吗?*He is an artist with a* ~. 他是别具风格的艺术家。***distinction without*** ~ 无聊的区别。***make a*** ~ 发生差别;使…有差别;(结果等)是重要的,有关系[影响](*One false step will make a great* ~. 失之毫厘,谬以千里。*Don't let it make any* ~. 没关系。*make a* ~ *between A and B* 使甲乙有别,对甲乙不一样)。***pay*** [***meet***] ***the*** ~ 付差额金。***seek common ground while reserving*** ~***s*** 求同存异。***settle*** ~***s*** 调停。***split the*** ~ **1.** 折中,妥协。**2.** 均分剩下的东西。**II** ***vt***. 〔罕〕区别,使有差别。

dif·fer·ent [ˈdifrənt; ˋdɪfərənt] ***a***. **1.** 不同的,不一致的,有差别的。**2.** 各种的,各式各样的。**3.** 〔美〕异常的。*That is a* ~ *pair of shoes*. 那是另外一件事。***be*** ~ ***from*** 和…不同,和…有别。**-ly** ***ad***.

dif·fer·en·ti·a [ˌdifəˈrenʃiə; ˏdɪfəˋrɛnʃɪə] ***n***. (*pl*. ***-ti·ae*** [-ʃiiː; -ʃɪi]) **1.** 差异。**2.**【逻】(同类的东西中使这一种有别于另一种的)特殊性。

dif·fer·en·ti·a·ble [ˌdifəˈrenʃiəbl, -ʃə-; ˏdɪfəˋrɛnʃɪəbl, -ʃə-] ***a***. **1.** 可鉴别的。**2.**【数】可微分的。**-bil·i·ty** [difəˌrenʃiəˈbiliti; dɪfəˏrɛnʃɪəˋbɪlətɪ] ***n***.

dif·fer·en·ti·al [ˌdifəˈrenʃəl; ˏdɪfəˋrɛnʃəl] **I** ***a***. **1.** 差别的,区别的;特定的。**2.**【数】微分的。**3.**【物、机】差动的,差速的,差示的。**II** ***n***. **1.** (铁路不同路线之间为保持运输平衡而规定的)运费差。**2.** (同一行业中熟练工和非熟练工的)工资差别。**3.**【数】微分。**4.**【机】差动器。~ **blood count** 白血球分类计数。~ **calculus**【数】微分。~ **diagnosis**【医】鉴别诊断。~ **equation** 微分方程式。~ **duties** 特定[差别]关税。~ **gear** 差动齿轮。~ **medium** 鉴别性培养基。~ **pressure** 分压,不均匀压力。~ **rate** (铁路的)特定运费率。~ **thermometer** 差示温度计。**-ly** ***ad***.

dif·fer·en·ti·ate [ˌdifəˈrenʃieit; ˏdɪfəˋrɛnʃɪˏet] ***vt***. **1.** 使有差别,区别,划分,区分。**2.** 使分化,使变异。**3.**【数】求…的微分。~ *one thing from another* 使甲乙互异。— ***vi***. **1.** 产生差别。**2.** 区分,区别。**3.**【生】分化,变异。

dif·fer·en·ti·a·tion [ˌdifəˌrenʃiˈeiʃən; ˏdɪfəˏrɛnʃɪˋeʃən] ***n***. **1.** 差别,区别;区分,划分。**2.**【生】分化,变异。**3.**【地】(从共同的岩浆产生出不同的岩石的)分异作用。**4.**【数】微分法。

dif·fi·cile [ˈdifisiːl; ˋdɪfəˋsil] ***a***. 〔F.〕困难的;难对付的。

dif·fi·cult [ˈdifikəlt; ˋdɪfɪkəlt] ***a***. **1.** 困难的,(工作等)艰难的。**2.** 执拗的,顽固的。*a* ~ *disposition* 执拗的性情。~ *of access* 难接近。~ *to answer* 难答。

dif·fi·cul·ty [ˈdifikəlti; ˋdɪfəklˌtɪ] ***n***. **1.** 困难;难事,难局,逆境;障碍。**2.** 异议;争论,纠葛。**3.** 〔常 *pl*.〕财政困难,(经济)拮据。***be in difficulties*** 财政困难,经济拮据。***make a*** ~ 不同意,反对。***make*** [***raise***] ***difficulties*** 刁难。***make no*** ~ ***in*** (*granting the request*) 立即同意[应允]。***tide over difficulties*** 渡过难关。***with*** ~ 好容易才,千辛万苦才。***without*** ~ 容容易易就…,轻易。

dif·fi·dence [ˈdifidəns; ˋdɪfədəns] ***n***. **1.** 缺乏自信。**2.** 羞怯,腼腆;谦虚。**3.** 〔古〕疑惑,猜疑。*with nervous* ~ 提心吊胆地。*with seeming* ~ 假装着害羞。

dif·fi·dent [ˈdifidənt; ˋdɪfədənt] ***a***. **1.** 缺乏自信的。**2.** 羞怯的,胆怯的。*He is* ~ *of his success*. 他对成功缺乏信心。**-ly** ***ad***.

dif·flu·ent [ˈdifluənt; ˋdɪfluənt] ***a***. **1.** 流出性的,分流性的 (*opp*. confluent)。**2.** 溶解的;溶化的。~ *rivers*

D

分流河。-ence [-əns; -əns] *n*. 1. 流出;分流。2. 溶解,潮解。

dif·fract [di'frækt; dɪ'frækt] *vt*. 分解;【物】(波等)绕射,衍射。-tion *n*. 绕射,衍射(*diffraction grating* [*fringe*] 衍射光栅[条纹])。-tive *a*. 折射的,衍射的。

dif·fuse [di'fjuːz; dɪ'fjuz] I *vt*. 1. 使(水分)渗出;(使气体等)扩散,发散。2. 散布(谣言等);普及(教育);传播(知识)。3.【物】使(光)漫射。— *vi*. 1. 扩散;渗出。2. 传播;散布。3.【物】漫射。II [-s] *a*. 1. 四散的;散乱的。2. (文章等)冗长的,啰嗦的,铺张的。~ *nebula* 弥漫星云。~ *sound* 漫射声。-ly *ad*. -ness *n*.

dif·fus·er, dif·fu·sor [di'fjuːzə; dɪ'fjuzə] *n*. 1. 散布者,传播者。2.【物】(使光线均匀分布的)漫射体。3.【机】扩散器。

dif·fus·i·ble [di'fjuːzəbl; dɪ'fjuzəbl] *a*. 会扩散的,会散开的;弥漫性的。-bil·i·ty [diˌfjuːzə'biliti; dɪˌfjuzə'bɪlətɪ] *n*. 散播力,散布性,弥漫性;【物】扩散率。

dif·fu·sion [di'fjuːʒən; dɪ'fjuʒən] *n*. 1. 散布,发散。2. 传播,普及。3. 冗长。4.【化】渗滤。5.【物】扩散,漫射。*the ~ of knowledge* 知识的传播。~ *of speech* 演说的冗长。~ *of light* 光线的漫射。

dif·fu·sive [di'fjuːsiv; dɪ'fjusɪv] *a*. 1. 散布性的,扩散的。2. (奉承话等)啰啰嗦嗦的,冗长的。

dig [dig; dɪg] I *vt*. (*dug* [dʌg; dʌg], [古] *~ged*; *dug*, [古] *~ged*; *~ging*) 1. 挖,掘(土),凿(井等),采掘(山芋、矿物等)。2. 探究(*up*; *out*)。3. [口](把指尖等)戳进,插进,刺入(*into*; *in*)。4. [美俚]理解。5. [美俚]赞成;喜欢。6. [美俚]看,看到。— *vi*. 1. 挖土;开凿,掘进,挖穿(*in*; *through*; *under*)。2. 探究,发掘(*for*; *into*)。3. [美俚]苦学,苦干,钻研(*at*)。4. [俚]住。~ ***a pit for*** 挖陷阱(陷人)。~ ***deep*** [美俚]挖深;掏出来。~ ***down*** 1. 挖倒,挖下,挖去。2. 掏腰包。~ ***down into sb.'s mind*** 探察某人心理。~ ***in*** 1. 挖进,埋进(肥料等)。2. 戳进。3. 苦学,苦干。4. 坚持主张。5. 开始吃。6. = ~ oneself in. ~ [***poke***] (*a person*) ***in the ribs*** 用指头戳(某人)胸膛。~ ***into*** 1. 掘进。2. 钻研。3. 用掉,用去。4. 吃。~ ***oneself in*** 挖战壕防守。~ ***out*** 1. 挖出;查出(事实)。2. [美口]慌慌忙忙走开[逃走]。~ ***one's way*** 挖进(*in*; *into*),挖出(*out*),挖穿(*through*)。~ ***over*** 探掘。~ ***up*** 1. 开垦(荒地等);采掘(山芋等)。2. 查出;(偶然)发现,找到,得到。3. [美俚]出钱,捐助,支付。4. 挑起(~ *up the hatchet* 挑起战端)。II *n*. [口] 1. 一挖;一戳;一撞。2. 挖苦,讽刺(*at*)。3. [美口]刻苦钻研的学生。4. (考古的)挖掘,挖掘地点。5. [*pl*.][英口]学生宿舍,单身宿舍;住处。

dig. = digest.

dig·a·mist ['digəmist; 'dɪgəmɪst] *n*. 再婚者。

dig·a·my ['digəmi; 'dɪgəmɪ] *n*. 再婚。-mous [-məs; -məs] *a*. 再婚的。

di·gas·tric [dai'gæstrik; daɪ'gæstrɪk] I *a*.【解】二腹的;二腹肌的。II *n*. (下颚的)二腹肌。

di·gen·e·sis [dai'dʒenisis; daɪ'dʒɛnɪsɪs] *n*.【生】(有性生殖和无性生殖的)世代交替。

di·gest [di'dʒest, dai-; dɪ'dʒɛst, daɪ-] I *vt*. 1. 消化,助消化。2. 玩味,领会,体会(文意)。3. 容忍,忍受,甘受(侮辱等)。4. (系统地)整理;汇编(法律);摘要。5.【化】浸煮,煮解。— *vi*. 1. 消化。2.【化】浸煮。*This food ~s well* [*ill*]. 这食品易[难]消化。*This conduct is more than I can ~*. 这种行为我忍受不了。II ['daidʒest; 'daɪdʒɛst] *n*. 1. 文摘;摘要。2. 法律汇编; [the D-] 罗马法典[公元六世纪罗马皇帝查士丁尼命令汇编的罗马法典,共五十卷]。

di·gest·er [di'dʒestə, dai-; də'dʒɛstə, daɪ-] *n*. 1. 消化者。2. 助消化的药[食品]。3. 汇编者。4.【化】浸煮器;蒸煮锅。

di·gest·i·ble [di'dʒestəbl, dai-; də'dʒɛstəbl, daɪ-] *a*. 1. 易消化的。2. 可摘要的。-bil·i·ty [diˌdʒesti'biliti; dəˌdʒɛstə'bɪlətɪ] *n*. 消化性[率]。

di·ges·tion [di'dʒestʃən, dai-; də'dʒɛstʃən, daɪ-] *n*. 1. 消化,消化力,消化作用。2. (精神上的)同化吸收,融会贯通。3.【化】浸煮(作用),浸提。4. 菌致分解[用细菌分解法处理污水]。*be easy* [*hard*] *of ~* 易[难]消化。*I have a weak* [*good*] ~. 我的消化力弱[强]。

di·ges·tive [di'dʒestiv, dai-; də'dʒɛstɪv, daɪ-] I *a*. 1. 有消化力的;助消化的;易消化的。2.【化】浸煮的。*He suffers from ~ trouble*. 他消化不好。~ *juice fluid* 消化液。~ *organs* 消化器官。II *n*. 消化剂。-ly *ad*. 在消化上,用消化作用。

dig·ga·ble ['digəbl; 'dɪgəbl] *a*. 可采掘的。

dig·ger ['digə; 'dɪgə] *n*. 1. 挖掘者;采金矿工。2. 地蜂,穴蜂(= ~ wasp)。3. 挖掘器。4. [口]澳洲人,澳洲兵;新西兰人。5. [澳]老兄,朋友。6. [美俚]扒手,为金钱而与男人交朋友或结婚的女人。7. [the D-] [美]专挖草木根吃的印第安人。8. [英史]掘地派成员[十七世纪英国的平均地权者开挖耕种某些公有土地,以抗议私有财产制度]。9. [美俚]为黄牛代购戏票的人。10. [美俚] [D-] 乐于帮助同伙的嬉皮士。

dig·ging ['digiŋ; 'dɪgɪŋ] *n*. 1. 挖掘,采掘。2. [*pl*.]开采物。3. 矿区,金矿。4. [*pl*.][美俚]住处,[英俚]公寓。

dight [dait; daɪt] *vt*. [古、诗]整顿;装饰;装备。

dig·it ['didʒit; 'dɪdʒɪt] *n*. 1. 手指,足趾。2. 一指之宽[约 3/4 英寸]。3.【天】太阳(或月亮)直径的 1/12[用作测定日蚀、月蚀的单位]。4. 阿拉伯数字[0,1,2,…有时将 0 除外,仅指 1 至 9]。★古人以指、趾计数,故称数字为 digit. *The number 301 contains three ~s*. 数字 301 是三位数。*binary* ~ 二进制数字[数位]。

dig·it·al ['didʒitl; 'dɪdʒətl] I *a*. 1. 手指的;指状的。2. 数字的,数据的。II *n*. 1. (钢琴等的)琴键。2. 手指。~ **audio tape** 数字音频磁带[一种音质极佳的微型盒带]。~ **camera** 数码照相机。~ **cash** 电子货币。~ **computer** 数字型电子计算机。[相对于 analogue computer 即模拟型电子计算机而言]。~ **highway** 信息(高速)公路。~ **TV** 数字电视。~ **superhighway** 信息高速公路。~ **videodisk** 数字视盘。

dig·i·tal·in [didʒi'tælin, -'teilin; ˌdɪdʒə'tælɪn, -'telɪn] *n*. 地支他灵,洋地黄苷,毛地黄苷。

dig·i·ta·lis [ˌdidʒi'teilis; ˌdɪdʒə'telɪs] *n*. 1.【植】毛地黄属。2. 毛地黄干叶;毛地黄制剂[强心剂]。

dig·i·tal·ize ['didʒitəlaiz; 'dɪdʒətlˌaɪz] *vt*. 用毛地黄治疗(心脏病)。**dig·i·tal·i·za·tion** [ˌdidʒitəlai'zeiʃən; ˌdɪdʒətəlaɪ'zeʃən] *n*.

dig·i·tate, dig·i·tat·ed ['didʒiteit, -id; 'dɪdʒətet, -ɪd] *a*. 1. 有指的,有趾的。2. 指状的,掌状的。~ *leaves* 掌状叶。

dig·i·ta·tion [didʒi'teiʃən; ˌdɪdʒɪ'teʃən] *n*. 指状分裂;指状突起。

dig·it·eer [ˌdidʒi'tiːə(r); ˌdɪdʒɪ'tɪə(r)] *n*. 电脑高手,电子计算机能手。

digiti- *comb*. *f*. 表示"指";"趾": *digiti*grade.

dig·i·ti·form [di'dʒitifɔːm; 'dɪdʒətəˌfɔrm] *a*. 指状的。

dig·i·ti·grade ['didʒitigreid; 'dɪdʒɪtəˌgred] I *a*.【动】(脚跟不落地而)用足趾行走的,趾行的。II *n*. 趾行动物[狗、猫、马等]。

dig·i·tize ['didʒiˌtaiz; 'dɪdʒəˌtaɪz] *vt*. 使计数化,使数字化,使成为数字。

dig·i·tox·in ['didʒi'tɔksin; ˌdɪdʒə'tɑksɪn] *n*. 毛[洋]地黄毒苷[用以制强心剂]。

di·glot ['daiglɔt; 'daɪglɑt] I *a*. 两种语言的,使用两种语言的。II *n*. 两种语言对照版本。

dig·ni·fied ['dignifaid; 'dɪgnəˌfaɪd] *a*. 有威风的,有尊严的;显贵的,高贵的。

dig·ni·fy ['dignifai; 'dɪgnəˌfaɪ] *vt*. (*-fied*; *-fy·ing*) 1. 使有威严,使高贵;授以荣誉。2. 把…夸大为。*to ~ cowardice by calling it prudence* 把怯懦美化为谨慎

dig·ni·ta·ry [ˈdignitəri; ˋdɪgnəˏtɛrɪ] **I** *n*. **1.** 高贵的人,高官显贵。**2.** 〔特指〕高僧。**II** *a*. 高官的,权贵的。

dig·ni·ty [ˈdigniti; ˋdɪgnətɪ] *n*. **1.** 威严,威风;端庄;尊严,高贵;体面。**2.** 高位,显职。**3.** 高官显贵。*impair one's* ~ 有伤体面。*a little on one's* ~ 有点摆架子。***be upon*** [***stand upon***] ***one's*** ~ 摆架子,闹气派。***beneath one's*** ~ 损害尊严,不合身分。***with*** ~ 庄严地;端着架子,神气十足地。

di·gox·in [daiˈgɔksin; daɪˋgɑksɪn] *n*. 【药】异羟基洋地黄毒苷〔作用较快的强心药〕,(商品名)地高辛,狄戈辛。

di·graph [ˈdaigrɑːf; ˋdaɪgræf] *n*. (读作一音的)复合字母〔如 ch, ea〕。

di·gress [daiˈgres; daɪˋgrɛs] *vi*. 脱轨,离题。~ *from the point* 离开要点。

di·gres·sion [daiˈgreʃən; daɪˋgrɛʃən] *n*. **1.** 离题;枝节话。**2.** 【天】偏离特定路线。*to return from the* ~ 言归正传,闲话休讲。

di·gres·sive [daiˈgresiv; daɪˋgrɛsɪv] *a*. 离题的,枝节的。**-ly** *ad*.

di·he·dral [daiˈhiːdrəl; daɪˋhidrəl] **I** *a*. 由两个平面构成的,二面的。**II** *n*. 【数】二面角 (= ~ angle);【空】上反角 (= positive ~);下反角 (= negative ~)。

di·hy·brid [daiˈhaibrid; daɪˋhaɪbrɪd] *n*. 【遗传】二对因子杂种〔杂合子〕。

di·hy·drate [daiˈhaidreit; daɪˋhaɪdret] *n*. 【化】二水合物。

di·hy·dro·chlo·ride [daiˌhaidrəˈklɔːraid; daɪˏhaɪdrəˋkloˏraɪd] *n*. 二氢氯化物;二盐酸化物。

di·hy·dro·strep·to·my·cin [daiˌhaidrəuˌstreptəuˈmaisin; daɪˏhaɪdroˏstrɛptəˋmaɪsɪn] *n*. 【药】双氢链霉素。

Di·jon [ˈdiːʒɔːŋ; ˋdiʒɔ̃ŋ] *n*. 第戎(迪戎)〔法国城市〕。

dik-dik [ˈdik-dik; ˋdɪk-dɪk] *n*. (非洲)小羚羊。

dike[1] [daik; daɪk] **I** *n*. **1.** 堤,堤防,堰堤。**2.** 沟,濠,渠。**3.** 【矿】岩脉。**4.** 障碍物。**II** *vt*. **1.** 用堤[濠沟]围绕。**2.** 开沟排水。

dike[2] [daik; daɪk] *n*. 搞同性恋的女人。**dik·ey** *a*.

dike[3] [daik; daɪk] *vt*. 〔美俚〕使穿得漂亮,打扮 (*out*, *up*)。*They were all* ~*d out for the party*. 他们都为赴晚会打扮得漂漂亮亮。

dike-grave [ˈdaikgreiv; ˋdaɪkˏgrev] *n*. **1.** (荷兰的)堤防监督。**2.** 〔英方〕(沼泽地区的)沟渠[堤防]监视官。

dik·tat [dikˈtɑːt; dɪkˋtɑt] *n*. (强加于战败国等的)单方面的苛刻解决条件。

dil. = 【化】dilute.

di·lac·er·ate [diˈlæsəˌreit; dəˋlæsəˏret] *vt*. 撕裂,裂碎。

di·lan·tin [daiˈlæntin; daɪˋlæntɪn] *n*. 【化、药】地仑丁,二苯乙内酰脲〔抗癫痫药〕。

di·lap·i·date [diˈlæpiˌdeit; dəˋlæpəˏdet] *vi*., *vt*. **1.** 使(局部)毁坏,(部分)损伤。**2.** 〔古〕浪费,乱花(钱财等)。

di·lap·i·dat·ed [diˈlæpideitid; dəˋlæpədetɪd] *a*. 破烂的(衣服等),要塌的(房子等);破落的,衰败的。*a* ~ *fortune* 衰败的家道。

di·lap·i·da·tion [diˌlæpiˈdeiʃən; dəˏlæpəˋdeʃən] *n*. **1.** 破烂,破败。**2.** 浪费,(家产的)荡尽。**3.** (崖岸等的)崩塌;崩塌物。**4.** (向居住教会房屋的圣职者索取的)房屋维修费。

di·lap·i·da·tor [diˈlæpideitə; dɪˋlæpəˏdetə˞] *n*. 损坏者;浪费者。

di·lat·a·ble [daiˈleitəbl; daɪˋletəbl] *a*. 会膨胀的,可扩张的。**-bili·ty** [daiˌleitəˈbiliti; daɪˏletəˋbɪlətɪ] *n*. 膨胀性[率]。

di·lat·ant [daiˈleitnt, di-; daɪˋletnt, dɪ-] **I** *a*. **1.** 膨胀的,有膨胀之势的。**2.** (颗粒物质)因变形而膨胀的。**3.** (胶状溶液)受压而凝固的。**II** *n*. 膨胀物。**-an·cy** *n*.

dil·a·ta·tion [ˌdaileiˈteiʃən; ˏdaɪləˋteʃən], **-la·tion** [ˌdaiˈleiʃən; ˏdaɪˋleʃən] *n*. **1.** 扩张,膨胀。**2.** 【医】扩张(症);扩张术。**3.** (说话、写文章的)铺叙,详述。

di·late [daiˈleit; daɪˋlet] *vt*. 使膨胀。*with* ~*d eyes* 瞪着眼睛。— *vi*. **1.** 扩张,膨胀。**2.** 详述。~ *on* [*upon*] *a subject* 对问题详加叙述。

di·la·tion [daiˈleiʃən; daɪˋleʃən] *n*. **1.** 膨胀,扩大。**2.** 【医】扩张(症)。

dil·a·tom·e·ter [ˌdiləˈtɔmitə, dailə-; ˏdɪləˋtɑmɪtə˞, daɪlə-] *n*. 【物】膨胀计。

di·la·tor [daiˈleitə; daɪˋletə˞] *n*. **1.** 使膨胀[扩张]的人。**2.** 【医】扩张器。**3.** 【解】扩张肌,开大肌。

dil·a·to·ry [ˈdilətəri; ˋdɪləˏtorɪ] *a*. 缓慢的,拖拉的。*a* ~ *measure* 拖延办法。**-to·ri·ly** *ad*. 迟迟,拖拖拉拉地。**-to·ri·ness** *n*.

di·lem·ma [diˈlemə, dai-; dəˋlɛmə, daɪ-] *n*. **1.** 【逻】(使对手在两个或多个对他不利的事物中进行选择的)双关论法,双刀论法;二难推论。**2.** 窘境,困境,进退两难。***be in a*** ~ = ***be on the horns of a*** ~ 进退维谷,左右为难。

dil·em·mat·ic [ˌdiləˈmætik; ˏdɪləˋmætɪk] *a*. **1.** 双关论法的。**2.** 左右为难的。

dil·et·tan·te [ˌdiliˈtænti; ˏdɪləˋtæntɪ] **I** *n*. (*pl*. ~*s*, *-ti* [-tiː; -ti]) **1.** 文学、艺术的爱好者。**2.** (艺术或科学的)业余爱好者,浅薄的涉猎者。**II** *a*. 爱好文艺的;业余的。**-tan·tish** [-ˈtæntiʃ; -ˋtæntɪʃ] *a*. 业余(性质)的。

dil·et·tant·ism [diliˈtæntizəm; ˏdɪləˋtæntɪzəm] *n*. 业余艺术;业余嗜好;业余知识。

dil·i·gence[1] [ˈdilidʒəns; ˋdɪlədʒəns] *n*. 勤勉,努力。*study with* ~ 勤奋学习。

dil·i·gence[2] [ˈdilidʒəns, F. diliʒɑ̃ːns; ˋdɪlədʒəns, dɪlɪʒɑ̃ːns] *n*. 四轮公共马车,驿站马车。

dil·i·gent [ˈdilidʒənt; ˋdɪlədʒənt] *a*. 勤勤恳恳的 (*in*);刻苦的,勤奋的。*He is* ~ *in his studies*. 他学习勤奋。**-ly** *ad*.

Dill [dil; dɪl] *n*. 迪尔〔姓氏〕。

dill[1] [dil; dɪl] *n*. **1.** 【植】莳萝。**2.** 莳萝子,莳萝叶〔可作香辣佐料〕。**3.** 莳萝泡菜 (= ~ pickle)。

dill[2] [dil; dɪl] *vt*. 〔英方〕安慰,使镇静。

Dil·lon [ˈdilən; ˋdɪlən] *n*. 狄龙〔姓氏〕。

Dil·ly, Dil·i [ˈdili; ˋdɪlɪ] *n*. 帝力〔东帝汶首都〕。

dil·ly [ˈdili; ˋdɪlɪ] *n*. 突出人物,优秀人物;突出事物。*a* ~ *of a movie* 优秀的电影。

dil·ly·dal·ly [ˈdilidæli; ˋdɪlɪdælɪ] *vi*. (*-lied*; *-ly·ing*) 吊儿郎当,闲混,闲逛。

dil·u·ent [ˈdiljuənt; ˋdɪljuənt] **I** *a*. 稀释用的。**II** *n*. 【医】稀释剂。

di·lute [daiˈljuːt, di-; daɪˋlut, dɪ-] **I** *vt*., *vi*. **1.** 冲淡,搀淡,稀释。**2.** (掺杂)使变薄弱。~ *wine with water* 用水把酒冲淡。*The quality of the novel is* ~*d by the bad writing*. 因写得不好而使小说质量有所减色。**II** *a*. 稀释的;淡的。~ *nitric acid* 稀硝酸。

di·lu·tion [daiˈljuːʃən, di-; daɪˋluʃən, dɪ-] *n*. **1.** 冲淡;稀释。**2.** 稀度,淡度。**3.** 稀释物。**4.** 削弱,削减。**5.** (把技术性操作分成若干加工过程而用生手替换熟手的)劳动力的削减 (= ~ of labour)。

di·lu·vi·al [daiˈljuːvjəl; daɪˋluvɪəl], **delu·vi·an** [-vjən; -vjən] *a*. **1.** (**Noah** 的)大洪水的。**2.** 【地】洪积(层)的。~ **deposits** [**formations**] 洪积层。~ **epoch** 【地】洪积世。

di·lu·vi·um [daiˈljuːvjəm, di-; daɪˋljuvɪəm, dɪ-] *n*. **1.** 冰河冲积物。**2.** 【地】洪积层。

Dilys [ˈdilis; ˋdɪlɪs] *n*. 迪莉斯〔女子名〕。

dim [dim; dɪm] **I** *a*. (*-mm-*) **1.** 微暗的,朦胧的;暗淡的,混沌的。**2.** 模糊不清的。**3.** 无光泽的,消光的。**4.** 迟钝的。*a* ~ *light* 微亮。*a* ~ *memory* 模糊的记忆。~ *prospects* 暗淡的前景。*take a* ~ *view of* 抱悲观[怀疑]的看法。***be*** ~ ***and remote*** 渺茫。**II** *vt*., *vi*. (*-mm-*) (使)暗淡;(使)朦胧,(使)模糊;(使)变朦胧。

Her eyes became ~*med with tears*. 她泪眼朦胧。~*out* 〔美〕熄灯,实行灯火管制。**III** ***n***. **1**. 〔古、诗〕暗淡。**2**. (汽车的)弱光前灯。~**box** 〔美俚〕**1**. 排解纠纷的人,和事佬。**2**. 出租汽车。~**-out** 灯火管制。~**wit** 〔美俚〕笨蛋,傻子。~**witted** ***a***. 〔美俚〕愚蠢的。

dim. = dimension; diminuendo; diminutive.

dime [daim; daɪm] ***n***. **1**. (美、加拿大)一角银币。**2**. 少数的钱。*a* ~ *a dozen* 便宜的,按堆卖的;容易获得的。***do not care a*** ~ 毫不在乎。***on a*** ~ **1**. 在极小的地方(*This car can turn on a* ~. 这车能在极小的地方转弯)。**2**. 立刻(*stopped on a* ~ 立刻停止)。~ **museum** 简陋的博物馆,收费极少的展览。~ **novel** 廉价小说〔多为黄色小说〕。~ **store** 一角商店〔出售五分、一角等廉价商品的商店〕。

di·men·hy·dri·nate [ˌdaimenˈhaidrəˌneit; ˏdaɪmɛnˋhaɪdrəˏnet] ***n***. 【药】茶苯醇胺,茶苯海明,乘晕宁,海晕宁。

D

di·men·sion [diˈmenʃən; dəˋmɛnʃən] **I** ***n***. **1**. 尺寸。**2**. 【数】次元,度(数),维(数)。**3**. 【物】因次,量网。**4**. 〔*pl*.〕容积;面积;大小,规模,范围。**5**. 〔*pl*.〕〔口〕女性的胸腰臀尺寸。*of great* [*vast*] ~*s* 非常大的;极重大的。*of one* ~ 线性的,一维的。*of three* ~*s* 立体的,三维的。*of two* ~*s* 平面的,二维的。*scheme* [*calamity*] *of vast* ~*s* 宏大的计划[范围广阔的灾害]。*The girl's* ~*s were 38-24-36*. 女孩的标准胸腰臀尺寸是 38-24-36 英寸。**II** ***a***. (石料、木材)切成特定尺寸的。~ *lumber* [*stone*] 切成特定尺寸的木材[石料]。**III** ***vt***. **1**. 使形成所需的尺寸。**2**. 在…上标出尺寸。

di·men·sion·al [diˈmenʃənəl; dɪˋmɛnʃənəl] ***a***. **1**. 尺寸的。**2**. 空间的。**3**. 【数】因次的;…次(元)的。*a two-* ~ *object* 平面。*a three-* ~ *picture* 立体影片。*two* [*three*]*-*~ 二[三]度空间的。~ **sound** 立体音响。

di·mer [ˈdaimə; ˋdaɪmɚ] ***n***. 【化】二聚物。**-mer·ic** [-ˈmerik; -ˋmɛrɪk] ***a***.

dim·er·ous [ˈdimərəs; ˋdɪmərəs] ***a***. **1**. 分成两部分的。**2**. (花的轮生体)有二基数的。**3**. (昆虫)有二跗节的。

dim·e·ter [ˈdimitə; ˋdɪmətɚ] ***n***. 二韵脚诗句[如:He is gone on the mountain. / He is lost to the forest.]。

di·meth·o·ate [daiˈmeθəeit; daɪˋmɛθəet] ***n***. 乐果(一种有机磷杀虫、杀螨剂)。

di·mid·i·ate [diˈmidiit; dɪˋmɪdɪˏet] **I** ***a***. **1**. 两分的,对开的,折半的。**2**. 【生】只一半发达的。**II** ***vt***. 〔古〕将…对分,将…折半。

di·min·ish [diˈminiʃ; dəˋmɪnɪʃ] ***vt***. 减少,减低(*opp*. increase);【建】使成尖顶;【乐】减半音。— ***vi***. 减少,缩小;【建】成尖顶。~***ed arch*** 平圆拱〔指高度不及宽度的一半的圆拱〕。~***ed fifth*** 【乐】减五度。***hide one's*** ~***ed head*** 失势退隐。~**ing returns** 报酬递减〔指资本和劳动力增加到一定程度后,生产率不能与资本和劳动力成比例地增加上去〕。**-ing** ***a***. 渐减的,递减的。

di·min·u·en·do [diˌminjuˈendəu; dəˏmɪnjuˋɛndo] ***ad***. 〔It.〕【乐】渐弱(= decrescendo)。

dim·i·nu·tion [ˌdimiˈnjuːʃən; ˏdɪməˋnjuʃən] ***n***. **1**. 减少,减缩,缩小。**2**. 【建】(柱子等的)逐渐变尖。

di·min·u·tive [diˈminjutiv; dəˋmɪnjətɪv] **I** ***a***. **1**. 小的,小型的。**2**. 【语法】指小的(*opp*. augmentative)。*a* ~ *suffix* 指小词尾[如:cigar*ette*]。**II** ***n***. **1**. 极小的人[物]。**2**. 【语法】指小词尾[如:bird*ie* stream*let*]。**3**. 爱称,昵称[如:Jack*ie*]。**4**. 小的人[东西]。

dim·is·so·ry [ˈdimisəri; ˋdɪməsərɪ] ***a***. **1**. 免职的;允许离开的。**2**. 【宗】准许迁往[调往]其他教区的。

dim·i·ty [ˈdimiti; ˋdɪmətɪ] ***n***. 凸纹条格细棉布。

dim·ly [ˈdimli; ˋdɪmlɪ] ***ad***. 暗淡,朦胧,模糊。

dim·mer [ˈdimə; ˋdɪmɚ] ***n***. **1**. 使变暗淡的人[物]。**2**. (舞台电灯的)减光器,调光器。**3**. 〔*pl*.〕减光车顶灯;(汽车上的)停车信号灯。

dim·mish [ˈdimiʃ; ˋdɪmɪʃ] ***a***. 暗淡的,朦胧的。

dim·ness [ˈdimnis; ˋdɪmnɪs] ***n***. **1**. 暗淡,朦胧,模糊。**2**. 蒙昧,愚钝。*the* ~ *of the room* [*one's memory*] 屋子阴暗[记忆淡薄]。

di·mor·phic, di·mor·phous [daiˈmɔːfik, -fəs; daɪˋmɔrfɪk, -fəs] ***a***. **1**. 【生】二态的,二形的。**2**. 【矿】双晶的。*a* ~ *flower* 二形花。**-phism** [-ˈmɔːfizəm; -ˋmɔrfɪzəm] ***n***. **1**. 【生】二态性,二态现象。**2**. 【矿】双晶现象。

dim·ple [ˈdimpl; ˋdɪmpl] **I** ***n***. **1**. 靥,酒窝;凹。**2**. 波纹,涟漪。**II** ***vi***., ***vt***. **1**. (使)现酒窝,(使)生酒窝。**2**. (使)起波纹。**-pled** ***a***. **1**. 有酒窝的。**2**. 起波纹的。

dim·ply [ˈdimpli; ˋdɪmplɪ] ***a***. **1**. 有酒窝的。**2**. 起波纹的。

DIN [din; dɪn] = 〔G.〕*Deutsche Industrie Normen* (= German Industry Standard) 德国工业标准。

din [din; dɪn] **I** ***n***. 噪音,喧嚣,鼓噪。**II** ***vi***. (***dinned***, ***din·ning***) 喧嚣,聒耳,嘈杂。*The noise* ~*ned in his ears*. 他听到聒耳声。*A hundred horns* ~*ned in protest*. 成百的喇叭齐鸣以示抗议。— ***vt***. 以喧声聒人,喋喋不休地说。~ ***something into sb.'s ears*** [***head***] 喋喋不休地说给某人听。

Di·na(h) [ˈdainə; ˋdaɪnə] ***n***. 黛娜〔女子名〕。

di·nar [diˈnɑː; dɪˋnɑr] ***n***. 第纳尔〔阿尔及利亚、伊拉克和南斯拉夫的货币单位〕。

din·dle [ˈdindl, ˈdinl; ˋdɪndl, ˋdɪnl] **I** ***vi***. 〔苏格兰、英方〕(由于巨响、惊吓等而)发颤,发抖。**II** ***n***. 〔苏格兰、英方〕抖动,震颤。

dine [dain; daɪn] ***vt***. **1**. 供吃;招待膳食;宴请。**2**. 可容…人用餐。~ *a famous scholar* 宴请一位出名的学者。*This table* ~*s twelve*. 这张餐桌能坐 12 人。*I request her to* ~ *with me tonight*. 今晚我请她吃饭。~ ***and wine*** (*a person*) 宴请(某人)。~ ***forth*** 出外吃晚饭。— ***vi***. 吃饭,进餐。~ ***on*** [***off***, ***upon***] (*a chicken*) 吃(鸡)。~ ***out*** [***in***] 在外[在家]吃饭。~ ***with Duke Humphrey*** 饿着。

din·er [ˈdainə; ˋdaɪnɚ] ***n***. **1**. 吃饭的(客)人。**2**. 〔美〕餐车。**3**. 餐车式的饭馆。~**-out** 常被宴请的人[饭局应酬多的人]。

di·ner·ic [daiˈnerik; daɪˋnɛrɪk] ***a***. 【物】(在同一容器中二液体间的)临界面的。

di·ner·o [diˈnɛərəu; dəˋnɛro] ***n***. 〔美口〕钱。

di·nette [daiˈnet; daɪˋnɛt] ***n***. **1**. (厨房旁边的)小吃饭间。**2**. 小吃饭间里的桌椅。

ding[1] [diŋ; dɪŋ] ***vi***. **1**. (钟等)叮当地响。**2**. 啰嗦,唠叨。**3**. 〔美俚〕打;扔;占上风;咒骂;冲撞。— ***vt***. 唠叨地讲。~ *into sb.'s ears* 唠唠叨叨地讲。

ding[2] [diŋ; dɪŋ] ***vi***. (***dang*** [dæŋ; dæŋ]) 〔Scot.〕(雨)猛下。

ding-a-ling [ˈdiŋəˈliŋ; ˋdɪŋəlɪŋ] ***n***. 〔俚〕笨蛋;怪人。

ding·bat [ˈdiŋbæt; ˋdɪŋbæt] ***n***. **1**. 东西,玩意儿(= dingus)。**2**. 〔美口〕(石子、木棍等)投掷物。**3**. 【印】(用于段落开始处的)装饰标志。

ding·dong [ˈdiŋˈdɔŋ; ˋdɪŋˋdɑŋ] **I** ***n***. 叮当,叮咚。**II** ***a***. 叮当作响的;(比赛等)激烈的。*a* ~ *race* [*fight*] (各方相继领先的)势均力敌的赛跑[激烈的战斗]。**III** ***ad***. 叮当作响地,使劲儿,拼命。*go* [*be*] *at it* ~ = *hammer away at it* ~ 〔俚〕拼命工作。*fall to work* ~ 拼命[认真]工作起来。**IV** ***vi***. 叮当作响。— ***vt***. 一再重复(以加深印象)。

dinge [dindʒ; dɪndʒ] ***n***. 〔美俚〕黑人。

din·ger [ˈdiŋgə; ˋdɪŋgɚ] ***n***. 〔美俚〕**1**. 非常奇特的事物。**2**. 铁路车站站长。

din·gey, din·ghy [ˈdiŋgi; ˋdɪŋgɪ] ***n***. (印度等)小船;舰载小艇;(附属大船的)供应小船;无甲板单桅比赛用小船;救生橡皮筏。

din·gi·ly [ˈdindʒili; ˋdɪndʒɪlɪ] ***ad***. 暗淡地;肮脏地;褴褛地。

din·gi·ness [ˈdiŋdʒinis; ˋdɪndʒɪnɪs] **n.** 暗淡;肮脏;褴褛。

D. Ing. = [拉] Doctor Ingeniariae 工程学博士(= Doctor of Engineering)。

Ding Jaw-jong **n.** 丁肇中(1936— ,物理学家,1976年与美国科学家黎希特(**Burton Ritcher**)发现"J粒子",同获诺贝尔物理奖)。

din·gle [ˈdiŋgl; ˋdɪŋgl] **n.** [诗]有树木的幽谷。

din·go [ˈdiŋgəu; ˋdɪŋgo] **n.** (澳洲)野狗。

ding·us [ˈdiŋgəs; ˋdɪŋgəs] **n.** [美俚]东西,玩意儿。

din·gy[1] [ˈdindʒi; ˋdɪndʒɪ] **a.** 1. 暗黑的。2. 肮脏的。3. 褴褛的。

din·gy[2] [ˈdiŋdʒi; ˋdɪŋdʒɪ] **n.** = dingey.

din·ing [ˈdainiŋ; ˋdaɪnɪŋ] **n.** 吃饭,进餐。~ **alcove** 小餐厅。~ **car** 餐车。~ **hall** 大餐厅。~ **room** 饭厅。~ **table** 餐桌。

dinitro- *comb. f.* 【化】二硝基:*dinitro*benzene.

di·ni·tro·ben·zene [daiˌnaitrəuˈbenziːn; daɪˏnaɪtroˋbɛnzin] **n.** 二硝基苯[用于染料,有机合成物]。

dink [diŋk; dɪŋk] **I** *a.* [Scot.] (衣着)整洁的。**II** *vt.* 1. 打扮,装饰。2. (网球)打靠近网边的吊球。**III** *n.* [美] (猎野鸭的)小船。

DINK, Dink, dink [diŋk; dɪŋk] **n.** 丁克族[夫妻都工作而无子女的一族]。

Din·ka [ˈdiŋkɑː; ˋdɪŋkɑ] **n.** 1. 丁卡人[居住在苏丹南部的苏丹黑种部族人]。2. 丁卡语。

dinkey [ˈdiŋki; ˋdɪŋkɪ] **n.** [美] 1. (铁道停车场作运输、调车等用的)小型机车。2. 小型电车。

dink·um [ˈdiŋkəm; ˋdɪŋkəm] **I** *n.* [澳俚]工作,劳动。**II** *a.* 纯粹的,真正的,可靠的,公正的。~ **oil** [澳俚]真情实况,真相。

dink·y [ˈdiŋki; ˋdɪŋkɪ] **I** *a.* 1. [英口]整洁的;可爱的;漂亮的。2. [口]小的;微不足道的。**II** *n.* = dinkey.

din·ner [ˈdinə; ˋdɪnɚ] **n.** 正餐,(现通例指)晚餐;午[晚]宴,宴会。★英美中级以下人家通例叫午餐为 dinner,中级以上人家则叫晚餐为 dinner. *ask sb. to* ~ 请某人吃饭。*give a* ~ 举办午[晚]宴。*at* ~ 吃着饭。*early* ~ 中饭。*late* ~ 晚饭。***after*** ~ , ***mustard*** 饭后上芥末;雨后送伞。***give a*** ~ ***for*** [***in honour of***] (*sb.*) 宴请(某人),特为(某人)请客。***make a good*** [***poor***] ~ 吃盛餐[便饭]。***sit down to*** ~ 入席。~ **bell** 开饭铃[钟]。~ **bucket** = pail. ~ **cloth** 正餐桌巾。~ **clothes** 餐服。~ **coat** [**jacket**] [英]男子无尾晚礼服[美国叫 tuxedo]。~ **dress** 一种半正式的妇女餐服[通常有袖或短外衣]。~ **fork** (通常有四个叉齿的)大桌叉。~ **hour** 正餐时间。~ **knife** 餐刀。~ **party** 宴会。~ **pail** 餐盒。~ **ring** 正式场合带的大戒指。~ **service** [**set**] 成套餐具。~ **table** 餐桌。~ **time** 正餐时间。~ **wagon** 1. (分层的)餐厅手推车。2. 双层食具柜。

dino- *comb. f.* 恐怖:*dino*saur.

di·noc·er·as [daiˈnɔsərəs; daɪˋnɑsərəs] **n.** 【古生】恐角兽。

di·no·flag·el·late [ˌdainəˈflædʒilit, -ˌleit; ˏdaɪnəˋflædʒəlɪt, -ˏlet] **n.** 腰皮鞭毛目动物。

di·nor·nis [daiˈnɔːnis; daɪˋnɔrnɪs] **n.** 【古生】恐鸟。

di·no·saur [ˈdainəsɔː; ˋdaɪnəˏsɔr] **n.** 【古生】恐龙。-**saur·i·an** [ˈdainəsɔːriən; ˏdaɪnəˋsɔrɪən] **n.**, **a.** 恐龙(的)。

di·no·there [ˈdainəθiə; ˋdaɪnəˏθɪr] **n.** 【古生】恐兽。

dint [dint; dɪnt] **I** *n.* 1. 打痕,凹痕。2. 打击。3. 暴力;力量。***by*** ~ ***of*** 凭…的力量,靠,凭借。**II** *vt.* 打凹,压凹。

di·oc·e·san [daiˈɔsisən; daɪˋɑsəsn̩] **I** *a.* 主教管区的。**II** *n.* 主教。

di·o·cese [ˈdaiəsis; ˋdaɪəsɪs] **n.** 主教管区。

di·ode [ˈdaiəud; ˋdaɪod] **n.** 【无】二极管。

di·o·done [ˈdaiədəun; ˋdaɪəˏdon] **n.** 【药】碘造影剂。

di·oe·cian, di·oe·cious [daiˈiːʃən, daiˈiːʃəs; daɪˋiʃən, daɪˋiʃəs] **a.** 【生】雌雄异株[体]的。

di·oe·cism [daiˈiːsizəm; daɪˋisɪzm̩] **n.** 【生】雌雄异株[体]。

di·oes·trum, di·es·trum [daiˈestrəm, -ˈiːs-; daɪˋɛstrəm, -ˋis-] **n.** 【生】间(动)情期。

Di·og·e·nes [daiˈɔdʒiniːz; daɪˋɑdʒəˏniz] **n.** 提奥奇尼斯[住在桶中白昼点灯寻找正人君子的古希腊哲学家,纪元前 412—323]。

Di·o·nys·i·a [ˌdaiəˈniziə; ˏdaɪəˋnɪzɪə] **n.** [*pl.*] 酒神节。-**c** [daiəˈniziæk; ˏdaɪəˋnɪzɪæk], -**n** [-iən; -ɪən] **a.** 酒神狄俄尼索斯的;酒神节的;狂欢的。

Di·o·ny·sus, Di·o·ny·sos [ˌdaiəˈnaisəs; ˏdaɪəˋnaɪsəs] **n.** 【希神】狄俄尼索斯[酒神]。

di·op·side [daiˈɔpsaid; daɪˋɑpˏsaɪd] **n.** 【矿】透辉石。

di·op·tase [daiˈɔpteis; daɪˋɑpˏtes] **n.** 【矿】透视石,绿铜矿,翠铜矿。

di·op·ter, di·op·tre [daiˈɔptə; daɪˋɑptɚ] **n.** (透镜的)屈光度。

di·op·tom·e·ter [ˌdaiɔpˈtɔmitə; ˏdaɪɑpˋtɑmɪtɚ] **n.** 屈光计。-**try** **n.** 屈光测量。

di·op·tric [daiˈɔptrik; daɪˋɑptrɪk] **a.** 屈光的,折光的。~ *glass* [*lens*] 屈光镜[透镜]。~ *strength* 焦度。~ *system* 屈光组。

di·op·trics [daiˈɔptriks; daɪˋɑptrɪks] **n.** 屈光学。

di·o·ra·ma [ˌdaiəˈrɑːmə; ˏdaɪəˋrɑmə] **n.** 1. (从小孔窥视的)透明幕上的画面,西洋景,洋片。2. 有人物塑像的缩型立体布景。3. 模拟动物野生状况的博物馆展览。

dio·ram·ic [ˌdaiəˈræmik; ˏdaɪəˋræmɪk] **a.**

di·o·rite [ˈdaiərait; ˋdaɪəˏraɪt] **n.** 【矿】闪长岩。

di·ox·ane [daiˈɔksein; daɪˋɑkˏsen] **n.** 【化】二氧杂环己烷[用做油脂溶剂]。

di·ox·ide [daiˈɔksaid; daɪˋɑksaɪd] **n.** 【化】二氧化物。

dip [dip; dɪp] **I** *vt.* (***dipped***, [古] ***dipt***; ***dip·ping***) 1. 浸,泡,蘸;(微微)弄湿,濡湿;浸染。2. 把(旗等)稍稍放下又急速升起[做信号或敬礼]。3. 汲出,汲取,舀 (*out*; *up*)。4. (把烛芯反复置于融蜡中以)浸制(蜡烛)。5. 为…施浸礼。6. (把猪羊等放在杀虫液里)浸洗。7. [口]使欠债[常用被动语态]。~ *out soup with a ladle* 用勺子舀[打]汤。~ *a curtsy* 屈膝行礼。*I am slightly ~ped.* 我有一点儿债。— *vi.* 1. 浸;(微微)一浸。2. 【空】(升前)急降。3. 沉,沉落;(地层)沉陷。4. (路)向下倾斜。5. (手)伸入(袋内),掏取,汲取。6. 浏览;稍加探究。7. [俚]扒窃。*The sun ~ped below the horizon.* 太阳落到地平线下了。~ ***into*** 1. 舀出;取出,掏出 (~ *into one's purse* 挥霍,乱花)。2. 看一看,查一查。3. 探究,细想 (~ *deep into the future* 细想将来)。4. 潜入。~ ***one's finger in*** 染指。**II** *n.* 1. 泡,浸渍,沾湿;洗浴。2. (汤等的)一勺;浸液,洗羊的消毒水;(布丁的)浇汁。3. (地、路等的)倾斜,凹下,洼,坑。4. 【空】(升前的)急降。5. (磁针的)倾角,俯角。6. (电线等下垂的)弛度。7. (双杠上的)双臂屈伸,拔双杠。8. 蜡烛。9. [美俚]扒手。*a* ~ *in price* 跌价。~ *of the needles* 磁针的俯角。***at the*** ~ 【海】(旗)微降[表示敬意]。***have a*** ~ ***in the sea*** 洗海水澡。~ **circle** 磁倾仪。~-**dye** *vt.* 浸染(针织物)。~ **grain** (木材的)曲走纹理。~ **needle** = dipping needle. ~ **net** 长柄的捞鱼网。**dipping needle** 【物】磁倾针。

di·par·tite [daiˈpɑːtait; daɪˋpɑrtaɪt] **a.** 分成几部分的。

di·pet·al·ous [daiˈpetələs; daɪˋpɛtələs] **a.** 【植】有两瓣的。

di·phase, di·pha·sic [ˈdaiˌfeiz, -ˈfeizik; ˋdaɪˏfez, -ˋfezɪk] **a.** 二相的。

di·phas·er [daiˈfeizə; daɪˋfezɚ] **n.** 二相发电机。

di·phen·yl [daiˈfenl, -ˈfiːn-; daɪˋfɛnəl, -ˋfin-] **n.** 【化】1. 联(二)苯。2. 二苯基。

di·phen·yl·a·mine [daiˌfenilәˈmiːn; daɪˏfɛnɪləˋmin] **n.** 二苯胺[用以制造炸药稳定剂和染料]。

di·phos·gene [daiˈfɔsdʒiːn, -ˈfɔz-; daɪˋfɑsdʒin, -ˋfɑz-] *n*. 双光气[在化学战中用作毒气]。

diph·the·ri·a [difˈθiəriə, dip-; dɪfˋθɪrɪə, dɪp-] *n*.【医】白喉。**-ri·al** [-riəl; -rɪəl], **-ric** [difˈθerik; dɪfˋθɛrɪk], **-rit·ic** [ˌdifθiˈritik, dip-; ˏdɪfθəˋrɪtɪk, dɪp-] *a*.(患)白喉的。

diph·the·roid [ˈdifθərɔid; ˋdɪfθəˏrɔɪd] **I** *a*. 白喉状的,白喉样的。**II** *n*. 假白喉。

diph·thong [ˈdifθɔŋ, ˈdip-; ˋdɪfθɔŋ, ˋdɪp-] *n*. **1.** 复合元音[oil 之 [ɔi] 等]。**2.**〔口〕复合元音词[oil 之 oi 等];元音连字[æ, œ 等]。**3.** 复合辅音[ch ([t] + [ʃ]), j ([d] + [ʒ]) 等]。**-al** *a*.

diph·thong·ize [ˈdifθɔŋgaiz; ˋdɪfθɔŋˏaɪz] *vt*. 使复合元音化;使照复合元音一样发音。— *vi*. 变成复合元音。

diph·y·cer·cal [ˈdifiˌsəːkl; ˋdɪfɪˏsɝkl̩] *a*.(鱼)双尾的,圆尾的。

di·phy·let·ic [ˌdaifaiˈletik; ˏdaɪfaɪˋlɛtɪk] *a*. 二源的[在血统的继承上有两个来源的]。

di·phyl·lous [daiˈfiləs; daɪˋfɪləs] *a*. 有两叶的。

di·phy·o·dont [daiˈfaiəˌdɔnt, diˈfiə-; ˋdɪfɪəˏdɑnt, dɪˋfɪə-] **I** *a*. 有两期牙齿的。**II** *n*. 有乳齿和永久齿两期牙齿的哺乳类动物。

dipl. = diplomat; diplomatic.

dipl(o)- *comb. f*. 双,复,重:*diplo*coccus.

di·ple·gi·a [daiˈpliːdʒiə; daɪˋplidʒɪə] *n*. 两侧瘫痪,两侧麻痹,双瘫。

di·plex [ˈdaipleks; ˋdaɪplɛks] *a*.【电】同向双工的,收发信号同时同向传送的。~ *telegraph* 单向双路电报。

dip·lo·blas·tic [ˌdipləˈblæstik; ˏdɪpləˋblæstɪk] *a*.【动】双胚层的。

dip·lo·coc·cus [dipləuˈkɔkəs; dɪpləˋkɑkəs] *n*. (*pl*. **-coc·ci** [-ˈkɔksai; -ˋkɑksaɪ]) 双球菌。

di·plod·o·cus [diˈplɔdəkəs; dɪˋplɑdəkəs] *n*. 梁龙[古生物恐龙的一种]。

dip·lo·ë [ˈdipləuiː; ˋdɪploˏi] *n*.(头颅骨里的)板障(骨)。**di·plo·ic** [diˈpləuik; dɪˋploɪk] *a*.

dip·loid [ˈdiplɔid; ˋdɪplɔɪd] **I** *a*. **1.** 二重的;两数的,二倍的。**2.** 二倍体的。**II** *n*. **1.**【生】二倍体,二倍染色体。**2.**(结晶)偏方 24 面体。

di·plo·ma [diˈpləumə; dɪˋplomə] **I** *n*. (*pl*. ~*s*,〔罕〕**-ma·ta** [-mətə; -mətə]) **1.** 特许证,执照。**2.** 毕业文凭,学位证书。**3.** 奖状。**4.** 公文;〔*pl*.〕古文书。**II** *vt*. 发给执照[学位证书等]。~ **mill**〔美俚〕滥发文凭的大学。~ **piece** 为文凭[证书]而写的论文。

di·plo·ma·cy [diˈpləuməsi; dɪˋploməsɪ] *n*. **1.** 外交;外交手腕。**2.** 交际手段;权谋。**3.** 外交使团。*shuttle* ~ 穿梭外交。*use* ~ 应用外交手腕。

dip·lo·mat [ˈdipləmæt; ˋdɪpləˏmæt] *n*. **1.** 外交官;外交家。**2.** 善于交际的人。

dip·lo·mate [ˈdipləmeit; ˋdɪpləˏmet] *n*. 领有文凭的专科医生,学位证书持有者。

dip·lo·mat·ese [ˌdipləməˈtiːz; ˏdɪpləməˋtiz] *n*. 外交语言。

dip·lo·mat·ic [ˌdipləˈmætik; ˏdɪpləˋmætɪk] *a*. **1.** 外交(上)的;有外交手腕的;外交使团的。**2.** 古抄本的;不改真本原样的。*the* ~ *body* [*corps*] 外交使团。*a* ~ *copy* 一字未改的抄稿[誊本]。~ *agent* 外交工作人员。~ *evidence* 文献上的证据。*resume* [*sever*] ~ *relations* 恢复[断绝]外交关系。~ **immunity** 外交豁免权。~ **pouch** 外交文件袋。~ **service** 外交官勤务。

dip·lo·mat·i·cal·ly [ˌdipləˈmætikəli; ˏdɪpləˋmætɪkl̩ɪ] *ad*. 外交上;用外交手腕。

dip·lo·mat·ics [ˌdipləˈmætiks; ˏdɪpləˋmætɪks] *n*. **1.** 古文书学。**2.** 外交手腕 (= diplomacy)。

dip·lo·ma·tism [dipˈləuməˌtizəm; dəpˋloməˏtɪzəm] *n*. **1.** 外交,外交活动。**2.** 外交手腕。

dip·lo·ma·tist [diˈpləumətist; dɪˋplomətɪst] *n*.〔主英〕= diplomat.

dip·lo·ma·tize, di·plo·ma·tise [diˈpləumətaiz; dɪˋploməˏtaɪz] *vi*. 运用外交方法,施展外交手腕;从事外交工作。— *vt*. **1.** 用外交方法处理。**2.**〔古〕给…颁发证书。

dip·lon [ˈdiplɔn; ˋdɪplɑn] *n*.【化】氘核。

dip·lont [ˈdiplɔnt; ˋdɪplɑnt] *n*.【动、植】二倍体。

di·plo·pi·a, dip·lo·py [diˈpləupiə, ˈdipləpi; dɪˋplopɪə, ˋdɪpləpɪ] *n*.(病)复视 (*opp*. haplopia)。

dip·lo·pod [ˈdipləˌpɔd; ˋdɪpləˏpɑd] *n*. 千足虫 (= millipede)。

di·plo·sis [diˈpləusis; dɪˋplosɪs] *n*.(染色体的)倍加作用。

dip·no·an [ˈdipnəuən; ˋdɪpnoən] *a*., *n*. 肺鱼类的;肺鱼。

Dip·noi [ˈdipnɔi; ˋdɪpnɔɪ] *n*.【动】肺鱼亚纲。

dip·o·dy [ˈdipədi; ˋdɪpədɪ] *n*. (*pl*. **-dies**)【韵】二重音脚。**di·pod·ic** [daiˈpɔdik; daɪˋpɑdɪk] *a*.

di·po·lar [daiˈpəulə; daɪˋpolɚ] *a*. 双极的(磁石)。

di·pole [ˈdaipəul; ˋdaɪpol] *n*.【物、化】**1.** 偶极。**2.** 偶极天线。

dip·per [ˈdipə; ˋdɪpɚ] *n*. **1.**(有柄的)勺。**2.**【摄】湿影液槽。**3.** 浸渍工人,浸制工人[如浸制蜡烛、火柴头等]。**4.**【鸟】川鸟类的鸟,善于潜水的鸟。**5.** 浸礼会会友。**6.**〔D-〕北斗七星。**7.** 读书很快的人。**8.**〔俚〕扒手。***the Big*** [***Great***] **D-** 北斗七星。***the Little D-*** 小北斗[小熊星座的七颗主星]。

dip·py [ˈdipi; ˋdɪpɪ] *a*. (**-i·er**; **-i·est**)〔俚〕**1.** 疯狂的。**2.** 愚蠢的,古怪的。*be* ~ *about peanuts* 嗜爱花生。*be* ~ *with love for her* 对她大为倾倒。

di·pro·pel·lant [ˌdaiprəˈpelənt; ˏdaɪprəˋpɛlənt] *n*.(火箭的)二元推进剂 (= bipropellant)。

dip·so·ma·ni·a [ˌdipsəuˈmeiniə; ˏdɪpsoˋmenɪə] *n*. 嗜酒狂,酒癖;【医】间发性酒狂。**-ni·ac** [-niæk; -nɪæk] **1.** *a*. 有间发性酒狂的。**2.** *n*. 嗜酒狂人。

dip·stick [ˈdipˌstik; ˋdɪpˏstɪk] *n*. **1.**(测量容器内液体深度的)量杆,量尺。**2.** 鼻烟棍 (= snuff stick)。

dipt [dipt; dɪpt]〔古〕dip 的过去式及过去分词。

Dip·ter·a [ˈdiptərə; ˋdɪptərə] *n*.〔*pl*.〕【虫】双翅目[包括苍蝇、蚊子等]。

dip·ter·al [ˈdiptərəl; ˋdɪptərəl] *a*. **1.**【虫】双翅类的。**2.**【植】(种子)有双翅的。**3.**【建】四周有两排柱子的。

dip·ter·an [ˈdiptərən; ˋdɪptərən] **I** *a*.【虫、植】= dipteral. **II** *n*. 双翅目的昆虫[包括苍蝇、蚊子]。

dip·ter·os [ˈdiptərɔs; ˋdɪptərɑs] *n*. 四周有两排柱子的建筑物。

dip·ter·ous [ˈdiptərəs; ˋdɪptərəs] *a*.【虫、植】= dipteral.

dip·tych [ˈdiptik; ˋdɪptɪk] *n*. **1.**〔古罗马〕可折合的双连记事板。**2.**(祭坛后的)可折合的双连画[雕刻]。**3.** 由两个平行的或相对的部分组成的东西。

dir. = director.

Di·rac [diˈræk; dɪˋræk] *n*. 迪拉克[姓氏]。

dir·dum [ˈdiədəm, ˈdəːdəm; ˋdɪədəm, ˋdɝdəm] *n*.〔苏格兰、英方〕**1.** 吵闹,喧嚣。**2.** 斥责。**3.** 厄运。

dire [ˈdaiə; daɪr] *a*. **1.** 可怕的;悲惨的;不吉利的。**2.** 迫切的,极端的。*a* ~ *need* 迫切的需要。**the** ~ **sister** 专管复仇的女神 (= the Furies)。

direc. prop. = [L.] *directione propria*【处方】依照适当指导。

di·rect [diˈrekt, dai-; dəˋrɛkt, daɪ-] **I** *a*. **1.** 笔直的,一直线的;正面的。**2.** 直接的。**3.** 直截了当的,直率的,明白的。**4.** 直系的,正统的。**5.**【语法】直接法的。**6.**【天】由西向东运行的。**7.**(不用媒染剂)直接染色的。*a* ~ *road* 直路。~ *rays* 直射光。~ *vision* 直视。~ *pressure* 正面追击;【物】定向压力。~ *proportion* 正比例。~ *tax* 直接税。~ *action* 直接作用;直接行动[如罢工

商品抵制等行动)。～ *relatives* 直系亲属。*a* ～ *address* 称呼。～ *motion* 顺行。**II** *ad*. 笔直,一直,直接。**III** *vt*. **1.** (把…)针对(某人),把…指向某人 (*at*; *to*; *towards*);暗指着说。**2.** 指挥,指导;【美剧、影】导演;命令;管理,掌管;支配。**3.** 指点某人,为某人,指示方向。**4.** 寄(信等)给,写寄发地址。*I* ～*ed my remarks to you*. 我的话是暗指你说的。～ *a business* [*campaign*] 指挥业务[战斗]。*a film* ～*ed by* ... 某人导演的影片。*Will you* ～ *me to the station*? 请问车站往哪里走? *D- the letter to my business address*. 请把这封信寄交我的办公地址。— *vi*. 指挥,指导,管理。*as* ～*ed* 照说明,按处方。～ **current**【电】直流电〔略作 D. C. 或 d. c.〕。～ **current dynamo** [**generator**] 直流发电机。～ **current motor** 直流电动机。～ **dye** 直接染料。～ **mail** (向广大群众投寄的)直接邮件。～ **method**【语】直接教学法。～ **primary** (**election**) 由选民直接投票的预选。～ **proportion**【数】正比例。～ **speech**【语法】直接引语。

di·rect·ed [di'rektid, 'dai-; də`rɛktɪd, `daɪ-] *a*. **1.** 有指导的;定向的。**2.**【数】标出(数、角、线段的)正负的。～ **number**【数】(有加减号的)有向数。～ **variants** 定向变异。

di·rec·tion [di'rekʃən, dai'-; də`rɛkʃən, daɪ`-] *n*. **1.** 方位,方向;范围,方面。**2.** 〔*pl*.〕指挥,指导;管理。**3.** 〔常 *pl*.〕指示,命令,吩咐;用法说明。**4.** 导演;(乐队)指挥。**5.** 寄发地址。**6.** 趋向,倾向。*Full* ～*s inside*. 内有详细说明。～ *finder* [*detector*]【无】测向仪。～ *finding* 定向。～ *finding station* 无线电测向站。～ *for use* 用法说明。*in all* ～*s* 四面八方,各方面。(*reforms*) *in many* ～*s* 各方面的(改革)。*in the* ～ *of* 向…方面。*take a new* ～ 有新倾向。*under the* ～ *of* 在…指导下。～ **angle**【数】方向角。

di·rec·tion·al [di'rekʃənəl, dai-; də`rɛkʃənḷ, daɪ-] *a*. **1.** 方向的。**2.**【无】指向的,定向的。～ **antenna** 定向天线。～ **derivative**【数】方向导数。～ **gyro**【空】陀螺方向仪。～ **radio** 无线电定向。

di·rec·tive [di'rektiv, dai-; də`rɛktɪv, daɪ-] **I** *n*. 〔美〕命令,训令,指令;方针。**II** *a*. **1.** 指导的,指挥的;管理的。**2.**【无】指向[定向]式的。*a* ～ *antenna* 定向天线。*rules* ～ *of our actions* 支配我们行动的法则。

di·rect·ly [di'rektli, dai-; də`rɛktlɪ, daɪ-] **I** *ad*. **1.** 径直的;直接地。**2.** 直截了当地,直率地。**3.** 正好地,恰好地。**4.** 不久;〔英〕立刻,立即。**II** *conj*. [常 'drekli; `drɛklɪ] 〔口〕一…(就)。*I will come* ～ *I have finished*. 我一完就来。

di·rect·ness [di'rektnis, dai-; də`rɛktnɪs, daɪ-] *n*. 直接;率直,坦白。*the* ～ *of manner* [*speech*] 态度[谈吐]坦率。

Di·rec·toire [di'rektwɑː; dɪ`rektwar] 〔F.〕 **I** *n*. (1795—1799 年法国革命政府的)五人执政内阁。**II** *a*. 法国五人执政内阁时期的〔尤指家具、衣服等的式样〕。

di·rec·tor [di'rektə, dai-; də`rɛktɚ, daɪ-] *n*. **1.** 指导员,指挥者;长官;理事,董事;校长,社长;(工厂的)厂长,(车间)主任。**2.**【剧】导演;【乐】指挥。**3.** (1795—1799 年法国革命政府的)执政官,行政委员。**4.**【医】有沟探针。**5.**【机】司动部分。**6.**【军】炮兵射击指挥仪。**7.**【无】引向器;导向器。*a board of* ～*s* 理事会,董事会。*an assistant* ～【影】助理导演。～ **circle** 准圆。～ **firing**【军】指挥仪射击。**D- General** 总裁,总监。～**'s chair** 导演椅〔一种可折叠的轻便椅〕。

di·rec·to·rate [di'rektərit, dai-; də`rɛktərɪt, daɪ-] *n*. **1.** 指导者(董事、导演等)的职位。**2.** 理事会,董事会。

di·rec·to·ri·al [diˌrek'tɔːriəl; dəˌrɛk`torɪəl] *a*. **1.** 指挥[指导]的,管理的。**2.** 指挥者的,管理者的。**3.** 〔D-〕(1795—1799 年法国革命政府的)执政内阁的。

di·rec·tor·ship [di'rektəʃip; də`rɛktɚˌʃɪp] *n*. 董事[理事、主任、社长等]的职务[任期]。

di·rec·to·ry [di'rektəri; də`rɛktərɪ] **I** *n*. **1.** 姓名地址录,工商人名录。**2.** (教堂的)礼拜规则书;(记载规则、指令等的)指南。**3.** 理事会,董事会;〔集合词〕一群董事[理事]。**4.** 〔D-〕 = Directoire. *a telephone* ～ 电话号码簿。**II** *a*. 指导的,指挥的,管理的。

di·rec·tress [di'rektris, dai-; də`rɛktrɪs, daɪ-] *n*. **1.** 女指导者;女董事。**2.** 女导演;女指挥。

di·rec·trix [di'rektriks, dai-; də`rɛktrɪks, daɪ-] *n*. (*pl*. ～*es* [-iz; -ɪz], *-trices* [-trisiːz; -trɪsiz]) **1.** 〔古〕 = directress. **2.**【数】准线。

dire·ful ['daiəful; `daɪrfəl] *a*. 可怕的;悲惨的;预兆不祥的。**-ly** *ad*.

dirge [dəːdʒ; dɝdʒ] *n*. **1.** 挽歌,悼歌。**2.** 凄凉的歌[诗、乐曲]。

dir·ham [diə'hæm; dɪr`hæm] *n*. **1.** 迪拉姆〔摩洛哥货币单位〕。**2.** 里亚尔的 1/100〔卡塔尔的货币名〕。

dir·i·gi·ble ['diridʒəbl; `dɪrədʒəbl] **I** *a*.【空】可操纵的。*a* ～ *torpedo* 可操纵的鱼雷。**II** *n*. 飞船,飞艇 (= ～ balloon)。

dir·i·ment ['dirimənt; `dɪrɪmənt] *a*. 使无效的。～ ***impediments***【法】(使结婚无效的)绝对障碍。

Dirk [dəːk; dɝk] *n*. 德克〔男子名, Derek 的异体〕。

dirk [dəːk; dɝk] **I** *n*. 短剑,匕首。**II** *vt*. 用短剑刺。

Dirk·sen ['dəːksn; `dɝksn] *n*. 德克森〔姓氏〕。

dirl [diəl, dəːl; dɪrl, dɝl] *vt*., *vi*. 〔苏格兰、北英方〕发颤,发抖。

dirn·dl ['dəːndl; `dɝndl] *n*., *a*. 紧身连衣裙。

dirt [dəːt; dɝt] *n*. **1.** 污物;烂泥;油垢;灰尘。**2.** 泥土;土地;【矿】含金土。**3.** 毫无价值的东西。**4.** 肮脏,下贱,卑鄙。**5.** 骂人话,恶言。**6.** 下流话,下流作品。**7.** 〔美俚〕闲谈,聊天;钱;糖;秘密情报;〔美乐俚〕 = blues. *treat a person like* ～ 视某人如草芥。*common as* ～ 草芥一样到处皆是的,平凡的。*yellow* ～ 〔蔑〕黄金。(*as*) ***cheap as*** ～ 极其便宜的。***cut*** ～ 〔美俚〕逃走。***do sb***. ～ 〔美〕用卑鄙手段[恶言恶语]陷害某人。***eat*** ～ 忍辱。***fling*** [***throw***] ～ ***at*** 臭骂。***hit the*** ～ 落在地上。***talk*** ～ 说下流话[猥亵话]。～**-cheap** *a*., *ad*. 极便宜的[地]。～ **bed**【地】泥土层。～ **eating** 食土癖。～ **farmer** 〔美口〕自耕农 (*opp*. gentleman farmer)。～ **floor** (屋内未铺地板的)泥土地面。～ **money** 〔英俚〕装卸污臭货物时额外付给码头工人的补贴。～ **pie** (小孩游戏做的)泥饼。～**-poor** *a*. 很穷的。～ **road** 〔美〕(未铺路面的)沙土路。～ **track** 沙土[煤渣]跑道。～ **wagon** 〔美〕垃圾车。

dirt·i·ly ['dəːtili; `dɝtɪlɪ] *ad*. 龌龊;卑鄙,下贱。

dirt·i·ness ['dəːtinis; `dɝtɪnɪs] *n*. 龌龊;卑鄙,下贱。

dirt·y ['dəːti; `dɝtɪ] **I** *a*. (*dirt·i·er*; *dirt·i·est*) **1.** 龌龊的,肮脏的,污秽的,不干净的;(原子核)污染的。**2.** (手段等)卑鄙的。**3.** 下流的,猥亵的。**4.** (钱财等)不正当的。**5.** 恶意的(话)。**6.** (脸色)难看的。**7.** (天气)恶劣的。**8.** (颜色等)浑浊的。**9.** (喇叭)声调邪乎的。**10.** 有毒瘾的,吸毒的 (*opp*. clean)。*That's a* ～ *shame*! 真丢脸! *a* ～ *fighter* 无耻的拳头选手。*a* ～ *crack* 〔美俚〕尖酸刻薄的话,挖苦话。*a* ～ *dig* 〔美俚〕刻薄嘴,骂人话。*a* ～ *trumpet* 声调邪乎的喇叭。***do one's*** ～ ***work for another*** 为某人效劳,做某人部下。***do the*** ～ ***on*** ... 对…干卑鄙的勾当。**II** *vt*. (*dirt·ied*; *dirt·y·ing*) 弄脏;沾污。～ *one's hands* 弄脏自己的手脚,有损于自己的人格。— *vi*. 变脏。～ **linen** 家丑。～ **money** [**gains**] 不义之财。～ **pool** 〔美俚〕不诚实的行为,不公正的竞技。～ **work** 〔美俚〕诈骗;不法行为。～ **wound** 已化脓的伤口。

Dis [dis; dɪs] *n*.【罗神】阎王;冥府,地狱。

dis. = 〔美〕 discharged; discipline; disconnect; discontinued; discount; distance; distribute.

dis-[1] *pref*. 〔动词词首〕 **1.** 表示"离开","分离": *dis*miss, *dis*perse. **2.** 表示"剥夺","除去": *dis*frock, *dis*bar. **3.** 表示"相反": *dis*able. **4.** 表示"未能","停止","拒绝":

D

*dis*satisfy, *dis*appear, *dis*allow. 5.〔形容词词首〕表示"不","非","相反":*dis*honest, *dis*satisfied, *dis*pleasing. 6.〔名词词首〕表示"相反","缺少":*dis*ease, *dis*union.

dis-[2] *pref*. = di-[2]:*dis*sylable.

dis, diss [dis; dɪs] *vt*. 对…不尊重,蔑视。

dis·a·bil·i·ty [ˌdisəˈbiliti; ˏdɪsəˋbɪlətɪ] *n*. 1. 无力,无能;残疾。2.【法】无能力,无资格。

dis·a·ble [disˈeibl; dɪsˋebl̩] *vt*. 1. 使不中用,使无能(*from doing*; *for*);使残废。2.【法】使无能力,使无资格。*Old age* ～*d him for hard labour*. 年迈使他不能胜任繁重工作了。*I was* ～*d from walking by a fall*. 我摔跤后连路也走不动了。*be* ～*d* 成残废;(军舰)失去战斗力。*a* ～*d soldier* 残废军人。*a* ～*d ship* 废船。**-ment** *n*. 无能;残废。

dis·a·buse [ˌdisəˈbjuːz; ˏdɪsəˋbjuz] *vt*. 去除…的错误想法,使省悟,纠正。～ *sb. of superstition* 破除某人迷信。

D

di·sac·cha·ride [daiˈsækəraid; daɪˋsækəˏraɪd] *n*. 二糖类〔如蔗糖、麦芽糖、乳糖〕。

dis·ac·cord [ˌdisəˈkɔːd; ˏdɪsəˋkɔrd] *vi*., *n*. 不一致,不和谐,不和;不同意。*Your theory* ～*s with my experience*. 你的理论和我的经验不一致。～*s among nations* 国家间的不和。

dis·ac·cred·it [ˌdisəˈkredit; ˏdɪsəˋkrɛdɪt] *vt*. 对(某人)不再信任;撤销对(某人)的授权,撤销对…的委托。～ *a diplomat* 对某外交官不再信任。

dis·ac·cus·tom [disəˈkʌstəm; dɪsəˋkʌstəm] *vt*. 使(对某事物)失去习惯,摆脱…的习惯。*In the country I was* ～*ed of rising late*. 我在农村去掉了晚起的习惯。

dis·ad·van·tage [ˌdisədˈvɑːntidʒ; ˏdɪsədˋvæntɪdʒ] **I** *n*. 1. 不利,不便;不利的处境[地位]。2. (名誉,信用等的)损害,损失。**be at a** ～ 处不利地位,吃亏。**sell goods to** ～ 吃亏卖出货物。**take sb. at a** ～ 突然[乘隙]打击某人。**to sb.'s** ～ = **to the** ～ **of** 对(某人)不利地。**II** *vt*. 使不利,使吃亏。*I was* ～*d by illness*. 我因病而处于不利地位。

dis·ad·van·taged [ˌdisədˈvɑːntidʒd; ˏdɪsədˋvæntɪdʒd] *a*. 社会地位低下的,被剥夺了基本权利的;生活条件差的。～ *children* 没有得到适当照顾的儿童。

dis·ad·van·ta·geous [ˌdisædvɑːnˈteidʒəs; ˏdɪsˏædvənˋtedʒəs] *a*. 不利的,吃亏的,有害的,不便的。*What is* ～ *to John may be advantageous to Henry*. 对约翰不利的事情也许对亨利有利。**-ly** *ad*. **-ness** *n*.

dis·af·fect [ˌdisəˈfekt; ˏdɪsəˋfɛkt] *vt*. 使疏远;使不满;使不忠。*The dictator's policies have soon* ～*ed the people*. 独裁者的政策很快就使人民大为不满。

dis·af·fect·ed [ˌdisəˈfektid; ˏdɪsəˋfɛktɪd] *a*. (对政府等)生厌的;不满的,不平的;不义的,不忠的。

dis·af·fec·tion [ˌdisəˈfekʃən; ˏdɪsəˋfɛkʃən] *n*. (尤指政治上的)不满,不平;厌恶;不服。*D- often leads to outright treason*. 政治上的不满常常导致断然的背叛。

dis·af·fil·i·ate [disəˈfilieit; dɪsəˋfɪlɪˏet] *vt*. 分离,拆散,使脱离关系。*He* ～*d himself from the church*. 他与教会脱离关系。— *vi*. 与…结束往来;与…脱离关系。**-a·tion** *n*.

dis·af·firm [ˌdisəˈfəːm; ˏdɪsəˋfɝm] *vt*. 1. 反驳,反对,拒绝。2.【法】否认;取消,废弃(以前的判决)。～ *a judicial decision* 取消判决。

dis·af·firm·ance, dis·af·fir·ma·tion [disəˈfəːməns, disæfəːˈmeiʃən; dɪsəˋfɝməns, dɪsæfɝˋmeʃən] *n*. 反驳;【法】否认;废弃。

dis·af·for·est [ˌdisæˈfɔrist, disəˈfɔrist; ˏdɪsəˋfɑrɪst, dɪsəˋfɑrɪst] *vt*. 1.【英法】把(森林地)开辟成不受森林法约束的普通地。2. 伐除…上的森林。**-a·tion** [ˌdisæˌfɔrisˈteiʃən; ˏdɪsæˏfɑrɪsˋteʃən] *n*.

dis·a·gree [ˌdisəˈgriː; ˏdɪsəˋgri] *vi*. 1. 不合,不对,不符合,不一致(*with*; *in*)。2. 争持,不同意(*with*)。3. 不适宜,有害(*with*)。*His conduct* ～*s with his words*. 他言行不一。*The food* ～*d with me*. 这食物对我不适合。

dis·a·gree·a·ble [ˌdisəˈgriːəbl; ˏdɪsəˋgriəbl̩] **I** *a*. 1. 不愉快的,讨厌的。2. 难对付的,难打交道的。*a thoroughly* ～ *person* 十分讨厌的家伙。**II** *n*.〔常 *pl*.〕讨厌的事,不愉快的事。

dis·a·gree·a·bly [ˌdisəˈgriːəbli; ˏdɪsəˋgriəbl̩ɪ] *ad*. 讨厌,无聊。

dis·a·gree·ment [ˌdisəˈgriːmənt; ˏdɪsəˋgrimənt] *n*. 1. 不一致,不调和;差异。2. 异议;不和,争论。3. 不适合,有害。*a* ～ *between accounts* 账目不一致。

dis·al·low [ˈdisəˌlau, dis-; ˋdɪsəˋlaʊ, dɪs-] *vt*. 不许,不准,不承认,驳回。～ *the veracity of a report* 不承认报告的真实性。**-ance** *n*.

dis·an·nul [ˌdisəˈnʌl; ˏdɪsəˋnʌl] *vt*. 取消,废弃。～ *a contract* 废除契约。

dis·a·noint [ˌdisəˈnɔint; ˏdɪsəˋnɔɪnt] *vt*. 不再把…奉若神明。～ *a king* 不把国王奉为神明。

dis·ap·pear [ˌdisəˈpiə; ˏdɪsəˋpɪr] *vi*. 1. 消失,消散。2. 失踪,绝迹。～ *from sight* 消失不见。～**ing bed** 立体多用床。**-ance** *n*.

dis·ap·point [ˌdisəˈpɔint; ˏdɪsəˋpɔɪnt] *vt*. 1. 使失望,使沮丧。2. 使(计划等)落空,打破…的念头,使受挫折。3. 对…失信。*be greatly* ～*ed to hear that* ... 听见…而大失所望。**be agreeably** ～**ed** 庆幸未如所想。**be** ～**ed in a person** [**thing**] 对某人[某事]失望。**be** ～**ed of one's purpose** [**hopes**] 目的[希望]落了空。

dis·ap·point·ed [ˌdisəˈpɔintid; ˏdɪsəˋpɔɪntɪd] *a*. 失望了的,受了挫折的;失恋的。*a* ～ *hope* 落空的希望。**-ly** *ad*.

dis·ap·point·ing [ˌdisəˈpɔintiŋ; ˏdɪsəˋpɔɪntɪŋ] *a*. 使人失望的,沮丧的,令人扫兴的,使人不痛快的。**-ly** *ad*.

dis·ap·point·ment [ˌdisəˈpɔintmənt; ˏdɪsəˋpɔɪntmənt] *n*. 1. 失望,失意,沮丧;挫折。2. 使失望的人[事情]。～ **in love** 失恋。**to one's** ～ 失望的是。

dis·ap·pro·ba·tion [ˌdisæprəuˈbeiʃən; ˏdɪsæprəˋbeʃən] *n*. 不认可,不答应,不赞成;指责,非难。

dis·ap·pro·ba·tive [disˈæprəubeitiv; dɪsˋæproˏbetɪv], **dis·ap·pro·ba·to·ry** [-bətəri; -ˏbetərɪ] *a*. 不赞成的,不答应的;对…表示不满的。*cast a* ～ *glance at the boy* 对小孩投以不赞成的眼光。

dis·ap·prov·al [ˈdisəˈpruːvəl; ˏdɪsəˋpruvl̩] *n*. 不准,不赞成;非难。*express* ～ *of the plan* 对计划表示不赞成。*shake one's head in* ～ 摇头表示不赞成。*All watched him with* ～. 大家都用非难的目光看着他。

dis·ap·prove [ˌdisəˈpruːv, dis-; ˏdɪsəˋpruv, dɪs-] *vt*. 不答应,不准,不赞成,不满,指责。*The court* ～*d the verdict*. 法庭不赞成陪审团的裁决。— *vi*. 不赞成,反对(*of*)。*I* ～ *of ladies' smoking*. 我反对妇女抽烟。**-prov·ing·ly** *ad*. 不以为然地,以为不可地。

dis·arm [disˈɑːm, diz-; dɪsˋɑrm, dɪz-] *vt*. 1. 缴械,解除…的武装;(劈剑)打落对方的武器。2. 缓和(敌意),冰释(疑虑);消除(怒气)。3. 取出…的信管。～*ed criticism by frank avowal of his errors* 坦率承认错误,避免了批评。— *vi*. 解除武装;裁减[废除]军备。

dis·ar·ma·ment [disˈɑːməmənt; dɪsˋɑrməmənt] *n*. 缴械;解除武装;裁军。*general and complete* ～ 全面彻底的裁减军备。～ *conference* 裁军会议。

dis·arm·ing [disˈɑːmiŋ; dɪsˋɑrmɪŋ] *a*. 使人消除敌意(或怀疑、怒气等)的。**-ly** *ad*.

dis·ar·range [ˈdisəˈreindʒ; ˋdɪsəˋrendʒ] *vt*. 扰乱,搅乱,弄乱。**-ment** *n*. 混乱,紊乱。

dis·ar·ray [ˈdisəˈrei; ˋdɪsəˋre] **I** *vt*. 1. 弄乱,搅乱。2.〔古〕脱去[剥去]衣服(*of*)。**II** *n*. 1. 混乱。2. 衣冠不整。

dis·ar·tic·u·late [ˈdisɑːˈtikjuleit; ˋdɪsɑrˋtɪkjəˏlet] *vt.*, *vi.* (使)关节脱离。**-la·tion** [ˌdisɑːˌtikjuˈleiʃən; ˏdɪsɑrˏtɪkjəˋleʃən] *n.*

dis·as·sem·ble [ˌdisəˈsembl; ˏdɪsəˋsɛmbl̩] *vt.* 拆卸,拆除,拆散;分解。

dis·as·sem·bly [ˌdisəˈsembli; ˏdɪsəˋsɛmblɪ] *n.* 拆卸,分解。

dis·as·sim·i·la·tion [ˌdisəˌsimiˈleiʃən; ˏdɪsəˏsɪmɪˋleʃən] *n.* 分解代谢,异化作用。

dis·as·sim·i·late [ˌdisəˈsimileit; ˏdɪsəˋsɪmɪˏlet] *vt.* 【生】使进行分解代谢。

dis·as·so·ci·ate [ˌdisəˈsəuʃieit; ˏdɪsəˋsoʃɪˏət] *vt.* = dissociate. **-a·tion** [ˌdisəˌsəuʃiˈeiʃən; ˏdɪsəˏsoʃɪˋeʃən] *n.* = dissociation.

dis·as·ter [diˈzɑːstə; dɪˋzæstɚ] *n.* 天灾,灾害;不幸,事故。~ *movie* 灾难电影(如 The Poseidon Adventure 等)。

dis·as·trous [diˈzɑːstrəs; dɪˋzæstrəs] *a.* 引起灾难的;悲惨的;损害重大的;不幸的。*with consequences* ~ *beyond imagination* 后果不堪设想。**-ly** *ad.*

dis·a·vow [ˈdisəˈvau; ˋdɪsəˋvaʊ] *vt.* 不承认,否认,推翻(前言),推卸(责任)。**-al** *n.*

dis·band [disˈbænd; dɪsˋbænd] *vt.*, *vi.* 解散,遣散(军队等)。**-ment** *n.*

dis·bar [disˈbɑː; dɪsˋbɑr] *vt.* 【法】取消律师资格。

dis·be·lief [ˈdisbiˈliːf; ˋdɪsbəˋlif] *n.* 不信。~ *in superstition* 不迷信。

dis·be·lieve [ˌdisbiˈliːv; ˏdɪsbəˋliv] *vt.*, *vi.* 不信,怀疑(*in*)。

dis·bench [disˈbentʃ; dɪsˋbɛntʃ] *vt.* 【英法】取消法律协会会员资格。

dis·bound [disˈbaund; dɪsˋbaʊnd] *a.* 装订损坏的。

dis·branch [disˈbrɑːntʃ; dɪsˋbræntʃ] *vt.* 1. 从…剪掉树枝。2. 分开,切断。

dis·bud [disˈbʌd; dɪsˋbʌd] *vt.* 1. 蔬芽,蔬蕾〔以改进花的质量〕。2. 除去(牛等的)幼角。

dis·bur·den [disˈbəːdn; dɪsˋbɝdn] *vt.* 1. 卸下(重担);摆脱,解除(烦闷等)。2. 说明,剖白(心地等)。~ *one's mind to* 向…吐露心怀。~ *a donkey* 卸下驴子的重担。~ *a person of grief* 解除某人的忧虑。— *vi.* 卸货。

dis·burse [disˈbəːs; dɪsˋbɝs] *vt.* 1. 支付,支出。2. 分配,分散。~*d $50,000 for roads* 支付5万美元来筑路。*Our troops were* ~*d over a wide area.* 我们的军队分布在广大地区。*She* ~*d the flowers to the children.* 她把花分给孩子们。**-ment** *n.* 1. 支付,支出。2. 付出款;开销。

disc[1] [disk; dɪsk] *n.* = disk. ~ **brake** 碟形制动器,圆盘式煞车。

disc[2] = discothèque〔此词不如 disco 常用〕。

disc. = discount; discover(ed).

disc·al [ˈdiskəl; ˋdɪskəl] *a.* 盘状的。

dis·calced [disˈkælst; dɪsˋkælst] *a.* (僧侣等)赤脚的;穿草鞋的(亦作 discalceate)。

dis·card I [disˈkɑːd; dɪsˋkɑrd] *vt.* 1. 放弃,抛弃。2. 解雇。3. (纸牌戏中)垫(牌)。~ *one for another* 舍甲求乙。— *vi.* 垫牌。**II** [ˈdiskɑːd; ˋdɪskɑrd] *n.* 1. 垫牌;垫出的牌。2. 抛弃;被抛弃的人[物]。***go into the*** ~ 被抛弃(*Sword and spear and battle-ax have gone into the* ~ *of time.* 刀枪剑戟已被时间所淘汰)。***throw into the*** ~ 〔美〕放弃。

dis·cern [diˈsəːn; dɪˋsɝn] *vt.* 1. 辨别,分清。2. 看出,认出。~ *good and evil* = ~ *good from evil* = ~ *between good and evil* 辨别善恶。~ *a distant object* 看出远处目标。~ *no difference* 看不出差别。— *vi.* 辨别。**-i·ble** *a.* 可辨别[看出]的。**-i·bly** *ad.* **-ing** *a.* 眼力好的,眼光敏锐的。**-ing·ly** *ad.* **-ment** *n.* 辨别(力);眼力;精明。

dis·cerp·ti·ble [diˈsəːptibl; dəˋsɝptəbl̩] *a.* 可分解的,可剖析的。**-bility** [-ˌsəːptiˈbiliti; -ˏsɝptɪˋbɪlətɪ] *n.*

dis·cerp·tion [diˈsəːpʃən; dɪˋsɝpʃən] *n.* 分离,割断;断片。

dis·charge [disˈtʃɑːdʒ; dɪsˋtʃɑrdʒ] **I** *vt.* 1. 发射(炮等),打(枪),射(箭)。2. 起,卸(货)。3. 排泄,排出,放出(水等)。4. 释放;解除,免除(义务等);遣散(军人),使退役;放走,放行,罢免,解雇。5. 尽(义务等),履行,践(约等);清偿(债务)。6. 【电】放(电)。7. (印染中)除去染料[颜色],漂白,拔染。8. 【法】撤销(命令)。~ *a bow* 开弓。~ *an arrow from a bow* 射箭。~ *a gun* 开炮。~ *a ship* 卸货。~ *one's duties* 尽责。*A chimney* ~*s smoke.* 烟囱冒烟。— *vi.* 1. 卸货,起货。2. (疮等)出脓,出水。3. (染料、墨水等)洇,沁,渗。4. 放电。5. (枪炮等)发射。~ (*sb.*) ***from*** (*service*; *office*; *hospital*; *prison*) 解(雇);免(职);使出(医院);使出(狱)。(*The river*) ~ (***itself***) ***into*** (*the sea*) (河)流注(海中)。~ ***oneself of one's duty*** 尽(义务)。**II** *n.* 1. 发射,射出。2. 起货,卸货。3. 流出,排泄;流量;排泄物。4. 免除,释放;退伍,退役;解雇,免职。5. 退伍[解职,释放]证明书。6. 履行;清账,清偿欠款;(担保的)解除。7. 【电】放电。8. 【纺】(印染中的)漂白(剂)。*be ready for the* ~ *from the hospital* 随时皆可出院。~ *from the ears* [*eyes, nose*] 耳屎[眼屎,鼻涕]。*the* ~ *of contract* 契约的解除。~ **gas** 废气。~ **jetties** 卸货码头。~ **liquid** 废液。

dis·charg·er [disˈtʃɑːdʒə; dɪsˋtʃɑrdʒɚ] *n.* 1. 发射者;发射装置;启动装置。2. 卸货人;开释人;履行者。3. 【电】放电器;避电器;火花间隙;【染】拔染剂。**static** ~ 静电放射器。

dis·ci·form [ˈdisifɔːm; ˋdɪsəˏfɔrm] *a.* 圆形的;椭圆形的。

dis·ci·ple [diˈsaipl; dɪˋsaɪpl̩] *n.* 1. 徒弟,门徒,信徒,弟子,追随者。2. 【宗】耶稣十二门徒之一。*a* ~ *of Freud* 弗洛伊德学说的信徒。*a* ~ *of the Hindus* 印度教徒。*the* (*twelve*) ~*s* 耶稣十二门徒。**-ship** *n.* 徒弟的身份;做徒弟的时期。

dis·ci·pli·nal [ˈdisiplinəl; ˋdɪsəplɪnl] *a.* 1. 训练上的。2. 纪律上的,惩戒的。

dis·ci·plin·ant [ˈdisiplinənt; ˋdɪsəplɪnənt] *n.* 1. 苦行者,苦行僧。2. 〔D-〕(西班牙古时基督教)鞭身教派教徒。

dis·ci·pli·nar·i·an [ˌdisipliˈnεəriən; ˏdɪsəplɪˋnɛrɪən] **I** *a.* 1. 训练上的。2. 训育的,惩戒性的,有关纪律的。**II** *n.* 1. 训练者。2. 严格执行纪律的人;严格的教员。*The teacher is a formidable* ~. 这位老师对纪律抓得很严。

dis·ci·pli·na·ry [ˈdisiplinəri; ˋdɪsəplɪnˏɛrɪ] *a.* 1. 训练上的。2. 纪律的;惩戒性的。~ *barracks* 【美军】惩戒所。*a* ~ *committee* 惩戒委员会。~ *punishment* 纪律处分。*take* ~ *action* 采取纪律措施,实行处分。**-ri·ly** *ad.*

dis·ci·pline [ˈdisiplin; ˋdɪsəplɪn] **I** *n.* 1. 训练,锻炼;(逆境等的)磨炼;修养;教养。2. 纪律,风纪;【宗】宗规,戒律。3. 训戒,惩戒;惩罚。4. 〔古〕学科。*courage without* ~ 匹夫之勇,蛮勇。*good* ~*s in an army* 一支军队的良好军纪。*school* ~ 校规,校训。*strict* ~ 严格的训练。*be under perfect* ~ 训练严格。*enforce* [*maintain*] ~ 坚持[维持]纪律。*a commission for* ~ *inspection* 纪律检查委员会。*keep one's passions under* ~ 节制情欲。**II** *vt.* 1. 训练,锻炼,操练。2. 训导,强使守纪律。3. 惩戒,惩罚。~ *oneself for an end* 为某一目的训练[锻炼]自己。~ *an outlaw* 强使一个亡命徒守纪律。*be* ~*d for one's failure* 因失败受罚。**-plin·a·ble** *a.* 可训练的;应惩罚的。

dis·cip·u·lar [diˈsipjulə; dəˋsɪpjəlɚ] *a.* 门徒的,信徒的,追随者的。

dis·claim [disˈkleim; dɪsˋklem] *vt.* 1. 放弃,【法】对…弃

D

权,不认领,不索取。2. 否认,不承认。～ *all participation* 否认参与其事。— *vi*. 1.【法】表示弃权。2.〔废〕否认有关系。**-a·tion** *n*. **-er** *n*. 1. 弃权;否认。2. 弃权者,否认者。

dis·cli·max [ˈdisˈklaimæks; ˋdɪsˋklaɪmæks] *n*. (由于耕种等而)破坏或改变生态平衡。

dis·close [disˈkləuz; dɪsˋkloz] *vt*. 1. 露出,泄露(秘密等)。2. 揭发,揭开,表明。～ *a secret* 泄露一个秘密。*The violets* ～ *their petals*. 紫罗兰绽开花瓣。*a* ～*d ballot* 无封投票。～ *one's intentions* 表明心意。

dis·clo·sure [disˈkləuʒə; dɪsˋkloʒɚ] *n*. 1. 泄露,暴露;(发明等的)公开。2. 揭发;显示;开诚布公的话。*make a* ～ *of* 暴露。

Disc·man [ˈdiskmən; ˋdɪskmən] *n*. CD随身听〔随身携带的激光唱碟放音机〕。

dis·co [ˈdiskəu; ˋdɪsko] *n*. 迪斯科 (= discothèque)。～**-beat** 强劲急促的迪斯科音乐节拍。～**-girl** 迪斯科女郎。～**-pub** 迪斯科酒吧。～**-set** 迪斯科乐队。

D

dis·cob·o·lus [disˈkɔbələs; dɪsˋkɑbələs] *n*. (*pl*. **-bo·li** [-bəlai; -bəlaɪ]) 1. (古代的)铁饼掷手;掷铁饼者。2. 〔D-〕铁饼掷手像〔公元前五世纪雕刻家 Myron 所作青铜像〕。

dis·cog·ra·phy [disˈkɔgrəfi; dɪsˋkɑgrəfɪ] *n*. 1. 唱片分类学。2. 唱片分类目录。**-ra·pher** *n*. 唱片分类目录编制者。

dis·coid [ˈdiskɔid; ˋdɪskɔɪd] **I** *a*. 1. 圆饼状的,盘状的。2.【植】花盘上的;只有管状小花的。**II** *n*. 圆饼状物。

dis·col·our, dis·col·or [disˈkʌlə; dɪsˋkʌlɚ] *vt*. 使变色;使褪色;污染,弄脏。*wallpaper* ～*ed by age* 褪色的陈年糊壁纸。— *vi*. 1. 变色;褪色,脱色。2. 污染,变脏。**-a·tion** [ˌdiskʌləˈreiʃən; ˏdɪskʌləˋreʃən] *n*. **-ment** *n*. 变色,褪色。

dis·com·bob·u·late [ˌdiskʌmˈbɔbjuleit; ˏdɪskəmˋbɑbjəˏlet] *vt*. 〔美口〕破坏,搞乱,扰乱,打乱(计划等)。*plans* ～*d by the turn of events* 因事态演变而遭打乱的计划。

dis·com·fit [disˈkʌmfit; dɪsˋkʌmfɪt] *vt*. 1. 破坏,搞乱,打乱(计划、目的等)。2. 使狼狈,使为难。3.〔古〕击溃,打败。*be* ～*ed by a question* 被质问得很狼狈。**-fi·ture** [-ˈkʌmfitʃə; -ˋkʌmfɪtʃɚ] *n*. 1. 为难,狼狈。2. 失望;挫折。3. 失败;溃败。

dis·com·fort [disˈkʌmfət; dɪsˋkʌmfɚt] **I** *n*. 1. 不舒适,不方便;困难。2. 不安;不愉快,烦闷。*neglect minor* ～*s* 对小小的不愉快不放在心上。**II** *vt*. 1. 使不安,使不愉快,使苦恼。2. 使不舒适,使不便。**-a·ble** *a*.〔古〕使人不舒适的;使人失望的。

dis·com·mend [ˌdiskəˈmend; ˏdɪskəˋmɛnd] *vt*. 1.〔罕〕不赞许。2.〔废〕劝说;非议,贬。

dis·com·mode [ˌdiskəˈməud; ˏdɪskəˋmod] *vt*. 1. 使不方便。2. 使为难,使烦恼。

dis·com·mod·i·ty [diskəˈmɔditi; dɪskəˋmɑdətɪ] *n*. 〔古〕1. 不便;不利。2. 无使用价值的东西。

dis·com·mon [disˈkɔmən; dɪsˋkɑmən] *vt*. 1. 把(公地)占为私有;剥夺…的公地使用权。2. (英牛津大学等)禁止(商人、市民等)和学生做买卖。

dis·com·pose [ˌdiskəmˈpəuz; ˏdɪskəmˋpoz] *vt*. 1. 使不安,使烦恼,使失常。2. 扰乱(秩序等)。*be* ～*d by bad news* 听到坏消息深感不安。**-pos·ed·ly** [-ˈpəuzidli; -ˋpozɪdlɪ] *ad*. 不安地,心绪不宁地。**-po·sure** [-ˈpəuʒə; -ˋpoʒɚ] *n*. 不安,烦乱,失常。

dis·con·cert [ˌdiskənˈsəːt; ˏdɪskənˋsɝt] *vt*. 1. 使为难,使困窘,使仓皇失措,使失常。2. 挫败,打乱(计划等)。*be* ～*ed by the unexpected question* 因遇到意想不到的问题而为难。**-ed** *a*. 心烦意乱的,不安的。**-ing·ly** *a*. **-ment** *n*. 失措;挫折。

dis·con·form·i·ty [diskənˈfɔːmiti; dɪskənˋfɔrmətɪ] *n*. 1.〔古〕不一致,不调合。2.【地】假整合。

dis·con·nect [ˌdiskəˈnekt; ˏdɪskəˋnɛkt] *vt*. 1. 分开,隔开,使(一物)与(另一物)分离(*from*; *with*)。2. 割断,切断(联络),挂断(电话),折断。～ *the telephone* 挂断电话。*We were* ～*ed*. 我们失去了联络。～ *the fuse from* [*with*] *a bomb* 从炸弹上卸下导火线。— *vi*. 1. 结束关系。2. 退隐,离群索居。～ *into silence* 隐居,销声匿迹。

dis·con·nect·ed [ˈdiskəˈnektid; ˏdɪskəˋnɛktɪd] *a*. 1. 断了联络的,分离的。2. 支离破碎的,无系统的,(演说等)乱七八糟的。～ *arguments* [*thoughts*] 首尾不一贯的论点[思想]。**-ly** *ad*. 无联络地,断断续续地。

dis·con·nex·ion, dis·con·nec·tion [ˌdiskəˈnekʃən; ˏdɪskəˋnɛkʃən] *n*. 分离;分开;断开,切断。*partial* ～【电】半断接(线)。

dis·con·so·late [disˈkɔnsəlit; dɪsˋkɑnsəlɪt] *a*. 1. 郁闷的,愁闷的;忧伤的。2. (前景等)阴暗的。～ *prospects* 暗淡的前景。*The team returned* ～ *from three losses*. 连输三场的球队归来时闷闷不乐。**-ly** *ad*. **-ness** *n*.

dis·con·tent [ˈdiskənˈtent; ˏdɪskənˋtɛnt] **I** *n*. 1. 不满;不平;不愉快。2. 不满的人。～ *among unemployed workers* 失业工人的不满。**II** *a*. 不满的,不安分的;不平的(*with*)。～ *with one's work* [*lot*] 对自己的工作[处境]不满意。**III** *vt*.〔通例用被动语态〕使不满意,使不平。*be* ～*ed with sb*. 对某人不满。**-ment** *n*.

dis·con·tent·ed [ˈdiskənˈtentid; ˋdɪskənˋtɛntɪd] *a*. 不平的;不满的。*For all their wealth, they were* ～. 他们尽管有钱,还是感到不满。**-ly** *ad*. **-ness** *n*.

dis·con·tin·u·ance [ˌdiskənˈtinjuəns; ˏdɪskənˋtɪnjuəns] *n*. 1. 停止,废止,中止,断绝。2.【法】(诉讼等的)撤销,(诉讼手续等的)中止。*the* ～ *of a business* 企业歇业。

dis·con·tin·u·a·tion [ˈdiskənˌtinjuˈeiʃən; ˋdɪskənˏtɪnjuˋeʃən] *n*. = discontinuance 1. *repeated* ～ *of work* 工程的多次停顿。

dis·con·tin·ue [ˈdiskənˈtinju(ː); ˏdɪskənˋtɪnju] *vt*. 1. 搁下,中止,停止;中断;暂停。2.【法】撤销(诉讼等);放弃(权利等)。～ *a newspaper* 停止订阅报纸。～ *a correspondence* 停止通信。— *vi*. 1. 中止,中断,停止,暂停。2. (报纸等)停刊。*This magazine will* ～. 这家杂志将停刊。

dis·con·ti·nu·i·ty [ˈdisˌkɔntiˈnju(ː)iti; ˏdɪskɑntəˋnuətɪ] *n*. 1. 断绝,中断;间断。2.【物】不连续性,突变性,突变点;【数】不连续点;断续函数。

dis·con·tin·u·ous [ˈdiskənˈtinjuəs; ˋdɪskənˋtɪnjuəs] *a*. 1. 不连续的,断断续续的;中断的。2. 突变的。～ *function*【数】不连续函数。**-ly** *ad*.

dis·co·phile [ˈdiskəfail; ˋdɪskəˏfaɪl] *n*. 唱片收藏[鉴别]家。

dis·cord I [ˈdiskɔːd; ˋdɪskɔrd] *n*. 1. 不和,倾轧。2. 不一致,不调和;【乐】不谐和(音)。3. 嘈杂声,喧闹。*marital* ～ 夫妇不和。*sow* ～ 挑拨。**be in** ～ **with** 和…闹别扭,与…不和。**the apple of** ～ 见 apple 条。**II** [disˈkɔːd; dɪsˋkɔrd] *vi*. 1. 不调和,不一致;倾轧,冲突(*with*; *from*)。2.【乐】不谐和,发乱音。

dis·cord·ance, dis·cor·dan·cy [disˈkɔːdəns, disˈkɔːdənsi; dɪsˋkɔrdəns, dɪsˋkɔrdənsɪ] *n*. 1. 不一致,不和,倾轧。2.【乐】(音的)不谐和;【地】不整一,不整合。

dis·cord·ant [disˈkɔːdənt; dɪsˋkɔrdənt] *a*. 1. 不一致的,不和的,倾轧的。2.【乐】不谐和的;【地】不整合的。～ *opinions* 众说纷纭,互不一致的意见。**-ly** *ad*.

dis·co·thèque [ˈdiskəteik; ˋdɪskətɛk] **I** *n*. 夜总会;(播放流行歌曲唱片的)"迪斯科"舞厅。**II** *vi*. 在迪斯科舞厅内跳舞。～ **dress** 迪斯科装(尤指一种底领、黑底色、底边有褶的短女装)。

dis·count [ˈdiskaunt; ˋdɪskaʊnt] **I** *n*. 1. 折扣,让头。2.【商】贴现,贴现率,折息,扣息。3. 不考虑,不重视,不全信。*5 percent* ～ *for cash* 现金付款,九五折优待。*an arithmetical* [*true*] ～ 真折扣。*a bank* ～ 银行贴现。*10 percent* ～ *on tickets* 票价打九折。*accept his story* *with some* ~ 打折扣听他的故事。*at 25%* ~打七五折。~ *of 10%* 九折。**at a** ~ 1.(股票等的处理)低于票面价格〔参看 at a premium〕,打折扣。2.(货物等的)跌价;无销路。3.不受重视,不受欢迎(*Superstitions are at a* ~ *today*. 迷信的习俗今天已不受欢迎)。**give** [**allow**, **make**] **a** ~ 打折扣(*on*)。**II** [ˈdiskaunt, disˈkaunt; ˋdɪskaʊnt, dɪsˋkaʊnt] **vt**. 1.打去(若干)折扣,打折扣买[卖];【商】把(票据等)贴现;(借款时)先扣(若干)利息。2.打着折扣听,不全信;低估;忽视,藐视。3.(通过事先采取行动)减弱(事件等的效果)。4.【台球】向(对方)让分。*be* ~*ed at 10% percent* 打九折。*The store* ~*ed all clothing for sale*. 该店的服装全部减价出售。~ *a politician* 对政客持怀疑态度。*They have* ~*ed the effect of a decline in the stock market*. 他们已经考虑到股票市场跌风的影响而事先作出估算。~ **bank** 贴现银行。~ **broke** 贴现掮客。~ **house** 廉价商店。~ **rate** 贴现率。**-er** *n*. =~ **house**.

dis·count·a·ble [ˈdiskauntəbl; ˋdɪskaʊntəbl] **a**. 1.可打折扣的;【商】可贴现的。2.该打折扣听的,不可全信的。

dis·coun·te·nance [disˈkauntinəns; dɪsˋkaʊntənəns] **I** **vt**. 1.使…丢脸,冷淡对待,使尴尬,使羞愧。2.不赞成,不支持,使泄气。*Teachers* ~*d smoking by the students*. 教师们反对学生们吸烟。*He survived every attempt to* ~ *him*. 在种种想叫他丢脸的打击面前,他挺过来了。**II** **n**. 不赞成,不支持。

dis·cour·age [disˈkʌridʒ; dɪsˋkɝɪdʒ] **vt**. (*opp*. encourage) 1.使受挫折;使沮丧,使泄气。2.劝阻,使打断念头;阻止,阻碍。*be* ~*d with life* 对生活失去信心。*Low prices* ~ *industry*. 低物价妨碍工业发展。~ *sb*. *from smoking* 劝阻某人吸烟。**-ment** **n**. 1.挫折,气馁,沮丧,失意。2.阻碍,拦阻(*give up* (*sth*.) *in complete* ~ 完全气馁而放弃不干(某事)。*Poor health is grave* ~. 身体不好是一个严重的障碍)。

dis·cour·ag·ing [disˈkʌridʒiŋ; dɪsˋkɝɪdʒɪŋ] **a**. 1.使人沮丧[气馁]的。2.阻止的。**-ly** *ad*.

dis·course [disˈkɔːs; dɪsˋkors] **I** **n**. 1.演说;【宗】讲道,说教。2.讲稿;论说,论文。3.〔古〕会话,谈话。4.【语法】叙述法。5.〔古〕推理能力。*make a stirring* ~ 作了一次激动人心的演讲。**II** **vi**. 1.讲演,论说(*on*; *upon*; *of*),说教,讲道。2.写论文,写讲稿。3.谈,讲,谈论。**D- on Method**《方法论》〔法国哲学家笛卡尔的著作〕。

dis·cour·te·ous [disˈkəːtjəs; dɪsˋkɝtɪəs] **a**. 1.不懂礼的,无礼的。2.粗鲁的。**-ly** *ad*. **-ness** *n*.

dis·cour·te·sy [disˈkəːtisi; dɪsˋkɝtəsɪ] **n**. 1.无礼貌,失礼(*opp*. courtesy)。2.粗鲁,鲁莽行为。

dis·cov·er [disˈkʌvə; dɪsˋkʌvɚ] **vt**. 1.看出,发现,看到。2.〔古〕现出,露出;显示,泄露;【象棋】(移开己方挡道棋子)将(对方)一军。~ *America* 发现美洲。*Try to* ~ *what is best to do*. 想办法找出最好的对策。*His poems* ~*ed vast realms of the spirit*. 他的诗显示出广阔的精神天地。**be** ~**ed**【剧】幕一开就在舞台上。~**ed check**【象棋】(移开己方的一子露出另一有攻击力的棋子)将(对方)一军。~ **oneself** 显露自己的身份,通名,自我介绍。— **vi**. 有所发现。**-able** *a*.

dis·cov·er·er [disˈkʌvərə; dɪsˋkʌvərɚ] **n**. 1.发现者,发见者。2.〔D-〕(美国的)"发现者"号卫星。~ *of electricity* 发现电的人。

dis·cov·ert [disˈkʌvət; dɪsˋkʌvɚt] **a**.【法】无夫的,(女子)未婚的,寡居的。

dis·cov·er·y [disˈkʌvəri; dɪsˋkʌvərɪ] **n**. 1.发见,发现,发觉。2.〔古〕显示,暴露,显露。3.(剧情的)发展。4.被发现的事物。5.【法】(审判前当事一方必须作出的)显示证据。~ *ship* 探险船。*make many discoveries about the heavenly bodies* 在天体方面有许多新发现。**D- Day**〔美〕美洲发现纪念日〔十月十二日〕。~ **well** 油田的第一口油井。

dis·cred·it [disˈkredit; dɪsˋkrɛdɪt] **I** **n**. 1.丧失信用,丧失信任。2.丧失名誉,丢脸,耻辱。3.不信,疑惑。*It is no* ~ *to him*. 那是无损于他的名誉的。*His theories met with general discredits*. 他的理论遭到普遍怀疑。**bring** ~ **on sb.'s name** 玷污某人名誉。**bring** ~ **on oneself** 使自己失信[丢脸]。**fall into** ~ 声名狼藉。**throw** [**cast**] ~ **on** [**upon**] 使人疑心…。**II** **vt**. 1.不信,怀疑;使成为不可信。2.损害…的信誉,丢…的丑。*an effort to* ~ *certain politicians* 设法使某些政界人士丧失信誉。*His behaviour* ~*s him*. 他的行为使他名誉扫地。*There was good reason to* ~ *the witness*. 有充足的理由怀疑证人。**-a·ble** *a*. 损害信用的,不名誉的;丢脸的,耻辱的。**-a·bly** *ad*.

dis·creet [disˈkriːt; dɪsˋkrit] **a**. 1.考虑周到的,用心深远的。2.慎重的,谨慎的,小心的。*He is very* ~ *in giving his opinions*. 他发表意见时十分慎重。*a* ~ *silence* 出于谨慎的沉默。**-ly** *ad*. **-ness** *n*.

dis·crep·an·cy [disˈkrepənsi; dɪsˋkrɛpənsɪ] **n**. 差异,矛盾;不符合,不一致。*a* ~ *between two versions of a story* 一篇故事两个不同讲法之间的差别。*There are obvious discrepancies between what you practice and what you preach*. 你言行不一。**-crep·ant** **a**. 互有差别的(*discrepant accounts* 互有差异的报道)。

D

dis·crete [disˈkriːt; dɪsˋkrit] **a**. 1.分离的,分立的;显然有别的。2.不连续的;【数】离散的;【哲】抽象的(*opp*. concrete)。*A nebula is really a* ~ *mass of innumerous stars*. 一团星云实际上是无数星体不连续的集合体。~ **quantity**【数】分离量。~ **smallpox**【医】稀疏性天花。~ **space**【物】离散空间。**-ly** *ad*.

dis·cre·tion [disˈkreʃən; dɪsˋkrɛʃən] **n**. 1.判断(力),辨别(力)。2.慎重,谨慎,考虑周到。3.(行动、判断或选择的)自由,自行裁决,斟酌;【法】任意决定权。4.〔古〕离散,间断,不连续。*D- is the better part of valour*. 考虑周到胜过勇敢。**act at** [**on**] **one's own** ~ 相机行事,自行决断。**age** [**years**] **of** ~【法】解事年龄,责任年龄,成年〔英国法律规定为14岁〕。**at** ~ 1.随意,任意。2.无条件(*be allowed to work overtime at* ~ 被允许自由加班。*surrender at* ~ 无条件投降)。**at the** ~ **of** 随…的意思,凭…自行处理。**be in** [**within**] **one's** ~ **to** (*do*)(做…)是某人的自由[权限]。**leave to sb.'s** ~ 交某人酌(办),任某人自由决定。**use one's own** ~ 依靠自己去判断。**with** ~ 慎重,审慎。

dis·cre·tion·al [disˈkreʃənl; dɪsˋkrɛʃənl̩], **dis·cre·tion·ar·y** [disˈkreʃnəri; dɪsˋkrɛʃənˏɛrɪ] **a**. 任意的,自由决定的。*a* ~ *power to act* 可自由采取行动的权力,可便宜行事权。~ **account** [**order**]【商】由经纪人[中间人]全权处理的资本帐户[自由裁决的定货]。~ **income** 可以自由处理的收入(指扣除纳税和衣食住等必需开支后的收入部分)。~ **principle** 独断主义。~ **wiring method**【电】选择布线法。

dis·crim·i·na·ble [disˈkriminəbl; dɪsˋkrɪmənəbl̩] **a**. 可区别的,可辨别的。

dis·crim·i·nant [disˈkriminənt; dɪsˋkrɪmənənt] **n**.【数】判别式。

dis·crim·i·nate [disˈkrimineit; dɪsˋkrɪməˏnet] **I** **vt**. 1.区别,鉴别,识别。2.区分出,辨出。*a mark that* ~*s the original from the copy* 使原本与抄本有所区别的特征。*He can* ~ *minute variations in tone*. 他能辨别出音调的细微变化。— **vi**. 1.识别,区别。2.分别对待,歧视,排斥。~ **against** 歧视,排斥(~ *against foreigners* 排外)。~ **between** (**one thing**) **and** (**another**) 区别开(一物)和(另一物)(~ *between right and wrong* 辨明是非)。~ **in favour** 优待(*He* ~*s in favour of his relatives*. 他优待自己的亲戚)。**II** [disˈkriminit; dɪsˋkrɪmənɪt] **a**. 1.能识别的,有分辨能力的。2.〔古〕明确的;显著的。*D- people choose carefully*. 有眼光的人作选择时总很细心。**-ly** *ad*.

dis·crim·i·nat·ing [disˈkrimineitiŋ; dɪsˋkrɪmə͵netɪŋ] ***a*.** **1.** 有辨别力的,有鉴别力的。**2.** 有差别的,区别对待的。**3.** 形成区别的,特征显著的。**4.** 辨别的,分析的。*a ~ tariff* (关税等的)差别税率。*a ~ test* 分析试验。*a ~ eye* 有鉴别力,有眼力。*~ audiences* 有鉴赏力的观众。*a ~ mark* 形成差别的标志。**-ly** ***ad*.**

dis·crim·i·na·tion [dis͵krimiˈneiʃən; dɪs͵krɪməˋneʃən] ***n*.** **1.** 辨别,区别,鉴别。**2.** 辨别力,识别力,鉴赏力,眼力。**3.** 不公平的待遇,差别对待,歧视,排斥。*racial and religious ~* 种族和宗教歧视。*a man of ~* 有眼光[见识]的人。*a policy of ~ against foreigners* 排外政策。*~ between right and wrong* 辨明是非。*bombing without ~* 狂轰滥炸。**-na·tor** [disˈkrimineitə; dɪsˋkrɪmə͵netɚ] ***n*.** **1.** 辨别者。**2.** 歧视者。**3.**【无】鉴频器。

dis·crim·i·na·tive [disˈkriminətiv; dɪsˋkrɪmənetɪv] ***a*.** **1.** 有辨别力的。**2.** 有区别的,差别分明的。**3.** 区别对待的,歧视的 (*the ~ features of man* 人的独有特征。*~ organs* 识别器官。*~ tariff* 差别关税)。

dis·crim·i·na·tor [disˈkrimineitə; dɪsˋkrɪmə͵netɚ] ***n*.** 辨别者。

dis·crim·i·na·to·ry [disˈkriminətəri; dɪsˋkrɪmənə͵torɪ] ***a*.** = discriminative.

dis·crown [disˈkraun; dɪsˋkraʊn] ***vt*.** 使退位,废黜…的王位。

dis·cul·pate [disˈkʌlpeit; dɪsˋkʌlpet] ***vt*.** 开脱…的罪责。

dis·cur·sion [disˈkəːʃən; dɪsˋkɝʃən] ***n*.** **1.** 东拉西扯的谈话[文章]等。**2.** (文章、谈话等的)散漫,东拉西扯,支离破碎。**3.**【哲】推论。

dis·cur·sive [disˈkəːsiv dɪsˈkɝsɪv] ***a*.** **1.** (谈话、文章等)散漫的,东拉西扯的,不着边际的,离题的。**2.**【哲】推论的 (*opp*. intuitive)。*a ~ talk* 漫无边际的谈话。**-ly** ***ad*.** **-ness** ***n*.**

dis·cus [ˈdiskəs; ˋdɪskəs] ***n*.** (*pl*. *~es* [-iz; -ɪz], ***dis·ci*** [ˈdiskai; ˋdɪskaɪ]) **1.**【体】铁饼;掷铁饼。**2.**【动】盘;盘域;【植】花盘。*the ~ throw(ing)* 掷铁饼。

dis·cuss [disˈkʌs; dɪsˋkʌs] ***vt*.** **1.** 议论;讨论,辩论。**2.** 论述,详述。**3.** 〔口〕津津有味地吃[喝]完;欣赏…的味道。**4.**【法】对(主要债务人)起诉。*~ what should be done* 讨论应该做什么。*They ~ed a bottle of wine*. 他们津津有味地喝完酒。*demand to ~ the principal debtor* 要求对主要债务人提起诉讼。— ***vi*.** 讨论;谈话。*~ with sb*. 和某人谈话。

dis·cuss·ant [disˈkʌsənt; dɪsˋkʌsənt] ***n*.** 应邀参加讨论的人,讨论会列席者。

dis·cus·sion [disˈkʌʃən; dɪsˋkʌʃən] ***n*.** **1.** 议论,讨论;辩论,审议。**2.** 详述,论述;〔口〕(对食品的)品尝,尝味 (*of*)。*a question under ~* 审议中的问题。*a bill down for ~* 一项被提出讨论的议案。

dis·dain [disˈdein; dɪsˋden] **I** ***vt*.** **1.** 轻蔑,鄙视,藐视,瞧不起。**2.** 不屑做。*~ a coward* 鄙弃懦夫。*~ a man for his snobbishness* 鄙视势利小人。*~ to reply an insult* 不屑于理睬别人的侮辱。— ***vi*.** 〔主美〕被轻蔑,遭鄙视。**II** ***n*.** 轻蔑,鄙视。*~ of riches* 鄙视财富。*be treated with ~* 遭人轻视。**-ful** ***a*.** 轻蔑的,藐视的,倨傲的 (*a ~ look* 蔑视的目光。*be ~ of danger* 无视危险)。**-ful·ly** ***ad*.**

dis·ease [diˈziːz; dɪˋziz] ***n*.** **1.** 病,疾病;【植】病害。**2.** (精神等的)病态,弊病。**3.** (酒等的)变质;(食物等的)腐败。**4.** 〔废〕不安。*an acute [chronic] ~* 急性[慢性]病。*a family ~* 遗传病。*foot-and-mouth ~*【兽医】口蹄疫。*tin ~* 铁皮的锈蚀。*the various ~s of civilization* 文明带来的弊害。**be cured of a ~** 治好病。**catch [suffer from, take] a ~** 患病。

dis·eased [diˈziːzd; dɪˋzizd] ***a*.** **1.** 有病的;【植】有病害的。**2.** 有弊病的;(精神等)病态的。*the ~ part* 患部。*a ~ society* 病态的社会。*a ~ mind* 病态心理。

dis·e·co·nom·ics [ˈdis͵ikəˈnɔmiks; ˋdɪs͵ikəˋnɑmɪks] ***n*.** 有害的经济政策。

dis·e·con·o·my [ˈdisi(ː)ˈkɔnəmi; ͵dɪsɪˋkɑnəmɪ] ***n*.** **1.** 不经济,成本(或费用)的增加。**2.** 使成本(或费用)增加的因素。

dis·em·bark [ˈdisimˈbɑːk; ͵dɪsɪmˋbɑrk] ***vt*.** 使离船上岸;(从船上)卸下。— ***vi*.** 离船登岸。**-a·tion** [͵disembɑːˈkeiʃən; ͵dɪsembɑrˋkeʃən] ***n*.**

dis·em·bar·rass [ˈdisimˈbærəs; ˋdɪsɪmˋbærəs] ***vt*.** 解脱,使摆脱(忧虑等),使脱离(困窘等);使安心。*He ~ed himself of his heavy coat*. 他脱下了沉重的外衣。*~ oneself from troublesome trivalities* 摆脱令人烦恼的琐事。**-ment** ***n*.**

dis·em·bod·y [ˈdisimˈbɔdi; ˋdɪsɪmˋbɑdɪ] ***vt*.** (***-bodied***; ***-bod·y·ing***) **1.** 使…脱离肉体,使不具形体〔主要以过去分词形式作修饰语用〕。**2.** 〔罕〕解散,遣散(军队)。*a disembodied soul* 脱离肉体的灵魂。**-bod·i·ment** ***n*.**

dis·em·bogue [͵disimˈbəug; ͵dɪsɛmˋbog] ***vi*.** **1.** (河水等)流出;流注 (*into*)。**2.** (内容等)倾吐出。**3.** 〔罕〕(船)驶出港湾。*a river that ~s into the ocean* 一条流入大洋的江河。— ***vt*.** (河流等)将(河水)倾吐出。*a river that ~s itself [its waters] into the ocean* 一条注入大洋的江河。

dis·em·bos·om [͵disimˈbuzəm; ͵dɪsəmˋbuzəm] ***vt*.** 说出,透露,公开(秘密等)。*~ oneself of a secret* 说出心中的秘密。*~ oneself* 说出心里话。*~ a secret* 透露秘密。

dis·em·bow·el [͵disimˈbauəl; ͵dɪsɪmˋbaʊəl] ***vt*.** ((英) ***-ll-***) **1.** 除去…的内脏,取出…的肠子。**2.** 取出…的内容。**3.** (蜘蛛)吐(丝)。*~ oneself* 剖腹自杀。**-ment** ***n*.**

dis·em·broil [͵disimˈbrɔil; ͵dɪsɛmˋbrɔɪl] ***vt*.** 排解…的纠纷,把…从纷扰中解脱。

dis·em·ployed [͵disimˈplɔid; ͵dɪsɛmˋplɔɪd] ***a*.** 失业的〔尤指由于技术、学识等方面不称职而失业的〕。

dis·en·chant [͵disinˈtʃɑːnt; ͵dɪsɪnˋtʃænt] ***vt*.** 使清醒,使摆脱幻想,使不再着迷。*The harshness of everyday reality ~ed him of his idealistic hopes*. 冷酷的日常现实使他从理想主义的幻梦中清醒过来。*He will be ~ed with her*. 他对她将不再着迷。**-ment** ***n*.**

dis·en·cum·ber [ˈdisinˈkʌmbə; ˋdɪsɪnˋkʌmbɚ] ***vt*.** 消除(成见等),摆脱(烦恼、负担等)。*~ the mind from prejudice* 消除成见。*~ one's mind from [of] cares* 消除烦恼。

dis·en·dow [ˈdisinˈdau; ˋdɪsenˋdaʊ] ***vt*.** 剥夺(教会、学校等的)捐款[基金]。**-ment** ***n*.**

dis·en·fran·chise [͵disinˈfræntʃaiz; ͵dɪsɪnˋfræntʃaɪz] ***vt*.** = disfranchise.

dis·en·gage [ˈdisinˈgeidʒ; ˋdɪsɪnˋgedʒ] ***vt*.** **1.** 放开,解开(束缚等),解除(契约等),使脱开(约束等)。**2.**【机】使(离合器等)分开;【军】使脱离(接触),使中止(战斗);【化】使分离,使游离,使离析。*~ a clutch*【机】使离合器分开。*~ oneself from the promise of marriage* 解除婚约。*She ~d quickly from his hold*. 她很快挣脱开他。*He accepted the invitation, but was later forced to ~ himself*. 他接受了邀请,但后来被迫失约。*Our army ~d the enemy*. 我军和敌军脱离了接触。**disengaging zone**【化】分离层。

dis·en·gaged [ˈdisinˈgeidʒd; ˋdɪsɪnˋgedʒd] ***a*.** **1.** 被解开的,已脱离的;已断绝关系的;已解除婚约的。**2.** 自由的,闲着的,空着的。**3.**【军】脱离接触的,【化】离析的,分离的;【机】脱开的。*I'll be ~ on Friday*. 我星期五就有空了。*Is this room ~?* 这房子空不空?

dis·en·gage·ment [͵disinˈgeidʒmənt; ͵dɪsɪnˋgedʒmənt] ***n*.** **1.** 解开,脱离。**2.** 解约;解雇。**3.** 闲暇,自由。**4.**【化】分离,离析;【军】脱离接触。*a ~ zone* 脱离接触区。

hours of ～ 空闲时间。

dis·en·tail [ˈdisinˈteil; ˋdɪsɛnˋtel] *vt*. 【法】解除(地产等的)限定继承权。

dis·en·tan·gle [ˈdisinˈtæŋgl; ˋdɪsnˋtæŋgl] *vt*. 解脱,解开(结扣等);解决(纠纷等);清理(破产的公司等)。～ *a complicated knot* 解开复杂的结扣。～ *oneself from the intrigues* 从勾心斗角中解脱出来。— *vi*. 1. (结扣等)解开。2. (纠纷等)解决。

dis·en·thral(l) [ˌdisinˈθrɔːl; ˏdɪsɛnˋθrɔl] *vt*. 使摆脱(奴役状态);使解除(束缚)。*be* ～*ed from morbid fantacies* 从病态的幻想中解放出来。**-ment** *n*.

dis·en·throne [ˌdisinˈθrəun; ˏdɪsɛnˋθron] *vt*. 废黜,使退位。**-ment** *n*.

dis·en·ti·tle [disinˈtaitl; dɪsɛnˋtaɪtḷ] *vt*. 【法】剥夺…的权利;剥夺…的官衔。～ *sb. to the right of inheritance* 剥夺某人的继承权。

dis·en·tomb [ˌdisinˈtuːm; ˏdɪsɛnˋtum] *vt*. 从坟墓中挖出;发掘。

dis·en·twine [ˌdisinˈtwain; ˏdɪsɛnˋtwaɪn] *vt*., *vi*. 解开;解决(纠纷),摆脱(瓜葛)。

di·sep·al·ous [daiˈsepləs; daɪˋsɛpələs] *a*. 【植】有两萼片的。

dis·e·quil·i·brate [ˈdisˌiːkwiˈlaibreit; ˋdɪsˏikwəˋlaɪbret] *vt*. 使失去平衡,打破…的平衡。**-bra·tion** *n*.

dis·e·qui·lib·ri·um [disˌiːkwiˈlibriəm; dɪsˏikwəˋlɪbrɪəm] *n*. (*pl*. ～*s*, *-ri·a* [-ə; -ə]) 不平衡;失去平衡〔尤指经济发展不平衡〕。

dis·es·tab·lish [ˈdisisˈtæbliʃ; ˏdɪsəˋstæblɪʃ] *vt*. 1. 使(教会)与政府分离。2. 废除(成规),打破…的现状;解除…的官职。～ *the authority of an outdated code* 废除过时的法典。**-ment** *n*.

dis·es·teem [ˌdisisˈtiːm; ˏdɪsəsˋtim] *vt*., *n*. 厌恶,轻视。

dis·fa·vour, dis·fa·vor [ˈdisˈfeivə; ˋdɪsˋfevɚ] **I** *n*. 1. 不赞成;厌弃;疏远,冷淡。2. 失众望,失宠。3. 不利。*He regarded my suggestions with* ～. 他不赞成我的建议。*The minister incurred the king's* ～. 这位大臣招致国王的冷遇。**be** [**live**] **in** ～ 过受气日子,失宠,不受欢迎,受冷遇。**fall** [**come**] **into** ～ 失宠,失众望,不受欢迎。**II** *vt*. 疏远,冷待;嫌弃。

dis·fea·ture [disˈfiːtʃə; dɪsˋfitʃɚ] *vt*. 毁损…的容貌。

dis·fig·ure [disˈfigə; dɪsˋfɪgɚ] *vt*. 1. 毁损…的外形[外貌],使破相,使变丑。2. 毁损…的优点[价值]。*Old towns* ～*d by tasteless new buildings*. 古老的城镇被平庸的新建筑弄得很难看。**-ment** *n*. 破相,外貌变丑;疵瑕;毁形。

dis·for·est [disˈfɔrist; dɪsˋfɔrɪst] *vt*. 采伐…的森林(= disafforest)。

dis·fran·chise [disˈfræntʃaiz; dɪsˋfræntʃaɪz] *vt*. 1. 褫夺…的公权[选举权]。2. 〔英〕剥夺(某地)选派议会议员的权利。**-ment** *n*.

dis·frock [disˈfrɔk; dɪsˋfrɑk] *vt*. 【宗】解除…的圣职。

dis·gorge [disˈgɔːdʒ; dɪsˋgɔrdʒ] *vt*. 1. 吐,呕吐出;吐出(脏物等)。2. (江河等)流出。*The soldiers had to* ～ *the jewels which they had plundered*. 士兵被迫交出抢劫的珠宝。*trains disgorging thousands of passengers* 有成千上万旅客下车的火车。— *vi*. 1. 呕吐。2. (河流等)流注。*where the river* ～*s into the sea* 河流入海的地方。

dis·grace [disˈgreis; dɪsˋgres] **I** *n*. 1. 失宠,受气;耻辱,出丑,丢脸。2. 丢脸的事,出丑的人。*the* ～ *of criminals* 罪犯身份的耻辱。*a humiliating* ～ 奇耻大辱。*Choose death before* ～. 宁死不屈。**be a** ～ **to** 是…的耻辱(*He is a* ～ *to his school*. 他给学校丢脸)。**bring** ～ **on** [**upon**] (*oneself*) 玷辱(自己),(自)失体面。**fall into** ～ (**with sb**.) (在某人面前)失宠。**in** ～ 失宠,受气;丢脸。**II** *vt*. 1. 玷污(名誉);使丢脸。2. 使失宠;贬黜。～ *oneself* 丢脸。～ *one's name* 玷污自己的名誉。*be* ～*d at court* 在宫廷中失宠。

dis·grace·ful [disˈgreisful; dɪsˋgresfəl] *a*. 可耻的,丢脸的,不光彩的,不名誉的。～ *behavior* 不光彩的行为。**-ly** *ad*. **-ness** *n*.

dis·grun·tle [disˈgrʌntl; dɪsˋgrʌntḷ] *vt*. 使不满,使不平;使不高兴。*He was* ～*d at their absence*. 他对他们的缺席不满。*members* ～*d with their president* 对会长不满的会员们。**-d** *a*. 不平的,不满的;不高兴的。**-ment** *n*.

dis·guise [disˈgaiz; dɪsˋgaɪz] **I** *n*. 1. 假装,伪装,幌子;化装服,伪装衣。2. 托辞,口实,借口。*throw off all* ～ 抛开一切假面具。*No words can be the* ～ *of base intentions*. 没有任何说法可以作为卑鄙用心的托辞。**in** ～ 假装的;伪装的(*a policeman in* ～ 便衣警察。*Misfortune might be a blessing in* ～. 因祸可能得福,塞翁失马安知非福)。**in** [**under**] **the** ～ **of** 1. 以…为口实,托辞…。2. 装做,假扮做。**make no** ～ **of one's feelings** 真情毕露。(*speak*) **without** ～ 摆明(说)。**II** *vt*. 1. 假装,假扮,佯装,扮作。2. 隐藏(真意等),隐瞒,掩饰。*The king was* ～*d as a peasant*. 国王假扮做农民。～ *oneself with a false mustache* 用假胡须化装。*a door* ～*d as a book-case* 做成书橱一样的门。*be* ～*d in* [*with*] *drink* 装醉。～ *one's age* 瞒岁数。～ *one's voice* 改变说话腔调。**-guis·ed·ly** *ad*.

dis·gust [disˈgʌst; dɪsˋgʌst] **I** *vt*. 1. 使作呕。2. 令人嫌恶,招人唾弃[反感]。*Your vacillations* ～ *me*. 你的优柔寡断使人讨厌。**be** ～**ed at** [**by**, **with**]... 嫌,讨厌,唾弃,对…作呕。**II** *n*. 1. 作呕。2. 厌恶,憎恶,反感(*at*; *for*; *towards*; *against*)。**take a** ～ **at** 嫌,讨厌…。**to one's** ～ 可厌的是;令人作呕的是。**-ed·ly** *ad*. **-ful** *a*. 1. 令人作呕的。2. 使人讨厌的。**-ing** *a*.

dish [diʃ; dɪʃ] **I** *n*. 1. 碟子,盘子。2. 盘菜;盘装食品;菜。3. 盘形,盘状(物)。4. 一盘的容量,满满一盘。5. 〔美俚〕漂亮的女人。6. 〔美俚〕心爱物;爱好。7. 下陷,凹处;【物】抛物面;【无】抛物面天线反射镜,卫星接收天线。*a meat* ～ 盛肉盘。*a wooden* ～ 木盘。*a* ～ *of beans* 一盘豆子。*a cold* ～ 冷盘(菜)。*Chinese* ～*es* 中国菜,中国口味。*a plain* [*dainty*] ～ 清淡的[好吃的]菜。*Rice is an inexpensive* ～. 大米是一种廉价食品。*an evaporating* ～ 蒸发皿。*one's favourite* ～ 爱吃的菜。*a standing* ～ 每日例菜;老生常谈,老调。*Mathematics is not my* ～. 我不喜欢数学。～ **of gossip** 闲谈。**eat off a** ～ 由盘中取食。**made** ～**es** 拼盘。**II** *vt*. 1. 把(食物)盛在碟[盘]子里。2. 使成盘形;把…挖空。3. 〔俚〕瞒,骗;打败,破坏,挫败(计划等)。～ *food onto plates* 把食物装进盘子里。*She* ～*ed him some breakfast*. 她用盘子给他装上早餐。— *vi*. 1. 成盘状,成中凹形。2. 闲谈。**be** ～**ed** 输了,完了。～ **it out** 〔口〕叱责;嚷叫;〔美俚〕处罚(*the woman* ～*ing it out to her children* 大声责骂孩子的妇女)。～ **sb. out of sth**. 骗去某人的某物。～ **out** 1. 上(菜),把(菜等)装盘端上;分配(饭菜等)。2. 〔喻〕托出,抛出;提供,发布(消息等)。3. 把…挖成空盘状。4. 滔滔不绝地讲。～ **up** 1. 把(食物)盛在盘里端出。2. (把故事等)说得动听(～ *up the story in a humorous way* 以幽默的语调把故事讲得娓娓动听)。～**cloth** (洗盘碟用的)抹布。～**cloth gourd** 丝瓜。～**clout** 1. = ～cloth. 2. 〔美俚〕软弱而愚蠢的人。～ **cross** 十字形盘碟架。～**pan** 洗碗碟等物的浅桶(～*pan hands* 家庭主妇因经常洗碗碟等而变粗糙的手)。～**rag** = ～cloth. ～ **ring** 环形盘垫。～**towel** 〔美〕(擦干碗碟的)抹布。～ **ware** 盛菜肴的盘碟。～**washer** 1. 洗盘子的人;洗碟机。2. 【鸟】鹡鸰。～**water** 1. 洗过盘子的脏水。2. 〔喻〕味道差的汤[茶]等;〔美俚〕没有力量的话,滥调(*dull as* ～*water* 十分枯燥乏味,令人厌烦)。**-ful** *n*. 满盘,一碟。

dis·ha·bille [ˌdisæˈbiːl; ˏdɪsəˋbil] *n*. 1. 衣着随便,穿着便服[睡衣等]。2. 便服。3. 邋遢,散漫;混乱,杂乱;(心

理)失常。*in* ～穿着便服,穿得很随便。

dis·ha·bit·u·ate [ˌdishəˈbitjueit; ˏdɪshəˋbɪtʃʊˏet] ***vt***. 使丢弃习惯。

dis·har·mo·ni·ous [ˌdisha:ˈməunjəs; ˏdɪsharˋmonjəs] ***a***. 不调和的,不谐和的。**-ly *ad***.

dis·har·mo·nize, dis·har·mo·nise [disˈha:mənaiz; dɪsˋharməˏnaɪz] ***vt***. 使不和谐。— ***vi***. 失去和谐。

dis·har·mo·ny [ˈdisˈha:məni; dɪsˋharmənɪ] ***n***. 不调和,不一致;不协调。

dis·heart·en [disˈha:tn; dɪsˋhartn̩] ***vt***. 使沮丧,使泄气,使垂头丧气。*He was ～ed at the result*. 这个结果使他垂头丧气。*be ～ed by the unlucky event* 因运气不佳而泄气。**-ing *a***. 使人沮丧的。**-ing·ly *ad***. **-ment *n***. 沮丧。

dished [diʃt; dɪʃt] ***a***. **1**. 凹,瘪,盘形凹陷的;(房间)有圆屋顶的,穹窿形的。**2**.〔俚〕筋疲力尽的。*a ～ face* 凹陷的脸。**3**.〔美俚〕完蛋了的,受挫折的。*～ bottom* 碟形底。

D

dis·her·i·son [disˈherizn; dɪsˋhɛrəzn̩] ***n***. 剥夺继承权。

di·shev·el [diˈʃevəl; dɪˋʃɛvl̩] ***vt***. ([英] ***-ll-***)弄乱,搅乱(头发等)。*The wind ～ed the papers on the desk*. 风把桌上的纸吹乱了。**-ed *a***. 散乱的;(头发等)乱蓬蓬的;服装不整洁的 (*dishevel appearance* 衣容不整洁)。

dis·hon·est [disˈɔnist; dɪsˋɑnɪst] ***a***. 不诚实的;不正直的;狡猾的,阴险的;不可靠的。*～ gains* 不正当收入,不义之财。**-ly *ad***.

dis·hon·es·ty [disˈɔnisti; dɪsˋɑnɪstɪ] ***n***. **1**. 不正直,不诚实;狡猾;阴险。**2**. 不诚实的行为。*a piece of ～* 一桩不老实的行为。*many dishonesties* 许多不诚实的行为。*a man of ～* 不诚实的人。

dis·hon·our, dis·hon·or [disˈɔnə; dɪsˋɑnɚ] **I *n***. **1**. 不名誉,丢脸;耻辱,侮辱。**2**.【商】(票据的)拒付,拒收。*I offered him no ～*. 我未曾侮辱他。*do sb. a ～* 侮辱人。*a notice of ～*【商】拒付通知。***be a ～ to*** 是…的耻辱。***bring sb. to ～*** 使蒙受耻辱。***To the ～ of ...*** 对…说来丢脸的是。**II *vt***. **1**. 使蒙受耻辱,侮辱,败坏(名誉)。**2**. 使(契约等)作废;【商】拒付,拒收(票据)。**3**. 奸污(妇女)。*a ～ed bill* 被拒收的票据。*a ～ed cheque* 空头支票。**-a·ble *a***. 不名誉的,耻辱的;卑鄙的,无耻的。**-a·bly *ad***.

dis·horn [disˈhɔ:n; dɪsˋhɔrn] ***vt***. 除去(动物的)角。

dish·y [ˈdiʃi; ˋdɪʃɪ] ***a***.〔美俚〕称心的,合意的;有吸引力的。

dis·il·lu·sion [ˌdisiˈlu:ʒən; ˏdɪsɪˋluʒən] **I *n***. 觉醒;幻灭。**II *vt***. 使觉醒,使幻灭,给…泼冷水。*Hamlet was ～ed in his mother*. 哈姆雷特对他母亲的幻想破灭了。***be ～ed with*** 对…大失所望。**-ize *vt***. **-ment *n***.

dis·in·cen·tive [ˌdisinˈsentiv; ˏdɪsɪnˋsɛntɪv] **I *n***. (生产等方面的)障碍因素。**II *a***. (对生产等)起阻碍作用的。

dis·in·cli·na·tion [ˌdisinkliˈneiʃən; ˏdɪsɪnkləˋneʃən] ***n***. 不喜欢,不愿,厌恶。*his ～ to the fair sex* 他对女性的厌恶。*have a ～ for work* 怕工作。***with ～*** 很勉强地 (*read a book with ～* 勉强地读书)。

dis·in·cline [ˈdisinˈklain; ˋdɪsɪnˋklaɪn] ***vt***. 使不愿,使无意于。*be ～d to* 无意于…。*feel ～d for any more sleep* 不想再睡了。*Your rudeness ～s me to grant your request*. 你的粗鲁态度使我不想答应你的要求。

dis·in·cor·po·rate [ˌdisinˈkɔ:pəreit; ˏdɪsɪnˋkɔrpəˏret] ***vt***. 解散(团体、公司、组织等)。

dis·in·fect [ˌdisinˈfekt; ˏdɪsɪnˋfɛkt] ***vt***. 给…消毒,给…灭菌;使洗净。*～ drinking water* 给饮用水消毒。**dis·in·fect·ant 1**. ***a***. 消毒的。**2**. ***n***. 消毒剂。**-fec·tion *n***. 消毒(作用),灭菌(法)。**-or *n***. 消毒器;消毒剂;消毒者。

dis·in·fest [ˌdisinˈfest; ˏdɪsɪnˋfɛst] ***vt***. 消灭(某处的)老鼠[跳蚤等];除去(庄稼等)的害虫。**-ant *n***. 除虫剂,杀虫剂。

dis·in·fla·tion [ˌdisinˈfleiʃən; ˏdɪsɪnˋfleʃən] ***n***. 通货收缩。**-ary *a***.

dis·in·for·ma·tion [disˌinfəˈmeiʃən; dɪsˏɪnfɚˋmeʃən] ***n***. 假情报[为迷惑敌方情报机关而故意泄露的虚假情报]。

dis·in·gen·u·ous [ˌdisinˈdʒenjuəs; ˏdɪsɪnˋdʒɛnjuəs] ***a***. 不真诚的,无诚意的,虚伪的;奸诈的,阴险的。**-ly *ad***. **-ness *n***.

dis·in·her·it [ˈdisinˈherit; ˋdɪsɪnˋhɛrɪt] ***vt***.【法】与…断绝父子关系,废(嫡);取消…的继承权。*～ed people* 被取消继承权的人们。**-ance *n***.

dis·in·sec·tion [ˌdisinˈsekʃən; ˏdɪsɪnˋsɛkʃən], **dis·in·sect·i·za·tion** [ˈdisinˌsektaiˈzeiʃən; ˋdɪsɪnˏsɛktaɪˋzeʃən] ***n***. (飞机、轮船等内部的)灭虫。

dis·in·te·grate [disˈintigreit; dɪsˋɪntəˏgret] ***vt***. **1**. 使崩溃,使瓦解。**2**. 使分裂,使分解,分化。*an empire ～d* 瓦解的帝国。*rocks ～d by frost and rain* 被风霜雨露剥蚀瓦解的岩石。*～ the enemy troops* 瓦解敌军。— ***vi***. **1**. 崩,碎,分裂,分解。**2**. 崩溃,溃散,瓦解 (*into*)。**3**.【原】蜕变,衰变。*The house gradually ～d with age*. 房屋因年久失修而逐渐倾颓。*The national economy ～d*. 国民经济崩溃了。**-gra·tor *n***. **1**. 造成分裂者,分裂因素。**2**. 粉碎机,解磨机;(造纸用)打浆机。

dis·in·te·gra·tion [disˌintiˈgreiʃən; dɪsˏɪntəˋgreʃən] ***n***. **1**. 分裂,分解,崩解。**2**. 瓦解,崩溃,溃散。**3**.【地】剥蚀;【原】裂变,衰变,蜕变。*the atmospheric ～ of rocks* 岩石的风化。*the ～ of a society* 社会的瓦解。*the ～ of personality* 人格分裂。*radioactive ～*【物】放射性蜕变。

dis·in·ter [ˈdisinˈtə:; ˋdɪsɪnˋtɝ] ***vt***. (***-rr-***) **1**. (从坟墓中或地下)掘出。**2**. 发掘出,揭露出。**-ment *n***.

dis·in·ter·est [disˈintrist; dɪsˋɪntərəst] **I *n***. **1**. 无利害关系。**2**. 无兴趣,不关心,冷淡。**II *vt***. 使无利害关系;使不关心。*～ oneself* 置身事外,采取不干涉态度。

dis·in·ter·est·ed [disˈintristid; dɪsˋɪntərəstɪd] ***a***. **1**. 无私心的,廉洁的,公平的。**2**.〔美口〕不关心的,不感兴趣的 (*～ aid* 无私的援助。*a ～ decision* 公平的决定)。**-ly *ad***. **-ness *n***.

dis·in·ter·me·di·a·tion [disˌintəmi:diˈeiʃən; dɪsˏɪntəmidɪˋeʃən] ***n***.〔美〕大量提款(指从储蓄银行中大量提款投入证券投资市场)。

dis·in·vest·ment [ˌdisinˈvestmənt; ˏdɪsɪnˋvɛstmənt] ***n***. 减少资本投资;变卖资本投资;抽回投资资本。

dis·jec·ta mem·bra [disˈdʒektə ˈmembrə; dɪsˋdʒɛktə ˋmɛmbrə] ***n***.〔L.〕〔*pl*.〕断片,残片;不连贯的引文。

dis·join [disˈdʒɔin; dɪsˋdʒɔɪn] ***vt***. 把…分开,拆散。— ***vi***. 分开。

dis·joint [disˈdʒɔint; dɪsˋdʒɔɪnt] ***vt***. **1**. 使关节脱位,使脱臼。**2**. 拆散(机械等)。**3**. 打乱(次序等)。— ***vi***. **1**. (关节等)脱位,脱臼。**2**. 分离,脱开。**-ed *a***. **1**. 关节脱臼的。**2**. 拆散了的,支离破碎的。**3**. 无条理的,无系统的。**-ed·ly *ad***. **-ed·ness *n***.

dis·junct I [disˈdʒʌŋkt; dɪsˋdʒʌŋkt] ***a***. **1**. 脱节的;不相连的。**2**.【乐】跳跃的。**3**.【动】(昆虫)头、胸和腹部由缢缩分开的。**II** [ˈdisdʒʌŋkt; ˋdɪsdʒʌŋkt] ***n***.【逻】选言肢。

dis·junc·tion [disˈdʒʌŋkʃən; dɪsˋdʒʌŋkʃən] ***n***. **1**. 分离,折断。**2**.【数】(计算机的)析取;逻辑加法;逻辑和;【逻】选言,选言判断;选言推理。

dis·junc·tive [disˈdʒʌŋktiv; dɪsˋdʒʌŋktɪv] **I *a***. **1**. 分离的,分离性的。**2**.【逻】选言的。**3**.【语】转折的;反意的。*a ～ proposition*【选】选言命题。*～ conjunctions* 转折连词。**II *n***. **1**.【语法】转折连词 (*but*; *yet* 等)。**2**.【逻】选言判断。

disk [disk; dɪsk] **I *n***. **1**. 圆盘;盘状,盘状物。**2**.【体】铁饼;[美]唱片。**3**.【植】花盘;【动】盘;【农】(圆盘)耙片。**4**.【自】(电子计算机的)数据存储盘;(照相排版机的)机盘。*the ～ of the sun* 太阳表面。*～ recording* 灌唱片。**II *vt***. **1**. 使成圆盘状。**2**. 用圆盘耙耕(地)。**3**. 灌

(唱片),把…录制成唱片。～ **harrow** 圆盘耙。～ **jockey** 〔美俚〕唱片节目播音员。～ **pack**【自】可换式磁盘组〔电子计算机的存储设备〕。

dis·like [dis'laik; dɪs`laɪk] ***n.*** 不喜欢,讨厌,反感。*likes and ～s* 喜欢与反感。*She has a ～ to [for; of] him.* 她不喜欢他。*I took an instant ～ to [for; of] him.* 我对他立刻产生了反感。

dis·limn [dis'lim; dɪs`lɪm] ***vt.*** 〔古〕使(画等的)轮廓模糊;使变模糊。

dis·lo·cate ['disləkeit; `dɪslo͵ket] ***vt.*** **1.** 使脱离原来位置;使(骨关节)脱位,使脱臼。**2.** 打乱…的正常秩序,弄乱…的位置;使混乱。*The glacier ～d the great stones.* 冰河搬动了巨石。*have [get] one's leg ～d* 腿关节脱臼。*～ one's shoulder* 肩关节脱臼。*Traffic was ～d by the accident.* 车祸使交通陷入混乱。*～ one's mind* 使心烦意乱。*strikes dislocating the economy* 打乱经济秩序的罢工。

dis·lo·ca·tion [ˌdisləˈkeiʃən; ͵dɪslo`keʃən] ***n.*** **1.**【医】脱位,脱臼;离位,转位,位移。**2.**【地】断层,断错;【物】位错。**3.** 混乱,打乱。*a disastrous economic ～* 灾难性的经济混乱。

dis·lodge [dis'lɔdʒ; dɪs`lɑdʒ] ***vt.*** **1.** 把…从住地[窝巢等处]逐出;【军】击退;赶走。**2.** 移去;取出。*～ a stone with one's foot* 用脚把石子踢开。*～ a beast* 把野兽从窝巢中逐出。*～ the enemy from their fortifications* 把敌人从碉堡中逐出。— ***vi.*** 从住处退出。**-ment** ***n.***

dis·loy·al [dis'lɔiəl; dɪs`lɔɪəl] ***a.*** 不忠的;无信义的;不贞的 (*to*)。*a ～ friend* 不忠诚的朋友。*be ～ to one's country* 叛国。*be ～ to the marriage bed* 不贞洁。**-ist** ***n.*** 不忠的人。**-ly** ***ad.*** **-ty** ***n.*** 不忠诚,不忠,无信义,不贞洁。

dis·mal ['dizməl; `dɪzməl] **I** ***a.*** **1.** 阴郁的,惨淡的,凄凉的;忧郁的,(叫声等)凄惨的。**2.** 沉闷的,无趣的。**3.** 〔废〕可怕的。*a ～ face* 忧郁的面孔。*a ～ room* 阴暗的房间。*the ～ days of winter* 萧瑟的冬天。*the ～ science* 沉闷的科学〔英美等国指政治经济学而言〕。*a ～ incidents* 不如意的事。**II** ***n.*** **1.** 〔美南部〕沼地。**2.** 〔the ～s〕〔口〕忧郁。**-ly** ***ad.***

dis·man·tle [dis'mæntl; dɪs`mæntl̩] ***vt.*** **1.** 拆除…的设备[装备、家具、防御工事]等。**2.** 拆掉…的覆盖物;剥掉…的衣服。**3.** 拆卸,拆散(机器等)。**4.** 摧毁,夷平。*～ a ship* 拆掉船上的装备。*～ a fortress* 拆除要塞的防御设备。*They ～d the machine and shipped it in pieces.* 他们把机器拆开,分成零碎部件运出。*The wind ～d the trees of their leaves.* 风把树上的叶子吹个精光。

dis·mask [dis'mɑːsk; dɪs`mæsk] ***vt.*** = unmask.

dis·mast [dis'mɑːst; dɪs`mæst] ***vt.***【海】(暴风、大炮等)打落[打断、吹断]桅杆。

dis·may [dis'mei; dɪs`me] **I** ***n.*** **1.** 灰心;沮丧,丧失勇气。**2.** 惊愕。*The enemy retreated in perfect ～.* 敌人沮丧地退去。*exclaim in ～* 惊愕得叫喊起来。*To my ～, this university was closed.* 使我沮丧的是,这所大学停办了。**II** ***vt.*** **1.** 使沮丧。**2.** 使惊愕。*The surprise attack ～ed the enemy.* 这次奇袭大灭了敌人的威风。*He was ～ed at the size of his adversary.* 对手的魁伟身材使他丧失了勇气。

dis·mem·ber [dis'membə; dɪs`mɛmbɚ] ***vt.*** **1.** 肢解,割断…的肢体。**2.** 割裂;把…撕碎;瓜分(国土等)。*The revolts ～ed the country.* 叛乱使国家四分五裂。*a ～-ed country* 一个被瓜分的国家。**-ment** ***n.***

dis·miss [dis'mis; dɪs`mɪs] ***vt.*** **1.** 使退去,让…走开,打发走。**2.** 遣散,解散(队伍等)。**3.** 解雇,把…免职;开除(学生等)。**4.** 放弃(企图等);断(念),消除(顾虑等),忘掉;草草了结(讨论中的问题等)。**5.**【法】驳回,拒绝受理。**6.** 搁置;不予考虑。*after school was ～ed* 放学以后。*～ a suitor* 拒绝求婚者。*She ～ed the class early.* 她早早下课。*～ an employee* 解雇雇员。*He was ～ed from the service for his careless behaviors.* 他因玩忽职守而被解除职务。*～ one's fear* 打消恐惧。*～ a suit* 对诉讼不予受理。— ***vi.*** (队伍等)解散。***D-!*** 〔口令〕散队! 解散! ***the ～***【军】解散口令。

dis·miss·al [dis'misəl; dɪs`mɪsl̩] ***n.*** **1.** 解雇;免职;开除。**2.** 退去,打发走;遣散;解散。**3.**【法】驳回,拒绝受理。**4.** 免职令;解雇通知;开除通告。

dis·miss·i·ble [dis'misəbl; dɪs`mɪsəbl] ***a.*** **1.** 可解雇的;可免职的。**2.** 可打发走的;可拒绝的;可不予考虑的。

dis·mis·sion [dis'miʃən; dɪs`mɪʃən] ***n.*** 〔罕〕= dismissal.

dis·mis·sive [dis'misiv; dɪs`mɪsɪv] ***a.*** **1.** 拒绝的;打发走的。**2.** 轻蔑的,瞧不起人的。*a curt ～ gesture* 轻蔑驱人之手势。*a ～ question* 盛气凌人的发问。

dis·mount ['dis'maunt; dɪs`maʊnt] **I** ***vt.*** **1.** 使下马,使下车;使(敌人、骑者等)摔下马来。**2.** (从支架,托座,台子等上)取下,卸下,拿下。**3.** 拆卸(机器等)。*The horse twisted, kicked and finally ～ed its rider.* 那匹马又蹦又跳,终于把骑手摔了下来。*～ a picture* 从画框里取下画。*～ a gun from its carriage* 从炮架上卸下大炮。— ***vi.*** (从车、马车上)下来 (*from*)。*～ from a horse* 下马。**II** ***n.*** 下马,下车;【体】跳下动作。***the ～***【军】下马令。

dis·na·ture [dis'neitʃə; dɪs`netʃɚ] ***vt.*** 使失去自然属性(或形态);使不自然。

Dis·ney[1] ['dizni; `dɪznɪ] ***n.*** **1.** 迪斯尼〔姓氏〕。**2. Walt ～** 瓦尔特·迪斯尼〔1901—1966,美国电影动画片设计家〕。

Dis·ney[2] ['dizni; `dɪznɪ] ***n.*** 迪斯尼动画片〔美国瓦·迪斯尼设计的电影动画片〕。

Dis·ney·land ['dizniˌlænd; `dɪznɪ͵lænd] ***n.*** 迪斯尼游乐园〔美国动画片制片人瓦·迪斯尼在洛杉矶附近设计的游乐场〕;〔喻〕奇妙的幻境。

dis·o·be·di·ence [ˌdisəˈbiːdjəns; ͵dɪsə`bidɪəns] ***n.*** 不服从,不顺从,违抗 (*to*);不孝。*～ to the law* 违抗法律。

dis·o·be·di·ent [ˌdisəˈbiːdjənt; ͵dɪsə`bidɪənt] ***a.*** 不顺从的,不服从的 (*to*);违法的,不孝的。*a ～ son* 不孝顺的儿子,逆子。**-ly** ***ad.***

dis·o·bey ['disə'bei; `dɪsə`be] ***vt.*** 不服从,违抗。*～ one's parents* 对双亲不孝。*～ a law* 违抗法律,— ***vi.*** 不听话;不顺从。*The son ～s.* 儿子不听话。

dis·o·blige ['disə'blaidʒ; `dɪsə`blaɪdʒ] ***vt.*** **1.** 使…失望,不满足…的愿望,对…不通融。**2.** 〔口〕使不便。**3.** 得罪,使生气。*We are sorry to ～ you, but the rooms you desire are already reserved.* 我们使您失望感到很抱歉,您要的房间已经被订出去了。*be ～d by a tactless remark* 因一句不得体的话而生气。*be ～d by an uninvited guest* 因为来了一位不速之客而被弄得很不方便。**-o·blig·ing** ***a.*** **1.** 不亲切的,不通融的。**2.** (作为邻居等)不考虑别人的。

dis·or·der [dis'ɔːdə; dɪs`ɔrdɚ] **I** ***n.*** **1.** 无秩序,混乱,杂乱;不合手续。**2.** 骚乱,纷扰。**3.** 小病,(身心机能的)失调。**4.**【化】无序。*a ～ in legal proceedings* 法律诉讼的不合手续。*the ～s in universities* 大学里的骚乱。*a mild stomach ～* 轻微的胃病。***in ～*** 混乱,紊乱 (*papers in ～* 胡乱堆放着的文件。*long hair in ～* 乱蓬蓬的长发)。***fall into ～*** 陷入混乱。***throw into ～*** 使混乱,把…卷入动乱。**II** ***vt.*** **1.** 扰乱,使混乱。**2.** 使(身心等)失调,使(神经等)错乱。**-ed** ***a.*** **1.** (秩序等)混乱的。**2.** (身心)失调的,有病的。*a ～ed stomach [liver]* 胃[肝]病。

dis·or·der·ly [dis'ɔːdəli; dɪs`ɔrdɚlɪ] **I** ***a.*** **1.** 无秩序的,不规则的,紊乱的。**2.** 骚乱的,无法无天的;【法】妨害治安的;伤风败俗的。*a ～ pile of clothes* 乱七八糟的一堆衣服。*charged with being drunk and ～* 被控告犯酗酒和妨害治安罪。**II** ***ad.*** 无秩序地,杂乱地。～ **conduct**【法】妨害治安行为。～ **house** 妓院,赌场。～ **per-**

D

son【法】妨害治安者,伤风败俗者。**-li·ness** *n*.

dis·or·gan·i·za·tion [disˌɔːgənaiˈzeiʃən; dɪsˏɔrgənəˋzeʃən] *n*. 分裂,瓦解;混乱,紊乱。

dis·or·gan·ize [disˈɔːgənaiz; dɪsˋɔrgəˏnaɪz] *vt*. 瓦解;打乱,使混乱。~ *a political party* 使一个政党瓦解。~ *a plan* 打乱一项计划。

dis·o·ri·ent [disˈɔːrient; dɪsˋɔrɪˏɛnt], **dis·o·ri·en·tate** [disˈɔːrienteit; dɪsˋɔrɪəntet] *vt*. **1**. 使不辨方向,使迷失方位。**2**. 使精神混乱〔尤指不辨时间、地点和人物等〕。*The strange streets ~ed him*. 生疏的街道使他迷路了。*a society ~ed by changing values* 由于价值观念不断改变而迷失方向的社会。*They became deeply intoxicated and totally ~ed*. 他们酩酊大醉,已经完全分不清东南西北了。**-a·tion** *n*.

dis·own [disˈəun; dɪsˋon] *vt*. **1**. 不承认…和自己有关系;否认…是自己的;声明与(子女等)脱离关系。**2**. 不承认…的权威性[正确性、有效性]等。~ *one's heirs* 宣布和自己的继承人断绝关系。~ *a letter* 否认是自己写的信。~ *the doctrine* 不承认那个学说是正确的。

D

dis·par·age [disˈpæridʒ; dɪsˋpærɪdʒ] *vt*. **1**. 轻蔑,轻视。**2**. 污蔑;贬损,指责。*Your behaviour will ~ the whole family*. 你的行为将使全家丢脸。*Don't ~ good manners*. 不要把礼貌不放在心上。**-ment** *n*. 轻蔑;贬损。

dis·par·ag·ing·ly [disˈpæridʒiŋli; dɪsˋpærɪdʒɪŋlɪ] *ad*. 轻蔑地;毁谤地。*speak ~ of a man* 说人坏话。

dis·pa·rate [ˈdispərit; ˋdɪspərɪt] **I** *a*. 根本不相同的;(种类)全异的;不能互相比拟的;【逻】异类的。~ *ideas* 根本不相同的看法。**II** *n*. 〔常 *pl*.〕无法比较的东西。**-ly** *ad*. **-ness** *n*.

dis·par·i·ty [disˈpæriti; dɪsˋpærətɪ] *n*. 不同,不等,不一致,不相称;悬殊。~ *in rank* 身份悬殊。*disparities between men and women* 男女差别。

dis·park [disˈpɑːk; dɪsˋpɑrk] *vt*. 开放(私人园地、猎苑等)改作别用。

dis·part[1] [disˈpɑːt; dɪsˋpɑrt] *vt*. 〔古〕使分离,使分裂。— *vi*. 〔古〕分裂,分离。

dis·part[2] [disˈpɑːt; dɪsˋpɑrt] *n*. 炮口与炮尾的中径差;炮口准星。

dis·pas·sion [disˈpæʃən; dɪsˋpæʃən] *n*. **1**. 不动感情,冷静。**2**. 公平,无偏见。

dis·pas·sion·ate [disˈpæʃənit; dɪsˋpæʃənɪt] *a*. **1**. 不动感情的,冷静的。**2**. 公平的,无偏见的。*a ~ critic* 一位不偏不倚的批评家。**-ly** *ad*. **-ness** *n*.

dis·patch [disˈpætʃ; dɪsˋpætʃ] **I** *n*. **1**. (迅速)发送,(火速)派遣。**2**. 急报,快信,急件,(新闻)电讯。**3**. (迅速)处理,速办;敏捷,急速。**4**. 调度,调遣。**5**. (即刻)处死,(就地)正法。**6**. 特电,特别公报。**7**. 运输行。*the date of the ~ of the parcel* 包裹发出的日期。*the Associated Press ~ from London (on) Oct. 19* 联合通讯社伦敦10月19日电。*quick ~ of business* 快速处理事务。*Proceed with all possible ~*. 火速进行。*a ~ carrier* 急件递送员。*the ~ of two companies to the front* 派遣两个连上前线。***be mentioned in ~es*** 【英军】因建立殊勋而在特别通报上受表彰。***send (sth.) by ~*** (某物)作快件寄发。***with ~*** 火速,从速。**II** *vt*. **1**. (火速)发出(信件,电讯等),(急速)送出(公文等),(快速)派出(军队等)。**2**. 快办,快速处理,迅速了结;〔口语〕匆匆吃完(饭等)。**3**. 调度,调遣。**4**. (迅速)处决(罪犯等)。~ *troops to the border* 火速向边界派出部队。*spy promptly ~ed* 被立即处决的间谍。~ *business* 赶快办完事情。~ *a meal* 三口并作两口地把饭吃完。~ *sb. on an errand* 差遣某人。— *vi*. 〔古〕赶快,匆忙做;就地处决人犯。~ **boat** (传送公文的)通讯快艇。~ **box** [**case**] 公文传送箱。~ **case** 公文包。~ **rider** 骑兵[摩托]通讯员。**-er** *n*. **1**. (急件等的)发送人。**2**. (火车,飞机等的)调度员。

dis·pel [disˈpel; dɪsˋpɛl] *vt*. (*-ll-*) **1**. 驱散(云、雾等)。**2**. 消除(疑虑等)。~ *vapors* 驱散雾气。~ *fears* 打消疑惧。*All doubts are now ~led*. 所有的怀疑这时都一扫而空。

dis·pen·sa·ble [disˈpensəbl; dɪsˋpɛnsəbl] *a*. **1**. 可有可无的,可省的,不重要的。**2**. (金钱等)可分与的。**3**. (罪恶等)可恕免的。**-sa·bil·i·ty**, **-ness** *n*. 可省去,非必需。

dis·pen·sa·ry [disˈpensəri; dɪsˋpɛnsərɪ] *n*. **1**. 配药处,药房。**2**. (免费或降价收费的)施药所。**3**. 诊疗所,门诊部。**4**. 〔美〕(酒类等的)配给处。~ **system** 〔美〕中央配给制度。

dis·pen·sa·tion [ˌdispenˈseiʃən; ˏdɪspənˋseʃən] *n*. **1**. 分配;分与;分配物。**2**. 【医】处方,配方。**3**. 【宗】天道,天命;天启。**4**. 施行,管理,处理;制度,体制。**5**. 【天主】(教会当局特许的对法律、誓言等的)豁免。**6**. 省却,免除,不用 (*with*)。*under the new ~* 按照新制度。*the ~ of Providence* 天意。*Total ~ of cigarettes can be difficult for a habitual smoker*. 吸惯烟的人要做到完全不吸烟不是一件容易的事。**-al·ism** *n*. 天命史观。

dis·pen·sa·to·ry [disˈpensətəri; dɪsˋpɛnsətorɪ] *n*. **1**. 药谱,药品说明书,药方解说。**2**. 〔古〕药房。

dis·pense [disˈpens; dɪsˋpɛns] *vt*. **1**. 分配,分给;发放(施舍物等)。**2**. 配(药),配(方);发(药)。**3**. 施与(恩惠等)。**4**. 实施,施行(法律等)。**5**. 免除,豁免(义务等)。~ *wisdom* 传播智慧。~ *a prize* 发奖。~ *the law without bias* 施政公允;执法如山。~ *a prescription* 配方。— *vi*. 〔古〕免除,特免。~ ***with*** **1**. 废,罢,省;免除 (*Let us ~ with formalities*. 我们别讲客套[免除礼节,节省手续])。**2**. 不需要,没有也行 (*I can ~ with an overcoat*. 我没有外套也行)。**3**. 豁免 (*~ with a penal statute* 免于按刑法规定追究责任)。

dis·pens·er [disˈpensə; dɪsˋpɛnsɚ] *n*. **1**. 药剂师,配药者。**2**. 执行者,管理者。**3**. 分与者;分配器;自动售货机。

dis·peo·ple [ˈdisˈpiːpl; ˋdɪsˋpipl] *vt*. = depopulate.

di·sper·mous [daiˈspəːməs; daɪˋspɝməs] *a*. 【植】双种子的。

dis·pers·al [disˈpəːsəl; dɪsˋpɝsl] *n*. = dispersion.

dis·perse [disˈpəːs; dɪsˋpɝs] **I** *vt*. **1**. 使疏散,使散开;冲散(敌军等);解散(集会等);驱散(云、雾等)。**2**. 传播(知识、病菌等);散布(谣言等);【物】使(光线)色散,使弥散。~ *the crowd* 驱散人群。*a book ~d throughout the world* 传布全世界的一本书。~ *knowledge* 传播知识。*the fog ~d by the wind* 被风驱散的雾气。*Her sweet words ~d his melancholy*. 她的温柔话语驱散了他的忧愁。— *vi*. **1**. 散开,分散,散去。**2**. (云、雾等)消散。*The smoke ~d into the sky*. 黑烟在天空中消散。*The crowd ~d*. 人群散去了。**II** *a*. 分散的;【物】弥散的。~ **system** 【化】分散体系。**-r** *n*. **1**. 分散剂。**2**. (蒸馏塔中的)泡罩。**3**. 扩散器,扩散装置。

dis·pers·ed [disˈpəːst; dɪsˋpɝst] *a*. 分散的,散开的。~ *element* (岩石、矿物中包含的)微量元素。~ *dye* 弥散性染料。**-ly** *ad*. 四散地,散乱地。

dis·per·sion [disˈpəːʃən; dɪsˋpɝʃən] *n*. **1**. 分散,散开;散布,传播;离散。**2**. 【物】弥散,色散;【化】分散作用;被分散物;分散相,分散体系;【医】(炎症等的)消散;【统】离中趋势。**3**. 〔the D-〕(犹太人的)离散异邦。*the ~ of heat* 热的扩散。*the ~ of an assembly* 集会的解散。~ ***on the ground*** 炮弹在地面上的散布。~ **error** (炮弹的)散布偏差。~ **zone** (炮弹的)散布区,弹着区。

dis·per·sive [disˈpəːsiv; dɪsˋpɝsɪv] *a*. **1**. 散,分散的,散乱的,弥散的,消散性的。**2**. 【物】色散的。*the ~ power of a lens* 透镜的色散率。*a ~ medium* 扩散媒介。**-ly** *ad*. **-ness** *n*.

dis·per·soid [disˈpəːsɔid; dɪsˋpɝsɔɪd] *n*. 【化】弥散体,分散体。

dis·pir·it [disˈpirit; dɪsˋpɪrɪt] *vt*. 使气馁,使沮丧。*be ~ed from further exertions by an unexpected blow*

由于在意外的打击下意气沮丧,不想再作进一步的努力。**-ed** *a*. 意气消沉的,垂头丧气的。**-ed·ly** *ad*.

dis·pit·e·ous [disˈpitiəs; dɪsˋpɪtɪəs] *a*. 〔古〕冷酷的,无情的,残忍的。

dis·place [disˈpleis; dɪsˋples] *vt*. **1**. 换置,移置;顶替,取代。**2**. 取代…的职位;迫使…离家[出国]。**3**.【化】置换,取代;【海】排(水)。**4**. 撤换,把…免职。*The ship* ~*s 500 tons*. 这条船排水量为 500 吨。*be* ~*d by the invaders* 被侵略者赶出家园。*huge rocks* ~*d by the earthquake* 因地震而移位的巨石。*Fiction* ~*s fact*. 虚构代替了事实。*Jet planes have* ~*d propeller ones*. 喷气式飞机取代了螺旋桨飞机。~ *an officer from a regiment* 撤换团里的一名军官。~**d mass**【地】移位岩体。~**d person**【国际法】(由于战争、政治迫害等被迫离开原居住地或本国的)难民〔略作 DP〕。**-r** *n*. **1**.【化】取代剂,置换剂。**2**. 取代者,取代物。**3**.【药】过滤器。

dis·place·ment [disˈpleismənt; dɪsˋplesmənt] *n*. **1**. 转位,移动;取代,置换;(人的)流离失所。**2**. 撤换,免职。**3**.【机】(活塞)排气量;【海】排水量〔一般指军舰的排水量;商船的排水量一般用 gross [net] ton(nage)〕。**4**.【化】置换(作用),取代(作用);【物】位移;【医】移位;【生】替位;【药】滤过;【地】(断层)移动。~ *nitration process*【化】取代硝化。~ **stress**【物】位移应力。~ **tonnage** 排水吨数。

dis·plant [disˈplɑːnt; dɪsˋplænt] *vt*. 〔废〕移植;移去;移置。

dis·play [disˈplei; dɪsˋple] **I** *vt*. **1**. 显示;展示,表现出。**2**. 展览,展出,陈列(商品等);展开(旗帜等),摊开(地图等)。**3**. 夸示,夸耀。**4**.【印】(用大号字)醒目地排印。~ *bravery* 表现出勇气。~ *fear* 流露出恐惧。~ *a new automobile* 展出新汽车。~ *one's learning* 卖弄学问。~ *a map* 摊开地图。~ *a sail* 张开风帆。~ ***one's wares*** 〔美俚〕显本领,露一手。**II** *n*. **1**. 显示;展示。**2**. 展览,陈列。**3**. 显示物;展览品,陈列品。**4**. 夸耀,夸示,虚饰。**5**.【印】醒目排印。**6**.【动】(雄性动物在繁殖期的)求偶夸耀行为。**7**. (用于电视电话、无线电传真等设备上的)显示器。*a great* ~ *of fireworks* 烟火大会。*a notable* ~ *of loyalty* 忠诚的明显表现。*be too fond of* ~ 太好卖弄。*a vulgar* ~ *of wealth* 庸俗地夸耀财富。~ *flight* 表演飞行。~ *sensitivity* 指示灵敏度。*make a* ~ *of* 夸耀;显示。*the* ~ *of national flag* 展开国旗。*foreign cars on* ~ 展出的外国汽车。~ **ad** 〔口〕(有别于分类广告、用醒目大字排印的)普通广告。~ **type**【印】(排广告等的)醒目大号铅字。~ **window** 展览橱窗。**-ed** *a*.【纹】(鸟的翼爪等)张开的。

dis·please [disˈpliːz; dɪsˋpliz] *vt*. 使不愉快,使不高兴;触怒,使发火。*be* ~*d with the work* 嫌工作不合心意。*be* ~*d at his conduct* 对他的行为感到不愉快。*His reply* ~*d the king*. 他的答复触怒了国王。— *vi*. 令人不快,使人生气。*Bad weather* ~*s*. 恶劣的天气令人不快。

dis·pleas·ing [disˈpliːziŋ; dɪsˋplizɪŋ] *a*. 使人不愉快的;令人发火的。*The noise was very* ~ *to him*. 噪音使他非常恼火。**-ly** *ad*.

dis·pleas·ure [disˈpleʒə; dɪsˋplɛʒɚ] *n*. **1**. 不愉快,不满意,不高兴。**2**. 发怒,生气。*incur* [*arouse*] *the* ~ *of* 触犯…,得罪…,伤…的感情。*take a* ~ *in* 对…觉得不高兴[生气]。

dis·plode [disˈpləud; dɪsˋplod] *vt*., *vi*. 〔废〕= explode.

dis·plume [disˈpluːm; dɪsˋplum] *vt*. 〔诗〕= deplume.

dis·port [disˈpɔːt; dɪsˋpɔrt] *vt*. 〔~ oneself〕嬉戏,玩耍;娱乐。~ *oneself to one's heart's content* 玩个痛快。— *vi*. 玩,游戏,娱乐。*He* ~*ed among books, radio and tape recorder*. 他以读书、听收音机和录音机自娱。

dis·pos·a·ble [disˈpəuzəbl; dɪsˋpozəbl] **I** *a*. **1**. 可(任意)处理的,用后就扔弃的。**2**. 可自由使用的;可供使用的。*a* ~ *paper plate* 用一次就扔掉的纸碟。*Every* ~ *vehicle was sent*. 所有能够用得上的车子都派出去了。**II** *n*. 〔美口〕使用后随即抛掉的东西(尤指容器等)。*Use returnables. Not* ~*s*. 请使用可回收容器,勿用需要抛掉的容器。~ **income** 可用收入〔指个人所得纳税以后的部分〕。~**weight** 飞机上遇紧急情况时可以丢弃的物件重量。

dis·pos·al[1] [disˈpəuzəl; dɪsˋpozl] *n*. **1**. 配置,布置,安排。**2**. 处置,处理。**3**. (财产等的)出售,让与。**4**. 支配权;(自由)处置权,(自由)使用权。*the* ~ *of troops* 部队的配置。*the* ~ *of waste material* 废料的处理。*land* ~ (放射性废料的)埋入地下。*the king's capricious* ~ *of offices* 国王授与官职,全凭一时之兴。~ *sth. by sale* 卖掉某物。***at one's*** ~ 随某人自由,由某人随意支配 (*My books are at your* ~. 我的书请你随意看好了)。***put*** [***leave***] ***sth. at one's*** ~ 把某物交某人自由处理。

dis·pos·al[2] [disˈpəuzəl; dɪsˋpozl] *n*. (厨房)垃圾粉碎机。

dis·pose [disˈpəuz; dɪsˋpoz] *vt*. **1**. 安排,配置,布置。**2**. 处置,处理。**3**. 使倾向于,使有意于 (*to sth*.; *to do*)。**4**. 〔古〕赋与。*outposts carefully* ~*d* 小心布置的岗哨。*The lamp was* ~*d on a table nearby*. 灯配置在附近的桌上。*Your words of cheer* ~ *me for the task*. 你的打气使我愿意接这项任务了。*He is well* [*ill*] ~*d to* [*towards*] *me*. 他对我有[没有]好感。— *vi*. 处置,处理;安排 (*of*)。~ ***of*** **1**. 处理,处置,安排;解决;办妥 (~ *of a business affair* 处理一件事务。~ *of oneself* 安排好自己,设法过日子。~ *of old clothes* 把旧衣服处理掉)。**2**. 卖掉,让与 (~ *of one's possessions* 卖掉个人的财产)。**3**. 除掉,干掉,杀掉 (~ *of the mice in the attic* 消灭阁楼上的老鼠)。**4**. 吃光,喝光 (~ *of some food* 吃一些食品)。***Man proposes. God*** ~***s***. 谋事在人,成事在天。

dis·posed [disˈpəuzd; dɪsˋpozd] *a*. **1**. 已处理了的。**2**. 性情…的。**3**. 有意于…;有…倾向,喜欢…。*ill* [*well*] ~ 脾气坏[好]的。*I am* ~ *to think so*. 我倾向于这样想,也许是这样。*I'm not* ~ *to argue with him*. 我不想和他争论。*He is* ~ *to take offence at trifles*. 他容易为一点小事发脾气。*a man* ~ *to meditate* 喜欢沉思默想的人。

dis·po·si·tion [ˌdispəˈziʃən; ˏdɪspəˋzɪʃən] *n*. **1**. 配置,安排;【军】部署,布置;〔*pl*.〕战略[战术]计划。**2**. 处理,处置;处置权,支配权。**3**.【法】(财产等的)让与。**4**. 性情,素质,气质;性质。**5**. 倾向,意向。**6**. 〔古〕神意,天命。*a girl with a pleasant* ~ 性格开朗的姑娘。*a* ~ *to gamble* 喜欢赌博。*the* ~ *of ice to melt when heated* 冰受热即溶解。*the* ~ *of furniture in the room* 房间里家具的布置。*a fair* ~ 处置公平。*the* ~ *of one's estate* 卖掉不动产。*funds at one's* ~ 可自行支配的资金。*the* ~ *of God* 神意,天命。**-al** *a*.

dis·pos·sess [ˌdispəˈzes; ˏdɪspəˋzɛs] *vt*. **1**. 剥夺,使不再占有,霸占 (*of*)。**2**. 撵走。~ *sb. of land* 夺去某人土地。~*ed refugees living in camps* 被逐出家园、住在帐篷里的难民。*men spiritually* ~*ed* 精神贫困的人。**-or** *n*. 霸占(他人财产、土地)的人。**-ion** *n*. **1**. 抢夺,霸占,强占。**2**. 驱逐。

dis·po·sure [disˈpəuʒə; dɪsˋpoʒɚ] *n*. 〔古〕**1**. 布置;安排;部署。**2**. 管理,处置。**3**. (财产的)出让。**4**. 免除。**5**. 支配权;安置权;管理权;控制权。**6**. 倾向,意向。**7**. 心境;性情;脾气。

dis·praise [disˈpreiz; dɪsˋprez] *n*., *vt*. **1**. 贬损,骂。**2**. 指责。*speak in* ~ *of* 指责,非难。

dis·prize [disˈpraiz; dɪsˋpraɪz] *vt*. 〔古〕贬价;贱视。

dis·prod·uct [disˈprɔdəkt; dɪsˋprɑdəkt] *n*. 有害产品(尤指由于生产者的疏忽而造成者)。

dis·proof [ˈdisˈpruːf; dɪsˋpruf] *n*. **1**. 反证,反驳。**2**. 反证物,反驳的证据。

dis·pro·por·tion [ˈdisprəˈpɔːʃən; ˏdɪsprəˋporʃən] **I** *n*.

D

不均衡,不相称,不相当,失调。*architectural* ～ 建筑上的不均衡。*a supply in* ～ *with the demand* 供求失调。**II** ***vt.*** 使失平衡,使不相称。**-a·ble** ***a.*** **-al** ***a.*** = disproportionate. **-a·tion** ***n.*** 【化】不均衡反应。

dis·pro·por·tion·ate [ˌdisprəˈpɔːʃənit; ˏdisprəˋporʃənɪt] ***a.*** 不均衡的,不匀称的,不相称的。**-ly** ***ad.***

dis·prove [disˈpruːv; dɪsˋpruv] ***vt.*** **1.** 证明…不成立,给与…反证。**2.** 驳斥,反驳。*I* ～ *his claim*. 我证明他提出的索赔要求不能成立。

dis·put·a·ble [disˈpjuːtəbl; dɪsˋpjutəbḷ] ***a.*** 有争论余地的,可质疑的 (*opp.* indisputable)。～ *statements* 可争论的说法。

dis·pu·tant [disˈpjuːtənt; dɪsˋpjutənt] **I** ***n.*** 争论者。**II** ***a.*** 争论的。

dis·pu·ta·tion [ˌdispju(ː)ˈteiʃən; ˏdɪspjuˋteʃən] ***n.*** 争论,议论;(大学中的)辩论。

dis·pu·ta·tious [ˌdispju(ː)ˈteiʃəs; ˏdɪspjuˋteʃəs] ***a.*** 爱议论的;爱争论的;争论的。～ *litigants* 爱争论的诉讼当事人。**-ly** ***ad.*** **-ness** ***n.***

dis·pu·ta·tive [disˈpjuːtətiv; dɪsˋpjutətɪv] ***a.*** **1.** 爱争论的,爱争辩的。**2.** 有关争论的。

dis·pute [disˈpjuːt; dɪsˋpjut] **I** ***vt.*** **1.** 驳斥,抗辩,对…提出质疑;争论,辩论。**2.** 反对,反抗,阻止。**3.** 争夺(土地、奖品、胜利等)。～ *a proposal* 辩论一项建议。～ *a will* 对遗嘱提出质疑。～ *every inch of ground* 寸土必争。～ *the enemy's advance* 阻止敌人推进。～ *a victory* [*prize*] *with sb*. 和某人争夺胜利[奖品]。— ***vi.*** **1.** 辩论,争论。**2.** 争吵。～ *with* [*against*] *sb. over* [*on*, *about*] *sth*. 与某人争论某事。～ *as to who is the greatest English poet* 争论谁是最伟大的英国诗人。**II** ***n.*** 议论,争论;辩驳,抗辩;争吵;争端。*a bitter* [*hot*] ～ 激烈的争论。*boundary* ～ 边界纠纷。*a labour* ～ 劳资纠纷,工潮。***beyond*** [***past***, ***without***, ***out of***] ～ 无争论余地;的确,无疑。***in*** [***under***] ～ (在)争论中的,未决的 (*a point in* ～ 争端)。**dis·put·a·tive** ***a.*** = disputatious. **-r** ***n.*** 争论者,争辩者。

dis·qual·i·fi·ca·tion [disˌkwɔlifiˈkeiʃən; dɪsˏkwɑləfəˋkeʃən] ***n.*** **1.** 无资格,不合格;取消资格。**2.** 使不合格的事物[原因]。*His* ～ *for the team was a bad knee*. 他没有资格参加运动队是因为膝关节有毛病。～ *from office* 没有资格担任公职。

dis·qual·i·fy [disˈkwɔlifai; dɪsˋkwɑləˏfaɪ] ***vt.*** (***-fied***; ***-fy·ing***) 使无资格,使不合格;使不能;【体】取消…的比赛资格。*Age disqualified him for the job*. 年岁过大使他失去做这项工作的资格[能力等]。*disqualified sb. from being a witness* 使某人失去充当证人的资格。～ *him from further participation in the game* 取消某人继续参加比赛的资格。

dis·qui·et [disˈkwaiət; dɪsˋkwaɪət] **I** ***vt.*** 使不安,使忧虑,使烦恼。～*ing rumours* 扰乱人心的谣言。*My heart is* ～*ed*. 我心中不安。**II** ***n.*** 不安,不平静,忧虑,烦恼。*be filled with* ～ 满心不安,满腹烦恼。*An uncertain but unceasing* ～ *is upon me*. 不知道什么缘故,我始终觉得心里七上八下的。**-ly** ***ad.***

dis·qui·e·tude [disˈkwaiitjuːd; dɪsˋkwaɪəˏtjud] ***n.*** 不安;忧虑。

dis·qui·si·tion [ˌdiskwiˈziʃən; ˏdɪskwəˋzɪʃən] ***n.*** **1.** 专题论文;学术讲演。**2.** 〔古〕(有系统的)研究。～ *on* [*about*] *a question* 关于某一问题的专题论文。

Dis·rae·li [dizˈreili; dɪzˋrelɪ] ***n.*** **1.** 迪斯雷利〔姓氏〕。**2.** **Benjamin** ～ 本杰明·迪斯雷利〔1804—1888, 英国著名政治家,小说家〕。

dis·rate [disˈreit; dɪsˋret] ***vt.*** 降价;降等;降级。～ *an officer* 把一个军官降职。

dis·re·gard [ˈdisriˈgɑːd; ˋdɪsrɪˋgɑrd] **I** ***vt.*** **1.** 不理,不顾,不管。**2.** 蔑视,轻视。*D- the footnotes*. 别去管那些脚注。*D-ing both hunger and fatigue, I traveled forward*. 我不顾饥饿和疲劳,继续向前走。～ *an invitation* 不把邀请放在心上。**II** ***n.*** 不理,不顾;蔑视,轻视。*have a total* ～ *for rank* 不计较地位。*This order was in* ～ *of the constitution*. 这项命令置宪法于不顾。**-ful** ***a.*** 轻视,忽视;不顾。

dis·rel·ish [disˈreliʃ; dɪsˋrɛlɪʃ] **I** ***n.*** 嫌恶,不喜欢,讨厌 (*for*)。*have a* ～ *for raw fish* 不喜欢吃生鱼。**II** ***vt.*** 嫌,讨厌。

dis·re·mem·ber [ˌdisriˈmembə; ˏdɪsrɪˋmɛmbɚ] ***vt.*** 〔口〕〔美方〕忘记,忘掉。

dis·re·pair [ˈdisriˈpɛə; ˏdɪsrɪˋpɛr] ***n.*** 失修,破损。*be in* (*a state of*) ～ (房屋等)年久失修,破损。*These houses have been allowed to fall into* ～. 听凭这些房屋破损。

dis·rep·u·ta·ble [disˈrepjutəbl; dɪsˋrɛpjətəbḷ] ***a.*** **1.** 名誉不好的,声名狼藉的。**2.** 不体面的,丢脸的。**3.** 破烂不堪的,难看的。*He looked* ～ *in his gray three days beard*. 他的灰白胡子三天没有刮,看起来不像样子。**-ta·bil·i·ty** ***n.*** 声名狼藉 (*a man of disreputability* 声名狼藉的人)。**-ness** ***n.***

dis·re·pute [ˈdisriˈpjuːt; ˏdɪsrɪˋpjut] ***n.*** 坏名声,声名狼藉;不体面,丢脸。***be in*** ～ 名声不好。***bring a man into*** ～ 使人声誉扫地。***incur*** ～ 招来坏名声,招来恶名。***fall into*** ～ 名誉变坏。

dis·re·spect [ˈdisrisˈpekt; ˏdɪsrɪˋspɛkt] **I** ***n.*** 失礼,失敬,无礼。*show* ～ *for one's seniors* 对长辈[上级]不尊重。**II** ***vt.*** 不尊敬,不尊重。～ *the law* 不尊重法律。**-a·ble** ***a.*** 不值得尊敬的。**-ful** ***a.*** 不敬的,失礼的,无礼的 (*a* ～*ful remark about teachers* 对老师不尊重地乱加议论)。**-ful·ly** ***ad.*** 失礼地,无礼地。

dis·robe [ˈdisˈrəub; dɪsˋrob] ***v.*** = undress.

dis·root [disˈruːt; dɪsˋrut] ***vt.*** 连根拔除,消除。*replace a* ～*ed tree* 补植一棵连根拔起的树。

dis·rupt [disˈrʌpt; dɪsˋrʌpt] **I** ***vt.*** **1.** 使分裂,使瓦解;破坏,使混乱。**2.** 打断,使中断。*The war* ～*ed the society*. 战争使社会陷入混乱。*Telephone service was* ～*ed for hours*. 电话中断了好几个小时。**II** ***a.*** 混乱的;瓦解的;中断的。**-er**, **-or** ***n.*** 造成混乱[破坏、分裂]者。

dis·rup·tion [disˈrʌpʃən; dɪsˋrʌpʃən] ***n.*** 分裂,破裂,瓦解;中断。*the* ～ *of rock* 岩石的破裂。*family* ～ 家庭破裂。*The state was in* ～. 国家处于分崩离析之中。**the D-** (1843年苏格兰教会的)大分裂。

dis·rup·tive [disˈrʌptiv; dɪsˋrʌptɪv] ***a.*** 分裂(性)的;破裂的;破坏性的。～ *activities* 破坏活动。～ **discharge** 【物】破裂放电,火花放电。**-ly** ***ad.***

dis·rup·ture [disˈrʌptʃə; dɪsˋrʌptʃə] ***n.*** = disruption.

dis·sat·is·fac·tion [ˈdisˌsætisˈfækʃən; ˏdɪssætɪsˋfækʃən] ***n.*** **1.** 不满,不平 (*with*; *at*)。**2.** 令人不满的事物。～ *with the present world* 对世道的不满。

dis·sat·is·fac·to·ry [ˈdisˌsætisˈfæktəri; ˏdɪssætɪsˋfæktərɪ] ***a.*** 令人不满的,使人不平的。～ *service* 令人不满的服务。

dis·sat·is·fy [ˈdisˈsætisfai; dɪsˋsætɪsˏfaɪ] ***vt.*** (***-fied***; ***-fy·ing***) 使不满,使失望,使不平,使不服〔通常多用被动语气〕。*a* ～*ing book* 一部不能令人满意的书。***be dissatisfied with*** [***at***] 不满于,对…不满。**-fied** ***a.*** 不满意的,不愉快的。

dis·sav·ing [disˈseiviŋ; dɪsˋsevɪŋ] ***n.*** 入不敷出;动用储蓄。

dis·seat [disˈsiːt; dɪsˋsit] ***vt.*** 〔古〕= unseat.

dis / sec = disintegrations per second【物】衰变/秒。

dis·sect [diˈsekt; dɪˋsɛkt] ***vt.*** **1.** 解剖;剖开,切开;【地】分割。**2.** 仔细分析。～*ed map* 明细地图。～*ed plateau* 【地】切割台地。～ *an idea* 仔细分析一种思想。— ***vi.*** **1.** 进行解剖。**2.** 进行仔细分析。～*ed leaf* 【植】深裂[多裂]叶。～**ing knife** [**room**]【医】解剖刀[室]。**-i·ble** ***a.*** 可解剖的,可仔细分析的。

dis·sec·tion [diˈsekʃən; dɪˋsɛkʃən] *n*. 1. 解剖;【地】切割作用。2. 详细分析。3. 解剖标本;【商英】分类。~ *of a human body* 人体解剖。*image* ~【物】析像,图像分析。

dis·sec·tor [diˈsektə; dɪˋsɛktɚ] *n*. 1. 解剖者;解剖学家。2. 解剖用具。3. 分析者。~ **tube**【物】析像管(= image ~).

dis·seise, dis·seize [ˈdisˈsiːz; dɪsˋsiz] *vt*.【法】霸占,强夺(*of*)。~ *sb. of his estate* 强占某人不动产。

dis·sei·see, dis·sei·zee [ˌdissiːˈziː; ˏdɪssiˋzi] *n*.【法】被强夺者,被侵占者。

dis·sei·sin, dis·sei·zin [disˈsiːzin; dɪsˋsizɪn] *n*.【法】霸占,侵占。

dis·sei·sor, dis·sei·zor [disˈsiːzə; dɪsˋsizɚ] *n*.【法】强夺者,侵占者。

dis·sem·ble [diˈsembl; dɪˋsɛmbl̩] *vt*. 1. 掩饰(感情、动机等)。2. 假装。3. 假装不见。~ *one's incompetence* 掩饰自己的无能。~ *innocence* 装出清白无辜的样子。—*vi*. 1. 掩饰;作伪,作假。2. 假装不知,装聋作哑。**-r** *n*. 作伪者,伪君子。

dis·sem·i·nate [diˈsemineit; dɪˋsɛməˏnet] *vt*. 1. 撒,播(种)。2. 传播,散布,普及。*the idea* ~*d by the newspaper* 报纸宣扬的观点。~ *Christianity* 传播基督教。— *vi*. 广为传播。**dis·sem·i·na·tion** [diˌsemiˈneiʃən; dɪˏsɛməˋneʃən] *n*. 播种;传播;散布。**-na·tor** *n*. 播种者,撒种者;传播者,散布者。

dis·sen·sion [diˈsenʃən; dɪˋsɛnʃən] *n*. 1. (意见等的)不一致,分歧。2. 不合;冲突,倾轧,纠纷。*sow* ~*s among* ... 在…当中挑拨离间。~ *between the two nations* 两国之间的纷争。

dis·sent [diˈsent; dɪˋsɛnt] I *vi*. 1. 持异议,有不同意见(*from*)。2. 〔英〕不信奉国教(*from*)。~ *from sb*. [*sb.'s views*] 不同意某人的观点。*pass without a* ~*ing voice* 一致通过。~ *from the Church of England* 不信奉英国国教。II *n*. 1. 不同意,异议(*from*)。2. 〔英〕反对国教;〔集合词〕不信奉国教者。*None of them dares even mutter* ~. 没有人敢说半个不字。**-er** *n*. 反对者;持异议者,持不同政见者;〔英〕〔通例 Dissenter〕不信奉国教者。

dis·sen·ti·ent [diˈsenʃiənt; dɪˋsɛnʃɪənt] I *a*. 不同意的。*The bill passed with one* ~ *vote*. 议案以一票反对被通过。II *n*. 不同意,异议;持不同意见者。

dis·sen·tious [diˈsenʃəs; dɪˋsɛnʃəs] *a*. 不和的,好争吵的;闹倾轧的。

dis·sep·i·ment [diˈsepimənt; dɪˋsɛpəmənt] *n*.【植、动】隔膜,隔壁;(植物的)子房中隔。

dis·sert [diˈsəːt; dɪˋsɝt], **dis·ser·tate** [ˈdisəteit; ˋdɪsɚˏtet] *vi*. 论述,论说;写论文,讲演。

dis·ser·ta·tion [ˌdisə(ː)ˈteiʃən; ˏdɪsɚˋteʃən] *n*. (专题)论述;论文,学位论文;学术讲演。*a doctoral* ~ 博士学位论文。

dis·serve [ˈdisˈsəːv; dɪsˋsɝv] *vt*. 损害,伤害,危害。~ *the society* 危害社会。

dis·serv·ice [ˈdisˈsəːvis; dɪsˋsɝvɪs] *n*. 损害,伤害,危害。*They do a great* ~ *to our society*. 他们给我们的社会带来很大危害。

dis·sev·er [disˈsevə; dɪˋsɛvɚ] *vt*. 分裂,分离;分割。~ *a chicken* 把鸡斩成小块。*A quarrel* ~*ed the two friends*. 一场争吵使两个朋友绝交了。— *vi*. 分离,分手。**-ance** [-ˈsevərəns; -ˋsɛvərəns], **-ment** *n*.

dis·si·dence [ˈdisidəns; ˋdɪsədəns] *n*. (意见等的)不同,不一致,异议。*political* ~ 政治意见的不同。**dis·si·dent** [ˈdisidənt; ˋdɪsədənt] 1. *a*. 持不同意见的(人)(*opinions dissident from ours* 和我们不同的意见)。2. *n*. 持不同意见者。

dis·sight [disˈsait; dɪsˋsaɪt] *n*. 〔罕〕难看的东西。

dis·sim·i·lar [diˈsimilə; dɪˋsɪmələ˞] *a*. 不同的,不一样的(*to*; *from*; *with*)。*The end would be* ~ *to the beginning*. 结局将不同于开始。**-ly** *ad*.

dis·sim·i·lar·i·ty [ˌdisimiˈlæriti; dɪˏsɪməˋlærətɪ] *n*. 不同,不相似;异点。*There are dissimilarities in our outlooks*. 我们的相貌有许多不同点。

dis·sim·i·late [diˈsimileit; dɪˋsɪməˏlet] *vt*. 1. 使不同,使有异点。2.【语】使异化。— *vi*. 1. 不同,有异点。2.【语】异化。

dis·sim·i·la·tion [ˈdisimiˈleiʃən; dɪˏsɪməˋleʃən] *n*. 1. 相异,异化(过程、作用、现象)。2.【生】异化作用(= catabolism);【语】(音的)异化(*opp*. assimilation)。

dis·si·mil·i·tude [ˌdisiˈmilitjuːd; ˏdɪsɪˋmɪləˏtjud] *n*. 相异,不同,异点;【修】对比。

dis·sim·u·late [diˈsimjuleit; dɪˋsɪmjəˏlet] *vt*. 假装(镇静),掩饰(感情等)。~ *fear* 掩饰恐惧,强作镇静。— *vi*. 作伪,作假。**-la·tion** *n*. **-la·tor** *n*. = dissembler.

dis·si·pate [ˈdisipeit; ˋdɪsəˏpet] *vt*. 1. 使(云雾等)消散,驱散(忧虑等)。2. 浪费(时间等),挥霍(金钱等)。~ *the mist* 驱散雾气。~ *the enemy force* 驱散敌军。~ *sorrows* 消除忧愁。~ *one's energy* 浪费精力。— *vi*. 1. 消散;【化】散逸。2. 放荡;浪费。*They* ~ *all night and sleep all day*. 他们白天睡觉,通夜鬼混。*Her anger was dissipating*. 她渐渐息怒。**-ed** *a*. 1. 被驱散的,【化】散失的。2. 浪费掉的。3. 放荡的。**-r, -tor** *n*. 浪子,败家子。

dis·si·pa·tion [ˌdisiˈpeiʃən; ˏdɪsəˋpeʃən] *n*. 1. 消散,分散;【化】散逸。2. 浪费;消耗,损耗。3. 放荡,闲游浪荡。4. 消遣,娱乐。*the* ~ *of a fortune* 挥霍。*the* ~ *of one's time* 浪费时间,虚度光阴。*My only* ~ *is angling*. 钓鱼是我唯一的消遣。~ **trail**【空】(喷气式飞机飞过后留下的)消散痕迹。

dis·si·pa·tive [ˈdisipeitiv; ˋdɪsɪpetɪv] *a*. 1. 消散的。2. 消耗(性)的,浪费的。3. 放荡的。~ *element*【无】耗能元件。

dis·so·cia·ble [diˈsəuʃiəbl; dɪˋsoʃɪəbl] *a*. 1. 可分离的;易分离的。2. 不调和的。3. 不爱交际的。*Worthy and unworthy motives are often not* ~. 高尚和不高尚的动机不是时常能够区别开来的。

dis·so·cial [diˈsəuʃəl; dɪˋsoʃəl] *a*. 1. 反社会的;自私的。2. 不爱交际的,孤僻的。*solitary* ~ *habits* 与世寡合的孤僻性格。

dis·so·cial·ize [diˈsəuʃiəlaiz; dɪˋsoʃɪəˏlaɪz] *vt*. 使不爱交际,使孤僻。

dis·so·ci·ate [diˈsəuʃieit; dɪˋsoʃɪˏet] *vt*. 1. 使分离,使脱离(*from*)。2.【化】使离解;【心】分裂(意识等)。~ *the two ideas* 分开两种观念。~ *oneself from the evil in one's past* 改邪归正。*It's difficult to* ~ *the man from his position*. 一想到这个人,就很难不同时想起他的职位。~*d personality*【心】分裂人格。— *vi*. 1. 分离,游离。2.【化】离解。

dis·so·ci·a·tion [diˌsəusiˈeiʃən; dɪˏsosɪˋeʃən] *n*. 1. 分解,分裂,分离。2.【生】离异,分化变异(体);【化】离解(作用);【心】分裂;【统】不相联。*the* ~ *of church and state* 政教分离。~ *of ideas* 观念的不相联。*electrolytic* ~【物】电离(作用)。

dis·so·ci·a·tive [diˈsəuʃiətiv; dɪˋsoʃɪetɪv] *a*. 1. 使分离的,分裂性的。2.【化】离解的;【心】分裂的;【生】离异的。~ *capture*【化】离解俘获。

dis·sol·uble [diˈsɔljubl; dɪˋsɑljəbl̩] *a*. 1. 可分解的,可分离的;(机构等)可解散的。2. (婚约、职务等)可解除的;(财产等)可清算的,(法律等)可取消的。3. 可溶解的,可液化的,可融解的。*Sugar is* ~ *in water*. 糖溶于水。

dis·sol·u·bil·i·ty [diˌsɔljuˈbiliti; dɪˏsɑljəˋbɪlətɪ] *n*. 可溶性;溶(解)度。

dis·so·lute [ˈdisəljuːt; ˋdɪsəˏlut] *a*. 放荡的;自甘堕落的。*a* ~ *crew* [*set of people*] 一群荒淫放荡的男女。

a brilliant and ~ writer 才气焕发而放荡不羁的[有才无德的]作家。**-ly** *ad*. **-ness** *n*.

dis·so·lu·tion [ˌdisəˈljuːʃən; ˏdɪsəˋluʃən] *n*. 1. 分解,分离。2. 溶解(作用),融化,液化。3. (婚约等的)取消,(职务等的)解除,(法律等的)废除;(公司等的)解散。4. (财产等的)清算;(债务等的)结清。5. (机能等的)消失,消亡,死亡。6. 腐朽,崩溃,解体。7. 〔废〕放荡。*the ~ of the partnership* 合作关系的取消。*the ~ of Parliament* 解散议会。*the ~ of the Republic* 共和国的崩溃。*the ~ of the body* 尸体的腐烂。

dis·solv·a·ble [diˈzɔlvəbl; dɪˋzɑlvəbl̩] *a*. 1. 可分解的。2. 可溶(解)的。3. 可解散的。**-ness**, **-a·bil·i·ty** [diˌzɔlvəˈbiliti; dɪˏzɑlvəˋbɪlətɪ] *n*. 可溶性。

dis·solve [diˈzɔlv; dɪˋzɑlv] *vt*. 1. 溶,使溶解,使融化,使液化。2. 使分解,使分离。3. 解散(议会等);【法】废除,撤消(法令等),取消(契约等),解除(婚约等)。4. 摧毁(希望等),打破(魔法等),揭开(秘密等),解开(谜语等)。5. 使感动,软化。6. 使(电影、电视画面)渐隐,使溶暗。*~ salt in water* 使盐溶于水。*~ sugar into syrup* 使糖融化为糖浆。*~ a bond* 解除契约。*~ Parliament* 解散议会。*~ sb.'s hopes* 使某人的希望破灭。*~ a spell* 破除魔法,解除符咒的魔力。*~ a marriage* 解除婚约。*~ the injunction* 取消禁令。*~ partnership* 散伙,拆伙。*Time ~s all things*. 时光使一切事务都难以永存。*be ~d in tears* 因感动而流泪。*~ one scene into another* 使(电影、电视等的)一个画面逐渐化入另一个画面。— *vi*. 1. 分解;崩溃。2. 溶解;融化。3. (议会等)解散;(婚约等)失效;(幻影等)消失。4. 动感情,软化。5. (电影,电视等画面)渐隐,溶暗。*Sugar ~s in liquid*. 糖溶于液体。*Ice ~s in the sun*. 冰在阳光下融化。*The assembly ~d*. 集会解散了。*Society must disintegrate once the family ~s*. 一旦家庭解体,社会也就必定崩溃。*She ~d in tears*. 她感动得泪流满面。*~ into water* 溶化成水。*~ into air* 在空气中消失。*~* ***out*** *[**in**]* (电影、电视等画面)溶出[入],化出[入]。— *n*. 【影】(电影、电视等画面的)渐隐,溶暗。**dissolving views** 【影】渐隐画面。

dis·solv·ent [diˈzɔlvənt; dɪˋzɑlvənt] *a*., *n*. = solvent.

dis·so·nance [ˈdisənəns; ˋdɪsənəns], **dis·so·nan·cy** [-si; -sɪ] *n*. 1. 不一致,不和谐。2. 【乐】不协和音。3. 倾轧,不和 (*opp*. consonance)。*cognitive ~* 认识上的分歧。

dis·so·nant [ˈdisənənt; ˋdɪsənənt] *a*. 1. 不调和的;不一致的。2. 【乐】不协和的;刺耳的。3. 倾轧的,不和的。*~ and loud voices* 又响又刺耳的声音。**-ly** *ad*.

dis·suade [diˈsweid; dɪˋswed] *vt*. 劝阻,劝止,劝戒 (*from*)。*~ a friend from joining a society* 劝阻朋友不参加某团体。*She was ~d from leaving home*. 她受到劝阻,没有离家出走。

dis·sua·sion [diˈsweiʒən; dɪˋsweʒən] *n*. 劝戒,告诫,制止。

dis·sua·sive [diˈsweisiv; dɪˋswesɪv] *a*. 劝戒的,劝阻的,告诫的。*be ~ of* 劝止。*make ~ gestures* 用手势劝阻。**-ly** *ad*. **-ness** *n*.

dis·syl·lab·ic [ˈdisiˈlæbik; ˏdɪsɪˋlæbɪk] *a*. 【语】双音节的。

dis·syl·la·ble [diˈsiləbl; dɪˋsɪləbl̩] *n*. 【语】双音节词,双音节式。

dis·sym·met·ri·c(al) [ˈdissiˈmetrik(əl); ˏdɪssɪˋmɛtrɪk(əl)] *a*. 1. 非对称的,不匀称的。2. (镜面内外、左右手等)相反对称的。3. 【化】对映形态的。

dis·sym·me·try [ˌdisˈsimitri; dɪsˋsɪmɪtrɪ] *n*. 1. 非对称(现象)。2. (镜面内外、左右手等的)相反对称。3. 【化】对映形态。

dist. = distance; distant; distinguish(ed); distributed; distribution.

dis·taff [ˈdistɑːf; ˋdɪstæf] **I** *n*. 1. (手工纺织用的)卷线杆。2. 针线活,女活,妇女工作,妇道。3. 〔集合词〕女性。4. 女人。*~ side* 母方,母系 (*opp*. spear side)。**II** *a*. 〔书〕女子的,女性的,妇道的。*cooking, sewing and such ~ matters* 做饭缝衣这类女活。**-er** *n*. 家庭中的女性。

dis·tal [ˈdistəl; ˋdɪstl̩] *a*. 【解】远端的,远侧的;末端的,末梢(部)的;【植】远基的,远轴的。*the ~ end of a bone* 骨头的末端部位。*~* **bite** 【牙科】远心咬合。

dis·tance [ˈdistəns; ˋdɪstəns] **I** *n*. 1. 距离,路程。2. 远隔,远离;远处,远方。3. (时间的)间隔,长远,长久。4. 悬殊。5. 隔阂,疏远。6. 【音】(二音间的)音程;【绘】远景;【拳击】规定的比赛时间。*The ~ between the two houses was exactly one mile*. 两座房屋正好相隔一英里。*What's the ~ from here to the station?* 从这里到车站有多远? *It's quite a ~ from here*. 离这里远得很。*A vast ~ of water surrounded the ship*. 船的四周都是辽阔的水面。*Every sound carries a great ~*. 每一种声音都传到远处。*the ~ between birth and death* 从生到死的这段时间。*a ~ of a century* 一世纪的间隔,经过一世纪。*Our philosophies are a long ~ apart*. 我们的哲学观点相去悬殊。*stare into the ~* 向远方凝视。*the extreme [middle] ~* (绘画的)远[中]景。*treat sb. with a little ~* 有点冷淡地对待某人。***a good ~ off*** 很远,远隔着。***at a ~*** 隔开一段距离,留有间隔,不挨近 (*look to advantage at a ~* 远看为好)。***at a respectful ~*** 敬而远之。***at this ~ of time*** 经过这样长一段时间 (*It's impossible to judge at this ~ of time*. 经过这样长一段时间以后,再想作出判断是不可能的了)。***be a great ~ away*** 离得很远。***be out of (striking) ~ (from...)*** 太远,难(打)到。***be within striking [hailing, hearing] ~*** (在)能打到[听到](的地方)。***from a ~*** 从远方 (*It's a very beautiful house, especially from a ~*. 这是一所漂亮的房子,从远处看尤其如此)。***go [last] the ~*** 做完,坚持干到最后一次。***in the ~*** 在远处,在很远的那边。***Keep at a ~!*** 别靠近! ***Keep ~*** 留间隔。***Keep sb. at a ~*** 与某人保持相当距离,敬而远之,疏远。***keep one's ~*** 避开,不接近 (*Keep your ~ from him*. 你不要接近他)。***know one's ~*** 知分寸,守本分。***to a ~*** 到远方 (*spread to a ~* 伸展到远方)。***within ... ~*** 在…距离内 (*within jumping ~* 在跳得到的地方)。**II** *vt*. 1. 隔开,把…放在一定距离之外;使显得遥远。2. 超过,赶过,胜过;(比赛中)把…甩在后面。*~ one's competitors* (竞赛中)把对手远远地甩在后面。*I feel I'm ~d by him in every respect*. 我感到自己在各方面都赶不上他了。*~* **learning** 远程教育(如电视教学等)。*~* **made good** 【海】直航距离〔从船经过的某一点至其现在位置之间的距离,以海里表示〕。*~* **medley** 等距离接力赛跑。*~* **post** (赛马时用的)距离标竿。*~* **recorder** 【无】遥测记录器。

dis·tant [ˈdistənt; ˋdɪstənt] *a*. 1. 远,远方的,远离的,远隔的;相距(若干路程)的。2. 冷淡的,疏远的,有隔阂的。3. (亲戚)远族的,远房的;(朋友等)泛泛之交的,交情不深的。4. 隐约的,不清晰的。*a ~ place* 远方。*a ~ view* 远景。*a ~ letter* 来自远方的信。*a ~ sound* 远处传来的声音。*~ ages* 往昔。*~ centuries past* 经过多少世纪。*10 miles ~ from here* 离这里十英里。*a ~ voyage* 远航。*a ~ politeness* 敬而远之。*a ~ air [manner]* 冷淡的态度。*a ~ connection [relative]* 远亲。*a ~ acquaintance* 点头之交。*one's ~ youth* 早已逝去的青年时期。*a ~ likeness [resemblance]* 约略相似。***at no ~ date*** 不日,日内。*~* ***crossing [hybridization]*** 【植】远缘杂交。***have not the most ~ idea (of a matter)*** 很不明白(某事)。***make a ~ allusion*** 迂回曲折地暗示。*~* **signal** 【铁路】预告信号。**-ly** *ad*. 远地,遥远地 (*be distantly related to* 和…是远亲)。

dis·taste [ˈdisˈteist; ˋdisˋtest] *n*. 厌恶;不爱吃[喝](*for*)。*He had hearty ~ for songs of pathos*. 他极不爱听感伤歌曲。*have a ~ for fish* 不爱吃鱼。

dis·taste·ful [disˈteistful; dɪsˋtestfəl] *a*. **1**. 味道不好的,不合口味的。**2**. 令人不愉快的,令人讨厌的 (*to*)。*a ~ medicine* 苦口的药。*I find him ~* . 我发现他很讨厌。*Drinking is ~ to me*. 我不喜欢喝酒。**-ly** *ad*. **-ness** *n*.

Dist. Atty. = District Attorney〔美〕地方检察官。

Dist. Ct. = District Court 地方法院。

dis·tem·per[1] [disˈtempə; dɪsˋtɛmpɚ] **I** *n*. **1**.【兽医】犬瘟热;马腺疫;兽类传染性卡他。**2**. 疾病〔尤指兽类疾病〕;不健康;(精神状态)不正常。**3**. (社会的)不安,骚动。*political ~* 政治骚乱。**II** *vt*. **1**. 使(精神等)失常,使(机能等)失调〔常用被动语态〕。**2**. 在…中造成动乱。*a ~ed fancy* [*illusion*] 由疾病引起的幻觉。

dis·tem·per[2] [disˈtempə; dɪsˋtɛmpɚ] **I** *n*. **1**. (壁画等用的)色粉颜料,胶画颜料。**2**.【化】水浆涂料。**3**. 胶画。**II** *vt*. **1**. 用胶画颜料画;用胶画颜料涂(壁等)。**2**. 用胶状物调制(颜料),把(蛋黄、胶水、颜料等)调制成胶画颜料。

dis·tend [disˈtend; dɪsˋtɛnd] *vi*. 扩张;膨胀。*The sea ~ed about them*. 海水在他们周围上涨。*Habitual overeating has ~ed his stomach*. 经常大吃大喝把他的胃口撑大了。

dis·ten·si·ble [disˈtensəbl; dɪsˋtɛnsəbl̩] *a*. 会膨胀的。**-bil·i·ty** *n*. 膨胀性,可张性。

dis·ten·sion, dis·ten·tion [disˈtenʃən; dɪsˋtɛnʃən] *n*. 膨胀(作用),胀大。~ *of the abdomen* 腹部的胀大。

dis·thene [ˈdisθiːn; ˋdɪsθin] *n*.【矿】蓝晶石。

dis·tich [ˈdistik; ˋdɪstɪk] *n*.【韵】(诗中押韵的)对联,对句。

dis·tich·ous [ˈdistikəs; ˋdɪstɪkəs] *a*.【植】对生的,双列的;【动】(触角等)变节的。~ *leaves*【植】双列叶。~ *antennae*【动】双节触角。

dis·til(l) [disˈtil; dɪsˋtɪl] *vt*. **1**. 蒸馏;用蒸馏法制造,用蒸馏法提取;蒸馏出 (*off*; *out*)。**2**. 提取…的精华。**3**. 使滴下。~ *whiskey from mash* 用麦芽汁蒸馏威士忌酒。~ *gasoline from crude oil* 从原油中蒸馏汽油。~ *out impurities* 蒸馏出杂质。*The cool of the night ~ the dew*. 深夜的寒气凝成露珠。*~ed liquors* 烧酒。*~ed water* 蒸馏水。~ *one's style* 使文体简洁。*A proverb ~s the wisdom of ages*. 谚语是许多世纪智慧的精华。—*vi*. **1**. 蒸馏。**2**. 滴下,渗出;凝成水滴。*Some water ~ed over the rocks from the moist undergrowth*. 岩石下潮湿的草丛使石上渗出水滴。

dis·til·land [ˈdistilænd; ˋdɪstəˏlænd] *n*.【化】被蒸馏物。

dis·till·ate [ˈdistilit, ˈdistileit; ˋdɪstɪlɪt, ˋdɪstɪlet] *n*. **1**. 蒸馏液,馏出物。**2**. 浓缩物;精华。*the ~ of their wisdom* 他们的智慧的精华,他们的心血的结晶。

dis·til·la·tion [ˌdistiˈleiʃən; ˏdɪstəˋleʃən] *n*. **1**. 蒸馏(作用);蒸馏法。**2**. 蒸馏液;蒸馏物。**3**. 精华,精萃。*dry* [*destructive*] ~【化】干馏(法)。*fractional* ~【化】分馏,分解蒸馏(法)。~ **column** [**tower**] 蒸馏塔。~ **plant** 蒸馏设备。~ **yield** 馏出体积。

dis·til·la·to·ry [disˈtilətəri; dɪsˋtɪlətorɪ] **I** *a*. 蒸馏(用)的。*a ~ vessel* 蒸馏器皿。**II** *n*. 蒸馏器;蒸馏场所。

dis·till·er [disˈtilə; dɪsˋtɪlɚ] *n*. **1**. 蒸馏者。**2**. 制酒者。**3**. 蒸馏器。*a whiskey ~* 威士忌酒制造者。*~'s grain* [*solubles*] 酒糟。

dis·till·er·y [disˈtiləri; dɪsˋtɪlərɪ] *n*. **1**. 蒸馏室。**2**. 酒厂。

dis·til(l)·ment [disˈtilmənt; dɪsˋtɪlmənt] *n*. 〔古〕蒸馏,蒸馏物,蒸馏液。

dis·tinct [disˈtiŋkt; dɪsˋtɪŋkt] *a*. **1**. 独特的,性质不同的 (*from*)。**2**. 清楚的,明显的;明确的;显著的。**3**. 难得的,不同寻常的。**4**. 〔诗、古〕修饰过的;富于变化的。*things similar in effect but wholly ~ in motive* 效果相似而动机不同的东西。*Gold is ~ from iron*. 金子和铁不同。*a neat ~ handwriting* 字迹清楚。*a ~ pronunciation* 发音清晰。*a ~ improvement of living conditions* 生活条件的显著改善。*His praise is a ~ honour*. 得到他的夸奖是一项难得的荣誉。~ **roots**【数】相异根,不等根。**-ly** *ad*. 清楚地,显然 (*be distinctly audible* 声音清晰)。**-ness** *n*.

dis·tinc·tion [disˈtiŋkʃən; dɪˋstɪŋkʃən] *n*. **1**. 差别,区别;区分。**2**. 特征,特性,个性。**3**. 优越,卓越;盛名。**4**. 殊动,大功,荣誉;勋章,荣誉称号。**5**.【电视】清晰度。**6**. 〔废〕分割,分离。*His ~ of sounds is excellent*. 他辨别声音的能力很强。*a ~ between what he says and what he does* 他的言行不一。*There is no ~ in his appearance*. 他的面貌没有什么特殊的地方。*Death comes to all without ~*. 人皆有一死。*draw* [*make*] *a clear ~ between right and wrong* 辨别是非[忠奸,正邪]。*gain* [*win*] ~ 出名,立功。*graduate from college with ~* 以优异成绩毕业。*serve with ~ in the war* 立下战功。*rise to ~* 出名。*a poet of ~* 名诗人。

dis·tinc·tive [disˈtiŋktiv; dɪsˋtɪŋktɪv] *a*. **1**. 区别的,鉴别性的。**2**. 独特的,有特色的。*the ~ stripes of the zebra* 斑马身上独特的条纹。~ **feature**【语】示差特征。~ **insignia**〔美陆军〕各(团或营的)队徽或队章。**-ly** *ad*. **-ness** *n*. 独特性。

dis·tin·gué [disˈtæŋgei; ˏdɪstæŋˋge] *a*. 〔F.〕(风度、服饰、容貌等)高贵的,高雅的,雍容华贵的。*a rather ~ foreign diplomat* 一位风度高雅的异国外交官。

dis·tin·guish [disˈtiŋgwiʃ; dɪsˋtɪŋgwɪʃ] *vt*. **1**. 区别;辨别,识别,判别。**2**. (通过耳、目等)辨认出。**3**. 把…分类。**4**. 使具有特色;使显著,使触目〔通常用 ~ oneself〕。~ *the sound of piano in an orchestra* 在乐队合奏中分辨出钢琴的声音。~ *good from evil* 分别善恶。~ *her from her sister* 辨别出她和她的妹妹。*I can't ~ things so far*. 那么远的东西我可分不清。*the geniality that ~ed him* 他那特有的亲切风度。*be ~ed for one's vices* 恶名昭著。~ *oneself in battle* 作战勇敢,战功卓著。~ *oneself by scholarship* 学问超群。*Let us ~ the various types of metaphor*. 我们把各种譬喻加以分类。—*vi*. 区别,辨别;识别。*His mind could no longer ~ between illusion and reality*. 他的头脑已经不再能分清幻觉和现实。**-a·ble** *a*. 可区别的,可辨别的;(通过耳、目等)可以辨认出的。

dis·tin·guish·ed [disˈtiŋgwiʃt; dɪsˋtɪŋgwɪʃt] *a*. **1**. 卓越的,卓著的。**2**. 以…出名的。**3**. 高贵的;(服饰、气度等)高雅的。*a ~ scholar* 知名学者。*a ~ old gentleman* 一位气度不凡的老先生。~ **marksman** 特等射手。~ **services** 特殊的功劳[贡献]。**D- Conduct Medal**〔英军〕殊功勋章。**D- Service Order**【美陆军】殊勋〔金十字〕勋章。

dis·tome [ˈdistəum; ˋdɪstom] *n*.【动】双盘吸虫〔肝蛭,肺蛭等〕。

dis·to·mi·a·sis [ˌdistəˈmaiəsis; ˏdɪstəˋmaɪəsɪs] *n*.【医】双盘吸虫病。

dis·tort [disˈtɔːt; dɪsˋtɔrt] *vt*. **1**. 使歪扭,弄歪(嘴脸、手足等)。**2**. 曲解,歪曲(事实等)。**3**. 使不正常。**4**.【电】使失真。*a mirror which ~s the features* 使人变相的镜,哈哈镜。*face ~ed with rage* 脸气得变了样。~ *the facts* 歪曲事实。*Arthritis ~ed his wrists*. 关节炎使他的手腕扭曲了。**-ed** *a*. 歪曲的;扭歪的;偏颇的。**-ed·ly** [-ˈtɔːtidli; -ˋtɔrtɪdlɪ] *ad*. 被歪曲地。

dis·tor·tion [disˈtɔːʃən; dɪsˋtɔrʃən] *n*. **1**. 歪扭,扭曲。**2**.【电】(信号、波形等的)失真;【物】(透镜成像产生的)畸变;【医】扭转,变形。**3**. 窜改,歪曲,曲解。*a gross ~ of the news* 大肆歪曲的报道。*frequency ~*【无】频率失真。*undergo a sudden ~* (脸等)突然变形。**-al** *a*.

dis·tor·tion·ist [disˈtɔːʃənist; dɪsˋtɔrʃənɪst] *n*. **1**. 漫画家。**2**. 擅长柔软体操[武艺、杂技]的人。

dis·tract [dis'trækt; dɪs`trækt] ***vt*.** **1.** 分散(注意力等),岔开(念头等)(*opp*. attract)。**2.**〔多用被动语态〕弄昏;使发狂,使精神错乱。**3.** 娱乐,消遣。*Reading ~s the mind from grief*. 读书解忧。*The music ~ed him from his work*. 乐声使他不能专心工作。*I'm ~ed with* [*by*] *anxiety*. 我焦急得发狂。*Grief drove him ~ed*. 悲伤使他发狂。~ *oneself by talking* 闲谈消遣。*I'm bored with bridge, but golf still ~s me*. 我已经玩厌了桥牌,但是还喜欢玩高尔夫球。

dis·tract·ed [dis'træktid; dɪs`træktɪd] ***a*.** **1.** 分神的,分散注意力的。**2.** 心烦意乱的,精神失常的,发狂的。*lend a very ~ attention* 根本心不在焉。*the ~ mother whose child had fallen ill* 因孩子生病而急得发狂的母亲。**-ly *ad*.**

dis·tract·ing·ly [dis'træktiŋli; dɪs`træktɪŋlɪ] ***a*.** **1.** 使人精神涣散的,使人分心的。**2.** 使人心烦意乱的,使人发狂的。

D

dis·trac·tion [dis'trækʃən; dɪs`trækʃən] ***n*.** **1.** 精神涣散,分心;使人分心的事情。**2.** 心乱,心烦;发狂,精神错乱。**3.** 消遣;娱乐。*a good place to study, free from ~* 一个不使人分心的良好的学习场所。*be driven to ~ by love* 爱得发狂。*The child will drive me to ~*. 这孩子闹得简直要使我发狂。*He listened with ~* . 他心不在焉地听着。*Fishing is his major ~* . 钓鱼是他的主要娱乐。**without ~ 1.** 全神贯注地,不分心地。**2.** 心不乱地。

dis·train [dis'trein; dɪs`tren] ***vt*.**【法】(为赔偿损失、担保债务等)扣押(财物)。~ *goods for an amercement* 为罚款而扣押财物。—***vi*.**【法】扣押 (*on*; *upon*)。**-ment *n*.**

dis·train·ee [ˌdistrei'niː; ˏdɪstre`ni] ***n*.**【法】财物被扣押者。

dis·train·er, dis·train·or [dis'treinə, ˌdistrei'nɔː; dɪs`trenɚ, ˏdɪstre`nɔ] ***n*.**【法】扣押他人财物者。

dis·traint [dis'treint; dɪs`trent] ***n*.**【法】扣押财物(行动,处分)。

dis·trait [dis'trei; dɪs`tre] ***a*.**〔F.〕(因烦恼、忧惧等而)心不在焉的〔形容女性时用 distraite〕。

dis·traught [dis'trɔːt; dɪs`trɔt] ***a*.** 心神错乱的;发狂的。~ *with terror* 恐怖得发狂。

dis·tress [dis'tres; dɪs`trɛs] **I *n*.** **1.** 苦恼,烦恼;悲痛,悲叹;使人悲痛[苦恼]的事情;(肉体的)苦痛。**2.** 贫苦,穷困。**3.** 灾殃,危难,不幸;【海】海难。**4.**【英法】扣押财物;被扣押的财物。*feel acute ~ at ...* 对…深感苦恼[悲痛]。*relieve ~ among the poor* 减轻穷人的痛苦。*an old story of a dame in ~* 少女落难之类老一套的故事。*a ship in ~* 失事的船只。*a signal of ~* 遇难信号。*levy a ~ upon* 对…实行扣押财物的处分。**II *vt*.** **1.** 使苦恼,使为难,使悲痛。**2.** 使贫困;使困苦。**3.**【法】扣押(财物)。~ *oneself* 焦虑,悲痛。~ *sb. into committing suicide* 因…的痛苦而自杀。~ **call** [**signal**] 遇险信号,求救信号〔即 SOS〕。~ **frequency**【无】遇险求救频率。~ **gun** [**flag**] 遇险[求救]号炮[信号旗]。~ **merchandize** 亏本出售的货物。~ **rocket** 遇难求救火箭。~ **selling** 廉价出售(以求现款)。~ **warrant**【法】扣押令。~**ed area** 灾区;经济萧条区。

dis·tress·ful [dis'tresful; dɪs`trɛsful] ***a*.** **1.** 苦难重重的,不幸的,悲惨的。**2.** 使人苦恼的;使人痛苦的。*the ~ circumstances of poverty and sickness* 贫病交加的不幸境遇。*a ~ cry* 惨叫。**-ly *ad*.**

dis·tress·ing [dis'tresiŋ; dɪs`trɛsɪŋ] ***a*.** 令人苦恼的;使人痛苦的。*the ~ news* 使人痛苦的消息。

dis·trib·u·ta·ry [dis'tribjutəri; dɪs`trɪbjutɛrɪ] ***n*.** (分出后不再流入本河的)分流 (*opp*. tributary)。

dis·trib·ute [dis'tribju(ː)t; dɪs`trɪbjut] ***vt*.** **1.** 分配,分给,分发,配给;〔古〕实施,颁布。**2.** 区分,把…分类。**3.** 分布,散布 (*over*)。**4.**【逻】周延;【电】配(电);【印】调(墨);拆(版)。~ *circulars* 散发传单。*a distributing centre* 集散地。*a distributing station* 配电站;图书配给站。~ *foodstuffs among the underfed people* 在饥民当中分发食物。~ *money to the poor* 向贫民发放救济金。~ *seed over a field* 在田间播种。*The guest ~d themselves in the garden*. 客人在花园里四处走动。*The process is ~d into three stages*. 工作进程分为三个阶段。*These plants were ~d into 22 classes*. 这些植物分为 22 类。~ *justice to the criminals* 对犯罪分子施行法律。— ***vi*.** 分配;散布;【数】分布。**dis·trib·u·tee** [disˌtribju'tiː; dɪsˏtrɪbju`ti]【法】分配遗产受益人。**-r *n*.** = distributor.

dis·tri·bu·tion [ˌdistri'bjuːʃən; ˏdɪstrə`bjuʃən] ***n*.** **1.** 分配,分发,配给;分配装置[系统];配给品;配给量;【经】配给方法,配给过程;分红;【法】(无遗嘱死亡者的)财产分配。**2.** 分布,配置,分布状态;【生】(生物的)分布范围;【无】频率分布。**3.** 分类,整理,区分。**4.**【电】配电;【机】配汽;【印】拆版;【逻】周延(性)。**5.** 销售。*the ~ of wealth* 财富的分配。*the accurate ~ of zoological specimens* 动物品种的精确分类。*live on charitable ~s alone* 完全依靠配给救济品生活。*the ~ of coniferous forests* 针叶林的分布范围。*the ~ of troops* 部队配置。*The ~ of our school paper is now 3000*. 我们校刊的发行量现在是 3000 份。*We have a good harvest but our ~ is bad*. 我们丰收了,但是产品卖不出去。~ **cost**【商】推销费用。~ **curve** [**function**]【统】分布曲线[函数]。

dis·trib·u·tism [dis'tribjutizəm; dɪs`trɪbjutɪzəm] ***n*.** 分产主义〔主张把私人财产,尤其是土地,重新进行分配〕。**-tist *n*.** 分产主义者。

dis·trib·u·tive [dis'tribjutiv; dɪs`trɪbjətɪv] **I *a*.** **1.** (关于)分配的;分布的。**2.**【逻】周延的;【语法】个体的,个别的。*a ~ agency for foodstuffs* 食品分配处。**II *n*.**【语法】个体词〔each, either, every 等〕。~ **education**〔常作 D- Education〕分配性教育〔学校与企业合办,把课堂教学与职业训练结合起来〕。~ **law**【数】分配律,布律。**-ly *ad*.**

dis·trib·u·tor [dis'tribjutə; dɪs`trɪbjətɚ] ***n*.** **1.** 分发者,分配者,配给者;散布者,分布者。**2.**【印】调墨胶辊;自动拆版机;拆版工人;【电】配电盘。**3.** 销售者;批发商。*oil ~*【机】分油器。~ **bar**【印】自动拆版装置。

dis·trict ['distrikt; `dɪstrɪkt] **I *n*.** **1.** 区;管区;行政区,市区。**2.** 地区,区域。**3.**〔美〕(各州众议员)选举区;〔英〕教区,分区。*a military ~* 军区。*a police ~* 警察管区。*a shopping ~* 商业学区。*a Congressional ~* 美国各州众议员选区。*an agricultural* [*wooded*] ~ 农业[山林]区。***the D- of Columbia*** 哥伦比亚特区〔美国首都华盛顿所在的行政区〕。**II *vt*.** 把…分区。*the new ~ing of the city* 城市重新分区。~ **attorney**〔美〕地方检察官。~ **council**〔英〕地方议会。~ **court**〔美〕地方法院。~ **heating** 分区供暖系统〔可供应同一地区内暖气或热水需求的中央系统〕。~ **man** 负责采访某一地区新闻的记者。~ **office**〔美〕县公署;地方分店。**D- Railway** (伦敦)郊区铁路。~ **school**〔美〕村立小学校。~ **tug** 港用拖船。~ **visitor** 教区牧师助理。

dis·trust [dis'trʌst; dɪs`trʌst] **I *n*.** 疑惑,不相信;不信任,猜疑。*have a ~ of sb*. 不信任某人。*His policy earned him the ~ of the Athenians*. 他的政策受到了雅典人的猜疑。**II *vt*.** 不信任,怀疑。~ *one's friend* 对朋友起疑心。**-ful *a*.** 不信任的,疑心重的 (*of*); 可疑的 (*A ~ful dog is the best watchdog*. 疑心重的狗是最好的看门狗)。**-ful·ly *ad*.**

dis·turb [dis'təːb; dɪ`stɝb] ***vt*.** **1.** 搅乱,扰乱;打扰。**2.** 使不安,使烦恼。**3.** 妨害,妨碍;侵犯(权利)。*Please don't ~ me while I am sleeping*. 我睡觉时请不要打扰我。~ *the peace*【法】扰乱治安。~ *the smooth surface of a lake* 搅乱平静的湖面。— ***vi*.** 妨碍睡眠[休息

等〕。**Do not** ～. 请勿打扰,现在恕不会客〔挂在会议室、旅馆房间门上用的字牌〕。～**ing force**【天】摄动力,扰力。**-er** *n*. 打扰者。

dis·turb·ance [dis'tə:bəns; dɪs\`tɚbəns] *n*. **1.** 动乱,变乱,骚乱。**2.** 烦闷;(心情)纷乱;(身心)失调。**3.**【无】干扰;【气】扰动;【地】(地壳的)局部运动。**4.**【法】侵犯(权利),妨害(治安)。*cause* [*make*, *raise*] *a* ～ 作乱,闹事,闹乱子。*quiet* [*suppress*] *a* ～ 平息骚动。*magnetic* ～ 磁场干扰。*political* ～ 政治骚乱。～ ***of apprehension*** [***attention***, ***intelligence***]【医】领悟[注意,心理]障碍。

dis·turbed [dis'tə:bd; dɪs\`tɚbd] *a*. **1.** 被打扰的;【天】受摄的。**2.** 不安的;心理失常的。**3.** 为心理失常者服务的。*the* ～ *children* 心理不正常的儿童。～ **body**【天】受摄体。～ **day** (地磁)受扰日。

dis·tyle ['distail; \`dɪstaɪl] **I** *n*.【建】双柱式门廊。**II** *a*.【建】双柱式的。

di·sul·fate, di·sul·phate [dai'sʌlfeit; daɪ\`sʌlfet] *n*.【化】**1.** 焦硫酸盐;二硫酸盐。**2.** 硫酸氢盐,酸式硫酸盐。

di·sul·fide, di·sul·phide [dai'sʌlfaid; daɪ\`sʌlfaɪd] *n*.【化】二硫化物。～ *oil* 含二硫化物的油。

dis·un·ion ['dis'ju:njən; dɪs\`junjən] *n*. **1.** 分离,分裂。**2.** 不一致,不统一;不和,倾轧。*the* ～ *of the body and soul* 肉体与灵魂的分离。*internal* ～ 内部倾轧。**-ism** *n*.【美史】(美国南北战争时主张南北分离的)分离主义。**-ist** *n*.【美史】分离主义者。

dis·u·nite ['disju:'nait; \`dɪsju\`naɪt] *vt*. **1.** 使分离。**2.** 使分裂;使起纷争;(使)不和。*The issue* ～*d the party members*. 该问题在党员中造成分裂。—*vi*. **1.** 分离。**2.** 分裂,不和。

dis·use ['dis'ju:s; \`dɪs\`jus] **I** *n*. 不用,废止,废弃。*The machine has become rusty from* ～. 机器已经因不用而生锈。*Traditional customs are coming* [*falling*] *into* ～. 老习惯正在破除。**II** ['dis'ju:z; \`dɪs\`juz] *vt*. 不用,废止;废弃。*a* ～*d car* 废车。*a* ～*d meaning of the word* 一个词的废义。**-d** *a*. 已不用的,已废止的,已废弃的。

dis·val·ue [dis'vælju:; dɪs\`vælju] **I** *vt*. **1.** 〔古〕轻视。**2.** 使减价。**II** *n*. **1.** 轻视。**2.** 贬值。

di·syl·lab·ic ['disi'læbik; \`dɪsə\`læbɪk] *a*. 双音节的。

di·syl·la·ble [di'siləbl; dɪ\`sɪləbl] *n*. 〔英〕= dissyllable.

ditch [ditʃ; dɪtʃ] **I** *n*. **1.** 水沟,渠。**2.** 壕沟。*fall into a* ～ 跌进沟里。***be driven to the last*** ～ 陷入绝境。***die in the last*** ～ 奋战而死。***the Big D-***〔美俚〕**1.** 大西洋。**2.** 巴拿马运河。***the D-***〔美空军俚〕英吉利海峡;北海。***the last*** ～ ***struggle*** 垂死挣扎,负隅顽抗。**II** *vt*. **1.** 在…开沟,在…挖壕沟;用壕沟围绕。**2.** 〔美〕使(火车)出轨,使(汽车)冲落沟内。**3.** 〔美俚〕摆脱,抛弃,甩开,避开(同伴等);逃避(责任)等。**4.** 使(飞机)迫降海上。*a pasture hedged and* ～*ed* 用树篱和沟渠围起来的牧场。*be* [*get*] ～*ed*〔美俚〕(飞机)迫降海上。*I* ～*ed that old hat of yours*. 我把你那顶旧帽子扔掉了。*He* ～*ed the cops by turning off his lights and driving down an alley*. 他关掉车灯,朝巷子深处驶去,想用这种办法逃开警察。— *vi*. **1.** 开沟,挖沟;修沟。**2.** 〔美〕(火车)出轨,(汽车)冲落沟内;(陆上飞机)迫降海上。～*ing device* (无人驾驶飞机的)迫降装置。*hedging and* ～*ing* 沟道和树篱的整修。～**-digger** **1.** 挖沟者。**2.** 做小工的人。**3.** 开沟机。～ **rider**〔美俚〕照管水渠的工人。～ **riding**〔美俚〕照管水渠的工作。～**water** *n*. 沟中死水 (*as dull as* ～*water* 完全停滞的;单调乏味的)。

ditch·er ['ditʃə; \`dɪtʃɚ] *n*. **1.** 挖沟者,掘壕者。**2.** 开沟机。**3.** 被迫使飞机降落水上的人。

di·the·ism ['daiθi(:)izəm; \`daɪθiɪzəm] *n*.【宗】善恶二神说,二神教。

dith·er ['diðə; \`dɪðɚ] **I** *n*. **1.** 发抖,颤抖。**2.** 〔口〕(因兴奋、恐怖等而引起的)慌乱。**3.**【物】高频振[脉]动。*have the* ～*s* 发抖。*throw sb. into a* ～ 使某人心慌意乱。*all of a* ～ 浑身发着抖。**II** *vi*. **1.** 〔方〕(因兴奋、恐怖等而)发抖,颤抖。**2.** 优柔寡断;犹豫不决,三心二意。*He sat there* ～*ing over his decision*. 他坐在那里拿不定主意。～ **motor** 高频振动用电机。～ **pump** 高频振动泵。

dithi(o)- *comb.f.*【化】联硫基;二硫代: *dithio*nate.

di·thi·o·nate [dai'θaiəneit; daɪ\`θaɪənet] *n*.【化】二硫磺酸盐,连二硫酸盐。

dith·y·ramb ['diθiræm*b*; \`dɪθɪræm*b*] *n*. **1.** 〔古希腊〕酒神赞歌。**2.** 〔书〕狂热的诗歌[演说、文章等]。

dit·ta·ny ['ditəni; \`dɪtənɪ] *n*.【植】**1.** 白鲜属植物。**2.** 苦牛至。

dit·to ['ditəu; \`dɪto] **I** *n*. (*pl*. ～*s*) **1.** 同上,同前〔略号作 d° 或 do 或"或",仅用于单据或表格中〕。**2.** 〔口〕同样的事物;一模一样的人;复制品。**3.** 〔*pl*.〕(衣裤)用同一种料子做的一套服装。*He is the* ～ *of his mother*. 他的长相和他的母亲一模一样。*a suit of* ～*s* = *a* ～ *suit* 用同一料子做的一套服装。***be in*** ～***s*** 穿着(衣裤)用同一种料子做的一套服装;对…表示完全同意。***say*** ～ ***to*** 对…表示同意。**II** *ad*. 如前所述,和以上所说一样地;同样地。*act* ～ 采取同样的行动,同样办理。**III** *vt*. **1.** 重复(别人的言论、行动等)。**2.** (在复印机上)复印。～**head** 应声虫,追随者。～ **machine** 复印机。～ **mark** "同上"符号。

dit·to·graph ['ditəgrɑ:f; \`dɪtəgræf] *n*. (书写、印刷中由疏忽而造成)重复的词,重复的字母。**-y** [di'tɔgrəfi; dɪ\`tɔgrəfɪ] *n*. (词或字母的)印重,写重,重复。

dit·ty ['diti; \`dɪtɪ] *n*. 小曲,小调。*a plaintive* ～ 一首伤感的小曲。～ **bag** (水手等的)针线包,针线盒。～ **box** **1.** 摄影道具箱。**2.** = ～ bag.

di·u·re·sis [ˌdaijuə'ri:sis; ˏdaɪju\`risɪs] *n*. (*pl*. *-re·ses* [-'ri:si:z; -\`risiz])【医】利尿;多尿。

di·u·ret·ic [ˌdaijuə'retik; ˏdaɪju\`retɪk] **I** *a*.【医】利尿的。**II** *n*. 利尿剂。

di·ur·nal [dai'ə:nl; daɪ\`ɝnl] **I** *a*. **1.** 每日的;【天】周日的。**2.** 昼间的,白天的 (*opp*. nocturnal)。**3.**【植】(花、叶等)昼开夜闭的;【动】(鸟等)昼出夜息的 (*opp*. nocturnal);(昆虫)只活一天的;【医】(病等)夜轻日重的。*the* ～ *round of the mailman* 邮递员每日的巡行。～ *task* 每日任务,日常工作。～ *noises* 白昼的喧闹。～ *flowers* 白天开的花。**II** *n*. **1.**【宗】每日祈祷书。**2.** 〔古〕日报,日记。**-ly** *ad*. **1.** 每日,天天。**2.** 只在白天。～ **cycle** 昼夜循环。～ **motion** 周日运动;(因地球自转而产生的星球每日似乎由东向西的)视移动。～ **tides** 潮汐。

div. = divide; dividend; divine; division; divisor; divorced.

di·va ['di:və; \`divə] *n*. 〔It.〕 (*pl*. ～*s*, ***di·ve*** ['di:vei; \`dive]) 歌剧女主角;主要女歌手;著名女歌唱家。

di·va·gate ['daivəgeit; \`daɪvəˏget] *vi*. **1.** 〔书〕流浪,漂泊。**2.** (说话)离题。**-ga·tion** [ˌdaivə'geiʃən; ˏdaɪvə\`geʃən] *n*.

di·va·lent ['daiˌveilənt; \`daɪˏvelənt] *a*. **1.**【化】(化合价)二价的。**2.**【生】(染色体)二价的。

di·van [di'væn; dɪ\`væn] *n*. **1.** (土耳其等国的)国务会议;(政府的)局。**2.** (土耳其等国的)国务会议室;接见厅;法庭;(海关等的)大楼。**3.** (一般的)会议;委员会。**4.** ['daivæn; \`daɪvæn] (靠墙放的)长沙发椅;沙发床。**5.** 烟茶室,咖啡室,…烟店。**6.** 波斯语诗集,阿拉伯语诗集。

di·var·i·cate [dai'værikeit; daɪ\`værɪket] **I** *vi*. **1.** (道路等)分为两叉。**2.**【动、植】(树枝、翅膀、羽毛等)分叉。**II** *a*.【生】(树枝、翅;羽等)分歧的,分叉宽阔的,展开的,**-ca·tion** [daiˌværi'keiʃən; daɪˏværə\`keʃən] *n*. 分叉,分歧;交叉点,意义暧昧;意见分歧。

D

dive [daiv; daɪv] **I** ***n*.** **1.** 潜水;【泳】跳水;【空】俯冲,(潜艇)下潜,急降。**2.** 猛冲,突然隐去;【拳】假装被击倒。**3.** 专心研究,探究。**4.** (气温、股票价格等的)暴落。**5.** 〔英〕(常指地下室中的)小饭馆;〔美口〕低级酒馆;赌窟;匪窝。*a fancy* ~【泳】花式跳水。*a nose* ~【空】俯冲。*Rail stocks took a* ~ *on the stock market*. 铁路股票在股票市场上暴跌。***make a* ~ *for sth*.** 冲过去拿(某物)。***take a* ~ *into*** (*the subject*) 埋头(该问题)中。**II** ***vi*.** (~***d***, **dove** [dəuv; dov]; ~***d***; ***div·ing***) **1.** (头朝下)跳入水中。**2.** (潜艇等)下潜,(飞机等)俯冲。**3.** (飞机)俯冲,(气温、物价等)突然下降。**4.** 突然潜匿;(手等)插入口袋;〔俚〕扒窃。**5.** 埋头研究。**6.** 〔美俚〕【拳】假装被打倒。~ *for pearls* 潜水取珍珠。~ *into a purse* 手伸进钱袋。~ *into the bushes* 潜入树丛中。~ *into* (*one's secret*) 探察(某人秘密)。—***vt*.** 使(潜艇等)下潜。~ *the submarine* 使潜艇下潜。~**-bomb** ***vt*.**, ***vi*.** 俯冲轰炸。~ **bomber** 俯冲轰炸机。~**keeper** 低级酒馆、赌窟等的老板。

D

div·er [ˈdaivə; ˋdaɪvɚ] ***n*.** **1.** 跳水者;潜水员;潜水采珠者。**2.** 潜水鸟;〔俚〕潜水艇;俯冲轰炸机。*a pearl* ~ 采珠人。~**'s connection** 潜水员的救难通知管。

di·verge [daiˈvəːdʒ; daɪˋvɝdʒ] ***vi*.** **1.** (道路等)分岔,分开;(意见等)分歧。**2.** 【生】趋异 (*opp*. converge);【数】(级数等)无极限,无限大。**3.** (点等)分出。**4.** 离(题),逸出(正轨) (*from*)。—***vt*.** 使岔开,使转向。**di·ver·ger** [daiˈvəːdʒə; daɪˋvɝdʒə] ***n*.** 〔美口〕富有幻想力的人 (*cf*. converger)。

di·ver·gence [daiˈvəːdʒəns; daɪˋvɝdʒəns] ***n*.** **1.** 分歧,分岔,分出 (*opp*. convergence)。**2.** 【生】趋异 (*opp*. convergence);【心】离散;【数、物】散度,开度;发散。**3.** 离题。*a* ~ *in opinion* 意见分歧。

di·ver·gent [daiˈvəːdʒənt; daɪˋvɝdʒənt] ***a*.** **1.** 叉开的,分歧的;背道而驰的。**2.** 【物、数】发散的;【生】趋异的。~ **adaptation** 【生】趋异适应。~ **pencil** 【物】发散光线锥。~ **series** 【数】发散级数。~ **squint** 【医】外斜视。

di·verg·ing [daiˈvəːdʒiŋ; daɪˋvɝdʒɪŋ] ***a*.** = divergent. ~ *star cluster*【天】散开星团。~ **lens** 【物】发散透镜。

di·vers [ˈdaivə(ː)z; ˋdaɪvɚz] **I** ***a*.** **1.** 若干,好几个。**2.** 〔古〕= diverse. ~ *articles* 若干物品。**II** ***pro*.** 若干人。*He chose* ~ *of them, who were asked to accompany him*. 他选择他们当中的几个人,要他们和他作伴。**III** ***n*.** 〔美俚〕指头。

di·verse [daiˈvəːs; daɪˋvɝs] ***a*.** **1.** 不同的,别的。**2.** 形形色色的,多种多样的。*He is of a* ~ *nature from the rest of his family*. 他和他家里别的人气质不同。~ *interpretations of these ideas* 对这些思想所作的多种多样的解释。**-ly** ***ad*.**

di·ver·si·fi·ca·tion [daiˌvəːsifiˈkeiʃən; daɪˏvɝsəfəˋkeʃən] ***n*.** **1.** 形形色色,多样化。**2.** 【商】(投资的)分散经营〔以避免单打一的经营有失败的风险〕。

di·ver·si·fied [daiˈvəːsifaid; daɪˋvɝsəfaɪd] ***a*.** **1.** 形形色色的,多样化的。**2.** (投资等)分散经营的。~ *investments* 分散经营的投资。~ *activity* 多种多样的活动。~ *economy* 多样化经济。~ *scenery* 绚丽多姿的风景。

di·ver·si·form [daiˈvəːsifɔːm; daɪˋvɝsəfɔrm] ***a*.** 各式各样的。

di·ver·si·fy [daiˈvəːsifai; daɪˋvɝsəˏfaɪ] ***vt*.** (**-*fied***; **-*fy·ing***) **1.** 使多样化,使不同。**2.** 把(资金)分散投资。~ *a course of study* 使课程多样化。~ *investments* 把资金分散投放。

di·ver·sion [daiˈvəːʃən; daɪˋvɝʃən] ***n*.** **1.** 转换,转移,转向;(河流、航线等的)改道;(资金等的)挪用;〔英〕(因修路等车辆)绕行,绕路。**2.** 消遣,娱乐。**3.** 【军】箝制,佯攻。*a flood* ~ *area* 分洪区。*a* ~ *of industry into the war effort* 工业转入作战生产。*Movies can be a worthwhile* ~. 电影可以成为一种有益的娱乐。

di·ver·sion·ar·y [daiˈvəːʃənəri; daɪˋvɝʃənˏɛrɪ] ***a*.** **1.** 转移注意力的。**2.** 【军】牵制性的,声东击西的。~ **tactics** 牵制战术,声东击西战术。

di·ver·sion·ist [daiˈvəːʃənist; daɪˋvɝʃənɪst] ***n*.** **1.** (政治上的)异端分子。**2.** 进行牵制活动者;在敌后活动者。

di·ver·si·ty [daiˈvəːsiti; daɪˋvɝsətɪ] ***n*.** **1.** 不同,异样,差异。**2.** 繁多,多种,多样,驳杂,参差。*a* ~ *of methods* 方法的多种多样。*a* ~ *of interests* 多种多样的趣味。~ *factor*【电】照强差异因素。

di·vert [daiˈvəːt; dəˋvɝt] ***vt*.** **1.** 使转向,使转换,使转移 (*from*; *to*);挪用(资金等);使(工作等)改行。**2.** 使消遣,使解闷,使娱乐。**3.** 【军】箝制,佯攻。~ *the course of a stream* = ~ *a stream from its course* 改变河道流向。~ *one's attention* 转移注意力。~ *children by telling stories* 讲故事逗乐孩子。*They were greatly* ~*ed by the play*. 这场戏使他们很开心。*She was trained as a doctor but* ~*ed to diplomacy*. 她是学医的,但是改行做外交工作了。

di·ver·tic·u·li·tis [ˌdaivəˈtikjuˈlaitəs; ˏdaɪvətɪkjuˋlaɪtəs] ***n*.** 【医】憩室炎。

di·ver·tic·u·lo·sis [daiˌvətikjuˈləusis; daɪvəˈtɪkjuˈlosɪs] ***n*.** 【医】憩室形成。

di·ver·tic·u·lum [ˌdaivəˈtikjuləm; ˏdaɪvəˋtɪkjuləm] ***n*.** (*pl*. **-*u·la*** [-lə; -lə])【解】憩室;支囊。

di·ver·ti·men·to [diˌveətiˈmentəu; dɪˏvɛrtɪˋmɛnto] ***n*.** (*pl*. **-*men·ti*** [-tiː; -ti], ~***s***)【乐】套曲;嬉游曲,赋格曲中的间插段;由多个乐章组成的旋律优美的轻音乐曲。

di·vert·ing [daiˈvəːtiŋ; daɪˋvɝtɪŋ] ***a*.** 有趣的,消愁解闷的。*a* ~ *caricature* 有趣的漫画。

di·ver·tisse·ment [daiˈvəːtismənt, F. divertisˈmɑ̃ŋ; daɪˈvɝtɪsmənt, dɪvertɪsˋmɑ̃ŋ] ***n*.** **1.** 娱乐;余兴[舞蹈等]。**2.** 【乐】= divertimento.

Di·ves[1] [ˈdaivz; ˋdaɪvz] ***n*.** 戴夫斯〔姓氏〕。

Di·ves[2] [ˈdaiviːz; ˋdaɪviz] ***n*.** 豪富,财主〔源出《圣经》《路加福音》〕。

di·vest [daiˈvest; daɪˋvɛst] ***vt*.** **1.** 剥去…的衣服。**2.** 剥夺。**3.** 摆脱。*The wind* ~*ed the trees of their leaves*. 风吹光了树的叶子。*be* ~*ed of one's coat* 被剥掉上衣。~ *sb. of his office* 撤销某人的职务。*He attempted to* ~ *himself of all responsibilities for the decision*. 他力图摆脱掉作出该项决定的一切责任。**-ment** ***n*.**

di·vest·i·ture [daiˈvestitʃə; daɪˋvɛstətʃɚ] ***n*.** **1.** 剥夺。**2.** 脱衣。

div·i [ˈdivi; ˋdɪvɪ] ***n*.** 〔英俚〕(消费合作社等的)红利。

di·vide [diˈvaid; dɪˋvaɪd] **I** ***vt*.** **1.** 分,区分,划分 (*into*)。**2.** 分配,分派,分给;分享,分担,分摊 (*with*; *between*; *among*)。**3.** 分开,隔开,隔离 (*from*)。**4.** 分裂,使对立;使(意见)分歧,离间(朋友);【化】分离。**5.** 【数】除;除尽;【机】在…上刻[分]度。~ *words between syllables* 给单词分音节。*Administratively, the country is* ~*d into counties*. 这个国家在行政区划分上分为许多郡。*The river* ~*s the city into two parts*. 那条河把市区分成两部分。*Opinions are* ~*d on that point*. 意见就在那一点上对立起来了。~ *ten dollars among five persons* 十块美元五个人分。~ *profits with the stock-holders* 和股东共分利润。*D- 6 by 3 and you get 2*. 给3除6得2。*9* ~*s 36*. 9能除尽36。~ *a sextant* 给六分仪分度。***be* ~*d against itself*** 发生内讧 (*If a house be* ~*d against itself, that house cannot stand*. 家不和,必自败)。—***vi*.** **1.** 分,分开。**2.** 分裂,(意见等)分歧。**3.** 【数】除,被除尽。**4.** (议会等)表决。~ *in one's mind* 内心徬徨,犹豫不决。*We all* ~ *equally*. 我们平等分配,各取一份。*The road* ~*s six miles from here*. 这条路在六英里之外有分岔。*He could add and subtract, but hadn't learned to* ~. 他会做加减法,但还没有学会除法。*Eight* ~*s by four*. 8能被4除尽。*Five will not* ~ *into nine*. 5除不尽9。*D-! D-!* (议会等中提出)表决! 表决! **II** ***n*.** **1.** 分,分配。**2.** 〔口〕分

裂。**3.** 分界;〔美〕分水岭。~ ***and rule*** 分而治之。***the Great D-*** **1.**〔美〕落矶山脉分水岭;主要分水岭。**2.** 大限;死;生死关头 (*cross the Great D-* 死)。

di·vid·ed [di'vaidid; də`vaɪdɪd] ***a*.** **1.** 被分割的;分离的;对立的,意见分歧的。**2.**【植】(叶)分裂的;全裂的。~ *circle*【机】刻度盘。~ *consonant*【语】分裂子音。~ *current*【物】分歧电流。~ *highway* (对行道分开的)分行公路。~ **payments** 分期付款。

div·i·dend ['dividend; dɪvə`dɛnd] ***n*.** **1.**【数】被除数 *opp*. divisor)。**2.** 红利,股息;利息;(破产时清算的)分配金。**3.** (一般的)份儿;报酬。*cum* [*ex*] ~〔英〕= ~ *on* [*off*]〔美〕有[无]股息。*stock* ~ 股息。*non-* ~ *payer* 无红股户。*Swimming is a fun, and gives you the* ~ *of better health*. 游泳既是娱乐,又有增进健康的好处。***declare a*** ~ 通告分红。~**-account** 股息账户。~**-cheque** 股息支票,股利券。~**-coupon** 股利券。~ **warrant** 股息单,领取股息通知单。

di·vid·er [di'vaidə; də`vaɪdə] ***n*.** **1.** 划分者;分割者;分裂者,离间者。**2.** 间隔物;分裂的原因。**3.** (割禾机等的)分切器;【数】除数;除法器;【电】分压器;【空】减速器。**4.**〔*pl*.〕划规,两脚规,分线规。*a pair of* ~*s* 一副两脚规。

di·vid·ing [di'vaidiŋ; də`vaɪdɪŋ] ***a*.** 起划分[区分、分割]作用的。*a* ~ *line* 分界线。~ **machine** [**engine**]【机】分度机,刻度机。~ **ridge** 分水岭。

div·i-div·i ['divi'divi; `dɪvɪ`dɪvɪ] ***n*.**【植】(南美热带产)鞣科芸实;鞣科芸实的豆荚〔含大量单宁酸,可供染色、鞣革用〕。

di·vid·u·al [di'vidjuəl; də`vɪdʒuəl] ***a*.**〔古〕**1.** 分开的;可分离的;可分割的。**2.** 各别的。**3.** 分配的,分享的。

Di·vi·na Com·me·dia [It. di'viːnaː kɔːm'meːdjaː; dɪ`vinɑ kɔm`medja]〔It.〕《神曲》〔意大利诗人但丁 (Dante, 1265—1321)的名著〕。

div·i·na·tion [ˌdivi'neiʃən; ˏdɪvə`neʃən] ***n*.** **1.** 占卜,卜卦。**2.** 先见;预言;预测。**3.** 直观的感知,本能的预知。*the* ~ *of the high priest* 大祭司的预言。

di·vine [di'vain; də`vaɪn] **I** ***a*.** **1.** 神的;神性的。**2.** 神授的,天赐的。**3.** 敬神的,奉为神的;神圣的。**4.** 神学的。**5.** 神妙的;绝世的,天才的,非凡的;〔俚〕好透了的。~ *song* 圣歌。~ *judgements* 神意。*a* ~ *call* 天命。*the* ~ *kingdom* 天国。*What* ~ *weather*! 多好的天气! ~ *beauty* 国色天香,绝代佳人。**II** ***n*.** **1.** 神学家,宗教学者。**2.** 圣职人员;牧师,教士,神父,祭司。**3.** 〔the D-〕神,上帝,造物主。**4.** 〔the ~〕(人性中)崇高的一面。*He hated the lust but admired the* ~ *in men*. 他憎恶人的肉欲,欣赏人性中神圣的一面。**III** ***vt*., *vi*.** **1.** 预测;占卜。**2.** 看穿,察觉;(凭直觉)推测,猜测。~ *sb.'s intention* 识破(看穿)某人企图。*He* ~*d from her look that something was in her mind*. 他从她的神色上看出她心上有事。***divining rod*** "魔杖"〔古代以迷信法探矿的一种木叉,据说寻得矿脉、水源等即自动弯曲云云〕。***the D- Being*** [***Father***] 神,上帝。***the D- Comedy*** = Divina Commedia. ***the*** ~ ***right of kings*** 帝王神权,王权神授说。~ **nature** 神性。~ **service** 礼拜式。**-r** ***n*.** 占卜者;预言者;推测者。**-ly** ***ad*.**

div·ing ['daiviŋ; `daɪvɪŋ] **I** ***a*.** **1.** 潜[跳]水的。**2.** 潜[跳]水用的。**II** ***n*.** 潜水;【泳】跳水。~ **bell** 潜水钟;〔美俚〕地下室酒馆。~ **board** 跳水板。~ **helmet** 潜水帽。~ **plane** (潜艇的)浮沉控制舵。~ **suit** [**dress**] 潜水服。

di·vin·i·ty [di'viniti; də`vɪnətɪ] ***n*.** **1.** 神性;神力,神威;神德。**2.** 〔the D-〕神,上帝;〔a ~〕(异教的)神;天使,神人。**3.** 神学;(大学的)神学院。**4.** 神奇,尽善尽美。*Doctor of D-* 神学博士〔略作 D. D.〕。*the* ~ *of Beethoven's music* 贝多芬乐曲的神奇力量。~ **calf** (作书籍封面用的)暗褐色小牛皮。~ **fudge** 奶油馅蛋糕。~ **school** 神学校。

di·vis·i·bil·i·ty [diˌvizi'biliti; dəˏvɪzə`bɪlətɪ] ***n*.** **1.** 可分割性,可分性。**2.**【数】可除尽,整约性,整除性。**3.**【物】(晶体的)解理性,可劈性。

di·vis·i·ble [di'vizəbl; də`vɪzəbl] ***a*.** **1.** 可分的,可分割的。**2.**【数】除得尽的 (*by*)。*12 is* ~ *by* 4. 12 可用 4 除尽。

di·vi·sion [di'viʒən; də`vɪʒən] ***n*.** **1.** 分,分开,分割;分划,区分。**2.** 分配;分派。**3.** 分裂,(意见)不一致,倾轧。**4.** 区域;〔英〕选区;部分,部门;(大学的)部;(政府机构等的)司,科。**5.** 间隔,隔墙,分界;标度。**6.**〔英〕(议会的)表决。**7.**【数】除法 (*opp*. multiplication)。**8.**【陆军】师;【海军】分舰队;海军航空兵分队。**9.**【园艺】分株;【生】门,类[科,属等]。**10.**【体】(按体重,年龄,技术等划分的)级,组。*the present* ~ *in our society* 当代社会的分裂。*take a* ~ 表决。~ *of business* 营业部。*cell* ~ 细胞分裂。*the sales* ~ *of the Ford Motor Go*. 福特汽车公司的销售部。*the D- of Humanities of the University of Chicago* 芝加哥大学人文科学部。~ *of officer*【美海军】分队长。~ *of function* 机能分工。~ *of labour*【经】分工。*the heavy weight* ~【拳】重量级。~ *of powers* (中央和地方或立法、司法、行政的)分权。~ **bell** 通知会场外议员即将表决的铃声。~ **sign** [**mark**]【数】除号。~ **wall** 界墙。

di·vi·sion·al [di'viʒənl; də`vɪʒənl] ***a*.** **1.** 分开的,分割的;分区的,分部的。**2.**【数】除法的;【陆军】师的;【海军】分(舰)队的。*a* ~ *commander* 师长。

Di·vi·sion·ism [di'viʒənizəm; də`vɪʒənɪzəm] ***n*.**【美术】点画派 (= Pointillism)。

di·vi·sive [di'vaisiv; də`vaɪsɪv] ***a*.** 引起分裂的,造成不和的。**-ly** ***ad*.** **-ness** ***n*.**

di·vi·sor [di'vaizə; də`vaɪzə] ***n*.**【数】除数,约数 (*opp*. dividend)。*common* ~【数】公约数。~ *of zero*【数】零因子。

di·vorce [di'vɔːs; də`vɔrs] **I** ***n*.** **1.**【法】离婚。**2.** 分离,脱离,(关系的)断绝 (*between*; *of*; *from*)。*the* ~ *rate* 离婚率。*get* [*obtain*] a ~ 获准离婚。~ *by consent* 协议离婚。*a* ~ *between thought and action* 思想与行动脱节。**II** ***vt*.** **1.** 与…离婚,使…离婚。**2.** 脱离,与…断绝关系;使分离,使脱节。*The judge* ~*d the couple*. 法官判决这对夫妇离婚。*She* ~*d her husband*. 她和丈夫离了婚。*He was* ~*d by his wife*. 他的妻子和他离婚了。*science* ~*d from religion* 和宗教脱离了关系的科学。~ *church from state* 使政教分离。*He is* ~*d from society*. 他脱离了社会。*Life and art cannot be* ~*d*. 生活与艺术不能脱离。~ *oneself* [*be* ~*d*] *from one's spouse* 和自己的配偶离婚。~ **court** 离婚裁决法庭。~ **mill** 〔口〕= ~ court. **-ment** ***n*.**

di·vor·cé [di'vɔːsei; dəˏvor`se] ***n*.**〔F.〕离了婚的男子。

di·vor·cée [di'vɔːsei; dəˏvor`se] ***n*.**〔F.〕离了婚的女子。

di·vor·cee [di'vɔːsiː; dəˏvor`si] ***n*.** 被离婚者;离了婚的人。

div·ot ['divət; `dɪvət] ***n*.** **1.**〔Scot.〕(一块)草皮。**2.**【高尔夫】(击球时球棒削起的)一块草根土。~ *digger*〔美〕= golfer.

di·vul·gate [di'vʌlgeit; də`vʌlget] ***vt*.**〔古〕公布,宣布。**-r** ***n*.** 公布者。**-ga·tion** ['divʌl'geiʃən; ˏdɪvəl`geʃən] ***n*.**

di·vulge [dai'vʌldʒ; də`vʌldʒ] ***vt*.** **1.** 泄漏(秘密等);揭发,暴露(隐私等)。**2.**〔古〕公布,宣布。~ *the source of one's information* 泄露情报来源。**-nce, -ment** ***n*.**

di·vulse [dai'vʌls; də`vʌls] ***vt*.**【医】撕开,扯裂。**-vul·sion** [-'vʌlʃən; -`vʌlʃən] ***n*.**【医】扯裂(术)。

div·vy ['divi; `dɪvɪ] **I** ***n*.**〔美俚〕(分得的)份儿。**II** ***vi*.** (*-vied*; *-vy·ing*) 拿一份,分享。—***vt*.** 分配,分摊 (*up*)。*They divvied up the profits among themselves*. 他们一伙瓜分利润。

D

di·wan [di'wɑːn; dɪ`wɑn] ***n.*** = dewan.
Dix·i·can ['diksikən; `dɪksɪkən] ***n.*** 美国南部各州的共和党人。
Dix·ie[1] ['diksi; `dɪksɪ] ***n.*** 迪克西〔女子名〕。
Dix·ie[2] ['diksi; `dɪksɪ] ***n.*** **1.** 〔美〕美国南部各州的别名;【美史】(美国南北战争期间参加南部同盟的)南部同盟诸州。**2.**【美史】南部同盟军军歌。~**crats** 〔*pl.*〕〔美〕南部各州的民主党党员。~ **Land** = ~ 1. ~**land** 〔美〕(源出美国新奥尔良地方的)半即兴式爵士音乐。
dix·ie ['diksi; `dɪksɪ] ***n.*** 〔英陆军俚〕(行军、露营等用的)大铁锅。~ **cup** (盛冰淇淋或其他饮料的)纸杯。
dix·it ['diksit; `dɪksɪt] ***n.*** 武断的讲话;独断的主张。
Dix·on [`diksn; `dɪksn] ***n.*** 狄克逊〔姓氏〕。
dix·y ['diksi; `dɪksɪ] ***n.*** = dixie.
D.I.Y. 〔英俚〕= do it yourself 自己动手。
diz·en ['daizn; `daɪzn] ***vt.*** 〔古〕= bedizen.
diz·zy ['dizi; `dɪzɪ] **I** ***a.*** (***-zi·er; -zi·est***) **1.** 头晕眼花的。**2.** (高度、速度等)使人眼花缭乱的。**3.** 〔美俚〕被弄糊涂的;昏头昏脑的,愚蠢的。*a* ~ *speed* [*height*] 使人头晕目眩的速度[高空]。*get* [*feel*] ~ 感到头晕。*The wet heat made him* ~. 蒸人的暑热使他头晕目眩。*He was* ~ *with shame*. 他羞愧得变糊涂了。*that* ~ *blonde* 那个愚蠢的金发女人。**II** ***vt.*** (***-zied; -zy·ing***) **1.** 使头晕眼花,使发昏。**2.** 使变糊涂。*prospects so brilliant as to* ~ *the mind* 如此美好的前途使头脑变得发晕了。**diz·zi·ly** ***ad.*** **diz·zi·ness** ***n.***
DJ = **1.** disc jockey 〔美俚〕无线电唱片音乐节目广播员。**2.** Dow Jones & Co. 〔美〕道·琼斯公司。
D.J. = **1.** District Judge 〔美〕地方初审法院法官。**2.** *Doctor Juris* (= Doctor of Law) 法学博士。
Dja·kar·ta [dʒə'kɑːtə; dʒə`kartə] ***n.*** 雅加达〔印度尼西亚首都〕。**-n** [-tən; -tən] ***n.*** 雅加达人。
djeb·el ['dʒebəl; `dʒɛbəl] ***n.*** 山,高山〔阿拉伯语裹常用于地名中〕(= jebel)。
djel·la·ba, djel·la·bah [dʒi'lɑːbə; dʒɪ`lɑbə] ***n.*** 结拉巴长袍〔伊斯兰教国家男女均穿着的宽敞长袍〕。
DJI = Dow-Jones Index 〔美〕道·琼斯指数〔以选取的若干工业、铁路、公用事业股票的每日平均价格为依据,据此计算出的证券的相对价格指数〕。
Dji·bou·ti [dʒi'buːti; dʒɪ`butɪ] ***n.*** **1.** 吉布提〔非洲〕。**2.** 吉布提〔吉布提首都〕。
dk. = deka; deck; dock.
dkg. = decagram(me)(s).
dkl. = decalitre.
dkm. = decametre.
D.L., DL = Deputy Lieutenant 〔英〕副郡长。
dl. = decilitre(s). **D/L** = 〔美〕 day letter; demand loan 活期贷款。
DL_{50} = 50% Lethal dose 致死中量,半致死量。
dld. = 〔美〕 delivered.
D.Lit(t)., D Lit(t) = Doctor of Literature 文学博士。
D.L.O. = Dead-Letter Office (无法投递的)死信招领处。
D.M. = Deputy Master (学院的)副院长。
D.M., DM = **1.** Doctor of Medicine 医学博士。**2.** Doctor of Mathematics 数学博士。**3.** 〔DM〕 deutsche mark 德国马克。
dm. = decimetre(s); delta metal; dram.
d/m = disintegrations per minute 衰变/分。
D.M.D. = Doctor of Dental Medicine.
D.M.E. = 【空】 distance measuring equipment 测距装置。
D.M.I. = Director of Military Intelligence. 〔英〕(帝国总参谋部)军事情报局局长。
dml. = demolition.
dmm. = decimillimetre(s).
D.M.S. = Doctor of Medical Science(s) 医学博士。
D.Mus., D Mus = Doctor of Music 音乐博士。
DMZ = demilitarized zone 非常军区。
D.N. = Daily News 〔美〕《每日新闻》。
d-n. = damn 〔委婉语〕。
DNA = **1.** deoxyribonucleic acid 【生化】去[脱]氧核糖核酸。**2.** deoxypentose-nucleic acid 去[脱]氧戊糖核酸。~ **fingerprint** DNA 指纹(印记);基因印记(检验法)〔通过检验血迹、精液等的细胞基因以判明身份〕。~ **profile** 【生化】DNA 基因图谱(鉴定)。~ **typing** DNA 定型。
D.N.ase [ˌdiːˌen'eis; ˏdiˏen`es] ***n.*** 脱氧核糖核酸酶 (= deoxyribonuclease)。
D.N.B. = 〔英〕 Dictionary of National Biography《英国人名词典》。
DNC = direct numerical control 【计】直接数字控制。
DNF = did not finish 未完成。
Dnie·per ['dniːpə; `dnipɚ] ***n.*** 第聂伯河〔欧洲〕。
D Notice 〔英〕 D 号通告,国防保密通告〔政府的一项备忘录,要求报纸不要刊登某些涉密消息,以确保国防安全〕。
do[1] [强 duː; 弱 du, də; du, dʊ, də] **I** ***vt.*** (***did*** [did; dɪd]; ***done*** [dʌn; dʌn]; 陈述语气第三人称单数现在式 ***does*** [强 dʌz, 弱 dəz; dʌz, dəz]) **1.** 行,为,作,做,办,干;尽(义务等),竭(力),担任,从事。~ *one's work* 干工作。~ *odd jobs* 干杂活,打零工。~ *business* 做买卖。~ *washing* 洗东西。*Who has done it?* 这是谁干的? ~ *the host* 做主人,当东。~ *one's duty* 尽义务。*crimes done deliberately* 蓄意犯罪。~ *a good deed* 行善,做好事。~ *penance* 忏悔。~ *one's best* [*utmost*] = ~ *the best one can* 竭尽所能。~ *one's worst* 捣乱。*What can I* ~ *for you?* 有什么事吗? 我能帮你干什么吗? (店员招呼顾客)要买什么吗? *I have much to* ~ *to pay my monthly bills*. 我应付每月的开支不是容易的。**2.** 完成,做完。*I have done reading*. 我已经看完书了。*You have done it very well*. 你做得很好。*Now you've done it*. 〔俚〕这可糟了! 可被你搞坏了! *But it was done now, and it could not be helped*. 生米已成熟饭,没有办法了。**3.** 给与;带来,产生;加以,使蒙受。*Too much exercise will* ~ *you harm*. 运动过度可能有害。*Such a book* ~*es credit to the writer*. 这样的书给作者带来声誉。*Will you* ~ *me a favor?* 能帮个忙吗? *It doesn't* ~ *any good*. 这不会有什么好处。~ *homage to* 对…表敬意。~ *sb. justice* 为某人说公平话;不亏待某人。**4.** 处理;修理;收拾(房间等);洗;整(容);预备(功课);解答(问题)。~ *the dishes* 洗碗碟。~ *one's face* 整容,化妆。~ *the flowers* 把花摆设好。~ *one's hair* 梳头发,做头发。~ *the room* [*kitchen*] 收拾房间[厨房]。~ *one's homework* 做作业,做功课。~ *English* 学英语,做英语作业。**5.** 翻译;改写;创作;抄,誊写。~ *a Latin passage into Chinese* 把一段拉丁文译成中文。~ *a poem into prose* 把诗改写成散文。*She* ~*es oil portraits*. 她创作油画肖像。*I have to* ~ *ten copies* 我得抄十份。**6.** 访问,游览,参观,逛。*They did London in five days*. 他们花五天时间游览伦敦。~ *the sights* 游览名胜。**7.** 适合,对…合宜,对…够用。*That would* ~ *me very well*. 那对我很适合,那好极啦。*Ten dollars will* ~ *me*. 十美元就够我用了。*Will this chair* ~ *you?* 这椅子行吗? **8.** 走过,跑过,跋涉。*He did 20 miles a day on foot*. 他一天走了二十英里。**9.** 扮演;上演;〔口〕装出〔一般接 the + 形容词〕。~ *Hamlet* 扮演哈姆雷特。*We did Othello* 我们演出《奥赛罗》。~ *the amiable* 装得和蔼可亲的样子。~ *the big* 充好汉。**10.** 煮,煎,烧。~ *the meat thoroughly* 把肉煮透。*steak done to a turn* 牛排煎得很好。**11.** 〔俚〕欺骗;打败。*I'm afraid (that) you've been done*. 我恐怕你已经受骗了。*be done for $ 500 at poker* 赌牌时被骗去 500 元。*That* ~*es me*. 那要叫我认输了。**12.** 〔俚〕待,对待;招待,款待。~ *sb. well* 优待某人;款待某人。"*I will* ~ *you next, please wait a minute.*" "请稍等

一下,接着就轮到你了。"〔理发师对顾客说的话〕。~ *oneself well* [*proud*] 生活阔绰,养尊处优。**13.**〔口〕使疲劳。*The long journey has done him*. 长途旅行使他疲劳不堪。**14.**〔口〕处置;〔口〕杀死。*If you stir, I will ~ you*.〔俚〕你要是动,我就干[杀]掉你。**15.**〔口〕服(刑);做满(任期)。~ *five years for forgery* 因犯伪造罪服刑5年。~ *a year as chairman of the club* 任俱乐部主席一年。**16.** 为(小说等)写评论。~ *the fiction for a newspaper* 专门为一家报纸写小说评论。—***vi*.** **1.** 做,行动,工作;进行;行事,表现。*Let us be up and ~-ing*. 打起精神来工作吧! ~ *like a gentleman* 做事正派。*When at* [*in*] *Rome*, ~ *as the Romans* ~. 入乡随俗。*He is ~ing very well at the Bar*. 他在律师界干的不错。*How shall we ~ for the great cost*? 我们怎么应付得了如此庞大的开支! ~ *without an automobile* 在没有汽车的情况下凑合着干。**2.**〔口〕发生。*There is nothing ~ing*! 没有发生什么事。*What's ~-ing at the office*? 办公室里出什么事了? **3.** 行,可以,适合,合用(*for*);够了。*This will never ~*. 这不中用,这个不行。*Any time will ~*. 什么时候都行。*This sum will ~ for the present*. 这笔钱暂时够用了。*It would never ~ to neglect official obligations*. 玩忽职守是绝对不行的。*That will ~*. 那就好了,够了。*These shoes won't ~ for mountaineering*. 这些鞋子不适合爬山。**4.** (植物等)生长,(健康等)进展。*Mother and child are ~ing fine*. 母亲和孩子的身体都很好。*Flax ~es well after wheat*. 收过小麦以后,亚麻长得不错。**5.** 办完,结束。*After she had done in the kitchen, she went out*. 她在厨房干完活以后就出去了。*His work is never done*. 他总是不把事情做完。*It is done*. 做完了。**be done with** 与…分手,结束(*I'm quite done with the girl*. 我和那个姑娘的关系彻底结束了)。**can ~ with** 将就,勉强能对付(*Can you ~ with cold mutton for lunch*? 你能凑合着吃点冷羊肉当午饭吗? *I can ~ with two meals a day*. 我一天只吃两顿饭也可以)。**could ~ with** 需要,希望得到(*I could ~ with a good rest*. 我希望好好休息一下。*You could ~ with a shave*. 你需要刮刮脸了)。~ **away with** **1.** 除去,废除。**2.** 干掉,杀死(*Trivial formalities have to be done away with*. 繁文缛节必须废除。~ *away with oneself* 自杀。*suspected of having done away with sb*. 有杀死某人的嫌疑)。~ **by** 对待,待(*He ~es well by a friend*. 他对朋友很好。*Do as you would be done by*. 你愿意别人怎样待你,你就怎样待别人)。~ **for** **1.**〔口〕杀死,除掉;毁掉,坏掉;累垮(*Once you are unemployed, you are done for*. 一旦失业,你就完了。*It was the shot that did for him*. 那颗子弹要了他的命)。**2.** 适合做(*You won't ~ for a lawyer*. 你不适合当律师)。**3.**〔英〕照料(家务),照顾,帮助(*She ~es for her brother*. 她给弟弟管家)。~ **in**〔俚〕**1.** 杀死,害死。**2.** 损坏,累垮。**3.** 欺骗(~ *oneself in* 自杀。~ *one's car in* 车子坏了。*be done in by the heat* 热坏了。*You'd better watch out, or you'll be getting done in*. 你得当心点,不然会受骗)。~ **it all**〔美俚〕服无期徒刑。~ **one's thing** 做自己喜欢做的事。~ **one's bit** 见 bit 条。~ **one's damnedest**〔俚〕苦干,拼命干。~ **off**〔古〕脱(~ *off one's clothes* 脱衣)。~ **or die** 干到底,决一死战,死而后已。~ **out** 打扫,收拾(~ *out a room* 收拾屋子)。~ **sb. out of** **1.** 驱逐某人。**2.** 欺骗某人(*He did me out of the job*. 他把我解雇了。*She did me out of several hundred dollars*. 她骗去了我几百元)。~ **over** **1.** 重做,改做。**2.** 重新装饰(房屋等)(~ *a room over* 重新装饰房间)。~ **sb. pround** 使某人感到荣幸。~ **time** 服徒刑(*It's hard to get a decent job once you've done time*. 一旦坐过牢,想再找个好工作就不那么容易了)。~ **to** 对待,处置(~ *to death*〔古〕处死)。~ **unto**〔古〕= ~ to. ~ **up** **1.** 包;捆(~ *up a parcel* 包包裹)。**2.** 扣,结扎(~ *up one's hair* 扎好头发。~ *up one's dress* 扣上衣服)。**3.** 整顿,修理,修饰;洗(~ *up one's shirts* 洗衬衫。*have one's house done up* 收拾屋子)。**4.**〔口〕使累垮,使极疲劳(*be done up with teaching all day* 教一天书下来累得要命)。**5.** 穿,打扮(*The waitresses are all done up in costumes*. 女服务员都穿着制服)。~ **well** **1.** 处置得当。**2.** (病人等)情况好;成功,发达;顺遂;成绩好。**3.** (植物)长得好(*He did well to refuse*. 他拒绝得好)。~ **with** **1.** 满足于,忍耐(*You must ~ with what you've got*. 你必须知足。*I can't ~ with his insolence*. 我忍受不了他的侮辱)。**2.** 与…相处(*It's difficult to ~ with her*. 和她不易相处)。**3.** 处置,对付(*What shall I ~ with a man like that*? 怎样对付这样一种人呢?)。~ **without** 省去,无需(*The store hasn't any, so you'll have to ~ without*. 店里没有,所以你就得将就一些了)。**Have done!** 停止!结束! **have done with** **1.** 办完,用完(*Have you done with the pen*? 你用好那支笔了吗?) **2.** 已和…无关,和…断绝关系(*I have done with her*. 我已和她断绝关系了)。**have to ~ with** 和…有关系[来往](*Smoking has a great deal to ~ with lung cancer*. 吸烟和肺癌有很大关系。*have nothing to ~ with* 和…无关系)。**How ~ you ~**? 您好〔被介绍时及别后重见打招呼时用语〕。**make ~ with** 将就,凑合着用(*She can't afford a new coat and so will have to make ~ with the old one*. 她买不起新外衣,只能凑合着用旧的了。

II *v*. substitute〔代动词,用来避免动词的重复〕。*Use a book as a bee does* (= uses) *flowers*. 像蜜蜂利用花一样地利用书吧。*Did you see him*? *Yes, I did* (= saw him). 你看见他了吗? 嗯,看见了。**So ~ I.** 我也是,我也如此(*You smoke sometimes, so ~ I*. 你有时吸烟,我也如此)。**So I ~.** 是的,不错(*You smoke sometimes*. — *So I ~*. 你有时吸烟吧。——是的)。

III *aux*. *v*. [强 duː, 弱 du, də, d; du, dʊ, də, d] **1.**〔构成疑问句〕。*Do you go*? 你去吗? *Did you go*? 你去了吗? **2.**〔与 not 连用构成否定句〕。*I did not* [*didn't*] *go*. 我没有去。*I ~ not* [*don't*] *know*. 我不知道。**3.**〔用于加强语气和倒装语序的句中〕。*I ~* [ˈduː; ˋdu] *think so*. 我的确是这样想的。*He did* [ˈdid; ˋdɪd] *come*. 他的确来过了。*Well ~ I remember it*. 那我是记得一清二楚。*Never did I see such a thing*. 我从来没有见过那样一种东西。**4.**〔命令和劝告〕。*Do not* [*don't*] *tell a lie*. 莫撒谎。*Do* [ˈduː; ˋdu] *come*. 请一定来。*Do* [ˈduː; ˋdu] *be quiet*. 务请肃静!

IV [ˈduː; ˋdu] ***n*.** (*pl*. ~*s*, ~*'s* [ˈduːz; ˋduz]) **1.** 要求做到的事。**2.**〔俚〕骗局,欺骗。**3.**〔英口〕宴会;庆祝会。**4.**〔英军俚〕交战。**5.**〔罕〕〔*pl*.〕处置;行动;〔英方〕骚动。**6.** 成功。**7.**〔*pl*.〕分配。*It's all a ~*. 这全是欺骗。*It was a tricky ~*. 这是一个狡猾的骗局。*We've got a ~ tonight*. 家里今晚请客。*make a ~ of it* 获得成功。*Fair do's*! 公平分配! ~ **one's ~** 做能做的事。**dos and don'ts** 善恶好歹;注意事项;习惯;规章制度(*Observe the following dos and don'ts*. 请遵守下列注意事项)。

do[2] [dəu; do] ***n*.**【乐】(全音阶的)第一音, do 音。

do. [ˈditəu; ˋdɪto] = ditto.

D/O, d.o. = delivery order.

D.O.A., DOA = dead on arrival 送达医院当即死去〔警察或验尸报告用语〕。

do·a·ble [ˈduːəbl; ˋduəbl̩] ***a*.** 可做的,做得到的,可行的。

doat [dəut; dot] ***vi*.** = dote.

do-all [ˈduːˌɔːl; ˋduˌɔl] ***n*.** 杂役,勤杂工。

dob·ber [ˈdɔbə; ˋdɑbɚ] ***n*.**〔美〕(钓丝上的)浮标,浮子。

dob·bin [ˈdɔbin; ˋdɑbɪn] ***n*.** 农用马,老驽马。

Do·ber·man pin·scher [ˈdəubəmən ˈpinʃə; ˋdobəmən ˋpɪnʃə] (一种德国品种的)多伯曼短毛猎犬。

do·bie [ˈdəubi; ˋdobɪ] ***n***. 〔美口〕 = adobe.

do·bla [ˈdəublɑː; ˋdoblɑ] ***n***. 多布拉〔西班牙古金币名〕。

do·bra [ˈdəubrə; ˋdobrə] ***n***. 多布猎〔葡萄牙几种古金币之一〕。

Dob·son [ˈdɔbsn; ˋdɑbsn] ***n***. 多布森〔姓氏〕。

do·by [ˈdəubi; ˋdobɪ] ***n***. 〔美口〕住处。

doc [dɔk; dɑk] ***n***. 〔美口〕 **1.** = doctor. **2.** 〔常 D-〕先生〔对医生、兽医的称呼〕。

do·cent [ˈdəusənt; ˋdosnt] ***n***. **1.** (美国某些大学的)代课教师。**2.** (大学)讲师。

do·ce·tic [dəuˈsiːtik; doˋsitɪk] ***a***. 基督幻影说的;基督幻影说者的。

Do·ce·tism [dəuˈsiːtizəm; dəˋsitɪzəm] ***n***. 【宗史】基督幻影说〔早期基督教的一种非正统学说,认为基督系幻影,无肉身〕。**Do·ce·tist** ***n***. 基督幻影说者。

doch-an-dor·rach [ˈdɔkənˈdɔrək; ˋdɔkənˋdɔrək] ***n***. 〔英方〕(临行时喝的)告别酒。

doc·ile [ˈdəusail; ˋdɑsl] ***a***. **1.** (学生等)容易教的,听话的,俯首贴耳的。**2.** (马等)驯良的,容易驾御的。**3.** 易处理的。*a ～ horse* 驯顺的马。*be ～ at school but unruly at home* 在学校里听话,在家里调皮。**-ly** ***ad***.

do·cil·i·ty [dəuˈsiliti; doˋsɪlətɪ] ***n***. 温顺;听话。*follow with ～* 俯首听命。

dock[1] [dɔk; dɑk] **I** ***n***. **1.** 船坞,修船所;〔常 *pl*.〕(附设码头,仓库等的)造船厂;〔美口〕码头,停泊处。**2.** 【铁路】终点站。**3.** 【空】飞机检修架,飞机库,飞机修配厂。**4.** (舞台下部的)布景存放处。*a wet* [*dry, floating*] *～* 泊船坞[干坞,浮坞]。*naval ～* 海军船坞。***in dry ～*** 〔俚〕失业。**II** ***vt***. **1.** 把(船)引入船坞[码头]。**2.** 在…设置船坞。**3.** 【宇航】使(太空飞行器)在外层空间相接。—***vi***. **1.** (船)进入船坞[码头]。**2.** 【宇航】(与另一飞船等)在外层空间相接,会合。**D- Board** 【海】港务局。**～ charge** [**dues**] 入坞费,码头费。**～hand** 码头工人。**～-man** ***n***. (*pl*. **～-*men***) = ～hand. **～master** 船坞长,造船厂厂长。**～side** ***n***. 码头边,码头侧邻区。**～-wallope** 码头上的短工,搬运工。**～ warrant** 船坞仓库存货凭单。**～yard** **1.** 造船厂,船舶修造厂。**2.** 海军船坞;〔英〕军舰修造所。**-ing** **1.** ***n***. 入坞。**2.** ***a***. 入坞的 (*～ accommodation* 入坞设备。*～ facilities* 泊船设备)。**-ize** ***vt***. 为(港口)设码头;在(河道等处)设船坞。

dock[2] [dɔk; dɑk] ***n***. 【植】 **1.** 酸模属草类;酸模。**2.** 草本植物。

dock[3] [dɔk; dɑk] **I** ***n***. **1.** 尾巴的骨肉部份。**2.** 剪短的尾,去毛的尾。**3.** (套在短尾上的)套尾皮袋。**II** ***vt***. **1.** 截去,剪短(尾巴等);把…的尾巴[短发]剪短。**2.** 削减,缩减(供应、工资等)。**3.** 剥夺,扣去…的应得工资[津贴等]。*～ a tail* 剪短尾巴。*～ the ears of cattle* 剪短牛耳。*～ a horse* 剪短马尾。*～ sb.'s wages* 削减某人的工资,使某人减薪。*～ an allowance* 削减津贴。*～ sb. a day's pay* 扣某人一天工资。*～ him of the pleasures of childhood* 剥夺他童年时代的欢乐。**～-tailed** ***a***. 尾巴剪短的。

dock[4] [dɔk; dɑk] ***n***. (刑事法庭的)被告席。***be in the ～*** 受审,处于被告席。**～ brief** 【法】(英国律师为贫苦被告进行的)免费辩护。

dock·age[1] [ˈdɔkidʒ; ˋdɑkɪdʒ] ***n***. **1.** 入坞费,码头费。**2.** 船坞设备。**3.** 入坞。

dock·age[2] [ˈdɔkidʒ; ˋdɑkɪdʒ] ***n***. **1.** (经费、工资等的)削减;缩减;扣除。**2.** (谷物中的)杂质。

dock·er[1] [ˈdɔkə; ˋdɑkɚ] ***n***. 〔英〕码头工人;船坞工人。

dock·er[2] [ˈdɔkə; ˋdɑkɚ] ***n***. **1.** 剪尾工。**2.** 剪尾器。

dock·et [ˈdɔkit; ˋdɑkɪt] **I** ***n***. **1.** (公文的)概略,摘要。**2.** 【法】判决摘要书;备审案件目录。**3.** (贴在货物等包装外皮上的)标签,签条。**4.** 应办事项(表);议事日程,记事条。**5.** 〔英〕(准备管制或稀缺物资的)购货证;关税完税证。**II** ***vt***. **1.** (在公文等上)附加提要。**2.** 在…上附加签条。**3.** 【法】把…记入[列入]应办案件表;给(判决等)作摘要。*judgments regularly ～ed* 按规定作出摘要的判词。*His papers were always neatly ～ed*. 他的论文总是附有眉目清楚的摘要。***clear the ～*** 结束所有案件的审理;〔喻〕结束,扫清(工作)。***on*** [***off***] ***the ～*** **1.** 【法】在[不在]审理中。**2.** 〔喻〕在〔不在〕审办[考虑]中。***trial ～*** 〔美〕备审案件目录。

doc·tor [ˈdɔktə; ˋdɑktɚ] **I** ***n***. **1.** 博士〔略作 D. 或 Dr.〕。**2.** 医生,医师,大夫;牙齿;兽医;巫医。**3.** 〔古〕学者,教师;【天主】权威神学家。**4.** 【机】校正器,调节器;临时应急工具[装置];〔口〕修理师;修理场,修理室。**5.** 〔海口〕大师傅〔船上或营地等对厨师的尊称〕。**6.** (钓鱼用的)人造彩色蝇。**7.** 【印】刮片,刮刀。**8.** 【化】(精炼石油用的)试硫液。**9.** 〔口〕凉爽的(海)风。*D- of Divinity* [*Laws, Literature, Medicine, Philosophy*] 神[法、文、医、哲]学博士。*a good-for-nothing ～* 庸医。*a chair ～* 修椅子的人,修椅工。*a car ～* 修车师傅。*～ knife* 刮刀。*～ solution* 【化】试硫液。*D- of the Church* (天主教的)权威神学家。*～ test* 【化】(汽油)含硫试验。*Doctors' Commons* (伦敦从前处理遗嘱、结婚、离婚等的)民法博士会馆。***～'s stuff*** 药剂。***practice as a ～*** 开业行医。***put the ～ on sb***. 欺骗某人。***see*** [***consult***] ***a ～*** 去就医,就诊。***sent for a ～*** 请医生(来),延医治疗。***When ～s differs*** 〔谑〕当大学者们产生意见分歧的时候。**II** ***vt***. **1.** 诊治,医治;为…充当医师。**2.** 修理,修复。**3.** 修正,改写(文稿等)。**4.** 〔口〕窜改(文件、账目等);搀混(酒等);阉割(家畜)。**5.** 授与…博士学位。*He ～ed his cold at home*. 他在家治感冒。*～ oneself for a cold* 给自己治感冒。*～ an old clock* 修理旧钟。*～ the play to suit the audience* 修改剧本以迎合观众。*～ the election returns* 窜改选举结果。*～ the fact on his passport* 窜改护照上的记录。*～ the drink with a stupefying dose* 在酒里掺麻醉剂。—***vi***. **1.** 行医,做医生。**2.** 〔方〕服药。*He ～ed in Europe before coming to the U.S.* 他来美国以前在欧洲当医生。**～blade** 【印】(改版用的)刮刀。**～ book** 《家医》,家用医书。**～ship** 博士学位。

doc·tor·al [ˈdɔktərəl; ˋdɑktərəl] ***a***. 博士的;学者的;权威的。*a ～ dissertation* [*thesis*] 博士论文。

doc·tor·ate [ˈdɔktərit; ˋdɑktərɪt] ***n***. 博士头衔[学位、资格]。

doc·to·ri·al [dɔkˈtɔːriəl; dɑkˋtorɪəl] ***a***. = doctoral.

doc·tress [ˈdɔktris; ˋdɑktrɪs] ***n***. 〔罕〕女医生;女博士;博士夫人。

doc·tri·naire [ˌdɔktriˈnɛə; ˏdɑktrɪˋnɛr] **I** ***n***. 空谈理论的人,教条主义者。**II** ***a***. 教条的,空谈理论的。*a ～ preacher* 一个空谈理论的说教者。**-nair·ism** [-ˈnɛərizəm; -ˋnɛrɪzəm] ***n***. 教条主义,空谈理论。

doc·tri·nal [dɔkˈtrainl; ˋdɑktrɪnl] ***a***. 教条的,教义的;学说上的。*a ～ dispute* 学说上的论争。**～ theology** 【宗】教义学。

doc·tri·nar·i·an [dɔktriˈnɛəriən; ˏdɑktrɪˋnɛrɪən] ***a***., ***n***. = doctrinaire. **-ism** ***n***. = doctrinairism.

doc·trine [ˈdɔktrin; ˋdɑktrɪn] ***n***. **1.** (宗教、政治方面的)教旨,教条;教义;原则;主义。**2.** 学说;〔口〕教训,训导。*Catholic ～s* 天主教教义。*the ～s of Freud* 弗洛伊德的学说。*religious ～s* 宗教教义。

doc·trin·ism [ˈdɔktrinizəm; ˋdɑktrɪnɪzəm] ***n***. 教义至上主义;对主义的信奉。**-trin·ist** ***n***. 教义至上主义者;主义的信奉者。

doc·u·ment [ˈdɔkjumənt; ˋdɑkjəmənt] **I** ***n***. **1.** 文献,文件;公文。**2.** 证件,证书,凭证。**3.** 记录影片,记实小说。**4.** 【海】船舶执照。*a diplomatic ～* 外交文件。*public ～s* 公文。*a ～ of searching* 搜查证。*a ～ of shipping* 装货单据。*a human ～* 人世间的记录。**II** [ˈdɔkjument; ˋdɑkjəˏmɛnt] ***vt***. **1.** 用文件[证书等]证明,为…提供文件[证书等]。**2.** 根据事实材料制作(影片等)。**3.** 【海】为(船舶)提供执照〔表明船的国籍、容量、所

有权等〕。*a ~ed vessel*〔美〕有执照的船。*a carefully ~ed biography* 有详细文献根据的传记。~ *a case* 为案件提供文件资料。

doc·u·men·tal [ˌdɔkjuˈmentəl; ˏdɑkjəˋmentl], **doc·u·men·ta·ry** [ˌdɔkjuˈmentəri; ˏdɑkjəˋmentərɪ] **I** *a*. **1.** 文件的;公文的;证书的。**2.** 记录的,记实的。*a ~ bill* [*draft*]【商】跟单汇票。*a ~ committee* 起草委员会。*a ~ film* 记录影片。*a ~ evidence* [*proof*] 文件证明。*a ~ history* 历史资料。**II** *n*.【影】记录片(= ~ film); 记实小说;【无】实况录音。**-men·ta·ri·ly** *ad*.

doc·u·men·ta·tion [ˌdɔkjumenˈteiʃən; ˏdɑkjəmenˋteʃən] *n*. **1.** 文件[证书等]的提供;参考文件[证件等]的利用。**2.** 提供的文件[证书等]。**3.** 与历史事实的相符。**4.** (利用微型照片复制等技术进行的)文献的编集,文件分类。

DOD = Department of Defense〔美〕国防部。

dod [dɔːd; dɑd] *vt*.〔英方〕剪(羊)毛。

do·dad [ˈduːdæd; ˋdudæd] *n*.〔美俚〕= doodad.

Dodd [dɔd; dɑd] *n*. 多德〔姓氏〕。

dod·der[1] [ˈdɔdə; ˋdɑdɚ] *vi*. **1.** (因年老、中风等而)摇晃,蹒跚;抖颤。**2.** 蹒跚而行。*an old man ~ing down the walk* 一个在人行道上摇摇晃晃行走的老人。**-y** [ˈdɔdəri; ˋdɑdərɪ] *a*. 衰老的,老迈的;蹒跚的。

dod·der[2] [ˈdɔdə; ˋdɑdɚ] *n*.【植】菟丝子,菟丝子属植物。

dod·dered [ˈdɔdəd; ˋdɑdɚd] *a*. **1.** (树木等)枯朽脱枝的。**2.** 衰弱的。

dodec(a)- *comb. f*. 十二: *dodeca*gon.

do·dec·a·gon [dəuˈdekəgən; doˋdɛkəˏgɑn] *n*.【数】十二角形,十二边形。**-al** [ˌdəudiˈkægənəl; dodɪˋkægənəl] *a*.

do·dec·a·he·dron [ˌdəudikəˈhedrən; ˏdodɛkəˋhidrən] *n*. (*pl*. ~s, *-dra* [-drə; -drə])【数】十二面体。

do·dec·a·phon·ic [dəuˌdekəˈfɔnik; doˏdɛkəˋfɑnɪk] *a*.【乐】十二音体系的。**-phonist** [-ˌfəunist; -fonɪst] *n*. 运用十二音体系作曲者。**-pho·ny** [-ˈfəuni; -ˋfonɪ], **-phonism** *n*. 十二音体系作曲法。

do·dec·a·style [dəuˈdekəstail; doˋdɛkəˏstaɪl] *n*.【建】十二柱式。

dod·gast·ed [dɔdˈgæstid; dɑdˋgæstɪd] *a*.〔俚〕被咒的;迷惑的。

Dodge [dɔdʒ; dɑdʒ] *n*. 道奇〔姓氏〕。

dodge [dɔdʒ; dɑdʒ] **I** *vi*. **1.** 躲开,闪开,避开。**2.** 掩饰,托词逃避,搪塞。*To avoid my friend, I ~d into the nearest café*. 为了避免和一个朋友见面,我躲进了最近的一家咖啡馆。*When asked a direct question, he ~s*. 当被问到一个明确的问题时,他就搪塞过去。—*vt*. 闪开,躲开,避开,摆脱。~ *a blow* 躲闪开打击。~ *a question* 回避问题。~ *a direct question* 把一个明确的问题搪塞过去。~ ***about*** 东躲西避。***dodging and dissembling*** 遮遮掩掩地。**II** *n*. **1.** 躲避;〔口〕推托,搪塞。**2.**〔俚〕妙计,窍门,诡计;新设计的装置[器具]。*by a swift ~ to the left* 很快向左一躲。*a ~ to win your confidence* 想赢得你的信任的一个诡计。~ *times*〔美〕闲暇,空闲时间。***be up to all ~s*** 诡计多端。***on the ~***〔英口〕搞鬼,蒙混;躲避;无固定住处(以逃避拘捕)。**dodg·er·y** *n*. **1.** 躲避。**2.** 推托。**3.** 用诡计,欺诈。

dodg·em [ˈdɔdʒim; ˋdɑdʒəm] *n*. (游乐园中的)电动躲闪车〔乘者相互躲让着行驶,躲闪不及常互相碰撞,源出 dodge them 一语,亦作~ car〕。

dodg·er [ˈdɔdʒə; ˋdɑdʒɚ] *n*. **1.** 躲闪者;推托者,蒙骗者。**2.**〔美〕传单,广告单。**3.**〔美南部〕玉米饼。**4.**〔澳〕一大块(面包等)。**5.**【船】船桥上的防浪屏。*a draft ~* 逃避服兵役者。*a tax ~* 逃税者。

Dodg·son [ˈdɔdʒsən; ˋdɑdʒsən] *n*. 道奇森〔姓氏〕。

dodg·y [ˈdɔdʒi; ˋdɑdʒɪ] *a*. **1.** 躲避的;推托的;会掩饰的。**2.**〔俚〕机警的,巧妙的。

do·do [ˈdəudəu; ˋdodo] *n*. (*pl*. ~s, ~es) **1.**【鸟】渡渡鸟〔原产于毛里求斯岛等地,已于十七世纪末绝种的一种鸽属巨鸟,性迟钝,不会飞〕;愚钝的人,落后者;〔俚〕不能单独飞行的飞行员。*The society is as dead as the ~*. 社交界一片死气沉沉。

dod·unk [ˈdɔdənk; ˋdɑdənk] *n*.〔美俚〕笨人。

Doe [dəu; do] *n*. 无名氏〔法院用语,用以指姓氏不明者,如 John Doe, Jane Doe (某约翰,某珍妮)〕。

doe [dəu; do] *n*. (*pl*. ~s,〔集合词〕~) **1.** 母鹿,母山羊,母羚羊,雌兔 (*opp*. buck)。**2.**〔美俚〕社交场合无男伴的女子。

do·er [ˈduːə; ˋduɚ] *n*. **1.** 行为者。**2.** 做(某事)的人,生长(好、坏)的动植物〔常用以构成复合词〕。**3.** 实干家。*He is a ~, not a talker*. 他是一个不说空话的实干家。*a good* [*poor*] *~* 发育良好[不良]的动[植]物。*an evil ~* 作恶者。*a ~ of good* 行善者,做好事者。

does [强 dʌz, 弱 dəz, dz; 强 dʌz, 弱 dəz, dz] do 的第三人称、单数、现在式。

doe·skin [ˈdəuskin; ˋdoˏskɪn] *n*. **1.** 母鹿[兔、羚羊、山羊]皮。**2.**【纺】仿鹿皮(织物);驼丝棉;〔*pl*.〕羊皮手套。

does·n't [ˈdʌznt; ˋdʌznt] = does not.

do·est [ˈdu(ː)ist; ˋduɪst]〔古、诗〕do[1]的第二人称、单数、现在式〔用于主语为 thou 时的场合〕。

do·eth [ˈdu(ː)iθ; ˋduɪθ]〔古、诗〕do[1]的第三人称、单数、现在式。

doff [dɔf; dɔf] **I** *vt*. **1.** 脱(帽、衣等)(*opp*. don)。**2.** 废除(习惯等)。**3.**【纺】落(纱);落(卷);落(筒)。~ *one's hat* 脱帽(敬意)。*D- your stupid habits and live*. 抛弃你的坏习惯好好生活吧。**II** *n*.【纺】落下的纱[卷等] **-er** *n*.【纺】**1.** 小滚筒,"道夫"。**2.** 落纱工。**3.** 落纱机。

do·fun·ny [ˈduːfʌni; ˋdufʌnɪ] *n*.〔美俚〕那个,那东西〔叫不出或想不起名称的东西,尤指小装饰品或一些新设计品〕。

dog [dɔg; dɔg] **I** *n*. **1.** 犬,狗;猎犬;犬科动物。**2.** (狼、狐等)雄兽,雄狗;类似犬的动物。**3.** 卑鄙的人,无赖;废物,没用的人。**4.**〔口〕(…样的)家伙〔常加形容词修饰〕;〔美〕装阔气;妄自尊大。**5.**【机】轧头,挡块,止动器;卡爪,棘爪;拔钉钳;搭钩;挂钩环,钩;【船】(水密门)夹扣。**6.**【天】〔the D-〕大犬座,小犬座。**7.** (炉中的)铁架。**8.**〔*pl*.〕〔美口〕小红肠;红肠夹心面包。**9.**〔*pl*.〕(人的)双脚。**10.**【气】假日,幻日;雾虹;(预示有雨的)小雨云。**11.**〔美俚〕(戏剧、音乐等的)失败之作;劣质品;滞销商品;亏本投资,贬值股票;丑妇;〔*pl*.〕破产,毁灭。**12.**〔美俚〕妓女。**13.**〔英俚〕〔the ~s〕跑狗比赛。*treat sb. like a ~* 把某人当狗一样对待。*a hunting ~* 猎犬。*a ~ fox* 雄狐。*a lazy ~* 懒家伙,懒骨头。*a lucky ~* 幸运儿。*a dead ~* 废料,没用的东西。*a dirty ~* 下流货。*a gay ~* 快活人儿。*Don't be a ~*. 不要这样卑鄙。*My ~s are burned up*. 我的两只脚都烧伤了。*She's been standing on her ~s all day*. 她已经站了一整天。*That used car you bought is a ~*. 你买的那辆旧车是件废物。***a dead ~*** 无用的东西。***a ~ in a blanket*** 葡萄卷饼,卷布丁。***a ~ in the manger*** 狗占马槽,占着茅坑不拉屎的人,自己干不了又不肯让位的人,占住自己不能享用的东西又不肯给别人享用的人。***a ~'s age***〔口〕好久好久。***Barking ~s do not*** [***seldom***] ***bite***. 叫狗不咬人,嘴狠手软,干叫唤不动手干。***be top ~*** 居于高位,居于支配地位。***be under ~*** 永远听人支配。***call off the ~*** **1.** 停止追逐[查询]。**2.** 岔开不愉快的谈话。***die like a ~*** = ***die a ~'s death*** 死得惨;死得可耻。~ ***and maggot***〔英军俚〕饼干和干酪。~ ***before its master***〔英俚〕大风前的巨浪。~***s of law*** 酷刑,苛法。~***s of war*** 战争惨祸,兵燹。***eat ~***〔美〕忍辱。***Every ~ has his day***. 凡人皆有得意时。***Give a ~ a bad*** [***ill***] ***name and hang him***. 谗言可畏,欲加之罪何患无辞。***get the ~***〔美〕胜,赢。***give*** [***throw***] ***sth. to the ~s*** **1.** 放弃,扔掉某物。**2.** 牺牲某物保护自己。***go to the ~s***〔口〕没落,堕落;灭亡;〔美〕努力全成泡影,失

败。*help a lame ~ over a stile* 助人渡过危难。*lead a ~'s life* (使某人)过苦日子。*lead sb. a ~'s life* 不停地烦扰某人使其生活充满苦恼。*Let sleeping ~s lie*. 莫惹睡狗,不要惹事生非。*Love me, love my ~*. 爱屋及乌。*not even a ~'s chance* 毫无机会。*put on (the) ~* 〔美俚〕耍威风,摆架子。*try it on the [a] ~* 1. 牺牲别人进行试验。2. 电影试演检验效果。*wake a sleeping ~* 惹事生非。

II *vt*. (-gg-) 1. 追猎;追随;尾随;跟踪,钉梢;(灾难等)紧紧缠住。2.【机】用钩抓住;用轧头夹住。*He kept ~ging my tracks all the way to London*. 他一直跟踪我到伦敦。~ *down*【海】用钩扣牢。~ *it* 1.〔俚〕打扮起来。2. 摆阔。3. 偷懒。

III *ad*.〔用作复合词〕极,非常。*I'm ~-tired*. 我累死了。~**berry**【植】山茱萸,山茱萸的籽实;挟木属植物。~**-biscuit** 喂狗的饼干;硬饼干。~**-box** 铁路上运狗的车厢。~**cart** 1. 狗拖的车。2. (二人背靠背坐的)单马拉双轮马车。~**-cheap** *a*., *ad*. 极便宜(地)。~ **clutch**【机】爪形夹盘,爪卡盘。~ **collar** 1. 狗项圈。2.〔俚〕(牧师等用的)项圈形胶领。3.〔口〕(用宝石等装饰的)项链。~**days** 1. 三伏天,大热天〔一般为 7 月 3 日—8 月 11 日〕。2. 无精打采的日子;无所作为的时期。~**-ear** *n*., *vt*. = ~'s-ear. ~**-eat-~** *n*., *a*. 狗咬狗(的),损人利己(的)(*a ~-eat-~ war* 狗咬狗的战争。*The only rule of the market place was ~-eat-~*. 市场上的唯一准则是损人利己)。~**face**〔俚〕士兵,步兵。~**fall** (摔跤时)双方同时倒地,平局。~ **fancier** 爱狗的人,狗商。~**-fight** *n*., *vi*. 1.【空】缠斗,混战。2. 狗打架,狗咬狗。~**fish**【动】角鲨,星鲨。~**hole** 1. 狗洞。2. 龌龊的房间。3.〔俚〕不安全的小煤矿。~**house** 1. 狗窝;小窝棚。2. 监狱的监视塔(*in the ~house*〔美俚〕丢脸,挨骂;受耻辱)。~ **Latin** 不规范的拉丁语。~ **lead** 狗绳,狗炼。~**-leg**, ~**-legged** *a*. (像狗的后腿一样)折曲的,罗圈腿(的)。~ **napper**〔美〕偷狗的人,狗贼。~ **paddle** 狗爬式游泳。~**-paddle** *vi*. 进行狗爬式游泳。~**robber**〔美〕军官的传令兵。~ **salmon**【动】鲑,大马哈鱼。~**'s-body** 1. 豆粉布丁。2.〔英海俚〕打杂;低级船员。~**'s chance** 极有限的一点机会。~**'s-ear** 1. *n*. (书页的)摺角。2. *vt*. 把(书页)摺角。~**'s-eared** *a*. (书页)摺角的;(书)翻旧了的。~**'s letter** 犬音字母〔指 r,尤指其发卷舌音时〕。~**'s nose** 啤酒与杜松子酒的混合饮料。~**shore**【船】(船下水前用的)支船木。~**-sick** 恶心的。~**-skin** 狗皮。~**sleep** 假寐,打盹,时常惊醒的睡眠。~ **spike** (铁路上的)狗头钉,钩头道钉。~**'s-tail**【植】洋狗尾草属植物。**D- Star** 1. 天狼星〔大犬座主星〕。2. 南河三〔小犬座主星〕。~**'s-tongue**【植】倒提壶属植物。~**'s tooth** (作男子衣料的)格子花呢。~**'s tooth violet**【植】山茨菇。~ **tag** 1. 狗牌,狗执照。2.〔军俚〕(战时士兵挂在颈上的)身分证明牌。~ **tent**〔军俚〕掩蔽帐篷。~**-tired** *a*. 极疲倦的。~**tooth** 1. 犬齿。2.【建】犬牙饰,四叶饰。~ **trick** 恶作剧。~**trot** *n*., *vi*. 小跑(*He ~trotted home*. 他小步跑回家)。~ **tune**〔俚〕二流歌曲。~**vane**【船】(桅上的)风向指示器。~**watch** 1.【海】(二小时换班的)折半轮值〔午后 4—6 时,6—8 时〕;夜班〔尤指最后一班〕。2.〔俚〕(报社记者等的)额外值班〔正班以外等待特殊重要消息的轮值〕。~**wood**【植】山茱萸,挟木属植物。**-dom** 1. 犬类。2. 犬性。3.〔集合词〕爱犬的人,爱玩狗的人。**-hood** *n*. 狗性。**-let**〔美〕小狗。**-like** *a*. 1. 狗一样的。2. 忠于主人的。

dog·ged [ˈdɔgid; ˋdɔgɪd] *a*. 1. 顽固的,固执的。2. 顽强的。*a ~ scholar* 坚持自己主张的学者。*resume one's ~ effort* 重新开始顽强的努力。*It's ~ as does it*. 有志者事竟成;坚持就是胜利。

dog·ger [ˈdɔgə; ˋdɔgɚ] *n*. 荷兰双桅渔船。*the D- Bank* (英国与丹麦之间的)陶格尔沙〔世界著名渔场之一〕。

dog·ger·el [ˈdɔgərəl; ˋdɔgərəl] I *n*. 歪诗,打油诗。II *a*. 1. (诗)拙劣的。2. 滑稽的。~ *lines of verse* 拙劣的诗句。

dog·ger·y [ˈdɔgəri; ˋdɔgəri] *n*. 1. 狗性;(狗一样)卑劣的行为。2.〔集合词〕狗。3. 乌合之众;暴徒。4.〔美俚〕小酒馆,下等酒吧间。

dog·gie [ˈdɔgi; ˋdɔgɪ] I *n*. 1. 小狗;〔儿〕狗。2.〔美俚〕红肠。II *a*. 爱狗的。~**bag** 狗食袋〔餐馆给顾客把残羹剩菜带回喂狗的袋子〕。

dog·gi·ness [ˈdɔginis; ˋdɔgɪnɪs] *n*. 像狗;爱狗;狗臭。

dog·gish [ˈdɔgiʃ; ˋdɔgɪʃ] *a*. 1. 狗的;狗一样的;卑鄙的。2. 脾气大的,泼辣的,爱吵闹的。3.〔口〕爱花俏的,浮华的。*a ~ temper* 坏脾气。**-ly** *ad*. **-ness** *n*.

dog·go [ˈdɔgəu; ˋdɔgo] *ad*.〔俚〕一动不动地;隐蔽地。*lie ~*〔英俚〕隐蔽,埋伏,一动不动地等候。

dog·gone [ˈdɔgɔn; ˏdɔgˋgɔn] I *a*.〔美俚〕1. 可恶的,讨厌的。2. 非常的,无比的。*That was a ~ insult*. 那是一个可恶的侮辱。II *int*.〔美俚〕讨厌! 可恶! 他妈的! 该死的! III *vt*.〔常用被动语态〕〔口〕咒骂。*I'll be ~d if I'll go*. 我要去就是混蛋,我决不去。*D- your silly ideas*. 去你的那套馊主意吧。IV *n*. 诅咒。V *ad*. 非常,极。*I've worked ~ hard in my life*. 我这辈子干的苦活儿可真够呛。

dog·gy [ˈdɔgi; ˋdɔgɪ] I *a*. 1. 狗的,狗一样的。2. 爱玩狗的。3.〔美俚〕时髦的,摆阔的。*a ~ smell* 狗臭。*the tweedy, ~ people* 衣着时髦的阔佬。II *n*. = doggie.

do·gie [ˈdəugi; ˋdogɪ] *n*.〔美方〕(牧场中)失去母牛的牛犊;孤犊儿。

dog·ma [ˈdɔgmə; ˋdɔgmə] *n*. (*pl*. ~s, ~ta [-tə; -tə]) 〔罕〕1. 教义,教理,教条;信条。2. 定论;独断论,武断的意见。*the ~ of the Assumption*【宗】关于圣母升天的教义。*a political ~* 政治信条。

dog·mat·ic, dog·mat·i·cal [dɔgˈmætik(əl); dɔgˋmætɪk(əl)] *a*. 1. 教条的,教义的。2. 教条主义的,独断论的。3. 固执己见的,武断的。*a ~ statement* 武断的说法。**dog·mat·i·cal·ly** *ad*. 独断地,专断地;教条式地。

dog·mat·i·cs [dɔgˈmætiks; dɔgˋmætɪks] *n*. 〔*pl*.〕【宗】教义学。

dog·ma·tism [ˈdɔgmətizəm; ˋdɔgməˏtɪzəm] *n*. 1. 教条主义。2. 武断,独断论。**dog·ma·tist** *n*. 1. 教条主义者,独断论者。2.【宗】教义学者。

dog·ma·tize, dog·ma·tise [ˈdɔgmətaiz; ˋdɔgməˏtaɪz] *vi*. 1. 教条式地说〔写,阐释〕,教条化。2. 武断,独断 (*on*; *about*)。—*vt*. 把…说成教条,使教条化。

do·good [ˈduːgud; ˋduˏgud] *a*.〔贬〕(空想)改良社会的。~ *schemes* 改良社会的空想方案。**-er** *n*.〔俚、蔑〕(空想的)社会改良家。**-ism** *n*. 空想的社会改良主义。

do·gy [ˈdəugi; ˋdogɪ] *n*. = dogie.

Doha [ˈdəuhə; ˋdohə] *n*. 多哈〔卡塔尔首都〕。

Do·her·ty [ˈdəuəti, dəuˈhəːti; ˋdoətɪ, doˋhɝtɪ] *n*. 多尔蒂〔姓氏〕。

doi·ly [ˈdɔili; ˋdɔɪlɪ] *n*. (垫碗碟或小摆设等的)小布巾;花边桌垫。

do·ing [ˈdu(ː)iŋ; ˋduɪŋ] *n*. 1. 做,干,实行。2.〔*pl*.〕行为,行动,举动,活动,所作所为。3.〔俚〕所需要的东西。4.〔*pl*.〕〔方〕做菜的材料。*Your misfortune is not of my ~*. 你的不幸不是我造成的。*daily ~s* 日常活动。*his ~s in England* 他在英国的活动。

doit [dɔit; dɔɪt] *n*. 1. 古荷兰小铜币。2. 小额,几文钱;小东西,琐事。*I don't care a ~ what he does*. 我对他干的事毫不放在心上。*not worth a ~* 毫无价值。

doit·ed [ˈdɔitid; ˋdɔɪtɪd] *a*. [Scot.] (老年人)昏愦的。

do-it-your·self [ˌduːitjɔːˈself; ˋduɪtjəˏsɛlf] *a*. (业余爱好者等)自制的,为业余爱好者设计成的。*a ~ kit for building a radio* 供业余爱好者装配收音机用的一套工具。**-er** *n*. 自己动手的人(指在家中自己制造和修理生活用具的人),自己动手的业余爱好者。

dol. = dollar(s).

do·lan·tin [dəˈlæntin; dəˋlæntın] ***n.*** 【药】盐酸地美罗,杜冷丁。

dol·ce [ˈdɔltʃi; ˋdoltʃ] ***a.***, ***ad.*** 〔It.〕【药】非常温柔的[地]。

dol·ce far ni·en·te [ˈdɔltʃi fɑː niˈenti; ˋdɑltʃıˏfɑr nıˋentı] 〔It.〕安逸,闲适。

dol·ce vi·ta [ˈdəultʃei ˈviːtɑː; ˋdoltʃeˋvitɑ] ***n.*** 〔It.〕放荡,淫乱。

dol·drums [ˈdɔldrəmz; ˋdɑldrəmz] ***n.*** 〔*pl.*〕 1. 郁闷,忧郁;沉闷;萎靡不振,无生气。2.【气】〔the ~〕赤道无风带。*be in the* ~ 意气消沉;【船】在无风带内。*August is a time of* ~ *for many enterprises*. 许多企业在八月份营业清淡。*in a state of mental* ~ 精神萎靡。

Dole [dəul; dol] ***n.*** 多尔〔姓氏〕。

dole[1] [dəul; dol] **I** ***n.*** 1. 施舍物,赈济品;(微少的)施舍。2.〔the ~〕〔英口〕失业救济。3.〔古〕命运。*Happy man may be his* ~!〔古、诗〕愿他幸福快乐。*the unemployment* ~ 失业救济。*on the* ~ 处于被救济状态。***draw the*** ~ 领失业津贴。**II** ***vt.*** 施舍,少量分发(*out*)。*The last of the water was* ~*d out to their thirsty crew*. 最后一点水被少量地分给干渴的船员。**doles·man** [ˈdəulzmən; ˋdolzmən] ***n.*** 接受施舍的人,领取失业救济的人。

dole[2] [dəul; dol] ***n.*** 〔古、诗〕悲哀,悲叹。*make one's* ~ 哀欢。**-ful** [-ful; -fəl], **-some** [-səm; -səm] ***a.*** 悲哀的;凄凉的(*a* ~*ful look* 悲哀的神色。*one's* ~*ful voice* 声音凄苦)。

dol·er·ite [ˈdɔlərait; ˋdɑləˏraıt] ***n.*** 【矿】1. 粗玄武岩。2.〔英〕辉绿岩(= diabase)。3.〔美〕(玄武岩一样的)深色火成岩。

dol·i·cho·ce·phal·ic [ˈdɔlikəuseˈfælik; ˋdɑlıˏkosəˋfælık] ***a.*** 【解】长头的〔头指数在 75 以下, *opp*. brachycephalic〕。

dol·i·cho·cra·ni·al [ˌdɔlikəuˈkreiniəl; ˏdɑlıkoˋkrenıəl] ***a.*** 【解】长颅的〔颅指数在 75 以下者〕。**-cra·nic** [-nik; -nık], **-cra·ny** [-ni; -nı] ***n.***

do·li·ne, do·li·na [dəˈliːnə; dəˋlinə] ***n.*** 【地】落水洞,石灰坑,斗淋。

do·little [ˈduːlitl; ˋdulıtl] ***n.*** 〔口〕游手好闲的人,懒汉。

Doll [dɔl; dɑl] ***n.*** 多尔〔女子名, Dorothy 的昵称〕。

doll [dɔl; dɑl] **I** ***n.*** 1. 玩偶,玩具娃娃。2. 貌美心拙的妇女。3.〔美俚〕姑娘,少女;美女。4.(对女子)有吸引力的男子。*in my* ~ *days* 在我当姑娘的时候,在我的少女时代。*in a world where women are only* ~*s* 在一个妇女仅是玩偶的世界里。~***'s face*** 美貌而呆板的面孔。~***'s house*** 玩偶之家;小住宅。***guys and*** ~***s*** 青年男女。**II** ***vt.***, ***vi.*** 〔美俚〕着意打扮,浓妆艳抹(*up*)。*be* ~*ed up in furs and diamonds* 用珠宝和皮大衣打扮得很漂亮。*This old woman* ~*s herself up like a young lady*. 这个老妇人总是漂漂亮亮地把自己打扮得像个少妇。~ **baby** 1. 洋娃娃。2. 情人,爱人。3. 漂亮可爱的少妇。~ **carriage** [**buggy**] 娃娃车。~**face** 娃娃脸(的成年人)。~**faced** ***a.*** 娃娃脸的。**-ish**, **-like** ***a.*** 玩偶似的,好看而没有头脑的。**-ishly** ***ad.***

dol·lar [ˈdɔlə; ˋdɑlɚ] ***n.*** 1. 美元〔符号为 $ 或 $〕。2. 元〔加拿大等国的货币单位,如加元,澳元等〕。3. 一元金币[银币,纸币];〔英俚〕五先令银币(= crown)。4.〔the ~s〕金钱,财富。5.【物】元(原子堆的反应性单位,指缓发中子产生的反应性)。*Hong Kong* ~ 港币。***bet one's bottom*** ~***s*** 〔美口〕确信,必然(*I'll bet my bottom* ~*s that he will succeed*. 我确信他必然成功)。~***-a-year man*** 〔美〕拿法定最低薪俸的现任官员。~***s to buttons*** [***doughnuts***]〔美俚〕确信,有把握(*It is* ~*s to doughnuts*. 的的确确。*I'll bet you* ~*s to doughnuts*. 我敢肯定)。***fell*** [***look***] ***like a million*** ~***s*** 〔美俚〕感觉[看上去]十分健康;(妇女)看上去特别吸引人。~***-a-year a.*** 只领象征性的菲薄薪金的。~ **area** 美元地区。~ **bloc** 美元集团。~ **diplomacy** 金元外交。~ **fish**【动】翻车鱼。~ **gap** [**shortage**] 美元亏空〔国际贸易中与美元地区相互贸易而入超〕。~ **mark** 美元符号(即 $ 或 $)。~(s)**-and-cent**(s) ***a.*** 纯经济的。**-wise** ***ad.*** 1. 以美元计算的(*How much does a million francs amount to* ~? 一百万法郎合多少美元)。2. 在财政方面。

doll·ish [ˈdɔliʃ; ˋdɑlıʃ] ***a.*** 玩偶似的;好看而没有头脑的。**-ly** ***ad.*** **-ness** ***n.***

dol·lop [ˈdɔləp; ˋdɑləp] ***n.*** 〔口〕1.(黏土、奶油等的)一块,一团。2. 少量,一点儿。~*s of mud* 泥团。*a* ~ *of soda water* 少量苏打水。

Dol·ly [ˈdɔli; ˋdɑlı] ***n.*** = Doll. ~ **Varden**(1870 年前后流行的)花布女服;饰花阔边女帽。

dol·ly [ˈdɔli; ˋdɑlı] **I** ***n.*** 1.〔儿〕(玩具)娃娃。2.【矿】(矿石的)捣碎棒;〔英方〕(洗衣用的)搅拌棒,捣衣杵。3.(车间运料用的)小轮手推车;(采石场的)窄轨小机车;移动式摄影车。4.(打桩用的)垫盘;【机】铆顶;抵座;(铁匠做钉头用的)型铁;(使用搅拌棒的)洗衣桶。**II** ***vt.*** 1. 用独轮车运(物)。2. 用搅拌棒洗(衣);用捣棒捣碎(矿石)。—***vi.*** 1.【影】推动移动式摄影车。2. 用捣棒捣碎矿石;用搅拌棒洗衣。~ ***in*** [***out***, ***back***] 向前[向后]推动移动式摄影车。~**man** 使用小轮手推车的搬运工。~**'s bird** 〔美俚〕打扮入时的漂亮姑娘。~ **shop** 1.〔美俚〕废品店,低级当铺。2.〔英口〕船具店(= marine store)。~ **shot**【影】移动式拍摄。~ **tub**(使用搅拌棒的)洗衣桶。

dol·man [ˈdɔlmən; ˋdɑlmən] ***n.*** 1. 土耳其长外套。2. 披肩式衣袖的女外衣。3. 骠骑兵的斗篷式短外衣。

dol·men [ˈdɔlmen; ˋdɑlmɛn] ***n.*** 【考古】石桌状墓标。

dol·o·mite [ˈdɔləmait; ˋdɑləmaıt] ***n.*** 【矿】白云石,白云岩。***the D-***(意大利东北部的)白云石山脉。**D- Alps** = the Dolomites. ~ **marble**【矿】粗粒白云石。**-mit·ic** [-ˈmitik; -ˋmıtık] ***a.*** 含白云石的。

do·lour, do·lor [ˈdəulə; ˋdolɚ] ***n.*** 〔诗〕悲哀,忧伤。***the*** ~***s of Mary*** 【宗】圣母玛利亚的悲哀。**dol·or·ous** [ˈdɔlərəs; ˋdɑlərəs] ***a.*** 〔诗〕(令人)忧伤的,(令人)悲哀的(*a dolorous melody* 感伤的曲调。*dolorous news* 令人悲哀的消息)。

dol·phin [ˈdɔlfin; ˋdɑlfın] ***n.*** 1.【动】海豚;海豚科动物。2.(码头的)系船柱;系船浮标。3.〔the D-〕【天】海豚座〔又作 Delphinus〕;〔俚〕= the Dorado.

dol·phin·ar·i·um [ˌdɔlfiˈnɛəriəm; ˏdɑlfıˋnɛrıəm] ***n.*** 海豚馆。

dolt [dəult; dolt] ***n.*** 呆子,笨蛋,傻瓜。

dolt·ish [ˈdəultiʃ; ˋdoltıʃ] ***a.*** 愚钝的,呆笨的。**-ly** ***ad.*** **-ness** ***n.***

do·lus [ˈdəuləs; ˋdoləs] ***n.*** 【法】恶意欺诈〔大陆法用语〕。*One is liable for* ~ *resulting in damages*. 一个人要对恶意欺诈造成的损害负法律责任。

DOM 〔美〕DOM 幻觉剂(= STP)。

Dom [dɔm; dɑm] ***n.*** 1. 阁下〔天主教高级修道士和圣职人员的尊称〕。2. = Don〔巴西,葡萄牙贵人名前的尊称〕。

dom. = 1. domain. 2. domestic. 3. dominion.

-dom *suf*. 1. 地位,职位;领域:earl*dom*, duke*dom*, king*dom*. 2. 状态,性质:wis*dom*, free*dom*. 3. 集团,界,派:official*dom*, Christen*dom*.

do·main [dəuˈmein; doˋmen] ***n.*** 1. 领土,版图;领地。2. 管区,势力圈;(特定动物等的)生长圈;(学问、活动等的)领域,范围;【物】磁区,畴;【数】域;整环。3. 产业,房地产;【法】土地[产业]所有权。4.【计】域名(= ~ name)。*the* ~ *of Great Britain* 英国的版图。*the* ~ *of science* 科学领域。*Geography is not within my* ~. 地理不是我的专长。*We enter the* ~ *of the pine trees*. 我们进入了松树生长带。***be out of one's*** ~ 非其所长。~ ***of use*** 【法】地上权。***eminent*** ~【法】(国家对一切产业的)支配权,征用权。~ **name**【计】域名。~ **theory**

【物】磁畴说。**-al, -ni·al** [də'meiniəl; də`menɪəl] ***a***. **1.** 属于某一领地[领域]的。**2.** 拥有领地的。

do·mal ['dəuml; `doml] ***a***.【语】卷舌的。

dome [dəum; dom] **I** ***n***. **1.** 圆屋顶,圆盖,窟窿;丘;【机】钟形汽室;【化】(蒸馏釜的)拱顶。**2.** 〔诗〕高楼,大厦,大教堂,殿宇。**3.** 〔美俚〕脑袋,头;狗的额头;油库。**4.**【地】穹地,穹丘;【化】(结晶的)坡面。*the great ~ of the sky* 广阔无垠的苍穹。*the ~ formed by the tree's branches* 树枝构成的圆顶。*that big ~ of yours* 〔俚〕你那个大脑袋。**II** ***vt***. **1.** 在…上加圆顶。**2.** 使成钟形;使呈穹状凸起。—***vi***. 成圆顶状,成穹状凸起。*His forehead ~d out in a curve*. 他的前额呈弯曲的半球形。~ **car** (装有玻璃圆顶供旅客观看沿途风景用的)圆顶游览车厢。**-d** ***a***. 圆顶的,圆盖形的,半球形的 (*a ~d roof* 圆形屋顶)。**-like** ***a***. 穹顶的。

Do·mes·day Book ['du:mzdei buk; `dumzde bʊk]【英史】(1086 年英王威廉一世颁布的)土地调查清册。

do·mes·tic [də'mestik; də`mɛstɪk] **I** ***a***. **1.** 家的,家里的,家庭的。**2.** 国内的,本国的,对内的。**3.** 热心家务的,不喜外出的;会持家的。**4.** 家养的,养驯了的 (*opp*. *wild*)。**5.** 自己制造的;国产的。~ *affairs* 家事;内政。~ *animals* 家畜。~ *economy* 家庭经济,家政。~ *life* 家庭生活。~ *expenses* 家用。*a ~ fowl* 家禽,鸡。*a ~ woman* 只关心家务事的女人,家庭妇女。~ *science* 家政学。~ *soap* 家用肥皂,洗衣皂。~ *loan* 内债。~ *mail* 国内邮件。~ *partner* (合资企业中的)国内合伙人,所在国合伙人;性伙伴,同居男女的一方。~ *violence* 家庭(内部的)暴力(行为)。~ *products* [*goods*] 国货,国产。~ *trade* 国内贸易。**II** ***n***. **1.** 家仆,佣人。**2.** 〔美〕〔*pl*.〕国货,本国产品。**3.** 家用织物。**-ti·ca·ble** ***a***. **1.** 易[可]养驯的;(植物)可移植的。**2.** 习于家居的。**-ti·cal·ly** ***ad***. 家庭式地,在家事上,适合家庭[国内]地。

do·mes·ti·cate [də'mestikeit; də`mɛstəket] ***vt***. **1.** 养乖,养驯(动物等);培养(野生植物)。**2.** 使喜爱家庭;使爱做家务。**3.** 使归化;使(移民等)服水土。**4.** 引入(国外习俗等)。**5.** 使受教化。~*d plants* 栽培植物。*Cats were ~d by the Egyptians*. 猫是由埃及人养驯的。~ *foreign customs* 引入外国习俗。—***vi***. **1.** (动物等)驯化。**2.** 喜爱家庭,喜爱做家务。**-ca·tion** [-'keiʃən; -`keʃən] ***n***. **-ca·tor** ***n***. **1.** 驯养者,驯化者。**2.** 使归化者。

do·mes·tic·i·ty [ˌdəumes'tisiti; ˏdomes`tɪsətɪ] ***n***. **1.** 对家庭生活的爱好,爱操持家务;深居简出。**2.** 家庭乐趣,家庭生活。**3.** 〔*pl*.〕家事,家务。*the domesticities* 家事,家务;家风。

Dom·ett ['dɔmit; `dɑmɪt] ***n***. 多米特〔姓氏〕。

dom·ic, dom·i·c(al) ['dəumik(əl); `domək(l̩)] ***a***. 圆顶式;有圆顶的。**-al·ly** ***ad***.

dom·i·cile ['dɔmisail; `dɑməsl] **I** ***n***. **1.** 住处,住所。**2.**【法】本籍,原籍。**3.**【商】期票支付场所。*a regular ~* 固定住所。~ *by birth* 原籍,出生地。~ *of choice*【法】选择居留地。~ *of origin* 原籍。**II** ***vt***. **1.** 决定(某人)住处,使定居。**2.** 指定(期票的)支付场所。*be ~d in* [*at*] 在(某处)住下来。~ *oneself* 定居下来。— ***vi***. 定居,安家。*I temporarily ~d with my aunt*. 我暂时和婶母住在一起。**-d** ***a***. **1.** (期票)指定支付地点的。**2.** 定居的。

dom·i·cil·i·ar·y [ˌdɔmi'siljəri; ˏdɑmə`sɪlɪˏɛrɪ] ***a***. **1.** 住处的,住所的。**2.** 户籍的。*a ~ register* 户籍。*a ~ visit* [*search*]【法】搜查住宅。

dom·i·cil·i·ate [ˌdɔmi'silieit; ˏdɑmə`sɪlɪˏet] ***vt***., ***vi***. = domicile. **-a·tion** ***n***.

dom·i·nance, dom·i·nan·cy ['dɔminəns, -si; `dɑmənəns, -sɪ] ***n***. **1.** 权势;统治,控制,支配。**2.** 优势,优越。**3.**【生】显性,优势度。*come under the ~ of* 沦于…的统治之下。

dom·i·nant ['dɔminənt; `dɑmənənt] **I** ***a***. **1.** 支配的,统治的;有权威的。**2.** 最有力的,占优势的;主要的;突出的,超群出众的。**3.** 居高临下的,高耸的。**4.**【生】显性的,优势的(*opp*. recessive);【乐】第五音的,属音的。*be in the ~ position* 居于支配地位。*the ~ party* 第一大党,多数党。*Writing has become his ~ interest*. 写作已成为他的主要兴趣。*a ~ mountain peak* 主峰。*the ~ chord*【乐】属和音。*the ~ chord of the ninth*【乐】第九属和音。**II** ***n***. **1.** 主因,要素,主要的人[物]。**2.**【生】显性性状;显性基因;优势种;【乐】全阶第五音,属音。~ **character**【生】显性性状。~ **mutant**【生】显性突变型[体]。~ **sex** 〔美俚〕女性。~ **tenement** [**estate**] ***n***.【法】承役地。

dom·i·nate ['dɔmineit; `dɑməˏnet] ***vt***. **1.** 把持,操纵,支配,统治;左右,控制。**2.** 优于,超出。**3.** 高出,俯视。~ *a country commercially* 控制一国的商业。*Dahlias ~ the garden*. 园子里开的大多都是大丽花。~ *one's passions* 抑制欲望。~*d by greedy egoism* 为贪婪的私欲所左右。~ *the conversation* 滔滔不绝地谈,不容他人插嘴。*The city is ~d by the castle*. 古堡俯视着城市。*a dominating position*【军】制高点。—***vi***. **1.** 有统治权力,居于支配地位;占优势 (*over*)。**2.** 巍然在上;高耸 (*over*)。*the castle dominating over the river* 高耸于河边的古堡。

dom·i·na·tion [ˌdɔmi'neiʃən; dɑmə`neʃən] ***n***. **1.** 把持,操纵,支配,统治;优势。**2.**【生】显性化。**3.** 〔*pl*.〕【宗】主天使〔天使分九阶三级三队,中级三队为主天使〕。*world ~* 世界霸权。*fall under the ~ of* 沦于…的支配[统治]之下。*the maternal ~* 母权统治。*the French ~ of the cinema* 法国在电影业中的优势地位。

dom·i·na·tive ['dɔmineitiv; `dɑməˏnetɪv] ***a***. 支配的,占优势的。

dom·i·na·tor ['dɔmineitə; `dɑməˏnetɚ] ***n***. **1.** 支配者,统治者;占优势者。**2.** 支配力,统治力。

dom·i·neer [ˌdɔmi'niə; ˏdɑmə`nɪr] ***vi***. **1.** 擅权,跋扈,作威作福 (*over*)。**2.** 高耸 (*over*)。~ *over one's inferiors* 对下级盛气凌人。—***vt***. **1.** 对…飞扬跋扈;对…盛气凌人。**2.** 高耸于…之上。~*ed by one's wife* 怕老婆,惧内。*The castle ~s the town*. 古堡高耸于城市之上。**-ing** ***a***. 盛气凌人的,飞扬跋扈的。

Dom·i·ni·ca [ˌdɔmi'ni:kə; ˏdɑmə`nikə] ***n***. 多米尼加(岛)〔西印度群岛〕。

do·min·i·cal [də'minikəl; də`mɪnɪkəl] ***a***.【宗】**1.** 主的,基督的。**2.** 主日的,星期日的。*the ~ prayer* 主祷文。*the ~ day* 星期日,主日。*the ~ year* 公元,公历。***the ~ letter*** 主日文字〔教会历上表示一月第一个星期日用的 A, B, C, D, E, F, G 七个字母,如某年一月一日是星期日,该年的主日字母即为 A; 一月二日为星期日,该年主日字母即为 B; 余类推〕。

Do·min·i·can[1] [də'minikən; də`mɪnɪkən] **I** ***a***.【天主】多明我会的。*the ~ Order*【宗】多明我会。**II** ***n***. 多明我会修道士。

Do·min·i·can[2] [də'minikən; də`mɪnɪkən] **I** ***a***. 多米尼加共和国的。**II** ***n***. 多米尼加共和国人。***the ~ Republic*** 多米尼加共和国〔拉丁美洲〕。

Dom·i·nic(k) ['dɔminik; `dɑmɪnɪk] ***n***. 多米尼克〔男子名〕。

Dom·i·nick ['dɔminik; `dɑmənɪk] ***n***.【动】= dominique[2].

dom·i·nie ['dɔmini; `dɑmənɪ] ***n***. **1.** 〔Scot.〕教员,老师。**2.** ['dəumini; `domɪnɪ] 〔美〕(荷兰改革派教会的)牧师;教士。

do·min·ion [də'minjən; də`mɪnjən] ***n***. **1.** 统治权,主权,支配;管辖 (*over*);【法】所有权。**2.** 〔常 *pl*.〕疆土,领土,版图;领地。**3.** 〔D-〕(英帝国的)自治领;加拿大。*have* [*hold*, *exercise*] *~ over* 具有对…的支配权,对…使行使统治权。*the overseas ~s* 海外领地。***D- Day*** 加拿大自治纪念日〔七月一日〕。***D- of Canada*** 加拿大

自治领〔俗简称 the D-〕。***D- Parliament*** 加拿大议会。***the Old D-*** 〔美〕Virginia 州的通称。

Dom·i·nique[1] [ˈdɔmiːk; ˌdɑməˋnik] ***n.*** 多米尼克(女子名)〔又作 Dominica〕。

Dom·i·nique[2] [ˈdɔmiːk; ˋdɑməˌnik] ***n.*** 【动】美国多米尼克肉卵兼用鸡。

do·min·i·um [dəˈminiəm; dəˋmɪnɪəm] ***n.*** 【法】所有权。

dom·i·no[1] [ˈdɔminəu; ˋdɑməˌno] ***n.*** (*pl.* ~*es*, ~*s*) **1.** 带有假面具的化装舞衣;(蒙住眼睛和部分面孔的)黑色假面具。**2.** 穿戴假面具化装舞衣的人。

dom·i·no[2] [ˈdɔminəu; ˋdɑməno] **I** ***n.*** 〔*pl.*〕**1.** 多米诺骨牌;多米诺牌戏。**2.** 〔*pl.*〕〔美俚〕牙齿。**3.** 〔俚〕打倒人的一击。*play* ~*s* 玩多米诺骨牌。***It's all ~ with*** (*sb.*). 〔俚〕(某人)完蛋了。**II** ***int.*** 不行! ~ **effect** 多米诺(骨牌)效应,一倒百倒,连锁效应。~ **theory** 多米诺(骨牌)理论〔指一国崩溃,其他邻国就会相继垮台的政治局面〕。

Do·mi·nus [ˈdəumiːnus, ˈdɔminəs; ˋdominʊs, ˋdɑmɪnəs] ***n.*** 〔L.〕上帝,主。

Dominus vo·bis·cum [vəuˈbiskum; voˋbɪskʊm] 〔L.〕上帝与你同在,上帝保佑你。

dom·sat [ˈdɔmˌsæt; ˋdɑmˌsæt] ***n.*** 国内通信卫星(= domestic satellite)。

Don[1] [dɔn; dɑn] ***n.*** 唐〔人名, Donald 的昵称〕。

Don[2] [dɔn; dɑn] ***n.*** 〔the ~〕顿河〔欧洲〕。

don[1] [dɔn; dɑn] ***vt.*** (**-nn-**) 〔书〕穿(衣),披(衣),戴(帽)(*opp.* doff)。~ *one's clothes* 穿上衣服。*Rioters ~ned handkerchiefs as gas masks.* 暴乱者扎上手帕捂住口鼻作为防毒面具。~ ***the spikes*** 〔美俚〕参加棒球比赛。

don[2] [dɔn; dɑn] ***n.*** 〔Sp.〕**1.** 〔D-〕唐〔意为"先生","阁下",西班牙人用在人名前的尊称〕。**2.** 西班牙贵族,绅士;(一般)西班牙人。**3.** 〔古〕大人物;〔俚〕名人,名家;专家(*at*)。**4.** (英大学尤指剑桥、牛津大学的)导师;特别研究员。*a ~ at cricket* 板球名手。**D- Juan** [dɔn ˈdʒuːən, Sp. don ˋhwɑːn; dɑnˋdʒuən, Sp. donˋhwɑn] **1.** 唐璜〔西班牙传说中的风流贵族〕;风流荡子。**2.** 英国诗人拜伦一部长诗的题目。

do·ña [ˈdəunjə; ˋdonjə] ***n.*** 〔Sp.〕**1.** 〔D-〕夫人,太太〔加在人名前的尊称〕。**2.** 西班牙女人。

do·na(h) [ˈdəunə; ˋdonə] ***n.*** 〔Pg.〕**1.** 〔D-〕太太,夫人〔加在人名前的尊称〕。**2.** 葡萄牙女人;〔英俚〕女人;情妇。

Don·ald [ˈdɔnəld; ˋdɑnəld] ***n.*** 唐纳德〔男子名〕。

Do·nar [ˈdəunə; ˋdonɚ] ***n.*** (日尔曼神话中的)雷神〔相当于北欧神话中的 Thor〕。

do·nate [dəuˈneit; ˋdonet] ***vt.*** 〔美〕捐赠,捐献;赠给,送。~ *blood to a blood bank* 向血库捐血。~ *1,000 dollars to an orphanage* 向孤儿院捐赠 1,000 美元。— ***vi.*** 捐赠,捐献(*to*; *towards*)。*They used to ~ to the Red Cross every year.* 他们每年捐钱给红十字会。

do·na·tion [dəuˈneiʃən; doˋneʃən] ***n.*** **1.** 捐赠,赠送,捐献。**2.** 捐赠物,赠品;捐款。*a blood ~* 捐血。*make* [*give*] a ~ 捐赠。*make ~s to the calamity fund* 为救灾基金捐款。

Don·a·tist [ˈdɔnətist; ˋdɑnətɪst] ***n.*** 多纳特斯教派〔四世纪北非的一个基督教派〕教友。**Don·a·tism** ***n.*** 多纳特斯派教义。

don·a·tive [ˈdəunətiv; ˋdonətɪv] **I** ***a.*** **1.** 赠与的,捐赠的。**2.** 【教会史】(圣职)直接授与的。*a ~ trust* 捐款托管。**II** ***n.*** 捐赠物;捐款。

do·na·tor [dəuˈneitə; ˋdonetɚ] ***n.*** **1.** 捐赠者,捐款人。**2.** 【化】= donor.

Don·bas(s) [dɔnˈbɑːs, ˈdɔnˌbɑːs; dɑnˋbas, ˋdɑnˌbas] ***n.*** 顿巴斯〔乌克兰煤田〕。

done [dʌn; dʌn] **I** do[1] 的过去分词。**II** ***a.*** **1.** 已完成的,完毕了的。**2.** 疲倦极了的,精疲力尽的。**3.** 烧熟了的〔通例用作复合词〕。**4.** 受了骗的;吃了亏的,负了伤的。**4.** 注定要完蛋的。**5.** 符合礼仪的,(趣味等)时行的,合时的。*Our work is ~.* 我们的工作做完了。*What ~ is ~.* 木已成舟。*half-~* 半熟的。*over-~* 煮得[烧得]过火的。*under ~* 煮得[烧得]夹生的。*The fish is ~.* 鱼烧好了。*too ~ to go any further* 累得不能再走了。*It isn't ~.* 这样做是失礼的,那已经不时行了。**III** ***ad.*** 〔美俚〕已经。***be ~ brown*** **1.** 烧成焦色。**2.** 上大当,受骗。***be ~ for*** **1.** 筋疲力竭。**2.** 身败名裂。**3.** 不行了,完了(*Three days without water and a man is ~ for.* 三天不喝水,人就完了)。***be ~ to the wide, be ~ up*** [***in***] 筋疲力尽,累透了。***Easier said than ~.*** 做比说难,说起来容易做起来难。***No sooner said than ~.*** 一说就做,说到做到。***D-!*** 好! 赞成! ***Well ~!*** 干得好! ***What's ~ cannot be undone.*** 事已定局,无可挽回;覆水难收。**-ness** ***n.*** 煮熟的程度。

do·nee [dəuˈniː; ˌdoˋni] ***n.*** 【法】受赠人(*opp.* donor)。

dong[1] [dɔŋ, dɔŋ; dɔŋ, dɑŋ] **I** ***n.*** (钟等的)当当声。**II** ***vi.*** (钟等)当当响。

dong[2] [dɔ(ː)ŋ; dɔŋ, dɑŋ] ***n.*** 盾〔越南货币单位〕。

don·ga [ˈdɔŋgə; ˋdɑŋgə] ***n.*** (非洲南部等的)小峡谷,山峡。

don·jon [ˈdɔndʒən; ˋdʌndʒən] ***n.*** (城堡)主楼,主塔〔dungeon 的古拼法〕。

don·key [ˈdɔŋki; ˋdɑŋki] **I** ***n.*** **1.** 驴子。**2.** 傻瓜;蠢驴;顽固的人。**3.** 〔美俚〕拖拉机。**4.** 〔美〕(1874 年以后)民主党的象征。(*as*) *stubborn* [*stupid*] *as a ~* 驴子般顽梗[愚蠢]的。**II** ***a.*** 【机】辅助的。*a ~ boiler* [*pump*] 辅助锅炉[泵]。*a ~ engine* 辅助机车;辅助发动机。~***'s years*** 〔口〕很长时期(*I haven't seen him for ~'s years.* 我好久没有看到他了)。***talk the hind leg off a ~*** 讲个不停。~ **act** 〔美俚〕蠢举,失策。~ **boiler** 辅助锅炉。~ **boy** **1.** 驴车夫。**2.** 轻便发动机操作者。~ **engine** 辅助发动机;轻便机车。~ **jacket** 女式防风厚上衣。~**man** 辅助发动机管理工。~ **pump** 辅助泵。~**'s breakfast** 〔美俚〕草垫。~**'s years** 很久,很长的时间。~**-work** 苦活;单调的日常工作。

Don·na [ˈdɔnə; ˋdɑnə] ***n.*** 唐娜〔女子名〕。

don·na [ˈdɔnə; ˋdɑnə] ***n.*** (*pl.* ***don·ne*** [ˈdɔni; ˋdɔnɪ]) 〔It.〕**1.** 〔D-〕夫人,女士〔加在已婚妇女名前的尊称〕。**2.** 意大利女子。

Don·ne [dʌn, dɔn; dʌn, dɑn] ***n.*** 多恩〔姓氏〕。

don·née [dɔːˈnei; dɔˋne] ***n.*** 〔F.〕(小说、戏剧等的)基本思想;(形成行动的)基本环境。

don·nered, don·nard [ˈdɔnəd; ˋdɑnɚd] ***a.*** 〔Scot.〕**1.** 眼花的,耀眼的。**2.** 迷乱的,茫然的。

don·nish [ˈdɔniʃ; ˋdɑnɪʃ] ***a.*** **1.** (英国)大学学监的,大学教师的。**2.** 卖弄学问的,学究式的。**-ly** ***ad.*** **-ness** ***n.***

don·ny·brook [ˈdɔnibruk; ˋdɑnɪbrʊk] ***n.*** 乱哄哄的争论,瞎吵,胡吵乱闹。*He was a center of a political ~.* 他是政治论战的中心人物。**D- Fair** 往时爱尔兰都柏林(Dublin)地区顿妮溪每年一次以酒色、赌斗著名的集市;扰嚷吵闹的地方。

do·nor [ˈdəunə; ˋdonɚ] ***n.*** **1.** 赠送人,捐款人。**2.** 【生】移植体;【物】施主;【化】给予体,供体;【医】供血者,输血者,(移植术中)皮肤[组织]供给者。**3.** 【法】(财产归属的)指定权。*a universal ~* 全适型供血者。*a skin ~* 捐皮者,供给皮肤者。*the ~ area* 【医】移植区。~ **egg** (人工受精中取自一妇女再植入另一妇女子宫内的)供体卵。

do·noth·ing [ˈduːˌnʌθiŋ; ˋduˌnʌθɪŋ] **I** ***a.*** **1.** 游手好闲的,什么也不做的,懒惰的。**2.** 无所作为的,无为主义的。**II** ***n.*** 懒鬼,饭桶。**-ism** ***n.*** **1.** 懒惰习性。**2.** (不愿打破现状的)无为主义。

Do·no·van [ˈdɔnəvən; ˋdɑnəvən] ***n.*** 多诺万〔姓氏,男子名〕。

Don Quix·ote [dɔnˈkwiksət; dɑnˋkwɪksət] ***n.*** **1.** 唐·吉诃德〔西班牙作家塞万提斯(Gervantes)所著同名小说

及其主人翁〕。2. 唐吉诃德式的人物,充满幻想的理想主义者。

don't [dəunt; dont] **I** = do not;〔卑,美方〕= does not. *Oh,* ~! 哎,不可以! 不行! *You know that,* ~ *you?* 你是知道的(是不是)。**II** *n*.〔谑〕禁止;〔*pl*.〕禁止事项。*a long list of* ~*s* 一长串禁止事项。~**-know** *n*. 未作决定的人;未定的事;未作决定的投票人;未定的选票。

do·nut [ˈdəuˌnʌt; ˋdoˏnʌt] *n*. = doughnut.

doo·dad, do·dad [ˈduːdæd; ˋdudæd] *n*.〔美俚〕装饰品;小玩意;花哨而不值钱的东西。*a kitchen full of the latest* ~*s* 满是新玩意[新装置]的厨房。

doo·dah [ˈduːdə; ˋdudə] *n*.〔俚〕激动,惊慌。*all of a* ~ 非常激动。

doo·dle[1] [ˈduːdl; ˋdudl̩] *n*.〔英口〕"V"型飞弹 (= buzz bomb)。

doo·dle[2] [ˈduːdl; ˋdudl̩] **I** *vi*. 1. 心不在焉地乱写乱画。2.〔美口〕漫不经心地弹奏。*He* ~*d during the whole lecture*. 他一整节课都在胡写乱画。—*vt*.〔方〕欺骗。**II** *n*. 1. 乱写乱画。2.〔美口〕傻瓜;吊儿郎当的人。

doo·dle[3] [ˈduːdl; ˋdudl̩] *n*. = doodlebug.

doo·dle·bug [ˈduːdlbʌg; ˋdudl̩ˏbʌg] *n*. 1.〔美方〕蚁狮〔一种蚁蛉科昆虫蛟蜻蛉的幼虫〕。2.〔古时用迷信方式探测地下矿产、水源等的〕风水卜杖。3.〔英口〕"V"型飞弹 (= buzz bomb)。4.〔军俚〕侦察车,战车。

doo·fun·ny, doo·hick·ey, doo·hi·ckus [ˈduːfʌni, ˈduːˌhiki, ˈduːˌhikəs; ˋdufʌnɪ, ˋduˏhɪkɪ, ˋduˏhɪkəs] *n*. = dofunny.

doo·lie[1], **doo·ly** [ˈduːli; ˋdulɪ] *n*.〔印〕轿子;轿式担架。

doo·lie[2] [ˈduːli; ˋdulɪ] *n*.〔口〕(美国)空军学院一年级生。

doom [duːm; dum] **I** *n*. 1. 命运;恶运;劫数;毁灭,死亡。2.【史】法令。3.〔古〕(不利的)判决,宣判。4.【宗】末日审判。*His* ~ *is sealed*. 他注定要遭恶运了,他已经在劫难逃了。*a sign of* ~ *and decay* 衰亡的征兆。*pass* [*pronounce*] ~ *of death on* [*upon*] *an offender* 判处罪犯死刑。***fall to*** [***go to, meet***] ***one's*** ~ 死,灭亡。~ ***and gloom*** 前景暗淡。***the day of*** ~ = doomsday. ***till the crack of*** ~ 直到世界末日。**II** *vt*. 1. 注定,命定。2. 判决,决定(命运等)。*be* ~*ed to failure* 注定要失败。*a* ~*ed vessel* 失事船,正在沉没中的船。~ *sb. to life imprisonment* 判处某人无期徒刑。~ *sb.'s penal servitude* 判某人服劳役。~ **palm**【植】埃及姜果棕。

dooms·day [ˈduːmzdei; ˋdumzˏde] *n*.【宗】最后的审判日,世界末日;〔古〕判决日。***till*** ~ 永远,直到世界末日。**D- Book** = Domesday Book. **D- Machine** 末日机器〔幻想中的一种能触发核武器毁灭世界而无人能加以阻止的机器〕。

door [dɔː, dɔə; dor, dɔr] *n*. 1. 门,户。2. 入口,门口;通道,门径,门路,关口。3. 一户,一家。4.【船、机】盖,口。*the front* [*back*] ~ 正[后]门。*a street* ~ 临街大门。*shut the* ~ *behind* [*after*] *him* 把他身后的门关上。*Mind the* ~! 注意门户! *Is the* ~ *to?* 是从这道门走吗? *three* ~*s off* 前面第三家。*next* ~ 隔壁。*live next* ~ *but one* 住在隔壁第二家。*a* ~ *to success* 成功之道。*the* ~ *to learning* 治学之道,学习的门径。*a manhole* ~【船】入孔盖,检修孔。***answer*** [***go to***] ***the*** ~ 应门,去开门(迎客)。***at death's*** ~ 命在旦夕,处在死亡边缘 (*She remained at death's* ~ *for weeks*. 她的生命好几个星期处在危险状态)。***at the*** ~ 1. 在门口,在入口处。2. 快,即将 (*stand at the* ~ 站在门口。*It's at our* ~*s*. 问题迫在眉睫,时间很紧迫)。***behind closed*** ~***s*** 秘密,私下,暗中 (*Family quarrels must be settled behind closed* ~*s*. 家丑不可外扬,家庭争端必须私下解决)。***close the*** ~ ***to*** 关上…的大门,使…成为不可能 (*His selfishness closes the* ~ *to our reconciliation*. 他的自私关上了我们和解的大门)。***close*** [***shut***] ***the*** ~ ***upon*** [***on***] 1. 把…拒于门外。2. 把…的门堵死 (*close the* ~ *upon all peddlers* 堵上门禁止通行。*The incident closed the* ~ *upon his promotion*. 这次事故使他不可能晋升了)。***darken the*** ~ 闯入。***from*** ~ ***to*** ~ 挨户,家家。***in*** ~***s*** 在家内,在屋内。***keep open*** ~***s*** 好客,款待客人。***lay*** (***blame***) ***at sb.'s*** ~ = ***lay*** (***blame***) ***at the*** ~ ***of sb***. 把(责任等)归咎于(*The blame of delinquency may be laid at the* ~ *of careless parents*. 少年犯罪可能要归咎于父母的放纵)。***lie at sb.'s*** ~ = ***lie at the*** ~ ***of*** (过失等)是某人造成的 (*One's mistakes generally lie at one's own* ~. 一个人犯错误多半是自己造成的)。***next*** ~ ***to*** 1. 邻接,在…的隔壁。2. 很像,几乎 (*Who lives next* ~ *to you?* 你的邻居是谁? *It costs you next* ~ *to nothing*. 这几乎不要你花钱)。***open a*** [***the***] ~ ***to*** [***for***] 欢迎,使…成为可能,向…开门,给…方便。***out of*** ~***s*** 在户外;在外,不在(家)。***point to the*** ~ 下逐客令。***put*** [***set***] ***sb. to the*** ~ 解聘,赶走。***see sb. to the*** ~ 送(客)。***show sb. the*** ~ 驱逐,撵走某人。***throw open the*** ~ ***to*** 对…敞开门户。***turn sb. out of*** ~***s*** 把某人撵出门外。***with closed*** ~***s*** 不公开地,秘密;独自。***with open*** ~***s*** 公开。***within*** ~***s*** 在屋内,在家里。***without*** ~***s*** 在户外。~ **alarm** [**bell**] 门铃。~**case** [**frame**] 门框。~ **chain** 门链〔使门只开一定宽度的防盗装置〕。~ **check** [**closer**] 自动闭门装置。~**-hinge** 门铰链。~ **holder** 门开后固定门扉的装置。~**keeper** 门警,门房。~**-key child** (父母整天都不在家的)带钥匙的孩子。~ **knob** 球形门把手。~**man** 看门人。~**mat** 1. (门口的)擦鞋棕垫。2.〔喻〕逆来顺受的人,被人欺侮的人 (*He's no* ~. 他可不是那种逆来顺受的人)。~ **money** 入场费。~**nail** 门上饰钉 (*as dead as a* ~*nail* 死定了)。~ **opener** 1. (消防队员用的)开门器。2. 推销员赠送的廉价礼物。~ **opening** 入口。~**plate** 门牌。~**post**【建】门柱。~**sill**【建】门槛。~**step** 1. 门阶。2. *vi*. & *vt*. (为推销、竞选等)挨户登门访问。~**stone** 门口铺石。~**stop** 1. 门垫〔防止门猛烈撞上的垫片〕。2. 制门器〔使门只开一定宽度的装置〕。~**-to-**~ 1. *a*. 挨门逐户的;(货物由发货场)直送用户的。2. *adv*. 挨户;送货上门地。~**way** 门口,出入口,〔喻〕入门 (*a doorway to success* 成功之道)。~**yard**〔美〕门前庭院。**-ed** *a*. 有门的。**-less** *a*. 没有门的。**-wards** *ad*. 向着房门。

doo·zer, doo·zy [ˈduːzə, ˈduːzi; ˋduzə, ˋduzɪ] *n*.〔美俚〕非常出色的人[东西]。

DOP = developing-out paper【摄】显像纸。

do·pa·mine [ˈdəupəˌmiːn; ˋdopəˏmin] *n*.【乐】多巴胺,多巴宁〔一种治脑神经病的药物〕。

dop·ant [ˈdəupənt; ˋdopənt] *n*.【物】掺杂剂,掺杂物。

dope [dəup; dop] **I** *n*. 1. 浓液,黏稠物,胶状物;【空】(涂机翼的)明胶,涂布油;浆料;〔美俚〕显影液。2.〔俚〕麻醉品,安眠药〔鸦片等〕;〔俚〕(赛马前给马服用的)兴奋剂;常服麻醉品的人,吸毒者。3. (制造炸药等用的)吸收剂,添加剂,填料〔锯屑等〕;(掺入汽油等的)防爆剂。4.〔美俚〕(加在冰淇淋上的)香汁[浇头],(任何)食品;〔美南部〕(没有酒精成份的)饮料〔尤指可口可乐〕。5.〔美俚〕(赛马成绩等的)预测,情报,内部消息,(给新闻记者的)特别情报[消息]。6.〔美俚〕傻子,笨蛋。7. 汽油。*a* ~*-peddler* 毒品贩子。*He could not sleep without* ~. 他不吃安眠药就睡不着觉。*Slip me the inside* ~. 给我透露一点内部消息。*have a* ~ *habit* 吸毒上瘾。*upset the* ~ 预测完全不对。*fire-proof* ~ 耐火涂料。**II** *vt*. 1. 在…上涂浓液;在…上涂明胶。2. 给(人等)吃麻醉品;偷偷给(马等)服兴奋剂;〔俚〕欺骗,麻痹。3.〔美俚〕(在饮料内)加酒精;(给发动机)上汽油;给(炸药等)加填料;【物】给(半导体)掺杂质。4.〔美俚〕预测(赛马等的结果)。5. 解(题)。~*d chemical*【物】掺杂元素。~*d fabric* 涂漆蒙布。~*d fuel* 加防爆剂的汽油。~*d glass* 掺杂玻璃。~ ***off***〔俚〕睡熟;昏昏沉沉。~ ***out*** 1. 解出

(谜等)。2.〔美俚〕预测;想出(方法等);拟出(计划等)。~ *addict* 吸毒成瘾者。~ **fiend**〔俚〕瘾君子,吸毒者。~ **room** 喷漆间。~**sheet**〔美俚〕比赛结果预测,(赛马的)内情简报。~ **shop**【空】上胶场。~ **story**(说明某一事实的背景、意义等的)辅助性报告。~ **transistor**【物】掺杂(质)晶体管。

dope·ster [ˈdəupstə; ˋdopstɚ] *n*.〔美俚〕(选举、赛马结果等的)预测家,内部消息供给人。*a political* ~ 政治行情预测家。

dope·y, dopy [ˈdəupi; ˋdopɪ] *a*.〔美俚〕1. 傻,笨,呆;迟钝的。2.(因经常服用麻醉品等而)昏昏沉沉的。

dop·pel·gäng·er [ˈdɔpəlˌgæŋə; ˋdɔpəlˏgæŋɚ] *n*.〔G.〕(迷信者认为存在的)活人的魂魄。

dopp·ler·ite [ˈdɔplərait; ˋdɑplərаɪt] *n*. 弹性沥青,橡皮沥青。

dor [dɔ:; dɔr] *n*. 1.【昆】欧洲粪金龟子(= ~beetle)。2. 飞时发嗡嗡声的昆虫。~**hawk**〔英方〕【动】欧洲夜莺,蚊母鸟。

Do·ra[1] [ˈdɔ:rə; ˋdɔrə] *n*. 多拉〔女子名, Dorothea 和 Theodora 的昵称〕。

Do·ra[2] [ˈdɔ:rə; ˋdɔrə], **D.O.R.A.**〔英〕(1914 年的)领土防御法(= the Defence of the Realm Act)。

do·ra·do [dəˈrɑ:dəu; dəˋrɑdo] *n*. 1.【动】鳍鳅。2.〔the D-〕【天】南剑鱼座。

Do·reen, Do·rene [dɔ(:)ˈri:n, ˈdɔ:ri:n; dɔˋrin, ˋdɔrin] *n*. 多琳〔女子名〕。

do·re·mi [ˌdəureiˈmi:; ˋdoˋreˋmi] *n*.〔美俚〕钱。

Do·ri·an [ˈdɔ:riən; ˋdɔrɪən] **I** *n*. 多利安人〔古希腊人的一支,居住在伯罗奔尼撒半岛、克里特岛等地〕。**II** *a*. 多利安人的;淳朴的。

Dor·ic [ˈdɔrik; ˋdɔrɪk] **I** *a*. 1. 多利安人的。2.(口音)土音重的。3.【建】陶立克式的〔纯朴、古老的希腊建筑风格〕。*the* ~ *order*【建】陶立克式。**II** *n*. 1.(古希腊的)多利克方言。2.(英语)方言土腔(尤指苏格兰方言)。3.【建】陶立克式。*speak in broad* ~ 满口乡下土腔。

Dor·is[1] [ˈdɔris; ˋdɔrɪs] *n*. 多丽丝〔女子名〕。

Dor·is[2] *n*. 多利士〔古希腊中部地区〕。

Dor·king [ˈdɔ:kiŋ; ˋdɔrkɪŋ] *n*.(英国多津地方出产的)肉用种五趾鸡。

dorm [dɔ:m; dɔrm] *n*.〔美口〕宿舍(= dormitory)。

dor·man·cy [ˈdɔ:mənsi; ˋdɔrmənsɪ] *n*. 1. 睡眠(状态);冬眠,休眠。2. 潜伏,蛰伏,静止,休止。

dor·mant [ˈdɔ:mənt; ˋdɔrmənt] *a*. 1. 睡着的,处于睡眠状态的;冬眠的,蛰伏的,休眠的。2. 静止的,休止的;潜伏的;(才能等)潜在的;(资金等)没有利用的;(权利等)尚待争取的。*the* ~ *economy* 停滞的经济。*A long* ~ *memory stirred*. 长期潜藏着的记忆复活了。~ *rights* 有待争取的权利。*a* ~ *project* 有待实现的计划。*the girl's* ~ *talent* 这个女孩子潜在的才能。***lie*** ~ 潜伏着;休眠着;冬眠着,蛰伏着。~ **capital** 游资。~ **buds**【植】休眠芽,潜伏芽。~ **seeds**【植】休眠种子。~ **partner**【商】匿名合伙人。~ **tree**【建】梁,楣。~ **volcano** 休眠火山。~ **window** 屋顶窗。

dor·mer [ˈdɔ:mə; ˋdɔrmɚ] *n*.【建】屋顶窗,老虎窗(= ~ window)。

dor·mice [ˈdɔ:mais; ˋdɔrmaɪs] *n*. dormouse 的复数。

dor·mi·tive [ˈdɔ:mitiv; ˋdɔrmətɪv] **I** *a*. 安眠的。**II** *n*. 安眠药,麻醉药。

dor·mi·to·ry [ˈdɔ:mitri; ˋdɔrməˏtorɪ] *n*. 1.(学校等的)宿舍;集体寝室。2.(在市内工作的人的)郊外住宅区。*a* ~ *town* 市郊住宅区。~ *suburb*(市内工作的人的)郊外住宅区。*a prosperous* ~ *community* 繁荣的市郊住宅区。

dor·mo·bile [ˈdɔ:məˌbi:l; ˋdɔrməˏbil] *n*. 行卧两用汽车,露营汽车。

dor·mouse [ˈdɔ:maus; ˋdɔrmaʊs] *n*.(*pl*. ***dor·mice*** [ˈdɔ:mais; ˋdɔrmaɪs])【动】睡鼠;〔喻〕爱睡的人。

dor·my [ˈdɔ:mi; ˋdɔrmɪ] *a*.(高尔夫)占先对方的穴数与尚待将球击入的穴数相等的。

dor·nick[1] [ˈdɔ:nik; ˋdɔrnɪk] *n*. 1. 花缎、锦缎和其他装饰织物的统称。2.(比利时制)多尼克地毯。

dor·nick[2] [ˈdɔ:nik; ˋdɔrnɪk] *n*.(适于投掷的)小石块。

Dor·o·the·a [ˌdɔrəˈθi:ə; ˏdɔrəˋθiə] *n*. 多萝西亚〔女子名〕。

Dor·o·thy [ˈdɔrəθi; ˋdɑrəθɪ] *n*. 多萝西〔女子名〕。~ **bag**〔英〕束口女提包。

dorp [dɔ:p; dɔrp] *n*.〔废〕村子,小村庄。

Dorr [dɔ:; dɔr] *n*. 多尔〔姓氏〕。

dors- *comb.f*. 背,脊: *dors*ad.

dor·sad [ˈdɔ:ˌsæd; ˋdɔrsæd] *ad*.【解、动】(身体)背部地,向后部。

dor·sal[1] [ˈdɔ:səl; ˋdɔrsl] **I** *a*. 1.【解、动】背的,脊的。2.【植】远轴的。3.【语】舌背音的。~ *fin* 脊鳍。~ *muscles* 背肌。~ *vertebrae*【解】胸椎。**II** *n*.【语】舌背音。

dor·sal[2] [ˈdɔ:səl; ˋdɔrsl] *n*. = dossal.

Dor·set(shire) [ˈdɔ:sit(ʃiə); ˋdɔrsɪt(ʃɪr)] *n*. 多塞特(郡)〔英格兰南部一郡〕。~ **Horn** 多塞特细毛羊。

dorsi-, dorso- *comb.f*. = dors-.

dor·si·ven·tral [ˌdɔ:siˈventrəl; ˏdɔrsɪˋventrəl] *a*. = dorsoventral.

dor·so·ven·tral [ˌdɔ:səuˈventrəl; ˏdɔrsoˋventrəl] *a*. 1.【植】有背腹性的。2.【动】背腹的,背腹可区辨的(= dorsiventral)。

dor·sum [ˈdɔ:səm; ˋdɔrsəm] *n*.(*pl*. ***-sa*** [-sə; -sə])〔L.〕1.【解】背(部)。2. 背面。*the* ~ *of the hand* 手背。3.【动】后缘〔鳞翅目的翅〕。

Dort·mund [ˈdɔ:tmənd; ˋdɔrtmənd] *n*. 多特蒙德〔德国城市〕。

dort·y [ˈdɔ:ti; ˋdɔrtɪ] *a*.〔Scot.〕坏脾气的;不高兴的。

do·ry[1] [ˈdɔ:ri; ˋdorɪ] *n*.(北美东海岸渔船上配备的)平底小船。

do·ry[2] [ˈdɔ:ri; ˋdorɪ] *n*.【动】1. 海鲂(= John D-)。2. 黄麻鲈。

D.O.S.〔美〕= doctor of osteopathetic science 整骨医学博士。

dos-à-dos [dəuzəˈdəu; dozəˋdo] **I** *ad*.〔F.〕背对背地。**II** *n*.(*pl*. ~ [-dəuz; -doz]) 1. 背对背长椅[马车]。2.〔美〕背对背双人舞。

dos·age [ˈdəusidʒ; ˋdosɪdʒ] *n*. 1. 下药,配药。2. 剂,剂量,服用量。3.(酒的)增味剂;增味;配料。

dose [dəus; dos] **I** *n*. 1.(药的)一服,一剂;药量,剂量。2. 苦药,讨厌的东西。3.(酒中的)配料,增味剂。4.(处罚等)一回,一次,一番。5.〔美俚〕花柳病,梅毒。6.【物】放射[辐射]剂量。*a* ~ *of medicine* 一服药。*take medicine in small* ~*s* 按小剂量服药。*administer a* ~ 投药。*a* ~ *of flattery* 一番奉承。*administer* ~*s of punishment* 施行惩罚。*a hard* ~ *to swallow* 一服难咽的苦药。*a* ~ *of hard work* 一项苦差事。*the maximum* [*minimum*] ~ 最大[最小]用量。*a lethal* [*fatal*] ~ 致死剂量。*lethal* ~ *50* 受照射者 50%死亡剂量。*lethal* ~ *50/30* 受照射者经过 30 天 50%死亡剂量。**II** *vt*. 1. 给…服药,给(药)。2. 把(药等)配分剂量。3. 在(酒)中加料。~ *a patient with quinine* 给病人服奎宁。*I* ~*d myself with hot milk*. 我拿热牛奶当药喝。*He* ~*d me with advice*. 他给我以劝告。~ *out powders* 把药剂配成(一定份量)。—*vi*. 服药。***like a*** ~ ***of salts***〔俚〕非常迅速地。~ *rate*【物】剂量率。**dosing tank** 量斗,投配器。

do·si·me·ter [dəuˈsimitə; doˋsɪmətɚ] *n*. 1.【物】放射性剂量仪;原子能辐射计。2.【化】剂量计,量筒,剂量仪器。

do·sim·e·try [dəuˈsimitri; doˋsɪmətrɪ] *n*. 1.(放射)剂量测定(法) 2. 药量测定。

doss [dɔs; dɑs] **I** *n*.〔英俚〕1. 简陋睡铺,(尤指小客栈的)床位。2. 睡眠。**II** *vi*. 1. 睡简陋床铺,住小客栈。2.

〔美〕睡。～ *down in a car* 倒在车子里睡一觉。～ *out* 露宿。～ **house** 〔俚〕小客栈;集体宿舍。

dos·sal, dos·sel [ˈdɔsəl; ˋdɑsəl] ***n*.** **1.** (祭坛后方或圣坛周围的)吊帐,垂帘,挂布,幔布。**2.** (椅子的)靠背饰布〔尤指国王座椅的靠背〕。

dos·ser [ˈdɔsə; ˋdɑsɚ] ***n*.** **1.** 驮筐,背筐。**2.** = dossal.

dos·si·er [ˈdɔsiei; ˋdɑsɪˏe] ***n*.** 〔F.〕(有关一事、一人的)全套档案。*a complete* ～ *on an individual* 关于某人情况的全套档案。*a criminal's* ～ 罪犯档案。

dos·sil [ˈdɔsl; ˋdɑsl] ***n*.** **1.** (桶等的)栓,塞子。**2.**【医】填入伤口的纱布。**3.**【印】(揩去铜板上余墨的)揩墨布卷。

dos·sy [ˈdɔsi; ˋdɑsɪ] ***a*.** 〔俚〕漂亮的,好看的。

dost [dʌst; dʌst] ***v*.** 〔诗、古〕(主语为 thou 时的) do 的第二人称、单数、现在式。

Dos·to·ev·sky [dɔstəˈjefski; dɑstəˋjɛfskɪ], **Fedor Mikhaylovitch** 费·米·杜斯妥也夫斯基〔1821—1881,俄国小说家〕。

D

Dot [dɔt; dɑt] ***n*.** 多特〔Dorothea 的昵称〕。

dot[1] [dɔt; dɑt] **I *n*.** **1.** 点;圆点;句点;【乐】附点〔音符后的一点,表示延长 1/2 拍〕。**2.** 一点点大的东西,小片,少量,小个子。**3.**【数】小数点;相乘的符号。*There are* ～*s of soot on the window sill*. 窗台上有一点烟灰。*Put a* ～ *on* [*over*] *the i*. 给字母 i 加上一点。*a* ～ *of butter* 一点儿奶油。*a mere* ～ *of a child* 小小的孩子。***in the year*** ～〔口〕老早以前。***off one's*** ～〔俚〕傻头傻脑的;发疯。***on the*** ～〔口〕按时;准时。***put*** ～***s on***〔口〕使倦怠[烦闷]。***to a*** ～〔美〕完全,全部(*be correct to a* ～ 完全正确)。***to the*** ～ ***of an i*** 一丝不苟地。**II *vt*.** (**-tt-**) **1.** 打点于;星罗棋布于,点缀;用点线表示。**2.**〔俚〕敲,打。*D- your i's and j's*. 写字时不要忘记在 i 和 j 字上打一点。*the sea* ～*ted with ships* 点缀着船只的海洋。*Trees* ～ *the landscape*. 树木点缀着景色。*Stars* ～ *the sky*. 星星缀满天空。*a* ～*ted note*【乐】附点音符。～ *a line across the page* 横贯书页划一条虚线。～ *sb*. *in the eye* 一拳打到某人眼上。*a* ～*ted line* 虚线。～ ***and carry one***〔做加法时〕逢十进位〔儿童用语〕。～ ***and go one*** **1.** = ～ and carry one. **2.** ***n*.** (拄着丁字杖走的)瘸子;一瘸一拐的步行声。**3.** ***a*., *ad*.** 一瘸一拐的[地]。～ ***down*** 暂且记下来。～ ***one's i's and cross one's t's*** 打 i 的点画 t 的横线;一笔不苟,详述。***sign on the*** ～***ted line***〔美〕在(信封、文件等留出供署名的)虚线上签名;〔喻〕全盘接受。～**-and-dash *a*.** **1.** 莫尔斯电码的。**2.** 一点一划相间的(～*-and-dash technique* 电报技术)。～ **mark** 刻印标记。～ **pattern**【无】光点图形。～**-sequential *a*.**【无】(彩色电视)点顺序制的。～ **weld**【机】点焊。

dot[2] [dɔt; dɑt] ***n*.**【法】嫁妆,嫁资,妆奁。**-al** [ˈdəutəl; ˋdəutəl] ***a*.**

dot·age [ˈdəutidʒ; ˋdotɪdʒ] ***n*.** **1.** 老耄,老糊涂。**2.** 溺爱,过分的偏爱。***be in one's*** ～ 年老昏愦。

do·tard [ˈdəutəd; ˋdotɚd] ***n*.** **1.** 年老昏愦的人,老糊涂。**2.** 溺爱者。

do·ta·tion [dəuˈteiʃən; doˋteʃən] ***n*.** **1.** 捐助。**2.** 基金。**3.** 天分,天资。

dote [dəut; dot] ***vi*.** **1.** 衰老,年老昏愦。**2.** 溺爱,过分偏爱(*on*; *upon*)。*She* ～*s on her youngest son*. 她溺爱最小的儿子。**dot·ing *a*.** 老糊涂的;溺爱的。**dot·ing·ly *ad*.** **dot·ing·ness *n*.**

doth [dʌθ; dʌθ]〔古、诗〕do 的第三人称、单数、现在式。

dot·tel [ˈdɔtl; ˋdɑtl] ***n*.** = dottle.

dot·ter [ˈdɔtə; dɑtɚ] ***n*.** **1.** 加点的人。**2.** 描点器;【军】(练习火炮瞄准的)点标器。

dot·tle [ˈdɔtl; ˋdɑtl] ***n*.** (烟斗中吸剩的)焦烟丝。

dot·ty [ˈdɔti; ˋdɑtɪ] ***a*.** **1.** 有点子的;点子多的。**2.** 有弱点的。**3.**〔口、方〕脚步不稳的。**4.**〔俚〕疯疯癫癫的,半痴的。*be* ～ *on one's legs* 脚步踉跄。*That's my* ～ *point*. 那是我的弱点。*be* ～ *about a lass* 迷恋一个姑娘。**dot·ti·ly *ad*.**

Dou·a·la [du(ː)ˈɑːlə; du(ʊ)ˋɑlə] ***n*.** 杜阿拉〔喀麦隆港市〕。

dou·ane [du(ː)ˈɑːn; duˋɑn] ***n*.** 〔F.〕海关。

Dou·ay, Dou·ai [duːˈei; duˋe] ***n*.** 杜埃〔法国地名〕。***the*** ～ ***Bible*** 杜埃版《圣经》〔罗马天主教会核定的英译本圣经,于 1582 及 1609—1610 年,由罗马天主教学者将新旧约分别从拉丁文译成英语,在法国 Douai 出版,又称 ～ *Version*〕。

doub·le [ˈdʌbl; ˋdʌbl] **I *a*.** **1.** 两倍的,加倍的。**2.** 双的,二重的,双重的;对,双,两,复。**3.** 双人用的;折叠式的。**4.** (意义)双关的;模棱两可的;表里不一的,两面派的,阴险的;一人演二角的。**5.**【植】重瓣的;【乐】低八度的;二拍子的。～ *pay* [*portion*] 双薪[份]。*a* ～ *axe* 双刃斧。*a* ～ *bed* 双人床。*a* ～ *blanket* 双连毯。*an egg with a* ～ *yolk* 双黄蛋。*a* ～ *bottom* (箱等的)夹底。*a* ～ *coating* 两道漆[粉刷]。*a* ～ *door* 双扇门。*a* ～ *eagle*【徽】双头鹰;〔美〕20 元金币。*serve a* ～ *purpose* 一举两得。*a* ～ *use* 双重用途。*a* ～ *flower*【植】重瓣花。～ *petunias* 重瓣矮牵牛花。*a* ～ *letter* (表示名词复数的)复写字母〔如 *ll*. = lines, *pp*. = pages, *LLD* = Doctor of Laws〕。*a* ～ *personality* 双重人格。～ *conduct* 两面派行为。*He wore a* ～ *face*. 他是一个两面派。～ *summer time*〔英〕(比标准时间快两个小时的)二重夏令时间。*a* ～ *suicide* 双双自杀,情死。*work* ～ *tides* [*shifts*] 昼夜不停地工作。*a* ～ *meaning* 语义双关。*a* ～ *interpretation* 双重解释。*a* ～ *rôle*【影】一人演二角。

II *n*. **1.** 双倍。**2.** 相似者,相似的人[物];幽灵;副本;【影】译制演员,配音演员,后备演员,替身;【剧】一人演二角的演员。**3.** 急转弯,突然转向;折回。**4.** (辩论等用的)诡计,谋略;回避。**5.** 褶子,褶儿;折叠,重叠。**6.**【印】排重,复印;【军】快步;〔*pl*.〕(网球等的)双打;【棒球】二垒打。**7.**【天】双星;【乐】变奏曲。**8.**〔美〕带厢房的房子。*pay* ～ 付双薪,加倍付酬。*Four is the* ～ *of two*. 4 是 2 的双倍。*Send me this sample in* ～. 把样品送两份给我。*This dress is the* ～ *of that*. 这件服装和那件一模一样。*He is the* ～ *of his cousin*. 他和他的表兄弟长得极相像。*make a* ～ 突然折回。*play a* ～ *game* 玩弄两面手法。*act as sb.'s* ～ 作为某人的后备演员。*a mixed* ～*s*【网球】男女混合双打。***at*** [***on***] ***the*** ～ 迅速地;【军】快步走。***come the*** ～ 摆弄,欺骗。～ ***or nothing*** [***quits***] (打赌等)要么债务加倍要么前账勾销,孤注一掷。***put a*** ～ ***on sb*.** 用计骗人。

III *ad*. **1.** 双倍地。**2.** 双重地。**3.** 双双地。*at* ～ *the speed* 用加倍速度。*pay* ～ *the price* 加倍付钱。*be* ～ *as many* [*much*] *as* ... 比…多一倍。*ride* ～ (二人)共骑一马。*see* ～ (酒醉眼花)看见重像。*He bent* ～ *with explosive laughter*. 他大笑得直不起腰来。***sleep*** ～ (二人)共睡一床。

IV *vt*. **1.** 是…的两倍,使加倍。**2.** 重复;折叠,把…对折;握(拳)。**3.** 替代(演员);兼演(两角);(在译制片中)为…配音。**4.**【海】绕过(岬角等)。**5.**【乐】使…高[低]八度。**6.** (辩论时)回避(要害问题等)。**7.**【牌】(以输赢加倍计算)叫(牌)。**8.** 使成伙伴,使合住[合骑等]。～ *a sum* 把数目加一倍。～ *one's efforts* 加倍努力。*The baby* ～*d its weight in a year*. 婴儿的体重一年增加了一倍。*Their fortune* ～*s ours*. 他们的财产比我们的多一倍。～ *the blanket* 把毯子对折起来。*He* ～*d his fists*. 他握紧双拳。～ *Cape Horn* 绕过合恩角。～ *a passenger with another* 使一旅客与另一旅客合住一室。～ *the parts of* (一人)兼演两个角色。— ***vi*.** **1.** 成两倍,增加一倍;【牌】加倍。**2.** 快步走[小跑]。**3.** 折叠起来;弯腰(*over*)。**4.** 急退,急转,突然迂回。**5.** 加倍使力,加倍努力。**6.** 替代演出(*for*);兼演两角(*as*);兼作(*as*)。**7.**【乐】兼奏(*on*)。**8.** (辩论等场合)用计。**9.**【牌】(将输赢加倍)叫牌。*His money* ～*d in three* *years*. 他的钱三年增加了一倍。~ *over with pain* 疼得弯下腰。*He* ~*d back by another road and surprised us*. 他从另一条路绕回来,突然出现在我们面前。*D*-!【军】快步走! *We* ~*d up the hill*. 我们一路小跑上了山。*The girl* ~*d as secretary and receptionist*. 那女孩兼做秘书和招待员。*The saxophonist* ~*s on drums*. 萨克斯管吹奏演员兼做鼓手。~ **back** 1. 向后折叠。2. 扭头往回跑。~ **in** 向内折叠。~ **in brass**〔美俚〕同时做两种工作,兼差;从两处拿钱。~ **over** 折起(书页等)(~ *over the edge before sewing* 衣服折起来缝边)。~ **up** 1. (旅客等)同住一室。2. 弯着身子(*He* ~*d up in agony*. 他痛得弯下了身子。~ *up with laughter* 笑弯了腰)。3. 折,摺;捏起(拳头)。~ **upon** 迂回;突然袭击(*upon one's steps* 折回原路行走,走回头路。~ *upon the enemy* 突然反击敌人)。~**-acting** *a*. 1.【机】双动的,往复式的。2. 双重作用的。~**-action** 1.【机】双向,双动。2. 双重作用。~**-banked** *a*. (艇等)双座的;(船舰等)双层的。~**-barrel** 1. *a*. = double-barrelled. 2. *n*. 双筒枪。~**-barrelled**,〔美〕**-reled** *a*. 1. (枪、望远镜等)双筒的。2. 双重的;有两种目的的;模棱两可的,暧昧的。3. 复姓的〔如 Forbes-Robertson〕。~**-bedded** *a*. 备有两张床的;备有双人卧铺的;双层床的。~ **beer** 双料啤酒。~**-bind** *n*. 1. 两难,左右为难。2. 窘境,困境。~ **bond**【化】双键。~**-breasted** *a*. (外衣等)双排扣的,对襟的。~**-chinned** *a*. 有双下巴的。~**-click**【计】*vt*. & *vi*. 双击(鼠标)。~**-clock** *vt*.〔美俚〕欺骗。~ **cover** 二盯一〔赛球时以两名队员盯住对方一名进攻手〕。~ **cross** 1. 出卖,欺骗,(有奖拳赛等约定要输而又打赢的)违约。2.【生】双杂交。~**-cross**〔美俚〕*vt*. 出卖,欺骗(朋友等)。~ **dagger**【印】双箭号。~**-dealer** 两面派,口是心非的人。~**-dealing** 1. *a*. 口是心非的,奸诈的,不诚实的。2. *n*. 两面派手法,奸诈。~**-decked** *a*. 双层结构的。~**-decker** 双层床,两层甲板的船;(铁路公路两用的)双层桥;双层电车[公共汽车];双层火室的汽机。~**dome**〔美俚〕智力甚高而格调高雅的人。~ **Dutch** 难以理解的东西,(尤指)莫名其妙的话。~**-dye** *vt*.【纺】染两次。~**-dyed** *a*. 1. 两次染色的,重染的。2. 罪恶昭彰的,坏透的。3. (信仰等)根深蒂固的。~ **eagle** 双鹰币〔美国金币,值 20 美元〕。~**-edged** *a*. 1. 双刃的。2. 模棱两可的。3. 双重目的的。4. 同时有好坏两方面影响的。~**ender** 两头构造相同之物[头尾同形船、两头机车、两头可开的电车等]。~ **entry** 复式簿记。~ **exposure**【摄】两次曝光的。~**-faced** *a*. 1. 有两面的;(布料等)两面可用的,两面一样好的。2. 口是心非的,伪善的。~ **feature** (一部)上下两集电影。~ **first**〔英大学〕1. 两门课考优等。2. 两门课优等生。~**-header**〔美〕1. 双车头火车。2.【棒球】连赛。~ **jeopardy** 双重告诉的危险。~**-jointed** *a*. 1. 双重关节的。2. (关节等)前后左右可以自由活动的。~**-leaded** *a*.【印】放宽行距的。~**-lock** *vt*. 上双锁于。~ **march**【军】跑步。~**-minded** *a*. 三心二意的;反复无常的。~ **negative**【语法】双重否定〔口语中用 I didn't hear nothing 之类,仍为否定意〕。~**-O** *n*.〔俚〕详细追究[检查]。~**-park** *vt*., *vi*. (把汽车)挨着其他汽车并排停放〔否则违章〕。~ **possessive**【语法】双重所有格〔如 He is a friend of father's. 他是我父亲的一位朋友〕。~**-quick** 1. *n*.【军】快步。2. *a*. 快步的;急速的。3. *ad*. (用)快步;迅速。4. *vi*. 快步前进。~ **ratio**【数】交比。~**-refine** *n*., *vt*. 再精炼,再精制。~**-ripper** [**-runner**]〔美〕双联雪橇。~ **room** 套间。~**-space** *vt*., *vi*. (在打字机上)隔行打印。~ **star**【天】双星。~ **take** 1.〔口〕先是一怔后来才恍然大悟(*do a* ~ *take* 先大吃一惊,后来才明白了)。2. 回头再看一看。~**-talk** 1. 不知所云的话。2. 含糊其词。~**-team** 1. *vt*.【体】双拦〔球赛时用两名队员拦阻对方一名进攻者〕。2. *vi*. 用两组牲口拉一部车;使用两倍兵力(*on*; *upon*)。~**think** 矛盾想法。~ **time** 1.【军】快步走。2. (加班等的)双工资。~**-time** 1. *vt*. 使快步走。2. *vi*. 快步行进。~**-tongued** *a*. 撒谎的,欺骗的。~**-track** *vt*. (使铁路)成双轨。~**tree** (马车的)双马轼。**-r** *n*. 1.【无】倍压器,倍频器。2.【纺】并线机。3.【自】倍增器,乘 2 装置。**-ness** *n*. 1. 加倍;二倍,双重,二重。2. 诡诈,欺骗。**-bly** *ad*. 1. 加倍。2. 二重,双重。3.〔古〕欺骗地(*be doubly cautious* 加倍小心)。

dou·ble en·ten·dre [ˈduːbl ɑ̃ːnˈtɑ̃ːndr; ˋdubl ˏɑ̃ˋtɑ̃dr] [F.] 1. (暗含下流,猥亵含义的)双关语。2. 含糊其词。*headlines containing double entendres* 含有暧昧词句的标题。

dou·ble·speak [ˈdʌblspiːk; ˋdʌblˏspik] *n*. 欺人之谈。

dou·blet [ˈdʌblit; ˋdʌblɪt] *n*. 1.〔古〕(十四至十六世纪欧洲的一种)男紧身上衣,马甲。2. 成对物;对偶物;〔*pl*.〕孪生子;【语】(同源异形或异义的)同源词〔如 cloak 和 clock, fashion 和 faction〕;〔*pl*.〕(骰子的)一对〔如一对么,一对五等〕。3. 一对中的一个,一对孪生子[同源词、骰子等]的一个。4.【印】排重的字句;【猎】(用双筒枪)同时打下的两只鸟。5.【物】(光谱)双(重)线;电子偶;偶极天线,偶极子,对称振子;双合透镜。~ **and hose** 男装;便装;工装。

dou·bling [ˈdʌbliŋ; ˋdʌblɪŋ] *n*. 1. 加倍,成双。2. 重叠;对折。3. (逃避追赶时等的)折回,往回跑,迂回,绕行,绕航。4.【化】再蒸馏;(橡胶的)重合,夹胶。5.【船】防护板,加强板。6. = doublure.

dou·bloon [dʌbˈluːn; dʌˋblun] *n*. 1. 旧时西班牙及中南美金币名。2.〔*pl*.〕〔美俚〕钱。

dou·blure [duːˈbljuə; duˋbljur] *n*.〔F.〕(衣服的)里子;(书籍的)封面衬裹。

doubt [daut; daʊt] **I** *n*. 1. 怀疑;疑惑,疑问。2.〔常 *pl*.〕疑惧。*a shadow of* ~ 有一点怀疑。*have grave* ~*s about* 对…有严重怀疑。**beyond** [**past**] (**all**) ~ 毫无疑问〔常用作插入语〕。**give sb. the benefit of the** ~ 对某人可疑处给与善意的解释,在证据不足时先假定某人是无辜的。**hang in** ~ 悬而未决(*His life hangs in* ~. 他的死活难以预料)。**in** ~ 1. 感到疑心,拿不准。2. 被怀疑,悬而未决(*His appointment to the position is still in* ~. 任命他担任那项职务还没有决定)。**make no** ~ **of** 毫不怀疑,确信。**no** ~ 1. 无疑地。2.〔口〕很可能。**throw** [**cast**] ~ **upon** 对…产生怀疑。**without** (**a**) ~无疑,的的确确。**II** *vt*. 1. 疑,怀疑;不信,拿不准〔后接名词从句时,肯定句用 whether, if, when, what 等,否定句及疑问句用 that, but, but that, 肯定句用 that 往往表示非常怀疑〕。*I* ~ *whether* [*if*] *he was there*. 我拿不准他在不在那里。*I do not* ~ (*but*) *that he was there*. 我相信他在那里。*I* ~ *that he will be there*. 我不相信他会到那里去[我看他多半不会去了]。~ *the truth of the story* 对那番话的真实性有怀疑。2.〔古、方〕怕,恐怕。*I* ~ *they will be too strong for us*. 我怕敌不过他们。—*vi*. 怀疑,不信(*about*; *of*)。*He* ~*ed of the importance of honesty*. 他不相信诚实有多么重要。**-able** *a*. 可疑的,令人怀疑的。**-ably** *ad*. 可疑地。**-er** *n*. 怀疑者。**-ing** *a*. 怀疑心重的,惴惴不安的(~*ing Thomas* 疑心重的人,多疑的人)。**-ing·ly** *ad*. 起怀疑心地,有怀疑地。**-ing·ness** *n*. 多疑。

doubt·ful [ˈdautful; ˋdaʊtfəl] *a*. 1. 怀疑的,拿不准的,不太相信的(*of*; *about*)。2. 可疑的,有疑问的;未必好的。3. 含糊的,暧昧的。4. 难以预料的,未定局的。*He is* ~ *of* [*about*] *the news*. 他怀疑那个消息不尽可靠。*I'm* ~ (*as to*) *what I ought to say*. 我拿不准该说些什么。*a* ~ *proposition* 可疑的命题。*a* ~ *character* 可疑的人物。*magazine of* ~ *taste* 内容不太好的[低级趣味的]杂志。*a* ~ *reply* 含糊的回答。*a* ~ *future* 难以预料的未来。**-ly** *ad*. **-ness** *n*.

doubt·less [ˈdautlis; ˋdaʊtlɪs] **I** *ad*. 1. 无疑地,必定。2.〔口〕很可能,多半。*D- he was the strongest*. 他无疑是最强有力的。*You have* ~ *seen it*. 你很可能已经看见

过它了。II *a*.〔罕〕无疑的。**-ly** *ad*. = ～. **-ness** *n*.

douce [duːs; dus] *a*.〔Scot.〕安详的;文静的;清醒的。**-ly** *ad*. **-ness** *n*.

dou·ceur [duːˈsəː; duˋsɚ] *n*.〔F.〕1. 酒钱,赏钱;贿赂。2.〔古〕和蔼可亲。

douche [duːʃ; duʃ] I *n*. 1.【医】灌洗(疗)法;冲洗,灌洗。2. 灌洗器,注水器。II *vt*. 灌洗;对…施行灌洗(疗法)。—*vi*. 施行灌洗疗法。

dough [dəu; do] *n*. 1. (揉好的)生面团。2. 生面团似的一团〔如揉好的陶土、油灰等〕。3.〔美俚〕钱,现钞。4.〔美口〕步兵〔~boy 的缩略形式〕。*a* ～*-brake* [*-kneader*, *-mixer*] 和面器,碾面机。*a* ～ *head*〔美〕面包厂。***in the*** ～〔美俚〕1. 兴旺;有钱,富有。2. 得胜,赢。***My cake is*** ～. 我的蛋糕还是生面团,我的计划失败了。***throw one's*** ～ ***around***〔美俚〕浪费金钱。**-boy** 1. 油炸面团;汤团。2.〔美口〕(第一次世界大战时出征的)美国步兵。~**foot**〔美口〕步兵。~**head**〔美俚〕傻瓜。

D

Dough·er·ty [ˈdəuəti; ˋdoɚtɪ] *n*. 多尔蒂〔姓氏〕。

dough·face [ˈdəufeis; ˋdofes] *n*.〔美俚〕1. 假面具。2.【美史】(南北战争时不反对南方蓄奴制的)亲南方的北方人[议员]。3. 优柔寡断的人,易受人左右的人。4. 生面团似的面孔。**-d** *a*.

dough·nut [ˈdəunʌt; ˋdonʌt] *n*. 1. 炸面饼圈。2. 环状物。3.〔美俚〕汽车轮胎;电子回旋加速室,环形室。～ **foundry** [**factory**]〔美俚〕小吃店。~**ing** "炸面包圈"手法(指多人簇拥在某一发言人身边在电视上作宣传的一种壮声势手法)。**-er·y** *n*.〔美俚〕= ～ foundry.

Dough·ty [ˈdauti; ˋdaʊtɪ] *n*. 道蒂〔姓氏〕。

dough·ty [ˈdauti; ˋdaʊtɪ] *a*.〔古、谑〕刚强的,勇猛的。～ **knights** 勇敢的骑士。**-ti·ly** *ad*. **-ti·ness** *n*.

dough·y [ˈdəui; ˋdoɪ] *a*. 1. 面团似的;黏成团的。2. 夹有生面的,半熟的。3. 苍白的;软弱的。*a* ～ *complexion* 苍白的面容。*a* ～ *consistency* 面团般的黏性。**dough·i·ness** *n*.

Doug·las(s) [ˈdʌgləs; ˋdʌgləs] *n*. 道格拉斯〔姓氏,男子名〕。～ **fir** [**pine**, **spruce**]【植】黄杉属;花旗松,洋松。

doum [duːm, daum; dum, daʊm] *n*.【植】埃及棕榈〔通常作 ～-palm〕。

doup·pi·o·ni, dou·pi·o·ni [ˌduːpiːˈəuniː; ˏdupiˋoni] *n*.【纺】双宫丝;双宫绸。

dour [duə; dur] *a*.〔Scot.〕1. 阴郁的;严厉的。2. 倔强的,执拗的。3. (土地)荒瘠不毛的,(岩石)嶙峋的。*a* ～ *warning* 严厉的警告。**-ly** *ad*. **-ness** *n*.

dou·rine [duˈriːn; duˋrin] *n*.〔F.〕【兽医】马交媾病,马花柳病。

douse [daus; daʊs] I *vt*. 1. 把…浸入(水中);在…上泼水,浇水。2.【海】急速收(帆等);放松(绳子等);关闭(舱窗等)。3.〔俚〕熄灭(灯、火等)。4.〔口〕脱(衣、鞋等)。～ *the clothes in soapy water* 把衣服浸入肥皂水。～ *the thirsty plant with water* 给干旱的植物浇水。～ *the lights* 熄灯。～ *a sail* 急速收帆。～ *a rope* 放松绳子。～ *my cap on entering the porch* 进入门廊时脱帽。—*vi*. 浸,泡;浇,洒,泼。II *n*. 1.〔英方〕一击。2. 浸,泡;浇,洒,泼,倾注。

douze·pers [ˈduːzˌpeəz; ˋduzˏpɛrz] *n*. *pl*. 1.【法史】十二名可入上院的贵族。2. (中古传奇)查理曼大帝的十二名骑士。

dove[1] [dʌv; dʌv] *n*. 1. 鸽;小野鸽〔亦作 *mourning dove*, *ring dove*, *rock dove*, *turtledove*〕。2.【宗】圣灵。3. 纯洁的人,天真无邪的人,温柔和蔼的人;〔昵称〕宝贝。4. 和平[纯洁、温柔、天真无邪]的象征。5.〔美〕(政界的)鸽派,主和派。6.【天】〔the D-〕天鸽座(= Columba)。*my* ～ 我的宝贝儿。*a soiled* ～ 娼妓。～ **colour** 暖灰色,淡红灰色。~**cot**, ~**cote** 鸽棚,鸽房(*flutter* [*cause a flutter in*] *the* ~*cots* 扰乱鸽棚,〔喻〕使平地起风波,无事生非)。~**-eyed** *a*. 目光柔和的。～ **gray** 一种紫灰色。**-let** 幼鸽,乳鸽。**-like** *a*. 鸽子般的。

dove[2] [dəuv; dov] *v*.〔美口,英方〕dive 的过去式。

dove·kie, dove·key [ˈdʌvkiː; ˋdʌvki] *n*.【动】1. 扁脚海雀。2. 海鸠。

Do·ver [ˈdəuvə; ˋdovɚ] *n*. 多佛〔英、美港市〕。***Strait of*** ～ 多佛海峡。***when*** ～ ***and Calais meet*** 永不,决不〔～ 和加来(Calais) 为英法两国隔海相望的二港市〕。～**'s powder**【药】阿片吐根散〔一种镇痛发汗剂〕。

dove·tail [ˈdʌvteil; ˋdʌvˏtel] I *n*.【木工】1. 鸠尾榫,楔形榫。2. 鸠尾接合(= ～ point)。II *vt*. 1. 用楔形榫接合,把…制成楔形榫。2. 使(事实、知识、计划等)相互吻合,使相呼应;和…吻合。～ *the end of a board* 把一块木板的末端做成鸠尾榫。～ *one's investigation into these sociological works* 把自己的研究纳进这些社会学著作的框框。—*vi*. 吻合,严丝合缝地嵌进。～ **joint**【木工】鸠尾榫,楔形榫。～ **groove** [**slot**]【机】燕尾槽。～ **machine** 制榫机。

dov·ish [ˈdʌviʃ; ˋdʌvɪʃ] *a*. 诉诸和平的。

dow [dau; daʊ] *vi*. (～*ed*, ***dought*** [daut; daʊt]; ～*ed*, ***dought***)〔主 Scot.〕得以,能够(= be able to)。

Dow [dau; daʊ] *n*.〔the ～〕【经】道琼斯平均指数。

Dow., **dow.** = dowager.

dow·a·ger [ˈdauədʒə; ˋdaʊədʒɚ] I *n*. 1. 王[公等]的未亡人;继承亡夫遗产[称号]的寡妇。2.〔口〕老年贵妇人。*a duchess* [*princess*] ～ 公爵[亲王]未亡人。*a queen* ～ (王国的)皇太后。*an empress* ～ (帝国的)皇太后。*a wealthy* ～ 一个有钱的年老贵妇人。II *a*. 王[公等]的未亡人的;年高贵妇的〔只作限定语用〕。*the* ～ *duchess* 公爵未亡人。*a* ～ *style of dress* 老年贵妇型服装。

dow·dy [ˈdaudi; ˋdaʊdɪ] I *a*. 1. (妇女)服装不整洁的,邋遢的。2. (服装等)式样俗气的;不美观的;过时的。II *n*. 邋遢女人。**dow·di·ly** *ad*. **dow·di·ness** *n*. **-ish** *a*. 有点邋遢的;有点俗气的。

dow·el [ˈdauəl; ˋdaʊəl] I *n*. 1.【木工】榫钉;夹缝钉;暗销。2.【建】传力杆,合缝钢条。*a plug* ～ (为装架子等而打入墙中的)木钉。II *vt*. (～(*l*)*ed*; ～(*l*)*ing*) 1. 用合板钉钉合;用(暗)销接合。2. 在…设置传力杆。

dow·er [ˈdauə; ˋdaʊɚ] I *n*. 1. 遗孀产〔寡妇应享受的一份亡夫遗产〕。2. 嫁妆,陪嫁。3. 天赋,天禀。II *vt*. 1. 给…(寡妇)以亡夫遗产。2. 给…以嫁妆。3. 赋与(才能)。

dow·er·y [ˈdauəri; ˋdaʊərɪ] *n*. = dowry.

dow·las [ˈdauləs; ˋdaʊləs] *n*. 1. (16、17 世纪英国产的)粗亚麻布。2. 粗棉布。

down[1] [daun; daʊn] I *ad*. (～*most*) 1. 向下(面);下,降;在下(面)。*come* ～ 下来;下(楼)来;(雨等)落下。*The ship went* ～ *with all on board*. 这条船连船带人都沉没了。*He is not* ～ *yet*. 他还没有下来呢。*Our lawn slopes* ～ *to the river*. 我们的草地向下倾斜到河边。*He is up, and* ～. 他起床下楼来了。*go* ～ *on one's knees* 跪下。*Sit* ～, *please*. 请坐下。*The sun is* ～. 太阳落山了。2. 倒下,病倒;放下。*The temple was thrown* ～ *by the earthquake*. 神庙被地震震塌了。*fall* ～ 跌倒。*Many are* ～ *with cold*. 很多人患感冒病倒了。*leave the blinds* ～ 放下百叶窗。*Put* ～ *your load and rest*. 放下扛着的东西歇一会儿。*They shouted* ～ *the opposition*. 他们以大喊大叫把反对派的声音压了下去。*The speaker was hissed* ～ *by the crowd*. 人群把演讲者嘘下台。3. (势头、程度等)减退,低落;(潮)退;(煮)干;(磨)碎;(价格)下降,(声音)由响到弱;(体积)由大到小;(数量)由多到少。*The wind went* ～. 风逐渐停了。*His passion has gone* ～. 他的情绪平静了下来。*boil* ～ 熬干,煮干。*grind* ～ 磨碎。*The tyres are* ～. 轮胎没气了。*get* ～ *sb.'s report to three pages* 把某人的报告压缩到三张纸。*Bread is* ～. 面包落价了。*The price of commodities have gone* ～. 商品降

价了。*Out patients are* ~ *a lot*. 门诊的病人数量大减。*Turn* ~ *the phonograph*. 把唱机开小一些。**4.**〔口〕潦倒;衰弱;(意气)消沉。*come* ~ *in the world* 没落,潦倒。*She is* ~ *in health*. 她身体衰弱。*The news put him* ~. 那个消息使他消沉下来了。**5.** (查究,追问)到底;(时间、顺序、地位等的)直到。*run* ~ *a thief* 穷追小偷。*The repair crew traced* ~ *the leak*. 修缮队查明漏水的地方。*We try to run* ~ *the rumour*. 我们竭力想查明谣言的出处。*every metal from gold* ~ *to lead* 从金到铅的每一种金属。*The art has passed* ~ *for centuries*. 这门手艺已经传下来好几百年了。*from 100* ~ *to 10* 从一百到十。~ *to page nine* 直到第九页。~ *to date* 直到今天。**6.** 用现金,现付。*pay* ~ 付现。*He paid $40* ~ *and $20 a month*. 他付定金40元,以后每月付20元。*ten dollars* ~ *and five dollars a week* 定金10元,以后一周付五元。**7.** 记[抄]到纸[账,文件等]上;约定,列入(计划)。*copy* ~ 抄,誊。*Write* ~ *the address*. 记下地址。*take* [*get*] ~ *sb.'s words* 记下某人讲的话。*Meeting is* ~ *for next week*. 约定下周会晤。*He is* ~ *to speak*. 预定他要发表讲演。**8.** 出(城),下(乡);(从首都)往内地;(从上游)至下游;(由北)往南;离开(大学);(从内陆)到海边;(列车等)下行,〔美〕(从西部)向东。*go* ~ *from town* 离城下乡。*go* ~ *to the store* (从住宅区等)去商店。*go* ~ *to Scotland* (由首都伦敦)去苏格兰。*live* ~ *in Florida* 住在南方的佛罗里达州。*We drove* ~ *from San Francisco to Los Angels*. 我们驱车从旧金山南下洛杉矶。*go* ~ *East* [*South*]〔美〕(从西部[北方])到东部[南方]。*a train going* ~ 下行列车。*go* ~ *from Oxford* (因毕业或退学)离开牛津(大学)。*Some twenty students have been sent* ~. 大约二十名学生停学[退学]。**9.**【印】付印,〔棒球俚〕出场。*The paper was* ~. 报纸已付印。*The edition has already gone* ~. 这一版已付印。**10.**〔加强语气〕完全,彻底;认真地;(办,料理,安顿)妥当。*get* ~ *to work* 认真工作。*wash* ~ *a car* 把车子彻底洗干净。*Let's settle* ~ *to studies*. 让我们安下心来读书。**11.**【海】往下风。*Put the helm* ~. = *D- with the helm*. 转舵向下风。***be*** ~ ***and out***〔口〕**1.**【拳】被击倒不能再战。**2.** 落魄,潦倒。***be*** ~ ***for*** 被列入计划[名单等];(议案)被发下(重新讨论)(*He was* ~ *for the competition*. 他被列入参加竞赛的名单)。***be*** ~ ***on*** [***upon***] 怒责;憎恶,轻视,痛恨;虐待,欺负(*We are* ~ *on him*. 我们很讨厌他)。***be*** ~ ***with*** 和…关系密切。~ ***below*** **1.** 在下面[楼下、甲板下、地面下等]。**2.**【宗】在地狱中。~ ***East***〔美〕在 New England 东部沿海地区。~ ***in the bushes*** [***mouth***]〔美口〕意气消沉;心灰意冷(*Why do you look so* ~ *in the mouth*? 你为什么显得这样消沉?) ~ ***to the ground*** 全然,完全(*That suits me* ~ *to the ground*. 那对我完全合适)。~ ***under*** 对跖地,地球底下的那一面〔从英国看指大洋洲说〕(*from* ~ *under* 从大洋洲方面;从地球底下的那一面)。***D- with*** **1.** 打倒。**2.** 拿下,放下,取下(*D- with your rifles*! 放下枪,缴枪! *D- with oars*! 放下桨! *D- with tyranny*! 打倒暴政! *D- with your money*! 交出钱来!)。***go*** ~ 下;(日)落;(船)下沉;(物价)下跌;(饮食等)能吃下,能吸收;(解释等)讲得通(*Such explanation will not go* ~. 那样的解释讲不通)。

II prep. 1. 下;往下方;沿着…往下。**2.** 顺(流)而下;在(河的)下游。**3.** (由郊区)进市区,(由住宅区)到商业区;在市区,在商业区。**4.** (时间上)自…以上。*ski* ~ *the slope* 沿着斜坡下滑。*run* ~ *the stairs* 下楼梯。*sail* ~ *the river* 沿河下航,顺流而下。*be situated* ~ *the river* 位于河的下游。*walk* ~ *the road* 沿着路走。*The custom remained the same* ~ *the ages*. 这个风俗自古以来一直没有变。~ (*the*) *wind* 顺着风向;在下风头。*live* ~ *town* 住在商业区。*drive* ~ *a street* 开车沿街驶去。

III a. (~***most***) **1.** 向下(方)的。**2.** 沿海的,河口地方的。**3.** 下行的;向南开的。**4.** 沮丧的,心灰意懒的。**5.** 现付的。**6.** 赌输的。**7.** 做完的,考虑好的;【赛马】下了赌注的;【体】(比对方)得分低。*a* ~ *elevator* 往下开的电梯。*a* ~ *look* 向下看。*the* ~ *trend of business* 商业的萧条趋势。*a* ~ *country*〔美〕滨海地方,河口附近地方。*a* ~ *grade* [*slope*]下坡。*a* ~ *platform* 下行车出发处。*a* ~ *train* [*bus*]下行列车[公共汽车]。*a* ~ *expression* 沮丧的表情。~ *payment* 定金;(分期付款的)初付款额。*be* ~ *three games* 负三局。*After an hour of poker, he was* ~ *$10*. 他玩一个小时牌输了10元。*with five* ~ *and one to go* 五件已做完,还剩下一件。

IV vt. 1.〔口〕打倒,击落,打下(鸟、飞机等);使屈服。**2.** 放下,扔下,丢下。**3.**〔英口〕咽下,吞下,忘掉(伤心事等)。~ *one's opponent* 把对手打翻在地。~ *a signal* 降下信号旗。*The anti-aircraft* ~*ed ten bombers*. 高射炮部队击落十架轰炸机。~ *a tankard of ale* 喝一大杯淡啤酒。~ ***tools*** 丢下工具,开始罢工。—**vi. 1.** 下降。**2.** (感情等)平息。**3.** (食物等)吃下;好吃。*Life will up and* ~. 人生总有沉浮。

V n. 1. 下位,下行;〔常 *pl*.〕倒霉,潦倒,落魄,失意;下降,衰落。**2.**〔口〕嫌恶,怨恨,憎恶。**3.** (广播剧等叙事而非对话时用的)低声调。**4.**〔美俚〕抑制剂,镇静剂。***have a*** ~ ***on*** 憎恶,怨恨。***ups and*** ~***s*** 浮沉,荣枯,盛衰。**~-and-out 1. *ad*.** = ~ and out. **2. *n*.** 穷愁潦倒的人;被击垮的人。**~-and-outer *n*.** = ~-and-out 2. **~-at-heel *a*.** 潦倒的,衣衫褴褛的。**~beat 1. *n*.**【乐】(指挥棒的)一挥;强拍;下降,衰落。**2.**〔口〕***a*.** 阴郁的,悲观的。**~burst**【气】下向风暴[指可能危及飞机的急速向下气流]。**~cast 1. *a*.** (眼睛)向下看的;唉声叹气的,垂头丧气的,萎靡不振的,衰颓的。**2. *n*.** 没落,灭亡;俯视;【地】下落,陷落;【矿】通风井,下风井。**~come *n*. 1.** 下降;衰落。**2.** = ~comer. **~comer** 下水管;落水管;下导管。**~draft** (烟囱的)倒灌风;向下通风;向下气流。**~-dressing** 便装。**~-Easter 1.**〔美〕新英格兰人,东部沿海地区的人[特指缅因州人]。**2.** 美国东部沿海地区造的船;从缅因州开出的船。**~fall** 堕落,滚落,陷落,落下;(雨等的)大下特下;(家、国等的)没落,灭亡,瓦解。**~-fallen *a*.** 坠落[陷落、没落、灭亡]的,已垮台的。**~grade 1. *a*.** 下坡的;衰落的。**2. *n*.** 下坡。**3. *vt*.** 降低(地位、级别、阶级等),贬低(他人);(美国政府文件)降低(保密级)。**~hearted *a*.**〔俚〕垂头丧气的,闷闷不乐的,无精打采的(*Are we* ~*hearted*?〔俚〕决不灰心!)。**~hill 1. *n*.** 下坡路(*the* ~ *of life* 晚年)。**2. *a*.** 倾斜的,下坡的;【滑雪】向下的。**3. *ad*.** 下坡;降下,向下(*go* ~ 下坡;衰颓,衰败)。**~hold 1. *n*.** 限制。**2. *vt*.** 减少。**~-home 1.** 美国南部的;南部气质的。**2.** 乡土的,淳朴的。**~lead**【无】(天线的)下引线。**~line *ad*.** 沿下行(铁路)线。**~load**【计】***vt*. & *vi*.** 下载。**~-market 1. *a*.** 低收入消费者的;低级的,低档次的。**2. *adv*.** 在低档货之列。**~ payment** 分期付款的首次交款。**~pipe** 水落管。**~-point *vt*.** 减少(配给品的份数)。**~pour *n*. 1.** (日光的)照射。**2.** 倾盆大雨。**~price *vt*.** 降低…的价格。**~range *a*., *ad*.**【宇】离开发射中心和沿着试验航向的[地]。**~right 1. *a*.** 明白的,露骨的;直率的,爽直的,坦白的;〔古〕真正的,纯粹的(*a* ~*right falsehood* 公然作伪。*a* ~*right no* 明确的否定。*a* ~*right sort of person* 脾气直率的人)。**2. *ad*.** 彻底,完全,干脆,真正(*He is* ~*right angry*. 他愤怒已极)。**~river 1. *a*.** 下游的。**2. *ad*.** 向下游。**~-scale *vt*.** 缩减…的规模。**~-side *n*. 1.** 底侧。**2.** 下降趋势。**3.** 阴暗面;缺点。**~size *vi*. & *vt*.** (在…)裁员,(对…)实行机构精简。**~spin** 急降。**~stage *n*., *a*., *ad*.** 舞台前方(的,地)。**~stair *a*.** 楼下的(*a* ~*stair room* 地下室)。**~stairs 1. *ad*.** 在楼下,往楼下(*come* ~*stairs* 下楼。*Downstairs the radio was singing*. 楼下的收音机正在播放歌曲。*kick* ~-

stairs 逐出家门)。**2.** ***a*.** = downstair. **3.** ***n*.** 楼下;〔美〕(戏院的)正厅。~**state** ***n*.**, ***a*.**, ***ad*.**〔美〕南部各州(的,地)。~**stater**〔美〕南部各州的人。~**stream** ***ad*.**, ***a*.** 顺流(的);在下游(的)。~**swing** 下降趋势。~**-the-line** ***a*.** 完全的,充分的;无保留的,真心诚意的。~**-throw** ***n*.** **1.**【地】陷落;下落地块 (*opp*. upthrow)。**2.** 投下;垮台;(声誉等的)低落。~**time** (工厂由于检修、待料等而暂时停工的)停工期[时间]。~**-to-earth** ***a*.** 切切实实的,脚踏实地的 (*a* ~*-to-earth appraisal of the situation* 对形势作切实的估计)。~**trodden** ***a*.** 被蹂躏的,被压制的。~**turn** ***n*.** **1.** 向下;下转,向下折曲。**2.** 下降趋势。~**wash** ***n*.** **1.** 从高处冲刷下来的物质。**2.**【空】下冲[洗]气流;下冲,下洗。~**wind** **1.** ***n*.** 顺风;下降气流。**2.** ***ad*.**, ***a*.** 顺风(的)。

down[2][daun; daʊn] ***n*.** **1.** 岗,丘,开阔的高地;〔美〕沙丘。**2.**〔*pl*.〕丘陵地,丘原,(适于牧羊的)丘陵地草原。**3.**〔D-〕(英国南部丘陵草原产的)塘种绵羊。***the D-s*** **1.** 英国东南部的丘陵草原。**2.** 多佛海峡的一部分〔为船舶停泊处〕。~**land** ***n*.** **1.** 山地牧场。**2.** 澳大利亚温带草原。**3.**【地】丘陵地。

down[3][daun; daʊn] ***n*.** **1.** (装被、褥等用的)鸭绒,绒毛;(鸟的)绒羽;柔毛。**2.** 汗毛,软毛,毳毛;(男孩脸上初生的)细软短须。**3.**【植】茸毛,(蒲公英等的)冠毛。

down·er [ˈdaunə; ˋdaʊnɚ] ***n*.**〔俚〕抑制剂,镇静剂〔如巴比妥盐、酒精饮料等〕。

Down·ing Street [ˈdauniŋ striːt; ˋdaʊnɪŋ strit] **1.** 唐宁街〔伦敦的一条街,英国首相官邸及一些主要政府机关所在地〕。**2.**〔口〕(英国的)首相,现内阁,现政府。

down·town **1.** [ˈdaunˈtaun; ˋdaʊnˋtaʊn] ***n*.**, ***a*.** (市中)商业区(的),闹市区(的)。**2.** [ˈdaunˈtaun; ˋdaʊnˋtaʊn] ***ad*.** 到[在]商业区。*go* [*live*] ~ 去[住在]商业区。*a* ~ *store* 闹市区的一家商店。*live in* ~ *New York* 住在纽约闹市区。

down·ward [ˈdaunwəd; ˋdaʊnwɚd] **I** ***a*.** **1.** 下方的,向下的,低下的。**2.** 下降的;下坡的;(市价)下跌的。*a* ~ *tendency* (物价的)跌势。*a* ~ *slope* 下坡。*He is on the* ~ *path*. 他正在走下坡路。**II** ***ad*.** = downwards. **-ly** ***ad*.** **-ness** ***n*.**

down·wards [ˈdaunwədz; ˋdaʊnwɚdz] ***ad*.** **1.** 向下;以下,往下。**2.** 趋向衰落,日趋没落,日益堕落。**3.** (年代等)以来,以后。*He lay face* ~ *on his bed*. 他脸向下伏在床上。*look* ~ 向下看。*As the river flows* ~, *it widens*. 这条河愈到下游愈宽。*be handed* ~ *from generation to generation* 世代相传,一代代地传下来。*boys of ten and* ~ 十岁以下的男孩。

down·y[1][ˈdauni; ˋdaʊnɪ] ***a*.** **1.** 长绒毛[茸毛]的;汗毛遍身的。**2.** 汗毛状的,茸毛似的;柔软的。**3.** 用绒羽制成的。**4.**〔俚〕狡猾的,机警的。*a* ~ *cloud* 绒毛状的云。*a* ~ *fellow* 狡猾的人。*a* ~ *pillow* 鸭绒枕头。***do the*** ~ 躺在床上睡觉。~ **mildew**【植】霜霉病,露菌病。**down·i·ly** ***ad*.** **down·i·ness** ***n*.**

down·y[2][ˈdauni; ˋdaʊnɪ] ***n*.** **1.** 丘陵草原性的。**2.** 丘陵起伏的。*a rolling* ~ *landscape* 丘陵连绵起伏的景色。

dow·ry [ˈdauəri; ˋdaʊrɪ] ***n*.** **1.** 嫁妆,嫁资。**2.** 天赋,天禀,才能。**3.**〔古〕寡妇(继承亡夫的一份)产业。**4.**〔古〕(丈夫给新娘的)财礼。

dowse[1][daus; daʊs] ***vt*.** = douse.

dowse[2][dauz; daʊz] **I** ***vi*.** (古时用迷信的)卜棒探寻水脉[矿脉]。— ***vt*.** 用卜棒找到(水脉等)。**II** ***n*.** (找寻矿脉等的)卜棒。

Dow·son [ˈdausn; ˋdaʊsn] ***n*.** 道森〔姓氏〕。

dox·ol·o·gy [dɔkˈsɔlədʒi; dɑksˋɑlədʒɪ] ***n*.**【宗】(礼拜式上唱的)荣光赞歌,荣耀颂。

dox·y[1], **dox·ie** [ˈdɔksi; ˋdɑksɪ] ***n*.**〔口〕**1.** 学说,见解。**2.** 宗教见解,宗教主张,教旨。

dox·y[2][ˈdɔksi; ˋdɑksɪ] ***n*.**〔俚〕**1.** 情妇。**2.** 淫妇;娼妓。

dox·y·cyc·line [dɔksiˈsaiklin; dɑksɪˋsaɪklɪn] ***n*.**【药】强力霉素。

doy·en [ˈdɔiən; ˋdɔɪən] ***n*.**〔F.〕(*fem*. ***doy·enne*** [dɔiˈjen; dɔɪˋjɛn]) **1.** (一个团体中的)老前辈,资格最老者,地位最高者。**2.** 历史最悠久者。*the D- of the Diplomatic Corps* 外交使团团长。*the* ~ *of the country's newspaper* 全国报纸当中最老的一家。

doy·enne [dɔiˈjen; dɔɪˋjɛn] ***n*.** (一个团体中的)女性老前辈,女性资格最老者。

Doyle [dɔil; dɔɪl] ***n*.** 多伊尔〔姓氏,男子名〕。

doz. = dozen(s).

doze[1][dəuz; doz] **I** ***vi*.** **1.** 打瞌睡,打盹。**2.** 迷迷糊糊,昏昏沉沉。~ *over a stupid book* 看着一本枯燥无味的书打瞌睡。*He* ~*d off during the sermon*. 他在听说教的时候直打盹。— ***vt*.** 在瞌睡中度过(时间)(*away*; *out*)。*He* ~*d away the afternoon*. 他在瞌睡中度过一下午。**II** ***n*.** 打瞌睡,打盹,假寐。*fall* [*go off*, *drop off*] *into a* ~ 打起瞌睡来。*drop back into a comfortable* ~ 舒舒服服地打个盹儿。

doze[2][dəuz; doz] ***vt*.** 用推土机清除[挖出、推平]。

doz·en [ˈdʌzn; ˋdʌzn] ***n*.** (*pl*. ~, ~*s*) **1.** 一打,十二个〔作为实数及作修饰语时,复数不加 s〕。**2.**〔~s〕若干,许许多多。*two* [*three*] ~ *eggs* 两[三]打鸡蛋。*four* ~ *of these eggs* 四打这种鸡蛋。*some* ~*s of eggs* 好几打鸡蛋。~*s of eggs* 几十个鸡蛋。*some* ~ (*of*) *eggs* 一打左右鸡蛋。*a* ~ *of eggs* 一打鸡蛋。*sell eggs by the* ~ 论打售蛋。*pack oranges in* ~*s* 按打包装橘子。*a round* ~ 整整一打。*a baker's* [*devil's*, *long*, *printer's*] ~ 十三个。~***s of times*** 屡次。(***talk***) ***thirteen*** [***nineteen***] ***to the*** ~〔英俚〕**1.** (说个)不停。**2.** (说得)过分地,迅速地。

doz·enth [ˈdʌznθ; ˋdʌznθ] ***num*.**〔俚〕= twelfth.

do·zer[1][ˈdəuzə; ˋdozɚ] ***n*.** 打瞌睡的人。

do·zer[2][ˈdəuzə; ˋdozɚ] ***n*.** 推土机。

doz·y [ˈdəuzi; ˋdozɪ] ***a*.** **1.** 想睡的,困倦的。**2.** (木材等)腐烂的。

DP = **1.** displaced person (由于战争或政治迫害等而逃离原居住地或本国的)难民。**2.** degree of polymerization【化】聚合度。**3.** Distributing Point【军】交付所,配给点[站]。**4.** data processing 数据处理。

d.p. = difference of potential【电】电位差,势差。

DPH, DPh(il), D. Ph(il). = Doctor of Philosophy 哲学博士。

D.P.H. = Doctor of Public Health 公共卫生博士。

D.P.I. = Director of Public Instruction〔美〕(海岸警卫队)公共教练处处长。

dpi = dots per inch【计】每英寸点数。

D.P.L. = Delta pine land cotton【纺】岱字棉。

dpm = disintegrations per minute 衰变/分。

DPN = diphosphopyridine nucleotide 二磷酸吡啶核苷酸。

DPRK = Democratic People's Republic of Korea 朝鲜民主主义人民共和国。

DPT = diphtheria pertussis tetanus 白喉、百日咳、破伤风混合血清。

dpt. = **1.** department. **2.** deponent.

Dr., **Dr** = Doctor.

dr. = **1.** debit. **2.** debtor. **3.** drachma(s). **4.** dram(s). **5.** drum.

drab[1][dræb; dræb] **I** ***n*.** **1.** 灰黄色,淡褐色。**2.**【纺】淡褐色厚呢。**3.** 单调,乏味,死气沉沉。*the* ~ *of country life* 蛰居乡间的单调生活。**II** ***a*.** **1.** 淡褐色的。**2.** 单调的。*a* ~ *life* 单调的生活。**-ly** ***ad*.** **-ness** ***n*.**

drab[2][dræb; dræb] **I** ***n*.** **1.** 邋遢女人。**2.** 淫妇;妓女。**II** ***vi*.** 嫖妓。

drab·bet [ˈdræbit; ˋdræbɪt] ***n*.** 家用本色斜纹亚麻布。

drab·ble [ˈdræbl; ˋdræbl̩] ***vt*.** 拖脏(衣服等),把(衣服等)弄得满是泥污。— ***vi*.** 拖泥溅水地走 (*through*); 在

浑水里钓鱼。

dra·cae·na [drəˈsiːnə; drəˋsinə] ***n.***【植】龙血树属植物。

drachm [dræm; dræm] ***n.*** **1.** = drachma. **2.** = dram.

drach·ma [ˈdrækmə; ˋdrækmə] ***n.*** (*pl.* ~ ***s***, ***drachmae*** [-miː; -mɪ]) **1.** 古希腊银币名。**2.** 德拉克马〔现代希腊货币单位〕。**3.** 古希腊衡量单位;现代衡量单位〔尤指 dram〕。

Dra·co [ˈdreikəu; ˋdreko] ***n.*** **1.** 〔the ~〕【天】天龙座。**2.** [d-]【动】飞龙。

Dra·co·ni·an [dreiˈkəunjən; dreˋkonjən], **Dra·co·nic** [dreiˈkɔnik; dreˋkɑnɪk] ***a.*** **1.** 古代雅典执政官德拉科的。**2.** 〔常 d-〕(法律等)严酷的,残酷的。*adopt ~ measures* 采取严厉措施。*face with the ~ law of ...* 面临着…的严酷法律。**-ism** ***n.*** 严刑峻法,严法重典主义。

dra·co·ni·an [dreiˈkəuniən; dreˋkonɪən], **dra·con·ic** [dreiˈkɔnik; dreˋkɑnɪk] ***a.*** 龙一样的。

drae·ger·man [ˈdreigəmæn; ˋdredʒə-mən] ***n.*** 矿工救护队队员。

draff [dræf; dræf] ***n.*** **1.** 渣滓,糟粕。**2.** (喂猪的)残羹剩饭,猪食。*D- is good enough for swine.* 喂猪只需用猪食〔意为不作不必要的浪费〕。**-y** ***a.*** 渣滓[糟粕]很多的,无价值的。

draft [drɑːft; dræft] **I** ***n.*** **1.** 选拔队,别动队,分遣队;(分遣队的)选拔;〔美〕征兵;(不经某人同意而要他出来竞选的)敦请。**2.** 汇票;付款通知单;(款项的)支取;〔喻〕强要,索取;耗完。**3.** 草稿,草案;图案,草图,轮廓。**4.** 牵引,拖,曳;牵伸,拉伸。**5.** 吸饮;一饮,一吸;汲出;(药水等的)一服;(捕鱼等的)一网,一网打获量。**6.**【海】(船的)吃水(深度)。**7.** 罅缝风,穿堂风,贼风,通风,气流;通风装置。★英国除 **1.** **2.** **3.** 用 draft 外,通例用 draught;美国除 **5.** 用 draught 外,通例用 draft. *a ~ system* 征兵制。*~ evasion* 逃避服兵役。*a telegraphic ~* 电(报)汇(款)。*a ~ for $100 on [upon] the bank* 一张向银行支取 100 元的汇票。*a rough ~ for [of] a speech* 讲话草稿。*the first ~* 初稿。*the ~ of a future building* 未来大厦的草图。*a beast of ~* 役畜,拉车的牲畜。*a ~ of air* 一阵风。*sit in a ~* 坐在通风处。*a ~ on sb.'s resources* 某人财力枯竭。*a vessel of 20 feet ~ [with a ~ of 20 feet]* 吃水 20 英尺的船。***at a ~*** 一口,一气。~ ***at B.O.*** (= booking office)【美剧】从卖座上看的演出成败情况。~ ***on demand*** 见票即付的汇票。***feel the ~*** 〔俚〕(手头)拮据。***make a ~ of money*** 提款。***make a ~ on a bank*** 向银行提款。***make a great ~ upon sb.'s confidence*** 死赖着要某人信任。***make out a ~ of*** (*the treaty*) 起草(条约)。***on ~*** 随时可从容器中汲出的 (*beer on ~* 桶装啤酒)。**II** ***vt.*** **1.** 选拔;选派;〔美〕征(兵)。**2.** 起草,拟(方案);画(草图,轮廓),为…打样,设计。**3.** 汲出。**4.** 在(石)上凿槽[琢边]。*~ a professional athlete* 选拔一个职业运动员。*He was ~ed into the army.* 他被征召入伍。*water ~ed by pumps* 用水泵汲出的水。*~ an act* 起草一项法案。**III** ***a.*** **1.** (马等)拉车用的,供役使的。**2.** (啤酒等)桶装的 (*opp.* bottled)。**3.** 正在起草中的。*~ beer* 桶装啤酒。*~ bill* 草案。*a ~ horse* 拉车的马,役马。**~-age** ***a.*** 〔美〕应征年龄的。**~ animals** 耕畜,役畜。**~ board** 〔美〕征兵局。**~ calls** 征兵人数。**~ dodger** 逃避服兵役者。**~ gauge** 风力计,风压表。**~ mark**【海】(船的)吃水线。**~ mill** = smokejack. **~nik** 〔美俚〕反征兵者。**~ tube** 汲管。**-ee** [drɑːfˈtiː; dræfˋti] ***n.*** 〔美口〕壮丁,应征入伍者。**-er** ***n.*** **1.** 起草者。**2.** 役马,拖车的马。

draft·ee [drɑːfˈtiː; dræfˋti] ***n.*** 被征召的士兵。

draft·ing [ˈdrɑːftiŋ; ˋdræftɪŋ] ***n.*** **1.** 起草。**2.** 制图。*~ committee* 起草委员会。*~ board* 绘图板。*~ paper* 绘图纸。*~ room* 绘图室。

drafts·man [ˈdrɑːftsmən; ˋdræftsmən] ***n.*** (*pl.* ***-men***) 起草人;制图员。**-ship** ***n.*** 制图技术[才能]。

draft·y [ˈdrɑːfti; ˋdræftɪ] ***a.*** 〔美〕通风的;通风良好的;有罅缝风吹入的。*a ~ room* 通风良好的屋子。**draft·i·ly** ***ad.*** **draft·i·ness** ***n.***

drag [dræg; dræg] **I** ***vt.*** (***-gg-***) **1.** 拖,曳;拖动,拖着(脚、尾巴等);硬拖(某人)做(某事)[至(某地)]。**2.** 打捞,(用捞锚等)探寻(水底等);用拖网捕捉。**3.** 耙(地),耙平。**4.** (在车轮上)装刹车。**5.** 〔美俚〕(去社交场合时)陪伴(女子);(讲话时)引入,带出。**6.** 〔美俚〕深深地吸(香烟)。**7.** 把(讨论等)拖长。**8.** 〔美俚〕厌烦[无聊]地度(时光)。*The ship ~s her anchor.* 船拖动了锚〔意为锚系不住船;已失去作用〕。*~ one's feet in the water* 在水中拖着脚步走。*~ sb. out of the room* 把某人拖出房间。*~ oneself through the day's work* 好不容易干完一天的活儿。*~ the lake for the body of the missing man* 打捞湖底搜寻失踪者的尸体。*He always ~s his Ph. D. into every discussion.* 他讨论发言的时候总是要生拉硬扯到他的哲学博士头衔。*~ the discussion out for three hours* 把讨论拖长到三个小时。—***vi.*** **1.** 拖曳;(原来下的锚)被拖动。**2.** 慢吞吞地走,拖沓,拖着脚步走 (*along*)。**3.** 拖宕,拖长。**4.** 用拖网[捞锚]探寻 (*for*)。**5.**【乐】拖长声音。**6.** 〔口〕(猛)吸(烟) (*on*)。*The minutes ~ like hours.* 一分钟长得像几小时,度日如年。*The negotiation ~ged on until July.* 谈判一直拖到七月份。*~ behind the party* 落在一行人后面。*a ~ging pain* 长时间的痛苦。*a ~ging market* 呆滞的市场。*~ on one's cigar* 吸上一支雪茄。*The book ~s.* 这本书冗长无味。*The door ~s.* 门呆得很〔不容易开关〕。~ ***a date*** 〔美俚〕带舞伴去参加舞会。~ ***a hoof*** 〔美俚〕跳舞。~ ***by*** (时间)一点一点地挨过去。~ ***down*** 〔俚〕挣工资;赚(钱)。~ ***in*** **1.** 把…拉进去。**2.** 硬把(某人)拉扯进(某事)。~ ***in*** (***by the head and shoulders***) ***a joke*** 牵强附会地插进一句(不恰当的)俏皮话。~ ***it*** 〔美俚〕走掉,跑掉;停止谈话;断绝关系;离职。~ ***on*** [***out***] 迁延,拖延;使拖延;拉长(声调等),拖长(字眼等);挨过。~ ***one's feet*** [***heels***] 〔美俚〕故意拖延。~ ***oneself along*** (慢吞吞地)拖着脚步走。~ ***through*** 好容易才完毕。~ ***up*** **1.** 拉上;拖上;拔出 (*~ up the roots of a tree* 把一棵树连根拔起)。**2.** 〔俚〕粗心大意地抚养(小孩) (*These children seem to have been ~ged up.* 这些小孩似乎是被胡乱带大的)。~ ***your freight*** 〔美俚〕出去!

II ***n.*** **1.** 拖曳物;拖网;捞锚;(四匹马拉的)双层马车;沉重的大耙;粗笨的橇,运货慢车;刮路机。**2.** 拖累物;阻碍物,累赘;极讨厌的人[物]。**3.** 齿扣,刹车,制动器;海锚;【空】阻力。**3.** 牵引;拖沓,拖延。**4.**【海】舳舻吃水差。**5.**【猎】(训练猎犬用的)人工臭迹;应用人工臭迹的行猎;野兽的臭迹。**6.** 〔美俚〕背景,(对人;机构等具有的)影响;势力。**7.** 〔俚〕(男穿)女装,(女穿)男装。**8.** 猛喝一口茶[酒],深吸一口烟。**9.** 〔美俚〕茶会,舞会;跳舞;有男子陪伴去参加舞会的女子。**10.** 〔美俚〕马路,街道。*the ~ of population growth on living standards* 人口增长对提高生活水平的阻碍。*His brother is a ~ to him.* 他的兄弟是他的一个累赘。*School is a ~ for some youngsters.* 学校是一些儿童很讨厌的地方。*Don't invite him — he's a ~.* 不要邀请他——他这个人讨厌极了。*walk with a ~* 慢吞吞地走。*take a long ~ on his cigar* 深深地吸一口雪茄烟。*the boys [girls] in ~* 穿女装的男孩[穿男装的女孩]。*He has ~ with the school authorities.* 他和学校当局很有些交情,他在学校当局那里说话挺管用。

III ***ad.*** 〔美俚〕带有女伴。*Are you going stag or ~?* 参加舞会你是单身去呢还是带着女伴去?

IV ***a.*** 〔美俚〕男穿女服的;女穿男服的。**~ anchor** **1.**【海】海锚,浮锚。**2.** 阻力;障碍。**~-and-drop**【计】拖放。**~ chain** **1.**【机】牵引链;刹车链。**2.** 〔喻〕障碍。**~line** **1.** 牵引绳索。**2.**【矿】索斗铲。**~ net** **1.** 拖网,捕捞网。**2.**

法网,〔美〕大举搜捕。～ **parachute** 阻力伞〔飞机降落于跑道时减速的尾伞〕。～ **queen** 〔美俚〕男扮女装的男性同性恋者。～ **race** 〔美俚〕(汽车拆卸减重后举行的)短程加速比赛。～**rope** (炮身等的)拖绳。～ **sail** 拖锚,浮锚。～**saw**【机】(锯长金属棒材用的)下料电锯。**dragging** *a*.

dra·gée [ˈdrɑːʒei; ˋdrɑʒe] *n*. 〔F.〕 **1**. 糖果〔多指装饰蛋糕的糖衣糖果〕。**2**.【药】糖衣药丸。

drag·gle [ˈdrægl; ˋdrægl] **I** *vt*. 拖脏,拖湿。— *vi*. **1**. (裙子等)拖曳;拖脏,拖湿。**2**. 慢吞吞前进,落后。～**tail** **1**. (拖着又长又脏的裙子的)邋遢〔不正派〕女人。**2**. 长裙拖地的女服。～**tailed** *a*. **1**. 拖着长裙子的。**2**. (妇女等)邋遢的,堕落的。**drag·gly** *a*. **1**. 拖脏的。**2**. 不整洁的。

drag·gy [ˈdrægi; ˋdrægɪ] *a*. **1**. 拖拉的;拖沓的。**2**. 死气沉沉的;沉闷的;无聊的。*a* ～ *market* 呆滞的市面。

drag·hound [ˈdræghaund; ˋdrægˏhaʊnd] *n*. 受过训练能循气味而追踪的猎狗。

D

drag·o·man [ˈdrægəumən; ˋdrægəmən] *n*. (*pl*. ～*s*, *-men*) (土耳其等近东诸国的)翻译,译员;向导。

drag·on [ˈdrægən; ˋdrægən] *n*. **1**. 龙。**2**. 飞龙旗。**3**. 凶暴的人;(年轻女子的)严格凶狠的监护人〔多指老太婆〕。**4**. 〔the D-〕【天】天龙座。**5**. (十七世纪前后口径大而枪身短的)龙骑枪;佩带龙骑枪的士兵。**6**.【动】飞龙〔蜥蜴的一种,有翼膜,能滑翔〕。**7**.【动】(一种善飞的)信鸽。**8**.【圣】海怪〔指鲸鱼,鲨鱼,鳄鱼;海蟒等〕。**9**.【军】装甲牵引车。**10**. "小龙"〔指亚洲新兴的经济腾飞的国家或地区〕。*the old D-* 魔王。*a regular* [*perfect*] ～ (年轻女子的)凶狠的伴婆。～ *'s blood* 龙血树树脂。～ *'s teeth* 〔英俚〕**1**. (多层排列的三角锥形)反坦克混凝土路障。**2**. 相互争斗的根源〔出自日尔曼神话: Cadmus 种下龙齿,化为武士相互砍杀〕。～**fly**【虫】蜻蜓。～**head**【植】青兰属植物。～**'s head**【天】升交点。～**'s tail**【天】降交点。～ **tree**【植】龙血树。

drag·on·et [ˈdrægənit; ˋdrægənɪt] *n*. **1**. 小龙,龙子。**2**.【动】鼠鰤,琴鰤 (*Callionymus lyra*)。

drag·on·nade [ˌdrægəˈneid; ˏdrægəˋned] **I** *n*. **1**. 〔*pl*.〕【法史】龙骑兵迫害〔法国国王路易十四使龙骑兵对新教徒进行迫害〕。**2**. 武力迫害,武力镇压。**II** *vt*. 用武力迫害。

dra·goon [drəˈguːn; drəˋgun] **I** *n*. **1**. 重骑兵;(持龙骑枪的)龙骑兵。**2**. 龙骑兵团〔英国一骑兵团名称〕。**3**. 凶汉,暴徒。**4**. (一种善飞的)信鸽。**II** *vt*. **1**. 用龙骑兵镇压。**2**. 武力迫害,暴力镇压。*The authorities* ～*ed the peasants into leaving their farms*. 当局用武力把农民驱离田庄。

drag·ster [ˈdrægstə; ˋdrægstɚ] *n*. 经改装〔拆卸减重〕而成的高速赛车。

drain [drein; dren] **I** *vt*. **1**. 排去(水等液体),排泄,放干 (*away*; *off*)。**2**. 喝干,倒空。**3**. 用完,花光。**4**. 使…某物枯竭;使…耗尽某物 (*of*)。～ *off the rain* 排掉雨水。～ *the flooded mine* 排干矿上的积水。～ *a glass of beer* 喝干一杯啤酒。～ *the cup of sorrow* [*pleasure*] *to the bottom* 备尝艰苦〔享尽快乐〕。*He* ～*ed the last of the whiskey into our glasses*. 他把最后一点威士忌酒都倒进我们的杯子里。*be* ～*ed of all strength* 筋疲力竭。～ *a country of its resources* 使国家资源枯竭。— *vi*. **1**. (水等液体)流掉,渐渐淌完 (*away*; *off*)。**2**. (土地)排水;(衣服、碗碟等)滴干。**3**. (资源等)逐渐枯竭。*The water will soon* ～ *away*. 水很快就会流掉。*His anger* ～*ed from him*. 他的怒气逐渐消失。*This land won't* ～. 这块田排不出水去。*This land* ～*s into the river*. 这块地的水排到河里。*Put the dishes on the board to* ～. 把碗碟放到板上滴掉水。*Hope and energy* ～ *away over the years*. 岁月逐渐使精力和希望枯竭了。**II** *n*. **1**. 排水渠;下水道,阴沟;〔*pl*.〕(建筑物的)排水系统。**2**.【医】引流,导液(管),排脓管。**3**. 排水,放干;(财富等的)外流,枯竭;耗费,负担。**4**. 〔口〕(酒的)一杯,一口。*the economic* ～ *of war* 战争的经济耗费。*Working too hard is a* ～ *on his strength*. 过分辛劳使他精力衰竭。***go down the*** ～ 〔俚〕**1**. (情况)愈来愈坏,(人)每况愈下。**2**. (资金等)被浪费;(计划等)失败,破产。***laugh like a*** ～ 〔口〕狂笑。～**board** (倾斜着放置洗过的碗碟以便把水滴尽的)滴水板。～**pipe** 排水管。～**pipe trousers** 瘦裤腿裤子。～**trap** (下水道等的)防臭阀。～**way** 泄水道。**-less** *a*. 〔书〕取之不竭的。

drain·age [ˈdreinidʒ; ˋdrenɪdʒ] *n*. **1**. 排水,放水;排水法;逐渐流出。**2**. 下水道;排水设备,排水系统。**3**. 水系,排水区域,流域。**4**. 阴沟水,(排出的)污水。**5**.【医】引流,导液(法)。～ *work* 排水工程。～ *and irrigation equipments* 排灌设备。～ **area** 排水面积〔区域〕;流域。～ **basin** (河流的)流域。～ **system** 排水系统;【地】水系。～ **tube**【医】导液管,引流管。～**way** 排水设施。

drain·er [ˈdreinə; ˋdrenɚ] *n*. **1**. 排水工,放水的人;下水道修建工。**2**. 排水器,滤干器;滴水板 (= drainboard)。

Drake [dreik; drek] *n*. **1**. 德雷克〔姓氏〕。**2**. **Sir Francis** ～ 杜雷克〔1540? —1596,英国航海家,最初环绕地球航行一周的人〕。

drake[1] [dreik; drek] *n*. **1**. 公鸭。**2**. (打水漂用的)石片。***play ducks and*** ～***s*** 玩打水漂游戏。～**stone** (打水漂用的)浮石片。

drake[2] [dreik; drek] *n*. **1**. (钓鱼用的)蜉蝣。**2**.【史】(17、18 世纪用的)小型火炮。

DRAM = dynamic random access memory【计】动态随机存取存储器。

dram [dræm; dræm] **I** *n*. **1**. 达姆〔常衡 = 1/16 ounce (= 1.771g.), 药衡 = 1/8 ounce (= 3.8879g.); 液量 = 1/8 ounce (= 0.0037 lit.)〕。**2**. (威士忌酒等的)少许,一口,微量。*a* ～ *drinker* 爱浅斟慢饮的人。*be fond of a* ～ 喜欢喝两口(酒)。*have not one* ～ *of learning* 一点学问也没有。**II** *vi*. (*-mm-*) 〔古〕少量饮酒。～**shop** 〔古〕小酒店。

dra·ma [ˈdrɑːmə; ˋdræmə] *n*. **1**. 剧本;一出戏;戏剧;戏曲。**2**. 〔the ～〕戏剧事业;戏剧艺术。**3**. (因有很多巧合和冲突而激动人心的)戏剧性事件,戏剧性场面。**4**. 戏剧效果,戏剧性。*the musical* ～ 音乐剧。*the poster* ～ 活报剧。*a poetic* ～ 诗剧。*the historical* ～ 历史剧。*the* ～ *of a murder trial* 审判一件凶杀案的戏剧性场面。*For God's sake, don't make a* ～ *about it*. 看在老天分上,不要大事宣扬这件事吧!

Dram·a·mine [ˈdræməmin; ˋdræməmɪn] *n*.【药】达姆明〔晕船药商标名〕。

dra·mat·ic [drəˈmætik; drəˋmætɪk] *a*. **1**. 戏剧的,剧本的;演剧的。**2**. 戏剧一样的,戏剧性的,激动人心的,引人注目的。*a* ～ *piece* 一个剧本。～ *art* 戏剧艺术。(*a*) ～ *performance* 演出。*a* ～ *critic* 剧评家。～ *poetry* 戏曲。～ *presentation* [*production*] 上演。～ *right* 上演权。*a* ～ *scene* [*event*] 戏剧性场面〔事件〕。*a* ～ *speech* 激动人心的演说。～ *colors* 引人注目的色彩。～ **present**【语法】戏剧手法的现在式〔描写过去事件为增强效果而用现在式〕。**-al·ly** *ad*.

dra·mat·ics [drəˈmætiks; drəˋmætɪks] *n*. 〔单复同〕 **1**. (特指业余的或学生的)演出;演剧活动。**2**. 演剧技术,舞台技术。**3**. 戏剧性的行为,作假。*amateur* ～ 业余演出活动。*His friends are tired of all his phony* ～. 他的朋友们对他那一套假做作都腻透了。

dram·a·tis per·so·nae (可略作 ***dram·pers***) [ˈdrɑːmətis pəːˈsəuniː; ˋdræmətɪs pɚˋsoni] 〔L.〕〔*pl*.〕【剧】 **1**. 登场人物,剧中人。**2**. 人物表。

dram·a·tist [ˈdræmətist; ˋdræmətɪst] *n*. 剧作家,剧本作者。

dram·a·ti·za·tion, dram·a·ti·sa·tion [ˌdræmətaiˈzeiʃən; ˏdræmətaɪˋzeʃən] *n*. **1**. 戏剧创作,戏剧化,戏剧性描写。**2**. (小说等的)改编为剧本。**3**. (由小说等)改编成的剧本。

dram·a·tize, dram·a·tise [ˈdræmətaiz; ˋdræmətaɪz] *vt*. **1.** (把小说等)改编为剧本。**2.** 演戏似地表现;把…戏剧化;使引人注目。*He ~s his woes with sobs and sighs*. 他像演戏似地又哭泣又叹气,来表现他的痛苦。— *vi*. **1.** 具有戏剧性;适于改编为剧本。**2.** (演戏似地)作假。*That incident would ~ well*. 那个事件很具有戏剧性。**-tiz·a·ble** *a*. **-tiz·er** *n*.

dram·a·turge [ˈdræmətəːdʒ; ˋdræmətɝdʒ], **dram·a·tur·gist** [ˈdræmətəːdʒist; ˋdræmətɝdʒɪst] *n*. 剧作家(= dramatist)。

dram·a·tur·gy [ˈdræmətəːdʒi; ˋdræmətɝdʒɪ] *n*. **1.** 剧作理论,剧本作法。**2.** 演出艺术。**-tur·gic, -gi·cal** [-ˈtuːdʒik(əl); -ˋtɝdʒɪk(əl)] *a*.

drank [dræŋk; dræŋk] drink 的过去式。

drape [dreip; drep] **I** *vt*. **1.** (用布等)覆盖,披盖;(随便地)披上(衣服等)。**2.** 悬挂;装饰。**3.** 把(衣服等)制成褶皱状。**4.** 【医】在(手术室等处)挂上消毒帷帘。*buildings ~d with flags* 用旗帜装饰起来的建筑物。*Don't ~ your feet over the chair*. 坐得端正些,不要把腿悬空架在椅子边上。*a cleverly ~d suit* 一件有漂亮褶皱的服装。— *vi*. **1.** (窗帘,饰帷等)优美地挂着。**2.** (衣服等)成褶皱状。*This silk ~s beautifully*. 这块丝绸有美丽的褶皱。**II** *n*. **1.** [*pl*.] 窗帘,布帘。**2.** 褶皱,裥。**3.** 服装式样。*the ~ of a skirt* 裙子的式样。

Dra·per [ˈdreipə; ˋdrepɚ] *n*. 德雷珀[姓氏]。

drap·er [ˈdreipə; ˋdrepɚ] *n*. 布店;绸布商。*a woollen ~* 呢绒商。*a ~'s* 布店。*go to the ~'s* 去布店(购买衣服)。

dra·per·y [ˈdreipəri; ˋdrepərɪ] *n*. **1.** 绸缎,呢绒,布匹;织物,服装。**2.** 绸缎业,布业;服装业;绸布店。**3.** [*pl*.] 帐帘,帷幔。**4.** (画像、雕像等上的)衣饰。~ *establishment* [*stores*] 绸布店。**-per·ied** *a*. 悬有(褶形)布帘的。

dras·tic [ˈdræstik; ˋdræstɪk] *a*. **1.** 激烈的,猛烈的;果断的。**2.** (法律等)严厉的。*apply ~ remedies* 下烈性药(下猛药)。*take ~ measures* 采取果断措施[激烈手段]。~ *purgatives* 猛泻药。*a ~ debate* 激烈的辩论。**-cal·ly** *ad*.

drat [dræt; dræt] *vt*. [口]咒骂[语气比 damn, confound 较为温和]。*D- it*! 讨厌! *D- the child*! 小鬼[妇女骂小孩的用语]! *D- you*! 讨厌! *D-, there goes another button*! 讨厌,又有一颗钮扣脱落了!

D ra·tion [ˈræʃən; ˋræʃən, ˋreʃən] 美国陆军的应急配给口粮。

draught [drɑːft; dræft] *n*., *v*., *a*. = draft.

draught·board [ˈdrɑːftbɔːd; ˋdræft͵bord] *n*. [英]跳棋盘(= [美] checkerboard)。

draught·i·ness [ˈdrɑːftinis; ˋdræftənɪs] *n*. 通风。

draught·i·ly [ˈdrɑːftili; ˋdræftəlɪ] *ad*. 通风地。

draughts [drɑːfts; dræfts] *n*. [*pl*.] [英]跳棋(= [美] checkers)。

draughts·man [ˈdrɑːftsmən; ˋdræftsmən] *n*. (*pl*. *-men*) **1.** 起草人;打样人;制图员。**2.** [英]跳棋棋子。

draught·y [ˈdrɑːfti; ˋdræftɪ] *a*. = drafty.

Dra·vid·i·an [drəˈvidiən; drəˋvɪdɪən] **I** *a*. (印度南部的)德拉维人[语]的。**II** *n*. 德拉维人[语]。~ **language** 德拉维语[流行于印度南部和斯里兰卡北部的一个语族]。

draw [drɔː; drɔ] **I** *vt*. (*drew* [druː; dru]; *drawn* [drɔːn; drɔn]) **1.** 拉,牵,曳,张(弓等)。**2.** 拔(牙、钉等),抽出(刀),从(容器等中)倒出(物品);取出(鸡等的)内脏。**3.** 惹,引,招,引起,招致,吸引(注意等)。**4.** 打(水),排干,汲出(水等液体);受,靠(人供给);领取,提取(钱款),获得(资源等),生(利),汲取(教训)。**5.** 描写;草拟,制订,拟(稿);描(图),绘制,画(线等),勾(轮廓)。**6.** 开给(汇票等),开立(票据等)。**7.** 抽(签),拈(阄)。**8.** 下(判断),引出(结论等),推断(结果等)。**9.** 吸进(空气);(船)吃水(深、浅)。**10.** 把…拉成丝,抽制(铁丝等);缩;扭歪(脸)[此义多用被动语态]。**11.** 使打成平局。**12.** [口]钓出,诱出(回话等),逗引…说话。**13.** 拖出;【猎】搜出(狐等);【医】抽(血),放(血);(用药)拔(脓);泡出(茶)味。**14.** 【机】退(火)。**15.** 【牌】吊(牌);补(牌)。~ *a wagon* 拉车。~ *a curtain* 拉幕。~ *a bow* 张弓。~ *a rope tight* 把绳子拉紧。*Music drew the shy girl out of her shell*. 音乐吸引那个害羞的姑娘走出了深闺。~ *a tooth* 拔牙。~ *water from a well* 从井里汲水。~ *a pond* 排干池塘里的水。~ *a cork from a bottle* 拔开瓶塞。~ *one's sword at* [*against*] *sb*. 拔剑指向某人。~ *sb.'s attention* 吸引某人注意。~ *sb. into conversation* 把某人引进谈话中来。~ *sb. on* 引某人谈(某事)。~ *a large audience* 吸引大量听众。~ *a vase* 画花瓶。~ *a character in a novel* 在小说中描绘一个人物。~ *a will* 立遗嘱。~ *a picture of* 描绘。~ *perpendicular lines* 画垂直线。~ *a comparison* [*parallel*, *distinction*] *between A and B* 比较[对比、区别]甲和乙。~ *a deep breath* 深深地吸一口气。~ *a sigh* 叹气。~ *one's first breath* 出生。~ *one's last* (*breath*) 咽气,死。~ *information from* 从…取得情报。~ *inspiration from Shakespeare* 从莎士比亚著作中汲取灵感。~ *a conclusion* 引出结论。~ *interest on a saving account* 储蓄生利。~ *a salary of $ 100 a week* 领取每周 100 美元的薪金。~ *trouble* 惹事。~ *a turkey* 掏出火鸡的内脏。~ *wire* 拉制金属丝。~ *filaments of molten glass* 把热熔玻璃拉成丝。~ *lots* 拈阄。~ *a prize* 抽彩票。*a face drawn with pain* 痛得扭歪了的脸。*The ship ~s six feet*. 这条船吃水六英尺。*The game was drawn*. 比赛打得不分胜负。— *vi*. **1.** 拉,牵,曳,拖;拉开,张满;汲取。**2.** 向(某处)移动,挨近,靠近,走近,靠拢(*to*; *towards*);(时间等)接近,逼近。**3.** 画,描;制图。**4.** 【医】(膏药等)吸脓,拔出牙齿。**5.** 拔刀,拔枪。**6.** 开立票据;支取;请求,征集,勒索。**7.** 缩,皱。**8.** (船)吃水(深,浅);(茶)泡开。**9.** (比赛)打成平局,不分胜负。**10.** 拈阄,抽签。**11.** 吸引人。**12.** (烟囱等)通风。**13.** (猎狗)追踪[接近]猎物。*all sails ~ing* 所有的帆都张开。*The carts ~ easily*. 这些车辆拉起来很轻便。*Night ~s nearer*. 夜色临近。~*ing at the well* 从井里汲水。~ *into the shore* 靠岸。*drew, aimed and fired* 拔出枪瞄准射击。*Like ~s to like*. 同声相应,同气相求。~ *for prize* 抽签得奖,抽彩票。*The draftsman ~s well*. 这个绘图员描图的技术好。*His face drew up*. 他的脸皱缩起来。*This cigar does not ~ well*. 这根雪茄不好抽。*The chimney ~s well*. 烟囱通风良好。*give the tea time to ~* 让茶慢慢泡开。*The play ~s well*. 这戏叫座。~ *on sb. for help* 要求某人给予帮助。~ *on one's imagination* 要求发挥想像力。*My shoes drew*. 我的鞋子缩小了。*They drew as many as four times that year*. 他们那一年四次打成平局。*This ship ~s deep*. 这船吃水深。~ ***a bead on*** 向…瞄准。~ ***a blank*** **1.** 抽空签。**2.** [口]失败,无所得。~ ***a full house*** 客满,剧场满座。~ ***ahead*** 【海】变成逆风。~ ***a longbow*** = ~ the longbow. ~ ***a term*** [美]被判徒刑。~ ***away*** (*from*) **1.** 拉走,引开;离开,退出。**2.** 拔出;(赛马、赛跑等)跑到前头,和(别人)拉开距离(*They started even but he soon drew away from the rest*. 他们起跑时不分先后,但他很快便跑到前面去了)。~ ***back*** **1.** 收回。**2.** 退回(转出口等的进口商品的关税)。**3.** 犹豫;退却,缩手不办。**4.** 拉开(幕布等)。~ ***bit*** [***bridle***, ***rein***] **1.** 勒住(马)。**2.** 减低速度;遏制。~ ***down*** **1.** 扯下,放下(~ *down the curtain* 闭幕)。**2.** 招来,惹,引起。**3.** 煮稠,熬干。~ ***first blood*** **1.** 发动初次攻击。**2.** 【美体】得第一名。~ ***forth*** 引出;博得(赞赏等)。~ ***in*** **1.** 拉入;引入,吸入,流入;收(网等);收回(借款等)。**2.** 引诱;诱致;使加入。**3.** 退缩;缩小;(天)黑了;(日)渐短。**4.** 紧缩(开支等),节减(~ *in a breath of fresh air* 吸一口新鲜空气。~ *in one's expenditure* 紧

缩开支。be drew in to buy 被骗去买某物)。～ ***iron***〔美俚〕(从口袋里)掏出枪来。～ ***it fine*** 1. (经费等)精打细算。2. 精确地区别;〔口〕吹毛求疵。～ ***it mild***〔口〕1. 心平气和地说;放谦虚一点。2. 不要吹;不要做得过火〔均为祈使语气〕。～ ***it strong*** 小题大做,夸张其词。～ ***level*** (*with*) 追上,赶上;扯平。～ ***lots*** [***cuts***] 抽签[抽签牌]。～ ***lots of water***〔美〕重要而有势力。～ ***near*** [***nigh***] 挨近,靠近。～ ***off*** 1. 放干,排掉(水等);脱去(手套等)。2. 消除(痛苦等)。3. 转移(他人注意力等)。4. 退走,撤退(军队等)。5. 从…中取出。～ ***on*** 1. 穿,戴 (～ *on a pair of boots* 穿靴。～ *on a pair of gloves* 戴手套)。2. 引起(战争等)。3. 引诱,勾引;招来。4. 依赖;靠;吸收。利用 (～ *on one's imagination* [*memory*] 凭想像力[记忆力]讲述)。5. 向…支取 (*He* ～*s $50 on his checking account*. 他从支票账上支付50美元)。6. 接近,挨近,靠近 (*He felt death* ～*ing on*. 他感到自己快死了)。～ ***oneself up*** (*to one's full height*) 立直,挺着胸脯;高视阔步。～ ***out*** 1. 拉长,拖长。2. 抽出;拔出;掏出;提出;【海】离(港等) (*from*);引出,诱出,诱使…说出。3. 使(队伍等)排列整齐。4. (日)渐长;(战争等)延长下去。5. 画,描;拟订,起草(计划)。～ ***over*** 拉下遮盖。～ ***round*** 围拢 (～ *round the fire* 围拢火炉)。～ ***ruin upon oneself*** 使自己身败名裂。～ ***short and long*** 抽签。～ ***the longbow*** 1. 吹牛,夸口。2.〔美〕(球等)玩得好,打得好。～ ***the pen*** [***quill***] ***against*** 写文章攻击…。～ ***to*** 近,快 (～ *to a close* 快完;收尾)。～ ***to a head*** (疮等)化脓;(阴谋等)成熟。～ ***together*** 聚拢,一齐挨近。～ ***up*** 1. 拽上,拉起(鱼网等);(把水)抽上。2. 正容;整(队)。3. 起草,写出,拟订。4. (车、马等)停住,使(车、马等)停住。5. 逼近 (*to*),追上 (*with*)。～ ***upon*** = ～ *on*.

II ***n***. 1. 牵引;抽出,拉,拖;服,吸。2. 拔出;拔牙,拔刀,拔枪;开弓;【医】(膏药等的)吸脓;支取,提(款)。3. 平局,和局,无胜负。4. 有吸引力的人[物];精彩节目。5. 抽签,拈阄;【牌】补进的牌。6.〔美〕吊桥的可吊起部分;〔口〕侦探;【地】冲沟,干涸的河谷。*take a* ～ *on his pipe* 吸一口烟。*end in a* ～ 终成平局,不分胜负。*The new play is a great* ～. 新戏非常叫座。***a sure*** ～ 肯定可搜出狐狸的地方;可引起议论之处。***be quick on the*** ～〔美俚〕反应敏捷。***beat to the*** ～ 先拔剑[枪];先下手。～ ***and quarter***〔古时刑罚〕四马分肢,肢解尸体。***play off a*** ～ 平局后加赛。～**back** ***n***. 1. 妨碍,障碍 (*to*)。2. 不利,失误;欠缺,缺点;弊端,瑕疵 (*in*)。3. 退款,退税。4.【机】回火。～**bar**【机】拉杆,导杆,挂钩。～**-bench**【机】拉丝机。～**boys**【纺】手工提花织物。～**-bridge** 吊桥。～**down** (水位)下降,消耗。～**knife,** ～**-shave** (两端有柄的)木工刮刀 (= drawing-knife)。～ **well** 吊桶井,深井。**-a·ble** ***a***.

draw·ee [drɔːˈiː; drɔˋi] ***n***.【商】(汇票等的)付款人,受票人 (*opp*. drawer)。

draw·er [ˈdrɔːə, drɔː; ˋdrɔɚ, drɔr] ***n***. 1. [ˈdrɔːə; ˋdrɔɚ] 拖曳者;【商】(汇票等的)出票人,开票人,制图人,【机】拉丝工;〔古〕酒馆侍者。2. [drɔː; drɔr] 抽屉;〔*pl*.〕橱柜。3. (*pl*. ～*s*) [drɔːz; drɔrz] 汗裤,衬裤。*a chest of* ～*s* 有抽屉的橱柜。*a pair of* ～*s* 一条衬裤。*bathing* ～*s* 游泳裤。***out of the bottom*** ～ 最低级的。

draw·gate [ˈdrɔːgeit; ˋdrɔˏget] ***n***. 运河中的水闸。

draw·ing [ˈdrɔːiŋ; ˋdrɔɪŋ] ***n***. 1. 延引,牵引;引诱。2. 抽签;拈阄。3.【机】拔丝;冲压成形。4. 描画,制图;图,图形;素描;图画。5.【纺】练条;【机】回火,退火。6. (支票等的)开发,付给;〔*pl*.〕〔英〕售得金额。*make a rough* ～ *of* 给…画草图。*a lineal* [*line*] ～ 素描。*a water-colour* ～ 水彩画。*a working* ～ 施工图。***in*** [***out***] ～ (不)合画法,画得(不)准确;和环境(不)相称。***make a*** ～ 打图样。～ **block** [**pad**] 图画纸本。～ **board** 制图板,画板。～ **card** (叫座的)节目[场面、演员等]。～ **compasses** 制图圆规。～ **knife** (两端有柄的)木工刮刀。～ **machine**【机】拔丝机。～ **mill** 拉丝厂。～ **paper** 图画纸,制图纸。～ **pen** 画图笔,鸭嘴笔。～ **pin** 图钉。～ **pump** 吸入[抽出]泵。～ **room** 1. 客厅;〔*pl*.〕聚集在客厅中的宾客;上流社会(人士)。2.〔美〕(火车的)特级专用车室。3.〔英〕(王宫中的)接见(室)。4.〔英〕制图室〔美国叫 drafting room〕(*hold a* ～ *room* 接见)。～**-room** ***a***. 客厅的;上流社会的。～ **table** 绘图桌。

drawl [drɔːl; drɔl] **I** ***vi***., ***vt***. 慢声慢气地说[唱](出),拉长腔调地说[唱](出),拖拖沓沓地说[唱](出)。*affected* ～*ing speech* 装腔作势的演说。**II** ***n***. 慢慢吞吞地说[唱];慢慢说出的话[唱出的调子]。*say in one's slow* ～ 拖长腔调说话。**-er** ***n***. **-ing·ly** ***ad***. **-y** ***a***.

drawn [drɔːn; drɔn] **I** draw 的过去分词。**II** ***a***. 1. (刀、剑等)拔出鞘的。2. 互无胜负的。3. (禽等)取出内脏的。4. (线等)画好的。5. 被吸引的。6. (钢丝等)被拔长的,延伸的,冷拉的。7. (脸等)扭歪的。*a* ～ *sword* 出鞘的剑。*a* ～ *fowl* 掏出内脏的鸡。*face* ～ *with pain* 痛得扭歪了的脸。～ **butter** (用面粉调成的)奶油酱。～ **game** 平局,和局。～ **steel** 拉制钢,冷拉钢。～ **work**【纺】抽花手工。

dray [drei; dre] **I** ***n***. 1. (没有边帮的)大车,载重(马)车。2. 粗陋的雪橇。**II** ***vt***. 用大车拖运。—***vi***. 赶大车;用大车运货。～ **horse** 重型挽马。～**man** (赶运货马车的)车夫。

dray·age [ˈdreiidʒ; ˋdreɪdʒ] ***n***. 1. 用马车拖运。2. 马车运货费。

Dray·ton [ˈdreitn; ˋdretn] ***n***. 1. 德雷顿〔姓氏〕。2. **Michael** ～ 米·德雷顿〔1563—1631,英国诗人〕。

dread [dred; drɛd] **I** ***vt***., ***vi***. 1. 恐怕,害怕,怕;担心,愁。2.〔古〕敬畏。～ *death* [*dying*, *to die*] 怕死。～ *meeting sb*. 怕见到某人。**II** ***n***. 1. 恐怖;担心,害怕。2.〔古〕敬畏。3. 畏惧的事物。*be in* ～ *of* 怕,担心。*have* ～ *of speaking in public* 害怕在大庭广众讲话。*Fire is a* ～. 水火无情,火是一件可怕的东西。**III** ***a***. 1. 令人恐惧的,非常可怕的。2. 可敬畏的。

dread·ful [ˈdredful; ˋdrɛdfəl] **I** ***a***. 1. 可怕的。2. 令人敬畏的。3.〔口〕讨厌的,糟透了的,丑陋的。*a* ～ *storm* 可怕的暴风雨。*a* ～ *hat* 难看的帽子。～ *cooking* 饭菜做得坏透了。**II** ***n***.〔英〕(趣味低级、售价便宜的)惊险小说[杂志]。*a penny* ～ 廉价惊险小说。**-ly** ***ad***. 可怕地;战战竞竞地;〔口〕特别,非常,极,极坏 (*be* ～*ly tired* 累极了)。

dread·naught, dread·nought [ˈdrednɔːt; ˋdrɛdˏnɔt] ***n***. 1. 耐用厚呢;厚呢大衣。2. 无所畏惧的人,勇士。3. [D-] (装备着旋转炮塔和大口径火炮的)无畏战舰,弩级战舰。

dream [driːm; drim] **I** ***n***. 1. 梦。2. 幻想,梦想;空想。3. 理想,愿望。4. 梦一样美好的人[物等],美景。*a hideous* ～ 恶梦。*It is beyond my* ～. 那是我梦想不到的。*a fond* ～ 一厢情愿的梦想。(*I wish you*) *sweet* ～*s* 晚安。*the land of* ～*s* 梦乡。*She is a perfect* ～. 她真是天仙一样的美女。***be*** [***live***, ***go about***] ***in a*** ～ 梦一样地过日子。***go to one's*** ～***s***〔诗〕入梦乡。***read a*** ～ 圆梦。***waking*** ～ 梦想,白日梦,幻想,空想。**II** ***vi***. (～***ed*** [dremt,〔罕〕driːmd; drɛmt, drimd], ～***t*** [dremt; drɛmt]; ～***ed***, ～***t***) 1. 做梦;梦见,梦到 (*of*; *about*)。2. 幻想,梦想;想像。3. 向往,渴望 (*of*)。4.〔与 little, not, never 等连用〕(很少,没有,决没有)想到。～ *of three mice* 梦见三只老鼠。*I never* ～*ed of it*. 我从没有想到过它。*Little did I* ～ *of succeeding so well*. 我很少想到会这样顺利。—***vt***. 1. 做(梦);梦见。2. 想像,幻想;臆想。3. (在空想中)虚度(光阴)。4.〔与 little, not, never 等连用〕(很少,没有,决没有)想到。～ *a happy dream* 做了一个快乐的梦。*Last night I* ～*ed you*. 我昨晚梦见你。～ *away one's time* 在空想中虚度光阴。*I never* [*little*] ～*t that* ... 我决没有[很少]想到…。～ ***up***〔口〕凭空想出;凭空捏造出。～ ***away***

[*out*] (*one's time*) 像梦一样地度过,虚度。~**boat** 〔美俚〕**1.** 理想的人[物];理想的情人。**2.** 同类事物中最好的。~ **factory 1.** 电影制片厂。**2.** 电影业。~**hole** (仓库等的)风窗,气窗。~**land 1.** 梦境,梦乡。**2.** 幻想世界。~ **reader** 圆梦者,详梦者。~**scape** 梦幻一般的景色。~ **team** "梦之队";最佳阵容,最佳组合。~ **world** = ~land. **-er** *n*. **1.** 做梦的人。**2.** 空想家,梦想家。**-ful** *a*. 梦多的;常易梦见的。**-less** *a*. 无梦的,梦不见的。**-like** *a*. 梦一般的;梦幻的,朦胧的。

dreamt [dremt; drɛmt] *v*. dream 的过去式及过去分词。

dream·y [ˈdriːmi; ˋdrimɪ] *a*. **1.** (人)喜欢幻想的。**2.** 梦幻般的,朦胧的,模糊的;(精神等)恍惚的。**3.** (乐曲等)悦耳的,轻柔的。**4.** 〔口〕漂亮的,顶呱呱的。**5.** 〔诗〕多梦的。*a* ~ *night's sleep* 多梦的一夜。*a* ~ *child* 喜欢幻想的孩子。*a* ~ *recollection of the event* 对那件事的模糊记忆。~ *music* 轻柔悦耳的音乐。*a* ~ *scheme* 充满幻想的计划。*He has a* ~ *new car*. 他有一辆顶漂亮的新车。**-i·ly** *ad*. **-i·ness** *n*.

drear [driə; drɪr] *a*. 〔诗〕= dreary.

drear·y [ˈdriəri; ˋdrɪərɪ] **I** *a*. **1.** 沉寂的,冷冷清清的;惨淡的,凄凉的;忧郁的。**2.** 沉闷的;枯燥的,无趣味的。**3.** 〔古〕悲哀的。*cheer a* ~ *mind* 使忧郁寡欢的心情振作起来。**II** *n*. 可怕的人物,可憎的人物〔多指历史名人〕。*a* ~ *tract of country* 荒凉的地方。*His speech was* ~. 他的讲演枯燥乏味。**-i·ly** *ad*. **-i·ness** *n*. **-i·some** *a*.

dredge[1] [dredʒ; drɛdʒ] **I** *n*. **1.** 疏浚机,挖泥机;挖泥船;捕捞船。**2.** (采牡蛎、捕鱼等用的)拖网,捞网。**3.** 悬浮矿石。~ *ore* 贫矿石。~ *pump* 疏浚泵;污水泵。**II** *vt*. **1.** 清淤,疏浚(河道等);挖掘(泥土等)。**2.** 用拖网捞取。—*vi*. 疏浚;挖泥;挖掘;捕捞。

dredge[2] [dredʒ; drɛdʒ] *vt*. (烹调时)把面粉撒(在食物上);撒(面粉)在食物上。~ *flour over meat* 把面粉撒在肉上。~ *meat with flour* 在肉上撒面粉。

dredg·er[1] [ˈdredʒə; ˋdrɛdʒɚ] *n*. **1.** 疏浚机,挖泥机;挖泥船;(捕牡蛎等的)采捞船。**2.** 疏浚工,挖泥工;使用拖网的渔夫。

dredg·er[2] [ˈdredʒə; ˋdrɛdʒɚ] *n*. (烹调时用的)撒粉器〔内装面粉、砂糖或其他调味品等,盖上有小孔〕。

dree [driː; dri] *vt*. 〔主 Scot.〕忍受,忍耐。~ ***one's weird*** 〔Scot.〕满足于自己的命运,安分守己。

dreg [dreg; drɛg] *n*. **1.** 〔常 *pl*.〕残滓,脚子;糟粕,渣滓;废物。**2.** 微量,少量的残剩物。*the* ~*s of society* 社会渣滓。*He left not a* ~ *in the glass*. 他把一杯水喝得点滴不剩。***drain*** [***drink***] ***to the*** ~***s*** 喝干;享尽(快乐等),受尽(痛苦等)。

dreg·gy [ˈdregi; ˋdrɛgɪ] *a*. (***-gi·er***; ***-gi·est***) 有渣滓的,脚子多的;浑浊的;污浊的。

Drei·bund [ˈdraibunt; ˋdraɪbʊnt] *n*. 〔G.〕三国同盟〔1882 年德、奥、意三国缔结的防守同盟〕。

D region [ˈdiː ˈriːdʒən; ˋdi ˋridʒən] 【气】D 区〔离地球表面约 60 到 90 公里高度处的电离层最低部分〕。

Drei·ser [ˈdraisə; ˋdraɪsɚ] *n*. **1.** 德赖瑟〔姓氏〕。**2.** **Theodore** ~ 西奥多·德莱塞〔1871—1945, 美国小说家〕。

drench [drentʃ; drɛntʃ] **I** *vt*. **1.** 使湿透,使浸透;浸泡。**2.** 使充满,使洋溢;包着,沐浴在…之下。**3.** 浸润;给(牲畜)灌药;〔古〕使饮。*be* [*get*] ~*ed with* [*by*] *rain* 被雨淋透。*be* ~*ed to the skin* [*through and through*] 全身湿透。*garment* ~*ed in blood* 鲜血染透的罩衣。*trees* ~*ed with sunlight* 沐浴在阳光下的树木。*a woman* ~*ed in black* 裹着黑衣的妇女。*a letter* ~*ed with a great longing for home* 充满思乡之情的一封信。**II** *n*. **1.** 弄湿,淋透;雨淋。**2.** 浸渍液;(制革时浸泡熟皮的)脱灰水。**3.** (喝)一大口;一服药水〔尤指给牲畜吃的药水〕。*a* ~ *of rain* 大雨倾盆。**drench·ing·ly** *ad*. 湿透地;大雨倾盆地。

drench·er [ˈdrentʃə; ˋdrɛntʃɚ] *n*. **1.** 〔口〕倾盆大雨。**2.** (给牲畜治病用的)灌药器。**3.** (制革行业用药液除去皮革石灰质的)脱灰工。

Dres·den [ˈdrezdən; ˋdrɛzdən] *n*. 德勒斯登〔德国城市〕。

dress [dres; drɛs] **I** *vt*. (~***ed***, 〔古〕 ***drest*** [drest; drɛst]; ~***ed***, ***drest***) **1.** 使穿衣,给…穿衣,打扮。**2.** 装饰,修饰;布置(橱窗等)。**3.** 加工(皮革等);梳理(头发),梳刷(马等);敷裹,包扎(伤处);烹调(饮食),做(菜)。**4.** 整顿(队伍)。**5.** 【矿】选(矿),洗(矿)。**6.** 修剪(树木等);给(土地)除草;为(庄稼)施肥;耕作(土地)。**7.** 使(石头、木材、织物等)表面平滑光泽。*a lady* ~*ed in black* 穿着丧服的妇女。~ *a baby* 给婴儿穿衣服。*be well* [*finely*] ~*ed* 衣着漂亮[讲究]。*get* ~*ed for a dinner party* 为出席宴会穿礼服。~ *a store window* 布置商店橱窗。~ *three chickens for dinner* 为晚餐做三只鸡。~ *meat* 做肉菜。~ *one's hair with taste* 头发的式样梳得秀气。~ *a horse* 给马梳刷。~ *one's wound* 给伤口包扎。~ *the ranks* 列队。~ *a field* 耕地。~ *a crop* 给作物除草施肥。—*vi*. **1.** 穿衣服;穿礼服;打扮,整装。**2.** 整队;【军】看齐。**3.** (鸡等)剖洗后的净重。*to* ~ *for the opera* 穿上看戏的服装。*We don't* ~ (*for dinner*). 我们(在家里晚餐)不穿礼服。~ *well* [*badly*] 衣着漂亮[难看]。*Wake up and* ~ *now!* 醒醒穿衣服吧! ~ *by* [*to*] *the right* 向右看齐。~ (*sb*.) ***down*** 〔口〕**1.** 梳刷(马)。**2.** 责骂;鞭打;【美体】打败(对方)。**3.** 把(鸡等)剖洗。~ ***oneself*** (外出时)换衣,打扮。~ ***out* 1.** 打扮。**2.** 装饰(船等)。**3.** 包扎(伤口)。~ ***ship* 1.** 【海】给船上挂彩旗。**2.** 【美海军】全舰挂国旗。~ ***up* 1.** (把…)打扮得漂漂亮亮,着盛装;化装。**2.** 整队。~ ***up like a plush horse*** [***Mrs. Astor's plush horse***] 〔美俚〕穿得过份考究。***Right*** — ~! 〔口令〕向右看——齐! **II** *n*. **1.** 衣服,服装;〔a ~〕女服,童装。**2.** 礼服,盛装。**3.** (鸟等的)羽毛;覆盖物;外表,形式。*try on a* ~ 试穿衣服。*the* ~ *of the 18th century* 18 世纪的服装。*an evening* ~ 晚礼服,燕尾服。*a morning* ~ 普通礼服。*a full* ~ 大礼服;正装。*no* ~ 服装不拘〔请帖中用语〕。*a bird in its summer* ~ 夏季羽毛丰满的鸟。*an old idea in a new* ~ 新瓶装旧酒;旧思想,新形式。**III** *a*. **1.** 女服的;童装的。**2.** 礼服的,盛装的。**3.** 需要穿礼服的。*girls in their* ~ *kimono* 穿着和服式女晨衣的姑娘。*a* ~ *dinner* 要求穿礼服的晚宴。~ **affair** 〔俚〕需要穿礼服的集会[场合]。~ **ball** 盛装舞会。~ **circle** 〔古〕二楼正座〔此处观众需穿晚礼服〕。~ **coat** 燕尾服。~ **form** (服装店橱窗中的)服装模特儿。~ **goods** (妇女、儿童用的)衣料。~ **guard** (女式脚踏车上的)护衣装置。~ **improver** 妇女托裙腰垫。~**make** *vi*. 做女服[童装]。~**maker** 女服[童装]裁缝。~**making** 女服[童装]制作业。~ **parade** 【军】正装阅兵式。~ **rehearsal** 【剧】彩排。~ **shield** (女人腋下的)汗垫。~ **shirt 1.** 礼服用衬衫。**2.** 〔美〕时髦男子。~ **suit** (一套)大礼服,(男子)晚礼服。~ **tie** 礼服用领带。~ **uniform** 〔美〕空军制服;陆军青色制服;海军青灰色冬制服。~**-up** *a*. 要求穿礼服的。

dres·sage [dreˈsɑːʒ, ˈdresɑːʒ; drɛˋsɑʒ, ˋdrɛsɑʒ] *n*. 〔F.〕**1.** 驯马表演。**2.** 驯马技术,对马的调教。

dress·er[1] [ˈdresə; ˋdrɛsɚ] *n*. **1.** (剧团的)服装员;装饰师;梳头师;〔口〕服装考究的人;穿…服装的人。**2.** 【纺】整经机;浆纱机;梳麻机。**3.** (树木)整枝剪;(石料、木材等的)打磨机;整形器;选矿机。**4.** 外科手术助手,敷裹员。**5.** 加工者;加工用具。*a fancy* ~ 服装迷。*a smart* ~ 服装漂亮的人。

dress·er[2] [ˈdresə; ˋdrɛsɚ] *n*. **1.** 食具柜;〔古〕案板,厨桌。**2.** 〔美〕梳妆台;镜台,化妆箱。~ **set** 全套梳妆用具。

dress·ing [ˈdresiŋ; ˋdrɛsɪŋ] *n*. **1.** 穿衣;衣服,服装;打扮,装束;装饰,修饰。**2.** (铸件等的)修整;(石料等的)修琢;(木材等的)打磨。**3.** (伤口的)包扎,敷裹;包扎用品,敷料,绷带。**4.** 烹调,做菜;(鸡鸭等的)剖洗。**5.** 调味品,加味品,填料。6. 追肥;(旱地用的)肥料。7.【矿】选矿。8.【军】整队;【纺】整理;上浆;梳棉。9.〔口〕申斥,责骂。~ **bag** [**case**] 化妆用品袋[盒]。~ **bell**【剧】整装铃。~-**down** *n*.〔口〕责骂;鞭打 (*get* [*receive*] *a dressing-down* 受到申斥)。~ **gown** [**robe**]〔主英〕晨衣,浴衣〔美国通例叫 bathrobe〕。~ **room** 化妆室;(舞台的)后台。~ **station**【军】(战地的)敷裹处,包扎处。~ **table** 化妆台,镜架台。~-**works** 选矿处。

dress·y [ˈdresi; ˋdrɛsɪ] *a*. 1. 讲究穿戴的,爱装饰的。2. (衣着)漂亮的,时髦的。**dress·i·ness** *n*.

drest [drest; drɛst] *v*.〔古、诗〕= dressed.

drew [druː; dru] I draw 的过去式。II *vi*. 1. 滴,滴下 (*from*); 湿透 (*with*)。2. 漏下,撒下。

drib [drib; drɪb] *n*.〔方〕点,滴;少量,微量〔主要用于片语 ~s and drabs 中〕。~*s and drabs* 点点滴滴;少量。

drib·ble [ˈdribl; ˋdrɪbl] I *vi*. 1. 滴下,点点滴滴地流。2. 淌口水,流涎。3. 慢慢流动;逐渐消散。4. (篮、足球等)带球,运球,短传。*uncontrollable dribbling of liquid* 难以控制的漏水。~ *at the mouth* 口角流涎。—*vt*. 1. 使滴,使淌(口水)。2. (篮、足球等)盘(球),带(球),运(球)。3. 逐渐发出 (*out*); 逐渐消磨 (*away*)。~ *water on a plant* 给植物洒水。~ *away one's time* [*energy*] 逐渐消磨掉时间[精力]。~ *out money to one's children* 一点一点地把钱花在子女身上。II *n*. 1. 滴;涓滴,少量。2.【体】盘球;带球,运球。3. 流涎。4. 微雨,毛毛雨。*call a plumber for* ~*s* 请管道工来修一下漏水的管子。*a* ~ *of revenue* 少量收入。*send money in* ~*s* 一点一点地送钱去。-**r** *n*. 1. 流口涎的人。2. 带球前进的运动员。

drib·(b)let [ˈdriblit; ˋdrɪblɪt] *n*. 1. 少量;少额。2. (液体的)涓滴。*by* [*in*] ~*s* 一点一点地,渐渐。*He felt a* ~ *of fear*. 他有点儿害怕。~*s coming through the ceiling* 渗过天花板滴下的水珠。~ **cone**【地】熔岩滴锥。

dried [draid; draɪd] I dry 的过去式及过去分词。II *a*. 干燥的,干缩的。~ *alum*【化】焦矾。~ *bêche-de-mer* 干海参。~ *beef* 牛肉干;〔美俚〕陈词滥调。~ *blood* 血粉(肥料)。~ *goods* 干货,干制品,干制海味。~ *milk* 奶粉。~-**up** *a*. 干缩的;干燥的 (*a dried-up water hole* 干了的水坑)。

dri·er [ˈdraiə; ˋdraɪɚ] *n*. 1. 干燥工。2. 干燥机。3. 干燥物;干料;【化】催干剂,干燥剂。

drift [drift; drɪft] I *n*. 1. 漂亮;(潮流的)推进力。2. 漂流物;吹积物;堆积物;【地】冰碛,漂砾。3. 倾向,趋势;动向。4. 大意,要点,要旨。5. (政策等的)坐观,放任自流。6. 流速;(船等的)流程,漂流距离;(滑车的)伸展距离。7. (仪表的)漂移;偏移;【海,空】偏航,偏流;(飞弹的)航差;【无】偏移;偏差。8.【矿】水平巷道;小平道。9.〔南非〕浅滩,滩。10.【机】冲头,冲孔器;打桩器。11.〔方〕(鸟等)群。*against the* ~ *of a current* 顶着潮流的压力。*be in a state of* ~ 心不自主,放任自流。*D- is as bad as unthrift*. 放任自流和浪费一样坏。*a policy of* ~ 放任主义[政策]。*a* ~ *of snow* [*leaves*] 吹积成的雪[树叶]堆。*the amount of* ~ (船的)漂流距离。*a* ~ *toward nationalism* 民族主义的倾向。*the* ~ *of an argument* 争论的要点。*catch the* ~ *of a talk* 抓住谈话的要点。*a* ~ *of ice* 流冰。*a* ~ *of sheep* 羊群。*the* ~ *of Nature* 造化的威力。*electronic* ~ 电子(仪器)的漂移。II *vt*. 1. 使漂流;使漂积[冲积];把…吹积;(吹积物等)覆盖。2.【机】(用冲头)冲孔。*The current* ~*ed the boat to sea*. 水流把船冲到海里去了。*a trail* ~*ed with leaves* 满是落叶的小道。*The wind* ~*ed the snow*. 风把雪吹成小堆。—*vi*. 1. 漂,漂流;漂移;游荡。2. 被吹积成堆。3. 心不由主地走;不知不觉地陷入 (*into*); 渐渐趋向 (*toward*)。*perfume* ~*ing into the room* 飘进屋里的香气。~ *toward ruin* [*bankruptcy*] 逐渐走向毁灭[破产]。*He* ~*ed from town to town*. 他在各个城市流浪。~*ing sand* 吹积成的沙堆。~ *apart from sb*. 逐渐疏远某人。~ *off to sleep* 慢慢地睡着了。~ *down the river* 顺流而下。~ (*along*) (*through life*) 随波逐流地过一辈子。~ *into* (*errors*) 不自觉地犯了错误。*let things* ~ 听天由命。~ **anchor**【海】浮锚。~ **angle**【海、空】偏航角,漂移角。~**bolt**【机】系栓。~ **bottle** 海流瓶[投入海中以测量海流]。~ **ice** 流冰,漂冰。~ **net**【海】漂网。~ **sand**【地】流沙。~ **sight**【航】偏流指示计。~ **space**【无】漂移空间。~ **tube**【无】漂移管。~**weed** 漂浮海草[藻]。~**wood** 1. *n*. 浮木;被扔弃的零星物品;寄生虫。2. *a*. 浮木的。**drift·y** *a*. 1. 漂移的;漂流的;流荡的。2. 吹积的。

drift·age [ˈdriftidʒ; ˋdrɪftɪdʒ] *n*. 1. 漂流(作用)。2. 漂流物;吹积物。3.【海】偏航,偏流,漂流偏差;(船的)流程;(子弹等受风影响的)偏差。

drift·er [ˈdriftə; ˋdrɪftɚ] *n*. 1. 漂流者,流浪者;漂流物;【军】漂流水雷。2. (带有漂网的)扫海船;漂网渔船,使用漂网的渔夫。3.【矿】架式钻机。

drill[1] [dril; drɪl] I *n*. 1.【军】操练,演习;(严格而有系统的)盘练,训练;〔英口〕教官。2.【机】钢钻,钻头;钻床,钻孔机;【矿】凿岩机。3.【动】(一种钻牡蛎壳破坏牡蛎繁殖的)海蜗牛,荔枝螺。4.〔英口〕正确的步骤,惯常的程序[手续]。*soldiers at* ~ 训练中的士兵。*gun* ~ 练炮。*a fire* ~ 消防训练。*a* ~ *in spelling* 拼写练习。*a* ~ *on pronunciation* 发音练习。*a twist* ~【机】麻花钻。*a three-fluted* ~【机】三槽钻头。*a heavy duty* ~ 重型钻床。*a rock* ~ 钎子。*know the* ~ *perfectly* 完全懂得规定的步骤。II *vt*. 1. 教练;(严格)训练;操练;练习;(通过反复教导)使牢记 (*into*)。2. (用钢钻)钻(孔);在…上(用钢钻)钻孔。3.〔美俚〕(用子弹)打穿,枪杀。4.〔美俚〕走,步行。~ *soldiers* 练兵。~ *schoolboys in grammar* 严格教学生练习语法。~ *an idea into sb*. 通过反复教导向某人灌输一种思想。~ *a board* 在板上钻孔。~ *holes an inch apart* 每隔一英寸钻一个孔。~ *sb. right between the eyes* 子弹正好穿过某人的两眼之间。*We had to* ~ *20 miles*. 我们得靠两条腿走二十英里了。—*vi*. 1. 操练;训练;做体操。2. 钻孔;钻通 (*through*)。3. (子弹等)穿过。4. (钻机、电话等)发出连续的嗡嗡声。~ *for oil* 钻探石油。*daylight* ~*ing into the room* 射入房间的日光。*The telephone started* ~*ing all of a sudden*. 电话突然嗡嗡响起来。~ **ammunition** 练习弹。~ **bit**【机】钻;钻头。~ **book** [**regulations**]【军】操典。~ **call** 出操号。~ **chulk**【机】钻夹头。~ **ground** 练兵场,操练场。~**log** 钻探剖面;岩心记录。~**master** 教练,【军】教官。~**press**【机】钻床。~-**ship** 钻探船,石油钻探平台。~ **team** (专为接受检阅等训练的)操典队。~ **tower** 消防训练塔。-**able** *a*.

drill[2] [dril; drɪl] I *n*. 1. 条播机。2. 条播沟。3. 条播种子,条播作物。II *vt*. 1. 条播(作为);在(土地)上条播。2. 用播种机播(种),用播种机撒(肥料)。~ *barley in rows* 条播大麦。~ *a hill with seedlings* 在小山上条植树苗。—*vi*. 条播,条植。

drill[3] [dril; drɪl] *n*.【纺】斜纹棉布[麻布];厚斜纹布。

drill[4] [dril; dril] *n*.【动】(西非的)鬼狒。

drill·ing[1] [ˈdriliŋ; ˋdrɪlɪŋ] *n*. 1. 钻孔;【矿】钻井;〔*pl*.〕钻屑,钻粉。2. 操练,训练。~ *machine* 钻床。~ *fluid* [*mud*] 钻探泥浆。

drill·ing[2] [ˈdriliŋ; ˋdrɪlɪŋ] *n*.【农】条播。*ridge* [*furrow*] ~ 垄[沟]播。

drill·ing[3] [ˈdriliŋ; ˋdrɪlɪŋ] *n*.【纺】斜纹布,卡其。

drill·ing[4] [ˈdriliŋ; ˋdrɪlɪŋ] *a*. 尖锐的,辛辣的。~ *eyes* 敏锐的目光。~ *taunt about politics* 辛辣的政治抨击。

drill·i·on [ˈdriliən; ˋdrɪlɪən] *n*.〔美俚〕天文数字。

dri·ly [ˈdraili; ˋdraɪlɪ] *ad*. 1. 干燥地。2. 冷冰冰地,冷淡地。3. 干巴巴地,枯燥无味地;不加渲染地 (= dryly)。

dri·me·ter [ˈdrimitə; ˋdrɪmətə] *n*. 含水量测定计;湿度计。

drink [driŋk; drɪŋk] **I** ***vt.*** (***drank*** [dræŋk; dræŋk]; ***drunk*** [drʌŋk; drʌŋk], 〔诗〕 ***drunk·en*** [ˈdrʌŋkən; ˋdrʌŋkən]) **1.** 饮,喝;喝干,喝完;〔~ oneself〕喝酒喝得…。**2.** 举杯祝贺,为…干杯。**3.** 吸入,(植物等)吸收(水分)。**4.** 把(金钱等)花在喝酒上;用喝酒打发掉(时间等)。**5.** 尽情欣赏,领略,陶醉 (*in*)。~ *a glass of milk* 喝一杯牛奶。*I could* ~ *the sea dry*. 我渴死了。*Let us* ~ *success to him*. 举杯祝他成功。~ *sb.'s health* 为某人的健康干杯。~ (*the toast of*) *the Queen* 为女王干杯。*The sunburnt sands drank water like a sponge*. 被太阳晒烫的沙子像海绵一样吸收水份。~ *air into his lungs* 吸一口气。~ *himself into oblivion* 喝得忘却一切。~ *one's troubles away* 以酒解忧。~ *one's income to the last penny* 喝光自己的收入。~ *the hours away* 喝酒消磨时间。~ *oneself drunk* 喝得大醉。~ *oneself into illness* 喝出病来。—***vi.*** **1.** 饮,喝。**2.** 喝酒;喝醉,酗酒。**3.** 吸,吸收 (*of*)。**4.** 干杯 (*to*)。**5.** 〔废〕喝起来有…味。~ *from a well* 喝井水。*eat and* ~ 饮食。*He never* ~*s*. 他从不喝酒。~ *deep of the Chinese culture* 深受中国文化的熏陶。*This whisky* ~*s well*. 这种威士忌酒味道不错。~ ***down*** **1.** (一口气)喝下。**2.** 以酒消(愁)。**3.** 喝到灌醉对方 (~ *down one's heartache* 以酒浇愁。~ *sb. down* 喝到使某人酒醉)。~ ***hard*** [***deep***, ***heavily***] 痛饮,大喝;酗酒。~ ***in*** 吸收;陶醉于 (*We drank in the beauty of the landscape*. 我们陶醉在美景中)。~ ***it*** 〔俚〕大喝。~ ***like a fish*** 牛饮,大口大口地喝。~ ***of*** 喝一口;分享一部分 (*He shall* ~ *of the cup*. 给他喝一口)。~ ***off*** 一气喝干。~ ***oneself out of a position*** 因为喝酒丢掉了差事。~ ***the cup of joy*** [***sorrow***] 享尽欢乐[尝尽酸辛]。~ ***to*** 举杯祝贺;为…干杯 (*I'll* ~ *to you*. 我要为你干杯)。~ (*sb.*) ***under the table*** = drink down 3. ~ ***up*** **1.** 喝干,喝完。**2.** 吸入,吸上来。**II** ***n.*** **1.** 饮料;酒。**2.** (酒等的)一口,一杯。**3.** 喝酒,酗酒。**4.** 〔the ~〕〔口〕(河、湖、海等的)一大片水〔尤指海洋〕。*soft* ~*s* (无酒精成分的)饮料。*strong* ~ 酒。~ *and tobacco* 烟酒。*D- was his downfall*. 酗酒是他垮掉的原因。*stand him a* ~ 请他喝一口酒。*Give me a* ~ *of milk*. 给我喝一口牛奶。*I will duck him in the* ~. 我要把他按进水里。*fall in the* ~ 落进水里。***a big*** ~ 〔美谑〕大河。***be fond of*** ~ 爱喝酒。***be given*** [***addicted***] ***to*** ~ 纵酒。***do a*** ~〔美〕喝酒。***have*** [***take***] ***a*** ~ 喝一杯。***in*** ~ 醉。***on the*** ~ 常常喝酒,有酒瘾。***take to*** ~ 喝(酒)上瘾。***the big*** ~〔美俚〕**1.** 大西洋或太平洋。**2.** 密西西比河。~ **money** [**penny**]〔古〕赏钱,酒钱,小账。~ **offering** 敬神酒,奠酒,祭献的酒。

drink·a·ble [ˈdriŋkəbl; ˋdrɪŋkəbḷ] **I** ***a.*** 可以饮的,饮用的。**II** ***n.*** 〔常 *pl.*〕饮料。*eatables and* ~*s* 食品和饮料。

drink·er [ˈdriŋkə; ˋdrɪŋkɚ] ***n.*** **1.** 饮者。**2.** 酒徒,醉翁。**3.** (给家禽喂水的)饮水器。*a great* [*hard*, *heavy*] ~ 酒豪,酒量大的人,酗酒者。*a little* [*small*] ~ 不爱喝酒的人,酒量小的人。*the* ~ *of the toast* 干杯者,举杯祝酒的人。

drink·er·y [ˈdriŋkəri; ˋdrɪŋkərɪ] ***n.*** 〔美〕酒店,酒吧间。

drink·ing [ˈdriŋkiŋ; ˋdrɪŋkɪŋ] **I** ***n.*** **1.** 喝,饮。**2.** (经常或过度的)喝酒。**3.** 〔美〕狂饮酒会。*give up* ~ 戒酒。**II** ***a.*** **1.** 适于饮用的。**2.** 喝酒用的。**3.** 有酒瘾的,喝酒的。*Is he a* ~ *man?* 他喜欢喝酒吗? *a* ~ *companion* 酒友。~ **bout** 宴会。~ **cup** 酒杯。~ **fountain** (公园、路旁公用的)喷嘴式饮水龙头。~ **paper** 吸水纸。~ **song** 祝酒歌。~ **water** 饮用水。

Drink·water [ˈdriŋkˌwɔːtə; ˋdrɪŋkˏwɔtɚ] ***n.*** 德林克沃特〔姓氏〕。

dri·og·ra·phy [draiˈɔgrəfiː; draɪˋɔgrəfi] ***n.*** 平版干胶印刷术。

drip [drip; drɪp] **I** ***n.*** **1.** 滴,点滴,水滴;滴下,滴滴答答〔水滴声〕;〔*pl.*〕滴下的液体[油汁等]。**2.** 【建】滴水,(屋)檐,滴水槽。**3.** 【机】滴水器;滴口;引管;采酸管。**4.** 【医】滴注(法);滴注器。**5.** 〔俚〕伤感,爱哭。**6.** 〔美俚〕平庸的人;使人厌烦的人;无聊的闲谈[劝告];恭维话。*in a* ~ 一滴一滴地。*fog* ~*s* 雾珠。*the irritating* ~ *of a faucet* 水龙头令人厌烦的滴水声。*intravenous* ~ 静脉滴注。**II** ***vi.*** (***drip·ped***, ***dript***; ***drip·ping***) **1.** 滴,滴下 (*from*); 湿透 (*with*)。**2.** 漏下,撒下。*sweat* ~*ping off one's brow* 额头滴下的汗珠。*The rain water* ~*s from the eaves*. 雨水滴下屋檐。*the cheeks* ~*ping with tears* 颊上满是泪珠。*The sunlight* ~*s over the house*. 阳光从房上漏下。*a story* ~*ping with love* 一个渗透着爱情的故事。— ***vt.*** 使滴下。*a dress* ~*ping moisture* 往下滴水珠的衣服。*Her fingers* ~*ped blood*. 她的手指滴血。~ **chamber** 排水室,沉淀池。~ **coffee** (用渗漏咖啡壶煮的)渗漏咖啡。~-~, ~-**drop** ***n.*** 不断的滴水;滴水穿石效应,潜移默化。~-**dry** **1.** [ˈdripdrai; ˋdrɪpdraɪ] ***a.*** (衣服)用快速晒干料子做的〔洗后不用绞干,可快速晒干〕。**2.** [ˈdripˈdrai; ˋdrɪpˋdraɪ] ***vi.*** (衣服)易快速晒干;晒干自挺。~-**feed** ***vt.*** 以静脉滴注法给(病人)输液。~ **mo(u)ld** 【建】滴水槽。~ **painting** 滴色画〔把颜料洒或滴在画布上而不用画笔的一种作画法〕;滴色画派。~ **pan** 【机】(车床等的)盛油[屑]盘。~**stone** ***n.*** **1.** 【建】滴水石。**2.** 【地】钟乳石,石笋。

drip·o·la·tor [ˈdripəleitə; ˋdrɪpəˏletɚ] ***n.*** 渗漏咖啡壶。

drip·ping [ˈdripiŋ; ˋdrɪpɪŋ] **I** ***n.*** **1.** 滴,滴下;滴水声。**2.** 〔常 *pl.*〕滴下物,水滴,液滴;(烧肉上的)油滴。**II** ***a.*** 水滴滴的,湿淋淋的。*a* ~ *day* 下雨天。***be*** ~ ***wet*** 淋透,湿透。~ **eaves** 【建】滴水檐。~ **pan** (烤肉等接油滴用的)油盘。

drip·py [ˈdripi; ˋdrɪpɪ] ***a.*** **1.** 滴水的。**2.** 多小雨的。**3.** 〔口〕容易伤感的。~ *weather* 经常下毛毛雨的天气。*a* ~ *love story* 感伤的爱情故事。

drive [draiv; draɪv] **I** ***vt.*** (***drove*** [drəuv; drʊv], 〔古〕 ***drave*** [dreiv; drev]; ***driven*** [ˈdrivn; ˋdrɪvṇ]; ***driv·ing***) **1.** 驱逐,赶,撵 (*along*; *away*; *back*; *down*; *in*; *off*; *out*; *forward*; *etc.*)。**2.** 赶(马车等);驾驶,开(汽车等);用车运,用车送。**3.** 逼迫,强迫,驱使,迫使,使不得不。**4.** 推动;推进;发动(机器等);运(笔);【无】激励。**5.** 努力经营,促使(成交)。**6.** 把(钉、桩等)打进 (*into*); 挖(隧道);钻(油井等);(在多山地区)开(路等)。**7.** 推迟,拖延。**8.** 【棒球】用力击(球),猛力掷(球);【网球】抽(球);发(急球);【高尔夫球】从球座打出。**9.** 从中轰出猎物。~ *away the flies* 赶走苍蝇。~ *off the pirates* 击退海盗。~ *a carriage* 赶马车。~ *a motorcar* 开汽车。~ *sb. home* 用车子送人回家。~ *a mule* 赶骡子。*a submarine* ~*n by nuclear power* 核动力驱动的潜艇。*Wind* ~*s the mill*. 风推动磨盘。~ *a nail into the wall* 把钉子敲进墙里。~ *a stone at the dog* 扔石头打狗。~ *a quill* 挥毫书写,拿鹅毛笔写字。~ *sb. mad with jealousy* [*to desperation*] 使某人嫉妒得发狂[绝望]。*The heat drove him to rest*. 酷热迫使他休息。*She was* ~*n to admit it*. 她被迫承认那件事。~ *a roaring trade* 生意兴隆。~ *a good bargain* 努力做成了一笔好生意。~ *a tunnel through a hill* 挖一条穿山隧道。~ *a railroad through a mountainous district* 横贯山区铺设一条铁路。~ *a wood* (打猎时)把林中的猎物哄赶出来。~ *one's departure to the last moment* 拖延行期直到最后一刻才动身。—***vi.*** **1.** 赶马车;开车;〔美口〕领到驾驶执照。**2.** 乘车,乘车旅行。**3.** 急驶,猛冲;(在外力推动下)急行。**4.** 努力争取。**5.** 【棒球】用力击球;猛力掷球;【网球】抽球;发急球。*learn how to* ~ 学开车。*In this state, you can't* ~ *until you are 18 years old*. 本州规定,年满十八岁方可领驾驶执照。*Do you ride or* ~? 骑马去还是开车去? *D- ahead!* 往前开! ~ *across the wilderness* 开车穿越荒原。*Rain*

drove into our faces. 雨猛打到我们脸上。*The ship drove before the wind*. 船顺风急驶。～ *in a carriage* 坐马车。～ *hard to make it a success* 努力争取成功。～ ***at*** 指望,打算,想(*I can't make out what he is driving at*. 我不明白他是什么打算)。～ ***away at*** 〔口〕一心做,拼命做。～ ***down*** 压低。～ (***sb.***) ***hard*** 强迫(某人)拼命工作。～ ***home*** 1. (把钉)敲进去。2. (摆清事实)使领会,使明白,使痛感。3. 用车把…送到家。～ ***into*** 1. 把…赶进去;(风等把…)吹积成。2. 把(功课等)灌输给。～ ***on the horn*** 〔俚〕乱揿(汽车)喇叭。***let*** ～ (***at***) 对准…打,照准…发射(*let* ～ *at the ball* 对准球一击)。
II n. 1. 驱逐,赶,撵,(猎物的)哄赶。2. 开车,驾驶马车[汽车]旅行;旅程。3.【机】传动,驱动;传动装置;【无】激励。4. 马车道,汽车路;(私宅内的)环形车路。5. 驱使;(被驱赶着走的)畜群。6. (木材的)流放,流运;(流运中的)木材。7. 冲力,动力;干劲;努力;魄力;精力。8. 倾向;趋势。9. 〔美〕(政治宣传、募捐等的)运动,热潮;竞争,廉价推销。10.【棒球】猛掷球,猛击球;【网球】抽球,发急球。11.【军】猛攻。12.【心】冲动,本能要求。*take* [*have, go for*] *a* ～ *in a motor-car* 乘汽车出游。*It's only a few minutes'* ～ *to the airport*. 坐车去机场几分钟就到了。*a* ～ *of cattle* 赶牲畜。*a* ～ *of logs* 流放木材。*the hunger* ～ 吃饱肚子的需求。*a sexual* ～ 性冲动。*a man with great* ～ 进取心强的人,干劲大的人。*a propaganda* ～ 宣传运动。*start a* ～ *to raise funds* 开展一项征募基金的运动。*His paintings has a* ～. 他的画有一种活力。*a* ～ *against Berlin* 猛攻柏林。*gear* ～ 齿轮传动。*chain* [*screw*] ～ 链[螺杆]传动。*front* [*rear*] ～ (汽车的)前[后]驱动。～**-by** 1. ***vt.*** 飞车而过(开枪射击)。2. ***n.*** 飞车射击。3. ***a.*** 草率从事的。～ **gear**【机】传[主]动齿轮,传动机构。～ **line** (汽车的)动力传动系统。～ **pipe** 自流井(竖管)。～ **pulse**【无】驱动脉冲。～ **shaft**【机】主动轴。～**-through** ***a.*** (入院做手术)快速出院的,短期的。～**way** 1. (由私人住房通到大路的)私人车道。2. 马路,汽车道。3. 〔美〕畜群道;马车道。～ **wheel**【机】主动轮,传动轮。**driv·a·ble, drive·a·ble** ***a.*** 1. 可驾驭的。2. (道路等)可供汽车行驶的。

drive-in [ˈdraivin; ˋdraɪv,ɪn] **I** ***n.*** 〔美〕(让顾客不下汽车即可吃饭、办事、看戏等的)路边饭店,路边银行;露天电影院。**II** ***a.*** (饭店、电影院等)路边服务式的;露天营业式的。*Drive-in business far exceeded walk-in business*. 露天营业式的生意远远压倒了室内服务式的生意。

driv·el [ˈdrivl; ˋdrɪvl] **I** ***vi.*** (***-l***(***l***)***-***) 1. 淌口水。2. 说蠢话,说糊涂话。3. 〔古〕喋喋不休地说。*a* ～*ling idiot* 说胡话的笨蛋。— ***vt.*** 1. 愚蠢地说。2. 浪费(时间、精力等)。～ *one's time* [*energy*] 浪费时间[精力]。**II** ***n.*** 1. 口水。2. 糊涂话。～ ***away*** 白费(时间等)。**-(l)er** ***n.*** 说胡话的人;呆子,糊涂虫。**-lin·ly** ***ad.***

driv·en [ˈdrivn; ˋdrɪvn] **I** drive 的过去分词。**II** ***a.*** 1. 被逼迫的,不得已的,被驱使的。2. 打入的。3. 吹积起来的。4.【机】从动的。～ **snow** 吹积的雪。*a* ～ *sense of obligation* 紧迫的责任感。*a* ～ *pile* 入土[打入]桩。～ **gear**【机】从动齿轮。～ **shaft**【机】从动轮。～ **wheel**【机】从动轮。

drive-on [ˈdraivˈɔn; ˋdraɪvˋɔn] ***a.*** (船等)可让汽车直接开上去的。

driv·er [ˈdraivə; ˋdraɪvɚ] ***n.*** 1. 驱逐者,驱赶者;(火车的)司机;(汽车等的)驾驶员;赶马车者。2.【机】传动轮,主动轮;推进器。3. 锤,夯,打桩机。4. 赶牲口的人;(监督奴隶等劳动的)监工。5. 激励器。6.【船】后桅斜桁帆,尾纵帆;【高尔夫球】长打棒。*a pile* ～ 打桩机。*a spike* ～ 钉锤。*a screw* ～ (螺丝)起子,改锥,旋凿。***the*** ～***'s seat*** 1. 驾驶座。2. 发号施令的地位,控制地位。～**'s license** (汽车)驾驶执照。**-less** ***a.*** 无人驾驶的。**-ship** (汽车)驾驶、保养和维修技术。

drive-up [ˈdraivˈʌp; ˋdraɪvˋʌp] ***a.*** 专为驾车者设计的(指驾车者毋需下车即可接受服务)。～ **window** (餐厅的)驾车者服务台。

driv·ing [ˈdraiviŋ; ˋdraɪvɪŋ] ***a.*** 1. 推动的,起推动作用的。2.【机】传动的;主动的。3. 猛冲的。4. 精力充沛的,有上进心的;(监工等对工人)苛刻的。5. 驾驶的,操纵的。*a* ～ *shaft* 驱动轴。～ *force* 推动力。*the* ～ *seat* 驾驶台,操纵台。*a* ～ *storm* 狂风暴雨。*a* ～ *young salesman* 精力充沛的年轻推销员。～ **axle** 主动轮。～ **band** [**belt**] 传动带。～ **box** 1. 司机台。2. 主动轴箱。～ **gear** 主动齿轮。～ **iron** 一种铁头高尔夫球棒。～ **licence** 驾驶执照。～ **shaft** 主动轮,传动轴。～ **wheel** (机械的)主动轮;(汽车的)驱动轮。

driz·zle [ˈdrizl; ˋdrɪzl] **I** ***n.*** 1. 细雨,毛毛雨,蒙蒙细雨。2. 细水珠。**II** ***vi.*** 下毛毛雨。*a drizzling rain* 蒙蒙细雨。*It* ～*s*. 下毛毛雨。— ***vt.*** 1. 细雨般地撒下。2. 用细水珠弄湿。**driz·zling·ly** ***ad.***

driz·zly [ˈdrizli; ˋdrɪzlɪ] ***a.*** 1. 下着蒙蒙细雨的。2. 毛毛雨似的。

dro·ger, dro·gher [ˈdrəugə; ˋdrogɚ] ***n.*** (西印度沿岸的)笨重的帆船,货船。

drogue [drəug; drog] ***n.*** 1. (捕鲸标枪末端的)浮标。2.【海】浮锚,海锚。3.【空】(飞机场上的)锥形风标。4.【空】(由飞机或降落伞牵引用于空战演习的)拖靶。5.【空】(空中加油飞机用的)漏斗形软管接头。6.【空】(减低飞行速度用的)减速小(降落)伞。

droit [drɔit; drɔɪt] ***n.*** 1. 权利;【法】法定所得。2. 〔*pl.*〕税,关税。3. 法律,法。*the* ～*s of Admiralty* 〔英〕捕获敌船(或从遇难船、弃船中所得的)财物收益享有权。

droit des gens [drwa dei ˈʒɑːn; drwa de ˋʒɑn] 〔F.〕国际法。

droit du sei·gneur [ˈdrɔit djuː seinˈjəː; ˋdrɔɪt dju senˋjɚ] 1. (封建领主对领地内新婚妇女蛮横索取的)初夜权。2. 任何蛮横索取的类似权利。

droll [drəul; drol] **I** ***vi.*** 〔古〕说笑话,开玩笑。～ *on* [*upon; at*] *sb*. 拿某人开玩笑。**II** ***a.*** 好笑的,滑稽的。**III** ***n.*** 逗人发笑的人;滑稽演员;小丑。**-ness** ***n.*** **-y** ***ad.***

droll·er·y [ˈdrəuləri; ˋdrolərɪ] ***n.*** 1. 滑稽(举动),诙谐。2. 笑话,滑稽话;滑稽戏;〔古〕漫画。

drome [drəum; drom] ***n.*** 〔口〕飞机场,航空港(= airdrome)。

-drome *comb. f.* 场: air*drome*, hippo*drome*, picture-*drome*.

drom·e·da·ry [ˈdrʌmədəri; ˋdrʌmədərɪ] ***n.***【动】单峰骆驼;(善跑的)乘骑骆驼。

drom·on(d) [ˈdrɔmən(d); ˋdrɑmən(d)] ***n.*** (中世纪地中海的)快速大帆船。

drom·om·e·ter [drəuˈmɔmitə; droˋmɑmɪtɚ] ***n.*** 速度计。

drone [drəun; dron] **I** ***n.*** 1. 雄蜂;〔喻〕懒人,寄生虫。2. (蜂等的)嗡嗡声;单调的低音;【乐】风笛的低音管;低音调;低音风笛。3. 言语单调的人;单调沉闷的话。4. 靶机,飞行靶标;(无线电遥控的)无人驾驶飞机。*a target* ～ 靶机。**II** ***vi.*** 1. (蜂、机械等)嗡嗡地响;用单调低沉的声音说话[唱歌],懒洋洋地说[唱]。2. 偷懒,混日子。*an aircraft droning through the stillness* 一架飞机打破寂静的嗡嗡声。*The old clergyman* ～*d on*. 那个老牧师懒洋洋地布道。— ***vt.*** 1. 用单调低沉的声音说出[唱出]。2. 懒洋洋地打发(日子)(*away*)。～ (*out*) *the sutras* 懒洋洋地讲经。**dron·ing·ly** ***ad.*** 嗡嗡地,单调低沉地;懒洋洋地;吊儿郎当地。

droog [druːg; drug] ***n.*** 流氓团伙成员。

drool [druːl; drul] **I** ***vi.*** 1. 〔英方、美〕= drivel. 2. 过分表示高兴。**II** ***n.*** = drivel. 糊涂话。

droop [druːp; drup] **I** ***vi.*** 1. (头、树枝等)低垂,下垂;(眼睛)朝下。2. (草木)枯萎;(人)衰弱,(精神)颓丧,(意气)消沉;〔诗〕(太阳等)落山,西沉。*with one's head* ～-

ing 低垂着头。*His spirits ~ed*. 他意气消沉。— **vt.** **1.** 使下垂;使(眼睛)朝下。**2.** 使颓丧。**II n.** **1.** 下垂,低垂。**2.** 颓丧。**3.** (声调的)低沉。*a ~ of the eyes* 眼睛俯视着。~ **nose** [**snout**] (飞机的)下垂式机头〔降落时飞机机头可下垂,使驾驶员获得更佳视野〕。

drop [drɔp; drɑp] **I n.** **1.** 滴;液滴,水滴。**2.** 〔*pl.*〕【药】滴剂;滴眼药。**3.** 微量,点滴;一口[杯]酒。**4.** 滴状物;耳坠;水果糖。**5.** 急降,降落;(物价)下跌,(生产)减低;败落,没落;落下距离,高低平面间的相差距离;(地面的)陷落深度;陡坡;【水】落差;【军】弹道降落距离。**6.** (绞刑台的)踏板;(绞刑犯的)吊起高度。**7.** (邮箱的)投信口;门上的锁孔盖;【建】吊饰;【机】落锤;(戏院的)垂幕;吊装布景。**8.** 中央保管所[仓库]。**9.** 降落伞部队;空投(物资)。**10.** 【橄榄球】投踢 (= drop-kick);【棒球】下曲球。**11.** 【机】轴吊距;【海】横帆的纵幅。**12.** 绞刑台。**13.** 刚出生的小动物;落果。**14.** 〔美俚〕(间谍等藏匿、传递情报的)情报点,秘密传递点。*a ~ of rain* [*water*] 雨[水]滴。*two ~s of quinine* 两滴奎宁。*a ~ of whisky* 一口威士忌酒。*a ~ of fever* 有一点发烧。*the ~ of tears* 落泪。*a ~ in prices* 跌价。*a ten feet ~* 十英尺的落下距离[落差]。*a sharp ~ to the lake* 斜向湖边的陡坡。*lemon ~s* 柠檬水果糖。*a persimmon ~* 树上落下的柿子。***a ~ in the bucket*** [***ocean***] 沧海之一粟。***at the ~ of a*** [***the***] ***hat*** 〔美俚〕一发信号就;随即,立刻;欣然 (*He used to fight at the ~ of a hat*. 他总是一看到信号就大打出手)。~ ***by*** ~ 一滴滴,一点点。***get*** [***have***] ***the ~ on*** (***sb.***) 〔美俚〕**1.** 先拔枪对准(某人),先发制(人)。**2.** 胜过(某人)。***have a ~ in one's eye*** 〔俚〕微醉,带醉。***take a ~*** 喝一杯 (*take a ~ too much* 喝醉了)。

II vt. (***dropped***, (罕) ***dropt*** [drɔpt; drɔpt]; ***drop·ping***) **1.** 使滴下,淌(汗等)。**2.** 垂下,放下;使落下,投下;空投;放低(声音等);降低(速度等)。**3.** (失手)落下,丢下;失落(钱包等)。**4.** 省略;遗漏。**5.** 丢开(话题等);改掉(习惯等);断绝(来往等)。**6.** 随便地说出,无意中漏出。**7.** (把信)投入(邮筒);(随便地)写、寄(信等)。**8.** 射落,打下(鸟等);击倒;〔俚〕杀掉。**9.** 降级;〔美〕解雇;开除(学生等)。**10.** 下(乘客),下(车);辞别(同行人)。**11.** (动物)下(崽),产(仔)。**12.** 【海】赶过,超越;使(岛等)从视线中消失。**13.** 【橄榄球】把落地球踢进(球门);【篮球】投球进(篮);【牌】吊出(王牌等)。**14.** 〔俚〕(赌博等)输(钱);(比赛)失(局等)。**15.** 把(鸡蛋)打入沸水中煮。**16.** 〔美俚〕吞服(丸药)。**17.** 退修(课程)。**18.** 将(衣服的滚边)放长。~ *lemon juice into tea* 给茶加柠檬汁。~ *sweat* [*blood*] 流汗[血]。~ *a bottle* 失手打破一个瓶子。*I must have dropped my wallet in the taxi*. 我必定是把皮夹子遗失在出租汽车里了。~ *a line* 垂钓。~ *a curtain* 落幕。~ *one's eyes* 垂下眼睛。*Let us ~ the subject*. 把这个问题放下吧。~ *one's speed by ten kilometers* 把每小时车速降低十公里。~ *smoking* 戒烟。~ *a hint* 暗示。~ *a sigh* (无意中)叹一口气。~ *sb. a line* 略写数语寄给[简告]某人。~ *sb. with a blow* 一拳把某人打倒在地。~ *one's voice to a whisper* 放低声音窃窃私语。~ *one's friend* 和友人断交。*be dropped from the club* 被俱乐部除名。*I'll ~ you at your door*. 我送你到家下车吧。~ *the ball through the basket* 投篮命中。~ *two games* 输掉两局。~ *a litter of six kittens* 下了一窝六只小猫。~ *300 combat troops* 空投下 300 支战斗部队。~ *the island* 船驶过的岛屿已从视线中消失。

— **vi.** **1.** 滴,滴落;降落,落下,落;(慢慢地)顺流而下(*down*);(话等)无意中漏出;〔美俚〕(罪犯等)落网。**2.** (价格)跌落;(声音等)变弱,变低。**3.** 倒下;倒毙;消失;完结,终止;(习惯等)停止,(交往等)断绝;(从窗口等)跳下。**4.** 下垂;下山,下车;降;访问 (*in*; *by*; *over*)。**5.** 落伍,落后。**6.** (猎犬找到猎物时)蹲下。**7.** (动物)下仔。**8.** 〔口〕(从比赛等中)退出。**9.** 【牌】被迫打出王牌。*Rain ~s from the cloud*. 云层中落下雨滴。~ *off a cliff* 从悬崖上坠下。*A pin could be heard to ~*. 一根针落在地上也听得见,寂静之极。~ *to the ground* 倒地。*There the matter dropped*. 事情到那一步就了结了。*Our correspondence has dropped*. 我们的通信中止了。*I will work till I ~*. 工作到死,鞠躬尽瘁。~ *from a race* 退出赛跑。~ *out of college* 退学。~ *from* [*out of*] *sight* 消失不见。*Her voice dropped*. 她的声音低下去了。~ *into reminiscence* 陷入回忆。~ *down a river* 慢慢地顺流而下。***be ready*** [***fit***] ***to ~*** 疲倦得要死。~ ***a brick*** 〔口〕失言,出错,出丑。~ ***across*** **1.** 偶然碰见。**2.** 谴责。~ ***asleep*** 睡着。~ ***astern*** 落在(他船)后面。~ ***a stitch*** (编织时)漏掉一针。~ ***away*** 一滴一滴落下;(一个个)走掉;(不知不觉间)跑掉 (*The guests ~ away one by one*. 客人一个个散了)。~ ***back*** **1.** 退后,后撤。**2.** 恢复旧习,故态复萌 (*into*)。~ ***behind*** [***back in line***, ***to the rear***] 落伍,落在后头。~ ***by*** 〔美〕顺便到(某处)去一下,随便访问一下。~ ***by*** ~ 一滴一滴地。~ ***dead*** 倒毙,暴死。~ ***down*** **1.** 倒下。**2.** (风等)突然停止。**3.** 沿(河)而下。~ ***in*** 〔口〕**1.** 顺便到(某处)访问 (*Please ~ in to tea*. 请随便来我家喝茶。~ *in on sb*. 偶然访问某人)。**2.** 偶然遇见 (*with*)。~ ***into*** **1.** 跌入,落入。**2.** 偶然进入 (~ *into a house* 偶然走进一所房屋)。**3.** 不知不觉地进入(某种状态),不知不觉地养成(习惯等) (~ *into sleep* 不知不觉地睡着了。~ *into a habit* 养成某种习惯。~ *into discussion* 不知不觉地谈论起来)。~ ***off*** **1.** (客)(一一)散去,走掉。**2.** 睡着。**3.** 衰落。**4.** 流出。**5.** 〔口〕死。***D- it***! 停止! 别闹了! 别那样了! ~ ***on*** [***upon***] 〔口〕严厉谴责。~ ***on one's knees*** 跪下。~ ***out*** **1.** 退出,脱离;(因不满传统制度而)退出正常社会,放浪形骸。**2.** 失落,落出。**3.** 消失,隐退 (*of*)。~ ***short*** **1.** 不足 (*of*)。**2.** 〔口〕暴死。~ ***the leather*** 〔美〕(篮球)投中得分。~ ***through*** 彻底失败。***let ~*** **1.** 忽略,遗漏。**2.** 放弃,撒手。~ **arch**【建】垂拱。~**-bottom** 活底,底卸式。~ **cloth** (家具等的)罩布。~ **curtain** 吊幕,垂幕。~**-front** ***a.*** 正面用铰链相接可放至水平位置的。~**-forge** ***vt.***【冶】用落锤锻造,锤锻,冲锻。~ **hammer**【机】落锤。~**head** **1.** 活动头〔使打字机或缝纫机头藏在台板下的活动装置〕。**2.** (汽车的)活动帆布车顶。~**-in** **1.** ***n.*** 偶然来访的客人;偶然到访的地方;〔美俚〕吸毒者的巢穴。**2.** ***a.*** 插入式的。~**-kick** ***n.***【橄榄球】踢落地球。~**leaf** ***a.*** (桌等)有折叠板的。~ **letter** 〔美〕由同一邮局收递的信件。~**light** 活动吊灯。~**-off** ***n.*** **1.** 陡坡。**2.** 衰减。~**-out** ***n.*** 〔美〕**1.** 中途退出;退学;落后。**2.** 中途退出者;退学者;落后者;因不满意传统制度而退出正常社会者,放浪形骸者。**3.** (磁带上的)信息漏失点。~ **press**【机】模锻压力机,落锤。~**scene** **1.** 垂幕吊装布景。**2.** 压台戏。**3.** 结局,最后下场。~ **shipment** 由厂方直接运给零售商的货物。~ **shot**【网球】扣球。~ **shutter** (旧式照相机上下滑动的)快门,开关。~**side** ***a.*** 侧卸的。~ **table** (一边连在墙上,使用时可放下的)连墙桌。~ **valve** (蒸汽机中上下活动的)活门,活阀。~ **window** (窗门可滑进窗框下面去的)伸缩窗。~ **wort**【植】六瓣合叶子。**-like** ***a.*** 水滴似的,滴状的。**-let** ***n.*** 微滴。

drop·line [ˈdrɔplain; ˋdrɑpˏlaɪn] ***n.*** (新闻)分成数行的横标题。

drop·page [ˈdrɔpidʒ; ˋdrɑpɪdʒ] ***n.*** **1.** (使用或操作时的)额外损耗量。**2.** (成熟前的)落果量。**3.** 〔总称〕落下的东西。

drop·per [ˈdrɔpə; ˋdrɑpɚ] ***n.*** **1.** 落下者,落下物。**2.** 滴管;(有滴管的)点药瓶。**3.** 【矿】分脉,支脉。~**-in** 〔美〕(习惯于)随便到人家串门子的人。

drop·ping [ˈdrɔpiŋ; ˋdrɑpɪŋ] ***n.*** **1.** 滴下;落下,降下;【军】空降,空投,伞降。**2.** 点滴;〔*pl.*〕滴下物;落下物。**3.** 〔*pl.*〕(鸟等的)粪;【纺】落棉,落毛。*animal ~s* 畜粪。~ **bottle**【医】点药瓶。~ **fire**【军】(步枪的)疏射。

~ **funnel** 滴液漏斗。~ **gear** 空投装置。~ **ground**【军】空投场。~ **satellite** (由运载器抛出的)抛射式人造卫星。

drop·si·cal [ˈdrɔpsikəl; ˋdrɑpsɪkl] ***a***.【医】水肿的,浮肿的;似水肿的;患水肿病的。**-ly** ***ad***. **-ness** ***n***.

drop·sied [ˈdrɔpsid; ˋdrɑpsɪd] ***a***. 患水肿病的。

drop·sonde [ˈdrɔpsɔnd; ˋdrɑpˏsɑnd] ***n***.【气】(由降落伞投下的)下投式探空仪。

drop·sy [ˈdrɔpsi; ˋdrɑpsɪ] ***n***.【医】水肿,浮肿,积水。

dropt [drɔpt; drɑpt] ***v***. drop 的过去式及过去分词〔罕用〕。

dros·er·a [ˈdrɔsərə; ˋdrɑsərə] ***n***. 茅膏菜属植物。

drosh·ky [ˈdrɔʃki; ˋdrɑʃkɪ] ***n***. (帝俄时代的)轻便马车,敞篷四轮马车。

dros·ky [ˈdrɔski; ˋdrɑskɪ] ***n***. = droshky.

dro·som·e·ter [drɔˈsɔmitə; droˋsɑmɪtɚ] ***n***.【气】露量计。

dro·soph·i·la [drəuˈsɔfilə; droˋsɑfələ] ***n***. (*pl*. ~**s**, **-lae** [-liː; -li]) **1**.【动】果蝇 (= fruit fly)。**2**. 〔D-〕【动】果蝇属。

dross [drɔs; drɔs] ***n***. **1**.【冶】浮渣;铁屑,铁渣。**2**. 渣滓;碎屑;杂质。**3**.【矿】劣质细煤。*transmute the ~ of reality into the gold of art* 把现实的渣滓熔炼为艺术的纯金。~ **coal** 渣煤,不粘(结性)煤。**-y** ***a***. **1**. 渣状的。**2**. 不纯的。**3**. 无价值的 (*the drossiest work* 最低劣的作品)。

drought [draut; draʊt], 〔诗, Scot., Ir., 美〕 **drouth** [drauθ; draʊθ] ***n***. **1**. 旱灾,干旱。**2**. 〔喻〕(长期的)缺乏。**3**. 〔古〕干渴;干燥。*a prolonged ~* 天久不雨,长期干旱。*a ~ of good writing* 长期缺乏好作品。~**-enduring** ***a***. 耐旱的。~**-resistant** ***a***. 抗旱的。

drought·y [ˈdrauti; ˋdraʊtɪ], 〔诗, 美〕 **drouth·y** [ˈdrauθi; ˋdraʊθɪ] ***a***. 干旱的;旱灾的;干燥的;〔古〕口渴的。**drought·i·ness**, **drouth·i·ness** ***n***.

drove[1] [drəuv; drov] ***v***. drive 的过去式。

drove[2] [drəuv; drov] **I** ***n***. **1**. (被赶着走的)畜群。**2**. (一道走或行动的)人群。**3**. (石匠的)平凿;(用平凿)凿平的石面。***in ~s*** 成群结队。**II** ***vt***. **1**. 赶(牲畜);(牲畜贩子)买卖(牲畜)。**2**. 用平凿凿(石料)。—***vi***. **1**. 赶牲畜。**2**. 用平凿凿石。~ **chisel** (石匠用的)平凿。~ **work** (经过粗凿的)凿平的石面。

dro·ver [ˈdrəuvə; ˋdrovɚ] ***n***. **1**. 赶家畜上市场的人。**2**. 牲畜商。

drown [draun; draʊn] ***vt***. **1**. 使溺死,淹死。**2**. 使湿透;淹没。**3**. 使沉溺于,使迷恋 (*in*)。**4**. 消(愁),解(闷)。**5**. (噪音等)盖掉(低声)。**6**. 搀淡,冲淡(饮料)。**7**. (加水)化开(生石灰)。*get* [*be*] *~ed* 淹死。*~ oneself in a river* 淹死在河里。*eyes ~ed in tears* 泪汪汪的眼睛。*be ~ed in wine* 恋酒贪杯。*be ~ed in sleep* 在酣睡中。*His voice was ~ed by the coughing of the audience*. 他的声音被听众的咳嗽声淹没了。*~ one's whisky* 冲淡威士忌酒。*~ one's sorrows* [*cares*] *in wine* 以酒消愁[解忧]。—***vi***. 淹死;沉没。*fall in the water and ~* 落水淹死。*The boat ~ed but we were saved*. 船沉了,但我们幸而获救。*a ~ing man* 快要淹死的人。~ ***out*** **1**. (洪水)把(人)赶跑。**2**. 把(另一声音)压倒[淹没、盖住]。***like a ~ed rat*** (湿得)像落汤鸡。~**ed valley** 被海水淹没而成为出海口或海湾的山谷。~**-proofing** 浮水法〔利用人体浮力长时间浮在水面上的技巧〕。**-er** ***n***. 溺死者。

drowse [drauz; draʊz] **I** ***n***. 瞌睡。**II** ***vt***. 使昏昏欲睡;糊里糊涂地度过 (*away*)。*a lecture that ~s the students* 使学生打瞌睡的讲演。*He ~d away the morning*. 他一上午都是昏昏沉沉的。—***vi***. **1**. 打盹儿,打瞌睡。**2**. 发呆;呆滞不动。*a village drowsing in the sun* 沉寂地躺在太阳光下的村庄。

drow·sy [ˈdrauzi; ˋdraʊzɪ] ***a***. **1**. 昏昏欲睡的,困倦的;打着瞌睡的。**2**. 催眠的;使人懒洋洋的。**3**. (街市等)沉寂的。**4**. 呆滞的。*feel ~* 昏昏欲睡。*~ spring weather* 使人懒洋洋的春天。*~ hills* 寂静的群山。~**-head** 瞌睡虫,爱瞌睡的人。**-si·ly** ***ad***. **-si·ness** ***n***.

drub [drʌb; drʌb] ***vt***. (**-bb-**) **1**. 用棒连续敲打。**2**. 打败(敌方),(愤慨时)踏响(地板等)。*~ a silly notion out of sb.'s head* 把一个糊涂念头从某人头脑中强行打消。*a book ~ed by every critic* 一本受到所有批评家抨击的书。— ***vi***. **1**. 敲击,连打。**2**. (用脚在地板等上)咚咚地踏。**drub·ber** ***n***. 敲打者;跺脚者。

drudge [drʌdʒ; drʌdʒ] **I** ***vi***. 做苦工 (*at*; *over*)。*~ at a tedious work* 干单调无味的苦活。—***vt***. 强使(某人)做苦工。**II** ***n***. **1**. 苦工,单调乏味的工作。**2**. 做苦工的人。**3**.【海】将官室[舰长室]的侍者;〔美俚〕生威士忌酒。*a daily ~* 枯燥无味的每日例行公事。**-r** ***n***. **drudg·ing·ly** ***ad***. 辛劳地;苦役般地;单调乏味地。

drudg·er·y [ˈdrʌdʒəri; ˋdrʌdʒərɪ] ***n***. 苦工,单调辛苦的工作。*farm ~* 农场上的苦活。*household ~* 繁琐的家务劳动。

drug [drʌg; drʌg] **I** ***n***. **1**. 药,药品,药物,药剂。**2**. 〔俚〕麻醉药品,麻醉剂,使人上瘾的毒品 (= narcotic ~s)。**3**. 〔*pl*.〕〔美〕卫生用品[牙刷、牙膏等]。**4**. 滞销货。*poisonous ~* 毒药。*This ~ will do you good*. 这种药能治你的病。*the ~ habit* 常用麻醉剂的习惯,吸毒瘾。*go on ~s* 吸毒。*a ~ in* [〔美〕 *on*] *the market* 滞销货。**II** ***vt***. (**-gg-**) **1**. 在(酒、食物等中)渗(麻醉药,下(麻醉)药于。**2**. 使服(麻醉)药,使麻醉。**3**. 使沉醉;毒化。*a cup of ~ged coffee* 一杯下了麻药的咖啡。*~ged sleep* 服下麻醉药后的熟睡。*She was ~ged against the pain*. 她服麻醉药止痛。*be ~ged with sleep* 睡觉太多而昏昏沉沉。—***vi***. 常用麻药;吸毒上瘾。~ **addict** 吸毒者,瘾君子。~**-fast** ***a***.【医】抗药性的,耐药性的。~**store** **1**. 药房。**2**. 〔美〕(出售药物而兼卖化妆品、纸烟、杂志的)杂货店。~**store cowboy** 〔美俚〕 **1**. 爱吹牛的年轻人。**2**. 在杂货店里混日子的年轻人。**3**. 讨女人欢喜的男人;女模女样的男子。~**store whisky** 用医师单方从药房里配来的威士忌酒。

drug·get [ˈdrʌgit; ˋdrʌgɪt] ***n***. **1**. 粗毛地毯[台毯],棉毛混纺地毯。**2**. (铺地板等用的)粗织物。**3**. (旧时作衣料用的)羊毛织物,棉毛混纺织物。

drug·gist [ˈdrʌgist; ˋdrʌgɪst] ***n***. 〔美〕〔Scot.〕 **1**. 药商。**2**. 药剂师。**3**. 〔美〕(卖药又兼卖糖果纸烟等的)杂货店老板。*~ rubber sundries* 〔*pl*.〕医用橡胶制品。

drug·gy [ˈdrʌgi; ˋdrʌgɪ] **I** ***n***. 〔美俚〕吸毒者。**II** ***a***. 吸毒后引起的。

drug·o·la [drʌgˈəulə; drʌgˋolə] ***n***. 〔美俚〕(毒贩付给警察等的)毒品贿,以毒品形式付给的贿赂。

dru·id, **Dru·id** [ˈdru(ː)id; ˋdruɪd] ***n***. **1**. (古代高卢、不列颠和爱尔兰等地凯尔特人中的)祭司,巫师,占卜者。**2**. (威尔斯等地的)诗人[音乐家]联谊会的主持人。**-ess** ***n***. (古代凯尔特人中的)女祭司,女巫师,女占卜者。**-ic**, **-dical** ***a***. **-ism** ***n***. (古代高卢、不列颠和爱尔兰等地凯尔特人中)由祭司[巫师、占卜者]举行的仪式。

drum[1] [drʌm; drʌm] **I** ***n***. **1**. 鼓。**2**. 鼓声,击鼓般的声音;麻鸦的叫声;〔古〕鼓手。**3**. 鼓状物;圆桶,汽油桶;【机】滚筒,鼓轮;卷线轴;绕线架;【建】(作石柱用的)鼓形石块;(支持圆屋顶的)鼓形墙壁;【解】鼓室;鼓膜;中耳;【动】鼓形共鸣器;(自动步枪的)转盘弹匣。**4**. 〔古〕夜会,(午后)茶会。**5**.【动】(发出鼓声的)石首鱼。*play* [*beat*] *the ~* 击鼓。*a double ~* 双面鼓。*a ~ of running feet* 奔跑的脚步声。*the ~ of a cicada* 蝉的共鸣器官。*a dozen ~s of lubricating oils* 十二桶润滑油。***beat*** [***rattle***] ***the*** [***a***] ***big ~*** (*for*; *about*) 为…鼓吹,为…做广告。***beat the ~*** 宣传。***with ~s beating and colours flying*** 军容威武。**II** ***vt***. (**-mm-**) **1**. 咚咚地敲打,连打,打响。**2**. 敲鼓奏(曲),敲出(曲调)。**3**. 生硬地教给(学问)。**4**. 〔美俚〕敲鼓招揽;鼓励,奖励。~ *a* *march* 击鼓奏进行曲。~ *a rhythm for dancers* 为跳舞的人击出鼓点。~ *one's fingers on the desk* 用手指敲桌子。~ *sb. from his work* 敲鼓把某人从工作岗位上召来。~ *sb. into action* 鼓动某人行动。~ *Latin into a boy* 硬叫孩子学拉丁文。—*vi*. **1.** 敲鼓,咚咚地敲。**2.** (鸟、昆虫振动翅膀等)发出嗡嗡声。**3.** 奔走招募;鼓吹(*for*)。~ *at the door* 咚咚咚地敲门。~ *on the floor* 咚咚咚地踏响地板。*The rain ~med*. 雨声滴答。~ *for a new film* 为新影片做广告。***a ~ming in the ears*** 耳鸣。***~ down*** (击鼓)使静默。***~ out*** 轰走;开除(*be ~med out of the university* 被开除出大学)。***~ up*** **1.** 招揽(顾客等);招募(新兵等)。**2.** 鼓励;激起(*~ up recruits* 招募新兵。*~ up customers* 招揽顾客。*~ up enthusiasm for the new policies* 激起支持新政策的热情)。~**beat** 鼓声。~**beater 1.** 鼓手,打鼓佬。**2.** 鼓吹者,支持者。~ **brake** 制动圆筒。~ **corps** 军乐队。~**-fed gun** 转盘式机枪。~**fire** (步兵进攻前的)猛烈炮火(*a ~fire of announcements* 连续发表强烈声明)。~**-fish**【动】石首鱼科的鱼。~**head 1.** *n*. 鼓面皮;【解】鼓膜;【机】绞盘头。**2.** (裁判等)即决的(*a ~head execution* 就地处决。*a ~head court-martial* 临时军事法庭)。~ **major 1.**【军】鼓手长。**2.** 行进军乐队指挥。~ **majorette** 军乐队女指挥。~ **printer** 滚桶印刷机。~ **stick 1.** 鼓槌。**2.**【烹】(煮熟的)家禽腿下部。~ **table** (三足)可旋转鼓形立橱。

drum² [drʌm; drʌm] ***n***. = drumlin.

drum·lin [ˈdrʌmlin; ˋdrʌmlɪn] ***n***.【地】(冰河漂积成的)鼓丘。

drum·mer [ˈdrʌmə; ˋdrʌmɚ] ***n***. **1.** 鼓手。**2.**〔美口〕旅行推销员。

Drum·mond [ˈdrʌmənd; ˋdrʌmənd] ***n***. 德拉蒙德〔姓氏〕。

drunk [drʌŋk; drʌŋk] **I** drink 的过去分词。**II** ***a***.〔多用作表语〕**1.** 酒醉的。**2.** 陶醉于(*with*)。*be ~ with* [*on*] *wine* 喝醉酒。*as ~ as a fiddler* [*lord, fish*] 大醉。*get beastly* [*blind, dead*] *~* 泥醉,烂醉。*be ~ with joy* 沉醉于欢乐之中。**III** ***n***. **1.** 醉汉。**2.**〔美口〕酒宴。**3.** 喝醉,酒醉状态。*be on a ~* 喝醉。*sleep off ~s* 睡觉解酒。~ **tank**〔谑〕醉汉拘留所。

drunk·ard [ˈdrʌŋkəd; ˋdrʌŋkɚd] ***n***. 酒鬼,醉汉。*play the ~* 发酒疯。*a chronic ~* 老酒鬼。~**'s chair** (英国18世纪时的一种)矮脚围椅。

drunk·en [ˈdrʌŋkən; ˋdrʌŋkən] ***a***. **1.**〔多作修饰语〕酒醉的;常醉的;爱喝酒的。**2.** 酒醉引起的。**3.** 像喝醉酒似的,摇摇晃晃的。*a ~ bum* [*sot*] 酒鬼。*a ~ brawl* 酒醉后的吵闹。*a ~ frolic* 酒醉后的胡闹。~ **saw**【机】切[开]槽锯。**-ly** ***ad***. 醉。**-ness** ***n***. **1.** 酩酊;醉态。**2.** 放荡,放纵。

drunk·o·meter [drʌŋˈkɔmitə; drʌŋˋkɑmɪtɚ] ***n***. (用呼出的气体测定司机等体内酒精含量的)测醉器。

dru·pa·ceous [druːˈpeiʃəs; druˋpeʃəs] ***a***. **1.**【植】核果(性)的。**2.** 结核果的。~ *fruit* 核果。~ *trees* 核果树。

drup·el, drupe·let [ˈdruːpəl, ˈdruːplit; ˋdrupəl, ˋdruplɪt] ***n***.【植】小核果。

Druse [druːz; druz] ***n***. 德鲁斯〔姓氏〕。

druse [druːz; druz] ***n***.【矿】晶簇,晶洞。

Drus(z)e [druːz; druz] ***n***. (叙利亚、黎巴嫩山区的)德鲁兹教派穆斯林。**Dru·s(z)i·an, Dru·s(z)e·an** [ˈdruːziən; ˋdruziən] ***a***.

druth·ers [ˈdrʌðəz; ˋdrʌðɚz] ***n***.〔美方〕(自由的)选择;偏爱。*If I had my ~, I'd go fishing*. 如果我能选择的话,我就去钓鱼。

DRV, DRVN = Democratic Republic of Vietnam 越南民主共和国。

dry [drai; draɪ] **I** ***a***. **1.** 干的,干燥的;无水分的,干透了的。**2.** (井、河等)干涸的,枯竭的;(气候)干旱的;无奶的;无泪的;无痰的,干咳的。**3.**〔俚〕口干的;〔美口〕禁酒的,赞成禁酒的(*opp*. wet)。**4.** 不新鲜的,陈的。**5.** 不用水操作的;不用润滑油的。**6.** 简慢的,冷淡的。**7.** 赤裸裸的,露骨的;不加渲染的;不带个人偏见的。**8.** 干巴巴的,枯燥无味的;(嗓音等)干涩的。**9.** (酒等)无甜味的,味淡的;(面包等)不涂奶油的。**10.**〔军俚〕空弹的,演习的。**11.** 无预期结果的,没有收获的。~ *air* 干燥的空气。~ *fish* 干鱼。*a ~ winter* 无雨的冬天。*a ~ bucket* 空桶,没有盛水的桶。*a ~ well* 枯井。*a ~ cow* 枯奶期的乳牛。~ *sobs* 没有眼泪的啜泣。~ *toast* 不涂奶油的烤面包。*with ~ eyes* 不流泪,冷然。~ *work* 使人累得口干燥的工作。*a ~ clutch* 不加润滑油的离合器。~ *wall construction* 不用灰浆的(预制件)筑墙法。*a ~ book* 枯燥无味的书。~ *thanks* 冷淡的感谢,客套。~ *facts* 毫无虚饰的事实。~ *humour* 一本正经地讲的笑话。*the ~ years of the great artists* 伟大艺术家作品贫瘠的时期。~ *lodging* 不供伙食的宿舍。*a ~ state* 禁酒的州。~ *firing* 射击演习。***a ~ eye*** 不流泪的眼睛,有泪不轻弹。***die a ~ death*** 老死。***~ as a bone*** 干透。***go ~***〔美〕颁布禁酒令。***not ~ behind the ears***〔美俚〕未成熟的,乳臭未干的,不懂事的。***row ~*** 划桨时不使水花溅起。***run ~*** **1.** (乳牛)不产奶。**2.** (河等)水干枯(*Most cows run ~ in about ten months*. 大部分乳牛有十个月不产奶。*This stream will never run ~*. 这条溪流永不会枯干)。

II ***vt***. (***dried; dry·ing***) **1.** 把…弄干,使干燥;晒干;揩干;排干(池塘等)。**2.** 使(乳牛)停止产奶。~ *the dishes* 揩干碗碟。~ *one's tears* [*eyes*] 擦干眼泪。~ *one's hand on a napkin* 用餐巾揩干手。—***vi***. 变干;干涸;干枯。~ ***out* 1.** 变干。**2.** 戒酒。~ ***up* 1.** 把…弄干,使干。**2.** 干涸;逐渐枯萎。**3.**〔俚〕停止讲话;(演员)忘记台词(*The spring dried up long ago*. 这泉水早就干涸了。*D- up*! 住嘴! *I wish the conversation would ~ up*. 我希望谈话不要再继续下去)。

III ***n***. **1.** (*pl*. ***dries***) 干燥(状态);干燥场;干裂,(石头的)裂缝;〔常 *pl*.〕干季。**2.** (*pl*. ***drys*** [draiz; draiz])〔美口〕禁酒主义者,赞成禁酒的人。***do a ~*** (演员)记不起台词。***in the ~*** 没有碰到雨,没有弄湿。~**ball** ***n***.〔美学俚〕死用功的学生。~ **battery** [**cell**] 干电池。~**-boned** ***a***. 皮包骨头的,骨瘦如柴的。~**-bones** 骨瘦如柴的人。~ **bread 1.** 没有涂奶油的面包。**2.** 陈面包。~**-bulb** ***a***. (寒暑表)干球式的(*a ~-bulb thermometer* 干球温度计)。~**-clean,** ~**-cleanse** ***vt***. 干洗(衣服)。~ **cleaner 1.** 干洗剂。**2.** 干洗商。~ **cup**【医】吸杯。~**-cure** ***vt***. 腌(鱼肉等)。~ **distillation** 干馏。~**-dock** ***vi***., ***vt***. (使)入干船坞。~ **dock** 干船坞。~**-farm 1.** ***vt***. 用旱作法栽培。**2.** ***vi***. 实行旱作法。~ **farming** 旱地耕作(法)。~ **fly** (钓鱼)假饵。~**foot** ***ad***. 不湿脚地。~ **goods**〔美〕绸缎呢绒类货品;〔英〕杂粮(等)。~ **hole**〔美〕笨人,蠢货。~ **ice**〔美〕干冰〔固体二氧化碳〕。~ **land 1.** 干旱地区。**2.** 陆地。~ **law**〔美俚〕禁酒法。~ **light 1.** 无阴影的光线。**2.** 公平的见解,公正无私。~ **measure** (度量衡)干量(*opp*. liquid measure)。~ **milk** 奶粉。~ **money** (小戏院等的)收入,售票所得。**D-Navy**〔美〕酒类缉私舰[艇]。~ **nurse** 保姆,保育人员(*opp*. wet nurse)。~**-nurse** ***vt***. 保育,抚育,当…的保姆[保育人]。~ **plate**【摄】干片。~**point 1.** ***n***. (不用酸的)铜版雕刻(术);铜版雕刻针;铜版画。**2.** ***vi***. 作铜版雕刻。~ **provisions** [**wares**] 食用干品[干货]。~ **resistance** 抗旱性。~ **rot 1.**【植】干腐病。**2.** 腐化(*Nepotism and lack of discipline often cause ~ rot in an organization*. 任人唯亲和缺乏纪律,往往造成一个组织的腐化)。~ **run**【军】空弹演习;假俯冲,假投弹。~**-salt** ***vt***. = ~-cure. ~**salter** 干货商。~**saltery** 干货业;干货店;干货类。~ **shampoo 1.** (头发)干洗。**2.** (酒精性)洗发水[粉]。~**-shod** ***a***., ***ad***. 不湿脚的[地],不湿鞋的[地]。~ **skim milk** 脱脂奶粉。~ **town**〔美〕禁酒市。~ **wall** 不涂泥灰的墙壁。~ **walling**【建】无浆砌

墙,干砌。～ **weight** 1.(脱水)干重。2.【空】(不包括汽油等在内的飞机的)自重。**-able** *a*. **-ness** *n*.

dry·ad, Dry·ad [ˈdraiəd; ˋdraɪəd] *n*. (*pl*. ～*s*, ～*es* [-ədiːz; -ədiz])【希神】林中女仙,树精。**-ic** [draiˈædik; draɪˋædɪk] *a*.

dry·as·dust [ˈdraiəzdʌst; ˋdraɪəzdʌst] **I** *a*. 枯燥无味的,兴味索然的;学究式的。**II** *n*.〔常 D-〕令人乏味的学究[考古学家、统计学家等]。

Dry·den [ˈdraidn; ˋdraɪdn̩] *n*. 1. 德赖登〔姓氏〕。2. **John** ～ 约翰·德赖登〔1631—1700,英国诗人、剧作家、批评家〕。

dry·er [ˈdraiə; ˋdraɪɚ] *n*. = drier.

dry·ly [ˈdraili; ˋdraɪlɪ] *ad*. = drily.

dry·o·pith·e·cine [ˌdraiəuˈpiθəˌsiːn, -ˌsain; ˏdraɪoˋpɪθəˏsin, -ˏsaɪn] **I** *a*.【考古】类人猿属的。**II** *n*.【考古】森林古猿。

Ds =【化】dysprosium〔一般作 Dy〕.

DS, D.S. =〔It.〕*dal segno* (= repeat from the sign)【乐】从记号𝄋处开始重复一遍; degree of substitution; Dental Surgeon; Distinguished Service; dry spinning.

d.s. = day's sight; days after sight.

d/s =【美军】day of supply;【化】disintegrations per second.

D S(c), D.S(c). = Doctor of Science 理学博士。

D.S.C. = Distinguished Service Cross〔英〕优异服务十字勋章。

DSIF = deep space instrumentation facility 深空探测设备。

DSIR =〔英〕Department of Scientific and Industrial Research〔英〕科学与工业研究总署。

D.S.M. =〔美〕Distinguished Service Medal〔美〕优异服务勋章。

D.S.O. =〔英〕(Companion of the) Distinguished Service Order; District Staff Officer.

d.s.p. = *decessit sine prole* (= died without issue).

DSRV = Deep Submergence Rescue Vehicle 深潜救助艇。

DST, D.S.T. 1. = daylight saving time 经济时〔即夏令时〕。2. = digital subscriber line【无】数字用户专线。

'dst = wouldst; hadst.

D.T. = 1. Daily Telegraph〔英〕《每日电讯报》。2. delirium tremens 震颤性谵妄。

d.t. = doubling time 加倍时间。

D T(h), D.T(h). = Doctor of Theology 神学博士。

D.T.'s [diːˈtiːz; diˋtiz]〔美俚〕= d.t.

DTV = digital TV 数码电视(机)。

Du. = Dutch; duke.

du·ad [ˈdjuːæd; ˋdjuæd] *n*. (一)对,一双。

du·al [ˈdju(ː)əl; ˋdjuəl] **I** *a*. 二的;二重的;二体的;二元的。～ *personality* 双重人格。**II** *n*.【语法】双数;【数】对偶。***the D- Monarchy*** 双重君主国〔指第一次世界大战前的奥匈帝国〕。～ **citizenship** 双重国籍。～ **control** 1. 双重管辖。2.【空】复式驾驶装置。～**-control machine** 复式驾驶(飞)机。～ **firing** (煤与石油)混合加热。～ **flying** 复式驾驶飞行;同乘飞行。～**-purpose** *a*. 1. 双重目的的,两用的。2.【农】(卵肉或乳肉)兼用的。

Du·a·la [duːˈɑːlɑː; duˋɑlɑ] *n*. = Douala.

du·al·in [ˈdjuːəlin; ˋdjuəlɪn] *n*. 双硝炸药。

du·al·ism [ˈdju(ː)əlizəm; ˋdjuəlɪzəm] *n*. 1. 二重,二体;两重性;二元性。2.【哲】二元论;【宗】(善与恶相斗争的)二神论。**du·al·ist** *n*. 1. 二元论者。2. 身兼二职的人。**-is·tic** [ˌdjuːəˈlistik; ˏdjuəlˋɪstɪk] *a*. 二重的;两重性的,二元性的;二元论的。**-is·ti·cal·ly** *ad*.

du·al·i·ty [dju(ː)ˈæliti; djuˋælɪtɪ] *n*. 1. 两重性,二元性。2.【物】二象性;【无】对偶(性)。

du·al·ize [ˈduːəˌlaiz; ˋduəˏlaɪz] *vt*. 使二元化,使具有二重性。

dub[1] [dʌb; dʌb] *vt*. (**-bb-**) 1. 授与…以称号,把…叫做;给…起浑名[绰号]叫…。2. 用剑拍肩授与…以骑士爵位。3. 涂油加工(皮革)。4. 把(木板)刮光,把(铁片等)锤平。5.【钓】装(假饵)于钓钩。6. 割去(小公鸡的)鸡冠。～ ***bright***【船】刨光(木船)壁面。～ ***out*** 弄平(木板等)。～ ***up***〔俚〕付清。

dub[2] [dʌb; dʌb] **I** *vt*., *vi*. (**-bb-**) 刺,戳;撞,敲 (*at*)。**II** *n*. 1. 刺,戳;撞,敲。2. 敲打声。

dub[3] [dʌb; dʌb] **I** *vt*. (**-bb-**) 1. 为(影片、广播节目等)配音;译制(影片)。2. 复制(录音、唱片等);把(音乐、对话等)灌进录音带。*Chinese-dubbed foreign films* 汉语配音译制的外国影片。**II** *n*. 配入影片声带中的对话[音乐等]。

dub[4] [dʌb; dʌb] *n*.〔美俚〕庸才,技艺拙劣的人[演奏者、运动选手](*at*)。

dub[5] [dʌb; dʌb] *n*.〔Scot.〕水池,水塘。

Dub. = Dublin.

dub. = dubious.

dub-a-dub [ˈdʌb-ə-dʌb; ˋdʌb-ə-dʌb] *n*. 1. (鼓的)咚咚声 (= rub-a-dub)。2. 鼓手。

Dubai [ˈdjuːbai; ˋdjubaɪ] *n*. 1. 迪拜〔组成阿拉伯联合酋长国的酋长国之一〕。2. 迪拜港〔阿拉伯联合酋长国港市〕。

dub·bing[1] [ˈdʌbiŋ; ˋdʌbɪŋ] *n*. 骑士爵位的授与。

dub·bing[2] [ˈdʌbiŋ; ˋdʌbɪŋ] *n*. (皮革用)防水油脂。

dub·bing[3] [ˈdʌbiŋ; ˋdʌbɪŋ] *n*. 1. 译制,配音。2. 复制的唱片。

du·bi·e·ty, du·bi·os·i·ty [dju(ː)ˈbaiəti, djuːbiˈɔsəti; djuˋbaɪətɪ, djubɪˋɑsətɪ] *n*. 1. 疑心,怀疑。2. 疑点,疑难。

du·bi·ous [ˈdjuːbjəs; ˋdjubiəs] *a*. 1. (对事情等)半信半疑的 (*of*; *about*);犹豫不决的。2. 可疑的,令人怀疑的。3. 暧昧的,含糊的。4. (命运等)未定的;(工作等)无把握的。*a* ～ *reply* 含糊的回答。*a* ～ *battle* 胜负难卜的战争。**-ly** *ad*. **-ness** *n*.

du·bi·ta·ble [ˈdjuːbitəbl; ˋdjubɪtəbl̩] *a*. 可疑的;不定的。**-ta·bly** *ad*.

du·bi·ta·tion [ˌdjuːbiˈteiʃən; ˏdjubəˋteʃən] *n*.〔古〕怀疑,半信半疑。**-ta·tive** *a*. 怀疑的,半信半疑的,踌躇不决的。

Dub·lin [ˈdʌblin; ˋdʌblɪn] *n*. 都柏林〔爱尔兰首都〕。

Du Bois [duːˈbɔiz; duˋbɔɪz] 1. 杜波依斯〔姓氏〕。2. **William Edward** ～ 威廉·爱·杜波依斯〔1868—1963,美国黑人学者,作家〕。

du·cal [ˈdjuːkəl; ˋdjukl̩] *a*. 公爵的;公爵似的;公爵领地的。

duc·at [ˈdʌkət; ˋdʌkət] *n*. 1. (中世纪流通欧洲各国的)达卡银币[金币]。2. 货币;〔*pl*.〕金钱,现款。3.〔美俚〕门票,入场券。

Du·ce [ˈduːtʃi, It. ˈduːtʃe; ˋdutʃɪ, ˋdutʃɛ] *n*. (*pl*. ～*s*, It. ***du·cei*** [ˈduːtʃi; ˋdutʃɪ])〔It.〕领袖;首领,独裁者。***Il*** [il; ɪl] ～"领袖"〔法西斯统治期间对墨索里尼的称呼〕。

duch·ess [ˈdʌtʃis; ˋdʌtʃɪs] *n*. 1. 公爵夫人;公爵未亡人;女公爵;(公国的)女大公。2. 气度威严的妇女。3.〔英俚〕叫卖小贩的妻子。

duch·y [ˈdʌtʃi; ˋdʌtʃɪ] *n*. 1. 公国,公爵领地。2. 英国王室直辖领地。

duck[1] [dʌk; dʌk] *n*. (*pl*. ～, ～*s*) 1. 鸭;家鸭;母鸭 (*opp*. drake);鸭肉。2.〔口〕亲爱的,宝贝。3. 有吸引力的人[物]。4.【体】鸭蛋,零分 (= ～-egg)。5. 跛子,瘸子 (= lame ～)。6.〔美俚〕家伙。*the domestic* [*wild*] ～ 家[野]鸭。*She's a perfect* ～. 她可爱极了。*a lame* ～ 瘸子;不能运行的船只。*a sitting* ～ 容易捕获的猎物;〔喻〕容易击中的目标。***be out for a*** ～ 吃鸭蛋[得零分]退场。***chance the*** ～ 好歹试一试。***dead*** ～ 注定已完蛋的人,无价值的东西。(***play***) ～(***s***) ***and drake***(***s***)

打水漂〔投石片滑行水面的游戏〕。~[~'s] *egg*〔俚〕【体】零分。~*'s quack*〔美俚〕极好的,很好的。*fine day for young* ~*s* 雨天。*fuck a* ~〔美俚〕他妈的,去你的。*in two shakes of* (*a*) ~*'s tail* 立刻,马上。*knee-high to a* ~ 很小的,微不足道的。*like* (*a*) ~ *in* (*a*) *thunder-storm* 惊慌失措。*like* (*a*) ~ *to water* (像鸭子入水)很自然地。*like water off* (*a*) ~*'s back* 毫无作用,毫无影响,漠不关心。*play* ~*s and drakes of* 1. 鲁莽地处理。2. 浪费,挥霍。3. 使混乱,给…造成困难。*take to* (*sth.*) *like a* ~ *to water* 极爱,最喜欢。*Will a* ~ *swim*? 那还用问吗?~ **ant** 白蚂蚁。~**bill** 1.【动】鸭嘴兽,多齿白鲟。2.【矿】鸭嘴装载机。~**billed** *a*.(嘴巴)像鸭嘴的。~**boards**〔*pl*.〕〔军俚〕(战壕或泥地上的)垫路木板。~ **hawk**〔美〕隼;〔英〕泽鹰。~**-legged** *a*. 短腿的。~**-legs** (鸭子似的)矮脚人。~**pin** 1. 滚球戏。2. (滚球戏用的)小柱子。~ **soup**〔美俚〕轻而易举的事;好欺侮的人。~**'s disease**〔谑〕短腿。~**weed**【植】(鸭爱吃的)浮萍属植物。

duck[2][dʌk; dʌk] *vi*. 1. 突然潜入水中;把头忽然插入水中;忽潜忽露。2. 急忙低头,急忙弯腰;躲避,回避;〔美口〕跑掉,逃走。~ *away from the ball* 避开球。~ **out**〔美口〕跑掉,逃走(*Let us* ~ *out of here*. 我们离开这儿吧)。—*vt*. 1. 把(人等)猛然按入水中;突然潜入(水中)。2. 突然低下(头),突然弯下(腰)。3.〔美口〕躲避,逃避;回避。~ *an embarrassing question* 回避令人难堪的问题。

duck[3][dʌk; dʌk] *n*. 1. (作衣料的)帆布;粗布。2.〔*pl*.〕〔口〕帆布裤子,帆布衣服。

duck[4][dʌk; dʌk] *n*.【美海军】水陆两用车;〔美空俚〕水陆两用飞机。

duck·er[1]['dʌkə; `dʌkɚ] *n*. 潜水人;潜水鸟。

duck·er[2]['dʌkə; `dʌkɚ] *n*. 养鸭人;猎野鸭人。

duck·ing ['dʌkiŋ; `dʌkɪŋ] *n*. 1. 钻入水中;全身湿透。2. 急低头;急弯腰。3. 猎野鸭;【拳】闪避;〔美俚〕帆布。~ **pond** 1. 猎鸭池。2. (古时一种惩罚人的)浸刑池。~ **stool**(古时惩罚泼妇用的)浸刑椅。

duck·ling ['dʌkliŋ; `dʌklɪŋ] *n*. 小鸭,子鸭。

duck·y ['dʌki; `dʌkɪ] I *n*.〔口〕亲爱的(=darling)。II *a*.〔美俚〕1. 漂亮的,迷人的,玲珑的,可爱的。2. 令人满意的。

duct [dʌkt; dʌkt] *n*. 1. 管,导管,输送管;槽,沟,渠道。2.【无】波道;【电】(电线,电缆等的)管道。*an ejaculatory* ~ 输精管。*a lachrymal* ~ 泪管。

-duct *comb. f*. 表示"管道","管": aqueduct, viaduct.

duc·tile ['dʌktail; `dʌktaɪl] *a*. 1. (金属等)易拉长的,延性的,可延展的;可锻的。2. (黏土等)可塑的,易变形的;柔软的。3. 易教的,驯良的。**-til·i·ty** [dʌk'tiliti; dʌk`tɪlətɪ] *n*. 1. 延性,延度。2. 可塑性;韧性;柔软。3. 柔顺,驯良。

duc·ti·lim·e·ter [dʌkti'limitə; dʌktɪ`lɪmɪtɚ] *n*. 塑性计。

duct·less ['dʌktlis; `dʌktlɪs] *a*. 无导管的。~ *gland*【解】无管腺,内分泌腺。

duc·tor ['dʌktə; `dʌktɚ] *n*. 印刷机的油墨滚筒。

duct·ule ['dʌktjul; `dʌktʊl] *n*. 小导管,小管道。

dud [dʌd; dʌd] I *n*. 1.〔俚〕〔*pl*.〕衣服;个人的衣服什物;〔罕〕破衣烂裳。2.〔军俚〕(没有爆发的)哑弹,瞎弹。3.〔俚〕假货,伪品;不中用的东西。4.〔俚〕失败,失望;无用的人,没有进取心的人。II *a*. 假的,不中用的。~ *coins* [*dollars*]〔美〕伪币。

dud·dy, dud·die ['dʌdi; `dʌdɪ] *a*.〔Scot.〕褴褛的,破烂的。

dude [dju:d; djud] *n*.〔美俚〕1. 纨袴子弟,花花公子,讲究穿戴的人。2.〔美方〕东部人,(休假时到西部牧场来的)东部旅行者。~ **hat**〔美俚〕高帽。~ **ranch**〔美西部〕(供东部人休假时游息的)休养农场;仿西部农场造的休养处。~ **wrangler** 带东部游客参观的牧童。

du·deen [du'di:n; du`din] *n*. =dudheen.

dudg·eon[1]['dʌdʒən; `dʌdʒən] *n*. 愤怒,愤恨。*in great* [*high, deep*] ~ 非常忿怒。

dudg·eon[2]['dʌdʒən; `dʌdʒən] *n*.〔废〕1. 匕首柄木。2. 黄杨木剑柄;黄杨木柄匕首。

du·dheen [du'di:n; du`din] *n*. [Ir.] 磁烟嘴,磁烟管。

dud·ish ['dju:diʃ; `djudɪʃ] *a*.〔美俚〕纨袴子弟的,花花公子般的,讲究穿戴的。

Dud·ley ['dʌdli; `dʌdlɪ] *n*. 达德利〔姓氏,男子名〕。

due [dju:; dju] I *a*. 1. (债款等)当付的,应该付给的;(票据等)到期(的),满期(的)。2. (车、船等按时间)应到达的;预期的,约定的〔只用作表语〕。3. 应有的;应做的;正当的,当然的;适当的,充分的;正式;照例。4. 应给与的,应归与的;起因于…,由于(*to*)。*the* ~ *date* (票据等的)付款日,满期日。*The bill is* ~ *on the 1st inst*. 这张支票本月一号到期。*We're* ~ *out*! 我们该走了! *He's about* ~. 他快来了。*When is the train* ~? 火车什么时候到? *a* ~ *margin for delay* 给意外延误留下足够的时间。*after* [*upon*] ~ *consideration* 经过充分考虑后。*protection due to their children* 应该给与孩子们的保护。~ *process* (*of law*), ~ *course of law* 正当法律手续。**be** ~ **to** 1. 由于(*The delay is* ~ *to the shortage of hands*. 事情耽搁下来是由于人手不足)。2. 应给,应归(*The credit is* ~ *to you*. 荣誉[功劳]应该归你)。3. 预定(*He is* ~ *to speak tonight*. 他预定今晚演说)。4. 应做的(*It is* ~ *to him to say so*. 他这样说是应该的)。5. 应付给的,欠的(*Ten dollars is* ~ *to you*. 欠你十元)。**become** ~ =fall ~. ~ **bill**〔美〕借据,借约。~ **from** 应收。**fall** ~ (票据)到期,满期。**in** ~ **course** 及时地;到一定时候,到适当时候。**in** ~ **form** 正式,照例。**in** ~ **time** 到时候就,在适当时候。**with** ~ **ceremony** 照正式仪式。**with** ~ **regard** [**respect**] **to** [**for**] 在给予…以应有尊重的情况下。II *ad*. (罗盘指针,方向等)正(南、北等)。*a* ~ *north wind* 正北风。*The wind is* ~ *east*. 风是正东风。III *n*. 1. 应得物,正当报酬,当然权利,应得权益。2.〔常 *pl*.〕应付款;税;费用;手续费;租费;会费。*give him more than his* ~ 给与他的过分多了,给与他的超过了他应得的。*harbour* ~*s* 入港费。*light* ~*s* 灯塔费。*club* ~*s* 俱乐部会费。**by** [**of**] ~〔古、诗〕当然。**for a full** ~【海】十分,完全;永久。**give sb. his** ~ 公平看待某人。**give the devil his** ~ 公平对待自己不喜欢的人。~ **date** (借据等的)到期日,应付款日期。

du·el ['dju(:)əl; `djuəl] I *n*. 1. 决斗。2. 竞争,斗争,抗争,〔美〕运动比赛。*fight a* ~ *with sb*. 与某人决斗。*challenge sb. to a* ~ 向某人提出决斗。*the* ~ 决斗法,决斗规则。*a* ~ *of wits* 斗智。*a verbal* ~ 舌战,论战。II *vi*. (*-l*(*l*)*-*) 决斗。**du·el·(l)ing** *n*. 决斗(术),斗争,抗争。

du·el·(l)er ['dju(:)ələ; `djuəlɚ] *n*.〔罕〕=duel(l)ist.

du·el·(l)ist ['dju(:)əlist; `djuəlɪst] *n*. 1. 决斗者。2. 斗争者,抗争者,角逐者。

du·el·lo [dju:'eləu; du`ɛlo] *n*. (*pl*. ~*s*, [It.] ***du·el·li*** [dju'eli; djʊ`ɛlɪ])〔It.〕1. 决斗(术)。2. 决斗规则。

du·en·na [dju(:)'enə; dju`ɛnə] *n*. 1. (西班牙家庭中的)保姆;(闺女的)陪媪。2. 女家庭教师。

du·et(t), ***du·et·to*** [dju(:)'et, dju(:)'etəu; dju`ɛt, dju`ɛto] *n*. 1.【乐】二重奏(曲),二重唱(曲);二重奏[唱]演出组。2. 双簧;对话;对骂。3. 一对,一双。**play a** ~ 演双簧,互相唱和。**duet·tist** *n*. 二重奏[唱]者。

Duff [dʌf; dʌf] *n*. 达夫〔姓氏〕。

duff[1][dʌf; dʌf] *n*. 1.〔英方〕生面团,揉面。2. (通常嵌有葡萄干等蒸制的)布丁。

duff[2][dʌf; dʌf] *n*.〔美俚〕臀部,屁股。*get off one's* ~ 抬起屁股,(久坐后)站起来。

duff[3][dʌf; dʌf] *n*. 1. (森林中的)枯枝落叶堆积层,地面

D

腐植质。2. 煤屑,炭粉。
duff[4][dʌf; dʌf] **I** *a*. 〔英俚〕(质量)低劣的;假的;不中用的。~ *gen* 〔罕俚〕不可靠的情报。**II** *n*. 无价值的东西,伪品,假货。
duff[5][dʌf; dʌf] *vi*. 〔俚〕1. 伪造;欺骗;把(旧货)装扮成新的。2. 〔澳〕在(偷来的家畜身上)重打烙印;偷(家畜)。
duf·fel, duf·fle [ˈdʌfəl, ˈdʌfl; ˋdʌfəl, ˋdʌfl] *n*. 1. 起绒粗呢。2. (运动员、野营者等的)一套轻便用具,一套衣物;〔美口〕露营用品。~ **bag** (装杂物的)军用帆布袋。
duff·er [ˈdʌfə; ˋdʌfɚ] *n*. 1. 废物,骗人货;伪币。2. 笨蛋,不中用的人。3. 〔俚〕兜售骗人货的小贩;〔*pl*.〕〔美俚〕参加走私的妇女;〔古〕行商。
Duf·fer·in [ˈdʌfərin; ˋdʌfərɪn] *n*. 达弗林〔姓氏〕。
dug[1][dʌg; dʌg] dig 的过去式及过去分词。
dug[2][dʌg; dʌg] *n*. (哺乳动物的)乳房,奶头。
du·gong [ˈdjuːgɔŋ; ˋdugɔŋ] *n*. 【动】儒艮,人鱼〔一种海生哺乳动物〕。
dug·out [ˈdʌgaut; ˋdʌg͵aʊt] *n*. 1. 独木舟。2. (太古人类居住的)岩洞;(挖在山坡或地下的)洞穴;【军】地下掩蔽部。3. 〔口〕(退役后的)复职军官;(超龄后)重新服役的军官。4. 【棒球】运动员休息室。
DUI = driving under the influence (或 intoxication) 酒后驾车。
du·i [ˈdjuːiː; ˋdjui] *n*. duo 的复数。
duke [djuːk; djuk] *n*. 1. 公,(公国的)君主;〔英〕公爵。2. 〔古〕司令官,首领,(古罗马的)省督。3. (公爵种)樱桃。4. 〔*pl*.〕〔口〕手,拳头。*the D- of Wellington* 威林顿公爵。*Put up your ~s!* 举起手来! *the Grand D-* 大公。*a* **~'s mixture** 〔美〕1. 集成物。2. 杂录,杂记。3. 混乱状态。***Royal D-*** 亲王兼公爵。
duke·dom [ˈdjuːkdəm; ˋdjukdəm] *n*. 1. 公爵领土,公国。2. 〔英〕公爵的地位〔身分〕。
Du·kho·bors [ˈduːkəbɔːz; ˋdukəbɔrz] *n*. 〔*pl*.〕【宗】杜霍波尔教派〔意为"灵魂力士派",俄国的一种否认正教仪式的教派信徒,1875 年从希腊教会分化出来〕。**Du·kho·bor·tsy** [ˌduːkəˈbɔːtsi; ͵dukəˋbɔrtsɪ].
D.U.K.W.S., Dukws [dʌks; dʌks] *n*. 水陆两用车〔美海军电报暗码代用语〕。
dul·cet [ˈdʌlsit; ˋdʌlsɪt] *a*. 1. (音乐等)美妙的,优美动听的。2. 赏心悦目的,好看的。3. 〔古〕美味的,可口的,有香味的。
dul·ci·an·a [ˌdʌlsiˈænə; ͵dʌlsɪˋænə] *n*. 【乐】(音调柔美似弦乐器的)风琴音栓。
dul·ci·fy [ˈdʌlsifai; ˋdʌlsəfaɪ] *vt*. (***-fied***; ***-fy·ing***) 1. 把…弄甜,加甜味于。2. 使愉快;使变温和。**-fi·ca·tion** [ˌdʌlsifiˈkeiʃən; ͵dʌlsɪfɪˋkeʃən] *n*.
dul·ci·mer [ˈdʌlsimə; ˋdʌlsəmɚ] *n*. 洋琴。
Dul·cin·e·a [dʌlsiˈniə; dʌlsəˋnɪə] *n*. 1. 达西尼亚〔小说《唐·吉诃德》中吉诃德先生心目中的情人〕。2. 〔d-〕理想中的情人。
du·li·a [duːˈlaiə; duˋlaɪə] *n*. 【天主】二等崇敬〔对于天使圣徒等的尊崇〕。
dull [dʌl; dʌl] **I** *a*. 1. 愚钝的,感觉迟钝的,呆笨的。2. 钝的,不快的,不锋利的 (*opp*. sharp)。3. (天气等)阴郁的,阴暗的;(颜色等)暗淡的。4. (市场等)呆滞的,萧条的;(谈话等)单调的,枯燥的,无聊的,沉闷的。5. (光等)模糊的。*a ~ child* 头脑迟钝的孩子。*a ~ edge* 钝刀。*be ~ of hearing* 耳朵不灵。*a ~ fire* 文火。*a ~ pain* 钝痛,隐痛。*a ~ day* 阴天。*a ~ town* 萧条的市镇。*Trade is ~*. 生意清淡。*a ~ book* 枯燥无味的书。*a ~ landscape* 单调的景色。**II** *vt*. 1. 把…弄钝。2. 使阴暗,使阴郁。3. 缓和,减轻(痛苦等)。4. 使迟钝;使呆滞。*~ a razor's edge* 把刀片弄钝了。*one's sense ~ed by his emotion* 因激动而造成的感觉迟钝。*~ sorrow* 减轻哀愁。—*vi*. 1. 变钝;变迟钝。2. (痛苦等)减少。3. 【纺】消光。~ ***the edge of*** 1. 弄钝刃口。2. 减弱(兴趣等)。~**-brained** *a*. 头脑迟钝的。~**-browed** *a*. 愁眉苦脸的,闷闷不乐的。~**-head** 傻瓜,笨蛋。~**-witted** *a*. 愚蠢的。**dul(l)·ness** *n*. **dul·ly** *ad*.
dull·ard [ˈdʌləd; ˋdʌlɚd] *n*. 笨蛋,蠢汉。
Dul·les [ˈdʌlis, ˈdʌləs; ˋdʌlɪs, ˋdʌləs] *n*. 1. 达勒斯,杜勒斯〔姓氏〕。2. **John Foster** ~ 约翰·福斯特·杜勒斯〔1888—1959,曾任美国国务卿〕。
dull·ish [ˈdʌliʃ; ˋdʌlɪʃ] *n*. 1. 有点钝的;迟钝的。2. 有点沉闷的。
dulse [dʌls; dʌls] *n*. 【植】掌状红皮藻。
du·ly [ˈdjuːli; ˋdjulɪ] *ad*. 1. 正当地,适当地;充分地。2. 及时,按时,准时。*Your letter is ~ to hand*. 来信已及时收到。*Eggs were ~ delivered*. 鸡蛋已按时运出。
Du·ma [ˈduːmə; ˋdumə] *n*. 杜马〔帝俄国会〕。
Du·mas [djuˈmɑː; djuˋmɑ] *n*. 1. 仲马〔法国姓氏〕。2. **Alexandre** ~ 大仲马〔1802—1870,世称 *Dumas père*,法国剧作家,小说家,著有《三剑客》、《基督山伯爵》等〕。3. **Alexandre** ~ 小仲马〔1824—1895,世称 *Dumas fils*,法国小说家及剧作家,为大仲马之子,其名著为《茶花女》〕。
Du Mau·ri·er [djuː ˈmɔriei; dju ˋmɔrɪ͵e] *n*. 杜莫里埃〔姓氏〕。
dumb [dʌm; dʌm] *a*. 1. 哑的,不能说话的。2. 沉默的,无言的。3. 无音的,无声的,不响的;打手势的,打哑语的。4. 口齿不清的,(在政府中)无代言人的,政治上无发言权的。5. 〔美口〕愚笨的。6. 没有动力的。*a ~ animal* 不会说话的畜牲。*be ~ from birth* 一生下来就是哑巴。*the deaf and ~* 聋哑人。*be* (*remain*) *~ on* (*sth*.) 闭口不提(某事)。*be struck ~* 吓呆,吓得目瞪口呆。~ ***down*** 降低…的难度。~ **barge** [**craft**] 无帆驳船,拖船。~**bell** 1. 【笨】哑铃。2. 〔美俚〕笨蛋。~ **bid** (拍卖时物主所定而不宣布的)内定底价。~ **bunny** [**head, ox, sock**] 〔美口〕笨蛋,蠢东西。~ **card** 方位盘。~ **chamber** 无出口的房间,闷室。~ **cluck** [**Dora**] 〔美口〕笨女人。~ **creatures** 动物,牲畜。~**found(er)** *vt*. =dumfound. ~ **piano** (练指用的)无声钢琴。~ **show** 默片,哑剧;手势。~**struck** [~**stricken**] *a*. 吓得目瞪口呆的。~ **waiter** 〔英〕回转式食品架;〔美〕送菜升降机。
Dum·bar·ton Oaks [dʌmˈbɑːtn əuks; ˋdʌmˋbɑrtn̩ oks] *n*. 敦巴顿橡树园〔在华盛顿郊区,1944 年 8 月—10 月间,中美英苏四国代表为筹备建立联合国举行会议的地方〕。
Dum·bo [ˈdʌmbəu; ˋdʌmbo] *n*. 〔美海军口〕救护(搜索)飞机。
dum·dum [ˈdʌmdʌm; ˋdʌmdʌm] *n*. 【军】(旧时一种杀伤力很强的软头)达姆弹 (= ~ bullet)。
dum(b)·found [ˈdʌmˈfaund; ͵dʌmˋfaʊnd] *vt*. 吓哑,吓呆,使发愣。**-ment** *n*.
dum(b)·found·er [ˌdʌmˈfaundə; ͵dʌmˋfaʊndɚ] *vt*. = dum(b)found.
dum·my [ˈdʌmi; ˋdʌmɪ] **I** *n*. 1. 〔口〕哑巴;经常沉默的人。2. 挂名代表;傀儡。3. (橱窗中的)模型人;(拍电影用的)假人;人形靶;模型发式;模型货样,样品;(书的)样本;【军】模拟弹;虚设物;模仿物。4. 〔主英〕橡皮奶头。5. 〔口〕笨蛋。6. (有凝汽器的)无声排汽机车。7. 【牌】(桥牌叫定后摊牌于桌上的)明家。*a wax ~* 蜡人。*a tailor's ~* 服装模型人。***sell the ~*** 【橄榄球】做递球假动作骗对方;〔喻〕声东击西。**II** *a*. 1. 摆样子的,做样品的,假的。2. 挂名的,傀儡的。*a ~ cartridge* 空弹。*a ~ bomb* (演习用的)模拟炸弹。*a ~ horse* 【体】木马。*a ~ director* 名义董事。*a ~ state* 傀儡国。**III** *vt*. (***-mied***; ***-my·ing***) 把(书、报等)做成大样 (*up*);把(书、报等)以大样印出 (*in*)。—*vi*. 1. 〔美俚〕装聋作哑,保守秘密 (*up*)。2. 〔澳方〕替别人占领土地。~**-head torpedo** (除去炸药的)演习用鱼雷。~ **run** 演习;排练。~ **variable** 【数】虚变量。
dump[1][dʌmp; dʌmp] *n*. 1. 铅制筹码。2. (已作废的)澳洲旧银币;〔口〕小钱;〔*pl*.〕金钱。3. (船上投环游戏用

的)绳圈;(造船用)短粗螺钉;球形糖果;〔古〕矮胖子。*not worth a* ~ 不值一文。*not care a* ~ 毫不介意。

dump[2][dʌmp; dʌmp] ***n*.** **1.**〔*pl*.〕〔口〕郁闷。**2.**〔古〕忧郁的曲调。***in the*** **~*s*** 不高兴,心情沮丧。

dump[3][dʌmp; dʌmp] **I** ***vt*.** **1.**〔主美〕倾倒(垃圾),倾卸(*out*);解雇;解除(合同等);使砰地落下,砰地放下(*down*);抛弃(废物,候选人等);〔口〕故意输掉(比赛等)。**2.**【商】(向海外)倾销;把(过剩移民)转送外国。**3.** 解雇,解(约)。**4.** 转嫁(责任等)。**5.**(电子计算机)转录,转储。—***vi*.** **1.** 砰地落下来。**2.** 卸货。**3.** 倾销。**II** ***n*.** **1.** 砰的一声。**2.** 卸货场所,垃圾场;(矿山的)渣坑。**3.**(射流)放空孔,排空孔;【自】(计算机的)转储,消除打印。**4.**(刚卸下的)货垛,煤堆,垃圾堆;【军】(弹药等的)临时堆积处。**5.**〔美俚〕破陋的房子[场所、街道]。~ **car**(铁道上的)倾斜车,自动卸货车。~ **cart** [**truck**] 倒垃圾车。

dump·age [ˈdʌmpidʒ; ˋdʌmpɪdʒ] ***n*.** **1.**〔美〕倾倒(垃圾等)。**2.** 垃圾。**3.** 垃圾倾倒权[费]。

dump·er [ˈdʌmpə; ˋdʌmpɚ] ***n*.**〔美〕**1.** 垃圾倾倒车;(倾卸车上的)倾卸装置;垃圾倾倒员。**2.** 倾销者。

dump·ing [ˈdʌmpiŋ; ˋdʌmpɪŋ] ***n*.** **1.** 倾倒(垃圾等),抛弃。**2.** 倾卸物,垃圾。**3.** 倾销。~ **device** 卸料装置。~ **field** 海外倾销市场。~ **ground** 垃圾倾倒场。

dump·ish [ˈdʌmpiʃ; ˋdʌmpɪʃ] ***a*.** 忧愁的,忧郁的。

dump·ling [ˈdʌmpliŋ; ˋdʌmplɪŋ] ***n*.** **1.**(有肉馅等的)汤团,团子;苹果布丁。**2.**〔口〕矮胖子;矮胖的动物。

dump·y[1][ˈdʌmpi; ˋdʌmpɪ] **I** ***a*.** 矮胖的,粗短的。*a* ~ *woman* 一个矮胖的女人。**II** ***n*.** 矮脚鸡。~ **level**(测量用的)定镜水准仪。**-i·ly** ***ad*.** **-i·ness** ***n*.**

dump·y[2][ˈdʌmpi; ˋdʌmpɪ] ***a*.** 忧郁的,不高兴的。

dun[1][dʌn; dʌn] **I** ***n*.** **1.** 催促者,纠缠不休者;讨债人。**2.** 催付,追收。**II** ***vt*.(-*nn*-)** **1.** 向…催讨。**2.** 向…纠缠不休,使烦恼。*a* ~*ning letter* 讨债信。~ *sb*. *for payment* 催某人还债。—***vi*.** 催债,讨债。**dun·ner** ***n*.** 讨债人。

dun[2][dʌn; dʌn] **I** ***a*.** **1.** 焦茶色的,暗褐色的。**2.**〔诗〕微暗的,阴暗的。~ *clouds* 阴沉沉的云朵。**II** ***n*.** **1.** 焦茶色,暗褐色。**2.** 暗褐色马。**3.**【动】蜉蝣的亚成虫;毛翅目昆虫。**4.** 暗褐色钓鱼假饵。**III** ***vt*.(-*nn*-)**使成暗褐色;腌(鳕等)成暗褐色。

Dun·bar [ˈdʌnbɑː; ˋdʌnbɑr] ***n*.** 邓巴〔姓氏〕。

Dun·can [ˈdʌŋkən; ˋdʌŋkən] ***n*.** **1.** 邓肯〔姓氏,男子名〕。**2.** **Isadora** ~ 伊萨多拉·邓肯〔1878—1927,美国女舞蹈家〕。**3.** ~ **I** 邓肯一世〔1034—1040 年在位,被马克白暗害的苏格兰国王〕。

dunce [dʌns; dʌns] ***n*.** 笨人;低能儿;劣等生。*an utter* ~ 十足的低能儿。

Dun·das [dʌnˈdæs, ˈdʌndæs; dʌnˋdæs, ˋdʌndæs] ***n*.** 邓达斯〔姓氏〕。

dun·der·head, dun·der·pate [ˈdʌndəhed, -peit; ˋdʌndɚˏhɛd, -pet] ***n*.** 傻瓜,蠢才。**-ed** ***a*.** 笨的,蠢的。

dune [djuːn; djun] ***n*.**(海边被风吹积成的)沙丘。~ **buggy** 沙滩车〔特别设计的轻型汽车,专供在沙丘或海滩上行驶〕。

Dun·e·din [dʌˈniːdin; dʌnˋidn̩] ***n*.** 达尼丁〔新西兰港市〕。

dung [dʌŋ; dʌŋ] **I** ***n*.** **1.**(牛马等的)粪;肥料。**2.**〔喻〕丑恶的东西。**II** ***vt*.** 给(地)施肥[上粪]。~ **beetle**【动】粪金龟子,蜣螂。~ **cart** 粪车。~ **depot** 粪池。~ **fly** 粪蝇。~ **fork** 粪耙。

dun·ga·ree [ˌdʌŋgəˈriː; ˏdʌŋgəˋri] ***n*.** **1.**(印度的)粗棉布,粗蓝斜纹布。**2.**〔*pl*.〕粗蓝布工装,粗布工作服。

dun·geon [ˈdʌndʒən; ˋdʌndʒən] ***n*.** **1.** 土牢,地牢。**2.**(欧洲中世纪的)城堡主楼,城堡主塔。

dung·hill [ˈdʌŋhil; ˋdʌŋˏhɪl] ***n*.** **1.** 粪堆,堆肥。**2.** 脏屋;脏物。**3.** 卑贱的状态[地位]。***a cock on his own*** **~, *a cock of the*** **~** 地头蛇,土霸王。~ **cock** [**fowl**](相对于"斗鸡"而言的)普通的农家公鸡。

dung·y [ˈdʌŋi; ˋdʌŋɪ] ***a*.** 到处是粪的;沾上粪的;粪一般的;肮脏的。

du·nite [ˈduːnait; ˋdunaɪt] ***n*.**【地】纯橄榄岩。

dun·i·was·sal [ˈduːniˈwɔsəl; ˋdunɪˋwɑsəl] ***n*.**〔Scot.〕二流绅士;(名门中)次子以下的子嗣。

dunk [dʌŋk; dʌŋk] ***vt*.** **1.**〔主美方〕(吃前)把(面包等)在汤[饮料]中浸一浸。**2.** 浸泡。~ *the curtains in the dye* 把窗帘布浸在染色液里。—***vi*.** 把自己浸入水中。*Let's* ~ *in the pool before dinner*. 我们饭前到池塘里泡一会儿。**-er** ***n*.**

Dun·kirk [ˈdʌnkəːk; ˋdʌnkɚk], **Dun·kerque** [F. ˋdʌnkəːk; ˋdʌnkɚk] ***n*.** **1.** 敦克尔克〔法国港市,1940 年英军被德军击败后从此处撤回本国〕。**2.** 类似敦克尔克的大溃退。

dun·lin [ˈdʌnlin; ˋdʌnlɪn] ***n*.**(*pl*. ~, ~*s*)【鸟】滨鹬。

Dun·lop[1][dʌnˈlɔp, ˈdʌnlɔp; dʌnˋlɑp, ˋdʌnlɑp] ***n*.** **1.** 邓洛普,邓禄普〔姓氏〕。**2.** **John Boyd** ~ 约翰·波义德·邓禄普〔1840—1921,英国发明家〕。

Dun·lop[2][ˈdʌnlɔp; ˋdʌnlɑp] ***n*.** **1.** 邓禄普车胎(= ~ tyre)。**2.**〔Scot.〕邓禄普干酪(= ~ cheese)。

Dun·more [dʌnˈmɔː; dʌnˋmɔr] ***n*.** 邓莫尔〔姓氏〕。

dun·nage [ˈdʌnidʒ; ˋdʌnɪdʒ] ***n*.** **1.** 手提行李。**2.**【海】(防止所装货物动摇损伤的)衬板,衬料[木屑等]。

Dunne [dʌn; dʌn] ***n*.** 邓恩〔姓氏〕。

dun·nite [ˈdʌnait; ˋdʌnaɪt] ***n*.** D 型炸药,苦味酸铵〔一种能打穿装甲的高性能炸药,为美国军官 B. W. Dunn 所发明〕。

dun·nock [ˈdʌnək; ˋdʌnək] ***n*.**【英,动】篱雀,岩鹨。

Duns·tan [ˈdʌnstən; ˋdʌnstən] ***n*.** 邓斯坦〔姓氏〕。

dunt [dʌnt; dʌnt] ***n*.** **1.**(陶器骤冷时的)爆裂。**2.**【空】与急降气流的碰击。

du·o [ˈdjuːəu; ˋdjuo] ***n*.**(*pl*. ~*s*, ***du·i*** [ˈdjuːiː; ˋdui]) **1.**【乐】二重唱,二重奏。**2.**(演员的)一对。*a comedy* ~ 一对滑稽演员。

duo- *comb*. *f*. 表示"二,双": *duo*logue.

du·o·cone [ˈdju(ː)əukəun; ˋdjuokon] ***n*.**【无】高低音扬声器。

du·o·dec·i·mal [ˌdju(ː)əuˈdesiməl; ˏdjuəˋdɛsəml̩] **I** ***a*.**【数】十二的;十二分之几的;十二进位制的。*the* ~ *system* 十二进位制。**II** ***n*.** **1.** 十二分之一。**2.**〔*pl*.〕【数】十二进位制。**-ly** ***ad*.**

du·o·dec·i·mo [ˈdju(ː)əuˈdesiməu; ˏdjuəˋdɛsəmo] **I** ***n*.**(*pl*. ~*s*) **1.**(纸张的)十二开 **2.**(书的)十二开本〔略作 12mo 或 12°,口语读作 twelve mo〕。**3.** 微小的东西;矮人。**II** ***a*.**(纸张)十二开的。

du·o·de·nal [ˌdju(ː)əuˈdiːnl; ˏdjuəˋdinl̩] ***a*.**【解】十二指肠的。

du·o·den·a·ry [ˌdju(ː)əuˈdiːnəri; ˏdjuəˋdɛnərɪ] ***a*.** = duodecimal.

du·o·de·ni·tis [ˌdju(ː)əudiˈnaitis; ˏdjuədɪˋnaɪtɪs] ***n*.**【医】十二指肠炎。

du·o·de·num [ˌdju(ː)əuˈdiːnəm; ˏdjuəˋdinəm] ***n*.**(*pl*. ~*s*, ***du·o·dena*** [ˌdju(ː)əuˈdiːnə; ˏdjuoˋdinə])【解】十二指肠。

du·o·di·ode [ˌdju(ː)əuˈdaiəud; ˏdjuəˋdaɪod] ***n*.**【无】双[孪]二极管。

du·o·graph [ˈdju(ː)əugrɑːf; ˋdjuəˏgræf] ***n*.**(照相制版)复影版。

du·o·logue [ˈdju(ː)əlɔg; ˋdjuəˏlɔg] ***n*.** **1.** 对话。**2.**(戏剧等的)对白;对话剧。

duo·mo [ˈdwɔːmɔː; ˋdwɔmə] ***n*.**(*pl*. ***-mi*** [-mi; -mɪ])[It.](意大利的)大教堂,中央教堂。

du·op·o·ly [djuˈɔpəli; djuˋɑpəlɪ] ***n*.** 两家卖主垄断市场的局面。

du·op·so·ny [djuˈɔpsəni; djuˋɑpsənɪ] ***n*.** 由两家买主独揽市场的局面。

D

du·o·rail [ˈdju(:)əureil; ˋdjuəˋrel] ***n***. 双轨铁路。

du·o·ser·vo [ˌdju(:)əuˈsəːvəu; ˏdjuəˋsɝvo] ***a***. 双力作用的。

du·o·tone [ˈdju(:)əutəun; ˋdjuəˏton] **I** ***a***. 同色浓淡双色调的;双色的。**II** ***n***. 【印】同色浓淡双色调套印法,双色网线版;双色套印画。

dup., **dupl.** = duplicate.

dup·a·ble [ˈdjuːpəbl; ˋdjupəbḷ] ***a***. 易受骗的。**dup·a·bil·i·ty** [ˌdjuːpəˈbiliti; ˏdjupəˋbɪlətɪ] ***n***.

dupe[1] [djuːp; djup] **I** ***n***. **1.** 被愚弄的人;容易受骗的人。**2.** 盲从者。**II** ***vt***. 欺骗,愚弄,蒙蔽。~ *sb. into doing sth.* 骗某人去做某事。

dupe[2] [djuːp; djup] ***n***., ***vt***. = duplicate (***n***., ***vt***.).

dup·er·y [ˈdjuːpəri; ˋdjupərɪ] ***n***. **1.** 诈欺;欺骗。**2.** 被愚弄,上当,受蒙蔽。

du·ple [ˈdjuːpl; ˋdjupḷ] ***a***. **1.** 二倍的,二重的,双的。**2.** 【乐】二拍子的。~ **time** [**measure**, **metre**] 【乐】二拍子〔2/2、2/4、2/8 拍等〕。

du·plet [ˈdjuːplit; ˋdjuplɪt] ***n***. 【原】粒子对,粒子偶;【化】电子对,电子偶。

du·plex [ˈdjuːpleks; ˋdjuplɛks] **I** ***a***. **1.** 二倍的,双的,二重的。**2.** 【机】双联式的,复式。**3.** 【讯】双向(通讯)的,(电报)双工的。**II** ***n***. **1.** 套楼公寓 (= ~ apartment)。**2.** 两户合住的房子 (= ~ house)。~ **apartment** (每套房间占有上下二层楼的)套楼公寓,楼中楼。~ **house** 〔美〕两户合住的房子。~ **pump** 联式泵。~ **paper** 双层纸。~ **telegraphy** 双工电报。

du·pli·cate **I** [ˈdjuːplikeit; ˋdjupləˏket] ***vt***. **1.** 使加倍,使成双。**2.** 使成双联式,使有正副两份,复制,复写,打印。**3.** 重叠,双折。**4.** 重演,重复。~*d agencies* 骈枝机关。~ *the document* 复制文件。*duplicating paper* 复写纸,打字纸。*He* ~*d his father's failure.* 他重蹈父亲的覆辙。**II** [ˈdjuːplikit; ˋdjupləkɪt] ***a***. **1.** 双的,二倍的,二重的。**2.** 双联的,双份的,复式的,成对的。**3.** 重复的;副的,做底子的,抄存的。*a* ~ *copy* 副本,复本。~ *copies* 正副两份。*a* ~ *ratio* 复比。*a* ~ *key* (另一把)备用钥匙。*a* ~ *letter* 信件留底。**III** [ˈdjuːplikit; ˋdjupləkɪt] ***n***. **1.** (绘画、相片等的)复制品;完全相似的对应物。**2.** 誊本,复本,抄件,副本,副件 (*opp.* original)。**3.** 对号牌子;当票。**4.** 同义语。**5.** 【牌】(桥牌比赛中的)换手重打。**6.** 一式两份。*made* [*done*] *in* ~ 制成一式两份。*type the letter in* ~ 把这封信打成一式两份。

du·pli·ca·tion [ˌdjuːpliˈkeiʃən; ˏdjupləˋkeʃən] ***n***. **1.** 加倍,二重,重复。**2.** 重叠,双折。**3.** 复制,打印;复制品。**4.** 【生】(由染色体迷乱造成的)部分遗传物质的复制,两岐。*save time by avoiding* ~ *of effort* 工作中避免重复以节约时间。

du·pli·ca·tor [ˈdjuːplikeitə; ˋdjupləketɚ] ***n***. **1.** 复印机。**2.** 复制者。

du·plic·i·ty [dju(:)ˈplisiti; djuˋplɪsətɪ] ***n***. **1.** 口是心非,不诚实,欺骗性。**2.** 二重性,重复。

Du Pont, **Du·pont** [djuːˈpɔnt; djuˋpɑnt] ***n***. 杜邦〔姓氏〕。

du·ra [ˈdjuərə; ˋdjurə] ***n***. 【解】硬脑[脊]膜 (= ~ mater)。

du·ra·ble [ˈdjuərəbl; ˋdjurəbḷ] **I** ***a***. **1.** 经久的,持久的。**2.** 坚牢的;耐用的。~ *goods* 耐用品。~ *cloths* 结实的衣料。*a* ~ *colour* 不易褪色的颜色。~ *peace* 持久的和平。**II** ***n***. 〔*pl*.〕耐久物品。~ **goods** 耐久货物,耐久品 (= ~s)。~ **press** 耐久性压制,风压〔用化学品在织物纤维上造成永久性的褶绉,略作 DP〕。**du·ra·bil·i·ty** [ˌdjuərəˈbiliti; ˏdjurəˋbɪlətɪ], **-ness** ***n***. **1.** 经久,坚牢。**2.** 持久性[力],耐久性[力]。**-bly** ***ad***. 经久,坚牢;持久。

du·ral [ˈdjuərəl; ˋdjurəl] ***a***. 【解】硬脑(脊)膜的。

du·ral·u·min [djuəˈræljumin; djʊˋræljʊmɪn] ***n***. (制飞机用的)硬铝,都拉铝。*a* ~ *bird* 铁鸟[飞机]。

du·ra ma·ter [ˌdjuərəˈmeitə; ˋdjuərəˋmetɚ] 〔L.〕【解】硬脑(脊)膜。

du·ra·men [djuəˈreimen; djʊˋremen] ***n***. 【植】心材。

dur·ance [ˈdjuərəns; ˋdjʊrəns] ***n***. **1.** 〔古〕(长期)监禁。**2.** 〔古〕持续。***in*** ~ (***vile***) 遭(非法)拘禁。

Du·rant(e) [djuˈrɑːnt, djuˈrænt; djʊˋrɑnt, djʊˋrænt] ***n***. 杜兰特〔姓氏〕。

du·ran·te vi·ta [djuˈræntiːˈvaitə; djʊˋræntiˋvaɪtə] 〔L.〕在有生之年。

du·ra·tion [djuəˈreiʃən; djʊˋreʃən] ***n***. **1.** 持久,持续。**2.** 持续时间,存在时间;期间。*a disease of long* ~ 长时间的疾病。*holidays of three weeks'* ~ 三周的假期。*the* ~ *of flight* 【空】续航时间。*a* ~ *record* 【空】续航记录。*the* ~ *of insurance* [*prescription*] 保险[有效]期间。*the* ~ *of day* 日照长度。*the* ~ *of life* 生存期间。*of long* [*short*] ~ 长[短]期的。***for the D-*** 〔俚〕战争未结束期间〔尤指第二次世界大战〕(*No vacations for the* ~. 战时一切假期取消)。**-al** ***a***.

dur·a·tive [ˈdjurətiv; ˋdjʊrətɪv] ***a***. 【语法】持续的,连续的。*the* ~ *aspect* 【语法】持续体,连续体。

Dur·ban [ˈdəːbən; ˋdɝbən] ***n***. 德班〔南非(阿扎尼亚)港市〕。

dur·bar [ˈdəːbɑː; ˋdɝbɑr] ***n***. **1.** (印度土邦君主等宫廷的)正式接见。**2.** (印度土邦君主等宫廷的)正式接见室。

dure [duə, djuə; dʊr, djʊr] ***a***. 〔古〕冷酷的,苛刻的。

du·ress(e) [djuəˈres; djʊˋrɪs] ***n***. **1.** 【法】强迫,胁迫;强制。**2.** (非法)监禁。***a plea of*** ~ 【法】向法庭提出申请,宣告以前的契约[声明等]系在被胁迫的情况下签订[发表]而现在要求宣告无效。***be held in*** ~ 在监禁中。~ ***of imprisonment*** 非法监禁。***under*** ~ 被迫,被劫持 (*a contract made under* ~ 被胁迫签订的契约)。

Dur·ham [ˈdʌrəm; ˋdɝəm] ***n***. **1.** 达累姆〔英格兰一郡及其首府名〕。**2.** 达累姆(产的)短角肉用牛。

du·ri·an [ˈduːriən; ˋdʊrɪən] ***n***. 【植】(马来群岛产的)榴连果;榴连树。

du·ri·crust [ˈdjuərikrʌst; ˋdjuərɪkrʌst] ***n***. 【地】硬壳,钙质壳。

dur·ing [ˈdjuəriŋ; ˋdjʊərɪŋ] ***prep***. 在…的期间;在…的时候。~ *the day* [*morning*, *evening*] (在)白天[早上,晚上]。~ *and after the crisis* 在危机期间和危机结束以后。~ *sb.'s absence* 某人不在的时候。

du·ri·on [ˈduːriən; ˋdʊrɪən] = durian.

dur·mast [ˈdəːmɑːst, -mæst; ˋdɝmɑst, -mæst] ***n***. 【植】栎属植物〔尤指柔毛栎〕。

durn [dəːn; dɝn] ***vt***., ***vi***. = darn.

du·ro [ˈduərəu; ˋdʊro] ***n***. (*pl*. ~**s**) 元〔西班牙和拉丁美洲一些国家的银元〕。

Du·roc (·jer·sey) [ˈdjuərɔk(ˈdʒəːzi); ˋdjʊrɑk(ˋdʒɝzɪ)] ***n***. 【动】(美国种体壮早熟的)短头红猪。

du·rom·e·ter [djuəˈrɔmitə; djʊˋrɑmɪtɚ] ***n***. 硬度计。

dur·ra [ˈdurə; ˋdʊrə] ***n***. 【植】(非洲原产、叶窄、株型中等的)食用高粱。

Dur·rell [ˈdərel; ˋdɝɛl] ***n***. 德雷尔〔姓氏〕。

Dur·res [ˈdurəs; ˋdʊrəs] ***n***. 都拉索〔阿尔巴尼亚港市〕。

durst [dəːst; dɝst] 〔古〕dare 的过去式。

du·rum [ˈdjuərəm; ˋdjʊrəm] ***n***. 硬粒小麦 (= ~ wheat)。

Dur·ward [ˈdəːwəd; ˋdɝwɚd] ***n***. 德沃德〔男子名〕。

Du·sham·be [duːˈʃɑːmbə; duˋʃɑmbə] ***n***. 杜尚别〔塔吉克城市〕。

dusk [dʌsk; dʌsk] **I** ***a***. 〔诗〕= dusky. **II** ***n***. **1.** 薄暮,黄昏。**2.** 幽暗;荫。*from dawn to* ~ 从黎明到黄昏。*at* ~ 在黄昏时刻。*in the* ~ *of the room* 在室内阴暗的光线中。**III** ***vt***. 使变成微黑[暗]。—***vi***. 变微暗[黑];接近黄昏。~ **action station** 【军】薄暮(对空)战斗配置。

dusk·y [ˈdʌski; ˋdʌskɪ] ***a***. **1.** 微暗的,暗淡的;微黑的。**2.** 暗黑的;黑黝黝的;阴暗的。**3.** 忧郁的。*a* ~ *brown*

深褐色。*a* ～ *frown* 愁眉不展。**-i·ly** ***ad***. **-i·ness** ***n***.

Dus·sel·dorf [ˈdusldɔːf; ˋdusl͵dɔrf] ***n***. 杜塞尔多夫〔德国城市〕。

dust [dʌst; dʌst] **I** ***n***. **1.** 尘,灰尘,尘土,尘埃。**2.** 〔英〕垃圾,废品;灰烬。**3.** 〔口〕金粉;粉末,粉剂;花粉。**4.** 〔诗〕遗骸,尸体;人体,人。**5.** 土,地面;葬地;废墟。**6.** 混乱,骚乱。**7.** 〔俚〕现金,钱。**8.** 〔古〕肉体。*sweep up* ～ 打扫灰尘。*insecticidal* ～ 杀虫粉。*gold* ～ 金粉。*the honoured* ～ 荣誉显赫的遗骸。*Down with the* [*your*] ～! 〔口〕拿出钱来! ***as dry as*** ～ 枯燥无味的。***be humbled in*** [***to***] ***the*** ～ 遭到奇耻大辱。***be out for*** ～ 努力挣钱。***bite the*** ～ 一败涂地;倒;倒毙,阵亡。***crumble to*** ～ 倒;垮;化为乌有。***eat*** ～ 含垢忍辱。***have a little*** ～ 交手,打一个回合。***in the*** ～ 死;屈辱。***lay the*** ～ (雨)压落尘埃。***lick the*** ～ **1.** 卑躬屈膝。**2.** = bite the ～. ***lie in the*** ～ **1.** 成为废墟。**2.** 战死。***make*** [***kick up***, ***raise***] ***a*** ～ **1.** 扬起灰尘。**2.** 引起骚动。***make the*** ～ ***fly*** 兴冲冲地干,蛮干。***out of the*** ～ 由灰尘中;由屈辱境遇中。***raise sb. from the*** ～ 提拔某人于寒微之中。***shake the*** ～ ***off one's feet*** = ***shake off the*** ～ ***of one's feet*** 愤然[轻蔑地]离去。***take the*** ～ ***of*** 落后,慢于,赶不上。***the*** ～ ***and heat of the day*** 鏖战;竞争激烈。***throw*** ～ ***in sb.'s eyes*** 〔口〕蒙蔽,欺骗。
II ***vt***. **1.** 掸(灰),打扫(灰尘)。**2.** 把…弄得满是灰尘,在…上撒粉;撒(粉等)。**3.** 使成为灰尘。**4.** 〔古〕使蒙满灰。～ *a table* 掸掉桌上的灰尘。～ *the snow from one's knees* 把膝上的雪花掸掉。～ *a cake with sugar* 在蛋糕上撒糖。～ *DDT over the floor* 在地板上撒滴滴涕。*hairs* ～*ed with grey* 斑白的头发。～ *oneself* 〔古〕弄得满身尘土。—***vi***. **1.** 扫除灰尘。**2.** 扬起灰尘。**3.** (鸟)沙浴。**4.** 〔美口〕急忙跑掉。～ ***'em off*** 〔美口〕用功。～ ***off*** 〔美口〕痛打,痛殴。～ ***sb.'s jacket*** [***coat***] ***for him*** 〔口〕打某人。～ ***the eyes of*** = ～ ***a person's eye*** 瞒,骗。～ **band** (表的)防尘圈。～ **bin** 垃圾箱。～ **bowl** (大草原中)久旱多尘暴的地区,"灰盆"地区。～ **bowler** 住在干旱多尘土地区的人。～ **brand** 〔英〕(麦子的)黑穗病。～ **cart** 垃圾车。～ **cloak** [**coat**] (防尘)罩衫。～ **coal** 粉煤。～**-coat** 风衣,轻便的防尘外衣。～**-colo(u)r** ***n***. 灰暗色。～ **counter** 【气象】计尘器。～ **cover 1.** (家具等的)布罩。**2.** (书的)护封。～ **devil** 【气】小尘暴,尘旋风。～ **disease** 〔口〕矽[硅]肺病。～ **explosion** 煤屑爆炸。～**-guard** (机器的)防尘板[罩]。～ **gun** 手提喷尘器。～**-heap 1.** 垃圾堆。**2.** 闲置,默默无闻 (*be consigned to* ～*heap* 受到冷落)。～ **jacket 1.** (书的)护封。**2.** (家具等的)防尘布套。～**man 1.** 清洁工。**2.** (童话中的)睡神,瞌睡虫。**3.** 【海】火夫。～**off** 〔美军俚〕救护用直升机。～**pan** 畚箕。～**proof** ***a***. 防尘的。～ **shot** 微型子弹。～ **storm** 【气】尘暴。～**up** 〔口〕争论,吵闹;打架;骚乱。～ **well** 冰川表面由沙土等形成的洞。～ **wrapper** = ～ jacket.

dust·er [ˈdʌstə; ˋdʌstɚ] ***n***. **1.** 打扫灰尘的人,打扫工。**2.** 掸子,掸帚;除尘器;畚箕,擦布,揩布。**3.** 撒粉器;撒(胡椒等的)粉瓶。**4.** 〔美〕防尘外衣,风衣。*a DDT* ～ 滴滴涕喷洒器。

dust·ing [ˈdʌstiŋ; ˋdʌstɪŋ] ***n***. **1.** 打扫,掸灰。**2.** 【海】(暴风雨中船的)颠簸。**3.** 拌药;撒粉;(火药等的)筛分;撒布;防腐粉 (= ～ powder)。**4.** 〔俚〕殴打,鞭打。*a* ～ *of powder* 撒粉。***give sb. a good*** ～ 痛打某人一顿。

dust·y [ˈdʌsti; ˋdʌstɪ] ***a***. **1.** 满是灰尘的,灰蒙蒙的。**2.** 土灰色的;(酒)浊的。**3.** 灰尘似的,粉状的。**4.** 枯燥无味的。**5.** 暧昧的;含糊的。**6.** 无价值的。*What a* ～ *answer!* 多含混的回答啊! *a* ～ *speech* 枯燥无味的演说。***not*** [***none***] ***so*** ～ 〔英俚〕还好。～ **miller 1.** 【植】耳状报春花 (= auricula)。**2.** (钓鲑等的)假饵钩。**3.** 〔美〕蠹蛾。

Dutch [dʌtʃ; dʌtʃ] **I** ***a***. **1.** 荷兰(人)的;〔美方、口〕德国人的。**2.** 荷兰语的。**3.** 荷兰制的;荷兰式的。**II** ***n***. **1.** 〔the ～〕荷兰人。**2.** 荷兰语;〔古〕(语言史上的)德国语。**3.** 〔the ～〕〔美方、口〕德国人。**4.** 〔美俚〕怒气,怒火。*double* ～ 糊涂话,莫名其妙的话。***beat the*** ～ 〔口〕做使人惊叹的事;干的事叫人莫名其妙 (*Well, you women do beat the* ～. 好了,好了,你们女人真叫人伤脑筋)。***go*** ～ 〔美口〕(聚餐等)各人自己付钱。***in*** ～ 〔美俚〕**1.** 丢脸,受气;为难,受窘。**2.** 得罪(上司等) (*get in* ～ *with sb*. 得罪了某人)。***talk to sb. like a*** ～ ***uncle*** 板着面孔唠唠叨叨地[严厉地]教训[责备]。～ **act** 〔美俚〕自杀。～ **auction** 喊价逐步减低的拍卖。～ **bargain** 酒席上讲成的买卖。～ **barn** 〔英〕干草棚。～ **butter** 人造奶油。～ **cheese** 荷兰(球状)干酪。～ **comfort** [**consolation**] 不幸时退一步着想而得到的安慰。～ **concert** 〔口〕乱七八糟的合唱。～ **courage** 酒后之勇,虚勇。～ **cousins** 老朋友。～ **door 1.** (上下两部分可各自分别开关的)两截门。**2.** (夹在杂志中可抽出的)散页广告。～ **foil** [**gold leaf**] 人造金箔。～ **lunch** [**supper**] 〔美〕聚餐式午餐[晚餐]。～ **metal** 荷兰合金,荷兰黄铜。～ **oven** (盖上加炭的)荷兰烤锅;(吊在火前烤的)铁皮烤肉匣;荷兰灶[撤火后用余热烧东西的灶]。～ **pink 1.** 一种黄色颜料。**2.** 〔俚〕血。～ **rush** 【植】木贼。～ **school** 〔美〕(以日常生活为题材的)荷兰画派。～ **telescope** 荷兰式望远镜[把凸透镜作物镜,凹透镜作目镜]。～ **tile** 饰瓦。～ **treat** [**party**] 〔美口〕(各人自己付钱的)聚餐。～ **uncle** 喋喋不休地教训人的人。～ **wife** 竹夫人[睡觉时减轻暑热用的藤具或竹具]。

Dutch·man [ˈdʌtʃmən; ˋdʌtʃmən] ***n***. **1.** (*pl*. **-men**) 荷兰人 (=〔美〕Hollander)。**2.** 〔美俚〕德国人。**3.** 【海】荷兰船;〔美俚〕德国船。**4.** (生于南非的)荷兰血统人。**5.** (芬兰以外的)北欧各国的海员。**6.** 〔d-〕塞孔堵洞物;遮盖物。***I'm a*** ～ (***if*** [***or***] ...) 〔发誓语〕如果…我就不是人! 决不会… (*It is true, or I'm a* ～. 我若说谎我就不是人。*You've passed the examination? Well, I'm a* ～! 你已经考试及格了! 我可不相信!)。

Dutch·man's-breech·es [ˈdʌtʃmənsbritʃiz; ˋdʌtʃmənz-ˋbrɪtʃɪz] ***n***. 〔*sing*., *pl*.〕【植】兜状荷包牡丹。

Dutch·man's-pipe [ˈdʌtʃmənsˈpaip; ˋdʌtʃmənsˋpaɪp] ***n***. 【植】美洲马兜铃。

du·te·ous [ˈdjuːtjəs; ˋdjutjəs] ***a***. 忠实的,顺从的,守本分的,尽职的。**-ly** ***ad***. **-ness** ***n***.

du·ti·a·ble [ˈdjuːtjəbl; ˋdjutɪəbl] ***a***. (货物)应缴税的;(输入品)应课关税的。～ *articles* [*goods*] 课税品。

du·ti·ful [ˈdjuːtiful; ˋdjutɪfəl] ***a***. 孝顺的;忠于职守的,守本分的;(对长上)必恭必敬的。*a* ～ *child* 听话的孩子。～ *attention* 恭敬地谛听,洗耳恭听。**-ly** ***ad***. **-ness** ***n***.

Dutt [dʌt; dʌt] ***n***. 达特〔姓氏〕。

du·ty [ˈdjuːti; ˋdjutɪ] ***n***. **1.** 义务,本份;责任;职责,职务,职能。**2.** 忠节,孝顺;恭敬,尊敬,敬意;义,谊。**3.** 税,关税;【机】功;能率;灌溉率;负荷,生产量;工作状态。**4.** 【军】任务,勤务;兵役;【宗】礼拜,(修行的)功课。**5.** 〔口〕(原指小孩的)拉屎。*one's maternal* ～ 做母亲的本份。*postmen's duties* 邮递员的职责。*filial* ～ 做子女的义务。*That's no part of my* ～. 那不是我管的事。*on radar* ～ *for two years* 当两年雷达兵。～ *call* 礼节性拜访。*customs duties* 关税。*export* [*import*] *duties* 出口[进口]税。*After graduation, he began his* ～. 他毕业后开始服兵役。***be in*** ～ ***bound to*** (***do sth.***) 有义务(做某事)。***do*** ～ ***as*** [***for***] 代…用,当…用 (*bookcases that do* ～ *as room dividers* 当分隔房间墙壁的书柜)。***do*** [***perform***] ***one's*** ～ **1.** 尽义务,尽职;尽(友)谊。**2.** 服兵役。～ ***of water*** 一定区域内某种作物所需灌溉的水量。***fail in one's*** ～ 失职。***off*** ～ 在工作时间外,不值班,不值勤;下班 (*go*[*come*] *off* ～ 下班)。***on*** ～ 在工作时间内,值班,值勤;上班 (*go on* ～ 上班)。***pay*** [***send***] ***one's*** ～ ***to*** 对…表示敬意。***take sb.'s*** ～ 替代某人的工作。～**-bound** ***a***. 义不容辞的。～**-free** ***a***.

D

无税的,免税的。~-**paid** *a*. 已完税的。~ **solicitor** 〔美〕(政府指定的)义务律师。

du·um·vir [dju(:)ˈʌmvə; djuˋʌmvɚ] *n*. (*pl*. ~*s* [-vəz; -vɚz], ***du·umvi·ri*** [dju(:)ˈʌmvirai; djuˋʌmvɪraɪ]) (古罗马)二头政治中的一个统治者;两人掌权统治者中的一个。

du·um·vi·rate [dju(:)ˈʌmvirit; djuˋʌmvərɪt] *n*. **1**. 二人共同负责的职务;二头政治。**2**. 共同统治的两个人。

du·vay [du:ˈvei; duˋve] *n*. 鸭绒被,羽绒被。

du·vet [dju:ˈvei; djuˋve] *n*. 〔F.〕鸭绒垫子。

du·ve·tyn, du·ve·tine, du·ve·tyne [ˈdu:vəti:n; ˋduvə͵tin] *n*. 【纺】起绒织物〔丝毛混纺品〕。

dux [dʌks; dʌks] *n*. (*pl*. ~*es*, ***du·ces*** [ˈdʌksiz; ˋdʌksɪz]) 〔Scot., N.Z., S. Afr.〕级长,班长。

D.V. = *Deo Volente* (〔L.〕=God willing; if God permits 如果上帝允许的话)。

DVD =digital videodisk 数字视盘。

DVD-ROM =digital videodisk read-only memory【计】数字只读光盘存储器。

D.V.M. =Doctor of Veterinary Medicine 兽医学博士。

d.w., dw =deadweight.

dwarf [dwɔ:f; dwɔrf] **I** *n*. **1**. 矮子。**2**. 矮小的动物[植物];矮生植物。**3**.【北欧神话】(善做金属小工艺品的)矮神。**4**.【天】矮星 (=~ star)。**II** *a*. 矮小的。*a* ~ *car* 小型汽车。**III** *vt*. 使矮小,使(发育、智能等)受阻碍;使相形见绌。~ *all one's rivals* 使所有的对手都相形见绌。*a* ~(*ed*) *tree* 盆栽树,盆景。—*vi*. 变矮小。~ **door** (活动门的下半截)小门。~ **star**【天】矮星。**-ism** *n*. **1**. 矮小。**2**.【植】矮态;【医】侏儒症。

dwarf·ish [ˈdwɔ:fiʃ; ˋdwɔrfɪʃ] *a*. 比较矮小的。

DWC =deadweight capacity【船】(总)载重吨位。

dwell [dwel; dwɛl] *vi*. (***dwelt*** [dwelt; dwɛlt], ~***ed***; ***dwelt***, ~***ed***) **1**.〔书〕住,居住,居留;寓于 (*at*; *in*, *on*)。**2**. (马跳障碍物时)踌躇。~ *at a place* 住在一个地方。*He has been* ~*ing for years in the same town*. 他在一个城市住了多年。~ *on the earth* 住在地球上。~ **on** [**upon**] **1**. 细想;详述;仔细研究;强调。**2**. 拖长(发音);仔细打量,盯着看。**3**. 减慢 (~ *on the pleasures of the past* 细想过去的欢乐。~ *on a stroke* 缓慢地荡桨。*Her eyes* ~ *on him*. 她盯着看他。~ *on a particular point in an argument* 详细阐述一个特殊论点。~ *on a syllable* 拖长一个音节)。**-er** *n*. **1**. 居住者,居民。**2**. (在障碍物前)踌躇不跳的马 (*city and town dwellers* 城镇居民)。

dwell·ing [ˈdweliŋ; ˋdwɛlɪŋ] *n*. **1**. 居住。**2**. 住宅,寓所;住处。*change one's* ~ 搬家。*a portable* ~ 活动房屋。*a modern* ~ 现代化住宅。~ **house** 住宅。~ **place** 住处。

dwelt [dwelt; dwɛlt] dwell 的过去式及过去分词。

D.W.I. =driving while intoxicated 酒后驾驶;(被指控)酒后开车的人。

Dwight [dwait; dwaɪt] *n*. 德怀特〔姓氏〕。

dwin·dle [ˈdwindl; ˋdwɪndl̩] *vi*. **1**. 减少,变小,缩小;变瘦。**2**. 衰落;变坏,退化。~ *in size* 体积缩小。~ *in numbers* 数量减少。~ *away into* [*to*] *nothing* 减少到零,化为乌有。~ *down to* 缩减到…。~ *into* 缩小成。~ *out* 逐渐消失。*His fame* ~*d*. 他的名声低落了。— *vt*. 使缩小,使减少。*Failing health* ~*d ambition*. 体弱雄心减。

DWT, D.W.T., dwt = deadweight ton(s)【船】(总)载重吨位。

dwt., dwt =pennyweight(s).

DX =distance【无】远距离(常用以表示远距离播送)。

DX., dx. =【讯】duplex.

Dy =【化】dysprosium.

dy =penny.

dy·ad [ˈdaiæd; ˋdaɪæd] **I** *n*. **1**. 二个,一对,一双。**2**.【数】并矢(量);【化】二价元素;【生】二分体,二分细胞。**3**.〔美口〕双边对话,双边会谈;双边关系。*a chromosome* ~ 二分染色体。**II** *a*. 二数的,二价的。**dy·ad·ic** [daiˈædik; daɪˋædɪk] **1**. *a*.【数】二数的,二进的;【化】二价的;二重(对称)的,双值的。**2**. *n*.【数】并矢式,并向量,双积。

Dy·a(c)k [ˈdaiæk; ˋdaɪæk] *n*. (婆罗洲的)达雅克人,达雅克语 (=Dayak)。

dy·ar·chy [ˈdaiɑ:ki; ˋdaɪɑrkɪ] *n*. =diarchy.

dyb·buk [ˈdaibək; ˋdaɪbək] *n*. (犹太民间传说)阴魂附体。

Dyce [dais; daɪs] *n*. 戴斯〔姓氏〕。

dye [dai; daɪ] **I** *vt*. 染,染上,把…染色,给…着色。~ *a dress green* 把衣服染成绿色。*A deep flush* ~*d her cheeks*. 她的双颊染上一层绯红。—*vi*. 着色,上色,染上颜色。*This cloth* ~*s easily*. 这种布容易上色。**be** ~**d in** (**the**) **grain** [**in the wool**] **1**. 生染;被染透。**2**.〔喻〕造成不可改变的结果。~ **well** [**badly**] 好[不好]染。**II** *n*. **1**. 染料,染液。**2**. 染色;色调。*acid* [*alkaline*, *basic*] ~*s* 酸性[碱性,盐基性]染料。*mordant* [*synthetic*] ~*s* 媒染[合成]染料。*take* ~ *well* 容易染色。(**scoundrel**) **of the blackest** [**deepest**] ~ 穷凶极恶的(无赖)。~**house** 染厂,染坊,染色间。~**jigger**【纺】染缸,卷染机。~ **marker** 海水染色剂〔投在海中使水变色作为标志的染料〕。~ **printing** 印染,印花。~**stuff** 染料;颜料;(橡胶的)染色剂。~ **vat** 染缸,染锅,染槽。~-**wood** 染料木。~-**works** 〔*sing*., *pl*.〕染厂。**-a·bil·i·ty** [-əˈbiləti; -əˋbɪlətɪ] *n*. 可染色性,可着色性。

dyed-in-the-wool [ˈdaid*i*nðəˈwul; ˋdaɪdnðəˋwʊl] *a*. **1**. 生染的,未纺织以前即染色的。**2**. 纯粹的,十足的,彻头彻尾的,难以改变的。

dye·ing [ˈdaiiŋ; ˋdaɪɪŋ] **I** *n*. 染色;染色法;染业。**II** *a*. 染色的。

dy·er [ˈdaiə; ˋdaɪɚ] *n*. 染色员,染工,染色师傅。

dy·er's-broom [ˈdaiəzbru:m; ˋdaɪɚzbrum] *n*.【植】染料木。

dy·er's-weed [ˈdaiəzwi:d; ˋdaɪɚz͵wid] *n*. **1**. 染料目(含染料的植物)。**2**.【植】一枝黄花属植物;一枝黄花。

dy·ing [ˈdaiiŋ; ˋdaɪɪŋ] **I** die 的现在分词。**II** *a*. **1**. 垂死的,快死的;临终的。**2**. 会死的,会灭亡的。**3**. (火)快熄灭的;快消灭的,行将完结的。**4**.〔口〕渴望,切盼,极想。*a* ~ *man* 快死的人。*one's* ~ *wish* 临终的心愿,遗嘱。*the* ~ *year* 年终岁尾。*a* ~ *fire* 行将熄灭的火。*the* ~ *moon* 下沉的月亮。*He is* ~ *to go*. 他很想去。**be** ~ **for** 对…想得要死。**to** [**till**] **one's** ~ **day** 直到老死。

dyke[1] [daik; daɪk] *n*.〔英〕=dike.

dyke[2] [daik; daɪk] *n*.〔俚〕爱搞同性爱的女性(尤指扮演男性角色者)。

dyn., dynam. =dynamics.

dyna-, dynam- *comb. f*. 力,动力: *dyna*mics.

dy·nam·e·ter [daiˈnæmitə; daɪˋnæmətɚ] *n*.【物】(望远镜的)倍率计。

dy·nam·ic, dy·nam·i·cal [daiˈnæmik, -kəl; daɪˋnæmɪk, -kəl] **I** *a*. **1**. 动力的,动力学的;力学(上)的;动(态)的;起动的。**2**. 有力的,有生气的;能动的;(工作)效率高的。**3**.【乐】力度;强弱法的。**4**.【医】机能(上)的。**5**.【哲】动力论的,力本论的。*a* ~ *personality* 活跃的性格。*a* ~ *atmosphere* 生气勃勃的景象。*a* ~ *population* 动态人口。**II** *n*.〔限指 dynamic〕(原)动力;动态。~ **agent** 起动的原因。~ **astronomy** 天体力学。~ **behavior** 能动行为。~ **characteristics**【讯】动态特性曲线。~ **electricity** 动力电。~ **elevation** 动力势差[位差]。~ **geology** 地质力学。~ **equilibrium** 动态平衡。~ **meteorology** 气象力学。~ **number** 重力势差[位差]数。**-al·ly** *ad*.

dy·nam·ics [daiˈnæmiks; daɪˋnæmɪks] ***n***. *pl*. **1.** 〔用作 *sing*.〕力学;动力学。**2.** 动力,原动力。**3.** 动态。**4.** 【乐】力度强弱法。

dy·na·mism [ˈdainəmizəm; ˋdaɪnə͵mɪzəm] ***n***. **1.** 【哲】物力论,力本学。**2.** 精力,活力;魄力,劲头。**-na·mist** ***n***. 物力论者。**-na·mis·tic** [ˌdaiəˈmistik; ͵daɪəˋmɪstɪk] ***a***.

dy·na·mi·tard [ˈdainəmitɑːd; ˋdaɪnəmɪtɑrd] ***n***. (为某一政治目的采取行刺等暴力行动而)使用炸药的人;〔美〕使用炸药的盗匪。

dy·na·mite [ˈdainəmait; ˋdaɪnəmaɪt] **I** ***n***. **1.** (一种爆炸力猛烈的)达那炸药,甘油炸药。**2.** 具有爆炸性的事[物];有潜在危险的人。**3.** 精力充沛的人。**4.** 〔俚〕毒品指海洛英等]。**II** ***vt***. **1.** (用炸药)炸破。**2.** 使完全失败。*Saboteurs* ~*d the dam*. 破坏者炸毁了堤坝。~**-laden** ***a***. (局势等)充满爆炸性的。

dy·na·mi·ter [ˈdainəmaitə; ˋdaɪnə͵maɪtɚ] ***n***. **1.** =dynamitard. **2.** 〔美俚〕野心勃勃的人。

dy·na·mo [ˈdainəməu; ˋdaɪnə͵mo] ***n***. **1.** 【电】发电机〔尤指直流发电机〕。**2.** 〔口〕勤奋肯干的人,精力充沛的人。*an alternating* [*direct*] *current* ~ 交[直]流发电机。*a compound* [*wound*] ~ 复绕[复激发]电机。*shunt* [*wound*] ~ 分绕[并励发]电机。~**-electric** ***a***. 电动的,机电的,机械能变为电能的,电能变为机械能的。

dy·na·mom·e·ter [ˌdainəˈmɔmitə; ͵daɪnəˋmɑmətɚ] ***n***. **1.** 测力计,拉力表。**2.** 功率计;动力计;电力测工仪。**-y** ***n***. 动力测定法。

dy·na·mo·tor [ˈdainəməutə; ˋdaɪnəmotɚ] ***n***. 【电】电动发电机。

dy·na·po·lis [daiˈnæpəlis; daɪˋnæpəlɪs] ***n***. (交通干线附近的)新兴城市。

dy·nast [ˈdinəst; ˋdaɪnæst] ***n***. (世袭王朝的)君主;统治者。

dy·nas·tic(al) [diˈnæstik(əl); daɪˋnæstɪk(əl)] ***a***. 朝代的;王朝的,皇朝的。

dy·nas·ty [ˈdinəsti, ˈdainəsti; ˋdɪnəstɪ, ˋdaɪnəstɪ] ***n***. **1.** 王朝,朝代。**2.** 王朝统治;世袭统治。**3.** 统治集团;统治家族。*the Ming* ~ 明王朝。

dy·nat·ron [ˈdainətrɔn; ˋdaɪnətrɑn] ***n***. 【无】(打拿)负阻管。

dyne [dain; daɪn] ***n***. 【物】达因〔力的单位〕。

Dy·nel [daiˈnel; daɪˋnɛl] ***n***. **1.** 【纺】迪尼尔〔美国制的一种合成纤维的商标名〕。**2.** 〔d-〕【纺】迪尼尔线;迪尼尔皮毛。

dy·no [ˈdainəu; ˋdaɪno] ***a***. 〔美口〕绝妙的。

dy·node [ˈdainəud; ˋdaɪnod] ***n***. 【无】**1.** 倍增器电极。**2.** 打拿极,中间极。

dys- *comb*. *f*. 恶化,不良;困难:*dys*function.

dys·cra·sia [disˈkreizjə; dɪsˋkreʒɪə] ***n***. 【医】体液不调,恶液质。**-cra·si·al, -cras·ic** ***a***.

dys·en·ter·y [ˈdisəntəri; ˋdɪsn͵tɛrɪ] ***n***. 痢疾。**-ter·ic** ***a***. 痢疾(性)的。

dys·func·tion [disˈfʌŋkʃən; dɪsˋfʌŋkʃən] ***n***. 【医】机能障碍,机能不良。**-al** ***a***.

dys·gen·ic [disˈdʒenik; dɪsˋdʒɛnɪk] ***a***. 【生】劣生的,遗传性状不良的。**-s** ***n***. 【生】劣生学。

dys·lex·i·a [disˈleksiə; dɪsˋlɛksɪə] ***n***. 【医】诵读困难。**-lex·ic** ***a***.

dys·lo·gi·a [disˈləudʒiə; dɪsˋlodʒɪə] ***n***. 【医】言语困难,难语症。

dys·lo·gis·tic [disləˈdʒistik; ͵dɪsloˋdʒɪstɪk] ***a***. 指责的,责难的;骂人的。~ *terms* 骂人的话,出口伤人。

dys·men·or·rhe·a [ˌdismenəˈriːə; ͵dɪsmɛnəˋriə] ***n***. 【医】痛经,月经困难。

dys·mne·si·a [disˈniːʒə; dɪsˋniʒə] ***n***. 【医】记忆障碍。

dys·pa·thy [ˈdispəθi; ˋdɪspəθɪ] ***n***. 〔古〕无情;反感。

dys·pep·sia [disˈpepsiə; dɪˋspɛpsɪə] ***n***. 消化不良,胃弱(*opp*. eupepsia)。

dys·pep·sy [disˈpepsi; dɪˋspɛpsɪ] ***n***. 〔方〕=dyspepsia.

dys·pep·tic [disˈpeptik; dɪˋspɛptɪk] **I** ***a***. **1.** 消化不良的,胃弱的;由消化不良引起的。**2.** 阴郁的,消沉的;易怒的。**II** ***n***. 消化不良的人。**-cal·ly** ***ad***.

dys·pha·gia [disˈfeidʒiə; dɪsˋfedʒɪə] ***n***. 【医】咽下困难。**dis·phagic** ***a***.

dys·pha·si·a [disˈfeiʒiə; dɪsˋfeʒɪə] ***n***. 【医】语言困难。

dys·pho·ni·a [disˈfəuniə; dɪsˋfonɪə] ***n***. 【医】发音困难。**disphon·ic** ***a***.

dys·pho·ri·a [disˈfɔːriə; dɪsˋforɪə] ***n***. 【医】烦躁不安。

dys·pla·si·a [disˈpleiziə, -ˈpleiʒə; dɪsˋplezɪə, -ˋpleʒə] ***n***. 【医】发育异常。**-plas·tic** [-ˈplæstik; -ˋplæstɪk] ***a***.

dysp·n(o)e·a [disˈpniːə; dɪspˋniə] ***n***. 【医】呼吸困难(*opp*. eupnea)。**-n(o)e·ic** [-ˈniːk; -ˋniɪk] ***a***.

dys·prax·i·a [disˈpræksiə; dɪsˋpræksɪə] ***n***. 【医】运动困难,运动障碍。

dys·pro·si·um [disˈprəusiəm; dɪsˋprosɪəm] ***n***. 【化】镝。

dys·to·cia [disˈtəuʃiə; dɪsˋtoʃɪə] ***n***. 【医】难产。

dys·to·pi·a [disˈtəupiə; dɪsˋtopɪə] ***n***. 非理想化的地方,糟透的社会;地狱般的处境(*opp*. utopia)。

dys·tro·phic [disˈtrɔfik; dɪsˋtrɑfɪk] ***a***. **1.** 营养不良的,营养障碍的。**2.** 发育不全的,畸形的;退化的。

dys·tro·phy [ˈdistrəfi; ˋdɪstrəfɪ] ***n***. 【医】营养障碍,营养不良。

dys·u·ri·a [disˈjuəriə; dɪsˋjʊrɪə] ***n***. 【医】排尿困难,尿痛。**dys·u·ric** ***a***.

Dyu·sham·be [dju(ː)ˈʃɑːmbə; djuˋʃɑmbə] ***n***. = Dushambe.

DZ = drop zone 空投(或伞降)地域。

dz. = dozen(s).

dzig·ge·tai [ˈdʒiˈgitai; ˋdʒɪgə͵taɪ] ***n***. (蒙古的)野驴。

E

E, e [iː; i] (*pl*. ***E's***, ***e's*** [iːz; iz]) **1.** 英文字母表第五字母。**2.** 【乐】E 调,E 音。**3.** E 字形。**4.** 〔美〕(顺序)第五等,(成绩)"劣等"〔注意,有时 E 也作成绩优等(excellent)的符号〕。**5.** = Ecstasy "摇头丸"〔一种能使吸食者产生灵魂出窍感觉的毒品〕。

E., e. = **1.** earth. **2.** east; eastern. **3.** engineer(ing).

e- *pref*. [i, ə; ɪ, ə] 表示"出","出自","外面","缺"等意:*e*ject, *e*radiate, *e*scribe, *e*dentate.

E-, e- *pref*. 表示"电子的"之意:E-book 电子书, E-business 电子商务, E-cash 电子货币, E-shopper 网上购物者, e-card 电子贺卡, e-journal 电子杂志。

EA = enemy aircraft 敌机。

ea. = each.

E.A.A. = Engineer in Aeronautics and Astronautics 航空学与航天学工程师。

each [iːtʃ; itʃ] **I** *a*. 各,各自的,每。~ *man* 各人。~ *side of the river* 河的两边。**II** *pro*. 每,各,各自。*E- (of us) has his likes and dislikes*. 各有各的好恶。*We ~ know what the other wants*. 我们彼此都知道各自的要求。*From ~ according to his ability and to ~ according to his work [needs]*. 各尽所能,按劳[需]分配。**III** *ad*. 各个地。*These books cost one dollar ~*. 这些书每本的价钱一美元。***bet ~ way*** 【赛马】赌两门。***~ and all*** 大家都,统统。***~ and every*** 每个都,人人都。***~ other*** 互相,彼此(*They help ~ other*. 他们互相帮助)。***on ~ occasion*** 每次。

Eads [iːdz; idz] *n*. 伊兹〔姓氏〕。

ea·ger [ˈiːgə; ˋigɚ] *a*. **1.** 〔多用作述语〕渴望,极想,热衷于(*after*; *about*; *for*)。**2.** 热切的,热情洋溢的。**3.** 〔古〕(寒气等)凛冽的;酷烈的;(气味等)浓烈的。*be ~ to do sth*. 极想做某事。*I am ~ for [after] news about them*. 我渴望得到有关他们的消息。*She is ~ in her studies*. 她热衷于学习。*one's ~ pursuit of pleasure* 一心追求享乐。*an ~ look* 热情洋溢的面孔,期待的神情。~ **beaver** (为讨好上司)干活特别卖力的人。**~-beaver** *a*. 巴结上司的,讨好卖乖的。**-ly** *ad*.

ea·ger·ness [ˈiːgənis; ˋigɚnɪs] *n*. 渴望;殷切;热忱;热情。*He had a great ~ to join the army*. 他(当时)满腔热忱想要参军。*The recruit was all ~ to go to the front*. 新入伍的战士迫切盼望上前线。

ea·gle [ˈiːgl; ˋigl̩] *n*. **1.** 鹰。**2.** 鹰徽;鹰旗。**3.** 〔美〕十元金币。**4.** 〔E-〕【天】鹰座。**5.** 〔E-〕密士失必州别名。~ **boat** 〔美〕小型反潜艇战舰。**~-eyed** *a*. 眼力锐利的,目光炯炯的。~ **owl** 【动】雕鸮。

ea·glet [ˈiːglit; ˋiglɪt] *n*. 小鹰。

ea·gre [ˈeigə, ˈiːgə; ˋegɚ, ˋigɚ] *n*. 〔方〕(河口的)海潮,潮。

EAL = **1.** Ethiopian Airlines 衣索比亚航空公司。**2.** Eastern Air Lines 〔美〕东方航空公司。

-ean *suf*. 作名词和形容词的词尾,表示"…的","属于…"。Europ*ean*, Aeg*ean*, trach*ean*.

E and OE, E. & O.E. = errors and omissions excepted 如有错漏,可予更改〔常印在账单上〕。

ear[1] [iə; ir] *n*. **1.** 耳朵。**2.** 听觉;听力;倾听;注意。**3.** 耳状物〔指水罐、茶杯等的把儿〕。**4.** 报头两端刊登小广告、天气预报的地方。***a flea in sb.'s ~*** 刺耳的话。***A word in your ~***. 我跟你私下讲句话。***about one's ~s*** (某人)陷于尴尬[麻烦等]处境(*bring the house about one's ~s* 遭全家反对)。***be all ~*** 〔口〕专心倾听。***be [go out] on one's ~s*** 〔美俚〕发怒;无礼。***bend sb.'s ~s*** 讲得使某人厌烦;和某人谈要事。***by the ~s*** (动物)相斗;(人)扭打,倾轧;不和(*set the whole neighbourhood by the ~s* 挑拨离间,使四邻不和。*fall together by the ~s* 打起来)。***close [stop] one's ~s to*** 完全不听。***fall on deaf ~s*** 不被理睬,不受注意。***feel one's ~s burning*** 感觉耳朵发烧(有人背地议论)。***get sb. on his ~*** 〔美俚〕使某人发火。***give sb. a thick ~*** 把(某人)打得鼻青脸肿。***give ~ to*** 听,倾听。***give one's ~s*** 不惜任何代价(要)。***have a good [poor] ~*** 听力好[不好]。***have an [no] ~ for music*** 懂[不懂]音乐。***have [hold, keep] an ~ to the ground*** 注意舆论等的动向,留心可能发生的事情。***have itching ~s*** 爱听新奇消息、闲话。***have [gain, win] sb.'s ~s*** 得到某人注意。***(go [through]) in at one ~ and out at the other*** 左耳进右耳出,听了就忘。***kick [throw] sb. out on his ears*** 突然解雇某人。***lend one's ~s to*** = ***give ~ to***. *over head and ~s* = *up to the ~s*. ***play [sing] by ~*** **1.** 不看乐谱演奏[歌唱]。**2.** 〔口〕临时应付事态〔事先没有计划〕。***prick up one's ~s*** 竖起耳朵听。***sleep upon both ~s*** 酣睡。***tickle sb.'s ~*** 巴结,奉承某人。***turn a deaf ~ to*** 装听不见[置若罔闻]。***up to the ~s*** 深陷(债务等)。***Walls have ~s***. 〔谚〕隔墙有耳。***(still) ~ behind the ~s*** 没有经验,缺乏训练。**~-ache** [ˈiəreik; ˋɪrˏek] 耳痛。~ **candy** 声音甜美的轻音乐。**~cap** 耳套。**~drop** 耳饰,耳坠。**~-drops** 耳药水。**~drum** 【解】耳鼓。**~flap** (帽子的)护耳。**~lap** **1.** = ~ flap. **2.** = ~ lobe. **3.** 外耳。~ **lobe** 耳垂。**~mark** **1.** *n*. (家畜耳朵上的)耳记;标记,特征(= dog-ear)。**2.** *vt*. (给家畜)打耳记;指定(资金等的)用途。~ **muffs** 〔*pl*.〕〔美〕(防寒用的)耳套。~ **phone** 耳机,译意风,收话器。**~pick** 耳挖勺。~ **piece** **1.** = ~phone. **2.** 眼镜架柄。**~phone** 耳机,耳塞;头戴受话器。**~-piecing** *a*. 刺耳的。**~-plug** (防水或防噪声的)耳塞。~ **reach** = ~shot. ~ **ring** 耳环。~ **shell** **1.** = abalone. **2.** 鲍鱼壳。**~shot** 听力所及的范围(*within [out of] the ~ shot of the alarm* 在听得见[听不见]警报器的地方)。~ **trumpet** (从前半聋人用的号筒形)助听器。**~wax** 耳垢。**~wig** **1.** *n*. 【动】蠼螋;偷听者;奉承者。**2.** *vt*. 在耳边说闲话(来打扰或企图影响某人)。

ear[2] [iə; ɪr] **I** *n*. **1.** (稻麦等的)穗。**2.** 〔*pl*.〕灯花。***be in the ~*** 正在抽穗。***come into ~s*** 抽穗。**II** *vi*. 抽穗。~ **developing stage** 孕穗期。

ear·bob [ˈiəbɔb; ˋɪrˏbɑb] *n*. 〔方〕耳环。

eared [iəd; ɪrd] *a*. **1.** 有耳朵的;…耳的。**2.** 有把儿的;…把的。**3.** 有穗的;…穗的。

ear·ful [ˈiəful; ˋɪrful] *n*. 〔口〕**1.** 听够了的话。**2.** 大量的新闻[闲话]。**3.** 耸人听闻的消息。**4.** 训斥。

Ear·hart [ˈɛəhɑːt; ˋɛrhɑrt] *n*. 埃尔哈特〔姓氏〕。

ear·ing [ˈiəriŋ; ˋɪrɪŋ] *n*. 【海】(横帆角上的)耳索。

earl [əːl; ɝl] *n*. (*fem*. **countess**)〔英〕伯爵〔相当于欧洲大陆的 count〕。**E- Marshal** 英国纹章院院长。

earl·dom [ˈəːldəm; ˋɝldəm] *n*. **1.** 伯爵爵位[身份]。**2.** 伯爵领地。

ear·less[1] [ˈiəlis; ˋɪrlɪs] *a*. **1.** 无耳的。**2.** 听觉不佳的。~ **seal** 【动】海豹科(*Phocidae*)动物。

ear·less[2] [ˈiəlis; ˋɪrlɪs] *a*. 无穗的。

ear·li·ness [ˈəːlinis; ˋɝlɪnɪs] *n*. 早,早期。

Ear·ly [ˈəːli; ˋɝlɪ] *n*. 厄利〔姓氏〕。

ear·ly [ˈəːli; ˋɝlɪ] (*opp*. late) **I** *a*. **1.** 早;(果实等)早熟的。**2.** 早日的,及早的。**3.** 早期的,很久以前的,古代的;近日的。*at an ~ date* 早日,在最近期间。*Please reply at your earliest convenience* 务请早日赐覆。~ *death* 早死,夭折。~ *maturity (of mind)* 思想早熟。~ *train* 早班车。~ *riser* 早起的人;~ *rising* 早起。~ *bird* 早起的人(*The ~ bird catches [gets] the worm*. 〔谚〕捷足先登)。~ *habits* 早起早睡的习惯。***E-Modern English*** 早期现代英语(十五世纪中叶至十八世纪中叶)。***It is ~ days yet*** (*to make up one's mind*). (要下决心)现在还为时过早。***one's ~ days*** 年轻时。***keep ~ hours*** 早睡早起。**II** *ad*. 早,先,初;幼小时候。*as ~ as May* 早在五月里。*Don't come too ~*. 不要来的太早。~ *in May* 五月初。***earlier on*** 以前,在更早的时候。***~ and late*** 从早到晚。***~ on*** 在早期。***~ or late*** 迟早,早晚。***E- sow, ~ mow***. 〔谚〕早种早收。***rise [get up] ~*** 早起。~ **ag(e)ing** 【医】早衰。~ **ambulation** 【医】(外科手术后)早期下床活动。~ **door** (剧院的)提早入座门。~ **rice** 早稻。**~-Victorian** *a*. 维多利亚王朝初期的;(英国)(作家等)旧式的。**~-warning radar** 预先[远程]警报雷达。

earn [əːn; ɝn] *vt*. **1.** 赚得,挣得。**2.** 获得,赢得,博得(名声)。*a well-~ed reward* 应得的报酬。*~ed income* 劳动收入。~ ***one's bread [living]*** 谋生,挣钱。~ ***one's***

own living 自食其力。

ear·nest[1]['ə:nist; ˋɝnɪst] **I** ***a*** . **1.** 热心的;诚挚的,真挚的,认真的。**2.** 重要的。**II** ***n*** . 热心;认真。***in*** ~ 诚挚,认真(*Are you in* ~ (*in what you say*)? 你(讲的话)当真吗? *It began raining in* ~ . 雨真的下大了)。***in good*** [***real***, ***sober***, ***sad***, ***dead***] ~ 一本正经地,非常认真地。**-ly** ***ad*** . **-ness** ***n*** .

ear·nest[2]['ə:nist; ˋɝnɪst] ***n*** . **1.** 定钱,保证金。**2.** 预兆。~ **money** 定钱,保证金。

earn·ings ['ə:niŋz; ˋɝnɪŋz] ***n*** . ***pl*** . 所得,收入,工资,报酬,利润。

Earp [ə:p; ɝp] ***n*** . 厄普〔姓氏〕。

earth [ə:θ; ɝθ] **I** ***n*** . **1.** 〔常 E-〕地球。**2.** 大地,陆地,地面,地上。**3.** 土壤,土。**4.** 【化】土类;泥。**5.** 世界人类;人的躯体。**6.** 尘世,人间,世间;世俗的事。**7.** 〔英〕(狐、獾等的)洞,穴。**8.** 【电】接地。**9.** 【化】难以还原的金属氧化物类〔如氧化铝、氧化钴等〕。*the whole* ~ 全人类。*be brought to* ~ 被击落在地上。*alkaline* ~ 【化】碱土。***be of the*** ~ 有点俗气。***break*** ~ 破土动工。***come back*** [***down***] ***to*** ~ 回到现实中来,不再幻想。***go the way of all the*** ~ 死。***go to*** ~ (狐等)躲入洞内。***move heaven and*** ~ (*to do sth.*) 竭力,用尽办法。***on*** ~ **1.** 在地球上,在人世间。**2.** 到底,究竟〔连用于 what; where; why; how 等词之后〕(*What on* ~ *are you?* 你究竟是什么人?)。**3.** 全然,一点也〔用于否定语后〕(*No use on* ~! 一点也没有用!)。***on God's*** ~ 普天之下。***put to*** ~ 【无】接地。***run to*** ~ = go to ~ . ***run ... to*** ~ 穷追(狐等)直至其洞内;查明,查出。***stop an*** ~ 堵塞狐(等)的洞穴。***take*** ~ 逃入洞内;隐匿。**II** ***vt*** . **1.** 把…埋入土中,用土掩盖,给…培土;把(萝卜等)保藏在土中(*up*)。**2.** 追(狐等)到洞内。**3.** 使(导体)接地〔美国用 ground〕。—***vi*** . (狐等)躲进洞内。~ **art** (对自然环境进行艺术加工的)地景艺术。~**-bag** 【军】砂袋,沙包。~**-based** ***a*** . 地面的。~**-bath** 泥浴。~**born** ***a*** . 地中生出的,生在地上的;人类的;世俗的。~**bound** ***a*** . **1.** 局限于地上的;世俗的;平凡的。**2.** 朝地球走的。**3.** 【电】接地的。~**-bred** ***a*** . 土生土长的;卑贱的;粗俗的。~**-closet** (用土覆盖粪便的)厕所(*opp*. water closet)。~ **fall** 塌方。~**flow** 【地】泥流。~ **inductor** 【电】地磁感应器。~**light** 【天】= ~ shine. ~**man** (*pl*. ***-men***) (科学幻想小说中登上其他天体的)地球人,地球上的来客。~ **metals** 碱(土)金属。~**mover** 挖土机。~**nut** 落花生。~ **oil** 〔古语〕石油。~ **plate** 【电】接地金属板。~ **resources satellite** 地球资源卫星。~ **satellite** 人造地球卫星。~ **science** 地球科学。~ **scraper** 刮土机。~**shaking** ***a*** . 翻天覆地的,震撼世界的,意义极其重大的。~**shine** ***n*** . 【天】大地光,地(球反)照〔指新月暗部所呈现的微光,系由地球反射的日光造成〕。~**-space** ***a*** . 地球-太空的。~ **station** (接受及转播外层空间传来的讯号的)地面通讯站。~ **time** 地球时〔用地球自转 24 小时作计算单位,以计算其他天体的时间〕。~ **wave** 地震波。~ **wire** 【电】地线。~**work** **1.** 土方(工程)。**2.** 土木工事;土垒;土炮台;土堤。**3.** 土石艺术〔利用泥土、石块等天然形态加工的艺术品〕。~**worm** 蚯蚓,蛐蟮;鄙夫,小人。~**ward(s)** ***ad*** . 向地面。

earthed [ə:θt; ɝθt] ***a*** . 接地的,通地的。

earth·en ['ə:θən; ˋɝθən] ***a*** . **1.** 土制的,土的,陶制的。**2.** 大地的,现世的。~ **ware** ***n*** . 〔集合词〕陶器。

earth·i·ness ['ə:θinis; ˋɝθɪnɪs] ***n*** . **1.** 土质,土性。**2.** = earthliness.

earthing ['ə:θiŋ; ˋɝθɪŋ] ***n*** . 【电】接地。

earth·li·ness ['ə:θlinis; ˋɝθlɪnɪs] ***n*** . 世俗,尘缘。

earth·ling ['ə:θliŋ; ˋɝθlɪŋ] ***n*** . 人类;俗人。

earth·ly ['ə:θli; ˋɝθlɪ] ***a*** . **1.** 地球的,地上的。**2.** 现世的,世俗的。**3.** 〔否定〕完全,一点也(= at all);〔疑问〕究竟(= on earth)。**4.** 〔古〕= earthy. *What* ~ *purpose can it serve?* 这究竟有什么好处呢? ~ *passions* 情欲。***have no*** ~ (***chance***) = ***not an*** ~ (***chance***) 〔英俚〕完全没有希望。***of no*** ~ ***use*** [***reason***] 完全没有用处[道理]。

earth·quake ['ə:θkweik; ˋɝθ͵kwek] ***n*** . **1.** 地震。**2.** 大变动,动乱。~ **bomb** 地震炸弹。~ **centre** 震源。~ **country** 震区。~ **weather** 地震前的异常天气。~**proof** ***a*** . 防震的。

earth·rise ['ə:θraiz; ˋɝθraɪz] ***n*** . 地出〔从月球或太空船上所见地球仿佛从月球地平线上升起的现象〕。

earth·y ['ə:θi; ˋɝθɪ] ***a*** . **1.** 土(状)的,土质的。**2.** 泥土气的;粗俗的;世俗的;现世的。**3.** 【化】土类的。~ **elements** 土族元素。~**iron ore** 泥状铁矿。

ease [i:z; iz] **I** ***n*** . **1.** 快活;安心;悠闲;自在。**2.** 容易,不费事。**3.** (衣服等)宽松。***at*** ~ **1.** = *stand at* ~ . **2.** 快活,自由自在,心情舒畅,安心。***be*** [***feel***] ***ill at*** ~ 不安心,局促不安,心神不宁。~ ***of mind*** 心情舒畅。***march at*** ~ 【军】常步走。***set sb.'s heart at*** ~ 使安心。***stand at*** ~ 【口令】稍息。***take one's*** ~ 休息,安心。***well at*** ~ 安心,畅快。***with*** ~ 容易。**II** ***vt*** . **1.** 使安逸,使畅快;使安心;减轻(痛苦等)。**2.** 放松(绳索等),使松动。**3.** 小心地搬。**4.** 〔谑〕抢,偷。~ *sb. of his purse* 抢人钱包。~ *sb.'s mind* 使安心。—***vi*** . **1.** 减轻,减缓(*off*; *up*)。**2.** 小心搬动。***E-all***! 【赛艇】停划! ~ ***down the speed*** 【海】减低速度 ***E- her***! 【海】慢开! ~ **nature** 解手。~ ***off*** [***away***] **1.** ***vi*** . (痛苦)渐减;【海】(索等)松弛。**2.** ***vt*** . 【海】放松;放开(小船)。**3.** 【商】(物价)松动[下跌]。~ ***one's mind*** 安心,宽心。~ ***oneself*** **1.** 泄愤,出气。**2.** = ~ nature. ~ ***out*** **1.** (以不伤和气的方式)解雇,使离任。**2.** 〔美运〕轻易得胜。***E- the helm*** [***rudder***]! 【海】回舵! ~**-up** ***a*** . 缓和的。

ease·ful ['i:zful; ˋizful] ***a*** . 安闲的,舒适的,轻松的,懒散的。**-ly** ***ad*** . **-ness** ***n*** .

ea·sel ['i:zl; ˋizl] ***n*** . 画架;黑板架。~ **picture** [***piece***] 画架画。

ease·ment ['i:zmənt; ˋizmənt] ***n*** . **1.** (苦痛等)减轻,(局势)缓和(的手段)。**2.** 便利;舒适。**3.** 【法】使用权,通行权。**4.** 附属建筑物。**5.** 使人舒适[便利]的东西。

eas·i·ly ['i:zili; ˋizɪlɪ] ***ad*** . **1.** 容易,不难。**2.** 顺利,流畅。**3.** 安逸。**4.** 远远;大大地。**5.** 多半,很可能。*It is* ~ *the best hotel*. 这无疑是最好的旅馆。*more* ~ *said than done* 〔谚〕说说容易实行难。*The train may* ~ *be late*. 火车多半要晚点。

eas·i·ness ['i:zinis; ˋizɪnɪs] ***n*** . **1.** 容易。**2.** 安乐,安逸。**3.** 轻松;从容。**4.** 温和。

east [i:st; ist] **I** ***n*** . **1.** 东,东方。**2.** 东边,东面。**3.** 〔the E-〕东方〔美语作 the Orient〕;〔美〕东部〔密士失必河以东〕。**4.** 〔诗〕东风。*the Far* [*Middle*, *Near*] *E-* 远[中、近]东。*go down E-* 〔美〕去东部。~ ***by north*** [***south***] 【海、测】东偏北[南]。***E- or west***, ***home is best***. 〔谚〕东好西好不如家好。***in the*** ~ (***of***) 在…的东部。[***on***, ***to***] ***the*** ~ ***of*** 在…的东方。**II** ***a*** . 东方的;从东方来的;东部的,东边的。**E- Central** (伦敦市)中央东部邮政区。**E- End** 伦敦东部(贫民区)。**E-Ender** 伦敦东部贫民。**E- India** = **E- Indies** 东印度群岛〔印度、印度支那及马来群岛的总称〕。**E- Indian** 东印度群岛的,东印度人。**E- Side** 纽约市东部(贫民区)。**III** ***ad*** . 向东,往东;在东方;从东方。

east·bound ['i:stˌbaund; ˋist͵baund] ***a*** . 东去的,向东行的。

East·er ['i:stə; ˋistɚ] ***n*** . 【宗】复活节。~ **Day** [**Sunday**] 复活节日〔春分满月后的第一个星期日〕。~ **dues** [**offering(s)**] 〔英〕复活节献金。~ **egg** 复活节彩蛋。~ **Monday** 复活节次日。~ **term** **1.** (英法院)4 月 15 日后约三个星期的开庭期。**2.** (英大学)复活节后约六个星期的时期,春季学期。~**tide** 【宗】复活节季节〔可分别指从复活节至升天节之间的四十天,或从复活节至圣灵降临节之间的五十天,或从复活节至三一节之间的五十七

E

天〕。～ **time** **1.** 复活节季节〔由复活节到圣灵降临节,共 50 日〕。**2.** = ～ week. ～ **week** 复活节一周间。

east·er·ly [ˈiːstəli; ˋistəːlɪ] **I** *a*. 东,向东方的;从东方来的。**II** *ad*. 向东方,从东方。**III** *n*. 东风;〔*pl*.〕东风带。

east·ern [ˈiːstən; ˋistəːn] **I** *a*. **1.** 东(方的);〔E-〕东方的,东部(地方)的。**2.** (风)从东吹来的。**3.** 朝东的。**II** *n*. **1.** 东方人。**2.** 东正教信徒。*the E- Church*【宗】东正教会。*the E- Empire*【史】东罗马帝国。*the E- Hemisphere* 东半球。*the E- States* 〔美〕东部各州。～ **larch**【植】美洲落叶松。～ **red-bud**【植】加拿大紫荆。～ **white pine**【植】美洲五针松。～ **most** *a*. 极东的,最东的。

east·ern·er [ˈiːstənə; ˋistənəː] *n*. **1.** 东方人。**2.** 〔E-〕〔美〕东部人,东部各州出身的人。

East·ern Sa·mo·a [ˈiːstən səˈməuə; ˋistəːn səˋmoə] *n*. 东萨摩亚〔南太平洋〕。

east·ing [ˈiːstiŋ; ˋistɪŋ] *n*. **1.**【海】东航〔偏东航行〕。**2.** (天体的)东进;(风向的)偏东。**3.** 东行航程。**4.** 朝东方向。

East·man [ˈiːstmən; ˋistmən] *n*. 伊斯曼〔姓氏〕。

east-north·east [ˈiːstˌnɔːθˈiːst; ˋistˏnɔrθˋist] **I** *n*.【海、测】东东北。**II** *a*., *ad*. **1.** 在东东北(的),向东东北(的)。**2.** 自东东北(的)。

east-south·east [ˈiːstˌsauθˈiːst; ˋistˏsaυθˋist] **I** *n*.【海、测】东东南。**II** *a*., *ad*. **1.** 在东东南(的),向东东南(的)。**2.** 自东东南(的)。

East Ti·mor [iːstˈtimɔːr; istˋtɪmor] *n*. 东帝汶〔亚洲〕。

east·ward [ˈiːstwəd; ˋistwəːd] **I** *a*. (向)东方的;朝东的。**II** *ad*. 朝东方,向东。**III** *n*. 东方,东部。**east·wards** *adv*. 向东。

east·ward·ly [ˈiːstwədli; ˋistwəːdlɪ] *ad*., *a*. **1.** 向东。**2.** 自东。

eas·y [ˈiːzi; ˋizɪ] **I** *a*. **1.** 容易的。**2.** 舒服的,安乐的,大方的;宽裕的;(衣服等)宽松的;懒散的,散漫的。**3.** 平缓的,从容的,缓慢的。**4.**【商】(物资)丰富的;(物价)便宜的;(银根)松动的 (*opp*. tight)。**5.** 平易的,(笔墨等)流畅的。**6.** 慈善的;温厚的。**7.**【牌】(无主桥牌局中的 A 牌)双方平等分配的。**8.** 随随便便的;易顺从的。*feel* ～ 舒服;安心。*Make your mind* ～. 请放心。*free and* ～ 悠然自得,毫不拘束。*E-*! 慢慢的,别急。～ *servicing* 小修。*Be* ～! 放心好了! ～ *chair* 安乐椅,圈椅。～ *dress* 便衣。～ *grace* 优雅。～ *labour*【医】顺产。*More easier said than done*. 说来容易做来难。～ ***on the ears*** 〔美俚〕好听的。～ ***on the eye(s)*** 〔美俚〕好看的。～ ***on the trigger*** 〔美俚〕易兴奋的,易怒的。～ ***to look at*** 〔美俚〕= ～ on the eyes. ***in*** ～ ***circumstances*** = on ～ street (又作 ***E- Street***)〔美口〕生活优裕,小康。***a woman of*** ～ ***virtue*** 水性杨花的女人。**II** *ad*. 〔口〕容易,轻易;慢慢,安然,悠然。*E- come*, ～ *go*. 〔谚〕来得容易花得快。～ ***ahead***! 〔口令〕轻步前进!【海】低速前进。***E- all***!【海】停桨! ～ ***does it***! 别急。***go*** ～ 别急! ***Stand at*** ～!【军】稍息! ***take things*** ～ = ***take it*** ～ 从容不迫,别急。**II** *n*. **1.** 〔口语〕暂时的休息,(桨手的)歇气。**2.** 〔美口〕易受欺骗的人,老好人。*without an* ～ 不停地。***take an*** ～ 歇一口气。～**-going** *a*. **1.** 逍遥自在的,悠闲的。**2.** 懒散的;不严肃的。**3.** (马)步子慢的。～ **meat** 〔英俚〕容易办的事。～ **mark** **1.** 〔美口〕(容易受骗的)老好人,傻瓜,糊涂虫。**2.** 容易达到的目标。～**money** [**dollars**] 〔美〕**1.** 来得容易的钱。**2.** 松动的银根,低利资金。～**-payment system**, ～**-purchase system** 分期付款购物法。

eat [iːt; it] *vt*. (***ate*** [eit; et]; ***eat·en*** [ˈiːtn; ˋitn]) **1.** 吃;喝(汤)。**2.** 蛀;腐蚀;消磨。～ *one's supper* 吃晚饭。～ *the soup first* 先喝汤。*posts* ～*en by termites* 被白蚁蛀蚀的柱子。—*vi*. **1.** 吃,吃饭。**2.** 吃起来有…的味道。**3.** 蛀坏,腐蚀 (*into*)。**4.** 〔美口〕发怒,生气。*be good to* ～ 可吃。～ *well* 好吃。*This cake* ～*s crisp* [*short*]. 这点心吃起来酥脆。*It* ～*s like fish*. 吃起来味道像鱼。～ ***away*** 侵蚀,蚕食;继续吃下去。～ ***in*** [***into***] 蛀坏;腐蚀;消耗(钱财)。～ ***its head off*** 〔指牛马等〕吃得多而又干不了活。～ ***of*** 〔古〕吃。～ ***off*** 咬掉〔腐蚀掉〕。～ ***one's fill*** 吃饱。～ ***one's heart out*** 烦恼,忧虑〔常含不必要的意思〕;默默伤心。～ ***one's terms*** [***dinners***] 学法律〔在英国学法律的学生必须每学期参加律师公会的聚餐三次以上,才取得律师资格〕。～ ***one's words*** 收回前言,俯首认错。～ ***out*** **1.** 出去吃饭。**2.** 吃光,侵蚀。～ ***sb. out of house and home*** 把人吃穷。～ ***the wind out of***【海】占他船的上风。～ ***out of another's hand*** 听命于某人。～ ***up*** **1.** 吃完;消耗 (～ *up one's savings* 耗尽积蓄)。**2.** 〔常用被动语态〕沉迷于,纠缠于 (*with*) (*be eaten up with pride* [*debt*] 自满极了[债务缠身])。**3.** 很快走完(距离) (*The road seems to be eaten up by him in half an hour*. 他好像半小时就走完了这段路)。***I'll*** ～ ***my hat*** [***boots, hands, head***] ***if*** 决不,决无,决非〔发誓语〕。***Well, don't*** ～ ***me***! 〔谑〕唷,别那么凶啊! ***What's*** ～***ing you***? 〔美口〕你生什么气? 你怎么啦?

eat·a·ble [ˈiːtəbl; ˋitəbl̩] **I** *a*. 可食用的,可吃的。**II** *n*. 〔*pl*.〕食物,食品。～*s and drinkables* 吃的和喝的。

eat·en [ˈiːtn; ˋitn̩] eat 的过去分词。

eat·er [ˈiːtə; ˋitəː] *n*. **1.** 吃的人(或动物)。**2.** 腐蚀物,腐蚀剂。

eat·er·y [ˈiːtəri; ˋitərɪ] *n*. 〔口〕小餐馆。

eat·ing [ˈiːtiŋ; ˋitɪŋ] **I** *n*. **1.** 吃。**2.** 食物。*good* ～ 好吃的东西。**II** *a*. **1.** 食用的。**2.** 可生吃的。**3.** 腐蚀的。～ *cares* 折磨人的心事。～ *apples* 供生吃的苹果 (*opp*. cooking apples)。～ **house** 饮食店,小餐馆,食堂。～**-out** 经常上馆子吃饭的习惯。

Ea·ton [ˈiːtn; ˋitn̩] *n*. 伊顿〔姓氏〕。

eats [iːts; its] *n*. 〔*pl*.〕〔口〕食物,饭食。

eau [əu; o] *n*. (*pl*. ***-x*** [əu; o]) 〔F.〕水。～ ***de Cologne*** [ˈəu de keˈləun; ˏo də kəˋlon] 科隆香水,花露水。～ ***de Nil*** [niːl; nil] (像尼罗河水一样的)深绿色。～ ***de vie*** [ˈəudviː; ˏodˋvi] 白兰地酒。～ ***douce*** [əu dus; o dus] 清水;软水。～ ***dure*** [əu dyr; o dyr] 硬水。～ ***sucrée*** [əu syˈkre; o syˋkrɛ] 糖水。

eaves [iːvz; ivz] *n*. 〔*pl*.〕屋檐。～**drop** **1.** *vi*. 偷听。**2.** *n*. 檐水。～**dropper** 偷听的人。

EB = eastbound 向东航行的。

E. B. = Encyclopaedia Britannica《大英百科全书》。

ebb [eb; ɛb] **I** *n*. **1.** 退潮,落潮 (*opp*. flood; flow)。**2.** 衰退,衰落。***Every tide has its*** ～. 〔谚〕凡事有盛必有衰。***at a low*** ～ 衰败,不振。***be at*** [***on***] ***the*** ～ (潮)正在退落;减少。～ ***and flow*** 潮涨退;盛衰;消长。***go out on the*** ～ (船)趁退潮出海。**II** *vi*. 退落;衰退,减退。～ ***away*** 逐渐衰退。～ **tide** 落[低]潮。

Eb·en·e·zer [ˌebiˈniːzə; ˏɛbɪˋnizəː] *n*. 埃比尼泽〔姓氏〕。

EbN, E by N = east by north 东偏北。

E-boat [ˈiːbəut; ˋiˏbot] *n*. 〔英〕(第二次世界大战期间的)敌方鱼雷快艇 (= enemy boat)。

eb·on [ˈebən; ˋɛbən] *a*. 〔诗〕= ebony.

Eb·on·ics [ˈebəniks; ˋɛbənɪks] *n*. 黑人英语。

eb·on·ite [ˈebənait; ˋɛbənˏaɪt] *n*. 硬橡胶,胶木。

eb·on·ize [ˈebənaiz; ˋɛbənˏaɪz] *vt*. 使成黑檀色;使像乌木(色)。

eb·on·y [ˈebəni; ˋɛbənɪ] **I** *n*. **1.**【植】乌木,黑檀。**2.** 〔E-〕柿属。**II** *a*. 乌木制的;黑檀色的,乌黑的。

EbS, E by S = east by south 东偏南。

e·bul·lience, e·bul·liency [iˈbʌljəns, -si; ɪˋbʌljəns, -sɪ] *n*. **1.** 沸腾;起泡。**2.** (感情的)奔放。**-lient** [-ljənt; -ljənt] *a*. **1.** 沸腾的。**2.** 热情奔放的。

e·bul·li·om·e·ter [iˌbʌliˈɔmitə; ɪˏbʌlɪˋɑmətəː] *n*. 沸点测定计。

e·bul·li·o·scope [iˈbʌliəskəup; ɪˋbʌlɪəˏskop] *n*. 沸点升高测定仪。

E

e·bul·li·os·co·py [iˌbʌliˈɔskəpi; ɪˌbʌlɪˋɑskəpɪ] ***n***. 沸点升高测定法。

eb·ul·lism [ˌebəˈlizəm; ˏɛbəˋlɪzəm] ***n***. 【医】体液起泡症〔由于气压突然减低,导致体内各种液体起泡〕。

eb·ul·li·tion [ˌebəˈliʃən; ˏɛbəˋlɪʃən] ***n***. 沸腾;鼓泡;(感情等)迸发。

e·bur·na·ted [ˈebəːneitid; ˋɛbɚnetɪd] ***a***. 像象牙一样坚硬结实的。

e·bur·na·tion [ˌebəˈneiʃən, ˌiːbəˈneiʃən; ˏɛbəˋneʃən, ˏibəˋneʃən] ***n***. 【医】象牙质性变。

e·bur·ne·an, e·bur·ne·ous [iˈbəːnjən, iˈbəːnjəs; ɪˋbɚnɪən, ɪˋbɚnɪəs] ***a***. **1**. (颜色)像象牙的。**2**. 用象牙制成的。

E.C. = **1**. Eastern Central〔英〕(伦敦)东部中央邮(政)区。**2**. Established Church【英宗】国教。

EC = European Community 欧洲(经济)共同体。

ec [ek; ɛk] ***n***. 〔俚〕经济学 (= economics)。

ec- *pref*. = ex-.

ECA = Economic Commission for Africa (of UN) (联合国)非洲经济委员会。

ECAFE = Economic Commission for Asia and the Far East (of UN) (联合国)亚洲及远东经济委员会。

é·car·té [eiˈkɑːtei; ˏekɑrˋte] ***n***. 〔F.〕一种两人玩的牌戏。

e·cau·date [iˈkɔːdeit; ɪˋkɔdet] ***a***. 【动】无尾的。

ec·bol·ic [ekˈbɔlik; ɛkˋbɑlɪk] **I** ***n***. 【医】催产药;流产剂。**II** ***a***. 催产的。

ec·ce [ˈekei, ˈeksi; ˋɛkɛ, ˋɛksɪ] ***int***. 〔L.〕看! 看呀! 瞧!

ec·ce homo [ˈeksiˈhəuməu; ˋɛksɪˈhomo]〔L.〕**1**. 瞧! 就是这个人!〔拉丁文《圣经》上彼拉多把荆冠戴在耶稣头上示众时说的话〕。**2**. 头戴荆冠的耶稣画像。

ec·cen·tric [ikˈsentrik, ek-; ɪkˋsɛntrɪk, ɛk-] **I** ***a***. **1**. 【数】不同圆心的 (*opp*. concentric); 【天】(轨道)不正圆的;【机】偏心的,离心的;偏心器的,偏心轮的。**2**. 目的[意思]不同的;(行为)异常的,反常的,偏执的。*an ~ person* 怪人。~ *conduct* 古怪行为。**II** ***n***. **1**. 怪人。**2**. 偏心圆;【机】偏心器,偏心轮;【天】离心圈。~ **angle**【数】离心角,偏心角。~ **anamoly**【天】偏近点角。**-cal·ly** [-kəli; -kəlɪ] ***ad***.

ec·cen·tric·i·ty [ˌeksenˈtrisiti; ˏɛksənˋtrɪsɪtɪ] ***n***. **1**. 反常,怪癖。**2**. 偏心,不同心,不对中;【数】偏心率;【机】偏心性。**3**. 偏心半径,偏心距,偏心度。

ec·chy·mo·sis [ˌekiˈməusis; ˏɛkəˋmosɪs] ***n***. 【医】瘀斑,皮下溢血,出血斑。

Eccl., **Eccles.** = Ecclesiastes.

eccl., **eccles.** = ecclesiastical.

ec·cle·si·a [iˈkliːʒiə; ɪˋklɪʒɪə] ***n***. (*pl*. ***-si·ae*** [-ʒiiː, -ziiː; -ʒɪi, -zɪi]) **1**. 古代雅典的人民会议。**2**. 【宗】教会会友,会众。

Ec·cle·si·as·tes [iˌkliːziˈæstiːz; ɪˏklizɪˋæstiz] ***n***. 【圣】《旧约·传道书》。

ec·cle·si·as·tic [iˌkliːziˈæstik; ɪˏklizɪˋæstɪk] **I** ***n***. (基督教的)牧师。**II** ***a***. = ecclesiastical.

ec·cle·si·as·ti·cal [iˌkliːziˈæstikəl; ɪˏklizɪˋæstɪkḷ] ***a***. 基督教会的 (*opp*. secular; lay)。~ **calendar** 教会历。~ **court** 宗教法庭。**-ly** ***ad***. 依照教会法式,教规上。

ec·cle·si·as·ti·cism [iˌkliːziˈæstisizəm; ɪˏklizɪˋæstəsɪzəm] ***n***. 教会中心主义;教(会统治)权。

Ec·cle·si·as·ti·cus [iˌkliːziˈæstikəs; ɪˏklizɪˋæstɪkəs] ***n***. 【宗】《圣经外传》〔或称《外经》,伪经中的一卷,亦作 Wisdom of Jesus〕。

ec·cle·si·ol·o·gy [iˌkliːziˈɔlədʒi; ɪˏklizɪˋɑlədʒɪ] ***n***. **1**. 教会学。**2**. 教堂建筑学。

ECCM = electronic counter-countermeasures 电子反干扰。

ec·crine [ˈekrin, ˈekrain; ˋɛkrɪn, ˋɛkraɪn] ***a***. (人体)汗腺分泌的。

ec·cri·nol·o·gy [ˌekriˈnɔlədʒi; ˏɛkrəˋnɑlədʒɪ] ***n***. 分泌学。

ec·dem·ic [ekˈdemik; ɛkˋdɛmɪk] ***a***. 【医】外来的。

ec·dys·i·ast [ekˈdiziæst; ɛkˋdɪzɪæst] ***n***. 〔谑〕脱衣舞女〔普通叫 stripteaser〕。

ec·dy·sis [ˈekdisis; ˋɛkdɪsɪs] ***n***. (*pl*. ***-dy·ses*** [-disiːz; -dɪsiz]) 【动】(蛇等的)蜕皮,(甲壳类的)脱壳;换羽。

ECE = Economic Commission for Europe (of UN) (联合国)欧洲经济委员会。

e·ce·sis [iˈsiːsis; ɪˋsisɪs] ***n***. 【动,植】定居。

ECG = electrocardiogram 心电图。

ech. = echelon.

ech·e·lette [ˌeʃəˈlet; ˏɛʃəˋlɛt] ***n***. 【物】红外光栅。

ech·e·lon [ˈeʃəlɔn; ˋɛʃəˏlɑn] **I** ***n***. **1**. 【军】梯队,梯阵;梯列。**2**. 组织系统中的等级,指挥阶层;(负有特殊责任而占据同一等级的)集团。**3**. 特勤部队。**4**. 【物】阶层光栅。*fly in ~* 梯队飞行。*a rear ~* 后方梯队。*in a higher ~* 在高级指挥阶层。*a maintain ~* 后勤保养队。**II** ***vt***. 使成梯队。*an army ~ed along the road* 沿公路排成梯队的大军。—***vi***. 排成梯队。~ **fire**【军】梯形炮火。~ **grating**【物】阶梯光栅。~ **lens**【光】阶梯透镜。

ech·e·ve·ri·a [ˌetʃiˈveriə, ˌek-; ˏɛtʃəˋvɛrɪə, ˏɛk-] ***n***. 【植】拟石莲花属 (*Echeveria*) 植物。

e·chid·na [eˈkidnə; iˋkɪdnə] ***n***. (*pl*. ***-s***, ***-nae*** [-niː; -ni]) 【动】针鼹。

ech·i·nate [ˈekineit; ˋɛkənet] ***a***. 布满刺针的;有刺的;棘皮的〔如豪猪〕(= ~d)。

e·chi·no·coc·cus [iˌkainəˈkɔkəs; ɪˏkaɪnəˋkɑkəs] ***n***. 【医】包虫,棘球蚴。~ **cyst** 包虫囊,棘球蚴囊。

e·chi·no·derm [iˈkainəˌdəːm; ɛˋkaɪnəˏdɝm] ***n***. (*pl*. ***ma·ta*** [-mətə; -mətə]) 【动】棘皮动物。

E·chi·no·der·ma·ta [iˌkainəˈdəːmətə; ɪˏkaɪnəˋdɝmətə] 〔*pl*.〕***n***. 【动】棘皮动物门。

e·chi·noid [iˈkainɔid, ˈeki-; ɪˋkaɪnɔɪd, ˋɛkə-] **I** ***a***. 【动】海胆类的,海胆状的。**II** ***n***. 【动】海胆类 (*Echinoidea*) 动物〔如海胆、饼海胆等〕。

Ech·i·noi·de·a [ˌekiˈnɔidiə; ˏɛkɪˋnɑɪdɪə] ***n***. 〔*pl*.〕【动】海胆纲。

echi·nu·late [iˈkinjulit; ɪˋkɪnjulɪt] ***a***. 【生】刺毛状的,小棘状的;有刺毛的。

e·chi·nus [iˈkainəs; ɛˋkaɪnəs] ***n***. (*pl*. ***-ni*** [-nai; -naɪ]) **1**. 【动】刺海胆。**2**. 【建】拇指圆饰。

ech·o [ˈekəu; ˋɛko] **I** ***n***. (*pl*. ***~es***) **1**. 回声,反响;共鸣,反映。**2**. 重复,摹仿;摹仿者;应声虫。**3**. 【韵】与上句末音押韵的诗句。**4**. 〔E-〕【希神】山林的女神。**5**. (雷达的)回波,反射波。***find an ~ in sb.'s heart*** 得人共鸣。***to the ~*** 大声,高声 (*applaud* [*cheer*] *to the ~* 大声喝彩)。**II** ***vt***. **1**. 使反响。**2**. 模仿,重复。**3**. 反射(声音等)响。~ *sb.'s words* 随声附和。—***vi***. **1**. 发出回声,共鸣 (*with*)。**2**. 重复。**3**. (桥牌战中)打出报信牌。~ **chamber** 回音室〔为制造回音及音响效果而特别设计的房间〕。~ **sounder** 回音测深器。

e·cho·ic [eˈkəuik; ɛˋkoɪk] ***a***. **1**. 回声的。**2**. 【语】像声的,拟声的。

ech·o·ism [eˈkəuizəm; ɛˋkoɪzəm] ***n***. 形声,像声,拟声。

ech·o·la·li·a [ˌekəˈleiliə; ˏɛkəˋlelɪə] ***n***. 模仿言语〔尤指精神不正常的一种症候〕。**-la·lic** [-ˈleilik; -ˋlelɪk] ***a***.

ech·o·lo·cate [ˌekəuˈləukeit; ˏɛkoˋloket] ***vi***., ***vt***. 【物】用回音测定(方向或距离),回波定(位)。

ech·o·lo·ca·tion [ˌekələˈkeiʃən; ˏɛkoloˋkeʃən] ***n***. 【物】回波定位(法)。

echt [ext; ɛxt] ***a***. 〔G.〕纯正的;实在的;可靠的。

ecks〔美〕= economics.

ECLA = Economic Commission for Latin America (of UN) (联合国)拉丁美洲经济委员会。

é·clair [F. eiˈklɛə; eˋklɛr] ***n***. 〔F.〕长圆形夹奶油的糖皮

E

小点心。

e·clair·cisse·ment [F. eiklɛəsiːsˈmɑ̃; eklɛrsisˋmɑ̃] ***n.*** 〔F.〕1. 说明,解释;澄清,明朗化。2. 〔E-〕启蒙运动。*come to an* ～ *with* 得人谅解。

ec·lamp·si·a [ekˈlæmpsiə; ɛkˋlæmpsɪə] ***n.***【医】惊厥,子痫。

é·clat [ˈeiklɑː; eˋklɑ] ***n.*** 〔F.〕光彩;喝彩;巨大成功;名誉,光荣。*a diplomatist of great* ～ 大名鼎鼎的外交家。*with great* ～ 在大声喝彩中;盛大地。

ec·lec·tic [ekˈlektik; ɪkˋlɛktɪk] **I** ***a.***【哲】折衷(主义)的。**II** ***n.*** 折衷主义者。*the E- School* 折衷(学)派。**-cally** ***ad.***

ec·lec·ti·cism [ekˈlektisizəm; ɛkˋlɛktɪˏsɪzəm] ***n.*** 折衷主义。

e·clipse [iˈklips; ɪˋklɪps] **I** ***n.*** 1.【天】蚀;(天体受到)遮蔽。2. 亮光的丧失,漆黑,晦暗;(名声等的)丧失,黯然无光。*an annular* ～ 环蚀。*a lunar* ～ 月蚀。*a partial* ～ 偏蚀。*a solar* ～ 日蚀。*a total* ～ 全蚀。***in*** ～ 1. 变暗;失去光彩。2. (鸟)失脱求爱美毛。***suffer an*** ～ 黯然失色。**II** ***vt.*** 1. (天体)蚀;遮蔽(天体)的光。2. 使失色;超越,盖过。

e·clip·tic [iˈkliptik; ɪˋklɪptɪk] ***n.***, ***a.***【天】黄道(的);日[月]蚀(的)。*obliquity of the* ～【天】黄赤交角。

ec·lo·gite [ˈeklədʒait; ˋɛklədʒaɪt] ***n.***【地】榴辉岩。

ec·logue [ˈeklɔg; ˋɛklɔg] ***n.*** (两牧童对话形式的)牧歌,田园诗。

e·clo·sion [iˈkləuʒən; ɪˋkloʒən] ***n.***【动】羽化;孵化。

ECM = 1. European Common Market 欧洲共同市场。2. electronic countermeasures 电子干扰。

eco- *pref.* 表示"生态(学)的": *eco*cide.

e·co·car[ˈekəukɑː;ˋɛkokɑr] ***n.*** (不污染环境的)生态汽车。

e·co·cide [ˈekəusaid, ˈiː-;ˋɛkosaid, ˋi-] ***n.*** 生态灭绝。

e·co·cline [ˈekəuklain, ˈiː-;ˋɛkoklaɪn, ˋi-] ***n.***【生】生态差型。

E. coli [iːˈkəulai; ɪˋkolaɪ] ***n.*** 大肠杆菌 (= Escherichia coli)。

ec·o·log·ic [ˌekəuˈlɔdʒik, ˌiː-;ˏɛkoˋlɑdʒɪk, ˏi-], **ec·o·log·i·cal** [ˌekəuˈlɔdʒikl, ˌiː-;ˏɛkoˋlɑdʒɪkl, ˏi-] ***a.*** 生态学的。～ **footprint** 生态足迹〔为提供食物、住房、交通、消费品和服务所必需的人均土地总面积,这是一种计算生态资源的方法〕。～ **terrorism** 生态恐怖主义〔指大肆破坏自然资源的行为〕。**-ly** ***ad.***

e·col·o·gy [i(ː)ˈkɔlədʒi; ɪˋkɑlədʒɪ] ***n.*** 1. 生态学;个体生态学。2.【社会学】环境适应学,社会生态学。3. 任何均衡的系统[制度等]。**Ecology Party** 生态保护激进组织(= Green Party)。**-o·gist** ***n.*** 生态学家。

econ. = economical; economics; economist; economy.

e·con·o·met·rics [iˌkɔnəˈmetriks; ɪˏkɑnəˋmɛtrɪks] ***n.*** 〔*pl.*〕〔作单数用〕计量经济学。**-met·ric** ***a.*** **-me·tri·cian** [-miˈtriʃən; -mɪˋtrɪʃən] ***n.*** 计量经济学家。

e·co·nom·ic [ˌiːkəˈnɔmik, ek-;ˏikəˋnɑmɪk, ɛk-] ***a.*** 1. 经济学的;经济(上)的;实用的。2. 〔罕〕经济的,节俭的。3.〔婉〕故意隐瞒的。***be*** ～ ***with truth*** 隐瞒事实真相。～ **agreement** 经济协定。～ **base** 经济基础。～ **blockade** 经济封锁。～ **botany** 实用植物学。～ **circles** 经济界。～ **crisis** 经济危机。～ **geography** 经济地理学。～ **lifelines** 经济命脉。～ **sanction** 经济制裁。

e·co·nom·i·cal [ˌiːkəˈnɔmikəl;ˏikəˋnɑmɪkl] ***a.*** 1. 节俭的,俭约的;经济的,合算的。2. 经济学上的。*an* ～ *stove* 经济火炉。*be* ～ *of energy* [*time*] 节省精力[时间]。**-ly** ***ad.***

e·co·nom·ics [ˌiːkəˈnɔmiks, ˈekəˈnɔmiks;ˏikəˋnɑmɪks, ˏɛkəˋnɑmɪks] ***n.*** 1. 经济学。2. (国家的)经济(状况);经济。

e·con·o·mism [i(ː)ˈkɔnəmizəm; ɪˋkɑnəmɪzm] ***n.*** 经济主义。

e·con·o·mist [i(ː)ˈkɔnəmist; ɪˋkɑnəmɪst] ***n.*** 1. 经济学家。2. 〔古〕节俭的人。

e·con·o·mis·tic [ˌi(ː)kɔnəˈmistik; ɪˏkɑnəˋmɪstɪk] ***a.*** 经济主义的。

e·con·o·mi·za·tion [iˌkɔnəmiˈzeiʃən; ɪˏkɑnəmɪˋzeʃən] ***n.*** 节约;节省。

e·con·o·mize [i(ː)ˈkɔnəmaiz; ɪˋkɑnəˏmaɪz] ***vt.***, ***vi.*** 更经济地使用[处理];节约,节省。

e·con·o·miz·er [i(ː)ˈkɔnəmaizə; ɪˋkɑnəˏmaɪzɚ] ***n.*** 1. 节俭者。2. 节约装置。3.【机】废气预热器;节油器;省煤器,节热器;废热锅炉。

e·con·o·my [i(ː)ˈkɔnəmi; ɪˋkɑnəmɪ] ***n.*** 1. 经济。2. 节约。3. (自然界的)法理,秩序,过程;组织;有机体。*domestic* ～ 家政(学);国内经济。*national* [*rural*] ～ 国民[农村]经济。*state-owned* ～ 国营经济。*political* ～ 政治经济学。*diversified* ～ 多种经营。*a man of* ～ 节俭的人。*practice* [*use*] ～ 节约,节省。*the* ～ *of nature* 自然界的秩序。*the* ～ *of a plant* 植物的机体。～ **class** 二等舱〔尤指客机舱位〕。

e·co·po·li·tics [ˌiːkəˈpolitiks;ˏikəˋpɑlɪtɪks] ***n.*** 1. 经济政治学。2. 生态政治学。

ECOSOC = Economic and Social Council (United Nations) (联合国)经济及社会理事会。

e·co·spe·cies [ˈiːkəuˌspiːʃi(ː)z, ˈekəu-; ˋikəˏspiʃɪz, ˋɛko-] ***n.***【生】生态种。**-spe·cif·ic** [-spiˈsifik; -spɪˋsɪfɪk] ***a.***

e·co·sphere [ˈiːkəusfiə; ˋikoˏsfɪr] ***n.*** 生态层〔海拔12,000英尺以下的空间,在此空间内,人类可不借助于氧气面罩等而自由呼吸〕。

e·co·sys·tem [ˌiːkəuˈsistəm;ˏikoˋsɪstəm] ***n.***【生】生态系(统)。

e·co·tone [ˈiːkəutəun; ˋikəton] ***n.***【生】交错群落(区)。

e·co·type [ˈiːkəutaip; ˋikətaɪp] ***n.***【生】生态型。**-typ·ic** [-ˌtipik; -ˏtɪpɪk] ***a.*** **-typ·i·cal·ly** ***ad.***

e·cra·seur [eikrəˈzəː; ekrəˋzɚ] ***n.*** 〔F.〕【医】绞勒器。

ec·ru [ˈeikruː; ˋɛkru] **I** ***n.*** 〔F.〕(生丝等的)淡褐色。**II** ***a.*** 未漂白的;本色的。

ECSC = European Coal and Steel Community 欧洲煤钢联营。

ec·sta·size [ˈekstəsaiz; ˋɛkstəˏsaɪz] ***vt.*** 使狂喜;使入迷。—***vi.*** 狂喜;入迷。

ec·sta·sy [ˈekstəsi; ˋɛkstəsɪ] ***n.*** 1. 狂喜;入迷;销魂;精神恍惚;(诗人的)忘我的境界。2. 〔E-〕摇头丸,"锁魂"丸〔一种毒品〕。***be in ecstasies over*** 对…心醉神迷。***get*** [***go***, ***be thrown***] ***into ecstasies*** 兴奋到极点,狂喜。***in an*** ～ ***of joy*** [***grief***] 高兴[悲伤]到极点。

ec·stat·ic [eksˈtætik; ɪkˋstætɪk] ***a.*** 欣喜若狂的;入迷的,出神的。**-cal·ly** ***ad.***

ec·thy·ma [ˈekθimə; ˋɛkθɪmə] ***n.***【医】深脓疱,臁疮。

ecto- *pref.* 表示"外面","外部"等意 (*opp.* endo-; ento-): *ecto*blast, *ecto*derm.

ec·to·blast [ˈektəublæst; ˋɛktəˏblæst] ***n.***【生】外胚层。

ec·to·chon·dral [ˌektəuˈkɔndrəl;ˏɛktəˋkɑndrəl] ***a.*** 在软骨表面上的。

ec·to·com·men·sal [ˌektəkəuˈmensl;ˏɛktəkəˋmɛnsl] ***n.***【生】外共栖。

ec·to·crine [ˈektəukriːn; ˋɛktəkrin] ***n.***【生】外分泌。

ec·to·derm [ˈektəudəːm; ˋɛktəˏdɝm] ***n.*** 1. 外胚层。2. 外层。**-al**, **-ic** ***a.***

ec·to·gen·e·sis [ˌektəuˈdʒenisis;ˏɛktəˋdʒɛnɪsɪs] ***n.***【生】体外发生。**-ge·net·ic** ***a.***

ec·tog·e·nous, **ec·to·gen·ic** [ekˈtɔdʒinəs, ˌektəˈdʒenik; ɛkˋtɑdʒənəs, ˏɛktəˋdʒɛnɪk] ***a.***【生】外生的。

ec·to·mere [ˈektəumiə; ˋɛktəmɪr] ***n.*** 外胚层裂球。**-mer·ic** [-ˈmerik, -ˈmiərik; -ˋmɛrɪk, -ˋmɪərɪk] ***a.***

-ec·to·my *comb. f.* 表示"切除术","截除术": append*ectomy*, tonsill*ectomy*.

ec·to·par·a·site [ˌektəuˈpærəsait;ˏɛktəˋpærəˏsaɪt] ***n.***【生】外寄生物。**-a·sitic** [-ˈsitik; -ˋsɪtɪk] ***a.***

ec·to·pi·a [ek'təupiə; ɛk'topɪə] *n*.【医】出位,异位,错位(=ectopy)。

ec·top·ic [ek'tɔpik; ɛk'tɑpɪk] *a*.【医】异位的。~ **pregnancy** 异位妊娠(=gestation)。~ **rhythm** 异位节律。

ec·to·plasm ['ektəuplæzəm; 'ɛktə,plæzəm] *n*.【生】外质(*opp*. endoplasm)。

ec·to·proct ['ektəuprɔkt; 'ɛktə,prɑkt] *n*.【动】外肛亚纲(*Ectoprocta*)动物。**-an** *a*.

ec·to·sarc ['ektəusɑːk; 'ɛktə,sɑrk] *n*.【生】外质(=ectoplasm)。

ec·to·therm ['ektəuθəːm; 'ɛktə,θɝm] *n*.【动】冷血动物,变温动物。

ec·to·troph·ic [ˌektəu'trɔfik; ˌɛktə'trɑfɪk] *a*.【植】外生的。~ *mycorrhiza* 外(生)菌根。

ec·to·zo·ic ['ektəuzəuik; 'ɛktə,zoɪk] *a*. 体外寄生虫的。

ec·to·zo·on [ˌektəu'zəuɔn; ˌɛktə'zoɑn] *n*. (*pl*. **-zo·a** [-'zəuə; -'zoə])【医】体外寄生虫。

ec·type ['ektaip; 'ɛktaɪp] *n*. 复制品;副本。

é·cu [ei'kjuː; e'kju] *n*. (*pl*. ***-cus*** [-'kjuː; -'kju]) [F.] 法国古金币;法国古银币〔尤指 17—18 世纪时流通者〕。

ECU = extreme closeup【影】极大特写镜头。

Ec·ua·dor [ˌekwə'dɔː, 'ekwədɔː; 'ɛkwə,dɔr] *n*. 厄瓜多尔〔拉丁美洲〕。

Ec·ua·do·ran [ˌekwə'dɔːrən; ˌɛkwə'dɔrən], **Ec·ua·dore·an**, **Ec·ua·do·ri·an** [-riən; -rɪən] **I** *n*. 厄瓜多尔人。**II** *a*. 厄瓜多尔的;厄瓜多尔人的。

e·cu·men·i·cal [ˌiːkju(ː)'menikəl; ˌɛkju'mɛnɪkəl] *a*. **1.** 普遍的,世界范围的。**2.** 全基督教的。

ec·u·men·i·cism [ˌiːkju'menisizəm; ˌɛkju'mɛnɛsɪzəm] *n*. = ecumenism.

ec·u·me·nic·i·ty [ˌiːkju(ː)mə'nisiti; ˌɛkjumɛ'nɪsətɪ] *n*. = ecumenism.

ec·u·men·ism ['ekjuminizəm; 'ɛkjumɪnɪzəm] *n*. **1.** 泛基督教主义。**2.** 泛宗教主义〔促进各种宗教信仰的人们的合作和谅解〕(=ecumenicity)。**-men·ist** *n*. 泛基督教[宗教]主义者。

E.C.W. = Emergency Conservation Work〔美旧〕自然资源紧急保护事业局。

ec·ze·ma ['eksimə, 'egzi-; 'ɛksɪmə, 'ɛgzɪ-] *n*.【医】湿疹。

ED, E.D. **1.** electron device 电子器件[装置]。**2.** erection deficiency【医】阳痿,勃起困难。

ed. = edited; edition; editor, education, educated.

-ed *suf*. **1.** 用以形成规则动词的过去式及过去分词:call>call*ed* [kɔːld; kɔld], talk>talk*ed* [tɔːkt; tɔkt], mend>mend*ed* ['mendid, -əd; 'mɛndid, -əd]。**2.** 附于名词后形成'…的','有…的'等意义的形容词:wing*ed* 有翼的。

e·da·cious [i'deiʃəs; ɪ'deʃəs] *a*. 贪吃的,食量大的。

e·dac·i·ty [i'dæsiti; ɪ'dæsətɪ] *n*. 贪食;狼吞虎咽。

E·dam ['iːdəm; 'idəm] *n*. 伊顿干酪〔荷兰制球形干酪,外涂红蜡,又叫 ~ cheese〕。

e·daph·ic [i'dæfik; ɪ'dæfɪk] *a*.【生态】土壤的。~ **formation** 土壤群系。

ed·a·phol·o·gy [edə'fɔlədʒi; ɛdə'fɑlədʒɪ] *n*. 土壤学。

e·da·phon ['edəfɔn; 'ɛdə,fon] *n*. 土壤微生物(群)。

E-day 英国加入欧洲共同市场日。

Ed.B. = Bachelor of Education 教育学士。

Ed.D. = Doctor of Education 教育学博士。

E.D.D. = English Dialect Dictionary《英语方言词典》。

Ed·da ['edə; 'ɛdə] *n*. 冰岛古代二文集之一。***the Elder*** [***Poetic***] ~ 冰岛古代诗集。***the Younger*** [***Prose***] ~ 冰岛古代文集。

Ed·die ['edi; 'ɛdɪ] *n*. 埃迪〔男子名,Edward 的昵称〕。

Ed·ding·ton ['ediŋtən; 'ɛdɪŋtən] *n*. 埃丁顿〔姓氏〕。

ed·do ['edəu; 'ɛdo] *n*. (*pl*. ~***es***)【植】芋。

Ed·dy ['edi; 'ɛdɪ] *n*. 埃迪〔姓氏〕。

ed·dy ['edi; 'ɛdɪ] **I** *n*. (水,风尘等的)漩涡,涡流。**II** *vt*., *vi*. (**-died**; **-dy·ing**) (使)起漩涡;(使)旋转。

e·del·weiss ['eidlvais; 'edl,vaɪs] *n*.【植】火绒草。

e·de·ma [i(ː)'diːmə; ɪ(i)'dimə] *n*. (*pl*. ***-ta*** [-tə; -tə])【医】水肿,浮肿。

E·den[1] ['iːdn; 'idn] *n*. **1.**【圣】(*Adam* 及 *Eve* 初住的)伊甸园。**2.** 乐园。

E·den[2] ['iːdn; 'idn] *n*. 伊登(艾登)〔姓氏〕。**Antony** ~ 艾登〔1897-1977,曾任英国首相〕。

e·den·tate [iː'denteit; ɪ'dɛntet] **I** *a*.【动】无齿的;贫齿类的。**II** *n*. 贫齿目动物。

e·den·tu·lous [iː'dentjuləs; ɪ'dɛntʃələs] *a*.【动】无齿的,无牙的。

Ed·gar ['edgə; 'ɛdgɚ] *n*. 埃德加〔男子名〕。

edge [edʒ; ɛdʒ] **I** *n*. **1.** 刀口,(刀)刃;锋;端;锐利。**2.** 边,棱,边缘,边界,界线,界限。**3.** 优势,优越条件。**4.** (声调、议论、欲望的)尖锐,强烈。**5.**〔喻〕〔美俚〕微醉状态。*cutting* ~ 切削刀。*chisel* ~ 凿锋。*the water's* ~ 水边。*gilt* ~*s* (书的)烫金边。~ *angle* 棱角。~ *ball*【体】边插球。*a decisive* ~ *in military strength* 军事力量的决定性优势。*His remark has a fine* ~ *of cynicism*. 他的话带着强烈的讽刺。***at hard*** ~ (练击剑时)用真剑;真刀真枪的[地]。***be on a razor's*** ~ 在锋口上;处境危急。***do the inside*** [***outside***] ~【溜冰】用冰刀里[外]刃滑。***give an*** ~ ***to*** **1.** 开(刀等的)刃。**2.** 加强,刺激。***give the*** ~ ***of one's tongue to*** 痛骂。***have an*** ~ ***on*** 有点醉(*He had an* ~ *on from beer*. 他喝了啤酒后微有醉意)。***have an*** ~ ***on*** [***over***] ***sb***.〔美〕**1.** 怀恨某人。**2.** 胜过某人。***not to put too fine an*** ~ ***upon it*** 率直地说。***on*** ~ **1.** 竖着,直放着。**2.** 易怒,紧张不安。**3.** 急切,热望,忍不住(*to do*)。***on the*** ~ ***of*** 快要,眼看。***put to the*** ~ ***of the sword*** 杀死。***set on*** ~ **1.** 把(书、箱子等)竖起来。**2.** 把…弄锐利。**3.** 使急躁,惹人生气(*set sb.'s nerves on* ~ 使人心烦意乱。*set sb.'s teeth on* ~ 使人倒牙;使人厌恶)。***take the*** ~ ***off*** **1.** 使钝,挫伤锐气。**2.** 使受挫折;减弱(胃口)。***turn the*** ~ ***of*** 弄钝…的锋芒,减弱…的锐气。**II** *vt*. **1.** 使(刀,剑)锋利,给(刀等)开刃。**2.** 给…镶边,滚边。**3.** 渐渐移近,挤进(*in*; *into*);挤掉(*out*; *off*);挤过(*through*)。**4.** 鼓励;催促;促(*on*)。—*vi*. **1.** 沿边移动,向边缘移动。**2.** 斜进,侧着身子进;渐进。~ ***along*** 侧着身子移动。~ ***away*** [***off***] 偷偷地离开;轻轻走开。~ ***down upon*** [***in***, ***with***] 徐徐斜行接近。~ ***in*** **1.** 插(话等)。**2.** 渐渐逼近。~ ***oneself into*** 挤进,插进。~ ***out*** **1.** (小心地)一步一步走出。**2.** 排挤;〔美〕微微胜过。~ ***out of*** 渐渐由…退出。~ ***up*** 由边上慢慢靠拢。~ **bone** *n*. (牛的)臀骨。~ **runner**【机】轮转机;碾子。~ **stone** **1.** (道路的)边缘石。**2.** (磨机的)立碾轮。**-less** *a*. 没刀刃的,钝的。

edg·ed ['edʒd, 'edʒəd; 'ɛdʒd, 'ɛdʒəd] *a*. **1.** 有刃的,有边的;锋利的。**2.**〔美俚〕微醉的。~ *tool* 有刃之物,利器。*play with* ~ *tool* 玩弄利刃;〔喻〕干危险的事。

edg·er ['edʒə; 'ɛdʒɚ] *n*. **1.** 轧边机。**2.** 磨边器。**3.**【机】弯曲模膛。**4.** (园林)旋转剪修器。

edge·ways, **edge·wise** ['edʒweiz, -waiz; 'ɛdʒ,wez, -,waɪz] *ad*. **1.** 刀刃(边缘)朝外(朝前)。**2.** 沿边;从旁边。**3.** 边对边地。*put* [*get*] *a word in* ~ 插嘴。

Edge·worth ['edʒwəːθ; 'ɛdʒ,wɝθ] *n*. 埃奇沃斯〔姓氏〕。

edg·i·ly ['edʒili; 'ɛdʒɪlɪ] *ad*. **1.** 锋利地,锐利地。**2.** 急躁地,易怒地。**3.** (绘画等的)轮廓过于分明地。

edg·ing ['edʒiŋ; 'ɛdʒɪŋ] *n*. **1.** (衣服的)边饰。**2.** 镶边,磨边;修剪(草坪的)边缘。~ **shears** (园林工人用)修边剪刀。

edg·y ['edʒi; 'ɛdʒɪ] *a*. **1.** 锋利的;泼辣的,尖锐的。**2.** (画)轮廓过于分明的。**3.** 神经紧张的,易激动的,急躁的。

edh [eð; ɛð] *n*. 古英语和冰岛语中所用的一个记号的名称〔表示 th 所发的舌齿摩擦音 [ð] 和 [θ]。现代英语以

E

th 代之〕(= eth)。

EDI = electronic data interchange 电子数据交换。

ed·i·bil·ity [ˌedi'biliti; ˏɛdɪˋbɪlətɪ] ***n*.** 可食用性。

ed·i·ble ['edibl; ˋɛdəbḷ] **I** ***a*.** 适合食用的,可以吃的。~ *oil and fat* 食用油脂。**II** ***n*.** 〔*pl*.〕食品。**-ness** ***n*.**

e·dict ['iːdikt; ˋidɪkt] ***n*.** 布告;命令。*an Imperial* (*a Royal*) ~ 敕令,诏书。**-al** [iː'diktəl; iˋdɪktəl] ***a*.** 布告的;法令的。

Edie ['iːdi; ˋidɪ] ***n*.** 伊迪〔男子名〕。

ed·i·fi·ca·tion [ˌedifi'keiʃən; ˏɛdəfəˋkeʃən] ***n*.** 教诲,启发,开导。

ed·i·fi·ca·to·ry ['edifikətəri; ˋɛdɪfɪkəˏtorɪ] ***a*.** 教导的,教诲的,启发的。

ed·i·fice ['edifis; ˋɛdəfɪs] ***n*.** **1.** 大建筑物,大厦。**2.** (知识的)体系,结构。

ed·i·fier ['edifaiə; ˋɛdəˏfaɪɚ] ***n*.** 教导者,启发者。

ed·i·fy ['edifai; ˋɛdəˏfaɪ] ***vt*.** (*-fied*; *-fy·ing*) **1.** 训导,教导,启发,使受熏陶〔常作反语用〕。**2.** 〔古〕建筑。

e·dile ['iːdail; ˋidaɪl] ***n*.** 营造官〔古罗马掌管公共建筑物、保安警察等的官吏〕(= aedile)。

Ed·in·burgh ['edinbərə; ˋɛdɪnˏbɝo] ***n*.** 爱丁堡〔英国城市〕。

Ed·i·son ['edisn; ˋɛdəsn] ***n*.** **1.** 爱迪生〔姓氏〕。**2.** **Thomas** ~ 陶迈斯·爱迪生〔1847—1931,美国发明家〕。

ed·it ['edit; ˋɛdɪt] **I** ***vt*.** **1.** 编辑,编排;校订,订正。**2.** 剪辑(影片;录音)。~ ***out*** (在编辑[剪辑]过程中)删除。**II** ***n*.** 编辑[校订]工作。

edit. = edited; edition; editor.

E·dith ['iːdiθ; ˋidɪθ] ***n*.** 伊迪丝〔女子名〕。

e·di·tion [i'diʃən; ɪˋdɪʃən] ***n*.** 版;版本;〔喻〕翻版。*the first* ~ 初版。*a cheap* ~ 廉价版。*a pocket* ~ 袖珍版。*rare* ~*s* 善本。*a popular* ~ 普及版。*a revised* (*and enlarged*) ~ 修订(增补)版。~ ***de luxe*** [də luks; də lʊks] 精装版,豪华版。~ **time** 报纸截稿时间(即印刷开始的时间,亦作 press time)。

e·di·tio prin·ceps [i'diʃiəu 'prinseps; ɪˋdɪʃɪo ˋprɪnseps] 〔L.〕初版,第一版。

ed·i·tor ['editə; ˋɛdɪtɚ] ***n*.** **1.** 编者,编辑;校刊者;校订者。**2.** 影片剪辑装置。**3.** 社论撰写人(=〔美〕editorial writer, 〔英〕leader writer)。*chief* ~ = ~ *in chief* (*pl. editors in chief*) 总编辑;主编,主笔。*a city* ~ 商业金融栏编辑。*a contributing* ~ 特约编辑。*a financial* ~ 〔美〕经济版编辑。*a managing* ~ 编辑主任,主编。

ed·i·to·ri·al [ˌedi'tɔːriəl; ˏɛdəˋtorɪəl] **I** ***a*.** **1.** 编辑的;编辑上的;主笔的,总编辑的。**2.** 〔美〕社论的。**II** ***n*.** 〔美〕(期刊的)社论。*an* ~ *article* 社论。*an* ~ *assistant* 编辑助理。*an* ~ *chair* 主笔职位。*an* ~ *office* 编辑室。*the* ~ *staff* 编辑部。*an* ~ *paragraph* [*note*] 短评。*an* ~ *writer* 〔美〕社论作者,主笔。~ **"we"** 编辑及作家用以代替"我"的"我们"(以避免"我"字用得太多或表示代表集体)。**-ly** ***ad*.** **1.** 在编辑上;以主笔身分。**2.** 以社论形式。

ed·i·to·ri·al·ist [ˌedi'tɔːriəlist; ˏɛdɪˋtorɪəlɪst] ***n*.** 社论作者。

ed·i·to·ri·al·ize [ˌedi'tɔːriəlaiz; ˏɛdəˋtorɪəlˏaɪz] ***vt*.**, ***vi*.** (*-iz·ed*; *-iz·ing*) **1.** (就某事)发表社论。**2.** (在报纸等的文章中)加编者按语。**-ali·za·tion** ***n*.** **-al·iz·er** ***n*.** 社论[编者按语]撰写者。

ed·i·tor·ship ['editəʃip; ˋədɪtəˏʃɪp] ***n*.** 编辑[主笔]的职位;编辑[校订]工作。

ed·i·tress ['editris; ˋɛdətrɪs] ***n*.** 女编辑,女校订。

Ed·mund ['edmənd; ˋɛdmənd] ***n*.** 埃德蒙〔男子名〕。

Ed·na ['ednə; ˋɛdnə] ***n*.** 埃德娜〔女子名〕。

E·do ['iːdəu; ˋido] ***n*.** **1.** 伊多人〔尼日利亚南部贝宁省人〕。**2.** 伊多语。

E·dom ['iːdəm; ˋidəm] ***n*.** **1.** 【圣】伊多姆〔即雅各之兄伊索〕。**2.** 伊多姆王国〔西南亚古王国名,在死海与亚喀巴湾之间〕。

E·dom·ite ['iːdəmait, -it; ˋidəˏmaɪt, -ɪt] ***n*.** 【圣】伊多姆的后裔;伊多姆人。**-it·ish** ***a*.**

EDP = electronic data processing 电子数据处理。

E.D.S. = English Dialect Society 英语方言学会。

EDT = Eastern Daylight Time 〔美〕东部夏季时间。

educ. = educated; education(al).

ed·u·ca·ble ['edjukəbl; ˋɛdʒəkəbḷ] ***a*.** 可教育的。**-bil·i·ty** [-'biliti; -ˋbɪlətɪ] ***n*.** 可教育性。

ed·u·cate ['edju(ː)keit, -dʒu(ː)-; ˋɛdʒəˏket, -dʒu-] ***vt*.** **1.** 教育;教导。**2.** 培养,训练。**3.** 送…上学,为…负担学费。~ *oneself* 自修。~ *one's taste in literature* 培养文学兴趣。~ *one's ear for music* 训练音乐欣赏能力。***be*** **~*d at*** [***in***] 在…受教育,在…读书(*be* ~*d at a college* 受大学教育)。**-ca·tor** ***n*.** 教师;教育(学)家。**-cat·ed** ['edju(ː)keitid; ˋɛdʒəˏketɪd] ***a*.** 受过教育的,有教育的,有训练的(*opp*. uneducated; illiterate)。**-catee** [-kei'tiː; -keˋti] ***n*.** 受教育者,学生。

ed·u·ca·tion [ˌedju(ː)'keiʃən; ˏɛdʒəˋkeʃən] ***n*.** **1.** 教育;训导;培养。**2.** 教育学,教授法。**3.** (蜜蜂、蚕等的)饲养;(动物等的)训练。*elementary* [*secondary, higher*] ~ 初等[中等、高等]教育。*general* ~ 普通教育。*get* [*receive*] *a medical* ~ 受医学教育。*moral* [*intellectual, physical*] ~ 德[智、体]育。*professional* ~ 专[职]业教育。

ed·u·ca·tion·al [ˌedju(ː)'keiʃənəl; ˏɛdʒəˋkeʃənḷ] ***a*.** 教育(上)的;有关教育的。*the* ~ *course* 学历。*an* ~ *worker* 教育工作者。*an* ~ *film* 教育影片。~ *expenses* 教育费。*an* ~ *undertaking* 教育事业。~ **park** 教育园〔大城市中为幼儿院至高等学校的学生开设的,公园式布局的教育设施〕。~ **television** 教育电视。**-ly** ***ad*.** 教育上,用教育方式。**-(al)ist** [-ʃən(əl)ist; -ʃən(ḷ)ɪst] ***n*.** 〔英〕**1.** 教师。**2.** 教育学家。

ed·u·ca·tive ['edju(ː)kətiv; ˋɛdʒəˏketɪv] ***a*.** 有教育意义的,起教育作用的。

e·duce [i(ː)'djuːs; ɪˋdjus] ***vt*.** **1.** 引出,唤起。**2.** 推断;演绎。**3.** 【化】离析。

e·du·ci·ble [i(ː)'djuːsibl; i(ɪ)ˋdjusəbḷ] ***a*.** 可引出的;可推断的。

e·duct ['iːdʌkt; ˋidʌkt] ***n*.** **1.** 【化】离析物,提出物,析出物。**2.** 推断。

e·duc·tion [i'dʌkʃən; ɪˋdʌkʃən] ***n*.** 引出,抽出;推断;【化】离析,析出。

e·duc·tor [i'dʌktə; ɪˋdʌktɚ] ***n*.** **1.** 喷射器。**2.** 析出物。

e·dul·co·rate [i'dʌlkəreit; ɪˋdʌlkəˏret] ***vt*.** 从…中除去酸类等杂质;【化】纯化。

EDVAC = electronic discrete variable automatic computer 电子数据计算机。

Edward (略 **Edw.**) ['edwəd; ˋɛdwɚd] ***n*.** 爱德华〔男子名;爱称 Ed, Eddie, Eddy, Ned, Neddie, Neddy, Ted, Teddie, Teddy〕。

Edwardian [ed'wɔːdjən; ɛdˋwordɪən] **I** ***a*.** (英王)爱德华时代的〔在建筑方面,特指爱德华一世、二世、三世;在文学、艺术方面,特指爱德华七世〕。**II** ***n*.** 爱德华七世时代(1901—1910)的人。

Ed·wards ['edwədz; ˋɛdwɚdz] ***n*.** 爱德华兹〔姓氏〕。

Ed·win ['edwin; ˋɛdwɪn] ***n*.** 埃德温〔男子名〕。

Ed·win·a ['edwinə; ˋɛdwɪnə] ***n*.** 埃德温娜〔女子名〕。

EE, E.E. = **1.** Electrical Engineer 电机工程师。**2.** Electrical Engineering 电机工程。**3.** Early English 早期英语。**4.** Envoy Extraordinary 特命公使。

e.e. = errors excepted. 如有错误,可予更正。

'ee [iː; i] ***pro*.** 〔口〕*ye* (= *you*)的简写。*Thank'ee*. 谢谢你。

-ee ***suf*.** 〔作名词的词尾〕**1.** 表示"受动者":less*ee* 租户,pay*ee* 收款人。**2.** 表示"动作者":absent*ee* 缺席者,

refugee 避难者。3. 表示"与人(或物)有关或相似": bargee 驳船船员, goatee 山羊胡子。

EE & MP, E.E. & M.P. = Envoy Extraordinary and Minister Plenipotentiary 特命全权公使。

EEC = European Economic Community 欧洲经济共同体。

EEG = electroencephalography.

eel [iːl; il] *n*. 1. 鳝鱼;鳝类;(醋中所生的)小线虫。2. 〔美俚〕精明油滑的人。~ **buck** [**pot**] 捕鳝笼。~ **grass** *n*. 【植】大叶藻。~ **spear** *n*. 捕鳝叉。~ **worm** *n*. 【动】小线虫,鳗蛔虫;线虫类 (Nematode) 动物〔一种植物寄生虫〕。

eel·pout [ˈiːlpaut; ˋilˏpaʊt] *n*. (*pl*. ~, ~*s*) 1. 锦鳚科(*Zoarcidae*)鱼。2. 江鳕,淡水鳕 (= burbot)。

eel·y [ˈiːli; ˋilɪ] *a*. 鳝鱼一样的;易滑脱的;油滑的。

e'en [iːn; in] *n*., *ad*. 〔诗〕= even(ing).

e'er [ɛə; ɛr] *ad*. 〔诗〕= ever.

-eer *suf*. 表示"从事…的人": auction*eer*, election*eer*, mountain*eer*.

ee·rie, ee·ry [ˈiəri; ˋɪrɪ] *a*. 〔Scot.〕1. 胆小的,害怕的。2. 阴森可怕的,怪诞的。**-ri·ly** *ad*. **-ri·ness** *n*.

E.E.T.S. = Early English Text Society 早期英语文本研究会。

ef- *pref*. 用于第一字母为 *f*- 的词前, = ex-[1].

eff. = efficiency.

ef·fa·ble [ˈefəbl; ˋɛfəbl] *a*. 〔古〕可说明[表述]的。

ef·face [iˈfeis; ɪˋfes] *vt*. 1. 消去,抹去;抹煞;使消灭。2. 忘却;漠视;使失色[相形见绌]。~ *oneself* 埋没自己,自卑;隐退。**-able** *a*. **-ment** *n*. **-r** *n*.

ef·fect [iˈfekt; əˋfɛkt] I *n*. 1. 结果。2. 效能,效果,效力,效应,作用,功效;影响。3. 感触,印象;外观,现象。4. 旨趣,意义。5. 实行,实施。6. (布的)花纹。7. 〔*pl*.〕物品,动产,家财。8. 〔*pl*.〕〔英〕仿制品。*cause and* ~ 因果。*curative* ~*s* 疗效。*general* ~ 大意,纲领。*household* ~*s* 家产,家具什物。*love of* ~ 爱面子,爱(修饰)外表。*no* ~*s* 无存款。*personal* ~*s* 私人财物,手提行李。*sound* ~*s* 音响效果。*three-dimensional* ~ 立体感。***be in*** (***full***) ~ 正在实行[厉行]。***bring*** [***carry***] ***into*** [***to***] ~ 实行,实现,贯彻。***come*** [***go***] ***into*** ~ 开始实施[生效]。***feel the*** ~***s of*** 痛感…。***for*** ~ 装门面。***give*** ~ ***to*** 实行,实施。***have an*** ~ ***on*** [***upon***] 对…有影响[效果]。***in*** ~ 实际上;总之;有效,生效。***of no*** ~ 无效;无益,不中用。***put into*** ~ 实行。***take*** ~ 奏效,见效,有效验,应验;生效。***to no*** ~ = ***without*** ~ 无效,不灵验。***to the*** ~ ***that*** ... 大意是说…,内容是(*A telegram to the* ~ *that* .... 电报大意是说…)。***to this*** [***that***, ***the same***] ~ 按这种[那种、同样]意思。***with*** ~ 有效地。II *vt*. 1. 产生,招致,导致,引起。2. 完成,达到,实现(目的等)。~ *a cure* 发挥治疗效果。~ *an insurance* 参加保险。**-or** *n*. 〔生〕效应器,效应基因。

ef·fec·tive [iˈfektiv; əˋfɛktɪv] I *a*. 1. 有效(力)的,灵验的;显眼的,〔美〕生效的,被实施的;【军】有战斗力的。2. 【经】实质上的;有实价的 (*opp*. potential, nominal)。3. 【军】精锐的。~ *horsepower* 【物】有效马力。~ *range* 有效射程。*an* ~ *shot* 命中(弹)。*an* ~ *landing area* 【空】安全降落区。*the* ~ *wind* 平均风速。~ *segregation* 【生】正分离。~ *coin* [*money*] 硬币。*the* ~ *strength of an army* 军队的战斗实力[有生力量]。***be far from*** ~ 很不得力。***become*** ~ 〔美〕(法令等)生效。***take*** ~ ***measures*** 采取有效措施。II *n*. 【军】〔*pl*.〕现役兵额,有生力量;精兵。**-ly** *ad*. 1. 有效地,有力地。2. 实际上。**-ness** *n*. 有效;有力。

ef·fec·tu·al [iˈfektjuəl; əˋfɛktʃʊəl] *a*. 有效的;有力的;灵验的。**-ly** *ad*. **-i·ty** [-ˈæliti; -ˋælətɪ] *n*. **-ness** *n*.

ef·fec·tu·ate [iˈfektjueit; əˋfɛktʃʊˏet] *vt*. 使有效,使实现;完成,贯彻。**-a·tion** *n*.

ef·fem·i·na·cy [iˈfeminəsi; əˋfɛmənəsɪ] *n*. 女人气,柔弱,娇气。

ef·fem·i·nate [iˈfeminit; əˋfɛmənɪt] I *a*. 女人似的,女人气的,柔弱的;娇气的。II [-neit; -net] *vt*., *vi*. (使)带女人气,(使)柔弱。**-ly** *ad*. **-ness** *n*.

ef·fen·di [eˈfendi; ɛˋfɛndɪ] *n*. 〔Turk.〕1. 阁下,先生,老爷〔政府官员的尊称,1935 年废止〕。2. (地中海东部各国的)权贵,有产者,学者。

ef·fer·ent [ˈefərənt; ˋɛfərənt] I *a*. 【生理】输出的,传出的;远心的 (*opp*. afferent)。II *n*. 【解】输出管,传出神经。~ **duct** 输出管。~ **nerve** 传出神经。

ef·fer·vesce [ˌefəˈves; ˏɛfəˋvɛs] *vi*. 1. 冒气泡,起泡沫;泡腾。2. 兴奋 (*with*)。**-ves·cence, -ves·cen·cy** [-sns, -snsi; -sns, -snsɪ] *n*.

ef·fer·ves·cent [ˌefəˈvesnt; ˏɛfəˋvɛsnt] *a*. 1. 起泡的,泡沫翻滚的。2. 奋发的。~ **granules** 【药】泡腾散粒剂。

ef·fete [eˈfiːt; ɛˋfit] *a*. 精力枯竭的;已衰老的;疲惫的,衰弱的;无能的。*an* ~ *system of education* 衰败的教育制度。

ef·fi·ca·cious [ˌefiˈkeiʃəs; ˏɛfəˋkeʃəs] *a*. 有效的;(药等)灵验的。**-ly** *ad*. **-ness** *n*.

ef·fi·ca·cy [ˈefikəsi; ˋɛfəkəsɪ] *n*. 效力,功效。

ef·fi·cien·cy [iˈfiʃənsi; əˋfɪʃənsɪ] *n*. 1. 功效。2. 效率;效能;实力,能力。3. 【物】性能。~ **apartment** 简易公寓〔带小厨房和卫生设备的小套房〕。~ **curve** 效率曲线。~ **engineer** [**expert**] (研究降低成本,提高功效的)效率技师[专家]。~ **test** 效率试验。

ef·fi·cient [iˈfiʃənt; əˋfɪʃənt] *a*. 1. 有效的,有力的;效率高的。2. 有实力的;有能力的,有本领的;能胜任的。~ *cause* 【哲】动因。**-ly** *ad*.

Ef·fie [ˈefi; ˋɛfɪ] *n*. 埃菲〔女子名, Euphemia 的昵称〕。

ef·fi·gy [ˈefidʒi; ˋɛfədʒɪ] *n*. 像,肖像,画像,雕像;模拟像。***burn*** [***hang***] ***sb***. ***in*** ~ 焚烧[绞死]某人的模拟像(以泄愤)。

ef·flo·resce [ˌeflɔ(ː)ˈres; ˏɛfloˋrɛs] *vi*. 1. 开花。2. 【化】风化;粉化;(盐)起霜。

ef·flo·res·cence, ef·flo·res·cen·cy [ˌeflɔ(ː)ˈresns, -si; ˏɛfloˋrɛsns, -sɪ] *n*. 1. 开花;开花期;花穗;(事业等)全盛(期)。2. 【化】风化;粉化;盐霜。3. 【医】疹,皮疹。

ef·flo·res·cent [ˌeflɔːˈresnt; ˏɛfloˋrɛsnt] *a*. 1. 开花的。2. (易)风化的;起霜的。3. 【医】发疹的;易发疹的。

ef·flu·ence [ˈefluəns; ˋɛflʊəns] *n*. 1. (液体、光、电等的)流出;发出,放出。2. 流出物,发射物。

ef·flu·ent [ˈefluənt; ˋɛflʊənt] I *a*. 流出的,发出的。II *n*. 1. 流出物,发出物。2. 排水渠,侧流。3. 〔*pl*.〕废水,污水。

ef·flu·vi·al [eˈfluːviəl; ɛˋfluvɪəl] *a*. 恶臭的。

ef·flu·vi·um [eˈfluːviəm; ɛˋfluvɪəm] *n*. (*pl*. **-vi·a** [-viə; -vɪə], ~*s*) 1. 臭气,恶臭;臭液。2. 【物】磁素,电素〔想像中磁、电微粒子〕。3. 【无】无声放电;(臭气、液体等)散[放]出。

ef·flux [ˈeflʌks; ˋɛflʌks] *n*. 1. 流出,涌出。2. 射流;流出量;流出物,【火箭】喷射气流,排出废气。3. 时间经过;满期,终了。

ef·fort [ˈefət; ˋɛfɚt] *n*. 1. 努力,尝试,尽力。2. 成就,努力的成果;杰作。3. 〔英〕(募捐等的)运动。4. 【机】作用力。5. 工作;工作研究计划。*a great oratorical* ~ 动人的演说,雄辩。*literary* ~*s* 文学作品。*mutual co-operation* ~ 共同合作的努力。*That's a pretty good* ~. 那是很大的成绩。*one's maiden* ~ 处女作。*propelling* ~ 推进力。*space* ~ 空间研究计划。*tractive* ~ 牵引力。***beyond human*** ~ 人力所不及。***by human*** ~ 用人力。~***s and resources*** 人力物力。***make additional*** ~***s*** 再接再厉。***make an*** ~ = ***make*** ~***s*** 努力作出 (*to*)。***make every*** ~ 力求,尽一切努力 (*to*);费尽心血。***redouble one's*** ~***s*** 加倍努力。***spare no*** ~***s*** 不遗余力。***with little*** ~ = ***without*** (***any*** [***an***]) ~ 不费力,不难,容易地。

E

ef·fort·less [ˈefətlis; ˋɛfɚtlɪs] *a*. **1**. 不努力的,不出力的。2. 不费力的,容易的。**-ly** *ad*. **-ness** *n*.

ef·front·er·y [iˈfrʌntəri; ɪˋfrʌntərɪ] *n*. 厚颜无耻。*have the* ~ (*to do sth*.) 厚着脸皮,居然。

ef·fulge [eˈfʌldʒ, i-; ɛˋfʌldʒ, ɪ-] *vt*., *vi*. (*-fulg·ed*; *-fulg·ing*) 照耀,(使)发闪光。

ef·ful·gence [eˈfʌldʒəns, i-; ɛˋfʌldʒəns, ɪ-] *n*. 光辉,灿烂。

ef·ful·gent [eˈfʌldʒənt; ɛˋfʌldʒənt] *a*. 辉煌的,灿烂的。**-ly** *ad*.

ef·fuse [eˈfjuːz, i-; ɛˋfjuz, ɪ-] **I** *vt*. **1**. 泻出;喷出;发散出;吐露。—*vi*. 泻出,流出;发出。**II** *a*. **1**. 【植】舒展的。**2**. 【动】豁开的〔指贝壳的唇边〕。

ef·fu·sion [iˈfjuːʒən, eˈf-; əˋfjuʒən, ɛˋf-] *n*. **1**. 喷发,溢出,流出;渗出物;【医】渗出;【机】泻流。**2**. 显露,流露,吐露(心情等)。*an* ~ *of blood* 出血,流血,杀害。~ *of blood in the brain* 脑溢血。*poetic* ~*s* 诗情奔放。*talk with an* ~ *of heart* 倾吐衷曲。*wild* ~*s of an angry man* 愤怒者的粗暴语言。

ef·fu·sive [iˈfjuːsiv; ɛˋfjusɪv] *a*. **1**. 充溢的,流出的,喷出的,涌出的,射流的。**2**. 吐露心情的,热情洋溢的。*be* ~ *in one's gratitude* 感谢不尽。*an* ~ *man* 热情洋溢的人。~ **rocks** 【地】喷发岩。**-ly** *ad*. **-ness** *n*.

eft [eft; ɛft] *n*. 【动】**1**. 〔美〕蝾螈。**2**. 〔古〕蜥蜴,水蜥。

EFTA = European Free Trade Association 欧洲自由贸易联盟。

eft·soon [eftˈsuːn; ɛftˋsun] *ad*. **1**. 〔古〕一会儿之后,立刻。**2**. 〔废〕经常;常常。**3**. 〔废〕又,再(= eftsoons)。

Eg. = **1**. Egypt; Egyptian. **2**. Egyptology.

e.g. = [L.] *exempli gratia* 例如(= for example)。

e·gad [iˈgæd; ɪˋgæd] *int*. 〔oh God 的委婉语〕天哪! 哎呀! 什么!

e·gal·i·tar·i·an [iˌgæliˈtɛəriən; ɪˏgælɪˋtɛrɪən] *a*. 平等主义的;平均主义的(= equalitarian)。**-an·ism** *n*. 平等[平均]主义(= equalitarianism)。

é·ga·li·té [eigɑːliˈtei; egɑlɪˋte] *n*. [F.] 平等。

e·gest [iːˈdʒest; iˋdʒɛst] *vt*. 【医】排出,排泄(*opp*. ingest)。**-ive** *a*.

e·ges·ta [iˈdʒestə; ɪˋdʒɛstə] *n*. 〔*pl*.〕排泄物;粪便;汗。

e·ges·tion [iːˈdʒestʃən; iˋdʒɛstʃən] *n*. 排出,排泄。

egg[1] [eg; ɛg] *n*. **1**. 蛋,鸡蛋;〔生〕卵,卵细胞;卵形物。**2**. 〔俚〕炸弹,手榴弹;鱼雷。**3**. 〔俚〕人,家伙。**4**. 〔俚〕没有意思的玩笑;拙劣的表演。*fertilized* ~ 【生】受精卵,孕卵。*raw* ~ 生蛋。*soft-boiled* ~ 半熟蛋。***a bad*** ~ 〔口〕**1**. 坏家伙。**2**. 失败的计划。***a good*** ~ 好人。***as full as an*** ~ ***is of meat*** = ***as full of meat as an*** ~ 塞满的;满满的。***as sure as*** ~***s is*** ~***s*** 确实,无疑。***break the*** ~***s in sb.'s pocket*** 破坏别人计划。***bring one's*** ~***s to a bad*** [***wrong***] ***market*** 失算,失败。~ ***and anchor*** [***dart***, ***tongue***] 【建】卵锚相间图案的花饰。***from the*** ~ ***to the apple*** 自始至终。***go lay an*** ~ 〔美〕别管闲事,滚开。***golden*** ~ 厚利。***good*** ~! 真好! ***have*** [***put***] ***all one's*** ~***s in one basket*** 孤注一掷。***have*** ~***s on the spit*** 正忙得不可开交。***in the*** ~ 未成熟的,尚在初期(***kill a plot in the*** ~ 防患于未然)。***lay an*** ~ **1**. 生蛋,下蛋。**2**. (飞机)扔炸弹。**3**. 〔俚〕(演出等)失败。***like as two*** ~***s*** 完全一样。***sit on*** ~***s*** 抱蛋,孵卵。***teach one's grandmother*** (***how***) ***to suck*** ~***s*** 班门弄斧。***tread*** [***walk***] ***upon*** ~***s*** 如履薄冰。***with*** ~***s on one's face*** 〔美〕受羞辱,处于窘困状态。~ **apple** = ~ plant. ~ **beater** [**whisk**] *n*. **1**. 打蛋器。**2**. 〔美俚〕直升机。~ **capsule** [**case**] 蛋壳。~ **cell** 【生】卵细胞。~ **coal** 小煤块。~**cup** *n*. (吃带壳蛋用的)蛋杯。~ **dance** 鸡蛋舞〔蒙上眼睛在放有鸡蛋的地上跳舞或头上顶蛋跳舞〕;非常吃力的事。~ **flip** = ~**head** 〔讽俚〕知识份子。~**nog(g)** *n*. 蛋酒。~ **plant** 茄子。~ **roll** 蛋卷。~**-shaped** *a*. 蛋形的;易碎的。~**shell** *n*. 蛋壳;淡黄色。~**shell china** 薄磁器。~**tooth** *n*. 〔动〕破卵齿。~ **tube** 【解】卵巢管。~ **white** 蛋白。

egg[2] [eg; ɛg] *vt*. **1**. 鼓动,煽动,怂恿(*on*)。**2**. 用蛋制作(食物)。**3**. 向人扔鸡蛋。~ ***sb***. ***on to do sth***. 怂恿某人干某事。

egg·er, **egg·ar** [ˈegə; ˋɛgɚ] *n*. 枯叶蛾科(*Lasiocampidae*)动物。

e·gis [ˈiːdʒis; ˋidʒɪs] *n*. = aegis.

eg·lan·tine [ˈegləntain; ˋɛglənˏtaɪn] *n*. 【植】**1**. 多花蔷薇。**2**. 忍冬属的一种。

EGO = eccentric geophysical observatory 偏心轨道地球物理观测卫星。

eg·o [ˈegəu, ˈiːgəu; ˋɛgo, ˋigo] *n*. (*pl*. ~*s*) **1**. 【哲】自我。**2**. 〔口〕自负;自私。*emancipation of* ~ 自我解放。~ **ideal** 【心】自我理想。~ **psychology** 自我心理学。~ **trip** 追求个人成就。~**-trip** *vi*. 表现自我,追求个人成就。~**-tripper** 追求个人成就者。

eg·o·cen·tric [ˌegəuˈsentrik, ˈiːg-; ˏɛgoˋsɛntrɪk, ˋig-] **I** *a*. 自我中心的;利己的。**II** *n*. 自我主义者,以我为中心的人。**-i·ty** [-ˈtrisiti; -ˋtrɪsɪtɪ] *n*. 自我中心,利己。

e·go·cen·tri·cal·ly [ˌegəuˈsentrikəli, ˌiːg-; ˏɛgoˋsɛntrɪkəlɪ, ˏig-] *ad*. 以自我为中心,利己地。

e·go·cen·trism [ˌegəuˈsentrizm, ˌiːg-; ˏɛgoˋsɛntrɪzm, ˏig-] *n*. 自我中心;自私自利。

eg·o·ism [ˈegəuizəm, ˈiːg-; ˋɛgoˏɪzəm; ˋig-] *n*. 【哲】自我主义;利己主义(*opp*. altruism);自私,利己心。*departmental* ~ 本位主义。*national* ~ 民族利己主义。

eg·o·ist [ˈegəuist, ˈiːg-; ˋɛgoɪst, ˋig-] *n*. 自我本位者;利己主义者;自私自利的人。**-tic**, **-ti·cal** *a*.

eg·o·ma·ni·a [ˌegəuˈmeiniə, ˈiːg-; ˋɛgoˋmenɪə, ˋig-] *n*. 自负[大]狂,自我中心狂。**-ni·ac** [-niæk; -nɪæk] *a*.

eg·o·tism [ˈegəutizəm, ˈiːg-; ˋɛgoˏtɪzm, ˋig-] *n*. **1**. 自我主义;自我中心癖〔满口不离 I 或 me 的习惯〕;自高自大。**2**. 利己主义,自私自利。**-tist** *n*.

eg·o·tis·tic, **-ti·cal** [ˈegəˈtistik, -tikəl, ˈiːg-; ˋɛgəˋtɪstɪk, -tɪkəl, ˋig-] *a*. **1**. 自我中心的;自高自大的。**2**. 利己主义的;自私的。**-ti·cal·ly** *ad*.

eg·o·tize [ˈegəutaiz, ˈiːg-; ˋɛgəˏtaɪz, ˋig-] *vi*. 〔罕〕老是谈论自己;自负,自私。

e·gre·gious [iˈgriːdʒəs; ɪˋgridʒəs] *a*. **1**. 〔蔑〕无比的;厉害的;惊人的。**2**. 〔古〕卓越的,显著的。*an* ~ *ass* [*fool*] 大傻瓜。**-ly** *ad*. **-ness** *n*. **1**. 非常,极坏。**2**. 〔古〕卓越,显著。

e·gress [ˈiːgres; ˋigrɛs] **I** *n*. **1**. 外出[退出]的行为[权利]。**2**. 出口,出路。**3**. 【天】终切。**II** *vi*. 外出。~ ***and ingress*** 出入。

e·gres·sion [i(ː)ˈgreʃən; ɪˋgrɛʃən] *n*. 外出,退出。

e·gret [ˈiːgret, ˈeg-; ˋigrɪt, ˋɛg-] *n*. **1**. 【鸟】白鹭,鹭鸶。**2**. 白鹭羽毛;羽毛装饰。**3**. 【植】冠毛。

E·gypt [ˈiːdʒipt; ˋidʒɪpt] *n*. 埃及〔非洲〕。

E·gyp·tian [iˈdʒipʃən; ɪˋdʒɪpʃən] **I** *a*. **1**. 埃及(人)的。**2**. 〔古〕吉普赛(人)的。**II** *n*. **1**. 埃及人;埃及语。**2**. 〔古〕吉普赛。***spoil the*** ~***s*** 【圣】夺取敌人财物。

E·gyp·tol·o·gy [ˌiːdʒipˈtɔlədʒi; ˏidʒɪpˋtɑlədʒɪ] *n*. 埃及学。

eh [ei; e] *int*. 啊? 嗯〔表示疑问、惊奇、询商等〕: *Wasn't it splendid*, ~? 难道不好,嗯?

EHF, **ehf** = extremely high frequency 【无】极高频。

EHP = effective horsepower 有效马力。

Ehr·lich [G. ˈeiliʃ; ˋerlɪʃ], **Paul** 埃尔利希〔1854—1915,德国细菌学家,606 的发明者〕。

e.h.t. = extra-high tension 超高压。

EHV = extra high voltage 【电】极高压。

E.I. = East India, East Indies. **1**. 东印度群岛。**2**. 东印度。

-eian *suf*. = -ean.

EIB(W) = Export-Import Bank (Of Washington) 〔美〕

(华盛顿)进出口银行。

ei·der [ˈaidə; ˋaɪdɚ] *n*.【鸟】绒鸭,绒鸭的绒毛。~ **down** 鸭的绒毛;鸭绒垫。~ **duck** 绒鸭。

ei·det·ic [aiˈdetik; aɪˋdetɪk] *a*.(印象)非常鲜明的,(印象)极为逼真的。**-i·cal·ly** *ad*.

ei·do·graph [ˈaidəugrɑːf; ˋaɪdəˏgræf] *n*. 伸缩画图器,图画缩放仪。

ei·do·lon [aiˈdəulon; aɪˋdolən] *n*.(*pl*. ~*s*, *-la* [-lə; -lə]) **1.** 幻象。**2.** 鬼怪。

Eif·fel [ˈaifəl; ˋaɪfl̩] **Tower** (巴黎)艾斐尔铁塔〔高984英尺〕。

ei·gen·func·tion [ˈaigənˌfʌŋkʃən; ˋaɪdʒənˏfʌŋkʃən] *n*.【数】特征函数,固有函数。

ei·gen·val·ue [ˈaidʒənvæljuː; ˋaɪdʒənˏvælju] *n*.【数】特征值,固有值。

eight [eit; et] **I** *num*. 八,第八(页等);八人,八个(东西)。*E- minus four equals four*. 八减四等于四。*We are* ~. 我们是八个人。~ *of them* 他们当中的八个人。*the* ~ *of them* 他们八个人。★注意二者的不同。*Book E-* 第八册。*section* ~ 第八节。**II** *n*. **1.** 八的记号。**2.** 八人[物]一组;(八人的)赛艇选手。**2.** 8字形(物);【溜冰】8字形花样。**3.** 八汽缸发动机,八汽缸汽车。**4.** 八点钟;八岁;八号衣服[鞋袜];(纸牌中的)8。~*-fifteen* 8点15分。*a piece of* ~ (西班牙从前的)8R (=8 reals) 银币。*at* ~ 在八点钟。~ **ball** **1.**【美撞球】标有8字的黑球〔把这个球最先打进袋里,就全盘算输〕。**2.**【无】无定向话筒。***be behind the*** ~ ***ball*** 〔美俚〕处境危险[非常不利]。~ **bells**【海】八击钟〔分别在四时半、八时半及十二时半各击钟一下,其后每半小时递增一击,逢四时、八时及十二时刚好八击〕。***in*** ~***s*** 用八个音节的诗行。***have one over the*** ~ 〔英俚〕醉得七颠八倒。***the Eights*** 牛津及剑桥两大学的划船比赛。~**-hour** *a*. 八小时制(~*-hour(s') day* 一日八小时劳动制。~*-hour labour* 八小时工作)。~ **pence** 八便士。~**-penny** *a*. 八便士的。

eight·ball [ˈeitbɔːl; ˋetˏbɔl] *n*. **1.** (美撞球戏中)有8字记号的球〔此球落入袋中即输〕。**2.** 〔美俚〕一种圆形扩音器。***behind the*** ~ 〔美俚〕处于不利地位。

eight·een [ˈeiˈtiːn, eiˈt-, ˈeit-; ˋeˋtin, eˋt-, ˋet-] **I** *num*. 十八,十八个。**II** *n*. 十八岁;十八的记号;十九世纪;十八点钟。~ *months* 一年半。*in the* ~*-fifties* 在十九世纪的五十年代〔略作 in the 1850's〕。

eight·een·mo [eiˈtiːnməu; eˋtinˏmo] *n*.【印】十八开本(=octodecimo)。

eight·eenth [ˈeiˈtiːnθ; ˋeˋtinθ] **I** *num*. **1.** 第十八,十八号。**2.** 十八分之一的。**II** *n*. **1.** 第十八。**2.** 十八分之一。**3.** (每月的)第十八日。

eight·fold [ˈeitfəuld; ˋetˏfold] *a*., *ad*. 八倍,八重。

eighth [eitθ; etθ] **I** *num*. **1.** 第八,八号。**2.** 八分之一的。*five* ~*s* 八分之五。**II** *n*. 第八个;八分之一;(每月的)第八日。~ **note**【乐】八分音符。~ **rest**【乐】八分休止符。**-ly** *ad*.

eight·i·eth [ˈeitiiθ; ˋetɪɪθ] **I** *num*. **1.** 第八十。**2.** 八十分之一的。**II** *n*. **1.** 第八十个。**2.** 八十分之一。

eight·score [ˈeitˈskɔː; ˋetˋskor] *n*. 一百六十。

eight·some [ˈeitsəm; ˋetsəm] *n*. 八人跳的苏格兰舞(=~ reel)。

eight·y [ˈeiti; ˋetɪ] **I** *num*. 八十,八十个。**II** *n*. 第八十;八十的符号。*the eighties* 八十多岁;八十年代;八十到九十的数目。~**-niner** [-ˈnainə; -ˋnaɪnɚ] 〔美〕1889年开始移入俄克拉荷马州的自耕农。~**-six** *vt*. 拒绝招待(顾客),恕不招待。

ei·kon [ˈaikɔn; ˋaɪkɑn] *n*. =icon.

Ei·leen [ˈailiːn; ˋaɪlin] *n*. 艾琳〔女子名〕。

Ein·stein [ˈainstain; ˋaɪnstaɪn] *n*. **1.** 爱因斯坦〔姓氏〕。**2. Albert** ~ 爱因斯坦〔1879—1955,物理学家,相对论的创立者。获1921年诺贝尔物理奖〕。~ **theory**【物】相对论。**-i·an** [ainsˈtainiən; aɪnsˋtaɪnɪən] *a*. 爱因斯坦(式)的;相对论的。

ein·stein·i·um [ainˈstainiəm; aɪnˋstaɪnɪəm] *n*.【化】锿。

Eir·e [ˈɛərə; ˋɛrə] *n*. 爱尔兰共和国的旧名称。

ei·re·ni·con [aiˈriːnikɔn; aɪˋrinɪkɑn] *n*. (宗教斗争中的)和解提议。

Ei·sen·how·er [ˈaizənhauə; ˋaɪznˏhauɚ] *n*. **1.** 艾森豪威尔〔姓氏〕。**2. Dwight** ~ 德怀特·艾森豪威尔〔1890—1969,美国第34任总统〕。~ **jacket** 男用短茄克〔原系军用茄克衫〕。

eis·tedd·fod [aiˈsteðvɔd; eˋstɛðvɑd] *n*. (*pl*. *-fods*, *-fod·an* [-dai; -daɪ]) 〔威尔斯〕(诗人、音乐家等的)艺术家年会。

ei·ther [ˈaiðə, ˈiːðə; ˋaɪðɚ, ˋiðɚ] **I** *a*. 两者之一的;(两者之中)随便哪一个的;两者中任何一方的。*sit on* ~ *side* 随便坐哪一边。*of* ~ *sex* 两性双方的。*curtains hanging on* ~ *side of the window* 挂在窗子两边的帘子。*E- view is correct*. 两种见解都对。~ ***way*** 总之;反正都;两边都(*abstain from voting* ~ *way* 两边的票都不投)。***in*** ~ ***case*** 两种情形都;反正。**II** *pron*. 两者中的任何一个。*E- (of them) will do*. (他们)随便哪个都行。**III** *conj*. 〔~... or...〕或…或…,不是…就是…,…呢还是…。*E- come in or go out*. 要末进来,要末出去。*E- you or I must go*. 你跟我总要有一个人去。**IV** *ad*. 〔与否定语连用〕**1.** 也(不…)。*If you do not go, I shall not* ~. 你不去,我也不去。*There is no time to lose,* ~. 再说,这又是刻不容缓的事。**2.** 而且还。*There was once a time, and not so long ago* ~. 有一次,而且还是不久以前。

ei·ther-or [ˈaiðərˈɔː, ˈiː-; ˋaɪðɚˋɔr, ˋi-] **I** *a*. 非此即彼的,二者择一的。**II** *n*. **1.** (自动控制)"异";按位加。**2.** 二者择一。

e·jac·u·late [iˈdʒækjuleit; ɪˋdʒækjəˏlet] *vt*., *vi*. **1.** 突然叫喊,短促地喊叫着说。**2.** 射出(精液等)。**-la·tion** *n*. **-la·tor** *n*. **1.** 突然叫喊者。**2.**【解】射出肌。

e·jac·u·la·to·ry [iˈdʒækjulətəri; ɪˋdʒækjələˏtorɪ] *a*. **1.** 喊叫的,用喊话方式说的。**2.**【生理】射精的。~ **duct** 射精管。

e·ject [iːˈdʒekt; iˋdʒɛkt] **I** *vt*. **1.** 逐出,撵出,驱逐,革(职),排斥。**2.** 喷出,吐出(烟的);发射,喷射。~ ***sb***. ***from*** 把(某人)赶出…。**II** *n*.【心】投射;推断的事物。

e·jec·ta [i(ː)ˈdʒektə; ɪˋdʒɛktə] *n*. 〔*pl*.〕喷出物,废物,渣。

e·jec·tion [i(ː)ˈdʒekʃən; ɪˋdʒɛkʃən] *n*. **1.** 逐出,赶出。**2.** 排出,推出;喷出,吐出;发射,喷射。**3.** 排出物,喷出物;射出物。~ **seat**【空】弹射座椅。

e·jec·tive [i(ː)ˈdʒektiv; ɪˋdʒɛktɪv] *a*. 排出的,喷出的;逐出的。

e·ject·ment [i(ː)ˈdʒektmənt; ɪˋdʒɛktmənt] *n*. **1.** 驱逐;排出,喷出。**2.**【法】收回不动产的诉讼。

e·jec·tor [i(ː)ˈdʒektə; ɪˋdʒɛktɚ] *n*. **1.** 驱逐者。**2.** 排出器[管];【机】弹射器,喷射器;喷射泵;【医】射出器;(塑料)推顶器。~ **pin** 顶杆,顶出销,退件销。~ **seat** = ejection seat.

e·ji·do [eˈhiːðɔː; ɛˋhiðo] *n*. (*pl*. ***-dos***) 〔Sp.〕(墨西哥农村的)合作农场。

EK = Eastman Kodak Company 〔美〕柯达公司。

eka- *pref*. 表示【化】"准"〔周期表中推定的某元素下一元素的暂用名〕。例: *eka*-aluminium 准铝〔即现在的 gallium〕。*eka*-element 待寻元素。

eke[1] [iːk; ik] *vt*. 〔古,方〕**1.** 放宽,放长。**2.** 增补,补充。~ ***out*** 弥补不足;辛辛苦苦维持(生活);节省地消费(~ *out one's salary with odd jobs* 做临时工弥补薪水的不足。~ *out a scanty livelihood* 勉勉强强过日子)。

eke[2] [iːk; ik] *ad*. 〔古〕又,也;加之。

EKG = electrocardiogram.

e·kis·tic·al [iˈkistikəl; ɪˋkɪstɪkl̩] *a*. 城市住区规划学的。

E

e·kis·ti·cian [iˈkistiʃən; ɪˋkɪstɪʃən] ***n*.** 城市住区规划学家。

e·kis·tics [iːˈkistiks; ɪˋkɪstɪks] ***n*.** 〔作单数用〕城市住区规划学;人类环境生态学。

ek·ka [ˈekɑː; ˋɛkɑ] ***n*.** 〔印度〕单座马车。

el [el; ɛl] ***n*.** **1.** 英语字母 L, l. **2.** 〔美口〕高架铁路(= elevated railroad)。

e·lab·o·rate [iˈlæbəreit; ɪˋlæbəˏret] **I** ***vt*.** **1.** 认真做;用心作;推敲(文章)。**2.** 详尽阐述。~ *a plan for* 为…精心拟定计划。~ *one's proposals* 阐述自己的建议。— ***vi*.** 增加细节,详细说明。~ *on* [*upon*] *a plan* 对计划作详细说明。**II** [iˈlæbərit; ɪˋlæbərɪt] ***a*.** **1.** 认真的,精心的,辛勤的。**2.** 精巧的,精细的,精益求精的;详尽的。**-ly** ***ad*.** **-ness** ***n*.** **1.** 苦心经营,费神。**2.** 认真作出,详尽发挥。**3.** 精致;缜密;精巧。

e·lab·o·ra·tion [iˌlæbəˈreiʃən; ɪˏlæbəˋreʃən] ***n*.** **1.** 认真做;精练,推敲。**2.** 精巧;细致的工作[作品]。**3.** 【生】同化作用〔食物进入体内后,由简单的物质变为复杂有机化合物的作用〕。

e·lab·o·ra·tive [iˈlæbərətiv; ɪˋlæbəˏretɪv] ***a*.** 认真做的,精练的,细致的。~ **faculty**【心】思考力。**-ly** ***ad*.**

e·lab·o·ra·tor [iˈlæbəreitə; ɪˋlæbəˏretɚ] ***n*.** **1.** 热心做事的人,苦心经营的人。**2.** 作详尽说明的人。

elaeo- *comb.f.* 表示"油":*elaeo*meter.

e·lae·om·e·ter [ˌeliˈɔmitə; ˏɛlɪˋɑmɪtɚ] ***n*.** 【化】油比重计。

el·ae·op·tene [ˌeliˈɔptiːn; ˏɛlɪˋɑptin] ***n*.** 【化】油萜(= eleoptene)。

elaio- *comb.f.* = elaeo-.

e·lai·o·my·cin [iˈleiəmaisin; ɪˋleəmaɪsɪn] ***n*.** 【药】油霉素,伊霉素。

elai·o·plast [iˈlaiəplæst; ɪˋlaɪəˏplæst] ***n*.** 【植】油质体。

E·lam [ˈiːləm; ˋiləm] ***n*.** 伊拉姆古国〔古代巴比伦以东的一个古王国〕。

E·lam·ite [ˈiːləmait; ˋiləmaɪt] **I** ***n*.** **1.** 伊拉姆古国人。**2.** 伊拉姆语。**II** ***a*.** 伊拉姆的;伊拉姆人的;伊拉姆语的。

E·lam·it·ic [ˌiːləˈmitik; ˏiləˋmɪtɪk] = Elamite.

é·lan [eiˈlɑ̃, eˋlɑ̃] ***n*.** 〔F.〕跃进;冲动,奔放。~ ***vital*** [viˈtʌl; vɪˋtʌl]【哲】生命的活力论。

e·land [ˈiːlənd; ˋilənd] ***n*.** 【动】(南非)大羚羊。

el·a·pid [ˈeləpid; ˋɛləpɪd] ***n*.** 眼镜蛇科的蛇。

el·a·pine [ˈeləpain; ˋɛləpaɪn] ***a*.** 眼镜蛇科的〔包括眼镜蛇;小尾眼镜蛇等〕。

e·lapse [iˈlæps; ɪˋlæps] **I** ***vi*.** (时间)经过,消失。*Three years have ~d.* 已经过去三年了。**II** ***n*.** (时间的)消逝。

e·las·mo·branch [iˈlæzməˌbræŋk, iˈlæs-; ɪˋlæzməˏbræŋk, ɪˋlæs-] **I** ***a*.** 【动】软骨鱼类(纲)的。**II** ***n*.** 软骨鱼类动物〔如鲨鱼、鳐鱼、鲼鱼等〕。

e·las·tic [iˈlæstik; ɪˋlæstɪk] **I** ***a*.** **1.** 有弹力[弹性]的。**2.** 伸缩自如的,灵活的。**3.** 机变的,轻快的。*an ~ body* 弹性体。~ *braces* 松紧吊裤带。~ *force* 弹力。*an ~ principle* 灵活性的原则。~ *ribbon* 松紧带。*an ~ temperament* 开朗的性格。**II** ***n*.** 橡皮线,松紧带,橡皮圈。~ **deformation**【无】弹性变形。~ **sides** (紧口靴)两边的松紧布;(两边有松紧布的)紧口靴。~ **side(d)** ***a*.** 两边有松紧布的(~ *side(d) boots* 紧口靴)。~ **tissue**【解】弹性(纤维)组织。**-al·ly** ***ad*.**

e·las·tic·ity [ˌelæsˈtisiti; ˏɪlæsˋtɪsɪtɪ] ***n*.** **1.** 弹力,弹性;伸缩力,伸缩性,灵活性。**2.** 开朗的性情。

e·las·ti·cize [iˈlæstisaiz; ɪˋlæstɪsaɪz] ***vt*.** (***-ciz·ed***; ***-ciz·ing***) 使弹性化。

e·las·ti·cized [iˈlæstisaizd; ɪˋlæstəˏsaɪzd] ***a*.** 用弹性线制成的。

e·las·tin [iˈlæstin; ɪˋlæstɪn] ***n*.** 【生化】弹性硬蛋白。

e·las·ti·vi·ty [ˌelæsˈtiviti; ˏelæsˋtɪvətɪ] ***n*.** 【物】倒电容系数,倒介电常数。**electric** ~ 介电常数的倒数。

e·las·to·mer [iˈlæstəmə; ɪˋlæstəmɚ] ***n*.** 【化】弹性体;高弹体。

e·las·to·plast [iːˈlæstəplæst; ɪˋlæstəˏplæst] ***n*.** **1.** 【化】弹性塑料。**2.** 弹性黏膏。**-ic** ***n*.**, ***a*.** 弹性塑料(的)。

e·late [iˈleit; ɪˋlet] **I** ***a*.** 〔古〕= elated. **II** ***vt*.** 使得意,鼓舞。***be ~d at*** [***by***, ***with***] 因…而得意洋洋。

e·lat·ed [iˈleitid; ɪˋletɪd] ***a*.** 欢欣鼓舞的,兴高采烈的,得意洋洋的。*an ~ look* 得意的样子。**-ly** ***ad*.** **-ness** ***n*.**

el·a·ter [ˈelətə; ˋɛlətɚ] ***n*.** **1.** 【植】弹丝。**2.** 【动】叩头虫(= elaterid)。

e·lat·er·id [iˈlætərid; ɪˋlætərɪd] **I** ***n*.** 叩头虫(= click beetle)。**II** ***a*.** 叩头虫科的。

e·lat·er·in [iˈlætərin; ɪˋlætərɪn] ***n*.** 【化】喷瓜素。

e·lat·er·ite [iˈlætərait; ɪˋlætəraɪt] ***n*.** 弹性沥青。

el·a·te·ri·um [ˌeləˈtiəriəm; ˏɛləˋtɪərɪəm] ***n*.** 西洋苦瓜素,喷瓜汁〔泻药或利尿药〕。

e·la·tion [iˈleiʃən; ɪˋleʃən] ***n*.** 兴高采烈,振奋;得意洋洋。***with great ~*** 怀着非常振奋的心情。

El·ba·san [ˌelbɑːˈsɑːn; ˏɛlbɑˋsɑn] ***n*.** 爱尔巴桑〔阿尔巴尼亚城市〕。

El·be [ˈelb; ˋɛlb] ***n*.** 〔the ~〕易北河〔欧洲〕。

El·bert [ˈelbət; ˋɛlbɚt] ***n*.** 埃尔伯特〔男子名, Albert 的异体〕。

el·bow [ˈelbəu; ˋɛlbo] **I** ***n*.** **1.** 肘;肘状物。**2.** (海岸线的)急弯,曲折。**3.** (椅子的)扶手;弯头;【建】肘形管,弯管,弯头。***at one's*** [***the***] ~ 在附近,在左右。***bend*** [***crook***, ***lift***] ***one's*** ~ 喝酒太多。***More*** [***All***] ***power to your ~!*** 祝你健康[成功]! ***out at*** (***the***) ***~s*** (上衣)露出肘部,衣衫褴褛;捉襟见肘,穷困。***rub*** [***touch***] ***~s with*** 与(人)交往。***shake the ~s*** 掷骰子,赌博。***up to the ~s in*** 忙着,埋头,专心(*We are up to the ~s in work.*我们正埋头工作)。**II** ***vt*.**, ***vi*.** 用肘推;挤进。~ ***off*** [***out***] 推开[推出]。~ ***one's way through*** (***a crowd***) 从人丛中挤过去。**~-bending** ***a*.** 〔美俚〕酗酒的。~ **board** 窗台(板)。**~chair** 扶手椅(= armchair)。~ **grease** 〔口〕使劲擦拭;苦干,重活,艰苦的工作。~ **joint** 弯管接头。~ **room** 活动余地,行动自由,自由行动的机会。~ **pipe** 【机】弯头。~ **union**【机】弯头套管。**-y** ***a*.** 用肘推的。

el·chee, el·chi [ˈeltʃi; ˋɛltʃɪ] ***n*.** (波斯与土耳其的)大使,使节。

el·co·sis [elˈkəusis; ɛlˋkosɪs] ***n*.** 【医】溃疡。

eld [eld; ɛld] ***n*.** 〔古、诗〕**1.** 从前,古代。**2.** 老年,高龄。

eld. = eldest.

eld·er[1] [ˈeldə; ˋɛldɚ] **I** ***a*.** 〔old 的比较级,但不能与 than 并用〕**1.** 年长的;资格老的。**2.** 从前的。**3.** 优先的。*one's ~ brother* [*sister*] 哥哥[姊姊]。**II** ***n*.** 年长者,长辈;族长;前人,祖先;(教会的)长老。~ *statesman* **1.** 政界元老,社会上有影响的人物。**2.** (日本史上天皇的)元老参事团参事。~ *times* 古时候。~ *title* 优先权。~ **care** ***n*.** 对穷苦老人的医疗照顾。

eld·er[2] [ˈeldə; ˋɛldɚ] ***n*.** 【植】接骨木。

el·der·ber·ry [ˈeldəˌberi; ˋɛldɚˏbɛrɪ] ***n*.** (*pl*. ***-ries***) **1.** 接骨木属植物,接骨木(= elder)。**2.** 接骨木属植物之果。

eld·er·ly [ˈeldəli; ˋɛldɚlɪ] ***a*.** 较老的,年长的。

eld·er·ship [ˈeldəʃip; ˋɛldɚˏʃɪp] ***n*.** 长辈;【宗】长老的职位。

eld·est [ˈeldist; ˋɛldɪst] ***a*.** 〔old 的最高级〕最年长的,最老的,领头的。~ *daughter* [*son*] 长女[子]。

ELDO = European Launcher Development Organization 欧洲发射工具发展组织。

El·don [ˈeldən; ˋɛldən] ***n*.** 埃尔登〔姓氏,男子名〕。

El Do·ra·do, El·do·ra·do [ˌel dəˈrɑːdəu; ˏɛl dəˋrɑdo] 〔Sp.〕(旧时西班牙征服者想像中的南美洲)黄金国;〔喻〕宝山,富庶之乡。

el·dritch [ˈeldritʃ; ˋɛldrɪtʃ] ***a*.** 〔Scot.〕怪异的,可怕的;有鬼怪出没的。

El·ea·nor [ˈelinə; ˋɛlɪnɚ] *n*. 埃莉诺〔女子名〕。

El·e·at·ic [ˌeliˈætik; ˏɛlɪˋætɪk] *a*. 伊利亚学派的〔公元前五、六世纪伊利亚的古希腊哲学流派〕。**-at·i·cism** *n*.

el·e·cam·pane [ˌelikæmˈpein; ˏɛləkəmˋpen] *n*.【植】土木香;用土木香根做香料作成的糖果。

elect. = electric; electrical; electrician; electricity.

e·lect [iˈlekt; ɪˋlɛkt] **I** *vt*. **1.** 推选;选(举)某人任某职。**2.** 作出(…的)选择;决定。～ *sb. to the presidency* [*to be president*] 选某人当总统。～ *to be a doctor* 决定当医生。—*vi*. **1.** 进行(投票)选举。**2.** 作出选择。***be ～ed*** 当选。***the ～ed*** 被选人;当选人。***the right to ～ and stand for election*** 选举权和被选举权。**II** *a*. 被选定的,当选的,当选而尚未就任的〔一般用于所修饰的名词之后〕。*the Mayor-*～ 当选市长。*the bride* ～ 被选中的未婚妻。**III** *n*.〔the ～〕**1.** 当选人,被选定的人。**2.** 特权集团;〔宗〕上帝的选民。

e·lec·tion [iˈlekʃən; ɪˋlɛkʃən] *n*. **1.** 选择。**2.** 选举,选出,当选。**3.** 选举权(利)。**4.**【神】神的选择。*carry an* ～ 当选。*an* ～ *address* 竞选演说。*an* ～ *campaign* 竞选运动。*a general* ～ 普选,大选。*a special* ～〔美〕补选〔在英国作 *by-*～〕。***stand for*** ～ 做候选人。**E-Day** 美国总统及国会议员选举日。**E- Year** (美国总统)选举年。

e·lec·tion·eer [iˌlekʃəˈniə; ɪˏlɛkʃənˋɪr] **I** *vi*. 为选举奔走,进行竞选活动。**II** *n*.〔英〕= -er 竞选的人。**-ing** *n*. 竞选活动。

e·lec·tive [iˈlektiv; ɪˋlɛktɪv] **I** *a*. **1.** 选举的,由选举产生的,有选举权的。**2.**〔美〕随意选择的 (*opp*. required);【化】有选择的。**II** *n*.〔美〕选修课程。～ **affinity**【化】有(选)择的亲和力。～ **course** 选修课程。～ **culture** 选择培养。～ **franchise** 选举权。～ **system** (学校的)选课制度。**-ly** *ad*. **-ness** *n*.

e·lec·tor [iˈlektə; ɪˋlɛktɚ] *n*. 选举人;〔美〕总统选举团成员;〔E-〕【史】选帝侯。

e·lec·to·ral [iˈlektərəl; ɪˋlɛktərəl] *a*. **1.** 选举的;选举人的。**2.**【史】〔E-〕选帝侯的。～ **college**〔美〕(由各州所选出的)总统选举团。～ **district** 选区。

e·lec·tor·ate [iˈlektərit; ɪˋlɛktərɪt] *n*. **1.** 选民(全体)。**2.** 选举区。**3.**【史】选帝侯的爵位[领土]。

electr. = electric(al); electricity.

E·lec·tra [iˈlektrə; ɪˋlɛktrə] *n*. **1.**【希神】厄勒克特拉〔阿加麦农 (Agamemnon)的女儿,曾在 Troy 战争中率领希腊军队〕。**2.** 女子名。～ **complex** *n*.【心】恋父(厌母)情结。

e·lec·tress [iˈlektris; ɪˋlɛktrɪs] *n*. **1.** 女选举人。**2.**【史】选帝侯的夫人。

e·lec·tric [iˈlektrik; ɪˋlɛktrɪk] **I** *a*. **1.** 电的;带电的;起电的,导电的,发电的,电动的。**2.** 令人激动的,紧张的,惊人的。**3.**〔美口〕(乐曲的)用电吉他演奏的。～ *eloquence* 惊人的口才。～ *performance* 惊人的表演。*an* ～ *atmosphere* 紧张的气氛。**II** *n*.〔口〕**1.** 带电物体。**2.** 电动车辆。～ **accumulator** 蓄电池。～ **appliances** 电气设备。～ **arc** 电弧。～ **beacon** 灯光信标。～ **bell** 电铃。～ **blanket** 电(热床)毯。～ **blue** 电光蓝色,铁蓝色。～ **bulb** 电灯泡。～ **capacity** = electrical capacity. ～ **car** [**vehicle**]电动汽车。～ **cell** 电池。～ **chair** 死刑电椅。～ **charge** 电荷。～ **circuit** 电路。～ **clock** 电钟。～ **current** 电流。～ **eel**【动】电鳗。～ **energy** 电能。～ **engineering** 电机工程。～ **eye** 光电池;电眼。～ **fan** 电风扇。～ **field** 电场。～ **furnace** 电炉。～ **generator** 发电机。～ **guitar**【乐】电吉他。～ **heater** 电热器;电炉。～ **iron** 电熨斗;电烙铁。～ **lamp** 电灯(泡)。～ **light** 电光〔注意, an ～ light 为“电灯”〕。～ **locomotive** 电力机车。～ **mains** 输电干线。～ **motor** 电动机。～ **organ** 电风琴。～ **outlet** 电源插座。～ **potential** 电位(势)。～ **power** 电力。～ **power house** [**station**] 发电厂。～ **railway** 电气铁路。～ **shock** 电震。～ **torch** 电筒。～ **tramway** 有轨电车。～ **vehicle** = ～ car. ～ **wave** 电波。～ **welding** 电焊。～ **wire** 电线。

e·lec·tri·cal [iˈlektrikəl; ɪˋlɛktrɪkl] *a*. **1.** 电力的,电动的,发电的;电气科学的。**2.** 令人激动的,紧张的,惊人的。～ **artifice**〔英军〕电气工匠兵。～ **capacity** 电容。～ **condenser** 电容器。～ **engineer** 电机工程师。～ **engineering** 电机工程。～ **transcription** 广播用唱片;录音广播。～ **image transmission** 传真(照片)。**-ly** *ad*. **-ness** *n*.

e·lec·tri·cian [ilekˈtriʃən; ɪˏlɛkˋtrɪʃən] *n*. 电工;电气技师;电学家。

e·lec·tric·i·ty [ilekˈtrisiti; ɪˏlɛkˋtrɪsətɪ] *n*. **1.** 电,电学。**2.** 电流,静电,电荷。**3.** 热心,强烈,紧张,高涨的情绪。*negative* ～ 负[阴]电。*positive* ～ 正[阳]电。*a machine run by* ～ 电动机器。

e·lec·tri·cize [iˈlektrisaiz; ɪˋlɛktrəˏsaɪz] *vt*. 充电。

e·lec·tri·fi·ca·tion [iˌlektrifiˈkeiʃən; ɪˏlɛktrəfəˋkeʃən] *n*. **1.** 起电;充电。**2.** 带电。**3.** 电气化。

e·lec·tri·fi·er [iˈlektrifaiə; ɪˋlɛktrəfaɪɚ] *n*.【电】起电器。

e·lec·tri·fy [iˈlektrifai; ɪˋlɛktrəˏfaɪ] *vt*. (*-fied*; *-fy·ing*) **1.** 使起电,使通电;使充电;使电气化。**2.** 使触电。**3.** 使震惊,使兴奋,使激动。*an electrified body* 带电体。～ *an audience* 使观众震动。

e·lec·trize [iˈlektraiz; ɪˋlɛktraɪz] *vt*. = electrify. **e·lec·tri·za·tion** [-ˈzeiʃən; -ˋzeʃən] *n*.

e·lec·tro [iˈlektrəu; ɪˋlɛktro] *n*. (*pl*. ～*s*)〔口〕= electroplate, electrotype.

e·lec·tro- [iˈlektrəu; ɪˋlɛktro] *comb. f*. 表示“电”,“电的”,“用电的”: *electro*analysis, *electro*form.

e·lec·tro·a·cous·tic, e·lec·tro·a·cous·ti·cal [iˈlektrəuəˈkuːstik, -əl; ɪˋlɛktroəˋkustɪk, -əl] *a*.【电】电声的;电声学的。*an* ～ *system* 电声系统。**-cal·ly** *ad*.

e·lec·tro·a·cous·tics [iˈlektrəuəˈkuːstiks; ɪˏlɛktroəˋkustɪks] *n*.〔作单数用〕电声学。

e·lec·tro·af·fin·i·ty [iˌlektrəuəˈfiniti; ɪˏlɛktroəˋfɪnətɪ] *n*.【化】电亲和势。

e·lec·tro·a·nal·y·sis [iˌlektrəuəˈnælisis; ɪˏlɛktroəˋnæləsɪs] *n*.【化】电解分析。**-lyt·i·cal** [-litikəl; -lɪtɪkəl] *a*.

e·lec·tro·bal·lis·tic [iˈlektrəubəlistik; ɪˋlɛktrobəlɪstɪk] *a*. 电弹道学的。**-cal·ly** *ad*.

e·lec·tro·bal·lis·tics [iˌlektrəubəˈlistiks; ɪˏlɛktrobəˋlɪstɪks] *n*.〔作单或复数用〕电子弹道学。

e·lec·tro·bath [iˈlektrəubɑːθ; ɪˋlɛktrəˏbɑθ] *n*.【化】电镀浴。

e·lec·tro·bi·ol·o·gy [iˌlektrəubaiˈɔlədʒi; ɪˏlɛktrobaɪˋɑlədʒɪ] *n*. 生物电学。

e·lec·tro·car·di·o·gram [iˌlektrəuˈkɑːdiəgræm; ɪˏlɛktroˋkɑrdɪəˏgræm] *n*.【医】心电图〔常略作 EKG, E.K.G., ECG〕。

e·lec·tro·car·di·o·graph [iˌlektrəuˈkɑːdiəgræf; ɪˏlɛktroˋkɑrdɪəˏgræf] *n*.【医】心电图描记器。

e·lec·tro·cau·ter·y [iˌlektrəuˈkɔːtəri; ɪˏlɛktroˋkɔtərɪ] *n*.【医】电烙术;电烙器。

e·lec·tro·chem·is·try [iˌlektrəuˈkemistri; ɪˏlɛktroˋkɛmɪstrɪ] *n*. 电化学。**-i·cal** *a*. **-i·cal·ly** *ad*.

e·lec·tro·con·vul·sive [iˈlektrəukənˈvʌlsiv; ɪˋlɛktrəkənˋvʌlsɪv] *a*. 导电痉挛的。～ **therapy** 导电痉挛疗法。

e·lec·tro·cul·ture [iˈlektrəuˌkʌltʃə; ɪˋlɛktroˏkʌltʃɚ] *n*. 用电刺激植物的生长。

e·lec·tro·cute [iˈlektrəukjuːt; ɪˋlɛktrəˏkjut] *vt*. **1.** 把…处电刑。**2.** 使触电致死。**e·lec·tro·cu·tion** *n*.

e·lec·trode [iˈlektrəud; ɪˋlɛktrod] *n*. **1.** 电极。**2.** 电焊条。*deflecting* ～【无】致偏电极。*focus(s)ing* ～【无】聚焦(电)极。*perforated* ～ 多孔电极。**-less** *a*. 无电极的。

e·lec·tro·de·pos·it [iˌlektrəudiˈpɔzit; ɪˏlɛktrodəˋpɑzɪt] **I** *n*. 电解沉积物。**II** *vt*. 电解沉积。

e·lec·tro·di·ag·no·sis [iˌlektrəuˌdaiəgˈnəusis; ɪˏlɛktroˏdaɪəgˋnosɪs] *n*. 电诊断(术)。

e·lec·tro·di·al·y·sis [iˌlektrəudaiˈælisis; ɪˏlɛktrodaɪˋæləsɪs] *n*. 【化】电渗析。**-a·lit·ic** [-əlitik; -əˋlɪtɪk] *a*.

e·lec·tro·dy·nam·ic [iˌlektrəudaiˈnæmik; ɪˏlɛktrodaɪˋnæmɪk] *a*. 电动力学的。**-s** [-ks; -ks] *n*. 电动力学。

e·lec·tro·dy·na·mom·e·ter [iˌlektrəuˌdainəˈnɔmətə; ɪˏlɛktroˏdaɪnəˋnɑmətɚ] *n*. 电动测功计,电功率计;力测电流计。

e·lec·tro·en·ceph·a·lo·gram [iˌlektrəuenˈsefələgræm; ɪˏlɛktroɛnˋsɛfələgræm] *n*. 【医】脑电图。

e·lec·tro·en·ceph·a·lo·graph [iˌlektrəuenˈsefələgræf; ɪˏlɛktroɛnˋsɛfələˏgræf] *n*. 脑电图描记器。**-ic** [-ik; -ɪk] *a*. **-y** [-i; -ɪ] *n*. 脑电图记录。

e·lec·tro·fax [iˌlektrəuˈfæks; ɪˏlɛktroˋfæks] *n*. 电子摄影。

e·lec·tro·form [iˈlektrəufɔːm; ɪˋlɛktrofɔrm] *vt*. 电铸。

e·lec·tro·funk [iˈlektrəufʌŋk; ɪˋlɛktrofʌŋk] *n*. (用电子乐器演奏的)电子(乡土)爵士乐。

e·lec·tro·gal·van·ize [iˌlektrəuˈgælvənaiz; ɪˏlɛktroˋgælvənaɪz] *vt*. 用锌电镀。

e·lec·tro·graph [iˈlektrəugrɑːf; ɪˋlɛktroˏgræf] *n*. **1.** 【讯】传真电报。**2.** 电刻器;电版机。**3.** 电图;X 光图像。**-ic** [-ik; -ɪk] *a*. 电图的,传真电报的。**-y** [-i; -ɪ] *n*. **1.** 电版术。**2.** 电版法传真。

e·lec·tro·ki·net·ics [iˌlektrəukiˈnetiks; ɪˏlɛktrokɪˋnɛtɪks] *n*. 电动学。

e·lec·tro·li·er [iˌlektrəuˈliə; ɪˏlɛktroˋlɪr] *n*. 枝形(吊式)电灯架。

e·lectro·lu·mi·nes·cence [iˌlektrəuˌluːməˈnesəns; ɪˋlɛktroˏluməˋnɛsəns] *n*. 【物】电致发光,场致发光。

e·lec·tro·lyse, e·lec·tro·lyze [iˈlektrəuˌlaiz; ɪˋlɛktrəˏlaɪz] *vt*. 电解。**-r** *n*. 电解池,电解槽;电解装置。

e·lec·trol·y·sis [ilekˈtrɔlisis; ɪˏlɛkˋtrɑləsɪs] *n*. **1.** 电解(作用),电蚀。**2.** 【医】用电针除去肿瘤、痣、毛发。

e·lec·tro·lyte [iˈlektrəulait; ɪˋlɛktrəˏlaɪt] *n*. 电解质,电离质,电解(溶)液。

e·lec·tro·lyt·ic [iˌlektrəuˈlitik; ɪˏlɛktrəˋlɪtɪk] *a*. 电解的;电解质的。～ **cell** 电解(电)池。～ **condenser** 电解容电器。～ **dissociation** 电离(作用)。～ **meter** 电解库仑计,电解库仑表。～ **rectifier** 电解(质)整流器。～ **refining** 电解法提纯,电解精练。

e·lec·tro·mag·net [iˈlektrəuˈmægnit; ɪˏlɛktroˋmægnɪt] *n*. 【物】电磁体,电磁铁。

e·lec·tro·mag·net·ic [iˈlektrəumægˈnetik; ɪˏlɛktromægˋnɛtɪk] *a*. 电磁的。～ **field** 电磁场。～ **spectrum** 电磁波频谱。～ **unit** 电磁单位。～ **wave** 电磁波。

e·lec·tro·mag·net·ics [iˈlektrəumægˈnetiks; ɪˏlɛktromægˋnɛtɪks] *n*. 〔作单数用〕电磁学。

e·lec·tro·mag·net·ism [iˈlektrəuˈmægnitizəm; ɪˏlɛktroˋmægnəˏtɪzəm] *n*. 电磁;电磁学。

e·lec·tro·mas·sage [iˌlektrəuˈmæsɑːdʒ; ɪˏlɛktroˋmæsɑdʒ] *n*. 【医】电推拿法,电按摩法。

e·lec·tro·me·chan·i·cal [iˌlektrəumiˈkænikəl; ɪˏlɛktroməˋkænɪkl] *a*. 电机的;电机学的。

e·lec·tro·me·chan·ics [iˌlektrəumiˈkæniks; ɪˏlɛktroməˋkænɪks] *n*. 〔作单数用〕电机学。

e·lec·tro·mer [iˈlektrəumə; ɪˋlɛktromɚ] *n*. 【物】电子异构体。

e·lec·trom·e·ter [ilekˈtrɔmitə; ɪˏlɛkˋtrɑmətɚ] *n*. 量电表,静电计。*a differential* [*quadrant*] ～ 差动[象限]静电计。

e·lec·tro·met·ric [iˈlektrəuˈmetrik; ɪˋlɛktrəˋmɛtrɪk] *a*. 电测(量)的。～ **titration** 【化】电势滴定。**-al** *a*. **-ally** *ad*.

e·lec·trom·e·try [ilekˈtrɔmitri; ɪˏlɛkˋtrɑmətrɪ] *n*. 电测,量电法,测电术。

e·lec·tro·mo·tive [iˈlektrəuməutiv; ɪˏlɛktrəˋmotɪv] *a*. 电动的。～ **force** 电动势。～ **series** 电动序。

e·lec·tro·mo·tor [iˌlektrəuˈməutə; ɪˏlɛktrəˋmotɚ] *n*. 电动机。

e·lec·tron [iˈlektrɔn; ɪˋlɛktrɑn] *n*. 【物】电子。*the* ～ *beam* 电子束。*the* ～ *theory* 电子(学)说。～ **accelerator** 电子加速器。～ **bomb** 镁壳燃烧弹。～ **camera** 电子摄影机。～ **gun** 电子枪。～ **lens** 电子透镜。～ **metal** (比铝轻的)镁合金。～ **microscope** 电子显微镜。～ **multiplier** 电子倍增器。～ **optics** 电子光学。～ **telescope** 电子望远镜。～ **tube** 电子管。～**-volt** *n*. 【物】电子伏(特)。

e·lec·tron·a·tion [iˌlektrəuˈneiʃən; ɪˏlɛktrəˋneʃən] *n*. 【化】增电子(作用)。

e·lec·tro·neg·a·tive [iˌlektrəuˈnegətiv; ɪˌlɛktrəˋnɛgətɪv] *a*. 【物】负电性的,阴电性的。

e·lec·tron·ic [ilekˈtrɔnik; ɪˏlɛkˋtrɑnɪk] *a*. 电子的,电子操纵的;用电子设备生产的;用电子设备完成的。～ **analog(ue) computer** 电子模拟计算机。～ **brain** [**calculator, computer**] 电脑[电子计算机]。～ **bulletin board** 电子公告板。～ **charge** 电(子)荷。～ **commerce** 电子商务〔在电脑上进行〕。～ **control** 电子控制。～**-controlled** *a*. 电子控制的。～ **data processing** 电子数据处理。～ **digital computer** 电子数字计算机。～ **discrete variable automatic computer** 电子数据计算机。～ **engineering** 电子工程学。～ (**super**) **highway** (由电脑联网传送信息的)电子(高速)公路。～ **image storage device** 电子录像设备。～ **intelligence** 〔美〕电子情报。～ **lash** 电子脚链〔监视犯人或假释犯的一种电子摇控装置〕。～ **mail** 电子邮件(＝E-mail)。～ **mail box** 电子(邮件)信箱〔电脑内用户使用的网址〕。～ **media** 电子舆论媒体〔指广播、电视〕。～ **music** 电子音乐。～ **numerical integrator and computer** 【美军】电子数字积分计算机。～ **organ** 电子琴。～ **smog** 电波烟雾(非离子放射污染)。～ **video recorder** 电子录像器。**-cal·ly** *ad*.

e·lec·tron·ics [ilekˈtrɔniks; ɪˏlɛkˋtrɑnɪks] *n*. **1.** 〔用作单数〕电子学。*molecular* ～ 分子电子学。**2.** 电子流行音乐。

e·lec·tro·os·mo·sis [ilektrəuɔzˈməusis; ɪˏlɛktroɑzˋmosɪs] *n*. 【物】电渗透。

e·lec·trop·a·thy [ilekˈtrɔpəθi; ɪˏlɛkˋtrɑpəθɪ] *n*. 【医】电疗学,电疗法。

e·lec·tro·phone [iˈlektrəufəun; ɪˋlɛktrəˏfon] *n*. 送话器。**-nic** [-nik; -nɪk] *a*. 电响的。

e·lec·tro·pho·re·sis [iˌlektrəufəˈriːsis; ɪˏlɛktrofəˋrɪsɪs] *n*. 电泳(法)。

e·lec·troph·o·rus [ilekˈtrɔfərəs; ɪˏlɛkˋtrɑfərəs] *n*. (*pl*. **-ri** [-rai; -ˏraɪ]) 【物】起电盘。

e·lec·tro·phys·i·ol·o·gy [ɪˌlektrəufiziˈɔlədʒi; ɪˏlɛktroˏfɪzɪˋɑlədʒɪ] *n*. 电生理学。

e·lec·tro·plate [iˈlektrəuˈpleit; ɪˋlɛktrəˏplet] **I** *vt*. 电镀。**II** *n*. **1.** 电镀物品;镀银餐具。**2.** 【印】电铸版。**-ting** [-tiŋ; -tɪŋ] *n*. 电镀术。

e·lec·tro·po·lar [iˌlektrəuˈpəulə; ɪˏlɛktrəˋpolɚ] *a*. 电极性的;电极化的。

e·lec·tro·pol·ish [iˈlektrəuˌpɔliʃ; ɪˋlɛktroˏpɑlɪʃ] *vt*. 电气抛光。

e·lec·tro·pos·i·tive [iˌlektrəuˈpɔzitiv; ɪˏlɛktrəˋpɑzətɪv] *a*. (*opp*. electronegative) **1.** 【物】正电性的,阳电性的。**2.** 【物】盐基性的,金属的。

e·lec·tro·re·fin·ing [iˌlektrəuriˈfainiŋ; ɪˏlɛktrorɪˋfaɪnɪŋ] *n*. 电解提纯;电精炼。

e·lec·tro·psy·chrom·e·ter [iˌlektrəusaiˈkrɔmitə; ɪˏlɛktrosaɪˋkrɑmɪtɚ] *n*. 电测湿度计。

e·lec·tro·scope [iˈlektrəuskəup; ɪˋlɛktrəˏskop] *n*.

【物】验电器。

e·lec·tro·sen·si·tive [iˌlektrəuˈsensitiv; ɪˏlɛktro-ˋsɛnsətɪv] *a*. 电敏感的。

e·lec·tro·shock [iˈlektrəuʃɔk; ɪˋlɛktrəˏʃɑk] *n*. 1. 电休克。2.【医】电震疗法,电休克疗法〔治疗精神病〕(= electrotherapy)。

e·lec·tro·sol [iˈlektrəusɔl; ɪˋlɛktrəˏsɑl] *n*.【化】电溶胶。

e·lec·tro·spin·o·gram [iˌlektrəuˈspainəgræm; ɪˏlɛktrə-ˋspaɪnəgræm] *n*.【医】脊髓电(流)图。

e·lec·tro·stat·ic(al) [iˈlektrəuˈstætik(əl); ɪˏlɛktrə-ˋstætɪk(l)] *a*. 静电的,静电学的。~ **generator** 感应起电机,静电发电机。~ **printing** 静电印刷,静电复印。~ **unit** 静电单位。**-cal·ly** *ad*.

e·lec·tro·stat·ics [iˈlektrəuˈstætiks; ɪˏlɛktrəˋstætɪks] *n*.〔用作单数〕静电学。

e·lec·tro·stric·tion [iˌlektrəuˈstrikʃən; ɪˏlɛktroˋstrɪkʃən] *n*.【物】电致收缩。

e·lec·tro·sur·ger·y [iˌlektrəuˈsəːdʒəri; ɪˏlɛktro-ˋsɝdʒərɪ] *n*.【医】外科透热法。

e·lec·tro·tech·nics [iˌlektrəuˈtekniks; ɪˏlɛktrəˋtɛknɪks] *n*.〔用作单数〕电工技术;电工学。

e·lec·tro·ther·a·py [iˌlektrəuˈθerəpi; ɪˏlɛktroˋθɛrəpɪ] *n*.【医】电疗法。

e·lec·tro·ther·mal, e·lec·tro·ther·mic [iˌlektrəu-ˈθəːməl, -mik; ɪˏlɛktroˋθɝməl, -mɪk] *a*. 电热的。

e·lec·tro·ther·mics [iˌlektrəuˈθəːmiks; ɪˏlɛktroˋθɝmɪks] *n*. 电热学。

e·lec·tro·tim·er [iˈlektrəuˈtaimə; ɪˋlɛktroˋtaɪmɚ] *n*. 定时继电器。

e·lec·trot·o·nus [ilekˈtrɔtənəs; ɪˏlɛkˋtrɑtənəs] *n*.【医】电紧张。

e·lec·tro·type [iˈlektrəutaip; ɪˋlɛktrəˏtaɪp] I *n*.【印】1. 电版;电铸版。2. 电铸术。3. 电版印刷物。II *vt*. 把…制成电版。—*vi*. 制电版。**-r** *n*. 电版技工。

e·lec·tro·va·lence [iˌlektrəuˈveiləns; ɪˋlɛktroˋveləns] *n*. 电价。

e·lec·tro·win·ning [iˌlektrəuˈwiniŋ; ɪˏlɛktroˋwɪnɪŋ] *n*.【冶】电解冶金法。

e·lec·trum [iˈlektrəm; ɪˋlɛktrəm] *n*. 1. 金银合金;镍银。2.【矿】银金矿。

e·lec·tu·a·ry [iˈlektjuəri; ɪˋlɛktʃʊˏɛrɪ] *n*.【药】干药糖剂。

el·ee·mos·y·nar·y [ˌeliiːˈmɔsinəri; ˏɛləˋmɑsnˏɛrɪ] I *a*. 1. 慈善的,施舍的。2. 受救济的;免费的。*an* ~ *corporation* 慈善团体。II *n*. 受救济的人。

el·e·gance [ˈeligəns; ˋɛləgəns] **-gan·cy** [-si; -sɪ] *n*. 1. 雅致,风雅,优美,高尚。2.〔主 *-cies*〕雅事,优雅的言谈[举动]。

el·e·gant [ˈeligənt; ˋɛləgənt] *a*. 优雅的,雅致的;优美的,高尚的;讲究的;〔口〕极好的,漂亮的,一流的。~ *arts* 高尚的艺术。*an* ~ *vase* 别致的花瓶。*an* ~ *writer* 格调高的作家。**-ly** *ad*.

el·e·gi·ac [ˌeliˈdʒaiək; ˏɛləˋdʒaɪæk], **el·e·gi·a·cal** [ˌeləˈdʒaiəkəl; ˏɛləˋdʒaɪəkl] I *a*. 1.〔希、罗诗〕挽歌的,哀歌的;挽(哀)歌体的。2. 挽(哀)歌式的。3. 悲哀的;哀怨的,忧伤的。II *n*. 1. 挽歌对句。2.〔*pl*.〕一连串的对句;排律诗。

el·e·gise [ˈelidʒaiz; ˋɛlɪdʒaɪz] *v*. = elegize.

el·e·gist [ˈelidʒist; ˋɛlɪdʒɪst] *n*. 挽歌作者。

e·le·git [iˈliːdʒit; ɪˋlidʒɪt] *n*.【法】(授权原告占有被告的财产直至债务还清的)扣押令。

el·e·gize [ˈelidʒaiz; ˋɛləˏdʒaɪz] *vt*. 作挽歌哀悼。—*vi*. 写哀歌 (*upon*)。

el·e·gy [ˈelidʒi; ˋɛlədʒɪ] *n*. 哀歌,挽歌。

e·lek·tron [iˈlektrɔn; ɪˋlɛktrɑn] *n*. = electron.

elem. = element; elementary; elements.

el·e·ment [ˈelimənt; ˋɛləmənt] *n*. 1. 要素;成分;(构成)部分;分子。2.【化】元素;【数】元,素;【机】单元;单体;【无】元件;【植】原种。3.【电】电池;电极;电阻丝。4. 生存环境,活动范围;本行,本领。5.〔*pl*.〕原理;初步;大纲。6.〔*pl*.〕自然力;暴风雨。7.【军】小队,分队。8.〔*pl*.〕【宗】(圣餐用)面包和葡萄酒。*the four* ~*s* (古希腊哲学家认为组成世界的地、水、火、风)四元素。*discontented* ~*s* 不平分子。*daughter* ~【物】子元素。*control* ~ 控制元件。*the* ~*s of grammer* 语法基础。***in one's*** ~ 在自己(活动)天地内,如鱼得水。***out of one's*** ~ 在自己活动天地外,不得其所,格格不入。***strife*** [***war***] ***of the*** ~***s*** 暴风雨。

el·e·men·tal [ˌeliˈmentl; ˏɛləˋmɛntl] I *a*. 1. 基本的,本质的;原理的;初步的。2.【化】元素的。3. 自然力的。4. 强大的,可怕的。~ *forces*〔古〕自然力。~ *studies* 初步研究。~ *strength* 威力。II *n*. 1. (古希腊)四元素的精灵。2.〔*pl*.〕基本原理。**-ism** *n*. 自然力崇拜。**-ly** *ad*.

el·e·men·ta·ry [ˌeliˈmentəri; ˏɛləˋmɛntərɪ] *a*. 1. 初步的,初等的;基本的,根本的,本质的。2. 自然力的。3. 单元的,单体的。4.【化】元素的。~ *arithmetic* 初等算术。~ *education* 初等教育。~ *knowledge* 基本知识。*an* ~ *school* 小学校。~ **particle**【物】基本粒子,元粒子。~ **species**【生】原种。~ **substances** 元素。**-ri·ly** [-rili; -rɪlɪ] *ad*. **-ri·ness** *n*.

el·e·mi [ˈelimi; ˋɛlɪmɪ] *n*.【化】橄榄树脂,榄香(脂)。

e·len·chus [iˈleŋkəs; ɪˋlɛŋkəs] (*pl*. **-chi** [-kai; -kaɪ]) *n*.【逻】反驳论证。*the Socratic* ~ 苏格拉底的问答法。

e·lenc·tic [iˈleŋktik; ɪˋlɛŋktɪk] *a*. 反驳论证的。

el·e·op·tene [ˌeliˈɔptiːn; ˏɛlɪˋɑptin] *n*.【化】油萜。

el·e·phant [ˈelifənt; ˋɛləfənt] *n*. 1. 象。2. 象牌图画纸〔28×23 英寸〕。***a white*** ~ 1. (泰国、印度视作神物的)白象。2. 累赘的珍品,沉重的包袱。***double*** ~ 倍大画图纸〔40×26½英寸〕。~ ***dugout***【军】大壕沟,大防空洞。***see the*** ~〔美俚〕开眼界,见世面。~**'s-ear**【植】1. 秋海棠。2. 天南星科芋属 (*colocasia*) 植物〔尤指野芋 (*colocasia antiquorum*)〕。~**'s-foot** *n*.【植】蒟蒻。~**'s trunk**〔主英、俚〕醉。

el·e·phan·ti·a·sis [ˌelifənˈtaiəsis; ˏɛləfənˋtaɪəsɪs] *n*.【医】象皮病。

el·e·phan·tine [ˌeliˈfæntain; ˏɛləˋfæntaɪn] *a*. 象(一样)的;巨大的;笨重的,粗笨的,累赘的。~ *humour* 笨拙的幽默。~ *movements* 迟钝的行动。~ *task* 累赘的任务。

el·eu·ther·o·ma·nia [iˌljuːθərəuˈmeiniə; ɪˏljuθərə-ˋmenɪə] *n*. 自由狂。

elev. = elevation.

el·e·vate [ˈeliveit; ˋɛləˏvet] *vt*. 1. 举起,抬高(声音、炮口等)。2. 提升,提拔。3. 鼓舞,振起;使(意气)激昂;使(思想等)向上[高尚]。*an elevating gear* (炮)俯仰装置。*an elevating plane* [*rudder*] 升降翼[舵]。*elevating thoughts* 高尚思想。

el·e·vat·ed [ˈeliveitid; ˋɛləˏvetɪd] I *a*. 1. 高的,升高的,提高的。2. 高尚的,严肃的。3. 欢欣的,振奋的。4.〔口〕有点醉的。II *n*.〔美口〕= ~ railroad. ~ **railroad**〔美〕高架铁路。~ **train**〔美〕高架(铁路)列车。

el·e·va·tion [ˌeliˈveiʃən; ˏɛləˋveʃən] *n*. 1. 高举,高升;【医】挺起,隆肿。2. 升级;上进,向上。3. 高尚。4. 高处,高地,高度;海拔;(枪炮的)仰角,射角;【测】标高。5.【建】正视图;立视图。

el·e·va·tor [ˈeliveitə; ˋɛləˏvetɚ] *n*. 1. 起重工人。2.〔美〕电梯,升降机 (=〔英〕lift);(飞机的)升降舵;(建筑施工的)起卸机;【医】起子,牙挺。3.〔美〕(备有起卸机的)谷仓。4.【解】提肌。*a belt* ~【讯】升降带。*a pneumatic* ~ 气压升降机。~ **operator** [**man, boy, girl**] 开电梯的人。~ **shaft** 电梯井。

el·e·va·to·ry [ˈeliveitəri; ˋɛlɪˏvetərɪ] *a*. 举起的。

e·lev·en [iˈlevən; ɪˋlɛvən] I *num*. 1. 十一,十一个。2. 第十一。II *n*. 1. 十一;十一个(人、东西)。2. 十一的记号。3. (足球、板球或曲棍球)球队。***be in the*** ~ 是球队

E

的队员。**the E-**【宗】耶稣的十一使徒〔犹大除外〕。**~-plus** *n*. 初中入学前预试〔英国私立学校对 11—12 岁学生升入初中前的预试,以决定其未来教育是否应为文科或理科〕。**~fold** *a*., *ad*. 十一倍的[地]。

e·lev·ens(es) [iˈlevnz(iz); ɪˋlɛvn̩z(ɪz)] *n*. 〔英口〕(午餐前吃的)茶点。

e·lev·enth [iˈlevənθ; ɪˋlɛvənθ] **I** *num*. **1.** 第十一。**2.** 十一分之一的。**II** *n*. **1.** 第十一。**2.** 十一分之一。**3.** (每月的)第十一日。*at the ~ hour* 在最后五分钟,刚好来得及,在危急的时候。**-ly** *ad*.

el·e·von [ˈelivɔn; ˋɛləvɑn] *n*. 【空】升降副翼。

ELF, elf = extremely low frequency 【无】极低频。

elf [elf; ɛlf] *n*. (*pl*. *elves*) **1.** 小精灵,小妖精。**2.** 矮子,小东西。**3.** 淘气鬼,小顽皮。**4.** 小兽,小虫。**5.** 小人,恶人。~ **bolt** 石镞。~**-fire** 鬼火。~ **land** 妖窟,魔境。~ **lock** 乱草蓬式的头发。~**-struck** *a*. 着迷的。**-like** *a*. 顽皮的,淘气的。

elf·in [ˈelfin; ˋɛlfɪn] **I** *a*. 小精灵的;小精灵一样的。**II** *n*. = elf.

elf·ish [ˈelfiʃ; ˋɛlfɪʃ] *a*. 小精灵一样的;顽皮的,淘气的,恶作剧的。**-ly** *ad*. **-ness** *n*.

El·gar [ˈelgə; ˋɛlgɚ] *n*. 埃尔加〔姓氏〕。

el·hi [ˈelhai; ˋɛlhaɪ] *a*. 〔美口〕中小学的,从一年级到十二年级的。

E·li·as [iˈlaiəs; ɪˋlaɪəs] *n*. 埃利阿斯〔男子名,爱称 Eliot〕。

e·lic·it [iˈlisit; ɪˋlɪsɪt] *vt*. 引出,探出(事实等);诱出(回答等)。~ *information by inquiring* 打听出,问出。~ *a laugh from somebody* 逗人发笑。~ *a reply* 诱使别人回答。

e·lic·it·a·tion [iˌlisiˈteiʃən; ɪˏlɪsəˋteʃən] *n*. 引出,导出,启发。*method of ~* 启发式。

e·lide [iˈlaid; ɪˋlaɪd] *vt*. **1.** 削减,删节;不考虑。**2.**【语音】省略(母音等)。**3.**【法】取消。

el·i·gi·ble [ˈelidʒəbl; ˋɛlɪdʒəbl̩] **I** *a*. **1.** 有被选举资格的。**2.** 适任的,合格的,适当的。**3.** 〔俚〕适龄的,年龄适当的。~ *for* [*to*] *membership* 可以作会员。**II** *n*. 合适的人。**el·i·gi·bil·i·ty** [ˌelidʒəˈbiliti; ˏɛlɪdʒəˋbɪlətɪ] *n*. **-bly** *ad*.

e·lim·i·na·ble [iˈliminəbl; ɪˋlɪmənəbl̩] *a*. **1.** 可消除的,可排除的。**2.**【数】可消去的。

e·lim·i·nant [iˈliminənt; ɪˋlɪmənənt] *n*. 【数】消元式,(消)结式。

e·lim·i·nate [iˈlimineit; ɪˋlɪməˏnet] *vi*. **1.** 除去,消灭,逐出,淘汰,排出 (*from*)。**2.**【数】消去。~ *errors of misprint* 消灭印刷错误。*wastes ~d from the body* 体内排出的废物。**e·limi·na·tion** *n*. 除去,消除,淘汰,排除(作用);【化】弃置;【数】消去,消元法 (~ *matches*【体】预赛,淘汰赛。*waste ~* 消灭浪费)。**e·lim·i·na·tor** 排除者;【电】消除器;【无】电源整流器 (*a battery ~* 代电池)。

e·lim·i·na·tive [iˈlimineitiv; ɪˋlɪmənetɪv] *a*. **1.** 抽出的,排出的,消除的。**2.** 不加考虑的;不受理的;略去的。**3.** (比赛)淘汰的。**4.**【数】消去的,相消的。**5.**【生理】排泄的 (= eliminatory)。

El·i·nor [ˈelinə; ˋɛlənɚ] *n*. 埃莉诺〔女子名〕。

ELINT, elint [ˈelint; ˋɛlənt] = electronic intelligence 〔美〕电子情报。*an ~ ship* 电子情报舰。

el·in·var [ˈelinvɑː; ˋɛlənvɑr] *n*. 【冶】镍铬恒性钢。

El·i·ot [ˈeljət; ˋɛljət] *n*. **1.** 艾略特〔姓氏〕。**2. George ~** 乔治·艾略特〔1819—1880,英国女作家〕。**3. Thomas Stearns ~** T.S. 艾略特〔1888—1965,美国出生的英国诗人、评论家〕。

E·lis·a·beth [iˈlizəbəθ; ɪˋlɪzəbəθ] *n*. 伊丽莎白〔女子名,Elizabeth〕。

E·lise [eˈliːz; ɛˋliz] *n*. 埃莉斯〔女子名, Elizabeth 的异体,= Elyse〕。

e·li·sion [iˈliʒən; ɪˋlɪʒən] *n*. 【语音】(母音、音节的)省略。

é·lite [eiˈliːt; eˋlit] *n*. 〔F.〕**1.** 〔集合词,作复数用〕精华;杰出人物,优秀分子,高贵的。**2.** 精锐部队。**3.** 一种打字机字母尺寸。*the ~ of society* 社会名流。***corp d'*** ~ [ˈkɔːdeiˈliːt; ˋkɔrdeˋlit] 精锐部队。

e·lit·ism [eiˈliːtizm, iˈliːtizm; eˋlitɪzm, ɪˋlitɪzm̩] **I** *n*. **1.** 杰出人物统治论;对杰出人物统治论的鼓吹。**2.** 高人一等的优越感。**e·lit·ist** *n*. **1.** 杰出人物中的一个。**2.** 杰出人物统治论的鼓吹者。**II** *a*. 具有高人一等优越感的。

e·lix·ir [iˈliksə; ɪˋlɪksɚ] *n*. **1.**【药】酏剂,甘香酒剂。**2.** 炼金药,长生不老药,灵丹妙药。~ ***vitae*** [ˈvaitiː; ˋvaɪtɪ] 长生不老药,仙丹 (= ~ *of life*)。

Eliz. = Elizabeth; Elizabethan.

E·liz·a·beth [iˈlizəbəθ; ɪˋlɪzəbəθ] *n*. 伊丽莎白〔女子名〕。

E·liz·a·be·than [iˌlizəˈbiːθən; ɪˏlɪzəˋbiθən] **I** *a*. 英国伊丽莎白女王的;伊丽莎白女王时代的。~ *sonnet* = Shakespearian sonnet. **II** *n*. 伊丽莎白一世时代的人〔尤指诗人,剧作家,政治家等〕。

elk [elk; ɛlk] *n*. (*pl*. ~**s**,〔集合词〕~) **1.**【动】麋,大角鹿 (=〔美〕moose;〔加拿大、北美〕wapiti)。**2.** 软鞣粗皮。~**hound** = Norwegian elkhound.

ell, el [el; ɛl] *n*. **1.** L 字母;L 状物;〔美〕(与正房成 L 形的)侧房。**2.** 古尺名〔英 = 45 英寸;Scot. = 37 英寸〕。***Give him an inch and he'll take an ~.*** 〔谚〕得寸进尺。

El·la [ˈelə; ˋɛlə] *n*. 埃拉〔女子名, Eleanor 的爱称〕。

El·len [ˈelin; ˋɛlɪn] *n*. 埃伦〔女子名, Helen 的异体〕。

El·lick [ˈelik; ˋɛlɪk] *n*. 埃利克〔男子名, Alexander 的爱称〕。

el·lipse [iˈlips; ɪˋlɪps] *n*. **1.**【数】椭圆,椭圆形。**2.** = ellipsis.

el·lip·sis [iˈlipsis; ɪˋlɪpsɪs] *n*. (*pl*. **-ses** [-siːz; -siz]) **1.**【语法】省略法。**2.**【印】省略符号〔—, …, * * * 等〕。

el·lip·so·graph [iˈlipsəgrɑːf; ɪˋlɪpsəˏgræf] *n*. 【数】椭圆规。

el·lip·soid [iˈlipsɔid; ɪˋlɪpsɔɪd] *n*. 【数】椭圆;椭(圆)球。~ *of stress* 应力椭(圆)面。

el·lip·tic [iˈliptik; ɪˋlɪptɪk] *a*. **1.** 椭圆(形)的。**2.** 省略法的;有省略处的。**-ti·cal·ly** *ad*.

el·lip·tic·i·ty [ˌelipˈtisiti; ɪˏlɪpˋtɪsətɪ] *n*. 【数】椭圆状;椭圆率。

El·lis [ˈelis; ˋɛlɪs] *n*. 埃利斯〔姓氏,男子名〕。

El·li·son [ˈelisn; ˋɛlɪsn] *n*. 埃利森〔姓氏〕。

Ells·worth [ˈelzwəːθ; ˋɛlzwɚθ] *n*. 埃尔斯沃斯〔姓氏,男子名〕。

elm [elm; ɛlm] *n*. 【植】榆,榆木。**-y** *a*. 多榆树的 (~ *bark beetle*【动】荷兰榆皮岬 (*Scolytus multistriat-us*))。

El·mer [ˈelmə; ˋɛlmɚ] *n*. 埃尔默〔男子名〕。

El Niño [elˈniːnjəu; ɛlˋninjo] *n*. 【气】"厄尔尼诺"现象。

el·o·cute [ˈeləkjuːt; ˋɛləkjut] *v*., *n*. 〔美〕演说。

el·o·cu·tion [ˌeləˈkjuːʃən; ˏɛləˋkjuʃən] *n*. **1.** 雄辩术,演说术。**2.** 朗诵法;发声法。*theatrical ~* 舞台发声法。**-ar·y** *a*. 演说上的;朗诵上的;发声上的。**-ist** *n*. 雄辩家,演说家,朗诵者;演说术[发声法]教师。

e·lo·de·a [iˈləudiə; ɪˋlodɪə] *n*. 水蕴草〔伊乐藻〕属 (*Elodea*) 植物。

é·loge [F. elɔːʒ; ɛˋloʒ] *n*. 〔F.〕悼词〔尤指新任法兰西科学院院士对已逝世的前任院士的悼念演说〕。

E·lo·him [eˈləuhim; ɛˋlohɪm] *n*. (希伯来圣经中所说的)神,上帝。

E·lo·hist [eˈləuhist; ɛˋlohɪst] *n*. 称"上帝"为"艾洛辛"的经典作者〔希伯来圣经某些篇章的作者,不称"上帝"为"耶和华",而称"艾洛辛"〕。**El·o·his·tic** [-tik; -tɪk] *a*.

e·loign, e·loin [iˈlɔin; ɪˋlɔɪn] **I** *vt*. **1.** 〔古〕(~ oneself) 使走掉;退隐。**2.** 带走(财产)。**3.**【法】将(私有财产)转移至管辖区域之外。**II** *n*. 【法】发还抵债物品。**-ment,**

-in·ment *n*.

E. long. = east longitude 东经。

e·lon·gate [ˈiːlɔŋgeit; ɪˋlɔŋget] **I** *vt*., *vi*. 拉长,(使)伸长;(使)延长。**II** *a*. 延长的;细长的。*an* ~ *leaf* 细长的树叶。**e·lon·ga·tion** [ˌiːlɔŋˈgeiʃən; ɪˏlɔŋˋgeʃən] *n*. **1.** 延长,伸长;延长线;伸张度。**2.**【天】距角。

e·lope [iˈləup; ɪˋlop] *vi*. **1.** (女人)私奔 (*with*)。**2.** 逃亡;出走。**-ment** *n*.

el·o·quence [ˈeləkwəns; ˋɛləkwəns] *n*. **1.** 雄辩;口才,辩才。**2.** 雄辩术;修辞法。*fiery* ~ 激烈的辩论。*a flow of* ~ 滔滔不绝的雄辩。***Facts speak louder than*** ~。事实胜于雄辩。

el·o·quent [ˈeləkwənt; ˋɛləkwənt] *a*. **1.** 雄辩的,善辩的,有口才的,有说明力的。**2.** 动人的,富于表情的,眉飞色舞的,意味深长的。**-ly** *ad*.

El·phin·stone [ˈelfinstən; ˋɛlfɪnstən] *n*. 埃尔芬斯通〔姓氏〕。

El Sal·va·dor [elˈsælvədɔː; ɛlˋsælvəˏdɔr] *n*. 萨尔瓦多〔拉丁美洲〕。

else [els; ɛls] **I** *a*. 〔常用于疑问代词和不定代词后,起形容词作用,意为 other〕另外的,别的,此外的,其他的。***What*** ~? 还有呢? *sb*. ~ 另外一个人。*sb*. ~*'s hat* 另外一个人的帽子。*Who* ~*'s*? = *Whose* ~? 另外什么人的呢? *What* ~ *do you want*? 你还要什么别的吗? *Who* ~ *is coming*? 还有谁来? *Nobody* ~ *knew*. 另外没有人知道。*What* ~ *shall I say*? 我还有什么可说呢? *What* ~ *can it be*? 不然是什么呢? ***nothing*** ~ ***than*** 仅有,只是 (*It is nothing* ~ *than a hat*. 这不过是一顶帽子罢了)。★不可说 any book else, any city else 等。**II** *ad*. 〔常用在疑问副词后〕另外,其他(时间、地方、方式)。*When* ~ *will you come again*? 你们什么时候还会来呢? *Where* ~ *might I find this book*? 别的什么地方我能找到这本书呢? *I went to the library and nowhere* ~. 我到图书馆去了,其他什么地方也没去。*How* ~ *can you hope to win*? 用其他方法[不这样]你怎么能够希望胜利呢? ***or*** ~ 〔前面加连词 or,构成复合连词,但 or 有时常被略去〕。**1.** 否则,要不然 (*Make haste*, (*or*) ~ *you will be late*. 赶快,要不然就晚了)。**2.** 〔威胁一定照办,否则…〕不然的话,哼! 否则给你个厉害看看 (*Do what I say*, *or* ~. 一定照我说的办,否则给你个颜色看看!)!

else·where [ˈelsˈhweə; ˋɛlsˏhwɛr] *ad*. 在别处,往别处,在另外一处。*You will have to look* ~ *for an answer*. 你一定要到别处去寻求答案。

El·sie [ˈelsi; ˋɛlsɪ] *n*. 埃尔西〔女子名, Elizabeth 的爱称〕。

ELSS = extravehicular life support system (宇航员的)舱外生命维持系统。

El·ton [ˈeltən; ˋɛltən] *n*. 埃尔顿〔男子名〕。

el·u·ate [ˈeljuit, ˈeljuwit, -ˌweit; ˋɛljuɪt, ˋɛljuwɪt, -ˏwet] *n*. 【化】洗出液。

e·lu·ci·date [iˈljuːsideit; ɪˋljusəˏdet] *vt*. 阐明,说明,解释。**-a·tion** [-ˈdeiʃən; -ˋdeʃən] *n*. **-tive, -to·ry** *a*. **-tor** *n*. 阐明者,解释者。

e·lu·cu·bra·tion [iˌluːkəˈbreiʃən; ɪˏlukəˋbreʃən] *n*. **1.** 刻苦钻研;苦思冥想。**2.** 苦心孤诣之作,苦心的著作。**3.** 〔常作 *pl*.〕〔谑〕学究气的作品。

e·lude [iˈljuːd; ɪˋljud] *vt*. **1.** 闪避,躲避(危险等);逃避(追捕等);避免。**2.** 难倒,使不懂。~ *sb.'s grasp* 逃脱,没有被人逮住。~ *the law* 规避法律。*The meaning* ~*s me*. 那个意义我摸不透。

El·ul [ˈelul; ˋɛlʊl] *n*. (犹太历)十二月。

e·lu·sion [iˈljuːʒən; ɪˋljuʒən] *n*. **1.** 逃避,回避。**2.** 搪塞,遁辞。

e·lu·sive [iˈljuːsiv; ɪˋljusɪv] *a*. **1.** 闪避的,逃避的。**2.** 无从捉摸的,油滑的;容易忘记的。**-ly** *ad*. **-ness** *n*.

e·lu·so·ry [iˈljuːsəri; ɪˋljusərɪ] *a*. 难以捉摸的,容易逃逸的。

e·lute [iˈljuːt; ɪˋljut] *vt*. 【化】洗提。**e·lu·tion** *n*.

e·lu·tri·a·te [iˈljuːtrieit; ɪˋljutrɪˏet] *vt*. 【矿】淘洗,淘析,淘选。**e·lu·tri·a·tion** [iˌljuːtriˈeiʃən; ɪˏljutrɪˋeʃən] *n*.

e·lu·vi·al [iˈljuːviəl; ɪˋljuvɪəl] *a*. 【地】残积的,淋滤的。

e·lu·vi·ate [iˈljuːvieit; ɪˋljuvɪet] *vi*. 【地】淋滤。

e·lu·vi·a·tion [iˌljuːviˈeiʃən; ɪˏljuvɪˋeʃən] *n*. 淋滤(作用)。

e·lu·vi·um [iˈljuːviəm; ɪˋljuvɪəm] *n*. 【地】残积层。

el·van [ˈelvən; ˋɛlvən] *n*. 【矿】淡英斑岩。

el·ver [ˈelvə; ˋɛlvɚ] *n*. 小鳗鱼。

elves [elvz; ɛlvz] elf 的复数。

elv·ish [ˈelviʃ; ˋɛlvɪʃ] *a*. = elfish.

El·y·ot [ˈeljət; ˋɛljət] *n*. 埃利奥特〔男子名〕。

É·ly·sée [ˌeiliːˈzei; eliˋze] *n*. 〔F.〕爱丽舍宫〔法国总统府〕。

E·ly·si·an [iˈliziən; ɪˋlɪʒən] *a*. 【希神】福地的;极乐的,天堂的,幸福的。~ ***Fields*** = Elysium. ~ ***joy*** 无上的快乐。

E·ly·si·um [iˈliziəm; ɪˋlɪʒɪəm] *n*. 【希神】福地;理想的乐土。

el·y·troid [ˈelitrɔid; ˋɛlɪtrɔɪd] *a*. 【生】似翅鞘的。

el·y·tron [ˈelitrɔn; ˋɛlɪˏtrɑn], **el·y·trum** [ˈelitrəm; ˋɛlɪˏtrəm] *n*. (*pl*. **-tra** [-trə; -trə]) 【动】鞘翅;膜质鳞,背鳞。

El·ze·vir [ˈelziviə; ˋɛlzəˏvɪr] **I** *n*. **1.** 埃利居维〔荷兰古籍印刷出版家,1592—1680〕。**2.** 埃利居维版本[铅字]。**II** *a*. 埃利居维版的。

em[1] [em; ɛm] *n*. **1.** 字母 M, m. **2.** 【印】全身〔12 点的字母 m〕。**3.** 欧美文字排版的字行长度单位。

em[2], **'em** [əm; əm] *pro*. 〔*pl*.〕〔口〕= them.

EM = **1.** electron microscope 电子显微镜。**2.** enlisted man [men]〔美〕士兵。

Em. = 【化】emanation; Emily; Emma; Emmanuel.

em- *pref*. **1.** 〔用于 b, m, p 前〕= en-[1]. **2.** 〔用于 b, m, p, ph 前〕= en-[2].

EMA = Electronic Missile Acquisition 导弹电子搜索系统。

e·ma·ci·ate [iˈmeiʃieit; ɪˋmeʃɪˏet] *vt*. **1.** 使憔悴,使衰弱,使消瘦。**2.** 减少,减弱(内容,效果,魅力等)。—*vi*. 消瘦,衰弱。**-d** *a*. 憔悴的,衰弱的,消瘦的。**-a·tion** [imeisiˈeiʃən; ɪmesɪˋeʃən] *n*. (因病或营养不良引起的)憔悴,消瘦。

e-mail, E-mail, email [ˈiːmeil; ˋimel] **I** *n*. 电子邮件。**II** *vt*. 给…发电子邮件。*She* ~*ed her husband that she had passed the entry examination*. 她发电子邮件告知其夫,她已通过了入学考试。**-er** *n*.

em·a·nant [ˈemənənt; ˋɛmənənt] **I** *a*. (气体、光等)发出的,发散的,放射的,流出的 (*from*)。*water* ~ *from the earth* 从地里流出的水。**II** *n*. 【数】放射式。

em·a·nate [ˈeməneit; ˋɛməˏnet] *vi*. **1.** (光、气体等)发出,发散,放射 (*from*)。**2.** 起源 (*from*)。*Fragrance* ~*d from flowers*. 香气从花中发散出来。

em·a·na·tion [ˌeməˈneiʃən; ˏɛməˋneʃən] *n*. **1.** 发散,放射。**2.** 由…发出的东西〔尤指人的美德、品质、精神力量〕。**3.** 【物】放射性的元素。

em·a·na·tive [ˈeməneitiv; ˋɛmənetɪv] *a*. 发(散)出的,放射性的,流出的。

e·man·ci·pate [iˈmænsipeit; ɪˋmænsəˏpet] *vt*. **1.** 解放 (*from*)〔尤指从法律、政治、道德等的约束中解放〕。**2.** 解脱(疑虑、迷信、偏见等)。**3.** 【法】使(孩子)脱离父母的管束(获得行动自主权)。

e·man·ci·pat·ed [iˈmænsipeitid; ɪˋmænsəˏpetɪd] *a*. 被解放的;不为习俗所拘束的,自由的,自主的。

e·man·ci·pa·tion [iˌmænsiˈpeiʃən; ɪˏmænsɪˋpeʃən] *n*. 解放;解脱。

E

e·man·ci·pa·tor [iˈmænsipeitə; ɪˋmænsɪpetɚ] *n*. 解放者。

e·man·ci·pa·to·ry [iˈmænsipeitəri; ɪˋmænsɪpəˏtorɪ] *a*. 解放的。

e·man·ci·pist [iˈmænsipist; ɪˋmænsəpɪst] *n*.【澳史】刑满释放犯。

e·mar·gi·nate [iˈmɑːdʒinit, -neit; ɪˋmɑrdʒnɪt, -net] *a*. (叶子、翅膀等)微缺的,凹缘的。

e·mas·cu·late [iˈmæskjuleit; ɪˋmæskjəˏlet] **I** *vt*. **1.** 给…去势,阉割,使柔弱。**2.** 减弱(文章语气等)。**II** [-lit; -lɪt] *a*. 阉割过的;无男子气的;删削了的。**e·mas·cula·tion** [iˌmæskjuˈleiʃən; ɪˏmæskjəˋleʃən] *n*. **e·mas·cu·la·tive** [iˈmæskjulətiv; ɪˋmæskjələtɪv], **-to·ry** [iˈmæskjuleitəri; ɪˋmæskjəletərɪ] *a*.

Emb. = Embassy.

emb. = embarkation.

em·balm [imˈbɑːm; ɪmˋbɑm] *vt*. **1.** 用防腐药物[香料等]保存(尸体)。**2.** 使不朽,使不被遗忘。**3.** 使充满香气。*fine sentiments ~ed in poetry* 保存在诗歌中的美好感情。**-ed** *a*. **1.** (尸体)被用防腐药物保存的。**2.** 充满香气的。**3.** 〔美俚〕喝得大醉的。**-ment** *n*.

em·bank [imˈbæŋk; ɪmˋbæŋk] *vt*. 筑堤(围绕,防护)。~ *a river* 筑河堤。**-ment** *n*. **1.** 筑堤。**2.** 堤;(铁路等的)路基 (*the* (*Thames*) *Embankment* 伦敦泰晤士河河堤)。

em·bar·ca·der·o [emˌbɑːkəˈderəu; ɛmˏbɑrkəˋdɛro] *n*. (*pl*. **-der·os**) 〔Sp.〕码头。

em·bar·ca·tion [ˌembɑːˈkeiʃən; ˏɛmbɑrˋkeʃən] *n*. = embarkation.

em·bar·go [emˈbɑːgəu; ɛmˋbɑrgo] **I** *vt*. **1.** 封(港),禁止(船只)出入港口;禁运,停止(通商)。**2.** 扣留征用(船只、货物)。**II** *n*. (*pl*. *~es*) **1.** 禁止出[入]港;战时封港令。**2.** 禁运(令),停止通商(令)。**3.** 禁止;限制;阻碍。~ *on* (*the export of*) *gold* = *gold* ~ 禁止黄金出口。***lay*** [***put***, ***place***] ***an*** ~ ***on*** (*a ship*) 禁止(船只)出入;实行禁运。***lay an*** ~ ***on*** [***upon***] ***free speech*** 限制言论自由。***lift*** [***take off***, ***remove***] ***the*** ~ ***on*** 解禁。***under an*** ~ 在禁运中。

em·bark [imˈbɑːk; ɪmˋbɑrk] *vi*. **1.** 上飞机,上船 (*on*)。**2.** 从事,开始 (*in*; *on*; *upon*)。**3.** 载客,装货,搭载。~ *in* [*on*] *a steamer* 上轮船。~ *for New Rork* 乘船去纽约。~ *in* [*on*] *matrimony* 开始过结婚生活。—*vt*. **1.** 载(客),装(货);使上船,使上飞机,搭载。**2.** 使从事,使着手。**3.** 邀(某人)入股,投资于(某企业)。*a ship ~ing passengers and cargo* 载客兼装货的船。~ *money in an enterprise* 投资于某企业。**-ka·tion** [-ˈkeiʃən; -ˋkeʃən] *n*. **1.** 乘飞机;乘船;装载(物)。**2.** (事业等的)开始,从事。**3.** 启程。

em·bark·ment [imˈbɑːkmənt; ɪmˋbɑːkmənt] *n*. = embarkation.

em·bar·ras [ɑ̃ŋbæˈrɑː; ɑ̃ŋbæˋrɑ] *n*. 〔F.〕障碍;混乱;窘迫。~ ***de choix*** [dəˈʃwɑː; dəˋʃwɑ] (因太多)难以选择。~ ***de richesse*** [də riˈʃes; də rɪˋʃɛs] 财富[东西]多得成了累赘。

em·bar·rass [imˈbærəs; ɪmˋbærəs] *vt*. **1.** 使窘迫,使困惑,使为难。**2.** 使穷困,使财政困难。**3.** 使(事件)发生纠纷,使(问题)复杂化。**4.** 使(行动)不便,妨碍,阻碍。*be* [*feel*] *~ed in the presence of strangers* 在生人面前局促不安。*The decline of sales ~ed the company*. 销路下降使公司陷于财政困难。~**-ment** *n*. 窘迫,困惑,为难。

em·bar·rass·ing [imˈbærəsiŋ; ɪmˋbærəsɪŋ] *a*. 令人为难的。~ *questions* 窘人的发问。**-ly** *ad*.

em·bas·sa·dor [imˈbæsədə; ɪmˋbæsədɚ] *n*. 〔古〕= ambassador.

em·bas·sage [ˈembəsidʒ; ˋɛmbəsɪdʒ] *n*. embassy (大使馆)的古变体。

em·bas·sy [ˈembəsi; ˋɛmbəsɪ] *n*. **1.** 大使馆。**2.** 大使的职务[地位]。**3.** 重任,差使。**4.** 使节;大使及其随员;大使馆全体人员。***go on an*** ~ 去当大使。***send sb. on a*** ~ 派某人出任大使。

em·bat·tle[1] [imˈbætl; ɛmˋbætl̩] *vt*. 〔一般用被动式〕**1.** 布阵,列阵,整军备战。**2.** 在…筑垒,设防于。

em·bat·tle[2] [imˈbætl; ɛmˋbætl̩] *vt*. 在…造城垛。

em·bat·tled [imˈbætld; ɛmˋbætl̩d] *a*. **1.** 摆好阵势的。**2.** 有城垛的,有雉堞墙的。

em·bat·tle·ment [imˈbætlmənt; ɪmˋbætl̩mənt] *n*. = battlement.

em·bay [imˈbei; ɛmˋbe] *vt*. **1.** 使(船)入湾;(风)把(船)吹进湾内。**2.** (像海湾那样)环抱,围住。**3.** 使成港湾。**-ment** *n*. **1.** 湾,湾形物。**2.**【地】形成港湾。

em·bed [imˈbed; ɪmˋbɛd] *vt*. (**-dd-**) 〔一般用被动式〕**1.** 栽种。**2.** 埋置,嵌进;【医】植入。**3.** 深留(记忆中)。*slug ~ded in the bone* 嵌进骨中的子弹。*These facts lie ~ded in his mind*. 这些事实牢牢印在他的心中。**-ment** *n*.

em·bel·lish [imˈbeliʃ; ɪmˋbɛlɪʃ] *vt*. **1.** 装饰,修饰,美化。**2.** 添加(故事的)细节;润色(文章)。**-ment** *n*.

em·ber [ˈembə; ˋɛmbɚ] **I** *n*. 〔*pl*.〕余火,余尽。**II** *a*. 【宗】四季大斋日的。~ *days* [*week*]【宗】四季大斋日[周]。

em·bez·zle [imˈbezl; ɪmˋbɛzl̩] *vt*. 侵吞;盗用;挪用(代保管的财务等)。~ *public funds* 挪用公款。**-ment** *n*. **-r** *n*. 盗用[侵吞、挪用]者。

em·bit·ter [imˈbitə; ɪmˋbɪtɚ] *vt*. **1.** 使变苦。**2.** 激怒,使怨恨。**3.** 加重(痛苦)。*Life is ~ed by disappointment*. 失望使得生活更难受。*Hops serve to ~ beer*. 酒花的作用是使啤酒发苦。**-ment** *n*.

em·blaze[1] [imˈbleiz; ɛmˋblez] *vt*. 〔古〕**1.** 照亮。**2.** 点燃。

em·blaze[2] [imˈbleiz; ɛmˋblez] *vt*. 〔废〕= emblazon.

em·bla·zon [imˈbleizən; ɛmˋblezn̩] *vt*. **1.** 以纹章装饰(盾等);用鲜艳颜色装饰。**2.** 颂扬,赞颂。**-ment** *n*. 描画纹章;装饰;颂扬。**-ry** *n*. 纹章描画(法);纹章[华美]装饰。

em·blem [ˈembləm; ˋɛmbləm] **I** *n*. **1.** 标志,象征。**2.** 纹章,徽章。**3.** 标记,典型;〔古〕寓意画。*The olive branch is an ~ of peace*. 橄榄枝象征和平。*a state* [*national*] ~ 国徽。~ *book* 寓意画集。**II** *vt*. 用图案[符号]表示,用象征表示。

em·blem·at·ic [ˌembliˈmætik; ˏɛmbləˋmætɪk] *a*. 作为象征的,作为标记的 (*of*)。*Whiteness is ~ of purity*. 白色是纯洁的象征。**-cal·ly** *ad*.

em·blem·a·tise *vt*. = emblematize.

em·blem·a·tist [emˈblemətist; ɛmˋblɛmətɪst] *n*. **1.** 徽章制作者[设计者]。**2.** 寓言作者。

em·blem·a·tize [emˈblemətaiz; ɛmˋblɛməˏtaɪz] *vt*. 标志,象征。

em·ble·ments [ˈemblimənts; ˋɛmblɪmənts] *n*. 〔*pl*.〕【法】庄稼;庄稼收益。

em·bod·i·ment [imˈbɔdimənt; ɪmˋbɑdɪmənt] *n*. 具体化,体现;化身,统一体。*an ~ of courage* [*health*] 勇敢[健康]的化身。

em·bod·y [imˈbɔdi; ɪmˏbɑdɪ] *vt*. (**-bod·ied**; **-bod·y·ing**) **1.** 使具体化,体现;使形象化。**2.** 使(精神等)肉体化。**3.** 归并。**4.** 包含,收录;【军】组编。~ *the feeling of the northland in his music* 在音乐中表现了北国情调。~ *troops in army corps* 把军队编成兵团。*This book embodies the works of many young writer*. 这本书收录了许多青年作家的作品。

em·bog [emˈbɔg; ɛmˋbɑg] *vt*. (**-gg-**) 使陷在泥沼中;〔喻〕使陷入困境。

em·bold·en [imˈbəuldən; ɪmˋboldn̩] *vt*. 给…壮胆,使更大胆,鼓励。*His kind manner ~ed her to ask for* *help*. 他的和蔼态度使她大起胆子开口求助。

em·bo·lec·to·my [ˌembəˈlektəmi; ˏɛmbəˋlɛktəmɪ] *n*. 【医】栓塞切除术。

em·bol·ic [emˈbɔlik; ɛmˋbɑlɪk] *a*. 1. 栓塞的,血栓病的。2. 内陷的,内褶的;内陷[褶]中的。

em·bol·ism [ˈembəlizəm; ˋɛmbəˏlɪzəm] *n*. 1. (古代历法中的)闰月。2. 【医】栓塞。**-ic** *a*. (*an embolismic month* [*year*] 闰月[年])。

em·bo·lus [ˈembələs; ˋɛmbələs] *n*. (*pl*. **-li** [-lai; -ˏlaɪ]) 【医】栓塞,栓子。

em·bo·ly [ˈembəli; ˋɛmbəlɪ] *n*. 【胚】内陷,内褶。

em·bon·point [F. ɑ̃bɔ̃ˈpwɛ̃; ɑ̃bɔ̃ˋpwæ] *n*. [F.] 〔通常指妇女肥胖的客气话〕发福。

em·bos·om [imˈbuzəm; ɪmˋbuzəm] *vt*. 1. 把…藏于怀内;拥抱;怀抱。2. 珍爱。3. 包围;遮掩,环绕。~ *hopes of success* 怀着成功的希望。*a house ~ed in trees* 树木围着的房子。*a village ~ed with hills* 群山环抱的村庄。

em·boss [imˈbɔs; ɪmˋbɔs] *vt*. 1. 用浮雕装饰;在(图案,花样等)作浮雕。2. 使凸出;(用模子)压花,压纹。~ *the paper with a design* 把图案压在纸上。~ *a pattern on metal* 在金属材料上作出凸花。*~ed cloth* 拷花布,压花布。~ *work* 浮雕细工。**-er** *n*. 1. 压花技工。2. 压花机。**-ing** *n*. 【工】凸花制法;【纺】浮雕印花,拷花,压花;【建】雕刻突饰。**-ment** *n*. 凸花装饰;浮雕工艺;浮雕花样 (*an embossment map* 立体地图)。

em·bou·chure [ˌɔmbuˈʃuə, ˈɔmbuˌʃuə; ˏɑmbuˋʃur, ˋɑmbuˏʃur] *n*. [F.] 1. 河口。2. 【乐】管乐器的吹口;管乐器吹奏法。

em·bour·geoise·ment [ˌembuəˈʒwɑːzmənt; ˏɛmburˋʒwɑzmənt] *n*. 资产阶级化,变成资产阶级;资产阶级习性。

em·bow [emˈbəu; ɛmˋbo] *vt*. 〔古〕把…成弓形,把…弄成弧形。**-ed** *a*. 弯曲的;弧形的。**-ment** *n*.

em·bow·el [imˈbauəl, em-; ɪmˋbauəl, ɛm-] *vt*. ([英] **-ll-**) 从(体内)取出肠子 (= disembowel)。

em·bow·er [imˈbauə, em-; imˋbauɚ, ɛm-] *vt*. 用树叶遮蔽;把…隐藏在树林中;(有树)围绕。—*vi*. 〔古〕栖息在亭子[树荫]中。

em·brace[1] [imˈbreis; ɪmˋbres] **I** *vt*. 1. 拥抱,抱。2. 包括,包含;包围,环绕。3. 皈依,信奉。4. 抓紧(机会),趁。5. 采用,接受。6. 参加,着手。7. 看出,领悟。*He ~d his son in his arms*. 他把儿子抱在怀里。~ *an opportunity* 利用机会。~ *a good chance* 抓住好机会。~ *soldier's life* 从军。—*vi*. 相抱。**II** *n*. 拥抱;包围;接受;领会;【动】交尾。

em·brace[2] [imˈbreis; ɪmˋbres] *vt*. 笼络[收买]陪审员。

em·brac·er[1] [imˈbreisə; ɪmˋbresɚ] *n*. 拥抱者。

em·brac·er[2], **em·brace·or** [imˈbreisə; ɪmˋbresɚ] *n*. 【法】笼络[收买]陪审员的人。

em·brac·er·y [imˈbreisəri; ɪmˋbresərɪ] *n*. 【法】笼络[收买]陪审员的行为。

em·branch·ment [imˈbrɑːntʃmənt, -ˈbræntʃ-; ɛmˋbrɑntʃmənt, -ˋbræntʃ-] *n*. 1. 分支,支脉;支流。2. 分支机构。

em·bran·gle [imˈbræŋgl; ɛmˋbræŋgl] *vt*. 使纠缠;搞乱;使困惑。**-ment** *n*.

em·bra·sure [imˈbreiʒə; ɛmˋbreʒɚ] *n*. 1. 【军】枪眼,炮眼,射击孔。2. 【建】漏斗状斜面墙。3. 【医】楔状隙。

em·bro·cate [ˈembrəukeit; ˋɛmbroˏket] *vt*. 【医】(以油膏、洗液等)涂擦。

em·bro·ca·tion [ˌembrəuˈkeiʃən; ˏɛmbroˋkeʃən] *n*. 1. 【医】涂擦。2. 涂擦剂。

em·broi·der [imˈbrɔidə; ɪmˋbrɔɪdɚ] *vt*. 1. 刺绣,在…上绣花。2. 修饰,润色,渲染。—*vi*. 刺绣,绣花。*an ~ing needle* 绣花针。**-er** *n*. 刺绣工。**-ess** *n*. 女刺绣工。

em·broi·dery [imˈbrɔidəri; ɪmˋbrɔɪdərɪ] *n*. 1. 刺绣,绣花。2. 粉饰,修饰;润色。~ **frame** 绣花架。

em·broil [imˈbrɔil; ɛmˋbrɔɪl] *vt*. 1. 使混乱,使纠缠,搅乱。2. 牵连,卷入。*be ~ed in a quarrel* 卷入争吵中。**-ment** *n*.

em·brown [imˈbraun, em-; ɛmˋbraun] *vt*. 使成褐色,使成棕色;使变深色。

em·bry·ec·to·my [ˌembriˈektəmi; ˏɛmbrɪˋɛktəmɪ] *n*. 【医】胎切除术〔尤指子宫外孕的胎切除术〕。

em·bry·o [ˈembriəu; ˋɛmbrɪo] **I** *n*. (*pl*. *~s*) 1. 【植】胚;【动】胚胎(对人来说,一般指三个月以内的胚胎)。2. 胚芽(时期),萌芽时期。*in* ~ 未发达的,初期的;萌芽时期的;在计划中的。**II** *a*. 1. 胚胎的,胚的。2. 胚芽(时期)的,未发达的,原始的,初期的。~ **grafting** 胚种嫁接。~ **sac** 【植】胚囊。

em·bry·og·e·ny [ˌembriˈɔdʒini; ˏɛmbrɪˋɑdʒənɪ] *n*. 【生】胚形成 (= embryogenesis)。**-o·gen·ic** [-ˈdʒenik; -ˋdʒɛnɪk], **-o·ge·net·ic** [-dʒəˈnetik; -dʒəˋnɛtɪk] *a*.

em·bry·oid [ˈembriɔid; ˋɛmbrɪɔɪd] *a*. 胚胎(状)的。

em·bry·o·logic [ˌembriəˈlɔdʒik; ˏɛmbrɪəˋlɑdʒɪk] *a*. 胚胎学的 (= bryological)。**-cal·ly** *ad*. **-gist** *n*. 胚胎学家。

em·bry·ol·o·gy [ˌembriˈɔlədʒi; ˏɛmbrɪˋɑlədʒɪ] *n*. 胚胎学,发生学。

em·bry·o·nal [ˌembriˈəunəl; ˋɛmbrɪonəl] *a*. = embryonic.

em·bry·on·ic [ˌembriˈɔnik; ˏɛmbrɪˋɑnɪk] *a*. 1. 胚胎的。2. 萌芽期的,初期的,未发达的。~ **layer** 【生】胚层。~ **membrane** 【解】胚膜。**-al·ly** *ad*.

em·bry·ot·o·my [ˌembriˈɔtəmi; ˏɛmbrɪˋɑtəmɪ] *n*. 【医】(难产时的)胎儿截割术,碎胎术。

em·bus [imˈbʌs; ɛmˋbʌs] *vt*., *vi*. 【军】(使)人员[物资等]被载上机动车辆。

em·bus·qué [F. ɑ̃byske; ɑ̃byskɛ] *n*. 【法】逃避兵役的人。

em·cee [ˈemˈsiː; ˋɛmˋsi] **I** *n*. 〔美口〕司仪〔master of ceremonies 的首字母 mc 的读音〕,电台节目主持人。**II** *vt*. 主持(电台节目等)。—*vi*. 当司仪。

e·meer [əˈmiə; əˋmɪr] *n*. = emir. **-ate** [-it; -ɪt] *n*. = emirate.

e·mend [i(ː)ˈmend; ɪˋmɛnd] *vt*. 校订,订正,改正,校勘,校正。~ *the text of a book* 校勘某书。~ *an author* 订正某作者著作。**-able** *a*.

e·men·date [ˈiːmənˌdeit; ˋimənˏdet] *vt*. 1. 校订,改正。2. 校勘,校正。**e·men·da·tor** *n*. 校订者,校勘者。**e·men·da·to·ry** [iˈmendəˌtəri; ɪˋmɛndəˏtorɪ] *a*.

e·men·da·tion [ˌiːmenˈdeiʃən; ˏimɛnˋdeʃən] *n*. 1. 修改;校订,订正。2. 被校订的地方。

EMER = emergency.

em·er·ald [ˈemərəld; ˋɛmərəld] **I** *n*. 1. 【矿】祖母绿,纯绿柱石。2. 绿宝石,绿刚玉。3. 鲜绿色。4. 【印】一种活字〔相当于 6½ 点〕。**II** *a*. 祖母绿(制)的;鲜绿(色)的;纯绿宝石制的。***the E- Isle*** 绿宝石岛〔爱尔兰别名〕。~ **green** 翠绿,巴黎绿〔图画颜料〕。~ **nickel** 翠镍矿。

em·er·ald·ine [ˈemərəldain; ˋɛmərəldaɪn] *a*. 祖母绿一样的,鲜绿的。

e·merge [iˈməːdʒ; ɪˋmɝdʒ] *vi*. 1. 出现,显露,现出。2. (自困境等中)摆脱;脱颖而出。3. 发生,暴露。~ *from* [*out of*] *water* 从水中现出。*The sun ~s from behind the clouds*. 太阳从云里露出。~ *from difficulties* 摆脱困境。~ *into a street* 在街上出现。

e·mer·gence [iˈməːdʒəns; ɪˋmɝdʒəns] *n*. 1. 出现,发生。2. 【植】突出体;(柑果的)瓤胞。3. 【虫】羽化。4. 【哲】突创论。

e·mer·gen·cy [iˈməːdʒənsi; ɪˋmɝdʒənsɪ] *n*. 突然事件;紧急情况,非常时期。*take ~ measures* 采取紧急措施。*be prepared* [*ready*] *for all emergencies* 以备万一。

in this ～ 在这个危急时刻。meet emergencies 采取应急措施。**in** [**on**] **an** ～ = **in case of** ～ 在危急时刻，万一发生事变。**rise to the** ～ 有应变之才，能够应付紧急事变。～ **act** 紧急法令。～ **airport** 应急机场。～ **brake** 紧急煞车。～ **bridge** 便桥。～ **call** 1. 紧急召集。2. 急诊。～ **case** 急诊病人。～ **crops** 救荒作物，短期作物。～ **door** [**exit**] 太平门。～ **fund** 应急基金。～ **man** 临时雇员；（球队等的）预备员，生力军。～ **staircase** 安全楼梯。～ **treatment**【医】紧急处理。

e·mer·gent [i'məːdʒənt; ɪ`mɝdʒənt] ***a.*** **1.** 发出的，现出的。**2.** 突现的，意外的；紧急的。**3.** 自然发生的。*the recently* ～ *countries* 新兴国家。～ **evolution**【生】突生进化。～ **year**（民族、国家等）计时开始的年代。

e·mer·i·tus [i(ː)'meritəs; ɪ`mɛrətəs] **I** ***a.*** 保留头衔而退休的，名誉的。*a professor* ～ = *an* ～ *professor* 名誉教授。**II** ***n.***（*pl.* ***-ti*** [-tai, -tiː; -taɪ; -ti]）（教授、教士等的）荣誉退休者。

e·mersed [i'məːst; ɪ`mɝst] ***a.***（水生植物）伸出水面的。

e·mer·sion [i(ː)'məːʃən; i`mɝʃən] ***n.*** **1.** 现出；浮出（*opp.* immersion）。**2.**【天】复现。

Em·er·son ['eməsn; `ɛmɚsn̩] ***n.*** **1.** 爱默生〔姓氏，男子名〕。**2. Ralph Waldo** ～ 爱默生〔1803—1882，美国评论家、哲学家、诗人〕。

em·er·y ['eməri; `ɛmərɪ] ***n.*** 粗金刚砂。～ **bag**（磨针用的）砂袋。～ **board** 砂板。～ **cloth** 砂布。～ **paper** 砂纸。～ **wheel** 砂轮。

em·e·sis ['eməsis; `ɛməsɪs] ***n.***【医】呕吐。

e·met·ic [i'metik; ɪ`mɛtɪk] **I** ***a.***【医】催吐的。**II** ***n.***【药】催吐药。**-al·ly** ***ad.***

em·e·tin(e) ['emətiːn; `ɛmətɪn] ***n.***【药】吐根碱，吐根素，依米丁。

é·meute [ei'məːt; e`mɝt] ***n.***〔F.〕起义；暴动。

E.M.F., EMF, e.m.f., emf = electromotive force 电动势。*back* [*counter*] ～ 反电势。

-emia ***n. suf.*** = -aemia.

e·mic·tion [i'mikʃən; ɪ`mɪkʃən] ***n.*** **1.** 排尿。**2.** 尿。

em·i·grant ['emigrənt; `ɛməgrənt] **I** ***a.***（向外国）移居的；移民的，侨居的。**II** ***n.*** 移民，侨民；迁徙的动物；移植的植物。*Japanese ～s for Brazil* 日本移居巴西的侨民。*～s from China* 来自中国的移民。

em·i·grate ['emigreit; `ɛmɪˏgret] ***vi.*** **1.** 移居（外国）。**2.**〔口〕搬出，迁出（*opp.* immigrate）。—***vt.*** 使移居，使迁出。

em·i·gra·tion [ˌemi'greiʃən; ˏɛmə`greʃən] ***n.*** 移居外国；〔集合词〕移民，侨民。～ *policy* 移民政策。

em·i·gra·to·ry ['emigrətəri; `ɛmɪgrəˏtorɪ] ***a.*** = migratory.

é·mi·gré ['emigrei; `ɛməgre] ***n.***〔F.〕移民；（因政治等原因而移居国外的）逃亡者，流亡者。

E·mile [ei'miːl; e`mil] ***n.*** 埃米尔〔男子名〕。

Emily, Emilie ['emili; `ɛmɪlɪ] ***n.*** 埃米莉〔女子名〕。

em·i·nence ['eminəns; `ɛmɪnəns] ***n.*** **1.** 高处，高地。**2.**【解】（骨的）隆起，隆凸。**3.** 高位，要职。**4.** 高超，卓越；著名；杰出，显赫。**5.**〔E-〕【天主】阁下〔对主教的尊称，前面加 Your, His〕。*a man of* ～ 名人。*have a position of* ～ *in the political world* 在政界居有显要地位。*attain* ～ *in literature* 在文学上享有盛名。

ém·i·nence grise [eimiːnɔns'griːz; eminɑns`griz] ***n.***〔F.〕（政界、政党的）幕后操纵者。

em·i·nen·cy ['eminənsi; `ɛmɪnənsɪ] ***n.*** = eminence.

em·i·nent ['eminənt; `ɛmɪnənt] ***a.*** **1.** 杰出的，卓越的。**2.** 著名的；显著的，突出的。～ *services* 功勋卓著。～ *statesman* 杰出的政治家。*a man of* ～ *impartiality* 大公无私的人。*be* ～ *as a speaker* 以演说家著称。～ **domain**【法】国家最高支配权；〔美〕土地征用权。～ **souls** 社会名流。**-ly** ***ad.***

e·mir [e'miə; ə`mɪr] ***n.*** **1.** 埃米尔〔某些穆斯林国家的首长（或王子、长官）〕。**2.** 穆罕默德后裔的尊称。**-ate** [e'miərit; ə`mɪrɪt] ***n.*** 埃米尔的统治，酋长国（*the United Arab Emirates* 阿拉伯联合酋长国）。

em·is·sa·ry ['emiseri; `ɛmɪˏsɛrɪ] **I** ***n.*** **1.** 使者，密使。**2.** 间谍。**II** ***a.*** 密使的；间谍的。

e·mis·sion [i'miʃən; ɪ`mɪʃən] ***n.*** **1.**（光、热、气体等的）发出，发射，射出，放射；传播。**2.**（纸币等的）发行；发行额。**3.** 发出物，放射物。**4.**【医】排出；遗精。～ **spectrum**【物】发射光谱。～ **theory**【物】微粒说。

em·is·sive [i'misiv; ɪ`mɪsɪv] ***a.*** 发出的，发射的，放射（性）的。～ *power*【物】发射力。

em·is·siv·i·ty [ˌemi'siviti; ˏɛmɪ`sɪvɪtɪ] ***n.*** 发射率，辐射系数。

e·mit [i'mit; ɪ`mɪt] ***vt.***（***-tt-***）**1.** 出（声），发，放（光等），发射，放射（热等）。**2.** 吐露（意见等）。**3.** 颁布（命令等）；发行（纸币等）。*The sun ～s light.* 太阳放出光。

e·mit·ron ['emitrɔn; `ɛmɪtrɑn] ***n.*** 光电摄像管。

e·mit·ter [i'mitə; ɪ`mɪtɚ] ***n.*** **1.** 辐射体，辐射源。**2.** 发射体，发射极。***beta*** ～ β辐射体。

Em·ma ['emə; `ɛmə] ***n.*** 埃玛〔女子名〕。

Em·(m)anuel [i'mænjuəl; ɪ`mænjʊəl] ***n.*** 伊曼纽尔〔男子名〕。

em·men·a·gogue [ə'menəgɔg; ə`mɛnəgɔg] ***n.***【药】通经药，调经药。

em·men·i·a [ə'meniə, ə'miː-; ə`mɛnɪə, ə`mi-] ***n.*** 月经。

em·mer ['emə; `ɛmə] ***n.*** 二粒小麦。

Em·met(t) ['emit; `ɛmɪt] ***n.*** 埃米特〔姓氏，男子名〕。

em·met ['emit; `ɛmɪt] ***n.***【动】〔方、古〕蚁。

em·me·tro·pi·a [ˌemə'trəupiə; ˏɛmə`tropɪə] ***n.***【医】正常眼，折光正常。

Em·my ['emi; `ɛmɪ] ***n.***（*pl.* ***-mies, -mys***）（美国电视艺术与科学学院对在电视节目安排、演技等方面有卓越成就者所颁发的）艾美金像奖。

e·mol·li·ent [i'mɔliənt; ɪ`mɑljənt] **I** ***a.*** 使（皮肤等）柔软的，有缓和作用的。**II** ***n.***【药】润肤剂，（皮肤的）缓和剂。

e·mol·u·ment [i'mɔljumənt; ɪ`mɑljʊmənt] ***n.*** 薪水，报酬。

Em·or·y ['eməri; `ɛmərɪ] ***n.*** 埃默里〔男子名〕。

e·mote [i'məut; ɪ`mot] ***vi.***〔美口〕表现感情（尤指演戏或像在演戏）。

e·mo·tion [i'məuʃən; ɪ`moʃən] ***n.*** **1.** 情感，情绪，感情。**2.** 感动，激动。*a man of strong ～s* 感情强烈的人。*with* ～ 感动地，激动地。**-less** ***a.*** 没有感情的，冷漠的。

e·mo·tion·al [i'məuʃənl; ɪ`moʃənl] ***a.*** **1.** 情绪的，感情的。**2.** 容易激动，易动感情的，感情脆弱的。**3.** 感动人的，激起感情的。*an* ～ *actor* 善于表情的演员。*an* ～ *state* 兴奋状态。～ **intelligence**【心】情感智力〔指与他人交往及控制自己感情的能力等〕。～ **quotient**【心】情商，情感商数〔指 ～ intelligence 的商数〕。**-ism** [-izm; -ˏɪzəm] ***n.*** 感情主义，唯情论，情绪表露。**-ist** [-ist; -ɪst] ***n.*** 容易动感情的人；感情主义者，唯情论者。**-i·ty** [iˌməuʃə'næliti; ɪˏmoʃə`nælətɪ] ***n.*** 激动；富于感情。**-ise, -ize** ***vt.*** 使带感情色彩；使动感情。**-ly** ***ad.***

e·mo·tive [i'məutiv; ɪ`motɪv] ***a.*** 感情的，情绪的；表现感情的。**-ly** ***ad.***

e·mo·tiv·i·ty [iməu'tiviti; ɪmo`tɪvətɪ] ***n.*** 感触性，易感性。

Emp. = Emperor; Empress.

e.m.p.【医】照方处理（= as directed）。

em·pale [im'peil; ɪm`pel] ***vt.*** = impale.

em·pan·el [im'pænl; ɪm`pænl̩] ***vt.***（〔英〕***-ll-***）把（某人）记入陪审员名单；选任（陪审员等）。

em·path·ic [em'pæθik; ɛm`pæθɪk], **em·pa·thet·ic** [ˌempə'θetik; ˏɛmpə`θɛtɪk] ***a.*** **1.**（美学上）移情作用的。**2.**【心】神入的。

em·pa·thize [ˈempəθaiz; ˋɛmpə͵θaɪz] ***vi***. 经历移情作用,感受移情作用。

em·pa·thy [ˈempəθi; ˋɛmpəθɪ] ***n***. **1.** 移情作用。**2.** 神入。

em·pen·nage [emˈpenidʒ; ɛmpɛˋnɪdʒ] ***n***. 【空】尾翼(面),尾部。

em·per·or [ˈempərə; ˋɛmpərɚ] ***n***. (*fem*. ***em·press***) 皇帝。***the Purple E-*** 深紫蝶。**-ship** ***n***. 皇帝的身份[地位,统治]。

em·per·y [ˈempəri; ˋɛmpərɪ] ***n***. 〔诗〕**1.** 帝国,帝权。**2.** 绝对统治权,权威。

emph. = emphasis, emphatic.

em·pha·sis [ˈemfəsis; ˋɛmfəsɪs] ***n***. (*pl*. ***-ses*** [-siːz; -siz]) **1.**【修】强调语势,强语气。**2.** 强调,着重,重点,重要性。**3.** (形、色等的)显著,鲜明。***lay*** [***place***, ***put***] ~ ***on*** [***upon***] 着重在;强调,加强(语气)。***speak with*** ~ 着重说。***underline words for*** ~ 在字下画线表示强调[重要]。

em·pha·size [ˈemfəsaiz; ˋɛmfə͵saɪz] ***vt***. **1.** 强调,着重。**2.** 使加强语气。**3.** 使(事实等)突出(或显得重要)。

em·phat·ic [imˈfætik; ɪmˋfætɪk] ***a***. **1.** 加强语气的,表现有力的,强调的。**2.** 显著的,显眼的。*an* ~ *denial* 断然的否认。*an* ~ *honour* 特殊的光荣。*an* ~ *victory* 大胜。**-cal·ly** ***ad***.

em·phy·se·ma [ˌemfiˈsiːmə; ͵ɛmfɪˋsimə] ***n***. 【医】气肿。*pulmonary* ~ 肺气肿。**-tous** [ˌemfiˈsemətəs; ͵ɛmfɪˋsɛmətəs] ***a***.

em·phy·teu·sis [ˌemfiˈtjuːsis; ͵ɛmfɪˋtjusɪs] ***n***. 【法】永佃权;永借权。

em·phy·teu·ta [ˌemfiˈtjuːtə; ͵ɛmfɪˋtjutə] ***n***. 【法】永久佃户;永借人。

em·pire [ˈempaiə; ˋɛmpaɪr] **I** ***n***. **1.** 帝国。**2.** 帝王统治(权);帝政;绝对统治权(*over*);(由某个人或集团控制的)大企业。*E- City* [*State*]〔美〕纽约市[州]。*E- Day*〔英〕帝国节〔5 月 24 日,1958 年改称 Commonwealth Day〕。*E- State Building* 纽约的帝国摩天大厦。*E- State of the South*〔美〕乔治亚州。*the E-* 神圣罗马帝国;英帝国;(拿破仑统治下的)法兰西第一帝国。**II** ***a***. **1.**〔E-〕法兰西第一帝国时期(1804—1815)的。**2.**〔E-〕(服装、家具等)法国十九世纪头三十年款式的。

em·pir·ic [emˈpirik; ɛmˋpɪrɪk] **I** ***n***. **1.** 凭经验办事的人,经验主义者。**2.**〔古〕庸医。**II** ***a***. = empirical.

em·pir·i·cal [emˈpirikəl; ɛmˋpɪrɪkl] ***a***. **1.** 以经验为根据的,经验主义的。**2.** 庸医的。~ **formula**【化】实验式,经验式。**-ly** ***ad***.

em·pir·i·cism [emˈpirisizəm; ɛmˋpɪrɪsɪzəm] ***n***. **1.**【哲】经验论(*opp*. rationalism);经验主义。**2.** 庸医的医法。

em·pir·i·cist [emˈpirisist; ɛmˋpɪrɪsɪst] ***n***. **1.** 经验主义者,经验论者。**2.** 庸医。

em·pir·i·o-crit·i·cism, **em·pir·i·o·crit·i·cism** [emˌpiriəuˈkritisizəm; ɛm͵pɪrɪoˋkrɪtɪsɪzəm] ***n***.【哲】经验批判主义。

em·pir·i·o-mo·nism [emˌpiriəuˈmɔnizəm; ɛm͵pɪrɪoˋmɑnɪzm] ***n***.【哲】经验一元论。

em·pir·i·o-sym·bo·lism [emˌpiriəuˈsimbəlizəm; əm͵pɪrɪoˋsɪmbəlɪzəm] ***n***.【哲】经验符号论。

em·place [imˈpleis, em-; ɪmˋples, ɛm-] ***vt***. **1.** 放,置。**2.**【军】放列,使(火炮)进入阵地。**-ment** ***n***. **1.** 定位置;【军】放列动作。**2.** 炮兵掩体,炮台,炮位。

em·plane [imˈplein; ɛmˋplen] ***vi***. 乘飞机。—***vt***. 使乘飞机,把…装入飞机。

em·ploy [imˈplɔi; ɪmˋplɔɪ] **I** ***vt***. **1.** 用,使用。**2.** 雇用。**3.** 使专心于,使忙于,使从事于。~ *one's time* 使用时间。*the* ~*ed* 雇工,雇员。*be* ~*ed* 被雇,受雇;从事。*be* ~*ed in drinking* 喝着酒。~ *everything in one's power* 尽一切方法。~ ***oneself in*** [***on***] …做(工作),从事,时间花(在…)。**II** ***n***. **1.** 使用。**2.** 雇用。**3.** 服务;工作;职业。*have many persons in one's* ~ 雇用着不少人。*in the* ~ *of sb*. = *in sb.'s* ~ 受某人雇用。***out of*** ~ 失业。

em·ploy·a·ble [imˈplɔiəbl; ɪmˋplɔɪəbl] ***a***. **1.** 能使用的。**2.** 可雇用的(尤指适于雇用的或满足起码雇用要求的)。**em·ploy·abil·i·ty** [imˌplɔiəˈbiliti; ɪm͵plɔɪəˋbɪlətɪ] ***n***.

employé [ɔmˈplɔiei; ɑmˋplɔɪe] ***n***. (*fem*. ***-ée*** [-ei; -eɪ]) [F.] = employee.

em·ploy·ee [ˌemplɔiˈiː, imˈplɔiiː; ͵ɛmplɔɪˋi, ɪmˋplɔɪ·i] ***n***. 雇员,雇工,受雇者。*office* ~*s* 职员。

em·ploy·er [imˈplɔiə; ɪmˋplɔɪɚ] ***n***. 雇主;雇用者。

em·ploy·ment [imˈplɔimənt; ɪmˋplɔɪmənt] ***n***. **1.** 使用,利用。**2.** 雇用。**3.** 工作,职业。**4.** 消遣。*the* ~ *of capital* 资金的运用。*the* ~ *of skilled labour* 熟练工人的雇用。*get* [*obtain*] ~ 就业。*lose* ~ 失业。***a blind alley*** ~ [***occupation***] 没有前途的职业[工作]。***in the*** ~ ***of*** 在…处工作,受雇于…。***out of*** ~ 失业,赋闲。***seek for*** ~ 找工作。***take*** (*sb*.) ***into*** ~ 雇用(某人)~ ***throw*** (*sb*.) ***out of*** ~ 解雇,取消(某人)差事。~ **agency** [**bureau**, **office**] 职业介绍所。 ~ **certificate** (学校发给适龄儿童可参加有酬工作的)从业证明书。~ **exchange**〔英〕(劳工部等设立的)职业介绍所。

em·poi·son [imˈpɔizn; ɛmˋpɔɪzn] ***vt***. **1.**〔古〕使有毒;使污染。**2.** 使怀恨,使狠毒。

em·po·ri·um [emˈpɔːriəm; ɛmˋporɪəm] ***n***. (*pl*. ~***s***, ***-ria*** [-riə; -rɪə]) **1.** 商场,商业中心。**2.**【商】商品陈列所,大百货店。

em·pow·er [imˈpauə; ɪmˋpaʊɚ] ***vt***. **1.** 授权,准许。**2.** 使能。~ *sb. to do sth*. 授权某人可做某事。*Science* ~*s man to conquer natural forces*. 科学使人类能征服自然。

em·press [ˈempris; ˋɛmprɪs] ***n***. 女皇;皇后。***an*** ~ ***dowger*** 皇太后。

em·presse·ment [F. ɑ̃ːpresˈmɑ̃; ɑ̃presˋmɑ̃] ***n***. [F.] 热诚,真挚。

em·prise, **em·prize** [imˈpraiz; ɛmˋpraɪz] ***n***.〔古、诗〕壮举;冒险;勇武。

emp·ti·ness [ˈem*p*tinis; ˋɛm*p*tɪnɪs] ***n***. **1.** 空虚;空腹;空处。**2.** 无智,无能。

emp·ty [ˈem*p*ti; ˋɛm*p*tɪ] **I** ***a***. **1.** 空的,空著的。**2.** 空虚的,空洞的。**3.** 无聊的,愚蠢的。**4.** 空闲的;无效的;徒劳的。**5.** 杳无人烟的,空寂的。**6.** (母畜)未怀孕的。**7.**〔口〕空腹的,饿着肚子的。**8.**【逻】无元的,无分子的。*An* ~ *bag will not stand up right*.〔谚〕空袋子,站不直;衣食足然后知礼义。*an* ~ *box* 空箱。~ *hours* 空闲时间。*an* ~ *house* 空屋。~ *lip service* 说得好听的空话。*an* ~ *talk* 空谈;废话。~ *promises* 空洞许诺。*feel* ~ 觉得饿了。*drink on an* ~ *stomach* 空着肚子喝酒。*an* ~ *idea* 愚蠢的想法。***be*** ~ ***of*** 无,缺,缺少(*a life* ~ *of happiness* 缺乏幸福的生活)。***come away*** ~ 空手而回。**II** ***n***.〔*pl*.〕空箱,空桶;空瓶;空车。**III** ***vt***. 弄空;用空;搬空,腾空,倒空(*out*)。~ *one's glass* 干杯。~ *a drawer* 把抽屉腾空。~ *a purse upon the table* 把钱袋里的钱统统倒在桌上。— ***vi***. (***-tied***; ***-tying***) **1.** 变空。**2.** 流注,注入。~ (*itself*) ***into*** (河)流入(大海)。~**-handed** ***a***. 空手的;徒手的;空手,空着手。~**-headed** ***a***. 没有头脑的,愚笨的。~ **word**【语法】虚词。**-ly** ***ad***. **-ing** ***n***. **1.** 倒出,空出。**2.** 倒出的东西。**3.**〔*pl*.〕〔美俚〕用啤酒糟做的酵素。

em·pur·ple [imˈpəːpl; ɛmˋpɝpl] ***vt***. 把…弄成[染成]紫色。

em·py·e·ma [ˌempaiˈiːmə; ͵ɛmpɪˋimə] ***n***. 【医】积脓;脓胸。

em·py·re·al [ˌempaiˈriːəl, emˈpiriəl; ɛmˋpɪrɪəl, ͵ɛmpəˋrɪəl] ***a***. 由净火形成的;最高天的,苍天的。

em·py·re·an [ˌempaiˈri(ː)ən, emˈpiriən; ͵ɛmpaɪˋrɪən,

ˌɛmˋpərɪən] **I** ***n*.**【宗】**1.** 最高天,上帝的住处。**2.** 苍天,太空。**II** ***a*.** = empyreal.

e·mu [ˈiːmjuː; ˋimju] ***n*.**【动】鸸鹋;高大而不会飞的鸟。

E.M.U., EMU, e.m.u., emu = electromagnetic unit(s) 电磁单位。

em·u·late [ˈemjuleit; ˋɛmjəˌlet] ***vt*.** **1.** 与…竞赛[竞争]。**2.** 努力赶上[超过]。**3.** 仿效。**4.**【自】仿真,使用仿真器仿效(另一计算机系统)。

em·u·la·tion [ˌemjuˈleiʃən; ˌɛmjəˋleʃən] ***n*.** **1.** 竞赛,竞争。**2.** 仿效。**3.**【自】仿真(技术)。*in a spirit of* ~ 以竞争的精神。*an* ~ *drive* 竞赛运动。

em·u·la·tive [ˈemjulətiv; ˋɛmjəletɪv] ***a*.** 竞争的,好胜的,不服输的。**-ly** ***ad*.**

em·u·la·tor [ˈemjuleitə; ˋɛmjəletɚ] ***n*.** **1.** 竞赛者,竞争者。**2.** 热心模仿的人。**3.**【自】仿真器,仿效器。

em·u·la·to·ry [ˈemjulətəri; ˋɛmjələˌtorɪ] ***a*.** 〔罕〕竞争的。

em·u·lous [ˈemjuləs; ˋɛmjələs] ***a*.** **1.** 好胜的,竞争心强的。**2.** 好仿效的。**3.** 渴望的。~ ***of*** **1.** 热心模仿。**2.** 渴望。**-ly** ***ad*.** **-ness** ***n*.**

e·mul·si·fi·a·ble [iˈmʌlsifaiəbl; ɪˋmʌlsəˌfaɪəbəl] ***a*.** 可乳化的 (emulsible)。

e·mul·si·fi·ca·tion [iˌmʌlsifiˈkeiʃən; ɪˌmʌlsəfəˋkeʃən] ***n*.**【化】乳化(作用)。

e·mul·si·fi·er [iˈmʌlsifaiə; ɪˋmʌlsəfaɪɚ] ***n*.**【化】乳化剂,乳化器。

e·mul·si·fy [iˈmʌlsifai; ɪˋmʌlsəˌfaɪ] ***vt*.** (***-fied; -fy·ing***) 使乳化。*a* ~*ing agent* 乳化剂。

e·mul·sion [iˈmʌlʃən; ɪˋmʌlʃən] ***n*.** 乳状液,乳胶;【医】乳剂。*sensitive* ~【摄】感光乳剂。

e·mul·sive [iˈmʌlsiv; ɪˋmʌlsɪv] ***a*.** **1.** 乳剂质的,乳化性的,生乳质物的。**2.** 能乳化的。

e·mul·soid [iˈmʌlsɔid; ɪˋmʌlsɔɪd] ***n*.**【化】乳胶(体)。

e·munc·to·ry [iˈmʌŋktəri; ɪˋmʌŋktərɪ] **I** ***a*.** 排泄用的。**II** ***n*.** 排泄器官。

en [en; ɛn] ***n*.** **1.** 字母 N 或 n. **2.**【印】对开〔em 全身的一半〕。

en [ɑ̃; ɑ̃] ***prep*.** 〔F.〕**1.** 在,在…中。**2.** 用。**3.** 像,如同。***en bloc*** [-ˈblɔk; -ˋblɑk] 总,全体 (*resign en bloc* 总辞职)。***en clair*** [-ˈklɛə; -ˋklɛr] 用普通文字,明码。***en famille*** [-fɑˈmiːjə; -fɑˋmijə] 在家,随意地,不拘礼地;一家人似地。***en fête*** [-ˈfet; -ˋfɛt] 过节(的),节日般(的)。***en garçon*** [ˈɑ̃ˌgɑːsɔ̃; ɑ̃ˌgarˋsɔ̃] (男子)独身。***en masse*** [-ˈmæs; -ˋmæs]〔法〕一同,一块儿;全部,整个地。***en passant*** [-ˈpɑsɑ̃; -ˋpɑsɑ̃] **1.** 顺便。**2.**【棋】吃掉一次进两格的敌卒〔敌卒已处于进一格便可吃掉的位置〕。~ ***prise*** [ɑ̃ˈpriːz; ɑ̃ˋpriz] 下棋处在容易被吃掉的地位。***en rapport*** [-rɑˈpɔə; -rɑˋpɔr] 同情;和谐,一致。***en règle*** [-ˈregl; -ˋrɛgl] 按部就班,照规则,正式。***en route*** [-ˈruːt; -ˋrut] 在途中 (*to*; *for*)。

en- *pref*. 〔在 p, b, m 前作 em-〕**1.** 加在名词前,表示"放进","放在…上面","走上","赋予":*en*case, *en*throne, *em*bus, *em*power. **2.** 加在名词或形容词前,表示"使成…":*en*slave, *em*bolden. **3.** 加在动词前,表示"在里面","包住":*en*fold; *en*wrap. ★en- 与 in- 常可通用,但在美国日常用语中多用 in-, 英国一般多用 en-:*in*quire, *en*quire; *in*close, *en*close.

-en *suf*. **1.** 加在形容词或名词后面构成动词,表示"弄","变","使","使有","变得","变得有":moist*en*, strength*en*, deep*en*, length*en*. **2.** 加在物质名词后构成形容词,表示"由…构成的","由…制成的":earth*en*, wood*en*. 在非重音音节的 r 后面作 -n:silver*n*. **3.** 加在不规则动词之后构成过去分词或形容词:spok*en*, fall*en*, beat*en*, drunk*en*. ★在这一类词中〔有的-en 可改为 -ed〔如 shap*en* > shap*ed*〕,有的是古语〔如 *graven*〕,有的已略去 e〔如 *sworn*〕。**4.** 加在名词之后构成复数名词:ash*en*, ox*en*. **5.** 加在名词之后构成阴性名词:vix*en*. **6.** 加在名词之后构成指小词:chick*en*, kitt*en*, maid*en*.

en·a·ble [iˈneibl; ɪnˋebl̩] ***vt*.** **1.** 使能够,使得,使成为可能。**2.** 授予…权力。~ *sb*. *to* (*do*) 使人能(做)…。*an enabling act* [*statue*] 授予权力的条令。

en·act [iˈnækt; ɪnˋækt] ***vt*.** **1.** 制定(法律);颁布;规定。**2.** 扮演;演出。*as by law* ~*ed* 如法律所规定。~*ing clauses*【法】说明法案制定经过的条文。**en·ac·tive** ***a*.** 有制定权的;制定法律的。**-ment** ***n*.** **1.** 制定(法律);颁布。**2.** 法令,条例,法规。**3.** (戏剧的)上演。

e·na·lite [ˈenəlait; ˋɛnəlaɪt] ***n*.**【矿】水矽[硅]钍铀矿。

en·am·el [iˈnæməl; ɪˋnæml̩] **I** ***n*.** **1.** 搪瓷,珐琅,瓷漆。**2.** 搪瓷制品。**3.** 指甲油。**4.** (牙齿的)珐琅质,釉质。**II** ***vt*.** (〔英〕***-ll-***) **1.** 给…上珐琅,在…涂瓷漆。**2.** 使光滑。**3.** 给…上彩色,彩饰。~**paint** 瓷漆。~ **ware** 搪瓷器皿。~ **wire** 漆包(电)线。

en·am·el·er, en·am·el·ler [iˈnæmlə; ɪˋnæml̩ɚ] ***n*.** 上釉工匠[技师](= enamelist 或 enamellist)。

en·am·o(u)r [iˈnæmə; ɪˋnæmɚ] ***vt*.** 使迷恋,使倾心。***be*** ~***ed of*** [*with*] 恋慕;迷恋;醉心于。

en·an·ti·o·morph [iˈnæntiəuˌmɔːf; ɛˋnæntɪəˌmɔf] ***n*.**【化】对映(结构)体。**-phic** ***a*.** **-phism** ***n*.**【化】对映性。

en·an·ti·op·a·thy [enæntiˈɔpəθi; ɛnˌæntɪˋɑpəθɪ] ***n*.** = allopathy.

en·an·ti·ot·ro·py [iˌnæntiˈɔtrəpi; ɛnˌæntɪˋɑtrəpɪ] ***n*.**【化】互变(现象),对映(异构)现象。

en·ar·gite [iˈnɑːdʒait; ɛˋnardʒaɪt] ***n*.**【矿】硫砷铜矿。

en ar·rière [F. ɑ̃nɑˈrjer; ɑ̃nɑˋrjɛr]〔F.〕**1.** 在后面;在…之后。**2.** 拖欠,拖延。

en·ar·thro·sis [ˌenɑːˈθrəusis; ˌɛnarˋθrosɪs] ***n*.** (*pl*. ***-ses*** [-siːz; -siz])【解】杵臼关节,球窝关节。

en bro·chette [F. ɑ̃ brɔˈʃet; ɑ̃ brɑˋʃɛt]〔F.〕在烤肉的铁扦子上烤。

en brosse [F. ɑ̃ˈbrɔs; ɑ̃ˋbrɑs]〔F.〕(毛发)刷状的。

enc. = enclosure(s).

en·cae·ni·a [enˈsiːniə; ɛnˋsinɪə] ***n*.** 〔*sing*., *pl*.〕**1.** 创立纪念;教堂奠基纪念。**2.** 〔E-〕牛津(或其他)大学校庆。

en·cage [inˈkeidʒ, en-; ɛnˋkedʒ] ***vt*.** 把…关进笼里,监禁。

en·camp [inˈkæmp; ɪnˋkæmp] ***vi*.** 扎营,露营。—***vt*.** 使扎营,使宿营。**-ment** ***n*.** **1.** 扎营,露营,野营。**2.** 扎营地,露营地。

en·cap·su·late [inˈkæpsəleit; ɛnˋkæpsəˌlet] ***vt*.** **1.** 把…包于胶囊等中。**2.** 压缩,节略 (= encapsule)。**-lant** ***n*.** 密封用的材料。**-la·tion** ***n*.**

en·car·nal·ize [inˈkɑːnəlaiz; ɛnˋkarnəˌlaɪz] ***vt*.** **1.** 使具肉体,使成化身。**2.** 具体化,体现,实现(理想等)。**3.** 使具肉感。

en·car·pus [enˈkɑːpəs; ɛnˋkarpəs] ***n*.**【建】垂花装饰。

en·case [inˈkeis; ɪnˋkes] ***vt*.** **1.** 把…装箱〔镶框子等〕。**2.** 把…包在…内。**-ment** ***n*.** **1.** 装箱;包装。**2.** 箱子,鞘,套子,袋子。

en·cash [inˈkæʃ; ɛnˋkæʃ] ***vt*.** 〔英〕兑现;付现。**-a·ble** ***a*.** **-ment** ***n*.** 兑现;付现;现金收纳。

en cas·se·role [enˈkæsirəul, F. ɑ̃ˈkɑːsrɔl; ɛnˋkæsɪrol, F. ɑ̃ ˋkɑsrɔl]〔F.〕用锅炖的;用锅盛出的(食物)。

en·caus·tic [enˈkɔːstik; ɛnˋkɔstɪk] **I** ***a*.** 带色陶土烧制的,蜡画法的。~ *brick* [*tile*] 彩砖[瓦]。~ *painting* 蜡画,瓷画。**II** ***n*.** 色蜡〔涂后用熨斗加热固定〕;蜡画。

-ence *suf*. 与形容词词尾 -ent 相对应的名词词尾,表示"动作"、"性质"、"状态"等:abs*ence*, dilig*ence*, indulg*ence*.

en·ceinte [enˈseint, F. ɑ̃ˈsɛːt; ɛnˋsent, F. ɑ̃ˋsɛt] **I** ***n*.** 〔F.〕墙;城廓;城内的地方;围。**II** ***a*.** 〔F.〕妊娠的,怀孕的。

En·cel·a·dus [enˈselədəs; ɛnˋsɛlədəs] ***n*.**【希神】恩塞拉

都斯〔反对宙斯的百手巨人之一〕。

en·ce·ni·a [en'siːniə; ɛn`siniə] ***n.*** = encaenia.

en·ce·phal·ic [ˌensi'fælik; ˏɛnsə`fælɪk] ***a.*** 脑的；头骨内的。

en·ceph·a·li·tic [enˌsefə'litik; ɛnˏsɛfə`lɪtɪk] ***a.***【医】脑炎的。

en·ceph·a·li·tis [ˌensefə'laitis; ˏɛnsɛfə`laɪtɪs] ***n.***【医】脑炎。*Japanese Type-B* ～ 流行性乙型脑炎。～ *lethargica* 昏睡性脑炎。

encephal(o)- *comb. f.* 表示"脑的"：*encephal*itis, *encephalo*graphy.

en·ceph·a·lo·gram [en'sefələ*u*græm; ɛn`sɛfələˏgræm] ***n.***【医】1. 脑电图（electroencephalogram 的缩写）。2. 脑蛛网膜下腔充气图相（pneumoencephalogram 的缩写）。

en·ceph·a·log·ra·phy [enˌsefə'lɔgrəfi; ɛnˏsɛfə`lɑgrəfɪ] ***n.***【医】脑照相术，气脑造影术。

en·ceph·a·lo·my·e·li·tis [enˌsefələ*u*maiə'laitis; ɛnˏsɛfələˏmaɪə`laɪtɪs] ***n.***【医】脑脊髓炎。

en·ceph·a·lon [en'sefələn; ɛn`sɛfəˏlɑn] ***n.*** (*pl.* ***-la*** [-lə; -lə])【解】脑。

en·chain [in'tʃein, en-; ɛn`tʃen] ***vt.*** **1.** 用链锁住，束缚。**2.** 抓牢，吸引住（注意力等）。**-ment** ***n.***

en·chant [in'tʃɑːnt; ɪn`tʃænt] ***vt.*** **1.** 对…施行魔法，用妖术迷惑。**2.** 使心醉，使销魂，使迷住。***an ～ed palace***（神话中的）魔宫。***be ～ed with*** [***by***] 被迷住。**-er** ***n.*** 妖人，巫士。**-ing** ***a.*** 迷惑的，迷人的；艳丽的，标致的。**-ing·ly** ***ad.*** **-ment** ***n.*** 妖术；迷惑；著迷；魅力。**-ress** ***n.*** 女巫；妖妇。

en·chase [in'tʃeis, en-; ɪn`tʃes, ɛn-] ***vt.*** 嵌，镶；浮雕，镂刻。

en·ch(e)i·rid·i·on [ˌenkaiə'ridiən; ˏɛnkaɪ`rɪdɪən] ***n.*** (*pl.* ～*s*, ***-rid·i·a*** [-'ridiə; -`rɪdɪə]) 手册，便览。

en·chi·la·da [ˌentʃi'lɑːdə; ˏɛntʃɪ`lædə] ***n.*** 墨西哥的一种卷肉玉米面饼。

en·chon·dro·ma [ˌenkɔn'drəumə; ˏɛnkɑn`dromə] ***n.*** (*pl.* ***-ma·ta*** [-mətə; -mətə], ***-mas***)【医】内生软骨瘤。**en·chon·drom·atous** [-'drɔmətəs, -'drəumətəs; -`drɑmətəs, -`dromətəs] ***a.***

en·cho·ri·al [en'kɔːriəl; ɛn`korɪəl] ***a.*** **1.** 某国特有的。**2.** 古埃及通俗文字的。

en·ci·na [en'siːnə; ɛn`sinə] ***n.*** = live oak.

en·ci·pher [in'saifə; ɪn`saɪfɚ] ***vt.*** 把（电文）译成密码。

en·cir·cle [in'səːkl; ɪn`sɝkl] ***vt.*** **1.** 环绕，围绕；包围。**2.** 围绕；一周。*a lake ～d with* [*by*] *woods* 树林环绕的湖。～ *the globe* 环绕地球〔特指外交，战略〕。**-ment** ***n.***

encl. = enclosure.

en·clasp [in'klɑːsp, en-; ɛn`klæsp] ***vt.*** 抱住，抱紧；握紧。

en·clave ['enkleiv F. ɑ̃klɑːv; `ɛnklev, F. ɑ̃klev] ***n.*** 插在别国领域中的领土，飞地。

en·clit·ic [in'klitik, en-; ɛn`klɪtɪk] **I** ***a.***【语法】与前一词结合的（*opp.* proclitic）〔例：cannot 的 not〕。**II** ***n.***【语法】前接成分。

en·close [in'kləuz; ɪn`kloz] ***vt.*** **1.**（用篱、墙等）围起，圈起，包围，围绕。**2.** 包，装。～ *the land with walls* 筑墙围地。*I ～ herewith a cheque for 10 pounds.* 随信附上十镑支票一张。***the ～d*** 附件。

en·clo·sure [in'kləuʒə; ɪn`kloʒɚ] ***n.*** **1.** 包围，围绕；封入。**2.** 包入物，封入物；附件。**3.** 圈占地，圈用地。**4.** 围墙，围栏。*prisoners-of-war* ～ 临时战俘营。

en·clothe [in'kləuð; ɛn`kloð] ***vt.***〔书〕= clothe.

en·cloud [in'klaud; ɪn`klaud] ***vt.***〔书〕阴云遮蔽，使天阴；使阴郁。

en·code [in'kəud; ɛn`kod] ***vt.*** 把（电文）译成电码〔密码〕～**r** ***n.*** 译电员；〔自动控制〕编码船。**-ment** ***n.***

en·co·mi·ast [en'kəumiæst; ɛn`komɪˏæst] ***n.*** 赞辞作者；赞美者；阿谀者。**-tic** ***a.*** **-ti·cal·ly** ***ad.***

en·co·mi·um [en'kəumjəm; ɛn`komɪəm] ***n.*** (*pl.* ～*s*, ***-mi·a*** [-miə; -mɪə]) 赞辞，颂词；称赞，赞美，推崇。

en·com·pass [in'kʌmpəs; ɪn`kʌmpəs] ***vt.*** **1.** 围绕，包围。**2.** 包含 **3.** 完成，贯彻。*be ～ed with perils* 被危险包围着。**-ment** ***n.***

en·core [ɔŋ'kɔː; `ɑŋkor] **I** ***n.*** 要求再演；重唱，重演。*get an* ～ 被要求重演。**II** ***int.*** 再来一个。**III** ***vt.*** 要求再演〔唱〕。

en·coun·ter [in'kauntə; ɪn`kauntɚ] **I** ***n.*** 遭遇；遭遇战，冲突。*an ～ action* 遭遇战。*an ～ of wits* 斗智。**II** ***vt.*** 遇见，碰见；邂逅相逢（友人等）。—***vi.*** 偶然遇见；遭遇；冲突（*with*）。～ **group** 病友谈心治疗小组〔美国现代的精神治疗方法，由患者互相畅谈内心感情〕。～ **parlour**〔英〕（与裸体妓女短暂在一处的）幽会小屋。

en·cour·age [in'kʌridʒ; ɪn`kɝɪdʒ] ***vt.*** 鼓励，怂恿，促进，支持，赞助。～ *sb. in his idleness* 助长某人的懒惰。～ *sb. to* (*do*) 鼓励某人（做）…。***be ～d by*** 受…鼓励〔鼓舞〕。**-ment** ***n.*** 奖励，鼓励；助长。**-ing** ***a.*** 鼓励的，赞助的，振奋人心的，令人欢欣鼓舞的。**-ing·ly** ***ad.***

en·crim·son [in'krimzn; ɛn`krɪmzn] ***vt.*** 使成深红色。

en·cri·nite ['enkrinait; `ɛnkrənaɪt] ***n.***【古生】石莲。

en·croach [in'krəutʃ; ɪn`krotʃ] ***vi.***（逐渐）侵入，侵犯；侵略，侵占；侵害；侵蚀（*on*; *upon*）。～ *on* [*upon*] *another nation's territory* 侵略别国领土。～ *on* [*upon*] *sb.'s right* 侵占他人权利。～ *upon sb.'s time* 占用别人时间。～ *upon the interests of sb. for one's own good* 损人利己。**-ment** ***n.*** **1.** 侵入，侵犯，侵害；侵蚀，蚕食。**2.** 侵占物，（海水的）侵蚀地。

en·crust [in'krʌst; ɪn`krʌst] ***vt.*** **1.** 把…包上外壳。**2.**（用宝石等）镶饰（表面）。—***vi.*** 长壳〔皮〕。**-ment** ***n.***

en·cul·tu·rate [in'kʌltʃəreit; ɛn`kʌltʃəˏret] **I** ***vt.*** 使适应时尚，使合时宜。**II** ***n.*** **-ra·tive** ***a.***

en·cum·ber [in'kʌmbə; ɪn`kʌmbɚ] ***vt.*** **1.** 妨碍，阻碍；拖累，打扰。**2.** 使负（债等）。**3.** 堆满（场所）（*with*）。*be ～ed with debts* 负债，为债务所累，*be ～ed with a big family* 为大家庭所累。*an estate ～ed with mortgages* 已抵押出去的地产。

en·cum·brance [in'kʌmbrəns; ɪn`kʌmbrəns] ***n.*** **1.** 妨碍，阻碍，阻碍物；累赘；家累。**2.**【法】（不动产方面的）债权。***without ～s*** 没有儿女的拖累。

ency(c)., **encycl.** = encyclop(a)edia.

-en·cy *suf.* 表示"性质"、"状态"的名词词尾：ag*ency*, depend*ency*.

en·cyc·lic, **en·cyc·li·cal** [en'siklik(əl), -'saik-; ɛn`sɪklɪk(l), -`saɪk-] **I** ***a.*** 传阅的，通谕的。**II** ***n.***（教皇的）通告，通谕。

en·cy·clo·p(a)e·di·a [enˌsaiklə*u*'piːdiə; ɪnˏsaɪklə`pidɪə] ***n.*** **1.** 百科全书；专科全书。**2.**〔E-〕（十八世纪）法国狄德罗（Diderot）与达朗贝（D'Alembert）合编的《百科全书》〔包含启蒙主义思想〕。

en·cy·clo·p(a)e·dic(al) [enˌsaiklə*u*'piːdik(əl); ɪnˏsaɪklə`pidɪk(l)] ***a.*** 百科全书的；包含各种学科的；广博的，渊博的。～ *knowledge* 渊博的知识。*an ～ mind* 博学的人。

en·cy·clo·pe·dism, **en·cy·clo·pae·dism** [enˌsaiklə*u*'piːdizəm; ɛnˏsaɪklə`pidɪzəm] ***n.*** **1.** 百科全书的知识，知识渊博。**2.**〔E-〕（法国十八世纪）《百科全书》派的观点。

en·cy·clo·p(a)e·dist [enˌsaiklə*u*'piːdist; ɛnˏsaɪklə`pidɪst] ***n.*** **1.** 百科全书编纂者。**2.**〔E-〕（法国十八世纪）《百科全书》派成员。

en·cyst [en'sist; ɛn`sɪst] ***vt.***【生】把…包在囊内。—***vi.***【生】被包在囊内。**-ment**, **-ta·tion** [ˌensis'teiʃən; ˏɛnsɪs`teʃən] ***n.*** 被囊作用。

end [end; ɛnd] **I** ***n.*** **1.** 端，尖，末端，终点。**2.** 边缘；极点，极限。**3.** 结局，结果。**4.** 目的。**5.** 最后，死。**6.**【纺】经纱

E

零头布,(丝的)头绪;〔*pl*.〕残片,残屑。7.〔美足球〕进攻、防守最前线两端位置上的球员。*As the year draws to its* ~ ....在这一年将要结束的时候…。*the* ~ *of the town* 市郊。~*s of a cigarette* ~ 香烟头。*one's journey's* ~ 旅行的目的地。*achieve* [*gain*, *win*] *one's* ~ 达到目的。*the East E-* (*of London*) 伦敦东区(劳动人民聚居区)。*the West E-* (*of London*) 伦敦西区(富人聚居区)。*The* ~ *crowns the work*. 〔谚〕工作贵在有始有终。*the supreme* ~ 最高目的。***a rope's*** ~ 1. (两端以线相连的)打人用的短绳。2. 绞索。***a shoemaker's*** ~ (带猪鬃的)绱鞋引线。***at a loose*** ~ 无固定职业,闲着。***at loose*** ~***s*** 1. 不安定。2. 混乱。***at the*** ~ 最后,终于。***at the*** ~ ***of*** 在…末端;在…的结尾。***at the*** ~ ***of one's forbearance*** [***patience***] 忍无可忍。***at the*** ~ ***of one's resources*** [***rope***, ***wits***] 山穷水尽[束手无策,智穷计尽]。***at the latter*** ~ 在末期。***be at an*** ~ 尽;完结,终了(*Our intercourse is at an* ~. 我们的交往至此为止)。***be on the receiving*** ~ 〔口〕1. 接收别人的礼物[善意]。2. 成为攻击目标。3.【体】处于接球的一方。***be the*** ~ ***of sb***. 成为致死的原因(*You'll be the* ~ *of me*. 你真是要我的命)。***begin*** [***start***] ***at the wrong*** ~ 一开头就错。***bring to an*** ~ 使结束。***the business*** ~ 起作用的一头(如针的尖、刀剑的锋)。***carry sth. through to the*** ~ 把某事进行到底。***come out at*** [***of***] ***the little*** ~ ***of the horn*** 说过的话没做到。***come to an*** ~ 完结,终了,告终。***come to a dead*** ~ 走投无路。***come to an untimely*** ~ 短命,夭折。***come to a sticky*** ~ 落得痛苦的下场。~ ***and aim*** 目的。~ ***for*** ~ 掉头,颠倒过来。***the*** ~***s of the earth*** 天涯海角。~ ***on*** 一端向前;正对着。~ ***to*** ~ 头尾连接,衔接。~ ***up*** 直立着。***for this*** ~ 因这目的,因此。***from*** ~ ***to*** ~ 从头到尾。***get*** [***have***] ***hold of the wrong*** ~ ***of the stick*** 完全误解。***get the better*** ~ ***of sb***. 机智胜人,占人上风。***go*** (***in***) ***off the deep*** ~ 1. 游泳时投入深水;冒险。2. 控制不住自己;发脾气。***have*** [***take***] ***an*** ~ 告终,终了。***have an*** ~ ***in view*** 有所企图。***have sth. at one's fingers'*** [***tongue's***] ~***s*** 熟练,精通。***have no*** ~ ***of a time*** 乐得忘记了时间。***in the*** ~ 终于,最后。***In the*** ~ ***things will mend***. 〔谚〕船到桥头自然直。***keep one's*** ~ ***up*** 乐观地战斗,坚持到底。***land in a dead*** ~ 陷入困境。***make an*** ~ ***of*** [***to***] 了结,结束,终止。***make both*** ~***s meet*** 使收支相抵,量入为出。***a means to an*** ~ 达到目的的手段。***meet one's*** ~ 死。(***be***) ***near one's*** ~ 快要死了。***no*** ~ 〔口〕无限,非常(*I'm no* ~ *glad*. 我非常快乐)。***no*** ~ ***of*** 〔口〕很多,非常(*have no* ~ *of money* 钱多得不得了。*think no* ~ *of oneself* 自命不凡。*no* ~ *of a fool* 大傻瓜。*no* ~ *of a fellow* 极好的人)。***on*** ~ 1. 竖着,笔直地。2. 继续,不停地(*work 10 hours on* ~ 连续工作十小时)。***play both*** ~***s against the middle*** 1. 为私利而脚踏两条船。2. 使人争吵而坐收渔人之利。***put an*** ~ ***to*** 结束,了结,停止。***right*** [***straight***] ***on*** ~ 继续,接连;立刻。***set one's hair on*** ~ 使人毛骨悚然。***to no*** ~ 无益,徒劳。***to that*** ~ 因为那个原故,为要达到那个目的(所以)。***to the*** ~ 到最后,始终。***to the*** (***bitter***, ***very***) ~ 到最后,到底,直到死。***to the*** ~ ***of time*** 永远。***to the*** ~ ***of the chapter*** 到最后,到底,直到死。***to the*** ~ ***that*** ... 为要,以便。***To what*** ~? 为什么? ***without*** ~ 无尽的,无穷的。***with this*** ~ ***in view*** 抱着这一目的。***world without*** ~ 永久,无穷。

II ***vt***. 1. 使完结,了结,终止。2. 使致死,杀。3. 竖立,使直立着。4. 成为…的结尾。*We* ~*ed the discussion on a note of optimism*. 我们以乐观的调子结束了这场讨论。*A bullet through the heart* ~*ed him*. 一颗子弹穿过心脏结束了他的生命。—***vi***. 1. 终止,完毕,结尾,收场。2. 死。*The road* ~*s here*. 这条路到此地就到头了。*All is well that* ~*s well*. 〔谚〕有好结果,就算好事。~ ***by doing***... 以…结束(*He* ~*ed by thanking the audience* 最后他向听众道谢,结束演出)。~ ***in*** 结果为…,终成,终归,终于。~ ***in bubble*** [***smoke***] 终归失败,终成泡影。~ ***off*** (***up***) 结束(~ *off one's talk with a joke* 用笑话结束讲话)。~ ***up*** 结束;完事;[俚]死。~ ***up with*** 以…而告终。~ ***with*** 以…完结[终止]。~**-all** 结尾,终结,收场;最终目的。~**-around** 循环。~ **consumer** [**user**] 目的用户〔指最终应用产品的人〕。~ **game** (棋赛等的)残局。~ **ga(u)ge**【机】端面规块。~ **leaf** = ~ paper. ~ **man** 1. 在一排末端的人。2.〔美〕(在化装演出黑人歌曲的剧团表演中)站在一排末端,同站正中扮领班者作滑稽对话的演员。~ **paper** (书的)衬页。~ **point** 终点。~**-point** ***n***.【数】端点。~ **product** 最后产物,最终结果。~**-result** 最终结果,归宿。~ **run** 〔美〕1.【体】打橄榄球时在自己一端抱球左右兜圈前冲的动作。2. 规避的伎俩。~**-stop** ***vt***. 突然结束。~ **table** (沙发旁的)茶几。~ **use** 最终用途。~**-user** ***n***. 目的用户。~ **zone**【足球】端区〔端线和球门线延长线至两边边线相交的区域〕。

end. = endorsed; endorsement.

en·dam·age [in'dæmidʒ; ɛn`dæmɪdʒ] ***vt***. 使损坏,伤害。

en·da·moe·ba, en·da·me·ba [ˌendə'miːbə; ˏɛndə`mibə] ***n***.【动】内变形虫属,内阿米巴属(*Endamoeba*)。**en·da·moe·bic** [-ik; -ɪk] ***a***.

en·dan·ger [in'deindʒə; ɪn`dendʒɚ] ***vt***. 危及,危害,使遭到危险。~ *one's life* 危及性命。~**ed species**【生】濒危物种。**-ment** ***n***.

en·darch ['endɑːk; `ɛndɑrk] ***a***.【植】内始式的。

end·brain ['endˌbrein; `ɛndˏbren] ***n***.【解】端脑(= telencephalon)。

en·dear [in'diə; ɪn`dɪr] ***vt***. 使受喜爱,使被爱恋。~ *oneself to one's friends* 受朋友们喜爱。**-ment** ***n***. 亲爱;亲爱的行为[表示]。

en·dear·ing [in'diəriŋ; ɪn`dɪrɪŋ] ***a***. 可爱的,惹人喜爱的。**-ly** ***ad***.

en·deav·o(u)r [in'devə; ɪn`dɛvɚ] **I** ***n***. 努力,尽力。***do one's*** (***best***) ~(***s***) 尽全力。***make every*** ~ 尽一切努力,不遗余力。**II** ***vi***. 尽力,竭力,努力,力图(*to do*)。~ ***after*** [***for***] 竭力想,争取。

en·dem·i·c(al) [en'demik(əl); ɛn`dɛmɪk(l)] **I** ***a***. 1. (动、植物)某些特产的;(风土人情的)某地[某民族]特有的。2. 地方病的。**II** ***n***. 1. 某地特产的植物[动物]。2. 地方病。**-ly** ***ad***. **en·demic·i·ty** [ˌendi'misiti; ˏɛndɪ`mɪsətɪ], **en·dem·ism** ***n***. 地方性;风土性。

en·der·mic [en'dəːmik; ɛn`dɝmɪk] ***a***.【医】经皮的,皮下的,经皮下吸收而作用的。***the*** ~ ***method***【医】皮下疗法。**-cal·ly** ***ad***.

En·ders ['endəz; `ɛndɚz] ***n***. 恩德斯〔姓氏〕。

En·di·cott ['endikət; `ɛndɪkət] ***n***. 恩迪科特〔姓氏〕。

end·ing ['endiŋ; `ɛndɪŋ] ***n***. 1. 终止,完了,收场,结局,结尾。2. 末期,最后。3. 死。4.【语法】词尾。*nerve* ~*s*【解】神经末梢。

en·dive ['endiv; `ɛndɪv] ***n***. 1. 〔美〕苣荬菜。2. 〔英〕= chicory

end·less ['endlis; `ɛndlɪs] ***a***. 1. 无尽的,无限的,无边的,无穷的;永远的;不断的。2.【机】环状的。*an* ~ *argument* 没完没了的议论。~ **band** 环带。~ **chain** 循环链。~ **saw** 环锯。~ **screw** 蜗杆。**-ly** ***ad***. **-ness** ***n***.

end·long ['endlɔːŋ; `ɛndˏlɔŋ] ***ad***. 〔古〕1. 纵长地。2. 竖立地,笔直地。

end·most ['end*m*əust; `ɛndˏmost] ***a***. 最末端的,极远的。

end(o)- *comb. f*. 表示"内","内部"(*opp*. ecto-): *endo*crine.

en·do·bi·ot·ic [ˌendəubai'ɔtik; ˏɛndobaɪ`ɑtɪk] ***a***.【生】寄生于宿主组织内的。

en·do·blast ['endəuˌblæst; `ɛndoˏblæst] ***n***. = endoderm.

en·do·car·di·al [ˌendəuˈkɑːdiəl; ˏɛndoˋkɑrdɪəl] *a*. 【解】**1**. 心脏内的。**2**. 心内膜的。

en·do·car·di·tis [ˌendəukɑːˈdaitis; ˏɛndokɑrˋdaɪtɪs] *n*. 【医】心内膜炎。

en·do·car·di·um [ˌendəuˈkɑːdiəm; ˏɛndoˋkɑrdɪəm] *n*. 【解】心内膜。

en·do·carp [ˈendəukɑːp; ˋɛndoˏkɑrp] *n*. 【植】内果皮。

en·do·cen·tric [ˌendəuˈsentrik; ˏɛndoˋsɛntrɪk] *a*. 【语】向心结构的。

en·do·com·men·sal [ˌendəukəˈmensl; ˏɛndokəˋmɛnsḷ] *n*. 【生】内共栖〔于宿主体内〕。

en·do·cra·ni·um [ˌendəuˈkreiniəm; ˏɛndoˋkrenɪəm] *n*. (*pl*. ***-ni·a*** [-ə;-ə], ***-ni·ums***) **1**. 【解】硬脑(脊)膜 (= duramater)。**2**. (昆虫头盖里的)幕骨。

en·do·crine [ˈendəukrain; ˋɛndoˏkraɪn] **I** *a*. 内分泌的, 内分泌腺的, 激素的。**II** *n*. 内分泌;内分泌腺, 激素。～ **disorders** 内分泌失调。～ **glands** 内分泌腺。

en·do·cri·nol·o·gy [ˌendəukraiˈnɔlədʒi; ˏɛndokraɪˋnɑlədʒɪ] *n*. 内分泌学。

en·do·derm [ˈendəudəːm; ˋɛndoˏdɝm] *n*. 【生】内胚层。

en·do·der·mis [ˌendəuˈdəːmis; ˏɛndoˋdɝmɪs] *n*. 【植】内皮层。

en·do·don·tics [ˌendəuˈdɔntiks; ˏɛndoˋdɑntɪks] *n*. 〔作单数用〕【医】(牙)根管治疗术 (= endontia)。**-don·tic** *a*. **-don·tist** *n*. (牙)根管治疗医师。

en·do·en·zyme [ˌendəuˈenzaim; ˏɛndoˋɛnzaɪm] *n*. 【生】(胞)内酶。

en·do·gam·ic [ˌendəuˈgæmik; ˏɛndoˋgæmɪk] *a*. **1**. 同族结婚的。**2**. 【植】同系配合的;同花传粉的。

en·dog·a·mous [enˈdɔgəməs; ɛnˋdɑgəməs] *a*. 同族通婚的。

en·dog·a·my [enˈdɔgəmi; ɛnˋdɑgəmɪ] *n*. **1**. 同族通婚。**2**. 【植】同系交配 (*opp*. exogamy)。

en·do·gen [ˈendədʒən; ˋɛndəˏdʒɛn] *n*. 【植】内生植物。

en·do·gen·ic [ˌendəuˈdʒenik; ˏɛndoˋdʒɛnɪk] *a*. 【地】内成的。

en·dog·e·nous [enˈdɔdʒənəs; ɛnˋdɑdʒənəs] *a*. **1**. 【生】内生的, 内长的, 内源的。**2**. 【地】内成的。～ **metabolism** 内源代谢。～ **plant** 单子叶植物。

en·dog·e·ny [enˈdɔdʒini; ɛnˋdɑdʒənɪ] *n*. 【生】内生, 内发, 内长, 内源;内生的细胞形成。

en·do·lymph [ˈendəulimf; ˋɛndoˏlɪmf] *n*. 【解】内耳膜迷路内的液体, 内淋巴。

en·do·me·tri·o·sis [ˌendəuˌmiːtriˈəusis; ˏɛndoˏmɪtrɪˋosɪs] *n*. 【医】子宫内膜异位。

en·do·me·tri·tis [ˌendəumiˈtraitis; ˏɛndomɪˋtraɪtɪs] *n*. 【医】子宫内膜炎。

en·do·me·tri·um [ˌendəuˈmiːtriəm; ˏɛndəˋmitrɪəm] *n*. 【解】子宫内膜。

en·do·mix·is [ˌendəuˈmiksis; ˏɛndoˋmɪksɪs] *n*. 【生】内融合, 内合。**-mic·tic** [-ˈmiktik; -ˋmɪktɪk] *a*.

en·do·morph [ˈendəumɔːf; ˋɛndəˏmɔrf] *n*. **1**. 【矿】内容矿物 (*opp*. perimorph) 〔指矿物内包含的另一矿体〕。**2**. 【物】内容体。**-ism** 【矿】内容现象, 内变质作用。

en·do·mor·phic [ˌendəuˈmɔːfik; ˏɛndoˋmɔrfɪk] *a*. **1**. 【矿】内容矿物的;内变质的。**2**. 【生】(胚胎的内胚层结构占优势的)腹体型的。**-phy** *n*.

en·do·mor·phism [ˌendəuˈmɔːfizm; ˏɛndoˋmɔrfɪzṃ] *n*. 【矿】内变质(作用)。

en·do·my·si·um [ˌendəˈmiziəm; ˏɛndəˋmɪzɪəm] *n*. 【解】内肌膜;肌纤维衣, 内衣。

en·do·neu·ri·um [ˌendəuˈnjuːriəm; ˏɛndoˋnjʊrɪəm] *n*. 【解】神经内膜。

en·do·par·a·site [ˌendəuˈpærəsait; ˏɛndoˋpærəˏsaɪt] *n*. 【动】内寄生虫, 内寄生物。

en·do·pep·ti·dase [ˌendəuˈpeptideis; ˏɛndoˋpɛptɪdes] *n*. 【化】肽链内切酶。

en·doph·a·gous [enˈdɔfəgəs; ɛnˋdɑfəgəs] *a*. 【动】内食的。

en·do·phyte [ˈendəufait; ˋɛndoˏfaɪt] *n*. 内生植物。**-phyt·ic** [-fitik; -fɪtɪk] *a*.

en·do·plasm [ˈendəuplæzəm; ˋɛndoˏplæzəm] *n*. 【生】内质 (*opp*. ectoplasm)。

en·do·pleu·ra [ˌendəuˈplurə; ˏɛndoˋplʊrə] *n*. 【植】内种皮。

en·dop·o·dite [enˈdɔpədait; ɛnˋdɑpədaɪt] *n*. 内肢;(昆虫的)内肢节。

en·do·proct [ˈendəuˌprɔkt; ˋɛndoˏprɑkt] *n*. 【动】内肛亚纲 (*Endoprocta*) 动物 (= entoproct)。

en·dors·a·ble [inˈdɔːsəbl; ɪnˋdɔrsəbḷ] *a*. 可背书的, 可背署的;可担保的;可承认的;可赞成的, 可批准的。

en·dorse [inˈdɔːs; ɪnˋdɔrs] *vt*. **1**. 【商】在(支票等)背面签名, 背书, 背署。**2**. 签署, 签注, 签收;批转, 批注(公文等)。**3**. 保证, 担保;承认, 赞成。**4**. 〔英〕在(驾驶员执照)上注明违章记录。**5**. 〔南非〕把(进入城市的黑人)强制送回农村 (*out*)。*have one's licence* ～*d* 〔英〕驾驶执照上被注明违章事件。～ ***off*** 背书证明支取一部分票面金额。～ ***over*** 背书(票据等)将所有权让与。**endorser**, **endorsor** *n*. 背书(让与)人。**endorsee** [ˌendɔːˈsiː; ˏɛndɔrˋsɪ] *n*. 被背书人, 受让人。

en·dorse·ment [inˈdɔːsmənt; ɪnˋdɔrsmənt] *n*. 背书;保证, 承证。～ *in blank* 无记名式背书。～ *in full* 记名背书。～ *to order* 指定背书。～ *without recourse* 无偿还背书。*qualified* ～ 有条件背书。

en·do·sarc [ˈendəusɑːk; ˋɛndoˏsɑrk] *n*. 【生】= endoplasm.

en·do·scope [ˈendəuskəup; ˋɛndəˏskop] *n*. 【医】内窥镜, 内镜。

en·dos·co·py [enˈdɔskəpi; ɛnˋdɑskəpɪ] *n*. 【医】内窥镜检查。

en·do·skel·e·tal [ˌendəuˈskelitl; ˏɛndəˋskɛlɪtḷ] *a*. 【解】内骨骼的。

en·do·skel·e·ton [ˌendəuˈskelitən; ˏɛndəˋskɛlətən] *n*. 【解】内骨骼 (*opp*. exoskeleton)。

en·dos·mo·sis [ˌendɔsˈməusis, -dɔz-; ˏɛndɑsˋmosɪs, -dɑz-] *n*. 【生】内渗 **en·dos·mot·ic** [-ˈmɔtik; -ˋmɑtɪk] *a*.

en·do·sperm [ˈendəuspəːm; ˋɛndəˏspɝm] *n*. 【植】胚乳。

en·do·sper·mous [ˌendəuˈspəːməs; ˏɛndəˋspɝməs] *a*. 【植】胚乳的。

en·do·spore [ˈendəuspɔː; ˋɛndoˏspor] *n*. 【生】**1**. 内生孢子。**2**. (孢子)内壁。**3**. (花粉粒)内壁。**-spor·ic** *a*.

en·dos·te·al [enˈdɔstiəl; ɛnˋdɑstɪəl] *a*. 【解】骨内(膜)的。

en·dos·te·um [enˈdɔstiəm; ɛnˋdɑstɪəm] *n*. (*pl*. ***-te·a*** [-tiə; -tɪə]) 【解】骨内膜。

en·do·ster·nite [ˌendəuˈstəːnait; ˏɛndəˋstɝnaɪt] *n*. 【动】腹内骨。

end·os·to·sis [ˌendɔsˈtəusis; ˏɛndɑsˋtosɪs] *n*. 【医】软骨骨化。

end·os·tra·cum [enˈdɔstrəkəm; ɛnˋdɑstrəkəm] (*pl*. ***-tra·ca*** [enˈdɔstrəkə; ɛnˋdɑstrəkə]) *n*. 【动】壳内层。

en·do·style [ˈendəstail; ˋɛndəstaɪl] *n*. 【动】内柱。

en·do·the·ci·um [ˌendəuˈθiːsiəm; ˏɛndoˋθisɪəm] *n*. (*pl*. ***-ci·a*** [-e; -ɛ]) 【植】(蒴)内层;药室内壁。

en·do·the·li·um [ˌendəuˈθiːliəm; ˏɛndoˋθilɪəm] (*pl*. ***-a*** [-ə; -ə]) *n*. 【解】内皮;【植】内种皮。

en·do·therm [ˈendəθəːm; ˋɛndəθɝm] *n*. 热血〔定温〕动物。**-al** [ˌendəuˈθəːməl; ˏɛndoˋθɝməl] *a*.

en·do·ther·mic [ˌendəuˈθəːmik; ˏɛndoˋθɝmɪk] *a*. 【化】吸热的 (= endothermal)。

en·do·tox·in [ˌendəuˈtɔksin; ˏɛndoˋtɑksɪn] *n*. 【医】内毒素。

en·do·tra·che·al [ˌendəu'treikiəl; ˏɛndo`trekɪəl] *a*. 【解】气管内的。

en·dow [in'dau; ɪn`daʊ] *vt*. 1. 捐赠基金[财产等]给(学校、医院等);留给(寡妇)一部分遗产。2. 授与,赋与(特权等)。~ *a school* 给学校捐赠基金。*an* ~*ed school* 拥有基金的学校。*He is* ~*ed with genius*. 他有天才。*She is richly* ~*ed by nature*. 她有极高天分,得天独厚。

en·dow·ment [in'daumənt; ɪn`daʊmənt] *n*. 1. 捐赠;捐款;基金;养老金。2. 天赋,天资。~ **assurance** [**insurance**] 人寿定期保险。~ **policy** 养老保险单。

en·drin ['endrin; `ɛndrɪn] *n*. 【化】艾氏剂,氯甲桥萘〔杀虫剂〕。

en·due [in'dju:; ɪn`dju] *vt*. 1. 授与,赋与(*with*)。2. 〔罕〕穿(衣);使穿上(*with*)。

en·dur·able [in'djuərəbl; ɪn`djʊərəbl̩] *a*. 1. 可忍受的。2. 能持久的。**-bly** *ad*. **-ness, en·dur·a·bil·i·ty** *n*.

en·dur·ance [in'djuərəns; ɪn`djʊrəns] *n*. 1. 忍耐(力)。2. 耐久,持久(力),持久性,耐久性。*beyond* [*past*] ~ 忍无可忍。*cold* ~ 耐寒性。~ **flight** 【空】持久飞行。~ **limit** 【机】疲劳极限。~ **test** 耐力试验。

en·dure [in'djuə; ɪn`djʊr] *vt*. 忍耐,忍受;容忍。*I can not* ~ *her*. 我讨厌她。~ *pain* 忍受痛苦。~ *heat* 耐热。—*vi*. 1. 忍受,忍耐。2. 支持,持久,持续。*as long as life* ~*s* 只要还有一口气。~ *to the end* 忍耐到底,坚持到最后。

en·dur·ing [in'djuəriŋ; ɪn`djʊrɪŋ] *a*. 持久的,永久的。~ *fame* 不朽的声名。**-ly** *ad*. **-ness** *n*.

en·dur·o [en'djuərəu; ɛn`djʊəro] *n*. (*pl*. **-dur·os**) (汽车、摩托车等的)长距离耐力赛。

end·ways, end·wise ['endweiz, 'endwaiz; `ɛndˏwez, `ɛndwaɪz] *ad*. 1. 竖着;末端朝前[上]。2. (两端)连接着;向着两端。3. 在末端。

En·dym·i·on [en'dimiən; ɛn`dɪmɪən] *n*. 【希神】安狄米恩〔月神戴安娜所爱的美貌牧童〕。

E.N.E., ENE, e.n.e. = east-northeast.

-ene *suf*. 【化】〔构成烯属烃和苯系烃的名词〕: benz*ene*.

E·ne·as, E·ne·id = Aeneas, Aeneid.

en·e·ma ['enimə, i'ni:mə; `ɛnəmə] *n*. 【医】灌肠(法);灌肠器;灌肠剂。*barium* ~ 钡灌肠。*saline* ~ 盐水灌肠。*soapsuds* ~ 肥皂水灌肠。

en·e·my ['enimi; `ɛnəmɪ] **I** *n*. 1. 敌人,仇敌;〔集合词〕敌军,敌舰;敌机;敌国。2. 危害物;大害。*an* ~ *worthy of one's steel* 劲敌,强敌。*the public* [*king's, Queen's*] ~ 公敌。*a lifelong* [*mortal, sworn*] ~ 不共戴天之敌,死敌。*an* ~ *alien* 敌国侨民。*Better an open* ~ *than a false friend*. 〔谚〕宁要公开敌人,不要虚伪朋友。**II** *a*. 敌人的,敌方的。***be an*** ~ ***to*** 危害;仇视。***be one's own*** ~ 自己害自己。***go over to the*** ~ 投敌,附敌。***the*** ~ 1. 敌(军)。2. 〔the E-〕恶魔。3. 〔口〕时间 (*How goes the* ~? 现在几点钟?)。***the great*** [***last***] ~ 死神。***the*** (***old***) ***E-*** = ***our ghostly*** ~ 恶魔。

en·er·get·ic [ˌenə'dʒetik; ˏɛnɚ`dʒɛtɪk] *a*. 1. (措施等)积极的,有力的。2. 精力旺盛的,精神饱满的。*an* ~ *effort* 积极努力。**-al** *a*. = energetic. **-al·ly** *ad*.

en·er·get·ics [ˌenə'dʒetiks; ˏɛnɚ`dʒɛtɪks] *n*. 〔用作单数〕力能学,能量学;动能学。

en·er·gid ['enədʒid; `ɛnɚdʒɪd] *n*. 【生】活质体。

en·er·gism ['enədʒizəm; `ɛnɚdʒɪzm] *n*. 活动主义,奋斗主义〔认为人生之至上幸福在于人的能力得到充分发挥的伦理学说,与 perfectionism 颇为接近〕。

en·er·gize ['enədʒaiz; `ɛnɚˏdʒaɪz] *vt*. 1. 加强;给与…以活力。2. 【物】给与…能量;给与…电压。—*vi*. 活动,用力,打起精神干。*To worry is often to* ~ *needlessly*. 忧虑往往是浪费精力。

en·er·gu·men [ˌenə:'gju:mən; ˏɛnɚ`gjumɛn] *n*. 【宗】1. 恶魔附身的人。2. 狂热的信徒,狂热的人。

en·er·gy ['enədʒi; `ɛnɚdʒɪ] *n*. 1. 干劲,活力。2. (语言、行为等的)生动。3. 〔*pl*.〕(个人的)精力;能力。4. 【物】能,能量。*What* ~ *you have*! 你真有精力呀! *be full of* ~ 精力旺盛。*act* [*speak*] *with* ~ 生气勃勃地干[说]。*conservation of* ~ 能量守恒,能量不灭。*kinetic* [*motive*] ~ 动能。*potential* [*latent*] ~ 势能。***apply*** [***devote, direct***] ***one's energies to*** 致力于。***brace one's energies*** 鼓起干劲,振作精神。~ **budget** 能源预算〔对一个生态系统中能源的收入、利用与损耗的计算〕。~ **level** 【物】能(量)级(位)。~ **paper** 纸片电池。

en·er·vate ['enə:veit; `ɛnɚˏvet] **I** *vt*. 使衰弱,削弱。*an enervating climate* 使人困倦的气候。**II** *a*. = enervated.

en·er·vat·ed ['enə:veitid; `ɛnɚˏvetɪd] *a*. 无力的,衰弱的。*an* ~ *style* 软弱无力的笔调。**-va·tion** *n*.

en·face [in'feis, en-; ɪn`fes, ɛn-] *vt*. 把(金额、日期、姓名等)填[印]在(票据等)上面,把(文字格式、备忘录等)写[印]在文件面上。*an* ~*d paper* 【商】具名支票。

en·fant [ɑ̃'fɑ̃; ɑ̃`fɑ̃] *n*. 〔F.〕小孩,儿童。

en·fants per·dus [F. ɑ̃fɑ̃ 'perdy; ɑ̃fɑ̃ `pɛrdy] 〔F.〕敢死队。

en·fant ter·ri·ble [F. ɑ̃fɑ̃ tɛribl; ɑ̃fɑ̃ tɛrɪbl̩] 〔F.〕1. 早熟的儿童〔说话或提问常使大人为难〕。2. 肆无忌惮的人。

en·fee·ble [in'fi:bl; ɪn`fibl̩] *vt*. 使衰弱,弄弱。**-ment** *n*.

en·feoff [in'fef, -'fi:f, en-; ɪn`fɛf, -`fif, ɛn-] *vt*. 【史】1. 封与…领地,授与…封地[采邑]。2. 转让,让渡。**-ment** *n*. 1. 领地的授与;授与领地的证书。2. 封地,采邑。

en·fet·ter [in'fetə, en-; ɪn`fɛtɚ, ɛn-] *vt*. 给…上脚镣;束缚;使做奴隶。

en·fi·lade [ˌenfi'leid; ˏɛnfə`led] **I** *n*. 1. 【军】纵射炮火,纵向射击。2. 易受纵射的地位。*an* ~ *barrage* 纵射弹幕。**II** *vt*. 对…进行纵射。

en·fin [F. ɑ̃fɛ; ɑ̃fɛ] *ad*. 〔F.〕终于,最后。

en·fleu·rage [ɑnflæ'rɑ:ʒ; ɑnflæ`rɑʒ] *n*. 〔F.〕花香吸取法。

en·fold [in'fəuld; ɪn`fold] *vt*. 〔主美〕1. 包,包进 (*in*; *with*)。2. 抱;拥抱。3. 折叠。

en·force [in'fɔ:s; ɪn`fors] *vt*. 1. 推行,厉行,实施(法律等)。2. 强迫,强制,强派。3. 坚持(要求、主张等)。~ *obedience to an order* 强迫服从命令。~ *obedience on* [*from, upon*] *sb*. 强迫某人服从。~*d education* 强迫教育,义务教育。

en·force·a·ble [in'fɔ:səbl; ɪn`forsəbl̩] *a*. 1. 可实施的。2. 可强行的,可压服的。3. (法律的)可强制服从的。**en·for·cibil·i·ty** *n*.

en·forc·ed·ly [in'fɔ:sidli; ɪn`forsɪdlɪ] *ad*. 强迫地。**-ment** *n*. 实施;〔古〕强制。**-r** *n*. 1. 实施[强制]者。2. (流氓集团内为维护黑规矩而设的)执法人。

en·frame [in'freim; ɛn`frem] *vt*. 装(画)在框内,给…配上框子。

en·fran·chise [in'fræntʃaiz, en-; ɪn`fræntʃaɪz, ɛn-] *vt*. 1. 释放(奴隶)。2. 给与…公民权[选举权、参政权];给与…自治权。**-ment** [-tʃizmənt; -tʃɪzmənt] *n*.

eng. = 1. engine; engineer; engineering. 2. engraved; engraver; engraving.

Eng. = England; English.

en·gage [in'geidʒ; ɪn`gedʒ] *vt*. 1. 〔多用被动语态〕使从事,使忙于 (*in*)。2. (用誓约、义务等)束缚,约束,保证(*oneself to do*);订婚 (~*d to*)。3. 保证。4. 雇,聘。5. 预约,定(戏座等)。6. (军队)交战,与…交战;使参加。7. 【机】使(齿轮等)咬合,衔接 (*with*)。8. 【建】使(柱)附墙。*Are you* ~*d*? 你有事吗? *Line* [*Number*] *is* ~*d*. (电话)占线了。~ *sb.'s attention* 惹人注意。*This seat is* ~*d*. 座已定出。~ *the enemy* 和敌人交战。—*vi*. 1. 约定,答应,允诺,保证 (*to do*; *for*)。2. 从事,参

加(*in*)。3. 交战(*with*)。4.【机】(齿轮等)咬合。**be ~d** [**~ oneself**] **in** 正做着,正忙[在做,在忙]。**be ~d** [**~ oneself**] **to** 同…订婚。**be ~d with** 正与…接洽。**~ for** 应承,保证;约定(*That's all I can ~ for*. 我能担保的只有这些)。**~ in** 从事,在忙;参加(*~ in teaching* 当教员)。**~** *in a game of tennis* 参加网球赛。

en·ga·gé [ɑ̃gɑːˈʒei; ɑ̃gɑˋʒe] **a.** 〔F.〕(在政治等事件中)完全卷入的。

en·gage·ment [inˈgeidʒmənt; ɪnˋgedʒmənt] **n.** 1. 约会,约定;约束,契约;预约。2. 婚约。3. 雇用,聘用期;职业。4. 义务;〔*pl*.〕债务。5.【军】战斗。6.【机】接合,咬合。*break one's ~* 毁约,违约。*fight several ~s* 打几仗。*fulfil one's ~* 践约。*meet one's ~s* 偿清债务。*a meeting ~* 遭遇战。*a minor ~* 小规模交火。*a naval ~* 海战。**be under an ~** (**to**)有约。**enter into** [**make**] **an ~** (**with**)同人定约。**~ ring** 订婚戒指。

en·gag·ing [inˈgeidʒiŋ; ɪnˋgedʒɪŋ] **a.** 吸引人的,迷人的,可爱的。**-ly ad.**

en·gar·land [enˈgɑːlənd; ɛnˋgɑrlənd] **vt.** 〔诗〕给…戴上花环。

Eng.D. = Doctor of Engineering 工程学博士。

en·gen·der [inˈdʒendə; ɪnˋdʒendɚ] **vt.** 使发生,使产生;惹起,酿成。—**vi.** 产生;形成。

engin. = engineer(ing).

en·gine [ˈendʒin; ˋɛndʒən] **I n.** 1. 机械,机器。2. 引擎,蒸汽机,发动机。3. 机车,车头。4. 工具;〔古〕方法,手段。*a Diesel* [*steam*] *~* 柴油[蒸汽](发动)机。*an internal combustion ~* 内燃机。*an auxiliary ~* 辅助发动机。*a dental ~* 钻牙机。*an ~ of torture* 刑具。*an ~ of warfare* 兵器,武器。*a fire ~* 救火车,灭火机。*a gasoline ~* 汽油机。*a pile ~* 打桩机。*a race ~* 比赛用汽车,赛车。*an empty ~* (未挂列车的)空车头。**II vt.** 给…安装发动机。**~ bearer** 发动机台。**~ driver** 〔英〕火车司机。**~ house** 救火车库;机车库。**~ lathe** 普通车床。**~man n.** = ~ driver. **~ room** 发动机房;轮机舱。**~ shed** 机车库。**~ turning** (纸币等上面的)机绘花纹。

en·gi·neer [ˌendʒiˈniə; ˏɛndʒəˋnɪr] **I n.** 1. 技师;工程师。2. 机械设计者,机车制造人。3. (轮船的)机师;〔美〕(火车的)司机;驾驶员。4. (海军的)轮机军官;(陆军的)工兵。*a civil ~* 土木工程师。*a naval* [*marine*] *~* 造船工程师。*a chief ~* 1. 总工程师。2. 轮机长。*a first ~* 一级机工。*a student ~* 见习技术员。*the Corps of E-s* 工兵部队。*the Royal E-s* 〔英〕皇家工兵。**~ in charge** 主管工程师。**~ in chief** 总工程师。**II vt.** 1. 设计,监督(工程等)。2. 操纵。3. 图谋,策划,策动。—**vi.** 做工程师。**~ship n.** 工程师职务[地位]。

en·gi·neer·ing [ˌendʒiˈniəriŋ; ˏɛndʒəˋnɪrɪŋ] **n.** 1. 工程(技术),工程学。2. 开车技术。3. 土木工程,工事。4. 操纵,管理。*civil* [*clectrical, mechanical, mining*] *~* 土木[电机,机械,采矿]工程(学)。*aeronautical* [*marine*] *~* 航空[轮机]工程。*the E-Corps* 工兵部队。*~ geology* 工程地质。*~ science* 技术科学。*a key ~ project* 关键工程。*military ~* 工兵学。*an ~ worker* 技工。*field ~* 安装技术。*rocket ~* 火箭技术。*Nature ~* 天工。

en·gine·ry [ˈendʒinəri; ˋɛndʒənrɪ] **n.** 1. 机械类。2. 武器。3. 谋略。

en·gird, en·gir·dle [inˈgəːd, -l; ɛnˋgɝd, -l] **vt.** 用带缠绕;围绕。

en·gla·cial [enˈgleiʃəl; ɛnˋgleʃəl] **a.** 冰川内的,冰河内的。

Eng·land [ˈiŋglənd; ˋɪŋglənd] **n.** 1. 英格兰〔英国的主要部分〕。2. (泛指)英格兰和威尔斯。3. (泛指)英国。

Eng·lish [ˈiŋgliʃ; ˋɪŋglɪʃ] **I a.** 1. 英格兰(人)的;英国(人)的。2. 英语的。**II n.** 1. 英语。2. 〔the ~〕英国人〔总称〕,英国人民;英军。3. 〔e-〕【印】十四点活字。4. 〔美〕(打网球、弹子球时的)旋转运动。*He is ~*. 他是英国人。*American ~* 美国英语。*Basic ~* 基本英语〔此处 Basic 系由 British *American Scientific International Commercial* 各词的第一字母组成〕。*current* [*present-day*] *~* 当代英语。*the king's* [*queen's*] *~* 纯正英语。*Middle ~* (约 1150—1475 年的)中世纪英语。*Modern ~* (约 1475 年以后的)近代英语。*Old ~* (约 450—1150 年的)古代英语。*spoken ~* 英语口语。*standard ~* 标准英语。**~ as she is spoke** 英语口语[语音]。**in plain ~** 直率地说,说得通俗些。**III vt.** 1. 把…译成英语。2. 使成英国式,使英国化。3. 〔e-〕使(球)旋转前进。**~ Channel** 英吉利海峡。**~ daisy**【植】雏菊(*Bellis perennis*)。**~ disease** 〔主英〕支气管炎。**~ horn** 英国管(中音双簧管)。**~ ivy** = ivy. **~ muffin** 英式松饼。**~ setter** 塞特狗,英国谍犬。**~ sonnet** 英国十四行诗。**~ sparrow** 家麻雀(*Passer domesticus*)〔产于欧洲,现今在北美极常见〕。**~ springer spaniel**【动】英国长耳跳犬。**~ toy spaniel**【动】英国长毛小犬。**~ walnut** 1. 胡桃树(*Fuglans regia*)。2. 胡桃。**-er n.** 英国人;翻译英语的人。**-ism n.** 1. 英语习惯用法。2. 英国方式,英国人的特点。**-ry n.** (特指住在爱尔兰的英格兰籍)英国人。

Eng·lish·man [ˈiŋgliʃmən; ˋɪŋglɪʃmən] **n.** (*pl*. **-men** [-mən, -men; -mən, -mɛn]) 1. 英吉利人,英国人;英国男子。2. 英国船只。**~'s tie** 锚结〔绳结的一种,又叫 anchor knot, fisherman's knot, true lover's knot, waterman's knot〕。

Eng·lish·ment [ˈiŋgliʃmənt; ˋɪŋglɪʃmənt] **n.** (外国著作的)英文版,英译本。

Eng·lish·wom·an [ˈiŋgliʃwumən; ˋɪŋglɪʃˏwumən] **n.** (*pl*. **-wom·en** [-wimin; -wɪmən])英国女人。

en·glut [inˈglʌt; ɛnˋglʌt] **vt.** 〔古、诗〕1. 吞下,咽下。2. 使充满,使吃饱。

en·gobe [ɔnˈgəub; ɛnˋgob] **n.**【化】釉底料。

en·gorge [inˈgɔːdʒ; ɛnˋgɔrdʒ] **vt.** 1. 喂饱;狼吞虎咽地吃。2. 使充血。*His eyes were ~d with blood*. 他双目充血。—**vi.** 1. 大吃,贪吃。2. 吮足血。**-ment n.** 饱食;【医】充血。

engr. = engineer; engraving.

en·graft [inˈgrɑːft, en-; ɪnˋgræft, ɛn-] **vt.** 1. 嫁接(树木)。2. 灌输(思想等),使记牢。3. 附加。**-a·tion, -ment n.**

en·grail [inˈgreil; ɛnˋgrel] **vt.** 使成锯齿状花边;使成波纹。**-ment n.**

en·grain [inˈgrein; ɪnˋgren] **I vt.** 1. 把(木材、纤维;纱、线等加工前)染色。2. 〔喻〕污染〔尤指性格、思想、习惯〕。**II a.** = engrained 生来的;沾染的,根深蒂固的。*an ~* [*~ed*] *habit* 积习,积癖。*~ed scoundrel* 不可救药的恶棍。*~ vices* 积弊。

en·grave [inˈgreiv; ɪnˋgrev] **vt.** 1. 雕上,刻上。2. 镌刻(铜版);(用雕刻铜版)印刷。3. 牢记,铭记(心上)。*~ a name on a stone* = *~ a stone with a name* 把名字刻在石头上。*be ~d on sb.'s memory* 给人留下深刻印象。

en·grav·er [inˈgreivə; ɪnˋgrevɚ] **n.** 雕刻师,雕刻工,镌版工。

en·grav·ing [inˈgreiviŋ; ɪnˋgrevɪŋ] **n.** 1. 雕刻,雕刻术。2. 雕板。3. 雕版印刷品;版画。

en·gross [inˈgrəus; ɪnˋgros] **vt.** 1. 用大字体写,正式誊清。2. 吸引(注意),占用(时间),使全神贯注。3. (以垄断方式)大量收购。*~ the conversation* 只顾一个人说,不让别人开口。*be ~ed in* 热中于,埋头,一心。**-ment n.**

en·gross·ing [inˈgrəusiŋ; ɪnˋgrosɪŋ] **a.** 使人全神贯注的;极有趣味的;非常吸引人的。*an ~ task* 迷人的工作。

en·gulf [inˈgʌlf; ɪnˋgʌlf] **vt.** 把…卷入旋涡;吞没。**-ment**

E

n.

en·hance [in'hɑːns; ɪn`hæns] *vt*. 1. 增加(价值、价格、力量、吸引力等),提高;增强。2. 夸张;宣扬。**-ment** *n*.

en·har·mon·ic [ˌenhɑː'mɔnik; ˏɛnhɑr`mɑnɪk] *a*.【乐】等音的。

ENIAC, eniac = electronic numerical integrator and computer 电子数字积分计算机。

E·nid ['iːnid; `ɪnɪd] *n*. 伊妮德〔女子名〕。

e·nig·ma [i'nigmə; ɪ`nɪgmə] *n*. 谜;难解的话[文章];不可解的事物[人物]。

e·nig·mat·ic(·al) [ˌenig'mætik(əl), ˌiːnig-; ˏɛnɪg`mætɪk(l̩), ˏinɪg-] *a*. 似谜的;令人迷惑的;神秘的。**-i·cal·ly** *ad*.

e·nig·ma·tize [i'nigmətaiz; ɪ`nɪgməˏtaɪz] *vt*. 使成谜;使不可解。

en·isle [en'ail; ɛn`aɪl] *vt*. 使成(孤)岛;使孤立。

en·jamb·ment, en·jambe·ment [in'dʒæmmənt, F. ɑ̃ʒɑ̃bmɑ̃; ɪn`dʒæmmənt, F. ɑ̃ʒɑ̃bmɑ̃] *n*. 〔诗〕(诗句的)跨行进行。

en·join [in'dʒɔin; ɪn`dʒɔɪn] *vt*. 1. 命令,吩咐;告诫;责成。2. 〔美〕禁止。~ *diligence on* [*upon*] *pupils* = ~ *pupils to be diligent* 叮嘱学生用功。

en·joy [in'dʒɔi; ɪn`dʒɔɪ] *vt*. 1. 享受…之乐,欣赏,喜爱。2. 享受,享有,取得。~ *swimming* 喜欢游泳。*How did you* ~ *your trip*? 旅行如何? ~ *cherry-blossom*(*s*) 欣赏樱花。~ *one's dinner* 饭吃得津津有味。~ *good health* 健康。~ *life* 享人生之乐。~ *the esteem of one's friends* 受到朋友们的敬重。~ ***oneself*** 过得快乐。**-a·ble** *a*. 愉快的,快乐的,有趣的。**-a·bly** *ad*. **-able** *a*. **-ness** *n*.

en·joy·ment [in'dʒɔimənt; ɪn`dʒɔɪmənt] *n*. 1. 享乐,欣赏;愉快,乐事。2. 享受,享有。*take* ~ *in* 喜欢,享受,欣赏。*be in the* ~ *of good health* 享有健康。

en·kin·dle [in'kindl, en-; ɛn`kɪndl̩] *vt*. 点着(火);使燃烧起来,激起(热情);挑起(战争等)。

enl. = enlarged; enlisted.

en·lace [in'leis; ɪn`les] *vt*. 1. 卷上,把…卷起来。2. 用带子捆扎。3. 围绕,缠绕。**-ment** *n*.

en·large [in'lɑːdʒ; ɪn`lɑrdʒ] *vt*. 1. 扩大,扩展,扩充;增大;【摄】放大。2. 〔美〕〔古〕释放。~ *one's views by reading* 以读书来开扩眼界。~ *one's house* 扩建房屋。*an* ~*d edition* 增订版。*an* ~*d photograph* 放大照片。— *vi*. 1. 扩展,扩大。2. 拉长说,详述(*on*; *upon*)。**-ment** *n*. 扩大,扩张;增补;【摄】放大;【医】增大,肥大,肿大。**-r** *n*. 1.【摄】放大机。2. 扩大者,增补者;详述者。

en·light·en [in'laitn; ɪn`laɪtn̩] *vt*. 1. 启发,开导;教导;〔口〕使明白,使领悟。2. 使摆脱偏见。3. 〔古〕照耀。~ *sb*. *on a subject* 使某人明白某问题。**-ed** *a*. 开通的,开明的,进步的,文明的;有知识的(*an* ~ *age* 文明时代)。**-ing** *a*. 1. 有启发作用的,使人领悟的。2. 〔古〕照耀的,照明的。**-ment** *n*.

en·light·en·ment [in'laitnmənt; ɪn`laɪtn̩mənt] *n*. 1. 启迪,启蒙,启发;教化,开导。2. 开明的状态。*the Enlightenment* (十八世纪欧洲的)启蒙运动。*the Age of Enlightenment* 启蒙时代。

en·link [in'liŋk; ɪn`lɪŋk] *vt*. 把…连接起来,使紧密联系(*with*; *to*)。

en·list [in'list; ɪn`lɪst] *vt*. 1. 使入伍;征募,招(兵)。2. 争取,谋取;获得(赞助等)。~ *sb*. *in an enterprise* 在事业上得到某人赞助。~ *the support of* 拉拢。*an* ~*ed man* 〔美〕士兵。—*vi*. 1. 应募;参加(*in*)。2. 协助,赞助,支持,偏袒。~ *as a volunteer* 当志愿兵。~ *in the army* 从军。~ *under the banner of revolution* 加入革命队伍。**-ment** *n*. 募兵;征募,入伍;服兵役期。

en·li·ven [in'laivən; ɪn`laɪvən] *vt*. 使快活,使有生气,给与生气;使生动;使活跃。

en·mesh [in'meʃ, en-; ɛn`mɛʃ] *vt*. 1. 把…绊在网上;使绊住。2. 使陷入。*be* ~*ed in difficulties* 陷入困难中。**-ment** *n*.

en·mi·ty ['enmiti; `ɛnmətɪ] *n*. 敌意,仇恨,憎恨;反目,不和。***at*** ~ ***with*** 与…不和。***have*** [***harbour***] ***no*** ~ ***against sb***. 对某人无冤无仇。

en·ne·ad ['eniæd; `ɛnɪˏæd] *n*. 1. 九个一组。2. [E-] (埃及的)九柱神。

en·ne·a·gon ['eniəgɔn; `ɛnɪəˏgɑn] *n*.【数】九角形,九边形。

en·ne·a·hed·ron [ˌeniə'hiːdrən; ˏɛnɪə`hidrən] *n*.【数】九面体。

en·ne·a·syl·la·ble [ˌeniə'siləbl; ˏɛnɪə`sɪləbl̩] *n*. 九音节。

en·no·ble [i'nəubl; ɪ`nobl̩] *vt*. 1. 使高贵;抬高。2. 把…列入贵族,给…授爵。**-ment** *n*.

en·nui [F. ɑ̃nyi, 'ɔnwiː; ɑ̃`nyi, `ɑnwi] *n*. 〔F.〕厌倦,倦怠,无聊。

E·noch ['iːnɔk; `inək] *n*. 伊诺克〔男子名〕。

e·nol ['iːnɔl, -nəul; `inɑl, -nol] *n*.【化】烯醇。**e·no·lic** [iː'nɔlik; i`nɑlɪk] *a*. **e·nol·i·za·tion** [ˌenəlai'zeiʃən; ˏɛnəlaɪ`zeʃən] *n*. 烯醇化(作用)。

e·nol·o·gy [iː'nɔlədʒi; i`nɑlədʒɪ] *n*. 葡萄酒酿制学。

e·nol·o·gist *n*. 葡萄酒酿制术研究者[专家]。

e·nor·mi·ty [i'nɔːmiti; ɪ`nɔrmətɪ] *n*. 1. 极恶,凶恶;暴行,大罪。2. 巨大,庞大。*the* ~ *of the crime* 罪恶深重。

e·nor·mous [i'nɔːməs; ɪ`nɔrməs] *a*. 1. 巨大的,庞大的。2. 无法无天的,罪大恶极的。*an* ~ *difference* 很大的分歧。~ *profits* 巨大的利益。*a man of* ~ *strength* 力气很大的人。**-ly** *ad*. **-ness** *n*.

e·nough [i'nʌf; ɪ`nʌf] **I** *a*. 充足的,足够的。~ *eggs*, *eggs* ~ 鸡蛋十分充足〔后者语气较弱〕。~ *noise to wake the dead* 吵得死人都不安。~ ***and to spare*** 绰绰有余。***more than*** ~ 太多。**II** *n*. 充足,满足,足够。*have* ~ *to eat* 有足够的东西吃。*E- of that*! 够了,别说了! *E- of this folly*! 不要再干这种傻事了! ***Cry*** '~'! 快认输吧! ***E- is as good as a feast***.【谚】饱食便是珍馐! 知足常乐。***have*** ~ ***to do*** 很吃力(*I had* ~ *to do to catch the tram*. 我好容易才赶上电车)。***have had quite*** [***about***] ~ ***of*** 感到厌烦。**III** *ad*. 〔用于被修饰语之后〕十分,充分,足,够。*I am warm* ~. 我够暖和的。*He was fool* (= *foolish*) ~ *to agree*. 他同意了,真够傻的。*She was clever* ~ *to take the management of her own house*. 她很能干,一定会管家。*The meat is roasted just* ~. 这肉烤得恰到好处。***Be good*** [***kind***] ~ ***to reply early***. 请早日赐覆。***be old*** ~ ***to*** 已经是可以…的年龄了。***can not*** ... ~ 无论怎样…都不够(*I cannot thank you* ~. 感谢不尽)。***curiously*** [***oddly***, ***strangely***] ~ 〔用作插入语〕说也奇怪,最奇怪的是。***sure*** ~ 确实,果然。***well*** ~ 1. 还不错,还可以。2. 相当;很,极。**IV** *int*. 够了! 别再说了!

e·nounce [i(ː)'nauns; ɪ`naʊns] *vt*. 1. 宣告,发表;声明,说明。2. 发声读出。**-ment** *n*.

En·o·vid ['iːnəvid; `inəvɪd] *n*. 女用口服避孕药〔商标名〕。

e·now [i'nau; ɪ`naʊ] *a*., *n*., *ad*. 〔古〕= enough.

en·phy·tot·ic [ˌenfai'tɔtik; ˏɛnfaɪ`tɑtɪk] *a*.【植】恒定流行的。

en·plane [en'plein; ɛn`plen] *vi*. 乘飞机(*cf*. deplane)。~ *for Europe* 乘飞机去欧洲。

en·quire [in'kwaiə; ɪn`kwaɪr] *vi*., *vt*. = inquire.

en·quir·y [in'kwaiəri; ɪn`kwaɪrɪ] *n*. = inquiry.

en·rage [in'reidʒ; ɪn`redʒ] *vt*. 触怒,激怒,使人愤怒。***be*** ~***d at*** [***by***] ***sth***. 对某事愤慨,为某事激怒。***be*** ~***d with sb***. 对某人发怒。**-d·ly** *ad*. **-ment** *n*.

en·rapt [in'ræpt; ɛn`ræpt] *a*. 狂喜的。

en·rap·ture [in'ræptʃə; ɪn`ræptʃɚ] ***vt.*** 使狂喜,使兴高采烈。**-d·ly *ad.***

en·reg·i·ment [in'redʒimənt; ɪn`rɛdʒɪmənt] ***vt.*** **1.** 把…编成联队。**2.** 把…严格地组织起来〔*cf.* regiment〕。

en·reg·is·ter [in'redʒistə; ɛn`rɛdʒɪstɚ] ***vt.*** 记录,登记。

en rè·gle [F. ɑ̃'regl; ɑ̃`rɛgl̩] 〔F.〕照规则,按规定。

en·rich [in'ritʃ; ɪn`rɪtʃ] ***vt.*** **1.** 使富裕,使丰富。**2.**【矿】富集。**3.** (使)充实。**4.** 使肥沃。**5.** 加浓。**6.** 浓缩。**7.** 装饰。~ *oneself at sb.'s expense* 损人肥己。~*ed bread* 营养面包。~*ed uranium*【原】浓缩铀。**-ment *n.*** **-er *n.*** **-ing·ly *ad.***

en·robe [in'rəub; ɛn`rob] ***vt.*** 使穿长袍。**-ment *n.***

en·rol(l) [in'rəul; ɪn`rol] ***vt.*** **1.** 把…记入名簿[清单、目录];登记,编入;使入会,使入学。**2.** 使入伍,使服兵役。~ *sb. as a member of a club* 吸收某人为俱乐部会员。~ *oneself in the army* 应征入伍,参军。**-ment *n.*** **1.** 登记,注册。**2.** 入伍,参军。**3.** 入会。**4.** 注册人数。

en·roll·ee [inˌrəu'liː; ɪnˏro`li] ***n.*** 被录用的人;入会者;被征入伍者;入学者。

en·root [in'ruːt, -'rut; ɪn`rut, -`rʊt] ***vt.*** 使根深蒂固,深植〔主要用作被动语态〕。

ens [enz; ɛnz] ***n.*** (*pl.* ***entia*** ['enʃiə; `ɛnʃɪə]) = entity.

Ens. = Ensign〔美〕海军少尉。

en·sam·ple [en'sɑːmpl; ɛn`sæmpl̩] ***n.*** 〔古〕= example.

en·san·guine [in'sæŋgwin; ɛn`sæŋgwɪn] ***vt.*** 血染,血污,血溅;使成血红色。

en·san·guined [in'sæŋgwind, en-; ɪn`sæŋgwɪnd, ɛn-] ***a.*** 血红色的。

en·sate ['enseit; `ɛnset] ***a.*** = ensiform.

en·sconce [in'skɔns; ɛn`skɑns] ***vt.*** **1.** 使安坐;安置。**2.** 隐藏。~ *oneself in* [*on*] 安坐于…,把自己安置于…。

en·seal [en'siːl; ɛn`sil] ***vt.*** 加封,封闭。

en·sem·ble [F. ɑ̃sɑ̃ːbl; ɑ̃sɑ̃bl̩] ***n.*** 〔F.〕 **1.** 全体,总体;总(体)效果。**2.** 全体演出,全体演出者。**3.**【乐】合唱,大合奏。**4.** 整套(衣服)。**5.** 剧团,歌舞剧,文工团。**6.**【自】集合,系集,信号群。~ **playing** 集体演出。

en·sep·ul·cher, en·sep·ul·chre [in'seplkə; ɛn`sɛpəlkɚ] ***vt.*** (***-che·red, -chred; -cher·ing, -chring***) 把…葬入坟墓;埋葬。

en·sheathe [in'ʃiːð; ɛn`ʃeð] ***vt.*** 把…插入鞘;用鞘套住。

en·shrine [in'ʃrain; ɪn`ʃraɪn] ***vt.*** **1.** 把…置于殿内祀奉;把…安置在龛内。**2.** 秘藏。*memories* ~*d in one's heart* 珍藏在内心中的回忆。**-ment *n.***

en·shroud [in'ʃraud, en-; ɪn`ʃraʊd, ɛn-] ***vt.*** **1.** 用寿衣包上。**2.** 隐蔽,包藏。*be* ~*ed in mist* 笼罩在雾中。

en·si·form ['ensifɔːm; `ɛnsɪˏfɔrm] ***a.***【植】剑形的。

en·sign ['ensain; `ɛnsaɪn] ***n.*** **1.** (表示职别等的)徽章。**2.** 旗,国旗;团旗。**3.** ['ensn; `ɛnsn] 军舰旗。**4.**〔美〕海军少尉;【英军】(从前做旗手的)步兵少尉〔现名 second lieutenant〕。*the national* ~ 国旗。***the blue*** ~ 英国海军预备舰舰旗。***the red*** ~ 英国商船旗。***the St. George's*** [***white***] ~ 英国军舰旗。***the white*** ~ 英国海军与皇家快艇中队旗。**-cy** ['ensainsi; `ɛnsaɪnsɪ] = **-ship *n.*** 少尉的职位[任务]。

en·si·lage ['ensilidʒ; `ɛnsl̩ɪdʒ] **I *n.*** 饲料青贮法;青贮饲料。**II *vt.*** 青贮(饲料)。

en·sile [en'sail; ɛn`saɪl] ***vt.*** 青贮(饲料)。

en·sky [in'skai; ɛn`skaɪ] ***vt.*** (***-skied, -skyed; -sky·ing***) **1.** 使耸入天际。**2.** 把…捧上天。—***vi.*** 耸入天际。

en·slave [in'sleiv; ɪn`slev] ***vt.*** **1.** 使做奴隶;征服。**2.** 强制,使盲从。*be* ~*d to a habit* 成为习惯的奴隶。**-ment *n.***

en·slav·er [in'sleivə; ɪn`slevɚ] ***n.*** 奴役者,征服者。

en·snare [in'snɛə; ɪn`snɛr] ***vt.*** **1.** 用绊子捕捉,绊住。**2.** 诱…入圈套;诱捕,诱惑,陷害。**-ment *n.***

en·snarl [in'snɑːl; ɛn`snɑrl] ***vt.*** 使缠结,使纠缠。

en·sor·cell, en·sor·cel [in'sɔːsl; ɛn`sɔrsəl] ***vt.*** (***-celled; -cell·ing, -cel·ing***)〔古〕**1.** 迷,迷惑;(妖言)惑(众)。**2.** 令人心醉,使人心荡神移,恼(人)。

en·soul [in'səul; ɛn`sol] ***vt.*** **1.** 使深入灵魂。**2.** 赋予…灵魂。

en·sphere [in'sfiə; ɛn`sfɪr] ***vt.*** **1.** 把…放置球中。**2.** 包围;使成球形。

en·sta·tite ['enstətait; `ɛnstətaɪt] ***n.***【地】顽火辉石(岩)(= protobastite)。

en·sue [in'sjuː, en-; ɛn`su] ***vi.*** 跟着发生;(…的)结果是…(*from*; *on*)。*the ensuing months* 随后数月。*the ensuing year* = *the year ensuing* 第二年。*Silence* ~*d.* 随即静默。*What will* ~ *from* [*on*] *this?* 这会产生什么结果呢? —***vt.***【圣】追求。

en·sure [in'ʃuə; ɪn`ʃʊr] ***vt.*** **1.** 保护,使安全(*against*; *from*)。**2.** 保证,担保;保险。~ *an income to sb.* 确保某人有一笔收入。*It will* ~ *you success.* 这将保证你成功。**-r *n.*** 保证者;保护者。

en·swathe [in'sweið; ɛn`sweð] ***vt.*** 绑;卷,缠。**-ment *n.***

ent. = entomology 昆虫学。

E.N.T. = ear, nose and throat 耳鼻喉。

-ent *suf.* **1.** 加在动词后构成形容词,表示"动作"、性质":insist*ent*. **2.** 加在动词后构成名词,表示"动作者"、"生效物":presid*ent*, solv*ent*.

en·tab·la·ture [en'tæblətʃə; ɛn`tæblətʃɚ] ***n.*** **1.**【建】柱上楣构,柱头盘。**2.** (机器部件等的)支柱。

en·ta·ble·ment [in'teiblmənt; ɛn`tebl̩mənt] ***n.*** **1.** = entablature. **2.** 承放雕像的平台。

en·tail [in'teil; ɪn`tel] **I *vt.*** **1.**【法】限定(继承人)。**2.** 遗留给,转给(弊害等)(*on*; *upon*)。**3.** 使蒙受,使产生,带来,引起;需要。~ *labour upon* 在…上要花费劳力。~ *great expense on sb.* 使某人承担大笔费用。**II *n.***【法】**1.** 限定继承权。**2.** 预定继承人的顺序。**-ment *n.***

en·ta·moe·ba [ˌentə'miːbə; ˏɛntə`mibə] ***n.*** (*pl.* ***-bae*** [-biː; -bi], ***-bas*** [-bəz; -bəz]) = endamoeba.

en·tan·gle [in'tæŋgl; ɪn`tæŋgl̩] ***vt.*** **1.** 使纠缠,缠住;使混乱。**2.** 使卷入,使陷入;连累。**3.** 困恼,迷惑。*be easily* ~*d by flattery* 易被甜言蜜语所迷惑。***be*** [***get***] ~***d in*** 给…缠住;被牵连,被卷入(*be* ~*d with sb.* 同某人有牵连)。

en·tan·gle·ment [in'tæŋglmənt; ɪn`tæŋgl̩mənt] ***n.*** **1.** 缠结;纠纷,混乱。**2.** 牵连。**3.** 为难。*barbed wire* ~*s* 带刺的铁丝网。

en·ta·sis ['entəsis; `ɛntəsɪs] ***n.***【建】凸肚状。

en·tel·e·chy [en'teləki; ɛn`tɛləkɪ] ***n.***【哲】**1.** 圆满实现。**2.** 生命原理。

en·tel·lus [en'teləs; ɛn`tɛləs] ***n.***【动】(印度的)瘤猿。

en·ten·te [F. ɑ̃tɑ̃ːt; ɑ̃tɑ̃t] ***n.*** 〔F.〕 **1.** (国家间的)协定,协商。**2.** 协约国;有协约关系的党派。~ ***cordiale*** [kɔr'djɑːl; kɔr`djɑl] 友好谅解。***E- cordiale*** (1904 年的)英法协约。***the*** (***Triple***) ***E-*** (1907 年的英、法、俄)三国协约。

en·ter ['entə; `ɛntɚ] ***vt.*** **1.** 入,进。**2.** 把…放进。**3.** 加入,参加;使加入,使入会,使入学。**4.** 编入;记入,登记,申报。**5.** 训练(狗、马等)。**6.**【法】提出。**7.** 开始。~ *the army* 参军。~ *a profession* 就业。~ *battle* 开始战斗。~ *details in a book* 把细目记入账簿。~ *a protest* 提出抗议;把抗议列入记录。~ *an action against sb.* 控告某人。~ *a ship* 申报船只入港。~ *an appearance* 到案,出庭;到场,出席。—***vi.*** **1.** 入;挤进。**2.**【剧】上[出]场。**3.** 参加,加入;入会,入学。~ *at the door* 从正门进来。~ *by a secret entrance* 偷进。~ *for* (*a race*) 参加(赛跑)。~ *for an examination* 投考。~ ***into*** **1.** 入,挤入;动手,开始(谈话等)。**2.** 成为…的一部分。**3.** 缔结(协约等)。**4.** 参加,参与(计划等)。**5.** 讨论(细节);着手处理。**6.** 考虑;体会;体谅,同情(~ *into sb.'s feelings* 体会某人心情。~ *into sb.'s troubles* 体谅别人困难。~ *into an agreement* 缔约)。~ ***on*** [***upon***] **1.** 动

手,开始。**2.** 入,投身于。**3.** 占有(土地、财产等)(~ *upon one's thirtieth year* 满 29 岁。~ *upon one's task* 动手工作。~ *upon a political career* 投身政界。~ *upon one's new duties* 开始担任新职)。~ ***one's head*** 想起,想到。~ ***up*** **1.** 把…正式记入账簿。**2.**【法】把…记入案件记录中。**-a·ble** ***a.***

enter- *comb.f.* = entero- 表示"肠的": *enter*itis, *entero*cele.

en·ter·ic [en'terik; ɛn`tɛrɪk] ***a.*** 肠的。~ **fever** 伤寒,肠热病。

en·ter·i·tis [ˌentə'raitis; ˏɛntə`raɪtɪs] ***n.***【医】肠炎。

en·ter·o- *comb.f.* "肠": *entero*cele.

en·ter·o·bi·a·sis [ˌentərəu'baiəsis; ˏɛntəro`baɪəsɪs] ***n.***【医】蛲虫病。

en·ter·o·cele ['entərəusiːl; `ɛntərəˏsil] ***n.***【医】肠疝,阴道后疝。

en·ter·o·co·li·tis [ˌentərəukə'laitis; ˏɛntərokə`laɪtɪs] ***n.***【医】小肠结肠炎。

en·ter·o·gas·trone [ˌentərəu'gæstrəun; ˏɛntərə`gæstron] ***n.***【医】肠抑胃素。

en·ter·o·ki·nase [ˌentərəu'kaineis, -'kineis; ˏɛntərə`kaɪnes, -`kɪnes] ***n.***【生化】肠致活酶。

en·ter·on ['entəˌrɔn; `ɛntəˏrɑn] ***n.*** 肠,消化道。

en·ter·os·to·my [ˌentə'rɔstəmi; ˏɛntə`rɑstəmɪ] ***n.***【医】肠造口术。

en·ter·o·to·my [ˌentə'rɔtəmi; ɛntə`rɑtəmɪ] ***n.***【医】肠切开术。

en·ter·prise ['entəpraiz; `ɛntɚˏpraɪz] ***n.*** **1.** (艰巨或带有冒险性的)事业,计划。**2.** 企[事]业单位。**3.** 企业心,事业心,进取心;冒险心;胆识。**4.** 兴办(企业);开创(事业)。*embark in* [*upon*] *an* ~ 举办企业。*free* ~ 自由企业。*a man of* ~ 有进取心的人。*a rash* ~ 轻率的计划。*a spirit of* ~ 事业精神。***undertake*** [***take on***] ***an*** ~ 创办事业。**-priser** ***n.*** = entrepreneur.

en·ter·pris·ing ['entəpraiziŋ; `ɛntɚˏpraɪzɪŋ] ***a.*** 有事业心的,有创业精神的,有积极性的,大胆的。*an* ~ *young man* 富有事业精神的青年人。~ *spirit* 事业心,冒险精神,积极性。**-ly** ***ad.***

en·ter·tain [ˌentə'tein; ˏɛntɚ`ten] ***vt.*** **1.** 招待,款待;使快乐;使感兴趣。**2.** 怀抱(希望等),含有(感情等)。**3.** 容纳,接受,答应(请求等),愿意考虑。*The play ~ed us very much.* 那个戏很有趣。~ *the proposal* 愿意考虑建议。*be ~ed at* [*to*] *dinner* 受款待,被宴请。~ *doubts* 怀疑。~ *hopes* 怀抱希望。~ *friends with music* [*refreshments*] 用音乐[茶点]招待朋友。—***vi.*** 进行招待[款待]的活动。~ ***angels unawares*** 招待某人而不知其为贵宾〔出自《圣经·希伯来书》〕。

en·ter·tain·er [ˌentə'teinə; ˏɛntɚ`tenɚ] ***n.*** **1.** 款待者。**2.** 演艺者〔尤指民歌手、舞蹈、喜剧演员等〕。

en·ter·tain·ing [ˌentə'teiniŋ; ˏɛntɚ`tenɪŋ] **I** ***a.*** **1.** 有趣的,使人愉快的;招待好的。**2.** 会应酬的。**II** ***n.*** 招待,款待。~ *expenses* 招待费,交际费。**-ly** ***ad.***

en·ter·tain·ment [ˌentə'teinmənt; ˏɛntɚ`tenmənt] ***n.*** **1.** 招待,款待;应酬;宴会;娱乐;游艺,余兴。**2.** 怀抱。**3.** 受理,采纳。**4.** 招待会,表演会,文娱节目。*a house of* ~ 娱乐场;旅馆;酒馆(等)。*a farewell* ~ 欢送会。*a musical* ~ 音乐演奏,音乐余兴。***give an*** ~ ***to sb.*** 招待(某人),宴请(某人)。***much to my*** ~ 最有趣的是。~ **tax** 娱乐捐。

en·thal·py ['enθælpi, en'θælpi; ɛn`θælpɪ, `ɛnθəlpɪ] ***n.***【化】热含量,焓。

en·thral(l) [in'θrɔːl; ɪn`θrɔl] ***vt.*** **1.** 迷惑,吸引住。**2.** 奴役,使做奴隶。*be ~ed by a novel* 被小说迷住。**-ing** ***a.*** **-ment** ***n.***

en·throne [in'θrəun; ɪn`θron] ***vt.*** **1.** 使登基,立…为王;【宗】使就任主教;给予…最高地位。**2.** 崇拜;尊崇。**-ment** ***n.***

en·thro·ni·za·tion [inˌθrəunai'zeiʃən; ɛnˏθronaɪ`zeʃən] ***n.*** = enthronement.

en·thuse [in'θjuːz; ɪn`θjuz] ***vi.***, ***vt.***〔口〕(使)表示热心;(使)变得热心。

en·thu·si·asm [in'θjuːziæzəm; ɪn`θjuzɪˏæzəm] ***n.*** **1.** 热心,热情,热诚(*for*)。**2.** 爱好的事物;〔古〕宗教狂,笃信。*Music is his great* ~. 音乐是他最爱好的东西。***be full of*** ~ ***about*** 热衷于。***an outburst of*** ~ 热情奔放。~ ***for*** (*sport*) (运动)热。***on momentary*** ~ 凭一时热情。***overflow with*** ~ 热情洋溢。***with*** ~ 热衷,热心。

en·thu·si·ast [in'θjuːziæst; ɪn`θjuzɪˏæst] ***n.*** **1.** 热心家,热情者,热衷者。**2.**〔古〕宗教狂。

en·thu·si·as·tic [inˌθjuːzi'æstik; ɪnˏθjuzɪ`æstɪk] ***a.*** 热心的,热情的;热烈的。**-cal·ly** ***ad.***

en·thy·meme ['enθimiːm; `ɛnθəˏmim] ***n.***【逻】省略推理法,省略三段论法。**en·thy·me·mat·ic** [ˌenθəmi'mætik; ˏɛnθəmɪ`mætɪk], **en·thy·mem·ic** [ˌenθi'miːmik; ˏɛnθɪ`mimɪk] ***a.***

en·tice [in'tais; ɪn`taɪs] ***vt.*** 引诱,怂恿。~ *away from* 从…诱出。~ ***sb. into doing*** [***to do***] 怂恿某人做…。**-ment** ***n.***

en·tic·ing [in'taisiŋ; ɪn`taɪsɪŋ] ***a.*** 迷人的,诱人的,动人心目的。**-ly** ***ad.***

en·tire [in'taiə; ɪn`taɪr] **I** ***a.*** **1.** 整个的,完全的;全部的,完整的;全体的。**2.** 纯粹的。**3.**【植】全缘的。**4.** (雄兽)没有阉过的。**II** ***n.***〔罕〕**1.** 整体;全部。**2.**〔英〕一种黑啤酒。**3.** 种马。~ *affection* 纯真的爱情。*an* ~ *horse* 没有阉过的马。**-ly** ***ad.*** 彻底地,完全地。**-ness** ***n.***

en·tire·ty [in'taiəti; ɪn`taɪrtɪ] ***n.*** 完全;全部,全体,总体。***in its*** ~ 整体,全部,全盘。***possession by entireties***【法】共同占有,(不可分的)所有权。

en·ti·ta·tive ['entitətiv; `ɛntɪtətɪv] ***a.*** 实体的,本质的。

en·ti·tle [in'taitl; ɪn`taɪtl] ***vt.*** **1.** 使…有资格(做某事);给与…权利[资格]。**2.** 给…定名,把…叫做。*His talent ~s him to command.* 他的才能使他有资格指挥。*be ~d to say that* 有资格说。*be ~d to praise* 值得表扬。*be ~d "Your Highness"* 被尊称为"殿下"。**-ment** ***n.*** 权利。

en·ti·ty ['entiti; `ɛntətɪ] ***n.*** **1.** 实体;统一体。**2.** 存在(物)。**3.** (有别于属性等的)本质。

en·to- *comb.f.* 表示"内": *ento*derm.

en·to·blast ['entəublæst; `ɛntəˏblæst] ***n.*** = endoblast.

en·to·derm ['entəudəːm; `ɛntəˏdɝm] ***n.*** = endoderm.

en·to·gas·tric [ˌentəu'gæstrik; ˏɛntə`gæstrɪk] ***a.*** 胃内的。

en·toil [in'tɔil; ɛn`tɔɪl] ***vt.***〔古、诗〕使入圈套;诱惑;陷害。

en·tomb [in'tuːm; ɪn`tum] ***vt.*** 埋葬;成为…的坟墓。**-ment** ***n.***

en·tom·ic(al) [in'tɔmik(əl); ɛn`tɑmɪk(l̩)] ***a.*** 昆虫的。

en·to·mo·log·ic [ˌentəumə'lɔdʒik; ɛntəmə`lɑdʒɪk] ***a.*** 昆虫学的。

en·to·mol·o·gist [ˌentəu'mɔlədʒist; ˏɛntə`mɑlədʒɪst] ***n.*** 昆虫学家,昆虫学者。

en·to·mol·o·gize [ˌentəu'mɔlədʒaiz; ˏɛntə`mɑlədʒaɪz] ***vi.*** **1.** 研究昆虫学。**2.** 采集昆虫。

en·to·mol·o·gy [ˌentəu'mɔlədʒi; ˏɛntə`mɑlədʒɪ] ***n.*** 昆虫学。*economic* ~ 实用昆虫学,经济昆虫学。

en·to·moph·a·gous [ˌentəu'mɔfəgəs; ˏɛntə`mɑfəgəs] ***a.***【动】食虫的。

en·to·moph·i·lous [ˌentəu'mɔfiləs; ˏɛntə`mɑfələs] ***a.***【植】虫媒的。*an* ~ *flower* 虫媒花。

en·to·moph·i·ly [ˌentəu'mɔfili; ˏɛntə`mɑfəlɪ] ***n.*** 昆虫传花粉作用。

en·to·mos·tra·can [ˌentəu'mɔstrəkən; ˏɛntə`mɑstrəkən] ***n.*** 切甲类(*Entomostraca*)动物。

en·to·phyte [ˈentəufait; ˋɛntəˏfaɪt] *n*. 内寄生植物。

en·to·plas·tron [ˌentəuˈplæstrən; ˏɛntəˋplæstrən] *n*. (*pl*. ***en·to·plastra*** [ˌentəuˈplæstrə; ˏɛntoˋplæstrə])【动】内腹甲。

en·tou·rage [ˌɔntuˈrɑːʒ; ˏɑntuˋrɑʒ] *n*. 〔F.〕1. (建筑物的)周围,环境。2. 随行人员,伴随者,近侍。

en·to·zo·a [ˌentəuˈzəuə; ˏɛntəˋzoə] *n*. entozoon 的复数。

en·to·zo·on [ˌentəuˈzəuɔn; ˏɛntəˋzoɑn] *n*. (*pl*. ***-zoa*** [-ˈzəuə; -ˋzoə]) 内寄生动物。**en·to·zo·al** [-əl; -əl], **en·to·zo·ic** [-ik; -ɪk] *a*.

en·tr'acte [ˈɔntrækt, ɔnˈtrækt; ˋɑntrækt, ɑnˋtrækt] *n*. 〔F.〕1. (多幕剧的)幕间休息。2. 幕间休息时的插演节目(如音乐、舞蹈等)。

en·trails [ˈentreilz; ˋɛntrəlz] *n*. 1. 〔*pl*.〕内脏;肠。2. (物体的)内部。

en·train[1] [inˈtrein; ɪnˋtren] *vt*. (用火车)输送(军队等)。—*vi*. 上火车。

en·train[2] [inˈtrein; ɪnˋtren] *vt*. 1. 〔罕〕拖。2. 产生,导致。3.【化】带走;使(空气)在混凝土中成气泡。*~ed oil* 带走的油。**-er** *n*.【化】夹带剂。

en·train·ment [inˈtreinmənt; ɪnˋtrenmənt] *n*.【化】雾沫。*dust* ~ 带走粉尘量。~ *phenomena* 卷吸现象。

en·tram·mel [inˈtræml; ɪnˋtræml̩] *vt*. (〔英〕***-ll-***) 纠缠;拘束,束缚;妨碍。

en·trance[1] [ˈentrəns; ˋɛntrəns] *n*. 1. 进入;入场;加入,入会;入学。2. 开始,着手。3. 就业,就职。4. (演员的)出场。5. 入场权;入场费;会费;学费。6. 入口,大门(口),楼梯口;【电】引入线。7. (海关)入港手续。8.【乐】起奏,起唱。9.【海】船头水线以下的部分。~ *examinations* 入学考试。~ *fee* [*money*] 入场费;会费;学费。~ *free* 免费入场。~ *requirements* 入学标准。***force an ~ into*** 闯进。***gain an ~*** 挤进去。***have free ~ to*** 可以自由进入…。***make*** [***effect***] ***one's ~*** 入场。***No ~***. 不准入内。

en·trance[2] [inˈtrɑːns; ɪnˋtræns] *vt*. 使出神,使神魂颠倒,使发迷;使狂喜。*be ~d with joy* 欢喜的发狂。*be ~d in thought* 想得出神。*be ~d with fear* 吓得魂不附体。**-ment** *n*.

en·tranc·ing [inˈtrɑːnsiŋ; ɪnˋtrænsɪŋ] *a*. 迷人的,使人神魂颠倒的。**-ly** *ad*.

en·trant [ˈentrənt; ˋɛntrənt] *n*. 1. 进入者。2. 新加入的人;新会员;(刚入大学的)新生;新就业者。3. 参加竞赛者。

en·trap [inˈtræp; ɪnˋtræp] *vt*. (***-pp-***) 1. 俘获,使陷罗网。2. 用计引诱,使堕术中。

en·treat [inˈtriːt; ɪnˋtrit] *vt*. 1. 恳求,请求。2. 〔古〕对待。~ *a favour of sb*. 请某人帮忙。~ *sb*. *for* [*to show*] *mercy* 求情。~ *sb*.*'s pardon* 请人原谅。*evil*(*ly*) ~ *sb*. 〔古〕虐待某人。—*vi*. 恳求,请求。**-ing·ly** *ad*. **-ment** *n*.

en·treat·y [inˈtriːti; ɪnˋtritɪ] *n*. 恳求,哀求。

en·tre·chat [ˌɑ̃trəˈʃɑː; ɑ̃trəˋʃɑ] *n*. 〔F.〕(芭蕾舞的)击足跳〔跃起两足腾空交叉数次〕。

en·tre·côte [F. ɑ̃trəkoːt; ɑ̃trəˋkot] *n*. 〔F.〕肋骨间的肉,去肋骨的肉片。

en·trée, en·tree [ˈɔntrei; ˋɑntre] *n*. 〔F.〕1. 入场;入场许可,入场权。2. 〔英〕鱼肉两正菜间的菜,〔美〕正菜。3.【乐】(舞剧的)开场舞,(歌剧的)开始乐章。

en·tre·mets [ˈɔntrəmei, 〔*pl*.〕ˈɔntrəmeiz; ˋɑntrəˏme, 〔*pl*.〕ˋɑntrəmez] *n*. 〔F.〕〔*sing*., *pl*〕正菜之外的菜;甜食。

en·trench [inˈtrentʃ; ɪnˋtrɛntʃ] *vt*. 1. 在…围以壕沟,用壕沟防护。2. 盘踞,固守,牢固树立。3. 深挖。—*vi*. 1. 侵犯,侵占。2. 〔古〕接近 (*on*; *upon*)。***be ~ed in*** ... 盘踞在…。~ ***oneself*** 挖壕沟自卫。***~ed within tradition*** 墨守惯例。**-ment** *n*. 1. 掘壕沟,筑垒。2. 壕沟,堡垒,阵地。3. 保护。4. 〔古〕侵犯。

en·tre nous [ɔːntrəˈnuː; ɑ̃trəˋnu] 〔F.〕(= *between ourselves*) 不要对外人说〔只限你我知道〕。

en·tre·pôt [ˈɔntrəpəu; ˋɑntrəˏpo] *n*. 〔F.〕1. 仓库;关栈;保税仓库。2. 货物集散地。~ **trade** 转口贸易。

en·tre·pre·neur [ˌɔntrəprəˈnəː; ˏɑntrəprəˋnɝ] *n*. 〔F.〕1. 企业家;创业人。2. 承包人;主办人;促进者。**-ship** *n*. 企业家(主办人等的)身分[地位、职权、能力]。

en·tre·sol [ˈɔntrəsɔl; ˋɛntrəˏsɑl] *n*. 〔F.〕【建】夹层,阁楼。

en·tro·py [ˈentrəpi; ˋɛntrəpɪ] *n*. 1.【物】熵。2.【无】平均信息量。

en·trust [inˈtrʌst; ɪnˋtrʌst] *vt*. 委托,付托;托。~ *sth*. *to sb*. = ~ *sb*. *with sth*. 把某物交给某人。**-ment** *n*.

en·try [ˈentri; ˋɛntrɪ] *n*. 1. 进入,入场;入城;(演员)出场。2. 入口;门口。3. 通道,路口;河口。4. 登记;记载;申报;记录;记载事项,项目,条目。5. 参加;(比赛的)参加人名单。6. (海关)报关手续,报单。7.【法】对土地的侵占;对家宅的侵入。8.【计】输入项目。*a triumphal* ~ 凯旋入城。*a port of* ~ 报关海港[口岸]。*double* [*single*] ~ 复[单]式簿记。*word* ~ (词典的)词条。~ ***for consumption*** 进口货物报单。~ ***for free goods*** 免税货物报单。***make an ~*** (***in***) 记入,登记。***make one's ~*** 出场。**~-level** *a*. 初级水平的,供初学者使用的,入门的。~**way** *n*. 入口通道。

en·twine [inˈtwain; ɪnˋtwaɪn] *vt*. 缠住,盘绕;纠缠。*a tree ~d with ivy* 爬满常春藤的树。—*vi*. 缠绕。**-ment** *n*.

en·twist [inˈtwist, en-; ɛnˋtwɪst] *vt*. 缠结;捻,搓。

e·nu·cle·ate [iˈnjuːklieit; ɪˋnjuklɪˏet] *vt*. 1. 〔古〕阐明。2.【医】摘出,剜出。3.【生】去核。**e·nu·cle·a·tion** *n*.

e·nu·mer·ate [iˈnjuːməreit; ɪˋnjuməˏret] *vt*. 1. 数,点。2. 枚举,列举。**e·nu·mer·a·ble** *a*. 可点数的,可列举的。**e·nu·mer·ation** [iˌnjuːməˈreiʃən; ɪˏnjuməˋreʃən] *n*. 1. 计算;列举。2. 详述;细目。3.【统】点查(*defy* ~ 不胜枚举, *the* ~ *method* 查点法)。**-a·tive** *a*. 计算的,计数的;列举的。

e·nun·ci·a·ble [iˈnʌnsiəbl, -ʃiː-; ɪˋnʌnsɪəbl, -ʃɪ-] *a*. 1. 可断言的,可阐明的,可系统表达的。2. 可宣布的;可发表的。3. 可清晰发音的。

e·nun·ci·ate [iˈnʌnsieit, -ʃi-; ɪˋnʌnsɪˏet, -ʃɪ-] *vt*. 宣布,发表(学说的),阐明(宗旨等)。—*vi*. (清晰)发音。**e·nun·ci·a·tion** [iˌnʌnsiˈeiʃən; ɪˏnʌnsɪˋeʃən] *n*. 1. 阐明;宣告;发表。2. 清晰发音。**e·nun·ci·a·tive** [iˈnʌnʃiətiv; ɪˋnʌnʃɪˏetɪv] *a*. 1. 阐明的;宣告的。2. 发音(清晰)的。**e·nun·ci·a·tor** *n*. 1. 阐明者,宣告者,陈述者。2. 发音清晰的人。

e·nure [iˈnjuə; ɪnˋjʊr] *vt*., *vi*. = inure.

en·u·re·sis [ˌenjuˈriːsis; ˏɛnjʊˋrisɪs] *n*.【医】遗尿(症)。

en·u·ret·ic [ˌenjuˈretik; ˏɛnjʊˋrɛtɪk] **I** *a*. 遗尿的。**II** *n*. 遗尿剂。

env. = envelope.

en·vei·gle [enˈviːgl; ɪnˋvigl] *vt*. = inveigle.

en·vel·op [inˈveləp; ɪnˋvɛləp] **I** *vt*. 1. 包,封;蔽。2.【军】包围。*an ~ing attack* 包围攻击。*be ~ed in* 被包围在。~ *oneself in a blanket* 包在毛毯中。**II** *n*. = envelope. ~ **table** (四边附有活动桌板的)摺叠式桌子。~ **top** 桌子四边作放大桌面用的摺叶。**-ment** *n*. 1. 封,包,包围。2. 封皮,封套。

en·ve·lope [ˈenvələup, ˈɔn-; ˋɛnvəˏlop, ˋɑn-] *n*. 1. 信封;纸袋;包封,封皮。2. 壳层,外壳。3.【数】包(络)线;包迹。4.【空】气囊;【天】包层;【生】包膜,包被。*floral* ~【植】花被。***push*** [***stretch***] ***the ~*** 逼人太甚。

en·ven·om [inˈvenəm, en-; ɛnˋvɛnəm] *vt*. 1. 置毒于,在…下毒。2. 使恶化;毒害。*an ~ed mind* 狠心。*~ed words* 恶毒的话。**en·ven·om·a·tion** [inˌvenəˈmeiʃən; ɪnˏvɛnəˋmeʃən] *n*. 毒化;投毒。

E

en·vi·a·ble [ˈenviəbl; ˋɛnvɪəbl] *a*. 引起妒忌的,值得羡慕的。**-ness** *n*. **en·vi·a·bly** *ad*.

en·vied [ˈenvid; ˋɛnvɪd] *a*. 被人妒忌的,被人羡慕的。

en·vi·er [ˈenviə; ˋɛnvɪr] *n*. 嫉妒者,羡慕者。

en·vi·ous [ˈenviəs; ˋɛnvɪəs] *a*. 忌妒的,猜忌的,艳羡的。*be ~ of sb. for his success* = *be ~ of sb.'s success* 忌妒[羡慕]某人的成功。~ *looks* 嫉妒的神情,羡慕的眼光。**-ly** *ad*. **-ness** *n*.

en·vi·ron [inˈvaiərən; ɪnˋvaɪərən] *vt*. 包围,围绕。*be ~ed with* [*by*] *enemies* 被敌人包围。

en·vi·ron·ment [inˈvaiərənmənt; ɪnˋvaɪrənmənt] *n*. **1**. 周围,围绕。**2**. 围绕物;环境,四周,外界。**3**. 环境艺术作品;环境戏剧(*cf*. environmental art)。*natural ~* 自然环境。*social ~* 社会环境。

en·vi·ron·men·tal [inˌvaiərənˈmentl; ɪnˏvaɪrənˋmɛntl] *a*. **1**. 环境的,环境产生的。**2**. 环境艺术的。*an ~ factor* 环境的因素。~ **art** 环境艺术〔一种以作品包围观众;而不是把作品固定在观众面前的艺术形式〕。~ **engineering** 模拟运转条件的技术;环境工程。~ **pollution** 环境污染。~ **radiation** 环境放射。~ **rape** 环境掠夺。~ **resistance** (限制人口增长的)环境阻力。~ **science** (研究环境污染等问题的)环境科学。**-ly** *ad*.

en·vi·ron·men·tal·ism [inˌvaiərənˈmentlizm, ɪnˏvaɪrənˋmɛntəlɪzəm] *n*. 【生】(同遗传论相对的)环境论〔认为环境系决定个体和群体发展的主要因素〕。

en·vi·ron·men·tal·ist [inˌvaiərənˈmentlist; ɪnˏvaɪrənˋmɛntlɪst] **I** *n*. **1**. 环境论者。**2**. 环境保护论者,研究环境问题的专家。**II** *a*. 环境论的,环境论者的。

en·vi·rons [ˈenvirənz, inˈvaiərənz; ˋɛnvɪrənz, ɪnˋvaɪrənz] *n*. 〔*pl*.〕附近,近郊,郊区。*the ~ of Paris* 巴黎郊区。

en·vis·age [inˈvizidʒ, en-; ɛnˋvɪzɪdʒ] *vt*. **1**. 正视,面对(事实等)。**2**. 想像;设想。**3**. 观察,展望。~ *realities* 正视现实。*programs ~d by the municipal authority* 市政当局拟议中的计划。**-ment** *n*.

en·vi·sion [inˈviʒən, en-; ɛnˋvɪʒən] *vt*. 想像,预见,展望。

en·voi [ˈenvɔi; ˋɛnvɔɪ] *n*. = envoy.

en·voy[1] [ˈenvɔi; ˋɛnvɔɪ] *n*. 使节;代表,使者;全权公使;外交官。*an Imperial ~* 钦差(大臣)。*a peace ~* 媾和使节。*a special ~* 特使。~ ***extraordinary and minister plenipotentiary*** 特命全权公使。**-ship** *n*. 使节身份。

en·voy[2] [ˈenvɔi; ˋɛnvɔɪ] *n*. (诗等的)跋,书后;(作为高潮的概括或献词的)结尾诗节。

en·vy [ˈenvi; ˋɛnvɪ] **I** *vt*. (*-vied*; *-vy·ing*) 羡慕,忌妒。*How I ~ you!* 我真羡慕您! —*vi*. 显示出羡慕[忌妒]。**II** *n*. **1**. 羡慕。**2**. 羡慕[忌妒]的对象。*be in ~ of sb.'s success* 羡慕某人的成功。***out of ~*** 出于忌妒[羡慕]。

en·wind [inˈwaind, en-; ɛnˋwaɪnd] *vt*. (*-wound*; *-winding*) 缠绕,包,卷。

en·womb [inˈwuːm; ɛnˋwum] *vt*. **1**. 深包,隐藏。**2**. 使包藏于子宫内。

en·wrap [inˈræp; ɛnˋræp] *vt*. (*-pp-*) **1**. 包裹,包围,围绕。**2**. 吸引住,使专心,使迷于。

en·wreathe [inˈriːð, en-; ɛnˋrið] *vt*. 用花圈围住[装饰];缠,绕(= inwreathe)。

en·wrought [inˈrɔːt; ɪnˋrɔt] *a*. = inwrought.

en·zo·ot·ic [ˌenzəuˈɔtik; ˏɛnzəˋɑtɪk] **I** *n*. 地方性动物病。**II** *a*. 地方性动物病的。

en·zy·got·ic [ˌenzaiˈɡɔtik; ˏɛnzaɪˋɡɑtɪk] *a*. 【生】同胚的,同一受精卵发生的。

en·zy·mat·ic [ˌenzaiˈmætik; ˏɛnzaɪˋmætɪk] *a*. 【生化】酶的,酶促的。**-al·ly** *ad*.

en·zyme [ˈenzaim; ˋɛnzaɪm], **en·zym** [-zim; -zɪm] *n*. 【化】酶。*digestive ~* 消化酶。*induced ~* 诱导酶。

en·zy·mic [enˈzaimik; ɛnˋzaɪmɪk] *a*. = enzymatic. **-al·ly** *ad*.

en·zy·mol·o·gy [ˌenzaiˈmɔlədʒi; ˏɛnzaɪˋmɑlədʒɪ] *n*. 酶(化)学。

eo- *comb. f*. 【地、考古】表示"始新","原始":*Eo*cene, *eo*hippus.

e·o·bi·ont [ˌi(ː)əuˈbaiənt; ɪəˋbaɪənt] *n*. 【生】生物前驱〔英国物理学家伯纳尔 (J.D. Bernal) 用语,假定生命起源于化学演变过程。生物前驱是生物具有生命前的一个发展期〕。

E·o·cene [ˈi(ː)əusiːn; ˋɪəˏsin] **I** *a*. 【地】始新世的,始新统的。**II** *n*. 〔the ~〕【地】始新世;始新统;始新世岩石。~ **epoch** 【地】始新世。~ **series** 始新统。

e·o·hip·pus [ˌi(ː)əuˈhipəs; ˏɪəˋhɪpəs] *n*. 【古生】始祖马(*Eohippus*)。

E·o·li·an [iːˈəuliən; iˋolɪən] *a*. = Aeolian.

E·ol·ic [iːˈɔlik; iˋɑlɪk] *n*., *a*. = Aeolic.

e·o·lith [ˈiːəuliθ; ˋiəˏlɪθ] *n*. 【考古】原始石器。

e·o·lith·ic [ˌiːəuˈliθik; iəˋlɪθɪk] *a*. 【地、考古】始石器时代的。

E.O.M. = end of month 月底。

e·on [ˈiːən, ˈiːɔn; ˋiən, ˋiɑn] *n*. 无限长的时代,永世 (= aeon)。

e·o·ni·an [iːˈəuniən; iˋonɪən] *a*. 永远的,永世的 (= aeonian)。

E·os [ˈiːɔs; ˋiɑs] *n*. 【希神】曙光女神,黎明女神〔相当于罗马神话的 Aurora〕。

e·o·sin(e) [ˈiːəsin; ˋiəsɪn] *n*. 【化】曙红,四溴萤光素;类似曙红的染料。

e·o·sin·o·phil [ˌiːəuˈsinəfil; ˏiəˋsɪnəfɪl], **e·o·sin·ophile** [-fail; -faɪl] *n*. 【生】嗜曙红。**e·o·sin·o·phil·ic** [-ˈfilik; -ˋfɪlɪk] *a*.

e·o·sin·o·phile [ˌiːəuˈsinəfail; ˏiəˋsɪnəfaɪl] *a*. 【化】易染曙红的。

e·os·phor·ite [iːˈɔsfərait; iˋɑsfəraɪt] *n*. 【矿】磷铝锰矿。

-eous 〔形容词词尾〕= -ous. **1**. 〔加在拉丁名词之后构成形容词〕: aqu*eous*, lign*eous*. **2**. 〔加在末尾为 -ty 的法语名词之后构成形容词〕: bount*eous*, dut*eous*. ★ right*eous*, court*eous* 等是在类推之下形成的; beaut*eous*, plent*eous* 等是诗歌用语。

E·o·zo·ic [ˌiːəuˈzəuik; ˏiəˋzoɪk] **I** *a*. 【地】始生代的,前寒武纪的。**II** *n*. 〔the ~〕始生代,前寒武纪。

ep- *pref*. 〔用于母音等 = epi-〕: *ep*enthesis.

E.P. = electroplate.

EPA = Environmental Protection Agency 〔美〕环境保护局。

e·pact [ˈiːpækt; ˋipækt] *n*. **1**. 闰余〔阳历一年间超过阴历的日数,通常为 11 日〕。**2**. 元旦月龄,岁首月龄〔阳历元旦回溯至阴历当月初一的日数〕。

ep·arch [ˈepɑːk; ˋɛpɑrk] *n*. **1**. (古希腊的)州长;(近代希腊的)县长。**2**. (东正教的)主教。

ep·arch·y [ˈepɑːki; ˋɛpɑrkɪ] *n*. **1**. (古希腊的)州;(近代希腊的)县。**2**. (东正教的)主教管区。

é·pa·ter [F. epɑˈte; ɛpɑˋtɛ] *vt*. 〔F.〕使吃惊,使震惊。

ep·aul(e)·ment [eˈpɔːlmənt; ɛˋpɔlmənt] *n*. 【建】肩墙。

ep·au·let(te) [ˈepəulet; ˋɛpəˏlɛt] *n*. 【军】肩章;肩章形的饰物。***win one's ~s*** 升为军官。

E.P.B. = Economic Planning Board 〔英〕经济计划局。

E.P.D. = excess profits duty 超额利润税。

é·pée [eiˈpei; eˋpe] *n*. 〔F.〕**1**. (击剑用的)剑。**2**. 尖剑术。

ep·ei·rog·e·ny [ˌepaiˈrɔdʒini; ˏɛpaɪˋrɑdʒənɪ] *n*. 【地】造陆作用。**e·pei·ro·gen·ic** [eˌpairəˈdʒenik; ɛˏpaɪrəˋdʒɛnɪk], **e·pei·ro·ge·net·ic** [-dʒiˈnetik; -dʒɪˋnɛtɪk] *a*.

ep·en·ceph·a·lon [ˌepenˈsefələn; ˏɛpənˋsɛfəlɑn] *n*. 【解】**1**. 后脑 (= hind brain)。**2**. 〔罕〕小脑。**-l·ic** *a*.

ep·en·dy·ma [eˈpendimə; ɛˋpɛndəmə] *n*. 【动】室管膜。

-al, -ry *a*.

e·pen·the·sis [e'penθisis; ɛ`pɛnθɪsɪs] *n*. (*pl*. **-ses** [-siːz; -siz]) 插入字母,增音。**e·pen·thet·ic** [ˌepən'θetik; ˏɛpən`θɛtɪk] *a*.

e·pergne [i'pəːn, F. e'pɛrn; ɪ`pɝn, e`pɛrn] *n*. 〔F.〕(餐桌中央的)饰架。

ep·ex·e·ge·sis [eˌpeksi'dʒiːsis; ɛˏpɛksɪ`dʒisɪs] *n*. 增词;附加说明。

ep·ex·e·get·ic(al) [eˌpeksi'dʒetik(əl); ɛpˏɛksɪ`dʒɛtɪk(l̩)] *a*. 增词的,附加说明的。

Eph. = Ephesians.

eph- *pref*. 〔用于 h 前〕(= epi-): *eph*emeral.

e·phah, e·pha ['iːfə; `ifə] *n*. 以砝〔古希伯来干量具名,约合⅓到一个蒲式耳〕。

e·phebe [i'fiːb, 'efiːb; ɪ`fib, `ɛfib] *n*. 男青年〔尤指古希腊刚成公民的男青年〕。

e·phe·bus [i'fiːbəs; ɪ`fibəs], **e·phebe** [i'fiːb, 'e-; ɪ`fib, `ɛ-] *n*. (*pl*. **-bi** [-bai; -baɪ]) 青年公民〔古雅典 18-20 岁接受体育和军事训练的男子〕。**e·phe·bic** *a*.

e·phed·rine, -drin [e'fedrin, 'efedriːn; ɛ`fɛdrɪn, `ɛfɛdrɪn] *n*. 【药】麻黄素,麻黄碱。

e·phem·er·a [i'femərə; ɪ`fɛmərə] *n*. (*pl*. **-s**, **-rae** [-riː; -ri]) 【虫】蜉蝣;短命的东西。

e·phem·er·al [i'femərəl; ɪ`fɛmərəl] **I** *a*. 朝生暮死的;短命的,暂时的。**II** *n*. **1**. 生命短暂的事物。**2**. 短生植物。*an* ~ *fever* 一日热。*an* ~ *flower* 一天就凋谢的花。~ *joys* 短暂的欢乐。**-ly** *ad*.

e·phem·er·al·i·ty [iˌfemə'ræliti; əˏfɛmə`rælətɪ] *n*. **1**. 短命,朝生暮死。**2**. (*pl*. **-ties** [-tis; -tɪs]) 生命短暂的事物。

e·phem·er·id [i'femərid; ə`fɛmərɪd] *n*. 【动】蜉蝣,蜉蝣目昆虫。

e·phem·er·is [i'feməris; ɪ`fɛmərɪs] *n*. (*pl*. **ephe·mer·ides** [ˌefə'merədiːz; ˏɛfə`mɛrɪdiz]) 【天】天体位置表;星历表。

e·phem·er·on [i'femərən; ɪ`fɛməˏrɑn] *n*. = ephemera.

E·phe·si·an [i'fiːʒiən; ɪ`fiʒən] **I** *a*. 以弗所的。**II** *n*. **1**. 以弗所人。**2**. 〔*pl*.〕【圣】《以弗所书》〔见《新约》〕。

Eph·e·sus ['efisəs; `ɛfəsəs] *n*. 以弗所〔小亚细亚古都〕。

eph·od ['efɔd, 'ɛfəd] *n*. 古时犹太教大祭司穿的法衣。

eph·or ['efɔ, -ə; `ɛfɔr, -ɚ] *n*. (*pl*. **-ors**, **-or·i** [-ərai; -əˏraɪ]) 古斯巴达五长官团长官。

E·phra·im ['iːfreiim; `ifrɪm] *n*. **1**. 【圣】伊弗列姆〔约瑟的次子〕。**2**. 以色列伊弗列姆部族人。**3**. 以色列王国。

ep·i- *pref*. 表示"在上";"在外";"在前";"在后";"在旁";"在其间";"除外"等〔母音前用 ep-, h 前用 eph-〕: *epi*blast, *epi*zoon.

ep·i·ben·thos [ˌepi'benθɔs; ˏɛpə`bɛnθɑs] *n*. 浅海生物。

ep·i·bi·ot·ic [ˌepibai'ɔtik; ˏɛpɪbaɪ`ɑtɪk] **I** *a*. **1**. 【生】外生的,体外生的。**2**. 残遗的。~ *species* 残遗种。**II** *n*. 残遗物;【生】残遗种。

ep·i·blast ['epiblæst; `ɛpəˏblæst] *n*. 【生】上胚层;外胚层。

e·pib·o·ly [i'pibəli; ɪ`pɪbəlɪ] *n*. 【胚】外包。**ep·i·bol·ic** [epi'bɔlik; ɛpɪ`bɑlɪk] *a*.

ep·ic ['epik; `ɛpɪk] **I** *n*. **1**. 叙事诗,史诗;写传说或历史中英雄事迹的诗。**2**. 史诗般的文艺作品。**II** *a*. **1**. 叙事诗的,史诗的。**2**. 英雄的,壮丽的;宏大的。~ **poem** 叙事诗 (= epic)。

ep·i·cal ['epikəl; `ɛpɪkl̩] *a*. = epic. **-ly** *ad*.

ep·i·ca·lyx [ˌepi'keiliks, -'kæliks; ˏɛpɪ`kelɪks, -`kælɪks] *n*. (*pl*. **-lyx·es**, **-lyces** [-liksiz, -lisiːz; -lɪksɪz, -lɪˏsɪz]) 【植】副萼。

ep·i·can·thus [ˌepi'kænθəs; ˏɛpɪ`kænθəs] *n*. 【医】内眦赘皮。**ep·i·can·thic** *a*.

ep·i·car·di·um [ˌepi'kɑːdiəm; ˏɛpɪ`kɑrdɪəm] *n*. (*pl*. **-di·a** [-diə; -dɪə]) 【解】心外膜,心包脏层。

ep·i·carp ['epikɑːp; `ɛpɪˏkɑrp] *n*. 【植】外果皮 (*opp*. endocarp)。

ep·i·ce·di·um [ˌepi'siːdiəm; ˏɛpə`sidɪəm] *n*. 悼歌,挽歌。

ep·i·cene ['episiːn; `ɛpəˏsin] **I** *a*. **1**. 【语法】两性通用的,通性。**2**. 【生】兼有两性的;无男女区别的;有女人气的。**II** *n*. **1**. 通性词。**2**. 兼有两性特征的人。

ep·i·cen·ter, 〔英〕**ep·i·cen·tre** ['episentə; `ɛpɪˏsɛntɚ] *n*. 【地】震中;中心,集中点。**-tral** *a*.

ep·i·cen·trum [ˌepi'sentrəm; ˏɛpɪ`sɛntrəm] *n*. (*pl*. **-tra** [-trə; -trə]) = epicenter.

ep·i·cist ['episist; `ɛpɪsɪst] *n*. 史诗作者,叙事诗人。

ep·i·cor·a·coid [ˌepi'kɔrəkɔid; ˏɛpɪ`kɑrəkɔɪd] **I** *a*. 【解】上喙突的。**II** *n*. 上喙骨。

ep·i·cot·yl [ˌepi'kɔtil; ˏɛpɪ`kɑtɪl] *n*. 【植】上胚轴。

ep·i·cot·yl·e·don·ar·y [ˌepikɔti'liːdnəri; ˏɛpɪkɑtɪ`lidn̩ərɪ] *a*. 上胚轴的。

ep·i·cra·ni·um [ˌepi'kreiniəm; ˏɛpɪ`krenɪəm] *n*. (*pl*. **-ni·a** [-ə; -ə]) 【解、昆】头盖。**ep·i·cra·ni·al** *a*.

ep·i·crit·ic [ˌepi'kritik; ˏɛpə`krɪtɪk] *a*. 【解】精微(感觉)的,细觉的。

Ep·ic·te·tus [ˌepik'tiːtəs; ˏɛpɪk`titəs] *n*. 埃皮克提图〔公元前一世纪时的希腊斯多噶派哲学家、教师〕。

ep·i·cure ['epikjuə; `ɛpɪˏkjʊr] *n*. **1**. 讲究饮食的人,美食家。**2**. 享乐主义者。

ep·i·cu·re·an [ˌepikjuə'riːən; ˏɛpɪkjʊ`riən] **I** *a*. **1**. 享乐主义的。**2**. 讲究饮食的。*an* ~ *feast* 丰盛的筵席。**II** *n*. **1**. 享乐主义者。**2**. 美食家。

Ep·i·cu·re·an·ism [ˌepikjuə'riənizəm; ˏɛpɪkjʊ`riənˏɪzəm] *n*. **1**. 伊比鸠鲁哲学;伊比鸠鲁学派。**2**. 信奉伊比鸠鲁哲学。**3**. 〔e-〕享乐主义;美食主义 (epicurism)。

ep·i·cur·ism ['epikjuərizəm; `ɛpɪkjʊˏrɪzəm] *n*. 享乐主义,美食主义。

Ep·i·cu·rus [ˌepi'kjuərəs; ˏɛpɪ`kjʊrəs] *n*. 伊比鸠鲁〔公元前 342? —270,古希腊杰出的唯物主义和无神论者〕。

ep·i·cy·cle ['episaikl; `ɛpəˏsaɪkl̩] *n*. **1**. 【天】本轮。**2**. 【数】周转圆。

ep·i·cy·clic [ˌepi'saiklik; ˏɛpə`saɪklɪk] *a*. **1**. 【天】本轮的。**2**. 【数】周转圆的。~ **train** 【机】周转轮系。

ep·i·cy·cloid(al) [ˌepi'saiklɔid(əl); ˏɛpɪ`saɪklɔɪd(l̩)] *n*. 【数】圆外旋轮线,外摆线。**-al** [ˌepisai'klɔidəl; ˏɛpɪsaɪ`klɔɪdl̩] *a*.

ep·i·deic·tic [ˌepi'daiktik; ˏɛpɪ`daɪktɪk] *a*. (文体、演讲等)富于词藻的;夸耀的。

ep·i·dem·ic [ˌepi'demik; ˏɛpə`dɛmɪk] **I** *n*. **1**. 流行病,传染病,时疫。**2**. (风尚等的)流行;(流行病的)蔓延。**II** *a*. **1**. 传染病。**2**. 流行性的。~ **catarrh** 流行性感冒。~ *encephalitis* 流行性脑炎

ep·i·dem·i·cal [ˌepi'demikəl; ˏɛpə`dɛmɪkl̩] *a*. = epidemic. **-ly** *ad*.

ep·i·de·mi·ol·o·gy [ˌepiˌdiːmi'ɔlədʒi, -ˌdemi-; ˏɛpɪˏdimɪ`ɑlədʒɪ, -ˏdɛmɪ-] *n*. 流行病学。**ep·i·de·mi·o·log·ic** [-ə'lɔdʒik; -ə`lɑdʒɪk], **ep·i·de·mi·o·log·i·cal** *a*. 流行病学的。**ep·i·de·mi·ol·o·gist** *n*. 流行病学家。

ep·i·den·drum [ˌepi'dendrəm; ˏɛpə`dɛndrəm] *n*. 【植】兰属 (*Epidendrum* 即 *Cymbidium*) 植物〔小花朵,主指美洲热带寄生兰〕。

ep·i·der·mal, ep·i·der·mic [ˌepi'dəːməl, -mik; ˏɛpə`dɝml̩, -mɪk] *a*. 【生】表皮的,外皮的。

ep·i·der·mis [ˌepi'dəːmis; ˏɛpə`dɝmɪs] *n*. 【解】表皮,外皮;【生】表皮层;(贝类的)壳。

ep·i·der·mi·za·tion [ˌepəˌdəːmi'zeiʃən; ˏɛpəˏdɝmɪ`zeʃən] *n*. 【医】皮肤移植。

ep·i·der·moid [ˌepi'dəːmɔid; ˏɛpɪ`dɝmɔɪd] *a*. 表皮状的,表皮性的 (= epidermoidal)。

ep·i·di·a·scope [ˌepi'daiəskəup; ˏɛpɪ`daɪəˏskop] *n*. 实

物幻灯机,透反射两用幻灯机。

ep·i·did·y·mis [ˌepiˈdidimis; ˏɛpəˋdɪdəmɪs] *n*. (*pl*. *ep·i·di·dym·ides* [-diˈdimidiːz; -dɪˋdɪmɪˏdiz])【解】附睾,副睾。**ep·i·did·y·mal** *a*.

ep·i·dote [ˈepidəut; ˋɛpɪˏdot] *n*.【矿】绿帘石。

ep·i·fo·cal [ˌepiˈfəukəl; ˏɛpəˋfokəl] *a*.【地】震中的。

ep·i·fo·cus [ˌepiˈfəukəs; ˏɛpɪˋfokəs] *n*.【地】震中。

ep·i·gam·ic [epiˈgæmik; ˏɛpəˋgæmɪk] *a*.【动】吸引异性的,诱惑性的。

ep·i·gas·tric [ˌepiˈgæstrik; ˏɛpəˋgæstrɪk] *a*.【解】上腹部的。

ep·i·gas·tri·um [ˌepiˈgæstriəm; ˏɛpɪˋgæstrɪəm] *n*. (*pl*. *ep·i·gas·tri·a* [ˌepiˈgæstriə; ˏɛpɪˋgæstrɪə])【解】上腹部;【动】第一腹片。

ep·i·ge·al, ep·i·ge·an [ˌepiˈdʒiːəl, -ən; ˏɛpɪˋdʒiəl, -ən] *a*. 1.【植】生于地上的,贴地生长的;(子叶)出土的。2.【动】栖息于地上[浅水中]的。

ep·i·gene [ˈepiˌdʒiːn; ˋɛpɪdʒin] *a*.【地】外成的。~ **rocks** 外成岩。

ep·i·gen·e·sis [ˌepiˈdʒenisis; ˏɛpəˋdʒɛnəsɪs] *n*. 1.【生】后成说,渐成说 (*opp*. preformation)。2.【矿】外成,外力变质。

ep·i·ge·net·ic [ˌepidʒiˈnetik; ˏɛpɪdʒɪˋnɛtɪk] *a*. 1. 外成的;具有外成性质的。2.【地】生于地表的;近地表生成的。3.【矿】后成的。

e·pig·e·nous [eˈpidʒinəs; ɪˋpɪdʒənəs] *a*.【植】附叶面生长的〔尤指某些真菌附在叶面上部生长的〕。

ep·i·ge·ous [ˌepiˈdʒiːəs; ˏɛpɪˋdʒiəs] *a*. = epigeal.

ep·i·glot·tic [ˌepiˈglɔtik; ˏɛpɪˋglɑtɪk] *a*.【解】会厌(软骨)的。

ep·i·glot·tis [ˌepiˈglɔtis; ˏɛpəˋglɑtɪs] *n*.【解】会厌,会厌软骨。

ep·i·gone [ˈepigəun; ˋɛpɪˏgon] *n*. (*pl*. ~*s*) (哲学、文艺等方面的)后继者,追随者;蹩脚的模仿者。

ep·i·gon·ic [ˌepiˈgɔnik; ˏɛpɪˋgɑnɪk] *a*. (哲学、文艺等方面)后继者的;追随着的;模仿者的。

ep·i·gram [ˈepigræm; ˋɛpəˏgræm] *n*. 警句;讽刺短诗。

ep·i·gram·mat·ic [ˌepigrəˈmætik; ˏɛpəgrəˋmætɪk] *a*. 警句的;讽刺诗的。**-al·ly** *ad*.

ep·i·gram·ma·tism [ˌepiˈgræmətizəm; ˏɛpəˋgræməˏtɪzəm] *n*. 警句的使用;警句文体。

ep·i·gram·ma·tist [ˌepiˈgræmətist; ˏɛpəˋgræmətɪst] *n*. 警句作者;讽刺诗作者。

ep·i·gram·ma·tize [ˌepiˈgræmətaiz; ˏɛpɪˋgræməˏtaɪz] *vt*. 1. 以警句形式表达。2. 把…写成讽刺短诗。—*vi*. 1. 作讽刺短诗。2. 写[说]警句。

ep·i·graph [ˈepigrɑːf; ˋɛpəˏgræf] *n*. 1. (墓碑、肖像等的)题字,碑文。2. (书前或章节前的)引语。

e·pig·ra·pher [eˈpigrəfə; ɛˋpɪgrəfɚ] *n*. 碑铭研究家,金石学家。

ep·i·graph·ic [ˌepiˈgræfik; ˏɛpɪˋgræfɪk] *a*. 铭文的;碑文的;与铭[碑]文有关的 (= exigraphical)。**-i·cal·ly** *ad*.

e·pig·ra·phist [eˈpigrəfist; ɛˋpɪgrəfɪst] *n*. = epigrapher.

e·pig·ra·phy [eˈpigrəfi; ɛˋpɪgrəfɪ] *n*. 1. 碑文,铭文。2. 碑铭学,金石学。

e·pig·y·nous [iˈpidʒinəs; ɪˋpɪdʒɪnəs] *a*.【植】(花被、雄蕊等)上位的。**e·pig·y·ny** *n*.

ep·i·la·tion [ˌepiˈleiʃən; ˏɛpɪˋleʃən] *n*.【医】脱毛(法);拔毛(术)。

ep·i·lep·sy [ˈepilepsi; ˋɛpəˏlɛpsɪ] *n*.【医】癫痫,羊痫疯。*masked* [*minor*] ~ 轻微的羊痫疯。

ep·i·lep·tic [ˌepiˈleptik; ˏɛpəˋlɛptɪk] I *a*. 癫痫的;患癫痫的。II *n*. 癫痫病人。

ep·i·lep·toid [ˌepiˈleptɔid; ˏɛpəˋlɛptɔɪd] *a*.【医】类癫痫的 (= epileptiform)。

ep·i·lim·ni·on [ˌepiˈlimniən; ˏɛpɪˋlɪmnɪən] *n*. (湖水的)上温层。

e·pil·o·gist [eˈpilədʒist; ɪˋpɪlədʒɪst] *n*. 1. 跋的作者,写结束语的人。2. 念收场白的演员。

ep·i·log(ue) [ˈepilɔg; ˋɛpəˏlɔg] *n*. 1. (文艺作品的)跋,后记,尾声,结尾部分。2. (戏剧、广播和电视节目的)收场白。

ep·i·mer, e·pi·mer·ide [ˈepimə, iˈpimərаid; ˋɛpəmɚ, ɪˋpɪmərаɪd] *n*.【化】差向[立体]异构体;差位[立体]异构体。

ep·i·mere [ˈepimiə; ˋɛpəmɪr] *n*.【解】(中胚层的)上段。

ep·i·my·si·um [ˌepiˈmisiəm, -ˈmiz-; ˏɛpɪˋmɪsɪəm, -ˋmɪz-] *n*. (*pl*. *-sia* [-ziə; -zɪə])【解】肌外膜。

ep·i·nas·ty [ˈepinæsti; ˋɛpəˏnæstɪ] *n*.【植】偏上性。**-tic** *a*.

ep·i·neph·rin(e) [ˌepiˈnefrin, -riːn; ˏɛpəˋnɛfrɪn, -rin] *n*.【生化】肾上腺素 (= adrenaline)。

ep·i·neu·ri·um [ˌepiˈnjuriəm, -ˈnur-; ˏɛpəˋnjʊrɪəm, -ˋnʊr-] *n*.【解】神经外膜。

ep·i·no·sic [ˌepiˈnɔsik; ˏɛpɪˋnɑsɪk] *a*. 不卫生的,有害健康的。

E·piph·a·ny [iˈpifəni; ɪˋpɪfənɪ] *n*. 1.【宗】(每年一月六日纪念耶稣显灵的)显现节。2.〔e-〕(神的)显现;(对事物真意的)领悟。

ep·i·phe·nom·e·non [ˌepifiˈnɔminən; ˏɛpɪfɪˋnɑmɪˏnɑn] (*pl*. *-na* [-nə; -nə]) *n*. 副现象,附带现象;【医】偶发症状。

e·piph·y·sis [iˈpifisis; ɪˋpɪfɪsɪs] *n*. (*pl*. *-ses* [-siːz; -siz])【解】1. 骺。2. 脑上体〔全称 ~ cerebri [ˈserəˌbrai; ˋsɛrəˏbraɪ]〕,松果体。**ep·i·phys·e·al, ep·i·phys·i·al** [ˌepiˈfiziəl; ˏɛpɪˋfɪzɪəl] *a*.

ep·i·phyte [ˈepifait; ˋɛpɪˏfaɪt] *n*. 1.【植】附生植物。2. (寄生于动物的)真菌。

ep·i·phy·tol·o·gy [ˌepifaiˈtɔlədʒi; ˏɛpɪfaɪˋtɑlədʒɪ] *n*. 植物流行病学。

ep·i·phy·tot·ic [ˌepifaiˈtɔtik; ˏɛpəfaɪˋtɑtɪk] I *a*. 植物流行病的。II *n*. 植物流行病。

ep·i·plas·tron [ˌepiˈplæstrən; ˏɛpɪˋplæstrən] (*pl*. ~*s*, *tra* [-trə; -trə]) *n*.【动】上腹甲。

ep·i·rog·e·ny [ˌepaiˈrɔdʒəni; ˏɛpaɪˋrɑdʒənɪ] *n*. = epeirogeny. **e·piro·gen·ic** [iˌpairəˈdʒenik; ɪˏpaɪrəˋdʒɛnɪk] *a*.

Epis(c) = Episcopal. **Epis(t)** = Epistle(s).

e·pis·co·pa·cy [iˈpiskəpəsi; ɪˋpɪskəpəsɪ] *n*.【宗】1. 主教制度;主教职位[任期]。2.〔the ~〕主教团。

e·pis·co·pal [iˈpiskəpəl; ɪˋpɪskəpl] *a*. 主教的;主教管辖的;〔E-〕主教派的。*the E- Church* 英国圣公会。*the Protestant E-Church* 美国圣公会。**-ly** *ad*.

e·pis·co·pa·li·an [iˌpiskəˈpeiliən; ɪˏpɪskəˋpelɪən] I *a*. 主教派的;圣公会的;〔E-〕新教徒主教教会的。II *n*. 主教派教友;圣公会教徒;主教制主义者。**-ism** *n*. 主教制主义。

e·pis·co·pate [iˈpiskəpit; ɪˋpɪskəpɪt] *n*. 主教职务[权限、任期];主教团;主教管区。

e·pis·cope [ˈepiskəup; ˋɛpɪskop] *n*. 不透明物投影放大器,反射投影机。

e·pi·si·ot·o·my [iˌpiːziˈɔtəmi; əˏpizɪˋɑtəmɪ] *n*.【医】会阴切开术。

ep·i·sode [ˈepisəud; ˋɛpəˏsod] *n*. 1. 插话,(小说中的)一段情节。2. (一系列事件中的)一个事件。3. (古希腊悲剧中)两段合唱间的部分。4.【乐】插部,间插段。5.【影】(回想式的)插话。6.【地】幕。

ep·i·sod·ic(al) [ˌepiˈsɔdik(əl); ˏɛpɪˋsɑdɪk(l̩)] *a*. 插曲的;插话(式)的;偶发的。**-al·ly** *ad*.

ep·i·some [ˈepəsəum; ˋɛpəsom] *n*.【生】因子附加体。

ep·i·spas·tic [ˌepiˈspæstik; ˏɛpɪˋspæstɪk] I *a*.【医】发泡的。II *n*. 发泡药。

ep·i·sperm [ˈepispəːm; ˋɛpəspɝm] *n*.【植】外种皮。

e·pis·ta·sis [iˈpistəsis; ɪˋpɪstəsɪs] ***n.*** 【遗】上位(遗传要素的)抑他性。
ep·i·stax·is [ˌepiˈstæksis; ˏɛpɪˋstæksɪs] ***n.*** 【医】鼻出血。
ep·i·ste·mic [ˌepiˈstiːmik; ˏɛpɪˋstimɪk] ***a.*** 认识的;与认识有关的。**ep·i·ste·mi·cal·ly** ***ad.***
e·pis·te·mo·log·i·cal [eˌpistiːməˈlɔdʒikəl; ɛˏpɪstiməˋlɑdʒɪkl̩] ***a.*** 认识论的。**-ly** ***ad.***
e·pis·te·mol·o·gy [iˌpistiˈmɔlədʒi; ɪˏpɪstəˋmɑlədʒɪ] ***n.*** 【哲】认识论。
ep·i·ster·num [ˌepisˈtəːnəm; ˏɛpəsˋtɝnəm] ***n.*** (*pl.* **-na** [-nə; -nə]) 1. 上胸骨。2. (海胆)上腹板。3. (昆虫)前侧片。**ep·i·ster·nal** ***a.***
e·pis·tle [iˈpisl; ɪˋpɪsl] ***n.*** 书信;书信体诗文; ***the E-*** 【圣】使徒书。***the E- side*** 【宗】祭坛右侧。
e·pis·tler [iˈpislə; ɪˋpɪstələ˞] ***n.*** 1. 书信作家。2. 〔通常用 E-〕举行圣餐礼时朗读《使徒书信》的人 (= epistoler [-tələ; -tələ])。
e·pis·to·lar·y [iˈpistələri; ɪˋpɪstəˏlɛrɪ] ***a.*** 书信的,尺牍的;尺牍体的,书信体的;用书信进行的。
e·pis·tome [ˈepistəum; ˋɛpəstom] ***n.*** 【动】(腕足类)口上突;(甲壳类)口上板;(甲壳类)口上区;(昆虫)口上片。
e·pis·tro·phe [iˈpistrəfi; ɪˋpɪstrəfɪ] ***n.*** 【修】结句反复;(诗歌各句末的)叠句。
ep·i·style [ˈepistail; ˋɛpɪˏstaɪl] ***n.*** = architrave.
ep·i·taph [ˈepitɑːf; ˋɛpəˏtæf] ***n.*** 墓志铭,墓志铭式的诗文。**-ial, -ic** ***a.*** **-less** ***a.***
e·pit·a·sis [iˈpitəsis; ɪˋpɪtəsɪs] ***n.*** (古典戏剧中)导致灾祸来临的高潮部分。
ep·i·tax·y [ˈepitæksi; ˋɛpɪtæksɪ] ***n.*** 【物】(晶体)取向附生,外延。**ep·i·tax·i·al, ep·i·tax·ic** ***a.***
ep·i·tha·la·mi·um, -mi·on [ˌepiθəˈleimiəm; ˏɛpɪθəˋlemɪəm] ***n.*** (*pl.* *~s*, ***-mi·a*** [-miə; -mɪə]) (祝贺新婚的)喜诗;颂歌。
ep·i·the·li·al [ˌepiˈθiːljəl; ˏɛpɪˋθilɪəl] ***a.*** 【生】上皮的;【植】皮膜的。**-i·za·tion** ***n.*** 【生】上皮新生,上皮形成。
ep·i·the·li·oid [ˌepiˈθiːliɔid; ˏɛpəˋθilɪɔɪd] ***a.*** 【生】上皮状的。
ep·i·the·li·o·ma [ˌepiθiːliˈəumə; ˏɛpəˋθilɪˋomə] ***n.*** (*pl.* ***-ma·ta*** [-mətə; -mətə], *~s*) 【医】上皮癌,上皮瘤。**-tous** ***a.***
ep·i·the·li·um [ˌepiˈθiːljəm; ˏɛpəˋθilɪəm] (*pl.* *~s*, ***-lia*** [-ljə; -lɪə]) ***n.*** 【生】上皮;【植】皮膜。
ep·i·the·lize [ˌepiˈθiːlaiz; ˏɛpəˋθilaɪz] ***vt.*** (治溃疡时)以上皮覆盖 (= epithelialize)。
ep·i·ther·mal [ˌepiˈθəːməl; ˏɛpəˋθɝməl] ***a.*** 【原】超热的;【地】浅成热液的。~ **neutron** 超热中子。
ep·i·thet [ˈepiθet; ˋɛpəˏθɛt] ***n.*** 1. 表示性质[属性]的修饰语。2. 称号,绰号。3. 【动、植】(一属中的)亚类名词。**-ic** ***a.*** 用性质形容词的。
e·pit·o·me [iˈpitəmi; ɪˋpɪtəmɪ] ***n.*** 1. 梗概,摘要,节录。2. 缩影。
e·pit·o·mize [iˈpitəmaiz; ɪˋpɪtəˏmaɪz] ***vt.*** 1. 作…的摘要。2. 使成…的缩影;集中体现。
e·p·i·zo·ic [ˌepiˈzəuik; ˏɛpəˋzoɪk] ***a.*** 【生】体表寄生的。**ep·i·zoite** [-ait; -aɪt] ***n.***
ep·i·zo·on [ˌepiˈzəuɔn; ˏɛpɪˋzoɑn] ***n.*** (*pl.* ***-zo·a*** [-ˈzəuə; -ˋzoə]) 【生】体表寄生动物,皮上寄生虫。
ep·i·zo·ot·ic [ˌepizəuˈɔtik; ˏɛpɪzəˋɑtɪk] ***n., a.*** 动物流行病(的)。**-al·ly** ***ad.***
ep·i·zo·ot·i·ol·o·gy [ˈepizəuˌɔtiˈɔlədʒi; ˋɛpɪzoˏɑtɪˋɑlədʒɪ] ***n.*** 兽疫学;动物流行病学。
e plu·ri·bus u·num [iːˈpluribəs ˈjuːnəm; iˋpluˋribəs ˋjunəm] [L.] 合众为一〔美国的铭语〕(= one out of many)。
ep·och [ˈiːpɔk, ˈepɔk; ˋipɑk, ˋɛpək] ***n.*** 1. 纪元,时代;时期。2. 值得纪念的事件[日期]。3. 【地】世,纪,期。4. 【物】初相;【天】历元;【电】(信号)出现时间,恒定相位延迟。***mark*** [***form***] ***an*** ~ (***in***)… (在…上)开辟新纪元。~**-making**, ~**-marking** ***a.*** 开新纪元的,划时代的,破天荒的。
ep·och·al [ˈepɔkəl; ˋɛpəkl̩] ***a.*** (新)时代的,划时代的,开新纪元的。**-ly** ***ad.***
ep·ode [ˈepəud; ˋɛpod] ***n.*** 1. 一种长短句相间的抒情诗。2. 古希腊抒情诗的第三部分。
ep·o·nym [ˈepəunim; ˋɛpəˏnɪm] ***n.*** 1. 名字被用来命名国家[地方等]的真人(或神话中的人)。2. 与某时期[运动,学说等]有关的人〔如构成 Elizabethan 一词的 Elizabeth〕。**-ic** ***a.***
e·pon·y·mous [iˈpɔniməs; ɛˋpɑnəməs] ***a.*** = eponymic.
e·pon·y·my [iˈpɔnimi; ɪˋpɑnəmɪ] ***n.*** 名祖命名法〔用本民族中一个真实的或神话的祖先名字作为本民族的名称的作法〕。
ep·oo·pho·ron [ˌepəˈɔfərɔn; ˏɛpəˋɑfərɑn] ***n.*** 【动】卵巢冠。
ep·o·pee [ˈepəupiː; ˋɛpəˏpi], **ep·o·poe·a** [ˈepəupiːə; ˋɛpəˏpiə] ***n.*** 史诗,叙事诗。
ep·os [ˈepɔs; ˋɛpɑs] ***n.*** 史诗,叙事诗,(口头传诵的)原始叙事诗;史诗事迹。
ep·ox·ide [eˈpɔksaid; ɛˋpɑksaɪd] ***n.*** 【化】环氧化物。
ep·ox·i·dize [eˈpɔksidaiz; ɛˋpɑksɪdaɪz] ***vt.*** 【化】使环氧化。
ep·ox·y [epˈɔksi; ɛpˋɑksɪ] **I** ***a.*** 环氧的。**II** ***n.*** 【化】环氧树脂。
eps. = envelopes.
ep·si·lon [epˈsailən; ˋɛpsələn] ***n.*** 1. 希腊语字母表第五字母〔E, ε=〔英〕短音 e〕。2. 【数】小的正数。
Ep·som [ˈepsəm; ˋɛpsəm] ***n.*** 1. 埃普索姆〔英国伦敦南面的城市〕。2. 埃普索姆的赛马场。
Ep·stein [ˈepstain; ˋɛpstaɪn] ***n.*** 1. 爱泼斯坦〔姓氏〕。2. **Jacob ~** 雅各·爱泼斯坦〔1880—1959,美国雕刻家〕。
E.P.T. = excess profits tax 超额利润税。
EPU = European Payments Union 欧洲支付同盟。
ep·u·rate [ˈepjuəreit; ˋɛpjuəˏret] ***vt.*** 提纯,精炼。
ep·u·ra·tion [ˌepjuəˈreiʃən; ˏɛpjuəˋreʃən] ***n.*** 1. 提纯。2. 清洗〔特指第二次世界大战后,法、意两国对官吏中法西斯党徒的刑事诉讼〕。
E.Q., EQ = emotional quotient 情商,情感商数。
eq. = equal; equalize; equation; equipment; equivalent.
eq·ua·bil·i·ty [ˌekwəˈbiliti, ˌiːk-; ˏɛkwəˋbɪlətɪ, ˏik-] ***n.*** 1. 平稳,稳定;均等。2. 平静。
eq·ua·ble [ˈekwəbl, ˈiːk-; ˋɛkwəbl, ˋik-] ***a.*** 1. 平均的,均等的,一样的。2. 均匀的。3. 稳定的;(性情)恬静的。4. (法律等)公平的。*a man of ~ temper* 性情平静的人。**-bly** ***ad.*** **-ness** ***n.***
e·qual [ˈiːkwəl; ˋikwəl] **I** ***a.*** 1. 相等的;平等的,均等的 (*to*; *with*);同等的;公平的;一样的。2. 平静的;平稳的。3. 势均力敌的;相当的。4. 适合的;胜任的,经得起的。*the principle of ~ opportunity* 机会均等主义。*~ opportunity employer* 〔美〕标榜招工一视同仁的雇主。*an ~ plain* 平原。**be ~ to** 1. 等于 (*The supply is ~ to the demand.* 供求相等。*Twice two is ~ to four.* 二个二等于四)。2. 赶得上,敌得过。3. 胜任,能干 (*He is ~ to anything.* 他事事能干)。4. 忍耐得住 (*be ~ to any trial* 经得起任何磨炼)。~ ***to the occasion*** 能应付局势 (*make a quick decision ~ to the occasion* 当机立断)。~ ***to the task*** 胜任。~ ***pay for ~ work*** 同工同酬。***in a firm, ~ tone*** 用坚定平稳的音调。***on an ~ footing*** 以平等地位对待,在同一立场上。***on ~ terms*** (***with***) (与…)平等相处。**II** ***n.*** 1. 地位相等的人,同辈。2. 对等的事物。*mix with one's ~s and betters* 跟同辈和长辈交往。*be the ~ of one's word* 守约。*have no ~ in music* 在音乐方面没有人比得上。***without*** (***an***) ~ 无敌。**III** ***vt.*** (〔英〕***-ll-***) 1. 抵得上,比得上。2. 等于。3. 〔古〕使相等,使平等;同样看待;照

E

样报答。*No man* ~*s him in strength*. 没有人比他气力大。~-**sign** [**mark**] *n*.【数】等号〔=〕。~ **time**〔美〕平等时间〔电台或电视台在另一天给予反对党同样长的发表政见的时间〕;〔喻〕均等的机会。

e·qual-ar·e·a [ˈiːkwəlˈeəriə; ˋikwəlˋɛərɪə] *a*. 等区的〔绘制地图投影上,子午线与纬线间地区按比例等于地球表面相应地区〕。

e·qual·i·tar·i·an [iˌkwɔliˈtɛəriən; ɪˏkwɑləˋtɛrɪən] **I** *a*. 平均主义的,平等主义的。**II** *n*. 平均主义者,平等主义者。**-ism** *n*. 平均主义,平等主义。

e·qual·i·ty [i(ː)ˈkwɔliti; i(ɪ)ˋkwɑlətɪ] *n*. **1**. 同等,平等,均一,均等;一样。**2**.【数】相等;等式。~ *between the sexes* 男女平等。*racial* ~ 种族平等。*the sign of* ~ 等号〔=〕。***be on an*** ~ ***with*** 和…同等。***the E-State***〔美〕(妇女在该处最先取得参政权的)怀俄明州。

e·qual·i·za·tion [ˌiːkwəlaiˈzeiʃən, -liˈz-; ˏikwəlaɪˋzeʃən, -ləˋz-] *n*. 相等;均等;平均。~ *of landownership* 平均地权。

e·qual·ize [ˈiːkwəlaiz; ˋikwəlˏaɪz] *vt*. **1**. 使相等,使平等。**2**. 补偿。**3**.【电】使均衡;调整。—*vi*. **1**. 相等,得到平衡。**2**.〔主英〕(与对方)打成平手,得分相等。

e·qual·iz·er [ˈiːkwəlaizə; ˋikwəlˏaɪzɚ] *n*. **1**. 使相等者,使平均者。**2**.【电】均压线;【自】补偿器;均衡器;平衡杆;平衡装置。

e·qual·ly [ˈiːkwəli; ˋikwəlɪ] *ad*. 相等地;平等地;公正地。

e·qua·nim·i·ty [ˌiːkwəˈnimiti, ekwə-; ˏikwəˋnɪmətɪ, ɛkwə-] *n*. 平静,沉着,镇定。***with*** ~ 沉着,泰然;安之若素。

e·quate [iˈkweit; ɪˋkwet] *vt*. **1**. 使相等。**2**. 使平均;同等看待。**3**.【数】把…作成等式。*Politics cannot be* ~*d with art*. 政治并不等于艺术。—*vi*. 等同。

e·qua·tion [iˈkweiʃən; ɪˋkweʃən] *n*. **1**. 平衡,均衡;平均,相等。**2**.【数】方程式,等式。**3**.【天】(时)差;均分,等分。**4**.【化】反应式。*algebraic* [*linear*, *simple*, *quadratic*, *cubic*, *simultaneous*] ~ 代数(一次,一元一次,二次,三次,联立)方程式。*differential* ~ 微分方程。*an identical* ~ 恒等式。~ ***of light***【天】光行时差。~ ***of payments*** 平均分期付款。~ ***of state***【物】物态方程式。~ ***of time***【天】时差。***personal*** ~【天】观测上的个人误差。

e·qua·tion·al [iˈkweiʃənəl; ɪˋkweʃənəl] *a*. **1**. 方程式的。**2**. 平均的。**3**.【语法】省略述语动词的。**-ly** *ad*.

e·qua·tor [iˈkweitə; ɪˋkwetɚ] *n*. **1**. (地球或天球的)赤道。**2**. (平分球形物体的面的)圆;(任何)大圆。*the celestial* ~ 天球赤道。*the earth's* [*terrestrial*] ~ 地球赤道。*the magnetic* ~ 地磁赤道。**-ward** *ad*. 朝赤道方向。

eq·ua·to·ri·al [ˌekwəˈtɔːriəl, iːk-; ˏɛkwəˋtorɪəl, ik-] **I** *a*. 赤道的;赤道附近的。~ *heat* 酷热。**II** *n*. 赤道仪。**E-Africa** 赤道非洲。~ **bulge** 赤道隆起带。~ **low** 赤道低压。~ **trough** 赤道槽。~ **telescope** 赤道仪。**-ly** *ad*.

E·qua·to·ri·al Guin·ea [ˌekwəˈtɔːriəlˈgini; ˏɛkwəˋtorɪəlˋgɪnɪ] *n*. 赤道几内亚〔非洲〕。

eq·uer·ry [ˈekwəri, iˈkweri; ˋɛkwərɪ, ɪˋkwɛrɪ] *n*. **1**. 马厩总管。**2**.〔英〕王室侍从。

e·ques·tri·an [iˈkwestriən; ɪˋkwɛstrɪən] **I** *a*. 马的,骑马的;骑术的,骑士(团)的。~ *feats* 马戏。~ *skill* 马术。*an* ~ *statue* 骑马塑像。**II** *n*. 骑马的人;骑手;马戏演员。**-ism** *n*. 马术。

e·ques·tri·enne [iˌkwestriˈen; ɪˏkwɛstrɪˋɛn] *n*. 骑马女人;女骑手;马戏女演员。

e·qui- *comb*. *f*. 表示"同等":*equi*distant.

e·qui·an·gu·lar [ˌiːkwiˈæŋgjulə; ˏikwɪˋæŋgjələ] *a*. 等角的。**-i·ty** *n*.

e·qui·axed [ˈiːkwiækst; ˋikwɪækst] *a*. 各方等大的〔特指金属晶粒〕。

e·qui·ca·lor·ic [ˌiːkwikəˈlɔrik; ˏikwɪkəˋlɑrɪk] *a*. (能产生)同等热量的。~ *diets* 同等热量的饮食。

e·qui·cen·ter, e·qui·cen·tre [ˈiːkwiˈsentə; ˋikwɪˋsɛntɚ] *n*.【数】等心。

e·qui·dis·tance [ˌiːkwiˈdistəns; ˏikwəˋdɪstəns] *n*. 等距离。

e·qui·dis·tant [ˌiːkwiˈdistənt; ˏikwəˋdɪstənt] *a*. **1**. 等距离的。**2**. (地图上所有方向的距离)同比例的。**-ly** *ad*.

e·qui·lat·er·al [ˌiːkwiˈlætərəl; ˏikwəˋlætərəl] **I** *a*.【数】**1**. 等边的,等面的。**2**. 两侧对称的。*an* ~ *figure* 等边形。**II** *n*. 等边形;(相应的)等边。~ **hyperbola** 直角变曲线,等轴双曲线。~ **triangle** 等边三角形。

e·quil·i·brant [iˈkwilibrənt; ɪˋkwɪləbrənt] *n*.【物】平衡力,均衡力。

e·qui·li·brate [ˌiːkwiˈlaibreit; ˏikwəˋlaɪbret] *vt*. 使平衡,使相称。—*vi*. 平衡,平均,相称。

e·quil·i·bra·tion [ˌiːkwilaiˈbreiʃən; ˏikwɪlɪˋbreʃən] *n*. 平衡,平均,均势,相称。

e·qui·li·bra·tor [ˌiːkwiˈlaibreitə; ˏikwɪˋlaɪbretɚ] *n*. 保持平衡的物;平衡装置。

e·quil·i·brist [i(ː)ˈkwilibrist; i(ɪ)ˋkwɪləbrɪst] *n*. 使自己保持平衡者〔如走钢丝的人〕。**-ic** *a*.

e·qui·lib·ri·um [ˌiːkwiˈlibriəm; ˏikwɪˋlɪbrɪəm] (*pl*. ~*s*, *-ri·a* [-riə; -rɪə]) *n*. **1**. 平衡,均衡,均势,相称。**2**. (心情的)平静。**3**. (判断的)不偏不倚。~ *constant*【化】平衡常数。*the* ~ *of demand and supply* 供求均衡。*indifferent* ~【物】随遇平衡。*the theory of* ~【哲】均衡论。

e·qui·mo·lal [ˌiːkwiˈməuləl; ˏikwɪˋmoləl] *a*.【化】克分子数相等的,重量克分子浓度相等的。

e·qui·mo·lar [ˌiːkwiˈməulə; ˏikwɪˋmolɚ] *a*.【化】克分子数相等的,体积克分子浓度相等的。

e·qui·mo·lec·u·lar [ˌiːkwiməuˈlekjulə; ˏikwɪməˋlɛkjʊlɚ] *a*.【化】等分子的,克分子数相等的。

e·qui·mul·ti·ple [ˌiːkwiˈmʌltipl; ˏikwɪˋmʌltəpl̩] *n*.〔常 *pl*.〕等倍数,等倍量。

e·quine [ˈiːkwain, ˈekwain; ˋikwaɪn, ˋɛkwaɪn] **I** *a*.【动】马的;似马的;马科的。**II** *n*. 马;马科动物。

e·quin·ia [iˈkwiniə; ɪˋkwɪnɪə] *n*. (马)鼻疽。

e·qui·noc·tial [ˌiːkwiˈnɔkʃəl; ˏikwəˋnɑkʃəl] **I** *a*. **1**.【天】二分点的;昼夜分线的;昼夜平分时的。**2**. 春分的,秋分的。**3**. (天球)赤道的。**II** *n*. **1**. 昼夜平分线,赤道。**2**.〔*pl*.〕春分[秋分]周内的暴风雨。*the autumnal* [*vernal*] ~ *point* 秋分[春分]点。~ **circle** [**line**]【天】天球赤道,昼夜平分线。~ **gales** (春分或秋分时的)暴风雨。**the** ~ **point** (春分或秋分的)二分点。~ **year** 分至年。

e·qui·nox [ˈiːkwinɔks; ˋikwəˏnɑks] *n*. **1**. 昼夜平分时,春[秋]分。**2**.【天】二分点。*the autumnal* ~ 秋分,秋分点。*the spring* [*vernal*] ~ 春分,春分点。

e·quip [iˈkwip; ɪˋkwɪp] *vt*. (*-pp-*) **1**. 配备,装备。**2**. 使作好(智力等方面的)准备,训练。~ *sb*. *for a trip* 给人准备行装。~ *a ship for a voyage* 装备船只出航。~ *sb*. *with learning* 教人学习。***be equipped with*** 安置着,装备着;身上穿着(*be* ~*ped with modern machinery* 配备着现代化机械)。~ ***oneself*** 整装,预备行装,收拾。

eq·ui·page [ˈekwipidʒ; ˋɛkwəpɪdʒ] *n*. **1**. 马车及仆从。**2**. (船、军队、士兵等的)装备,设备,用具。**3**.〔古〕成套用品。**4**. (贵族的)随员,扈从。*a dressing* ~ 一套化妆用品。*a tea* ~ 一套茶具。

e·qui·par·ti·tion [ˌiːkwipɑːˈtiʃən; ˏikwəpɑrˋtɪʃən] *n*.【物、化】均分,均隔,匀布,匀配。~ *of energy*【物】能量的平均分配。

e·quip·ment [iˈkwipmənt; ɪˋkwɪpmənt] *n*. **1**.〔常 *pl*.〕设备,装备,配件,配备物品。**2**. (一个企业除房地产以外的)固定资产。**3**. (工作必需的)知识,技能,修养。**4**. (火

车)车辆;(汽车等)运输配备。*laboratory* ~ 实验室设备。*a machinery* ~ *plant* 机械装配厂。*military* ~*s* 军事装备。*the necessary* ~*s for a voyage* 航海必需的装备。*soldier's* ~ 士兵的装备。~ *and parts* 器材。

e·qui·poise [ˈekwipɔiz; ˋɛkwə͵pɔɪz] **I** *n*. **1.** 相称,平衡。**2.** 平衡物;平衡力;平衡锤。**II** *vt*. **1.** 使相称;使平衡。**2.** 使相持不下。

e·qui·pol·lence, e·qui·pol·len·cy [ˌiːkwiˈpɔləns, -si; ͵ikwəˋpɑləns, -sɪ] *n*. **1.** 均等,均势。**2.**【逻】(概念、判断的)等值,同义。

e·qui·pol·lent [ˌiːkwiˈpɔlənt; ͵ikwəˋpɑlənt] **I** *a*. **1.** (大致)相等的,均等的。**2.**【逻】等值的,同义的。**II** *n*. = equivalent.

e·qui·pon·der·ance, e·qui·pon·der·an·cy [ˌiːkwiˈpɔndərəns, -si; ͵ikwɪˋpɑndərəns, -sɪ] *n*. 等重;均衡,平衡。

e·qui·pon·der·ant [ˌiːkwiˈpɔndərənt; ͵ikwɪˋpɑndərənt] **I** *a*. 等重的,均衡的。**II** *n*. 等重物,均衡物。

e·qui·pon·der·ate [ˌiːkwiˈpɔndəreit; ͵ikwɪˋpɑndər͵et] *vi*., *vt*. (使)均重;(使)均力;(使)平衡。

e·qui·po·ten·tial [ˌiːkwipəuˈtenʃəl; ͵ikwɪpoˋtɛnʃəl] *a*. **1.** 潜力均等的,均势的。**2.**【物】等电位的,等能的,等势的,恒势的。**-i·ty** [-ˈæliti; -ˋælɪtɪ] *n*.

Eq·ui·se·tum [ˌekwiˈsiːtəm; ͵ɛkwəˋsitəm] *n*.【植】**1.** 木贼属。**2.** [e-] (*pl*. ~*s*, *-ta* [-tə; -tə]) 木贼;间荆。

eq·ui·ta·ble [ˈekwitəbl; ˋɛkwɪtəbl] *a*. **1.** 公平的,公正的,合理的。**2.**【法】衡平法上(有效)的。~ **right** 在衡平法上的权利。**-ness** *n*. **-bly** *ad*.

eq·ui·tant [ˈekwitənt; ˋɛkwətənt] *a*.【植】跨状的,套折的。

eq·ui·ta·tion [ˌekwiˈteiʃən; ͵ɛkwɪˋteʃən] *n*. 骑马;骑马术。

eq·ui·tes [ˈekwitiːz; ˋɛkwɪ͵tiz] *n*. [*pl*.]【罗马史】特权市民阶层成员;骑士阶层

eq·ui·ty [ˈekwiti; ˋɛkwətɪ] *n*. **1.** 公平,公正。**2.**【法】衡平法[指补充成文法或普通法的公平原则,必要时以纠正用法不公];衡平法上的权利。**3.** [口](应付款额之外的)财产净价。**4.** [英] [*pl*.] (无固定利息的)股票,证券。**5.** [E-] [英]演员工会。~ ***of redemption*** 衡平法上关于赎回担保物的权利。~ ***of a statute***【法】法律条文的解释。~ **capital** **1.** 投资于新企业的资本。**2.** (资本)净值。~ **stock** 股东手上持有的股票。

equiv. = equivalent.

e·quiv·a·lence, e·quiv·a·len·cy [iˈkwivələns, -si; ɪˋkwɪvələns, -sɪ] *n*. **1.** 均等,相等,相当。**2.**【化】等价,化合价相当;当量。**3.** 等值;等量。**4.** (语词的)同义;同类。**5.**【数】等势;等效。**6.**【地】等时代。~ **gate**【计】"同"门。

e·quiv·a·lent [iˈkwivələnt; ɪˋkwɪvələnt] **I** *a*. **1.** 相当的,相同的,同等的。**2.**【化】等价的,当量的;【数】等价的;等量的;等势的;【物】等效的;【数】等面积的,等体积的。**3.** 同意义的 (*to*)。**II** *n*. **1.** 同等物;【数】等价,等值,等价物,等值物;等量物;相当物。**2.** 同义词,对应词句 (*of*)。**3.**【化】当量;克当量;等量。**4.**【地】同期地层。*a square* ~ *to a triangle* 同三角形等积的正方形。*five pounds or its* ~ *in books* 五镑或相当于五镑价值的书籍。*chemical* ~ 化学当量。*electrochemical* ~ 电化当量。*transmission* ~【电】传输衰耗等效值。*be* ~ *to* 等于;相当于。~ **circuit** 等效电路。~ **electrons** 同科电子。~ **focal length**【物】等值焦距。~ **lens** 等焦透镜。~ **mass** 等效质量。~ **weight** 当量。**-ly** *ad*.

e·quiv·o·cal [iˈkwivəkəl; ɪˋkwɪvəkl̩] *a*. **1.** 歧义的,语义双关的,多义的。**2.** 暧昧的,含糊的,可疑的。**3.** 不肯定的,不明确的。~ **term** 多义名词。**-ly** *ad*. **-ness** *n*.

e·quiv·o·cal·i·ty [iˌkwivəˈkæliti; ɪ͵kwɪvəˋkælətɪ] *n*. **1.** 多义;暧昧;含糊,模棱两可。**2.** 可疑性。**3.** 不肯定性。

e·quiv·o·cate [iˈkwivəkeit; ɪˋkwɪvə͵ket] *vi*. 躲闪;推诿;含糊其词;说话支吾,态度暧昧。

e·quiv·o·ca·tion [iˌkwivəˈkeiʃən; ɪ͵kwɪvəˋkeʃən] *n*. 推诿;躲闪;说话支吾;含糊其词;暧昧。***fallacy of*** ~【逻】一语多义的谬误;名词多义的谬误。

e·quiv·o·ca·tor [iˈkwivəkeitə; ɪˋkwɪvəketɚ] *n*. 说话支吾的人。

eq·ui·voque, eq·ui·voke [ˈekwivəuk; ˋɛkwə͵vok] *n*. 两义语,双关话;模棱两可;文字游戏。

E·quu·le·us [iˈkwjuːliəs; ɪˋkwjulɪəs] *n*. [the ~]【天】小马(星)座。

E·quus [ˈiːkwəs; ˋikwəs] *n*. [L.]【动】马属。

ER = emergency room 急救室。

er [əː, ə; ɚ, ə] *int*. [表示踌躇不决]呃,啊,这。

Er【化】元素铒的符号 (= erbium)。

E.R. = **1.** East Riding (of Yorkshire) 东赖丁(英国约克郡的一个行政区)。**2.** East River 东河[纽约市]。

-er *suf*. **1.** 加在名词、形容词、动词和动词词组构成的复合词后,构成名词。(a) 表示"…的人[动物、植物]": hunt*er*, sing*er*, woodpeck*er*. (b) 表示"…的东西[器具、机械]","…的事情": gasburn*er*, eyeopen*er*. (c) 表示"…的物质","…剂": deodoriz*er*. (d) 表示"…(地方)的人","…居民": London*er*, western*er*; cottag*er*, villag*er*. (e)表示"参与…的人","造…的人","…商","…研究者","…学者": farm*er*, garden*er*, hatt*er*, geograph*er*. (f) [在近代口语中] ① 构成该动作的名词: backhand*er* (= back-handed blow), din*er* (= dining car). ② 构成来自数词的名词: fiv*er* (= 5 pound [dollar] note), tenn*er*. ③ 使其他词尾的名词带有口语意味: Rugg*er* (= *Rugby football*), Socc*er* (= *association football*). **2.** 加在古法语名词或形容词的后面: carpent*er*, pott*er*, sampl*er*. **3.** 加在形容词[副词]的后面构成比较级。(a)使单音节形容词,或末尾为 -y, -ly, -le, -er, -ow的双音节形容词,或其他少数形容词[尤其是重音在最末音节上的形容词]成为比较级 (*cf*. -est): rich*er*, lazi*er*, likeli*er*, tender*er*, seren*er*, narrow*er*. 但在诗中及古体散文中,也有自由用其他形容词构成比较级的。(b) 使末节不是 -ly 的(主要是与形容词同形的)副词构成比较级: hard*er*, fast*er*, soon*er*. **4.** 构成有动作意义的名词: rejoind*er*, supp*er*. **5.** 表示动作发生多次或反复发生。(a)原为动词: wand*er* (< wend), wav*er* (< wave). (b)原为拟声语: chatt*er*, twitt*er*, flick*er*, glitt*er*.

e·ra [ˈiərə; ˋɪrə] *n*. **1.** 纪元;年代,时代。**2.**【地】代。*inaugurate* [*mark*] *a new* ~ 开[划]新纪元。*before* [*in*] *the Christian* ~ 公元前[后]。

ERA, E.R.A. = **1.** Emergency Relief Administration [美旧]紧急救济署。**2.** engine-room artifier【海】机舱机电军士。

e·ra·di·ate [i(ː)ˈreidieit; i(ɪ)ˋredɪ͵et] *vt*. 发射,放射,辐射。**e·ra·dia·tion** [iˌreidiˈeiʃən; ɪ͵redɪˋeʃən] *n*.

e·rad·i·ca·ble [iˈrædikəbl; ɪˋrædɪkəbl̩] *a*. 可以根除的,可以消灭的。

e·rad·i·cate [iˈrædikeit; ɪˋrædɪ͵ket] *vt*. 连根拔除;根除,扑灭,使…断根。

e·rad·i·ca·tion [iˌrædiˈkeiʃən; ɪ͵rædɪˋkeʃən] *n*. 根除,扑灭,消灭。

e·rad·i·ca·tive [iˈrædikətiv; ɪˋrædɪkətɪv] *a*. 根除的,消灭的。*an* ~ *medicine* 根治药。

e·rad·i·ca·tor [iˌrædiˈkeitə; ɪ͵rædɪˋketɚ] *n*. **1.** 根除者。**2.** 除草器。**3.** 去墨水液,褪色灵。

e·ras·a·ble [iˈreizəbl; ɪˋrezəbl̩] *a*. 擦得掉的,可消除的,可删去的。

e·rase [iˈreiz; ɪˋres] *vt*. **1.** 擦掉,揩掉;消除(电子计算机中的记忆);涂掉,删掉(字句等)。**2.** 清除;除去。**3.** 忘掉 (*from*);[美俚]杀死,暗杀掉。*The pencil marks were* ~*d*. 铅笔痕迹被擦去。~ *the recording* 抹去录音,洗掉录音。—*vi*. **1.** 容易被擦掉[抹掉]。**2.** 擦,抹。**eras-**

E

ing head (录音机的)抹音磁头。

e·ras·er [iˈreizə; ɪˋresɚ] *n*. 1. 涂消者;【无】消磁器,抹音头。2. 消除用具;挖字刀,消字灵,橡皮擦,黑板擦。3. 〔美〕(在拳击中)打倒对手的猛击。

e·ra·sion [iˈreiʒən; ɪˋreʒən] *n*. 1. 擦抹,删去。2.【医】刮除术。

E·ras·mian [iˈræzmiən; ɪˋræzmɪən] *a*., *n*. 〔荷兰〕伊拉斯姆斯学派(的);伊拉斯姆斯的弟子(的);伊拉斯姆斯风(的)。

E·ras·tian [iˈræstʃən; ɪˋræstʃən] **I** *a*. 伊拉斯图(Thomas Erastus)的。**II** *n*. 伊拉斯图派,国家全能论者。**-ism** *n*. 国家全能论。

e·ra·sure [iˈreiʒə; ɪˋreʒɚ] *n*. 擦掉;删去,删去部分〔语句〕;涂擦痕迹。

er·bi·um [ˈəːbiəm; ˋɝbɪəm] *n*.【化】铒。

ere [ɛə; ɛr] **I** *prep*. 〔诗、古〕在…以前。~ *long* 不久,一会儿。**II** *conj*. 〔诗〕1. 在…之前。2. 与其。~ *it is too late* 趁着还不太晚。*He will die*, ~ *he will yield*. 他宁死不屈。

Er·e·bus [ˈeribəs; ˋɛrəbəs] *n*.【希神】(人世与地狱之间的)黑暗区域。*as dark as* ~ 漆黑。

e·rect [iˈrekt; ɪˋrɛkt] **I** *a*. 1. 直立的;【征】垂直的;(头、手等)朝上举的;直竖的。2. 〔古〕不屈的,坚毅的;谨慎的。3.【医】勃起的。*A flagpole stands* ~. 旗竿笔直地竖着。*an* ~ *figure* (直)立像。*an* ~ *image* 正像。*with* (*every*) *hair* ~ 毛发直竖。*with tail* ~ 竖着尾巴。**II** *vt*. 1. 使直立,树立,竖。2. 建立,设立;创立(理论等);安装(机械等)。3.【生】把(种)升为(属),提升。4.【数】作(垂直线) 5.【医】使勃起。*an* ~*ing shop* 装配车间。~ *a house* 建造房子。~ *a monument* 立纪念碑。~ *oneself* 站起来。— *vi*.【医】勃起。**-ly** *ad*. **-ness** *n*.

e·rec·tile [iˈrektail; ɪˋrɛktɪl] *a*. 直立的竖得起来的,立得起来的;【医】有勃起能力的。~ *tissue* 勃起组织。

e·rec·tion [iˈrekʃən; ɪˋrɛkʃən] *n*. 1. 直立;树立,建设;设立;架设;【机】安装,装配。2. 建设物,建筑物。3.【医】勃起。

e·rec·tive [iˈrektiv; ɪˋrɛktɪv] *a*. 直立的,竖起的;建立的。

e·rec·tor [iˈrektə; ɪˋrɛktɚ] *n*. 1. 建立者,设立者。2.【机】安装工人,装配工人;安装器。3.【解】竖立肌。~ **muscle** *n*.【解】竖立肌。

ere·long [ɛəˈlɔŋ; ɛrˋlɔŋ] *ad*. 〔古〕不久,即刻。

er·e·ma·cau·sis [ˌeriməˈkɔːsis; ˏɛrɪməˋkɔsɪs] *n*.【化】慢性氧化。

er·e·mite [ˈerimait; ˋɛrəˏmaɪt] *n*. 隐士。

er·e·mit·ic [ˌeriˈmitik; ˏɛrəˋmɪtɪk] *a*. 隐士式的。

er·em·u·rus [ˌeriˈmjurəs; ˏɛrəˋmjʊrəs] *n*. (*pl*. *-u·ri* [-ai; -aɪ])【植】独尾属(*Eremurus*)植物。

ere·now [ˌɛəˈnau; ˏɛrˋnaʊ] *ad*. 〔古、诗〕从前;至此,至今。

e·rep·sin [iˈrepsin; ɪˋrɛpsɪn] *n*.【生化】肠肽酶。

er·e·thism [ˈeriθizəm; ˋɛrɪθɪzm] *n*.【医】兴奋增盛,过敏。

ere·while [ɛəˈhwail; ˏɛrˋhwaɪl] *ad*. 〔古〕片刻前,不久前。

Er·furt [ˈɛəfuət; ˋɛrfurt] *n*. 埃尔富特〔德国城市〕。

erg [əːg; ɝg] *n*.【物】尔格〔功的单位〕。

erg(o)-[1] *comb*. *f*. = work.

erg(o)-[2] *comb*. *f*. = ergot.

er·go [ˈəːgəu; ˋɝgo] *ad*. 〔L.〕所以,因此。

er·go·graph [ˈəːgəgrɑːf; ˋɝgoˏgræf] *n*. 测力器,示功器。

er·gom·e·ter [əːˈgɔmitə; ɝˋgɑmətɚ] *n*. 测力计,测功计。

er·gom·e·try [əːˈgɔmitri; ɝˋgɑmətrɪ] *n*.【物】测力学,测功学。

er·gon [ˈəːgɔn; ˋɝgɑn] *n*. 1.【物】尔刚〔用热表示的功的单位〕。2. = erg.

er·go·nom·ic·al [ˌəːgəuˈnɔmikəl; ˏɝgəˋnɑmɪkl] *a*. 人体功率学的;工作环境改造学的。

er·go·nom·ics [ˌəːgəuˈnɔmiks; ˏɝgəˋnɑmɪks] *n*. 〔用作单数〕(生物)工效学;人体功率学;〔尤指〕工作环境改造学。

er·go·nom·ist [ˌəːgəuˈnɔmist; ˏɝgəˋnɑmɪst] *n*. 工作环境改造学家,(生物)工效学家。

er·go·no·vine [ˌəːgəuˈnəuviːn; ˏɝgəˋnovin] *n*.【化】麦角新碱。

er·go·pho·bia [ˌəːgəuˈfəubiə; ˏɝgəˋfobɪə] *n*.【医】厌恶工作的病态。

er·gos·ter·ol [əːˈgɔstərɔl; ɝˋgɑstəˏrol] *n*.【生化】麦角甾醇。

er·got [ˈəːgət; ˋɝgət] *n*. 1. 麦角,麦角碱,麦角菌。2.【农】(植物的)麦角病。**-ism** *n*.【医】麦角中毒。

er·got·a·mine [əˈgɔtəmiːn; ɝˋgɑtəˏmin] *n*.【药】(治周期性偏头痛的)麦角胺。

Er·ic, Er·ik [ˈerik; ˋɛrɪk] *n*. 埃里克〔男子名〕。

E·rid·a·nus [iˈridənəs; ɪˋrɪdənəs]【天】〔the ~〕波江(星)座。

Er·ie [ˈiəri; ˋɪrɪ] *n*. 〔美〕1. 伊利市。2. 伊利湖〔北美洲〕。3. 伊利运河。4. 伊利人(北美印第安人中的一支)。*on the* ~ 〔美俚〕1. 竖起耳朵听,偷听。2. 躲藏。

e·rig·er·on [iˈridʒərɔn; ɪˋrɪdʒərɑn] *n*.【植】加拿大蓬(= Erigeron canadense)。

Er·in [ˈiərin; ˋɪrɪn] *n*. 〔诗〕爱尔兰。*Sons of* ~ 爱尔兰人。

E·rin·ys [iˈrinis, iˈrainis; ɪˋrɪnɪs, ɪˋraɪnɪs] *n*. (*pl*. ***E·rin·yes*** [iˈriniiːz; ɪˋrɪnɪˏiz])【希神】(复仇的女神)伊莉妮丝。

e·ri·om·e·ter [ˌeriˈɔmetə; ˏɛrɪˋɑmɛtɚ] *n*. 纤维细度测定器。

E·ris [ˈeris; ˋɛrɪs] *n*.【希神】厄里斯〔司争吵、不和的女神〕。

er·is·tic [eˈristik; ɛˋrɪstɪk] **I** *a*. 争论的。**II** *n*. 1. 争论者。2. 争论;辩论术。**-al·ly** *ad*.

Er·i·tre·a [ˌeriˈtriə; ˏɛrɪˋtriə] *n*. 厄立特里亚〔埃塞俄比亚北部邻国,濒临红海〕。**-n** 1. *a*. 厄立特里亚的。2. *n*. 厄立特里亚人。

erk [əːk; ɝk] *n*. 〔英〕1. (英国空军中军阶最低的)空军兵,地勤人员。2. 〔口〕无用的蠢人。

Er·lan·ger [ˈəːlæŋə; ˋɝlæŋɚ] *n*. 厄兰格〔姓氏〕。

Er·len·mey·er [ˈəːlənmaiə; ˋɝlənˏmaɪɚ] **flask**【化】锥瓶,锥形烧瓶;爱伦美氏(烧)瓶。

erl·king [ˈəːlkiŋ; ˋɝlˏkɪŋ] *n*.【北欧神话】妖王。

ERM = exchange rate mechanism【经】汇率转换机制。

er·mine [ˈəːmin; ˋɝmɪn] **I** *n*. (*pl*. *~s*, 〔集合词〕~)【动】1. 貂;扫雪鼬;貂皮。2. 标志法官地位和贵族身分的貂皮袍;【徽】白底黑斑的毛皮。***wear the*** ~ 就任法官职务。**II** *a*. 〔诗〕纯白的;纯洁的。

er·mined [ˈəːmind; ˋɝmɪnd] *a*. 穿貂皮袍的;以貂皮装饰的。

-ern *suf*. 表示"方位":east*ern*, west*ern*.

ern(e) [əːn; ɝn] *n*. 海鹰。

Er·nest [ˈəːnist; ˋɝnɪst] *n*. 欧内斯特〔男子名〕。

Er·nes·tine [ˈəːnəstiːn; ˋɝnəstin] *n*. 欧内斯婷〔女子名〕。

e·rode [iˈrəud; ɪˋrod] *vt*. 1. 侵蚀,腐蚀。2. 腐蚀出,侵蚀成。*metals* ~*d by acids* 被酸腐蚀的金属。— *vi*. 受侵蚀,遭腐蚀。

e·rod·ent [iˈrəudənt; ɪˋrodənt] **I** *a*. 侵蚀的,腐蚀的。**II** *n*.【医】腐蚀药。

e·rod·i·ble [iˈrəudəbl; ɪˋrodəbl] *a*. 会被腐蚀的;受到腐蚀的。

e·rog·e·nous [iˈrɔdʒinəs; ɪˋrɑdʒənəs] *a*. = erotogenic.

E·ros [ˈirɔs, ˈerɔs; ˋɪrɑs, ˋɛrɑs] *n*. 1.【希神】爱神厄洛斯。2. 性欲,性爱。3. 精力,生命力。

e·rose [iˈrəus; ɪˋros] *a*. **1.** 不整齐的。**2.**【植、虫】啮蚀状的。

e·ro·sion [iˈrəuʒən; ɪˋroʒən] *n*. **1.** 腐蚀,侵蚀(作用)。**2.**【医】糜烂,齿质腐损。

e·ro·sive [iˈrəusiv; ɪˋrosɪv] *a*. 腐蚀性的,侵蚀性的。

er·o·te·sis [ˌerəˈtiːsis; ˏɛrəˋtisɪs] *n*.【修】反问法。

e·rot·ic [iˈrɔtik; ɪˋrɑtɪk] **I** *a*. 性爱的,色情的;性欲的,情欲上的。**II** *n*. **1.** 情诗。**2.** 好色之徒。**-cal·ly** *ad*.

e·rot·i·ca [iˈrɔtikə; ɪˋrɑtɪkə] *n*. 〔*pl*.〕〔用作单数或复数〕色情书籍,色情画。

e·rot·i·cism [iˈrɔtisizəm; ɪˋrɑtəˏsɪzəm] *n*. = erotism.

er·o·tism [ˈerətizəm; ˋɛrətɪzəm] *n*. **1.** 色情性,好色。**2.** 性欲;性冲动;性行为。**3.**【医】性欲亢进。

e·ro·to·gen·ic [iˌrɔtə*u*ˈdʒenik; ɪˏrɑtəˋdʒɛnɪk] *a*. 性感应区的。

e·ro·to·ma·ni·a [iˌrəutəuˈmeiniə; ɪˏrotəˋmenɪə] *n*.【医】色情狂。

ERP, E.R.P. = European Recovery Program〔美〕欧洲复兴计划(即马歇尔计划)。

err [əː; ɝ] *vi*. **1.** 犯错误,错。**2.** 做坏事。**3.**〔古〕入歧途,漫游。*To ~ is human*.〔谚〕人孰无过。~ ***from the truth*** 违背真理。~ ***from the right path*** 误入歧途。~ ***in believing*** 误信。~ ***on the safe side*** 错也保险。~ ***on the side of lenity*** [***severity***] 失之过宽[过严]。

er·ran·cy [ˈeransi; ˋɛrənsɪ] *n*. 错误状态;犯错误的倾向;违背常规的事。

er·rand [ˈerənd; ˋɛrənd] *n*. **1.** 差使;差事;〔古〕使命。**2.**〔古〕口信。*a fool's ~* 徒劳的事。***go on a fool's*** [***gawk's***] ~ 白白受累,无谓奔走。***go on an ~ for sb***. 为某人办事。***run*** (***on***) **~s** 跑腿。***send sb. on an ~*** 差使某人。~ **boy** 使童。

er·rant [ˈerənt; ˋɛrənt] **I** *a*. **1.** (冒险)周游的,漂泊的,漫游的。**2.** 走错了的;错误的,迷路的。**3.** 无定的,移动的。~ *conceptions* 谬见。**II** *n*. 游侠。**-ly** *ad*.

er·rant·ry [ˈerəntri; ˋɛrəntrɪ] *n*. **1.** (中世纪骑士的)冒险周游;游侠行为。**2.**〔总称〕游侠。

er·ra·ta [eˈrɑːtə; ɛˋrɑtə] *n*. erratum 的复数。

er·rat·ic [iˈrætik, eˈr-; əˋrætik] **I** *a*. **1.** 飘忽不定的;(行为等)古怪的,反常的;(心意、爱情等)乖僻的,反复无常的。**2.**【天】轨道无定的;【地】漂移性的;【医】间断无定的,不规律的;游走的。**II** *n*. **1.** 奇人,怪人;反复无常的人。**2.**【地】漂砾。~ **blocks** [**boulders**]【地】漂砾;漂块。**an ~ star** 游星。**-cal·ly** *ad*. **-ism** *n*.

er·ra·tum [eˈrɑːtəm; ɛˋrɑtəm] *n*. (*pl*. ***-ta*** [-tə; -tə]) (书写或印刷中的)错误;〔*pl*.〕勘误表。

er·rhine [ˈerain; ˋɛraɪn] **I** *n*.【医】催嚏剂,引涕剂。**II** *a*. 催嚏的,引涕的。

err·ing [ˈəːriŋ; ˋɝɪŋ] *a*. 做错了事的;有罪过的;走入歧途的。**-ly** *ad*.

er·ro·ne·ous [iˈrəunjəs, eˈr-; əˋronjəs, ɛˋr-] *a*. 错误的,不正确的。~ *opinions* 错误意见。**-ly** *ad*. **-ness** *n*.

er·ror [ˈerə; ˋɛrɚ] *n*. **1.** 错误;失错。**2.** 谬见,误想;误信;误解。**3.** 罪过。**4.**【数】误差;【法】误审,违法;(棒球中的)错打。*commit* [*make*] *an ~* 犯[出]错。*correct ~s* 改正错误。*a clerk's* [*clerical*] ~ 笔误。*mean ~s* 标准误差。***a writ of ~***【法】(推翻错误原判的)再审命令。*nature's ~* 天生畸形。***in ~*** 弄错了的;错误地。***~s of commission*** [***omission***] 违犯[疏忽]罪。***fall into ~*** 误入歧途。***nature's ~*** 天生畸形。**-less** *a*. 无错误的,正确的。

er·satz [G. ɛəˈzæts; ɛrˋzɑts] **I** *n*. 〔G.〕代用品。**II** *a*. 代用的,人造的,合成的。

Erse [əːs; ɝs] **I** *n*. (苏格兰高地或爱尔兰的)克尔特语,盖耳语。**II** *a*. 盖耳语的。

Er·skin(e) [ˈəːskin; ˋɝskɪn] *n*. 厄斯金〔姓氏〕。

erst [əːst; ɝst] *ad*. 〔古〕以前,从前,往昔。

erst·while [ˈəːst*h*wail; ˋɝstˏ*h*waɪl] **I** *ad*. 从前,往昔。**II** *a*. 以前的,从前的,原来的。

ERTS = Earth Resources Technology Satellites 地球资源技术卫星(计划)。

er·u·bes·cence [ˌeruːˈbesns; ˏɛrʊˋbɛsəns] *n*. 变红,发红,脸红。

er·u·bes·cent [ˌeruːˈbesnt; ˏɛrʊˋbɛsənt] *a*. 发红的,略带红色的;变红的;脸红的。

e·ruct, e·ruc·tate [iˈrʌkt, -teit; ɪˋrʌkt, -tet] *vt*. 使打嗝;嗝出;喷出。—*vi*. 打嗝,嗳气。

e·ruc·ta·tion [ˌiːrʌkˈteiʃən; ˏirʌkˋteʃən] *n*. **1.** 嗳气,打嗝儿。**2.** (火山等的)喷出;喷出物。**-tive** *a*.

er·u·dite [ˈeru(ː)dait; ˋɛrʊˏdaɪt] **I** *a*. 博学的,有学问的。*an ~ commentary* 学者的评论。**II** *n*. 饱学之士,有学问的人。**-ly** *ad*. **-ness** *n*.

er·u·di·tion [ˌeru(ː)ˈdiʃən; ˏɛrʊˋdɪʃən] *n*. 博学;学识;学问。**-al** *a*.

e·rum·pent [iˈrʌmpənt; ɪˋrʌmpənt] *a*. 突然现出的;【植】裂出的,迸出的。

e·rupt [iˈrʌpt; ɪˋrʌpt] *vi*. **1.** (火山等)迸发,喷出,爆发。**2.** (人从房子里)涌出;(牙齿)冒出;(皮肤)发疹子。—*vt*. 喷发;喷射出。**-i·ble** *a*.

e·rup·tion [iˈrʌpʃən; ɪˋrʌpʃən] *n*. **1.**【地】喷发;(战争、感情等)爆发,迸发。**2.**【医】疹,发疹;(牙齿)萌出。**3.** 喷出物。**-al** *a*.

e·rup·tive [iˈrʌptiv; ɪˋrʌptɪv] **I** *a*. **1.** 喷出的,爆发的,喷发的。**2.**【地】火山喷出的。**3.**【医】疹的,发疹性的。~ *fountain* 喷泉。**II** *n*. 火成岩,喷发岩(= ~ rock)。**-ly** *ad*. **-ness** *n*.

E.R.V. = English Revised Version〔*cf*. Revised Version of the Bible〕.

Er·vin [ˈəːvin; ˋɝvɪn] *n*. 欧文〔姓氏,男子名〕。

Er·vine [ˈəːvin; ˋɝvɪn] *n*. 欧文〔姓氏〕。

Er·win [ˈəːwin; ˋɝwɪn] *n*. 欧文〔姓氏〕。

-er·y *suf*. **1.**〔加于名词或形容词之后〕表示"性质","行为","习性"等: brav*ery*, snobb*ery*. **2.**〔加于动词之后〕表示"职业","技术"等: arch*ery*, fish*ery*, surg*ery*. **3.**〔加于动词之后〕表示"厂","店","场所"等: bak*ery*, groc*ery*. **4.**〔加于名词之后〕表示"…类的产品": machin*ery*, pott*ery*. **5.**〔加于名词之后〕表示"集体": soldi*ery*. **6.**〔加于动词之后〕表示"境遇","身份","状况": drudg*ery*, slav*ery*.

e·ryn·go [iˈriŋgəu; ɪˋrɪŋgo] *n*. (*pl*. ***-goes***)【植】**1.** 刺芹属(*Eryngium*)植物。**2.**〔废〕海滨刺芹的糖煮根〔原用作春药〕。

er·y·sip·e·las [ˌeriˈsipiləs; ˏɛrəˋsɪpləs] *n*.【医】丹毒。

er·y·sip·e·loid [ˌeriˈsipilɔid; ˏɛrəˋsɪpəˏlɔɪd] *n*.【医】类丹毒。

er·y·the·ma [ˌeriˈθiːmə; ˏɛrəˋθimə] *n*. (*pl*. ***-ma·ta*** [-tə, -tə])【医】红斑,红皮病。

e·ryth·rism [iˈriθrizəm; ɪˋrɪθrɪzm] *n*. 异常红〔尤指哺乳动物的毛发和鸟羽〕。**-al, er·y·thris·tic** [-ˈθristik; -ˋθrɪstɪk] *a*.

e·ryth·rite [iˈriθrait; ɪˋrɪθraɪt] *n*.【化】**1.** 钴华。**2.** 赤丁四醇,赤藓(糖)醇。

e·ryth·ri·tol [iˈriθrəˌtəul; ɪˋrɪθrəˏtol] *n*.【化】赤藓醇,丁四醇,赤藻糖醇。

e·ryth·ro- *comb.f*. 表示"红","赤": *erythro*mycin.

e·ryth·ro·blast [iˈriθrəublæst; ɪˋrɪθrəˏblæst] *n*.【生】成红血(球)细胞,有核红血球。**-ic** *a*.

e·ryth·ro·blas·to·sis [iˌriθrəublæsˈtəusis; ɪˏrɪθroˏblæsˋtosɪs] *n*.【医】**1.** 骨髓成红血细胞增多症。**2.** 胎儿、婴儿成红血细胞增多症。

e·ryth·ro·cyte [iˈriθrəusait; ɪˋrɪθroˏsaɪt] *n*.【医】红(血)细胞,红血球。**e·ryth·ro·cyt·ic** [-ˈsitik; -ˋsɪtɪk] *n*.

e·ryth·ro·cy·tom·e·ter [iˌriθrə*u*saiˈtɔmitə; ɪˏrɪθrosaɪˋtɑmətɚ] *n*.【医】红(血)球计数器。

er·y·throid [ˈeriθrɔid; ˋɛrɪθrɔɪd] *a*. **1.** 色调微红的。**2.**

属于红血球的,属于成红血球的原生细胞的。

e·ryth·ro·my·cin [iˌriθrəuˈmaisin; ɪˌrɪθroˋmaɪsɪn] ***n.*** 【医】红霉素。

er·y·thron [ˈeriθrɔn; ˋɛrɪθrɔn] ***n.*** 【解】红血球系统。

e·ryth·ro·phyll [iˈriθrəfil; ɪˋrɪθroˌfɪl] ***n.*** 【生化】叶红素。

e·ryth·ro·poi·e·sis [iˌriθrəupɔiˈiːsis; ɪˌrɪθropɔɪˋisɪs] ***n.*** 【医】红(血)细胞生成,红血球生成。**e·ryth·ro·poi·et·ic** [-pɔiˈetik; -pɔɪˋɛtɪk] ***a.***

er·y·throp·(s)i·a [ˌeriˈθrɔp(s)iə; ˌɛrəˋθrop(s)ɪə] ***n.*** 【医】红视症。

e·ryth·ro·sin [iˈriθrəusin; ɪˋrɪθrosɪn] ***n.*** **1.** 【化】赤鲜红;四碘萤光素。**2.** 【纺】新品酸性红(=erythrosine)。

Es=【化】einsteinium.

es- *pref.* ex- 的异体: *es*cape, *es*cheat.

-es *suf.* **1.** 〔加于词尾为 s, z, sh, ch, o, y 的大多数名词之后,构成复数〕: glass*es*, fuzz*es*, bush*es*, peach*es*, hero*es*, lodi*es*, loav*es*. **2.** 〔加于词尾为 s, z, sh, ch 等动词之后,构成现在时陈述语气第三人称单数〕: buzz*es*, reach*es*.

ESC = Economic and Social Council (United Nations) (联合国)经济及社会理事会。

E

es·ca·drille [ˌeskəˈdril; ˌɛskəˋdrɪl] ***n.*** 〔F.〕 **1.** (六机编成的)飞行小队。**2.** (八艘舰艇组成的)海军分队。

es·ca·lade [ˌeskəˈleid; ˌɛskəˋled] **I** ***vt.*** (用梯子)攀登;【军】(用云梯)爬(城)。**II** ***n.*** **1.** 爬云梯,用云梯爬墙。**2.** 活动人行道。

es·ca·late [ˈeskəleit; ˋɛskəˌlet] ***vi.*** **1.** 乘自动梯上升;像乘自动梯上升。**2.** (战争)逐步升级。**3.** 迅速上涨,飞快增加〔如物价、工资等〕。—***vt.*** 使逐步上升。**es·ca·la·tion** [ˌeskəˈleiʃən; ˌɛskəˋleʃən] ***n.***

es·ca·la·tor [ˈeskəleitə; ˋɛskəˌletɚ] **I** ***n.*** **1.** 【建】自动楼梯。**2.** (规定工资定期按生活费用)上下调整的条款。**II** ***a.*** (规定工资、价格定期按比例)上下调整的。~ *clauses* 伸缩条款。

es·cal·lo·ni·a [ˌeskəˈləuniə; ˌɛskəˋlonɪə] ***n.*** 【植】鼠刺属植物;〔E-〕鼠刺属。

es·cal·(l)op [isˈkɔləp; ɛˋskɑləp] ***n.*** =scallop.

es·cap·a·ble [iˈskeipəbl; ɪˋskepəbl] ***a.*** 可以避免的;可以逃脱的。

es·ca·pade [ˌeskəˈpeid; ˌɛskəˋped] ***n.*** **1.** 越轨行为,恶作剧。**2.** 逃走,逃避。

es·cape [iˈskeip; ɪˋskep] **I** ***vi.*** **1.** 逃走,逃亡;逃脱,逃逸;逃避;避免。**2.** (液体等)漏出,漏气。**3.** (栽培植物)长成野生植物。*The gas is escaping somewhere.* 煤气有个地方漏气了。~ *from prison* 越狱。— ***vt.*** **1.** 避开,避免。**2.** 漏掉;疏忽,忘记。**3.** 逸出;从…发出。*narrowly* [*barely*] ~ *death* [*being killed*] 死里逃生。*Nothing ~s you!* 你真细心! *A groan ~d his lips.* 他不禁哼了一声。*an ~d convict* 越狱逃犯。~ *one's lips* 脱口而出。*His name ~s me.* = *His name ~s my memory.* 他的名字我记不起来了。~ *sb.'s notice* 未被别人注意。**II** ***n.*** **1.** 逃避;逃亡;漏出,逸出。**2.** 逃亡手段;避难装置;逃路。**3.** 【机】排气管。**4.** 野化植物,退化植物。**5.** 【建】出口。*an air* ~ 放气管。*a narrow* [*hairbreadth*] ~ 九死一生。***have an*** ~ 逃走。***have one's*** ~ ***cut off*** 被切断逃路。***make good one's*** ~ = ***effect one's*** ~ 逃脱。***make one's*** ~ 逃走。~ **artist** **1.** (魔术师或杂技演员等)有脱身术的人。**2.** 善于越狱的人。~ **canal** 排水渠。~ **clause** (契约等的)例外条款。~ **hatch** (危急时的)逃生出口;出路,办法。~ **literature** 逃避现实的文学。~ **mechanism** 【心】逃避不愉快的现实的方法。~ **pipe** 放出管。~**-proof** ***a.*** 防逃脱的。~ **shaft** 【矿】太平竖井,安全竖井。~ **stair** 太平梯。~ **valve** 安全阀,放出阀,保险阀。~ **velocity** 【物】(火箭)第二宇宙速度,逃逸速度,脱离速度,克服地心吸力的速度。~ **way** 逃路;太平门,太平梯。~ **wheel** 【机】擒纵轮(=scape wheel)。

es·cap·ee [iˌskeiˈpiː, e-; ɪˌskeˋpi, ɛ-] ***n.*** 逃脱者〔尤指越狱犯人〕。

es·cape·ment [iˈskeipmənt; ɪˋskepmənt] ***n.*** **1.** 擒纵机;(钟、表等的)司行轮,摆轮;(打字机等上面的)棘轮装置。**2.** 〔罕〕逃跑;〔古〕逃路,出口。

es·cap·ism [iˈskeipizəm; əˋskepɪzəm] ***n.*** **1.** 逃避现实,空想,幻想。**2.** 逃避现实的文学[艺术]。

es·cap·ist [iˈskeipist; əˋskepɪst] **I** ***n.*** 逃避现实的人。**II** ***a.*** 逃避现实的。~ *literature* 逃避现实的文学。

es·ca·pol·o·gy [ˌeskəˈpɔlədʒi; ˌɛskəˋpɑlədʒɪ] ***n.*** 逃脱法,逃脱术。

es·car·got [F. eskarˋgəu; ɛskarˋgo] ***n.*** 〔F.〕 蜗牛〔尤指食用蜗牛〕。

es·ca·role [ˈeskərəul; ˋɛskərol] ***n.*** 【植】菊苣,茅菜。

es·carp [iˈskɑːp; ɛˋskɑrp] **I** ***vt.*** 使成急斜面。**II** ***n.*** 【建】内壕,壕沟内岸。**-ment** ***n.*** 急斜面;悬崖。

-esce *suf.* 〔用在拉丁语系动词之后〕表示"开始…","…起来","渐渐…","…化"(等): conval*esce*, efferv*esce*.

-escence *suf.* 构成与 -escent 结尾的形容词相对应的名词,表示"作用","变化","过程","状态"等: conval*escence*, lumin*escence*.

-escent *suf.* 构成形容词,表示"…期的","…性的": adol*escent*, recrud*escent*.

esch·a·lot [ˈeʃəlɔt; ˋɛʃəˌlɑt] ***n.*** =shallot.

es·char [ˈeskɑː; ˋɛskɑr] ***n.*** 【医】焦痂。

es·cha·rot·ic [ˌeskəˈrɔtik; ˌɛskəˋrɑtɪk] **I** ***a.*** 【医】生焦痂性的,腐蚀性的。**II** ***n.*** 苛性剂,腐蚀剂。

es·cha·to·log·i·cal [ˌeskətəˈlɔdʒikəl; ˌɛskətəˋlɑdʒɪkl] ***a.*** 【宗】末世学的。

es·cha·tol·o·gy [ˌeskəˈtɔlədʒi; ˌɛskəˋtɑlədʒɪ] ***n.*** 【宗】末世学〔研究人类和世界终局的神学〕。

es·cheat [isˈtʃiːt; ɛsˋtʃit] **I** ***vi.***, ***vt.*** 【法】(把)(无继承人的土地或财产)归属国家[领主或国王];充公。**II** ***n.*** **1.** (土地或财产的)归还国家,充公。**2.** 归还的财产;没收地。

Esch·e·rich·i·a [ˌeʃəˈrikiə; ˌɛʃəˋrɪkɪə] ***n.*** 【微】埃希氏菌属。~ **coli** 大肠埃希氏菌,大肠杆菌。

es·chew [isˈtʃuː; ɪsˋtʃu] ***vt.*** 【修】避开;戒绝。~ *wine* [*evil*] 戒酒[避开罪恶]。

esch·scholt·zia [eˈʃɔltsiə; ɛˋʃɑltsɪə] ***n.*** 【植】花菱草,花菱草属植物。

es·clan·dre [esˈklɑːndr; ɛsˋklændr] ***n.*** 〔F.〕 丑闻;纷扰。

es·co·lar [ˈeskəˌlɑː; ˋɛskəˌlɑr] ***n.*** 玉梭鱼(*Ruvettus pretiosus*)〔产于大西洋热带地区〕。

es·cort [iˈskɔːt; ɪˋskɔrt] **I** ***vt.*** 护卫,护送,伴随。**II** [ˈeskɔːt; ˋɛskɔrt] ***n.*** **1.** 警卫,护送。**2.** 护卫队,仪仗兵;护送者,护卫者;伴随者;护航舰[机]。*a convoy* ~ 车运警卫部队。~ *carrier* 护航用小型航空母舰。*an* ~ *of jet fighters* 喷气战斗机护航队。*conduct* ~ *operations* 护航。*under the* ~ *of* 在…护送下。

e·scribe [iˈskraib; ɪˋskraɪb] ***vt.*** 【数】旁切。*an ~d circle* 旁切圆。

es·cri·toire [ˌeskriˈtwɑː; ˌɛskrɪˋtwɑr] ***n.*** 〔F.〕写字台。

es·crow [ˈeskrəu; ˋɛskro] ***n.*** 【法】(由第三者保存,待条件完成后即交受证人的)证书[契据]。~ **agreement** [**bonds**] 有条件转让契约[债券]。

es·cu·do [esˈkuːdəu; ɛsˋkudo] ***n.*** (*pl.* ~*s*) 埃斯库多〔葡萄牙及智利等国的货币单位〕。

es·cu·lent [ˈeskjulənt; ˋɛskjulənt] **I** ***a.*** 适于食用的。**II** ***n.*** 食用品〔尤指蔬菜〕。

es·cutch·eon [isˈkʌtʃən; ɪsˋkʌtʃən] ***n.*** **1.** 用纹章装饰的盾。**2.** 盾形物,盾纹面;昆虫小盾片。**3.** (船尾标志船名的)楯部。**4.** 锁眼盖孔罩。*a* (***dark***) ***blot on*** [***in***] ***one's*** ~ 名誉上的污点。

E.S.E., **ESE**, **e.s.e.** = east-southeast.

-ese *suf.* **1.** 〔接在地名之后〕表示"…语","…人",

Chinese, Japanese. 2. 〔接在作家人名之后〕表示"…风格的","…体的","…笔调的": Carlylese, Johnsonese.

es·er·ine [ˈesəriːn; ˋɛsərin] *n.* = physostigmine.

es·kar, es·ker [ˈeskə; ˋɛskɚ] *n.* 【地】蛇形丘。

Es·ki·mo [ˈeskiməu; ˋɛskɪˏmo] I *n.* (*pl.* ~, ~*s*, ~*es* [-z; -z]) 爱斯基摩人[语、狗]。II *a.* 爱斯基摩的。~ **dog** 北极狼犬。~ **pie** 〔美〕紫雪糕。**-an** [ˌeskiˈməuən; ˏɛskɪˋmoən] *a.*

ESL = English as a second language 英语作为第二语言。

Es·mond(e) [ˈezmənd; ˋɛzmənd] *n.* 埃斯蒙德〔男子名〕。

e·soph·a·ge·al [iːˌsɔfəˈdʒiːəl; ˏisəˋfædʒiəl] *a.* 【解】食管的。

e·soph·a·go·scope [iːˈsɔfəgəskəup; iˋsɑfəgəˏskop] *n.* 食管镜,食道窥镜。

e·soph·a·gus [iːˈsɔfəgəs; iˋsɑfəgəs] *n.* (*pl.* **-gi** [-dʒai; -dʒaɪ]) 【解】食管。

es·o·ter·ic [ˌesəuˈterik; ˏɛsəˋtɛrɪk] I *a.* 1. 深奥的;难解的。2. 秘密的;机密的。3. 秘教的 (*opp.* exoteric); (弟子)受秘传的;限于少数人的。II *n.* 受秘传的人。**E-Buddhism** 密教。

es·o·ter·i·ca [ˌesəuˈterikə; ˏɛsəˋtɛrɪkə] *n.* 〔*pl.*〕秘(密)事;秘书;秘教;秘传。

es·o·tro·pi·a [ˌesəuˈtrəupiə; ˏɛsəˋtropɪə] *n.* 【医】辐辏性斜视,内斜视。

ESP = extrasensory perception 超感官知觉,超感觉力。

esp. = especially.

es·pa·drille [ˈespədril; ˋɛspəˋdrɪl] *n.* 登山帆布鞋,帆布便鞋。

es·pal·ier [isˈpæljə; ɪsˋpæljɚ] I *n.* 树墙,树棚;墙式果树,棚式果树。~ **growth form** 匍匐生长型。II *vt.* 1. 给(果树等)支棚架。2. 使(果树等)成匍匐状。

es·pa·ña [esˈpɑːnjɑː; ɛsˋpɑnjɑ] 〔Sp.〕= Spain.

es·pa·ñol [espɑːˈnjɔːl; ɛspɑˋnjɔl] I *n.* 1. 西班牙语。2. (*pl.* **-ñoles** [-ˈnjɔːles; -ˋnjɔlɛs]) 西班牙人。II *a.* 西班牙人的,西班牙语的,西班牙的。

es·par·to [esˈpɑːtəu; ɛsˋpɑrto] *n.* 〔Sp.〕【植】(可制纸、席的)茅草 (= ~ grass)。

es·pe·cial [isˈpeʃəl; ɪsˋpɛʃəl] *a.* 特别的;特殊的。*a matter of ~ importance* 特别重大的事件。*in* ~ 特别,格外,尤其。

es·pe·cial·ly [isˈpeʃəli; ɪsˋpɛʃəlɪ] *ad.* 特别,格外,尤其。★口语中常把 especial(ly) 说成 special(ly).

Es·pe·ran·tist [ˌespəˈræntist; ˏɛspəˋræntɪst] I *n.* 世界语学者[提倡者]。II *a.* 世界语的,世界语学者的。

Es·pe·ran·to [ˌespəˈræntəu; ˏɛspəˋrænto] *n.* 世界语〔1887 年波兰人 Zamenhof 用 Dr. Esperanto 为笔名发表〕。

es·pi·al [isˈpaiəl; ɪsˋpaɪəl] *n.* 侦察;监视;发觉。

es·piè·gle·rie [F. espjegləˈriː; ɛspjɛgləˋri] *n.* 〔F.〕恶作剧;顽皮,淘气。

es·pi·o·nage [F. ˌespiəˈnɑːʒ, ˈespiənidʒ; ˏɛspɪəˋnɑʒ, ˋɛspɪənɪdʒ] *n.* 〔F.〕侦察,监视;谍报;间谍活动。*electronic ~ equipment* 电子侦察设备。

es·pla·nade [ˌespləˈneid; ˏɛspləˋned] *n.* 1. (一般指为散步、驱车游玩的)平地,广场;(尤指海滨、湖边供游人散步的)大道。2. 【军】(要塞与市镇间的)空地。

es·pous·al [isˈpauzəl; ɪˋspauzl] *n.* 1. (对主义、事业等的)拥护,支持。2. 〔常 *pl.*〕订婚或订婚仪式;结婚,婚礼。

es·pouse [isˈpauz; ɪˋspauz] *vt.* 1. 信仰,拥护,采纳(主义、学说等)。2. 嫁娶〔尤指娶妻〕。

es·pres·si·vo [ˌespreˈsiːvəu; ˏɛsprɛˋsivo] *a.*, *ad.* 〔It.〕【乐】富于表情的[地]。

es·pres·so [eˈspresəu; ɛˋsprɛso] *n.* (*pl.* ~*s*) 蒸馏咖啡〔用蒸汽加压煮出的咖啡〕。

es·prit [ˈespriː; F. esˈpri; ɛˋspri; ɛsˋprɪ] *n.* 〔F.〕精神;活气;才智。~ ***de corps*** [dəˈkɔː; dəˋkor] 集体精神,团结精神。~ ***de lois*** [dəˈlwɑː; dəˋlwɑ] 法律的精神。~ ***fort*** [fɔːr; fɔr] 意志坚强的人;自由思想家。

es·py [isˈpai; əsˋpaɪ] *vt.* (**-pied**) 1. (偶然)看出;发现(缺点等)。2. 窥探。

Esq. = Esquire.

-esque *suf.* 表示"…式的","…风格的","…似的": arabesque, picturesque.

Es·qui·mau [ˈeskiməu; ˋɛskəˏmo] *n.* (*pl.* **-x** [-məuz; -ˏmoz]) *a.* = Eskimo.

es·quire [isˈkwaiə; əsˋkwaɪə] I *n.* 1. 〔英〕先生。★信中或正式文件中用于男子姓名以后的尊称;略作 Esq. 或 Esqre (写作 John Smith, Esq.; 头衔写作 John Smith, Esq. M.A.); 美国有时仅用 esquire 称呼律师。2. 〔英〕(地位在骑士之下的)乡绅。3. (中世纪骑士的)扈从。4. 〔古〕地主,绅士。II *vt.* 1. 在(收件人姓名)后用先生的称号;称…为先生。2. 护送。

ESRO = European Space Research Organization 欧洲太空研究组织。

ess [es; ɛs] *n.* (*pl.* ~*es* [ˈesiz; ˋɛsɪz]) 1. 字母 S, s. 2. s 形物件。

ESS = Economic and Scientific Section 经济与科学部。

-ess *suf.* 1. 〔加在名词之后〕表示"阴性": poetess, actress. 2. 〔加在形容词之后,构成抽象名词〕: duress, largess.

es·say [ˈesei, ˈesi; ˋɛse, ˋɛsɪ] I *n.* 1. (文艺上的)随笔,漫笔;小品文,短论〔理论性强的学术论文叫 treatise, dissertation〕。2. 尝试,企图 (*at*); 试验。3. (未被接受的)邮票[纸币]的图案印刷样张。II [eˈsei, ˈesei; əˋse, ɛˋse] *vt.* 试;企图。~ **question** (同填充题、是非题相对而言的)问答题。**-ist** *n.* 随笔[小品文等]作者。

es·se [ˈesi; ˋɛsɪ] *n.* 〔L.〕【哲】存在。*in* ~ 存在着。

Es·sen [ˈesn; ˋɛsn] *n.* 埃森〔德国〕。

es·sence [ˈesns; ˋɛsns] *n.* 1. 【哲】本质 (*opp.* phenomenon); 真髓,精髓,精华,要素。2. 香气;香油,香精,香料。~ *of mint* 薄荷精,薄荷油。*in* ~ 本质上;大体上。*of the* ~ 绝对不可缺的。**-d** *a.* 香料的,香气的。

es·sen·tial [iˈsenʃəl; əˋsɛnʃəl] I *a.* 1. 本质的;实质上的,实在的。2. 根本的,必需的;主要的,紧要的 (*to*)。3. 理想中的,完美的。4. 提炼的,精华的;【乐】基本的;【医】特发的,原发的。~ *elements* 要素。~ *ingredients* 主要成分。II *n.* 〔常 *pl.*〕本质;要点,要素,要件。~*s of English Grammar* 英语语法要点。~*s of life* 生活必需品。~ **anemia** 原发性贫血。~ **character** 【生】种特征。~ **disease** 【医】原发病。~ **harmony** 【乐】基本和声。~ **oil** 【化】(香)精油,香料油。~ **proposition** 【逻】本质的命运。**-ly** *ad.* 本质上;本来;根本。

es·sen·tial·ism [iˈsenʃəlizəm; əˋsɛnʃəˏlɪzəm] *n.* 【哲】本质先于存在论。**-tial·ist** *n.* 本质先于存在论者。

es·sen·ti·al·i·ty [iˌsenʃiˈæliti; əˏsɛnʃɪˋælətɪ] *n.* 1. 本性,本质。2. 重要性;要点。

es·sen·tial·ize [iˈsenʃəlaiz; əˋsɛnʃəˏlaɪz] *vt.* 1. 提炼出,使精炼。2. 扼要地表达,讲明…的本质,用基本形式阐述。

es·ses [ˈesiz; ˋɛsɪz] *n.* 连写的 ss〔ess 的复数〕。

es·so·nite [ˈesənait; ˋɛsənaɪt] *n.* 【地】钙铝榴石。

EST = eastern standard time 〔美〕东部时间。

est. = 1. established. 2. estimate; estimated. 3. Erhard Seminars Training (艾哈德式的一种激励身心的训练)。

-est *suf.* 1. 〔接在大多数单音节的、某些双音节的和少数多音节的形容词和副词之后,构成最高级〕表示"最": hardest, noblest, politest, laziest. ★用法大体上如 -er; 比较级不用 -er 的 barren, fragile 等词,最高级也常有采用 -est 的〔末节为 -id 的词,如 limpid, 也一样〕; 另外,如 beautiful 这种三音节以上的词,在诗里差不多全可自由应用 -est. 2. 〔在诗歌与古语中,接在与 Thou

连用的动词之后,构成陈述语气第二人称单数〕: Thou sing*est*.

estab. = established.

es·tab·lish [is'tæbliʃ; əs`tæblɪʃ] ***vt*.** **1.** 建立,树立,设立,创立;建设,开设;制定,规定。**2.** 安顿,安排,安置;使开业;使定居;使固定。**3.** 确定,证实;使承认,使认定,分办。**4.** 使(教会)成国教。~ *sb. in business* 使人立足商界。~ *a claim to* 确定有权…。~ *a law* 制定法律。~ *oneself as physician* 开业行医。—***vi*.** (植物等)移植生长。**-able** ***a*.**

es·tab·lished [is'tæbliʃt; əs`tæblɪʃt] ***a*.** **1.** 被设立的;确定的;被制定的;被认定了的;既定的。**2.** 国定的。**3.** 【植】移植生长的。*an* ~ *clerk* 常设办事员。*an old* ~ *shop* 老铺,老店。*an* ~ *customs* 成例,常规。*an* ~ *fact* 既成事实。*an* ~ *variety* 移植的品种。*an* ~ *invalid* 慢性病人。~ *reputation* 定评。***the E- Church*** 英国国教。

es·tab·lish·er [is'tæbliʃə; əs`tæblɪʃə] ***n*.** 创办者,建立者。

es·tab·lish·ment [is'tæbliʃmənt; əs`tæblɪʃmənt] ***n*.** **1.** 确定;设置,制定;设立,建立,开设,创设。**2.** 建立的机构;家庭,产业;机关,商店,学校(等);〔英〕研究所。**3.** 制度,编制。**4.** 定薪,(固定的)收入;定职;定员;定居。**5.** 【植】移植生长。**6.** 〔the E-〕权力机构[体制];当局;习俗社会。*keep a large* ~ 拥有巨大家业。*an ammunition* ~ 弹药库。*industrial and mining* ~*s* 工矿企业。*a manufacturing* ~ 工业公司。*business* ~*s* 商店。*the E- newspaper* 官方报纸。*an atomic energy* ~ 原子能科学研究所。*peace* [*war*] ~【军】平时[战时]编制。***the Civil Service E-*** 〔英〕文职定额。***the*** (***Church***) ***E-*** (英国)国教。***the*** ~ ***of the port*** 标准潮讯,潮候时差。~ **period**【生】成林期。

es·tab·lish·men·tar·i·an [isˌtæbliʃmən'tɛəriən; əsˏtæblɪʃmen`tɛrɪən] **I** ***n*.** **1.** 国教信徒,国教主义者。**2.** 拥护既成权力体制的人。**II** ***a*.** **1.** 国教的,国教信徒的。**2.** 拥护既成权力体制的。

es·ta·mi·net [estɑːmiː'ne; ˏɛstəmi`nɛ] ***n*.** 〔F.〕小咖啡馆,小酒吧,小餐馆。

es·tan·cia [es'tɑːnsjɑː; ɛs`tɑnsjɑr] ***n*.** 〔Sp.〕(拉美的)大庄园〔尤指大牧场〕。

es·tate [is'teit; əs`tet] ***n*.** **1.** 财产;遗产;房地产。**2.** 〔古〕身分,地位;家产。**3.** 生活状况;等级;集团;情况,状态。**4.** 财产权,所有权。**5.** 庄园,种植园。**6.** 人生阶段。*a housing* ~ 居民区。*an industrial* ~ 工业区。*landed* ~ 地产。*personal* ~ 动产。*real* ~ 不动产。*a tea* ~ 茶树种植园。*the third* ~ 第三等级〔指平民〕;(法国革命前的)中产阶级。*the fourth* ~〔谑〕第四等级〔指新闻界记者〕。*the fifth* ~ 第五等级〔指科学界〕。~ ***for life*** [***years***] 终身[定期]财产。~ ***in fee*** 世袭领地。~ ***upon condition*** 有条件的遗产。***reach*** [***come to***] ***man's*** [***woman's***] ~ 成年。***suffer in one's*** ~ 家道艰难。***the Three E-*** (***of the Realm***) (封建时代欧洲的)贵族、僧侣和庶民;〔英〕僧侣上院议员、贵族上院议员与下院议员。***wind up an*** ~ 清算死者[破产人]的财产。~ **agent**〔英〕**1.** 土地管理人。**2.** 地产掮客。~ **car**〔英〕客货两用轿车。~ **duty** [**tax**] 财产税,遗产税。**-d** [-id; -ɪd] ***a*.** 有财产的,有产业的,有地产的。

Es·tates-Gen·er·al [i'steits'dʒenərəl; ə`stets`dʒɛnərəl] 三级会议〔法国 1789 年革命前的立法机构〕。

es·teem [is'tiːm; əs`tim] **I** ***n*.** **1.** 尊重,尊敬。**2.** 〔古〕评价。***as a mark*** [***token***] ***of*** ~ 以表敬意。***gain*** [***get***] ***the*** ~ ***of*** 受人尊敬。***have a great*** ~ ***for*** 对…大为敬佩。***hold sb. in*** ~ 尊重;尊敬。***in my*** ~ 照我想[看]。**II** ***vt*.** **1.** 尊重。**2.** 认为;〔古〕评价。*I shall* ~ *it* (*as*) *a favour if* ... 若蒙…,不胜感谢。*an* ~*ed favor*【美商】订购信。*your* ~*ed letter* 尊函。

Es·telle [es'tel; ɛs`tɛl] ***n*.** 艾丝特尔〔女子名〕。

es·ter ['estə; `ɛstə] ***n*.** 【化】酯。~ **value** 酯化值。

es·ter·ase ['estəreis; `ɛstəres] ***n*.** 【化】酯酶。

es·ter·i·fy [es'terifai; ɛs`tɛrɪˏfaɪ] ***vt*.**, ***vi*.** (***-fied***; ***-fying***)【化】(使)酯化。**-fi·ca·tion** [-fi'keiʃən; -fɪ`keʃən] ***n*.** 【化】酯化。

Esth. = Esther, Esthonia.

Es·ther ['estə; `ɛstə] ***n*.** **1.** 埃丝特〔女子名〕。**2.** 以斯帖〔《圣经》犹太女王名〕。**3.** 〔the E-〕【圣】《以斯帖书》。

es·the·si·a [es'θiːʒə, -ʒiə; ɛs`θiʒə] ***n*.** 感觉,感知;感觉力,知觉性。

es·the·si·om·e·ter [esˌθiːziː'ɔmitə; ɛsˏθizɪ`ɑmətə] ***n*.** 【医】触觉测量器。

es·thete ['iːsθiːt, 'es-; `ɛsθit] ***n*.** **1.** 唯美主义者。**2.** 审美家;美学家 (= aesthete)。

es·thet·ic(al) [iːs'θetik(əl), es-; ɛs`θɛtɪk(l̩)] ***a*.** 美的;美学的,审美的;艺术的 (= aesthetic(al))。~ **forest** 风景林。**-al·ly** ***ad*.**

es·the·ti·cian [ˌesθi'tiʃən; ˏɛsθə`tɪʃən] ***n*.** 审美学者,审美学家 (= aesthetician)。

es·thet·i·cism [iːs'θetisizəm; ɛs`θɛtəˏsɪzəm] ***n*.** 唯美主义;审美眼光;美的嗜好 (= aestheticism)。

es·thet·ics [iːs'θetiks; ɛs`θɛtɪks] ***n*.** 〔用作单数〕美学 (= aesthetics)。

Es·tho·ni·a [es'təuniə; ɛs`tonɪə], **Es·tho·ni·an** [-niən; -nɪən] ***n*.** = Estonia. **-n** ***a*.**, ***n*.** = Estonian.

es·ti·ma·ble ['estiməbl; `ɛstəməbl̩] ***a*.** **1.** 值得尊重的;可估计的。**2.** 〔古〕有价值的,可贵的。**-ness** ***n*.** **-bly** ***ad*.**

es·ti·mate I ['estimeit; `ɛstəˏmet] ***vt*.** **1.** 估计,估算;估价;估量。**2.** 评价,评断。**3.** 〔古〕尊重。*an* ~*d sum* 估计总数。~ *the loss at 1,000 yuan* 估计损失为一千元。—***vi*.** 估计,估价。**II** ['estimit; `ɛstəmɪt] ***n*.** **1.** 估计;预测;〔英〕〔*pl*.〕预算,预算额;预算书;估价单;(从典型统计得出的)数值。**2.** 评价,判断。*an intelligence* ~ 情报[敌情]判断。*a rough* ~ 据粗略的估计。***at a moderate*** ~ 照适中的估计。***by*** ~ 照估计。***form an*** ~ ***of*** 给…作一估计;评价。***the E-*** 〔英〕财政收支概算。**-d** ***a*.**

es·ti·ma·tion [ˌesti'meiʃən; ˏɛstə`meʃən] ***n*.** **1.** 估计,评价。**2.** 预算,预算额;概算。**3.** 尊重,尊敬。**4.** 意见,判断。**5.** 【化】估定;测定。*in my* ~ 据我估计,我认为。*in the* ~ *of the law* 从法律上来看。***full*** [***rise***] ***in the*** ~ ***of the public*** 在公众心目中的评价下降[上升]。***held in high*** ~ 极受尊重。

es·ti·ma·tive ['estimətiv; `ɛstəˏmetɪv] ***a*.** **1.** 有估计能力的。**2.** 可用以估计的;能作出判断的。~ *figure* 估计的数字。

es·ti·ma·tor ['estimeitə; `ɛstəˏmetə] ***n*.** 估计者;估计量。

es·ti·val [iːs'taivəl; `ɛstəvl̩] ***a*.** = aestival.

es·ti·vate ['estiveit; `ɛstəˏvet] ***vi*.** **1.** 消夏。**2.** 【动】夏眠,夏蛰。

es·ti·va·tion [ˌesti'veiʃən; ˏɛstə`veʃən] ***n*.** **1.** 【动】夏眠,夏蛰。**2.** 【植】花被卷叠式;夏眠〔指生态〕(= aestivation)。

es·to·ca·da [ˌestə'kɑːdə; ɛstə`kɑdə] ***n*.** (斗牛结束阶段的)刺牛。

Es·to·ni·a [es'təunjə; ɛs`tonɪə] ***n*.** 爱沙尼亚〔国名,位于波罗的海沿岸〕。

Es·to·ni·an [es'təunjən; ɛs`tonɪən] **I** ***a*.** **1.** 爱沙尼亚(人)的。**2.** 爱沙尼亚语[文化]的。**II** ***n*.** **1.** 爱沙尼亚人。**2.** 爱沙尼亚语。

es·top [is'tɔp; ɛs`tɑp] ***vt*.** (***-pp-***) **1.** 【法】禁止翻供。**2.** 〔古〕堵塞,遮拦。**3.** 防止,禁止 (*from*)。

es·top·page [is'tɔpidʒ; ɛs`tɑpɪdʒ] ***n*.** **1.** 【法】禁止翻供。**2.** 堵塞,阻止。

es·top·pel [is'tɔpəl; ɛs`tɑpl̩] ***n*.** 【法】禁止翻供。

es·to·vers [es'təuvəz; ɛ`stovəz] ***n*.** 〔*pl*.〕【法】(法律上准许的)必需供给品〔如给租户作燃料或修理用的木材,

给离婚妻子的赡养费〕。

es·trade [es'trɑːd; ɛs`trɑd] *n*. 台,坛。

es·tra·di·ol [ˌestrə'daiəul, -ɔːl; ˏɛstrə`daɪol, -ɑl] *n*.【化】雌二醇。

es·trange [is'treindʒ; ə`strendʒ] *vt*. **1.** 使疏远;离间。**2.** 隔离;使离开(习惯了的环境等)。**3.** 转用,移用。*be* [*become*] *~d from each other* 互相疏远。*~ oneself from* 同…疏远起来。**-d** *a*. **-ment** *n*.

es·tray [i'strei; ɪ`stre] **I** *n*. **1.** 他去的人;不见了的东西。**2.**【法】无人认领的走失家畜;无主的走失家畜。**II** *vi*. 〔古〕迷路,走失。

es·treat [is'triːt; ɪs`trit] **I** *n*.【法】(关于罚款等判决记录的)副本,抄本。**II** *vt*. 抄(判决记录);(按副本)追收(罚款等)。

es·tri·ol ['estraiəul; `ɛstraɪˏol] *n*.【生化】雌三醇。

es·tro·gen ['estrədʒən; `ɛstrədʒən] *n*.【生化】雌(性)激素。

es·tro·gen·ic [ˌestrə'dʒenik; ˏɛstrə`dʒɛnɪk] *a*.【生化】雌激素的,促进发情的。

Es·tron ['iːstrən; `istrɑn] *n*. 醋酸纤维。

es·trone ['estrəun; `ɛstron] *n*.【生化】雌素酮。

es·trous ['iːstrəs, 'es-; `istrəs, `ɛs-] *a*.【动】发情期的,有发情期特征的。**~ cycle**【动】发情周期。

es·trum ['iːstrəm; `istrəm] *n*. = oestrum 或 estrus.

es·trus ['iːstrəs, 'es-; `istrəs, `ɛs-] *n*.【动】发情期。

es·tu·ar·i·al [ˌestju'ɛəriəl; ˏɛstjʊ`ɛrɪəl] *a*. 三角港的,三角湾的,河口湾的,港湾的。

es·tu·ar·ine ['estjuːərin, -ain; `ɛstʃʊəˏrɪn, -aɪn] *a*. **1.** 江河口的;江河湾的;港湾的。**2.** (江河口、江河湾、港湾等)沉积的。

es·tu·ar·y ['estjuəri; `ɛstʃʊərɪ] *n*. 三角湾,河口湾,港湾。**~ deposit** 港湾沉积。

E.S.U., ESU, e.s.u. = electrostatic unit 静电单位。

e·su·ri·ence, e·su·ri·en·cy [i'sjuəriəns, -si; ɪ`sjʊrɪəns, -sɪ] *n*. **1.** 饥饿,贪吃,暴食。**2.** 贪心,贪婪。

e·su·ri·ent [i'sjuəriənt; ɪ`sjʊrɪənt] *a*. **1.** 饥饿的;暴食的,贪吃的。**2.** 贪心的。

ESV = earth satellite vehicle 人造地球卫星。

ET = eastern time〔美〕东部时间。

E.T. = **1.** English Translation. **2.** electric telegraph. **3.** 〔美〕electric transcription.

E.T. ['iːtiː; `iti] *n*. extraterrestrial 之缩写,《外星人》〔美国的一部科学幻想影片〕。

-et[1] *suf*. **1.**〔主要加在法语的名词之后〕表示"小":bull*et*, fill*et*, isl*et*, sonn*et* (但 hatch*et*, pock*et*, pack*et* 等已失去"小"的意义). **2.** 表示"组","组合":oct*et*, quart*et*.

-et[2], **-ete** *suf*. 表示"…者","做…的人":aesth*ete*, athl*ete*, po*et*.

et [et; ɛt] *conj*.〔L.〕和,以及 (= and)。**~ *al*.** [ˌet'æl; ˏɛt`æl] **1.** = ~ alibi. **2.** = ~ alii. **~ *seq* (*q*).** = ~ ***sq* (*q*).** = ~ ***sequentes*** [***sequentia***] [et'sikwentiːz, -ʃiə; ɛt`sɪkwɛntiz, -ʃɪə] 以及下列等等,参看以下某句[某页] (= and those that follow)。

ETA = estimated time of arrival 估计的到达时间。

e·ta ['iːtə; `itə] *n*. 希腊语字母表第七字母〔H, η, 相当英语的长音 e〕。

et alibi [et'ælibai; ɛt`ælɪbaɪ]〔L.〕以及其他地方 (= and elsewhere)。

et alii [et'æliai; ɛt`ælɪaɪ]〔L.〕以及其他人等 (= and others)。★ et alii 一般指人,指物时用 etc.

et·a·mine ['etəmiːn; `ɛtəmin] *n*.【纺】纱罗;筛绢。

é·tape [ei'tæp; e`tæp] *n*.〔F.〕**1.** 兵站;宿营地。**2.** 一日的行程。

é·tat ['etɑː; `ɛtɑ] *n*.〔F.〕**1.** 国家。**2.** = estate.

é·ta·tisme, e·ta·tism [ei'tɑːtizəm; e`tɑtɪzəm] *n*.〔F.〕国家社会主义,国家主义。

e·ta·tist, é·ta·tiste [ei'tɑːtist; e`tɑtɪst] **I** *a*. (拥护)国家社会主义的,(拥护)国家主义的。**II** *n*. 国家社会主义者,国家主义者。

état-major [ˌetɑːmɑː'ʒɔːr; ˏetɑmɑ`ʒɔr] *n*.〔F.〕【军】参谋;参谋部。

etc. =〔L.〕*et cetera* (常读作 *and so forth*).

et cet·er·a [it'setrə; ɪt`sɛtərə]〔L.〕等等,以及其他〔指人时用 et al.〕。

et·cet·e·ras [it'setrəz; ɪt`sɛtrəz] *n*.〔*pl*.〕其他种种东西,等等东西。*these* ~ 这种种东西。*100 dollars without* ~ 一百美元整。

etch [etʃ; ɛtʃ] **I** *vt*. **1.** 蚀刻,浸蚀。**2.** 刻划,描述。**3.** 铭刻。—*vi*. 进行蚀刻。**II** *n*. 腐蚀剂,蚀刻剂。*mass* ~ (晶体的)粗蚀。

etch·ant ['etʃənt; `ɛtʃənt] *n*. 蚀刻剂。

etch·er ['etʃə; `ɛtʃɚ] *n*. 蚀刻技工;蚀刻器。

etch·ing ['etʃiŋ; `ɛtʃɪŋ] *n*. **1.** 蚀刻法;蚀刻(铜)版画;蚀镂术。**2.** 蚀刻画,蚀刻版,蚀刻版印刷品。*close* [*rough*] ~ (晶体的)精[粗]蚀。*electrochemical* ~ 电化浸蚀,电抛光。**~ figure** 蚀像。**~ ground** 蚀刻底子。**~ needle** 蚀刻用钢针。

ETD = estimated time of departure 估计的离开时间。

e·ter·nal [i'təːnl; ɪ`tɝnl] *a*. **1.** 永远的,永久的;不变的,不朽的。**2.**〔口〕不停的,没完没了的。~ *death* 死灰。~ *life* 永生。~ *truth* 永恒的真理。*the* ~ *triangle* 三角恋爱。***the E-***【宗】上帝。***the E- City*** 不朽的都市〔指罗马〕。**-ly** *ad*. **-ity, -ness** *n*.

e·ter·na·lize [i'təːnəlaiz; ɪ`tɝnəlˏaɪz] *vt*. 使永恒,使无穷,使不朽。

e·ter·ni·ty [i(ː)'təːniti; i(ɪ)`tɝnətɪ] *n*. **1.** 无始无终,无穷无尽,永恒。**2.**【宗】来世;永生;永劫。***an ~ box***〔俚〕棺材。***send sb. to ~*** 送某人上西天。***through all ~*** 永远,万古千秋。

e·ter·nize [i(ː)'təːnaiz; i(ɪ)`tɝnaɪz] *vt*. 使永恒,使无穷,使不朽。**e·ter·ni·za·tion** [i(ː)ˌtəːnai'zeiʃən; i(ɪ)ˏtɝnaɪ`zeʃən] *n*.

E·te·sian [i'tiːziən; ɪ`tiʒən] **I** *a*. 一年一次的。**II** *n*.〔常 *pl*.〕(定期发生的)地中海季风。

eth. = ethical; ethics.

-eth *suf*. **1.**〔加于以母音结尾的基数词以后,构成序数词〕:fortι*eth*. **2.**〔古〕〔加于动词之后,构成第三人称单数现在时〕:ask*eth*; go*eth*.

eth·ane ['eθein; `ɛθen] *n*.【化】乙烷。

eth·a·no·ic [ˌeθə'nəuik; ˏɛθə`noɪk] *a*. **~ acid**【化】醋酸,乙酸。

eth·a·nol ['eθənɔːl, -nəul; `ɛθənol, -nol] *n*.【化】**1.** 醇。**2.** 乙醇;酒精 (= alcohol)。

eth·a·nol·a·mine ['eθənəu'læmiːn; `ɛθənə`læmin] *n*.【化】乙醇胺;胺基乙醇。

Eth·el ['eθəl; `ɛθəl] *n*. 埃塞尔〔女子名〕。

eth·ene ['eθiːn; `ɛθin] *n*.【化】乙烯 (= ethylene)。

e·the·o·gen·e·sis [ˌiːθiəu'dʒenisis; ˏiθɪə`dʒɛnɪsɪs] *n*.【生】雄体单性生殖。

e·ther ['iːθə; `iθɚ] *n*. **1.**【物】以太,能媒。**2.**【化】醚;乙醚。**3.**〔诗〕上空,苍天。**4.**【哲】灵气;气氛。**~net**【计】以太网(局域网)。**~ wave** 以太波。**-ish, -like** *a*.

e·the·re·al, e·the·ri·al [i'θiəriəl; ɪ`θɪrɪəl] *a*. **1.** 空气一样的;轻飘的,稀薄的。**2.** 天上的,太空的;灵气的;微妙的。**3.**【物】以太的。**4.**【化】用醚制的,醚(性)的。**~ oil** 香精油。**-ity** *n*. **-ly** *ad*.

e·the·re·al·i·za·tion [iˌθiəriəli'zeiʃən; ɪˏθɪrɪəlɪ`zeʃən] *n*. **1.** 轻飘化,稀薄化。**2.** 微妙化。**3.** 醚化,气化。

e·the·re·al·ize [i(ː)'θiəriəlaiz; i(ɪ)`θɪrɪəlaɪz] *vt*. **1.** 使轻飘,使稀薄。**2.** 使微妙。**3.** 使成醚;气化。

Eth·er·ege ['eθəridʒ; `ɛθərɪdʒ] *n*. 埃瑟里奇〔姓氏〕。

e·the·ri·al [i'θiəriəl; ɪ`θɪrɪəl] *a*. = ethereal.

e·ther·i·fy [i'θerifai; ɪ`θɛrəˏfaɪ] *vt*.【化】醚化。

e·ther·i·za·tion [ˌiːθərai'zeiʃən; ˏiθəraɪ`zeʃən] *n*.【医】

麻醉。

e·ther·ize [ˈiːθəraiz; ˋiθə͵raɪz] *vt*.【医】用醚麻醉。**-r** *n*. 麻醉剂。

eth·ic [ˈeθik; ˋɛθɪk] **I** *a*. = ethical. **II** *n*. = ethics.

eth·i·cal [ˈeθikəl; ˋɛθɪkl̩] *a*. **1.** 伦理的,道德的;伦理学(上)的;合乎道德的。**2.** (药品)合乎规格的,凭处方出售的。*an* ~ *principle* 道德原则。~ *culture* 伦理教育。~ **dative**【语法】心性与格〔*Knock me at the door*. 中之 *me* 表示间接关系人的受格,加强叙述的语气〕。~ **drug** [**pharmaceutical**] 凭处方出售的药品。~ **genitive**【语】泛指的第二人称的所有格。~ **hacker** 文明黑客〔指努力探索电脑系统安全的弱点,但并非旨在破坏而是要修补这些安全弱点的电脑能手〕。~ **investment** 讲究道德原则的投资〔要审查所投资的企业或项目是否符合道德原则〕。**-ly** *ad*. **-ness** *n*.

eth·i·cal·i·ty [͵eθiˈkæliti; ͵ɛθɪˋkælətɪ] *n*. 伦理性。

eth·i·cian [eˈθiʃən; ɛˋθɪʃən] *n*. = ethicist.

eth·i·cist [ˈeθisist; ˋɛθɪsɪst] *n*. 伦理学家 (= ethician)。

eth·i·cize [ˈeθisaiz; ˋɛθɪ͵saɪz] *vt*. 使伦理化;使变得道德的,认为…合乎伦理。

eth·ics [ˈeθiks; ˋɛθɪks] *n*. **1.** 伦理学。**2.** 伦理,道德。**3.** 伦理学书籍[论文];伦理观,道德标准。*practical* ~ 实用伦理学。*medical* ~ 行医道德。*press* ~ 新闻道德。

eth·i·nyl [eˈθainl; ɛˋθaɪnl̩] *n*.【化】乙炔基。

E·thi·op(e) [ˈiːθiɔp; ˋiθɪ͵ɑp] *n*., *a*. 〔古〕= Ethiopian.

E·thi·o·pi·a [͵iːθiˈəupjə; ͵iθɪˋopɪə] *n*. 埃塞俄比亚(衣索比亚)〔非洲〕。

E·thi·o·pi·an [͵iːθiˈəupjən, -piən, ͵iθɪˋopɪən, -pɪən] **I** *a*. 埃塞俄比亚的,埃塞俄比亚人的,埃塞俄比亚语的。**II** *n*. **1.** 埃塞俄比亚人,埃塞俄比亚语,**2.** (泛指)黑人。

E·thi·op·ic [͵iːθiˈɔpik, -ˈəupik; ͵iθɪˋɑpɪk, -ˋopɪk] **I** *a*. 埃塞俄比亚语的;埃塞俄比亚人的;埃塞俄比亚的。**II** *n*. 埃塞俄比亚语。

eth·moid [ˈeθmɔid; ˋɛθmɔɪd], **eth·moi·dal** [-dəl; -dl̩] **I** *a*.【解】筛状的;筛骨的。**II** *n*. 筛骨。

eth·narch [ˈeθnɑːk; ˋɛθnɑk] *n*. (拜占庭帝国等的)总督。**-y** *n*. 总督的职位[身份、统治权、管辖区]。

eth·nic [ˈeθnik; ˋɛθnɪk] **I** *a*. = ethnical. **II** *n*. 少数民族的成员,种族集团的成员。~ **cleansing** 种族清洗。

eth·ni·cal [ˈeθnikəl; ˋɛθnɪkl̩] *a*. **1.** 种族的,种族上的,人种学的。**2.** 异教徒的。~ *nation* 部落民族。~ *psychology* 种族心理学。**-ly** *ad*.

eth·nic·i·ty [eθˈnisiti; ɛθˋnɪsətɪ] *n*. 种族划分;种族关系。

eth·no- *comb*. *f*. 表示"人种","种族","民族": *ethno*graphy.

eth·no·cen·tric [͵eθnəuˈsentrik; ͵ɛθnəˋsɛntrɪk] *a*. 种族[民族]中心主义的,种族[民族、集团]优越感的。**-al·ly** *ad*.

eth·no·cen·trism [͵eθnəuˈsentrizəm; ͵ɛθnəˋsɛntrɪzm] *n*. 种族[民族]中心主义,种族[民族、集团]优越感。

eth·nog·e·ny [eθˈnɔdʒini; ɛθˋnɑdʒɪnɪ] *n*. 人种起源学。

eth·nog·ra·pher [eθˈnɔgrəfə; ɛθˋnɑgrəfɚ] *n*. 人种史[人种论]研究者,人种史[人种论]学家。

eth·no·gra·phic(al) [͵eθnəuˈgræfik(əl); ͵ɛθnəˋgræfɪk(l̩)] *a*. 人种学的。

eth·nog·ra·phy [eθˈnɔgrəfi; ɛθˋnɑgrəfɪ] *n*. 人种史,人种论。

ethnol. = ethnologic; ethnology.

eth·no·log·ic(al) [͵eθnəuˈlɔdʒik(əl); ͵ɛθnəˋlɑdʒɪk(l̩)] *a*. 人种学的,民族学的;人类文化学的。**-al·ly** *ad*.

eth·nol·o·gist [eθˈnɔlədʒist; ɛθˋnɑlədʒɪst] *n*. 人种学家,民族学家;人类文化学家。

eth·nol·o·gy [eθˈnɔlədʒi; ɛθˋnɑlədʒɪ] *n*. 人种学,民族学;人类文化学。

eth·no·psy·chol·o·gy [͵eθnəusaiˈkɔlədʒi; ͵ɛθnəsaɪˋkɑlədʒɪ] *n*. 人种心理学,民族心理学。

et hoc genus omme [et ˈhɔk ˈdʒiːnəs ˈɔmniː; ɛt ˋhɔk ˋdʒinəs ˋɑmni] 〔L.〕诸如此类 (= and all that kind of thing)。

e·thol·o·gy [iˈθɔlədʒi; ɪˋθɑlədʒɪ] *n*.【生】(个体)生态学。**-gi·c(al)** *a*. **-gi·cal·ly** *ad*. **-gist** *n*. (个体)生态学研究者。

e·thos [ˈiːθɔs; ˋiθɑs] *n*. **1.** 道德本质,气质。**2.** 民族精神,时代思潮;社会风气。**3.** 文学作品中的客观因素〔指比决定人的行为的思想、感情更有普遍性的理性特征〕。

eth·yl [ˈeθil, ˈiːθail; ˋɛθɪl, ˋiθaɪl] *n*. **1.**【化】乙基,乙烷基。**2.** 四乙铅〔加在汽油中的防爆剂〕。**3.** 含四乙铅的汽车燃料。~ **acetate** 醋酸乙酯,乙酸乙酯。~ **alcohol** 乙醇。~ **cellulose**【化】乙基纤维素。~ **ether** = ether.

eth·yl·ate [ˈeθileit; ˋɛθəlet] **I** *vt*.【化】使引入乙烷基类,使成乙醇。**II** [-lit; -lɪt] *n*. 乙醇盐。**-tion** *n*.

eth·yl·ene [ˈeθiliːn; ˋɛθə͵lin] *n*.【化】乙烯,伸乙基。~ **dichloride** 二氯化乙烯。~ **glycol** 乙二醇,甘醇。~ **oxide** 乙烯化氧,环氧乙烷。

eth·yl·i·dene [əˋθilidiːn, əˋθɪlɪ͵din] *n*. 亚乙基。

e·thy·nyl [eˈθainl; ɛˋθaɪnl̩] *n*.【化】乙炔基。

-etic *suf*. 〔构成形容词或名词〕: em*etic*, gen*etic*.

e·ti·o·late [ˈiːtiəuleit; ˋitɪə͵let] *vt*. **1.** 使(叶子等)变白。**2.** 使变苍白;使衰弱;使(工业等)萎靡。**3.** 使褪色。— *vi*. 变白;变苍白;褪色。

e·ti·o·la·tion [͵iːtiəuˈleiʃən; ͵itɪəˋleʃən] *n*. **1.** 遮断日光使植物变白的方法;叶子等因不受日光而变白。**2.** 褪色;萎靡。

e·ti·ol·o·gy [͵iːtiˈɔlədʒi; ͵itɪˋɑlədʒɪ] *n*. = aetiology.

et·i·quette [͵etiˈket, ˈetiket; ͵ɛtɪˋkɛt] *n*. **1.** 礼仪,礼节,仪式,典礼。**2.** 格式;成规。*a breach of* ~ 失礼。*be against the* ~ *of the game* 违反比赛规则。*It is against* ~ *to do so*. 这样做是违反礼仪的。*diplomatic* ~ 外交礼节。*legal* [*medical*] ~ 法律[医务]界成规。

et·na [ˈetnə; ˋɛtnə] *n*. 酒精煮水器〔来自西西里岛 Etna 火山之名〕。

ETO = European Theatre of Operation (第二次世界大战时的)欧洲战区。

E·ton [ˈiːtn; ˋitn̩] *n*. **1.** 〔英〕伊顿〔伦敦西面一市镇〕。**2.** 伊顿公学〔培养英国上层政界人物的一所中学〕(= ~ college)。**3.** 〔*pl*.〕伊顿公学男生制服 (= ~ clothes) *go into* ~*s* 开始穿伊顿公学的制服,进伊顿公学。~ **collar** 白色硬宽领。~ **crop** (女子头发的)男孩发型。~ **jacket** [**coat**] 伊顿公学式短上衣。

E·to·ni·an [iːˈtəuniən; iˋtonjən] **I** *a*. 伊顿公学的。**II** *n*. 伊顿公学学生。

E·tru·ri·a [iˈtruəriə; ɪˋtrurɪə] *n*. 伊顿鲁里亚〔意大利中部的古国〕。

E·trur·i·an [iˈtruəriən; ɪˋtrurɪən], **E·trus·can** [iˈtrʌskən; ɪˋtrʌskən] **I** *a*. 伊特鲁里亚人[语]的。**II** *n*. 伊特鲁里亚人;伊特鲁里亚语。

-ette *suf*. 〔加在名词以及少数形容词之后〕**1.** 表示"微小": cigar*ette*, statu*ette*. **2.** 表示"女性": suffrag*ette*. **3.** 表示"仿制品","代用品": leather*ette*. **4.** 表示"组","组合": quart*ette*.

E.T.U. = Electrical Trades Union 〔英〕电气工会。

é·tude [eˈtjuːd; ɛˋtjud] *n*. 〔F.〕练习;(绘画等的)习作;【乐】练习曲。

é·tui, e·twee [eˈtwiː; əˋtwi] *n*. (*pl*. ~*s*) (放化妆品、针线等的)小盒子。

ETV = educational television 教育电视。

-ety *suf*. 构成表示"状态"、"性质"的抽象名词: vari*ety*, sobri*ety*.

etym. = etymology.

et·y·mo·log·i·cal [͵etiməˈlɔdʒikəl; ͵ɛtəməˋlɑdʒɪkl̩] *a*. **1.** 词源学的,语源学的。**2.** 词源的,语源的。*an* ~ *dictionary* 语源词典。**-ly** *ad*.

et·y·mol·o·gist [͵etiˈmɔlədʒist; ͵ɛtəˋmɑlədʒɪst] *n*. 词源

[语源]学家,词源[语源]研究者。

et·y·mol·o·gize [ˌetiˈmɔlədʒaiz; ˏɛtəˋmɑləˏdʒaɪz] ***vt.*** 发现(某词)的词源[语源]。—***vi.*** 研究词源[语源];探溯词源[语源]。

et·y·mol·o·gy [ˌetiˈmɔlədʒi; ˏɛtəˋmɑlədʒɪ] ***n.*** **1.** 词源,语源。**2.** 词源[语源]学。

et·y·mon [ˈetimɔn; ˋɛtəmɑn] ***n.*** (*pl.* ***-ma*** [-mə; -mə]) **1.** 词的原形,词源,词根。**2.** 词的原义。

Eu=【化】europium 铕。

EU=European Union 欧洲联盟,欧盟。

eu- *pref.* 表示"善良","美好","优美"(*opp.* dys-);"真正":*eu*pepsia, *eu*phony; *eu*bacteria; *eu*ploid.

Eu·bac·te·ri·a [ˌjuːbækˈtiəriə; ˏjubækˋtɪrɪə], **Eu·bac·te·ri·ales** [juːˌbæktiəriˈeiliːz; juˏbæktɪrɪˋeliz] ***n.*** 〔*pl.*〕【微】真细菌类。

Eu·bac·te·ri·um [ˌjuːbækˈtiəriəm; ˏjubækˋtɪrɪəm] ***n.*** Eubacteria 的单数。

Eu·boe·a [juːˈbiːə; juˋbiə] ***n.*** (希腊东部的)优比亚岛〔埃维厄岛〕。

eu·caine [juːˈkein, ˈjuːkein; juˋken, ˋjuken] ***n.*** 优卡因〔成药名〕。

eu·ca·lypt [ˈjuːkəlipt; ˋjukəlɪpt] ***n.*** =eucalyptus.

eu·ca·lyp·tol, eu·ca·lyp·tole [ˈjuːkəˈliptəul, -tɔːl; ˏjukəˋlɪptol, -tɔl] ***n.*** 【化】桉树脑。

eu·ca·lyp·tus [ˌjuːkəˈliptəs; ˏjukəˋlɪptəs] ***n.*** (*pl.* ~***es***, ***-ti*** [-tai; -taɪ]) 桉树;〔E-〕桉树属。~ **oil**【化】桉树油。

eu·cha·ris [ˈjuːkəris; ˋjukərɪs] ***n.*** 【植】桉树属(*Eucharis*)植物。

Eu·cha·rist [ˈjuːkərist; ˋjukərɪst] ***n.*** **1.** 【宗】圣餐;圣餐中用的面包和葡萄酒;圣体。**2.** 〔e-〕感恩祈祷。**-ic(al)** ***a.***

eu·chre [ˈjuːkə; ˋjukɚ] **I** ***n.*** 〔美〕尤卡牌战〔二至四人打三十二张牌的纸牌战〕。**II** ***vt.*** (玩尤卡牌战时趁对方疏忽时)打赢;〔口〕智胜,打败;欺骗,耍弄。**-d** ***a.***

eu·chro·ma·tin [juːˈkrəumətin; juˋkromətɪn] ***n.*** 【生】常染色质。

eu·chro·mo·some [juːˈkrəuməsəum; juˋkroməsom] ***n.*** 【生】常染色体。

eu·cil·i·ate [juːˈsiliːit; juˋsɪlɪɪt] ***n.*** 【动】真纤毛亚纲(*Euciliata*)动物。

Euck·en [ˈɔikən; ˋɔɪkən], **R.** 欧肯〔1846—1926, 德国哲学家〕。

eu·clase [ˈjuːkleis; ˋjukles] ***n.*** 【地】蓝柱石。

Eu·clid [ˈjuːklid; ˋjuklɪd] ***n.*** **1.** 欧几里得〔古希腊数学家〕。**2.** 欧几里得几何学。

Eu·clid·e·an, Eu·clid·i·an [juːˈklidiən; juˋklɪdɪən] ***a.*** 【数】欧几里得的。~ **geometry** 欧几里得几何,欧氏几何。~ **space** 欧几里得空间,欧氏空间。

eu·col·loid [ˈjuːkəlɔid; ˋjukəlɔɪd] ***n.*** 【化】真胶体。

eu·d(a)e·mon·ism [juːˈdiːmənizəm; juˋdimənɪzm̩] ***n.*** 【哲】幸福论。

eu·d(a)e·mon·ist [juːˈdiːmɔnist; juˋdimɑnɪst] ***n.*** 幸福论者,幸福主义者。

eu·di·om·e·ter [ˌjuːdiˈɔmitə; ˏjudɪˋɑmətɚ] ***n.*** 【化】空气纯度测定管。

eu·di·o·met·ric(al) [ˌjuːdiəˈmetrik(əl); ˏjudɪəˋmɛtrɪk(l̩)] ***a.*** 气体测定法的,量气管的。**-al·ly** ***ad.***

eu·di·om·e·try [ˌjuːdiˈɔmitri; ˏjudɪˋɑmətrɪ] ***n.*** 【化】气体测定(法),空气纯度测定法。

Eu·gene [ˈjuːdʒiːn, juːˈdʒiːn; juˋʒin, ˋjudʒin] ***n.*** 尤金〔男子名〕。

Eu·ge·ni·a [juːˈdʒiːniə; juˋdʒinɪə] ***n.*** 尤金妮亚〔女子名〕。

eu·gen·ic [juːˈdʒenik; juˋdʒɛnɪk] ***a.*** 优生学的。**-i·cal·ly** ***ad.***

eu·gen·i·cist [juːˈdʒenisist; juˋdʒɛnəsɪst] ***n.*** 优生学家。

eu·gen·ics [juːˈdʒeniks; juˋdʒɛnɪks] ***n.*** 优生学,人种改良学。

eu·gen·ist [ˈjuːdʒinist; ˋjudʒənɪst] ***n.*** =eugenicist.

eu·ge·nol [ˈjuːdʒinɔl, -nəul; ˋjudʒənɔl, -nol] ***n.*** 【化】丁子香酚。

eu·gle·na [juːˈgliːnə; juˋglinə] ***n.*** 眼虫属(*Euglena*)动物。

eu·he·dral [juːˈhiːdrəl; juˋhidrəl] ***a.*** 【物】全形的,自形的。

eu·he·mer·ism [juːˈhiːmərizəm; juˋhimərɪzəm] ***n.*** 神话即历史论〔纪元前300年希腊哲学家 Euhemerus 的学说,认为神话来源于人间英雄的史实〕。

eu·he·mer·ist [juːˈhiːmərist; juˋhimərɪst] ***n.*** 神话即历史论者。

eu·he·mer·is·tic [juːˌhiːməˈristik; juˏhiməˋrɪstɪk] ***a.*** (基于)神话即历史论的。**-al·ly** ***ad.***

eu·he·mer·ize [juːˈhiːməraiz; juˋhiməraɪz] ***vt.*** 以神话即历史的观点解释(神话等)。

eu·la·chon [ˈjuːləˈkɔn; ˋjuləˋkɑn] ***n.*** =candlefish.

eu·la·mel·li·branch [ˌjuːləˈmelibræŋk; ˏjuləˋmɛləbræŋk] ***n.*** 真瓣鳃类(*Eulamellibranchia*)动物。**-bran·chi·ate** [-ˈbræŋkiːit; -ˋbræŋkɪɪt] ***n.***, ***a.***

eu·lo·gist [ˈjuːlədʒist; ˋjulədʒɪst] ***n.*** 颂扬者,作颂诗的人。

eu·lo·gis·tic(al) [ˌjuːləˈdʒistik(əl); ˏjuləˋdʒɪstɪk(l̩)] ***a.*** 颂扬的,歌功颂德的。**-cal·ly** ***ad.***

eu·lo·gi·um [juːˈləudʒiəm; juˋlodʒɪəm] ***n.*** (*pl.* ~***s***, ***-gi·a*** [-dʒiə; -dʒɪə]) 〔拉〕=eulogy.

eu·lo·gize [ˈjuːlədʒaiz; ˋjulədʒaɪz] ***vt.*** 称赞,颂扬。

eu·lo·gy [ˈjuːlədʒi; ˋjulədʒɪ] ***n.*** **1.** 颂词;颂文〔尤指对一位刚去世的人歌功颂德的演说、文章〕。**2.** 称赞,颂扬。***chant the*** ~ ***of sb.*** 赞颂某人。***pronounce sb.'s*** ~ = ***pronounce a*** ~ (***up***) ***on sb.*** 对某人致颂词。

Eu·men·i·des [juːˈmenidiːz; juˋmɛnədiz] ***n.*** 〔*pl.*〕【希神】复仇三女神(=Furies)。

eu·my·cete [juˈmaisiːt; juˋmaɪsit] ***n.*** 真菌。

Eu·nice [ˈjuːnis; ˋjunɪs] ***n.*** 尤妮斯〔女子名〕。

eu·nuch [ˈjuːnək; ˋjunək] ***n.*** 阉人;太监,宦官。

eu·on·y·mus [juːˈɔniməs; juˋɑnəməs] ***n.*** 【植】卫矛属(*Euonymus*)植物。

eu·pa·to·ri·um [ˌjuːpəˈtɔːriəm; ˏjupəˋtɔrɪəm] ***n.*** 【植】泽兰属(*Eupatorium*)植物〔包括雾花泽兰、贯叶泽兰等〕。

eu·pat·rid [juːˈpætrid, ˈjuːpətrid; juˋpætrɪd, ˋjupətrɪd] ***n.*** (*pl.* ***-rid·ae*** [-ridiː; -rɪdi] ***-rids***) 〔E-〕(古雅典)世袭贵族。

eu·pep·si·a [juːˈpepsiə; juˋpɛpʃɪə] ***n.*** 【医】消化(力)良好(*opp.* dyspepsia)。

eu·pep·tic [juːˈpeptik; juˋpɛptɪk] ***a.*** **1.** 【医】消化良好的;助消化的。**2.** 乐观的,愉快的。

eu·phau·si·id [juˈfɔːziːid; juˋfɔzɪɪd] ***n.*** 【动】磷虾目(*Euphausiacea*)动物(=euphausid)。

euphem. =euphemism; euphemistic(ally).

Eu·phe·mia [juːˈfiːmiə; juˋfimɪə] ***n.*** 尤菲米亚〔女子名〕。

eu·phe·mism [ˈjuːfimizəm; ˋjufɪˏmɪzəm] ***n.*** 【修】委婉说法;委婉话,婉言。

eu·phe·mis·tic [ˌjuːfəˈmistik; ˏjufəˋmɪstɪk] ***a.*** 婉言的;委婉的。**-cally** ***ad.***

eu·phe·mize [ˈjuːfimaiz; ˋjufəˏmaɪz] ***vi.***, ***vt.*** 委婉地说,用委婉的话说。

eu·phen·ics [juˈfeniks; juˋfɛnɪks] ***n.*** 〔用作单数〕(用化学药物操纵父母的遗传基因来进行的)人种改良运动。

eu·phon·ic(al) [juːˈfɔnik(əl); juˋfɑnɪk(l̩)] ***a.*** 声音和谐的,悦耳的;语音好的。**-al·ly** ***ad.***

eu·pho·ni·ous [juːˈfəuniəs; juˋfonɪəs] ***a.*** 好听的,悦耳的,声音和谐的。**-ly** ***ad.***

eu·pho·ni·um [juːˈfəuniəm; juˋfonɪəm] ***n.*** 【乐】次中音

号。

eu·pho·nize [ˈjuːfənaiz; ˋjufəˏnaɪz] *vt*. 使(声音)和谐,使(语音)悦耳。

eu·pho·ny [ˈjuːfəni; ˋjufənɪ] *n*. **1**. (声音、语音的)和谐,悦耳。**2**. 和谐的声音;悦耳的语音。

eu·phor·bi·a [juˈfɔːbiə; juˋfɔrbɪə] *n*. 大戟属植物,大戟(=spurge)。

eu·pho·ri·a [juːˈfɔːriə; juˋforɪə] *n*. **1**. 【心】幸福感。**2**. 【医】欣快,精神愉快。

eu·pho·ri·ant [juˈfɔːriənt; jʊˋforɪənt] *n*. 【医】安乐药,欣快剂。

eu·phor·ic [juːˈfɔrik; juˋfɑrɪk] *a*. 欣快症的;欣快的。

eu·pho·tic [juˈfəutik; jʊˋfotɪk] *a*. 【生态】(水域的)光亮带的,透光层的。

eu·phra·sy [ˈjuːfrəsi; ˋjufrəsɪ] *n*. 【植】小米草。

Eu·phra·tes [juːˈfreitiːz; juˋfretiz] *n*. 幼发拉底河〔亚洲〕。

eu·phroe [ˈjuːfrəu, -vrəu; ˋjufro, -vro] *n*. (船帆、帐篷等的)绳索收紧器。

Eu·phros·y·ne [juːˈfrɔsiniː; juˋfrɑsənɪ] *n*. 【希神】赐人欢乐与美丽的三女神之一〔另两女神为 Aglaia 和 Thalia〕。

eu·phu·ism [ˈjuːfjuːizəm; ˋjufjuɪzm] *n*. 绮丽体;浮华的词句。

eu·phu·ist [ˈjuːfjuːist; ˋjufjuɪst] *n*. 用浮华词句的人。

eu·phu·is·tic [ˌjuːfjuːˈistik; ˏjufjuˋɪstɪk] *a*. 夸饰的,浮华的;绮丽体的。**-cal·ly** *ad*.

eu·plas·tic [juˈplæstik; jʊˋplæstɪk] **I** *a*. 【生理】易形成组织的;易变成组织的。**II** *n*. 能成组织的物质。

eu·ploid [ˈjuːplɔid; ˋjuplɔɪd] *a*. 整倍体的。**-y** *n*.

eup·ne·a, eup·noe·a [jupˈniːə, ˈjuːpniə; jʊpˋnɪə, ˋjupnɪə] *n*. 〔废〕【医】平静呼吸。

Eur. = Europe; European.

Eur·af·ri·ca [juəˈræfrikə; jʊˋræfrɪkə] *n*. 欧非共同体。

Eur·ail·pass [juəˈreilpɑːs; jʊˋrelpæs] *n*. 全欧火车特价证〔一种向旅欧游客提供的全欧铁路通用的廉价车票〕。

Eur·a·sia [ˈjuəˈreiʒə, -ʃə; jʊˋreʒə, -ʃə] *n*. 欧亚(大陆)。

Eur·a·sian [juəˈreiʒiən, -ʃən; jʊˋreʒɪən, -ʃən] **I** *a*. 欧亚(大陆)的;欧亚混血的。**II** *n*. 欧亚混血人。*the ~ Continent* 欧亚大陆。

EURATOM, Euratom [juərˈætəm; jʊˋrætəm] = European Atomic Energy Community 欧洲原子能发展组织。

eu·re·ka [juəˈriːkə; jʊˋrikə] *int*. 〔希〕我知道了! 有了! 〔阿基米德发现王冠所含纯金量时的欢呼〕。

eu·rhyth·mic [juːˈriðmik; juˋrɪðmɪk] *a*. **1**. (建筑式样)匀称的,协调的。**2**. 韵律体操的;艺术体操的。

eu·rhyth·mics [juːˈriðmiks; juˋrɪðmɪks] *n*. 〔作单数用〕韵律体操,艺术体操〔用即兴音乐伴奏〕。

eu·rhyth·my [juˈriðmi; jʊˋrɪðmɪ] *n*. **1**. 韵律运动。**2**. 匀称,和谐,协调。

Eu·rip·i·des [juəˈripidiːz; jʊˋrɪpɪdiz] 欧里庇得斯(480—406B.C.,古希腊悲剧作家)。

Eu·rip·i·de·an [juəˌripiˈdiən; jʊˏrɪpɪˋdɪən] *a*. 欧里庇得斯的,欧里庇得斯悲剧的。

eu·ri·pus [juˈraipəs; jʊˋraɪpəs] *n*. (*pl*. *-pi* [-pai; -paɪ]) 潮急水险的海峡,险流海峡。

Eu·ro [ˈjuərəu; ˋjʊro] *n*. 欧元。~**land** 欧元区。

Eu·ro·bond [ˈjuərəubɔnd; ˋjʊrəˏbɑnd] *n*. (美国公司以美元在国外买卖并计息的)欧洲债券。

Eu·roc·ly·don [juˈrɔklildɔn; jʊˋrɑklɪˏdɑn] *n*. **1**. 【圣】地中海的东北暴风。**2**. 暴风。

Eu·ro·crat [ˈjuərəukræt; ˋjʊrəkræt] *n*. 欧洲经济共同市场的官员或代表。

Eu·ro-cur·ren·cy [ˈjuərəuˈkʌrənsi; ˋjʊrəˋkʌrənsɪ] *n*. 欧洲货币。

Eu·ro·dol·lar [ˈjuərəudɔlə; ˋjʊrədɑlɚ] *n*. 欧洲美元〔美国在欧洲银行和借贷机关流通的美元〕。

eu·ro·ky [ˌjuˈrəuki; jʊˋrokɪ], **eu·ry·o·ky** [ˌjuriːˈəuki; ˏjʊrɪˋokɪ] *n*. 【生】广适性。**eu·rokous** [-kəs; -kəs], **eu·ry·o·kous** [-ˈəukəs; -ˋokəs] *a*.

Euromart [ˈjuərəmɑːt; ˋjʊrəˏmɑrt] = European Common Market 欧洲共同市场。

Eu·ro·pa [juəˈrəupə; jʊˋropə] *n*. 【希神】欧罗巴〔被宙斯化作白牛劫走的腓尼基公主〕。

Eu·rope [ˈjuərəp; ˋjʊrəp] *n*. 欧洲。

Eu·ro·pe·an [ˌjuərəˈpiːən, jɔːr-; ˏjʊrəˋpiən] **I** *a*. 欧洲的;全欧的;欧洲人的。**II** *n*. **1**. 欧洲人。**2**. 拥护参加欧洲经济共同体的人。~ *Atomic Energy Community* 欧洲原子能组织。~ *Common Market* 欧洲共同市场。~ **community** 欧洲共同体〔由欧洲经济共同体、欧洲原子能组织、欧洲煤钢联营于 1967 年组成〕。~ *Economic and Monetary Union* 欧洲经济货币同盟。~ *Economic Community* 欧洲经济共同体。~ *plan* 欧洲旅馆收费制〔以日计旅馆费中包括房间和服务费,膳食费另算〕(*opp*. American plan)。~ *Recovery Plan* 欧洲复兴计划。*E- Theatre of War* 欧洲战区。

Eu·ro·pe·an·ism [ˌjuərəˈpiːənizəm; ˏjʊrəˋpiənɪzm] *n*. 欧洲主义;欧洲人的特征(指传统、习惯、思想、特性等)。

Eu·ro·pe·an·i·za·tion [ˌjuərəˌpiənaiˈzeiʃən; ˏjʊrəˏpiənaɪˋzeʃən] *n*. 欧化。

Eu·ro·pe·an·ize [ˌjuərəˈpiːənaiz; ˏjʊrəˋpiənˏaɪz] *vt*. 使欧化,使具有欧洲风味。

eu·ro·pi·um [juəˈrəupiəm; jʊˋropɪəm] *n*. 【化】铕。

Eu·ro·po- *comb.f.* 表示"欧洲": *Europo-*centric.

Eu·ro·po-cen·tric [juəˌrəupəˈsentrik; jʊˏropəˋsɛntrɪk] *a*. 欧洲中心主义的。

Eu·ro·po-cen·trism [juəˌrəupəˈsentrizəm; jʊˏropəˋsɛntrɪzəm] *n*. 欧洲中心主义。

Eu·ro·sis [ju(ː)ˈrəusis; jʊˋrosɪs] *n*. 欧洲危机。

Eu·ro·vi·sion [ˈjuərəviʒən; ˋjʊrəvɪʒən] *n*. 欧洲电视节目交换制。

eu·ry·bath [ˈjuəribɑːθ; ˋjʊrɪbɑθ] *n*. 【生】(海洋的)广深水性生物。**-ic** [-ˈbæθik; -ˋbæθɪk] *a*.

Eu·ryd·i·ce [juəˈridisi(ː); jʊˋrɪdəsi(ɪ)] *n*. 【希神】(歌手俄耳甫斯之妻)欧律狄斯。

eu·ry·ha·line [ˌjuəriˈheilain, -lin; ˏjʊrəˋhelaɪn, -lɪn] *a*. 【生】广盐性的。

eu·ry·hy·gric [ˌjuəriˈhaigrik; ˏjʊrɪˋhaɪgrɪk] *a*. 【生】耐广湿性的。

eu·ryph·a·gous [juːˈrifəgəs; juˋrɪfəgəs] *a*. 【生】广食性的。

eu·ryp·ter·id [juːˈriptərid; juˋrɪptərɪd] *n*. 【古生】广翅鲎。

eu·ry·therm [ˈjuəriθəːm; ˋjʊrɪθɝm] *n*. 广温性生物。**-al, -ic, -ous** *a*.

eu·ryth·mic, eu·ryth·mi·cal [juəˈriðmik, -kəl; jʊˋrɪðmɪk, -kəl] *a*. = eurhythmic.

eu·ryth·mics [juəˈriðmiks; jʊˋrɪðmɪks] *n*. = eurhythmics.

eu·ryth·my [juəˈriðmi; jʊˋrɪðmɪ] *n*. = eurhythmy.

eu·ry·top·ic [ˌjuəriˈtɔpik; ˏjʊrɪˋtɑpɪk] *a*. 【生】广适性的。**-i·ty** [ˈjuəritəuˈpisiti; ˋjʊrɪtoˋpɪsətɪ] *n*.

eu·sol [ˈjuːsɔl; ˋjusɑl] *n*. 【药】优苏消毒水。

Eus·tace [ˈjuːstəs; ˋjustəs] *n*. 尤斯塔斯(男子名)。

Eu·sta·chi·an [juːsˈteiʃiən; juˋsteʃɪən] *a*. (16 世纪意大利解剖学家)欧斯塔奇 (Eustachi)的;欧氏的。~ **tube** 【解】耳咽管,欧氏管。

eu·sta·cy [ˈjuːstəsi; ˋjustəsɪ] *n*. 【地】海面升降,海面变化。

eu·stat·ic [juːˈstætik; juˋstætɪk] *a*. 海面升降的,海面变化的。**-cal·ly** *ad*.

eu·stele [ˈjuːstiːl, juˈstiːli; ˋjustil, jʊˋstilɪ] *n*. 【植】真中柱。

eu·tec·rod [juːˈtekrɔd; juˋtɛkrɑd] ***n.***【机】共晶焊焊条。

eu·tec·tic [juːˈtektik; juˋtɛktɪk] **I** ***a.***【化】低共熔的；易熔的；共晶的。**II** ***n.*** 低共熔混合物，共晶体。～ **alloy** 低共熔合金。～ **point**【化】低共熔点。

eu·tec·toid [juːˈtektɔid; juˋtɛktɔɪd] **I** ***n.***【化、冶】类低共熔体，共析。**II** ***a.*** 类低共熔体的，共析的。

Eu·ter·pe [juːˈtəːpi; juˋtɝpɪ] ***n.***【希神】司音乐及抒情诗的女神。**-an** [-ən; -ən] ***a.***

eu·tha·na·si·a [ˌjuːθəˈneiziə; ˏjuθəˋneziə] ***n.*** **1.** 安然去世，无痛苦的死亡。**2.**（为结束不治之症患者的痛苦施行的）无痛苦致死术；安乐死。

eu·then·ics [juːˈθeniks; juˋθɛnɪks] ***n.***〔用作单数〕优境学〔通过改善生活状况以改良人种的研究〕。

eu·the·ri·an [juːˈθiriən; juˋθɪrɪən] **I** ***n.*** 真兽亚纲动物。**II** ***a.***【动】真兽亚纲的。

eu·to·ci·a [juːˈtəuʃiə, -siə; juˋtoʃɪə, -sɪə] ***n.***【医】安产，顺产。

Eu·to·pi·a [juːˈtəupiə; juˋtopɪə] ***n.*** 乌托邦。

eu·troph·ic [juˈtrɔfik, -ˈtrəufik; juˋtrɑfɪk, -ˋtrofɪk] **I** ***a.*** **1.** 富营养的〔湖泊等有充足养料可供藻类生长〕。**2.** 发育营养正常的。**II** ***n.*** 改进营养的药物。～ **lack**【地】富营养湖。

eu·troph·i·cate [juˈtrɔfikeit; juˋtrɑfɪket] ***vi.*** 使超营养；藻类污染。

eu·troph·i·ca·tion [juˌtrɔfiˈkeiʃən; juˏtrɑfɪˋkeʃən] ***n.*** 超营养作用。

eux·e·nite [ˈjuːksinait; ˋjuksɪnaɪt] ***n.***【矿】黑稀金矿。

Eux·ine [ˈjuːksin, -sain; ˋjuksɪn, -saɪn] **Sea** 黑海的古称（= the Black Sea）。

E.V. = English Version (of the Bible)（《圣经》的）英译本。

EV = electric vehicle 电动汽车。

EVA = extravehicular activity【宇】太空人在飞船外的活动，出舱活动。

E·va [ˈiːvə; ˋivə] ***n.*** 伊娃〔女子名，Eve 的异体〕。

evac. = evacuation.

e·vac·u·ant [iˈvækjuənt; ɪˋvækjʊənt] **I** ***a.***【医】促进排泄的，通便的。**II** ***n.*** 泻药；利尿剂。

e·vac·u·ate [iˈvækjueit; ɪˋvækjuˏet] ***vt.*** **1.** 抽空，除清；排泄，泻出（粪便等）。**2.** 搬空，腾出（房子等）；（有组织地）撤退；疏散。～ *water from a pond* 抽干池水。～ *a city* 从城市中疏散人口。—***vi.*** **1.** 撤走，撤离，疏散。**2.** 大小便。

e·vac·u·a·tion [iˌvækjuˈeiʃən; ɪˏvækjuˋeʃən] ***n.*** **1.** 腾出；撤退；（空袭时的）疏散。**2.** 抽空；排泄，排泄物。～ *hospital* 后送医院。～ *of bowels* 大便。

e·vac·u·ee [iˌvækjuˈiː; ɪˏvækjʊˋi] ***n.*** 撤退者，被疏散者。

e·vad·a·ble [iˈveidəbl; ɪˋvedəbḷ] ***a.*** 可逃避的，可规避的。

e·vade [iˈveid; ɪˋved] ***vt.*** 逃避，躲避（攻击等），避免（困难等）；回避，忌避；避开（质问等）；漏（税）。～ *a question* 避免答覆问题。～ *paying one's debts* 逃债。～ *(paying) taxes* 漏税，偷税。～ *(military) service* 逃避兵役。*a term that* ～*s definition* 难下定义的词。～ *discovery* 难发现。—***vi.*** 躲避；逃避；规避。**-r** ***n.*** 躲避者，规避者。**e·vad·ing·ly** ***ad.***

e·vag·i·nate [iˈvædʒineit; ɪˋvædʒɪnet] ***vt.***【生】使（管状器官）外翻；翻转。**e·vag·i·na·tion** ***n.***【生】外翻，外翻部分。

e·val·u·ate [iˈvæljueit; ɪˋvæljʊˏet] ***vt.*** **1.** 对…估价，对…作评价。**2.**【数】求…的值。

e·val·u·a·tion [iˌvæljuˈeiʃən; ɪˏvæljʊˋeʃən] ***n.*** **1.** 估价，评价。**2.**【数】赋值，值的计算。

ev·a·nesce [ˌiːvəˈnes; ˏɛvəˋnɛs] ***vi.*** 渐渐消失，消散。

ev·a·nes·cence [ˌiːvəˈnesns; ˏɛvəˋnɛsṇs] ***n.*** **1.** 消失，消散；幻灭。**2.** 消失性，消散性，瞬息。

ev·a·nes·cent [ˌiːvəˈnesnt; ˏivəˋnɛsṇt] ***a.*** **1.**（印象等）渐渐消失的。**2.** 快消灭的；短暂的，瞬息的。**3.** 纤细的，轻盈的。**4.**【植】（叶脉）隐失的。**5.**【数】无限小的。

e·van·gel [iˈvændʒel; ɪˋvændʒəl] ***n.*** **1.**〔古〕基督救世的福音。**2.**〔E-〕【圣】四福音书之一。**3.** 喜信，佳音。**4.** = evengelist.

e·van·gel·ic(al) [ˌiːvænˈdʒelik(əl); ˏivænˋdʒɛlɪk(ḷ)] **I** ***a.*** **1.** 福音（传道）的。**2.**〔常 -ical〕福音派的新教会的。**3.** E- 英国低教会的。**4.** 衷于传道的。**II** ***n.*** [-icəl; -ɪcəl] 福音派信徒。**-cal·ly** ***ad.***

e·van·gel·i·cal·ism [ˌiːvænˈdʒelikəlizəm; ˏivænˋdʒɛlɪkəlɪzṃ] ***n.*** 福音主义，福音派教义的信仰。

E·van·ge·line [iˈvændʒiliːn; ɪˋvændʒəlin] ***n.*** 伊凡洁琳〔女子名〕。

e·van·gel·ism [iˈvændʒelizəm; ɪˋvændʒɛˏlɪzṃ] ***n.*** **1.** 福音传道，传播福音。**2.** 传道狂似的热情。**3.** = evangelicalism.

e·van·gel·ist [iˈvændʒilist; ɪˋvændʒəlɪst] ***n.*** **1.** 福音传教士。**2.**〔E-〕【圣】《福音书》的著者。

e·van·gel·ize [iˈvændʒilaiz; ɪˋvændʒəˏlaɪz] ***vi.*** 宣讲福音，传教。—***vt.*** **1.** 对…宣讲福音。**2.** 使信奉基督教。

e·van·ish [iˈvæniʃ; ɪˋvænɪʃ] ***vi.***〔诗〕消失；消灭。**-ment** ***n.***

Ev·ans [ˈevənz; ˋɛvənz] ***n.*** 埃文斯〔姓氏〕。

e·vap·o·ra·ble [iˈvæpərəbl; ɪˋvæpərəbḷ] ***a.*** 易蒸发的；挥发的。

e·vap·o·rate [iˈvæpəreit; ɪˋvæpəˏret] ***vt.*** **1.** 使蒸发；通过升华使（金属等）沉淀。**2.** 使除去水分，使脱水。**3.** 发射（电子）。**4.** 使消失，消灭。*water* ～*d by heat* 被热蒸发的水。— ***vi.*** 蒸发，挥发，发散蒸气，〔口〕消失，〔谑〕（人）失踪，死亡，〔美俚〕跑掉，逃掉。

e·vap·o·rat·ed [iˈvæpəreitid; ɪˋvæpəretɪd] ***a.*** 浓缩的，脱水的，蒸发干燥的。～ **milk** 淡炼乳。～ **vegetable** 脱水蔬菜。

e·vap·o·ra·ting [iˌvæpəˈreitiŋ; ɪˏvæpəˋretɪŋ] ***a.*** 蒸发用的。～ **column**【化】浓缩柱，蒸浓柱。～ **dish**【化】蒸发皿。

e·vap·o·ra·tion [iˌvæpəˈreiʃən; ɪˏvæpəˋreʃən] ***n.*** **1.** 蒸发（作用），发散，升华沉淀作用。**2.** 脱水（法）。**3.** 蒸气。**4.**（电子的）发射。**5.** 蒸发量。**6.** 消散。～ **cooling** 蒸发冷却。～ **gum test**（石油）蒸发胶质试验。～ **nucleon**【原】蒸发核子。

e·vap·o·ra·tive [iˈvæpəreitiv; ɪˋvæpəˋretɪv] ***a.*** 蒸发的，使蒸发的，蒸发产生的。～ *power* 蒸发力。

e·vap·o·ra·tor [iˈvæpəreitə; ɪˋvæpəˋretɚ] ***n.*** 蒸发器。

e·vap·o·rim·e·ter [iˌvæpəˈrimitə; ɪˏvæpəˋrɪmɪtɚ] ***n.*** 蒸发计。

e·vap·o·ro·graph [iˈvæpərəgrɑːf; ɪˋvæpərəgræf] ***n.***【物】蒸发成像仪。

e·vap·o·trans·pi·ra·tion [iˌvæpəuˌtrænspiˈreiʃən; ɪˏvæpoˏtrænspəˋreʃən] ***n.*** 土壤水分蒸发蒸腾损失总量。

e·vap·o·trans·pire [iˌvæpəuˈtrænspaiə; ɪˏvæpoˋtrænspaɪr] ***vt.*** 使（土壤中的水分）蒸发，蒸腾。

E·varts [ˈevəts; ˋɛvəts] ***n.*** 埃瓦茨〔姓氏〕。

e·va·sion [iˈveiʒən; ɪˋveʒən] ***n.*** **1.** 逃避，规避，回避；（税的）偷漏。**2.** 遁辞，借口推诿。～ *tactics*【军】规避战术。～ *of responsibility* 逃避责任。～ *of taxes* = *tax* ～ 偷税。*take shelter in* ～*s* 找借口规避。

e·va·sive [iˈveisiv; ɪˋvesɪv] ***a.*** **1.** 逃避的，偷漏的，托辞的，推诿的，躲躲闪闪的。**2.** 不可捉摸的。*an* ～ *action*【军】规避动作。*an* ～ *answer* 含糊的回答。*an* ～ *talk* 躲躲闪闪的谈话。**-ly** ***ad.*** **-ness** ***n.***

Eve [iːv; iv] ***n.*** **1.** 伊芙〔女子名〕。**2.** 夏娃〔基督教《圣经》中人类的女始祖，亚当之妻，见《创世纪》〕。***daughters of*** ～ 女人。

eve [iːv; iv] ***n.*** **1.** 节日前夕。**2.**（重大事件的）关头〔前夕〕。**3.**〔诗〕傍晚。*on the* ～ *of the battle* 战役前夕。

E

Christmas E- 圣诞节前夜,圣诞之夜〔12 月 24 日〕。*New Year's E-* 除夕。*on St. Tib's E-* 永远不,决不会〔*St. Tib* 为虚构的圣徒名,日历中无此节日〕。

e·vec·tion [iˈvekʃən; ɪˋvɛkʃən] ***n.*** 【天】出差。~ *in latitude* 黄纬出差。~ *of the moon* 月球出差。

Ev·e·line [ˈiːvlin; ˋivlɪn] ***n.*** 伊芙琳〔女子名〕。

Ev·e·lyn [ˈiːvlin, ˈev-; ˋivlɪn] ***n.*** 伊夫林〔姓氏〕。

e·ven[1] [ˈiːvən; ˋivən] **I** ***a.*** **1.** 平的,平坦的,平滑的。**2.** 一样的,一致的;均匀的;同一的;同一水准的,高低相同的(*with*)。**3.** 不曲折的,无凹陷的,连贯的。**4.** 单调的;平凡的。**5.** (心气)平静的,平稳的。**6.** 公平的;平等的,对等的。**7.** 【数】偶数的,双数的(*opp.* odd)。**8.** 整的,无零头的,恰好的。~ *country* 平坦的原野。~ *money* 同额赌注。*an* ~ *surface* 平滑的表面。*This will make all* ~. 这样就扯平了。*The snow is* ~ *with the window.* 雪同窗子一般齐。*an* ~ *color* 匀净的颜色。*an* ~ *tenor of life* 单调的生活。*an* ~ *bargain* [*exchange*] 公平交易。*an* ~ *money* 相等的赌注。~ *grain* 【植】均匀纹理。*an* ~ *temper* 温和的性情。*an* ~ *number* 偶数。*an* ~ *mile* 整整一英里。**be** [**get**] ~ **with** (*sb.*) **1.** 和(某人)扯平,不亏欠(某人)。**2.** 向(某人)报复。***break*** ~〔口〕不赔不赚,不输不赢。***evenly*** ~ 能再分的偶数〔4 除得尽〕。***odd and*** ~ 猜单双。***make*** ~ 排字时把最后一行排足。***of*** ~ ***date*** 【法、商】同一日期的,即日。***unevenly*** ~ 不能再分的偶数〔2 除得尽而 4 除不尽〕。***with the*** ~ ***hand*** 公平。**II** ***vt.*** **1.** 把…弄平坦。**2.** 使平均;使相等。~ *the edges by trimming them* 修剪边缘。—***vi.*** **1.** 变平坦。**2.** 变相等。~ ***up*** 使平均;使平衡;使整齐。~ ***up on*** 〔美〕报复。**-handed** ***a.*** 公平的,大公无私的。**-minded** ***a.*** 沉着的,泰然自若的。**-tempered** 性情平和的。**-ly** ***ad.*** **-ness** ***n.***

e·ven[2] [ˈiːvən; ˋivən] ***ad.*** **1.** 〔加强语气〕即使…也,连…还,甚至,也,都,还。**2.** 〔与比较级连用〕更加,愈加。**3.** 〔古〕正,恰恰,刚刚;即,就是。*E- children can understand it.* 连小孩子都知道的。*E- Homer sometimes nods.* 〔谚〕智者千虑,必有一失。*E- woods have ears.* 〔谚〕隔墙有耳。*I* ~ *lent him my own books.* 我甚至把自己的书也借给他了。*He went away* ~ *as you came.* 你一来他就走了。*He did* ~ *better.* 他甚至做得更好。~ **as** **1.** 正在…时(*E- as she spoke, it began to snow.* 恰恰在她说话的时候,天下雪了)。**2.** 正如(*It happened* ~ *as I expect.* 情况正如我预料的那样)。~ ***if*** = ~ ***though*** 即使…也。***never*** ~连…也不。~ ***now*** **1.** 甚至现在还。**2.** 〔诗〕恰恰现在。~ ***so*** **1.** 即使如此。**2.** 〔古〕正是那样。~ ***then*** 甚至那时候都,连…都。***or*** ~ 乃至,以至。

e·ven[3] [ˈiːvən; ˋivən] ***n.*** 〔诗〕傍晚,黄昏(= evening)。~**fall** ***n.*** 〔诗〕黄昏。

eve·ning [ˈiːvniŋ; ˋivnɪŋ] ***n.*** **1.** 傍晚,黄昏,晚。**2.** 〔方〕午后〔从中午到黄昏〕。**3.** 晚年;衰退期,末期。**4.** 晚会。*an* ~ *edition* 夕刊。~ *gown* 女夜礼服。*an* ~ *paper* 晚报。*an* ~ *school* 夜校。*the* ~ *star* 晚星,金星。~ *student* 夜校学生。*the* ~ *of life* 晚年。*Good* ~! 晚安! ~ *by* ~ 天天晚上。~ *coat* 燕尾服。~ *glow* 夕阳。***go out*** ~***s*** 〔美〕= *go out in the* ~ 晚上出去,在黄昏时候出去。***make an*** ~ ***of it*** 玩个通宵。***of an*** ~往往在晚上。***on*** [***in***] ***the*** ~ ***of*** 在…日的傍晚。***towards*** ~ 快黑的时候。**-s** ***ad.*** 每晚,在绝大多数晚间。~ **dress** [**clothes**] 夜礼服。~ **gown** 女夜礼服。~ **prayer** 〔常作 E- P-〕= evensong. ~ **primrose** 【植】月见草,待宵草。~ **wear** 晚礼服。

e·ven·song [ˈiːvənˌsɔːŋ; ˋivənˏsɔŋ] ***n.*** **1.** 【天主】晚祷,晚课(= vespers)。**2.** 【英国教】晚祷。**3.** 黄昏时唱的歌。**4.** 〔古〕黄昏。

e·ven-ste·ven, e·ven-ste·phen [ˈiːvnˈstiːvn; ˋivənˋstivən] ***a.*** 〔口〕比分相等的,半斤八两的;各半的。

e·vent [iˈvent; ɪˋvɛnt] ***n.*** **1.** 事件;事情;事变;大事。**2.** 偶然事件,可能发生的事。**3.** 活动,经历。**4.** 〔古〕结局。**5.** 【体】项目〔尤指重要比赛〕。**6.** 【法】诉讼[判决]的结果。*It was quite an* ~. 那确实是件大事。*current* ~*s* 时事。*a double* ~ 双打比赛。*prophesy* [*wise*] *after the* ~ 事后诸葛亮。*field and track* ~ 田径赛。*a target* ~ 射靶比赛。*a team* ~ 团体赛。***at all*** ~***s*** = ***in any*** ~ 无论怎样。***in either*** ~ 无论是这样还是那样。***in no*** ~ 决不能。***in that*** ~ 在那时候,在那种场合;如果那样。***in the*** ~ **1.** 结果,终于。**2.** 〔美〕如果。***in the*** ~ ***of*** 万一在…的时候,若…—…。***in the*** (***natural***) ***course of*** ~***s*** 按自然趋势。***pull off the*** ~ 比赛得奖。~ **counter** 信号计数器。~ **movie**(投入巨资制作的有宏大场面的)电影"大片"。

e·vent·ful [iˈventful, -fəl; ɪˋvɛntfəl] ***a.*** 事故多的;重大的。*an* ~ *year* 多事之秋,多事的一年。**-ly** ***ad.*** **-ness** ***n.***

e·ven·tide [ˈiːvəntaid; ˋivənˏtaɪd] ***n.*** 〔诗〕黄昏。

e·vent·less [iˈventlis; ɪˋvɛntlɪs] ***a.*** 无大事的,平静无事的。

e·ven·tra·tion [ˌiːvenˈtreiʃən; ˏivɛnˋtreʃən] ***n.*** 【医】腹脏突出。

e·ven·tu·al [iˈventjuəl; ɪˋvɛntʃuəl] ***a.*** **1.** 最后的。**2.** 可能发生的,万一的。**-ly** ***ad.*** 最后,终于。

e·ven·tu·al·i·ty [iˌventjuˈæliti; ɪˏvɛntʃuˋælətɪ] ***n.*** 偶然性;不测事件。*provide against eventualities* 以备万一。

e·ven·tu·ate [iˈventjueit; ɪˋvɛntʃuˏet] ***vi.*** **1.** 结果,终归(*in*)。**2.** 〔美〕发生,起。~ *well* [*ill*] 结果好[不好]。

ev·er [ˈevə; ˋɛvɚ] ***ad.*** **1.** 〔表示否定、疑问和比较〕曾经,这以前。*Nothing* ~ *happens in this village.* 这个村里从来没有发生事情。*Have you* ~ *seen* [*Did you* ~ *see*] *a tiger?* 你以前见过老虎没有? *Have you* ~ *been there?* 以前你到过那里吗? *Did you* ~? = *Did you* ~ *see* [*hear*] *the like?* 这种事你听[看]过吗? *the nicest thing* ~ = *that* ~ *was on record* 迄今最好的东西。**2.** 〔表示不耐烦等语气〕可能,总会。*Is he* ~ *at home?* 他也有在家的时候吗? **3.** 〔表示条件、威胁等语气〕假如,要是。*If the band* ~ *plays again, we will dance.* 要是乐队再演奏的话,我们就跳个舞。*If I* ~ *catch him.* 我要是抓到他的话,哼〔就决不饶他〕! **4.** 〔表示肯定,现在一般用 always〕常是,老是,始终,不断;永远是。*work hard as* ~一向勤奋。*do better than* ~做得比一向更好了。*He is* ~ *repeating the same words.* 他总是重复同样的话。*Yours* ~ = *E- yours* 〔信末语〕你永久的朋友。**5.** 〔加强 as...as〕尽量。*Be as quick as* ~ *you can!* 尽量赶快。**6.** 〔加强疑问词或最高级形容词,表示惊奇〕究竟,到底。*Which* ~ *way did he go?* 他究竟上哪一边去了? *What* ~ *can it be?* 那到底是什么? *Why* ~ *didn't you say so?* 你究竟为什么不那样讲? **7.** 〔加强 so, such 等〕非常。~ ***such a nice man*** 非常好的人。***as*** ~ 仍旧;照常。~ ***after*** [***afterwards***] 打那以后,以后老是。~ ***and again*** = ~ ***and anon*** 〔古〕时时,常常。~ ***since*** 从…以来(*I have known him* ~ *since he was a boy.* 从他是孩子的时候起,我就认识他了)。~ ***so*** 〔口〕大大,非常(*The patient is* ~ *so much better.* 病人好得多了。*Thank you* ~ *so much.* 非常感激你。*I like it* ~ *so much.* 我非常喜欢它)。~ ***such*** 〔口〕很…的(*It is* ~ *such a tool.* 这工具很有用)。***for*** ~ 永远。〔俚〕一直(*He would go on talking for* ~. 他一直不停地讲下去)。***for*** ~ ***and*** ~ = ***for*** ~ ***and a day*** 永远。***hardly*** [***scarcely***] ~ 难得,几乎从不。***seldom, if*** ~ 就是有也极少见。~**-normal granary** 〔美〕美联邦政府为调节粮价或应荒年之需而收购的剩余农产品。

ever- *comb. f.* 〔放在形容词或动词现在分词之前,构成复合形容词〕表示"常": *ever*-active; *ever*-present; *ever*-changeful, *ever*-increasing.

ev·er·bloom·ing [ˈevəˈbluːmiŋ; ɛvəˋblumɪŋ] ***a***. 四季开花的。

Ev·er·est [ˈevərist; ˋɛvrɪst] ***n***. 埃佛勒斯峰〔即珠穆朗玛峰〕。

Ev·er·ett [ˈevərit; ˋɛvərɪt] ***n***. 埃弗雷特〔姓氏,男子名〕。

ev·er·glade [ˈevəgleid; ˋɛvə˒gled] ***n***. 〔美〕湿地,沼泽地。*the E-* 美国佛罗里达州南部大沼泽地。

ev·er·green [ˈevəgriːn; ˋɛvə˒grin] **I** ***a***. 常绿的(*opp*. deciduous)。**II** ***n***. 常绿植物,常绿树;〔*pl*.〕(装饰用的)常绿树枝。*E- State* 〔美〕华盛顿州的别名。

ev·er·last·ing [ˌevəˈlɑːstiŋ; ˏɛvəˋlæstɪŋ] **I** ***a***. **1**. 永久的,耐久的,不朽的,无穷的。**2**. 不断的;冗长的,使人厌烦的。**3**.【植】干后花的形状颜色不变的。**II** ***n***. **1**. 永久,无穷。**2**. 〔英〕牢固耐久的毛呢。**3**.【植】蜡菊,蝶须,鼠曲草。***from*** ～ ***to*** ～ 永远无穷地。***the E-*** 上帝,神。～ **cloth**【纺】永固缎纹织物。～ **cotton homespun**【纺】耐用的手工棉织品。～ **flower**【植】干后花的形状颜色不变的植物〔尤指季生菊科植物如蜡菊、灰毛菊等〕。～ **peas** 阔叶山黧豆。**-ly** ***ad***. **-ness** ***n***.

ev·er·more [ˌevəˈmɔː; ˏɛvəˋmɔr] ***ad***. 始终;永远;将来,今后。***for*** ～永远。

e·ver·si·ble [iˈvəːsibl; ɪˋvɝsəbl̩] ***a***.【生】可外翻的,可翻转的。

e·ver·sion [iˈvəːʃən; ɪˋvɝʃən] ***n***.【生】外翻,翻转。～ *of the eyelids* 眼睑外翻。

e·vert [i(ː)ˈvəːt; ɪ(i)ˋvɝt] ***vt***. **1**. 使(眼睑等)外翻,使翻转。**2**. 〔古〕颠覆,推翻。

e·ver·tor [iˈvəːtə; ɪˋvɝtɚ] ***n***.【解】外转肌,外翻肌。

ev·er·y [ˈevri; ˋɛvrɪ] ***a***. **1**. 所有的,一切的。**2**. 无论哪个…都,凡…无不。**3**. 充分的,一切可能的。**4**. 〔与数词连用时,可用复数〕每。～ *one of them* 他们全都。*E- one thinks in his way*. 〔谚〕仁者见仁,智者见智。*I wish you* ～ *success*. 祝你事事如意。～ *day* 每日,天天。～ *four days* = ～ *fourth day* 每隔三日,每逢第四日。*have* ～ *reason* 有充分理由。～ *third man* 每三个人中有一个人。～ ***bit*** 从每一点,全部,完全。～ ***man Jack*** = ～ ***mother's son*** 人人,无例外地。～ ***now and again*** [***then***] = ～ ***once in a while*** [***way***] 时时,偶尔,间或。～ ***other*** [***second***] **1**. 每隔(～ *other day* 每隔一天),**2**. 所有其他。～ ***so often*** 〔口〕时时。～ ***time*** 每次,总是;每逢,每当。～ ***way*** = *in* ～ *way*. ～ ***which way*** 〔美〕**1**. 四面八方。**2**. 散乱(*Rail-roads cross the country in* ～ *which way*. 铁路四通八达纵横全国)。***in*** ～ ***way*** 在每一方面,从各方面来看。***not*** ～…不见得。(*E-couple is not a pair*. = *Not* ～ *couple is a pair*. 〔谚〕成双未必能配对)。★ **1**. all 是对复数普通名词的总括性修饰语。every 是个别性的同时又是总括性的修饰语;each 则纯粹是个别性的。**2**. ～和 each 的意思都是"每一"或"每个",但～更强调全体或全部,而 each 更强调个人或各别。此外,～只作形容词,而 each 除了作形容词外,还可用作代词和副词。**3**. all 和～虽有共同意义,但今日如说 "All are happy." 仍不如说 "Everybody is happy." 为普通。**4**. ～本应作单数处理,但在口语中因接用复数代名词而可作复数处理: Everyone of them took off their hats.

eve·ry·bod·y [ˈevribɔdi, ˈevribədi; ˋɛvrɪ˒bɑdɪ; ˋɛvrɪ˒bədɪ] ***pron***. 每人,人人。～ *else* 所有别人(= *all the others*)。★～ 跟 *everyone* 同义,但在口语中 ～ 用得较广。

eve·ry·day [ˈevridei; ˋɛvrɪˋde] ***a***. **1**. 每日的。**2**. 日常的,平常的,普通的。～ *affairs* 日常琐事。～ *clothes* 便服。～ *English* 日常用英语。*an* ～ *occurrence* 日常的事。～ *people* 普通人。*the* ～ *world* 人世间。

eve·ry·how [ˈevrihau; ˋɛvrɪ˒haʊ] ***ad***. 各种各样地;各方面地。

Eve·ry·man [ˈevrimæn; ˋɛvrɪ˒mæn] ***n***. **1**. 15 世纪道德剧中的主人公。**2**. 〔e-〕平常人,普通人。

eve·ry·one [ˈevriwʌn; ˋɛvrɪ˒wʌn] ***pron***. = everybody.

eve·ry·place [ˈevripleis; ˋɛvrɪ˒ples] ***ad***. = everywhere.

eve·ry·thing [ˈevriθiŋ; ˋɛvrɪ˒θɪŋ] ***pron***. **1**. 凡事,事事,万事,万物。**2**. (有关的)一切;最重要的东西。*be* ～ *to sb*. 某人认为是最重要的。*before* ～ 在一切之上,比什么都重要。*E- has its time*. 〔谚〕物各有时。*E- is good for something*. 〔谚〕天生一物必有用。*Use is* ～. 实用最重要。*The book did* ～ *but sell*. 这本书就是卖不出去。*To know* ～ *is to know nothing*. 〔谚〕样样都通,样样稀松。***and*** ～ 等等。***like*** ～ 猛烈地,拼命地。

eve·ry·way [ˈevriwei; ˋɛvrɪwe] ***ad***. **1**. 不管从哪方面来看;全然。**2**. 各式各样的方法。*This candidate is* ～ *better than that one*. 这个候选人比那个更好。*They tried* ～ *to find the solution*. 他们想尽办法来解决问题。

eve·ry·when [ˈevriwen, -hwen; ˋɛvrɪ˒hwɛn] ***ad***. 经常地,时时地。

eve·ry·where [ˈevri*h*wɛə; ˋɛvrɪ˒hwɛr] ***ad***. 处处,到处,无论什么地方。

eve·ry-whith·er [ˈevriˌhwiðə; ˋɛvrɪ˒hwɪðə] ***ad***. 到处,各处;每一个方向。

e·vict [iˈvikt; ɪˋvɪkt] ***vt***. **1**. (依法)收回(租屋、租地等)。**2**. 驱逐,赶出(房客等)。～ *tenant from a house* 把房客赶出屋外。

e·vic·tion [i(ː)ˈvikʃən; i(ɪ)ˋvɪkʃən] ***n***. **1**. (租地、租房等的)收回。**2**. (租户等的)驱逐,赶出。*an* ～ *man* 赶房客搬家的人。

e·vic·tor [i(ː)ˈviktə; ɪˋvɪktɚ] ***n***. 驱逐者;收回者。

ev·i·dence [ˈevidəns; ˋɛvədəns] **I** ***n***. **1**. 根据,证据。**2**. 形迹,迹象,痕迹。**3**.【法】证据,证人;证词。**4**. 明白,明显,显著。*circumstantial* ～ 间接(根据情况的)证据。*collateral* ～ 旁证。*conclusive* ～ 确定证据。*documentary* ～ 书面证据。*external* ～ 外来的证据。*historical* ～ 历史上的证据。*internal* ～ 内在的证据。*material* ～ 物证。*oral* [*parol*] ～ 口头证据。*verbal* ～ 证言。***bear*** ～ 作证。***bear*** [***give, show***] ～ ***of*** 有…的迹象。***call sb. in*** ～ 叫某人作证。～***s of debt*** 借据。***give*** ～ 作证,提供证据。***in*** ～ 明显的,显而易见的(*The child was nowhere in* ～. 到处都看不到那个小孩)。***turn King's*** [***Queen's***, 〔美〕***State's***] ～ 作检举同犯的证人;供出对同犯不利的证据。**II** ***vt***. **1**. 证明。**2**. 显示。

ev·i·dent [ˈevidənt; ˋɛvədənt] ***a***. 明白的,明显的。*with* ～ *prids* 得意扬扬地。**-ly** ***ad***.

ev·i·den·tial [ˌeviˈdenʃəl; ˏɛvəˋdɛnʃəl] ***a***. 证据上的;作为证据的,证明的。**-ly** ***ad***.

ev·i·den·tia·ry [ˌeviˈdenʃəri; ˏɛvəˋdɛnʃərɪ] ***a***. = evidential.

e·vil [ˈiːvl; ˋivl] **I** ***a***. **1**. 邪恶的;有害的。**2**. 不幸的,不吉利的。**3**. 可厌的,不愉快的。**4**. 〔古〕低劣的。**5**. 〔美俚〕失望的,发怒的。**6**. 〔美俚〕(表演等)有刺激性的。～ *days* 厄运。～ *devices* 奸计。*an* ～ *life* 不幸的生活。～ *news* [*tidings*] 噩耗,凶讯。～ *thoughts* 邪念。～ *tongue* 谗言;谗言者。***in an*** ～ ***hour*** 在不幸的时刻。***an*** ～ ***eye*** 恶毒[凶狠]的目光。***the E- One***【宗】魔鬼。**II** ***n***. **1**. 邪恶;弊病;不幸。**2**. 诽谤,恶言。**3**.【医】瘰疬(= king's ～)。*good and* ～ 善恶。*Of two* ～*s choose the less*. 〔谚〕两害相权取其轻。*the social* ～ 社会的罪恶,卖淫。*The* ～*s we bring on ourselves are the hardest to bear*. 〔谚〕自作孽不可活。***do*** ～ 干坏事。***return good for*** ～ 以德报怨。***with*** ～ ***in one's heart*** 不怀好意。**III** ***ad***. 恶毒地。*E- to him that* ～ *thinks* 邪念伤身。***speak*** ～ ***of*** 诽谤。～**-disposed** ***a***. 性恶的。～**doer** 作恶的人,坏人。～**doing** 坏事,恶劣行为。～**-eyed** ***a***. 目光恶毒的,目光凶狠的。～**-minded** ***a***. **1**. 狠毒的,恶毒的;(带有)恶意的。**2**. 好色的。～**-starred** ***a***. 不幸的。**-ly** ***ad***. **-ness** ***n***.

E

e·vince [iˈvins; ɪˋvɪns] *vt*. 表示;表明;显示。

evin·ci·ble [iˈvinsəbl; ɪˋvɪnsəbḷ] *a*. 可表明的,可证明的。

e·vin·cive [iˈvinsiv; ɪˋvɪnsɪv] *a*. 证明性的,表明性的,显示的。

e·vi·rate [ˈiːvireit, ˈev-; ˋivɪret, ˋɛv-] *vt*. 1.〔罕〕阉割。2.〔喻〕使软弱。

e·vis·cer·ate [iˈvisəreit; ɪˋvɪsə͵ret] *vt*. 1. 取出…的内脏。2. 抽去…的精华,挫伤…元气。3. 摘除(病人)器官。 **e·vis·cer·a·tion** [i͵visəˈreiʃən; ɪ͵vɪsəˋreʃən] *n*. 内脏摘除术。

ev·i·table [ˈevitəbl; ˋɛvətəbḷ] *a*. 可避免的。

ev·o·ca·tion [͵evəuˈkeiʃən; ͵ɛvoˋkeʃən] *n*. 1. 引起,唤起。2.【法】案件的移送,调案。3.〔古〕召唤;招魂。4.【动】(胚胎中的)唤起。

e·voc·a·tive [iˈvɔkətiv, iˈvəu-; ɪˋvɑkətɪv, ɪˋvo-] *a*. 唤起…的,引起…的 (*of*)。~ *words* 引起回忆或感情的言语。*The perfume was ~ of spring*. 那种香味令人想起了春天。**-ly** *ad*. **-ness** *n*.

ev·o·ca·tor [ˈevəkeitə; ˋɛvə͵ketɚ] *n*. 1. 招魂者。2. (印象或记忆的)唤起人。

e·voc·a·to·ry [iˈvɔkətəri; ɪˋvɑkətərɪ] *a*. = evocative.

e·voke [iˈvəuk; ɪˋvok] *vt*. 1. 召唤(死者灵魂等)。2. 唤起;引起,招致。3.【法】移送(案件到上级法院)。~ *admiration* [*surprise, a smile, protests, memories of the past*] 引起羡慕[惊奇、微笑,抗议、对过去的回忆]。

e·vo·lute [ˈiːvəluːt, ˈev-; ˋivəlut] I *n*. 1.【数】渐屈线,法包线,缩闭线。2.【机】展开线。II *a*.【植】展开的,反卷的(*opp*. involute)。

e·vo·lu·tion [͵iːvəˈljuːʃən, ͵evəˈljuːʃən; ͵ivəˋluʃən, ɛvəˋljuʃən] *n*. 1. 发展,发育;开展。2. (气体等的)放出;散出,放出物,散出物。3. 发生;演变;【生】演化,进化;进化论(*opp*. creationism)。4.【生】种族发生,系统发育;个体发生;个体发育。5.【天】(天体)形成。6.【数】开方。7.〔军〕按计划行动,位置变换。8. (跳舞等的)规定动作。*an ~ unit* 〔军〕机动单位。*the theory* [*doctrine*] *of ~* 进化论。**-al, -ary** *a*. 发展的;进化(论)的;展开的。**-ism** *n*. 进化论,进化主义 (*opp*. creationism)。

e·vo·lu·tion·ist [͵iːvəˈljuːʃənist; ͵ivəˋljuʃənɪst] I *n*. 进化论者。II *a*. 进化的,进化论的,进化论者的 (= evolutionistic [͵iːvə͵ljuːʃəˈnistik; ͵ivə͵ljuʃəˋnɪstɪk])。

e·vo·lu·tive [͵iːvəˈluːtiv, ˈev-; ɛvəˋlutɪv, ˋɛv-] *a*. (促进)发展的,(促进)进化的。

e·volve [iˈvɔlv; ɪˋvɑlv] *vt*. 1. 发展,展开,使逐渐形成。2. 使进化。3. 引伸出。4. 放出,发出(热等)。5.【化】离析。—*vi*. (情节等)进展;发展;进化。**-ment** *n*. 展开,发达;进化;发生。

EVR = electronic video recorder [recording] 电子录影机[录影]。

e·vul·sion [iˈvʌlʃən; ɪˋvʌlʃən] *n*. 拔出,拔去,强拔。

ev·zone [ˈevzəun; ˋɛvzon] *n*. 希腊精锐部队中的步兵。

EW = 1. electronic warfare 电子战。2. emergency ward 急诊病房。3. enlisted woman [women] 女兵。

E·we [ˈei͵wei; ˋe͵we] *n*. 1. 埃维人〔居住于迦纳、多哥境内和达荷美边境的黑人种族〕。2. 埃维人讲的克瓦(Kwa)语。

ewe [juː; ju] *n*. 母羊。~ *lamb* 小母羊。***one's ~ lamb*** 自己最珍视的东西。

Ew·ell [ˈjuːəl; ˋjuəl] *n*. 尤厄尔〔姓氏〕。

ewe-neck [ˈjuːnek; ˋjunɛk] *n*. (马和狗的)母羊式脖颈。**-ed** [-nekt; -nɛkt] *a*.

ew·er [ˈjuːə; ˋjuɚ] (盛洗脸水用的)大口水罐。

e·wig·keit [ˈeivigkait; ˋevɪgkaɪt] *n*. 〔G.〕永远,永久。***in*** [***into***] ***the ~*** 〔谑〕在[进入]未知的领域[虚无缥渺]中。

EWR = early-warning radar 预先警报雷达,远程警戒雷达。

ex[1] [eks; ɛks] *n*. (*pl*. **~es**) 1. 英语 x 字母。2. X 形状的东西。

ex[2] [eks; ɛks] *n*. 〔口〕离了婚的配偶。

ex[3] [eks; ɛks] I *n*. 〔口〕考试。II *vt*. 考试。

ex [eks; ɛks] ***prep***. 〔L.〕1. 由,从;为,因。2.【商】无,不;未 (*opp*. cum);在(船上、码头)交货。3.〔美〕大学某班级中途退学的。~ ***animo*** [ˈænimәu; ˋænɪmo] 衷心的(地)。~ ***bond*** 完税后关栈交货。~ ***cathedra*** [͵ekskəˈθiːdrə; ˋɛkskəˋθidrə] 权威性地,用职权。~ ***dividend*** 无红利〔略作 ~ div. 或 x-d.〕。~ ***interest*** 无股息〔略 ~ int. 或 x-i.〕。~ ***libris*** [ˈlaibris; ˋlaɪbrɪs] (某某)藏书。~ ***new*** 〔英〕无权要求新股。~ ***officio*** [ˈeksəˈfiʃiəu; ɛksəˋfɪʃɪo] 依据职权,当然(成员等)。~ ***parte*** [ˈekspɑːti; ˋɛkspɑrtɪ] 片面的,一方面的。~ ***pede Herculem*** [eksˈpiːdiˈhəːkjuləm; ɛksˋpidɪˋhɝkjʊləm] 由部分可知全体。~ ***pier*** [***quay, wharf***] 码头交货。~ ***post facto*** [ˈekspəustˈfæktəu; ˋɛkspostˋfækto]【法】在事后;溯及既往地。~ ***rail*** 铁路旁交货。~ ***rights*** 无新股特权〔略 Ex R.〕。~ ***ship*** 船上交货。~ ***store*** 仓库交货;〔美〕店铺交货。~ ***voto*** [ˈvəutəu; ˋvoto] 由于许愿;(许愿用的)供品。~ ***warehouse*** 仓库交货。***Yale ~ '47***. 耶鲁大学一九四七班肄业。

Ex. = Exodus.

ex. = 1. examined. 2. example. 3. exception. 4. exchange. 5. excluding. 6. excursion. 7. executed; executive. 8. exempt. 9. exercise. 10. exhibit. 11. export. 12. express. 13. extra. 14. extract. 15. extremely.

ex- *pref*. 1. = forth, without, thoroughly 等。★ex- 仅可接用于母音字母和 h, c, p, q, s, t 之前;f 之前用 ef-, 其他子音字母前用 e- (略去 x): *ex*asperate, *ex*clude; *ef*ferent, *e*ducate. 2. 加在名词以前,表示"以前的","前任的": *ex*-premier, *ex*-pow. 3. = out, away, off. ★母音字母前用 ex-; 子音字母前用 ec-: *exo*dus, *exo*rcize; *ecc*entric, *ec*stasy. 4. = exo.

ex·ac·er·bate [eksˈæsə(ː)beit; ɛkˋsæsɚ͵bet] *vt*. 1. 使(病等)更重[恶化],加深(痛苦等)。2. 激怒,使烦恼。

ex·ac·er·ba·tion [eks͵æsə(ː)ˈbeiʃən; ɛks͵æsɚˋbeʃən] *n*. 1. 增剧,加重。2. 激怒,愤激。3.【医】病势加重,剧变,恶化。

ex·act[1] [igˈzækt; ɪgˋzækt] *a*. 1. 精密的,准确的。2. 严格的,严正的;严厉的。3. 严密的。~ *discipline* 严格的纪律。*the ~ sciences* 精密科学。*the ~ sum* 准确的金额。*an ~ translation* 确切的翻译。***be ~ to a cent*** 算得一分不差。~ ***to the letter*** 原本原样,极正确。~ ***to the life*** 和实物丝毫不差。***to be ~*** 精确地说〔插入语〕。~ **differential**【数】恰当微分。~ **science** 精密科学(如物理、数学、化学等)。

ex·act[2] [igˈzækt; ɪgˋzækt] *vt*. 1. 勒索(钱财等),强要。2. 强制,逼使(服从等)。3. 急需,需要。*The task ~s the closest attention*. 这个工作需要周密注意。~ *payments* 强要报酬。

ex·act·a·ble [igˈzæktəbl; ɪgˋzæktəbḷ] *a*. 可以强取的,可以强求的。

ex·act·ing [igˈzæktiŋ; ɪgˋzæktɪŋ] *a*. 1. 严格的,难以取悦的。2. 强索的,横征暴敛的。3. 吃力的。*an ~ microbe* 对生存条件要求极高的微生物。~ *work* 费力的工作。~ *terms* 苛刻的条件。**-ly** *ad*. **-ness** *n*.

ex·ac·tion [igˈzækʃən; ɪgˋzækʃən] *n*. 1. 强求,勒索。2. 苛刻的要求。3. 苛捐杂税。

ex·ac·ti·tude [igˈzæktitjuːd; ɪgˋzæktə͵tjud] *n*. 1. 正确,精确。2. 精密;严正,严格。

ex·act·ly [igˈzæktli; ɪgˋzæktlɪ] *ad*. 1. 确切地,精确地,恰好。2. 十分。3. = yes. ***not ~*** 不全是,未必就(*Those are not ~ the same*. 那些并不完全一样)。~ ***true*** 千真万确。

ex·act·ness [igˈzæktnis; ɪgˋzæktnɪs] *n*. = exactitude.

ex·ac·tor [igˈzæktə; ɪgˋzæktɚ] ***n.*** 勒索者;强征捐税的人。

ex·ag·ger·ate [igˈzædʒəreit; ɪgˋzædʒə,ret] ***vt.*** **1.** 夸张,夸大。**2.** 使过大,使增大。~ *an illness* 夸大病情。*shoes exaggerating the size of his feet* 使他的脚显得特别大的鞋子。—***vi.*** 夸张,夸大,言过其实。

ex·ag·ger·at·ed [igˈzædʒəreitid; ɪgˋzædʒə,retɪd] ***a.*** **1.** 夸张的,言过其实的。**2.** 过大的,逾常的。*an* ~ *sense of one's importance* 自视过高。**-ly** ***ad.***

ex·ag·ger·a·tion [ig,zædʒəˈreiʃən; ɪg,zædʒəˋreʃən] ***n.*** 浮夸,夸张;(艺术等的)夸张手法。

ex·ag·ger·a·tive [igˈzædʒəreitiv; ɪgˋzædʒə,retɪv] ***a.*** 夸张的,夸大的,小题大做的,言过其实的。**-ly** ***ad.***

ex·ag·ger·a·tor [igˈzædʒə,reitə; ɪgˋzædʒərtɚ] ***n.*** 夸张者。

ex·al·bu·mi·nous [,eksælˈbjuːminəs; ,ɛksælˋbjumənəs] ***a.***【植】无胚乳的。~ **seed** 无胚乳种子。

ex·alt [igˈzɔːlt, eg-; ɪg,zɔlt, ɛg-] ***vt.*** **1.** 高举,升起。**2.** 抬高(地位等),提高(权力等)。**3.** 褒奖,捧。**4.** 加强(想像力等),激发,发扬;加浓(色彩等)。**5.** 使高兴,使得意。*He was ~ed to the skies.* 他被捧上天了。*We were ~ed by his poems.* 他的诗激发了我们的想像力。

ex·al·ta·tion [,egzɔːlˈteiʃən; ,ɛgzɔlˋteʃən] ***n.*** **1.** 高举;升高。**2.** 提拔;晋升。**3.** 兴奋,得意。**4.**【冶】纯化;【化】炼浓。~**register** 缴款通知书。

ex·alt·ed [igˈzɔːltid; ɪgˋzɔltɪd] ***a.*** **1.** 高贵的;高尚的,(目的等)崇高的。**2.** 得意扬扬的,兴奋的。~ *personages* 高贵人士。

ex·am [igˈzæm, eg-; ɪgˋzæm] ***n.*** 〔口〕考试 (= examination)。

exam. = examination; examined.

ex·a·men [egˈzeimen; ɛgˋzemɛn] ***n.*** 批判性研究;详细探索。

ex·am·i·na·ble [igˈzæminəbl; ɪgˋzæmɪnəbl̩] ***a.*** **1.** 可考查的,可检查的。**2.** 在审查范围内的。

ex·am·i·nant [igˈzæminənt; ɪgˋzæmɪnənt] ***n.*** 主考人,审问者;检察人;审查人。

ex·am·i·na·tion [ig,zæmiˈneiʃən; ɪg,zæmɪˋneʃən] ***n.*** **1.** 考试 (*in*)。**2.** (问题等的)检讨,考察;检查;审查,调查;检定,检验;观察。**3.** 审问。**4.** 检察;诊察。*an* ~ *in geography* 地理考试。*a civil service* ~ 文官考试。*an entrance* ~ 入学考试。*a medical* ~ 诊察。*a physical* ~ 体格检查。~ *papers* 试卷。*an oral* [*verbal*] ~ 口试。*a written* ~ 笔试。~ ***in chief***【法】己方律师对证人所作的直接讯问〔*cf.* cross-examination〕。~ ***of party***【对】对方的讯问。~ ***of the voir dire*** [,vwarˈdiːr; vwarˋdir]【法】对方对被传讯证人预先所作的讯问。***an*** ~ ***of the witness***【法】律师对证人的质询。***go in*** [***up***] ***for one's*** ~ 受考,应试。***make an*** ~ ***of*** 检查。***on*** ~ 一经检验,察看时。***pass*** [***fail in***] ***an*** ~ 考试及格[不及格]。***sit for an*** ~ 应该。***take an*** ~ 参加考试。***under*** ~ 在调查[检查]中。***undergo an*** ~ 受检查[诊察]。**-al** ***a.***

ex·am·i·na·to·ri·al [ig,zæminəˈtɔːriəl; ɛg,zæmənəˋtorɪəl] ***a.*** **1.** 检查的,审查的;考试的。**2.** 主考人的。

ex·am·ine [igˈzæmin; ɪgˋzæmɪn] ***vt.*** **1.** 调查,检查,审查;检验,检定;观察,研究。**2.** 考试。**3.** 审问(*on*)。**4.** 诊察。*E- yourself.* 你反省反省吧。~ *one's own heart* [*conscience*] 扪心自问,反省。—***vi.*** 调查 (*into*);审问。~ *into a matter* 调查事实。**examining judge** 预审法官。

ex·am·i·nee [ig,zæmiˈniː; ɪg,zæmɪˋni] ***n.*** 参加考试的人;受审查的人。

ex·am·in·er [igˈzæminə, eg-; ɪgˋzæmɪnɚ, ɛg-] ***n.*** **1.** 检查员,审查人。**2.** 主考人。**3.** 检察官。*customs* ~ 海关检查员。*satisfy the ~s* 考试[审查]及格。

ex·am·ple [igˈzɑːmpl; ɪgˋzæmpl̩] **I** ***n.*** **1.** 例证,实例;标本,样本。**2.** 范例;典型,模范,榜样;例题。**3.** 先例;儆戒。*E- is better than precept.* 〔谚〕身教胜于言教。***as an*** ~ = ***by way of*** ~ 例如,举例来说。***be an*** ~ ***to*** 是…的教训。***beyond*** [***without***] ~ 无先例的,空前的,未曾有的。~***s of the great masters*** 名家作品。***follow the*** ~ ***of*** 照…的榜样,以…作模范。***for*** ~ 例如。★日常用语中常说作 for instance. ***give*** [***take***] ***an*** ~ 举例;示范。***give*** [***set***] ***a good*** ~ ***to*** 以身作则。***make an*** ~ ***of sb.*** 惩一儆百。***take*** ~ ***by*** 临摹。**II** ***vt.*** 〔废〕作为…的示范〔常用被动语态〕。

ex·an·i·mate [igˈzænimit; ɪgˋzænɪmɪt] ***a.*** **1.** 已死的,无生命的。**2.** 没精神的,没生气的;意气消沉的。

ex·an·i·ma·tion [ig,zæniˈmeiʃən; ɪg,zænɪˋmeʃən] ***n.*** **1.**【医】死;假死,昏厥。**2.** 沮丧,意气消沉。

ex·an·them [egˈzænθim; ɛkˋzænθɪm] ***n.***【医】**1.** 皮疹,皮肤溃烂。**2.** 疹。

ex·an·the·ma [,eksænˈθiːmə; ,ɛksænˋθimə] ***n.*** (*pl.* ***-mas***, ***-them·atas*** [-ˈθemətəz; -ˋθɛmətəz]) ***n.***【医】**1.** 皮疹。**2.** 疹。

ex·arch[1] [ˈeksɑːk; ˋɛksark] ***n.*** **1.** (东罗马帝国的)总督。**2.** (东正教的)大主教;主教特派使节。

ex·arch[2] [ˈeksɑːk; ˋeksark] ***a.***【植】外始式的。

ex·arch·ate [ˈeksɑːkeit; ˋɛksarket] ***n.*** 东罗马帝国总督[东正教主教等]的权限[职位、管区]。

ex·ar·tic·u·la·tion [,eksɑː,tikjuˈleiʃən; ,ɛksar,tɪkjuˋleʃən] ***n.***【医】**1.** 脱白。**2.** 关节截断。

ex·as·per·ate [igˈzɑːspəreit; ɪgˋzæspə,ret] **I** ***vt.*** **1.** 激怒,使恼怒。**2.** 加剧,加重,使恶化。**II** ***a.*** [igˈzɑːspərit; ɪgˋzɑspərɪt] **1.** 被激怒的,恼怒的。**2.**【生】具硬突起的,(表面)粗糙的。**ex·as·per·at·ed·ly** ***ad.***

ex·as·per·at·er [igˈzɑːspəreitə; ɪgˋzɑspə,retɚ] ***n.*** 激怒他人者。

ex·as·per·at·ing [igˈzɑːspəreitiŋ; ɪgˋzɑspəretɪŋ] ***a.*** 使人恼怒的,激怒人的。**-ly** ***ad.***

ex·as·per·a·tion [ig,zɑːspəˈreiʃən; ɪg,zæspəˋreʃən] ***n.*** **1.** 愤激,激昂,愤怒。**2.** 激化,恶化;加剧。

exc. = **1.** excellent. **2.** except; excepted; exception. **3.** exchange.

Ex·cal·i·bur [eksˈkælibə; ɛksˋkælɪbɚ] ***n.*** (传说中)英国国王亚瑟王的神剑。

ex ca·the·dra [,ekskəˈθiːdrə; ɛkskəˋθidrə] 〔L.〕有权威的,有权力的〔尤指教皇的诏书〕。

ex·ca·vate [ˈekskəveit; ˋɛkskə,vet] ***vt.*** **1.** 开凿,挖掘。**2.** 掘出,发掘。—***vi.*** **1.** 凿,掘开。**2.** 变成空洞。

ex·ca·va·tion [,ekskəˈveiʃən; ,ɛkskəˋveʃən] ***n.*** **1.** 开凿;发掘;挖掘;挖土,剜通。**2.** 穴,洞;坑道,开凿成的山路。**3.**【考古】出土文物,发掘物。

ex·ca·va·tor [ˈekskəveitə; ˋɛkskə,vetɚ] ***n.*** **1.** 开凿者;发掘者。**2.** 挖掘器;挖土机;电铲。**3.** (牙科用的)钻孔器。

ex·ceed [ikˈsiːd; ɪkˋsid] ***vt.*** **1.** 超过(限度、范围)。**2.** 越出。**3.** 胜过,优于,凌驾。*a task that ~s one's ability* 不能胜任的工作。~ *by five dollars* 超出五美元。~ *one's authority* [*instructions*] 越权。~ *sb. in courage* 勇气过人。~ *the speed limit* 超出驾驶速率限制。—***vi.*** (数量、程度)超过其他,领先,突出。~ *in size* 规模突出。**-a·ble** ***a.*** **-er** ***n.***

ex·ceed·ing [ikˈsiːdiŋ; ɪkˋsidɪŋ] **I** ***a.*** **1.** 超越的,胜过的。**2.** 非常的;极度的。**II** ***ad.*** 〔古〕= -ly. **-ly** ***ad.***

ex·cel [ikˈsel; ɪkˋsɛl] ***vt.*** (***-ll-***) 优于,超过。~ *sb. in knowledge* 学识过人。—***vi.*** 胜过其他,突出;擅长。~ *in* (*at*) *swimming* 擅长游泳。*She ~s as a dancer.* 她擅长跳舞。

ex·cel·lence [ˈeksələns; ˋɛksələns] ***n.*** **1.** 优越,优秀,杰出,卓越;〔*pl.*〕优点,长处。**2.** 〔E-〕阁下 = excellency. ~ *in English* 擅长英语,英语优良。

ex·cel·len·cy [ˈeksələnsi; ˋɛksələnsɪ] ***n.*** **1.** 〔E-〕阁下;

E

被尊称为"阁下"的人。2.〔常 *pl*.〕优点;美德(= excellence)。*Your E-* 阁下〔直接称呼时指 *you*〕。*His E-* 阁下〔间接提到时指 *he*, *him*〕。*Their Excellencies* 阁下〔间接提到时指 *they*, *them*〕。★ 原用于王族的尊称,目前限用于大臣、大使、全权公使、使节、总督等,美国亦用于总统、州长以及外国大使;其夫人称作 Your E-, Her E-.

ex·cel·lent [ˈeksələnt; ˋɛksələnt] ***a***. 优秀的,卓越的,杰出的;优良的,精良的,极好的。**-ly** ***ad***.

ex·cel·si·or [ekˈselsiɔː; ɛkˋsɛlsɪɔr] **I** ***n***. 1.〔美〕(填塞用的)木丝,细刨花。2.【印】3 点活字。**II** ***int***. 精益求精〔商标用语、箴言等〕。*the E- State* 美国纽约州(的别名)。***as dry as*** ~ 干透了的。

ex·cept [ikˈsept; ɪkˋsɛpt] **I** ***prep***. 除…之外。*We all failed* ~ *him*. 我们都失败了,只有他除外。~ ***for*** 只有,除了…以外(*The carpet is good* ~ *for its price*. 地毯很好,只是价钱太高)。~ ***that*** 除了,只是〔后接名词子句〕。★ ~ 跟 besides 意义不同。例如"We all agreed ~ him."是说"我们都同意,只有他不同意"。"We all agreed besides him."是说"我们都同意,他也同意"。**II** ***conj***. 1.〔古〕除非,如果不是(= unless)。2. 只是,要不是,除…以外。*I would go* ~ *it's too far*. 要不是路太远,我就去了。**III** ***vt***. 把…除去,把…除外(*from*)。*The minors are* ~*ed from the regulation*. 未成年者不在此限。*nobody* ~*ed* 无人例外。*present company* ~*ed* 目前在场者除外。—***vi***. 反对(*to*; *against*)。~ *to a statement* 反对某项声明。~ *against a witness* 对证人提出异议。**-a·ble** ***a***. 可例外的,可除外的。

ex·cep·tant [ekˈseptənt; ɛkˋsɛptənt] **I** ***a***. 例外的;除外的。**II** ***n***. 例外者。

ex·cept·ing [ikˈseptiŋ; ɪkˋsɛptɪŋ] **I** ***prep***.〔用于句首或 not, without, always 后面〕除…外。*E- his son*, *they are all right*. 除了他的儿子以外,他们大家都好。*Everyone helped*, *not* ~ *John*. 每个人都帮了一把手,连约翰也不例外。**II** ***conj***.〔古〕= except. ***conj***.

ex·cep·tion [ikˈsepʃən; ɪkˋsɛpʃən] ***n***. 1. 例外;除外,除去。2.【法】抗告;异议,不服,反对。*Every rule has its* ~*s*. 任何规则均有例外。***by way of*** ~ 作为例外。***liable*** [***subject***] ***to*** ~ 容易遭到反对的,会引起异议的。***make an*** ~ ***of*** 把…作为例外。***make no*** ~***s*** 一视同仁,一样看待。***take*** ~ 1. 反对,表示异议。2. 有反感。***take*** ~ ***at*** 发怒,生气。***take*** ~ ***to*** [***against***] 对…提出异议。***without*** ~ 一概,全都;无例外地。***with the*** ~ ***of*** 除…外。**-al·ly** ***ad***. **-less** ***a***. 无例外的。

ex·cep·tion·a·ble [ikˈsepʃənəbl; ɪkˋsɛpʃənəbḷ] ***a***. 可以反对[抗议]的,会引起反对的。**-ness** ***n***.

ex·cep·tion·al [ikˈsepʃənl; ɪkˋsɛpʃənḷ] ***a***. 1. 例外的,特别的。2. 格外的,异常的,稀有的,较优的。*a man of* ~ *talent* 具有特殊才能的人。~ *promotion* 破格提升。**-ly** ***ad***. **-ness** ***n***.

ex·cep·tion·al·ism [ikˈsepʃənəlizəm; ɪkˋsɛpʃənəlɪzəm̩] ***n***. 例外论。

ex·cep·tion·ali·ty [ikˌsepʃənˈæliti; ɪkˏsɛpʃənˋælətɪ] ***n***. 1. 例外,除外。2. 异常,特别,优越。

ex·cep·tive [ikˈseptiv; ɛkˋsɛptɪv] ***a***. 1. 形成例外的,特殊的,有除外含意的(如前置词 but, except, save 等)。2.〔古〕好反对的,吹毛求疵的。*an* ~ *clause* 除外条款。

ex·cerpt I [ˈeksəːpt; ˋɛksɚpt] ***n***. (*pl*. ~*s*, *-ta* [-ə; -ə]) 摘录,摘要;节录;抽印。**II** [ekˈsəːpt; ɛkˋsɚpt] ***vt***. 摘录,摘要;引用,删节。**-er**, **-or** ***n***. 摘录者,引用者。**-ible** ***a***. 可摘录的。

ex·cerp·ta [ikˈsəːptə; ɪkˋsɚptə] ***n***. ***pl***. 摘要,大纲,摘录。

ex·cerp·tion [ekˈsəːpʃən, ik-; ɛkˋsɚpʃən, ɪk-] ***n***. 摘录,摘要;节录。

ex·cess [ikˈses; ɪkˋsɛs] **I** ***n***. 1. 过量;过剩。2. 超过,超越。3. 超过数量。4. 过度,(饮食等)无节制。5.〔*pl*.〕过分行为,暴行。*an* ~ *of enthusiasm* 过分热心。*an* ~ *of exports* [*imports*] 出[入]超。*an* ~ *of supply over demand* 供过于求。*an* ~ *of* $ *100 over the estimate* 比预算超额 100 美元。~ *of authority* 越权。***go*** [***run***] ***to*** ~ 走极端。***in*** ~ 过度。***in*** ~ ***of*** 超过。(*smoke*) ***to*** ~ (吸烟)过度。***with*** ~ ***of joy*** 因过度高兴。**II** [ˈikses; ɪˋksɛs] ***a***. 过量的,超过限额的,过量的。*an* ~ *fare* 补票费。~ **insurance** 超过损失保险。~ **issue** (纸币的)额外发行。~ **luggage** 超重行李。~**-profits tax** 超额利润税。~ **reserve** (现金的)超额储备。

ex·ces·sive [ikˈsesiv; ɪkˋsɛsɪv] ***a***. 1. 过多的,过度的,极端的。2. 份外的,额外的。**-ly** ***ad***. **-ness** ***n***.

Exch. = exchange; exchequer.

ex·change [iksˈtʃeindʒ; ɪksˋtʃendʒ] **I** ***vt***. 1. (以某物与另一物)交换,调换(*for*)。2. 互换,交流,交易。3. 兑换。~ *one's labour for money* 以劳动换取报酬。~ *blows* 互殴。~ *civilities* 互相行礼。—***vi***. 1. 兑换(*for*)。2. 交换;调换(职位、任务)(*from*; *into*)。~ *from* [*out of*] *one ship into another* 从甲船换乘乙船。**II** ***n***. 1. 交换,互换。2. 交流,交易。3. 兑换、汇兑;汇划。4. 汇兑行情,兑换率,汇水,贴水。5.〔*pl*.〕(票据)交换总额。6. 交换品,〔特指〕交换书刊。7. 交易所。8.〔英〕职业介绍所。9. 电话局,电话交换台。*an* ~ *of goods* 物资交流。*an* ~ *of prisoners* 交换俘虏。~ *of views* 交换意见。*foreign* ~ 外汇。*domestic* [*internal*] ~ 内汇。*a post* ~〔美〕陆军消费合作社(*PX*)。*a bill of* ~ 汇票。*the rate* [*course*] *of* ~ (= ~ *rate*) 外汇率[行情、比价]。*a set of* ~ 联单汇票[双联或三联]。*the first* [*second*, *third*] *of* ~ 第一[第二、第三]联汇票。*the cotton* ~ 棉花交易所。*a labour* 〔英〕职业[劳工]介绍所。*short* ~ 短期汇票。*a stock* ~ 证券交易所。*a* [*central*] *telephone* ~ 中央电话局。*E- is no robbery*.〔谑〕交换不是掠夺〔为不公平交换辩解的话〕。***in*** ~ ***for*** 换,调。***make an*** ~ 交换。***value in*** [***of***] ~ 交换价值(= ~ value)。~ **area** (电话)通话区。~ **broker** 证券交易所经纪人;汇兑掮客。~ **control** 外汇管理。~ **girl** 女接线员。~ **professor** 交流讲学教授。~ **quotations** 外汇行情。~ **rate** 汇率。~ **student** (两国间)交换的留学生。~ **table** 汇兑换算表。

ex·change·a·bil·i·ty [iksˌtʃeindʒəˈbiliti; ɪksˏtʃendʒəˋbɪlətɪ] ***n***. 可交换性,可交易性。

ex·change·a·ble [iksˈtʃeindʒəbl; ɪksˋtʃendʒəbḷ] ***a***. 可交换的;可兑换的;可转换的(*for*)。~ **value** 交换价值。

ex·chang·ee [ˌekstʃeinˈdʒiː; ˏɛkstʃenˋdʒi] ***n***. 被交换者,交换的学生[教授、俘虏等]。

ex·chang·er [iksˈtʃeindʒə; ɪksˋtʃendʒɚ] ***n***. 交换器。

ex·cheq·uer [iksˈtʃekə; ɪksˋtʃɛkɚ] ***n***. 1. 国库;资金;财源〔口〕(个人的)财力。2.〔E-〕【英史】税务法庭〔专管王室岁入并审理有关案件,1873 年归并高等法院 = Court of E-〕。3.〔E-〕〔英〕财政部。*His* ~ *is low*. 他的经济状况不好。*Chancellor of the E-*〔英〕财政大臣。**E- Bill**〔英〕财政部证券。**E- Bond**〔英〕国库债券。

ex·cide [ikˈsaid; ɪkˋsaɪd] ***vt***. 割掉,切开。

ex·cip·i·ent [ikˈsipiənt; ɪkˋsɪpɪənt] ***n***.【药】赋形剂。

ex·cis·a·ble [ikˈsaizəbl; ɪkˋsaɪzəbḷ] ***a***. 应纳国产货物税[执照税]的。

ex·cise[1] [ekˈsaiz; ɛkˋsaɪz] **I** ***n***. 1. (国产)货物税;消费税;(生产、贩卖)执照税。2.〔the E-〕(英国的)国产税务局〔现名 Commissioners of Customs and E-〕。~ *duties* 消费税。***the*** ~ ***law***〔英〕酿酒法;〔美〕执照法。**II** ***vt***. 1. 向…征收国产税[消费税]。2.〔英方〕向…索取高价。**-man** ***n***. (*pl*. *-men*)〔英古〕消费税征收官员(= E- officer)。

ex·cise[2] [ekˈsaiz; ɛkˋsaɪz] ***vt***. 1. 删去(文章等)…切除。2.【动、植】在…上开槽,切开。

ex·ci·sion [ekˈsiʒən; ɪkˋsɪʒən] ***n***. 1. 删除。2.【医】切除

(术)。3.【宗】逐出教会。

ex·cit·a·bil·i·ty [ikˌsaitəˈbiliti; ɪkˏsaɪtəˋbɪlətɪ] *n* 1.【物】可激发性。2.【医】兴奋性,敏感性;【生理】(感官的)刺激反应性。

ex·cit·a·ble [ikˈsaitəbl; ɪkˋsaɪtəbl̩] *a*. 易激动的;敏感的。**-bly** *ad*.

ex·cit·ant [ˈeksitənt; ɛkˋsaɪtənt] I *a*. 有刺激性的,使兴奋的。II *n*. 刺激物;兴奋剂。

ex·ci·ta·tion [ˌeksiˈteiʃən; ˏɛkaɪˋteʃən] *n*. 1. 刺激,兴奋,激发,鼓舞。2.【物】激发;【电】激励、励磁。3.【植】激感(现象)。

ex·cit·a·tive [ekˈsaitətiv; ɛkˋsaɪtətɪv] *a*. 1. 刺激性的,兴奋性的,有刺激作用的;激发的。2.【电】励磁的。

ex·cit·a·to·ry [ekˈsaitətəri; ɛkˋsaɪtəˏtorɪ] *a*. 1. = excitative. 2. 显示兴奋的,有激动迹象的。

ex·cite [ikˈsait; ɪkˋsaɪt] *vt*. 1. 刺激;使兴奋;使激动。2. 激励;鼓励,激发,唤起(注意等),引起(兴趣);煽动,3.【电】激起(电流)。4.【摄】使感光。*The good news ~d everybody*. 好消息使每一个人都很兴奋。~ *admiration* 引起羡慕。~ *jealousy in sb*. 引起某人嫉妒。~ *a nerve* 刺激神经。~ *heat by friction* 摩擦生热。—*vi*.〔口〕兴奋,激动。*Don't* ~. 冷静点! (= *Don't* ~ *yourself*.)。**get ~d at** [**by**, **about**, **over**] 因…而激动[兴奋]起来。

ex·cit·ed [ikˈsaitid; ɪkˋsaɪtɪd] *a*. 1. 激昂的,激动的,兴奋的。2.【物】激发的,励磁的。~ **state**【物】受激态。**-ly** *ad*. 激昂,兴奋。

ex·cite·ment [ikˈsaitmənt; ɪkˋsaɪtmənt] *n*. 1. 刺激,兴奋,振奋;激昂,奋激;骚动。2. 刺激的事物。*at a high pitch of* ~ 极度激动[兴奋]。*great* ~ *caused by the fire* 由火灾引起的骚动。*be flushed with* ~兴奋得脸色发红。**in** ~兴奋地,激动地。

ex·cit·er [ikˈsaitə; ɪkˋsaɪtɚ] *n*. 1. 刺激者;刺激物。2.【电】励磁机;【无】激励器;主控振荡器;辐射器;主控振荡槽路。

ex·cit·ing [ikˈsaitiŋ; ɪkˋsaɪtɪŋ] *a*. 1. 令人兴奋的,使人激动的。2.【电】励磁的。~ *news* 令人兴奋的消息。**-ly** *ad*.

ex·cit·on [ˈiksitɔn; ˋɪksɪtɑn] *n*.【物】激子。**-ic** [ˌiksiˈtɔnik; ɪksɪˋtɑnɪk] *a*. **-ics** *n*.〔用作单数〕【物】激子学。

ex·ci·tor [ikˈsaitə; ɪkˋsaɪtɚ] *n*. 1. = exciter. 2.【解】兴奋反射神经。

excl. = exclusive.

ex·claim [iksˈkleim; ɪksˋklem] *vt*., *vi*. 惊叫,呼喊,大声说。~ ***against*** 指责。~ **at** [**on**, **upon**] 抗议。~ ***in*** [***with***] ***delight*** 欢呼。~ **over** 感叹。**-er** *n*.

ex·cla·ma·tion [ˌekskləˈmeiʃən; ˏɛkskləˋmeʃən] *n*. 1. 惊叫,呼喊。2. 感叹;【语法】感叹词;【修】咏叹法。***the note*** [***point***] ***of*** ~ = ***the*** ~ ***mark*** [***point***] 感叹号〔!〕。

ex·clam·a·to·ry [eksˈklæmətəri; ɪkˋsklæməˏtorɪ] *a*. 叫喊的;感叹的;咏叹式的。

ex·clave [ˈekskleiv; ˋɛksklev] *n*. 飞地〔在别国境内的某国领土〕。

ex·clo·sure [iksˈkləuʒə, eks-; ɪksˋkloʒɚ, ɛks-] *n*. 围地〔尤指为防止家畜或野兽侵入而栅起来的地方〕。

ex·clude [iksˈkluːd; ɪksˋklud] *vt*. 1. 拒绝;排除,排斥;把…除外。2. 驱除,赶出。~ *sb*. *from membership in a society* 拒绝接纳某人入会。~ *immigrants from a country* 不许移居入境。*There were fifteen present excluding myself*. 除我以外,有十五人出席。*None of these three can be* ~*d*. 这三者缺一不可。*the law of* ~*d middle*【逻】排中律。~ **sb**. **from** 不准进;把…赶出;剥夺(某人…的权利);拒绝(某人入会等)。~ ***the possibility of*** 排除…的可能性。

ex·clu·sion [iksˈkluːʒən; ɪksˋkluʒən] *n*. 1. 拒绝,杜绝;除去,排除,排斥;赶出。2. 被排除在外的事物。***the*** ~ ***policy*** 闭关政策。***to the*** ~ ***of*** 把…除外;排斥。~ **clause** 契约中声明不属保险范围事项的条款。~ **principle**【物】(泡利)不相容原理(= Pauli ~ principle)。**-ar·y** *a*.

ex·clu·sion·ism [iksˈkluːʒənizəm; ɪkˋskluʒənˏɪzəm̩] *n*. 排外主义,闭关主义;排他主义。

ex·clu·sion·ist [iksˈkluːʒənist; ɪksˋkluʒəˏnɪst] I *n*. 排他主义者。II *a*. 排他主义的。~ *attitude* 闭关自守的态度。

ex·clu·sive [iksˈkluːsiv; ɪksˋklusɪv] I *a*. 1. 除外的;排外的,排他的,(俱乐部等)不公平的,势利的,非大众化的。2. 孤高的。3. 独占的;独有的,唯一的;专有的,专属的。4. 全部的。5.〔美〕时髦的。6. (商店、商品等)高级的,价格高的,别处没有的。7. 不计及,不算入(*of*)(*opp*. inclusive). *an* ~ *aggressive bloc* 排他性的侵略集团。*an* ~ *agency policy* 独家代理政策。~ *jurisdiction* 专辖权。~ *of expenses* 除去费用不算。~ *privileges* 独有的特权。~ *rights for the sale of* 专售权。*an* ~ *selling agency* 独家经销店。*an* ~ *school* (限上层阶级子弟入学的)专设学校。~ *species*【植】确限种,专见种。~ *voice*【法】否认权,否决权。*an* ~ *hotel* 高级旅馆。*be* ~ *in manner* 态度傲慢。~ **of** 除;不算,不计(*opp*. inclusive of)(*from 10 to 21* ~ 从11到20〔10和21除外〕)。II *n*. 1. 独家新闻。2. 专有权。3. 孤傲者。4.【数】不可兼。**-ly** *ad*. **-ness** *n*.

ex·clu·siv·ism [iksˈkluːsivizəm; ɪksˋklusɪvɪzəm̩] *n*. = exclusionism.

ex·clu·siv·ist [iksˈkluːsivist; ɪksˋklusɪvɪst] *n*. 排他主义者。

ex·clu·siv·is·tic [iksˌkluːsiˈvistik; ɪksˏklusɪˋvɪstɪk] *a*. 排他主义的。

ex·clu·siv·i·ty [ˌeksklu:ˈsiviti; ˏɛkskluˋsɪvətɪ] *n*. 排外,排外主义;排他性,排他主义〔尤指搞宗派,拉山头,或闭关自守〕。

ex·cog·i·tate [eksˈkɔdʒiteit; ɛksˋkɑdʒətet] *vt*. 想出,设计,发明。

ex·cog·i·ta·tion [eksˌkɔdʒiˈteiʃən; ɛksˏkɑdʒɪˋteʃən] *n*. 1. 想出,设计,设法。2. 计划,计策,方案。

ex·cog·i·ta·tive [eksˈkɔdʒiteitiv; ɛksˋkɑdʒətetɪv] *a*. 想出的,计划的,发明的。

ex·com·mu·ni·cate [ˌekskəˈmjuːnikeit; ˏɛkskəˋmjunəˏket] I *vt*. 1. 把…革出教门,剥夺(教友)特权(如在教堂结婚、埋葬、领受圣餐等)。2. 开除(会籍等)。II *a*. 被革出教门的(= excommunicated)。III *n*. 被革出教门的人。

ex·com·mu·ni·ca·tion [ˈekskəˌmjuːniˈkeiʃən; ˏɛkskəˏmjunəˋkeʃən] *n*. 革出教会;革出教会的公告。*major* [*greater*] ~ 大革出〔开除教籍〕。*minor* [*lesser*] ~小革出〔只停止领圣餐〕。

ex·com·mu·ni·ca·tive [ˌekskəˈmjuːnikətiv; ˏɛkskəˋmjunəˏketɪv] *a*. 革出教会的;开除的。

ex·com·mu·ni·ca·tor [ˌekskəˈmjuːnikeitə; ɛkskəˋmjunəˏketɚ] *n*. 革出教会者,开除者。

ex·co·ri·ate [eksˈkɔːrieit; ɛkˋskorɪˏet] *vt*. 1. 剥(皮),磨掉,擦伤(皮肤等)。2. 严厉指责。

ex·co·ri·a·tion [eksˌkɔːriˈeiʃən; ɛksˏkorɪˋeʃən] *n*. 1. 剥皮,擦伤皮肤。2. 严厉指责。3.【医】表皮脱落。

ex·cre·ment [ˈekskrimənt; ˋɛkskrɪmənt] *n*. 排泄物;粪便。**-tious** *a*.

ex·cres·cence [iksˈkresns; ɪksˋkrɛsns] *n*. 赘疣,瘤;多余的东西。

ex·cres·cen·cy [iksˈkresnsi; ɪksˋkrɛsnsɪ] *n*. = excrescence.

ex·cres·cent [iksˈkresənt; ɪksˋkresənt] *a*. 1. 赘生的,无用的,多余的。2.【语】赘音的。

ex·cre·ta [eksˈkriːtə; ɛksˋkritə] *n*.〔*pl*.〕【生理】排泄物

〔特指汗、尿、粪便等〕。

ex·crete [eks'kriːt; ɛks`krit] *vt*.【生理】排泄;分泌〔*cf*. secrete〕。

ex·cre·tion [eks'kriːʃən; ɛks`kriʃən] *n*. **1**. 排泄;分泌〔*cf*. secretion〕。**2**. 排泄物;分泌物。

ex·cre·tive [eks'kriːtiv; ɛks`kritɪv] *a*. 排泄的;分泌的,促进排泄[分泌]的;有排泄力的。

ex·cre·to·ry [eks'kriːtəri; ɛks`krɪˏtorɪ] *a*. 有排泄功能的,排泄的。~ **cells** 排泄细胞。~ **ducts** 排泄管。~ **organ** 排泄器官。

ex·cru·ci·ate [iks'kruːʃieit; ɪks`kruʃɪˏet] *vt*. **1**. 使苦恼[痛苦]。**2**. 〔古〕拷打;折磨。

ex·cru·ci·at·ing [iks'kruːʃieitiŋ; ɪks`kruʃɪˏetɪŋ] *a*. **1**. 使苦恼的;极痛苦的;难忍受的。**2**. 极度的,剧烈的。**-ly** *ad*.

ex·cru·ci·a·tion [iksˌkruːʃi'eiʃən; ɪks`kruʃɪ`eʃən] *n*. **1**. 苦恼,剧痛;折磨。**2**. 〔古〕酷刑,拷问。

ex·cul·pate ['ekskʌlpeit; `ɛkskʌlˏpet] *vt*. 开脱,申明…无罪,辩白。~ *oneself from a charge of theft* 辩白自己无盗窃嫌疑。

ex·cul·pa·tion [ˌekskʌl'peiʃən; ˏɛkskʌl`peʃən] *n*. 开脱,申明无罪;辩白;辩明无罪,昭雪。

ex·cul·pa·to·ry [iks'kʌlpətəri; ɪks`kʌlpəˏtorɪ] *a*. 开脱罪责的;辩明无罪的。

ex·cur·rent [eks'kʌrənt; ɛks`kɝənt] *a*. **1**. 流出的。**2**.【植】(茎)贯顶的,(树形)尖塔状的,(叶脉)延伸的。

ex·curse [iks'kəːs; ɪks`kɝs] *vi*. **1**. 旅行,游览。**2**. 说话[作文]离题。**3**. 〔罕〕徘徊。

ex·cur·sion [iks'kəːʃən; ɪk`skɝʒən] *n*. **1**. 短途旅行,游览。**2**. 旅行团,游览团。**3**. 离题。**4**.【机】冲程。【物】漂移,偏移。**5**.【医】肺的一个完全呼吸动作。*amplitude* ~【物】振幅偏移。*an* ~ *bus* [*train*] 游览汽车[列车]。*go on* [*for*] *an* ~ *to* = *make* [*take*] *an* ~ *to*. 到…去旅行。~ *rates* 游览收费率。**-al**, **-ary** *a*. **-ist** *n*. 短途旅行者,游览者。

ex·cur·sive [iks'kəːsiv; ɪks`kɝsɪv] *a*. **1**. 好旅行的。**2**. 容易离题的。**3**. 散漫的。*an* ~ *conversation* 漫谈。~ *reading* 涉猎性的阅读。**-ly** *ad*. **-ness** *n*.

ex·cur·sus [eks'kəːsəs; ɛks`kɝsəs] *n*. (*pl*. ~, ~*es*) **1**. 余论,补论;附注;补注;追记。**2**. 枝节的话,离题的话。

ex·cus·a·ble [iks'kjuːzəbl; ɪks`kjuzəbl̩] *a*. 情有可原的,可以饶恕的,可申辩的,不无理由的。**-bly** *ad*. **-ness** *n*.

ex·cus·a·to·ry [iks'kjuːzətəri; ɪks`kjuzəˏtorɪ] *a*. 辩解的,表示歉意的。

ex·cuse [iks'kjuːz; ɪks`kjuz] **I** *vt*. **1**. 原谅,宽恕。**2**. 免除,宽免。**3**. 为…辩解,表白;成为…的理由。*E- me*. 对不起〔离开、打断别人说话、表示不同意或举止失礼时的道歉话〕。*E- me for interrupting you*. = *E- my interrupting you*. 原谅我打扰你了。*If you'll kindly* ~ *me* 请原谅…。~ *sb*. *for being late* 原谅某人迟到。*Sickness* ~*s his absense*. 他是因病才缺席的。~ ***oneself*** **1**. 为自己辩解。**2**. 说声"对不起"就(要)走开 (*She* ~*d herself to us*. 她说声"对不起"就离开我们了)。~ ***oneself for*** 替自己辩解。~ ***oneself from*** 谢绝,托故推辞,申明不能。~ ***sb***. ***from*** (*attendance*) 允许某人不(出席)。**II** [-'kjuːs; -`kjus] *n*. **1**. 原谅,饶恕。**2**. 辩解;解释;理由。**3**. 托辞,借口。**4**. 〔*pl*.〕道歉,歉意。**5**. 请假条。*That is no* ~ *for your being late*. 那不能成为你迟到的理由。***an*** ~ ***for being*** [***existence***] 存在的理由。***be ill at making*** ~***s*** 不善辩解。***in*** ~ ***of*** 为…辩明。***make one's*** ~***s*** 辩解,推托。***make some*** ~ (***for***) 找借口。***without*** ~ 无故。

ex·cus·sio [eks'kʌʃiəu; ɛk`skʌʃɪo] *n*.【法】向保证人要求履行保证义务前,尽量设法从债务人要债。

ex-di·rec·to·ry [ˌeksdi'rektəri; ˏɛksdɪ`rɛkˏtorɪ] *a*. 〔英口〕电话簿上找不到的,未登记的。

ex·e·at ['eksiæt; `ɛksɪæt] *n*. 〔英〕**1**. 短期离校的许可。**2**. 牧师调换教区的许可。

ex·ec [ig'zek; ɪg`zɛk] *n*. **1**. 〔美口〕行政长官。**2**. 〔美口〕主任参谋,副舰长。

exec. = executive; executor.

ex·e·cra·ble ['eksikrəbl; `ɛksɪkrəbl̩] *a*. **1**. 该诅咒的,讨厌的,可恶的。**2**. (天气、食物等)恶劣的。**-bly** *ad*. **-ness** *n*.

ex·e·crate ['eksikreit; `ɛksɪˏkret] *vt*. **1**. 诅咒,咒骂。**2**. 憎恶,嫌恶。—*vi*. 咒骂。**-cra·tion** *n*. **1**. 诅咒,咒骂。**2**. 憎恶,嫌恶。**3**. 被诅咒的事物,嫌恶物;咒语。**-cra·tive**, **-cra·to·ry** *a*.

ex·e·cut·a·ble ['eksikjuːtəbl; `ɛksɪkjutəbl̩] *a*. 可执行的,可实行的,可以作成的。

ex·ec·u·tant [ig'zekjutənt; ɪg`zɛkjʊtənt] *n*. **1**. 实行者,执行者。**2**.【乐】演奏者。

ex·e·cute ['eksikjuːt; `ɛksɪˏkjut] *vt*. **1**. 实行,实施,执行;履行;贯彻,完成。**2**. 作成,制成(美术品等);奏(乐曲),演(剧)。**3**. 〔英〕让渡(财产);经过签名盖章等手续使(法律文件等)生效。**4**. 对…执行死刑,处决。~ *the captain's command* 执行船长命令。~ *a deed* 签名使契据生效。~ *fire*【军】开火。~ *one's* [*duties*] *office* 尽职。~ *the part of Hamlet* 扮演哈姆雷特。~ *a painting* [*statue*] 创作一幅画[一件雕像]。~ *one's promises* 践约,履行契约。~ *an estate* 让渡财产。~ *a will* 使遗嘱生效。***be summarily*** ~***d*** 就地正法,当场处决,立即处死。

ex·e·cu·tion [ˌeksi'kjuːʃən; ˏɛksɪ`kjuʃən] *n*. **1**. 实行,履行,执行;贯彻。**2**. 执行死刑;强制执行;执行命令。**3**. 作成,完成;签名盖印使法律文件生效;执行法律。**4**. 扮演,演奏,(演奏)技巧,手法。**5**. 成功,奏效;效果;(武器的)杀伤力。*forcible* ~ 强制执行。*The* ~ *leaves much to be desired, though the idea is good*. 设想虽好,执行起来很难如愿。~ *by hanging* 绞刑。***carry*** [***put***] ***into*** ~ 实行,实施。***do*** ~ 奏效,见效;(武器有)摧毁作用 (*He did great* ~ *among the cakes*. 他吃掉很多饼)。***Every shot did*** ~. 百发百中。***E- Dock***【英史】(泰晤士(*Thames*)河畔处决海盗等的)死刑码头。***make good*** ~【军】摧毁;使敌方受重大损失。***put to*** ~ 处死刑,执行死刑。~ **sale**【法】强制拍卖。

ex·e·cu·tion·er [ˌeksi'kjuːʃənə; ˏɛksɪ`kjuʃənɚ] *n*. **1**. 死刑执行人;刽子手。**2**. (遗嘱、判决等的)执行人。

ex·ec·u·tive [ig'zækjutiv; ɪg`zɛkjʊtɪv] **I** *a*. **1**. 执行的,实行的,实施的,有执行权力[手腕]的;行政(上)的。**2**. 行政官的;总经理的。~ *authorities* 行政当局。*an* ~ *branch* [*department*] **1**. 行政部门。**2**.【海】作战部。~ *committee* 执行委员会。~ *board* 理事会。~ *council* 咨询会议,行政会议,最高行政会议。*an* ~ *officer* = exec. **II** *n*. **1**. 行政部门;行政官;执行委员会。**2**.【美商】总经理,董事。***the*** (***Chief***) ***E-*** 〔美〕总统;州长;〔英〕国王。~ **agreement** 〔美〕(政府行政部门就例行事务同外国政府签订的)行政协定。**E- Mansion** 〔美〕总统官邸;州长官邸。**E- Order** 〔美〕总统命令 (=〔英〕*Order in Council*). ~ **part** 〔美〕(远离市中心的)商业机构办公区。~ **session** 〔美〕(参议院的)秘密会议。

ex·ec·u·tor [ig'zekjutə; ɪg`zɛkjətɚ] *n*. **1**.【法】指定遗嘱执行人。**2**. ['eksikjuːtə; `ɛksɪˏkjutɚ] 执行者。*a literary* ~ (遗嘱上指定的)遗著保管人。**-ship** [ig'zekjutəʃip; ɪg`zɛkjətɚˏʃɪp] *n*. (遗嘱)执行人的职务。

ex·ec·u·to·ri·al [igˌzekju'tɔːriəl; ɪgˏzɛkjə`torɪəl] *a*. 执行者的;执行上的。

ex·ec·u·to·ry [eg'zekjutəri; ɛg`zɛkjəˏtorɪ] *a*. **1**. 执行上的,行政上的;实施中的。**2**.【法】(契约等)将来有效的。

ex·ec·u·trix [ig'zekjutriks; ɪg`zɛkjətrɪks] *n*. (*pl*. ~*es*, ***-tri·ces*** [-traisiːz; -traɪsiz])【法】女遗嘱执行人。

ex·e·dra [ikˈsiːdrə, eksi-; ɪkˋsidrə, ˋɛksi-] *n*. (*pl*. *-drae* [-driː; -dri]) (古希腊的)对话间;座谈馆大楼;室外讨论会场。

ex·e·ge·sis [ˌeksiˈdʒiːsis; ˏɛksəˋdʒisɪs] *n*. (*pl*. *-ses* [-siːz; -siz]) (对《圣经》等宗教经典的)注释;注解。

ex·e·gete [ˈeksidʒiːt; ˋɛksəˏdʒit] *n*. (《圣经》等宗教经典的)注释学者,评注家。

ex·e·get·ic [ˌeksiˈdʒetik; ˏɛksəˋdʒɛtɪk] *a*. (关于《圣经》等宗教经典的)注释的。**-cal·ly** *ad*.

ex·e·get·ics [ˌeksiˈdʒetiks; ˏɛksəˋdʒɛtɪks] *n*. (《圣经》等宗教经典的)注释学,训诂学。

ex·em·pla [igˈzemplə; ɪgˋzɛmplə] *n*. exemplum 的复数。

ex·em·plar [igˈzemplə; ɪgˋzɛmplɚ] *n*. 模范;典型;标本,样本。

ex·em·pla·ry [igˈzempləri; ɪgˋzɛmplərɪ] *a*. 1. 值得模仿的,典型的,示范的。2. 惩戒性的。~ *conducts* 模范行为。~ *punishments* 作为惩戒的处罚。~ **damages** 【法】惩罚性赔偿〔超过实际损失的赔偿〕。**-ri·ly** *ad*. **-riness** *n*.

ex·em·pli·fi·ca·tion [igˌzemplifiˈkeiʃən; ɪgˏzɛmpləfəˋkeʃən] *n*. 1. 举例,例证,例示;模范,适例。2.【法】核正誊本,正本。

ex·em·pli·fy [igˈzemplifai; ɪgˋzɛmpləˏfaɪ] *vt*. (**-fied**) 1. 举例证明[解释];示范;作…的范例。2.【法】复印;制成核正誊本。

ex·em·pli gra·ti·a [igˈzemplaiˈgreiʃiə; ɪgˋzɛmplaɪˋgreʃɪə] 〔L.〕假如(= for example, 略作 e.g.)。

ex·em·plum [igˈzempləm; ɪgˋzɛmpləm] *n*. (*pl*. *-pla* [-plə; -plə]) 1. (中世纪布道时讲的)劝喻性故事。2. 例证,范例。

ex·empt [igˈzem*p*t; ɪgˋzɛm*p*t] I *vt*. 免除,豁免(*from*). ~ *sb*. *from an examination* 免考。II *a*. 被免除的,被豁免的(*from*). *commodities* ~ *from taxes* 免税商品。III *n*. 被免除(义务、责任)的人;免税人。

ex·empt·i·ble [igˈzem*p*tibl; ɪgˋzɛm*p*təbl̩] *a*. 可享豁免权的。

ex·emp·tion [igˈzempʃən; ɪgˋzɛmpʃən] *n*. 1. 免除;豁免,免税〔尤指部分所得税〕。2. 取得豁免的原因。~ *from taxation* 免税。

ex·en·te·rate [ekˈsentəreit; ɛkˋsɛntəˏret] *vt*. 1. 〔罕〕除去[取出]…的肠子;(蜘蛛)吐(丝)。2.【医】摘除(某器官)。**-ter·ation** [ekˌsentəˈreiʃən; ɛkˏsɛntəˋreʃən] *n*.

ex·e·qua·tur [ˌeksiˈkweitə; ˏɛksɪˋkwetɚ] *n*. 〔L.〕= Let him perform. (驻在国政府发给他国领事或商务代表的)许可证书。

ex·e·quies [ˈeksikwiz; ˋɛksɪkwɪz] *n*. exequy 的复数。

ex·e·quy [ˈeksikwi; ˋɛksɪkwɪ] *n*. 〔*pl*.〕葬礼,殡仪,出殡行列。

ex·er·cis·a·ble [ˈeksəsaizəbl; ˋɛksɚˏsaɪzəbl̩] *a*. 可行使的,可实行的,可运用的;可操作的,可履行的。

ex·er·cise [ˈeksəsaiz; ˋɛksɚˏsaɪz] I *n*. 1. (精力等的)运用,使用;实行;执行。2. 演习,操练;训练;〔常 *pl*.〕运动,体操。3. 习题,练习,课程;(声乐、器乐的)练习曲。4. 〔古〕礼拜;修行。5. 〔*pl*.〕〔美〕典礼,仪式;传统[习惯]做法。6. 学术辩论;(授学位前的)口试。*an* ~ *book* 练习簿。~ *in mathematics* 数学习题。~ *of the memory* 记忆力的锻炼。*graduating* ~*s* 毕业典礼。*gymnastic* ~*s* 体操,健身操。*military* ~*s* 军事演习,军事操练。*opening* ~*s* 开会仪式。*public* ~*s* (音乐等的)公演,大会。*a religions* ~ 礼拜。**do one's** ~ 做功课。**take** ~ 运动。II *vt*. 1. 实行;行使(职权等);使活动,运用;发挥(力量)。2. 练习,训练,操练。3. 使受(影响等)。4. 使烦恼,使操心,使忧虑。~ *a power* 行使权力。~ *pressure* 施加压力。~ *judgement* 运用判断力。— *vi*. 练习;运动。**be ~d about sth**. 为某事担忧[操心]。**~ oneself in** 练习…。

ex·er·cis·er [ˈeksəsaizə; ˋɛksɚsaɪzɚ] *n*. 1. 行使职权的人。2. 受训练者。3. 体育机械。4. 训练马的马夫。

ex·er·ci·ta·tion [egˌzəːsiˈteiʃən; ɪgˏzɝsəˋteʃən] *n*. 1. 〔古〕练习;训练;实习。2. (能力、权力等的)运用,行使。3. 演说练习;论文习作。

ex·ergue [ekˈsəːg; ɛkˋzɝg] *n*. 钱币等反面底线下刻记年月日或铸造局的地方。

ex·ert [igˈzəːt; ɪgˋzɝt] *vt*. 1. 用(力),尽(努力等),行使(职权等)。2. 发挥(威力等),使受(影响等)(*on*; *upon*). ~ *an influence* 施加影响。~ *all one's powers* 尽全力。~ **oneself** 努力,尽力,出力(~ *oneself to the utmost* 尽全力)。

ex·er·tion [igˈzəːʃən; ɪgˋzɝʃən] *n*. 1. 努力,尽力。2. 行使,运用。**be no ~ to** 不费力(*It's no ~ to him to lift the stone*. 他不用费力就把那块石头举起来)。**use [make, put forth] ~s** 尽力。

ex·er·tive [igˈzəːtiv; ɪgˋzɝtɪv] *a*. 努力的,费劲的,尽力的。

ex·es [ˈeksiz; ˋɛksɪz] *n*. 〔*pl*.〕〔口〕费用(= expenses)。

ex·e·unt [ˈeksiʌnt, -ənt; ˋɛksɪʌnt, -ənt] *vi*. 〔L.〕【剧】(某些演员)退场〔*cf*. exit〕。~ *omnes* [ˈɔmniːz; ˋɑmniz] 全体退场,全体下。

ex·fil·trate [eksˈfiltreit; ɛksˋfɪltret] *vi*., *vt*. 〔美军俚〕偷偷溜出(敌占区),偷越过(敌方封锁线)。

ex·fil·tra·tion [ˌeksfilˈtreiʃən; ˏɛksfɪlˋtreʃən] *n*. 偷偷越过(封锁线等)。

ex·fo·li·ate [eksˈfəulieit; ɛksˋfolɪˏet] *vt*. 像鳞片般剥下;使成片状。—*vi*. (岩面、皮肤等)剥落;【植】片状剥落;【动】鳞片样脱皮;【地】页状剥落;【医】表皮脱落。

ex·fo·li·a·tion [eksˌfəuliˈeiʃən; ɛksˏfolɪˋeʃən] *n*. 1. 剥落;【医】表皮剥落;剥落物。2. 分层(丝织品的)茸毛。

ex-GI [ˈeksdʒiːˈai; ˋɛksˏdʒiˋaɪ] *n*. 〔美俚〕复员军人。

exgra·tia [eksˈgreiʃiə; ɛksˋgreʃɪə] *a*., *ad*. 〔L.〕作为优惠的[地];【商】通融的[地]。

ex·hal·ant, ex·hal·ent [eksˈheilənt, egˈzei-; ɛksˋhelənt, ɛgˋze-] I *a*. 呼气的;发散(性)的,蒸发(性)的。II *n*. 呼吸气管;发散管,蒸发管。

ex·ha·la·tion [ˌeks*h*əˈleiʃən, egzə-; ˏɛksəˋleʃən, ˏɛgzə-] *n*. 1. 呼气;蒸发,(气味等的)发散;(怒气等的)发泄。2. (气体等)发散物;薄雾。

ex·hale [eksˈheil, egˈzeil; ɛksˋhel, ɪgˋzel] *vt*. 1. 呼(气)(*opp*. inhale)。2. 放出(蒸气);发散出(香味);发泄(怒气)。3. 使蒸发。4.【医】渗出。—*vi*. 1. 呼气。2. 散发,蒸发。

ex·haust [igˈzɔːst; ɪgˋzɔst] I *vt*. 1. 用尽,耗尽(资源等)。2. 排出(空气),抽空,空出(容器等);汲干。3. 提尽(可溶解的物质)。4. 使筋疲力尽,使疲惫不堪〔多用 ~ *oneself* 或被动语态〕。5. 彻底研究,详论。~ *the water of a well* 把井水抽干。~ *oneself walking* 走累。*feel quite* ~*ed* 感到累极了。*be* ~*ed by disease* 病得毫无力气。*be* ~*ed with toil* 劳累不堪。—*vi*. 1. 排出。2. 排气。II *n*. 1. 排出;抽空。2. 排气装置。3. (排出的)废气。*an* ~ *pipe* [*valve*] 排气管[阀]。~ *steam* [*gas*] 废气。

ex·haust·ed [igˈzɔːstid; ɪgˋzɔstɪd] *a*. 1. 耗尽的,枯竭的。2. 筋疲力尽的。~ *tea* 泡得无味的茶。*an* ~ *well* 枯井。

ex·haust·er [igˈzɔːstə; ɪgˋzɔstɚ] *n*.【机】排气机,抽风机。

ex·haust·i·bil·i·ty [igˌzɔːstəˈbiliti; ɪgˏzɔstəˋbɪlətɪ] *n*. 可空竭;可用尽。

ex·haust·i·ble [igˈzɔːstəbl; ɪgˋzɔstəbl] *a*. 可空竭的;可耗尽的,用得尽的。

ex·haust·ing [igˈzɔːstiŋ; ɪgˋzɔstɪŋ] *a*. 1. 使耗尽的。2. 使筋疲力尽的。**-ly** *ad*.

ex·haus·tion [igˈzɔːstʃən; ɪgˋzɔstʃən] *n*. 1. 枯竭,用尽。2. 排空,抽空。3. 疲惫,衰竭。4. 彻底的研究,详尽的论述。

ex·haus·tive [ig'zɔːstiv; ɪg`zɔstɪv] *a*. 1. (论述等)详尽的;无遗漏的,彻底的。2. 消耗的,使枯竭的。**-ly** *ad*. **-ness** *n*.

ex·haust·less [ig'zɔːstlis; ɪg`zɔstlɪs] *a*. 用不完的,不会枯竭的。**-ly** *ad*. **-ness** *n*.

ex·her·e·date [eks'herideit; ɛks`hɛrə,det] *vt*. 剥夺…的继承权。

ex·hib·it [ig'zibit; ɪg`zɪbɪt] **I** *vt*. 1. 表明,显示,显出。2. 陈列,展览;〔罕〕公演。3. 【法】提出(证据等)。4. 【医】〔废〕用(药)。~ *great bravery* 表现英勇。~ *a charge* 提出控诉。~ *a prize* 提供奖金。—*vi*. 开展览会;(产品、作品)展出。~ ***wares*** 〔美俚〕参加比赛,露一手。**II** *n*. 1. 展出;展览会。2. 陈列品,展览品。3. 【法】证件,证物。**-ant, -er** *n*. = exhibitor.

ex·hi·bi·tion [ˌeksi'biʃən; ˏɛksə`bɪʃən] *n*. 1. 表明,显示。2. 陈列,展览。3. 【法】(证据等的)提出。4. 展览会,展览品,陈列品。5. (英国大学)奖学金。6. 〔美〕(毕业典礼的)游艺会。*a competitive* ~ 评比会。*an art* ~ 美术展览会。~ *flight* 【空】表演飞行。~ *game* [*match*] 表演赛。***make an ~ of oneself*** 丢脸,出丑。***place*** [***put***] ***sth. on ~*** 展出某物。

ex·hi·bi·tion·er [ˌeksi'biʃənə; ˏɛksə`bɪʃənɚ] *n*. 1. 展出者。2. 〔英〕得到奖学金的大学生。

ex·hi·bi·tion·ism [ˌeksi'biʃənizəm; ˏɛksə`bɪʃənˏɪzəm] *n*. 1. 【医】下体裸露癖。2. 表现癖。

ex·hi·bi·tion·ist [ˌeksi'biʃənist; ˏɛksə`bɪʃənɪst] *n*. 1. 【医】下体裸露癖患者。2. 好表现的人。

ex·hib·i·tive [ig'zibitiv; ɪg`zɪbɪtɪv] *a*. 供展览的,起显示作用的;能表示…的 (*of*)。

ex·hib·i·tor [ig'zibitə; ɪg`zɪbɪtɚ] *n*. 1. 展出者,展出厂商;展览会参加者。2. 电影院老板[经理]。3. 奖学金捐赠人。4. 提供者,提出者〔= exhibiter〕。

ex·hib·i·to·ry [ig'zibitəri; ɪg`zɪbɪtorɪ] *a*. 1. 展览的。2. 显示的,表示的。

ex·hil·a·rant [ig'zilərənt; ɪg`zɪlərənt] **I** *a*. 令人高兴[兴奋]的。**II** *n*. 令人兴奋的东西,兴奋剂。

ex·hil·a·rate [ig'ziləreit; ɪg`zɪlə,ret] *vt*. 使高兴;使兴奋。**-d** *a*.

ex·hil·a·rat·ing [ig'ziləreitiŋ; ɪg`zɪlə,retɪŋ] *a*. 使人高兴的,令人兴奋的。*an ~ drink* 提神的饮料[指酒]。**-ly** *ad*.

ex·hil·a·ra·tion [igˌzilə'reiʃən; ɪgˏzɪlə`reʃən] *n*. 高兴,兴奋。**-ra·tive, -ra·to·ry** [ig'ziləreitiv, -rətəri; ɪg`zɪləretɪv, -rətorɪ] *a*. 令人高兴的,令人兴奋的。

ex·hort [ig'zɔːt; ɪg`zɔrt] *vt*. 1. 力劝;告诫;勉励。2. 倡导。—*vi*. 劝告。**-hor·ta·tion** *n*. 劝勉;告诫。**-hor·ta·tive, -hor·ta·to·ry** *a*. 劝勉的;告诫的。**-er** *n*. 劝勉者,告诫者,倡导者。

ex·hume [eks'hjuːm, ig'zjuːm; ɪk`sjum, ɪg`zjum] *vt*. 1. (从坟墓内)掘出(尸体等)。2. 〔喻〕发掘(被遗忘的东西)。**-hu·ma·tion** [ˌekshjuː'meiʃən; ɛkshju`meʃən] *n*. 发掘;掘墓。

ex·i·gence, -cy ['eksidʒəns, -si; `ɛksədʒəns, -sɪ] *n*. 1. 危急,紧急,迫切。2. 〔常 *pl*.〕迫切的需要,严酷的要求。3. 危机,危急关头,非常时期;急变;急事;困境。***in this extreme ~*** 在这危急关头。***meet the exigencies of the times*** 应付当前的危局。***suit the ~*** 应急。

ex·i·gent ['eksidʒənt; `ɛksədʒənt] *a*. 1. 紧急的,危急的。2. (生活)艰苦的;苛求的。*be ~ of money* 急需金钱。

ex·i·gi·ble ['eksidʒibl; `ɛksədʒəbl] *a*. 可要求的,可强索的 (*from*; *against*)。

ex·i·gu·i·ty [ˌeksi'gju(ː)iti; ˏɛksə`gjuətɪ] *n*. 微小;不足;贫乏。*an ~ of budget* 过少的预算。

ex·ig·u·ous [eg'zigjuəs; ɛg`zɪgjuəs] *a*. 细小的,微小的。*a merely ~ income* 微薄的收入。**-ly** *ad*. **-ness** *n*.

ex·ile ['eksail, egz-; `ɛksaɪl, `ɛkz-] **I** *n*. 1. 流放,放逐,充军;流亡,亡命。2. 充军者,流犯;流亡者;亡命者。***go into ~*** 逃亡。***live in ~*** 流亡(异乡)。**II** *vt*. 放逐,处…以流刑,使充军,发配。~ ***oneself*** 亡命(国外)。

ex·il·ian [eg'ziliən, ek'siliən; ɛg`zɪlɪən, ɛk`sɪlɪən], **exil·ic** [eg'zilik, ek's-; ɛg`zɪlɪk, ɛk`s-] *a*. 放逐的,亡命的。

ex·il·i·ty [eg'ziliti, ek'sil-; ɛg`zɪlətɪ, ɛk`sɪl-] *n*. 〔废〕微薄;微小;细微。

EXIM = Export-Import Bank 〔美〕进出口银行。

ex·int. = ex interest 无利息。

ex·ist [ig'zist; ɪg`zɪst] *vi*. 1. 存在,有。2. 生存;活着。~ ***actually*** 实际存在。~ ***as*** 作为…而存在,以…形态存在。~ ***in*** 存在于…中。~ ***on*** 靠…生活[生存]。

ex·ist·ence [ig'zistəns; ɪg`zɪstəns] *n*. 1. 存在,实在,继续存在。2. 生存,生活,生活方式。3. 实体,存在物,生物。*a precarious* [*hollow*] ~ 朝不保夕的[空虚的]生活。*a struggle for ~* 生存竞争。*be taxed out of ~* 因税重而绝迹。***bring*** [***call***] ***into ~*** 使发生,使产生,使成立。***come into ~*** 产生;成立。***in ~*** 现存的;存在的 (*the most miserable being in ~* 世上最不幸的人。*the only copy to be known in ~* 海内孤本)。***put out of ~*** 绝灭,使绝遗迹。

ex·ist·ent [ig'zistənt; ɪg`zɪstənt] **I** *a*. = existing. **II** *n*. 生存者,存在的事物。

ex·is·ten·tial [ˌegzis'tenʃəl; ˏɛgzɪs`tɛnʃəl] *a*. 1. 关于存在的,依据存在经验的。2. 【哲】存在主义的。3. 【逻】存在判断的。*an ~ proposition* 存在判断的命题。**-ism** *n*. 【哲】存在主义。**-ist** *n*. 【哲】存在主义者。

ex·ist·ing [ig'zistiŋ; ɪg`zɪstɪŋ] *a*. 存在的,现存的,实在的 (*opp*. extinct);现行的,目前的。*the ~ circumstances* [*condition*] 现状,现况。~ *equipments* 原[现]有设备。*the ~ situation* 当前形势。

ex·it ['eksit, 'egzit; `ɛksɪt, `ɛgzɪt] **I** *n*. 1. 出口,出路,太平门。2. 【电】引出端;排气管。3. 外出;离去;死亡;【剧】退场 (*opp*. entrance)。***make one's ~*** 退出;退场;去世。**II** *vi*. 1. 退出,离去。2. 死,去世。

ex·it ['eksit; `ɛksɪt] *vi*. 〔L.〕【剧】退场〔*cf*. exeunt; *opp*. enter〕.

ex li·bris [eks'laibris; ɛks`laɪbrɪs] *n*. 〔*sing*., *pl*.〕藏书签。

ex li·brist [eks'laibrist; ɛks`laɪbrɪst] *n*. 藏书签搜集者。

exo- *comb*. *f*. 表示"外","外部": *exo*ergic, *exo*skeleton.

ex·o·at·mos·phere [ˌeksəu'ætməsfiə; ˏɛkso`ætməsfɪr] *n*. 外大气圈,外逸层〔地球大气圈的最高层〕。

ex·o·bi·ol·o·gy [ˌeksəubai'ɔlədʒi; ˏɛksobaɪ`ɑlədʒɪ] *n*. 外(层)空(间)生物学〔探索地球之外存在生物的可能性的科学〕;宇宙生物学。**-o·log·i·cal** *a*. **-o·log·ist** *n*. 外空生物学家。

ex·o·carp ['eksəukɑːp; `ɛksə,kɑrp] *n*. 【植】外果皮(= epicarp)。

ex·o·cen·tric [ˌeksəu'sentrik; ˏɛkso`sɛntrɪk] *a*. 【语】离心结构的。

ex·o·coe·lom [ˌeksəu'siːləm; ˏɛkso`siləm] *n*. 【生】胚外体腔。

ex·o·crine ['eksəkrain; `ɛksəkraɪn] **I** *a*. 【医】外分泌的。**II** *n*. 外分泌腺。

ex·o·der·mis [ˌeksəu'dəːmis; ˏɛkso`dɝmɪs] *n*. 【植】外皮层。

ex·o·don·tia [ˌeksə'dɔnʃə; ˏɛksə`dɑnʃə] *n*. 拔牙术;拔牙学。

ex·o·don·tics [ˌeksəu'dɔntiks; ˏɛkso`dɑntɪks] *n*. 〔*pl*.〕【医】拔牙学(= exodontia)。**-don·tist** *n*. 拔牙专家。

ex·o·dus ['eksədəs; `ɛksədəs] *n*. 1. 离去,退出;(移民等大批)出国。2. 〔E-〕古代以色列人出埃及。3. 〔E-〕【圣】《出埃及记》。

ex·o·er·gic [ˌeksəu'əːdʒik; ˏɛkso`ɝdʒɪk] *a*. 【物】放能的。

ex of·fi·ci·o [ˌeks əˈfiʃiəu; ˏɛks əˋfiʃɪˏo] **I** *ad*. 依据职权地。**II** *adj*. 职权上的。

ex·og·a·my [eksˈɔgəmi; ɛksˋɑgəmɪ] *n*. 1. 异族结婚;外婚 (*opp*. endogamy)。2. 【生】异系交配。**-o·gam·ic, -a·mous** [ˈeksəuˈgæmik, ekˈsɔgəməs; ˋɛksoˋgæmɪk, ɛksˋɑgəməs] *a*.

ex·o·ge·nic [ˌeksəuˈdʒenik; ˏɛksoˋdʒɛnɪk] *a*. = exogenous.

ex·og·e·nous [ekˈsɔdʒinəs; ɛkˋsɑdʒɪnəs] *a*. 1. 外部发生的,外源的。2. 【生】外因的。**-ly** *ad*.

ex·on·er·ate [igˈzɔnəreit; ɪgˋzɑnəˏret] *vt*. 1. 证明…无罪;开释;昭雪。2. 免除(义务等),解除(责任等)。~ *sb. from blame* 宽免某人的罪责。

ex·on·er·a·tion [igˈzɔnəreiʃən; ɪgˏzɑnəˋreʃən] *n*. 免罪,昭雪;免除,解除。

ex·on·er·a·tive [igˈzɔnəreitiv; ɪgˋzɑnəˏretɪv] *a*. 1. 免罪的,免咎的。2. 免除(义务)的,解除(责任)的。

ex·oph·thal·mos [ˌeksɔfˈθælməs; ˏɛksɑfˋθælməs] *n*. 【医】眼球突出症(= exophthalmus, exophthalmia). **-thal·mic** *a*.

ex·op·lasm [ˈeksəuplæzəm; ˋɛksəˏplæzəm] *n*. 【生】外质。

ex·op·o·dite [ikˈsɔpədait; ɪkˋsɑpədaɪt] *n*. 【动】外肢,外肢节。

exor. = executor.

ex·o·ra·ble [ˈeksərəbl; ˋɛksərəbl̩] *a*. 心软的,容易说服的。

ex·or·bi·tance [igˈzɔːbitəns; ɪgˋzɔrbətəns] *n*. 1. (价格、收费、要求等的)过高,过度。2. (倾向、性情的)过分。3. 〔古〕无法无天;混乱。

ex·or·bi·tant [igˈzɔːbitənt; ɪgˋzɔrbətənt] *a*. 过高的,过度的,过分的。**-ly** *ad*.

ex·or·cise, ex·or·cize [ˈeksɔːsaiz; ˋɛksɔrˏsaɪz] *vt*. 驱除(妖魔等);从…驱魔 (*out of*; *from*). **-ment** *n*. **-r** *n*. = exorcist.

ex·or·cism [ˈeksɔːsizəm; ˋɛksɔrˏsɪzəm] *n*. 驱邪,袚魔。

ex·or·cist [ˈeksɔːsist; ˋɛksɔrsɪst] *n*. 袚魔师,大法师。

ex·or·di·al [ekˈsɔːdiəl; ɛkˋsɔrdɪəl] *a*. 绪言的,绪论的;开端的。

ex·or·di·um [ekˈsɔːdiəm; ɪgˋzɔrdɪəm] *n*. (*pl*. ~s, **-di·a** [-diə; -dɪə]) 1. (事物的)发端;开端。2. (论文的)绪言。

ex·o·skel·e·ton [ˌeksəuˈskelitn; ˏɛksoˋskɛlətn] *n*. 【解】外骨骼,皮骨骼。**-e·tal** [-tl; -tl̩] *a*.

ex·os·mo·sis [ˌeksɔsˈməusis; ˏɛksəsˋmosɪs] *n*. 外渗。**-mot·ic** [-ˈmɔtik; -ˋmɑtɪk] *a*.

ex·o·sphere [ˈeksəsfiə; ˋɛksəsfɪr] *n*. 【气】外逸层。

ex·o·spore [ˌeksəuˈspɔː; ˋɛksəsˏpɔr] *n*. 【植】1. 外生孢子;(孢子)外壁。2. 分生孢子(= conidium)。

ex·os·to·sis [ˌeksɔsˈtəusis; ˏɛksɑsˋtosɪs] *n*. (*pl*. **-ses** [-siːz; -siz]) 【医】外生骨疣。

ex·o·ter·ic [ˌeksəuˈterik; ˏɛksəˋtɛrɪk] *a*. 1. 外面的,外界的。2. 对外行开放的;公开的。3. 易懂的,通俗的;大众化的。~ *doctrine* 公开的教义[主义]。**-cal·ly** *ad*.

ex·o·ther·mic [ˌeksəuˈθəːmik; ˏɛksoˋθɝmɪk] *a*. 放热的 (= exothermal)。

ex·ot·ic [igˈzɔtik; ɪgˋzɑtɪk] **I** *a*. 1. 外来的,外国产的 (*opp*. indigenous)。2. 异国情调的;异乎寻常的;〔口〕奇异的;吸引人的。3. 脱衣舞的。4. 【物】极不稳定的,极难俘获的。**II** *n*. 1. 舶来品;外来物;外来品种;外来语。2. 脱衣舞女(~ dancer)。**-cal·ly** *ad*.

ex·ot·i·ca [igˈzɔtikə; ɪgˋzɑtɪkə] *n*. 〔*pl*.〕舶来品;古董,珍品;奇风异俗。

ex·ot·i·cism, ex·ot·ism [igˈzɔtisizəm, ˈegzətizəm; ɪgˋzɑtɪˏsɪzm, ˋɛgzətɪzəm] *n*. 1. 异国趣味,异国情调。2. 外来物;外来语。3. 外国化倾向;对外国事物的兴趣。

ex·o·tox·in [ˌeksəuˈtɔksin; ˏɛksoˋtɑksɪn] *n*. 【生化】(菌体)外毒素,外泌毒。

ex·o·tro·pi·a [ˌeksəuˈtrəupiə; ˏɛksəˋtropɪə] *n*. 【医】外斜视。

EXP = experimental.

exp. = expense; expiration; export; exportation; express.

ex·pand [iksˈpænd; ɪkˋspænd] *vt*. 1. 扩大(范围等);使增加;扩张;使膨胀。2. 展开,张开。3. 扩充,使发展;【释】扩编。4. 【数】展开。5. 详述,引伸,写出(缩体)。~ *one's knowledge* 增长知识。~ *the business* 扩展企业。*birds ~ing its wings* 展开双翼的飞鸟。—*vi*. 1. 扩大,扩张。2. 伸展,张开,延伸;膨胀 (*opp*. contract)。3. 扩充;发展(*into*)。4. 详述,引伸(*on*; *upon*)。5. 变得和蔼,感到舒畅。*The saplings have ~ed into trees*. 苗木已长成树。**-er, -or** *n*. 扩张器;扩管器;扩口器。

ex·pand·ed [iksˈpændid; ɪkˋspændɪd] *a*. 1. 膨胀的;被扩大的;被延伸的;(花瓣)展开的。2. 【印】宽体的 (= extended)。~ *wings* 展开的翅膀。*an ~ program* 一项扩大了的计划。~ **cinema** 舞台电影,综合演出〔电影与舞台剧混合的演出〕。~ **metal** 网形铁。~ **plastics** 泡沫塑料(亦称 foamed plastics)。~ **rubber** 多孔橡胶。

ex·panse [iksˈpæns; ɪkˋspæns] *n*. 1. 辽阔,广袤,太空,穹苍。2. 膨胀,扩张,展开。*the boundless ~ of the Pacific* 浩瀚无垠的太平洋。*the blue* ~碧空。

ex·pan·si·bil·i·ty [iksˌpænsəˈbiliti; ɪkˏspænsəˋbɪlətɪ] *n*. 扩张性;膨胀性,延伸性。

ex·pan·si·ble [iksˈpænsəbl; ɪkˋspænsəbl̩] *a*. 易扩张的;能延伸的;能膨胀的。*the ~ force of ice* 冰的膨胀力。

ex·pan·sile [iksˈpænsail; ɪkˋspænsaɪl] *a*. 易膨胀的;膨胀性的。~ *movement* 膨胀运动。

ex·pan·sion [iksˈpænʃən; ɪkˋspænʃən] *n*. 1. 张开,伸展。2. 扩大;扩建;展开;发展。3. 广袤,辽阔。4. 扩张物,扩大部分。5. (讲题等的)详述,阐述。6. 扩张。7. 【物】膨胀;【数】展开(式)。*the ~ of currency* 通货膨胀。*territorial ~* (= ~ of territory) 领土扩张。*arms* [*armaments*, *military*] ~ 扩张军备。*the rate of ~* 膨胀率。*volume ~*体积膨胀;响度扩大。~ **joint** 【建】伸缩(接)缝。**-ism** *n*. 1. (通货的)膨胀论。2. (领土等的)扩张主义。**-ist** 1. 通货膨胀论者,扩张主义者。2. 扩张主义的。

ex·pan·sion·ar·y [iksˈpænʃənəri; ɪkˋspænʃənɛrɪ] *a*. 引向膨胀的;扩大性的;扩张性的。

ex·pan·sive [iksˈpænsiv; ɪkˋspænsɪv] *a*. 1. 易扩张的,膨胀性的。2. 辽阔的,浩瀚的。3. 胸襟开阔的,豁达的;滔滔不绝的。4. 豪华的。5. 【心】自大狂的;趾高气扬的。*an ~ forehead* 宽阔的前额。~ *delusion* 自大狂。**-ly** *ad*. **-ness** *n*.

ex par·te [ˈeksˈpɑːti; ɛksˋpɑrtɪ] 〔L.〕偏袒的,单方面的;片面的。

ex·pa·ti·ate [eksˈpeiʃieit; ɛkˋspeʃɪˏet] *vi*. 1. 细说,详述 (*on*; *upon*). 2. 漫游。**-a·tion** *n*. [eksˌpeiʃiˈeiʃən; ɛkˏspeʃɪˋeʃən] **-a·to·ry** *a*.

ex·pa·tri·ate I [eksˈpætrieit; ɛksˋpetrɪˏet] *vt*. 1. 把…逐出国外。2. 〔~ oneself〕移居国外,放弃国籍。—*vi*. 放弃国籍;移居国外。**II** [eksˈpætriit; ɛkˋspætrɪɪt] *a*. 被逐出国外的,移居国外的。**III** [eksˈpætriit; ɛkˋspetrɪɪt] *n*. 被逐出国外的人,移居国外的人。

ex·pa·tri·a·tion [eksˌpætriˈeiʃən; ɛksˏpetrɪˋeʃən] *n*. 1. 放逐国外。2. 移居国外;【法】脱离原国籍。

ex·pect [iksˈpekt; ɪkˋspɛkt] *vt*. 1. 期待,预期,预料 (*sth*., *that*). 2. 指望[要求]某人做某事 (*to do*),期望某人如何;预期某事(发生、出现等)。3. (对某人)有…期望[要求] (*sth. of sb*.) . 4. 〔口〕想,料想,以为。*I ~ed you yesterday*. 我当你昨天会来的。*Don't ~ me*. 别指望我(来)吧。*I will do what is ~ed of me*. 我当尽我的本分。*I ~ (that) he will come*. 我想他会来

E

的。*I shall not* ～ *you till I see you*. 便中随时请来好了。～ *sb. home at six o'clock* 期望某人六点钟回家。*That must be* ～*ed*. 那是当然的。*I* ～ *to go there*. 我想到那里去。*Will he come today?* — *I* ～ [*don't* ～] *so*. 他今天会回来吗? ——我想会来[不会来]。— *vi*. 1.〔废〕等待;逗留; 2.〔口〕怀孕。***as one might*** ～ 人们预料得到。***as was*** ～***ed*** (= ***as might have been*** ～***ed***) 果不其然,不出所料,如预期的那样。***be*** ～***ing*** 〔口〕(不久)要生孩子了〔*cf*. expectant〕。～ ***an act of God*** 〔美俚〕希望生个孩子。

ex·pect·ance, ex·pect·an·cy [iks'pektəns, -ənsi; ɪk`spectəns, -ənsɪ] *n*. 1. 预期,期望,期待。2. 期望的东西。*life* ～估计寿命。***be on the very tiptoe of*** ～ 焦急地等待。

ex·pect·ant [iks'pektənt; ɪk`spektənt] I *a*. 1. 预期的,期望的;期待的。2.【法】推定的,有继承权而期待占有的;【医】期待自然复原的。*an* ～ *attitude* 观望态度。*an* ～ *mother* 孕妇。*an* ～ *method* [*treatment*]【医】自然疗法,期待疗法。II *n*. 1. 期待者。2. 预定任用者。3.【数】期望值。**-ly** *ad*.

ex·pec·ta·tion [ˌekspek'teiʃən; ˏɛkspɛk`teʃən] *n*. 1. 期待,期望;所希望的东西。2.〔*pl*.〕前程,(发迹,继承遗产的)希望。3. 估计。4. 期待疗法。5.【数】期望值。***against*** [***contrary to***] ～出乎预料。***answer*** [***meet***] ***sb.'s*** ～ (= ***come up to sb.'s*** ～) 不负所望。***beyond*** ～ 料想不到地。～ ***of life*** 平均寿命 (= life expectancy)。***fall short of*** [***do not come up to***] ***sb.'s*** ～ 辜负期望;使人失望。***have*** [***entertain, cherish***] ***great*** ～***s*** 抱有极大的希望。***in*** ～指望中的。***in*** ～ ***of*** 预料着,指望着。***a man of*** (***great***) ～***s*** 有承受巨大遗产或取得高位希望的人。

ex·pec·ta·tive [iks'pektətiv; ɪk`spektətɪv] *a*. 期待中的;等待的。

ex·pec·to·rant [iks'pektərənt; ɪk`spɛktərənt] I *a*.【医】祛痰的。II *n*. 祛痰剂。

ex·pec·to·rate [eks'pektəreit; ɛk`spɛktəˏret] *vt*. 咳出,吐(痰、血、唾液等)。— *vi*. 吐痰,咳痰。～ ***phlegm*** [***blood***] 吐痰[血]。

ex·pec·to·ra·tion [eksˌpektə'reiʃən; ɛkˏspɛktə`reʃən] *n*. 1. 吐痰,咳(出)痰。2. 咳出物;唾液。

ex·pe·di·ence, ex·pe·di·en·cy [iks'piːdiəns, -ənsi; ɪk`spidɪəns, -ənsɪ] *n*. 1. 便利,方便;得策,上策。2. 权宜手段[办法];权宜之计。

ex·pe·di·ent [iks'piːdiənt; ɪk`spidɪənt] I *a*. 1. 方便的,便利的,有利的;得当的,适当的。2. 权宜的,临时的。*Do whatever is* ～. 权宜处置,怎么方便就怎么办。*measures* ～ *for public welfare* 有利公共福利的办法。*It is* ～ *that he should go*. 他最好还是走。II *n*. 应急办法,权宜手段。*He is full of* [*fruitful in*] ～*s*. 他办法多。*a temporary* ～ 临时办法。*resort to an* ～ 使手段。

ex·pe·di·en·tial [iksˌpiːdi'enʃəl; ɛksˏpidɪ`ɛnʃəl] *a*. 权宜之计的,为了便利的。*an* ～ *policy* 权宜之策。

ex·pe·dite ['ekspidait; `ɛkspɪˏdaɪt] I *vt*. 1. 加快,促进;迅速做好(工作等)。2. 派遣;发送,急送。II *a*. 1. 没有阻碍的。2. 迅速的。3. 便当的。**-ly** *ad*.

ex·pe·dit·er ['ekspidaitə; `ɛkspɪˏdaɪtɚ] *n*. 快干者,促进派,(企业和国家急要工程的)督办员,计划督办专员。

ex·pe·di·tion [ˌekspi'diʃən; ˏɛkspɪ`dɪʃən] *n*. 1. 远征,征伐;探险。2. 远征队,探险队。3. 迅速。*the Northern E-* (中国)北伐战争。*an arctic* ～北极探险。*go* [*start*] *on an* ～ 去远征[探险]。*join an* ～ 参加远征队[探险队]。***go on a fishing*** ～ 〔美〕摸底,试探一下。***use*** ～ 从速,赶快。***with*** ～ 赶紧。

ex·pe·di·tion·ar·y [ˌekspi'diʃənəri; ˏɛkspɪ`dɪʃənˏɛrɪ] I *a*. 远征的;探险的。*an* ～ *force* 远征军。II *n*. 远征队员,探险队员。

ex·pe·di·tious [ˌekspi'diʃəs; ˏɛkspɪ`dɪʃəs] *a*. 迅速的,急速的,敏捷的,效率高的。*an* ～ *messenger* 急使。～ *measures* 应急手段。**-ly** *ad*. **-ness** *n*.

ex·pel [iks'pel, eks-; ɪk`spɛl, ɛks-] *vt*. (**-ll-**) 1. 赶出;驱逐;开除。2. 射出(子弹等),排出(气体等)。*He was* ～*led from the school*. 他被学校开除了。*bullets* ～*led from the gun* 从枪中射出的子弹。**-la·ble** *a*. 可驱逐的,应开除的,可击退的。**-ler** *n*. 驱逐者,开除者。**-lee** *n*. 被驱逐出国者。

ex·pel·lant, ex·pel·lent [iks'pelənt; ɪk`spɛlənt] I *a*. 驱逐的,有驱除力的。II *n*. 驱除剂,排毒剂。*mosquito* ～驱蚊药水。

ex·pend [iks'pend; ɪk`spend] *vt*. 1. 使用,花费(金钱、劳力、时间等);用光,耗尽。2.【海】把(暂时不用的绳)绕在桅杆上。— *vi*.〔罕〕花钱。～ ***time*** [***money***] ***in*** [***on***] 把时间[金钱]花费在…上。★ ～ 与 spend 是同义词,"花钱"普通用 spend money。

ex·pend·a·ble [iks'pendəbl; ɪk`spɛndəbḷ] I *a*. 1. 可消费的,可消耗的。2.【军】消耗性的。～ *equipment* 使用一次的设备。～ *pattern material* 可熔化模型材料。II *n*.〔常 *pl*.〕(战争中的)消耗品,牺牲者。

ex·pend·i·ture [iks'penditʃə; ɪk`spɛndɪtʃɚ] *n*. 1. (时间、劳力、金钱等的)支出,花费。2. 消费;开销;费用,经费。3. 支出额,消费额。*a useless* ～ *of time* 时间的浪费。*annual* ～ 岁出。*current* ～ 经常费。*extraordinary* ～ 临时支出。*ordinary* ～ 经常支出。*revenue and* ～ 收支。

ex·pense [iks'pens; ɪk`spɛns] *n*. 1. (时间、精力、金钱等的)消耗,花消,消费。2. (无形的)损失;牺牲。3.〔常 *pl*.〕费用;(额外)开支。4. 费钱的东西。*household* [*domestic*] ～*s* 家用。*sundry* [*miscellaneous*] ～*s* 杂费。*running* [*current*] ～*s* 经常费。*incidental* ～*s* 临时费。*school* ～*s* 学费。*travelling* ～*s* 旅费。***at a great*** ～ 以巨大费用。***at any*** ～无论花费多少。***at his*** [***her, my***] ～嘲弄他[她,我等] (*They have a good laugh at his* ～. 他们嘲笑他)。***at one's own*** [***public***] ～自[公]费 (*He went abroad at his own* ～. 他自费出国)。***at the*** ～ ***of*** 以…为代价;由…出钱;牺牲… (*He attained his goal at the* ～ *of others*. 他牺牲别人来达到自己的目的)。***cut down*** [***curtail***] ***one's*** ～***s*** 节省开支。***free of*** ～免费。***go to*** ～ 花钱,用钱,出钱。***meet one's*** ～***s*** 足够开支。***put sb. to*** ～使人花钱,使某人负担用费,使破财。***regardless of*** ～不计钱财,不惜花费。***spare no*** ～不惜花费。～ **account** 支出账目;报销账单。～ **allowance** 交际费,额外开支。

ex·pen·sive [iks'pensiv; ɪk`spɛnsɪv] *a*. 费钱的;昂贵的,高价的;浪费的,奢侈的 (*opp*. inexpensive). *an* ～ *mode of living* 奢侈的生活方式。*That will come very* ～. 那是很费钱的。**-ly** *ad*. **-ness** *n*.

ex·pe·ri·ence [iks'piəriəns; ɪk`spɪrɪəns] I *n*. 1. 经验,体验。2. 见识,经历,阅历。3.〔*pl*.〕【宗】灵性的感受。*E- is the mother of science* [*wisdom*]. 〔谚〕经验为学问之母。*an unpleasant* ～一次不愉快的经历。*a man of vast worldly* ～富有处世经验的人。*have* ～ *with* (*persons*) 和(某些人)打交道有经验。～ *in teaching* 教学经验。***E- keeps a clear school***. 经验学校学费高;苦头吃得多,学问也增多。***E- teaches***. = ***E- does it***. 经验使人聪明。II *vt*. 1. 经验,体验。2. 感受,经历。3. (从经验中)知道,发现。*be thoroughly* [*poorly*] ～*d in* 在…方面十分有[缺乏]经验。～ *great pleasure* 觉得很快活。～ ***religion*** 〔美俚〕获得信仰。～ **meeting**【宗】宗教座谈会,灵性交流会;祈祷。～ **table** (根据人寿保险公司资料拟出的)寿命估计表,死亡率统计表。**-a·ble** *a*. **-less** *a*. **-r** *n*.

ex·pe·ri·enced [iks'piəriənst; ɪk`spɪrɪənst] *a*. 有经验的,经验丰富的;老练的,熟练的。*have an* ～ *eye* 有眼光,看得准。

ex·pe·ri·en·tial [iksˌpiəriˈenʃəl; ɪkˏspɪrɪˋɛnʃəl] *a*. 经验(上)的,由经验得到的,来自经验的,从经验出发的。～ *philosophy* 经验哲学。**-ism** *n*. 经验主义。**-ist** *n*. 经验主义者。**-ly** *ad*.

ex·per·i·ment [iksˈperimənt; ɪkˋspɛrəmənt] **I** *n*. 实验;试验;尝试 (*of*). *a scientific* ～ 科学试验,科学仪器设备。*a new* ～ *in education* 教育上的新尝试。～ *farm* 试验农场。～ *station* 试验站。***make*** [***try***] ***an*** ～ ***on*** [***in with***] 做…实验。***prove by*** ～ 实验证明。**II** [-ment, -mɛnt] *vi*. 做实验,进行试验;尝试 (*on*; *with*; *in*). **-a·tive** *a*. **-a·tor, -er, -or** *n*. 实验者。

ex·per·i·men·tal [eksˌperiˈmentl; ɪkˏspɛrəˋmɛntḷ] **I** *a*. 实验(上)的;试验性的;经验上的。～ *parthenogenesis* 人工单性生殖,人工孤雌生殖。*an* ～ *farm* 试验农场。～ *psychology* 实验心理学。～ *science* 实验科学。**II** *n*. 〔*pl*.〕实验性的东西。**-ism** *n*. 实验主义,经验主义。**-ist** *n*. 实验者,试验者;实验主义者,经验主义者。**-ize** *vi*. 实验。**-ly** *ad*.

ex·per·i·men·ta·tion [eksˈperimenˈteiʃən; ɛkˏspɛrəmɛnˋteʃən] *n*. 1. 实验,试验。2. 实验法。

ex·pert [ˈekspəːt; ˋɛkspɝt] **I** *n*. 1. 老手,熟手,内行,专家 (*in*; *at*); 技师。2.【法】鉴定人。3.【军】特等射手。*a language* [*linguistic*] ～ 语言学专家。*a mining* ～ = *an* ～ *on mining* 矿山技师。**II** *a*. 1. 熟练的,老练的。2. 精巧的,巧妙的。(*in*; *at*; *with*). 3. 专家的,内行的,专门的。*an* ～ *accountant* 会计师。*an* ～ *botanist* 植物学专家。～ *evidence*【法】鉴定人的证明,鉴定。*an* ～ *witness*【法】鉴定者。***be*** ～ ***in*** [***at***]…在…方面是专家。**-y** *ad*. **-ness** *n*.

ex·pert·ise [ˌekspəˈtiːz; ˏɛkspɚˋtiz] *n*. 1. 专门技能,专门知识。2. 专家评价,鉴定。

ex·pert·ize [ˈekspətaiz; ˋɛkspɚˏtaɪz] *vt*., *vi*. (对…)提出专业性意见[鉴定]。

ex·per·to cre·di·te [eksˈpəːtəuˈkrediti; ɛksˋpɝtoˋkrɛdəti] 〔L.〕相信有经验者的话 (= believe in the expert)。

ex·pi·a·ble [ˈekspiəbl; ˋɛkspɪəbḷ] *a*. 可赎的,可抵偿的。

ex·pi·ate [ˈekspieit; ˋɛkspɪˏet] *vt*. 赎,抵偿,补偿。～ *oneself* 赎罪,偿罪。～ *sin* (*a crime*) 赎罪,赎前愆。**-a·tion** *n*. 赎罪,消孽 (～ *of the sins of the dead* 超度死者。*in* ～ *of one's sin* 赎罪)。**-a·tor** *n*. 赎罪者。**-a·to·ry** *a*. 赎罪的。

ex·pi·ra·tion [ˌekspaiəˈreiʃən; ˏɛkspəˋreʃən] *n*. 1. 呼出空气,呼气〔*cf*. inspiration〕; 呼出物,嘘出的声音。2.〔古〕断气,死亡。3. 终止,届满,截止,满期 (*of*)。*at the* ～ *of three years* 三年期满后。*at the* ～ *of a contract* 合同到期后。

ex·pir·a·to·ry [iksˈpaiərətəri; ɪkˋspaɪrəˏtorɪ] *a*. 吐气的,呼气的。～ *movement* 深呼吸运动。

ex·pire [iksˈpaiə, eks-; ɪkˋspaɪr, ɛks-] *vi*. 1. 吐气,呼气。2. 断气,死;消灭。3. 满期,届满。*The lease* ～*s in a month*. 租约再过一个月就到期了。—*vt*.〔罕〕吐出;排出。

ex·pir·ee [ˌekspəˈriː; ɛˏkspaɪˋri] *n*. = emancipist.

ex·pi·ry [iksˈpaiəri; ɪkˋspaɪrɪ] *n*. 1. 终止;完满;满期。2. 呼气。3.〔古〕死亡,断气。***at the*** ～ ***of the term*** 期满。

ex·pis·cate [eksˈpiskeit; ɛkˋspɪsket] *vt*.〔Scot.〕查出,探出;搜出。**-ca·tion** *n*. **-ca·to·ry** *a*.

ex·plain [iksˈplein; ɪkˋsplen] *vt*. 1. 说明,阐明;解释。2. 说明…的理由,替…辩解。～ *one's behaviour* 为自己的行为作辩解。*Please* ～ *yourself*. 1. 请你把意思说清楚。2. 请你讲讲你为什么要那样做。—*vi*. 1. 说明,阐明。2. 辩解。～ ***away*** 巧辩过去,把…解释清楚,把…解释过去。～ ***oneself*** 为自己的行为作解释;说明自己心意[立场]。～ ***...as...*** 把…解释为。**-a·ble** *a*. **-er** *n*.

ex·pla·na·tion [ˌekspləˈneiʃən; ˏɛkspləˋneʃən] *n*. 1. 解释,注释;说明。2. 辩解,剖白。3. (消除误会后)和解。*notes in* ～ 注解。***by way of*** ～ 作说明。***come to an*** ～ ***with sb***. 与人交谈后消除了误会。***in*** ～ ***of*** 来解释,来说明。

ex·plan·a·tory [iksˈplænətəri; ɪkˋsplænəˏtorɪ] *a*. 解释的,说明的;辩明的 (*of*). ～ *notes* 注释。～ **title**【影】字幕。**-a·to·ri·ly** *ad*. **-a·to·ri·ness** *n*.

ex·plant [eksˈplɑːnt; ɛkˋsplænt] *vt*.【医】外植,移植。—*n*. 外植体。**-plan·ta·tion** [-plɑːnˈteiʃən; -plænˋteʃən] *n*.

ex·ple·tive [eksˈpliːtiv; ˋɛksplitɪv] **I** *a*. 补足的,附加的;多余的。**II** *n*. 1. 虚词,语助词;(无意义的)惊叹语;赌咒发誓语。2. 填补物,附加物。

ex·ple·to·ry [ˈeksplətəri; ˋɛkspləˏtorɪ] *a*. 补充的,附加的,多余的。

ex·pli·ca·ble [ˈeksplikəbl; ˋɛksplɪkəbḷ] *a*. 可解释的,可说明的,可辩明的 (*opp*. inexplicable).

ex·pli·can·dum [ˌeksplәˈkændəm; ˏɛkspləˋkændəm] *n*. (*pl*. ***-da*** [-də; -də]) (哲学讨论中)待解决的术语或陈述。

ex·pli·cate [ˈeksplikeit; ˋɛksplɪˏket] *vt*. 1. (详尽地)解释,说明,阐明。2. 引申,发展(概念等)。

ex·pli·ca·tion [ˌeksplìˈkeiʃən; ˏɛksplɪˋkeʃən] *n*. 1. 解释,说明;(观点的)阐明。2. (花等的)张开。

ex·pli·ca·tion de texte [ˌekspliːkɑːˈsjuŋ dəˈtekst; ˏɛksplɪkɑˋsuŋ dəˋtɛkst]〔F.〕对文艺作品各部分的精细分析。

ex·pli·ca·tive, -to·ry [eksˈplikətiv, eksˈplikətəri; ɛksplɪˏketɪv, ˋɛksplɪkəˏtorɪ] *a*. 阐明意义的;说明的,解释的。

ex·plic·it [iksˈplisit; ɪkˋsplɪsɪt] *a*. 1. 明白的,明确的 (*opp*. implicit). 2. 直爽的,不隐讳的。3. 显然可见的。4. (租金等)须直接付款的。～ *definition*【数】显定义。～ *cost* 直接以货币支付的成本。～ *function*【数】显函数。*an* ～ *statement* 明确的声明。～ *faith* [*belief*] 彻底了解教义后的明确的信仰。*be* ～ *in one's statement* 率直陈述。**-ly** *ad*. **-ness** *n*.

ex·plode [ikˈspləud; ɪkˋsplod] *vt*. 1. 使爆炸,爆破;使爆发。2. 破除(迷信等),打破,推翻(学说等)。3. 发(p, b, t 等)爆裂音。—*vi*. 爆炸,爆破,爆发;激发,迅猛地发展。*an exploding population* 激增的人口。*exploding atom* 爆裂原子。～ *with laughter* 哄笑。

ex·plod·ed [iksˈpləudid; ɪkˋsplodɪd] *a*. 爆炸[爆破]了的;(理论、学说等)被推翻的,(迷信等)被打破的。～ **view** (机器的)部件分解图。

ex·plod·er [iksˈpləudə; ɪkˋsplodɚ] *n*. 1. 爆炸者,爆破手。2. 爆炸物。3. 信管,雷管;爆炸,爆炸装置;放炮器;清除器。

ex·ploit[1] [ˈeksplɔit; ˋɛksplɔɪt] *n*. 功绩,功劳,勋绩。*the* ～ *of the famous heroes* 著名英雄们的丰功伟绩。

ex·ploit[2] [ikˈsplɔit; ɪkˋsplɔɪt] *vt*. 1. 利用;利用…谋私利。2. 剥削。3. 开发,开拓。～ *an office* [*a business*] 利用职权(以营私舞弊)。～ *the coal fields* 开采煤田。**-a·ble** *a*. 能利用的,能开发的;可剥削的。**-age** *n*. 利用,开发;剥削。**-er** *n*. 剥削者;开发者。

ex·ploi·ta·tion [ˌeksplɔiˈteiʃən; ˏɛksplɔɪˋteʃən] *n*. 1. 利用,非法利用。2. 剥削。3. 开发,开拓。4. 宣传,广告。～ *of oil wells* 利用油井资源。～ *of man by man* 人剥削人。

ex·ploit·ee [ˌeksplɔiˈtiː; ˏɛksplɔɪˋti] *n*. 被剥削者;被榨取者。

ex·ploi·(ta·)tive [ikˈsplɔi(tə)tiv; ɛkˋsplɔɪ(tə)tɪv] *a*. 1. 开发的。2. 剥削的;利用的〔特指天然资源的滥用〕。

ex·plo·ra·tion [ˌeksplɔːˈreiʃən; ˏɛkspləˋreʃən] *n*. 1. 勘探,探测,测定。2. 探险;调查。3.【医】(伤处等的)探查;

(伤情)探查术。*pressure* ～ 压力分布测定。*space* ～ 星际探索,宇宙空间探索。

ex·plor·a·tive [iks'plɔːrətiv; ɪk`splɔrətɪv], **ex·plor·atory** [iks'plɔːrətəri; ɪk`splorə,torɪ] *a*. **1**. 勘探的;探测的。**2**. 爱探究的,爱调查的。～ *operation on stomach* 开腹检查。

ex·plore [iks'plɔː; ɪk`splɔrɪ] *vt*. **1**. 勘探,探测;测定,在…探险。**2**. 调查。**3**.【医】探查(伤处等);探索,研究。～ *the Antarctic regions* 南极地区考察[探险]。—*vi*. 探测;考察;探险;【医】探查。*an exploring party* [*team*] 探测队,考察队。*an exploring tube*【医】探测管。

ex·plor·er [iks'plɔːrə; ɪk`splorə] *n*. **1**. 探测员,探险者。**2**. 探矿机,探测线圈;【医】探针;【空】搜索机。**an Arctic** ～ 北极探险家。

ex·plo·sim·e·ter [ˌikspləu'simitə; ˏɛksplo`sɪmətə] *n*. 爆炸测定计。

ex·plo·sion [iks'pləuʒən; ɪk`sploʒən] *n*. **1**. 爆炸,炸裂;爆炸声。**2**. 扩张,激增;(感情等的)爆发。**3**.【语】爆破。*air* [*subsurface*] ～ 空中[地下]爆炸。*nuclear* ～ 核爆炸。*a population* ～ 人口爆炸。～ **chamber** (发动机的)燃烧室。～ **gas turbine** 爆燃式燃气轮机。

ex·plo·sive [iks'pləusiv; ɪk`splosɪv] **I** *a*. **1**. 爆炸(性)的,爆发(性)的。**2**. 暴躁的。**3**.【语】爆破音的。**4**. 极易引起争论的。*Gunpowder is* ～. 火药容易爆炸。*an* ～ *substance* 易爆炸物。*an* ～ *temper* 暴躁易怒的性格。**II** *n*. **1**. 易爆炸物,炸药,爆破器材。**2**.【语】爆破音(p, b, t, d, k, g 等音)。*packages of* ～*s* 炸药包。～ **bullet** 炸裂弹。～ **compartment** 炸药室。～ **engine** 爆发内燃机。～ **forming** 爆炸成型。～ **rivet** 炸药铆钉。～ **train** 导火药,分段装药,传爆系统。**-ly** *ad*. **-ness** *n*.

ex·po ['ekspə; `ɛkspə] *n*.〔美口〕博览会,展览会。

ex·po·nent [eks'pəunənt; ɪk`sponənt] **I** *n*. **1**. (学说、理论等的)代表者,倡导者,拥护者。**2**. 典型,样品。**3**. 说明者,解说员;演奏者。**4**.【数】指数;幂。*an* ～ *of Darwin's theory* 达尔文理论的倡导者。*an* ～ *of self-education* 自学成材的代表。*fractional* ～【数】分数指数。**II** *a*. 阐述的,说明的,讲解的。

ex·po·nen·tial [ˌekspəu'nenʃəl; `ɛkspo`nɛnʃəl] **I** *a*. 指数的,幂的。～ *curve* 指数曲线。～ *function* 指数函数。～ *sum* 指数和,三角和。**II** *n*. 指数。*complex* ～ 复指数。**-ly** *ad*.

ex·po·nen·ti·a·tion [ˌekspəunənʃi'eiʃən; ˏɛkspoˏnɛnʃɪ`eʃən] *n*.【数】取幂。

ex·port ['ekspɔːt; `ɛksport] **I** *n*. **1**. 输出,出口。**2**. 出口货;〔*pl*.〕输出额。**3**.【无】呼叫,振铃。*an* ～ *bill* 出口单。～ *business* 出口事业。～ *duty* [*tax*] 出口税。*an excess of* ～*s* 出超。～ *trade* 出口贸易。～ *trader* 出口商人。～ *surplus* 出超。*invisible* ～*s* 无形输出〔指船舶,保险、国外投资等的收入〕。***be engaged in*** ～ 做出口贸易。**II** *a*. 输出的,出口的。**III** [iks'pɔːt; ɪks`port] *vt*. **1**. 输出,出口(*opp*. import). **2**. 带走,运走,排出。～ *industrial goods* 输出工业品。*waste products* ～*ed by blood from the tissues* 由血液从身体内排出的废物。—*vi*. 输出物资。

ex·port·a·ble [iks'pɔːtəbl; ɛks`portəbl] *a*. 可出口的。

ex·por·ta·tion [ˌekspɔː'teiʃən; ˏɛkspor`teʃən] *n*. **1**. 输出,出口。**2**. 出口商品。**3**.【无】呼叫,振铃。

ex·port·er [iks'pɔːtə; ɪk`sportə] *n*. 出口商;输出者,输出国。

ex·pos·al [iks'pəuzəl; ɪk`spozəl] *n*. = exposure.

ex·pose [iks'pəuz; ɪk`spoz] *vt*. **1**. 使暴露,使曝露(在日光、风雨等之中)。**2**.【摄】使曝光,使感光。**3**. 陈列(货物),露出。**4**. 揭露,揭发,揭穿(秘密等)。**5**. 使遭受,招惹,招致(攻击、危险等)。**6**.【史】扔弃(婴儿)〔如古代斯巴达人将弱婴弃置户外〕。～ *one's skin to the sun* 使皮肤晒到太阳。*a situation* ～*d to every wind* 四面受风的地位。*a house* ～*d to the west* 西晒[正西]的房子。～ *a plot* 揭穿阴谋。～ *a card* 亮牌。*be* ～*d to danger* 可能遭受危险。～ *oneself to ridicule* 使自己受嘲弄。～ ***... to*** 使…受到;使…朝向…。

ex·po·sé [eks'pəuzei; ɛkspo`ze] *n*.〔F.〕(事实的)陈述;(丑事、真相等的)暴露,揭露。

ex·posed [iks'pəuzd; ɪk`spozd] *a*. 无掩蔽的;暴露的,显露的。*an* ～ *position* 位置显露。～ *wiring* 明线。**-ness** *n*.

ex·po·si·tion [ˌekspə'ziʃən; ˏɛkspə`zɪʃən] *n*. **1**. 解释,注释;解说,说明。**2**. 展览,陈列;展览会,博览会。**3**. 暴露,曝光。**4**.【剧】展示部分〔阐明情节、人物等〕。**5**.【乐】呈示部。

ex·pos·i·tive [iks'pɔzitiv; ɪk`spazətɪv] *a*. 讲解的,评注的,说明的,叙述的。

ex·pos·i·tor [iks'pɔzitə; ɪk`spazɪtə] *n*. 解释者,解说员,说明者,评注者。

ex·pos·i·to·ry [iks'pɔzitəri; ɪk`spazɪˏtorɪ] *a*. = expositive.

ex post fac·to ['eks pəust'fæktəu; `ɛks post`fækto]〔L.〕事后的,有追溯效力的,在事后。*an* ～ *law* 有追溯效力的法律。

ex·pos·tu·late [iks'pɔstjuleit; ɪk`spastjʊˏlet] *vi*. 劝导,忠告(*about*; *for*; *on*). ～ ***with sb. on*** [***about***] 告诫某人…。

ex·pos·tu·la·tion [ikˌspɔstju'leiʃən; ɪkˌspastjʊ`leʃən] *n*. 劝导,忠告。

ex·pos·tu·la·tor [iks'pɔstjuleitə; ɪk`spastjʊletə] *n*. 劝导者,忠告者。

ex·pos·tu·la·to·ry [iks'pɔstjulətəri; ɪk`spastjʊləˏtorɪ] *a*. 告诫的。

ex·po·sure [iks'pəuʒə; ɪk`spoʒə] *n*. **1**. 曝露;曝晒;揭发。**2**.【摄】曝光;胶卷[软片]张数;曝光时间。**3**. (房屋的)朝向,方位。**4**. 商品的陈列。**5**.【史】(婴儿的)曝弃。～ *meter* 曝光表。*correct* ～ 适度曝光。*There are three* ～*s left on this film*. 这个胶卷剩下三张没拍。

ex·pound [iks'paund; ɪk`spaʊnd] *vt*. **1**. 详细说明(理论),陈述;为…辩护[解释]。**2**. 解释(经典)。—*vi*. 阐述;解释,说明。**-er** *n*. 陈述者,说明者。

ex·press [iks'pres; ɪk`sprɛs] **I** *vt*. **1**. 表示,表现,表达〔*cf*. suppress; impress〕。**2**.【数】用符号表示。**3**. 榨出,压出。**4**. 用快邮寄出;〔美〕快运,快汇。～ *regret* 表示遗憾。～ *oneself* 表达自己的意思。～ *oneself* (*as*) *satisfied* 表示满意。～ *oneself in English* 用英语说。～ *the juice from grapes* 榨葡萄汁。～ *the letter* 寄快信。**II** *a*. **1**. 明白表示的;明确的。**2**. 一模一样的。**3**. 专门的,特殊的。**4**. 快速的;快递的。*an* ～ *provision* (法律)明文条款。*an* ～ *ticket* 快车票。*an* ～ *letter*〔英〕快信。～ *post* [*mail*] 快递邮件。*an* ～ *telegram* 急电。*You are the* ～ *image of your father*. 你跟你父亲一模一样。***at*** ～ ***speed*** 火急。***by his*** ～ ***consent*** 经他特别许可。***for the*** ～ ***purpose of*** 特为,特意。**III** *ad*. 乘快车;用快递方式。**IV** *n*. **1**.〔英〕专差;专差急送的文件。**2**. 快运,快汇;快递(业务)。**3**. 快运货物,快汇款。**4**. 快车。**5**.〔美〕快运公司。***by*** ～ 乘快车;用快递方式。～ **bullet** 猎枪子弹。～ **company**〔美〕快递公司。～ **delivery**〔英〕快件〔美国叫 special delivery〕。～ **highway** 高速公路。～ **rifle** 高速猎枪。～ **train** 特别快车。～ **way** = ～ highway. **-a·ble** *a*. = **-i·ble**. **-less** *a*. **-ly** *ad*.

ex·press·age [iks'presidʒ; ɛk`sprɛsɪdʒ] *n*.〔美〕(小件包裹的)快递业务;(小额款项的)快汇业务;快递费。

ex·press·i·ble [iks'presəbl; ɪk`sprɛsəbl] *a*. **1**. 可表示的,可表达的。**2**. 可榨出的。

ex·pres·sion [iks'preʃən; ɪk`sprɛʃən] *n*. **1**. 表现,表示,表达。**2**. 词句;语句,措辞,说法。**3**. 表情,脸色,态度;腔调,声调。**4**.【数】式,符号。**5**. (油的)榨出,压榨。**6**.【生】表现度。*emotional* ～ 表情。*a happy* ～ 妙言。*an odd* ～ 怪话。*the* ～ *of the eye* 眼睛表情,眼色。*a* *smiling* ～ 笑脸。**beyond** [*past*] ～ 形容不出,无法表达。**find** ～ (*in*)(在…中)表现出来…,表现在…。**give** ～ **to** 表达,反映(*give the fullest* ～ *to their initiative* 充分表现他们的积极性)。～ **mark**【乐】表示感情色彩的符号。**-al** *a*. 表现的;表情的。**-ism** *n*.【美】表现主义;表现派。**-ist** 1. *n*.【美】表现主义者,表现派。2. 表现派的〔亦作 expressionistic〕。**-less** *a*. 缺乏表情的,呆板的。

ex·pres·sive [iks'presiv; ɪk`sprɛsɪv] *a*. 表现…的,表示…的,富于表情的;意味深长的(*of*)。～ *eyes* 富于表情的眼睛。*be* ～ *of feeling* 表现感情。*words* ～ *of gratitude* 表示感谢的话。**-ly** *ad*. **-ness** *n*.

ex·pres·siv·i·ty [ˌekspre'siviti; ˏɛksprɛ`sɪvətɪ] *n*. 1. 善于表达,表达性。2.【生】(基因的)表现度。

ex·press·ly [iks'presli; ɪk`sprɛslɪ] *ad*. 1. 明白地,清楚地。2. 特别地,特意地,专门地。

ex·press·man [iks'presmæn; ɪk`sprɛsmæn] *n*. (*pl*. **-men**) 运送员,递送员。

ex·pres·so [ek'spresəu; ɛk`sprɛso] *n*. = espresso.

ex·pro·pri·ate [eks'prəuprieit; ɛk`spropriˏet] *vt*. 1. 没收(财产等);征用(土地)。2. 让渡(所有权)。3. 把(他人财产)转到自己名下,把…据为己有。4. 剥夺…的所有权。*The state* ～*d the king*. 国家没收了国王的财产。**-a·tion** *n*. (土地的)征用。**-a·tor** *n*. 剥夺者,没收者,征用者。

ex·pul·sion [iks'pʌlʃən; ɪk`spʌlʃən] *n*. 1. 逐出,驱逐,开除。2. 排气。*the* ～ *of sb. from school* 某人被开除学籍。*the* ～ *of air from the lungs* 从肺中排出空气。

ex·pul·sive [iks'pʌlsiv; ɪk`spʌlsɪv] *a*. 驱逐的;开除的。

ex·punc·tion [ik'spʌŋkʃən; ɪk`spʌŋkʃən] *n*. 1. 涂抹,拭去;删除,勾销,擦去。2. 取消,抹煞。*make some* ～*s* 略加删节。

ex·punge [eks'pʌndʒ; ɛk`spʌndʒ] *vt*. 1. 涂掉;删去;抹掉。2. 消灭,除去(*from*)。～ *certain passages from the record* 从纪录中删去几段。

ex·pur·gate ['ekspəːgeit; `ɛkspɚˏget] *vt*. 使纯洁,删去(书籍的不妥处)。*an* ～*d edition* 删改本;洁本。

ex·pur·ga·tion [ˌekspəː'geiʃən; ˏɛkspɚ`geʃən] *n*. 删改。

ex·pur·ga·tor ['ekspəːgeitə; `ɛkspɚˏgetɚ] *n*. (书籍的)删改者。

ex·pur·ga·to·ri·al, ex·pur·ga·to·ry [eksˌpəːgə'tɔːriəl, eks'pəːgətəri; ɛkˏspɝgə`torɪəl, ɛks`pɝgəˏtorɪ] *a*. 删改的。***Expurgatory Index*** 禁书目录。

ex·qui·site ['ekskwizit; `ɛkskwɪzɪt] **I** *a*. 1. 精致的,精巧的,优美的,优雅的。2. 微妙的;细腻的;敏锐的。3. (痛苦等)剧烈的,(快乐等)非常的。～ *works of art* 绝妙的艺术品。*an article of* ～ *workmanship* 精致的工艺品。*a man of* ～ *taste* 趣味优雅的人。～ *pain* 剧痛。**II** *n*. 过分讲究穿戴的人。*the young* ～*s* 过于讲究打扮的年轻人。**-ly** *ad*. **-ness** *n*.

exr. = executor.

exrx. = executrix.

ex·san·gui·nate [eks'sæŋgwineit; ɛks`sæŋgwɪˏnet] *vt*.【医】给…除血[驱血];使无血。**-na·tion** [eks'sæŋgwi'neiʃən; ɛks`sæŋgwɪ`neʃən] *n*.

ex·san·guine [eks'sæŋgwin; ɛks`sæŋgwɪn] *a*. 无血的,贫血的。

ex·scind [ek'sind; ɛk`sɪnd] *vt*. 切开,割去;除去。

ex·sect [ek'sekt; ɛk`sɛkt] *vt*. 切去,割去;根除。**-section** *n*.

ex·sert [ek'səːt; ɛk`sɝt] *vt*.【生】使突出,使伸出。

ex·sert·ed [ek'səːtid; ɛk`sɝtɪd] *a*.【生】伸出的。

ex-serv·ice ['eks'səːvis; `ɛks`sɝvɪs] *a*. 退役的;退伍的。

ex·serv·ice·man ['eks'səːvismæn; `ɛks`sɝvɪsmæn] *n*. (*pl*. **-men** [-men; -mɛn]) 退役军人,复员军人〔*cf*. veteran〕。

ex·sic·cate ['eksikeit; `ɛksɪˌket] *vt*. 使干燥,使干涸。—*vi*. 变干燥,变干涸。

ex·sic·ca·tion [ˌeksi'keiʃən; ˏɛksɪ`keʃən] *n*. 干燥(法);除湿作用,干燥作用。

ex·sic·ca·tive [eks'sikətiv; ɛks`sɪkətɪv] **I** *a*. 使干燥的,除湿的。**II** *n*. 干燥剂。

ex·sol·dier ['eks'səuldʒə; `ɛks`soldʒɚ] *n*. 退伍[退役]军人。

ex·stip·u·late [eks'stipjulit; ɛks`stɪpjʊlɪt] *a*.【植】无托叶的。

ex·stro·phy ['ekstrəfi; `ɛkstrəfɪ] *n*.【医】(器官的)外翻〔尤指膀胱外翻〕。

ext. = extension; exterior; external; extinct; extra; extract.

ex·tant [eks'tænt; ɛk`stænt] *a*. 1. 现存的,尚存的。2. 〔古〕突出的,显著的。

ex·ta·sy ['ekstəsi; `ɛkstəsɪ] *n*. = ecstasy.

ext. dia. = external diametre 外径。

ex·tem·po·ra·ne·ous [eksˌtempə'reinjəs; ɛkˏstɛmpə`renɪəs] *a*. 1. 临时作成的,脱口而出的,即席的。2. 不用讲稿的,善于即席讲话的。3. 临时的,权宜之计的。*an* ～ *speech* 即席演说。*an* ～ *shelter* 临时遮蔽所。**-ly** *ad*.

ex·tem·po·ra·ry [iks'tempərəri; ɪk`stɛmpəˏrɛrɪ] *a*. = extemporaneous. **-rar·i·ly** *ad*. 即席,当场。

ex·tem·po·re [eks'tempəri; ɛk`stɛmpərɪ] **I** *a*. 临时作成的,无准备的;当场的,即席的。**II** *ad*. 无准备地,临时地;即席地,当场地。**III** *n*. 即席之作,即兴诗文。

ex·tem·po·ri·za·tion [eksˌtempərai'zeiʃən; ɪkˏstɛmpərə`zeʃən] *n*. 即席作成;即席之作;即兴诗[文]。

ex·tem·po·rize [eks'tempəraiz; ɛk`stɛmpəˏraɪz] *vt*., *vi*. 临时制作,当场作成;即席发(言),即兴演奏,即兴创作。

ex·tend [iks'tend; ɪks`tɛnd] *vt*. 1. 伸出(手等);伸展。2. 延(期);延长(铁路)。3. 扩充,扩大,扩展;发挥(力量);延续。4. 拉长,拉开(绳子等)。5. 寄与,给予(同情等)。6. 把(速记等)译出;详细写出。7. 致(祝辞)。8. 提供,赠送(招待券)。9. 〔英〕【法】估价;扣押,没收(土地、房产等)。10.【军】疏开,散开,展开。11.【数】开拓。12. 使(竞赛者)拼命〔常用被动语态〕。13. 搀杂(…以增加数量)。14. 会计把(数字)转入另一栏,算出…的总额,写出…的总额。～ *one's visit for a few days longer* 把访问期延长几天。～ *a building* 增建。～ *liquor* 用水掺酒。～ *an invitation* [*one's congratulations*] *to* 向…发出邀请[致贺]。*Both man and horse* ～*ed themselves* [*were* ～*ed*]. 人马竭尽全力。—*vi*. 1. 伸展;扩充,延长;延伸;绵亘,连续。2.【军】疏开,散开,展开。*The strike* ～*ed over ten weeks*. 罢工继续了十个星期。

ex·tend·ed [iks'tendid; ɪk`stɛndɪd] *a*. 1. 伸开的,展开的。2. 延长的,继续的。3. (势力)扩大的;扩张的;(意思)引伸的。4.【印】(铅字)宽体的。*an* ～ *battle line* 拉长了的战线。～ **bonds** 延期偿付的债券。～ **formation** [**order**]【军】疏开队形。～ **play** 慢速唱片,密纹唱片。～ **type** 宽体铅字。

ex·tend·er [iks'tendə; ɪk`stɛndɚ] *n*. 1. 补充剂,增量剂。2. 补充部分,延伸部分。

ex·tend·i·ble, ex·ten·si·ble [iks'tendəbl, -səbl; ɪk`stɛndəbl̩, -səbl̩] *a*. 可伸长的,可延长的,可扩张的。**-ness** *n*.

ex·ten·si·bil·i·ty [ikˌstensə'biləti; ɪkˏstɛnsə`bɪlətɪ] *n*. 延伸性,伸展性,伸长率,延伸度,可扩张性。

ex·ten·sile [eks'tensail; ɛk`stɛnsɪl] *a*. 1.【动】可伸展的,(爪子)伸长出来的。2. = extensible.

ex·ten·sion [iks'tenʃən; ɪk`stɛnʃən] *n*. 1. 伸长,伸展,延长,延伸,扩展,扩大;广度,范围。2. 延期;〔美〕(房屋的)增建部分,(铁路等的)延长线,(电话的)分机;增设部分;附加物。3. (语句等的)铺张。4.【物】广延性。5.【军】延伸。6.【医】牵伸术;伸直;(病变)蔓延,扩展。7.【商】延期还债认可书。8.【逻】外延(*opp*. intension);【数】开拓;广延性。9. 会计从另一栏转来或算出的金额。*an* ~ *of a loan* 借款的延期偿还。*a university* ~ 大学的附设部分(如函授班、夜校等)。~ **course** 大学函授班[夜校等]开设的课程。~ **instrument** 附加仪表,外接仪器。~ **ladder** (消防用)伸缩梯。~ **line** 分机线。~ **set** (电话)分机。~ **spring** 牵簧。~ **student** 在大学的附设部分(如函授班、夜校等)接受教育的学生。~ **table** (可以加装活动板的)伸缩桌。~ **telephone** 电话分机。~ **work**【军】疏开工事。

ex·ten·sion·al [iksˈtenʃənəl; ɪkˋstɛnʃənəl] ***a***. 1.【逻】外延的。2. 延伸的,客观现实的;具体的,事实的。

ex·ten·si·ty [iksˈtensiti; ɛkˋstɛnsətɪ] ***n***. 1. 扩张;扩大。2.【心】(空间知觉的)延长性。

ex·ten·sive [iksˈtensiv; ɪkˋstɛnsɪv] ***a***. 1. 广阔的,广大的,广博的;(交易等)大量的;范围广泛的。2.【物】广延的;【逻】外延的。3.【农】粗放的(*opp*. intensive)。~ *knowledge* 广博的知识。*an* ~ *order* 大批定货。~ *reading* 泛读,粗读;博览群书。~ *cultivation* 粗放的耕作。**-ly** ***ad***. **-ness** ***n***.

ex·ten·som·e·ter [ˌekstenˈsɔmitə; ˏɛkstɛnˋsɑmətɚ] ***n***.【机】伸长计。

ex·ten·sor [iksˈtensə; ɪkˋstɛnsɚ] ***n***.【解】伸(张)肌(*opp*. flexor)。

ex·tent [iksˈtent; ɪkˋstɛnt] ***n***. 1. 广度,宽度,长度,一大片(土地)。2. 分量,程度;区域,范围,界限,限度。3.【逻】外延。4.【法】扣押,扣押令;〔美〕临时所有权令;〔英古〕土地估价。*interior* ~【数】内延。*unlimited* ~ 无限空间。*a vast* ~ *of land* 广大的土地。*the full* ~ *of the park* 公园的全景。~ *of the error* 误差量。*the* ~ *of one's patience* 忍耐限度。***to a certain*** ~ 在一定程度上,有点儿,多少,稍稍。***to a great*** [***large***] ~ 大部分,大大,在很大程度上。***to some*** ~ 在某种程度上,多少,有点儿,有些。***to such an*** ~ ***that*** 达到这样的程度以至。***to that*** ~ 达到那种程度。***to the*** ~ ***of*** [***that***] 达到…的程度。***to the utmost*** [***full***] ~ 到极点,极端;尽可能,尽力。

ex·ten·u·ate [iksˈtenjueit; ɪkˋstɛnjʊˏet] ***vt***. 1. 掩饰(坏事);(用借口来)减轻(罪过)。2.〔废〕低估,藐视。3.〔古〕使细弱。*Nothing can* ~ *his base conduct*. 他的卑鄙行为无可掩饰。*try to* ~ *one's guilt* 试图减轻罪责。

ex·ten·u·at·ing [eksˈtenjueitiŋ; ɛkˋstɛnjʊˏetɪŋ] ***a***. 使减轻的,情有可原的。~ *circumstances*【法】可使罪行减轻的情况。**-ly** ***ad***.

ex·ten·u·a·tion [iksˌtenjuˈeiʃən; ɪkˏstɛnjʊˋeʃən] ***n***. 1. 减轻;酌量。2.【电】降低;衰减。*plead circumstances in* ~ *of one's guilt* 请求酌情减轻罪行。

ex·ten·u·a·tive [eksˈtenjueitiv; ɛkˋstɛnjʊˏetɪv] ***a***. = extenuating.

ex·ten·u·a·to·ry [iksˈtenjuətəri; ɪkˋstɛnjuəˏtorɪ] ***a***. 减轻的;可酌量的。*an* ~ *defense* 有助于减罪的辩护。

ex·te·ri·or [eksˈtiəriə; ɪkˋstɪrɪɚ] **I** ***a***. 1. 外面的,外部的;外表上的,表面的(*opp*. inward)。2. 外界的,外在的(*opp*. internal, intrinsic)。3. 对外的,外交上的;外国的,外来的,外用的。*an* ~ *angle*【数】外角。~ *lines*【军】外线。*an* ~ *policy* 对外政策。**II** ***n***. 1. 外部,外面,表面,外形,外观。2.【影、剧】户外布景;【影】外景(*opp*. interior)。*a good man with a rough* ~ 外貌粗鲁而内心善良的人。**-ly** ***ad***.

ex·te·ri·or·i·ty [eksˌtiəriˈɔriti; ɪkˏstɪrɪˋɑrətɪ] ***n***. = externality.

ex·te·ri·or·ize [eksˈtiəriəraiz; ɪkˋstɪrɪəˏraɪz] ***vt***. 1. = externalize. 2.【医】用手术从腹中取出…。**-i·za·tion** ***n***.

ex·ter·mi·nate [iksˈtəːmineit; ɪkˋstɝmɪˏnet] ***vt***. 消灭,扑灭,根绝。

ex·ter·mi·na·tion [iksˌtəːmiˈneiʃən; ɪkˏstɝmɪˋneʃən] ***n***. 根除,灭绝,消灭,扑灭。

ex·ter·mi·na·tor [iksˈtəːmineitə; ɪkˋstɝmɪˏnetɚ] ***n***. 1. 扑灭者,根绝者。2. 根绝物(指杀虫剂等)。

ex·ter·mi·na·to·ry [iksˈtəːminətəri; ɪkˋstɝmənəˏtorɪ] ***a***. 扑灭的,绝灭的,根绝的。

ex·tern [ˈekstəːn; ˋɛkstɝn] **I** ***a***. = external. **II** ***n***. 1. 走读生。2. 住院外的医生(*opp*. intern);住院外的医科实习生。

ex·ter·nal [eksˈtəːnl; ɪkˋstɝnl] **I** ***a***. 1. 外部的,外面的;【哲】外界的,客观的,物质的。2. 表面上的(*opp*. intrinsic);肤浅的,浅薄的,形式上的。3. 对外的;外国的;偶然的。4.【医】外用的。~ *diametre* 外径。~ *evidence* 外证。~ *grinding machine* 外圆磨床。*the* ~ *world* 外界,客观世界。*an* ~ *loan* [*debt*] 外债。~ *parameter* 外界参数。~ *temperature* 外界温度,室外温度,周围温度。~ *trade* 对外贸易。~ *remedies* 外用药。**II** ***n***. 1. 外部,外面。2.〔*pl*.〕外形,外貌,外观;形式;外部情况。*judge by* ~*s* 从外观上判断。~**-combustion engine** 外燃(发动)机。~ **examination** 由校外人士主持的考试。~ **fertilization** 卵细胞体外人工授精。~ **galaxy**【天】(银)河外星系。~ **respiration**【医】外呼吸。~ **student** (获准入学并可参加学位考试的)校外学生。~ **works**【物】外功。**-ly** ***ad***.

ex·ter·nal·ism [eksˈtəːnəlizəm; ɛkˋstɝnəlɪzm] ***n***. 1. 形式主义;讲究外表,拘泥形式。2.【哲】现象论,外在性,客观性,外在化。

ex·ter·nal·i·ty [ˌekstəːˈnæliti; ˏɛkstɝˋnælətɪ] ***n***. 1. 外表,外貌,外部事物。2.【哲】客观存在性,外在性,客观性。3. 形式主义,讲究外表。

ex·ter·nal·i·za·tion [eksˌtəːnəlaiˈzeiʃən; ɛkˏstɝnəlaɪˋzeʃən] ***n***. 1. 客观化,客观性;外表化,外表性。2. 仅具外表形式。3. 客观[外表]化的事物。

ex·ter·nal·ize [eksˈtəːnəlaiz; ɪkˋstɝnəlaɪz] ***vt***. 1. 赋与…以形体;使客观化,使形像化,使具体化。2. 以外因说明。*Language* ~*s thought*. 语言使思想具体化。~ *sb.'s failure* 把某人的失败归咎于外因。

ex·terne [eksˈtəːn; ɛkˋstɝn] ***n***., ***a***. = extern.

ex·ter·o·cep·tor [ˌekstərəuˈseptə; ˏɛkstərəˋseptɚ] ***n***. 外感受器。

ex·ter·ri·to·ri·al [ˌeksteriˈtɔːriəl; ˏɛkstɛrəˋtorɪəl] ***a***. = extraterritorial. **-ly** ***ad***.

ex·ter·ri·to·ri·al·i·ty [ˈeksteriˌtɔːriˈæliti; ˋɛkstɛrəˏtorɪˋælətɪ] ***n***. = extraterritoriality.

ex·tinct [iksˈtiŋkt; ɪkˋstɪŋkt] **I** ***a***. 1. 已消灭的,(火等)已熄灭的。2. (生物)已绝种的,已灭绝的。3. (官职等)已废除的。4.【法】已过时效的,失效的。*an* ~ *family* 已绝嗣的家族。*an* ~ *species* 已灭绝的物种。*an* ~ *volcano* 死火山。**II** ***vt***.〔古〕使熄灭;使灭绝,消灭。

ex·tinc·tion [iksˈtiŋkʃən; ɪkˋstɪŋkʃən] ***n***. 1. (权利等的)消灭,(生物等的)灭绝;(火等的)熄灭;(法律等的)废除。2.【物】消光;自屏;衰减。~ *coefficient*【物】消光系数。

ex·tinc·tive [iksˈtiŋktiv; ɪkˋstɪŋktɪv] ***a***. 使熄灭的,使消灭的,使灭绝的。

ex·tin·guish [iksˈtiŋgwiʃ; ɪkˋstɪŋgwɪʃ] ***vt***. 1. 熄(灯),灭(火),熄灭(希望等)。2. 消灭,扑灭。3. 废除;压制;使沉默。4. 使销声匿迹;使暗淡;使失色。5.【法】偿清。6. 使失效,废除,取消。~ *one's hope* 使希望破灭。*She was* ~*ed by her sisters*. 她的姐妹使她相形见绌。~ *one's opponents with a single word* 一句话把对方说得哑口无言。**-a·ble** ***a***. 可熄的;会绝灭的;可扑灭的。**-er** ***n***. 1. 消灭者。2. 消除器;熄灯器;灭火器。**-ment** ***n***. 消灭;熄灭;绝灭;偿清。

ex·tir·pate [ˈekstəːpeit; ˋɛkstɚˏpet] ***vt***. 1. 根除,根绝,绝灭,扑灭。2.【医】摘出,切除。~ *weeds* [*evils*] 根除杂草[弊端]。~ *superstition* 破除迷信。**-pa·tion** ***n***.

ex·tir·pa·tor [ˈekstəːpeitə; ˋɛkstə·ˏpetə·] ***n.*** 根绝者;扑灭者。

extn. = extraction.

ex·tol(l) [iksˈtɔl; ɪkˋstɑl] ***vt.*** 赞美,称赞,颂扬;吹捧。~ ***sb. to the skies*** 把某人捧上天。**-ment** ***n.***

ex·tol·ler [iksˈtɔlə; ɪkˋstɑlə·] ***n.*** 赞美者;吹捧者。

ex·tort [iksˈtɔːt; ɪkˋstɔrt] ***vt.*** **1.** 强夺;敲诈,勒索(*from*);强求,逼迫。**2.** 曲解,牵强附会。*He ~ed a promise from me.* 他硬要我答应。~ *a bizzare sense from the few words* 对片言只字作牵强附会的曲解。**-ive** ***a.***

ex·tor·tion [iksˈtɔːʃən; ɪkˋstɔrʃən] ***n.*** 强夺;敲诈,勒索;【法】恐吓取财。**-ar·y, -ate** ***a.*** 强夺的;敲诈的,横征暴敛的。**-er, -ist** ***n.*** 强求者;敲诈勒索者。

ex·tra [ˈekstrə; ˋɛkstrə] **I** ***a.*** **1.** 额外的,附加的,补充的。**2.** 另外收费的。**3.** 特大的;特优的,特级的。*an ~ loss* 额外损失。*an ~ train* 加车。*an ~ allowance* 特别津贴。*an ~ edition* 特号,临时增刊。~ *news* 号外。~ *girls* [*ladies*] 临时女演员。*an ~ hand* 临时工。*Dinner 5 s., wine ~.* 晚餐五先令,酒资在外。*without ~ charge* 不另收费。*It is nothing ~.* 没有什么了不起的。**II** ***n.*** **1.** 外加物;赠品,附加物;额外人手[津贴];(报纸的)号外。**2.** 特号;特级品。**3.**【影】临时演员〔*cf.* supernumerary〕。**4.**【板球】额外得分。*a real ~* 上等产品〔广告用语〕。**II** ***ad.*** **1.** 额外地,另外地。**2.** 格外地,非常地。~ *good wine* 特好葡萄酒。*an ~ special (edition)* 最后版晚报特刊。*be charged ~* 额外收费。*try ~ hard* 特别尽力地试试看。~**-base hit**【棒球】本垒打。~ **bold** ***n.***【印】超黑体字,特黑体字。~**-fine** ***a.*** 超级的,极好的。~**-hard** ***a.*** 异常硬的,超硬的。~**-heavy** ***a.*** 特重的,超重的,超功率的。

extra- *pref.* 一般加在形容词之前表示"外","额外","格外","临时","超出":*extra*-fine, *extra*territorial.

ex·tra·ca·non·i·cal [ˌekstrəkəˈnɔnikl; ˏɛkstrəkəˋnɑnɪkl̩] ***a.***【宗】未入圣典的;非钦定著作之列的。

ex·tra·cel·lu·lar [ˌekstrəˈseljulə; ˏɛkstrəˋsɛljulə·] ***a.***【生】细胞外的(*opp.* intra-cellular)。

ex·tract I [iksˈtrækt; ɪkˋstrækt] ***vt.*** **1.** (用力)拔出,抽出。**2.** 分离出,提取,蒸馏出,榨出。**3.** 摘出(要点),引用。**4.** 推断出。**5.**【数】开(方),求(根)。**6.**【军】退(弹)。~ *a tooth* 拔牙。*I could ~ no information from him.* 我从他那里一点儿消息也打听不出来。~ *the root* 开方,求根。**II** [ˈeks-; ˋɛks-] ***n.*** **1.** 抽出物;提出物,蒸馏品,精华,汁;【药】浸膏。**2.** 拔萃;摘录,摘记,抄。~ *of beef* = *beef ~* 牛肉汁。~ *of roses* 玫瑰精。*make ~s* 精选,摘要。**-able, -ible** ***a.***

ex·tract·ant [iksˈtræktənt; ɪkˋstræktənt] ***n.*** 提取剂,分馏物。

ex·trac·tion [iksˈtrækʃən; ɪkˋstrækʃən] ***n.*** **1.** 抽出,拔出。**2.**【化】提取(法);萃取(法);回收物,提出物;精炼。**3.** 精选,摘要。**4.** 血统,家世,出身。**5.**【数】开方,求根。*spirit of the first ~* 原汁酒。*a man of foreign ~* 外国(血统的)人。*~s from a book* 一本书的内容摘录。*an ~ of 81 percent* 百分之八十一的出粉率,八一粉。*the ~ of root*【数】开方法,求根法。~ **column** 提取塔。~ **rates** 提取率。

ex·trac·tive [iksˈtræktiv; ɪkˋstræktɪv] **I** ***a.*** **1.** 可提出的;可抽出的。**2.** 消耗资源的。**II** ***n.*** = extract. ~ *industries* 天然产业[矿业、农业、渔业等]。*an ~ process* 抽提[提炼]过程。

ex·trac·tor [iksˈtræktə; ɪkˋstræktə·] ***n.*** **1.** 提取者。**2.** 抽出器;分离器;精选者;【医】提出器,拔出器;【军】退子钩;退弹簧,退壳器;【林】推子钩;脱模工具。*an air ~* 抽气机。*an electrostatic stalk ~* (茶叶)静电拣梗机。*an ~ groove* 弹底槽。

ex·tra·cur·ric·u·lar, ex·tra·cur·ric·u·lum [ˌekstrəkəˈrikjulə, -ləm; ˏɛkstrəkəˋrɪkjulə·, -ləm] ***a.*** **1.** 正课以外的。**2.** (娱乐等)业余的。**3.** (活动等)逾矩的,本分以外的。~ *activities* 课外活动。~ *athletics* 课外体育运动。

ex·tra·dit·a·ble [ˈekstrədaitəbl; ˋɛkstrəˏdaɪtəbl] ***a.*** 可引渡的。

ex·tra·dite [ˈekstrədait; ˋɛkstrəˏdaɪt] ***vt.*** 引渡(外国的罪犯);送还(逃犯)。**-tra·di·tion** ***n.***

ex·tra·dos [eksˈtreidɔs; ɛkˋstredɑs] ***n.***【建】(拱的)拱背线,外弧面,外曲线(*opp.* intrados)。

ex·tra·es·sen·tial [ˈekstrəiˈsenʃəl; ˋɛkstrəɛˋsɛnʃəl] ***a.*** 非主要的,本质以外的,非必要的。

ex·tra·ga·lac·tic [ˌekstrəgəˈlæktik; ˏɛkstrəgəˋlæktɪk] ***a.*** 银河系外的,(银)河外的。~ *light* 银河以外传来的光。~ *nebula* [*system*] 河外星系,河外星云。~ *space* 河外太空。

ex·tra·ju·di·cial [ˌekstrədʒu(ː)ˈdiʃəl; ˏɛkstrədʒuˋdɪʃəl] ***a.*** 法院职权以外的,法律外的;非正式的。**-ly** ***ad.***

ex·tra·le·gal [ˌekstrəˈliːgəl; ˏɛkstrəˋligl̩] ***a.*** 越出法律范围的;法外的;未经法律规定的。**-ly** ***ad.***

ex·tra·li·mit·al [ˌekstrəˈlimitəl; ˏɛkstrəˋlɪmɪtl̩] ***a.*** (有机体、物种等)在某区域内不存在的。

ex·tral·i·ty [eksˈtræliti; ɛksˋtræləti] ***n.*** 治外法权(= extraterritoriality)。

ex·tra·mar·i·tal [ˌekstrəˈmæritl; ˏɛkstrəˋmærətl̩] ***a.*** 婚姻外的,私通的,通奸的。

ex·tra·mun·dane [ˌekstrəˈmʌndein; ˏɛkstrəˋmʌnden] ***a.*** 超现实世界的,地球以外的;宇宙外的。

ex·tra·mu·ral [ˌekstrəˈmjuərəl; ˏɛkstrəˋmjʊrəl] ***a.*** **1.** 墙外的;城外的。**2.** 大学外的。**3.** (非校队参加的)校际比赛的。~ *activities* 校外活动。~ *classes* 校外班。~ *hospital treatment* (医)院外治疗。*an ~ lecture* 为校外编写的讲义;(对校外人作的)公开讲授。~ *teaching* [*courses*] 大学对外课程。

ex·tra·ne·ous [eksˈtreinjəs; ɛkˋstrenɪəs] ***a.*** **1.** 体外的,外部的;外来的。**2.** 范围外的,局外的,无关的,不重要的,枝节的。~ *help* [*interference*] 外来援助[干涉]。~ ***to the subject*** 无关本题的。~ **reflex**【心】新异反射。~ **stimul**【心】新异刺激。~ **substance**【医】异物。**-ly** ***ad.*** **-ness** ***n.***

ex·tra·net [ˈekstrənet; ˋɛkstrənɛt] ***n.***【计】外联网。

ex·tra·nu·cle·ar [ˌekstrəˈnjuːkliə; ˏɛkstrəˋnjuklɪr] ***a.***【生、物】核外的。

ex·tra·of·fi·cial [ˌekstrəəˈfiʃəl; ˏɛkstrə·əˋfɪʃəl] ***a.*** 职务外的,职权外的。

ex·traor·di·na·ry [iksˈtrɔːdənəri; ɪkˋstrɔrdnˏɛrɪ] ***a.*** **1.** 非常的,异常的,非凡的,卓绝的。**2.** 意外的,离奇的,可惊的;特别的。**3.** [ekstrəˈɔːdinəri; ɛkstrəˋɔrdɪnərɪ] 特命的,特派的;临时的。*a woman of ~ beauty* 非常美丽的女人。*an ~ event* 异常事件。*do ~ things* 干怪事。~ *rays*【物】非常光线。*an ~ session* 临时议会。*an ambassador* [*envoy*] ~ 特使。**-ar·i·ly** ***ad.*** **-ariness** ***n.***

ex·trap·o·late [eksˈtræpəleit; ɛksˋtræpəˏlet] ***vt.***, ***vi.*** **1.**【数】外推。**2.** 推断;判定。**3.** 推测,推论。**-o·la·tion** ***n.*** 推断,推知;【数】外推法。**-o·la·tive** ***a.***

ex·tra·sen·so·ry [ˌekstrəˈsensəri; ˏɛkstrəˋsɛnsərɪ] ***a.***【心】超感觉的。~ *perception*【心】超感官知觉,超感觉力。

ex·tra·so·lar [ˌekstrəˈsəulə; ˏɛkstrəˋsolə·] ***a.*** 太阳系以外的。

ex·tra-spe·cial [ˌekstrəˈspeʃəl; ˏɛkstrəˋspɛʃəl] ***a.*** 〔口〕异常优秀的,特别优良的。

ex·tra·sys·to·le [ˌekstrəˈsistəliː; ˏɛkstrəˋsɪstəli] ***n.***【医】(心脏)期前收缩。**-sys·tol·ic** [-sisˈtɔlik; -sɪsˋtɑlɪk] ***a.***

ex·tra·ter·res·tri·al [ˌekstrətəˈrestriəl; ˏɛkstrətəˋrɛstrɪəl] **I** ***a.*** 地球外的,行星际的,大气圈外的,宇宙的。**II** ***n.*** 外星人,外星球的生物。

E

ex·tra·ter·ri·to·ri·al [ˌekstrəˌteriˈtɔːriəl; ˋɛkstrəˏtɛrɪˋtorɪəl] *a*. 治外法权的。**-ly** *ad*.

ex·tra·ter·ri·to·ri·al·i·ty [ˌekstrəˌteriˌtɔːriˈæliti; ˏɛkstrəˏtɛrəˏtoriˋælətɪ] *n*. 治外法权。

ex·tra·u·ter·ine [ˌekstrəˈjuːtərin; ˏɛkstrəˋjutərɪn] *a*. 子宫外的。~ *pregnancy* 子宫外孕。

ex·trav·a·gance [iksˈtrævigəns; ɪkˋstrævɪgəns], **ex·trav·a·gan·cy** [-si; -sɪ] *n*. **1**. 奢侈,挥霍,铺张,浪费。**2**. 过分(的事情)。**3**. 放纵的言行。*check* [*avoid*] ~ 制止[防止]浪费。*with* ~ 过度地,过分地。

ex·trav·a·gant [iksˈtrævəgənt; ɪkˋstrævəgənt] *a*. **1**. 过度的,过分的。**2**. 放肆的。**3**. 奢侈的,浪费的。**4**. 〔古〕游荡的。*an* ~ *price* 过高的价格。*load sb*. *with* ~ *praise* 过分赞扬某人。~ *in conduct* 行为放肆。~ *in dress* 穿着奢华。~ *habit* 奢侈的习惯。

ex·trav·a·gan·za [eksˌtrævəˈgænzə; ɛkˏstrævəˋgænzə] *n*. **1**. 狂文,狂诗,狂曲,幻想曲,滑稽剧。**2**. 狂妄的言行。**3**. (电影、体育比赛等)铺张华丽的表演。

ex·trav·a·gate [iksˈtrævəgeit; ɪkˋstrævəˏget] *vi*. 〔罕〕漂泊,放浪;越轨。

ex·trav·a·sate [eksˈtrævəseit; ɛkˋstrævəˏset] **I** *vt*. 使(血液等由脉管中)渗出;使(熔岩等)溢出。~*d blood* 淤血。—*vi*. 外渗,外沉,溢出。**II** *n*. 渗出液。

ex·trav·a·sa·tion [eksˌtrævəˈseiʃən; ɛkˏstrævəˋseʃən] *n*. **1**. 【医】外渗,外沉,外渗液;溢血。**2**. 【地】熔岩外喷;(熔岩等的)溢出。

ex·tra·vas·cu·lar [ˌekstrəˈvæskjulə; ˏɛkstrəˋvæskjələ˞] *a*. 脉管外的;血管外的;导管外的。

ex·tra·ve·hic·u·lar [ˌekstrəviˈhikjulə; ˏɛkstrəvɪˋhɪkjələ˞] *a*. (太空人)在太空(飞)船外部活动(使用)的;太空(飞)船外的。

ex·tra·ver·sion [ˌekstrəˈvəːʒən; ˏɛkstrəˋvɝʒən] *n*. = extroversion.

ex·tra·vert [ˈekstrəvəːt; ˋɛkstrəˏvɝt] *n*. = extrovert.

ex·tre·ma [iksˈtriːmə; ɪkˏstrimə] *n*. extremum 的复数。

ex·tre·mal [iksˈtriːməl; ɪkˋstriməl] *n*. 【数】极值曲线,致极函数。

ex·treme [iksˈtriːm; ɪkˋstrim] **I** *a*. **1**. 极端的;过激的(*opp*. moderate)。**2**. 极限的,非常的。**3**. 尽头的,末端的。**4**. 〔古〕最后的,临终的。*the* ~ *end of a rope* 绳索的末端。~ *measures* 极端手段。~ *old age* 极高龄。*an* ~ *case* 极端的例子。~ *unction* 【天主】临终涂油礼。~ *value* 【数】极值。*in one's* ~ *moments* 临终时刻。*the* ~ *hour of life* 临终。*the* ~ *lefts* 极左派。*the* ~ *penalty* (*of law*) 极刑。**II** *n*. **1**. 极端;末端。**2**. 〔*pl*.〕两极端。**3**. 〔*pl*.〕困境。**4**. 【数】极限值,外项;【逻】(三段论法结论中的)小词或大词〔*cf*. middle〕。*the* ~*s of fortune* 盛衰荣枯。***be in*** ~***s*** 处困境。*Extremes meet*. 两极相通,物极必反。***go from one*** ~ ***to the other*** 从一个极端转到另一个极端。***go to*** ~***s*** = ***run to an*** ~ 走极端。***go to the*** ~ ***of*** 采用…的极端手段。***in*** (***the***) ~ 极端,非常,很。~ **sports**【体】极限运动〔难度极大且具有危险性的运动〕。**-ness** *n*.

ex·treme·ly [iksˈtriːmli; ɪkˋstrimlɪ] *ad*. 极端地,非常地。~ *high frequency* 【无】甚高频。

ex·trem·ism [iksˈtriːmizəm; ɪkˋstrimɪzəm] *n*. 极端主义。

ex·trem·ist [iksˈtriːmist; ɪkˋstrimɪst] **I** *n*. 过激主义者,极端分子。**II** *a*. 极端主义的,过激论的。

ex·trem·i·ty [iksˈtremiti; ɪkˋstrɛmətɪ] *n*. **1**. 末端,尽头;极端,极度。**2**. 〔常 *pl*.〕困迫,绝境。**3**. 〔常 *pl*.〕最后手段,非常手段。**4**. 最后;〔常 *pl*.〕临终。**5**. 肢,手,足。*at the* ~ *of* 在…的尖端[末端]。*be in dire* ~ 极端困迫。*be reduced* [*driven*] *to* (*the last*) ~ [*extremities*] 陷入困境。*resist to the last* ~ 反抗到底,抵抗到最后。*the extremities* (人的)四肢,手足。***expect the*** ~ 作赴死准备,作万一准备。***proceed*** [***go***] ***to extremities*** 采取最后手段。

ex·tre·mum [ikˈstriːməm; ɪkˋstriməm̩] *n*. (*pl*. **-trema** [-mə; -mə])【数】极值。

ex·tri·ca·ble [ˈekstrikəbl; ˋɛkstrɪkəbl] *a*. 摆脱得了的;能救出的;能脱险的 (*opp*. inextricable)。

ex·tri·cate [ˈekstrikeit; ˋɛkstrɪˏket] *vt*. **1**. 救出,使脱离 (*from*)。**2**. 【化】放出,游离。**3**. 分辨出。~ ***oneself*** [***itself***] ***from*** [***out of***] 从…中脱离,摆脱。

ex·tri·ca·tion [ˌekstriˈkeiʃən; ˏɛkstrɪˋkeʃən] *n*. **1**. 救出,脱出。**2**. 【化】游离,放出。

ex·tri·ca·tor [ˈekstriˌkeitə; ˋɛkstrɪˏketə˞] *n*. **1**. 救出者,解脱者。**2**. 【化】游离器。

ex·trin·sic [eksˈtrinsik; ɛkˋstɪnsɪk] *a*. **1**. 外在的,非本质的 (*opp*. intrinsic, essential)。**2**. 附带的,外来的,外赋的;体外的。*That's something* ~ *to the subject*. 那是对本题无关宏旨的东西。**-cal·ly** *ad*.

extro- *pref*. = extra.

ex·trorse [eksˈtrɔːs; ɛkˋstrɔrs] *a*. 【植】(花药)向外的,外向的,外倾的 (*opp*. introrse)。**-ly** *ad*.

ex·tro·ver·sion [ˌekstrəuˈvəːʃən; ˏɛkstroˋvɝʃən] *n*. (*opp*. introversion)【医】外翻;【心】外向性。**-ver·sive** *a*. (*opp*. introversive)。

ex·tro·vert [ˈekstrəuvəːt; ˋɛkstroˏvɝt] **I** *n*. (*opp*. introvert)【心】外向性格的人。**II** *a*. 外向性的。**III** *vt*. 使成外向性格。**IV** *vi*. 变成外向性格。**-ish** *a*. 有点外向性。

ex·trude [eksˈtruːd; ɛkˋstrud] *vt*. **1**. 挤压,模压。**2**. 使(熔浆等)流出。**3**. 逐出 (*from*)。~ *tubing* 自模型内挤压出管子。—*vi*. 突出,伸出;挤压成形。**-r** *n*. 挤压机。

ex·tru·sion [eksˈtruːʒən; ɛkˋstruʒən] *n*. **1**. 挤压,挤压成形;挤出。**2**. 逐出。**3**. 【地】(熔岩的)喷出;突出,伸出。~ **flow** 挤力流。~ **moulding** 挤压模塑法。~ **press** 挤压机。~ **stress** (塑性变形的)挤压应力。

ex·tru·sive [eksˈtruːsiv; ɛkˋstrusɪv] **I** *a*. **1**. 挤出的;冲出的;迸出的;势在冲出的。**2**. 【地】喷出的;火山的。~ *rock* 火山岩,喷出岩。**II** *n*. 喷出岩体。

ex·tu·bate [eksˈtjuːbeit; ɛkˋstjubet] *vt*. 从(身体某部)除管〔如气管〕。**-ba·tion** *n*. 【医】除管法。

ex·u·ber·ance [igˈzjuːbərəns; ɪgˋzjubərəns], **ex·u·ber·an·cy** [-si; -sɪ] *n*. **1**. 繁茂,丰富。**2**. 充沛,充溢。~ *of foliage* 枝叶繁茂。

ex·u·ber·ant [igˈzjuːbərənt; ɪgˋzjubərənt] *a*. **1**. 茂盛的,繁茂的,丰富的。**2**. (感情等)充溢的;(活力)充沛的,(精神)旺盛的,(词藻)过于华丽的,极度的。~ *growth* 繁茂生长。~ *spirits* 兴高采烈。*an* ~ *imagination* 丰富的想像。**-ly** *ad*.

ex·u·ber·ate [igˈzjuːbəreit; ɛgˋzjubəˏret] *vi*. **1**. 充溢,富于,充满;显得茂盛。**2**. 沉溺 (*in*)。

ex·u·date [ˈeksjudeit; ˋɛksjuˏdet] *n*. 渗出物,渗出液,流出物。*cellular* ~ 细胞渗出液。

ex·u·da·tion [ˌeksjuːˈdeiʃən; ˏɛksjuˋdeʃən] *n*. **1**. 渗出(液),分泌(物),流出(物),溢泌(物)。**2**. 【冶】(跑铁水)胀箱;(打箱过早)跑火。*tin* ~ 锡汗。

ex·u·da·tive [igˈzjuːdətiv; ɪgˋzjudətɪv] *a*. 渗出的,流出的,溢泌的。

ex·ude [igˈzjuːd; ɪgˋzjud] *vt*. **1**. 使渗出;使流出。**2**. 使发散。~ *sweat* 流汗。—*vi*. **1**. 渗出;流出。**2**. 发散。

ex·ult [igˈzʌlt; ɪgˋzʌlt] *vi*. 欢跃;狂喜。~ *at* [*in*] *a triumph* 为胜利而狂喜。*She* ~*ed to find that she had succeeded*. 她为自己的大功告成而狂喜。*an* ~*ing heart* 欢跃[得意]的心情。

ex·ult·ance, ex·ult·an·cy [igˈzʌltəns, -ənsi; ɪgˋzʌltn̩s, -ənsɪ] *n*. = exultation.

ex·ult·ant [igˈzʌltənt; ɪgˋzʌltənt] *a*. 兴高采烈的,欢欣鼓舞的,耀武扬威的。**-ly** *ad*.

ex·ul·ta·tion [ˌegzʌlˈteiʃən; ˏɛgzʌlˋteʃən] *n*. 大喜,狂喜,欢跃;得意。

ex·um·brel·la [ˌeksʌmˈbrelə; ˏɛksʌmˋbrɛlə] *n*.【动】上伞(水母伞顶部)。

ex·urb [ˈeksəːb; ˋɛksɚb] *n*. 城市远郊富裕阶层住宅区。**-an** *a*. 城市远郊的。

ex·ur·ban·ite [ekˈsəːbənait; ɛkˋsɚbəˏnaɪt] **I** *n*. 城市远郊富裕居民〔尤指办公在市内,住在市郊的商人等〕。**II** *a*. 城市远郊的;城市远郊居民的;有城市远郊特点的。

ex·ur·bi·a [ekˈsəːbiə; ˋɛksəbɪə] *n*. (总称)城市远郊。

ex·u·vi·ae [igˈzjuːviiː; ɪgˋzjuvɪi] *n*. 〔*pl*.〕蜕(蛇、蝉等脱下的皮壳);〔喻〕空壳,残骸。

ex·u·vi·al [igˈzjuːvjəl; ɪgˋzjuvɪəl] *a*. 蜕皮性的。~ **glands**【动】蜕皮腺。

ex·u·vi·ate [igˈzjuːvieit; ɪgˋzjuvɪˏet] *vi*., *vt*. 脱(壳),蜕(皮)。

ex·u·vi·a·tion [igˌzjuːviˈeiʃən; ɪgˏzjuvɪˋeʃən] *n*. **1**. 脱壳,蜕皮,脱皮;蝉蜕;蜕下的皮[壳等]。

ex·vo·to [eksˈvəutəu; ɛkˋsvoto]〔L.〕**I** *n*. 还愿的奉献物。**II** *a*. 许愿的,还愿的。

ex·works [eksˈwəːks; ɛkˋswɚks] *ad*.〔口〕出厂(指出厂价格或价值等)。*put down the price* ~ 压低出厂价格。

exx. = examples.

-ey *suf*. (用于末字母为 *-y* 的词后) = -y[1]: clay*ey*.

ey·as [aiəs; ˋaɪəs] *n*. (巢中的)雏鸟;雏鹰。

eye [ai; aɪ] **I** *n*. (*pl*. ~*s* 〔古〕***ey·en*** [ˈaiən; ˋaɪən]) **1**. 眼睛,目。*blind in one* ~ = *lose an* ~ 一目失明。*compound* ~*s* (昆虫的)复眼。*the naked* ~ 肉眼。*Where are your* ~*s*? 难道你看不见? *His* ~*s are bigger than his belly*. 他眼馋肚饱。*What the* ~ *does not see, the heart does not grieve over*. 眼不见,心不烦。*Eyes, front*!【军】向前看! *Eyes left* [*right*]!【军】向左[右]看齐! **2**.〔常 *pl*.〕眼神,眼睛的表情。**3**. 视觉,视力;眼力,鉴别力,眼光,观察力。*have a straight* ~ 能看出某物是否直或正的眼力。*have an* ~ *for the beautiful* 有审美眼光。*have an* ~ *in one's head* 颇有眼光。**4**. 见解,观点;判断。*in sb.'s* ~ 照某人看来,按某人的看法。*in the* ~(*s*) *of* (*the*) *law* 从法律观点上看。**5**. 注视,注意,注目。*keep one's* ~ *on the picture* 盯着图画看。*keep one's* [*both*] ~*s open* 提防,当心。**6**. 眼状物;洞;孔;环;圈;(鱼卵、虫卵的)小黑点;色斑;(孔雀的)翎眼;眼状斑点;针眼;锚眼;钩眼;靶心;(索端的)索眼;圆窗。**7**.【气】风眼,风吹来的方向。*the* ~ *of a hurricane* 飓风眼,飓风中心部的平静区域。**8**.〔美俚〕侦探;私人侦探。**9**.【植】(马铃薯等的)芽眼,花心;(菊科的)花盘;【微】眼点;【物】光电池,光电管。*a magic* ~ 电眼,电子射线管。***All my*** ~ (***and Betty Martin***) = ***all the eye*** 或 ***all in the eye*** 〔英〕瞎说,胡扯,无聊。***an evil*** ~ 狠毒的眼光。***an*** ~ ***for an*** ~ = ~ ***for*** ~ 以眼还眼;报复。***an*** ~ ***in the sky*** 〔美俚〕侦察卫星。***apply the blind*** ~ 假装没看见。***be all*** ~***s*** 非常留意,注视。***be bright in the*** ~ 〔口〕喝醉。***before*** [***under***] ***sb.'s very*** ~***s*** 当某人面前。***black sb.'s*** ~ = ***give sb. a black*** ~ 把某人的眼眶打青。***by the*** ~ 用眼睛估计,凭眼力。***cast an*** ~ ***at*** [***over***] ***sth***. 对某物随便看一眼。***cast sheep's eyes on sb***. 对某人飞媚眼。***catch sb.'s*** ~(***s***) 引某人注意。***catch*** [***strike***] ***the*** ~ 显眼。***clap*** [***set, lay***] ~***s on*** 看到。***close one's eyes*** 死,逝世。***close*** [***shut***] ***one's*** ~***s to*** 拒绝注意。***cry one's*** ~***s out*** 哭得很伤心。***do sb. in the*** ~ 〔俚〕骗人,愚弄人。***dust the*** ~***s of*** 欺骗,蒙蔽。***easy as my*** ~ 易如反掌。***easy on the*** ~***s*** 〔俚〕悦目的,诱人的。***feast one's*** ~***s on*** 饱眼福。***fix one's*** ~***s on*** 盯,凝视。***get*** [***have***] ***one's*** ~ ***well in*** (射击等)看得很准,(运动员)能用眼跟上球的方向。***give an*** ~ ***to*** 照看,注意。***give sb. the*** (***glad***) ~ 〔美〕对人做媚眼。***half an*** ~ 随便一看 (*if you had half an* ~ 假若你稍加注意)。***have all one's*** ~***s about*** 谨防,当心。***have an*** ~ ***to*** **1**. 照看,注意。**2**. 以…为目的。***have an*** ~ ***on*** [***upon***] 照看,注意。***have*** ~***s at the back of one's head*** 能看到一切。***have*** ~***s for*** 〔口〕对…极感兴趣;注意。***have in one's*** ~ 心目中有…;考虑。***hold the public*** ~ 吸引世人眼目。***in a pig's*** ~ 〔美俚〕永不,决不。***in sb.'s mind's*** ~ 在想像中,在心目中。***in the*** ~ ***of the wind*** = ***in the wind's*** ~【海】逆风。***in the*** ~***s of*** = ***in one's*** ~***s*** 在…的心目中,在…的眼里。***in the public*** ~ 常公开露面〔在电视或报纸上〕;人人皆知。***keep an*** [***one's***] ~ ***on*** [***upon***] = ***have one's*** ~***s on*** **1**. 照看。**2**. 密切注意。***keep an*** ~ [***one's*** ~***s***] ***out for*** 注意,记住。***keep one's*** ~***s peeled*** [***open, skinned***] 时刻提防。***look sb. in the*** ~ 无畏惧[无愧]地正视某人。***make*** ~***s at sb***. 向某人送秋波;对…使眼色。***make sb. open his*** ~***s*** 使人吃惊。***meet sb.'s*** ~***s*** (偶尔)引起某人注意。***Mind your*** ~! 〔口〕注意! 当心! ***My*** ~(***s***)! 〔俚〕天啦! 嗳唷!〔表示赞叹、反对、惊讶〕。***never take one's*** ~***s off*** 目不转睛。***one's*** ~***s draw*** [***gather, pick***] ***straw*** 〔废〕昏昏欲睡。***open sb's*** ~***s*** (***to***) 使某人认清。***put a finger in one's*** ~ 哭。***put one's*** ~ ***together*** 入睡。***run one's*** ~***s through*** [***over***] 浏览。***see*** ~ ***to*** ~ ***with*** 跟…意见一致。***see with one's own*** ~***s*** 亲眼看见。***set an*** ~ ***by*** 对…非常喜爱;极尊重。***spit in the*** ~ ***of*** 藐视,蔑视。***the blind man's*** ~***s*** 瞎子用的拐杖。***the*** ~ ***of day*** [***the morning, heaven***] 〔诗〕太阳。***the*** ~***s of night*** [***heaven***] 〔诗〕星。***the*** ~***s of a ship*** 船头;锚索眼。***to one's mind's*** ~ 在心眼儿上,在心目中,在想像中。***to the*** ~ **1**. 从表面上看来。**2**. 当面,公然。***turn a*** [***one's***] ***blind*** ~ ***to*** 对…熟视无睹。***up to one's*** [***the***] ~***s in*** **1**. 极忙,埋头(工作)。**2**. 深陷(债务中)。***wipe one's*** ~***s*** **1**. 抢在某人前面打别人瞄准的猎物。**2**. 使人看到自己的狂妄。***with all one's*** ~***s*** 拼命,仔细。***with an*** ~ ***on*** [***to***] 指望着,着眼于,为了要…。***with dark*** [***cold, dry***] ~***s*** 冷眼。***with half an*** ~ 一看就…〔不用细看〕(*That can be seen with half an* ~. 那是显而易见的事)。***with one's*** ~***s open*** **1**. 明明知道。**2**. 注意。***with one's*** ~***s shut*** 不注意,胡乱地。***with open*** ~***s*** 明知故犯。***worth a Jew's*** ~ 〔古〕极为贵重。**II** *vt*. (~*d*; ***ey***(***e***)·***ing***) **1**. 看,观看;偷看;盯着看,注视,凝视。**2**. 在…打眼。~ *sb. askance* 用眼睛瞟人,斜着眼睛看人。~ *narrowy* 细看。~ *sb. jealously* [*with jealousy*] 嫉视某人。~ *a needle* 打针眼。~**ball** **1**. *n*. 眼球;瞳子 (~ *ball to* ~ *ball* 面对面的[地])。**2**. *vt*.〔美俚〕打量;用眼睛瞪(某人)使之慑服。~**bank**【医】眼库。~**bath** 洗眼杯。~**beam**〔古〕目光。~**bolt**【机】有眼螺栓,吊环螺栓。~**bright**【植】小米草〔过去认为对眼疾具有疗效〕。~**brow** **1**. *n*. 眉毛;【建】滴水;窗眉;【纺】飞花 (*knit the* ~*brows* 皱眉头。*raise the* ~*brow* 扬起眉毛;怀疑、吃惊的表情)。**2**. *vt*. (皱起眉头)瞪(~ *brow sb. out of the room* 把(某人)瞪出房间)。~ **candy** 令人赏心悦目的人[物]。~**-catcher** *n*. 特别引人注目的事物,醒目广告。~**-catching** *a*.〔美口〕引人注目的。~ **chart** 视力检验表。~ **cup** = ~-bath. ~**dropper** *n*.【医】滴管。~**drops** 眼药水,洗眼水。~**end** *n*. 有眼端。~**fidelity** 映像保真性,保真度。~**glass** **1**. 镜片;〔*pl*.〕眼镜,夹鼻眼镜。**2**. (望远镜等装置中的)目镜。**3**. 洗眼杯。~**-grabber** 引人注目的事物。~ **graffing** 芽眼嫁接法。~**hole** 眼窝;窥视孔;(针等的)眼。~**-in-the-sky** 空中监视。~**joint** *n*. 眼榫接合。~**-lash** 睫毛。~**let**, ~ **let hole** 孔眼;小孔;(皮鞋等的)带眼;金属套圈;窥视孔;枪眼,炮眼,(孔眼)锁缝。*vt*. 打小孔。~**letting** 用空心铆钉接合板材。~**lid** 眼睑;可调节喷口的半圆形调节片;可调节喷口 (*hang* (*on*) *by the* ~ *lids* 一发千钧。*in the batting of an* ~ *lid* 转瞬间。*lower* ~ *lid* 下眼睑。*upper* ~ *lid* 上眼睑)。~**liner** 描眼膏。~ **measurement** 目测。~**-mo** 携带式(电视)摄影机。~**opener** *n*. **1**. 使人惊奇的事物,有启发的

事物,迷人的人[物]。2.〔美俚〕起床喝的醒眼酒。~-**opening** *a*. 使人惊奇的,有启发性的。~-**piece** 目镜。~-**popping**〔美〕使人吃惊的。~**reach** = ~ shot. ~**rhyme** 不完全韵〔拼写相近,但发音各异的词,如 lone, none〕。~**servant**, ~**server**〔古〕当面勤快而背地懒惰的佣人。~**service**〔古〕1. 当面勤快而背地偷懒的帮佣。2. 敬仰的目光。~**shade** 眼罩, ~**shadow** 眼影膏。~**shot** 眼界,视野;视力,眼力;一瞥;见解(*beyond* ~ *shot* = *out of* ~ *shot* 在视界之外,不可见的地方。*in* [*within*] ~ *shot* 在视界之内)。~**sight** 视觉,视力,眼力;眼界;见解,观察。~**socket** *n*. 眼窝。~**some** *a*.〔美〕媚人的,可爱的。~**sore** 刺眼的东西。~**spot**【动】1. 眼点。2. 眼状色斑。~**stalk**【动】眼柄。~**strain** 眼疲劳。~**strings** 眼肌肉,眼神经。~**tooth** (*pl*. ~ *teeth*) 上颌犬牙(*cut one's* ~*teeth* 懂事,长大。*draw sb.'s* ~*teeth* 挫人的傲气)。~**wall**【气】眼壁〔飓风风眼外围的漏斗状云层(= wall cloud)〕. ~**wash** 1. 眼药水。2.〔俚〕奉承;欺诈。~**water** 眼药,洗眼药水;泪。~**wear** 双目镜。~**wink** 眨眼;一瞬;瞥见。~**winker** 睫毛,落入眼中的微粒。~**witness** 目击者,见证人。-**less** *a*. 1. 无眼的,瞎的。2. 盲目的,卤莽的。

eyed [aid; aɪd] *a*. 1. …眼的。2. 有孔眼的。3. 有眼状花纹的。4. 有(某种特点的)眼睛的;有眼状斑纹的。*blue*-~ 蓝眼睛的。

eye·ful [ˈaiful; aɪ`fʊl] *n*. 1. 满眼。2. 被完全看到的东西。3.〔俚〕值得一看的人[物]。*get* [*have*] *an* ~〔口〕好好看一下,看个够。*The bottle cap popped off and he got an* ~ *of beer* 瓶盖噗地一声掉了,他看见一满瓶啤酒。

eye ground [ˈaiˈgraund; `aɪˏgraʊnd] *n*. 眼底。

ey·en [ˈaiən; `aɪən] *n*. eye 的古体和方言体的复数。

Eye·tie [ˈaiti; `aɪtɪ] I *n*.〔英俚〕意大利人。II *a*. 意大利的〔带贬意,源于 Italian 的头两个字母〕。

ey·ot [eit, ˈeiət; `aɪət, et] *n*.〔英方〕= ait.

eyre [ɛə; ɛr] *n*.【史】巡回;巡回法院。*judices in* ~ 巡回法官。

ey·rie, ey·ry [ˈɛəri; `ɛrɪ] *n*. = aerie.

ey·rir [ˈeiriə; `erɪr] *n*. (*pl*. **au·rar** [ˈaurɑː; `aurɑr]) 奥拉〔冰岛货币名,等于 1/100 克朗〕。

EZ = 1. eastern zone 东区。2. electrical zero【电】电零点。

E·ze·ki·el [iˈziːkjəl; ɪ`zikɪəl] *n*. 1. 伊齐基尔〔姓氏〕。2.【圣】以西结〔希伯来预言家〕。3.【圣】《以西结书》〔旧约〕。

Ez·ra [ˈezrə; `ɛzrə] *n*. 1.【圣】以斯拉〔纪元前六世纪希伯来预言家〕。2.【圣】《以斯拉书》〔旧约〕。3. 男子名。

F

F, f [ef; ɛf] (*pl*. **F's, f's** [efs; ɛfs]) 1. 英语字母表第六字母。2. 第六。3.〔F〕【乐】F 音, F 调。4.〔F〕F 字形。5.〔F.〕〔美〕(学业成绩)劣,不及格 (failure) 的符号。6.【摄】光圈数 (f-number) 的符号。**F holes** (提琴上的) F 形孔眼。**F sharp** ($F^{\#}$) 升 F 调。

F = 1.【化】fluorine. 2.【生】(generation of) filial offspring;【植】子代〔F_1杂种子1代; F_2杂种子2代〕;【动】世代〔*cf*. f = force〕。

F. = 1. Fahrenheit. 2. Father. 3. Fellow. 4. Final (dividend). 5. France. 6. French; Friday.

F, F/, f, f/, f., f:, etc. 见 *f-number* 条。

f. = and the following (page) (*pl*. ***ff***.).

f. = 1. farad. 2. farthing. 3.【美军】fast. 4. fathom. 5. feet. 6. feminine. 7. field. 8. florin. 9. folio. 10. following. 11. foot. 12. *forte*.【棒球】13. foul(s). 14. franc(s). 15. from.

FA, F.A. = 1. field artillery 野战炮;野战炮兵。2. fine arts 美术。3. Football Association (英国)足球协会。4. field ambulance 战地救护车;野战救护队。5. first aid【医】(对病人的)急救。

fa [fɑː; fɑ] *n*.【乐】全音阶的长音阶第四音。

f.a.a., FAA = free of all average 一切海损均不赔偿。

F.A.A. = Fleet Air Arm〔英〕海军航空兵。

FAA = Federal Aviation Administration〔美〕联邦航空局。

F.A.A.A.S. = Fellow of the American Association for the Advancement of Science 美国科学促进会会员。

F.A.A.S./C. = Free from All Average Seizure and Capture 因船只被扣留与被掳掠而造成的损失及一切海损均不赔偿。

F.A.A.S./C. *including* **R.D.C.** = Free from All Average Seizure and Capture Including Running Down Clause 因船只被扣留与被掳掠而造成的损失及一切海损(包括碰撞损失)均不赔偿。

FAB = Foreign Affairs Bureau 外事局。

fab [fæb; fæb] *a*.〔口〕惊人的,极好的,难以置信的〔fabulous 的缩略〕。

fa·ba·ceous [fəˈbeiʃəs; fə`beʃəs] *a*. 1.【植】豆科植物的。2.(蚕)豆状的。

fab·by [ˈfæbi; `fæbɪ] *a*.〔口〕顶呱呱的,好极了的;妙极了的。

Fa·bi·an [ˈfeibjən; `febɪən] I *a*. 1. 古罗马大将费边(Fabius)式的,使敌人疲于奔命的,以逸待劳的,持久的〔cf. Fabius〕. 2. 费边社(社员)的。~ **Society** 费边社〔1884 年在伦敦成立,主张以渐进的方法实现社会主义的团体〕。II *n*. 费边社社员;费边主义者。-**ism** *n*. 费边主义;持久战术。-**ist** 1. *n*. 费边主义者。2. *a*. 费边主义的。

Fa·bi·us [ˈfeibjəs; `febɪəs] *n*. 费比乌斯〔? —203 B.C., 罗马大将,以避免与敌作战和采取拖延政策的战略使敌师劳而无功,终于战胜迦太基军队〕。

fa·ble [ˈfeibl; `febl] I *n*. 1. 寓言,童话〔*cf*. allegory, parable〕。2.〔集合词〕神话,传说。3. 荒唐故事,无稽之谈。4.〔古〕(史诗、剧本等的)情节。5. 人人谈论的话题。*celebrated in* ~ 传闻中大名鼎鼎的。**Aesop's** ~**s** 伊索寓言。**old wive's** ~**s** 闲话,奶奶经。II *vi*. 讲故事,编寓言。— *vt*. 虚构(故事),杜撰,煞有介事地讲。-**r** *n*. = fabulist.

fa·bled [ˈfeibld; `febld] *a*. 1. 寓言中的,故事中有名的。

2. 虚构的,荒唐无稽的;神话般的、传说式的。a ~ *chest of gold* 虚构的所谓金箱。*a* ~ *goddess* 传说中的女神。

fab·li·au [ˈfæbliəu; ˋfæblɪo] *n*. (*pl*. **-aux** [-ˌəuz; -ˏoz]) (中世纪法国文学体裁)诗体短篇小说,韵文故事。

Fa·bre [ˈfɑːbə; ˋfɑbɚ], **J.H.** 法布尔〔1823—1915, 法国昆虫学家〕。

fab·ric [ˈfæbrik; ˋfæbrɪk] *n*. 1. 构造物,建筑物;工厂;结构;(社会等的)组织;【地】组构。2. 编织品,织物;纤维品;织法;质地。*aeroplane* ~【空】飞机蒙布。*the* ~ *of society* = the social ~ 社会组织。*a cloth of exquisite* ~ 织法精美的布。*soil* ~ 土壤结构。*synthetic* ~*s* 合成纤维织物。*woolen* [*silk*] ~*s* 毛[丝]织品。~ **glove** 毛线手套。~ **proofing** 布上涂胶。**-a·ble** *a*. 可成型的,可塑造的。

fab·ri·cant [ˈfæbrikənt; ˋfæbrəkənt] *n*. 〔罕〕厂商,制造商,工厂主。

fab·ri·cate [ˈfæbrikeit; ˋfæbrɪˏket] *vt*. 1. 构成;组成;〔美〕制作,建造。2. 捏造,伪造,杜撰。3. 创立(理论等)。~ *a document* 伪造文书。~ *new theories* 创立新理论。~ *automobiles* 制造汽车。*a* ~*d building* 装配式房屋。*a* ~*d ship* 组合船。**-ca·tion** [ˌfæbriˈkeiʃən; ˏfæbrɪˋkeʃən] *n*. **-ca·tor** *n*. 1. 捏造者。2. 装配工;修整工。3. 金属加工厂。

Fab·ri·coid, Fab·ri·koid [ˈfæbrikɔid; ˋfæbrɪˏkɔɪd] *n*. 〔商标名〕(做书面等用的)漆布,人造革,防雨布。

fab·roil [ˈfæbrɔil; ˋfæbrɔɪl] *n*. 纤维胶木。

Fab. Soc. = Fabian Society〔英〕费边社。

fab·u·list [ˈfæbjulist; ˋfæbjəlɪst] *n*. 1. 寓言作家。2. 虚构情节的人。

fab·u·los·i·ty [ˌfæbjuˈlɔsiti; ˏfæbjəˋlɑsətɪ] *n*. 1. 神话;寓言性质;虚构性;无稽。2.〔古〕耸人听闻之言。

fab·u·lous [ˈfæbjuləs; ˋfæbjələs] *a*. 1. 寓言般的。2. 传说上的,神话中的。3. 荒唐无稽的;难以相信的;无比的,非常的。4. 编写寓言的。5.〔口〕极好的。*a* ~ *price* (近乎荒唐的)非常昂贵的价格。~ *wealth* 巨富。*a* ~ *writer* 寓言作家。*a* ~ *bird* 一种传说中的鸟。~ **age** (一个国家开国初期的)神话时代。**-ly** *ad*. **-ness** *n*.

FAC = Foreign Affairs Commitee 外交委员会。

fac. = 1. facsimile. 2. factor. 3. factory. 4. faculty.

fa·cade, fa·çade [fəˈsɑːd; fəˋsɑd] *n*. 1.【建】正面。2. 外表,外观;虚伪,浮面,(掩饰真相的)门面。*maintain a* ~ *of wealth* 保持富有的门面。

fa·cad·ism [fəˈsɑːdizəm; fəˋsɑdɪzm] *n*. 保存旧门面〔翻新旧建筑时保存原有旧门面以保持老风貌的一种做法〕。

face [feis; fes] **I** *n*. 1. 脸,面孔;面貌,样子;面子,威信。2. 愁容,苦脸;〔口〕老面皮,厚脸皮。3. 外观,形势,局面。4. 面前,眼前。5. 面(部),表面;前面,正面;【物】萤光面;(钟表等的)字盘;(器具的)使用面。6.【军】方阵的一面。7.【商】票面,额面;(文件的)字面。8.【印】版面;【矿】(煤矿等的)采掘面;(矿石等的)晶面;【机】(刀具的)切削面。9. 面部化妆。10. 面具。*a sad* ~ 愁容。*a smiling* ~ 笑脸。*save one's* ~ 保全面子。*lose one's* ~ 丢脸。*the right* [*wrong*] ~ 表[反]面。*with a smile on one's* ~ 面带笑容。*the* ~ *of the note* 票面额。*a* ~ *of placid contentment* 一副怡然自得的外表。*the funny* ~*s* 假面具〔儿童玩具〕。*get one's* ~ *on* 作好面部化妆。***a smooth face*** 1. 没有胡子的脸。2. 讨好的面孔。***accept the*** ~ ***of*** 保全[维护]…的面子;偏袒,偏爱。***at*** [***in, on***] ***the first*** ~ 初初一看,乍看之下。***before sb.'s*** ~ 当着某人的面。~ ***to*** ~ 面对面。***fall on one's*** ~ 脸朝下倒下,(彻底)失败。***feed one's*** ~〔美俚〕吃饭。***fly from the*** ~ ***of men*** 无面目见人。***fly in the*** ~ ***of*** 悍然不顾;公然抗拒。***grind the*** ~***s of the poor*** 压榨穷人。***have*** (***the wind***) ***in one's*** ~ 朝着,逆着(风)。***have two*** ~***s*** 怀二心;口是心非;耍两面派;(语言)暧昧。***hide one's*** ~ ***from*** 不理睬。***in sb.'s*** ~ 正对着;当面。***in the*** ~去你的〔表示蔑视和不满〕! ***in the*** ~ ***of*** 1.〔英〕在…前面;面临。2. 不避,不惧;不管,不顾,尽管 (*in* (*the*) ~ *of the world* 公然,在众目睽睽下)。3. 反对 (*fly in the* ~ *of* 公开反抗)。***in the*** (***very***) ~ ***of day*** [***the sun***] 公然,在光天化日之下。***keep a straight*** ~ 不露笑容,板着面孔。***laugh in sb.'s*** ~ 当面嘲笑某人。***lift sb.'s*** ~ 为人整容〔尤指消除面部皱纹的整容外科〕。***look sb. in the*** ~ = ***look in sb.'s face*** 瞧着某人的脸,正视。***make a long*** ~ 拉下脸来,板着脸。***make*** ~***s*** [***a*** ~] 做苦脸;做鬼脸。***on*** [***upon***] ***the*** ~ ***of*** (***a document, etc.***) 1. (文件等的)字面上,由句法上看。2. 明明,可见 (*The story is false on the* ~ *of it.* 这个故事明明是假的)。***on the*** (***mere***) ~ ***of it*** (单)由外表判断,一看就…。***open one's*** ~〔美俚〕开口,说。***pull*** [***put***] ***a long*** ~ = make a long ~. ***pull*** ~***s*** [***a*** ~] = *make* ~*s*. ***put a bold*** ~ ***on*** 对…装做满不在乎。***put a good*** ~ ***on*** 1. 给…装面子,粉饰,对…抱乐观态度,对…装作无事。***put a new*** ~ ***on*** 使局面一新,使面目一新。***run one's*** ~〔美俚〕硬要赊欠。***set*** [***put***] ***one's*** ~ ***against*** 抵制,坚决反对。***set one's*** ~ ***to*** [***towards***] 1. 向…方面。2. 着手;决心。***show one's*** ~ 露面,出面。***slap sb. in the*** ~ 打人耳光;侮辱人。***stare sb. in the*** ~ 1. 盯着人的脸看。2. 就在眼前,迫在眉睫。***straighten one's*** ~ 板起面孔。***to sb.'s*** ~ 对着某人,向某人,在某人前面,当面。***turn*** ~ ***about*** 背转过去,调转方向。***turn one's*** ~ ***away*** 背过脸去。***wear a long*** ~ = ***make a long*** ~. **II** *vt*. 1. 面向,面对,对着。2. 对抗,抵抗;毅然承受,勇敢承当(难局等)。3. 给…包面;用…抹盖,涂上;把…的表面弄平,削平(石等)。4. 使转向;命令(队伍)转变方向;翻开(牌面)。5. 染(茶等的)色;镶(衣)边。~ *the wall* 向着墙壁。*be* ~*d with danger* 面临危险。*The picture* ~*s page 8*. 插图在第 8 页对面。*a house facing the street* 临街的房屋。*a wall* ~*d with concrete* 水泥覆面的墙壁。—*vi*. 1. 面对着 (*on*; *to*)。2.【军】〔口令〕向…转! 3. 朝某一方向。*About* ~!〔口令〕向后转! *Left* [*Right*] ~! 向左[右]转! ~ ***about*** [***round***] (使)转过身来,改变主意 (*He* ~*d his men about*. 他命令他的队伍向后转)。~ ***sb. down*** 用目光压倒,降伏,挫败。~ ***it*** [***a matter***] ***out*** 坚持到底,不让步。***F- off!*** (冰上曲棍球)比赛开始! ~ ***off*** (在一场力量、耐力等的考验中与对手)对抗。~ ***sth. out*** 把某事坚持到底。~ ***the music*** 毅然面对难局;经受谴责,临危不惧。~ ***the world*** 见世面。~ ***up*** 着色,把表面弄得好看些。~ ***up to*** 大胆面向;正面对付。***Let's*** ~ ***it.***〔美口〕面对现实(不要躲避退缩)吧;尽力对付吧。~**-ache**【医】面部神经痛。~**-around** *n*. 转变方向[态度]。~**bone** 颧骨。~ **book** 肖像影集。~ **brick**【建】面砖。~**card** (纸牌中 K, Q, J 三种)人头牌。~**-centred** *a*.【物】(原子)面心的 (~-*centred crystal* 面心晶体)。~ **cloth** 面巾 (= wash-cloth)。~**-cream** 润肤香脂。~ **down** 1. *ad*. 面朝下地。2. *n*.〔美口〕= ~ off. 3. 摊牌。~ **fly** 牛蝇。~ **goods** 光洁毛织物。~ **guard** (厂矿,击剑等用的)护面具,面罩。~**-harden** *vt*.【冶】使(铁合金)表面硬化。~**-lifting** 1. (除去面部皱纹的)整型外科手术;整型。2. (建筑物、汽车等的)改建,翻新(门面)。~ **mask** 1. 面罩。2. 面模。~**-off** *n*. 1. (冰上曲棍球)开球。2. 对峙,敌对;摊牌;面对面的会议[争论、谈判]。~ **par** 票面价格。~ **plate** 1.【机】面板,花盘。2. (电灯开关等上的)护板,盖板。~ **powder** 搽脸香粉。~**-saver**〔美俚〕保全面子的事。~**-saving** *a*. 保全面子的。~ **time** 1. (在电视或公众场合的)露脸;曝光;亮相。2. (社交场合的)会面。3. (雇员在老板面前卖力工作的)做表面文章。~**-to-**~ *a*., *ad*. 面对面的[地]。~**-up** *ad*. 面朝上的。~ **value** 1. (钞票,债券等的)票面价值。2. 表面价值 (*take a promise at* ~ *value* 把一项诺言信以为真)。

F

faced [feist; fest] *a*. 〔多用以组成复合词〕具有…脸型的,有…表面的,有…贴边的。*a marble-～ brick building* 大理石面的砖房。*a neatly-～ terrace* 表面整齐的地坛。*round-～* 圆脸蛋的。*satin-～ lapels* 缎子面的翻领。*straight-～* 板面孔的。

face·less [ˈfeislis; ˋfeslɪs] *a*. **1**. 没脸面的。**2**. 面目不明的;缺乏鲜明个性的;没有个性的;匿名的。

fac·er [ˈfeisə; ˋfesɚ] *n*. **1**. 化妆师,美容师;对物品表面进行加工的人,用来覆盖或加工物品表面的材料。**2**. 〔口〕(拳击的)面部打击。**3**. 〔英口〕意外事故;意外障碍,大打击。**4**. 【机】铣刀盘;平面铣刀。

fac·et [ˈfæsit; ˋfæsɪt] **I** *n*. **1**. (宝石等的)小平面,刻面;平圆面。**2**. (事物的)方面。**3**. (昆虫的)小眼面。**4**. 【建】柱槽筋,凸线。**II** *vt*. 在(钻石上)刻面。**facet(t)ed eyes** 复眼。**facet(t)ed pebbles** 棱石。

fa·ce·ti·ae [fəˈsiːʃiˌiː; fəˋsiʃɪˏi] *n*. 〔*pl*.〕 **1**. 滑稽言语,诙谐。**2**. 〔书〕(黄色下流的)滑稽书,淫书。

fa·ce·tious [fəˈsiːʃəs; fəˋsiʃəs] *a*. **1**. 滑稽的,好笑的。**2**. 爱开玩笑的。**-ly** *ad*. **-ness** *n*.

fa·ci·a [ˈfæʃə; ˋfæʃɪə] *n*. = fascia.

fa·cial [ˈfeiʃəl; ˋfeʃəl] **I** *a*. 面部的,颜面的。**II** *n*. 〔美俚〕面部按摩;美容。*a ～ layer* 表面的一层。*～ expression* 面部表情。～ **angle** 颜面角;(结晶的)面角。～ **cream** 雪花膏;香脂。～ **index** (测定面部长宽比率的)面长指数。～ **nerve** 面神经。～ **neuralgia** 【医】面神经痛。～ **tissue** 纸巾,擦面用的薄纸。

fa·ci·es [ˈfeiʃiiːz, ˈfeiʃiːz; ˋfeʃɪiz, ˋfeʃɪz] *n*. 〔*pl*.〕〔单复同〕 **1**. 颜面,外观;外表。**2**. 【生态】演替系列混优种社会,演替系列变群丛。**3**. 【地】相。**4**. 【医】面色;表面。

fac·ile [ˈfæsail, ˈfæsil; ˋfæsl, ˋfæsɪl] *a*. **1**. 容易的;轻快的;轻便的。**2**. 机敏的;流畅的。**3**. 易亲近的;温和的;易打交道的。*a ～ task* 容易的工作。*a ～ liar* 随口撒谎的人。*a ～ style* 流畅的文体。*She has a ～ tongue*. 她口齿流利,能说会道。*He is ～ tool*. 他容易被人利用。**-ly** *ad*.

fa·c'i·le prin·ceps [ˈfæsiliˈprinseps; ˋfæsəlɪˋprɪnsɛps] 〔L.〕稳得第一的,独占鳌头。*In that special field of science he is ～, and has left all competitors behind*. 在这一专门的科学领域中,他是出类拔萃的,使其他的竞争者望尘莫及。

fa·cil·i·tate [fəˈsiliteit; fəˋsɪləˏtet] *vt*. **1**. 使容易,使顺当。**2**. 助长,促进。*The broken lock ～d my entrance into the empty house*. 门锁坏了,使我得以进入这个空屋。★此词不以人作主语。**-ta·tion** [-ˈteiʃən; -ˋteʃən] *n*.

fa·cil·i·ty [fəˈsiliti; fəˋsɪlətɪ] *n*. **1**. 容易,简易,轻便。**2**. 机敏,灵巧,流畅。**3**. 〔常 *pl*.〕方便,便利,设备,器材,工具,装置;机构。**4**. 和善,柔和。*facilities of travelling* 旅游设施[机构]。*servicing facilities* 辅助设备;维护设备。*homing ～* 归航设备。*monetary facilites* 金融机关。～ ***and difficulty*** 顺利和困难。***give*** [***accord***, ***afford***] ***facilities for*** 给与…方便。***with ～*** **1**. 容易。**2**. 流利。

fac·ing [ˈfeisiŋ; ˋfesɪŋ] *n*. **1**. 【建】饰面,面层,覆盖面;敷面物,面料;面饰;墙面。**2**. (衣服等的)镶边,贴边,滚条。**3**. 【机】衬片;刮面;刮面法。**4**. 【军】〔*pl*.〕(军服的)领章,袖章。**5**. (茶等的)着色,色料。**6**. 【军】转变队列方向,看齐。*a cement ～* 水泥墙面。***go through one's ～s*** 被考试;受训练。***put sb. through his ～s*** 训练,教练(某人);考验某人的本领。～ **slip** 邮包上注明目的地、日期等的标签。～ **tool** 【机】车面刀。

facs = facilities.

fac·sim·i·le [fækˈsimili; fækˋsɪməlɪ] **I** *n*. **1**. (通讯)传真。**2**. 复制,摹写,摹本。*documents reproduced in ～* 和原件惟妙惟肖的文件复制本。***in ～*** 逼真,毫不走样,惟妙惟肖。**II** *vt*. 复制,摹写。～ **paper** 传真感光纸。～ **telegraph** 传真电报。～ **transmission** [**broadcasting**] 电传真迹,电话传真(简称 Fax.)。

fact [fækt; fækt] *n*. **1**. 事实,实际,实情。**2**. 犯罪行为。**3**. 论据;证据。*an established ～* 既定事实。*The ～ (of the matter) is that ...* 事实上是。*Facts are stubborn (things)*. 〔谚〕事实是改变不了的。*Facts speak louder than words*. 事实胜于雄辩。*the hard ～s* 现实。*His ～s are open to question*. 他的论据有问题。***after*** [***before***] ***the ～*** 犯罪后[前],作案后[前] (*an accessary after the ～* 事后从犯)。***as a matter of ～*** 事实是,事实上。***bring out the ～s and reasons*** 摆事实,讲道理。***～s of life*** **1**. 性知识。**2**. 严酷的现实。***～s on file*** 小资料。***from the ～ that ...*** 从…的事实上来看。***in ～*** 其实,事实上,实际上;总之。***be caught in the ～*** 当场被捕。***in point of ～*** 实际上。***turn the ～s upside down*** 颠倒黑白。**～-finder** *n*. 事实调查者。**～-finding** *n*., *a*. 进行实际调查(的) (*a ～ finding committee* 调查委员会)。

fac·ta [ˈfæktə; ˋfæktə] *n*. factum 的复数。

fac·tion [ˈfækʃən; ˋfækʃən] *n*. **1**. 宗派,派别,小集团。**2**. 派系纠纷,内讧。*sb.'s own ～* 某人的嫡系。**-al**, **-ary**, *a*. **-alism** *n*. 派别的活动;小团体主义,宗派主义。**-ist** *n*. 宗派[小团体]主义者。

-fac·tion *suf*. 加在词尾为 -fy 的动词后,形成表示其作用的名词: satis*faction*.

fac·tion·eer [ˌfækʃəˈniə; ˏfækʃəˋnɪɚ] *vi*. 搞派系斗争。

fac·tious [ˈfækʃəs; ˋfækʃəs] *a*. **1**. 闹派别的;好捣乱的。**2**. 起于派别的;由于搞宗派而产生的。**-ly** *ad*. **-ness** *n*.

fac·ti·tious [fækˈtiʃəs; fækˋtɪʃəs] *a*. **1**. 人为的,人工的。**2**. 装成的,不自然的;虚构的;假的。**-ly** *ad*. **-ness** *n*.

fac·ti·tive [ˈfæktitiv; ˋfæktətɪv] **I** *a*. 【语法】作为的,使役的。*a ～ verb* (直接受词后须加补语的)使役动词。**II** *n*. 使役格。

fac·tor [ˈfæktə; ˋfæktɚ] **I** *n*. **1**. 〔英〕经销人;(代客买卖收取佣金的)经纪人;代理商;代办人;〔Scot.〕土地经管人。**2**. 要素,因素;原动力。**3**. 【物】系数,率;【数】因子,因数;【化】当量换算因数;【生】遗传因子,基因;【摄】曝光系数。**4**. 倍;乘数;商。*amplification ～* (电子管的)放大系数。*common ～* 公因子,公因素。*the copper ～* 含铜率。*engagement ～* 【机】接触比,重叠系数。*～ of safety* 安全系数。*the ～ of shape* 【林】形数。*increase by a ～ of five* 增加四倍。*the key ～* 关键。*the plant* [*utility*] *～* 设备使用率。*resolution into ～s* 因数分解。*the visibility ～* 视度。*3 and 5 are ～s of 15*. 三和五是十五的因子。**II** *vt*. **1**. 【数】把…化为因子[因数]。**2**. 为…充当代理商;代理经营;代管(产业)。～ ***out*** 析出因数。～ **group** 【数】商群。～ **ring** 【数】商环。

fac·tor·age [ˈfæktəridʒ; ˋfæktərɪdʒ] *n*. **1**. 代理[经纪]行业。**2**. 佣金。

fac·to·ri·al [fækˈtɔːriəl; fækˋtɔrɪəl] **I** *a*. **1**. 代理商的;工厂的。**2**. 【数】因数的;阶乘的。**II** *n*. 【数】阶乘;【统】阶乘积。*the ～ of 4* 四的阶乘。～ **experiment** 析因实验。～ **function** 阶乘函数。

fac·tor·ize [ˈfæktəraiz; ˋfæktəraɪz] *vt*. 【数】把…化为因子[数]。**-tor·i·za·tion** [ˌfæktəraiˈzeiʃən; ˏfæktərəˋzeʃən] *n*.

fac·to·ry [ˈfæktəri; ˋfæktərɪ] *n*. **1**. 工厂,制造厂。**2**. 〔古〕代理店。*an atomic-energy ～* 原子能发电站。*～ costs* 制造成本。*a ～ girl* 女工。*a ～ hand* 职工,工人。*The F- Law* [*Acts*] 工厂法。～ **farming** 工厂化牲畜[家禽]饲养业。～ **ship** (设有鱼类加工设备的)加工渔船。～ **town** 工业区,工厂区。

fac·to·tum [fækˈtəutəm; fækˋtotəm] *n*. **1**. 什么都得干的雇员[仆人];勤杂人员;打杂的人。**2**. 【印】特大型花体大写字母。

fac·tu·al [ˈfæktjuəl; ˋfæktʃʊəl] *a*. 事实上的,实在的。*～ writing* (某人的)手笔,真迹。**-i·ty** [ˌfæktjuˈæliti; ˏfæktʃjʊˋælətɪ] *n*. 实在性。**-ly** *ad*. **-ness** *n*.

F

fac·tu·al·ism [ˈfæktjuəlizəm; ˋfæktʃuəlɪzəm] *n*. 尊重事实,求实精神。

fac·tum [ˈfæktəm; ˋfæktəm] *n*. 〔L.〕(*pl*. **-ta** [-tə; -tə])【法】**1**. 事实;行为。**2**. 呈文,事实陈述书,辩驳书。**3**. (遗嘱的)正式订立。

fac·ture [ˈfæktʃə; ˋfæktʃɚ] *n*. **1**. 〔古〕制造;(制)成品。**2**. 制法〔尤指艺术品表面的加工〕。

fac·u·la [ˈfækjulə; ˋfækjʊlə] *n*. (*pl*. **-lae** [-liː; -li])【天】(太阳的)光斑〔*cf*. macula〕。**-lar**, **-lous** *a*.

fac·u·lae [ˈfækjuˌli; ˋfækjʊˏli] *n*. facula 的复数。

fac·ul·ta·tive [ˈfækəltətiv; ˋfæklˏtetɪv] *a*. **1**. 特许的,特准的。**2**. 任意的,随意的。**3**. 能力上的,机能上的。**4**.【生】兼性的。~ *money* 特准发行的货币。*a* ~ *course* 选修课程。~ **parasite**【生】兼性寄生物,兼性寄生菌。~ **plant**【植】不定型植物。**-ly** *ad*.

fac·ul·ty [ˈfækəlti; ˋfækl̩tɪ] *n*. **1**. 能力,才能;官能,机能;〔美〕技能,手腕。**2**. 特权;特许;权能。**3**. 〔英〕(大学的)专科,系,院;全院〔系〕教授;〔美〕教授会,教职员。**4**. 任何一种专业的全体从业人员,公会。*the* ~ *of memory* 记忆力。*the imaginative* ~ 想像力。*a housekeeper of notable* ~ 极能干的女管家。*the students and* ~ 全院师生。*the F- of Engineering* 工学院。*the medical* ~ 医界同仁。**collect one's faculties** 镇定下来。

fad [fæd; fæd] *n*. **1**. 一时流行的风尚;一时的爱好。**2**. 一时的怪念头。**-dish**, **-dy** *a*. 爱新奇的,一时流行的。**-di·ly** *ad*. **-dism** *n*. 一时的狂热性;追随时尚。**-dist** *n*. 爱新奇的人,好事的人。

FAD = flavin adenine dinucleotide.【生化】黄素腺嘌呤二核苷酸。

fade[1] [feid; fed] *vi*. **1**. 褪色;失去光泽。**2**. 凋落,枯谢;衰老,憔悴。**3**. 渐淡,渐渐消失。**4**. 〔美俚〕离开,跑掉,逃掉。*The flowers have* ~*d*. 花已凋零。*All memory of his boyhood has* ~*d from his mind*. 他已经记不清自己童年时代的情景。—*vt*. 使褪色;使凋谢;使衰老。*a carpet* ~*d by the sun* 被晒得褪了色的地毯。~ *in* [*out*]【影】(使)渐现[隐];【无】(使)(声音)渐高[消]。~ **away** *n*. 逐渐消失。~ **cream** 淡化霜,增白霜〔一种能抑制皮肤黑色素的美容霜〕。~**-in**【影】渐现,淡入;【无】(声音)渐高。~**-out**【影】渐隐,淡出;【无】(声音)渐消。~**-over**【影】淡入淡出。~**proof** *a*. 不褪色的。**-r** 音量[光量]调节器,混频电位器。

fade[2] [fɑːd; fɑd] *a*. **1**. 乏味的,平淡的。**2**. 〔废〕萎谢褪色的,憔悴的。

fade·less [ˈfeidlis; ˋfedlɪs] *a*. 不凋谢的;不褪色的;不衰落的。**-ly** *ad*.

fa·do [ˈfɑːduː; ˋfɑdu] *n*. 思乡曲〔葡萄牙民歌,带有忧郁、怀乡情调〕。

fae·cal [ˈfiːkəl; ˋfikl̩] *a*. = fecal.

fae·ces [ˈfiːsiːz; ˋfisiz] *n*. 〔*pl*.〕= feces.

fa·e·na [fəˈeina; fəˋena] *n*. 〔Sp.〕(斗牛的)连续劈刺〔斗牛士在击杀牛前炫示技能的劈刺动作〕。

fa·er·ie, **fa·er·y** [ˈfeiəri, ˈfɛəri; ˋfeərɪ, ˋfɛrɪ] **I** *n*. (*pl*. ***fa·er·ies***) **1**. 妖精之国,仙境。**2**. 〔古〕妖精。**II** *a*. 妖精(一样)的;梦幻的。

Faer·oes [ˈfɛərəuz; ˋfɛroz] *n*. 法罗群岛〔大西洋北部〕。

Faer·o·ese [ˌfɛərəˈiːz; ˏfɛroˋiz] **I** *n*. **1**. 法罗群岛的居民。**2**. 法罗语。**II** *a*. **1**. 法罗群岛居民的。**2**. 法罗语的。

fag [fæg; fæg] **I** *vt*. (**-gg-**) **1**. 使疲劳。**2**. 磨损,拆散(绳索的末端)。**3**. (英国公学中旧生)强迫(新生)跑腿。—*vi*. **1**. 拼命劳动(*at*),做苦工。**2**. 替旧生跑腿。***be fagged out*** 疲劳极了。~ ***away*** 辛辛苦苦地做工。~ ***out*** **1**. 使筋疲力尽。**2**.【板球】使做外野手。**II** *n*. **1**. 〔英〕苦工;做苦工的人;疲劳。**2**. (英国学校中受旧生使唤的)当值新生。**3**. 烟头,布头。**4**. 〔美俚〕搞同性恋关系的男子。*It is too much* (*of a*) ~. 那是(一件)受不了的苦活。~ **end** **1**. 绳索的散端,末端,零头;烟头;布头(等)。**2**. 残渣,废渣。**3**. 〔美俚〕上当,吃亏(*get the* ~ *end* 上了当)。**-gy** *a*. 〔美俚〕男性同性恋的;女性化的。

fag·got [ˈfægət; ˋfægət] **I** *n*. **1**. 柴把,柴捆;束枝条。**2**.【冶】成束熟铁块,束铁。**3**. 〔英〕(加调味品的)烤肝片。**4**. 长条抽线,束芯装饰针迹。**II** *vt*., *vi*. **1**. 捆,束。**2**. 用花式针迹接(缝)。~ **vote** 〔英〕(把一人财产暂时分与数人使享有选举权而进行的)结伙选举。~ **voter** 结伙投票人。**-ry** 〔美俚〕男性同性恋。**-y** 〔美俚〕男性同性恋的;(男子)女性化的。

fa·gin [ˈfeigin; ˋfegɪn] *n*. 小偷把头;教唆犯〔原为狄更斯小说 *Oliver Twist* 中的人物〕。

fag·ot [ˈfægət; ˋfægət] 〔美〕= **faggot**.

fag·ot·ing, **fag·got·ing** [ˈfægətiŋ; ˋfægətɪŋ] *n*. **1**. 宽格花边抽花手工。**2**. 花式针迹接缝。

Fahr. = Fahrenheit.

Fahr·en·heit [ˈfærənhait, ˈfɑːr-; ˋfærənˏhaɪt, ˋfɑr-] *n*., *a*. 华氏温度计(的)。*the* ~ *scale* 华氏温标。*a* ~ *thermometer* 华氏温度计。

fa·ience [faiˈɑːns; faɪˋɑns] *n*. 〔F.〕彩釉陶器。

fail [feil; fel] **I** *vi*. **1**. 失败,不及格(*opp*. succeed, pass);(判断)错误,不中目标。**2**. 〔与 of 或不定式连用〕不能,不(做),忘记。**3**. (分量)不足,缺乏(*in*);(作物)歉收。**4**. (健康等)衰退,衰弱,停止作用;(水)断,风(停)。**5**. 倒闭,破产。**6**. (后嗣)全无,绝。*He* ~*s in truthfulness*. 他不够老实。*She never* ~*s to write me every week*. 她永不忘记每周给我写信。*I* ~ *to see*. 我弄不懂。*The wind* ~*ed*. 风停了。*Water supply has* ~*ed*. 供水中断。— *vt*. **1**. 使失望;辜负;无助于,丢弃;不履行,玩忽。**2**. (考试)失败,不及格;〔口〕(考试人)不录取(考生),把(考生)评为不及格。*Words* ~*ed me at the last minute*. 到最后的时候我说不出话来了。*Time would* ~ *me to tell of it*. 没有那么多的时间去谈。*I* ~*ed exam in geography*. 我地理考试不及格。*The teacher* ~*ed me in physics*. 老师评我物理考试不及格。***Don't* ~ *to*** 务必,一定(*Don't* ~ *to write me*. 不要忘了给我写信)。~ ***of*** 不能达到,缺乏…能力(*The debater's argument* ~*ed of logical connection*. 辩论者的论点缺乏逻辑的连贯性)。***never* ~ *to*** (*do*) 必定(*He never* ~*s to come on Sunday*. 他星期天准来)。**II** *n*. **1**. 失败,失误;不及格;不及格者。**2**.【商】(期货交割)失期。***without* ~** 必定,务必。~**-out** *n*. 故障后果。~**-safe** **1**. *a*. (核弹运载机等)具有安全装置的;故障(自动)保险的。**2**. *vt*., *vi*. (使)具有自动保险装置。**F-Safe** (核弹运载机等的)自动保险装置。~**test** *n*. (零件故障)可靠性试验。

fail·ing [ˈfeiliŋ; ˋfelɪŋ] **I** *n*. 缺点,弱点,短处;失败。**II** *prep*. **1**. 如果没有…。**2**. 如果在…中失败。*F- good weather, the lecture will be held indoors*. 如果天气坏,讲演会改在室内举行。*F- election, she will return to her law practice*. 如果竞选失败,她将重操旧业去当律师。**III** *a*. 失败的,减弱中的,衰退中的。

faille [feil, fail; fel, faɪl] *n*.【纺】罗缎。

fail·ure [ˈfeiljə; ˋfeljɚ] *n*. **1**. 失败(*opp*. success);不及格。**2**. 不足,缺乏;衰退;【医】衰竭。**3**. 不履行,玩忽。**4**. 破产,倒闭;(银行等的)无力支付。**5**. 失败的事;失败者。**6**.【物】失效;【机】断裂,破坏,变钝。*F- is the mother of success*. = *F- teaches success*. 〔谚〕失败是成功之母。*a* ~ *of rain* 雨量缺乏。~ *in duty* 不尽职。*a crop* ~ = (*a*) ~ *of crops* 收成不好,歉收。~ *of electricity* 停电。*a* ~ *of issue* 无后(嗣)。~ *of eyesight* 视力减退。*He is a* ~ *as a teacher*. 他教书不行。*heart* ~【医】心力衰竭。*a social* ~ (社会上的)失败者。***end in* ~ = *meet with* ~** 终归失败。***invite* ~** 招致失败。

fain [fein; fen] **I** *a*. **1**. 〔古、诗〕乐意的,愿意的。**2**. 〔古〕不得不的,勉强的〔仅用作述语〕。*He was* ~ *to submit*. 他只好服从。**II** *ad*. 〔诗、古〕欣然,乐意〔与 *would* 连用〕。*I would* ~ *help you*. 我乐意帮助你。

fain(s) [fein(z); fen(z)] *int*. 〔英学俚〕免除。*Fain*(*s*)

F

I keeping goal! 可别叫我守球门。

fai·né·ant [ˈfeniənt; F. fɛneɑ̃; ˋfɛnɪənt, F. fɛneɑ̃] **I** *a*. 〔F.〕懒惰的。**II** *n*. 懒人。

faint [feint; fent] **I** *a*. **1.** 软弱的,无力的;无勇气的,怯懦的。**2.** 轻微的,稀薄的,暗淡的,模糊的。**3.** 〔只用作述语〕将昏倒似的。**4.** 闷人的。~ *resistance* 微弱的抵抗。*a* ~ *heart* 懦夫,胆小鬼。*a* ~ *smell* 闷人的气味。~ *lines* [*rulings*](练习本等上的)淡色横格。***be*** ~ ***with hunger*** 饿得头晕眼花。***feel*** ~ 感到头昏眼花。**II** *vi*. **1.** 头晕,昏过去 (*away*)。**2.** 渐渐不明,消失;〔古〕衰弱;颓丧。**III** *n*. 昏厥;眼花。***go off in a*** ~ 昏过去。***fall*** (***down***) ***in a dead*** ~ 昏倒,不省人事。**-ly** *ad*. **-ness** *n*. (*be attacked with faintness* 昏过去)。~**-ruled** *a*. (纸张)印有淡色横格的。

faint·heart [ˈfeinthɑːt; ˋfenthɑrt] **I** *n*. 懦夫,优柔寡断的人,窝囊废。**II** *a*. 懦怯的;没有决断的;胆小的;羞怯的。

faint·heart·ed [ˈfeintˈhɑːtid; ˋfentˋhɑrtɪd] *a*. 懦怯的,缺乏决断的;胆小的;羞怯的。**-ly** *ad*. **-ness** *n*.

faint·ing [ˈfeintiŋ; ˋfentɪŋ] **I** *n*. 昏倒,昏厥。**II** *a*. 昏倒的。~ **fit**[**spell**] 昏厥。**-ly** *ad*.

faint·ish [ˈfeintiʃ; ˋfentɪʃ] *a*. **1.** 发呆的;像要昏过去似的。**2.** (记号等)略为模糊的;(光线等)微弱的。**-ness** *n*.

faints [feints; fents] *n*. 〔*pl*.〕(蒸馏威士忌时最初和最后滴出的)劣质酒精。

fair[1] [fɛə; fɛr] *n*. **1.** 〔英〕定期集市,庙会。**2.** 义卖市场。**3.** 商品展览会,展销会,商品交易会。*World's F-* 万国博览会。*China's Export Commodities F-* 中国出口商品交易会。*a country* ~ 本乡物资交易会。*village* ~ 农村集市。*hold a* ~ *to raise money* 举办义卖筹款。*vanity* ~ 浮华市集,名利场。***a day after the*** ~ = ***a day too late for the*** ~ 过迟,太晚。~ **ground** 〔常 *pl*.〕集市场地,赛马场。

fair[2] [fɛə; fɛr] **I** *a*. **1.** 〔古诗〕美丽的;女性的。**2.** (水等)清澈的,清洁的;(笔迹等)鲜明的;洁白的,干净的。**3.** (头发)金色的 (*opp*. dark);(皮肤)白嫩的。**4.** (风等)畅快的;爽朗的,(天气等)好的,顺畅的;(前途等)有希望的。**5.** 正当的;公平的,合理的,正派的 (*opp*. foul)。**6.** 平坦的,平滑的。**7.** 还可以的,相当的。**8.** 充足的,不少的。**9.** 嘴甜的,说着好听的。**10.** 按法律可以捕猎的;可以据理攻击的。*a* ~ *lady* 美妇人。~ *weather* 好天气。~ *income* 相当高的收入。*a* ~ *crop* 还不错的收成。~ *average quality*【商】中等品。*one's* ~ *name* [*fame*] 清白的名声。*a* ~ *month* 整整一个月。*a* ~ *one* 美人。*a* ~ *way* 坦途。~ *words* 花言巧语。*a* ~ *field and no favour* 公平无私,对双方都不偏袒。***be*** ~ ***game for ridicule*** 活该成为嘲笑的对象。***be*** ~ ***in one's dealing*** 处置公平。***be in a*** ~ ***way to*** 有希望,很可能。***by*** ~ ***means*** 秉公。***by*** ~ ***means or foul*** 千方百计,不择手段。~ ***and softly*** 态度好些;稳重一些。~ ***and square*** 光明正大的,磊落坦率的;公正地,公道地。~ ***to middling*** 〔口〕中常的;过得去,还算好。***see*** ~ ***play*** 公平裁判;公平对待,公平处理。***to be*** ~ 说良心话。***write a*** ~ ***hand*** 写一笔好字。**II** *ad*. **1.** 好,清楚,明白。**2.** 谦和,恳切。**3.** 正直;光明正大,公平;漂亮。**4.** 幸亏,好在;顺利,有望。**5.** 直,挺直地,朝正面,正。**6.** 十分。*deal* ~ *with sb*. 公平待人。*fall* ~ 直挺挺地倒下去。*play* ~ 光明正大地比赛,公开合理地处理(等)。*speak sb*. ~ 彬彬有礼地对人讲话。*strike sb*. ~ *on the chin* 不偏不歪地打在某人下巴上。*write out* ~誊清。***bid*** ~ ***to*** (***do***) 很有希望。**III** *n*. **1.** 〔古、诗〕佳人;爱人;美好的事物。**2.** 〔the ~〕女性。**3.** 〔古〕幸运。***for*** ~ 〔美口〕完全地,肯定的。***see*** ~ 〔俚〕= see ~ play. ***through*** ~ ***and foul*** (***weather***) 在任何情况下。**IV** *vt*. **1.** 誊清。**2.** 使表面平顺;【船,空】把…作成流线型,减阻,整流。—*vi*. 〔英方〕(天气)好转。~ **ball**【棒球】正打球,线内球。~ **catch** (足球)侵人犯规。~ **copy** 誊正本,校正本;【印】清样。~**-faced** *a*. 白嫩的;美貌的;好看的。~ **game 1.** 准予捕猎的鸟兽。**2.** 有正当理由可追击[攻击、研究]的对象。~**-haired** *a*. 金发的;〔口〕被宠爱的。~**-haired boy** 〔美俚〕宠儿,红人。~ **lead** 引线孔,引出管。~ **light** *n*. 〔英〕门顶窗,气窗 (= transom window)。~ **minded** *a*. 公正的,没有偏见的。~ **play** 正派的比赛;公平合理[正大光明]的处理[态度],公平;漂亮。~ **sex** 妇女,女性〔与定冠词连用〕。~ **shake** 〔美〕公平待遇。~**-spoken** *a*. 谈吐文雅的,彬彬有礼的,和蔼的;亲切的;嘴甜的。~**-trade** *vt*. 规定(商品)的最低零售价,按公平交易约定(买卖)。~**-trade agreement** 〔美〕互惠贸易协定,(厂商与零售商所订)不擅自降低零售价格的协定。~ **way** 航路,水路;【空】水上飞机用水面跑道;【高尔夫球】(球的)正规通路;球座与终点间的草地 (*a* ~ *way topnotcher* 高尔夫球名手)。~**-weather** *a*. 只适宜于好天气的;只适宜于顺利时候的(*a* ~*-weather sailor* 仅能在风平浪静时值勤的水手。~*-weather friends* 可共安乐而不可共患难的朋友)。

Fair·bank(s) [ˈfɛəbæŋk(s); ˋfɛrbæŋk(s)] *n*. 费尔班克(斯)〔姓氏〕。

fair·ground [ˈfɛəgraund; ˋfɛrˏgraund] *n*. 举行赛会的场地;露天市场;露天马戏场。

fair·i·ly [ˈfɛərili; ˋfɛrɪlɪ] *ad*. 仙女似地;优雅地,身姿绰约地。

fair·ing[1] [ˈfɛəriŋ; ˋfɛrɪŋ] *n*. 市场上买的礼物,酬谢物。***get one's*** ~***s*** 获得应得的报酬。***give sb. his*** ~ 给人以应得的报酬。

fair·ing[2] [ˈfɛəriŋ; ˋfɛrɪŋ] *n*. 【空】整流片;整流罩;【机】减阻装置。

fair·ish [ˈfɛəriʃ; ˋfɛrɪʃ] *a*. 相当的;还算大[好]的。

fair·ly [ˈfɛəli; ˋfɛrlɪ] *ad*. **1.** 公正地,正当地。**2.** 明白地,清楚地。**3.** 适当,相当。**4.** 完全,简直。*write* ~ 写清楚。~ *good* 还好。*I* ~ *cried with joy*. 我简直高兴得叫了起来。***act*** ~ ***by all men*** 〔谚〕一视同仁。***be*** ~ ***beside oneself*** 简直疯了。***be*** ~ ***under way*** 在顺利航行中;完全就绪。~ ***and squarely*** 光明正大。

fair·ness [ˈfɛənis; ˋfɛrnɪs] *n*. **1.** 晴朗。**2.** 公平。**3.** 〔诗、古〕美丽,洁白。**4.** (头发的)金黄色。**5.** 顺畅,适当。***in*** ~ ***to*** 为了对…做到公平合理。~ **doctrine** 〔美〕(电台,电视台为辩论双方提供同等机会的)公平经营原则。

fair·y [ˈfɛəri; ˋfɛrɪ] **I** *n*. **1.** 妖精;仙女。**2.** 〔美俚〕漂亮姑娘。**3.** 〔美俚〕妖里妖气的男子;搞同性恋爱的男子。**II** *a*. **1.** 妖精(一样)的;仙女似的。**2.** 幻想中的。**3.** 美丽的,小巧玲珑的,可爱的;优雅的。*a* ~ *lamp* [*light*] 彩色小灯。*a* ~ *shape* 优美的姿态。~ **circle** 仙女环蘑菇〔迷信传说中认为由于仙女跳舞,而在茂草中丛生如环的蘑菇,故名〕。~**dom** *n*. = fairyland. ~ **godmother** (危难时提供及时帮助的)慷慨朋友,救星。~ **hood 1.** 妖精气质,魔性。**2.** 〔集合词〕妖精们。~**land** *n*. 仙境,奇境;胜地。~**like** *a*. 妖精一样的,仙女般的。~ **ring** = ~ circle. ~ **shrimp**【动】无甲目 (Anostraca) 动物;丰年虫。~ **tale 1.** 神话故事,童话。**2.** 谎言。

fait ac·com·pli [ˌfetəkumˈpliː; fɛtakumˋpli] 〔F.〕既成事实。

Faith [feiθ; feθ] *n*. 费丝〔女子名〕。

faith [feiθ; feθ] **I** *n*. **1.** 信用,信任。**2.** 信仰,信心;信条,教义,教(派)。**3.** 约,誓约。**4.** 信义,忠实,诚实,诚意。**5.** 〔the F-〕宗教信仰〔指基督教信仰〕。*in bad* ~ 不诚实地。*in good* ~ 真诚地。***break*** ~ 背弃信仰,不守信义。***break one's*** ~ 背信食言。***by my*** ~ = ***by the*** ~ ***of my fathers*** [***body, love***] = upon my ~. ***engage*** [***pledge, plight***] ***one's*** ~ 担保,发誓,答应。***give one's*** ~ 担保,断定地。***have*** ~ ***in*** 相信。***have no*** ~ ***in*** 不相信。***i' faith*** = ***in*** ~! 实在,真,真正。***keep*** ~ 忠于信仰,遵守信义。***lose*** ~ ***in*** 对…失去信念。***my*** ~ = in ~. ***on the*** ~ ***of*** 靠着…的信用,由…的保证。***pin one's*** ~ ***on*** [***to***] 绝对信任,深信不疑。***put*** ~ ***in*** 相信,

信任。***upon my*** ～ 我担保,一定。**II** ***int*.** 真正,真。～ ***cure*** [***healing***] (用宗教,祷告等迷信方法的)信仰医疗。～ **healer** 实行信仰疗法的人。

faith·ful [ˈfeiθf*u*l; ˋfeθfəl] **I** ***a*. 1.** 忠实的,忠诚的;贞节的;信仰坚定的。**2.** 可靠的;正确的。**II** ***n*.** 〔the ～〕〔集合词〕信徒。**-ness** ***n*.** 诚实;正确。

faith·ful·ly [ˈfeiθf*u*li; ˋfeθfulɪ] ***ad*. 1.** 忠实地;诚心诚意地。**2.** (对契约等)切实遵守地。*deal* ～ *with* 诚恳地对待。*promise* ～〔口〕坚决保证,明确约定。***Yours*** ～ = ***F- yours*** 你的忠实的〔信尾用语〕。

faith·less [ˈfeiθlis; ˋfeθlɪs] ***a*. 1.** 无信义的,不忠实的;不贞的。**2.** 靠不住的。**3.** 没有信仰的。**-ly** ***ad*.** **-ness** ***n*.**

fai·tour [ˈfeitə; ˋfetɚ] ***n*.** 〔古〕骗子;流氓。

fake[1] [feik; fek]〔口〕**I** ***n*. 1.** 冒充,诈骗;冒牌货,骗人货。**2.** 魔术用具;假动作,假消息。**3.** 捏造者;〔美〕骗子。**II** ***a*.** 假的,冒充的,骗人的。～ *diamonds* 假钻石。*a medical* ～ 冒牌医生。**III** ***vt*. 1.** 伪造;捏造 (*up*)。**2.** 假装,装做。**3.** 即席演奏。～ *an accompaniment* 即席伴奏。～ (*up*) *a report* 捏造报告。～ *illness* 装病。— ***vi*.** 作伪,造假货。*She's not sick; she's just faking*. 她没有病,是在装假呢。～ ***a curtain*** 【美剧】(特雇观众所作的)假捧场。～ ***it up*** 涂抹,装饰。～ ***sb. out***〔口〕以欺骗、讹诈手法胜过某人。～ **book** (盗印的只印有简单乐谱的)流行歌曲集。

fake[2] [feik; fek] **I** ***n*.** 【海】盘索;【电】线圈;软焊料。**II** ***vt*.** 卷(绳索)。

fake·ment [ˈfeikmənt; ˋfekmənt] ***n*.** 〔口〕蒙骗;骗人货。

fa·keer [fəˈkiə; fəˋkɪr] ***n*.** = fakir[1].

fak·er [ˈfeikə; ˋfekɚ] ***n*.** 〔口〕**1.** 骗子;卖假货的小贩。**2.** 骗人货,伪造物。

fak·er·y [ˈfeikəri; ˋfekərɪ] ***n*. 1.** 伪造,捏造;伪装。**2.** 假货,赝品。

fa·kir[1] [fəˈkiə, ˈfeikiə; fəˋkɪr, ˋfekɪr] ***n*.** (伊斯兰教或印度教的)游方修士,托钵僧。

fak·ir[2] [ˈfeikə; ˋfekɚ] ***n*.** = faker.

fa-la, fal-la [fəˈlɑː, ˈfɑːlɑː; fəˋlɑ, ˋfɑlɑ] **1.** (古歌谣结尾音节)叠用词。**2.** (古代歌谣的)叠用曲。

Fa·lange [Sp. feˈlæŋhei, ˈfeilændʒ; feˋlæŋhe, ˋfelændʒ] ***n*.** (西班牙)长枪党。

Fa·lan·gist [fəˈlændʒist; fəˋlændʒɪst] ***n*.** 长枪党党员。

Fa·la·sha [fɑːˈlɑːʃə; fɑˋlɑʃə] ***n*.** 法拉沙人〔住在埃塞俄比亚,信奉犹太教的含族人〕。

fal·ba·la [ˈfælbələ; ˋfælbələ], **fal·be·lo** [ˈfælbeləu; ˋfælbelo] ***n*.** (女子衣、裙等上的)荷叶边。

fal·cate(d) [ˈfælkeit(id); ˋfælket(ɪd)] **I** ***a*.** 【植,动】镰刀状的。*a* ～ *leaf* 镰刀状叶片。**II** ***n*.** 镰刀形。

fal·chion [ˈfɔːltʃən; ˋfɔltʃən] ***n*. 1.** (中世纪的)弯形大刀,偃月刀。**2.** 〔诗〕刀,剑。

fal·ci·form [ˈfælsifɔːm; ˋfælsɪˌfɔrm] ***a*.** 镰刀形的。

fal·con [ˈfælkən, ˈfɔːlkən; ˋfælkən, ˋfɔlkən] ***n*. 1.** 【动】隼,(猎鹰的)母鹰。**2.** (15—17世纪用的)轻炮。**-er** ***n*.** 养猎鹰的人;鹰猎者。**-et** ***n*. 1.** 小隼,小鹰。**2.** 轻炮。

fal·con-gen·tle [ˈfɔːlkənˈdʒentl, ˈfɔːkən-; ˋfɔlkənˋdʒentḷ, ˋfɔkən-] ***n*.** 【动】雌苍鹰,雌隼。

fal·con·ry [ˈfɔːlkənri; ˋfɔlkənrɪ] ***n*. 1.** 猎鹰训练术。**2.** 鹰猎。

fal·cu·la [ˈfælkjulə; ˋfælkjulə] ***n*.** (*pl*. ***-lae*** [-liː; -li]) (猫等的)钩爪。

fal·de·ral [ˈfældəˈræl; ˋfældəˌræl], **fal·de·rol** [ˈfældəˈrɔl; ˋfældəˋrɑl] ***n*. 1.** 细小的装饰品。**2.** 无意义的重复 **3.** 废话。

fald·stool [ˈfɔːldstuːl; ˋfɔldˌstul] ***n*. 1.** (主教等坐的)折椅。**2.** (英国国教的)跪拜台;读经台。

Fa·ler·ni·an [fəˈləːniən; fəˋlɝnɪən] ***n*.** (意大利 Campania 地方的)费勒年(山)葡萄酒。

Falk·land Is·lands [ˈfɔːklændˈailændz; ˋfɔklændˋaɪləndz]〔与 the 连用〕福克兰群岛(即马尔维纳斯(Malvinas)群岛)〔大西洋〕。

Falk·ner [ˈfɔːknə; ˋfɔknɚ] ***n*.** 福克纳〔姓氏〕。

fall [fɔːl; fɔl] **I** ***vi*.** (***fell*** [fel; fɛl]; ***fall·en*** [ˈfɔːlən; ˋfɔlən]) **1.** 落下;散落,(毛发等)脱落;降落;(水银柱等)下降;(物价)下落,跌落;(帘、幕等)放下,垂下;(眼睛、脸色)下沉;(河流)流下,灌注,(地面等)倾斜。**2.** 倒下,摔倒;趴下;塌倒;崩解;瓦解,垮台。**3.** 陷落;失足。**4.** 堕落;(女人)失身。**5.** 死,战死。**6.** (精神等)衰退;(洪水等)减退,(风力)减弱;(潮水)退落。**7.** (瞌睡)沉沉,(恐怖)逼人;(光线等)当头。**8.** (小羊等)生下。**9.** (言语)漏出。**10.** 忽然…起来,…出来,…下来 (*to*)。**11.** 陷于(某种状态),变化,成为。**12.** (事故)发生;(时候)到来,正当,适逢;轮(到)。**13.** 属于;分为(…类)。**13.** 落入,留传给;(重音等)落在…上。**14.** (谈话等)停止。**15.** 〔美俚〕被捕,落网。*The barometer is* ～*ing*. 气压正在下降。*The rain* ～*s*. 下雨了。*The curtain* ～*s*. 幕落。*Night* ～*s*. 夜色降临。*The fortress fell*. 要塞失守了。～ *in battle* 战死。～ *to sb.'s gun* 被人击毙。～ *to the river* 向河边倾斜。～ *within the jurisdiction of* 属于…管辖范围。*It* ～*s to our lot to do this*. 该我们来做这件事了。*His countenance* [*face*] ～*s*. 他脸色一沉。*His spirits fell at the news*. 他听到那个消息时垂头丧气。～ *asleep* 睡着,入睡。～ *ill* 病倒。～ *into step* 进入同步。～ *out of step* 失去同步。*He suddenly fell grave*. 他突然板起了面孔。*Not a word* ～*s from her lip*. 她一言不发。*The bill* ～*s due next week*. 支票在下周到期。*The shot* ～*s wide of* (*its*) *mark*. 那一枪没有打中。*She was tempted and fell*. 她被引诱而堕落。*The light fell on my book*. 灯光正照到我的书上。*The conversation fell suddenly*. 谈话声突然停止。*The novel* ～*s into six parts*. 小说分为六部分。*He fell thrice for theft*. 他因盗窃被捕过三次。～ ***a sacrifice*** [***victim***] ***to*** 成为…的牺牲品。～ ***aboard*** 【海】(与他船)相撞。～ ***across*** 碰见。～ ***among*** 遇见(盗匪等)。偶然陷入…之中。～ ***apart*** 崩溃,土崩瓦解。～ ***at sb.'s feet*** 拜倒在某人脚下。～ ***away*** **1.** 疏远,背叛,变节;背离;(客人等)减少。**2.** 渐退,隐退,消失。**3.** 消瘦;变弱;死。**4.** 分裂,(各级)分开,散开,排出。**5.** 变懒,变懈怠。**6.** (地势)倾斜。～ ***back*** 撤退,后退;退让;退缩;违约,不履行。～ ***back on*** [***upon***] 退守,撤退到…线;投靠,求助于。～ ***behind*** **1.** 落后,跟不上。**2.** 拖欠。～ ***beyond*** 属于…外,在…外。～ ***down*** (向下游)流下;〔美俚〕失败 (～ *down on a job* 工作失败)。～ ***flat*** 失败,达不到预期结果。～ ***for***〔美俚〕**1.** 被迷住,爱上。**2.** 受骗上当。～ ***from*** **1.** 由…滚落下来;(由…口里)露出。**2.** 〔古〕背叛(～ *from favour* 失宠)。～ ***home*** (木材或船侧上部)向里弯。～ ***in*** **1.** (屋顶等)塌陷,往里坍塌;(眼等)洼下,凹进去。**2.** 【军】排队,站队;集合。**3.** 一致,符合。**4.** 终止;(土地等)租借期满;(土地等)可以利用。～ ***in for*** 参与,享受(～ *in for a share* 可分一份)。～ ***in*** [***to***] ***pieces*** 粉碎,破碎不堪。～ ***into*** **1.** 陷入(网等)中;陷入(坏习惯等)中,变成(～ *into line* 同人站成一排;跟人步调一致)。**2.** 渐渐(～ *into decay* 渐渐荒废)。**3.** 开始(～ *into conversation with* 和…谈起话来)。**4.** 流入。**5.** 分成,分解(成几部分)(～ *into four divisions* 分四个部分)。～ ***in with*** **1.** 偶然碰见。**2.** 同意;赞成。**3.** 符合;适合。～ ***off*** **1.** 下降,跌落。**2.** 离开;疏远;叛离。**3.** 减退,销路减少;衰退;堕落。**4.** 【海】偏向下风,(船只)不易驾驶,(飞机)侧降。～ ***on*** [***upon***] **1.** 开始(行动);进攻,袭击。**2.** (节日)正当,适逢。**3.** 忽然看出来,想起来。**4.** (灾难等)临头,落在…上(～ *on the ball*〔美〕开始用功。～ *on one's feet* [*legs*] 侥幸避免危难。～ *on one's sword* 自刎。～ *upon one's knees* 跪下)。～ ***on stony ground*** (计划等)落空。～ ***out*** **1.** 起纠纷,争吵(*They often* ～ *out over some trifling matter*. 他们常常因小事争吵)。**2.** 落下,脱落;【军】离队,原地解散。**3.** 发生(…事),结果(是)(*It fell out that* ... 结果…)。**4.** 离

F

队;【军】原地解散。~ ***out of*** 放弃(习惯等)。~ ***over*** **1**. 落在…上;落在…外。**2**. 向前摔倒。**3**. (头发)披在(肩)上。~ ***over one another*** 〔美〕争夺,竞争,争先恐后。~ ***over oneself*** **1**. 跌跤。**2**. 拼命赶。~ ***short*** (***of***) (…)缺乏;(…)不足;(子弹等)达不到(目标)。~ ***through*** 落空,失败。~ ***to*** **1**. 着手。**2**. 开始用餐。**3**. 争吵起来。**4**. 开始攻击。**5**. (门等自动)关起来(*Let us* ~ *to*! 大家吃吧! ~ *to work* 动手工作。~ *to reading* 读起书来)。~ ***to the ground*** 落在地上;(计划等)落空。~ ***under*** **1**. 受(影响、检查等)。**2**. 归入(…部,类等);属于(~ *under sb.'s notice* 受某人注意,被某人看见)。~ ***within*** 属于,该当,适合。—***vt***. 〔美、英方〕击倒,斫倒(树木)。**II** ***n***. **1**. 落下,坠落;(温度等的)下落,降落;(物价的)跌落;落差;降雨(量),降雪(量);(河水)流入,流下,倾泻;〔常 *pl*.〕瀑布。**2**. 〔树的〕采伐,采伐量。**3**. 跌倒,摔倒;陷落;塌倒;瓦解,崩颓;灭亡,战死。**4**. (对诱惑等的)屈服;堕落。**5**. 减退,衰退;(潮的)退落;(太阳的)没落。**6**. 【地】倾斜,斜度;【矿】冒落。**7**. (兽的)下仔;(羊等的)一胎。**8**. 〔美〕秋天〔落叶期之意〕。**9**. 下垂物;向下飘荡的服装,领子的翻下部分,(女帽上的)罩纱,(外衣的)宽下摆,大裤脚;(钢琴的)盖子。**10**. 【摔跤】把对手摔倒;一局摔角。**11**. 【机】(滑车上的)拉绳,起重机绳;〔*pl*.〕【海】(放救生艇的)吊绳,辘绳。**12**. 【猎】陷阱;〔美口〕被捕。**13**. 【语】降调;【乐】乐曲终止。*Pride will have a* ~. 骄者必败。*A* ~ *into the pit, a gain in your wit*. 吃一堑,长一智。*the F-* (*of man*) 【宗】人的堕落。*a heavy* ~ *of rain* [*snow*] 大雨[雪]。*a sharp* ~ *of temperature* 温度的剧降。*a waterfall with a* ~ *of 100 metres*. 落差一百公尺的瀑布。*in the* ~ *of 1980* 〔美〕一九八〇年秋天。*the* ~ *of leaves* 落叶;秋天。~ *of the hammer* (拍卖时)击锤成交。~ *and spring yoke* 〔美〕老少悬殊的婚姻。***have a*** ~ 〔美俚〕被捕。***nod to its*** ~ 摇摇欲坠。***ride for a*** ~ **1**. 乱骑马。**2**. 闯乱子,准会失败。***take a*** ~ 被打倒。***try a*** ~ ***with*** 同某人较量一番。**III** ***a***. 〔美〕秋天的,秋季的,秋天播种的;秋天成熟的;(衣服等)秋天用的。~ *fashions* 秋季畅销货。~ *goods* 秋季货品。~ *wheat* 冬小麦。~**age** **1**. 伐木。**2**. 〔集合词〕伐下的树枝。~ **away** ***n***. 【宇】(火箭各级的)分开,散开,排出。~ **back** **1**. 后备物。**2**. 撤退;退路。~**fish** 【动】风鱼(*semotilus corporalis*)〔产于美国东北部清澈的江河湖海中〕。~ **guy** 〔美俚〕(无法脱身的)替罪羊,替死鬼,背黑锅者。~ **line** **1**. 【地】瀑布线。**2**. (滑雪的)直接下滑线。~**-off** ***n***. **1**. 下降,减少。**2**. 【宇】(火线各级的)分开,散开,排出。~ **out** ***n***. **1**. 【原】微粒回降;回降物,放射性落尘。**2**. 意外的副产品,附带成果。**3**. 剩余物,残渣(*radio active* ~ *out* 放射性微粒回降。*a* ~ *out shelter* 微粒掩蔽所)。~**-pipe** 水落管。~**-trap** 陷阱。~ **up** 放射性落尘对海洋地区的污染。~ **wind** 【气】下降风,下吹风。

fal·la·cious [fəˈleiʃəs; fəˋleʃəs] ***a***. **1**. 谬误的。**2**. 虚妄的;靠不住的,令人失望的。~ *hopes* 渺茫的希望。**-ly** ***ad***. **-ness** ***n***.

fal·la·cy [ˈfæləsi; ˋfæləsɪ] ***n***. 谬误,谬见,谬论,错误。*a pathetic* ~ (诗人认为万物都有感情的)感伤的谬妄。

fal-lal [ˌfælˈlæl; ˏfælˋlæl] ***n***. (服装上的)装饰品。

fal·lal·er·y [fælˈlæləri; fælˋlælərɪ] ***n***. 俗气的装饰品;虚饰。

fall·en [ˈfɔːlən; ˋfɔlən] **I** fall 的过去分词。**II** ***a***. **1**. 落下来的;倒了的。**2**. 陷落了的;已垮台的。**3**. 堕落了的;灭亡的;破落了的;已死的。**4**. 憔悴的。~ *angel* 沦落的天使;恶魔。*a* ~ *woman* 堕落的女人。*persons* ~ *in battle* 降亡者。*the* ~ 阵亡者。~ *cheeks* 憔悴的双颊。

fall·er [ˈfɔːlə; ˋfɔlɚ] ***n***. **1**. 伐木者。**2**. 【纺】(走锭纺纱机的)坠杆。

fal·li·bil·i·ty [ˌfæliˈbiliti; ˏfæləˋbɪlətɪ] ***n***. 易错;易受骗;虚妄。

fal·li·ble [ˈfæləbl; ˋfæləbḷ] ***a***. 易犯错误的;易受骗的;难免有错误的。*All men are* ~. 人皆有过。**-ness** ***n***. **-li·bly** ***ad***.

fall·ing [ˈfɔːliŋ; ˋfɔlɪŋ] **I** ***n***. **1**. 落下,堕落,下降。**2**. 洼进,凹陷;崩塌;垮台;陷落。**3**. 堕落。*the* ~ *of the leaf* 落叶时节,秋天。**II** ***a***. **1**. 落下的;垂下的;跌落的。**2**. 衰退的;变衰弱的。**3**. 〔美方〕(天气)像要下雨[下雪]似的。*a* ~ *intonation* [*tone*] 降调。~ *market* 【商】疲软的行市。~ **away** 反叛,叛教,叛党,脱党,变节。~ **in** 垮下,陷下〔*cf*. fall in〕。~ **leaf** 【空】落叶式降落〔一种特技表演〕。~ **off** 衰落,衰败;(销路等的)减少(*a* ~ *off place* 〔美〕穷乡僻壤)。~ **out** 争执,冲突,不和。~ **sickness** 〔罕〕癫痫。~ **sluice** 自动水闸。~ **star** 流星。~ **stone** 陨石。

Fal·lo·pi·an [fəˈləupiən; fəˋlopɪən] **tube** ***n***. 【解】输卵管,喇叭管。

fal·low[1] [ˈfæləu; ˋfælo] **I** ***a***. (田地)休闲中的,荒芜的;(精神,智力等)松弛的,不活跃的;不熟练的。*lie* ~ (田地)在休闲中。*lay land* ~ 休闲田地。**II** ***n***. 休闲地;休闲。**III** ***vt***. 使(翻耕后的土地)休闲。*land in* ~ 休闲地。*green* ~ 绿肥作物休闲地。*black* ~ 秋耕休闲地。*occupied* ~ 半休闲。**-ness** ***n***.

fal·low[2] [ˈfæləu; ˋfælo] ***a***. 淡棕色的。~ **deer** 【动】黇鹿(*Dama dama*)〔产于欧洲,夏天皮毛发黄,起白斑〕。

false [fɔːls; fɔls] **I** ***a***. (*opp*. true) **1**. 虚伪的,虚假的,捏造的;撒谎的,不诚实的;错误的。**2**. 不正的,非法的。**3**. 假造的;摹造的,人造的。**4**. 临时的,补助的。**5**. 【乐】不合调的。***be*** ~ ***of heart*** 不老实。***be*** ~ ***to*** = *prove* ~ *to*. ***bear*** [***give***] ~ ***witness*** 作假见证。***prove*** ~ ***to*** (背信)出卖;违背;辜负,欺骗。***sail*** [***take***] ***under*** ~ ***colours*** 挂别国国旗航行;冒充。**II** ***ad***. 欺诈地;叛卖地。***play sb***. ~ 欺骗,出卖。~ **acacia** 【植】刺槐。~ **accusation** [**charge**] 诬告。~ **alarm** **1**. 假警报,一场虚惊。**2**. 昙花一现的人物。~ **arrest** 【法】(个人之间的)非法拘留。~ **attack** 【军】佯攻。~ **attic** 【建】假(屋)顶层。~ **bottom** **1**. (盒子等的)活底。**2**. (威士忌酒杯的)假底。~ **card** 为迷惑对方而出的牌。~ **eggplant** 【植】假茄子。~ **face** 假面具。~ **front** 骗人的外表。~ **fruit** 【植】假果。~ **hair** 假发。~ **imprisonment** 非法监禁。~ **jaw** 【机】虎钳口。~**-hearted** ***a***. 奸诈的,不诚实的,虚伪的。~**hood** (*opp*. truth) 错误;虚伪,虚妄;撒谎;谎言(*tell a* ~*hood* 撒谎)。~ **keel** 【船】副龙骨,保护龙骨。~ **papers** (船只为欺骗而携带的关于所运货物和目的地等的)伪证件。~ **position** 与心意[原则]相反的地位[立场];尴尬的地位[处境]。~ **pretenses** 【法】欺诈,诈骗(财物)。~ **pride** 妄自尊大。~ **ribs** 【解】假肋。~ **roof** 屋顶状天花板。~ **smut** 【农】稻曲病。~ **start** 【体】错误的起步;慌张失措的开始。~ **statement** 伪证。~ **step** **1**. 失足;绊倒。**2**. 社交性错误,不正当行为。~ **tooth** 假牙,义齿。~ **window** 【建】假窗,配景窗。~ **work** 【建】脚手架,建筑架,工作架,临时支撑。**-ly** ***ad***. 不正,误,不诚实;虚妄(*be falsely accused* 被诬告)。**-ness** ***n***. 虚伪;欺骗。

fal·set·tist [fɔːlˈsetist; fɔlˋsɛtɪst] ***n***. 假嗓子歌手。

fal·set·to [fɔːlˈsetəu; fɔlˋsɛto] **I** ***n***. (*pl*. ~*s*) 〔It.〕假声,假嗓子〔*cf*. head voice〕;假嗓子歌手。*in* ~ 用假声。**II** ***a***. 用假声的。**III** ***ad***. 用假声地。~ **tone** 假声[嗓子]。

fals·ies [ˈfɔːlsiːz; ˋfɔlsɪz] ***n***. 〔*pl*.〕〔美口〕妇女衬胸〔为使胸部丰满而衬在乳罩内的乳房形衬垫物〕。

fal·si·fi·ca·tion [ˌfɔːlsifiˈkeiʃən; ˏfɔlsɪfɪˋkeʃən] ***n***. **1**. 弄虚作假;伪造;窜改;歪曲。**2**. 证明为虚伪,证明为无根据。~ *of accounts* 造假账。~ *of wine* 酒里掺水作假。

fal·si·fier [ˈfɔːlsiˌfaiə; ˋfɔlsɪˏfaɪr] ***n***. 伪造者;窜改者;弄虚作假的人,撒谎的人。

fal·si·fy [ˈfɔːlsiˌfai; ˋfɔlsɪˏfaɪ] ***vt***. (**-*fied***; **-*fy·ing***) **1**. 窜改,伪造(文件等);歪曲。**2**. 证明…是假的[错的]。**3**. 搞错,误用。~ *certificates* 伪造执照。~ *records* 窜改

F

记录。～ *a statement* 证明论述有误。*Her hopes have been falsified*. 她的希望已落空。—*vi*. 作假,撒谎。

fal·si·ty [ˈfɔːlsiti; ˋfɔlsətɪ] ***n***. 虚伪,不真实;欺诈;谎言。

Fal·staff [ˈfɔːlstɑːf; ˋfɔlstɑf], **Sir John** 约翰·福斯泰夫〔莎士比亚戏剧中一个肥胖、机智、乐观、爱吹牛的武士〕;爱吹牛的人。**-i·an** [-iən; -ɪən] ***a***. 像福斯泰夫(一样)的。

falt·boat [ˈfɑːltbəut; ˋfɑlt,bot] ***n***. 可以折叠的小艇。

fal·ter [ˈfɔːltə; ˋfɔltɚ] **I** ***vi***. **1**. 蹒跚,踉跄,摇晃。**2**. 颤抖,支吾,结巴。**3**. 逡巡,踌躇,迟疑;畏缩;(记忆力等)不确定,不稳定。—***vt***. 结结巴巴地说 (*out*)。**II** ***n***. **1**. 摇晃。**2**. 支吾,结巴。**3**. 踌躇,逡巡;不稳。

fal·ter·ing [ˈfɔːltəriŋ; ˋfɔltərɪŋ] ***a***. **1**. 踉跄的,摇晃的;不稳的。**2**. 颤抖的,支吾的。**3**. 踌躇的。*speak in a* ～ *voice* 用颤抖[吞吞吐吐]的声音说。**-ly** ***ad***.

F.A.M., F. and A.M. = Free and Accepted Masons〔英〕共济会。

fam. = familiar; family.

fa·ma·cide [ˈfeiməsaid; ˋfemə,saɪd] ***n***. 【法】毁谤者。

fame [feim; fem] **I** ***n***. **1**. 名声,声望。**2**. 〔古〕传闻,风声。*a house of ill* ～ 妓院。*ill* ～ 污名,恶评,丑闻。*undying* ～ 不朽之名。**II** ***vt***. **1**. 使出名,扬…的名。**2**. 〔古〕盛传。***come to*** ～ = ***win*** ～ 成名。

famed [feimd; femd] ***a***. 闻名的,有名的,出名的。***be*** ～ ***for*** 给…出名。

Fa·meuse [fəˈmuːz; fəˋmuz] ***n***. 晚熟的美国红苹果〔又名 snow apple〕。

fa·mil·ial [fəˈmiljəl; fəˋmɪljəl] ***a***. **1**. 家庭的;涉及家庭的。**2**. 某家特有的。

fa·mil·iar [fəˈmiljə; fəˋmɪljɚ] **I** ***a***. **1**. 亲密的,交情好的。**2**. 常见的,流行的。**3**. 熟悉…的,精通…的(*with*)。**4**. 世所周知的,人人知道的 (*to*)。**5**. 平常的,普通的,通俗的;非正式的。**6**. (男女间)亲昵;过分亲密,放肆。**7**. 家族[庭]的。～ *friends* 亲密的朋友。*a* ～ *song* 流行歌曲。*a* ～ *phrase* 惯用词句。*things* ～ *to us* 我们所熟悉的事物。*be* ～ *with English* 通晓英语。*a* ～ *essay* 小品文,随笔。*He made himself much too* ～ *with the girl*. 他对这位姑娘太放肆了。***be*** ～ ***with*** **1**. 同…相好。**2**. 精通,熟习。***be on*** ～ ***terms with*** 因…交情好,同…熟识。～ ***spirit*** = familiar ***n***. 5. ***make oneself*** ～ ***with*** 同…好[熟悉]起来,同…亲近起来。**II** ***n***. **1**. 亲友。**2**. 常客。**3**. 高级官吏的家属。**4**. 【天主】教皇[主教]的仆人。**5**. 传说中供女巫差遣的妖精。**-ly** ***ad***.

fa·mil·i·ar·i·ty [fəˌmiliˈæriti; fə,mɪlɪˋærətɪ] ***n***. **1**. 亲密,亲近;融洽。**2**. 熟悉,精通。**3**. 深交,不客气。**4**. 〔*pl*.〕爱抚;放肆的言行。*show thorough* ～ *with a language* 十分精通某种语言。***F- breeds contempt***. 〔谚〕亲昵引起轻视,近之则不逊。

fa·mil·iar·i·za·tion [fəˌmiljəraiˈzeiʃən; fə,mɪljəraɪˋzeʃən] ***n***. **1**. 亲密;熟识。**2**. (思想等的)通俗化。

fa·mil·iar·ize [fəˈmiljəraiz; fəˋmɪljə,raɪz] ***vt***. **1**. 使亲密,使熟习,使熟知;使精通。**2**. 使尽人皆知,使通俗化(*to*)。～ ***oneself with*** 精通,熟习。

fam·i·lism [ˈfæmilizəm; ˋfæməlɪzəm] ***n***. 家庭主义〔强调家庭感情;以家庭为基本单位的社会结构〕。**-lis·tic** [ˌfæmiˈlistik; ,fæməˋlɪstɪk] ***a***.

fam·i·ly [ˈfæmili, ˈfæməli; ˋfæmlɪ, ˋfæməlɪ] **I** ***n***. **1**. 家,家庭;〔集合词〕家庭成员,家属,子女;亲属。**2**. 氏族,家族,亲族。**3**. 〔美〕阁员,(特指国务部的)同僚;派别。**4**. 门第,家系;〔英〕门阀,名门。**5**. 人种,种族,民族。**6**. 系;族;科;【语】语族。**7**. 〔美俚〕(黑手党等犯罪集团的)行动小组。*His* ～ *is an old one*. 他的家庭是一个旧式家庭。*My* ～ *are all well*. 我全家都好。*the President's official* ～ 〔美〕总统的全体阁僚。*the Indo-European* ～ 印欧语族。*the Teutonic* ～ 条顿民族。*the chromium* ～ 【化】铬族。*the Kantian* ～ 康德学派。*the cat* ～ 【动】猫科。***a happy*** ～ **1**. 幸福家庭。**2**. 相安无事处于同一牢笼的不同类动物。***in a*** ～ ***way*** **1**. 像家人一样随便,不拘形式地。**2**. 怀孕。***in the*** ～ ***way*** 〔美〕怀孕。***of*** (***good***) ～ 出身门第很高的。***run in the*** ～ (性格特征等)为一家所共有,世代相传 (*A gift for music runs in that* ～ *.* 那一家人人有音乐天才)。**II** ***a***. 家庭的,家族的。*a* ～ *likeness* 亲属之间的相似,隐约的相似。～ **allowance** (工资外的)家庭津贴。～ **Bible** 家用大型《圣经》。～ **butcher** 供应家庭的肉商〔区别于供应军队等〕。～ **circle** 家庭中常来的亲友们;【剧】家庭包厢。～ **coach** 〔英〕**1**. 有顶大马车。**2**. 一种罚金游戏。～ **credit**(为有孩子或多子女的低收入家庭提供的)家庭社会保险津贴。～ **dissensions** 家庭纠纷。**F-Division** 〔英〕(处理离婚、收养等方面诉讼的)高级民事法庭。～ **doctor** 家庭特约医师。～ **farm** 家庭农场。～ **friend** 世交;与全家人都来往的朋友。～ **hotel** (特别优待一家人住宿的)家庭旅馆。～ **hour** 〔美〕全家看电视时间(常在下午7—9时)。～ (**care**) **leave**〔为照顾婴儿或家中病人而请的〕家务假。～ **man** **1**. 爱管家务[关心家庭]的人。**2**. 有老婆孩子的人。～ **name** 姓。～ **planning** 计划生育。～ **room** 供一家人公用的起居室。～ **selection** 谱系选择。～**-sensitive** ***a***.(电影、电视等删除掉暴力与色情内容而使)全家可观看的。～ **skeleton** 不愿外扬的家丑。～ **style** 家庭式用餐法〔把大盘菜依次传递,自己拨取食物的进餐法〕。～ **ties** 家累。～ **tree** 家系图。～ **way** 怀孕。*She is in the* ～ *way again*. 她又怀孕了。*She got herself in a* ～ *way*. 她有喜了。

fam·ine [ˈfæmin; ˋfæmɪn] ***n***. **1**. 饥荒。**2**. 〔古〕饥饿。**3**. 极度缺乏。*a coal* ～ 煤荒。*a water* ～ 水荒。*die of* ～ 饿死。～ **prices** 缺货时的高价。

fam·ish [ˈfæmiʃ; ˋfæmɪʃ] ***vt***. 使饿,使饥饿;〔古〕使饿死〔多用被动语态〕。*be* ～*ed for food* 缺粮挨饿,断炊。*be* ～*ed to death* 饿死。*I'm* ～*ing*. 〔俚〕我饿坏了。*a* ～*ing wind* 冷得要命的风。—***vi***. 饿,挨饿;〔古〕饿死。

fa·mous [ˈfeiməs; ˋfeməs] ***a***. **1**. 有名的,出名的,驰名的(*for*)。**2**. 〔口〕极好的。*a* ～ *scenic spot* 有名的风景区。*a* ～ *appetite* 胃口极好。*a* ～ *performance* 精彩的演出。***be a*** ～ ***hand at*** = ***be*** ～ ***at*** 是…的名手,善于。**-ly** ***ad***. **1**. 著名地。**2**. 非常,很。**3**. 〔口〕挺好。**4**. 以引用名言的方式。**-ness** ***n***.

fam·u·lus [ˈfæmjuləs; ˋfæmjʊləs] ***n***. (*pl*. **-li** [-lai; -laɪ]) (中世纪巫师或学者的)助手;侍从。

fan[1] [fæn; fæn] **I** ***n***. **1**. 扇子;风扇,鼓风机。**2**. 簸箕;扬谷机;(风车的)定风翼;【空】螺旋桨,螺旋桨叶片。**3**. 扇状物(如孔雀尾,棕榈树叶等)。*a draft* ～ 喉风机,通风扇。*an electric* ～电风扇。*an exhaust* ～ 抽风机,排气风扇。*a folding* ～ 折扇。**II** ***vt***. (**-nn-**) **1**. 煽;煽动;激起。**2**. (用扇子)驱走;簸(谷);扬去(糠等)。**3**. 煽燃。**4**. 把(翅膀等)张开成扇形。**5**. 〔美俚〕拍打,鞭打;搜查;〔美俚〕连续急速扫射。**6**. 〔美俚〕搜查。～ *a fire* 煽火使旺。～ *the flies from the food* 从食物上扇走苍蝇。—***vi***. 飘动,拍翅;成扇形。～ ***away*** 煽去。～ ***in*** 煽进。～ ***oneself*** 扇扇子。～ ***out*** 【军】成扇形散开;【讯】分开(电缆心)。～ ***the flame*** 煽动情绪。～**-in** 【计】输出,输出端数。～**light** ***n***. 【建】楣窗,扇形气窗 (=〔美〕transom)。～**like** ***a***. **1**. 像扇的,像风扇般转动的。**2**. 折叠的。～**-out** 【计】输出,输出端数。～ **palm** 【植】扇叶棕榈。～**-shaped** ***a***. 扇形的。～ **tracery** 【建】扇形(花)格架。～ **truss** 【建】扇形桁架。

fan[2] [fæn; fæn] ***n***. 〔美俚〕(运动,影迷,球迷)狂热爱好者;狂慕者。*a film* [*movie*] ～ 影迷。～ **mail** (影迷、球迷等写来的)表示敬慕的信。

fa·nat·ic(al) [fəˈnætik(əl); fəˋnætɪk(əl)] **I** ***n***. 狂热宗教徒,狂信者;入迷的人。**II** ***a***. 狂信的,狂热的,入迷的。**-i·cal·ly** ***ad***.

fa·nat·i·cism [fəˈnætisizəm; fəˋnætɪsɪzəm] ***n***. 狂信,狂热。

fa·nat·i·cize [fəˈnætisaiz; fəˋnætɪsaɪz] ***vt***., ***vi***. (使)狂

F

信;(使)变成狂信者;(使)变狂热。

fan·cied [ˈfænsid; ˋfænsɪd] ***a.*** 幻想的,空想出来的。

fan·ci·er [ˈfænsiə; ˋfænsɪə˞] ***n.*** **1.** 空想家。**2.** 懂得一些窍门的行家;巧妙的设计师。**3.** …迷。**4.** (鸟兽的)饲养行家。*a bird* ~ 养鸟迷;养鸟行家。

fan·ci·ful [ˈfænsifʊl; ˋfænsɪfʊl] ***a.*** **1.** 爱空想的;富于想像力的。**2.** 幻想中的。**3.** 奇异的。**-ly** ***ad.*** **-ness** ***n.***

fan·cy [ˈfænsi; ˋfænsɪ] **I** ***n.*** **1.** 想像(力)。**2.** 幻想。**3.** 嗜好,爱好;嗜好品。**4.** 〔集合词〕〔the ~〕嗜好者,玩赏者;〔特指〕拳击爱好者;鸟兽(饲养)爱好者。**5.** (玩赏动物)珍奇品种培育(法)。**6.** 花式;花式织物,花式货品。**7.** 〔古〕爱。*a passing* ~ 一时的爱好。*a wild* ~ 不着边际的空想。***after one's*** ~ 合自己心意。***be full of fancies*** 幻想多;异想天开。***catch*** [***please***, ***strike***, ***suit***, ***take***] ***the*** ~ ***of*** 投合…的心意,吸引。***go off into wild flights of*** ~ 胡思乱想;异想天开。***have a*** ~ ***for*** 爱好,爱上,入迷。***have a*** ~ ***that*** 总觉得要[想]~ ***see in*** ~ 想像。***strike sb.'s*** ~ 投合某人心意。***take a*** ~ ***to*** [***for***] 爱好,爱上。***to one's*** ~ 合自己心意。**II** ***a.*** **1.** 煞费心机的,别出心裁的(*opp.* plain)。**2.** 装潢用的;花式的,杂色的;变种的,品种珍奇的。**3.** 空想的,幻想的;异想天开的;异常的,特别的。**4.** 〔美口〕(水果等)特选的,特制的,高档的。**5.** (价格)高昂的;供应高价品的。*a* ~ *ball* 化装跳舞会。~ *birds* 珍奇鸟类。*a* ~ *box* 装璜特别好看的商品盒子。~ *buttons* 饰钮。~ *cakes* 花式糕点。~ *coal* 上等煤,精选煤。~ *diving* 花式跳水。~ *dress* (化装舞会等的)奇异服装。*a* ~ *fair* 〔英〕小商品市场。~ *fishes* 观赏鱼。~ *fresh fruits* 特级鲜果。~ *goods* 花哨的小工艺品。*a* ~ *price* 十分昂贵的价格。**III** ***vt.*** (***-cied***; ***-cy·ing***) **1.** 想像,设想,幻想,妄想。**2.** 想…;爱好,欢喜。**3.** 认为,相信;〔俚〕自命为,自以为。**4.** (为玩赏而)饲养,培养(变种动植物等)。*He fancies himself* (*to be*) *ill.* 他以为自己病了。*I* ~ *he will come.* 我想他会来的。*He fancies himself* (*to be*) *an authority.* 他自以为是个权威。*I rather* ~ *he won't come.* 我总以为他不会来。*She fancies herself still young.* 她以为自己还年轻哩。*I don't* ~ *this place at all.* 我一点也不喜欢这个地方。*Don't you* ~ *anything?* (问病人等)你想吃点什么吗? ***F-*** (***that***)! 真想不到! 奇怪! ***F- his believing it!*** 谁想得到他竟会相信! — ***vi.*** 想像,幻想。***Just*** ~! = ***Only*** ~! 想想看! 奇怪! ~**-bred** ***a.*** **1.** 由幻想而产生的。**2.** (动物)品种优良的。~ **dan** 〔美俚〕华而不实的人,喜欢耍花架子的运动员。~ **dive** 花式跳水。~**-free** ***a.*** **1.** 任凭想像随意驰骋的。**2.** 未婚的,情窦未开的,天真无邪的。~ **house** 妓院。~ **man** **1.** 情夫。**2.** 靠女人倒贴而生活的男子。~**sick** ***a.*** 害相思病的。~ **woman** [**girl**, **lady**] **1.** 情妇。**2.** 妓女。~**work** 钩编织品,刺绣品。

F.and A.M. = Free and Accepted Masons 〔英〕共济会。

fan·dan·gle [fænˈdæŋgl; fænˋdæŋgl] ***n.*** **1.** 〔美俚〕(华丽但不值钱的)小装饰品。**2.** 〔俚〕胡闹,荒唐事。

fan·dan·go [fænˈdæŋgəu; fænˋdæŋgo] ***n.*** (*pl.* ~*s*) **1.** (一种轻快的)西班牙舞(曲),方登戈舞(曲)。**2.** 胡闹,荒唐事。

fan·dom [ˈfændəm; ˋfændəm] ***n.*** 全体运动迷,全体球迷,全体影迷。

fane [fein; fen] ***n.*** **1.** 〔古、诗〕神庙。**2.** 〔古〕教堂。

fan·fare [ˈfænfɛə; ˋfænˏfɛr] **I** ***n.*** **1.** (喇叭、铜鼓的)嘹亮的吹奏声。**2.** 鼓吹,夸耀。**II** ***vt.*** 热闹地介绍[宣布]。*make* [*raise*] *a big* ~ 大吹大擂。

fan·fa·ron [ˈfænfərɔn; ˋfænfəˏrɑn] ***n.*** **1.** 吹牛者,大言不惭者。**2.** = fanfare.

fan·fa·ron·ade [ˌfænfærəˈnɑːd; ˏfænfærəˋnɑd] ***n.*** **1.** 浮夸,吹牛。**2.** = fanfare.

Fang [fæŋ; fæŋ] ***n.*** **1.** (分布在非洲几内亚湾东部海岸的)芳族,芳人。**2.** 芳人讲的班团语。

fang [fæŋ; fæŋ] **I** ***n.*** **1.** (犬、狼等的)尖牙;狼牙,尖齿;(蛇的)毒牙。**2.** 牙根。**3.** (牙状的)尖端;(工具等的)齿,爪。**II** ***vt.*** **1.** 以尖牙咬;在…上长有尖牙状物。**2.** 灌水引动(水泵)。*rocks* ~*ed with icicles* 上有尖牙状冰柱的岩石。

fanged [fæŋd; fæŋd] ***a.*** 有尖牙的,有毒牙的。

fan·gle [ˈfæŋgəl; ˋfæŋgəl] ***n.*** 新型。*new* ~ *of dresses* 新款式的服装。

fan·ion [ˈfænjən; ˋfænjən] ***n.*** (士兵或测量员作为标志用的)小旗,测量旗。

fan·jet [ˈfænˌdʒet; ˋfænˏdʒɛt] ***n.*** **1.** 【机】涡轮通风器。**2.** 【空】鼓风式喷气飞机。

fan·ner [ˈfænə; ˋfænə˞] ***n.*** **1.** 扇风者。**2.** 鼓风机,扬谷机。

Fan·nie [ˈfæni; ˋfænɪ] ***n.*** = Fanny.

fan·nings [ˈfæniŋs; ˋfænɪŋs] ***n.*** 〔*pl.*〕 **1.** 簸出物;筛出的粗茶叶。**2.** (交换机电缆的)扇形编组。

Fan·ny [ˈfæni; ˋfænɪ] ***n.*** 芬妮〔女子名, Frances 的昵称〕。

fan·ny [ˈfæni; ˋfænɪ] ***n.*** (*pl.* ***-nies***) 〔俚〕臀部;屁股。~**pack** 腰包〔紧在腰带上的钱包〕。

fan·on [ˈfænən; ˋfænən] ***n.*** **1.** (祭师做弥撒时带的)臂巾。**2.** (教皇做弥撒时穿的)披肩。

fan·tab·u·lous [fænˈtæbjuləs; fænˋtæbjʊləs] ***a.*** 〔美俚〕极好的,极妙的。

fan·tad [ˈfæntæd; ˋfæntæd] ***n.*** = fantod.

fan·tail [ˈfænteil; ˋfænˏtel] ***n.*** **1.** 扇状尾部。**2.** 【动】扇尾金鱼;扇尾鸽。**3.** 【建】鸠尾榫。**4.** 【船】鸭尾艄。**5.** (运煤工戴的)扇形帽。~ *deck* 船尾甲板。**-ed** ***a.*** 扇形尾的。

fan·ta·si·a [fænˈteizjə, -ˈtɑː-; fænˋtezjə, -ˋtɑ-] ***n.*** **1.** 【乐】幻想曲。**2.** 幻想作品。

fan·ta·size [ˈfæntəsaiz; ˋfæntəˏsaɪz] ***vt.***, ***vi.*** 幻想,梦想。**-ta·sist** [-sist; -sɪst] ***n.*** 幻想家,梦想家。

fan·tasm [ˈfæntæzm; ˋfæntæzm] ***n.*** **1.** 幻影;鬼。**2.** 幻想,幻觉;空想(= phantasm)。

fan·tas·ma·go·ri·a [fænˌtæzməˈgɔːriə; fænˏtæzməˋgɔrɪə] ***n.*** = phantasmagoria.

fan·tast [ˈfæntæst; ˋfæntæst] ***n.*** 幻想家,空想家;神经不正常的人。

fan·tas·tic, fan·tas·ti·cal [fænˈtæstik, -tikəl; fænˋtæstɪk, -tɪkəl] **I** ***a.*** **1.** 空想的,异想天开的。**2.** 奇异的,古怪的。**3.** 极大的,大得难以相信的。~ *reasons* 奇怪的理由。**II** ***n.*** 〔古〕古怪的人。**-ti·cal·ly** ***ad.*** **-ism** ***n.***

fan·tas·ti·cal·i·ty [fænˌtæstiˈkæliti; fænˏtæstɪˋkælətɪ] ***n.*** **1.** 怪异的,奇异。**2.** 奇谈;怪事。

fan·tas·ti·cate [fænˈtæstikeit; fænˋtæstɪˏket] ***vt.*** 使成为荒谬(的梦想)。**-ca·tion** [fænˌtæstiˈkeiʃən; fænˏtæstɪˋkeʃən] ***n.***

fan·tas·ti·co [fænˈtæstikəu; fænˋtæstɪko] ***n.*** 可笑的怪人。

fan·ta·sy [ˈfæntəsi, -zi; ˋfæntəsɪ, -zɪ] **I** ***n.*** **1.** 空想,幻想。**2.** 怪念头,想入非非。**3.** 想像力的产物;离奇的图案,奇妙的设计。**4.** 【乐】幻想曲;幻想作品。**5.** 观赏硬币〔专供收藏;并无流通使用价值〕。**II** ***vt.*** (***-sied***; ***-sy·ing***) 想像;幻想;对…进行幻想。— ***vi.*** **1.** 空想,幻想,梦想。**2.** 奏幻想曲。~ **land** 梦境,幻想世界,幻境。

Fan·te(e), Fan·ti [ˈfæntiː; ˋfæntɪ] ***n.*** 〔*sing.*, *pl.*〕(西非洲、迦纳的)芬堤族;芳堤语。***go*** ~ (欧洲人)芬堤化,遵从西非当地的风俗习惯。

fan·toc·ci·ni [ˌfæntəˈtʃiːniː; ˏfæntəˋtʃinɪ] ***n.*** 〔*pl.*〕〔It.〕木偶,傀儡;木偶戏,傀儡戏。

fan·tod [ˈfæntɔd; ˋfæntɑd] ***n.*** 焦燥不安;神经紧张。*the* ~*s* 焦急不安状态。

fan·tom [ˈfæntəm; ˋfæntəm] ***n.*** = phantom.

fan·wise [ˈfænˌwaiz; ˋfænˏwaɪz] ***ad.***, ***a.*** (展开)成扇形(的)。

fan·wort [ˈfænˌwəːt; ˋfænˏwɝt] ***n.*** 【植】水盾草属(= cabomba)。

Fany, F.A.N.Y. = First Aid Nursing Yeomanry〔英〕急救护士队。

FAO, F.A.O. = Food and Agriculture Organization (联合国)粮食及农业组织。

F.A.P. = First Aid Post 急救所[站]。

FAQ = **1.** fair average quality【商】中等品。**2.** free at quay 码头交货(价格)。**3.** frequently asked question【计】(网上)常问的问题。

fa·quir [ˈfɑːkiə, fəˈkiə; ˋfɑkɪr, fəˋkɪr] ***n.*** = fakir[1].

far [fɑː; fɑr] **I** ***a.*** (***far·ther*** [ˈfɑːðə; ˋfɑrðə], ***fur·ther*** [ˈfəːðə; ˋfɝðɚ]; ***far·thest*** [ˈfɑːðist; ˋfɑrðɪst], ***fur·thest*** [ˈfəːðist, ˋfɝðɪst]) **1.** 远隔的;离得远的,上远路的,长途的。**2.** 较远的,远处的。**3.** 久远的,上了年纪的。*a ~ country* 遥远的国家。*a ~ traveller* 远行者。*the ~ side of the room* 屋子的那一边。*the ~ side of a horse* 马的右边,下马的那边[上马由左边]。*a statesman of ~ sight* 目光远大的政治家。*the F- East* 远东。*the ~ past* 太古时候,很久以前。*the F- West* (尤指美国)西部地方。**II** ***ad.***〔比较形同上〕**1.**〔地点〕远,远隔,远在。★口语中表示地点时。far 主要用于疑问句和否定句,肯定句中的表现方式是: We went a long way〔书面语… went far〕。The house is a long way off〔书面语… is far〕。**2.** (时间)遥远,久远。**3.** (程度)很,极,大,…得多,*~ ahead* 远在前面。*~ away* [*off*] 远隔,在老远处。*the ~ distant past* 久远以前,*~ back in the past* 远古,在很久以前。*as ~ back as the 18th century* 远在十八世纪。*go so ~ as to* 竟然到…的地步,甚至…。*~ into the night* 到深夜。*~ better* 好得很。*I cannot say how ~ his story is true.* 我不能说他的话可靠到什么程度。***a ~ cry*** 距离很远;大不相同(*It is a ~ cry to London.* 到伦敦很远。*It is a ~ cry from a magic lantern to television.* 电视与幻灯大不相同)。***as ~ as*** **1.** 远到,直到(*go as ~ as Africa* 远至非洲)。**2.** 就;尽;至于(*as ~ as possible* 尽可能,尽量)。***as ~ as in me lies*** 尽我的力量。***as*** [***so***] ***~ as it goes*** 就现状来说,就其本身而言。***as ~ as I know*** 就我所知(= so ~ as I know)。***by ~*** (修饰比较级,最高级,表示数量,程度等)…得多;尤其;更(*This is by ~ the best.* 这个尤其好)。***~ and apart*** 远离着,远隔着。***~ and away*** 非常;大大,…得多,肯定的,无疑地(*He is ~ and away the greatest poet living.* 他是目前最最伟大的诗人)。***~ and near*** [***nigh***] 远近,到处,四面八方。***~ and wide*** 遍,广泛地,到处。***~ be it from me*** 我决不会。(***few and***) ***~ between*** 极少,偶尔。***~ from*** **1.** 远离。**2.** 决不,决没有,完全不(*~ from Paris* 远离巴黎的地方。*It's ~ from perfect.* 那还远远算不上完善)。***~ from it!*** 差得远呢! (***be***) ***~ gone*** (病等)更加厉害;大醉;(欠债)更多。***~ out***〔美俚〕**1.** 不寻常的。**2.** (政见等)极端的。**3.** 奥秘的,秘传的。***from ~*** 从远处。***from ~ and near*** 从各处;远近都…。***go ~*** **1.** 成功,成名。**2.** 长时间保持,大有帮助。***go ~ towards*** 大有助于,大有贡献于。***go ~ with*** 很能感动…,对…有巨大力量[影响]。***how ~*** **1.** (离…)多远(*How ~ is it to the office?* 离办公室多远?)。**2.** 到什么程度[范围](*I don't know how ~ to trust them.* 我不知道应该相信他们到什么程度)。***in so ~ as*** (表示程度、范围)就…,尽…,至于。***so*** [***thus***] ***~*** 到目前(此地)为止;就此范围[程度]来说。***So ~, so good.*** 到现在为止,一直都还不错。***so ~ as*** 尽…说,就…说;只就…说(*So ~ as I know.* 就我知道的说)。***so ~ as ... concerns*** 就…说。***~-away*** [ˈfɑːrəˈwei; ˋfɑrəˋwe] ***a.*** **1.** 远方的;老早老早以前的。**2.** (眼色、神情等)走神的,恍惚的。***~-back a.*** **1.** 古时的。**2.** 遥远的。***~-between a.*** **1.** 隔离的,远隔的。**2.** 稀有的。***~-end*** (线路或电路的)远端。***~-famed a.*** 驰名的,闻名的。***~-fetched a.*** 强词夺理的,牵强附会的。***~-flung a.***〔书〕广泛的,漫长的,辽阔的。***~-going a.*** 范围广泛的。***~-gone a.*** **1.** (病等)日益加重的。**2.** 遥远的。**3.** 疲乏不堪的。**4.** 已耗损的。***~most a.*** 遥远的。***~-off*** [ˈfɑːrɔːf; ˋfɑrɔf] ***a.*** 远方的,远隔的;遥远的。***~-out a.*** **1.** 在太空远处的。**2.**〔喻〕远离常规[传统方式]的;非常新颖的;先锋派(艺术)的。***~-outer*** 远离常规的人,反传统的人。***~-point*** 视远点〔眼睛看物的极限点〕。***~-ranging a.*** 远程的。***~-reaching a.*** 深远的,效果[影响]大的;广泛的(*~-reaching designs* 远大的计划)。***~-red a.***【物】远红外的。***~ right*** 极右分子[主义]。***~-right a.*** 极右的。***~-seeing a.*** 看得远的,目光远的;想得周到的;有先见之明的。***~-sighted a.*** 远视的,有先见之明的;【医】远视的。***~-sightedness*** 远视,远见。***-ness n.***

far. = **1.** farad. **2.** farthing.

far·ad [ˈfærəd; ˋfærəd] ***n.*** 法拉〔电容单位〕。***-a·ic*** [-ˈdeiik; -ˋdeɪk], ***-ic*** [fəˈrædik; fəˋrædɪk] ***a.*** 感应电流的。***-ism*** [ˈfærədizəm; ˋfærədɪzəm] ***n.*** 感应电应用,感应电疗法。

Far·a·day [ˈfærədi, -dei; ˋfærədɪ, -de] ***n.*** **1.** 法拉第〔姓氏〕。**2. Michael ~** 法拉第〔1791~1867,英国物理学家、化学家〕。**3.**〔f-〕【电】法拉第〔电量单位〕。***~ dark space***【物】法拉第暗区。***~ disk***【物】法拉第圆盘。***~ effect***【物】法拉第效应。

far·a·dism [ˈfærədizəm; ˋfærəˏdɪzəm] ***n.*** **1.** 感应电流,感应电学。**2.** 感应电治疗。

far·a·dize [ˈfærədaiz; ˋfærədaɪz] ***vt.***【医】用感应电治疗[刺激]。***-za·tion*** [ˌfærədaiˈzeiʃən; ˏfærədaɪˋzeʃən] ***n.*** 感应电疗法。

farce [fɑːs; fɑrs] **I** ***n.*** **1.** 滑稽戏,笑剧。**2.** 滑稽,可笑的事物,冒充的东西。**3.** 馅儿。**II** ***vt.*** **1.** 使带滑稽趣味,使(演说、作品等)有趣味。**2.**〔古〕填塞;(用香料等)增进…的口味。

far·ceur [fɑːˈsəː; fɑrˋsɝ] ***n.***〔F.〕**1.** 丑角,滑稽角色;笑剧作家。**2.** 爱说笑话的人。

far·ci·cal [ˈfɑːsikəl; ˋfɑrsɪkəl] ***a.*** 笑剧的,滑稽戏的,滑稽的。***-ly ad.*** ***-ness n.***

far·ci·cal·i·ty [ˌfɑːsiˈkæliti; ˏfɑrsɪˋkælətɪ] ***n.*** 滑稽剧性质;滑稽性,滑稽味。

far·ci(e) [fɑːˈsiː; fɑrˋsi] ***a.*** 有馅的。

far·cy [ˈfɑːsi; ˋfɑrsɪ] ***n.*** **1.** (马的)鼻疽;马皮疽。**2.** 家畜慢性放线菌病。

far·del [ˈfɑːdl; ˋfɑrdḷ] ***n.***〔古〕**1.** 捆,包;包袱;重担。**2.** 不幸,灾祸。

fare [fɛə; fɛr] **I** ***n.*** **1.** 运费,车费,船费。**2.** 乘客。**3.** 伙食。**4.** (渔船的)捕获量。**5.** 精神食粮。*a single* [*double*] *~* 单程[来回]票价。*a bill of ~* 菜单。*coarse ~* 粗食。*simple* [*homely*] *~* 家常便饭。**II** ***vi.*** **1.** 过日子,生活;受招待。**2.**〔主语为 it〕(事)进行得(好,坏),处境(好,坏),结果(如何)。**3.** 吃,进食。**4.**〔古〕去,前进,旅行。*How did you ~ in Paris?* 您在巴黎生活如何? *How ~s it with you?* 你近来怎样? 你好吗? ***~ forth***〔古〕动身,去。***~ ill*** 倒楣,过无聊日子;(事业等)吃亏,失败。***~ well*** 走运;过得好;(事业)顺遂,成功。***F- you well!***〔古〕= farewell. ***You may go farther and ~ worse.***〔谚〕越走得远可能越倒楣〔劝人知足常乐;安于现状语〕。

far·er [ˈfɛərə; ˋfɛrɚ] ***n.*** 旅行者。

fare-thee-well [ˌfɛəðiːˈwel; ˏfɛrðiˋwɛl], **fare-you-well** [ˌfɛəjəˈwel; ˏfɛrjuˋwɛl] ***n.*** 极度;完善。*to a ~* 尽善尽美;登峰造极。

fare·well [ˈfɛəˈwel; ˋfɛrˋwɛl] **I** ***int.*** 再见,再会,一路平安。**II** ***a.*** 告别的,送行的。*a ~ address* 告别辞。*a ~ dinner* 饯行宴会。*a ~ meeting* 欢送会。*a ~ present* 告别礼物。**III** ***n.*** **1.** 告别。**2.** 欢送会。**3.** 告别辞。***bid ~*** 辞行。***make one's ~s*** 道别,告辞。***~ to life*** 辞世,死。***take a ~ of*** 向…辞行。***take one's ~*** 辞行,告

别。

fare·well-to-spring [ˈfɛəˈweltəˈspriŋ; ˋfɛrˋweltəˋsprɪŋ] *n*.【植】可爱高代花(*Godetia amoena*)〔产于美国西部〕。

fa·ri·na [fəˈrainə, fəˈriːnə; fəˋraɪnə, fəˋrinə] *n*. 1. 谷粉。2. 淀粉。3. 粉状物质。4.【植】花粉。

far·i·na·ceous [ˌfæriˈneiʃəs; ˌfærɪˋneʃəs] *a*. 1. 谷粉制的。2. 含淀粉的。3. 粉状的。

far·i·nose [ˈfærinəus; ˋfærɪˌnos] *a*. 1. 产粉的,含粉的,粉质的。2.【动、植】具粉的,被粉的。

far·kle·ber·ry [ˈfɑːklberi; ˋfɑrklˌbɛrɪ] *n*.【植】白莓(*Vaccinium arboreum*)〔美国南部的一种灌木〕。

farl(e) [fɑːl; fɑrl] *n*.〔Scot.〕燕麦薄饼;薄饼。

Far·ley [ˈfɑːli; ˋfɑrlɪ] *n*. 法利〔姓氏〕。

farm [fɑːm; fɑrm] **I** *n*. 1. 农场,农庄;农田;农场住宅,农家。2. 饲养场,畜牧场。3.〔美〕别墅。4.【英史】地租;出租田地;包租区。5.〔美〕(棒球联合总会所属主要任务为训练新队员的)棒球分会。6. 育儿所,托儿所。*a state* ~ 国营农场。*F- Credit Administration*〔美〕农场贷款署。*a fruit* ~ 果园。*a wheat* ~ 小麦地。*a chicken* [*poultry*] ~ 养鸡场。**II** *vt*. 1. 耕作,耕种,在…上经营农场;饲养(家畜等)。2. 佃出,出租;招人承包,包出(工件、活计、收租税等)(*out*). 3. 寄养(幼儿等)(*out*)。4. 把(囚犯等)作为劳动力出租(*out*)。5. 使(地力)耗尽。~ *out the right to collect taxes* 包出收税权。*She ~ed out the baby with her mother*. 她把婴儿放在母亲家寄养。— *vi*. 耕作,经营农物[畜牧场],务农。~ *for a living* 以农为生。~ *upon one's own land* 自耕。~ **bloc**【美政】(国会中由各农业州议员组成的)农业集团。~ **crops** 农作物。~ **hand** 农业工人,农场工人;雇农。~**house** *n*. 农场住宅;农家。~ **implements** [**tools**] 农具。~ **labourer** = ~**hand**, ~**land** 农田。~ **machinery** 农业机械。~ **produce** 农产品。~ **stead**〔主英〕(包括住宅在内的)农场。~ **work** 农业劳动,农活。~**yard** 农家庭院。

farm·er [ˈfɑːmə; ˋfɑrmɚ] *n*. 1. 经营农业者,农场主〔*cf*. peasant〕,农夫。2.(租税等的)包收人。3. 幼儿代养人。*a landed* [*tenant*] ~ 自耕[佃]农。*Farmer's Association* 农会。**an afternoon** ~ 拖拖拉拉的人。**a dirt** ~〔美口〕自耕农;小农。**gentleman** ~ 乡绅,从事农业的贵族。~**like** *a*. 农夫般的

farm·er·ette [ˌfɑːməˈret; ˌfɑrməˋrɛt] *n*.〔美口〕农场女工,农妇。

farm·ing [ˈfɑːmiŋ; ˋfɑrmɪŋ] **I** *n*. 1. 农业,农作,耕作;饲养(家禽)。2.(租税等的)包收。3. 寄养幼孩。*mechanized* ~ 机耕。*small peasant* ~ 小农经济。*tank* ~ (用溶液培养植物的)无土栽培法。**II** *a*. 农业的;农场的。*the busy* [*slack*] ~ *season* 农忙[闲]季节。~ *implements* 农具。~ *land* 耕地。*a* ~ *region* 农业区。~ *system* 农作制度,农场管理制度〔*cf*. cropping system〕。

far·o [ˈfɛərəu; ˋfɛro] *n*.【牌】菲罗〔一种类似牌九的简单赌博〕。~ **bank** 玩菲罗牌战的赌场。

fa·rouche [fəˈruːʃ; ˌfəˋruʃ] *a*. 1. 桀骜不驯的,凶猛的。2. 缺乏社交风度的;粗野失礼的;缺乏教养的。

far·ra·gi·nous [fəˈreidʒinəs; fəˋredʒɪnəs] *a*. 杂凑成的,混杂的,乱七八糟的。

far·ra·go [fəˈrɑːgəu; fəˋrago] *n*. (*pl*. ~*es*) 拼凑,大杂烩,混杂物。

Far·rar [fəˈrɑː; fəˋrɑr] *n*. 法勒〔姓氏〕。

Far·rell [ˈfærəl; ˋfærəl] *n*. 法雷尔〔姓氏〕。

far·ri·er [ˈfæriə; ˋfærɪr] *n*.〔英〕1. 钉马掌[马蹄铁]的铁匠。2. 马医;兽医。3.【军】管理军马的骑兵下士。

far·ri·er·y [ˈfæriəri; ˋfærɪərɪ] *n*.〔英〕马掌钉法;兽医术。2. 马掌铺,马掌厂。

far·row [ˈfærəu; ˋfæro] **I** *n*. 一胎猪;猪下仔。*10 at one* ~ 一胎生下十只小猪。**II** *vt*. (猪)产(一胎猪崽)。— *vi*. (猪)产崽(*down*)。

fart [fɑːt; fɑrt] **I** *n*.〔卑〕1. 屁。2. 傻老头。**II** *vt*., *vi*. 放(屁)。

far·ther [ˈfɑːðə; ˋfɑrðɚ]〔far 的两种比较级形式之一,另一形式为 further〕**I** *a*. 1. 再过去点的,再远点的;再进一步的,更往前一点儿的。2. 进一步的,另外的〔通常也用 further〕. *the* ~ *side of the hill* 山那边。*make no* ~ *objection* 不再刁难[反对]。**II** *ad*. 1. 再过去点,再远点,再往前一点儿。2. 加之,更,还,并且〔通常也用 further〕。*I can go no* ~. 我不能再走了。***I'll see you ~ first***. 我才不干呢! ~ **on** 1.(说明等)在下面;在后面。2. 更远些,再往前些(*The village is about three miles* ~ *on*. 村子还在前面三英里左右的地方)。**No** ~! 够了! 到此为止! **until** ~ **notice** 等到另行通知时。**wish sb**. ~ 但愿某人[物]不在那里就好了。**F- India** 印度支那。

far·ther·most [ˈfɑːðəməust; ˋfɑrðɚˌmost] *a*. 最远的。

far·thest [ˈfɑːðist; ˋfɑrðɪst]〔far 的两种最高级形式之一,另一种形式为 furthest〕**I** *a*. 最远的,顶远的。*the* ~ *corner of the country* 最遥远的角落;最偏远的地方。**II** *ad*. 最远;最大程度地,最大限度地。*the seat* ~ *from the door* 离门最远的坐位。*the* ~ *thing from the ordinary* 最不寻常的事。**at** (**the**) ~ 最远也不过;顶多也不过,至迟也不过。

far·thing [ˈfɑːðiŋ; ˋfɑrðɪŋ] *n*. 1. 法新〔1961 年以前的英国铜币,等于四分之一便士〕。2.〔主要用于否定句〕一点儿,极少量。*the uttermost* ~ 最后一个铜板。**doesn't matter a** ~ 无关紧要,不足轻重。**have not a** ~ 一文不名。**not care a** ~ 毫不在乎。**not worth a** ~ 毫无价值,一文不值。

far·thin·gale [ˈfɑːðiŋgeil; ˋfɑrðɪŋˌgel] *n*. (十六、七世纪妇女撑开裙子用的)鲸骨衬箍;用鲸骨箍等撑大的裙子。

FAS = Federation of Amrican Scientists 美国科学家联合会。

FAS, f. a. s. = free alongside ship【商】船边交货(价格)。

fas·ces [ˈfæsiːz; ˋfæsiz] *n*.〔*pl*.〕1.〔用作单或复,其原来的单数形 fascis 较罕用〕〔L.〕束棒,权标〔古罗马高级执法官吏的权标,形状为一束棍棒,中有一柄露出的斧头,为"法西斯"一词的来源〕;权威的标记。2. 意大利法西斯党的标志。

fas·ci·a [ˈfæʃiə; ˋfæʃɪə] *n*. (*pl*. ***fas·ci·ae*** [ˈfæʃiiː; ˋfæʃɪi])〔常 *pl*.〕1. 带,饰带。2.【医】绷带。3.【建】挑口饰,(柱顶)盘座面。4.(店门上的)招牌。5.〔英〕汽车仪表板。6.【解】筋膜;【动】(昆虫的)横带。~ **board** 1.【建】挑口板。2.〔英〕汽车仪表板。

fas·ci·ate [ˈfæʃiˌeit; ˋfæʃɪˌet] *a*. 1. 用带子捆束的。2.【植】扁化的;生长于束簇内的;簇生的。3.【动】具横带的(= fasciated)。

fas·ci·cle [ˈfæsikl; ˋfæsɪkl] *n*. 1. 小束,一簇。2.【植】(花、叶等的)束,球,簇;密伞花序;簇生叶,丛生花。【解】(神经、肌肉的)束。3.(书刊的)一卷,一分册。**-d** *a*. 成束的,簇生的。

fas·cic·u·lar [fəˈsikjulə; fəˋsɪkjulɚ] *a*. 1.【解】(成)束的。2.【植】簇生的;维管束的。~ *fibres* 束状纤维。**-ly** *ad*.

fas·cic·u·late(d) [fəˈsikjulit(id); fəˋsɪkjuˌlet(ɪd)] *a*. = fascicular. **-lated·ly** *ad*.

fas·cic·u·la·tion [fæˌsikjuˈleiʃən; fæˌsɪkjuˋleʃən] *n*. (成)束状;【植】簇生。

fas·ci·cule [ˈfæsikjuːl; ˋfæsɪˌkjul] *n*. 1.(书籍的)分册。2.【解】(神经、肌肉的)束。

fas·cic·u·lus [fəˈsikjuləs; fəˋsɪkjuləs] *n*. (*pl*. ***fas·cic·u·li*** [fəˈsikjulai; fəˋsɪkjulaɪ]) 1.【解】(神经、肌肉的)束。2.(书籍的)分册。

fas·ci·nate [ˈfæsineit; ˋfæsɪnˌet] *vt*. 1. 迷住,使神魂颠倒,强烈地吸引住(蛇睨视青蛙等),蛊惑;使吓呆。*The* *boy was ~d by the toys*. 小孩被玩具迷住了。*The snake ~d its prey*. 蛇(用目光)吓住它要捕食的动物。— *vi*. 迷人,极度吸引人。

fas·ci·nat·ing [ˈfæsineitiŋ; ˋfæsn͵etɪŋ] *a*. 魅惑的,使人神魂颠倒的,妖媚的。**-ly** *ad*.

fas·ci·na·tion [ˌfæsiˈneiʃən; ͵fæsnˋeʃən] *n*. 1. 迷惑力,魅力。2. 迷恋,神魂颠倒;强烈爱好。

fas·ci·na·tor [ˈfæsineitə; ˋfæsɪ͵netɚ] *n*. 1. 魅惑者,迷人者;妖艳迷人的妇女;魔术师。2. 网眼毛线披巾。

fas·cine [fæˈsiːn; fæˋsin] *n*. 1. (护堤岸用的)柴笼;(垫沟,加固战壕等用的)柴捆,木把,捆。2.【林】粗杂材。

fas·cis [ˈfæsis; ˋfæsɪs] *n*. fasces 的单数〔罕用〕。

fas·cism [ˈfæʃizəm; ˋfæʃ͵ɪzəm] *n*. 〔常作 F-〕法西斯主义。

Fa·scis·mo [It. faˈʃisməu; faˋʃɪsmo] *n*. 〔It.〕= Fascism.

fas·cist [ˈfæʃist; ˋfæʃɪst] **I** *n*. 法西斯主义者,法西斯分子。**II** *a*. 法西斯主义的,法西斯主义者的。**-ic** [fəˈʃistik; fəˋʃɪstɪk] *a*. **-i·cal·ly** *ad*.

Fa·scis·ta [fæˈʃistə; fæˋʃɪstə] *n*. 〔It.〕【史】1. 意大利法西斯党党员。2. 意大利法西斯党,法西斯蒂。

Fa·scis·ti [fæˈʃistiː; fæˋʃɪsti] *n*. Fascista 的复数。

fas·cist·i·za·tion [fəˌʃistaiˈzeiʃən; fə͵ʃɪstaɪˋzeʃən] *n*. 法西斯化。

fash [fæʃ; fæʃ] **I** *vt*. 〔Scot.〕使困恼,使困窘,使烦恼。~ ***oneself*** 谋虑;气恼。~ ***one's beard*** [***head***, ***thumb*** 等] 烦恼。**II** *n*. 烦恼,焦虑;使人厌烦的人[物]。

fash·ion [ˈfæʃən; ˋfæʃən] **I** *n*. 1. 时髦,时兴;风气,潮流;时新式样;时兴货品;〔集合词〕上流社会,社交界,时髦人物,红人。2. 制法,方法,风格,方式;式样;型式;〔古〕种类。*It is not the* ~ *to* (*do*). …现在通常不时兴了。*the world of* ~ 社交界。*people of* ~ 社会名流。*a man of* ~ 有名人物,时下名流。*He did it after* (*in*) *his own* ~. 他照自己的办法做了。*behave in a strange* ~ 举动奇怪。*the modern* ~ 摩登式样。*the present* ~ 时式。***after*** [***in***] ***a*** [***some***] ~ 多少,勉强,好歹还…一点(*He knows English after a* ~. 他多少懂一点英语)。***after the*** ~ ***of*** 照着,模仿。***be all the*** ~ 极时髦,风行一时。***be in*** (***the***) ~ 时新,合乎时尚。***be*** (***all***) ***the*** ~ 完全迎合时好,极时新。***be out of*** (***the***) ~ (人或物)不合时尚。***bring into*** ~ 使流行(起来)。***come into*** ~ 流行起来,正流行。***follow the*** ~ 赶时髦。***go out of*** ~ (渐渐)过时。***in*** (***the***) ~ 时新的,投合时好的。***in the old*** ~ 照旧,照老样。***in this*** ~ 照这样。***the latest*** ~ ***in*** (*shoes*) 最新流行式样的(鞋子)。***make*** ~ 作样子。***set*** [***lead***] ***the*** ~ 开风气之先,率先兴起新花样,创先例。**II** *vt*. 1. 形成,铸成,造,作(*into*; *to*)。2. 使适合,使适应(*to*);改变,改革。~ *a vase from clay* = ~ *clay into a vase* 用黏土做一个花瓶。~ *a whistle out of a piece of wood* 用木头做一个哨子。*doctrines ~ed to the varying hour* 因时而变的理论。~ *sb. into a good teacher* 把某人培养成一名优秀教师。~ **book** 时装录。~ **designer** 时装设计师。~ **house** 高档时装店。~ **monger** 赶时髦的人。~ **plate** 1. 时装样片。2. 衣着时髦的人。~ **plate stem**【船】(钢板)组成船首柱。~ **show** 时装表演。~ **statement** 个性化服饰〔通过衣着、仪表表现个性〕。**-ist**超级时尚迷,拼命追求时髦的人。**-less** *a*.

-fash·ion *comb. f*. 加在名词之后,表示"…式的": *crab-~*, *Japanese-~*.

fash·ion·a·ble [ˈfæʃənəbl; ˋfæʃənəbl] **I** *a*. 1. 时髦的;流行的,时新的。2. 社交界的;合乎上流社会口味的。3. (价格昂贵)高级的。*a* ~ *dressmaker* 时装裁缝。*a* ~ *restaurant* 高级饭馆。***become*** ~ ***for a time*** 风靡一时。**II** *n*. 时髦人物,场面人物。**-bly** *ad*. **-ness** *n*.

-fash·ioned [ˈfæʃənd; ˋfæʃənd] *comb. f*. 〔加在形容词或副词之后,作为形容词〕表示"…式的";"…作成的","…形的": *old-~* 老式的。*carefully-~* 精心作成的。

fast[1] [fɑːst; fæst] **I** *a*. 1. 紧(*opp*. loose),牢实的,坚牢的,粘得紧的,坚固的;固定的。2. 忠实的,可靠的。3. 耐久的;不褪色的;抗(酸等)的。4. (运动)激烈的,(睡眠)香甜的。5. 迅速的(*opp*. slow);(钟表)走得快的;敏捷的。6. 贪快乐的,放荡的。7. (球拍等)弹力好的;【摄】感光快的,曝光时间短的。*The door is* ~. 门关着。*a* ~ *colour* 经久不变的颜色。*a* ~ *fight*【美体】激烈的比赛。~ *friends* 可靠的朋友。~ *friendship* 忠实的友情。*a* ~ *grip* 紧紧一握。*a* ~ *highway* 高速公路。*a* ~ *life*〔美〕放荡的生活。*a* ~ *liver* 生活放荡的人。*a* ~ *track* 快行道。*a* ~ *train* 快车。*a* ~ *trip* 短期旅行。*a* ~ *woman* 放荡的女人。***a*** ~ ***one*** 1. (棒球中的)急球。2. 〔俚〕骗局,诡计。3. 黄色笑话。***as*** ~ ***as one's legs could carry*** (***one***) 拼命跑。***be*** ~ ***in growth*** 成长迅速。***be*** ~ ***with*** (*gout*) 因(痛风)而动不得。~ ***and hard*** 牢固稳定的,一成不变的。***lay*** ~ ***hold on*** = take ~ hold of. ***make*** ~ 把…拴紧[关紧];把…打上结扣,系,拴(*make a door* ~ 把门关紧)。***pull a*** ~ ***one*** 欺骗。***take*** ~ ***hold of*** 紧紧握住,抓牢。**II** *ad*. 1. 紧紧地,牢固地。2. 酣畅地,(睡)熟。3. 〔古、诗〕紧迫地,逼近地(*by*; *beside*; *upon*);接连不断地,紧接着。4. 快,速。5. 放荡。*F- bind*, ~ *find*. 〔谚〕藏得好,丢不了。*speak* ~ 说得快。*It is raining* ~. 阴雨连绵。***live*** ~ 生活放荡;滥费精力。***play*** ~ ***and loose*** (***with***) 反复无常,靠不住。***stand*** ~ 不后退,屹立不动;不让步。~ **ball**【棒球】快速直球。~ **break** 1. (篮球的)快攻,快速突破。2. (比赛的)迅速开始。~**-breeder** (**reactor**)【物】快中子增殖反应堆。~ **buck**〔美俚〕轻易得来的钱,来路不明的钱。~ **counter**〔美〕伪报选举票数者;诡计多端的人;骗子。~**-fingered** *a*. 1. 非法的,不合法的。2. 聪明的,巧妙的。3. 狡猾的。~**-food** *a*. 供应汉堡包之类现成或快速食物的。~**-forward** 1. *n*. (录音机的)快进键;快进(功能)。2. *vt*., *vi*. (使)快进,加快。~ **groove** 唱片末尾的深槽。~ **lane** 1. 快车道。2. (在竞争中)导致暴富的快节奏生活。~**-moving** *a*. 1. 快速移动的。2. (小说等)情节紧凑的。~ **one**〔俚〕1. 欺诈行为。2. 黄色笑话。~**-stepping** *a*. 1. (马等)快速的。2. 积极的。~**-talk** *vt*. 花言巧语地企图说服[影响]。~ **time** 夏季时间(= daylight-saving time)。~ **track** 快行道。

fast[2] [fɑːst; fæst] **I** *vi*. 1. 斋戒,禁食,绝食。2. 节制饮食;忌食某些食物。**II** *n*. (宗教上的)禁食,齐戒;绝食;斋期,禁食期,绝食期。***break one's*** ~ 1. 开斋。2. 吃早餐。~ ***on bread and water*** 过清水面包的斋戒生活。***keep*** [***observe***] ***a*** ~ 守斋,断食。~ **day** 斋戒日,禁食日。

fast·back [ˈfɑːstbæk; ˋfæstbæk] *n*. (向尾部倾斜的)长坡度的汽车顶;有长坡度车顶的汽车。

fas·ten [ˈfɑːsn; ˋfæsn̩] *vt*. 1. 把…结牢[拴住];锁,闩(门);(用钉等)钉牢,使固定;加固;上紧,扣紧(钮子等)。2. 把(眼睛等)盯住(*on*)。3. 把…归于,把…加在(*on*; *upon*)。4. 使(颜色)不褪。~ *the documents* ~ *together* 把文件扎成一捆。~ *one's eyes on sb*. 把眼睛盯住某人。~ *one's shoes* 结上鞋带。*a rope ~ed to the post* 拴在柱子上的绳索。~ *the dyes into the cloth* 使布深染而不褪色。*She ~ed herself on him*. 她缠住他不放。~ *a crime on sb*. 归罪于某人。— *vi*. 1. 握牢,抓牢;坚持,集中注意力于。2. (门等)关紧。*The door will not* ~. 门关不上。~ ***a quarrel upon sb***. 跟某人吵闹。~ ***down*** (把箱盖等)钉上,盖紧;确定。~ ***in*** 关进,装进。~ ***off*** (打结、用针把线)扣牢。~ ***on*** [***upon***] 握住,抓住,捉牢;盯住[纠缠]不放;一口咬定;牢牢注意;~ ***up*** 使固着,使拴紧;捆,扎;钉牢。

fas·ten·er [ˈfɑːsnə; ˋfæsnɚ] *n*. 1. 扣件,钮扣,揿钮,钩扣,扣钉,卡子,夹子,持着器;钉书机。2. 结扎者,结扎工。*belt* ~ 皮带扣,引带扣。*slide* [*zip*] ~ 拉链。

F

snap ~ 按扣,子母扣。*paper* ~ 书钉。

fas·ten·ing [ˈfɑːsniŋ; ˋfæsnɪŋ] ***n*.** **1.** 扣紧,扎牢。**2.** 扣件,拴扣物(如锁、闩、钩、扣、钉等)。

fas·ti [ˈfæstai; ˋfæstaɪ] ***n*.** 〔*pl*.〕〔L.〕(古罗马的)行事日历,岁时纪,年代纪。

fas·tid·i·ous [fæsˈtidiəs; fæsˋtɪdɪəs] ***a*.** **1.** 爱挑剔的,难讨好的,过分讲究的。**2.** (微生物等)需要复杂营养的。*be* ~ *about one's food* 挑食。**-ly *ad*. -ness *n*.**

fas·tig·i·ate, -i·a·ted [fæsˈtidʒiit(id), -eit(id); fæsˋtɪdʒɪɪt(ɪd), -et(ɪd)] ***a*.** 锥状的,倾斜的;【植】帚状的;【动】圆束状的。**-ate·ly *ad*.**

fas·tig·i·um [fæsˈtidʒiəm; fæˋstɪdʒɪəm] ***n*.** **1.** (疾病的)危急时刻,高峰期。**2.**【解】(第四脑室的)尖顶。**3.**【建】屋脊。

fast·ing [ˈfɑːstiŋ; ˋfæstɪŋ] **I *n*.** 禁食。*F- comes after feasting*. 〔谚〕开头大吃大喝,最后忍饥挨饿。**II *a*.** 禁食的。~ **blood-sugar level**【医】(空腹时的)血糖水平。~ **cure** 禁食疗法。

fas·tish [ˈfɑːstiʃ; ˋfɑstɪʃ] ***a*.** **1.** 相当迅速的,还快的。**2.** 有些放荡的。

fast·ness [ˈfɑːstnis; ˋfæstnɪs] ***n*.** **1.** 坚固,坚牢;固定,固着。**2.**【纺】坚牢度;不褪色性;抗(毒)性。**3.** 迅速,急速。**4.** 放荡。**5.** 要塞,堡垒。*acid* ~ 耐酸性。~ *to light* 耐光性,不褪色。~ *to washing* 耐洗度。

fas·tu·ous [ˈfæstjuəs; ˋfæstʃʊəs] ***a*.** **1.** 高傲的,傲慢的。**2.** 浮夸的,虚饰的。

fat [fæt; fæt] **I *a*.** **1.** 肥胖的,丰满的 (*opp*. lean, thin)〔*cf*. stout〕;多脂肪的,(肉等)肥的;(猪等)养肥了的。**2.** (煤)含沥青的;〔美〕(松等)树脂多的;黏性好的。**3.** (土地等)肥沃的;(工作等)优厚的;收益多的,有利的,富裕的,兴旺的;(嗓音)圆润的;(香味)浓郁的。**4.**【印】粗笔画的,黑体的。**5.** 迟钝的,愚钝的。*a* ~ *dividend* 优厚的红利。~ [*poor*] *lime* 纯[劣]质石灰。*a* ~ *salary* 高薪。*Laugh and grow* [*be*] ~. 心宽体胖。~ *soil* 沃土。*a* ~ *page* (空白部分多,对印刷所)有利的版面。*a* ~ *year* 丰年。***a* ~ *lot*** 〔口〕〔反〕不多,少,一点也不(*You know a* ~ *lot about it*. 你一点儿也不懂)。***cut it* (*too*)** ~〔俚〕做得太过分;夸示。***cut up*** ~〔俚〕留下大笔遗产。***get* [*grow*]** ~ 发胖。***have a* ~ *chance of*** 〔俚〕〔反〕机会不多,希望不大。**II *n*.** **1.** 肥肉 (*opp*. lean),脂肪(质);油脂。**2.** 最好部分;优厚的工作。**3.**【剧】要角。**4.** 肥胖。**5.** 养肥可供销售的食用动物;树脂多的树。**6.** 多余额,积余,储备。**7.**〔俚〕钱。*be somewhat inclined to* ~ 略为显得肥胖。**(*All*) *the* ~ *is in the fire*.** **1.** 生米已成熟饭,事情已无可挽回。**2.** 危机迫在眉捷。***chew the* ~** 〔俚〕闲聊,嚼舌头。***fry the* ~ *out of*** 〔美俚〕摊派勒索。***live on one's own* ~** 吃老本。***live on* [*eat*] *the* ~ *of the land*** 极奢侈。**III *vt*.** **1.** 养肥 (*out*; *up*)。**2.** 用油脂处理(皮革)。**3.** 在…加入脂肪。— ***vi*.** 长肥。***kill the fatted calf for sb*.** 宰肥牛欢迎某人,热诚欢迎某人。~ **back** **1.** 腌用猪板油。**2.** (炼油或作肥料用)步鱼 (= menhaden)。~**-brained *a*.** 愚笨的。~ **cat** 〔美俚〕**1.** 政治运动中出资多的人,对政治家(或政党)给予财政支援的大亨。**2.** 有钱有势的人。**3.** 洋洋自得的懒汉。~ **city** 〔美俚〕极舒适的生活环境,富裕。~ **deposit** 脂肪沉积体。~ **farm** 〔美俚〕减肥中心。~ **head** 呆子,傻瓜。~ **headed *a*.** 傻头傻脑的。~ **part** 〔美剧俚〕重要角色。~ **stock** 供食用的家畜。~ **type**【印】黑体。~**-witted *a*.** 愚笨的;傻的,鲁钝的。**-less *a*. -ly *ad*. -ness *n*.**

fa·tal [ˈfeitl; ˋfetl] ***a*.** **1.** 命中注定的;避免不了的;必然的。**2.** 生死[成败]攸关的;致命的 (*to*)。**3.** 毁灭性的;铸成不可挽回的错误的;悲惨的,不祥的;严重的,意外的。*a* ~ *blow* 致命的打击。*a* ~ *disease* 不治之症。*a* ~ *wound* 致命伤。*a blow* ~ *to one's prospects* 危害前途的巨大打击。~ ***and neglected*** 造成严重后果的疏忽 (= fatally neglected)。~ ***shears*** 死。***the* ~ *sisters*** 命运三女神〔*cf*. the Fates〕. ***the* ~ *thread*** 生命线,生命,命脉。**-ly *ad*. -ness *n*.**

fa·tal·ism [ˈfeitəlizəm; ˋfetˏlɪzəm] ***n*.**【哲】宿命论。

fa·tal·ist [ˈfeitəlist; ˋfetlɪst] ***n*.** 宿命论者。

fa·tal·is·tic [ˌfeitəˈlistik; ˏfetˋlɪstɪk] ***a*.** 宿命的,宿命论的。~ *attitude* 听天由命的态度。**-ti·cal·ly *ad*.**

fa·tal·i·ty [fəˈtæliti, fei-; fəˋtælətɪ, fe-] ***n*.** **1.** 宿命,天数,命运,命数。**2.** 灾难,惨事;惨死;死亡(事故)。***by a strange*** ~ 由于不可捉摸的命运。~ **rate** 致死率。

fa·tal·ize, fa·tal·ise [ˈfeitəlaiz; ˋfetəlaɪz] ***vt*.** **1.** 使倾向宿命论。**2.** 使受命运支配。— ***vi*.** 倾向宿命论。

Fa·ta Mor·ga·na [ˈfɑːtə mɔːˈgɑːnə; ˋfɑtə mɔrˋgɑnə] 〔It.〕**1.** (英国神话传说中)亚瑟王 (King Arthur) 的妹妹变成的妖精。**2.** 〔f- m-〕空中楼阁(特指西西里海岸上的海市蜃楼)。

fate [feit; fet] ***n*.** **1.** 命运,宿命。**2.** 灾难,死亡,灭亡。**3.** 结局;(正常发展的)可预期演变。**4.** 〔the (three) Fates〕【希、罗神】命运三女神。*There is no escape* [*flying*] *from* ~. 〔谚〕在劫难逃。**(*as*) *sure as*** ~ 一定,千真万确地。***decide* [*fix*, *seal*] *one's*** ~ 决定将来命运。***go to one's*** ~ 自趋灭亡。***meet one's*** ~ 死;送命。***the irony of*** ~ 命运的播弄。

fat·ed [ˈfeitid; ˋfetɪd] ***a*.** 宿命的,命运决定了的。*be* ~ *to be hanged* 注定要被绞死。*one's* ~ *lot* 宿命。

fate·ful [ˈfeitful; ˋfetful] ***a*.** **1.** 决定命运的;重大的,决定性的。**2.** 致命的,带来灾难的。**3.** 预言性的。**-ly *ad*. -ness *n*.**

fa·ther [ˈfɑːðə; ˋfɑðɚ] **I *n*.** **1.** 父亲;〔口〕爸爸〔妻子对公公,女婿对岳丈通常也这样称呼〕;义父,继父。**2.** 族长;祖先;前辈,长辈。**3.** 〔F-〕圣父,上帝。**4.** 神父;教父;师傅;修道院长;早期基督教作家。**5.** 〔英〕(议会等的)元老;前辈,长者;创造人,开山祖师,鼻祖;根源。**6.** 父亲的身分[情分],父(性)爱。**7.** 〔*pl*.〕(古罗马的)元老院议员。*Is your* ~ *a glazier*? 〔谑〕你父亲是装玻璃的么?〔指责别人挡了光线〕。*The child is* ~ *of* [*to*] *the man*. 〔谚〕从小看大,三岁看老。*Like* ~, *like son*. 〔谚〕有其父必有其子。*The wish is* ~ *to the thought*. 希望是思想之父;有什么希望就有什么想法。~*s of a city* 城市的耆老。*the F- of English poetry* 英国诗歌之父(指乔叟)。*F- of the City* 市参议员。***be a* ~ *to*** 像爹一样对待…。***be gathered to one's* ~*s*** 去见祖宗,死。***F- Christmas*** 〔英〕圣诞老人。~ ***of the Bar*** 年长律师。***sleep* [*lie*] *with one's* ~*s*** 埋葬在故乡。***the F- of lies*** 魔鬼。***the F- of lights*** 上帝。***the* ~ *of his country*** 国父。***the F- Thames*** 泰晤士河。***the F- of waters*** 江河之父(指伊洛瓦底江,尼罗河或密西西比河)。***the Holy F-*** 教皇。***the Pilgrim Fathers***【英史】最初移居美国的清教徒。**II *vt*.** **1.** 做…的父亲,生(孩子);创作,产生(新著作等);创立(计划等)。**2.** 自认是…的父亲;自认是…的作者[创立人](等)。**3.** 像父亲一样对待,保护;治理。**4.** 确定(作品等)的作者;确定(儿童的)生父;确定(罪行的)责任。*He* ~*ed two sons*. 他生了两个儿子。~ *an orphan* 收养孤儿。*Investigations* ~*ed the baby on him*. 调查结果证明他就是那孩子的生父。~ *a crime upon the suspect* 确定该嫌疑犯即是作案者。~ **confessor**【天主】听忏悔的神父 (= ghostly ~)。~**-hood** 父亲的身分[资格];父性;父权;父道。~ **image** [**figure**] 父亲般的人物,长者;(精神分析学中所指)被人当做父亲看待的人。~**-in-law** (*pl*. **fathers-in-law**) 岳父;公公;舅父;〔俚〕干爹;〔古、罕〕继父。~ **land** 祖国。~ **right** **1.** 父权。**2.** 父系继承权。**F-'s Day** 〔美〕父亲节(每年六月的第三个星期日)。~ **ship** = ~-hood. **F- Time** 时光老人〔拟人化说法〕。**-less *a*.** 没有父亲的,生父不明的。**-like *a*., *ad*.** 父亲般的[地]。

fa·ther·ly [ˈfɑːðəli; ˋfɑðɚlɪ] **I *a*.** **1.** 父亲的。**2.** 父亲般的;爱护的;慈祥的。**II *ad*.** 父亲般地。**-li·ness *n*.**

fath·om [ˈfæðəm; ˋfæðəm] **I *n*.** (*pl*. ~*s*, 〔集合词〕~)

1. 英寻(测量水深用的长度单位,合 6 英尺,或 1.829 米)。2.〔英〕剖面为一平方英寻的(木材)量。*piled* ~ 劈柴层积(〔英〕= 6×6×6 英尺)。**II** *vt*. 1. 测(水)深。2. 推测,领会,看穿。*I can not* ~ *his meaning*. 我领会不透他的意思。~ *the universe* 探索宇宙。**III** *vi*. 测深;进行探索。**-a·ble** *a*. 深度可测的;可以了解的。

fa·thom·e·ter [fæˈðɔmitə; fæˋðɑmətɚ] *n*.【海】回音测深仪,水深计。

fath·om·less [ˈfæðəmlis; ˋfæðəmlɪs] *a*. 1. 深不可测的;无法估量的。2. 无法了解的。*the* ~ *depths of the ocean* 无法测量的海洋深处。~ *motives* 无法理解的动机。**-ly** *ad*. **-ness** *n*.

fa·tid·ic [fəˈtidik, fei-; fəˋtɪdɪk, fe-] *a*. 预言的;先见的(= fatidical)。

fat·i·ga·ble [ˈfætigəbl; ˋfætɪgəbl̩] *a*. 可使之疲劳的;易疲劳的。**-bil·i·ty** [ˌfætigəˈbiliti; ˏfætɪgəˋbɪlətɪ] *n*.

fa·tigue [fəˈtiːg; fəˋtig] **I** *n*. 1. 疲乏,劳累;劳苦;累活。2.【机】(金属屡经打击等后的)疲劳。3.【医】(组织、器官等对刺激失去反应能力的)疲劳。4.【军】(军务以外的)杂役劳动。5.〔*pl*.〕【军】(士兵服杂役等时穿的)工作服。*auditory* ~【医】听觉疲劳。*photoelectric* ~【物】光电疲乏。~ *strength* 疲劳强度。~ *tester* 疲乏试验器。**II** *vt*. 把(金属材料)弄疲劳,使疲乏。*feel* ~*d* 感到疲劳。— *vi*. 1. 疲劳。2. (士兵)担任杂役。~ **clothes** [**dress**]【军】工作服,劳动服装。~ **duty**【军】勤务。~ **party**【军】劳动队,杂役班。**-less** *a*. 不知疲劳的。

Fa·ti·ma [ˈfætimə; ˋfætɪmə] *n*. 1. 法蒂玛〔606? —632,穆罕默德的女儿〕。2. 法国神话故事中专杀妻子的"蓝胡子" (bluebeard)的第七个妻子;好奇心重的女人。

Fat·i·mid [ˈfætimid; ˋfætɪmɪd], **Fat·i·mite** [-ˌmait; -ˏmaɪt] **I** *a*. 1. (穆罕默德女儿)法蒂玛后裔的。2. 法蒂玛王朝(公元 909—1171)的。**II** *n*. 法蒂玛王朝君主;法蒂玛的后裔。

fat·ling [ˈfætliŋ; ˋfætlɪŋ] *n*. 肥畜,养肥备宰的幼畜。

fat·so [ˈfætsəu; ˋfætso] *n*.〔口〕胖家伙〔作称呼用,含贬义〕。

fat-sol·u·ble [ˈfætˌsɔljubl; ˋfætˏsɑljubl̩] *a*. 脂溶的,可溶于油脂的。

fat·ten [ˈfætn; ˋfætn] *vt*. 1. 催肥,养肥(*up*)。2. 使(变)肥沃。3. 使充实,使增多。~ *one's child up with milk* 给孩子吃牛奶让他发胖。— *vi*. 1. 长肥;变肥沃。2. 发财致富。3. 增大,增多,变充实。**-a·ble** *a*.

fat·ten·er [ˈfætnə; ˋfætənə] *n*. 1. 养肥禽畜的人。2. 养肥后供宰杀的禽畜。

fat·tish [ˈfætiʃ; ˋfætɪʃ] *a*. 较肥的,稍肥的。

fat·ty [ˈfæti; ˋfætɪ] **I** *a*. (*-ti·er*; *-ti·est*) 1. 脂肪(质)的,油脂的,油腻的。2. 肥胖的。3.【医】脂肪过多的。**II** *n*.〔口〕胖子〔称呼用〕。~ **acid**【化】脂肪酸。~ **compound**【化】脂肪族化合物。~ **degeneration**【医】脂肪变性。~ **liver**【医】脂肪肝。**fat·ti·ness** *n*.

fa·tu·i·ty [fəˈtju(ː)iti; fəˋtjuətɪ] *n*. 1. (自以为是的)愚蠢。2. 蠢事。

fat·u·ous [ˈfætjuəs; ˋfætʃuəs] *a*. 1. 愚蠢的,荒唐的,虚妄的。2. 虚幻的,空虚的。*a* ~ *attempt* 妄举。~ *fires* 鬼火。*a* ~ *smile* 傻笑。**-ly** *ad*. **-ness** *n*.

fat·wa [ˈfʌtwɑː; ˋfʌtwɑ] *n*.〔阿拉伯〕伊斯兰教法学家所作的裁决;(上述裁决中的)死刑令〔如霍梅尼对作家拉什迪所下的死刑令〕。

fau·bourg [ˈfəubuəg, -bəːg; foˋbug, -bɚg] *n*.〔F.〕(特指巴黎的)郊区,近郊。

fau·cal [ˈfɔːkl; ˋfɔkəl] **I** *a*. 咽门的;喉音的。**II** *n*. 咽喉软颚音。

fau·ces [ˈfɔːsiːz; ˋfɔsiz] *n*. (*pl*.)【解】咽门,喉头。

fau·cet [ˈfɔːsit; ˋfɔsɪt] *n*.〔美〕1. (放水)旋塞,龙头。2. (连接管子的)承口,插口。~ *joint* 套筒接合。

fau·cial [ˈfɔːʃəl; ˋfɔʃəl] *a*. 咽门的。

faugh [fɔː; fɔ] *int*. 哼,呸〔表示轻视、厌恶〕。

Faulk·ner [ˈfɔːknə; ˋfɔknɚ] *n*. 1. 福克纳〔姓氏〕。2. **William** ~ 威廉·福克纳〔1897～1962,美国小说家,1949 年诺贝尔文学奖金获奖者〕。**-i·an** (有关美国现代著名作家)福克纳的;福克纳风格的。

fault [fɔːlt; fɔlt] **I** *n*. 1. 过失,过错;罪过,责任。2. 缺点,缺陷,瑕疵。3. (猎狗的)失去嗅迹。4.【电】故障,误差;漏电;【地】断层。5.【网球】发球出界;犯规。*Faults are thick where love is thin*.〔谚〕一朝情义淡,样样不顺眼。~ *detection*【机】探伤。*The* ~ *is his own*. 这是他自己的错。*a grave* ~ *in a theory* 理论上的重大缺陷。*a* ~ *in the machine* 机械故障。*image* ~【物】像差,影像失真。*numerical* ~*s* 数值误差。***a* ~ *on the right side*** 因祸得福。***be at*** ~ 1. (猎犬追捕猎物等时)失去嗅迹,踌躇不前;不知所措,正在为难。2. 出毛病,有故障。3. = in fault (*My memory is at* ~. 我想不起来了)。***find*** ~ ***in*** 看出…缺点。***find*** ~ ***with*** 找…的岔子。***have no*** ~ ***to find with*** 无错可寻。***hit off a*** ~ (猎狗)闻出(曾一度错失的)嗅迹。***in*** ~ 有过错,有责任(*Who is in* ~ ? 是谁的不是?)。***to a*** ~ 过度,极端(*He is kind to a* ~. 他过分老实)。***whip a*** ~ ***out of sb***. 鞭打某人使之改过。***with all*** ~***s*** 不保证商品没有缺点。***without*** ~〔古〕无误,确实。**II** *vi*. 1.【地】产生断层;有断层余迹。2. 发球出界;犯规。3.〔方〕责备,挑剔。4.〔古〕犯错误,做错。— *vt*. 1. 找…的岔子,挑剔;〔方〕责备。2.【地】使产生断层。3. 把…做错。*He* ~*ed my speech in two ways*. 他认为我的讲话有两点不妥。~ *one's performance* 表演发生失误。~**age**〔集合词〕【地】断层。~ **block**【地】(两个断层间的)零乱岩石。~-**finder** 1. 吹毛求疵者,喜欢挑剔的人。2.【机】故障探测器。~-**finding** 1. *n*. 挑剔,找岔子。2. *a*. 吹毛求疵(的),喜欢挑剔的。

fault·i·ly [ˈfɔːltili; ˋfɔltɪlɪ] *ad*. 有过失地;不完善地;该指责地。

fault·i·ness [ˈfɔːltinis; ˋfɔltɪnɪs] *n*. 有过失,有瑕疵[缺陷];不完善;可指责。

fault·less [ˈfɔːltlis; ˋfɔltlɪs] *a*. 无过失的;无缺点的;完善无缺的。**-ly** *ad*. **-ness** *n*.

fault·y [ˈfɔːlti; ˋfɔltɪ] *a*. (*fault·i·er*; *-i·est*) 有过失的,有缺点的;有毛病的;有错误的,该指责的;不完善的。*a* ~ *argument* 有漏洞的论点。*a* ~ *memory* 记忆力失常。*a* ~ *sentence* 病句。~ **coal** 劣质煤。~ **insulator** 故障绝缘子。

faun [fɔːn; fɔn] *n*.【罗神】半人半兽状的神。

fau·na [ˈfɔːnə; ˋfɔnə] *n*. (*pl*. ~*s*, *-nae* [ˈfɔːniː; ˋfɔnɪ]) 1. (一个地区或时代的)全部动物;动物区系;动物群。2. 动物志〔*cf*. flora〕。*marine* ~ 水产动物。*the* ~ *of the Ice Age* 冰河时代的动物。

fau·nal [ˈfɔːnəl; ˋfɔnəl] *a*. 1. 动物区系的;动物群的。2. 动物志的。**-ly** *ad*.

fau·nist [ˈfɔːnist; ˋfɔnɪst] *n*. 动物区系研究者。

fau·nis·tic(al) [fɔːˈnistik(əl); fɔˋnɪstɪk(əl)] *a*. 动物区系(研究)的,动物区系研究者的。

Faust [faust; faust] *n*. 浮士德〔欧洲中世纪传说中的人物,为获得知识和权力,向魔鬼出卖自己的灵魂。德国作家歌德曾创作同名诗剧〕。**-i·an** *a*.

faute de mieux [fəut də ˈmjəː; fot dəˋmjɚ]〔F.〕因别无更好的东西(= for want of sth. better)。

fau·teuil [ˈfəutəːi; ˋfotəl] *n*.〔F.〕1. 扶手椅。2. 戏院正厅前座。

fau·vism [ˈfəuvizm; ˋfovɪzm̩] *n*.〔常用 F-〕野兽派画风[思潮、艺术家]。**fau·vist** *n*. 野兽派画家。

faux [fəu; fo] *a*.〔F.〕虚假的;人为的;人造的。

faux pas [ˈfəu ˈpɑː; ˋfo ˋpɑ] (*pl*. ***faux pas*** [fəuˈpɑːz; foˋpɑz])〔F.〕1. 过失;失着。2. 违反习俗[礼节]的举动[言语]。3. (特指妇女的)失足。

fa·vel·a [fɑːˈvelɑː; fɑˋvɛlɑ] *n*.〔Pg.〕(巴西城市近郊的)贫民窟[区]。

F

fa·ve·o·late [fəˈviəˌleit; fəˋviəˏlet] *a*. 蜂窝状的;有蜂窝状小孔的,有气泡的。

fa·vo·ni·an [fəˈvəuniən; fəˋvonɪən] *a*. 〔诗〕1. 西风的。2. 温和的。

fa·vo(u)r [ˈfeivə; ˋfevɚ] **I** *n*. 1. 厚爱,恩惠,照顾,亲切;〔*pl*.〕(女人对男人的)委身。2. 偏袒,偏爱。3. 利益;赞成,支持,提倡,许可,宽恕。4. (表示好意或爱情的)礼物,纪念章,徽章,花结。5. 〔古〕信函。6. 〔古〕容貌。*I shall esteem it a* ～ *if* ... 若蒙…不胜荣幸。*your* ～ *of yesterday* 昨日尊函。*a wedding* ～ 婚礼用的花束、彩球(等)。*under the* ～ *of night* 趁黑夜。***ask a*** ～ ***of*** 请帮忙,请照顾。***ask the*** ～ ***of an early reply*** 请早赐复。***be*** [***with***] ～ ***of*** ... …敬烦…转交〔信封上用语〕。***be incapable of appreciating sb.'s*** ～ 不识抬举。***by*** [***with***] ***your*** ～ 对不起;冒昧的说。***curry*** ～ (***with sb.***) 拍人马屁,求宠于人。***do sb. a*** ～ 帮某人的忙,答应某人的请求,接济某人。***find*** ～ ***with*** [***in the eyes of***] ***sb***. 得某人的宠爱[欢心]。***heap*** ～***s upon*** 给予许多帮忙[好处]。***in*** ～ 时兴,流行 (*What is now in* ～? 现在流行的是什么?)。***in*** ～ ***of*** 1. 赞成,支持 (*I am in* ～ *of woman's suffrage*. 我赞成妇女参政)。2. 有利于 (*The score was 80 to 78 in* ～ *of the guest team*. 比分为八十比七十八,客队获胜)。3. 付与 (*cheque to be drawn in* ～ *of sb*. 开一张支票付给某人)。***in*** (***high***) ～ ***with*** 得人欢心,受人宠爱。***in sb.'s*** ～ 得某人好感[欢心]。***in popular*** ～ 得舆论拥护。***out of*** ～ ***with*** 失宠,被嫌弃,不流行。***show undue*** ～ ***to*** 偏爱,偏袒。***stand high in sb.'s*** ～ = *in sb.'s* ～. ***the last*** [***ultimate***] ～ 女人以身相许。***win sb.'s*** ～ 得某人欢心[好感]。**II** *vt*. 1. 赞成,赞助,帮忙。2. 便于,有利于;促进。3. 惠赐,惠赠 (*with*)。4. 偏袒,偏爱;善为照顾。5. 证实(理论等)。6. 〔口〕容貌像。～ *a proposal* 赞成提案。*Fortune* ～*s the brave*. 〔谚〕幸运找勇士。*The market* ～*s the buyers*. 行市对买方有利。*Will you* ～ *us with a song?* 给我们唱一个歌,好吗? *Trusting to be* ～*ed with your further orders*. 今后尚希源源定购。*The weather* ～*ed us*. 天公作美。*The boy* ～*s his father*. 这男孩长得像他父亲。*The man* ～*ed his sprained foot when he walked*. 那人走路时对他那只扭伤的脚很小心。***Favoured by*** ... 敬烦…转交〔信封上用语〕。

fa·vo(u)r·a·ble [ˈfeivərəbl; ˋfevərəbl] *a*. 1. 顺利的;良好的;有利的,有望的。2. 好意的,赞成的。3. 起促进作用的。4. 讨人喜欢的,赢得赞同的。*a* ～ *answer* 满意的答复。*a* ～ *balance of trade* 贸易顺差。*a* ～ *opportunity* 好机会。*a* ～ *wind* 顺风。*be* ～ *to a scheme* 赞成计划。***be*** (***not***) ～ ***for*** (不)利于 (*be* ～ *for a start* 利于起程)。***take a*** ～ ***turn*** (形势等)好转。**-a·bly** *ad*. **-ness** *n*.

fa·vo(u)red [ˈfeivəd; ˋfevɚd] *a*. 1. 怀有好意[好感]的。2. (受)优惠的;有利的;有才能的;有某种特权的。3. 〔作复合词用〕有…容貌的。*the most-*～*-nation clause* 最惠国条款。*ill-*～ 丑陋的。*well-*～ 标致的。**-ly** *ad*. **-ness** *n*.

fa·vo(u)r·er [ˈfeivərə; ˋfevərɚ] *n*. 宠爱者;照顾者;支持者;赞成者。

fa·vo(u)r·ing [ˈfeivəriŋ; ˋfevərɪŋ] *a*. = favo(u)rable. ～ *winds* 顺风。

fa·vo(u)r·ite [ˈfeivərit; ˋfevərɪt] **I** *n*. 1. 亲信,受宠信者。2. 受人特别喜爱的人[物];〔美〕党内有声望的政治家。3. 有希望的获胜者(尤指马)。*She is a general* ～. 人人都喜欢她。*The* ～ *came in third*. 被认为最有获胜希望的人[马]结果跑了第三名。**II** *a*. 中意的;心爱的。*one's* ～ *author* 自己喜欢的作家。*one's* ～ *book*(*s*)自己爱读的书。*a* ～ *child* 特别受宠爱的孩子。***be a*** ～ ***with*** 是…的宠儿,在…面前走红运[吃香]。***fortune's*** ～ 幸运儿。～ ***son*** 1. (由于有成就而受到乡里尊敬的)名人。2. 州[市]政界领袖拥护的候选人(如总统候选人)。***the*** ～ (比赛中的)红马;红选手。

fa·vo(u)r·it·ism [ˈfeivəritizəm; ˋfevərɪtˏɪzəm] *n*. 偏袒,偏爱,徇私。*It was thought that most promotions vere based on* ～. 人们认为,这次提职大部分都不公平。～ *towards one's townsmen* 同乡观念。

fa·vus [ˈfeivəs; ˋfevəs] *n*. 〔L.〕【医】黄癣,毛囊癣。

Fawkes [ˈfɔːks; ˋfɔks] *n*. 福克斯〔姓氏〕。

fawn[1] [fɔːn; fɔn] **I** *n*. 1. 小鹿;小山羊,小动物。2. 鹿毛色,淡黄褐色。***in*** ～ (鹿)怀着小鹿。**II** *vi*. 生小鹿[小山羊、小动物]。— *vt*. 生(小鹿、小山羊或小动物)。**III** *a*. 淡黄褐色的。～ **lily**【植】赤莲属植物;〔尤指〕美洲赤莲。

fawn[2] [fɔːn; fɔn] *vi*. (狗等)摇尾乞怜;讨好,奉承 (*on*; *upon*)。**-er** *n*. 摇尾乞怜者;奉承者。**-ing** *a*. 摇尾乞怜的,奉承的。**-ing·ly** *ad*. **-ing·ness** *n*.

fax [fæks; fæks] **I** *n*. 1. 传真(照片、文件)〔facsimile 的缩略词〕。2. 电视(传真)画面;复印本。**II** *vt*. 给(某人)发传真。～**-mail** (无线电)传真邮件。～ **modem**【电信】传真调制解调器。

fay[1] [fei; fe] *n*. 〔诗〕仙女;小妖精。

fay[2] [fei; fe] *n*. 〔古〕信仰〔发誓语〕。***by my*** ～ 我保证,一定。

fay[3] [fei; fe] *vt*., *vi*. 【船】接合;合榫。～ ***in*** [***with***] (与)…恰相吻合。

Fay(e) [fei; fe] *n*. 费伊〔女子名 Faith 的昵称〕。

faze [feiz; fez] **I** *vi*. 〔美俚〕打扰,惊扰,使为难;使担忧〔多用于否定句中〕。*The news did not* ～ *him*. 这个消息不会使他担心。**II** *n*. 混乱,狼狈;忧虑。

FB = 1. fire brigade 消防队。2. flying boat 水上飞机,飞船。3. freight bill 运货单。4. fullback (足球)后卫;后卫的位置。

F.B.A. = Fellow of the British Academy 不列颠学会会员。

FBI = 1. Federal Bureau of Investigation 〔美〕联邦调查局。2. Federation of British Industries 英国工业联合会。

FBM = 1. foot board measure (量木材用的)板尺。2. fleet ballistic missile 舰队弹道导弹。

FBR = fast breeder reactor 快中子增殖反应堆。

FBS = forward-based system【军】前沿配置系统;前沿武器系统。

FC = 1. fire control 消防;【军】实施射出;射击指挥;火力控制;(用电子仪器等进行的)射击控制。2. football club 足球俱乐部。3. foot-candle【物】英尺烛光〔照度单位〕。4. free church 独立教会。5. Fighter Command【美军】战斗机指挥部。

fc = franc.

f.c. = 1. fire control 火灾控制。2. follow copy【印】见原稿。

FCA = Farm Credit Administration 〔美〕农业信贷署。

F.C.A. = Fellow of Chartered Accountants 〔英〕特许会计师学会会员。

fcap, fcp = foolscap.

F.C.C. = 1. Federal Communications Commission 〔美〕联邦电信委员会。2. First Class Certificate 一级证件。3. Food Control Committee 〔英〕粮食管制委员会。

F.C.S. = Fellow of the Chemical Society 〔美〕化学学会会员。**f.c.s.** = free of capture and seizure【保险】拘捕和扣留除外。

F.D. = 〔L.〕*fidei defensor* (= Defender of the Faith).

F/D = 1. Free Docks 船坞交货。2. Forward Delivery【商】定期交货;来日交货。

FDA = Food and Drug Administration 〔美〕食品及药物管理局。

FDC = fleur de coin (钱币)新铸的。

FE = Far East.
Fe = 【化】〔L.〕*ferrum* (= iron) 元素铁的符号。
feal [fiːl; fil] *a*.〔古〕忠实的,诚实的。
fe·al·ty [ˈfiːəlti; ˋfiəltɪ] *n*. 1.【英史】(臣仆对封建主的)忠诚。2.〔诗〕信义,诚实。
fear [fiə; fɪr] **I** *n*. 1. 恐怖,畏惧。2. 忧虑,担心,顾虑,不安。3.(对神的)敬畏。4. 可能,机遇。5. 令人害怕的事物。*He was overcome by* ～. 他吓坏了。*She could not speak for* ～. 她吓得说不出话来。*full of hopes and* ～*s* 充满希望和顾虑。*No* ～!〔口〕没事儿! 当然不会那样! 不会(那样)的! *There is no* ～ *of their losing the battle*. 他们不会打败仗的。*There is not much* ～ *of that*. 那件事不大有可能发生。***for*** ～ ***of*** 因为怕,以免。***for*** ～ ***that*** [***lest***] 生怕,以免。***from*** ～ 由于恐惧。***go about in*** ～ ***of one's life*** 害怕会送命。***have a*** ～ ***that ...*** 胆心,怕(发生某事)。***in*** ～ ***and trembling*** 胆颤心惊,提心吊胆。***out of*** ～ = *from* ～. ***with*** ～ 吓得,怕得。***strike*** ～ ***into*** 使…感到害怕。***without*** ～ ***or favour*** 公平,秉公。**II** *vt*. 1. 恐怕,害怕。2. 畏敬。3. 担忧。—*vi*. 1. 害怕。2. 忧虑。*I* ～ (*that*) *he will get ill*. 我担心他要生病了。*I* ～ *it's too late*. 我怕太迟了。*Never* ～! 不怕! 放心好了! ★口语中一般不说 fear 而说 be afraid (of).
fear·ful [ˈfiəful; ˋfɪrfəl] *a*. 1. 吓人的;可怕的。2.〔口〕非常的,厉害的。3. 害怕的,担心的,胆怯的。*be* ～ *to look upon* 看起来可怕。*be* ～ *of falling* 怕摔倒。*be* ～ *to speak* 不敢讲话。***be*** ～ ***that*** [*lest*] ... 担心,害怕…。**-ness** *n*.
fear·ful·ly [ˈfiəfuli; ˋfɪrfəlɪ] *ad*. 1. 可怕地。2. 胆怯地。3.〔口〕非常地,十分。～ *busy* 忙极了。
fear·less [ˈfiəlis; ˋfɪrlɪs] *a*. 无畏的,大胆的。*be* ～ *of* 不怕…。**-ly** *ad*. **-ness** *n*.
fear·nought, -naught [ˈfiənɔːt; ˋfɪrˏnɔt] *n*. 1. 粗绒大衣呢,粗绒大衣呢外套。2.【纺】开毛机,和毛机。
fear·some [ˈfiəsəm; ˋfɪrsəm] *a*. 1. 可怕的,吓人的。2. 胆小的,羞怯的。**-ly** *ad*. **-ness** *n*.
fea·sance [ˈfiːzəns; ˋfizns] *n*.【法】实现条件;履行义务。
fea·si·bil·i·ty [ˌfiːzəˈbiliti; ˏfizəˋbɪlətɪ] *n*. 现实性;可行性。
fea·si·ble [ˈfiːzəbl; ˋfizəbl] *a*. 1. 可实行的,行得通的。2. 可能(有)的,有理的。3. 可用的,适宜的。*a* ～ *plan* 可以实行的计划。*a road* ～ *for travel* 适于旅行[可通行]的道路。**-si·bly** *ad*. **-ness** *n*.
feast [fiːst; fist] **I** *n*. 1.(宗教上的)节日;节期,祝典。2. 筵席;宴会,酒席。3. 欢乐,娱乐;赏心乐事。*a death's head* [*a skeleton*] *at the* ～ 扫兴的人[事]。*a* ～ *for the eyes* 赏心悦目的事。*immovable* ～*s* 固定节日〔如圣诞节〕。*movable* ～*s* 活动节日〔如复活节〕。*a* ～ *for the gods* 精美的饮食;使人愉快的事物。*a* ～ *of fat things* 山珍海味的酒席。*A cheerful look makes a dish a* ～.〔谚〕脸上笑嘻嘻,便饭成筵席。***a Dutch*** ～ 主人先醉的酒宴。***a*** ～ ***of eyes*** 眼福。***a*** ～ ***of reason and a flow of soul*** 富有教益的谈话;非常美妙的谈话。***Enough is as good as a*** ～. 饱食即美餐;知足常乐。***give*** [***make***] ***a*** ～ 请客。***make a*** ～ ***of*** [***upon***] 大吃,饱吃。***make*** ～〔古〕吃酒席,作乐。***the*** ～ ***of trumpets*** 犹太人的新年。**II** *vi*. 1. 摆节筵;参加宴会;赴宴。2. 享受。～ *on rare books* 愉快地读到大量珍本书籍。*F- today and fast tomorrow*.〔谚〕今朝大吃大喝,明日忍饥挨饿。—*vt*. 1. 宴请。2. 使享受,使精神愉快。～ *one's friends* 宴请朋友。～ *one's eyes on the beautiful scenes* 饱览美景。～ ***a night away*** 通宵宴饮。～ ***at the public crib*** 尸位素餐,(尤指)拿干薪。～ ***one's eyes*** (***up***) ***on*** 以…大饱眼福。**-less** *a*.
feast·er [ˈfiːstə; ˋfistɚ] *n*. 欢宴者。
feat[1] [fiːt; fit] *n*. 1. 卓绝的手艺,技术,本领;武艺。2. 功绩,功劳,〔特指〕武功。*laudable* ～*s* 可称颂的事迹。～*s in* [*of*] *arms* 武功。～*s of horsemanship* 马术。
feat[2] [fiːt; fit] *a*.〔古〕1. 灵巧的。2. 漂亮的,整洁的。3. 合适的。**-ly** *ad*.
feath·er [ˈfeðə; ˋfɛðɚ] **I** *n*. 1. 羽毛,翎毛;羽饰;箭羽。2.(同样)毛色;种类。3. 鸟;〔集合词〕禽类〔*cf*. fur〕。4.(宝石等的)羽状瑕疵;【无】羽状回波;轻如羽毛的东西;零杂废物。5.(划船)桨叶的水平运动;(潜艇上潜望镜引起的)微波。6.【建】榫牙。7.【机】滑键;(铸件的)周缘翅片。8. 服装,服饰。9. 状态,心情。*Fine* ～*s make fine birds*.〔谚〕佛靠金装,人靠衣装。*I am not of that* ～. 我不是那种人。*Birds of a* ～ *flock together*.〔谚〕物以类聚。*fur, fin and* ～ 兽类、鱼类和鸟类。***a*** ～ ***in one's cap*** [***hat***] 值得夸耀的事;荣誉。***be spitting*** ～*s* 大怒。***birds of a*** ～ 同一类人,一丘之貉。***crop sb.'s*** ～*s* 杀某人的威风。***cut a*** ～ 船头破浪前进。***in*** ～ 有羽毛[羽饰]的。***in full*** ～ (雏等)长满了毛的;盛装;精神抖擞。***in good*** [***high, fine, full***] ～ 身强力壮,兴高采烈。***knock sb. down with a*** ～ 使人十分惊奇。***make the*** ～***s fly***〔美口〕1. 工作得很起劲。2. 用激烈的语言或使用武力对付;引起争斗[争吵]。***not a*** ～ ***to fly with*** 一文不名,一筹莫展。***not care a*** ～ 毫不介意。***rise at a*** ～〔美口〕一碰就冒火。***ruffle one's*** ～*s* 发怒。***ruffle sb.'s*** ～*s* 激怒某人。***show the white*** ～ 示弱。***singe one's*** ～*s* 损害自己的名誉;使自己受损失;事业失败。***smooth sb.'s rumpled*** ～*s* 稳住情绪,使平息怒气。***wag the*** ～ 炫耀自己的身分。**II** *vt*. 1. 给装上羽毛,用羽毛装饰,用羽毛覆盖;在…上装箭羽。2. 使(桨)与水面平行;【空】使(螺桨)顺流交距,使(旋翼)周期变距。3. 射掉(飞禽的)羽毛。4.(用楔形部件)使连接。～ *an arrow* 上箭翎。～ ***one's nest*** 贮备;肥私囊。—*vi*. 1. 长羽毛;成羽毛状;像羽毛似的动摇。2. 使桨与水面平行;【空】(螺桨)顺流交距;(旋翼)周期变距。～ ***out*** 1. 长出羽毛。2.(边缘、末端)稀疏开来;飘散开来。3. 减弱;逐渐消失。～ ***up to***〔美俚〕追求(女友)。～ **bed** 1. 羽毛褥垫,安有羽毛褥垫的床。2. 安适的处境,闲职。3. 因轮藻丛生而形成的羽毛状池底[湖底]。～ **bed** 1. *vi*. 要求资方限产超雇,担任闲职。2. *vt*. 同意限产超雇,使成闲职;以政府津贴资助。3. *a*. 要求限产超雇的;因限产超雇而闲散的(*a* ～ *bed soldier* 职务闲散的士兵;放荡的人;嫖客)。～**bedding** 限产超雇(法)〔指工会为减少失业,在劳资合同中责成资方限制产量,或超额雇用工人〕。～ **bone** (用家禽羽茎制成的)鲸须代用品。～ **brain** [～**head**, ～**pate**] 愚蠢的人,轻浮的人。～-**brained** [～**headed**, ～**pated**] *a*. 轻率的,愚笨的。～ **duster** (羽毛)扫帚。～ **edge** 1. *n*.(木板、剃刀等的)薄边。2. *vt*. 把(木板的边)削薄。～-**footed**, ～-**heeled** *a*. 脚步很轻的;飞毛腿的,轻捷如飞的。～-**light** *a*. 轻如羽毛的。～ **palm** 羽叶棕榈,～ **star**【动】毛头星〔海百合纲动物〕。～ **stitch** 1. *n*.(毛线衣的)羽状针织法。2. *vi*., *vt*. 把(毛衣等)织成羽状。～ **weight** 1. *n*. 较轻的人[物];不重要的人[物];【拳】次轻级选手。2. *a*. 轻的;次轻级的;轻微的,琐细的。～ **wit** 愚人,笨蛋,低能者。**-like** *a*. 1. 轻如羽毛的。2. 羽毛状的。
feath·ered [ˈfeðəd; ˋfɛðəd] *a*. 1. 有羽毛的。2. 附装羽毛的;用羽毛装饰的。3. 羽毛状的;鸟一样飞得快的。4. 边沿刨薄的。*the* ～ *tribe* 鸟类。*a* ～ *board* 边沿刨薄的木板。
feath·er·i·ness [ˈfeðərinis; ˋfɛðərɪnɪs] *n*. 1. 长着羽毛(或羽状物)。2. 羽毛状。3. 轻软。
feath·er·ing [ˈfeðəriŋ; ˋfɛðərɪŋ] *n*. 1. 羽毛。2. 羽饰。3. 羽状物;(狗脚等的)丛毛。4.【建】叶瓣饰。5.【乐】(提琴)轻柔运弓法。
feath·er·less [ˈfeðəlis; ˋfɛðəlɪs] *a*. 没有羽毛的。**-ness** *n*.
feath·er·y [ˈfeðəri; ˋfɛðərɪ] *a*. 1. 生羽毛[羽状物]的。2. 羽毛似的(雪片等)。3. 轻软的。
fea·ture [ˈfiːtʃə; ˋfitʃə] *n*. 1. 形状,外形;特色;(特指)好

F

看的外表;〔pl.〕脸形;五官;面目,容貌,面貌,相貌。2. 脸面的一部〔口、鼻、耳等〕。3. 部件,零件。4. 一条,一项。5. 特点,要点,性能。6. 地势,地形。7. (电影)正片;故事片。8.【剧】特别演出;(期刊的)特写,特辑。*the geographical ~s of a district* 一个地区的地理特征。*a ~ of the Sunday supplement* 星期日增刊上的一节特写。*a ~ film* 故事片,艺术片。*a man of handsome* [*poor*] *~s* 面貌美好[丑陋]的男子。*Her eyes are her best ~.* 她的眼睛是她最好看的部分。***make a ~ of*** 以…为特色[号召]。**II** ***vt*.** 1. 使有特色,使成为,的特征;描写…的特征。2.〔美〕以…作为号召物;使成为特色;以…作为报纸杂志等的特写;以…作为重要文章;给予(某事件、某文章等)以显要地位;【影】使(演员)主演。3.〔俚〕想像。4.〔口〕面貌相…。*a film featuring famous actresses* 以著名女演员作为号召的影片。*The mother was ~ed in the son.* 儿子长得很像母亲。*Can you ~ smoking here?* 在这种场合吸烟,你能想像吗?— ***vi*.** 起重要作用,作重要角色。~ **film** 正片;故事片。~**-length** ***a*.** (电影)达到正片(应有)长度的;(投稿文字)达到专题文章应有长度的。~ **story** 报章杂志中的特写文章。**-less** ***a*.** 没有特色的,平淡无奇的。

fea·tured [ˈfiːtʃəd; ˋfitʃəd] ***a*.** 1. 面貌秀丽的。2. 作为特色[号召物]的。3. 有…面貌特征的。*a ~ actor* 主要演员。*sharp-~* 面部轮廓分明的。~ **cast**【影】主要演员阵容。~ **story** (报刊)特载;特别详细的报导。

fea·tu·rette [ˌfiːtʃəˈret; ˏfitʃəˋrɛt] ***n*.**【影】短故事片,短艺术片。

F

feaze[1] [fiːz, feiz; fiz, fez] ***vt*.** = faze.

feaze[2] [fiːz; fiz] ***vt*., *vi*.**【海】解开。

Feb. = February.

feb·ri- *comb. f.* = fever.

fe·brif·ic [fiˈbrifik; fɪˋbrɪfɪk] ***a*.**〔古〕发烧的,发热的。

fe·brif·u·gal [fiˈbrifjugəl, ˌfebriˈfjuːgəl; fɪˋbrɪfjugəl, ˏfɛbriˋfjugəl] ***a*.**【医】退热的,解热的。

feb·ri·fuge [ˈfebrifjuːdʒ; ˋfɛbrɪˏfjudʒ] **I** ***n*.**【医】退热药,解热剂。**II** ***a*.** 退热的。

fe·brile [ˈfiːbrail, ˈfeb-; ˋfibraɪl, ˋfɛb-] ***a*.**【医】热病的;发热的。

Feb·ru·ar·y [ˈfebruəri; ˋfɛbrʊˏɛrɪ] ***n*.** 二月。~ *fills dyke.*〔谚〕二月雨雪多,沟渠流成河。*All the months in the year curse a fair ~.*〔谚〕二月天气好,全年气候糟。

FEC = Federal Exchange Commission〔美〕联邦交易委员会。

fec. = fecit.

fe·cal [ˈfiːkəl; ˋfikḷ] ***a*.** 粪便的;排泄物的;糟粕的,渣滓的。

fe·ces [ˈfiːsiːz; ˋfisiz] ***n*.**〔pl.〕粪便,排泄物;渣滓。

fe·cit [ˈfiːsit; ˋfisɪt]〔L.〕(某某)画,(某某)作(= he [she] made [did] it)〔略作 fec.〕。*John Jones ~ = fec. John Jones* 约翰·琼斯画[作]。

feck·less [ˈfeklis; ˋfɛklɪs] ***a*.**〔Scot.〕1. 没有气力的,没有精神的。2. 不中用的,无益的。3. 不负责任的。*two years of ~ negotiations* 拖了两年的毫无结果的谈判。**-ly** ***ad*.** **-ness** ***n*.**

fec·u·la [ˈfekjulə; ˋfɛkjulə] ***n*.** (*pl*. ***-lae*** [-liː; -lɪ]) 1. 淀粉。2. 沉渣。3. 虫粪。

fec·u·lence [ˈfekjuləns; ˋfɛkjuləns] ***n*.** 1. 污秽,混浊。2. 污物;渣滓。

fec·u·len·cy [ˈfekjulənsi; ˋfɛkjʊlənsɪ] ***n*.** = feculence.

fec·u·lent [ˈfekjulənt; ˋfɛkjʊlənt] ***a*.** 1. 污秽的,混浊的。2. 粪便的;排泄物的。

fe·cund [ˈfiːkənd, ˈfe-; ˋfikənd, ˋfɛ-] ***a*.** 1. 生殖力旺盛的。2. 多产的;丰饶的,肥沃的;创造力旺盛的。*a ~ mind* 创造力旺盛的头脑。

fe·cun·date [ˈfiːkəndeit, ˈfe-; ˋfikənˏdet, ˋfɛ-] ***vt*.** 1.【动】使受孕;使受胎。2. 使多产,使丰饶,使肥沃。3.【植】使结实。**-dation** [ˌfiːkənˈdeiʃən; ˏfikənˋdeʃən] ***n*.**

fe·cun·di·ty [fiˈkʌnditi; fɪˋkʌndətɪ] ***n*.** 1. 多产,富饶,肥沃。2.【动】生育力,产卵力。3.【植】结实性;结实力。*~ of imagination* 想像力丰富。

fed[1] [fed; fɛd] feed 的过去式及过去分词。**-up·ness** 1. 过饱;吃饱。2. 极度厌倦。

fed[2] [fed; fɛd] ***n*.**〔美俚,常作 F-〕联邦调查局人员;联邦政府(工作人员)。***the F-***〔美〕联邦储备制(= the Federal Reserve System)。

Fed.〔美〕= Federal; Federation.

fe·da·yee [feˈdɑjiː; fɛˋdɑji] ***n*.** (*pl*. ***-yeen*** [-ˈiːn; -ˋin])〔Ar.〕(尤指反对以色列的)阿拉伯突击队队员。

Fed·er·a·cy [ˈfedərəsi; ˋfɛdərəsɪ] ***n*.** (*pl*. ***-cies*** [-siz; -sɪz]) 联盟;联邦。

fed·er·al [ˈfedərəl; ˋfɛdərəl] **I** ***a*.** 1. 同盟的,联合的。2. 联邦的,联邦制的;〔美〕联邦政府的,中央政府的;〔F-〕【美史】南北战争时北部联邦同盟的。***make a F- case out of sth.***〔美俚〕过分夸大[强调]某事重要。**II** ***n*.** 1. 联邦主义者。2.〔F-〕【美史】北部联邦同盟盟员;联邦政府战士;联邦政府拥护者。**F- agent**〔美〕联邦调查局人员。**F- Aviation Commission**〔美〕联邦航空委员会。**F- Bureau of Investigation**〔美〕联邦调查局。**F- city** 联邦城(美国首都华盛顿市的别名)。**F- Constitution** 美国宪法。**F- Court**〔美〕联邦法院。**F- Government** (of the U.S.) 美国(中央)政府(*opp*. State Government)。**F- Labor Union**〔美〕联邦工会。**F- Reserve Bank**〔美〕联邦储备银行。**F- Reserve Board**〔美〕联邦储备委员会,联邦储备银行董事会。**F- Trade Commission**〔美〕联邦贸易委员会。**-ese** 美联邦政府的官式用语或行为。**-ism** ***n*.** 联邦制;〔F-〕【美史】联邦主义。**-ist** 1. ***n*.** 联邦主义者;〔F-〕【美史】北部联邦同盟盟员。2. ***a*.** (拥护)联邦制的;北部联邦同盟盟员的。**-ly** ***ad*.** 在全联邦范围内;在联邦政府一级。

fed·er·al·i·za·tion [ˌfedərəlaiˈzeiʃən; ˏfɛdərəlaɪˋzeʃən] ***n*.** 联邦化,同盟化;置于联邦政府权力之下。

fed·er·al·ize [ˈfedərəlaiz; ˋfɛdərəlˏaɪz] ***vt*.** 1. 使成联邦,使成联邦制。2. 把…置于联邦政府权力之下。3. 使结成同盟。

fed·er·ate **I** [ˈfedərit; ˋfɛdərɪt] ***a*.** 同盟的,联合的;联邦制度(下)的。**II** [ˈfedəreit; ˋfɛdəˏret] ***vt*., *vi*.** (使)联合;(使)结成同盟[联邦]。

fed·er·a·tion [ˌfedəˈreiʃən; ˏfɛdəˋreʃən] ***n*.** 1. 同盟,联盟。2. 联邦;联邦政府。**-ist** 联合主义者;联邦论者。

fed·er·a·tive [ˈfedərətiv; ˋfɛdəˏretɪv] ***a*.** 1. 联合的,联盟的。2.〔美〕有关整个国家的;有关外交和国家安全的。**-ly** ***ad*.**

fedex, fedEx [ˈfedeks; ˋfɛdɛks] **I** ***n*.** 联邦快递(公司)。**II** ***vt*.** 快递。

FEDOM =〔F.〕Fonds Européen de Développement pour les Pays et Territoires d'Outre-Mer 欧洲海外开发基金组织(= European Development Fund for Overseas Countries and Territories)。

fe·do·ra [fiˈdɔːrə; fɪˋdɔrə] ***n*.**〔美〕折顶弯帽檐软呢帽。

fee [fiː; fi] **I** ***n*.** 1. 报酬;薪水;公费;手续费;税;会费,学费,报名费,入场费。2. 赏金,小账。3.【史】(封建时代的)采邑,封地。4. 永租地;永业田,世袭地。5. 所有权;继承财产。*a doctor's ~ for a visit* 医生的出诊费。*a monthly ~* 月薪。*a license ~* 牌照费。*a membership ~* 会费。*a school* [*tuition*] *~* 学费。*~ of permit* 执照税,牌照税。***hold in ~*** (***simple***) 拥有无条件继承的权利。**II** ***vt*.** 1. 给…发薪水,给…小费,向…交手续费,缴(会费)[学费](等)。2.〔英〕雇用,聘请。~ **absolute**【法】无条件继承权。~ **simple**(处置权不受限制的)土地绝对所有权;无条件继承的不动产(权)〔继承人身份不受限制〕,继承者身分不受限制的不动产权。~**-splitting** 病人介绍费(向医生介绍病人的佣金)。~ **tail** (限定继承人的)土地所有权;具有一定身分的人才能继承的土地。

～-TV 收费电视,投币电视。

Fee·bie [ˈfiːbiː; ˋfibi] ***n***. 〔美俚〕联邦调查局人员。

fee·ble [ˈfiːbl; ˋfibl] ***a***. (***-bler***; ***-blest***) 1. 无力的,虚弱的。2. 软弱的;微弱的;(声、光等)轻微的。*a ～ reason* 薄弱的理由。*a ～ joke* 不高明的俏皮话。*a ～ brain* 低能。～**-minded** ***a***. 意志薄弱的,无决断的;低能的。**-ness** ***n***.

fee·blish [ˈfiːbliʃ; ˋfiblɪʃ] ***a***. 有点弱的。

fee·bly [ˈfiːbli; ˋfiblɪ] ***ad***. 柔弱地,无力地;微弱地。

feed[1] [fiːd; fid] fee 的过去式及过去分词。

feed[2] [fiːd; fid] **I** ***vt***. 1. 给…饮食,给…东西吃;给(婴儿)喂奶。2. 喂养,饲养,使吃草,放牧(家畜),用…作牧场(*down*). 3. (机器、煤炉等)加上(油、煤等)(*with*);【物】馈给(信号);通过线路向电台传送(节目)以供广播。4. 悦(目),娱(耳);满足(欲望等);(用希望)安慰,使高兴(*with*)。5. 〔口〕给(演员)提台词。6. (足球)传(球)。7. 培养,增长,煽动(某种情绪)。*F- a cold and starve a fever*. 〔谚〕受寒要吃,发烧要饿。*～ wheat to cattle* = *～ cattle with wheat* 用小麦喂牛。*～ down the grassy land* 把(牛)放进草地吃草。*～ the fire with fuel* 给火加燃料。*be well* [*poorly*] *fed* 吃得好[差]。*better fed than taught* 养而不教。*Well fed, well bred*. 吃得饱,懂礼貌[衣食足而后礼义兴]。***be fed up with*** 〔美俚〕吃…吃得过饱;厌倦(*I'm fed up with your grumbling*. 我对你的牢骚已经听厌了)。～ ***oneself*** 自己吃。～ ***one's face*** 〔美俚〕吃饭。～ ***out*** 催肥。～ ***the flame of jealousy*** [***anger***] 使更加嫉妒[愤怒]。～ ***to market*** 养肥出售。～ ***up*** 供给食物[营养];养肥;使吃饱。～ ***with the money*** 贿赂。— ***vi***. 1. 吃饭,进餐;吃东西,靠…生活,用…做食料;流入,进入。2. 【物】馈入。*What time do we ～? 我们什么时候开饭? He ～s on hope*. 他靠希望支撑着生活。～ ***at the high table*** = ～ high. ～ ***at the public trough*** 〔美〕吃公家饭,尸位素餐。～ ***high*** [***well***] 吃得好。～ ***on*** 吃…过日子;用…喂养(鸟兽等)(*～ on grass* 靠吃草生活。*～ on hope* 寄托于希望)。**II** ***n***. 1. 喂养,饲养。2. 饲料,饲草,草料;〔口〕饭食,吃饭。3. 【机】进刀;传送,送料,上料,加水;馈电,供电;【机】送料管,运料槽。4. 〔英口〕【剧】提台词〔特指提供给喜剧演员的笑料〕。5. 〔口〕一餐,丰盛的一餐。*～ for horses* 马料。*a ～ of oats* 燕麦的一次喂用量。*have a ～* 吃饲料。*have a good ～* 吃一顿丰盛的宴席。*automatic ～* 【机】自动进刀,自动进给。*clockwork ～* 钟表的发条。*cylinder ～* 气缸进气。*hydraulic ～* 【机】水力进给,液压进刀,液压输送。*jump ～* 【机】(仿形切削的)快速越程,中间越程。*shunt ～* 【电】关联馈电。*tape ～* 磁带卷盘。*work ～* 【机】工件进程。***at one ～*** 一顿。***be off one's ～*** 胃口不好。***be on the ～*** (鱼)在找吃,正吃着。***be out at ～*** (牛等)在牧场上吃着草。～**-back** 1. 【电】反馈,回授。2. 回复,反应,反作用。3. 成果,资料(*negative ～-back* 负反馈。*positive ～-back* 正反馈)。～**-back** ***a***. 【电】反馈的。～ **bag** (系在马口下的)饲料袋(*put on ～ bag* 〔俚〕吃饭)。～ **belt** 【机】进料皮带。～ **bin** 供应仓库。～**-box** 料箱;【纺】喂毛盒。～ **cable** 【电】馈电电缆,电源电缆。～**-in** 1. ***n***. 【电】馈入。2. ***n***. 施食(集会)。3. ***a***. 【机】进给的,进料的。～ **pipe** 供水管;送料管。～ **pump** 给水泵,进水泵,进料泵。～ **stock** (送入机器或加工厂的)原料。～ **stuff** 饲料,饲料中的营养成分。～ **system** 送料系统。～**-tank** 给水箱。～ **through** 引线,馈入装置;连接线。～ **trump** 中注管。～ **water** (供给锅炉烧成水蒸汽的)给水。～ **well** 给水井。

feed·er [ˈfiːdə; ˋfidɚ] ***n***. 1. 给食者;喂食者;供应者;饲养员;煽动者,怂恿者,填鸭式教人的人。2. 寄食者,使唤人;食客。3. 奶瓶;〔英〕围涎;秣槽,料箱,4. 支流;【矿】支脉;【铁路、空】支线;【电】馈(电)线。5. 进料器;进刀装置;给水器;加煤器;加油器。6. 配角;(主要剧情中的)陪衬情节。*a large* [*gross, prodigious*] *～* 大肚汉。～ **line** [**road**] (铁路的)支线。

feed·ing [ˈfiːdiŋ; ˋfidɪŋ] **I** ***n***. 1. 喂食,饲养,给食。2. 送料,进料。3. 牧场。*Is there good ～ here?* 这里的伙食好吗? **II** ***a***. 1. 喂食的,饲养的,给食的。2. 【机】进给的,进料的。～ **adaptation** 摄食适应。～ **bottle** (喂孩子的)奶瓶。～ **migration** (鱼类的)就食洄游。～ **storm** 越来越厉害的暴风雨。～ **stuffs** 〔美〕饲料。

fee-faw-fum [ˈfiːˈfɔːˈfʌm; ˋfi ˋfɔ ˋfʌm], **fee-fo-fum** [ˈfiːˈfɔːˈfʌm; ˋfiˋfɔˋfʌm] **I** ***int***. 唬唬唬! 〔童话中表示要吃人的喊声,用以恐吓儿童〕。**II** ***n***. 1. 吓人的话,(只能吓唬儿童的)胡言乱语。2. 嗜杀成性的人,食人魔鬼。

feel [fiːl; fil] ***vt***. (***felt*** [felt; fɛlt]; ***felt***) 1. 触,摸;试探。2. 感觉,觉得;感知。3. 【军】侦探(敌情等)。4. 想,认为,以为(*that*). 5. (无生物)受到…的作用,受影响于。6. 〔～ oneself〕有…的感觉。*～ sb.'s pulse* 按脉;试探某人的意图。*～ a friend's death* 痛惜友人的死亡。*～ music* 为音乐所感动。*I ～ that you are right*. 我以为你说得对。*The ship ～s the helm*. 船随舵转动。*She felt herself slighted*. 她感到自己受轻视。— ***vi***. 1. 有感觉;有感情作用。2. 摸上去有…感觉;像要。3. 体谅,同情。4. 摸索着寻找。*Ice and snow ～ cold*. 冰雪摸上去是冷的。*This room ～s hot*. (人在)这间屋子里觉得热。*～ bad* 有病;心情不好。*～ sad* 觉得心酸。*～ sure* 有把握。*～ one's pocket for a dime* 在衣袋里摸找角币。*Can animal ～?* 动物有感情吗? ～ ***about*** [***after***] 摸索,探寻,探查。～ ***as if*** [***though***] 觉得仿佛。～ ***at home*** 畅快,舒松。～ ***cheap*** 觉得丢脸。～ ***empty*** 觉得饿。～ ***for*** 1. 侦探(敌情);探摸。2. 同情,体谅(*～ for thc poor* 同情穷人)。～ ***free to*** 可以随便。～ ***funny*** 感到不舒服,总觉得不对劲儿。～ ***... in one's bones*** 深切感到。～ ***like*** 1. 像要…似的(*It ～s like rain*. 像要下雨似的)。2. 摸上去像是…(*It ～s like glass*. 那摸上去像玻璃)。～ ***like a boiled rag*** 觉得很不舒服,觉得虚弱无力。～ ***like a fighting cock*** 精神健旺。～ ***like a fish out of water*** 如鱼出水,感到不得其所。～ ***like a million dollars*** 〔美口〕感觉身体[精神]很好。～ ***like ...ing*** 觉得想…(*I don't ～ like taking a walk*. 我不想散步。*～ like putting one on* 〔美〕很想上前帮助一下)。～ ***like*** [***quite***] ***oneself*** 觉得自在舒畅,沉着,镇定。～ ***low*** 意气消沉。～ ***mean*** 〔美〕感觉难为情。～ ***of*** 〔美〕摸摸看。～ ***one's legs*** [***feet, wings***] 相信自己的能力,自信。～ ***one's way*** 摸索着走;行动谨慎。～ ***out*** 探明,摸清。～ ***seedy*** 觉得不舒服。～ ***shaky*** 感到没有把握;感到不舒服。～ ***slack*** 没精打采。～ ***strongly about*** 对…抱有明确的态度。～ ***the need of*** [***for***] 对…感到需要。～ ***up*** [***equal***] ***to*** 〔口〕以为能承担,觉得能够胜任(*I don't ～ up to a long hike today*. 我今天不能走远路)。～ ***with*** 同情。**II** *n*. 触,摸;触觉,感觉;感受。*Let me have a ～*. 让我摸一摸。***get the ～ of sth***. 掌握[学会,熟悉]某事。***to the ～*** 在触觉上(*rough to the ～* 摸起来很粗糙)。

feel·er [ˈfiːlə; ˋfilɚ] ***n***. 1. 试探手段;探试者;试探器;探针。2. 触角;触毛,触须。3. 【机】测隙规,厚薄规。4. 【军】侦察兵,探子。5. 【无】灵敏元件。6. 〔美俚〕手指。*a gauge ～* 千分垫尺。***put forth*** [***send out*** 或 ***throw out***] ***a ～*** (用言语或动作)探听别人的反应;伸出触角(进行试探)。～ **gauge** 【机】测隙规,厚薄规。～ **pin** 【医】探针。～ **plug** 【机】探视孔。

fee·lie [ˈfiːliː; ˋfili] **I** ***n***. 多感觉艺术品[物品];多感觉宣传媒介〔指同时可以看见形像,闻到气味;有时并能听见音响的艺术品〕。**II** ***a***. (艺术品)多感觉的。

feel·ing [ˈfiːliŋ; ˋfilɪŋ] **I** ***n***. 1. 感触,感觉;知觉。2. 〔常 *pl*.〕感情,心情,情绪。3. 同情,怜悯,体谅。4. (对艺术等的)感受,敏感,鉴赏力。5. 恶感,反感。6. 看法,感想,(对市场行情的)预感。7. 气氛,(艺术品的)情调。*speak with ～s* 带着感情说。*hurt sb.'s ～s* 伤人感情。8. 事物给人的感觉。*good* [*ill*] *～* 好感[恶感]。*a man of fine ～* 会体谅人的人。*a man of ～* 易于伤感[富有同

F

情心]的人。*a man without any* ～*s* 毫无感情的人。*Monday* ～ 不爱工作的情绪。*public* ～ 人心。*No hard* ～*s*. 没有恶意。***appeal to sb.'s better*** ～***s*** 诉诸某人的良心。***be dead*** [***lost***] ***to all*** ～ 麻木不仁。***enter into sb.'s*** ～***s*** 表同情,体谅。***entertain a*** ～ ***against sb***. 对某人怀恨在心。***have a*** ～ ***for*** 对于…有一种体会(*She has a deep* ～ *for beauty in nature*. 她对大自然的美有很深的感受力)。***have a*** ～ ***of*** [***that***] 觉得。***have mixed*** ～***s*** 悲喜交集。***have no*** ～ ***for*** 对…不同情。***one's better*** ～***s*** 良心,天良。***relieve one's*** ～ 发泄感情,泄愤。***show much*** ～ ***for*** 对…大表同情。**II** ***a***. **1**. 富于感情的;富于同情心的。**2**. 衷心的。**3**. 动人的。**4**. 表达感情的。*a* ～ *story* 动人的故事。*a* ～ *heart* 多情善感。*a* ～ *glance* 含情脉脉的一瞥。***in a*** ～ ***way*** 富有感情[同情]地,谆谆地,恳切地。**-ful** ***a***. 充满感情的。**-less** ***a***. **1**. 没有感情的。**2**. 没有知觉的。**-ly** ***ad***. **-ness** ***n***.

feet [fiːt; fit] ***n***. foot 的复数。***die on one's*** ～ 垮台;倒塌。～ ***of clay*** **1**. 伟人或受崇拜者不为人所知的弱点。**2**. 意料之外的严重缺点[错误](*give the appearance of having* ～ *of clay* 显示出出人意外的弱点)。***vote with one's*** ～ 离去[避开]以表示不赞同。～**-first** ***ad***. **1**. 脚先入水地。**2**. 〔美俚〕死(*be carried out* ～*-first* 死掉被抬走)。**-less** ***a***. 无足的。

feeze [fiːz, feiz; fiz, fez] **I** ***vt***. **1**. 〔废、方〕驱,驱逐;吓唬;打;惩罚。**2**. 打扰;妨碍,为难(= faze)。**II** ***n***. **1**. 〔英方〕冲击,猛冲,磨擦。**2**. 〔口〕惊慌,激动。

F

feign [fein; fen] ***vt***. **1**. 装作,假装。**2**. 伪造(文件等),捏造(故事等)。～ *oneself sick* = ～ *that one is sick* 装病。～ *ignorance* 假装不知。— ***vi***. 做假,佯装。**-ed** ***a***. **1**. 假装的,做作的。**2**. 虚构的。

feigned·ly [ˈfeindli; ˋfendlɪ] ***ad***. 假装地,装聋作哑地。

feint [feint; fent] **I** ***n***. **1**. (诱骗敌方的)佯攻;牵制运动。**2**. 假托,伪装。***by way of*** ～ 用声东击西的策略。***make a*** ～ ***of ...ing*** 装作(*make a* ～ *of studying hard* 装作用功读书)。**II** ***vi***. **1**. 装作,假装。**2**. 佯攻,虚击(*at*; *on*; *upon*; *against*)。**III** ***a***., ***ad***. 虚假的(地);不鲜明的(地),淡淡的(地)。～ *lines* 淡格子线。*an exercise book ruled* ～ 画有淡格线的练习簿。

feis [feʃ; feʃ] ***n***. (爱尔兰或其他地方的爱尔兰裔人一年一度的)文化艺术节。

feist [faist; faɪst] ***n***. 〔美方〕小狗;无用的人,脾气坏的人。

feist·y [ˈfaisti; ˋfaɪstɪ] ***a***. 〔美口,方〕**1**. 精力充沛的;活跃的,坐立不安的。**2**. 爱争吵的,好斗的。

feld·spar [ˈfeldspɑː; ˋfɛldˏspɑr] ***n***. 【矿】长石。

feld·spath·ic [feldˈspæθik; fɛldˋspæθɪk] ***a***. 【矿】长石(质)的;含长石的;像长石的。

feld·spath·oid [feldˈspæθɔid; fɛldˋspæθɔɪd] ***n***. 【矿】似长石。

fe·li·cif·ic [ˌfiːliˈsifik; ˏfilɪˋsɪfɪk] ***a***. 造福的;带来幸福的。

fe·lic·i·tate [fiˈlisiteit; fəˋlɪsəˏtet] ***vt***. 庆祝;庆幸;庆贺,祝贺。～ *a friend on* [*upon*] *his success* 祝贺友人成功。*He* ～*d himself that he had passed the entry examination*. 他庆幸自己通过了入学考试。

fe·lic·i·ta·tion [fiˌlisiˈteiʃən; fəˏlɪsəˋteʃən] ***n***. 祝贺,庆祝,〔常 *pl*.〕祝词。*offer one's* ～*s* 道贺;致祝词。

fe·lic·i·tator [fiˈlisiteitə; fəˋlɪsəˏtetɚ] ***n***. 祝贺者。

fe·lic·i·tous [fiˈlisitəs; fəˋlɪsətəs] ***a***. **1**. 巧妙的,适当的(措词等);善于措词的。**2**. 〔罕〕可喜的,幸运的。**-ly** ***ad***. **-ness** ***n***.

fe·lic·i·ty [fiˈlisiti; fəˋlɪsətɪ] ***n***. **1**. 幸福,幸运。**2**. (言词等的)巧妙,适切。**3**. 巧妙[得当]的语言。***rare*** ～ ***of phrase*** 稀有的佳句。***with*** ～ 巧妙;得体。

fe·lid [ˈfiːlid; ˋfilɪd] ***n***. 【动】猫科动物。～ *leo* 狮。

Fe·lidae [ˈfiːlidiː; ˋfilədi] ***n***. 〔*pl*.〕【动】猫科。

fe·line [ˈfiːlain; ˋfilaɪn] **I** ***a***. **1**. 猫的,猫科的。**2**. 猫一样的;狡诈的;阴险的。**II** ***n***. 猫科动物。～ *amenities* 笑里藏刀。

fe·lin·i·ty [fiˈliniti; fɪˋlɪnətɪ] ***n***. 猫的特性,猫一样的残忍[阴险]性。

Fe·lix [ˈfiːliks; ˋfilɪks] ***n***. 费利克斯〔男子名〕。

fell[1] [fel; fɛl] fall 的过去式。

fell[2] [fel; fɛl] **I** ***vt***. **1**. 砍倒(树等);弄倒;打倒。**2**. 把(破缝边缘)缝平。**II** ***n***. **1**. (树等)一季的采伐量。**2**. 折进(边缘)缝平,(衣服等的)平缝。

fell[3] [fel; fɛl] ***a***. 〔古、诗〕残忍的,凶恶的,残暴的,致命的;尖锐的,剧烈的。*a* ～ *and barbarous enemy* 凶恶野蛮的敌人。*a* ～ *disease* 致命的病。**-ness** ***n***.

fell[4] [fel; fɛl] ***n***. **1**. 兽皮,毛皮,生皮。**2**. (人的)皮肤。**3**. 羊毛,毛丛,发丛。*a* ～ *of hair* 乱蓬蓬的头发,发绺。～**monger** ***n***. 皮货商,生皮商,毛皮商。

fell[5] [fel; fɛl] ***n***. **1**. 〔北英〕高沼;丘原。**2**. 〔用作地名〕荒山,…岗,…丘陵。

Fell [fel; fɛl] ***n***. ***feel Dr***. ～ ***towards sb***. 不知为什么总觉得讨厌某人〔来自 Thomas Brown 的诗句: I do not love thee, Dr. Fell, / The reason why I cannot tell〕.

fel·lah [ˈfelə; ˋfɛlə] ***n***. (*pl*. ～*s*, 〔古〕～*in*, ～*een* [ˈfeləˈhiːn; ˋfɛləˋhin]) (埃及等地的)农夫〔贫苦雇农〕。

fel·ler[1] [ˈfelə; ˋfɛlɚ] ***n***. **1**. 伐木者,采伐者,樵夫;伐木者。**2**. 平缝工,接缝工;(缝纫机的)平缝装置。

fel·ler[2] [ˈfelə; ˋfɛlɚ] ***n***. 〔俚〕= fellow.

fel·loe [ˈfeləu; ˋfɛlo] ***n***. 车轮外围,车辖辘,轮缘,轮网。

fel·low [ˈfeləu; ˋfɛlo] **I** ***n***. **1**. 同伴,伴侣;帮手;同事,同辈;同类,酒友。**2**. 同等者,匹敌者,对手;同代人;一员;类似的人[物];一对中的一个。**3**. [常 ˈfelə; ˋfɛlə]〔口〕小伙子,家伙;某个人;男朋友。**4**. (英大学的)特别研究生;〔英〕(由毕业生中选出的管理学校的)大学评议员;(得奖学金的)特等校友,特别研究生。**5**. 〔F-〕(学会中地位较高的)特别会员。～*s at school* 同学。～*s in arms* 战友。～ *feeling* 同情,相互了解。*pass all one's* ～*s* 超过同辈。～*s of Shakespeare* 莎士比亚同时代的人们。*His shoes are not* ～*s*. 他的鞋不是一对。*a good* [*jolly*] ～ 有趣味的人,酒友。*that* ～ 那家伙。*my dear* [*good*] ～ 亲爱的朋友,老兄。*poor* ～ 可怜的家伙。**II** ***a***. 同伴的,同事的;同在一处的;同道的。*a* ～ *countryman* 同国人,同胞。*a* ～ *passenger* 同车[船]旅客。*a* ～ *soldier* 战友。*a* ～ *student* 同学。～ *sufferers* 难友。*a* ～ *townsman* 同乡。～ *traders* 同行。～ **commoner** **1**. 〔英〕得与特别研究生共食的大学生。**2**. 同桌吃饭的人;同一权利的享有者。～ **creature** **1**. (动物的)同类。**2**. 人类,同胞。～**-man** 人,同胞。～ **traveller** **1**. 旅伴。**2**. (政治上的)同路人,同情者。～**-travelling** ***a***. (政治上)同路的。

fel·low·ship [ˈfeləuʃip; ˋfɛloˏʃɪp] **I** ***n***. **1**. 伙伴关系,交情,友谊。**2**. 共处,共同,协力,提携(*in*; *of*). **3**. 会,团体;(基督徒的)团契。**4**. (英大学)特别研究生的地位[补助费];大学评议员的地位[报酬];(学会)特别会员的地位。**II** ***vt***., ***vi***. (〔美〕***-pp-***)〔美〕参加(教会团体)。***be admitted to*** ～ 获准入会。***bear sb***. ～ 与某人有交谊。***give*** [***offer***] ***the right hand of*** ～ 同人结交;准许入伙。

fel·ly[1] [ˈfeli; ˋfɛlɪ] ***n***. = felloe.

fel·ly[2] [ˈfeli; ˋfɛlɪ] ***ad***. 〔古〕剧烈地;残酷地。

fe·lo-de-se [ˈfiːləudiˈsiː, ˈfeləu-; ˋfilodiˋsi, ˋfɛlo-] ***n***. (*pl*. ***fe·lo·nes-de-se*** [fiˈləuniːzdiˈsiː; fɪˋlonizdɪˋsi], ***fe·los-de-se*** [ˈfiːləuzdiˈsiː; ˋfilozdɪˋsi]〔L.〕【法】**1**. 自杀者。**2**. 〔仅用 *sing*.〕自杀。

fel·on[1] [ˈfelən; ˋfɛlən] **I** ***n***. 重罪人,重罪犯。**II** ***a***. 〔诗〕残忍的,凶恶的。

fel·on[2] [ˈfelən; ˋfɛlən] ***n***. 【医】瘭疽;甲沟炎;指头脓炎。

fe·lo·ni·ous [fiˈləunjəs, -niəs; fəˋlonɪəs, fɛ-] ***a***. 有重罪的;【法】重罪(犯)的;〔主诗〕凶恶的。～ **homicide** 【法】谋杀。**-ly** ***ad***. **-ness** ***n***.

fel·on·ry [ˈfelənri; ˋfɛlənrɪ] *n*. 〔集合词〕重罪犯;犯人们。

fel·o·ny [ˈfeləni; ˋfɛlənɪ] *n*. 【法】重罪 (*opp*. misdemeanor)。***compound a*** ～【法】受到赔偿而不起诉,私了案件。～ ***murder*** 犯另一重罪时的凶杀(如强奸后杀死被害者)。

fel·site [ˈfelsait; ˋfɛlsaɪt] *n*. 【矿】霏细岩,致密长石。**fel·sit·ic** *a*.

fel·spar [ˈfelspɑː; ˋfɛl͵spɑr] *n*. 〔英〕= feldspar.

fel·stone [ˈfelstəun; ˋfɛlston] *n*. = felsite.

felt[1] [felt; fɛlt] feel 的过去式及过去分词。*a*. 可以[显然]感觉到的。*a* ～ *earthquake* 感觉得到的地震。*a* ～ *want* 迫切的需要。

felt[2] [felt; fɛlt] **I** *n*. 毛毡;毛布;毡制品;油毛毡。**II** *a*. 毡制的。*a* ～ *hat* 毡帽。**III** *vt*. 1. 把…制成毡。2. 用毡遮盖,使粘结。— *vi*. 成毡,粘结起来。

felt·ed [ˈfeltid; ˋfɛltɪd] *a*. 1. 毡制的。2. 用毡覆盖的。3. 粘结起来的。～ *cloth* 薄毡料。

felt·ing [ˈfeltiŋ; ˋfɛltɪŋ] *n*. 1. 制毡法。2. 制毡材料。3. 毡。～ *products* 毡制品。

Fel·ton [ˈfeltən; ˋfɛltən] *n*. 费尔顿〔姓氏〕。

felt·y [ˈfelti; ˋfɛltɪ] *a*. 1. 毡状的。2. = felted.

fe·luc·ca [feˈlʌkə; fɛˋlʌkə] *n*. (地中海沿岸的)二桅[三桅]小帆船。

fem [fem; fɛm] **I** *n*. 〔美俚〕女子。**II** *a*. 〔美俚〕女性化的,女人似的。**F- Lib**, **Femlib** 〔美〕妇解,妇女解放运动。

fem. = female, feminine.

fe·male [ˈfiːmeil; ˋfimel] **I** *a*. (*opp*. male) 1. 女性的。2. 雌的;【植】雌性的,雌蕊的。3. 【机】阴的,内空的,凹的。4. 女人似的,柔弱的。*the* ～ *sex* 女性,女人。*a* ～ *operative* 女工。*a* ～ *flower* 雌花。*a* ～ *joint* 套筒接合。*a* ～ *screw* 阴螺丝,内螺丝。**II** *n*. 1. 女子。2. 牝兽,雌禽,雌性动物。3. 雌性植物,雌株。～ **condom** 女用避孕套。～ **fern** 【植】蹄盖蕨,欧洲蕨。～ **impersonator** 男扮女的演员。～ **sapphire** 淡色蓝宝石。～ **suffrage** 妇女参政权[选举权]。～ **voice** 【乐】女声。

feme [fiːm, fem; fim, fɛm] *n*. 【法】女子;妻子。～ **covert** 有夫之妇,已婚妇女。～ **sole** 【法】1. 未婚女子,独身女子。2. 寡妇,财产权独立的妻子。

fem·i·na·cy [ˈfeminəsi; ˋfɛmɪnəsɪ] *n*. (*pl*. **-cies** [-siz; -sɪz]) 女性,女人的气质,女人的特性。

fem·i·nal·i·ty [ˌfemiˈnæliti; ͵fɛməˋnælətɪ] *n*. 1. 女性;妇女的特性。2. 女用小型物品。

fem·i·ne·i·ty [ˌfemiˈniːiti; ͵fɛməˋniətɪ] *n*. = femininity.

fem·i·nie [ˈfemini; ˋfɛmɪnɪ] *n*. 〔集合词〕女性。

fem·i·nine [ˈfeminin; ˋfɛmənɪn] **I** *a*. 1. 女性的,女人的。2. 妇女似的;娇柔的;柔弱的。3. 【语法】阴性的〔*cf*. masculine〕。4. 【诗】句尾有一多余轻音节的,弱韵的。～ *beauty* 女性美。*the* ～ *gender* 阴性。**II** *n*. 1. 女性,温柔的女性。2. 【语法】阴性;阴性词。～ **caesura** 不是紧接重音的诗行中断。～ **rhyme** 弱韵〔押韵的双音节字的第二音节为非重音,如 motion; 或三音节的第二,三音节为非重音,如 happily〕。**-ly** *ad*. **-ness** *n*.

fem·i·nin·i·ty [ˌfemiˈniniti; ͵fɛmɪˋnɪnətɪ] *n*. 1. 女性,女人的特性;温柔,柔弱。2. 〔集合词〕妇女。

fem·i·nism [ˈfemiˌnizəm; ˋfɛmə͵nɪzəm] *n*. 1. 男女平等主义;争取女权运动。2. 女性。3. 女人用的语言。

fem·i·nist [ˈfeminist; ˋfɛmɪnɪst] *n*. 男女平等主义者,争取女权运动的人。

fe·min·i·ty [fiˈminiti; fɪˋmɪnətɪ] *n*. = femininity.

fem·i·nize, **feminise** [ˈfemiˌnaiz; ˋfɛmə͵naɪz] *vt*., *vi*. 1. (使)女性化;【生】(使)雌性化 (*opp*. masculinize)。2. (在某一地区或职业等方面)(使)妇女占多数。**femi·ni·za·tion** [ˌfeminaiˈzeiʃən; fɛmɪnaɪˋzeʃən] *n*.

femme [fem, F. fam; fɛm, fam] *n*. 1. 【法】妻子。2. 〔美俚〕女子;在女子同性恋中充当女性角色者。

femme de cham·bre [F. fam də ʃɑ̃ːbr; fam də ʃɑbr] (*pl*. ***femmes de chambre***) 〔F.〕女仆,侍女,女服务员〔*cf*. chambermaid〕。

femme fa·tale [F. ˌfamˈfatal; ͵famfaˋtal] (*pl*. ***femmes fa·tales*** [F. ˌfamfaˈtal; ͵famfaˋtal]) 〔F.〕荡妇〔尤指引诱男人堕落的女人〕。

fem·o·ral [ˈfemərəl; ˋfɛmərəl] *a*. 大腿的,股骨的。～ **artery** 【解】股动脉。

fem·to- *comb*. *f*. 表示"毫微微"(=10^{-15}),"尘"。

fe·mur [ˈfiːmə; ˋfimə] *n*. (*pl*. ～*s*, ***fem·o·ra*** [ˈfemərə; ˋfɛmərə]) 【解】股骨;腿;(昆虫的)腿节。

fen[1] [fen; fɛn] **I** *n*. 沼泽;沼泽群落。***the Fens*** 英国剑桥郡附近的低地。**II** *vt*., *vi*. 〔方〕= fend. ～ **fire** 沼地磷火。～ **land** *n*. 沼泽地。～ **man** *n*. 沼泽居民。～ **pole** 〔英方〕(沼地居民用的)跳沟撑竿。

fen[2] [fen; fɛn] = fain[2].

fen[3] [fən; fən] *n*. 〔Chin.〕分。

fe·na·gle [fəˈneigl; fɪˋnegl] *vi*., *vt*. = finagle.

fence [fens; fɛns] **I** *n*. 1. 栅栏,篱笆;围墙。2. 自卫术;剑术。3. (机械的)防护物;〔古〕防壁,防护。4. 巧辩词令。5. 〔俚〕买卖贼赃的人;赃品买卖处,贼市,黑货市场。6. 〔*pl*.〕〔美〕政党组织,政治利益。*a thorn* ～ 刺篱。*a stone* ～ 石头围垣。*a sunk* ～ (不遮住视线的)矮篱,矮墙。～ *riders* 〔美〕修理牧场围墙的工人;骑墙派。*a master of* ～ 剑术家;雄辩家。*No* ～ *against a flail* [*an ill fortune*]. 〔谚〕恶运难逃。***be on both sides of the*** ～ 两面讨好。***be on sb.'s*** ～ 帮助[卫护]某人。***be*** [***sit***, ***stand***] ***on the*** ～ 观望形势,抱骑墙态度。***be on the other side of the*** ～ 加入反对方面。***be on the same side of the*** ～ 站在同一立场上,和某方一致。***descend*** [***come down***] ***on the right side of*** ～ 附和胜方。***make*** [***walk like***] ***a Virginia*** ～ 〔美俚〕东倒西歪地走。***mend*** [***look after***] ***one's*** ～***s*** 修补篱笆;〔美〕(国会议员)改善自己政治地位。**II** *vi*. 1. 击剑。2. 搪塞,闪开。3. 筑围墙,用栅栏防护。4. (马)跳过栅栏。5. 〔俚〕买卖赃物。—*vt*. 1. 用墙围住,用栅栏防御[护]。2. 防御,防护;〔古〕防止。3. (用栅栏)隔开,栏开,使成禁猎区。4. 买卖(赃物)。～ ***about*** [***up***] 用栅栏围起来。～ ***in*** 围进。～ ***off*** [***out***] 挡开,架开,用栅(墙,篱笆等)隔开。～ ***round*** 搪塞开,用围墙围住。～ ***with*** 搪塞(～ *with a question* [*questioner*] 避免正面答复)。～**-hanger** 未打定主意的人,犹豫不决者。～**-mending** 〔美〕改善恶化的政治关系。～**-off** *n*. (击剑比赛中)和局后的加赛。～ **rider** 〔美〕1. 修理牧场围墙的工人。2. 骑墙派。～ **shop** 黑货[赃品]商店。～**-sitter** 骑墙派。～**-straddler** 〔美俚〕两面讨好者。～ **time** [**month**, **season**] 禁猎[渔]期。**-less** *a*. 没有围墙的;〔诗〕不设防的。

fenc·er [ˈfensə; ˋfɛnsɚ] *n*. 1. 剑术师,击剑家。2. 篱笆匠。3. 能跳过篱笆的马。*a good* ～ 善于越过篱笆的良马。

fenc·ible [ˈfensəbl; ˋfɛnsəbl] **I** *a*. 1. 可以防卫的。2. 〔Scot.〕能保卫国家的,具有服兵役资格的。3. 国防军的。**II** *n*. 【史】〔主 Scot.〕国防军士兵。

fenc·ing [ˈfensiŋ; ˋfɛnsɪŋ] *n*. 1. 击剑,剑术。2. 辩论,巧妙的搪塞。3. 栅栏,围墙,篱笆。4. 筑栅栏的材料。5. 买卖赃物。～ **cully** 〔英俚〕窝藏赃物者。～ **den**[**ken**] 〔俚〕窝藏赃物的场所。～ **foil** 练习剑。～ **master** 击剑教练(员)。

fend [fend; fɛnd] *vt*. 1. 闪避,挡开(武器等)。2. 〔古〕防御,保护。3. 〔英方〕供养。— *vi*. 〔口〕1. 努力,力争。2. 供养,照料。～ ***for*** 筹措;扶养(～ *for oneself* 自己谋生;照料自己)。～ ***off*** 挡开,架开;避开(灾祸等)。

fend·er [ˈfendə; ˋfɛndɚ] *n*. 1. 防御者,防护板,防御物。2. 火炉围栏。3. (车辆的)挡泥板。4. 〔英〕(电车、机车等的)缓冲装置,救护装置〔*cf*. 〔美〕bumper〕。～ **beam** (船舷上的)护舷物;(铁路终点的)止车障。～ **board** 挡

泥板。~ **pile** 护舷棒。~ **stool**〔英〕炉围前的脚凳。**-less** *a*. 无防撞物[防护板]的,无挡牌的。

fen·es·tel·la [ˌfenisˈtelə; ˏfɛnəˋstɛlə] *n*. (*pl*. **-lae** [-liː; -li])【建】小窗,窗状壁龛。

fe·nes·tra [fiˈnestrə; fəˋnɛstrə] *n*. (*pl*. **-trae** [-triː; -tri]) **1.**【解】窗。~ **cochleae** 耳蜗窗。~ **rotunda** 圆窗。**2.**【动】明斑(蛾类翅上的透明斑点)。

fe·nes·trate [fiˈnestrit; fɪˋnestret] *a*. **1.**【动】具透明点的。**2.**【植】具窗孔的,网状的。

fe·nes·trat·ed [fiˈnestreitid, ˈfenistreitid; fiˋnɛstretɪd, ˋfɛnɪstretɪd] *a*. **1.** 有窗孔的;有口的;有孔的。**2.**【生】穿孔的;具透明点的 (= fenestrate)。

fen·es·tra·tion [ˌfenisˈtreiʃən; ˏfɛnɪsˋtreʃən] *n*. **1.**【建】窗户配列。**2.**【医】(耳科手术中的)开窗术。

Fe·ni·an [ˈfiːnjən; ˋfinjən] **I** *n*. **1.** 芬尼亚〔传说中的爱尔兰古代勇士〕。**2.** 芬尼亚运动(指十九世纪爱尔兰争取民族独立的反英运动)成员。~ ***Brotherhood*** 芬尼亚运动。**II** *a*. 芬尼亚运动(成员)的。**-ism** *n*. 芬尼亚共和主义。

fenks [feŋks; fɛŋks] *n*. 〔*pl*.〕(作肥料以及制作普鲁士蓝用的)鲸油渣。

fen·nec, fen·nek [ˈfenək; ˋfɛnɛk] *n*.【动】耶狐 (*Fennecus zerda*)〔产于北非和阿拉伯的一种大耳大眼淡黄色小狐〕。

fen·nel [ˈfenl; ˋfɛnl] *n*.【植】茴香(属)。~ **oil** 茴香油。~ **water** 茴香水〔用作兴奋剂等〕。~ **flower**【植】黑种草属。

fen·ny [ˈfeni; ˋfɛnɪ] *a*. **1.** 沼泽性的,沼泽多的。**2.** 生长在沼泽地带的。

fen·u·greek [ˈfenjugriːk; ˋfɛnjʊˏgrik] *n*.【植】胡芦巴〔一种豆科植物〕。

Fen·wick [ˈfenik, ˈfenwik; ˋfɛnɪk, ˋfɛnwɪk] *n*. 芬威克〔姓氏〕。

feod [fjuːd; fjud] *n*. 采邑,领地。

feoff [fef, fiːf; fɛf, fif] **I** *n*. 采邑,领地。**II** *vt*. 把采邑[领地]授与[出售给](某人)。

feoff·ee [feˈfiː, fiːˈfiː; ˏfeˋfi, ˏfiˋfi] *n*. **1.** 领受采邑者,不动产承受人。**2.** 公共不动产管理人。

feof·fer [ˈfefə, ˈfiːfə; ˋfefɚ, ˋfifɚ] *n*. = feoffor.

feoff·ment [ˈfefmənt, ˈfiːf-; ˋfɛfmənt, ˋfif-] *n*. **1.** 采邑授与。**2.**【法】土地及其他不动产的交付[让与]。**3.** 不动产交付证。

feof·for [feˈfɔː, fiːˈfɔː; fɛˋfɔr, fiˋfɔr] *n*. **1.** 采邑授与者。**2.** 不动产赠与[让与]人。

FERA = Federal Emergency Relief Administration〔美旧〕联邦紧急救济署。

fe·ra·cious [fəˈreiʃəs; fəˋreʃəs] *a*. 〔罕〕多产的;丰富的。**fe·rac·i·ty** [-ˈræsiti; -ˋræsətɪ] *n*.

fer·ae na·tur·ae [ˈfiəri nəˈtjuəriː; ˋfɪrɪnəˋtjuri] 〔L.〕**1.** 野生的。**2.**【法】不属于私产的(野生动物)。

fe·ral [ˈfiərəl; ˋfɪrəl] *a*. 野生的,野蛮的,凶悍的。

fer·bam [ˈfəːbæm; ˋfɝbæm] *n*.【化】富尔邦〔果树杀虫剂〕;二甲胺基荒酸铁〔用作杀真菌剂〕。

fer·ber·ite [ˈfəːbərait; ˋfɝbəraɪt] *n*.【矿】钨铁矿。

fer-de-lance [ˌfεədəˈlɑːns; ˏferdəˋlans] *n*.【动】枪头蛇,矛头蛇〔美洲产大毒蛇〕。

Fer·di·nand [ˈfəːdinənd; ˋfɝdn̩ˏænd] *n*. 费迪南〔男子名〕。

fere [fiə; fɪə] *n*. 〔古〕**1.** 同伴,伙伴。**2.** 配偶〔夫或妻〕。

fer·e·to·ry [ˈferiˌtəri; ˋferəˏtorɪ] *n*. **1.**【宗】放圣骨的神龛,(教堂内)安设神龛的地方。**2.** 棺架,尸架。

Fer·gus [ˈfəːgəs; ˋfɝgəs] *n*. 费格斯〔姓氏〕。

Fer·gu·s(s)on [ˈfəːgəsn; ˋfɝgəsn] *n*. 费格森〔姓氏〕。

fe·ri·a [ˈfiəriə; ˋfɪrɪə] *n*. (*pl*. ~***s***, ***-ri·ae*** [-iː; -i]) **1.** 〔*pl*.〕(古罗马)假日;节日。**2.**【宗】(星期六或星期日以外,尤指宗教节日或节日前夕以外的)平日。**-al** *a*.

fe·rine [ˈfiərain; ˋfɪraɪn] *a*. = feral.

Fe·rin·ghee, Fe·rin·gi [fəˈriŋgi; fəˋrɪŋgɪ] *n*. 〔印蔑〕欧洲人;欧亚混血儿;(尤指)在印度出生的葡萄牙人。

fer·i·ty [ˈferiti; ˋfɛrɪtɪ] *n*. 凶残;野性;未驯化。

fer·ma·ta [fəˈmɑːtə; fəˋmɑtə] *n*.【乐】**1.** 延音。**2.** 延长号(𝄐)或(𝄑)。

fer·ment [ˈfəːment; ˋfɝmɛnt] **I** *n*. **1.** 酶,酵素。**2.** 发酵。**3.** 扰动,骚动。*Yeast is a* ~. 酵母是一种发酵剂。*cause national* ~ 引起举国骚动。***be in a*** ~ 在动乱中。**II** [fəːˈment; fɚˋmɛnt] *vt*., *vi*. (使)发酵;(使)激动,(使)骚动。**-ta·ble** *a*. 发酵性的,可发酵的。**-ta·tion** [ˌfəːmenˈteiʃən; ˏfɝmɛnˋteʃən] *n*. 发酵;激动,激昂,纷扰,人心骚动。**-ta·tive, -tive** *a*. 发酵性的,有发酵力的。

fer·mi [ˈfεəmi, ˈfəː-; ˋfɛrmi, ˋfɝ-] *n*.【物】费密〔长度单位,等于 10^{-13} 厘米〕。

fer·mi·on [ˈfεəmiːɔn; ˋfɛrmiˏɑn] *n*.【原】费米子〔属费米系统的粒子〕。

fer·mi·um [ˈfεəmiəm; ˋfɛrmɪəm] *n*.【化】镄。

fern [fəːn; fɝn] *n*.【植】蕨(纲),蕨类植物。*royal* ~ (蕨类植物)王紫萁。~ **bracken,** ~ **brake** 蕨;羊齿丛。~ **owl**【动】欧夜鹰。~ **seed** 蕨孢子。

fern·er·y [ˈfəːnəri; ˋfɝnərɪ] *n*. **1.** 蕨类种植处,蕨类种植盆。**2.** 簇生的蕨。

fer·ni·co [ˈfəːnikəu; ˋfɝnɪko] *n*.【冶】费镍钴〔铁镍钴合金〕。

fern·y [ˈfəːni; ˋfɝnɪ] *a*. 蕨的,像蕨的,多蕨的。

fe·ro·cious [fəˈrəuʃəs; fəˋroʃəs] *a*. **1.** 凶猛的,野蛮的,残暴的。**2.** 〔口〕非常的,十分强烈的。*a* ~ *appetite* 特大的胃口。*a* ~ *look* [*feature*] 凶恶的相貌。*a* ~ *bore* 一个十分令人讨厌的家伙。**-ly** *ad*. **-ness** *n*.

fe·roc·i·ty [fəˈrɔsiti; fəˋrɑsətɪ] *n*. **1.** 凶猛,野蛮,残暴。**2.** 暴行。

-fer·ous *suf*. 通常接在 i 以后,构成形容词,表示"含…的","生…的","产…的": pesti*ferous*, coni*ferous*, auri*ferous*.

fer·ox [ˈferɔks; ˋfɛrɑks] *n*. 〔英〕大湖鳟,猛鲑。

fer·rate [ˈfereit; ˋfɛret] *n*.【化】高铁酸盐,铁(III)酸盐。

fer·re·dox·in [ˈferəˌdɔksin; ˋfɛrəˏdɑksɪn] *n*.【生化】铁氧化还原蛋白。

fer·rel [ˈferəl; ˋfɛrəl] *n*. = ferrule.

fer·re·ous [ˈferiəs; ˋfɛrɪəs] *a*. **1.** 铁(制)的,铁色的,铁质的,含铁的。**2.** 硬如铁的。~ **metals** 黑色金属〔*cf*. non-~ metals〕。

fer·ret[1] [ˈferit; ˋfɛrɪt] **I** *n*. **1.**【动】(猎兔用的)白鼬,雪貂。**2.**【动】(美西部)黑脚黄鼬。**3.** 搜索者,侦探。**II** *vt*., *vi*. 用雪貂(把兔等由隐藏处)驱出,搜出;搜寻。~ ***about*** 四处搜寻。~ ***for*** 探索。~ ***out*** 探索出,搜出;肃清。***go ferreting*** 带着雪貂去打猎。

fer·ret[2], **fer·ret·ing** [ˈferit, -iŋ; ˋfɛrɪt, -ɪŋ] *n*. 细布[丝]带。

fer·ret·y [ˈferiti; ˋfɛrɪtɪ] *a*. 白鼬似的;搜索者似的;喜欢窥视的。

fer·ri- *comb*. *f*.【化】表示"含(正)铁的": *ferric*, *ferri*ferous.

fer·ri·age [ˈferiidʒ; ˋfɛrɪɪdʒ] *n*. **1.** 摆渡;渡船业。**2.** 摆渡费。

fer·ric [ˈferik; ˋfɛrɪk] *a*. **1.** 铁的,含铁的。**2.**【化】(正)铁的,三价铁的。~ **oxide** 三氧化二铁,氧化铁。~ **sulphate** 硫酸铁。

fer·ri·cy·a·nide [ˌferiˈsaiənaid; ˏfɛrɪˋsaɪənaɪd] *n*.【化】氰铁酸盐,氰铁化物。

fer·rif·er·ous [feˈrifərəs; fɛˋrɪfərəs] *a*. 含铁的,含有三价铁的。

fer·ri·mag·net·ism [ˌferiˈmægnitizəm; ˏfɛrɪˋmægnətɪzəm] *n*. 铁淦氧磁性。

Fer·ris wheel [ˈferis; ˋfɛrɪs] 阜氏转轮〔游艺场中供人乘坐可以飞快转动的玩具〕。

fer·rite [ˈferait; ˋfɛraɪt] *n*.【化】**1.** 铁素体,纯粒铁,纯铁

体。2. 铁酸盐。3. 铁氧体,铁淦氧。

fer·ro- *comb. f.* 1. 表示"铁": *ferro*concrete. 2. 表示"铁和…": *ferro*chrome. 3. 表示"亚铁": *ferro*cyanide.

fer·ro·al·loy [ˌferəuˈæləi; ˏfɛroˋæləɪ] ***n.*** 【化】铁合金。

fer·ro·chro·mi·um [ˌferəuˈkrəumiəm; ˋfɛroˋkromɪəm] ***n.*** 铬铁(合金)(= ferrochrome)。

fer·ro·con·crete [ˌferəuˈkɔnkriːt; ˏfɛroˋkɑnkrit] ***n.*** 【建】钢[铁]筋混凝土,钢骨水泥。

fer·ro·cy·a·nide [ˌferəuˈsaiənaid, -nid; ˏfɛroˋsaɪənaɪd, -nɪd] ***n.*** 【化】氰亚铁酸盐,亚铁氰化物。

fer·ro·e·lec·tric [ˌferəuiˈlektrik; ˏfɛroɪˋlɛktrɪk] ***n.***, ***a.*** 【物】铁电体(的);强介质(的)。

fer·ro·mag·ne·sian [ˌferəumægˈniːʃən; ˏfɛromægˋniʒən] **I** ***a.*** 【矿】含铁和镁的。*a ~ mineral* 铁镁矿物。**II** ***n.*** 铁镁矿物。

fer·ro·mag·net·ic [ˌferəumægˈnetik; ˏfɛromægˋnɛtɪk] ***a.*** 铁磁(性)的。**-mag·net·ism** [-ˈmægnitizəm; -ˋmægnətɪzəm] ***n.***

fer·ro·man·ga·nese [ˌferəuˈmæŋgəniːz, -niːs; ˏfɛroˋmæŋgəˏniz, -ˏnis] ***n.*** 铁锰合金,锰铁。

fer·ro·mo·lyb·de·num [ˌferəuməˈlibdinəm; ˏfɛroməˋlɪbdənəm] ***n.*** 【冶】钼铁,钼钢。

fer·ro·nick·el [ˌferəuˈnikl; ˏfɛroˋnɪkl] ***n.*** 【冶】镍铁,铁镍剂。

fer·ro·phos·phor·ous [ˌferəuˈfɔsfərəs; ˏfɛroˋfɑsfərəs] ***n.*** 【冶】磷铁。

fer·ro·pseu·do·brook·ite [ˌferəuˌsuːdəuˈbrukait; ˏfɛroˏsudoˋbrʊkaɪt] ***n.*** 月铁板钛矿〔由阿波罗 11 号太空飞船带回地球的月球矿物〕。

fer·ro·sil·i·con [ˌferəuˈsilikən; ˏfɛroˋsɪləkən] ***n.*** 【化】矽[硅]铁。

fer·ro·type [ˈferəutaip; ˋfɛrotaɪp] **I** ***n.*** 【摄】铁板照相(法)。**II** ***vt.*** 用铁板给(照片)上光。

fer·rous [ˈferəs; ˋfɛrəs] ***a.*** 1. 铁的,从铁得来的。2.【化】亚铁的,二价铁的。~ ***and non-*** ~ ***metals*** 黑色及有色金属。~ **nitrate** 硝酸亚铁。~ **oxide** 氧化亚铁。~ **sulphate** 硫酸亚铁。

fer·ru·gin·o·si·ty [feˌruːdʒiˈnɔsiti; fɛˏrudʒɪˋnɑsətɪ] ***n.*** 含铁性。

fer·ru·gi·nous [feˈruːdʒinəs; fɛˋrudʒənəs] ***a.*** 1. 铁(质)的,含铁的。2. 铁锈色的,赤褐色的。*a ~ spring* 含铁矿泉。

fer·rule [ˈferuːl; ˋfɛrul] **I** ***n.*** 1. (装于手杖、木柄、伞柄等顶端起加牢作用的)金属箍,金属包头。2.【机】套圈,箍。**II** ***vt.*** 用箍镶。

fer·rum [ˈferəm; ˋfɛrəm] ***n.*** 〔L.〕【化】铁。

fer·ry [ˈferi; ˋfɛrɪ] **I** ***n.*** 1. 渡口;渡船;摆渡权。2.〔美〕(出厂飞机的)现场输送〔指把飞机从接收地飞送至使用地等〕。*row the travelers over the* ~ 用摆渡船把旅客送过渡口。***take the*** [***charon's***] ~ 死。**II** ***vt.*** 1. 用船过渡,(用船等)运送,运输。2.用飞机运送。~ *the traveler across a river* 用船把旅客摆渡过河。— ***vi.*** 1. 乘渡船,摆渡;(小船)来往于渡口(*upon*)。2. 乘飞机飞渡。~ *across the river* 乘船渡河。~ **boat** ***n.*** 渡船。~ **bridge** (上下渡船用的)浮桥;列车轮渡。~ **house** 1. 候船室。2. 渡船船夫室。~ **man** ***n.*** 渡船工人。~ **pilot** (把出厂飞机开到使用现场的)飞机驾驶员。~ **steamer** 渡轮。

fer·ti·gate [ˈfəːtigeit; ˋfɝtɪget] ***vt.*** 水肥混合灌溉,水肥滴灌〔用加了化肥的水通过塑料管道灌溉〕。

fer·ti·ga·tion [ˌfəːtiˈgeiʃən; ˏfɝtɪˋgeʃən] ***n.*** 滴灌施肥。

fer·tile [ˈfəːtail; ˋfɝtl] ***a.*** (*opp.* sterile) 1. 肥沃的,丰饶的;多产的,丰富的 (*of*; *in*)。2.【生】能生育的,有繁殖力的;已受孕[受精]的。3.【原】可变成裂变物质的。~*egg* 受精卵。*a ~ land* [*soil*] 肥地。*a ~ plain* 沃野。~ *pollen* 能育花粉。~ *shower* 及时雨。*a ~ mind* 想像力丰富的头脑。*be ~ in expedients* 会临机应变的。*be ~ of imagination* 想像力丰富。~ **material**【原】(通过中子诱发核反应可变成裂变性燃料的)可转换物质〔如铀 238〕;燃料源物质;变成核燃料的中子吸收剂。**-ly** ***ad.*** **-ness** ***n.***

fer·til·i·ty [fəːˈtiliti; fɝˋtɪlətɪ] ***n.*** (*opp.* sterility) 1. 肥沃,丰饶;肥力,肥(沃)度;(土地的)生产力。2.【生】能育性,繁殖力。3. (思想等的)丰富。*the soil* ~ 土壤肥力。~ **agent** 致育因素。~ **drug** (催女性排卵以医治不孕症的)受胎药。

fer·ti·li·za·ble [ˈfəːtilaizəbl; ˋfɝtḷˏaɪzəbḷ] ***a.*** 可施肥的,可受精的。

fer·ti·li·za·tion [ˌfəːtilaiˈzeiʃən; ˏfɝtləˋzeʃən] ***n.*** 1. 肥沃化,施肥(法);丰饶化。2.【生】受孕[受精](作用,现象)。

fer·til·ize, fer·ti·lise [ˈfəːtilaiz; ˋfɝtlaɪz] ***vt.*** 1. 使肥沃,使丰饶,使多产。2.【生】使受孕[受精]。~*d eggs* 受精卵。— ***vi.*** 施肥。

fer·til·iz·er [ˈfəːtiˌlaizə; fɝtlˏlaɪzɚ] ***n.*** 1. 肥料(特指化学肥料)。2. 受精媒介物(如蜂、虫、鸟、风、水等)。*additional* ~ 追肥。*ground* ~ 基肥。

fer·til·i·zin [fəːˈtilizin; ˋfɝtḷˏaɪzɪn] ***n.*** 【生】受精素。

fer·u·la [ˈferulə; ˋfɛrulə] ***n.*** (*pl.* ***-lae*** [-liː; -li]) 1.【植】阿魏。2. = ferule[1].

fer·ule[1] [ˈferuːl; ˋfɛrul] **I** ***n.*** (责打学生用的)戒尺;〔喻〕责罚;纪律。***be under the*** ~ 在教师鞭策之下;受人支配。**II** ***vt.*** 用教鞭责打(手心)。

fer·ule[2] [ˈferuːl; ˋfɛrul] ***n.***, ***vt.*** = ferrule.

fer·ven·cy [ˈfəːvənsi; ˋfɝvənsɪ] ***n.*** 1. 炽热。2. 热情,热心,热烈。

fer·vent [ˈfəːvənt; ˋfɝvənt] ***a.*** 1. 炽热的。2. 热情的,热心的,热烈的,强烈的。~ *heat* 白热。~ *hatred* 痛恨。~ *love* 热爱。*a ~ soul* 热情的人。**-ly** ***ad.***

fer·vid [ˈfəːvid; ˋfɝvɪd] ***a.*** 1.〔诗〕炽热的。2. 热烈的,热情的;激烈的。~ *loyalty* 赤胆忠心。**-ly** ***ad.*** **-ness** ***n.***

fer·vid·i·ty [fəːˈviditi; fəˋvɪdətɪ] ***n.*** 1. 炽热。2. 热心,热烈。

fer·vo(u)r [ˈfəːvə; ˋfɝvɚ] ***n.*** 1. 高温。2. 强烈的感情,激情,热情。

F.E.S. = Fellow of the Entomological Society 昆虫学会会员。

Fes·cen·nine [ˈfesiˌnain, -nin; ˋfɛsəˏnaɪn, -nɪn] ***a.*** 〔常用 f-〕粗俗的;猥亵的;下流的。

fes·cus [ˈfeskjuː; ˋfɛskju] ***n.*** 1. 教鞭,指示棒。2.【植】羊茅,酥油草。

fess(e) [fes; fɛs] ***n.*** 【纹】(徽章中横跨盾形中央的)中线,中横带。

fes·ta [ˈfestə; ˋfɛstɑ] ***n.*** 〔It.〕喜庆日,节日。

fes·tal [ˈfestl; ˋfɛstḷ] ***a.*** 节日的;喜庆的,欢乐的。*a ~ day* 节日。*a ~ mood* 节日气氛[情绪]。**-ly** ***ad.***

fes·ter [ˈfestə; ˋfɛstɚ] **I** ***n.*** 1. 脓疮,溃烂。2. (怨恨等)郁积,恶化。**II** ***vt.***, ***vi.*** 1. (使)溃烂,(使)化脓。2. (使)烦恼,(使)恶化。*Jealousy ~ed his mind.* 嫉妒使他苦恼。

fes·ti·nate [ˈfestineit, -nit; ˋfɛstəˏnet, -nɪt] **I** ***vt.***, ***vi.*** 〔罕〕赶紧,使赶快。**II** ***a.*** [ˈfestinit; ˋfɛstənɪt]〔罕〕急急忙忙的,匆忙的。*a ~ gait* 匆忙的步伐。

fes·ti·na·tion [ˌfestiˈneiʃən; ˏfɛstəˋneʃən] ***n.*** 行走急促〔尤指某些神经疾病症状〕。

fes·ti·val [ˈfestəvəl; ˋfɛstəvl] **I** ***a.*** 节日的,喜庆的。**II** ***n.*** 1. 节日,喜庆日;庆祝典礼。2. 贺宴;会演;(定期)音乐节。*a ~ atmosphere* 节日的气氛。

fes·tive [ˈfestiv; ˋfɛstɪv] ***a.*** 节日的,过节似的;喜庆的;欢乐的。*the ~ board* 筵席。*a ~ mood* 节日气象。*a ~ season* 节期。**-ly** ***ad.***

fes·tiv·i·ty [fesˈtiviti; fɛsˋtɪvətɪ] ***n.*** 1. 节日,喜庆日;喜庆,欢乐。2.〔*pl.*〕祝宴,庆祝典礼。

fes·toon [fesˈtuːn; fɛsˋtun] **I** ***n.*** 1. 花彩;穗边窗帘[门

F

帘]。2.【建】垂花饰。3. 花彩装饰物;彩旗。II *vt*. 1. 给…结彩,在…饰以花彩。2. 使成花彩形。**-e·ry** *n*.〔集合词〕(一团)花丝;彩饰。

Fest·schrift [ˈfestˌʃrift; ˋfɛstˏʃrɪft] *n*. (*pl*. **-schrift·en** [-ˈʃriftn; -ˏʃrɪftn̩], **-schrifts**)〔亦 f-〕纪念册;(专为纪念某著名学者由其同事、学生等写成的)纪念文集。

fet·a (cheese) [ˈfetə; ˋfɛtə] (用羊奶做的)希腊白软干酪。

fe·tal [ˈfiːtl; ˋfitl̩] *a*. 胎儿的;胎的。~ **hemoglobin** 胎儿血红素。~ **membrane** 胎膜。~ **position** 胎儿(状)姿势,(调气养身的)打坐。

fe·ta·tion [fiːˈteiʃən; fiˋteʃən] *n*. 怀孕,受胎;胚胎发育。

fetch[1] [fetʃ; fɛtʃ] I *vt*. 1. 拿来,拿去;请来;接去。2.【海】到达;赶上(别的船)。3. 使发生;使出(血),使流(泪),使吐(气);使发出(喊声等)。4. 卖得(好价钱)。5.〔口〕给以打击,杀死。6.〔俚〕吸引,使发生兴趣。7. 激恼。8. 推导出,演绎出。9. 使信服 (*round*)。10.〔方〕使苏醒。~ *a doctor* 请医生来。*Please* ~ *me the pen*. 请把笔给我拿来。~ *the harbour* (船)到港。~ *way*【海】开始航行。*The call* ~*ed him at once*. 一喊他就来了。~ *a sigh* 发叹息声。~ *a good price* 卖好价钱。*This old watch won't* ~ *you much*. 你这只旧表卖不出多少钱。*The beauty of the lake* ~*ed her completely*. 湖光美景完全吸引了她。*The film* ~*ed the public*. 影片博得好评,受人欢迎。*A little flattery will* ~ *him*.〔美俚〕稍一奉承他就软化了。—*vi*. 1. 取,拿来,带来。2.【海】航行,前进;绕道走 (*about*; *round*)。3. (猎犬)叼回猎物。4.〔方〕到达,抵达。*They* ~*ed home after a long ride*. 他们坐了很久的车之后,终于到家了。*To* ~!〔命令猎犬〕去(把猎物叼回来)! ~ *headway* [*sternway*] 前进[后退]。~ **about** 迂回。~ **again**〔古〕使复活,使苏生。~ **and carry** 1. (猎犬)把打死的猎物叼回。2. 传播小道消息。3. 当听差[仆役],打杂 (*for*)。~ **around** 1. 使确信,说服。2. 使复活。~ **away** (桌上的物品因船只颠簸等而)滑离原处。~ **down** 打下(射击物);减轻(刑罚等);落(价)。~ **in** 拉进;招徕。~ **off** 1. 使摆脱窘境。2. 杀死。3. 一口气喝光。~ **out** 使显出(光彩等);拿出;引出。~ **to** 使苏醒。~ **up** 1. 拿出,想起;引起,产生。2. 收回,取回(失品)。3. 呕吐;扶养,养育。4.〔方〕苏醒。5.【海】到达,停止,忽然停止 (~ *up all standing* 船驶上暗礁时,风帆未下而忽然停止)。~ **up with** 追到,赶上。~ **way** = ~ **away**. II *n*. 1. 拿取,拿来。2. 行程,(对岸)两点间的距离;风浪区。3. 诡计,谋略。4.〔古〕(想像力等的)作用,范围。*a far* [*long*] ~ 一段远距离。*the* ~ *of a bay* 海湾的全长度。~**-up** *n*. 突然的停止。**-er** *n*. 取物的人,请人的人。

fetch[2] [fetʃ; fɛtʃ] *n*. 1. (迷信者所说的)生魂,活人的魂,人将死时的离魂。2. 相同物。*be the exact* ~ *of* 和…一模一样。~ **candle** [**light**] (迷信者所说的)人将死时从其家中飘向墓地的鬼火。

fetch·ing [ˈfetʃiŋ; ˋfɛtʃɪŋ] *a*.〔口〕动人的,吸引人的,迷人的。**-ly** *ad*.

fête, fete [feit; fet] I *n*. 1. 节日,喜庆日;盛大招待会,盛宴;游园会。2. 生日。*a national* ~ 国庆节日。*a garden* [*lawn*] ~〔美〕游园会。II *vt*. 款待,盛宴招待;给以巨大荣誉。~ **champêtre** 〔F.〕游园大会。~ **day** 节日;庆祝日〔生日等〕。

fet·e·ri·ta [ˌfetəˈritə; ˏfɛtəˋrɪtə] *n*.【植】非洲芦粟〔原产非洲,美国西南部种植为饲料,粒大,色白〕。

fe·tial [ˈfiːʃəl; ˈfiʃəl] I *n*. (古罗马主持外交谈判,宣网战争等职务的)外事祭司团成员。II *a*. 1. 古罗马祭司团的;古罗马祭司团职务的。2. 外交的,处理国家关系事务的。

fe·ti·a·lis [ˌfiːʃiˈeilis; ˏfiʃɪˋelɪs] *n*. (*pl*. **-a·les** [-liːz; -liz]) = fetial.

fe·tich(e) [ˈfiːtiʃ, ˈfet-; ˋfitɪʃ, ˋfɛt-] *n*. = fetish.

fet·ich·ism [ˈfetiʃizəm; ˋfɛtɪʃɪzəm] *n*. = fetishism.

fet·ich·ist [ˈfetiʃist; ˋfɛtɪʃɪst] *n*. = fetishist.

fet·i·cide [ˈfiːtisaid; ˋfitəˏsaɪd] *n*. 杀胎,堕胎 (= foeticide)。

fet·id [ˈfetid, ˈfiː-; ˋfɛtɪd, ˋfi-] *a*. 发臭的,腐臭的。**-ly** *ad*. **-ness** *n*.

fe·tip·a·rous [fiːˈtipərəs; fiˋtɪpərəs] *a*. (有袋动物等)胎儿发育完全前生产的。

fet·ish [ˈfiːtiʃ, ˈfetiʃ; ˋfitɪʃ, ˋfɛtɪʃ] *n*. 1. 物神,崇拜物。2. 偶像,迷信。3.【心】物恋的对象。4. 物神崇拜的仪式。***break with*** ~ 破除盲目崇拜。***make a perfect*** ~ ***of*** 盲目崇拜。

fet·ish·ism [ˈfiːtiʃizəm, ˈfe-; ˋfitɪʃɪzm̩, ˋfɛ-] *n*. 1. 物神崇拜,拜物教。2. 迷信,盲目崇拜。3.【心】(由异性的局部肢体或所用物件得到变态性欲满足的)物恋。

fet·ish·ist [ˈfiːtiʃist, ˈfe-; ˋfitɪʃɪst, ˋfɛ-] *n*. 1. 物神崇拜者;拜物教徒。2.【心】恋物欲者。

fet·ish·is·tic [ˌfetiˈʃistik; ˏfɛtɪʃˋɪstɪk] *a*. 1. 拜物教(徒)的;盲目崇拜的。2.【心】物恋的。

fet·lock [ˈfetlɔk; ˋfɛtˏlɑk] *n*. 1. 距毛,(马蹄上部的)丛毛。2. (生距毛处的)球节。3. (生距毛的)肢关节。***hairy about*** [***at***; ***in***] ***the*** ~***s***〔俚〕没教养的,没礼貌的。

fe·tol·o·gy [fiːˈtɔlədʒi; fiˋtɑlədʒɪ] *n*.【医】胎儿学。**-ogist** 胎儿学者。

fe·tor [ˈfiːtə, ˈfiːtɔː; ˋfitɚ, ˋfitɔr] *n*. 奇臭,恶臭。

fet·ter [ˈfetə; ˋfɛtɚ] I *n*.〔*pl*.〕脚镣;囚禁;束缚,羁绊。*No man loves his* ~*s, be they made of gold*.〔谚〕金铸的脚镣也没人喜好。***be in*** ~***s*** 上着脚镣,被囚禁着。II *vt*. 给…上脚镣,束缚。*be* ~*ed by tradition* 受传统的束缚。~ **bush** *n*.【植】1. (美国)亮叶南烛 (*Lyonia lucida*). 2. 美国马醉木 (*Pieris floribunda*). ~**lock** 1. = fetlock. 2. (马的) D 字形脚镣; D 字形徽章。

Fet·tes [ˈfetis; ˋfɛtɪs] *n*. 费蒂斯〔姓氏〕。

fet·tle [ˈfetl; ˋfɛtl̩] I *n*. 1. 状态,情绪。2. 涂炉床材料。***in good*** [***fine***] ~ 神采奕奕,兴高采烈。II *vt*. 1.〔英方〕修补,整顿。2. 殴打。3.【冶】用矿渣等涂(炉床)。—*vi*.〔英方〕1. 准备好。2. 纷扰,小题大做。**-r** *n*. 修理工,保养工。

fet·tling [ˈfetliŋ; ˋfɛtlɪŋ] *n*.【冶】涂炉床材料〔如矽[硅]石〕。

fet·tuc·ci·ne, fet·tu·ci·ne, fet·tu·ci·ni [ˌfetuːˈtʃiːniː; ˏfɛtəˋtʃini] *n*. [It.]〔*pl*.〕〔作单数用〕奶油酱汁面条。

fe·tus [ˈfiːtəs; ˋfitəs] *n*. 胎儿 (= foetus)。

fet·wa [ˈfetwə; ˋfɛtwə] *n*. (根据伊斯兰教法规所作的)判决。

feu [fjuː; fju] I *n*.〔Scot.〕【法】永久租借(权);永久租借地;封地。II *vt*. 准许永久租借。

feud[1] [fjuːd; fjud] I *n*. (部落或家族之间的)世仇;仇恨;不和;争执,纠纷。***be at*** ~ ***with*** 与人不和。***deadly*** ~ 不共戴天之仇,世仇。***sink a*** ~ 尽释前嫌;捐弃旧怨,言归于好。II *vi*. 长期不和;经常争吵。*spend one's time* ~*ing with the neighbours* 经常和街坊争吵。

feud[2] [fjuːd; fjud] *n*. (封建制度下的)封地,采邑。

feu·dal[1] [ˈfjuːdl; ˋfjudl̩] *a*. 1. 封建的;封建制度[时代]的。2. 封地的,采邑的。*the* ~ *age* [*days*, *times*] 封建时代。*the* ~ *system* 封建制度。*a* ~ *lord* 封建主,诸侯。~ *estates* 封地,采邑。**-ist** *n*. 1. 封建主义者。2. 研究封建制度的学者。**-ly** *ad*.

feu·dal[2] [ˈfjuːdl; ˋfjudl̩] *a*. 世仇的;不和的,争吵的。**-ist** *n*. 结下世仇的人。

feu·dal·ism [ˈfjuːdəlizəm; ˋfjudl̩ˏɪzəm] *n*. 1. 封建主义,封建制度。2. 寡头制度。*industrial* ~ 工业上的寡头制度。

feu·dal·is·tic [ˌfjuːdəˈlistik; ˏfjudl̩ˋɪstɪk] *a*. 封建制度的,封建主义(者)的。

feu·dal·i·ty [fjuːˈdæliti; fjuˋdælətɪ] *n*. 1. 封建制度,封建性。2. 封地,采邑。

feu·dal·ize [ˈfjuːdəlaiz; ˋfjudl̩ˏaɪz] *vt*. 对(土地)实行封

建制度,使为领地。**-za·tion** [ˌfjuːdəlaiˈzeiʃən; ˏfjudl̩əˋzeʃən] ***n*.** 封建化。

feu·da·to·ry [ˈfjuːdətəri; ˋfjudəˏtorɪ] **I *a*. 1.** 封建的,臣属的,受有封地的。**2.** (邦土)隶属于外国的。**II *n*. 1.** 封建领主,诸侯,家臣。**2.** 封邑。

feu de joie [ˌfəː də ˈʒwɑː; ˏfɚ dəˋʒwɑ] 〔F.〕 **1.** 大篝火(= bonfire)。**2.** 礼炮(= fire of joy)。

feud·ist [ˈfjuːdist; ˋfjudɪst] ***n*. 1.** 研究封建法的专家。**2.** 〔美〕结下世仇的人;仇敌。

Feu·er·bach [G. ˈfɔiərbah; ˋfɔɪərbah] **L. A.** 费尔巴哈〔1804—1872,德国哲学家〕。

fe·il·le·ton [ˈfəːitɔŋ; ˋfɚɪtɔŋ] ***n*.** 〔F.〕 **1.** (报纸的)副刊,小品栏,文艺栏;小品文。**2.** 连载小说,通俗小说。

feuil·le·ton·ist [ˈfɔijətənist; ˋfɔɪjətənɪst] ***n*.** (报刊的)小品栏作家,文艺栏作家,连载小说作家,法国报刊副刊[专栏]作家。

fe·ver [ˈfiːvə; ˋfivɚ] **I *n*. 1.** 发热,发烧;热度。**2.** 热病。**3.** 狂热;兴奋。~ *and ague* 疟疾。*hectic* ~ 消耗热,痨病热,潮热。*intermittent* ~ 间歇热。*quartan* ~ 间三日疟,四日疟。*scarlet* ~ 猩红热。*typhoid* ~ 伤寒。*yellow* ~ 黄热病。***be in a* ~ *of impatience*** 焦虑不安。***run a* ~** 发烧。***send sb. into a* ~ *of excitement*** 使人非常激动。**II *vt*. 1.** 使发烧;使患热病。**2.** 使兴奋[发狂]。~ **blister** [**sore**]【医】唇疱疹,口角疱疹(= cold sore)。~ **few**【植】小白菊。~ **heat** 发烧时的体温;高度兴奋,狂热。~ **pitch** 高度兴奋,狂热。~ **therapy**【医】高烧疗法〔提高患者体温以消灭病菌的一种旧疗法〕。~ **trap** 使人容易发热病的地方,瘴疠之地。~ **tree**【植】蓝桉。~ **ward** 隔离病房。~ **weed**【植】刺芹属植物。~ **wort**【植】抱茎莛子藨。**-ed *a*.** 发烧的;高度兴奋的。

fe·ver·ish [ˈfiːvəriʃ; ˋfivərɪʃ] ***a*. 1.** 发烧的,有热病症状的;热病的。**2.** 容易引起热病的,热病蔓延的。**3.** 兴奋的,狂热的,焦躁的。~ *activities* 疯狂的活动。*with* ~ *excitement* 极端兴奋地。**-ly *ad*. -ness *n*.**

fe·ver·ous [ˈfiːvərəs; ˋfivərəs] ***a*.** = feverish. **-ly *ad*.**

few [fjuː; fju] **I *a*.** (~*er*; ~*est*) **1.** 〔无冠词 a (否定用法)〕少数的,很少,几乎没有 (*opp*. many) 〔*cf*. little〕。**2.** 〔a ~ (肯定用法)〕有些,几个(*opp*. none) 〔*cf*. a little〕。*I have* ~ *friends*. 我朋友很少,我几乎没有朋友。*a man of* ~ *words* 沉默寡言的人。*I have a* ~ *friends*. 我有少数几个朋友。*in a* ~ *days* 过几天,在两三天内。**II *n*. 1.** 〔无冠词(否定用法)〕很少数,几乎没有。**2.** 〔*a* ~ (肯定用法)〕少数,几个。**3.** 〔the ~〕(对"多数"说的)少数。***a* ~ 1.** 几个,两三个(*A* ~ *of them come*. 他们来了几个人。*A faithful* ~ *remain*. 只剩下不多几个忠诚的友人[同道])。**2.** 〔俚〕一点点;〔反语〕很多,的确。***a good* ~ = *quite a* ~, *not a* ~, *some* ~** 〔美语〕不少,相当多。***at the* ~*est*** 至少。***a very* ~** 极少数。***every* ~ *days*** [***minutes***, ***weeks***] 每隔几天[分钟、星期]。~ ***and far between*** 稀少,隔很久才发生的。~ ***or no*** [***none***] 几乎没有。***no* ~*er than*** 不下于,多达。***only a* ~** 仅仅少数,一点点。***to name*** (***only***) ***a* ~** 〔插入语〕(仅)举几个为例。

few·ness [ˈfjuːnis; ˋfjunɪs] ***n*.** 少,少数。

few·trils [ˈfjuːtrilz; ˋfjutrɪlz] ***n*.** 〔*pl*.〕〔英方〕(琐碎的)小事;小物件;少量。

fey [fei; fe] ***a*.** 〔Scot.〕 **1.** 该死的;垂死的。**2.** 像垂死的人一样心乱的。**3.** 发狂似的。**4.** 奇异的,古怪的。**5.** 能看见神仙的。**6.** 非现世的。

fez [fez; fɛz] ***n*.** (*pl*. ***fez·zes*** [ˈfeziz; ˋfɛzɪz]) 土耳其帽。

ff. = **1.** 〔It.〕【乐】*fortissimo*. **2.** folios 面数;页数。**3.** following (pages) 以下(各页)。

F/F = full(y) fashioned【纺】全成形的。

FF = functional food 保健食品。

FFA, f.f.a. = **1.** foreign freight agent 国外货运代理人。**2.** free from alongside 船边交易(价格)。**3.** free fatty acid【生化】自由脂肪酸,游离脂肪酸。

F.F.A. = fellow of the Faculty of Actuaries 〔英〕保险统计师公会会员。

F.F.P.S. = Fellow of the Faculty of Physicians and Surgeons 〔英〕内外科医师公会会员。

F.F.V. 〔美俚〕 = (a member of one of the) First Families of Virginia 贵族,俗不可耐的绅士;贵族派头的,俗不可耐的。

F.G. = **1.** Fire Guards 〔英〕义勇消防队。**2.** foot-guards 〔英〕近卫步兵。

FGA, f.g.a. = **1.** foreign general agent 国外一般代理人。**2.** foreign general average 国外共同海损险。**3.** free of general average 共同海损不保在内。

FGCM = field general court-martial 战地高等军事法庭。

F.G.S. = fellow of the geological society (of London) 〔英〕(伦敦)地质学会会员。

F.G.S.A. = Fellow of the Geological Society of America 美国地质学会会员。

FH, F.H. = fire hydrant 消防栓,消防龙头,灭火龙头。

FHA = **1.** Farmers Home Administration 〔美〕农家信贷管理局。**2.** Federal Housing Administration 〔美〕联邦住房管理局。**3.** Future Homemakers of America 〔美〕美国未来家庭主妇协会。

F.H.S. = Fellow of the Horticultural Society 〔美〕园艺学会会员。

FHWA = Federal Highway Administration 〔美〕联邦公路局。

F.I. = Falkland Islands 福克兰群岛(即马尔维纳斯群岛)〔大西洋〕。

f.i. = for instance 例如。

F.I.A. = Fellow of the Institute of Actuaries 〔英〕保险统计学会会员。

fi·a·cre [fiːˈɑːkə; fiˋɑkə] ***n*.** 法国出租小马车。

fi·an·cé [fiˈɑ̃nsei, Am. ˌfiənˈsei; fɪˋɑ̃nse, ˏfɪənˋse] ***n*.** 〔F.〕未婚夫。

fi·an·cée [fiˈɑ̃nsei, Am. ˌfiənˈsei; fɪˋɑ̃nseɑ̃, ˏfɪənˋse] ***n*.** 〔F.〕未婚妻。

fi·as·co [fiˈæskəu; fɪˋæsko] ***n*.** (*pl*. ~***s***, ~***es***)(演奏等的)大失败;(特指)大为丢脸[出丑]的失败。***end in a* ~** 以完全失败告终。

FIAT [fiət, ˈfiːæt; fiət, ˋfiæt] = *Fabbrica Italiana Automobile Torine* 〔It.〕飞雅特汽车公司。

fi·at [ˈfaiæt, -ət; ˋfaɪæt, -ət] **I *n*. 1.** 命令,法令。**2.** 许可,认可。**II *vt*. 1.** 认可。**2.** 以命令宣布。~ **money** 〔美〕不兑换纸币,流通券。

fib[1] [fib; fɪb] **I *n*.** 小谎,无伤大雅的谎话。**II *vi*.** 撒小谎。**fib·ber *n*.** 惯撒小谎的人。

fib[2] [fib; fɪb] **I *n*.** 〔英〕一拳,一击。**II *vt*.** 击。

fi·ber [ˈfaibə; ˋfaɪbɚ] ***n*.** 〔美〕 = fibre. **~ed *a*.** = fibred. **~fill** = fibrefill. **~-op·tic** = fibre-optic. ~ **optics** = fibre optics.

fi·ber·ize [ˈfaibəraiz; ˋfaɪbərˏaɪz] ***vt*., *vi*.** (使)成纤维,(使)纤维化。

fibr- *comb. f*. 表示"纤维": *fibr*in.

fi·bre [ˈfaibə; ˋfaɪbɚ] ***n*. 1.** 纤维,纤维质;纤维制品,纤维板,硬纸板。**2.**【植】须根,木纹;〔口〕筋。**3.** 性格,素质,骨气。*bast* ~【植】韧皮纤维。*nerve* ~【解】神经纤维。*synthetic* ~ 合成纤维。*a fabric of coarse* [*fine*] ~ 质地粗[细]的织物。*a man of real* ~ 有骨气的男子。~**-board *n*.** 硬纸板;纤维板。~**fill *n*.** (被褥等的)纤维填塞物;合成纤维棉絮。~**glass** 玻璃纤维,玻璃丝。~**-optic *a*.** 纤维光学的。~ **optics 1.** 纤维光学。**2.** 用于纤维光学的纤维。~**scope** (利用光学纤维对胃等进行检查的)纤维镜。**-d *a*.** 含纤维的,纤维质的。**-less *a*.** 无纤维的;无骨气的。

fi·bri·form [ˈfaibrifɔːm; ˋfaɪbrəform] ***a*.** 纤维状的,像

纤维的。

fi·bril [ˈfaibril; ˋfaɪbrəl] ***n*. 1.** 小纤维。**2.**【动】纤丝,原纤维。**3.** 根毛。**-lar, -lar·y** ***a*.**

fi·bril·late [ˈfaibrileit; ˋfaɪbrɪlet] **I** ***a*.** 有原纤维的,有纤维组织的。**II** ***vt*., *vi*. 1.** (使)形成原纤维。**2.** (使)(心脏)作纤维性颤动。

fi·bril·la·tion [ˌfaibriˈleiʃən; ˏfaɪbrɪˋleʃən] ***n*.**【医】纤维性颤动。

fi·bril·li·form [faiˈbrilifɔːm; faɪˋbrɪləform] ***a*.** 小纤维状的。

fi·bril·lose [ˈfaibriləus; ˋfaɪbrɪlos] ***a*.** 小纤维的,发丝的,根毛的;似小纤维的,似发丝的,似根毛的。

fi·brin [ˈfaibrin; ˋfaɪbrɪn] ***n*. 1.**【生化】(血)纤维蛋白。**2.**【植】麸植。

fi·brin·o·gen [faiˈbrinədʒən; faɪˋbrɪnədʒən] ***n*.**【医】(血)纤维蛋白原。

fi·brin·o·gen·ic [ˌfaibrinəuˈdʒenik; ˏfaɪbrɪnoˋdʒɛnɪk] ***a*. 1.** 纤维蛋白原的。**2.** 可形成纤维蛋白原(= fibrinogenous)。

fi·bri·nol·y·sin [ˌfaibrinəuˈlaisin; ˏfaɪbrɪnoˋlaɪsɪn] ***n*.**【生】(血)纤维蛋白溶酶。

fi·bri·nol·y·sis [ˌfaibrinəuˈlaisis; ˏfaɪbrɪnoˋlaɪsɪs] ***n*.**【生】纤维蛋白溶解。**-lyt·ic** [-ˈlitik; -ˋlɪtɪk] ***a*.**

fi·brin·ous [ˈfaibrinəs; ˋfaɪbrɪnəs] ***a*.** 纤维蛋白的;纤维蛋白状的;含纤维蛋白的。

fi·bro·blast [ˈfaibrəublɑːst; ˋfaɪbrəblæst] ***n*.**【生】纤维原细胞。**-blas·tic** [ˌfaibrəuˈblɑːstik; ˏfaɪbroˋblɑstɪk] ***a*.**

F

fi·bro·cyte [ˈfaibrəusait; ˋfaɪbrosaɪt] ***n*.**【生】纤维(母)细胞。

fi·broid [ˈfaibrɔid; ˋfaɪbrɔɪd] **I** ***a*.** 纤维状的;纤维性的;由纤维组织的。**II** ***n*.**【医】纤维瘤。

fi·bro·in [ˈfaibrəuin; ˋfaɪbroɪn] ***n*.**【生化】丝纤朊,丝(心)蛋白。

fi·bro·ma [faiˈbrəumə; faɪˋbromə] ***n*.** (*pl*. **~ta** [-tə; -tə], **~s**)【医】纤维瘤。**-tous** ***a*.**

fi·bro·sis [faiˈbrəusis; faɪˋbrosɪs] ***n*.**【医】纤维变性,纤维化。

fi·bro·si·tis [ˌfaibrəuˈsaitis; ˏfaɪbrəˋsaɪtɪs] ***n*.**【医】纤维织炎。

fi·brous [ˈfaibrəs; ˋfaɪbrəs] ***a*. 1.** 含纤维的,纤维状的。**2.** 能分成纤维的。**3.** 坚韧的,有筋骨的。*the ~ husk of coconut* 椰子的纤维质外壳。~ **glass** 纤维玻璃,玻璃丝。~ **roots**【植】纤维根,须根。~ **tumour**【医】纤维肿(瘤)。**-ly** ***ad*.** **-ness** ***n*.**

fi·bro·vas·cu·lar [ˌfaibrəuˈvæskjulə; ˏfaɪbroˋvæskjələ˞] ***a*.**【植】纤维管(组织)的。

fib·ster [ˈfibstə; ˋfɪbstə˞] ***n*.** 惯撒小谎的人。

fib·u·la [ˈfibjulə; ˋfɪbjələ] ***n*.** (*pl*. **~s**, **-lae** [-liː; -li]) **1.**【解】腓骨。**2.** (古希腊、罗马的)饰针,别针。**-r** ***a*.**

F.I.C. = Fellow of the Institute of Chemistry〔英〕化学学会会员。

-fic *suf*. 构成形容词,表示"…化的","引起…的","做成…的":speci*fic*, terri*fic*.

-fi·ca·tion *suf*. 〔使末尾为 -fy 的动词变成名词〕表示"形成","…化":magni*fication*.

fi·celle [fiˈsel; fɪˋsɛl] ***a*.** 灰褐色的。

fiche [fiːʃ; fɪʃ] ***n*. 1.** 卡片。**2.** 微缩胶片(= microfiche)。

Fich·te [G. ˈfixtə; ˋfɪxtə], **J.G.** 费希特〔1762—1814,德国哲学家〕。

fich·u [ˈfiːʃuː; ˋfiʃu] ***n*.** 三角形女用薄围巾。

fick·le [ˈfikl; ˋfɪkl̩] ***a*.** 轻浮的,反复无常的,易变的。**-ness** ***n*.**

fi·co [ˈfiːkəu; ˋfiko] ***n*.** (*pl*. **~es**) **1.**〔古〕无价值的东西;不足道的事。**2.**〔废〕= fig〔表轻蔑的手势〕。

fic·tile [ˈfiktail; ˋfɪktl̩] **I** ***a*. 1.** 可塑造的,塑造的。**2.** 陶器的,黏土制的。**3.** 顺从的。*a ~ deity* 泥菩萨。*~ ware* 陶器。**II** ***n*.** 陶制器。

fic·tion [ˈfikʃən; ˋfɪkʃən] ***n*. 1.** 小说;虚构的文学作品〔包括小说,剧本等〕。**2.** 编造,想像,虚构;捏造。**3.** 编造的谎话。**4.**【法】假定,拟制。*Fact* [*Truth*] *is stranger than ~* .〔谚〕事实比小说还奇怪。**-eer** ***n*.** (特指粗制滥造的)小说作家。**-er**, **-ist** ***n*.** 小说家〔特指长篇小说作家〕。

fic·tion·al [ˈfikʃənəl; ˋfɪkʃənəl] ***a*.** 虚构的;小说的。**-ly** ***ad*.**

fic·tion·al·ize [ˈfikʃənəlaiz; ˋfɪkʃənəˏlaɪz] ***vt*.** 把…编成小说,使小说化(= fictionize)。**-i·za·tion** [ˌfikʃənəlaiˈzeiʃən; ˏfɪkʃənəlaɪˋzeʃən] ***n*.**

fic·ti·tious [fikˈtiʃəs; fɪkˋtɪʃəs] ***a*. 1.** 虚构的,编造的,想像的;虚伪的。**2.** 假定的,虚设的。**3.** 小说式的。*a ~ bill* [*paper*] 空头支票。*a ~ character* 虚构人物。*a ~ name* 假名。*a ~ price* 虚价。*~ transactions*【商】买空卖空。~ **person**【法】法人。~ **year**[**star**]【天】假想年[天体]。**-ly** ***ad*.** **-ness** ***n*.**

fic·tive [ˈfiktiv; ˋfɪktɪv] ***a*. 1.** 虚构的;想像上的,假定的。**2.** 用想像力进行创作的。~ *tears* 虚情假义的眼泪。**-ly** ***ad*.**

fid [fid; fɪd] ***n*. 1.** 支撑材,固定材;楔状铁栓。**2.**【船】桅栓。**3.** (解绳用的)硬木钉。

-fid *suf*. 表示"…分的","…叉的";【植】"…裂的":bi*fid*, tri*fid*.

fid. = fiduciary.

fid·dle [ˈfidl; ˋfɪdl] **I** ***n*. 1.**〔口〕提琴,提琴类乐器。**2.**【海】防食器滚落的餐具框、栏。**3.** 欺骗行为。***as fit as a ~*** [***flea***] 神采奕奕。***hang up the ~*** 隐退;住手不干。***hang up one's ~ when one comes home*** 在外谈笑兴致高,回家闷头睡懒觉。***have a face as long as a ~*** 板着面孔。***play first ~*** 做领头人,当第一把手,带头。***play second ~*** 做第二把手,充当副手。***play third ~*** 当第三把手,当配角。**II** ***int*.** = ~ sticks. **III** ***vt*. 1.** 用提琴演奏。**2.** 虚度(时光)。**3.**〔俚〕欺骗,伪造(账目等)。— ***vi*. 1.**〔口〕拉提琴。**2.** 虚度光阴,鬼混。**3.** (胡乱地,神经质地)摸弄;玩弄,瞎摆弄。*F- while Rome is burning*. 尽管大难临头,依然歌舞升平。*Stop fiddling around and get to work*. 别再鬼混,去干活吧!~ ***about*** [***around***] 闲逛,混日子。~ ***with*** (胡乱)玩弄,抚摸(*He keeps fiddling with the dials on the radio, he is sure to put it out of order*. 他老是玩弄收音机上的刻度盘,一定会把它弄坏的)。~**back** ***n*.** 小提琴形状的东西。~ **bow** 提琴弓。~ **case** 提琴匣。~**deedee** ***n*.** ***int*.** 胡说,无聊话。~**-faddle**〔口〕**1.** ***n*.** 无聊话,琐碎小事;懒人。**2.** ***a*.** 无聊的,为琐事操心的。**3.** ***int*.** 胡说! **4.** ***vi*.** 无事忙;胡扯。~**head 1.** (提琴头状的)船首饰。**2.** (蕨类植物幼苗的)卷牙(= crosier)。~ **pattern** (刀、叉等柄部的)提琴形。~**stick 1.** 提琴弓。**2.** 无聊事(*not care a ~ stick* 毫不在乎)。~**sticks** ***int*.** 胡说! ~**wood**【植】**1.** 美洲热带地区马鞭草料(*Verbenaceae*)植物或其硬木材。**2.** 同科的其他种树。

fid·dler [ˈfidlə; ˋfɪdlə˞] ***n*. 1.** 拉小提琴的人。**2.** 爱玩乐的人;游手好闲的人;(账目等的)弄虚作假者。**3.** = ~ crab. ***pay the ~*** 承担后果;负担玩乐的费用。~ **crab**【动】招潮属(*Uca*)蟹〔雄蟹的螯一大一小〕,招潮(蟹)。~**'s green**【海】水手的天堂〔指海员上岸饮酒作乐〕。

fid·dley [ˈfidli; ˋfɪdlɪ] ***n*.** = fidley.

fid·dling [ˈfidliŋ; ˋfɪdlɪŋ] ***a*.** 无用的,无足轻重的。

fi·de·i·com·mis·sar·y [ˌfaidiaiˈkɔmisəri; ˏfaɪdɪaɪˋkɑməˏsɛrɪ] **I** ***n*.** (*pl*. **-sar·ies**) 非继承人而经立遗嘱人指定受馈赠者。**II** ***a*.** 命继承人将财产的一部分赠与他人之遗嘱的。

fi·de·ism [ˈfiːdeiˌizm, ˈfaidiːˌizm; ˋfideˏɪzm, ˋfaɪdiˏɪzm] ***n*.**【哲】唯信仰论,信仰主义。**fi·de·is·tic** [ˌfiːdeiˈistik; ˏfideˋɪstɪk] ***a*.** **fi·de·ist** ***n*.** 信仰主义者。

fi·del·i·ty [fiˈdeliti, fai-; fɪˋdɛlətɪ, faɪ-] *n*. **1**. 忠诚,忠实(*to*)。**2**. 真实,翔实;(画等的)逼真度。**3**. (收音、录音设备等的)保真度,重现精度。*a high* ~ *amplifier* 高保真度放大器。~ *to a principle* 忠于原则。*report with* ~ 如实报告。*reproduce (the Ms.) with complete* ~ (照原稿)原样复制。**high** ~ (收、录音设备等的)高保真度[略作 hi-fi]。

fidg·et [ˈfidʒit; ˋfɪdʒɪt] **I** *vi*. 坐立不安,烦躁。— *vt*. **1**. 使烦躁,使坐立不安。**2**. (心不在焉地或心烦意乱地)摆弄。**II** *n*. 〔常 *pl*.〕坐立不安,烦躁;烦躁不安的人。***be in a*** ~ 忐忑不安。***give sb. the*** ~***s*** 使人烦躁不安。***have the*** ~***s*** 心神不安,担心。

fidg·et·y [ˈfidʒiti; ˋfɪdʒɪtɪ] *a*. 坐立不安的,烦躁的;为小事操心的。**-i·ness** *n*.

fid·i·bus [ˈfidibəs; ˋfɪdɪbəs] *n*. (点火用的)纸捻。

fid·ley [ˈfidli; ˋfɪdlɪ] *n*. 【船】锅炉舱顶棚;锅炉(舱)栅。

FI.DO, fi·do [ˈfaiˌdəu; ˋfaɪˏdo] *n*. (飞机跑道使用的)火焰驱雾法(= Fog Investigation Dispersal Operations)。

fi·do [ˈfaidəu; ˋfaɪdo] *n*. 有铸造缺陷的硬币〔系 freaks, irregulars, defects 和 oddities 四词的首字母缩合词〕。

fi·du·cial [fiˈdjuːʃəl; fɪˋduʃəl] *a*. **1**. 【测】基准的。**2**. 有信仰的。**3**. 可靠的,信用的。*a* ~ *line* [*point*] 基准线[准点]。*a* ~ *mark* 准标。

fi·du·ci·ar·y [fiˈdjuːʃəri; fɪˋdjuʃɪˏɛrɪ] **I** *a*. **1**. 信用的,信托的。**2**. 受信托的。**3**. 信用发行的。~ *capacity* [*character*] 受托人身分。*a* ~ *guardian* 受托监护人。*a* ~ *institution* 信用机关。~ *issue* (纸币的)信用发行。*a* ~ *loan* 信用贷款。~ *notes* 无现金储备而发行的纸币。~ *property* 受托保管的财产。*a* ~ *relation* 信托关系。**II** *n*. 被信托者,受托人。**-ar·i·ly** *ad*.

fi·dus A·cha·tes [ˈfaidəs əˈkeitiːz; ˋfaɪdəs əˋketiz] 〔L.〕忠实的朋友;忠实的追随者;忠仆。

fie [fai; faɪ] *int*. 呸! ***Fie upon you!*** 去你的! ***Fie, for shame!*** 呸,不要脸!

fief [fiːf; fif] *n*. 采邑,封地。

fie-fie [ˈfaifai; ˋfaɪˏfaɪ] *a*. 不像样子的,出丑的。

Field [fiːld; fild] *n*. 菲尔德〔姓氏〕。

field [fiːld; fild] **I** *n*. **1**. 原野,旷野;(海、空、冰雪等的)茫茫一片。**2**. 田地,牧场;割草场;〔*pl*.〕〔集合词〕土地,田野;(地上的)庄稼。**3**. 广场,工作场。**4**. (矿物的)产地,煤田,油田。**5**. 战斗,战役;战场,战地,作战训练[演习]区域。**6**. 【体】(跑道以内的)运动场;田赛场(*opp*. track),赛球场,【棒球】外场;(全体)外场守场员;(全体)运动员;(全体)游猎者;【赛马】(热门马以外的)马。**7**. 活动地,舞台;范围,方面,界(如学术界)。**8**. 【物】场;力场;区;【数】域;(望远镜等的)视界,视域。**9**. (画等的)底子,【影,电视】画面,镜头。**10**. 影响人们行为的各种因素的综合;环境。**11**. 扫描场〔尤指隔行扫描制的半帧〕;【计】信息[符号]组,字段。*beast of the* ~ 野兽。*a* ~ *of sea* [*sky*] 海域[天空]。*a snow* ~ 雪原。*a wheat* ~ 小麦地。*a coal* ~ 煤田。*a bleaching* ~ 漂白场。*a flying* ~ 飞机场。*a good* ~ 坚强的选手阵容。*gravitational* ~ 重力场,引力场。*a hard-fought* ~ 激战(地)。*magnet* ~ 磁场。*a maiden* ~ 未采的油田[矿区]。*real number* ~ 【数】实数域。*root* ~ 【数】根域。*a single* ~ 一个对一个地打,单打。*terraced* ~*s* 梯田。*the* ~ *of battle* 战场。~ *of force* 【物】力场。*a* ~ *of research* 研究范围。*a new* ~ *of inquiry* 研究的新领域。*a* ~ *of observation* [*view, vision*] 视界;视野。*the visual* ~ 视界,雷达可见区。***be in the*** ~ **1**. 从军,参战,参加竞赛。**2**. 【物】在某种物理能的作用范围内。***be out in left*** ~ 〔美俚〕发疯。***conquer the*** ~ 获胜,占优势。***enter the*** ~ 上场,上阵。***fair*** ~ ***and no favour*** 均等的比赛条件,公平无私。~ ***of fire*** 【军】射界。~ ***of honour*** 决斗场,战场。***hold*** [***keep, maintain***] ***the*** ~ 守住阵地。***in one's own*** ~ 在自己本行内。***in the*** ~ **1**. 实地,在现场。**2**. 在某一行中。***lead the*** ~ 带头追猎。***leave sb. a clear*** ~ 给人行动自由。***leave sb. the*** ~ 输给某人。***leave the*** ~ ***open*** 不加干涉。***lose the*** ~ 败退。***play the*** ~ 〔美俚〕交好几个异性朋友;避免对专一的对象承担义务。***take the*** ~ 出阵,开战。***take to the*** ~ 接防,接守。***win the*** ~ 〔古〕取得胜利,获胜。**II** *vt*. **1**. (棒球、板球运动中)接[截](球),守(球)。**2**. 使(球队或球员)入场,把…投入战场。**3**. 把(谷物等)曝露场上。**4**. 当场圆满答复。— *vi*. (棒球赛等)担任外场员或守队队员;【赛马】冷门马。**III** *a*. **1**. 田间的,野生的;野外的。**2**. 实地的。~ *care* 田间管理。~ *crops* 大田作物。~ *flowers* 野花。~ *operations* 野外作业。*a* ~ *worker* 实地工作者。~ **allowance** (军官)战地津贴。~ **ambulance** 战地救护车,野战救护队。~ **army** 野战军。~ **artillery** 〔总称〕野战炮,野战炮兵。~ **ball** 【棒球】外野球。~ **book** 野外工作记录本。~ **capacity** 土壤容水量。~ **corn** 饲料玉米。~ **day** **1**. 野外演习日。**2**. 户外集会。**3**. 体育比赛日。**4**. 野外科学活动日。**5**. 特别愉快的时刻,获得意外成功的时刻。**6**. 有重要活动的日子。~ **dressing** (战场上的)应急治疗。~ **driver** 〔美〕兜捕无主家畜的警察。~ **editor** 〔美〕(报馆的)地方通讯员;外埠通讯员。~ **effect transistor** 【无】场效果晶体管。~ **event** 【体】田赛。~ **exercise** 野外演习。~ **glasses** 双筒望远镜。~ **goal** **1**. (橄榄球)射中可得三分的球。**2**. (篮球)投进得二分的球。~ **grade** 【军】校级。~ **gun** 野战炮。~ **hand** **1**. (农场的)农工。**2**. 〔美〕干农活的黑人。~ **hockey** 曲棍球(= hockey)。~ **hospital** 野战医院。~ **house** (运动场周围的)更衣室[贮藏室]等房屋。~**-ice** 【地】冰原冰。~ **lens** **1**. 【物】向场(透)镜。**2**. (显微镜等的)物镜。~ **mail** 军邮。~ **man** (*pl*. **-men**) 外务员〔推销员或其他不在公司内从事业务活动的人员〕。~ **magnet** 【物】场磁体,场磁铁。~ **marshal** (英)陆军元帅,最高级陆军将官。~ **mouse** 野鼠,田鼠。~ **music** **1**. 军乐队员〔号手、鼓手等〕。**2**. 军乐。~ **night** 有重要活动的夜晚。~ **officer** 陆军校级军官。~ **pea** 【植】紫花豌豆。~ **piece** 野战炮。~ **ration** 战地口粮。~ **secretary** 地方联络员。~**-sequential** *a*. 【无】(彩色电视)场序制的,帧序制的。~ **service** 野战勤务。~**s-man** *n*. = ~er. ~ **sparrow** 【动】原野春雀(*Spizella pusilla*)〔北美的一种褐色白肚麻雀〕。~ **sports** **1**. 野外运动。**2**. 田赛。~ **strip** 拆卸检修(枪炮)。~ **survey** 实地调查,实地考察。~ **telegraph** 军用电报,野战电报机。~ **telegraphy** 军用电报学。~**-test** *vt*. 对…作现场试验[工作试验,野外试验]。~ **theory** 【物】场论。~ **trial** 猎狗的现场追猎试验。~ **trip** (学生)校外旅行考察,(科研人员)社会调查。~ **umpire** 【棒球】垒裁判员。~**ward(s)** *ad*. 向原野,向田野。~ **winding** 【物】(磁)场绕组。~ **work** [**survey, study**] **1**. 野战工事。**2**. 野外测量[考察],实地调查,现场工作。**-er** *n*. (棒球、板球的)外场员,守队队员。

field·er [ˈfiːldə; ˋfildɚ] *n*. 【棒球、板球】外场员,外野手;守队队员。~***'s choice*** 外场员的自由选择〔不扔球给一垒而扔给其他的垒〕。

field·fare [ˈfiːldˌfεə; ˋfildˏfɛr] *n*. (冬季迁飞英国的)北欧鹅。

Field·ing [ˈfiːldiŋ; ˋfɪldɪŋ] *n*. **1**. 菲尔丁〔姓氏〕。**2**. **Henry** ~ 亨利·菲尔丁〔1707—1754,英国小说家〕。

field·ing [ˈfiːldiŋ; ˋfildɪŋ] *n*. 【棒球】守备。

fiend [fiːnd; find] *n*. **1**. 魔鬼;[the F-] 魔王。**2**. 恶毒的人,刻毒鬼。**3**. 〔俚〕…迷,…狂。**4**. 能手,神手。*a dance* ~ 跳舞迷。*an opium* ~ 鸦片鬼。*a theatre* ~ 戏迷。*a* ~ *at mathematics* 数学能手。**-like** *a*. 恶魔似的。

fiend·ish [ˈfiːndiʃ; ˋfindɪʃ] *a*. 恶魔(似)的;恶毒的,残忍的。**-ly** *ad*. **-ness** *n*.

fierce [fiəs; fɪrs] *a*. **1**. 残忍的,凶猛的。**2**. 猛烈的。**3**. 〔英方〕精力旺盛的。**4**. 狂热的,强烈的。**5**. 〔美〕令人难受的,讨厌的。~ *anger* 愤怒。~ *look* 可怕的样子。~ *heat* 酷暑。*a* ~ *offensive* 猛攻。*a* ~ *tempest* 狂风

F

暴雨。~ *pain* 剧痛。**-ly** *ad*. **-ness** *n*.

fi·e·ri fa·ci·as [ˈfaiərai ˈfeiʃiæs; ˋfaɪəraɪ ˋfeʃɪæs]〔L.〕【法】强制执行命令,扣押债务人动产令〔略 *fi. fa.*〕。

fi·er·y [ˈfaiəri; ˋfaɪərɪ] *a*. (***fier·i·er***; ***-i·est***) **1**. 火的,火焰的;燃烧的;火似的;如火如荼的。**2**. (眼光)炯炯有神的。**3**. 热烈的,激烈的,急躁的,(马等)暴躁的。**4**. 易燃烧的,易爆炸的。**5**. 红肿的,火热的,火红的。~ *eyes* 闪闪发光的眼睛。~ *winds* 热风。~ *heat* 炎热。~ *red* 火红色。~ *revolutionary struggles* 轰轰烈烈的革命斗争。*a* ~ *speech* 激昂的演说。*a* ~ *steed* [*courser*] 悍马。*a* ~ *taste* 刺激性的味道。~ *temper* 暴躁的脾气。*a* ~ *sore* 红肿。***go through a ~ trial*** 经过千锤百炼。~ **cross 1**. 焦十字,血十字〔四端烧焦或染血的木十字架,古苏格兰高地人氏族出战的信号〕。**2**. 火十字〔四端燃烧的木十字架,美国迫害黑人的三 K 党持之以制造恐怖〕。**fi·er·i·ly** *ad*. **fi·er·i·ness** *n*.

fi·es·ta [ˈfiːestɑː, fiˈestə; ˋfiɛstɑ, fiˋɛstə] *n*. **1**. 宗教节日。**2**. 喜庆日子;假日。

fi. fa. [ˈfaifei; ˋfaɪfe] =〔L.〕*fieri facias*.【法】扣押债务人动产令。

fife [faif; faɪf] **I** *n*. (主指军乐队的)笛子。**II** *vi*., *vt*. 吹(笛子),用笛子吹奏(歌曲)。~ **rail**【海】桅脚栅栏,桅边系索杆。

fif·er [ˈfaifə; ˋfaɪfɚ] *n*. 吹笛人,笛手。

FIFO [ˈfaifəu; ˋfaɪfo] = first in first out 先进先出。

fif·teen [ˈfifˈtiːn; ˋfɪfˋtin] **I** *num*. 十五。**II** *n*. **1**. 十五;十五个(人、物);十五岁;十五点钟(即下午三点);十五的记号。**2**. 十六世纪。**3**. (网球赢得第一球的得分叫法)15点,一分。**4**.〔英〕橄榄球队〔由 15 人组成〕。*in the ~ fifties* 在十六世纪五十年代。~ **all** (在一盘网球中)双方各得一分。~ **forty** (在一盘网球中)发球人得 15 点,接球人得 40 点,即 1 比 3。~ **love** (在一盘网球中)发球人得 15 点,接球人得 0 点,即 1 比 0。~**fold** *a*., *ad*. 十五倍。

fif·teenth [ˈfifˈtiːnθ; ˋfɪfˋtinθ] **I** *num*. **1**. 第十五。**2**. 十五分之一。**II** *n*. **1**. 每月的第十五日。**2**.【乐】(第)十五度音程。

fifth [fifθ; fɪfθ] **I** *num*. **1**. 第五。**2**. 五分之一。**II** *n*. **1**.〔美〕五分之一加仑(瓶)。**2**. 每月的第五日。**3**.【乐】五度音程,五度和音,第五音,属音。**4**.〔*pl*.〕五级品。**5**.〔F-〕= Fifth Amendment. *the ~ act* 第五幕;终幕;(人生的)晚境。*one ~* 五分之一。*three ~s* 五分之三。*augmented* [*diminished*] ~【乐】增[减]五度。*smite* (*under*) *the ~ rib* 刺死,给以致命打击。**F- Amendment**《美国宪法修正案》第五条〔规定不得强迫刑事犯罪者自证其罪〕。**F- Avenue** (美国纽约市最繁华的)第五号街。~ **column** 第五纵队。~ **columnism** 第五纵队战术,利用内奸。~ **columnist** 第五纵队队员。**F- Monarchy**【宗】基督的王国。**F- monarchy men**【英史】十七世纪热烈盼望基督再次降临的基督教徒。**F- Republic** (法兰西)第五共和国〔成立于 1958 年〕。~ **wheel 1**. 半拖车接轮;转向轮;试验(汽车行车距离的)专用轮。**2**. 备用轮。**3**. 多余的人[物]。**-ly** *ad*.

fif·ti·eth [ˈfiftiiθ; ˋfɪftɪɪθ] *num*., *n*. 第五十;五十分之一。

fif·ty [ˈfifti; ˋfɪftɪ] **I** *num*. 五十,五十个。**II** *n*. **1**. 五十个人[物];五十岁;五十的记号。**2**.〔*pl*.〕五十年代;〔*pl*.〕五十到五十九岁的时期。*in nineteen ~* 在 1950 年。*the fifties* 五十几(岁);(一世纪中的)五十年代。*in the nineteen fifties* (略 1950's) 在二十世纪五十年代。**III** *a*. 许多的。*I have ~ things to tell you*. 我有许多话要和你说。

fif·ty-fif·ty [ˈfiftiˈfifti; ˋfɪftɪˋfɪftɪ] *a*., *ad*.〔口〕均摊,各半。*go ~ with sb*. 与人平分(损失均摊)。*on a ~ basis* 平分,对等。

fif·ty-fold [ˈfiftifəuld; ˋfɪftɪˏfold] *a*., *ad*. 五十倍。

fig[1] [fig; fɪg] *n*. **1**.【植】无花果,无花果树,无花果属植物。**2**. 少许,一点儿;无价值的东西,琐事。**3**.〔美〕(烟草等的)小片。**4**. 表轻蔑的手势〔把拇指夹在两指之间或塞入口中〕。***A ~ for this***! 有什么了不起! ***Adam ~*** 香蕉。***Chinese ~*** 柿子。~***'s end*** 无价值的东西。***not care a ~*** 毫不在乎。***not worth a ~*** 毫不足取,一文不值。~ **eater**【动】无花果虫〔成虫靠食成熟水果为生,也称 green June kettle〕。~ **leaf 1**. 无花果叶。**2**. (雕塑)裸体像的遮羞叶,遮羞布。~ **marigold**【植】日中花属(松叶菊属)植物。~ **tree** 无花果树。~ **wasp**【动】无花果小蜂,榕小蜂。

fig[2] [fig; fɪg]〔口〕**I** *n*. **1**. 服装。**2**. 健康状况。***be in full ~*** 盛装。***be in good ~*** 情况好,精神好。**II** *vt*. (***-gg-***) 使盛装,打扮。~ *out* [*up*] *a horse* 把马装饰起来。

fig. = figurative(ly); figure(s).

fight [fait; faɪt] **I** *vi*. (***fought*** [fɔːt; fɔt]; ***fought***) **1**. 打仗,搏斗,打架。**2**. 战斗,奋斗,斗争。**3**. 当职业拳击手。— *vt*. **1**. 与…作战,打(仗)。**2**. 争取,争夺。**3**. 使斗,斗。**4**. 指挥,操纵。~ *a battle* 打一仗。~ *the enemy head on* 正面进攻敌人,打硬仗。~ *the fire* [*gale*] 与火灾[烈风]战斗。~ *gun* 指挥开炮。~ *a prize* 夺奖。*The captain fought his ship well*. 舰长出色地指挥军舰作战。~ ***back*** 抵抗,还击。~ ***down*** 打败,压服。~ ***for a cause*** 为主义战斗。~ ***for existence*** 为生存而斗争。~ (***for***) ***one's own hand*** 争夺私利。~ ***hand to hand*** 短兵相接。~ ***it out*** 打个青红皂白,一决雌雄。~ ***like kilkenny cats*** 死拼,斗得两败俱伤。~ ***off*** 打退;竭力摆脱,克服。~ ***on*** 继续战斗,继续斗争。~ ***out*** 打出结果。~ ***shy*** (***of***) **1**. 回避,躲避。**2**. 避开正面搏斗(*The boy ~s shy of girls*. 这个男孩子怕和女孩子接触。~ *shy of an invitation* 谢绝邀请)。~ ***to a finish*** 打到底。~ ***together*** 打成一团。~ ***tooth and nail*** 狠狠地打;拼命干。~ ***under way*** (军舰)边走边打。~ ***up against*** 与…力战[苦斗]。**II** *n*. **1**. 战斗;搏斗;争吵,打架;斗争,竞争。**2**. 战斗力,斗争性,斗志。**3**. 拳击赛。*a free ~* 乱斗。*a hand to hand ~* 格斗,肉搏战。*a prize ~* 职业拳击赛。*a running ~* 追击战。*a sham ~* 假打;〔英〕模拟战。*a stand up ~* 光明正大的战斗。*a straight ~* 一对一的二人竞选。*a ~ for higher wages* 为增加工资而斗争。*They have plenty of ~ in them*. 他们斗志旺盛。*take the ~ out of the enemy troops* 瓦解敌军斗志。***give*** [***make***] ***a ~*** 打一仗。***put up a good ~*** 善战,善斗。***show ~*** 显示斗志,不示弱。~**-back** *n*. 回击,反击。~**-off** *n*. (拳击等的)决赛。

fight·er [ˈfaitə; ˋfaɪtɚ] *n*. **1**. 战士,兵士;斗争者,奋斗者。**2**.【空】战斗机,歼击机。**3**. 好斗的人。**4**. (职业)拳击手。*an escort ~* 护航战斗机。*a jet ~* 喷气式战斗机。~**-bomber** 战斗轰炸机。~ **escort** (护送轰炸机的)护航战斗机。~**-interceptor** 战斗截击机。~ **plane** 战斗机,歼击机。

fight·ing [ˈfaitiŋ; ˋfaɪtɪŋ] **I** *a*. **1**. 战斗的,斗争的,搏斗的。**2**. 适于战斗的。**3**. 好战的,好斗的。**4**. 容易引起争斗的,挑战性的。*in ~ condition* 处在适于战斗的状态,斗志旺盛。~ *words* 挑战性的话,招引是非的话。**II** *n*. 战争,战斗,作战。*a ~ field* 战场。*hand-to-hand ~* 短兵相接,肉搏战。*house-to-house ~* = *street ~* 巷战。~ *formation* 战斗队形。~ *men* 战斗员,战士。~ *spirit* 战斗意志。~ **chance** 经过努力获得成功的机会。~ **chair** 搏斗椅,钓鱼椅〔牢固钉在船上供钓鱼者与上钩的鱼搏斗的坐椅〕。~ **cock** 斗鸡,好斗的人(*feel like a ~ cock* 觉得斗志昂扬。*live like ~ cocks* 过奢侈生活)。**F- French** (在第二次世界大战中,巴黎沦陷后继续抗战的)战斗的法国人。~ **top** 军舰桅顶上的轻武器发射台[观测台]。

fig·ment [ˈfigmənt; ˋfɪgmənt] *n*. 虚构;虚构的事物。

fig·u·line [ˈfigjulin, -ˈlain; ˋfɪgjəlɪn, -ˋlaɪn] **I** *a*.〔罕〕陶土的;陶土状的;陶制的。**II** *n*. 陶[瓷]器,陶瓷像。

fig·ur·a·bi·li·ty [ˌfigjurəˈbiliti; ˏfɪgjʊrəˋbɪlətɪ] *n*. 能成形性,能定形性。

fig·ur·a·ble [ˈfigjurəbl; ˋfɪgjʊrəbl̩] *a*. 能成形的,能定形的。

fig·u·ral [ˈfigjurəl; ˋfɪgjərəl] *a*. 1. 人物[动物]形像的。2. (绘画等)以人物[动物]形像构成的;以人物[动物]形像来表现的。3. 比喻的。*the ~ representation* 人物画像。

fig·u·rant [ˈfigjurənt; ˋfɪgjərænt] *n*. 〔F.〕(芭蕾舞的)一般(男)演员;配角。

fig·u·rante [ˌfigjuˈrɑːnt; ˏfɪgjəˋrænt] *n*. 〔F.〕(芭蕾舞的)一般女演员;女配角。

fig·u·ra·tion [ˌfigjuˈreiʃən; ˏfɪgjəˋreʃən] *n*. 1. 定形,成形(作用,过程)。2. 外形,轮廓。3. 比喻表达法。4. 图案装饰法,图案[符号]表现法;图像,形像。5.【乐】(音、旋律的)修饰。

fig·u·ra·tive [ˈfigjurətiv; ˋfɪgjərətɪv] *a*. 1. 比喻的,形容的(*opp*. literal); 修饰多的,比喻多的,词藻华丽的,象征性的。2. 用图形[形像]表现的。*the ~ art* 造形美术[绘画与雕刻]。*a ~ design* 象征的设计。*in a ~ sense* 在比喻的意义上。*a ~ style* 华丽的文体。**-ly** *ad*. **-ness** *n*.

fig·ure [ˈfigə, Am. ˈfigjər; ˋfɪgjɚ, ˋfɪgɚ] **I** *n*. 1. 外形,形状,外观;姿态。2. 画像,塑像。3. 图形,图案;插图;图表。4. 人影,人形;人物。5. 风度,态度,样子。6. 数字,位数;符号;数值;价格,〔*pl*.〕计算,算术;【几何】图形。7. 修辞手段,修辞格;【逻】(三段论法的)格;【乐】音型;(舞蹈中的)舞步形式,(溜冰,飞行的)花样,花式;动作所形成的轨迹。*a woman of good ~* 身材好看的女人。*a slender ~* 苗条的身段。*a fine ~ of a man* 优美的体态。*a half-length ~* 半身像。*a rectangular ~* 矩形。*the great ~s of history* 历史上的大人物。*a ~ of fun* 滑稽有趣的人物。*a person of ~* 地位高的人。*significant ~s* 有效数字。*double* [*three*] *~s* 两[三]位数。*an income of five ~s* 五位数字[数以万计]的收入。*cite* [*give*] *~s* 列举数字。***be good at ~*** 会计算。***cut* [*make*] *a ~*** 露头角。***cut* [*make*] *a brilliant* [*conspicuous, fine, good, great, splendid*] *~*** 露头角,出风头。***cut* [*make*] *a poor* [*little, ridiculous, sorry*] *~*** 出丑。***cut no ~*** 〔美〕没有什么突出表现,默默无闻。***do things on the big ~*** 〔美〕大干特干。***~ of merit*** 【物】灵敏值,优质。***~ of speech*** 形像化说法,形像化比喻。***get* (*sth*.) *at a low* [*high*] *~*** 低价[高价]买得(某物)。***Go ~***. 请参见数据〔文章中用语〕。***go* [*come*] *the big* [*whole*] *~*** 〔美〕干到底,彻底地干。***in round ~s*** 用整数表示;大概,总而言之。***keep one's ~*** 保持体态苗条。***lay ~*** (画家用的)人体模型;虚构人物;傀儡。***make an imposing ~*** 仪表堂堂。***miss a* [*one's*] *~*** 〔美〕失算,铸成大错。**II** *vt*. 1. 用图表示;用塑像等形像表现;描写。2. 加图案于,画图案于,加花样于。3. 想像。4. 表示,象征,用比喻表现。5. 用数字表示;计算;估计。6. 〔口〕推测,判断,认为。7. 懂,领会。*~ the loss* 计算亏损。*Saints ~d on the wall*. 画在壁上的圣徒像。*the ~ cloth* 印花布。*I ~ he got angry*. 我想他是生气了。*He ~d himself a good scholar*. 他自以为很有学问。*She ~d the whole scheme at once*. 她立刻就懂得了整个计划。— *vi*. 1. (作为…而)出现;扮演;突出,显露头角。2. 计算。3. 考虑,估计。4. 跳某种(花式)舞步。5. 〔美俚〕有道理,合乎情理。*He ~d in the war*. 他在战争中出了名。*~ largely in a narrative* 在故事中极突出。*~ for an election* 筹划选举。*Sure, that ~s*. 没错,那是合情合理的。***~ as*** 扮演…角色。***~ for*** 谋取,企图获得。***~ in*** 1. 算进。2. 参加。***~ on*** 1. 依赖,指望。2. 仔细考虑;计划;估计。***~ out*** 1. 算出,作出。2. 估计,推测;解决;了解。3. 〔口〕确定;发现,想出。***~ out at*** 总共…,合计…。***~ up*** 〔美〕总计。**~ eight** 8字形(如绳结、溜冰花式;飞行花式等)。**~-of-eight knot** 八字结〔绳结的一种〕。**~ skating** 花式溜冰。**~some** *a*. 有些显著的。

fig·ured [ˈfigəd; ˋfɪgjɚd] *a*. 1. 有形状的,有图形表示的。2. 有花纹的,带图案的;富有文采的;【乐】华丽的,加了花的。**~ fabrics** 有花纹的织品。**~ iron** 型钢。**~ satin** 花缎。

fig·ure·head [ˈfigəhed; ˋfɪgjɚˏhɛd] *n*. 1. 船头雕饰;破浪神的雕像。2. (有名无实的)傀儡领袖。3. 〔谑〕嘴脸。

fig·u·rine [ˈfigjuriːn; ˋfɪgjərin] *n*. 小人像。

fig·wort [ˈfigwəːt; ˋfɪgˏwɝt] *n*. 【植】玄参,玄参属植物。

Fi·ji [fiːˈdʒiː, ˈfiːdʒi; fiˋdʒi, ˋfidʒɪ] *n*. 1. 斐济〔西太平洋〕。2. 斐济人,斐济语。

Fi·ji·an [fiːˈdʒiːən; fiˋdʒiən] *a*., *n*. 1. (西太平洋)斐济群岛(的);斐济群岛人(的)。2. 斐济语(的)。

fi·la [ˈfailə; ˋfaɪlə] *n*. filum 的复数。

fil·a·gree [ˈfiləgriː; ˋfɪləgri] *n*. = filigree.

fil·a·ment [ˈfiləmənt; ˋfɪləmənt] *n*. 1. 细丝,丝状体。2.【纺】长丝;单纤维。3.【植】(雄蕊的)花丝。4.【电】灯丝;丝极;游丝。**~ breakdown**【电】灯丝击穿。**~ current** 灯丝电流。**-ed** *a*. 有细丝的。

fi·lar [ˈfailə; ˋfaɪlɚ] *a*. 1. 线的,丝的;丝状或多线物的。2. (测微计的)视界里划有细线的。

fi·lar·i·a [ˈfilɛəriə; ˋfɪlɛrɪə] *n*. 【动】(寄生人体内的)丝虫。

fi·lar·i·al [fiˈlɛəriəl; fɪˋlɛrɪəl] *a*. 丝虫的,带丝虫的,丝虫引起的。*~ disease*【医】丝虫病。

fil·a·ri·a·sis [ˌfiləˈraiəsis; ˏfɪləˋraɪəsɪs] *n*. 【医】丝虫病。

fil·a·ture [ˈfilətʃə; ˋfɪlətʃɚ] *n*. 1. 缫丝。2. 缫丝机。3. 缫丝厂,制丝厂。**~ silk** 机缫生丝,厂丝。

fil·bert [ˈfilbət; ˋfɪlbɚt] *n*. 1.【植】欧洲榛,欧洲榛果实,榛果实。2. 〔美俚〕狂热者。*a football ~* 足球迷。

filch [filtʃ; fɪltʃ] *vt*. 偷窃(小物品)。— *vi*. 小摸小偷。**-er** *n*. 小偷。

file[1] [fail; faɪl] **I** *n*. 1. 纸夹,文件夹。2. 钉成册的文件,档案,卷宗,案卷,合订本。3.【计】外存贮器,存贮带。4. 行列;【军】纵列(*opp*. rank)。5. (象棋盘上的)纵线。*~ computer* 编目计算机。*a column of ~s* 若干纵列组成的队伍〔如三路或四路纵队〕。*a ~ of men* 执行任务的二人小分队。*a blank ~*【军】(无后列时的)单列。*main ~* 主文件;主存贮器。***~ by ~*** 一列一列,陆续。***half a ~*** 二人小分队中的一人。***in ~*** 排成二列纵队;挨次,鱼贯地。***in single* [*Indian*] *~*** 成一路纵队,成单行。***keep on* [*in*] *a ~*** 合订保存;归档。***on ~*** 合订成册,存档。**II** *vt*. 1. 按次序订存,编档保存,汇存。2. 〔美〕提起,提出。3. 命令(军队等)排成纵队行进。4. 用电报[话]发稿。*~ an information* 起诉,告发。*~ a complaint with the authorities* 向当局申诉。— *vi*. 排成纵队前进;申请 (*for*); 备案作候选人。*F- left* [*right*](口令)各队向左(右)(走)! ***~ away* [*off*]** 排成纵队出发。***~ in*** 鱼贯而入,陆续编入。***~ out*** 鱼贯而出。**~ clerk** 档案[卷宗]管理员。**~ closer** (负责保持队形整齐的)队列官。**~ memory** 外存贮器。**~ signal** 档案分类标签。

file[2] [fail; faɪl] **I** *n*. 1. 锉刀。2. 〔英俚〕滑头。*block ~* 大方锉。*a close ~* 吝啬鬼。*an old* (*a deep*) *~* 老滑头。***bite* [*gnaw, lick*] *a ~*** 自找苦吃;徒劳。**II** *vt*. 锉;磨炼(品性等);推敲(文章等)。*~ one's fingernails* 锉指甲。— *vi*. 用锉刀锉。***~ away* [*off*]** 锉去(锈等)。***~ down*** (用锉)锉开,锉坏。***~ one's teeth*** 锉牙齿;咬牙切齿。***~ out*** 锉出。

file·fish [ˈfailˌfiʃ; ˋfaɪlˏfɪʃ] *n*. 【动】1. 鲀。2. = triggerfish.

fil·e·mot [ˈfilimɔt; ˋfɪləˏmɑt] *n*., *a*. 枯叶色(的);黄褐色(的)。

fi·let [fiˈlei, ˈfiːlei; fɪˋle, ˋfɪle] *n*. 〔F.〕1. 肉片,鱼片。2. 方网眼花边 (= ~ lace)。*~ net* 方网眼的网。**~ de sole** 鲽鱼片。**~ mignon** 烤里脊肉片。

fil·i·al [ˈfiljəl; ˋfɪljəl] ***a*.** **1.** 子女的,孝顺的。**2.**【生】子代的,后代的。~ *affection* 子爱。~ *duty* 做儿女的义务。~ *obedience* 孝顺。~ *piety* 孝道。*a* ~ *generation*【生】杂交后代,子代。***first*** ~ 杂交第一代,子一代〔略作 F_1〕。***second*** ~ 子二代〔略: F_2〕。**-ly** ***ad*.** **-ness** ***n*.**

fil·i·ar·chy [ˌfiliˈɑːki; ˏfɪlɪˋɑkɪ] ***n*.** (父母、祖父母等长辈围着子女或孙儿女转的)"小皇帝"现象。

fil·i·ate [ˈfilieit; ˋfɪlɪˏet] ***vt*.** **1.** = affiliate. **2.**【法】确定(私生子的)父亲。

fil·i·a·tion [ˌfiliˈeiʃən; ˏfɪlɪˋeʃən] ***n*.** **1.** 父子关系;【法】私生子父亲的鉴定;私生子的确认。**2.** 起源,由来;血统,出身;(语言等的)分支。**3.** 关系的确定。*determine the* ~ *of a language* 确定一种语言的来源。~ *of manuscripts* 对手稿的鉴定。

fil·i·beg [ˈfilibeg; ˋfɪləˏbɛg] ***n*.** 〔Scot.〕 = kilt.

fil·i·bus·ter [ˈfilibʌstə; ˋfɪləˏbʌstɚ] **I** ***n*.** **1.**【史】掠夺兵,暴兵;海盗。**2.** 〔美〕(用冗长的发言)妨碍会议的议员;会议妨碍行为。**II** ***vt*.,** ***vi*.** **1.** 掠夺,侵夺。**2.** 〔美〕(因发言冗长)妨碍(会议的进程)。

fil·i·cide [ˈfiliˌsaid; ˋfɪlɚˏsaɪd] ***n*.** **1.** 杀子女者。**2.** 杀子女的行为。**fil·i·cid·al** ***a*.**

fil·i·cite [ˈfilisait; ˋfɪlɪˏsaɪt] ***n*.** 蕨类化石。

fil·i·form [ˈfilifɔːm; ˋfɪlɪfɔrm] ***a*.** 丝状的,线状的,纤维状的。

fil·i·gree [ˈfiləgriː; ˋfɪləˏgri] **I** ***n*.** **1.** 金银细丝工艺。**2.** 华而不实的东西。**II** ***a*.** 金银细丝工艺的。~ *work* 金银细丝工艺(制品)。**III** ***vt*.** **1.** 用金银细丝饰品装饰。**2.** 用华而不实的饰品装饰。

F

fil·ing [ˈfailiŋ; ˋfaɪlɪŋ] ***n*.** **1.** 锉;锉磨;锉法。**2.** 〔常 *pl*.〕锉屑。*iron* ~*s* 铁锉屑。

Fil·i·pine [ˈfiliˌpiːn; ˋfɪləˏpin] ***a*.** = Philippine.

Fil·i·pi·no [ˌfiliˈpiːnəu; ˏfɪləˋpino] **I** ***n*.** (*pl*. ~*s*) (尤指信基督教的)菲律宾人。**II** ***a*.** = Philippine.

fill [fil; fɪl] **I** ***vt*.** **1.** 注满,装满,装填,填充。**2.** (风)张满(帆),使(帆背)受风。**3.** 充满,充实(知识等);普及。**4.** 使满足;使吃饱。**5.** 占(地位);补(缺),填(空),任(职)。**6.** 〔美〕满足(要求等);供应(定货);执行(命令等)。**7.** 配(药方)。**8.** 把…搀成杂质品。~ *the heart with hope* 使心里充满希望。*a meal that* ~*s sb*. 一顿饱餐。~ *an office satisfactorily* 尽职。~ *an order* 供应定货。~ *a prescription* 照方配药。— ***vi*.** **1.** 充满。**2.** 张满帆。**3.** 堵塞。*The well* ~*s with water*. 井里充满了水。*The sails* ~*ed*. 船张满帆。*My heart* ~*ed at the words*. 听到那话,我心中感到难过。~ ***away***【海】转帆向风,顺风前进。~ ***in*** 填充,装满;填写 (~ *in an application* 填申请书)。~ (***sb*.**) ***in about*** [***on***] ... 〔美口〕对(某人)提供关于…的情况。~ ***one's mind*** 充实知识,学习。~ ***sb.'s place*** 代替。~ ***out*** **1.** ***vt*.** 使充分,使完全;使充实;使扩张,使膨胀;倾注(酒等);〔美〕填满(空白)。**2.** ***vi*.** 满杯;长大;变圆;长胖。~ ***the bill*** 如约完成;满足需要,最为适合。~ ***up*** **1.** ***vt*.** 装满,填满;补足;填写。**2.** ***vi*.** 充满;(戏院等)客满;填塞,淤塞。~ ***up time*** 消磨时光。**II** ***n*.** **1.** 充满,饱满。**2.** 填塞物;填土,填方,路堤。*a* ~ *of tobacco* 一袋烟,一烟斗烟草。***drink*** [***eat***] ***one's*** ~ ***of*** 喝[吃]饱。***have one's*** ~ ***of sorrow*** 饱经忧患。***take one's*** ~ ***of rest*** 充分休息。***grumble one's*** ~ 发够牢骚。***weep one's*** ~ 尽情地哭。

fil·la·gree [ˈfiləgriː; ˋfɪləˏgri] ***n*.,** ***a*.,** ***vi*.** = filigree.

fill-dike [ˈfildaik; ˋfɪlˏdaɪk] **I** ***n*.** 春汛,桃花汛〔又称 *February* ~〕。**II** ***a*.** 春汛到来的,沟渠满溢的。

fille [ˈfiːjə; ˋfijə] ***n*.** 〔F.〕少女,姑娘,女儿。

filled [fild; fɪld] ***a*.** 满的,填满的;充气的;加载的。~ **gold** 镀金的金属〔铜、铁、铅等〕。~ **milk** 加有植物油脂的牛乳。~ **soap** 杂质肥皂。

fill·er [ˈfilə; ˋfɪlɚ] ***n*.** **1.** 装填者,斟酒人;注入器,漏斗;填充物。**2.** (杂志的)补白;电影补白短片。**3.** 雪茄烟心;(自来水笔的)吸墨管。**4.** 〔*pl*.〕【化】填料。**5.** (计算机的)进位填充数,填充位。*a tank* ~ (油箱的)注油孔。

fil·lér [ˈfiːleə; ˋfilɛr] ***n*.** (*pl*. ~(***s***))〔Hung.〕菲勒〔匈牙利货币名,等于 1/100 福林〕。

fil·let [ˈfilit; ˋfɪlɪt] **I** ***n*.** **1.** 带子,带状物。**2.** 头带,束发带。**3.** 肉片,鱼片。**4.**【建】平缘,木摺;突出横饰线。**5.** (书面等上的)饰线,轮廓线。**6.**【机】嵌条,内圆角。**7.**【解】襻,丘系;〔*pl*.〕(马、牛等的)腰部。*a* ~ *of veal* [*mutton*] 小牛[羊]肉片,里脊片。*light* ~ 浅角焊缝。**II** ***vt*.** **1.** 用带束(发),给…加边线。**2.** 把(鱼肉)切片。**3.** 修(图)。~*ed angle* [*corner*] 圆角[内圆角]。

fil·li·beg [ˈfiliˌbeg; ˋfɪlɪˏbɛg] ***n*.** = filibeg (= kilt).

fil·li·bus·ter [ˈfilibʌstə; ˋfɪləˏbʌstɚ] ***n*.,** ***v*.** = filibuster.

fill-in [ˈfilˌin; ˋfɪlˏɪn] **I** ***n*.** **1.** (暂时)补缺者;替工;临时填补物。**2.** 〔美口〕(有关事实的)摘要。**3.** 在等待时间所作的消遣。**II** ***a*.** 临时补缺的。

fill·ing [ˈfiliŋ; ˋfɪlɪŋ] ***n*.** **1.** 装满,填装;填补。**2.** 填料;填土。**3.** (糕点内的)馅。**4.** (织品的)纬纱,浆料。*gap* ~ 填缝。*gas* ~ 充气。*shell* ~ 外壳安装。~ **pressure** 充填压力,充气压力,填料压力。~ **station** 〔美〕(汽车)加油站;〔美俚〕小城市。

fil·lip [ˈfilip; ˋfɪləp] **I** ***n*.** **1.** 弹指,轻拍。**2.** 刺激 (*to*)。**3.** 琐碎东西,小事,琐事。*make a* ~ 弹一弹,拍一拍。*a* ~ *to the memory* 唤起记忆的东西。***not worth a*** ~ 毫不足取。**II** ***vt*.** **1.** 用指头弹 (*away*; *down*; *forth*; *off*)。**2.** 激励,刺激。~ *sb.'s memory* 唤起记忆。~ *sb.'s spirits* 使某人振作精神。— ***vi*.** 弹指。

fil·li·peen [ˌfiliˈpiːn; ˏfɪlɪˋpin] ***n*.** = philopena.

fil·lis·ter [ˈfilistə; ˋfɪlɪstɚ] ***n*.** **1.** (刨凹槽用的)凹刨。**2.**【建】凹槽;刨槽,开槽。~ **plane**【木工】槽口刨。

Fill·more [ˈfilmɔː; ˋfɪlmor] ***n*.** 菲尔莫尔〔姓氏〕。

fil·ly [ˈfili; ˋfɪlɪ] ***n*.** **1.** 小母马(*opp*. colt)。**2.** 〔口〕精神十足的小姑娘。

film [film; fɪlm] **I** ***n*.** **1.** 薄层,薄膜;薄雾,轻烟;细丝状的东西。**2.**【摄】感光乳剂,照相软片,电影胶片;影片。**3.** 〔*pl*.〕〔集合词〕电影。**4.** (眼中的)薄翳。*carbon resistance* ~【电】炭膜电阻。*a* ~ *of gossamer* 蜘蛛丝。*a roll* [*spool*] of ~ 一卷胶片。*a magnetic* ~ (录音)磁带。*a silent* ~ 无声电影,默片。*a sound* ~ 有声影片。*a talkie* ~ 有声对白影片。*a documentary* [*feature*] ~ 纪录[故事]片。*a three-dimensional* ~ 立体电影。~ *actor* [*actress*] 电影男[女]演员。~ *cutter* 电影剪辑员。~ *play* 电影剧本。*have a* ~ *over the eyes* 看不清楚。**II** ***vt*.,** ***vi*.** **1.** (在…上)蒙上薄膜;(使)生薄膜;(使)变朦胧。**2.** (把…)摄成影片;(使小说)电影化。~**-card** = fiche. ~**dom** 电影业,电影界 (= ~land) ~**-fan** 电影迷。~**goer** 看电影者,电影观众。~**graph** 电影胶片,录音设备。~**let** 短小的影片。~ **maker** **1.** 电影制作人,制片家,电影导演。**2.** (照片的)软片制作者。~ **noir** 黑暗电影,富实电影。~ **pack** 盒装胶卷。~**set** **1.** ***n*.** 电影布景。**2.** ***vt*.**【印】(照相版印刷术中)对(书稿等)作照相排版。~ **star** 电影明星。~ **strip** 幻灯胶片;(教学用)电影胶片;连续幻灯片。~ **studio** 电影制片厂。

film·craft [ˈfilmˌkrɑːft; ˋfɪlmˏkræft, -ˏkrɑft] ***n*.** 电影摄制艺术。

film·ic [ˈfilmik; ˋfɪlmɪk] ***a*.** 电影的,有关电影的,有关电影摄制术的。

film·ize [ˈfilmaiz; ˋfɪlmaɪz] ***vt*.** 〔美〕把…改编成电影;使电影化。

film·o·graph·y [filˈmɔgrəfi; fɪlˋmɑgrəfɪ] ***n*.** **1.** (某一导演执导的或某名演员主演的)影片集锦。**2.** 影片评介。

film·y [ˈfilmi; ˋfɪlmɪ] ***a*.** (***film·i·er***; ***-i·est***) **1.** 薄膜[细丝](状)的,薄膜[细丝]形成的。**2.** 蒙蒙薄雾的,朦胧的。~ *ice* 薄冰。~ *clouds* 淡淡的云彩。**-i·ness** ***n*.**

fi·lo·po·di·um [ˌfiləˈpəudiəm, ˌfailə-; ˏfɪləˋpodɪəm, ˏfaɪlə-] ***n*.** (*pl*. ***-di·a*** [-ə; -ə])【生】丝状假足。

fi·lose [ˈfailəus; ˋfaɪlos] *a*. 丝状的,线状的;有线状突出的。

fil·o·selle [ˌfiləˈsel; ˏfɪləˋsɛl] *n*. [F.]锈花绒[丝]线。

fils [fiːs; fis] *n*. 〔F.〕儿子〔区别同名父子时附加于儿子名字之后的用语, = Jr.〕〔*cf*. père〕。***Dumas*** ~ 小仲马。

fil·ter [ˈfiltə; ˋfɪltɚ] **I** *n*. **1**. 滤器,滤纸,过滤用料[砂、炭等]。**2**. 【无】滤波器;【物】滤光镜,滤色器。*acoustic* ~ 消声器。*bacterial* ~ 细菌滤器。*infrared* ~ 红外滤光器。**II** *vt*. 过滤,用过滤法除去。— *vi*. **1**. 过滤(*through*)。**2**. 渗入,(消息)走漏(*out*; *through*; *into*)〔*cf*. infiltrate〕。**3**. 〔英〕(车辆在十字路口)开入另一车道。~ **bed** 滤垫,滤水池。~ **centre** 资料处理中心,情报[资讯]整理处。~ **cigarette** 过滤嘴香烟。~ **paper** 滤纸(尤指定量滤纸)。~ **passer** 滤过性病毒。~ **press** 【化】压滤器,鱼油压榨机。~ **tip** **1**. 香烟过滤嘴。**2**. 带过滤嘴的香烟。~**-tipped** *a*. 有过滤嘴的。

fil·ter·a·ble [ˈfiltərəbl; ˋfɪltərəbḷ] *a*. 可过滤的。~ **virus** 过滤性病毒。**-a·bil·i·ty** [ˌfiltərəˈbiliti; ˏfɪltərəˋbɪlətɪ] *n*.

filth [filθ; fɪlθ] *n*. **1**. 污物,污秽。**2**. 淫猥,猥亵语。**3**. 道德败坏。~ *disease* (由于不洁而引起的)肮脏病。

filth·y [ˈfilθi; ˋfɪlθɪ] *a*. (***filth·i·er***; ***-i·est***) **1**. 不洁的,污秽的。**2**. 丑恶的;猥亵的;道德败坏的。*a* ~ *lane* 肮脏的陋巷。***be*** ~ ***with dough*** 〔美俚〕有钱的。***be*** ~ ***with money*** 有钱的。~ **lucre** **1**. 不义之财。**2**. 〔蔑〕臭钱。~ **pelf** 〔废〕= ~ lucre. **-i·ly** *ad*. **-i·ness** *n*.

fil·tra·ble [ˈfiltrəbl; ˋfɪltrəbḷ] *a*. = filterable. **-bil·i·ty** *n*.

fil·trate [ˈfiltreit; ˋfɪltret] **I** *vt*., *vi*. 过滤。**II** *n*. 滤液,滤过的水。

fil·tra·tion [filˈtreiʃən; fɪlˋtreʃən] *n*. 过滤;渗入。*automatic* (*centrifugal*) ~ 自动(离心)过滤。

fi·lum [ˈfailəm; ˋfaɪləm] *n*. (*pl*. **-la** [-lə;-lə]) 【解】丝状部分;丝。

fim·bri·ate [ˈfimbrieit; ˋfɪmbrɪˏet] **I** *a*. **1**. 【生】有毛缘的。**2**. 用花带镶边的。**II** *vt*. **1**. 使有毛缘。**2**. 【纹】在…上镶以窄边。

Fin. = Finland; Finnish.

fin. = **1**. finance; financial. **2**. finish; finished. **3**. finis.

fin [fin; fɪn] **I** *n*. **1**. 鳍,鱼翅;鳍状物。**2**. 手,臂。**3**. 【海】(潜水艇的)鳍板,水平舵;【火箭】舵;【空】稳定器,安定翼;【军】弹尾;【机】翅,尾翼,周缘翅片;散热片。**4**. 〔美口〕(人的)头。**5**. 汽车尾部的突起装饰物。**6**. = flipper. *the anal* [*caudal*, *dorsal*, *pectoral*, *ventral*] ~ 臀[尾、脊、胸、腹]鳍。~, *fur and feather* 鱼类,兽类与鸟类。*a cooling* ~ 冷却片。*damping* ~ 阻尼片。*rear* ~ 尾翼。*Shark's* ~ 鲨鱼翅。***Tip*** [***give***] ***us your*** ~. 〔俚〕让我们握手。**II** *vt*., *vi*. (**-nn-**) **1**. 把(鳍)切下。**2**. (猛烈地)拍动(鳍)。**3**. 给…装上翅片[鳍板]。~ **keel** (游艇等的)鳍状龙骨。~ **ray** 鳍棘〔鱼鳍的软骨组织〕。

fin·a·ble [ˈfainəbl; ˋfaɪnəbḷ] *a*. **1**. 可罚款的,该罚款的。**2**. 可精制的,可提炼的。**-ness** *n*.

fi·na·gle [fiˈneigl; fɪˋnegḷ] *vt*. 〔口〕用计取得[办妥];骗取,诈取,诱取。**-r** *n*.

fi·nal [ˈfainl; ˋfaɪnl] **I** *a*. 最终的,最后的,终极的;结局的,结果的;决定性的。*the* ~ *ballot* 决选投票。*the* ~ *cause* 【哲】终极原因;目的。*a* ~ *clause* 【语法】目的子句。~ *game* [*contest*] 决赛。*a* ~ *issue* 最后结果。*the* ~ *round* 决赛。***in the*** ~ ***analysis*** 归根到底。**II** *n*. 结局,〔口〕(报纸的)末版,〔常 *pl*.〕〔美俚〕【体】决赛;最后[期终]考试。*the tennis* ~*s* 网球决赛。***prepare for the*** ~***s*** 准备参加期终考试。***run*** [***play***] ***in the*** ~***s*** 参加决赛。**F- Solution** 最后解决〔指纳粹对犹太人的大规模屠杀或任何一种种族灭绝运动〕。~ **thrill** 〔美俚〕死亡。

fi·na·le [fiˈnɑːli; fɪˋnɑlɪ] *n*. **1**. 结局,收尾。**2**. 【乐】终曲。**3**. 最后一幕;大团圆。

fi·nal·ist [ˈfainəlist; ˋfaɪnḷɪst] *n*. 【体】决赛选手。

fi·nal·i·ty [faiˈnæliti; faɪˋnælətɪ] *n*. **1**. 最后,定局,结尾。**2**. 最后的事物,最后的言行回答。**3**. 【哲】目的性,终极性。*an air of* ~ 最后的态度,摊牌的神气。*speak with* ~ 断言,咬定说。

fi·nal·ize [ˈfainəlaiz; ˋfaɪnḷˏaɪz] *vt*. 使落实;使完成;把…最后定下来。**-za·tion** [ˌfainəlaiˈzeiʃən; ˏfaɪnəlaɪˋzeʃən] *n*.

fi·nal·ly [ˈfainəli; ˋfaɪnḷɪ] *ad*. **1**. 最后,最终。**2**. 决定性地;不可更改地。

fi·nance [faiˈnæns, fi-; faɪˋnæns, fɪ-] **I** *n*. **1**. 财政,金融,财政学。**2**. 〔*pl*.〕岁入,财源,资金。*public* ~ 国家财政。*the Minister of F-* 财政部部长。*the Ministry of F-* 财政部。~ *bill* 财政法案。~ *company* 信贷公司。**II** *vt*. **1**. 为…供给资金,给…通融资金。**2**. 赊货给…。~ *an enterprise* 供给企业资金。— *vi*. 掌握财政,处理财务。~ **bill** **1**. (议会的)拨款法案。**2**. (银行之间的)业务往来汇票。**fi·nanc·ing** *n*. 资金的筹措,理财。

fi·nan·cial [faiˈnænʃəl, fi-; faɪˋnænʃəl, fɪ-] *a*. **1**. 财政(上)的,财务(上)的,金融(上)的。**2**. (会员)缴费的〔*cf*. honorary〕。~ *ability* 财力。~ *adjustment* 财政整理。~ *affairs* 财务。~ *capital* 金融资本。~ *circles* = *the* ~ *world* 金融界。*the* ~ *condition* [*situation*] 财政状况。~ *crisis* 财政危机,金融恐慌。*a* ~ *magnate* 金融巨头。*a* ~ *man* 财政家。*a* ~ *member* 普通会员。~ *reports* 会计报告。~ **statement** 资产负债表;借贷对照表;财政报告。~ **year** 〔英〕会计年度(=〔美〕fiscal year)。**-ly** *ad*.

fin·an·cier **I** [faiˈnænsiə, fi-; ˏfaɪnənˋsɪr, ˏfɪ-] *n*. 财政官,财政家;金融家,资本家。**II** [ˌfainənˈsiə; ˏfaɪnənˋsɪr] *vt*. 对…提供资金,通融资金给;〔美〕骗取。— *vi*. 〔罕〕筹划财政,管理财务;从事(不正当的)金融活动。

fin·back [ˈfinˌbæk; ˋfɪnˏbæk] *n*. 【动】鳁鲸属动物〔尤指长须鲸〕。

fin·ca [ˈfiːŋkɑː; ˋfiŋkɑ] *n*. 〔Sp.〕(西班牙或拉美的)种植园,庄园;地产。

finch [fintʃ; fɪntʃ] *n*. 【动】雀科鸣禽(如燕雀、金翅雀等)。

find [faind; faɪnd] **I** *vt*. (***found*** [faund; faʊnd]; ***found***) **1**. 找到;获得;发现;(偶然)看见;拾得,遇见。**2**. 想出,(炮弹等)打中;(锚)到达(海底)。**3**. 觉得,发觉;找出,查明。**4**. 供给;供应;筹措(资金等)。**5**. 【法】断定,裁决,宣判。**6**. (江、河等)自然地形成,流向。**7**. 学会使用;恢复使用。~ *sb*. *dead* 发现某人死了。~ *sb*. *dying* 发现某人奄奄一息。~ *a good friend in sb*. 发现某人是个好朋友。*Water* ~*s its own level*. 水往低处流。*A bomb found him*. 炸弹打中了他。~ *time to do sth*. 有时间做某事。~ *food for friend* 供给朋友食物。~ *money for a plan* 为一项计划,筹措经费。*Experience helped the young birds to* ~ *its wings*. 经验使小鸟学会用翅膀飞起。*The judge found the thief guilty*. 法官判决小偷有罪。~ *expression in* 在…表现出来。~ *it difficult to explain* 觉得难以说明。~ *tea for workmen* 给工人弄茶喝。*It will be found that* ... 下面将指出…。~ *sb*. *guilty* 断定某人有罪。~ *the cubic root of* 求…的立方根。— *vi*. **1**. 作出判断。**2**. 找到猎物。***all*** [***everything***] ***found*** (工资以外)供给全部膳宿(*wages $ 20 a month and all* ~ 工资每月二十元,另供膳宿)。***be found in*** [***at***] 在某地,到某地。***be well found in*** 在…方面设备齐全[修养很高]。***cannot*** ~ ***it in one's heart to*** ... 不忍心…。~ ***fault with*** 吹毛求疵。~ ***favour in the eyes of*** 得到(某人的)看重。~ ***favour with*** 得宠。~ ***for*** [***against***] ***the defendant*** 下有利[不利]于被告的判决。~ ***it in one's hearts to*** ... 有意,想。~ ***it*** (***to***) ***pay*** = ~ (***that***) ***it pays*** 看来合算(有利)。~ ***one's account in*** 认为…有利,由…得利。

F

~ *one's feet* [*legs*] 在社会上站稳;对自己的能力有把握。~ *one's place in a book* 在书中找到要找的一处。~ *one's tongue* [*voice*] 讲得出话,恢复说话能力。~ *one's way* 到达 (*How did it* ~ *its way into print*? 怎么会付印的?)。~ *one's way out of* 由…(脱离)出来。~ *oneself* 1. 发觉自己的处境。2. (对于健康等的)自我感觉。3. 发现自己的特长并加以发挥。4. 自备衣食 (*three shillings a day and* ~ *yourself* 一天的报酬三先令,衣食自理)。~ *out* 发现,找出;猜着;想出;揭发(坏人等)。~ *sb. in* 供给某人(衣、食、费用等)。~ *up* 〔英方〕找出。~ *what o'clock it is* 查明事实真相。**II** *n*. 发现,发现物,拾得物,掘获物,被发觉的人材。*have* [*make*] *a great* ~ 有大发现,找出贵重宝物。*a sure* ~ 一定能发现狐狸等的地方;〔俚〕必能找到的人[物]。

find·er [ˈfaində; ˋfaɪndɚ] *n*. 1. 发现者。2. 探测器;瞄准装置;寻像器;选择器,寻线机,测距器。*a fault* ~ 障碍寻找器,障碍位置测定仪。*a height* ~ 测高仪。*a range* ~ 测距仪,测远仪。*a view* ~ 寻像器,取景器。~**'s fee** 中间人佣金;财务经纪费。

fin de siè·cle [F. fɛ̃dəsjɛkl; fæ̃dəˋsjɛkl] **I** *n*. 〔F.〕世纪末〔特指风气颓废的 19 世纪末〕。**II** *a*. 世纪末的,颓废的。

find·ing [ˈfaindiŋ; ˋfaɪndɪŋ] *n*. 1. 发现;发现的东西。2. 〔*pl*.〕结论;研究结果;【法】判决,(陪审员的)评定;(委员会等的)审查结果。3. 〔*pl*.〕〔美〕(服装,鞋,首饰制造用的)零件材料及工具。*a* ~ *store* 零件材料商店。

fine[1] [fain; faɪn] **I** *a*. (*fin·er*; *fin·est*) 1. 美好的,美丽的,优良的。2. (天气)晴朗的,令人愉快的。3. 精制的;华美的;纯洁的;优雅的。4. 稀薄的,细致的,细微的,纤细的。5. (刀)锐利的;(感觉)敏锐的,(区别)微小的。6. 纯粹的;成色好的。*a* ~ *character* 品格高尚的人。~ *chemicals* 精制化学药品。*a* ~ *day* 晴天。*a* ~ *distinction* 细微的差别。~ *dust* [*powder*] 细粉。*a* ~ *ear* 听觉灵敏。*a* ~ *edge* 利刃。~ *fibrous cotton* 细绒棉。*A* ~ *friend you have been*. 〔谑〕你真够朋友。~ *gold 18 carats* 十八开金。~ *grain* 细密的纹理。~ *linen* [*thread*, *china*] 细麻布[纱线,瓷器]。~ *measuring instrument* 精密量具。*a* ~ *mind* 聪明的头脑。~ *ore* 【矿】细矿粉。*a* ~ *pen* 笔头细的钢笔。*a* ~ *pencil* 画细线用的铅笔。~ *rain* 细雨。*a* ~ *sense of humour* (深具)幽默感。~ *skin* 细嫩的皮肤。~ *sugar* [*salt*] 精制糖[盐]。~ *tea* 高级茶叶。*have a* ~ *time* 〔俚〕过得高兴。*a* ~ *view* 壮观,壮丽的景色。~ *weather* 好天气。~ *words* 漂亮话。~ *workmanship* 精巧的制作。*as* ~ [*fit*] *as a fiddle* 很健康,精神好。*as* ~ *as silk* 柔软如丝;身体好。*F- feathers make* ~ *birds*. 〔谚〕人要衣装,佛要金装。*F- words dress ill deeds*. 〔谚〕口里仁义道德,心中男盗女娼。***F- excuse***! 〔反〕好个辩护! ~ ***feathered friend*** 〔美俚〕好朋友〔略带讽刺意味〕。~ ***paper*** [***bill***] 有信用的支票。~ ***thing*** 〔美俚〕好个东西〔表示厌恶的反语〕。***the New York finest*** 〔美俚〕纽约的警察。***not to put too*** ~ ***a point upon it*** 直截了当地说。***one*** ~ ***day*** [***morning***] 有一天,有一次〔讲故事时常用的开场白,有时也说明将来要发生不吉利的事〕。***one of these*** ~ ***days*** 改天,总有一天。***say*** ~ ***things about*** 恭维。**II** *n*. 晴天,好天气。***get home in the*** ~ 天晴时到家,顺利。(***in***) ***rain or*** ~ 不拘晴雨〔*cf*. rain or shine〕。**III** *ad*. 〔口〕巧妙,很好,精巧地,细微地。*talk* ~ 说得好。***cut*** [***run***] ***it*** [***things***] (***right***) ~ 精打细算,(时间等)扣得紧,几乎不留余地。**IV** *vt*. 1. 把…提纯,澄清,精制,使精细。2. 使稀薄,使细小。— *vi*. 1. 变好,变纯;变精致。2. 变稀薄。3. (天气)转晴。~ ***away*** [***down***, ***off***] 渐好;渐纯;缩小;渐渐消失。~ **arts** 美术(指绘画、雕刻、建筑、诗歌、音乐等)。~**-comb** *vt*. 仔细搜查。~**-cut** 1. *a*. (烟草)细切的。2. *n*. 烟丝。~**-draw** (**-drew**, **-drawn**) *vt*. 1. 细缝,密缝。2. 拉细(铁丝等)。3. 仔细讨论。~**-drawn** *a*. 1. 细(密)缝的,拉细了的;过于精致的。2. (推理等)微妙的;(运动员)体重减轻了的。~**-grained** *a*. (木材、皮革等)纹理细密的。~ **print** (契约等)有限制性质的附属细则〔因其印刷字体较正文为小,故名〕。~**spun** *a*. 细纺的,拉细的,脆弱的;过分琐细的 (*a* ~ *spun theory* 空洞的理论)。~ **structure** 微观[显微]结构。~**-tooth comb** = ~**-toothed comb** 细齿梳子 (*go over with a* ~*-tooth comb* 仔细检查;搜查)。~**-tune** *vt*. 精密[仔细]调校;仔细[妥贴]安排。~**-tooth-comb** *vt*. = 仔细搜查 (= ~-comb)。

fine[2] [fain; faɪn] **I** *n*. 1. 罚款。2. 【法】(获得或更新租契时交纳的)地租。3. 终结〔现限用于 in ~ 这一习语中〕。***in*** ~ 最后,总而言之。**II** *vt*., *vi*. (对…)处以罚款。

fi·ne[3] [ˈfiːne; ˋfine] *n*. 〔It.〕【乐】终止,完。*Al F-* 到末尾。

fine·a·ble [ˈfainəbl; ˋfaɪnəbl̩] *a*. = finable.

fine·ly [ˈfainli; ˋfaɪnlɪ] *ad*. 精细地,美好地。

fine·ness [ˈfainnis; ˋfaɪnnɪs] *n*. 1. 优良,精致。2. 细微,细度。3. 敏锐。4. 纯度;成色。5. 光洁度。~ **ratio** 【航】细度比,径长比〔指流线型飞机机身长度同宽度的比例〕。

fin·er·y[1] [ˈfainəri; ˋfaɪnərɪ] *n*. 1. 漂亮服装;美观的装饰品。2. 〔罕〕华丽,时髦。

fin·er·y[2] [ˈfainəri; ˋfaɪnərɪ] *n*. 【冶】精炼炉。

fines [ˈfainz; ˋfaɪnz] *n*. 〔*pl*.〕【矿】细粒〔尤指经过筛选的碎石〕。

fi·nesse [fiˈnes; fɪˋnɛs] **I** *n*. 1. 手腕,手段,技巧;策略。2. 在桥牌中先出小牌,保留好牌以赢牌的手法,偷牌。*the* ~ *of love* 恋爱手腕。**II** *vt*. 1. 用手段实现,用巧计战胜。2. 保留大牌而先出(小牌)。~ *sb.'s rights away* 骗取他人权利。— *vi*. 1. 施巧计。2. 【牌】偷牌。~ *for the Jack* 把 J 牌偷打出去,偷跑 J 牌。

fin·ger [ˈfiŋgə; ˋfɪŋgɚ] **I** *n*. 1. 指头,手指〔一般指拇指以外的手指〕。2. 指状物;(手套的)指部;(钟表的)指针。3. 一指之阔〔约 $\frac{3}{4}$ 英寸〕;一中指之长〔约 $4\frac{1}{2}$ 英寸〕。4. 【乐】运指法。5. 〔美俚〕警察,告密的人。6. 〔美俚〕伸出中指表示侮辱的手势。*Better a* ~ *off than aye wagging*. 〔谚〕长痛不如短痛。*the first* [*index*] ~ 食指。*the little* [*small*] ~ 小指。*the middle* [*long*] ~ 中指。*the ring* ~ 无名指。*spring* ~ 弹簧夹。*His* ~*s are all thumbs*. 他笨手笨脚。(***a***) ~ ***on the wall*** 灾难的预兆。***burn one's*** ~***s*** (管闲事)吃亏。***by a*** ~***'s breadth*** 差一点,险些。***by the*** ~ ***of God*** 靠神力。***count on the*** ~ 搬着指头计算。***crook one's little*** ~ 〔俚〕喝酒。***cross one's*** ~***s*** 把一个手指交叉放在同一只手的另一手指上〔迷信者认为这样可以逢凶化吉〕。***dig one's*** ~ ***in*** 染指。***give sb. the*** ~ 〔美俚〕使某人失败;让某人倒楣;亏待某人;侮辱某人。***have a*** ~ ***in the pie*** 参与,染指。***have at one's*** ~***s' ends*** [~ ***ends***, ~ ***tips***] 熟识,精通。***in sb.'s*** ~ 在某人掌握中,听某人支配。***lay*** [***put***] ***a*** [***one's***] ~ ***on sb***. 触犯,干涉。***lay*** [***put***] ***a*** [***one's***] ~ ***on sth***. 1. 明白指出,记得。2. 发现,找到。***let sth. slip through one's*** ~***s*** 放走,放过,漏掉。***look through one's*** ~***s at*** 假装没有看见。***My little*** ~ ***told me***. 我当然知道。***not lift*** [***stir***] ***a*** ~ ***to help*** 一点不肯帮忙。*one's* ~*s itch to do sth*. 手痒,急于想干某事。***put one's*** ~ ***in*** 染指。***put one's*** ~ ***in one's eyes*** 哭泣。***put one's*** ~ [~***s***] ***in the fire*** 自讨苦吃。***put the*** ~ ***on*** 〔美俚〕向当局指明犯罪罪犯[场所];指名告发。***rap sb.'s*** ~***s*** 处分某人,申斥某人。***slip between*** [***through***] ***sb.'s*** ~ 从某人的指缝中溜掉;(机会)被某人错过。***snap one's*** ~ ***at*** 打榧子〔向人捻拇指作响,表示轻蔑,不在乎等〕。***stick in*** [***to***] ***sb.'s*** ~ 被人中饱[侵吞]。***to the*** ~ ***nail*** 完全。***turn*** [***twist***, ***wind***, ***wrap***] ***sb. round*** [***around***] ***one's*** (***little***) ~ 把某人玩弄于股掌之上,任意摆布[支配]某人。***with a wet*** ~ 不费力地。***with one's*** ~ ***in one's mouth*** 1. 一事无成。2. 傻里傻气。***work one's*** ~ ***to the bone*** 不住手地工

F

作。II *vt*. 1. 用指头摸弄[触碰,捻摸]。2. 接受(贿赂等);偷。3. 用指头做;【乐】用手指弹[奏];在乐谱上标明(指法符号)。4.〔美俚〕尾随,监视;指责,告发。5. 指出,指认。6. 像手指般伸进。— *vi*. 1. 用手指触碰。2. 用手指弹奏。3. 像手指般伸出。~ **alphabet** [**language**] 手势语〔*cf*. dactylology〕。~ **board** 1. (提琴等的)指板;(钢琴等的)键盘。2. = ~ post. ~ **bowl** [**glass**] (饭后用)洗指钵。~**-breadth** 指宽,指幅〔约为 ¾ 英寸到 1 英寸宽〕。~**fish**【动】海星。~ **food** (在正式宴会上可用手指拿取送入口中的)手拿食物。~**hold** *n*. 1. 以指支持。2. 微弱的支持。~ **hole** (管乐器、电话机等上的)指孔。~ **man**〔美俚〕(盗贼等的)眼线。~ **mark** 指迹。~**nail** 指甲。~ **paint** 作手指画用的颜料。~**-paint** *vi*., *vt*. 用手指画(画)。~ **painting** 1. 指画法〔用手指、手、胳臂代替笔刷来涂抹颜料〕。2. 指画。~**-parted** *a*. 如手指状辐射的。~ **plate** (门等表面上)防止被手指染污的防护板[层]。~**-pointing** 指责,责难。~ **post** 1. 指路牌,指向柱。2. 指南。~ **print** 1. *n*. 指纹,手印;〔喻〕特征。2. *vt*. 打下[取下]…的指纹印;(依据独特的标记)辨识出。~ **reading** 盲人摸读法〔*cf*. braille〕. ~ **stall** *n*. 护指套。~ **wave** 手指卷发〔指仅用手指、梳子等使头发呈波浪形,与电烫相区别〕。**-less** *a*.

fin·gered [ˈfiŋgəd; ˋfɪŋgɚd] *a*. 1. 有指的;【植】指状的;掌状的。2. 用手指弹奏的;被手指污染的。3.〔用以构成复合词〕表示"有…指的","手指…的"。*a* ~ *citron* 佛手柑。*five-*~ 有五指的。*He was light-*~. 他手指纤巧;他手脚不干净(好偷东西)。~ *roots* 指状根。

fin·ger·ing[1] [ˈfiŋgəriŋ; ˋfɪŋgərɪŋ] *n*. 1. 用手指抚摸;用手指弹奏。2.【乐】指法;指法符号。

fin·ger·ing[2] [ˈfiŋgəriŋ; ˋfɪŋgərɪŋ] *n*. (织袜用)细绒线。

fin·ger·ling [ˈfiŋgəliŋ; ˋfɪŋgɚlɪŋ] *n*. 1. 小东西,微不足道的东西,小事。2. 长不及一指的小鱼。

fin·ger·tip [ˈfiŋgətip; ˋfɪŋgɚˏtɪp] *n*. 1. 指尖。2. (射箭等用的)指尖套。***have sth. at one's*** ~***s*** 1. 手头掌握了某物。2. 精通某事。***to one's*** [***the***] ~***s*** 完全地,彻底地(*He was a gentleman to his* ~*s*. 他是十足的绅士)。

fin·i·al [ˈfainiəl; ˋfaɪnɪəl] *n*. 1.【建】叶尖饰,尖顶饰。2. 物件顶端的装饰品。

fin·i·cal [ˈfinikəl; ˋfɪnɪkəl] *a*. = finicky. **-ly** *ad*. **-ity**, **-ness** *n*.

fin·ick·ing [ˈfinikiŋ; ˋfɪnɪkɪŋ] *a*. = finicky.

fin·ick·y [ˈfiniki; ˋfɪnɪkɪ] *a*. 苛求的,过于挑剔的;过于讲究的。**fin·ick·i·ness** *n*.

fin·i·kin [ˈfinikin; ˋfɪnɪkɪn] *a*. = finicky.

fin·ing [ˈfainiŋ; ˋfaɪnɪŋ] *n*. 1. (酒等的)澄清;(金属的)精制。2.〔*pl*.〕(酒等的)澄清剂。

fi·nis [ˈfainis, ˈfiːnis; ˋfaɪnɪs, ˋfɪnɪs] *n*.〔L.〕(书、电影等的)终止,终结;(生命的)结束〔时常印在书的结尾,表示"本书完"〕。

fin·ish [ˈfiniʃ; ˋfɪnɪʃ] I *vt*. 1. 完毕,完成,结束;使…毕业,使…卒业。2. 磨光,【机】给…抛光;给…最后加工;润饰,修整,整理。3. 用完,吃光。4.〔口〕杀掉,结束掉;累死;彻底征服,压服。~ *doing sth*. 做完某事。*Where were you* ~*ed*? 你是哪里毕业的? ~ *sb. with a single blow* 一拳打死某人。*I am* ~*ed*. 我准备完毕了;我累坏了。*The house will soon be* ~*ed*. 房子快要完工了。*be* ~*ed to gauge* 按尺寸精确加工。*surface* ~ 表面光洁度;表面抛光。*My arguments* ~*ed him*. 我的一番道理说得他哑口无言。— *vi*. 终了,完结;死;【体】到终点 (*up*)。~ ***off*** 1. 完成,结束;用完;吃完。2.〔口〕致…于死地,杀死。~ ***up*** 1. 完成。2. 吃光;用尽。~ ***up with*** 以…结束。~ ***with*** 1. 完成,结束。2. 和…断绝关系。II *n*. 1. 结束,最后阶段;终点;完蛋的原因;〔美俚〕死,毁灭。2. 完结,完成;完美;最后一道工序;抛光;【建】终饰;(态度等的)文雅。***be in at the*** ~ 猎获猎物时亲自在场;〔喻〕目睹(比赛,战斗等的)最后情形。***fight to a*** [***the***] ~ 打到底。~ **allowance**【机】加工余量。~ **line**〔美〕决胜线,(赛跑或赛马等的)终点线。

fin·ished [ˈfiniʃt; ˋfɪnɪʃt] *a*. 1. 完成了的,完结了的。2. 精巧的,制作完美的。3.〔美俚〕死了的;完蛋了的。~ *goods* 完美的成品,精制品。~ *products* 成品。*a* ~ *gentleman* 文雅绅士。~ *manners* 彬彬有礼。

fin·ish·er [ˈfiniʃə; ˋfɪnɪʃɚ] *n*. 1. 修整工,完工者;精加工工具。2. 精作机,精轧机,末道清棉机。3. 决定性的打击,决定性的事件。*the* ~ *of the law*〔谑〕死刑执行人,刽子手。

fin·ish·ing [ˈfiniʃiŋ; ˋfɪnɪʃɪŋ] I *a*. 最后的。II *n*. 完成修整,精加工;结尾,结束。~ **block** 拉细丝机。~ **coat** (墙壁)最后一道涂工。~ **material**【建】装饰材料。~ **metal** 精炼金属。~ **school** (青年妇女的)进修学校,家事学校。~ **touch** [**stroke**] (绘画等)最后修饰的笔触。

fi·nite [ˈfainait; ˋfaɪnaɪt] I *a*. 有限的;【语法】限定的;【数】有穷的,有尽的。II *n*.〔the ~〕有限(性);〔集合词〕有限物。~ **decimal** 有尽小数。~ **induction** 数学归纳法。~ **progression** [**series**] 有限级数。~ **verb** 限定动词。**-ly** *ad*. **-ness** *n*.

fin·i·tude [ˈfainitjuːd; ˋfɪnətjud] *n*. 有限,限定。

fink [fiŋk; fɪŋk] I *n*.〔美俚〕1. 工贼。2. 告密者。3. 可鄙的家伙,讨厌的家伙,乞丐。II *vi*. 1. 告发同党。2. 破坏罢工。3.〔美俚〕退缩,撤退;惨败。~**-out** *n*.〔美俚〕1. 大失败,大出丑。2. 退出;退缩。

Fin·land [ˈfinlənd; ˋfɪnlənd] *n*. 芬兰〔欧洲〕。**Fin·land·i·zation** 芬兰化。

Fin(n) [fin; fɪn] *n*. 芬兰人。

Finn [fin; fɪn] *n*. 芬兰人。

fin·nan had·die [ˌfinən ˈhædi; ˏfɪnən ˋhædɪ], **fin·nan-had·dock** [-ˈhædək; -ˋhædək] *n*.【动】熏鳕鱼。

finned [find; fɪnd] *a*. 1. 有鳍的;有鳍状物的。2.〔用以构成复合词〕(有)…鳍的。*long-*~, *short-*~.

fin·ner [ˈfinə; ˋfɪnɚ] *n*. = finback.

Finn·ic [ˈfinik; ˋfɪnɪk] *a*. 1. 芬兰人的。2. 芬兰语(族)的。

fin·nick·y [ˈfiniki; ˋfɪnɪkɪ] *a*. = finicky.

Finn·ish [ˈfiniʃ; ˋfɪnɪʃ] I *a*. 1. 芬兰的,芬兰人的。2. 芬兰语的。II *n*. 芬兰语。

Fin·no-U·gric [ˈfinəuˈjuːgrik, -ˈuː-; ˋfɪnoˋjugrɪk, -ˋu-] I *a*. 芬兰—乌戈尔语系的。II *n*. 芬兰—乌戈尔语系 (= Finno-Ugrian)。

fin·ny [ˈfini; ˋfɪnɪ] *a*. (***-ni·er***; ***-ni·est***) 1. 有鳍的;鳍状的。2.〔诗、谑〕鱼类的;多鱼的。*the* ~ *deep* 多鱼的深海。*the* ~ *tribe* 鱼族[类]。

fi·noc·chi·o [fiˈnəukiːəu; fɪˋnokio] *n*.【植】茴香。

Fin·sen [ˈfinsən; ˋfɪnsən] *n*. **F- light** [**lamp**] 水银弧光灯。

f.i.o. = free in and out 船方不负担装卸货费用。

fiord [fjɔːd; fjord] *n*. (尤指挪威海岸的断岩峭壁间的)峡湾;峡江 (= fjord)。

fi·o·rin [ˈfaiərin; ˋfaɪərɪn] *n*.【植】小糠草。

fio·ri·tu·ra [ˌfjɔriːˈtuːrɑː; ˏfjɔrɪˋturɑ] *n*. (*pl*. ***-tu·re*** [-re; -rɛ])【乐】装饰音。

fip·pence [ˈfipəns; ˋfɪpəns] *n*.〔英口〕= fivepence.

fip·pen·ny [ˈfipini, ˈfipni; ˋfɪpɪnɪ, ˋfɪpnɪ] **bit** *n*. 五便士币〔1857 年前在美国流通的西班牙银币,约合六美分〕。

fip·ple [ˈfipl; ˋfɪpl̩] **flute**【乐】直笛。

fir [fəː; fɝ] *n*. 1.【植】冷杉属 (Abies);枞;松科常绿树(如黄杉等)。2. 冷杉木,枞木。~**-apple**, ~**-ball**, ~**-cone** *n*. 冷杉球果。~ **needle** 冷杉针叶,枞叶。~ **tree** 冷杉,枞树。

FIR = food-irradiation reactor 食物辐射(杀菌)用反应堆。

fire [ˈfaiə; ˋfaɪr] I *n*. 1. 火,火焰;火灾;燃烧;炉火,烽火。2. 射击;火力。3. 火花,闪光;光辉。4. 热情,热烈,热心;生气;(诗等的)灵感。5. 发烧,发热,炎症。6. 火刑;磨难,迫害。7.〔诗〕星。*A burnt child dreads the*

F

~.〔谚〕儿童被火烧,见火就逃跑;惊弓之鸟[吃过亏的人]格外胆小。*He who plays with ~ gets burned.* 玩火者必自焚。*It is too warm for ~.* 天气暖和不必生火。F-! 起火了! *council ~* 印地安人在会议时点的篝火。*F- and water are good servants, but bad masters.*〔谚〕水火是良仆,也能成恶主。*F- that's closest kept burns most of all.*〔谚〕火闷得越紧,烧起来越凶。*The ~ which lights [warms] us at a distance will burn us when near.*〔谚〕火在远处是明灯,到了近处烧死人。*ground ~* 地面火力。*heavenly ~s, ~s of heaven*〔诗〕星星。*liquid ~*〔口〕烈性酒。*open [cease] ~* 开[停]火。*rapid ~*(轻武器或自动武器的)速射。*the ~ of a diamond* 钻石的光辉。*the ~ of lightning* 闪电光。*the ~ of love* 爱火,热烈的爱。*a speech lacking ~* 缺乏热情的演说。*full of ~* 充满热情[愤恨]。*Keep away from ~!* 切勿近火。*the ~s of persecution* 残酷的迫害。*Soft ~ makes sweet malt.*〔谚〕慢工出细活。***amid ~ and thunder*** 轰轰烈烈。***a running ~*** 1. 连发,连射。2. 一连串的批评指责。***between two ~s*** 腹背受敌,在两面夹攻中。***blow the ~*** 挑唆,煽动。***build a ~ under oneself*** 作法自毙。***by ~ and sword*** 杀人放火,使用残暴方法。***carry ~ in one hand and water in the other*** 两面三刀。***catch ~*** 着火。***~ and fag(g)ot*** 火刑。***fight ~ with ~*** 以火攻火,以毒攻毒。***~ and brimstone*** 1. 地狱里的磨难。2. 见鬼! ***~ and fury*** 炽烈奔放的感情。***flash [shoot] ~*** 眼中冒火,怒目相对。***go through ~ and water*** 赶汤蹈火。***hang ~***(火器)发射不出,迟缓发射;(作事)犹豫不决;延迟。***Hermes's ~*** = St. Elmo's ~. ***hold ~*** 忍着不表态。***Kentish ~*** 1. 长时间的鼓掌。2. 一片反对声。***lay a ~*** 预备生火。***lift ~***【军】1. 延伸射击。2. 中止射击。***make a ~*** 生火。***miss ~***(枪炮)打不响;失败。***nurse a ~*** 1. 看管火。2. 烤火。***on ~*** 燃烧着;兴奋着,热中。***on the ~***〔美俚〕在考虑[审议]中。***open ~*** 1. 开火。2. 开始。***play with ~*** 玩火,轻举妄动。***pour oil on ~*** 火上加油。***pull (a game etc.) out of the ~*** 转败为胜。***pull [snatch] sb. out of the ~*** 把某人救出火坑。***put to ~ and sword*** 又烧又杀。***save sth. out of the ~*** 把东西(从火中)抢救出来。***set ~ to = set on ~*** 放火烧,使燃烧;使兴奋,使激动。***set the Thames [river] on ~*** 作惊人之举。***show sth. the ~*** 把某物稍稍热一下。***St. Anthony's ~***【医】丹毒。***St. Elmo's ~*** 桅顶(飞机翼尖、塔尖等的)电辉火。***stand ~*** 冒着炮火;忍受批评。***stir the ~*** 拨火。***strike ~***(用火石)打火;(用火柴)擦火。***take ~*** 着火燃烧;激动起来。***the sacred ~*** 1. 真挚的爱,神圣的爱。2. 天才。***under ~*** 在炮火下;受到攻击。**II *vt*.** 1. 烧、点(火),生(炉子)。2. 烧(瓦等);烤(茶等)。3.〔口〕扔、投(石头等)。4. 射击,打(枪),开(炮);炸破;使爆发。5. 激发(感情等)。6. 使发光辉。7.【兽医】(用烙铁)烧灼。8.〔美俚〕解雇,撵走 (*out*)。~ *a house* 烧房子。~ *a salute* 放礼炮。~ *questions at sb.* 向某人提出(许多)质问。~ *sb. with anger* 激怒某人。~ *the blood of* 使热血沸腾。~ *the imagination* 激发想象力。—***vi*.** 1. 着火,燃烧。2. 激动。3.〔口〕扔石头(等)。4. 发射,开火,开炮 (*at*; *into*; *on*; *upon*)。F-! 开火! ~ *back in self-defence* 自卫还击。***be ~d (out)***〔俚〕被解雇。~ ***at*** 对…开枪,向…射击。~ ***away*** 1. 继续射击。2.〔口〕开始像连珠炮似地谈话或提问。~ ***off*** 1. 发炮,开炮。2. 使爆炸,炸掉。3. 熄灭(火)。4. 开口。5. 发射(火箭等)(~ *off questions* 提问题)。~ ***on*** = ~ *at*. ~ ***out***〔美〕撵走,解雇。~ ***up*** 1. 发动(机器);生火。2. 突然发怒。~ **action**【军】火力交锋,火战。~ **alarm** 火警警钟,火警;报火机。~ **ant**【动】火蚁,火伤蚁〔美国南部的一种有害昆虫;人被咬后,有火辣的感觉〕。~**-arm**〔常 *pl*.〕火器,手枪,步枪,轻武器。~ **apparatus** 消防设备。~**back** 1. (反射炉火的)背壁。2.【动】(背部火红的)南豆雉。~**-ball** 1. 火球;流星;〔诗〕太阳;【军】(从前的)燃烧弹。2.〔美口〕干劲十足的人。~ **balloon**(下部置火使球内空气因热而上升的)热气球;(升至高空后才爆炸燃烧的)流星火花。~ **bar** 炉条。~**base**【军】火力基地,重火力点。~**-bird** 1.【动】火红鸟。2. 无线电信管。~ **blast [blight]**【植病】火疫。~**boat** 消防艇,救火船。~ **bomb**【军】燃烧弹。~ **bomb *vt*.** 用燃烧弹轰击。~ **box** 1.【机】机车锅炉炉膛,燃烧室。2. 盛放火警报警器的箱子。~**brand** 1. 火把。2. 放火者;煽动叛乱者,挑动争执者。~**break** 森林的防火线〔森林或草原上清除掉树木或草皮,以防野火蔓延的空旷地带〕。~**brick**(耐)火砖。~**brigade**〔英〕消防队;〔美军俚〕特速紧急分遣队。~**bug**〔美〕萤火虫;〔美口〕放火者,纵火狂。~ **call** = ~ alarm. ~ **chief** 消防署署长。~ **clay**(耐)火泥,耐火(黏)土。~ **coat** 氧化膜。~ **company** 1. 消防队。2.〔英〕火险公司。~ **control** 1.【军】实施射击,射击指挥,火力控制,射击控制。2. 消防。~ **control system** 射击指挥系统,射击指挥仪。~ **cracker** 爆竹,爆鞭。~**-cure *vt*.** 用烟熏(烟草等)。~**-damp**【化】(煤矿内的)碳化氢,沼气。~ **department** 消防署。~**dog**(炉中的)柴架,炭架。~ **door** 防火门,炉门。~**drake**, ~**dragon**(北欧神话中的)喷火龙。~ **drill** 消防演习;(工厂、学校等的)防火训练。~**-eater** 1. 吞火魔术师。2. 爱打架的人,暴性子。~**-eating *a*.** 强暴的,咄咄逼人的,好战的。~ **engine** 1. 救火车。2.〔泛指〕消防车〔运送消防队员和消防设备到火警现场的卡车等〕。~ **escape**(防火)太平门[梯],安全出口。~ **extinguisher** 灭火器。~ **fight** 交火。~ **fighter**〔美〕消防人员;〔美〕(空袭时的)临时消防员。~ **fighting** 消防活动。~**flood** 注火法〔一种石油开采程序〕。~ **fly** 萤火虫。~ **grate** 炉篦,炉条,火床。~**guard** 1. 火炉栏。2. = ~ break. ~ **hose** 救火蛇管,水龙带。~**house** = ~ station. ~ **hydrant** 消防栓,消防龙头,灭火龙头。~ **insurance** 火(灾保)险。~ **irons** 火炉用具(如火钳、通条、火铲等)。~ **ladder** 太平梯,消防梯。~ **lane** = ~ break. ~**light**(炉)火光。~ **lighter** 引火物。~ **line** 1. = ~ break. 2.〔常 *pl*.〕(火灾现场的)消防警戒线,交通封锁线。3. (草原、森林等的)火灾最前线。~**lock** 火炮。~**man**(*pl*. ~**men**) 1. 司炉工,烧火工人。2. 消防队员。3.【矿】救火员,爆破工,煤矿煤气检查员,通风员。~ **marshal**〔美〕消防队长。~**-new *a*.** 崭新的(= brand-new)。~ **office**〔英〕火灾保险公司。~ **pan**〔英〕火铲,火斗,火盆。~**place** 壁炉,炉床。~**plug** 灭火塞,消火栓。~ **policy** 火(灾保)险单。~ **position** 发射阵地;战斗姿态。~**power**【军】1. 火力。2. 火量〔单位时间发射炮弹数与重量〕。~**proof** 1. ***a*.** 耐火的,防火的。2. ***vt*.** 使耐火,使防火。~**proofing** 使防火,耐火,耐火装置[材料]。~**raising**〔英〕放火。~ **resistance** 耐火度。~ **room** 锅炉间,火室。~ **sale** 火灾中受损物品的减价销售。~ **screen** 火障,炉围。~ **ship**(火攻敌舰用的)火攻船。~**side** 1. ***n*.** 炉边;家;家庭;〔古〕家属。2. ***a*.** 炉边的,亲切的,毫无拘束的 (*the president's ~side chat* (美国)总统的炉边谈话)。~**station** 消防站。~ **step**(战壕里射击时用的)踏垛。~**-stone** 燧石,耐火岩石,耐火黏土,黄铁矿。~**storm**(原子弹爆炸等引起的)风暴性大火。~**teazer**〔英俚〕烧炉员。~ **thorn** 火棘属植物。~ **tower** 森林火警瞭望塔。~**trap** 无太平门的建筑物,易遭火灾的建筑物。~**trench**【军】散兵壕。~ **truck**【美】救火车。~ **wall** 防火墙,隔火墙;(电脑内联网设置的)防侵入"防火墙"。~**warden**〔美〕防火监查员;【林】防火瞭望员。~**-watcher** 火灾警戒员。~ **water**〔口〕烈烟。~**weed**(火烧过后长出的杂草)火草。~**wood** 木柴;〔英〕柴火。~**work** 1.〔*pl*.〕焰火,花火;烽火。2.【军】烟火信号弹。3.〔常 *pl*.〕激情的表现。4. 才气的焕发。~ **worship** 拜火,拜火教。**-less *a*.**

Fi·ren·ze [It. fi'rendze; fi`rendzɛ] ***n*.**〔It.〕= Florence.

fir·er [ˈfaiərə; ˋfaɪrɚ] ***n*.** **1.** 点火者,放火者,烧火工人。**2.** 开炮者,点火物。**3.** 火器,枪炮。*a quick* ～ 速射炮。*a single* ～ 单发枪。

fir·ing [ˈfaiəriŋ; ˋfaɪrɪŋ] ***n*.** **1.** 点火;(茶的)烘烤;(陶器等的)烧成。**2.** 射击。**3.** 燃料。**4.** 添煤,司炉。**5.** 〔口〕解雇。**6.**【无】触发。～ *practice* 开炮演习。～ **iron** (兽医用的)烙针。～ **line** 第一线;【军】火线;前线部队。～ **order** (发动机的)发火次序。～ **party** **1.** 葬礼时的鸣枪队。**2.** 行刑队。～ **pin** (枪炮的)撞针。～ **point** 油的发火点;(打靶时的)发射位置。～ **range** **1.** 靶场,火箭试射场。**2.** 射程。～ **squad** = ～ party. ～ **step** (战壕内射击时登上的)踏垛 (= fire step)。

fir·kin [ˈfəːkin; ˋfɝkɪn] ***n*.** **1.** 费尔金〔英国容量单位,合九加仑〕。**2.** (装油脂用,容量为8—9磅的)小木桶。

firm[1] [fəːm; fɝm] **I** ***a*.** **1.** 坚固的,坚牢的;稳固的。**2.** 坚定的,坚决的。**3.**【商】固定的 (*opp*. optional); (货币)坚挺的(*opp*. easy, weak 疲软),稳定的;(金融等)紧缩的。～ *belief* 确信。～ *friendship* 牢不可破的友谊。～ *ground* 陆地。～ *step* 坚定的步伐。***as*** ～ ***as a rock*** 坚如磐石。***be*** ～ ***on one's legs*** 站稳。***be on*** ～ ***ground*** 脚踏实地;在稳固的基础上。**II** ***ad*.** 稳固地,坚定地。*hold* ～ 固守。*stand* ～ 站稳。**III** ***vt*., *vi*.** 使(变)坚固,使(变)坚实、使(变)稳定。～**ware**【计】固件;稳固设备(的微程序控制);(用器件实现的)操作系统;微程序语言。

firm[2] [fəːm; fɝm] ***n*.** **1.** 商号,商行;公司。**2.** 工作集体〔如一组医生〕。*trading* ～*s* 商行。*a printing* ～ 印刷公司。*a long* ～ 〔英〕(骗取货物而不付钱的)滑头商号。

fir·ma·ment [ˈfəːməmənt; ˋfɝməmənt] ***n*.** 苍穹,天空。**-al** ***a*.**

fir·man [fəːˈmɑːn, ˈfəːmən; ˋfɝmən, fɚˋmɑn] ***n*.** **1.** (土耳其皇帝等颁发的)诏书。**2.** 许可证;执照;护照。

firm·er [ˈfəːmə; ˋfɝmɚ] ***n*.** (木工所用的)凿子[圆凿]。

firm·ly [ˈfəːmli; ˋfɝmlɪ] ***ad*.** 断然地,坚定地,坚固地。

firm·ness [ˈfəːmnis; ˋfɝmnɪs] ***n*.** 坚固,坚定,稳固。

firn [fəːn; fɝn] ***n*.**【地】冰原,永久积雪〔俗名万年雪〕。

fir·ry [ˈfəːri; ˋfɝrɪ] ***a*.** (***-ri·er***; ***-ri·est***) **1.** 冷杉木制的;枞木制的。**2.** 多冷杉的,多枞的。

first [fəːst; fɝst] **I** ***num*.** 第一。**II** ***a*.** **1.** 最初的,最早的。**2.** 最上等的,第一流的。**3.** 基本的,概要的。**4.** 高音(调)的。*Judge not of men and things at* ～ *sight*. 〔谚〕对人对事慢评论,初次印象未必真。*the* ～ *coat* (油漆等的)底涂,底层。*the* ～ *impression* 最初印象。*the* ～ *instance*【法】初审。*the* ～ *snow of the season* 初雪。*the* ～ *train* 头班车。*the* ～ *two days* = 〔古〕*the two* ～ *days* 头两天。***at*** ～ ***hand*** 直接。***at*** ～ ***sight*** [***blush***] 乍看;一见就。***at the*** ～ ***opportunity*** 一有机会就。***for the*** ～ ***time*** 第一次。***in the*** ～ ***place*** [***instance***] 首先。***on the*** ～ ***fine day*** 天一晴就。***take the*** ～ ***opportunity*** 一有机会就。***the F- Commoner*** 〔英〕下议院议员。***the*** ～ ***form*** 〔英〕(中等学校的)一年级。***the*** ～ ***thing*** 〔俚〕首先。**III** ***n*.** **1.** 最初,第一;第一位。**2.** 每月的第一日,一号。**3.**【乐】高音部。**4.** 第一等,头等,优等,甲等;〔*pl*.〕一级品。**5.** (棒球的)第一垒。**6.**【汽车】起码[最慢]速度。*get* [*take*] *a* ～ 考第一。*come in* ～ 跑第一。*May* (*the*) ～ = *the* ～ *of May* 五月一日。***at*** (***the***) ～ 首先。***be the*** ～ ***to*** (***do***) 最先…的。***from*** ～ ***to last*** 自始至终。***from the*** ～ 从头,自始。***the F-*** 〔英〕九月一号〔鹧鸪开猎日〕。**IV** ***ad*.** **1.** 第一,最初,首先。**2.** 宁可。*safety* ～ 安全第一。*F- come,* ～ *served*. 〔谚〕先到先招待。*stand* ～ 站在最前面。*He said he would die* ～. 他说他宁愿死掉(也不作那样的事)。～ ***and foremost*** 首先,第一。～ ***and last*** 总的说来。～, ***midst and last*** 彻头彻尾,始终,一贯。～, ***last and all the time*** 〔美〕始终一贯,绝对。～ ***of all*** 第一,首先。～ ***off*** 首先。～ ***or last*** 〔古、罕〕早晚,迟早。～ **aid** 急救处理。～**-aid** ***a*.** 急救的(*a* ～*-aid kit* 急救药箱)。～ **base**【棒球】一垒 (*get to* ～ *base* 〔俚〕获得初步成功,完成了第一步)。～**-begotten** ***a*.** 最初生产的。～ **blood** (在拳击等搏斗中)最初出血;〔喻〕从对手方面取得的最初胜利。～**born** **1.** ***a*.** 初生的;最年长的。**2.** ***n*.** 长子[女];最初的结果。～ **cause** **1.** 首要原因;根源。**2.**【神】〔F- C-〕上帝,造物主。～**-chop** ***a*.** 〔Ind.〕 = ～**-class** **1.** ***a*.** 头等的;第一类的;〔口〕最好的(*a* ～*-class carriage* 头等车。*a* ～*-class paper* 信用优良的支票)。**2.** ***ad*.** 乘头等舱[车];作为第一类邮件;〔口〕极好 (*He plays* ～*-class*. 他演得顶好。*travel* ～*-class* 乘头等车旅行)。～**comer** 第一个来客,先到的人。～ **cousin** 堂兄弟姐妹,表兄弟姐妹。～ **day** 星期日〔一周的第一天,基督教公谊会用语〕。～**-day cover**【邮】首日封。～**-degree** ***a*.** **1.** 最低级的,最轻度的;【医】第一度的 (～*-degree burn* 第一度灼伤)。**2.** 最高级的,一级的,最严重的 (～*-degree combat readiness* 一级战斗状态)。**F- Empire** (法兰区)第一帝国〔1804—1815〕。～ **estate** 第一等级(僧侣)〔欧洲封建时代的三个等级之一,其他两个等级是贵族和庶民〕。～ **family** **1.** 美国最早移民的黑裔。**2.** 总统的家族。～ **finger** 食指。～**-foot** [Scot.] 元旦日第一个来客。～ **floor** **1.** 〔美〕一楼。**2.** 〔英、欧〕二楼。～ **fruits** 前初的结果,初次收获。～**-generation** ***a*.** 第一代的〔**1.** 指出生在外国的入籍公民。**2.** 有时指父母入籍后出生的公民〕。～**hand** **1.** ***a*.** 第一手的,直接的,亲自得到的。**2.** ***ad*.** 直接地。**F- International** 第一国际(1864—1876)。～ **lady** 〔常作 F- L-〕第一夫人,总统夫人,元首夫人。～ **lieutenant** **1.** (美陆军)中尉。**2.** (美海军)中尉〔负责舰只或海军站的维修和保养〕。～**-line** ***a*.** **1.**【军】第一线的。**2.** 头等的,最重要的。～ **mate** [**officer**]【海】大副。～ **name** 〔美〕一个人姓名中的名字,教名 (=given name)。～**name** ***vt*.** 不以姓而以名相称。～ **night** (戏剧或歌剧等的)首夜演出。～**-nighter** 经常观看首夜演出者。～ **offender**【法】初犯。～ **papers** 〔美国〕要求加入某国国籍的初步申请书。～ **person** **1.**【语法】第一人称。**2.** 用第一人称叙述的文体。～ **point of Aries**【天】春分点。～ **quarter** **1.** 上弦日子〔指阴历每月初八前后〕。**2.** 上弦月。～**-rate** **1.** ***a*.** 第一等的,最上等的。**2.** ***ad*.** 〔口〕非常(好)地(*feel* ～*-rate* 觉得精神极好)。**3.** ***n*.** 一级战舰;一流人物。～**-rater** 一流人物;一级品。～ **reading** (议会审议议案时的)正式初读。**F- Republic** (法兰西)第一共和国〔1792—1804〕。～**-run** ***a*.** 〔美〕头轮的〔指电影院〕。～**-runner** 〔美〕头轮电影院。**F- Sea Lord** 〔英〕海军部军事委员会第一军事委员。～ **sergeant** (美陆、海军)军士长。～**-strike** ***a*.** (核战争中的)第一次核打击的。～**-strike capability** 第一次核打击能力。～**-string** ***a*.** **1.**【体】正式(队员)的〔区别于候补(队员)的〕。**2.** 第一流的,优秀的。～**-time** ***a*.** 初次的。**F- Triumvirate** (古代罗马的)前三雄执政〔指凯撒、庞培和克拉苏的三头执政团〕。～ **water** (特指钻石、珍珠等)最好品质,最纯洁的光泽,优等。

first·ling [ˈfəːstliŋ; ˋfɝstlɪŋ] ***n*.** 〔常 *pl*.〕初生产物,初次收获;初产的幼畜;最初结果。

first·ly [ˈfəːstli; ˋfɝstlɪ] ***ad*.** 第一,首先。★列举条目时常作:～, secondly, thirdly, ... lastly.

firth [fəːθ; fɝθ] ***n*.** [Scot.] = frith.

fisc [fisk; fɪsk] ***n*.** **1.** 古罗马的皇室财库。**2.** 国库,王室的财库。

fis·cal [ˈfiskəl; ˋfɪskəl] **I** ***a*.** **1.** 国库的。**2.** 〔美〕财政上的;会计的。*a* ～ *policy* 财政政策。～ *resources* 财源。**II** ***n*.** **1.** 财政部长;(苏格兰等的)检察官;(西班牙及葡萄牙的)检察长。**2.** 印花税票。**3.** 财政年度,会计年度。～ **accountability**(政府对公共支出须作出合理解释的)财政责任。～ **agent** 财务代理人[银行、商行]。～ **law** 会计法。～ **stamp** 印花税票。～ **year** 会计年度,财政年度。

Fish [fiʃ; fɪʃ] ***n*.** 菲什〔姓氏〕。

fish [fiʃ; fɪʃ] **I** ***n.*** (*pl*. *~es*,〔集合词〕~) **1.** 鱼;〔集合词〕鱼类;鱼肉。★说鱼的若干种类时用 fishes, 说几条鱼不用复数;鱼肉是不可数名词,无复数。**2.**〔口〕(特殊的)人物,家伙,东西。**3.**【海】钓锚器;撑夹桅杆的加固夹箍;【建】接合板,夹片,鱼尾板;悬鱼饰;【天】〔the Fish-(es)〕双鱼宫。**4.**【军口】鱼雷。**5.**〔美口〕新囚犯;生手,笨蛋;容易受骗的人。**6.**〔美俚〕〔谑〕天主教徒。**7.**〔美俚〕美元。*eat three ~* 吃三条鱼。*lots of ~* 许多鱼。*F- begins to stink at the head*.〔谚〕上梁不正下梁歪,鱼要腐烂头先坏。*Gut no ~ till you get them*. = *Never fry a ~ till it is caught*.〔谚〕鱼未捉到,别忙煎鱼。*He who would catch ~ must not mind getting wet*.〔谚〕捉鱼不要怕湿脚。*If you swear you will catch no ~*.〔谚〕咒骂不解决问题。*It is a silly ~, that is caught twice with the same bait*.〔谚〕智者不上两回当。*Never offer to teach ~ to swim*.〔谚〕别班门弄斧。*a big ~* 大亨,大人物。*a cool ~* 无耻之徒。*a dull ~* 钝汉。*a loose ~* 放荡鬼。*a queer ~* 怪人,莫明其妙的家伙。***a ~ out of water*** 离水的鱼,不得其所的人。***All is ~ that comes to his net***. 到手的都要,便宜事来者不拒。***as dumb*** [***mute***] ***as a ~*** 默不作声。***big ~ in a little pond*** 矮子里头的高个子。***catch ~ with a silver hook*** 钓不到鱼之后花钱买鱼(冒充是自己钓的)。***cry stinking ~*** 拆自己的台。***drink like a ~*** 牛饮。***drunk as a ~*** 大醉。***eat ~ on Fridys*** 斋戒日吃鱼〔有些基督教信徒在星期五不食肉,作为守斋〕。***feed the ~es*** 晕船;葬身鱼腹。***~ and chips***〔主英〕炸鱼加洋芋片。***have other ~ to fry***〔口〕别有要事。***hook*** [***land***] ***one's ~*** 如愿以偿。***make ~ of one and flesh*** [***fowl***] ***of another*** 厚此薄彼。***neither ~, flesh, nor fowl*** [***nor good red herring***] 非驴非马,不伦不类。(***a***) ***pretty*** [***nice***] ***kettle of ~*** 混乱;乱七八糟。***The best ~ smell when they are three days old***.〔谚〕鱼过三天就要臭;久居别家招人嫌。***The best ~ swim*** [***are***] ***near the bottom***.〔谚〕好鱼居水底,要得宝物不容易。***There's as good ~ in the sea as ever came out of it***.〔谚〕有水何患无鱼。***Venture a small ~ to catch a great one***.〔谚〕虾子钓鲤鱼,吃小亏占大便宜。**II** ***vt*.** **1.** 在(…中)捕鱼,钓(鱼),捉(鱼),捕(鱼)。**2.** 捞出,搜出,查出,摸出。**3.**【海】加夹箍夹牢;【工】用接合板连接[加固];将(锚)吊起。**4.**〔美俚〕奉承,巴结。*~ a pond* 在池塘里捕鱼。*~ trout* 钓鳟鱼。— ***vi*.** **1.** 捕鱼。**2.** 搜查(*after*),探查,采(珊瑚等)。*~ for a living* 捕鱼谋生。***~ in the air*** 缘木求鱼。***~ in troubled waters*** 混水摸鱼,趁火打劫。***~ or cut bait*** 要就大干要就不干。***~ out*** [***up***] (从水中)吊起;捞出,搜出;把鱼捕尽。~ **ball** [**cake**] 鱼丸子。~ **beam** 下部鼓出的桁梁。~**bone** ***n*.** 鱼骨。~ **bowl** **1.** 玻璃鱼缸。**2.** "玻璃鱼缸"场所〔喻一举一动易为人所知的地方〕。~ **crow**【动】渔鸦。~ **culture** [**breeding**] 养鱼法。~ **culturist** 养鱼家。~**-eye**【摄】(指镜头)超广角的〔视角特别广阔的〕;用超广角镜头拍摄的。~ **farm** 养鱼场。~ **farming** 养鱼(法)。~ **flake**〔Can.〕晒鱼台。~ **flour** 鱼粉。~ **fork** 鱼叉;鱼钩。~ **fry** **1.** 炸鱼。**2.** 吃炸鱼的野餐。**3.** 鱼苗。~ **globe** 金鱼缸。~ **glue** 鱼胶。~ **hawk**【动】鱼鹰,鹗。~**-hook** 鱼钩,钓钩;【船】钓锚钩子。~**-in** 集体进入禁区钓[捕]鱼示威〔表示反对将该地列为钓[捕]鱼禁区〕。~ **joint** 夹板接合。~ **kettle** 有柄的椭圆形煮鱼锅。~ **knife** 鱼刀,食鱼用刀。~ **ladder** 鱼梯〔使鱼逐级向上游过水闸或瀑布的一系列台阶式水道〕。~**like** ***a*.** 鱼似的;冷淡的。~**-line** ***n*.** 钓丝。~ **meal** 鱼粉肥料,鱼粉饲料。~**monger**〔主英〕鱼贩子。~**net** **1.** 鱼网。**2.**【军】伪装网。~ **paper** 青壳纸,鱼膏纸。~ **plate** 接合板;(铁轨接头处用的)鱼尾(夹)板。~**pond** 养鱼塘;〔谑〕海。~**pot** 捕鱼笼。~**pound** ***n*.**〔方〕(捕鱼)潜网;鱼梁。~ **protein concentrate** (作食品用)精制鱼蛋白粉。~**-skin** 鱼皮,(尤指)鲨鱼皮。~**skin disease**【医】鱼鳞癣(= ichthyosis)。~ **slice**〔英〕(侍者用)分鱼刀;煎鱼锅铲。~**sound** ***n*.** 鱼鳔。~ **stick**〔美〕炸鱼排〔一种长方形裹着面包粉的油炸鱼排或鱼饼〕。~ **story**〔口〕牛皮,大话,靠不住的故事。~ **strainer** (从锅里捞鱼的)笊篱。~ **tackle** 收锚复滑车。~**tail** **1.** ***a*.** 鱼尾状的。**2.** ***v*.** 摆尾飞行(~*tail burner* 鱼尾状煤气喷火口。~*tail wind* 扰乱弹道的不定风)。~ **torpedo** 鱼雷。~**way** = ~ ladder. ~**weir** 鱼梁。~**wife**, ~**woman** 卖鱼妇;骂街的泼妇。~**works**〔*sing*., *pl*.〕鱼场设备;水产制品厂。~ **worm** 蚯蚓 (= angle worm)。

fish-blood·ed [ˈfiʃˈblʌdid; ˋfɪʃˋblʌdɪd] ***a*.** 冷血的,无情的。

Fish·er [ˈfiʃə; ˋfɪʃɚ] ***n*.** 菲舍〔姓氏〕。

fish·er[1] [ˈfiʃə; ˋfɪʃɚ] ***n*.** **1.** 渔夫;渔船。**2.**【动】食鱼貂;以鱼为食的兽。*a ~ of men*〔谑〕传教师。***the great ~ of souls*** 撒旦,魔鬼。

fish·er[2] [ˈfiʃə; ˋfɪʃɚ] ***n*.**〔英俚、古〕一镑纸币。

fish·er·man [ˈfiʃəmən; ˋfɪʃɚmən] ***n*.** **1.** 捕鱼人。**2.** 渔船。~*'s bend* 渔人结。

fish·er·y [ˈfiʃəri; ˋfɪʃərɪ] ***n*.** **1.** 渔业,水产业。**2.** 渔场。**3.** 打鱼执照,捕鱼权。**4.** 渔业公司;养鱼术。*the pearl ~* 采珠场。

fish·i·fy [ˈfiʃifai; ˋfɪʃɪfaɪ] ***vt*.**〔美俚〕为…供应鱼,使有鱼。

fish·ing [ˈfiʃiŋ; ˋfɪʃɪŋ] ***n*.** **1.** 钓鱼,捕鱼;捕鱼权。**2.** 鱼尾接口。~ **banks** [**ground**] 渔场。~ **boat** 渔船。~ **expedition** **1.** 审前盘问。**2.** 非法调查。~ **line** 钓丝。~ **net** 渔网。~ **pole** 钓竿〔只有竿、钩和钓丝的简单钓竿〕。~ **population** 渔民。~ **rod** 分节活动钓竿。~ **season** 渔汛期。~ **tackle** 钓具。

fish·y [ˈfiʃi; ˋfɪʃɪ] ***a*.** (*-i·er*; *-i·est*) **1.** 鱼的,多鱼的;鱼肉做的,鱼似的。**2.** 腥臭的。**3.** (眼光)模糊的;〔俚〕可疑的,靠不住的。*a ~ translation* 不忠实的翻译。*There's something ~ about it*. 这里面有鬼。**fish·i·ly** ***ad*.** **fish·i·ness** ***n*.**

fisk [fisk; fɪsk] ***n*.** = fisc.

fissi- *comb*. *f*. 表示"分裂","裂变": *fissi*le, *fissi*parous.

fis·sile [ˈfisail; ˋfɪsaɪl] ***a*.** **1.** 易分裂的,可分裂的。**2.**【原】裂变的。~ *material* 可裂变物质,核燃料。

fis·sil·i·ty [fiˈsiliti; fɪˋsɪlətɪ] ***n*.**【原】可裂变性。

fis·sion [ˈfiʃən; ˋfɪʃən] **I** ***n*.** **1.** 裂开,分裂。**2.**【生】分裂生殖。**3.**【原】(核)裂变。*a ~ bomb* (裂变式)原子弹。*~ product* 裂变产物。*reproduction by ~* 分裂繁殖。*atomic ~* 原子分裂。*uranium ~* 铀核裂变。**II** ***vt*.**, ***vi*.**【原】(使)裂变。~**-track dating method**【地】裂变迹定年法。

fis·sion·a·ble [ˈfiʃənəbl; ˋfɪʃənəbl̩] **I** ***a*.** 可分裂的,可裂变的。**II** ***n*.**〔常 *pl*.〕可裂变物质。**-bil·i·ty** ***n*.**

fis·sip·a·rous [fiˈsipərəs; fɪˋsɪpərəs] ***a*.**【生】分裂生殖的。**-ly** ***ad*.** **-ness** ***n*.**

fis·si·ped [ˈfisiped; ˋfɪsɪped] **I** ***a*.**【动】裂足的,叉指的(= fissipedal.) **II** ***n*.** 裂脚类动物〔包括猫、狗等〕。

fis·si·ros·tral [ˌfisiˈrɔstrəl; ˏfɪsɪˋrɑstrəl] ***a*.**【动】**1.** 宽阔而深裂的(指某些鸟类的喙)。**2.** 有裂喙的〔如褐雨燕、欧夜鹰〕。

fis·sure [ˈfiʃə; ˋfɪʃɚ] **I** ***n*.** **1.** 裂缝;裂隙。**2.** (思想、观点等的)分歧。**3.**【解】裂纹,沟。**4.**【医】裂伤。*anal ~* 肛裂。**II** ***vt*.**, ***vi*.** (使)裂开。

fist [fist; fɪst] **I** ***n*.** **1.** 拳头;〔口〕手。**2.**〔口〕笔迹 **3.**【印】指标参见号。*clench* [*double*] *one's ~* 握拳。*Give us your ~*. 让我们握握手。*write a good* [*an ugly*] *~* 字写得好[丑]。***grease sb.'s ~*** 向某人行贿。***make good*** [***poor***] ***~ at*** [***of***] 做得成功[不成功]。***the mailed ~*** 暴力,武力威胁。**II** ***vt*.** **1.** 用拳打。**2.** 紧握;掌管(风帆等),把(手)握成拳头。~ **fight** 打架。~ **law** 暴力主义。**-ed** ***a*.** **1.** 有拳头的;握成拳头的。**2.**〔组成

合词〕: close- [tight-] fisted 吝啬的,手紧的。
fist·ful [ˈfistful; ˋfɪstfʊl] **n**. = handful.
fist·i·a·na [ˌfistiˈænə; ˏfɪstɪˋenə] **n**. 拳击界。
fist·ic(al) [ˈfistik(əl); ˋfɪstɪk(əl)] **a**. 〔口〕拳击的,拳术的。*a ~ arena* 拳赛场。*a ~ populace* 拳赛迷。
fist·i·cuff [ˈfistiˌkʌf; ˋfɪstɪˏkʌf] **n**. **1**. 拳的一击。**2**. 〔*pl*.〕互殴,乱斗。***come to ~s*** 打起架来。
fis·tu·la [ˈfistjulə; ˋfɪstʃʊlə] **n**. (*pl*. *~s*, *-lae* [-liː; -li]) **1**. 【动】细管,喙管。**2**. 【医】瘘(管)。**-r a**.
fis·tu·lous [ˈfistjuləs; ˋfɪstʃʊləs] **a**. **1**. 烟斗状的,管状的;管子做的,有管的。**2**. 【医】瘘管(状)的 (= fistular)。
fist·y [ˈfisti; ˋfɪstɪ] **a**. = fistic(al).
fit[1] [fit; fɪt] **I vt**. (*-tt-*) **1**. 适合。**2**. 使适合,使适应;使(服装等)合身;使合格,使胜任;〔美〕使准备(投考)。**3**. 为…提供设备,供给 (*with*)。**4**. 耕(地)。*This coat does not ~ me*. 这件上衣我穿着不合身。*~ a coat on sb*. 给某人试上衣样子。*~ the dress to the figure* 量体裁衣。*~ students for college* 训练学生使能升入大学。— **vi**. **1**. 适合;调和,配合;(服装等)合身,合适;适应。**2**. 〔美〕准备(投考)。*Her clothes ~ well*. 她的衣服很合身。*The window ~s badly*. 这窗户关不上。*~* ***in*** **1**. 使适合,使顺应。**2**. 适合;调和(*~ in with its surroundings* 适应环境)。*~* ***into*** 顺应,调和。*~* ***like a glove*** 完全合适。*~* ***on*** **1**. 装上;把…置于原处(*~ the lid on* 把盖子盖上)。**2**. 试穿(*have one's new coat fitted on* 试穿新上衣)。*~* ***oneself for*** 作好…的准备。*~* ***out*** **1**. 使装备齐全,准备好。**2**. 办妥(*~ out a ship for a voyage* 把船装备好以便远航)。*~* ***the cap on*** 认为所指的是自己。*~* ***up*** 准备,装备,设备(*fit up the house with electric light* 给房子安装电灯)。**II a**. **1**. 适当的,相称的,合适的,适宜的(*for*; *to*)。**2**. 胜任的,合格的;有准备的。**3**. 〔口〕几乎要…的。**4**. 〔俚〕健康的,结实的。*be not ~ to be seen* 样子见不得人。*the survival of the fittest* 适者生存。*I walked till I was ~ to drop*. 我走到快累倒才停。*laugh ~ to burst oneself* 捧腹大笑。*Is he ~ for work* [*to travel*] *yet?* 他还能工作[旅行]吗? ***as ~ as a fiddle*** [***flea***] 很健康,神采奕奕。***be ~ for*** 适于,适合。***feel ~*** 精神极好。*~* ***to be tied*** 大发脾气(*She looked ~ to be tied*. 她看上去气得要命)。*~* ***to kill*** 极度地,大大地(*The girl was dressed up ~ to kill*. 这女孩浓妆艳抹)。***keep ~*** 保持健康。**III ad**. 适合地,恰当地;适时地〔仅用于下列成语〕: ***see*** [***think***] *~* ***to*** (***do***)... 认为应当(做…)。**IV n**. **1**. 适当,妥当;合身。**2**. 〔俚〕(投考)准备 (*for*)。**3**. 【机】配合;密接部。*force ~* 压入配合。*shrink ~* 冷缩配合。*This coat is an easy* [*a bad*, *a poor*] *~*. 这件衣服合身[不合身]。
fit[2] [fit; fɪt] **n**. **1**. (病的)发作,惊厥,(婴儿的)惊风。**2**. (感情的)激发;一时高兴。*a ~ of epilepsy* 癫痫发作。*have ~s of coughing* 一阵阵咳嗽。*fall down in a ~* 昏倒。*a ~ of fury* 勃然大怒。*a ~ of industry* 一时的勤勉。***beat*** [***knock***] ***sb***. ***into ~s*** 彻底打败某人。***by ~s*** (***and starts***) 凭一时高兴,忽冷忽热地,一阵阵地。***give sb***. ***~s*** [***a ~***] 〔口〕使某人大吃一惊;使某人大发脾气。***go into ~s*** (因癫痫等)昏过去。***have*** [***throw***] ***a ~*** 〔口〕大发脾气,大为不安。***in a ~ of rage*** [***anger***] 一时气愤。***scream oneself into ~s*** 狂叫,拼命叫。***when the ~ is on sb***. 当某人一时高兴时。
fit[3] [fit; fɪt] **n**. 〔古〕**1**. 诗歌;故事。**2**. (诗歌的)一节。
Fitch [fitʃ; fɪtʃ] **n**. **1**. 菲奇〔姓氏〕。**2**. **John ~** 约翰·菲奇〔1743—1798,美国汽船发明者〕。
fitch [fitʃ; fɪtʃ] **n**. 【动】鸡鼬,鸡貂;鸡鼬毛。
fitch·et [ˈfitʃit; ˋfɪtʃet], **fitch·ew** [ˈfitʃu; ˋfɪtʃʊ] **n**. = fitch.
fit·ful [ˈfitful; ˋfɪtfəl] **a**. 发作的;间歇的;不定的。*a ~ breeze* 一阵阵微风。*a ~ gleam* 忽明忽灭的光。*a ~ wind* 方向不定的风。*a ~ worker* 忽作忽息的工人。**-ly ad**. **-ness n**.
fit·i·fied [ˈfitifaid; ˋfɪtɪfaɪd] **a**. 〔美〕**1**. 癫痫的。**2**. 行为古怪的,反复无常的。
fit·ly [ˈfitli; ˋfɪtlɪ] **ad**. 适合地,合宜地,适时的。
fit·ment [ˈfitmənt; ˋfɪtmənt] **n**. **1**. 家具,设备。**2**. 〔*pl*.〕附件,配件(= fittings)。
fit·ness [ˈfitnis; ˋfɪtnɪs] **n**. **1**. 适当,恰当,合理。**2**. 健康。*the ~ of things* 事物的合情合理。*~* **centre** 健身中心。*~* **test** 健康检查。*~* **walking** 健身快步走。
fit-out [ˈfitəut; ˋfɪtaʊt] **n**. (旅行等的)准备;装备。
fit·ted [ˈfitid; ˋfɪtɪd] **a**. 按实物尺寸做的。*~ bed sheets* 与床身宽长一致的床单。*a ~ coat* 定做的上衣。
fit·ter [ˈfitə; ˋfɪtɚ] **n**. **1**. 装配钳工。**2**. 裁剪和试样的服装工人。**3**. 〔*pl*.〕破片,碎片。*~'s shop* 装配车间。
fit·ting [ˈfitiŋ; ˋfɪtɪŋ] **I n**. **1**. 配合,装配,装修。**2**. (衣样的)试穿。**3**. 〔*pl*.〕【机】用具;零件,附件,(接头)配件。**4**. 家具,装置,设备,器材。*a ~ shop* 装配车间;装配厂。*be ready for a ~* 准备试衣。*gas and electric-light ~s* 煤气和电灯设备。*~* **school** 〔美〕补习学校。**II a**. 适当的。**-ly ad**. **-ness n**.
fit-up [ˈfitʌp; ˋfɪtʌp] **n**. 〔英〕(可以带着走的)临时舞台装置[道具]。*a ~ company* 流动剧团。
Fitz- [fits-; fɪts-] **pref**. 表示"…的儿子"〔*cf*. Mac-, Mc-, O'-〕, 旧时用来表示王族的庶子: *Fitz*roy (国王的庶子), *Fitz*clarnece (Clarnece 公爵的庶子)。
Fitz·ger·ald [fitsˈdʒerəld; fɪtsˋdʒerəld] **n**. 菲茨杰拉德〔姓氏〕。
Fitz·john [fitsˈdʒɔn; fɪtsˋdʒɑn] **n**. 菲茨章〔姓氏〕。
Fitz·roy [fitsˈrɔi; fɪtsˋrɔɪ] **n**. 菲茨罗伊〔姓氏〕。
five [faiv; faɪv] **I num**. 五,五个;第五。**II n**. **1**. 五岁;五点钟;(牌的)五点;【板球】得五分;5 镑钞票;〔*pl*.〕5 号大小的手套[鞋袜、衣服等]。**2**. 〔俚〕〔*pl*.〕五厘公债(等);〔美〕五人篮球队;五个一组的东西。*~ and twenty = twenty-five* 二十五。*a bunch of ~s* 手,拳头。*~ senses* 五官。*~*-**by**-*~* **a**. 〔美俚〕矮胖的。*~*-**case note** 〔美俚〕五元钞。**F- Civilized Nations** 【史】北美易洛魁 (Cherokee) 族五个印第安部落联盟。*~*-**fold a**., **ad**. 五倍,五重。*~* **hundred** 五百;五百分〔纸牌游戏〕。*~*-**o'clock shadow** (清晨刮脸的人)傍晚已经长出的微微一层髭须。*~* **o'clock tea** 午后茶点。*~*-**ouncers** 〔*pl*.〕〔美俚〕拳,一拳。*~*-**pence** 〔英〕五便士〔口 fippence〕;〔美〕5 分(铜币)。*~*-**penny a**. 〔英〕五便士的。*~* **percents** 〔*pl*.〕五厘利债券;股息五厘的股票。*~*-**spot** **1**. 五点的纸牌。**2**. 〔美俚〕五元钞票。*~*-**star a**. 五个星的;五星级的;第一流的 (*a ~-star general* 美国的五星上将。*a ~-star film* 第一流影片)。**F- Towns** 英国五大陶瓷名城。
five-and-dime [ˈfaivənˈdaim; ˋfaɪvənˋdaɪm] **n**. 〔美俚〕专售廉价商品的商店。
five-and-ten-cent (**store**) [ˈfaivnˈtenˈsent; ˋfaɪvnˋtenˋsent] 〔美俚〕廉价品商店;五分一角钱商店。〔亦作 five-and-ten, five-and-dime.〕
five-fin·ger [ˈfaivˌfiŋgə; ˋfaɪvˏfɪŋgɚ] **n**. 【植】**1**. 委陵菜属(= cinquefoil)。**2**. 高报春(= oxlip)。**3**. 五叶地锦(= Virginia creeper)。**4**. 任何掌状裂叶或花冠的植物。
fiv·er [ˈfaivə; ˋfaɪvɚ] **n**. 〔英俚〕五镑钞;〔美〕五元钞。
fives[1] [faivz; faɪvz] **n**. 〔*pl*.〕〔用作单数〕〔英〕(二人或四人对墙投击的)手球。
fives[2] [faivz; faɪvz] **n**. (马等的)腺疫,传染性卡他。
five·shoot·er [ˈfaivˌʃuːtə; ˋfaɪvˏʃutɚ] **n**. 左轮枪。
fix [fiks; fɪks] **I vt**. **1**. 使固定;安装。**2**. 集中注意于,盯住,凝视。**3**. 打定(主意),抱定(宗旨);牢记。**4**. 决定;确定;规定。**5**. 阉割。**6**. 使固定;【化】使凝固,使不挥发;【摄】定(影)。**7**. 安排;准备。**8**. 〔美口〕调整,整理;修理。**9**. 〔口〕拉拢,收买,操纵,贿赂。**10**. 〔口〕打败;偿清。**11**. 烧(火);封(火)。**12**. 【生】(为显微镜检查等目的而)固定(机体,组织等)。*bacteria that ~ nitrogen* 固氮菌。*~*

all the blame on sb. 把过失都推给某人。～ *bayonets* 上刺刀。～ *one's attention on* [*upon*] 集中注意力于…。～ *one's gaze* [*eyes*] *on* [*upon*] 注视。～ *sb*. *with one's eyes* 用眼睛盯牢某人。～ *a machine* 修理机器。～ *a jury* 买通陪审团。～ *one's account* 清账。— *vi*. 1. 固着;固定。2.【化】凝固,不挥发。3. 注目。4. 决定,选定;〔美口〕准备,打算。*She is* ～*ing to go skating*. 她正准备去滑冰。～ **it** 〔美口〕处理。～ **on** [**upon**] 决定(～ *on a date for the meeting* 决定开会日期)。～ **out** 把船具备齐,准备出航。～ **up** 1. 安顿住处。2.〔美口〕修理,修补;解决,商妥;组织,编成。3. 打扮妥当(～ *up a dispute* 排解争端。～ *up sb*. *for the night* 安顿某人过夜。～ *sb*. *up with a job* 安排某人工作)。**II** *n*. 1. (船只、飞机等的)方位,定位。2.〔美口〕困境。3.〔美俚〕(比赛等)通过作弊预先安排好的结果[定局]。4.〔俚〕(吸毒者的)自我毒品注射。*navigator* ～ 领航坐标。*radar* [*radio*] ～ 雷达[无线电]定位。***be in a*** (***pretty***) ～ 束手无策,进退两难。***get oneself into a bad*** ～ 陷入困境。***in a fine*** ～ 情况好。***out of*** ～ 〔美俚〕(钟表等)不准;(身体)不舒服。

fix·a·ble [ˈfiksəbl; ˋfɪksəbl] *a*. 可固定的。

fix·ate [ˈfikseit; ˋfɪkset] *vt*., *vi*. 1. (使)凝视;(使)注意。2. (使)固定下来。

fix·a·tion [fikˈseiʃən; fɪkˋseʃən] *n*. 1. 固定;凝固。2. 凝视。3.【心】(青春早期的)固恋。4.【摄】定相;定影。～ *of tissues*【生】组织固定法。

fix·a·tive [ˈfiksətiv; ˋfɪksətɪv] **I** *a*. 1. 固着的,固定的。2. 定色的,防挥发的,防止褪色的。**II** *n*.【生、化】固定剂,固着剂;【摄】定影液。

F

fix·a·ture [ˈfiksətʃə; ˋfɪksətʃɚ] *n*. 发蜡。

fixed [fikst; fɪkst] *a*. 1. 固定的;确定的,不变的,固执的。2.【化】凝固的,不易挥发的。3.〔美口〕(在经济上)处境…的。4.〔美俚〕(比赛等)通过作弊预先安排好结果的。*a* ～ *deposit* 定期存款。*a* ～ *fact* 〔美〕确定事实。*a* ～ *gun*【军】固定机枪。*a* ～ *income* 固定收入。*a* ～ *point* 警察常驻的地方。～ *par of exchange* 汇兑的法定平价。*a* ～ *oil* 不挥发性油,固定油。*well* ～ 〔美〕生活宽裕。～ **assets** 固定资产(*opp*. current assets)。～ **capital** 固定资本〔*cf*. circulating capital〕。～ **charge** 固定支出。～ **cost** 固定成本〔不因生意大小而变动的成本〕。～ **idea**【心】固执的思想;固定妄想。～ **price** 定价,标价。～ **property** 不动产。～ **rate** 固定汇率。～ **satellite** 固定人造卫星(如通讯卫星)。～ **star** 恒星。

fix·ed·ly [ˈfiksidli; ˋfɪksədlɪ] *ad*. 固定地;不变地;决心地;集中地。

fix·ed·ness [ˈfiksidnis; ˋfɪksɪdnɪs] *n*. 1. 固定性,稳定性,耐挥发性。2. 固定的东西。

fix·er [ˈfiksə; ˋfɪksɚ] *n*. 1. 固定器。2.【摄】定影剂。3. 维修工,保全工。4.〔美口〕向警察行贿[说项]者,在政党中奔走调停者。5.〔美俚〕贩毒的人。

fix·ing [ˈfiksiŋ; ˋfɪksɪŋ] *n*. 1. 固着,固定;【摄】定影,定相。2. 修理,整理。3.〔*pl*.〕〔美〕设备;装饰;〔美口〕(菜肴的)配料;调味品,花色配菜。*a* ～ *salt* (盐基性的)定色剂。*roast turkey and all the* ～*s* 烤火鸡以及配菜。～ **solution**【摄】定影液。

fix·i·ty [ˈfiksiti; ˋfɪksətɪ] *n*. = fixedness.

fixt [fikst; fɪkst] 〔诗〕fix 的过去式及过去分词。

fix·ture [ˈfikstʃə; ˋfɪkstʃɚ] *n*. 1. 固定,固定状态;固定物;【机】装置器,工件夹具。2.〔*pl*.〕【法】(不动产的)固定附着物〔房屋、树木等〕。3.【商】定期放款,定期存款。4. 运动会举行日;比赛项目。5. 固定在某地[某项工作]的人。*an A*-～ A 形电杆;A 形支柱。*gas* ～*s* 煤气设备。*racing* ～*s* 赛马日期。

fiz [fiz; fɪz] *n*., *v*. = fizz.

fiz·gig [ˈfizgig; ˋfɪzgɪg] *n*. 1.〔古〕轻浮的女子。2. 发嘶嘶声的烟火。3. 旋转的儿童玩具。4. 鱼叉。

fizz [fiz; fɪz] **I** *n*. 1. 嘶嘶声。2. 活跃。3.〔美〕发泡性饮料(特指香槟酒等)。**II** *vi*. 1. 嘶嘶地响[发泡]。2. 兴奋,高兴。～ **water** 〔美〕苏打水〔*cf*. soda water, soda pop〕。

fiz·zle [ˈfizl; ˋfɪzl] **I** *n*. 1. 嘶嘶声。2.〔美口〕失败。**II** *vi*. 1. 发嘶嘶声。2.〔口〕失败。～ **out** (燃烧物着水时)"嘶"的一声熄掉;〔口〕(计划等)失败。

fiz·zy [ˈfizi; ˋfɪzɪ] *a*. (-*zi*·*er*; -*zi*·*est*) 发嘶嘶声的,起泡的。*a* ～ *drink* 汽水(或汽酒等)。

fjeld [fjeld; fjɛld] *n*. (北欧诸国的)荒瘠高原。

fjord [fjɔːd; fjɔrd] *n*. = fiord.

fl. = 1. florin. 2. floruit. 3. flourished. 4. flower. 5. fluid.

Fl. = Flanders; Flemish.

Fla. = Florida.

flab [flæb; flæb] *n*.〔口〕松弛的肌肉。

flab·ber·gast [ˈflæbəgɑːst; ˋflæbɚ͵gæst] *vt*.〔口〕使发愣,使大吃一惊。

flab·by [ˈflæbi; ˋflæbɪ] *a*. 1. 不结实的;松软的;松弛的。2. 无力的;软弱的。～ *muscles* 松弛的肌肉。**flab·bi·ly** *ad*. **flab·bi·ness** *n*.

fla·bel·late [fləˈbeleit; fləˋbɛlet], **fla·bel·li·form** [fləˈbeləfɔːm; fləˋbɛləfɔrm] *a*. 扇形的。

fla·bel·lum [fləˈbeləm; fləˋbɛləm] *n*. (*pl*. -*bel*·*la* [-ə; -ə]) 1. 教皇仪仗扇。2.【解】扇状器官[结构]。

flac·cid [ˈflæksid; ˋflæksɪd] *a*. 1. (肌肉等)不结实的,松弛的。2. 软弱的。-**ly** *ad*. -**cid·i·ty** [flækˈsiditi; flækˋsɪdətɪ], -**ness** *n*.

flack[1] [flæk; flæk] **I** *n*.〔美俚〕1. (剧团等的)新闻宣传员;广告代理人;(演员等的)宣传员(= press agent)。2. 广告,宣传。**II** *vi*. 作(剧团等的)新闻宣传员等(*for*)。-**er·y** 广告宣传;大肆宣传。

flack[2] [flæk; flæk] *n*. = flak[2].

fla·con [ˈflækn; ˋflækn] *n*. 香水瓶;小玻璃瓶。

flag[1] [flæg; flæg] **I** *n*. 1. 旗〔*cf*. banner, ensign, pennant, standard, colours〕;【海】司令旗,旗舰旗;旗舰。2. (狗、鹿等的)茸尾。3.〔*pl*.〕(鹰等)脚部长羽,(鸟的)次级飞羽。4. 报头(印刷报名处)。*a black* ～ 黑旗〔海盗旗或升在监狱外宣布执行死刑的旗〕。*a yellow* ～ 黄旗,检疫旗。*a white* ～ (表示投降、休战、求和的)白旗。***a*** ～ ***of convenience***【海】方便旗(指在外国登记船只而悬挂该国国旗)。***dip the*** ～ 将旗降下又立即升起以表示敬意。***drop the*** ～ 落旗〔赛跑出发与决胜时的信号〕。～ ***of truce*** 休战旗〔向敌人表示希望谈判的白旗〕。***hang*** [***show***] ***the white*** ～ 竖白旗,投降。***haul down one's*** ～ 投降。***hoist a*** ～ ***half-mast high*** 下半旗致哀。***hoist one's*** ～ (舰队司令等)升旗开始就职。***keep the*** ～ ***flying*** 坚持战斗。***strike*** [***lower***] ***the*** [***one's***] ～ 降旗表示敬礼[投降];【海】舰队司令等降旗离职。***under the*** ～ ***of*** 在…旗帜下。**II** *vt*. (-*gg*-) 1. 在…上升旗,悬旗于。2. 用旗发出(信号),用旗通报[指挥等];打旗号[手势]使(车等)停下(*down*)。3.〔美军〕加旗形标识于(档案、卡片等以防止改动)。～ *a train* 打旗号指挥火车。～ *down a train* 打旗号使火车停下。～ *down a taxi* 打手势让出租汽车停止。～ *sb*. *a taxi* 为某人叫来一辆出租汽车。～ *the streets* 街上到处悬挂出旗帜。～-**boat** (做赛船目标的)旗艇;司令艇。～ **captain**【军】旗舰舰长。～ **camer** 国家航空公司。～ **commander**【军】海军中校参谋。～ **day** 1.〔英〕(卖旗募捐的)旗日。2.〔F- D-〕〔美〕国旗制定纪念日(六月十四日)。～ **fall** 旗下挥(表示比赛开始)。～ **lady** 〔美〕女信号旗手。～ **lieutenant**【军】海军上尉参谋,海军将官的副官。～ **list** 海军将官名册。～**man** 信号兵,信号旗手,(铁道等的)信号工。～ **officer** 海军将官。～**pole** = ～staff. ～ **rank** 海军将官级军衔。～**ship** 旗舰;〔喻〕(同类事物中)最优秀或最重要的一个。～**staff** 旗竿。～ **station** (铁道上的)旗站,信号停车站。～**stop** 信号停车站〔公共汽车、火车

等见停车信号方停车的地方)。~-**wagger** *n*.〔主澳〕=~-waver. ~**wagging**〔军俚〕摇旗信号;(挑战性质的)豪言壮语。~-**waver** 摇旗者;沙文主义者;摇旗呐喊的人,宣传鼓动者;激起沙文主义情绪的东西(如歌曲等)。~-**waving** 沙文主义情绪[宗派意识]的强烈表现[煽动]。

flag[2][flæg; flæg] I *n*. 1. (铺路用的)石板,扁石。2.〔*pl*.〕石板路。II *vt*. (-*gg*-)用石板铺。~**stone**(铺路用的)石板,扁石。

flag[3][flæg; flæg] *n*. 1.【植】菖蒲;鸢尾;香蒲。2. 菖蒲叶[花]。

flag[4][flæg; flæg] *vi*. (-*gg*-) 1. (帆等)无力地垂下,(草木等)萎垂。2. (力气、兴趣、热情等)松弛,减弱,衰退;失去吸引力。

fla·gel·la [flə'dʒelə; flə`dʒɛlə] *n*. flagellum 的复数。

flag·el·lant ['flædʒilənt; `flædʒələnt] I *n*.【宗】鞭打自己以求赎罪的宗教教徒。II *a*. 1. 自行鞭打的。2. 严厉抨击的。

flag·el·late ['flædʒeleit; `flædʒəlet] I *vt*. 鞭打。II *a*. 1.【动】有鞭毛的,鞭毛形的。2.【植】有鞭状匍匐枝的。III *n*. 鞭毛藻,鞭毛虫。-**la·tor** *n*.

flag·el·la·tion [ˌflædʒe'leiʃən; ˏflædʒə`leʃən] *n*. 1. 鞭身,鞭打〔尤指宗教悔过和变态性欲等行为〕。2.【动】鞭毛的发生。

flag·el·la·tor ['flædʒeˌleitə; `flædʒɛˌletɚ] *n*. 鞭打者。-**y** *a*. 鞭打的。

fla·gel·li·form [flə'dʒelifɔːm; flə`dʒɛlɪˏfɔrm] *a*. 鞭状的;细长的。

fla·gel·lum [flə'dʒeləm; flə`dʒɛləm] *n*. (*pl*. ~*s*, -*gella* [-lə; -lə]) 1.【动】鞭毛,鞭状体;(昆虫触角的)鞭节。2.【植】鞭状匍匐枝。3.〔谑〕鞭子。

flag·eo·let [ˌflædʒə'let; ˏflædʒə`lɛt] *n*. 1. 六孔竖笛,哨笛。2. (风琴的)音栓。

Flagg [flæg; flæg] *n*. 弗拉格〔姓氏〕。

flag·ging[1]['flægiŋ; `flægɪŋ] *n*. 1. 石板路。2.〔集合词〕(铺路用的)石板。

flag·ging[2]['flægiŋ; `flægɪŋ] I *a*. 1. 下垂的。2. 萎靡不振的,松弛的,逐渐衰退的。II *n*. 下垂,松弛。-**ly** *ad*.

flag·gy[1]['flægi; `flægɪ] *a*. (岩石)会裂成扁石的;(土地)多扁石的。

flag·gy[2]['flægi; `flægɪ] *a*. 多菖蒲的,菖蒲状的。

fla·gi·tious [flə'dʒiʃəs; flə`dʒɪʃəs] *a*. 明目张胆为非作歹的,罪大恶极的,邪恶无耻的,狂暴残虐的。-**ly** *ad*. -**ness** *n*.

flag·on ['flægən; `flægən] *n*. (有把的)酒壶[瓶],大肚酒瓶。

fla·grance ['fleigrəns; `flegrəns] *n*. 臭名远扬,罪恶昭彰,明目张胆。

fla·grant ['fleigrənt; `flegrənt] *a*. 罪恶昭彰的,臭名远扬的;公然的,明目张胆的。*a* ~ *offence* 明目张胆的罪行。*a* ~ *sinner* 明目张胆的为非作歹者。-**ly** *ad*.

fla·gran·te de·lic·to [flə'grænti də'liktəu; flə`grænti dɪ`lɪkto]〔L.〕当场。*be caught* ~ 被当场抓住。

flag-smut [flægsmʌt; flægsmʌt]【植】秆黑粉病。

flail [fleil; flel] I *n*. 1. 连枷;古代一种类似连枷的武器。2. 扫雷装置。II *vt*., *vi*. 用连枷打(谷类);鞭打,抽打。~ **joint**【解】连枷关节。~ **tank** 扫雷坦克。

flair [flɛə; flɛr] *n*. 1. 嗅觉。2. (某种)天资,(天生的)才能。3.〔口〕鉴别力,眼力。***have a*** ~ ***for*** 对…有鉴别力,有…的天资。

flak[1][flæk; flæk] *n*. = flack[1].

flak[2][flæk; flæk] *n*. 1. 高射炮火力;高射炮。2. 恶评,谴责,谩骂;激烈的争论,反对。*a* ~ *area* 防空火力区。~ *installation* 高射炮掩体。*a* ~ *ship* [*train*] 防空军舰[火车]。~ **jacket** [**suit**] 1. (飞行员的)护身衣。2. (警察的衬有钢片的)防弹背心。

flake[1][fleik; flek] I *n*. 1. 薄片。2. 火星,火花。3.【动】肌隔;【植】花瓣带条纹的石竹。4.〔美俚〕怪人。5.〔美俚〕(警察为了完成工作任务,用以充数的)"涉嫌"逮捕。~ *of snow* 雪片。*soap* ~*s* 肥皂片。*corn* ~*s* 玉米片。*huge* ~*s of flames* 火舌。***fall in*** ~***s*** 一片片地降落。II *vt*. 1. 使成薄片。2. 像雪片般覆盖。—*vi*. 1. 剥落(*away*; *off*)。2. 雪片似地降下。~**board** 用碎木片胶压成的木板;刨花板。~ **white**【化】碳酸铅白。

flake[2][fleik; flek] *n*. 1. 晒鱼架;食品搁架。2. (修船时用的)舷侧踏板。

flake[3][fleik; flek] *n*., *vt*. = fake[2]. ~ ***out***〔俚〕1. 因疲劳而入睡。2. 昏过去,不省人事。3. 离去;消失。

fla·ko ['fleikəu; `fleko] *a*.〔美俚〕喝醉了的。

flak·y ['fleiki; `flekɪ] *a*. (***flak·i·er***; ***-i·est***) 1. 薄片状的。2. 易成薄片的,易剥落的。3.〔美俚〕极古怪的,与常人不同的。**flak·i·ly** *ad*., **flak·i·ness** *n*.

flam [flæm; flæm] I *n*.〔口〕谎话;欺诈;诡计。II *vt*. (-*mm*-) 欺骗。~ *sb*. *off with lies* 用谎话骗人。*Stop your* ~*ming*! 别胡说。

flam·bé [flɑːŋ'bei; flɑŋ`be] I *a*. (食物)燃烧着的〔指端上桌的食物是浸在燃烧着的白兰地、兰姆酒内的〕。II *n*. 浸在燃烧着的酒内的食物。

flam·beau ['flæmbəu; `flæmbo] *n*. (*pl*. ~*s*, ~*x* [-z; -z]) 1. 火炬。2. 华丽的大烛台。

flam·boy·ance [flæm'bɔiəns, -si; flæm`bɔɪəns, -sɪ] *n*. 1. 火红。2. 艳丽。3. 过分华丽,装饰得过火。

flam·boy·ant [flæm'bɔiənt; flæm`bɔɪənt] I *a*. 1. 过分华丽的。2. 艳丽的。3. 火焰似的。4. 火红色的。5.【建】火焰式的。6. 夸张的,虚饰的。II *n*. 火焰色红花。-**architecture** 火焰式建筑〔15—16 世纪流行于法国,多采用火焰形或波状曲线〕。-**ly** *ad*.

flam·doo·dle ['flæmˌduːdl; `flæmˏdudl] *n*.〔美俚〕1. 小物件,小玩意。2. (愚蠢的)胡说。3. 吹牛;欺骗。

flame [fleim; flem] I *n*. 1. 火焰;光辉,光芒;【火箭】火舌。2. 热情,激情。3.〔俚〕爱人,情人。4.〔口〕(电脑网络上的)不礼貌函件。*the* ~ *of sunset* 火红的晚霞。~*s of anger* 怒火。*an old* ~ *of mine* 我从前的情人。***burst into*** ~(*s*) 烧起来。***commit sth. to the*** ~*s* 把某物丢在火中,烧掉,付之一炬。***fan the*** ~ 激起热情;煽动。***in*** ~*s* 燃烧着。II *vi*. 发火焰;燃烧,闪耀,发光;(激动地)爆发。*Her face* ~*d with shame*. 她的脸儿羞得通红。—*vt*. 1. 烧,加热,点燃,激起。2. 发出(烽火、火焰等)信号。3.〔口〕(在网上)向(他人)发不礼貌函件。~ ***up*** [***out***, ***forth***] 烧起来;极度兴奋,激怒;面孔发红。~ **bomb** 火焰炸弹。~-**colo(u)red** *a*. 火红的。~ **furnace** 反射炉。~-**out** (喷气发动机)熄火;燃烧中断。~ **projector**, ~ **thrower** 火焰喷射器。~**proof** *a*. 1. 耐火的。2. 防火的。~ **tracer** 曳光弹。~ **tree** 凤凰木。

fla·men ['fleimen; `flemɛn] *n*. (*pl*. ~*s*, ***fla·mi·nes*** ['flæminiːz; `flæmɪniz]) (古罗马的)祭司。

fla·men·co [flə'meŋkəu; flə`mɛŋko] *n*. (*pl*. ~*s*) (西班牙安达鲁西亚地区吉普赛人的一种顿足拍手的)弗拉曼柯舞[歌曲、乐曲]。

flam·ing ['fleimiŋ; `flemɪŋ] *a*. 1. 火焰熊熊的,燃烧灼热的。2. 火红的,火焰般的,烂漫的。3. 热情的,激情的。4. 夸张的。*a* ~ *August* 赤日炎炎的八月。~ *eyes* 热情的眼光。*a* ~ *speech* 热烈的演说。~ **onions**〔军俚〕火球形的高射炮火。-**ly** *ad*.

fla·min·go [flə'miŋgəu; flə`mɪŋgo] *n*. (*pl*. ~*s*, ~*es*)【动】火烈鸟。

Fla·min·i·an [flə'miniən; flə`mɪnɪən] **Way** 弗拉米尼乌斯大道〔罗马监察官弗拉米尼乌斯(Flaminius)于公元前 220 年修成的大道,从罗马通到阿里米尼乌姆〕。

flam·ma·ble ['flæməbl; `flæməbl] *a*. 易燃的〔现今工商业界文件中多用之代 inflammable, 因后者虽同义,但其词首 in-易引起误解〕。-**bil·i·ty** [ˌflæmə'biliti; ˏflæmə`bɪlətɪ] *n*. 易燃性。

flam·men·wer·fer ['flæmənvɛəfə; `flæmənvɛrfɚ] *n*. [G.]火焰喷射器(= flame projector)。

F

flam·y [ˈfleimi; ˋflemɪ] ***a***. 〔罕〕火焰(似)的。

flan [flæn, flɑːn; flæn, flɑn] ***n***. **1**. (硬币)坯子;【机】毛坯。**2**. 〔主英〕果馅饼。

Flan·a·gan [ˈflænəgən; ˋflænəgən] ***n***. 弗拉纳根〔姓氏〕。

Flan·ders [ˈflɑːndəz; ˋflandəz] ***n***. 佛兰德〔中世纪欧洲一伯爵领地,包括现比、法、荷等地区,为第一次世界大战激战地〕。

flâ·ne·rie [ˈflɑːnəriː; ˋflanəri] ***n***. 〔F.〕无目的闲步;游手好闲,无所事事。

flâ·neur [flɑːˈnəː; flaˋnɚ] ***n***. 〔F.〕无目的闲步者,懒人,游手好闲的人。

flange [flændʒ; flændʒ] **I** ***n***. **1**. 【机】法兰(盘);凸缘;边凸缘制造机。**2**. (铁路轨的)宽底。**3**. 【建】(梁)翼缘。*a ~ coupling* 凸缘联轴节。*a mounting ~* 安装盘。*~ of bush* 衬套凸缘。*~ wheel* 轮缘。**II** ***vt***. 在…上安装凸缘。*a ~d wheel* 凸缘轮。

flang·er [ˈflændʒə; ˋflændʒɚ] ***n***. **1**. 【机】凸缘制造机。**2**. 凸缘工人。**3**. (铁道)排雪板。

flank [flæŋk; flæŋk] **I** ***n***. **1**. 协腹,腰窝。**2**. 【建】厢房,侧翼建筑物。**3**. 【军】侧翼,翼侧。**4**. 【机】齿腹,面,齿侧。**5**. 【激光】脉冲波前。*cover a ~* 掩护侧面。*a ~ attack* [*fire*] 翼侧攻击[侧射]。*the left* [*right*] *~* 左[右]翼。***in ~*** 从侧面,在侧面。***take in ~*** 侧击。***turn the ~ of the enemy*** 由侧面包抄敌人。**II** ***vt***. **1**. 在…的侧面。**2**. 守[攻击、绕过]…的侧面。*a road ~ed with trees* 一边有树的道路。—***vi***. **1**. (堡垒等)和…的侧面相接(*on*; *upon*)。**2**. 占领两翼阵地。~ **speed** (船的)全速。

flank·er [ˈflæŋkə; ˋflæŋkɚ] ***n***. **1**. 【军】侧堡,侧面堡垒;〔*pl*.〕侧卫。**2**. 【足球】侧翼后卫运动员(= ~ back)。

flan·nel [ˈflænl; ˋflænl̩] **I** ***n***. **1**. 法兰绒;绒布;〔*pl*.〕法兰绒衣服〔如衬衫、运动衣、裤等〕。**2**. 〔俚〕(骗人的)花言巧语;花招。*cotton ~* 绒布。**II** ***a***. 法兰绒制的。**III** ***vt***. (〔英〕***-ll-***) **1**. 用法兰绒擦[包]。**2**. 使穿法兰绒衣服。—***vi***. 〔俚〕耍花招。~**board** (作教学用具的)法兰绒板,绒布面揭示板〔可把用法兰绒包着的字母、阿拉伯数字等按压于其上〕。~ **cake** 〔美〕烤软饼。~**-mouthed** ***a***. **1**. 口齿不利落的,乡土音很重的。**2**. 油嘴滑舌的,花言巧语的;耍花招的;爱吹牛的(人)。**-ly** ***a***. 法兰绒制的;像法兰绒一样的。

flan·nel·et(te) [ˌflænəˈlet; ˏflænəˋlɛt] ***n***. 绒布,棉法兰绒。

flan·nel·graph [ˈflænlgrɑːf; ˋflænl̩græf] ***n***. 可按压在绒布板上的示教图。

flap [flæp; flæp] **I** ***vt***. (***-pp-***) **1**. 拍打,拍击;拍动(翅膀),扑动。**2**. 拍打(蚊、蝇等);使(帆、帘子等)拍动。**3**. 把(帽边等)拉下。**4**. 合上,叠起,扔弃。—***vi***. **1**. 拍动,摆动,飘动。**2**. 拍翅飞行。**3**. 垂下。**4**. 乱吹,讲空话。**5**. 〔俚〕激动起来,被搞糊涂。~ ***about*** 〔俚〕闲聊,讲空话。~ ***away*** [***off***] 拍走,拍去;拍着翅膀飞去。~ ***down*** 垂下。~ ***out*** 扑灭(灯火)。**II** ***n***. **1**. 拍动。**2**. 拍击;鼓翼。**3**. 垂下物;前襟的翻褶;袋口盖;(帽)边;信封口盖。**4**. 【机】(整流罩、散热器等的)风门片,鱼鳞片,瓣。**5**. (折叠式桌子的)折板,铰链板;(活板门的)活板;【造纸】挡水板;【空】襟翼,阻力板。**6**. (鱼鳃)盖;(狗等)下垂的长耳;(菌类)张开的伞。**7**. 【医】(手术后遗下或移植用的)瓣。**8**. 〔口〕兴奋,恐慌。**9**. 〔口〕空袭(警报)。*a ~ in the face* 打在脸上的一巴掌。*a ~ pocket* 有盖衣袋。*air ~* 风门片,鱼鳞片。***be in a ~*** 在激动中,慌作一团。***get into a ~*** 激动[慌乱]起来。~ **door** 吊门,活板门。~ **dragon** 抢葡萄干游戏(snap dragon 的原名)。~**-eared** ***a***. 大耳朵的,耳朵下垂的。~ **gasket** 平垫圈。~**jack** 〔英方、美〕**1**. 薄煎饼。**2**. (随身携带的)粉盒。~**-mouthed** ***a***. (狗等)嘴唇下垂的。~**-seat** 折椅。

flap·doo·dle [ˈflæpˌduːdl; ˋflæpˏdudl̩] ***n***. 〔俚〕蠢话,胡说,瞎扯。

flap·pable [ˈflæpəbl; ˋflæpəbl̩] ***a***. 缺乏自信的,性格软弱的;容易心慌的。

flap·per [ˈflæpə; ˋflæpɚ] ***n***. **1**. 拍击者;拍击物;〔俚〕手。**2**. 苍蝇拍;(吓鸟的)叫子。**3**. 片状悬垂物。**4**. 阔鳍,鳍状肢,鸭脚板,橡皮脚掌。**5**. 〔俚〕还不能飞的雏鸟;(不懂世故的)小姑娘;〔美俚〕摩登女郎,轻佻女郎。**6**. 唤起记忆的人[物]。~ **bracket** [**seat**] 机器脚踏车后面的座位。~ **vote** 〔英口〕妇女选举权。**-ish** ***a***. 〔美俚〕**1**. 小姑娘的。**2**. (女子)轻佻的。

flare [flɛə; flɛr] **I** ***n***. **1**. 摇曳的火焰,闪烁的火光,闪光(信号);曳光管;照明弹;(太阳的)耀斑,色球爆发。**2**. (突然)烧起;(怒气等的)爆发;(衣裙的)张开;炫耀,夸示。**3**. 【摄】翳雾斑;【物】物镜反射光斑。**4**. (船只水线以上)船侧外倾。**5**. (足球的)短横传。**6**. 〔*pl*.〕喇叭裤。*landing ~s* 着陆照明弹;机场着陆照明灯火。**II** ***vi***. **1**. (火焰)摇曳,闪闪地燃烧(*about*; *away*; *out*),闪烁。**2**. (裙子等)张开。**3**. (船侧)外倾。—***vt***. **1**. 使闪亮,使闪闪燃烧。**2**. 用闪光作信号;夸示。**3**. 使(裙子)张开。**4**. 使(船侧)外倾。~ ***out*** 突然闪亮;突然发怒。~ ***up*** 突然烧起来;突然发怒;忽然喧嚷起来。~**back** **1**. 火舌回闪,炮尾焰。**2**. 短暂而意外的重新出现。~ **bomb** 照明弹。~**-out** ***n***. (飞机着陆前的)滑行平飞,拉平。~ **path** 【空】照明跑道。~ **pistol** 闪光信号枪。~ **point** 【化】燃烧点,着火点。~**-up** **1**. (突然)焚烧;(信号的)闪光。**2**. 激怒。**3**. (一时的)盛况;狂欢。**4**. 已平静后的突然爆发。

flar·ing [ˈflɛəriŋ; ˋflɛrɪŋ] ***a***. **1**. 闪耀的;发光的,闪烁的。**2**. 花哨的。**3**. 外倾的;曲线形的,喇叭状张开的。**-ly** ***ad***.

flash [flæʃ; flæʃ] **I** ***vt***. **1**. 使闪光,使闪烁;反照,反射(*back*)。**2**. 晃;迅速传达出去,拍出,发出(电报等)。**3**. 使闪现;把(发亮的东西)晃一下,亮出一下;使掠过(心头)(*into*; *upon*)。**4**. 灌水使(船)浮过障碍物,用水突然灌注。**5**. 〔口〕炫耀,卖弄。**6**. 将(玻璃)展成薄片;给(玻璃)镶盖。**7**. 给(房顶)加覆盖物。~ *a glance* [*a look*, *one's eyes*] *at* 用眼瞟一下,看一眼。*The news was ~ed across* [*over*] *the country*. 消息闪电般传遍全国。*His eyes ~ed defiance*. 他眼中显现出反抗的神色。—***vi***. **1**. (电光等)一闪;(火药等)忽然烧起来(*off*; *out*; *up*);(刀等)晃一晃。**2**. 忽然显现,突然出现(*forth*; *in*; *out*)。**3**. 忽然想起;(机智、才能等)突然显现。**4**. 飞驰,掠过。**5**. (河水等)冲泻,泛滥,暴涨。**6**. 〔美俚〕(服迷幻药后)感到恍恍惚惚。~ ***by*** [***past***] 一闪而过的。~ ***it away*** 〔俚〕炫耀,招摇。~ ***on*** **1**. 立刻心领神会。**2**. 〔美俚〕(服迷幻药后)感觉飘飘然。~ ***one's stuff*** 【美体】显出本领。~ ***out*** [***up***] 勃然发怒。~ ***upon*** 闪现心头,掠过心头,忽然想起。**II** ***n***. **1**. 闪光,闪发,焕发。**2**. 刹那,一瞬间。**3**. 浮华,浮夸,华而不实;衣饰漂亮的人。**4**. 灌注的水,堰闸。**5**. 【摄】闪光,闪光灯下摄成的照片。**6**. 速报,急报,简短电讯。**7**. 惹人注目的东西[人物]〔尤指优秀动员〕。**8**. 【军】徽章,肩章。**9**. (混合酒的)色料。**10**. (盗贼等的)隐语,黑话。*a ~ of hope* 一线希望。*~ of lightning* 闪电。*~ of merriment* 刹那的欢乐。*~ of wit* 灵机一动,突然出现的机智。***a ~ in the pan*** 空枪;昙花一现(的人)。***in a ~*** 即刻,一刹那间。**III** ***a***. **1**. 闪光的,闪耀的,一闪而过的。**2**. 浮华的,浮夸的,华而不实,假的。**3**. 盗贼的,流氓的。**4**. 〔俚〕(旅馆等)高级的。**5**. 火速的;暴涨的。**6**. (相机)带有闪光设备的。*~ language* 隐语。*~ money* [*note*] 假钱[钞票]。~**back** (电影的)闪回;(小说等的)倒叙;火舌回闪;(服迷幻药后)幻觉重现。~**-bang** 闪爆弹〔一种能发出闪光和巨响使人眩晕的防暴手榴弹〕。~**board** (调节水位的)闸板。~ **bomb** 闪光炸弹。~ **bulb** (照相用)闪光灯(泡)。~ **burn** (原子弹等的)闪光灼伤。~ **card** 单词数目抽认卡〔上面写有单词、数目等的卡片。教师逐一揭示,要求学生立即回答〕。~**-cook** ***vt***. 快速煮食。~ **cube** 立体闪光灯。~**-dry** ***vt***. 使快干。~ **flood** 暴洪〔暴雨造成的急发性大洪水〕。~-**forward** (小说、电影等)提前叙述未来事件。~ **gun**【摄】(闪光灯的)闪光操纵器,闪光粉点燃器。~ **house** (歹徒出入的)巢穴;魔窟。~ **lamp**【摄】闪光灯。~**light** 1.(灯塔、机场等的)闪光信号灯;手电筒。2.【摄】闪光,闪光电。3. 闪光灯下摄成的照片。~-**man** 1.(通匪)劣绅。2.(拳赛的)赞助者。~ **memory**【计】快闪内存,闪存。~**over**【电】飞弧,闪络,跳火。~ **photolysis**【化】闪光分解。~ **picture** 用闪光灯拍的照片。~ **point** (油的)燃烧点,发火点;(战争等的)爆发点。~**tube** 闪光管。

flash·er [ˈflæʃə; ˋflæʃɚ] *n*. 1. 闪光物;〔古〕华而不实的人物;【电】闪烁装置。2. 自动断续装置。

flash·ing [ˈflæʃiŋ; ˋflæʃɪŋ] I *n*. 1. 闪光,炫耀。2.(坝水的)决放,(河水的)暴涨;【化】急骤蒸发。3. 玻璃镶色。4.(房屋的)金属盖片,防雨板。II *a*. 闪烁的。*a* ~ *lantern* 闪光灯。*a* ~ *light* 闪光。~ **point** = flash point.

flash·y [ˈflæʃi; ˋflæʃɪ] *a*. (*flash·i·er*; *-i·est*) 1. 闪光的;瞬间的,昙花一现的。2. 浮华的,仅是外表好看的,华而不实的。3.(脾气等)暴烈的。**-i·ty** *ad*. **-i·ness** *n*.

flask [flɑːsk; flæsk] *n*. 1. 瓶,长颈瓶。2.【化】烧瓶。3.(携带用)扁瓶。4.(打猎用的)火药筒。5.【机】沙箱,砂型。

flask·et [ˈflɑːskit; ˋflæskɪt] *n*. 1. 小瓶。2.〔古〕浅篮。3.(洗衣服用的)衣篮。

flat[1] [flæt; flæt] *n*. 1.〔英罕〕地板;(房屋的)一层。2. 一套房间;〔*pl*.〕分宅公寓〔美国高级公寓叫 apartment house〕。3.(轮船的)平台,甲板。**-let**〔英〕小套间。

flat[2] [flæt; flæt] I *a*. (~*ter*; ~*test*) 1. 平的,平坦的,扁平的。2. 浅的。3. 伸平的,平展的。4.(图画等)平板的;(颜色等)单调的,不鲜明的;【摄】无深浅反差的。5. 意气消沉的,无精打采的,单调的,无聊的;〔美俚〕没有钱的,不名一文的。6.(啤酒等)走了气的。7.(市面)呆滞的,萧条的,不景气的;(价钱)无涨落的。8. 淡然的;直率的,直截了当的。9.【乐】降音的,降音号的。10.【语】平舌的;浊音的,带声的 (*opp*. sharp);【语法】无语尾变化的。11.(风帆)绷紧的。12.【军】(弹道等)低平的。*crops* ~ *after a storm* 暴风雨后庄稼倒伏。*knock* ~ 把人打倒在地。*a* ~ *price* (各种商品)一样的价格。*a* ~ *rate of 3%* 一律百分之三。*feel* ~ 感觉无聊。*a* ~ *lie* 弥天大谎。*The market is* ~. 市面萧条。*Prices are* ~. 物价平平。*a* ~ *denial* [*refusal*] 断然否认[拒绝]。***become*** ~ 泄气。***lay a city*** ~ 把城市夷为平地。***That's*** ~. 当然;绝对这样。II *ad*. 1. 匍匐地,平直地。2. 完全地;断然地,干脆地,直截了当地。3. 恰恰,正好。4.【金融】无(利)息地。*tell sb*. ~ 明白地告诉某人。~ *and plain* 简单明了,直截了当。*ten dollars* ~ 拾元整。~ *aback* 吓了一跳。*the bond are sold* ~ 公债无息出售。***be*** ~ ***broke*** 完全破产。***fall*** ~ 跌倒;完全失败;全无效果,全无好评 (*fall* ~ *on the audience* 毫不动人)。III *n*. 1. 平面;平面图;坪,平地;浅滩,低湿平地。2. 平坦部分;扁平的东西;平底船;平底篮。3.〔俚〕(容易受骗的)傻子,蠢汉;泄气轮胎。4.【乐】降半音,降音号[b];【建】平顶;【机】台面;【剧】背景屏。(***draw***) ***from the*** ~ 按照图样(描摹) (*opp*. from the round 按照实物)。***in the*** ~ 在纸上;平面图的 (*opp*. in the round, in relief)。***join the*** ~***s*** 使(故事等)首尾呼应;装出始终如一的样子。***on the*** ~ = in the ~. **IV** *vt*. (*-tt-*) 1. 使平;使降音。2. 使(图画等)平淡。3.〔美〕丢弃(恋人)。—*vi*. 1. 变平,变平淡。2.【乐】降音。~ *out* 〔美〕渐薄;打错主意,终无结果,虎头蛇尾。~ **bed**, ~-**bed** 1. *a*. 平板卡车(拖车等)的;【印】平面印刷机的。2. *n*. 平板卡车(拖车等);平面印刷机。~**boat** (浅水)平底船。~-**bottomed** *a*. 平底的。~**car**〔美〕(无盖平板)货车。~ **file** 扁锉。~-**fish** 比目鱼,平鱼,鲽鱼。~**foot** 1. (*pl*. ~*feet*) 平底脚。2. (*pl*. ~*foots*) 警察。~-**footed** 1. *a*. 平底脚的;拖着脚步走的;站稳脚跟的;果断的,无准备的。2. *ad*. 直截了当地,决意地 (*come out* ~-*footed*〔美俚〕打开天窗说亮话)。~-**hat** *vi*.【航】贴地飞行,不顾死活地低飞。~**head** 1.〔美俚〕傻子,无知识的人。2.(铆钉等的)扁平头。**F-head** 北美印第安人。~**iron** 熨斗。~ **knot** 旋圆两角结,缩帆结,平结 (= reef knot)。~**line** 1. *n*.(人死后脑电图呈现的)平线。2. *vi*.〔婉〕死亡。3. *a*.(脑电图)呈平直线的。~**ling(s)** *ad*.〔废、英方〕1. 直挺挺地。2. 以(刀剑等的)扁平面打击。~**long** *a*.〔废〕用(刀剑的)扁平面打击 (*a* ~ *long blow* 用刀剑的扁平面给予的一击)。~-**out** *a*. 1. 以最快速度的,以最大努力的。2. 十足的,不折不扣的。~ **pad**〔美口〕固定的导弹发射平台。~-**panel display**【电信】(比电视显像管薄得多的)平板显示屏。~ **race** (无障碍物的)平地赛跑。~-**riser** 垂直起飞飞机。~-**roofed** *a*.(建筑物等)平顶的。~ **silver**〔美〕银质餐具。~ **spin** 1.(飞机的)水平螺旋。2.〔美俚〕精神错乱。~ **tire** 已爆破[无气]的车胎;〔美〕不中用的人,不善交际的人。~**top** 1. 平顶建筑物。2.〔美俚〕航空母舰。~**ware** 盘碟类,银质餐具。~**ways** *ad*. 平面向下,平面与另一物接触着。~**woods** 地势平坦低洼处的树林。~**work** 通常用机械方法熨烫的毛巾、床单、衣服等。~**worm** 扁虫,扁平无环节的寄生虫。~**wise** *ad*. = ~ways.

flat·ly [ˈflætli; ˋflætlɪ] *ad*. 1. 水平地;平伏地,匍匐地。2. 平淡地,单调地。3. 断然地,直截了当地。*refuse* ~ 断然拒绝。

flat·ness [ˈflætnis; ˋflætnɪs] *n*. 1. 平坦,平滑。2. 直率,果断。3. 无变化,单调。4.(音的)低沉;(市况的)萧条。

flat·ten [ˈflætn; ˋflætn̩] *vt*. 1. 使平,弄平。2. 使倒伏。3.【乐】使发低半音。4. 使无光泽。5.【拳】打倒。6. 压缩(编制等),精简(机构等)。~ *one's opponent* 打倒对手。—*vi*. 1. 变平。2. 倒伏。3. 变单调;变呆板。4.【乐】发低半音。~ *out* 1. 打平,辗平。2. 变平;【空】取水平姿式。

flat·ten·er [ˈflætnə; ˋflætnɚ] *n*.【冶】压延工,压延机。

flat·ten·ing [ˈflætəniŋ; ˋflætənɪŋ] *n*. 整平,扁率。~ *oven*【化】平板(玻璃)炉。

flat·ter[1] [ˈflætə; ˋflætɚ] *vt*. 1. 奉承,谄媚,阿谀。2. 使满意,使高兴。3.(画像等的形象)美于(真人[实物])。*Oh, you* ~ *me*. 啊! 你恭维我了。*His portrait* ~*s him*. 他的画像比他本人漂亮。*The music* ~*ed his ears*. 音乐使他听得满意。***feel oneself's highly*** ~***ed*** 得意洋洋。~ ***oneself that*** 自以为,对自己(某方面)估价过高(*She* ~*ed herself* (*that*) *She might win the prize*. 她自以为会获奖)。

flat·ter[2] [ˈflætə; ˋflætɚ] *n*. 1.【机】平面锤;压平机,拉扁钢丝模,扁条拉模,扁平槽。2. 敲平的人。

flat·ter·er [ˈflætərə; ˋflætərɚ] *n*. 奉承[拍马]的人。*When* ~*s meet, the devil goes to dinner*.〔谚〕马屁精聚会的时候,魔鬼就无事可做了〔指吹牛拍马,使人丧失理智,必然产生恶果,就连魔鬼也不能干出更坏的事情来,因而赴宴去了〕。

flat·ter·ing [ˈflætəriŋ; ˋflætərɪŋ] *a*. 1. 谄媚的,讨好的,奉承的。2. 讨人喜欢的。3.(画像等)比本人[实物]好看的。~ *prospects* 有希望的前途。*a* ~ *review* 捧场性的书评。*a* ~ *tongue* 甜嘴蜜舌。**-ly** *ad*.

flat·ter·y [ˈflætəri; ˋflætərɪ] *n*. 1. 谄媚,恭维,巴结。2. 恭维话,谄媚的举动。***be proof against*** ~ 不为阿谀所动。***be hood-winked by*** ~ 被捧得昏头昏脑。

flat·tie, flat·ty [ˈflæti; ˋflætɪ] *n*. 1. 平的东西。2. 平跟[无跟](拖)鞋。3. 美国东部的平底船。4.〔美俚〕警察。5.〔美俚〕无立体感的老式电影。

flat·tish [ˈflætiʃ; ˋflætɪʃ] *a*. 1. 稍平的。2. 有点单调[呆板]的。

flat·u·lence [ˈflætjuləns; ˋflætjələns], **flat·u·len·cy** [-si; -sɪ] *n*. 1.【医】肠胃气胀。2. 浮夸,空谈,吹虚;自负。

F

flat·u·lent [ˈflætjulənt; ˋflætjələnt], **flat·u·ous** [ˈflætjuəs; ˋflætjuəs] *a*. 1. 肠胃气胀的。2.（食物）能使肠胃气胀的。3. 浮夸的，空谈的，吹虚的；自负的。**-ly** *ad*.

fla·tus [ˈfleitəs; ˋfletəs] *n*. 1. 气息；一阵风。2. 肠胃气。

Flau·bert [fləuˈbɛr; ˏfloˋbɛr], **Gustave** 福楼拜〔1821—1880，法国小说家〕。

flaunt [flɔːnt; flɔnt] I *vt*. 1.（耀武扬威地）挥舞（旗帜等）。2. 宣扬，夸示，标榜。3.〔美〕藐视。—*vi*. 1.（旗等）飘扬，招展。2. 招摇，夸耀。II *n*. 1. 飘扬，招展。2. 夸示，夸耀；招摇。

flaunt·ing [ˈflɔːntiŋ; ˋflɔntɪŋ] *a*. 招摇的，夸耀的，洋洋得意的。**-ly** *ad*.

flaunt·y [ˈflɔːnti; ˋflɔntɪ] *a*. = flaunting.

flau·tist [ˈflɔːtist; ˋflɔtɪst] *n*. = flutist.

fla·va·none [ˈfleivənəun, ˈflævə-; ˋflevənon, ˋflævə-] *n*.【化】黄烷铜（衍生物）。

fla·ves·cent [fləˈvesnt; fləˋvɛsənt] *a*. 变黄色的，成黄色的。

fla·vin(e) [ˈfleivin, ˈflæ-; ˋflevɪn, ˋflæ-] *n*. 1.【生化】（核）黄素。2.【化】栎（黄）素染料；吖啶黄素。

fla·vo·dox·in [ˌfleivəuˈdɔksn; ˏflevoˋdɑksn̩] *n*. 黄素氧还蛋白。

fla·vone [ˈfleivəun, ˈflævəun; ˋflevon, ˋflævon] *n*.【化】黄铜（衍生物）。

fla·vo·nol [ˈfleivənɔl; ˋflevəˏnol] *n*.【化】黄铜醇（衍生物）。

fla·vo·pro·tein [ˌfleivəuˈprəutiːn; ˏflevoˋprotin] *n*.【化】黄素蛋白。

fla·vo·pur·pu·rin [ˌfleivəuˈpəːpərin; ˏflevoˋpɚpjərɪn] *n*.【化】黄红紫素。

fla·vo(u)r [ˈfleivə; ˋflevɚ] I *n*. 1. 味，滋味。2. 风味，情趣，风趣。3.〔古〕香味，气味。*give a ~ to* 加风味，使有风味。II *vt*. 1. 给…添风味[添情趣、添风趣]。2. 给…增加香气，给…调味。~ *the cake with chocolate* 在蛋糕里加巧克力提味。**-ed** *a*. 1. 提味的。2. 风味…的（*chocolate-~ed cake* 有巧克力味道的蛋糕）。**-ing** *n*. 调味；佐料，调味料，香料。**-less** *a*. 无味的；无风趣的。**-ous** *a*. 味浓的；有香味的；有风趣的。

flaw[1] [flɔː; flɔ] I *n*. 1. 裂缝。2. 瑕疵，缺点。3.（使证件等因而失效的）缺陷。*a ~ in an otherwise perfect character* 白璧之瑕，美德中仅有的缺点。II *vt*., *vi*. 1.（使）生裂缝，（使）有裂纹。2.（使）（证件等）因有缺陷而失效。~ **detector** 探伤仪。**-ed** *a*. 有裂纹的；有瑕疵的；有缺陷的。

flaw[2] [flɔː; flɔ] *n*. 一阵狂风；短暂的风暴。

flaw·less [ˈflɔːlis; ˋflɔlɪs] *a*. 无裂隙的，无瑕疵的，完美无缺的。**-ly** *ad*. **-ness** *n*.

flax [flæks; flæks] *n*. 1.【植】亚麻；亚麻皮，亚麻纤维。2. 亚麻布。3. 像亚麻的植物。***quench smoking*** ~ 使有希望的事夭折〔flax 的原意是烛芯，这个短语的意思是使火光熄灭了〕。~ **brake**, ~ **breaker** 剥麻机，亚麻碎茎机。~**seed** 亚麻籽[仁]。

flax·en [ˈflæksən; ˋflæksən] *a*. 亚麻的，亚麻制的；亚麻[淡黄]色的。~ *hair* 浅黄色的头发。

Flax·man [ˈflæksmən; ˋflæksmən] *n*. 弗拉克斯曼〔姓氏〕。

flax·y [ˈflæksi; ˋflæksɪ] *a*. 亚麻的，似亚麻的；淡黄色的。

flay [flei; fle] *vt*. 1. 剥…的皮。2. 抢夺，掠夺。3. 严厉批评。~ ***a flint*** 极吝啬，一钱如命。~**flint**〔古〕吝啬鬼，敲诈者。**-er** *n*. 剥皮者；抢劫者；痛责者。

flea [fliː; fli] *n*. 1. 跳蚤，蚤目的昆虫。2.（伤害植物叶、芽的）叶甲科的昆虫（= flea-beetle）。*a sand ~* 沙蚤。*a water ~* 水蚤。***a ~ in one's*** [***the***] ***ear*** 刺耳话，讥讽。***send sb. away with a ~ in his ear*** 用讥讽话气走某人。***skin a ~ for its hide*** 贪得无厌，爱财如命。~-**bag**〔美俚〕1. 睡袋（= sleeping bag）；床铺。2.〔美俚〕跳蚤窝〔条件很差的低廉旅馆〕。3. 生蚤的动物。4. 邋遢的老妇人。~ **bane**【植】飞蓬（属）。~-**beetle** 叶甲科甲虫。~-**borne** *a*. 蚤传播的。~ **circus**（受过训练的）跳蚤杂技表演〔西方狂欢节的助兴节目之一〕。~ **collar**（围在家畜颈上而内藏灭蚤药的）杀蚤圈。~**hopper**【动】跳盲蝽〔棉作物害虫〕。~ **market** 欧洲街道上的廉价品和旧货市场。~-**pit**〔俚〕被认为有跳蚤或臭虫等的场所（如小旅店、电影院等）。~**wort**【植】1. 欧洲桂根旋复花。2. 欧洲亚麻子车前。

flea·bite [ˈfliːbait; ˋflibaɪt] *n*. 1. 蚤咬，蚤咬的疤痕。2. 小痛痒；小麻烦；少量的花费。3.（白马的）小褐斑。*The cost is a mere ~*. 这点费用算不了什么。*Your misfortune is but a ~ to mine*. 和我比起来，你的不幸不值一提。

flea-bit·ten [ˈfliːbitn; ˋfliˏbɪtn̩] *a*. 1. 被蚤咬的；生蚤的。2.（马等）有红棕色斑点的。

fleam [fliːm; flim] *n*. 1.（兽医用的）放血针，刺血针；【医】静脉切开刀。2. 锯齿口和锯条面所成的角。

flèche [fleiʃ; flɛʃ] *n*.〔F.〕1.【筑城】凸角堡。2.【建】（歌德式教堂的）尖顶塔。

fleck [flek; flɛk] I *n*. 1.（皮肤上的）斑，雀斑。2.（色、光的）斑纹，斑点。3. 微粒，小片。II *vt*. 使起斑点。*a sky ~ed with clouds* 白云朵朵的天空。**-less** *a*. 无斑点的，无缺点的。**-y** *a*. 斑纹点点的。

fleck·er [ˈflekə; ˋflɛkɚ] *vt*. = fleck.

flec·tion [ˈflekʃən; ˋflɛkʃən] *n*.〔美〕= flexion. **-al** *a*. **-less** *a*.

fled [fled; flɛd] flee 的过去式及过去分词。

fledge [fledʒ; flɛdʒ] I *vt*. 1. 把（小鸟）喂养到长羽毛。2. 用羽毛盖上；在…上装上羽毛。~ *an arrow* 在箭上装羽毛。— *vi*.（小鸟）长羽，（幼虫）长翅。II *a*. 羽毛丰满的，能飞的。**-d** *a*. 羽毛丰满的；快会飞的。**-less** *a*. 还没有生羽毛的。

fledg(e)·ling [ˈfledʒliŋ; ˋflɛdʒlɪŋ] *n*. 羽毛未丰的小鸟；乳臭小儿。~ *poets* 初出茅庐的诗人。

flee [fliː; fli] *vi*. (***fled*** [fled; flɛd]; ***fled***) 1. 逃走（*from*; *before*）；逃避，逃出（*from*）。2. 消失，消散。~ *from temptation* 避免诱惑。*Life had* [*was*] *fled*. 死亡，断气。— *vt*. 避开，逃避。~ *the dangerous place* 逃离险地。~ *the presence of one's teacher* 避开老师。*F- temptation*! 避开诱惑！

fleece [fliːs; flis] I *n*. 1. 羊毛。2. 一只羊一次所剪的毛。3. 羊毛状物〔如白云、白雪、蓬发等〕。4.【纺】绒头织物，长毛大衣呢，粗梳回丝。~ *fabric* 起绒织物。***the Golden F-***【希神】金羊毛〔*cf*. Argo 条〕。(***the Order of***) ***the Golden F-*** 金羊毛勋章〔旧时奥地利、西班牙的最高勋章〕。II *vt*. 1. 剪（羊）毛。2. 诈取。3.（羊毛般）盖满，装饰。~ *sb. of all he possesses* 骗取某人全部所有。*a sky ~d with white clouds* 白云如絮的天空。**-able** *a*. 1. 可以剪取的。2. 易受欺骗的。**-d** *a*.【纺】（针织物）布面起绒的。

fleec·y [ˈfliːsi; ˋflisɪ] *a*. (***fleec·i·er***; ***-i·est***) 羊毛质的；羊毛似的；披盖有羊毛的。~ *clouds* 如絮的白云。**-i·ly** *ad*. **-i·ness** *n*.

fleer[1] [fliə; flɪr] I *vi*.〔方〕露牙微笑，作鬼脸表示轻蔑（*at*）。—*vt*. 嘲笑。II *n*. 嘲笑，挖苦的言语[表情]。

fle·er[2] [ˈfliːə; ˋfliɚ] *n*. 逃走者。

fleet[1] [fliːt; flit] *n*. 1. 舰队。2. 船队；（飞机的）机队；（汽车、战车等的）车队。3.〔the ~〕海军兵力；海军。4.〔英〕连成一排的捕鱼网（具）；有一百只钩子的钓索。*a combined ~* 联合舰队。*a ~ in being* 现有舰队。*a ~ of airplanes* = *an air* [*aerial*] ~【军】大机群。*a ~ of trucks* [*taxis*] 卡车队[出租汽车队]〔指某一单位的全部车辆〕。***Admiral of the F-***〔英〕海军元帅。**F- Admiral**〔美〕海军五星上将；〔英〕海军总司令。~ **air arm** 海军航空兵部队。~ **base** 舰队基地。~ **captain**〔英〕舰队参谋长。~ **engagement** 舰队战斗。~ **fighter** 海军战

斗机。~-**owned** *a*.(出租汽车等)由公司拥有和经营的。

fleet[2][fliːt; flit] *vi*. 1. 疾飞,掠过。2.【海】(船员)变换位置。3.〔古〕(时间)飞逝。—*vt*. 1. 消磨(时间)。2.【海】变换(位置)。3. 放下(铰盘的索、缆等)。~ *aft the crew* 把船员调到船尾。

fleet[3][fliːt; flit] *a*. 1.〔诗、书〕快速的,敏捷的。2. 短暂的,转瞬即逝的。*be ~ of foot* 腿快。~-**foot(ed)** *a*. 走路快的,快腿的。-**ly** *ad*. -**ness** *n*.

fleet[4][fliːt; flit] **I** *a*. 浅的。*a ~ soil* 浅土,薄土。**II** *ad*. 浅,不深地。*plow ~* 浅耕。*sow ~* 浅种。

fleet[5][fliːt; flit] *n*.〔英方〕1. 小湾;小河。2.〔the F-〕(伦敦)弗利特河。**F- marriage** 在弗利特河一带由名誉极坏的教士主持的秘密结婚。**F- Street** (伦敦报馆集中的)伦敦弗利特街;(英国)伦敦新闻界;新闻记者〔这条街因河而得名,一般误译为"舰队街"〕。**F- Streeter** 伦敦新闻界人士。

fleet·ing [ˈfliːtiŋ; ˋflitɪŋ] *a*. 飞逝的,短暂的,飞跑的。~ **target**【军】瞬间目标。-**ly** *ad*. -**ness** *n*.

Fleet·wood [ˈfliːt-wud; ˋflit-wʊd] *n*. 弗利特伍德〔姓氏〕。

Flem. = Flemish.

Flem·ing [ˈflemiŋ; ˋflɛmɪŋ] *n*. 佛兰德人。

Flem·ish [ˈflemiʃ; ˋflɛmɪʃ] *n*., *a*. 佛兰德(的);佛兰德人(的);佛兰德语(的)。~ **bond**【建】荷兰式砌合。~ **brick** 镶路硬砖。~ **coil**【海】平放在甲板上类似蒲团的绳圈。~ **knot** 水手常用的"8"字形绳结。

flench [flentʃ; flɛntʃ], **flense** [flens; flɛns] *vt*. 剥鲸鱼或海豹的皮,取鲸鱼或海豹的油。

flesh [fleʃ; flɛʃ] **I** *n*. 1. 肉;肉食〔现多说 meat〕;(和鱼肉 fish、鸟肉 fowl 区别说的)兽肉。2. 肉体;肌肤。3. 肉欲,情欲;人性;人情。4. 血肉之躯,肉身。5. 果肉;菜蔬的鲜嫩部分。6. 肉色。7. 亲属;亲骨肉〔主要用于片语中〕;众生,一切生物。*the pleasures of the ~* 肉体的快乐。*after the ~* 照凡人地,世俗地,粗鄙地。*all ~* 众生;人类。*be made one ~* = *become one ~* 成为一体,结为夫妇。~ *and blood* 1. 血肉;肉体;人性;人类。2.〔作表语用〕现世的,现实的。~ *and fell* 全身;完全地。*gain ~* = *make ~*. *go the way of all ~* 逝世,死亡。*grow in ~* 发胖。*in ~* 肥胖的。*in the ~* 1. 以肉体形式;活着的。2. 亲身,本人。*live on ~* 以肉食为主。*lose ~* 变瘦,消瘦。*make ~* 长肉,发胖。*make sb.'s ~ creep* 使人战栗,令人毛骨悚然。*one's (own) ~ and blood* 亲骨肉,亲属。*pick up ~* 病愈后长胖。*proud ~*【医】浮肉,赘肉。*put on ~* = make ~. *the arm of ~* 人力,人的努力。**II** *vt*. 1. 用肉喂养(猎狗等);使尽量吃肉。2. 使(猎狗等)闻到肉味。3. 使(兵士等)惯于血战。4. 使长肉,使发胖 (*up*);〔喻〕赋予…以血肉,使形像生动。5. (制革)刮去(皮上)的肉。6.〔古〕使满足。—*vi*.〔口〕长肉,发胖。~-**and-blood** *a*. 血肉般的;确有其人的,真实的。~-**colo(u)red** *a*. 肉色的。~-**eater** 食肉者,食肉动物。~-**eating**, ~-**feeding** *a*. 食肉的。~-**fallen** *a*. 骨瘦如柴的。~ **fly** 麻绳。~ **peddler**〔美俚〕戏院的代理人。~**pot** 肉锅;〔*pl*.〕丰盛的饮食[物质生活],奢侈的生活,寻欢作乐的场所 (= *the ~ pots of Egypt*)。~-**printing** 鱼肉印象法〔电子追踪或记录鱼肉的蛋白质模式,用以进行辨别或研究〕。~ **side** 兽皮贴肉的一面。~ **tights** (演员穿的)肉色紧身衣。~-**tint**【绘】人体的肤色,肉色。~ **wound** 轻伤。

esh·er [ˈfleʃə; ˋflɛʃɚ] *n*. 1. (皮革的)刮肉人;去肉工具。2.〔主 Scot.〕肉店,屠户。

esh·i·ness [ˈfleʃinis; ˋflɛʃɪnɪs] *n*. 多肉,肥胖。

esh·ing [ˈfleʃiŋ; ˋflɛʃɪŋ] *n*. 1.〔*pl*.〕(制革时)刮肉。2.〔*pl*.〕(演员穿的)肉色紧身衣。3. (牲畜身上)肥肉和瘦肉的分布;长膘能力。

esh·less [ˈfleʃlis; ˋflɛʃlɪs] *a*. 1. 瘦弱的。2. 无肉体的,非物质的。

esh·ly [ˈfleʃli; ˋflɛʃlɪ] *a*. (-**li·er**; -**li·est**) 1. 肉体的。2. 肉欲的,肉感的,刺激感官的。3. 多肉的。4. 尘世的。*the ~ envelope* 肉体,躯壳。**fresh·li·ness** *n*.

flesh·y [ˈfleʃi; ˋflɛʃɪ] *a*. (**flesh·i·er**; -**i·est**) 1. 肉的,似肉的。2. 多肉的,肥胖的。3.【植】肉质的。~ *fruit* 肉果。

fletch [fletʃ; flɛtʃ] *vt*. 装上羽毛〔如装箭羽〕。

Fletch·er [ˈfletʃə; ˋflɛtʃɚ] *n*. 1. 弗莱彻〔姓氏、男子名〕。2. **John ~** 约翰·弗莱彻〔1579—1625,英国剧作家〕。3. **John Gould ~** 约翰·古尔德·弗莱彻〔1886—1950 美国诗人〕。

Fletch·er·ism [ˈfletʃerizəm; ˋflɛtʃərɪzəm] *n*.〔美〕细嚼进食健康论[法]。

fleur-de-lis [ˌfləːdəˈliː, -ˈliːs; ˌflɝdəˋli, -ˋlis] *n*. (*pl*. ***fleurs-de-lis*** [-lis, -liːz; -lɪs, -liz], **-*li'ses*** [-ˈliːsiz; -liˋsɪz]) 1.【植】鸢尾。2. 艺术上的鸢尾花形,鸢尾[百合]花形纹章。3. 法国王室纹章 (= fleur-de-lys)。

fleur·et [ˈfluərit; ˋflurɪt] *n*. 1. 小花形装饰。2. 小剑;(击剑比赛用尖端为一小球的)钝头剑。

fleu·ry [ˈfluəri; ˋflurɪ] *a*. 饰以鸢尾花徽记的。

flew [fluː; flu] fly[1]的过去式。

flews [fluːz; fluz] *n*.〔*pl*.〕(猎犬等的)上唇两旁的下垂部分。

flex [fleks; flɛks] **I** *vt*., *vi*. 1. 弯曲(关节)。2. 折曲(地层)。~ *one's muscles*〔美俚〕显示力量。**II** *n*. 1. 弯曲,折曲。2.〔主英〕【电】花线,皮线。

flex. = flexible. ~ **place** 弹性工作制〔工作地点〕。

flex·i·bil·ity [ˌfleksəˈbiliti; ˌflɛksəˋbɪlətɪ] *n*. 1. 柔屈性,挠性,柔(韧)性。2. 机动性,灵活性。3. 弹性,塑性;(光的)折射性。

flex·i·ble [ˈfleksəbl; ˋflɛksəbl̩] *a*. 1. 易弯的,挠性的。2. 柔韧的;柔顺的。3. 灵活的。~ **(lamp) cord**【电】花线,皮线。~ **coupling**【机】弹性联轴节,活动耦合。~ **pressure** 流体压力。~ **rule** 软尺,卷尺。~ **tube** 挠性管。**flexibly** *ad*.

flex·ile[ˈfleksail; ˋflɛksɪl] *a*. = flexible.

flex·ion [ˈflekʃən; ˋflɛkʃən] *n*. 1. 弯曲;弯曲部;弯曲度。2.【语法】曲折,词尾变化。-**al** *a*. 可弯曲的;【语法】屈折的,词尾可变化的。-**less** *a*.

flex·o·me·ter [flekˈsɔmitə; flɛkˋsɑmɪtɚ] *n*. 挠度计,曲率计。

flex·or [ˈfleksə; ˋflɛksɚ] *n*.【解】屈肌 (*opp*. extensor)。

flex·time [ˈflekstaim; ˋflɛkstaɪm] *n*. (职工)自定时间上班制。

flex·u·ose [ˈflekjuəus; ˋflɛkjʊos], **flex·u·ous** [ˈflekjuəs; ˋflɛkjʊəs] *a*. 1. 弯曲的。2. 动摇不定的。3.【植】锯齿状的,波状的。

flex·u·os·i·ty [ˌflekjuˈɔsiti; ˌflɛkjʊˋɑsətɪ] *n*. 屈曲,弯曲。

flex·ure [ˈflekʃə; ˋflɛkʃɚ] *n*. 1. 屈曲,挠曲,弯曲(部)。2. 折褶。3.【数】歪度。4.【物】弯曲,曲率。5.【地】单斜挠曲。~ **coast**【地】单褶海岸。

flib·ber·ti·gib·bet [ˈflibətiˈdʒibit; ˋflɪbɚtɪˋdʒɪbɪt] *n*. 1. 轻浮、不负责任的人。2. 爱散布流言蜚语的人。

flic·flac [ˈflikˌflæk; ˋflɪkˏflæk] *n*. 1. (朝后翻的)筋斗。2. 一种舞步。

flick[1][flik; flɪk] **I** *n*. 1. (用鞭子)轻打;(用手指)轻弹;(用手帕等)轻拂。2. (击球时手腕等)抽动。3. 轻弹声。4. (溅着的)污点。*a ~ of the whip* 鞭子的轻轻一挥。**II** *vt*. 1. 轻轻鞭打。2. 弹掉 (*away*)。3. 轻轻拂去(灰尘) (*off*)。~ *the dust from one's shoes* 从鞋子上轻轻拂去灰尘。—*vi*. 1. 轻击,轻拂,轻弹。2. (翅)拍动;(旗)飘扬。~ **knife** 弹簧折刀 (= switch-blade knife)。

flick[2][flik; flɪk] *n*.〔英俚〕〔常 *pl*.〕1. 电影 (*cf*. flicker[1])。2.【军】照见(指探照灯照见空中飞机);照见瞬间;(口令)集中照射。

flick·er[1][ˈflikə; ˋflɪkɚ] **I** *n*. 1. 闪烁,摇;忽隐忽现;扑动。2.〔美俚〕假装昏倒的乞丐。3.〔*pl*.〕〔美俚〕电影。

F

4. 〔~s〕〔美俚〕电影制片业。**II** ***vi*.** **1.** 明灭不定,闪烁;闪变。**2.** (旗等)飘扬,(树叶等)摆动。**3.** 〔美俚〕昏倒,假装昏倒。*The fire ~s low*. 炉火颤动欲灭。—***vt*.** 使闪烁;使颤动。

flick·er[2] [ˈflikə; ˋflɪkɚ] ***n*.** 〔美〕金翼啄木鸟。

flick·er·ing [ˈflikəriŋ; ˋflɪkərɪŋ] ***a*.** 扑动的;闪烁的,摇曳的,忽隐忽现的。**-ly *ad*.**

Flick·er·tail State [ˈflikəˌteil; ˋflɪkɚˏtel] 〔美〕北达科他州〔别号〕。

flick·er·y [ˈflikəri; ˋflɪkərɪ] ***a*.** 忽明忽灭的,不稳定的。

flied [flaid; flaɪd] 〔美〕 fly 的过去式及过去分词。

fli·er [ˈflaiə; ˋflaɪɚ] ***n*.** = flyer.

flight[1] [flait; flaɪt] **I** ***n*.** **1.** 飞行,飞翔;(鹰对猎物的)追赶。**2.** (候鸟等的)迁徙;飞行的一群。**3.** (光阴)飞逝。**4.** (思想等的)飞跃,奔放,(才智等的)焕发。**5.** 航程,飞行距离;飞翔力;定期客机,班机;搭机航行。**6.** (阶梯的)一段,楼梯;【体】(跳栏的)一组跨栏;(箭等的)连发,齐发。**7.** 射远竞赛。**8.** 飞行小队。*air patrol* ~ 空中巡逻飞行。*circular* [*circuitous*] ~ 回旋飞行,圆圈飞行。*cosmic* [*space*] ~ 宇宙[太空]飞行。*dipping* ~ 俯冲飞行。*horizontal* [*level*] ~ 水平飞行。*interplanetary* [*interstellar*] ~ 星际航行。*inverted* ~ 倒飞。*longdistance* ~ 长距离飞行。*manned space* ~ 载人太空飞行。*night* [*nocturnal*] ~ 夜间飞行。*nonstop* ~ 不着陆飞行。*round-the-world* ~ 环球飞行。*soaring* ~ 滑翔飞行。*trick* ~ 特技飞行。*a* ~ *of swallows* 一群飞燕。***a* ~ *of ambition*** 野心勃勃。***a* ~ *of fancy*** 奇想,想入非非。***in the first* ~** 〔口〕占首位;领先。***make* [*take*] *a* ~** 飞行;飞翔。***a* ~ *of stairs*** 一段楼梯。***the* ~ *of time*** 光阴流逝,时光荏苒。***wing a* [*one's*] ~** 飞行。**II** ***vt*.** **1.** 射击(飞鸟);使(鸟)惊起。—***vi*.** (鸟)成群飞翔;(候鸟)迁徙。~ **arrow** 远箭。~ **bag** 航空手提包;印有航空公司名字的旅行袋。~ **chart** 航空地图。~ **commander** 〔英〕空军中校。~ **control** **1.** (地面对飞机的)飞行指挥,飞行控制。**2.** 地面飞行指挥站。~ **course** 航线。~ **crew** 〔集合词〕飞行人员。~ **deck** (航空母舰上的)飞行甲板;若干飞机内的仪器舱。~**deliver** ***vt*.** 把(飞机)直接从飞机制造厂驾驶送往战地机场。~ **engineer** 【航】机上机械员。~ **feather** (鸟翼的)拨风羽。~ **formation** **1.** 飞行编队。**2.** 空军小队。~ **indicator** 陀螺地平仪。~**leader** 【航】飞行队队长;编队长;分队长。~ **lieutenant** 〔英〕空军上尉。~ **line** **1.** (机场的)飞机保养场。**2.** 飞行路线。~ **log** 飞行记录簿。~ **map** 航空照像用地图。~ **nurse** 机上护士。~ **officer** 〔美〕空军军官。~ **path** (飞机、飞弹等的)飞行路线,航迹。~ **pay** [**skins**] 飞行津贴。~ **personnel** 〔集合词〕飞行人员。~ **recorder** 飞行自动记录仪。~ **refuel(l)ing** 空中加油。~ **route** 飞行路线。~ **sergeant** 〔英〕空军上士。~ **shooting** (射箭的)射远比赛。~ **simulator** (地面上训练飞行人员的)飞行摹拟装置。~ **status** 飞行资格。~ **strip** 着陆场,简便机场。~ **surgeon** 航空军医,空军医生。~**-test** ***vt*.** 对(飞机)进行飞行试验,试飞。~ **time** 飞行时间,开始飞行的时间。~**worthy** ***a*.** 能够飞行的;可在航空飞行中使用的。**-less** ***a*.** 不能飞行的。

flight[2] [flait; flaɪt] ***n*.** **1.** 溃逃,逃走。**2.** (资金等的)外逃。~ *of capital* 资金外流。***put* [*turn*] *to* ~** 迫使溃逃。***seek safety in* ~** 溜之大吉。***take* (*to*) ~** = ***betake oneself to* ~** 逃之夭夭。**-ism** ***n*.** 逃跑主义。

flight·y [ˈflaiti; ˋflaɪtɪ] ***a*.** **1.** 好作奇想的;反复无常的;轻浮的;不负责任的;不认真的。**2.** 有些疯癫的;愚蠢的;发痴的。**-i·ly** ***ad*.** **-i·ness** ***n*.**

flim·flam [ˈflimflæm; ˋflɪmflæm] **I** ***n*.** **1.** 诡计,欺诈,欺骗。**2.** 呓语,梦话,胡言乱语。**II** ***vt*.** (*-mm-*) 〔口〕欺骗,欺诈。**III** ***a*.** **1.** 欺诈的。**2.** 胡言乱语的。

flim·flam·mer [ˈflimflæmə; ˋflɪmflæmɚ] ***n*.** 〔口〕骗子。

flim·sy [ˈflimzi; ˋflɪmzɪ] **I** ***a*.** (*-si·er*; *-si·est*) **1.** 薄的,薄弱的。**2.** 浮夸的。**3.** 没有价值的,不足取的。*a ~ excuse* 站不住脚的辩解。**II** ***n*.** **1.** 薄纸。**2.** (新闻记者用的)薄纸原稿。**3.** 〔俚〕钞票。**4.** 电报。**-si·ly** ***ad*.** **-si·ness** ***n*.**

flinch[1] [flintʃ; flɪntʃ] **I** ***vi*.** 退缩,畏缩 (*from*)。**II** ***n*.** 退缩,畏缩。

flinch[2] [flintʃ; flɪntʃ] ***v*.** = flense.

flin·ders [ˈflindəz; ˋflɪndɚz] ***n*.** 〔*pl*.〕破片,碎片。*break* [*fly*] *into ~s* 破碎。

fling [fliŋ; flɪŋ] **I** ***vt*.** (***flung*** [flʌŋ; flʌŋ], ***flung***) **1.** 扔,抛,掷,丢;摔倒;摔下 (*off*)。**2.** 关进 (*into*)。**3.** 急伸,挥动。**4.** 急派(军队等);急送(武器)。**5.** 乱花(钱财等);〔书〕发出。**6.** 〔美俚〕尝试。— ***vi*.** **1.** 猛冲,突进,突然走开 (*away*; *forth*; *off*; *out*)。**2.** 骂,嘲笑。**3.** (马)暴跳 (*about*; *out*)。~ ***about*** 跳来跳去;抛散。~ ***aside*** 丢弃。~ ***away*** 抛弃;愤然离开;跳出;浪费;放过(机会等)。~ ***caution to the wind*** 鲁莽,轻率。~ ***down*** 摔倒,打倒。~ ***sth. in sb.'s teeth*** 当面斥责。~ ***off*** 甩掉;逃脱;冲出;挫败。~ ***one's arms about*** 左右上下挥动双臂。~ ***one's clothes on*** = ~ ***oneself into one's clothes*** 匆匆披上衣服。~ ***oneself about in one's anger*** 气得暴跳如雷。~ ***oneself into*** 跳进,一屁股坐进;投身。~ ***oneself on* [*upon*] *sb.'s mercy*** 完全听任别人处置。~ ***out*** 投出;冲出;粗声大气地骂;(马)又踢又跳。~ ***over*** 〔俚〕离弃。~ ***the door open*** 猛然把门推开。~ ***to the four winds*** 抛到九霄云外,不再考虑。~ ***up*** 抛弃,放弃。**II** ***n*.** **1.** 扔,掷,抛;(马的)跳,踢。**2.** 谩骂,讽刺,攻击。**3.** 跳舞。**4.** 〔美俚〕尝试。**5.** 放肆,放纵。*the Highland* ~ 苏格兰舞。***at one* ~** 一下子,一气,一举。***have a* ~ *at sb*.** 挖苦某人。***have a* ~ *at sth*.** 试图做某事。***have one's* ~** 花天酒地,尽情放荡。***in full* ~** 莽撞地,猛然地;猛(跑)。

Flint [flint; flɪnt] ***n*.** 弗林特〔姓氏〕。

flint [flint; flɪnt] ***n*.** **1.** 燧石,打火石。**2.** 坚硬的东西。*a ~ and steel* 打火用具。*a heart of* ~ 冷酷的心,铁石心肠。***fix sb.'s* ~ *for him*** 惩罚某人。***get one's* ~ *fixed*** 〔美〕受处分。***get* [*wring*] *water from a* ~** 缘木求鱼。***old* ~** 老吝啬鬼。***set one's face like a* ~** 打定主意,坚决不变。***skin* [*flay*] *a* ~** 贪鄙,一钱如命。~ **corn** 【植】硬粒玉米〔一种印第安种玉米,粒极硬。粒端不凹进去〕。~ **glass** 火石玻璃,氧化铅玻璃。~**-hearted** ***a*.** 冷酷无情的。~ **knapper** 燧石匠。~**lock** 燧发机;燧发枪。~**stone** 燧石,打火石。~ **ware** 〔美〕石器。

flint·y [ˈflinti; ˋflɪntɪ] ***a*.** (***flint·i·er***; ***-i·est***) 燧石的,燧石似的;强硬的,坚硬的。*a ~ heart* 冷酷的心。**-i·ly** ***ad*.** **-i·ness** ***n*.**

flip[1] [flip; flɪp] **I** ***vi*.** (***-pp-***) **1.** 用指头弹;轻轻打。**2.** (用鞭子等)抽。**3.** 叭嗒叭嗒地动;翻动纸张。**4.** 跳上车。**5.** 起强烈反应。**6.** 〔美俚〕失去自制力;入迷;精神失常发疯。~ *at an ass with a whip* 用鞭子抽驴子。— ***vt*.** **1.** 用指轻弹,轻击。**2.** (用鞭)抽打;急速挥动(扇子等);急拉(鱼饵)。**3.** 翻动(纸牌等)。**4.** 跳上(行驶中的车辆)。~ *the ash from one's cigarette* 弹去烟头上的灰。~ ***the pigskin*** 〔美〕(足球)递球。~ ***up*** 掷钱币(按正反面决定事)。**II** ***n*.** **1.** 抛,弹;轻打。**2.** 〔口〕(短距离)飞行[传球]。**3.** 筋斗。~ **chip** 【计】叩焊,(反装)晶片,倒装片(法)。~ **phone** 翻盖式移动电话。~ **side** 〔美口〕(唱片的)背面〔尤指所录乐曲不太有名的一面〕;〔喻〕对等人物。**-per** ***n*.** 〔俚〕炒股高手。

flip[2] [flip; flɪp] ***n*.** (加有香料的)饮料酒〔如啤酒、葡萄酒、苹果酒等〕。

flip[3] [flip; flɪp] ***a*.** (***flip·per***, ***flip·pest***) 〔美俚〕 flippant.

flip-flap [ˈflipˌflæp; ˋflɪpˏflæp] ***n*.** **1.** 啪嗒啪嗒的响声。**2.** 爆竹,烟火。**3.** 触发器,触发电器。**4.** 〔俚〕(向后翻,手足轮流触地的)后空筋斗。**5.** (游乐场内装有座椅的)旋转器[电子飞船等]。

flip-flop [ˈflipˌflɔp; ˋflɪpˏflɑp] **I** ***n*.** 1. (杂技的)后空筋斗。2. (观点的)突然大转变。3. 啪嗒啪嗒的响声。4.【电】触发器;触发电路,双稳态多谐振荡器。**II** ***vi*.** (*-pp-*) 1. 翻后空筋斗。2. 观点突然改变。3. 啪嗒啪嗒作声。**III** ***ad*.** 发出啪嗒声地。

flip·pan·cy [ˈflipənsi; ˋflɪpənsɪ] ***n*.** 1. 轻率,无礼。2. 轻率无理的言语[行动]。

flip·pant [ˈflipənt; ˋflɪpənt] ***a*.** 1. 轻率的,无礼的。2.〔古〕能说会道的。**-ly *ad*.**

flip·per [ˈflipə; ˋflɪpɚ] ***n*.** 1. 阔鳍,(海豹、海象等的)鳍状肢。2.〔俚〕手。3. (潜水时缚在脚上的)鸭脚板,橡皮脚掌。

flip·per·ty-flop·per·ty [ˈflipətiˈflɔpəti; ˋflɪpətɪˋflɑpətɪ] ***a*.** 松弛下垂的,(帽子等)耷拉着的。

flirt [flɜːt; flɝt] **I** ***vt*.** 1. 用指弹起;忽然扔掉。2. 摆动,挥动。—***vi*.** 1. 摆动,飘动。2. 调情 (*with*); 玩弄。3. 不认真考虑,不严肃对待。**II** ***n*.** 1. 急投;摆动。2. 调情的人,卖弄风情者。

flir·ta·tion [fləːˈteiʃən; ˋflɝˋteʃən] ***n*.** (男女之间的)挑逗,调情。

flir·ta·tious [ˈfləːˈteiʃəs; flɝˋteʃəs] ***a*.** 爱调情的,轻佻的。

flit [flit; flɪt] **I** ***vi*.** (*-tt-*) 1. 飞速飞过,掠过,飞来飞去 (*about*; *by*; *to and fro*); 轻轻走过。2. 死亡。3. 迁移,离开;(悄悄)搬走。*make* [*take*] *moonlight flitting* (为躲债)乘夜搬走。~ ***about*** 翱翔。~ ***by*** [***past***] 迅速飞过。~ ***to and fro*** 飞来飞去。**II** ***n*.** 1. 飞去;夜逃;偷偷搬家。2.〔美俚〕男子同性恋者。~ **gun** 喷雾器。

flitch [flitʃ; flɪtʃ] **I** ***n*.** 1. 腌猪肋肉。2. (熏制或供熏制用的)(大比目鱼)鱼块;鲸油脂块。3.【建】贴板,桁板。4. (木材的)背板,料板。~ ***of Dunmow*** = ***Dunmow*** ~ 英国 Dunmow 地方赠给终年和睦的夫妇的腌猪肉。**II** ***vt*.** 把(鱼)切成块;把(木材)截成板。~**ed beam**【建】合板梁。

flite [flait; flaɪt] **I** ***vi*.** 〔Scot.〕争吵,相骂。**II** ***n*.** 争吵,相骂。

flit·ter [ˈflitə; ˋflɪtɚ] **I** ***vi*.** 飞来飞去,匆忙来往。**II** ***n*.** 一掠而过的人[物];避债夜逃者 (= moonlight ~)。~**mouse** (*pl*. ~***mice***)【动】蝙蝠。

fliv·ver [ˈflivə; ˋflɪvɚ] **I** ***n*.** 1.〔美俚〕廉价小汽车;〔谑〕一般汽车,小吨位驱逐舰,小飞机;海军小艇;不值钱的东西。2. 失败,挫折。3. 欺骗。**II** ***vi*.** 1. 失败,挫折。2. 乘坐廉价小汽车[飞机]。

flix [fliks; flɪks] ***n*.** 毛皮;海狸绒。

flk. =〔美军〕flank.

float [fləut; flot] **I** ***vi*.** 1. 漂浮,浮起 (*opp*. sink); 飘流,漂流。2. (谣言等)散布。3. (公司)成立;(计划)实行。4. (票据)流通。5. (货币)浮动。6. 在数处投票;漂荡;旅行。7. 犹豫不决 (*between*)。8. 悠哉游哉地生活,对世事不关心,逍遥度日。~ *before one's eyes* [*mind*] 浮现眼前[心中]。~ *through life* 悠游岁月。— ***vt*.** 1. 使漂浮;使浮动;使漂流。2. 淹没,以水注满。3. 创立(公司);实行(计划);筹(款);使(计划等)获得支持。4. 发行(公债等)。5. (泥水工)把(灰泥等)用镘刀摊平。6. 散布(谣言)。7. 使(货币)浮动。8. 使平滑。*a ship* ~*ed by the tide* 因涨潮而浮起的船。~ *a loan* 发行公债,筹集贷款。~ *an issue of stock* 发行一批股票。~ ***off*** (搁浅的船)浮起。**II** ***n*.** 1. 漂浮。2. 浮游物;浮萍,浮冰;木筏,浮码头;浮船坞;浮筒;浮标;水箱浮球,救生圈;【机】浮体;(钓鱼用的)浮子;(鱼的)浮囊。3. (水车的)蹼板,承水板;(轮船的)轮翼。4.【空】(水上飞机的)浮舟。5. (泥水工的)镘刀,单纹锉刀。6. (装运展览物的)平台卡车;彩车;花车;活动模型。7.【经】(货币等的)浮动。8.〔常 *pl*.〕(舞台的)脚灯。9. (织物上的)浮丝,织疵,跳花。10. 土地许可证。11. 运煤车。12.〔英〕(店铺每晨开始营业时备用作找付等用的)周转零钱。*a joint currency* ~ 货币共同浮动。***on the*** ~ 漂浮着。~**-board** (水车的)蹼板,承水板;(轮船等的的)轮翼。~ **bridge** 浮桥;(铁路轮渡的)固定浮坞。~ **finish**【建】镘修整,浮镘出面。~ **grass** 水草。~ **period**〔美〕课间休息。~**plane** 水上飞机,浮筒飞机。~**stone** (磨砖用的)磨石;轻石,浮石。~ **valve** 浮阀。

float·a·ble [ˈfləutəbl; ˋflotəbl] ***a*.** 1. 能浮起的。2. (水道)可航行的,可飘送木排的。3.【矿】可浮选的。

float·age [ˈfləutidʒ; ˋflotɪdʒ] ***n*.** 1. 漂浮,浮力。2. 漂浮物〔尤指从失事船只中漂出的破烂物〕。3. (船体的)浮出水面部分。4. 对漂浮物的占有权。5. 火车轮渡费。

float·a·tion [fləuˈteiʃən; floˋteʃən] ***n*.** 1. 漂浮;(船的)下水。2.【矿】浮选(法)。3. (公债等的)发行;(公司等的)设立;创业;(计划的)实行。*the* ~ *of a loan* 筹资。*the centre of* ~ 浮体的重心。*oil* ~ 浮油选矿。~ **balance** 浮力秤。~ **oil** 浮选油。

float·er [ˈfləutə; ˋflotɚ] ***n*.** 1. 漂浮者;漂浮物;〔美〕浮尸;浮子;浮标。2.〔口〕游民;〔美〕流动选民;流动工,临时工。3. (公司的)发起人;(债券等的)发行人。4. (公认为有可靠担保物的)流通证券。5. (运输货物的)保险。6. 镘工。7. (未决定投任何一方票的)浮动选民[投票人] (= floating voter)。9.〔美俚〕(受雇)于同一次选举中在多处作非法投票的人。10. 警察限令某人离开城镇的命令。

float·ing [ˈfləutiŋ; ˋflotɪŋ] ***a*.** 1. 漂浮的,浮动的,流动性的。2.【医】游离的。3. 移动的;不定的。4. (涂工的)第二道(漆等)。5. (船货)未到埠的,在海上的,在运输中的。~ *address* 浮动地址,可变通信处。~ *exchange rate* 浮动汇率。~ *capital* 游资,流动资本。*a* ~ *debt* 流动债务,短期债务。~ *money* 游资。*a* ~ *pier* [*stage*] 浮码头。*the* ~ *population* 流动人口。~ *tool*【机】浮动工具。~ *trade* 海上贸易。~ **aerodrome** 水上飞机。~ **algae**【植】浮游藻类。~ **anchor** 浮锚,海锚。~ **assets** 流动资产。~ **axle** 浮轴。~ **barge** (海洋)钻井浮船。~ **battery** 1. 浮动蓄电池;浮置[浮充]电池组。2. (设于船上或筏上的)流动炮台。~ **body**【物】浮体。~ **bridge** 浮桥;缆索渡船。~ **cargo** 未到埠船货。~ **crane** 水上起重机。~ **debt** 流动债务,短期债务。~ **decimal**【计】浮动小数点。~ **(dry)dock** 浮(船)坞。~ **gang** (铁路)机动养路队。~ **island** 1. 浮岛;浮动花园;浮在水面上的大片植物。2. 奶油和蛋白盖面的蛋糕。~ **kidney**【医】浮动肾。~ **light** 浮标灯;灯船;桅顶灯;夜间用救命浮标。~ **pier** 浮码头。~**-point *a*.**【数】浮点的。~ **policy** 总保险单,船名未详保险(证书),预定保险(证书)。~ **population** 流动人口。~ **rate** 浮动汇率。~ **rib** 浮肋。~ **voter** = floater 7.

floc [flɔk; flɑk] ***n*.** 1. (浮悬的)絮状物。2. 棉丛,丛毛;棉屑;毛屑;棉绒;毛绒 (= flock)。

floc·ci [ˈflɔksai; ˋflɑksaɪ] floccus 的复数。

floc·ci-nau·ci-ni·hi·li-pi·li-fi·ca·tion [ˌflɔksiˌnɔːsiˌnaihiliˌpailifiˈkeiʃən; ˏflɑksɪˏnɔsɪˏnaɪhɪlɪˏpaɪlɪfɪˋkeʃən] ***n*.**〔英谑〕(把什么都看得毫无价值的)藐视一切的心理[行为、脾气]。

floc·cose [ˈflɔkəus; ˋflɑkos] ***a*.** 羊毛状的;【植】被丛卷毛的。

floc·cu·late [ˈflɔkjuleit; ˋflɑkjəlet] **I** ***vt*., *vi*.** 絮凝,絮结。**II** ***n*.** 絮凝物;絮结体。**-la·tion** [ˌflɔkjuˈleiʃən; ˏflɑkjəˋleʃən] ***n*.** **-lator *n*.**

floc·cule [ˈflɔkjuːl; ˋflɑkjul] ***n*.** 絮状物;絮凝粒,絮状沉淀。

floc·cu·lence [ˈflɔkjuləns; ˋflɑkjələns] ***n*.** 1. 丛毛状。2. 羊毛状。3. 絮凝性,絮结性。

floc·cu·lent [ˈflɔkjulənt; ˋflɑkjələnt] ***a*.** 1. 丛毛状的。2. 羊毛状的。3.【动】丛毛的。4. 絮凝的,絮结的。

floc·cu·lus [ˈflɔkjuləs; ˋflɑkjələs] ***n*.** 〔L.〕(*pl*. ***-li*** [-lai; -laɪ]) 1.【解】(小脑的)绒球。2. 绒毛,絮状物。3.【天】(太阳表面的)谱斑。

floc·cus [ˈflɔkəs; ˋflɑkəs] ***n*.** (*pl*. ***floc·ci*** [ˈflɔksai;

F

ˋflɑksaɪ]) 绒毛丛;绒毛团;【气】絮状云;【植】丛卷毛。

flock[1] [flɔk; flɑk] **I** ***n*.** **1.** (禽、畜等的)群,羊群。**2.** 人群;(对牧师而言的)教徒;(对父母而言的)子女;(对老师而言的)学生。**3.** 大量,众多。*a whole* ~ *of visitors* 一大群访问者。*a* ~ *of pamphlets* ~ 一大堆小册子。***come in*** **~*s*** 成群涌来,纷至沓来。**~*s and herds*** 羊和牛,家畜。***flower of the*** ~ 鹤立鸡群,某一集团中出类拔萃的人物。***fire into the wrong*** ~ 打错目标。***It is a small*** ~ ***that has not a black sheep*. = *There is a black sheep in every*** ~. 〔谚〕人多必有败类。**II** ***vi*.** 聚集,成群(*together*);成群地去[来](*about*; *after*; *into*; *to*; *in*; *out*)。*People ~ed to see her*. 人们成群结队地去看她。*Sheep usually* ~ *together*. 羊通常总是成群的。~**master** 羊群牧主,牧群管理人。

flock[2] [flɔk; flɑk] **I** ***n*.** **1.** 棉丛;丛毛。**2.** 棉屑;毛屑。**3.** 棉绒;毛绒。**II** ***vt*.** 用毛[棉]屑装填;在…处植绒。~**bed** 有毛[棉]屑垫子的床。~**paper** (糊墙用的)毛面纸。**-ing** ***n*.** 植绒花纹。

flock·y [ˈflɔki; ˋflɑkɪ] ***a*.** 羊毛状的;绒毛丛生的,毛茸茸的。

floe [fləu; flo] ***n*.** 大片浮冰,浮冰块。~ **berg** 冰山。

flog [flɔg; flɑg] ***vt*.** (**-gg-**) **1.** 鞭打;鞭挞。**2.** (抽打似地)扔放(钓丝)。**3.** 驱使,迫使。**4.** 〔英俚〕非法出售。**5.** 〔俚〕打败,胜过。**6.** 严厉批评。~ *a horse along* 策马前进。~ *laziness out of sb*. 驱策某人使不再懒惰。~ *Latin into sb*. 使人强记拉丁文。~ ***a dead horse*** 徒劳无益。~ ***a willin horse*** (不必要地)强迫勤奋的人,滥加驱使。

flog·ging [ˈflɔgiŋ; ˋflɑgɪŋ] ***n*.** 鞭打,笞打。

flong [flɔŋ; flɑŋ] ***n*.** 【印】作纸型用的纸版。

flood [flʌd; flʌd] **I** ***n*.** **1.** 洪水,水灾。**2.** 溢流,涨水,潮水最高点,泛滥,汹涌。**3.** 〔诗〕河,湖,海。**4.** 充溢,丰富;大量,一大阵,滔滔不绝。**5.** 〔口〕泛光灯,探照灯(= ~ light)。*ebb and* ~ 低潮与高潮。*golden* ~ 一片阳光。~*s of ink* 连篇累牍。~*s of rain* 倾盆大雨。*a* ~ *of anger* 怒气的爆发,大发雷霆。*a* ~ *of light* 一大片明亮的光线。*a* ~ *of tears* 泪如泉涌。*a* ~ *of words* 滔滔不绝;洋洋数千言。***the F-*** = *Noah's* ~ 【圣】(旧约创世纪中所载)挪亚(*Noah*)遭逢的大洪水。***at the*** ~ 正当高潮;在恰好时机。~ ***and field*** 海陆。***go through fire and*** ~ 赴汤蹈火。***in*** ~ 洋溢,滔滔,大量;泛滥。***take at the*** ~ 利用有利时机。***throw a*** ~ ***of light on sth*.** 充分阐明。**II** ***vt*.** **1.** 淹没,使泛滥;涨满(河床)。**2.** 用水浇灌,灌溉。**3.** 涌到;冲进。*Applicants* ~ *the office*. 申请者挤满办事处。~*ed districts* 水灾区域。*be* ~*ed with letters* 信件像潮水般涌来。—***vi*.** **1.** 发大水,泛滥;(潮)涨。**2.** 涌到(*in*)。**3.** 【医】患子宫出血,血崩。*Applicants* ~*ed in*. 申请者如潮水般涌来。~ **control** 治洪,防洪,洪水调节〔如修理水闸、水库、河堤等〕。~**gate** **1.** 水门,水闸门;防洪闸门。**2.** (怒气等的)制约。**3.** 大量。~ **level** 最高洪水位,洪水警戒线。~**light** **1.** ***n*.** 泛光灯,泛光照明,探照灯。**2.** ***vt*.** 泛光照明,用泛光[探照]灯照亮。~**lighting** 泛光照明。~**lit** ***a*.** 泛光灯照耀的。~**mark** 满潮线。~ **plain** 泛滥平原;涝原,漫滩。~ **tide** 涨潮(*opp*. ebb tide);高峰。~**water** 洪水。~**way** 分洪河道。~**wood** 〔美〕漂流木,浮木。

flood·ing [ˈflʌdiŋ; ˋflʌdɪŋ] ***n*.** **1.** 泛滥;灌溉。**2.** 充溢。**3.** 【化】溢流;(分馏时的)液阻现象;(油漆干燥或加热时的)变色。**4.** 【医】血崩;产后出血。~ **irrigation** 漫灌。

flood·om·e·ter [flʌˈdɔmitə; flʌˋdɑmɪtɚ] ***n*.** 潮洪水位测量仪。

floo·ey, floo·ie [ˈflu:i; ˋfluɪ] ***ad*.** 〔常与 go 连用〕糟,不行(= blooey)。

floor [flɔ:, flɔə; flor, flɔr] **I** ***n*.** **1.** 地板,地面。**2.** (楼房的)层。**3.** (船底的)肋板。**4.** (海洋、山洞等的)底。**5.** 议员席;经纪人席。**6.** 发言权,发言机会。**7.** 表演场地。**8.** 最低数值[限度](*opp*. ceiling)。*dirt* ~ (没有铺装的)泥地面。*a dressing* ~ 整理车间。*a moulding* ~ 翻砂车间。*a naked* ~ 未铺地毯的地板。*the* ~ *of bridge* 桥面。*a competition* ~ 室内比赛场。*founding* ~ 造型工地。*a threshing* ~ 打谷场。*the basement* ~ 地下室。*the top* ~ 顶楼。*the first* [*second*] ~ 〔英〕二[三]楼;〔美〕一[二]楼。*The Senate from New York has the* ~. 该纽约州参议员发言了。*a price* ~ 底价,最低价格。***get*** [***be let***] ***in on the ground*** ~ 〔美口〕在有利条件下参加某种事业;站在同等地位获得同等权利。***be on the*** ~ **1.** 正在发言[讨论]中。**2.** 【影】正在拍摄中。***cross the*** ~ ***of the House*** 议员从一党派转变到另一党派。***get*** [***obtain***] ***the*** ~ 获得发言权。***give the*** ~ ***to*** 给予发言权。***go on the*** ~ 【影】开始拍摄。***have the*** ~ 有发言权。***mop*** [***wipe***] ***the*** ~ ***with sb*.** 把某人打得大败。***take the*** ~ 〔美〕起立发言;参加讨论;参加跳舞。**II** ***vt*.** **1.** 在…上铺地板[基面]。**2.** 〔英〕罚…坐地板。**3.** 打倒;〔口〕打败,难倒,使认输。**4.** 〔英俚〕做完(考卷等)。**5.** 〔美口〕把…减到最低限度,把(汽车加速器等)压到最低一挡。~ ***sb*. *with one blow*** 一拳把人打翻在地。~ ***an examination paper*** = ~ ***the paper*** 圆满答完考卷。***get*** **~*ed*** 被打败,被压服。~ **action** 议会采取的行动。~**board** **1.** 适合做地板用的木材。**2.** 一块地板(常指可以掀起的活动地板)。**3.** 汽车底部板。~ **broker** 交易所场内经纪人。~**cloth** 铺地板的漆布;(揩地板的)拖布。~ **exercise** 自由体操,地面体操〔不用器械,在地毯上表演各种芭蕾舞式动作以及翻筋斗,用手倒立等〕。~ **frame** 【机】地轴承架。~ **knob** (装在地板上的)门碰头。~ **lamp** 落地灯。~ **leader** (议会的)政党头目。~ **manager** **1.** 〔美〕政党提名大会中候选人的助选员。**2.** 百货大楼中分管一层楼面业务的经理。~ **partner** (经纪行派驻在交易所中的)驻所经纪人。~ **plan** 【建】楼面布置图。~ **price** 最低价,廉价。~ **push** 闸刀开关。~ **sample** 商店中做样品用过的商品(常廉价出售)。~ **sheet** 踏板。~ **show** (舞厅里的)余兴表演。~ **slab** (铺设水泥楼面、地面的)水泥板。~ **space** 地板[楼面]面积;设备占用面积。~**-through** (占有大楼整个一层楼面的)公寓住所。~ **time** 空闲时间。~ **trader** 交易所场内商人。~**walker** 〔美〕(百货商店中的)巡视员〔其职务为引导顾客,防备窃贼和监督店员等〕(= 〔英〕 shop walker)。~ **wax** 地板蜡。**-less** ***a*.** 无地板的。

floor·age [ˈflɔ:ridʒ; ˋflorɪdʒ] ***n*.** **1.** 地板[楼面]面积;设备占用面积(= floor space)。**2.** 做地板的材料。

floor·er [ˈflɔ:rə; ˋflorɚ] ***n*.** **1.** 铺地板者。**2.** 把人打倒的一击;使人沮丧的消息;难以置辩的论据。**3.** 难以解答的试卷,难题。

floor·ing [ˈflɔ:riŋ; ˋflorɪŋ] ***n*.** **1.** 室内地面;铺地板。**2.** 铺地板的材料。~ **block** 嵌木地板。~ **saw** 企口锯〔锯条两边都有锯齿的手锯〕。

floo·sie, floo·sy, floo·zie, floo·zy [ˈflu:zi; ˋfluzɪ] ***n*.** 〔美俚〕行为不检点[名声不好]的妇女;妓女。

flop [flɔp; flɑp] **I** ***vi*.** (**-*pp*-**) **1.** 鼓翼;扑拍,跳动。**2.** 啪嗒躺下[放下、坐下];〔美俚〕上床。**3.** 突然转变。**4.** 彻底失败。~ *down on one's knees* 噗通一声跪下。~ *into an armchair* 蓦地坐到扶手椅子里。— ***vt*.** 啪啪地翻动;噗地一声放下。~ *the pages of a book* 啪啪作响地翻书页。**II** ***ad*.** 噗地一声,恰巧。*fall* ~ *into the water* 噗通一声落到水里。*fall* ~ *on one's face* 噗地一声向前扑倒。**III** ***n*.** **1.** 噗通(声);啪嗒(声);落下。**2.** 大失败;失败者。**3.** 〔美俚〕床;躲避处;过夜。~**-eared** ***a*.** (猎犬等)耳朵下垂的。~**house** 〔美口〕**1.** (按床位收费的)小客栈。**2.** 监狱。~**-nik** 〔美俚〕失败了的卫星。~**-valve** 瓣。

flop·o·ver [ˈflɔpˌəuvə; ˋflɑpˏovɚ] ***n*.** 【电视】场频不稳〔电视图像因受干扰而上下跳动〕。

flop·per [ˈflɔpə; ˋflɑpɚ] ***n*.** **1.** (拍动翅膀学飞的)幼禽。**2.** 〔美俚〕变节者。**3.** 伪造事故骗钱的人。

flop·py [ˈflɔpi; ˋflɑpɪ] ***a*.** (**-*pi·er*; *-pi·est***) 〔口〕**1.** 松

软的。2. 松懈的;懒散的。~ disc (储存电子计算机数据的)软磁盘。-pi·ly ad. -pi·ness n.

flop·ti·cal [ˈflɔptikəl; ˋflaptɪkl] n.【计】(大小和软盘相似,可容纳 20—25 兆信息量的)软光盘,软光碟。

flor. = floruit.

Flo·ra [ˈflɔːrə; ˋflorə] n. 1. 弗洛拉〔女子名〕。2.【罗神】花神。

flo·ra [ˈflɔːrə; ˋflorə] n. (pl. ~s, ~e [-riː; -ri]) 1. 植物群;(某一地域的)全部植物。2. 植物区系;植物志。

flo·ral [ˈflɔːrəl; ˋflorəl] a. 1. 花(一样)的。2. 植物(群)的;植物区系的。3.〔F-〕花神的。~ *designs* 花卉图案。*a ~ emblem* (代表一国、一州等的)象征之花。~ *envelope* 花被,花盖。*a ~ offering* 花制赠品。~ **clock** 花钟。~ **leaf** 花叶,苞片。~ **zone** 植物带。-ly ad.

Flor·ence [ˈflɔrəns; ˋflɔrəns] n. 1. 弗洛伦斯〔女子名〕。2. 佛罗伦斯〔意大利城市〕。

Flor·en·tine [ˈflɔrəntain; ˋflɔrəntaɪn] I a. 1. 佛罗伦斯的。2. 佛罗伦斯画派的。II n. 1. 佛罗伦斯人。2.〔f-〕佛罗伦斯厚绸,精纺背心呢,(夏季)斜纹裤料。

flo·res [ˈfləuriz; ˋflorəs, -ɪz, flɔr-] n.〔作单数用〕【化】华(如汞华)。

flo·res·cence [flɔːˈresns; floˋrɛsn̩s] n. 1. 开花,开花期。2. 兴盛[全盛]时期。

flo·res·cent [flɔːˈresnt; floˋrɛsn̩t] a. 1. 开花的,开花期的。2. 全盛时期的。

flo·ret [ˈflɔːrit; ˋflorɪt] n. 1.【植】(菊科植物的)小花。2.【纺】绢丝。~ **silk** 优级绢丝。~ **yarn** 绢棉混纺纱。

Flo·rey [ˈflɔːri, ˈfləuri; ˋflorɪ, ˋflorɪ] n. 弗洛里〔姓氏〕。

flori- *comb. f.* 表示"花","像花": *flori*ated, *flori*culture.

flo·ri·at·ed [ˈflɔːrieitid; ˋflorɪetɪd] a. 有花卉装饰的。-a·tion n.

flo·ri·bun·da [ˌflɔːriˈbʌndə; ˏflorɪˋbʌndə] n.【植】花束玫瑰〔人工培植的一种具有一簇簇花束的玫瑰〕。

flo·ri·cul·tur·al [ˌflɔːriˈkʌltʃərəl; ˏflorɪˋkʌltʃərəl] a. 花卉栽培的。

flo·ri·cul·ture [ˈflɔːriˌkʌltʃə; ˋflorɪˏkʌltʃɚ] n. 花卉栽培,园艺。

flo·ri·cul·tur·ist [ˌflɔriˈkʌltʃərist; ˏflorɪˋkʌtʃərɪst] n. 花卉栽培家。

flor·id [ˈflɔrid; ˋflɔrɪd] a. 1. 华丽的,丰富多彩的;(绘画等)富丽的,(文章等)词藻华丽的。2. 红润的,血色好的。3. 花哨的,浮华俗气的。4.〔古〕像花一样的,用花装饰的。*a ~ prose style* 华丽体(文章)。*a ~ writer* 词藻华丽的作家。-ly ad. -ness n.

Flor·i·da [ˈflɔridə; ˋflɔrədə] n. 佛罗里达〔美国州名〕。~ **Keys** 佛罗里达州南部一狭长的珊瑚岛群。~ **Strait** 佛罗里达海峡。**f- water** 花露水。

Flori·dan [ˈflɔridən; ˋflɔrɪdən], **Flo·rid·i·an** [ˈflɔridiən; ˋflɔrɪdɪən] I a. 佛罗里达州的,佛罗里达人的。II n. 佛罗里达州人。

flo·rid·i·ty [flɔˈriditi; flɔˋrɪdətɪ] n. 1. 华丽,绚丽。2. 鲜艳。3. 花哨。

flo·rif·er·ous [flɔːˈrifərəs; floˋrɪfərəs] a.【植】有花的,开花的,多花的。-ly ad. -ness n.

flor·i·gen [ˈflɔːridʒən, ˈflɔ-; ˋflorɪdʒən, ˋflɔ-] n.【植】成花素。-ic a.

flo·ri·le·gi·um [ˌflɔːriˈliːdʒiəm; ˏflorɪˋlidʒɪəm] n. (pl. -gia [-dʒiə; -dʒɪə]) 1. 花谱,群芳谱。2. 名诗选,作品集锦;佳作选集。

flor·in [ˈflɔrin; ˋflɔɪn] n. 1.〔1252 年发行于佛罗伦斯的〕一种金币。2. 英国的一种银币(值二先令)。3. 欧洲国家不同时代所用的金币或银币。

flo·rist [ˈflɔrist; ˋflɔrɪst] n. 1. 种花者,花匠。2. 花商;花店。3. 花卉研究者。

flo·ris·tic [flɔːˈristik; floˋrɪstɪk] a. 1. 花的。2. (关于)植物种类地理学的。-ti·cal·ly ad.

flo·ris·tics [flɔːˈristiks; floˋrɪstɪks] n. pl.〔用作单数〕植物种类地理学。

-florous *suf.* 表示"…花的": uni*florous*.

flo·ru·it [ˈflɔːrjuit; ˋflorʊɪt] n.〔L.〕在世期,活跃时期〔用于生死年月不能确定的场合;略作 fl(or), 如: fl. A. D. 63—110〕;全盛时期。

flo·ry [ˈflɔːri; ˋflorɪ] a. = fleury.

flos·cu·lar [ˈflɔskjulə; ˋflaskjulɚ] a. 花的,有小花的。

flos·cule [ˈflɔskjuːl; ˋflaskjul] n. 小花。

flos·cu·lous [ˈflɔskjuləs; ˋflaskjuləs] a. = floscular.

flos fer·ri [ˈflɔs ˈferai; ˋflas ˋfɛraɪ] n.【地】文石华,铁华,霰石华。

floss [flɔs; flas] I n. 1. (蚕茧外的)乱丝,绪丝。2. 绣花丝线。3. 细绒线。4. 絮状物,木棉。5.【植】绒毛,(玉米等的)黍须。6.【冶】(浮于熔化金属表面的)浮滓。7. (清除牙缝中食物碎屑的)牙缝拉线(= dental ~)。*candy* ~ 棉花糖。II vi. 使用牙缝拉线清除牙垢。~**silk** n. 乱丝,绪丝;丝绵;丝线。

floss·y [ˈflɔsi; ˋflasɪ] I a. (*floss·i·er*; *-i·est*) 1. 乱丝的,绪丝的。2. 丝绵似的;轻软的,毛茸茸的。3.〔美俚〕迷人的,装饰华丽的,穿得漂亮的。II n.〔美俚〕1. 浓妆艳抹的轻浮女子。2. 任何女子 (= flossie)。

flo·tage [ˈfləutidʒ; ˋflotɪdʒ] n. = floatage.

flo·ta·tion [fləuˈteiʃən; floˋteʃən] n. = floatation.

flo·til·la [fləuˈtilə; floˋtɪlə] n. 1. 小舰队。2. 海军纵队。3. 船队。*a destroyer ~* 驱逐舰队。*a torpedo-boat ~* 鱼雷艇队。

flot·sam [ˈflɔtsəm; ˋflatsəm] n. 1. (失事船只的)残骸和漂出物。2.〔集合词〕流浪者。3. 零碎东西;废物,废料。~ *and jetsam* 1. (失事船只的)残骸和漂出物。2. 流浪者。3. 零碎东西;废物。

flot·san [ˈflɔtsən; ˋflatsən] n. = flotsam.

flounce[1] [flauns; flaʊns] I n. (裙子的)荷叶边。II vt. 给(裙子等)镶荷叶边。

flounce[2] [flauns; flaʊns] I vi. 1. 肢体乱动,挣扎。2. 跳动,暴跳。3. 猝然离开 (*away*; *out*; *about*)。~ *away* [*off*] 挣脱。II n. 肢体乱动,急动,急转;暴跳。

flounc·ing [ˈflaunsiŋ; ˋflaʊnsɪŋ] n. 荷叶边;做荷叶边的料子。

floun·der[1] [ˈflaundə; ˋflaʊndɚ] I vi. 1. 挣扎 (*in*), 肢体乱动,踉跄。2. 着慌,勉强应付,行为[言语]错乱。~ *through* 胡乱地做完 (*The frightened girl ~ed through her song*. 那着慌的女孩胡乱地唱完了她的歌)。II n. 挣扎,踉跄前进。

floun·der[2] [ˈflaundə; ˋflaʊndɚ] n. (pl. ~s,〔集合词〕~)【动】比目鱼,鲽形目鱼。

flour [flauə; flaur] I n. 1. 面粉;谷粉;粉,粉末。2. 粉状物质。*emery ~* 金钢砂粉。*wood ~* 木屑。II vt. 1. 在…撒粉。2.〔美〕把…研成粉。— vi. 碎成粉。~ **bag** 面粉袋。~ **mill**,〔美〕~**ing mill** 面粉厂。

flour·ish [ˈflʌriʃ; ˋflʌrɪʃ] I n. 1. 挥动,挥舞。2. 华丽的辞藻,丰富多彩。3. 花字;花边;花饰;雕花。4. 丰富多彩[热闹]的演奏[歌唱];【乐】有震颤音的花腔。5. 繁荣,茂盛;兴旺。6. 戏剧性动作。*She went away with a ~ of bonnet*. 她挥挥帽子走掉了。*a ~ of trumpets* 响亮喧闹的喇叭声;〔喻〕大事件开场前的大肆宣扬。*in full ~* 全盛,极盛;盛行。*with a ~ of trumpets* 自吹自擂地,耀武扬威地。II vt. 1. 挥舞;摇动(旗等)。2. 夸示。3. 以颜色[花纹等]装饰;以花体字作…的装饰。~ *one's wealth* 夸耀豪富。— vi. 1. 茂盛,繁荣,繁盛。2. 活跃,盛行,享有盛名。3. 手舞足蹈。4. 写花体字;使用华丽词句;花言巧语。5.【乐】奏[唱]得精彩响亮。*It's one thing to ~ and another to fight*. 舞剑是一回事,战斗是另一回事。

flour·ish·ing [ˈflʌriʃiŋ; ˋflʌrɪʃɪŋ] a. 1. 繁茂的,繁生的。2. 繁荣的,兴盛的;茂盛的,蒸蒸日上的,欣欣向荣的。-ly ad.

F

flour·y [ˈflauəri; ˋflaʊrɪ] *a*. 面粉的；粉状的；多粉的。

flout [flaut; flaʊt] **I** *vt*. 藐视，轻视，嘲笑。— *vi*. 表示轻蔑。**II** *n*. 嘲笑；侮慢，表示轻蔑的言行。**-ing·ly** *ad*.

flow [fləu; flo] **I** *vi*. **1**. 流，流动。**2**. (血液等)流通，循环。**3**. 流过；川流不息；(时间)飞逝；(言语等)流畅。**4**. (衣服、头发等)飘动，飘拂，(旗等)飘扬。**5**. 流出，涌出。**6**. (潮)涨 (*opp*. ebb)。**7**. 出血，行经。**8**. 充满，斟满，富有。**9**. 〔古〕泛滥。**10**. 来自。*Blood will* ～. 一定会流血生事。— *vt*. 溢过，淹没；使泛滥，使充溢。～ ***away*** 流走；流逝。～ ***down*** 流下。～ ***in*** 流入。～ ***like water*** (酒)源源不绝。～ ***out*** 流出。～ ***over*** 横流，溢出，泛滥。～ ***over into*** 涌入。**II** *n*. **1**. 流，流水，迳流，气流。**2**. 流出，流入，流动；川流不息。**3**. 流量，消耗量；流速，流率；生产量。**4**. 涨潮。**5**. 〔常 *pl*.〕(特指尼罗河的)泛滥。**6**. 洋溢，饱满，丰满。**7**. 滔滔，流畅。**8**. (衣服、头发等的)飘动，飘拂；(旗等的)飘扬。**9**. 【医】月经 (= menstrual ～)。*soil* ～【地】流砂。*a* ～ *of eloquence* 口若悬河。*a* ～ *of ten gallons a second* 每秒十加仑的流率[量]。*a good* ～ *of milk* 丰富的挤奶量。*ebb and* ～ 涨落，盛衰，消长。*The tide is on the* ～. 正在涨潮。*a* ～ *of spirits* 精神饱满，兴致勃勃。*a* ～ *of soul* 推心置腹，融洽的交谈。～ *of talk* [*conversation, words*] 健谈，善于词令，滔滔不绝。*the* ～ *of time* 时光流逝。*a* ～ *of traffic* 车水马龙。～ **chart** [**sheet**] 生产流程图，作业图，生产过程图解。～**-line**【地】流理〔火成岩的纹理〕。～**meter** 流量表，流量计，流速计。～ **rate** 流速；流量。

flow·age [ˈfləuidʒ; ˋfloɪdʒ] *n*. **1**. 流动，流出，泛滥。**2**. 泛滥的河水，积水，溢出的液体，流出物。**3**. 【地】(岩石形状的)渐变。

Flow·er [ˈflauə; ˋflaʊɚ] *n*. 弗劳尔〔姓氏〕。

flow·er [ˈflauə; ˋflaʊɚ] **I** *n*. **1**. 花；花卉；花状装饰物。**2**. 精华 (*of*)。**3**. 开花，盛开。**4**. 少壮，青春，盛年，盛时。**5**. 〔*pl*.〕词藻。**6**. 〔*pl*.〕【化】华；(发酵时的)泡沫；〔古〕月经。*printer's* ～【印】(用于章末卷尾作为补白的)尾花图饰。*the language of* ～*s* 用花表达的话，以花作象征的意义。*the national* ～ 国花。*The* ～*s are out*. 花开了。*the* ～ *of the youth of the country* 国家的优秀青年。*the* ～ *of scholarship* 学界精华。～*s of sulphur* 硫华。*No* ～*s*. 花圈敬辞〔讣文上谢绝赠送花圈的用语〕。～*s of speech* 华丽的词藻(常含讽刺意味)。***in*** (***full***) ～ 开着花；盛开，怒放。***in the*** ～ ***of life*** (***one's age***) 在青春时代。**II** *vt*. 用花装饰；使开花。— *vi*. 开花；成长，兴旺。～ **arrangement** 插花术。～ **bed** 花坛。～ **child** 〔美俚〕花孩〔嬉皮士的一种，常戴花象征爱〕。～**-de-luce**【植】鸢尾。～ **girl** 卖花女；在新娘前撒花的女孩。～ **head**【植】头状花序 (= head)。～**-of-an hour**【植】野西爪苗 (*Hipiscus trionum*)。～ **people** = ～ children (～ child 的复数)。～ **piece** 花卉画，花卉装饰。～**pot** 花盆，花钵。～ **power** 花的力量〔意即爱的力量，是 ～ children 的口号〕。～ **show** 花卉展览。～ **stalk** 花柄，花梗。**F- state** 花州〔美国佛罗里达州的别号〕。～ **thinning**【园艺】疏花。**-less** *a*. 无花的，隐花的。**-like** *a*. 像花一样的。

flow·er·age [ˈflauəridʒ; ˋflaʊərɪdʒ] *n*. **1**. 花〔总称〕。**2**. 开花。

flow·ered [ˈflauəd; ˋflaʊɚd] *a*. **1**. 有花的。**2**. 以花形图案装饰的。

flow·er·er [ˈflauərə; ˋflaʊərɚ] *n*. **1**. 开花的植物。**2**. (陶瓷、刺绣等的)描花人。*an abundant* ～ 花多的树。*an early* [*a late*] ～ 开花期早[晚]的花。

flow·er·et [ˈflauərit; ˋflaʊərɪt] *n*. 小花；【建】小花饰。

flow·er·ing [ˈflauəriŋ; ˋflaʊərɪŋ] *a*. 开花的。*a* ～ *plant* 显花植物。～ **crab**【植】多花海棠。～ **peach**【植】碧桃。～ **quince 1**. 【植】贴梗海棠。**2**. 贴梗海棠果。

flow·er·y [ˈflauəri; ˋflaʊərɪ] *a*. (***-er·i·er***; ***-i·est***) **1**. 花的，花似的。**2**. 花多的；用花装饰的。**3**. 词藻华丽的。～ *language* 词藻丰富的语言。**-er·i·ly** *ad*. **-er·i·ness** *n*.

flow·ing [ˈfləuiŋ; ˋfloɪŋ] *a*. **1**. 流动的；如流的；(轮廓等)圆滑的，流畅的，连续不断的。**2**. 飘垂的。**3**. 上涨的。～ *lock's* 垂发。～ *tide* 涨潮。***a land*** ～ ***with milk and honey*** 【圣】流乳与蜜的地方，鱼米之乡。***sail with a*** ～ ***sheet*** [***sail***]【海】放松帆脚减少风力，慢航。～ **well** 自喷井，自流井。**-ly** *ad*. **-ness** *n*.

flown[1] [fləun; flon] fly[1] 的过去分词。

flown[2] [fləun; flon] *a*. **1**. (陶瓷)涂有晕色的。**2**. 〔古〕满溢的。

fl. oz. = fluidounce.

F.L.S. = Fellow of the Linnean Society 〔英〕林奈学会会员。

flt. 【美军】= **1**. fleet. **2**. flight. **3**. float.

flu [flu:; flu] *n*. 〔口〕【医】流行性感冒 (= influenza)。

flub [flʌb; flʌb] **I** *vt*., *vi*. (***-bb-***) (把工作等)搞坏；弄糟，做错。**II** *n*. 〔口〕错误，过失。

flub·dub [ˈflʌbdʌb; ˋflʌbˏdʌb] *n*. **1**. 糊涂话；空话，哗众取宠的话。**2**. (俗气的)艳丽服装。**3**. 〔美俚〕笨拙，蠢少年。～ ***and gulf*** 〔美〕夸大的空话，胡说八道。

fluc·tu·ate [ˈflʌktjueit; ˋflʌktjʊˏet] *vi*. **1**. 波动，起伏，涨落；【物】脉动；(市价等)变动。**2**. (意见等)动摇不定。—*vt*. 使波动，使起伏。*a fluctuating market* 变动的行市。～ ***between hopes and fears*** 忽喜忽忧。

fluc·tu·a·tion [ˌflʌktjuˈeiʃən; ˏflʌktjʊˋeʃən] *n*. **1**. 波动，起伏，涨落；【物】脉动。**2**. 动摇不定，踌躇。**3**. 【生】仿徨变异。

flue[1] [flu:; flu] *n*. **1**. 烟道，暖气管。**2**. (管风琴的)唇管，唇管口。**3**. 〔俚〕(当铺中传送抵押品至收藏处的)滑槽，斜槽。***in*** [***up***; ***upon***] ***the*** ～ 进了当铺；死了。～ **pipe** (管风琴的)唇管。

flue[2] [flu:; flu] *n*. 绒毛；毛屑，棉屑。

flue[3] [flu:; flu] *n*. 拖网；挂网；(任何)渔网。

flue[4] [flu:; flu] *vt*., *vi*. (使)成喇叭形。

flue[5] [flu:; flu] *n*. = flu.

flue-cured [ˈflu:kjuəd; ˋflukjʊɚd] *a*. (烟草)烤干的。

flue·gel·horn, flu·gel·horn [ˈflu:glˌhɔ:n; ˋflugl ˏhɔrn] *n*. 【乐】夫吕号〔一种铜管乐器，结构和音调与短号差不多〕。

flu·en·cy [ˈflu(:)ənsi; ˋfluənsɪ] *n*. 流畅，流利。～ ***of speech*** 口齿流利。***with*** ～ 流畅地，滔滔不绝。

flu·ent [ˈflu(:)ənt; ˋfluənt] **I** *a*. **1**. 流畅的，流利的。**2**. 畅流的，液态的。*speak* ～ *English* 说流利的英语。*a* ～*-speaker* 口若悬河的演说家。*a* ～ *writer* 文笔流畅的作家。**II** *n*. 【数】变数，变量。**-ly** *ad*.

flu·er·ic [ˈflu:ərik; ˋfluərɪk] *a*. = fluidic.

flu·er·ics [ˈflu:əriks; ˋfluərɪks] *n*. = fluidics.

flue·y [ˈflu:i; ˋfluɪ] *a*. 绒毛似的，蓬松的。

fluff [flʌf; flʌf] **I** *n*. **1**. 织物上的绒毛，柔毛；汗毛。**2**. 蓬松物。**3**. 说错；错误；〔美俚〕(戏剧、广播中)念错台词。**4**. 〔俚〕青年女子。**5**. 没有价值的东西[言语]。**II** *vi*. **1**. 起毛，变松。**2**. 说错；念错台词，忘记台词；出错；搞糟。— *vt*. **1**. 使起毛；抖开。**2**. 〔美俚〕说错；念错(台词)，忘记(台词)；搞糟。

fluff·y [ˈflʌfi; ˋflʌfɪ] *a*. **1**. 绒毛状的，有绒毛的；柔软的；蓬松的。**2**. 错乱的；糊涂的。～ **cellulose**(不含热量或营养成份的)代食品。**fluff·i·ness** *n*.

flu·id [ˈflu(:)id; ˋfluɪd] **I** *n*. 流体，液。*body* ～ 体液。*cooling* ～ 冷却液。**II** *a*. **1**. 流动的；流体的；液体的。**2**. 容易[可]变动的；不固定的。**3**. 容易变成现金的；可以另派用处的。**4**. 流畅的。*a* ～ *analogue computer* 射流模拟计算机。～ *battle lines* 非固定作战线。～ *assets* 流动资产。～ *capital* 流动资本。*a* ～ *style* 流畅的文体。～ **drachm** [**dram**] 流量打兰(药衡名)。～ **drive** 【机】液压传动。～ **extract** 【药】流浸膏剂。～ **mechanics** 水力学，流体力学。～ **ounce** 液量英两，液量盎司〔美国合 29.4 毫升，英国合 28.4 毫升〕。～ **pressure** 流体压

力,流体静力学压力。**-ly** *ad*.

flu·id·ic [flu'idik; flʊ`ɪdɪk] *a*. 流体性的;射流的。

flu·id·ics [flu'idiks; flʊ`ɪdɪks] *n*. 〔用作单数〕射流[流体]学;射流技术。

flu·id·i·fy [flu(:)'idifai; flu`ɪdə,faɪ] *vt*. 液化;使成流体。— *vi*. 1. 流体化。2. 积满液体。

flu·id·i·ty [flu(:)'iditi; flu`ɪdətɪ] *n*. 流动性,流度;流质;液流度,液性。

flu·id·ize ['flu:idaiz; `fluədaɪz] *vt*. (*-ized*; *-iz·ing*) 1. 使液化,流化,使流质化。2. 用高速气流输送,使悬浮在气流中加以运送。**-za·tion** *n*.

flu·id·on·ics [,flu:i'dɔniks; ,fluə`dɑnɪks] *n*. *pl*. = fluidics.

fluke[1] [flu:k; fluk] *n*. 1. 锚爪,锚钩;(鱼叉等的)倒钩。2. 鲸尾叶突。

fluke[2] [flu:k; fluk] I *n*. 1. (撞球)侥幸的击中。2. 幸运,侥幸成功。3. 偶然事件;倒楣,意外挫折。*win by a* ~ 侥幸得胜。II *vt*. 侥幸击中,侥幸做成。— *vi*. 侥幸成功,意外受挫。

fluke[3] [flu:k; fluk] *n*. 1. 【动】比目鱼,鲽形目的鱼。2. 肝蛭,吸虫。*blood* ~*s* 血吸虫。

fluk·ic·ide ['flu:kisaid; `flukɪsaɪd] *n*. 【药】杀吸虫剂。

fluk·y ['flu:ki; `flukɪ] *a*. (*fluk·i·er*; *-i·est*) 1. 〔口〕侥幸的,靠运气的。2. 偶然的,变化不定的。**-i·ly** *ad*. **-i·ness** *n*.

flume [flu:m; flum] I *n*. 〔美〕 1. 斜槽;渡槽,流水槽,滑运沟。2. 峡流。*go* [*be*] *up the* ~ 〔美俚〕倒楣,垮台。II *vi*. 利用水槽,建造水槽。— *vt*. 用水槽运送(木材等)。~ **ride**〔美〕水槽急流滑水〔游乐场游人从高坡斜槽滑水的娱乐〕。

flum·mer·y ['flʌməri; `flʌmərɪ] *n*. 1. 面粉糊;冻状食品;柔软易食的食物(尤指燕麦粥、乳蛋黏糊;乳蛋甜点心)。2. 假恭维,废话。

flum·mox ['flʌməks; `flʌməks] I *vt*. 〔俚〕使狼狈,使失措,使慌乱。~ *sb*. *by the lip* 说得(人)狼狈而退。II *n*. 失败。

flump [flʌmp; flʌmp] I *n*. 〔口〕砰的一声,砰然落下。*fall with a* ~ 砰的一声倒落。II *vt*. 砰地放下。— *vi*. 砰地落下[移动]。

flung [flʌŋ; flʌŋ] fling 的过去式及过去分词。

flunk [flʌŋk; flʌŋk] I *n*. 〔美俚〕(考试等)失败,不及格。~ *in an examination* 考试不及格。II *vi*., *vt*. (使)失败;放弃。*She* ~*ed English*. 她英语没有考及格。~ *out* 考试不及格而退学。**-ee** [flʌŋ'ki:; flʌŋ`ki] *n*. 因考试不及格而退学者,因工作不力而被解职者。

flun·k(e)y ['flʌŋki; `flʌŋkɪ] *n*. 1. (穿制服的)仆从,奴才,走狗。2. 马屁精,势利小人。**-ism** *n*. 奴才相,奴才气,奴才作风。

flu·or ['flu(:)ɔ:, 'flu(:)ə; `fluɔr, `fluɚ] *n*. = fluorite.

fluor- *comb*. *f*. 1. 表示"氟": *fluor*ide. 2. 表示"荧光": *fluor*escent.

flu·o·resce [fluə'res; fluə`rɛs] *vi*. 发荧光。

flu·o·res·ce·in [fluə'resi:in; ,fluə`rɛsɪɪn] *n*. 【化】荧光素;荧光黄。

flu·o·res·cence [fluə'resns; ,fluə`rɛsns] *n*. 荧光(性)。

flu·o·res·cent [fluə'resnt; ,fluə`rɛsnt] I *a*. 1. 荧光的,发荧光的。2. 外表华丽的;光辉四射的。3. 〔美口〕容光焕发的。II *n*. 〔美口〕荧光灯。~ **lamp** [**light**, **tube**] 荧光灯,日光灯。~ **screen** 荧光屏。

flu·o·res·cer [fluə'resə; fluə`rɛsɚ] *n*. 荧光增白剂。

flouri- *comb*. *f*. 表示"荧光": *fluori*meter.

fluor·i·date ['flu(:)ərideit, 'flɔ:-; `fluərə,det, `flɔ-] *vt*. 向(饮水等)中加氟化物(以防儿童蛀齿)。**-da·tion** [-'deiʃən; -`deʃən]

flu·or·ide ['flu(:)əraid; `fluə,raid] *n*. 【化】氟化物。

flu·o·ri·dize ['flu(:)əridaiz; `fluərədaɪz] *vt*. 用氟化物处理。**-di·za·tion** [-dai'zeiʃən; -daɪ`zeʃən] *n*. **-r** *n*. 1. 氟化剂。2. (纺织品上可防水防油的)氟化面层。

flu·o·rim·e·ter [,flu(:)ə'rimitə; ,fluə`rɪmɪtə] *n*. = fluorometer.

fluor·i·nate ['flu(:)ərineit; `fluərənet] *vt*. 1. 氟化。2. = fluoridate. **-na·tion** *n*.

flu·o·rine ['flu(:)əri:n; `fluərin] *n*. 【化】氟。

flu·o·rite ['flu(:)ərait; `fluə,raɪt] *n*. 【矿】萤石,氟石。

fluoro- *comb*. *f*. = fluor-.

flu·o·ro·car·bon [,flu(:)ərə'kɑ:bən; ,fluərə`kɑrbən] *n*. 【化】碳氟化合物。

flu·o·rog·ra·phy [flu(:)ə'rɔgrəfi; fluə`rɑgrəfi] *n*. 荧光屏图像摄影术 (= photofluorography)。

flu·o·rom·e·ter [,flu(:)ə'rɔmitə; ,fluə`rɑmɪtɚ] *n*. 荧光(测定)计;氟量计。**-metric** [,flu(:)ərə'metrik; ,fluərə`mɛtrɪk] *a*. **-metry** [-tri; -trɪ] *n*.

fl·u·o·ro·plas·tic [,flu(:)ərə'plæstik; ,fluərə`plæstɪk] *n*. 【化】氟塑料。

flu·o·ro·poly·mer [fluə(:)ə'pɔlimə; ,fluəə`pɑlɪmɚ] *n*. 【化】含氟聚合物。

fluor·o·scope ['flu(:)ərəskəup; `fluərə,skop] I *n*. 荧光镜[屏];荧光检查器。II *vt*. 用荧光镜检查。

fluor·o·scop·ic [,flu(:)ərə'skɔpik; ,fluərə`skɑpɪk] *a*. 荧光镜的,荧光检查法的。**-i·cal·ly** *ad*.

flu·o·ros·co·py [flu(:)ə'rɔskəpi; ,fluə`rɑskəpɪ] *n*. 1. 荧光学。2. 荧光屏检查;X 线透视(法),透视检查。**-copist** *n*. 透视科医师。

flu·o·ro·sis [,flu(:)ə'rəusis; ,fluə`rosɪs] *n*. 【医】(慢性)氟中毒。

flu·or·spar ['flu(:)əspɑ:; `fluə,spɑr] *n*. 【矿】= fluorite.

flur·ried ['flʌrid; `flɝɪd] *a*. 混乱的,慌张的。*in a* ~ *manner* 慌慌张张地。

flur·ry ['flʌri; `flɝɪ] I *n*. 1. 阵风,急风。2. 暴雨,风雪。3. 慌张;(时间的)混乱。4. (股票市场行情等)短时间波动。*in a* ~ 慌慌张张。II *vt*. 使激动[慌张],搅乱;使混乱。— *vi*. 慌张,匆忙。

flush[1] [flʌʃ; flʌʃ] I *vi*. 1. 奔流,涌进;泛滥,充溢。2. (脸色等)骤然发红;发亮;辉耀。3. (植物)冒新芽。*No tide* ~*es through this narrow inlet*. 这小湾潮水涌不过来。*Her face* ~*ed with anger*. 她气得满脸通红。— *vt*. 1. 淹没;用水冲洗。2. 使脸红;使骤然发红。3. 激励,使得意。4. 使植物冒芽。*Shame* ~*ed his cheeks*. 他羞得两颊通红。*be* ~*ed with victory* 因胜利而洋洋得意。II *n*. 1. 奔流;冲洗;水车排出的水;涨水。2. (草木的)冒芽,新芽;新鲜;旺盛;激增。3. (脸的)晕红;〔诗〕(云的)霞光,(夕阳等的)辉耀。4. 【医】(热病等的)发烧;升火。5. (感情的)激发,兴奋。*the* ~ *of grass* 嫩草。*the first* ~ *of spring* 春天萌发的嫩草。*the* ~ *of dawn* 朝霞。*the* ~ *of hope* 希望的曙光。***young shoots in full*** ~ 嫩芽盛发。***in the very*** ~ ***of youth*** 风华正茂。***in the full*** ~ ***of triumph*** 在胜利的欢欣鼓舞中。~ **gate** (水库等的)溢洪道[水门等]排水装置。~ **tank** (抽水马桶上的)水箱[水柜]。~ **toilet** 抽水马桶。

flush[2] [flʌʃ; flʌʃ] I *a*. 1. 洋溢的,注满的,泛滥的。2. 精力充沛的,有生气的。3. 丰富的;富裕的,有钱的。4. 挥霍的,浪费的。5. 齐平的,同平面的,同高的 (*with*);【印】左面每行排齐的,没有缩排 (indention) 的。6. 直接的。*a blow* ~ *in the face* 正中脸部的一击。*be* ~ *of* [*with*] *money* 钱多。*be* ~ *with one's money* 挥霍钱财。*The door is* ~ *with the casing*. 门跟门框严丝合缝。*The river is* ~ *with its banks*. 河水齐岸。II *ad*. 1. 齐平地,严丝合缝地。2. 直接地。*a book cut* ~ 切齐的书。*a line set* ~ 【印】(边部与其他行)排齐的一行。III *vt*. 1. 弄平,嵌平,使齐平。2. 【印】把(左面)排齐。~ **deck** (船的)平甲板。~**-decker** 平甲板船。

flush[3] [flʌʃ; flʌʃ] I *vi*. (鸟等)惊起,惊飞,赶鸟。— *vt*. 使(鸟等)惊飞。II *n*. 飞起,一阵子飞起的鸟群;赶鸟。

F

flush[4][flʌʃ; flʌʃ] ***n***. (纸牌戏中的)一手同花的五张牌。*a royal* ～ 最强的一手牌〔以 A 打头的同花顺次五张牌〕。*a straight* ～ 次强的一手牌〔同花顺次的五张牌〕。***a*** ～ ***sequence*** 同花顺。

flush·er [ˈflʌʃə; ˋflʌʃɚ] ***n***. **1**. (阴沟、马路等的)冲扫者。**2**. 冲洗装置。

flush·ing [ˈflʌʃiŋ; ˋflʌʃɪŋ] ***n***., ***a***. 抽水冲洗(的)。～ **box** [**cistern**, **tank**] = flush tank.

flus·ter [ˈflʌstə; ˋflʌstɚ] **I** ***vt***. 扰乱,使惊惶失措;使酩酊。— ***vi***. 混乱,慌张,惊惶失措;喝醉。**II** ***n***. 混乱,慌张;醉。*all in a* ～ 惊慌失措。

flus·ter·a·tion [ˌflʌstəˈreiʃən; ˏflʌstəˋreʃən], **flus·tra·tion** [ˌflʌsˈtreiʃən; ˏflʌsˋtreʃən] ***n***. 慌乱,惊慌失措;酩酊大醉。

flute [fluːt; flut] **I** ***n***. **1**. 【乐】长笛;长笛吹奏者;(风琴的)长笛音。**2**. (女服的)管状裙褶。**3**. (柱上的)凹槽。**4**. 笛状物(如细长酒杯、细长面包等)。**5**. 【机】(刀具)出屑槽;【纺】沟槽。**II** ***vi***. 吹长笛;发笛声。— ***vt***. **1**. 用长笛吹(歌曲);用长笛般的声音歌唱[说话、吹口哨]。**2**. 在…上刻凹槽。**-like** ***a***. 像长笛(音)的。

flut·ed [ˈfluːtid; ˋflutɪd] ***a***. **1**. (似)笛声的。**2**. 有凹槽的。～ *twist drill* 【机】麻花钻。～ *columns* 刻有凹槽的柱子。*the* ～ *notes of the birds* 小鸟清脆的啭鸣。

flut·er [ˈfluːtə; ˋflutɚ] ***n***. **1**. 刻凹槽的人;刻凹槽的器具。**2**. 〔古〕长笛吹奏者。

flut·ey [ˈfluːti; ˋflutɪ] ***a***. (***flut·i·er***, ***flut·i·est***) 像长笛声的,柔和而清亮的。

flut·ing [ˈfluːtiŋ; ˋflutɪŋ] ***n***. **1**. 发长笛声,吹长笛。**2**. (刻)凹槽[沟槽]。**3**. 凹槽装饰。

flut·ist [ˈfluːtist; ˋflutɪst] ***n***. 长笛吹奏者。

flut·ter [ˈflʌtə; ˋflʌtɚ] **I** ***vi***. **1**. 拍翅振翼;(旗帜)飘扬。**2**. 颤动,(心)急跳,(脉搏)浮动。**3**. (心绪)不宁,坐立不安。**4**. 〔口〕对人进行测谎。*He* ～*ed about the room nervously*. 他心绪不宁地在房间里徘徊。— ***vt***. **1**. 振(翼);拍(翅)。**2**. 扰乱;使不安。**II** ***n***. **1**. 振翼;飘扬。**2**. 不安,焦急,波动。**3**. (身体部分的)病态阵跳。**4**. 〔英俚〕投机,小赌。**5**. 颤振。**6**. 图像跳动,脉冲干扰,放音失真。**7**. 对…进行测谎。*the* ～ *of wings* 翅膀的拍动。***all in a*** ～ 心慌意乱。***cause*** [***make***] ***a great*** ～ 轰动一时。***fall into a*** ～ 心慌意乱。***in a*** ～ 心里卜卜跳。***put sb. in*** [***into***] ***a*** ～ = ***throw sb. into a*** ～ 使忐忑不安。～ **computer** 颤动(摸拟)计算机。～ **kick** (爬泳或仰泳时小腿部的)浅打水。～ **wheel** (置于水槽底部的)水轮。**-er** ***n***. **-ing·ly** ***ad***.

flut·y [ˈfluːti; ˋflutɪ] ***a***. (***flut·i·er***; ***-i·est***) 笛声一样的;嘹亮的 (= flutey)。

flu·vi·al [ˈfluːviəl; ˋfluvɪəl] ***a***. **1**. 河的,河流的。**2**. 生在河中的。**3**. 河流冲刷作用形成的。～ *navigation* 河道航行。～ *plants* 河生植物。～ *soil* [*deposits*] 冲积土[物]。

flu·vi·a·tile [ˈfluːviətail; ˋfluvɪətaɪl] ***a***. = fluvial.

flux [flʌks; flʌks] **I** ***n***. **1**. 流,流出;流动。**2**. 涨潮。**3**. 不断的变动,波动。**4**. 【物】流量,通量,电通量,磁通量。**5**. 熔解,熔融;助熔剂;焊剂。**6**. 【医】异常溢出;腹泻。*luminous* ～ 【物】光通量。*radiant* ～ 【物】辐射通量。*soldering* ～ 焊剂。***be*** [***remain***] ***in*** (***a state of***) ～ 动荡不定,不断变动。～ ***and reflux*** (潮水的)涨落;(势力的)不断消长。**II** ***vt***. **1**. 熔化,使熔解。**2**. 用助熔剂处理。— ***vi***. **1**. (潮)涨;流出。**2**. 熔化。～ **density** 【物】通量密度。～ **gate** 地球磁力磁向测量仪,磁门。～ **meter** 磁通(量)计。

flux·ion [ˈflʌkʃən; ˋflʌkʃən] ***n***. **1**. 流动。**2**. 不断变化,转变。**3**. 【数】微分,流数。*the method of* ～*s* (牛顿的)流数法。

flux·ion·al [ˈflʌkʃənl; ˋflʌkʃənəl], **-ar·y** [-nəri; -nərɪ] ***a***. **1**. 流动的,变动的,不定的。**2**. 【数】微分的,流数的。～ **analysis** [**calculus**] 【数】流数术,微积分。

fly[1][flai; flaɪ] **I** ***vi***. (***flew*** [fluː; flu]; ***flown*** [fləun; flon]) **1**. 飞 (*about*; *away*; *forth*; *off*; *out*),飞行;驾驶飞机,坐飞机旅行。**2**. 飞跑;(时间等)飞逝;飞散,碎,(门)突然打开;突然…起来;〔古〕突击,扑向 (*at*; *on*, *upon*)。**3**. 奔逃,逃走〔过去式和过去分词要用 fled〕;消失;褪色。**4**. (旗帜、衣服等)飘动,飞舞。**5**. (在棒球中)打飞球〔过去式和过去分词要用 flied〕。**6**. 放鹰打猎。*The delegation flew from London to New York*. 代表团由伦敦飞往纽约。*She simply flew down the street*. 她沿着大街飞奔而去。*Fly for a doctor*! 快去请医生! *Time flies like an arrow*. 光阴似箭。*The dog flew at me*. 狗向我扑来。— ***vt***. **1**. 飞,驾驶,空运。**2**. 放(风筝、鸟等)。**3**. (坐飞机)飞过。**4**. 使(旗帜)飘扬。**5**. 逃避,逃出,从…逃开〔过去式和过去分词一般用 fled〕。～ *the approach of danger* 逃避危险。～ *the country* 亡命国外。～ ***a kite*** **1**. 放风筝。**2**. 试探舆论。**3**. 开空头支票。～ ***about*** 翱翔;飞散。～ ***apart*** 飞散,粉碎。～ ***around*** [***round***] 〔美口〕飞绕,飞来飞去。～ ***at*** 扑向;责骂。～ ***at high game*** 胸怀大志;情绪高涨。～ ***blind*** 盲目飞行,完全靠仪表飞行。～ ***high*** = ～ at high game. ～ ***in pieces***, ～ ***into fragments*** = ～ apart. ～ ***in the face of*** 勇敢反抗,违反。～ ***into*** 突然发作 (～ *into a passion* [*rage*] 勃然大怒。～ *into raptures* 欣喜若狂)。～ ***low*** 谦卑;销声匿迹。～ ***off*** 飞速跑掉;飞出;挥发。～ [***go***] ***off at a tangent*** 说话离题,突然改变行径。～ [***go***, ***slip***] ***off the handle*** 〔俚〕死去;发脾气。～ ***on*** [***upon***] = ～ at. ～ ***one's flag*** (海军司令官)升司令旗,就司令职。～ ***open*** (门)突然打开。～ ***out*** **1**. 冲出,激怒。**2**. 升(旗)。～ ***right*** 〔美俚〕为人正派。～ ***round*** (轮子)急转。～ ***short of*** 未达到应有水准。～ ***the iron beam*** 沿铁路飞行。～ ***to arms*** 急忙去拿武器,急忙作战斗准备。～ ***to sb.'s arms*** 投入某人怀抱。～ ***up*** 突然大怒。***Go*** ～ ***a kite***! 〔美俚〕走开!去你的! ***let*** ～ 放,射,投射 (*let* ～ *an arrow* 射出一箭)。***let*** ～ ***at*** 向…发射,向…射击;骂。***make the dust*** [***feathers***, ***fur***] ～ 引起动乱。***make the money*** ～ 浪费金钱,挥霍。***send sb.*** ～***ing*** 逐出;驱散;解雇。***send sth.*** ～***ing*** 乱抛。***with flags*** ～***ing*** = with flying colours. **II** ***n***. **1**. 飞,飞行;飞行距离,飞程。**2**. 〔*pl*. flys〕〔英〕轻便旅行马车。**3**. (服装的)钮扣遮布;(帐篷的)门帘;(旗帜的)外端[布幅]。**4**. 〔*pl*.〕(舞台上部)布景控制处。**5**. 【机】飞轮,整速轮;【印】(印刷机上的)拨纸器;(织机的)飞梭,锭翼,锭壳;【纺】飞花,落棉,飞毛;(棒球中的)飞球。*have a* ～ 作一次飞行。***on the*** ～ **1**. 在飞行中。**2**. 〔美俚〕匆忙地。**3**. 无所事事,在街头游荡,作乐。**4**. 狡猾地,诡诈地。～ **ash** 飞灰,煤灰〔尤指污染空气者〕。～**away** **1**. ***a***. 过于宽大的;(衣服)不合身的;轻浮的,轻率的;尖形的,翅状的;(造好的飞机)随时可以出厂的,包装好准备空运的。**2**. ***n***. 轻浮的人;过于宽大;不合身的衣服;直接飞离飞机制造厂的新飞机;海市蜃楼;(单杠运动中的)翻筋斗跳下。～ **ball** (棒球中的)飞球。～**-bar** (造纸用的)飞刀。～**boat** **1**. 航行荷兰沿岸的平底船。**2**. 快艇。～ **bomb** 飞弹。～**-boy** 〔美俚〕空军人员,飞机驾驶员。～**by**, ～**-by** ***n***. (*pl*. ***-bies***) 飞机或太空飞船的越过定点〔指定地点〕;飞越。～**-by-night** **1**. ***n***. (夜间在外不归的)夜游神;〔俚〕夜间潜逃的逃债者。**2**. ***a***. 钱款上靠不住的,骗人的,无信用的。～**-cruise** ***n***. 空海联航站。～ **front** 掩襟。～ **girl** 风骚的时髦女郎。～**ladder** 云梯顶部。～**leaf** ***n***. (*pl*. ***-leaves***) (书籍前后的)空白页,衬页。～**-man** (*pl*. ***-men***) **1**. 出租马车车夫。**2**. (舞台上的)道具管理员。～**over** **1**. 〔英〕立体交叉路跨线桥。**2**. (飞机)飞越,(举行庆典时的)低空编队飞行。～**past** 〔美〕 **1**. 立交桥。**2**. (阅兵时的)空中分列式。～ **post** ***vt***. 仓卒地张贴(传单等)。～ **sheet** 广告,传单,小册子。～**-tipping** 〔英〕在街上乱倒垃圾废物。～**way** 候鸟飞行路线。～**wheel** 【机】飞轮,整速轮。

fly[2][flai; flaɪ] ***n***. (*pl*. ***flies*** [flaiz; flaɪz]) **1**. 蝇,苍蝇。

F

2.(有透明翼的)飞虫。3. 植物的蝇害,虫害。4.(钓鱼用的)假蚊钩。*a* ~ *in amber* 琥珀中的化石蝇,〔喻〕保存得很好的珍贵遗物。*a* ~ *in the ointment* 美中不足,杀风景的(小)事情。*a* ~ *on the wheel* 过分自恃的人。*break* [*crush*] *a* ~ *on the wheel* 小题大作;杀鸡用牛刀。*Don't let flies stick to your heels*.〔口〕别磨蹭,快点。*Let that* ~ *stick in* [*to*] *the wall*.〔Scot.〕对这件事[问题]不要再谈了。*rise to the* ~ (鱼)上钩;(人)上当。*There are no flies on sb*. [*sth*.].〔俚〕1.(某人)很灵活[机灵]。2.(某人)可信赖。3.(某物、某事)没有弊病,不必生疑。~ **agaric** [**amanita**]【植】蛤蟆菌。~**bane** 灭蝇草;灭蝇药。~**blow** 1. *n*. 卵,麻蝇的幼蛆。2. *vt*. (*-blew*; *-blown*) 产蝇卵在…,使生蛆;玷污(声誉等)。~**blown** *a*. 被蝇卵弄脏了的,生了蛆的;(声誉)被玷污了的。~ **book** 假蚊钩盒。~**-cast** *vi*. 用假蚊钩钓鱼。~**catcher** 1.【动】鹟科食虫鸟。2.【植】捕蝇草。~**-fish** *vi*. 用假蚊钩钓鱼。~**-fisher** 用假蚊钩钓鱼的人。~**-flap** 蝇拍。~ **net** 防虫网。~**paper** 粘蝇纸,毒蝇纸。~**rod** 假蚊钩钓鱼竿。~**speck** 1. *n*. 蝇屎污点,小污斑,小点,小团。2. *vt*. 使玷上小污点。~ **swatter** 蝇拍。~**-trap** 1. 捕蝇器。2. 捕蝇草属植物。~**weight** *n*. 1. 最轻级(拳击选手)。2. 小东西,无足轻重的东西。

fly[3] [flai; flaɪ] *a*.〔俚〕伶俐的;敏捷的,敏锐的。~ *cop* 便衣侦探。

fly·a·ble [ˈflaiəbl; ˋflaɪəbl] *a*.(天气等)适于飞行的,适航的;(飞机等)可以在空中飞行的。

fly·er [ˈflaiə; ˋflaɪɚ] *n*. 1. 飞鸟;航空器,飞行物。2. 飞行者,飞行员。3. 能飞跑的动物;快马。4. 快艇;快车。5.【纺】锭翼,锭壳。6.【建】梯级。7. 跳,跃起。8.〔美口〕投机,孤注一掷。9.〔美〕(广告)传单。10.〔口〕野心勃勃的人。*take a* ~ (滑雪赛中)从跳板上飞跳;〔喻〕冒险行事。

fly·ing [ˈflaiiŋ; ˋflaɪɪŋ] I *a*. 1. 飞的,飞行的,飞行员的。2. 飘扬的,飞舞的。3. 飞似的,飞速的。4. 临时的,短暂的。5. 到处流传的。6. 逃亡的。*a* ~ *formation* 飞行队形。*a* ~ *suit* 飞行服。~ *time* 飞行时间。~ *corps* 飞行队,航空队。~ *man* 飞行员,航空员。~ *ship* 飞船。~ *visit* 走马观花的访问[参观]。*with colours* ~ = *with* ~ *colours* 完全胜利,大获成功。II *n*. 1. 飞行,飞跑。2. 飞散物。3.〔*pl*.〕【纺】飞毛,飞花。~ **blowtorch**〔美俚〕喷气式战斗机。~ **boat** 飞船;水上飞机。~ **bomb**【军】飞弹。~ **bridge**【海】浮桥,舰桥,船上驾驶台。~ **buttress**【建】拱扶垛,飞拱。~ **coffin**〔美俚〕滑翔机;飞机。~ **colours** 1. 迎风飘扬的旗。2. 显著的胜利,巨大成功。~ **column**【军】快速突击部队,别动队。~ **crane** (用直升飞机作成的)飞行起重机。~ **dog** 吸血蝙蝠。**F- Dutchman** 1.(传说中)注定要永远在海上飘流直至最后审判日的荷兰水手。2. 鬼船。~ **ferry** 滑钢渡,系留渡(指由钢索控制、借水流推动往返于两岸的渡船)。~ **field** 小型机场〔供小型飞机起落和小检修的机场〕,飞行场。~ **fish**【动】文鳐鱼,飞鱼。**F-Fortress** 飞行堡垒〔第二次世界大战中美国使用的 B—17 远距离重轰炸机〕。~ **fox**【动】狐蝠〔产于非洲、澳洲和南亚,头像狐,食果类〕,大蝙蝠亚目动物。~ **frog**【动】大蹼树蛙〔产于东印度〕。~ **gurnard**【动】豹魴鮄。~ **jib** 船首斜桅帆,三角帆。~ **jump**, ~ **leap** 助跑跳高。~ **lemur**【动】猫猴〔东南亚树居的一种哺乳动物〕。~ **louse** 小型飞机。~ **machine** 航空机〔指飞机、飞船等〕。~ **mare**【摔跤】后背包。~ **off** 起飞;离舰。~ **officer**〔英〕空军中尉。~ **phalanger**【动】大洋洲袋鼯。~ **picket** (罢工时由工会派至各处劝说工人参加罢工的)流动宣传员。~ **rings** 吊环。~ **saucer** "飞碟",真相未明的空中飞行物(= UFO)。~ **school** 飞行学校,航空学校。~ **spot scanning**【电视】高速点扫描法。~ **squad** (警察等的)紧急行动小组。~ **squadron** 1. 机动舰队。2.(由受过专门训练的工人组成的)机动工组。~ **squirrel**【动】1. 北美鼯鼠。2. = ~ phalanger. ~ **start** 1.【体】疾足起步法〔先开始起跑,到起步线时全力飞跑〕。2. 任何迅速的开始。~ **windmill**〔美俚〕直升飞机。

Flynn [flin; flɪn] *n*. 弗林〔姓氏〕。

flyte [flait; flaɪt] *vi*. = flite.

FM = 1. Field Marshal〔英〕陆军元帅。2. frequency modulation【物】调频,频率调制。3. foreign mission 外交使团。

Fm = fermium【化】元素镄的符号。

fm. = 1. fathom. 2. from.

f.m.〔处方〕作成混合剂。

FMI =〔F.〕*Fonds Monetaire Internatinal* 国际货币基金组织(= International Monetary Fund)。

f-num·ber [ˈefˌnʌmbə; ˋɛfˏnʌmbɚ] *n*.【摄】光圈数。

FO, F.O. = 1. field officer【军】校官。2. Foreign Office (英国等的)外交部。3. field order 野战命令。4. Flying Officer〔英〕空军中尉。5. forward observer【军】前进观察员。

fo. = folio.

FOA = Foreign Operations Administration〔美〕援外事务管理署。

foal [fəul; fol] I *n*. 驹(尤指一岁以下的马、驴、骡)。II *vt*., *vi*. 生(驹)。*be in* [*with*] ~ (马)怀驹。~**foot** = coltsfoot.

foam [fəum; fom] I *n*. 1.〔只用单数〕泡沫;(马等的)涎沫[大汗]。2. 泡沫材料,泡沫状物,泡沫橡皮;泡沫塑料。3.〔诗〕海。*in a* ~ (马等)浑身是汗。*sail the* ~ 航海。II *vi*. 1. 起泡沫;(马等)出汗珠。2. 冒口水。3.(浪)汹涌。— *vt*. 使起泡沫,使成泡沫状物。~*ing ale* 起泡的啤酒。~ *at the mouth* (狗等)口吐泡沫(发怒)。~ *away* [*off*] 成泡沫消失。~ *over* 起泡溢出。~**ed concrete**【建】泡沫混凝土。~**ed plastics** 泡沫塑料[塑胶],多孔塑料。~ **rubber** 泡沫橡皮,海绵橡皮。**-less** *a*. 无泡沫的。**-like** *a*. 像泡沫的。

foam·y [ˈfoumi; ˋfomɪ] *a*. (*foam·i·er*; *-i·est*) 起泡沫的,布满泡沫的,泡沫一样的。**-i·ly** *ad*. **-i·ness** *n*.

FOB, f.o.b. = free on board【商】船上交货,离岸价格。

fob[1] [fɔb; fɑb] I *n*. 1.(男裤上的)表袋。2.(怀表上的)表链及饰物。II *vt*. (*-bb-*) 把…装在表袋中。~**-chain** 表链及饰物。

fob[2] [fɔb; fɑb] *vt*. (*-bb-*)〔古〕欺骗。~ *off* 1. 搪塞。2. 把冒充品当真品推销。3. 摈弃。~ *sth*. *inferior* [*spurious*] *off upon sb*. = ~ *sb*. *off with sth*. *worthless* 用劣货骗人。~ *sb*. *off with empty promises* 用空洞的诺言搪塞人。

FOBS = fractional orbit(al) bombardment system 部分轨道袭击系统〔一种核武器袭击系统,核弹头由绕地球运行的空间航空器发射,以避免被雷达发现〕。

FOC, f.o.c. = free of charge 免费。

fo·cal [ˈfəukəl; ˋfokəl] *a*. 1.【物】焦点的,(集中)在点上的,有焦点的。2.【医】病灶的,病灶性的。~ **distance** [**length**]【物】焦距。~ **infection**【医】病灶性感染。~ **plane**【物】焦平面。~ **point** 焦点。**-ly** *ad*.

fo·cal·ize, fo·cal·ise [ˈfəukəlaiz; ˋfokəlaɪz] *vt*. 1. 使聚焦,使集中在焦点上。2. 调节(焦距),使(注意等)集中。— *vi*. 聚焦,调焦距;集中注意。**-i·za·tion** [ˌfəukəlaiˈzeiʃən; ˏfokəlaɪˋzeʃən] *n*. **-r** *n*.【无】聚焦设备,聚焦装置。

Foch [fəuʃ; fɔʃ], **Ferdinand** 福煦〔1851—1929,法国元帅,第一次世界大战联军总司令〕。

fo·ci [ˈfəusai; ˋfosaɪ] *n*. focus 的复数。

Focke [fɔk; fɑk] *n*. 福克〔姓氏〕。

fo·co [ˈfəukəu; ˋfoko] *n*.〔Sp.〕"中心",游击活动中心。

fo·com·e·ter [fəuˈkɔmitə; foˋkɑmɪtɚ] *n*. 焦距计[仪]。

fo'c's'le [ˈfəuksl; ˋfoksl̩] *n*. = forecastle.

fo·cus [ˈfəukəs; ˋfokəs] I *n*. (*pl*. *fo·cus·es*, *fo·ci* [ˈfəusai; ˋfosaɪ]) 1.【物】焦点。2.【物】焦距;聚焦,对焦

点,配光,对光。3.(活动兴趣等的)中心。4.【医】病灶。5.(地震的)震源。*the ~ of the world's attention* 世界注意的中心。*principal ~*【物】主焦点。*real* [*true*] *~*【物】实焦点。*virtual ~*【物】虚焦点。*the ~ of a disease* 病的主要患部。*the ~ of an earthquake* 震源。***bring into ~ = bring to a ~*** 使集中在焦点上配光,对光。***in ~*** 焦点对准,清晰。***out of ~*** 焦点没有对准,模糊。**II** ***vt***.(〔英〕***-ss-***)1.使聚焦,对焦。2.调节镜头、焦距等。3.集中注意力于。4.使限制于小区域。— ***vi***.聚焦,注视,调焦距;限制于小区域。**~ing cloth**【摄】遮光黑布。**~ electrode**【无】聚焦电极。**~ing glass** [**screen**]【摄】调焦距用的毛玻璃。

fod·der [ˈfɔdə; ˋfɑdɚ] **I** ***n***.1.饲料。2.创作素材。3.〔美俚〕弹药。4.无价值的人。*~ crops* 饲料作物。***cannon ~*** 炮灰。***cut one's own ~*** 〔美〕管自己事,自己的谋生。**II** ***vt***.用饲料喂(家畜)。**-less** ***a***.没有饲料的。

foe [fəu; fo] ***n***.1.敌人;仇敌(*opp*. friend),敌军,敌兵;(比赛的)敌手,对手。2.危害物。*a ~ worthy of sb.'s steel* 劲敌,强敌。***our*** [***the arch***] ~【宗】魔鬼。

foehn [fein, G. fəːn; fen, G. fɚn] ***n***. = föhn.

foe·man [ˈfəumən; ˋfomən] ***n***.(*pl*. ***-men***)〔古、诗〕敌兵,敌人。

foe·tal [ˈfiːtl; ˋfitl] ***a***. = fetal.

foe·ta·tion [fiːˈteiʃən; fiˋteʃən] ***n***. = fetation.

foe·ti·cide [ˈfiːtisaid; ˋfitə͵saɪd] ***n***. = feticide.

foe·tid [ˈfetid, ˈfiːt-; ˋfɛtɪd, ˋfit-] ***a***. = fetid.

foe·tor [ˈfiːtə; ˋfitə] ***n***. = fetor.

foe·tus [ˈfiːtəs; ˋfitəs] ***n***. = fetus.

F

fog[1] [fɔg; fɑg] **I** ***n***.1.雾。2.烟雾,尘雾。3.【摄】(底片的)雾翳;(影像的)模糊。4.(灭火机喷出的)泡沫,喷雾。5.困惑,迷惑不解,迷惘。*a dense ~* 大雾,浓雾。*the ~ of war* 战云。***be lost in a ~*** 如坠五里雾中,困惑不解。**II** ***vt***.1.以雾笼罩。2.使困惑,使迷惘。3.【摄】使模糊,使起雾翳。— ***vi***.1.被雾笼罩。2.(在铁路沿线)设立浓雾信号。3.(植物因湿度过大而)烂死(*off*)。4.【摄】(影片)模糊,有雾翳。**~ alarm** 浓雾警报。**~ bank** (海上)雾堤。**~ bell**【海】雾钟〔海岸等处所设,起雾时用以报警〕。**~bound** ***a***.(船只)因浓雾而进退不得的。**~-bow** 雾虹。**~ broom** 除雾机。**~ buoy**【海】雾标〔装有铃或自动汽笛,起雾时用以使船拉开距离〕。**~ circle** = ~-bow. **~dog** 雾层(~ bank)中的明亮处。**~drip** 有雾时树上滴下的水滴。**~eater** 1. = ~-bow. 2.雾中升起的满月。**~horn** 雾角(雾中警号);粗而响的噪音。**~light** 汽车在雾中行驶时的灯光。**~ signal** 浓雾信号,雾中信号。**~ siren**, **~ whistle** 浓雾警笛;雾中警笛。**-less** ***a***.无雾的。

fog[2] [fɔg; fɑg] ***n***.1.割后再生的草。2.(地上未割的)过冬草,冬季原野上的枯草。3.〔方〕苔藓。

fo·gey [ˈfəugi; ˋfogɪ] ***n***. = fogy.

fog·gy [ˈfɔgi; ˋfɑgɪ] ***a***.(***-gi·er***; ***-gi·est***)1.有雾的,多雾的。2.(玻璃等)不明净的。3.朦胧的。4.【摄】模糊的,有雾翳的。*a ~ night* 浓雾弥漫之夜。*a ~ idea* 模糊不清的思想。*have not the foggiest idea of ...* 丝毫不懂…的意义。**F- Bottom** 雾谷〔指美国国务院,常用以讽刺其发言人发布的话或其政策之含混不清〕。**fog·gi·ly** ***ad***. **fog·gi·ness** ***n***.

fo·gram [ˈfəugræm; ˋfogræm], **fo·grum** [-grʌm; -grʌm] ***n***.守旧的人,过时的人。

fo·gy [ˈfəugi; ˋfogɪ] ***n***.〔俚〕守旧者,老古板〔通常说 *old ~*〕。**-ish** ***a***.守旧的,古板的。**-ism** ***n***.守旧(思想、作风),古板(性格)。

foh [fɔː; fɔ] ***int***. = faugh.

Föhn [fein, G. fəːn; fen, G. fɚn] ***n***.〔G.〕【气】(阿尔卑斯山北部盆地的)暑热南风。

foi·ble [ˈfɔibl; ˋfɔɪbl] ***n***.1.(性格上的)弱点,小缺点。2.刀剑的前段〔指中段到刀尖,杀伤力不强部分〕(*opp*. forte)。

foil[1] [fɔil; fɔɪl] **I** ***n***.1.箔,金属薄片。2.(镜底的)银箔,(宝石等的)衬底。3.衬托物,陪衬的角色;烘托,衬托。4.【建】叶形饰。5.水翼(= hydrofoil);气垫船。*gold ~* 金箔。*tin ~* 锡箔。***serve as a ~ to*** 做陪衬。**II** ***vt***.1.铺箔于,垫箔于。2.用…陪衬,衬托。3.【建】给…加上叶形饰。

foil[2] [fɔil; fɔɪl] ***n***.1.钝头剑,练习剑。2.〔*pl*.〕(使用钝头剑的)击剑比赛;击剑术。

foil[3] [fɔil; fɔɪl] **I** ***vt***.1.挫败;打破(对方策略)。2.(打猎时)搞乱(臭迹[足迹])。***be ~ed in ...*** 失败。**II** ***n***.1.猎兽的足迹。2.〔古〕击退。***break her ~*** (猎物)奔回原路逃跑。***put to the ~*** 挫败,击退。***run*** (***upon***) ***the ~*** (猎物)再在原路上奔跑使猎犬迷惑。

foiled [fɔild; fɔɪld] ***a***.【建】有叶形饰的。

foil·ing[1] [ˈfɔiliŋ; ˋfɔɪlɪŋ] ***n***.【建】叶形饰。

foil·ing[2] [ˈfɔiliŋ; ˋfɔɪlɪŋ] ***n***.(猎物的)臭迹。

foils·man [ˈfɔilzmən; ˋfɔɪlzmən] ***n***.(*pl*. ***-men*** [-mən; -mən])击剑运动员;击剑手。

foin [fɔin; fɔɪn] ***vi***., ***n***.〔古〕【击剑】刺。

Fo·ism [ˈfəuizəm; ˋfoɪzəm] ***n***.(中国的)佛教。

foi·son [ˈfɔizn; ˋfɔɪzən] ***n***.1.〔古〕丰收,丰饶,大量。2.〔Scot.〕营养;精力;力气;智力。

Fo·ist [ˈfəuist; ˋfoɪst] ***n***.中国佛教徒。

foist [fɔist; fɔɪst] ***vt***.1.偷偷塞进,私自增加(*into*; *in*)。2.偷偷安插(人);骗卖(假货等);冒称(作品)是某人所作(*on*; *upon*)。*~ sth*. (*off*) *on sb*. 把某物骗售给某人。

fol. = 1. folio. 2. following.

fo·late [ˈfəuleit; ˋfolet] **I** ***a***.【生化】叶酸的。**II** ***n***.叶酸盐。

fold[1] [fəuld; fold] **I** ***n***.1.折,折叠。2.褶痕,褶层,褶页。3.(蛇,蝇等的)一卷,一团。4.(起伏地的)凹处,洼;〔*pl*.〕(地形的)重叠起伏;【地】褶皱。5.【动】(腕足类的)中隆。6.【解】褶。*Another ~ give a 32mo*. 再一折就是32开。**II** ***vt***.1.折叠;对折(*back*; *in*; *over*; *together*; *up*)。2.合拢;交叠;叉手,盘(脚)。3.抱住。4.和入,掺入,在(食物)中拌进(作料)。5.包,笼罩。6.关掉,结束掉。*~ a letter* 将信折起来。*The bird ~s its wings*. 鸟收拢翅膀。*~ one's arms* 两臂抱拢〔多指袖手旁观〕。*~ one's hands* 两手抱住(无所作为)。*~ sb. in one's arms* 抱住某人。*hills ~ed in the mist* 雾气笼罩的群山。— ***vi***.1.折叠起来,对折起来。2.彻底失败;(戏剧等)因生意清淡而停演。*~* ***down*** [***back***](将书页)折过来,折进去。*~* ***up*** 1.折起。2.放弃。3.倒塌;〔俚〕倒闭,破产。***with ~ed arms*** 两臂交叉抱着〔多指袖手旁观〕。***with ~ed hands*** 两手抱在一起(一无作为)。**~out** ***n***.(书中的)折页。

fold[2] [fəuld; fold] **I** ***n***.1.羊栏。2.羊群。3.〔集合词〕(具有共同信仰的)信徒。***return to the ~*** 浪子回头。**II** ***vt***.把…关进栏内。

-fold *suf*. 加在数词之后,表示"倍","重":three*fold*, mani*fold*。★现在表示倍数意义的词一般多用 -ple, -ble 等拉丁词尾:tri*ple*, tre*ble*, quadru*ple* 等;词尾为 -fold 的词多用作比喻或副词。

fold·a·way [ˈfəuldəwei; ˋfoldəwe] ***a***.可折叠存放的。*a ~ cot* 折叠小床。*a ~ ladder* 折梯。

fold·boat [ˈfəuldˌbəut; ˋfold͵bot] ***n***.折艇。

fold·er [ˈfəuldə; ˋfoldə] ***n***.1.折叠者,折叠机。2.文件夹。3.〔美〕折叠式印刷品。4.〔*pl*.〕折叠式眼镜。

fold·e·rol [ˈfɔldərɔl; ˋfɑldə͵rɑl] ***n***. = falderal.

fold·ing [ˈfəuldiŋ; ˋfoldɪŋ] ***a***.可折叠的,折叠式的;(丝绸)起绉的。**~ bed** 折叠床。**~ bridge** 开合桥。**~ chair** 折叠椅。**~ doors** 〔*pl*.〕双扇门,折门。**~ fan** 折扇。**~ money** 〔美〕纸币;巨款。**~ rule** 折尺。**~ screen** 折叠屏风。**~ stair** 折梯。**~ stool** 折凳。**~ top** (汽车的)折叠式车顶。

Fo·ley [ˈfəuli; ˋfolɪ] ***n***.富利〔姓氏〕。

Fol·ger [ˈfəuldʒə; ˋfoldʒɚ] ***n***.福尔杰〔姓氏〕。

fo·li·a [ˈfəuliə; ˋfolɪə] *n*. folium 的另一复数形式。

fo·li·a·ceous [ˌfəuliˈeiʃəs; ˏfolɪˋeʃəs] *a*. 1. 叶的;叶状的,有叶状器官的。2. 层状的,(岩石等)分成薄层的。

fo·li·age [ˈfəuliidʒ; ˋfolɪɪdʒ] *n*. 1. 〔集合词〕(树的)叶子。2. 【建】叶饰。~ **leaf** 营养叶。~ **plant** 观叶植物。

fo·li·aged [ˈfəuliidʒd; ˋfolɪɪdʒd] *a*. 有叶的。*dark-*~ 树叶浓密的。

fo·li·ar [ˈfəuliə; ˋfolɪɚ] *a*. 叶的,叶状的,叶质的。

fo·li·ate I *vt*. [ˈfəulieit; ˋfolɪˏet] 1. 把…打成箔;涂箔(在镜背等)。2. 【建】使加叶饰。3. 把(书籍的)页数〔非面数〕编号。— *vi*. 1. 分裂成薄片。2. 生叶。**II** *a*. [ˈfəuliit; ˋfolɪɪt] 1. 【植】有叶的;如叶的;【动】叶状的。2. 打成薄片的;层状的。

fo·li·a·tion [ˌfəuliˈeiʃən; ˏfolɪˋeʃən] *n*. 1. 生叶。2. 【植】叶卷叠式,幼叶卷叠式。3. 打成箔,涂箔。4. 【建】叶状饰。5. (书籍)标记页数。

fo·li·a·ture [ˈfəuliətʃə; ˋfolɪətʃɚ] *n*. 〔罕〕= foliage.

fo·lic acid [ˈfəulik ˈæsid; ˋfolɪk ˋæsɪd] 【生化】叶酸。

fo·lie à deux [fəuˌliː ɑː ˈdəː; foˏli ɑ ˋdɚ] (两个接近的人的)病态感应,感应性神经病。

fo·lie de gran·deur [fəuˌliːdəgrɑːnˈdəː; foˏlidəgrɑnˋdɚ] 〔F.〕权势狂、自大狂。

fo·li·ic·o·lous [ˌfəuliːˈikələs; ˏfolɪˋɪkələs] *a*. 【生】叶上生的,寄生在叶上的〔如地衣、菌类、藻类等〕。

fo·lin·ic [fəuˈlinik; foˋlɪnɪk] **acid** *n*. 【化】醛叶酸,柠胶(因)素。〔= citrovorum factor〕。

fo·li·o [ˈfəuliəu; ˋfolɪˏo] **I** *n*. (*pl*. ~*s*) 1. (纸张的)对折,对开〔*cf*. quarto, sexto, octavo, duodecimo, sextodecimo, octodecimo〕;对开本的书。2. 【印】只有一个编码的正反两面,一张。3. 张数号,页码。4. (写本的)一页。5. 单位字数〔计算文件字数的单位,英国通常为 72 字或 90 字,美国为 100 字〕。~ *volumes* = *volumes* (*in*)~ 对开本。*in* ~对开。**II** *a*. 对褶的,对开的。**III** *vt*. 编…的页码(张数号)。

fo·li·o·late [ˈfəuliəleit; ˋfolɪəlet] *a*. 具小叶的。

fo·li·ole [ˈfəuliəul; ˋfolɪˏol] *n*. 小叶;【动】叶状突。

fo·li·ose [ˈfəuliəus; ˋfolɪos] *a*. 叶子覆盖的;多叶的。

fo·li·um [ˈfəuliəm; ˋfolɪəm] *n*. (*pl*. ~*s*, *-li·a* [-ə; -ə]) 1. 【地】薄层。2. 【数】叶形线。

folk [fəuk; fok] **I** *n*. (*pl*. ~*s*, ~) 1. (常~*s*, 〔古、方〕~)人们。2. 〔口〕家属,亲戚;正派的人们。3. 〔古〕民族,种族。4. 人民,世人。*fine* ~*s* 名流。*town* ~(*s*) 城市人。*country* ~(*s*) 乡下人。*our* ~*s* 乡亲们。*my* ~*s* (全家)亲属们。*one's* ~*s* 家属。*the old* ~(*s*) 老人们。*the young* ~*s* 儿女。*your young* ~*s* 你家孩子们。*just* ~*s* 〔口〕厚道热肠的人,淳朴的人。**II** *a*. 民间的。~ **custom** 民间习俗。~ **dance** 土风舞。~ **etymology** 民俗语源,通俗词源;文字的通俗变化〔如 bridegome 变化 bridegroom, asparagus 变为 sparrow-grass 等〕。~**lore** 民间创作;民间传说;民俗学。~**lorist** 民间传说研究者,民俗学者。~ **medicine** 土法治疗,民间疗法。~**moot**, ~**mote** 〔废〕【史】(市、郡等的)群众大会。~ **music** 民间音乐。~**nik** 〔俚〕民间歌手,民歌爱好者。~-**rock** 民歌风摇摆舞音乐。~**say** 〔美〕俗话。~ **song** 民歌。~ **state** 由一个民族组成的国家。~ **story**, ~ **tale** 民间故事,传说。~**ways** 社会习俗,民间风俗习惯。

Folke·stone [ˈfəukstən; ˋfokˏstən] *n*. 福克斯通〔英肯特州一港口〕。

Fol·ke·ting, ***Fol·ke·thing*** [ˈfəulkətiŋ, Dan. ˈfɔlgəteŋ; ˋfolkətɪŋ, Dan. ˋfɑlgəteŋ] *n*. 〔Dan.〕1. (1953 年以前的)丹麦议会的下院。2. (现在)丹麦一院制议会。

folk·sy [ˈfəuksiː; ˋfoksɪ] *a*. (*-si·er*; *-si·est*) 〔美口〕1. 爱交际的,友好的。2. 随便的,无拘束的。3. 有民间风味的。~ **musical compositions** 有民间风味的音乐作品。**-i·ness** *n*.

foll. = following (words, pages 等)。

fol·li·cle [ˈfɔlikl; ˋfɑlɪkl] *n*. 1. 【解】(小)囊,滤泡,卵泡。2. 【植】蓇葖。**a hair** ~毛囊。~ **mite** 【动】蠕形螨〔一种毛孔寄生虫〕。~-**stimulating hormone** 【生】滤〔卵〕泡刺激素,促卵泡激素,促卵(成熟)激素。

fol·lic·u·lar [fəˈlikjulə; fəˋlɪkjəlɚ] *a*. 【解】小囊的,滤泡的,卵泡的;【植】蓇葖的。

fol·lic·u·late(d) [fəˈlikjuleit(id); fəˋlɪkjəlet(ɪd)] *a*. = follicular.

fol·lic·u·lin [fəˈlikjulin; fəˋlɪkjəlɪn] *n*. 【生化】卵巢滤泡激素,经酮(= estrone)。

fol·lies [ˈfɔliz; ˋfɑlɪz] *n*. 〔用作单数〕活报剧;时事讽刺剧。

fol·low [ˈfɔləu; ˋfɑlo] **I** *vt*. 1. 跟着,跟随;接着,跟着发生,继…之后;(地位)在…之后。2. 追赶,追求。3. 顺…前进。4. 因…而起,是必然结果。5. 信奉,追随,遵循;听从(忠告等)。6. 仿效,照。7. 从事。8. 注视;倾听;注意(事态的发展等)。9. (在理解上)跟得上;听得懂;领悟,了解。*Spring* ~*s winter*. 冬去春来。*F- this road to the corner*. 顺着这条路到转角处。*I do not quite* ~ *you*. 我听不大懂你的话。*Are you* ~*ing* (*me*)? 你听清楚没有? ~ *the argument easily* 那个议论容易理解。~ *the world's affairs* 注意世界局势。— *vi*. 跟着,跟随,随后,继;结果发生;因而当然,那么…就。*Go on ahead and I'll* ~。前面走着吧,我跟着你。*It* ~*s* (*from this*) *that*... 由此得出,可见。**as** ~**s** 如下,如次(*She wrote as* ~*s*. 她写的内容如下。*It reads as* ~*s*. 全文如下)。★主句的主语不论是单数还是复数,通常都不用 as ~. ~ ***a course of action*** 采取一定行动。~ ***sb. about*** 跟踪,尾随。~ ***in*** [***out***] 跟着某人进去[出来]。~ ***after*** 紧跟,追求,力求达到。~ ***a lead*** 【牌】跟牌;跟着。~ ***in sb.'s steps*** 照某人成例,继某人衣钵。~ ***in the wake of*** 踏着…的足迹,继承着…的意愿;仿效。~ ***knowledge*** 求学。~ ***my leader*** = ~-my-leader. ~ on 紧接着;继续下去。~ out 贯彻,进行到底;查明。~ the band 〔美〕追随群众;赶时髦。~ the drum 从军。~ the lead of sb. 效法某人。~ the stage 做演员。~ through 〔体〕(完成球棒或球拍击球后的)弧形动作;完成;坚持到底。~ up 1. 趁(机)。2. 穷追;贯彻到底。3. (足球队员)靠近盘球人作后援;【医】(在诊断或治疗后)随访(~ *up a victory* 乘胜穷追。~ *up a blow* 连打。~ *up work* 贯彻工作)。***in what*** ~***s*** 在下文中。**II** *n*. 1. 跟随,追随。2. (撞球)跟球。3. 〔口〕添菜。~-**my-leader** (游戏)(跟领头人一样动作,错则受罚的)猴子学样。~-**on** 1. *n*. 随后发生的事;继任者。2. *a*. 后继的,随后发生的。~-**scene** [**shot**] 【影】跟镜头场面。~-**the-leader** = ~-my-leader. ~-**through** (球打出后的)后续打姿;(一个举动的)最末部分;继续完成最后的行动。

fol·low·er [ˈfɔləuə; ˋfɑloɚ] *n*. 1. 跟随者;追随者;跟踪者。2. 随员;部下;信从者,信徒。3. 〔英〕(特指女仆人的)情人。4. 【火箭】跟踪装置。5. 【机】从动件,从动轮,随动件。6. (契据的)附页。*unwilling* ~*s* 胁从分子。

fol·low·ing [ˈfɔləuiŋ; ˋfɑləwɪŋ] **I** *a*. 1. 接着的,其次的。2. 后面的;以下的,下述的。3. 【海】(风)后面吹来的;(潮水)后面涌来的。*in the* ~ *year* = *in the year* ~第二年。*on the* ~ *day* = *on the day* ~在第二天。**II** *n*. 1. 随员,部属,追随者。2. 〔the ~〕以下所说。*a political leader with a large* ~拥有大批追随者的政治领袖。**III** *prep*. 在…以后。*F- the meeting, a dinner was given*. 会见后举行宴会。~ **in range** 【火箭】远距离跟踪。

fol·low-up [ˈfɔləuʌp; ˋfɑloˏʌp] **I** *n*. 1. 跟踪。2. 【医】(诊断或治疗后对病人进行的)定期复查,随访。3. (报纸或广播的)补充[继续]报导。4. 【机】随动装置。5. 【商】经常发出的广告信。**II** *a*. 重复的;补充的;继续的,接着的。~ *pressure* 自动加压(法)。*a* ~ *instruction* 补充指示。*a* ~ *letter* 补充寄来的信。*the* ~ *survey* 继续

F

观察。～ **system** 连续通信劝购法。～ **units**【军】后续部队。

fol·ly [ˈfɔli; ˋfɑlɪ] *n*. **1**. 愚笨,愚蠢。**2**. 愚行,傻念头。**3**.〔古〕罪恶,放荡。**4**. 花费巨大而无益的事,华而不实的大建筑〔常冠以设计者名字,例 *Allen's F-*〕。**5**.〔*pl*.〕时事讽刺剧。*commit a* ～作蠢事。*The follies of youth are food for repentance in old age*.〔谚〕年轻时胡闹,年老时烦恼。

Fol·som [ˈfɔlsəm, ˈfəul-; ˋfɑlsəm, ˋfol-] **man** 佛索姆人〔冰河时代晚期居住在北美的一种人〕。

Fo·mal·haut [ˈfəumlˌhɔːt; ˋfomlˏhɔt] *n*.〔天〕北落师门〔南鱼座 α〕。

fo·ment [fəuˈment; foˋment] *vt*. **1**.【医】热敷,热罨。**2**. 酝酿,煽动,挑起。～ *dissension* 挑拨离间,散布不和。～ *a mutiny* 煽动哗变。**fo·men·ta·tion** [ˌfəumenˈteiʃən; ˏfomenˋteʃən] *n*. **-er** *n*. 挑唆者。

fond [fɔnd; fɑnd] *a*.〔常用作述语〕**1**. 喜欢,爱好(*of*)。**2**. 宠爱的,溺爱的。**3**. 不大可能实现的。*be* ～ *of fishing* 爱钓鱼。*a* ～ *mother* 慈母。*a* ～ *dream* 黄粱美梦。

fon·dant [ˈfɔndənt; ˋfɑndənt] *n*. 奶油软糖,奶油软糖馅。

fon·dle [ˈfɔndl; ˋfɑndl̩] *vt*. 爱抚;〔古〕溺爱…。—*vi*. 爱抚(*with*; *together*)。

fon·dling [ˈfɔndliŋ; ˋfɑndlɪŋ] *n*. **1**. 爱抚。**2**. 被宠爱的人[动物]。

fond·ly [ˈfɔdli; ˋfɑndlɪ] *ad*. **1**. 亲爱地。**2**. 愚蠢地,毫无头脑地。*as I* ～ *imagined* 像我以前傻想的那样。～ *hope* 妄想;一厢情愿的希望。

fond·ness [ˈfɔndnis; ˋfɑndnɪs] *n*. **1**. 喜欢,嗜好(*for*)。**2**. 宠爱;溺爱。**3**. 傻想法,轻信。***have a*** ～ ***for*** 爱好。

fon·du(e) [fɔnˈduː; fɑnˋdu] *n*.【烹】**1**. 酒味(融化)干酪酱。**2**. 干酪煎肉丁。**3**. 松脆干酪酥。

fons et o·ri·go [ˈfɔnz et əˈraigəu; ˋfɑnz ɛt əˋraɪgo]〔L.〕本源,根源。

font[1] [fɔnt; fɑnt] *n*. **1**.【宗】洗礼盘,圣水器。**2**.(煤油灯的)油壶。**3**.〔诗〕源泉。

font[2] [fɔnt; fɑnt] *n*. 美【印】(同一型号的)一副铅字,全副铅字(= fount)。*a wrong* ～ 非同一型号的铅字〔略 w.f.〕。～**ware**【计】字型[字体]软件〔指可为不通用的奇特字母或字体排版的软件〕。

Fon·taine·bleau [ˈfɔntinbləu; ˋfɑntɪnblo] *n*. 枫丹白露〔法国北部一城市〕。

font·al [ˈfɔntl; ˋfɑntl̩] *a*. **1**. 源泉的,本源的。**2**. 洗礼的。

fon·ta·nel(le) [ˌfɔntəˈnel; ˏfɑntəˋnɛl] *n*.【解】囟门。

food [fuːd; fud] *n*. **1**. 食物,食品,粮食,食料;养料。**2**. 精神食粮,材料,资料。*animal* [*vegetable*] ～ 肉[素]食。*canned* ～ 罐头食品。*mental* [*intellectual*] ～ 精神食粮。*non-staple* [*subsidiary*] ～ 副食品。*spiritual* ～ 精神食粮。～ *for poetry* 诗的素材。***be*** [***become***] ～ ***for fishes*** 葬身鱼腹,淹死。***be*** ～ ***for worms*** 死亡。～ ***and drink*** 饮食。～ ***for powder*** 炮灰,〔蔑〕兵士。～ ***for thought*** [***meditation***] 思考的材料。～ **card** [**coupon**] 粮票,饭票。～ **chain** [**cycle**]【生态】食物链。～ **court**(商场内饮食摊位集中的)小吃街,饮食区。～ **web** 食物网。～ **office**〔英〕粮食管理局。～ **poisoning** 食物中毒。～ **pyramid**【生态】食物金字塔。～ **science** 食物营养学。～ **stamp**(发给失业人口等免费或廉价的)食物券。～**stuff** 食品,粮食。**-less** *a*. 缺量的,断炊的。

foo·fa·raw [ˈfuːfərɔː; ˋfufəˏrɔ] *n*.〔美俚〕**1**. 多余装饰品;(服装等的)褶边;饰边。**2**. 大惊小怪。

fool[1] [fuːl; ful] **I** *n*. **1**. 笨人,傻子,白痴。**2**. 受愚弄[欺骗]的人。**3**.(已往王侯雇养的)小丑,弄臣。**4**. 有癖好的人。*Fool's haste is no speed*.〔谚〕欲速则不达。*a chess playing* ～ 棋迷。*an April* ～ 愚人节被愚弄的人。***act*** [***play***] ***the*** ～ 当傻瓜,做蠢事,装傻样;扮演丑角,逗人乐。***All Fool's Day*** 愚人节〔四月一日〕。***be a*** ～ ***for one's pains*** 徒劳。***be a*** ～ ***to*** 比不上。***be*** ～ ***enough to do*** 笨到做…。***be no*** [***nobody's***] ～ 很精明。***be the*** ～ ***of fate*** 被命运愚弄。***A*** ～***'s bolt is soon shot***. 蠢人往往一下子把箭射完〔指蠢人不善于把握时机地逐步运用力量,不善于节约精力、金钱等〕。***make a*** ～ ***of*** 愚弄。***make a*** ～ ***of oneself*** 闹笑话。***play the*** ～ ***with*** 欺瞒;使失败,弄坏。***go*** [***be sent***] ***on a*** ～***'s errand*** 去[被派去]作无谓奔走。**II** *vt*. **1**. 愚弄;欺骗。**2**. 浪费,虚度。— *vi*. **1**. 闹笑话;开玩笑;干傻事。**2**. 游手好闲;瞎弄。*Stop* ～*ing*! 别闹笑话了。*He is only* ～*ing*. 他不过是开玩笑罢了。***be badly*** ～***ed*** 上大当。～ ***about*** = ～ ***around***〔美口〕闲游,瞎干涉,多管闲事。～ ***away*** 浪费(时间、金钱等)。～ (***sb***.) ***into*** 骗人作…。～ (***sb***.) ***out of*** 骗取某人(财物等)。～ ***with*** 玩弄。**III** *a*.〔美口〕愚蠢的。～ **duck**【动】(北美出产的)赤鸭。～**hardy** *a*. 有勇无谋的,蛮干的。～ **hen**〔美〕松鸡。～**proof** *a*. **1**.〔俚〕傻瓜也明白[会干]的,极简单明了的。**2**. 有安全装置的。～**'s gold**【矿】黄铁矿,黄铜矿。～**'s paradise**(实际是荒唐无聊的)自以为非常幸福[有意义]的处境。

fool[2] [fuːl; ful] *n*.〔英〕(煮熟的)糖水水果拌奶油。

fool·er·y [ˈfuːləri; ˋfulərɪ] *n*. 愚蠢的思想[谈吐、行动]。

fool·ing [ˈfuːliŋ; ˋfulɪŋ] *n*. **1**. 戏弄,开玩笑。**2**. 轻浮的行为。

fool·ish [ˈfuːliʃ; ˋfulɪʃ] *a*. 愚蠢的;鲁莽的,可笑的,荒谬的。*Better a witty fool than a* ～ *wit*.〔谚〕宁做聪明的傻子,不做愚蠢的聪明人。***cut*** [***make***] ***a*** ～ ***figure*** 闹笑话。～ **powder**〔美俚〕海洛因。**-ly** *ad*. **-ness** *n*.

fool·oc·ra·cy [fuːˈlɔkrəsi; fuˋlɑkrəsɪ] *n*. 愚人统治,愚人统治集团。

fools·cap [ˈfuːlzkæp; ˋfulzkæp] *n*. **1**. 丑角帽;(罚不用功的学生戴的)圆锥形纸帽。**2**. [ˈfuːlskæp; ˋfulskæp](约 13×16 英寸)大页书写纸。

fool's-pars·ley [ˈfuːlzˈpaːsli; ˋfulzˋpɑrslɪ] *n*.【植】毒欧芹。

foot [fut; fʊt] **I** *n*. (*pl*. *feet* [fiːt; fit]) **1**. 脚,足。**2**. 步调,脚步。**3**.〔集合词〕步兵。**4**.(器物的)足部;(山)麓;帆的下缘。**5**. 底部,底座,最下部;压脚板;末尾。**6**. 呎,英尺(=12 英寸,$\frac{1}{3}$码,0.3048 米)。★作长度单位时,前为数词,单数也可用作复数。例:two foot six = two feet six (inches). **7**.【韵】音步。**8**.(*pl*. *foots*)渣滓,沉淀物;粗糖,油糟。**9**.【动】跗节。**10**.【植】花梗,发状根。*have a light* ～ 脚步轻。*have leaden* [*heavy*] *feet* 脚步沉重,行动迟缓。*the* ～ *of a bed* 床头的对面一端〔*opp*. the head of a bed 床头;床的脚为 the legs of a bed〕。*the* ～ *of the list* 表列的下端。*the 42nd* ～ 步兵第 42 团。～ *and horse* 步兵与骑兵。*at the* ～ *of a hill* 在山脚。*at the* ～ *of a class* 全班的最后一名。*fleet* [*swift*] *of* ～ 行动敏捷,健步如飞。*Better the* ～ *slip than the tongue trip*. = *Better to slip with the* ～ *than with the tongue*.〔谚〕宁可失脚滑倒,不可随口失言。***at a*** ～***'s pace*** 用步行速度,常步。***at sb.'s feet*** 在某人脚下[门下、手下](*sit at sb.'s feet* 拜某人为师)。***be carried out with one's feet foremost*** 被抬出去埋葬。***be sure of*** ～ 踏实。***betray*** [***display***, ***show***] ***the colven*** ～ 露马脚。***bring sb. to his feet*** 扶起某人。***carry*** [***sweep***, ***take***] ***sb. off his feet*** 使人兴奋,使人狂热。***catch sb. on the wrong*** ～ 使人措手不及。***change*** ～ [***feet***] 换脚,换步。***drag one's feet*** **1**. 拖着脚步走。**2**. 故意拖拉,迟缓误事。***drop*** [***fall***] ***on one's feet*** 运气好,没有跌着;安然脱险,幸免于难。***feel one's feet*** [***legs***, ***wing***] 感到有把握。***feet of clay*** 泥足,外强中干的,不堪一击的(*a colossus with feet of clay* 泥足巨人)。***find one's feet*** 开始站稳;能独立行动。***find*** [***get***, ***know***, ***take***] ***the length of sb.'s*** ～ 抓到某人的弱点。～ ***by*** ～ 一步一步;逐渐。～ ***to*** ～ 短兵相接。***have a*** ～ ***in the dish*** 有一份,获得立足点。***have cold feet*** 害怕,胆寒,畏缩,不敢上阵。***have*** [***with***] ***one*** ～

in the grave 风烛残年,离死不远。***have one's*** ～ ***into*** 插足。***have*** [***put, set***] ***one's*** ～ ***on the neck of sb.*** 压服某人。***have two left feet*** 笨极了。***jump*** [***spring***] ***to one's feet*** 突然站起来,跃起。***keep one's feet*** 站稳。***lay sth. at sb.'s feet*** 把某物献在某人脚下。***lift off one's feet*** (被水等)冲[撞]倒。***measure another man's*** ～ ***by one's own last*** 以己度人。***miss one's*** ～ 失脚,踏空,走乱步子。***my*** [***me***] ～! 〔口〕怪啦! 胡说! 去你的! ***not to lift*** [***move, stir***] ***a*** ～ 一步也不动。***off one's feet*** 躺着,坐着,跌倒;不知所措;措手不及;不能控制自己。***on*** ～ 步行;在进行中(*go on* ～ 走着去。*set a plan on* ～ 实施计划)。***on one's feet*** 站起;健康复原,经济独立,自立。***pull*** ～ 逃走。***put one's best*** ～ ***foremost*** [***forward***] 争先快走;全力以赴。***put*** [***set***] ***one's*** ～ ***down*** 立定脚跟;坚持立场;拿定主张。***put one's*** ～ ***in*** [***into***] ***it*** 〔口〕弄糟,闹笑话,引起麻烦。***put one's feet up*** 〔口〕双腿平搁起来休息。***raise sb. to his feet*** 扶起某人。***rise*** [***spring, struggle***] ***to one's*** ～ 站起。***rush sb. off his feet*** 使某人措手不及。***scrape one's feet*** 用脚擦地作声。***set*** ～ ***in*** 进入。***set*** ～ ***on*** 踏上。***set on*** ～ 着手。***set sb.*** [***sth.***] ***on his*** [***its***] ***feet*** 使某人[物]独立生存[存在]下去。***shoot oneself in the*** ～搬起石头砸自己的脚。***sling a nasty*** ～〔俚〕跳舞跳得到家。***sweep sb. off his*** ～ 使某人大为激动〔不能控制自己〕。***take to one's feet*** 走出,步行,走去。***trample*** [***tread***] ***under*** ～ 践踏,蹂躏;虐待。***under sb.'s*** ～ [***feet***] 屈服于人,唯命是从。***with both feet*** 强烈地,坚决地。***with one's feet foremost*** 死去。***with one's wrong*** ～ ***foremost*** 心情不好。**II** ***vt.*** **1.** 踏在…上,在…上走,在…上跳;跳(舞)。**2.** 〔口〕结(账),付(款)。**3.** 给(袜子等)换底。**4.** (鹰等)以爪捕捉。～ *the road* 走路。～ *the floor* 跳舞。～ (*up*) *an account* 结算账目。～ *a bill* 付账。— ***vi.*** **1.** 步行;踏拍子;跳舞。**2.** 〔俚〕合计;共达。**3.** (船等)前进。～ *up to $500*. 共计五百元。～ *it* 〔口〕走着去,跳舞。～ ***up*** 〔口〕凑成,凑足。～**-and-mouth disease** (牛羊等的)口蹄疫。～**bath** 洗脚;脚盆。～**-board** (马车、汽车等的)踏脚板;床靠脚一端的竖板。～**-boy** 小听差。～ **brake** 脚踏闸,脚踏式制动器。～ **bridge** 人行小桥。～**-candle** 【物】英尺烛光[烛光亮度]。～**-dragging** ***n.*** 〔美俚〕迟疑不决,拖延。～**-drill** 【军】徒手训练。～ **drop** 垂足病。～**fall** 脚步,脚步声。～ **fault** (网球)发球犯规;(排球)脚过中线。～**gear** 鞋袜。**F-Guards** (英国)近卫步兵连。～**hill** 山麓小丘,〔常 *pl.*〕山脉的丘陵地带。～ **hold** 立足点,【军】据点。～**-in-mouth** ***a.*** 口不择言的;措词尖锐的。～**lights** 〔*pl.*〕【剧】舞台上的脚光;舞台;演戏(*appear before the* ～ *lights* 上台演戏。*behind the* ～*-lights* 在观众席上。*get across* [*over*] *the* ～*lights* 演出受欢迎。*smell of the* ～ *lights* 像在做戏,装模作样。*smell the* ～ *lights* 变成戏迷)。～ **man** 步兵;(穿号衣的)马夫,男仆。～**-mark** 足迹。～**note** **1.** ***n.*** (书中的)脚注。**2.** ***vt.*** 为…作脚注。～**pace** **1.** 常步,慢步。**2.** 【建】梯台。～**pad** **1.** (徒步的)拦路盗贼〔*cf.* highwayman〕。**2.** (软降落宇航器腿上防止在星球表面上陷入的)防陷足垫。～**page** 男仆。～ **passenger** 步行者,行人。～**path** **1.** 步道,人行道。**2.** 小路。～**plate** (火车司机室内的)踏板。～**-pound** 【物】磅〔能的单位〕。～**-poundal** 【物】呎磅达〔功的单位〕。～**-pound-second** 呎磅秒单位制。～**-print** **1.** 足迹,脚印。**2.** 太空飞船或飞弹等的预定着陆点。**3.**【计】底面积〔电脑所占的桌面面积〕。～**-pump** 脚踏泵。～**-race** 竞走。～ **rail** 【矿】轨蹼,轨脚。～**rest** 搁脚板。～**-rope** 【海】(水手收帆时站的)脚缆,脚踏索,帆的下缘索。～ **rot** **1.** 【植】根腐病。**2.** 【兽医】腐蹄病。～ **rule** 一英尺长的直尺。～ **soldier** 步兵。～**sore** ***a.*** 走痛了脚的。～**stalk** 【植】叶柄;花梗;【动】肉茎。～**stall** 【建】基脚;墩柱。～**step** 脚步;脚步声;足迹;【机】垫轴台,轴承架(*follow* [*walk*] *in sb.'s* ～*-steps* 步某人的后尘)。～**stock** = tailstock. ～**stone** 基石;墓基。～**stool** **1.** 脚台,脚凳。**2.** 〔美〕地,大地。～**-sure** ***a.*** 脚步稳的,踏实的。～**-ton** 呎吨[能量单位]。～ **wall** 底帮,底壁,下盘;基础墙。～ **warmer** 暖脚物。～**way** 人行道。～**wear** = footgear. ～**well** (汽车中安设用脚操纵的脚闸、风门踏等机件,驾驶者放腿脚的)搁脚处。～**work** **1.** 【体】步法。**2.** 要跑腿的工作。～**worn** ***a.*** **1.** 走累的。**2.** 被脚踏磨损的(～ *worn stairs* 磨损的楼梯)。

foot·age [ˈfutidʒ; ˋfʊtɪdʒ] ***n.*** 以英尺计的长度[呎数];(影片等总长度的)英尺数。【矿】进呎。

foot·ball [ˈfutbɔːl; ˋfʊtbɔl] ***n.*** **1.** 足球〔美国通常指橄榄球〕,足球运动,足球的球。**2.** 玩物,玩弄物;被踢来踢去的难题[悬案]。*American* ～美式足球,橄榄球。*Association* ～英式足球〔又称 soccer〕。*Rugby* ～橄榄球。*a* ～ *fiend* 〔美〕足球迷。***become a*** ～ ***of*** 变成玩弄品。***play*** ～ 踢足球;对难办的事采取踢皮球的态度。

foot·ball·er [ˈfutbɔːlə; ˋfʊtbɔlɚ], **foot·ball·ist** [-ist; -ɪst] ***n.*** 足球[橄榄球]运动员。

foot·cloth [ˈfutˌklɔθ; ˋfʊtˏklɔθ] ***n.*** (*pl.* ***-cloths*** [-ˌklɔːðz, -ˌklɔːθs; -ˏklɔðz, -ˏklɔθs]) **1.** 马披巾。**2.** 〔罕〕地毯;毯。

foot·ed [ˈfutid; ˋfʊtɪd] ***a.*** **1.** 有足的;有多足的。**2.** 有某种足或足型的〔用以构成有连字符的复合词〕。*four-*～ 四足的。

foot·er [ˈfutə; ˋfʊtɚ] ***n.*** **1.** 〔常用以构成复合词〕高…英尺的人,长…英尺的东西。**2.** 步行者。**3.** 〔英俚〕足球赛。*a six* ～身高六英尺的人。

foot·fall [ˈfutfɔːl; ˋfʊtˏfɔl] ***n.*** 脚步;脚步声。

foot·ing [ˈfutiŋ; ˋfʊtɪŋ] ***n.*** **1.** 立足处,立脚点。**2.** 立场,基础,地位;【建】底脚。**3.** 关系,交情。**4.** 合计,总额。**5.** 场地情况。**6.** 入会费,入社费,入学费。**7.** 【军】编制。*Mind your* ～. 当心脚下,别跌倒。*be on a friendly* ～ *with sb.* 跟某人关系好。***get*** [***gain, obtain***] ***a*** ～ 取得地位。***keep one's*** ～站稳,坚守立场。***lose*** [***miss***] ***one's*** ～ 跌跤;丧失立场。***on a peace*** [***war***] ～按平时[战时]编制。***on an equal*** ～平等对待。***on one*** [***a, the same***] ～ ***with*** 以同等资格。***pay*** (***for***) ***one's*** ～缴入会费,纳费入伙。～ **course** 【建】基础层。

foot·le [ˈfuːtl; ˋfutl] **I** ***n.*** 蠢话,傻事。**II** ***vi.*** **1.** 说蠢话,做傻事。**2.** 浪费时间。

foot·less [ˈfutlis; ˋfʊtlɪs] ***a.*** **1.** 无脚的。**2.** 无基础的,无支撑的。**3.** 〔诗〕人迹未到的。**4.** 〔口〕笨拙的,无能的,无益的。

foot·ling [ˈfutliŋ; ˋfʊtlɪŋ] ***a.*** 〔口〕**1.** 愚蠢的。**2.** 不关重要的,琐细的;微不足道的。

foot·lock·er [ˈfutlɔkə; ˋfʊtˏlɑkɚ] ***n.*** 【美军】士兵个人用品箱,床脚箱〔置于床脚的美士兵个人用品箱〕。

foot·loose [ˈfutˌluːs; ˋfʊtˏlus] ***a.*** 到处走动的;随心所欲的。

foot·sie, foot·sy [ˈfutsi; ˋfʊtsi] ***n.*** (*pl.* ***-si·es***) 〔儿〕脚儿。***play*** ～ (***with***) 〔口〕**1.** (在桌下)柔情地碰碰腿儿[膝]。**2.** 调情;暗中勾搭,搞秘密交易。

foot·slog [ˈfutˌslɔg; ˋfʊtˏslɑg] ***vi.*** (***-gg-***) 在泥泞中行进。**-ger** ***n.*** 长途步行者;步兵。

foo·ty [ˈfuti; ˋfutɪ] ***a.*** (***foo·ti·er; -i·est***) **1.** 微不足道的,无足轻重的。**2.** 肯定很糟的,褴褛的。

foo·zle [ˈfuːzl; ˋfuzl] **I** ***vt., vi.*** (尤指在高尔夫球中)笨拙地打(球等);笨拙地做(事);(把…)弄糟。**II** ***n.*** **1.** 不高明的一击,笨拙的动作。**2.** 〔口〕笨人。

fop [fɔp; fɑp] ***n.*** 纨袴子弟,花花公子。

fop·ling [ˈfɔpliŋ; ˋfɑplɪŋ] ***n.*** 〔古〕= fop.

fop·per·y [ˈfɔpəri; ˋfɑpərɪ] ***n.*** 纨袴习气。

fop·pish [ˈfɔpiʃ; ˋfɑpɪʃ] ***a.*** 浮华的,有纨袴子弟习气的。**-ly** ***ad.*** **-ness** ***n.***

FOR, f.o.r. = free on rail 【商】火车上交货(价格)。

for [强 fɔː; fɔr, 弱 fə; fɚ] **I** ***prep.*** **1.** 〔表示目标、去向〕向,往。*leave* [*sail*] ～ *London* 动身[坐船]到伦敦去。

passengers ～ *New York* 到纽约去的旅客。*the train* ～ *Paris* 开往巴黎的火车。*He is getting on* ～ *forty*. 他快四十岁了。*Now* ～ *it*! 走吧！开动吧！*a change* ～ *the better* 好转。*a change* ～ *the worse* 恶化。**2.** 〔表示愿望、爱好、特长等〕倾向于，对于。*have a liking* ～ *music* 爱好音乐。*have respect* ～ *one's teachers* 尊敬老师。*long* ～ *freedom* 渴望自由。*an eye* ～ *beauty* 审美眼光。**3.** 〔表示目的〕为了。*a house* ～ *rent* 〔美〕房屋出租。*not* ～ *sale* 非卖品。*die* ～ *one's country* 为祖国牺牲。*go out* ～ *a walk* 出去散步。*struggle* ～ *existence* 生存竞争。*shout* ～ *help* 大声呼救。*send* ～ *a doctor* 叫人去请医生。*Oh*, ～ *a glass of water*! 啊，有一杯水就好了。**4.** 〔表示理由、原因〕因为。*My head aches* ～ *want of sleep*. 我因为睡眠不足而头痛。～ *fear of* 唯恐。**5.** 代，替，代表。*a substitute* ～ *butter* 奶油代用品。*speak* ～ *sb*. 代某人说话〔辩白〕。**6.** 〔表示等价、报酬、赔偿或比例关系〕交换。*I gave a dollar* ～ *it*. 我用一块钱弄到手的。*sell* ～ *a dollar* 一块钱卖掉了。*give blow* ～ *blow* 以打还打。*answer point* ～ *point* 逐点答复。*translate word* ～ *word* 逐字翻译。**7.** 〔表示时间、距离、数量等〕历经，达，计。～ *hours* ［*days*, *years*］有(好)几小时［(好)几天，(好)几年］。*the meeting lasted* (～) *an hour* 会议继续了一小时。*run* (～) *a mile* 跑一英里路。★ 在上述情形下，*for* 常可略去。**8.** 〔表示关联〕关于，说到。*He has no equal* ～ *running*. 讲到赛跑，他是无敌的。～ *my part* 至于我，讲到我。*So much* ～ *today*. 今天就讲［做］这么多。**9.** 〔表示赞成、支持〕拥护，有利于(*opp*. against)。*They are all* ～ *him*. 他们都支持他。*vote* ～ *sb*. 投某人的票。**10.** 〔表示身分等〕看作，当作，作为。*be hanged* ～ *a pirate* 被当作海盗绞死。*be mistaken* ～ *a Japanese* 被误认为是日本人。*They knew it* ～ *a fact*. 他们知道那是事实。*It was built* ～ *a pleasure boat*. 这条船是作为游艇建造的。**11.** 〔表示让步〕虽然，尽管。*F- all his wealth* , *I don't like him*. 尽管他那样有钱，我并不喜欢他。**12.** 〔表示与具体条件作比较〕比起来，考虑到，就…而言。*It is rather cold* ～ *April*. 拿四月来讲，天气算冷了一点。*clever* ～ *one's age* 拿年龄来说就算聪明的了。**13.** 〔表示对象〕属于…的，给…的。*a present* ～ *you* 送给你的礼物。**14.** 〔表示用途〕适于…的。*fit* ～ *food* 适于作食物。**15.** 〔与名词或代词等连用，后接动词不定式起主语［宾］语、定语、状语作用〕。*F- them to surrender would be impossible*. 要他们投降是不可能的。*make way* ～ *the car to pass* 给汽车让路。*The book is too difficult* ～ *me to read*. 这本书太艰深，我读不下去。*It is time* ～ *him to go*. 他该走了。(***as***) ～ ***me*** 讲到我。***be*** ～ ***it*** 1. 赞成。2. 势必受罚。～ ***all*** 无论…怎样(*F- all you say*, *I still like him*. 不管你怎样说，我仍然喜欢他)。～ ***all I care*** 我管不着，与我无关。～ ***all I know*** 也许，或许。～ ***all that*** 虽然如此，还是。～ ***all time*** 永久。***F- crying out loud***! 〔美口〕真想不到！见鬼！去你的吧！有这种事么！〔用于表示惊诧、不快〕。～ ***days*** (***and days***) ***on end*** 永远，老是。～ ***it*** 1. 应付的(手段、方法)。2. 因此。3. 快要发生麻烦，就要挨骂。4. 〔美〕(兵士)接到行动命令(*There is nothing* ～ *it but to wait*. 除等待外别无办法。*be worse* ～ *it* 因此更糟。*be in* ～ *it* 骑虎难下；势必要受罚)。～ ***one*** 至少有一个，举一个作例子〔用作插入语〕(*I*, ～ *one*, *object to it* 至少我是反对那样做的)。～ ***oneself*** 为自己；亲自；独自。～ ***one thing*** 第一〔表示列举〕；原因之一是〔用作插入语〕。**II** ***conj***. 因为。*We can't go*, ～ *it is raining*. 天下雨，我们不去了。★ 用来说明理由，比 because 更为正式，但语气较弱，一般不用于句首，口语中也多不用。回答 why 引导的问题时，要用 because.

for- *pref*. **1.** 表示"禁止"，"拒绝"，"蔑视"，*for*bear, *for*bid, *for*go. **2.** 表示"破坏"：*for*do, *for*swear. **3.** 表示"极度"，"过度"(= all over, thoroughly)：*for*gather, *for*lorn, *for*worn. **4.** = fore-：*fore*cast.

for. = foreign; forestry.

fo·ra [ˈfɔːrə; ˋfɔrə] ***n***. forum 的另一复数形式。

for·age [ˈfɔridʒ; ˋfɔrɪdʒ] **I** ***n***. **1.** 粮秣；饲料。**2.** 粮秣的搜索［征发］。***be on the*** ～ (牛马)正在找饲料，(兵)正在征发粮秣。**II** ***vt***., ***vi***. **1.** 搜索［征发］粮秣。**2.** 给(马)吃草料。**3.** 〔古〕蹂躏，掠夺。～ *among papers* 乱翻文件。～ *about* ［*around*］*in a drawer* 在抽屉里乱翻。～ ***for oneself*** 自行采购(粮秣)；用现成食品当饭食；自行谋生。～ **acre** 饲料亩〔牧场饲料作物的计算单位，等于牧场总面积乘饲料作物所占百分比，例如：10 英亩×30%密度 = 3 饲料亩〕。～ **cap** 〔英〕步兵便帽。

for·ag·er [ˈfɔridʒə; ˋfɔrɪdʒɚ] ***n***. **1.** 粮秣征发员。**2.** 〔*pl*.〕成散开横队的骑兵。

fo·ra·men [fəˈreimen; foˋremən] ***n***. (*pl*. ***fo·ram·i·na*** [fəˈræminə; fəˋræmɪnə]) 【动、植】孔。～ **magnum** (昆虫的)后头孔；(枕骨)大孔。

fo·ram·i·nate(d) [fəˈræminit(id); fəˋræmɪˏnet(ɪd)] ***a***. 〔罕〕有孔的；有小孔的；多孔的。

for·a·min·i·fer [ˌfɔːrəˈminifə, ˌfɔ-; ˏfɔrəˋmɪnəfɚ, ˏfɑ-] ***n***. (*pl*. ***fo·ram·i·nif·er·a*** [fəˌræmiˈnifərə; fəˏræməˋnɪfərə]) 【动】有孔虫目。**fo·ram·i·nif·er·al**, **fo·ram·i·nif·er·ous** ***a***.

for·as·much [fərəzˈmʌtʃ; fərəzˋmʌtʃ] ***conj***. 由于，鉴于〔与 as 连用〕(= since, considering that)。

FORATOM = 〔F.〕*Forum Atomique Européen* 欧洲原子能公司(= European Atomic Forum)。

for·ay [ˈfɔrei; ˋfɔre] ***n***., ***vt***., ***vi***. 侵略，掠夺；摧残，蹂躏。*make* ［*go on*］*a* ～ 进行袭击［劫掠］。

forb [fɔːb; fɔrb] ***n***. 〔美〕一种阔叶、开花的非禾本牧草；任何非草本的药用植物。

for·bade [fəˈbeid; fɚˋbed], **for·bad** [-ˈbæd; -ˋbæd] forbid 的过去式。

for·bear[1] [fɔːˈbeə, fɔrˋbɛr] ***vi***. (***-bore*** [fɔːˈbɔː; fɔrˋbɔr]; ***-borne*** [fɔːˈbɔːn; fɔrˋbɔrn]) 忍耐，容忍(*with*)；克制，节制，戒(*from*)。— ***vt***. 抑制，节制；忍住，忍受，忍耐。～ (*from*) *complaining* 不发牢骚。～ *to go into details* 不准备详细说。*I cannot* ～ *to go into details*. 我不得不详细说。*She could not* ～ *crying out*. 她禁不住叫喊出来。～ *with sb*. ［*sth*.］容忍某人［某事］。***bear and*** ～ [ˈfɔːbeə; ˋfɔrbɛr] 忍了又忍。

for·bear[2] [ˈfɔːbeə; ˋfɔrˏbɛr] ***n***. = forebear.

for·bear·ance [fɔːˈbeərəns; fɔrˋbɛrəns] ***n***. **1.** 忍耐，克制。**2.** 【法】债务偿还期的延缓。**3.** 放弃执行某些权利。*at the end of one's* ～ 忍无可忍。*F- is no* (*ac*) *quittance* 〔谚〕不催账不等于取消账。

for·bear·ing [fɔːˈbeəriŋ; fɔrˋbɛrɪŋ] ***a***. 能忍耐的；宽容的。**-ly** ***ad***.

For·bes [fɔːbz, ˈfɔːbis; fɔrbz, ˋfɔrbɪs] ***n***. 福布斯〔姓氏〕。

for·bid [fəˈbid; fɚˋbɪd] ***vt***. (***-bad*** [fəˈbæd; fɚˋbæd], ***-bade*** [fəˈbeid; fɚˋbed]; ***-bid·den*** [fəˈbidn; fɚˋbɪdn]; ***~ding***) **1.** 禁止，不许。**2.** 妨害，阻止。*Cameras are forbidden*. 禁止拍照。*Parking forbidden*! 禁止停车！～ *sb*. *the house* 不许某人进屋来。～ *sb*. *to smoke* 禁止某人吸烟。*Time* ～*s*. 时间不许可。*High walls* ～ *all approach*. 高墙遮断，难以接近。*The storm* ～*s us to proceed*. 暴风雨阻止我们前进。**God** ［**Heaven**, **The saints**］～！但愿不这样！决没有(那样的事)(*God* ～ *that he should injure you*! 他决不会害你的！)。

for·bid·dance [fəˈbidəns; fɚˋbɪdns] ***n***. 禁止；禁令。

for·bid·den [fəˈbidn; fɚˋbɪdn] **I** forbid 的过去分词。**II** ***a***. 被禁止的。**F- City** 紫禁城。～ ［**prohibited**］**degrees** 【法】禁婚亲等。～ **fruit** 【宗】禁果；因被禁止反而更想弄到手的东西。～ **ground** ［**zone**］禁区。

for·bid·ding [fəˈbidiŋ; fɚˋbɪdɪŋ] ***a***. 可怕的，令人难亲近的；凶险的。*a* ～ *countenance* ［*look*］严峻的面貌。**-ly**

F

ad. -ness *n*.

for·bore [fɔːˈbɔː; fɔrˋbor] forbear[1] 的过去式。

for·borne [fɔːˈbɔːn; fɔrˋborn] forbear[1] 的过去分词。

for·by(e) [fɔːˈbai; fɔrˋbai] **I** *ad*., *prep*.〔古, Scot.〕而且;除…外。**II** *a*. 不同寻常的,极好的。

force[1][fɔːs; fors] **I** *n*. **1**. 力,势。**2**. 体力,气力,精力,魄力。**3**. 暴力,压力;兵力,武力。**4**.〔*pl*.〕部队,军队,兵力。**5**. 势力,威力;【法】效力的约束,实施。**6**.(语言、文字等的)确切意义,实质;要点;影响力,说服力,主动性。**7**.【物】…力;势能。~ *of character* 人格的力量。*the ~ of habit* 习惯势力。*the ~s of nature* 自然力。*the ~ of public opinion* 舆论的威力。*with the ~ of a thunderbolt* 以雷霆万钧之力。*a 12 ~* [*12th-~*] *typhoon* 十二级台风。*the air ~* 空军。*the armed ~s* 军队。*an assault ~*【军】突击队。*brutal ~* 暴力。*centrifugal ~* 离心力。*centripetal ~* 向心力。*democratic ~* 民主势力。*feudal ~* 封建势力。*interatomic ~* 原子间力。*the land ~* 陆军。*magnetic ~* 磁力。*the naval* [*sea*] ~ 海军。*the* [*police*] ~〔集合词〕警察。*the productive ~s* 生产力。*the relation of ~s* 力量的对比。*the social ~s* 社会势力。*a striking ~* 机动兵力。***a ~ to be reckoned with*** 不可忽视的力量。***by main ~*** 用蛮力,全靠气力;凭暴力,强迫。***by* (*the*) *~ of*** 由于,迫于;通过,靠…的力量(*by ~ of arms* 用武力。*by ~ of habit* 由于习惯。*by ~ of circumstances* 由于环境。*by ~ of contrast* 通过对比)。***by* [*with*] *~ and arms*** 用武力。***cease to be in ~*** 失效。***come* [*enter*] *into ~*** 实行,生效。***in ~*** **1**. 有效,在有效期中。**2**. 大举,大批地,大规模地。***in full ~*** 用全力;发挥充分威力。***in great ~*** 大举,大批地;精力充沛地。***join ~ with*** (军队)会师;(同人)联合,(与人)通力合作。***of no ~*** 无效。***put in* [*into*] *~*** 施行,实施。***remain in ~*** 在有效期中,仍然有效。***resort to ~*** 诉诸武力。***put up a show of ~*** 示威。***take by ~***【军】夺取,武力侵占。***with all one's ~*** 尽全力,竭力。***with much ~*** 极有力地,效力卓著地。**II** *vt*. **1**. 强制,迫使,逼迫。**2**. 强力夺取,攻克。**3**. 强行,强加。**4**. 推动。**5**. 竭力提高,抬高,加快。**6**. 勒索;强奸。**7**. 迫使(对手)出某张牌,迫出(某张牌)。**8**.(通过温室栽培等)促成(植物)早熟[发育、生长];加速(学生的)学业。~ *sb. to do* [*into doing, into an action*] 强迫某人做某事。*They were ~d to leave the town*. 他们被迫离开该城。~ *an action*【军】迫使敌人作战。~ *an entry* 强行进入。~ *a passage* 强行通过。~ *one's strength* 硬使劲。~ *a smile* 强颜欢笑,苦笑。~ *one's voice* 提高嗓门。~ *one's appetites* 勉强吃,硬吃。~ ***one's way into*** 闯进。~ ***one's way through a crowd*** 由人群中挤过去。~ ***sb.'s hand*** 逼使摊牌;逼人过早行动。~ ***the bidding*** (拍卖时)抬价。~ ***the game*** (板球赛时)硬冒险。~ ***the pace*** [***running***](赛跑时)为使对手疲劳而尽力快跑。~ **fan** 鼓风机。~**-feed** *vt*. 强喂(食物);强灌(食物)〔尤指直插管灌送食物〕;强使接受。~ **feed**【机】压力润滑,压力进给。~**-in-being** 可随时作战的军事力量。~**-land** *vi*. 强迫降落;强行登陆。~**-out**【棒球】封死。~ **pump** 压力泵,压力水泵。**-less** *a*. 无力的,较弱的。

force[2] [fɔːs; fors] *n*.〔北英〕瀑布。

forced [fɔːst; forst] *a*. **1**. 强迫的,强制的。**2**. 用力的。**3**. 勉强的,不自然的。~ *analogy* 牵强附会。*a ~ smile* 苦笑。*a ~ style* (文体)矫揉造作。~ *tears* 假哭,硬挤出的几滴眼泪。~ **draught** (锅炉等的)鼓风,压力通风。~ **loan** 义务公债。~ **landing** 强行登陆;(飞机)迫降。~ **march** 强行军。~ **oscillation** [**vibration**]【物】强迫振动[振荡]。~ **quotations**【商】限价。~ **sales** (为清偿债务而进行的)拍卖。**-ly** *ad*.

force de frappe [fors də ˈfrɑːp; fors də ˋfrɑp]〔F.〕打击力量〔尤指法国的核打击[威摄]力量〕。

force·ful [ˈfɔːsful; ˋforsfʊl] *a*. 强有力的,坚强的;有说服力的。**-ly** *ad*. **-ness** *n*.

force ma·jeure [fɔːs mɑːˈʒəː; fɔrs maˋʒɝ]〔F.〕不可抗力〔如天灾等〕。

force·meat [ˈfɔːsmiːt; ˋfɔrs͵mit] *n*. 加调味料的肉馅、五香碎肉(= farcemeat)。

for·ceps [ˈfɔːseps; ˋfɔrsɛps] *n*. (*pl*. ~, **-ci·pes** [-səpiːz; -səpiz]) **1**. 镊子,钳子。**2**.【动】(昆虫的)尾铗。**3**.【解】钳状体。

for·ci·ble [ˈfɔːsəbl; ˋforsəbl̩] *a*. **1**. 强有力的,有说服力的。**2**. 强暴的,强迫的。~ *detention* 扣留。*a ~ entry into* 强行闯入,非法侵入。~ *execution* 强制执行。~**-feeble** *a*. 外强中干的,貌似强大而实际虚弱的。**-bil·i·ty** [ˌfɔːsəˈbiliti; ˏfɔsəˋbɪlətɪ] *n*. **-ness** *n*. **-bly** *ad*.

forc·ing [ˈfɔːsiŋ; ˋforsɪŋ] **I** *n*. **1**. 强制,强夺。**2**.【农】催熟栽培。**II** *a*. **1**. 强迫的,施加压力的。**2**. 促成植物早熟的。~ **bed** 温床。~ **crops** [**culture**]【农】催熟作物[栽培]。~ **house** 温室,温床。~ **pump** = force pump.

for·ci·pate(d) [ˈfɔːsipeit(id); ˋfɔrsə͵pet(ɪd)] *a*. 钳状的。

for·close [fɔːˈkləuz; fɔrˋkloz] *v*. = foreclose.

for·clo·sure [fɔːˈkləuʒə; fɔrˋkloʒɚ] *n*. = foreclosure.

Ford[1][fɔːd; fɔrd] *n*. **1**. 福特[姓氏]。**2**. **Henry ~** 亨利·福特〔1863—1947,美国汽车制造厂商〕。**3**. **G. R. ~** 杰鲁·福特〔美国第38任总统〕。

Ford[2][fɔːd; fɔrd] *n*. **1**. 福特牌汽车。**2**.〔f-〕时髦式样。**Fordize** *vt*. **1**. 大量生产(标准化的产品)。**2**. 使(人员、生产方法等)标准化(以提高生产效率)。

ford [fɔːd; fɔrd] **I** *n*. 浅滩,津渡,可涉水而过的地方。**II** *vt*., *vi*. 涉(水)。~ ***over*** 涉水而过。**-able** *a*. 可以涉水而过的。**-less** *a*. 不能涉水而过的,没有浅滩的。

for·do [fɔːˈduː; fɔrˋdu] *vt*. (**-did** [fɔːˈdid; fɔrˋdɪd]; **-done** [fɔːˈdʌn; fɔrˋdʌn]) 毁坏;使疲乏〔只用过去分词〕。**for·done** *a*.〔古〕筋疲力尽的。

fore[1][fɔː, fɔə; for, fɔr] **I** *a*. **1**. 前面的(*opp*. hind, back, aft)。**2**. 先前的。*the ~ part of an aircraft* 飞机的前部。**II** *ad*. 在前面,在船头。**III** *prep*., *conj*.〔方〕在前。**IV** *n*. 前部;头;前桅;(马等的)前腿。***at the ~*** (信号旗)悬在前桅上,在最前。***come to the ~*** 发作,涌现出来,出人头地;惹人注意。***to the ~*** **1**. 在前面,在显著地位。**2**. 在场;立即有用;(钱等)在手边。**3**. 活着。~ **edge** (与书脊相对的)书的前页边。~**-end** *n*. **1**. 枪托前半部。**2**.【船】前端。**3**. 春季。~ **painting** (印在书的前页边上的)页边画饰。

fore[2][fɔː, fɔə; for, fɔr] *int*. (打高尔夫球时的叫声)前面的人让开!〔后面又有人要击球了〕。

fore- *pref*. **1**. 表示"先","前","预": *fore*arm, *fore*cast, *fore*see. **2**. = *for-*; *fore*close.

fore-and-aft [ˈfɔːrəndˈɑːft; ˋfɔrəndˋɑft] *a*.【海】从船首到船尾的;纵向的。*a ~ sail* 纵帆〔*cf*. square sail〕. *a ~-rig* 纵帆装置。

fore-and-aft·er [ˈfɔːrəndˈɑːftə; ˋforənd͵æftɚ] *n*.【海】**1**. 舱口盖纵梁。**2**. 有纵帆装置的船。

fore·arm[1][ˈfɔːrˌɑːm; ˋfɔr͵ɑrm] *n*.【解】前臂。

fore·arm[2][fɔːˈɑːm; fɔrˋɑrm] *vt*. 预先武装,使预作准备。

fore·bear [ˈfɔːbɛə; ˋforbɛr] *n*.〔常 *pl*.〕祖先,祖宗。

fore·bode [fɔːˈbəud; fɔrˋbod] *vt*. **1**. 预示;预知。**2**. 预感。— *vi*. **1**. 预言。**2**. 有预感。

fore·bod·ing [fɔːˈbəudiŋ; fɔrˋbodɪŋ] *n*. 预报,预示;(特指凶事的)预知,预感。

fore·body [ˈfɔːˌbɔdi; ˋfɔr͵bɑdɪ] *n*. 船身前半部;水上飞机的前机身;弹体前部。

fore·brain [ˈfɔːˌbrein; ˋfɔr͵bren] *n*.【解】**1**. 前脑。**2**. 壮年人发达的脑部〔包括间脑和大脑半球〕。

fore·cab·in [ˈfɔːˌkæbin; ˋfɔr͵kæbɪn] *n*. 前部船舱〔通常是二等舱〕。

fore·cad·die [ˈfɔːˌkædi; ˋfor͵kædɪ, ˋfɔr-] *n*. (高尔夫)

F

在前面球洞拣球的球僮。

fore·cast [ˈfɔːkɑːst; forˋkæst] **I** *vt*. (~, ~*ed*; ~, ~*ed*) 预测;预报(天气)。**II** *n*. 预测;预报。*a weather* ~ 天气预报。

fore·cas·tle [ˈfəuksl; ˋfoksl] *n*. (轮船的)船首楼,(船首楼内的)水手舱。*a* ~ *deck* 船首楼甲板。

fore·close [fɔːˈkləuz; forˋkloz] *vi*. 【法】(因超过限期等)取消赎取权。— *vt*. **1.** 【法】取消(抵押人的)赎取权。**2.** 逐出;排除。**3.** 妨碍;结束,停止(讨论等)。**4.** 要求独占。

fore·clo·sure [fɔːˈkləuʒə; forˋkloʒɚ] *n*. **1.** 拒斥。**2.** 【法】丧失赎取权。

fore·course [ˈfɔːkɔːs; ˋforkors] *n*. 【海】前桅(最下一个)大横帆。

fore·court [ˈfɔːkɔːt; ˋforkort] *n*. 前院。

fore·date [fɔːˈdeit; forˋdet] *vt*. 倒填(契据等的)日期(= antedate)。

fore·deck [ˈfɔːdek; ˋforˏdɛk] *n*. 【海】前甲板。

fore·do [fɔːˈduː; forˋdu] *vt*. 〔古〕= fordo.

fore·doom [fɔːˈduːm; forˋdum] *vt*. 注定…要遭遇不幸。

fore·fa·ther [ˈfɔːˌfɑːðə; ˋforˏfɑðɚ] *n*. 〔常 *pl*.〕祖先,祖宗;前人。**F-s' Day** 〔美〕(每年 12 月 22 日纪念英国清教徒于 1620 年在美洲登陆的)祖先纪念日。

fore·feel [fɔːˈfiːl; forˋfil] *vt*. (***-felt*** [-ˈfelt; -ˋfɛlt]; ***-felt***) 预感到。

fore·fend [fɔːˈfend; forˋfɛnd] *vt*. = forfend.

fore·fin·ger [ˈfɔːˌfiŋgə; ˋforˏfɪŋgɚ] *n*. 示指,食指。

fore·foot [ˈfɔːfut; ˋforˏfut] *n*. (*pl*. ***fore·feet*** [ˈfɔːfiːt; ˋforfit]) **1.** (兽等的)前脚。**2.** 【船】龙骨前端部。

fore·front [ˈfɔːfrʌnt; ˋforˏfrʌnt] *n*. 最前部,最前线;(活动、趣味等的)中心。*bring to* [*place in*] *the* ~ 放在显著地位,使成为活动[注意]中心。

fore·gath·er [fɔːˈgæðə; forˋgæðɚ] *vi*. = forgather.

fore·gift [ˈfɔːgift; ˋforˏgɪft] *n*. 【法】租赁押金,押租。

fore·glance [ˈfɔːglɑːns; ˋforˏglæns, ˋfor-] *n*. **1.** 朝前看。**2.** 预见,先见。

fore·go[1] [fɔːˈgəu; forˋgo] *vt*., *vi*. (***-went*** [-ˈwent; -ˋwɛnt]; ***-gone*** [-ˈgɔn; -ˋgɑn]) 在前,居先,先行。*the* ~*ing statement* 前面所述。

fore·go[2] [fɔːˈgəu; forˋgo] *vt*. (***-went*** [-ˈwent; -ˋwent]; ***-gone*** [-ˈgɔn; -ˋgɑn]) = forgo.

fore·go·er [fɔːˈgəuə; forˋgoɚ] *n*. **1.** 先行的人[物];带头的猎犬。**2.** 先例。**3.** 前人,前辈。**4.** 祖先。

fore·gone [fɔːˈgɔn; forˋgɔn] **I** forego[1]和 forego[2]的过去分词。**II** *a*. **1.** 过去的;早先的。**2.** 预先决定的,确定要发生的;(结局)必不可免的。*a* ~ *conclusion* 定论;不可避免的结果。

fore·ground [ˈfɔːgraund; ˋforˏgraʊnd] *n*. (*opp*. background) **1.** (图画等的)前景。**2.** 最显著的地位。*keep oneself in the* ~ 站在前面,处在最显著的地位。

fore·gut [ˈfɔːgʌt; ˋforˏgʌt] *n*. 【解】前肠。

fore·hand [ˈfɔːhænd; ˋforˏhænd] **I** *n*. **1.** 前方。**2.** 马体前部。**3.** (网球等的)正手打。**II** *a*. **1.** 前方的;预先的。**2.** 正手打的。*a* ~ *payment* 预付款。*a* ~ *stroke* 正手一击。

fore·hand·ed [fɔːˈhændid; ˋforˋhændɪd] *a*. **1.** 及时的;合时宜的。**2.** 节俭的。**3.** 〔美〕富裕的。**4.** (网球等的一击)正手打的。**-ly** *ad*. **-ness** *n*.

fore·head [ˈfɔrid, ˈfɔːhed; ˋfɔrɪd, ˋforˏhɛd] *n*. **1.** 额,脑门。**2.** 前部。

for·eign [ˈfɔrin; ˋfɔrɪn] *a*. **1.** 外国的;外交的。**2.** 外国来[产]的;外省的,外地的;〔美〕他州的,本州管辖外的。**3.** 别家工厂[公司、企业]的;他人的。**4.** 〔医〕外来的;异质的。**5.** 无关的,不相干的。*a* ~ *country* [*land*] 外国。*a* ~ *debt* [*loan*] 外债。*a* ~ *deposit* 国外存款。*the F- Office* (英国等的)外交部。~ *languages* 外国语。~ *students* 外国留学生。~ *policy* 外交政策,对外政策。~ *relations* 外交关系。~ *trade* 国际贸易,对外贸易。~ *affairs* 外交事务。*the F- Affairs Board* 外事局。*a* ~ *agency* 国外代理店。~ *aid* 外援。~ *capital* 外资。~ *goods* 外国货。*a* ~ *visitor* 外宾。*a* ~ *car* [*line*] 别家公司的车辆[铁路]。~ *body* [*substance*] 异物。~ *protein* 异体蛋白。~ *seeds* 混杂种子。~ *to the question* 与本问题无关。***the Minister for*** [***of***] ***F- Affairs*** = ***F- Minister*** 外交部长。***the Ministry for*** [***of***] ***F- Affairs*** 外交部。~**-born** *a*. 在外国出生的(*the* ~*-born* 从外国来的移民)。~ **correspondent** 驻外记者。~ **exchange** 外汇〔外币、期票、汇票、支票、电汇、邮汇等的统称〕。~ **exchange control** 外汇管制。~**-flag** *a*. (飞机等)在外国登记的,(船等)挂外国国旗的。~ **legion** 外国志愿军。~ **mission** **1.** 宗教使团〔基督教在国外的传教机构〕。**2.** 驻外使团;出国谈判代表团。~ **pollen** 外来花粉。**F- Service** (美国国务院的)外事处。~ **settlement** 租界,外国人居留地。**-ize** *vt*., *vi*. (使)外国化。**-ness** *n*.

for·eign·er [ˈfɔrinə; ˋfɔrɪnɚ] *n*. **1.** 外国人。**2.** 外人,陌生人。**3.** 外国船;外来物,进口货物;(非本土的)外来动植物。

fo·reign·ism [ˈfɔːrinizm; ˋfɔrɪnɪzm] *n*. **1.** 外国的习语,外来语。**2.** 外国习俗,外国作风[派头]。

fore·judge[1] [fɔːˈdʒʌdʒ; forˋdʒʌdʒ] *vt*. 【法】(由法庭判决)驱逐,逐出,剥夺(某种权利)。**-(e)ment** *n*. 驱逐的判决。

fore·judge[2] [fɔːˈdʒʌdʒ; forˋdʒʌdʒ] *vt*. 臆断;未经审问就判断。

fore·know [fɔːˈnəu; forˋno] *vt*. (***-knew*** [fɔːˈnjuː; forˋnju]; ***-known*** [fɔːˈnəun; forˋnon]) 预知。

fore·knowl·edge [fɔːˈnɔlidʒ; forˋnɑlɪdʒ] *n*. 预知,先见之明。

for·el [ˈfɔrəl; ˋfɔrəl] *n*. **1.** (作书皮用的)羊皮纸。**2.** 书套,书壳。

fore·la·dy [ˈfɔːˌleidi; ˋforˏledɪ] *n*. (*pl*. ***-la·dies***) = forewoman.

fore·land [ˈfɔːlənd; ˋforlənd] *n*. **1.** (堤岸、墙壁的)前沿,前地。**2.** 地角。**3.** 海岬;滨海地带(*opp*. hinterland)。

fore·leg [ˈfɔːleg; ˋforˋlɛg] *n*. (兽的)前腿。

fore·limb [ˈfɔːlim; ˋforlɪm] *n*. 【解】前肢,上肢。

fore·lock[1] [ˈfɔːlɔk; ˋforˏlɑk] *n*. 额发,额毛〔尤指马等的〕。*take* [*seize*] *time* [*an opportunity*, *an occasion*] *by the* ~ 抓牢时机,乘机。

fore·lock[2] [ˈfɔːlɔk; ˋforˏlɑk] **I** *n*. 【机】开口销,扁销。**II** *vt*. 用开口销[扁销]拴住。

fore·man [ˈfɔːmən; ˋformən] *n*. **1.** (*pl*. ***-men***) 首席陪审员。**2.** 工头,监工,领班。

fore·mast [ˈfɔːmɑːst; ˋforˏmæst] *n*. 【海】前桅。*the* ~ *seaman* [*man*, *hand*] 前桅员;普通水手[水兵]。

fore·milk [ˈfɔːmilk; ˋformɪlk] *n*. 初乳。

fore·most [ˈfɔːməust; ˋforˏmost] **I** *a*. **1.** 最初的,最前的。**2.** 第一流的;主要的。**II** *ad*. 首先,第一。***first and*** ~ 首先,第一。***head*** ~ 轻率地。

fore·moth·er [ˈfɔːˌmʌðə; ˋforˏmʌðɚ] *n*. 女祖先。

fore·name [ˈfɔːneim; ˋforˏnem] *n*. (姓前的)名,教名〔如 John Brown 中的 John〕。

fore·named [ˈfɔːneimd; ˋforˏnemd] *a*. 〔美〕前面举出[提到]的。

fore·noon [ˈfɔːnuːn; ˋforˏnun] **I** *n*. 午前,上午。**II** *a*. 上午的,午前的。~ **watch** 【海】上午八时至十二时的守望。

fore·no·tice [ˈfɔːˈnəutis; ˋforˋnotɪs] *n*. 预告。

fo·ren·sic [fəˈrensik; fəˋrɛnsɪk] **I** *a*. **1.** 法庭的。**2.** 公开辩论[讨论],论争的。~ *ability* [*eloquence*] 辩才。**II** *n*. **1.** 辩论练习。**2.** 辩论学,辩论术。~ **chemistry** 法律化学,刑事侦破化学,化学破案术。~ **medicine** 法医学。~ **psychiatry** 法医心理分析学。**-cal·ly** *ad*.

fore·or·dain [ˌfɔːrɔːˈdein; ˏforɔrˋden], **fore·or·di·nate** [fɔːrˈɔːdineit; forˋɔrdɪnet] *vt*. 预先注定。

fore·or·di·na·tion [ˌfɔːrɔːdiˈneiʃən; ˏfɔrɔrdəˋneʃən] ***n.*** 预先注定。
fore·part [ˈfɔːpɑːt; ˋfɔˏpɑrt] ***n.*** **1.** 前部。**2.** (时间的)前段。
fore·passed, fore·past [fɔːˈpɑːst, -ˈpæst; fɔrˋpɑst, -ˋpæst] ***a.*** 〔罕〕过去的;既往的。
fore·paw [ˈfɔːpɔː; ˋfɔrˏpɔ] ***n.*** (动物的)前爪。
fore·peak [ˈfɔːpiːk; ˋfɔrˏpik] ***n.*** 【船】船首舱。
fore·plane [ˈfɔːplein; ˋfɔrˏplen] ***n.*** **1.** 粗刨。**2.** 【宇】前缘舵,前舵。
fore·quar·ter [ˈfɔːˌkwɔːtə; ˋfɔrˏkwɔrtɚ] ***n.*** **1.** 前槽肉〔牛、羊等腰板以上前半截的四分之一部分〕。**2.** 〔*pl.*〕(马等的)前身(包括前腿)。
fore·reach [fɔːˈriːtʃ; fɔrˋritʃ] ***vt.*** **1.** (帆船)追过。**2.** 赶上。**3.** 超出。—***vi.*** (帆船)凭惯性继续前进。
fore·run [fɔːˈrʌn; fɔrˋrʌn] ***vt.*** (***-ran*** [fɔːˈræn; ʃɔrˋræn]; ***-run***; ***-run·ning***) **1.** 在前跑,先走。**2.** 预报,预示。**3.** 赶过,超过。
fore·run·ner [ˈfɔːˌrʌnə; ˋfɔrˏrʌnɚ] ***n.*** **1.** 先驱者;(提前赶到的)通报者。**2.** 前兆。**3.** 祖先。
fore·said [ˈfɔːˌsed; ˋfɔrˏsɛd] ***a.*** 〔罕〕前述的;上述的(= aforesaid)。
fore·sail [ˈfɔːseil, -sl; ˋfɔrˏsel, -sl] ***n.*** 【海】(横帆船的)前桅帆。
fore·see [fɔːˈsiː; fɔrˋsi] ***vt.*** (***-saw*** [-ˈsɔː; -ˋsɔ]; ***-seen*** [-ˈsiːn; -ˋsin]) 预见到,预知,看穿。—***vi.*** 有先见之明。**-able** ***a.*** 可预见到的。**-r** ***n.*** 预言者,有先见之明的人。**-ing·ly** ***ad.*** 有预见地。
fore·shad·ow [fɔːˈʃædəu; fɔrˋʃædo] ***vt.*** 预示,预兆。*Dark clouds ~ a storm.* 乌云预示暴风雨。
fore·shank [ˈfɔːʃæŋk; ˋfɔrʃæŋk] ***n.*** **1.** (牛的)上前腿。**2.** 上前腿肉。
fore·sheet [ˈfɔːʃiːt; ˋfɔrˏʃit] ***n.*** 【船】前桅帆脚索。**2.** 〔*pl.*〕前板,艇首坐位。
fore·shock [ˈfɔːʃɔk; ˋfɔrˏʃɑk] ***n.*** (大地震前的)预震。
fore·shore [ˈfɔːʃɔː; fɔrˋʃɔr] ***n.*** **1.** (高潮线和低潮线之间的)前滩。**2.** 海滩。
fore·short·en [fɔːˈʃɔːtn; fɔrˋʃɔrtn] ***vt.*** **1.** (在绘画中)按远近比例缩小(图形)。**2.** 省略,缩短。
fore·show [fɔːˈʃəu; fɔrˋʃo] ***vt.*** (***~ed***; ***-shown*** [-ˈʃəun; ˋʃon])预示,预告,预报。
fore·side [ˈfɔːsaid; ˋfɔrˏsaɪd] ***n.*** 〔罕、古〕前部;上部。
fore·sight [ˈfɔːsait; ˋfɔrsaɪt] ***n.*** **1.** 先见。**2.** 深谋远虑。**3.** 远景;【测】前视。**4.** (枪炮上的)瞄准器,准星。
fore·sight·ed [ˈfɔːsaitid; ˋfɔrˏsaɪtɪd] ***a.*** 有先见之明的;深谋远虑的。
fore·skin [ˈfɔːskin; ˋfɔrˏskɪn] ***n.*** 【解】包皮。
fore·speak [fɔːˈspiːk; ˋfɔrˋspik] ***vt.*** (***-spoke*** [-ˈspəuk; -ˋspok], 〔古〕***-spake*** [-ˈspeik; -ˋspek]; ***-spoken*** [-ˈspəukn; -ˋspokn], 〔古〕***-spoke***; ***-speaking***) 〔罕〕**1.** 预告;预言;预示。**2.** 预先提出申请或要求;预约。
For·est [ˈfɔrist; ˋfɔrɪst] ***n.*** 福雷斯特〔姓氏,男子名〕。
for·est [ˈfɔrist; ˋfɔrɪst] **I** ***n.*** **1.** 森林,山林。**2.** (英国)皇家狩猎场。*a ~ fire* 森林火灾。*a ~ of masts* 林立的桅杆〔指大量的船只〕。**II** ***vt.*** 在…造林;使长满树林,使成为森林。~ **fly** 【昆】马风蝇。~ **ranger** 林警,森林保护员。~ **reserve** 〔美〕保护林,保存林。
fore·stage [ˈfɔːsteidʒ; ˋfɔrˏstedʒ] ***n.*** (幕前的)舞台前部。
for·est·al [ˈfɔristl; ˋfɔrɪstl] ***a.*** (有关)森林的。
fore·stall [fɔːˈstɔːl; fɔrˋstɔl] ***vt.*** **1.** 抢先,占先;先下手。**2.** 阻止。**3.** 垄断,屯积。
for·est·a·tion [ˌforisˈteiʃən; ˏfɔrɪsˋteʃən] ***n.*** 造林(法),植林。
fore·stay [ˈfɔːstei; ˋfɔrˏste] ***n.*** 【船】前桅支索。
fore·stay·sail [fɔːˈsteiseil, -sl; fɔrˋstesel, -sl] ***n.*** 【海】前支索的三角帆。
For·est·er [ˈfɔristə; ˋfɔrɪstɚ] ***n.*** 福雷斯特〔姓氏〕。
for·est·er [ˈfɔristə; ˋfɔrɪstɚ] ***n.*** **1.** 林务员。**2.** 林中居民;林中禽兽。**3.** 【动】(虎蛾科的)林蛾。
for·est·ry [ˈfɔristri; ˋfɔrɪstrɪ] ***n.*** **1.** 森林学。**2.** 林业。**3.** 森林,森林地带。
fore·taste [ˈfɔːteist; ˋfɔrˏtest] **I** ***n.*** **1.** 试食,先尝,预尝到的滋味。**2.** 预感。**II** ***vt.*** 先尝,试吃。
fore·tell [fɔːˈtel; fɔrˋtɛl] ***vt.***, ***vi.*** (***-told*** [-ˈtəuld; -ˋtold]; ***-told***) 预言,预示,预兆。**-er** ***n.***
fore·thought [ˈfɔːθɔːt; ˋfɔrˏθɔt] **I** ***n.*** **1.** 事先的考虑,预谋。**2.** 深谋远虑。**II** ***a.*** 预谋的,预先计划好的。
fore·thought·ful [ˈfɔˌθɔːtfl; ˋfɔˏθɔtfəl] ***a.*** 深谋远虑的;慎重的。**-ly** ***ad.***
fore·time [ˈfɔːtaim; ˋfɔrtaɪm] ***n.*** 已往,过去,往昔。
fore·to·ken [ˈfɔːtəukən; ˋfɔrtokən] **I** ***n.*** 预兆,征兆。**II** [-ˈtəukən; -ˋtokən] ***vt.*** 预示。
fore·told [fɔːˈtəuld; fɔrˋtold] foretell 的过去式和过去分词。
fore·tooth [ˈfɔːtuːθ; ˋfɔrˏtuθ] ***n.*** (*pl.* ***-teeth***) 门牙,前齿。
fore·top [ˈfɔːtɔp, -təp; ˋfɔrtɑp, -təp] ***n.*** **1.** 前发,额发;(马的)额毛。**2.** 【船】前桅楼;前桅平台。
fore-top·gal·lant [ˌfɔːtɔpˈgælənt; ˏfɔrtɑpˋgælənt] ***a.*** 在前桅中段以上的。~ **sail** 前桅上桅帆。
fore·top·mast [fɔːˈtɔpmɑːst; fɔrˋtɑpmæst] ***n.*** 【船】前桅的中段。
fore-top·sail [fɔːˈtɔpseil; fɔrˋtɑpsel] ***n.*** 【海】前桅中桅帆。
fore·type [ˈfɔːtaip; ˋfɔrˏtaɪp] ***n.*** 前面的典型,原型,前例,范例。
for·ev·er [fəˈrevə; fəˋrɛvɚ] **I** ***ad.*** 〔美〕永远,不绝,不断。*go away ~* 一去不复返。*She's ~ complaining.* 她总是发牢骚。★ 英国通常分写作 for ever. ***~ and a day*** = ***~ and ever*** = ***~ and ~*** = 〔书〕***~ and aye*** 永久,永远。**II** ***n.*** 〔the ~〕永远。
for·ev·er·more [fəˈrevəˈmɔː; fəˋrɛvɚˋmɔr] ***ad.*** 永远〔语气比 forever 更强〕。
fore·warn [fɔːˈwɔːn; fɔrˋwɔrn] ***vt.*** 预先警告。*Forewarned is forearmed.* 〔谚〕警惕即警备。
fore·went [fɔːˈwent; fɔrˋtɛnt] forego 的过去式。
fore·wing [ˈfɔːwiŋ; ˋfɔrwɪŋ] ***n.*** 【动】前翅。
fore·wom·an [ˈfɔːwumən; ˋfɔrwumən] ***n.*** (*pl.* (***-wom·en*** [-ˈwimin; -ˋwɪmɪn]) **1.** 女工头,女领班。**2.** 女首席陪审员。
fore·word [ˈfɔːwəːd; ˋfɔrˏwɝd] ***n.*** 前言,序言。
fore·worn [fɔˈwɔːn; fɔrˋwɔrn] ***a.*** 极疲倦的 (= forworn)。
fore·yard [ˈfɔːjɑːd; ˋfɔrjɑrd] ***n.*** 【海】前桅的最下桅桁。
for·feit [ˈfɔːfit; ˋfɔrfɪt] **I** ***vt.*** (因被罚而)丧失(所有权);(因犯罪等而)失去(职位、生命等);(因过劳等而)失掉(健康等)。*~ one's life on the battlefield* 阵亡。*~ a motor licence* 汽车执照被没收。**II** ***a.*** 丧失了的,被没收了的。**III** ***n.*** **1.** 罚金,没收物。**2.** (权利、名誉、生命等的)丧失。**3.** 〔*pl.*〕罚物游戏。***be the ~ of one's crime*** (以生命)抵罪。
for·fei·ture [ˈfɔːfitʃə; ˋfɔrfɪtʃɚ] ***n.*** **1.** (地位、权利、生命等的)丧失。**2.** 没收。**3.** 没收物;罚金。
for·fend [fɔːˈfend; fɔrˋfɛnd] ***vt.*** **1.** 〔古〕禁止;防止,避开。**2.** 〔美〕保护。*God* [*Heaven*] *~!* = God forbid.
for·fi·cate [ˈfɔːfikit, -keit; ˋfɔrfɪkɪt, -ket] ***a.*** (某些鸟尾)分岔的。
for·gat [fɔːˈgæt; fəˋgæt] forget 的古体。
for·gath·er [fɔːˈgæðə; fɔrˋgæðɚ] ***vi.*** **1.** 聚会。**2.** 偶然遇见 (*with*)。**3.** 交往 (*with*)。
for·gave [fəˈgeiv; fəˋgev] forgive 的过去式。
forge[1] [fɔːdʒ; fɔrdʒ] **I** ***n.*** **1.** 铁工厂,锻工车间。**2.** 锻炉,熔铁炉。**3.** (思想等的)锻炼。*a boiler ~* 锅炉锻工车

间。*a portable* ～ 轻便锻炉。**II** *vt.*, *vi.* **1.** 打(铁),锻制。**2.** 锻炼。**3.** 编造(故事等);伪造(文书等)。**-able** *a.* 可锻造的。

forge[2] [fɔːdʒ; fɔrdʒ] *vi.* (坚定地)勉力前进。～ *ahead* (不停地)努力前进;(赛跑)努力赶上,领先 (～ *ahead with our work* 把我们的工作大力向前推进)。

forg·er [ˈfɔːdʒə; ˋfɔrdʒɚ] *n.* **1.** 伪造者。**2.** 锻工。

for·ger·y [ˈfɔːdʒəri; ˋfɔrdʒərɪ] *n.* **1.** 伪造,伪造签字。**2.** (文件)伪造罪,伪造物。

for·get [fəˈget; fɚˋgɛt] *vt.* (**-got** [-ˈgɔt; -ˋgɑt], **-gat** [fəˈgæt; fɚˋgæt]; **-got·ten** [-ˈgɔtn; -ˋgɑtn̩],〔诗〕**-got**; **-get·ting**) **1.** 忘掉,忘记 (*opp.* remember)。**2.** 忽略,疏忽掉。*Don't* ～ *me to your brother.* 别忘记代我问候你的兄弟。～ *one's keys* 忘带钥匙;忘记钥匙在那里。— *vi.* 遗忘,忘记。*F- about it.* 不要介意。**forgive and** ～ 不念旧恶,不记仇。**F- it.**〔美〕不用谢了,别再提了。～ **oneself** **1.** 忘我。**2.** 忘乎所以。**3.** 奋不顾身。**4.** 昏过去。

for·get·ful [fəˈgetful; fɚˋgɛtfəl] *a.* (*opp.* mindful) **1.** 健忘的。**2.** 不留心的,疏忽的。**3.**〔古〕使人忘记的,易忘的。*be* ～ *of one's sleep and meals* 废寝忘食。**-ly** *ad.* **-ness** *n.*

for·ge·tive [ˈfɔːdʒətiv; ˋfɔrdʒətɪv] *a.*【古】**1.** 能发明创造的。**2.** 富有想像力的。

for·get-me-not [fəˈgetminɔt; fɚˋgɛtmɪˏnɑt] *n.*【植】毋忘(我)草。

for·get·ta·ble [fəˈgetəbl; fəˋgɛtəbl̩] *a.* **1.** 易被忘记的。**2.** 可以忘记的。

F

for·get·ter [fəˈgetə; fɚˋgɛtɚ] *n.* 健忘者,容易忘记的人。

forg·ing [ˈfɔːdʒiŋ; ˋfɔrdʒɪŋ] *n.* **1.** 锻造(法)。**2.** 锻件。

for·giv·a·ble [fəˈgivəbl; fəˋgɪvəbl̩] *a.* 可宽恕的。

for·give [fəˈgiv; fɚˋgɪv] *vt.* (**-gave** [-ˈgeiv; -ˋgev]; **-giv·en** [-ˈgivn; -ˋgɪvn̩]) **1.** 原谅,饶恕,宽恕。**2.** 免除(债务等)。*Pray* ～ *me!* 请原谅我吧! *You are forgiven.* 你得到宽恕了。～ *sb. his debts* 豁免某人的债务。

for·give·ness [fəˈgivnis; fɚˋgɪvnɪs] *n.* 饶恕,宽恕;宽大。*ask for* ～ 请求宽恕。*be full of* ～ 十分宽大。

for·giv·ing [fəˈgiviŋ; fɚˋgɪvɪŋ] *a.* 宽大的;仁慈的。**-ly** *ad.* **-ness** *n.*

for·go [fɔːˈgəu; fɔrˋgo] *vt.* (**-went**; **-gone** [-ˈgɔn; -ˋgɔn]) **1.** 摒绝,放弃,对…断念;谢绝。**2.**〔古〕从…离开。

for·got [fəˈgɔt; fɚˋgɑt] forget 的过去式及过去分词。

for·got·ten [fəˈgɔtn; fɚˋgɑtn̩] **I** forget 的过去分词。**II** *a.* 被忘却的。*a* ～ *man* 被遗忘的人〔如因失业而脱离原来的社会生活的人〕。

for·int [ˈfɔrint; ˋfɔrɪnt] *n.*〔Hung.〕福林〔匈牙利货币单位〕。

fo·ris·fa·mil·i·ate [ˌfɔrisfəˈmilieit; ˏfɔrɪsfəˋmɪlɪet] *vt.* (**-at·ed**; **-at·ing**)【法】使离父母而独立;父母在世时使(儿女)继承产业。— *vi.* 放弃对父母产业更多的继承。

for·judge [fɔːˈdʒʌdʒ; fɔrˋdʒʌdʒ] *vt.* = forejudge.

fork [fɔːk; fɔrk] **I** *n.* **1.** 餐叉;肉叉;叉子;耙。**2.** 树叉,木叉;分岔;分歧点,岔路;支流。**3.**【乐】调音叉。**4.** 叉状闪电。**5.** (象棋中)同时可攻两个棋子的棋着。**6.** 二者之间的选择。*a knife and* ～ 一副刀叉。**play (a good) knife and** ～ (因胃口好而)饱餐一顿。**II** *vi.* 分歧,分叉。— *vt.* **1.** 用叉叉起,用叉抛举(干草等);用耙耙。**2.** 使成叉形。**3.** (象棋中)同时进攻(两个棋子)。**4.**〔口〕交付,支付,放弃。～ **out** [**over**, **up**]〔俚〕交出,支付。～ **dinner** [**luncheon**] (食物都已切好,只须用叉即可进食的)叉餐。～ **lift** 叉式升降装卸车,铲车。～**tailed** *a.* (鸟)尾巴开叉的。

forked [fɔːkt; fɔrkt] *a.* 有叉的。～ *lightning* 叉状闪电。*three-* ～ 三叉的。～ **chain**【化】侧链。～ **tongue** 谎言,假话。～**-tongued** *a.* 不诚实的,骗人的。**-ly** *ad.* **-ness** *n.*

fork·y [ˈfɔːki; ˋfɔrkɪ] *a.* (**fork·i·er**, **fork·i·est**) = forked. **fork·i·ness** *n.*

for·lorn [fəˈlɔːn; fɚˋlɔrn] *a.* **1.** 绝望的;被遗弃的;孤独无助的;可怜的;凄凉的。**2.**〔诗〕被剥夺的 (*of*)。**be** ～ **of hope** 绝望。～ **hope** **1.** 敢死队。**2.** 冒险事业;没有成功希望的事业。**3.** 渺茫的希望。**-ly** *ad.*

form [fɔːm; fɔrm] **I** *n.* **1.** 形态;形状;样子,外貌;【哲】形式 (*opp.* content)。**2.** 人影,物影。**3.** 格式;表格纸 (=〔美〕blank)。**4.** 型;方式;种类。**5.** (人的)姿态,神气,精神;健康状态。**6.** 态度;礼节;仪式。**7.** 结构,组织。**8.**〔英〕条凳。**9.** (学校的)年级。**10.**【语法】形式,词形。**11.**【物】(晶)面式;【印】印版;【机、建】型,模壳。**12.** (野兔等的)窝,洞。*I see a* ～ *in the dark.* 我在黑处看见一个人影。*fill in* [*out*] the ～ 填表。*an order* ～ 定(货)单。*a telegraph* ～ 电报纸。*attach importance to* ～ 着重形式。*a matter of* ～ 形式上的问题。*an established* ～ 一定的方式。*bad* ～ 失礼举动,粗鲁行为。*good* ～〔英〕有礼貌的态度,端正的行动方式。*a* ～ *of address* 称呼。*the* ～ *of government* 政体。**after the** ～ **of** 照…的格式。**be in (good)** ～ (运动员等)竞技状态良好。**for** ～**'s sake** 为了划一形式,形式上。**minute** ～**s of life** (微)生物。**in due** ～ 正式地,照规定的格式。**in** ～ 形式上。**in great** ～ 精神饱满。**in the** ～ **of** 用…的形式。**in** [**under**] **various** ～**s** 用种种形式。**lose one's** ～ = **out of** ～ (运动员)情绪失常。(**run**) **true to** ～ 一如往常,一贯。**take the** ～ **of** 取…的形式,表现为。**II** *vt.* **1.** 形成,养成,塑造。**2.** 构成,成立,组织。**3.** 作出,想出。**4.**【语法】构(词),造(句)。**5.** 结成(同盟)。**6.**【军】排成;编成 (*up*)。～ *the dough into loaves* 把面粉团做成面包。*The House is not yet* ～*ed.* 议会还没有组成。～ *fours* 成四列。— *vi.* **1.** 形成,产生。**2.**【军】排队。～ *into line* 排成队。～ *itself into* 成…形。～ *part of* 成为…的组成部分。～ *the character* 陶冶品性。～ **action**【法】诉讼手续[程序]。～ **class**【语】形式类,形(态)类。～**fitting** *a.* (衣服)贴身的。～ **genus**【动】形态属。～ **letter** 格式信件〔内容已印好,只需填写日期、收信人、地址等〕。～ **piston**, ～ **plunger**【机】模塞;阳模。**-ing** *n.* 成形,成型,模铸。**-less** *a.* 无形状的,无定形的。

form- *comb. f.* 表示【化】"甲酸","甲酰","甲醛","甲醛": *form*aldehyde, *form*ate.

-form *suf.* 表示"具有…形式的;有形状的": vermi*form*; uni*form*; multi*form*.

for·mal [ˈfɔːməl; ˋfɔrml̩] **I** *a.* **1.** 正式的。**2.** 礼节上的,仪式上的;郑重其事的。**3.** 形态的,外形的;形式上的;拘泥形式的,刻板的。**4.** 布置整齐的,有条理的。**5.** 正规的,合乎规格的。**6.**【语言】规范化的,书面语的,正规的〔非俗语、俚语的〕。*a* ～ *receipt* 正式收据。*a* ～ *call* 正式访问。*a* ～ *manner* 郑重其事的态度。～ *logic* 形式逻辑。*a* ～ *resemblance* 外形上的类似。～ *obedience* 表面服从。**II** *n.* **1.**〔美〕须穿礼服的社交集会。**2.**〔口〕夜礼服。**go** ～〔口〕穿夜礼服。**-ness** *n.*

form·al·de·hyde [fɔːˈmældihaid; fɔrˋmældəhaɪd] *n.*【化】甲醛。

for·ma·lin [ˈfɔːməlin; ˋfɔrməlɪn] *n.*【化】甲醛液,福尔马林。

for·mal·ism [ˈfɔːməlizəm; ˋfɔrməˋlɪzəm] *n.* 形式主义,拘泥形式。

for·mal·ist [ˈfɔːməlist; ˋfɔrməlɪst] **I** *n.* 拘泥形式的人;形式主义者。**II** *a.* 拘泥形式的,形式主义的。**-ic** [ˌfɔːməˈlistik; ˏfɔrməˋlɪstɪk] *a.* 形式主义的。

for·mal·i·ty [fɔːˈmæliti; fɔrˋmælətɪ] *n.* **1.** 拘泥形式,拘谨。**2.** 礼节,俗套。**3.**〔*pl.*〕正式手续。*trivial formalities* 烦琐的礼节。**go through** [**check in**] **formalities** 办理(飞机等)的乘坐手续。**without** ～ 不拘形式地。

for·mal·ize [ˈfɔːməlaiz; ˋfɔrml̩ˏaɪz] *vt*. 1. 使成正式。2. 使具有形式,形式化。— *vi*. 拘泥形式。**-i·za·tion** [ˌfɔːməlaiˈzeiʃən; ˏfɔrməlaɪˋzeʃən] *n*. 形式化;正式化。

for·mal·ly [ˈfɔːməli; ˋfɔrməlɪ] *ad*. 1. 正式地。2. 遵照一定格式地。3. 形式上。

for·mant [ˈfɔːmənt; ˋfɔrmənt] *n*. 【语言】1. 共振峰。2. 构形成分。

for·mat [ˈfɔːmæt, -mɑːt; ˋfɔrmæt, -mɑt] I *n*. 1. (出版物的)开本,版式〔*cf*. folio〕。2. 【自】(数据安排的)形式。3. (电视播送或硬币设计等的)组织[安排、布局]的总计划。II *vt*. 设计;构成;安排〔包括制作的全过程,但特别着重制成品的形式〕。

for·mate[1] [ˈfɔːmit; ˋfɔrmet] *n*. 【化】蚁酸盐;甲酸酯。

for·mate[2] [ˈfɔːmeit; ˋfɔrmet] *vi*. 【空】飞机加入编队,编队飞行。

for·ma·tion [fɔːˈmeiʃən; fɔrˋmeʃən] *n*. 1. 构成,形成;设立;编制。2. 组织,构造;形态;形成物,构造物;【军】编队,队形;兵团。3. 【地】层;组;【生】社区;(植物)群系。*heat of* ~【化】形成热,生成热。*close* ~【军】密集队形。*dispersed* [*open*] ~【军】疏开队形。*fighting* [*battle*] ~【军】战斗队形。*rock* ~【地】岩层。*skirmish* ~【军】散兵线。~ *flight* [*flying*]【军】编队飞行。**-al** *a*.

form·a·tive [ˈfɔːmətiv; ˋfɔrmətɪv] I *a*. 1. 形成的,构成的。2. 造型的。3. 【语法】构词(用)的。*a* ~ *period* 发育期。*the* ~ *arts* 造型艺术。~ *technique* 造形[型]技术,造形[型]工艺。II *n*. 构词要素〔指词首、词尾等, = ~ element〕;用构词要素构成的词。~ **cell**【动】形成细胞,毛原细胞。~ **period**【生】形成期。~ **tissue** [**layer**]【生】形成组织[层]。

forme [fɔːm; fɔrm] *n*. 【英印】印版。

form·er[1] [ˈfɔːmə; ˋfɔrmɚ] *n*. 1. 构成者,创造者。2. 【机】模型,样板,成形[型]设备。3. 【无】线圈架。4. 〔英〕公学及其他中等学校的学生。*fifth* ~*s* 五年级学生。

for·mer[2] [ˈfɔːmə; ˋfɔrmɚ] *a*. 1. 以前的,从前的。2. 在前的;[美]前任的。*in* ~ *times* 从前。*in the* ~ *case* 在前一例[情况]。*the* ~ 前者 (*opp*. latter)。**-ly** *ad*.

for·mic [ˈfɔːmik; ˋfɔrmɪk] *a*. 1. 蚂蚁的。2. 【化】甲酸的,蚁酸的。~ **acid** 甲酸。

For·mi·ca [fɔːˈmaikə; fɔrˋmaɪkə] *n*. 佛米卡〔一种做桌面等的抗热塑料薄板的商标名〕。

for·mi·car·y [ˈfɔːmikəri; ˋfɔrməkɛrɪ] *n*. 蚁巢,蚁山。

for·mi·cate [ˈfɔːmikeit; ˋfɔrmɪket] *vi*. 像蚂蚁一样爬行;群集。

for·mi·ca·tion [ˌfɔːmiˈkeiʃən; ˏfɔrmɪˋkeʃən] *n*. 【医】(皮肤上的)蚁走感。

for·mi·da·ble [ˈfɔːmidəbl; ˋfɔrmɪdəbl̩] *a*. 1. 可怕的,可畏的。2. 难以应付的;庞大的。*a* ~ *enemy* 强敌。*a* ~ *task* 难应付的工作。**-ness** *n*. **-bly** *ad*.

form·less [ˈfɔːmlis; ˋfɔrmlɪs] *a*. 无形状的,无定形的。**-ly** *ad*.

For·mo·sa [fɔːˈməusə; fɔrˋmosə] *n*. 〔废〕"福摩萨"〔16世纪葡萄牙对台湾的称呼〕。

for·mu·la [ˈfɔːmjulə; ˋfɔrmjələ] I *n*. (*pl*. ~*s*, *-lae* [-liː; -li]) 1. 公式,程式;定则,方案。2. 【医】配方,处方。3. (政治口号等的)提法,表述,套语,惯用语句。4. 【宗】信仰表白书。5. 【化】式;【数】公式。*a* ~ *for making soap* 肥皂制法[配方]。~ *of integration* 积分公式。*a binominal* ~【数】二项式。*a legal* ~ 法律上的惯用语句。*a molecular* ~【化】分子式。*a structural* ~【化】结构式,构造式。II *a*. (赛车)方程式的(指赛车要符合规定的体积,重量及汽缸容量等)。~ **investing** 方程式投资〔按方程式计划进行的一种投资方法〕。~ **translation**【计】公式翻译,公式转换〔用以编写科技等计算程序的一种计算机语言〕。

for·mu·lar·i·za·tion [ˌfɔːmjuləraiˈzeiʃən; ˏfɔrmjələraɪˋzeʃən] *n*. 公式化。

for·mu·lar·ize [ˈfɔːmjuləraiz; ˋfɔrmjələraɪz] *vt*. = formulate.

for·mu·lar·y [ˈfɔːmjuləri; ˋfɔrmjəlɛrɪ] I *n*. 1. 公式汇编。2. 配方书,处方集,药典。3. 有关宗教礼节[仪式]的书。II *a*. 1. 公式的。2. 仪式上的。3. 配方的。

for·mu·late [ˈfɔːmjuleit; ˋfɔrmjəˏlet] *vt*. 1. 把…作成公式,用公式表示。2. 对…作简洁陈述,有系统的表达。**-la·tion** [ˌfɔːmjuˈleiʃən; ˏfɔrmjəˋleʃən] *n*.

for·mu·lism [ˈfɔːmjulizəm; ˋfɔrmjəlɪzm̩] *n*. 公式主义。

for·mu·list [ˈfɔːmjulist; ˋfɔrmjəlɪst] *n*. 公式主义者。

for·mu·lis·tic [ˌfɔːmjuˈlistik; ˏfɔrmjəˋlɪstɪk] *a*. 公式主义(者)的。

for·mu·lize [ˈfɔːmjulaiz; ˋfɔrmjəˌlaɪz] *vt*. = formulate. **-za·tion** [ˌfɔːmjulaiˈzeiʃən; ˏfɔrmjəlaɪˋzeʃən] *n*.

for·myl [ˈfɔːmil; ˋfɔrmɪl] *n*. 【化】甲酰。

For·nax [ˈfɔːnæks; ˋfɔrnæks] *n*. 【天】天炉(星)座。

for·ni·cate [ˈfɔːnikeit; ˋfɔrnəˏket] *vi*. (未婚者之间或与未婚者)私通。**-tion** [ˌfɔːniˈkeiʃən; ˏfɔrnɪˋkeʃən] *n*. **-tor** *n*.

for·nix [ˈfɔːniks; ˋfɔrnɪks] *n*. (*pl*. ***for·ni·ces*** [-nisiːz; -nɪsiz])【解】穹隆,穹。

for·ra(r)d·er [ˈfɔrədə; ˋfɔrədɚ] *ad*. 〔英口〕更往前。***get no*** ~ 不再前进。

for·rel [ˈfɔrəl; ˋfɔrəl] *n*. = forel.

for·sake [fəˈseik; fɚˋsek] *vt*. (***-sook*** [-ˈsuk; -ˋsuk]; ***-sak·en*** [-ˈseikən; -ˋsekən]; ***-saking***) 1. 舍弃,放弃,丢弃。2. 革除(旧风习等);抛弃(坏习惯)。

for·sak·en [fəˈseikən; fɚˋsekən] forsake 的过去分词。

for·sook [fəˈsuk; fɚˋsuk] *v*. forsake 的过去式。

for·sooth [fəˈsuːθ; fɚˋsuθ] *ad*. 〔反〕的确,真的,当然〔表示轻蔑、讥刺〕。

for·spent [fɔːˈspent; fɔrˋspent] *a*. 〔古〕疲倦已极的。

for·stall [fɔːˈstɔːl; fɔrˋstɔl] = forestall.

For·ster [ˈfɔːstə; ˋfɔrstɚ] *n*. 福斯特〔姓氏〕。

for·swear [fɔːˈswɛə; fɔrˋswɛr] *vt*. (***-swore*** [-ˈswɔː; -ˋswɔr]; ***-sworn*** [-ˈswɔːn; -ˋswɔrn]) 1. 发誓抛弃,断然放弃(坏习惯等)。2. 发誓否认,背(誓),背弃(信义)。*The old man forswore smoking*. 那老人下决心戒烟。~ *an oath* 背弃誓言。— *vi*. 作伪证,发假誓。~ ***oneself*** 发伪誓,作伪证。

for·sworn [fɔːˈswɔːn; fɔrˋswɔrn] forswear 的过去分词。*a*. 发了假誓的,做了伪证的。

for·syth·i·a [fɔːˈsaiθjə; fɚˋsɪθɪə] *n*. 【植】连翘(属)。

fort [fɔːt; fɔrt] I *n*. 1. 要塞,堡垒。2. 〔美〕(从前和印第安人交易的)市集,(设有碉堡的)边界贸易站。***hold the*** ~ 1. 守住堡垒。2. 坚决不让步。3. 处理日常事务;维持现状。II *vt*. 设要塞保卫。**F- Knox** 诺克斯堡〔美国联邦政府的黄金贮存地〕。

fort. = 1. fortificatin. 2. fortified.

for·ta·lice [ˈfɔːtəlis; ˋfɔrtəlɪs] *n*. 小碉堡,外堡;〔古、诗〕要塞。

Fort-de-France [fɔːt də ˈfrɑːns; fɔrt de ˋfrɑns] 法兰西堡〔马提尼克岛首府〕。

forte [fɔːt; fɔrt] *n*. 1. 长处,拿手好戏。2. 刀身的最强部〔自中央至刀柄〕(*opp*. foible)。*Cooking is her* ~. 她擅长烹调。

forte [ˈfɔːti; ˋfɔrtɪ] I *a*. 〔It.〕【乐】强音的 (*opp*. piano)。II *ad*. 用强的,加强。III *n*. 强音部。~ ***possible*** 最强。~**-piano**【乐】*ad*., *a*. 强而转弱。

forth [fɔːθ; forθ] I *ad*. 1. 向前,向前方。2. 以后。3. 向外,由隐而显。*burst* ~ (芽、蕾)绽开;(火山等)爆发。*stretch* ~ *one's arms* 伸出胳臂。*sway back and* ~ 前后摇动。*put* ~ *leaves* 发芽。*from this time* ~ 今后,从此以后。***and so*** ~ 等等。***right*** ~ 立刻。***so far*** ~ 到那儿为止,单就那些来说。***so far*** ~ ***as*** …到…的程度 (*so far* ~ *as you work* 你工作多少就…)。II ***prep***. 〔古〕出于,来自。*go* ~ *the house* 从屋里出去。

F

forth·com·ing [fɔːθˈkʌmiŋ; ˋforθˋkʌmɪŋ] I *a*. 1. 即将到来的,即将出现的。2. 现有的,随时可得的。3. 愿意帮助的,乐于供给消息的。*the ~ holidays* 即将到来的假日。*The funds are not ~*. 资金尚未筹得。II *n*. 来临,临近。

forth·put·ting [ˈfɔːθˌputiŋ; ˋforθ͵putɪŋ, ˋforθ-] *a*. 〔美〕爱管闲事的。

forth·right [ˌfɔːθˈrait; ͵forθˋraɪt] I *ad*. 1. 〔古〕立刻,径直地。2. 直率地。*He told us ~ just what his objections were*. 他有什么不同的意见,都坦率地向我们讲了。II *a*. 1. 直接的。2. 直率的。*It's sometimes difficult to be ~ and not give offence*. 又直率又不得罪人,这有时很难办到。III *n*. 〔古〕直路。

forth·with [ˈfɔːθˈwiθ; ͵forθˋwɪθ] I *ad*. 立刻。*Any member guilty of such conduct will be suspended ~*. 凡犯有类似错误的人,得立刻停止其会员资格。II *n*. 〔美俚〕必须立即执行的命令。

for·ti·eth [ˈfɔːtiiθ; ˋfortɪɪθ] *n*., *num*. 〔the ~〕第四十(个);四十分之一(的)。

for·ti·fi·a·ble [ˈfɔːtifaiəbl; ˋfortəfaɪəbl̩] *a*. 宜于设防的,可以弄巩固的。

for·ti·fi·ca·tion [ˌfɔːtifiˈkeiʃən; ͵fortɪfəˋkeʃən] *n*. 1. 筑城,筑垒,设堡;筑城学[术]。2. 〔常 *pl*.〕防御工事。3. 堡垒,要塞。4. (酒精、维生素)含量的增加,强化。

for·ti·fi·er [ˈfɔːtifaiə; ˋfortəfaɪɚ] *n*. 1. 筑城者,设防者。2. 增强的人[物];强化物。3. 〔谑〕(用强壮剂泡的)含酒精饮料,滋补酒。

for·ti·fy [ˈfɔːtifai; ˋfortə͵faɪ] *vt*. (*-fied*; *-fy·ing*) 1. 在…设要塞,在…建防御工事。2. 加强(体力、结构等);使(意志等)坚定。3. 在(食物中)增加酒精[维生素等]的含量。*a fortified port* 军港。*a fortified town* 设防都市。*a fortified zone* 要塞地带。*powdered milk fortified with vitamins* 加有维生素的奶粉。— *vi*. 筑防御工事。~ *oneself* 加强自己意志,喝酒提神。

for·tis [ˈfɔːtis; ˋfortɪs] I *a*. 【语音】强音的〔指收紧发音器官肌肉而发出的,如绝大多数清辅音性的爆破音〕。II *n*. 强音〔收紧发音器官肌肉发出的音〕。

for·tis·si·mo [fɔːˈtisiməu; forˋtɪsə͵mo] I *ad*. 〔It.〕【乐】用最强音,极强〔略为 *ff*.〕。II *a*. 【乐】极强的。

for·ti·tude [ˈfɔːtitjuːd; ˋfortə͵tjud] *n*. 坚强意志[精神],坚忍,刚毅。*intestinal ~* 坚忍不拔的精神。***bear a calamity with ~*** 毅然忍受灾祸。

for·ti·tu·di·nous [ˌfɔːtiˈtjuːdinəs; ͵fortəˋtjudɪnəs] *a*. 坚忍不拔的,刚毅的,顽强的。

Fort-La·my [fɔːrlɑːˈmiː; forlɑˋmi] *n*. 拉密堡〔乍得城市〕。

fort·night [ˈfɔːtnait; ˋfortnaɪt] *n*. 〔主英〕两星期〔*cf*. sennight.〕。*a ~'s holiday* 两个星期的休假。*Monday ~* 两星期以前[以后]的星期一。*today* [*this day*] ~ 两个星期以前[以后]的今天。

fort·night·ly [ˈfɔːtˌnaitli; ˋfort͵naɪtlɪ] I *a*. 〔主英〕每两星期一次的。*a ~ review* 一种双周(评论)刊物。II *n*. 双周刊。III *ad*. 隔两周,每两星期地。

For·tran, for·tran [ˈfɔːtræn; ˋfortræn] *n*. 【计】1. 公式变换 (= formula transformation)。2. 公式翻译,公式译码(资料处理) (= formula translation)。3. 公式转换器,公式翻译程序 (= formula translator)。

for·tress [ˈfɔːtris; ˋfortrɪs] I *n*. 要塞;堡垒;安全地带。*Flying F-* 〔美〕空中堡垒。*a floating ~* 军舰。*an impregnable ~* 难以攻陷的要塞。II *vt*. 1. 在…设置要塞。2. 用要塞保卫。

for·tu·i·tism [fɔːˈtju(ː)itizəm; forˋtju(ə)͵tɪzəm] *n*. 【哲】偶然论。

for·tu·i·tist [fɔːˈtju(ː)itist; forˋtjuətɪst] *n*. 偶然论者。

for·tu·i·tous [fɔːˈtju(ː)itəs; forˋtjuətəs] *a*. 1. 偶然的,意外的。2. 幸运的。**-ly** *ad*. **-ness** *n*.

for·tu·i·ty [fɔːˈtjuiti; forˋtjuətɪ] *n*. 1. 偶然事件;偶然机会。2. 偶然性。

for·tu·nate [ˈfɔːtʃənit; ˋfortʃənɪt] *a*. 1. 幸运的,侥幸的。2. 带来幸运的。*a ~ man* 幸运的人。*a ~ star* 吉星。*the ~* 幸运者。*be ~ in one's son* 幸而有个儿子。***be born under a ~ star*** 生来有福。**-ly** *ad*.

for·tune [ˈfɔːtʃən; ˋfortʃən] I *n*. 1. 运气;幸运;命运。2. 财产,巨富;〔古〕女财主,女继承人。3. 〔F-〕司命运的女神。*F- favours the bold* [*brave*]. 〔谚〕勇者成功。*F- is easily found, but hard to be kept*. 〔谚〕找到幸福容易,维持幸福困难。*a man of ~* 财主。*marry a ~* 和有钱的女子结婚。***be in good*** [***bad***] ~ 运气好[坏]。***by good ~*** 幸好。***come into a ~*** 继承一笔财产。***have a ~*** 有财产。***have ~ on one's side*** 走红运。***have good*** [***bad***] ~ 运气好[坏]。***have the ~ to do*** 幸而…。***if ~ favours*** 如果运气好。***make a ~*** 发财。***make one's ~*** 成功立业,发迹;发财。***push one's ~*** 追求名利,努力抬高自己地位。***seek one's ~*** 找出路。***spend a small ~ on*** (*books*) 〔口〕把一大笔钱花在(书)上。***tell sb.'s ~s*** 为某人算命。***tempt ~*** 蔑视命运,冒险。***try one's ~*** 碰运气。II *vt*. 〔古〕给…大宗财富,给…带来幸运。— *vi*. 〔古、诗〕偶然发生;偶然偶见 (*upon*)。***It ~d that*** …偶尔。~ **cookie** 占卜饼〔一种夹层饼,其中夹有写着预言吉凶祸福或格言等的小纸片〕。~ **Fortune 500** 《财富》500 强〔指美国 Fortune 杂志每年评出的全球最大的 500 家企业〕。~ **hunter** 追求有钱女子的男子。~ **hunting** 为了财产而追求有钱的女子。~**-teller** 算命卖卜者。~ **telling** 算命卖卜。**-less** 不幸的,无财产的。

for·ty [ˈfɔːti; ˋfortɪ] I *num*. 四十,四十个;第四十。II *n*. 1. 〔*pl*.〕四十年代,四十到十九岁的时期。2. 四十岁。3. 【网球】三分。*Life begins at ~*. 〔谚〕人生始于四十。*a man of ~* 四十岁的人。*After ~* 四十岁以后。*in nineteen ~* 在 1940 年。*in the nineteen forties* 在二十世纪四十年代〔略 1940's 或 1940s〕。***like ~*** 〔美口〕非常,猛烈地。***over*** [***under***] ~ 四十岁以上[以下]。***Roaring Forties*** 大西洋南纬 40°至 50°之间风浪特大的海域。the Forties 苏格兰东北岸与挪威西南岸之间的海域〔因该区域水深 40 呎以上而得名〕。~ **wink** 〔口〕小睡(特指午睡)。

for·ty·ish [ˈfɔːtiiʃ; ˋfortɪɪʃ] *a*. 近四十岁的,四十岁左右的。

for·ty-eight·mo [ˈfɔːtiˈeitməu; ˋfortɪˋetmo] *n*. 四十八开本,四十八开的纸张[页面]。

for·ty-five [ˈfɔːtiˈfaiv; ˋfortɪˋfaɪv] I *num*. 四十五,四十五个。II *n*. 1. 45″ 口径手枪(常作 0.45,意为 0.45cm.)。2. (每分钟)四十五转唱片(常写作 45)。***the Forty-five*** 【英史】詹姆士二世党徒的 1745 年叛乱。

for·ty-nin·er [ˈfɔːtiˈnainə; ˋfortɪˋnaɪnɚ] *n*. 〔美〕1849 年涌往加利福尼亚州淘金的人。

fo·rum [ˈfɔːrəm; ˋforəm] *n*. (*pl*. ~*s*, ***fo·ra*** [ˈfɔːrə; ˋforə]) 1. 古罗马城镇的广场[市场]。2. 论坛;会议场;法庭。3. 座谈会,讨论会;评论;评判;(广播、电视的)专题讲话[座谈]节目。4. 制裁。*the ~ of conscience* 良心的制裁。*the ~ of public opinion* 舆论的评判。**the F-** 古罗马会议广场(遗址)。***the Forum*** 古罗马城大广场(遗址)。

for·ward [ˈfɔːwəd; ˋforwɚd] I *ad*. 1. 向前,前进 (*opp*. backward)。2. 【海】在船头,向船头 (*opp*. aft)。3. 今后,将来。4. 出来,出现,表面化。*F-!* 【军】前进! *from this time ~* 今后。*backward(s) and ~(s)* 来回地,前前后后。***carriage ~*** 运费由收货人照付。***date ~*** 【商】预填日期,填未来的日期〔如期票上所填若干日之后的日期〕。***help ~*** 促进。***look ~*** 向前看;期待,希望 (*look ~ to sb.'s visit* 等待某人来访)。***put ~*** 提出(计划、意见等)。***put*** [***set***] ***oneself ~*** 出面,挺身而出。***rush ~*** 冲向前。***send ~*** 打发;发出。II *a*. 1. 前方的;前面的。2. 【海】船前部的。3. 前进的,进步的,急进的。4. 在时令前的,过早的;早熟的。5. 热心的,争先恐

后的;鲁莽的,唐突的。6.【商】预约的,预定的,预先的,期货的。a ~ *contract* 预约。a ~ *crop* 早熟作物。a ~ *march* 进军。a ~ *payment* 预付货款。~ *prices* [*rates*] 期货价格。a ~ *rally* 【军】前方集结地区。*the* ~ *ranks* 先头部队。*the* ~ *rale* 带头作用。a ~ *school* 促进派,急进派,求进取的一派。a ~ *spring* 早来的春天。a ~ *pupil* 名列前茅的学生。**be ~ in** [*with*] **one's work** 工作有进展。**be ~ to help** 助人为乐。**III** *n*. 1.(足球、篮球等的)前卫,前锋。2. 期货;远期外汇。**IV** *vt*. 1. 促进,助长;促成,推进(计划等);促进(植物)发育[*cf*. force]。2. 转交(信件)、寄出(信件);送到,运送(货物)。3.【装订】把(书帖)叠齐订好[为粘贴封面作好准备]。~ *a plan* 推进一项计划。*Please* ~ *my mail to my new address*. 本人已迁居,来信请转新址。*Please* ~! 请转交! ~ **buying** 购买期货。~ **delivery** 【商】定期[来日]交货。~ **echelon** 【美军】先头部队;先遣指挥部。~**-looking** *a*. 高瞻远瞩的,进取的。~ **pass** 【橄榄球】前进传球。~ **quotation** 【商】期货报价。~**-thinking** = ~-looking.

for·ward·er [ˈfɔːwədə; ˋfɔrwədɚ] *n*. 1. 发运人(尤指报关行,运输代理人,运输代理行)。2.【装订】把书帖订好(交付粘贴封面)的工人。

for·ward·ing [ˈfɔːwədiŋ; ˋfɔrwədɪŋ] *n*. 1. 推进;促进。2. 寄送,托运;运输。~ **agency** 运输行。~ **agent** 运输商。~ **business** 运输业。~ **station** 运转站。

for·ward·ly [ˈfɔːwədli; ˋfɔrwədlɪ] *ad*. 1. 向前地;争先恐后地。2. 鲁莽地,唐突地。3. 在前部。

for·ward·ness [ˈfɔːwədnis; ˋfɔrwədnɪs] *n*. 进取(心);急切,热心;早熟;鲁莽,唐突。

for·wards [ˈfɔːwədz; ˋfɔrwədz] *ad*. = forward (*ad*.)。

for·wea·ried [fɔːˈwiərid; fɔrˋwɪrɪd] *a*.〔古〕极疲倦的。

for·went [fɔːˈwent; fɔrˋwɛnt] forgo 的过去式。

for·why [fɔːˈwai, -ˈhwai; fɔrˋwaɪ, -ˋhwaɪ] **I** *ad*.〔废方〕为什么。**II** *conj*.〔废〕因为。

for·worn [fɔːˈwɔːn; fɔrˋwɔrn] *a*.〔古〕极疲倦的。

for·zan·do [fɔːˈtsaːndəu; fɔrˋtsando] *a*., *ad*. = sforzando.

FOS, f. o. s. = free on steamer【商】轮船上交货(价格)。

Fos·dick [ˈfɔzdik; ˋfɑzdɪk] *n*. 福斯迪克〔姓氏〕。

fos·sa [ˈfɔsə; ˋfɑsə] *n*. (*pl*. **fos·sae** [ˈfɔsiː; ˋfɑsi])【解】窝,凹。*the nasal* ~ 鼻窝。

fos·sate [ˈfɔseit; ˋfɑset] *a*.【解】凹的,有窝的。

foss(e) [fɔs; fɔs] *n*. 1. 城壕,护城。2.【地】海渊。3.【解】= fossa.

fos·sette [fɔˈset; fɑˋsɛt] *n*. 1.(齿冠等上的)小凹,小窝。2. 酒窝,笑窝。

fos·sick [ˈfɔsik; ˋfɑsɪk] *vi*. 1.〔Aus.〕淘金。2. 寻觅,搜求。~ *for clients* 招揽顾客。— *vt*. 1. 采掘(金矿等)。2. 寻觅。

fos·sil [ˈfɔsl; ˋfɑsl̩] **I** *a*. 1. 从地下发掘出来的;化石的。2. 属于旧时代的;陈腐的;不合时宜的。**II** *n*. 1. 化石。2.〔口〕旧事物,旧制度。3. 老顽固,守旧者;习语中保存的旧词(如 to and fro 中的 fro)。~ **botany** 古植物学,化石植物学。~ **fuels** (煤、石油、天燃气等)矿物燃料。~ **ivory** (古象的)化石象牙。~ **oil**〔美〕(石油的旧称)矿油。~ **remains** (动物的)化石遗体。~ **study** 化石研究。

fos·sil·ate [ˈfɔsileit; ˋfɑsəˌlet] *vt*. = fossilize.

fos·sil·a·tion [ˌfɔsiˈleiʃən; ˌfɑsəˋleʃən] *n*. = fossilization.

fos·sil·if·er·ous [ˌfɔsiˈlifərəs; ˌfɑsəˋlɪfərəs] *a*. 产化石的,含化石的。

fos·sil·ize [ˈfɔsilaiz; ˋfɑslˌaɪz] *vt*. 1. 使成化石。2. 使(头脑等)陈腐,使僵化,使落伍。—*vi*. 1. 变成化石。2. 僵化,陈腐,过时。3.〔口〕搜集化石标本。**-za·tion** [ˌfɔsilaiˈzeiʃən; ˌfɑsilaiˋzeʃən] *n*. 化石作用。

fos·si·lol·o·gy [ˌfɔsiˈlɔlədʒi; ˌfɑsəˋlɑlədʒɪ] *n*. 化石学,古生物学。

fos·so·ri·al [fɔˈsɔːriəl; fɑˋsɔrɪəl] *a*.【动】掘土的,适于掘地的。~ *animals* 掘土动物。~ *claws* 适于掘土的爪。

Fos·ter [ˈfɔstə; ˋfɑstɚ] *n*. 福斯特〔姓氏,男子名〕。

fos·ter [ˈfɔstə; ˋfɑstɚ] *vt*. 1. 养育,抚育〔但并不在法律上认作继承人,与 adopt 有别〕。2. 鼓励;扶植;促进(发育)。3. 怀抱(希望等)。~ *a spirit of righteousness* 发扬正气。~ *a child* 收养一个小孩。~ *an evil thought* 心怀恶意。~ *the sick* 照料病人。~ **brother** [**sister**] 在同一家庭中养育的(但不是同父母的)弟兄[姐妹]。~ **child** 养子,养女。~ **daughter** 养女。~ **earth** 培养土。~ **father** 养父。~ **home** 寄养别人孩子的家庭。~ **mother** 养母。~**-mother** *vt*. 收养,抚养。~ **parents** 养父母。~ **son** 养子。

fos·ter·age [ˈfɔstəridʒ; ˋfɔstərɪdʒ] *n*. 1. 养育,寄养。2. 养子[女]身分。3. 助长,鼓励,促进。

fos·ter·er [ˈfɔstərə; ˋfɑstərɚ] *n*. 养育者;鼓励者。

fos·ter·ling [ˈfɔstəliŋ; ˋfɔstɚlɪŋ] *n*. 养子,养女。

fou [fuː; fu] *a*.〔Scot.〕喝醉的。

fou·droy·ant [fuːˈdrɔiənt; fuˋdrɔɪənt] *a*. 1. 闪电似的,使人眼花缭乱的,引起敬畏的。2.【医】急性的,暴发的。~ **paralysis**【医】急性麻痹。

fouet·té [fweˈtei; fwɛˋte] *n*.〔F.〕(芭蕾舞)单腿快速转身。

fou·gasse [fuːˈgɑːs; fuˋgɑs] *n*.〔F.〕【军】定向地雷。

fought [fɔːt; fɔt] fight 的过去式及过去分词。

fought·en [ˈfɔːtn; ˋfɔtn̩] *a*.〔古〕曾为战场的。*a* ~ *field* 古战场。

foul [faul; faʊl] **I** *a*. 1. 肮脏的,腐烂的;有恶臭的。2.(管道等)淤塞的;(船底等)粘满海藻;贝壳的;有触礁[撞碰]危险的;(水、空气等)污浊的。3.(绳子等)缠结难解的。4.(天气)恶劣的,不利航行的,逆风的;(疾病等)严重的,凶险的。5. 卑鄙的,丑恶的;(言语等)下流的。6. 丑陋的,难看的;讨厌的,令人作呕的。7.【体】违反规则的,犯规的,不正当的。8.【印】错误百出的。9.(船只)相撞的;与…冲突的 (*of*)。~ *linen* (要洗的)脏衣。*a* ~ *smell* [*taste*] 恶臭的气味[味道]。~ *breath* 臭气。*a* ~ *chimney* 阻塞不通的烟囱。*a ship* ~ *of a rock* 撞在岩石上的船。*a* ~ *deed* 恶劣的行为。*a* ~ *language* = *a* ~ *tongue* 下流话。*a* ~ *journey* 不愉快的旅行。~ *murder* 用卑鄙的手段诱杀。~ *weather* 恶劣的天气。*cut the* ~ *rope* 把纠缠着的绳子割开。***be ~ with*** 给…弄脏。***by fair means or*** ~ 不择手段地。***get*** ~ (绳索)纠缠,缠住。***in the teeth of a ~ wind*** 向着猛烈的逆风。**II** *ad*. 1. 碰撞地;争执不和地。2. 不正当地,犯规地。***fall*** [***go, run***] ~ ***of*** 1. 船只相撞。2. 争吵。***play sb***. ~ 用卑鄙手段对待某人。**III** *n*. 1. 脏东西;逆境。2. 碰撞;缠结。3.(在比赛中)犯规。***claim a*** ~【体】声明对方犯规,表示胜利无效。***through ~ and fair*** = ***through fair and*** ~ 在任何情形下,不管顺利或困难。**IV** *vt*. 1. 污染,弄脏。2. 使纠缠;使壅塞;阻碍。3. 船只相撞,碰撞。4.(在比赛中)犯规。*It is an ill bird that* ~*s its own nest*.〔谚〕家丑不可外扬〔原意为任何鸟都不肯把自己的巢弄脏〕。~ *sb*.*'s name* 损坏某人名誉。~ *one's hand with* ... 被…把手弄脏,因参与…而弄臭名誉。— *vi*. 1. 腐败,腐烂。2.(绳索、链条等)纠结,缠住;(管道、枪筒等)壅塞。3. 船只碰撞。4.【体】犯规。~ ***out*** 1.〔美〕比赛中因犯规过多而被罚出场。2.【棒球】因击出的界外球被接住而出局。~ ***up***〔美俚〕弄糟,搞坏。~**-brood** (蜜蜂的)幼虫腐臭病〔由细菌引起,分为两种。一种叫欧腐病,一种叫美腐病〕。~ **ball**【棒球】界外球。~ **bill (of health)** 瘟疫流行地所发健康证书。~ **coast** (暗礁多的)危险海岸。~ **ground** (暗礁多的)危险海底。~ **line** 犯规线,罚球线。~**-mouthed** [~**-spoken**, ~**-tongued**] *a*. 说话不干净的,嘴巴臭的。~ **play** 1.【体】犯规。2. 欺诈,卑鄙手段 (*opp*. fair play)。~ **proof**【印】毛样。~ **shot** (篮球)罚球;罚球所

得的一分（= free throw）。～ **stroke** 犯规的击球。～ **talk** 猥亵的谈话。～ **tip**【棒球】触击球。～**-up**〔口〕**1.** 拙劣的工作。**2.** 混乱，故障，乱七八糟。**-ly** *ad*. 下流地；粗鄙地；讨厌的。**-ness** *n*.

fou·lard [fuːˈlaːd; fuˋlard] *n*. 印花薄软绸；软绸手帕[领带、领巾]。

foul·ing [ˈfauliŋ; ˋfaulɪŋ] *n*.（水管、枪筒等中的）污垢。

fou·mart [ˈfuːmaːt; ˋfumart] *n*.【动】鸡貂。

found[1] [faund; faʊnd] find 的过去式和过去分词。*a*.（文艺作品等）找到的，拾得的，拣到的，自然形态的〔不是创作的，而是由艺术家对天然物或已有的文字材料加工完成的〕。～ **object** 拾得艺术品。～ **poem** 拾得诗〔把现成的散文词句重新安排而成为诗的形式〕。

found[2] [faund; faʊnd] *vt*. **1.** 为（建筑物等）打基础；建立，创办（学校等）。**2.** 树立，创（学说）。**3.** 以…为（论点、作品等）的根据；把（论点、作品等）建立在…的基础上（*on*; *upon*）。～ *a family* 建立家庭。～ *a hospital* [*university*] 创办一所医院[大学]。*a novel* ～*ed on fact* 根据事实写成的小说。*well* ～*ed* 十分有根据的。*ill* ～*ed* 根据不可靠的。*laws* ～*ed on human experience* 以人类经验为根据的法律。～ *one's claim on facts* 把自己的主张建立在事实材料的基础上。

found[3] [faund; faʊnd] *vt*. 铸造；熔铸。～ *a bell* 铸钟。～ *glass* 制玻璃。*a* ～*ing furnace* 铸造炉，熔炉。*metal* ～*ing* 金属熔铸。

found[4] [faund; faʊnd] **I** *a*.〔英〕（对房客等）不另加费供应的，已包括在价款[租金等]之内的〔通常置于句子末尾〕。*Room to let, laundry* ～. 房间出租，洗衣不另收费。**II** *n*. 不另外收费的供应品[服务等]，（工资以外）另行供给的膳食[住宿等]。*Maid wanted, good salary and* ～. 征求女佣，高工资并供给食宿（等）。

foun·da·tion [faunˈdeiʃən; faunˋdeʃən] *n*. **1.** 建设，创设，创立。**2.** 基础，根本；根据；地基，地脚。**3.** 基金；捐款；用捐款创办的事业；慈善机关；财团，基金会。**4.**（编织品的）模型；（衣服的）衬里；帽心。*a stone* ～ 石基。*a frame* ～【机】架座，机架，地脚。***be on the*** ～ 由基金维持。***lay the*** ～ ***for*** [***of***] 给…打下基础。***strike at the*** ～ [***root***] ***of sth***. 要毁灭某事物。***without*** ～ 无根据的。～ **cream** 粉底霜。～ **field** 种子田。～ **garment** 紧身褡，妇女胸衣。～ **hospital** 慈善医院。～ **member**〔英〕（团体等的）发起人，创办人，基本会员。～ **muslin**（上胶的）硬衬里细纱。～ **net**（上胶的）粗网眼纱。～ **school** 靠基金维持的学校。～ **stone** 基石；基础，根源。**-al** *a*. 基本的，基础的。**-er**〔英〕公费生。**-less** *a*.

found·er[1] [ˈfaundə; ˋfaʊndɚ] *n*. 奠基者，创立者，创办人。～**-member**（团体等的）创办人，发起人。～**s' shares**〔英〕（公司等的）发起人股份。

found·er[2] [ˈfaundə; ˋfaʊndɚ] *n*. 铸造工，翻砂工；铸件。

found·er[3] [ˈfaundə; ˋfaʊndɚ] **I** *vi*. **1.**【海】沉没。**2.** 失败，垮掉。**3.**（土地等）陷落；掉进（泥淖等里）（*in*）；（房屋等）倒塌。**4.**（马等）摔倒。**5.**（马）患蹄叶炎。— *vt*. **1.** 使沉没。**2.** 使摔倒，弄跛（马脚）；使倒塌，使垮掉。**3.** 破坏，损害。**II** *n*.（马的）蹄叶炎，胸肌风湿（= chest ～）。

foun·der·ous [ˈfaundərəs; ˋfaʊndərəs] *a*. 泥泞的，易使人摔倒的（= foundrous）。*a* ～ *road* 泥泞的道路。

found·ling [ˈfaundliŋ; ˋfaʊndlɪŋ] *n*. 弃儿，拾来的小儿。～ **hospital** 育婴院。

found·ress [ˈfaundris; ˋfaʊndrɛs] *n*. 女奠基人，女创立者，女创办人。

found·ry [ˈfaundri; ˋfaʊndrɪ] *n*. **1.** 铸造，翻砂。**2.** 铸工厂；玻璃（制造）厂；铸工车间。*an iron* ～ 翻砂厂。*a glass* ～ 玻璃厂。*a type* ～ 铸字所。～ **goods** 铸件。～ **iron** [**pig**] 生铁。～ **proof**【印】（打纸型版前的）清样。～ **worker** 铸造工人，翻砂工人。

fount[1] [faunt; faʊnt] *n*. **1.**〔诗〕泉，源泉。**2.**〔口〕（油灯上的）贮油罐；（自来水笔的）墨水管。**3.**〔美俚〕餐馆内出售苏打水、冰淇淋等的小卖部（= soda fountain）。

fount[2] [faunt; faʊnt] *n*.〔英〕【印】（字体、大小都一样的）一套活字（= font[2]）。

foun·tain [ˈfauntin; ˋfaʊntn] *n*. **1.** 泉水，喷泉。**2.** 人造喷泉，人造喷泉装置，饮用喷泉（= drinking ～）；喷水池；喷水塔。**3.** 源泉，根源。**4.** 液体贮藏器（如墨水管，油罐等）。**5.** 出售汽水的柜台（= soda ～）。*a* ～ *of wisdom* 知识的源泉。*poison the* ～*s of trust* 损坏信用。***F- of Youth*** 青春泉，长生不老泉〔传说此泉在美洲和西印度群岛，饮此泉者有病治病，无病可返老还童〕。～**head** 水源；根源，本源（*trace an error to its* ～ *head* 追究错误的根源）。～ **pen** 自来水钢笔。～ **shell** 大海螺。

four [fɔː; for] **I** *num*.（基数）四，四个〔用作基数词可以单独表示数的概念；也可以同表示人或事物的词连用，起数量限定作用〕；第四〔用于表示章、节等词之后〕。*Six minus two equals* ～. 六减二等于四。～ *Chapters* 四章。*Chapter* ～ 第四章。**II** *n*. **1.** 四人小组；（套在车上的）四匹马。**2.** 四的记号；（骰子的）四点；（钟点的）四时；四岁。**3.**〔*pl*.〕四厘公债。**4.**（口）四桨小艇；四桨小艇艇员；〔*pl*.〕四桨小艇竞赛。**5.**〔*pl*.〕【军】四路纵队。**6.**〔*pl*.〕【机】四汽缸发动机；四汽缸汽车。*a column of* ～*s* 四路纵队。*a child of* ～ 四岁的孩子。～*-and-twenty* = *twenty-*～ 二十四。***a coach and*** ～ 四匹马拉的大马车。***Form*** ～***s***！〔口令〕排成四列纵队！***Fours right*** [***left***]！（口令）排成四列向右[左]转！***in*** ～***s*** **1.** 每组[批]四个。**2.** 一柄四叶。***on all*** ～***s*** **1.** 匍匐，爬着。**2.** 完全一致的，完全吻合的（*No simile runs on all* ～*s*. 任何比喻都有出入）。～ **ale**〔英古〕一夸脱四便士的啤酒。～**-bagger**〔口〕（棒球中的）全垒打。～**-by-two** 擦枪布。～**colour** *a*.【印】四色的，四色版的，四色版印刷的〔指在印刷过程中用黄、红、蓝、黑四块分色印版表达出任何颜色〕。～**-clour problem**【数】四色难题〔指以四种颜色绘制地图、而不得让同一种颜色的地区相邻的数学难题〕。～**-cornered** *a*. 有四个角的；四方的；有四人参加的。～**-coupled** *a*. 有两对轮子的。～**-course** *a*. **1.** 四样的，（菜等）四道的。**2.**【农】四年轮作的。～**-cycle** *n*.（内燃机的）四冲程循环。～**-dimensional**，～**dimensioned** *a*.【数】四维的。～**-eyes**〔美俚〕〔蔑〕戴眼镜的人，四眼先生；四眼田鸡。～**-flush** *vi*.〔美俚〕虚张声势，吹牛。～ **flush**【牌】四张同花明牌、一张不同花暗牌的一手牌。～**flusher**〔美俚〕虚张声势的人，吹牛的人。～**-foot way**【英铁路】四英尺轨距。～**-footed** *a*. 四足的。～**-handed** *a*. 有四只手的；（游戏）四人玩的；四人一组的；【乐】（钢琴谱）二人合奏的。**F- Horsemen**【圣】（指战争、饥馑、瘟疫、死亡四大害的）四骑士。～ **hundred**〔也作 F- H-〕名士，名流〔前面加 *the*，原指纽约的四百知名人士，通指当地的名士、名流〕。～**-in-hand** **1.** *n*. 一人驾驶的四马马车；活结领带。**2.** *a*. 四马拉的。**3.** *ad*. 一人驾驶四马马车。～**-leaf clover**【植】四叶苜蓿〔被看作幸运的象征〕。～**-letter** *a*.〔美〕庸俗的，下流的，黄色的。～**-letter word** 四字母忌讳词〔与性或大便有关，通常由四个字母构成的单音节的词，一般都忌讳不说〕。～**-o'clock** [fɔːrəˈklɔk; forəˋklɑk]【植】紫茉莉；【动】食蜜鸟。～**-part** *a*.【乐】四部合唱的。～**pence**〔英〕四便士；（从前的）四便士银币。～**penny** **1.** *a*.〔英〕四便士的（*a* ～ *penny loaf of bread* 四便士一个的面包）。**2.** *n*.（从前的）四便士银币 = ～-ale. ～**-plex** 四单元住宅楼。～**ply** *a*.（羊毛等）四股的；（木材等）四层的。～**-poster** 四柱卧床。～**-pounder**【军】发射四磅炮弹的火炮；四磅重的面包（等）。～**score** *n*.，*a*. 八十。～**-seater** 可坐四人的车辆。～**square** *a*. 方的；基础巩固的，坚定不移的；直率的。～**-star** *a*.〔美〕优良的，最上等的；〔美〕四星级军衔的（*a* ～*-star general*〔美军〕陆军四星上将）。～**-striper**〔美俚〕海军上校。～**-stroke cycle**【机】四冲程循环。～**-way** *a*. 四面皆通的（～*-way pipe* 四通管）；由四人参加的。～**-wheel** *a*. 四轮的。～**-wheeler** 四轮出租马车。～**-fold** *a*.，*ad*. 四倍，四重。～**-some** *n*. 四人一组;(游戏中,特指高尔夫球中的)双打;参加双打者。

four·chette [fuəˈʃet; furˋʃɛt] ***n*.** **1.** (手套的)指叉。**2.**【解】阴唇小带。

Four·drin·i·er [fuəˈdriniə; fʊrˋdrɪnɪɚ] ***n*.,*a*.** 佛氏造纸机(的)。

4-F [ˈfɔːrˈef; ˋfɔrˋɛf] ***n*.** 〔美〕选拔征兵制体检不合格者。

four·gon [furˈgɔːn; furˋgɔn] ***n*.** 〔F.〕行李车。

Fou·rier [ˈfuriei; ˋfʊrɪɚ] ***n*.** **1.** 傅立叶〔姓氏〕。**2. François Marie Charles ~** 弗朗瓦斯·马利·沙利·傅立叶〔1772—1837,法国空想社会主义者〕。**3. Jean ~** 季恩·傅里叶〔1768—1830,法国数学家,物理学家〕。**~ series**【数】傅里叶级数。**~'s equation**【数】傅里叶方程式。

Fou·ri·er·ism [ˈfuriərizəm; ˋfʊrɪə͵rɪzəm] ***n*.** 傅立叶(F.M. Charles Fourier)的空想社会主义,傅立叶主义。

Fou·ri·er·ist [ˈfuriərist; ˋfʊrɪərɪst], **Fou·ri·er·ite** [ˈfuriərait; ˋfʊriərait] ***n*.** 傅立叶主义者。

four·ra·gère [fuːrɑːˈʒɛə; furaˋʒɛr] ***n*.** 〔F.〕【军】(军服的)彩色肩带(尤指某一部队全体的功勋肩带)。

four·some [ˈfɔːsəm; ˋforsəm, fɔr-] ***n*.** **1.** 四人一组。**2.** (每边两人的)双打。

four·teen [fɔːˈtiːn; forˋtin] **I** ***num*.** 十四,十四个;第十四。**II** ***n*.** 十四的记号;十四岁,十四点钟,十五世纪。*in ~ forty* 在1440年。*in the ~ forties* 在十五世纪四十年代。

four·teenth [fɔːˈtiːnθ; forˋtinθ] **I** ***num*.** 第十四(个);十四分之一(的)。**II** ***n*.** 每月的第十四日。

fourth [fɔːθ, fɔrθ] **I** ***num*.** **1.** 第四(个)。**2.** 四分之一(的)。**II** ***n*.** 每月的四日;【乐】四度音程,四度和音,第四音;〔*pl*.〕【商】四级品。*a ~ part* 四分之一。***the (glorious) F- = the F- of July*** 美国独立纪念日。**~-class** **1.** ***a*.** 第四类邮件的;邮包的。**2.** ***ad*.** 以第四类邮件发送;以邮包发送。**~ dimension** (长、宽、高三维之外的)第四维〔在相对论中指时间〕。**~-dimensional** ***a*.** 第四维的。**~ estate** 〔常用 F- Estate〕新闻界,报界。**~ market** 〔美〕第四市场〔投资者之间直接进行的未挂牌证券的交易〕。**F- Republic** (法国)第四共和国(1947—1958)。**F- World** 第四世界(泛指资源贫乏的发展中国家)。

fourth·ly [ˈfɔːθli; ˋforθlɪ] ***ad*.** 第四。

fou·ter, fou·tre [ˈfuːtə; ˋfutɚ] ***n*.** 〔废〕无价值的东西〔强烈轻蔑语的婉转说法〕。

fo·ve·a [ˈfəuviə; ˋfovɪə] ***n*.** (*pl*. ***fo·ve·ae*** [-iːiː;-͵i], ~*s*) **1.**【解】凹,窝。**2.** 中央凹(= fovea centralis)。**fo·ve·al** [-əl; -əl], **fo·ve·ate** [-it,-eit; -ɪt, -et] ***a*.** **fo·ve·i·form** [-ifɔːm; -ɪfɔrm] ***a*.**

fo·ve·o·la [fəˈviələ; fəˋvɪələ] ***n*.** (*pl*. ***-lae*** [-͵liː; -͵li], ~*s*)【解】小凹(= foveole)。**fo·ve·o·late** [-lit, -leɪt; -lɪt, -let], **fo·veo·lat·ed** [ˈfəuviəleitid; ˋfovɪə͵letɪd] ***a*.**

fowl [faul; faʊl] **I** ***n*.** (*pl*. ~*s*,〔集合词〕~) **1.** 鸡;家禽〔鸭、鹅、火鸡等〕;家禽肉。**2.** 〔前加修饰语〕…鸟;〔古、诗〕鸟。*a barndoor* [*barnyard*, *domestic*] *~* 鸡。*~ of the air* 飞鸟。*keep ~s* 养鸡。*fish, flesh, and ~* 鱼,肉,鸡。*neither fish, flesh, nor ~* 不伦不类的,非驴非马的。*game ~* 猎禽。*guinea ~*【动】珍珠鸡。*sea ~* 海鸟。*water ~* 水鸟。*wild ~* 野鸟。**II** ***vi*.** 捕鸟,打鸟。**~ cholera** 鸡霍乱,家禽霍乱症。**~-house** 鸡窝。**~ pest [plague]** 家禽的瘟症。**~-run** 〔英〕养鸡场。**~ variola** 家禽痘疮,家禽疮疹。

Fow·ler [ˈfaulə; ˋfaʊlɚ] ***n*.** 福勒〔姓氏〕。

fowl·er [ˈfaulə; ˋfaʊlɚ] ***n*.** 捕鸟者。

fowl·ing [ˈfauliŋ; ˋfaʊlɪŋ] ***n*.** 捕鸟,打鸟。**~ piece** 鸟枪,猎枪。

Fox[1] [fɔːks; fɑrks] ***n*.** **1.** 福克斯人〔美国的一支印第安人〕。**2.** 福克斯语〔福克斯人、索克人等所操的阿尔衮琴语〕。

Fox[2] [fɔːks; fɑrks] ***n*.** **1.** 福克斯〔姓氏〕。**2. Charles James ~** 查理·詹姆士·福克斯〔1749—1806,英国政治家〕。

fox [fɔks; fɑks] **I** ***n*.** **1.** 狐;狐皮。**2.** 狡猾的人。**3.** 〔美俚〕大学新生。**4.**【海】(多根绳子搓成的)绳索。*a white ~* 白狐。*~ farming* 养狐业。*an old ~* 老狐狸;老奸巨猾;狡猾的(老)人。***~ and geese*** 〔棋类〕狐入鹅群。***~ and hounds*** 猎狗追狐(游戏)。***play the ~*** 玩滑头,假装。***set a ~ to keep one's geese*** 引狼入室。***When the ~ preaches, take care of your geese.*** 〔谚〕狐狸在说教,当心鹅被盗。**II** ***vi*.** **1.** 捕狐,猎狐。**2.** 用狡计,欺诈。**3.** (书页等)变色,褪色;(啤酒等)变酸。—***vt*.** **1.** 使(书页等)生斑变色〔常用过去分词〕。**2.** 使(啤酒等)变酸。**3.** 〔口〕欺骗。**4.** 为(皮鞋)换面。**5.** 使醉。*be badly ~-ed* (书页等)颜色变得很厉害。**Foxbat** 狐蝠〔北约指原苏联米格25飞机的暗语〕。**~-bolt** 开尾螺栓。**~ brush** 狐尾。**~ earth** 狐穴。**~-fire** ***n*.** 狐火〔腐烂树木发出的磷火〕。**~-glove**【植】毛地黄属,(中药)熟地。**~ grape**【植】美国蘡薁(*Vitis Labrusca*)〔产于北美洲南部〕。**~-hole**【军】单人战壕,散兵坑。**~-hound** 狐猴,捕狐的猎狗。**~ hunt** 猎狐。**~ hunter** 猎狐者。**~-pass** 〔美俚〕失言,失礼(= faux pas)。**~'s sleep** 假睡;假装的漠不关心。**~ snake**【动】黄背锦蛇(*Elaphe Vulpina*)。**~ squirrel**【动】黑松鼠(*Sciurus niger*)〔产于北美东部〕。**~tail** 狐尾;【植】狐尾状植物〔尤指看麦娘、狗尾草等〕,石松。**~tail lily** 独尾属植物。**~tail millet** 小米,谷子,粟。**~ terrier** 猎狐小狗〔目前多半养着玩〕。**~trot** **1.** ***n*.** (骑马的)快步;狐步舞(曲);〔F-〕通讯中用于代表字母f的词。**2.** ***vi*.** 跳狐步舞。**~ wedge** 扩裂楔。**~wood** 褪色的木材。

foxed [fɔkst; fɑkst] ***a*.** **1.** (书页等)变了色的,生褐斑的。**2.** (皮鞋)修过面的。**3.** (啤酒等)变酸了的。**4.** 受骗的。

fox·ing [ˈfɔksiŋ; ˋfɑksɪŋ] ***n*.** 鞋面皮;鞋面修补用皮。

fox·y [ˈfɔksi; ˋfɑksɪ] ***a*.** (***fox·i·er***; ***-i·est***) **1.** 狐似的,狡猾的。**2.** 赤褐色的,狐色的。**3.** 变了色的,有褐斑的。**4.** (啤酒等)酸的,有气味的。**5.** 〔美〕时髦的,迷人的,性感的。**6.** (油画)红色过强的。**-i·ly** ***ad*.** **-i·ness** ***n*.**

foy [fɔi; fɔɪ] ***n*.** 〔主 Scot.〕**1.** 告别宴会;饯行宴会;临别赠品。**2.** 秋收结束的会餐;打鱼季节结束的会餐。

foy·er [ˈfɔiei; ˋfɔɪɚ] ***n*.** 〔F.〕**1.** 灶,炉。**2.** (剧场、旅馆等的)门厅,休息室。

FP = **1.** fireplug 消火栓。**2.** fully paid 全数付讫。**3.** floating policy 总保(险)单。**4.** foot-pound【物】英尺磅。

F.P. = **1.** field punishment 战地惩戒。**2.** fireplug 消防栓。**3.** fission product 裂变产物。**4.** former pupil 从前的学生。

fp = **1.** freezing point【物】冰点,凝固点。**2.** footpound 英尺-磅(功的单位)。**3.** foolscap 大页书写纸。

f.p. = **1.** feed pump 供给泵。**2.** flask point 闪(燃)点。

FPA, fpa = free of particular average【商】单独海损不赔。

FPC = fifth protein concentrate 蛋白鱼粉。

fpc, F.P.C. 〔美〕= Federal Power Commission【美】联邦动力委员会。

F.P.D. = fully paid 全数付讫。

f.p.m., fpm = feet per minute 英尺/分。

FPO = **1.** field post office 战地邮局。**2.** 〔美〕fleet post office 舰队邮局。

F.P.S. = Fellow of the Philological Society 〔英〕语文学会会员。

fps =【物】**1.** feet per second 英尺/秒。**2.** foot-pound-second 英尺磅秒单位制的。**3.** frames per second (电视图像的)每秒帧数。

fpsps = feet per second per second 每秒每秒英尺(= ft/s^2)

Fr. = **1.** Father. **2.** France; French. **3.** 〔G.〕*Frau*. **4.** Friar. **5.** Friday.

Fr = francium【化】元素钫[金法]的符号。
fr. = **1.** fragment. **2.** franc(s). **3.** frequent. **4.** from.
Fra [frɑː; frɑ] *n*.〔It.〕兄弟〔用在教士姓名前,作称呼用〕。
fra·cas [ˈfrækɑː; ˋfrækɑ] *n*. (*pl*. ~ [ˈfrækɑːz; ˋfrækɑz]; ~*es* [-kəsiz; -kəsɪz]) 喧嚷,吵闹。
frac·tion [ˈfrækʃən; ˋfrækʃən] *n*. **1.** 小部分,碎片,片断。**2.** 一些,一点儿。**3.**【化】分馏,分层,分级。**4.**【宗】圣餐面包分切式。**5.**【数】分数。*a common* [*vulgar*] ~ 普通分数。*a compound* [*complex*] ~ 繁分数。*a mixed* ~ 带分数。*a decimal* ~ 小数。*a proper* [*improper*] ~ 真[假]分数。*a* ~ *closer* 稍微靠近一点。*by* ~*s* 有余数的,不完全的。*crumble into* ~*s* 碎成片片。*in a* ~ *of a second* 一秒钟的若干分之几,一转眼的工夫。*not a* ~ *of* 一点也没有。*not by a* ~ 一点也不。*to a* ~〔口〕道道地地,百分之百地。
frac·tion·al [ˈfrækʃənl; ˋfrækʃənl] *a*. **1.** 零碎的,断片的。**2.**【数】分数的,小数的,有零数的;不足买卖单位的。**3.**【化】分馏的,分级的。*a* ~ *expression* 分数式。~ **column** 分馏塔,分馏柱。~ **currency** 辅币。~ **distillation**【化】分馏(作用)。~ **electric motor** 小马力电动机。~ **error** 相对误差,部分误差。~ **tower** = ~ column.
frac·tion·al·ize [ˈfrækʃənəlaiz; ˋfrækʃənəˏlaɪz] *vt*. 把…分成分数;把…分成部分 (= fractionize)。**frac·tion·al·i·za·tion** [ˌfrækʃənəlaiˈzeiʃən; ˏfrækʃənəlaɪˋzeʃən] *n*. = fractionization.
frac·tion·ar·y [ˈfrækʃənəri; ˋfrækʃənərɪ] *a*. = fractional.
frac·tion·ate [ˈfrækʃəneit; ˋfrækʃənet] *vt*. **1.**【化】使分馏。**2.** 把…分级,把…分成几部分。*a fractionating column* 分馏柱。*a fractionating tower* 分馏塔。**frac·tion·a·tion** [ˌfrækʃəˈneiʃən; ˏfrækʃəˋneʃən] *n*.【化】分馏(法);分层分离,分级分离,份化。**frac·tion·a·tor** *n*.【化】分馏器。
frac·tious [ˈfrækʃəs; ˋfrækʃəs] *a*. **1.** 倔强的。**2.** 易怒的;脾气不好的。**3.** 任性的。**-ly** *ad*. **-ness** *n*.
frac·tog·ra·phy [frækˈtɔgrəfi; frækˋtɑgrəfɪ] *n*. 金属断面显微镜观察。**-phic** [ˌfræktəˈgræfik; ˏfræktəˋgræfɪk] *a*.
frac·ture [ˈfræktʃə; ˋfræktʃɚ] **I** *vt*., *vi*. (使)破裂;(使)折断;(使)断裂。**II** *n*. **1.** 破裂,折断,断裂。**2.** 裂痕,裂缝,裂面。**3.**【医】挫伤,骨折。**4.**【矿】断口;【地】断层。*a comminuted* ~ 粉碎骨折。*a compound* ~ 复合骨折。**frac·tur·a·tion** [ˌfræktʃəˈreiʃən; ˏfræktʃəˋreʃən] *n*.【地】岩层断裂。
frac·tus [ˈfræktəs; ˋfræktəs] *n*.【气】(碎积云或碎层云的)碎云(类)。
frae [frei; fre] *prep*.〔Scot.〕从,自。
frae·num [ˈfriːnəm; ˋfrinəm] *n*. (*pl*. *frae·na* [ˈfriːnə; ˋfrinə]) = frenum.
frag·ging [ˈfrægiŋ; ˋfrægɪŋ] *n*.〔美军俚〕士兵(用手榴弹等杀伤性炸弹)杀伤军官的行为。
frag·ile [ˈfrædʒail; ˋfrædʒəl] *a*. **1.** 脆的,易碎的。**2.** 脆弱的,虚弱的。~ *health* 虚弱的体质。**-ly** *ad*. **-ness** *n*. = fragility.
fra·gil·i·ty [frəˈdʒiliti; frəˋdʒɪlətɪ] *n*. **1.** 脆弱;虚弱。**2.** 脆性,脆度,易碎性。
frag·ment [ˈfrægmənt; ˋfrægmənt] **I** *n*. **1.** 碎屑,碎片,破片,断片。**2.** 未完稿,断简残篇。*lie in* ~*s* 已成破片。*reduce to* ~*s* 弄碎。**II** *vi*., *vt*. (使)成碎片,(使)分裂。
frag·men·tal [frægˈmentl; frægˋmentl] *a*. = fragmentary.
frag·men·tar·y [ˈfrægməntəri; ˋfrægmənˏtɛrɪ] *a*. **1.** 破片的,断片的。**2.** 残缺不全的,不连续的。**3.**【地】碎屑质的,断岩的。~ *memories* 片断的回忆。~ *ejecta*【地】喷屑。~ *rocks*【地】碎屑岩。**-tar·i·ly** *ad*. **-tar·i·ness** *n*.
frag·men·tate [ˈfrægmənteit; ˋfrægmənˏtet] *vt*., *vi*. (使)成碎片(使)碎裂。
frag·men·ta·tion [ˌfrægmenˈteiʃən; ˏfrægmənˋteʃən] *n*. **1.** 破碎,碎裂。**2.**【生】(染色体)断裂。*a* ~ *bomb* 杀伤炸弹。~ **damage** 破片杀伤。~ **effect** 破片杀伤效果。~ **grenade** 碎裂手榴弹。~ **shell** 杀伤炮弹。
frag·ment·ize [ˈfrægməntaiz; ˋfrægmənˏtaɪz] *vt*., *vi*. = fragmentate. **-za·tion** *n*.
fra·grance [ˈfreigrəns; ˋfregrəns] **fra·gran·cy** [-si; -sɪ] *n*. 芳香,香气,香味。
fra·grant [ˈfreigrənt; ˋfregrənt] *a*. 芬芳的,香的。**-ly** *ad*.
frail[1] [freil; frel] **I** *a*. **1.** 脆弱的,虚弱的。**2.** 意志薄弱的,不坚定的。~ *happiness* 暂时的幸福。**II** *n*.〔美俚〕少女,少妇。**-ly** *ad*. **-ness** *n*.
frail[2] [freil; frel] *n*. **1.** 灯心草篓〔用以装无花果、葡萄干等〕。**2.** 灯心草篓的容量〔约 32、56 或 75 磅〕。
frail·ty [ˈfreilti; ˋfreltɪ] *n*. **1.** 脆弱,虚弱。**2.** 意志薄弱。**3.** 弱点,过失。*F-, thy name is woman*. 弱者,你的名字是女人〔莎士比亚剧作《哈姆雷特》中的名句〕。
fraise[1] [freiz; frez] *n*. **1.**【军】(钢丝网或木桩构成的)障碍物。**2.** (16 世纪欧洲流行的)皱领。
fraise[2] [freiz; frez] **I** *n*.【机】铣刀,绞刀,扩孔钻。**II** *vt*.【机】绞(孔),用绞刀扩大。
fraises des bois [freiz de ˈbwɑ; frez de ˋbwɑ]〔F.〕野生草莓。
frak·tur [frɑːkˈtuə; frɑkˋtur] *n*. 德文尖角体的活字。
F.R.A.M. = Fellow of the Royal Academy of Music〔英〕皇家音乐院会员。
fram·a·ble [ˈfreiməbl; ˋfreməbl] *a*. **1.** 可构造的,可组织的,可制订的。**2.** 可想像的。**3.** 可装配框子的。
fram·b(o)e·si·a [fræmˈbiːziə; fræmˋbiʒɪə] *n*.【医】雅司病,热带性类梅毒。
fram·boise [frɔːnˈbwɑːz; frɔnˋbwɑz] *n*.〔F.〕悬钩子白兰地酒。
frame [freim; frem] **I** *n*. **1.** 机构;组织;系统。**2.** 结构,框架,构架,骨架,骨骼。**3.** 体格,身躯。**4.** 精神状态,心情。**5.**【园艺】温床,阳畦;船的肋骨;【印】排字台,活字架;【机】架,座;【影】画面,镜头;【电视】帧。**6.**【美俚】桥牌比赛,职业拳击赛的一个回合,棒球的一局。**7.**〔美俚〕诬陷 (= ~-up)。*backing* ~【摄】安片框。*cant* ~【船】斜肋骨。*a missile* ~【军】飞弹弹体。*a pea* ~ 豌豆架。*square* ~【船】直肋骨。*the* ~ *of government* 政府机构。*a man of gigantic* [*massive*] ~ 体格魁梧的人。~ ***of axes***【数】坐标系统。~ ***of mind*** 心情,心境。~ ***of reference*** **1.**【数、物】参考系(统),参考坐标[标架],坐标系(统),读数[计算]系统,空间坐标,基准标架。**2.** 观点,理论。***out of*** ~ 纷乱,无秩序。***sheriff's picture*** ~ 绞索。**II** *a*.〔美〕木造的,木结构的。~ *building* [*dwelling*, *house*] 木造房屋。**III** *vt*. **1.** 编制,组织。**2.** 构造;给…装框子[装架子]。**3.** 作出,拟定,想像,设计,计划。**4.** 使适合 (*for*)。**5.** 讲出,说出。**6.**〔口〕捏造(事件),陷害,诬陷。**7.**〔古〕举步走向 (*toward*)。*a lake* ~*d in woods* 树木环抱着的湖。~ *a lie* 编谎话。~ *a plan* 拟定计划。*be* ~*d*〔美〕陷入圈套。— *vi*. (计划等)有成功希望。***be not*** ~***d for*** 不适于;经不起,受不了。~ ***to oneself*** 想像。~ ***well*** 有才能,有希望 (*He* ~*s well in speaking*. 他有希望作演说家)。~ **aerial** [**antenna**]【无】框形天线。~ **relay**【无】帧中继。~ **saw** 框锯。~**-up**〔美俚〕阴谋;诬害。~**work** 构架(工程),结构,框架;机构,组织。**-r** *n*. **-less** *a*.
fram·ing [ˈfreimiŋ; ˋfremɪŋ] *n*. **1.** 结构,组织,编制。**2.** 框架;骨骼。**3.** 计划,构想。**4.**【电视】图框配合;成帧,按帧调节光栅,调节帧频稳定图像。
franc [fræŋk; fræŋk] *n*. 法郎〔法国、比利时、瑞士等国的货币单位〕。
France[1] [frɑːns; fræns] *n*. **1.** 法朗士〔姓氏〕。**2.** **Anatole**

～ 阿纳多勒·法朗士〔1844—1924,法国小说家,批评家〕。

France[2] [frɑːns; fræns] *n*. 法国,法兰西。

Fran·ces [ˈfrɑːnsis; ˋfrænsɪs] *n*. 弗朗西丝〔女子名〕。

fran·chise [ˈfræntʃaiz; ˋfræntʃaɪz] **I** *n*. **1**. 选举权;公民权,市民权,参政权;【史】(某种)豁免权。**2**. 特许行使特权的地区;避难所。**3**. 〔美〕(私人公司或社团所享有的)某种特许权。**4**. 保险契约规定的免赔限度,免赔额。**5**. 控制权,管辖范围。**II** *vt*. **1**. 给…以特(许)权。**2**. 赋与…以选举权〔市民权、公民权、参政权〕。**-chi·see** [ˌfræntʃaiˈziː; ˏfræntʃaɪˋzi] *n*. 大公司的联营店;获特许经营联营店者。

Fran·cis [ˈfrɑːnsis; ˋfrænsɪs] *n*. 弗朗西斯〔男子名〕。

Fran·cis·can [frænˈsiskən; frænˋsɪskən] **I** *a*. 【宗】方济各会的。**II** *n*. 方济各会的修道士。

Fran·cis·co [frænˈsiskəu; frænˋsɪsko] *n*. 弗朗西斯科〔男子名,Francis 的异体〕。

fran·ci·um [ˈfrænsiəm; ˋfrænsɪəm] *n*. 【化】[钫]。

Franck [frɑːŋk; fræŋk; frɑŋk, fræŋk] *n*. **1**. 弗朗克〔姓氏〕。**2**. **James** ～ 詹·弗朗克〔1882—1964,出生于德国的美国物理学家,诺贝尔奖金获得者〕。

Fran·co [ˈfrɑːŋkəu; ˋfrɑŋko], **Francisco** 佛朗哥〔1892—1975,西班牙军人,国家元首(1939—1975)〕。

Fran·co- *comb. f*. 表示"法国(的)": the *Franco-*Prussian War 普法战争。

fran·co·lin [ˈfræŋkəulin; ˋfræŋkəlɪn] *n*. 【动】鹧鸪。

Fran·co·phile, Fran·co·phil [ˋfræŋkəufail, -fil; ˋfræŋkəˏfaɪl, -fɪl] **I** *a*. 亲法国的。**II** *n*. 亲法分子。

Fran·co·phobe [ˈfræŋkəufəub; ˋfræŋkəˏfob] **I** *a*. 厌恶法国的,恐惧[仇视]法国的。**II** *n*. 恐法(分子),仇视法国者。**Fran·co·phobia** [-fəubiə; -fobɪə] *n*. 厌恶[仇视]法国,恐法病。

Fran·co·phone [ˈfræŋkəufəun; ˋfræŋkəˏfon] **I** *n*. 说法语者(尤指在通用两种以上语言的国家里) **II** *a*. 〔常 f-〕说法语的。

Fran·co·phon·ic [ˌfræŋkəuˈfəunik; ˏfræŋkəˋfonɪk] *a*. 〔或 f-〕说法语的。

Fran·co·pho·nie [ˌfrænkəuˈfəuni; ˏfrænkəˋfonɪ] *n*. 〔或 f-〕**1**. 〔集合词〕法语国家;说法语社会。**2**. 法语国家[社会]文化;法语国家[社会]共同体。

franc-ti·reur [frɔːntiˈrœːr; frɔntɪˋrœr] *n*. (*pl*. ***francs-ti·reurs*** [frɔːntiˈrœːr; frɔntɪˋrœr]) 〔F.〕(法国非正规军的)义勇兵,游击队员。

fran·gi·bil·i·ty [ˌfrændʒiˈbiliti; ˏfrændʒəˋbɪlətɪ] *n*. **1**. 脆弱,脆弱性。**2**. 易脆性,脆度。

fran·gi·ble [ˈfrændʒəbl; ˋfrændʒəbl] *a*. **1**. 脆弱的。**2**. 易碎的。～ **grenade** 【军】烧夷弹〔俗名 Molotov cocktail 或 gasoline bomb〕。

fran·gi·pane [ˈfrændʒipein; ˋfrændʒɪˏpen] *n*. = frangipani.

fran·gi·pan·i [ˌfrændʒiˈpæni; ˏfrændʒɪˋpænɪ] *n*. **1**. 【植】鸡蛋花,鸡蛋花属植物;从鸡蛋花提炼出的香料。**2**. 杏仁酥。

Fran·glais [frɔːnˈglei; frɔnˋgle] *n*. 〔F.〕(法语中的)英语外来语〔尤指美语外来语〕。

Frank[1] [fræŋk; fræŋk] *n*. 弗兰克〔男子名〕。

Frank[2] [fræŋk; fræŋk] *n*. **1**. 法兰克人〔古代日尔曼民族的一支〕。**2**. 〔近东各地的〕西欧人。**3**. 〔诗〕法兰西人。

frank [fræŋk; fræŋk] **I** *a*. **1**. 率直的,直言不讳的,坦白的。**2**. 【医】症状明显的。*a* ～ *avowal of guilt* 坦白认罪。*to be* ～ *with you* 坦白对你说,老实说〔插入语〕。**II** *n*. **1**. 免费邮寄特权。**2**. 免费寄发签字[印戳]。**3**. 免费递送的邮件。**III** *vt*. **1**. 免费邮寄。**2**. 在(信件)上盖免费递送或邮资已付印戳。**3**. 许…免费通行。**4**. 特许自由出入。**5**. 释放,豁免。～**ing-machine** 自动邮资盖印机。

Frank·en- [ˈfræŋkən; ˋfræŋkən] *comb. f*. 【生】转基因的〔源自 Frankenstein,详见下条〕。～**food** 转基因食品。～**tomato** 基因改变了的番茄。

Frank·en·stein [ˈfræŋkənstain; ˋfræŋkənˏstaɪn] *n*. **1**. 法兰肯斯坦〔英国女作家 Mary Wollstonecraft Shelley (1797—1851) 所著小说中主人公,系一生理学家,曾制造一怪物,后为此怪物所毁灭〕。**2**. 作法自毙的人;毁掉创造者自己的事物;人形怪物。*a* ～*'s monster* 自己所创造反而毁灭自己的恶魔;自找的烦恼。**-i·an** *a*.

Frank·fort [ˈfræŋkfət; ˋfræŋkfɚt] *n*. **1**. (莱茵河畔)法兰克福〔德国城市〕(= ～ on the Main 或〔G.〕*Frankfurt am Main*) **2**. (奥得河畔)法兰克福〔德国城市〕(= ～ on the Oder 或〔G.〕*Frankfurt an der Oder*)。**3**. 〔f-〕= frankfurter. ～ **black** (铜版印刷用)黑色油墨。

frank·furt(er), frank·fort(er) [ˈfræŋkfət(ə); ˋfræŋkfɚt(ɚ)] *n*. 猪牛肉混合香肠。

frank·in·cense [ˈfræŋkinˌsens; ˋfræŋkɪnˏsɛns] *n*. 乳香。～ **oil** 【化】蓝丹油。

Frank·ish [ˈfræŋkiʃ; ˋfræŋkɪʃ] **I** *a*. **1**. 法兰克人的,法兰克族的。**2**. 法兰克语的;法兰克文化的。**3**. 西欧人的。**II** *n*. 法兰克语。

Frank·lin, Frank·lyn [ˈfræŋklin; ˈfræŋklɪn] *n*. **1**. 富兰克林〔姓氏,男子名〕。**2**. **Benjamin** ～ 富兰克林〔1706—1790,美国政治家,科学家〕。～ **stove** 富兰克林炉〔一种壁炉状铸铁火炉〕。

frank·lin [ˈfræŋklin; ˋfræŋklɪn] *n*. **1**. (中世纪英国非贵族出身的)小地主。**2**. 〔主英〕拥有土地的富农。

frank·lin·ite [ˈfræŋklinait; ˋfræŋklɪˏnaɪt] *n*. 【矿】锌铁矿,锌铁尖晶石。

frank·ly [ˈfræŋkli; ˋfræŋklɪ] *ad*. 率直地,坦白地,真诚地。～ *speaking* 老实说,坦率说〔用作插入语〕。

frank·ness [ˈfræŋknis; ˋfræŋknɪs] *n*. 率直,坦白。

frank·pledge [ˈfræŋkpledʒ; ˋfræŋkˏplɛdʒ] *n*. **1**. 【英史】十家连保制。**2**. 实施连保的十家。**3**. 实施连保的十家成员(指十二岁以上的男子)。

Franks [fræŋks; fræŋks] *n*. 弗兰克斯〔姓氏〕。

fran·se·ri·a [frɑːnˈsiəriə; frɑnˋsɪrɪə] *n*. 【植】弗氏菊〔菊科植物,产于美国西部,以西班牙植物学家弗兰塞里 (*Antonio Franseri*)命名〕。

fran·tic [ˈfræntik; ˋfræntɪk] *a*. **1**. 狂乱的;疯狂的。**2**. 〔口〕厉害的,非常的。*be in a* ～ *hurry* 急如星火。*be* ～ *with pain* 痛得发狂,剧痛。**-(al)ly** *ad*. **-ness** *n*.

frap [fræp; fræp] *vt*. (用绳索等)捆牢,收紧。

frap·pé [ˈfræpei; ˋfræpe] **I** *a*. 〔F.〕冷却的,冰过的。**II** *n*. 冰镇冷饮,刨冰冷饮。*wine* ～ 冰镇葡萄酒。

Fra·ser, Fra·zer [ˈfreizə; ˋfrezɚ] *n*. 弗雷泽〔姓氏〕。

frat [fræt; fræt] *n*. = fraternity.

fra·te [ˈfrɑːtei; ˋfrɑtɛ] *n*. (*pl*. ***fra·ti*** [ˈfrɑːti; ˋfrɑtɪ]) 〔It.〕= friar.

fra·ter[1] [ˈfreitə; ˋfretɚ] *n*. 〔废〕修道院食堂或斋堂。

fra·ter[2] [ˈfreitə, ˈfrɑːtə; ˋfretɚ, ˋfrɑtɚ] *n*. **1**. (宗教团体或兄弟会的)兄弟;会友。**2**. 〔废〕托钵僧,修道士。

fra·ter·nal [frəˈtəːnl; frəˋtɝnl] *a*. **1**. 兄弟的,兄弟般的,友爱的。**2**. 〔美〕兄弟会的,共济会的。*a* ～ *association* [*order*, *society*] 〔美〕兄弟会,共济会。～ *affection* [*love*] 友爱。～ **twins** 【生】异卵双生。**-ly** *ad*.

fra·ter·ni·ty [frəˈtəːniti; frəˋtɝnətɪ] *n*. **1**. 兄弟关系,友爱;博爱。**2**. 同行朋友,同仁;会友,社友。**3**. 兄弟会,共济会。**4**. 〔美〕大学生联谊会〔美国男学生中略带秘密性的组织,女学生的此类组织则称 Sorority,它们多以两个或三个希腊字母为其名称〕。**5**. (动物)一次交配所生的全部幼畜。*freedom* [*liberty*], *equality and* ～ 自由,平等,博爱。*the* ～ *of the Press* 报界同仁。*the angling* ～ 钓鱼的朋友。～ **house** 〔美〕大学生联谊会会所。

frat·er·nize, frat·er·nise [ˈfrætənaiz; ˋfrætɚˏnaɪz] *vi*. **1**. 亲如兄弟,亲近。**2**. 和敌兵[敌国国民]亲善(特指被占领国国民)。**3**. 〔美俚〕(第二次世界大战中及战后)士兵和敌国国民发生性行为。— *vt*. 使亲善,使亲如兄弟。**-za·tion** [ˌfrætənaiˈzeiʃən; ˏfrætɚnaɪˋzeʃən] *n*.

frat·ri·ci·dal [ˌfreitriˈsaidl, ˌfræ-; ˏfretrɪˋsaɪdl, ˏfræ-] *a*. 杀兄弟[姊妹]的;杀同胞的。*a* ~ *war* [*struggle*] 内战,自相残杀的战争。

frat·ri·cide [ˈfreitrisaid, ˈfræ-; ˋfretrɪˏsaɪd, ˋfræ-] *n*. 1. 杀兄弟[姊妹]的行为。2. 杀害兄弟[姊妹]者。

Frau [frau; fraʊ] *n*. (*pl*. ~*s*, 〔G.〕 ***Frau·en*** [ˈfrauən; ˋfraʊən]) 〔G.〕 1. 夫人〔和英语 Mrs. 相当〕; 妻。2. 〔口〕德国女人。

fraud [frɔːd; frɔd] *n*. 1. 欺骗,欺诈;舞弊;欺诈行为,骗局。2. 骗子;伪品。*actual* ~ = ~ *in fact* 有意的欺骗。*constructive* [*legal*] ~无意[合法]的欺骗。*pious* ~ 善意的欺骗。***in*** ~ ***of*** = ***to the*** ~ ***of*** 【法】为了诈骗…。

fraud·u·lence [ˈfrɔːdjuləns; ˋfrɔdjələns], **fraud·u·len·cy** [-si; -sɪ] *n*. 欺骗性,欺诈。

fraud·u·lent [ˈfrɔːdjulənt; ˋfrɔdjələnt] *a*. 1. 欺骗性的,欺诈的。2. 骗得的。**-ly** *ad*.

fraught [frɔːt; frɔt] I *a*. 〔仅用作述语〕 1. 〔古〕积载着…的,装着…的。2. 充满…的;隐藏着…的 (*with*)。*a policy* ~ *with danger* 充满危险的政策。*a ship* ~ *with precious wares* 满载着贵重货物的一条船。II *n*. 货物,装载物。

fräu·lein [ˈfrɔilain; ˋfrɔɪlaɪn] *n*. (*pl*. ~*s*, 〔G.〕 ~) 1. 〔G.〕小姐〔与英语 miss 相当〕。2. 〔口〕(德国)姑娘。3. (英国人家庭中的)德国保姆[家庭教师]。

frax·i·nel·la [ˌfræksiˈnelə; ˏfræksɪˋnɛlə] *n*. 【植】白藓。

fray[1] [frei; fre] I *vt*. 1. 擦,磨;磨损(布边等),擦破(绳子的末端)以致纤维散开。2. 使(关系、神经等)紧张。*Long wear had* ~*ed the cuffs of his old shirt*. 他那件旧衬衫穿的时间太久,袖口都磨破了。*The edge of the carpet was* ~*ed into a fringe*. 地毯的边缘被散编成一绺绺流苏。— *vi*. 被磨损,被擦断。II *n*. (织物等的)磨损处。

fray[2] [frei; fre] I *n*. 1. 吵闹;打架。2. 争论,辩论。***be eager for the*** ~ 〔书〕希望发生事端,唯恐天下不乱。II *vt*. 〔古〕吓唬,使惊恐。— *vi*. 〔古〕吵架,打架。

fray·ing [ˈfreiiŋ; ˋfreɪŋ] *n*. 织物磨损后落下的碎片,摩擦后落下的东西。

fra·zil [ˈfreizl; ˋfrezl] *n*. 河底所结的冰。

fraz·zle [ˈfræzl; ˋfræzl] I *vt*., *vi*. 1. 磨损,磨破,(使)变破烂。2. (使)疲倦。II *n*. 1. 磨破。2. 磨损的边缘。3. 疲倦。***be beaten to a*** ~ 被打得死去活来。***be worn to a*** ~ 1. 被穿破。2. 疲惫不堪。

fraz·zled [ˈfræzld; ˋfræzld] *a*. 1. 〔口〕穿破了的,磨损了的。2. 疲惫的。3. 〔美俚〕喝醉了的。

FRB = Federal Reserve Board [Bank] 〔美〕联邦储备委员会[银行]。

FRC = 1. Federal Radio Commission 〔美旧〕联邦无线电委员会。2. Foreign Relations Committee 〔美〕外交委员会。

FRCM = Fellow of the Royal College of Music 〔英〕皇家音乐学院会员。

freak[1] [friːk; frik] I *n*. 1. 奇想,任性,异想天开。2. 反常行为,怪诞行为。3. 畸形的人(物)。4. 〔美俚〕吸毒成瘾者。5. …爱好者,热心者。6. 嬉皮士,颓废分子;逃避现实的人。*human* ~*s* 畸形的人们。*a* ~ *of nature* 畸形的人[物],天生的畸形。~*s of weather* 天气反常。*out of mere* ~完全出于想入非非。II *a*. 反常的,奇特的。~ *shapes* 奇形怪状。III *vi*., *vt*. 〔仅用于 ~ out 成语中〕。~ ***out*** 〔俚〕 1. (因服毒品等而)产生幻觉[逃避现实]。2. 成为颓废派。3. 使处于极度兴奋中。4. 行动反常。~***-out*** 1. 吸毒引起的幻觉。2. 通过吸毒逃避现实,通过吸毒逃避现实的人。3. 嬉皮士集会。4. 反常的行动。~ ***show*** (狂欢节余兴的)畸形人表演。

freak[2] [friːk; frik] I *vt*. 使…上有斑点[条纹]。II *n*. 斑点,条纹。**-ed** *a*. 有斑点的,花的,有条纹的。

freak·ish [ˈfriːkiʃ; ˋfrikɪʃ] *a*. 1. 异想天开的。2. 捉摸不定的。3. 畸形的,反常的,奇特的。**-ly** *ad*. **-ness** *n*.

freck·le [ˈfrekl; ˋfrɛkl] I *n*. 雀斑;斑点。II *vi*., *vt*. (使)生斑点,(使)生雀斑。

freck·ly [ˈfrekli; ˋfrɛklɪ] *a*. (*-li·er*; *-li·est*) 多雀斑的。

freak·y [ˈfriːki; ˋfrikɪ] I *a*. 〔美俚〕吸毒(者)的,逃避现实的。II *n*. 吸毒者。

Fre·da [ˈfriːdə; ˋfridə] *n*. 弗丽达〔女子名 Winifred 的昵称〕。

Fred·er·ic(k), **Fre·dric(k)** [ˈfredrik; ˋfrɛdrɪk] *n*. 弗雷德里克〔男子名〕。

Fred·er·i·c(k)a [ˌfredəˈriːkə; ˏfrɛdəˋrikə] *n*. 弗雷德丽卡〔女子名〕。

free [friː; fri] I *a* (*fre·er*; *fre·est*) 1. 自由的,自主的;自立的。*a* ~ *action* 自由行动。~ *competition* 自由竞争。*as* ~ *as the wind* 自由自在,行动自由。*You are* ~ *to go or stay*. 去留随你的便。2. 自动的;任意的,奔放的;直率的,不客气的。*of one's own* ~ *will* 自发的,自动的。*I am* ~ *to confess*. 我直率地承认。~ *spirit* 奔放不羁的精神。3. 随意的,自如的;(文章等)流利的;不拘泥于文字的(*opp*. literal)。~ *verse* 自由体诗歌。~ *translation* 意译。*a* ~ *style of writing* 流畅的文体。4. 不拘束的,随便的;大方的;不吝啬的。~ *manners* 态度大方。*be* ~ *with* [*of*] *one's money* 用钱大方。5. 空闲的 (*opp*. busy); (房屋、空间等)空余的。*Are you* ~? 你现在有空吗? *Have you any rooms* ~? 你有空房间吗? 6. 自由开放的,畅通无阻的。*a* ~ *port* 自由(贸易)港。*The way is* ~ *for an advance*. 此路通行无阻。7. 免费的;免税的。*admission* [*admittance*] ~免费入场。~ *medical care*. 公费医疗。*a* ~ *school* 免费学校。~ *of charge*(*s*) 免费。*free goods* 免税品。8. 免…的,无…的 (*from*; *of*)。*an ice-*~*harbour* 不冻港。*an interest-*~*loan* 无息贷款。*a nuclear-weapon-* ~ *zone* 无核武器区。9. 【化】单体的,游离的;【植】分离的,离生的,特生的。~ *nitrogen* 游离氮。~ *oxygen* 游离氧。~ *state* 游离状态。10. (土地等)易于耕作的;(石头等)易于凿取的。11. 顺风的。12. 【语言】(重音等)自由的,不固定的。13. 丰富的,富足的。~ *living* 优裕的生活。14. (线条等)优美的;(姿势等)潇洒的。~ *lines and curves* 优美的线条和曲线。~ *gestures and movements* 潇洒的手势和动作。15. (绳索等)未固定的;悬空的。*the* ~ *end of a rope* 绳子未系住的一端。16. 在场者均参加的。*a* ~ *fight* 一场混战。~ ***alongside ship*** 【商】船边交货〔略 f. a. s.〕。~ ***and easy*** 不拘仪式的,随便的。~ ***from*** 无…的,不受…影响的(*a day* ~ *from wind* 无风的日子)。~ ***of*** 1. 无…的,摆脱了…的;离开,在…外的(~ *of duty* 免税。~ *of a burden* 无负担。*the sea* ~ *of ice* 无流冰的海。*The train was not* ~ *of the station yet*. 火车还没有离开车站)。2. 可自由进入并使用的 (*be* ~ *of a friend's house* 可自由使用朋友的房屋)。~ ***of all average*** 【商】一切海损不保在内。~ ***on board*** 【商】船上交货〔略 f. o. b.〕。~ ***on rail*** 【商】火车上交货〔略 f. o. r.〕。***get*** ~ 获得自由 (*of*)。***give sb. a*** ~ ***hand*** 给与某人行动自由,听其自由处置。***give*** [***spend***] ***with a*** ~ ***hand*** 随便花钱。***have a*** ~ ***hand*** 有行动自由。***have one's hands*** ~ 1. 可以自由行动。2. 无事。***make sb.*** ~ ***use of*** 使某人自由使用,使某人自由出入。***make sb.*** ~ ***of the city*** 给某人市民权。***make*** ~ ***with*** 随意使用。***set*** ~ 释放,解放。II *ad*. 1. 自由地,无阻碍地。2. 一帆风顺地。3. 免费地。*Members are admitted* ~会员免费入场。*The yacht was sailing* ~ *over the sea*. 游艇在海上顺风行驶。III *vt*. (~*d*; ~*ing*)解放,释放,使自由;解救,使摆脱 (*from*; *of*); 清除。~ *the land from oppression* 把国家从压迫下解放出来。~ *oneself from one's difficulties* 从困难中解脱出来。~ ***agent*** 有自主权力的人;(可解约加入他队的)自由身职业运动员。

~ **air** 大气,大气层的空气。~**-and-easy** 〔口〕可以自由抽烟的音乐会(在酒吧间的)聚餐;下流音乐厅[酒馆]。~ **association**【心】自由联想〔让病人把所想到的不论什么念头和回忆,都毫无掩饰地说出来,以此发现和明确内心被压抑的内容〕。~ **beach** 允许裸体的沙滩,裸体浴沙滩区。~ **bench**【法】寡妇财产。~**board**【船】杆弦高度,杆弦。~**boot** *vi*. 做海盗,干抢劫勾当。~**booter** 海盗,海盗似的冒险家。~**booting** *a*., *n*. 干抢劫勾当(的);掠夺行为(的)。~**born** *a*. 生而自由的,自由民的,自由民生养的。~ **charge**【电】自由电荷。~**-choice** *a*. 由牲口任意选择饲料的。**F-Churches** (由英国国教分离出来的)独立教会。~**coinage**【经】自由铸造货币的制度。~ **companion** (中世纪的)雇佣兵。~ **delivery** 免费邮递。~**-drop 1**. *n*. (不用降落伞的)自由空投(物)。**2**. *vt*. 自由空投。~ **education** 公费教育。~ **energy**【物】自由能。~ **enterprise** 私营企业自由竞争(论)〔美国资本家主张政府尽可能少地限制私营企业自由竞争的论点或做法〕。~ **fall 1**. (跳伞的)自由降落;降落伞张开以前的降落。**2**. (火箭等的)惯性运动。~**-fire zone**【军】格杀区〔在该区内,任何移动的物体均将被轰击〕。~ **flight** (火箭的)无动力飞行〔指燃料耗尽或断绝后的飞行〕。~**-flight** *a*. 无动力飞行的。~**-for-all 1**. *n*. 自由参加的比赛;可以自由发表意见的争论;大吵大闹,打群架。**2**. *a*. 对任何人都开放的。~**-for-aller** *n*. 〔英俚〕不择手段的谋取私利者。~**-form** *a*. 形式[造型]自由的;线条不规则的;独创性的;反传统的;任意的。~ **frequence**【物】固有频率,自然频率。~ **goods 1**. 免税品。**2**. 不需成本的原料〔空气、水等〕。~**hand** *a*. 不用仪器而随手画出的(*a* ~ *hand drawing* 徒手画,写意画)。~ **hand** 自由行动。~**handed** *a*. 不拘束的;慷慨的;用钱大方的。~**hearted** *a*. 坦白的,爽朗的,大方的,感情用事的。~ **hold** 地产[职位等]的自由保有权,完全保有的地产。~ **holder** 不动产的所有人,世袭地的保有人。~ **house** 可卖各种牌子酒的酒店。~ **hydrogen**【化】有效氢,游离氢。~ **labour 1**. 自由人的劳动(与奴隶劳动相对而言)。**2**. 〔集合词〕不属于工会的工人。~ **lance** (中世纪的)自由骑士,游勇;自由行动者;(无固定职业,以卖文、卖艺为生的)自由作家[演员]。~**-lance 1**. *vi*. 做自由作家[演员]。**2**. *a*. 自由作家[演员]的。~ **list** 免费入场名单,(期刊的)赠阅名单,免税品一览表。~ **liver** 讲究吃喝玩乐的人。~**-living** *a*. **1**. 喜欢吃喝玩乐的。**2**.【生】独立生存的,非寄生的,非共生的。~ **load** *vi*. 利用别人慷慨而占便宜;吃白食。~**loader** 利用别人慷慨而占便宜的人,揩油者,经常吃白食者。~**loading** *a*. 利用别人慷慨而占便宜的。~ **love** 非法同居;(不受婚姻和法律约束的)两性自由离合论。~**man** (*pl*. *-men*) 自由民享有市民特权的人,荣誉市民。~ **market** 自由市场。~**-martin** (同公牛孪生的)无生殖机能的小雌牛。~**mason** (中世纪的)石工工会会员;〔F-〕共济会(Free & Accepted Masons)会员。**F- masonry** *n*. **1**. 共济会规章[制度],共济会仪式,共济会成员。**2**. 〔f-〕同病相怜。~**minded** *a*. 无精神负担的。~ **oscillation**【物】自由振动。~ **press** 出版自由。~ **radical**【原】自由基,游离基。~**-return** *a*.【宇】自动重返大气层的。~ **rider** 非工会会员但享受工会活动成果的工人。~ **silver**〔美〕银币的自由铸造。~ **soil** 无奴隶制的地方;(美国南北战争前禁止蓄用奴隶的)自由地区,自由土地。~ **speech** 言论自由。~**-spoken** *a*. 直言不讳的,讲话坦率的。~**standing** *a*. (雕刻、建筑物等)独立的,自力撑持的。**F- State 1**. (美国南北战争前的)自由州,不蓄奴地区。**2**. 爱尔兰自由邦。~**stone 1**. *n*. 易切石,软性石;核与肉容易分离的果实。**2**. *a*. (果实等)容易与核分离的。~ **style**【游】自由式。~**-swimming** *a*. (动物)能自由浮游的,能游泳的。~**swinging** *a*. 大胆的,直率的,不考虑个人的。~ **thinker** 理性主义者;唯理论者,【宗】自由思想家。~ **thinking** *a*. 自由思想的(尤指宗教上)。~ **thought** (十八世纪不受传统宗教思想束缚的)自由思想。~ **throw**【篮球】罚球。~**-tongued** *a*. 说话不当心的。~ **trade** 自由贸易。~ **trader** 自由贸易主义者;〔废〕走私者。~ **university** 自由大学〔主要由学生们自己组织的独立大学或学院,学生可自由选课,不分班级〕。~ **verse** (不受格律约束的)自由诗。~ **vibration**【物】自由振动。~ **ware**【计】免费软件。~ **way 1**. 快车道。**2**. 不收养路费的公路。~ **wheel** *vi*. **1**. 靠惯性滑行。**2**. 随心所欲[放任自流]地生活[行动]。~ **wheel** (自行车的)飞轮,【机】滑轮。~ **wheeling 1**. *n*. 惯性滑行。**2**. *a*. 惯性滑行的;放任自流的,随心所欲的。~**-will** *a*. 自由的,随心所欲的;自愿的,出乎自由意志的。~ **will** 自愿,自由意志;【哲】自由意志论。~**-wool** 净毛。~ **zone** 堆放免付关税货物的地区。

free·bie, free·by [ˈfriːbi; ˋfribɪ] *n*. (*pl*. *-bies*) 〔美俚〕**1**. 免费赠品〔如戏院赠票〕;不劳而获的东西。**2**. 施与[接受]免费赠品者。

Freed·heim [ˈfriːdhaim; ˋfridhaɪm] *n*. 弗里德海姆〔姓氏〕。

freed·man [ˈfriːdmən; ˋfridmən] *n*. (*pl*. *-men*) **1**. (由奴隶解放出来的)自由民。**2**. 法律上解除了约束的人。

free·dom [ˈfriːdəm; ˋfridəm] *n*. **1**. 自由;自主;自由身分。**2**. 〔使用等的〕自由权。**3**. 直率,放肆,过分亲密。**4**. 特权,特许;免除,解脱 (*from*)。**5**.【物】自由度。**6**. (动作等的)优美,(生活的)优游闲适。*necessity and* ~【哲】必然和自由。*the Four Freedoms* (1941 年美国总统罗斯福提出的所谓"言论自由、信仰自由、免于匮乏、免于恐惧"的)四大自由〔即 ~ *of speech*, ~ *of worship*, ~ *from want*, ~ *from fear*〕。~ *of assembly* 集会自由。~ *of conscience* 信仰自由。~ *of the will* 意志自由。~ *of the air*【军】空战主动权。~ *of the city* (赠与外宾的)荣誉市民权。~ *of the press* 出版自由。~ *of the seas*【国际公法】战时中立国船只的自由航海权,商船自由航海权。~ *from care* 放心。~ *from taxation* 免税。*take* [*use*] ~*s with sb*. 对某人放肆。*with* ~ 自由地。~**-fighter** 争取自由的战士。**F- Ride** 〔亦作 f- r-〕〔美〕"自由乘客"运动〔为争取公民权利故意乘坐黑人白人同车同船的各种交通工具去南部各州,要求废除车船种族隔离的示威运动〕。**F- Rider** 〔亦作 f- r-〕参加"自由乘客"运动的民权工作者。

free·ly [ˈfriːli; ˋfrilɪ] *ad*. **1**. 自由地,随意地。**2**. 直率地,不客气地。**3**. 慷慨地,豪爽地。**4**. 免费地。

Free·man [ˈfriːmən; ˋfrimən] *n*. 弗里曼〔姓氏,男子名〕。

free·ness [ˈfriːnis; ˋfrinɪs] *n*. **1**. 自由。**2**. 直率;随意。**3**. 大方。**4**. 排水度。

free·si·a [ˈfriːʒiə, -siə; ˋfriʒɪə, -sɪə] *n*.【植】小苍兰属。

Free·town [ˈfriːtaun; ˋfriˏtaʊn] *n*. 自由城(弗里敦)〔狮子山国首都〕。

freeze [friːz; friz] **I** *vi*. (*froze* [frəuz; froz]; *fro·zen* [ˈfrəuzən; ˋfrozən]; *freez·ing*) **1**. 冷冻,凝固,结冰。**2**. 冻僵,冰冷。**3**. 战栗,颤抖;〔美口〕木立不动。*It froze hard last night*. 昨夜冰冻得厉害。*I am simply freezing*. 我简直冻僵了。— *vt*. **1**. 使冷冻,使结冰,使凝冻;冷藏。**2**. 使冻僵,使冻伤,使冻死。**3**. 使沮丧。**4**. 冻结(存款、工资、物价等)。~ *ice cream* 制冰淇淋。~ *sb*. *with a frown* 皱起眉头使某人沮丧[吓退]。~ [***be frozen***] ***to death*** 冻死。~ ***sb*.*'s blood*** = ***make sb*.*'s blood*** ~ 使某人毛骨悚然[吓得不能动弹]。~ (***on***) ***to*** 〔口〕**1**. 贴紧,搂紧。**2**. 抓紧。~ ***out* 1**. 冻干。**2**. 〔口〕(用冷淡态度)使人无地自容,逼走某人。~ ***over*** 全面结冰。~ ***together*** 冻结在一起。~ ***up* 1**. (使)冻结。**2**. (态度等)变呆板[冷淡,僵硬]。**II** *n*. **1**. 结冰,凝冻;冻结。**2**. 严寒期。~**-dry** *vt*.【化】冷冻干燥,冻干〔在高度真空内将冷冻状态的食物等干燥,特别用以保存食物〕。~**-dryer** 冻干机。~**-etching** 冷裂法〔将标本速冻后割裂,借以显示其内部立体结构以便观察〕。~**-frame**【影,电视】静止镜头。

freez·er [ˈfriːzə; ˋfrizɚ] *n*. **1**. 制冰淇淋者,冷藏工人。**2**.

F

冷冻装置,冷冻机,冷藏车,冷藏库,电冰箱。

freez·ing [ˈfriːziŋ; ˋfrizɪŋ] I *a*. 1. 凝冻的,极冷的。2. 使人打冷颤的;极冷淡的。3. 结冰的;冷冻用的。*a* ~ *machine* 冷冻机。II *ad*. 冷冻一样地。*be* ~ *cold* 冷冻一样地冷。III *n*. 冻结,结冰(作用)。~ **drizzle** 冻毛雨。~ **mixture** 冷却剂,冷冻混合物。~ **point**【物】冰点,凝冻点。**-ly** *ad*.

freight [freit; fret] I *n*. 1.〔英〕船运货物,运输〔美国兼指空运、陆运〕。2. 货运。3. 运费。4.〔美〕货运列车 (= ~ train)。~ *rates* 运费率。*volume of* ~ 货运量。***by*** ~〔美〕用普通货车运送。***dead*** ~ 空舱费。***drag*** [***pull***] ***one's*** ~〔美俚〕离开,出发。~ ***forward*** 运费由提货人支付。~ ***paid*** 运费付讫。~ ***prepaid*** = ***advanced*** ~ 运费先付。II *vt*. 1. 运送。2. 装货于,充满。3. 出租[租用](船、车)。~ **agent** 运输行。~ **car**〔美〕(一节)货车 (=〔英〕goods waggon)。~ **engine** 货运机车〔注意其牵引力而不重视其速度〕。~ **house** 货栈,堆栈。~ **liner**〔英〕集装箱货运列车。~ **ton** [**tonnage**] 容积顿(数)。~ **train**〔美〕货运列车 (=〔英〕goods train)。

freight·age [ˈfreitidʒ; ˋfretɪdʒ] *n*. 1. 货运。2. 运费。3. 运送的货物。

freight·er [ˈfreitə; ˋfretɚ] *n*. 1. 租船人;装货人,货主;承运人。2. 货船,运货机。

frem·i·tus [ˈfremitəs; ˋfrɛmətəs] *n*.【医】震颤。

Fre·mont [friˈmɔnt; friˋmɑnt] *n*. 弗里蒙特〔姓氏〕。

fre·na [ˈfriːnə; ˋfrinə] frenum 的复数。

French[1] [frentʃ; frɛntʃ] *n*. 弗伦奇〔姓氏〕。

French[2] [frentʃ; frɛntʃ] I *a*. 法国的,法兰西的;法语的;法国人的;法国式的。II *n*. 1. 法语。2.〔the ~〕〔集合词〕法国人。***pedlar's*** ~ 窃贼的行话。~ **bean**〔英〕菜豆。~ **bulldog** 法国老虎狗,法国哈巴狗。~ **Canadian** 1. 法裔加拿大人。2. 加拿大法语 (= Canadian French)。~ **chalk** 滑石,滑石粉。~ **Community** 法兰西共同体〔1958 年成立,参加者有法国、中非共和国、查德、刚果(布)、加彭、马尔加西和塞内加尔等〕。~ **cuff** 双袖口,翻边袖口。~ **curve** 曲线板,曲线规。~ **doors** 法(式)双扇玻璃门。~ **dressing** 法式色拉调料。~ **endive**【植】菊苣嫩叶。~ **fry**〔常用 f- fry〕【烹】炸得松脆的;法(国)式洋芋丝(片)〔俗称~ fries〕。~ **gray** [**grey**] 浅灰色。~ **heel** 法式高弯跟(女鞋)。~ **horn**【乐】法国号。~ **ice cream** 法式冰淇淋〔用鸡蛋和高脂肪奶油做成〕。~ **knot** 法式花芯刺绣针迹;法式线结〔将线绕针数次而缝成的花式结〕。~ **leave** 不辞而别〔源出法国 18 世纪的习俗,参加宴会的客人可不辞而别〕(*take* ~ *leave* 不辞而别)。~ **letter**〔英俚〕避孕套。~**man** (*pl*. ***-men***) 法国人。~ **marigold**【植】万寿菊。~ **pastry** 法式点心。~ **polish** 法国磨光漆。~**-polish** *vt*. 在…上加法国漆。~ **pox** 梅毒。~ **Revolution** 法国大革命(1789—1799)。~ **roll** 花卷蛋糕。~ **roof** 法式屋顶。~ **seam**【纺】来去(线)缝,法式接缝。~ **telephone** 法式电话机〔早期电话机的一种〕。~ **toast** 蘸牛奶、鸡蛋后轻炸的面包片。~ **window** 双扇落地玻璃门〔一般通至阳台〕。~ **woman** *n*. (*pl*. ***-wo·men***) 法国女人。

French·i·fy [ˈfrentʃifai; ˋfrɛntʃɪˏfaɪ] *vt*. 使法国化。**-fi·ca·tion** *n*.

French·less [ˈfrentʃlis; ˋfrɛntʃlɪs] *a*. 不懂法语的。

French·y [ˈfrentʃi; ˋfrɛntʃɪ] I *a*. (***French·i·er***; ***-i·est***) 1. 法国式的。2.〔美俚〕轻松愉快的;嘻笑作乐而不严肃的;轻率的。II *n*.〔口〕法国人。**French·i·ly** *ad*. **French·i·ness** *n*.

fre·net·ic [friˈnetik; friˋnɛtɪk] *a*. 1. 非常激动的。2. 发狂的 (= phrenetic)。**-al** *a*.〔古〕= phrenetic.

fren·u·lum [ˈfrenjuləm; ˋfrɛnjuləm] *n*. (*pl*. ~*s*, ***-la*** [-lə; -lə]) 1.【解】小系带。2.【动】(昆虫的)翅缰。

fre·num [ˈfriːnəm; ˋfrinəm] *n*. (*pl*. ***fre·na*** [ˈfriːnə; ˋfrinə], ~*s*) 1.【解】系带。2.【动】(蔓足类的)系褶;(昆虫的)系带。

fren·zied [ˈfrenzid; ˋfrɛnzɪd] *a*. 狂乱的,狂暴的,疯狂似的。*make* ~ *efforts* 拼命挣扎[用力]。~ *rage* 狂怒。**-ly** *ad*.

fren·zy [ˈfrenzi; ˋfrɛnzɪ] I *vt*. (***-zied***; ***-zy·ing***)〔主用被动语态〕使狂乱,使发狂。*become frenzied* 发狂。*be frenzied with joy* 狂喜。II *n*. 狂乱,疯狂似的激动。*drive sb. to* ~使某人发狂。*in a* ~发狂,在狂乱中。*in the* ~ *of the moment* 在一时狂怒中。*work oneself into a* ~渐渐狂暴起来。**-zi·ly** *ad*.

fre·on [ˈfriːɔn; ˋfriɑn] *n*.【化】氟里昂〔商标名〕氟氯烷〔一种无色气体冷冻剂〕。

freq. = frequency; frequent; frequentative; frequently.

fre·quence [ˈfriːkwəns; ˋfrikwəns] *n*. = frequency.

fre·quen·cy [ˈfriːkwənsi; ˋfrikwənsɪ] *n*. 1. 屡次,频仍,频繁。2. (脉搏等的)次数,出现率;频度;【物】频率,周率。*audio* ~音频。*a high* [*low*] ~高[低]频。*the* ~ *of earthquakes in Japan* 地震在日本的频繁发生。*mean* [*median*] ~中频。*resonance* [*resonant*] ~谐振频率,共振频率。*ultrahigh* ~超高频。*ultralow* ~超低频。*very high* ~甚高频。*very low* ~甚低频。~ **band**【无】频带,波段。~ **changer** [**converter**]【电】换频器,变频器。~ **channel**【电视】频道。~ **curve**【统】频数曲线。~ **distribution**【统】频数分布;频率分布。~ **divider** 分频器。~ **meter**【电】频率[周率]计。~ **modulation**【电】调频,频率调制;调频播送。~ **selection**【电】频差法分辨。

fre·quent [ˈfriːkwənt; ˋfrikwənt] I *a*. 1. 屡次的,常见的;频繁的。2. (脉搏等)急促的,快的。*a* ~ *caller* [*visitor*] 常客。*a* ~ *occurence* 经常发生的事情。*a coast with* ~ *lighthouses* 灯塔密布的海岸。II [fri(ː)ˈkwent; fri(ɪ)ˋkwɛnt] *vt*. 1. 常去,时常出入于。2. 与…时常交际[来往]。*Tourists* ~ *the district*. 游客常去那个地方。*I know him, but I don't* ~ *him much*. 我认识他,但不常往来。~ *learned men* [*good company*] 与学者[正派朋友]交往。**-ly** *ad*.

fre·quen·ta·tion [ˌfriːkwenˈteiʃən; ˏfrikwɛnˋteʃən] *n*. 常去,经常来往[出入]。

fre·quen·ta·tive [friˈkwentətiv; friˋkwɛntətɪv] I *a*. 多次的,反复表示的。II *n*.【语法】反复动词〔如 chatter 是 chat 的反复动词〕(= ~ verb)。

fre·quent·er [friˈkwentə; friˋkwɛntɚ] *n*. 常客,常往来的人。

frère [frer; frɛr] *n*.〔F.〕(*pl*. ~*s* [frer; frɛr]) 1. 兄弟;团友,社友。2. (天主教的)修士。

fres·co [ˈfreskəu; ˋfresko] I *n*. (*pl*. ~*es*, ~*s*) 1. (湿绘)壁画法。2. 壁画。***paint in*** ~作壁画。II *vt*. 在…作壁画,用壁画法画出,作壁画。

fresh [freʃ; frɛʃ] I *a*. 1. 新产生的,新制的;新获得的;新近的,新到的。2. 清新的;生气勃勃的,强健的,气色好的,鲜艳的,鲜嫩的。3. 清洁的;清凉的。4. 新鲜的,无咸味的 (*opp*. salt);未加盐(腌)的,生的。5. 无经验的,不熟练的;新入学的,新进的 (*opp*. old)。6.〔俚〕微醉的;〔美俚〕莽撞的,放肆的,无礼的(尤指对异性)。7.【气】疾(风);【海】迅速的。8. 外加的,另外的,进一步的。9. (谈话等)有创见的,有启发性的。10. (母牛)开始有奶的,新近产犊的。*news* ~ *and* ~最新消息。~ *flowers* 鲜花。~ *fish* 鲜鱼,生鱼。~ *fruit* 新鲜水果。*feel* ~觉得清新[爽快]。*make a* ~ *start* 从新开始。~ *troops* 生力军。*a* ~ *hand* 无经验者,生手。*a* ~ *recruit* 新兵。*He's a bit* ~. 他有点醉了。***as*** ~ ***as lark*** [***a daisy***] 精神饱满的。***be*** ~ ***in mind*** [***memory***] 记忆犹新。***break*** ~ ***ground*** 开垦生荒地;着手新事业。~ ***from school*** [***the country***] 刚由学校[乡下]出来。***F-paint!*** 油漆未干! ***get*** ~〔美俚〕厚脸起来;变得无礼。***green and*** ~ 生的;不熟练的;幼稚的。***in the*** ~ ***air***

在户外。*throw* ～ *light on* 提供新情况。II *ad*. 刚,新,才。III *n*. 1. (河流的)暴涨,泛滥。2. (流入咸水中的)淡水流。3. 〔学俚〕新生。4. (一天、一年等的)开始。*in the* ～ *of the morning* 清晨。～**-blown** *a*. (花)刚开的。～ **breeze**【气】清劲风(五级风)。～**-caught** *a*. 刚捕获的。～**-coined** *a*. (硬币)新铸造的。～ **gale**【气】强风(八级风)。～ **man** (*pl*. **-men**) 大学新生,一年级生;新手,生手。～**-run** *a*. (鱼)新由海中进到淡水中的。～ **water** *a*. 1. 淡水的(～ *water fish* 淡水鱼。～ *water fishery* 淡水养鱼业。*a* ～ *water lake* 淡水湖)。2. 只习惯于淡水航行的,无经验的,不熟练的。3. 〔美俚〕内地的,不知名的(～ *water college* 内地大学)。～**-water eel**【动】鳗鲡属。**-ness** *n*.

fresh·en [ˈfreʃn; ˋfrɛʃn] I *vt*. 1. 使新鲜。2. 使清爽,使有精神;把(自己)盥洗一番 (*up*)。3. 使变淡,去…的盐分。4. 添(饮料)。*The rest* ～*ed my spirit*. 我休息后精神饱满。— *vi*. 1. 变新鲜。2. 变活泼。3. (风)变强。4. 咸味变淡。5. (母牛)开始有奶,产犊。～ *the way* 增加船行速度。～ *up* 1. 弄新鲜,变新鲜。2. 盥洗打扮。**-er** *n*. 1. 清凉剂(如饮料等)。2. 〔英俚〕新学生;新手。

fresh·et [ˈfreʃit; ˋfrɛʃɪt] *n*. 1. (因下雨、融雪而引起的)河水暴涨。2. 流入海中的淡水流。

fresh·ly [ˈfreʃli; ˋfrɛʃlɪ] *ad*. 1. 新近;刚才。2. 精神饱满地;气息清新地,活泼地。

Fres·nel [freiˈnel, F. freˈnɛl; freˋnɛl], **Augustin Jean** 夫瑞奈[1788-1827,法国物理学家]。～ **mirrors**【光】夫瑞奈式镜。【物】夫瑞奈区。

fret[1] [fret; frɛt] I *vt*. (**-tt-**) 1. 使焦急,使烦恼。2. 腐蚀,侵蚀,使消损,使磨损。3. 侵蚀成…。4. (风等)使(水面)起浪。*a knife fretted with rust* 锈坏了的小刀。～ *oneself* 烦闷,焦急。～ *oneself ill* 急出病来。～ *oneself to death* 急死。～ *one's health away* [*out*] 烦坏了健康。— *vi*. 1. 焦急,烦恼。2. 侵蚀。3. 消损,磨损。4. (水面)起浪。～ *over mistake* 为错误而焦急。～ ***and fume*** 焦急。～ ***the bit*** (马)咬嚼子。～ ***away*** [***out***] ***one's life*** 在烦闷中过日子。II *n*. 1. 谋急,烦恼。2. 腐蚀(处);磨损处。***in a*** ～ = ***on the*** ～ 焦急,烦闷。

fret[2] [fret; frɛt] I *n*. (弦乐器指板上定音的)档子。II *vt*., *vi*. (**-tt-**) 把(弦)压在档子上。

fret[3] [fret; frɛt] I *n*.【建】回纹饰;网状饰物。II *vt*. (**-tt-**) 用回纹装饰。～**-saw** 网丝锯,线锯。～**work**【建】浮雕细工。

fret·ful [ˈfretful; ˋfrɛtfụl] *a*. 1. 谋急的,烦恼的。2. (水面)起波纹的;(风)一阵阵的。**-ly** *ad*. **-ness** *n*.

fret·ty [ˈfreti; ˋfrɛtɪ] *a*. (**-ti·er**; **-ti·est**) 1. = fretful. 2. 有回纹装饰的。

Freud [frɔid; frɔɪd], **Sigmund** 弗洛伊德〔1856—1939,奥地利精神病学家〕。

Freud·i·an [ˈfrɔidjən; ˋfrɔɪdjən] I *a*. 弗洛伊德的,弗洛伊德学说[学派]的,精神[心理]分析学的。II *n*. 弗洛伊德派,精神[心理]分析学家。～ **slip** 无意中泄露真实欲望的漏嘴。**-ism** *n*. 弗洛伊德学说[学派],精神[心理]分析学。

Fri. = Friday.

fri·a·bil·i·ty [ˌfraiəˈbiliti; ˏfraɪəˋbɪlətɪ] *n*. 脆性,易碎性。

fri·a·ble [ˈfraiəbl; ˋfraɪəbḷ] *a*. 易(粉)碎的,脆的。*a* ～ *rock* 松散岩石。

fri·ar [ˈfraiə; ˋfraɪɚ] *n*. (天主教的)男修士,行乞修士。*The* ～ *preached against stealing and had a goose* [*pudding*] *in his sleeve*. 〔谚〕口里仁义道德,心里男盗女娼。～**bird** 蜜鸟〔产于澳洲和西南亚,头部光光无羽毛〕。～**'s balsam** 安息香酊。～**'s lantern** 鬼火 (= ignis fatuus)。

fri·ar·y [ˈfraiəri; ˋfraɪərɪ] I *n*. 男修道院。II *a*. 男修道院的,男修士的。

frib·ble [ˈfribl; ˋfrɪbḷ] I *n*. 1. 无聊的人,轻佻的人。2. 无聊的事,无聊的行为。II *vi*. 做无聊的事;浪费时间。

fric·an·deau [ˈfrikændəu; ˋfrɪkændo] *n*. (*pl*. ～*x*, ～*z*) 〔F.〕油焖[烤]小牛肉[其他肉类]。

fric·an·do [ˈfrikændəu; ˋfrɪkənˏdo] *n*. (*pl*. = ～*es*) fricandeau.

fric·as·see [ˌfrikəˈsi:; ˏfrɪkəˋsi] I *n*. 〔F.〕油焖[油煎]原汁肉块。II *vt*. 油焖[油煎](原汁肉块)。

fric·a·tive [ˈfrikətiv; ˋfrɪkətɪv] I *a*.【语音】摩擦的,由摩擦产生的。～ **consonants** 摩擦子音。II *n*.【语音】摩擦音。

Frick(e) [frik; frɪk] *n*. 弗里克〔姓氏〕。

fric·tion [ˈfrikʃən; ˋfrɪkʃən] *n*. 1. 摩擦,阻力。2. 倾轧,冲突,不和 (*between*)。3. 擦热皮肤。*moist* ～【医】湿擦。～ **ball**, ～**-ball** (轴承中的)滚珠。～ **band**【矿】摩阻带。～ **brake** 摩擦制动器,摩擦刹车。～ **clutch** 摩擦离合器。～ **cone** 摩擦(锥)轮。～ **drive** 摩擦传动。～ **gear(ing)** 摩擦传动装置。～ **monger** 挑拨离间,制造不和的人。～ **tape** (导体外面包的)绝缘胶布;摩擦带。

fric·tion·al [ˈfrikʃənəl; ˋfrɪkʃənəl] *n*. 摩擦的,由摩擦而生的。～ **electricity** 摩擦电。～ **resistance** 摩擦阻力。**-ly** *ad*.

Fri·day [ˈfraidi; ˋfraɪdɪ] *n*. 星期五。*Black* [*Good*] ～ 耶稣受难日〔复活节前的星期五〕。*Man F-* 忠仆〔F- 原为《鲁滨逊漂流记》中一个忠于鲁滨逊的仆人的名字〕。**-s** *ad*. 星期五,每星期五。

fridge [fridʒ; frɪdʒ] *n*. 〔主英口〕电冰箱,冷冻机。

fried [fraid; fraɪd] I fry[1]的过去式及过去分词。II *a*. 1. 油煎的。2. 〔美俚〕喝醉了的。～ **cake** 油煎饼,炸面圈。～ **shirt** 〔美俚〕浆得笔挺的衬衫。

friend [frend; frɛnd] I *n*. 1. 友人,朋友 (*opp*. foe, enemy)。2. 〔称呼语〕朋友〔常作 My ～〕;〔英〕下议院议员间的称呼〔常作 My honourable ～〕;〔英〕法院律师间的称呼〔常作 My learned ～〕。3. 自己人;支持者,赞助者,同情者;助手,随从;〔*pl*.〕〔Scot.〕近亲,家属。4.【宗】公谊会(the Society of friends)教友。5. 有帮助的事物[本质]。*A* ～ *in need is a* ～ *indeed*. 〔谚〕患难朋友才是真朋友。*Old* ～*s and old wine are best*. 〔谚〕陈酒味醇,老友情深。*The best of* ～*s must part*. 〔谚〕天下无不散的筵席。*a boy* [*girl*] ～男[女]朋友。*bosom* [*close, great, good, sworn*] ～*s* 好朋友,心腹朋友。*My shyness here is my best* ～. 我的腼腆在这里对我很有好处。***a*** ～ ***at*** [***in***] ***court*** 有势力的朋友,好门路。***be*** [***make***] ～***s with*** 跟…要好,跟…做朋友。***keep*** ～***s with*** 跟…保持友好。***make*** ～ ***again*** 言归于好,重修旧好。***make*** ～***s of*** 和…为友,引…为同党。***part*** ～***s*** 不伤感情地分手(*Let us part* ～*s*. 让我们好聚好散)。II *vt*. 〔诗〕与…为友 (= befriend)。

friend·less [ˈfrendlis; ˋfrɛndlɪs] *a*. 没有朋友的,无依无靠的。**-ness** *n*.

friend·ly [ˈfrendli; ˋfrɛndlɪ] I *a*. (**-li·er**; **-li·est**) 1. 友好的;朋友似的,亲密的。2. 有帮助的,互助的。*a* ～ *game* [*match*] 友谊赛。*a* ～ *nation* 友邦。*a* ～ *shower* 及时雨。*a* ～ *society* 〔英〕互助会。～ *troops* 友军。***be*** ～ ***to*** 赞成。***be on*** ～ ***terms with*** = ***have*** ～ ***relations with*** 跟…友好。II *ad*. 友好地;朋友般地。～ **action** [**suit**] 目的在于解决疑点的友好诉讼。**-li·ly** *ad*. **-li·ness** *n*.

friend·ship [ˈfrendʃip; ˋfrɛndʃɪp] *n*. 友谊,友情;亲睦。*a* ～ *visit* 友好访问。***strike up a*** ～做起朋友来,建立友谊。

fri·er [ˈfraiə; ˋfraɪɚ] *n*. = fryer.

Frie·sian [ˈfri:ʒən; ˋfriʒən] *a*. = Frisian.

frieze[1] [fri:z; friz] I *n*. 起绒粗呢。II *vt*. 使(布上)起绒毛。～ **flannel** 棉毛法兰绒。

frieze[2] [fri:z; friz] *n*.【建】(柱的)中楣;带状装饰。～ **panel** 束腰板。～ **rail** 上腰板。

frig·ate [ˈfrigit; ˋfrɪgɪt] *n*. 1. (十八、十九世纪装有大炮

F

的)快速帆船。**2.** 驱逐领舰。**3.** 护卫舰,护航舰。～ **bird**【动】军舰鸟〔热带猛禽〕。

frig [frig; frɪg] *vt.* (**-gg-**)〔俚、卑〕与(女子)发生性行为。

frig(e) [fridʒ; frɪdʒ] *n.*〔英口〕冰箱(= refrigerator)。

frig·ging [ˈfrigiŋ; ˋfrɪgɪŋ] *a.*〔俚〕他妈的〔一个意义笼统的粗野的字眼〕(= damned)。

fright [frait; fraɪt] **I** *n.* **1.** 恐怖。**2.** 可怕的东西;难看的人。*a perfect* ～极可怕;丑陋的人。***die from*** [***of***] ～吓死。***get*** [***have***] ***a*** ～ 大吃一惊。***give a*** ～ 使某人受惊。***in a*** ～ 在惊恐之下。***take*** ～ ***at*** 因某事惊恐。**II** *vt.*〔诗〕= frighten.

fright·en [ˈfraitn; ˋfraɪtn] *vt.* 使惊惧,吓唬。～ *a child into fits* 把小孩吓得抽风[不知人事]。～ *sb. out of an evil practice* 吓掉某人的坏习惯。～ *sb. into submission* 吓某人服从。～ *sb. away* 把某人吓走。— *vi.* 惊恐,害怕。*I don't* ～ *easily.* 我不会轻易就害怕。***be*** ～***ed at*** 受…惊吓,看见…大吃一惊。***be*** ～***ed of***〔口〕害怕,对…感到恐惧(*The child has always been* ～ *of the dark.* 这孩子一直怕黑暗)。***be*** ～***ed out of one's wits*** 被吓呆。

fright·ful [ˈfraitful; ˋfraɪtful] *a.* **1.** 可怕的,令人毛骨悚然的。**2.** 讨厌的,丑恶的。**3.**〔俚〕非常的。*have a* ～ *time* 真觉得不愉快。*a* ～ *bore*〔俚〕极讨厌的人。*a* ～ *scandal* 非常丢脸的事。**-ly** *ad.* **1.** 可怕地。**2.**〔俚〕非常地。**-ness** *n.* **1.** 恐怖;丑恶。**2.** (对占领地人民的)残暴政策。

frig·id [ˈfridʒid; ˋfrɪdʒɪd] *a.* **1.** 寒冷的。**2.** 冷淡的,生硬的。**3.** 索然无味的。**4.**【医】(妇女)性欲冷淡的〔*cf.* impotent〕。*the* ～ *zones* 寒带。*a* ～ *manner* 冷淡的态度。**-ly** *ad.* **-ness** *n.*

Frig·id·aire [ˌfridʒiˈdɛə; ˏfrɪdʒɪˋdɛr] *n.*〔美〕电冰箱〔原为一种商标名称〕。

fri·gid·i·ty [friˈdʒiditi; frɪˋdʒɪdətɪ] *n.* **1.** 寒冷;冷淡。**2.** 索然无味。**3.**【医】(妇女)性欲冷淡。

frig·o·rif·ic [ˌfrigəˈrifik; ˏfrɪgəˋrɪfɪk] *a.* 致冷的;冷冻的;冷却的。

frig·o·rim·e·ter [frigəˈrimitə; frɪgəˋrɪmətɚ] *n.* 低温计。

fri·jol(e) [ˈfri:həul; ˋfrihol] *n.* (*pl.* ***fri·joles*** [-z;-z])【植】豇豆。～ **refritos** 炒豆〔墨西哥和美国南部常吃的一种菜豆〕。

frill [fril; frɪl] **I** *n.* **1.** 褶边。**2.**【摄】胶片边缘的皱褶。**3.**【动】壳皱。**4.**〔*pl.*〕〔俚〕摆架子;〔美〕虚饰。**4.**〔美俚〕女孩,妇女。***put on*** ～***s***〔俚〕摆架子,装腔作势。**II** *vi.* (胶片边缘)起皱褶。— *vt.* 在…上加褶边。**-ed** *a.* 有饰边的。**-er·y** *n.* 衣褶边。

frill·ies [ˈfriliz; ˋfrɪlɪz] *n. pl.*〔俚〕镶有褶边的裙子。

frill·y [ˈfrili; ˋfrɪlɪ] *a.* 镶褶边的。

fringe [frindʒ; frɪndʒ] **I** *n.* **1.** (地毯等的)穗,须边,流苏;缘饰。**2.** (森林等最外面的)边缘;〔喻〕(知识等的)初步,皮毛。**3.** (动植物的)伞;缘缨。**4.** 前刘海。**5.**【物】(光线中的)条纹。**6.** 略知皮毛的人。**7.** = ～ benefit. *a* ～ *of* (*beard*) 一嘴(胡子)。*the mere* ～*s of philosophy* 哲学的皮毛。*diffraction* ～【物】衍射条纹,绕射条纹。*interference* ～【物】干涉条纹。**II** *vt.* **1.** 给…加穗饰。**2.** 使成为缘饰,成为…的边缘。*houses fringing the road on either side* 点缀在路两边的房屋。**III** *a.*〔美〕**1.** 边缘的,外围的。**2.** 次要的,附加的。～ **area**【无】线条区,电视接收边缘区,散乱边缘区,干扰区域。～ **benefit** (工资外的)补贴〔如年金、工资照付的假期、保险金等〕。～ **theatre**〔英〕**1.** (多上演实验性剧本且票价低廉的)末流戏院。**2.** (末流戏院上演的)实验戏剧。～ **tree**【植】流苏树属植物(尤指美国流苏树)。**-less** *a.* **-like** *a.*

fringed [frindʒd; frɪndʒd] *a.* = fringy. ～ **gentian**【植】穗裂龙胆〔产于美国北部和加拿大〕。～ **polygala**【植】少叶远志〔产于北美东部〕。

fring·ing [ˈfrindʒiŋ; ˋfrɪndʒɪŋ] *n.*【无】**1.** 边缘现象,散射现象,边缘通量(的形式)。**2.** 彩色电视中同步不够时用转盘调整色帧。～ **reef**【地】靠近海岸而与海岸平行的珊瑚礁,裙礁,岸礁,边礁。～ **sea** 边缘海。

Fringlish [ˈfriŋgliʃ; ˋfrɪŋglɪʃ] *n.*〔或 f-〕法国化英语,夹有法语的英语。

fring·y [ˈfrindʒi; ˋfrɪndʒɪ] *a.* (***fring·i·er***; ***-i·est***) 穗状的,有穗状缘饰的。

frip·per·y [ˈfripəri; ˋfrɪpərɪ] *n.* **1.** (衣服等)俗气的装饰;(文体等)拙劣的修饰。**2.** 浮夸;无聊的东西。

Fris·bee [ˈfrizbi:; ˋfrɪzbi] *n.*〔美〕〔或 f-; frisby〕飞盘〔塑料制圆盘形往来投掷的玩具,后发展成为运动器具〕。

Fris·co [ˈfriskəu; ˋfrɪsko] *n.*〔美口〕= San Francisco.

fri·sé [friˈzei; frɪˋze] *n.* (家具包面用的)卷毛厚绒织物。

fri·sette [friˈzet; frɪˋzɛt] *n.*〔罕〕妇女额前卷发,前刘海。

fri·seur [friˈzə:; frɪˋzɚ] *n.*〔F.〕(为妇女理发的)理发师。

Fri·sian [ˈfriziən; ˋfrɪʒən] **I** *a.* **1.** 法里孙群岛的。**2.** 法里孙人的。**3.** 法里孙语的。**II** *n.* **1.** 法里孙人;法里孙群岛人。**2.** 荷兰北部古条顿人。**3.** 法里孙语〔与古英语有关系的法里孙的西日耳曼语〕。～ **Islands** 法里孙群岛〔北欧德国、荷兰及丹麦沿海一带的群岛〕。

frisk [frisk; frɪsk] **I** *n.* **1.** (猫儿等)欢跃,蹦跳;快活的时刻。**2.**〔俚〕搜身。**II** *vi.* 欢跃,跳跳蹦蹦。— *vt.* **1.** (轻快地)摇动。**2.**〔俚〕搜查(身体)。**3.**〔俚〕扒窃。

fris·ket [ˈfriskit; ˋfrɪskɪt] *n.*【印】夹纸框。

frisk·y [ˈfriski; ˋfrɪskɪ] *a.* (***frisk·i·er***; ***-i·est***) 欢跃的,活泼的。**-i·ly** *ad.* **-i·ness** *n.*

fris·son [friˈsɔn; frɪˋsɑn] *n.* (*pl.* ～*s* [-ˈsɔn; -ˋsɑn])〔F.〕(由激动、恐惧或喜悦引起的)颤抖(尤指阅读惊险小说等引起的感觉)。

frit [frit; frɪt] **I** *n.* 玻(璃)料;烧料。**II** *vt.* 烧结,用加热方法处理(玻璃料)。～ **fly** 一种小蝇(小麦害虫)。

frith [friθ; frɪθ] *n.* 河口,海口,海湾。

frit·il·lar·y [friˈtiləri; frɪˋtɪlˏɛrɪ] *n.* **1.**【植】贝母属。**2.**【动】豹纹蝴蝶。

frit·ter¹ [ˈfritə; ˋfrɪtɚ] *n.* **1.** 油炸馅饼。**2.**〔*pl.*〕鲸油渣(可作肥料)。*apple* ～*s* 油炸苹果馅饼。*oyster* ～*s* 油炸牡蛎馅饼。

frit·ter² [ˈfritə; ˋfrɪtɚ] **I** *vt.* **1.** 剁碎,弄碎。**2.** (一点一点地)浪费掉(*away*)。**II** *n.* 碎片。

fritz [frits; frɪts] **I** *n.*〔常 F-〕〔俚、贬〕德国人〔*cf.* Johk Bull〕;德国兵;德国飞机[潜艇等]。***on the*** ～〔美俚〕坏掉,不行了,有毛病。***on the terrific*** ～ 破烂不堪,要大大修理。**II** *vi.*〔美俚〕损坏[仅用于下列成语]:～ ***out*** (机器等)损坏,发生故障。

friv·ol [ˈfrivəl; ˋfrɪvəl] *vt.*, *vi.* (〔英〕***-ll-***)〔俚〕浪费时间(*away*),闲混,做无聊的事。

fri·vol·i·ty [friˈvɔliti; frɪˋvɑlətɪ] *n.* **1.** 轻佻,轻浮。**2.** 轻薄的话[举动]。

friv·o·lous [ˈfrivələs; ˋfrɪvələs] *a.* **1.** 轻佻的。**2.** 琐碎的,无意义的。**-ly** *ad.* **-ness** *n.*

fri·zette [friˈzet; frɪˋzɛt] *n.* = frisette.

friz, frizz¹ [friz; frɪz] **I** *n.* (*pl.* ***friz·zes***) 卷曲,卷结,卷曲的东西(如头发)。**II** *vt.*, *vi.* (***frizzed***; ***frizz·ing***) (使)卷曲,(使)卷结,(使)起绒毛。～**zing machine**【纺】卷结机,起球机。

frizz² [friz; frɪz] *vi.* (油炸物时)吱吱吱地响。

friz·zle¹ [ˈfrizl; ˋfrɪzl̩] **I** *n.* 卷发,小卷结,卷曲的状态。**II** *vt.*, *vi.* = friz.

friz·zle² [ˈfrizl; ˋfrɪzl̩] *vt.*, *vi.* (把肉等)炸焦,炸酥,炸得吱吱发响。

friz·zly, friz·zy [ˈfrizli, -zi; ˋfrɪzlɪ, -zɪ] *a.* 卷结的,鬈发的。

fro¹ [frəu; fro] *ad.* 向那边;向后。***to and*** ～ 往复,来回,前前后后。

fro² [frə, frəu; frə, fro] *prep.*〔英方〕= from.

Fro [frəu; fro] *n.*〔美俚〕非洲发型 = Afro.

Fro·bish·er [ˈfrəubiʃə; ˋfrobɪʃɚ] ***n***. 弗罗比舍〔姓氏〕。

frock [frɔk; frɑk] **I** ***n***. **1.** (妇女、小儿的连衣裙式)长衣。**2.** 长工作服;(船员的)毛绒卫生衣。**3.** 僧袍。**4.** 〔英〕长礼服式军服。**5.** 〔英〕= ~ coat. **II** ***vt***. **1.** 使穿长工作服[礼服,长衣服]。**2.** 授与…圣职。~ **coat** (男子)长礼服。

froe [frəu; fro] ***n***. 劈板斧〔柄与斧背成直角〕,锛。

Froe·bel [ˈfrəːbəl; ˋfrebəl], **Friedrich** 弗勒贝尔〔1782—1852,德国教育家,幼稚园创办人〕。

Froe·bel·lism [ˈfrɔːbəlizəm; ˋfrobəˏlɪzəm] ***n***. 弗勒贝尔的教育主张;弗勒贝尔式教育法。

frog [frɔg; frɑg] **I** ***n***. **1.** 蛙。**2.** 关节窝;(马蹄底中部的)蹄楔。**3.** 【铁路】辙叉,道岔。**4.** (腰皮带上的)挂剑圈,挂武器环。**5.** 盘花饰扣。**6.** 插花用底盘。**7.** (提琴弓上的)紧弦螺母。**8.** 〔F-〕〔贬〕法国佬,法国话。~ ***in the throat*** 嘎嘎声。**II** ***vi***. **1.** 捉青蛙。**2.** 〔美俚〕骗。~**eater** 食蛙者;〔F-〕〔贬〕法国人。~**fish** 【鱼】躄鱼科的鱼;鮟鱇鱼。~ **hair** 〔美俚〕用于政治竞选的钱。~ **hopper** 【动】沫蝉,吹沫虫。~ **hopping tactics** 【军】跳进战术,跳岛战术。~ **kick** 【体】蛙泳的蹬夹动作。~**-man** (*pl*. **-men**)蛙人;潜水员。~**-march** ***n***., ***vt***. 蛙式抬运〔使犯人面朝下平伏,由四人提着四肢行走〕。~ **spawn** 【植】红藻。

frog·gy [ˈfrɔgi; ˋfrɑgɪ] **I** ***a***. 多蛙的;蛙似的。**II** ***n***. 〔儿〕蛙;〔F-〕〔俚、贬〕法国人。

Froh·man [ˈfrəumən; ˋfromən] ***n***. 弗罗曼〔姓氏〕。

frol·ic [ˈfrɔlik; ˋfrɑlɪk] **I** ***n***. **1.** 嬉戏,玩乐。**2.** 狂欢的聚会。**II** ***vi***. (***frol·icked***; ***-ick·ing***) 嬉戏,玩闹。**III** ***a***. 〔古、诗〕嬉戏的,快乐的。~ **pad** 〔美俚〕夜总会,舞厅。**frol·ick·er** ***n***.

frol·ic·some [ˈfrɔliksəm; ˋfrɑlɪksəm] ***a***. 〔废〕嬉戏的,爱闹着玩的。**-ly** ***ad***. **-ness** ***n***.

from [强 frɔm, 弱 frəm, frm; frɑm, frəm, frm] ***prep***. **1.** 〔表示动作的起点〕从,自。*fall* ~ *the sky* 从天上落下。*jump* (*down*) ~ *a window* 从窗口跳下。*part* ~ *a friend* 跟朋友分离。(*re*)*move* ~ *one place to another* 从甲地迁到乙地。*set out* ~ *London* 从伦敦出发。~ *door* [*house*] *to door* [*house*] 挨门挨户。~ *place to place* 从一处到另一处,一处一处地。**2.** 〔表示顺序的起点〕从。*count* ~ *one to ten* 从一数到十。~ *childhood* 从幼年时起。~ *now on* 从今以后。~ *1st October* 从十月一日起。~ *that time onward* 从那时以后。~ *birth till death* 从生到死。~ *the beginning* 自始。~ *beginning to end* 自始至终。~ *time to time* 时时。**3.** 〔表示变更、转变的原来状态〕从。*awake* ~ *a dream* 从梦中醒来。*recover* ~ *illness* 从病中恢复。*go* ~ *bad to worse* 愈来愈坏。**4.** 〔表示距离、间隔〕*away* ~ *home* 离开家。*five years* ~ *now* 今后五年。*be absent* ~ *school* 缺课。*rest* ~ *work* 工作后〔(暂时)搁起工作〕休息。*How far is it* ~ *here?* 离开这里多远? **5.** 〔表示差异、区别、选择〕*differ* ~ *others* 跟别的不同。*know right* ~ *wrong* 辨别是非。*distinguish good* ~ *bad* 区别好坏。*choose* ~ 从…中选择。**6.** 〔表示解除、除去、停止、阻碍、防止、阻止〕*be expelled* ~ *school* 被学校开除。*take 3* ~ *10* 十减去三。*cannot refrain* ~ *laughing* 忍不住笑。*be prevented* ~ *coming in* 被阻止入内。*save oneself* ~ *falling* 使自己免于摔倒。**7.** 〔表示出处、来源、根源、根据〕*a letter* ~ *a friend* 朋友的来信。*quotations* ~ *Shakespeare* 引自莎士比亚的文句。*judge* ~ *sb.'s conduct* 根据某人的行为来判断。*People expect much* ~ *him*. 人们对他期望很大。~ *what I have heard* 根据我所听到的。**8.** 〔表示原因、动机、理由〕*die* ~ *cholera* 患霍乱而死。*act* ~ *a sense of duty* 出于责任感而行动。*suffer* ~ *influenza* 患流行性感冒。**9.** 〔表示原料、材料〕*make wine* ~ *grapes* 用葡萄酿酒。*Steel is made* ~ *iron*. 钢是生铁炼成的。★在制造过程中,原料形状或性质不变的用 of, 例如:That bridge is made of steel. 那座桥是用钢造的。**10.** 〔用于表示时间和地点的副词和前置词前〕从,自。~ *above* [*below*] 自上[下]。~ *within* [*without*] 从内[外]。~ *far and near* 从远处和左近。*choose a book* ~ *among these* 从这些书籍中选一册。~ *before the war* 自从战前。*speak* ~ *behind the door* 从门后说话。~ *over the sea* 从海外。~ *under the table* 从桌下。~ *of old* 自古以来。~ ***way back*** 从很久以前。~**-scratch** ***a***. 白手起家的,从零开始的。

fro·mage [frɔːˈmaːʒ; frɔˋmɑʒ] ***n***. 〔F.〕= cheese.

frond [frɔnd; frɑnd] ***n***. **1.** (羊齿,棕榈,海草等的)叶子。**2.** 【植】叶状体,植物体。**3.** 〔诗〕叶;棕榈复叶。**-age** ***n***. 〔集合词〕叶丛,茂盛的叶。

fron·des·cence [frɔnˈdesns; frɑnˋdɛsns] ***n***. **1.** 【植】发叶过程,发叶状态,发叶期。**2.** 叶子,叶丛。**-des·cent** ***a***.

fron·dose [ˈfrɔndəus; ˋfrɑndos] ***a***. 【植】叶状体的;有叶的;多叶的。

frons [frɔnz; frɑnz] ***n***. 【动】(昆虫的)额。

front [frʌnt; frʌnt] **I** ***n***. **1.** 前部,前面;正面;(剧场的)正面[前面]座位〔也可指全部观众席位〕(*opp*. back, rear)。**2.** 【军】前线;战线,战地;【政】阵线。**3.** (房屋的)正面,门面,方向;(道路、河、海等的)边;〔the ~〕〔英〕海滨人行道。**4.** (妇女的)额前头发;(衬衫的)硬衬胸;领结;(祭坛前面的)帷子(等)。**5.** 门面;相貌,模样儿;装模作样,厚脸皮;〔诗〕额。**6.** 【语】舌前,硬颚;舌前音。**7.** 【气】锋〔冷热空气团分界处〕。**8.** (企业、团体等的)挂名负责人,出面人物;幌子,掩护物。**9.** 〔美〕现况,现状。**10.** 〔美〕前面的那位〔指最近边的服务员,常于呼唤时用〕。*a question at the* ~ 当前的问题。*the east* ~(房屋的)东面。*a river* ~ 河边。*a united* ~ 联合战线。*cold* ~【气】冷锋。***be at the*** ~ 在前线。***bring to the*** ~ 使出名。***change*** ~ 改变看法[态度],【军】变换方向。***come to the*** ~ 出名;变得明显,引人注目。***false*** ~ 假外表;骗人的企图。~ ***to*** ~ 〔古〕面对面。***get in*** ~ ***of oneself*** 〔美口〕赶紧。***go to the*** ~ 上前线,出征。***have the*** ~ (*to do*) 居然有脸,竟好意思…。***head and*** ~ 主要部分。***in*** ~ 在前方,在正对面;在人注意的地方。***in*** ~ ***of*** 在…的前面。***out*** ~ 在观众席上。***present*** [***put on***, ***show***] ***a bold*** ~ ***on*** 装出勇敢大胆的样子。***put a bold*** ~ ***on*** 勇敢地对付。***put up a*** ~ 设门窗;装饰门面。***to the*** ~ 在场,还活着。***up*** ~ **1.** 在前面。**2.** 预先。**II** ***a***. **1.** 前面的,最前的;正面的。**2.** 【语】舌前的。*the* ~ *row* 前排。*a* ~ *door* 前门。**III** ***ad***. 在[向]前面。*Eyes* ~! (口令)向前看! **IV** ***vt***. **1.** 面向;对抗。**2.** 【语】把…发成舌前音,把(发音部位)移前。**3.** 【军】向着(敌军等的)正面。**4.** 装饰…的正面。**5.** 把…附在前面(*with*)。**6.** 领导(乐队)。*The hotel* ~*s the sea*. 饭店面临大海。~ *difficulties* 正视困难,不怕艰难。*Marble will* ~ *the building*. 大楼的正面将以大理石作装饰。— ***vi***. **1.** 面对(*on*)。**2.** 为…作掩护(*for*)。*The house* ~*s on the sea*. 房屋面向大海。~ ***for*** 〔美俚〕主办,后援,推荐;对…负责。~**bencher** (英国下院的)前座议员,前排席位议员。~ **edge** 前沿,光锋。~**-end processor** 【计】前端处理机〔将数据从终端设备发送到计算机又发送回终端设备的数据处理系统中的一个装置〕。~ **lash** 〔美〕(对不利的强烈反应所作的)对应反应(以便起抵销或中和作用)。~ **line** 前线,第一线。~**-line** ***a***. 前线的,第一线的。~ **man** (企业、团体的)挂名负责人,出面人物。~ **matter** 书籍正文前的材料〔序言、目录、用法说明等〕。~ **money** 〔美〕预付款,定购货款。~ **office** **1.** (公司的)董事会,理事会。**2.** (机关、企业中的)全体决策人员。~ **page** **1.** (书的)标题页。**2.** (报纸)头版。~**-page** **1.** ***a***. 有在头版上登载价值的;重要的,轰动的。**2.** ***vt***. 把…登在头版上。~ **room** 前屋(尤指起坐室)。~ **runner** **1.** 比赛中领先者。**2.** 遥遥领先者〔如赛马〕。~ **view** 正面图,正视图。

front·age [ˈfrʌntidʒ; ˋfrʌntɪdʒ] ***n***. **1.** (房屋的)正面,前

F

面;正面宽度;面对方向,眼界。2. 路边地,河边地,屋前空地。3.【军】扎营地。-r n. 临街[临河]空地的所有者。

fron·tal [ˈfrʌntl; ˋfrʌntl] I a. 1. 前面的,正面的 (*opp.* back; rear)。2. 额部的,前额的。*a* ~ *attack* 正面攻击。II n. 额骨;额前装饰物(如发带,头帕);(祭坛前面的)帷子;(房屋的)正面,(门、窗上面的)人字形小墙(檐),三角楣。~ **bone** 额骨。~ **fog**【气】锋面雾。~ **lobe**【解】额叶。**-ly** *ad*.

fron·tier [ˈfrʌntjə, ˈfrɔn-; ˋfrʌntɪɚ, ˋfrɑn-] I n. 1. 边疆;边界,边缘。2. 新开辟地,边地;〔美〕边疆城市。3. 〔常 *pl*.〕(知识等的)尚待开发的领域。*the* ~*s of medicine* [*science*] 医学[科学]新领域。II a. 1. 边疆的。2. 新垦地的,边地的。~ *guards* 边防战士。*a* ~ *town* 边疆城市。~ **spirit** 〔美〕开拓精神;进取精神;美国西部开发时期的边民精神。

fron·tiers·man [ˈfrʌntjəzmən; frʌntɪrˋzmən] n. (*pl*. *-men*) 〔美〕边疆居民;边疆开发者。

fron·tis·piece [ˈfrʌntispiːs, ˈfrɔn-; ˋfrʌntɪsˏpis, ˋfrɑn-] I n. 1. (书籍的)卷首插画;〔罕〕扉页。2.【建】主立面,正门;(门、窗上面的)饰壁,人字形小墙(檐),三角楣。3. 〔俚〕脑门,天庭。II vt. 1. 给(书)加进卷首插画。2. 把…画入卷首插图。

front·less [ˈfrʌntlis; ˋfrʌntlɪs] a. 1. 无前部的,无正部的。2. 〔古〕无耻的。

front·let [ˈfrʌntlit; ˋfrʌntlɪt] n. 1. 额带,额饰;【宗】额上护符;(兽类或禽类的)前额。2. 祭坛前面帐子上的飘带。

fron·to·gen·e·sis [ˌfrʌntəuˈdʒenisis; ˏfrʌntoˋdʒɛnɪsɪs] n.【气】锋生(作用)。

fron·tol·y·sis [frʌnˈtɔlisis; frʌnˋtɑlɪsɪs] n.【气】锋消(作用)。

fron·ton [ˈfrɔntɔn, Sp. frəunˈtəun; ˋfrɑntɑn, Sp. fronˋton] n. 1. 回力球场。2. 〔墨西哥〕回力球戏 (= jai alai)。

frore [frɔː, frɔə; frɔr, fror] a. 〔诗、古〕霜冻的;极冷的。

frosh [frɔʃ; frɑʃ] n. 〔美口〕大学一年级生。

Frost [frɔst; frɑst] n. 1. 弗罗斯特〔姓氏〕。2. **Robert Lee** ~ 罗伯特·弗罗斯特〔1874—1963,美国诗人〕。

frost [frɔst, frɔːst; frɑst, frɔst] I n. 1. 霜;霜柱;结霜;冰冻,严寒;冰点以下的温度。2. (态度、感情等的)冷淡,冷酷。3. 〔俚〕(演剧、出版物宴会、旅行等的)失败;扫兴。*a heavy* [*hard, severe*] ~酷寒。*ten degrees of* ~冰点下十度。*The dance turned out a* ~. 舞蹈节目完全失败。***a dead*** ~ 〔俚〕彻底失败。~ ***in the ground*** 地中霜柱,地面冻结。***Jack F-*** 霜精,严寒。II vt. 1. 在…上覆以霜;霜害(植物等);〔喻〕使意气沮丧。2. 使(玻璃、金属等表面)无光泽,使(头发)霜白;在(糕饼等上)加糖霜。3. 在(马蹄铁上)加钉防滑。— vi. 〔罕〕1. 起霜,受冻。2. (油漆的表面等)干成霜状。*It* ~*s*. 下霜。~**-bite** 1. n. 冻伤,霜害。2. vt. 冻伤,使遭霜害。~ **bite boating** 〔美〕冬季赛艇运动。~ **biter** 〔美〕冬季赛艇运动用的赛艇。~**biting** = ~ bite boating. ~ **bitten** a. 1. 受霜害的;被冻伤的;生冻疮的(*get one's limbs* ~ *bitten* 手脚全生冻疮)。2. 冷酷无情的,冷淡的。~**-bound** a. 1. (土地等)冰冻的。2. 冷冰冰的,不热情的。~ **fish**【动】1. = tomcod. 2. 初霜时节出现的几种鱼。~ **flower**【植】紫苑属。~**-hardy** a. 抗寒的,耐寒的。~ **heave** (道路的)冻胀,冰冻隆胀。~ **line**【气】霜线。~ **snow** 冰晶。~**work** (窗上冻结的)霜花;(银器等的)霜花纹装饰。~**less** a. 无霜的,无霜冻的。

frost·ed [ˈfrɔstid; ˋfrɔstɪd] I a. 1. 霜盖着的;冻结了的;受了霜害的;冻伤了的;(蔬菜等)经过快速冰冻的。2. (须、发等)变白了的;(糕饼)盖有霜状混合物的;(玻璃、金属等)霜状表面的,无光泽的,磨砂的。3. (态度等)冷淡的。*a* ~ *bulb* 磨砂灯泡。~ *glass* 毛玻璃,磨砂玻璃。*a pair of* ~ *jeans* 一条水磨牛仔裤。II n. (牛奶、糖浆、冰淇淋等做的)一种甜饮料。

frost·ing [ˈfrɔːstiŋ; ˋfrɔstɪŋ] n. 1. 糖霜〔糖、奶油、调料、水或其他汁、蛋白等的混合物,用作糕点面上的盖浇物〕。2. (玻璃、金属等的)磨砂面。3. 玻璃粉、油彩等的混合物〔作装璜用〕。

frost·y [ˈfrɔsti; ˋfrɑstɪ] a. 1. 霜冻的,下霜的,严寒的;冻结的;霜似的,霜白的。2. 冷淡的,无情的。3. (须、发等)白的、灰白的;〔喻〕年老的。*the* ~ *years of life* 老年。*a* ~ *smile* 冷笑。*give sb. a* ~ *stare* 冷冷地凝视某人。**-i·ly** *ad*. **-i·ness** n.

froth [frɔθ, frɔːθ; frɑθ, frɔθ] I n. 1. 泡,泡沫;口边白沫。2. 渣滓,废物。3. 浅薄的意见,空想,空谈。*a lot of verbal* ~花言巧语。~ *at the mouth* 嘴角上的涎沫。II vt. 1. 使生泡沫。2. 用轻松的东西装饰。— vi. 起泡沫。~**-blower** 〔英谑〕爱喝啤酒的人。

froth·y [ˈfrɔθi; ˋfrɔθɪ] a. 1.起泡沫的;多泡沫的。2. 空虚的,浅薄的。3. 质料轻薄的。*a* ~ *orator* 空话连篇的演说者。**-i·ly** *ad*. **-i·ness** n.

Froude [fruːd; frud] n. 弗鲁德〔姓氏〕。

frou·frou [ˈfruːfruː; ˋfruˏfru] n. 1. (女子丝绸裙子等的)沙沙声。2. (能发沙沙声的)下摆垂饰;(女子服装上)过分多的装饰〔如穗边、丝带、褶边等〕。3. 〔口〕过分精致。

frounce [frauns; fraʊns] I vt., vi. 〔废〕(使)卷曲,(使)卷缩。II n. 〔古〕虚夸的展示。

frow[1] [frau; fraʊ] n. 1. 荷兰[德国]妇女。2. 妇女,妻子。

frow[2] [frəu; fro] n. = froe.

fro·ward [ˈfrəuəd; ˋfroɚd] a. 1. 难驾驶的;桀骜不驯的。2. 〔古〕不利的。**-ly** *ad*. **-ness** n.

frown [fraun; fraʊn] I n. 皱眉,蹙额。~*s of fortune* 倒运。II vi. 1. 皱眉,蹙额。2. 皱眉头表示厌恶[反对] (*at*; *on*; *upon*)。— vt. 1. 用皱眉蹙额对…表示不满。2. 皱眉蹙额表示(不满)。~ *sb. into silence* 皱眉使某人闭嘴。~ *one's displeasure* 皱眉表示不快。~ ***down*** 用皱眉蹙额压制住(反对者等使不敢讲话)。

frowst [fraust; fraʊst] I n. 〔英口〕屋内的闷热,霉臭,陈腐的气味。II vi. 〔英〕闷居室内。

frowst·y [ˈfrausti; ˋfraʊstɪ] a. 〔口〕闷热的,霉臭的。

frow·zy, -sy [ˈfrauzi, ˋfraʊzɪ] a. 1. 霉臭的;难闻的;闷热的。2. 邋遢的。**frowz·i·ly** *ad*. **-i·ness** n.

froze [frəuz; froz] freeze 的过去式。

fro·zen [ˈfrəuzn; ˋfrozn̩] I freeze 的过去分词。II a. 1. 冰冻的。2. 冻结的。3. 冻僵[冻伤、冻死]了的。4. 极冷的。5. 冷淡的。6. 〔美〕(事实、真理等)不可推翻的,不容否认的。~ *bean curd* 冻豆腐。~ *custard* 冰冻乳蛋糕。~ *food* 冰冻食品。~ *meat* 冻肉。~ *plants* 冻伤的植物。*a* ~ *section* 冰冻切片。*a* ~ *stream* 冻了冰的河流。*the* ~ *zones* 寒带。*the* ~ *limit* 〔口〕令人无法容忍的限度。~ **assets**【商】冻结资产。~ **credits** 冻结债务。~ **frame** (电影等的)静止镜头 (= freeze frame)。~ **loans** 呆账。~ **sleep**【医】冷眠疗法;超低体温。~ **sucker** 冰棍,棒冰。**-ly** *ad*. 冷淡地;〔美〕顽固地。

frs. = francs.

F.R.S., FRS = Fellow of the Royal Society 〔英〕皇家学会会员。

frt. = freight.

fruc·tif·er·ous [frʌkˈtifərəs; frʌkˋtɪfərəs] a.【植】结果实的。

fruc·ti·fi·ca·tion [ˌfrʌktifiˈkeiʃən; ˏfrʌktɪfɪˋkeʃən] n.【植】结实;果实;结实器官。

fruc·ti·fy [ˈfrʌktifai; ˋfrʌktəfaɪ] vi., vt. (*-fied*)【植】(使)结果实。

fruc·tose [ˈfrʌktəus; ˋfrʌktos] n.【化】果糖,左旋糖。

fruc·tu·ous [ˈfrʌktjuəs; ˋfrʌktjuəs] a. = fruitful.

frug [fruːg; frug] I n. 扭摆舞〔摇摆舞的一种,着重腰身,头部,肩臂的扭动。脚腿几乎不动〕。II vi. 跳扭摆舞。

fru·gal [ˈfruːgəl; ˋfrugl̩] a. 节俭的;俭朴的。*be* ~ *of* 节约。**-ly** *ad*.

fru·gal·i·ty [fruːˈgæliti; fruˋgæləti] ***n.*** 节俭;俭朴。

fru·giv·o·rous [fruːˈdʒivərəs; fruˋdʒɪvərəs] ***a.*** 【动】食果实(为生)的。

fruit [fruːt; frut] **I** ***n.*** **1.** 实,果实〔*cf.* berry, capsule, drupe, legume, nut, pome〕;水果。★单数也可用作集合名词;复数指各种水果;作为食品时 fruit 是不可数名词。**2.**〔*sing.*, *pl.*〕结果,效果;〔常 *pl.*〕产品,(…的)产物;收获;〔*pl.*〕收入,利益;〔古〕小孙;年幼的人;小兽。**3.**〔美俚〕下流家伙,搞同性恋爱的男子;精神不正常的人。**4.**〔美俚〕容易受骗的人。*Forbidden ~ is sweet.*〔谚〕禁果分外甜〔被禁止的东西更加吸引人〕。*fresh* [*dried*] ~鲜[干]果。*preserved* ~果脯。*bear* ~结果实,发生效果。*the ~s of one's labour* 劳动果实。*the ~ of the body* [*loins*, *womb*] 子女。*the ~s of the earth* [*ground*] 土地的产物,农作物。***eat the bitter ~ of one's own doings*** [***making***] 自食其果。***Old ~!***〔英口〕喂,老兄〔对好朋友的招呼〕。***top one's ~*** 把好水果盖在坏水果上面,粉饰门面。**II** ***vi.***, ***vt.*** (使)结果实。~ **bat**【动】大蝙蝠亚目〔如:狐蝠〕。~-**bearer** 结果实的树。~**cake** 嵌有水果[葡萄干等]的糕饼,水果蛋糕。~ **cocktail** [**cup**] 糖水水果[餐前或餐后小吃]。~ **fly** 实蝇科的小蝇;果蝇。~ **juice** 水果汁。~ **knife** 水果刀。~-**machine**〔口〕吃角子老虎〔即 slot machine, 因为滚筒上绘有各种水果,故名〕。~ **piece** 水果的静物画[雕刻]。~ **ranch** (大)果园。~ **seeder** 水果去核器。~ **sugar** 果糖。~ **tree** 果树。~**wood** (做家具、镶板等的)果木。~ **zone** 果树带。

fruit·age [ˈfruːtidʒ; ˋfrutɪdʒ] ***n.*** **1.** 果实。**2.** 果实产量;〔集合词〕水果。**3.** 结果实,结子;结果,成果,产物。

fruit·ar·i·an [fruːˈtɛəriən; fruˋtɛrɪən] ***n.*** 用果实当常食的人,果实主义者。

fruit·ed [ˈfruːtid; ˋfrutɪd] ***a.*** **1.** 结有果实的。**2.** 加水果调味的。

fruit·er [ˈfruːtə; ˋfrutə˞] ***n.*** **1.** 水果装运船。**2.** 果树。**3.** 果树栽培者,果农。

fruit·er·er [ˈfruːtərə; ˋfrutərə˞] ***n.***〔主英〕水果商。

fruit·er·ess [ˈfruːtəris; ˋfrutərɪs] ***n.***〔英〕女水果商。

fruit·ful [ˈfruːtful; ˋfrutfəl] ***a.*** **1.** 果实累累的,多产的;肥沃的;丰饶的。**2.** 效果好的,收益多的。*a session ~ in great measures* 重要议案多的议会。*a ~ occupation* 收入多的职业。*a ~ vine* 结得多的葡萄;多产的女人。**-ly** ***ad.*** **-ness** ***n.***

fruit·ing [ˈfruːtiŋ; ˋfrutɪŋ] **body**【生】子实体。

fru·i·tion [fru(ː)ˈiʃən; fru(ʊ)ˋɪʃən] ***n.*** **1.** 结果实。**2.** 成就,实现。**3.** 享有,享受。*the ~ of one's studies* 研究的成果。***be brought to*** = ***come to ~*** (计划等)可以实现,有结果,有收获。

fruit·less [ˈfruːtlis; ˋfrutlɪs] ***a.*** **1.** 不结果实的。**2.** 无效[结]果的;无益的。**-ly** ***ad.*** **-ness** ***n.***

fruit·y [ˈfruːti; ˋfrutɪ] ***a.*** **1.** 果实状的;有水果香味的;(葡萄酒)有葡萄味的。**2.** 丰腴的,(声音)圆润的。**3.**〔美俚〕(故事等)有趣味的。**4.**〔美俚〕猥亵的,粗俗的;精神不正常的;搞男性同性恋的;(男子)女模女样的。

fru·men·ta·ceous [ˌfruːmenˈteiʃəs; ˏfrumenˋteʃəs] ***a.*** 小麦[谷类]的;谷类[小麦]制的;似谷类[小麦]的。

fru·men·ty [ˈfruːmənti; ˋfruməntɪ] ***n.***〔英〕牛奶麦粥。

frump [frʌmp; frʌmp] ***n.*** **1.** 服装邋遢的女人。**2.**〔常 *pl.*〕〔英方〕情绪不好,不高兴。**3.** 守旧者,老古董,老顽固。

frump·ish [ˈfrʌmpiʃ; ˋfrʌmpɪʃ] ***a.*** **1.** (妇女)衣服邋遢的。**2.**〔古〕脾气坏的。**-ly** ***ad.*** **-ness** ***n.***

frump·y [ˈfrʌmpi; ˋfrʌmpɪ] ***a.*** = frumpish. **-i·ly** ***ad.*** **-i·ness** ***n.***

Frun·ze [ˈfrunze; ˋfrunzɛ] ***n.*** 伏龙芝〔吉尔吉斯城市〕。

frus·ta [ˈfrʌstə; ˋfrʌstə] frustum 的复数。

frus·trate [frʌsˈtreit; frʌsˋtret] **I** ***vt.*** **1.** 挫败(敌人);破坏(计划等),阻挠。**2.** 使失败,使落空。***be ~d in*** 在…方面归于失败;终成画饼。**II** [ˈfrʌstrit; ˋfrʌstrɪt] ***a.*** **1.**〔古〕无益的,无效的。**2.** 受挫折的;被破坏的;失败了的。**3.** 沮丧的。

frus·tra·tion [frʌsˈtreiʃən; frʌsˋtreʃən] ***n.*** 挫折,失败,落空。

frus·tule [ˈfrʌstʃuːl; ˋfrʌstʃul] ***n.***【植】(矽[硅])藻细胞。

frus·tum [ˈfrʌstəm; ˋfrʌstəm] ***n.*** (*pl.* **~s**, **-ta** [-tə; -tə]) **1.**【数】平截头体。**2.**【建】柱身。~ *of a cone* 圆锥截体。

fru·tes·cent [fruːˈtesnt; fruˋtɛsn̩t] ***a.***【植】灌木的,灌木状[性]的。

fru·tex [ˈfruːteks; ˋfrutɛks] ***n.*** (*pl.* **-ti·ces** [-tisiːz; -tɪsiz])【植】灌木。

fru·ti·cose [ˈfruːtikəus; ˋfrutəˏkos] ***a.***【植】灌木的,灌木状的。

fry[1] [frai; fraɪ] **I** ***vt.***, ***vi.*** (***fried***; ***fry·ing***) **1.** 用油煎,用油炸;烤;炒。**2.**〔美俚〕(使)被处电刑。~ ***in one's own grease*** 作法自毙,自作自受。~ ***the fat out of*** (*business men*, *etc.*)【美政】使(实业家等)出钱。*have other fish to ~* 别有要事〔见 fish 条〕。**II** ***n.*** **1.** 油炸物;〔英〕油炸杂碎。**2.**〔美〕油煎品聚餐[野餐]。**3.**〔口〕烦恼,愤激。*a fish ~*备有油炸鱼的野餐会。~**pan**〔美〕= ~**ing pan.**

fry[2] [frai; fraɪ] ***n.*** 〔*sing.*, *pl.*〕**1.** 鱼秧,鱼苗,小鱼。**2.** 鱼苗群。**3.** 小生物群〔蜂、蛙等〕。*small* [*lesser*, *young*] ~ **1.** 小鱼群。**2.**〔蔑〕小崽子,后生小子。**3.** 零杂物件。

Fry(e) [frai; fraɪ] ***n.*** 弗赖伊〔姓氏〕。

fry·er [ˈfraiə; ˋfraɪə˞] ***n.*** **1.** 做油炸食品的人。**2.** 油炸锅。**3.** (适于)油炸的食品(如小鸟、鱼等)。

fry·ing pan [ˈfraiiŋ pæn; ˋfraɪɪŋ pæn] ***n.*** 油炸锅。***leap*** [***jump***] ***out of the ~ into the fire*** 跳出油锅落入烈火,境遇越来越糟。

FRZ = freeze.

FS = **1.** field service 野战勤务。**2.** Fleet Surgeon 海军军医。

F.S. = **1.** factor of safety 安全系数。**2.** finisher scutcher【纺】末道清棉机。

F.S.A. = **1.** Farm Security Administration〔美旧〕农户社会保险局。**2.** Federal Security Agency〔美旧〕联邦社会保险署。**3.** Fellow of the Society of Arts 艺术学会会员。

FSCC = Federal Surplus Commodities Corporation〔美旧〕联邦剩余商品公司。

F.S.E. = Fellow of the Society of Engineers〔英〕工程学会会员。

FSH = follicle-stimulating hormone【生】滤[卵]泡刺激素。

FSI = free standing insert〔附在报纸插页广告上的〕购物折扣优惠券。

FSLIC = Federal Savings and Loan Insurance Corporation〔美〕联邦储蓄贷款保险公司。

FSO = foreign service officer〔美〕驻外使领馆官员;外事官员。

F.S.S. = Fellow of the (Royal) Statistical Society〔英〕(皇家)统计学会会员。

ft. = **1.** foot; feet. **2.** fort.

FTC = **1.** Federal Trade Commission〔美〕联邦贸易委员会。**2.** Flying Training Command〔英〕飞行训练司令部。

fth(m). = fathom 英寻〔测海深单位〕。

ft-lb = foot-pound 英尺-磅。

ft./s. = feet per second 英尺/(每)秒。

fub·sy [ˈfʌbzi; ˋfʌbzɪ] ***a.***〔英方〕肥胖的,矮胖的。

fuch·sia [ˈfjuːʃə; ˋfjuʃə] **I** ***n.*** **1.**【植】倒挂金钟属;灯笼海棠。**2.** 紫红色。**II** ***a.*** 紫红色的。

fuch·sin(e) [ˈfuːksin; ˋfuksɪn] ***n.***【化】(碱性)品红,玫苯胺红。

fu·ci [ˈfjuːsai; ˋfjusaɪ] fucus 的复数。

fuck [fʌk; fʌk] **I** *vt*. **1.** 〔俚〕(男子)与…性交。**2.** 欺骗。**3.** 利用,占…的便宜。— *vi*. 〔俚〕性交。~ ***about*** [***around***] 〔俚〕乱管闲事;胡闹。~ ***a duck*** 〔俚〕他妈的;去你的。~ ***it*** 〔俚〕**1.** 嗳呀,滚开。**2.** 算了吧;别啰嗦了。~ ***off*** [***up***] **1.** 〔俚〕走开。**2.** 浪费时间。**3.** 嘲弄;吊儿郎当。**4.** 闯祸;搞糟;犯错误;使计划失败。***F- you*** (***charley***)! 〔俚〕滚你的! **II** *n*. 〔俚〕**1.** 性交。**2.** 些微,一点。*I don't give a* ~. 我才不管哩。**III** *int*. 〔俚〕他妈的! 混帐! 滚开! ~**off**, ~**up** *n*. 〔俚〕**1.** 大错误。**2.** 老犯错误的人。

fucked [fʌkt; fʌkt] *a*. 〔俚〕**1.** 受骗的,上当的。**2.** 失败的;弄死了的。~ ***out*** 〔俚〕精疲力竭的。~ ***up*** 〔俚〕**1.** 混乱的,乱七八糟的。**2.** (不必要地)被弄复杂了的。**3.** 因个人(生活)问题而陷于窘境的。

fuck·ing [ˈfʌkiŋ; ˋfʌkɪŋ] **I** *n*. 〔俚〕性交。**II** *a*. = fucky.

fuck·y [ˈfʌki; ˋfʌkɪ] *a*. 〔俚〕**1.** 该死的。**2.** 难做的,难完成的。**3.** 低劣的,讨厌的,丑恶的。**4.** 乱七八糟的。

fu·coid [ˈfjuːkɔid; ˋfjukɔɪd] **I** *a*. 海草的,似海草的(尤指岩草)。**II** *n*. 海草(尤指岩草,马尾藻属等的粗海藻)。

fu·cus [ˈfjuːkəs; ˋfjukəs] *n*. (*pl*. ~*es*, *fu·ci* [ˈfjuːsai; ˋfjusaɪ]) 【植】石衣藻属。

fud [fʌd; fʌd] *n*. = fuddy-duddy (*n*.)

fud·dle [ˈfʌdl; ˋfʌdl] **I** *vt*. **1.** 使醉。**2.** 使迷糊。— *vi*. **1.** 参加饮宴;常喝酒。**2.** 大醉。~ ***away*** 醉中度日。~ ***oneself*** (因醉)昏迷。~ ***one's cap*** [***nose***] 大醉。**II** *n*. **1.** 烂醉。**2.** 糊涂,一团糟。*a* ~ *of dirty clothes* 一堆脏衣服。***be on the*** ~ 大醉。

fud·dy-dud·dy [ˈfʌdiˌdʌdi; ˋfʌdɪˏdʌdɪ] **I** *n*. 〔俚〕**1.** 爱唠叨的人;吹毛求疵的人。**2.** 老派[守旧]的人;老古董。**II** *a*. 保守的,古板的,老派的。

fudge [fʌdʒ; fʌdʒ] **I** *n*. **1.** 梦话,胡言;捏造的话。**2.** (报纸中临时插入,常用另一种颜色印出的)特载。**3.** 奶油巧克力软糖。**II** *int*. 胡说! **III** *vt*. **1.** 蒙混,捏造;骗(*up*)。**2.** 对…敷衍应付。— *vi*. **1.** 胡说八道。**2.** 弄虚作假。**3.** 推诿 (*on*)。~ *on an exam* 考试作弊。~ ***and mudge*** 不表态;模棱两可;推托。

Fueh·rer [ˈfjuərə; ˋfjʊrərə] *n*. 〔G.〕= Führer.

Fu·e·gi·an [fuːˈeidʒiən; fuˋedʒɪən] **I** *a*. **1.** 火地岛(Tierra del Fuego)的。**2.** 火地岛(印地安)人的;火地岛文化的。**II** *n*. 火地岛人。

fu·el [ˈfjuəl; ˋfjʊəl] **I** *n*. **1.** 燃料,柴炭。★指燃料种类时为可数名词。**2.** 刺激物。*atomic* ~ 原子燃料。*gaseous* [*solid*] ~气体[固体]燃料。*heavy* ~柴油,燃料油。*jet* ~喷气式发动机燃料。*liquid* [*wet*] ~液体燃料。~ *alcohol* 燃料酒精,动力酒精。~ *capacity* 燃料容量。~ *economizer* 省油器。~ *gas* 燃气。~ *oil* 燃料油。~ *pump* 燃油泵。~ *ratio* 燃烧率。~ *ship* 油船。***add*** ~ ***to the fire*** [***flames***] 火上加油。**II** *vt*., *vi*. (〔英〕*-ll-*)(给…)加[供给]燃料,(给船等)上煤,(给…)加油。~ **cell**, ~**-cell** 燃料电池〔可不断将一种燃料如氢的化学能直接转变为电能〕。~ **gauge** 量油计,油规,油表。**-er** 使用特制混合燃料的赛车。

fu·el·(l)ing [ˈfju(ː)əliŋ; ˋfju(ʊ)əlɪŋ] *n*. 加燃料,加油。*a* ~ *station* 加油站,燃料供应站。

fug [fʌg; fʌg] **I** *n*. **1.** 〔主英〕(室内的)闷浊或暖和空气。**2.** (室隅、桌下等的)尘土和垃圾。**II** *vi*. 待在门窗关闭的房屋中。— *vt*. 使(房间等)空气闷浊。**-gy** *a*.

fu·ga·cious [fju(ː)ˈgeiʃəs; fjuˋgeʃəs] *a*. **1.** 易逃避的,难捕捉的;瞬息即逝的,一时的。**2.** 【植】先落的,早谢的。~ *leaves* 〔植〕早落叶。**-ly** *ad*. **-ness** *n*.

fu·gac·i·ty [fju(ː)ˈgæsiti; fju(ʊ)ˋgæsətɪ] *n*. 挥发性;逸性,逸度。

fu·gal [ˈfjuːgəl; ˋfjugəl] *a*. 【乐】赋格曲(性质)的。**-ly** *ad*.

-fu·gal *comb*. *f*. 表示"离开": centri*fugal*, febri*fugal*.

-fuge *comb*. *f*. 表示"驱逐";"逃走";"避开": febri*fuge*, re*fuge*, vermi*fuge*.

fug·gy [ˈfʌgi; ˋfʌgɪ] *a*. **1.** 空气闷浊的;闷热的。**2.** 爱住暖屋的。

fu·gi·tive [ˈfjuːdʒitiv; ˋfjudʒətɪv] **I** *a*. **1.** 逃亡的。**2.** 飘泊的,流浪的。**3.** 不固定的,一时的,(诗文)即兴的,偶成的。*a* ~ *soldier* 逃兵。~ *colours* 易褪的颜色。~ *verses* 即兴诗。~ *essays* 随笔。~ *ideas* 偶感。**II** *n*. **1.** 逃亡者,亡命者,被放逐者。*a* ~ *from justice* 逃犯。**2.** 难以捕捉的东西。~ **sorties** 〔罕〕(飞离基地以躲避敌机攻击的)避战飞行。**-ly** *ad*. **-ness** *n*.

fu·gle [ˈfjuːgl; ˋfjugl] *vi*. 〔古〕担任示范兵,作为示范者演示;作向导;以身作则地指导。**-man** *n*. **1.** 【军】示范兵。**2.** 领导者,示范者。

fugue [fjuːg; fjug] *n*. 〔F.〕**1.** 【乐】赋格曲〔一种多声部的乐曲,在五度上模仿并用复调方法发展主题〕。**2.** 【心、医】浮客症,神游(症)〔患者患病时,行为似乎是正常的,但痊愈后,对其行为失却记忆能力〕。

fugu·ist [ˈfjuːgist; ˋfjugɪst] *n*. (擅长)赋格曲的作曲家。

Füh·rer [ˈfjuərə; ˋfjurɚ] *n*. **1.** 〔G.〕元首〔纳粹党魁希特勒的称号〕。**2.** 〔f-〕独裁者,暴君。

Fu·ji(san) [ˈfuːˈdʒiː(ˈsɑːn); ˋfuˋdʒi(ˋsɑn)], **Fu·ji·ya·ma** [ˌfuːdʒiˈjɑːmɑː; ˏfudʒɪˋjɑmɑ] *n*. 〔Jap.〕富士山〔日本〕。

Fu·ku·o·ka [ˌfuːkəˈəukə; ˏfukʊˋokə] *n*. 〔Jap.〕福冈〔日本港市〕。

-ful *suf*. **1.** 加在名词之后,构成形容词,表示"充满","…多的","赋有…性质的": shame*ful*, beauti*ful*. **2.** 加在动词之后,构成形容词,表示"容易…的": forget*ful*. **3.** 加在名词之后,构成名词,表示"满","容量": mouth*ful*.

Fu·la [ˈfuːlɑː; ˋfulɑ] *n*. (*pl*. ~*s*, ~) **1.** 弗拉人〔西非黑人与高卡索瓦人混血血统的穆斯林牧民〕。**2.** 弗拉语〔属尼日尔-刚果语〕(= Fulah, Ful)。

Fu·la·ni [ˈfuːləni; ˋfulənɪ] *n*. (*pl*. ~*s*, ~) = Fula 〔奈及利亚北部一带用语〕。

Ful·bright [ˈfulbrait; ˋfulˏbraɪt] **I** *a*. 傅尔布莱特奖学金的,享有傅尔布莱特奖学金的。**II** *n*. 傅尔布莱特奖学金〔因美国阿肯色州参议员傅尔布莱特 1946 年提出之法案而得名。按该法案规定,此奖金的基金大部是靠美国向国外推销剩余物资而来。美国政府以此作为对外交换学者、教师等的奖学金〕。~ **Act** 傅尔布莱特法案。

ful·crum [ˈfʌlkrəm; ˋfʌlkrəm] *n*. (*pl*. ~*s*, ***-cra*** [-krə; -krə]) **1.** 【机】支点,支柱,支轴。**2.** 【动】喙基骨,转节,舌骨,棘状鳞。**3.** 【植】叶附属物。*a* ~ *bearing* 支点承座,刀口承。

ful·fil(l) [fulˈfil; fʊlˋfɪl] *vt*. **1.** 履行(条约、义务),遵守,执行(命令等)。**2.** 完成(计划等),做完(工作)。**3.** 满(期)。**4.** 达到(目的);应验(预言等);满足(希望)。**5.** 使臻于完善;〔~ oneself〕充分发挥潜在的能力。~ *one's duty* 履行义务。~ *one's promise* 兑现诺言。~ *one's expectations* 满足愿望。~ *a task ahead of schedule* 提前完成任务。*She succeeded in* ~*ing herself as an actress*. 她作为演员充分发挥了自己的才能。**-ment** *n*.

ful·gent [ˈfʌldʒənt; ˋfʌldʒənt] *a*. 〔诗〕光辉的,灿烂的。**-ly** *ad*.

ful·gu·rate [ˈfʌlgjuəreit, ˈful-; ˋfʌlgjəret, ˋful-] *vi*. 闪耀,闪烁。— *vt*. 【医】用电灼治疗。**-ration** *n*.

ful·gu·rat·ing [ˈfʌlgjuəˌreitiŋ; ˋfʌlgjʊəˏretɪŋ] *a*. 【医】(病痛)突然剧烈发作的,钻心的 (= fulgurant)。*a* ~ *pain* 突如其来的剧痛。

ful·gu·rite [ˈfʌlgjuərait; ˋfʌlgjʊəˏraɪt] *n*. 【地】闪电熔岩。

ful·gu·rous [ˈfʌlgjuərəs; ˋfʌlgjʊərəs] *a*. 闪电似的,满布闪电的;闪光的。

ful·ham [ˈfuləm; ˋfʊləm] *n*. 〔俚〕(赌博中作弊用的)灌过铅的骰子,假骰。

fu·lig·i·nous [fjuːˈlidʒinəs; fjuˋlɪdʒənəs] *a*. **1.** 充满烟

灰的,像烟灰的,烟垢的。**2.** 乌黑的,阴暗的。

full[1][ful; fʊl] **I** ***a*.** **1.** 充满的,装满的。**2.** 充分的,丰富的;挤满的;(吃、喝等)尽兴的,**3.** (精神)饱满的。**4.** 完全的,完美的;(资格)正式的;最高度的;(花)盛开的。**5.** 又胖又圆的,(脸)丰满的;(衣服)宽松的,多皱褶的。**6.** (光线)强烈的;(颜色)纯正的;(声音)洪亮的。**7.** (酒)醇厚的。**8.** 同父同母的。**9.** 详尽的,完备的。*He that is ~ of himself is very empty*. 〔谚〕人若十分自恃,必定十分无知。*F- Admiral* 〔美〕海军上将。~ *charge* 【军】全装(弹)药。~ *daylight* 大白天。~ *experience* 丰富的经验。~ *blood* 纯种;同父母,同胞。*a ~ figure* 又圆又胖的身体。*F- General* 〔美〕四星上将。*a ~ harvest* 丰收。*a ~ life* 经历丰富的一生。*a ~ man* 完人。~ *marks* 满分。~ *maturity* 完全成熟,壮年。*a ~ meal* 丰盛的一餐。*a ~ member* 正式会员。*a ~ mile* 整整一英里。~ *pay* 全薪。~ *professor* 〔美〕正教授。*a ~ report* 详细的报告。~ *score* 【乐】总谱。*a ~ size* 原尺寸,原大。~ *speed* 全速。~ *speed* [*steam*] *ahead* 【海】全速前进。*a ~ stomach* 满腹。~ *strength* 全力;【军】满员。~ *summer* 盛夏。*My heart is too ~ for words*. 我激动得说不出话来。*a ~ voice* 洪亮的嗓音。*a ~ bust* 丰满的胸部。*eat till one is ~* 吃饱肚子。***as ~ as an egg is of meat*** = 〔美〕***as ~ as a tick*** 塞得满满的。***at ~ length*** 手脚充分伸直地;尽量详尽地。***be ~ of*** 充满…(的)。***be ~ of one's own affairs*** = ***be ~ of oneself*** 只为自己打算。***be ~ of vigour and vitality*** 朝气蓬勃,精力充沛。***be ~ of years and honours*** 德高望重。***~ to overflowing*** [***the brim***] 满得不能再满。***~ up*** 〔俚〕**1.** 客满;吃饱;装满。**2.** 激动得要流泪。***in ~ activity*** [***blast, chisel, play, swing***] 正达到极点,正起劲。***in ~ feather*** [*fig*] 盛装;穿着全套礼服;精神饱满;很有钱。***turn*** (***it***) ***to ~ account*** 充分利用。**II** ***n*.** **1.** 充分,完全,全部。**2.** 极盛时,极点。*I cannot tell you the ~ of it*. 我不能完全告诉你。***at*** (***the***) ***~*** 在达到最高点,在完满状态中。***in ~*** 详细地(填写姓名等);全部地(*payment in ~*全付,付足)。***the ~ of the moon*** 满月时。***to the ~*** 充分地,十足地。**III** ***ad*.** **1.** 充分地,完全地。**2.** 恰恰,直接地。**3.** 极其,十分。~ *six miles* 整整六英里。*hit sb. ~ on the nose* 正打在某人鼻子上。***~ and by*** 〔美〕扯满篷。***~ as useful as*** 完全同…一样有用。***~ fain*** 非常喜欢,极想。***~ many*** 〔诗〕很多的。***~ out*** 以最大能量;最快地。***~ soon*** 立即。***~ well*** 很,充分地。**IV** ***vt*.** 把(衣服)裁宽大些,把(裙子)缝出皱褶。— ***vi*.** 满;(衣服)宽大;〔美〕(月)圆。~ **age** 成年。~**back** (足球)后卫,后卫的位置。~ **binding** (书籍的)全皮装订。~**-blooded** ***a*.** **1.** 多血质的,精力旺盛的。**2.** 情欲强烈的。**3.** 非混血的,纯种的。**4.** 内容充实的,有力的。**5.** 真正的,道地的。~**-blown** ***a*.** (花)盛开的;充分发展的,成熟的;(帆)张满的(~*-blown dignity* 神气活现。*a ~-blown power plant* 大型配套发电厂)。~**-bottomed** ***a*.** (船)底部宽阔的,容量大的;(假发)长而垂到肩背的。~ **brother** [**sister**] (同父母)亲兄弟[姐妹](*opp*. half brother [sister])。~ **dress** 礼服;(船只等)挂满旗。~**-dress** ***a*.** 礼服的,(宴会等)应穿礼服的;正式的,大规模的(*a ~-dress debate* 〔英〕议会的正式辩论。*a ~-dress operation* 大规模作战。*a ~-dress rehearsal* 正式排演,彩排。~*-dress talks* 正式会谈)。~ **face** **1.** ***n*.** (人的)正面像;黑体铅字。**2.** ***ad*.** 向正面,面对面。~**-court press**(篮球比赛中的)全场紧逼;〔喻〕全面攻势。~**-faced** ***a*.** 圆脸的,肥头肥脑的;圆满无缺的;(月等)向正面的;【印】黑体的。~**-fledged** ***a*.** 羽毛丰满的;发育充分的,经过充分训练的;有充分资格的。~**hand** 【牌】三张同点和两张同点的一组牌。~**-hearted** ***a*.** 全心全意的,诚恳的。~ **house** **1.** 客满,满座。**2.** = ~ **hand**. ~**-length** **1.** ***a*.** 全身的,全长的;标准长的,未删节的;大型的。**2.** ***n*.** 全身像。~ **load** 满载。~ **moon** 满月,望月。~**-mouthed** ***a*.** (牛等)牙齿齐全的;(狗等)大声叫的,(演讲)声音宏亮的;(文体等)刚劲的。~ **name** (连名带姓的)全名。~ **nelson** 【摔跤】双肩下握颈翻,里外肩下握颈翻。~ **page** ***a*.** 全页的,整版的。~ **sail** 【海】**1.** 帆数齐全。**2.** 风帆全张。**3.** 全速(行驶)。~ **score** 【乐】总谱。~ **stop** [**point**] 句号,句点。~ **text** 全文。~**-throated** ***a*.** 高声喧嚷的,声音宏亮的。~ **throat** 〔美口〕全力声援。~ **tide** 全潮。~**-time** ***a*.** 全部时间的,专职的(~*-time teacher* 专任教员)。~**-timer** 全日班学生〔*cf*. half-timer 选读生〕。

full[2][ful; fʊl] ***vt*.** 【纺】蒸洗,漂洗〔使毛织品紧密〕;缩绒,缩呢。~*ing clay* 漂土,漂泥。*a ~ing mill* 漂洗机。

full-bod·ied [ful'bɔdid; fʊl`bɑdɪd] ***a*.** **1.** 身体丰硕的,魁伟的。**2.** (指酒)醇厚的,强烈的。*a ~ wine* 醇酒。

full-di·men·sion·al ['fuldi'menʃənəl; `fʊldə`mɛnʃənl] ***a*.** **1.** 完全发展的;全部实现的。**2.** 无所不包的,包括各方面的。

Ful·ler ['fulə; `fʊlə] ***n*.** 富勒〔姓氏〕。

full·er[1]['fulə; `fʊlɚ] **I** ***n*.** **1.** 【冶】套柄铁锤,套锤。**2.** 用套锤锻成的槽(尤指马蹄铁上的槽)。**II** ***vt*.** 用套锤锻制,用套锤在…上开槽。

full·er[2]['fulə; `fʊlɚ] ***n*.** 【纺】蒸洗工,缩绒工。~**'s earth** 漂(白)〔一种软质黄色泥,可去衣上油渍〕。

full-fash·ioned ['ful'fæʃnd; `fʊl`fæʃənd] ***a*.** (袜子、毛衣)紧身的。

full·ness ['fulnis; `fʊlnɪs] ***n*.** **1.** 满,充满。**2.** 成熙。**3.** 充实,丰富。**4.** (光的)强烈,(声音的)洪亮,(颜色的)纯度,深度,浓度。【物】丰满度。**5.** 丰满,圆胖。**6.** 发胀。*a ~ of sleeves* 宽袖。*a great ~ of face* 肥头大脸。***in its ~*** 十分,完全。***in the ~ of one's heart*** 满腔热情;无限感慨。***in the ~ of time*** 在成熟的时候,在预定的时候。

full-rigged ['ful'rigd; `fʊl`rɪgd] ***a*.** **1.** (指船)桅帆众多齐备的。**2.** 全副装备的;装备齐全的。

full-scale ['ful'skeil; fʊl`skel] ***a*.** **1.** 照原物尺寸的,足尺的。**2.** 极大限度的;完全彻底的;全面的。*a ~ drawing* 与原物大小一致的图形。~ *warfare* 全面战争。

full·y ['fuli; `fʊlɪ] ***ad*.** 充分地,完全地;足足;至少。*be ~ paid up* 全部付讫。~ *refined wax* 精制蜂蜡。*It is ~ proved that*. …事实已充分证明…。*The journey will take ~ two hours*. 走这一趟足足要花两小时。

ful·mar ['fulmə; `fʊlmɚ] ***n*.** 【动】(北海)臭鸥,管鼻鹱。

ful·mi·nant ['fʌlminənt; `fʌlmɪnənt] ***a*.** **1.** 电闪雷鸣的,轰鸣的。**2.** 【医】(疾病)急性的,爆发性的。

ful·mi·nate ['fʌlmineit; `fʌlməˏnet] **I** ***vt*.** **1.** 使轰鸣,使爆炸。**2.** 怒骂,怒喝。— ***vi*.** **1.** 轰鸣。**2.** 爆炸。**3.** (疾病)爆发。**4.** 怒喝。**II** ***n*.** 【化】雷酸盐;雷汞。*mercury ~* 雷酸汞。*silver ~* 雷酸银。**ful·mi·na·tion** [ˌfʌlmi'neiʃən; ˏfʌlmɪ`neʃən] ***n*.** **1.** 猛烈爆发。**2.** 严厉谴责。

ful·mi·nat·ing ['fʌlmineitiŋ; `fʌlmɪnetɪŋ] ***a*.** **1.** 爆炸发光的,起爆的。**2.** 呵斥的。**3.** (疾病)暴发性的。~ **cap** 雷帽,雷汞爆管。~ **compound** 【化】雷酸盐。~ **powder** 雷爆(火)药(尤指雷粉)。

ful·mi·na·tor ['fʌlmineitə; `fʌlmɪnetɚ] ***n*.** **1.** 轰鸣者。**2.** 怒喝者,大声呵斥者;谴责者。

ful·mi·na·to·ry ['fʌlmineitəri; `fʌlmɪnətorɪ] ***a*.** **1.** 轰鸣的,爆炸的。**2.** 怒喝的,谴责的。

ful·mine ['fʌlmin; `fʌlmɪn] ***vt*., *vi*.** 〔罕、诗〕= fulminate.

ful·min·ic [fʌl'minik; fʌl`mɪnɪk] ***a*.** 爆炸性的。~ ***acid*** 【化】雷酸。

ful·ness ['fulnis; `fʊlnɪs] ***n*.** = fullness.

ful·some ['fulsəm; `fʊlsəm] ***a*.** (谄媚等)因过分做作而显得可厌的,令人作呕的。**-ly** ***ad*.** **-ness** ***n*.**

Ful·ton ['fultən; `fʊltən] ***n*.** 富尔顿〔姓氏〕。

ful·vous ['fʌlvəs; `fʌlvəs] ***a*.** 暗黄色的,黄褐色的。

fu·made [fjuː'meid; fju`med] ***n*.** 烟熏鲱鱼。

F

fu·mar·ic [fjuˈmærik; fjʊˋmærɪk] **acid**【化】夫马酸,延胡索酸,反式丁烯二酸,紫槿酸。

fu·ma·role [ˈfjuːmərəul; ˋfjuməˏrol] *n*.【地】(火山区的)喷气坑,气孔。

fu·ma·to·ri·um [ˌfjuːməˈtɔːriəm; ˏfjuməˋtɔrɪəm] *n*. (*pl*. ~*s*, *-to·ri·a* [-ˈtɔːriə; -ˋtɔrɪə])密封熏蒸所,熏蒸器。

fu·ma·to·ry [ˈfjuːmətəri; ˋfjuməˏtorɪ] **I** *a*. 熏烟的。**II** *n*. 熏蒸室,烟熏室。

fum·ble [ˈfʌmbl; ˋfʌmbl̩] **I** *vi*. **1**. 摸索;乱摸(*for*; *after*)。**2**. 笨手笨脚地摸弄。**3**. 犯大错。**4**. 失球,接漏球。— *vt*. **1**. 瞎摸,笨手笨脚地做。**2**. 失(球),接漏(球)。~ *about* 瞎摸,摸弄;失错。~ *at* [*with*] *a lock* 摸索着(对不准匙孔地)开锁。**II** *n*. **1**. 摸索,乱摸;笨手笨脚的处理;失错。**2**. 失球,接漏球。**-r** *n*. 摸索着,笨手笨脚的人,工作拙劣的人。**-bling** *a*.

fume [fjuːm; fjum] **I** *n*. **1**. 〔常 *pl*.〕烟气;香气,臭气;熏烟;水蒸气;烟雾。**2**. 激昂,激怒。~*s of heat* 闷人的热气。***be in a*** ~ 愤怒,怒气冲冲。***put sb. in a*** ~ 激怒某人。**II** *vt*. **1**. (用烟)熏。**2**. 烘制(木材等)。**3**. 蒸发,冒(烟、气等)。**4**. 烧(香)。— *vi*. **1**. 冒烟。**2**. (烟等)上升;蒸发。**3**. 发怒。

fumed [fjuːmd; fjumd] *a*. 熏过的。~ *oak* 氨熏橡木〔氨熏使橡木颜色变深〕。

fu·mi·gant [ˈfjuːmigənt; ˋfjumɪgənt] *n*. 熏蒸剂;【医】熏剂。

fu·mi·gate [ˈfjuːmigeit; ˋfjumɪˏget] *vt*. **1**. (为杀虫等)用烟熏;熏蒸消毒。**2**. 烧(香)。**-tion** [ˌfjuːmiˈgeiʃən; ˏfjumɪˋgeʃən] *n*. 熏蒸(消毒),熏蒸法;烧香。**-tor** *n*. 烟熏者;烟熏器;熏蒸消毒器。

fu·mi·to·ry [ˈfjuːmitori; ˋfjumɪˏtorɪ] *n*.【植】蓝堇属。

fum·y [ˈfjuːmi; ˋfjumɪ] *a*. 冒烟的;发蒸气的;烟雾状的。

fun [fʌn; fʌn] **I** *n*. **1**. 嬉戏,娱乐,玩笑,兴趣。**2**. 有趣的人物[事物]。*be fond of* ~爱闹着玩。*be full of* ~很好玩,极有趣。*Swimming is good* ~. 游泳很有趣味。*Skating is great* ~. 滑雪太有意思了。*Your friend is great* ~. 你的朋友真是个有趣的人。***do not see the ~ of*** 不懂得…的趣味,不以为有趣。***for*** [***in***] ~ 开玩笑,不是认真的。~ ***and games*** 〔口〕欢乐,开玩笑。***for the ~ of it*** [***the thing***] 为了取笑,当作玩耍。***have*** ~ 作乐,玩乐。***like*** ~ **1**. 〔口〕有力地;迅速地(*It sells like* ~. 很快就卖完)。**2**. 〔美俚〕(着重地表示否定或怀疑)不像是真的,不能相信;绝不可能;完全不是(这样)。***make ~ of*** = ***poke ~ at*** 嘲弄,取笑。***What*** ~! 多么有趣! **II** *vi*. (*-nn-*)〔口〕开玩笑,说笑。**III** *a*. **1**. 有趣的,奇妙的。**2**. 供娱乐用的,为玩玩用的。~**about** 游乐或赛车用小型汽车。**F- City** 游乐城〔纽约市的别号〕。~ **fair 1**. 〔英〕公共露天游乐场。**2**. (教堂等为筹款举办的)儿童游乐集市。~ **fur** (供非正式场合穿着的)低廉毛皮[人造毛皮]外衣。~ **house** 游乐园〔由各种玩乐设备组成的游乐场所〕。~ **run**(为募捐举行的)公益长跑活动。

fu·nam·bu·list [fju(ː)ˈnæmbjulist; fjʊ(u)ˋnæmbjəlɪst] *n*. 走钢丝的杂技演员。

Fun·chal [funˈʃɑːl; funˋʃɑl] *n*. 丰沙尔〔马德拉群岛首府〕。

func·tion [ˈfʌŋkʃən; ˋfʌŋkʃən] **I** *n*. **1**. 功能,官能,机能,作用。**2**. 〔常 *pl*.〕职务,职责。**3**. 庆祝仪式;(盛大的)集会,宴会。**4**.【数】函数;与其他因素有密切关系的事。*The ~ of the ear is to listen*. 耳的功能是听。*the ~ of education* 教育的功能。*discharge one's* ~*s* 尽职。*the ~s and powers of the National Congress* 全国代表大会的职权。*a controllable* ~【火箭】遥控程序。*public* [*social*] ~招待会,文娱晚会,社交集会。*vital* ~*s* 生命机能。**II** *vi*. (器官等)活动,(机器等)运行,发挥作用。~ *as teacher* 担任教师。*a sofa* ~*ing as a bed* 兼当床用的沙发。*The lathe doesn't ~ well*. 这台车床有毛病。~ *digit* [*letter*]【计】操作数码[字码]。~ **space**【数】函数空间。~ **word**【语】(主要表示语法关系的)功能词。

func·tion·al [ˈfʌŋkʃənl; ˋfʌŋkʃənl̩] *a*. **1**. 官能的,机能的。**2**. 在起作用的;职务上的。**3**.【数】函数的。**4**.【建】从使用的观点设计[构成]的。**5**. 有多种用途的;可改变用途的。**6**. 可使用的,可操作的。~ **disease** 官能病(*opp*. organic disease)。~ **disorder** 机能紊乱;机能障碍。~ **food** 保健食品。~ **furniture** 实用的家具。~ **group**【化】官能团,功能团。~ **illiterate** (看不懂与本职工作有关的指示、指令的)半文盲,职务文盲。~ **shift**【语】词性转换。**-ism** *n*.【心、建】机能主义〔心理学上指思想和行动的过程,是人的整个机体的反应;建筑学上指讲求实用,而不注重外观〕。**-ist** *n*. 机能主义者。**-ly** *ad*.

func·tion·ar·y [ˈfʌŋkʃənəri; ˋfʌŋkʃənˏɛrɪ] *n*. 工作人员,职员,官员。*a petty* ~小职员。*a public* ~公务员。

func·tion·ate [ˈfʌŋkʃəneit; ˋfʌŋkʃənet] *vi*. = function (*vi*.)。

func·tor [ˈfʌŋktə; ˋfʌŋktɚ] *n*. **1**. 起功能作用的东西。**2**.【数】函子;算符。

fund [fʌnd; fʌnd] **I** *n*. **1**. 资金,基金,专款。**2**. 〔*pl*.〕〔the ~s〕(国家的)财源;〔英〕公债。**3**. 〔*pl*.〕存款,现款。**4**. 储备,蕴藏。**5**. 特别基金管理机构。*a ~ of knowledge* 丰富的知识。*idle* ~*s* 游资。*public welfare* ~*s* 公益金。*a reserve* ~公积金。*a scholarship* ~奖学金基金。*a sinking* ~偿债基金。~*s for the living of troops* 军队的生活费。***in*** ~***s*** 有钱;有资本。***out of*** ~***s*** 缺钱。***the*** (***public***) ~***s*** 公债。**II** *vt*. **1**. 换(短期借款)为长期公债。**2**. 〔英〕投(资金)于公债。**3**. 把…列作为基金[专款]。**4**. 为…提供基金,储存(一笔钱款)以资生息。~**-holder** *n*. 公债持有人,证券持有人。~**-raiser** 基金筹措者。~**raising** 基金筹措。~**-raising** *a*. 基金筹措的。

fun·da·ment [ˈfʌndəment; ˋfʌndəmənt] *n*. **1**. 臀部,肛门。**2**. 基础,基本原理。

fun·da·men·tal [ˌfʌndəˈmentl; ˏfʌndəˋmɛntl̩] **I** *a*. **1**. 基础的,基本的,根本的,重要的;原始的,主要的。**2**.【物】基频的,基谐波的;【乐】基音的。*a ~ change* 根本变化。*a ~ function*【数】特征函数。*a ~ law* 根本法则,基本定律;基本法。*a ~ rule* 基本原则。**II** *n*. **1**. 原理,原则,基本,根本,基础。**2**.【乐】基音;【物】基频,基谐波。~ **bass**【乐】根音低音部,根音低音。~ **frequency**【物】基频。~ **particle**【物】基本粒子(= elementary particle)。~ **star**【天】基本星。**-ism** *n*.【宗】原教旨主义〔相信《圣经》所说的事情都是真实的,并认为这一点对基督教来说是最基本的〕。**-ist 1**. *n*. 原教旨主义者。**2**. *a*. 原教旨主义的。**-ly** *ad*.

fun·da·men·tal·i·ty [ˌfʌndəmenˈtæliti; ˏfʌndəmɛnˋtælətɪ] *n*. 基本性,根本状态;重要性。

fund·ed [ˈfʌndid; ˋfʌndɪd] *a*. 成为有固定利息的长期借款的,以公债形式投资的。~ **debt** [**liability**] (期限一年以上的)长期借款。

fun·dus [ˈfʌndəs; ˋfʌndəs] *n*. (*pl*. ***fun·di*** [ˈfʌndai; ˋfʌndaɪ]) [L.]【解】底,底部,基底。~ *uteri* 子宫底。

fu·ner·al [ˈfjuːnərəl; ˋfjunərəl] **I** *n*. **1**. 葬礼;送丧行列(= ~ procession);追悼会。**2**. 〔喻〕不愉快的事;操心的事,有关系的事。*a state* ~国葬。*attend a* ~参加丧礼。**II** *a*. 葬礼的;出殡用的;出殡时的。*a ~ ceremony* [*service*] 丧礼。*a ~ director* 〔美〕丧葬承办人。*a ~ march* 丧礼进行曲。*a ~ oration* 悼词。*a ~ procession* [*train*] 送葬行列。*a ~ urn* 骨灰瓮。***None of your*** ~! 那不是你的事(与你无关)。***That's your*** ~. 那是你的事(与我无关)。~ **home** [**parlor**] 殡仪馆。

fu·ner·ar·y [ˈfjuːnərəri; ˋfjunərərɪ] *a*. (有关)殡葬的。*a ~ urn* 骨灰瓮。

fu·ne·re·al [fju(ː)ˈniəriəl; fju(ʊ)ˋnɪrɪəl] *a*. 丧葬似的;悲哀的;阴森的,严肃的。~ *garments* 丧服。

F

fun·gal [ˈfʌŋgəl; ˋfʌŋgəl] *a*. = fungous.
fun·gi [ˈfʌndʒai, ˈfʌŋgai; ˋfʌndʒaɪ, ˋfʌŋgaɪ] *n*. fungus 的复数。
fungi- *comb. f.* 表示"真菌": *fungi*cide.
fun·gi·ble [ˈfʌndʒibl; ˋfʌndʒɪbl] **I** *a*. 可代替的;【法】可互换的〔指可用一物代替他物偿债〕。**II** *n*.【法】(偿还债务时所用的)代替物。
fun·gi·cide [ˈfʌndʒisaid; ˋfʌndʒɪ͵saɪd] *n*. 杀真菌剂。
fun·gi·form [ˈfʌndʒifɔːm; ˋfʌndʒɪ͵fɔrm] *a*. 真菌状的。
fun·gin [ˈfʌndʒin; ˋfʌndʒɪn] *n*. 菌纤维素。
fun·giv·or·ous [fʌnˈdʒivərəs; fʌnˋdʒɪvərəs] *a*. 食真菌的。
fun·go [ˈfʌŋgəu; ˋfʌŋgo] *n*. 飞球〔指打棒球的人自掷自打,让守野的人练习接球〕。*a* ~ *hit* 大飞球。*a* ~ *bat* [*stick*] 练习打球的棒。
fun·goid [ˈfʌŋgɔid; ˋfʌŋgɔɪd] **I** *a*. 似真菌的;有真菌特征的。**II** *n*. 真菌。
fun·gous [ˈfʌŋgəs; ˋfʌŋgəs] *a*. **1.** 如真菌的;真菌状的;因真菌引起的。**2.** 倏生倏灭的,忽然产生又迅速消失的。
fun·gus [ˈfʌŋgəs; ˋfʌŋgəs] **I** *n*. (*pl*. ~*es*, *fungi* [ˈfʌŋgai; ˋfʌŋgaɪ]) **1.** 真菌〔包括霉菌、酵母菌和伞菌等〕。**2.** 突然发生的暂时现象。**3.**【医】海绵肿。**II** *a*. = fungous.
fu·ni·cle [ˈfjuːnikl; ˋfjunɪkl] *n*. = funiculus.
fu·nic·u·lar [fju(ː)ˈnikjulə; fju(ʊ)ˋnɪkjələ˞] **I** *a*. **1.** 索状的,索带的。**2.** 用缆索运转的。**3.**【解】索的,脐带的,精索的。*a* ~ *machine* 吊重机。*a* ~ *polygon* 索多边形。*a* ~ *railway* 缆索铁道。**II** *n*. 缆车道 (= ~ railway).
fu·nic·u·lus [fju(ː)ˈnikjuləs; fju(ʊ)ˋnɪkjələs] *n*. (*pl*. *-cu·li* [-lai; -laɪ]) **1.**【解】索,脐带,精索。**2.**【植】珠柄。**3.**【动】白索。**4.**【生】菌丝索。**5.**〔罕〕细绳索。
Funk [fʌŋk; fʌŋk] *n*. 芬克〔姓氏〕。
funk[1] [fʌŋk; fʌŋk] **I** *n*.〔口〕**1.** 恐怖,惊慌。**2.** 胆小鬼。***be in a blue*** ~ 不胜惊恐;意志消沉。***be in a*** ~ 畏缩,害怕。***put sb. in*** [***into***] ***a*** ~ 使某人吓得要命。**II** *vi*., *vt*. **1.** (使)害怕;(使)畏缩。**2.** 怕(事)。~ *out of a fight* 怕打架而走开。~ *a difficulty* 害怕困难,逃避困难。~ **hole** 防空壕;逃避所。~ **money** (转移国外以获取高利的)流动资金。
funk[2] [fʌŋk; fʌŋk] **I** *n*.〔美俚〕**1.** 刺鼻的味道,霉味。**2.** 早期的爵士音乐。**3.** 畸形艺术 (= ~ art)。**II** *vt*. **1.** 向…喷烟,以烟扰乱(某人);使闻到刺鼻的味道。**2.** 吸(烟斗)。— *vi*. **1.** 抽烟,吸烟。**2.** 发出刺鼻臭味。~ **art** 畸形艺术,恶臭艺术〔以古怪、肮脏的物品拼凑成的一种所谓的"艺术作品"〕。
fun·ky[1] [ˈfʌŋki; ˋfʌŋkɪ] *a*. 胆战心惊的;害怕的。
fun·ky[2] [ˈfʌŋki; ˋfʌŋkɪ] *a*.〔美俚〕**1.** 有恶臭的,刺鼻的。**2.** 有早期爵士音乐味道的,质朴的。**3.** (模样或作风)古怪的。**4.** 极好的。
fun·nel [ˈfʌnl; ˋfʌnl] **I** *n*. **1.** 漏斗。**2.** 漏斗形物,通风筒;【矿】通风井。**3.** (火车等的)烟囱。**4.**〔美俚〕酒鬼。**II** *vt*. (〔英〕*-ll-*) **1.** 把…灌进漏斗。**2.** 使成漏斗形。**3.** 使汇集。— *vi*. **1.** 成漏斗形,逐渐变窄[宽]。**2.** 经过漏斗。**3.** 汇集。~ **cloud**【气】漏斗云。~**form** *a*. 漏斗状的。~ **hood** 烟囱帽。~**-shaped** *a*. 漏斗(状)的。~**-tube** 漏斗管。**-like** *a*. 像漏斗的。
fun·nelled [ˈfʌnld; ˋfʌnld] *a*. **1.** 有漏斗的。**2.** 漏斗状的。**3.** 有…烟囱的〔构成复合词〕。*a two-* ~ *steamer* 双烟囱轮船。
fun·nies [ˈfʌniz; ˋfʌnɪz] *n*.〔*pl*.〕〔美口〕连环漫画;新闻漫画栏。
fun·ni·ly [ˈfʌnili; ˋfʌnɪlɪ] *ad*. 有趣地,好笑地,滑稽地;〔口〕奇怪地。~ ***enough*** 说来真奇怪〔插入语〕。
fun·ni·ment [ˈfʌnimənt; ˋfʌnɪmənt] *n*. 笑话,滑稽动作。
fun·ny[1] [ˈfʌni; ˋfʌnɪ] **I** *a*. **1.** 有趣的,好笑的,滑稽的。**2.** 有病的,不舒服的。**3.** 狡猾的,欺骗(性)的,可疑的,不光明的。**4.**〔口〕稀奇的,古怪的。**5.**〔美〕粗野的,无礼的。*a* ~ *column* 漫画栏。*a* ~ *business* 怪事,不道德的行为。*a* ~ *thing* 古怪的事。*There is sth*. ~ *about it*. 那真有点蹊跷。***a*** ~ ***way to behave*** 奇怪的行动。***feel*** = ***go all*** ~ (觉得)身体不对劲;(觉得)情形古怪。***get*** ~ ***with***〔口〕对人十分不敬。**II** *n*. **1.** 滑稽人物。**2.**〔常 *pl*.〕滑稽连环漫画栏。**3.** 笑话,有趣的故事。*make a* ~ 说个笑话。~**-bone** (受触时发麻的)肘部尺骨端,笑骨。~ **business**〔口〕**1.** (小丑等)引人捧腹的动作;胡闹。**2.** 欺骗;不道德行为。~ **car** 一种比赛用的腊肠形汽车。~ **farm** 精神病院。~**man** (*pl*. *-men*)〔美口〕丑角,滑稽演员;爱说笑话的人。~**-money 1.**〔美、加俚〕膨胀的通货,滥发的货币。**2.** 伪钞;收不回来的钱,对有倒闭危险的企业的投资。~ **paper** 报纸的滑稽漫画和字谜栏。**-niness** *n*.
fun·ny[2] [ˈfʌni; ˋfʌnɪ] *n*.〔英〕(比赛用)单人双桨小艇。
fun·ster [ˈfʌnstə; ˋfʌnstə˞] *n*.〔美〕爱逗人笑的人,幽默家,喜剧演员。
fur [fəː; fɝ] **I** *n*. **1.** 毛,软毛;毛皮;〔*pl*.〕兽皮,皮货,毛皮制品,皮衣[袭],毛皮手套(等)。★要与 leather (没有毛的皮革)区别。**2.** 毛皮兽,软毛兽。**3.**【医】舌苔。**4.** (桃的)茸毛。**5.** 锅垢,水锈。*a* ~*-puller* 剥皮匠。*a* ~*-trader* 毛皮商。~ *lining* 毛皮里子。~ ***and feather*** 禽兽。***hunt*** ~ 猎野兔。***mane the*** ~ ***fly*** 闹出乱子,引起争吵。***stroke the*** ~ ***the wrong way*** 抚摸倒毛,惹怒人。**II** *vt*. (*-rr-*) **1.** 用毛皮护覆,用毛皮给…镶里。**2.** 使生水垢;除去(锅上的)水垢;使长舌苔。**3.**【建】给…钉上板条。*Hard water* ~*s the kettle*. 硬水使水壶生水垢。*become furred in influenza* 因感冒长了舌苔。— *vi*. 长舌苔;生水垢。~ **piece** 皮领;皮披肩。~ **seal** 海狗;海獭。

F

fur. = 1. furlong. 2. furnish(ed). 3. further.
fu·ran [ˈfjuərən, fjuˈræn; ˋfjurən, fjʊˋræn], **fu·rane** [ˈfjuərein; ˋfjuren] *n*.【化】呋喃,氧(杂)茂。
fu·ra·zol·i·done [ˌfjuərəˈzɔlidəun; ˏfjurəˋzɑlɪdon] *n*.【药】呋喃唑酮,痢特灵。
fur·be·low [ˈfəːbiləu; ˋfɝbɪ͵lo] **I** *n*. **1.** (女服的)裙褶,褶饰,边饰。**2.**〔*pl*.〕花哨庸俗的装饰。**II** *vt*. **1.** 给…加裙褶[裙饰]。**2.** 用花哨庸俗的东西装饰。
fur·bish [ˈfəːbiʃ; ˋfɝbɪʃ] *vt*. **1.** 研磨,磨光 (*up*)。**2.** 刷新,翻新,修复,温习 (*up*)。
fur·cate [ˈfəːkeit; ˋfɝket] **I** *a*. 分叉的,叉形的。**II** *vi*. 分叉,分歧。**-d** *a*. 成叉形的。
fur·ca·tion [fəːˈkeiʃən; fɝˋkeʃən] *n*. 分叉。
fur·cu·la [ˈfəːkjulə; ˋfɝkjələ] *n*. (*pl*. *-lae* [-liː; -li])【解、动】叉突;Y 腺;弹器;叉骨。**-r** *a*.
fur·cu·lum [ˈfəːkjuləm; ˋfɝkjələm] *n*. (*pl*. *-la* [-lə; -lə]) = furcula.
fur·fur [ˈfəːfə; ˋfɝfɚ] *n*. (*pl*. ~*es* [-fəriːz; -fəriz]) 皮屑,头屑。
fur·fu·ra·ceous [ˌfəːfjuˈreiʃəs; ˏfɝfjʊˋreʃəs] *a*. **1.** 糠的,似糠的;麸的,似麸的。**2.** 多(头)皮屑的。
fur·fu·ral [ˈfəːfəræl; ˋfɝfəræl] *n*.【化】糠醛;呋喃亚甲基。
fur·fu·ran [ˈfəːfəræn; ˋfɝfəræn] *n*. = furan.
fu·ri·ous [ˈfjuəriəs; ˋfjʊrɪəs] *a*. **1.** 暴怒的,狂怒的。**2.** 狂暴的,猛烈的。**3.** 喧闹的。*be* ~ *with sb*. [*at sth*.] 对某人[某事]大发雷霆。*a* ~ *sea* 怒涛汹涌的海。***run at a*** ~ ***pace*** 飞跑。***grow fast and*** ~ 疯狂起来。**-ly** *ad*. **-ness** *n*.
furl [fəːl; fɝl] **I** *vt*., *vi*. 卷收(风帆等),收(伞),拉拢(窗帘);卷起,折起。~ *a flag* 叠好旗帜。~ *an umbrella* 收伞。*This umbrella doesn't* ~ *neatly*. 这把伞收不整齐。**II** *n*. **1.** 卷,折,收拢。**2.** 一卷东西。
fur·long [ˈfəːlɔŋ; ˋfɝlɑŋ] *n*. 浪(英国长度单位, = $\frac{1}{8}$ 英里)。

fur·lough [ˈfəːləu; ˋfɝlo] **I** ***n*.** (军人、官吏的)休假。**II** ***vt*.** **1.** 给予休假。**2.** 强迫…休假,使停职,暂时解雇。***be on*** ~ 在休假中。***go home on*** ~ 休假回国[家]。

fur·me(n)·ty [ˈfəːməti, -mən-; ˋfɝmətɪ, -mən-] ***n*.** = frumenty.

furn. = **1.** furnished. **2.** furniture.

fur·nace [ˈfəːnis; ˋfɝnɪs] **I** ***n*.** **1.** 炉子;熔炉;高炉。**2.** 极热的地方。**3.** 磨炼;艰难。*an atomic* [*a nuclear*] ~ 原子反应堆,核反应堆。*blast* ~【冶】鼓风炉,高炉。*an electric* ~ 电炉。*electric-arc* ~【冶】电弧炉。*induction* ~【冶】感应炉。*open hearth* ~【冶】平炉。*a reverberating* ~反射炉。***be tried in the*** ~ 受磨炼。**II** ***vt*.** 在炉中烧热(金属)。~ **coke** 冶金焦炭。~ **heating** 暖气炉,暖房法。~**man** 炉前工。

Fur·ness [ˈfəːnis; ˋfɝnɪs] ***n*.** 弗尼斯〔姓氏〕。

fur·nish [ˈfəːniʃ; ˋfɝnɪʃ] ***vt*.** **1.** 供给,供应,提供。**2.** 装备,布置,装修(房屋)。~ *sb. with sth.* = ~ *sth. to sb.* 供给某人某种东西。*a well ~ed shop* 货物齐全的商店。*Furnished rooms to let.* 备有家具的房间出租。***be ~ed with*** 备有。~ ***out*** 补充;使完备〔指房屋的设备〕。**-er** ***n*.** 供给者;(承办家具陈设的)家具商。**-ing** ***n*.** 〔*pl*.〕设备,家具;陈设品;〔美〕服饰品。

fur·ni·ture [ˈfəːnitʃə; ˋfɝnɪtʃɚ] ***n*.** 〔集合词〕**1.** 家具,器具。**2.** 设备,装修。**3.** 附属品,内容(*of*)。**4.**【印】空铅,填充材料。~ *and fixtures* 家具什物。*the* ~ *of one's mind* 知识,见闻,思想。*the* ~ *of one's pocket* 钱财。*the* ~ *of one's shelves* 书籍。***remove*** ~ (替人)搬家〔指一种行业〕。

Fur·ni·val(l) [ˈfəːnivəl; ˋfɝnɪvəl] ***n*.** 弗尼瓦尔〔姓氏〕。

fu·ror [ˈfjuərɔː; ˋfjurɔr] ***n*.** 〔L.〕**1.** 狂怒。**2.** 热烈的感谢[赞扬]。**3.** (对某事的)狂热。***create a regular*** ~ (演出等)得到热烈的赞扬。~ ***poeticus*** 诗迷,诗痴。

fu·ro·re [fjuːˈrɔːri; fjuˋrɔrɪ] ***n*.** 〔It.〕**1.** = furor. **2.**【乐】热烈,激情。***make a*** ~ 轰动一时。

fu·ro·se·mide [fjuəˈrəusəmaid; fjʊˋrosəmaɪd] ***n*.**【药】速尿(灵),腹胺酸,利尿磺胺。

furred [fəːd; fɝd] ***a*.** **1.** 毛皮制的;用毛皮镶边的;用毛皮作衣服里子的。**2.** (野兽)有毛皮的。**3.** 穿毛皮的,穿轻裘的。**4.** 有舌苔的。**5.** 钉上板条的。

fur·ri·er [ˈfʌriə; ˋfɝrɪɚ] ***n*.** **1.** 皮货商人。**2.** 毛皮加工者。**3.** 缝制[修补、改制]毛皮衣服的人。

fur·ri·er·y [ˈfəːriəri; ˋfɝrɪərɪ] ***n*.** **1.** 〔废〕毛皮,皮货。**2.** 皮货业;毛皮业。

fur·ring [ˈfəːriŋ; ˋfɝrɪŋ] ***n*.** **1.** 毛皮镶边,毛皮衬里。**2.** 锅垢。**3.**【建】垫高料,钉板条。**4.**【医】舌苔。**5.** 船旁衬木、衬条。~ **tile** 墙面磁砖。

fur·row [ˈfʌrəu; ˋfɝo] **I** ***n*.** **1.** 沟,犁沟,垄沟。**2.** 耕地,农田。**3.** 航迹;车辙,(脸上的)皱纹。*make deep ~s in the road* (车等)在路上留下深深的轮沟。***draw a straight*** ~ 老实地过日子。***plough a lonely*** ~ 孤独行动。**II** ***vt*.** **1.** (用犁)开(沟),给(田)作垄。**2.** 使起皱纹。**3.** 〔诗〕(破浪)前进。*a brow ~ed with sorrows* 因忧患而生皱纹的前额。*a ~ed field* 畦田。— ***vi*.** **1.** 〔口〕犁地。**2.** 起皱纹。~ **drilling** 沟播。~ **irrigation** 沟灌。~ **opener** 开沟器。~ **slice** 犁块。**-less** ***a*.** 无沟的,无皱纹的。**-y** ***a*.** 有沟的,多皱纹的。

fur·ry [ˈfəːri; ˋfɝɪ] ***a*.** **1.** 毛皮的;毛皮制的;毛皮似的。**2.** 穿毛皮的;镶毛皮的;衬毛皮的。**3.** 水垢多的。**4.** 有舌苔的。**5.** 〔美俚〕可怕的;毛骨悚然的。

fur·ther [ˈfəːðə; ˋfɝðɚ] 〔far 的两种比较级形式之一,另一形式为 farther〕**I** ***a*.** **1.** 〔表示距离和时间〕更远的,较远的。**2.** 〔表示程度〕更进一步的,深一层的。**3.** 更多的,此外的。*on the* ~ *side* 在那一边。~ *news* 续报。**II** ***ad*.** **1.** 更远,更进一步。**2.** 而且。*I can walk no* ~. 我不能再走了。*inquire* ~进一步探讨。*He said that he couldn't find it, and* ~, *that nobody would ever find it.* 他说他找不到那件东西,而且也不会有人找得到它。***for*** ~ ***details*** 至于详细情形(则请…)。~ ***on*** 再向前(进)。***till*** ~ ***notice*** 另候通知。***I'll see you*** ~ ***first.*** (那种事)我决不干〔~ 是 in hell 的委婉话〕。***to be*** ~ ***continued*** (未完)待续。(***to***) ***go*** ~ ***and fare worse*** 越搞越糟(不如安于现状)。**III** ***vt*.** 促进,推动。~**more** ***ad*.** 而且。~**most** ***a*.** 最远的(= furthest)。~**some** ***a*.** **1.** 〔Scot.〕冒失的,鲁莽的。**2.** 〔古〕有利的,有帮助的,起促进作用的。

fur·ther·ance [ˈfəːðərəns; ˋfɝðərəns] ***n*.** 助长,促进,推动。

fur·thest [ˈfəːðist; ˋfɝðɪst] 〔far 的两种最高级形式之一,另一形式为 farthest〕**I** ***a*.** 最远的。**II** ***ad*.** 最远地,最大程度地,最大限度地。

fur·tive [ˈfəːtiv; ˋfɝtɪv] ***a*.** **1.** 偷偷摸摸的,鬼鬼祟祟的。**2.** 偷来的。*a* ~ *glance* 偷看,窥。*a* ~ *look* 贼头贼脑的脸色。*be* ~ *in one's actions* 行动鬼祟。**-ly** ***ad*.** **-ness** ***n*.**

fu·run·cle [ˈfjuərʌŋkl; ˋfjʊrʌŋkl] ***n*.**【医】疖。

fu·run·cu·lar [fjuəˈrʌŋkjulə; fjʊˋrʌŋkjələ], **fur·un·cu·lous** [fjuəˈrʌŋkjuləs; fjʊˋrʌŋkjələs] ***a*.**【医】疖的。

fu·run·cu·lo·sis [fjuˌrʌŋkjuˈləusis; fjʊˏrʌŋkjəˋlosɪs] ***n*.**【医】疖病。

fu·ry [ˈfjuəri; ˋfjʊrɪ] ***n*.** **1.** 愤怒,狂怒。**2.** (病状,天气等的)凶险,猛烈。**3.** 〔F-〕【罗神】复仇三女神之一;〔*pl*.〕冤魂。**4.** 泼妇。***be haunted by the furies of*** 被…的冤魂纠缠。***fly into a*** ~ 大怒。***in a*** ~ 在狂怒中。***like*** ~ 〔口〕猛烈地(*work like* ~猛干。*rain like* ~下暴雨)。***the*** ~ ***of the elements*** 狂风暴雨。

furze [fəːz; fɝz] ***n*.**【植】荆豆(属)。

fur·zy [ˈfəːzi; ˋfɝzɪ] ***a*.** 荆豆茂盛的,像荆豆属植物的。

fu·sain [fjuˈzein; fjʊˋzen] ***n*.** **1.** 炭画笔。**2.** 炭笔画。**3.** 炭素。

fu·sar·i·um [fjuːˈzæriəm; fjuˋzærɪəm] ***n*.**【生】镰刀霉。~ **wilt** 镰刀霉属枯凋症。

fus·cin [ˈfʌsin; ˋfʌsɪn] ***n*.**【生化】暗褐菌素;【医】视褐素。

fus·cous [ˈfʌskəs; ˋfʌskəs] ***a*.**【生】暗褐色的。

fuse[1] [fjuːz; fjuz] **I** ***vt*., *vi*.** **1.** 熔化。**2.** 熔合。**3.** (政党等)联合,合并,融合。**4.** 由于保险丝烧断而电路不通。*All the lights have ~d.* 由于保险丝烧断,电灯都灭了。**II** ***n*.**【电】保险丝,熔丝,熔断器。***have a short*** ~ 〔美〕脾气急躁;容易发怒。***blow a*** ~ 使保险丝熔断;〔口〕勃然大怒。~**-link** 熔线,熔断片,熔丝链。~ **wire** 作保险丝用的金属丝;保险丝,熔丝,熔(断)线。

fuse[2] [fjuːz; fjuz] **I** ***vt*.** 给…装信管,给…装导火线。**II** ***n*.** 信管,导火线,引线。*a non-delay* [*time*] ~瞬发[定时]引信。

fused [fjuːzd; fjuzd] ***a*.** **1.** 熔融的,熔凝的。**2.** 融合的,合并的。~ **quartz** 熔凝石英,熔凝水晶。~ **salt** 熔盐。

fu·see [fjuːˈziː; fjuˋzi] ***n*.** **1.** 耐风火柴。**2.** (铁路等的)带色闪光信号〔危险信号〕。**3.** (钟表的)均力圆锥轮。**4.**【宇】火箭发动机点火器。**5.** 雷管。**6.** (马脚上的)骨瘤。

fu·se·lage [ˈfjuːzilɑːʒ; ˋfjuzḷɑʒ] ***n*.** **1.**【空】飞机机身。**2.**【宇】火箭的外壳;弹体,壳体。~ **cover** 机身外壳。

fu·sel [ˈfjuːzəl; ˋfjuzəl] **oil** ***n*.**【化】杂醇油。

fu·si·bil·i·ty [ˌfjuːzəˈbiliti; ˏfjuzəˋbɪlətɪ] ***n*.** (可)溶性,溶度。

fu·si·ble [ˈfjuːzəbl; ˋfjuzəbḷ] ***a*.** 可溶解的;易熔的。*a* ~ *alloy* [*metal*] 易熔合金[金属]。

fu·si·form [ˈfjuːzifɔːm; ˋfjuzɪˏfɔrm] ***a*.**【生】纺锤状的;两端尖的;流线形的,梭形,橄榄形。~ **root**【植】纺锤根。

fu·sil [ˈfjuːzil; ˋfjuzɪl] ***n*.** (旧式)燧发枪,明火枪。

fu·sil·ier, fu·si·leer [fjuːziˈliə; ˏfjuzɪˋlɪr] ***n*.**【史】燧发枪兵;〔*pl*.〕〔英〕明火枪团。

fu·sil·lade [ˌfjuːziˈleid; ˏfjuzɪˋled] **I** ***n*.** **1.** 一齐射击,排枪。**2.** 一连串的猛烈批评。*a* ~ *of questions* 连珠炮似的质问。**II** ***vt*.** 以排枪射击,以排炮轰击。

fu·sion [ˈfjuːʒən; ˋfjuʒən] ***n*.** **1.** 熔解,熔化;【物】(核)聚

变,合成。2.〔美〕融合;(政党等的)合并,联合。*the heat of* ～熔化热。*the point of* ～ = ～ *point* 熔点。*atomic* [*nuclear*] ～核聚变,核熔合。*thermonuclear* ～热核反应。～ **administration**〔美〕联合政府。～ **bomb** 热核弹,氢弹。～ **frequency**(电视中视觉的)停闪频率。～ **nucleus**【物】融合核。～ **welding** 熔融焊,熔焊(接)。

fu·sion·ism [ˈfjuːʒənizəm; ˋfjuʒənɪzm̩] *n*. 党派大联合论。**fu·sion·ist** *n*., *a*.

fuss [fʌs; fʌs] **I** *n*. 1. 忙乱,激动;大惊小怪。2. 吹捧,过分体贴。3. 大惊小怪的人。4. 抗议;争吵。*What's all the* ～? 你们在乱七八糟地忙些什么? ～ *and feathers* 大吹大擂,夸示,炫耀。*get into a* ～ 焦急,忙乱。*kick up a* ～〔美俚〕制造麻烦〔如表示抗议等〕;骚乱〔如打架等〕。*make a* ～ = *make too much* ～小题大做,无事自扰。*make a* ～ *of sb*. 对某人过分关心[照料]。*make a* ～ *over* 大肆吹捧。*make a great* ～ *about nothing* [*trifles*] 小题大做。**II** *vi*. 1. 忙乱,大惊小怪,小题大做,(不停地,东转西转地)忙忙碌碌(*about*; *up and down*)。2. 奉承,过分关心;特别考究。3. 烦恼;抱怨;唠叨。4.〔美俚〕追求女人。— *vt*. 1. 使无事自扰;使急躁。2.〔美俚〕追求,与(女子)约会。～ *around*〔美口〕无意义,无目的地忙乱。～ **budget**〔口〕大惊小怪[小题大做,终日忙忙碌碌]的人,爱挑剔的人(尤指年老的泼妇)。～**pot** = ～**budget**.

fuss·y [ˈfʌsi; ˋfʌsɪ] *a*. 1. 爱大惊小怪的,爱小题大做的;过分操心的。2.(衣着、字句等上)充分讲究的。*as* ～ *as a hen with one chick* 在小事上瞎忙。**-ily** *ad*. **-i·ness** *n*.

fus·tet [ˈfʌstet; ˋfʌstɛt] *n*.【植】黄栌。

fus·tian [ˈfʌstiən; ˋfʌstʃən] **I** *n*. 1. 粗斜纹布,纬起毛织物,纬起绒织物。2. 夸大的话,(文词的)浮夸。**II** *a*. 1. 粗斜纹布制的。2. 浮夸的,夸大的;无价值的。

fus·tic [ˈfʌstik; ˋfʌstɪk] *n*.【植】黄颜树〔桑树〕;黄颜木;(黄颜木制成的)黄色染料。

fus·ti·gate [ˈfʌstigeit; ˋfʌstɪˏget] *vt*. 1. 用棍子打。2. 猛烈抨击。**fus·ti·ga·tion** [ˌfʌstiˈgeiʃən; ˏfʌstɪˋgeʃən] *n*. **fus·ti·ga·to·ry** *a*.

fus·ty [ˈfʌsti; ˋfʌstɪ] *a*. 1. 发霉的;陈腐的。2. 古板的;过时的。**-i·ly** *ad*. **-i·ness** *n*.

fut [fʌt; fʌt] *n*., *ad*. = phut.

fut. = future.

fu·thark [ˈfuːθɑːk; ˋfuθɑrk] *n*. 北欧古字母〔由起首六个字母 f、u、p(th)、a(或 o)、r、k(或 c)而得名〕(= futharc; futhorc; futhork)。

fu·tile [ˈfjuːtail, Am. -til; ˋfjutaɪl, -tɪl] *a*. 1. 无用的,无益的。2.(人)没出息的;轻浮的。3.(事)不足道的,无关紧要的。**-ly** *ad*. **-ness** *n*.

fu·til·i·tar·i·an [ˌfjuːtiliˈtɛəriən; ˏfjutɪləˋtɛrɪən] **I** *a*. 悲观的,认为一切都是没有价值[空忙一场]的。**II** *n*. 悲观主义者。**-ism** *n*. 悲观主义,万事皆空论。

fu·til·i·ty [fju(ː)ˈtiliti; fju(ʊ)ˋtɪlətɪ] *n*. 1. 无用,无益。2. 无益的事。3. 轻浮的言行。

fut·tock [ˈfʌtək; ˋfʌtək] *n*.【船】(艉上的)复肋材。

fu·tur·am·a [ˌfjuːtʃəˈræmə; ˏfjutʃəˋræmə] *n*. 未来世界展示。

fu·tur·am·ic [ˌfjuːtʃəˈræmik; ˏfjutʃəˋræmɪk] *a*. 未来型的,设计新颖的。

fu·ture [ˈfjuːtʃə; ˋfjutʃɚ] **I** *n*. 1. 未来,将来。2. 前途,远景。3.〔*pl*.〕【商】期货,期货交易。4.〔俚〕未婚夫,未婚妻。5.【语】将来时,将来式。～ *delivery* 期货交割。*have a* ～ 有前途,将来有希望。*have no* ～没有前途,前途无望。*deal in* ～*s* 作期货交易。*for the* ～ = *in* ～. *in* (*the*) ～ 将来,今后。★ in the ～比 in ～常用。*in the near* [*no distant*] ～ 在不久的将来。**II** *a*. 未来的,将来的;【语法】将来时的。～ *life* 来世。～ *ages* [*generations*] 后代,后世。～ **perfect**【语法】未来完成式。～ **shock** 未来休克〔对于迅速变化客观环境的不能适应〕。**-less** *a*. 没有前途的,前途无望的。

fu·tur·ism [ˈfjuːtʃərizəm; ˋfjutʃərɪzəm] *n*.【文艺】未来主义〔二十世纪初始于意大利的绘画、音乐、文学流派,抛弃传统手法。强调表现当代生活中机器代替一切的忙乱现象〕。

fu·tur·ist [ˈfjuːtʃərist; ˋfjutʃərɪst] **I** *n*. 1. 未来主义者,未来派文艺家。2. 相信《圣经》预言会实现的基督教徒。3. 未来学家。**II** *a*. 未来主义的,未来派的。

fu·tur·is·tic [ˌfjuːtʃəˈristik; ˏfjutʃəˋrɪstɪk] *a*. 1. 未来的。2. 未来派(艺术)的;未来主义的。**-ti·cal·ly** *ad*.

fu·tur·is·tics [ˌfjutʃuˈristiks; ˏfjutʃʊˋrɪstɪks] *n*. 未来学。

fu·tu·ri·ty [fjuːˈtjuəriti; fjuˋtʃʊrətɪ] *n*. 1. 未来,将来。2. 未来性。3.〔*pl*.〕未来的事物,远景。～ **industry** 未来工学〔未来的科技发展将会造成的工业〕。～ **race** 优胜者早已排定的比赛〔尤指赛马〕。

fu·tu·rol·o·gy [fjuːtʃəˈrɔlədʒi; fjutʃəˋrɑlədʒɪ] *n*. 未来学〔研究未来科技发展及其对社会之影响的一门科学〕。**fu·tu·rol·o·gist** *n*. 未来学家。

fuze [fjuːz; fjuz]〔美〕= fuse[2].

fu·zee [fjuːˈziː; fjuˋzi] *n*. = fusee.

fuzz [fʌz; fʌz] **I** *n*. 1. 微毛,细毛,茸毛,绒毛。2.〔美俚〕警察,侦探。**II** *vi*. 成绒毛状。— *vt*. 1. 使长绒毛。2. 使模糊。～**box**, ～**tone**(装在电吉他上的)嗡声箱,哑音器〔作用在于使音乐稍变粗哑〕。～**buster** 超速侦测器。～**word** 含糊其辞。

fuzz·ball [ˈfʌzbɔːl; ˋfʌzbɔl] *n*.【植】马勃菌,牛尿菌。

fuzz·y [ˈfʌzi; ˋfʌzɪ] *a*. 1. 有茸毛的,覆着细毛的,如茸毛的。2. 不清楚的。*a* ～ **photo** 模糊的照片。～ **logic** 模糊逻辑。～ **math** 模糊数学。**fuzz·ily** *ad*. **fuzz·i·ness** *n*.

FV, f. v. = 〔L.〕*folio verso* 见本页背面(= on the back of the page)。

F.W.A. = Federal Works Agency〔美旧〕联邦工程局。

F.W.B. = four wheel brakes 四轮制动器。

F.W.D. = four wheel drive 四轮驱动。

Fwd Ech = Forward Echelon 先头梯队。

FX = Foreign Exchange 外汇。

F.Y. = Fiscal Year〔美〕财政年度。

-fy *suf*. 表示"弄成","变成","…化": beauti*fy*, magni*fy*.

fyce [fais; faɪs] *n*. 小狗(= feist)。

FYI, fyi = for your information 供参考。

fyke [faik; faɪk] *n*. 长袋鱼网(=～ net)。

fyl·fot [ˈfilfɔt; ˋfɪlfɑt] *n*. 卍字形。

fytte [fit; fɪt] *n*.〔口〕诗歌的一节。

fz. = fuze.

F.Z.S. = Fellow of the Zoological Society〔英〕动物学学会会员。

G

G, g [dʒiː; dʒi] (*pl.* ***G's***, ***Gs***, ***g's***, ***gs*** [dʒiːz; dʒiz]) 英语字母表的第七个字母。**1.** 〔G〕G 字形物。**2.** 【乐】G 调, G 音。**3.** 【物】〔g〕重力加速度 (acceleration of gravity) 的符号。**4.** 〔G〕〔美〕学业成绩优良 (good) 的符号。**5.** 〔g〕【心】普通[一般]智力 (general intelligence) 的符号。**6.** 第七。**7.** 〔G〕〔美俚〕一千美元。**8.** 〔美〕〔G〕(电影) G 级的, 男女老少均可观看的。**9.** 〔G〕【电】导电性 (conductance) 的符号。*G class* 第七级。*hard g* 发音为 [g; g] 的 *g*. *soft g* 发音为 [dʒiː; dʒi] 的 *g*. **G flat** (G^b) 变 G 调。**G major** G 大调。**G minor** G 小调。**G sharp** ($G^\#$) 升 G 调。

G = **1.** generator. **2.** German. **3.** Germany. **4.** giga 十亿。**5.** Gossypium 棉属。**6.** grid. **7.** Gulf. **8.** 【军】gun.

G. = **1.** German. **2.** George. **3.** special gravity. **4.** Gulf.

g. = **1.** game. **2.** ga(u)ge. **3.** gender. **4.** genitive. **5.** 〔美〕gold. **6.** grain. **7.** gram(s). **8.** grand. **9.** guide. **10.** guinea. **11.** gulf.

GA = gibberellic acid.

GA, G.A. = **1.** General Agent; General Assembly. **2.** General Average. **3.** General of the Army.

Ga =【化】gallium. 元素镓的符号。

Ga. = **1.** Georgia. **2.** Gallic.

gab [gæb; gæb] **I** ***n.*** **1.** 〔主 Scot.〕废话, 空谈, 唠叨。**2.** 【机】(偏心盘杆的) 凹节。**3.** 〔Scot.〕嘴。*Stop* [*Stow*] *your* ~ ! 住嘴! ***blow the*** ~ 泄露秘密, 告密。***have the gift of*** (***the***) ~ 能说会道, 有口才。**II** ***vi.*** (***-bed***; ***-bing***) 空谈, 闲聊, 唠叨。~ **session** 〔美俚〕长时间的闲聊。

gab·ar·deen, gab·ar·dine [ˌgæbəˈdiːn, ˈgæbə-; ˏgæbə-ˋdin, ˋgæbə-] ***n.*** **1.** 【纺】斜纹呢, 华达呢〔俗称轧别丁〕。**2.** (中世纪犹太人穿的) 宽大长外套。

gab·ber [ˈgæbə; ˋgæbɚ] ***n.*** 唠叨的人; 闲聊的人。

gab·ble [ˈgæbl; ˋgæbḷ] **I** ***vt.*** 喋喋不休地讲; 急促不清地说。— ***vi.*** **1.** 唠叨。**2.** (鹅、鸭等) 发出咯咯声。**II** ***n.*** **1.** 急促不清的话; 无意义的话。**2.** (鸡鸭等发出的) 咯咯声。**-bler** ***n.***

gab·bro [ˈgæbrəu; ˋgæbro] (*pl.* ~***s***) ***n.*** 【地】辉长岩。**gab·broic** [gæˈbrəuik; gæˋbroɪk] ***a.***

gab·by [ˈgæbi; ˋgæbɪ] ***a.*** 〔口〕爱说话的, 多嘴的。

ga·belle [gæˈbel; gəˋbɛl] ***n.*** 〔F.〕〔古〕**1.** 税, 国税。**2.** 法国大革命前的盐税。

gab·er·dine [ˈgæbədiːn, ˌgæbəˈdiːn; ˏgæbɚˋdin, ˋgæbɚ-din] ***n.*** **1.** 工作服。**2.** = gabardine.

gab·er·lun·zie [ˌgæbəˈlʌnziː; ˏgæbɚˋlʌnzɪ] ***n.*** 〔Scot.〕乞丐。

Ga·be·ro·nes [ˌgɑːbəˈrəunəs; ˏgɑbəˋronəs] ***n.*** 加贝罗内斯〔博茨瓦纳的首都 Gaborone 的旧名〕。

gab·fest [ˈgæbfest; ˋgæbfɛst] ***n.*** 〔美口〕**1.** 长时间的闲谈。**2.** (社交中) 非正式的聚谈。

ga·bi·on [ˈgeibiən; ˋgebɪən] ***n.*** **1.** (盛土石用的) 枝条筐。**2.** (筑堤、坝等用的) 金属条筐。

ga·bi·on·ade [ˌgeibiəˈneid; ˏgebɪəˋned] ***n.*** 用盛装土石的筐垒成的堤[墙]。

ga·ble [ˈgeibl; ˋgebḷ] ***n.*** 【建】山墙, 三角墙; 三角形的建筑部分。~ **end** 山贴端。~ **roof** 【建】人字屋顶, 三角屋顶。~ **window** 山墙窗; 三角窗。

ga·bled [ˈgeibld; ˋgebḷd] ***a.*** 有山墙的, 人字形的。

ga·blet [ˈgeiblit; ˋgeblɪt] ***n.*** 【建】花山头。

Ga·bon [F. gaˈbõ; gaˋbõ] ***n.*** 加蓬(加彭)〔非洲〕。

Gab·o·nese [ˌgɑːbəˈniːz; ˏgæbəˋniz] ***n.*** 加蓬人。

Ga·boon [gəˈbuːn; gəˋbun] ***n.*** = Gabon.

ga·boon [gəˈbuːn; gəˋbun] ***n.*** 〔方〕痰盂。

Ga·bri·el [ˈgeibriəl; ˋgebrɪəl] ***n.*** **1.** 盖布里尔〔男子名〕。**2.** 【宗】(替上帝把好消息报告世人的天使) 加百利。**3.** 〔美俚〕(爵士乐队中的) 号手。

Ga·bun [gəˈbuːn; gəˋbun] ***n.*** = Gabon.

ga·by [ˈgeibi; ˋgebɪ] ***n.*** 〔英方〕蠢货, 傻瓜。

gad[1] [gæd; gæd] **I** ***n.*** **1.** 【矿】钢楔, 小钢凿。**2.** 〔方〕(赶牛用的) 刺棒, 棍。**II** ***vt.*** (***-dd-***) **1.** 用刺棒刺。**2.** 【矿】用钢楔凿碎或弄松(矿石)。

gad[2] [gæd; gæd] **I** ***n.*** 闲逛, 游荡。**II** ***vi.*** (***-dd-***) **1.** 游荡, 闲荡 (*about*; *abroad*; *out*)。**2.** 追求刺激。**3.** 蔓延。*a gadding plant* 蔓生植物。***be on*** [***upon***] ***the*** ~ 游荡着。

gad[3], **Gad** [gæd; gæd] ***int.*** 〔古〕嘿! *By* ~! 天哪! 哎呀!

gad·a·bout [ˈgædəbaut; ˋgædəbaʊt] **I** ***n.*** 游手好闲的人。**II** ***a.*** 游荡的; 游手好闲的。

gad·a·rene [ˌgædəˈriːn; ˏgædəˋrin] ***a.*** 〔常 G-〕猛冲的; 急速的; 头朝下的。

gad·di [ˈgʌdi; ˋgʌdɪ] ***n.*** 〔印〕**1.** 君主座席的垫子。**2.** 〔喻〕王座, 王位, 宝座; 王权。

gad·fly [ˈgædflai; ˋgædflaɪ] ***n.*** **1.** 【动】虻, 牛虻。**2.** 讨厌的人。**3.** 强烈的刺激[冲动]。

gadg·et [ˈgædʒit; ˋgædʒɪt] ***n.*** 〔口〕**1.** 小机件, 小配件; 小装置。**2.** 新发明, 小玩意儿。**3.** 〔喻〕诡计, 圈套。

gadg·e·teer [ˌgædʒəˈtiə; ˏgædʒəˋtɪɚ] ***n.*** 制造小机件的人; 设计新玩意儿的人。

gadg·et·ry [ˈgædʒitri; ˋgædʒətrɪ] ***n.*** **1.** 小机件; 小玩意儿〔总称〕。**2.** 专心琢磨新玩意儿; 爱搞小发明。

Ga·dhel·ic [gəˈdelik; gəˋdɛlɪk] ***a.***, ***n.*** = Goidelic.

ga·did [ˈgeidid; ˋgedɪd] ***n.*** 鳕科 (*Gadidae*) 鱼。

ga·doid [ˈgeidɔid; ˋgedɔɪd] **I** ***n.*** 【鱼】鳕鱼。**II** ***a.*** 鳕科的, 似鳕的。

gad·o·lin·ite [ˈgædəlinait; ˋgædəlɪnaɪt] ***n.*** 【矿】矽[硅]铍钇矿。

gad·o·lin·i·um [ˌgædəˈliniəm; ˏgædəˋlɪnɪəm] ***n.*** 【化】钆。

ga·droon [gəˈdruːn; gəˋdrun] ***n.*** 圆模雕刻装饰; (银器上的) 卵形凹凸刻纹。**-ing** ***n.***

gad·wall [ˈgædwɔːl; ˋgædwɔl] ***n.*** (*pl.* ~***s***, ~) 【动】漈凫 (*Anas strepera*)〔产于美洲北部淡水区〕。

gad·zooks [ˌgædˈzuːks; ˏgædˋzuks] ***int.*** 〔常 G-〕〔古〕该死〔轻微的诅咒〕。

gae[1] [gei; ge] ***vi.*** (***gaed*** [geid; ged]; ***gaen*** [gein; gen]; ***gae·ing***) 〔Scot.〕= go.

gae[2] [gei; ge] 〔Scot.〕give 的过去式。

Gae·a [ˈdʒiːə; ˋdʒiə] ***n.*** 【希神】盖娅〔大地女神〕。

Gael [geil; gel] *n*. (苏格兰高地及爱尔兰等地的)盖尔人。

Gael·ic [ˈgeilik; ˋgelɪk] **I** *a*. 盖尔族的,盖尔语的。**II** *n*. 盖尔语。

gaff[1] [gæf; gæf] **I** *n*. **1**. 鱼叉,鱼钩,钩竿。**2**. (爬电杆用的)攀钩;(肉铺的)挂钩。**3**.【海】桅斜桁。**4**. (装在斗鸡距上的)铁距。**5**. 〔俚〕骗人的秘密机关;欺骗,愚弄,花招。**6**. 〔美俚〕苦难,苦境,刑罚;嘲笑,挖苦。**7**. = gaffe. ***blow the*** ～ 〔俚〕泄露秘密。***get*** [***give***] ***sb***. ***the*** ～ 〔美〕刺激某人。***stand the*** ～ 〔美俚〕忍受痛苦[惩罚]而毫不怯懦。**II** *vt*. 用鱼叉捕(鱼),用鱼钩钓上来;〔俚〕欺骗。～**-rigged** *a*. 主帆上有斜桁的。～ **sail**【海】斜桁帆。～**-top sail**【海】斜桁上帆。

gaff[2] [gæf; gæf] *n*. 〔英俚〕低级娱乐场,低级戏院[舞厅]〔通常叫做 penny gaff〕.

gaffe [gæf; gæf] *n*. 〔F.〕过失,不慎的言行,出丑。

gaf·fer [ˈgæfə; ˋgæfɚ] *n*. **1**. 〔贬、谑〕老头子〔对乡下老人的称呼。*cf*. gammer〕. **2**. 〔英〕工头,雇主。**3**. 经理,马戏团领班;(电影、电视的)照明电工。*G- Johnson* 约翰逊老头。

gag [gæg; gæg] **I** *n*. **1**. 塞口的东西,(牲畜的)口衔。**2**. 对言论自由的压制;(议会)限制辩论时间,终止辩论。**3**.【医】张口器。**4**. 插科打诨,逗乐。**5**. 〔俚〕欺诈,哄骗。*place* [*put*] *a* ～ *upon freedom of speech* 压制言论自由。**II** *vt*. (**-gg-**) **1**. 塞住…的口;【医】用张口器使(患者)张开口。**2**. 压制…的言论自由,限制…的发言。**3**. 给(表演)加笑料。**4**. 〔俚〕欺诈,瞒。**5**. 关闭(阀门等)。— *vi*. **1**. (俚)插科打诨。**2**. 窒息,作呕。**3**. 〔俚〕欺骗。～ **bit** (驯马用的)衔铁。～ **law** [**rule**] 限制言论[讨论]自由的法令(尤指在立法机关里讨论某问题)。～**man** *n*. 笑料的设计人,插科打诨的演员。～ **order** 〔美〕禁止报导令,禁止公开评论令。～ **rein** 马缰。

ga·ga [ˈgɑːgɑː; ˋgɑgɑ] **I** *a*. **1**. 糊涂的;愚蠢的。**2**. 狂热的。**II** *n*. 低级的观众。

gage[1] [geidʒ; gedʒ] **I** *n*. **1**. 抵押品,担保品。**2**. (表示挑战扔下的)帽子[手套等];挑战,挑衅。***in*** ～ ***of*** … 作为抵押。***throw down a*** ～ 挑战。**II** *vt*. 〔古〕以…作抵押;以…打赌。

gage[2] [geidʒ; gedʒ] *n*., *vt*. **1**. 〔美〕= gauge. **2**.【海】吃水;(对于风及他船的)相对位置。

gage[3] [geidʒ; gedʒ] *n*. = greengage.

Gage [geidʒ; gedʒ] *n*. 盖奇〔姓氏〕。

gag·er [ˈgeidʒə; ˋgedʒɚ] *n*. = gauger.

gag·ger [ˈgægə; ˋgægɚ] *n*. **1**. 箝住别人口的人,塞口的东西。**2**. 插科打诨的演员,讲笑话的人。**3**.【机】铁骨。**4**.【交】校正轨距的工人。

gag·gle [ˈgægl; ˋgægl̩] **I** *n*. **1**. (鹅等的)一群。**2**. (杂乱的)一堆,一簇。**3**. 〔贬〕一群饶舌的妇女。*a* ～ *of reporters and photographers* 乱哄哄的一群记者和摄影师。**II** *vi*. (鹅等)嘎嘎地叫。— *vt*. 咯咯地叫出[说出]。

gag·ster [ˈgægstə; ˋgægstɚ] *n*. 开玩笑的人,插科打诨的演员,笑话的作者。

gahn·ite [ˈgɑːnait; ˋgɑnaɪt] *n*.【矿】锌尖晶石。

Gai·a [ˈgeiə, ˈgaiə; ˋgeə, ˋgaɪə] = Gaea.

gai·ety [ˈgeiəti; ˋgeətɪ] *n*. **1**. 愉快的神情,欢乐的气氛。**2**. 〔常 *pl*.〕狂欢,乐事。**3**. (服装的)华美。

gai·ly [ˈgeili; ˋgelɪ] *ad*. **1**. 快活地。**2**. 华丽地。

gain[1] [gein; gen] **I** *vt*. **1**. 获得;博得,挣得;赢得,打胜(战争、官司)。**2**. 吸引;争取…(到一边),说服。**3**. (尤指通过努力)到达(目的地)。**4**. 增加,增进;(钟、表等)走快(*opp*. lose)。～ *one's living* 谋生。～ *the summit* 到达山顶。*My watch* ～*s five minutes a day*. 我的表每天快五分钟。— *vi*. **1**. 得利,得益。**2**. 前进,进步。**3**. 增加,增重,增进。**4**. (钟、表等)快走。～ ***by comparison*** [***contrast***] 比较[对比]之下显出其长处。～ ***ground*** 进展,占优势。～ ***headway*** 前进。～ ***in*** 获得,增长(～ *in health* 增进健康。～ *in influence* 影响增长)。～ ***on*** [***upon***] **1**. 蚕食,侵入。(*The sea* ～*s on the land*. 海水侵入陆地)。**2**. 接近,逼近,赶上。**3**. 占优势,超过,胜过。(*The days are* ～*ing on the night*. 白天渐渐比夜晚长了)。**4**. 得欢心,巴结上。～ ***one's ends*** 达到目的。～ ***one's point*** 贯彻自己意见。～ ***over*** 说服,拉拢过来。～ ***speed*** 渐渐增加速度。～ ***strength*** 力量增加;(风力等)渐强。～ ***the ear of*** 得人倾听。～ ***the wind*** 占他船的上风。～ ***time*** **1**. (钟、表等)走得快。**2**. (用拖延等办法)争取时间。**II** *n*. (*opp*. loss) **1**. 获利,获得。**2**. 得益,利益。**3**. 〔*pl*.〕收益,利润;报酬,奖金。**4**. 增大,增加,增进。**5**.【无】增益,放大,增量。*be blinded by the love of* ～ 利令智昏。*Ill-gotten* ～*s never prosper*. 〔谚〕不义之财,发不了家。*No* ～*s without pains*. 〔谚〕不劳则无获。*a* ～ *to one's happiness* 幸福的增进。～ **control**【无】增益调整。～ **day** 盈余日〔地球自转一周所剩的时日〕。

gain[2] [gein; gen] **I** *n*.【建】**1**. (木料上或墙上的)腰槽。**2**. 雄榫上的斜肩。**II** *vt*. 在…上开腰槽,用腰槽连接。

gain·a·ble [ˈgeinəbl; ˋgenəbl̩] *a*. 可得到的,能赢得的。

gain·er [ˈgeinə; ˋgenɚ] *n*. **1**. 获得者,得益者,胜利者(*opp*. loser)。**2**.【体】后滚翻花式跳水。***come off a*** ～ 结果获得胜利。

Gaines [geinz; genz] *n*. 盖恩斯〔姓氏〕。

gain·ful [ˈgeinful; ˋgenfəl] *a*. **1**. 有利益的,有报酬的。**2**. 唯利是图的。**-ly** *ad*. **-ness** *n*.

gain·ings [ˈgeiniŋz; ˋgenɪŋz] *n*. 〔*pl*.〕收入,收益,利益,奖金,奖品。

gain·less [ˈgeinlis; ˋgenlɪs] *a*. 无利可图的;一无所获的,没有进展的。

gain·ly [ˈgeinli; ˋgenlɪ] *a*. 优美的,秀丽的。

gain·say [geinˈsei; genˋse] **I** *vt*. (**-*said*** [-ˈseid, -ˈsed; -ˋsed, -ˋsɛd]; **-*say·ing***)〔主要用于疑问句和否定句〕**1**. 否定,否认。**2**. 反驳,反对。*There is no* ～*ing his honesty*. 他的诚实是不可否认的。**II** *n*. 否认,矛盾。***beyond*** ～ 无可否认,不容置疑。

Gains·bor·ough [ˈgeinzbərə; ˋgenz,bɝə] *n*. 盖恩斯伯勒〔姓氏〕。

(')gainst [geinst; genst] ***prep***., ***conj***. 〔诗〕= against.

gait[1] [geit; get] **I** *n*. **1**. 步态,步法。**2**. (走、跑等的)速度。***gang one's ain*** [***own***] ～ 〔Scot.〕走自己的路,我行我素。***slacken one's*** ～ 放慢步行速度。**II** *vt*. 训练(马的)步法。

gait[2] [geit; get] *n*.【纺】穿经;花纹循环。

gai·ted [ˈgeitid; ˋgetɪd] *a*. 有…步伐的。*heavy-*～步履沉重的。

gai·ter [ˈgeitə; ˋgetɚ] *n*. **1**. 鞋罩,绑腿。**2**. 高帮松紧鞋,绑腿式长统靴。***be ready to the last*** ～ ***button*** 有充分准备,已准备完毕。

Gait·skell [ˈgeitskəl; ˋgetskl̩] *n*. 盖茨克尔〔姓氏〕。

gal[1] [gæl; gæl] *n*. 〔俚〕= girl.

gal[2] [gæl; gæl] *n*.【物】伽〔加速度单位〕。

Gal. = Galatian(s).

gal. = **1**. gallery. **2**. gallon.

ga·la [ˈgɑːlə; ˋgɑlə] **I** *n*. **1**. 庆祝,节日。**2**. 〔古〕盛装。**3**. 〔英〕运动盛会。**II** *a*. 节日的,欢乐的。*a* ～ *day* 庆祝日,节日。*a* ～ *dress* 节日服装,漂亮服装。

gal·a·bi·a, **gal·a·bi·ya** [gɑːˈlɑːbiə; gɑˋlabɪə] *n*. 盖拉布衣〔阿拉伯国家的人特别是农民穿的长棉大褂〕。

ga·lac·ta·gogue [gəˈlæktəgɔg; gəˋlæktəgɑg] **I** *a*.【医】催奶的。**II** *n*. 催乳剂。

ga·lac·tic [gəˈlæktik; gəˋlæktɪk] *a*. **1**. 乳的,乳汁的;【医】催乳的。**2**.【天】银河的。**3**. 极大的,巨额的。～ **circle** [**system**]【天】银河圈[系]。～ **cluster**【天】银河星团。～ **noise**【无】银河(星系射电)噪声,银河系射频辐射。～ **structure**【天】银河的结构。

ga·lac·t(o) [gəˈlækt(ə); gəˋlækt(ə)] *comb*. *f*. 表示"乳的": *galactose*.

gal·ac·tom·e·ter [ˌgæləkˈtɔmitə; ˏgæləkˋtɑmətɚ] *n.* = lactometer.

ga·lac·tor·rhe·a [gəˌlæktəˈriə; gəˏlæktəˋriə] *n.*【医】乳溢。

ga·lac·tose [gəˈlæktəus; gəˋlæktos] *n.*【化】半乳糖。

ga·lac·to·se·mi·a [gəˌlæktəˈsiːmiə; gəˏlæktəˋsimɪə] *n.*【医】半乳糖血。

ga·lac·to·side [gəˈlæktəsaid; gəˋlæktəˏsaɪd] *n.*【化】半乳糖苷。

ga·lah [gəˈlɑː; gəˋlɑ] *n.*【动】凤头鹦鹉 (*Kakatoë roseicapilla*)〔产于澳洲,粉灰色,澳大利亚内陆到处可见,作观赏鸟〕。

ga·lan·gal [gəˈlæŋgl; gəˋlæŋgl] *n.* **1.**【植】高良姜 (*Alpinia officinarum*); 山奈 (*Kaempteria galanga*). **2.** 莎草属植物〔如高莎草 (*Cyperus longus*)〕.

gal·an·tine [ˈgælənˌtiːn; ˋgælənˏtin] *n.* 〔F.〕(肉或鸡肉去骨加香料扎紧煮熟后做成的)冻肉卷。

ga·lan·ty show [gəˈlænti ˈʃəu; gəˋlæntɪ ˋʃo] 影子戏。

gal·a·te·a [ˌgæləˈtiə;ˏgæləˋtiə] *n.* (作海魂衫童装用的)条纹花布。

Ga·la·tia [gəˈleiʃə; gəˋleʃə] *n.* 加拉太〔小亚细亚中部一古国〕。

Ga·la·tian [gəˈleiʃən; gəˋleʃən] **I** *a.* 加拉太的,加拉太人的。**II** *n.* 加拉太人。***The ~s***【圣】《加拉太书》。

gal·a·vant [ˈgæləvænt; ˋgæləˏvænt] *vi.* = gallivant.

ga·lax [ˈgeilæks; ˋgelæks] *n.*【植】加腊克斯 (*Galax aphylla*)〔产于美国东南部,为常绿灌木,开小白花,叶子有光泽。常用以编织花圈〕。

gal·ax·y [ˈgæləksi; ˋgæləksɪ] *n.* **1.** 〔the G-〕银河;银河系;〔*pl.*〕河外星系。**2.** 人才荟萃,一群显赫的〔出色的〕人物;一系列光彩夺目的东西。*a ~ of talent* [*beauties*] 一群才子[美女]。

gal·ba·num [ˈgælbənəm; ˋgælbənəm] *n.*【化】古蓬香脂,波斯树脂。

G

Gal·braith [gælˈbreiθ; gælˋbreθ] *n.* 加尔布雷斯〔姓氏〕。

gale[1] [geil; gel] *n.* **1.** 大风(尤指风速每小时在 30 至 60 英里的大风);暴风。**2.** 〔口〕(突发的)一阵。**3.** 〔诗〕微风。*a fresh ~* 强风。*a moderate ~* 疾风(即七级风)。*a strong ~* 烈风(九级风)。*a whole ~* 狂风(十级风)。*a ~ of wind* 一阵大风。*~s of laughter* 阵阵笑声。

gale[2] [geil; gel] *n.*【植】香杨梅。

gale[3] [geil; gel] *n.* 〔英〕(租金的)定期交付。*a hanging ~* 租金欠交。

ga·le·a [ˈgeiliə; ˋgelɪə] *n.* (*pl.* **-le·ae** [-liiː; -ləi]) **1.**【植】盔瓣。**2.**【动】(昆虫的)外颚叶。**3.**【医】帽状头痛膜。

ga·le·ate(d) [ˈgeiliit(id); ˋgelɪˏet(ɪd)] *a.* 盔状的,戴盔的。

ga·lee·ny [gəˈliːni; gəˋlinɪ] *n.*【英动】珠鸡 (= guinea fowl)。

Ga·len [ˈgeilin; ˋgelɪn] *n.* 盖伦〔男子名〕。

Ga·len [ˈgeilin; ˋgelɪn] *n.* **1. Clandius ~** 克莱迪斯·盖伦〔130? —200?,古希腊名医〕。**2.** 〔谑〕医生,郎中,草药医生。

ga·le·na [gəˈliːnə; gəˋlinə] *n.*【矿】方铅矿。

Ga·len·ic [gəˈlenik; gəˋlɛnɪk] *a.* **1.** 古希腊医生盖伦的,盖伦医说的。**2.**【药】草本制剂的。

ga·len·i·cal [gəˈlenikəl; geˋlɛnəkəl] **I** *n.*【药】草本制剂。**II** *a.* = Galenic.

Ga·len·ism [ˈgeilənizəm; ˋgelənˏɪzəm] *n.* (古希腊名医)盖伦的医术,医学理论。**-ist** *n.* 奉行盖伦医学理论的人。

ga·len·ite [gəˈliːnait; gəˋlinaɪt] *n.* = galena.

Ga·li·bi [gɑːˈliːbi; gɑˋlibɪ] *n.* (*pl.* **~s**, **~**) 加利比人〔圭亚那的一支印第安人〕。

Ga·li·cia [gəˈliʃiə; gəˋlɪʃɪə] *n.* **1.** 加利西亚省〔西班牙西北部一省〕。**2.** 加利西亚地区〔原为奥匈帝国领土,后分属波兰和前苏联〕。

Ga·li·cian [gəˈliʃən; gəˋlɪʃən] **I** *a.* **1.** (西班牙)加利西亚地方的;加利西亚人的;加利西亚语的。**2.** (波兰)加利西亚地方的,加利西亚人的。**II** *n.* **1.** 西班牙加利西亚人[居民]。**2.** 西班牙加利西亚语的葡萄牙方言。**3.** 波兰的加利西亚人[居民]。

Gal·i·le·an[1] [ˌgæliˈli(ː)ən; ˏgæləˋliən] **I** *a.* (巴勒斯坦北部)加利利的。**II** *n.* **1.** 加利利人[居民]。**2.** 基督教徒。***the ~*** 耶稣。

Gal·i·le·an[2] [ˌgæliˈli(ː)ən; ˏgæləˋlɪən] *a.* (意大利物理学家和天文学家)伽利略的。**~ telescope** 伽利略望远镜。

Gal·i·lee [ˈgæləˌliː; ˋgæləˏli] *n.* 加利利〔巴勒斯坦北部的古罗马地名〕。***Sea of ~*** 〔以〕太巴列湖 (= Lake Tiberias)。

gal·i·lee [ˈgæləliː; ˋgæləli] *n.* 〔英〕(教堂的)门廊;(塔的)前厅,门厅。

Gal·i·le·o [ˌgæləˈliːəu; gæləˋlio], **Gal·i·le·i** 伽利略〔1564—1642,意大利物理学家和天文学家〕。

gal·i·ma·ti·as [ˌgæliˈmeiʃiəs, -ˈmætiəs; ˏgæləˋmeʃɪəs, -ˋmætɪəs] *n.* 胡说八道,胡言乱语。

gal·in·gale [ˈgæliŋgeil; ˋgælɪŋˏgel] *n.*【植】**1.** (英国)高莎草。**2.** = galangal.

gal·i·ot [ˈgæliət; ˋgælɪət] *n.* = galliot.

gal·i·pot [ˈgæliˌpɔt; ˋgælɪˏpɑt] *n.*【化】海松树脂。

gall[1] [gɔːl; gɔl] *n.* **1.** 胆汁;胆囊,胆。**2.** 苦物,苦味。**3.** 恶毒,刻薄,怨恨。**4.** 〔口〕厚脸,无耻。***dip one's pen in ~*** 写恶毒文章。***~ and wormwood*** 最令人厌恶的东西。***have the ~ to do*** 〔美俚〕居然有脸做某事。***in the ~ of bitterness*** 吃苦受难。**~ bladder** 胆囊。**~-stone**【医】胆石。

gall[2] [gɔːl; gɔl] *n.* **1.**【植】(虫)瘿〔植物受到虫害等引起的瘤状物〕。**2.** 五倍子,没食子。*Chinese ~* 五倍子。**~-fly**【动】五倍子虫。**~ gnat** [**midge**]【动】瘿蚊。**~-mite**【动】瘿螨。**~ wasp**【动】瘿蜂。

gall[3] [gɔːl; gɔl] **I** *n.* **1.** (马的)鞍伤,擦伤。**2.** 瑕疵,缺点。**3.** 苦恼,苦恼的原因。**4.** 磨损的地方;(树丛等的)光秃处。**II** *vt.* **1.** 擦伤,擦破;磨损。**2.** 使烦恼,激怒。**3.** 伤害(某人)感情,侮辱。— *vi.* **1.** 被擦伤,被擦破,被磨损。**2.**【机】(因摩擦过度而)咬紧。

gall. = gallon.

Gal·la [ˈgælə; ˋgælə] *n.* (*pl.* **~s**, **~**) **1.** 盖拉人〔埃塞俄比亚南部和索马里毗连的农、牧民〕。**2.** 盖拉语。

Gal·la(g)·her [ˈgæləhə; ˋgæləhɚ] *n.* 加拉赫〔姓氏〕。

gal·lant [ˈgælənt; ˋgælənt] **I** *a.* **1.** 勇敢的;豪侠的,有义气的。**2.** 服饰华丽的,堂皇的,壮丽的,雄壮的,雄伟的。**3.** [gəˈlænt, ˈgælənt; gəˋlænt, ˋgælənt] 对女子殷勤的;好色的。*the honourable and ~ member* (英议会)军人身分的议员。*~ adventures* 艳遇,爱情奇遇。***make a ~ show*** 装饰华丽。**II** *n.* **1.** 豪侠。**2.** 时髦人士。**3.** [gəˈlænt; gəˋlænt] 对妇女献殷勤的男人;情郎。**III** *vt.* **1.** 向(女子)献殷勤。**2.** 护卫,陪送(女子)。— *vi.* 求爱,调情 (*with*)。**~ show** = galanty show. **-ly** *ad.*

gal·lant·ry [ˈgæləntri; ˋgæləntrɪ] *n.* **1.** 勇敢,豪侠;勇敢的言行。**2.** (对女子的)殷勤言行;对女子的尊崇。**3.** 风流事件;淫荡。

Gal·la·tin [ˈgælətin; ˋgælətɪn] *n.* 加勒廷〔姓氏〕。

Gal·le [ˈgɑːlə; ˋgɑlə], **Johann Gottfried** 约翰·戈特弗里德·伽拉〔1812—1910,德国天文学家,海王星的发现者〕。

gal·le·ass, gal·li·ass [ˈgæliˌæs; ˋgælɪˏæs] *n.* (16—17 世纪航行于地中海的,有侧炮的)三桅军舰〔通常用奴隶划桨〕。

gal·le·in [ˈgæliːin, ˈgæliːn; ˋgælɪɪn, ˋgælin] *n.*【化】棓因;棓子色素。

gal·le·on [ˈgæliən; ˋgælɪən] *n.* (15—18 世纪用做军舰或商船的)西班牙大帆船。

gal·ler·ia [gælə'riːə; gælə`riə] *n*.〔意〕(有屋顶的)拱廊商街。

gal·ler·ied ['gælərid; `gælərɪd] *a*. **1**. 有柱廊的,有看台的;有画廊的;有长廊的。**2**. 有地下通道的;有地道的。

gal·ler·y ['gæləri; `gælərɪ] *n*. **1**. 看台,旁听席,(教堂、议院等的)边座,楼座;(剧场中票价最低的)廉价座,顶层楼座。**2**. 观众,听众。**3**. 回廊,走廊;阳台;游廊;穿廊。**4**. 美术馆,美术品陈列室;画廊;〔集合词〕展出中的[收存中的]美术品。**5**. 摄影室;(射击等的)练习室;【海】船尾看台。**6**. (要塞的)地道,地下通道;(水道工程的)暗渠;【矿】水平巷道,平巷,横坑道。*the distinguished guest's* ~贵宾席。*the press* ~记者席。*the public* ~旁听席。***the National G-*** (伦敦的)国家美术馆。***the rogues'*** ~ (警察部门等的)案犯照片栏。***a*** ~ ***hit*** [***shot***, ***stroke***] 卖弄技巧的表演,争取观众喝彩的表演。***bring down the*** ~ 博得满场喝彩。***play to the*** ~ 讨好观众的表演,迎合低级趣味。**II** *vt*., *vi*. (在…)建筑长廊[游廊];(在…)挖地道, ~ **forest** (沿海岸线生长而不向内陆伸展的)海边森林。~**-gods**〔美俚〕顶楼观众。~ **goer** 常去美术馆的人。**-ite** *n*. 顶层楼座的观众。

gal·let ['gælit; `gælɪt] **I** *n*. 碎石,石片。**II** *vt*. 把碎石嵌入…。

gal·ley ['gæli; `gælɪ] *n*. **1**. (古代用奴隶等划桨的)单层甲板大帆船;(古希腊、罗马的)军舰。**2**. 军舰舰长用的大划艇;(船舰、飞机上的)厨房。**3**. 【冶】长方形炉;【印】长方形活字盘,长条校样。***be sent to the*** ~***s*** 被罚作划船苦工。~ **proof**【印】长条(校样)。~ **range** (船)厨房炉灶。~ **slave 1**. 划船的囚犯[奴隶]。**2**.〔美俚〕印刷商。**3**. = drudge. ~**-west** *ad*.〔美俚〕粉碎性地,彻底地,毁灭性地(*knock* ~*-west* 彻底打败(对方),打得(对方)落花流水)。~ **worm**【动】马陆 (= millipede)。

gal·li·am·bic [ˌgæli'æmbik; ˏgælə`æmbɪk] **I** *a*.【韵】抑抑扬扬格的。**II** *n*. 抑抑扬扬格的诗。

gal·li·ard ['gæljəd; `gæljɚd] **I** *n*. **1**. 愉快而勇敢的人。**2**. (十六、七世纪时流行的)轻快活泼的法国双人舞。**II** *a*.〔古〕愉快的,活泼的。

gal·li·ass ['gæliæs; `gælɪæs] *n*. = galleass.

Gal·lic ['gælik; `gælɪk] *a*. **1**. 高卢的,高卢人的。**2**. 法国的,法国人的。

gal·lic[1] ['gælik; `gælɪk] *a*. 虫瘿的,五倍子的,棓子的。~ **acid** 棓酸;五倍子酸,鞣酸;没食子酸;镓酸。

gal·lic[2] ['gælik; `gælɪk] *a*.【化】正镓的,三价镓的。~ **compound**【化】正镓化合物。

Gal·li·can ['gælikən; `gælɪkən] **I** *a*. **1**. = Gallic. **2**. 法国天主教的;(1870 年以前法国天主教徒中)主张限制教皇权力的。**II** *n*. **1**. 法国天主教徒。**2**.【宗】教皇权力限制主义者。**-ism** *n*. (1862 年在法国掀起的)主张限制教皇权力的天主教自治运动。

Gal·li·ce, gal·li·ce ['gælisi(:); `gæləsi] *ad*.〔L.〕用法语;法语化地。

Gal·li·cism, gal·li·cism ['gælisizəm; `gæləˏsɪzəm] *n*. **1**. 法语的成语性词语,法语风格;法语成语[表达方式]。**2**. 法国习惯,法国思维方法。

Gal·li·cize, gal·li·cize ['gælisaiz; `gæləˏsaɪz] *vt*., *vi*. (使)法国化,(使)具有法国风。

gal·li·gas·kins [ˌgæli'gæskinz; ˏgælɪ`gæskɪnz] *n*. **1**.〔*pl*.〕(16—17 世纪用的)宽裤。**2**. (一般的)灯笼裤。**3**.〔英方〕(打猎等用的)皮绑腿。

gal·li·mau·fry [ˌgæli'mɔːfri; ˏgælə`mɔfrɪ] *n*. **1**. 混合,杂凑。**2**. 烧杂烩,炒什锦。

gal·li·na·cean [ˌgæli'neiʃən; ˏgælə`neʃən] **I** *n*.【动】鹑鸡类〔鸡、鹧鸪等〕。**II** *a*. = gallinaceous.

gal·li·na·ceous [gæli'neiʃəs; ˏgælə`neʃəs] *a*. **1**. 家禽的。**2**. 鹑鸡类的。

gall·ing ['gɔːliŋ; `gɔlɪŋ] *a*. **1**. 擦伤的,擦痛的。**2**. 激怒的,烦恼的。**-ly** *ad*.

gal·li·nip·per ['gælinipə; `gælɪˏnɪpɚ] *n*.〔美口〕巨蚊;叮咬人厉害的昆虫。

gal·li·nule ['gælinjuːl, -ˌnuːl; `gæləˏnjul, -ˏnul] *n*. 秧鸡科 (*Rallidae*) 动物(尤指鷭 (*Gallinula chloropus*))。

Gal·li·o ['gæliəu; `gælɪo] *n*. **1**.【圣】迦流〔亚该亚的总督,拒绝过问宗教争端〕。**2**.〔喻〕躲避分外事的职员。

gal·li·ot ['gæliət; `gælɪət] *n*. **1**. (旧时地中海的)一种帆桨并用的平底小快艇。**2**. 单桅轻快的荷兰商船[渔船]。

gal·li·pot[1] ['gælipɔt; `gæləˏpɑt] *n*. **1**. 陶制药罐。**2**.〔古〕药剂师。

gal·li·pot[2] ['gælipɔt; `gæləˏpɑt] *n*. = galipot.

gal·li·um ['gæliəm; `gælɪəm] *n*.【化】镓。~ **arsenide** 砷化镓〔一种合成化合物,主要用作半导体材料〕。

gal·li·vant [ˌgæli'vænt; ˏgælə`vænt] *vi*. **1**. 游荡,闲逛;陪异性游荡。**2**. 寻欢作乐;找刺激。

gall·nut ['gɔːlnʌt; `gɔlˏnʌt] *n*. 五倍子,没食子。

Gal·lo- *comb*. *f*. 表示"法国的" (= Gallic 或 French): *Gallo-Briton* 法英的。

gal·lo·glass ['gæləuˌglæs; `gæloˏglæs] *n*. 古爱尔兰酋长的武装随从,保镖。

Gal·lo·ma·ni·a [ˌgælə*u*'meinjə; ˏgælə`menɪə] *n*. 崇拜法国,法国迷。

gal·lon ['gælən; `gælən] *n*. 加仑〔液体 = 4 夸脱 (quarts),〔英〕固体 = 1/8 蒲式耳 (bushel)〕。*the British imperial* ~ 英制加仑〔= 4.546 升〕。*the wine* [*Winchester*] ~美制加仑〔= 3.7853 升〕。

gal·lon·age ['gælənidʒ; `gælənɪdʒ] *n*. **1**. 加仑量,加仑数。**2**.〔美〕汽油消费量。

gal·loon [gə'luːn; gə`lun] *n*. **1**. 细带,绦带。**2**. 金银丝带,金银花边。**-ed** *a*.

gal·lop ['gæləp; `gæləp] **I** *n*. **1**. (马四脚同时离地的)飞跑。**2**. 骑马奔跑。**3**.〔口〕快步;急驰,飞奔。*a canterbury* ~小跑。*a snail's* ~〔谑〕慢吞吞地走。(***at***) ***a full*** ~ 飞跑,用最大速度。***go at a*** ~ 用尽速力跑去。***go for a*** ~ 去跑一趟;骑马跑一阵。**II** *vt*. **1**. 使(马等)飞跑。**2**. 迅速运送。— *vi*. **1**. (马等)飞跑。(时间)飞驰。**2**. 匆匆地说[读]。**3**. 匆忙地做。~ ***through*** [***over***] ***a book*** 急促地读书。~ *through one's work* 急匆匆地把活儿做完。~**ing consumption**【医】奔马痨,急性肺结核。~**ing dominoes**〔美俚〕骰子。

gal·lo·pade [gælə'peid; ˏgælə`ped] *n*. 四分之二拍的轻快横步舞(曲)。

gal·lop·er ['gæləpə; `gæləpɚ] *n*. **1**. 骑马飞跑的人;飞跑的马。**2**.【军】传令官,副官。**3**.【军】轻野炮,轻便炮车。

Gal·lo·phil(e) ['gælə*u*fail; `gæləˏfaɪl] **I** *n*. 爱好法国的人,亲法者。**II** *a*. 亲法的。

Gal·lo·phobe ['gælə*u*fəub; `gæləˏfob] **I** *n*. 憎恶法国的人,恐法症者。**II** *a*. 恐法的,憎恶法国的。

Gal·lo·pho·bi·a [ˌgæləu'fəubjə; ˏgælə`fobɪə] *n*. 憎恶法国,恐法症。

gal·lous ['gæləs; `gæləs] *a*.【化】亚镓的。

Gal·lo·way ['gæləwei; `gæləˏwe] *n*. **1**. 加洛韦〔苏格兰西南部地名〕。**2**. 加洛韦马〔一种产于该地体型小但强壮的马〕;加洛韦牛〔一种产于该地黑毛的肉用牛〕。

gal·low·glass ['gæləuˌglæs; `gæloˏglæs] *n*. = galloglass.

gal·lows ['gæləuz; `gæloz] **I** *n*. (*pl*. ~*es*, ~) **1**. 绞刑架;绞台。**2**. 挂牌架,(体操用的)铁杆架;【海】吊杆。**3**. 绞刑,应受绞刑的人。**4**.〔*pl*.〕〔方〕(裤子的)吊带,背带。***cheat the*** ~ 逃脱绞刑,逃避死罪。***come to*** [***die on***] ***the*** ~ 被绞死。***have a*** ~ ***look*** = ***have the*** ~ ***in one's face*** 有被绞死的面相,有不得善终的脸相。***The*** ~ ***groans for him*** [***you***]. 绞架在等着他[你]呢。**II** *a*. 该绞死的;穷凶极恶的,坏透的;非常的。~ **bird** 应处绞刑的犯人;穷凶极恶的人。~ **bitts**〔*pl*.〕【海】甲板中央的双柱吊架。~ **humo(u)r**〔美〕凄惨的幽默;充满怨恨的幽默。~ **look** 犯死罪的面相。~**-ripe** *a*. 应处绞刑的。

G

～ **tree** 绞刑架,绞台。

Gal·lup [ˈgæləp; ˋgæləp] ***n*.** **1.** 盖洛普〔姓氏〕。**2.** **George H.** ～ 盖洛普〔美国民众舆论的统计家〕。～ **poll** (美国)盖洛普民意测验〔通过对一部分人进行典型调查以了解民意的方法〕。

gal·lus·es [ˈgæləsiz; ˋgæləsız] ***n*.** 〔*pl*.〕〔美方〕(裤子的)吊带,背带。

gal·ly [ˈgæli; ˋgælı] ***vt*.** (**-lied**, **ly·ing**)〔主方〕吓唬,恐吓。

Ga·lois [gælˈwɑː; ˏgalˋwa], **Evariste** 伽罗瓦〔1811—1832,法国数学家〕。～ **equation** 伽罗瓦方程。～ **field** 有限域[体],伽罗瓦域。～ **theory** 伽罗瓦理论。

ga·loot [gəˈluːt; gəˋlut] ***n*.** **1.** 〔美俚〕蠢货,傻瓜。**2.** 无经验的青年海员。

gal·op [ˈgæləp; ˋgæləp] **I** ***n*.** = gallopade. **II** ***vi*.** 跳四分之二拍的轻快舞蹈。

ga·lore [gəˈlɔː, -ˈlɔə; gəˋlɔr, -ˋlor] **I** ***ad*.** 多,许多,丰盛。***with beef and ale*** [***beer***] ～ 酒菜丰盛。**II** ***n*.** 〔罕〕丰富,充足。*in* ～丰富。

ga·losh [gəˈlɔʃ; gəˋlɑʃ] ***n*.** 〔*pl*.〕(长统橡皮)套鞋。**-ed** ***a*.** 穿长统橡皮套鞋的。

gals. = gallons.

Gals·wor·thy [ˈgɔːlzwəːði, ˈgælzwəːði; ˋgɔlzwɚðı, ˋgælzwɚðı] **1.** ***n*.** 高尔斯沃西[高尔斯华绥]〔姓氏〕。**2.** **John** ～ 约翰·高尔斯华绥〔1867—1933,英国小说家,剧作家〕。

Galt [gɔːlt; gɔlt] ***n*.** 高尔特〔姓氏〕。

Gal·ton [ˈgɔːltən; ˋgɔltn̩] ***n*.** **1.** 高尔顿〔姓氏〕。**2.** **Sir Francis** ～ 高尔顿〔1822—1911,为达尔文的表弟,1883年创优生学,对指纹学,数学,气象学均有贡献〕。

ga·lumph [gəˈlʌmf; gəˋlʌmf] ***vi*.** 得意洋洋地走,昂首阔步地前进。

galv. = **1.** galvanic. **2.** galvanism. **3.** galvanized.

G

Gal·va·ni [gælˈvɑːni; gælˋvɑnı], **Luigi** 卢杰·贾法尼〔1737—1798,意大利解剖医学家,电流发现人〕。

gal·van·ic [gælˈvænik; gælˋvænık] ***a*.** **1.** 以化学方法产生电流的。**2.** 触电似的;惊起的,激励的。**3.** (笑等)不自然的。～ **battery** [**cell**] 原电池(组)。～ **belt** (医疗用)电带。～ **current** 直流,动电电流。～ **electricity** 动电。～ **pile** 电堆。～ **shock** 电休克。

gal·va·nism [ˈgælvənizəm; ˋgælvəˏnızəm] ***n*.** **1.** 由原电池产生的电。**2.** 流电学。**3.** 【医】流电疗法。**4.** 有力,有劲。

gal·va·nist [ˈgælvənist; ˋgælvənıst] ***n*.** 流电学家。

gal·va·nize [ˈgælvənaiz; ˋgælvəˏnaız] ***vt*.** **1.** 通电流于。**2.** 电镀,给(铁等)镀锌。**3.** (用电)刺激,使兴奋,激励。*the ～d iron* 镀锌铁皮,白铁皮,马口铁。***be*** ～ ***to*** [***into***] ***life*** 受刺激而活跃起来。**-ni·za·tion** [ˌgælvənaiˈzeiʃən; ˏgælvənaiˋzeʃən] ***n*.**

gal·va·niz·er [ˈgælvənaizə; ˋgælvəˏnaızə] ***n*.** **1.** 电镀工;电镀器。**2.** 激励者。

gal·va·no- *comb. f*. 表示"电的","电流的"(= galvanic 或 galvanism): *galvano*meter, *galvano*plasty.

gal·van·o·graph [gælˈvænəgrɑːf; gælˋvænəgræf] ***n*.** 【印】电铸版;电铸版印刷品。

gal·va·nog·ra·phy [ˌgælvəˈnɔgræfi; ˏgælvəˋnɑgrəfı] ***n*.** 电铸制版术。

gal·va·no·mag·net·ic [ˌgælvənəuˈmægˈnetik; ˏgælvənomægˋnetık] ***a*.** 电磁的。

gal·va·nom·e·ter [ˌgælvəˈnɔmitə; ˏgælvəˋnɑmətə] ***n*.** 电流计,电表。*a ballistic* ～冲击电流计。*Einthoven* ～弦线检流计。*a tangent* ～正切电流计。

gal·va·no·plas·tics [ˌgælvənəuˈplæstiks; ˏgælvanoˋplæstıks], **gal·va·no·plas·ty** [-ti; -tı] ***n*.** 电铸(制版法),电镀法。

gal·va·no·scope [ˈgælvənəuskəup; ˋgælvənəˏskop] ***n*.** 验电(流)器,检流器。**-ic** ***a*.**

gal·ways [ˈgɔːlweiz; ˋgɔlwez] ***n*.** 〔*pl*.〕〔俚〕连鬓胡子。

Gal·we·gian [gælˈwiːdʒən; gælˋwidʒıən] **I** ***a*.** (苏格兰)加洛维区的;加洛维区人的。**II** ***n*.** 加洛维人,加洛维区居民。

gal·yak, gal·yac [ˈgæljæk; ˋgæljæk] ***n*.** 羔皮。

gam[1] [gæm; gæm] **I** ***n*.** **1.** 【海】鲸鱼群。**2.** (捕鲸船间的)交际性访问,联欢,〔美方〕(陆上的)联欢,聚会。**II** ***vi*.** (**-mm-**) **1.** (像鲸鱼一样)成群,聚拢,聚集。**2.** (捕鲸船员)在海上交际,联欢。— ***vt*.** **1.** (在海上)与…联欢。**2.** 闲聊以消磨(时间)。

gam[2] [gæm; gæm] ***n*.** 〔美俚〕腿(尤指女人健美的腿)。

GAM = guided aircraft missile 机载导[飞]弹。

Ga·ma [ˈgɑːmə; ˋgɑmə], **Vasco de** 伽马〔1469? —1524,葡萄牙航海家。首先经海路到达印度〕。

ga·ma [ˈgɑːmə; ˋgɑmə] **grass** 【植】鸭茅状磨擦禾(*Tripsacum dactyloides*)〔产于美洲,为饲料草〕。

gamb, gambe [gæmb, gæm; gæmb, gæm] ***n*.** (兽的)腿,胫。

gam·bade [gæmˈbeid; gæmˋbed], **gam·ba·do** [-ˈbeidəu; -ˋbedo] ***n*.** (*pl*. ～*s*, ～*es*) **1.** (马的)跳跃。**2.** 奇怪举动,荒唐行为,戏谑,恶作剧。**3.** 长裹腿,长统靴。

gam·be·son [ˈgæmbsən; ˋgæmbəsən] ***n*.** 中世纪软铠甲〔革制品或布中有填塞物的布制品〕。

Gam·bi·a [ˈgæmbiə; ˋgæmbıə] ***n*.** 冈比亚(甘比亚)〔非洲〕。**-an** ***n*.** 冈比亚人。

gam·bi(e)r [ˈgæmbiə; ˋgæmˏbır] ***n*.** 棕儿茶,黑儿茶。

gam·bit [ˈgæmbit; ˋgæmbıt] ***n*.** **1.** (国际象棋中牺牲一卒以取得优势的)起手着法。**2.** (交易等的)开始,开场白。**3.** 策略,策划占人上风的一着。

gam·ble [ˈgæmbl; ˋgæmbl] **I** ***vi*.** **1.** 赌,赌博。**2.** 投机;孤注一掷,冒险。— ***vt*.** **1.** 赌输;以…打赌。**2.** 冒…的险。～ *at cards* 打纸牌。～ *in stocks* [*rice*, *gold*] 做股票[大米、黄金]投机。～ ***away*** 乱花,滥用;赌输掉。～ ***on*** 〔俚〕信任,靠牢。～ ***oneself out of house and home*** 赌得倾家荡产。**II** ***n*.** **1.** 赌博,赌。**2.** 投机;冒险。***on the*** ～ 因赌,贪赌。**-some** ***a*.** 爱赌的;喜欢投机的。

gam·bler [ˈgæmblə; ˋgæmblɚ] ***n*.** 赌钱者,赌徒;投机商人。

gam·bling [ˈgæmbliŋ; ˋgæmblıŋ] ***n*.** 赌博,投机,冒险。～**-den** ***n*.** 赌场。～ **hell** [**house**]〔口〕赌窟。～ **joint** 赌场。

gam·bly [ˈgæmbli; ˋgæmblı] ***a*.** 碰运气的。

gam·boge [gæmˈbuːʒ; gæmˋbuʒ] ***n*.** **1.** 【化】藤黄胶脂。**2.** 橙黄色。

gam·bol [ˈgæmbəl; ˋgæmbəl] **I** ***n*.** 欢跃,跳跃;嬉戏。**II** ***vi*.** (〔英〕**-ll-**)欢跃,跳跃;嬉戏。

gam·brel [ˈgæmbrəl; ˋgæmbrəl] ***n*.** **1.** 【动】(马等的)跗关节。**2.** (肉店等的)挂肉钩架。**3.** 【美建】复斜屋顶〔又称 ～ roof 或 curb roof〕。

gam·bu·si·a [gæmˈbjuːʒə, -ʒiə; gæmˋbjuʒə, -ʒıə] ***n*.** 【动】食蚊鱼(*Gambusia affinis*)。

game[1] [geim; gem] **I** ***n*.** **1.** 游戏;娱乐;戏谑;运动。**2.** (运动、棋类等的)比赛,竞赛;(比赛中的)一盘,一场,一局;胜利;比分,得分,比赛成绩。**3.** 〔*pl*.〕比赛会,运动会。**4.** 游戏用具,比赛器具;比赛方式;比赛规则。**5.** 计划,事业。**6.** 花招,诡计,策略。**7.** 〔集合词〕猎物,野味;(鹄等的)群;野外游戏[游猎、鹰狩等]。**8.** 追求物,目的物。**9.** 胆量,勇气。**10.** 〔口〕行当,职业。*What a* ～! 多精彩的比赛啊! 多么有趣! *a close* ～接近的比分。*an advertising* ～广告竞争。*a* ～ *not worth the candle* 得不偿失。*How is the* ～? 胜负如何? *The* ～ *is 4 all* [*7 to 6*, *love three*]. 比赛成绩是4比4[7比6,0比3]。*The* ～ *is up* [*over*]. 无成功希望;一切都完了。*One careless move loses the whole* ～. 〔谚〕一着不慎,满盘皆输。*None of your* ～*s*! 别耍花招了! *That's a* ～ *two people can play*. 这一套你会我也会。*That's not the*

~！那样干不对。*The same old* ~！又是那一套老玩意儿！惯用伎俩！*winged* ~可猎鸟类。*big* ~【猎】巨兽［狮、虎等］；巨大的目标，冒险的事业。*fair* ~ 非禁猎的鸟兽；正当目的物；攻击的对象。*forbidden* ~ 禁猎的鸟兽。***ahead of the*** ~〔美口〕（特别在赌博中）处于赢家地位。***be on*** [***off***] ***one's*** ~（马、选手等）竞技状态好［不好］。***fly at high*** ~ 胸怀大志。***fly at higher*** ~ 怀有更大的抱负；得陇望蜀。***force the*** ~（板球等中）冒险快速得分。~ ***and*** ~ = ~ ***all*** 一比一。~ ***and*** (***set***)【网球】比赛完结。***a*** ~ ***of chance*** 碰运气取胜的游戏。***a*** ~ ***of skill*** 凭技术取胜的游戏。***give the*** ~ ***away*** 露馅。***have a*** ~ ***with*** 蒙蔽，瞒骗。***have the*** ~ ***in one's hands*** 有必胜把握。***make*** ~ ***of*** 嘲笑，捉弄。***play a dangerous*** ~ 干冒险玩意儿。***play a deep*** ~ 背地捣鬼。***play a double*** ~ 耍两面派。***play a good*** [***poor***] ~赌法高明［笨拙］。***play a losing*** [***winning***] ~ 作无［有］胜利希望的比赛；干明知无益［有利］的事。***play a waiting*** ~ 待机下手。***play sb.'s*** ~ = ***play the*** ~ ***of sb.*** 无意中给别人占了便宜。***play the*** ~ 按规则玩游戏；做事光明正大，守规矩。***see through sb.'s*** ~ 看穿某人诡计。***speak in*** ~ 说着玩，开玩笑。***spoil the*** ~ 弄坏（事情）。***throw up the*** ~ 罢手，认输。**II** ***a.*** **1.** 关于猎获物的，关于野味的。**2.** 斗鸡似的；雄纠纠的，勇敢的，倔强的。**3.** 对…有兴趣的，爱。~ *pie* 野味馅饼。***be*** ~ ***for*** [***to do***] ***anything*** 对什么都有兴趣。***die*** ~ 死斗，死拚；奋斗到底。**III** ***vi.*** 打赌，赌输赢。— ***vt.*** 赌输（*away*）。~ **acts** 狩猎条例。~**-bag** ***n.*** 猎袋。~ **ball** **1.** 决胜负的一球。**2.**（送给球员或教练的）得胜纪念球。~ **bird** 猎鸟，猎禽，法律许可捕猎的鸟类。~ **breaker**（橄榄球）决胜的关键球；得关键分的球员。~ **cock** 斗鸡。~ **fish** 供捕钓的鱼（尤指上钓时猛烈挣扎者）。~ **fowl** 斗鸡；猎鸟。~**-keeper** 猎物看守人；猎场看守人。~ **land** 猎场。~ **laws** 狩猎法。~ **licence** **1.** 许可狩猎；狩猎执照。**2.** 买卖野味许可（证）。~ **plan** 精心策划的行动。~ **preserver** 猎区经营者。~ **room** 娱乐室。~**s master**〔英〕体育［体操］教师。~ **tenant** 猎场［渔场］承租人。~ **theory** 策略运筹法［学］，形势运筹学〔运用数学分析的方法去选择最好的策略以求在比赛、战争，商业等上缩小损失或转小胜为大胜的方法，也叫 theory of game〕。

game² [geim; gem] ***a.***〔口〕跛的，瘸的；残废的，受伤的。

gam·e·lan [ˈgæməlæn; ˋgæməlæn] ***n.*** 嘎麦兰〔印尼器乐大合奏，中有竹木琴，锣和其他打击乐器〕。

game·ly [ˈgeimli; ˋgemlɪ] ***ad.*** 雄赳赳地，兴致勃勃地。

game·ness [ˈgeimnis; ˋgemnɪs] ***n.*** 勇气，兴致勃勃。

games·man·ship [ˈgeimzmənʃip; ˋgemzmən͵ʃɪp] ***n.***（运动、比赛中）致胜绝招，小动作。

game·some [ˈgeimsəm; ˋgemsəm] ***a.*** 爱玩耍的，爱闹着玩的，快乐的。**-ly** ***ad.*** **-ness** ***n.***

game·ster [ˈgeimstə; ˋgemstɚ] ***n.*** 赌棍，赌徒。

gam·e·tan·gi·um [ˌgæmiˈtændʒiəm; ͵gæməˋtændʒɪəm] ***n.***（*pl.* ***-gi·a*** [-ə; -ə]）【植】配子囊。

gam·ete [gəˈmiːt; ˋgæmit] ***n.***【生】配子。

ga·me·to·cyte [gəˈmiːtə*u*sait; gəˋmitə͵saɪt] ***n.***【生】配子母细胞。

ga·me·to·gen·e·sis [gəˌmiːtə*u*ˈdʒenisis; ͵gæmətəˋdʒenəsɪs] ***n.*** 配子发生。**-gen·ic** [-ˈdʒenik; -ˋdʒɛnɪk], **gam·e·tog·e·nous** [ˈgæmiˈtɔdʒinəs; ˋgæmɚˋtɑdʒənəs] ***a.*** **gam·e·tog·e·ny** [-ni; -nɪ] ***n.***

gam·e·tog·o·ny [ˌgæməˈtɔdʒəni; ͵gæməˋtɑdʒənɪ] ***n.*** 有性生殖。

ga·me·to·phore [gəˈmiːtəfɔː; gəˋmitə͵fɔr] ***n.***【植】配子托。**-phoric** ***a.***

ga·me·to·phyte [gəˈmiːtəfait; gəˋmito͵faɪt] ***n.***【植】配子体。

gam·ic [ˈgæmik; ˋgæmɪk] ***a.***【生】受精后方可发育的，受精的。

gam·i·ly [ˈgeimili; ˋgeməlɪ] ***ad.*** 勇敢地；大胆地。

gam·in [ˈgæmin; ˋgæmɪn] ***n.***〔F.〕**1.** 流浪儿；顽童。**2.** 妖冶的女人。

gam·ine [gæˈmiːn; gæˋmin] ***n.***〔F.〕**1.** 女流浪儿；女顽童。**2.** 妖冶的女人。

gam·i·ness [ˈgeiminis; ˋgemənɪs] ***n.*** 勇敢。

gam·ing [ˈgeimiŋ; ˋgemɪŋ] ***n.*** 赌博。~ **house** 赌场。~ **table** 赌台。

gam·ma [ˈgæmə; ˋgæmə] ***n.*** **1.** 希腊语的第三个字母（Γ, γ =〔英〕G, g）；第三位的东西；【虫】γ 纹蛾；【天】（亮度居于第三位的）γ 星。**2.**〔*pl.*〕γ 量，微克（=100 万分之一克）。**3.**【物】伽马（磁场强度单位 = 10^{-5} 奥斯特）。**4.**【摄】灰度（非线性）系数。~ **decay**【物】γ 衰变。~ **globulin** γ 球蛋白。~(-) **interferon** ***n.*** γ－干扰素〔一种淋巴激活素，用以治疗癌症〕。~ **knife**【医】γ 手术刀，伽玛刀〔可使发出的 γ 射线束聚焦，放射外科上用于治疗脑瘤等〕。~ **minus** 仅次于第三等。~ **plus** 稍高于第三等。~ **ray**【物】**1.** 光（量）子。**2.** γ 射线。~ **ray astronomy** γ 射线天文学。~ **sonde** γ 探空仪。

gam·ma·di·on [gəˈmeidiɔn; gəˋmedɪɔn] ***n.***（*pl.* ***-di·a*** [-diə; -dɪə]）（由 Γ 形成的）卐字形，卍字形。

gam·mer [ˈgæmə; ˋgæmɚ] ***n.***〔英〕乡下老太婆〔*cf.* gaffer〕。

gam·mex·ane [ˈgæmeksein; ˋgæmɛksen] ***n.***【化】六氯化苯，六六六杀虫剂。

gam·mon¹ [ˈgæmən; ˋgæmən] **I** ***n.***〔英口〕胡说八道；欺骗。**II** ***int.*** 胡说八道！**III** ***vi.*** 说瞎话；装假。— ***vt.*** 欺骗，愚弄。~ ***and patter*** **1.** 废话。**2.** 隐语；行话。

gam·mon² [ˈgæmən; ˋgæmən] **I** ***n.*** 腌猪腿，熏腿；熏制五花肉。**II** ***vt.*** 把…制成腊肉。~ ***and spinach*** 腊肉烧菠菜。

gam·mon³ [ˈgæmən; ˋgæmən] **I** ***n.***（西洋双陆棋戏中的）全胜〔即在对方未弃一子前即取得胜利〕；连赢两盘。**II** ***vt.***（以全胜［连赢两盘］）击败，打败（对方）。

gam·mon⁴ [ˈgæmən; ˋgæmən] ***vt.***【海】把（船首斜桅）缚在船头上。

gam·my [ˈgæmi; ˋgæmɪ] ***a.***〔英方〕跛的；残废的〔尤指腿而言〕。

gam·o- *comb. f.* 表示 **1.**【生】"雌雄合体"。**2.**【植】（器官的）结合：*gamo*genesis, *gamo*petalous.

gam·o·gen·e·sis [ˌgæmə*u*ˈdʒenisis; ͵gæməˋdʒɛnɪsɪs] ***n.***【生】有性生殖。

gam·o·pet·al·ous [ˌgæmə*u*ˈpetələs; ͵gæməˋpɛtələs] ***a.***【植】合瓣的。

gam·o·phyl·lous [ˌgæmə*u*ˈfiləs; ͵gæməˋfɪləs] ***a.***【植】合被（片）的。

gam·o·sep·al·ous [ˌgæmə*u*ˈsepələs; ͵gæməˋsɛpələs] ***a.***【植】合萼的。

-gamous *comb. f.* 表示"…婚的"，"…性的"：bi*gamous*, poly*gamous*.

gamp [gæmp; gæmp] ***n.***〔英〕笨重的大伞。

gam·ut [ˈgæmət; ˋgæmət] ***n.*** **1.**【乐】音阶；长音阶；全音域。**2.**〔喻〕整个领域，全体。*the complete* ~ *of the spectrum* 光谱波长的全区域。*the whole* ~ *of experience* 所有经验。*run the* ~ *of dissipation* 极端放荡。*run the* ~ *of emotions* 百感交集。

gam·y [ˈgeimi; ˋgemɪ] ***a.*** **1.** 猎物多的。**2.** 有煮野味香味的。**3.** 有胆量的，好斗的。**4.** 下流的，猥亵的。

-gamy *comb. f.* 表示"…婚"：bi*gamy*, poly*gamy*.

gan, 'gan [gæn; gæn] ***v.***〔古、诗〕gin³的过去式。

Gan·da [ˈgændə; ˋgændə] ***n.***（*pl.* ~*s*, ~）**1.** 干达人〔乌干达南部的农民〕。**2.** 干达语〔属班图语系〕。

gan·der [ˈgændə; ˋgændɚ] **I** ***n.*** **1.** 雄鹅。**2.** 蠢汉。**3.**〔俚〕一看，一眼。***see how the*** ~ ***hops***〔美口〕观望，看风使舵。***take a*** ~ 看一看。**II** ***vi.***〔方〕漫步，游荡。

Gan·dhi [ˈgændiː; ˋgɑndɪ] **1.** 甘地〔印度姓氏〕。**2.** **Mohandas** ~ 莫汉达斯·甘地〔1869—1948，印度民族主义

G

领袖和社会改革家,有圣雄甘地之称〕。3. **Indira** ～ 英迪拉·甘地夫人〔1917—1984,尼赫鲁之女,担任印国大党领袖、政府总理等职,1984 年遇刺身亡〕。4. **Rajiv** ～拉吉夫·甘地〔1944—1991,英迪拉之子,为国大党领袖,自1984 年任总理,1991 年 5 月 22 日大选时遇刺身亡〕。

Gan·dhi·ism [ˈgændiizəm; ˋgændɪ͵ɪzəm] ***n*.** (印度甘地提出运用"非暴力抵抗"和"不合作运动"来实现民族解放的)甘地主义。

gan·dy [ˈgændi; ˋgændɪ] **dancer** 〔俚〕(美国)铁路工段工人;季节流动工。

ga·nef, ga·nof [ˈgɑːnəf; ˋgɑnəf] ***n*.** 〔美俚〕贼。

gang[1] [gæŋ; gæŋ] **I** ***n*.** **1.** 一队,一群;(盗贼等的)一帮;(儿童等的)一伙。**2.** (工具、机械等的)一套。**3.** 〔美俚〕棒球队。**4.** 〔美俚〕大量。*a* ～ *of thieves* 一帮贼。*a chain* ～系成一串的囚犯。*the* ～ *of roughs* 暴力集团。**II** ***vt*.** **1.** 把…编成班组。**2.** 〔口〕合伙攻击。**3.** 使成套。— ***vi*.** 〔美〕成群结队;作伴 (*with*)。～ ***up*** 〔美口〕成群结队;勾结起来;聚集,集合。～ ***up on*** [***against***] 〔美俚〕成群结队的对抗[攻击]。～ ***up with*** 〔美俚〕同…联合起来一致行动。～**buster** 〔美俚〕打击流氓组织的执法人员。～ **control** 【机】共轴控制。～ **drill** 【机】排式钻床;排式钻头。～ **hook** 〔美〕(钓鱼竿的)联钩,串钩。～ **land** 〔美俚〕盗贼充斥的街区;黑社会。～ **maintenance**, ～ **master** 把头;工长。～ **mill** 框锯制材厂。～ **milling** 多刀铣削,排铣。～ **plough** [**plow**] 多铧犁。～ **saw** 框锯,排锯。～ **shag** 〔美俚〕爵士乐即席演奏会;淫乱的聚会。～ **socket** 联通插座。～ **switch** 联动[同轴]开关。～ **war** (歹徒之间的)打群架;火拼。～**-up** ***n*.** **1.** 联合(以对付某人或某国)。**2.** 攻击。

gang[2] [gæŋ; gæŋ] ***n*.** = gangue.

gang[3] [gæŋ; gæŋ] **I** ***n*.** 〔Scot.〕路,路程。**II** ***vi*.** 〔Scot.〕去,行走。～ ***agley*** 〔Scot.〕(计划等)出差错。～ ***one's ain gait*** 按自己的意思行事。

G

gang·board [ˈgæŋbɔːd; ˋgæŋ͵bord] ***n*.** 【海】**1.** (船首楼与船尾楼间的狭窄的)道板,(上甲板两侧的)过道。**2.** (上下船的)跳板,梯板。

gange [gændʒ; gændʒ] ***vt*.** 用细金属线加固(钓钩[钓线])。

gang·er [ˈgæŋə; ˋgæŋɚ] ***n*.** 〔英〕把头,工头。

Gan·ges [ˈgændʒiːz; ˋgændʒiz] ***n*.** 恒河〔发源于喜马拉雅山,流经印度和孟加拉〕。

gan·gli·a [ˈgæŋgliə; ˋgæŋglɪə] ***n*.** ganglion 的复数。

gan·gli·at·ed [ˈgæŋgliˌeitid; ˋgæŋglɪ͵etɪd] ***a*.** 有神经节的 (= gangliate).

gan·gling [ˈgæŋgliŋ; ˋgæŋglɪŋ] ***a*.** 瘦长的;身材难看的。

gan·gli·on [ˈgæŋgliən; ˋgæŋglɪən] ***n*.** (*pl*. ～*s*, *-gli·a* [-gliə; -glɪə]) **1.** 【解】神经节。**2.** 【医】腱鞘囊肿。**3.** (活动、力量、兴趣等的)中心。

gan·gli·on·ate, gan·gli·on·at·ed [ˈgæŋgliəneit, -tid; ˋgæŋglɪən͵et, -netɪd] ***a*.** = gangliate.

gan·gli·on·ic [ˌgæŋgliˈɔnik; ͵gæŋglɪˋɑnɪk] ***a*.** 神经节的。

gan·gly [ˈgæŋli; ˋgæŋlɪ] ***a*.** = gangling.

gang·plank [ˈgæŋplæŋk; ˋgæŋ͵plæŋk] ***n*.** 〔美〕= gangboard.

gan·grel [ˈgæŋgrəl; ˋgæŋgrəl] ***n*.** 〔Scot.〕流浪汉,乞丐。

gan·grene [ˈgæŋgriːn; ˋgæŋgrin] **I** ***n*.** **1.** 【医】坏疽。**2.** 腐败,堕落。**II** ***vi*.** 生坏疽,腐烂。— ***vt*.** 使生坏疽,使腐烂。

gan·gre·nop·sis [ˌgæŋgreˈnɔpsis; ͵gæŋgreˋnɑpsɪs] ***n*.** 【医】走马疳,口颊坏疽。

gan·gre·nous [ˈgæŋgrinəs; ˋgæŋgrɪnəs] ***a*.** 【医】坏疽性的。

gangs·man [ˈgæŋzmən; ˋgæŋzmən] ***n*.** (*pl*. *-men*) **1.** = ganger. **2.** = gangster.

gang·ster [ˈgæŋstə; ˋgæŋstɚ] ***n*.** 〔美〕匪徒,歹徒,恶棍。～**dom** 〔集合词〕匪徒,歹徒,恶棍;黑社会。**-ism** ***n*.** 〔美〕歹徒的犯罪行为。

Gang·tok [ˈgʌŋtɔk; ˋgʌŋtɑk] ***n*.** 甘托克〔锡金首都〕。

gangue [gæŋ; gæŋ] ***n*.** 【矿】脉石,矿石中的杂质,矿物渣,尾矿。

gang·way [ˈgæŋwei; ˋgæŋ͵we] **I** ***n*.** **1.** 通路。**2.** (剧场、音乐厅等座位间的)过道。**3.** 〔英〕下议院中划分前后座位的通道。**4.** (运输木材的)倾斜道。**5.** 【矿】主巷道,主运输平巷;木桥。**6.** 【船】舷门,舷梯。跳板 (= gangboard). **7.** (工地上临时搭建的)木板路。***bring to the*** ～(把水手)拉到舷门鞭打。***members above*** [***below***] ***the*** ～ 英国议会下院中同其所属政党政策意见较一致[不甚一致]的议员。**II** ***int*.** 闪开! 让路! ～ **ladder** 舷梯。

gan·is·ter, gan·nis·ter [ˈgænistə; ˋgænɪstɚ] ***n*.** **1.** 【地】致密矽[硅]岩。**2.** 【冶】矽[硅]石〔酸性炉衬料〕。～ **brick** 矽[硅]砖。～ **sand** 矽[硅]粉,石英砂。

gan·ja, gan·jah [ˈgɑːndʒə; ˋgɑndʒɑ] ***n*.** **1.** 大麻。**2.** 烟熏过的大麻叶和花(尤指卷作香烟状作为麻醉药吸食的大麻叶和花) (= marijuana)。

gan·net [ˈgænit; ˋgænɪt] ***n*.** **1.** 【动】塘鹅。**2.** 〔俚〕贪婪的人。**-ry** ***n*.**

gan·oid [ˈgænɔid; ˋgænɔɪd] **I** ***n*.** 【鱼】硬鳞鱼,光鳞鱼。**II** ***a*.** (鱼)硬鳞的,光鳞的。*a* ～ *scale* 硬鳞。

gan·o·in [ˈgænəuin; ˋgænoɪn] ***n*.** (鱼鳞的)闪光质,硬鳞质。

gant·let[1] [ˈgɔːntlit; ˋgæntlɪt] ***n*.** = gauntlet[1].

gant·let[2] [ˈgɔːntlit; ˋgɑntlɪt] **I** ***n*.** **1.** (已往军队中使犯人走在两排人中间受鞭打的)夹笞刑。**2.** 交叉射击,交叉火网。**3.** 【铁路】(二线经过桥或隧道时的)汇合的一段轨道,套式轨道的套叠处。～ *track* 套式轨道。***run the*** ～ 受夹笞刑;受夹攻,遭受严格考验。**II** ***vt*.** 使(轨道等)套叠。

gant·line [ˈgæntˌlain; ˋgænt͵laɪn] ***n*.** 【海】桅顶吊索。

gan·try [ˈgæntri; ˋgæntrɪ] ***n*.** **1.** 桶架。**2.** 【机】龙门起重机;(起重机的)构台[门架]。**3.** 【铁路】跨轨信号架。**4.** 【宇】导弹拖车。**5.** 火箭平台〔具有多层平台并可移动,用以吊竖火箭及发射前检修〕。～ **crane** 高架龙门起重机,跨线起重机。

Gan·y·mede [ˈgænimiːd; ˋgænə͵mid] ***n*.** **1.** 【希神】甘尼米〔宙斯神的侍酒童子〕。**2.** 〔谑〕侍酒少年,侍者。**3.** 【天】木星的第三卫星。

ganz·feld [ˈgɔntsˌfelt; ˋgɔnts͵fɛlt] ***a*.** (中和外界刺激因素的)超感官知觉全域试验的。

GAO = General Accounting Office 〔美〕总审计局。

gaol [dʒeil; dʒel] **I** ***n*.** 牢狱,监狱。*be sent to* ～入狱。***deliver a*** ～ 提审监狱中的全部罪犯。***in*** ～ 在押。**II** ***vt*.** 监禁,使…下牢,把…关进监狱。★美国用 jail [dʒeil; dʒel],英国在正式文件中用 gaol,一般文字中 gaol 与 jail 通用。～**-bird** 囚犯;惯犯;恶棍,无赖。～ **delivery** **1.** 越狱,劫狱。**2.** 【英法】提审囚犯出清监狱。～ **fever** (从前在监狱中流行的)恶性伤寒。～ **sentences** 徒刑。

gaol·er [ˈdʒeilə; ˋdʒelɚ] ***n*.** 监狱看守。

gaol·er·ess [ˈdʒeiləris; ˋdʒelərɪs] ***n*.** 监狱女看守。

gap [gæp; gæp] **I** ***n*.** **1.** (墙壁、篱笆等的)裂口,裂缝;豁口,缺口。【军】突破口。**2.** (意见的)龃龉,分歧;隔阂,距离,差距。**3.** 山峡,隘口。**4.** 间隙;【机】火花隙;【空】(双翼机的)翼隔。**5.** (文章等中的)脱漏,中断;(知识等的)空白,缺陷。*a* ～ *in historical records* 史料的中断。*credibility* ～ 信用差距。*generation* ～代沟〔不同代的人之间的思想隔阂〕。～*s between teeth* 齿缝。*the* ～ *between imports and exports* 进出口差额。***bridge*** [***close, fill, stop, supply***] ***a*** ～ 填补空白,弥补缺陷。***stand in the*** ～ 首当其冲,挺身阻挡。**II** ***vt*.** (*-pp-*) 使豁裂,使生罅隙。— ***vi*.** 豁开。～**-filler** ***n*.** 【无】雷达辅助天线。～**-toothed** ***a*.** (由于缺牙)齿缝很大的。

Gap·a [ˈgæpə; ˋgæpə] ***n*.** 地对空无线电导航飞行器。

gape [geip; gep] I *n*. 1. 张口,打呵欠。2. 张口呆看。3. 豁口。4.【动】嘴裂,喙裂;口张时的阔度。*the* ~*s* (家禽的)张口病;〔谑〕打一阵呵欠。II *vi*. 1. 张大嘴;打呵欠。2. (地面等)开裂;裂开。3. 目瞪口呆地凝视。~ *after* [*for*] 渴望得到。~ *at* 张口结舌地看,吃惊地呆看。~-**mouthed** *a*. 张开大嘴的。~ **worm** (引起家禽患张口病的)线虫。

gap·er [ˈgeipə; ˋgepɚ] *n*. 1. 张口呆看的人。2. 打呵欠的人。3. 印度阔嘴鸟;张口蛤蜊。4.〔美俚〕镜子。

gape·seed [ˈgeipsiːd; ˋgepˏsid] *n*. 〔英方〕注目;引起注意的人[事]。*buy* [*seek*, *sow*] ~〔讽〕在市场上闲逛,在市场上呆看。

gapped [gæpt; gæpt] *a*. 豁裂的,有缺口的。

gap·py [ˈgæpi; ˋgæpɪ] *a*. 罅隙多的;有裂口的;脱节的。

gar [gɑː; gɑr] *n*. (*pl*. ~, ~*s*)【动】1. 雀鳝。2. = needlefish.

GAR = guided aircraft rocket 机载飞弹。

gar·age [ˈgærɑːʒ, -ridʒ; ˋgærɑʒ, -rɪdʒ] I *n*. 汽车库,汽车间;(汽车)修车场;飞机库。II *vt*. 把(汽车)开进车库[修理厂]。~**man** 汽车库工人,汽车修理厂工人。~ **sale** 车库买卖〔在卖主家进行的现场旧货出售,因多在卖主家的车库前进行,故名〕。

garb[1] [gɑːb; gɑrb] I *n*. 1. 服装(尤指某一种人穿的服装);装束。2. 外表,外衣。*in clerical* ~ 牧师服,僧袍。*fantastic* ~ 奇装异服。*in the* ~ *of a sailor* 穿着水手服。*Hamlet in Chinese* ~ 中译本《哈姆雷特》。II *vt*. 〔常用被动语态或接 oneself〕穿,装扮。~ *oneself as a sailor* 打扮成水手模样。*be elegantly* ~*ed* 衣着雅致。

garb[2] [gɑːb; gɑrb] *n*.【徽】麦束。

gar·bage [ˈgɑːbidʒ; ˋgɑrbɪdʒ] *n*. 1. 残羹剩菜;丢弃的食物;〔美俚〕食品。2. 废料,脏东西。3. 浮游于太空的失去作用的人造卫星[火箭]。4. 无用的数据。*the* ~ *heap of history* 历史的垃圾堆。*literary* ~无聊读物。~ **can** [**truck**] 垃圾箱[车]。~ **in/out**【计】无用(信息)输入/输出〔由于输入错误数据,电脑输出也随之无效〕。

gar·ban·zo [gɑːˈbænzəu, Sp. gɑːˈvɑːθəu, -səu; gɑrˋbænzo, Sp. gɑrˋvɑθo, -so] *n*. (*pl*. ~*s*) 〔Sp.〕【植】鹰嘴豆,埃及豆,雏豆 (= chick-pea)。

gar·ble [ˈgɑːbl; ˋgɑrbl] *vt*. 1. 断章取义,任意窜改(原文等)。2. 无意中歪曲[混淆](事实,意思等)。3. 〔罕〕精选,筛选。

gar·board [ˈgɑːbɔːd, -bɔəd; ˋgɑrˏbɔrd, -ˏbord] *n*.【船】(贴近龙骨的)龙骨翼板〔又称 ~ strake〕。

Gar·ci·a [ˈgɑːʃjə; ˋgɑrʃjə] *n*. 加西亚〔姓氏〕。

gar·çon [garˈsɔ̃; garˋsɔ̃] *n*. (*pl*. ~*s*) 〔F.〕(旅馆中的)男服务员;少年。

gar·dant [ˈgɑːdənt; ˋgɑrdənt] *a*. = guardant.

gar·den [ˈgɑːdn; ˋgɑrdn] I *n*. 1. 庭园;花园;菜园;果园。2. 〔*pl*.〕公园,(动、植物)园;露天饮食店。3. 〔*pl*.〕〔英〕(一排或数排房屋并种有树木的)…广场,…街。土地肥沃的地区,精耕细作的土地。4. 〔G-〕〔美〕新泽西州的别名。5. 〔the G-〕伊壁鸠鲁 (Epicurus) 学派。*Everything in your* ~ *is nice*. 你家园子里的一切都是好的〔反语,其真实含义为:"别把你家的一切都看得那么美!"〕。*a back* ~ 后花园。*botanical* [*zoological*] ~*s* 植[动]物园。*a kitchen* ~菜园。*a market* ~供应市场菜蔬、花果的农圃。*nursery* ~苗圃。*a public* ~公园。*Queen's G-* 女王广场。***common or*** ~ 普通的,平凡的。***G- of Eden*** (《圣经》中所说亚当和夏娃所住的)伊甸园,没有罪恶的圣洁之地。***lead sb. up*** [***down***] ***the*** ~ (***path***) 使迷惑,诱人误入歧途。***the G- of the Gods*** (美国 *Colorado Springs* 市附近的)奇岩园地带。II *a*. 1. 花园的,果园的。2. 花园似的,风光优美的。3. 生长于园中的,在园中栽培的〔相对于野生的而言〕。4. 普通的,平凡的,老一套的。III *vi*. 栽培花木,从事园艺。~ *for pleasure* 栽培花木以自娱。— *vt*. 把…开辟为花园[菜园、果园]。~ **apartments** 花园公寓〔周围有草坪或绿树荫封的公寓〕。~ **balsam** 凤仙花 (*Impatiens balsamian*)。~ **city** 花园城市。~ **cress**【植】独行菜 (*Lepidium sativum*)〔偶尔用在沙拉菜中〕。~ **engine** 庭园用小型抽水机。~ **frame** 栽培植物用框架。~ **glass** (罩植物用的)钟形玻璃罩。~ **hiliotrope**【植】缬草 (*Valeriana officinalis*)〔花极芳香,根味极辛烈。曾用作药草〕。~ **party** 游园会。~ **plant** 栽培植物。~ **plot** 园地。~ **seat** 庭园坐椅;〔英〕公共汽车顶层坐位。**G- State** 花园州〔美国新泽西州的别称〕。~ **stuff** 蔬菜,水果。~-**variety** *a*. 普通的,平凡的,老一套的。

Gar·den [ˈgɑːdn; ˋgɑrdn̩] *n*. 加登〔姓氏〕。

gar·dened [ˈgɑːdnd; ˋgɑrdnd] *a*. 有花园的。

gar·den·er [ˈgɑːdnə; ˋgɑrdnɚ] *n*. 园丁,花匠;菜农;园艺爱好者。*a jobbing* ~临时园林工人。*a nursery* ~苗圃经营者。*a market* ~菜农。

gar·de·ni·a [gɑːˈdiːniə; gɑrˋdinɪə] *n*.【植】栀子;〔G-〕栀子属。

gar·den·ing [ˈgɑːdniŋ; ˋgɑrdnɪŋ] *n*. 园艺(学)。

Gar·di·ner [ˈgɑːdnə; ˋgɑrdnə] *n*. 加德纳〔姓氏〕。

Gard·ner [ˈgɑːdnə; ˋgɑrdnə̩] *n*. 加德纳〔姓氏〕。

gar·dy·loo [ˌgɑːdiˈluː; ˏgɑrdɪˋlu] *int*. 泼水啰!〔古时英国爱丁堡居民向窗外泼水而向行人发出警告声〕。

gare·fowl [ˈgɛəfaul; ˋgɛrˏfaul] *n*.【鸟】大海鸦。

gar·fish [ˈgɑːfiʃ; ˋgɑrˏfɪʃ] *n*.【动】长嘴硬鳞的鱼(如颌针鱼)。

gar·ga·ney [ˈgɑːgəni; ˋgɑrgənɪ] *n*.【动】巡凫 (*Anas querquedula*)。

gar·gan·tu·an [gɑːˈgæntjuən; gɑrˋgæntʃuən] *a*. 庞大的,巨大的〔该词源于 *Gargantua*, 他是法国讽刺作家拉伯雷 (*Rabelais*) 在其作品《巨人传》中所描写的一个食欲巨大的国王〕。

gar·get [ˈgɑːgit; ˋgɑrgɪt] *n*. (牛、猪等的)喉肿;乳房炎。

gar·gle [ˈgɑːgl; ˋgɑrgl] I *vt*., *vi*. 1. 漱(喉)。2. (漱口时从喉底)发出(咕噜声)。II *n*. 1. 含漱剂。2. 漱口声,咕噜声。

gar·goyle [ˈgɑːgɔil; ˋgɑrgɔɪl] *n*. 1.【建】(哥德式建筑上)怪形生物状的滴水嘴[承溜口]。2. 奇形怪状的雕刻像。3. 面貌古怪的人。

Gar·i·bal·di [ˌgæriˈbɔːldi; ˏgærəˋbɔldɪ], **Giuseppe** 加里波底〔1807—1888,意大利将军和民族主义的领袖〕。

gar·i·bal·di [ˌgæriˈbɔːldi; ˏgærəˋbɔldɪ] *n*. 1. (女人、小儿用的)红色阔罩衫〔最初系仿照加里波底之红衫军所穿红色军服式样〕。2. 〔美〕加利福尼亚红鱼。3. 夹有酸栗果酱的饼干。

gar·ish [ˈgɛəriʃ; ˋgɛrɪʃ] *a*. 耀眼的;(服装等)过于艳丽的,华丽而俗气的;(文章等)华美的,华而不实的。-**ly** *ad*. -**ness** *n*.

gar·land [ˈgɑːlənd; ˋgɑrlənd] I *n*. 1. 花环,花冠;【建】华饰;【海】索环。2. 胜利和荣誉的象征。3. 〔古〕诗歌选集。***carry away*** [***gain***, ***win***] ***the*** ~ 获胜,夺得锦标。II *vt*. 1. 给…饰以花环;给…带上花环。2. 把…做成花环。

Gar·land [ˈgɑːlənd; ˋgɑrlənd] *n*. 加兰〔姓氏,男子名〕。

gar·lic [ˈgɑːlik; ˋgɑrlɪk] *n*. 蒜,大蒜。*a clove of* ~一瓣大蒜。***be*** ~ ***for dessert*** 〔俚〕最不受欢迎的东西。**gar·lick·y** *a*. 大蒜一样的,有大蒜气味的;吃大蒜的。

gar·ment [ˈgɑːmənt; ˋgɑrmənt] I *n*. 1. 衣服,(尤指)外衣;外套;长袍。2. 〔*pl*.〕服装,衣着。3. 外观,外表;(物件的)包皮。II *vt*. 穿〔主用过去分词形式〕。*a lady* ~-*ed in silk* 一位穿着绸衣服的女士。~ **bag** 装衣服的塑料袋。**G- Center** 服装中心〔美国纽约曼哈坦区内服装工厂和时装商店林立的街区〕。

gar·ner [ˈgɑːnə; ˋgɑrnɚ] I *n*. 1. 〔诗〕谷仓。2. 蓄积,积累物。II *vt*. 1. 〔诗〕贮藏,积累。2. 〔美口〕得…分[票]。

Gar·ner [ˈgɑːnə; ˋgɑrnɚ] *n*. 加纳〔姓氏〕。

gar·net[1] [ˈgɑːnit; ˋgɑrnɪt] *n*. 1.【矿】石榴石。2. 石榴红

G

(色)。~-**berry** *n*.【植】红醋栗。~ **laser** 石榴石光激射器。~-**paper** 用石榴石细砂做的砂纸。

gar·net[2] [ˈgɑːnit; ˋgɑrnɪt] *n*.【船】装货用的滑车。

gar·ni [gɑːˈniː; gɑrˋni] *a*. (为食品)添配料的。

gar·ni·er·ite [ˈgɑːniərait; ˋgɑrnɪəˏraɪt] *n*.【矿】矽[硅]镁镍矿。

gar·nish [ˈgɑːniʃ; ˋgɑrnɪʃ] **I** *n*. **1.** 装饰品;(文章的)修饰;华丽的词藻。**2.**【烹】配菜,配头。**II** *vt*. **1.** 装饰,文饰。**2.** 给…(点)加配菜,给…加配头。**3.**【法】= garnishee. ***swept and ~ed*** 扫除干净,布置一新。

gar·nish·ee [ˌgɑːniˈʃiː; ˏgɑrnɪˋʃi] **I** *n*.【法】(接到扣押令的)第三债务人。~ *order* 扣押令。**II** *vt*. (***-nish·eed***; ***-nish·ee·ing***) 通知(受托人)扣押债务人的财产;向(第三债务人)下达扣押令;扣押(债务人的财产);扣发(债务人的工资)。

gar·nish·er [ˈgɑːniʃə; ˋgɑrnɪʃɚ] *n*. **1.** 装饰者。**2.**【法】通知扣押债权者。

gar·nish·ment [ˈgɑːniʃmənt; ˋgɑrnɪʃmənt] *n*. **1.** 装饰,装饰品。**2.**【法】扣押债权的通知,(对第三者债务人发出的)出庭命令。

gar·ni·ture [ˈgɑːnitʃə; ˋgɑrnɪtʃɚ] *n*. **1.** 装饰品,摆设。**2.** 服装,服饰。**3.**【烹】配头,配菜。

ga·rot(t)e [gəˈrɔt; gəˋrɑt] *n*., *vt*. = garrotte.

GARP = Global Atmospheric Research Program 全球大气研究方案。

gar·pike [ˈgɑːˌpaik; ˋgɑrˏpaɪk] *n*.【鱼】雀鳝。

gar·ran [ˈgærən; ˋgærən] *n*. = garron.

gar·ret[1] [ˈgærət, -rit; ˋgærət, -rɪt] *n*. **1.** 屋顶层,顶楼,阁楼,亭子间。**2.**〔俚〕头。*be wrong in the* ~头脑有毛病。*have one's* ~ *unfurnished* 头脑空虚,没学识。***from cellar to*** ~ = ***from*** ~ ***to cellar*** [***kitchen***] 整幢房屋,屋里上上下下。

gar·ret[2] [ˈgærət, -rit; ˋgærət, -rɪt] *vt*.【建】(用小石)填塞缝隙。

Gar·ret(t) [ˈgærət; ˋgærət] *n*. 加勒特〔男子名〕。

gar·ret·eer [ˌgærəˈtiə; ˏgærəˋtɪr] *n*. **1.** 住顶楼的人。**2.** 穷文人;亭子间作家。

gar·ri·son [ˈgærisn; ˋgærəsn] **I** *n*. **1.** 守备队,卫戍部队,警备队,驻军。**2.** 要塞,驻防地,卫戍区。***be sent into*** ~ 奉派防守。***go into*** ~ 去接防。***in*** ~ 驻防,接防。***on*** ~ ***duty*** 负责防守。**II** *vt*. 派兵驻守;把…派作守备队。~ **artillery** 要塞炮兵。~ **cap**【美军】**1.** 军便帽,船形帽 (= overseas cap). **2.** 军帽 (= service cap). **Gfinish** (赛马临近终点时优胜骑手从后面作的)终点冲刺。~ **hospital** 卫戍医院。~ **town** 有军队驻守的城镇。

Gar·ri·son [ˈgærisn; ˋgærəsn] *n*. 加里森〔姓氏〕。

gar·ron [ˈgærən; ˋgærən] *n*. 矮马。

gar·rot(t)e [gəˈrɔt; gəˋrɑt] **I** *n*. **1.** 螺环绞刑〔西班牙的一种绞刑,行刑时旋紧套于犯人颈上的螺钉〕;螺环绞具。**2.** (偷袭敌人时用以勒杀敌方哨兵等的)绞颈索。**3.** 勒杀抢劫。**II** *vt*. (***-rot·(t)ed***; ***-rot·(t)ing***) **1.** 处…以螺环绞刑。**2.** (用绞颈索等)勒…的咽喉(使失去抵抗力)。**3.** 勒杀抢劫。

gar·rot·(t)er [gəˈrɔtə; gəˋrɑtɚ] *n*. 绞杀者;勒杀抢劫的强盗。

gar·ru·li·ty [gəˈruːliti; gəˋrulətɪ] *n*. 饶舌,喋喋不休。

gar·ru·lous [ˈgæruləs; ˋgærələs] *a*. **1.** 饶舌的,絮聒的,喋喋不休的。**2.** (鸟)叽叽喳喳的;(流水)潺潺不息的。**-ly** *ad*. **-ness** *n*.

gar·ter [ˈgɑːtə; ˋgɑrtɚ] **I** *n*. **1.**〔*pl*.〕吊袜带。★英国多半说 suspenders. **2.**〔英〕〔the G-〕嘉德勋章〔最高勋章〕,嘉德勋位。**3.**〔海俚〕〔*pl*.〕脚镣。*G- King of Arms* 英国勋章院的主管人。**II** *vt*. **1.** 用袜带系紧。**2.** 授给…嘉德勋位。~ **belt** 吊袜带。~ **snake** (美国无毒)花蛇。~ **stitch** (织物的)平针织法,平针图案。

garth [gɑːθ; gɑrθ] *n*. **1.**〔古〕庭院,花园;围场。**2.** 修道院内的空地。**3.** 为捕鱼而筑起的坝[堰],鱼梁。

Garth [gɑːθ; gɑrθ] *n*. 加斯〔姓氏,男子名〕。

Gar·y [ˈgeəri; ˋgɛrɪ] *n*. 盖里〔姓氏,男子名〕。

gas [gæs; gæs] **I** *n*. (*pl*. ~**es** [ˈgæsiz; ˋgæsɪz]) **1.** 气,气体,气态〔*cf*. fluid; solid〕. **2.** 可燃气,煤气,沼气;【矿】瓦斯。**3.**【军】毒气 (= poison gas);毒瓦斯,(麻醉用的)笑气。**4.** 煤气灯;〔美口〕汽油,(汽车等的)油门。**5.**〔俚〕空谈,吹牛。**6.**〔美俚〕令人愉快的人[事];使某人受到很大影响的人[事]。*Air is a mixture of ~es*. 空气是多种气体的混合物。*laughing* ~笑气(即一氧化二氮)。*marsh* ~沼气。*natural* ~天然气。*nerve* ~神经毒气。*poison* ~毒气。*a* ~ *projectile* 毒气弹。*tear* ~催泪性毒气。*light the* ~点亮气灯;点燃煤气灶。***step on the*** ~〔美〕踏动(汽车的)加速器;加速,赶紧,加油干。***turn down the*** ~ 扭小气灯。***turn on the*** ~ 开煤气;〔口〕打开话匣子;吹牛。***turn out*** [***off***] ***the*** ~ 关掉煤气;〔口〕关掉话匣子,停止吹牛。**II** *vi*. **1.** 发散气体。**2.** 给汽车加油。**3.** 使用毒气。**4.**〔口〕空谈,乱吹牛。— *vt*. **1.** 供给…煤气,给…灌充煤气,给(汽车)加油。**2.** 向…放毒气;用毒气攻击[杀伤]。**3.**【纺】用煤气烧去[处理](布毛等)。**4.**〔美口〕使获得快感,使开心,使兴奋。*be ~sed* 中毒气。~ *the yarn* 烧去纱上的毛头。~ ***up*** **1.**〔美口〕给汽车加油。**2.**〔美俚〕开着(汽车的)油门(以备随时开走)。~ **bacillus** 产气荚膜(梭状芽胞)杆菌,韦氏杆菌。~ **bag** (气球的)气囊;〔俚〕饶舌者,话匣子,废话连篇的人。~ **black** 炭黑 (= carbon black). ~ **bomb** [**shell**] 毒气(炸)弹。~ **bracket** 煤气灯管。~ **burner** 煤气灶,煤气灯;煤气喷嘴,煤气火焰。~ **chamber** 死刑毒气室;(苹果等的)贮藏室。~ **coal** (适于提炼煤气的)气煤。~ **coke** 煤气焦炭。~ **constant** 气体常数。~ **current** 离子电流。~-**eater** 耗油量大的汽车。~ **engine** 内燃机,气体发动机。~ **field** 天然气田。~ **fire** 煤气取暖器。~-**fired** *a*. 烧煤气的,以煤气为燃料的。~ **fitter** 煤气装置人;承装煤气的店家。~ **fitting** 煤气装置工程;〔*pl*.〕煤气装备。~ **fixture** 煤气灯装置。~ **furnace** 煤气发生炉,煤气炉。~ **gangrene**【医】气菌坏疽。~ **helmet** [**mask**] 防毒面具。~ **holder** 煤气库,煤气罐;贮气柜[器]。~ **house** 煤气库;〔喻〕贫民区;〔美俚〕化学实验室。~ **jet** 煤气喷嘴,煤气火焰。~-**laser** 气体激光器[雷射]。~ **law** 气体定律。~ **light** 煤气灯光;气灯。~ **lighter** 煤气点燃器;打火机。~ **liquor** 煤气液,液化气。~ **lit** *a*. 以煤气灯照明的,广泛使用煤气灯的。~ **log** (煤气炉子的)燃烧嘴。~ **main** 煤气总管。~ **man** 煤气工人;煤气收费员;【矿】通风员,瓦斯检查员。~ **mantle** 煤气网罩。~ **meter** **1.** 煤气表,气量计。**2.** 贮气器,煤气罐 (*lie like a* ~ *meter* 乱撒谎)。~ **motor** 煤气(发动)机。~ **oil** 瓦斯油,粗柴油。~ **oven** 煤气灶。~ **pipe** (煤)气管。~ **plant**【植】白鲜 (*Dictamnus albus*)〔开白色或浅红色花朵,芳香。炎热的夜晚则放出可燃气体〕。~ **poker** *n*. 煤气点火棒。~ **producer** 煤气发生炉。~ **proof** *a*. 防毒气的,不透气的。~ **ring** (有环形喷火头的)煤气灶。~ **station**〔美〕(汽油)加油站。~ **stove** 煤气炉。~-**tar** 煤焦油。~ **tight** *a*. 不透气的,气密的,密封的。~ **turbine** 燃气轮机,燃气透平。~ **well** 天然气井。~ **works**〔*pl*.〕〔作 *sing*. 用〕**1.** 煤气厂。**2.**〔英俚〕下议院。

GAS = gasoline.

gas·a·ter·ia [ˌgæsəˈtiəriə; ˏgæsəˋtɪrɪə] *n*.〔美俚〕(汽车的)自动加油站。

Gas·con [ˈgæskən; ˋgæskən] **I** *n*. **1.** (以夸口著名的法国)加斯科尼 (*Gascony*) 人。**2.**〔g-〕夸口的人,吹牛的人。**II** *a*. **1.** 加斯科尼的,加斯科尼人的。**2.**〔g-〕夸口的,吹牛的。**-ism** *n*. 夸口,吹牛。

gas·con·ade [ˌgæskəˈneid; ˏgæskəˋned] *n*., *vi*. 自夸,吹牛。

Gas·co·ny [ˈgæskəni; ˋgæskənɪ] *n*. 加斯科尼〔法国西南部一地区〕。

gas·e·i·ty [gæˈsiːiti; gæˋsiətɪ] *n*. 气态。

gas·e·lier [ˌgæsəˈliə; ˏgæsəˋlɪr] **n.** 枝形煤气吊灯。
gas·e·ous [ˈgæsiəs, ˈgeizjəs; ˋgæsɪəs, ˋgezjəs] **a.** **1.** 气体的,气态的。**2.** 无实质的,空虚的。**3.** 过热的。**4.** 〔美俚〕不可靠的。~ *density* 气体密度。*a* ~ *mixture* 气体混合物。~ *steam* 过热蒸气。**-ness** **n.**
ga·ser [ˈgeizə; ˋgezɚ] **n.** 【物】γ射线激射器。
gash[1] [gæʃ; gæʃ] **I** **n.** **1.** 深长的伤口[切痕]。**2.** (地面等的)裂缝。**3.** 划开。**II** **vt.**, **vi.** (在…上)划深长切口,划开。
gash[2] [gæʃ; gæʃ] **a.** 〔英俚〕【海】多余的,备用的。
gash[3] [gæʃ; gæʃ] **a.** 〔Scot.〕**1.** 衣冠楚楚的。**2.** 伶俐的,干净利落的。
gas·i·fi·a·ble [ˈgæsifaiəbl; ˋgæsəfaɪəbl] **a.** 可气化的。
gas·i·fi·ca·tion [ˌgæsifiˈkeiʃən; ˏgæsəfəˋkeʃən] **n.** 气化(作用)。
gas·i·fi·er [ˈgæsifaiə; ˋgæsəfaɪɚ] **n.** 气化器,燃气发生器。
gas·i·form [ˈgæsifɔːm; ˋgæsəˏfɔrm] **a.** 气体的,气态的。
gas·i·fy [ˈgæsifai; ˋgæsəˏfaɪ] **vt.**, **vi.** (***-fied***; ***-fy·ing***) (使)气化;(使)成为气体。
Gas·kell [ˈgæskəl; ˋgæskəl] **n.** 加斯克尔〔姓氏〕。
gas·ket [ˈgæskit; ˋgæskɪt] **n.** **1.** 【海】束帆索。**2.** 【机】垫圈,垫片。
gas·kin [ˈgæskin; ˋgæskɪn] **n.** **1.** 〔*pl.*〕〔废〕(十六世纪前后的)灯笼裤;(打猎用的)皮绑腿。**2.** (马或其他有蹄类动物的)后大腿。
gas·less [ˈgæslis; ˋgæslɪs] **a.** 无气体的,不用气体的。
gas·o·gene [ˈgæsədʒiːn; ˋgæsəˏdʒin] **n.** **1.** (小型)煤气发生器。**2.** (小型)汽水制造机。
gas·o·hol [ˈgæsəˈhɔl; ˋgæsəˋhɔl] **n.** 酒精汽油。
gas·o·lier [ˌgæsəˈliə; ˏgæsəˋlɪə] **n.** = gaselier.
gas·o·line, gas·o·lene [ˈgæsəliːn, ˌgæsəˈliːn; ˋgæsəlin, ˏgæsəˋlin] **n.** 〔美〕汽油。★英国叫 petrol。*gelatinized* [*jellied*] ~凝固汽油 (= napalm)。*a* ~ *bomb* 汽油弹。~ **mileage** 汽车耗1加仑汽油平均所行的英里数。
gas·om·e·ter [gæˈsɔmitə; gæˋsɑmətɚ] **n.** **1.** 气量计;煤气计算表。**2.** 贮气器,煤气罐。
gas·om·e·try [gæˈsɔmitri; gæˋsɑmətrɪ] **n.** 气体计量。
gasp [gɑːsp; gæsp] **I** **vi.** **1.** 喘,喘气;透不过气。**2.** 热望,切望 (*after*; *for*)。— **vt.** 喘着气说,气吁吁地说 (*out*)。~ ***one's life away*** ~ = ~ ***out one's life*** = ~ ***one's last*** 死去。~ ***up*** 咽气,断气。**II** **n.** 喘气;屏息,透不过气。***at one's last*** ~ 奄奄一息。***at the last*** ~ **1.** 奄奄一息。**2.** 最后一刻,最后。***prolong one's last*** ~ 苟延残喘。***to the last*** ~ 到死为止。
G.A.S.P. = Group Against Smoke and Pollution 反烟反污染组织。
gasp·er [ˈgɑːspə; ˋgæspɚ] **n.** **1.** 喘气者。**2.** 〔俚〕廉价香烟。
gasp·ing [ˈgɑːspiŋ; ˋgæspɪŋ] **a.** 气喘的,痉挛的,阵发性的。**-ly** **ad.**
gassed [gæst; gæst] **a.** 〔美俚〕喝醉酒的。
gas·ser [ˈgæsə; ˋgæsɚ] **n.** **1.** 〔俚〕爱夸夸其谈的人,爱吹牛的人。**2.** 天然气井。**3.** 〔俚〕出类拔萃的人,非常有趣的事。
Gas·ser [ˈgæsə; ˋgæsɚ] **n.** 加瑟〔姓氏〕。
gas·si·ness [ˈgæsinis; ˋgæsənɪs] **n.** **1.** 气态,充满气体。**2.** 爱说空话,夸夸其谈,吹牛。
gas·sing [ˈgæsiŋ; ˋgæsɪŋ] **n.** **1.** 用煤气处理,烧(布毛)。**2.** 毒气战;放毒气。**3.** 〔俚〕瞎聊天。**4.** 充气,放气,出气。**5.** 起气泡,真空管中出现气体。
gas·sy [ˈgæsi; ˋgæsɪ] **a.** **1.** 气体的,气状的;充满气体的。**2.** 专好吹牛的,(话等)夸大的。
gaster-, gastero- *comb. f.* 表示"胃的": *gastero*poda.
gas·ter·o·pod [ˈgæstərəpɔd; ˋgæstərəˏpɑd] **n.** 【动】腹足纲软体动物〔如螺蛳等〕。
gastr-, gastri- *comb. f.* 表示"胃的": *gastr*ectomy, *gastri*tis.
gas·trae·a [gæsˈtriːə; gæsˋtriə] **n.** 【动】原肠祖,原肠幼虫。
gas·tral·gi·a [gæsˈtrældʒiə; gæsˋtrældʒɪə] **n.** 【医】胃痛。
gas·trec·ta·sia [ˌgæstrekˈteiʒə; ˏgæstrɛkˋteʒə] **n.** 胃扩张 (= gastrectasis)。
gas·trec·to·my [gæsˈtrektəmi; gæsˋtrɛktəmɪ] **n.** (*pl.* ***-mies***) 【医】胃切除术。
gas·tric [ˈgæstrik; ˋgæstrɪk] **a.** 胃的。~ **fever** 胃热;(尤指)伤寒。~ **juice** 胃液。~ **ulcer** 胃溃疡。
gas·trin [ˈgæstrin; ˋgæstrɪn] **n.** 【生化】胃泌(激)素。
gas·tri·tis [gæsˈtraitis; gæsˋtraɪtɪs] **n.** 胃炎。
gastro- *comb. f.* 表示"胃的": *gastro*enteritis.
gas·tro·cam·e·ra [ˌgæstrəuˈkæmərə; ˏgæstroˋkæmərə] **n.** 胃内摄影机。
gas·tro·col·ic [ˌgæstrəuˈkɔlik; ˏgæstroˋkɑlɪk] **a.** 胃和结肠的;附于胃和结肠的。~ **omentum** 【生】胃结系膜。
gas·tro·derm [ˈgæstrəuˌdəːm; ˋgæstroˏdɝm] **n.** 内胚层 (= endoderm)。
gas·tro·en·ter·it·ic [ˌgæstrəuinˈteritik; ˏgæstroɪnˋtɛrətɪk] **a.** 胃肠的。
gas·tro·en·ter·i·tis [ˌgæstrəuˌentəˈraitis; ˏgæstroˏɛntəˋraɪtɪs] **n.** 【医】胃肠炎。
gas·tro·en·ter·ol·o·gy [ˌgæstrəuˌentəˈrɔlədʒi; ˏgæstroˏɛntəˋrɑlədʒɪ] **n.** 【医】胃肠病学。**-o·gist** **n.**
gas·tro·in·tes·ti·nal [ˌgæstrəuinˈtestənl; ˏgæstroɪnˋtɛstənl] **a.** 胃肠的。
gas·tro·lith [ˈgæstrəliθ; ˋgæstrəlɪθ] **n.** 【医】胃石。
gas·trol·o·ger [gæsˈtrɔlədʒə; gæsˋtrɑlədʒɚ] **n.** 烹调学家,美食学家。
gas·trol·o·gist [gæsˈtrɔlədʒist; gæsˋtrɑlədʒɪst] **n.** = gastrologer.
gas·trol·o·gy [gæsˈtrɔlədʒi; gæsˋtrɑlədʒɪ] **n.** 烹调学,美食学。
gas·tro·nome [ˈgæstrənəum; ˋgæstrənom], **gas·tron·o·mer** [gæsˈtrɔnəmə; gæsˋtrɑnəmɚ], **gas·tron·o·mist** [gæsˈtrɔnəmist; gæsˋtrɑnəmɪst] **n.** 善于烹调的人,考究饮食的人。
gas·tro·nom·ic(al) [ˌgæstrəuˈnɔmik(əl); ˏgæstrəˋnɑmɪk(əl)] **a.** 烹调法的。*a* ~ *emporium* 〔美俚〕餐馆;公寓。
gas·tron·o·my [gæsˈtrɔnəmi; gæsˋtrɑnəmɪ] **n.** 烹调法。
gas·tro·pod [ˈgæstrəpɔd; ˋgæstrəˏpɑd] **n.** = gasteropod.
gas·tro·scope [ˈgæstrəskəup; ˋgæstrəˏskop] **n.** 【医】胃(窥)镜。
gas·trot·o·my [gæsˈtrɔtəmi; gæsˋtrɑtəmɪ] **n.** 【医】胃切开术。
gas·tro·trich [ˈgæstrətrik; ˋgæstrətrɪk] **n.** 【动】腹毛类(*Gastrotricha*)动物。
gas·tro·vas·cu·lar [ˌgæstrəuˈvæskjulə; ˏgæstroˋvæskjəlɚ] **a.** 【动】**1.** 具消化及循环功能的。**2.** 具有消化及循环双重功能的器官的。~ **cavity** 【动】腔肠,消化循环腔,胃脉管腔。
gas·tru·la [ˈgæstrulə; ˋgæstrʊlə] **n.** (*pl.* ***-lae*** [-liː; -li]) 【动】原肠胚。
gas·tru·la·tion [ˌgæstruˈleiʃən; ˏgæstrʊˋleʃən] **n.** 【医】原肠胚形成。
gat[1] [gæt; gæt] **n.** 〔美俚〕左轮手枪。
gat[2] [gæt; gæt] 〔古〕get 的过去式。
gat[3] [gæt; gæt] **n.** (山峡或沙洲间的)狭航道。
gate[1] [geit; get] **I** **n.** **1.** 大门,扉,篱笆门,门扇。**2.** 闸门;城门;洞门;隘口,峡道。**3.** 【冶】浇注道,浇口,切口;【无】门电路,选通电路,选通脉冲,启开脉冲,时间限制电路。**4.** (运动会、展览会等的)门票收入;观众数;入场费。**5.** 〔英〕伦敦 Billingsgate, Newgate 等的略称。**6.** 锯架。**7.**

电影放映机镜头窗口。8.〔俚〕解雇。*a folding* ～折叠门,活栅门。*a turnpike* ～征收通行税的关卡。*go* [*pass*] *through the* ～(*s*) 进门。*enter at a* ～从大门进去。*There was a* ～ *of thousands*. 观众数以千计。***at the*** ～(***s***) ***of death*** 奄奄一息。***crash the*** ～〔俚〕擅自入场。***get the*** ～〔美〕被赶出,被解雇。***give sb. the*** ～〔美〕迫令退席;解雇。***keep the*** ～ 守门。***open a*** ～ ***to*** [***for***] 大开方便之门,给…以机会。***the*** ～ ***of horn*** 应验的梦兆,角门。***the*** ～ ***of ivory*** 不应验的梦兆,牙门〔据神话传说,应验的梦自角门入,不应验的梦自牙门入〕。**II** ***vt***. 1. 在…装门。2.(英大学)禁止(学生)外出。3. 用门控制。～ **bill** (英大学)迟到登记簿;迟到罚金。～**-crash** ***vi***.〔俚〕无券入场,擅行入场。～**-crasher**〔俚〕无券入场者,擅行入场的人。～**d community**(富人居住的)封闭式社区。～**event**【体】入围赛。～**fold** 折叠插页。～**house** 1. 城门上面或旁边的屋子;门楼。2. 门房。3. 水电站闸门上的控制室。～**keeper** = ～ **man** 看门人,门警,门房。～**-leg(ged) table** 折叠式桌子。～ **meeting** 收费的运动会。～ **money** 入场费。～**post** 门柱 (*between you and me and the* ～*post* 极秘密的,严守秘密的)。～**tender**〔美〕看守铁路平交道栏栅的人。～ **tower** 门楼。～**way** 门口,入口,通路;手段。**-less** ***a***. 无门的。

gate² [geit; get] ***n***. 1.〔古〕街道,路〔一般作地名用,如 kirk*gate*〕。2.〔方〕方式,方法。

-gate *comb. f.* "…门"〔表示丑闻之意,源出 Watergate〕; Whitewater*gate* 白水丑闻。

Gates [geits; gets] ***n***. 盖茨〔姓氏〕。

gath·er ['gæðə; `gæðɚ] **I** ***vt***. 1. 集合,聚集;搜集。2. 摘,摘取,采集;征收(税等)。3. 蓄积;累积;增长。4. 皱(眉);缝(衣褶)。5. 抱,围住,拉紧。6. 得出(印象、感想等);推断;推测 (*that*)。7. 鼓起(勇气);恢复(健康);振作(精神)。8.【火箭】导入,引入。～ *crops* 收庄稼。～ *flowers* 采花。～ *experience* 积累经验。～ *speed* 加速。～ *strength* 恢复体力。～ *taxes* 收税。～ *up one's tools* 收拾起工具。*The demand* ～*ed weight*. 要求渐渐增强了。～ *one's brows* 皱眉。— ***vi***. 1. 聚集,蓄积;增长,增加。2. 皱,缩。3.(疮)化脓,出头。4.【海】逼近,接近(目标)。*The dusk is* ～*ing*. 暮色渐浓。***be*** ～***ed to one's fathers*** [***people***] 见老祖宗去。～ ***breath*** 喘过气来。～ ***colour*** 血气变好。～ ***flesh*** 长肉,发胖。～ ***ground*** 得势。～ ***head*** 化脓;(暴风雨等)力量增强。～ ***in*** 收获;〔口〕拾得。～ ***in upon*** (轮齿)咬合。～ ***one's energies*** 集中精力,尽力。～ ***one's wits*** 聚精会神。～ ***oneself up*** [***together***] 鼓起勇气,打起精神。～ ***out*** 选出。～ ***together*** 集合,集聚,收集。～ ***up*** 收集;总括(事件);蜷缩(手、脚等);集中力量;培垄。～ ***volume*** 增大,变大。～ ***way***【海】开动,开始移动。**II** ***n***. 1. 聚集;收缩。2.〔常 *pl*.〕衣褶,折裥。**-a·ble** ***a***. 可收集的,可积聚的。**-er** ***n***. 收集者。

gath·er·ing ['gæðəriŋ; `gæðrɪŋ] ***n***. 1. 聚集;集会。2. 搜集,采集;积聚,积累。3. 化脓;脓疮。4. 捐赠,捐款。5.(印好后依页码次序折叠成的)毛书。6. 衣褶。*a social* ～社交聚会,联欢会。～ **coal** (使火终夜不熄的)封火煤。～ **cry** 战斗召集令。～ **ground** 水源地。

Gat·ling gun ['gætliŋ gʌn; `gætlɪŋ gʌn] 格林炮;格林式机枪〔美国 *R. F. Gatling* 所发明〕。

GATT = General Agreement on Tariffs and Trade 关税及贸易总协定。

gauche [gəuʃ; goʃ] ***a***.〔F.〕不善交际的;不灵活的;笨拙的,不机智的。**-ly** ***ad***. **-ness** ***n***.

gau·che·rie [ˌgəuʃə'riː; ˏgoʃə`ri] ***n***. 1. 笨拙。2. 笨拙举动。

Gau·cho ['gautʃəu; `gaʊtʃo] ***n***. (*pl*. ～*s*) 高卓人〔南美洲草原地带的牧人,多系西班牙人和印第安人的混血种〕。

gaud [gɔːd; gɔd] ***n***. 1. 花哨而俗气的装饰品;不值钱的小玩意。2.〔*pl*.〕庸俗的排场[宴会、仪式]。

gau·de·a·mus [ˌgaudei'ɑːmus, ˌgɔːdiː'eiməs; ˏgɔdɪ`ema ˏgaude`ɑmus] ***n***. 尽情欢乐(尤指高等学校学生的乐)。

gaud·er·y ['gɔːdəri; `gɔdərɪ] ***n***. 浮夸的外观;华丽的装。

gaud·y¹ ['gɔːdi; `gɔdɪ] ***a***. (衣服、装饰、文风)炫丽的,俗的,华而不实的。**-i·ly** ***ad***. **-i·ness** ***n***.

gaud·y² ['gɔːdi; `gɔdɪ] ***n***.〔英〕(英国大学中每年举行一的)宴会,招待会。

gauf·fer ['gɔːfə; `gɔfɚ] ***n***., ***vt***. = goffer.

gauge [geidʒ; gedʒ] **I** ***n***. 1. 规,量规,量器,量计,表。标准尺寸,标准规格;(金属片等的)厚度,(枪炮的)口径(电线等的)直径。3. 容量,范围。4.【建】茸脚(铺覆瓦,石板等的外露部分);(铁路的)轨距,(汽车等两侧轮间的)轮距;【印】版面宽度。5.(估计、判断等的)方法手段,标准。6.【纺】隔距。7.【海】= gage². ★美国在海用语以外亦拼作 gage. *an altitude* ～高度计。*a broad* ～宽轨。*a go* ～通过规。*a level* ～水准仪。*a marking* ～(木工的)划线器。*a narrow* ～窄轨。*a n go* ～不通过规。*a pressure* ～压力计。*a rain* ～雨器。*a remote transmitting* ～遥测仪。*a screw pit* ～螺距规。*a slide* ～游标卡尺。*the standard* ～标轨距(=1.435米)。*a water* ～水位表,水标尺。*a win* ～风速计。***get the*** ～ ***of*** 探测意向。***have the lee*** ～ 在…的下风;较…不利。***have the weather*** ～ ***of*** 在…上风;较…有利。***take the*** ～ ***of*** 估计,估价。**II** ***vt***. 测,量;估计,估价。2. 使成标准尺寸;使合标准。**block** 规矩块。～ **cock** 试水位旋塞。～ **glass** (锅炉)位玻璃管,量液玻璃管。～ **group**【物】规范群。～ **la**【建】挂瓦条。～ **lathe**【机】样板车床。～ **length** 标距,量。～ **line** 轨线;计量管;密度。～ **pile**【建】定位桩。**pressure** 表压。～ **reel** ***n***.【纺】纤度计。～ **stuff**【建】饰石膏。～ **table** 计量表,校正表。～ **theory**【物】(试确立引力、电磁力、强力和弱力之间相互关系的)规范论。**-a·ble** ***a***. 可计量的,可测量的。

gaug·er ['geidʒə; `gedʒɚ] ***n***. 1. 计量者;计量器。2. (内货物税的)收税官。

gaug·ing ['geidʒiŋ; `gedʒɪŋ] ***n***. 规测,用规检验,测量,准。～ **rod** 计量竿,探测杆,表尺。

Gaul [gɔːl; gɔl] ***n***. 1. 高卢〔占有今意大利北部、法、比、等国,属古罗马帝国一部分〕。2. 高卢人。3. 法国人。

Gau·lei·ter ['gauˌlaitə; `gaʊˏlaɪtɚ] ***n***.〔G.〕1. (纳德国的)省长,地方长官。2.〔喻〕土皇帝,小暴君。

Gaul·ish ['gɔːliʃ; `gɔlɪʃ] **I** ***a***. 1. 高卢的,高卢人的;高语的。2. 法国人的。**II** ***n***. 高卢语。

Gaull·ism ['gɔːlizəm; `gɔlɪzəm] ***n***. 戴高乐主义。

Gaull·ist ['gɔːlist; `gɔlɪst] **I** ***n***. 戴高乐派。**II** ***a***. 戴高主义的。

gault [gɔːlt; gɔlt] ***n***.【地】重黏土。～ **clay** 重黏土,泥灰黏土。～ **stage**【考古】(早白垩世晚期的)高尔特阶。

gaul·the·ri·a [gɔːl'θiəriə; gɔl`θɪrɪə] ***n***.【植】冬青(*Gaultheria procumbens*),平铺白珠树。

gaunt [gɔːnt; gɔnt] ***a***. 1. 瘦削的,憔悴的。2. 萧瑟的,凉的。**-ly** ***ad***. **-ness** ***n***.

gaunt·let¹ ['gɔːntlit; `gɔntlɪt] ***n***. 1. (铠甲的)铁护手;铠。2. (骑马、击剑等用的)长手套;(防护手套;长手的)腕部。***take*** [***pick***] ***up the*** ～ 应战;护卫。***thr*** [***fling***] ***down the*** ～ 挑战。

gaunt·let² ['gɔːntlit; `gɔntlɪt] ***n***. = gantlet².

gaun·try ['gɔːntri; `gɔntrɪ] ***n***. = gantry.

gaur [gauə; gaʊr] ***n***. (*pl*. ～, ～*s*)【动】⿰牛曷 (*Bibos ga rus*)〔印度野牛,为世界最大的牛〕。

gauss [gaus; gaʊs] ***n***.【物】高斯〔磁感应强度单位,磁通密度单位〕。～**'s system of unit** 高斯单位制。～ **nu ber** 高斯随机数。～ **theorem** 高斯定理。**-age** ***n***. 高数。

Gauss·i·an ['gausiən; `gaʊsɪən] ***a***. 高斯的。～ **cu**

G

【统】高斯曲线。

auze [gɔːz; gɔz] *n*. 1. (棉、丝等织成的)薄纱,罗纱布;网纱。2. 薄雾。*wire* ～铁纱。～ **room** 滤尘间。

auz·y [ˈgɔːzi; ˋgɔzɪ] *a*. 罗纱似的;轻薄透明的。*a* ～ *mist* 薄雾。**-i·ly** *ad*. **-i·ness** *n*.

a·vage [gəˈvɑːʒ; gəˋvɑʒ] *n*.【医】管饲法。

ave [geiv; gev] give 的过去式。

av·el [ˈgævəl; ˋgævəl] **I** *n*. 1.〔美〕(法官、会议主席等用的)小槌;拍卖槌。2. 石匠用的大槌。**II** *vi*. 敲小槌(催促通过议案、要求注意等)。— *vt*. (用敲小槌)强行通过(议案等),要求(注意)。

a·vi·al [ˈgeiviəl; ˋgevɪəl] *n*.【动】1. 恒河鳄 (*Gavialis gangeticus*)。2. 马来鳄 (*Tomistoma schlegeli*)。

a·vot(te) [gəˈvɔt; gəˋvɑt] **I** *n*. (起源于法国农村的)加伏特舞(曲)。**II** *vi*. 跳加伏特舞。

awk [gɔːk; gɔk] **I** *n*. 笨人;腼腆的人。***a*** ～***'s errand*** 徒劳。**II** *vi*. 发呆地看着。

awk·y [ˈgɔːki; ˋgɔkɪ] **I** *a*. 愚钝的,笨拙的,腼腆的。**II** *n*. 笨人,腼腆的人。**-i·ness** *n*.

ay [gei; ge] **I** *a*. (～*er*; ～*est*) 1. 快乐的,快活的(人、性格、举动等);轻快的,欢快的。2. 华丽的,花哨的;衣服漂亮的。3.〔婉〕淫荡的,放荡的,〔俚〕同性恋的。4.〔美俚〕脸皮厚的,冒失的。～ *colors* 鲜艳的颜色。*a* ～ *lady* 荡妇。～ *quarters* 风化区。～ *science* 诗,(特指)情诗。***go*** ～ = ***lead a*** ～ ***life*** 过放荡生活。**II** *n*. 同性恋者。～ **cat**〔美卑〕小流氓,盗匪的小喽啰,新流浪人。～ **dog**〔美俚〕纵情逸乐者,追求声色者。～ **plague** 同性恋瘟疫〔指爱滋病〕。**-ness** *n*.

ay [gei; ge] *n*. 盖伊〔女子名〕。

ay·e·ty [ˈgeiəti; ˋgeətɪ] *n*. = gaiety.

ay-Pay-Oo [ˈgeiˈpeiˈuː; ˋgeˋpeˋu] *n*. 格别乌〔1922—1935 年间的苏联国家政治保安部〕。

y·wings [ˈgeiˌwiŋz; ˋgeˏwɪŋz] *n*.【植】少叶远志 (*Polygala paucifolia*)〔产于美国南部和加拿大〕。

z. = gazette; gazetter.

a·za·bo [gəˈzeibəu; gəˋzebo] *n*. (*pl*. ～*s*, ～*es*)〔美古俚〕人,家伙〔常用于贬意〕。

ze [geiz; gez] **I** *vi*. (在感慨、惊异、欢喜下)瞪看,凝视;注视 (*at*; *into*; *on*; *upon*)。★在好奇、惊恐、愚钝、挑战、无礼等表现下时普通用 stare. ～ *at scenery* 注视景色。～ *into the sky* 凝视天空。～ ***after sb***. 目送某人。～ ***round*** 左顾右盼,四处观望。**II** *n*. 凝视;注视。***at*** ～ 瞪着。***fix one's*** ～ ***upon*** 瞪着看。**-r** *n*. 凝视者。

a·ze·bo [gəˈziːbəu; gəˋzɪbo] *n*. (*pl*. ～*s*, ～*es*) 1. 塔楼,阳台,凉亭;信号台。2.〔美俚〕= gazabo.

ze·hound [ˈgeizˌhaund; ˋgezˏhaund] *n*.〔古〕锐目猎犬〔凭视力而不是嗅觉猎取野物,如灵猩〕。

·zelle [gəˈzel; gəˋzel] *n*.【动】瞪羚;〔喻〕羚羊企业〔指在某个领域捷足先登,因而赚了大钱的企业〕。～-***eyed*** 眼睛像瞪羚似的。

·zette [gəˈzet; gəˋzet] **I** *n*. 1.〔英〕公报;(牛津大学等的)学报。2. 新闻纸,报纸;(作报纸名)…新闻,…报。*an official* ～正式公报。*London G-* 伦敦公报。*appear* [*be*] *in the* ～ = *be named in the* ～; *go into the* ～; *have one's name in the* ～被宣告破产。**II** *vt*.〔英〕公告;在公报上发表;正式任命。***be*** ～***d out*** 被公布辞职。***be*** ～***d to*** (*a post*) 在公报上被任命(担任某项职务)。

z·et·teer [ˌgæziˈtiə; ˏgæzəˋtɪr] *n*. 1. 地名词典;地名索引。2.〔古〕公报记者。

z·o·gene [ˈgæzədʒiːn; ˋgæzəˏdʒin] *n*. = gasogene.

z·pa·cho [gɑːzˈpɑːtʃəu, *Sp*. gɑːθˈpɑːtʃəu; gɑzˋpɑtʃo, *Sp*. gɑθˋpɑtʃo] *n*.〔Sp.〕西班牙凉菜汤〔番茄、黄瓜片、胡椒、洋葱、油、醋等合烧成〕。

·zump [gəˈzʌmp; gəˋzʌmp] **I** *vt*. 向…抬价敲诈(尤指房屋议定价格后再抬价)。**II** *n*. 欺诈,敲诈。

.B. = Great Britain.

B 一种神经性毒气的代号。

G.B.E. = Knight (Dame) Grand Cross of the Order of the British Empire 英帝国大十字最高级(女)勋爵士。

G.C. = George Cross〔英〕乔治十字勋章。

G.C.A., **GCA** = ground controlled approach【空】地面控制进场。

G.C.B. = Knight Grand Cross of the Bath〔英〕巴斯大十字最高级勋爵士。

G.C.D., **GCD**, **g.c.d.** = greatest common divisor【数】最大公约数。

G.C.F., **GCF**, **g.c.f.** = greatest common factor【数】最大公因子。

G.C.H. = Knight Grand Cross of the Hanoverian Order〔英〕汉诺威大十字最高级勋爵士。

GCI = ground controlled interception【军】地面控制截击。

G clef【乐】高音谱记号(𝄞)。

G.C.M., **g.c.m.** = greatest common measure【数】最大公约数,最大公测度。

G.C.M.G. = Knight Grand Cross of St. Michael and St. George〔英〕圣迈克尔和圣乔治大十字最高级勋爵士。

GCR = ground control(led) radar 地面控制雷达。

G.C.R. = gas-cooled reactor 气(体)冷(却)式反应堆。

GCT = Greenwich Civil Time 格林威治民用时。

G.C.V.O. = Knight (Dame) Grand Cross of the Royal Victorian Order〔英〕维多利亚大十字最高级(女)勋爵士。

G.D. = 1. Grand Duchess 大公爵夫人;女大公爵。2. Grand Duchy 大公国;大公爵领地。3. Grand Duke 大公爵;大公。

Gd = 1. gadolinium【化】钆。2. Guard 卫兵,警卫。

g / d = **gram(me)s per denier** 克/旦。

Gdansk, **Gdańsk** [gəˈdɑːnsk, *Pol*. gˈdaɲsk; gəˋdɑnsk, *Pol*. gˋdaɲsk] *n*. 格但斯克〔旧称 Danzig 但泽〕〔波兰港市〕。

GDI = gasoline direct injection 汽油直射(发动机)。

GDP = gross domestic product 国内生产总值。

G.D.P. = Guanosine diphosphate【生化】磷酸鸟苷酸。

GDR = the German Democratic Republic 德意志民主共和国,即东德(1990 年与联邦德国 the Federal Republic of Germany) 合并。

gds, **gds.** = **goods** [*pl*.] 货物,商品。

Gdy·nia [gəˈdinjə; gəˋdɪnjə] *n*. 格丁尼亚〔波兰港市〕。

GE, **GEC** = General Electric Company〔美〕通用电气公司。

Ge[1] = germanium【化】元素锗的符号。

Ge[2] [ʒei; ʒe] *n*. 热依语〔巴西南美印第安的一个语族名〕。

ge·an·ti·cli·nal [dʒiˌæntiˈklainl; dʒɪˏæntəˋklaɪnl] **I** *n*.【地】地背斜 (= geanticline). **II** *a*. 地背斜的,地背斜属性的。

ge·an·ti·cline [dʒiˈæntiklain; dʒɪˋæntəklaɪn] *n*.【地】地背斜,大背斜。

gear [giə; gɪr] **I** *n*. 1.【机】齿轮,(齿轮)传动装置,齿链;排挡。2.〔古〕衣服;甲胄与武器。3. 家具;财物,动产。4. 工具,用具;马具;船具;【火箭】起落架。5.〔英口〕胡说。6.〔英口〕行为,事件。*bevel* ～伞形齿轮。*bottom* ～低速挡,末挡。*helical* ～斜齿轮。*high* ～【机】高速挡〔口〕高速度。*hunting* ～打猎用具。*low* ～【机】低速挡〔口〕低速度。*magnetic* ～磁力离合器。*remote-control* ～遥控装置。*reverse* ～倒车挡;反向齿轮。*steering* ～转向装置。*telemetering* ～遥测装置。*top* ～高速挡,末挡。***get*** [***put***] ***into*** ～ = ***throw into*** ～ 开动机器;着手工作。***get out of*** ～ = ***throw out of*** ～ 断开传动装置;使混乱。***in*** ～ 1. (机器)开得动,运转顺利;情况正常。2. (齿轮)搭上,联结上(发动机)。***in high*** ～ 开高速齿轮,热烈地进行。***out of*** ～ 1. (齿轮)脱开。2. (机器)开不动;情况混乱,出毛病。***shift*** ～***s*** 1. 换挡,变速。

2. 改变方式[办法、调子]。II *vt*. 1. 把齿轮装上(机器等),使扣上齿轮;开动(机器等)。2. 给…装上马具(*up*)。3. 使适合(*to*)。— *vi*. 1. (齿轮)扣上(*into*);(机器)开动。2. 适合,一致(*with*)。~ ***down*** 挂慢挡,减小速度。~ ***level*** 挂平挡。~ ***up*** 挂快挡,增加速度;促进。~**box** *n*. 齿轮箱,变速箱。~ **case** 齿轮箱 ~**-driven** *a*. 齿轮转动的。~**housing** *n*. 齿轮箱壳。~ **lever** 变速杆。~ **shaper** 插齿机,刨齿机。~**shift**【机】变速,换挡,变速装置。~ **wheel**【机】齿轮。

gear·ing [ˈgiəriŋ; ˋgɪrɪŋ] *n*. 1.【机】传动装置,齿轮装置。2. 传动,啮合。*feed* ~进刀传动装置。*link* ~联杆传动装置。*spiral* ~螺旋齿轮装置。

geck·o [ˈgekəu; ˋgɛko] *n*. (*pl*. ~*s*, ~*es*)【动】守宫,壁虎。

gee[1] [dʒiː; dʒi] *n*. 1. 英语字母 G, g. 2.〔美俚〕一千元。3.〔美俚〕人,家伙。

gee[2] [dʒiː; dʒi] *int*.〔美俚〕哎呀! ~ ***whiz(z)*** 哎呀〔表示惊奇、兴奋等〕。

gee[3] [dʒiː; dʒi] I *int*. (驭马快走用语)叽骂! II *vi*., *vt*. 向右! (*opp*. haw) III *n*. = gee·gee.

gee[4] [dʒiː; dʒi] *n*. "奇"导航系统〔英国的双曲线导航系统〕。

gee[5], **gee-gee** [dʒiː, ˈdʒiːdʒiː; dʒi, ˋdʒidʒi] *n*.〔儿〕马。

G8, G-8 西方八大(工业)国〔指美、英、德、法、意、加、日和俄罗斯,原无俄国,每年开一次峰会。参见 G7〕。

geeho [ˈdʒiːˈhəu; ˋdʒiˋho] = gee[3].

geek [giːk; gik] *n*.〔美俚〕1. 人,家伙。2. 傻子。3. 表演低级惊险节目的演员〔如咬下活鸡头,吞蛇等〕,艺人,吞蛇(等)演员。~ **show** 低级惊险节目的表演(如吞蛇等)。

gee-pole [ˈdʒiːpəul; ˋdʒipol] *n*. 橇的舵棍。

geese [giːs; gis] *n*. goose 的复数。

gee·ser [ˈgiːzə; ˋgizɚ] *n*. = geezer.

gee-up [ˈdʒiːˈʌp; ˋdʒiˋʌp] *int*. = gee[3].

Ge·ez [giːˈez; giˋɛz] *n*. (埃塞俄比亚的)古闪语(~ Ethiopic)。

gee·zer [ˈgiːzə; ˋgizɚ] *n*.〔俚〕古怪的老头儿,老家伙;〔罕〕古怪的老太太。

ge·gen·schein [ˈgeigənʃain; ˋgegənʃaɪn] *n*.〔亦作 G-〕【天】对日照。

Ge·hen·na [giˈhenə; gɪˋhɛnə] *n*.【犹史】(耶路撒冷附近的)欣嫩子谷(*Hinnom*);地狱;焦热地狱。

Gei·ger [ˈgaigə; ˋgaɪgɚ], **Hans** 盖革〔1882—1947,德国物理学家〕。~ **counter**【物】(测定放射能的)盖革计数器。~**-Müller counter**【物】盖革-穆勒计数器。

Gei·gers [ˈgaigəz; ˋgaɪgɚz] *n*. *pl*.〔俚〕放射能微粒子。

gei·sha [ˈgeiʃə; ˋgeʃə] *n*. (*pl*. ~*s*)〔Jap.〕艺妓。

Geiss·ler tube [ˈgaislə ˈtjuːb; ˋgaɪslɚˋtjub]【物】(真空放电实验用的)盖斯勒管〔H. Geissler (1814—1879)为德国机械师,该管发明人〕。

Geist [gaist; gaɪst] *n*.〔G.〕灵魂,理智性;精神,时代精神。

gel [dʒel; dʒɛl] I *n*. 冻胶,凝胶(体);定型发胶。II *vi*. (***-ll-***) 成冻胶,胶化。

Ge·län·de·läu·fer [gəˈlendəlɔifə; gəˋlɛndəlɔɪfɚ] *n*.〔G.〕越野滑雪者。

Ge·län·de·sprung [gəˈlɛndəʃpruŋ; gəˋlɛndəʃpruŋ] *n*.〔G.〕【滑雪】越野飞跳。

ge·la·ti [dʒiˈlɑːtiː; dʒəˋlɑti] *n*. 意大利果子露〔全脂牛奶加糖和明胶等调制成〕(= gelato)。

gel·a·tin [ˈdʒelət*i*n; ˋdʒɛlətn̩], **gel·a·tine** [ˌdʒeləˈtiːn; ˏdʒɛləˋtin] *n*. 1. 胶;明胶;动物胶;胶质。2. 凝胶体,果子冻。3. (舞台照明用的)彩色透明滤光板。*explosive* [*blasting*] ~【化】爆炸胶。~ **paper** 照相软片片基。~ **plate**【摄】干板。~ **process**【印】胶板。**vegetable** ~ 植物胶,琼脂,洋菜。

ge·lat·i·nate [dʒiˈlætineit; dʒəˋlætəˏnet] *vt*., *vi*. (使)成为明胶,(使)成胶体。

ge·la·tin·i·form [ˌdʒeləˈtinifɔːm; ˏdʒɛləˋtɪnəˏfɔrm] *a*. 胶状的。

ge·lat·i·nize [dʒiˈlætinaiz; dʒɪˋlætəˏnaɪz] *vt*. 1. 使成明胶,使成胶状。2.【摄】涂明胶于。— *vi*. 成明胶,成胶状。

ge·lat·i·n(o)- *comb*. *f*. 表示"胶": *gelatin*oid, *gelatin*ous.

ge·lat·i·noid [dʒiˈlætinɔid; dʒəˋlætəˏnɔɪd] I *a*. 似胶的;胶状的。II *n*. 胶状物质。

ge·lat·i·nous [dʒiˈlætinəs; dʒəˋlætənəs] *a*. 1. 凝胶的;含凝胶的。2. 凝胶状的,胶冻状的,胶黏的。

ge·la·tion [dʒiˈleiʃən; dʒɛˋleʃən] *n*. 1. 冻结,凝结。2. 凝胶化(作用),胶凝(作用)。

geld[1] [geld; gɛld] *n*.【英史】(古代英国地主向君主缴纳的)贡赋(亦作 gelt, gheld)。

geld[2] [geld; gɛld] *vt*. (~*ed*, ***gelt*** [gelt; gɛlt]; ~***ed***, ***gelt***) 1. 给…去势,阉割;割去…的卵巢。2. 剥夺,减弱;删去(书等的)一部分内容。~ *a book* 对一本书任意删削。**-er** *n*. 阉割者。**-ing** *n*. 1. 阉过的牲畜(尤指骟过的马)。2. 去势的人,太监。

gel·id [ˈdʒelid; ˋdʒɛlɪd] *a*. 冰冷的,冻结的,冷淡的。**-li·i·ty** [-ˈliːditi; -ˋlɪdətɪ] *n*. **-ly** *ad*. **-ness** *n*.

gel·ig·nite [ˈdʒelignait; ˋdʒɛlɪgˏnaɪt] *n*. 葛里炸药〔由硝铵、硝酸、甘油和木浆混合制成〕;炸胶。

gel·se·mi·um [dʒelˈsiːmiəm; dʒɛlˋsimɪəm] *n*.【植】1. 常绿钩吻(*Gelsemium sempervirens*). 2. 常绿钩吻根。

gelt[1] [gelt; gɛlt] geld[2]的过去式及过去分词。

gelt[2] [gelt; gɛlt] *n*. 1. = geld[1]. 2.〔俚〕金钱。

GEM = ground effect machine 气垫车,气垫船。

gem [dʒem; dʒɛm] I *n*. 1. 宝石;宝物,珍宝;精华,佳作。2.【印】四点活字。3.〔美〕松饼,软面包。4. 受尊重[被喜爱]的人。5. 花苞,嫩芽。*a* ~ *of a boy* 宝贝男孩。***G- of the mountains***. 山中宝石〔美国爱达荷州的别名〕。II *vt*. 用宝石装饰,用宝石镶嵌。III *a*. (珠宝)最佳品质的。**-less** *a*. **-like** *a*.

Ge·ma·ra [gəmɑːˈrɑː; gəmɑˋrɑ] *n*.《犹太教法典》(Talmud) 的注释篇。

gem·el [ˈdʒeməl; ˋdʒɛməl] *a*. 双生的;成对的。

gem·i·nate [ˈdʒeminit; ˋdʒɛmənɪt] I *a*.【生】双生的,成双的,成对的。~ *fertilization* 对生受精。II [-neit; -net] *vt*., *vi*. (使)加倍,(使)重复,(使)成对。**-na·tive** [ˌdʒemiˈneitiv; ˏdʒɛməˋnetɪv] *a*.

gem·i·na·tion [ˌdʒemiˈneiʃən; ˏdʒɛməˋneʃən] *n*. 1. 加倍,重复。2.【语】子音(字母)的重复。

Gem·i·ni [ˈdʒeminai; ˋdʒɛməˏnaɪ] *n*.〔作单数用 *sing*.〕【天】双子座;双子宫〔黄道第三宫〕。

gem·ma [ˈdʒemə; ˋdʒɛmə] *n*. (*pl*. ***-mae*** [-miː; -mi])【植】叶芽,无性芽;【生】胞芽,(真菌的)芽孢。

gem·man [ˈdʒemən; ˋdʒɛmən] *n*.〔美黑人方言〕= gentleman.

gem·mate [ˈdʒemit; ˋdʒɛmet] I *a*. 有芽的,发芽繁殖的。II [-meit; -met] *vi*. 发芽,发芽繁殖。**-ma·tion** [dʒeˈmeiʃən; dʒɛˋmeʃən] *n*. **-mative** [ˈdʒemeitiv; ˋdʒɛmetɪv] *a*.

gem·mif·er·ous [dʒeˈmifərəs; dʒɛˋmɪfərəs] *a*. 1. 产宝石的。2. 发芽的,发芽繁殖的。

gem·mip·a·rous [dʒeˈmipərəs; dʒɛˋmɪpərəs] *a*. 发芽的,发芽繁殖的。

gem·ol·o·gy, gem·mol·o·gy [dʒeˈmɔlədʒi; dʒɛˋmɑlədʒɪ] *n*. 宝石学。**-mol·o·gist** *n*. 宝石学家。

gem·mu·la·tion [ˌdʒemjuˈleiʃən; ˏdʒɛmjəˋleʃən] *n*.【生】萌芽,生芽。

gem·mule [ˈdʒemjuːl; ˋdʒɛmjul] *n*. 1.【植】= gemma. 2.【动】胚芽;芽球。

gem·my [ˈdʒemi; ˋdʒɛmɪ] *a*. 宝石多的;镶宝石的;光辉灿烂的。

ge·mot, ge·mote [giˈməut; gəˋmot] *n*. (在诺曼人征服

英国前的)英国早期自由民立法大会;自由民法庭。

gems·bok [ˈgemzbɔk; ˋgɛmz,bɑk] ***n***. (南非的)大羚羊。

gem·stone [ˈdʒemˌstəun; ˋdʒɛm,ston] ***n***. 宝石。

ge·müt·lich [giˈmjuːtliʃ; gɪˋmjutlɪʃ] ***a***. 〔G.〕适意的;愉快的;舒服的;可亲的。

gen [dʒen; dʒɛn] **I** ***n***. 〔英军俚〕情报 (= *gen*eral information). **II** ***vt***., ***vi***. (给…)提供情报 (*up*)。

Gen. = **1**. General. **2**. Genesis. **3**. Geneva; Genevan.

gen. = **1**. gender. **2**. genera. **3**. general(ly). **4**. generator. **5**. generic. **6**. genitive. **7**. genus.

-gen *suf*. 表示 **1**.【化】"产生": hydro*gen*, nitro*gen*. **2**.【植】"生长": acro*gen*, endo*gen*.

ge·nappe [ʒeˈnæp; dʒəˋnæp] ***n***. 光滑绒线[纱线]。

gen·ba·ku-sho [ˈgenˌbɑːˌkuˈʃəu; ˋgɛn,bɑ,kʊˋʃo] ***n***. 〔日〕原子辐射病。

gen·darme [ˈʒɑːndɑːm; ˋʒɑndɑrm] ***n***. 〔F.〕(*pl*. ~*s*) **1**. 宪兵。**2**. 〔美俚〕警察。**3**. 山脊突岩。

gen·dar·me·rie, ***gen·darm·er·y*** [ʒɑːnˈdɑːməri; ʒɑnˋdarmərɪ] ***n***. 〔F.〕宪兵队。

gen·der[1] [ˈdʒendə; ˋdʒɛndɚ] ***n***. **1**.【语法】性。**2**. 〔口〕性 (= sex). *the common* [*neuter*] ~通〔中〕性。*the masculine* [*feminine*] ~阳[阴]性。*grammatical* ~ 语法的性。*natural* ~自然的性。~ **gap** 两性见解差距,性沟。**-ed** ***a***. 性别化的,带性别色彩的。**-ist** ***a***. 带有性别歧视的。**-ize** ***vi***., ***vt***. (使)性别化,(使)带上性别色彩。**-less**【语法】无性的。

gen·der[2] [ˈdʒendə; ˋdʒɛndɚ] ***vt***., ***vi***. 〔诗〕= engender.

gene [dʒiːn; dʒin] ***n***.【生】基因。*dominant* ~显性基因。~ **deletion**【生】基因删除。~ **insertion**【生】基因插入。~ **pool**【生】基因库,基因总汇。~ **bank** 基因银行。~ **therapy**【生】基因治疗。

geneal. = genealogy.

ge·ne·a·log·i·cal [ˌdʒiːnjəˈlɔdʒikəl; ,dʒɪnɪəˋlɑdʒɪkəl] ***a***. 家系的;家谱的;系统的,系谱的。*a* ~ *table* 家谱,系谱。*a* ~ *tree* 家系图;(动物等演化发展的)系统树。**-ly** ***ad***.

ge·ne·al·o·gist [ˌdʒiːniˈælədʒist; ,dʒɪnɪˋælədʒɪst] ***n***. 家系学者,系谱学者。

gen·e·al·o·gize [ˌdʒiːniˈælədʒaiz; ,dʒɪnɪˋælədʒaɪz] ***vt***. 追溯…的系谱。— ***vi***. 制定系谱。

ge·ne·al·o·gy [ˌdʒiːniˈælədʒi; ,dʒɪnɪˋælədʒɪ] ***n***. **1**. 家系,血统;系统。**2**. 家谱。**3**. 系谱学。

gen·e·ra [ˈdʒenərə; ˋdʒɛnərə] genus 的复数。

gen·er·a·ble [ˈdʒenərəbl; ˋdʒɛnərəbl̩] ***a***. 可生殖的,可生育的。

gen·er·al [ˈdʒenərəl; ˋdʒɛnərəl] **I** ***a***. (*opp*. special) **1**. 一般的,综合的,通用的。**2**. 普通的,广泛的,通常的。**3**. 全体的,总的;全面的,普遍的;概括的,大概的,大体的,笼统的;简略的。**4**.【陆军】将官级的。**5**. 〔用于职衔后〕总…,…长。*the* ~ *affair* 总务。*the* ~ *opinion* 一般舆论。*a* ~ *attack* 总攻击,全面进攻。~ *knowledge* 一般知识,常识。*a* ~ *meeting* 大会,全会。~ *principles* 原则,总则,通则。*a* ~ *outline* 大纲,概要。*the* ~ *programme* 总纲。*the* ~ *public* 公众,大众。~ *readers* 一般读者。*the* ~ *welfare* 公共福利。*a* ~ *war* 全面战争。*a* ~ *rainfall* 普遍降雨。*a* ~ *verdict*【法】一般评决。*the Attorney G-* (美国的)司法部长,(英国的)总检查长。*consul* ~总领事。*secretary*-~ 秘书长。***as a*** ~ ***rule*** 原则上,一般地说。***for the*** ~ ***good*** 为公益。***in a*** ~ ***way*** 一般说来。**II** ***n***. **1**. 〔英、美〕陆军[空军]上将,将军。**2**. 战略[战术]家。**3**.【宗】会长,团长。(救世军的)最高司令。**4**. 〔the ~〕〔古〕一般,全体,全面 (*opp*. particular); 〔古〕一般人,庶民。**5**. 〔主 *pl*.〕通则,一般原则 (*opp*. particulars). **6**. 〔英口〕勤杂员。*G- of the air force* 〔美军〕空军五星上将。*G- of the Armies*【美军】三军五星上将,三军元帅〔1919 年美国给珀辛 (J.J.Pershing) 授的特别军衔〕。*G- of the army*【美军】陆军五星上将。***in*** ~ 一般;大体上(*people in* ~普通老百姓)。***in the*** ~ 概括的说;全面;普通。**G-American** 〔美〕普通美语,美国普通话〔以示有别于新英格兰和南部各州绝大多数人所说的英语,现已趋统一〕。~ **anesthesia** 全身麻醉。~ **armistice** 全面停战。**G-Assembly** 联合国大会;(美国的)州议会。~ **average**【保险】共同海损。~ **cargo** 一般货物。~ **computer** 通用计算机。~ **concept** [**idea**, **notion**]【逻】普通概念。~ **course** 普通科。**G- Court 1**. (美国殖民地时代行使有限司法权的)州议会。**2**. 美国新罕布什尔州和麻萨诸塞州的)州议会。~ **court-martial** 最高军事法庭。~ **dealer** 〔英〕杂货商。~ **delivery** 〔美〕留局待领邮件。~ **editor** 总编辑。~ **education** 普通教育。~ **election** 普选。~ **headquarters**【军】野战总司令部。~ **hospital** 综合性(军)医院。~ **line** 总路线。~ **offensive** 全面进攻。~ **officer** 将级军官。~ **order**【军】一般命令;卫兵守则。~ **pardon** 大赦。~ **paresis** [**paralysis**]【医】全身麻痹,全瘫。~ **post** 〔主英〕**1**. (邮件)上午第一次的发送。**2**. 职务的大变动。**G- Post Office** 邮政总局。~ **practitioner** 普通医生〔各科病症均看,为专科医生之对〕。~**-purpose** ***a***. 用途多的,通用的,万能的(~*-purpose digital computer* 通用数字计算机)。~ **radiation** 连续辐射。~ **semantics**【语】普通语义学。~ **servant** 勤杂女工。~**ship** ***n***. 将军的地位[身分];将帅的风度;将才;军略,韬略。~ **staff**【军】总参谋部。~ **store** [**shop**] 百货店,百货公司。~ **strike** 总罢工。~ **term**【逻】全称名辞,【数】公项;〔*pl*.〕笼统的话。

gen·er·al·cy [ˈdʒenərəlsi; ˋdʒɛnərəlsɪ] ***n***. 将军的地位[任期,职权,军衔]。

gen·er·al·is·si·mo [ˌdʒenərəˈlisiməu; ,dʒɛnərəˋlɪsə,mo] ***n***. (*pl*. ~*s*) 大元帅;最高统帅,总司令。

gen·er·al·ist [ˈdʒenərəlist; ˋdʒɛnərəlɪst] ***n***. 知识渊博者,经验丰富的人,多面手。**-ism** ***n***. 知识渊博;多面手,通才。

gen·er·al·i·ty [ˌdʒenəˈræliti; ,dʒɛnəˋrælətɪ] ***n***. **1**. 一般,一般性,普遍性;通则。**2**. 概括,概要,梗概。**3**. 大部分,大多数。*come down from generalities to particulars* 从略说大概转到详述细节。*a rule of great* ~普遍性的法则。*the* ~ *of people* 一般人,多数人。

gen·er·al·i·za·tion [ˌdʒenərəlaiˈzeiʃən; ,dʒɛnərəlaɪˋzeʃən] ***n***. **1**. 一般化,普遍化。**2**. 概括,综合,总结;归纳;法则化。**3**. 广义;概说;概念,通则。*Don't be hasty in* ~. 不要急于笼统地下结论。

gen·er·al·ize [ˈdʒenərəlaiz; ˋdʒɛnərə,laɪz] ***vt***. **1**. 使一般化。**2**. 概括,综合;归纳。**3**.【美】强调…的基本特征[一般性]。**4**. 推广,普及。~ *the use of video* 普及电视。~ *a conclusion from a collection of facts* 从一大堆事实中归纳出结论。— ***vi***. 形成概念,笼统地表达;延及全身。

gen·er·al·ly [ˈdʒenərəli; ˋdʒɛnərəlɪ] ***ad***. **1**. 大概,普通。**2**. 通常,一般。**3**. 广泛地,普遍地。~ *speaking* 一般地说。*She is* ~ *here on Sunday*. 她星期天通常在这里。*It is* ~ *believed that* .... 普遍认为。

gen·er·ate [ˈdʒenəˌreit; ˋdʒɛnə,ret] ***vt***. **1**. 生殖,生育。**2**. 产生,发生(光、热、电等)。**3**.【数】生成,形成〔通过点、线、面的活动生成线、面[体]〕。**4**. 引起,招来;酿成,导致。**generating station** [**plant**] 发电厂[站]。**generating line**【数】母线,生成线。

gen·er·a·tion [ˌdʒenəˈreiʃən; ,dʒɛnəˋreʃən] ***n***. **1**. 代〔约30年〕,世代,时代;同时代的人。**2**. 一代[一世]。**3**. 生殖,生育;发生,产生。**4**.【数】(面、体、线的)形成。**5**. 完善化阶段,完善化方案,完善化的模型;发展阶段。*a* ~ *ago* 约三十年前。*alternation of* ~*s*【生】世代交替。*the present* ~现代;现代人。*the last* [*past*] ~上一代。*the first* ~第一代 (*the first* ~ *university students* 第一代大学生). *future* ~*s* 后代。*the beat* ~"垮掉的一代"〔美国青年中的颓废派〕。*the rising* [*coming*] ~

下一代。the younger [older] ~年轻[年老]的一代。 **for ~s** 一连好几代,祖祖辈辈。**~ after ~ = from ~ to ~** 世世代代。**Generation E** 年轻企业家一代。**~ gap** "代沟"〔不同辈份的人,如青年与老年在人生观、行为举止、习惯爱好和心理状态之间的差异〕。**Generation X**〔美〕无名的一代,X一代〔指出生于1965—1976年间的美国人,源出作家 Douglas Coupland 发表于 1991 年的一部同名小说〕。

gen·er·a·tive [ˈdʒenərətiv, -reit-; ˋdʒɛnə͵retɪv, -rət-] *a*. 1. 生产的,有生产力的。2. 生殖的,有生殖力的。3. 生成语法的。~ **cell** 生殖细胞。~ **force** [**power**] 发生力,生殖力。~ **fuel** 再生燃料。~ **grammar**【语】生成语法,孳生语法。~ **organs** 生殖器官。

gen·er·a·tor [ˈdʒenəreitə; ˋdʒɛnə͵retə] *n*. 1. 产生者,生殖者,创始者。2. 发电机,发生器。3.【乐】基础低音。4. = generatrix. *an A.C.* ~交流发电机。*a D.C.* ~直流发电机。*an electric* ~发电机。*a gas* ~煤气发生器。*an induction* ~感应发电机。*a shunt* ~分[并]激发电机。*a steam* ~汽锅,蒸汽发生器。*a thermo* ~温差电堆,热电堆,热偶电池。*a timing* ~定时信号振荡器。

gen·er·a·trix [͵dʒenəˈreitriks; ͵dʒɛnəˋretrɪks] *n*. (*pl*. *-tri·ces* [-trisiːz; -trɪsiz])【数】(产生线、面、体的)母点,母线,母面。

ge·ner·ic [dʒiˈnerik; dʒəˋnɛrɪk] I *a*. 1.【生】属的,类的。2. 一般的,普通的(*opp*. specific)。3. (商品)未注册的;不受商标注册保护的。4.【语法】全称的,总称的。*a ~ name* 属名。*the ~ singular* [*plural*] 全称单数[复数]。*the ~ person* 全称人称〔one, you 等〕。II *n*. = *a ~ drug* 未注册的药品(如 aspirin)。**-ness** *n*.

ge·ner·i·cal [dʒiˈnerikəl; dʒəˋnɛrɪkəl] *a*. = generic. **-ly** *ad*.

G

gen·er·i·type, gen·er·o·type [dʒiˈnerətaip; dʒəˋnɛrətaɪp] *n*.【生】属典型种。

gen·er·os·i·ty [͵dʒenəˈrɔsiti; ͵dʒɛnəˋrɑsətɪ] *n*. 1. 宽大;慷慨大方。2.〔*pl*.〕宽大[侠义]的行为,慷慨的行为。3. 丰饶。

gen·er·ous [ˈdʒenərəs; ˋdʒɛnərəs] *a*. 1. 宽大的,慷慨的,大方的。2. 丰盛的,丰富的。3. 肥沃的;(色彩、酒味)浓的;浓厚的,浓重的。*a ~ harvest* 丰收。*a ~ nature* [*spirit*] 宽大的性格。*~ and selfless assistance* 慷慨无私的援助。*a ~ fare* [*table*] 丰盛的菜。***be ~ with one's money*** 用钱大方。***of ~ amount*** 大量的。***of ~ size*** 十分大的。**-ly** *ad*. **-ness** *n*.

gen·e·sis [ˈdʒenisis; ˋdʒɛnəsɪs] *n*. (*pl*. ***gen·e·ses*** [-siːz; -siz]) 1. 创始,发生;起源。2.〔G-〕【圣】《创世纪》。

-genesis *comb*. *f*. 含有 genesis 意义的名词词尾;abio*genesis*, partheno*genesis*.

gen·et[1] [ˈdʒenit; ˋdʒɛnɪt] *n*. 1.【动】香猫,麝(香)猫。2. 麝猫皮。

gen·et[2] [ˈdʒenit; ˋdʒɛnɪt] *n*. = jennet.

ge·net·ic, ge·net·i·cal [dʒiˈnetik(əl); dʒəˋnɛtɪk(əl)] *a*. 1. 遗传(学)上的。2. 发生的,发展的;创始的。~ **code**【生】遗传密码。~ **copying** 遗传复制。~ **engineer** 遗传工程学家。~ **engineering** 遗传工程。~ **fingerprint** 基因指纹〔可在血液、皮肤、精液、头发等中检测到的遗传特征〕。~ **fingerprinting** 基因指纹鉴定〔法医通过检测血液等组织中的遗传特征来确定有关人员身份等〕。~ **marker** 遗传标识。~ **material**【生】遗传物质。~ **mother** 基因母亲〔提供卵子给他人生育但自身并不参加此种孕育的妇女〕。~ **profile**【医】基因档案。~ **relationship** 亲缘关系。~ **system** 遗传系统。**-i·cal·ly** *ad*.

ge·net·i·cist [dʒiˈnetisist; dʒəˋnɛtəsɪst] *n*. 遗传学家。

ge·net·ics [dʒiˈnetiks; dʒəˋnɛtɪks] *n*. 遗传学。

ge·ne·va [dʒiˈniːvə; dʒəˋnɪvə] *n*. (荷兰)杜松子酒。

Ge·ne·va [dʒiˈniːvə; dʒəˋnivə] *n*. 日内瓦。*the ~ agreement* 日内瓦协议。*the ~ Conventions* 日内瓦公约。*Lake ~* 日内瓦湖。~ **bands** 日内瓦加尔文派牧师祭衣的白领带。~ **Cross** 红十字。~ **gown** 日内瓦加尔文派牧师穿的黑色宽袖长祭衣。

Ge·ne·van [dʒiˈniːvən; dʒəˋnivən], **Gen·e·vese** [͵dʒeniˈviːz; ͵dʒɛnəˋviz] I *a*. 1. 日内瓦的,日内瓦人的。2.【宗】加尔文教派的。II *n*. 1. 日内瓦人。2. 加尔文派教徒。

Ge·nève [F. ʒəˈnɛːv; ʒəˋnɛːv] *n*. 〔F.〕 = Geneva.

Gen·e·vese [͵dʒinəˈviːz; ͵dʒɪnəˋviz] *a*., *n*. 〔F.〕 = Genevan.

Gen·e·vieve [ˈdʒenəviːv; ˋdʒɛnəviv] *n*. 吉纳维夫〔女子名〕。

Gen·ghis Khan, Jen·ghiz Khan [ˈdʒeŋgiz ˈkɑːn; ˋdʒɛŋgɪz ˋkɑn] *n*. 成吉思汗〔1162—1227,蒙古帝国的开国皇帝,即元太祖〕。

ge·nial[1] [ˈdʒiːnjəl, -niəl; ˋdʒinjəl] *a*. 1. 有利于生活和生长的;温暖的,温和的;宜人的,舒适的,愉快的。2. 亲切的,和蔼的,友好的。3. 显示天才的。4.〔罕〕婚姻的;生殖的,生产的。5.〔罕〕天生的,天然的。*a ~ climate* 温和的气候。*~ instinct* 生殖本能。*~ smiles* 亲切的微笑。*~ sunshine* 和煦的阳光。**-ly** *ad*. **-ness** *n*.

ge·ni·al[2] [dʒiˈnaiəl; dʒəˋnaɪəl] *a*.【解】颏的。

ge·ni·al·i·ty [͵dʒiːniˈæliti; ͵dʒinɪˋælətɪ] *n*. 1. 温暖,温和;舒适。2. 亲切,和蔼;亲切的言行。

ge·ni·al·ize [ˈdʒiːniə͵laiz; ˋdʒinɪə͵laɪz] *vt*. 使适宜于动植物生长;使宜人;使温暖。

gen·ic [ˈdʒenik; ˋdʒɛnɪk] *a*.【生】基因的;基因性的;由基因引起的;遗传的。

ge·nic·u·late(d) [dʒiˈnikjulit(id); dʒəˋnɪkjəlɪt(ɪd)] *a*. 1.【生】有膝状关节的。2. (弯如)膝状的。

ge·nie [ˈdʒiːni; ˋdʒinɪ] *n*. (*pl*. ~*s*, ***ge·ni·i*** [-niai; -nɪaɪ]) = jinni.

ge·ni·i [ˈdʒiːniai; ˋdʒinɪ͵aɪ] genius 和 genie 的复数。

ge·nis·ta [dʒiˈnistə; dʒɪˋnɪstə] *n*.【植】金雀花。

gen·i·tal [ˈdʒenitl; ˋdʒɛnətl̩] I *a*. 生殖的;生殖器的。*the ~ organs* 生殖器,外阴部。II *n*.〔*pl*.〕(外)生殖器,外阴部。~ **gland** 生殖线。

gen·i·ti·val [͵dʒeniˈtaivəl; ͵dʒɛnəˋtaɪvl̩] *a*.【语法】属格的,所有格的。

gen·i·tive [ˈdʒenitiv; ˋdʒɛnətɪv] I *a*.【语法】属格的,所有格的。*the ~ case* 属格,所有格〔英语所有格又叫 the possessive case〕。II *n*. 属格,所有格,属于属格[所有格]的词[词组]。

genito- *comb*. *f*. 表示"生殖","生殖器": *genito*urinary.

gen·i·to·u·ri·nar·y [͵dʒenitəuˈjuərinəri; ͵dʒɛnətoˋjʊrɪ͵nɛrɪ] *a*. 泌尿生殖器的。*~ organs* 泌尿生殖器。

gen·ius [ˈdʒiːnjəs, -iəs; ˋdʒinjəs, -ɪəs] *n*. (*pl*. ~*es*, ***ge·ni·i***) [ˈdʒiːniai; ˋdʒinɪaɪ] 1. 天才,天资,天赋,天分,才华,创造能力。2. 天才人物,才子,奇才。3. (时代)精神,思潮,倾向;(人种,语言等的)特征,特质;(某地方的)风气。4. (*pl*. genii)〔常 G-〕守护神。5. 神仙,恶魔;对人有好或坏影响的人。*an infant ~* 神童。*a man of ~* 天才。*the ~ of modern civilization* 近代文明的特征。*be influenced by the ~ of* 受…风气所影响。*bear the impress of ~* 带有天才的迹象。*have a ~ for poetry* 有诗才。***one's evil ~*** 附身恶魔;给与坏影响的人。***one's good ~*** 护身神;给与好影响的人。~ **loci** [ˈləusai; ˋlosaɪ] (某地的)守护神;(某地的)风气。

genl. = general.

Gen·o·a [ˈdʒenəuə; ˋdʒɛnoə] *n*. 热那亚〔意大利港市〕。

gen·o·cide [ˈdʒenəusaid; ˋdʒɛnə͵saɪd] *n*. 种族灭绝;灭种的罪行。**-cid·al** [͵dʒenəˈsaidl; ͵dʒɛnəˋsaɪdl] *a*.

Gen·o·ese [͵dʒenəˈiːz; ͵dʒɛnəˋiz] I *a*. 热那亚的;热那亚人的。II *n*. (*pl*. ~) 热那亚人,热那亚市民。

ge·nome [ˈdʒiːnəum; ˋdʒinom] *n*. 基因组,染色体组。**-nom·ic** [-ˈnəumik, -ˈnɔmik; -ˋnomɪk, -ˋnɑmɪk] *a*.

gen·o·type [ˈdʒenətaip; ˋdʒeno͵taɪp] *n*.【生】1. 基因型;遗传型。2. 属典型种,属模式种。**-typ·ic(al)** [-ˈtipik(əl); -ˋtɪpɪk(əl)] *a*. **-typ·ical·ly** *ad*.

-genous *comb. f*. 表示"…生的","…发生的";"…生长的": nitro*genous*, auto*genous*.

Ge·no·va [ˈdʒenəuvɑ; ˋdʒenovɑ] [It.] = Genoa.

gen·re [ʒɑːŋr; ʒɑŋr] *n*.〔F.〕1. (文艺作品的)类型,(诗、剧、小说、散文的)体裁。2. 风俗画,世态画〔又作 ~ painting〕。

gens [dʒenz; dʒɛnz] *n*. (*pl*. ***gen·tes*** [ˈdʒentiːz; ˋdʒɛntiz]) 1. (古罗马或古希腊的)氏族。2. 氏族(尤指父系氏族)。~ **togata**〔L.〕古罗马公民。

Gen Serv = General Service【军】普通勤务。

gent [dʒent; dʒɛnt] *n*.〔卑、谑〕男人,绅士;人,家伙〔是 gentleman 的缩略语〕。~***s*** (店铺中)男宾部 (*~s' hairdresser* 男宾理发部)。***the G-s***〔口〕男厕所。

gen·ta·mi·cin, gen·ta·my·cin [ˌdʒenˌtɑːˈmaisin; ͵dʒɛn͵tɑˋmaɪsɪn] *n*.【药】庆大霉素。

gen·teel [dʒenˈtiːl; dʒɛnˋtil] *a*. 1. 有礼貌的,有教养的;有上流社会特点的,适合上流社会的。2.〔口〕优雅的,文雅的,有品格的。3. 时髦的;〔反〕装绅士派头的,赶时髦的,摆架子的。***do the*** ~ 装气派。***live in*** ~ ***poverty*** 穷人摆阔。**-ly** *ad*. **-ness** *n*. **-ism** *n*.〔书〕雅语〔如用 stomach 替代 belly〕。

gen·tes [ˈdʒentiːz; ˋdʒɛntiz] gens 的复数。

gen·tian [ˈdʒenʃiən; ˋdʒɛnʃən] *n*. 1.【植】龙胆属植物,龙胆。2. 龙胆健胃剂。~ **bitter** 龙胆苦味汁[健胃剂]。~ **violet**【化】龙胆紫。

gen·tile [ˈdʒentail; ˋdʒɛntaɪl] **I** *n*. 1. (犹太人眼中的)异邦人;非犹太人(尤指基督教徒)。2. 异教徒。3.〔美〕〔常 G-〕非摩门教徒。4.【语法】说明民族[国籍]的词。**II** *a*. 1. (犹太人眼中的)异邦人的,非犹太人的。2. 异教徒的。3. 非摩门教徒的。4. 氏族的,部落的;民族的。5.【语法】说明民族[国籍]的。~**dom** *n*. (犹太人眼中的)异邦;异邦人;异教徒。

gen·ti·lesse [ˈdʒentiles; ͵dʒɛntl̩ˋɛs] *n*.〔古〕良好的教养。

gen·ti·li·tial [ˌdʒentiˈliʃəl; ͵dʒɛntəˋlɪʃəl] *a*. 国家的,民族的;部落的;家族的。

gen·til·i·ty [dʒenˈtiliti; dʒɛnˋtɪlətɪ] *n*. 1. 名门,上流阶层。2. 文雅,优雅;绅士气派。3.〔讽〕装绅士派头,充上流阶层。4.〔古〕出身高贵;绅士们。*shabby* ~摆阔气,硬要面子。

gen·tis·ic [dʒenˈtisik, -ˈtiz-; dʒɛnˋtɪsɪk, -ˋtɪz-] **acid**【化】龙胆酸。

gen·tle [ˈdʒentl; ˋdʒɛntl̩] **I** *a*. 1. 文雅的,有礼貌的。2. 柔和的;轻柔的;(坡等)和缓的;不猛烈的,(药等)温和的。3. 生长名门的,上流阶层的。4. 驯服的,温顺的。5.〔古〕慷慨的,高尚的,豪侠的。6. 有身份的,有带徽章资格的。*a* ~ *blow* 轻轻一击。*a* ~ *rain* 细雨。*a* ~ *smile* 温柔的微笑。~ *in action* 行动和缓。~ ***and simple*** 贵贱,上下各阶层。***G- Reader*** (***and Kind Heart***) 敬爱的读者〔著者对读者的称呼〕。***of*** ~ ***birth*** = ***of*** ~ ***blood*** 出身名门的。***the*** ~ ***craft*** [***art***] 钓鱼;制鞋业。***the*** ~ ***passion*** 恋爱。***the G- People***〔美俚〕鼓吹非暴力主义的温和派。***the*** ~ ***sex*** 女性 (*opp*. sterner sex)。**II** *n*.〔古〕绅士;(作鱼饵用的)蛆。**III** *vt*. 1. 使高贵。2. 使文雅,使温和,使柔和。3. 驯服(马等);抚弄,轻拍。~ **breeze**【气】微风(三级风)。~ **folk(s)** *n*.〔*pl*.〕有身份的人,上流人士。~**-hearted** *a*. 心肠软的。~**hood** *n*. 名门世族;绅士派头。**-ness** *n*.

gen·tle·man [ˈdʒentlmən; ˋdʒɛntl̩mən] *n*. (*pl*. **-men**) 1. 绅士;有身份的人,上流人士。2.〔男子尊称〕阁下。3. (中国旧时的)士大夫;【法】社会贤达〔证明文件上用语〕。4. (达官贵人的)随从,侍从。5.〔*pl*.〕(商业信函中的称呼)先生们 (= Sirs 或 Dear Sirs)。6.【英史】(非贵族但有使用家徽特权的)乡士〔有时略作 Gent,附加名后表示身份〕。7.〔*pl*.〕男厕所。8.〔美〕议员。*a coloured* ~〔美讽〕有色绅士,黑人。*a country* ~乡绅,乡下地主。*a fine* ~时髦绅士;花花公子。*a walking* ~【剧】配角。***a*** ~ ***at large***〔谑〕失业者,无职业者。***a*** ~ ***in brown***〔谑〕臭虫。***a*** ~ ***in waiting*** (英王的)侍从。***a*** ~ ***of fortune*** 海盗;骗子。冒险家 (= adventurer)。***a*** ~ ***of the press*** 新闻记者。***a*** ~ ***of the road*** [***pad***] 拦路强盗,游民,乞丐;出门兜揽生意的人。***a*** ~ ***of the*** (***long***) ***robe*** 律师,教士。***a*** ~ ***of the three outs***〔谑〕(无现钱、无袖肘、无信用的)三无绅士。***a*** ~ ***of virtu*** 古董家,古玩专家。***a*** ~***'s*** [***gentlemen's***] ***agreement*** 君子协定。***a*** ~***'s*** ~ 侍从,男仆。***my*** ~ 那家伙,此人。***the*** ~ ***from*** ***...***〔美〕(从某州)选出的(众议院)议员。***the*** ~ ***in black*** 恶魔。***the old*** ~〔谑〕恶魔。~**-at-arms'** *n*. (英国国王的)卫士。~**-farmer** *n*. (*pl*. ***gentlemen-farmers***) (占有土地,不劳动,只管经营、管理的)乡绅。~ **like** *a*. = *gentlemanly*. ~ **ranker** 有军籍的绅士。~**-pensioner** = ~-at-arms. ~**ship** *n*. 绅士身份。~ **usher**〔英〕门役,拜谒者的引见人。

gen·tle·man·ly [ˈdʒentlmənli; ˋdʒɛntl̩mənlɪ] *a*. 绅士的,绅士派头的。**-li·ness** *n*.

gen·tle·wom·an [ˈdʒentlwumən; ˋdʒɛntl͵wʊmən] *n*. (*pl*. **-wom·en** [-ˌwimin; -͵wɪmən]) 1. 有身份的妇女,女士,贵妇人。2. (王室、贵族的)侍女,女仆。~**like** *a*. **-li·ness** *n*. **-ly** *a*.

gen·tly [ˈdʒentli; ˋdʒɛntlɪ] *ad*. 1. 文雅地,温柔地,有礼貌地。2. 柔和地、轻轻地、渐渐地。3. 出身高贵地,有教养地。*G-!* 慢点儿! *be* ~ *born* 出身名门的,有身份的。*smile* ~嫣然一笑。*The road sloped* ~ *to the lake*. 路缓缓地向湖边倾斜下去。

gen·try [ˈdʒentri; ˋdʒɛntrɪ] *n*. 1. 贵族们,绅士们;〔英〕(仅次于贵族的)绅士阶级,上等人士;可以使用纹章的平民〔多为大地主〕。2.〔谑、蔑〕人们,伙伴。*evil* ~*s* 劣绅。***the flash*** ~ 盗贼们,流氓们。***the*** ~ ***of the press*** 新闻界人士。***the light-fingered*** ~ 扒手们。***the silk-stocking*** ~ 富人,财主。***these*** ~〔蔑〕这些家伙。

gents [dʒents; dʒɛnts] *n*. gent 的复数。

ge·nu [ˈdʒiːnjuː, ˈdʒen-; ˋdʒinju, ˋdʒɛn-] *n*. (*pl*. ***genu·a*** [ˈdʒenjuə; ˋdʒɛnjuə])【解】1. 膝。2. 膝状部分。

gen·u·flect [ˈdʒenju(ː)flekt; ˋdʒɛnjʊ͵flɛkt] *vi*. 1. 曲膝,跪拜(尤指做礼拜时)。2. 屈服,屈从。

gen·u·flec·tion, gen·u·flex·ion [ˌdʒenju(ː)ˈflekʃən; ͵dʒɛnjʊˋflɛkʃən] *n*. 曲膝;屈服,屈从。

gen·u·flec·tor [ˈdʒenju(ː)flektə; ˋdʒɛnjʊflɛktɚ] *n*. 曲膝者;屈服者,屈从者。

gen·u·ine [ˈdʒenjuin; ˋdʒɛnjʊɪn] *a*. 1. 真正的 (*opp*. sham, counterfeit)。2. 坦率的,真诚的,真心诚意的。3. 血统纯粹的,纯种的。*a* ~ *Rubens* 鲁本兹亲笔画。*a* ~ *signature* 亲笔签名。*a* ~ *writing* 真迹,墨宝。*a* ~ *skeptic* 十足的怀疑论者。*a* ~ *breed* 纯种。**-ly** *ad*. **-ness** *n*.

ge·nus [ˈdʒiːnəs; ˋdʒinəs] *n*. (*pl*. ***gen·er·a*** [ˈdʒenərə; ˋdʒɛnərə], ~*es*) 1. 种类,类;【生】属。2.【逻】类,类概念。***the*** ~ ***Homo*** 人类。

-geny *suf*. 表示:"起源","产生";"发展": anthropo*geny*, pro*geny*.

Gen X = Generation X。

geo- *comb. f*. 表示"地球","土地": *geo*centric, *geo*logy.

geo [gjəu; gjo] *n*.〔Scot.〕海湾。

Geo. = George.

geo·an·ti·cline [ˌdʒi(ː)əuˈæntiklain; ͵dʒioˋæntɪklaɪn] *n*.【地】地背斜。

ge·o·board [ˈdʒi(ː)əubɔːd; ˋdʒɪobɔd] *n*. 几何板〔供学生学习几何的一种教具,为一方形板,上面立着一排排小细柱,以橡皮筋绕在小柱上即可绕出各种几何图形〕。

ge·o·cen·tric [ˌdʒi(ː)əuˈsentrik; ͵dʒioˋsɛntrɪk] *a*. 以地球为中心的 (*opp*. heliocentric); 从地心出发计算[观

察]的;地心的。*the* ～ *theory* 地球中心说,地心说。～ **latitude** [**longitude**] 地心纬度[经度]。～ **parallax** 地心视差。～ **zenith** 地心天顶。**-al·ly** *ad*.

ge·o·cen·tric·ism [ˌdʒi(ː)əuˈsentrisizəm; ˏdʒioˋsentrəsɪzəm] *n*. 地球中心说。

ge·o·chem·is·try [ˌdʒi(ː)əuˈkemistri; ˏdʒioˋkemɪstrɪ] *n*. 地球化学。**-ical** *a*. **-ist** *n*.

ge·o·chro·nol·o·gy [ˌdʒi(ː)əukrəˈnɔlədʒi; ˏdʒiokrəˋnɑlədʒɪ] *n*. 地质年代学。**-chron·o·log·i·cal** [-ˌkrɔnəˈlɔdʒikl; -ˏkrɑnəˋlɑdʒɪkl] *a*.

ge·o·chro·nom·e·try [ˌdʒi(ː)əukrəˈnɔmitri; ˏdʒiokrəˋnɑmɪtrɪ] *n*. 地球测时学。**-no·met·ric** [-krɔnəˈmetrik, -ˌkrəunə-; -krɑnəˋmetrɪk, -ˏkronə-] *a*.

ge·o·cide [ˈdʒi(ː)əusaid; ˋdʒiosaɪd] *n*. 地球末日。

ge·o·co·ro·na [ˌdʒi(ː)əukəˈrəunə; ˏdʒiokəˋronə] *n*. 地华〔地球大气最外层,主要含氢〕。

geod. = geodesy; geodetic.

ge·ode [ˈdʒi(ː)əud; ˋdʒiod] *n*. 【地】晶洞,晶球。空心石核。**-od·ic** [dʒi(ː)ˈɔdik; dʒiəˋɑdɪk] *a*.

ge·o·des·ic [ˌdʒi(ː)əuˈdesik; ˏdʒiəˋdɛsɪk] **I** *a*. **1**. 大地测量学的。**2**. 【数】(最)短线的。**II** *n*. 【数】= ～ line. ～ **circle** 短程圆。～ **dome** 【建】网格球形顶。～ **line** 测地线;短程线。

geo·des·i·cal [ˌdʒi(ː)əuˈdesikəl; ˏdʒiəˋdɛsɪkəl] *a*. = geodesic.

ge·od·e·sy [dʒi(ː)ˈɔdisi; dʒiəˋɑddəsɪ] *n*. 大地测量学。*astronomical* ～天文大地测量学。

ge·o·det·ic(al) [ˈdʒi(ː)əuˈdetik(əl); ˏdʒiəˋdɛtɪk(əl)] *a*. = geodesic (*a*.). **-i·cal·ly** *ad*.

ge·o·det·ics [ˌdʒi(ː)əuˈdetiks; ˏdʒiəˋdɛtɪks] *n*. = geodesy.

ge·o·dy·nam·ic(al) [ˌdʒi(ː)əudaiˈnæmik(əl); ˏdʒiodaɪˋnæmɪk(əl)] *a*. 地球动力学的。

ge·o·dy·nam·ics [ˌdʒi(ː)əudaiˈnæmiks; ˏdʒiodaɪˋnæmɪks] *n*. *pl*. 〔用作单〕地球动力学。

ge·o·e·lec·tric [ˌdʒi(ː)əuiˈlektrik; ˏdʒioɪˋlɛktrɪk] *a*. 【物】地电的。

Geof·frey [ˈdʒefri; ˋdʒɛfrɪ] *n*. 杰弗里〔男子名〕。

geog. = geographer; geographic(al); geography.

ge·og·nos·tic(al) [ˌdʒiːəgˈnɔstik(əl); ˏdʒiəgˋnɑstɪk(əl)] *a*. 地球构造学的。**-ti·cal·ly** *ad*.

ge·og·no·sy [dʒiˈɔgnəsi; dʒɪˋɑgnəsɪ] *n*. 地球构造学。

ge·og·ram [ˈdʒi(ː)əugræm; ˋdʒiogræm] *n*. 地球环境制图。

ge·og·ra·pher [dʒiˈɔgrəfə; dʒɪˋɑgrəfɚ] *n*. 地理学者,地理学家。

ge·o·graph·ic(al) [ˌdʒiəˈgræfik(əl); ˏdʒiəˋgræfɪk(əl)] *a*. 地理学的,地理的。～ **distribution** 地理分布。～ **features** 地势。～ **information systems** *n*. 电子地图技术;地理信息系统〔可缩写为 GIS〕。～ **latitude** 地理纬度。～ **mile** 地理英里〔赤道上经度一分的长度,约1,854米〕。～ **north** 正北。～ **strategic point** 战略地点。**-i·cal·ly** *ad*.

ge·og·ra·phy [dʒiˈɔgrəfi; dʒɪˋɑgrəfɪ] *n*. **1**. 地理学。**2**. 地理,地形,地势(*of*)。**3**. 地志,地理书。**4**. (生产、建筑等的)配置,布局。*applied* ～商业地理。*botanical* ～植物分布学。*human* ～人文地理学。*physical* ～地文学,自然地理。*political* ～政治地理学。*the* ～ *of Asia* 亚洲地理,亚洲地形。*lessons in* ～地理课程。

ge·oid [ˈdʒiːɔid; ˋdʒiɔɪd] *n*. 【地】**1**. 像地体,大地水平面。**2**. 地球体,地球形。

geol. = geologic(al); geologist; geology.

ge·o·log·ic(al) [dʒiəˈlɔdʒik(əl); ˏdʒiəˋlɑdʒɪk(əl)] *a*. 地质学的,地质的。*a* ～ *survey* 地质调查。～ **chronology** 地质编年学。～ **section** 【地】地质剖面。**-i·cal·ly** *ad*.

ge·ol·o·gist [dʒiˈɔlədʒist; dʒɪˋɑlədʒɪst] *n*. 地质学者,地质学家。

ge·ol·o·gize [dʒiˈɔlədʒaiz; dʒɪˋɑləˏdʒaɪz] *vi*. 研究地质(学);搜集地质标本。— *vt*. 对(某地)作地质调查。

ge·ol·o·gy [dʒiˈɔlədʒi; dʒɪˋɑlədʒɪ] *n*. **1**. 地质学。**2**. (某一地区的)地质。**3**. 地质学的著作。*economic* ～应用地质学。*historical* ～地史学。*structural* ～构造地质学。

geom. = geometer; geometric(al); geometry; geometrician.

ge·o·mag·net·ic [ˌdʒiːəumægˈnetik; ˏdʒiomægˋnɛtɪk] *a*. 地磁的。～ **storm** (地)磁暴。**-net·ism** *n*. 地磁;地磁学。

ge·o·man·cy [ˈdʒi(ː)əumænsi; ˋdʒiəmænsɪ] *n*. 泥土占卜〔拿一把土撒在地上,按形成的形状进行占卜,或按在地上任意画的线或形状进行占卜〕。**-man·tic** [-ˈmæntik; -ˋmæntɪk] *a*.

ge·o·me·chan·ics [ˌdʒi(ː)əumiˈkæniks; ˏdʒiomɪˋkænɪks] *n*. 地球力学,地质力学。

ge·om·e·ter [dʒiˈɔmitə; dʒɪˋɑmətɚ] *n*. **1**. = geometrician. **2**. 【动】尺蠖。

ge·o·met·ric [dʒiəˈmetrik; ˏdʒiəˋmɛtrɪk] *n*. 有几何图形的东西。

ge·o·met·ric(al) [dʒiəˈmetrik(əl); ˏdʒiəˋmɛtrɪk(əl)] *a*. **1**. 几何学的,几何图形的。**2**. 按几何级数增长的。～ **stairs** 弯曲的楼梯。～ *ornaments* 几何图形装饰。～ **mean** 【数】几何平均数,等比中项[中数]。～ **progression** [**series**] 几何级数,等比级数。～ **projection** 几何投影。～ **worm** 【动】尺蠖。**-ri·cal·ly** *ad*.

ge·om·e·tri·cian [ˌdʒiəuməˈtriʃən; ˏdʒiəməˋtrɪʃən] *n*. 几何学者,几何学家。

ge·om·e·trid [dʒiˈɔmitrid; dʒɪˋɑmətrɪd] *n*., *a*. 尺蠖(的)。

ge·om·e·trize [dʒiˈɔmitraiz; dʒɪˋɑmətraɪz] *vt*. 用几何图形表示,使符合几何原理和定律。— *vi*. 研究几何学,按几何学方法或原理工作。

ge·om·e·try [dʒiˈɔmitri; dʒɪˋɑmətrɪ] *n*. **1**. 几何学。**2**. 几何形状。**3**. 几何学著作。*analytical* ～解析几何。*descriptive* ～图形几何,画法几何。*Euclidean* ～欧氏几何。*non-Euclidean* ～非欧几何。*plane* ～平面几何。*solid* ～立体几何。*spherical* ～球面几何。

ge·o·mor·phic [ˌdʒi(ː)əuˈmɔːfik; ˏdʒiəˋmɔrfɪk] *a*. 地形的;地形学的。

ge·o·mor·phol·o·gist [ˌdʒi(ː)əumɔːˈfɔlədʒist; ˏdʒiomɔrˋfɑlədʒɪst] *n*. 地形学家。

ge·o·mor·phol·o·gy [ˌdʒiːəumɔːˈfɔlədʒi; ˏdʒiomɔrˋfɑlədʒɪ] *n*. 地形学。**-pho·log·ic** [-ˌmɔːfəˈlɔdʒik; -ˏmɔrfəˋlɑdʒɪk]. **-pho·log·i·cal** *a*.

ge·oph·a·gy [dʒiˈɔfədʒi; dʒɪˋɑfədʒɪ] *n*. 食土,食土癖。

ge·o·phone [ˈdʒi(ː)əufəun; ˋdʒiəˏfon] *n*. 地音探听器,地震检波器。

ge·o·phys·ics [ˌdʒi(ː)əuˈfiziks; ˏdʒioˋfɪzɪks] *n*. 地球物理学。**-i·cal** *a*. **-i·cal·ly** *ad*. **-i·cist** *n*. **-i·cal warfare** 地球物理战〔如枯叶战,黄雨战〕。

ge·o·phyte [ˈdʒiːəfait; ˋdʒiəˏfaɪt] *n*. 地下芽植物。

ge·o·po·lit·i·cal [ˌdʒi(ː)əupəˈlitikl; ˏdʒiəpəˋlɪtɪkl] *a*. 地理政治论的,地缘政治学的。**-ly** *ad*.

ge·o·pol·i·ti·cian [ˌdʒi(ː)əuˌpɔliˈtiʃən; ˏdʒioˏpɑləˋtɪʃən] *n*. 地理政治论者,地缘政治学家。

ge·o·pol·i·tics [ˌdʒi(ː)əuˈpɔlitiks; ˏdʒioˋpɑlətɪks] *n*. 地理政治论,地缘政治学。

ge·o·pon·ic [ˌdʒi(ː)əuˈpɔnik; ˏdʒiəˋpɑnɪk] *a*. **1**. 耕作的,农业的。**2**. 〔谑〕乡间的,田园的。

ge·o·pon·ics [ˌdʒi(ː)əuˈpɔniks; ˏdʒiəˋpɑnɪks] *n*. **1**. 耕作,农业。**2**. 〔谑〕乡间,田园。

ge·o·probe [ˈdʒiːəprəub; ˋdʒiəprob] *n*. 地球探测火箭。

ge·o·ra·ma [ˌdʒiəˈrɑːmə; ˏdʒiəˋrɑmə] *n*. (由内面观赏的)内侧绘有世界地理实景的空心大圆球。

Geor·die[1] [ˈdʒɔːdi; ˋdʒɔrdi] *n*. 〔Scot.〕= collier.

Geor·die[2] [ˈdʒɔːdi; ˋdʒɔrdi] *n*. George 的爱称。

George[1] [dʒɔːdʒ; dʒɔrdʒ] *n*. 乔治〔姓氏,男子名;爱称 Geordie, Georgie, Dod, Doddy〕。*St*. ～英国的守护神。*St*. *G～'s day* 圣乔治日〔四月二十三日〕。**By ～** 确实,实在〔发誓或感叹〕。～ ***Cross*** [***Medal***] 乔治十字勋章〔英国王乔治六世 1940 年颁发的表彰英勇行为的勋章〕。***Let ～ do it***.〔美俚〕让别人去干吧!

George[2] [dʒɔːdʒ; dʒɔrdʒ] *n*. **1**. (英国嘉德勋章的两种图案之一)骑马降龙宝像。**2**. (英国有圣乔治像的)半克朗货币。**3**. 〔g-〕褐色陶制大水壶。**4**. 〔g-〕〔英俚〕(飞机的)自动驾驶仪。*a brown* ～褐色陶制容器。

George·town [ˈdʒɔːdʒtaun; ˋdʒɔrdʒtaʊn] *n*. **1**. 乔治敦〔圭亚那首都〕。**2**. 乔治敦〔开曼群岛(英)首府〕。**3**. 美国华盛顿哥仑比亚特区内的住宅区。

George Town [ˈdʒɔːdʒ ˈtaun; ˋdʒɔrdʒ ˋtaʊn] 乔治市〔即 Penang 槟城〕〔马来西亚港市〕。

geor·gette [dʒɔːˈdʒet; dʒɔrˋdʒɛt] *n*. 乔其绉纱(= ～ crepe)。

Geor·gia[1] [ˈdʒɔːdʒjə; ˋdʒɔrdʒjə] *n*. 乔治娅〔女子名〕。

Geor·gia[2] [ˈdʒɔːdʒjə; ˋdʒɔrdʒjə] *n*. **1**. 乔治亚〔美国南部之一州〕。**2**. 格鲁吉亚〔国名〕。

Geor·gian [ˈdʒɔːdʒjən; ˋdʒirdʒən] **I** *a*. **1**. (英国)乔治一世至四世统治时期的;(英国)乔治五世统治时期的。**2**. 格鲁吉亚的,格鲁吉亚人的,格鲁吉亚语的。**3**. (美国)佐治亚州的,佐治亚州人的。**II** *n*. **1**. 格鲁吉亚人;格鲁吉亚语。**2**. 佐治亚州人。

Geor·gi·(a)na [dʒɔːˈdʒiːnə; dʒɔrˋdʒinə] *n*. 乔治(亚)娜〔女子名〕。

geor·gic [ˈdʒɔːdʒik; ˋdʒɔrdʒɪk] **I** *n*. 田园诗。***The Georgics*** 《农事诗》〔古罗马诗人维吉尔(Virgil)所作的田园诗〕。**II** *a*. 农业(业)的。

Geor·gie [ˈdʒɔːdʒi; ˋdʒɔrdʒɪ] *n*. 乔吉〔George 的爱称〕。

ge·o·sci·ence [ˌdʒi(ː)əuˈsaiəns; ˏdʒioˋsaɪəns] *n*. 地学,地球科学。

ge·o·sci·en·tist [ˌdʒi(ː)əuˈsaiəntist; ˏdʒioˋsaɪəntɪst] *n*. 地球学家。

ge·o·space [ˈdʒi(ː)əuspeis; ˋdʒiospes] *n*. 地球空间(轨道)。

ge·o·stat·ic [ˌdʒi(ː)əuˈstætik; ˏdʒiəˋstætɪk] *a*. 地压的;【建】耐地压的。～ **curve** 地压曲线。

ge·o·stat·ics [ˌdʒiəuˈstætiks; ˏdʒiəˋstætɪks] *n*. *pl*. 〔用作单〕刚体力学。

ge·o·sta·tion·ar·y [ˌdʒi(ː)əuˈsteiʃənəri; ˏdʒioˋsteʃənərɪ] *a*. (人造卫星等)对地静止的,对地同步的。～ **orbit** (人造卫星的)对地静止轨道。

ge·o·stra·te·gic [ˌdʒi(ː)əustrəˈtiːdʒik; ˏdʒiostrəˋtidʒɪk] *a*. 地理战略论的,地缘战略学的。

ge·o·strat·e·gist [ˌdʒi(ː)əuˈstrætidʒist; ˏdʒioˋstrætədʒɪst] *n*. 地理战略论者,地缘战略学家。

ge·o·strat·e·gy [ˌdʒi(ː)əuˈstrætidʒi; ˏdʒioˋstrætədʒɪ] *n*. 地理战略论,地缘战略学。

ge·o·stroph·ic [ˌdʒi(ː)əuˈstrɔfik; ˏdʒiəˋstrɑfɪk] *a*. 【气】地转的,因地球自转引起的。～ **current** 地转(海)流。～ **flow** 地转流。～ **wind** 地转风。**-i·cal·ly** *ad*.

ge·o·syn·cli·nal [ˌdʒi(ː)əusinˈklainəl; ˏdʒiosɪnˋklaɪnəl] **I** *a*. 地槽的,大向斜的,地向斜的。**II** *n*. = geosyncline.

ge·o·syn·cline [ˌdʒi(ː)əuˈsinklain; ˏdʒioˋsɪnklaɪn] *n*. 【地】地槽,大向斜。

ge·o·tax·is [ˌdʒi(ː)əuˈtæksis; ˏdʒioˋtæksɪs] *n*. 趋地性。**-tac·tic** [-ˈtæktik; -ˋtæktɪk] *a*. **-tac·ti·cal·ly** *ad*.

ge·o·tec·ton·ic [ˌdʒi(ː)əutekˈtɔnik; ˏdʒiotɛkˋtɑnɪk] *a*. 大地构造的。～ **geology** 大地构造地质学。**-al·ly** *ad*.

ge·o·ther·mal [ˌdʒi(ː)əuˈθəːməl; ˏdʒioˋθɝməl], **ge·o·ther·mic** [ˌdʒi(ː)əuˈθəːmik; ˏdʒioˋθɝmɪk] *a*. 地热的,有关地热的(= geothermal). ～ **gradient** 【地】地温梯度〔每趋向地心 60 英尺,温度升高华氏一度〕。**-al·ly** *ad*.

ge·o·trop·ic [ˌdʒi(ː)əuˈtrɔpik; ˏdʒiəˋtrɑpɪk] *a*. 向地性的。**-al·ly** *ad*.

ge·ot·ro·pism [dʒiˈɔtrəpizəm; dʒiˋɑtrəˏpɪzəm] *n*. 【生】向地性。*negative* ～负向地性,背地性。*positive* ～正向地性。

Ger. = German; Germany.

ger. = gerund.

ge·rah [ˈgiːrə; ˋgirə] *n*. **1**. 一种古希伯来银币。**2**. 格拉〔古希伯来衡器名,等于 1/20 谢克尔(*shekel*)〕。

Ger·ald [ˈdʒerəld; ˋdʒɛrəld] *n*. 杰拉尔德〔男子名〕。

Ger·al·dine [ˈdʒerəldiːn, ˈdʒerəldain; ˋdʒɛrəldɪn, ˋdʒɛrəldaɪn] *n*. 杰拉尔丁〔女子名〕。

ge·ra·ni·ol [dʒəˈreiniːɔːl; dʒəˋrenɪol] *n*. 【化】牻牛儿醇。

ge·ra·ni·um [dʒɪˈreinjəm, dʒəˈr-; dʒəˋrenɪjəm, -nɪəm] *n*. 【植】牻牛儿苗属,老鹳草属,〔G-〕老鹳草属。～ **oil** 草叶油。

Ger·ard [ˈdʒerɑːd, dʒəˈrɑːd; ˋdʒɛrɑrd, dʒəˋrɑrd] *n*. 杰勒德〔姓氏,男子名〕。

ger·ber·a [ˈgəːbərə; ˋgɝbərə] *n*. 【植】非洲菊(*Gerbera jamesonii*)。

ger·bil, **ger·bille** [ˈdʒəːbl; ˋdʒɝbl̩] *n*. 【动】沙鼠亚科(*Gerbillinae*)动物;沙鼠。～**tube** 沙鼠通道〔联接两座或多座建筑物的空中走廊,多用玻璃或塑料封闭〕。

ger·ent [ˈdʒiərənt; ˋdʒɪrənt] *n*. 〔罕〕有职有权者;经营管理者;统治者。

ger·e·nuk [ˈgeərəˌnuk, gəˈrenək; ˋgeərəˏnʊk, gəˋrɛnək] *n*. 【动】长颈羚(*Litocranius walleri* = giraffe antelope)。

ger·fal·con [ˈdʒəːˌfɔːlkən, -ˌfɔːk-; ˋdʒɝˏfɔlkən, -ˏfɔk-] *n*. 【动】(冰岛产的)大隼。

Ger·hard [ˈgəːhɑːd; ˋgɝhɑrd] = Gerald.

ger·i·at·ric [ˌdʒeriˈætrik; ˏdʒɛrɪˋætrɪk] *a*. 老年病学的,老年的,衰老的。

ger·i·a·tri·cian [ˌdʒeriəˈtriʃən; ˏdʒɛrɪəˋtrɪʃən] *n*. 老年病学家(= geriatrist)。

ger·i·at·rics [ˌdʒəriˈætriks; ˏdʒərɪˋætrɪks] *n*. *pl*. 〔用作单〕老年病学。

ger·i·at·rist [ˌdʒeriˈætrist; ˏdʒɛrɪˋætrɪst] *n*. = geriatrician.

germ [dʒəːm; dʒɝm] **I** *n*. **1**. 微生物,细菌,病菌,病原菌。**2**. 【生】幼芽,胚芽,胚原基。**3**. 起源,根源;萌芽。*the* ～ *of life* 生命的根源。**be in** ～ 处于萌芽状态,处在不发达阶段。**II** *vi*. 〔喻〕发芽,萌芽;发生。～ **carrier** 带菌者。～ **cell** 生殖细胞。～**free** *a*. 无菌的;(实验动物)在无菌状态下生长的。～ **layer** 胚层。～**-plasm(a)** 种质。～**-proof** *a*. 抗菌的。～ **theory** 【生】生源说,【医】病菌说,微生物说。～**warfare** 细菌战争。～ **weapon** 细菌武器。

Germ. = German; Germany.

Ger·man [ˈdʒəːmən; ˋdʒɝmən] **I** *a*. **1**. 德意志的,德国的。**2**. 日耳曼人的,德国人的。**3**. 日耳曼语的,德语的。**II** *n*. **1**. 德意志人;德国人;日尔曼人。**2**. 日尔曼语,德语。**3**. 〔g-〕(一种复杂的)德国华尔兹舞,德国华尔兹舞舞会。*High* ～高地德语〔现在的标准德语〕。*Low* ～低地德语〔包括 Frisian, Dutch, Flemish 等〕。～ **measles** 【医】风疹。～ **Ocean** 北海 = North Sea. ～ **sausage** 德国香肠,大腊肠。～ **shepherd** (**dog**) 德国牧羊犬〔也叫(～)police dog〕。～ **silver** 锌白铜〔镍、锌、铜的合金〕。～ **text** 德文式黑体字。～ **wool** 细毛线。

ger·man [ˈdʒəːmən; ˋdʒɝmən] *a*. **1**. 同父母的,同祖父母的,同外祖父母的〔常用连词符号附加在被修饰的名词后面〕。**2**. 〔罕〕= germane. *brothers* [*sisters*]-～胞弟兄〔姐妹〕。*cousins*-～嫡堂弟兄〔姐妹〕。

ger·man·der [dʒəːˈmændə; dʒəˋmændɚ] *n*. 【植】**1**. 石蚕属,香科属。**2**. 水苦荬属,婆婆纳属〔尤指 ～ speedwell〕。

ger·mane [dʒəːˈmein; dʒɚˋmen] *a*. 1. (议论等)切题的，关系密切的。2. (比喻等)恰当的，贴切的 (*to*)。*a remark hardly ~ to the question* 同问题不大有关的话。**-ly** *ad*.

Ger·man·ic [dʒəːˈmænik; dʒɚˋmænɪk] **I** *a*. 1. 德意志的，德国的；德国人的，德语的。2. 日耳曼人的，日耳曼语(系)的，条顿民族的。**II** *n*. 日耳曼语(系)〔印欧语系中的重要分支，包括现代英语、德语、荷兰语、佛兰芒语、冰岛语、挪威语以及哥特语等〕。

Ger·man·ism [ˈdʒəːmənizəm; ˋdʒɚmənɪzm] *n*. 1. 日耳曼[德意志]精神，日耳曼气质；日耳曼式，日耳曼倾向；日耳曼主义。2. 日耳曼词语；德语习语，德语特色。

Ger·man·ist [ˈdʒəːmənist; ˋdʒɚmənɪst] *n*. 1. 德语学家，德意志文学专家，德意志主义者。2. 日耳曼语学者，日耳曼文学专家。

ger·ma·nite [ˈdʒəːmənait; ˋdʒɚmə͵naɪt] *n*. 【矿】锗石。

ger·ma·ni·um [dʒəːˈmeiniəm; dʒɚˋmenɪəm] *n*. 【化】锗。~ **transistor** 锗晶体管。

Ger·man·ize [ˈdʒəːmənaiz; ˋdʒɚmə͵naɪz] *vt*. 1. 使德意志化。2. 把…译成德语。— *vi*. 具有德意志方式[习惯、态度]。**-i·zation** *n*.

Germano- *comb. f*. (= German)：*Germano*phobia.

Ger·man·o·ma·ni·a [͵dʒəːmənəuˈmeinjə; ͵dʒɚmənəˋmenjə] *n*. 崇拜德国，德国迷。

Ger·man·o·phil(e) [dʒəːˈmænəufail; dʒɚˋmænə͵faɪl] *n*.，*a*. 亲德派(的)，德国崇拜者(的)。

Ger·man·o·phobe [dʒəːˈmænəufəub; dʒɚˋmænə͵fob] *n*.，*a*. 恐惧和仇恨德国的人(的)。

Ger·man·o·pho·bi·a [dʒəːˈmænəufəubiə; ͵dʒɚmənəˋfobɪə] *n*. 恐德病，仇德狂。

Ger·ma·ny [ˈdʒəːməni; ˋdʒɚmənɪ] *n*. 德意志，德国。

ger·men [ˈdʒəːmen; ˋdʒɚmen] *n*. (*pl*. ~*s*; **-mi·na** [-minə; -mɪnə]) 1. 【植】蕾，幼芽，子房。2. 【动】生殖腺。

ger·mi·ci·dal [͵dʒəːmiˈsaidəl; ͵dʒɚməˋsaɪdl] *a*. 杀菌(剂)的，有杀菌力的。

ger·mi·cide [ˈdʒəːmisaid; ˋdʒɚmə͵saɪd] *n*. 杀菌剂。

Ger·mi·nal [ˈdʒəːminl; ˋdʒɚmɪnl] *n*. 〔F.〕 1. 播种月〔阳历 3 月 21 日至 4 月 19 日〕；法国革命历第 7 月。2. [g-] 树发芽时，春天。

ger·mi·nal [ˈdʒəːminl; ˋdʒɚmənl] *a*. 1. 胚种的，幼芽的。2. 原始的，初期的。~ *ideas* 原始观念。~ **area** 胚盘。~ **cell** 生殖[发]细胞。~ **disc**【生】胚盘。~ **furrow** 生殖槽。~ **layer** 胚层，生发层。~ **selection** 配子选择，生殖质淘汰。~ **vesicle** 胚核，胚胞。**-ly** *ad*.

ger·mi·nant [ˈdʒəːminənt; ˋdʒɚmənənt] *a*. 1. 发芽的；有发育力的。2. 开始的，发端的。

ger·mi·nate [ˈdʒəːmineit; ˋdʒɚmə͵net] *vi*. 1. 发芽，萌芽，发育。2. 发生，发展。*Seeds ~ in the spring*. 种子在春天发芽。— *vt*. 1. 使发芽；使发育。2. 使发生，使发展。*Seeds are ~d by warmth and moisture*. 温暖的气候和水分促使种子发芽。**germinating ability** [**capacity**] (种子)发芽力。**germinating viability** 发芽势。

ger·mi·na·tion [͵dʒəːmiˈneiʃən; ͵dʒɚməˋneʃən] *n*. 萌芽，发生。~ **percentage** 发芽率。

ger·mi·na·tive [ˈdʒəːmi͵neitiv; ˋdʒɚmə͵netɪv] *a*. 发芽的，有发育力的。

ger·mi·na·tor [ˈdʒəːmi͵neitə; ˋdʒɚmə͵netɚ] *n*. 1. 使发芽[发育]的人[物]。2. 种子发芽力测定器。

geront(o)- *comb. f*. 表示"老人"，"老年"：*geronto*logy.

ger·on·toc·ra·cy [͵dʒerənˈtɔkrəsi; ͵dʒɛrənˋtɑkrəsɪ] *n*. 1. 老人政府；老人统治。2. (*pl*.) 老人组成的统治集团。

ge·ron·to·c·rat·ic [dʒə͵rɔntəuˈkrætik; dʒə͵rɑntəˋkrætɪk] *a*.

ger·on·tol·o·gy [͵dʒerənˈtɔlədʒi; ͵dʒɛrənˋtɑlədʒɪ] *n*. 老人学，老人病学。**-to·log·i·cal** *a*. **-o·gist** *n*. 研究老人病学的专家。

ge·ron·to·mor·pho·sis [dʒə͵rɔntəuˈmɔːfəsis; dʒə͵rɑntəˋmɔrfəsɪs] *n*. 【医】特化进化。

ge·ron·to·pho·bia [dʒə͵rɔntəˈfəubiə; dʒə͵rɑtəˋfobɪə] *n*. 恐老症；憎老症，憎恨老人。

Ger·ry [ˈgeri; ˋgɛrɪ] *n*. 格里〔姓氏，男子名〕。

ger·ry·man·der [ˈdʒerimændə; ˋgɛrɪ͵mændɚ] **I** *vt*. 〔美〕(为本党利益)不公正地改划(州、县等的选区)；任意改划(一地区的选区)以谋取利益。— *vi*. 不公正地划分选区。**II** *n*. 不公正地划分的选区。

gers·dorff·ite [ˈgerz͵dɔːfait; ˋgɛrz͵dɔrfaɪt] *n*. 【矿】砷硫镍矿，辉砷镍矿。

Gersh·win [ˈgəːʃwin; ˋgɚʃwɪn] *n*. 格什温〔姓氏〕。

Ger·trude [ˈgəːtruːd; ˋgɚtrud] *n*. 格特鲁德〔女子名〕。

Ger·ty [ˈgəːti; ˋgɚtɪ] *n*. 格蒂〔女子名 Gertrude 的昵称〕。

ger·und [ˈdʒerənd; ˋdʒɛrənd] *n*. 1. 【语法】(由动词加 -ing 形成的)英语动名词。2. 【语法】拉丁动名词。~**-grinder** 1. 拉丁语教师。2. 学究式的老师。

ge·run·di·al [dʒiˈrʌndiəl; dʒəˋrʌndɪəl] *a*. 【语法】动名词的。**-ly** *ad*.

ger·un·di·val [͵dʒerənˈdaivəl; ͵dʒɛrənˋdaɪvəl] *a*. 【语法】动形词的，动词状形容词的。**-ly** *ad*.

ge·run·dive [dʒiˈrʌndiv; dʒəˋrʌndɪv] **I** *a*. = gerundial. **II** *n*. 1. 【语法】拉丁动形词。2. (其他语言中)类似拉丁动形词的形式。

ges·ne·ri·a [gesˈniəriə; gɛsˋnɪərɪə] *a*. 【植】苦苣苔科的。

ges·so [ˈdʒesəu; ˋdʒɛso] *n*. (绘画、雕刻用的)石膏粉。

gest(e) [dʒest; dʒɛst] *n*. 1. 〔古〕武侠(故事)(尤指中世纪用韵文写的故事)。2. 英勇行为，冒险活动，奇遇。

ge·stalt [gəˈʃtælt; gəˋʃtɑlt] *n*. 〔G.〕 (*pl*. ~***en*** [-ən; -ən]) 【心】完形，经验的整体。**G- psychology** 形态心理学〔又译格式塔心理学，为现代欧美资产阶级心理学主要派别之一〕。

Ge·sta·po [geˈʃtɑːpəu; gəˋʃtɑpo] *n*. 〔G.〕盖世太保〔纳粹德国的秘密国家警察，源自德语的 Geheime *Staat*polizei〕。

Ges·ta Ro·ma·no·rum [ˈdʒestə͵rəuməˈnɔːrəm; ˋdʒɛstə͵roməˋnɔrəm]《古罗马人记事》〔用拉丁文写出的一部十三、四世纪欧洲故事集〕。

ges·tate [ˈdʒesteit; ˋdʒɛstet] *vt*.，*vi*. 1. (使)怀孕，妊娠。2. 酝酿，孕育。

ges·ta·tion [dʒesˈteiʃən; dʒɛsˋteʃən] *n*. 1. 妊娠(期)，怀孕(期)。2. 酝酿，孕育。

ges·tic [ˈdʒestik; ˋdʒɛstɪk]，**ges·tic·al** [-əl; -əl] *a*. 与身体动作有关的(尤指跳舞时)。

ges·tic·u·late [dʒesˈtikjuleit; dʒɛsˋtɪkjə͵let] *vi*. 用姿势[动作]示意，打手势。— *vt*. 用姿势[动作]表达(意思)。

ges·tic·u·la·tion [dʒes͵tikjuˈleiʃən; dʒɛs͵tɪkjəˋleʃən] *n*. 用动作[姿势]示意，打手势。

ges·tic·u·la·tive [dʒesˈtikjuleitiv; dʒɛsˋtɪkjə͵letɪv]，**ges·tic·u·la·tory** [dʒesˈtikjulətəri; dʒɛsˋtɪkjələtərɪ] *a*. 打手势的，做手势的。

ges·tic·u·la·tor [dʒesˈtikjuleitə; dʒɛsˋtɪkjəletɚ] *n*. 用姿势[动作]示意的人，打手势的人。

ges·ture [ˈdʒestʃə; ˋdʒɛstʃɚ] **I** *n*. 1. 姿势，手势。2. 〔古〕仪态，举止，样子。3. 姿态，表示(尤指友好的表示)。4. 【计】光笔指令。*a fine ~* 雅量。*a warlike ~* 耀武扬威，挑衅的姿态。**II** *vi*.，*vt*. = gesticulate. ~ **language** 手势语。~ **politics** 手势政治〔指只追求宣传效果的政治活动〕。

Ge·sund·heit [gəˈzunthait; gəˋzunthaɪt] *int*. 〔G.〕为你的健康干杯!〔祝酒词〕；祝你健康!〔对刚打喷嚏的人祝愿语〕。

get [get; gɛt] **I** *vt*. (**got** [gɔt; gɑt]；〔美、古〕 ***got·ten*** [ˈgɔtn; ˋgɑtn]；***getting***) 1. 获得；赚得；赢得，博得，取得。~ *a first prize* 获得头奖。~ *a lot of money* 得到许多钱。~ *more than one bargained for* 得到意外收获；碰到意外不愉快的事。~ *a living* 谋生。~ *fame* [*credit*，*glory*] 获得名誉[信任、荣誉]。~ *knowledge* 获取知识。2. 收到，接到。*Did you ~ my letter*? 你收

到我的信了吗？～ *a telegram* 接到一封电报。**3.** 生(病)，得(病)，感染上(病)；(毒品等)使上瘾。～ *the measles* 出痧子。～ *a film* 迷上一部电影。**4.** 挨(打等)，〔口〕受(罚)，被判(刑)。～ *a blow on the head* 头上挨了一拳。〔口〕受罚，受苦；被判刑。～ *three months* 被处徒刑三月。～ *the sack* 〔口〕被解雇。**5.** 买，定购。*Where did you* ～ *that hat?* 你在哪里买到这顶帽子的？**6.** 拿；搞到，弄来。*Go* ～ *your exercise book*. 把你的作业本拿来。*G- me some food*. 给我弄点吃的来。**7.** 抓住，捕捉。*The police got the thief*. 警察捉住了小偷。**8.** 赶上，搭上(车、船等)。*hurry to* ～ *train* 急着去赶火车。**9.** 〔完成式 have got〕有。*I've got very little money*. 我没有多少钱。**10.** 〔完成后接不定式 have got to = have to〕得，该，不得不。*I've got to go to the doctor's*. 我得去看医生了。**11.** 使达到(某种状态、地位、场所等)，使产生(某种结果)。～ *the breakfast ready* 准备好早饭。～ *the sum right* 把数目弄对。*add 2 and 2 to* ～ *4* 二加二等于四。**12.** 使怀孕；〔常用于动词〕生，使生(仔)。～ *a woman with child* 使女人怀孕。**13.** 说服，劝说。*I got him to do homework*. 我说服他去做功课。**14.** 〔口〕理解，了解；暗记。*I can't* ～ *you*. 我不明白你的意思。～ *the verse by heart* 把诗背熟。**15.** 〔后接以过去分词作补足语的受语〕使［要］…如何；把…了。～ *one's hair cut* 理发。～ *one's coat mended* 修补上衣。*I got my arm broken*. 我把手臂弄断了。～ *oneself elected* 使自己选上。★参见释义 11. 有类似处。**16.** 〔美〕迷人，吸引人，惹人欢喜。*The place doesn't* ～ *me altogether*. 这地方一点也不吸引我。*Her singing* ～*s me*. 她的歌唱迷住了我。**17.** 〔口〕打；击中；使受伤，杀死。*The blow got him in the mouth*. 一拳打中他的嘴巴。*It* ～*s them in the end*. 终于弄死了他们。**18.** 〔口〕吃；准备饭菜。～ *lunch at the inn* 在旅馆吃中饭。**19.** 使为难，问倒；使烦恼。*This problem* ～*s me*. 这问题难住我了。**20.** 收听，(电话)接通。*Please* ～ *me London*. 请给我接通伦敦。**21.** 【棒球】使对方球员下场。**22.** 报复。*I'll* ～ *you yet!* 早晚要给你点颜色看看！— *vi*. **1.** 得，成为…，开始…起来。*It's getting dark* [*late, cold*]. 天渐黑［晚、冷］起来。～ *into rage* 生起气来。～ *to be friends* 做起朋友来。*They got talking together*. 他们谈起话来了。*How did you* ～ *to know that I was here?* 你怎么知道我在这儿？*He soon* ～*s to like it*. 他不久就喜欢上它。**2.** 到达；去；进去。*The train* ～*s here at one o'clock*. 火车一点钟到这里。**3.** 〔与过去分词构成被动式〕被，受。～ *beaten* 挨揍。～ *caught in the rain* 遇上雨。～ *drunk* [*hurt*] 喝醉［受伤］了。*He got laughed at* [*punished, scolded*]. 他被人嘲笑［处罚，责备］。**4.** 〔美方〕勉勉强强…，好容易…。*I got to come*. 我总算来了。**5.** 〔俚〕赶快走开；(命令)去！滚！停止！*tell sb. to* ～叫某人立刻走开。**6.** 获得财产，赚到钱。～ ***about*** **1.** 走动；旅行，往来。**2.** (消息等)传开。**3.** 忙于工作，参加社会活动。**4.** (病后)下床活动了。～ ***above oneself*** 变得自高自大。～ ***abroad*** (消息等)传开。～ ***across*** **1.** 使通过。2. 讲清楚，使人了解(～ *sb. across the street* 带某人过马路。～ *one's idea across to the audience* 使听众理解自己的想法)。～ *after* 〔美口〕**1.** 训诫，攻击。**2.** 敦促，再三要求。～ ***ahead*** 进步，获得成功(～ *ahead with one's career* 事业有进展)。～ ***ahead and do it*** 〔美〕快干。～ ***ahead of*** 赶过，胜过。～ ***along*** **1.** 过活，过日子。**2.** 团结，和好相处 (*together; with*)。**3.** 有起色，进步；成功。**4.** 〔口〕〔主要用于祈使句〕走开，出去；胡说 (*How are you* ～*ting along* [*on*]? 你近来怎么样？～ *along* (*well*) *together* 相处得很好。*G- along with you!* 〔口〕滚开！去你的！胡说！)。～ ***among*** 加入。～ ***around*** 〔美〕**1.** 往来，走动。**2.** (消息等)传开。**3.** 避开(法律等)。**4.** 参加社会活动；忙于工作。**5.** (用哄骗、奉承等)说服，影响，智胜(某人)。～ ***at*** **1.** 到达；拿得到，够得着。**2.** 抓住；看出，了解。**3.** 〔口〕贿赂，收买 (*The mayor has been got at*. 市长已受贿赂)。**4.** 〔俚〕挖苦，攻击；欺骗。**5.** 意指 (*What are you* ～*ting at?* 你说这话是什么意思?)。～ ***away*** **1.** 离开，逃脱；出发。**2.** 把…送出。～ ***away with*** (***sth.***) **1.** 拿走，抢走，带走。**2.** 〔俚〕卷(款)潜逃。**3.** 避开责备［惩罚］(*The thief got away with my watch*. 那贼把我的手表偷走了)。～ ***away with it*** 侥幸成功；逃脱处罚。***Get away*** [***along, out***] ***with you!*** 〔口〕滚开！去你的！～ ***back*** **1.** 取回。**2.** 回来。**3.** 送回。**4.** 〔俚〕报复 (*on*) (～ *back one's own on sb*. 对某人进行报复)。～ ***back at*** 报复(～ *back at sb. for doing sth*. 为某人所做某事对他实行报复)。～ ***behind*** **1.** 落后。**2.** 拖欠。**3.** 看穿，看透(～ *behind sb.'s tricks* 看穿某人诡计)。**4.** 回避。**5.** 〔美〕支持，撑腰。～ ***by*** **1.** 走过，通过。**2.** 〔美〕勉强混过去，侥幸成功。～ ***clear of*** 脱离，摆脱，避开，还清(债务)。～ ***done with sth.*** 做完，结束。～ ***down*** **1.** 落下，降下；下车。**2.** 写下。**3.** 放下，咽下。**4.** 使沮丧，使抑郁。**5.** 开始认真对待，开始认真考虑 (*to*)。～ ***down on*** 〔美〕产生恶感，开始不喜欢。～ ***even with*** 〔俚〕报复 (*I'll* ～ *even with him sooner or later*. 我迟早要向他报复)。～ ***forward*** 进步；促进。～ ***going*** **1.** 〔美口〕开始，动手，采取行动。**2.** 〔美俚〕离开，出去。～ ***hep*** 〔美俚〕知道，熟悉起来；真相大白。～ ***hold of*** 获得，找到；接触。～ ***hold of the wrong end of the stick*** 根本弄错，完全误解。～ ***home*** **1.** 回家，到家。**2.** 达到目的。**3.** 言语中肯。～ ***in*** **1.** 进入，到达。**2.** 收(庄稼)；收集(税收、捐款等)。**3.** 插入；安排进…。**4.** 请…来做。**5.** 当选为议员(～ *in on time* 准时到达。～ *in for Chester* 当选为赤斯特选区议员。～ *in the New Year goods* 进年货。～ *in a word edgeways* 从旁插句话)。～ ***into*** **1.** 进入；穿上。**2.** (酒劲)冲脑。**3.** 成癖；陷于。**4.** 研究(～ *into a mess* [*muddle, scrape*] 〔口〕把事情搞糟。～ *into positions* 【军】进入阵地。～ *into trouble* 陷入麻烦。*The wine got into his head*. 他酒力发作了)。～ ***in with*** **1.** 和…好起来。**2.** 【海】靠近。～ ***it*** 〔口〕**1.** 懂得。**2.** 挨骂，受处分。～ ***it hot*** 〔口〕挨一顿痛骂，大受申斥。～ ***it on*** 〔美俚〕兴奋，激动。～ ***it right*** 正确理解，使人了解清楚。～ ***left*** 失败，吃亏，上当。～ ***next to*** **1.** 知道(某事)。**2.** 结识(某人)。～ ***nowhere*** (使)无进展，(使)无效。(使)无成就(*It will* ～ *you nowhere*. 这样不会对你有好处)。～ ***off*** **1.** 下来，下车；脱下(衣服等)。**2.** 卖出(货物)；发出(电报、信件等)。**3.** 〔口〕说(笑话)。**4.** 使入睡。**5.** 出发，起飞、离去。**6.** 逃脱，避开；免脱处罚［不幸、损失等］。**7.** 〔美〕弄好；〔美俚〕弄错。**8.** 〔美俚〕吸毒后感到飘飘然；处于快感中。(*tell sb. where he* ～*s off* 斥责某人)。～ ***off by heart*** 背诵。～ ***off on the right*** [***wrong***] ***foot*** 出师顺利［不利］。～ ***off one's chest*** 尽情倾诉，倾吐衷情。～ ***off the air*** 〔美俚〕广播结束。～ ***off to sleep*** 入睡。～ ***off with*** 〔俚〕和异性亲热起来。～ ***on*** **1.** 上马，上车；穿上，安上。**2.** 进步 (*with*)；繁荣，成功。**3.** 过日子，生活；相好，相投 (*with; together*) (～ *on in the world* 发迹，出头。～ *on in years* 上年纪。～ *on like a house on fire* 进展迅速顺利。*have got 'em all on* 〔口〕穿上最好的衣服，打扮得漂漂亮亮)。～ ***on for*** [***to, toward***] 靠近，接近，快要 (*It is* ～*ting on for midnight*. 快到半夜了。*He's* ～*ting on for seventy*. 他近七十岁了)。～ ***on the air*** 〔美〕开始广播［播音］。～ ***on to*** 〔美〕**1.** 识破，理解，明白过来。**2.** 同…接触。～ ***on sb.'s feet*** (尤指说话时)站起来；恢复。～ ***on the move*** 开始活动。～ ***one's*** [***his, hers, yours, theirs***] 得到应有的报酬，受到应得的惩罚 (*John will* ～ *his when his father learns that he did not attend school today*. 当约翰的父亲知道约翰今天逃学时，他准会挨骂)。～ ***one's skates on*** 赶快。～ ***out*** **1.** 走出，离开；摆脱；〔命令语气〕出去！(*G- out!* 滚!)。**2.** 泄露，显露。**3.** 取出；拔出；发现。**4.** 说出，公布；出版；抛出(股票)。～ ***out of*** **1.** 由…出来。**2.** 逐渐放弃(恶习)；避免。

G

3. 拔出;弄出。4. 问出,打听出(~ *out of control* 失去控制。~ *out of one's duties* 逃避职责。~ *out of hand* 控制不了,管不住了。*I could ~ nothing out of him*. 我从他嘴里什么也问不出)。~ ***outside of***〔俚〕吃,喝(*The snake got outside of a frog*. 蛇吞下了一只青蛙)。~***over*** 1. 越过,爬过(墙等)。2. 克服(困难)。3. 走完;完成。4. 回避,逃避(法律、规则等)。5. 痊愈,复原。6. 默认;原谅;断念;忘记过去;混过(时间)。7.〔俚〕欺骗;消灭(证据等)。8.〔俚〕说服,使了解。~ ***rid of*** 摆脱,解脱;除去。~ ***right down to cases***〔美口〕考虑基本问题。~ ***round*** = ~ ***around***. ~ ***round the table*** 使敌对各方坐下谈判。***G- set!***【体】准备! ~ ***sth. down cold*** [***pat***]〔美口〕完全了解,知道得一清二楚。~ ***somewhere*** 使有成效,使有进展。~ ***there***〔美〕成功,达到目的。~ ***the weight of one's feet*** [***legs***] 坐下[躺下]休息。~ ***through*** 1. 了结,办完。2. (使)通过(议案);及格。3. 用完,花光。4. 达到目的;成功(*with*);熬过(一段时期)。5. 打通(电话)。~ ***to*** 1. 到达,接触到。2. 开始。3.〔美口〕收买。~ ***to first base***〔美口〕成功。~ ***together*** 1. 收集,积累。2. 聚集,集会。3.〔口〕取得一致意见,同意。~ ***under*** 镇压,控制。~ ***under way*** 出发;出动,(船)开动。~ ***up*** 1. (使)起床,(使)起立,爬上;登上;骑上(马);逼近。2. (风等)变大;变烈;使(神经)兴奋[紧张]。3. 飞出,跳出。4. 准备,安排,组织,起草;编纂,出版。5. 钻研。6. 整理,修整,打扮,理发。7. 增进(健康);演出(戏剧)。8.〔对马吆喝〕走! 9. 玩弄(诡计等)。~ ***up and*** ~〔口〕赶快走。~ ***up and go*** 精力,魄力,主动精神(*With his ~ up and go, he ought to be a success as a manager*. 以他的精力来说,他理当是一位成功的经理)。~ ***up early*** 早起;有进取心。~ ***used to*** 惯于。~ ***well*** 痊愈,复原。~ ***wind of*** 听见,风闻。~ ***wise to***〔美俚〕懂得,晓得。~ ***with it***〔美俚〕赶上时髦,不落伍。**II** ***n***. 1.【畜】幼畜,(动物的)子。2.〔英俚〕私生子。3. (煤炭)产量。4. 赢利;薪资。*What's your weeks ~?* 你的周薪多少? ~**-off** (飞机的)起飞。~**-out** 1. 脱身;脱逃;〔美俚〕退路。2. 亏盈相抵(*as all ~-out*〔美口〕极顶,最大程度)。~**-rich-quick** ***a***. 想发横财的。~**-together** 1. ***n***. (非正式的)会谈,会商;〔美〕联欢会;集会。2. ***a***. 协议的;会商的;大群人的。~**up** 1.〔口〕装束,打扮,风度。2. 式样,格式。3. (书籍的)装订。4.〔美〕野心,精力。~**-up-and-go** ***a***. 干劲十足的,有进取心的。

ge·ta [ˈgetə, -ɑː; ˋgɛtə, -ɑ] ***n***. (*pl*. ~, ~*s*)〔Jap.〕木屐。

get·at·a·ble [getˈætəbl; gɛtˋætəbl] ***a***. 1. 可到达的,可接近的,可获得的。2. 能懂的。**-bil·l·ty** ***n***.

get·a·way [ˈgetəˌwei; ˋgɛtəˏwe] ***n***. 1.〔口〕(盗贼等的)逃亡,逃走。2. (赛马、汽车的)起跑,开始。3.【空】最小飞机速度。*a car with a good ~* 一辆起动快的汽车。*make a* [*one's*] ~逃走;【军】突围。~ **day** (运动会等)赛会的最后一天。

Geth·sem·a·ne [geθˈsemәni; gɛθˋsɛmənɪ] ***n***. 1. (耶路撒冷附近的)客西马尼园〔据传是耶稣被捕处〕。2.〔g-〕使人受精神折磨的地方[经验]。

get·(t)a·ble [ˈgetəbl; ˋgɛtəbl] ***a***. 能得到的,能到手的。

get·ter [ˈgetə; ˋgɛtɚ] ***n***. 1. 获得者。2. (电子管的)收气剂;收气器。3. 吸气剂,吸气器。4. 采矿工,采煤工。5. 采煤机。6.〔加〕毒饵。

Get·ty(s) [ˈgeti(z); ˋgɛtɪ(z)] ***n***. 格蒂(斯)〔姓氏〕。

Get·tys·burg [ˈgetizˌbəːg; ˋgɛtɪzˏbɝg] ***n***. 葛底斯堡〔美国城市〕。~ **Address** (1863 年美国总统林肯所作的)葛底斯堡演说〔其中有"民治,民有,民享"(by the people, of the people, for the people)这一名句〕。

Ge·um [ˈdʒi(ː)əm; ˋdʒiəm] ***n***.【植】水杨梅属;〔g-〕水杨梅。

Gev. = giga-electron-volt.

gew·gaw [ˈgjuːgɔː; ˋgjugɔ] **I** ***n***. 华而不实的东西,小玩意儿。**II** ***a***. 外表好看的,华而不实的。

gey [gei; ge] **I** ***a***.〔Scot.〕相当的;颇多的。**II** ***ad***.〔Scot.〕十分,非常。

gey·ser[1] [ˈgaizə; ˋgaɪzɚ] ***n***. 1. 间歇(喷)泉。2.〔英〕[ˈgiːzə; ˋgizə] 水的(蒸气)加热器,(浴室里的)热水锅炉。

gey·ser[2] [ˈgiːzə; ˋgizɚ] ***n***. = geezer.

gey·ser·ite [ˈgaizərait; ˋgaɪzəˏraɪt] ***n***.【矿】矽[硅]华〔某种间歇(喷)泉周围的沉积物〕。

GFE = government furished equipment 政府提供的设备,官方设备。

G-film [ˈdʒiːfilm; ˋdʒifɪlm] ***n***. G 级电影,男女老少均可观看的电影。

G-force [ˈdʒiːfɔːs; ˋdʒiˏfɔrs] ***n***. 1. 地心引力。2. 火箭或飞机改变速度时人体的反应力。

GFR = German Federal Republic.

G.F.T.U. = General Federation of Trade Unions〔英〕工会总联合会。

G.G. = Grenadier Guards 英国近卫军步兵联队。

g.gr. = great gross【商】十二罗(= 1,728 个)。

GHA = Greenwich hour angle【海】格林威治时角。

Gha·na [ˈgɑːnə; ˋgɑnə] ***n***. 加纳(迦纳)〔非洲〕。

Gha·na·ian [gɑːˈneiən; gɑˋneən] **I** ***a***. 加纳的,加纳人的。**II** ***n***. 加纳人。

ghar·ry [ˈgæri; ˋgærɪ] ***n***. (印度等地的)马车。

ghast·ful [ˈgɑːstful, ˈgæ-; ˋgɑstfəl, ˋgæ-] ***a***.〔古〕可怕的。**-ly** ***ad***.

ghast·ly [ˈgɑːstli, ˈgæ-; ˋgɑstlɪ, ˋgæ-] **I** ***a***. 1. 鬼一样的,苍白的。2. 恐怖的,可怕的。3.〔口〕糟透的,坏透的。4. 极大的。*The dinner was ~*. 晚饭坏透了。*a ~ failure* 大失败。**II** ***ad***. 鬼一样地,可怕地。**-li·ness** ***n***.

gha(u)t [gɔːt; gɔt] ***n***.〔印度英语〕1. 山路;〔*pl*.〕山脉(尤指印度南部沿海的山脉)。2. (上下码头、浴场等的)石阶。***a burning ~*** 河旁边的火葬场。

gha·zi [ˈgɑːziː; ˋgɑzi] ***n***. 1. (击败异教徒的)伊斯兰教勇士。2. (土耳其的)最高领袖〔给凯旋的苏丹或将军上的尊号〕。

ghee [giː; gi] ***n***. (做菜用的)印度酥油〔用水牛的乳制成〕。

gher·kin [ˈgəːkin; ˋgɝkɪn] ***n***. 1. (一种做泡菜用的)小黄瓜。2. 嫩黄瓜。

ghet·to [ˈgetəu; ˋgɛto] **I** ***n***. (*pl*. ~*s*, *-ti* [ˈgetiː; ˋgɛti]) 1. (城市中)犹太居民区。2. (城市中因社会、经济压力而形成的)少数民族聚居区。3.〔美〕城市中的黑人,波多黎各人等的集中居住区。**II** ***vt***. = ghettoize. ~ **act** 种族隔离法。

ghet·to·ize [ˈgetəuaiz; ˋgɛtoaɪz] ***vt***. 1. 用压力使集中居住。2. 使成为少数民族聚居区。**-i·za·tion** [ˌgetəuaiˈzeiʃən; ˏgɛtoaɪˋzeʃən] ***n***. 强迫集中居住。

ghet·to·lo·gist [geˈtɔlədʒist; gɛˋtɑlədʒɪst] ***n***. 研究城市少数民族居住区情况的专家。

ghil·lie [ˈgiliː; ˋgɪli] ***n***. 1. 活结无舌鞋。2. = gillie.

ghost [gəust; gost] **I** ***n***. 1. 鬼,幽灵。2. 灵魂。3. 阴影;幻象。4. (光学和电视上的)双重图像,散乱的光辉,反常回波。5.【冶】鬼线。6.〔口〕(美术、文艺的)代笔人。7. 微量,一点儿。8.〔美〕"影子"〔指被算作出席或出勤而实际旷课或旷工者〕。*look like a ~* 看起来像鬼一样。*a ~ of a smile* 一丝丝微笑。***give*** [***yield***] ***up the ~*** 死。***have not the ~ of a chance*** = ***have not a ~ of a show***〔美〕毫无希望。***lay a ~*** 把鬼撵跑,镇鬼。***play ~ to sb***. 替某人代笔。***raise a ~*** 使鬼魂出现,召鬼。***the Holy G-***【宗】圣灵。***when the ~ walks*** 出鬼;〔俚〕(剧院)发薪水的时候。**II** ***vi***.〔美口〕替人代笔;(鬼一样)作祟。— ***vt***. 1. 为某人代作(文章、作品等)。2. 像鬼一样出没于(某地)。3. (旷课学生)被算作出席;(旷工者)被算作出勤。~ **candle** (点在死者周围的)避邪烛。~ **cell**【动】血影细胞。~ **dance**〔美〕(十九世纪北美印第安人的)鬼神舞。~**like** ***a***. 像鬼一样的。~ **station** 鬼站〔已停用或无职工驻守的火车站〕。~ **town**〔美〕被遗弃城市

的遗迹。～ **word** 幽灵词〔因误读、误写而造出来的词,别字〕。

ghost·ly [ˈgəustli; ˋgostlɪ] *a*. **1**. 鬼的;幽灵的,鬼一样的;朦胧的,可怕的。**2**. 〔古〕灵魂的,精神上的,宗教上的。**3**. 代人捉刀的。*our* ～ *enemy* 恶魔。*the* ～ *hour* 半夜。～ **adviser** [**director**, **father**] 听忏悔的神父。～ **comfort** (牧师对忏悔者或将死者的)精神安慰。**-li·ness** *n*.

ghost·write [ˈgəustˌrait; ˋgostˏraɪt] *vi*. (*-wrote* [-rəut; -rot]; *-writ·ten* [-ˌritn; -rɪtn]; *-writ·ing*) 受雇代为作文[作画] (*for*). — *vt*. 为人代写(作品等)。

ghost·writ·er [ˈgəustˌraitə; ˋgostˏraɪtɚ] *n*. 捉刀人,受雇作文[作画]的人。

ghost·y [ˈgəusti; ˋgostɪ] *a*. 鬼的,幽灵的;鬼似的,幽灵似的。

ghoul [guːl, gaul; gul, gaul] *n*. **1**. (东方神话中的)食尸鬼。**2**. 盗尸人。**3**. 以恐吓人为乐的歹徒。

ghoul·ish [ˈguːliʃ; ˋgulɪʃ] *a*. 食尸鬼似的;残忍的。**-ly** *ad*.

GHQ, **G.H.Q.** = general headquarters 统帅部,总司令部。

ghyll [gil; gɪl] *n*. 〔英方〕= gill².

GI¹, **G.I.** [ˈdʒiːˈai; ˋdʒiˋaɪ] **I** *n*. (*pl*. *GI's*, *G.I.'s*) 〔美口〕**1**. (陆军)兵士。**2**. (发给士兵的)军用品 (= government issue). **II** *a*. **1**. 兵士的。**2**. 军用的。**3**. 符合军事法规的;要求严守军纪的。*an ex-GI* 退役军人。*GI shoes* 军鞋。**III** *vt*. (*GI'd*; *GI'ing*) 为准备接受军事检查而对(营房等)大扫除。**IV** *ad*. 严格按照军事法规地。～ **Jane** [**Jill**, **Joan**] 美国女兵。～ **Joe** 〔俚〕美国兵;丘八(尤指第二次世界大战时的美国兵)。

GI² = **1**. galvanized iron. **2**. gastrointestinal. **3**. general issue. **4**. government issue.

gi. = gill(s) 及耳(液量单位, $\frac{1}{4}$ pint)。

gi·ant [ˈdʒaiənt; ˋdʒaɪənt] **I** *n*. **1**. 巨人;大汉。**2**. 巨兽;巨树,巨物。**3**. 卓越人物。***the G-'s Causeway*** 巨人堤道〔北爱尔兰安特里姆郡的岬,有上千的玄武岩小圆柱〕。**II** *a*. 巨大的,伟大的。*a* ～ *crab* 大蟹。～ **gum** 杏仁桉。～ **killer** 〔美〕重量拳击家,凶猛的拳击家。～ **panda** 大熊猫。～ **redwood** 【植】世界爷。～ **star** 【天】巨星。～('s) **stride** (公园里的)旋转秋千。～ **swing** 伏虎〔体育用具〕。～**like** *a*. 巨人般的。

gi·ant·ess [ˈdʒaiəntis; ˋdʒaɪəntɪs] *n*. 女巨人。

gi·ant·ism [ˈdʒaiəntizəm; ˋdʒaɪəntɪzm] *n*. **1**. 巨大,庞大。**2**. 【医】巨大畸形;巨大发育,巨大症。

gia·our [ˈdʒauə; ˋdʒaur] *n*. 邪教徒〔穆斯林对非伊斯兰教徒、基督教徒的蔑称〕。

Giauque [dʒiˈəuk; dʒiˋok] *n*. 吉奥克〔姓氏〕。

gib¹ [gib; gɪb] **I** *n*. 【机】凹字楔,扁栓,夹条。**II** *vt*. (*-bb-*) 用扁栓[夹条]固定。

gib² [gib; gɪb] *n*. **1**. 咪咪〔指所呼唤的猫〕。**2**. (阉过的)公猫。

Gib. = Gibraltar.

gib·ber [ˈdʒibə; ˋdʒɪbɚ] **I** *vi*. 急促不清楚地说话,(猴子)叽叽喳喳地叫。**II** *n*. = gibberish.

Gib·ber·el·la [ˌdʒibəˈrelə; ˏdʒɪbəˋrɛlə] *n*. 赤霉菌属。

gib·ber·el·lic [ˌdʒibəˈrelik; ˏdʒɪbəˋrɛlɪk] **acid** 【化】赤霉酸。

gib·ber·el·lin [ˌdʒibəˈrelin; ˏdʒɪbəˋrɛlɪn] *n*. 【药】赤霉素,吉贝素。

gib·ber·ish [ˈdʒibəriʃ, ˈgib-; ˋdʒɪbərɪʃ, ˋgɪb-] *n*. 急促而不清楚的话;无意义的声音。

gib·bet [ˈdʒibit; ˋdʒɪbɪt] **I** *n*. **1**. 绞架。**2**. 绞刑。**3**. (起重机的)臂。**II** *vt*. **1**. 绞死,吊死。**2**. 把(某人)吊在示众架上;当众侮辱,使出丑。*die on the* ～被绞死。

gib·ble-gab·ble [ˈgiblˌgæbl; ˋgɪblˏgæbl̩] *n*. = gabble.

gib·bon [ˈgibən; ˋgɪbən] *n*. 长臂猿。

Gib·bon(s) [ˈgibən(z); ˋgɪbən(z)] *n*. 吉本(斯)〔姓氏〕。

gib·bose [ˈgibəus; ˋgɪbos] *a*. = gibbous.

gib·bos·i·ty [giˈbɔsiti; gɪˋbɑsətɪ] *n*. **1**. 凸状;隆起。**2**. 驼背。**3**. 【天】凸圆。

gib·bous [ˈgibəs; ˋgɪbəs] *a*. **1**. 凸面的;隆起的。**2**. 驼背的。**3**. 【天】凸圆的。**4**. (月球、行星)光亮部分大于半圆的。*the* ～ *moon* 凸月。**-ly** *ad*.

Gibbs [gibz; gɪbz] *n*. 吉布斯〔姓氏〕。

gibbs·ite [ˈgibzait; ˋgɪbˏzaɪt] *n*. 【矿】水铝矿,三水铝矿,三水铝石。

gibe [dʒaib; dʒaɪb] **I** *vt*., *vi*. 嘲笑 (*at*). **II** *n*. 嘲笑。**gib·ing·ly** *ad*.

Gib·e·on·ite [ˈgibiənait; ˋgɪbɪənˏaɪt] *n*. 【圣】基遍人,贱民,苦力。

gib·er [ˈdʒaibə; ˋdʒaɪbɚ] *n*. 嘲笑者。

gib·let [ˈdʒiblit; ˋdʒɪblɪt] *n*. (禽类的心、肫等)杂件。

Gi·bral·tar [dʒiˈbrɔːltə; dʒɪˋbrɔltɚ] *n*. **1**. 直布罗陀。**2**. 要塞地。***the Straits of*** ～ 直布罗陀海峡。**-i·an** *n*. 直布罗陀的居民。

Gib·son¹ [ˈgibsn; ˋgɪbsn̩] *n*. 吉布森〔姓氏〕。

Gib·son² [ˈgibsən; ˋgɪbsən] *n*. 〔亦 g-〕吉布森鸡尾酒〔一种马提尼鸡尾酒,由艾酒、杜松子酒等混合而成〕。～ **girl** 吉布森式女孩〔指美国插图画家吉布森 (C. D. Gibson, 1867—1944) 绘画中的十九世纪九十年代的美国女孩的形象〕。

gi·bus [ˈdʒaibəs; ˋdʒaɪbəs] *n*. (歌剧中用的)折叠礼帽。

gid [gid; gɪd] *n*. (羊的)回旋病。

gid·dap [giˈdæp; gɪˋdæp] *int*. = giddyap.

gid·dy [ˈgidi; ˋgɪdɪ] **I** *a*. **1**. 发晕的;眼花缭乱的。**2**. 令人发晕的。**3**. 急速旋转的。**4**. 轻率的,轻浮的。*a* ～ *girl* 轻浮的姑娘。*feel* ～发晕。*a* ～ *head* 轻率的人,浮躁的人。*a* ～ *goat* 〔俚〕呆子。*a* ～ *round of pleasures* 接踵而至使人应接不暇的快乐。**II** *vi*., *vt*. (*-died*; *-dy·ing*) (使)眩晕;(使)急速旋转。～**-brained** *a*. 轻率的,浮躁的。～**-go-round** 〔英口〕旋转木马 (= merry-go-round). **gid·di·ly** *ad*. **gid·di·ness** *n*.

gid·dy·ap [ˌgidiˈæp; ˏgɪdɪˋæp] *int*. 走吧! 快! 快! 驾! 〔对马的吆喝〕(= giddyup, giddap)。

Gid·e·on [ˈgidiən; ˋgɪdɪən] *n*. 吉迪恩〔男子名〕。

gie [giː, gi; gi, gɪ] *n*. 〔Scot.〕= give.

Giel·gud [ˈgi(ː)lgud; ˋgilgud] *n*. 吉尔古德〔姓氏〕。

Gif·ford [ˈgifəd; ˋgɪfɚd] *n*. 吉福德〔男子名〕。

gift [gift; gɪft] **I** *n*. **1**. 赠送;赠与权;赠品,礼物。**2**. 天赋,才能,天资。*birthday* ～*s* 寿礼,生日礼物。*of many* ～*s* 多才多艺。*Christmas* ～圣诞节礼品。*Gifts from enemies are dangerous*. 〔谚〕敌人的礼物是收不得的。***a Greek*** ～ 图谋害人的礼物。***at a*** ～ 白送(*I wouldn't have* [*take*] *it at a* ～. 白送我也不要)。***by*** [***of***] ***free*** ～ 白送,免费赠送。***Christmas G-!*** 〔美南部〕恭贺圣诞! ***Cordelia's*** ～ 妇女温柔的声音。***have the*** ～ ***of*** (***the***) ***gab*** 能说会道。***the*** ～ ***of tongues*** 学语言的天才。***in sb.'s*** ～ = ***in the*** ～ ***of sb***. 有赠与权。**II** *vt*. **1**. 赠送,授予。**2**. 天赋(权利、才能等)。*be* ～*ed with talents* 有才能。～**-book** *n*. 礼节书。～ **coupon** (**certificate**) (百货公司等发的)礼券,赠券。～**-enterprise** 附送赠品的买卖。～ **horse** 馈赠的马,〔转义〕价值有问题的礼物 (*Don't look a* ～ *horse in the mouth*. 〔谚〕送来的礼别挑剔)。～ **shop** 手工艺品店,礼品店。～**-wrap** *vt*. (以装潢花纸、丝绸等)包装(作礼品用的)商品。

gift·ed [ˈgiftid; ˋgɪftɪd] *a*. 有天才的,天禀的。

gift·ie [ˈgifti; ˋgɪftɪ] *n*. 〔Scot.〕才能,能力。

gig¹ [gig; gɪg] **I** *n*. **1**. 旋转物。**2**. 轻便二轮马车。**3**. 小快艇,比赛快艇。**4**. 【矿】轮子坡,小水仓。**5**. 两层罐笼,吊桶。**6**. 怪人。**II** *vi*. (*-gg-*) 〔常作～ it〕坐小快艇;乘轻便二轮马车。～ **lamps** 〔俚〕眼镜。

gig² [gig; gɪg] *n*. 【纺】刺果起绒机。(= ～ mill)。

gig³ [gig; gɪg] **I** *n*. 鱼叉;(钓鱼用)排钩。**II** *vt*. (*-gg-*) **1**. 用鱼叉叉(鱼)。**2**. 〔美〕戳;刺激,激励。— *vi*. 用鱼叉叉

G

鱼。

gig[4][gig; gɪg] **I** ***n*.** (军队、学校等的)记过。**II** ***vt*.** 给…以记过处分。

gig[5][gig; gɪg] ***n*.** 〔美俚〕**1.** 爵士音乐演奏会。**2.** 演奏爵士音乐的职业。**3.** 活儿。

giga- *comb.f.* 表示"京","千兆","十亿"(10^9): *giga*cycle.

gi·ga·cy·cle [ˈdʒigəˌsaikl; ˋdʒɪgəˏsaɪkl] ***n*.** 千兆周。

giga-electron-volt [ˈdʒigə-iˈlektrɔn-vəult; ˋdʒɪgə-ɪˋlɛktrɑn-volt] ***n*.** 十亿[千兆]电子伏。

gi·ga·hertz [ˈdʒigəˌhəːts; ˋdʒaɪgəˏhɝts] ***n*.** 千兆赫(兹)〔频率单位〕(= gigacycle)。

gi·gan·te·an [ˌdʒaigænˈtiən, dʒaiˈgæntiən; ˏdʒaɪgænˋtiən, dʒaɪˋgæntɪən] ***a*.** 巨人似的;巨大的。

gi·gan·tesque [ˌdʒaigænˈtesk; ˏdʒaɪgænˋtɛsk] ***a*.** 巨人似的,适于巨人的;庞大的。

gi·gan·tic [dʒaiˈgæntik; dʒaɪˋgæntɪk] ***a*.** 巨大的;庞大的,巨人似的。**-al·ly** ***ad*.** **-ness** ***n*.**

gi·gan·tism [ˈdʒaigæntizm; dʒaɪˋgæntɪzm] ***n*.** **1.** 巨大,庞大。**2.** 【医】巨人症,巨大发育,巨大畸形 (= giantism)。

gi·gan·tom·a·chy [ˌdʒaigænˈtɔmæki; ˏdʒaɪgænˋtɑməkɪ] ***n*.** **1.** 〔G-〕【希神】巨人对天神的搏斗。**2.** 巨人与巨人的战争;巨人集团之间的战争;大国间的战争。

gi·ga·ton [ˈdʒigəˌtʌn; ˋdʒɪgəˏtʌn] ***n*.** 十亿吨级〔热核武器爆炸力的计算单位,指相当于十亿吨级梯恩梯炸药的当量〕。

gig·git [ˈgigit; ˋgɪgɪt] ***vt*.** 〔美〕赶快运 (*away*)。— ***vi*.** 赶快去。

gig·gle [ˈgigl; ˋgɪgl] ***n*.**, ***vi*.** 吃吃地笑,痴笑。~ **gas** 〔美俚〕笑气。~ **smoke** 〔美俚〕大麻。~ **soup** [**water**] 〔美俚〕酒。**gig·gly** ***a*.**

gig·let [ˈgiglet; ˋgɪglɪt], **-lot** [-lət; -lət] ***n*.** 痴笑的女孩。

gig·man [ˈgigmən; ˋgɪgmən] ***n*.** (*pl*. ***-men***) 马车主;市侩。

gig·man·i·ty [gigˈmæniti; gɪgˋmænətɪ] ***n*.** 市侩阶层,庸夫俗子。

GIGO = garbage in, garbage out 【计】无用输入,无用输出。

gig·o·lo [ˈdʒigələu; ˋdʒɪgəˏlo] ***n*.** **1.** 舞男。**2.** 靠女人倒贴而生活的男子。

gig·ot [ˈdʒigət; ˋdʒɪgət] ***n*.** (熟的)羊腿,鹿腿。*a* ~ *sleeve* 羊脚形袖子。

gigue [ʒiːg; ʒig] ***n*.** 〔F.〕【乐】吉格舞曲〔尤指古典音乐组曲中的一个乐章〕。

Gi·la [ˈhiːlə; ˋhilə] ***n*.** 【动】(美国西南部产的)大毒蜥 (= ~ monster)。

Gil·bert [ˈgilbət; ˋgɪlbɚt] ***n*.** 吉尔伯特〔姓氏,男子名〕。

gil·bert [ˈgilbət; ˋgɪlbɚt] ***n*.** 【电】吉伯〔磁通势单位,等于 0.796 安匝〕。

Gilbert and Ellice Islands [ˈgilbət ənd ˈelis ˈailəndz; ˋgɪlbɚt ənd ˋɛlɪs ˋaɪləndz] 吉尔伯特和埃利斯群岛〔西太平洋〕。

Gil·ber·ta [gilˈbəːtə; gɪlˋbɝtə] ***n*.** 吉尔伯塔〔女子名〕。

Gil·ber·ti·an [gilˈbəːtjən; gɪlˋbɝtɪən] ***a*.** 英国喜歌剧作家吉尔伯特 (Gilbert) 派的;滑稽的,诙谐的。

gild[1][gild; gɪld] ***vt*.** (~***ed***, ***gilt*** [gilt; gɪlt]; ~***ed***, ***gilt***) **1.** 给…镀金,给…贴上金箔。**2.** 使光彩夺目。**3.** 修饰,虚饰。**4.** 使有钱,使阔气。*the sky ~ed by the morning sun* 被朝阳染成金色的天空。~ ***the lily*** 作不恰当的修饰,画蛇添足。~ ***the pill*** 把不愉快的事情弄得使人容易接受;美化劣质;粉饰太平。~ ***the refined gold*** 锦上添花,多此一举。

gild[2][gild; gɪld] ***n*.** = guild.

Gil·da [ˈgildə; ˋgɪldə] ***n*.** 吉尔达〔女子名〕。

gild·ed [ˈgildid; ˋgɪldɪd] ***a*.** **1.** 镀金的,涂金色的。**2.** 修饰的,虚饰的。**3.** 有钱的,阔气的。*a* ~ *frame* 金色镜框。*a group of* ~ *youths* 一群纨绔子弟。~ *vices* 阔佬们的消遣。~ *vanities* 夸耀富贵的虚荣。**G- Chamber** 英国上议院。~ **spurs** 金马刺〔爵士徽章〕。

gild·ing [ˈgildiŋ; ˋgɪldɪŋ] ***n*.** **1.** 镀金,上金粉。**2.** 镀金材料,金箔,金粉。**3.** 虚饰,粉饰。*chemical* [*electric*] ~ 电镀金。~ ***metal*** 手饰铜。

Giles [dʒailz; dʒaɪlz] ***n*.** 贾尔斯〔姓氏,男子名〕。

Gi·lhe·ney [giˈliːni; gɪˋlinɪ] ***n*.** 吉利尼〔姓氏〕。

Gill[1][dʒil; dʒɪl] ***n*.** 〔有时 g-〕少女;女情人。*Every Jack has his* ~. 破锅不愁无烂盖,男人自有女人爱。*Jack and* ~ 青年男女。

Gill[2][gil, dʒil; gɪl, dʒɪl] ***n*.** 吉尔〔女子名〕。

gill[1][gil; gɪl] **I** ***n*.** **1.** 〔常 *pl*.〕鱼鳃,(水生动物的)呼吸器。**2.** 【植】层,褶片;菌褶。**3.** (鸡,火鸡等的)垂肉,颐下肉。**4.** 〔常 *pl*.〕(人的)腮;〔美俚〕嘴巴。***look blue*** [***green, white, yellow***] ***about the ~s*** 血色不好[面有菜色,面如土色,垂头丧气]。***look rosy about the ~s*** 血色好。***turn red in the ~s*** 发怒。***look white about the ~s*** (因惊吓或患病而)脸色苍白。**II** ***vt*.** **1.** 除去(鱼的)鳃和肚杂;除去(菌褶)。**2.** 用刺网捕(鱼)。— ***vi*.** (鱼)被刺网捕住。~ **cleft** [**slit**] 鳃裂 (= visceral cleft)。~ **fungus** 伞菌。~ **net** 【海】刺网。

gill[2][gil; gɪl] ***n*.** **1.** (树木茂盛的)峡谷。**2.** (峡谷中的)溪流。

gill[3][dʒil; dʒɪl] ***n*.** 及耳〔液量单位 = $\frac{1}{4}$ pint〕。

Gil·lette [ˈgilit, giˈlet; ˋgɪlɪt, gəˋlɛt] ***n*.** 吉勒特〔姓氏〕。

Gil·lian [ˈdʒiliən; ˋdʒɪlɪən] ***n*.** 吉琳〔女子名 = Juliana〕。

gil·lie, gil·ly [ˈgiliː; ˋgɪlɪ] ***n*.** (*pl*. ***gil·lies***) **1.** (苏格兰高地的)游猎侍从;游猎向导。**2.** (旧时苏格兰高地的)氏族首长侍从;男仆。

Gil·ling·ham [ˈgiliŋəm; ˋgɪlɪŋəm] ***n*.** 吉林厄姆〔姓氏〕。

gil·ly·flow·er [ˈdʒiliflauə; ˋdʒɪlɪˏflauɚ] ***n*.** 【植】**1.** 紫罗兰花。**2.** 桂竹香。**3.** 麝香石竹。**4.** 一种锥状苹果。

Gil·man [ˈgilmən; ˋgɪlmən] ***n*.** 吉尔曼〔姓氏〕。

Gil·mer [ˈgilmə; ˋgɪlmɚ] ***n*.** 吉尔默〔姓氏〕。

Gil·pin [ˈgilpin; ˋgɪlpɪn] ***n*.** 吉尔平〔姓氏〕。

gilt[1][gilt; gɪlt] gild 的过去式及过去分词。**I** ***a*.** 镀金的,涂金的;金色的。**II** ***n*.** **1.** 镀金材料,镀金涂层。**2.** 炫目的外表。**3.** 〔口〕金钱。***take the ~ off the gingerbread*** 剥去金箔,剥去美丽的外衣,把真相暴露出来。***The ~ is off*.** 假象消失。~**-edged** ***a*.** **1.** 金边的。**2.** (证券等)上等的。**3.** (演员等)阵容极强的,最好的 (*~-edged securities* 【商】信用可靠的证券,金边证券。*a ~-edged theatrical cast* 极佳的演员阵容)。~**head** 【动】鸟颊鱼。~ **warrant**〔英〕金边认股证〔持证者可优先或以优待价格购买金边证券〕。

gilt[2][gilt; gɪlt] ***n*.** 小母猪。

gim·bal [ˈdʒimbəl; ˋdʒɪmbəl] ***n*.** 〔常 *pl*.〕**1.** (使罗盘等平衡的)平衡环 (= ~ring);常平架。**2.** 【机】万向接头。~ **error** 框架误差。

gim·baled [ˈdʒimbəld; ˋdʒɪmbəld] ***a*.** 装有万向接头[常平架]的。~ **engine** 换向发动机。

gim·crack [ˈdʒimkræk; ˋdʒɪmˏkræk] **I** ***a*.** 华而不实的。**II** ***n*.** 小玩意儿,华而不实的东西。**-crack·ery** [-krækəri; -ˏkrækərɪ] ***n*.** 〔集合词〕华而不实的东西。

gim·el [ˈgiml; ˋgɪml̩] ***n*.** 希伯来语的第三个字母。

gim·let [ˈgimlit; ˋgɪmlɪt] **I** ***n*.** 手钻,手锥,螺丝锥。**II** ***vt*.** 用螺丝锥(把孔眼)钻透。**III** ***a*.** **1.** 有钻孔能力的,锐利的。**2.** 有钻劲的。*eyes like ~s* 敏锐的目光。~**-eyed** ***a*.** 目光锐利的。

gim·mal [ˈgiml, ˈdʒim-; ˋgɪml̩, ˋdʒɪm-] ***n*.** 双连环;连环套。

gim·me [ˈgimi; ˋgɪmɪ]〔俚〕= give me.

gim·mer [ˈgimə; ˋgɪmɚ] ***n*.** **1.** 〔英方〕小母羊。**2.** 〔贬〕女人。

gim·mick [ˈgimik; ˋgɪmɪk] **I** ***n*.** **1.** 〔口〕(轮盘赌具、魔术师道具等的)暗机关。**2.** 骗人玩意儿;鬼花招;〔俚〕产品

广告噱头;竞选宣传伎俩。3. 巧妙的小机械;小发明;诀窍。II *vt*. 〔口〕在…(轮盘赌、魔术道具等)上暗设机关。**-y** *a*. (赌具等)暗设机关的,(道具等)使用巧妙手法的。

gim·mick·ry [ˈgimikri; ˋgɪmɪkrɪ] *n*. 〔口〕1. 花招;伎俩。2. 耍花招;玩弄伎俩 (= gimmickery)。

gimp[1] [gimp; gɪmp] I *n*. 1. (用以装饰衣服、窗帘等的)嵌心丝带。2. 经过加固的钓鱼丝。II *vt*. 用嵌心丝带装饰(衣服等)。

gimp[2] [gimp; gɪmp] *n*. 〔美口〕精神,活力。

gimp[3] [gimp; gɪmp] I *n*. 瘸子;跛行。II *vi*. 瘸着走,跛行。**-y** *a*. 跛的,瘸的。

gin[1] [dʒin; dʒɪn] I *n*. 1. 弹棉机,轧花机。2. 打桩机,三脚起重机。3. 陷阱;网,渔网。II *vt*. 1. 轧(棉)。2. 用陷阱(网)捕捉。*cotton ginning factory* 轧棉厂。**ginned cotton** 皮棉(*cf*. unginned cotton 籽棉)。

gin[2] [dʒin; dʒɪn] *n*. 1. 杜松子酒,荷兰酒。2. 〔美俚〕烈酒。~ ***and it*** 杜松子酒和苦艾酒混合的饮料。~**-fizz** 杜松子酒汽水。~ **mill** 〔美俚〕低级酒店。~**-palace** 豪华的酒店。~ **rummy** 金罗美〔一种牌戏〕。

gin[3] [gin; gɪn] *vi*., *vt*. (***gan*** [gæn; gæn]; ***gun*** [gʌn; gʌn]) 〔古、诗〕开始。

gin·gel·li, gin·gel·ly [ˈdʒindʒili; ˋdʒɪndʒəlɪ] *n*. = gingili.

gin·ger [ˈdʒindʒə; ˋdʒɪndʒɚ] I *n*. 1. 生姜,姜。2. 姜黄色;〔英俚〕(头发的)赤色,赤毛(人)。3. 〔口〕精神,气魄。*put some ~ into* 鼓起干劲来,加把劲。*There is no ~ in him*. 他没有勇气[气魄、精神]。II *vt*. 1. 使有姜味。2. 使有活力,鼓舞。~ **ade** = ~ beer. ~ **ale** 姜麦酒。~ **beer** 姜啤酒。~ **brandy** 姜汁白兰地。~**-bread** 1. *n*. 姜饼;华而不实的东西,俗气的装饰。2. *a*. 华而不实的,俗气的。~**bread nut** 姜汁饼干。~ **bread plum** [**tree**] 埃及棕榈。~**bread work** 华而不实的装饰。~ **bread trap** 〔口〕嘴。~ **cordial** 姜汁柠檬葡萄水。~ **group** 〔英〕(议员中的)鞭挞政府派。~ **nut** = gingerbread nut. ~ **pop** = ~ ale. ~ **race** [**root**] 姜根。~ **snap** = ~nut. ~ **wine** 姜水甜酒。

gin·ger·ly [ˈdʒindʒəli; ˋdʒɪndʒəlɪ] *a*., *ad*. 小心翼翼的[地];兢兢业业的[地]。**-i·ness** *n*.

gin·ger·y [ˈdʒindʒəri; ˋdʒɪndʒərɪ] *a*. 1. 姜(似)的;辛辣的。2. 姜色的;〔英〕(头发)红的。3. 有精神的。

ging·ham [ˈgiŋəm; ˋgɪŋəm] I *n*. 1. 条格平布,方格花布。2. 〔口〕伞。II *a*. 方格花布做的。

gin·gi·li [ˈdʒindʒili; ˋdʒɪndʒəlɪ] *n*. 1. 芝麻 (= sesame)。2. 芝麻油。

gin·gi·val [dʒinˈdʒaivəl; dʒɪnˋdʒaɪvəl] *a*. 齿龈的,齿槽的,龈的。

gin·gi·vi·tis [ˌdʒindʒiˈvaitis; ˏdʒɪndʒəˋvaɪtəs] *n*. 【医】龈炎。

ging·ko [ˈgiŋkəu; ˋgɪŋko] *n*. (*pl*. ***~es***) 1. 【植】银杏,白果树。2. 〔G-〕银杏属。

gin·gly·mus [ˈdʒiŋglimәs; ˋdʒɪŋglɪməs] *n*. (*pl*. ***-mi*** [-mai; -maɪ]) 【解】铰状关节,屈戌关节。

gink [giŋk; gɪŋk] *n*. 〔美俚〕怪人,家伙。

gink·go [ˈgiŋkgəu; ˋgɪŋkgo] (*pl*. ***~es***) *n*. 〔美〕= gingko.

gin·ner [ˈdʒinə; ˋdʒɪnɚ] *n*. 机器轧棉工人。**-y** *n*. 轧花厂。

gin·seng [ˈdʒinseŋ; ˋdʒɪnsɛŋ] *n*. 人参。

gio [gjəu; gjo] *n*. = geo.

Gio·con·da, La [dʒəuˈkɔndə, It. dʒəuˈkoundɑː; dʒoˋkɑndə, It. dʒoˋkondɑ] 蒙娜·丽莎〔意大利画家达芬奇的名画,通常叫做 Mona Lisa〕。

gio·co·so [dʒəuˈkəusəu; dʒəˋkoso] *a*., *ad*. 【乐】谐谑的(地),愉快的(地),戏嬉的(地)。

gip [dʒip; dʒɪp] I *vt*., *vi*. 〔美俚〕骗,诓骗。II *n*. 骗子。

gi·pon [dʒiˈpɔn, ˈdʒipɔn; dʒɪˋpɑn, ˋdʒɪpɑn] *n*. = jupon.

gip·po [ˈdʒipəu; ˋdʒɪpo] *n*. 〔英俚〕肉汤;炖肉。

Gip·py [ˈdʒipi; ˋdʒɪpɪ] *n*. 〔英俚〕埃及兵;埃及香烟;吉普赛人。~ **tummy** (在热带国家旅游者患的)腹泻病。

gip·sy, gyp·sy [ˈdʒipsi; ˋdʒɪpsɪ] I *n*. 1. 〔常 G-〕吉普赛人;〔G-〕吉普赛语。2. 像吉普赛人的人,黑脸妇女,顽皮[动人]的姑娘。3. 【海】绞绳筒,手推绞盘。II *a*. 吉普赛式的;流浪的。III *vi*. 过吉普赛式的生活;过流浪生活,野餐旅行。~ **bonnet** (妇女、小儿用的)宽边帽。~ **cab** 〔美俚〕流动兜客的出租汽车。~ **caravan** 吉普赛式轿车。~ **leave** 〔美俚〕不告而别。~ **moth** 【动】舞毒蛾。~ **rose** 【植】山葡萄。~ **table** 三脚小圆桌。~ **wheel** 锚链轮。~ **winch** 【海】手推绞盘。**-hood** *n*. 吉普赛生涯;吉普赛人身分。**-dom** *n*. 吉普赛生涯,吉普赛人。**-fy** *vt*. 使吉普赛化。**-ish** *a*. 吉普赛人似的。**-ism** *n*. 吉普赛人的生活方式。

gi·raffe [dʒiˈrɑːf; dʒəˋræf] *n*. (*pl*. ~, ~***s***) 1. 【动】长颈鹿。2. 〔G-〕【天】鹿豹座。**-ish** *a*.

gi·ran·do·la, gir·an·dole [dʒiˈrændələ, ˈdʒirəndəul; dʒəˋrændələ, ˋdʒɪrəndol] *n*. 1. 多枝烛台。2. 旋射焰火。3. 旋转喷水嘴。4. (周围镶有小宝石的)耳环。

Gi·rard [dʒiˈrɑːd; dʒəˋrɑrd] *n*. 吉拉德〔姓氏〕。

gir·a·sol(e) [ˈdʒirəˌsɔl, -ˌsəul; ˋdʒɪrəˏsɑl, -ˏsol] *n*. 1. 【矿】青蛋白石。2. 【植】菊芋。

gird[1] [gəːd; gɝd] (~***ed***, ***girt*** [gəːt; gɝt]; ~***ed***, ***girt***) *vt*. 1. 缠,束;佩(剑)。2. 装备;赋与(权力) (*with*)。3. 围绕,包围着 (*with*)。4. 〔~ oneself〕准备 (*for*)。*The climber ~ed himself with a rope*. 登山者以绳束腰。*a sea-girt island* 四面临海的岛屿。*to be girt with supreme power* 被赋与最高权力。*The soldiers girt themselves up for battle*. 士兵们准备投入战斗。~ *on a sword* [*one's armour*] 佩剑[佩带甲胄]。~ ***oneself*** = ~ (***up***) ***one's loins*** 准备行动。— *vi*. 准备。

gird[2] [gəːd; gɝd] I *vi*. 嘲笑 (*at*)。— *vt*. 嘲笑。II *n*. 嘲笑。**-ing·ly** *ad*.

gird·er [ˈgəːdə; ˋgɝdɚ] *n*. 【建】纵梁,大梁,撑柱,撑杆,大型工字梁。*a framed* ~ 构桁。~ **truss** 梁构桁架。**-less** *a*.

gir·dle[1] [ˈgəːdl; ˋgɝdl] I *n*. 1. 带,腰带。2. 环形物,围绕物。3. 【解】(支持四肢的)带。4. 【植】环形带,成带现象;环剥,环状剥皮。5. 【建】(抱)柱带。6. 〔美〕(女子的)紧身褡。7. 宝石与镶嵌底板接触处的边缘。*the pelvic* [*hip*] ~ 腰带。*the shoulder* ~ 肩带。***have*** [***hold***] ... ***under one's*** ~ 使服从,率领。***make*** [***put***] ***a*** ~ ***round*** 绕…一周;围绕。***under sb.'s*** ~ 在某人控制下。***within the*** ~ ***of*** 被…环绕着的。II *vt*. 1. 用带束,拿带缠 (*round*; *in*; *about*)。2. 围,包围。3. 环剥(树皮),剥去(树)的一圈皮。

gir·dle[2] [ˈgəːdl; ˋgɝdl] *v*. 〔Scot.〕= griddle. ~ **cake** 〔Scot.〕用浅锅烘的饼 (= griddle-cake)。

gir·dler [ˈgəːdlə; ˋgɝdlɚ] *n*. 1. 把树咬成环槽的甲虫。2. 做腰带的人。3. 束缚[围绕]的人[物]。

girl [gəːl; gɝl] *n*. (*opp*. boy) 1. 姑娘,女孩子,少女,未婚女子。2. 女儿。3. 女仆,保姆。4. 女职员,女店员;女演员。5. 〔口〕情人,女朋友。6. 〔和年龄无关只表示亲爱的称呼〕小姐,阿姊,阿姨。*a bachelor* ~ 独身女子。*a chit* [*slip*] *of a* ~ 黄毛丫头,瘦长的姑娘。*a fancy* ~ [*lady*, *woman*] 1. 情妇。2. 妓女。*a gaiety* ~ 杂耍女艺人。*the* ~*s* (全家的)女儿们。*a shop* ~ 女店员。*the principal* [*leading*] ~ 女主角。*one's best* ~ 情人。***a*** ~ ***about*** [***of***] ***the town*** 妓女。~ ***next door*** 普普通通的女孩。***my dear*** ~ 亲爱的姑娘〔对妻的爱称〕。***old*** ~ 老太婆〔对妇女或母马的爱称或蔑称〕。~ **Friday** 女事务员,能干的女助手。~ **friend** 1. 〔口〕未婚妻,女情人。2. 女性朋友。~ **guides** 〔英〕女童子军。~ **scouts** 〔美〕女童子军。

girl·cott [ˈgəːlkət; ˋgɝlkət] *n*. 〔美口〕(妇女们)联合抵制(某人、某事物等)。

girl·hood [ˈgəːlhud; ˋgɝlhʊd] ***n*.** **1.** 少女身分;姑娘时代。2.〔集合词〕姑娘们。

girl·ie [ˈgəːli; ˋgɝlɪ] **I** ***n*.** **1.**〔爱〕姑娘,女人。**2.**〔俚〕妓女。**II** ***a*.**(杂志、电影)有裸体或半裸体女子图片[镜头]的。

girl·ish [ˈgəːliʃ; ˋgɝlɪʃ] ***a*.** **1.** 少女的;少女似的。**2.** 少女时期的。**-ly** ***ad*.** **-ness** ***n*.**

gir·ly [ˈgəːli; ˋgɝlɪ] ***a*.** **1.** = girlish. **2.** = girlie(*a*.)

girn [ˈgəːn; ˋgɝn] ***n*., *vi*., *vt*.**〔英方〕咆哮。

gi·ro [ˈdʒaiərəu; ˋdʒaɪro] ***n*.** = autogiro.

Gi·ro [ˈdʒairəu; ˋdʒaɪro] ***n*.**(各国银行使用电子计算机处理的)邮政转账服务。

Gi·ronde [dʒiˈrɔnd; dʒɪˋrɑnd] ***n*.**(法国大革命时代的)吉伦特党。

Gi·ron·dist [dʒiˈrɔndist; dʒɪˋrɑndɪst] **I** ***n*.** 吉伦特党员;稳健主义者。**II** ***a*.** 吉伦特党的;稳健主义的。

girt[1] [gəːt; gɝt] gird 的过去式及过去分词。

girt[2] [gəːt; gɝt] **I** ***n*.** = girth. **II** ***vt*.** **1.** 束,缠,绕。**2.** 用肚带束,给…束肚带。**3.** 量…的围长。— ***vi*.** 围长为。

girth [gəːθ; gɝθ] **I** ***n*.** **1.**(马等的)肚带。**2.**(树干、人腰身的)围长;【建】围梁,船壳围长。**3.** 尺寸,大小。*a man of large* ~粗腰身的人。*a tree 16 feet in* ~树身粗 16 英尺的树。**II** ***vt*.** **1.** 围绕,包围。**2.** 给…上肚带,给…紧肚带。**3.** 给…量围长。— ***vi*.** 围长为。

gi·sarme [giˈzaːm; gɪˋzarm] ***n*.**(早期步兵使用的)战斧。

gis·mo [ˈgizməu; ˋgɪzmo] ***n*.**〔俚〕= gizmo.

Gis·sing [ˈgisiŋ; ˋgɪsɪŋ] ***n*.** **1.** 吉辛〔姓氏〕。**2. George Robert** ~乔治·罗伯特·吉辛〔1857—1903, 英国小说家〕。

gist [dʒist; dʒɪst] ***n*.** **1.** 要点,要旨。**2.** 诉讼依据;诉讼主因。

git [git; gɪt] ***vt*., *vi*.**〔方〕= get.

git·tern [ˈgitəːn; ˋgɪtɝn] ***n*.** 吉特恩〔类似吉他的一种古弦乐器〕。

give [giv; gɪv] **I** ***vt*.** (***gave*** [geiv; gev]; ***giv·en*** [ˈgivn; ˋgɪvn]; ***giv·ing***) **1.** 送给,给。*I gave the boy a book. I gave a book to the boy*. 我给男孩一本书。**2.** 授予,赋予,赐予(地位、头衔、名誉等)。*The law ~s citizens the right to vote*. 该法律给公民选举的权利。*be ~n the title of* 被授予…称号。*G- a rogue rope enough and he will hang himself*.〔谚〕坏人必自取灭亡。**3.** 作出;举出;显示出;载入;提出,表示出。~ *an account of* 说明。~ *examples* 举例。~ *a guess* 猜一猜。~ *a suggestion* 提出建议,建议。~ *a try* 试一试。~ *signs of an illness* 显示出病兆。*This word is not ~n in the dictionary*. 这个词没有载入词典。*The thermometer ~s 30° in the shade*. 在阴凉处温度计上是摄氏三十度。*gave him her confidence* 向他表示她的信任。**4.** 致(谢),转达(问候),贺(喜);提议为…干杯。~ *thanks* 感谢,致以感谢。*G- my love* [*compliments*, *regards*] *to your mother*. 请问候你的母亲。*I* ~ *you joy*. 恭喜恭喜。*I('ll)* ~ *you Mr. X*. 为恭贺 X 先生干杯吧。**5.** 交付;委托;让出;嫁出。~ *the porter one's bag to carry* 把包交给搬行李工人提。~ *a daughter in marriage* 把女儿嫁出去。**6.** 卖与;交换。*I will* ~ *it for 5 dollars*. 五块钱我就卖。*I will* ~ *5 dollars for it*. 我出五块钱买。**7.** 献身于,致力于。~ *one's mind to a matter* 为某件事费心。~ *one's life to study* 为学问而献身。**8.** 产生,得出;发,生;引起。*Trees* ~ *fruit*. 树结果子。*Cows* ~ *milk* 奶牛产奶。*4 divided by 2* ~*s 2*. 二除四得二。**9.** 说,宣告;发出。*Judgment was ~n against the plaintiff*. 作出原告败诉的裁决。~ *a cry* 喊叫,大叫一声。~ *orders* 发出命令。*The umpire gave him out*. 裁判员宣告他出界。*The sun ~s lights*. 太阳发出光。**10.** 作为…的源泉[来源];给(病人)服(药);把(病)传染给;为…生子女;使…生子女。~ *pleasure* 带来欢乐。*You have ~n me your cold*. 你把伤风传染给我了。*She gave him four sons*. 她给他生了四个儿子。*He gave her two daughters*. 他使她生了两个女儿。**11.** 举行,主办(音乐会、宴会);演出。**12.** 施以(惩罚);把…强加于。**13.** 完成(一次具体的动作或努力)~ *a kick* [*kiss*, *sly look*, *jump*] 踢[吻、睨视、跳]。**14.** 假定,假想〔主用过去分词〕。*Given health*, *I can finish the work*. 若是身体好,我可以完成那项工作。**15.** 被认为是,被归于。*The pamphlet has been given to his pen*. 据说这册子是他写的。**16.** 规定,限定;指定。*He gave us Sunday as our day of meeting*. 他指定星期日为我们的集会日。**17.** 使接触到…;使能够…;使可见…。~ *sb. to understand sth*. 使某人理解某事。*The window ~s the meadow*. 隔窗可见草地。**18.** 牺牲,失去。*She gave one eye in the accident*. 她在事故中失去一只眼睛。**19.** 为…把电话接到…。*G- me the service desk*, *please*. 请接服务台。**20.** 介绍。*Ladies and gentleman*, *I* ~ *you the Governor of Washington*. 女士们,先生们,我请华盛顿州州长和诸位见面。**21.** 描述。~ *the scenery of London* 描述伦敦风光。— ***vi*.** **1.** 捐助,赠送。~ *generously to charity* 慷慨捐助。**2.**(色)褪,(天气)变暖和;(冰等)融解。*The winter is giving*. 冬天(的寒冷)渐渐和缓了。*The frost did not* ~ *all day*. 霜终日不化。**3.** 投降,屈服,让步。*The Iron Army never* ~*s*. "铁军"永不退却。**4.**(地等受压力)坍下,凹下;(木器等)弯曲;(沙发等)有弹性;(螺钉等)松动。*The foundations are giving*. 地基陷下去了。*This sofa ~s comfortably*. 这张沙发的弹性好,坐起来舒服。*His knees gave*. 他瘫了。**5.** 干缩,湿坏。**6.** 面向,通达。*a wicket giving into an avenue* 通到林荫路的小门。**7.**〔美俚〕发生,进行。*He demanded to know what gave*.〔美俚〕他要求知道发生了什么。**8.** 适应,顺应。*She gave to the motion of the horse*. 她适应马的动作。~ ***a bit*** [***piece***] ***of one's mind*** 直言不讳。~ ***about*** 公布,传播(谣言)。~ ***and take*** 公平交换;互让;交换意见。~ ***as good as one gets*** 回敬,以牙还牙。~ ***away*** **1.** 让掉,赠送;分送,分发。**2.**〔俚〕无意中泄露(机密),露马脚。**3.** 出卖(朋友)。**4.**(在结婚仪式中)将(新娘)引交新郎。**5.** 放弃,牺牲(~ *away a good chance of success* 错过成功的良机)。**6.** 垮,倒。~ ***back*** **1.** 归还;返回,报复。**2.** 后退,往后站;凹陷。~ ***down***(牛等)使(奶)流出。~ ***for*** 牺牲,交换(~ *one's life for the country* 为国牺牲)。~ ***forth*** 发出(气味、声音等);发表,公布。~ ***in*** **1.** 提出(文件等),交上。**2.** 屈服,退让(*to*)。**3.** 宣布,表示。~ ***into***(过道等)通向。~ ***it to sb*.**〔口〕痛骂,狠揍。~ ***lessons*** [***instruction***] ***in***(*mathematics*)教授(数学)。***G- me*** …. **1.** 给我…。**2.** 我愿…,我比较喜欢(*G- me liberty*, *or* ~ *me death*.〔谚〕不自由,毋宁死。*G- me the good old times!* 怀念从前。*G- me Bach and Mozart*, *not these modern composers*. 我喜欢巴哈和莫扎特,不喜欢这些近代的作曲家)。~ ***off*** 放出,发散(水蒸气等)。~ ***on*** [***upon***](门,窗等)向着(~ *on* (*to*) *the garden* 通向花园)。~ ***oneself away*** 露马脚,现原形。~ ***oneself out to be*** [***as***] 自称为。~ ***oneself over to*** 沉迷于(恶习等)。~ ***oneself to*** **1.** 专心于,迷恋(~ *oneself to one's work body and soul* 一心一意埋头工作)。**2.** 沾染(恶习等)。~ ***oneself up*** **1.** 决心;断念,想开(*for*)。**2.** 埋头,专心于(*to*)(~ *oneself up to study* 专心读书)。**3.** 自首,投降。~ ***out*** **1.** 分发。**2.** 公布,发表(~ *out the news* 公布消息)。**3.** 放出,发出。~ *out a good heat* 发出很大热量。**4.** 精疲力竭。**5.** 缺乏,用尽。(*The water supply at last gave out*. 水的供给终于断绝了)。**6.** = give. ~ ***over*** **1.** 不再做,停止做(*doing*)。**2.** 放纵。**3.**〔古〕宣布(病人)无可救药。**4.** 托付,委托。**5.** 停息(*She gave herself over to laughter*. 她纵声大笑。~ *over a patient for dead* 认为病人无可救药。~ *over trying to convince sb*. 不再想去说服某人。*The rain gave over*. 雨停了)。~ ***sb. best*** 承认某

人的优点。~ *sb*. *his due* [*own*] 公平对待某人。~ *sb*. *to understand that* …使人确信…,使人了解…。~ *sb*. *what for* 〔口〕责骂某人,痛打某人。~ *the devil his due* 对坏人也要实事求是。~ **up** 1. 放弃,扔弃;停止,中止,断绝(~ *up smoking* 戒烟)。2. 对…断念,对…放弃希望(~ *sb*. *up for lost* 对某人已不抱任何希望了)。3. 引渡(罪人)。4. 投降;自首(*The enemy gave up*. 敌人投降了。*The criminal gave himself up*. 罪犯自首了)。5. 让与(~ *up one's seat to the old* 给老人让座)。~ **upon** = ~ on. ~ **way** 1. 坍塌,垮下,毁坏;退让,屈服;让路,让步(*to*)。2. 划起(船)来,用力划。3. (股票)跌价。4. 忍不住(~ *way to tears* 忍不住落泪)。*What* ~*s*? 〔美俚〕出什么事了? **II** *n*. 1. 弹性;可弯性;可让性。2. (精神、性格等的)适应性。3. 给予。*There is no* ~ *in a stone floor*. 石头铺的地面毫无弹性。

give-and-take [ˈgivənˈteik; ˋgɪvənˋtek] **I** *n*. 1. 公平交换;互让。2. 交换意见。**II** *a*. 1. 公平交换的;互让的。2. 交换意见的。

give·a·way [ˈgivəwei; ˋgɪvəˏwe] *n*. 1. 泄露机密。2. (招徕顾客的)赠品;(电台中的)有奖问答节目。

giv·en [ˈgivən; ˋgɪvən] give 的过去分词。**I** *a*. 1. 一定的,特定的。2. 给予的,赠送的。3. 〔数学推理等的独立用法,表示条件〕已知的,假设的。4. 爱好的,喜欢的,习惯的(*to*)。5. (文件等于…)签订的。*within a* ~ *period* 在一定期间内。*meet at a* ~ *time and place* 在约定的时间和地点会面。*G- x, it follows that* .... 已知 x, 则可推出…。*G- a protracted war*, ... 只要是长期战争,…。*I am not* ~ *that way*. 我不是干那种事的人。*be* ~ *romantically*. 生性浪漫。*G- under my hand and seal this 10th day of May 1980 in* .... 一九八〇年五月十日在…亲笔签订。**be** ~ **to** 喜欢,癖好(*be much* ~ *to reading and studying* 喜欢看书学习)。**II** *n*. (推理过程中的)已知事物。*It's taken as a* ~. 这被认为已知。~ **name** 教名,名字〔不包括姓氏〕。

giv·er [ˈgivə; ˋgɪvɚ] *n*. 给的人,赠送者。*an alms* ~ 施舍者。

giv·ing [ˈgiviŋ; ˋgɪvɪŋ] *n*. 给予物,礼物。

giz·mo, gis·mo [ˈgizməu; ˋgɪzmo] *n*. 小物件,新玩意儿;小发明。

giz·zard [ˈgizəd; ˋgɪzɚd] *n*. 1. (鸟等的)砂囊,胗。2. 〔口〕喉咙,胃。***fret one's*** ~ 苦恼。***stick in sb.'s*** ~ 难被某人消化,不合某人口味。

Gjino·kast·ër [ˌgjiːnəuˈkɑːstə; ˏgjinoˋkɑstɚ] *n*. 吉诺卡斯特〔阿尔巴尼亚城市〕。

GK. = Greek.

GL = gun laying (radar) set 炮瞄雷达。

Gl =【化】glucin(i)um 元素铍之符号。

gla·bel·la [gləˈbelə; gləˋbɛlə] *n*. (*pl*. **-lae** [-iː; -ɪ])【解】眉间。**-r** *a*.

gla·brate [ˈgleibreit, -brit; ˋglebret, -brɪt] *a*. 1. 无毛的,几乎无毛的,平秃的。2. (老年或到成熟期时)变光秃的。

gla·bres·cent [gleiˈbresənt; gleˋbrɛsn̩t] *a*. 有点光秃的;变光秃的。

gla·brous [ˈgleibrəs; ˋglebrəs] *a*. 无毛的,光滑的。

gla·cé [glæˈsei; glæˋse] *a*. 〔F.〕1. (布、皮革等)光滑的,磨光的。2. (水果)加糖霜的,糖渍的。3. 冰冻的。

gla·cial [ˈgleisjəl; ˋgleʃəl] *a*. 1. 冰的;冰状的。2. 冰河的,冰河时期的。3. 冰冷的,冷淡的。4. 像冰河运动般缓慢的。5.【化】结晶状的。*a* ~ *wind* 凛冽的寒风。*a* ~ *stare* 冷冰冰的瞪上一眼。~ *progress* 极缓慢的进展。~ **acetic acid** 冰醋酸。~ **deposits** 冰河堆积物。~ **epoch** [**era, period**] 冰河时期。~**-lake** 冰川湖。~ **meal** 冰河作用所形成的细石粉。**-ist** *n*. 冰河学家,冰河学者。

glac·i·ate [ˈgleisieit; ˋgleʃɪˏet] *vt*. 1. 使结冰,使冻结;使冰河化。2. 以冰[冰河]覆盖。3. 使受冰河作用 — *vi*. 被冰覆盖。**-d** *a*. 冰冻的;冰封的;【地】受冰河作用的。(~*d rock*【地】冰擦岩)。**-a·tion** *n*. 冰河作用,冰河化,冰蚀。

glac·ier [ˈgleiʃə; ˋglɛʃɚ] *n*. 冰河,冰川。~ **avalanche**【地】冰崩。~ **plain** 冰川平原。

glac·i·er·et [ˌglæsjəˈret, ˌglei-; ˏglæsjəˋrɛt, ˏgle-] *n*. 小冰河,小冰川。

glac·i·ol·o·gy [ˌgleisiˈɔlədʒi; ˏglesɪˋɑlədʒɪ] *n*. 1. 冰河学,冰川学。2. 冰河造成的地理特征。

glac·is [ˈgleisis; ˋglesɪs] *n*. (*pl*. ~**es**, ~ [ˈglæsiz; ˋglæsɪz]) 1. 缓斜坡;堡垒前的斜坡。2. 缓冲地区,缓冲国。

glad [glæd; glæd] *a*. 1. 〔用作述语〕高兴,欢喜,乐意。2. 令人高兴的,使人愉快的。3. 充满欢乐的;兴高采烈的。4. (风光)明媚的,(景色)美丽的。~ *of heart* 欣然。*I am* ~ *of it*. 那很好。(*I am very*) ~ *to see you*. 看到你很高兴。*I should be* ~ *to know* .... 〔反、谑〕我倒想知道…。*a* ~ *spring morning* 春光明媚的早晨。~ *air* [*looks*] 笑容。~ *smile* 欣然微笑。~ *tidings* 好消息。~ **eye** 〔口〕秋波;媚眼(*give the* ~ *eye* 送秋波,用眼色挑逗)。~ **hand** (带有某种动机或虚情假意的)热情欢迎[打招呼]。~**-hand** *vt*., *vi*. 欢迎,招呼。~ **hander** 〔美口〕(虚情假意的)欢迎者[打招呼的人]。~ **rags** 〔美俚〕盛装,夜礼服。**-ly** *ad*. **-ness** *n*.

glad·den [ˈglædn; ˋglædn̩] *vt*., *vi*. (使)欢喜。

glade [gleid; gled] *n*. 1. 林中空地[通道]。2. 沼泽地。

glad·i·ate [ˈglædieit, ˈgleidiit; ˋglædɪɪt] *a*.【植】剑状的。

glad·i·a·tor [ˈglædieitə; ˋglædɪˏetɚ] *n*. 1. (古罗马的)斗剑者,角斗士。2. 争论者。3. 格斗者(尤指职业拳击者)。

glad·i·a·to·ri·al [ˌglædiəˈtɔːriəl; ˏglædɪəˋtorɪəl] *a*. 1. 斗剑(者)的,格斗(者)的。2. 争论(者)的。

glad·i·o·la [ˌglædiˈəulə; ˏglædɪˋolə], **glad·i·ole** [ˈglædiəul; ˋglædɪol] *n*. = gladiolus.

glad·i·o·lus [ˌglædiˈəuləs; ˏglædɪˋoləs] *n*. (*pl*. ~**es**, **-li** [-lai; -laɪ]) 1.【植】唐菖蒲。2.【解】胸骨体。

gla·di·us [ˈgleidiəs; ˋgledɪəs] *n*. 古罗马军队的短剑。

glad·some [ˈglædsəm; ˋglædsəm] *a*. 令人高兴的,快乐的,愉快的。~ *tidings* 喜讯。**-ly** *ad*. **-ness** *n*.

Glad·stone[1] [ˈglædstən; ˋglædstən] *n*. 1. (由中部对开的)旅行提包〔又名~ bag〕。2. (游览用)四轮双人马车。

Glad·stone[2] [ˈglædstən; ˋglædstən] *n*. 1. 格拉德斯通〔姓氏〕。2. **William Ewart** ~ 威廉·尤尔特·格拉德斯通〔1809—1898,英国政治家,于 1868—1894 年间四度任英国首相〕。

Glad·ys [ˈglædis; ˋglædɪs] *n*. 格拉迪斯〔女子名〕。

glai·kit, glai·ket [ˈgleikit; ˋglekɪt] *a*. 〔主 Scot.〕愚蠢的;轻浮的;轻佻的。

glair [glɛə; glɛr] **I** *n*. 1. (用于釉光或釉浆的)蛋白。2. (用蛋白制成的)釉光,釉浆〔作装订书本等用〕。3. 蛋白状黏液。**II** *vt*. 在…涂蛋白。

glair·e·ous [ˈglɛəriəs; ˋglɛrɪəs], **glair·y** [-ri; -rɪ] *a*. 涂蛋白的,蛋白状的,蛋白质的。

glaive [gleiv; glev] *n*. 〔古、诗〕剑;(特指)阔剑。

glam [glæm; glæm] *n*. 有钱的中年人〔指有潜在购买力的经济一般较富裕的中年人〕。

glam·or [ˈglæmə; ˋglæmɚ] *n*. 〔美〕= glamour.

glam·or·ize [ˈglæməraiz; ˋglæməraɪz] *vt*. 1. 〔口〕使有魔力,使迷人。2. 美化,把…理想化。

glam·o(u)r [ˈglæmə; ˋglæmɚ] **I** *n*. 1. 魔法,魔术;魔力。2. 魄力;(诗等的)迷人的神韵〔意境〕。***cast a*** ~ ***over*** 迷惑,使对…着迷。**II** *vt*. 迷惑,迷住。~ **boy** 〔美〕美男子。~ **girl** 迷人的姑娘。~ **puss** 愚美人。~ **stock** 〔美〕热门股票。

glam·o(u)r·ous [ˈglæmərəs; ˋglæmərəs] *a*. 富有魔力的,迷人的。

glance[1][glɑːns; glɑns] ***n*.** **I** **1.** 匆匆一看,一瞥,扫视;眼色。**2.** 一闪;闪光。**3.** (炮弹等的)斜飞,侧过。**4.**〔古〕约略提及,影射。*One ~ was enough*. 看一眼就够了。***at a ~ = at the first ~*** 一看就,一见就;初看。***cast hostile ~s upon*** 敌视,仇视。***exchange ~s*** 互相使眼色。***give*** [***take***] ***a ~ at*** [***to, of, into, over***] 对…匆匆一看,瞥一眼。***steal a ~ at*** 偷偷一看。***with a keen ~*** 以敏锐的一瞥。**II** ***vi*.** **1.** 匆匆一看,一瞥,扫视(*at*; *over*)。**2.** 约略提到;影射(*at*; *over*)。**3.** (枪弹等)擦过,掠过(*aside*; *off*)。**4.** 闪耀,发光。— ***vt*.** **1.** (把眼睛等)向…晃一眼,扫视。**2.** 使反射,投射(光线)。**3.** 影射,暗示。~ ***down*** [***up***] 朝下[朝上]一看,俯[仰]身一瞥。~ (***one's eyes***) ***over*** [***through***] 粗略一看,浏览。

glance[2][glɑːns; glɑns] **I** ***n*.** 【矿】辉矿类。*lead ~* 方铅矿。*silver ~* 辉银矿。**II** ***vt*.** 使发光,磨光。~ **coal** 镜煤;无烟煤。~ **copper** 辉铜矿。

glanc·ing [ˈglɑːnsiŋ; ˋglɑnsɪŋ] ***a*.** **1.** 粗略的,随便的。**2.** 偶尔的,间接的。~ **angle**【光】掠射角。**-ly** ***ad*.**

gland[1][glænd; glænd] ***n*.** **1.**【解】腺。*a ductless ~* 无管腺。*the lacrimal ~s* 泪腺。*the salivary ~s* 唾腺。*the sweat* [*sudoriferous*] *~s* 汗腺。*thyroid ~* 甲状腺。**2.**【植】(分泌蜜等的)腺。

gland[2][glænd; glænd] ***n*.**【机】密封压盖,填料盖,密封盖。*a labyrinth ~* 迂回密封盖,曲折密封盖,迷宫式密封盖。*packing ~* 压垫盖,填料盖。*a steam valve ~* 汽阀压盖。

glan·dered [ˈglændəd; ˋglændɚd] ***a*.**【兽医】患鼻疽(病)的。

glan·ders [ˈglændəz; ˋglændɚz] ***n*.**〔用作单〕【兽医】鼻疽病,马鼻疽。**-dered** [-dəd; -dɚd], **-der·ous** [-dərəs; -dərəs] ***a*.** 患鼻疽病的。

glan·des [ˈglændiːz; ˋglændiz] ***n*.** glans 的复数。

glan·di·fer·ous [glænˈdifərəs; glænˋdɪfərəs] ***a*.** 结坚果的。

G

glan·di·form [ˈglændifɔːm; ˋglændəˏfɔrm] ***a*.** **1.** 腺状的。**2.** 坚果状的。

glan·du·lar [ˈglændjulə; ˋglændjəlɚ] ***a*.** **1.** 腺的,含腺的,有腺的特征[功能]的。**2.** 天生的,固有的。**3.** 性的。*a ~ dislike for cat* 天生不喜欢猫。*~ relationship* 性关系。~ **cancer**【医】腺癌。~ **fever** 传染性单核白血球增多(= infectious mononucleosis)。~ **swelling**【医】腺肿。**-ly** ***ad*.**

glan·dule [ˈglændjuːl; ˋglændjul] ***n*.**【解】小腺。

glan·du·lif·er·ous [ˌglændjuˈlifərəs; ˏglændjəˋlɪfərəs] ***a*.** 有小腺的。

glan·du·lous [ˈglændjuləs; ˋglændjələs] ***a*.** = glandular. **-ness** ***n*.**

glans [glænz; glænz] ***n*.** (*pl*. ***glan·des*** [ˈglændiːz; ˋglændiz])【解】阴茎头;阴蒂头。~ **clitoridis** 阴蒂头。~ **penis** 龟头。

glare[1][glεə; glεr] **I** ***n*.** **1.** 闪耀,闪光;眩目的光,强烈的光。**2.** 显眼;炫耀;著名。**3.** 瞪眼。*the ~ of the footlights* 舞台上耀眼的灯光。***in the full ~ of publicity*** 非常显眼,在众目睽睽之下。**II** ***vi*.** **1.** 发耀眼的光,发强烈的光,闪耀。**2.** 瞪(*at*; *on*; *upon*)。— ***vt*.** **1.** 用目光表示(嫌恶、轻视)。**2.** 使反射。

glare[2][glεə; glεr] **I** ***n*.**〔美〕(冰等的)平滑光亮的表面。**II** ***a*.** 亮晶晶的,光滑的。~ **ice** 光滑而发亮的冰。

glare·less [ˈglεəlis; ˋglεrlɪs] ***a*.** 不刺目的。

glar·ing [ˈglεəriŋ; ˋglεrɪŋ] ***a*.** **1.** 耀眼的,闪闪发光的。**2.** 瞪眼的,怒目而视的。**3.** 炫耀的,显眼的;突出的。**4.** 粗俗的,俗气的。~ *errors* 大错。*a ~ lie* 露骨的谎话。**-ly** ***ad*.** **-ness** ***n*.**

glar·y[1][ˈglεəri; ˋglεrɪ] ***a*.** = glaring.

glar·y[2][ˈglεəri; ˋglεrɪ] ***a*.**〔美〕光滑的。

Gla·ser [ˈgleizə; ˋglezɚ] ***n*.** 格莱泽〔姓氏〕。

Glas·gow [ˈglɑːsgəu; ˋglɑsgo] ***n*.** 格拉斯哥〔英国城市〕。

glas·nost [ˈglɑːsnɔst; ˋglɑsnɔst] ***n*.**〔俄〕(政治上的)公开性。

glass [glɑːs; glæs] **I** ***n*.** **1.** 玻璃,玻璃状物。**2.**〔集合词〕玻璃制品,玻璃器具,料器;玻璃暖房(= ~ house)。**3.** 玻璃杯;一杯的量;酒杯。**4.** 镜子,望远镜,显微镜,晴雨表,温度表,砂漏,钟表的玻璃盖;玻璃框,车窗。**5.**〔*pl*.〕眼镜。*crown ~* 冕玻璃(硬性光学玻璃)。*cut ~* 雕花玻璃,车玻璃。*flint ~* 燧石玻璃(软性光学玻璃)。*frosted* [*mat*] *~* 磨沙玻璃,霜化玻璃。*ground ~* 毛玻璃,磨口玻璃。*optical ~* 光学玻璃。*organic ~* 有机玻璃。*plate ~* 板玻璃。*pyrex ~* 派来克斯玻璃(原商品名,一种耐热玻璃)。*spun ~* 玻璃丝。*stained ~* 彩画玻璃。*toughened ~* 钢化玻璃,淬火玻璃。*wire*(*d*) *~* 嵌丝玻璃。*a ~ of wine* [*water*] 一杯酒[水]。*enjoy a ~ now and then* 时常喝酒。*look in the ~* 照镜子。*The ~ is at fair*. 晴雨表上显示"天晴"。*dinner* [*table*] *~* 玻璃餐具。*~ and china* 料器和瓷器。***be fond of one's ~*** 爱喝酒,爱杯中物。***clink ~es*** 碰杯。***flinch one's ~*** 故意不把酒喝干。***have had a ~ too much*** 喝多了,喝醉了。***look through blue ~es*** 悲观地看事物。***look through green ~es*** 羡慕[妒忌]地看事物。***look through rose-coloured ~es*** 乐观地看事物。***raise one's ~ to*** 为某人的健康干杯。***under ~***【园艺】在温室中。**II** ***vt*.** **1.** 给…镶玻璃,用玻璃覆盖;把…装在玻璃器里。**2.** 使平滑如玻璃。**3.**〔常作 ~ *oneself*〕映照,反映。**4.** 用望远镜瞭望。**5.** 使滞钝无光。~ *a window* 给窗户上玻璃。*~ed fruits* 密封于玻璃容器中的水果。*eyes ~ed by boredom* 因厌倦而滞钝无光的眼睛。*The flowers ~ themselves in the pool*. 花影映照在池中。— ***vi*.** **1.** 成玻璃状,(目光等)变迟钝。**2.** 用望远镜瞭望。**~-arm** 容易发酸[麻木]的胳臂。~ **blower** 吹玻璃工人。~ **case** 玻璃橱柜。~ **ceiling** 玻璃天花板〔指公司中对女职员晋级的封顶〕。~ **cloth** 揩玻璃的布;玻璃纤维织布;涂有玻璃粉的织物;玻璃沙布。~ **culture** 温室栽培。~ **cutter** 划玻璃的人;划玻璃的刀。~ **dust** (研磨用的)玻璃粉。~ **eye** **1.** 马眼黑内障病。**2.** 玻璃制假眼睛。**3.** 一片眼镜;〔*pl*.〕一副眼镜。~ **fibre** 玻璃纤维。**~-glaze** 玻璃釉。**~-glazed** ***a*.** 浓釉的。**~-house** **1.** 玻璃厂,玻璃店。**2.** 温室,玻璃房子。**3.**〔英俚〕军事监狱。**4.**〔口〕飞机驾驶员座位;装有玻璃天棚的摄影室(*Those who live in ~ houses should not throw stones*.〔谚〕自己有短处就别揭别人的疮疤)。~ **jaw**〔美俚〕拳击选手经不起打击的下颌。**~maker** ***n*.** 玻璃工匠,玻璃器皿工匠。**~making** ***n*.** 玻璃制造工艺[工业]。**~-man** ***n*.** 玻璃商人;装玻璃的工人;玻璃制造者。~ **paper** 玻璃沙纸,沙皮。~ **snake** 一种尾脆似玻璃的蛇蜥属(*Ophisaurus*)动物。**~ware** 料器,玻璃器皿。~ **wool** 玻璃棉,玻璃绒,玻璃丝。**~work** **1.** 玻璃制造业;玻璃制品。**2.**〔常 *pl*.〕玻璃工厂。**~worm** ***n*.** 箭虫(= arrowworm)。**~wort** ***n*.**【植】欧洲海蓬子〔烧成灰可作玻璃原料〕;钾猪毛菜。**-less** ***a*.** 没有玻璃的,未装玻璃的。

Glass [glɑːs; glæs] ***n*.** 格拉斯〔姓氏〕。

Glass·boro [ˈglæsbəːrə; ˋglæsbɚrə] ***n*.** 葛拉斯堡罗〔美国城市〕。

glass·ful [ˈglɑːsful; ˋglɑsfʊl] ***n*.** 一杯的容量。

glass·ine [glæˈsiːn; glæˋsin] ***n*.** 玻璃纸。

glass·y [ˈglɑːsi; ˋglɑsɪ] ***a*.** **1.** 玻璃质的,玻璃状的。**2.** (眼睛)呆滞的,没有神采的。**3.** 透明如玻璃的,平稳如镜的。*a ~ surface* 镜一样的平面。**~-eyed** ***a*.** 眼睛无神的;目光呆滞的。**-ily** ***ad*.** **-iness** ***n*.**

Glas·we·gian [glæsˈwiːdʒjən; glæsˋwidʒjən] **I** ***a*.** 格拉斯哥的。**II** ***n*.** 格拉斯哥市民。

glau·ber·ite [ˈglaubərait; ˋglaʊbəraɪt] ***n*.**【化】钙芒硝。

Glau·ber's salt [ˈglaubəz ˈsɔːlt; ˋglaʊbɚz ˋsɔlt]【化】芒硝,结晶硫酸钠,〔口〕元明粉。

glau·co·ma [glɔːˈkəumə; glɔˋkomə] ***n*.**【医】青光眼,绿内障。**-tous** [-təs; -təs] ***a*.** (患)青光眼的。

glau·co·nite [ˈglɔːkənait; ˋglɔkənaɪt] ***n***. 【地】海绿石。

glau·cous [ˈglɔːkəs; ˋglɔkəs] ***a***. **1**. 淡灰蓝色的,淡灰绿色的。**2**. 【植】表面具白霜的。~ **gull** 【动】北极鸥〔产于北极〕。

glaum [glɔːm; glɔm] ***vt***., ***vi***. 〔美俚、英方〕抢,夺,偷。

glaze [gleiz; glez] **I** ***vt***. **1**. 镶玻璃于,装玻璃于。**2**. 打光,擦亮;给…上釉;把…弄光滑。**3**. 在(油漆物上)涂透明[半透明]色料。**4**. 在(食物表面)浇糖浆。**5**. 使(眼睛)蒙上薄翳。**6**. 铺一层薄冰于。*~d bricks* 琉璃砖。*~d frost* 雨淞。*~d paper* 有光纸。*~d printing paper* 道林纸。*~d tiles* 琉璃瓦。— ***vi***. **1**. 变光滑;变明亮,变成薄膜状。**2**. (眼光)变呆,变模糊。~ ***in*** 把…围在玻璃中,用玻璃盖上。**II** ***n***. **1**. 釉料,上光料。**2**. 光滑面,光滑层,薄冰层。**3**. (眼光的)呆钝;(眼睛的)翳子。**4**. 上釉,上光。**5**. 【气】雨淞。**6**. 【烹】(浇在食物表面的)冻胶,糖浆。~ **wheel** 研磨轮,研光轮。

glaz·er [ˈgleizə; ˋglezɚ] ***n***. 上釉工人,打光工人;上光机,轧光机。

gla·zier [ˈgleizjə; ˋgleʒɚ] ***n***. **1**. 釉工;光布工。**2**. 装玻璃的人。*Is your father a ~?* [*Your father was a bad ~.*]〔谑〕你老子是装玻璃的吗? [你老子是个蹩脚的装玻璃工。]〔意指:你怎么挡人光线呢,难道你的身体是玻璃的吗?〕。~**'s diamond** 划玻璃刀。**-ziery** ***n***. 〔集合词〕**1**. 釉工。**2**. 装玻璃工。

glaz·ing [ˈgleiziŋ; ˋglezɪŋ] ***n***. **1**. 玻璃装配(业)。**2**. 玻璃工艺;玻璃制品。**3**. 上釉。**4**. 釉;上光料。~ *calender* 【纺】轧光机,擦光机。

glaz·y [ˈgleizi; ˋglezɪ] ***a***. **1**. 玻璃似的。**2**. 上过釉的。**3**. (目光)无神的。

G.L.C. = Greater London Council 大伦敦市议会。

GLCM = ground-launched cruise missile 地面发射的巡航导弹。

gleam [gliːm; glim] **I** ***n***. **1**. 闪光,微光。**2**. (感情等的)闪现;短暂微弱的显现。**3**. 反光。*a ~ of hope* 一线希望。*a ~ of anticipation in his eyes* 他眼中闪烁着期待的目光。*the first ~s of day* 曙光。*the ~ of dawn in the east* 东方的晨曦。**II** ***vi***. **1**. 发微光,闪烁。**2**. (感情等的)闪现。— ***vt***. 使发微光,使闪烁,隐约地显现。

gleam·y [ˈgliːmi; ˋglimɪ] ***a***. 发微光的,发闪光的。

glean [gliːn; glin] ***vt***. **1**. 拾(落穗);收拾(遗留在田地的)庄稼。**2**. 搜集(新闻、资料等)。**3**. 发现,查明。~ *a field* 拾一块地上的残穗。— ***vi***. 拾落穗;搜集新闻[资料]。**-er** ***n***. 搜集人;拾落穗的人。**-ing** ***n***. **1**. 拾落穗,搜集。**2**. 〔*pl*.〕搜集物;(资料、传闻等的)拾遗。

glebe [gliːb; glib] ***n***. **1**. 教会附属地;圣职领耕地。**2**. 〔诗〕土地,耕地。**3**. 【矿】含矿地带。

glede [gliːd; glid], **gled** [gled; glɛd] ***n***. 【动】鸢〔产于欧洲〕。

glee [gliː; gli] ***n***. **1**. 高兴,快乐,狂欢。**2**. 【乐】(无伴奏的男声)合唱曲。***full of ~*** = ***in high ~*** 欢天喜地。~ **club** 合唱队。

gleed [gliːd; glid] ***n***. 〔方〕一块燃烧着的煤。

glee·ful [ˈgliːful; ˋglifəl] ***a***. 极高兴的,开心的;令人愉快的。~ *news* 喜讯。***in ~ mood*** 高高兴兴地。**-ly** ***ad***. **-ness** ***n***.

glee·man [ˈgliːmən; ˋglimən] ***n***. (*pl*. ***-men***) 〔古〕吟游诗人。

Gleep [gliːp; glip] ***n***. 【原】低功率石墨实验性原子反应堆〔*g*raphite *l*ow *e*nergy *e*xperimental *p*ile〕.

glee·some [ˈgliːsəm; ˋglisəm] ***a***. = gleeful.

gleet [gliːt; glit] **I** ***n***. **1**. 【医】后淋,慢性淋病性尿道炎。**2**. (牲口等的)慢性鼻腔炎。**II** ***vi***. 排出黏薄液体。**-y** ***a***. 后淋的,淋病状。

gleg [gleg; glɛg] ***a***. 〔Scot.〕警惕的,灵敏的;敏锐的。

glen [glen; glɛn] ***n***. 峡谷,幽谷。~ 〔G-〕 **plaid** 格伦乌夸特方格呢〔也叫 Glenurquhart plaid〕。

Glen(n) [glen; glɛn] ***n***. 格伦〔姓氏,男子名〕。

Glen·da [ˈglendə; ˋglɛndə] ***n***. 格伦达〔女子名〕。

Glen·gar·ry [glenˈgæri; glɛnˋgærɪ] ***n***. (*pl*. ***-ries***)〔有时用 g-〕苏格兰便帽(呈船形,帽后有二短飘带,系高地人所戴 = ~ bonnet)。

gle·noid [ˈgliːnɔid; ˋglinɔɪd] ***a***. 【解】(有)浅窝的,关节窝的。~ **cavity** 关节腔。

gley [glei; gle] ***n***. 潜育层(土壤)。

gli·a [ˈglaiə, ˈgliːə; ˋglaɪə, ˋgliə] ***n***. 神经胶质 (= neuroglia). **-al** ***a***.

gli·a·din [ˈglaiədin; ˋglaɪədɪn] ***n***. 【生化】**1**. 麦醇溶蛋白,麦胶蛋白。**2**. 醇溶谷蛋白。

glib [glib; glɪb] ***a***. (***glib·ber***, ***glib·best***) **1**. 能说会道的,口齿流利的。**2**. (动作)轻巧的;浮浅的;随便的。**3**. 〔古〕光滑的。*a ~ talker* 伶牙俐齿的谈话者。~ *answers* 敏捷的回答。**-ly** ***ad***. **-ness** ***n***.

glide [glaid; glaɪd] **I** ***n***. **1**. 滑行;滑动。**2**. 流逝,消逝。**3**. 【空】滑翔;【船】滑行台,滑道;【地】滑裂带。**4**. 【语】滑音,滑移;【乐】滑音,延音。**5**. 静悄悄的流水。**II** ***vi***. **1**. 流动,滑动;滑行。**2**. 悄悄走,溜走。**3**. 【空】滑翔。**4**. 渐变,渐消 (*into*)。— ***vt***. 使滑动,使滑行。~ ***by*** [***on***] (时间等)悄悄过去(溜走)。~ **bomb** ***vt***., ***vi***. 下滑轰炸。~ **bomb** 滑翔式炸弹。~ **path** 【空】**1**. 滑翔台。**2**. 滑翔航道。~ **slope** 滑翔斜率,滑翔道。~ **vehicle** 滑翔导弹。

glid·er [ˈglaidə; ˋglaɪdɚ] ***n***. **1**. 滑行者,滑动物。**2**. 【空】滑翔机;【海】滑行艇。**3**. (露台等处的)吊椅。**4**. 【宇】滑翔导弹,可收回的卫星。*a ~ bomb* 滑翔式炸弹。~ *troops* 滑翔部队。*a winged rocket-assisted ~* 火箭加速滑翔机。

glid·ing [ˈglaidiŋ; ˋglaɪdɪŋ] ***a***. 滑行的,滑翔的。*a ~ way of walking* 像滑行似的步伐。~ **angle** 【空】下滑角。**-ly** ***ad***.

glim [glim; glɪm] ***n***. **1**. 〔俚〕灯火,蜡烛,灯笼。**2**. 眼睛。**3**. 模糊的感觉;微弱的迹象;少许,微量。**4**. 一瞥,看一看。***douse*** [***dowse***] ***the ~*** 〔俚〕熄灯。

glim·mer [ˈglimə; ˋglɪmɚ] **I** ***n***. **1**. 微光,薄光,闪光。**2**. 模糊的感觉[概念];轻微的表露。**3**. 少许,微量。**4**. 【矿】云母 (= mica)。**5**. 〔*pl*.〕〔俚〕眼睛。*a ~ of hope* 一线希望。*have a ~ing of* 模模糊糊地知道。*a ~ of intelligence* 很少一点情报。**II** ***vi***. **1**. 发微光。**2**. 朦胧出现。***go ~ing*** 渐渐消失。

glimpse [glimps; glɪmps] **I** ***n***. **1**. 一瞥,瞥见 (*at*; *of*)。**2**. 模糊的感觉;隐约的显现。**3**. 〔古〕闪光。***at a ~*** 一瞥之间。***catch*** [***get***] ***a ~ of*** 瞥见。***~s of the truth*** 一孔之见。***the ~s of the moon*** **1**. 夜间世界。**2**. 世事,俗事。**II** ***vt***., ***vi***. 瞥见;〔诗〕闪现。

glint [glint; glɪnt] **I** ***vi***. **1**. 闪耀,反射;发微光。**2**. (箭一样)飞出,掠过。**3**. 窥视;闪现。— ***vt***. 使发光,使闪光,使反射。**II** ***n***. **1**. 闪光;微光。**2**. 短暂微弱的显露。**3**. (雷达的)回波起伏。

gli·o·ma [glaiˈəumə; glaɪˋomə] ***n***. (*pl*. ***-ma·ta*** [-mətə; -mətə]) 【医】神经胶质瘤。**-ous** ***a***.

glis·sade [gliˈsɑːd; glɪˋsɑd] **I** ***n***. **1**. (登山者沿覆雪斜坡)滑降。**2**. (芭蕾舞)横滑步。**II** ***vi***. **1**. 滑降。**2**. 跳横滑步舞。

glis·san·do [gliˈsɑːndəu; glɪˋsɑndo] **I** ***n***. (*pl*. ***-di*** [-diː; -dɪ], *~s*) 【乐】**1**. 级进滑奏,滑音,滑唱。**2**. 有级进滑奏的乐段。**II** ***a***., ***ad***. 滑奏的[地],滑音的[地],滑唱的[地]。

glis·sé [gliˈsei; glɪˋse] ***n***. 〔F.〕(芭蕾舞)横滑步。

glist [glist; glɪst] ***n***. **1**. 闪耀。**2**. 云母。

glis·ten [ˈglisn; ˋglɪsn] **I** ***vi***. 发光,辉耀,闪烁;反光。**II** ***n***. 闪光;反光;光辉。

glis·ter [ˈglistə; ˋglɪstɚ] ***n***., ***vi***. 〔古〕 = glisten, glitter.

glitch [glitʃ; glɪtʃ] ***n***. **1**. 〔美俚〕晦气;过失;处置失当;小故障,小事故,小技术问题。**2**. 假电子讯号。**3**. 【天】(中子星)自转突快。

G

glit·ter [ˈglitə; ˋglɪtɚ] I *n*. 1. 光辉,灿烂。2. 发光的小东西。II *vi*. 1. 闪烁,闪闪发光。2. 华丽夺目,炫耀。*All is not gold that* ~*s*.【谚】闪闪发光者未必尽黄金。~ **ice**〔Can.〕【气】雨淞〔雨水速冻而成的晶亮的冰〕。~ **rock**(由服饰华丽的男乐师演奏的)闪烁摇滚乐。

glit·te·ra·ti [ˌglitəˈrɑːti; ˏglɪtəˋrætɪ] *n*. *pl*.〔总称〕知名人士;国际上层社会人士。

glit·ter·ing [ˈglitəriŋ; ˋglɪtərɪŋ] *a*. = glittery. **-ly** *ad*.

glit·ter·y [ˈglitəri; ˋglɪtərɪ] *a*. 晶亮的,灿烂的。

Gloag [gləug; glog] *n*. 格洛格〔姓氏〕。

gloam [gləum; glom] I *vi*.〔主 Scot.〕暗下来,变朦胧。II *n*.〔诗〕= gloaming.

gloam·ing [ˈgləumiŋ; ˋglomɪŋ] *n*. 黄昏,薄暮。*in the* ~ *of one's life* 在晚年。

gloat [gləut; glot] I *vi*. 1. 幸灾乐祸地注视;爱慕地凝视。2. 得意地看[思索];贪婪地瞪视 (*on*; *over*; *upon*)。~ *on* [*upon*] *a heap of treasure* 瞪着一堆财宝。~ *over sb.'s misfortune* 幸灾乐祸。II *n*. 1. 得意的注视;沾沾自喜。2. 爱慕的凝视;垂涎。3. 幸灾乐祸的观望。**-er** *n*.

gloat·ing [ˈgləutiŋ; ˋglotɪŋ] *a*. 心满意足的。*a* ~ *smile* 得意的微笑。**-ly** *ad*.

glob [glɔb; glɑb] *n*. (浓流体或半固体的)团块。

glob·al [ˈgləubəl; ˋglobəl] *a*. 1. 球面的,球状的;全球的。2. 世界的。3. 总体的,普遍的,综合的。*take a non-stop* ~ *flight* 作一次环绕世界一周的不着陆飞行。*a* ~ *system of communication* 全球通信系统。*the* ~ *consciousness* 全球意识。*a* ~ *war* 一场全球战争。*the* ~ *sum* 总计 (= total sum). ~ **tectonics**【地】板块构造(论)。~ **village** 地球村〔指将来电子交通传播发达,全球距离日益缩小,犹如一个村庄〕。~ **warming**(由温室效应导致的)全球气候变暖。**-ly** *ad*.

glob·al·ism [ˈgləublizm; ˋglobɪlɪzm̩] *n*.〔美〕(看问题等着眼于全世界)全球性,全球观念;全球性干涉政策。**-ist** *a*., *n*. 赞成奉行全球性干涉政策的(人)。

G

glo·bal·ize [ˈgləubəlaiz; ˋglobəˏlaɪz] *vt*. 使全球化。*the* ~*d economy* 全球化了的经济。**-i·za·tion** [ˌgləubəlaiˈzeiʃən; ˏglobəlaɪˋzeʃən] *n*. 全球化。

glo·bate [ˈgləubeit; ˋglobet] *a*. 球状的。

globe [gləub; glob] I *n*. 1. 球;球状物。2. [the ~] 地球,世界。3. 天体。4. 地球仪,天体仪。5. 球形容器,灯罩,灯泡。6.【解】眼球。7. (象征王权的)小金球。*the terrestrial* ~地球。*a terrestrial* ~地球仪。*a celestial* ~天球仪。*the use of the* ~*s* (从前的)天文、地理仪器示教法。*the whole habitable* ~全世界。II *vt*., *vi*. (使)成球状。~ **amaranth**【植】千日红。~ **artichoke** = cardoon. ~**fish**【动】河豚。~**flower**【植】金莲花。~ **lightning**【气】球状闪电。~**-mallow**【植】球葵。~**-trotter**〔口〕(短期的)环球旅行家。~**-trotting** 1. *n*. (短期)环球旅行。2. *a*. 环球旅行的。~ **valve**【机】球(形)阀。

glo·big·er·i·na [gləuˌbidʒəˈrainə; gloˏbɪdʒəˋraɪnə] *n*. (*pl*. **-rinae** [-ˈrainiː; -ˋraɪni])【地】抱球虫。

glo·bin [ˈgləubin; ˋglobɪn] *a*.【生】珠蛋白。

glo·boid [ˈgləubɔid; ˋglobɔɪd] I *a*. 球状的。II *n*. 球状体。

glo·bose [ˈgləubəus; ˋglobos] *a*. 球状的,球形的。

glo·bos·i·ty [gləuˈbɔsiti; gloˋbɑsətɪ] *n*. 球状,球形。

glob·u·lar [ˈglɔbjulə; ˋglɑbjəlɚ] *a*. 1. 球状的,地球状的。2. 世界范围的。3. 由小球聚集成的;有小球的。4. 完整的。~ *masses of fish eggs* 聚集成块的球状鱼卵。~ **chart** 球面投影地图。~ **projection** 球面投影法。~ **proteins** 球蛋白。~ **sailing**【海】球面航行。**-ly** *ad*. **-ness** *n*.

glob·u·lar·i·ty [ˌglɔbjuˈlæriti; ˏglɑbjəˋlærətɪ] *n*. 球状,球形。

glob·ule [ˈglɔbjuːl; ˋglɑbjul] *n*. 1. 小球。2. 液滴,血球,药丸。

glob·u·lin [ˈglɔbjulin; ˋglɑbjəlɪn] *n*.【生化】球蛋白,球朊。

glob·u·lous [ˈglɔbjuləs; ˋglɑbjələs] *a*. = globular.

glo·chid·i·ate [gləuˈkidiət; gloˋkɪdɪət] *a*.【植】有钩毛的。

glo·chid·i·um [gləuˈkidiəm; gloˋkɪdɪəm] *n*. (*pl*. **-chidi·a** [-ˈkidiə; -ˋkɪdɪə]) 1.【植】钩毛。2.【动】河蚌幼虫;瓣钩幼虫 (*Unionidae*)。

glock·en·spiel [ˈglɔkənspiːl; ˋglɑkənspil] *n*.【乐】1. 钟琴。2. 钟组乐器,编钟。

glögg, glogg [glɔːg; glɔg] *n*. 瑞典式热饮〔把酒、白兰地与糖和香料等温热,再加葡萄干和杏仁作配料〕。

glom [glɔm; glɑm] *vt*., *vi*.〔美俚〕= glaum.

glom·er·ate [ˈglɔmərit; ˋglɑmərɪt] *a*.【植、解】团集的。

glom·er·a·tion [ˌglɔməˈreiʃən; ˏglɑməˋreʃən] *n*. 1. 聚成团;结成团块;做成球状。2. 团块;球状物。

glo·mer·u·late [glɔˈmerjulit; glɑˋmerjəlɪt] *a*. 作团伞状的。

glom·er·ule [ˈglɔməruːl; ˋglɑmərul] *n*. 1.【植】团伞序。2. = glomerulus.

glo·mer·u·lo·ne·phri·tis [gləuˈmerjuˌləunefˈraitis; gloˋmɛrjʊˏlonɛfˋraɪtɪs] *n*.【医】血管球性肾炎。

glo·mer·u·lus [gləuˈmerjuləs; gloˋmerjʊləs] *n*. (*pl*. **-li** [-lai; -laɪ])【医】1. 小球。2. 血管(小)球。**-u·lar** [-lə; -lɚ] *a*.

glon·o·in [ˈglɔnəuin; ˋglɑnoɪn] *n*. 硝化甘油,甘油三硝酸酯 (= nitroglycerin)。

gloom [gluːm; glum] I *n*. 1. 黑暗,幽暗,朦胧;〔诗〕幽暗处,背阴处。2. 忧郁,悲哀;意气消沉。3.〔Scot.〕忧郁的面貌。*in the green* ~*s of the forest* 林中绿荫处。*A* ~ *fell over the household*. 全家黯然忧伤。***cast a*** ~ ***over*** 使忧郁,使阴暗。***chase one's*** ~ ***away*** 解闷,消愁。~ ***and doom*** 前途暗淡。***in the*** ~ 在幽暗中。II *vi*. 1. 变黑暗,变阴郁。2. 变忧郁 (*over*)。3. 现愁容,做苦脸 (*at*; *on*)。— *vt*. 1. 使暗,使朦胧。2. 使忧郁。3. 忧伤地说。

gloom·y [ˈgluːmi; ˋglumɪ] *a*. 1. 暗的,黑暗的,阴暗的。2. 阴郁的,忧闷的;令人沮丧的;脾气不好的。3. 没希望的,前途暗淡的。*take a* ~ *view of* 对…悲观。**-i·ly** *ad*. **-i·ness** *n*.

glop [glɔp; glɑp] *n*.〔美俚〕1. 软胶质物;浓流体物。2. 乏味的东西。**glop·py** [-i; -ɪ] *a*.

Glo·ri·a [ˈglɔːriə; ˋglɔrɪə] *n*.〔L.〕1. (基督教用拉丁语,开始的)《荣耀颂》歌。2.《荣耀颂》的曲调。3. [g-] 赞颂光荣。4. [g-] (神像等背后的)后光,光轮。5. [g-] 丝毛交织薄绸。~ ***in excelsis*** (用于赞美诗)荣耀归于上帝。~ ***Patri*** (用于赞美歌)荣耀归于圣父。~ ***tibi*** (用于回答)荣耀归于您。

glo·ri·fy [ˈglɔːrifai; ˋglɔrəˏfaɪ] *vt*. (**-fied**; **-fy·ing**) 1. 赞美,崇拜。2. 颂扬,夸赞。3. 给予…光荣,使增光。4. 〔口〕装饰;使(普通或低劣的东西)美观,美化,使有魅力,使有吸引力, 5. 使光辉灿烂,使光彩夺目。*A large chandelier* ~*s the whole room*. 枝形大吊灯使整个房间光亮夺目。*a recipe for* ~*ing pancakes* 使薄煎饼好看的制法。~ *oneself* 自夸。**-fi·ca·tion** [ˌglɔːrifiˈkeiʃən; ˏglɔrəfəˋkeʃən] *n*. 1. 赞美,颂扬。2. 美化。3. 〔美口〕祝贺,庆祝。

glo·ri·ole [ˈglɔːriəul; ˋglɔrɪol] *n*. (神像等背后的)光轮,后光。

glo·ri·ous [ˈglɔːriəs; ˋglɔrɪəs] *a*. 1. 光荣的;荣耀的。2. 壮丽的;辉煌的,灿烂的。3.〔口〕令人愉快的,极好的。4.〔讽〕可怕的。5. 有点儿醉的,酒后放纵的。*a* ~ *day* 光荣的日子;好天气。*a* ~ *death* 光荣的牺牲。~ *fun* 非常有趣。*a* ~ *mess* [*muddle*, *row*] 乱七八糟。*a* ~ *view* 壮观,绝景。***have a*** ~ ***holiday*** [***weekend***] 过一个愉快的假日[周末]。***the*** ~ ***Fourth*** 美国独立纪念日(7月4日)。**-ly** *ad*.

glo·ry [ˈglɔːri; ˋglɔrɪ] **I** ***n*. 1.** 光荣,荣誉;(对神的)赞美。**2.** 荣耀的事,可赞美的事,可夸耀的事。**3.** 壮观,壮丽,美观。**4.**【宗】天上的荣光;天国的荣誉。**5.** 繁荣,昌盛。**6.** 兴致勃勃,得意洋洋。**7.** (神像等的)后光,光轮。**8.** 日华,月华;日冕。*be in one's* ~ 在极得意时。*cover oneself with* ~ 满载荣誉,取得辉煌胜利。***Eternal*** ~ ***to*** …永垂不朽。***go to*** ~ 升天,死。***return with*** ~ 凯旋。***send sb. to*** ~〔谑〕送某人归天,处死。***the old G-*** 美国国旗。**II** ***vi*.** (***-ried***; ***-ry·ing***) 欢跃,狂喜;自豪,得意。~ *in one's victory* 因胜利而得意洋洋。~ *in doing sth*. [*to do sth*.] 为做某事而自豪。~ ***in honest poverty*** 甘守清贫。~ ***in one's own disgrace*** 丢了脸还自鸣得意。~ ***to do*** [***in doing***] ***sth*.** 为做某事而自豪。**III** ***int*.**〔俚〕哎呀! 要命!〔表示惊叹、欢喜,也说成 G-be!〕。~**-box**〔澳、新西兰〕嫁妆箱[盒]。~ **hole 1.**〔口〕放杂物的橱[抽屉、房间]。**2.** (玻璃熔化炉的)炉口;观察孔,火焰窥孔。

Glos. = Gloucestershire.

gloss[1] [glɔs; glɑs] **I** ***n*. 1.** (表面的)平滑,光泽,光彩。**2.** 平滑的表面。**3.** 虚饰,假象。*the* ~ *of varnished furnitures* 上漆家具的平滑表面[光泽]。*a* ~ *of respectability* 装得道貌岸然。***put*** [***set***] ***a*** ~ ***on*** 使…具有光泽,润饰…。**II** ***vt*. 1.** 给…加光泽,给…上釉。**2.** 掩饰;掩盖(*over*)。— ***vi*.** 发光。~ ***over one's faults*** 掩盖错误。~ **paint** 上光漆。

gloss[2] [glɔs; glɑs] **I** ***n*. 1.** (书边或行间对难字难句的)注解,解释,评注。**2.** 曲解。**3.** 词汇表,集注,夹加于行间的注释性译文。**II** ***vt*. 1.** 注解,注释;评注。**2.** 曲解;搪塞。— ***vi*.** 作注释,写评注。

gloss. = glossary.

gloss-, glosso- *comb. f*. 表示 **1.** "舌":*gloss*algia. **2.** "语言":*glosso*logy.

glos·sa [ˈglɔsə; ˋglɑsə] ***n*.** (*pl*. ~*s*, ~*sae* [-siː; -si])【解】舌;【动】(昆虫的)中唇舌。

glos·sal [ˈglɔːsəl; ˋglɔsəl] ***a*.** 舌的。

glos·sar·i·al [glɔˈsɛəriəl; glɑˋsɛrɪəl] ***a*.** 词汇的;词汇表的。*a* ~ *index* 词汇索引。

glos·sa·ry [ˈglɔsəri; ˋglɑsərɪ] ***n*.** 难字[专业词,外来语]汇编,集注,词汇表。**-rist** [ˈglɔsərist; ˋglɑsərɪst] ***n*.** 词汇表编辑者;词汇注解者。

glos·sa·tor [glɔˈseitə; glɑˋsetə˞] ***n*.** 注释者,评注者,注解者。

glos·sec·to·my [glɔˈsektəmi; glɑˋsɛktəmɪ] ***n*.** 舌切除术。

glos·si·na [glɔˈsainə, glɔˈsiːnə; glɑˋsaɪnə, glɑˋsinə] ***n*.**【动】舌蝇,采采蝇(= tsetse fly)。〔G.〕毒蝇属。

glos·si·tis [glɔˈsaitis; glɑˋsaɪtɪs] ***n*.**【医】舌炎。

glos·sog·ra·pher [glɔˈsɔgrəfə; glɑˋsɑgrəfə˞] ***n*.** = glossarist.

glos·so·la·li·a [ˌglɔsəuˈleiliə; ˏglɑsoˋlelɪə] ***n*.**【医】言语不清。

glos·so·pha·ryn·geal [ˈglɔsəuˌfærinˈdʒiːəl; ˏglɑsoˏfærɪnˋdʒɪəl] ***a*.**【解】舌咽的。~ **nerve**【解】舌咽神经。

glos·sot·o·my [glɔˈsɔtəmi; glɑˋsɑtəmɪ] ***n*.**【解】舌切开术。

gloss·y [ˈglɔsi; ˋglɑsɪ] **I** ***a*. 1.** 有光泽的,光滑的。**2.** 虚饰的,浮华的;似是而非的。*a* ~ *surface* 光滑的表面。~ *deceit* 似是而非的欺骗。**II** ***n*. 1.**〔口〕有光纸印刷的杂志 **2.**【摄】印在光纸上的相片。**-i·ly** ***ad*.** **-i·ness** ***n*.**

glost [glɔst; glɑst] ***n*. 1.** 釉。**2.** 上釉的瓷器。

glott-, glotto- *comb. f*. 表示"语言":*glotto*logy.

glot·tal [ˈglɔtl; ˋglɑtl] ***a*. 1.**【解】声门的。**2.**【语】自声门发出的。~ **stop**【语】声门塞音。

glot·tis [ˈglɔtis; ˋglɑtɪs] ***n*.** (*pl*. ~***es***, ***-ti·des*** [-diːz; -diz])【解】声门。

glot·to·chro·nol·o·gy [ˌglɔtəukrəˈnɔlədʒi; ˏglɑtokrəˋnɑlədʒɪ] ***n*.**【语】同源语言演变史学。

Glouces·ter [ˈglɔstə; ˋglɑstə˞] ***n*. 1.** 格罗斯特〔英国格罗斯特郡的首府〕。**2.** 格罗斯特干酪〔= ~ cheese〕. *single* ~(用脱脂乳制成的)次级干酪。*double* ~(用全脂乳制成的)一级干酪。

Glouces·ter·shire [ˈglɔstəʃiə; ˋglɑstə˞ˏʃɪr] ***n*.** 格罗斯特郡〔英国西南部的一郡〕。

glove [glʌv; glʌv] **I** ***n*. 1.** 手套(一般指五指分开的。*cf*. mitten)。**2.** 棒球手套;拳击手套(= boxing ~)。*a pair of* ~*s* 一副手套。*Excuse my* ~*s*. (握手时的客套话)对不起,没有脱手套。***be hand and*** [***in***] ~ ***with*** 与…合作,与…亲密无间。***bite one's*** ~ 复仇。***fit like a*** ~ 恰恰相合。***go for the*** ~***s*** 孤注一掷。***handle*** [***treat***] ***with*** (***kid***) ~***s*** 灵活处理。***handle without*** ~***s*** 严厉对待。***put on the*** ~***s***〔口〕拳击。***take off the*** ~***s*** (争吵)认真起来。***take up the*** ~ 应战。***The*** ~***s are off*** 认真起来。***throw down the*** ~ 挑战。***without*** ~***s*** = ***with the*** ~***s off*** 毫不留情地。***worth his fielder's*** ~ 能干的。**II** ***vt*. 1.** 给戴手套。**2.** 作…的手套。~ **box 1.** 手套箱。**2.** = ~ compartment. **3.** 处理放射性物质的手套式密闭室。~ **compartment** (汽车仪表盘上)存放零星杂物的凹处。~ **fight** (戴手套的)拳击(*opp*. prize fight)。~ **money** 贿赂。~ **sponge** 一种形似手套的劣质海绵。**-less** ***a*.** 不戴手套的。**-like** ***a*.** 像手套的。

glov·er [ˈglʌvə; ˋglʌvə˞] ***n*.** 手套制造人;手套商。

Glov·er [ˈglʌvə; ˋglʌvə˞] ***n*.** 格洛弗〔姓氏〕。

glow [gləu; glo] **I** ***vi*. 1.** 灼热;发白热光;燃烧〔*cf*. *blaze*〕;放光,发热。**2.** (运动后)身体发热;(面色等)发红;(眼)发亮。**3.** (怒火等)燃烧,(感情等)洋溢。**4.** 鲜艳夺目,显示浓艳的颜色。~ *with enthusiasm* 热情洋溢。~ *with health* 脸色红润,容光焕发。~ *with pride* 得意洋洋。**II** ***n*. 1.** 白热,灼热;光辉。**2.** 热烈,激情,喜悦。**3.** (色彩、印象等的)鲜明;(脸上的)红光,红晕。*the* ~ *of sunset* 晚霞。*the* ~ *of happiness* 幸福的喜悦。***all of a*** ~ = ***in a*** ~〔口〕热烘烘;红彤彤。~ **discharge** 辉光放电。~ **lamp** 辉光灯,辉光放电管。~ **watch** 夜光表。~**worm** 萤火虫。

glow·er[1] [ˈgləuə; ˋgloə˞] ***n*.**【电】炽热体;灯丝。

glow·er[2] [ˈglauə; ˋgloə˞] **I** ***vi*.** 怒视,凝视(*at*). **II** ***n*.** 怒视,凝视。**-ing·ly** ***ad*.**

glow·ing [ˈgləuiŋ; ˋgloɪŋ] ***a*. 1.** 白热的;通红的;灼炽的。**2.** (色彩)鲜明的,光辉的;强烈的。**3.** 热心的,热烈的。**4.** 脸色红润的,容光焕发的。*give a* ~ *account of* 热烈赞赏。~ *cheeks* 红润的两颊。~ *colours* 光彩夺目的颜色。*a* ~ *example* 光辉榜样。*a* ~ *patriot* 热烈的爱国者。~ **furnace** 淬火炉。**-ly** ***ad*.**

glox·in·i·a [glɔkˈsinjə; glɑkˋsɪnjə] ***n*.**【植】大岩桐;〔G-〕大岩桐属。

gloze [gləuz; gloz] ***vt*. 1.** 护(短),掩饰(错误)(*over*)。**2.**〔古〕注解,说明(*on*; *upon*)。— ***vi*. 1.** 谄媚。**2.**〔古〕评解,说明。**gloz·ing·ly** ***ad*.**

GLR = gun laying radar 炮瞄雷达。

glu. = glutamic acid【生化】麸酸,麸胺酸,谷氨酸。

glu·ca·gon [ˈgluːkəgɔn; ˋglukəgɑn] ***n*.**【生化】升血糖激素,胰高血糖素。

glu·cide [ˈgluːsaid; ˋgluˏsaɪd] ***n*.** 糖精。

glu·ci·num [gluːˈsainəm; gluˋsaɪnəm], **glu·cin·i·um** [gluːˈsiniəm; gluˋsɪnɪəm] ***n*.**【化】铍〔铍 beryllium 的别名〕。

glu·co·nate [ˈgluːkəneit; ˋglukənet] ***n*.**【化】葡萄糖酸盐[酯]。

glu·co·ne·o·gen·e·sis [ˌgluːkəuniəˈdʒenisis; ˏglukoniəˋdʒɛnəsɪs] ***n*.** = glyconeogenesis.

glu·con·ic [gluːˈkɔnik; gluˋkɑnɪk] **acid**【化】葡萄糖酸。

glu·co·pro·tein [ˈgluːkəuˈprəutiːn, -tiːin; ˏglukoprotin, -tɪn] ***n*.** = glycoprotein.

glu·cose [ˈgluːkəus; ˋglukos] ***n*.**【化】葡萄糖,右旋糖。

glu·co·side [ˈgluːkəsaid; ˋglukəˏsaɪd] ***n*.**【化】葡萄糖

G

苷，糖苷。

glue [gluː; glu] **I** *n*. **1.** 胶，胶水。**2.** 各种胶粘物。*stick like* ~ *to sb*. 缠住某人不放。**II** *vt*. **1.** 粘上；使粘牢。**2.** 在…上涂胶水。~ *two pieces of wood together* 把两片木头粘起来。~ ***one's ears to*** 贴着耳朵听。~ ***one's eyes on*** 盯着看。~ **pot** 胶锅。~ **water** 胶水。

glue·y [ˈglu(ː)i; ˋgluɪ] *a*. 胶的，胶质的；胶粘的。

glum [glʌm; glʌm] *a*. 阴郁的，闷闷不乐的，愁容满面的。**-ly** *ad*. **-ness** *n*.

glu·ma·ceous [gluːˈmeiʃəs; gluˋmeʃəs] *a*. 【植】**1.** 有颖（片）的。**2.** 颖（片）状的。

glume [gluːm; glum] *n*. 【植】颖，颖片。*an empty* ~ 护颖。~ **spot** 颖枯病。**-like** *a*.

glump·y [ˈglʌmpi; ˋglʌmpɪ] *a*. 〔口〕= glum.

glut [glʌt; glʌt] **I** *n*. **1.** 吃得过多，饱食。**2.** 充斥；供过于求。*a* ~ *of fruit* 水果太多了。**II** *vt*. **1.** 使满足；使吃饱；使厌腻。**2.** 使（市场）充斥。— *vi*. 狼吞虎咽。~ *oneself with food* 吃得太饱。~ *one's eyes* 看够，大饱眼福。~ *one's revenge* 出够了气。~ *the market* 使存货过剩。

glu·ta·mate [ˈgluːtəmeit; ˋglutəˌmet] *n*. 【化】麸胺［谷氨］酸盐［酯］。

glu·tam·ic [gluːˈtæmik; gluˋtæmɪk] **acid** 【化】麸胺酸，谷氨酸。

glu·ta·mine [ˈgluːtəmiːn; ˋglutəmin] *n*. 【化】麸醯胺酸，谷氨酰胺。

glu·ta·thi·one [ˌgluːtəˈθaiəun; ˌglutəˋθaɪon] *n*. 【生化】麸胱甘肽。

glu·te·al [gluːˈtiəl, ˈgluːti-; gluˋtɪəl, ˋglutɪ-] *a*. 【解】臀的，臀肌的。

glu·te·lin [ˈgluːtəlin; ˋglutḷɪn] *n*. 【化】小麦谷蛋白，谷蛋白。

glu·ten [ˈgluːtən; ˋglutn] *n*. 【化】面筋，麸质。~ **bread** （供糖尿病人吃的）麸质面包，面筋面包。~ **flour** （大部分面粉已被除去的）麸质面粉。

glu·ten·ous [ˈgluːtnəs; ˋglutṇəs] *a*. 麸质多的。

glu·te·us [ˈgluːtiəs; gluˈtiəs] *n*. (*pl*. ***glu·tei*** [gluːˈtiːai; gluˋtiaɪ]) 【解】臀肌。

glu·ti·nos·i·ty [ˌgluːtiˈnɔsiti; ˌglutəˋnɑsətɪ] *n*. 黏质，黏性。

glu·ti·nous [ˈgluːtinəs; ˋglutɪnəs] *a*. 黏的，黏质的；【植】有黏液的。~ *rice* 糯米。**-ly** *ad*. **-ness** *n*.

glut·ton[1] [ˈglʌtn; ˋglʌtn] *n*. **1.** 贪吃的人，饕餮，食量大的人。**2.** 〔口〕对…入迷的人，酷爱…的人。*a* ~ *of books* 手不释卷的人。*a* ~ *for work* 闲不住的人。*a* ~ *for punishment* 不怕挨打的拳击家。

glut·ton[2] [ˈglʌtn; ˋglʌtṇ] *n*. 【动】狼獾。

glut·ton·ize [ˈglʌtənaiz; ˋglʌtəˌnaɪz] *vt*. 狼吞虎咽，大吃。— *vi*. 吃得过多。

glut·ton·ous [ˈglʌtənəs; ˋglʌtnəs] *a*. 贪吃的；食量大的；贪婪的。***be*** ~ ***of*** 贪。**-ly** *ad*.

glut·ton·y [ˈglʌtəni; ˋglʌtənɪ] *n*. 暴饮暴食，贪食。

gly. = 【化】glycine.

glyc·er·al·de·hyde [ˌglisəˈældihaid; ˌglɪsəˋældəˌhaɪd] *n*. 【化】甘油醛。

glyc·er·ate [ˈglisəreit; ˋglɪsəret] *n*. 【化】甘油酸盐；甘油酸酯。

gly·cer·ic [gliˈserik; glɪˋsɛrɪk] **acid** 【化】甘油酸。

glyc·er·ide [ˈglisəraid; ˋglɪsəˌraɪd] *n*. 【化】甘油酯。**-id·ic** [-ˈridik; -ˋrɪdɪk] *a*.

glyc·er·in(e) [ˈglisərin; ˋglɪsərɪn], **glyc·er·ol** [ˈglisərɔl; ˋglɪsərɑl] *n*. 【化】甘油，丙三醇。

glyc·er·in·ate [ˈglisərineit; ˋglɪsərɪnet] *vt*. 用甘油处理。**-i·na·tion** [ˌglisəriˈneiʃən; ˌglɪsərəˋneʃən] *n*.

glyc·er·yl [ˈglisəril; ˋglɪsərɪl] *n*. 【化】甘油基。

gly·cine [ˈglaisiːn; ˋglaɪsin] *n*. 【化】甘胺酸，胺基醋［乙］酸。

glyc(o)- *comb*. *f*. 表示“糖”，“糖原”，“甘味”，“甘油”：*glyco*genesis.

gly·co·bi·ol·o·gy [ˈglaikəubaiˌɔlədʒi; ˋglaɪkəuˌbaɪɑlədʒɪ] *n*. 【生】糖原生物学〔专门研究复糖和碳水化合物在活的有机体内之作用〕。

gly·co·coll [ˈglaikəkɔl; ˋglaɪkəkɑl] *n*. 【化】= glycine.

gly·co·gen [ˈglikəudʒen; ˋglaɪkədʒən] *n*. 【化】肝糖，糖原。

gly·co·gen·e·sis [ˌglaikəuˈdʒenisis; ˌglaɪkəˋdʒɛnəsɪs] *n*. 【生化】肝糖生成（作用），糖原生成（作用）。

gly·co·gen·ic [ˌglaikəuˈdʒenik; ˌglaɪkəˋdʒɛnɪk] *a*. 【生化】生肝醣的，生糖原的。

gly·col [ˈglaikɔl, -kəul; ˋglaɪkɑl, -kol] *n*. 【化】乙二醇；〔口〕甘醇。

gly·col·(l)ic [glaiˈkɔlik; glaɪˋkɑlɪk] *a*. 乙二醇的。~ **acid** 乙醇酸。

gly·col·y·sis [glaiˈkɔlisis; glaɪˋkɑləsɪs] *n*. 【生化】（糖原）酵解，糖酵解。**-co·lyt·ic** [ˌglaiˈkəuˈlitik; ˌglaɪkəˋlɪtɪk] *a*.

gly·co·ne·o·gen·e·sis [ˌglaikəuniːəˈdʒenisis; ˌglaɪkəˌnioˋdʒɛnəsɪs] *n*. 【生化】醣新生，糖原异生（作用）。

gly·co·pro·tein [ˌglaikəuˈprəutin, -tiːin; ˌglaɪkəˋprotɪn, -tiɪn] *n*. 【生化】醣蛋白，糖蛋白，糖（多）肽。

gly·co·side [ˈglaikəˌsaid; ˋglaɪkəˌsaɪd] *n*. 【生化】醣［糖］苷。**-sid·ic** [-ˈsidik; -ˋsɪdɪk] *a*.

gly·co·su·ri·a [ˌglaikəˈsjuəriə; ˌglaɪkəˋsjuərɪə] *n*. 【医】糖尿病。

gly·cyr·rhi·za [ˌglisiˈraizə; ˌglɪsəˋraɪzə] *n*. 【植】甘草。

Glyn [glin; glɪn] *n*. 格林［姓氏］。

gly·ox·al [glaiˈɔksæl; glaɪˋɑksæl] *n*. 【化】乙二醛。

glyph [glif; glɪf] *n*. **1.** 【建】束腰竖沟。**2.** 雕像，雕刻的文字。**3.** 表达信息的符号〔如指路牌上的箭头号等〕。**-ic** *a*. 雕刻的。

glyph·o·graph [ˈglifəgrɑːf; ˋglɪfəˌgræf] **I** *n*. 【印】电刻版。**II** *vt*., *vi*. 电刻。**-er** [gliˈfɔgrəfə; glɪˋfɑgrəfəˏ] *n*. 电刻者。**-ic** [ˌglifəˈgræfik; ˌglɪfəˋgræfɪk] *a*. 电刻版的。

glyph·og·ra·phy [gliˈfɔgrəfi; glɪˋfɑgrəfɪ] *n*. 电刻术。

glyp·tic [ˈgliptik; ˋglɪptɪk] *a*. **1.** 雕刻的；雕刻宝石的。**2.** 【矿】有花纹的。**-s** *n*. 〔用作单数〕雕刻术；宝石雕刻术。

glyp·to·dont [ˈgliptədɔnt; ˋglɪptəˌdɑnt] *n*. 【动】（古代动物）雕齿兽。

glyp·tog·ra·phy [glipˈtɔgrəfi; glɪpˋtɑgrəfɪ] *n*. 宝石雕刻术；宝石雕刻学。

GM = **1.** General Manager 总经理。**2.** General Motors Corporation〔美〕通用汽车公司。**3.** guided missile 飞［导］弹。

G.M. = **1.** good middling〔美〕三级棉。**2.** Grand Master（棋类）特级大师。**3.** George Medal〔英〕乔治勋章。

gm. = gram(me) 克（重量单位）。

G-man [ˈdʒiːmæn; ˋdʒiˌmæn] *n*. (*pl*. ***-men***) 美国联邦调查局(FBI)的调查员，密探（= Government man）。

G.M.B., **g.m.b.** = good merchantable brand 上好可销商品。

GMC = General Motors Corporation〔美〕通用汽车公司。

G.M.C. = General Medical Council〔英〕全国医学总会。

Gmc, **Gmc.** = Germanic.

GMT = Greenwich mean time 格林威治平时〔*cf*. GCT〕。

gnar, **gnarr** [nɑː; nɑr] *vi*. (***-rr-***)〔罕〕咆哮，吼（= gnarl）。

gnarl[1] [nɑːl; nɑrl] **I** *n*. （木材的）节，瘤。**II** *vt*. **1.** 扭，拗。**2.** 使有节。— *vi*. 生节。

gnarl[2] [nɑːl; nɑrl] *vi*. = gnar(r)。

gnarl·y [ˈnɑːli; ˋnɑrlɪ], **gnarled** [nɑːld; nɑrld] *a*. **1.** 节

多的,瘤多的,扭曲的。2. 脾气乖僻的。**-i·ness** *n*.

gnash [næʃ; næʃ] **I** *vt*. 切齿,咬(牙)啮。～ *one's teeth* 咬牙切齿。— *vi*. (由于愤怒或痛苦而)咬牙。**II** *n*. 咬。

gnat [næt; næt] *n*. 1. 〔英〕蚊子;咬人的小昆虫。2. 小烦扰,琐碎的事。～*'s heel* 〔美〕极少量的。～*'s whistle* 〔美〕好东西。*strain at a ～ and swallow a camel* 小事拘谨而大事糊涂,见小不见大。～**-robot** 微型医用机器人〔可用于体内探查和施行手术〕。～**-strainer** 见小不见大的人。

gnath·ic [ˈnæθik; ˋnæθɪk] *a*. 颚的,颌的。～ **index** 颌〔颚〕指数〔鼻沟至后脑壳中缝的距离与后脑壳中缝至齿中缝的距离之比〕。

gnath·ism [ˈnæθizəm; ˋnæθɪzəm] *n*. 颌〔颚〕部突出。

gna·thite [ˈneiθait, ˈnæθait; ˋneθaɪt, ˋnæθaɪt] *n*. 颌〔颚〕形附器,口器。

gna·th·i·tis [næˈθaitis; næˋθaɪtɪs] *n*. 【医】颌炎。

gna·thon·ic [næˈθɔnik; næˋθɑnɪk] *a*. 〔罕〕讨好的,奉承的。

gnaw [nɔː; nɔ] *vt*. (～*ed*; ～*ed*, *gnawn*) 1. 咬,啃;咬断。2. 使腐蚀;侵蚀;消耗。3. 使苦恼,折磨。— *vi*. 1. 咬,齿啃 (*at*; *into*)。2. 侵蚀,消耗。3. 折磨,苦恼。*Anxiety and distress ～ed at his heart*. 焦虑和烦恼使他痛苦。～ **away** [**off**] 咬去。～ **through** 咬断,咬穿。**-er** *n*. 咬者,蚀坏者,啮齿类动物。

gnaw·ing [ˈnɔːiŋ; ˋnɔɪŋ] **I** *n*. 咬,不断的苦痛。**II** *a*. 咬的;使人苦恼的。*a ～ animal* 啮齿动物。**-ly** *ad*.

GND = ground 地;接地。

gneiss [nais; naɪs] *n*. 【地】片麻岩。**-ic, -y** *a*.

gneiss·oid [ˈnaisɔid; ˋnaɪsɔɪd] *a*. 像片麻岩的,片麻岩状的。

gneiss·ose [ˈnaisəus; ˋnaɪsos] *a*. 片麻岩的。

GNI = gross national income 国民总收入。

gnoc·chi [ˈnɔkiː, ˈnɔː-, It. ˈnjəukkiː; ˋnɑki, ˋnɔ-, It. ˋnjokki] *n*. 形状不一的饺子[洋芋]〔蘸酱油吃〕。

gnome[1] [nəum; nom] *n*. 格言。

gnome[2] [nəum; nom] *n*. 1. (传说中居于地下保护财宝和矿藏的)地精,土地神。2. 矮子,侏儒。

gno·mic(al) [ˈnəumik(əl); ˋnomɪk(əl)] *a*. 1. 格言的,用格言的,爱写格言诗的。2. 【语法】(时态)表示永恒真理的。*gnomic poetry* (希腊的)箴言诗。**-mi·cal·ly** *ad*.

gnom·ish [ˈnəumiʃ; ˋnomɪʃ] *a*. 地精的,地精似的;好戏耍的。

gno·mon [ˈnəumɔn; ˋnomɑn] *n*. 1. (日晷的)晷针,指时针。2. 【数】磬折形〔自平行四边形的一角截去一较小平行四边形后的图形〕。

gno·mon·ic [nəuˈmɔnik; noˋmɑnɪk] *a*. 1. 指时针的。2. 【天】用日晷仪测时的。3. 【数】磬折形的。～ **projection** [**chart**] 心射切面投影(图)。

gno·mon·ics [nəuˈmɔniks; noˋmɑnɪks] *n*. 〔用作单数〕日晷测时学;日晷制造法。

gno·sis [ˈnəusis; ˋnosɪs] *n*. 【宗】灵知,神秘的直觉。

Gnos·tic [ˈnɔstik; ˋnɑstɪk] **I** *a*. 1. (相信神秘直觉说的早期基督教)诺斯替教派的,诺斯替派教徒的。2. 〔g-〕有灵知的;聪明的。**II** *n*. 诺斯替教徒。

Gnos·ti·cism [ˈnɔstisizəm; ˋnɑstɪsɪzəm] *n*. 【宗史】诺斯替教。

GNP = gross national product 国民生产总值[毛额]。

G.N.R. = Great Northern Railway 〔美〕大北铁路。

gnu [nuː, njuː; nu, nju] *n*. (*pl*. ～*s*, 〔集合词〕～) 【动】牛羚,角马。

GO = General Orders 【军】一般命令;卫兵守则。

go [gəu; go] **I** *vi*. (*went* [went; wɛnt]; *gone* [gɔn; gɑn]; 第二人称单数现在式〔古〕 *go·est* [ˈgəuist; ˋgoɪst]; 第三人称单数现在式 *goes* [gəuz; goz], 〔古〕 *go·eth* [ˈgəuiθ; ˋgoɪθ]) 〔*cf*. going 及 gone〕 1. 去,走;旅行;前进。～ *abroad* 出国。～ *a walk* 去散步。～ *by train* [*car*, *air*, *water*] 乘火车[汽车,飞机,船]去。～ *on foot* 走路去。～ *on a journey* 去旅行。～ *the same way* 向同一方向走。～ *hunting* [*swimming*, *shopping*, *fishing*, *etc*.] 打猎[游泳、买东西、钓鱼等]去。*Who ～es* (*there*)? 〔哨兵喝问用语〕(是)谁? *Go*. (赛跑口令)跑! ～ *the shortest way* 走捷径。*You may ～ further and fare worse*. 〔谚〕走得越远,情形越坏。2. 离去,离开;死;垮,坏;放弃,停止存在,消失。*It is really time for us to ～*. 我们该走了。*All hope is gone*. 一切希望都完了。*How goes the time*? 什么时候了? *Poor Tom is gone*. 可怜的汤姆死了。*First the sails and then the masts went*. 先是帆坏了,随后桅杆也断了。*The meat is ～ing*. 肉要坏了。*The bank may ～ any day*. 这家银行随时可能倒闭。*His sight is going*. 他的眼力不行了。*These slums have to ～*. 这些贫民窟必须拆除。3. 处于…状态;处于一般的状况。～ *armed* 携带武器,武装着。～ *hungry* 挨饿。～ *in rags* 衣衫褴褛。*She has gone six months with child*. 她怀孕六个月了。*forget how the song goes* 忘记歌是怎样唱的。*as things ～* 从一般情况来看。4. 流传,流行;通用。*as the saying ～es* 像俗话说的那样。*The story ～es that* 据说…。*It ～es as follows* 如下所说。*as* [*so*] *far as it ～es* 就现在来说。*The sovereign ～es throughout the British Isles*. 英镑在英伦诸岛通用。5. 发生;进展;变为,成为。*What's ～ing on*? 发生了什么事? *All things went well*. 一切都好。*How are things ～ing*? 形势怎么样了? ～ *mad* 发狂。～ *blind* 变瞎。～ *to pieces* 破碎,垮台。6. 运转,运行;起作用;走动着。*The clock does not ～*. 钟不走了。*The car ～es by electricity*. 这车是用电开动的。*Her tongue ～es nineteen to the dozen*. 她喋喋不休说个没完。7. 遵照…行动 (*by*)。*a good rule to ～ by* 应该遵守的良好规则。*What he says ～es*. 他说话算数。8. 放置,装入,纳入;(算术的)除得。*Where are the forks to ～*? 叉子放在哪里? *The boots will not ～ into the bag*. 靴子装不进袋里去。*Six into twelve ～es twice*. 六除十二得二。*Six into five won't ～*. 六除五不能除。9. 响,发音;(钟)报点。～ *bang* [*crack*] 破裂[爆裂],砰[啪]地响。*It has just gone six*. 才敲过六点钟。10. (时间)消逝,过去,(距离)走过,经过。*The evening went pleasantly enough*. 晚上过得很愉快。*ten days to ～ before Easter* 还有十天到复活节。*There are eight miles to ～*. 还有八英里。11. 归,落入…手。*The prize went to his rival*. 奖品落入对方手中去了。12. 诉诸。～ *to war* 诉诸武力,发动战争。～ *to law* 诉诸法律,起诉。13. 总共,合成。*How many ounces ～ to the pound*? 多少英两是一磅? *qualities that ～ to make a hero* 有助于造就一个英雄的品质。14. 通到,到达,延伸至。*The road ～es to Rome*. 这条路通罗马。*His land ～es almost to the river*. 他的田几乎一直延伸到河边。*His knowledge fails to ～ very deep*. 他的知识不很精深。15. 花费。*His spare money ～es on books*. 他多余的钱都花在买书上。16. 卖,卖得(…价)。*The house went cheap*. 这房子卖得很便宜。*The eggs went for 3s. a dozen*. 鸡蛋一打卖三先令。17. 相配;(诗、歌词)有节奏;(与曲调)相配 (*to*)。18. 称为,叫做;冒(名)。*He ～es by a name of Henry*. 他名叫亨利。～ *under a false name* 用假名。19. 有,备有〔主用现在分词形式〕。*There's sure to be some sort of dinner ～ing*. 肯定会有一顿饭吃吃的。20. 招惹。*Don't ～ to trouble*. 不要惹麻烦。21. 〔用以加强否定的命令语气〕。*Don't ～ and make a fool of yourself*. 别去干蠢事。22. 〔美方〕想。*I didn't ～ to do it*. 我没有想做那样的事。23. 〔用进行时态,后接不定式〕将要,打算。*It's ～ing to rain*. 快要下雨了。*We're ～ing to call a meeting to discuss it*. 我们准备开会讨论一下。*as* [*so*] *far as it ～es* 就现状来说,就其本身而言。～ *a long way in* [*towards*] (*doing sth*.) 大有效力,大大有用处 (*The president's statement* *went a long way towards reassuring the nation*. 总统的话在提高全国人民的信心方面收效甚大)。～ **about** 1. 四处走动,走来走去。2. 着手(工作)。3. (谣言等)流传。4.【海】掉转船头;【军】折回 (～ *about to do* 打算做。*Go about your business*! 走开,干你的事去! *A story is ～ing about that ....* 风传…)。～ **after** 追求。～ **against** 违背,反对;不利于 (*The case went against him*. 这案子作出了对他不利的裁决)。～ **ahead** 继续前进,取得进展。～ **all lengths** 干到底。～ **all out** = ～ **all-out** 全力以赴,鼓足干劲。～ **along** 前进。～ **along with** 陪[随]…一起去;赞同,同意。**Go along with you**! 〔口〕去你的! ～ **and ...** 〔口〕去…,糊里糊涂地…(*I have gone and done it*. 我糊里糊涂就那样做了。*Go and be miserable*! 去受罪吧!)。～ **around** 〔美〕= ～ round. ～ **at** 〔口〕扑过去,攻击;兴冲冲开始干(～ *at it hammer and tongs* 大干而特干)。～ **away** 离开;带走,拐逃 (*with*)。～ **back** 1. 回来;追溯到 (*to*);回顾。2. 走下坡路(*The old tree is ～ing back*. 这棵老树不行了)。～ **back of** 〔美口〕调查,研究。～ **back on** [**from**, **upon**] 破坏,背(约),背叛;〔美〕遗弃。～ **bad** (食品、蛋等)坏掉。～ **before** 走在前面;居先,超过。～ **behind** 1. 调查,摸底;进一步斟酌。2. 亏本。～ **between** 做中间人。～ **beyond** 超出,越过。～ **blooey** 爆炸;出毛病。～ **by** 1. 走过,过去。2. 以…为根据(作判断)。3. 〔美〕顺道访问。4. 受…所控制。5. 称为,名叫(*as time goes by* 随着时间的过去。*let an opportunity ～ by* 放过机会。*Years have gone by*. 经过多年。*I ～ by what I hear*. 我依据听到的作判断)。～ **down** 1. 下去,(价格等)下跌;(船只)沉没,(飞机)坠落,(日,月)落下;继续到 (*to*);(风、浪等)平静下来;(潮、肿等)减退,消退。2. 被记下,被载入。3. 倒下,垮台,破产。4. 〔口〕咽下;被接受,受欢迎 (*with*)。5. (英大学)退学,离校(～ *down in history as a hero* 作为英雄留名史册。*The pill won't ～ down*. 这药丸无法下咽。*The film went down well with the audience*. 影片大受观众欢迎)。～ **down hill** 走下坡路。～ **dry** 〔美〕禁酒。～ **easy** 慢慢来,不紧张。～ **far** 价值大,效力大;成功,大有前途。～ **far toward**(**s**)大大有助于。～ **flat out** 全力以赴,鼓足干劲。～ **flooey** = ～ blooey. ～ **flop** 失败。～ **for** 1. 去拿,去找,去喊,去请,尽力求得,2. 〔美〕拥护,支持,偏袒。3. 被认为,适用于。4. 〔口〕猛烈攻击,袭击;【剧】批评 (*It ～es for you too*. 这对你也是适用的。*A dog went for him*. 狗向他冲了过来。～ *for a doctor* 去请医生。～ *for each other in the papers* 在报上互相攻讦)。～ **for little** 被认为不大有用。～ **for much** [**nothing**] 被认为大有用处[毫无用处]。～ **forth** 1. 出发。2. 发布;发表。～ **forward** 1. 前进。2. 发生。～ **free** 被释放;被解放。～ **fut** [**phut**] 〔俚〕(车胎等)破裂,泄气;失败,成泡影。～ **glimmering** 〔口〕逐渐消灭,化为乌有。～ **gold**(唱片)上金榜;成为金榜唱片。～ **halves** [**shares**] 彼此一半,平分。～ **hang** 不再被关心,被忘却。～ **hard with sb**. 使某人为难。～ **home** 1. 回家。2. 击中,命中。～ **ill** (事态)恶化。～ **ill with** 对…不利。～ **in** 1. 进入;放得进;参加。2. (纸牌赌博中)开价。3. 天体被云遮盖。4. (钱)用于。5. (板球战等)开始一局比赛。～ **in at** 〔口〕激烈打击。～ **in for** 〔口〕赞成,支持;寻求,追求,沉迷在…;参加(～ *in for an examination* 参加考试。～ *in for swimming* 热爱游泳。～ *in for technical innovations* 搞技术革新)。～ **in with** 参加,加入。**Going**! **Going**! **Gone**! 要卖了! 要卖了! 卖掉了! 〔拍卖用语〕。～ **into** 1. (门等)通着;进入。2. 加入;参与。3. 查究。4. 成为。5. 说到,涉及。6. 穿…的服装,(尤指)穿(孝)。7. 采取…态度,进入…状态(～ *into action* 行动起来。～ *into the army* 参军。～ *into details* 深入细节。～ *into mourning* 戴孝。～ *into production* 投入生产。～ *into a rage* 大发雷霆)。～ **it** 〔口〕1. 使劲儿干,莽撞。2. 放荡;挥霍。～ **it alone** 单干。～ **it blind** 〔口〕瞎干。～ **it strong on sth**. 热烈赞许某事物。～ **near to do sth**. 几乎做某事。～ **off** 1. 经过,进行得 (*well*; *badly*)。2. (枪)打出,(炸弹)爆炸,(话等)冒出。3. 〔口〕(食物)变坏。4. 睡着,昏过去。5. 逃走,离去,走掉;(演员)退场,下。6. 〔口〕(女儿)出嫁;渐渐忘怀;死;卖掉 (*Her voice is ～ing off*. 她的嗓子坏了。～ *off into a faint* 昏过去。～ *off into a fit of laughter* 哄然大笑。～ *off into wild flights of fancy* 开始胡思乱想。～ *off at high prices* 高价卖出)。～ **off with** 拿走,抢走,拐走。～ **on** 1. 往前走;继续…下去 (*with*; *doing*);日子过得(*well*, *badly* 等)。2. 〔口〕胡作非为(*shamefully* 等)。3. 责骂 (*at*)。4. 出场,上台。5. 可穿用。6. 发生。7. 〔口〕接近。8. 依据。9. 受救济(*He is four going on five*. 他四岁多快五岁了。*Go on with your work*. 接着干下去。～ *on raining all day* 雨整天下个不停。～ *on to say* 接着说。*These gloves won't ～ on*. 手套戴不上去)。**Go on**! 〔口〕接下去! 〔反〕别胡说啦! ～ **on for** 接近。～ **out** 1. 出去,出国,(妇女)离家外出工作。2. (火、灯)熄,灭。3. 退职,辞职;下台;不再流行,(衣着式样等)过时。4. 出版。5. (时间)过去。6. 出去交际。7. 罢工。8. 〔美〕垮下,倒塌。9. 〔美〕参加选拔。10. 向往,充满同情(～ *out of one's mind* 发狂。～ *out of print* 绝版)。～ **out for** 拚命取得。～ **over** 1. 越过,渡过;转向 (*to*),改变立场。2. 温习,仔细检查。3. (车)翻倒。4. 延期。5. 〔美口〕很受欢迎,成功。6. 走完。～ **over big** 〔美口〕大受欢迎,大成功。～ **partners** 共同出资。～ **round** 1. 迂回走,四处走动。2. (传食物等)使人人分到。3. 顺便访问。4. (带子)长得够绕一圈;足够分配。～ **slow** 慢慢走,怠工。～ **so far as to say it** = ～ **the length of saying it** 甚至说那样的话。～ **some** 〔美口〕做了不少,得了不少。～ (**sb**.) **one better** 〔美俚〕胜过某人。～ **steady** 〔美俚〕成为关系相当确定的情侣。～ **the whole hog** [**figure**] 全力以赴。～ **through** 1. 通过,经过。2. 修毕,受(考试等);经历,忍受。3. 用光,荡尽。4. (书)突破(第…版)。5. 完成,贯彻 (*with*)。6. 仔细检查。**Go to**! 〔古〕去你的! ～ **to** 1. 相当于。2. 付出。～ **to bat for** 〔美口〕为人辩护判决。～ **together** 陪同,相配;〔口〕恋爱。～ **too far** 过火,走极端。～ **under** 沉没;没落,破产;失败,屈服;〔美俚〕死。～ **up** 1. 上升;〔英〕上大学,上城市去;腾贵;烧起来;爆炸。2. 〔美〕破产;死;〔美〕失败;走向舞台正面的里头。～ **uphill** 走上坡路。～ **upon** 1. 据…来判断(行动)。2. 着手。～ **west** 1. 死,上西天。2. (钱)完了。～ **with** 1. 陪…同行,同…一致,同…调和;跟…谈恋爱。2. 带有。3. 领会,了解。4. 〔主美〕对付,处理。～ **without** 缺少;没有…而忍受过去。～ **without saying** 不待说。～ **wrong** 1. 走错路,误入歧途。2. 出毛病,失败。**Here ～es**. 瞧,开始了。**leave ～ of** 松手放开。**let ～** 1. 松手,放开。2. 释放。3. 解雇。4. 放弃;忘记。**let ～ with** 尽情地(说、叫喊等)。**let oneself ～** 发脾气。**There you ～ again**. 你这一套又来了。**What ～es**? 〔美俚〕发生了什么事? — **vt**. 〔口〕1. 忍受;享受;买得走〔常用于否定结构〕。2. 〔口〕打赌,叫牌,出价。3. 承担责任。4. 生产。*I will ～ you a shilling*. 我和你赌一个先令吧。*I can't ～ her music*. 她的音乐我听不下去。*I can't ～ the price*. 我出不起这价钱。**II n**. (*pl*. ～**es**) 1. 去,进行。2. 〔口〕事情〔特指困难事情〕,难关,约定的事情。3. 〔the ～〕时髦。4. 〔口〕精神,精力。5. 〔口〕成功。6. 拳击比赛;比赛。7. 〔口〕(酒的)一杯;(食物的)一份。8. 试一下;干一下;一口气。9. (英大学)学位考试。*a capital ～* 妙极了。*first ～* 〔口〕首先。*Here's a ～*! = *What a ～*! 这事真难办! *a near ～* 侥幸逃脱难关。*a jolly* [*pretty*, *queer*, *rum*] ～怪事。*It's no ～*. 〔口〕不行,没希望。*It is a ～*. 好吧,就这样决定。*He's plenty of ～ in him*. 他劲头十足。*itch to have a ～ at it* 跃跃欲试。**at** [**in**] **one ～** 一口气。**be all** [**quite**] **the ～** 〔口〕风行一时。**be full of ～** 精力

充沛。*come and* ～ 来往。*from the word* ～〔美口〕从一开始。*full of* ～ 精神旺盛。*make a* ～ *of it*〔美〕成功,干好。*on* [*upon*] *the* ～ 1. 在进行,在活动;刚要动身。2. 衰微。3. 有醉意。*the little* [*great*] ～(剑桥大学)学士学位预[正]考。**III** *a*. 好的,运行良好的;〔美口〕一切正常的,可以开始的;【宇航】可随时发射的。**IV** *int*. (赛跑口令)跑。*On your mark! Get set! Go!* 各就各位! 预备! 跑! ～ **condition** 【宇】待飞,待发。～**-no-**～ *n*. (太空飞船等)飞或不飞的最后决定;事情的最后决定。～ **side** 【机】通过端。

Go·a [ˈgəuə; ˋgoə] *n*. 果阿〔印度一地区〕。

go·a [ˈgəuə; ˋgoə] *n*. 【动】藏原羚,藏黄羊(*Procapra picticaudata*)〔产于我国西藏的一种棕灰色的长毛小羚羊〕。～ **powder** (采自巴西 araroba 树上的)苛柸粉〔对皮肤病有特效〕。

goad [gəud; god] **I** *n*. 1. (赶家畜用的)刺棒。2. 使痛苦[烦恼]之物;激励物,刺激物。**II** *vt*. 1. 用刺棒驱赶(家畜)。2. 激励,刺激,煽动;策动;唆使。～ *sb. to do* [*into doing*] *sth*. 唆使某人做某事。～ *sb. to* [*into*] *fury* 使某人发怒。

goaf [gəuf; gof] *n*. = gob 2.

go-a·head [ˈgəuəˌhed; ˋgoəˏhɛd] **I** *a*. 1. 〔美口〕前进着的;进取的;有冒险精神的。2. 可通行的。*a vigorous* ～ *company* 一个兴旺发达的公司。～ *signal* 放行信号。**II** *n*. 1. 许可,放行信号。2. 进取心;活力,精力。

goal [gəul; gol] *n*. 1. (赛跑等的)终点。2. (足球等运动的)球门;守门员。3. 门球;门球得分。4. 目的,目标;目的地。*get* [*kick, make, score*] *a* ～ 打进一个门球,得一分。*win by two* ～*s* 以两球获胜。*one's* ～ *in life* 人生目的。*move* [*shift*] *the* ～*s* 中途改变目标,出尔反尔。～**-directed** *a*. 有目的的,有用意的。～**keeper** (足球等运动的)守门员。～ **line** (足球等运动的)门线。～**-line stand** 负隅顽抗。～**-mouth** (足球等运动的)球门区。～ **post** (足球等运动的)门柱。～ **post mast** 【船】龙门架桅。～**tender** = ～keeper.

goal·ee, goa·lie [ˈgəuli; ˋgolɪ] *n*. 〔口〕= goalkeeper.

goal·tend·ing [ˈgəulˌtendiŋ; ˋgolˏtɛndɪŋ] *n*. 1. (足球等的)守门。2. (趁球快进入对方篮筐时所作的)扰乱投篮。

go-a·round [ˈgəu-əˌraund; ˋgo-əˏraund] *n*. 1. 回合;激烈争论。2. 躲闪,拖延。3. 回旋。

go-as-you-please [ˈgəuəzjuˈpliːz; ˋgoəzjuˋpliz] *a*. 无拘束的,随意的。

goat [gəut; got] *n*. 1. 【动】山羊。2. 〔the G-〕【天】山羊座;摩羯宫。3. 坏人(*opp*. sheep);色鬼。4. 〔俚〕替罪羊,牺牲品。5. 【铁路】道岔扳子,转辙机。*act* [*play*] *the* (*giddy*) ～ 胡闹。*get sb.'s* ～ 使人发怒,使人焦急,触怒。*ride the* ～ 加入秘密团体。*separate the sheep from the* ～*s* 把好人和坏人区别开。～ **antelope** 【动】山羚羊〔特性介于山羊和羚羊之间的几种动物,如亚洲的苏门羊和斑羚〕。～**god** 【希神】(人身羊足、头上有角的)畜牧神,潘神 = Pan. ～**herd** 牧山羊人。～**skin** 山羊皮;山羊皮制品,羊皮囊。～**sucker** 【动】夜鹰。～**'s wool** 不存在的东西。**-ish** *a*. 1. 山羊似的。2. 好色的,淫荡的。

goat·ee [gəuˈtiː; goˋti] *n*. 山羊胡子。

goat·fish [ˌgəutˈfiʃ; ˏgotˋfɪʃ] *n*. (*pl*. ～, ～*es*) 【动】羊鱼科(*Mullidae*)鱼;羊鱼。

goat·ling [ˈgəutliŋ; ˋgotlɪŋ] *n*. (1—2 岁的)小山羊。

goats·beard [ˈgəutsˌbiəd; ˋgotsˏbɪəd] *n*. 【植】1. 绥升麻。2. 波罗门参属(*Tragopogon*)植物。

goat's-rue [ˈgəutsˌruː; ˋgotsˏru] *n*. 【植】1. 美洲灰叶(*Tephrosia virginiana*)。2. 山羊豆(*Galega officinalis*)。

goat·y [ˈgəuti; ˋgotɪ] *a*. = goatish.

gob[1] [gɔb; gɑb] **I** *n*. 1. 黏块[如痰块]。2. 【矿】(填废坑用的)矿渣;矿内废石;采空区。3. 〔*pl*.〕许多,大量。**II** *vi*. 吐;吐痰。

gob[2] [gɔb; gɑb] *n*. 〔俚〕嘴。～**-stopper** 棒棒糖,大块硬糖。

gob[3] [gɔb; gɑb] *n*. 〔美俚〕水兵。

go·ban(g) [gəuˈbæŋ; goˋbæŋ] *n*. (日本用围棋盘下的)五子棋。

gob·bet [ˈgɔbit; ˋgɑbɪt] *n*. 1. 〔古〕一片,一块〔尤指生肉或食物〕;一堆。2. 一口(食物)。3. (尤指在考试中供考生翻译或评论而摘录的)片段引文;乐章的片断。

gob·ble[1] [ˈgɔbl; ˋgɑbl] *vt*., *vi*. 1. 狼吞虎咽。2. 〔美俚〕急急抓住;任意花完(*up*)。3. 如饥似渴地阅读(*up*)。**-r** *n*. 狼吞虎咽的人。

gob·ble[2] [ˈgɔbl, ˈgɑbl] **I** *vi*. 发出火鸡般的咯咯叫声。**II** *n*. (火鸡的)咯咯声。**-r** *n*. 公火鸡。

gob·ble·dy·gook [ˈgɔbldiˈguk; ˋgɑbldɪˋguk] *n*. 〔俚〕浮夸,冗繁而费解的语言[文章];官腔;官样文章(= gobbledegook)。

Gob·e·lin [ˈgəubəlin; ˋgobəlɪn] **I** *a*. 巴黎哥白林染织厂制双面挂毯的。**II** *n*. 哥白林厂制壁饰花毯。*the* ～ *tapestry* 壁饰花毡。～ **blue** 暗青绿色。

gobe·mouche [gəubˈmuːʃ; gobˋmuʃ] *n*. (*pl*. ～*s* [-muːʃ; -muʃ])〔F.〕轻信小道消息的人。

go-be·tween [ˈgəubiˌtwiːn; ˋgobɪˏtwin] *n*. 1. 掮客,媒人,中间人。2. 【电】连接杆,连接环,中间节,中间网路。

Go·bi [ˈgəubi; ˋgobɪ] *n*. 〔the ～〕戈壁沙漠,戈壁滩。

go·bi·oid [ˈgəubiːˌɔid; ˋgobɪˏɔɪd] **I** *a*. 【动】1. 虾虎鱼的。2. 似虾虎鱼的。**II** *n*. 虾虎鱼。

gob·let [ˈgɔblit; ˋgɑblɪt] *n*. 高脚杯;〔诗〕酒杯。～ **cells** 【医】杯状细胞。

gob·lin [ˈgɔblin; ˋgɑblɪn] *n*. 妖魔,恶鬼。**-ry** *n*. 〔集合词〕鬼怪集团。

go·bo [ˈgəubəu; ˋgobo] *n*. (*pl*. ～*s*, ～*es*) 1. (摄影机的)透视遮光片,(摄影机镜头周围的)遮光黑布。2. 麦克风纯音片,麦克风话筒上排除杂音的遮布。

go·boon [gɔˈbuːn; gɑˋbun] *n*. 〔俚〕痰盂。

go·by [ˈgəubi; ˋgobɪ] *n*. (*pl*. **-bies**, 〔集合词〕～) 【动】(虾虎鱼科的)刺鳍鱼,刺虾虎鱼。

go-by [ˈgəubai; ˋgobaɪ] *n*. 〔口〕假装不见;不理。*give sb. the* ～ 对某人冷淡。

GOC, G.O.C. = 1. Gulf Oil Company〔美〕海湾石油公司。2. Government of Congo 刚果政府。3. Ground Observer Corps〔美〕地面观察队(勤务)。

GOC(inC), G.O.C.(-in-C.) = General Officer Commanding(-in-Chief) 总指挥官。

go-cart [ˈgəukɑːt; ˋgokɑrt] *n*. 1. 小儿学步车;(折叠式)婴儿轻便车。2. 手推车。3. 早期的轻便马车。4. 微型竞赛汽车(= kart)。

god [gɔd; gɑd] *n*. 1. 〔G-〕上帝,造物主。2. 〔有时作 G-〕神;男神(*opp*. goddess)。3. 神像,偶像;神化的人[物];被极度崇敬的人[物]。4. 〔*pl*.〕戏院顶层楼座观众。*G- helps those who help themselves*. 〔谚〕自助者神助之。*He that serves G- for money will serve the devil for better wages*. 〔谚〕为钱侍奉上帝,为更多的钱就会给魔鬼卖力。*When G- would destroy a man he first makes him mad*. 〔谚〕上帝毁灭人,先使他发狂。*Whom the* ～*s love die young*. 〔谚〕好人寿不长。*a feast for the* ～*s* 丰盛的酒席。*a sight for the* ～*s* 壮观。*a* (*little*) *tin* ～ 受到过分尊敬的人,自命不凡的人。*act of G-* 【法】天灾,不可抗力。*By* (*my*) *G-*! 的的确确。*for God's sake* 看在上帝面上。*G-! = Good G-! Great G-! My G-! Oh, G-!* 天啊! 啊呀! *Thank G-! = G- be thanked!* 幸亏! 谢天谢地! *G- bless me* [*my life, my soul, you, etc.*]! 〔表示惊讶〕啊呀! 喔唷! 吓我一跳。*G- bless you* [*him*]! 愿上帝保佑你[他]! *G- damn you!* 天杀的! 该死的! *G- forbid!* 上天不容! *G- forfend!* 上天不容,决无此事。～ *from the machine* 意外的救星〔源出古希腊戏剧中经常以机关推出的扮天神的角色〕。*G- grant* …! 但愿…! *G- help* *him*! 唉,真可怜! ***G- knows when*** [***where, why, what***] 天晓得,谁也不晓得。***G- knows*** (*that*) 确确实实…。***G- speed you***! 祝你一路平安! ***G- willing*** 如果情形允许的话。***G- wot*** 〔古〕天知道。***So help me G-***! 的的确确! 老天爷在上,决无半点假话! ***the ~ of day*** 太阳神 (Apollo, Phoebus)。***the ~ of fire*** 火神 (Vulcan)。***the ~ of heaven*** 天神 (Zeus, Jupiter)。***the ~ of hell*** 地狱神 (Pluto)。***the G- of Host*** 【圣】万军之主耶和华。***the ~ of love*** 爱神 (Cupid = the blind ~)。***the ~ of marriage*** 月下老人 (Hymen)。***the ~ of the sea*** 海神 (Poseidon, Neptune)。***the ~ of war*** 战神 (Ares, Mars)。***the ~ of wine*** 酒神 (Bacchus, Dionysus)。***the ~ of this world*** 魔王。***make a ~ of one's belly*** 一味追求吃喝。***on God's earth*** 世界上。***under ~*** 就人间而言。***with ~*** 和上帝一块;死了。***wrestle with G-*** 热忱祈祷。***Ye ~s*** (***and little fishes***)! 〔口〕怎么搞的! **II** ***vt***. 神化,把…崇拜为神。~ *it* 做神,俨然以神自居。~**-awful** ***a***. 非常可怕的,可憎的。~ **booster** 〔美俚〕牧师。~**box** 〔美俚〕教堂,礼拜堂。~**child** 教子,教女。~**daughter** 教女。~**father** **1**. ***n***. 教父;洗礼时名字被用以命名的人。**2**. ***vt***. 作…的教父。~**-fearing** ***a***. 敬神的,虔敬的。~**-forsaken** ***a***. 为神所抛弃的,堕落的,凄凉的,邪恶的,倒霉的。~**given** ***a***. **1**. 天赐的。**2**. 极受欢迎的;恰当的;应时的。~**head** 神性;神格;神。**Godman** 基督;神人。~**mother** 教母。~ **parent** 教父母。**God's acre** 墓地〔尤指教堂墓地〕。**God's book** 《圣经》。**God's (own) country** 天府之邦,乐土,故乡,祖国。**God's earth** 全世界。~**send** 天赐;意外得来的所需之物。**God's foolstool** 〔口〕大地,地。**God's gift** 天赐。**God's image** 人体。~**son** 教子。~**speed** 成功,幸运;天惠(*bid sb. ~ speed* 祝某人成功;祝某人一路平安)。**God's plenty** [**quantity**] 〔口〕许多,丰盛。**God's truth** 绝对真理。**-hood** ***n***. 神性,神格。**-less** ***a***. **1**. 没有神的。**2**. 不敬神的,不信神的。**3**. 邪恶的。**-like** ***a***. 神似的,上帝般的;庄严的;神圣的。**-ship** ***n***. 神道,神性,神位,神,上帝。**-ward(s)** ***ad***. 向神,对神。

god·damn(ed) [ˈgɔdˈdæm(*d*); ˋgɑdˋdæm(*d*)] ***a***. **1**. 该死的,讨厌的。**2**. 十足的,完全的。

God·dard [ˈgɔdəːd, ˈgɔdɑːd; ˋgɑdɚd, ˋgɑdɑrd] ***n***. 戈达德〔姓氏〕。

god·dess [ˈgɔdis; ˋgɑdɪs] ***n***. **1**. 女神。**2**. 非凡的女子;绝世美女。*the ~ of corn* 司五谷的女神 (Demeter, Ceres)。*the ~ of heaven* 天后,天之女神 (Hera, Juno)。*the ~ of hell* 地狱的女神 (Persephone, Proserpine)。*the ~ of love* 爱的女神 (Aphrodite, Venus)。*the ~ of the moon* 月的女神 (Artemis, Diana)。*the ~ of war* 战争的女神 (Bellona)。*the ~ of wisdom* 智慧的女神 (Athena, Minerva)。

go·det [ˌgəuˈdet; ˏgoˋdɛt] ***n***. 〔法〕(填补、加固或放大衣服的)三角形布料。

go·de·ti·a [gəuˈdiːʃə; goˋdiʃə] ***n***. 【植】高代花。

go-dev·il [ˈgəudevl; ˋgodɛvl̩] ***n***. **1**. 拖木橇,运石车。**2**. 刮管器,冲棍。**3**. 油井爆破器,坠撞器。

god·fa·ther [ˈgɔdˌfɑːðə; ˋgɑdˏfɑðə] **I** ***n***. **1**. 教父。**2**. 监护人。**3**. 〔美俚〕(黑手党下属组织的)首领。**II** ***vt***. 当…的教父;作…的监护人。

God·frey [ˈgɔdfri; ˋgɑdfrɪ] ***n***. 戈弗雷〔男子名〕。

god·less [ˈgɔdlis; ˋgɑdlɪs] ***a***. **1**. 没有神的。**2**. 不信神的,不虔诚的。**3**. 邪恶的。**-ly** ***ad***. **-ness** ***n***.

god·like [ˈgɔdlaik; ˋgɑdlaɪk] ***a***. 如神的,上帝般的;神圣的,庄严的。

god·ling [ˈgɔdliŋ; ˋgɑdlɪŋ] ***n***. 【宗】小神。

god·ly [ˈgɔdli; ˋgɑdlɪ] ***a***. 敬神的,信神的;〔古〕神圣的;虔诚的。*the ~* 〔讽〕善男信女。**-li·ness** ***n***.

God·man [ˈgɔdmən; ˋgɑdmən] ***n***. 戈德曼〔姓氏〕。

Go·dol·phin [gəˈdɔlfin; gəˋdɑlfɪn] ***n***. 戈多尔芬〔姓氏〕。

go·down [ˈgəudaun; ˋgodaʊn] ***n***. (印度、菲律宾等地的)仓库。

God·win [ˈgɔdwin; ˋgɑdwɪn] ***n***. 戈德温〔姓氏〕。

god·wit [ˈgɔdwit; ˋgɑdwɪt] ***n***. 【动】(塍鹬属中的)长嘴涉水鸟。

go·er [ˈgəuə; ˋgoɚ] ***n***. **1**. 去的人;行人,路人。**2**. 走动的人[车,马,钟表等]。**3**. 常去…的人〔常作 *comb. f*.〕。*a film ~* 经常看电影的人。*comers and ~s* 来往的人。*a good* [*poor*] ~ 走得好[不好]的马[钟等]。

Goe·the [ˈgəːtə; ˋgɝtə], **Johann Wolfgang von.** 约翰·沃尔夫冈·歌德〔1749—1832,德国诗人、剧作家、小说家、哲学家〕。

Goe·the·an, Goe·thi·an [ˈgəːtiən; ˋgɝtɪən] **I** ***a***. 歌德的,歌德派的,歌德风格的。**II** ***n***. 歌德崇拜者。

goe·thite [ˈgəuθait, ˈgəːtait; ˋgoθaɪt, ˋgɝtaɪt] ***n***. 【矿】针铁矿。

gof·fer, go·fer [ˈgəufə; ˋgofɚ] **I** ***n***. **1**. (衣服等的)襞,皱褶。**2**. 烫皱褶用的烫斗。**II** ***vt***. 在…上作皱褶,在…上作出波纹,作出浮花。*~ed cloth* 轧纹布,拷花布。*~ed edges* (书籍的)锯齿状浮雕花边。*~ed paper* 皱纹纸。

go-ga(u)ge [ˈgəugeidʒ; ˋgogedʒ] ***n***. 【机】过端量规,通过规。

go-get·ter [ˈgəuˈgetə; ˋgoˋgɛtɚ] **I** ***n***. **1**. 能干而有上进心的人。**2**. 火箭自动制导的控制装置。**II** ***a***. **1**. 摇摆舞的,跳摇摆舞小舞场的。**2**. 最时髦的。**3**. 活跃的,乱窜的,无节制的。

gog·gle [ˈgɔgl; ˋgɑgl̩] **I** ***vi***., ***vt***. 转动[凸出]眼珠,瞪眼看,斜眼看。**II** ***n***. **1**. 瞪眼,转动眼珠。**2**. 〔*pl*.〕遮风镜;〔俚〕眼镜;【机】护目镜。**III** ***a***. (眼珠)突出的,转动的,瞪住的。~**-box** ***n***. 〔英俚〕电视机。~**-eye** ***n***. 【动】弹突鱼类〔如岩鲈〕。~**-eyed** ***a***. 眼睛转动的;眼珠凸出的;瞪眼的。

gog·let [ˈgɔglit; ˋgɑglɪt] ***n***. 〔印〕冷冰瓶。

go-go [ˈgəuˌgəu; ˋgoˏgo] **I** ***a***. **1**. 摇摆舞的;和跳摇摆舞的人有关的;摇摆舞音乐唱片的;摇摆舞厅的。**2**. 〔俚〕活泼的;有力的;时髦的。**3**. 赌博性投资的。**II** ***n***. **1**. 摇摆舞。**2**. 赌博性投资 (= ~ fund)。

Go·gol [ˈgɔgəl; ˋgɑgəl], **Nikolai Vasilievitch** 果戈理〔1809—1852,俄国小说家、剧作家〕。

Goi·del [ˈgɔidəl; ˋgɔɪdəl] ***n***. 盖尔人;讲戈伊德尔语的人。

Goi·del·ic [gɔiˈdelik; gɔɪˋdɛlɪk] **I** ***a***. **1**. 盖尔人的。**2**. 戈伊德尔语的。**II** ***n***. (包括爱尔兰的、苏格兰的、马恩岛的)戈伊德尔语族。

go·ing [ˈgəuiŋ; ˋgoɪŋ] **I** go 的现在分词。**II** ***a***. **1**. 进行中的;运转中的;营业中的;营业发达的。**2**. 活着的,存在的。**3**. 现行的;流行中的。*a ~ concern* 营业发达的商行[公司]。*the ~ prices* 时价。*the best novelist ~* 当今活着的最好小说家。*There is cold beef ~*. 有现成的冷牛肉。*the ~ rate* 现行率。~ ***and coming*** 逃脱不了 (*get sb. ~ and coming* 使某人无路可逃)。~ ***strong*** 〔美〕成功,进行顺利。***in ~ order*** 正常运转。***get ~*** 〔口〕= set ~。***get sb. ~*** 〔俚〕使某人激动,使某人发怒。~ (***on***) 接近,快到(某一年龄或时间)(*She is ~ on seventeen*. 她快十七岁了)。***keep ~*** 继续(运转,谈话);维持。***set ~*** **1**. 使运转,开动。**2**. 实行。**3**. 出发 (*set the clock ~* 开钟)。**III** ***n***. **1**. 行走,出行。**2**. 出发,动身。**3**. 进展的情况;工作[行驶]的方法[速度];工作的条件。**4**. (走路、赛跑、开车等时)地面[路面]的状况。**5**. 【建】(梯段的)级距;级长。**6**. 〔常 *pl*.〕行为,举动。*heavy ~* 缓慢的进展。*rough ~* 困难的进程;(比赛运动中的)苦战。*a safe ~ and return* 平安出发与归来。*The ~ was very hard over this mountain road*. 在这山路上行走很吃力。***go while the ~'s good*** 及时离开,及时行动。~ **away** 出发度蜜月。~**-over** ***n***. 〔美口〕**1**. 彻底检查,彻底审查。**2**. 申诉,痛打。~**s-on** ***n***. 〔口〕**1**. 勾当,(坏)举动,品行,(不良)行为〔常与 such, strange 等词连用〕。**2**. 事件,发生的情况。

goi·tre, goi·ter [ˈgɔitə; ˋgɔɪtɚ] ***n*.**【医】甲状腺肿。**goi·tered *a*.**

goi·trous [ˈgɔitrəs; ˋgɔɪtrəs] ***a*.**【医】甲状腺肿的。

gok [gɔk; gɑk] *vt*. (***gokked*; *gok·king***)〔美俚〕完全懂得,彻底了解。

G.O.K. = God only knows〔美俚〕天晓得。

go-kart [ˈgəuˌkɑːt; ˋgoˏkɑrt] ***n*.** 微型竞赛汽车。

Gol·con·da [gɔlˈkɔndə; gɑlˋkɑndə] ***n*. 1.** 戈尔康达〔印度南部古都,曾以出产金钢石著名〕。**2.** 丰富的矿藏,大财源。

gold [gəuld; gold] **I *n*. 1.** 金,黄金;金币。**2.** 财富;财宝;黄金一样贵重[富丽]的东西。**3.** 金色,金黄色。**4.** 包金,镀金;金粉,金钱,金箔。**5.** (射箭的)金色靶心。**6.** 金牌,金质奖章。*age of* ~黄金时代 (= golden age)。black ~黑金,石油。*cloth of* ~金线织物。*dead* ~无光泽的金子。*fool's* ~〔美〕看来像黄金的矿,黄铁矿 (= iron pyrites)。*greed of* ~黄金欲。*a heart of* ~一颗高贵的心。*She is pure* ~. 她纯洁无瑕。*a voice of* ~金嗓子,优美的声音。*the old* ~古金色,暗黄褐色。***as good as*** ~ (小孩)很乖。***be worth one's weight in*** ~ 非常有价值,非常有裨益。***gild refined*** ~ 画蛇添足,多此一举。***go*** ~获金唱片奖。***go off*** ~ 废除金本位。***make a*** ~ 射中靶心。***on a*** ~ ***basis*** 用金本位。**II *a*. 1.** 金的,金制的,含金的。**2.** 金色的。**3.** 金本位的。~ **amalgam** 金汞膏。~ **bank**〔美〕国立银行。~ **bar** 金条。~**-beater** 金箔工。~ **beatle**【动】金甲虫。~ **bloc** 金本位国家集团。~**-brick 1.** ***n*.**〔口〕假金砖,赝品,虚有其表的东西;〔美俚〕懒汉,(军队中)逃避工作的人。**2.** ***vt*.**〔美俚〕欺骗,以高价出售劣货。**3.** ***vi*.**〔军俚〕偷懒,不尽职,逃避工作,吊儿郎当。~**bug 1.** = ~ beatle. **2.**〔美俚〕主张金本位的人。~ **bullion** 金块。~ **card** 金卡〔可透支的信用卡〕。~ **certificate** 金券。**G- Coast 1.** 黄金海岸(非洲加纳的旧称)。**2.**〔美口〕富豪住宅区。~ **coin** 金币。~**-collar *a*.**金领阶层的,高层专业技术人员的 (*a* ~*-collar worker* 一位金领阶层人士)。~ **content** 含金量。~**-crest**【动】戴菊(鸟名)。~ **currency** 金本位货币。~ **digger 1.** 金矿工人;淘金者。**2.**〔口〕以美色骗取男人钱财的女子。~ **digging** 找金矿;淘金;淘金地带。~ **dust** 砂金。~ **exchange standard** 金汇兑本位制。~ **fever** 淘金热。~ **field** 采金地。~**-filled *a*.** 镀金的,包金的。~ **finch**【鸟】金翅雀。~**fish** 金鱼。~ **foil** 金箔。~ **guarantee clause** 黄金保值条款。~ **lace** 金线带。~ **leaf** 金叶。~ **medal** 金牌,金质奖章。~ **mine** 金矿,金山;宝库。~ **parity** 黄金平价。~ **point** 黄金点〔相当于金的熔点或 1064.43℃〕。~ **plate** 金制餐具;镀金的材料。~ **record**〔美〕金唱片〔赠给大获成功的歌星的纪念性镀金唱片〕。~ **reserve** 黄金储备。~ **rush** 抢购黄金;涌往新金矿,淘金热。~ **size** (贴饰金叶的)胶粘剂。~ **standard** 金本位。~ **star** 金星〔美军官兵阵亡的标志〕。~**stone**【地】沙金石。~ **thread**【植】黄连属 (*coptis*) 植物〔尤指格林兰黄连 (*coptis groenlandica*)〕。

gol·darn [ˈgɔlˈdɑːn; ˋgɑlˋdɑrn] *vt*., *a*., *ad*.〔美俚〕= damn, damned.

gold·en [ˈgəuldən; ˋgoldn̩] ***a*. 1.** 金色的,金黄色的。**2.** 金的,金制的。**3.** 产金的。**4.** (机会)宝贵的,贵重的;绝好的;(时代等)隆盛的。**5.** 第五十周年的。~ **age** 黄金时代;退休职工〔多作修饰语用〕。~ **ager**〔口,也作 G-A-〕老人家,老大爷,老公公〔尤指六十五岁以上老人或上了年纪退休的老人〕。~ **apple 1.**【希神】(导致众女神争夺的)金苹果。**2.** 西红柿,番茄。**3.** (英王加冕时所用象征王权的)珠宝。~ **aster**【植】金菊属 (*Chrysopsis*) 植物。~ **balls** 当铺招牌;当铺。~ **bantan corn** 金黄短穗玉米。~ **bowl 1.** 金鱼缸。**2.** 无法躲人耳目的地方,大庭广众。~ **boy** 有名声的男子,有成就的男子。~ **calf** 金犊〔古代以色列人崇拜的偶像〕;金钱崇拜。~ **chain** = laburnum. **G- Delicious** (美国产苹果)金冠,黄元帅。~ **eagle** 鹫 (Aquila chrysaëtos)。~ **exile** 黄金流放〔指被流放者在境外过着舒适而安全的生活,亦即当寓公,此类人员多为原政界高层人士〕。~**-eye**【动】鹊鸭,白鹁鸭。**G- Fleece 1.**【希神】金羊毛〔传说 Jason 乘 Argo 号船只远征 Colchis 时带回的宝物〕。**2.** 金羊毛骑士章〔西班牙等国最高勋位〕。**G- Gate** 金门〔美国旧金山入口处海峡名〕。~ **girl** 有名声的女子,有成就的女子。~ **goal** 金球〔足球比赛加时赛中决定胜负的一记进球〕。~ **glow**【植】金光菊 (*Rudbeckia laciniata*)。~ **goodbye** 黄金送别〔指公司付给高层雇员的丰厚退休金〕。~ **goose** 金鹅〔希腊寓言中每天能产一金蛋的神鹅,其主人妄想一次取得全部金蛋,将鹅杀掉,结果一无所得〕。~ **handshake** 丰厚的退休金[退伍奖金]。**G- Horn** (土耳其的)伊斯坦布尔港。~ **hour** 最佳治疗时间〔指受伤后未被耽误而获得有效治疗的时间〕。~ **hours** 幸福日子。~ **jubilee** 五十周年,金婚礼。~ **key** 贿赂。~ **knop**〔英〕瓢虫。~ **mean 1.** 中庸(之道)。**2.** = ~ section. ~**-mouthed *a*.** 雄辩的。~ **number**【天】黄金数。~ **oldie,** ~ **oldy** 曾风靡一时的(仍为人喜爱的)作品。~ **opinions** 盛赞,高度评价。~ **opportunity** 绝好的机会,良机。~ **parachute** 退休高层人员之优厚津贴。~ **pheasant** 绵鸡。~**remedy** 灵药。~ **retriever** 黄毛猎犬〔指任何一种猎取禽兽的厚黄毛猎犬〕。~**rod *n*.**【植】一枝黄花属 (*Solidago*) 植物;黄花。~**rule** 金箴〔语出圣经《马太福音》,指所谓推己及人的箴言〕。~ **saying** 金玉良言。~**-seal**【植】白毛茛 (*Hydrastis canadensis*)〔产于美洲,原大量用于医药〕。~ **section**〔美术〕黄金分割〔即矩形短边与长边之比等于长边与长短二边和之比〕。**G- State** 金山州〔美国加利福尼亚州的别名〕。~ **shackle** 金镣铐〔指公司为留住职员而付给的丰厚薪金等,亦作~handcuffs〕。~ **standard** 参比标准。~ **syrup** 黄色糖浆。~ **warbler**【动】金莺。~ **wedding** 金婚〔结婚 50 周年纪念〕。

Golden [ˈgəuldən; ˋgoldən] ***n*.** 戈尔登〔姓氏〕。

gold·ie [ˈgəuldi; ˋgoldɪ] ***n*.**〔美〕金奖唱片(集)。

Gold·i·locks [ˈgəuldiˌlɔks; ˋgoldəˏlɑks] ***n*. 1.** 金发姑娘〔民间故事中到三个狗熊家作客的小姑娘〕。**2.**〔g-〕有黄头发的人。**3.** 金发状毛茛。

Gol·ding [ˈgəuldiŋ; ˋgoldɪŋ] ***n*.** 戈尔丁〔姓氏〕。

gold·smith [ˈgəuldsmiθ; ˋgoldsmɪθ] ***n*.** 金饰工;金首饰商。~ **beetle**【动】金工甲虫。

Gold·smith [ˈgəuldsmiθ; ˋgoldsmɪθ] ***n*. 1.** 戈德史密斯〔姓氏〕。**2. Oliver** ~奥列弗·戈德史密斯〔1730?—1774,生于爱尔兰的英国剧作家,小说家〕。

go·lem [ˈgəulem; ˋgolɛm] ***n*. 1.** (十六世纪希伯来传说中的)有生命的假人。**2.** 机器人。

Golf [gɔlf; gɔlf] 通讯中用于代表字母 g 的词。

golf [gɔlf; gɔlf] **I *n*.** 高尔夫球。**II *vi*.** 打高尔夫球。~ **club 1.** 高尔夫球棍。**2.** 高尔夫球俱乐部。~ **course** [**links**] 高尔夫球场。~ **widow** 因丈夫迷恋高尔夫球而常独居的妇女。**-er *n*.** 打高尔夫球的人。

Gol·gi [ˈgəuldʒi; ˋgoldʒɪ] ***n*. 1.** 高尔基〔姓氏〕。**2. Camillo** ~〔1844—1926,意大利解剖学家与病理学家〕。~ **apparatus**【生】高尔基体 (= Golgi body)。

gol·gio·some [ˈgɔldʒiəsəum; ˋgɑldʒɪəsom] ***n*.**【生】高尔基体。

Gol·go·tha [ˈgɔlgəθə; ˋgɑlgəθə] ***n*. 1.**【宗】各各他〔耶稣被钉死的地方〕。**2.**〔g-〕墓地,受难地,殉教处。

gol·iard [ˈgəuljəd; ˋgoljəd] ***n*.** 学生流浪诗人〔指中世纪晚期写拉丁文讽刺诗的流浪学生,常身兼行吟诗人和小丑〕。**-iardic** [-ˈjɑːdik; -ˋjɑrdɪk] ***a*.**

Go·li·ath [gəˈlaiəθ; gəˋlaɪəθ] ***n*. 1.**【圣】(非利士勇士)歌利亚;〔喻〕巨人。**2.**〔g-〕移动式大型起重机 (= ~ crane)。~ **beetle**【动】(非洲产的)花金龟科大甲虫。~ **heron**【动】(非洲产的)巨苍鹭。

Go·light·ly [gəˈlaitli; gəˋlaɪtlɪ] ***n*.** 戈莱特利〔姓氏〕。

gol·li·wog(g) [ˈgɔliwɔg; ˋgɑlɪwɑg] ***n*. 1.** 奇形怪状的黑面木偶。**2.** 奇形怪状的人。

G

gol·ly[1] [ˈgɔli; ˋgɑlɪ] *int*. 〔口〕天哪!〔惊讶、发誓声,又作 By [my] ~!〕。

gol·ly[2] [ˈgɔli; ˋgɑlɪ] *n*. = golliwog.

go·losh(e) [gəˈlɔʃ; gəˋlɑʃ] *n*. = galosh.

go·lup·tious [gəˈlʌpʃəs; gəˋlʌpʃəs], **go·lop·tious** [gəˈlɔpʃəs; gəˋlɑpʃəs] *a*. 〔谑〕可口的,好吃的,使人高兴的。

G.O.M. = Grand Old Man〔英〕英国首相格莱斯顿(Gladstone)的尊称。

gom·been [gɔmˈbiːn; gɑmˋbin] *n*. 〔Ir.〕高利贷。~**-man** *n*. 放高利贷者。

gom·broon [gɔmˈbruːn; gɑmˋbrun] *n*. 龚布龙陶瓷〔波斯产的一种白色半透明陶瓷〕。

gom·er·al, gom·er·el [ˈgɔmərəl; ˋgɑmərəl], **gom·er·il** [-əril; -ərɪl] *n*. 〔Scot.〕蠢汉。

Go·mor·rah, Go·mor·rha [gəˈmɔrə; gəˋmɑrə] *n*. **1.** 【圣】(古代的)蛾摩拉城〔因其居民罪恶深重而与 Sodom 城同时被神毁灭〕。**2.** 罪恶的城市。

gom·phi·a·sis [gɔmˈfaiəsis; gɑmˋfaɪəsɪs] *n*. 【医】牙松动。

gom·pho·sis [gɔmˈfəusis; gɑmˋfosɪs] *n*. 【解】嵌合。

go·mu·ti [gəuˈmuːti; goˋmutɪ] *n*. 【植】**1.** 桄榔(*Arenga pinnata*)〔产于马来亚〕;桄榔纤维。**2.** 西谷椰子(*Metroxylon sagu*)〔产于马来亚〕。

-gon *comb. f*. 表示"…角形": hexa*gon*, poly*gon*.

go·nad [ˈgəunæd; ˋgonæd] *n*. 【生化】性腺,生殖腺,卵巢,睾丸。**-al, -i·al, -ic** *a*.

gon·a·do·tro·phin, [ˌgɔnədəuˈtrəufin; ˏgɑnədoˋtrofɪn], **gon·a·dotro·pin** [ˌgɔnədəuˈtrəupin; ˏgɑnədoˋtropɪn] *n*. 【生化】促性腺激素。

gon·a·do·tro·pic [ˌgɔnədəuˈtrɔpik; ˏgɑnədoˋtrɑpɪk] *a*. 【生化】促性腺的。~ *hormone* 促性腺激素。

Gond [gɔnd; gɑnd] *n*. 龚德人〔印度中部的德拉维地族的一部〕。

Gon·di [ˈgɔndi; ˋgɑndɪ] *n*. **1.** 龚德语〔印度中部的德拉维地的方言群〕。**2.** 该方言群的主要方言。

gon·do·la [ˈgɔndələ; ˋgɑndələ] *n*. **1.** (意大利威尼斯的)平底狭长小船。**2.** 大型平底船;游览船。**3.** 敞篷车。**4.** (飞船等的)吊舱;吊篮。**5.** (设在商店中央的)商品陈列台。**6.** (运输混凝土的)带斥兜的卡车。

gon·do·lier [ˌgɔndəˈliə; ˏgɑndəˋlɪə] *n*. (意大利威尼斯的)平底船船夫。

Gond·wa·na·land [gɔndˈwɑːnəlænd; gɑndˋwɑnəlænd] *n*. 冈瓦纳大陆〔假定性的大陆名称,包括现今印度、澳大利亚、亚洲、南美洲和南极洲,约在古生代时分离开来〕。

gone [gɔn, gɔːn; gɔn, gɑn] **I** go 的过去分词。**II** *a*. **1.** 过去的,已往的;…前的,以前的;刚过完…的。**2.** 垂死的,死了的。**3.** 无望的;无可挽救的。**4.** 遗失了的;衰败的。**5.** 虚弱无力的,发晕的。**6.** 用光了的。**7.** 〔口〕入迷的,一往情深的(*on*; *upon*)。**8.** 〔美俚〕怀孕的;喝醉的。**9.** 〔美俚〕极好的,第一流的。*dead and* ~死了。*past and* ~过去的,一去不复返的。*these ten years* ~以往的十年。*on Monday* ~ *five weeks* 五个星期以前的星期一。*be eight years* ~刚过八周岁。*a* ~ *feeling* [*sensation*] 虚飘飘的感觉,发晕的感觉。*She's six months* ~. 她怀孕六个月了。**be dead ~ in love** 深陷情网中。**be far ~ 1.** (病、债、夜、骄傲、爱情、疲倦等)到了很深程度。**2.** 深深卷入某事。**Be ~!** 〔口〕走开。**be ~ of** [**with**] 变成,结果是(*What has* ~ *of him*? 他结果怎样? 他情况怎样?)。**be ~ on sb**. 倾心爱某人,迷恋某人。**G- with the wind**. 随风而逝,往事如过眼云烟〔美国小说《飘》的原文名〕。~ **case** 无可挽救的事;没有希望的人。~ **fishing** 〔美俚〕闲散的,悠闲的;旷工的。~ **goose** [**gosling**] 〔美口〕毫无希望的事;无可挽救的人。**-ness** [ˈgɔnnis; ˋgɑnnɪs] *n*.

gon·ef [ˈgɔnif; ˋgɑnɪf] *n*. 〔俚〕= ganef.

gon·er [ˈgɔnə; ˋgɑnɚ] *n*. 〔口〕无可挽救的人[物],失败者,落魄者;临死的人。

Gon·er·il [ˈgɔnəril; ˋgɑnərɪl] *n*. 贡纳梨〔莎士比亚的《李尔王》中李尔的长女名,被作为冷酷、不孝的典型〕。

gon·fa·lon [ˈgɔnfələn; ˋgɑnfələn] *n*. (中世纪意大利各城邦用的)旌旗。

gon·fa·lon·ier [ˌgɔnfələˈniə; ˏgɑnfələˋnɪə] *n*. 旗手;(中世纪意大利各城邦的)长官。

gon·fa·non [ˈgɔnfənən; ˋgɑnfənən] *n*. **1.** = gonfalon. **2.** (悬于船等横杆上的)旗。

gong [gɔŋ; gɔŋ] **I** *n*. **1.** 锣。**2.** 皿形钟、铃。**3.** 〔俚〕奖章,辈章,纪念章。**4.** (钟等用以报时的)鸣钟弹簧。**II** *vi*. **1.** 打锣。**2.** (交通警)鸣锣阻止汽车前进。~ **buoy** 锣标〔装有铜锣的浮标〕。**-like** *a*.

Gon·go·rism [ˈgɔŋgərizəm; ˋgɑŋgərɪzəm] *n*. (西班牙诗人)龚果拉(Gongora, 1561—1627)的风格;文字交错缠结而华美瑰丽的风格。

gong·ster [ˈgɔŋstə; ˋgɑŋstɚ] *n*. 〔俚〕用锣声指挥交通的警察。

go·nid·i·um [gəuˈnidiəm; goˋnɪdɪəm] *n*. (*pl*. **-nid·i·a** [-ˈnidiə; -ˋnɪdɪə]) 【生】**1.** 藻(细)胞。**2.** 微生子。**-i·al** *a*.

go·ni·om·e·ter [ˌgəuniˈɔmitə; ˏgonɪˋɑmɪtɚ] *n*. **1.** 角度计,测角计,测向计。**2.** 【无】天线方向性调整器。

go·ni·o·met·ric(al) [ˌgəuniəˈmetrik(əl); ˏgonɪəˋmɛtrɪk(əl)] *a*. 测角的,测角计的。**-cal·ly** *ad*.

go·ni·om·e·try [ˌgəuniˈɔmitri; ˏgonɪˋɑmətrɪ] *n*. 角度测定,测角(术);测向(术)。

go·ni·on [ˈgəuniˌɔn; ˋgonɪˏɑn] *n*. (*pl*. **-ni·a** [-niə; -nɪə]) 【解】下颌角点。

gon·na [ˈgɔnə; ˋgɑnə] 〔美俚〕= going to.

gono- *comb. f*. 表示"性的","生殖的": *gono*phore.

go·no·cho·rism [ˌgɔnəuˈkəurizəm; ˏgɑnoˋkorɪzəm] *n*. 【生】雌雄异体。

gon·o·coc·cus [ˌgɔnəuˈkɔkəs; ˏgɑnoˋkɑkəs] *n*. (*pl*. **-coc·ci** [-ˈkɔksai; -ˋkɑksaɪ]) 【微】淋球菌。

gon·o·cyte [ˈgɔnəsait; ˋgɑnəsaɪt] *n*. 【生】生殖母细胞。

gon·of, gon·oph [ˈgɔnəf; ˋgɑnəf] *n*. 〔俚〕= ganef.

gon·o·phore [ˈgɔnəfɔː; ˋgɑnəfɔr] *n*. **1.** 雌雄蕊柄;生殖体。**2.** (软水母群的)无性繁殖芽体。**-phor·ic** [-ˈfɔːrik; -ˋfɔrɪk], **go·nopho·rous** [gəˈnɔfərəs; gəˋnɑfərəs] *a*.

gon·o·pore [ˈgɔnəpɔː; ˋgɑnəpɔr] *n*. 【生】生殖孔。

gon·or·rh(o)e·a [ˌgɔnəˈriːə; ˏgɑnəˋriə] *n*. 淋病。

gon·or·rh(o)e·al [ˌgɔnəˈriːəl; ˏgɑnəˋriəl] *a*. 淋病的,淋毒性的。

-gony *comb. f*. 构成名词,表示"…发生";"…起源": cosmo*gony*, theo*gony*.

goo [guː; gu] *n*. 〔美俚〕**1.** 雾;黏性物质,甜腻的东西。**2.** 伤感,令人厌恶的自作多情。**3.** 甜言蜜语。

goo·ber [ˈgu(ː)bə; ˋgubɚ] *n*. (美国中部及南部)落花生〔又叫 ~ pea〕。

good [gud; gʊd] **I** *a*. (**bet·ter** [ˈbetə; ˋbɛtɚ]; **best** [best; bɛst]) (*opp*. bad) **1.** 好的,良好的;漂亮的,优美的。**2.** 愉快的,幸福的。**3.** 善良的,有品德的;仁慈的,宽大的。**4.** 技能好的,有本事的;老练的;有资格的(*at*)。**5.** 真正的;健全的,无损伤的,完美的;新鲜的。**6.** 强壮的,结实的,坚牢的。**7.** 有效的;适当的,合适的;正当的,有利的,有益的(*for*)。**8.** 有信用的,可靠的;有根据的,真实的。**9.** 可敬的;〔反〕好(一个)。**10.** 充足的,十足的;丰富的;肥沃的;相当的。**11.** 有趣的。**12.** 亲密的。**13.** 上流社会的;有教养的。**14.** 忠实的;虔诚的。*a* ~ *few* 〔口〕相当多。*a* ~ *joke* 逗人乐的笑话。*a* ~ *match* 劲敌;佳偶。*a* ~ *200 pounds* 足足二百磅。*a* ~ *year* 丰年。~ *debts* 能收回的贷款。~ *faith* 正直,诚实。~ *form* 〔英〕正规礼节。~ *land* 肥沃的土地。~ *life* 道德的生活;幸福的生活。~ *looks* 美貌。~ *luck* 幸运。~ *money* 优良货币。~ *nature* 好性格,温厚。*a* ~ *reason* 正当的理由。*a* ~ *saying* 名言。~ *thing* 有利的交易,投机;名言;〔*pl*.〕好吃的东西。*my* ~ *sir* [*la-*

dy]〔讽〕我的老爷[太太]。*your* ～ *selves* 贵店,贵社。*I'll be* ～! 我以后不淘气了〔孩子对父母、老师悔过语〕。**as** ～ **as ...** 和…一样,事实上等于(*He is as* ～ *as dead*. 他和死了一样)。**as** ～ **as a play** 非常有趣。**as** ～ **as gold** 1.(孩子)很乖的,规规矩矩的。2. 极贵重的。3. 十分可靠的(*His promise is as* ～ *as gold*. 他的保证非常可靠)。**as** ～ **as one's word** 守约,践约。**Be** ～!〔口〕放乖些! **be** ～ **at ...** 善于…(*He is* ～ *at figures* [*painting*, *describing*, *etc*.]. 他善于计算[绘画、描写等])。**be** ～ **enough to** = **be so** ～ **as to** 请…(*Be* ～ *enough to shut the door*. 请把门关上)。**be** ～ **for** 1. 值…,有支付…能力的。(*be* ～ *for a 100 dollars* 有支付一百元的能力)。2. 有效的,对…有用的;对…有益(*Exercise is* ～ *for health*. 运动有益健康)。**be** ～ **to** 1. 适于(*This water is* ～ *to drink*. 这水可喝)。2. 对…厚道(*He has always been* ～ *to me*. 他对我总是很好)。**G- afternoon**! [gud,ɑːftə'nuːn; gʊd,ɑftə`nun]您好吧! ['gud,ɑːftə'nuːn; `gʊd,ɑftə`nun] 再会〔午后用〕。～ **and**〔美〕非常,全然;充分(*He was* ～ *and mad*. 他完全疯了。*I'm* ～ *and ready*. 我充分准备好了)。～ **and hard**〔美〕彻底。**G- day**! [gud'dei; gʊd`de] 您好! ['gud'dei; `gʊd`de] 再见! **G- evening**! [gud'iːvniŋ; gʊd`ivnɪŋ] 您好! ['gud'iːvniŋ; `gʊd`ivnɪŋ] 再会! **G- for you** [**him**]〔美口〕干得好! 真运气! **G- morning**! [gud'mɔːniŋ; gʊd`mɔrnɪŋ] 您好! 早安! ['gud'mɔːniŋ; `gʊd`mɔrnɪŋ] 再见!〔午前用〕。**G-morrow**!〔古〕= Good morning. **G- night**! [gud'nait; gʊd`naɪt] 晚安! 明天见! 再会!〔夜晚用〕。～ **offices** 调停,调停人的作用;(有势力者的)影响。～ **Samaritan** 厚道的外人。～ **turn** 好意(*One* ～ *turn deserves another*. 有好心应当有好报)。～ **word** 好话,推荐之辞(*say a* ～ *word for sb*. 替某人说好话)。**have a** ～ **mind to** 相当想。**have a** ～ **night** 睡得好。**have a** ～ **time** (*of it*) 过得愉快,玩得高兴。**hold** ～ (*for*) 对…有效,对…适用。**in** ～ **time** 刚好,及时地;迅速地。**make** ～ 1. 履行;证明。2. 补偿,弥补;支付。3. 维持,保持(地位等)。4.〔美〕成功。**Do you** ～!〔反〕这对你好处多着呢! **not** ～ **enough to** (*do*)〔口〕没有…的价值,不值得做。**Not so** ～!〔口〕糟透了! **on** ～ **terms** 相处得好,和睦。**see** ～ **to do** 认为做某事适当。**too** ～ **to be true** 哪有这么好的事。**II** *n*. 1. 善,善良,美德(*opp*. evil, harm)。2. 利益,好处,幸福。3.〔the ～〕好人(*opp*. the bad, the wicked)。4. 好事,好结果。*for our* ～为我们好。～ *and evil* 善与恶。*What* ～ *is it*? = *What is the* ～ *of it*? 那有什么好处? *What is the* ～ *of the haste*? 急有什么用? **after no** ～ 不怀好意,想干坏事。**be some** [**much**] ～ 有点[极有]好处。**come to** ～ 得好结果。**come to no** ～ 结果不好。**do** ～ **to** 对…做好事;对…有益[有效]。**do sb.** ～ 对某人有益。**for** ～ (**and all**) 永久地,一劳永逸地(*I am going for* ～ *and all*. 我一去就不回了)。**for** ～ **or for evil** 不论好坏。**Much** ～ **may it do you**!〔反〕这对你好处多着呢! **no** ～ 没用;〔美口〕不好,不行。**to the** ～ 1. 有好处。2.【商】在贷方,纯益;净赚,多出来(*We were 100 dollars to the* ～. 我们赚了 100 美元)。**up to no** ～ = **after no** ～. **III** *ad*. = well. **G- Book**【宗】《圣经》。～ **cheer** 1. 作乐,闹饮。2. 美酒佳肴;大吃大喝。3. 神采奕奕,意气风发,兴致勃勃。**G- Conduct Medal**【美军】品德优良奖章。～ **cop bad cop**〔美口〕软硬兼施的,恩威并重的。～ **fellow** 热诚而令人感到亲切的人。～**-fellowship** *n*. 亲密;融洽;善于应酬。～**-for-nothing**, ～**-for-nought** 1. *a*. 无益的,无用的。2. *n*. 无用的人,饭桶。～**-hearted** *a*. 好心肠的,仁慈的。～**-humo(u)red** *a*. 心情好的,愉快的;脾气好的。～ **Joe** 好好先生。～**-looker**〔俚〕美人。～**-looking** *a*. 标致的,美貌的。～**man** 1.〔古〕家长,户主,丈夫,良人。2. 先生〔次于 gentleman 的敬称,= mister, 用于人名前〕。～**-natured** 性格好的,温厚的。～**-neighbo(u)r** *a*. 睦邻的。～**-neighbo(u)rhood**, ～**-neighbo(u)rliness**, ～**-neighbo(u)rship** 睦邻关系。～ **neighbo(u)r policy** 睦邻政策。～ **people** 仙女们。～ **sense** 判断力强,机智。～**-sized** *a*. 宽阔的;大的;相当大的;大号的。～**-tempered** *a*. 性格好的,和蔼的。～**time Charlie**〔口〕逍遥派,无忧无虑的、寻欢作乐的人。～ **use** (语文的)标准用法。～**wife**〔Scot.〕夫人,主妇,太太〔次于 lady 的敬称, = mistress, 用于人名前〕。～**-will** 1. 好意,友好,亲善 (*to*); 诚意,热心(*an ambassador of* ～ *will* 亲善使节)。2.【商】信誉,招牌。

good-by(e) ['gud'bai; gʊd`baɪ] **I** *int*. 再见! **II** [gud'bai; gʊd`baɪ] *n*. 告别;告别辞。*have several* ～*s to say* 要到好几处告别。*kiss sb*. ～吻别某人。*kiss sth*. ～无可奈何地失去某物。*say* ～ *to sb*. 向某人告别。*wave* ～挥手告别。

good·ish ['gudiʃ; `gʊdɪʃ] *a*. 还好的。

good·ly ['gudli; `gʊdlɪ] *a*. (**-li·er**; **-li·est**) 1. 美丽的,优美的。2. 好的,不错的。3. 颇大的,颇多的。**-li·ness** *n*.

good·ness ['gudnis; `gʊdnɪs] *n*. 1. 善良;仁慈;善行,美德;优点。2. 真髓,(食品的)养分;精华。3.〔作感叹词〕= God. *boil all the* ～ *out of coffee* 把咖啡的香味都煮跑了。**for** ～**' sake** 看在老天爷面上。**G- knows**! 天晓得! 实实在在说。**G- me**! 天哪! 啊呀!〔表示惊讶〕。**have the** ～ **to** (*do*) 有…的好意。**in the name of** ～ 实实在在。**Thank** ～! 谢天谢地! **wish to** ～ 希望,但愿(*I wish to* ～ *that* .... 我非常想…)。

goods [gudz; gʊdz] *n*.〔*pl*.〕1. 商品,货物〔美国说 freight〕。★不与数目字连用。2. 动产。3.〔the ～〕〔美口〕本领;不负所望的人[物]。*capital* ～生产资料。*consumer* ～消费品。*damaged* ～残损货品。*fancy* ～化妆品,装饰品,时髦商品。～ *agent* 运输行。～ *in stock* 存货。～ *of first* [*second*] *order* 直接[间接]必需品。*green* ～新鲜蔬菜;〔美俚〕伪钞。*printed* ～印花布。*semi-finished* ～半成品。*shaped* ～定型制品。**a piece of** ～〔贬〕人〔特指少女〕。**by** ～ 用货车装运。**catch sb. with the** ～ 人赃俱获。**deliver the** ～ 交货;〔喻〕履行诺言,不负所望。**get the** ～ **on sb.**〔美俚〕在某人身上发现罪证。～ **and chattels**【法】私人财物,全部动产。**have all one's** ～ **in the window** 肤浅,华而不实,虚有其表。**have the** ～ 有才华,有充分资格。**He is the** ～. 他就是合适的人。**know one's** ～〔俚〕精通本行业务。～**agent** 运货代理人。～ **train** 货物列车〔美国说 freight train〕。

good·y[1] ['gudi; `gʊdɪ] *n*. 1.〔古〕〔常加在姓氏前〕(下层社会的)妇女,老妇人。2.〔美〕(哈佛大学)打扫宿舍的女人。

good·y[2] ['gudi; `gʊdɪ] *n*.〔主 *pl*.〕〔口〕1. 好吃的东西,糖果,甜食。2. 精品,佳作。3. 英雄,好汉 (*opp*. baddy)。

good·y[3] ['gudi; `gʊdɪ] **I** *a*.〔口〕伪善的,假道学的。**II** *ad*. 伪善地,假道学地。**III** *n*. 伪善者,假道学。～-～ 1. *a*. 伪善的,假正经的。2. *n*. 伪善的,假君子。**G-Two-Shoes** 伪善的人。

good·y[4] ['gudi; `gʊdɪ] *int*. 好啊〔孩子气地表示高兴〕!

Good·year ['gudjə(ː); `gʊdjɪr] *n*. 1. 古德伊尔〔姓氏〕。2. **Charles** ～查理·古德伊尔〔1800—1860, 发明硬橡皮的美国人〕。

goo·ey ['guːi; `guɪ] *a*.〔美俚〕1. 黏的,甜腻的。2. 过份伤感的。

goof [guːf; guf] **I** *n*.〔美俚〕1. 傻瓜,糊涂虫。2. 大错,疏忽。**II** *vi*. 1. 出大错。2. 闲荡,混日子 (*off*)。— *vt*. 弄糟,搞坏(事)。～ **off** 浪费时间,工作吊儿郎当。～ **up** 把事情弄糟,出大错。～**ball**〔俚〕1. 兴奋剂;催眠药片;镇静剂。2. 饭桶,神经失常的人〔也作 ～ ball〕。～**-off** 1. 工作不负责任的人,吊儿郎当的人。2. 休息时间。

goof·er ['guːfə; `gufɚ] *n*.〔美俚〕容易受骗的人,傻瓜。

go-off [gəu'ɔ(ː)f; go`ɔf] *n*.〔口〕出发;着手,开始。**at one**

~ 一次,一举,一气。*succeed* (*at*) *the first* ~ 一举成功。

goof·y [ˈguːfi; ˋgufɪ] *a*. 〔美俚〕愚蠢的。**-i·ly** *ad*. **-i·ness** *n*.

goo·gly [ˈguːgli; ˋguglɪ] *n*. 【曲棍球、板球】曲球〔先转向一方,继而飞向另一方的球〕。

goo·gol [ˈguːgɔl; ˋgugɑl] *n*. **1**. 大数,后面带有 100 个零的数〔常作 10^{100}〕;10 的一百次方。**2**. 巨大数目。

goo·gol·plex [ˈguːgɔlpleks; ˋgugɑlplɛks] *n*. 【数】$10^{10^{100}}$

goo-goo[1] [ˈguːguː; ˋgugu] *a*. 爱慕的,色情的。~ **eyes** 媚眼。

goo-goo[2] [ˈguːguː; ˋgugu] *n*. 〔美〕主张[进行]政治改良的人。

gook[1] [gu(ː)k; gʊk] *n*. 〔美俚、蔑〕外国人〔尤指菲律宾人,太平洋群岛人,日本人等黄种人或棕种人〕。

gook[2] [gu(ː)k; guk] *n*. 甜腻的东西= goo. **-y** *a*.

goon [guːn; gun] *n*. **1**. 〔美俚〕蠢汉;古怪的人。**2**. (受雇恐吓工人的)打手,暴徒。**3**. 粗鲁的人,无赖。~ ***squad*** (破坏罢工的)打手队。

goo·ney [ˈguːni; ˋgunɪ] **bird** 【鸟】黑脚信天翁。(Diomedea nigripes, goony bird)。

goop[1] [guːp; gup] *n*. **1**. 举止粗鲁的孩子。**2**. 〔俚〕笨蛋。**3**. 平淡无趣的人。

goop[2] [guːp; gup] *n*. 〔美俚〕胶状半流体。**-y** *a*.

goo·san·der [guːˈsændə; guˋsændɚ] *n*. 【动】秋沙鸭。

goose [guːs; gus] **I** *n*. (*pl*. ***geese*** [giːs; gis]) **1**. 鹅;雌鹅(*opp*. gander);鹅肉。**2**. (*pl*. ~*s*) (成衣铺的)弯把熨斗。**3**. 呆头鹅,傻瓜。**4**. 〔俚〕(鹅叫一样的)奚落声,倒彩。*The older the ~ the harder to pluck*. 〔谚〕年纪越大,越是一毛不拔。*The old woman is picking her geese*. 下雪了[儿语]。***a wild ~ chase*** 徒劳的追求,无益的举动。*All his geese are swans*. **1**. 夸大自己的长处。**2**. 敝帚自珍。***all right on the ~ = be sound on the ~*** 〔美〕稳健,持正统观念。***as silly*** [***stupid***] ***as a ~*** 蠢极了。***cannot say bo*** [***boh, boo***] ***to a ~*** 〔口〕胆小怕事。***chase the wild ~*** 徒劳的追求,无益的举动。***cooked*** [***gone***] ~ 无可救药的人,没有希望的事。***cook one's*** (***own***) ~ 自己害自己;毁掉自己的希望[机会、计划]。***cook sb.'s ~*** 〔俚〕干掉[杀死]某人;挫败某人的计划[希望]。***get the ~*** 〔俚〕被听众[观众]喝倒彩。***give ... the ~*** 〔美俚〕加快速度。***the ~ that lays the golden eggs*** 摇钱树,财源。***kill the ~ that lays the golden eggs*** 杀鸡取卵;只顾眼前利益,不顾长远利益。***like geese on a common*** 自由自在地闲逛。***make a ~ of sb.*** 瞒骗某人,愚弄某人。***shoe the ~*** 徒劳无益,白费气力。***swim like a tailor's ~*** 〔谑〕沉下去。***The ~ hangs*** [***honks***] ***high***. 〔美俚〕前途有望,形势大好。***turn geese into swans*** 把蠢鹅说成天鹅,言过其实。**II** *vt*. **1**. 突然开大(汽车等的)油门;推动,促进。**2**. 〔俚〕对(某人)发嘘嘘声〔表示反对〕。~ **barnacle** 【动】茗荷儿(gooseneck barnacle)。~ **egg** 鹅蛋;〔美俚〕零分;〔美俚〕青肿块。~**flesh** 鸡皮疙瘩(*I am ~flesh all over*. 我浑身起鸡皮疙瘩)。~**foot** *n*. (*pl*. ~*foots*)【植】藜。~**gog** *n*. 〔英口〕= gooseberry. ~ **grass** 【植】蟋蟀草,牛筋草。~**herd** 牧鹅人。~**neck** 鹅头颈;【机】鹅颈管[钩],S形弯曲管;台灯的活动灯架(~ *neck lamp* 有活动灯架的台灯)。~ **pimples** = ~ flesh. ~ **quill** 鹅毛管;鹅毛笔。~ **skin** = ~ flesh. ~ **step** 正步;步法教练。~**-step** *vi*. **1**. 正步,进行步法教练。**2**. 按上级命令行动。

goose·ber·ry [ˈguzbəri; ˋguzˏbɛrɪ] *n*. 【植】**1**. 醋栗,鹅莓;茶藨子。**2**. 醋栗果实;醋栗酒。**3**. (陪伴年轻女人到交际场所的)女伴。***play ~*** 任社交场合少女的监护人;插在两个想单独在一起的人(如情侣)之间。***play*** (***up***) ***old ~ with*** 击败;制止。~ **fool** 醋栗果酱 (= jam)。

goos·er·y [ˈguːsəri; ˋgusərɪ] *n*. **1**. 养鹅场。**2**. 〔集合词〕鹅群。

goos·ey[1], **goos·ie** [ˈguːsi; ˋgusɪ] *n*. **1**. 〔儿〕鹅。**2**. 傻瓜。

goos·ey[2], **goos·y** [ˈguːsi; ˋgusɪ] *a*. **1**. 像鹅一样的,傻头傻脑的。**2**. 神经质的。

GOP = Grand Old Party 美国共和党的别称。

go·pher[1] [ˈgəufə; ˋgofɚ] **I** *n*. **1**. (北美产的)地鼠,金花鼠;(美国南部)可以食用的龟;(无毒)穴居大土蛇 (= ~ snake)。**2**. [G-]【计】地鼠程序〔许多图书馆在因特网上使用的一种卡片索引程序〕。**3**. [G-]〔美俚〕明尼苏达州人。**II** *vi*. 〔美〕挖洞;拚命采掘。

go·pher[2] [ˈgəufə; ˋgofɚ] *n*. **1**. 【圣】歌斐木〔挪亚制方舟的木材〕。**2**. 【植】美洲香槐。

go·pher[3] [ˈgəufə; ˋgofɚ] *n*., *vt*. = gof(f)er.

go·ral [ˈgɔːrəl; ˋgɔrəl] *n*. 【动】斑羊。

gor·bli·my, gor·bli·mey [gɔːˈblaimi; gɔˋblaɪmɪ] *int*. 〔英口〕哎呀! 糟了。

gor·cock [ˈgɔːkɔk; ˋgɔrkɑk] *n*. 红色雄松鸡。

Gor·di·an [ˈgɔːdiən; ˋgɔrdɪən] *a*. 古代弗吕加国王戈尔地雅斯 (Gordius) 的。~ ***knot*** **1**. 【希神】戈尔地雅斯难结〔按神谕,能解开此结者即可为亚细亚国王,后此结被亚历山大大帝解开〕;〔喻〕难解的结,难办的事,棘手问题。**2**. (问题或故事情节的)关键,焦点。***cut the ~ knot*** 用大刀阔斧的方法解决困难问题,快刀斩乱麻。**g- worm** 【动】金线虫〔一种昆虫寄生虫〕。

Gor·don [ˈgɔːdn; ˋgɔrdn] *n*. **1**. 戈登〔姓氏,男子名〕。**2**. **Charles George** ~ 查理·乔治·戈登〔1833—1885,英国军人,曾协助满清政府镇压太平天国起义,后在远征 Sudan 中战死〕。

gore[1] [gɔː; gɔr] *n*. 流出的血,血块。

gore[2] [gɔː; gɔr] **I** *n*. (衣服或帆上加缝的)三角形布条;衽,裆;三角形地带。**II** *vt*. 用三角形布条缝上,把…裁成三角形。

gore[3] [gɔː; gɔr] *vt*. (用枪)刺破;(用角)抵伤;(礁石)撞通(船身)。

gorge [gɔːdʒ; gɔrdʒ] **I** *vi*. 狼吞虎咽,拚命吃。**II** *vt*. 使吃饱;使塞足,使注满。***be ~d with = ~ oneself with*** 吃饱。**III** *n*. **1**. 咽喉;胃;咽下物。**2**. 峡,峡谷;【筑城】背面出入口;(代替钓钩的)吞饵。**3**. 贪吃,饱吃。**4**. 障碍物。*a full ~* 一肚皮,满腹。***cast*** [***heave***] ***the ~ at = cast up the ~ at*** 见到;就吐;唾弃。***one's ~ rises at*** …见了发呕,极端厌恶。***raise*** [***rouse, stir***] ***the ~*** 激怒。

gor·geous [ˈgɔːdʒəs; ˋgɔrdʒəs] *a*. **1**. 华丽的,豪华的。**2**. 〔英口〕极好的,漂亮的。*He is perfectly ~ as Romeo*. 他演罗密欧演得真好。**-ly** *ad*. **-ness** *n*.

gor·ger·in [ˈgɔːdʒərin; ˋgɔrdʒərɪn] *n*. 【建】柱颈。

gor·get [ˈgɔːdʒit; ˋgɔrdʒɪt] *n*. **1**. 护喉甲胄。**2**. 领子。**3**. (女子穿戴的)护颈胸布。**4**. (鸟、兽的)颈部杂色。**5**. 【医】有槽导子。~ **patch** 【军】领章。

Gor·gi·o [ˈgɔːdʒiəu; ˋgɔrdʒɪo] *n*. (*pl*. ~*s*) 非吉普赛人〔吉普赛人用语〕。

Gor·gon [ˈgɔːgən; ˋgɔrgən] *n*. **1**. 【希神】三个蛇发女怪之一〔人一见她即化为石〕。**2**. [g-] 令人作呕的人[景象],丑妇。**-i·an** *a*.

gor·go·nia [gɔːˈgəuniə; gɔrˋgonɪə] *n*. 【动】柳珊瑚属。

gor·gon·ize [ˈgɔːgənaiz; ˋgɔrgəˏnaɪz] *vt*. 使吓呆;睨视使化为石。

Gor·gon·zo·la [gɔːgənˈzəulə; ˏgɔrgənˋzolə] *n*. (意大利米兰)葛更佐拉(村)白干酪,羊乳制的上等干酪。

gor·hen [ˈgɔːˌhen; ˋgɔrˏhɛn] *n*. 【动】牝山鸡,牝红松鸡;母松鸡。

Go·ri [ˈgɔːri; ˋgɔrɪ] *n*. 哥里[格鲁吉亚城市]。

go·ril·la [gəˈrilə; gəˋrɪlə] *n*. **1**. 【动】大猩猩。**2**. 〔美俚〕貌似大猩猩的人;丑恶的人。**3**. 〔美俚〕凶手,打手。**4**. 〔美俚〕引起轰动的影片或唱片。

gor·i·ly [ˈgɔːrili; ˋgɔrəlɪ] *ad*. 血淋淋地,残忍地,骇人听闻地。

Gor·ki [ˈgɔːki; ˋgɔrkɪ], **Maxim** 马克西姆·高尔基〔1868—1936,俄国文学家〕。

gor·mand [ˈgɔːmənd; ˋgɔrmənd] ***n.*** = gourmand.

gor·mand·ize, gor·mand·ise [ˈgɔːməndaiz; ˋgɔrmən͵daɪz] **I** ***vi.*** 狼吞虎咽。— ***vt.*** 拚命吃,吞食。**II** ***n.*** 〔罕〕讲究饮食,大吃大喝。

gor·mand·iz·er, gor·mand·is·er [ˈgɔːməndaizə; ˋgɔrmən͵daɪzɚ] ***n.*** 贪吃的人,讲究饮食的人。

gorm·less [ˈgɔːmlis; ˋgɔrmlɪs] ***a.*** 〔英方〕智力迟钝的;愚蠢的。

gorse [gɔːs; gɔrs] ***n.*** 【植】荆豆。

gors·y [ˈgɔːsi; ˋgɔrsɪ] ***a.*** 荆豆(多)的。

Gor·ton [ˈgɔːtn; ˋgɔrtn] ***n.*** 戈顿〔姓氏〕。

go-round [ˈgəuraund; ˋgoraʊnd] ***n.*** 〔美俚〕**1.** 争论激烈的会议。**2.** 表演;轮班。**3.** 周游一圈。

gor·y [ˈgɔːri; ˋgɔrɪ] ***a.*** **1.** 血淋淋的,沾满鲜血的。**2.** 残酷的,流血的。**3.** 骇人听闻的。

gosh [gɔʃ; gɑʃ] ***int.*** 〔表示惊讶的叹词,为 God 的变体〕。(***by***) ~ 天哪,啊呀。

gos·hawk [ˈgɔsˌhɔːk; ˋgɑs͵hɔk] ***n.*** 【动】苍鹰。

Go·shen [ˈgəuʃən; ˋgoʃən] ***n.*** 【圣】歌珊地〔出埃及前以色列人所居住的埃及北部的肥沃牧羊地〕;〔喻〕丰饶之地,乐土。

gos·ling [ˈgɔzliŋ; ˋgɑzlɪŋ] ***n.*** **1.** 小鹅。**2.** 笨人,傻瓜;毛娃娃。***shoe the*** ~ = shoe the goose. **~-grass** = goose-grass.

go-slow [ˈgəuˈsləu; ˋgoˋslo] **I** ***a.*** 故意拖延的。*a ~ strike* 怠工。**II** ***n.*** 怠工。

gos·pel [ˈgɔspəl; ˋgɑspəl] **I** ***n.*** **1.** 福音;【基督】[G-]《圣经·新约》中的《约翰(马太;马可;路加)福音》;福音书中的一节。**2.** 真理,真实。**3.** 主义,教理,信条。**4.** 〔美〕黑人福音音乐〔一种黑人宗教音乐〕。*the G- according to St. John* 【圣】《约翰福音》。*go forth and preach G-* 宣传福音。*the ~ of efficiency* 效率主义。*the ~ of laissez faire* 放任主义。*the ~ of simple life* 简朴生活之道。*the ~ of soap and water* 清洁主义。*the ~ for the day* 圣餐式中所读的福音书章节。***take sth. as [for]*** ~ 把…认为真理。~ **oath** 手按福音书宣誓。~ **pusher**, ~ **shark** 〔美俚〕牧师。~ **shop** 〔英蔑〕美以美派教堂。~ **side** 教堂祭坛北侧。~ **truth** 福音书中的真理,像福音一样真实的东西。**II** ***a.*** 福音的,传播福音的。

gos·pel·(l)er [ˈgɔspələ; ˋgɑspəlɚ] ***n.*** 圣餐式中读福音书的人;福音宣传者,传道师。*a hot* ~热心的信徒,狂热的宣传者。

gos·po·din [gɔspɑˈdʒin; ͵gɔspɑˋdɜin] ***n.*** (*pl.* ***-da*** [-dɑː; -dɑ]) 〔Russ.〕…先生〔俄语尊称词〕。

gos·port [ˈgɔspɔːt; ˋgɑspɔrt] ***n.*** (飞机座舱间的)通话软管。

Goss(e) [gɔs; gɑs] ***n.*** 戈斯〔姓氏〕。

gos·sa·mer [ˈgɔsəmə; ˋgɑsəmɚ] **I** ***n.*** **1.** 游丝。**2.** 薄纱,新娘面纱。**3.** 纤细的东西;空幻的东西。**4.** 薄雨衣。**II** ***a.*** 轻而薄的,薄弱的;幻影似的。*a ~ justification* 站不住脚的辩解。**-ed, -y** ***a.***

gos·san [ˈgɔsn; ˋgɑsn] ***n.*** 【矿】铁帽。

gos·sip [ˈgɔsip; ˋgɑsɪp] **I** ***n.*** **1.** 街谈巷议,闲谈;闲话,流言蜚语。**2.** 碎嘴子,饶舌者。**3.** 漫笔,随笔。**4.** 〔古、英方〕密友。**II** ***vi.*** 聊天;说(别人的)闲话。*Gossiping and lying go hand in hand.* 〔谚〕说短道长,必然撒谎。~ **column** (报纸上的)闲话栏。**-er** = ~ **monger** ***n.*** 爱闲聊的人,搬弄是非者。**-ist** 闲话栏作家。**-y** ***a.*** 爱闲谈的;爱说闲话的;漫谈式的。

gos·soon [gɔˈsuːn; gɑˋsun] ***n.*** 〔Ir.〕小伙子;服务员。

got [gɔt; gɑt] get 的过去式及过去分词。

got·cha [ˈgɔtʃə; ˋgɑtʃə] 〔口〕= (I have) got you(我)抓住你的把柄了。~ **journalism** 专门揭人疮疤的新闻报道。

Gö·te·borg [ˈjeitəbɔːg; ˋjetəbɔrg] ***n.*** 哥德堡〔瑞典港市〕。

Goth [gɔθ; gɑθ] ***n.*** **1.** 哥德人;哥德族〔古代日尔曼族的一支〕。**2.** 野蛮人;粗野的人。

Goth., goth. = Gothic.

Goth·am [ˈgəutəm; ˋgotəm] ***n.*** **1.** (英国传说中的)愚人村。**2.** 英国 Newcastle 市的别名。**3.** [ˈgəuθəm; ˋgoθəm] 〔美〕纽约市的别名。***the wise men of*** ~ 愚人。

Goth·am·ite [ˈgəutəmait; ˋgotə͵maɪt] ***n.*** **1.** 愚人村的村民;愚人。**2.** [ˈgəuθəmait; ˋgoθə͵maɪt] 〔谑〕纽约人。

Goth·ic [ˈgɔθik; ˋgɑθɪk] **I** ***a.*** **1.** 哥德人的,哥德族的;哥德语的。**2.** 〔有时作 g-〕中世纪的,野蛮的,粗鄙的。**3.** 【建】哥德式的。**4.** 【印】哥德体的,〔英〕黑体的。**5.** 〔有时作 g-〕哥德式小说体的。**II** ***n.*** **1.** 哥德语。**2.** 【建】哥德式,尖拱式建筑。**3.** 【印】哥德体字,黑体字〔英国叫 black letter〕。~ **arch** 尖端拱门。~ **architecture** 哥德式建筑。~ **type** 黑体。**-al·ly** ***ad.***

Goth·i·cism [ˈgɔθisizəm; ˋgɑθəsɪzəm] ***n.*** **1.** 哥德词语;哥德式倾向。**2.** 【建】哥德式建筑。**3.** 〔常作 g-〕野蛮,粗野。**4.** 【印】哥德体,黑字体。

Goth·i·cize [ˈgɔθisaiz; ˋgɑθə͵saɪz] ***vt.*** 〔常作 g-〕使具有哥德风格,使哥德化。

Goth·ick [ˈgɔθik; ˋgɑθɪk] ***a.*** 描写恐怖和凄凉体裁的;有可怖的中世纪气氛的。

Goth·ish [ˈgɔθiʃ; ˋgɑθɪʃ] ***a.*** 野蛮的,粗野的。

go-to-meet·ing [ˈgəutəˈmiːtiŋ; ˋgotəˋmitɪŋ] ***a.*** **1.** 常到教堂去的,虔诚的。**2.** (衣服)节日穿的。**3.** (举止等)极恰当的。

got·ta [ˈgɔtə; ˋgɑtə] 〔俚〕= (have) got to

got·ten [ˈgɔtn; ˋgɑtn] get 的过去分词。★英国除作 ill-gotten 应用外是古语,美国现在仍通用。*It has ~ to be quite late.* 太晚了。

got·up [ˈgɔtˈʌp; ˋgɑtˋʌp] **I** ***a.*** 做成的,人工的;假的。*a ~ affair* 故意造成的事件,圈套,鬼把戏。*a ~ match* 讲好了输赢的比赛。*hastily* ~匆忙做成的。**II** ***n.*** 〔口〕一步登天的人,暴发户。

gouache [guˈɑːʃ; gʊˋɑʃ] ***n.*** 〔F.〕树胶水彩画法;树胶水彩画;树胶水彩画颜料。

Gou·da [ˈgaudə; ˋgaʊdə] ***n.*** 荷兰扁圆形干酪。

gouge [gaudʒ; gaʊdʒ] **I** ***n.*** **1.** 凿,圆凿。**2.** 〔美口〕圆凿工艺;圆槽,凿孔;【地】断层泥。**3.** 〔美口〕欺诈;骗子。**II** ***vt.*** **1.** 用圆凿打(眼)。**2.** 用大拇指抠出(眼珠子)。**3.** 〔美口〕欺诈。~ ***out*** 凿制(软木塞子等);(用大拇指)抠出(眼珠子);挖开。

Gough [gɔf; gɑf] ***n.*** 高夫〔姓氏〕。

gou·lash [ˈguːlæʃ; ˋgulæʃ] ***n.*** **1.** 浓味蔬菜炖肉〔又称 Hungarian goulash〕。**2.** 【牌】重新分牌。

Gould(e) [guːld; guld] ***n.*** 古尔德〔姓氏〕。

goup [guːp; gup] ***n.*** 〔美俚〕(巧克力糖浆之类的)黏液。

gou·ra·mi [ˈgurəmi, guˈrɑːmi; ˋgurəmɪ, gʊˋrɑmɪ] ***n.*** (*pl.* ~(*s*)) 【动】**1.** 丝足鱼,吻口鱼(*Osphronemus goramy*)〔产于东南亚〕。**2.** 丝足鱼属的鱼。

gourd [guəd; gurd] ***n.*** **1.** 【植】葫芦属植物,葫芦。**2.** 葫芦制成的容器。**3.** 葫芦形的细颈瓶。*the bottle [white-flowered]* ~葫芦。*the snake* ~蛇瓜。*the Spanish* ~南瓜。*the sponge [towel]* ~丝瓜。*the white* ~冬瓜。**-ful** ***n.*** 一葫芦的量。

gourde [guəd; gurd] ***n.*** 古德〔海地货币和硬币名〕。

gour·mand [ˈguəmənd; gurmənd] ***n.*** **1.** 贪吃的人。**2.** 美食家,讲究饮食的人。**-ism** ***n.*** 美食主义。

gour·mand·ise [guəmənˈdiːz; gurmənˋdiz] ***n.*** 〔F.〕= gormandise.

gour·met [ˈguəmei; ˋgurme] ***n.*** 讲究吃的人,食物品尝家。~ **powder** 味精。

goût [guː; gu] ***n.*** 〔F.〕**1.** 味道。**2.** 趣味,嗜好。**3.** 鉴赏力。

gout [gaut; gaʊt] ***n.*** **1.** 【医】痛风。**2.** 〔古、诗〕(血的)滴,块。*rich [poor] man's* ~因营养过多[不足]而得的痛风。~ **fly** 【动】麦秆蝇。

gout·y [ˈgauti; ˋgaʊtɪ] ***a.*** 像痛风病的;患痛风病的,因痛风而肿胀的。**-i·ly** ***ad.*** **-i·ness** ***n.***

G

Gov., **gov.** = government; governor.

gov·ern [ˈgʌvən; ˋgʌvɚn] ***vt*.** **1.** 统治;统辖;执掌(政权等)。**2.** 支配;管理;左右,指挥,指导。**3.** 抑制,遏制,压制(感情等)。**4.** 运转(机械、船);调节,控制。**5.**【语法】(尤指动词或介词)支配(受词)。*the ~ing class* 统治阶级。*a ~ing body* 管理机构,(会议的)执行机构。*a ~ing principle* 指导原则[精神]。~ ***oneself*** 克制。— ***vi*.** 统治;控制,调节。

gov·ern·a·bil·i·ty [ˌgʌvənəˈbiliti; ˏgʌvɚnəˋbɪlətɪ] ***n*.** 统治的可能性。

gov·ern·a·ble [ˈgʌvənəbl; ˋgʌvɚnəbl] ***a*.** 可统治的,可支配的。

gov·ern·ance [ˈgʌvənəns; ˋgʌvɚnəns] ***n*.** **1.** 统治,管理,支配。**2.** 统治方式,管理方法。

gov·ern·ess [ˈgʌvənis; ˋgʌvɚnɪs] **I** ***n*.** **1.** 家庭女教师。**2.** 女统治者;女管理者;总督[州长]夫人。*a daily* ~每日来的家庭女教师。*a resident* ~在学生家中住宿的家庭女教师。*a nursery* ~保姆。**II** ***vi*.** 做家庭女教师;做保姆。~ **car** [**cart**]〔英〕面对面坐的轻便二轮马车。

gov·ern·ment [ˈgʌvənmənt; ˋgʌvɚnmənt] ***n*.** **1.** 政治;政体;政权;管理,支配。**2.** 政厅;〔G-〕政府,〔英〕内阁。**3.** 行政管理区域。**4.**【语法】支配。**5.** 政治学。**6.**〔美〕〔*pl*.〕政府证券。*constitutional* ~立宪政治。*democratic* ~民主政治。*the local* ~地方政府。*form a G-*〔英〕组阁。~ **board** (交易所的)公债部。~ **bond** 公债。**G- House** (旧时英国殖民地等的)政府大厦,总督官邸。**~-in-exile** ***n*.** 流亡政府。~ **issue**〔美〕政府发给军人的供给品(如被服、装备等)〔略作 G. I.〕;(成批制成的)现成物品。~ **man** 官吏;支持政府者。~ **offices** 官厅,机关。~ **officials** 官吏,官员。~ **school** 公立学校。~ **securities** [**papers**]【商】政府证券[公债]。

gov·ern·men·tal [ˌgʌvənˈmentl; ˏgʌvɚnˋmɛntl] ***a*.** 统治的;政治上的;政府的,官设的。**-ism** ***n*.** 政府至上主义。**-ly** ***ad*.**

gov·ern·men·tese [ˌgʌvənmenˈtiːz; ˏgʌvɚnmɛnˋtiz] ***n*.** 官话,官腔。

gov·er·nor [ˈgʌvənə; ˋgʌvənɚ] ***n*.** **1.** 统治者,管辖者。**2.** 地方长官,总督,县长,市长(等);〔美〕州长,(要塞等的)司令官;〔英〕狱长。**3.**〔英〕(组织、机构等的)主管人员(如银行总裁、学校董事等)。**4.**〔英口〕父亲;头领;老板,〔称呼〕先生。**5.**【机】节速器,调节器;【电】调节用变阻器,控制器。**6.** (钓鱼的)假蚊钩。*the board of ~s* 理事会。*Look here, G-!* 喂! 老板! *an electric* ~电气节速器。*a pendulum* ~【机】摆调节器。*a throttling* ~【电】节流调速器。**~-general** (*pl*. **~s-general**)〔英〕总督。**~-generalship** 总督的职位[任期]。**~-ship** 统治者的职位[任期]。

Govt., **govt.** = government.

gow [gau; gaʊ] ***n*.**〔美俚〕麻醉品〔如鸦片等〕。

gow·an [ˈgauən; ˋgaʊən] ***n*.**〔Scot.〕【植】春白菊,英国普通雏菊。

Gow·er(s) [gɔə(z); ˋgoɚ(z)] ***n*.** 高尔(斯)〔姓氏〕。

gowk [gauk; gaʊk] ***n*.**〔方〕**1.** 杜鹃,布谷鸟。**2.** 傻子。***give sb. the*** ~ 愚弄某人。

gown [gaun; gaʊn] **I** ***n*.** **1.** 长外衣,长袍;睡衣。**2.** (教授、毕业生等穿的)大学礼服;教士服;法官服;文官服〔对军服而言〕。**3.**〔the ~〕(穿着职业服装的)教士,法官(等)。**4.**〔集合词〕大学的学生和教师。**5.** (古代罗马市民的)外衣,罩袍;〔诗〕和平之衣。*an academic* ~大学礼服。*an evening* ~(女人)晚礼服。***arms and*** ~ 战争与和平。***in wig and*** ~ 穿着法官服。***take*** [***wear***] ***the*** ~ 做教士,当律师。***town and*** ~ (英国牛津和剑桥的)城镇居民和大学中的人。**II** ***vt*.**〔主用 *p. p.*〕穿长外衣,穿法衣,着大学礼服。*a ~ed war* 法庭上的争辩。

gowns·man [ˈgaunzmən; ˋgaʊnzmən] ***n*.** (*pl*. **-men**) **1.** 穿长袍式礼服的人(如法官、教士、律师等)。**2.** 大学师生。

gow·ster [ˈgaustə; ˋgaʊstɚ] ***n*.**〔美俚〕吸大麻的人;吸毒品者。

gox [gɔks; gɑks] ***n*.** 气态氧 (= gaseous oxygen)。

goy [gɔi; gɔɪ] ***n*.** 非犹太人,异教徒。

goy·im [ˈgɔiim; ˋgɔɪɪm] ***n*.**〔*pl*.〕非犹太人。

GP = general audience, parental guidance suggested GP 级电影[指适合一般观众观看,但建议父母对儿童观众加以指导的电影]。

G.P., **g.p.** = **1.** general paresis 全身瘫痪。**2.** =〔英〕general practitioner 普通医生。**3.** = *Gloria Patria* (= Glory to the Father) 荣耀归于天父。**4.** = Graduate in Pharmacy 药学毕业生。

gp. = group.

g.p. =【物】gauge pressure. 表压,计示压力。

GP bomb = general purpose bomb〔美〕普通炸弹,杀伤爆炸炸弹。

g.p.d. =【纺】grams per denier.

g.p.d., **gpd** = gallons per day.

g.p.h. [**m.**, **s.**] = gallons per hour [minute, second].

gpl = grams per litre.

gpmt. =【美军】groupment.

G.P.O., **GPO** = General Post Office〔英〕邮政总局。

G.P.O. = General Post Office; Government Printing Office.

GPS = **1.** Global Positioning System 全球卫星定位系统。**2.** = global positioning satellite 全球定位卫星。

G.P.U., **GPU** [ˈdʒiː piː ˈjuː, ˈgei ˌpei ˈuː; ˋdʒi pi ˈju, ˋge ˏpe ˋu] = Gay-Pay-Oo.

GQ. = general quarters【美军】战舰的战备状态。

G.Q.G. = Grand Quarter General.

GR. =【军】**1.** general reserve 总预备队。**2.** gunnery range 射击场。

Gr. = Grecian; Greece; Greek.

gr. = **1.** grade. **2.** grain(s). **3.** gram(me)(s). **4.** grammar. **5.** great. **6.** gross. **7.** group.

Gr. Br., **Gr. Brit.** = Great Britain 大不列颠。

G.R. **1.** = *Georgius Rex* (King George). **2.** = General Reserve.

Graaf·i·an [ˈgrɑːfiən; ˋgrɑfɪən] ***a*.** (荷兰解剖学家)格拉夫(R. de Graaf) 的。~ **follicle** [**vesicle**]【解】囊状卵泡。

grab [græb; græb] **I** ***vt*.** (***grabbed***; ***grab·bing***) **1.** 攫取,抓取;抓住。**2.** 抢夺,霸占。**3.**〔俚〕对…产生强烈的感情影响。**4.**〔美俚〕匆忙上(车)。~ *a bus* 赶搭公共汽车。— ***vi*.** **1.** 抓住,抓牢 (*at*; *for*; *onto*)。**2.** 急促行动。**3.** (马)后蹄踢着前蹄。~ ***and keep*** 强取豪夺。~ ***at*** 抓住不放。~ ***hold of*** 抓紧。~ ***off***〔美口〕抢得。**II** ***n*.** **1.** 抓取,抢夺,不法所得。**2.**【机】抓扬机,挖掘机,抓斗,抓岩机,钻具打捞器。*make a* ~ *at a rope* 抓住绳索。***have*** [***get***] ***the*** ~ ***on sb***.〔俚〕占得较…有利的地步,强过,胜过。***up for ~s***〔俚〕供人竞购(以售给出价最高者)。**~-all** ***n*.** 贪心汉;〔口〕杂物袋;(海岸附近的)固定鱼网。~ **bag**, ~ **box**〔美〕摸彩袋。~ **hook** 起重钩。~ **line**, ~ **rope** (船等)作扶手用的绳子 (= guest-rope)。~ **sample**【化】定时取集的样品。

grab·ber [ˈgræbə; ˋgræbɚ] ***n*.** **1.** 抢夺的人。**2.** 贪心汉,唯利是图的人。

grab·ble [ˈgræbl; ˋgræbḷ] ***vi*.** **1.** 摸索。**2.** 匍匐,爬 (*for*)。— ***vt*.** 夺取。

grab·by [ˈgræbi; ˋgræbɪ] ***a*.** 贪婪的。

gra·ben [ˈgrɑːbən; ˋgrɑbən] ***n*.**【地】地堑,断层沟。~ **fault** 地堑断层。

Grace [greis; gres] ***n*.** 格雷斯[姓,女子名]。

grace [greis; gres] **I** ***n*.** **1.**【宗】(神的)恩惠,恩典,感化;恩宠,慈悲;天惠,天恩;(对神的)皈依。**2.**【法】特权,特赦权;【商】缓期,宽限。**3.** (动作、体态、结构等的)优美,优雅;(说话、举止)斯文,温雅;美德,美容;〔*pl*.〕风度,魅力。4. 善意,恩赐;情理,体面(感);〔古〕宽厚,仁慈。5.【宗】(饭前或饭后的)感恩祷告。6.【乐】装饰音。7.(英国牛津和剑桥大学)评议会的表决。8.〔G-〕阁下,夫人〔对公爵、公爵夫人、大主教等的尊称,前加 *His*, *Her*, *Your* 等〕。*an act of* ～恩典;(议会颁布的)大赦令。*I cannot with any* ～ *ask him*. 我没有脸去问他。*Every lover sees a thousand* ～*s in the beloved object*. 情人眼里出西施。**airs and** ～**s** 装腔作势,做作的派头。**a saving** ～ 可以弥补缺点的优点,可取之处。**be in a state of** ～【宗】蒙受天恩。**by** ～ **of** 承蒙,多承。**days of** ～(票据付款的)宽限日期。**fall from** ～ 堕落,犯罪;失去天恩。**good** ～**s** 好意,友谊;宠爱。**have the** ～ **to** (*do*) 有…的雅量,爽爽快快地…;有勇气…(*have the* ～ *to apologize* 通情达理地道歉)。**insinuate oneself into the good** ～**s of sb**. 巧妙地博得某人欢心。**in sb.'s good** [**bad**] ～**s** 受某人照顾[白眼]。**in this year of** ～〔讽〕在基督教存在了这么久的现在尚且…。**keep in sb.'s good** ～**s** 讨好,求宠。**make one's** ～**s** 行礼。**say** ～ 做祷告。**sue for** ～ 请求照顾。**the** (*three*) **Graces**【希神】司美丽、温雅、欢乐的三女神〔即 Aglaia, Euphrosyne 和 Thalia〕。**the year of** ～ 公元。**with a bad** [**an ill**] ～ 勉强地,不情愿地。**with a good** ～ 高兴地,欣然地。**with an easy** ～ 态度自若。**II** *vt*. 1. 装饰,使优美(*with*)。2. 使增光,使有荣誉;惠赐。3.【乐】缀…以装饰音。*a character* ～*d by every virtue* 十全十美的人物。**Will you** ～ **our party with your presence**? 如蒙光临,不胜荣幸。～ **cup** 1. (感恩祷告后用的)祝酒杯。2. (宴会等的)最后一次祝酒。～ **note(s)**【乐】装饰音。～ **period** (缴保险费等的)宽限期。

grace·ful [ˈgreisful; ˋgresfəl] *a*. 1. 优美的,雅致的。2. 得体的,适度的。*a* ～ *letter of thanks* 得体的感谢信。*as* ～ *as a swan* 姿态优美,举止端庄。**-ly** *ad*. **-ness** *n*.

grace·less [ˈgreislis; ˋgreslɪs] *a*. 1. 不优美的,不雅致的。2. 粗俗的,粗鄙的。3. 缺德的,邪恶的,堕落的。**-ly** *ad*. **-ness** *n*.

Gra·ci·a [ˈgreiʃiə; ˋgreʃɪə] *n*. 格雷西亚〔女子名〕。

gra·ci·as [ˈgrɑːθiɑːs, -siː-; ˋgrɑθɪɑs, -si-] *int*. 〔Sp.〕谢谢!

Gracie [ˈgreisi; ˋgresɪ] *n*. 格雷西〔女子名, Grace 的昵称〕。

grac·ile [ˈgræsail; ˋgræsaɪl] *a*. 1. 细长的,纤弱的。2. 纤细优美的,苗条高雅的。**-ness** *n*.

gra·cil·i·ty [grəˈsiliti; grəˋsɪlətɪ] *n*. 1. 细弱,纤弱;苗条。2. (文体的)简洁。

gra·ci·o·so [ˌgreiʃiˈəusəu, grɑːsi-; grɑˋθjəusəu; ˏgreʃəˋoso, grɑsɪ-, grɑˋθjoso] *n*. 〔Sp.〕(西班牙喜剧中的)丑角;小丑。

gra·cious [ˈgreiʃəs; ˋgreʃəs] **I** *a*. 1. 宽厚的,仁慈的;有礼貌的,谦和的;庄重的〔常指皇族人士,如 His ～ Majesty〕。2. 亲切的,和蔼的;态度自若的。3. 优美的,雅致的;高雅的,潇洒的。4. 〔古〕幸运的,愉快的,神圣的。*It's* ～ *of you to come*. 承蒙光临。**II** *int*. 〔表示惊骇等〕 **Good** [**My**] ～! = **G- Heaven** [**me, goodness**]! 嗳呀! 天呀! 天哪! **-ly** *ad*. **-ness** *n*.

grack·le [ˈgrækl; ˋgrækḷ] *n*. 【动】鹩哥,紫拟椋鸟(*Quiscalus quiscula*)〔产于美洲〕。

grad [græd; græd] *n*. 〔美口〕毕业生,校友(graduate 的缩略)。

grad. = gradient; graduate(d)。

gra·date [grəˈdeit; ˋgrədet] *vi*., *vt*. 1. (使)(色彩)渐次变浓[变淡],(使…)显出层次来。2. 顺次配列,(把…)分等级。

gra·da·tim [grəˈdeitim; greˋdetɪm] *ad*. 〔L.〕渐渐地,徐徐地,一步步地。

gra·da·tion [grəˈdeiʃən; greˋdeʃən] *n*. 1. 分等,分级。2. 〔*pl*.〕等级,阶段。3. 渐变;(颜色等的)层次;【美】浓淡法。4.【语】母音交替。**-al** *a*. 有次序的,分等级的;逐渐变化的。**-al·ly** *ad*.

grade [greid; gred] **I** *n*. 1. 等级,级别;阶段;程度,标准,水平。2. 〔美〕(中小学的)年级;某一年级的学生。3. 〔*pl*.〕〔美〕小学校(=～ school)。4. (学校考试的)评分等级。5. 〔主美〕坡度,斜坡,倾斜度。6.【畜】改良杂种。7.【语】母音交替。*a poor* ～ *of tea* 低级茶。～ *A eggs* 甲级鸡蛋。*teach in the* ～*s* 做小学教师。**at** ～〔美〕在同一水准面上。**make the** ～ 1. 上陡坡。2. 达到标准;成功。**on the down** ～ 走下坡路,在衰败中。**on the up** ～ 走上坡路,在兴盛中。**up to** ～ 合格。**II** *vt*. 1. 定…的次序,定…的等级,给…分类,给…分级。2. 〔美〕减缓(坡度);【地】均夷;使(色调)渐浓[渐淡]。3. 给…记分数。4.【畜】通过杂交改良(*up*)。— *vi*. 1. 属某种等级。2. (颜色等)渐次调和[变化]。～ **crossing**〔美〕(铁道、公路等的)平面交叉。～ **label(l)ing**〔美〕商品质量的标签说明。～**mark** 1. *n*. 表示货品等级的记号。2. *vt*. 在…上作货品等级的记号。～ **school**〔美〕小学。～ **separation** 立体交叉〔指两条路以不同高度相交的交叉点〕。～ **teacher**〔美〕小学教师。

grad·er [ˈgreidə; ˋgredɚ] *n*. 1. 分类者;分类机。2. 〔美〕(小学校的)…年级生。*a fifth* ～五年级生。

grade·ly [ˈgreidli; ˋgredlɪ] *a*. 〔英方〕1. 极好的,十足的。2. 漂亮的,好看的。3. 恰当的,真正的。

gra·di·ent [ˈgreidiənt; ˋgredɪənt] **I** *a*. 1. 倾斜的。2.【动】步行的,能步行的。**II** *n*. 1. 〔英〕(道路的)倾斜度,坡度,坡路。2.【物】梯度,陡度,(温度、气压等的)变化率,梯度变化曲线。

gra·di·en·ter [ˈgreidjəntə; ˋgredjəntɚ] *n*. 倾斜测定器,倾斜计,水准仪,水平计。

gra·din [ˈgreidin; ˋgredɪn], **gra·dine** [grəˈdiːn; grəˋdin] *n*. 1. 阶梯的一级,阶梯座位的一排。2.【宗】祭坛后方的坛。

grad·ing [ˈgreidiŋ; ˋgredɪŋ] *n*. 1.【工】平地面,减少斜度。2. 分品,分级,分段,校准。3. 粒度。

gra·di·om·e·ter [ˌgreidiˈɔmitə; ˏgredɪˋɑmətɚ], **gra·dom·e·ter** [grəˈdɔmitə; grəˋdɑmətɚ] *n*. 倾斜仪,坡度测定仪。

grad·u·al[1] [ˈgrædʒuəl, ˈgrædjuəl; ˋgrædʒuəl, ˋgrædjuəl] *a*. 1. 渐次的,逐渐的。2. 渐进的;渐升[降]的;倾斜度小的。*a* ～ *slope* 缓坡,倾斜度不大的山坡。*the* ～ *increase of production cost* 生产成本的逐渐增加。**-ness** *n*. **-ly** *ad*.

grad·u·al[2] [ˈgrædjuəl; ˋgrædjuəl] *n*. 【天主】1. 弥撒圣歌〔圣餐后对唱的赞美诗 = ～ psalms〕。2. 弥撒圣歌集。**-ly** *ad*. **-ness** *n*.

grad·u·al·ism [ˈgrædʒuəˌlizəm, -djuəlizəm; ˋgrædʒuəˏlɪzəm, -djuəlɪzəm] *n*. 渐进主义。**-al·ist** *n*., *a*. 渐进主义者(的)。**-al·is·tic** *a*.

grad·u·ate [ˈgrædjueit; ˋgrædjuˏet] **I** *vt*. 1. 〔美〕授与…学位,准予…毕业。2. 给(量杯等)标上刻度;在(表、尺等上)分度。3. 给(学生)分级。4. (用蒸发办法)使浓缩。*The university* ～*d 150 students last year*. 该大学去年有 150 名学生毕业。*She was* ～*d with honours from Harvard University*. 她以优异成绩毕业于哈佛大学。*a ruler* ～*d in centimeters* 刻度为公分的尺。— *vi*. 1. 〔英〕大学毕业,取得学位(*at*),〔美〕毕业(*from*);取得资格(*as*; *in*)。2. 渐次变为(*into*);渐次消逝(*away*)。**II** [ˈgrædʒuət, ˈgrædjuət; ˋgrædʒuət, ˋgrædjuət] *n*. 1. 大学毕业生;〔美〕毕业生(*of*; *in*)。2.【化】量筒,量杯。**III** *a*. 1. 得学士称号的,为大学毕业生设立的。2. 刻度的,分等的。～ **course**〔美〕研究生课程。～ **nurse** 受过正式训练的护士。～ **students**〔美〕研究生。～ **school**〔美〕研究院。

grad·u·at·ed [ˈgrædjueitid; ˋgrædjuˏetɪd] *a*. 1. 分度的,刻度的。2. 分等的。3. 毕业了的。*a* ～ *glass* 刻度杯,量杯。～ *taxation* 累进税。

G

grad·u·a·tion [ˌgrædjuˈeiʃən; ˏgrædʒʊˋeʃən] ***n*.** **1.** 毕业,授学位,得学位。**2.** 毕业典礼,授学位典礼。**3.**〔*pl*.〕表示经纬度的线;刻度;分划,分度。**4.** 分等级。**5.** 浓缩。～ **exercises**〔美〕毕业典礼。

grad·u·a·tor [ˈgrædjueitə; ˋgrædʒʊˏetɚ] ***n*.** 分度器;刻度器;刻度员。

gra·dus [ˈgreidəs, ˈgrædəs; ˋgredəs, ˋgrædəs] ***n*.** **1.** 诗韵辞典〔尤指写拉丁、希腊语诗歌用的格律〕。**2.** (由浅入深的)钢琴练习曲集。

Grae·cism [ˈgriːsizəm; ˋgrisɪzm] ***n*.** =〔英〕Grecism.

Grae·co- *comb. f.*〔英〕= *Greco-*.

Graf [grɑːf; grɑf] ***n*.** (*pl*. ***Graf·en*** [-n; -n̩])〔G.〕(德国、奥地利、瑞典等国的)伯爵。

graf·fi·to [grəˈfiːtəu; grəˋfito] ***n*.** (*pl*. ***-ti*** [-tiː; -ti]) (古墓、古墙上的)粗糙雕刻;现代在墙壁等处的乱涂。～ **pollution** 涂写污染〔指在公共场所乱涂乱写〕。

graf·fi·ti [grəˈfiːti; grəˋfiti] ***vt*.** 在…上涂鸦。

graf·fi·tist [grəˈfiːtist; grəˋfitɪst] ***n*.** (在公共场所的墙壁等处)乱涂乱写者。

graft[1] [grɑːft; grɑft] **I** ***n*.** **1.** 接穗,嫁接;嫁接植物;嫁接法。**2.**【医】移植,移植片,移植物。**2.**〔美口〕贪污,受贿;(贪污所得的)赃品。***take*** ～贪污。**II** ***vt*., *vi*.** **1.** 接枝,嫁接 (*in*; *into*; *on*; *upon*)。**2.** 用嫁接法种植。**3.**【医】移植(皮、肉)。**4.**〔美口〕贪污,受贿。～ **copolymer** 接枝共聚物。～ **hybrid** 嫁接杂种。

graft[2] [grɑːft; grɑft] ***n*.** **1.**〔英〕一铲可以挖起的土的深度。**2.** 弯口铁铲。

graft·age [ˈgrɑːftidʒ, ˈgræftidʒ; ˋgrɑftɪdʒ, ˋgræftɪdʒ] ***n*.**【植】**1.** 嫁接,嫁接术。**2.** 嫁接后的状态。

graft·er [ˈgrɑːftə; ˋgrɑftɚ] ***n*.** **1.** 嫁接者,移植者。**2.**〔美口〕贪污分子,受贿者。

graft·ing [ˈgrɑːftiŋ; ˋgrɑftɪŋ] ***n*.** 嫁接法;【医】移植法。～ **clay** 覆盖于接穗和砧木连接处的黏土。

Gra·ham(e) [ˈgreiəm; ˋgreəm] ***n*.** 格雷厄姆〔姓氏,男子名〕。

gra·ham [ˈgreiəm; ˋgreəm] ***a*.** 用未筛过的面粉制作的,全麦粉的。～ **bread**〔美〕(美国 S. Graham 创制的)营养黑面包。～ **flour**〔美〕(富有营养价值的)粗面粉,全麦面粉。

grail[1] [greil; grel] ***n*.** **1.** 杯;盘 (= platter)。**2.** 长期向往的事物。***the*** [***Holy***] ***G-*** (中世纪传说中)耶稣在最后晚餐时所用的杯[盘]。

grail[2] [greil; grel] ***n*.** = gradual psalms.

grail[3] [greil; grel] ***n*.**〔诗〕砾石,鹅卵石。

grain [grein; gren] **I** ***n*.** **1.** 谷物,粮食〔英国叫 corn〕;谷类植物。**2.** 谷粒,籽粒。**3.** (沙、金、盐等的)粒,颗粒,晶粒。**4.** 些微,一点儿〔主要用于否定句〕。**5.** (木材、大理石等的)纹理;皮革的正面,粒面。**6.** 脾气,特性,癖性。**7.** 谷〔英美重量最低单位,略作 gr. = 64.8 毫克或 1/7,000 磅〕。**8.** 胭脂虫;(用胭脂虫制的)红色染料;不褪色染料;〔古〕颜色,色调。**9.**〔*pl*.〕麦芽渣,酒糟。*a* ～ *distillery* 酒精厂。*a* ～ *of rice* 米粒;(瓷器上的)透明碎米花。*coarse* ～粗粮,杂粮。*refined* ～细粮。(*food*) ～*s* 粮食。*woods of fine* [*coarse*] ～细[粗]纹木材。*There isn't a* ～ *of truth in what he said*. 他说的全不是真话。***against the*** ～ **1.** 逆纹理。**2.**〔喻〕不合脾气地,违反意愿地。***a*** ～ ***of mustard seed*** 发展前途极大的小东西。***a*** ～ ***of wheat in a bushel of chaff*** 徒劳,毫无结果,无济于事。***dye in*** ～ 生染,用不褪色染料染。***in*** ～ 深红的;根深蒂固的;十足的;坏透的;天生的 (*knave* [*rogue*] *in* ～生来的大坏蛋)。***with a*** ～ ***of salt*** = ***with some*** ～***s of allowance*** 有保留地,不全信地,打上几分折扣(处理)。***without a*** ～ ***of ...*** 一点也没有 (*a boy without a* ～ *of common sense* 一点道理都不懂的小男孩)。**II** ***vt*.** **1.** 把…作成细粒。**2.** 把…漆[画]成木纹,使(皮等)表面粗糙。**3.** 染透。**4.** 刮去(皮上的)毛。— ***vi*.** 成为细粒。～ **alcohol** 乙醇,酒精。～ **elevator**〔美〕谷塔,谷仓。～ **field** 庄稼(田)地。～ **leather** 粒面向外的皮革。～ **rust** 谷物锈病。～**sick** (牛的)瘤胃扩张症。～ **side** 皮革粒面。～ **sorghum** 高粱。**-less** ***a*.** 没有谷粒的,没有纹理的。

grained [greind; grend] ***a*.** 粒状的,有纹的。**-ness** ***n*.**

grain·er [ˈgreinə; ˋgrenɚ] ***n*.** **1.** 脱毛器,刮毛刀;鞣皮剂。**2.** 漆[画]木纹者;起纹器。

grains [greinz; grenz] ***n*. *pl*.**〔作单数用〕双齿[多齿]鱼叉。

grain·y [ˈgreini; ˋgrenɪ] ***a*.** **1.** 谷粒多的。**2.** 粒状的,粒面的;木纹状的。**3.** 有细粒的。**-i·ness** ***n*.**

graip [greip; grep] ***n*.**〔Scot.〕(叉肥料或掘马铃薯等用的)三齿[四齿]叉。

Gral·la·to·res [ˌgræləˈtɔːriːz; ˏgræləˋtɔriz] ***n*. *pl*.**【动】涉禽类。

gral·la·to·ri·al [ˌgræləˈtɔːriəl; ˏgræləˋtɔrɪəl] ***a*.**【动】涉禽类的。

gram[1] [græm; græm] ***n*.** **1.**【植】鹰嘴豆。**2.** 绿豆。

gram[2] [græm; græm] ***n*.** 克〔重量单位,略作 g.〕。～ **atom**【化】克原子。～ **calorie** 克卡〔热量单位〕。～ **equivalent**【化】克当量。～ **molecule**【化】克分子。

gram. = grammar; grammarian; grammatical.

-gram[1] *comb. f.* 表示"克":kilo*gram*.

-gram[2] *comb. f.* 表示"书写物","字":tele*gram*.

gra·ma, gram·ma [ˈgrɑːmə, ˈgræmə; ˋgrɑmə, ˋgræmə] ***n*.**〔美〕【植】格兰马草 (= ～ grass)。

gram·a·ry(e) [ˈgræməri; ˋgræmərɪ] ***n*.**〔英古〕魔术。

gra·mer·cy [grəˈməːsi; grəˋmɝsɪ] ***int*.**〔古〕**1.** 多谢! **2.** 天哪!

gram·i·ci·din [ˌgræmiˈsaidin; ˏgræməˋsaɪdn̩] ***n*.**【药】短杆菌肽。

gram·i·na·ceous [ˌgræmiˈneiʃəs; ˏgræməˋneʃəs], **gra·min·e·ous** [grəˈminiəs; grəˋmɪnɪəs] ***a*.** **1.** 草的;草似的。**2.** 草多的;草绿色的。**3.** 禾本科的。

gram·i·niv·o·rous [ˌgræmiˈnivərəs; ˏgræməˋnɪvərəs] ***a*.** 吃草的,草食的。

gram·ma·log(ue) [ˈgræməlɔg; ˋgræməlɑg] ***n*.** (速记中)用简略记号表示的字[词]。

gram·mar [ˈgræmə; ˋgræmɚ] ***n*.** **1.** 语法;语法学;语法书。**2.** 语法现象,(个人的)语法知识,文理。**3.** (学术的)基本原理;入门,初阶。*general* [*philosophical*, *universal*] ～一般语法学。*historical* ～历史语法学。*His* ～ *is shocking*. 他的文句糟极了,他的文理极差。*a bad* [*good*] ～不正确的[正确的]说法。*a G- of Science*《科学初阶》。～ **school** **1.**〔英〕语法学校〔十六世纪以前以教拉丁文为主,后变为中学,教授语言、历史和自然科学等〕。**2.**〔美〕初级中学。

gram·mar·i·an [grəˈmɛəriən; grəˋmɛrɪən] ***n*.** 语法学者;语法教师。

gram·mat·i·cal [grəˈmætikəl; grəˋmætɪkl̩] ***a*.** 语法的,语法上的;合语法的。～ *gender* 语法上的性。*a* ～ *sense* 字面的意义,语法上的意义。**-ly** ***ad*.** **-ness** ***n*.**

gram·mat·i·cize [grəˈmætisaiz; grəˋmætɪsaɪz] ***vt*.** 使合语法。— ***vi*.** **1.** 讨论语法问题。**2.** 卖弄语法知识。

gramme [græm; græm] ***n*.** = gram[2].

gram·my [ˈgræmi; ˋgræmɪ] ***n*.**〔口〕= **1.** gramophone. **2.** grandmother.

Gram-neg·a·tive [ˈgræmˈnegətiv; ˋgræmˋnɛgətɪv] ***a*.**〔亦作 g-〕【医】革兰氏阴性的。

gram·o·phone [ˈgræməfəun; ˋgræməfon] ***n*.** 留声机。*sing into the* ～灌唱片,灌音。**-phon·ic** [ˌgræməˈfɔnik; ˏgræməˋfɑnɪk] ***a*.** **-i·cally** ***ad*.**

Gram-pos·i·tive [ˈgræmˈpɔzətiv; ˋgræmˋpɑzətɪv] ***a*.**〔亦作 g-〕【医】革兰氏阳性的。

gramps [græmps; gramps] ***n*.**〔俚〕= grandfather.

gram·pus [ˈgræmpəs; ˋgræmpəs] ***n*.** **1.**【动】逆戟鲸,鲩。**2.**〔口〕呼吸[打鼾]声音粗大的人。*blow* [*puff*, *snore*] *like a* ～鼾声如雷。

Gram's method [græmz'meθəd; græmz`mεθəd] 革兰氏染色法〔研究细菌的一种染色法〕。

Gram stain [græm stein; græm sten] ***n.*** 细菌染色液。

gran turismo [græn tuə'rizməu; græn tʊ`rɪzmo] ***n.*** (*pl.* ***gran turismos***)〔It.〕(制造标准比得上赛车的)高级跑车。

gran·a·dil·la [ˌgrænə'dilə; ˏgrænə`dɪlə] ***n.***【植】西番莲属(*Passiflora*)植物的食用果实。

gran·a·ry ['grænəri; `grænərɪ] ***n.*** 谷仓,粮仓;产粮区。*a grand* ～天然粮仓;鱼米之乡。

Gran Cha·co ['grɑːn 'tʃɑːkəu; `grɑn `tʃɑko]〔常与 the 连用〕(南美洲亚热带地区,横贯阿根廷、玻利维亚、巴拉圭的)大厦谷。

grand [grænd; grænd] **I** ***a.*** **1.** 盛大的,宏大的;堂皇的,雄伟的。**2.**〔口〕富丽的,漂亮的,豪华的。**3.**〔用于头衔〕最高的,首要的;伟大的,杰出的;崇高的,尊贵的。**4.**(最)重要的,重大的;大的,主要的(*opp.* petit, petty, common)。**5.** 总括性的,全部的,完全的。**6.**【乐】大合奏用的,全…。**7.**〔口〕快乐的,极好的。**8.**(亲属关系中)(外)祖…;(外)孙…。*a* ～ *air* 堂皇的气派,堂堂仪表。*a* ～ *character* 崇高的人格。～ *climax* 顶点,最高潮。*a* ～ *committee* 英国下议院审议法律、贸易法案的两个常设委员会之一。～ *entrance* 大门。*a* ～ *lady* 贵妇人。*a* ～ *man* 伟人;名人。～ *manner* =～ style. *a* ～ *mistake* 大错误。～ *question* 重大问题。～ *relief* 高浮雕。～ *sight* 壮观。*a* ～ *style* 庄重的文体。*the* ～ *total* 总计。*a* ～ *view* 壮丽的景色。*It will be* ～ *if you can come.* 你要是能来,那就再好没有了。***do the*** ～〔口〕装模作样,摆架子。***have a*** ～ ***time*** 过得极愉快。***live in*** ～ ***style*** 过豪华生活。***the G- National*** 英国利物浦每年举行一次的野外障碍赛马。***the G- Old Man***【英史】英国首相格拉德斯通(Gladstone)的尊称。***the G- Old Party*** 美国共和党的别称(略作 GOP)。***the*** ～ ***slam*** **1.**〔美俚〕(桥牌等的)满贯;(运动比赛等的)全胜。**2.**【棒球】全垒打,本垒打,也叫 ～***-slammer***. **II** ***n.*** **1.** 大钢琴(=～ piano). **2.**〔美俚〕〔单复同〕一千元(钞票)。～**aunt** 叔祖母,伯祖母,姑婆,舅婆,姨婆。～**baby** 小孙子,小孙女(即婴孩期的 ～child)。**G- Canal** **1.** 中国大运河〔杭州—通县〕。**2.** 意大利威尼斯主运河。**G- Canyon** 美国科罗拉多河流域的大峡谷。～**child** (*pl.* ～***children***) 孙子,孙女,外孙。**G- Cross** 英国大十字勋章。～**daughter** 孙女,外孙女。～**dad**, ～**-dad**〔口〕爷爷。～**daddy** = grandfather. ～**-ducal** ***a.*** 大公的,大公国的。～ **duchess** 大公夫人;大公爵夫人;女大公爵。～ **duchy** (大公辖下的)公国;大公爵领地。～ **finale**(戏剧、运动会等的)高潮性结尾。～ **juror** 大陪审官。～ **jury** 大陪审团〔由 12 人以上组成的审查罪案团体,负责罪案的审查事项,如证据充分,则提请小陪审团审理〕。～ **larceny**【法】**1.** 大盗窃案罪〔美国法定额各州不一,一般为 25—60 美元,为小盗窃罪(petit larceny)之对〕。**2.**(不拘数目,不用武力,人对人进行的)敲诈,勒索。～ **lodge**(共济会等秘密团体的)总部。～**ma**, ～**ma(m)ma**〔口〕奶奶,外婆。～ **master** **1.** 大师〔最高棋手等的称号〕。**2.**〔G- M-〕【英史】骑士团团长;(共济会等秘密团体分支组织的)领导人。**G- Monarch** 法国路易十四国王。～**nephew** 侄孙,侄外孙。～**niece** 侄孙女,侄外孙女。～ **opera** 大歌剧〔无对白,全部为歌唱〕。～ **orchestra** 大型管弦乐队,交响乐队。～**pa**, ～**papa**〔口〕爷爷,外公。～ **parent** ***n.*** 祖父母,外祖父母。～ **piano** 大钢琴,三角钢琴。～ **right and left**【民间舞蹈】反向圆转〔两组成圆形交织,作反向圆转〕。～**sire**〔古〕祖父;祖先;老者。～ **slam** **1.**(桥牌等)大满贯(全赢 13 墩牌)。**2.**【体】全胜。～**son** 孙子,外孙。～ **tour** **1.** 教育旅行〔旧时英国贵族子弟到欧洲大陆旅行,以完成自己的教育阶段〕。**2.** 与此类似的旅行。**3.** 有向导的参观〔如对建筑物等〕。～**uncle** 伯祖父,叔祖父,外伯祖,外叔祖。**-ness** ***n.*** 宏大;壮观;伟大;堂皇;庄严;华丽。

gran·dam, **gran·dame** ['grændæm, -dəm; `grændæm, -dəm] ***n.***〔古〕祖母,外祖母;老太婆,老妇人。

grande [grɑːnd; grɑnd] ***a.***〔F.〕重大的,宏大的,盛大的,显要的。～ **dame** 贵妇。～ **passion** 寝食俱废的恋爱。～ **toilette** 大礼服。

gran·dee [græn'diː; græn`di] ***n.*** **1.** 大公,(西班牙及葡萄牙的)最高贵族。**2.** 高官,显贵。

gran·deur ['grændʒə; `grændʒɚ] ***n.*** **1.** 宏伟庄严;壮观。**2.** 豪华,富丽堂皇。**3.** 伟大,崇高。*full of power and* ～威武雄壮。*with* ～隆重的。

grand·fa·ther ['grændˌfɑːðə; `grændˏfɑðɚ] ***n.*** **1.** 祖父,外祖父。**2.** 老大爷。**3.** 祖先。*a great* ～曾祖父。～ **clause**〔美〕**1.** 老祖父条款〔规定南北战争前享有选举权的白人后代,即使没有文化也有选举权〕。**2.**(某些法律中的)不追溯条款。～**('s) clock** 有摆的座钟。**-ly** ***a.*** 祖父的,祖父似的,慈祥的。

grand·folks ['grændfəuks; `grændfəuks] ***n.*** (外)祖父母辈。

gran·dil·o·quence [græn'diləkwəns; græn`dɪləkwəns] ***n.*** 夸大,夸张

gran·dil·o·quent [græn'diləkwənt; græn`dɪləkwənt] ***a.*** 夸张的,夸大的。*Indeed, no eulogy could be more* ～ *than this.* 真是恭维备至。**-ly** ***ad.***

gran·di·ose ['grændiəus; `grændɪos] ***a.*** **1.** 雄伟的,宏大的,壮观的。**2.** 铺张的,夸大的,浮夸的,自以为是的,沾沾自喜的, **-ly** ***ad.***

gran·di·os·i·ty [ˌgrændi'ɔsiti; ˏgrændə`ɑsətɪ] ***n.*** **1.** 宏大,辉煌;堂皇。**2.** 夸张;铺张;浮夸;沾沾自喜。

gran·dio·so [grɑːn'djəusəu; ˏgrændi`oso] ***a.***, ***ad.***〔It.〕【乐】雄伟的〔地〕,壮丽的〔地〕,崇高的〔地〕。

grand·ly ['grændli; `grændlɪ] ***ad.*** 宏伟地;堂皇地;盛大地;崇高地;华丽地。

grand mal ['græn 'mæl; `græn `mæl]〔F.〕【医】癫痫大发作。

grand monde [ˌgrɑːn 'mɔnd; ˏgrɑn `mɔnd]〔F.〕上流社会。

grand·moth·er ['grændˌmʌðə; `grændˏmʌðɚ] **I** ***n.*** **1.** 祖母,外祖母。**2.** 老奶奶。**3.** 女祖先。*a great* ～曾祖母。***teach one's*** ～ ***(how) to suck eggs*** 教训长辈;班门弄斧。***Tell that to your*** ～. 胡说。***This beats my*** ～. 吓了一跳。**II** ***vt.*** 娇养,溺爱;悉心照料。～ ***the cups*** 弄湿茶托以防杯滑。**-ly** ***a.*** 祖母似的,慈祥的,溺爱的,唠叨的。

grand prix [grɑːn 'priː; grɑn `pri]〔F.〕头等奖,最高奖。

grand siècle [grɑːn si'ekl; grɑn sɪ`εkl̩]〔F.〕古典时代,黄金时代〔尤指法国的十七世纪〕。

grand·stand ['grændstænd; `grændstænd] **I** ***n.*** **1.**(体育场的)正面看台,大看台。**2.** 坐在正面观众席上的观众。**II** ***vi.***〔口〕为博取观众喝采而卖弄技巧。～ **play** **1.**(比赛时为博取观众喝采的)卖弄技巧。**2.**〔喻〕哗众取宠的言行;做作的举动。**-er** ***n.*** 为博取观众喝采而卖弄技巧的运动员。

grange [greindʒ; grendʒ] ***n.*** **1.**〔英〕庄园;地主的住宅;〔古〕谷仓;(庄园、修道院的)附属农场。**2.**〔G-〕〔美〕格兰其〔成立于 1867 年的美国全国性保护田庄农民利益的秘密组织,正式名称为"农人协进会"〕。

grang·er ['greindʒə; `grendʒɚ] ***n.*** **1.**〔美〕"格兰其"成员,"农人协进会"会员。**2.** 庄稼汉,农夫;农场管家。

grang·er·ism ['greindʒərizəm; `grendʒəˏrɪzəm] ***n.*** 转载别本书上的插图。

grang·er·ize ['greindʒəraiz; `grendʒəˏraɪz] ***vt.*** **1.** 插入(由别本书上剪来的插图)。**2.** 从(书中)剪下插图。**-i·za·tion** ***n.*** **-iz·er** ***n.***

gra·nif·er·ous [grə'nifərəs; grə`nɪfərəs] ***a.*** 结谷粒的,结颗粒状果实的。

gran·ite ['grænit; `grænɪt] ***n.*** **1.** 花岗岩,花岗石。**2.** 坚

G

如磐石,坚韧不拔。*gneissic* ～片麻状花岗岩。***as hard as*** ～ 像岩石一样坚硬的。***bite on*** ～ 白费气力,徒劳无功。***the G- City*** 苏格兰阿伯丁市的别名。***the G- State*** 美国新罕布什尔州的别名。～ **boys**〔美〕新罕布什尔州人(的绰号)。～**ware** 有花岗石斑纹的陶器;涂灰色珐琅的铁器。～**-wash** ***n***.(花岗)石洗,石磨〔将蓝色劳动布放在有粗糙石块的水中洗涤,使织物经磨损后显出淡色条纹,用以制作牛仔服〕。

gra·nit·ic [grəˈnitik; grəˋnɪtɪk] ***a***. 花岗岩(似)的;由花岗岩形成的。

gra·nit·i·form [græˈnitifɔːm; græˋnɪtəfɔrm] ***a***. 花岗石状的。

gran·it·oid [ˈgrænitɔid; ˋgrænɪtɔɪd] ***a***. 花岗岩状的;有花岗岩结构的。

gra·niv·o·rous [grəˈnivərəs; grəˋnɪvərəs] ***a***. 食谷的,食种子的。

gran·nie, gran·ny [ˈgræni; ˋgrænɪ] **I** ***n***. **1.**〔口〕奶奶,外婆。**2.** 老妈妈,老奶奶。**3.** 婆婆妈妈的人;唠叨挑剔的人。**4.**〔美〕接生婆。**5.** = ～'s knot. ***～'s knot*** 松 8 字结〔*cf*. reef knot〕. ***teach one's*** ～ (***how***) ***to suck eggs*** = teach one's grandmother (how) to suck eggs. **II** ***a***. 祖母装的,松身密实装的。～**-bashing** ***n***. **1.** 虐待老人。**2.** 访老助老〔一种帮助老人的社区服务〕。～ **dress** (从颈部一直达到踝部的松身密实装,祖母装。～ **glass** (外形类似过去老年妇女使用的)仿老式金丝眼镜。**G-Smith** 澳大利亚的绿苹果。～ **track** 女儿责任制〔由妇女承担起照料父母之责任〕。

gran·o·lith [ˈgrænəliθ; ˋgrænəlɪθ] ***n***. 人造铺地石。**-ic** ***a***.

gran·o·phyre [ˈgrænəfaiə; ˋgrænəfaɪr] ***n***.【地】花斑岩,文像斑岩。**-phyr·ic** [-ˈfiərik; -ˋfɪərɪk] ***a***.

grant [grɑːnt; grænt] **I** ***vt***. **1.** 许可,答应,承认。**2.** 授与,让渡,转让。**3.** 假定,姑且承认。～ (*sb*.) *a request* 接受(某人)要求。～ *a pension* 给予退休金。*I* ～ *you*. 就算你对。*This* ～*ed*, *what next*? 就算这样,下文呢? ～(***ing***) ***that*** ... = ～***ed that*** ...假定…,即使…。***take it for*** ～***ed*** 认为当然 (= accept as true)。**II** ***n***. **1.** 许可;答应;承认。**2.** 授与,让渡;转让证书。**3.** 授给物,转让权;补助金。～ ***in aid*** (***of***) (…的)补助金。***in*** ～【法】凭证件才能让渡的(财产)。～**-aided** ***a***. 受补助的(～*-aided school* 接受公共基金资助的学校)。**-a·ble** ***a***. 可同意的,可授与的,可转让的。**-ed·ly** ***ad***.

Grant [grɑːnt; grænt] ***n***. **1.** 格兰特〔姓氏,男子名〕。**2.** **Ulysses Simpson** ～ 尤利塞斯·辛普森·格兰特〔1822—1885,美国南北战争时北军总司令,第十八任总统〕。

gran·tee [grɑːnˈtiː; grɑnˋti] ***n***.【法】被授与者,受让人。

Gran·tham [ˈgrænθəm; ˋgrænθəm] ***n***. 格兰瑟姆〔姓氏〕。

grant-in-aid [ˈgrɑːntinˈeid; ˋgræntɪnˋed] ***n***. (*pl*. ***grants-in-aid***) (中央对地方的)拨款;补助金,助学金。

grant·man [ˈgrɑːntmən; ˋgræntmən] ***n***. 申请补助费专家。～**ship** 懂得如何申请到补助费的本领。

gran·tor [grɑːnˈtɔː, ˈgrɑːntə; grænˋtɔr, ˋgræntɚ] ***n***.【法】授与者,让与者。

gran·u·lar [ˈgrænjulə; ˋgrænjəlɚ] ***a***. 颗粒状的,粒面的,由小粒形成的。～ **lid**【医】沙眼。～ **structure**【农】(土壤的)团粒结构。**-i·ty** [ˌgrænjuˈlæriti; ˏgrænjəˋlærətɪ] ***n***. 颗粒状,颗粒度,颗粒性。**-ly** ***ad***.

gran·u·late [ˈgrænjuleit; ˋgrænjəˏlet] ***vt***. 使成颗粒,使成粒状;使表面粗糙,使表面成粒面。— ***vi***. 形成颗粒,表面变粗糙。～**d glass** 麻面玻璃。～**d leather** 珠皮。～**d fertilizer** 颗粒肥料。～**d sugar** 砂糖。

gran·u·la·tion [ˌgrænjuˈleiʃən; ˏgrænjəˋleʃən] ***n***. **1.** 形成颗粒,形成粒面,表面粗糙。**2.**【医】肉芽,颗粒;肉芽形成。～ **tissue**【病理】肉芽组织。

gran·u·la·tor [ˈgrænjuleitə; ˋgrænjəˏletɚ] ***n***. 砂糖成粒器;使形成颗粒的东西[人]。

gran·ule [ˈgrænjuːl; ˋgrænjʊl] ***n***. **1.** 颗粒,细粒。**2.** 粒状斑点。**3.**【天】(日面的)米粒,粒状斑。

gran·u·lite [ˈgrænjulait; ˋgrænjəlaɪt] ***n***.【地】白粒岩,粒变岩。**-litic** [-ˈlitik; -ˋlɪtɪk] ***a***.

gran·u·lo·cyte [ˈgrænjuləusait; ˋgrænjələsaɪt] ***n***.【医】粒性白血球。**-lo·cyt·ic** [-ləuˈsitik; -ləˋsɪtɪk] ***a***.

gran·u·lo·cy·to·pe·nia [ˌgrænjuləuˌsaitəˈpiːniə; ˏgrænjələˏsaɪtəˋpinɪə] ***n***.【医】粒细胞减少。

gran·u·lo·ma [ˌgrænjuˈləumə; ˏgrænjəˋlomə] ***n***. (*pl*. ～***s***, ***-ma·ta*** [-mətə; -mətə])【医】肉芽肿,肉芽瘤。**-tous** ***a***.

gran·u·lo·ma·to·sis [ˌgrænjuləuməˈtəusis; ˏgrænjəlomə ˋtosɪs] ***n***.【医】肉芽肿症。

gran·u·lose [ˈgrænjuləus; ˋgrænjəˏlos] **I** ***n***.【化】淀粉糖。**II** ***a***. = granular.

gran·u·lous [ˈgrænjuləs; ˋgrænjələs] ***a***. 颗粒状的,有颗粒的。

gra·num [ˈgreinəm; ˋgrenəm] ***n***.【生】叶绿体基粒。

grape [greip; grep] ***n***. **1.** 葡萄。**2.** 葡萄色,深紫色。**3.**〔the ～〕葡萄酒。**4.**〔*pl*.〕(马脚上生的)葡萄疮;(牛的)结核病。**5.**【军】葡萄弹。～ *juice* 葡萄汁。***sour*** ～***s*** 酸葡萄〔指可望而不可及的东西〕。***the*** ～ = ***the juice of the*** ～葡萄酒。～ **brandy** 葡萄白兰地酒。～ **cure** 葡萄疗法。～**fruit**【植】葡萄柚。～ **hyacinth**【植】麝香兰属(*muscari*)植物。～ **ivy**【植】菱叶白粉藤(*Cissus rhombifolia*)〔产于南美北部,为常见的园庭植物〕。～ **shot**【军】葡萄弹。～**stone** 葡萄核,葡萄种子。～ **sugar** 葡萄糖。～**vine** **1.** 葡萄藤;葡萄树。**2.**〔美俚〕传闻,谣言;小道消息的流传;秘密情报的口头传递。**3.** 一种花式滑冰的动作;一种摔跤动作。～**vine telegraph** 小道消息的不胫而走。

grap·er·y [ˈgreipəri; ˋgrepərɪ] ***n***. 葡萄园;葡萄温室。

graph[1] [grɑːf; grɑf] **I** ***n***. **1.**【数】曲线图;坐标图,图表。**2.** 统计曲线。**II** ***vt***. 用图表表示,把…绘入图表。～ **paper** 图纸,坐标图纸,标绘图纸。～**ing calculator** 绘图计算器〔一种学生用的微型计算机〕。

graph[2] [grɑːf; grɑf] **I** ***n***. 胶版。**II** ***vt***. 用胶版印刷。

graph[3] [grɑːf; grɑf] ***n***.【语】**1.** 词的拼法。**2.** 表示音素的最小字母单位。

-graph *comb*. *f*. 表示 **1.** "写、画、记录的用具": phono*graph*, tele*graph*. **2.** "写[画、记录]的结果": auto*graph*, photo*graph*.

graph·eme [ˈgræfiːm; ˋgræfim] ***n***.【语】**1.** 字母。**2.** (字母的)书写单位;(音素的)图形单位。

-graph·er *comb*. *f*. 表示"书写者","描绘者","记录者": photo*grapher*, biblio*grapher*.

graph·ic(al) [ˈgræfik(əl); ˋgræfɪk(əl)] ***a***. **1.** 书写的,绘画的;印刷的,雕刻的。**2.** (叙述等)写实的,绘画似的,生动的。**3.** 图的,图解的;用图表示的;用文字表示的。～ *error* 笔误。～ *method* 图解法。*the* ～ *arts* 书画刻印艺术。～ **algebra** 图解代数学。～ **formula**【化】图解式,结构式。～ **novel** 连环画小说。**-ly** ***ad***. **-ness** ***n***.

graph·ics [ˈgræfiks; ˋgræfɪks] ***n***. *pl*.〔用作单数〕**1.** (建筑或工程的)绘图学,制图学。**2.** 图解计算,图式计算;(可用人工操作的)电子计算机图解法。**3.**【语】书法,字体。

graph·ite [ˈgræfait; ˋgræfaɪt] ***n***.【化】石墨,黑铅,炭精;铅笔粉。*colloidal* ～胶体石墨。～ *electrode*【电】石墨电极。*live* [*dead*] ～含〔不含〕铀石墨。～ **moderated reactor**【原】石墨减速反应堆。

graph·i·tize [ˈgræfitaiz; ˋgræfətaɪz] ***vt***. **1.** 使石墨化。**2.** 在…内(或上)涂石墨,在…内充石墨。**-i·ti·za·tion** [ˌgræfitaiˈzeiʃən; ˏgræfətaɪˋzeʃən] ***n***.

graph·i·toid [ˈgræfitɔid; ˋgræfətɔɪd] ***a***. 石墨状的。

graph·ol·o·gy [græˈfɔlədʒi; græˋfɑlədʒɪ] ***n***. **1.** 笔迹学。**2.** 图解法。

graph·o·scope [ˈgræfəskəup; ˋgræfəskop] ***n***. 电子计算

机显示器。

graph·o·type [ˈgræfətaip; ˋgræfətaɪp] ***n***. 白垩凸板。

-graph·y *comb. f*. 表示 **1**.“书法”;“写法”;“图示法”: photo*graphy*. **2**. “志”,“记”: geo*graphy*, biblio*graphy*.

grap·nel [ˈgræpnəl; ˋgræpnəl] ***n***. **1**. 小锚,四爪锚〔又叫 ~ *anchor*〕。**2**. (锚形)铁爪篱。

grap·pa [ˈgrɑːpɑ; ˋgrɑpɑ] ***n***. 〔It.〕白兰地酒。

grap·ple [ˈgræpl; ˋgræpl] **I** ***vt***. **1**. 抓住,捉牢。**2**. (用铁爪篱)钩住(敌船等)。**3**. 与…扭打,与…格斗。— ***vi***. **1**. 用铁锚[铁钩]钩住。**2**. 揪扭,扭打;搏斗(*with*)。~ *an enemy* 与敌人格斗。~ ***difficulties*** 与困难作斗争。~ *with problems* 尽力解决问题。**II** ***n***. **1**. 抓机,抓斗。**2**. 紧握;揪扭,扭打,格斗。**3**. = grapnel. ***come to ~s with*** **1**. 与…格斗。**2**. 尽力从事[对付]。

grap·pler [ˈgræplə; ˋgræplɚ] ***n***. **1**. 抓钩器,抓钩者。**2**. 格斗者。**3**. 〔俚〕手。

grap·pling [ˈgræpliŋ; ˋgræplɪŋ] ***n***. = grapnel. ~ **iron** (打捞用的)抓机;(使船只泊下的)铁钩。

grap·to·lite [ˈgræptəlait; ˋgræptəlaɪt] ***n***. 【动】笔石〔属于腔肠动物的一种化石〕。**-lit·ic** ***a***.

grap·y [ˈgreipi; ˋgrepɪ] ***a***. (***grapi·er***; ***grap·i·est***) **1**. 葡萄(似)的。**2**. 由葡萄制成的,有葡萄(酒)味的。**3**. 【医】生了葡萄疮的。

GRAS = Generally Recognized as Safe 一般安全〔美国食品药物管理局使用的检验标记,表示食品无害人体,安全可用〕。

gra·ser [ˈgreizə; ˋgrezɚ] ***n***. 【物】伽玛(γ)射线激光器。

grasp [grɑːsp; græsp] **I** ***vt***. **1**. 抓住,握紧,抱住。**2**. 领会,理解。~ *the argument* 对论点有所了解。— ***vi***. 抓牢,紧握。***G- all, lose all***. 〔谚〕样样抓,样样差;贪多必失。~ ***at*** 去抓,攫取。~ ***at a straw*** 捞救命稻草。~ ***the nettle*** 迎着艰险上,挺身应付难局。**II** ***n***. **1**. 抓;把握,紧握。**2**. 权力;统制,支配。**3**. 理解;理解力。**4**. 把手,柄,(剑等的)把。*a mind of wide* ~有多方面理解力的头脑。***beyond one's*** ~ 手[能力]达不到,不能理解的,鞭长莫及。***have a good ~ of*** 深刻了解。***in the ~ of*** 在…掌握中。***keep a firm ~ on*** 抓紧。***within one's*** ~ 手[能力]达得到,能理解的。

gras·pa·ble [ˈgrɑːspəbl; ˋgræspəbḷ] ***a***. 能理解的,可以懂的。

grasp·ing [ˈgrɑːspiŋ; ˋgræspɪŋ] ***a***. **1**. 抓的,握的。**2**. 贪婪的。**-ly** ***ad***. **-ness** ***n***.

grass [grɑːs; græs] **I** ***n***. **1**. 草;牧草;牧草地,牧场;草地,草原。**2**. 〔*pl*.〕【植】禾本科植物;〔*pl*.〕草叶;〔俚〕龙须菜,芦笋,莴苣,(色拉中的)生菜。**3**. 草绿时节,春天。**4**. 【矿】矿山地面,矿井地面。**5**. 〔英俚〕(印刷厂的)临时排字工作,临时工作。**6**. 【无】噪音细条,(雷达屏上的)“毛草”。**7**. 〔俚〕大麻〔北美产的毒品〕。**8**. 闲居(处)。*All flesh is* ~. 人尽如草,终必枯亡。~ *family* 禾本科植物。*a* ~ *lamb* 牧放中出生的小羊。*a horse five years old next* ~来春五岁的马。*While the* ~ *grows the horse* [*steed*] *starves*. 〔谚〕远水不救近火。***be at*** ~ = ***be out at*** ~ **1**. 在牧放中。**2**. 闲着(休假,失业等)。**3**. 【矿】离开矿井,在露天。***between*** [***betwixt***] ~ ***and hay*** 〔美〕在儿童与成人之间的青少年。***bring to*** ~ 把(矿)运出井外。***come to*** ~ 走出矿井外。***cut one's own*** ~ 〔口〕自食其力。***cut the ~ from under sb.'s feet*** 妨碍某人;挫败某人。***go to*** ~ **1**. (家畜)上牧场去。**2**. 〔口〕歇工,休假;退休;死去。**3**. 〔口〕被打倒(*Go to* ~! 去你的! 见你的鬼!)。***hear the ~ grow*** 极端敏感。***hunt*** ~〔口〕一败涂地,被打倒。***Come*** [***Keep***] ***off the*** ~. **1**. (布告)勿踏草地。**2**. 谨慎小心。***lay down in*** ~ (在地上)铺上草皮,使成草地。***let no ~ grow under one's feet*** 不错过机会,说干就干。***put*** [***send, turn out***] ***to*** ~ **1**. 把…赶到牧场,放牧。**2**. 辞退,解雇;强迫退休。**II** ***vt***. **1**. 用草覆盖;使长草,在…撒草种。**2**. 使吃草,放牧。**3**. 在草上晒;把…摊开在草地上。**4**. 〔英〕打倒;把(鱼)钓上岸来;打落(飞鸟)。***be ~ed down*** 用草覆盖着,埋在草下。***be ~ed over*** 完全被草盖上。— ***vi***. **1**. (家畜)在牧场上吃草。**2**. 长满草。**3**. 〔美俚〕告密,当告密者。~**-blade** 草叶。~ **character** (汉字的)草书。~ **cloth** **1**. 亚麻布等。**2**. 草编物。~ **cutter** 割草机。~ **green** 草绿色。~**-green** ***a***. **1**. 草绿色的。**2**. 绿草如茵的。~ **hand** **1**. (汉字的)草书。**2**. 〔英俚〕(印刷厂的)临时排字工。~**hopper** **1**. 蚱蜢,蝗虫。**2**. 小型侦察机。**3**. 〔美〕吸大麻烟的人。**4**. 〔美俚〕警察;告密者。~**land** 牧场;草地;草原。~**plot** 草地。~ **roots** **1**. 草根。**2**. 农牧地区;〔集合词〕农牧民。**3**. 基础,根本;基层,基层群众(*cadres at ~ roots level* 基层干部)。~**-roots** ***a***. 〔美口〕农牧地区的,乡下的;农民的,来自民间的;基层的,基层群众的。~ **skiing** 滑草(运动)〔长满青草或覆盖着稻草的斜坡上滑下的运动〕。~ **snake** (无毒)青草蛇。~ **snipe** 红胸滨鹬(= pectoral sandpiper)。~ **tree** **1**. 黄胶草属〔百合科植物,产澳洲,茎木质粗短,顶端密生长叶,可产香树脂〕。**2**. 澳洲千年木〔龙舌兰科植物〕,~ **widow** 离了婚的女人,跟丈夫分居的女人。~ **widower** 离了婚的男人,跟妻子分居的男人。~**work** 〔英〕[矿]坑外作业。**-less** ***a***. 不长草的,没有草的。**-like** ***a***.

grass·y [ˈgrɑːsi; ˋgræsɪ] ***a***. **1**. 草深的,草多的。**2**. 草似的,草绿色的。**3**. 食草的。**-i·ness** ***n***.

grat [græt; græt] greet[2]的过去式。

grate[1] [greit; gret] **I** ***n***. **1**. 炉格,炉篦,炉栅。**2**. 火炉,壁炉。**3**. 格栅,格子。**4**. 【矿】篦条筛,固定筛。**II** ***vt***. 在…上装炉格,在…上装格栅。**-d** ***a***. 有格栅的,有炉格的。**-less** ***a***. 无格栅的,无炉格的。

grate[2] [greit; gret] ***vt***. **1**. 磨擦,轧。**2**. 擦碎;磨损。**3**. 使谋急,激怒。~ *the teeth* 把牙磨得嘎嘎响。— ***vi***. **1**. 磨擦;轧,擦得嘎嘎嘎地响(*against*; *on*; *upon*)。**2**. 激怒,使人烦躁。*noises grating upon the ears* 刺耳的噪音。

G-rated [dʒiː-ˈreitid; dʒi-ˋretɪd] ***a***. (电影)G级的,成年与儿童都适宜观看的。

grate·ful [ˈgreitful; ˋgretfʊl] ***a***. **1**. 感恩的,感谢的。**2**. 愉快的,爽快的;可喜的。*a* ~ *letter* 道谢的信。*a* ~ *odo(u)r* 爽快的气味。***be ~ to sb***. 感谢某人(*for*)。***make a ~ acknowledgement for*** 对…表示衷心的感谢。**-ly** ***ad***. **-ness** ***n***.

grat·er [ˈgreitə; ˋgretɚ] ***n***. **1**. 磨碎[擦碎]东西的人[工具]。**2**. 磨光机;擦菜板;粗齿木锉。

grat·i·cule [ˈgrætikjuːl; ˋgrætɪkjul] ***n***. **1**. 十字线,分度线,标线(片)。**2**. 【地】量板;(绘制地图用的)方格图。

grat·i·fi·ca·tion [ˌgrætifiˈkeiʃən; ˏgrætəfəˋkeʃən] ***n***. **1**. 满足,喜悦;使人满足[喜悦]的事物。**2**. 报酬,奖金。**3**. 满足感。*Your praise gives me much* ~. 承您夸奖,十分高兴。

grat·i·fy [ˈgrætifai; ˋgrætəfaɪ] ***vt***. **1**. 使满足。**2**. 使喜悦,使高兴。**3**. 〔古〕报酬,奖赏。*I was gratified to learn that your son had passed the entrance examination*. 得悉令郎已通过入学考试,我十分高兴。~ *one's thirst for money* 满足金钱欲。**-fi·er** ***n***. 使人感到满足的人[事物]。

grat·i·fy·ing [ˈgrætifaiiŋ; ˋgrætəfaɪɪŋ] ***a***. 可喜的,令人满足的。~ *results* 可喜的成绩。**-ly** ***ad***.

grat·in [ˈgrætn; ˋgrætn] ***n***. 〔F.〕奶汁烤菜(法),表面有一层焦花面包和干酪屑的食物,焦黄面包和干酪屑涂层。

grat·ing[1] [ˈgreitiŋ; ˋgretɪŋ] ***n***. **1**. 格栅,格子;(船上作地板或透光用的)格子板,格子盖。**2**. 【物】光栅。*diffraction* ~衍射光栅,绕射栅。*echelette* ~红外光栅。*wire* ~线栅。

grat·ing[2] [ˈgreitiŋ; ˋgretɪŋ] **I** ***a***. 刺耳的,使人烦躁的,讨厌的。**II** ***n***. 摩擦,摩擦声。**-ly** ***ad***.

gra·tis [ˈgreitis; ˋgretɪs] **I** ***ad***. 免费。*sent the sample* ~ 免费赠送样品。*be admitted* ~受免费招待。***free*** ~

for nothing〔口、谑〕白送。**II** *a*.〔多作表语〕免费的。*Entrance is* ～. 入场免费。

grat·i·tude [ˈgrætitjuːd; ˋgrætətjud] *n*. 感谢;谢意;礼物。*We can hardly express our* ～ *to you for your timely help*. 对于你们的及时帮助,我们很难表达我们的感激之情。***devoid of all*** ～ 忘恩负义。***in token of one's*** ～ 借表谢意。***out of*** ～ 出于感激。***with*** ～ 感谢。

Grat·tan [ˈgrætn; ˋgrætn] *n*. 格拉顿〔姓氏〕。

gra·tu·i·tous [grəˈtju(ː)itəs; grəˋtjuətəs] *a*. 1. 免费的;无偿的。2. 无必要的,无故的,无理由的。～ *service* [*help*] 免费服务[无偿援助]。～ *blessing* 天恩。*a* ～ *liar* 无故扯谎的人。～ **contract**【法】单方面受益的契约。～ **utility**【经】自然效用。**-ly** *ad*. **-ness** *n*.

gra·tu·i·ty [grəˈtjuːiti; grəˋtjuətɪ] *n*. 1. 赏金,小费。2.【军】退伍金;养老金。*No gratuities accepted*. 不收小费。

grat·u·late [ˈgrætjuleit; ˋgrætʃəˏlet] *vt*.〔古〕祝,贺。

grat·u·la·tion [ˌgrætjuˈleiʃən; ˏgrætʃəˋleʃən] *n*.〔古〕祝贺;满足。

grat·u·la·to·ry [ˈgrætjuleitəri; ˋgrætjʊletərɪ] *a*.〔古〕祝贺的。

grau·pel [ˈgraupəl; ˋgraʊpəl] *n*.【气】霰;软雹。

Grau·stark [ˈgraustaːk; ˋgraʊstɑrk] *n*. 空想中的浪漫世界,高度浪漫主义的作品。

gra·va·men [grəˈveimen; grəˋvemɛn] *n*. (*pl*. ～*s*, *-va·mi·na* [-ˈveiminə; -ˋvemɪnə]) 1. 不平,诉苦。2.【法】控诉理由。*the* ～ *of a charge* 控诉的要点。

grave[1] [greiv; grev] *n*. 1. 坟墓;墓穴;墓碑;墓石。2. 死;墓地;埋葬…的地方。3.〔英方〕菜窖。***as secret*** [***silent***] ***as the*** ～ (对秘密)守口如瓶。***beyond the*** ～ 死后,在阴间。***dig one's*** ～ ***with one's teeth*** 为口腹伤生。***dig one's own*** ～ 自掘坟墓。***dread the*** ～ 怕死。***find one's*** ～ ***in*** (*someplace*) 死在(某处)。～ ***of reputations*** 丢脸的地方[原因]。***have*** [***with***] ***one foot in the*** ～ 一只脚在棺材里,离死不远。***in one's*** ～ 已死。***make sb. turn in his*** ～ 做出使死者不安的事,说出使死者不安的话。***on this side of the*** ～ 在人世间。***silent as the*** ～ 1. 没有一点声音;像坟墓那样寂静。2. 一言不发,守口如瓶。***sink into the*** ～ 死。***sb. walking across*** [***on, over***] ***my*** ～ 有人在我坟头上走动〔无故打冷颤时的迷信说法〕。～**clothes**〔*pl*.〕尸衣,寿衣。～**digger** 掘墓人;【动】埋葬虫。～ **goods** 陪葬的贵重物品。～ **robber** 盗墓贼。

grave[2] [greiv; grev] **I** *a*. 1. 重大的,重要的;严重的。2. 严肃的,认真的;庄重的;沉着的;沉重的。3. (颜色等)朴素的。4.【语】低沉的,抑音的(*opp*. acute)。*a* ～ *international situation* 严重的国际局势。*look* ～面孔严肃。*a* ～ *man* 沉着的人。*as* ～ *as a judge* 板着面孔。**II** *n*.【语】抑音〔= ～ accent〕。**-ly** *ad*. **-ness** *n*.

grave[3] [greiv; grev] *vt*. (～*d*; ～*d*, ***graven***)〔古〕雕,刻;铭记 (*in*; *on*)。*be graven on one's heart* 铭记在心。— *vi*. 雕刻。

grave[4] [greiv; grev] *vt*. 对(船底)作清洗并涂上沥青等涂料。

gra·ve [ˈgraːvei; ˋgrave] *a*., *ad*.〔It.〕【乐】沉重,庄重;极慢。

grav·el [ˈgrævəl; ˋgrævəl] **I** *n*. 1.〔集合词〕砂砾,砾石。2.【地】砂石,砾。～ *bed* 砾层。3.【医】尿砂。*auriferous* ～含金砾,金砂。*pay* ～有开采价值的砂金。***scratch*** ～〔美口〕飞跑;为生活奔忙。**II** *vt*. (〔英〕*-ll-*) 1. 铺石子(在路上)。2.〔口〕困住,使着慌。3. (因砂粒嵌入蹄内)使(马)跛足。4.〔美口〕使发怒,激怒。5.〔废〕使(船)搁浅在沙滩上。～ *a road* 以沙砾铺路。***be*** ～***led for sth***. 因为某事感到为难。～**blind** *a*. 几乎失明的,快瞎的。～ **crusher**〔俚〕步兵。～ **pit** 碎石坑,碎石采掘场。～ **road** 碎石路。～**stone** 卵石。～**-voiced** *a*. 声音粗哑的。～ **walk** 砂砾小路。**-ly** *a*. 砂砾多的,铺砂砾的,由砂砾形成的;【医】尿砂的。

grav·en [ˈgreivən; ˋgrevən] grave[3]的过去分词。*a*. 雕刻的,铭记在心上的,不可磨灭的。～ *image* 雕像,偶像。

Gra·ven·hurst [ˈgreivənhəːst; ˋgrevənhɝst] *n*. 格雷文赫斯特〔加拿大市镇;白求恩大夫故乡〕。

Grav·en·stein [ˈgraːvenˌstain; ˋgrævenˏstaɪn] *n*. 伏花皮(晚熟)品种苹果。

grav·er [ˈgreivə; ˋgrevɚ] *n*. 雕刻刀,雕刻工具;〔古〕= engraver.

Graves[1] [graːvz; grɑvz] *n*. (法国)格老弗白葡萄酒。

Graves[2] [greivz; grevz] *n*. 格雷夫斯〔姓氏〕。

graves [greivz; grevz] *n*. *pl*. = greaves.

grave·side [ˈgreivˌsaid; ˋgrevˏsaɪd] **I** *n*. 墓边。**II** *a*. 在墓旁的;在墓旁发生的。

grave·stone [ˈgreivˌstəun; ˋgrevˏston] *n*. 墓石,墓碑。

grave·yard [ˈgreivˌjaːd; ˋgrevˏjɑrd] *n*. 墓地。～ **shift** [**watch**]【矿】(由午夜零时至上午八时的)末班作业;〔美口〕夜班。

grav·ics [ˈgræviks; ˋgrævɪks] *n*. 重力场学。

grav·id [ˈgrævid; ˋgrævɪd] *a*. 妊娠中的。**-vid·i·ty** [græˈviditi; grəˋvɪdətɪ] *n*. **-ly** *ad*. **-ness** *n*.

gra·vim·e·ter [grəˈvimitə; grəˋvɪmətɚ] *n*.【物】1. 重力计,比重计 (= *gravity meter*)。2. 引力测量仪。

grav·i·met·ric [ˌgræviˈmetrik; ˏgrævəˋmɛtrɪk] *a*. (测定)重量的;重量分析的 (= gravimetrical)。**-met·ri·cal·ly** *ad*.

gra·vim·e·try [grəˈvimitri; grəˋvɪmətrɪ] *n*. 重量[密度]测定;重量分析法;重力测量学。

grav·ing[1] [ˈgreiviŋ; ˋgrevɪŋ] *n*. 雕刻品;〔古〕雕刻。

grav·ing[2] [ˈgreiviŋ; ˋgrevɪŋ] *n*. 船底的清洗和涂油。～ **dock** 干船坞。

grav·i·sphere [ˈgrævisfiə; ˋgrævɪsfɪr] *n*.【宇】(太空中某一区域的)引力范围。

grav·i·tate [ˈgræviteit; ˋgrævəˏtet] *vi*. 1. 受重力作用,受引力作用,自然被吸引。2. 沉淀;沉降。3. 倾向 (*to*; *towards*)。*If you all* ～ *to one side, you'll upset the boat*. 如果大家都移向一边,船就要翻了。*The population* ～*s towards the town*. 人口有集中都市的倾向。— *vt*. 使受重力吸引而移动,吸引。

grav·i·ta·tion [ˌgræviˈteiʃən; ˏgrævəˋteʃən] *n*. 1. 万有引力,地心吸力,重力。2. 引力作用;吸引力;下沉;(自然的)倾向,趋势。*the law of* ～引力定律。*terrestrial* ～地球引力。*theory of* ～重力论。*universal* ～万有引力。

grav·i·ta·tion·al [ˌgræviˈteiʃənəl; ˏgrævəˋteʃənəl] *a*.【物】万有引力的,地心吸力的。～ **collapse**【物】引力坍陷。～ **constant**【物】引力常数。～ **field**【物】引力场,重力场。～ **pull** (星球等对另一物体的)引力作用。～ **wave**【物】引力波,重力波。**-ly** *ad*.

grav·i·ti·no [ˌgrævəˈtiːnəu; ˏgrævəˋtino] *n*. (*pl*. *-nos*)【物】引力微子〔一种假设的基本粒子〕。

grav·i·ton [ˈgrævitɔn; ˋgrævətən] *n*.【物】重力量子,引力子。

grav·i·ty [ˈgræviti; ˋgrævətɪ] *n*. 1. 认真,严肃,庄重。2. 重要性,严重性;危险性。3. 重量。4.【物】重力,引力,地心吸力。5.【乐】(音调的)低沉。*acceleration of* ～重力加速度。*the centre of* ～重心,重点。*specific* ～比重。*null* [*zero*] ～无重力,失重。***keep one's*** ～ 持重,不苟言笑。～ **cell** 重力电池。～ **feed** 自重供给,自重进料〔借自身的重力作用以供给燃料、原料等〕。～ **knife** (朝下一摔即可启开的)重力弹簧刀。～ **meter** 重力计,比重计。～ **wave** (液体表面的)重力波;引力场变化波。

gra·vure [grəˈvjuə; grəˋvjur] *n*. 1. 照相凹版,照相凹版印刷术。2. 照相凹版印刷品。

gra·vy [ˈgreivi; ˋgrevɪ] *n*. 1. 肉汁,肉卤。2.〔美俚〕非法所得的钱;容易挣得的钱;额外的收益。***by*** [***good***] ～

G

〔美口〕哎呀！好家伙。***dip in the*** ～〔美俚〕分肥，揩公家的油。～ **boat** 上肉汁用的船形盘。～ **soup** 肉羹。～ **train**〔美俚〕容易捞到钱的活儿，工作清闲而报酬优厚的职务。

gray [grei; gre]〔美〕= grey. ～ **area** 灰区〔指难以界定其学科性质的知识领域或难以界定其准确范畴的事物或现象〕。～ **diplomat**〔美俚〕灰色外交家〔指军舰〕。～**-flanneled** *a*.〔美俚〕广告商的，广告业的。**G- Lady**〔美〕红十字会义务女护士。～**-legs** *n*.〔美俚〕西点军官学校的全体学员。～ **mail** 证言泄漏政府机密而受威胁。～ **market** 灰市〔私人输入商品之市场〕。～ **matter 1.**（脑的）灰白质。**2.**〔美俚〕人脑；智力，主意，点子（*loan sb*. ～ *matter* 给某人出主意）。

Gray [grei; gre] *n*. **1.** 格雷〔姓氏，男子名〕。**2. Thomas** ～ 托马斯·格雷〔1716—1771，英国诗人，其名作为《墓畔哀歌》〕。

gray·ling [ˈgreiliŋ; ˋgrelɪŋ] *n*.【动】**1.** 茴鱼。**2.** 眼蝶科灰色[棕色]蝴蝶。

Gray·son [ˈgreisn; ˋgresn̩] *n*. 格雷森〔姓氏〕。

gray·wa·ter [ˈgreiˌwɔːtə; ˋgreˏwɔtɚ] *n*.〔美〕可循环水，可再利用的废水。

Graz [grɑːts; grɑts] *n*. 格拉次〔奥地利城市〕。

graze[1] [greiz; grez] **I** *vi*. **1.** 喂草，放牧；吃草。**2.**〔谑〕吃饭。**3.**〔口〕零碎进食〔指西方妇女中日益流行的以吃零食当饭吃而不再吃正餐的趋势〕。**4.**〔口〕（看电视时）不断地更换频道。— *vt*. **1.** 使吃青草，放牧。**2.** 在…放牧。～ **cattle** 放牛。～ **a field** 把一块地用作放牧的草场。**II** *n*. 放牧，畜牧；牧草。***send sb. to*** ～ 赶出某人。

graze[2] [greiz; grez] **I** *vt*. **1.** 轻擦；擦破（皮肤）。**2.** 擦过，掠过。— *vi*. 轻轻擦过（*along*; *against*; *by*）。**II** *n*. **1.** 擦过，轻触。**2.** 擦伤。**3.**【军】瞬发。

gra·zier [ˈgreizjə; ˋgreʒɚ] *n*.〔英〕畜牧业者。

gra·zier·y [ˈgreizjəri; ˋgreʒərɪ] *n*. 畜牧业。

graz·ing [ˈgreiziŋ; ˋgrezɪŋ] *n*. **1.** 放牧，放牧法。**2.** 牧场；牧草。～**-land** *n*. 畜牧场，放牧地。

gra·zi·o·so [grɑːˈtsjəusəu; grɑˋtsjoso] *a*., *ad*.〔It.〕【乐】优美；幽雅；柔和。

Gr.Br(it). = Great Britain【地】**1.** 大不列颠（岛）。**2.** 英国。

grease [griːs; gris] **I** *n*. **1.**（炼出的）动物脂，油脂；【机】脂膏，滑脂；（作颜料溶剂用的）脂油；〔古〕脂肪。**2.** 羊毛的脂肪成分；未脱脂羊毛。**3.**【兽医】马踵炎。**4.**〔美俚〕牛油。**5.**〔美俚〕硝化甘油，甘油炸药。**6.**〔俚〕贿赂。*axle* ～轴用润滑脂。*silicon* ～矽[硅]脂，矽[硅]润滑油。*wool in the* ～未脱脂羊毛。***Elbow*** ～ ***gives the best polish***.〔谚〕苦干出好活。***fry*** [***stew***] ***in one's own*** ～ 自作自受。***in*** ～ = ***in pride*** [***prime***] ***of*** ～ 打猎时禽兽正肥，正好屠宰。***melt one's*** ～ 使完了劲。**II** [griːz, griːs; griz, gris] *vt*. **1.** 给…涂油，搽油；用油弄脏；涂油润滑。**2.** 贿赂。**3.** 使（马）患踵炎症。～ ***it in***〔美俚〕使飞机顺利着陆。～ ***sb.'s palm*** [***hand***] 用金钱影响…；贿赂，收买。～ ***the fat pig*** [***sow***] 管闲事。～ ***the skids for***〔美口〕促使…垮台。～ ***the wheels*** 给车轮上油；行贿使事情好办。～**ball**〔美俚〕**1.** 意、西、希、葡等国人血统的美国人。**2.** 皮肤润滑的人。～ **box**（车轴上的）润滑油箱。～**burner**〔美口〕厨子〔尤指做油煎食品的厨子〕。～**bush** = ～wood. ～ **cup**【机】牛油杯，滑脂杯。～ **gun 1.**【机】滑脂枪，注油枪。**2.**〔美俚〕快速发射自动手枪；M3式手提机枪。～ **heel** 马踵炎。～ **job**〔美俚〕（飞机）平稳顺利地着陆。～ **monkey**〔美俚〕机械工人〔尤指汽车或飞机的检修工〕。～ **paint**（化妆用的）油彩。～**proof** *a*. 防油脂的，耐油脂的，不吸收油脂的。～ **wood 1.**【植】黑肉叶刺茎藜类植物。**2.** 黑肉叶刺茎藜（Sarcobatus vermiculatus）〔产于美国西部沙漠地带，常用作饲料〕。

greased [griːzd; griːst; grizd, grist] *a*. **1.**〔美俚〕灌足酒的，醉的。**2.**（马）患肿炎症的。***like*** ～ ***lightning*** 风驰电掣地。

grease·less [ˈgriːslis; ˋgrislɪs] *a*. 没有油脂的。**-ness** *n*.

greas·er [ˈgriːzə; ˋgrizɚ] *n*. **1.** 涂油[上油]工人；擦拭工人。**2.** 加润滑脂的器具。**3.**（轮船的）伙夫长。**4.**〔美俚〕贿赂者。**5.**〔美俚、蔑〕墨西哥、拉丁美洲人血统的美国人。

greas·y [ˈgriːsi, ˈgriːzi; ˋgrisɪ, ˋgrizɪ] *a*. **1.** 多脂的，油脂性的，油腻腻的；（羊毛）未脱脂的。**2.** 油滑的；滑的；泥泞的。**3.**【海】（天气）恶劣的，阴沉的。**4.** 会逢迎人的，谄媚的。**5.**【兽医】患踵炎症的。*The road is* ～ [ˈgriːzi; ˋgrizɪ]. 路滑。*The candle is* ～ [ˈgriːsi; ˋgrisɪ]. 蜡烛一燃烧便滴下油脂。～ **grind**〔美俚〕用功的学生。～ **pole**（游戏用的）滑棒。～ **spoon**〔美俚〕下等餐馆。**-ily** *ad*. **-i·ness** *n*.

great [greit; gret] **I** *a*. **1.** 大的，巨大的。**2.** 很多的；充足的，十足的，非常的。**3.** 伟大的，杰出的；优异的，显著的；贵族的，高尚的。**4.** 重大的；主要的；长久的；强烈的。**5.**〔口〕了不起的，绝妙的，非常愉快的，令人满意的。**6.** 精通的，熟悉的，熟练的。**7.** 真正的，名副其实的。**8.**（字母）大写的。**9.**〔口〕多么…〔用在其他形容词前面，表示惊讶、愤怒、轻蔑等〕。*live to a* ～ *age* 活到很大年纪。*a* ～ *chair* 靠椅。*in* ～ *detail* 十分详尽地。*a* ～ *family* 名门望族。*the* ～ *house* 村中最大富豪。～ *ladies* 贵妇人。*the* ～ *majority* 大部分，大多数。*a truly* ～ *man* 真正的伟人。*a* ～ *occasion* 节日，盛典；重大时机。～ *pain* 剧痛。*a* ～ *play* 盛大的演出。*have a* ～ *time* 过得很愉快。*That's* ～! 好得很！真了不起！～ *toe* 拇趾 = big toe. *the* ～ *unpaid*〔英谑〕〔集合词〕无俸法官。*the* ～ *unwashed*〔谑〕（旧社会中的）穷苦老百姓，下层社会。*a* ～ *while* (*ago*) 很久（以前）。*a* ～ *word among scientists* 科学家爱用的一个词。*the* ～ *world* 上流社会，贵族社会。***be*** ～ ***at*** [***in***]〔口〕善于；精通（*be* ～ *at tennis* 网球打得很好）。***be*** ～ ***on***〔口〕**1.** 对…很熟悉的。**2.** 热衷于…的（*be* ～ *on science fiction* 爱读科学幻想小说，科学幻想小说迷）。***be*** ～ ***with* 1.** 为某种感情所激动。**2.**〔英古〕怀孕的（*be* ～ *with anger* 大为生气。*be* ～ *with child* 怀孕）。***G- Big***〔美俚〕很大，巨大的。***G- God***! [***Caesar***! ***Heavens***! ***Scott***! ***Snake***! ***Sun***!] 啊呀！〔表示惊叹、谴责、惋惜等〕。***have a*** ～ ***mind to*** 想…得不得了。***have a*** ～ ***notion to*** 常爱想…。***no*** ～***. matter*** 不重要；无关紧要。***no*** ～ ***scratch*** [***shakes***, ***thing***,〔美俚〕***shucks***] 平常得很，没有什么了不起。***the G- Beyond*** 来生，来世。***the G- Day*** [***Assize***, ***Inquest***]【宗】世界末日大审判。***the G- Depression***（1929年资本主义世界的）大萧条。**II** *n*. **1.** 全部，全体。**2.**〔通常作 the ～〕大人物，大事。**3.**〔美俚〕大师，名家。**4.**〔*pl*.〕〔英俚〕牛津大学学士学位考试。〔尤指古典文学和哲学的考试〕。***a*** ～ ***of***〔美口〕大部分，许多。～ ***and small*** 大人物和小人物；贵贱上下。***in the*** ～ 总括。**III** *ad*.〔口〕很好地，成功地。*Things are going* ～. 事情进展顺利。～ **ape** 类人猿（灵长目猩猩科和长臂猿科动物的总称，指长臂猿、猩猩、黑猩猩及大猩猩等而言）。～ **auk** 大海鸟（*Pinguinus impennis*）〔原产于北大西洋，一八四四年后已灭绝〕。～**-aunt** = grandaunt. **G- Basin** 美国西部大盆地。**G- Bear**【天】大熊座。**G- Beyond** 阴间，彼岸。**G- Bible** 一五三九年 Coverdale 译的《圣经》。**G- Britain** 大不列颠。～ **calorie**（热量单位）大卡。**G- Charter**【英史】大宪章。～ **circle** 大圆〔尤指地球表面的大圆，即地球面上通过球心的平面切成的圆〕。～**est common divisor** [**factor**, **measure**]【数】最大公约数。～ **coat** 厚大衣。**G- Dane** 丹麦种大猎犬。**G- Dipper**【天】北斗七星。**G- Divide 1.** 北美（洲）大陆分水岭〔指落基山脉〕。**2.**〔常作 g- d-〕分水岭，分水界。**3.** 分界线；生死线（*cross the G- Divide* 死）。～ **forty days** 由复活节至升天节的四十日。～ **game 1.** 高尔夫球。**2.** 间谍活动。～ **hearted** *a*. 心胸开阔的，宽宏大量的。～ **go**〔英俚〕**1.** 牛津大学文学士[数

G

学士]的最终考试。**2.** 文学士[数学士]的课程。～ **gross** 大箩〔量词,等于12箩〕。～ **horned owl**【动】猫鸮(*Bubo virginianus*)〔产于北美,头上有两撮黑羽毛〕。～ **hundred**〔英〕一百二十。～**nephew** = grandnephew. ～-**niece** = grandniece. ～**power** 强国,大国。～-**power** *a*. 强国的,大国的。～-**power chauvinism** 大国沙文主义。～ **pox**〔美俚〕梅毒。～ **primer**【印】十八点活字。**G- Society 1.** 大社会〔美国总统约翰逊提出的社会福利计划〕。**2.** 社会整体。～-**seal** 国玺,御玺。**G- Seal 1.** 英国掌玺大臣。**2.**〔g- s-〕国玺。～ **uncle** = granduncle. **G- Wall** 中国的万里长城。**G- War** 第一次世界大战。**G- Week** = Holy Week. **G- White Way** 不夜街〔纽约市百老汇大街的剧院区〕。～ **year** 柏拉图年〔等于25,800年〕。

great- *comb. f.* 用在由 *grand* 构成,并表示亲属关系的复合词前,表示更远一辈的亲属关系。*a* ～-*grandfather*; *a* ～-*grandson*.

great·en [ˈgreitən; ˋgretn̩] *vt., vi.* (使)变得更加伟大[重大]。

great-grand·child [ˌgreit-ˈgræntʃaild;ˏgret-ˋgræntʃaɪld] *n.* (*pl.* -**children**) **1.** 曾孙,外曾孙 (= great-grandson)。**2.** 曾孙女,外曾孙女 (= great-granddaughter)。

great-grand·par·ent [ˌgreitˈgrændˌpɛərənt; ˏgret-ˋgrændˏpɛrənt] *n.* **1.** 曾祖,外曾祖 (= great-grandfather)。**2.** 曾祖母,外曾祖母 (= great-grandmother)。

great·ly [ˈgreitli; ˋgretlɪ] *ad.* **1.** 大大地,非常地。**2.** 崇高地。

great·ness [ˈgreitnis; ˋgretnɪs] *n.* **1.** 大,巨大。**2.** 高尚,伟大。

greave [griːv; griv] *n.*〔常 *pl.*〕胫甲,护胫。

greaves [griːvz; grivz] *n.*〔*pl.*〕**1.** 油渣。**2.**【冶】金属渣。

grebe [griːb; grib] *n.*【动】䴙䴘。

G

Gre·cian [ˈgriːʃən; ˋgriʃən] **I** *a.* 希腊(式)的。★除指建筑、容貌及成语外,一般用 Greek. **II** *n.* **1.** 希腊人。**2.** 希腊语学家。～ **bend**〔英〕1870年前后妇女中间流行的、上身微向前屈的步行姿势。～ **knot**〔英〕(女人脑后的)发髻。～ **nose** 悬胆鼻,鼻梁笔直的鼻子。～ **profile** 鼻梁笔直的脸部侧面轮廓。～ **slippers**〔英〕东方式的拖鞋。-**ize** *vt.* 使希腊化,使具希腊特征。

Gre·cism [ˈgriːsizəm; ˋgrisɪzm̩] *n.* **1.** 希腊词语,希腊习语。**2.** 希腊文化,希腊精神。

Gre·cize [ˈgriːsaiz; ˋgrisaɪz] *vt., vi.* (使)希腊化;(使)有希腊风格;(把…)译成希腊语。

Gre·co- *comb. f.* 表示"希腊": *Greco*-Roman.

Gre·co-Ro·man [ˈgriːkəuˈrəumən;ˏgrikoˋromən] *a.* 属希腊和罗马的,受希腊和罗马影响的。

gree[1] [griː; gri] *n.*〔废〕好意。**do** [**make**] ～〔古〕以德报怨。

gree[2] [griː; gri] *n.*〔Scot.〕优越;杰出;胜利。

gree[3] [griː; gri] *vt., vi.* (使)同意。

Greece [griːs; gris] *n.* 希腊〔欧洲〕。

greed [griːd; grid] *n.* 贪心,贪婪。

greed·y [ˈgriːdi; ˋgridɪ] *a.* **1.** 贪吃的。**2.** 贪心的,贪婪的 (*for*; *after*; *of*)。**3.** 渴望的,热望的 (*of*; *for*)。*be* ～ *of gain* [*honours*] 贪财[名]。*be* ～ *to do sth.* 渴望[急欲]做某事。-**i·ly** *ad.* -**i·ness** *n.*

Greek [griːk; grik] **I** *a.* **1.** 希腊(人)的;希腊语的;希腊式的。**2.**【宗】东正教的;希腊正教的。～ *architecture* 希腊式建筑。***gay*** ～**s** 快活的人,游手好闲的人。***Greekless*** ～ 只根据译本进行的希腊文学研究。**II** *n.* **1.** 希腊人;希腊语;具有古代希腊人精神的人;希腊正教会成员;〔美俚〕大学生联谊会会员。**2.** 难懂的事。**3.**〔主俚〕骗子。***be all*** ～ ***to*** 完全不懂,一窍不通 (*That's all* ～ *to me.* 我完全不懂)。***When*** ～ ***meets*** ～, ***then comes the tug of war.***〔谚〕两雄相遇,其斗必烈。～ **calends** 从不,永不 (*She will do it on the* ～ *calends.* 她决不会这样做)。～ **Catholic 1.** 希腊正教会成员。**2.** 做罗马天主教礼拜仪式的正教会成员。～ **Church** 东正教会。～ **cross** 四臂一样长的十字架。～ **Fathers** 希腊正教会神父。～ **fire** (从前海战时所用的)燃烧物。～ **fret**【建】格子细工;回纹饰。～ **gift** 别有用心的礼物。～ **god** 美男子。～-**letter** *a.* (大学)联谊会的(～-*letter fraternity*〔美〕用希腊语字母命名的联谊会)。

Gree·l(e)y [ˈgriːli; ˋgrilɪ] *n.* 格里利〔姓氏〕。

green [griːn; grin] **I** *a.* **1.** 绿色的,青色的。**2.** 未成熟的;年青的;无经验的;易受骗的,天真的。**3.** 未加工的;未处理过的;(木材等)未干的;(酒)不陈的;(鱼)未到产卵期的;(蟹)未到脱壳期的;未训练过的。**4.** 新的,新鲜的;活生生的。**5.** 活泼的,精神旺盛的,青春的。**6.** (脸色)发青的,苍白的。**7.**〔口〕妒忌的。**8.** 青葱的;无雪的,温暖的 (*opp.* white)。**9.**〔口〕就绪的,顺利的。**10.** 反对环境污染的,主张环境保护和维持生态平衡的。*a* ～ *eye* 妒忌的眼睛。*a* ～ *wound* 未愈合的伤口。*a* ～ *old age* 老当益壮。*a* ～ *winter* 温暖的冬天。～ *cheese* 未熟的干酪。～ *corn* (做菜用的)嫩玉米。～ *crop* 青菜〔*cf.* white crop, root crop〕;绿肥。～ *duck* 子鸭。～ *feed* [*fodder*] 青饲料。～ *glass* 瓶料玻璃;～ *manure* 绿肥。～ *recollections* 记忆犹新。***as*** ～ ***as grass*** 幼稚,无经验。～ ***in earth*** 刚埋葬不久。～ ***with envy*** 十分妒嫉。***in the*** ～ ***wood*** [***tree***] 在青春旺盛的时代。**keep the memory** ～ 永记不忘。**II** *n.* **1.** 绿色,青色;草地;绿色物质,绿色颜料。**2.**〔英〕〔*pl.*〕蔬菜;〔*pl.*〕(装饰用的)青枝绿叶;绿叶花环。**3.**〔口〕青春,生气。**4.** 绿色徽章;〔*pl.*〕绿色党,爱尔兰国民党。**5.** 公有草地,草坪;高尔夫球(的)终打地区 (= putting ～)。**6.**〔美俚〕钱;低级的大麻叶(毒品);〔*pl.*〕性交。***Do you see any*** ～ ***in my eye?*** 你以为我可欺吗? ***in the*** ～ 血气方刚的,少壮时代的。**III** *vt.* 使成绿色;〔俚〕欺骗。— *vi.*〔罕〕成为绿色,变绿。～ **algae**【植】绿藻门 (*Chlorophyta*)。～ **back** 美钞。～ **bag 1.** 旧时律师用以装文件的绿色布袋[小箱]。**2.** 律师。～ **bean** 青豆。～ **belt** (环城)绿化地带。**G- Berets** "绿色贝雷帽"〔美国陆军的特种部队〕。～-**blind** *a.* 绿色盲的。～ **blindness** 绿色盲。～ **book** (英、意等国政府内载供讨论的提议的)绿皮书;(华盛顿)的社交名册。～ **brier** 绿蔷薇〔美国东部产〕。～ **card**〔美〕绿卡〔发给墨西哥等国的入境临时作工许可证,亦指在美国的永久居留权身份证〕。～ **charge** 未混合的火药。**G- Cloth 1.** 英国宫廷事务部供应局。**2.**〔g- c-〕赌台。～ **cross**【军】窒息剂,绿十字毒气。～ **dragon**【植】龙根天南星 (*Arisaema dracontium*)〔产于美洲〕。～ **drake**【动】蜉蝣。～-**eyed** *a.* 绿眼睛的;嫉妒的 (*the* ～-*eyed monster* 嫉妒). ～ **finch**【动】(欧洲产的)绿黄色雀科鸣鸟。～ **fingers**〔英口〕园艺技能。～ **fly**〔英〕绿色蚜虫。～ **foxtail**【植】狗尾草。～ **gage**【植】青梅子,青李子。～**goods 1.** 新鲜货,蔬菜。**2.**〔美俚〕伪钞。～ **grocer**〔英〕蔬菜水果商人,菜贩。～**grocery**〔英〕**1.** 蔬菜水果业。**2.** 蔬菜水果店。**3.**〔集合词〕蔬菜,水果。～ **hand 1.** 生手,没有经验的人。**2.**〔方〕园艺技能。～**heart** *n.*【植】产于热带美洲的绿心硬木。～**horn** 生手,未经世故的人;容易上当的糊涂虫;〔口〕新到的移民。～**keeper** 高尔夫球场看守人。～ **lead ore**【矿】磷铅矿,水晶矿。～**let** *n.* = vireo. ～ **light** (交通信号)绿灯;放行,准许 (*get the* ～ *light* 获准,准予通行。*give the* ～ *light to sb.* 给某人开绿灯,纵容某人)。～ **line**【军】轰炸线;敌我分界线。～ **lung**〔英〕(城市中的)公园;绿化区。～ **man**【海】新来水手。～ **mold** 绿霉。～ **money** 绿币〔小型社区内一种非现金支付手段,如以劳务、货物作偿付手段等〕。～ **monkey**【动】青猴 (*Cercopithecus sabaeus*)〔产于非洲的长尾小猴,毛色微青〕。**G- Mountain Boys** 青山军〔美国独立战争中由艾丹·爱伦组织的佛蒙特士兵〕。**G- Mountain State** 美国佛蒙特州别名。～ **onion** 大葱,青蒜。～ **peak**【动】绿色啄木鸟。～ **pepper**【植】灯笼椒,青辣椒 (*Capsicum frutescens var. fascicu-*

latum). ~ **politics** 绿色政治运动〔指进行反对战争、鼓吹保护生态环境等的政治活动〕。~ **power**〔美〕金钱的力量。~ **revolution** 绿色革命〔由于粮食作物新品种的发展和农业技术的改进,引起收成的极大增长〕。~-**room** 演员休息室;(工厂内的)原料贮存室。~-**sand**【地】海绿石砂;【机】新取砂,湿砂〔铸造用〕。~-**shank**【动】青足鹬。~ **sea**【海】冲击船首的巨浪。~ **sick** *a*.【医】患萎黄病的;【植】患缺绿病的。~ **sickness**【医】萎黄病,绿色贫血;【植】缺绿病。~ **soap** 绿肥皂〔治皮肤病用的一种软皂〕。~**stick**【医】旁弯骨折。~ **stick fracture**【医】半骨折;骨裂;~**stone**【地】粗玄岩,绿岩,软玉。~**stuff** 蔬菜;草木。~-**sward** 草地,草皮。~**tail** *n*.【动】步鱼。~ **tea** 绿茶。~ **thumb** 种植技能,园艺技能。~ **turtle**【动】绿蠵龟(*Chelonia mydas*)。~ **vitriol**【化】绿矾。~ **washing** 绿色外衣〔指某些公司为掩盖起污染环境行为而假惺惺地赞助环保活动〕。~**weed**【植】染料木。~**wood** 新材,生材;绿林(*go to the* ~ *wood* 落草,做绿林豪客)。

Green [griːn; grin] *n*. 1. 格林〔姓氏〕。2. **John Richard** ~ 约翰·里查·格林〔1837—1883,英国历史家〕。3. **Julian** ~ 朱利安·格林〔1900—,美国小说家〕。

Green·a·way [ˈgriːnəwei; ˋgrinəwe] *n*. 格里纳韦〔姓氏〕。

green·er [ˈgriːnə; ˋgrinə-] *n*. 1. 〔俚〕新来谋事的外国人。2. 生手。

green·er·y [ˈgriːnəri; ˋgrinərɪ] *n*. 1. 〔集合词〕绿叶,绿树。2. = greenhouse.

green·house [ˈgriːnhaus; ˋgrin͵haus] *n*. 1. 玻璃暖房,温室。2. 〔军俚〕周围有玻璃的座舱;轰炸员舱。~ **effect** (地球大气层吸收太阳红外辐射,引起地球表面增加的)温室效应。~ **gas** 温室(效应)气体〔主要指二氧化碳〕。

green·ie [ˈgriːni; ˋgrinɪ] *n*. 〔美俚〕绿丸〔运动员为增加气力而在赛前服用的兴奋剂〕。

green·ing [ˈgriːniŋ; ˋgrinɪŋ] *n*. 1. 绿化。2. 青皮苹果。

green·ish [griːniʃ; ˋgrinɪʃ] *a*. 带绿色的。

Green·land[1] [ˈgriːnlənd; ˋgrinlənd] *n*. 格林兰〔姓氏〕。

Green·land[2] [ˈgriːnlənd; ˋgrinlənd] *n*. 格林兰(岛)〔丹麦〕。-**er** *n*. 格林兰人。-**ish** *a*.

green·ling [ˈgriːnliŋ; ˋgrinlɪŋ] *n*. 【动】六线鱼〔产于北太平洋〕。

green·ly [ˈgriːnli; ˋgrinlɪ] *ad*. 1. 绿色地。2. 新鲜地;旺盛地。3. 不熟练地。

green·mail [ˈgriːnmeil; ˋgrinmel] *n*. 大量收购股票。

green·ness [ˈgriːnnis; ˋgrinnɪs] *n*. 1. 绿色。2. 新鲜。3. 未熟练。

green·ock·ite [ˈgriːnəˌkait; ˋgrinə͵kaɪt] *n*. 【矿】硫镉矿。

Gree·nough [ˈgriːnəu; ˋgrino] *n*. 格里诺〔姓氏〕。

Green·wich [ˈgrinidʒ; ˋgrɪnɪdʒ] *n*. (伦敦)格林尼治〔英国伦敦东南一市镇,为本初子午线所经过的地方〕。~ **mean time** 格林尼治平时(略作 GMT)。~ **Royal Observatory** 格林尼治天文台。~ **time** 世界标准时。~ **Village** (美国纽约市曼哈顿下城之一区,为作家、艺术家等聚居的)格林尼治村。

green·y [ˈgriːni; ˋgrinɪ] *a*. (***green·i·er***, ***green·i·est***)〔口〕= greenish.

greet[1] [griːt; grit] *vt*. 1. 向…致敬〔意〕,向…问好,迎接,欢迎。2. (景象、声音等)映入(眼帘),收入(耳中)。~ *a distinguished guest with loud applause* 以热烈的掌声欢迎贵宾。~ *sb. by saying "Good morning!"* 向某人说"早上好!"致意问候。*be* ~*ed with hisses* 被嘘。*A roaring sound* ~*ed his ears*. 隆隆的响声传入他耳朵。*A surprising view* ~*ed her eyes*. 一个奇异的景象呈现在她眼前。

greet[2] [griːt; grit] *vi*. (***grat*** [græt; græt]; ***grut·ten*** [ˈgrʌtn; ˋgrʌtn])〔Scot.〕哭泣,悲伤。

greet·ing [ˈgriːtiŋ; ˋgritɪŋ] *n*. 1. 敬礼。2. 〔常 *pl*.〕问候话,欢迎辞。~ **card** (生日、节日等的)贺片。

greg·a·rine [ˈgregərain, -ərin; ˋgrɛgəraɪn, -ərɪn] I *n*.【动】簇虫(*Gregarinida*)。II *a*. 簇虫的(= gregarinian)。

gre·gar·i·ous [greˈgeəriəs; grɪˋgɛrɪəs] *a*. 1. 【动】爱群居的,群居(性)的;【植】聚生的,簇生的。2. 爱社交的,集体性的。-**ly** *ad*. -**ness** *n*.

gre·go [ˈgriːgəu, ˈgrei-; ˋgrigo, ˋgre-] *n*. (地中海东岸诸国人民所穿的)有头巾的粗布短外衣;粗布大外衣。

Gre·go·ri·an [greˈgɔːriən; grɛˋgorɪən] I *a*. 罗马教皇格利高里的。II *n*. 格利高里圣歌。~ **calendar** (现在通用的)阳历,西历。~ **Chant** 以教皇格利高里命名的无伴奏齐唱圣歌。~ **style** 新历。~ **telescope** 反射望远镜〔苏格兰数学家约翰·格利高里发明的一种望远镜〕。~ **tones** 格利高里圣歌曲调。

Greg·o·ry [ˈgregəri; ˋgrɛgərɪ] *n*. 格利高里〔姓氏,男子名〕。**G- powder** 以大黄为主的泻药。

greige [greiʒ; greʒ] I *n*. 1. 本色布,本色纱。2. 灰褐色。II *a*. 灰褐色的。

grei·sen [ˈgraizn; ˋgraɪzn̩] *n*. 【地】云英岩。

gre·mi·al [ˈgriːmiəl; ˋgrimɪəl] *n*. 【宗】(主教做弥撒时披的)膝衣。

grem·lin [ˈgremlin; ˋgrɛmlɪn] *n*. 〔英军俚〕1. (二次大战中传闻常和飞机捣蛋的)小妖精。2. (使事情不能顺利进行的)小捣蛋鬼。3. 冲浪新手。

Gre·na·da [grəˈneidə; grəˋnedə] *n*. 格林纳达〔拉丁美洲〕。

gre·nade [griˈneid; grɪˋned] *n*. 1. 手榴弹〔通常称 hand-~〕;枪榴弹〔又名 rifle-~〕。2. 灭火弹;催泪弹。~-**discharger** [**launcher**] 枪榴弹发射器。

gren·a·dier [ˌgrenəˈdiə; ͵grɛnəˋdɪr] *n*. 1. 掷弹兵。2.【动】长尾鳕科深海鱼。3. (南非)织布鸟属的鸟。***G-s*** 英国近卫步兵第一团〔又称 **G- Guards**〕。

gren·a·dine[1] [ˈgrenədiːn; ˋgrɛnədin] *n*. 五香小牛肉,五香鸡。

gren·a·dine[2] [ˈgrenədiːn; ˋgrɛnə͵din] *n*. 1. (做窗帘用的)薄纱;紧拈细丝线。2. 杂质品红。

gren·a·dine[3] [ˈgrenədiːn; ˋgrɛnədin] *n*. 石榴汁。

Gren·fell [ˈgrenfel; ˋgrɛnfɛl] *n*. 格伦费尔〔姓氏〕。

Gren·ville [ˈgrenvil; ˋgrɛnvɪl] *n*. 格伦维尔〔姓氏〕。

Gresh·am [ˈgreʃəm; ˋgrɛʃəm] *n*. 1. 格雷沙姆(格雷欣)〔姓氏〕。2. **Thomas** ~ 汤马斯·格雷欣〔1519—1579,英国财政学家〕。~**'s law**【经】格雷欣法则〔劣币驱逐良币的法则〕。

gres·so·ri·al [greˈsɔːriəl; grɛˋsorɪəl] *a*. 【动】(鸟类等的脚)适于步行的。

Gret·a [ˈgretə; ˋgrɛtə], **Gretch·en** [ˈgretʃən; ˋgrɛtʃən] *n*. 女子名〔Margaret 的爱称〕。

grew [gruː; gru] grow 的过去式。

grey, 〔美〕 **gray** [grei; gre] I *a*. 1. 灰色的,灰白的,本色的。2. 灰暗的,阴沉的,阴暗的。3. 灰白头发的;衰老的;老练的,成熟的。4. 古代的,古老的,太古的。5.【经】半黑市性质的。6. (人)匿名的,无法查明身分的。7. (教士)穿灰色衣服的。8. 界限不明的,介于两者之间的。~ *experience* 老练。~ *hair* 灰白头发。~ *hairs* 〔喻〕老年。~ *iron* 灰口铁。~ *sister* =~ friar sister. *the* ~ *past* 古代。II *n*. 1. 灰色,鼠色。2. 灰色颜料;灰色动物〔特指马〕;灰色衣服;本色布。3. 微明,黎明;黄昏;阴冷的光。4. 〔黑人俚〕白人。*the* ~ *of the morning* 黎明。*be dressed in* ~穿着灰色服装。*in the* ~ (布)未加漂白。*the* (**Scots**) ***Greys*** (骑青灰马的英国)苏格兰龙骑兵第二团。III *vt*., *vi*. (使)变成灰色。~ **area**〔英〕灰区〔指就业率颇低,但并非低至可供政府特别补助的区域〕。~**back** *n*. 灰背类动物〔鸟类、鱼类、鲸类等中任何背带灰色者,如小鲛、鳐类、鸭等〕。~**beard** *n*. 1. 白胡子老人。2. 石制大酒壶。3.【植】灰色地衣。~ **cells** = ~ matter. ~ **cloth** 本色布。~**coat** *n*. 〔英〕1. 穿灰衣服的人。2.(英国昆布兰郡的)义勇骑兵。～ **collar** 灰领职工〔指服务与维修性行业职工〕。～ **drake**【动】灰蜉蝣。～ **economy** 灰色经济〔指介于进入官方统计数字中的正常经济活动和黑市交易之间的经济活动,如受私人雇佣、兼干第二职业等〕。～ **eminence** 心腹人物;暗中掌权的人 = eminence grise. ～**fish**【动】绿鳕,星鲨。～ **friar** 方济各会(Franciscan)修道士。～ **goods** 本色布。～ **goose**【动】灰雁。～**-haired**, ～**-headed** *a*. 白头的;老的;老练的(*in*);古老的。～ **hen**【动】黑琴鸡。～**lag** *n*. =～ goose. ～ **literature** 灰色文献〔指散发给公众的各种产品信息,使用手册等非正式出版物〕。～ **mare** 比丈夫强的妻子,雌老虎。～ **matter** 1.(脑的)灰质。2.头脑。3.智力。～ **mullet**【动】鲻鱼。～ **sister** 方济各会女修道士。～ **squirrel** 灰松鼠(*Sciuru carolinensis*)〔原产于美国〕。～**stone**【地】灰色火山岩,玄武石。～ **wacke** 硬砂岩,杂砂岩。～ **whale**【动】灰鲸(*Eschrichtius glancus*)〔产于北太平洋,黑色带白斑〕。～ **wolf**【动】灰狼(*Canis lupus*)〔产于北半球北部,特性是群出觅食〕。

Grey [grei; gre] *n*. 格雷〔姓氏〕。

grey·cing [ˈgreisiŋ; ˋgresɪŋ] *n*. 〔英国〕= greyhound-racing.

grey·hound [ˈgreiˌhaund; ˋgreˏhaʊnd] *n*. 1.(身体瘦长、善于赛跑的狗)灵猩,〔G-〕灰狗(为美国著名长途汽车公司名称)。2.远洋快轮。～ **racing** 赛狗,跑狗。

grey·ish [ˈgreiiʃ; ˋgreɪʃ] *a*. 带灰色的。

grey·ly [ˈgreili; ˋgrelɪ] *ad*. 灰;晦暗地。

grey·ness [ˈgreinis; ˋgrenɪs] *n*. 灰色,本色。

grib·ble [ˈgribl; ˋgrɪbl] *n*.【动】蚀船虫,船蛆〔能在水下蛀坏船只的一种蛀虫〕。

grid [grid; grɪd] *n*. 1.格子,格栅。2.(蓄电池的)铅板。3.【无】栅级。4.铁道网;【电】电力网;〔英〕(全国)高压输电网,电(视)台网。5.〔美俚〕橄榄球场;橄榄球。6.地图的坐标方格;(照相排字机的)字格。7.(烘烤面包等用的)铁篦子。～ **bias** 栅偏压。～ **circuit** 栅极电路。～ **current** 栅极电流。～ **leak**【电】栅漏。

grid·der [ˈgridə; ˋgrɪdɚ] *n*. 〔美俚〕橄榄球运动员。

grid·dle [ˈgridl; ˋgrɪdl] I *n*. 1.(烤饼用的)烤盘。2.〔美〕薄烤饼(=～ cake)。3.【矿】(选矿用的)筛子,大孔筛。II *vt*. 1.用烤板烤。2.筛。～**-hot** *a*. 刚出笼的,刚做成的。

gride [graid; graɪd] I *vi*. 嘎吱嘎吱地切[刮、擦、轧](*along*; *through*)。II *n*. 擦刮声,轧轧声。

grid·i·ron [ˈgridˌaiən; ˋgrɪdˏaɪɚn] *n*. 1.(烧鱼肉等有柄的)烤架,铁丝格子。2.【海】格子船台,船架。3.(舞台上承受升降布景装置的)梁格结构。4.栅形补偿摆(=～ pendulum)。5.格状物,格状结构。6.〔美俚〕美国国旗。6.〔美俚〕橄榄球场;橄榄球。7.(停货车等的)侧道〔=～ siding〕;高压输电网。*be on the* ～ 受迫害,受苦。*lay sb*. *on the* ～ 嘲笑,取笑某人。

grid·lock [ˈgridlɔk; ˋgrɪdlɑk] *n*. 1.(棋盘式街道的)交通大堵塞。2.拥塞停滞。

grief [griːf; grif] *n*. 1.悲伤,忧伤,伤心事;〔美口〕困难;麻烦。2.痛苦,不幸,灾难。*bring sb*. *to* ～使受伤;使失败,使陷悲境。*come to* ～受伤;受欺负;出毛病,失败;遭难。*die of* ～气死。*Good* [*Great*] ～ 哎呀!〔表示惊奇,惊恐等的惊叹语〕。*smile at* ～ 不过度悲伤,达观。

grief-strick·en [ˈgriːfˌstrikn; ˋgrifˏstrɪkn̩] *a*. 忧伤的;极为悲痛的;悲伤的。

griev·ance [ˈgriːvəns; ˋgrivəns] *n*. 1.不平,不满。2.抱怨,牢骚;冤苦悲叹。3.〔罕〕伤害;苦难。*nurse* (*hare*) *a* ～ *against sb*. 怀恨某人,不满某人。*pour out* ～诉苦。*rip up old* ～s 重提旧怨。～ **committe** (由工会或劳资双方组成的)劳资协调委员会。

grieve[1] [griːv; griv] *vt*. 使悲伤,使忧伤,使痛心。— *vi*. 悲伤,悲叹(*at*; *for*; *over*; *about*)。

grieve[2] [griːv; griv] *n*. 〔方〕农场管理者,监工。

griev·ous [ˈgriːvəs; ˋgrivəs] *a*. 1.悲痛的,痛苦的。2.可叹的;痛心的。3.〔古〕极恶的。4.剧烈的,严重的,难忍的。*a* ～ *crime* 罪大恶极。*a* ～ *cry* 痛哭。*a* ～ *fault* 重大过失。～ *news* 噩耗。～ *pain* 剧痛。**-ly** *ad*.

griff [grif; grɪf] *n*. = griffin[2].

griffe[1] [grif; grɪf] *n*. 〔美〕黑白混血儿。

griffe[2] [grif; grɪf] *n*.【建】虎爪饰〔用于立柱基础处的装饰〕。

grif·fin[1] [ˈgrifin; ˋgrɪfɪn] *n*. 1.【希神】鹫头飞狮。2.看守者。3.(年青女子的)陪媪。4.【动】秃鹰类。*the G-* 伦敦的鹫头飞狮纪念碑。

grif·fin[2] [ˈgrifin; ˋgrɪfɪn] *n*. 1.〔印〕新来的欧洲人,生手。2.〔美俚〕= griffe[1].

Grif·fin [ˈgrifin; ˋgrɪfɪn] *n*. 格里芬〔姓氏〕。

Grif·fith(s) [ˈgrifiθ(s); ˋgrɪfɪθ(s)] *n*. 格里菲斯〔姓氏〕。

grif·fon [ˈgrifən; ˋgrɪfən] *n*. 1. = griffin[2]. 2.体格结实的比利时种小狗。3.粗毛短绒的长头猎狗。～ **vulture** 秃头鹫。

grift [grift; grɪft] I *n*. 〔俚〕骗人行为。II *vt*. 〔俚〕诈骗。

grift·er [griftə; ˋgrɪftɚ] *n*. 〔俚〕赌棍,骗子,小偷。

grig [grig; grɪg] *n*. 〔方〕1.蟋蟀;蚱蜢。2.〔英〕小鳗。3.轻松愉快的人。*as merry* [*lively*] *as a* ～ 非常快活。

Gri·gnard reagent [griːˈnjɑːd riːˈeidʒənt; griˋnjɑrd riˋedʒənt]【化】格林亚试剂。

gri·gri, gree·gree [ˈgriːgriː; ˋgrigri] *n*. 〔美南部〕黑人的咒文[崇拜物]。

grill [gril; grɪl] I *n*. 1.烤架,铁丝格子。2.炙烤的肉类食物。3. = grillroom. 4. = grille. *put sb*. *on the* ～〔美〕严刑审讯某人。II *vt*. 1.(在烤架上)炙烤。2.〔美〕使受酷热;用炙烤来折磨。3.〔美口〕(警察)严厉盘问。4.〔美橄榄球〕训练。5.用条花邮戳盖消(邮票)。— *vi*. 1.受烤,受炙。2.〔美口〕受严厉盘问。～**room** *n*. 烤肉处;(供应烤肉的)小餐厅,小饭店。

gril·lage [ˈgrilidʒ; ˋgrɪlɪdʒ] *n*. (软地上作建筑物基础的)格排垛,格床。

grille [gril; grɪl] *n*. 1.格栅,铁格子。2.(银行出纳台上的)格子窗。3.(养鱼的)孵卵器。

grilled [grild; grɪld] *a*. 1.装有栅格的。2.在烤架上烤的;烙的。

grilse [grils; grɪls] *n*. (*pl*. ～)【动】幼鲑。

grim [grim; grɪm] *a*. 1.严厉的,冷酷的,残忍的。2.坚强的,不屈的。3.可怕的;讨厌的。4.不祥的,邪恶的。～ *courage* 坚韧不拔的勇气。*a* ～ *smile* [*laugh*] 狞笑。*the* ～ *reality* 冷酷的现实。*a* ～ *war* 残酷的战争。*hold on like* ～ *death* 死不放手。**-ly** *ad*. **-ness** *n*.

gri·mace [griˈmeis; grɪˋmes] I *n*. 愁眉苦脸;(做作出来的)怪相;鬼脸。*make* ～*s* 作怪相。II *vi*. 皱着眉头,作怪相。

gri·mal·kin [griˈmælkin; grɪˋmælkɪn] *n*. 1.老雌猫。2.心毒的老太婆。

grime [graim; graɪm] I *n*. 尘垢,灰尘;(道德上的)污点。II *vt*. (灰尘等)弄脏。**Grimes Golden** 黄色苹果(晚秋品种)。

Grimm [grim; grɪm], **Jakob Ludwig Karl** 雅可伯·路德维奇·卡尔·格林〔1785—1863〕, **Wihelm Karl** 威廉·卡尔·格林〔1786—1859〕〔两兄弟,德国语言学家,童话作家〕。

grim·y [ˈgraimi; ˋgraɪmɪ] *a*. (***grim·i·er***; ***-i·est***) 积满污垢的,肮脏的。**grim·i·ly** *ad*. **grim·i·ness** *n*.

grin [grin; grɪn] I *n*. (因苦痛或愤怒)龇牙咧嘴;露着牙齿笑。*sardonic* ～冷笑。***on the*** (***broad***) ～ 笑嘻嘻,露齿而笑。II *vi*. 露出牙齿(*with*);露着牙齿笑(*at*)。～ ***and bear it*** 苦笑着忍受,逆来顺受。～ ***like a cheshire cat*** 咧着嘴傻笑。

grind [graind; graɪnd] I *vt*. (***ground*** [graund; graʊnd],〔罕〕～***ed***) 1.磨碎;碾成(*into*);转动,推摇(磨等)。2.磨快,磨光,磨薄。3.用手摇风琴演奏。4.折磨,虐待,使苦恼。5.〔口〕刻苦学习,苦心教授。6.咬牙;

嘎吱嘎吱地擦。～ *balls for bearings* 磨轴承滚珠。～ *one's teeth* 磨牙齿,咬牙切齿。～ *sb. in Latin* 教某人苦学拉丁语。— ***vi.*** **1.** 碾;碾碎;磨碎;可磨。**2.** 苦干,苦学(*at*; *for*; *up*)。**3.** 摩擦得嘎嘎响。**4.** (跳舞时)扭摆屁股。*The truck ground to a stop.* 卡车嘎的一声煞住。*Though the mills of God ～ slowly, yet they ～ exceeding small.* 〔谚〕天网恢恢,疏而不漏。～ *away at English studies* 刻苦钻研英语。～ **down** 碾碎;折磨;虐待(*be ground down by poverty* 受穷苦的折磨)。～ **gerunds** 〔美口〕在学校教书。～ ***one's heel into*** 把脚跟踩进(砂等中)。～ **out** **1.** 碾成。**2.** 单调地演奏手摇风琴。**3.** 苦吟(诗句)。～ ***the faces of the poor*** 压榨贫民。～ ***up*** 碾成粉,擂碎。***have an ax(e) to ～*** 别有私图。**II** ***n.*** **1.** 碾,磨,碾声,磨声,摩擦声,研细的程度。**2.** 苦差使,枯燥的工作;刻苦,用功。**3.** 〔美〕刻苦用功的学生。**4.** 〔美俚〕开玩笑,讥讽;开玩笑的人。**5.** 〔英〕步行锻炼,越野障碍赛马[赛跑]。*a greasy* ～〔美俚〕埋头读书的学生。*the daily* ～〔口〕日常工作。

grin·de·li·a [grinˈdiːljə, -ˈdiːliə; grɪnˋdiljə, -ˋdilɪə] ***n.*** 【植】胶草(*Grindelia camporum*)〔茎和叶可作药用〕。

grind·er [ˈgraində; ˋgraɪndɚ] ***n.*** **1.** 磨工。**2.** 磨的上段;上磨扇;臼齿;〔*pl.*〕〔口〕牙齿。**3.** 研磨机,粉碎机,磨床。**4.** 〔口〕用功学生;为人作考试准备的教师。**5.** 〔美方〕夹心面包。*cylindrical* ～外圆磨床。*high-precision* ～高精度磨床。*percussion* ～撞碎机。*swinging* ～摇摆研磨机。*universal internal* ～万能内圆磨床。***take a*** ～ 把左手拇指按在鼻头上,用右手在胸前作出磨磨的样子以表示嘲笑。～**'s asthma**【医】磨工气喘,因吸入灰屑所致的肺部疾患。

grind·er·y [ˈgraindəri; ˋgraɪndərɪ] ***n.*** **1.** 磨工车间。**2.** 〔英〕革制品用具[原料]～ **warehouse** 皮鞋用具店。

grind·ing [ˈgraindiŋ; ˋgraɪndɪŋ] **I** ***a.*** **1.** 磨的,适合于磨的。**2.** 折磨人的;难熬的。～ *toothache* 难忍的牙痛。～ *poverty* 赤贫。～ *tyranny* 暴政。**II** ***n.*** 粉碎,研磨;摩擦;〔口〕填鸭式教学。～ **machine** 磨床。～ **wheel** 砂轮。**-ly** ***ad.***

grind·stone [ˈgraindstəun; ˋgraɪndˏston] ***n.*** 磨石;【机】砂轮形磨石。***hold*** [***keep***] ***one's*** [***sb.'s***] ***nose to the*** ～ 不断折磨自己[某人],使自己[某人]埋头辛苦地劳动。

grin·go [ˈgriŋgəu; ˋgrɪŋgo] ***n.*** (*pl.* ～*s*)〔蔑〕外国佬〔尤指在拉丁美洲的英国人和美国人〕。

grin·ner [ˈgrinə; ˋgrɪnɚ] ***n.*** 露着牙齿笑的人,龇牙咧嘴的人。

grin·ning [ˈgriniŋ; ˋgrɪnɪŋ] ***a.*** 露齿而笑的,龇牙咧嘴的。**-ly** ***ad.***

grip[1] [grip; grɪp] **I** ***n.*** **1.** 紧握,抓牢;握法;(互相道贺时的)亲密握手;(秘密团体等的)握手暗号。**2.** 【机】柄,夹,把手。**3.** 吸引力;掌握,支配,控制。**4.** 理解力。**5.** 〔美〕手提包,旅行包;〔美剧〕道具管理员,布景管理员。**6.** 痉挛;流行性感冒。*cable* ～电缆扣。*vice* ～虎钳夹口。*wedge* ～楔形夹。*a bulldog* ～紧握不放。***be at*** ～***s*** 互相揪着搏斗。***be at*** ～***s with*** 勉力对付(*be at* ～*s with the subject* 钻研问题)。***be in the*** ～ ***of*** 被…支配。***come*** [***get***] ***to*** ～***s*** (***with***) 揪扭,扭在一起;开始努力对付。***have a good*** [***poor***] ～ ***on a situation*** 善于[不会]掌握形势。***have a*** ～ ***on an audience*** 掌握听众心理,能吸引观众。***lose*** ～ ***of one's audience*** 使听众扫兴。***lose one's*** ～ 放手。**II** ***vt.*** (～***ped***, 〔古〕***gript*** [gript; grɪpt]; ～***ping***) **1.** 握住,牢牢抓住;吸住(注意力)。**2.** (机器等)扣住,煞住。**3.** 领会,了解,把握。～ **brake** 手煞车。～**-and-grin** **1.** ***n.***(政客等的)握手微笑的镜头。**2.**(政客等为拍照而)摆出握手微笑姿态的。

grip[2] [grip; grɪp] ***n.*** = grippe.

grip[3] [grip; grɪp] ***n.*** 〔英〕小阳沟。

gripe [graip; graɪp] **I** ***n.*** **1.** 紧握,抓住;掌握;支配。**2.** 〔*pl.*〕〔口〕肠绞痛,腹绞痛。**3.** 不平,愤怒。**4.** 把手,柄。**5.** 【机】离合器;制动器。**6.** 船首添材,屈曲部前材;〔*pl.*〕艇索,绊带。***come to*** ～***s*** 互相揪扭。***in the*** ～ ***of*** 被抓牢;在…掌握中的,在…把持下的。**II** ***vt.*** **1.** 握紧,捉牢;扭紧。**2.** 使肠痛。**3.** 〔美俚〕激怒,使苦恼,压迫。— ***vi.*** **1.** 抓牢。**2.** 肠痛。**3.** 〔美俚〕诉苦,发牢骚。**4.** 【海】逆风航行。

grip·er [ˈgraipə; ˋgraɪpɚ] ***n.*** 〔美俚〕爱发牢骚的人。

grippe [grip, griːp; grɪp, grip] ***n.*** 〔F.〕【医】流行性感冒。

grip·per [ˈgripə; ˋgrɪpɚ] ***n.*** **1.** 握者。**2.** 夹具;【机】抓器,抓爪。

grip·ping [ˈgripiŋ; ˋgrɪpɪŋ] ***a.*** **1.** 抓的,夹的。**2.** 引人注意的,扣人心弦的。*a* ～ *story* 扣人心弦的故事。～ **device**【机】夹具,固定器。**-ly** ***ad.*** **-ness** ***n.***

grip·ple [gripl; ˋgrɪpl] ***a.*** 〔英方〕吝啬的;贪婪的。

grip·sack [ˈgripsæk; ˋgrɪpsæk] ***n.*** 〔美〕手提包,旅行包。

gript [gript; grɪpt] ***v.*** 〔古〕grip 的过去式及过去分词。

gri·saille [griˈzeil; grɪˋzel] ***n.*** 〔F.〕浮雕式灰色装饰画[画法];(玻璃等上的)纯灰色画。

Gri·sel·da [griˈzeldə; grɪˋzɛldə] ***n.*** **1.** 格里塞尔达〔女子名〕。**2.** 温顺的女人。

gris·eo·ful·vin [ˌgriziːəuˈfulvin; ˏgrɪzioˋfulvɪn] ***n.*** 【药】灰黄霉素。

gris·e·ous [ˈgrisiəs, ˈgriz-; ˋgrɪsɪəs, ˋgrɪz-] ***a.*** 灰色的〔特指珠灰色〕。

gri·sette [griˈzet; grɪˋzɛt] ***n.*** 〔F.〕(法国的)女工,女店员。

gris-gris [ˈgriːgriː; ˋgrigri] ***n.*** (*pl.* ～)格哩格哩〔伏都教的一种符箓、咒文、咒语〕。

gris·kin [ˈgriskin; ˋgrɪskɪn] ***n.*** 〔英〕(猪腰部的)五花肉。

gris·ly [ˈgrizli; ˋgrɪzlɪ] ***a.*** (相貌)可怕的;〔口〕讨厌的。**-i·ness** ***n.***

grist [grist; grɪst] ***n.*** **1.** 制粉用谷类;谷粉;酿造用麦芽;一次所碾的谷;一次所磨的粉。**2.** 〔美〕大量,许多。**3.** 有利的东西。***All is*** ～ ***that comes to his mill.*** 〔谚〕到他磨里的东西全会变成粉,他善于利用一切机会[事物]。***bring*** ～ ***to the mill*** 有利,能赚钱。～ ***to*** [***for***] ***sb.'s mill*** 对…有利的东西。～**mill** 磨坊。

gris·tle [ˈgrisl; ˋgrɪsl̩] ***n.*** (牛等的)软骨。***in the*** ～ 骨头还软的,未成熟的。

gris·tly [ˈgrisli; ˋgrɪslɪ] ***a.*** 软骨质的;软骨状的;由软骨形成的。**-tli·ness** ***n.***

grit [grit; grɪt] **I** ***n.*** **1.** 粗砂,砂砾,砂粒。**2.** = ～stone. **3.** 〔口〕刚毅,坚韧,勇气。*a hone of good* ～优质磨石。*Americans of the true* ～道地的美国人。***hit the*** ～〔美俚〕走路,跋涉。***put*** (***a little***) ～ ***in the machine*** 破坏正常工作,捣乱。**II** ***vi.*** (**-tt-**) 发轧轧声。— ***vt.*** **1.** 轧,研磨,摩擦。**2.** 在…上铺砂砾。～ *the teeth* 咬牙。～**stone** ***n.*** 粗(角)砂岩,天然磨石。

grits [grits; grɪts] ***n.*** *pl.* 〔用作单或复〕**1.** 粗碾小麦[谷类];去壳但未碾制的燕麦。**2.** 〔美〕玉米片;玉米粥。

grit·ty [ˈgriti; ˋgrɪtɪ] ***a.*** **1.** 粗砂质的,砂多的;砂砾的。**2.** 刚强的,勇敢的,坚韧不拔的。**-ti·ly** ***ad.*** **-ti·ness** ***n.***

griv·et [ˈgrivit; ˋgrɪvɪt] ***n.*** 〔F.〕素领猴(*Cercopithecus aethiops*)〔一种产于非洲的长尾猴〕。

griz·zle[1] [ˈgrizl; ˋgrizl] ***vi.*** 〔英口〕**1.** 烦恼,烦躁。**2.** (小孩)啼哭,使人烦躁的哭泣。

griz·zle[2] [ˈgrizl; ˋgrɪzl] **I** ***vi.***, ***vt.*** (使)成灰色。**II** ***a.*** 灰色的。**III** ***n.*** **1.** 灰白头发,灰色假发。**2.** 灰色,有灰色光斑的色调。**3.** 灰色(或有灰白花斑的)图案[动物]。**4.** 含硫次煤。**5.** 烧得不透的砖,灰色次砖。

griz·zled [ˈgrizld; ˋgrɪzl̩d] ***a.*** **1.** 灰色的,灰白的;斑白的。**2.** 灰白头发的。

griz·zly [ˈgrizli; ˋgrɪzlɪ] **I** ***a.*** 灰色的,带灰色的;灰色头发的。**II** ***n.*** **1.** 灰熊(= ～ bear)。**2.** 【矿】格筛。

grm. = gram(s).

groan [grəun; gron] **I** ***vi.*** **1.** 哼,呻吟,发呻吟声。**2.** 苦恼,烦闷(*beneath*; *under*; *with*)。**3.** 渴望(*for*)。—

vt. 哼着说（*out*）；用不满意的呻吟声反对。~*ing board* 摆满菜肴的桌子。~ *under the heavy tax* 在重税下痛苦呻吟。*The shelf ~s with books*. 书架堆满书而嘎吱作声。~ **sb. down** 发哼哼声阻止某人讲话。~ ***inwardly*** 内心痛苦。**II** *n*. 呻吟，呻吟声；哼声。

groat [grəut; grot] *n*. **1.**（英国从前的）四便士银币。**2.** 小额，少量。***not care a*** ~ 毫不介意。***not worth a*** ~ 一文不值。

groats [grəuts; grots] *n*.〔*pl*.〕去壳的谷粒；去壳并弄成碎片的燕麦[小麦、大麦等]。

gro·cer [ˈgrəusə; ˋgrosɚ] *n*. 食品商，杂货商。~**'s itch**（因长期接触螨类引起的）皮炎。

gro·cer·y [ˈgrəusəri; ˋgrosərɪ] *n*. **1.**〔美常用 *pl*.〕食品，杂货。**2.** 食品杂货业。**3.**〔美〕食品杂货店；〔美南部〕小酒馆。

gro·ce·te·ri·a [ˌgrəusəˈtiəriə; ˏgrosəˋtɪrɪə] *n*.（由顾客自行取货后到柜台付款的）食品杂货自助商店。

grog [grɔg; grɑg] **I** *n*. **1.** 掺水烈酒。**2.**（喝掺水烈酒的）饮酒会。**3.**【冶】耐火材料，熟料，陶渣。*half and half* ~酒水各半的淡酒。**II** *vi*. 喝掺水烈酒。— *vt*. 用热水注入(空酒桶)浸出一点酒。~ **blossom** 酒糟鼻子。~ **brick** 耐火砖。~ **shop** *n*.〔英〕(低级)小酒馆。

grog·ger·y [ˈgrɔgəri; ˋgrɑgərɪ] *n*.〔古〕小酒馆。

grog·gy [ˈgrɔgi; ˋgrɑgɪ] *a*. **1.**〔古〕喝醉酒的。**2.** 不稳的，摇摇晃晃的。**3.**（马等）脚步不稳的；踉踉跄跄的。**4.**〔美口〕头昏眼花的。**-gi·ly** *ad*. **-gi·ness** *n*.

grog·ram [ˈgrɔgrəm; ˋgrɑgrəm] *n*. **1.** 丝和马海毛[羊毛]混纺的粗织物。**2.** 丝毛混纺的衣服。

groin [grɔin; grɔɪn] **I** *n*. **1.**【解】腹股沟，鼠蹊。**2.**【建】穹棱，拱肋，交叉拱。**3.** = groyne (*n*.)。**II** *vt*. **1.** 使成穹棱，在…上盖拱肋。**2.** = groyne (*vt*.)。

grok [grɔk; grɑk] *vt*., *vi*.（***grokked***, ***grok·king***）〔美俚〕(由于移情作用而)透悉[彻悟]。

Gro·lier [ˈgrɔːliə; ˋgrolɪɚ] *a*. 法国十六世纪藏书家格罗里(Grolier de Servières) 的。~ **binding** 有金丝交错的美丽考究的装订。

grom·met [ˈgrɔmit; ˋgrɑmɪt] *n*. **1.**【海】索眼，索环。**2.** 金属孔眼。**3.**【机】垫圈；【电】橡皮套管。

grom·well [ˈgrɔmwəl, -wel; ˋgrɑmwəl, -wɛl] *n*.【植】紫草（*Lithospermum officinale*）。

groom [grum, gruːm; grum, grʊm] **I** *n*. **1.** 马夫。**2.** 新郎 (= bridegroom)。**3.** 英国王宫侍从官。**4.**〔古〕男仆。**II** *vt*. **1.** 喂(马)，刷(马)。**2.** 修饰，使整洁。**3.**〔美〕培训；推荐(候选人)。*an impeccably ~ed woman* 打扮得十分干净的妇女。*be ~ed as a presidential candidate* 被推荐作总统候选人。*be well* [*badly*] *~ed* 修饰得整洁[不整洁]。— *vi*. 进行修饰。~**'s cake**（宝塔形的）结婚蛋糕。

grooms·man [ˈgrumzmən; ˋgrumzmən] *n*.（*pl*. ***-men***）（在婚礼上）陪伴新郎者，伴郎，男傧相(又叫 bestman)。

groove [gruːv; gruv] **I** *n*. **1.** 槽，沟；车辙；沟纹，纹道。**2.** 常规，成规，惯例。**3.** 最佳状态，得心应手的状态；使人愉快的东西，适合能力和兴趣的职位；合适的位置。**4.**【解】(器官、骨的)沟；【印】(铅字末端的)槽；【建】企口。*nail* ~【解】甲沟。*oil* ~(润滑)油槽。*His mind works in a narrow* ~. 他心地狭隘。***fall*** [***get***] ***into a*** ~ 落入老一套，习惯于老一套。***in the*** ~ **1.** 得心应手，处于最佳状态。**2.**（歌曲等）流行的；完美的。**3.** 合时，赶时髦。**II** *vt*. **1.** 在…作槽；在…挖沟。**2.**〔美俚〕灌(唱片)。**3.**〔美俚〕高度欣赏；使感到愉快。— *vi*.〔美俚〕极度享受。~**d pulley**【机】槽轮。**-less**, **-like** *a*.

groov·er [ˈgruːvə; ˋgruvɚ] *n*. 挖槽者，挖槽工具，挖槽机。

groov·y [ˈgruːvi; ˋgruvɪ] *a*. **1.** 沟的，槽的。**2.** 常规的，千篇一律的。**3.** 最佳状态的，〔美俚〕绝妙的。**4.**（歌曲等）流行的。**-i·ness** *n*.

grope [grəup; grop] *vi*. **1.**（暗中）摸索。**2.** 探索（*after*; *for*）。~ *about for information* 到处搜集情报。~ *for a clue* 找线索。— *vt*. 用手摸索。~ *one's way* 摸着走；摸索解决办法。

grop·ing·ly [ˈgrəupiŋli; ˋgropɪŋlɪ] *ad*. 摸索着；暗中摸索一样地。

gros·beak [ˈgrəusbiːk; ˋgrosˏbik] *n*.【动】锡嘴雀；蜡嘴雀。

gro·schen [ˈgrəuʃən; ˋgroʃən] *n*.（*pl*. ***-schen***）**1.** 格罗升〔奥地利货币和硬币名，等于一先令的 1/100〕。**2.** 格罗升〔德国曾使用过的一种币面价值多种的小银币〕。

gros de Lon·dres（或 ***lon·dres***）[grəu də ˈlɔːndrə; gro də ˋlɔndrə]【纺】伦敦横棱绸。

gros de Naples [grəu də nɑːpl; gro də nɑpl̩]〔F.〕（意大利那不勒斯产）厚重丝织物。

gros·grain [ˈgrəugrein; ˋgrogren] *n*.【纺】厚斜纹绸，罗缎。

gross [grəus; gros] **I** *a*. **1.** 粗壮的，肥大的；魁伟的。**2.** 显著的；严重的；恶劣的。**3.** 浓厚的，稠密的；茂盛的。**4.** 粗劣的，粗糙的；油腻的。**5.** 感觉迟钝的，不敏感的；（不用显微镜）肉眼看得见的。**6.** 粗俗的，粗鲁的，下流的。**7.** 总的，全体的；毛重的（*opp*. net）。**8.** 世俗的，肉体的。*a ~ blunder* [*error*] 严重的错误。*a ~ body* 肥壮的身体。~ *darkness* 一团漆黑。*a ~ fog* 浓雾。~ *income* 总收入。~ *industrial output value* 工业总产值。~ *losses* 毛损。~ *proceeds* 总货价收入。~ *profit* 毛利，总利润。~ *sales* 销售总额。~ *vegetation* 茂盛的草木。**II** *n*. **1.** 总额，全部。**2.**〔*sing*., *pl*.〕罗(=12打)。***a great*** ~ 十二罗(=1728个)。***a small*** ~ 十打(=120个)。***by the*** ~ 按罗；整批，全数；大量。***in*** ~【法】绝对独立的。***in*** (***the***) ~ **1.** 大体上，一般地。**2.** 批发，整批。**III** *vt*.〔口〕(未扣除各项费用之前)总共赚得。~ **domestic product** 国内生产总值〔即国民生产总值减去外国投资的净收益〕。~ **dynamics** 一般动力学。~ **feeder** **1.** 喜欢吃粗糙或油腻食物的人。**2.** 大量耗用肥料的植物。~ **national product** 国民生产总值〔简称 GNP〕。~ **ton** **1.** 长吨，英吨(=2,240磅)。**2.**（船的）总吨位。~ **weight**（包括容器、包装等在内的货物）毛重。**-ly** *ad*. **-ness** *n*.

gross·er [ˈgrausə; ˋgrausɚ] *n*.〔美俚〕赚钱的作品〔如电影等〕。

gros·su·lar·ite [ˈgrɔsjulərait; ˋgrɑsjʊləraɪt] *n*.【地】钙铝榴石。

Gros·venor [ˈgrəuvnə; ˋgrovnɚ] *n*. 格罗夫纳〔姓氏〕。

grosz [grəuʃ; groʃ] *n*.（*pl*. ***grosz·y*** [-i; -ɪ]）格罗希〔波兰货币名和硬币名，等于一兹罗提（*zloty*）的 1/100〕。

grot [grɔt; grɑt] *n*.〔诗〕= grotto.

Grote [grəut; grot] *n*. 格罗特〔姓氏〕。

gro·tesque [grəuˈtesk; groˋtɛsk] **I** *a*. **1.** 奇异的，奇形怪状的；怪诞的，可笑的。**2.** 风格特殊的。**II** *n*. **1.** 奇形怪状的人[物、图形等]；（文学、艺术上的）奇异风格；风格奇异的作品。**2.**〔英〕【印】粗黑体字〔美国称 gothic〕。**-ly** *ad*. **-ness** *n*.

gro·tes·quer·ie, **gro·tes·quer·y** [grəuˈteskəri; groˋtɛskərɪ] *n*. **1.** 奇形怪状的东西。**2.** 奇特，怪诞。

grot·to [ˈgrɔtəu; ˋgrɑto] *n*.（*pl*. *~es*, *~s*）**1.** 洞穴。**2.**（人工开挖的用于避暑或娱乐的）洞室。

grouch [grautʃ; graʊtʃ] **I** *n*.〔美口〕**1.** 牢骚，怨气。**2.** 脾气坏的人。**II** *vi*.〔美口〕闹别扭，发牢骚。

grouch·y [ˈgrautʃi; ˋgraʊtʃɪ] *a*. 脾气坏的，爱闹别扭的。

ground[1] [graund; graʊnd] grind 的过去式及过去分词。*a*. 碾碎了的，磨过的，磨成粉的。~ *and polished piston*【机】研磨活塞。~ **glass** **1.** 磨砂玻璃，毛玻璃。**2.** 微粒玻璃，玻璃粉。~ **rice** 米粉。

ground[2] [graund; graʊnd] **I** *n*. **1.** 地，地面；土地，地产；场；运动场，广场；〔*pl*.〕庭园，场地。**2.** 底；水底，海底；【矿】脉石，母岩；矿区；〔*pl*.〕渣滓，沉淀物。**3.** 基础；〔常 *pl*.〕理由，根据，原因；借口；立场，意见。**4.** 地域，范围；

面积;土壤。5. 阵地。6.【美】底子;底色;〔*pl*.〕【建】底材;(铜版术)(涂在版面上的)防蚀剂。7.【电】接地;地线。8.【海】= groundage. *a classic* ~文物胜地,古迹。*fishing* ~*s* 渔场。*grazing* ~*s* 牧场。*a parade* ~练兵场,阅兵场。*a parking* ~停车场。*recreation* ~*s* 运动场。*weapons proving* [*testing*] ~*s* 武器试验场。*coffee* ~*s* 咖啡渣。*What* ~ *have you for thinking so?* 你有甚么理由这样想? *The* ~ *here is stony*. 这里的地面多石。*a blue pattern on white* ~白地蓝花纹。***above*** ~ 活着,在世上。***beat over the old*** ~ 旧调重弹。***be dashed to the*** ~ 一败涂地,遭受挫折。***be off the*** ~ 站在一边,不妨碍。***be on the*** ~ 1. 在场。2. 在地上。3. 在决斗。***below*** ~ 死掉,被埋葬。***bite the*** ~ 大败,倒下,死去。***break fresh*** [***new***] ~ 开垦处女地,开辟新天地。***break*** ~ 1. 耕田;破土,动工,开业。2.【海】开船。***bring to the*** ~〔方〕埋葬。***broken*** ~ 新开垦土地,凸凹不平之地。***come*** [***go***] ***to the*** ~ 失败;灭亡。***common*** ~ 共同立场,一致点(*seek common* ~ *while reserving differences* 求同存异)。***cover*** (***the***) ~ 1. 走完一段路程,旅行。2. 包括,涉及(*The report covers much* ~. 报告涉及面很广)。3. (工作)有所进展;充分地处理(某个题目)。***cut the*** ~ ***from under sb.'s feet*** 拆某人的台,破坏某人计划;使某人议论站不住脚。***debatable*** ~ 1. 发生争执的土地。2. 争论点。(***down***) ***to the*** ~〔口〕在各方面,彻底地。***fall on stony*** ~ 无效,没有结果。***fall to the*** ~ 坠地;失败,成画饼。***forbidden*** ~ 禁区。***from the*** ~ ***of one's*** [***the***] ***heart*** 出自心底,衷心地。***from the*** ~ ***up*** 1. 从头开始,从基本点着手。2.〔美〕= down to the ~. ***gain*** [***gather, get***] ~ 占领阵地;占优势;流行;有进步,获得进展。***gain*** ~ ***on*** [***upon***] 1. 压制,侵占。2. 逼近,接近。***gain*** ~ ***with sb***. 同某人搞熟。***get*** ~ ***of*** 1. 蚕食。2. 优于。3. 甩开(追者)。***get off the*** ~ 1. 飞起,进行顺利。2. (报刊等)开始发行,(事业等)着手,开始。***give*** ~ = lose ~. ***go to*** ~ (狐狸)逃入地穴。***Hit the*** ~!【军】卧倒! ***hold*** [***keep, maintain, stand***] ***one's*** ~ 1. 坚守阵地。2. 坚持主张;站稳立场。***jumping-off*** ~【军】进攻基地,据点,战略基地。***kiss the*** ~ 匍伏;屈辱。***lose*** ~ 退却,让步;失利;衰落。***mop*** [***wipe***] ***the*** ~ ***with sb***.〔俚〕击倒某人,把某人打得一败涂地。***on delicate*** ~ 处境微妙。***on even*** ~ 在同样基础上。***on firm*** ~ 处于安全地位。***on one's own*** ~ 在行。***on the*** ~(***s***) ***of*** 由于,根据,以…为理由[借口]。***raze to the*** ~ 夷为平地。***run into the*** ~ 1. 做得过头,夸张。2. 把事情弄糟。***shift one's*** ~ 改变主张,改变立场。***smell the*** ~ 船因水浅而失速;船擦底。***suit down to the*** ~ 完全适合,完全令人满意。***take*** ~ 占领阵地。***take the*** ~ 搁浅。***to*** ~ 进洞,躲起来。***touch*** ~ 1. 船擦水底。2. 触及实质性问题。***tread on delicate*** ~ 接触微妙问题,碰到棘手问题。***tread the*** ~ 步行,走路。***worship the*** ~ ***sb. treads on*** 十分钦佩某人,拜倒在某人脚下。**II** ***vt***. 1. 在…基础上树立,把(论据等)放在…基础上,给…打基础(*on*; *in*)。2. 教给…基本知识,使…受初步训练(*in*)。3. 把…放在地上,使落地;放下(武器)。4.【电】使接地。5.【美】给…上底色。6. 使搁浅。7. 使停飞[停驶等]。~ *arms* 放下武器,投降。*The boat was* ~*ed*. 船搁浅了。*I* ~*ed my argument on my own experience*. 我的论点是以自己的亲身经验为依据的。***be*** ~***ed on*** 以…为基础,根据。***be well*** [***ill***] ~***ed in*** 在…方面很有[没有]基础[根据]。— ***vi***. 1. 有基础。2.【海】搁浅;【空】着陆。~**-air** ***a***. 陆空的。~**-air communication** 陆空通讯联络。~ **alert**【空】地面待命,(军事机场的)戒备状态。~ **antenna** 地面天线。~ **ash**【植】白腊树幼树,白腊树手杖。~ **bait** 投饵〔投到水面的鱼饵〕。~ **bass**【乐】基础低音。~ **beetle**【动】步行虫〔一种在山岩下生活的昆虫,夜出捕食其他小虫子〕。~ **berry**【植】刺悬钩子(*Rubus hispidus*)。~ **box** (花坛镶边或用作篱围的)矮脚黄杨。~**-breaker** 创始者,改进者。~ **bridge** (沼地上)木棒铺成的路。~ **cherry**【植】酸浆属(*Physalis*)植物(= *Husktomato*)。~ **circle** (齿轮的)基圆。~ **coat** 底涂层。~ **colour** 底涂色。~ **control**【空】地面控制,地面制导设备。~ **control approach** (恶劣气候下由雷达引导的)地面控制进场。~ **cover**【植】1. 地被植物。2. (森林中幼树以外的)矮小植物。~ **crew**【空】地勤人员。~ **echo** 地面回波。~ **effect** (航空器接近地面飞行时升力增加的)地面效应。~ **effect machine** 气垫船[车]。~ **fertilizer** 基肥。~ **fir**【植】石松属(Lycopodium)植物〔如,卷柏状石松(L. Selago)和王柏(L. Obscurum)〕。~ **fire** 地面(对空)火力。~**fish** 底栖鱼类。~ **floor** 1.〔英〕楼房底层(=〔美〕first floor)。2. 有利地位,优先机会(*get in on the* ~ *floor* 取得有利地位)。~ **fog**【气】低雾。~ **game**〔英〕猎兽[鹿,兔等]。~ **gripper** = ~ crew. ~ **hemlock**【植】加拿大紫杉(Taxus canadensis)〔产于美国东北〕。~ **hog**【动】美国土拨鼠。~ **hog day**〔美〕二月二日圣烛节〔传说土拨鼠于该日结束冬眠出洞〕。~ **ivy**【植】欧亚活血丹。~ **landlord**〔英〕房产地主。~ **level** 1. 地平面。2. = ~ state. ~**line** 基线,地平线。~ **linkup** 空降部队与地面部队的会合。~ **loop**【空】地转〔飞机滑行时因失去控制而引起的猛烈旋转〕。~**man** 球场管理员。~**-mass** ***n***.【地】石基。~ **meristem**【植】基本分生组织。~ **mine** 海底水雷。~ **net** 拽网,拖网。~ **note**【乐】基音,基础低音。~**nut**【植】1. (北美产)野豆。2. 野豆块茎(可供食用)。3. 落花生。~ **observer**【军】地面观察员,对空监视哨。~ **pea** 落花生。~ **pine**【植】扁叶石松。~ **personnel** = ~ crew. ~ **plan** 1. 平面图;底层设计图。2. 初步计划,根本计划。~ **plane** (透视画中的)地平面。~**-plane antenna** 水平极化天线。~ **plate**【电】接地板。~ **plum**【植】粗果黄芪(*Astragalus crassicarpus*)。~ **rent** 地租。~ **return**【电】地回路,地面反射。~ **rule** 1.【棒球】场(地)规则,【体】球场规则。2. 为任何一项活动制定的一套规则。~ **sea** (飓风和地震引起的)海啸。~ **sheet** 铺在地上的防潮布。~(**s**) **keeper** (运动场地,田庄,墓园等的)看管。~(**s**) **man** = ~(s) keeper. ~ **speed**【空】(飞机的)对地速度。~ **squirrel**【动】黄鼠属(Citellus)动物。~ **staff**〔英〕1. = ~ crew. 2. 全体职业板球运动员。~ **state**【物】(原子的)基态。~ **swell** 1. = ~ sea. 2.【地】地隆。3. 数量、程度、力量等的突然大幅度增长。~**-test** ***vt***. 对(飞机、火箭等)作地面试验。~**-to-air** = surface-to-air. ~**-to-**~ = surface-to-surface. ~ **torpedo** 海底水雷。~ **troops** 地面部队。~ **water** 地下水,潜水。~ **wave**【电】地波。~ **wire**【电】地线。~**work** 基础,基本成分,基本原理。~ **zero**【军】(核)爆心投影点;(炸弹的)着地点;一片空白。

ground·age [ˈgraundidʒ; ˋgraʊndɪdʒ] ***n***.〔英〕船舶进港费,停泊费。

ground·ed [ˈgraundid; ˋgraʊndɪd] ***a***. 1. 有基础的,根深蒂固的。2.【电】接地的。~ **antenna** 接地天线。~ **base** 基极接地。~**-base transistor** 共基极晶体管。~ **collector** 共集极接地。~ **emitter** 发射极接地。~ **grid** 接地栅极,抑制栅极。**-ly** ***ad***. **-ness** ***n***.

ground·er [ˈgraundə; ˋgraʊndə] ***n***.【棒球】(沿地面跳滚的)滚地球(= ~ ball)。

ground·ing [ˈgraundiŋ; ˋgraʊndɪŋ] ***n***. 1. (画、刺绣等的)底子。2. 基础训练;初步。3.【海】搁浅。4.【电】接地,通地。

ground·less [ˈgraundlis; ˋgraʊndlɪs] ***a***. 没有根据的,没有理由的。**-ly** ***ad***. **-ness** ***n***.

ground·ling [ˈgraundliŋ; ˋgraʊndlɪŋ] ***n***. 1. 栖息地上[地下]的动物;栖息水底的鱼;匍匐植物。2. 剧场中廉价座位的观众;缺乏鉴赏力的人。3. 在陆地上生活[工作]的人(*opp*. one in aircraft)。

ground·sel[1] [ˈgraunsl; ˋgraʊnsl̩] ***n***.【植】千里光属(*Senecio*)植物。

G

ground·sel[2] ['graundsəl; `graʊndsəl], **ground·sill** [-sil; -sɪl] *n*.【建】作基础的木材,木结构的最下部分,地槛。

group [gru:p; grup] I *n*. 1. 群;批,簇。2. 集团,团体,小组。3.【化】基,团,组;(周期表的)属,族。4. (雕塑等的)群像。5.【地】界。6. (英、美的)空军大队。7. 〔G-〕【宗】牛津团契。*a* ~ *of people* 一群人。*the grain* ~谷类。*blood* ~血型。**a ginger** ~ 要求政府采取坚决行动的议员,起推动作用的政党骨干小组。**a pressure** ~〔美〕(对国会等施加影响的)压力集团。~ **by** ~ 分批地。**in a** ~ = **in** ~**s** 成群地。II *vt*. 1. 集合,使成一团(*with*)。2. 组合,配合(*together*)。3. 把…分类。— *vi*. 成群;聚集,类集。~ **captain** 〔英〕空军上校。~ **commander** 空军大队长。~ **formation**【军】大队编队(飞行)。~ **insurance** 集体人寿保险。~ **leader** 小组长。~ **let** 〔美〕小群。~ **medicine** 1. 医生会同用药;集体制药。2. 集体用药。~ **mind**【心】团体心理。~ **psychology** 群众心理学。~ **representation** 职业代表制〔不同于区域代表制〕。~ **theory**【数】群论。~ **therapy** [**psychotherapy**]【医】集体治疗,心理治疗〔把同病患者编组,指导他们互相诉说苦恼,互相批评,解除精神负担〕。~**think** *n*. 小集团思想〔指集体内成员在思想观点上的一致〕。~ **velocity**【物】波群速度。~**ware**【计】群件,组软件〔指一组组相关的数据包软件〕。~ **work** 社会团体福利工作〔组织社会团体开展文化娱乐等活动〕。

group·er ['gru:pə; `grupɚ] *n*. (*pl*. ~(*s*)) 1.【动】鲈科鱼。2. 〔G-〕【宗】牛津团契成员。3. 〔美俚〕参加集体淫乱活动的人。

grou·pie[1] ['gru:pi; `grupɪ] *n*. 〔美俚〕追随歌星的青年女子;明星倾慕者。

grou·pie[2] ['gru:pi; `grupɪ] *n*. 〔主美口〕联营集团。

group·ing ['gru:piŋ; `grupɪŋ] *n*. 1. 集团。2.【统】归组。*tactical* ~【军】战斗编组。**ability** ~能力分组。

grouse[1] [graus; graʊs] *n*. (*pl*. ~)【动】松鸡。*a black* ~黑琴鸡。*a hazel* ~榛鸡。*a red* ~红松鸡。

grouse[2] [graus; graʊs] I *vi*. 〔英俚〕发牢骚,抱怨。II *n*. 1. 委屈,不平,牢骚话。2. 爱发牢骚的人。

grous·er[1] ['grausə; `graʊsɚ] *n*. 1. (拖拉机等的)履带齿片。2. (稳定钻机、船只等用的)临时桩。

grous·er[2] ['grausə; `graʊsɚ] *n*. 爱发牢骚的人。

grout[1] [graut; graʊt] I *n*. 1.【建】薄胶泥,薄浆,石灰浆。2. 〔英〕〔常 *pl*.〕渣滓。II *vt*.【建】给…灌浆。~**ing machine** 水泥搅拌机。

grout[2] [graut; graʊt] *vt*., *vi*. (猪)用鼻子拱(泥土等)。

grout·y ['grauti; `graʊtɪ] *a*. 〔方〕暴躁的,易怒的,脾气不好的;抑郁的,含怒的,不高兴的。

grove [grəuv; grov] *n*. 小树林,树丛,园林。*an orange* ~一片小橘林。-**less** *a*. 无树林的。

grov·el ['grɔvl; `grɑvl] *vi*. 1. 趴,匍匐。2. 卑躬屈节。~ **in the dust** [**dirt**] 趴在地上;摇尾乞怜。

grov·el(l)·er ['grɔvlə; `grɑvlɚ] *n*. 1. 趴着的人。2. 卑躬屈节的人。

grov·el(l)·ing ['grɔvliŋ; `grɑvlɪŋ] *a*. 1. 趴着的。2. 奴颜婢膝的。-**ly** *ad*.

Grover ['grəuvə; `grovɚ] *n*. 格罗弗〔男子名〕。

Grove(s) [grəuv(z); grov(z)] *n*. 格罗夫(斯)〔姓氏〕。

grov·y ['grəuvi; `grovɪ] *a*. 树丛的,林木的。

grow [grəu; gro] *vi*. (**grew** [gru:; gru]; **grown** [grəun; gron]) 1. 生长;成长,发育;发芽,苗长。2. 长大,增加,变强。3. 〔后接形容词、副词、成语等〕渐渐变得。4. 形成,产生。*Great oaks from little acorns* ~. 〔谚〕万丈高楼平地起。~ *weary* 变疲乏。~ *old* [*rich*] 变老[富]。— *vt*. 培育;栽培;培养,使增长;使发展。~ *a beard* 留胡子。~ *roses* 种玫瑰。~ **down** [**downwards**] 变小;减少。~ **in** 增加(~ *in beauty* [*strength*, *wisdom*] 增加美丽[力量、智慧])。~ **in** [**into**] 长成。~ **on** [**upon**] 1. (感觉、习惯等)加深对…的影响(*The smoking habit grew on me*. 我渐渐有烟瘾了)。2. (书、画等)渐渐把人迷住,渐渐使人爱好(*The picture* ~*s on him*. 他渐渐爱起那张画来)。~ **out** 出芽,发芽。~ **out of** 1. 抛弃;戒除。2. 长大而穿不上衣服。3. 源出,来自,起因于(~ *out of bad habits of his boyhood days* 戒除幼时的坏习惯。*The book grew out of a series of lectures*. 这书是由一系列讲稿编写而成的。*Soon, she grew out of her clothes*. 不久,她便长得高大而穿不上原先的衣服了)。~ **together** 长合,愈合。~ **up** 长大,成人;发生,滋长。~ **up like mushrooms** 像雨后春笋般地滋长。

grow·a·ble ['grə*u*əbl; `groəbl] *a*. 可种植的。

grow·er ['grəuə; `groɚ] *n*. 1. (以某种特殊方式生长的)植物。2. 种植者,栽培者,饲养者。*a fast* [*slow*] ~早熟[晚熟]植物。*a cotton* ~棉农。*a livestock* ~饲养员。

grow·ing ['grəuiŋ; `groɪŋ] I *n*. 成长,发育,发达。II *a*. 1. 成长中的;发育中的;发育旺盛的;增长中的。2. 促进发育的,适于生长的。~ **pains** 1.【医】发育性痛,发身期痛〔青少年的一种关节痛〕;发育期感情上的失去平衡。2. (企业等)早期发展过程中经历的困难。~ **point**【植】生长点。~ **season** 生长期。~ **weather** 促进谷物生长的气候。-**ly** *ad*.

growl [graul; graʊl] I *n*. (动物、人、雷等的)低沉的怒吼,隆隆声;咆哮;不平。II *vi*. 嗥叫,咆哮(*at*);怒吼;鸣不平;(雷)发隆隆声。— *vt*. 咆哮着说,发牢骚地说(*out*)。

growl·er ['graulə; `graʊlə] *n*. 1. 嗥叫的动物;咆哮的人。2. 〔英俚〕四轮马车。3. 小冰山。4.【电】短路线圈测试仪,电机转子试验装置。5. 〔美俚〕啤酒罐。**rush the** ~〔美俚〕1. 带着酒具到酒店打酒。2. 大量喝酒。

growl·er·y ['grauləri; `graʊlərɪ] *n*. 1. 嗥叫(声);咆哮;轰鸣(声)。2. 发牢骚的地方,私室。

growl·ing ['grauliŋ; `graʊlɪŋ] *a*. 狺狺叫的,咆哮的;隆隆响的。-**ly** *ad*.

grown [grəun; gron] grow 的过去分词。*a*. 1. 已成长的,成熟的。2. 被…长满的。*a well-* ~ *tree* 生意盎然的大树。*a* ~ *man* 成年人。*a grass-* ~ *place* 一处长满青草的地方。~-**up** *n*. 成年人。

growth [grəuθ; groθ] *n*. 1. 生长,成长,发育,发展。2. 栽培,培养。3. 生长物,产物;【医】瘤,赘生物。4.【经】(资本价值与收益的)预期增长。*a* ~ *of weeds* 杂草丛生。*evil* ~*s* 弊病。**of foreign** ~ 外国培植的。**of home** ~ 本国培植的。**of one's own** ~ 自己栽培的。**reach full** ~ 充分发育,成熟。~ **centre** 培训中心。~ **factor**【生】生长因子,生长因素〔食品里促进正常发育的有机体〕。~ **fund** 发展基金〔投资公司〕。~ **industry** 发展特快的新行业。~ **rate** 生长率,增长率。

groyne [grɔin; grɔɪn] I *n*.【建】防波堤,折流坝。II *vt*. 给…(海滩等)筑防波堤。

grub [grʌb; grʌb] I *vt*. (-**bb**-) 1. 掘出(树根、树桩等),掘除(*up*; *out*)。2. 费力查出,找出(记录等)。3. 〔俚〕养活,供给吃住。— *vi*. 1. 挖地;(掘除树根等)开地。2. 尽心查找(*for*)。3. 做苦工,孜孜从事(*along*; *away*; *on*)。4. 〔俚〕吃。~ *up weeds* 根除杂草。~ *about among records* 翻查记录。II *n*. 1.【动】蛆蛴螬。2. 做苦工的人,穷苦文人。3. 邋遢人。4. 〔俚〕食物。5. 板球中的滚球。~ **ax(e)** [**hoe**, **hook**] 鹤嘴锄。~ **saw** 锯石头用的手锯。~ **screw** 无头[平头]螺丝,木螺丝。**G- Street** 1. (伦敦的)格拉布街〔以前英国穷苦文人集居的街道,即现在的弥尔顿街〕。2. 〔集合词〕穷文人,廉价小说。~-**street** *a*. 穷文人的,低级作品的。

grub·ber ['grʌbə; `grʌbɚ] *n*. 1. 掘树根的人[工具];【农】碎土机。2. 作苦工的人。

grub·by ['grʌbi; `grʌbɪ] *a*. 1. 生蛆的。2. 污秽的,邋遢的。3. 卑鄙的。**grub·bi·ly** *ad*. **grub·bi·ness** *n*.

grub·stake ['grʌbsteik; `grʌbˏstek] I *vt*. 〔美方〕(以分其所获物为条件)供给(探矿者)以资金、衣物、伙食。II *n*. 1. (供给探矿者的)资金[物品]。2. 贷款。-r *n*. 贷款者。

grudge [grʌdʒ; grʌdʒ] I *vt*. 1. 羡慕,嫉妒。2. 吝惜,不愿给。~ *the time* 爱惜时间。*I ~ going*. 我不想去。*I ~ his going*. 我不愿意他去。— *vi*. 1. 嫉妒。2. 〔古〕鸣不平。II *n*. 怨恨,妒嫉;恶意。***bear*** [***owe***] ***sb. a ~*** 对某人怀恨在心。***hold*** [***have***] ***a ~ against sb***. 怀恨某人。

grudg·ing [ˈgrʌdʒiŋ; ˋgrʌdʒɪŋ] *a*. 吝啬的,不愿的;勉强的;怀恨的。*a ~ praise* 勉强的赞扬。*be ~ of money* 吝啬,爱财如命。-ly *ad*.

grue [gruː; gru] I *vi*. 〔方〕(因害怕或寒冷而)发抖,战栗。II *n*. 1. 一阵战栗。2. 可怕的性质[影响]。3. 〔Scot.〕一点,一粒。4. 〔Scot.〕薄浮冰,雪。

gru·el [ˈgruəl, ˈgruil; ˋgruəl, ˋgruɪl] I *n*. 1. 麦片粥,稀糊。2. 〔英口〕严厉的惩罚。***get*** [***have***, ***take***] ***one's ~*** 〔古〕受重罚;被击败;被处死。***give sb. his ~*** 〔口〕给予严重惩罚;击败;处死某人,干掉某人。II *vt*. (〔英〕-*ll*-) 重罚,使极度疲劳。

gru·el·(l)ing [ˈgruəliŋ; ˋgruəlɪŋ] I *n*. 痛打,惩罚。II *a*. 使极度疲劳的,激烈的。

Gru·en·ther [ˈgrʌnθə; ˋgrʌnθɚ] *n*. 格仑瑟〔姓氏〕。

grue·some [ˈgruːsəm; ˋgrusəm] *a*. 可怕的,令人毛骨悚然的。-ly *ad*. -ness *n*.

gruff [grʌf; grʌf] *a*. 1. 态度生硬的,粗暴的;脾气坏的。2. 声音粗哑的。***as ~ as a bear*** 粗暴,粗鲁。-ly *ad*. -ness *n*.

gruff·ish [ˈgrʌfiʃ; ˋgrʌfiʃ] *a*. 1. 有点粗暴的,有点生硬的。2. (声音)有点粗哑的。

grum [grʌm; grʌm] *a*. (***grum·mer***; ***grum·mest***) 〔罕〕忧郁的,沉闷的。

grum·ble [ˈgrʌmbl; ˋgrʌmbl̩] I *vi*. 1. 鸣不平,发牢骚;诉委屈 (*at*; *about*; *over*)。2. 咕哝,嘟囔。3. (雷等)隆隆响。— *vt*. 1. 抱怨 (*out*)。2. 嘟囔地说出。~ *one's complaint* 发牢骚。II *n*. 1. 不平,怨言。2. (雷等的)隆隆声。**grum·bly** *a*.

grum·bler [ˈgrʌmblə; ˋgrʌmblɚ] *n*. 爱发牢骚的人。

grum·bling·ly [ˈgrʌmbliŋli; ˋgrʌmblɪŋlɪ] *ad*. 喃喃抱怨者,嘟嘟囔囔地。

grume [gruːm; grum] *n*. 1. 【医】凝块。2. 黏液。

grum·met [ˈgrʌmet, -it; ˋgrʌmet, -ɪt] *n*. = grommet.

gru·mous [ˈgruːməs; ˋgruməs] *a*. 1. 【植】成聚团颗粒的。2. 像血块一样的;像黏液的。

grump [grʌmp; grʌmp] I *n*. 1. 〔常 *pl*.〕一阵坏脾气,发火。2. 脾气坏的人。II *vi*. 抱怨,嘀咕,发牢骚。

grump·ish [ˈgrʌmpiʃ; ˋgrʌmpɪʃ] *a*. = grumpy.

grump·y [ˈgrʌmpi; ˋgrʌmpɪ] *a*. 性情粗暴的,脾气坏的。-i·ly *ad*. -i·ness *n*.

Grun·dy [ˈgrʌndi; ˋgrʌndɪ] *n*. 〔常作 Mrs. G-〕心胸狭窄、拘泥礼俗、事事好挑剔他人的人〔原为 Tom Morton 所作喜剧 "Speed the Plough" (1798)中的人物,其邻居 Dame Ashfield 事事怕她挑剔,以致谨小慎微〕。***offend one's ~*** 伤害一般人的感情。***What will Mrs. ~ say***? 别人会怎样说呢?

Grun·dy·ism [ˈgrʌndiizəm; ˋgrʌndɪɪzm] *n*. (因害怕他人挑剔而谨小慎微的)拘泥礼节,因袭主义。

grunge [grʌndʒ; grʌndʒ] *n*. 〔美俚〕蹩脚货;难看的或乏味的东西。

grun·ion [ˈgrʌnjən; ˋgrʌnjən] *n*. (*pl*. ~(*s*)) 【动】叫嗓鱼 (*Leuresthes tenuis*) 〔产于美国加利福尼亚海岸〕。

grunt [grʌnt; grʌnt] I *vi*. 1. (猪等)作咕噜声,打哼哼。2. 发哼声,咕哝〔表示不满、不同意、疲劳等〕。— *vt*. 咕哝着说出 (*out*)。II *n*. 1. (猪等的)哼声。2. 咕哝,牢骚。3. 〔美俚〕电气线路工助手。4. 〔美俚〕猪肉。5. = grunter. 6. 〔美军俚〕步兵,海军陆战队〔越南战争中用语〕。

grunt·er [ˈgrʌntə; ˋgrʌntɚ] *n*. 1. 像猪一样哼的动物。2. 【动】石鲈。3. 哼哼的人,咕哝的人。4. 〔美俚〕摔跤运动员。

grunt·ing [ˈgrʌntiŋ; ˋgrʌntɪŋ] *a*. 呼噜的,咕哝的。~ ***ox*** 【动】牦牛 (= yak)。-ly *ad*.

grunt·ling [ˈgrʌntliŋ; ˋgrʌntlɪŋ] *n*. 小猪。

grutch [grʌtʃ; grʌtʃ] 〔英方〕I *vi*. 1. 抱怨,发牢骚。2. 勉强地给或准许。II *n*. 不满,嫌隙,积怨。

gru·yère [gruːˈjɛə; gruˋjɛr] *n*. (瑞士)格里尔干酪。

gr. wt. = gross weight 毛重。

gryph·on [ˈgrifən; ˋgrɪfən] *n*. = griffin[1].

grys·bok [ˈgraisbɔk; ˋgraɪsbɑk] *n*. 【动】南非产灰色小羚羊。

Gs. = guilders.

gs. = guineas.

G.S. = 1. General Secretary 总书记,秘书长。2. General Service 普通勤务。3. General Staff 总参谋部。4. Girl Scouts 〔美〕女童子军。5. ground speed.

g.s. = 1. grandson. 2. ground speed.

GSC = General Staff Corps 【军】参谋团。

G-7 = Group of Seven 西方七大(工业)国集团〔英、美、法、德、意、加、日七国〕。

GSM = global system for mobile communication 【电信】全球通(通信系统)。

G.S.O. = General Staff Officer 〔英〕(陆军)参谋部参谋。

GST = Greenwich sidereal time 格林尼治恒星时。

G-string [ˈdʒiːstriŋ; ˋdʒistrɪŋ] *n*. 1. 【乐】小提琴的 G 弦。2. (系在腰上遮盖外阴部的)兜裆布〔为美洲印第安人和脱衣舞表演者所穿用〕。

G-suit [ˈdʒiːˌsjuːt; ˋdʒiˏsjut] *n*. (飞行员或宇航员的)抗超重飞行衣,抗过载飞行衣〔亦作 gravity suit 或 anti-G suit〕。

GSV = guided space vehicle 导航太空航行器。

G.T. = gross ton.

GT = Gran Turismo 高级跑车。

gt. = 1. gilt. 2. great. 3. gutta.

g.t. = gilt top 【印】天金。

Gt. Br., **Gt. Brit.** = Great Britain 1. 大不列颠(岛)。2. 英国。

G.T.C., **g.t.c.** = good till cancelled, or countermanded 【商】取消[定货]前有效。

gtd = guaranteed.

GTP = Guanosine triphosphate 【化】三磷酸鸟苷。

gua·ca·mo·le [ˌgwɑːkəˈməulei; ˏgwɑkəˋmole] *n*. 色[沙]拉调味酱汁。

gua·cha·ro [ˈgwɑːtʃəˌrəu; ˋgwɑtʃəˏro] *n*. (*pl*. ~*s*) 【动】油鸱 (*Steatornis caripensis*) 〔产于南美,为夜游飞禽,肉可食,油可点灯〕。

gua·co [ˈgwɑːkəu; ˋgwɑko] *n*. 【植】马兜铃属植物〔美洲热带地方所产的一种可治蛇毒的树〕。

Gua·da·la·ja·ra [ˌgwɑːdɑːlɑːˈhɑːr; ˏgwɑdələˋhɑrə] *n*. 瓜达拉哈拉〔墨西哥城市、西班牙城市和省名〕。

Gua·de·loupe [ˌgwɑːdəˈluːp; ˏgwɑdəˋlup] *n*. 哥德洛普(岛)〔法〕〔拉丁美洲〕。

guai·ac [ˈgwaiæk; ˋgwaɪæk] *n*. 【植】1. 神圣愈疮木 (*Guaiacum sanctum*); 愈疮木 (*Guaiacum officinale*)。2. = guaiacum.

guai·a·col [ˈgwaiəˌkəul, -ˌkɔl; ˋgwaɪəˏkol, -ˏkɑl] *n*. 【化】邻甲氧基苯酚,愈疮木酚。

guai·a·cum [ˈgwaiəkəm; ˋgwaɪəkəm] *n*. 【植】愈疮木属木材。

Guam [gwɑːm; gwɑm] *n*. 关岛〔西太平洋〕。**Guam·a·ni·an** [gwɑːˈmeiniən; gwɑˋmenɪən] *n*. 关岛人。

guan [gwɑːn; gwɑn] *n*. 【动】冠雉〔产于中南美,以果类为食物〕。

gua·na [ˈgwɑːnɑː; ˋgwɑnɑ] *n*. = iguana.

gua·na·co [gwəˈnɑːkəu; gwəˋnɑko] *n*. (*pl*. ~*s*) 【动】

G

(南美安第斯山区野生的)红褐色美洲驼。

gua·nay [gwəˈnai; gwəˋnaɪ] ***n.***【动】冠鸬鹚(*Phalacrocorax bougainvillii*)〔产于秘鲁和智利。该地鸟粪主要来源于这种鸟〕。

gua·neth·i·dine [guəˈneθidiːn; guəˋnɛθɪdin] ***n.***【药】胍乙啶。

guan·i·dine [ˈgwaːnidiːn, -din; ˋgwanɪdin, -dɪn] ***n.***【化】胍。~ **nitrate** 硝酸胍。

gua·nine [ˈgwaːniːn; ˋgwanin] ***n.***【化】鸟嘌呤。

gua·no [ˈgwaːnəu; ˋgwano] **I** ***n.*** **1.**(秘鲁产)海鸟粪,鸟粪石。**2.**鱼肥,人造氮肥。**II** ***vt.*** 在…上施鸟肥[鱼肥]。

Guan·tá·na·mo [gwaːnˈtaːnaːməu; gwanˋtanamo] ***n.*** 关塔那摩〔古巴城市〕。

guar [gwaː; gwa] ***n.***【植】瓜尔豆(*Cyamopsis tetragonoloba*),产于美国西南部,作饲料用)。

guar. = guarantee(d)。

Gua·ra·ní [ˌgwaːraːˈniː; ˏgwaraˋni] ***n.*** **1.**(*pl.* ***-nis***, ***-ni***)瓜拉尼人〔居住在巴拉圭河和大西洋之间的南美印第安人〕。**2.**瓜拉尼语。**3.**〔g-〕(*pl.* ***-nis***)瓜拉尼〔巴拉圭货币单位,等于100分〕。

guar·an·tee [ˌgærənˈtiː; ˏgærənˋti] **I** ***n.*** **1.**保证,担保。**2.**保证人〔法律上用 guarantor〕。**3.**接受保证的人。**4.**抵押品,担保物。*offer one's house as a* ~ 以房屋作抵押。***stand*** ~ ***for*** 做保人。**II** ***vt.*** **1.**保证,担保。**2.**〔口〕包,管保。*I* ~ *his success.* 我包他成功。***be*** **~*d against*** [***from***] ***loss*** 保证不受损失。~ ***sb. against*** [***from***] ***a risk*** 保证某人不出危险。~ **fund** 保证基金。~ **engineer** 造船公司派在新船上进行观察,以便随时作机件修整的工程师。

guar·an·tor [ˌgærənˈtɔː; ˋgærəntɚ] ***n.***【法】保证人。

guar·an·ty [ˈgærənti; ˋgærəntɪ] **I** ***n.***【法】**1.**保证;保证书。**2.**抵押品,担保物。**3.** = guarantor. **II** ***vt.*** = guarantee. ~ **money** 保证金。

guard [gaːd; gard] **I** ***n.*** **1.**警卫;警戒;看守。**2.**防卫者;看守者;哨兵,卫兵,〔集合词〕警卫队;〔the G-〕(英国等的)皇家禁卫军;【海】护航舰。**3.**防护装置;(车的)挡泥板;(枪的)保险;(刀、叉、剑等柄上的)护板。**4.**(击剑、拳击等的)防护姿势,防护术。**5.**〔英〕列车员(=〔美〕conductor);(列车上的)司门员;制动手。**6.**(篮球、足球等的)卫,后卫。*the advance* [*rear*] ~ 前[后]卫。*life* ~ 救生员。*mud* ~ 挡泥板。***catch sb. off***(***his***)~ 乘某人不备。***come off*** ~【军】离防,下防。***drop*** [***lower***] ***one's*** ~ 丧失警惕。***get past sb.'s*** ~ 冲破某人的防御。~ ***of honour*** 仪仗队。***Imperial G-*** 警卫兵。***keep*** [***mount, stand***] ~ 站岗,守卫,放哨。***keep sb. under close*** ~ 把某人置于严密监视下。***off one's*** ~ 疏忽,不提防。***on*** ~ 值班,当班,提防着。***on one's*** ~ 警戒,提防。***put*** [***throw***] ***sb. off his*** ~ 使某人不提防。***put*** [***set***] ***sb. on*** (***his***) ~ 使某人提防。***relieve*** [***change***] ~ 接防站岗,换岗。***row the*** ~ 用小船在军舰周围巡逻。***run the*** ~ 偷过哨兵线。***stand*** ~ ***over*** 派人看守。***stand*** [***be, lie***] ***on*** [***upon***] ***one's*** ~ 警戒,提防。***the Life Guards*** 〔英〕禁卫骑兵第一、第二团。***the Royal Horse Guards*** 〔英〕禁卫骑兵第三团。**II** ***vt.*** **1.**防守,警卫,守卫。**2.**看守,监视。**3.**给…加保护装置,对…进行校正检查。**4.**谨慎使用(言词等)。**5.**【医】对…配用矫正剂。~ *a fortress* 防守要塞。~ *one's reputation* 维护自己的名誉。*The lunatic was carefully ~ed.* 对疯子严加看守。— ***vi.*** **1.**防卫,警惕,预防(*against*)。**2.**警卫,看守。**3.**(击剑时)取守势。~ *against disease* 预防疾病。~ **band** **1.**(电讯)防护频带。**2.**(录音磁带等的两磁迹间的)保护间距。~ **boat** 警戒艇;巡逻艇。~ **book** (钉线上衬有厚线条的)剪贴簿,相片簿。~ **cell**【植】保护细胞。~ **chain** 表链。~ **duty**【军】警卫职务。~ **flag**【军】(警戒舰的)值班旗。~ **hair**【动】保护鬃毛。~**-house** = ~room. ~ **mount** 卫兵交班礼。~**-officer**【军】联络官。~**-rail** (铁道)护轨;栏杆。~ **ring** 护圈;防止戒指脱落的指环。~ **room** **1.**卫兵室,警卫室。**2.**禁闭室。~ **ship** 警戒舰。~ **tent** 岗篷。

guard·ant [ˈgaːdnt; ˋgardn̩t] ***a.***【纹】兽面为正面而兽身为侧面的。

guard·ed [ˈgaːdid; ˋgardɪd] ***a.*** **1.**被保护着的。**2.**被看守着的。**3.**谨慎的。*a* ~ *answer* 谨慎的回答。*The warehouse is* ~. 库房有人看守。**-ly** ***ad.*** **-ness** ***n.***

guard·ee [ˈgaːdiː; ˋgardi] ***n.***〔英口〕衣冠楚楚的卫兵。

guard·er [ˈgaːdə; ˋgardɚ] ***n.*** 守卫者,卫兵;看守人[物]。

guard·i·an [ˈgaːdjən; ˋgardɪən] **I** ***n.*** **1.**保护者,保卫者;保管者,管理员。**2.**【法】监护人(*opp.* ward)。**3.**方济各修道院院长。**4.**【英史】贫民救济委员。**5.**〔G-〕(用于报刊名)卫报。~ ***ad litem*** (未成年被告的)诉讼监护人。**II** ***a.*** 守护的。~ **angel** 守护天使。~ **deity** 守护神。~ **saint** 守护圣徒。

guard·i·an·ship [ˈgaːdiənʃip; ˋgardɪənˏʃɪp] ***n.*** 保护,守护;监护人的职责[身份]。***under the*** ~ ***of*** 在…保护下。

guard·less [ˈgaːdlis; ˋgardlɪs] ***a.*** 无警戒的,无保护的。

guards·man [ˈgaːdzmən; ˋgardzmən] ***n.*** (*pl.* ***-men***) **1.**卫兵,哨兵。**2.**〔英〕禁卫军官兵;〔美〕国民警卫队员。

Guar·ne·ri [gwaːˈneriː; gwarˋnɛri] ***n.***〔It.〕瓜奈里家族〔意大利克雷莫纳的小提琴制造家族〕。

Guar·ner·i·us [gwaːˈneriəs; gwarˋnɛrɪəs] ***n.*** 瓜奈里小提琴。

Gua·te·ma·la [ˌgwætiˈmaːlə; ˏgwatəˋmalə] ***n.*** **1.**危地马拉〔拉丁美洲〕。**2.**危地马拉(城)〔危地马拉首都〕(= ~ City)。

Gua·te·ma·lan [ˈgwætiˈmaːlən; ˋgwatəˋmalən] **I** ***a.*** 危地马拉的,危地马拉人的。**II** ***n.*** 危地马拉人。

gua·va [ˈgwaːvə; ˋgwavə] ***n.***【植】番石榴,芭乐。

Guay·a·quil [ˌgwaiəˈkiːl; ˏgwaɪəˋkil] ***n.*** 瓜亚基尔〔厄瓜多尔港市〕。

gua·yu·le [gwaːˈjuːl; gwaˋjul] ***n.*** **1.**【植】(美洲热带的)银胶菊。**2.**银菊胶〔银胶菊的脂,可作橡胶代用品〕。

gub·bins [ˈgʌbinz; ˋgʌbɪnz] ***n.*** *pl.*〔用作单或复〕**1.**〔英口〕(小)装置;(小)配件。**2.**〔英口〕不值钱的东西;废物;碎块;果皮。**3.**〔英口〕傻瓜。**4.**〔美俚〕食物;吃剩的东西。

gu·ber·na·to·ri·al [ˌgjuːbənəˈtɔːriəl; ˏgjubɚnəˋtɔrɪəl] ***a.*** **1.**统治者的;地方长官的;总督的。**2.**〔美〕州长的。

guck [gʌk; gʌk] ***n.***〔俚〕浓胶黏性物质。

gud·dle [ˈgʌdl; ˋgʌdl̩] ***vt.***, ***vi.***〔Scot.〕(用手在溪边石缝里)摸(鱼)。**-r** ***n.***

gudg·eon[1] [ˈgʌdʒən; ˋgʌdʒən] ***n.*** **1.**【动】钩鱼〔作鱼饵用〕。**2.**容易受骗的人,傻子。**3.**饵,诱饵。

gudg·eon[2] [ˈgʌdʒən; ˋgʌdʒən] ***n.***【机】**1.**耳轴。**2.**舵枢。

Gue·bre, Gue·ber [ˈgiːbə, ˈgei-; ˋgibɚ, ˋge-] ***n.*** 拜火教徒。

guel·der-rose [ˈgeldəˈrəuz; ˋgɛldɚˋroz] ***n.***【植】荚蒾,绣球花(= snowball)。

Guelph, Guelf [gwelf; gwɛlf] ***n.*** 中世纪意大利的教皇党员〔参看 *Ghibelline*〕。

Guen·e·vere [ˈgwenəviə; ˋgwɛnəvɪə] ***n.*** 格纳维尔〔女子名〕。

gue·non [gəˈnəun; gəˋnon] ***n.***〔F.〕长尾猴属(*Cercopithecus*)动物〔包括青猴(*C. sabaeus*);黑长尾猴(*C. aethiops*)〕。

guer·don [ˈgəːdən; ˋgɝdən] **I** ***n.***〔诗〕报酬,奖赏。**II** ***vt.***〔诗〕酬劳,奖赏。**-less** ***a.*** 无报酬的。

gue·ri·don [ˈgeridən; ˋgɛrɪdən] ***n.***〔F.〕作摆设的小桌子。

Guern·sey [ˈgəːnzi; ˋgɝnzɪ] ***n.*** **1.**(英国海峡中的)耿济岛(Isle of ~)。**2.**耿济种乳牛。**3.**〔g-〕黑色厚毛线衫。

guer·(r)il·la [gəˈrilə; gəˋrɪlə] ***n.*** **1.**游击队员;〔常 *pl.*〕游击队。**2.**〔古〕游击战〔现多用 ~ war〕。*a* ~ *area* 游击区。~ *band* 游击队。*a* ~ *detachment* 游击支队。

～ *forces* 游击队。～ **strike** 未经工会同意的罢工。～ **tactics** 游击战术。～ **theatre** 流动剧团,街头活报演出队。～ **war** [**warfare**] 游击战。**-ism** *n*. 游击主义,游击战。

guess [ges; gɛs] Ⅰ *vt*. 1.推测,猜测。2.猜对,猜中(谜等)。3.〔口〕以为,相信。～ *a riddle* 猜中谜语。*I* ～ *it's going to rain*. 我想天快下雨了。— *vi*. 猜 (*at*); 推测。～ *at a riddle* 猜谜。*I* ～ *not*. 决不是那样。*I can't even* ～ *at what you mean*. 我猜不着你的意思。***keep sb.*** ～***ing*** 使人捉摸不定。Ⅱ *n*. 推测,猜测。***at a*** ～ = ***by*** ～ 依推测,照估计。***by*** ～ ***and by god*** [***gosh***] 凭瞎猜,凭粗略估计。***It's anybody's*** ～. 这是谁也拿不准的事。***miss one's*** ～ 推测错。***My*** ～ ***is that****....* 我认为…。***One man's*** ～ ***is as good as another's***. 猜测终究是猜测。～**-rope**, ～**-warp** *n*. = guest rope. ～ **stick** 〔俚〕尺,计算尺。～ **who** 〔美俚〕不认识的人。～**work** 推测。

gues(s)·ti·mate [ˈgestimit; ˋgɛstəmet] Ⅰ *n*. 〔美俚〕瞎猜,瞎估计。Ⅱ [-meit; -ˏmet] *vt*. 〔美俚〕瞎猜,瞎估计。

guest [gest; gɛst] Ⅰ *n*. 1.客人,宾客。2.旅客,宿客,顾客。3.客串演员,特约演员。4.【动】寄生生物,寄生虫;【植】寄生植物。*a distinguished* ～ 贵宾。*a state* ～ 国宾。*the* ～ *of honour* 正餐的主宾。*an unbidden* ～ 不速之客。*house* ～ 留宿的宾客。Ⅱ *vt*. 招待,款待。— *vi*. 1.做客。2.〔美俚〕在无线电节目中客串演出。～**chamber** 客房。～ **flag** 客旗〔挂在游艇上表示主人不在但有客人在船中的长方形白旗〕。～**house** 宾馆,招待所,高级寄宿舍。～ **member** 特邀代表。～ **mineral** 寄生矿物。～ **night** (大学,俱乐部等)招待来宾的夜晚。～ **players** 特邀选手。～ **room** = ～chamber. ～ **rope** 1.扶手绳。2.(稳定拖船的)辅助缆索。～ **speaker** 邀请来的演说者。～ **worker** (在德国工作的)外籍工人。**-less** *a*. **-ship** *n*.

Guest [gest; gɛst] *n*. 格斯特〔姓氏〕。

guest·ship [ˈgestʃip; ˋgɛstʃɪp] *n*. 客人身份。

Gue·va·ra [geˈvɑːrɑː; gɛˋvɑrɑ], **Ernesto** 格瓦拉〔1928～1967,出生于阿根廷的拉丁美洲革命家〕。**-ist** 格瓦拉主义者。

guff [gʌf; gʌf] *n*. 〔美俚〕胡说,瞎扯;闲聊。

guf·faw [gʌˈfɔː; gʌˋfɔ] Ⅰ *n*. 哄笑,大笑。Ⅱ *vi*. 哄笑,大笑。— *vt*. 大笑着说。

gug·gle [ˈgʌgl; ˋgʌgl̩] *vi*., *n*. = gurgle.

GUI = graphical user interface【计】图形用户界面。

Gui·an·a [giˈænə, gaiˈænə; gɪˋænə,ˋgɪɑnə] *n*. 圭亚那〔拉丁美洲〕。

gui·chet [ˈgiːʃei; ˋgiʃe] *n*. 〔F.〕售票窗口;格子窗口。

guid·a·ble [ˈgaidəbl; ˋgaɪdəbl̩] *a*. 可指导的。

guid·ance [ˈgaidəns; ˋgaɪdns] *n*. 1.向导,指引,指导。2.导航;制导。3.【机】导槽,导板,导管。*traffic* ～ 交通管理。*vocational* ～ 业务辅导。***under sb.'s*** ～ 在某人指导下。～ **system**【宇】制导系统。

guide [gaid; gaɪd] Ⅰ *n*. 1.引导,指导。2.领路人,导游者,向导;指导者,指挥者。3.【军】向导舰;〔*pl*.〕基准兵,标兵。4.〔英〕女童子军。5.规准,指针。6.(旅行、游览)指南;入门书;路标。7.【机】导轨,导沟,导杆;【电】导路;导体;导引物;【自】波导,导向装置;【医】导子,标。*a* ～ *fossil* 标准化石。*A G- To English Grammar*《英语语法入门》。***G- center***!【军】向中看齐〔向中央基准兵看齐〕! ***G- left*** [***right***]!【军】向左[右]看齐! Ⅱ *vt*. 1.引导。2.指导,指挥;支配(思想感情等),左右(人的行为);管理;指示。3.教导,辅导。～ *him in his studies* 辅导他学习。～ *the state* 治理国家。*be* ～*d by one's sense of duty* 在责任感支配下。～ **bar** [**rod**]【机】导杆。～ **bearing**【机】导引轴承。～ **board** 路牌。～**book** 旅行指南,参考手册。～ **dog** 盲人引路犬。～ **flag**【军】标旗,指示旗。～ **line** 1.指导路线,方针;准则,指标。2. 指路绳。3.【印】样张,样行;标线。～**post** 路标。～ **rope** 导绳。～ **way**【机】导沟,导向槽。～ **word**【印】眉题〔印在书眉上标明本页内容的词〕。

guided [ˈgaidid; ˋgaɪdɪd] *a*. 有领导的;制导的。～ **missile** 飞弹。～ **wave** 被导波,循轨波。

guid·ing [ˈgaidiŋ; ˋgaɪdɪŋ] *n*. 导向,定向;制导,导航;导波,控制。～ **hole** 中导孔,导孔。～ **principles** 指导方针。～**rod** 标杆。

GUIDO, Guido [ˈgaidəu; ˋgaɪdo] *n*. 〔美〕太空飞行工程师;导航控制中心负责人。

gui·don [ˈgaidən; ˋgaɪdən] *n*. 1.队旗;长标旗。2.旗手。

g(u)ild [gild; gɪld] *n*. 1.(互助性质的)协会;(中世纪的)行会,同业公会,基尔特。2.【植】依赖植物集团。*the* ～ *mentality* [*outlook*] 行会主义。～ **socialism** 行会社会主义;基尔特社会主义。

guil·der [ˈgildə; ˋgɪldɚ] *n*. = gulden.

guild·hall [ˈgildˌhɔːl; ˋgɪldˏhɔl] *n*. 1.(中世纪的)同业公会会所,会馆。2.市政厅;〔the G-〕伦敦市政厅。

guilds·man [ˈgildzmən; ˋgɪldzmən] *n*. (*pl*. ***-men*** [-mən; -mən]) 同业公会会员,行会会员。

guile [gail; gaɪl] *n*. 狡猾;诡计。**-less** *a*. 坦率的,正直的。

guile·ful [ˈgailful; ˋgaɪlfəl] *a*. 狡诈的,诡计多端的。**-ly** *ad*. **-ness** *n*.

Guillaume [giˈjəum; giˋjom], **Charles Edouard** 查利·吉永〔1861—1938,法国物理学家,曾获 1920 年诺贝尔物理奖〕。

guil·le·mot [ˈgilimɔt; ˋgɪləˏmɑt] *n*.【动】海雀科的鸟,海鸠。

guil·loche [giˈləuʃ; gɪˋloʃ] *n*.【建】扭索饰。

guil·lo·tine [ˌgiləˈtiːn, ˈgil-; ˋgɪləˏtin] Ⅰ *n*. 1.断头台。2.【机】截切机,闸刀。3.【物】截流器。4.【医】铡刀,环状刀。*tonsil* ～ 扁桃体铡除刀。5.(议会)中止辩论〔指在预定时间对议案等进行表决〕。Ⅱ *vt*. 1.把…送上断头台,把…处斩刑。2.【医】用截切机截断。3.对(议案)中止辩论而付表决。～ **amputation**【医】外科截断术。

guilt [gilt; gɪlt] *n*. 1.罪,罪过,罪行。2.内疚,有罪感。*The evidence proved his* ～. 证据已证明他有罪。～ ***by association*** 牵连犯罪。～ **complex**【心】犯罪情结〔老感到自已有罪的变态心理〕。

guilt·i·ly [ˈgiltili; ˋgɪltəlɪ] *ad*. 有罪地,有罪似地。

guilt·i·ness [ˈgiltinis; ˋgɪltənɪs] *n*. 有罪;罪恶。

guilt·less [ˈgiltlis; ˋgɪltlɪs] *a*. 1.无罪的;无辜的。2.〔口〕不知的,无经验的;没有 (*of*)。*be* ～ *of writing poems* 不会作诗。*windows* ～ *of glass* 没有玻璃的窗子。**-ly** *ad*. **-ness** *n*.

guilt·y [ˈgilti; ˋgɪltɪ] *a*. 1.有罪的,犯了错误的。2.自觉有罪的,内疚的。～ *behaviour* 犯罪行为。*have a* ～ *conscience* 自疚,问心有愧。*wear a* ～ *look* 露出内疚的神色。***be found*** ～ 被判决有罪。***be*** ～ ***of*** 犯…罪(*be* ～ *of murder* 犯杀人罪)。***be inwardly*** ～ 理亏心虚。～ ***of death*** 〔古〕应处死刑。***plead not*** ～ 不服罪。

guimp(e) [gimp, gæmp; gɪmp, gæmp] *n*. (女用)带袖内衣。

Guin·ea [ˈgini; ˋgɪnɪ] *n*. 几内亚〔非洲〕。

guin·ea [ˈgini; ˋgɪnɪ] *n*. 1.畿尼〔旧时英国金币,合 21 先令〕。2.〔口〕= ～ fowl. **G- corn**【植】高粱,蜀黍。～ **fowl**【动】(珍)珠鸡。～ **grains**【植】药用卡满龙种子(= grains of paradise)。～ **grass**【植】羊草。～ **hen** 1.雌(珍)珠鸡;(珍)珠鸡。2. = ～ fowl. ～ **pig**【动】豚鼠,天竺鼠;供科学实验的人[物]。**G- worm** 麦地那龙线虫。

Guin·ea-Bis·sau [ˈginibiˈsəu; ˋgɪnɪbɪˋso] *n*. 几内亚比绍〔非洲〕。

Guin·e·an [ˈginiən; ˋgɪnɪən] Ⅰ *a*. 几内亚的,几内亚人的。Ⅱ *n*. 几内亚人。

Guin·ness [ˈginis; ˋgɪnɪs] *n*. (爱尔兰产)黑啤酒。

gui·pure [giːˈpjuə; gɪˋpjur] *n*. 网络花边,凸纹花边。

guise [gaiz; gaɪz] Ⅰ *n*. 1.态度,外观。2.伪装,借口。3.

〔古〕服装,打扮。*in* [*under*] *the* ～ *of* 扮作;以…为幌子(*under the* ～ *of friendship* 假借友谊的名义。*in the* ～ *of a monk* 扮作和尚)。II *vt*., *vi*.〔英方〕伪装。

gui·tar [gi'tɑː; gɪ`tɑr] I *n*. 六弦琴,吉他。*electric* ～ 电吉他。II *vi*. 弹吉他。**-ist** [gi'tɑːrist; gɪ`tɑrɪst] *n*. 弹吉他的人。

gui·tar·fish [gi'tɑːfiʃ; gə`tɑrfɪʃ] *n*.【动】犁头鳐。

gu·lar ['gjuːlə, 'guː-; `gjulə, `gu-] *a*. 喉的,喉上的。

gulch [gʌltʃ; gʌltʃ] *n*.〔美〕深谷,峡谷,冲沟〔尤指金矿地的急流河床〕。

gul·den ['guldən; `gʊldən] *n*. (*pl*. ～*s*, ～) 盾(荷兰货币单位)。

gules [gjuːlz; gjulz] *n*., *a*.【纹】红色(的)。

gulf [gʌlf; gʌlf] I *n*. 1.(比 bay 大而深入陆地的)海湾,内海,湾。2.深渊;深坑,鸿沟;漩涡,涡。3.(感情、意见等的)悬殊,分歧,隔阂 (*between*)。4.〔诗〕深海。*a great* ～ *fixed* 歧异,不可逾越的鸿沟。*the* ～ *between the rich and the poor* 贫富之间的悬殊。**the** ～ **below** 地狱。**the G- States**〔美〕墨西哥湾沿岸各州。**the G- Stream** 墨西哥湾流〔由墨西哥湾向北流至大西洋的水流〕。**the G- War** 海湾战争〔1991 年 1—2 月由美国领导的 28 国军事联盟发动"沙漠风暴行动",战争历时六周,结束了伊拉克对科威特的占领〕。II *vt*. 吞没,使深深卷入,卷进。～ **weed**【植】果囊马尾藻。

gulf·y ['gʌlfi; `gʌlfɪ] *a*. 多漩涡的;多深坑的。

gull[1] [gʌl; gʌl] *n*.【动】鸥。

gull[2] [gʌl; gʌl] I *n*. 1.〔古〕欺诈。2.容易受骗的人,笨蛋。II *vt*. 欺骗。～ *sb*. *into buying rubbish* 骗人买无用的东西。～ *sb*. *out of his money* 骗人钱。

Gul·lah ['gʌlə; `gʌlə] *n*. (美国东南部的)嘎勒族黑人,嘎勒英语。

gul·let ['gʌlit; `gʌlɪt] *n*. 1.【解】食道,咽喉,咽。2.海峡,水道。3.锯齿间空隙。4.【建】水落管,水槽。

gul·li·bil·i·ty [ˌgʌli'biliti; ˌgʌlə`bɪlətɪ] *n*. 易受欺骗。

gul·li·ble ['gʌlibl; `gʌləbl̩] *a*. 容易受骗的,容易上当的,轻信的。**-bly** *ad*.

gull·ish ['gʌliʃ; `gʌlɪʃ] *a*. 笨的,呆的。

Gul·li·ver's ['gʌlivəz; `gʌlɪvəz] **Travels**《格列弗游记》〔英国作家 Jonathan Swift 的名作,其中有关于大人国和小人国的描写〕。

gul·ly[1] ['gʌli; `gʌlɪ] I *n*. 1.沟渠,阴沟;(干涸的)沟壑,溪谷,涧谷。2.【建】集水沟,雨水口,檐槽。3.【板球】后方右侧场地。II *vt*. (*-lied*; *-ly·ing*) 1.水流冲成(沟渠)。2.在…开沟。～ **drain**【建】下水道。～ **hole**【建】沟渠;集水孔。

gul·ly[2] ['gʌli; `gʌlɪ] *n*.〔英方〕大刀。

gu·los·i·ty [gjuː'lɔsiti; gju`lɑsətɪ] *n*. 贪婪,食欲过度。

gulp [gʌlp; gʌlp] I *vt*. 1.吞;狼吞虎咽地吃,一口吞下。2.抑制,忍住(眼泪等)。— *vi*. 1.吞下,狼吞虎咽。2.喘不过气来,哽塞。～ *down sobs* 吞声饮泣。II *n*. 1.吞咽。2.一口吞下的量,一大口。*swallow at one* ～ 一口吞下,一饮而尽。**-ing·ly** *ad*.

gum[1] [gʌm; gʌm] I *n*. 1.树胶,树脂。2.橡胶;〔美〕弹性树胶;橡胶树,产树胶的树,3.〔*pl*.〕〔美〕高统橡胶套鞋(= ～ boots)。4.〔美〕橡皮糖,口香糖(= chewing ～)。5.眼屎;病树的分泌物。II *vt*. (*-mm-*) 1.在…涂树胶。2.用树胶粘合(*down*; *together*; *up*)。3.〔美俚〕欺骗。～ *down the flap of an envelope* 用胶粘好信封的盖口。*The boy's pocket was all gummed up with candy*. 这个男孩的口袋全被糖弄粘了。— *vi*. (果树因病)分泌树液,(树)分泌树胶;结胶;发黏。～ *up* 1.粘合。2.〔美俚〕弄坏,搞乱。～ **ammoniac** (= ammoniac) 1. *n*. 氨草胶。2. *a*. 氨的,氨性的,含氨的。～ **arabic** 阿拉伯树胶。～ **boots**〔美〕长统橡胶套鞋。～ **dragon** = ～ tragacanth. ～ **drop** 橡皮软糖。～ **elastic** 弹性橡胶(即生橡胶)。～ **foot**〔美俚〕便衣警察。～ **resin**【化】树胶脂。～ **tragacanth**【化】龙胶,黄蓍胶。～ **tree**【植】桉树,产橡胶的树(*up a* ～*-tree* 不上不下,进退两难)。～ **water** 阿拉伯胶溶液,胶水。～ **wood** 橡胶树木料。

gum[2] [gʌm; gʌm] I *n*.〔常 *pl*.〕齿龈;牙床。II *vt*. (*-mm-*) 1.锉深(锯)齿。2.用牙床咀嚼。*beat* [*bump*] *one's* ～*s*〔美俚〕唠叨,饶舌。～ **boil** 齿龈脓肿。

gum[3] [gʌm; gʌm] *n*.〔英方、俚〕上帝(= God)(用于咒诅,发誓)。*By* ～! 我敢向天发誓,确确实实。*My* ～! 天啊! 啊呀!〔表示痛苦、悲哀或愤怒等〕。

gum·bah [guːm'bɑː; gum`bɑ] *n*.〔美俚〕老朋友,死党〔黑社会用语〕。

gum·ball ['gʌmbɔːl; `gʌmbɑl]〔美俚〕I *n*. 警车顶灯。II *vi*. (警车)亮着顶灯行驶。

gum·bo ['gʌmbəu; `gʌmbo] *n*. (*pl*. ～*s*) 1.【植】秋葵;秋葵荚。2.〔美〕浓汤。3. 强黏土(= ～ soil)。4.〔G-〕〔美〕(路易斯安那州和西印度群岛的法国移民和黑人用的)法语方言。

gum·ma ['gʌmə; `gʌmə] *n*. (*pl*. ～*s*, ～*ta*)【医】梅毒瘤,树胶状肿。**-tous** [-təs; -təs] *a*.

gum·mi·ness ['gʌminis; `gʌmənɪs] *n*. 树胶状,树胶质;黏性,黏着性。

gum·ming ['gʌmiŋ; `gʌmɪŋ] *n*. 1.结胶,胶合。2.【植】流胶症。3.【印】(在石版上)涂胶。4. 树胶的采集。

gum·mite ['gʌmait; `gʌmaɪt] *n*.【矿】脂铅铀矿。

gum·mo·sis [gə'məusis; gə`mosɪs] *n*.【植】流胶;流胶病。

gum·mous ['gʌməs; `gʌməs] *a*. 树胶质的,树胶状的。

gum·my ['gʌmi; `gʌmɪ] *a*. 1.树胶状的;树胶制的。2. 含树胶的;胶黏的。3. (脚)树胶状肿的。4.〔美俚〕拙劣的,讨厌的。～ *bark* 分泌树胶的树皮。～ *ankles* 肿胀的足踝。～ **tumour**【医】梅毒瘤,树胶状肿。

gump [gʌmp; gʌmp] *n*.〔方〕笨蛋。

gump·tion ['gʌmpʃən; `gʌmpʃən] *n*. 1.〔口〕精明能干,通晓事理。2. 事业心,进取精神。3. 调合颜料的溶剂。**-less** *a*.

gump·tious ['gʌmpʃəs; `gʌmpʃəs] *a*. 精力充沛的,非常能干的,机灵的。

gum·shoe ['gʌmˌʃuː; `gʌmˏʃu] I *n*. 1. 橡胶套鞋。2.〔*pl*.〕橡胶底帆布鞋。3.〔俚〕侦探。II *vi*.〔美俚〕轻声走路,偷偷地走;侦察。III *a*.〔美俚〕偷偷地进行的。～ **man**〔美俚〕侦探,警察。

gun [gʌn; gʌn] I *n*. 1.炮,枪,猎枪;〔美口〕手枪。2. 枪状物;〔美俚〕毒品注射器;(杀虫用)喷雾器。3.(信号枪、礼炮的)鸣放。4.〔美俚〕罪犯;扒手;强盗。5.〔谑〕烟斗。6. 猎枪手。7.(引擎的)油门,风门。*a salute of twenty-one* ～*s* 二十一响礼炮。*When* ～*s speak it is too late to argue*.〔谚〕大炮说话时,争辩已太迟。*an air* ～ 汽枪。*a cement* ～ 水泥喷枪。*electron* ～【无】电子枪。*a heavy field* ～ 重炮。*heavy mountain and field* ～*s* 山野重炮。*a machine* ～ 机关枪。*a plasma* ～ 等离子枪。*a spray* ～【机】喷枪。*a squirt* ～ 水枪。*a welding* ～ 焊接喷灯,焊接喷枪。*a big* [*great*] ～〔俚〕大人物,高级军官。*as sure as a* ～ 不错,的确。*beat* [*jump*] *the* ～〔俚〕(赛跑时)未听发令枪响就起跑,抢跑;行动过早。*blow great* ～*s* 刮大风。*carry too many* [*the biggest*] ～*s* (在议论、竞赛等中)占上风。*give it the* ～ 开动,加快。*go great* ～*s* 快速有成效地干。～*s and butter* 既要大炮又要牛油的政策,军事与经济发展并重的政策。*spike sb.'s* ～ 击败某人,挫败某人。*stick* [*stand*] *to* [*by*] *one's* ～(*s*) 坚守阵地,固执己见。*under the* ～*s* 在严密监视下。II *vt*. (*-nn-*) 1.〔美口〕向…开枪。2.〔美口〕开大(引擎,汽车等的)油门。*The guard was gunned down*. 卫兵被射倒。～ *the engine* 开大引擎的油门。—*vi*.〔美口〕1. 拿枪射击;用枪打猎。2. 开大油门前进。～ *for* 1.用枪搜索;捕杀。2.〔美俚〕寻求,争取。*That guy was gunning for a rise*. 那家伙在想办法升官。～ **barrel** 枪筒;炮筒。～**boat** 炮舰(～ *boat diplomacy* 炮舰外交)。～ **captain** (海军中的)炮

G

长。～ **car** 铁道运炮车。～ **carriage**【军】炮车,炮架。～ **case** 1.猎枪套。2.〔英俚〕法官头巾。～**cotton**【军】火棉,强棉药。～ **crew**〔集合词〕炮手,机枪手。～ **dog** 猎犬。～ **fight** 1.*n*. 手枪格斗。2. *vi*. (两人之间)用手枪格斗,枪战。～**fighter** 用手枪格斗的人;(美国西部的)枪战能手。～**fire** 1.炮击,炮火。2.【军】号炮;号炮时。～ **flint** 枪机燧石。～ **harpoon** 用射鲸炮发射的鱼叉。～ **house** 炮塔,炮室。～**-howitzer** 加农榴弹炮。～**-layer** 瞄准手,射击手。～**lock** 炮机,枪机。～**man** 带枪者;(罢工时的)带枪纠察员;〔美俚〕带手枪的歹徒;枪炮工人。～ **metal** 炮铜〔铜锡锌合金〕。～ **moll**〔美俚〕带枪歹徒的女帮凶[情妇]。～**-pit** 火炮掩体。～**play** 手枪战〔如在歹徒警察之间发生的手枪战〕。～**-point** 枪口〔主要用在 *at gunpoint* (在枪口威胁下)这个片语里〕。～**pointer** 方向瞄准手。～**port** (军舰的)炮眼,炮门。～**powder** 1.黑色火药,有烟火药。2. 中国珠茶 (= ～ powder tea)。～ **rack** 墙上的枪架。～ **room** 1.私宅中的藏枪室;枪炮陈列室。2. (英国军舰上的)下级军官住所。～ **runner** 军火走私者。～ **running** 军火走私。～ **ship**〔美军俚〕武装直升飞机。～**shot** 1.(自炮内射出的)炮弹。2. 射击,炮击。3. (枪、炮的)射程 (*within* ～ *shot* 在射程内。*out of* ～ *shot* 在射程外)。～**-shy** *a*. 怕枪炮声的,风声鹤唳的,(猎犬、马等)被枪炮声吓坏的。～**sight** 瞄准器,标尺。～**slinger**〔俚〕带枪的歹徒,带枪的狗腿子。～**smith** 枪炮工人。～**-stock** 枪托。～**toting** *a*. 经常携带和使用枪枝的。

gung ho [ˈgʌŋˈhəu; ˋgʌŋˋho]〔美俚〕1. 同心协力的。2. 热心。3. 热情地干。

gun·ite [ˈgʌnait; ˋgʌnaɪt] *n*. 喷枪,水泥枪〔G-〕古耐特〔一种喷枪或水泥枪商标〕。

gunk [gʌŋk; gʌŋk] *n*.〔俚〕油腻物,胶黏物质,浓糊状物质。～ **hole** (上有顶篷的)小船坞,小船停泊处。**-y** *a*.

gun·nage [ˈgʌnidʒ; ˋgʌnədʒ] *n*. (军舰的)火炮量。

gunned [gʌnd; gʌnd] *a*. 装备有大炮的;带枪的。*a ship heavily* ～ 装备多门火炮的船舰。*over-* [*under-*]～ 装备火炮过多[不足]的。

gun·nel[1] [ˈgʌnəl; ˋgʌnəl] *n*. = gunwale.

gun·nel[2] [ˈgʌnəl; ˋgʌnəl] *n*.【动】(北大西洋产的)锦鳚科鱼。

gun·ner [ˈgʌnə; ˋgʌnɚ] *n*. 1.炮兵,炮手,火炮瞄准手;飞机上的枪炮手。2. 管理军械(库)的海军准尉。3. 猎枪手。***kiss*** [***marry***, ***be married to***] ***the*** ～***'s daughter***〔海军俚〕〔谑〕(水兵)被绑在大炮上鞭打。

gun·ner·a [ˈgʌnərə; ˋgʌnərə] *n*.【植】根乃拉草;〔G-〕根乃拉草属。

gun·ner·y [ˈgʌnəri; ˋgʌnərɪ] *n*. 1.射击。2. 射击技术,枪炮操作与射击法。3.〔集合词〕重炮,枪炮。～ **jack** [**lieutenant**]〔英俚〕炮术练习舰上的射击检查官。～ **ship** 炮术练习舰。

gun·ning [ˈgʌniŋ; ˋgʌnɪŋ] *n*. 1.射击。2. 打猎。3. 用枪搜索捕杀。*go* ～ 去打猎。

gun·ny [ˈgʌni; ˋgʌnɪ] *n*. 1.粗黄麻布。2. 黄麻麻袋。～**-bag** [**sack**] 黄麻麻袋。

gun·sel [ˈgʌnsl; ˋgʌnsl̩] *n*.〔俚〕1. 娈童〔指被人作为女性玩弄的男子〕2. 带枪的歹徒,带枪的狗腿子。

Gun·ter [ˈgʌntə; ˋgʌntɚ] *n*. 1.冈特〔姓氏〕。2. **Edmund** ～ 埃德蒙·冈特〔1581—1626,英国数学家〕。***according to*** ～〔美〕精确地 (= according to Cocker)。**Gunter's chain** 冈特氏测链〔长 66 英尺〕。

gun·ter [ˈgʌntə; ˋgʌntɚ] *n*. 1.【海、测】冈特氏尺规〔又叫 Gunter's scale〕。2.【海】中桅;中桅帆。

Gun·ther [ˈgʌnθə; ˋgʌnθɚ] *n*. 冈瑟〔姓氏〕。

gun·wale [ˈgʌnəl; ˋgʌnəl] *n*. 船舷的上缘。～ ***down*** [***to***] 船舷和水面相平。～ ***under*** 舷边没入水面以下。

gun·yah [ˈgʌnjə; ˋgʌnjə], **gun·yeh** [-je; -jɛ] *n*. 澳洲土人小屋。

gup [gʌp; gʌp] *n*.〔度用英语〕闲话,闲谈,〔英口〕蠢话。

gup·py[1] [ˈgʌpi; ˋgʌpɪ] *n*.【动】孔雀鱼 (*Lebistes reticulatus*)〔西印度群岛产,胎生、观赏、食蚊小鱼〕。

gup·py[2] [ˈgʌpi; ˋgʌpɪ] *n*. 有通气管的流线型潜艇〔是 *g*reater *u*nderwater *p*ropulsive *p*ower + *-y* 的缩略词〕。

gurge [gəːdʒ; gɝdʒ] I *n*. 漩涡。II *vi*. (液体)形成漩涡。

gur·gi·ta·tion [gəːdʒiˈteiʃən; gɝdʒəˋteʃən] *n*. 1.(液体的)漩涡,(波涛似的)沸腾;翻滚。2. 沸腾声。

gur·gle [ˈgəːgl; ˋgɝgl̩] I *vi*. 1.汩汩地流。2. (人高兴时从喉咙中)发咯咯声;(流水)作汩汩声。— *vt*. 1.使发汩汩声。2. 咯咯地发出(声响)。～ *one's delight* 发出咯咯的笑声。II *n*. 1.汩汩声。2. 咯咯声。～*s of delight* 咯咯的笑声。

gur·goyle [ˈgəːgɔil; ˋgɝgɔɪl] *n*. = gargoyle.

gur·jun [ˈgəːdʒʌn; ˋgɝdʒən] *n*.【植】(东印度)陀螺状羯布罗香。

Gur·kha [ˈguəkə; ˋgʊrkə] *n*. 1.(尼泊尔的)廓尔喀人。2. 英国[印度]军队中的尼泊尔籍士兵。～ **regiments** (英国陆军中)廓尔喀人组成的团。

gur·nard [ˈgəːnəd; ˋgɝnɚd], **gur·net** [ˈgəːnit; ˋgɝnɪt] *n*. (*pl*. ～*s*,〔集合词〕～)【动】鲂鮄科海鱼,绿鳍鱼。

gur·rah [ˈgʌrə; ˋgʌrə] *n*. (印度的)土瓮。

gur·ry [ˈgʌri; ˋgʌrɪ] *n*. 鲸鱼的碎肉,鱼的碎肉。

gu·ru [ˈguruː; ˋguru] *n*. 1.【印度教】个人的宗教教师[指导]。2. (受下级崇敬的)领袖,头目;〔美俚〕头面人物,权威。

Gus [gʌs; gʌs] *n*. 格斯〔男子名〕(Augustus 的爱称)。

gu·san·o [guˈsɑːnəu; guˋsɑno] *n*.〔古巴人用语〕虫豹,蛆虫〔指逃亡到美国的古巴人〕。

gush [gʌʃ; gʌʃ] I *n*. 1.涌出,喷出,迸出。2. (感情的)冲动;洋溢的热情。3. 洋洋洒洒的文章,滔滔不绝的讲话。*a* ～ *of enthusiasm* 热情进发。*gas* ～【油】汽喷。II *vt*. 1.涌出,喷出,迸出。2. 洋洋洒洒地写,滔滔不绝地说。*The gaping wound* ～*ed forth* [*out*] *with blood*. 伤口大量出血。—*vi*. 1.涌出,喷出,迸出。2. 过分表露感情;洋洋洒洒地写,滔滔不绝地讲。～ *over film stars* 不停地谈电影明星。

gush·er [ˈgʌʃə; ˋgʌʃɚ] *n*. 1.迸出物。2. 喷油井。3. 容易动感情的人;滔滔不绝的说话者。

gush·ing [ˈgʌʃiŋ; ˋgʌʃɪŋ] *a*. 1.涌出的,喷出的,迸出的。2. 过分热情的,容易动感情的,滔滔不绝的。**-ly** *ad*. **-ness** *n*.

gush·y [ˈgʌʃi; ˋgʌʃɪ] *a*. 1.迸发的,喷出的;流出的。2. 过分多情的。**-i·ly** *ad*. **-i·ness** *n*.

gus·set [ˈgʌsit; ˋgʌsɪt] I *n*. 1.(用以填补、加固或放大衣服的)三角形布料。2.【机】角撑板,角板。3. 楔形土地。II *vt*. 1.在…缝三角形布料。2. 给…装上角撑板。

gus·set·ed [ˈgʌsitid; ˋgʌsɪtɪd] *a*. 1.缝有三角形布料的。2. 装有角撑板的。

gus·sie, gus·sy [ˈgʌsi; ˋgʌsɪ] *vt*., *vi*. (把…)打扮得花枝招展 (*up*)。

gust[1] [gʌst; gʌst] *n*. 1.阵风;一阵狂风。2. (雨、火、烟、雹、声音等)突发的一阵;(感情)进发。*a* ～ *of rage* 勃然大怒。*a* ～ *of rain* 一阵暴雨。*a* ～ *of wind* 一阵风。

gust[2] [gʌst; gʌst] I *n*. 1.〔古〕味觉,味感。2. 风味,嗜好。***have a*** ～ ***of*** 嗜好,欣赏。II *vt*.〔Scot.〕尝尝,享受。

Gus·ta [ˈgʌstə; ˋgʌstə] *n*. 女名〔Augusta 的爱称〕。

gus·ta·tion [gʌsˈteiʃən; gʌsˋteʃən] *n*. 尝味,味觉。

gus·ta·to·ry [ˈgʌstətəri; ˋgʌstə͵torɪ] *a*. 味觉的。*the* ～ *bud* 味蕾。*the* ～ *cell* 味觉细胞。*the* ～ *nerve* 味觉神经。

Gus·ta·vus [gəsˈtɑːvəs; gəsˋtɑvəs] *n*. 古斯塔夫斯〔男子名〕。

gus·to [ˈgʌstəu; ˋgʌsto] *n*. (*pl*. ～*s*) 1.爱好,嗜好,趣味。2. 热忱,兴致勃勃。3.〔古〕滋味。4. 艺术风格。***enjoy the full*** ～ ***of***〔古〕充分领略。***with enormous*** ～

兴致勃勃地,津津有味地。

gust·y [ˈgʌsti; ˋgʌstɪ] ***a*.** 1.阵风的;多阵风的,起大风的。2.迸发的。**-i·ly *ad*. -i·ness *n*.**

gut [gʌt; gʌt] **I *n*.** 1.肠子,〔*pl*.〕内脏,〔口〕肚子;〔美俚〕香肠。2.〔*pl*.〕内容,内部的主要部分;本质,实质。3.〔*pl*.〕〔俚〕精神,毅力,耐久力,勇气,厚脸,无礼。4.(提琴、网球拍等的)肠线,(钓鱼钩上用的)丝线。5.狭水道,海岬,海峡;弯头,狭巷,狭道。*the blind* ~ 盲肠。*the large* [*small*] ~ 大[小]肠。*surgical* ~ 外科缝合用的羊肠线。~ *ache* 肚子痛。*a* ~ *fighter* 顽强的对手。*a* ~ *issue* [*question*] 关键问题。~ *language* 粗话。***a man of* [*with*] *plenty of* ~*s*** 颇有胆量的人。***get down to the* ~*s of a matter*** 触及问题的实质。***hate sb.'s* ~*s*** 〔俚〕恨透了某人。***have no* ~*s in sth*.** 毫无内容。***have the* ~*s to do* [*say*] *sth*.** 〔美〕有做[说]某事的勇气。***not fit to carry* ~*s to a bear*** 1.太不中用。2.不能作食物。***run sb. through the* ~** 折磨某人。***spill one's* ~** 〔美俚〕告密,翻肠倒肚地全部说出。***sweat one's* ~*s out*** 拚命干。***tear the* ~*s out of sb*.** 耗尽某人精力。***tear the* ~*s out of sth*.** 阉割精华,使化为乌有。**II *vt*.** 1.取出(鱼等的)内肠。2.损毁(房屋等的)内部装置,抽去(书籍等的)主要内容。3.〔口〕狼吞虎咽。**III *a*.** 〔美俚〕深有感触的,激起感情的;直觉的。~ **course** 〔美俚〕容易的课程。~ **scrapper** 〔美俚〕提琴师。

gut·buck·et [ˈgʌtbʌkit; ˋgʌtˏbʌkɪt] ***n*.** 缓慢淫荡的四步爵士舞曲。

Gu·ten·berg [ˈguːtnbəːg; ˋgutnˏbɝg], **Johannes** 古腾堡〔1400—1467,德国活版印刷发明人〕。

gut·less [ˈgʌtlis; ˋgʌtlɪs] ***a*.** 没有勇气的,懦怯的。

guts·y [ˈgʌtsi; ˋgʌtsɪ] ***a*.** 〔俚〕有勇气的,有力量的。

gut·ta [ˈgʌtə; ˋgʌtə] ***n*.** (*pl*. ***gut·tae*** [ˈgʌtiː; ˋgʌti]) 1.滴,滴状物。2.【建】圆锥饰。3.【化】古塔胶,杜仲胶,〔用于补牙或作绝缘体〕。~**-percha** 杜仲胶,古塔胶。~**-percha tree** 杜仲树。

gut·tate [ˈgʌteit; ˋgʌtet] ***a*.** 滴状的;有(彩色)斑点的。**gut·tation** [gʌˈteiʃən; gʌˋteʃən] ***n*.**

gua·ta·tim [gəˈteitəm; gəˋtetəm] ***ad*.** 【处方】一滴一滴地 (=drop by drop)。

gut·ter [ˈgʌtə; ˋgʌtɚ] **I *n*.** 1.水槽,檐槽。2.沟,边沟,街沟,明沟。3.【印】排版上的隔条;(装订)左右两页间的空白。4.贫民区,贫民窟。*caves* ~【建】天沟。*children of the* ~ 流浪儿。*vent* ~ 通风道。***be born in the* ~** 出身贫贱。***lap the* ~** 〔俚〕酩酊大醉。***rise from the* ~** 从微贱中发迹。***take a child out of the* ~** 收养穷苦小孩。**II *vt*.** 1.在…开沟。2.为…装檐槽。~ *a new building* 给新楼装导水槽。—***vi*.** 流,淌蜡,(烛火)风中摇晃。~ *down* [*out*] 1.逐渐变弱熄灭。2.默默无闻地结束。~**-bird *n*.** 1.麻雀。2.声名狼藉的人。~ **child** 流浪儿。~ **film** 迎合低级趣味的电影。~ **language** 〔美俚〕脏话。~**man** 1.清除阴沟的人。2.摊贩。~ **press** 迎合低级趣味的报纸。~**snipe** 流浪儿,穷途末路的人。

gut·tle [ˈgʌtl; ˋgʌtl] ***vt*., *vi*.** 狼吞虎咽。**-r *n*.** 贪吃者。

gut·tur·al [ˈgʌtərəl; ˋgʌtərəl] **I *a*.** 1.喉的,咽喉的。2.【语】颚音的,喉音的。3.发出不愉快声音的。~ *sounds* 喉音。*the* ~ *speech of the Germans* 德国人多喉音的说话。**II *n*.** 【语】颚音,喉音〔如 g, k 等〕;颚音字母[符号]。**-ism *n*.** 颚音的性质[习惯]。**-ize *vt*.** 使发颚音,使颚音化。**-ly *ad*. -ness *n*.**

gut·ty [ˈgʌti; ˋgʌtɪ] ***a*.** 1.大胆的,生气勃勃的。2.感触很深的,挑动性的。

guy[1] [gai; gaɪ] **I *n*.** 1.〔英〕盖伊·福克斯 (Guy Fawkes) 的模拟像〔Guy Fawkes 为火药阴谋案的主犯,每年十一月五日焚烧其模拟像以示庆祝〕。2.怪人;服装奇异的人。3.〔美俚〕家伙,人,小伙子,朋友。*a little* ~ 矮子。*a queer* ~ 怪人。*a regular* ~ 虚有其表的人。*a right* ~ 〔美〕可靠的人。*a smart* ~ 自作聪明的人,精明的家伙。*a tough* ~ 硬汉。**II *vt*.** 1.〔英〕把(某人)制成模拟像嘲弄。2.嘲笑,挖苦。3.糟蹋。

guy[2] [gai; gaɪ] **I *n*.** 〔俚〕逃走,逃亡。*do a* ~ 逃亡。*give the* ~ *to* 逃出,摆脱。**II *vi*.** 逃走。

guy[3] [gai; gaɪ] **I *n*.** 【海】支索,牵索,张索;【电】天线拉线。**II *vt*.** 用支索撑住,加固。

Guy [gai; gaɪ] ***n*.** 盖伊〔男子名〕。

Guy·a·na [gaiˈɑːnə, gaiˈænə; gaɪˋanə, gaɪˋænə] **I. *n*.** 1.圭亚那〔拉丁美洲〕。2.圭亚那人。**II.** *a*. 圭亚那的。

guy·ot [giːˈəu; ˋgaɪət] ***n*.** 海底平顶山,桌状山。

guz·zle [ˈgʌzl; ˋgʌzl] ***vi*., *vt*.** 大吃大喝,吃光喝光。~ *one's money* 大吃大喝花光金钱。**guzzler *n*.** 酒鬼,大吃大喝的人。

Gwen [gwen; gwɛn] ***n*.** 格温〔女子名〕〔Gwendolyn 的爱称〕。

Gwen·do·lyn [ˈgwendəlin; ˋgwɛndəlɪn] ***n*.** 格温多琳〔女子名〕。

G.W.R. =Great Western Railway.

gwyn·i·ad [ˈgwiniæd; ˋgwɪnɪæd] ***n*.** (英国淡水湖产)鳟类小鱼。

gybe [dʒaib; dʒaɪb] **I *vi*., *vt*.** (使)(帆)随风向自一舷移向他舷,将帆自一舷移向他舷以变更(船的航道) (=jibe)。**II *n*.** 1.帆的方向改变。2.航道的改变。***jerk a* ~** 伪造执照。

gym [dʒim; dʒɪm] ***n*.** 〔口〕1.体育馆。2.体操,体育课。~ **shoe** 球鞋,橡胶底运动鞋。~ **suit** 运动衣。

gym·kha·na [dʒimˈkɑːnə; dʒɪmˋkɑnə] ***n*.** 运动会。

gym·na·si·a [dʒimˈneiziə; dʒɪmˋnezɪə] ***n*.** gymnasium 的复数。

gym·na·si·al [dʒimˈneɪziəl; dʒɪmˋnezɪəl] ***a*.** (德国或欧洲其他某些国家)大学预科的。

gym·na·si·arch [dʒimˈneiziɑːk; dʒɪmˋnezɪɑrk] ***n*.** (古希腊的体育,竞技和学校的)监理官。

gym·na·si·ast [dʒimˈneiziæst; dʒɪmˋnezɪæst] ***n*.** 1.(德国等欧洲国家的)预科学生。2.运动家。

gym·na·si·um [dʒimˈneiziəm, gimˈnɑːziəm; dʒɪmˋnezɪəm, gɪmˋnɑzɪəm] ***n*.** (*pl*. ***gym·na·si·a*** [-ˈneiziə; -ˋnezɪə] 或 ~*s*) 1.体育馆,健身房。2.〔有时 G-〕(德国或欧洲其他某些国家的)大学预科,准备进大学的高级中学。

gym·nast [ˈdʒimnæst; ˋdʒɪmnæst] ***n*.** 体操教员,体育家。

gym·nas·tic [dʒimˈnæstik; dʒɪmˋnæstɪk] **I *a*.** 体操的,体育的,锻炼精神的。~ *apparatus* 体操用具。**II *n*.** 锻炼课程。**-tical·ly *ad*.**

gym·nas·tics [dʒimˈnæstiks; dʒɪmˋnæstɪks] ***n*.** 〔*pl*.〕1.〔作单数用〕体育。2.〔作复数用〕体操。~ **team** 体操队。

gym·no- *comb.f*.【生】表示"裸": *gymno*sperm.

gym·nos·o·phist [dʒimˈnɔsəfist; dʒɪmˋnɑsəfɪst] ***n*.** 古印度实行裸体的苦行者;裸体主义者。

gym·no·sperm [ˈdʒimnəuspəːm; ˋdʒɪmnəspɝm] ***n*.** 【植】裸子植物 (*opp*. angiosperm)。**-ous *a*. -y *n*.**

gym·no·tus [dʒimˈnəutəs; dʒɪmˋnotəs] ***n*.** (*pl*. ***-ti*** [-tai; -taɪ])【动】电鳗。

gymp [gimp; gɪmp] ***n*.** =gimp.

gyn- *pref*.〔用于元音前〕=gyno-: *gyn*archy.

G.Y.N. =gyn(a)ecology.

gyn·ae·ce·um [ˌgainiˈsiːəm, ˌdʒai-; ˏgaɪnəˋsiəm, dʒaɪ-] ***n*.** (*pl*. ***-ce·a*** [-ˈsiːə; -ˋsiə]) 1.(古希腊、古罗马的)闺房,女眷内室。2.【植】=gynoecium.

gyn·ae·co- *comb.f*. 表示"女性";"雌性": *gynaeco*logy.

gyn·(a)e·coc·ra·cy [ˌgainiˈkɔkrəsi, ˌdʒai-; ˏgaɪnəˋkɑkrəsɪ, dʒaɪ-] ***n*.** 妇人政治;女权政治。

gy·n(a)e·col·o·gy [ˌgainiˈkɔlədʒi, ˌdʒai-; ˏgaɪnəˋkɑlədʒɪ, dʒaɪ-] ***n*.** 妇科学。**gy·n(a)e·col·o·gist** [-dʒist; -dʒɪst] ***n*.** 妇科医生。

gy·nan·der [gaiˈnændə, dʒai-; gaɪˋnændɚ, dʒaɪ-] ***n*.** 【生】雌雄嵌体。

gyn·an·dro·morph [gaiˈnændrəˌmɔːf, dʒai-; gaɪˋnændrəˏmɔr, dʒaɪ-] *n*. 【生】雌雄嵌体。**-phic**, **-phous** *a*. **-phism**, **-phy** *n*.

gy·nan·drous [gaiˈnændrəs, dʒai-; gaɪˋnændrəs, dʒaɪ-] *a*. 【植】雌雄蕊合体的。

gyn·an·dry [gaiˈnændri, dʒai-; gaɪˋnændrɪ, dʒaɪ-] *n*. 〔罕〕女性假两性畸形。

gyn·arch·y [ˈdʒinɑːki, ˈdʒai-; ˋdʒɪnarkɪ, ˋdʒaɪ-] *n*. (*pl*. **-arch·ies**) 妇女执政,妇女政治。

gynec-, **gyneco-** *comb.f.* = gynaec-, gynaeco-.

gyn·e·coid [ˈgainikɔid, ˈdʒaini-; ˋgaɪnɪkɔɪd, ˋdʒaɪnɪ-] *a*. 妇女的,女性的,有女性特征的。

gyn·e·pho·bi·a [ˌgainiˈfəubiə, ˌdʒaini-; ˏgaɪnɪˋfobɪə, dʒaɪnə-] *n*. 恐女病。

gyn·i·at·rics [ˌgainiˈætriks, dʒai-; ˏgaɪnəˋætrɪks, dʒaɪ-] *n*. 〔作单数用〕【医】妇科疗法。

gynic [ˈgainik, ˈdʒai-; ˋgaɪnɪk, ˋdʒaɪ-] *a*. 女子的,女性的 (*opp*. andric)。

gyn·o- *comb.f.* 表示"女性的","雌性的": *gyno*phore.

gy·noc·ra·cy [gaiˈnɔkrəsi, dʒai-; gaɪˋnɑkrəsɪ, dʒaɪ-] = gyn(a)ecocracy.

gy·noe·ci·um [gaiˈniːsiəm, dʒai-; gaɪˋnɪsɪəm, dʒaɪ-] *n*. (*pl*. **-ci·a** [-siə; -sɪə]) 【植】雌蕊群。

gyn·o·phore [ˈgainəufɔː; ˈdʒainəu-; ˋgaɪnəfor, ˋdʒaɪnə-] *n*. 【植】雌雄柄。**-phor·ic** *a*.

gyn·o·ste·gi·um [ˌgainəuˈstiːdʒiəm, ˌdʒai-; ˏgaɪnəˋstidʒɪəm, ˏdʒaɪ-] *n*. 【植】合蕊冠。

gyn·o·ste·mi·um [ˌgainəuˈstiːmiəm, ˌdʒai-; ˏgaɪnəˋstimɪəm, ˏdʒaɪ-] *n*. 【植】合蕊柱。

-gyn·ous *comb.f.* 表示"女": poly*gynous*.

gyp[1] [dʒip; dʒɪp] *n*. 〔英〕(剑桥大学等的)校工。

gyp[2] [dʒip; dʒɪp] *n*. 〔口〕〔英〕苦难。***give sb.*** ～ 严厉地责备[处罚,击败]某人,使某人活受罪。

gyp[3] [dʒip; dʒɪp] **I** *n*. 〔俚〕欺骗,骗局,骗子。**II** *vt*., *vi*. (*gypped*; ～*ping*) 骗,欺骗。**III** *a*. 〔美俚〕**1**. 商业性的,旨在获取利润的。**2**. 欺骗的,不诚实的。～ **artist** 〔美俚〕骗子手。～ **joint** 〔美俚〕骗钱的赌场[商店等]。

gyps. = gypsum.

gyp·s(e)·ous [ˈdʒips(i)əs; ˋdʒɪpsɪəs] *a*. 石膏状的,含有石膏的。

gyp·sif·er·ous [dʒipˈsifərəs; dʒɪpˋsɪfərəs] *a*. 含石膏的,产生石膏的。

gyp·site [ˈdʒipsait; ˋdʒɪpsaɪt] *n*. 土石膏。

gyp·sog·ra·phy [dʒipˈsɔgrəfi; dʒɪpˋsɑgrəfɪ] *n*. 石膏雕刻,石膏雕刻术。

gyp·soph·i·la [dʒipˈsɔfilə; dʒɪpˋsɑfɪlə] *n*. 【植】丝石竹属 (*Gypsophila*) 植物〔如满天星 (*G. paniculata*)〕。

gyp·sous [ˈdʒipsəs; ˋdʒɪpsəs] *a*. = gypseous.

gyp·sum [ˈdʒipsəm; ˋdʒɪpsəm] **I** *n*. **1**. 【矿】石膏。**2**. 【农】石膏肥料。**3**. 【建】灰泥板,灰胶纸柏板。**II** *vt*. **1**. 给(农田)施石膏肥料。**2**. 用石膏处理。

gyp·sy [ˈdʒipsi; ˋdʒɪpsɪ] *n*. 〔美〕= gipsy.

gyr- *comb.f.* 表示"旋转","环": *gyr*ate.

gy·ral [ˈdʒaiərəl; ˋdʒaɪrəl] *a*. **1**. 旋转的,回旋的。**2**. 【解】脑转的。

gy·rate [ˈdʒaiərit; ˋdʒaɪreɪt] **I** *a*. 旋转的;【植】螺旋状的。**II** [ˌdʒaiəˈreit; ˏdʒaɪəˋret] *vi*. 旋转。

gy·ra·tion [dʒaiəˈreiʃən; dʒaɪˋreʃən] *n*. **1**. 旋转,回旋。**2**. 【动】螺层。**-al** *a*.

gy·ra·to·ry [ˈdʒaiərətəri; ˋdʒaɪrəˏtorɪ] *a*. 旋转的。

gyre [ˈdʒaiə; dʒaɪr] **I** *vi*. 〔诗〕= gyrate. **II** *n*. **1**. 线圈。**2**. = gyration.

gy·rene [ˌdʒaiəˈriːn; dʒaɪˋrin] *n*. 〔美俚〕海军陆战队成员。

gyr·fal·con [ˈdʒəːfɔːlkən; ˋdʒɝˏfɔlkən] *n*. 【动】矛隼 (*Falco rusticolous*)〔产于两极地带的一种巨雕〕。

gyro [ˈdʒaiərəu; ˋdʒaɪəro] *n*. (*pl*. ～*s*) **1**. = gyrocompass. **2**. = gyroscope. **3**. 自转旋翼飞机 (= autogyro)。～ **control** 【空】陀螺仪。～ **horizon** 陀螺地平仪。

gy·ro- *comb.f.* 表示"环";"回转": *gyro*magnetic, *gyro*scope.

gy·ro·com·pass [ˈdʒaiərəuˌkʌmpəs; ˋdʒaɪroˏkʌmpəs] *n*. 回转罗盘,陀螺罗盘。

gy·ro·cop·ter [ˈdʒaiərəuˌkɔptə; ˋdʒaɪrəˏkɑptɚ] *n*. (只载一名乘客的)旋翼飞机。

gy·ro·dy·nam·ics [ˈdʒaiərəudaiˈnæmiks; ˋdʒaɪrədaɪˋnæmɪks] *n*. 陀螺动力学。

gyr·o·dyne [ˈdʒaiərəudain; ˋdʒaɪrədaɪn] *n*. 旋翼式螺旋桨飞机。

gy·ro·graph [ˈdʒaiərəugrɑːf; ˋdʒaɪərəgræf] *n*. 转数记录器。

gy·roi·dal [ˌdʒaiəˈrɔidl; dʒaɪˋrɔɪdḷ] *a*. 螺旋形的,回转的。

gy·ro·mag·net·ic [ˌdʒaiərəumægˈnetik; ˏdʒaɪromægˋnɛtɪk] *a*. 【物】回转磁的。

gy·ro·pi·lot [ˈdʒaiərəuˌpailət; ˋdʒaɪrəˏpaɪlət] *n*. (陀螺)自动驾驶仪。

gy·ro·plane [ˈdʒaiərəuˌplein; ˋdʒaɪrəˏplen] *n*. 旋翼飞机。

gy·ro·scope [ˈdʒaiərəuˌskəup, ˈgaiə-; ˋdʒaɪrəˏskop, ˋgaɪə-] *n*. 陀螺仪,回转仪。**gy·ro·scop·ic** [ˌdʒaiərəuˈskɔpik; ˏdʒaɪrəˋskɑpɪk] *a*.

gy·rose [ˌdʒaiəˈrəus; ˋdʒaɪros] *a*. 【植】前后屈曲的,波状的。

gy·ro·sta·bi·liz·er [ˈdʒaiərəuˈsteibəˌlaizə; ˋdʒaɪrəˋstebəˏlaɪzɚ] *n*. 【海】陀螺稳定器。

gy·ro·stat [ˈdʒaiərəustæt, ˈgaiə-; ˋdʒaɪrəˏstæt, ˋgaɪ-] *n*. 回转轮,回转仪,陀螺仪。

gy·ro·stat·ic [ˌdʒaiərəuˈstætik; ˏdʒaɪrəˋstætɪk] *a*. 回转轮的,回转仪的,陀螺仪的,旋转学的。

gy·ro·stat·ics [ˌdʒaiərəuˈstætiks; ˏdʒaɪrəˋstætɪks] *n*. *pl*. 〔作单数用〕旋转学。

gy·rus [ˈdʒaiərəs; ˋdʒaɪrəs] (*pl*. **gy·ri** [-rai; -raɪ]) *n*. 【解】脑回。

gyve [dʒaiv; dʒaɪv] **I** *n*. 〔常 *pl*.〕〔古、诗〕脚镣;手铐。**II** *vt*. 把(某人)钉上镣,给(某人)戴上手铐。

H

H, h [eitʃ; etʃ] (*pl*. **H's, Hs, h's, hs** [ˈeitʃiz; ˋetʃɪz]) **1**. 英语字母表的第八个字母。**2**. H形物。*an H-beam steel* H形钢条。*an H-Post* H形电杆。***drop one's h's*** 不发h音〔如伦敦方言中把 *hat* [hæt; hæt] 读作 *'at* [æt; æt]]。～ ***hour***【军】发起攻击的时间;特定军事行动开始的时刻。

H = 【电】henry; 【化】hydrogen; 【物】磁场密度(intensity of magnetic field), 地磁水平分量(the horizontal component of terrestrial magnetism); 〔表示铅笔芯硬度的符号〕= hard(ness); 〔俚〕heroin.

H[1] = 【化】protium. **H**[1+] = 【物】proton. **H**[2] = 【化】deuterium. **H**[3] = 【化】tritium.

h., H. = harbour; hard; hardness; heavy sea; height; high; hence; 【棒】hit(s); horns; hour(s); howitzer; humidity; hundred; husband.

H.A. = Heavy Artillery; High Altitude; Hockey Association.

h.a. 〔L.〕= this year 今年,本年度。

ha [hɑː; hɑ] **I** ***int.*** 哈! 〔表示惊愕、快乐、疑惑、踌躇等〕。**II** ***vi.*** "哈!"地叫一声。**III** ***n.*** "哈!"的一声。

ha. = hectare(s).

haaf [hɑːf; hɑf] ***n.*** (苏格兰 Shetland 或 Orkney 诸岛附近的)深海渔场。

haar [hɑː; hɑr] ***n.*** 〔Scot.〕冷海雾〔伴随有毛毛雨的湿冷海雾〕。

Ha·bak·kuk [ˈhæbəkək; ˋhæbə͵kʌk] ***n.*** **1.** 【犹太教】哈巴谷〔公元前七世纪希伯来的一先知〕。**2.**【宗】(《旧约全书》中的)《哈巴谷书》〔记载哈巴谷的预言〕。

Ha·ba·na [Sp. aˈbana; Sp. aˋbana] ***n.*** 哈瓦那〔古巴首都〕(= Havana)。

ha·ba·ne·ra [ˌhɑːbəˈnerə, Sp. ˌabaˈnera; ͵hɑbəˋnɛrə, Sp. ͵abaˋnɛra] ***n.*** **1.** 哈巴涅拉舞〔类似探戈舞的一种动作缓慢的古巴舞蹈〕。**2.** 哈巴涅拉舞曲。

hab. corp. = habeas corpus.

hab·da·lah [ˌhɑːvdɑːˈlɑː, Eng. hɑːvˈdɔːlə; ͵hɑvdɑˋlɑ, Eng. hɑvˋdɔlə] ***n.*** 〔常作 H-〕【犹太教】安息日结束仪式。

ha·be·as cor·pus [ˈheibjəs ˈkɔːpəs; ˋhebjəs ˋkɔrpəs] 〔L.〕【法】**1.** 人身保护令〔要求把拘留或监禁的人限时送交法院处理的法令〕(= a writ of habeas corpus)。**2.** 人身保护权。***Habeas Corpus Act*** 人身保护法〔英王查理二世于 1679 年颁布实施〕。

H

hab·er·dash [ˈhæbədæʃ; ˋhæbə͵dæʃ] ***vi.*** (男子)打扮,修饰。

hab·er·dash·er [ˈhæbədæʃə; ˋhæbə͵dæʃə] ***n.*** **1.** 〔英〕针线等缝纫用品商。**2.** 〔美〕男子服饰用品商。

hab·er·dash·er·y [ˈhæbədæʃəri; ˋhæbə͵dæʃərɪ] ***n.*** **1.** 男子服饰用品;缝纫用品。**2.** 〔英〕针线等缝纫用品店[业];〔美〕男子服饰用品店[业]。

hab·er·geon [ˈhæbədʒən; ˋhæbə͵dʒən] ***n.*** (中世纪武士穿的高领无袖的)短锁子甲。

hab·ile [ˈhæbil; ˋhæbl̩] ***a.*** 〔书〕能干的,熟练的。

ha·bil·i·ment [həˈbilimənt; həˋbɪləmənt] ***n.*** **1.** 〔*pl.*〕服饰,装备。**2.** 〔*pl.*〕(适合某一场合或职位穿着的)制服,礼服;〔谑〕衣服。**-ed** ***a.*** 穿着衣服[礼服等]的;盛装的。

ha·bil·i·tate [həˈbiliteit; həˋbɪlətet] ***vi.*** 具备资格〔尤指德国大学中的教师资格等〕。—***vt.*** **1.** 〔美方〕对(矿山)投资和提供设备。**2.** 给…穿衣。**3.** 使合格;使有能力。**-ta·tion** [həˌbiliˈteiʃən; hə͵bɪləˋteʃən] ***n.*** **-ta·tive** [həˌbiliˈteitiv; hə͵bɪləˋtetɪv] ***a.***

hab·it [ˈhæbit; ˋhæbɪt] **I** ***n.*** **1.** 习惯,癖好。**2.** 脾性,性情;(动,植物的)习性,常态。**3.** 体质,体格。**4.** 举止,行为。**5.** 〔古〕服装;法衣,骑装。**6.** 毒瘾。*H- is second nature.* 〔谚〕习惯成自然。*early ~s* 早起的习惯。*the ~ of getting up late* 晚起的习惯。*sober ~s* 滴酒不尝的习惯。*a man of gouty ~* 易得痛风病的人。***be in a*** [***the***] ***~ of*** 有某种习惯[脾气],惯于。***be off the ~*** 〔美俚〕**1.** 戒掉毒瘾。**2.** 吸毒者未受毒品的影响,清醒着。***break off a*** [***the***] ***bad ~ of*** 改掉坏习惯。***fall*** [***get***] ***into a*** [***the***] ***~ of*** 养成某种习惯。***get sb. into the ~ of*** 使某人养成某种习惯。(***do sth.***) ***from force of ~*** 出于习惯势力(做某事)。***have a*** [***the***] ***~ of*** = *be in a* [*the*] *~ of*. ***~ of body*** 体质。***~ of mind*** 心情,性格。***kick the ~*** 〔美俚〕戒掉嗜好〔尤指毒瘾〕。***out of ~*** 出于习惯。**II** ***vt.*** **1.** 装扮,穿着。**2.** 〔古〕住在。*be ~ed in* 穿着…。~**-forming** ***a.*** 成习惯的,成癖的,使人上瘾的,使之成嗜好的(*a ~-forming drug* 会使人上瘾的麻醉毒品)。

hab·it·a·bil·i·ty [ˌhæbitəˈbiliti; ͵hæbɪtəˋbɪlətɪ] ***n.*** 可居住性,适于居住。

hab·it·a·ble [ˈhæbitəbl; ˋhæbɪtəbl̩] ***a.*** 可居住的,适于居住的。**hab·it·a·bly** ***ad.*** **-ness** ***n.*** = habitability.

hab·it·ant [ˈhæbitənt; ˋhæbɪtənt] ***n.*** 居住者,居民。

hab·i·tant [ˈhæbitɔ̃ːŋ; ˋhæbɪtɔ̃ːŋ] ***n.*** 〔F.〕**1.** 讲法语的加拿大人(又指魁北克乡村地区讲法语的居民)。**2.** 美国路易斯安那州的法裔农民。

hab·i·tat [ˈhæbitæt; ˋhæbɪtæt] ***n.*** **1.** (动、植物生长的)自然环境[地区]。**2.** 聚集处,住所,居住地。**3.** 经常发现某种事物的地方。**4.** 海底实验室人员居住的加压舱,海底实验室。

hab·i·ta·tion [ˌhæbiˈteiʃən; ͵hæbɪˋteʃən] ***n.*** **1.** 居住。**2.** 〔书〕住所,住宅。**3.** 聚居地。*a house fit for ~* 适于居住的房屋。

ha·bit·u·al [həˈbitjuəl; həˋbɪtʃʊəl] ***a.*** 日常的,平常的;惯常的,习惯的。*~ practice* 习惯的做法,惯技。*a ~ criminal* 惯犯。*a ~ cinema-goer* 经常看电影的人。*a ~ liar* 惯于说谎的人。**-ly** ***ad.*** **-ness** ***n.***

ha·bit·u·ate [həˈbitjueit; həˋbɪtʃʊ͵et] ***vt.*** **1.** 使习惯于。**2.** 〔古〕常去。***be ~d to*** (***sth.***) 惯于…(*He was ~d to hard work.* 他已经习惯于干重活)。***~ oneself*** (***sb.***) ***to*** (***sth.***) 使自己[某人]习惯于某事物。—***vi.*** (吸毒)上瘾。

ha·bit·u·a·tion [heˌbitjuˈeiʃən; hɛ͵bɪtʃʊˋeʃən] ***n.*** **1.** 成为习惯。**2.** (对麻醉品等的)适应;毒瘾。

hab·i·tude [ˈhæbitjuːd; ˋhæbɪtjud] ***n.*** 〔古〕= habit 1., 2., 3.

ha·bit·u·é [həˈbitjuei; həˋbɪtʃʊe] ***n.*** 〔F.〕**1.** 常客,熟客。**2.** 有毒瘾的人。

hab·i·tus [ˈhæbitəs; ˋhæbɪtəs] ***n.*** (*pl.* ***hab·i·tus*** [-tuːs; -tus]) **1.** 习惯,癖,嗜好,【植、动】习性。**2.** 体型,体质。

H.A.C. = **1.** Hague Arbitration Convention. **2.** Honourable Artillery Company. **3.** Hughes Aircraft Corporation.

ha·chure [hæˈʃjuə; hæˋʃjʊr] **I** ***n.*** 〔F.〕(图上表示阴影的)影线;(地图上表示山岳的)蓑状线。**II** ***vt.*** 用蓑状线画。

ha·ci·en·da [ˌhæsiˈendə; ͵hɑsɪˋɛndə] ***n.*** 〔Sp.〕**1.** (西班牙及中、南美的)大庄园,种植园,牧场,工厂,矿山。**2.** (上述农场或牧场里的)主要住宅。

hack[1] [hæk; hæk] **I** ***vt.*** **1.** 乱劈,乱砍。**2.** 平(地),翻(地),耙(地),碎土播(种)(*in*)。**3.** 整修(篱笆、墙面等)。**4.** (打橄榄球时)故意踢对方的外胫;(打篮球时)拉[打]对方的手。**5.** 〔美方〕对付;宽容。**6.** 胡乱删改。*~ in oat* 碎土播种燕麦。—***vi.*** **1.** 砍,劈。**2.** 不断地干咳。**3.** 〔英方〕说话结巴。**4.** (运动中)踢对方的手[脚]犯规。*~ a hacking cough* 不断地干咳。**II** ***n.*** **1.** 劈,砍。**2.** 劈或砍的工具,鹤嘴锄。**3.**【机】格架。**4.** 砍痕,伤痕;(运动中)打手,踢胫。**5.** 干咳。**6.** 〔英方〕说话结巴。**7.** 〔美方〕穷迫,困窘。**8.** (对海军军官的)营房拘禁。***have sb. under ~*** 把某人拘禁在营房内。***put sb. under ~*** 使某人张口结舌。***take a ~ at*** 尝试。~**-file** 刀锉。~ **hammer** 劈石斧。~**saw** 弓锯,钢锯。~**watch** 航行表。**-er** ***n.***

hack[2] [hæk; hæk] **I** ***n.*** **1.** 出租的马,骑用的马,役马;驽马,老马。**2.** 出租马车;〔口〕出租汽车,出租马车的车夫,出租汽车司机。**3.** 干苦活的雇工,受雇做乏味工作的文人,以赚钱为目的的劣等艺术家。4.〔美俚〕警察;监狱看守;看守人;(货物列车尾部的)守车。5.〔美〕唯命是听的政党工作人员。6.〔美俚〕娼妓。*a Grubstreet* ~ = *a* ~ *writer* 雇佣的穷文人。*political* ~ 政治仆从。**II** *a*. 1. 出租的;用旧了的。2.(文人等)被雇佣的;雇佣文人做的。3. 陈旧的,陈腐的。*a* ~ *job* 卖苦力的工作,苦工。**III** *vt*. 1. 出租(马等)。2. 雇(人)作苦工;雇(人)写文章。3. 用旧,使变陈腐。4.【计】非法侵入(他人计算机网络并进行破坏)。— *vi*. 1. 用普通速度骑马〔尤指租用的马〕(*along*)。2.〔口〕驾驶出租马车[汽车]。3.【计】非法侵入(他人计算机网络并进行破坏)。~**man** *n*. 出租汽车司机;出租马车的车夫。~**stand** *n*.〔美〕出租汽车[马车]停车处。~**work** *n*.(为了挣钱的)卖文工作;(为了卖钱的)劣等作品。

hack[3] [hæk; hæk] *n*. 1.(鱼等的)晒架;晒砖场。2. 饲草架。3.【猎】饲鹰板。4.【机】格架。*be at* ~ (还未去猎过食物的小鹰)在饲养训练中。*live at* ~ *and manger* 过优裕的生活。

hack·a·more [ˈhækəmɔːə; ˋhækəmor] *n*.(美西部驯马用的)马勒。

hack·ber·ry [ˈhækbəri; ˋhækˏbɛrɪ] *n*. 1. 朴属植物〔产于美洲的树,其果实小如樱桃,可食用〕。2. 朴树木,朴果。

hack·but [ˈhækbʌt; ˋhækˏbʌt] *n*. 一种老式手枪;一种火绳枪。

hack·but·eer, back·but·ter [ˌhækbəˈtiːə, ˈhækbətə; ˏhækbəˋtiɚ, ˋhækbətɚ] *n*. 火绳枪射手,火枪手。

hack·er [ˈhækəː; ˋhækɚ] *n*. 黑客〔指非法侵入他人计算机网络并进行各种破坏者〕。

hack·er·y [ˈhækəri; ˋhækərɪ] *n*.(印度的)双轮牛车。

hack·ie [ˈhæki; ˋhækɪ] *n*.〔口〕出租汽车司机。

hack·le[1] [ˈhækl; ˋhækl] **I** *n*. 1.(梳麻或生丝用的)刷梳;麻栉;(栉梳机的)针排。2.(雄鸡、雄孔雀颈上的)纤毛〔制蚊钩用〕,禽鸟颈毛。3.〔*pl*.〕(狗等)颈背部竖起的毛;〔喻〕脾气,暴怒。4.(钓鱼用的)蝇钩,假蚊钩。*get sb.'s* ~*s up* 使某人发怒。*with one's* ~*s up* 勃然大怒,怒得毛发倒竖。**II** *vt*. 梳理;为(假蚊钩)装上颈毛。

hack·le[2] [ˈhækl; ˋhækl̩] **I** *vt*. 乱砍,乱劈,剁碎,砍掉。**II** *n*. 锯齿形。

hack·ly [ˈhækli; ˋhæklɪ] *a*. 粗糙的,参差不齐的;锯齿状的。

hack·ma·tack [ˈhækmətæk; ˋhækməˏtæk] *n*. 1.【植】(产于美国北部、加拿大等地的)落叶松(= tamarack)。2.【植】一种杨树(= balsam poplar)。

hack·ney [ˈhækni; ˋhæknɪ] **I** *n*. 1. 普通乘用的马或挽马;出租马。2. 出租马车;出租汽车。3. 作苦工的人。**II** *a*. 1. 出租的,被雇用的。2. 陈腐的,平常的。**III** *vt*. 1. 出租(马、马车等)。2. 滥用,虐使;用旧,使变陈腐。~ **carriage** [**coach**] 出租马车。

hack·neyed [ˈhæknid; ˋhæknɪd] *a*. 陈腐的,平常的。*a* ~ *phrase* [*tune*] 陈词滥调。*a* ~ *comparision* 陈旧的比喻。

had [强 hæd, 弱 həd, əd; 强 hæd, 弱 həd, əd] have 的过去式及过去分词。*be had* 受骗,上当,被利用。~ *as good* (*do*) 不如,宁可 (~ *as good study English instead of Russian* 宁可学英语而不学俄语)。~ *as lief* [*soon*]〔古〕〔书〕毋宁,宁可 (*I* ~ *just as lief* [*soon*] *stay out of the quarrel*. 我宁可置身争论之外)。~ *best* (*do*) 最好 (*We* ~ *best go at once*. 我们最好马上走)。~ *better* (*do*) 最好 (*You* ~ *better go*. 你还是走好)。~ *better have done* …做了就好了 (*You* ~ *better have gone already*. 你早就应该走了〔可惜没有走〕)。~ *better not* (*do*) 最好不要 (*He* ~ *better not remain here*. 他还是不留在这里好)。~ *it not been for* 若非,假使没有。~ *like to* 差不多,几乎就…了。~ *need* (*to*) (*do*) 应当 (*You* ~ *need to do your best*. 你应当尽最大的努力)。~ *rather* (*do*) 还是…的好。~ *rather... than* 宁可…也不愿;与其…宁可 (*I* ~ *rather undertake some purposeful labour than stay idle*. 我宁可做些有意义的劳动也不愿闲着)。~ *sooner ... than* 宁可…也不愿;比…更喜欢 (*He* ~ *sooner live in the countryside than in the city*. 他宁肯住在乡下,不愿住在城里)。

ha·dal [ˈheidl; ˋhedl] *a*. 超深渊的,大洋深处六千公尺以下水层的。

had·a·way [ˌhædəˈwei; ˏhædəˋwe] *int*.〔英方〕快干!抓紧干!

had·die [ˈhædi; ˋhædɪ] *n*.〔Scot.〕= haddock.

had·dock [ˈhædək; ˋhædək] *n*.(*pl*. ~*s*,〔集合词〕~)【动】(产于北大西洋的)小口鳕,黑线鳕。

hade [heid; hed] **I** *n*.【地】断层余角,伸角,伸向。**II** *vi*. 垂直倾斜。

Ha·des [ˈheidiːz; ˋhediz] *n*. 1.【希神】冥王哈得斯。2.〔h-〕〔口〕地狱,冥府。

hadj [hædʒ; hædʒ] *n*. = hajj.

hadj·i [ˈhædʒi(ː); ˋhædʒi] *n*. = haji, hajji.

Had·ley [ˈhædli; ˋhædlɪ] *n*. 哈德利〔姓氏〕。

had·n't [ˈhædnt; ˋhædnt] = had not.

Ha·dow [ˈhædəu; ˋhædo] *n*. 哈多〔姓氏〕。

had·ron [ˈhædrən; ˋhædrɑn] *n*.【物】强子。**-ic** [hæˈdrɔnik; hæˋdrɑnɪk] *a*.

hadst [强 hædst, 弱 hədst; 强 hædst, 弱 hədst]〔古〕have 的单数第二人称过去式〔与主语 thou 连用〕。

hae [hei, hæ; he, hæ] *vt*.〔Scot.〕有。

Haeck·el [ˈhekəl; ˋhɛkəl] *n*. 1. 海克尔〔姓氏〕。2. **Ernst Heinrich** ~ 厄恩斯特·海因里奇·海克尔〔1834—1919,德国生物学家〕。

haem- *comb. f*. = haema-, haemat-, haemato-, haemo-, hem-, hema-, hemat-, hemato-, hemo-, 表示"血":*haem*al, *haema*toma.

haema- *comb. f*. = haem-.

hae·mal [ˈhiːməl; ˋhiməl] *a*. 1. 血(液)的;血管的。2. 位于心脏与大血管一侧的。

hae·mat·ic [hiːˈmætik; hiˋmætɪk] **I** *a*. 血的,血液的;多血的;对血液起作用的。**II** *n*. 补血剂,清血药。**hae·mat·ics** *n*. 血液学。

hae·ma·tin(e) [ˈhiːmətin; ˋhimətɪn] *n*. 1.【生化】正铁血红素。2.【化】苏木因,氧化苏木精。

hae·ma·tite [ˈhiːmətait; ˋhimətaɪt] *n*.【矿】赤铁矿,红铁矿。

haemato- *comb. f*. = hemato-.

hae·ma·to·blast [ˌhiːmətəuˈblæst; ˏhimətoˏblæst] *n*.【解】1. 血小板。2. 成血细胞。**-ic** *a*.

haem·a·to·cele [ˈhiːmətəusiːl; ˋhimətosil] *n*.【医】血囊肿,积血。

hae·ma·to·cyte [ˈhiːmətəusait; ˋhimətosaɪt] *n*.【解】血球,血细胞。

haem·a·tol·o·gy [ˌheməˈtɔlədʒiˌ hiː-; ˏhɛməˋtɑlədʒɪ, ˏhi-] *n*. 血液学,血液病学。

hae·ma·to·ma [ˌhiːməˈtəumə; ˏhiməˋtomə] *n*.(*pl*. **-ta** [-tə; -tə], ~*s* [-z; -z])【医】血肿。

haem·a·to·ther·mal [ˌhiːmətəuˈθəːməl; ˏhimətoˋθɝməl] *a*. 恒温动物的(= hematothermal)。

Hae·ma·tox·y·lin [ˌhiːməˈtɔksilin; ˏhiməˋtɑksɪlɪn] *n*.【化】苏木精。

hae·ma·tox·y·lon [ˌhiːməˈtɔksilɔn; ˏhiməˋtɑksɪlɑn] *n*. = logwood.

haem·a·tu·ri·a [ˌhiːməˈtjuəriə; ˏhiməˋtjʊrɪə] *n*.【医】血尿(症)。

haemo- *comb. f*. = hemo-.

hae·mo·cyte [ˈhiːməusait; ˋhimosaɪt] *n*.【医】血球,血细胞。

hae·mo·dy·nam·ics [ˌhiːməudaiˈnæmiks; ˏhimodaɪˋnæmɪks] *n*.【医】血流动力学。

H

hae·mo·glo·bin [ˌhiːməuˈgləubin; ˏhimoˋglobɪn] *n*. 【生化】血红素;血红蛋白。

hae·mo·ly·sin [ˌhiːmuˈlaisin; ˏhimuˋlaɪsɪn] *n*. 【医】溶血素。

hae·mol·y·sis [hiːˈmɔlisis; hɪˋmɑlɪsɪs] *n*. (*pl*. *-ses* [-siːz; -siz]) 【医】溶血(作用),血球溶解。

hae·mo·phil·i·a [ˌhiːməuˈfiliə; ˏhimoˋfɪlɪə] *n*. 【医】血友病。

hae·mo·phil·i·ac [ˌhiːməuˈfiliæk; ˏhimoˋfɪlɪæk] *n*. 【医】血友病患者。

haem·or·rhage [ˈhemәridʒ; ˋhɛmәrɪdʒ] **I** *n*. **1.** 【医】出血。**2.** 〔口〕大量流失。*cerebral* ~ 大脑出血,脑溢血。*internal* ~ 内出血。**II** *vi*. 【医】出血。**haem·or·rhag·ic** [ˌheməˈridʒik; ˏhɛməˋrɪdʒɪk] *a*.

haem·or·rhoid [ˈhemərɔid; ˋhɛməˏrɔɪd] *n*. 〔*pl*.〕【医】痔疮。*external* [*internal*] ~*s* 外[内]痔。

hae·mo·sta·sia, hae·mosta·sis [ˌhiːməuˈsteiʒə, hiːˈmɔstəsis; ˏhimoˋsteʒə, hiˋmɑstəsɪs] *n*. 【医】止血(法)。

hea·mo·stat [ˈhiːməustæt; ˋhimoˏstæt] *n*. 【医】止血器,止血剂。

hae·mo·stat·ic [ˌhiːməuˈstætik; ˏhimoˋstætɪk] **I** *a*. 止血的,能够止血的。**II** *n*. 【医】止血剂。

hae·mu·re·sis [ˌhiːmjuəˈresis; ˏhimjuˋrɛsɪs] *n*. 【医】血尿 (= haematuria)。

hae·res [ˈhiːriːz; ˋhiriz] *n*. (*pl*. ***hae·re·des*** [ˈhiːriːdiːz; ˋhiridiz]) 【法】继承人(= heir)。

Haes [heiz; hez] *n*. 黑斯〔姓氏〕。

haf·ni·um [ˈhæfniəm; ˋhæfnɪəm] *n*. 【化】铪。

haft [hæft; hæft] **I** *n*. (工具或武器的)柄,把。**II** *vt*. 给…装柄,为…配把。

hag[1] [hæg; hæg] *n*. **1.** 女妖,母夜叉。**2.** 女巫。**3.** 凶相丑恶的老妇人。**4.** 【动】八目鳗类鱼。~**born** *a*. 女巫生的。~**ridden** *a*. 为恶梦所扰的。~**seed** *n*. 女巫的子女。

hag[2] [hæg; hæg] 〔英方〕 **I** *n*. **1.** 沼地,沼泽中的硬地。**2.** 砍伐,标记出来以待砍伐的树木;〔集合词〕砍倒的树。**II** *vt*. 砍,劈。

Ha·gar [ˈheigɑː; ˋhegɑr] *n*. **1.** 【圣】夏甲〔亚伯拉罕之妾,亚伯拉罕之妻萨拉出于妒嫉将其驱入沙漠〕。**2.** 女子名。

hag·ber·ry [ˈhægberi; ˋhægˏbɛrɪ] *n*. = hackberry.

hag·but [ˈhægbʌt; ˋhægˏbʌt] *n*. = hackbut.

hag·fish [ˈhægfiʃ; ˋhægˏfɪʃ] *n*. (*pl*. ~, ~*es*) 【动】盲鳗〔一种口圆牙利的海鱼,能穿入其他鱼类体内并吞食之〕。

Hag·ga·da, Hag·ga·dah [həˈgɑːdə; həˋgɑdə] *n*. (*pl*. **-ga·doth** [-ˈdəuθ; -doθ]) **1.** 【宗】〔常用 h-〕(犹太教法典中解释某些戒律的)寓言、传说等;犹太教法典中载有上述传说的章节。**2.** 逾越节在纪念出埃及的宴会上讲的《出埃及记》故事;载有上述故事及礼仪的书。**hag·gad·ic** [həˈgɑːdik, -gædik; həˋgɑdɪk, -ˋgædɪk] *a*.

hag·ga·dist [həˈgɑːdist; həˋgɑdɪst] *n*. 犹太教法典中解释戒律的传说的著者[研究者]。**-dis·tic** [ˌhægəˈdistik; ˏhægəˋdɪstɪk] *a*.

Hag·gai [ˈhægeiai; ˋhægəˏaɪ] *n*. **1.** 【宗】哈该〔公元前六世纪希伯来一先知〕。**2.** 《旧约全书》中的《哈该书》〔记载哈该的预言〕。

hag·gard [ˈhægəd; ˋhægəd] **I** *a*. **1.** 憔悴的,形容枯槁的;消瘦的。**2.** 样子凶暴的。**3.** 难驯服的,未驯服的,(鹰)成年被捕的。~ *hawks* 野鹰。**II** *n*. 未驯服的鹰;悍鹰。**-ly** *ad*. **-ness** *n*.

Hag·gard [ˈhægəd; ˋhægəd] *n*. 哈格德〔姓氏〕。

hag·gis [ˈhægis; ˋhægɪs] *n*. 一种苏格兰布丁〔把牛(羊)肉杂碎与麦片等放在羊肚中烹煮的食品〕。

hag·gish [ˈhægiʃ; ˋhægɪʃ] *a*. 老丑妇似的,母夜叉似的,女巫似的。

hag·gle [ˈhægl; ˋhægl] **I** *vi*. (就价格、条件等)争论,争辩;讨价还价 (*about*; *over*; *for*; *with*)。~ *over the price* 讨价还价,讲价钱。—*vt*. **1.** 乱砍,乱劈。**2.** 〔古〕(因争论而)烦恼;使疲惫。**II** *n*. 争论;讨价还价。

hagi- *comb*. *f*. "圣徒的";"神圣的": *hagi*archy.

hag·i·arch·y [ˈhægiɑːki; ˋhægɪˏɑrkɪ] *n*. 圣徒[教士]统治;圣徒等级组织。

hagio- *comb*. *f*. = hagi-: *hagi*ology.

Hag·i·og·ra·pha [ˌhægiˈɔgrəfə; ˏhægɪˋɑgrəfə] *n*. 犹太教《圣经》的第三部分。

hag·i·og·ra·pher [ˌhægiˈɔgrəfə; ˏhægɪˋɑgrəfə] *n*. **1.** 犹太教《圣经》第三部分的作者。**2.** 圣徒传记作者。

hag·i·og·ra·phist [ˌhægiˈɔgrəfist; ˏhægɪˋɑgrəfɪst] *n*. = hagiographer.

hag·i·og·ra·phy [ˌhægiˈɔgrəfi; ˏhægɪˋɑgrəfɪ] *n*. **1.** 圣徒生平的写作与研究;圣徒传记。**2.** 理想化的传记,偶像化的传记。**hag·i·o·graph·i·c(al)** [ˌhægiəˈgræfik(əl); ˏhægɪəˋgræfɪk(əl)] *a*.

hag·i·ol·a·try [ˌhægiˈɔlətri; ˏhægɪˋɑlətrɪ] *n*. 圣徒崇拜。**hag·i·ol·a·ter** [-ˈɔlətə; -ˋɑlətə] *n*. 圣徒崇拜者。**hag·i·ol·a·trous** [-ˈɔlətrəs; -ˋɑlətrəs] *a*.

hag·i·ol·o·gy [ˌhægiˈɔlədʒi; ˏhægɪˋɑlədʒɪ] *n*. **1.** 圣徒传记文学,圣徒传记研究。**2.** 圣徒名单。**hag·i·o·log·i·c(al)** [ˌhægiˈɔlədʒik(əl); ˏhægɪˋɑlədʒɪk(əl)] *a*. **hag·i·ol·o·gist** [ˌhægiˈɔlədʒist; ˏhægɪˋɑlədʒɪst] *n*. 圣徒传记研究者。

hag·i·o·scope [ˈhægiəskəup; ˋhægɪəskop] *n*. 中世纪教堂内壁上的窄窗〔由此可以见主祭坛〕。

Hague [heig; heg] *n*. 〔the ~〕海牙〔荷兰中央政府所在地〕。~ **Tribunal** 海牙国际仲裁法庭。

hah [hɑː; hɑ] *int*., *n*. = ha.

ha-ha[1] [hɑ(ː)ˈhɑː hɑˋhɑ] **I** *int*. 哈哈! 〔表示嘲笑等〕。**II** *n*. 哈哈的笑声;〔美俚〕(对某人的)嘲笑。*give sb*. *the merry* ~ 嘲笑某人。

ha-ha[2] [ˈhɑːhɑː; ˋhɑhɑ] *n*. (造在花园界沟里不遮挡视线的)隐篱,暗墙(= sunk fence)。

hah·ni·um [ˈhɑːniːəm; ˋhɑnɪəm] *n*. 铧〔原子序数为 105,原子量 260,符号为 Ha 的人造超铀元素〕。

haick [heik; hek] *n*. = haik.

Hai·fa [ˈhaifə; ˋhaɪfə] *n*. 海法〔以色列港市〕。

haik [haik; haɪk] *n*. (阿拉伯人的)白布大罩衣。

hai·ku [ˈhaikuː; ˋhaɪku] *n*. 〔Jap.〕 **1.** 俳句〔由五、七、五共十七字组成的短诗〕。**2.** 俳句诗。

hail[1] [heil; hel] **I** *n*. **1.** 雹,冰雹。**2.** 像雹子般落下的东西。*a* ~ *of blows* [*curses*] 一阵打击[咒骂]。*a* ~ *of bullets* 一阵弹雨。**II** *vt*. 使像雹子般落下。~ *blows* [*curses*] *down on sb*. 给某人一顿痛打[一通臭骂]。—*vi*. 下雹;冰雹般落下来。~**stone** (一粒)冰雹。~**storm** 下雹,雹暴。

hail[2] [heil; hel] **I** *vt*. **1.** 向…高呼,为…欢呼;向…欢呼致敬。**2.** 招呼。~ *sb*. (*as*) *King* 欢呼拥立某人为国王。~ *a taxi* 叫出租汽车。— *vi*. 招呼;(向过往船只)打信号招呼。~ ***from*** ... **1.** (船)自…来。**2.** 出生地是…(*She* ~*s from London*. 她是伦敦人。~ *from all corners of the country* 来自全国各地)。**II** *n*. 高呼,欢呼,招呼;欢迎。***within*** ~ 在能听到呼叫的距离内〔尤指招呼船〕,在近处。**III** *int*. 〔书、诗〕万岁! *All* ~! = *Hail to you*! 万岁。*Hail Columbia* 〔美俚〕 **1.** 揍,骂 (*give sb*. *Hail Columbia* 狠揍[臭骂]某人)。**2.** 喧闹。***Hail Mary***! 【天主】万福马利亚。~**-fellow** = ~**-fel-low-well-met** **1.** *a*. 友好的,很亲密的 (*be* ~*-fellow with everybody* 跟谁都很要好)。**2.** *n*. 密友。

hail·er [ˈheilə; ˋhelə] *n*. **1.** 欢呼者;打招呼者。**2.** (海军船舰等上的)手提扩音器(= bullhorn)。

hail·y [ˈheili; ˋhelɪ] *a*. 雹子(一样)的;夹有冰雹的。

hair [hɛə; hɛr] *n*. **1.** 〔集合词〕毛发,头发,汗毛。**2.** 毛状物;毛状金属丝;毛发织物;【植】茸毛。**3.** 一丝丝,些微。*grey* ~*s* 白发;老年。*a fine coat of* ~ (马等)一身好

毛。*against the* ～〔古〕违背本意,不合本性。*a* ～ *in one's neck* 麻烦事。*a* ～ *to make a tether of* 〔Scot.〕小题大作。*be not worth a* ～ 一钱不值。*both of a* ～ 同类,一丘之貉。*bring sb.'s grey* ～*s* (*in sorrow*) *to the grave* 使老人忧心至死。*bush* [*head*, *shock*] *of* ～ 浓浓的头发。*by* (*the turn of*) *a* ～ 差一点儿,险些儿,几乎。*comb* [*stroke*] *sb.'s* ～ *for him* 严责某人。*do up one's* ～ 梳头。*fell of* ～ 耷拉下来的头发,发绺。*get* [*have*, *take*] *sb. by the short* ～*s* 〔俚〕任意摆布某人,完全操纵某人;抓住某人辫子。*get in sb.'s* ～ 〔美俚〕触怒,使烦恼。*hang by a* (*single*) ～ 千钧一发,岌岌可危。*have grey* ～ 满头白发。*have grey* ～*s* 有些白头发。*have one's* ～ *cut* 剪发,理发。*in one's* ～ 光着头。*in the* ～ 1. 毛向外的。2. 兽皮有毛的。*Judas* ～ 红头发。*keep your* ～ *on* 〔俚〕保持镇静! 别发火! *let one's* (*back*) ～ *down* 1. 将头发散开。2. 〔口〕举止随便,不拘礼节。3. 直言不讳。*Let your* ～ *dry*. 〔俚〕别那么神气,别那么拿架子。*lose one's* ～ 1. 头变秃。2. 发怒。*make sb.'s* ～ *curl* = *make sb's* ～ *stand on end* 使人毛骨悚然。*not touch a* ～ *of sb.'s head* 不动某人一根汗毛。*not turn a* ～ = *without turning a* ～ 不动声色,镇定自若。*put* [*turn*] *up one's* ～ (少女成年后)梳拢头发。*smooth* [*stroke*] *sb.'s* ～ *the wrong way* = *stroke sb. against the* ～ 使某人恼怒。*split* ～*s* (*over sth.*) 作无益的细微分析,无故挑剔。*stroke sb. with the* ～ 〔Scot.〕安抚。*Take a* ～ *of the dog that bit you*. 〔谚〕以毒攻毒;用酒解酒。*tear one's* [*the*] ～ 扯头发〔表示悲伤、焦急、忿怒〕。*to* (*the turn of*) *a* ～ 完全一样,丝毫不差。*wear one's* (*own*) ～ 不戴假发。～**ball** 毛球,毛团〔常见于牛、猫等胃中的毛团块,因牛、猫等爱舐毛而把毛吃入胃中,渐聚之而成团〕。～**breadth** 1. *n*. 一发之差,极微小的距离(*by a* ～*breadth* 一发之差,间不容发。*within a* ～*breadth of sth*. 差一点就…)。2. *a*. 一发之间的,间不容发的(*a* ～*breadth escape* 九死一生,死里逃生)。～**brush** 发刷,毛刷。～**clippers** 〔*pl*.〕发剪。～**cloth** 1. 毛布〔马毛[驼毛等]与绒布的织物,用于制家具套等〕。2. 粗毛织衬衣。～ **cut** 1. 理发。2. 发式。～**cutter** 理发员。～**do** 〔口〕1. (女人的)梳发,烫发。2. (女人)做头发,头发梳法。～**dresser** 1. 理发员。2. 梳头者。～**dressing** 理发,梳头;理发业(～*dressing saloon* 理发厅)。～**dryer** 吹风器。～**dye** 染发药水。～ **extension** 假发固定法〔假发和真发的织结〕。～ **felt** 毛毡。～ **hygrometer** 毛发湿度计。～**lace** 发带,头带。～**line** 1. 极细的线;细缝;细微的差别。2. (字画等的)纤细笔画。3. 【纺】细线条,线条精纺呢。4. 头型轮廓,发型轮廓。5. 【军】瞄准线;〔*pl*.〕光学仪器所用叉线(*to a* ～*line* 精密地)。～ **net** 发网。～ **oil** 发油。～ **pencil** 画笔。～**piece** *n*. 1. 男子的(遮秃)假发。2. 女式假发。～**pin** 1. *n*. 发夹;夹叉,簪;发夹状的东西;道路的急转弯;〔美俚〕女人,女学生。2. *a*. U 字形的(*a* ～*pin bend* 陡路上的; *U* 字形转弯的路)。～ **powder** 发粉。～**-raiser** 令人惊的故事;使人毛骨悚然的东西[事情]。～**-raising** *a*. 〔口〕使人毛发竖起的,恐怖的。～ **restorer** 生发药。～**s breadth** = ～breadth. ～ **seal** 海驴,海豹。～ **side** 【机】(皮带的)毛面。～ **slide** 发夹。～ **space** 【印】字间最小间隔。～**splitter** 专爱拘泥小节的人,爱吹毛求疵的人。～**splitting** *n*., *a*. 拘泥小节(的),吹毛求疵(的)。～**spring** 【机】游丝;细弹簧。～ **streak** 【动】窄尾小灰蝶〔一种翼上有细纹的蝴蝶〕。～ **stroke** (字、画的)细笔画;【印】细线。～**tail** 带鱼。～**-thin** *a*. 细如毛发的。～ **trigger** 微火触发器。～**-trigger** *a*. 1. 一触即发的,即时的。2. 一碰就坏的。～**-weaving** (尼龙)假发植入(术)。～**worm** = gordian worm. **-ed** *a*. 具有(某种)头发的(*fair-haired* 金发的。*short-haired* 短发的)。**-less** *a*. 无毛的,无发的,秃顶的。**-like** *a*. 毛发似的,极细的。

hair·tic·i·an [hɛəˈtiʃiən; hɛrˋtɪʃɪən] *n*. 〔美〕发型师。

hair·y [ˈhɛəri; ˋhɛrɪ] *a*. 1. 毛发的,多毛的,毛厚的。2. 发状的,毛似的。3. 〔美俚〕粗鲁的;可怕的,令人沮丧的。4. 〔美俚〕(笑话等)陈腐不堪的。～ *about* [*at*, *in*] *the fetlocks* [*heel*] 没有教养的,没有礼貌的。～**-chested** *a*. 粗壮的。～**-heeled** [-hiːld; -hild] *a*. 〔俚〕没有教养的,没有礼貌的。～ **velch** 【植】长柔毛野豌豆〔叶子带毛,开小朵蓝花,种植作饲料用〕。**hair·i·ly** *ad*. **hair·i·ness** *n*.

Hai·ti [ˈheiti; ˋhetɪ] *n*. 海地〔拉丁美洲〕。

Hai·tian [ˈheiʃən; ˋheʃən] I *n*. 1. 海地人。2. 海地人讲的法语(= Haitian Creole)。II *a*. 海地的,海地人的。

hajj [hædʒ; hædʒ] *n*. 【宗】(伊斯兰教的)麦加朝圣。

haj·ji, haj·i [ˈhædʒi(ː); ˋhædʒi] *n*. 哈吉〔曾赴麦加朝过圣的穆斯林的荣誉称号〕。

hake [heik; hek] *n*. 【动】狗鳕,无须鳕。

ha·keem [hɑːˈkiːm; hɑˋkim] *n*. (伊斯兰教国家的)学者;医生。

Ha·ken·kreuz [ˈhɑːkənkrɔits; ˋhɑkənkrɔɪts] *n*. 〔G.〕卐字〔德国纳粹党党徽〕。

ha·kim[1] [ˈhɑːkiːm; ˋhɑkim] *n*. (伊斯兰教国家的)地方长官;法官。

ha·kim[2] [hɑːˈkiːm; hɑˋkim] = hakeem.

Hak·ka [ˈhɑːkˈkɑː; ˋhɑkˋkɑ] *n*. 〔汉〕客家〔古代移居闽、粤等地的中原人的后裔〕;客家人;客家语。

Hak·luyt [ˈhækluːt; ˋhæklut] *n*. 1. 哈克路特〔姓氏〕。2. **Richard** ～ 理查德·哈克路特〔1552? —1616,英国地理学及历史学家〕。

Ha·ko·da·te [ˌhækəuˈdɑːti; ˋhakoˋdɑtɛ] *n*. 函馆〔日本港市〕。

Ha·ko·ne [ˈhɑːkəne; ˋhɑkənɛ] *n*. 箱根〔日本城镇;著名风景区〕。

hal- *comb. f*. 〔后接母音〕= halo-: *hal*ite; *hal*ide.

Hal [hæl; hæl] *n*. 哈尔〔男子名, Henry 的昵称〕。

Ha·la·kha, Ha·la·cha [ˌhɑːlɑːˈhɑː, həˈlɑːhə; ˏhɑlɑˋhɑ, həˋlɑhə] *n*. (*pl*. **-la·khot**, **-la·chot** [-ˈhəut; -ˋhot]) 1. 〔常用 h-〕犹太教法典异传(未载入圣经的戒律和教规)。2. 犹太教法典中载有上述戒律和教规的章节。

ha·la·khist, ha·la·chist [ˈhɑːləhist, həˈlɑːhist; ˋhɑləhɪst, həˋlɑhɪst] *n*. 犹太教法典异传的叙述[编写]者。

ha·la·ha(h) [həˈlɑːlə; həˋlɑlə] *n*. (*pl*. ～, ～*s*) 赫拉勒〔沙特阿拉伯货币单位,等于 100 里亚尔〕。

ha·la·tion [həˈleiʃən; həˋleʃən] *n*. 【物】晕影,晕光作用。

hal·berd [ˈhælbə(ː)d; ˋhælbɚd] *n*. 戟〔十五和十六世纪使用的一种枪钺合一的兵器〕。

hal·berd·ier [ˌhælbəːˈdiə; ˏhælbɚˋdɪr] *n*. 戟兵。

halbert [ˈhælbə(ː)t; ˋhælbɚt] *n*. = halberd.

hal·cy·on [ˈhælsiən; ˋhælsɪən] I *n*. 1. 【动】翠鸟,鱼狗。2. 传说中的太平鸟〔巢居海上,冬至产卵时海波平静〕。II *a*. 1. 翠鸟的;翠鸟产卵期的。2. 平静的。3. 愉快的。4. 富饶的。～ *days* 1. 冬至前后十四日间海上平静的日子。2. 宁静幸福的日子,太平时代。

Hal·dane [ˈhɔːldein; ˋhɔlden] *n*. 霍尔丹〔姓氏〕。

hale[1] [heil; hel] *a*. (尤指老人)强壮的,矍铄的。～ *and hearty* 矍铄的,老当益壮的。**-ness** *n*.

hale[2] [heil; hel] *vt*. 强拉,硬拖。

Hale-Bopp [ˈheilbɔp; ˋhelbɑp] *n*. 【天】海尔-波普彗星〔出现于 1997 年,据说上次出现于 4200 年之前,下次将于 4397 年前后出现〕。

Hale(s) [heil(z); hel(z)] *n*. 黑尔(斯)〔姓氏〕。

hal·er [ˈhɑːlə; ˋhælɚ] *n*. (*pl*. **-er·u** [-əruː; -əru], ～*s*) 赫勒〔捷克货币名称,为 1/100 克朗〕。

half [hɑːf; hæf] I *n*. (*pl*. **halves** [hɑːvz; hævz]) 1. 半,一半;一部分。2. 半小时;半英里;半品脱;半价票;〔美〕半美元;半学年,一学期。3. (球赛的)半场,半局,半盘,半回合。4. (足球)中卫(= halfback); (运动中的)配手,合作者。5. (高尔夫球赛等)相同得分。6. (尤指打

H

官司的)一方。~ *past four* =〔美〕~ *after four* 四点半钟。[*The*] ~ *of four is two*. 四的一半是二。~ *and* ~ 一半一半,各半。*H- a loaf is better than none*.〔谚〕面包半个别嫌少,总比没有面包好。*Never do things by halves*.〔谚〕做事不可半途而废。*one* ~ 二分之一,一半。*one's better* ~〔谑〕妻子。*one's worse* ~〔谑〕丈夫。*The first blow* [*stroke*] *is* ~ *the battle*.〔谑〕良好的开端,就是成功的一半。*The* ~ *is more than the whole*.〔谚〕过犹不及。*the other* ~ (穷人眼中的)有钱人;(有钱人眼中的)穷人。*too long by* ~ 长了一半。*two pounds and a* ~ = *two and a* ~ *pounds* 两磅半。*the summer* ~ 夏天开始的半学年。***and a*** ~ 非常困难的(*That is a job and a* ~. 那是非常困难的工作)。***by*** ~ 1. 只一半。2.〔反〕非常,极,过分(*too clever by* ~ 聪明过度)。***by halves*** 不完全(*do sth. by halves* 做事情半途而废,做事不彻底)。***cry halves*** 要求平分。***cut in*** ~ = ***cut in*** (***to***) (***two***) ***halves*** 切成两半。***divide sth. into halves*** 把…分成两半。***go halves with sb. in sth.*** 与(某人)平分(某物)。***in*** ~ [***halves***] 成两半。***not*** (***the***) ~ ***of*** 仅仅是次要部分,仅仅是小部分(*That's not* ~ *of the story*. 那还仅仅是事情的一小部分〔严重的事还在后面呢〕)。***on*** (***the***) ***halves*** 平分,对分。***see with*** ~ ***an eye*** 一看就明白。***time and a*** ~ 在平时工资外另加 50%。***to*** (***the***) ***halves*** 1. 到半途;不完全。2.〔美〕利益均分。***with*** [***have***] ~ ***a mind*** [***notion***] ***to*** (***sth.***) 对…半心半意。**II** *a*. 1. 一半的。2. 一部分的;不完全的。*a* ~ *share* 半分儿。*a* ~ *sheet of paper* 半张纸。~ *a dozen* = *a* ~ *dozen* 半打,六个。~ *an hour* =〔美〕*a* ~ *hour* 半小时。~ *knowledge* 一知半解,半瓶醋。*a* ~ *smile* 微笑,欲笑不笑。~ *the number* 半数。*work* ~ *shift* 上半班。**III** *ad*. 1. 一半地。2. 部分地,不完全地。3. 相当地〔常与否定词连用,表示相反的意思〕。~ *in doubt* 半信半疑。*Well begun is* ~ *done*.〔谚〕好的开始等于成功的一半。~ *dead* 累的要命。~ ***as much*** [***many***] ***again as*** 一倍半,多一半。~ ***as much*** [***many***] ***as*** 只有一半,少一半。~ ***green*** 半生的,半腌的。~ ***shot*** 半醉的。***I*** ~ ***wish...*** 我很想。***more than*** ~ 非常。***not*** ~ 1. 一点也不(*not* ~ *bad* 一点也不坏,相当好。*Her singing isn't* ~ *bad*. 她唱得很不坏)。2.〔俚〕极其,非常(*He didn't* ~ *swear*. 他骂得很凶。*Do you like beer?* — *Oh, not* ~! 你喜欢(喝)啤酒吗?—喜欢极了!)。~**-and-**~ 1. *n*. 两种成分各半的东西;淡烈两种啤酒各半的混合酒;奶油和全脂牛奶各半的混合物;混血儿。2. *a*. 两者各半的;不三不四的,不伦不类的。3. *ad*. 等量地,各半地。~**-assed**〔俚〕*a*. 1. 杂乱的;没有完整计划的;没有意义的。2. 不称职的;不够格的;能力差的。3. 不现实的。~**back** *n*. (足球的)中卫。~**-baked** *a*. 1. 半生不熟的。2. 不成熟的,思虑不缜密的(~*-baked ideas* 不成熟的意见。*a* ~*-baked scheme* 不周密的计划)。3. 浅薄的,无经验的(*a* ~*-baked youth* 初出茅庐的青年。*a* ~*-baked film critic* 半瓶醋的影评家)。~**beak** *n*. 鱵科(*Hemiramphidae*)鱼〔一种下颚特别长的热带小海鱼〕。~ **binding** 半精装。~**-blood** *n*. 同父异母,同母异父;杂种,混血儿。~**-blooded** *a*. 杂种的,混血的。~ **blue**〔英〕(给次要运动员的)半蓝徽章。~ **boot** 半高统靴。~**-bound** *a*. 1. 半精装的。2.【化】半化合的。~**-box** 无盖轴箱。~**-breadth** (船的)中轴距离。~**-bred** *a*. 1. 混血的,杂种的。2. 教养不足的,粗野的。~**-breed** 1. *n*. 杂种,混血儿〔尤指美洲印第安人与白种人的后代〕。2. *a*. 杂种的,混血的。~ **brother** 异父[异母]兄弟。~ **calf** 犊皮背精装。~**-caste** *n*., *a*. 欧亚混血儿(的);混血儿(的)。~**-cell**【化】半电池。~ **cock** (枪)处于半击发状态,机头半张开(*go off at* ~ *cock* =〔美〕*go off* ~*-cocked* 还没有开保险就发射,动手过早)。~**-cocked** *a*. (枪)处于半击发状态的;行动过早的,仓促行事的。~**-cooked** *a*. 半熟的;〔美〕尚未成熟的。~**-cracked** *a*. 笨的,蠢的。~ **crown** 半克朗〔英国旧银币名,合 2 先令 6 便士〕。~ **deck** 商船上见习生的宿处。~ **dollar**〔美〕半元银币,五十分。~**-done** *a*. 半成的;不完全的;半熟的。~ **eagle**〔美〕(从前的)五元金币。~**-evergreen** *a*.【植】半长青的。~ **gainer**【体】面对池反身直体跳水。~**-hardy** (植物等)能经受一般寒冷的,需要防低温[霜雪]的。~**-hearted** *a*. 无兴趣的,不热心的,半心半意的。~ **hitch** (容易解开的)简单结子。~**-holiday** 半日假。~**-hour** 1. *n*. 三十分钟,半小时。2. *a*. 半小时的,每半小时的。~**-hourly** *a*., *ad*. 每半小时的[地]。~ **hunter** 双盖怀表。~**-length** 1. *a*. 半身的。2. *n*. 半身像,半身画像。~**-life**【原】半衰期〔放射性同位素分裂[从生物体中排出]一半量的时间〔也作 ~ life 或 ~ life period〕〕。~**-light** 淡灰色光。~ **line**【数】半直线。~**-long** *a*.【语】半长音的。~**-mast** 1. *vt*. 下半(旗)。2. *n*. 半旗位置(*fly* [*hang*, *hoist*] *a flag at* ~*-mast* 下半旗。~*-mast high* 在半旗位置)。~ **measures** 姑息手段,折衷办法。~**-moon** 半月;半月形。~ **mourning** 比黑色浅的(如灰、白、紫色的)丧服;穿浅色丧服时期。~ **nelson** (摔跤)扼颈(*get a* ~ *nelson on sb*. 把某人完全压住)。~ **note**【乐】二分音符。~ **nut**【机】对开螺母,开缝螺母,闸瓣,闸瓦。~ **pay** 半薪。~**-pay** *a*. 领半薪的(*place sb. on the* ~*-pay list*〔英〕令某人支半薪休职)。~**penny** [ˈheipəni; ˋhepənɪ] 1. *n*. (*pl*. ~***pence*** [ˈheipəns; ˋhepəns], ~ ***pennies***) 半便士;〔口〕铜币。2. *a*. 半便士的;便宜的,没价值的(~*penny under the hat* 一种骗钱的下等赌博。*not a* ~*penny the worse* 毫不逊色,一点也不差。*three* ~*pence* 一便士半。*receive more kicks than* ~*pence*〔口〕没有受奖反而更加倒霉。*turn up* [*come back*] *again like a bad* ~*penny* 来得不是时候)。~**pennyworth** *n*. 半便士的东西;极少量。~ **pint** 1. 十六分之一加仑。2.〔美俚〕个子矮小的人;微不足道的人。~**-price** *ad*. 半价。~ **rest**【乐】二分休止符。~**-round** 1. *a*. 半圆的,半月形的。2. *n*. 半球。~**-seas-over** *a*. 1.【海】航行到半途的。2.〔口〕半醉的。~ **sister** 异父[异母]姊妹。~ **size** 上身短的(或身体矮小的)妇女的衣服尺寸。~**-slip** 无上身衬裙。~ **sole** 鞋前掌。~**-sole** *vt*. 给(鞋)打前掌。~ **sovereign** 半金镑〔英国旧币名,等于旧币 10 先令〕。~**-staff** *n*., *vt*. = ~-mast. ~ **step**【军】小步,快步;【乐】半音(程)。~**-stuff** (造纸用)半纸料。~ **tide** 半潮〔满潮与退潮间的一半〕。~**-timber(ed)** *a*.【建】(房屋等)半露木的。~**-time** 1. 半工半薪。2. (比赛中的)半场休息时间(*be on* ~*-time* 做半工支半薪。*What is the score at* ~*-time?* 上半场比分多少?)。~**-timer** 以一半时间做工的人;〔英〕半工半读的学生。~ **tint** 中间色调;(水彩)薄涂。~ **title** (书籍)印在扉页上的书名。~**tone** 1. *n*.【印】照相铜版;网目铜版,中间色调;【乐】半音。2. *a*. 照相铜版的;中间色调的(~*tone process* 网目铜版制版术)。~**-track** 1. *n*. 半履带式,半履带式车辆〔尤指一种轻装甲车〕。2. *a*. 半履带式的。~**-truth** *n*. 部分真实的陈述[报导],欺骗性的半真半假的陈述[报导]。~**volley** *n*., *vt*.【体】球一着地立即打出[踢出]。~**way** 1. *ad*. 半途;不彻底地;几乎,快要(*meet sb.* ~*way* 在半路迎接[迎战]某人;迎合[迁就]某人。*meet trouble* ~*way* 杞忧,自寻烦恼。*I have* ~*way decided to go*. 我已差不多决定要去了)。2. *a*. 中间的,半途的,不彻底的(*a* ~*way house* 位于两城镇之间的旅店;妥协方案,折衷办法;为吸毒者设立的戒瘾治疗中心;为长期监禁或住院治疗者设立的重返社会训练所。*a* ~*way inn* 中途客栈。~*-way measures* 不彻底的办法,折衷的办法 = half measures)。~**-wit** 笨蛋。~**-witted** *a*. 鲁钝的,迟钝的。~**-yearly** *a*., *ad*. 每半年的[地]。

half·y [ˈhɑːfi; ˋhæfɪ] *n*.〔美俚〕没有腿的残废人。

hal·i·but [ˈhælibət; ˋhæləbət] *n*. (*pl*. ~*s*,〔集合词〕~)【动】庸鲽,大比目鱼。

H

hal·ide [ˈhælaid; ˋhælaɪd] I *n*.【化】卤化物。II *a*. = haloid.

hal·i·dom [ˈhælidəm; ˋhælɪdəm], **hal·i·dome** [ˈhælidəm, -dəum; ˋhælɪdəm, -dom] *n*.〔古〕圣物;圣宝。***by my*** ～ 誓必,一定。

hal·i·eu·tic [ˌhæliˈjuːtik; ˏhælɪˋjutɪk] *a*. 钓鱼的。

hal·i·eu·tics [ˌhæliˈjuːtiks; ˏhælɪˋjutɪks] *n*. 钓鱼技术;钓鱼论。

Hal·i·fax[1] [ˈhælifæks; ˋhælɪfæks] *n*. **1**. 哈利法克斯〔加拿大港市〕。**2**. 哈利法克斯〔英国城市〕。

Hal·i·fax[2] [ˈhælifæks; ˋhælɪˏfæks] *n*. 哈利法克斯〔姓氏〕。

hal·ite [ˈhælait; ˋhælaɪt] *n*.【化】石盐,岩盐。

hal·i·to·sis [ˌhæliˈtəusis; ˏhælɪˋtosɪs] *n*.【医】口臭。

Hal·i·ver [ˈhælivə; ˋhælɪvɚ] *n*.〔美〕比目鱼肝油。

hall [hɔːl; hɔl] *n*. **1**.〔常作 H-〕(政治团体、工会等的)本部,总部,办公大楼。**2**. 会馆,会场,会堂;展览厅;娱乐场。**3**.〔常作 H-〕〔美〕(大学的)学部大楼,教学大楼,讲堂,学生宿舍。**4**.〔英〕(大学的)大餐厅,公共食堂。**5**. 地主庄园的主要建筑,(已往王公贵族的)府第,宅邸。**6**. 门厅,过道,走廊。*a banquet* ～ 宴会厅。*a dance* ～ 跳舞厅。*a music* ～ 音乐堂。*a lecture* ～ 大讲堂。*a servants'* ～ 仆役室。*a taxi-dance* ～〔美〕有舞女伴舞的舞厅。***H- of Fame*** **1**. 纽约市纪念美国名人的纪念馆;名人遗物收藏馆。**2**. 杰出人物。～***s of ivy***〔美〕高等学校。***the City*** [***Town***] ***H-*** 市政厅。***the H- of Mirrors*** (温莎宫的)镜厅。***the Science H-***〔美〕科学大楼。～**-bedroom** 廊底小卧室〔尤指楼上走廊尽头间隔出来的小卧室〕。～**man** **1**. 门侍。**2**.〔美〕没有加入大学生联谊会的学生。～**mark** **1**. *n*. (伦敦金业工会证明金银纯度的)检验印记;质量证明;标志,特点。**2**. *vt*. 在…上盖检验印记。～**stand** 衣帽架。～ **tree** 柱式衣帽架〔尤指大厅入口处者〕。～**way**〔美〕门厅,过道。

Hall [hɔːl; hɔl] *n*. 霍尔〔姓氏,男子名〕。

hal·lah [ˈhɑːlə; ˋhɑlə] *n*. (犹太人安息日和假日吃的)白面包卷。

Hal·lam [ˈhæləm; ˋhæləm] *n*. 哈勒姆〔姓氏〕。

Hal·leck [ˈhælik; ˋhælɪk] *n*. 哈利克〔姓氏〕。

hal·lel [hɑːˈleil, ˈhɑːlel; hɑˋlel, ˋhɑlɛl] *n*. (犹太教在某些节日中诵咏的)《诗篇》第 13 到 118 篇。

hal·le·lu·iah, hal·le·lu·jah [ˌhæliˈluːjə; ˏhæləˋlujə] *n*., *int*. 哈利路亚〔犹太教和基督教的欢呼用语,意为"赞美神"〕。～**girl**, ～**lass**〔谑〕救世军女工作人员。

Hal·ley [ˈhæli; ˋhælɪ] *n*. 哈利〔姓氏〕。

Halley [ˈhæli; ˋhælɪ] *n*. **1**. 哈雷〔姓氏〕。**2**. **Edmund** ～ 埃德蒙德·哈雷〔1656—1742,英国天文学家〕。～**'s comet** 哈雷彗星。

hal·liard [ˈhæljəd; ˋhæljɚd] *n*. = halyard.

hal·lo(a) [həˈləu; həˋlo] I *int*. 喂! 啊呀! II *n*. "喂"的一声,"啊呀"的一声。III *vt*., *vi*. 对…叫一声喂!

hal·loo [həˈluː; həˋlu] I *int*. 喂! 嗨! 驰!〔嗾狗声和引人注意的喊声〕。II *vt*., *vi*. 大声喊叫,高声嗾使。III *n*. 高呼。***Do not*** ～ ***until you are out of the wood(s)***.〔谚〕未离险境,别先高兴。

hal·low[1] [ˈhæləu; ˋhælo] I *vt*. 把…视为神圣;尊敬;把…献给神。II *n*. 圣人,圣徒。

hal·low[2] [həˈləu; həˋlo] *int*., *v*., *n*. = halloo.

hal·lowed [ˈhæləud; ˋhælod] *a*. **1**. (被视为)神圣的;被尊为神圣的。**2**. 受崇拜的。*the* ～ *traditions from the past* 神圣的古老传统。**-ly** *ad*. **-ness** *n*.

Hal·low·een [ˈhæləuˈiːn; ˋhæloˋin] *n*. 万圣节前夕〔指十月三十一日夜晚,儿童可以纵情玩乐〕。

Hal·low·mas [ˈhæləumæs; ˋhælomæs] *n*. 万圣节〔指十一月一日〕。

Hall·statt [ˈhɑːlstɑːt; ˋhɑlstɑt] *a*. 欧洲铁器时代早期的〔约公元前八世纪到四世纪〕。～ **civilization** 欧洲铁器时代早期文化〔Hallstatt 系奥地利一村庄名,该处曾有考古发现〕。

hal·lu·ci·nate [həˈluːsineit; həˋlusnˏet] *vt*., *vi*. (使)生幻觉。

hal·lu·ci·na·tion [həˌluːsiˈneiʃən; həˏlusnˋeʃən] *n*. 幻觉,错觉。**-nato·ry** [-təri; -tərɪ] *a*. 幻觉的,妄想的。

hal·lu·ci·no·gen [həˈluːsinədʒen, ˌhæljuˈsinədʒen; həˋlusənədʒɛn, ˏhæljuˋsɛnədʒɛn] I *n*.【乐】幻觉剂。II *a*. 引起幻觉的。

hal·lu·ci·no·sis [həˌluːsiˈnəusis; həˏlusəˋnosɪs] *n*.【医】幻觉病。

hal·lux [ˈhæləks; ˋhæləks] *n*. (*pl*. **-lu·ces** [-jusiːz; -jəsiz])【解】拇趾,大趾;鸟的后趾。

halm [hɑːm; hɔm] *n*. = haulm.

hal·ma [ˈhælmə; ˋhælmə] *n*. (棋盘有 256 目的)一种跳棋。

ha·lo [ˈheiləu; ˋhelo] I *n*. (*pl*. ～(*e*)*s*) **1**. (日月等的)晕,晕圈。**2**. 神像后的光环。**3**. 荣光,光辉。**4**.【解】乳晕,乳头轮。II *vt*. 使有晕圈,以光圈围绕(*Rainbows* ～*ed the waterfalls*. 彩虹给瀑布围上了光圈)。— *vi*. 成晕圈。

halo- *comb*. *f*.〔后接辅音〕**1**. 表示"盐":*halo*phyte. **2**. 表示"卤":*halo*genide.

hal·o·bi·ont [ˌhæləuˈbaiənt; ˏhæloˋbaɪɑnt] *n*.【动】(海中的)适盐生物。

hal·o·bi·os [ˌhæləuˈbaiəs; ˏhæloˋbaɪəs] *n*. 海洋生物。

hal·o·gen [ˈhælədʒen; ˋhælədʒən] *n*.【化】卤(素)。～ *acid* 氢卤酸。

hal·o·ge·nate [ˈhælədʒəneit; ˋhælədʒəˏnet] *vt*. **1**. 卤化,卤代。**2**. 加卤,卤合。**hal·o·ge·na·tion** *n*.

hal·o·gen·ide [ˈhælədʒənaid; ˋhælədʒənaɪd] *n*.【化】卤化物。

hal·o·ge·ton [ˈhælədʒətən, həˈlɔdʒitən; ˋhælədʒətɑn, həˋlɑdʒɪtɑn] *n*.【植】盐生草(*Halogeton glomeratus*)〔产于美国西部〕。

hal·oid [ˈhælɔid; ˋhælɔɪd] I *a*.【化】卤(族)的,含卤(素)的;似海盐的。II *n*. 卤化物;海盐。

hal·o·me·ter [hæˈlɔmitə; hæˋlɑmɪtɚ] *n*.【化】盐量计。

hal·o·mor·phic [ˌhæləˈmɔːfik; ˏhæləˋmɔrfɪk] *a*. (土壤)在中性环境(或碱性盐)中形成的。**-phism** *n*.

hal·o·phile [ˈhæləfail; ˋhæləˏfaɪl] *n*. 嗜盐生物,适于在盐质环境中生长的动植物。**hal·o·phil·ic** [-ˈfilik; -ˋfɪlɪk], **ha·loph·i·lous** [həˈlɔfiləs; həˋlɑfɪləs] *a*.

hal·o·phyte [ˈhæləfait; ˋhæləˏfaɪt] *n*.【植】盐土植物。

hal·o·thane [ˈhæləθein; ˋhæləˏθen] *n*.【化】卤(化)乙烷〔其气体可作吸入麻醉剂〕。

Hal·ste(a)d [ˈhɔːlstid, ˈhælsted; ˋhɔlstɪd, ˋhælstɛd] *n*. 霍尔斯特德〔姓氏〕。

halt[1] [hɔːlt; hɔlt] I *n*. **1**. 暂停前进,止步。**2**. 休息;立定。**3**. (铁路)临时站;电车站。***bring to a*** ～ 使停止。***call*** [***cry***] ***a*** ～ 命令停止;命令立定(*call a* ～ *to attacks* 命令停止进攻)。***come to a*** ～ = ***make a*** ～ 停止。II *vi*. **1**. 站住,立定,休息。**2**. 停止;暂停前进。～ *for a rest* (军队)停下来休息。— *vt*. **1**. 止住,使停止。**2**. 使驻扎。～ *the troops for a rest* 命令军队停下来休息。*a* ～*ing place* 驻军地;休息地。

halt[2] [hɔːlt; hɔlt] I *n*., *a*.〔古〕跛(的)。II *vi*. **1**. 踌躇不前;吞吞吐吐地说。**2**. (韵文等)欠完整,有缺点。**3**.〔古〕跛行。～ *between two opinions* 拿不定主意。～ *in one's speech* 讲话吞吞吐吐。*A poor argument* ～*s*. 论点拙劣,漏洞百出。

hal·ter[1] [ˈhɔːltə; ˋhɔltɚ] I *n*. **1**. (牛马等的)笼头,缰绳。**2**. 绞索;绞刑。**3**. (女用)三角背心。***come to the*** ～ 被处绞刑。***put a*** ～ ***round one's own neck*** 自己套上绞索,作茧自缚。***stretch a*** ～ 受绞刑。II *vt*. **1**. 给…套上笼头[系上缰绳]。**2**. 绞死。**3**. 束缚,抑制。～**-break** *vt*. 使(马)带惯笼头。

hal·ter[2] [ˈhɔːltə; ˋhɔltɚ] *n*. 跛行者,踌躇者。

H

hal·ter[3] [ˈhɔːltə; ˋhɔltɚ] ***n***. (*pl*. ～*es*) (昆虫的)平衡棒,平衡器。

halt·ing[1] [ˈhɔːltiŋ; ˋhɔltɪŋ] ***a***. 跛的。**-ly *ad*. -ness *n*.**

halt·ing[2] [ˈhɔːltiŋ; ˋhɔltɪŋ] ***a***. 踌躇的;不完整的。*speak in a* ～ *way* 说话吞吞吐吐。

ha·lutz [hɑːˈluːts; hɑˋluts] ***n***. (*pl*. ***ha·lutz·im*** [hɑːluːtˈsiːm; hɑlutˋsim]) 哈鲁茨〔以色列农业居民点中最早移入的犹太拓荒者〕。

hal·vah, hal·va [hɑːlˈvɑː; hɑlˋvɑ] ***n***. 哈发糕〔用芝麻、面和蜜糖作馅的点心,源出土耳其〕。

halve [hɑːv; hæv] ***vt***. **1**. 把…分成相等的两部分。**2**. 使平均分担。**3**. 将…减半。**4**. 【建】把…开半对搭。～ ***a hole with***【高尔夫球】和对方以同一打击数打进洞穴。～ ***a match***【体】打成平手。

halves [hɑːvz; hævz] half 的复数。

halv·ing [ˈhɑːviŋ; ˋhævɪŋ] ***n***. 二等分;【建】半开胶合。

hal·yard [ˈhæljəd; ˋhæljɚd] ***n***. 【海】扬帆绳,旗绳,升降索。

ham[1] [hæm; hæm] **I *n***. **1**. 火腿;〔*pl*.〕〔美〕火腿(夹心)面包。**2**. 〔*pl*.〕膝腘,(兽类的)后踝,腿臂。**3**. 〔美俚〕表演过火的演员。**4**. 〔俚〕爱做作的人。**5**. 〔美〕无线电收发报业余爱好者。***squat on one's*** ～***s*** 蹲下。**II *a***. **1**. 过火的,做作的;蹩脚的。**2**. 搞业余无线电收发报的。**III *vt*., *vi***. (***-mm-***) (使)表演过火。～**-and-egger *n***.〔俚〕**1**. 普通人。**2**. 不出众的拳击师。～**-and-eggery *n***.〔俚〕小饭店,简易餐柜。～**-and-eggs *a***. 日常的,普通的。～**-fisted**, ～**-handed *a***.〔主英〕**1**. 拳头很大的。**2**. 〔俚〕笨拙的。

ham[2] [hæm; hæm] ***n***. (旧时的)小镇;村庄。

Ha·ma [ˈhæmə; ˋhæmə] ***n***. 哈马〔叙利亚城市〕。

ham·a·dry·ad [ˌhæməˈdraiəd; ˏhæməˋdraɪəd] ***n***. **1**. 【希神】树精。**2**. (印度等地产的)一种眼镜蛇(= king cobra)。**3**. 阿拉伯狒狒(*Comopithecus hamadryas*)〔产于阿拉伯和北非〕。

ha·mal [həˈmɑːl; həˋmɑl] ***n***. (土耳其等中东国家的)搬运工人,搬行李的人。

Ha·man [ˈheimən; ˋhemən] ***n***. 海曼[哈曼]〔姓氏〕。

ha·mate [ˈheimeit; ˋhemet] ***a***. 【解】(骨)钩状的。

Ham·burg [ˈhæmbəːg; ˋhæmbɚg] ***n***. **1**. 汉堡〔德国港市〕。**2**. (欧洲种)红冠青脚鸡。**3**. = ～ steak. ～ **steak** 〔美〕**1**. 碎牛肉。**2**. 牛肉饼,汉堡牛排〔碎牛肉煎成的圆饼〕。**3**. 夹牛肉饼的面包片;汉堡包。

ham·burg·er [ˈhæmbəːgə; ˋhæmbɚgɚ] ***n***. **1**. = Hamburg steak. **2**. 被打得遍体鳞伤的拳击手。***make*** ～ ***out of*** (***sb***.) 〔美俚〕把人打得一塌糊涂。～ **steak** = Hamburg steak.

hames [heimz; hemz] ***n***. 〔*pl*.〕马颈轭。

ham·fat·ter [ˈhæmfætə; ˋhæmˏfætɚ] ***n***.〔美俚〕拙劣的演员。

Ham·il·ton[1] [ˈhæmiltən; ˋhæmḷtən] ***n***. 汉密尔顿〔姓氏,男子名〕。

Ham·il·ton[2] [ˈhæmiltən; ˋhæmḷtən] ***n***. 汉密尔顿〔加拿大港市,百慕达群岛首府〕。

Ham·il·to·ni·an [ˌhæmilˈtəuniən; ˏhæmɪlˋtonɪən] **I *a***. 【史】汉密尔顿主义的。**II *n***. 【史】汉密尔顿的追随者。

Ham·il·to·ni·an·ism [ˌhæmilˈtəunjənizəm; ˏhæmɪlˋtonjənɪzəm] ***n***. 【史】汉密尔顿主义〔美国联邦党领导人汉密尔顿(1757-1804)的政见,主张建立中央集权的联邦政府等〕。

Ham·ite [ˈhæmait; ˋhæmaɪt] ***n***. 含米特人〔分居于东非和北非的含族黑人〕。

Ham·it·ic [hæˈmitik; hæˋmɪtɪk] **I *a***. 含米特人的;含米特语族的,含米特语的。**II *n***. 含米特语。

ham·let [ˈhæmlit; ˋhæmlɪt] ***n***. 村子;〔英〕(无教堂的)小村庄。

Ham·let [ˈhæmlit; ˋhæmlɪt] ***n***. **1**. 哈姆雷特〔莎士比亚悲剧剧名和该剧主人翁〕。**2**. 〔喻〕优柔寡断的人。～ ***without the Prince of Denmark*** = ～ ***with*** ～ ***left out*** 没有主人公的戏,去掉了本质的东西。

Ham·lin [ˈhæmlin; ˋhæmlɪn] ***n***. 哈姆林〔姓氏〕。

ham·mal [həˈmɑːl; həˋmɑl] ***n***. = hamal.

ham·mam [ˈhæməm; ˋhæməm] ***n***. 土耳其浴室,蒸气浴室。

ham·mer [ˈhæmə; ˋhæmɚ] **I *n***. **1**. 槌,铁锤,榔头。**2**. 【机】唇锤,杵锤。**3**. (会议主席或拍卖人用的)小木槌。**4**. 槌状物,(电铃的)小槌子,锣锤;【乐】音槌。**5**. (火器的)击铁。**6**. 【体】链球。**7**. 【解】(中耳的)锤骨。*a soldering* ～ 烙铁。*a steam* ～ 蒸汽锤。～ *throwing* 掷链球。***be*** [***go***] ***at it*** ～ ***and tongs*** 闹哄哄地激烈殴斗[争辩]。***between*** (***the***) ～ ***and*** (***the***) ***anvil*** 腹背受敌,两面被夹攻。***be*** [***go, come***] ***under the*** ～ 被拍卖。***bring*** [***send***] ***sth***. ***to the*** ～ 拿…去拍卖。～ ***and tongs*** 〔口〕猛烈地,全力地,劲头十足地,以雷霆万钧之势。***knight of the*** ～ 铁匠。***up to the*** ～ 极好的,无可疵议的。**II *vt***. **1**. 锤击,锤薄;使锤成;把…锤进。**2**. (用拳头)痛打。**3**. 〔口〕(用炮)猛轰使惨败。**4**. 〔英〕(交易所中敲榔头)宣布(某人、公司等)已无偿还能力。**5**. 〔俚〕严厉批评,攻击。**5**. (辩论时)提出(有力理由等);硬性灌输〔常与 home 连用〕。～ *a box together* 钉成一个箱子。～ *an idea into sb.'s head* 硬向某人灌输某种观念。～*-ed finish of stone* 锤琢过的石材。— ***vi***. 接连锤打。***give sb. a good*** ～***ing*** 痛打某人一顿。～ ***at*** **1**. 一再敲打。**2**. 不断研究,埋头于…。**3**. 接连说明。～ ***away at*** 连连敲打;刻苦钻研,反复谈论(～ *away at the same point* 老是强调同一观点)。～ ***down*** 用锤钉上。～ ***in*** (***to***) 用锤敲进。～ ***out*** **1**. 锤薄;锤平。**2**. 苦心想出;推敲出。**3**. 敲出(音调等)。**4**. 调整,消除。～ **beam**【建】椽尾(小)梁。～ **blow** 锤打,猛击。～**cloth *n***. 马车夫座位上的布篷。～**fish**【动】撞木鲛,双髻鲨。～**-harden *vt***. 用锤打紧(金属等)。～**head** **1**. 锤头。**2**. 【动】撞木鲛,双髻鲨。**3**. 〔美俚〕笨蛋,傻子,白痴。～**-headed *a***. 有锤状头的;钝的。～ **lane**〔美俚〕(超级公路的)快车道。～ **lock**【摔跤】把对方的手扭到背后。～**man**, ～**smith** 锻工。～ **throw**【体】掷链球。～ **toe** **1**. 趾骨锤状变形。**2**. 锤状趾。

ham·mer·ing [ˈhæməriŋ; ˋhæmərɪŋ] ***n***. 锤击。*cold* ～ 冷锻。

ham·mer·less [ˈhæməlis; ˋhæmɚlɪs] ***a***. **1**. 无锤的。**2**. 【军】内击铁的(指击铁在枪的内部)。～ *gun* 暗机枪。

ham·mock[1] [ˈhæmək; ˋhæmək] ***n***. 吊床。*lash* [*sling*] *a* ～ 结绑[吊挂]吊床。～ **chair** 帆布椅。**-like *a***.

ham·mock[2] [ˈhæmək; ˋhæmək] ***n***. = **1**. hummock. **2**. 美国南方肥沃的高地。

Ham·mond [ˈhæmənd; ˋhæmənd] ***n***. 哈蒙德〔姓氏〕。

ham·my[1] [ˈhæmi; ˋhæmɪ] ***a***. 有火腿香味的。

ham·my[2] [ˈhæmi; ˋhæmɪ] ***a***. 〔俚〕演技拙劣的;(把角色)演得过火的。**ham·mi·ly *ad*. ham·mi·ness *n*.**

Hamp·den [ˈhæm*p*dən; ˋhæm*p*dən] ***n***. 汉普登〔姓氏〕。

ham·per[1] [ˈhæmpə; ˋhæmpɚ] **I *vt***. 妨碍,阻挠,牵制。*be* ～*ed by a big, heavy overcoat* 为一件沉重的大衣所累。**II *n***. **1**. 【海】(平时不可少而暴风雨时则成累赘的)船具。**2**. 阻碍物;足械。**-ed·ly *ad*. -ed·ness *n*. -er *n*.**

ham·per[2] [ˈhæmpə; ˋhæmpɚ] **I *n***. 有盖提篮;篮装食品[礼品]。**II *vt***. 把(食品)装入篮内。*a* ～ *of wine* 一篮子酒。

Hamp·ton [ˈhæmptən; ˋhæmptən] ***n***. 汉普顿〔姓氏〕。

ham·shack·le [ˈhæmʃækl; ˋhæmˏʃækl] ***vt***. **1**. 把(牛马等的)头用绳绑在前足上。**2**. 束缚。

ham·ster [ˈhæmstə; ˋhæmstɚ] ***n***. 【动】仓鼠。

ham·string [ˈhæmstriŋ; ˋhæmstrɪŋ] **I *n***. 【解】腘旁腱;【动】(兽类的)后腿腱。**II *vt***. (～***ed***, ***ham·strung*** [ˈhæmstrʌŋ; ˋhæmstrʌŋ]) **1**. 割断…的腿筋;使残废。**2**. 减弱…的活动能力。

ham·u·lus [ˈhæmjuləs; ˋhæmjʊləs] ***n***. (*pl*. ***-li***

[ˈhæmjulai; ˋhæmjulaɪ]) **1.**【解】钩。**2.**【动】钩形突；小钩。

Han [hæn; hæn] ***n.*** (*pl.* ~(*s*))〔中〕**1.**【史】汉代（= *the* ~ *Dynasty*）。**2.** 汉族，汉人。**3.** 汉水。

han·a·per [ˈhænəpə; ˋhænəpɚ] ***n.*** 文件筐。

Han·cock [ˈhænkɔk; ˋhænkɑk] ***n.*** 汉考克〔姓氏〕。

Hand [hænd; hænd] ***n.*** 汉德〔姓氏〕。

hand [hænd; hænd] **I** ***n.*** **1.** 手；(猴子等的)脚；(一般四足兽的)前脚。**2.** (钟表的)指针，(工具等的)把，柄。**3.** 手状物；(香蕉等的)一扇；(烟叶的)一束。**4.**〔常 *pl.*〕握有；管理；支配；权力；(古代罗马法律中规定的)夫权。**5.** 人手，职工，雇员；船员。**6.** 支援，帮助，参加；插手，干预。**7.** 技巧，手艺，手法。**8.** 笔迹，书法；签名。**9.** 方，侧；方面。**10.** 答允；婚约。**11.**【牌】手中的牌；打牌人；牌戏的一盘。**12.** 一掌之宽〔约英寸，量马高度用〕。**13.**〔口〕拍手喝采。**14.** (摸皮革、织物等的)手感。*a bench* ~ 钳工。*a* ~ *of banana* 一扇香蕉。*blind* ~ 模糊不清的笔迹。*the hidden* ~ 看不见的势力，幕后操纵者。*the last* ~ 最后几笔，定稿前的润色。*an old parliamentary* ~ 精通议院事务的人。~ *of writ* [*write*]〔Scot.〕笔迹，字体。*the minute* [*hour*] ~ (钟表的)分[时]针。*factory* ~*s* 工人。*an indicator* ~ 指针。*His* ~ *is in.* 他在不断地练习。*His* ~ *is out.* 他不行。*My* ~*s are tied.* 我的权力极其有限。*write a good* ~ 写得一笔好字。*ask for a girl's* ~ 向女子求婚。***A clean*** ~ ***wants no washing.***〔谚〕手上不沾污〔指罪恶、坏事等〕，不必多洗刷。***cool*** ~ 冒失鬼。***a crack*** [***good, great***] ~ 行家，熟手。***a dead*** ~【法】没有让渡权的所有主。***extra*** ~***s*** 临时工。***a free*** ~ 放手处理的权力（*allow sb. a free* ~ *in his work* 让某人放手工作）。***a fresh*** [***green***] ~ 生手。***a good*** [***poor***] ~ ***at*** 巧[拙]于。***a*** ~***'s turn*** 小事（*not do a* ~*'s turn* 易如反掌的事都不做）。***a nap*** ~ 一手好牌；有利的地位。***a numb*** ~ 笨人。***all*** ~***s***【海】全体船员；【口】全体人员。***all*** ~***s to the pump***(*s*) 大家都来帮忙。***an old*** ~ 内行，过来人。***at first*** ~ 直接（*knowledge at first* ~ 第一手知识）。***at*** ~ **1.** 在手边，在近处。**2.** 即将到来（*live close at* ~ 住在附近。*The autumn harvest is at* ~. 秋收即将到来）。***at second*** ~ **1.** 经过他人一道手的，第二手的；间接的。**2.** 旧的，用过的。***at the*** ~(*s*) ***of sb.*** = ***at sb.'s*** ~(*s*) **1.** 在某人手下。**2.** 出自某人之手（*suffer cruel exploitation at the* ~*s of the slaveholders* 受奴隶主残酷剥削）。***bathe*** [***dip***] ***one's*** ~***s in blood*** 双手沾满鲜血，成为杀人犯。***bear*** [***lend***] ***a*** ~ (***in***) 参加。***bear*** [***lend***] ***a*** ~ (***with***) 帮助，出一把力。***be even*** ~***s with sb.***〔Scot.〕向某人报复，同某人算账。***be out of sb.'s*** ~***s*** 某人不能控制[处理、负责]。***bite the*** ~ ***that feeds one*** 忘恩负义，恩将仇报。***by*** ~ **1.** 用手的，手工的；用手递交的。**2.** (婴儿)用牛奶抚养的（*bring up a child by* ~ 亲手把孩子抚养成人；不用人奶喂大小孩。*deliver a letter by* ~ 信由专人递送。*made by* ~ 手工制的）。***by the*** ~***s of*** 经…的手。***by the left*** ~ **1.** 贵族男子娶非贵族女子所生的；门第不相称的夫妇所生的。**2.** 私生的。***by the strong*** ~ 强制地。***change*** ~***s***（财产等)转换所有者，易手。***check one's*** ~***s in*** 拒绝做某事；认输。***come to*** (***one's***) ~(*s*) 拿到手，收到。***cross sb.'s*** ~ **1.** (用钱币)在某人手心中划十字〔指把钱币付给算命者〕。**2.** 贿赂。***die by one's own*** ~ 自杀。***do not lift a*** ~ 不努力，不动手，不试一下；懒。***eat*** [***feed***] ***out of sb.'s*** ~ 完全顺从某人，唯某人之命是从。***fall*** [***get***] ***into sb.'s*** ~***s*** [***the*** ~***s of sb.***] 落到某人手里。***fight*** ~ ***to*** ~ 短兵相接，肉搏。***fold one's*** ~***s*** 叉着手，袖手旁观。***force sb.'s*** ~ (在作好准备前)强迫某人行动[表态]。***from*** ~ ***to*** ~ 从甲手到乙手，传递。***from*** ~ ***to mouth*** 做一天吃一天，现挣现吃，刚够糊口。***gain*** [***get, have***] ***the upper*** ~ ***of*** 占优势，占上风。***get a big*** ~〔美〕受到热烈鼓掌；大受欢迎。***get*** ~ 得手，得势。***get*** [***have***] ***one's*** ~ ***in*** **1.** 使自己熟习。**2.** 插手。~ ***oneself in*** ~ 控制自己。***get sth. off one's*** ~***s*** 摆脱某事，摆脱对某事的责任。***give one's*** ~ ***on a bargain*** 保证履行契约。***give one's*** ~ ***to sb.*** **1.** 向某人伸出手。**2.** (女子)答应和某人结婚。***give sb. a*** ~ 帮助某人。***give sb. a*** [***the***] ***glad*** ~〔俚〕欢迎。***grease the*** ~ ***of sb.*** 买通，向人行贿。~ ***and foot*** 手脚一齐，完全地；尽力地（*bind sb.* ~ *and foot* 把某人完全捆住）。~ ***and*** [***in***] ***glove with*** 亲密地；勾结着（*have all along worked* ~ *in glove with sb.* 一直与某人狼狈为奸）。~ ***in*** ~ **1.** 手拉手。**2.** 联合（*act* ~ *in* ~ 联合行动）。~ ***over fist*** **1.** 不费气力地，大量地。**2.** = ~ ***over*** ~。~ ***over*** ~ **1.** (粑绳等时)一把一把往上。**2.** 稳妥而迅速地(前进)。***Hands are full.*** 很忙。~***s down*** **1.** 不费气力地，容易地。**2.** 无疑地。***Hands off!*** 请勿动手。***Hands off...!*** 不许干涉(他)！***Hands up!*** **1.**〔要对方不抵抗的命令〕举起手来！**2.** 举手赞成。~ ***to fist***〔口〕亲密的[地]；齐心协力的[地]。~ ***to*** ~ 逼近地。~ ***under*** ~ 左右手替换着(由绳子上降落)。***have a good*** ~ 有一手好牌。***have a*** ~ ***in*** 干与，参与，插手。***have a*** ~ ***like a foot*** 笨手笨脚。***have an open*** ~ 慷慨。***have long*** ~***s*** 很有势力。***have*** [***hold, keep***] (***sb.***) (***well***) ***in*** ~ 掌握，支配(某人)。***have one's*** ~***s free*** **1.** 空着手，无事干。**2.** 可以自由行动。***have one's*** ~***s full*** 手头事很多，很忙。***heavy on*** [***in***] ~ (马等)难驾驭；(人)难应付。***hold*** ~***s*** 手搀手。***hold one's*** ~ 迟迟不下手。***hold up one's*** ~***s*** 举手(投降)。***in*** ~ **1.** 现有，在手头。**2.** (工作)正在进行。**3.** 控制住（*have the situation well in* ~ 完全掌握着局势）。***in the*** ~***s of ...*** 在…掌握中；交托给。***join*** ~***s*** (***with***) **1.** 同…携手，联合。**2.** 同…合伙开店。**3.** 同…结婚。***keep a slack*** ~ 放松缰绳；漫不经心地管理。***keep*** [***have***] ***one's*** ~ ***in*** 不断练习，使技能不荒疏。***keep one's*** ~ [***a firm*** ~] ***on*** 牢牢地控制着。***kiss*** ~***s*** [***the*** ~] 吻君王的手〔一种礼仪〕。***kiss one's*** ~ ***to*** 向…飞吻。***lay*** (***violent***) ~***s on oneself*** 自杀。***lay*** ~***s on*** [***upon***] ***sb.*** **1.** 袭击某人。**2.**【宗】对…行按手礼。***lay*** ~***s on*** [***upon***] ***sth.*** 拿住，抓住；找到。***lay one's*** ~ ***on the table*** = *show one's* ~. ***lie on sb.'s*** ~(*s*) **1.** (商品)在某人手中未脱手；(物件)在某人手中未用掉。**2.** (时间)使某人感到无聊。***lift a*** [***one's***] ~ [***against***] 打，威胁。***lift one's*** ~***s*** 举手宣誓。***light in*** ~ (马等)易于驾驭。***lose the upper*** ~ 失去优势。***make a*** ~ 成功；得利。***Many*** ~***s make light work.***〔谚〕人多好办事。***marry with the left*** ~ 与门第比自己低的人结婚。***off*** ~ 马上，立即，事前无准备地。***off sb.'s*** ~***s*** 脱手，卸脱责任。***offer one's*** ~ **1.** 伸出手来(准备握手)。**2.** 向女人求婚。***offer*** [***give***] ***sb. the right*** ~ ***of fellowship*** **1.** 同某人结交。**2.** 同意某人入伙。***on all*** ~***s*** = ***on*** [***at***] ***every*** ~ 在各方面；一般。***on either*** ~ 在两边中的任何一边。***on*** ~ **1.** 现有，在手头。**2.**〔美〕在近处，即将发生。**3.**〔美〕出席，到场。***on sb.'s*** ~***s*** 在某人手里；由某人负责照管（*She has many patients on her* ~*s.* 她有许多病人要她照顾。*Time hangs heavy on one's* ~*s.* 时间慢得令人难过）。***on the left*** [***right***] ~ (***of***) 在…的左[右]边。***on the mending*** ~ 在好转中。***on the one*** ~, ... ***on the other*** (~) 一方面…，另一方面。***on the other*** ~ 从另一方面来说，相反，反之。***one's right*** ~ 右手；得力助手。***out of*** ~ **1.** 即时。**2.** 脱手；告终。**3.** 难对付；难控制。***overplay one's*** ~ **1.** 过高地估计自己。**2.** 做得过分。***play a good*** ~ (牌)玩得精明。***play a lone*** ~ 单干。***play for one's own*** ~ 为自己的利益打算[行动]。***play into sb.'s*** ~***s*** = ***play into the*** ~***s of sb.*** 因失算而使某人占了便宜。***play one's*** ~ ***for all it is worth*** 尽全力。***play one's*** ~ ***heavily*** 做得过火。***pump sb.'s*** ~〔美〕使劲同某人握手。***Put not your*** ~ ***between the bark and the tree.***〔谚〕少管闲事。***put one's*** ~ ***in***

H

[*into*] ***a hornet's nest*** 惹祸,树敌。***put*** [*set*, *turn*] ***one's ~ to sth.*** [*the plough*] 着手一项工作。***Put your ~ no further than your sleeve will reach.***〔谚〕量入为出。***raise one's ~ against*** = *lift one's ~ against*. ***read sb.'s ~*** 看某人的手相。***ready to one's ~*** = *under one's ~*. ***rub one's ~s*** 因高兴而搓手。***serve sb. ~ and foot*** 勤勤恳恳为某人服务。***set one's ~ to*** 1. 着手,从事于。2. 在…上面签字,批准,承认。***shake sb.'s ~*** = ***shake ~s with sb.***, ***shake sb. by the ~*** 同某人握手。***show one's ~*** 摊牌;摆计划;表示态度。***sit on one's ~s***〔美俚〕1. (观众等)不鼓掌。2. (应当采取行动时)踌躇不前。***slack ~*** 玩忽,不留心。***stay one's ~*** 不作某事。***stay sb.'s ~*** 使某人住手。***strengthen sb.'s ~*** (*s*) 增强某人实力,使某人得以采取强有力的行动。***strike ~s*** 约定。***take a ~ in*** [*at*] 参加,和…发生关系。***take in ~*** 1. 处理;照料。2. 控制;承担。3. 尝试。***the upper ~*** 优势。***throw in one's ~*** 放弃,退出竞选。***throw up one's ~s*** 绝望地放弃。***tip one's ~*** 摊牌,表明态度。***to ~*** 1. 近在手边。2. 收到,占有(*your letter to ~* = *yours to ~*【商】来函收到)。***try one's ~ at*** 试试。***under one's ~*** 在手边,就可使用,来得及。***under one's ~ and seal*** 经签名盖章。***upon ~*** = *on ~*. ***wash one's ~s*** 1. 洗手。2. 解手,上厕所。***wash one's ~s of*** 不再管或负责某事;和…断绝关系。***wash one's ~s with invisible soap and imperceptible water*** 以无形的肥皂和水洗手〔意为由于紧张等而搓手〕。***win a lady's ~*** 赢得某女子同意结婚。***with a bold ~*** 大胆地。***with a firm ~*** 坚决地。***with a free ~*** 1. 慷慨地,不吝惜地。2. 浪费地,无节制地。***with a heavy ~*** 1. 粗手粗脚地,粗枝大叶地。2. 高压地,严厉地。***with a high ~*** 武断地,用高压手段。***with an iron ~*** 严厉地,以铁腕。***with an iron ~ in a velvet glove*** 外柔内刚地,口蜜腹剑地。***with a strong ~*** 决断地,强硬地。***with clean ~s*** 清白无罪地,廉洁地。***wring one's ~s over sth.*** 为某事苦恼地绞扭着手。**II** *vt*. 1. 交付;传递给(*to*)。2. 用手搀扶,用手帮助(*to*; *into*; *out of*; *across*; *over*)。3.【海】卷叠(风帆)。~ *a lady into a bus* 搀扶一位女士上公共汽车。~ *a letter to her* 递给她一封信。~ *sb. a surprise* 使某人大吃一惊。~ ***a good line***〔美〕所有功课都考得很好。~ ***around***〔美〕= ~ round. ~ ***back*** 交回。~ ***down*** 1. 传下来。2. 宣布(判决等)(~ *traditions down to us* 把传统传给我们)。~ ***in*** 交进,交上。~ ***into*** 扶进,扶上车。~ ***it to sb.***〔美俚〕承认某人的长处,给某人应得的荣誉。~ ***off***【橄榄球】用手推开对手。~ ***on*** (***to sb.***) 依次传递,传给后代。~ ***out*** 1. 拿出来。2. 分,分派。3. 施舍。~ ***over*** 1. 送交(当局等)。2. 移交,让与(~ *sb. over to the police* 把某人送交警察)。~ ***round*** 顺次传递;分交。~ ***up*** 交给,呈上;告密。~**arm** (手)枪。~ **ax** [**axe**] 手斧〔旧石器时代的一种石器〕(= broad hatchet)。~**bag** 手提包;旅行包。~ **baggage** 手提行李。~**ball** 手球,手球游戏;手触球犯规。~**barrow** (前后两人推运的)平台车,手推车;(两边有柄的)抬物架。~**bell**【乐】手摇铃。~**bill** 传单,招贴,广告。~**blown** *a*.〔指玻璃器皿〕吹制的。~**book** 手册,便览,指南;〔美〕赛马手册。~ **brake** 手煞车。~**-breadth** 一手之宽〔从二英寸半到四英寸〕,手掌宽。~ **canter**【马术】缓跑,小跑。~ **car**〔美〕铁路上所用手摇[机动]四轮小车。~**cart** 手车,手推车。~**clap** 拍手。~ **clasp** 握别,握手礼。~ **computer** 手摇计算机。~**craft** 1. *n*. 手工,手工艺。2. *vt*. 用手工制作。~**crafted** *a*. 手工的,手工艺的。~**crank** 手动曲柄。~**cuff** 1. *n*.〔常 *pl*.〕手铐。2. *vt*. 给…上手铐。~ **drill**【机】手摇钻。~**fast** 1. *n*. 握手约;婚约;握紧,抓牢。2. *a*.〔古〕握手定约的;订过婚约的。3. *vt*.〔古〕握手约定,使定婚约,使行定婚典礼。~**-feed** *vt*. (~**-fed**) 用手喂。~ **gallop** (马的)慢跑。~**-glass** 有柄小镜;(阅读用)有柄放大镜。~**-grenade** 手榴弹。~**grip** 1. 紧握;握手。2. 柄,把。3.〔*pl*.〕扭打;肉搏(*come t*[o] *~grips* 开始搏斗)。~**gun** 手枪。~**held** 掌上电脑。~**hold** 1. 把握;紧握。2. 把手,把柄;(攀登时)可用手抓住的东西。~**-holding** *n*. 关怀备至,手把手的指导。~**-in-~** *a*. 1. 手牵手的,亲密的。2. 并进的。~**-jack** 手力起重器,手力千斤顶。~**-knitted** *a*. 手编的。~ **lamp** 手提灯。~ **language** 手势语。~ **level**【测】手持水平仪。~ **line** 手钓丝。~**loom** 手织机。~**-luggage** 手提行李。~**made** 1. *a*. 手工的,手制的(*opp*. machine made)。2. *n*. 手工制品。~**maid**, ~**- maiden**〔古〕侍女,女仆,婢女;〔喻〕陪衬性的东西。~**-me-down** 1. *a*.〔口〕现成的〔常指价廉而劣等的〕;用旧的。2. *n*.〔口〕现成的衣服,旧衣服;旧事物。~ **money** 定钱,保证金。~**off**【体】后卫传球组织进攻。~ **organ** 手摇风琴。~**out** 1. 施舍物;救济品。2. (政府、政界人物)交给新闻界发表的声明[报导]。3. (用作宣传、讲授的)小册子,传单,讲义。~**over** *a*. 移交的(*~over procedure* 移交手续)。~ **perforator** 三柱凿孔机。~**-pick** 1. *n*.【矿】手镐。2. *vt*. 用手选出;精心挑选,精选。~**-picked** *a*. 精选的;〔美〕第一流的。~**-play** 互殴,扭打。~ **post** 路标。~**pump** 手压泵。~**rail** 栏杆,扶手。~**-reared** *a*. 一手养大的。~**-receiver**【讯】手持受话器。~**-running** *ad*.〔方、口〕持续地,不中断地。~**saw** 手锯,小锯。~**'s breadth** *n*. = ~-breadth. ~ **screw** 1. 手旋螺钉。2. 木工用的夹子,夹钳。~**scrub** = nailbrush. ~**s-down** *a*. 1. 垂手可得的,轻而易举的。2. 无疑的。~**set**【讯】送受话器,手机。~**sewn** *a*. 手工缝制的。~ **shake** 握手。~**-shaker** 善于打交道的人。~**s-off** *a*. 不干涉的,不干预的,不插手的。~ **s-on** *a*. 插手的,亲自参加的。~**-sort** *vt*. 手拣,用手分类。~ **spike** 杠,推杆。~ **spring** (以手着地的)翻斤斗。~ **staff** 连枷柄。~[...] *n*.【体】倒立。~**'s turn** 一举手之劳的帮助(*She did not do a ~'s turn*. 她一点忙也不帮)。~ **tape** 远距离皮卷尺。~**taut**, ~**-tight** *a*.【海】用手劲尽量拉紧的。~**-to-~** *a*. 1. 短兵相接的,肉搏的。2. 一个一个传下去的。~**-to-mouth** *a*. 过一天算一天的;勉强糊口的。~ **trolley hoist** 手动架空绞车。~ **truck** 手车,手推车。~ **vice** 手钳。~ **vote** 举手选举。~**wheel** 手轮,操纵轮,驾驶盘,转向盘。~**-work** 手工,精细工艺。~**-worked** *a*. 手工制成的。~**woven** *a*. 手织的。~**writing** 1. 笔迹,手迹。2. 手写稿(*the ~writing on the wall* 不祥之兆,灾祸的预兆)。~**written** *a*. 手写的,用笔写的。~**-wrought** *a*. = handworked.

h. and c. = hot and cold.

hand·ed [ˈhændid; ˋhændɪd] *a*. 1. 惯用…手的。2. 有…手的。3. 有…人参加的。*right-~* 惯用右手的。*short-~* 人手不足的。*two-~* 有两只手的。*a three-~ game* 三人玩的游戏。~**-down** *a*. 传下来的。**-ness** *n*. 惯用左手[右手]。

Han·del [ˈhændl; ˋhændl] *n*. 1. 汉德尔〔姓氏〕。2. **George Frederick ~** 韩德尔〔1685—1759,生于德国的英国作曲家〕。

hand·ful [ˈhændful; ˋhændfʊl] *n*. 1. 一把,一握。2. 少数,少量,一小撮。3.〔口〕难以控制的人[动物];麻烦的事。

hand·i·cap [ˈhændikæp; ˋhændɪˏkæp] **I** *n*. 1. 障碍,不利条件。2. (为使得胜机会均等,给强者以不利条件,给弱者以有利条件的)赛马或其他竞赛。3. (在强、弱手竞赛中)给弱者的有利条件,给强者的不利条件。**II** *vt*. (**-pp-**) 1. 妨碍,使不利。2. 给(竞赛中强手)不利条件;使(竞赛中弱手)获得优待。***the handicapped*** (身体或精神上有缺陷的)残疾人。

hand·i·cap·per [ˈhændikæpə; ˋhændɪˏkæpɚ] *n*. 1. 在竞技中规定有利[不利]条件的人员。2. 根据以往记录和竞技条件预测赛马胜负的新闻记者。

hand·i·craft [ˈhændikrɑːft; ˋhændɪˏkræft] *n*. 1. 手工,手工艺。2. 手工艺业。3. 手工艺品。*a ~ worker* 手工

H

业工人。

hand·i·crafts·man [ˈhændikrɑːftsmən; ˋhændɪ͵kræftsmən] (*pl*. **-men** [-men; -mɛn]) ***n*.** 手工业者;手工艺人。

hand·i·cuff [ˈhændiˌkʌf; ˋhændɪ͵kʌf] ***n*.** 用手打;〔*pl*.〕扭打。

hand·ie-talk·ie [ˈhændiˌtɔːki; ˋhændɪ͵tɔkɪ] ***n*.** 手提式步话机。

hand·i·ly [ˈhændili; ˋhændɪlɪ] ***ad*.** 巧妙地;敏捷地;便利地。

hand·i·ness [ˈhændinis; ˋhændɪnɪs] ***n*.** 巧妙;敏捷;轻便。

hand·i·work [ˈhændiwəːk; ˋhændɪ͵wɝk] ***n*.** **1.** 手工,工艺品(= handwork)。**2.** (某人)亲手做的事情。

hand·ker·chief [ˈhæŋkətʃif; ˋhæŋkɚtʃɪf] ***n*.** (*pl*. **~s**, **-chieves** [-tʃiːvz; -tʃivz]) **1.** 手帕。**2.** 头巾,围巾。*a pocket* ~ 手帕。*a neck* ~ 围巾。***throw the ~ to sb*.** (游戏时)丢手帕给某人要他追自己;〔喻〕暗示看中某人。

han·dle [ˈhændl; ˋhændl̩] **I** ***n*.** **1.** 柄,把手;曲柄;摇柄。**2.** (摸皮革、织物等的)手感。**3.** 把柄,可乘之机,口实。**4.** 〔口〕头衔,称号。**5.** (赛马等时投下的)赌金总额。*a crank* ~ 手摇曲柄。*a hammer* ~ 榔头柄。*a* ~ *to one's name* 〔口〕头衔〔如 Lord, Dr. 等〕。*an operating* ~ 控制柄,操纵手摇柄。*a starting* ~ 起动曲柄。***fly off* [*at*] *the* ~** 〔美口〕冒火,自制不住。***give a ~ for* [*to*]** 使人有可乘之机,给人以口实。***go off the ~*** 〔口〕死。***the ~ of the face*** 〔谑〕鼻子。***throw the ~ after the blade*** 赔,吃亏了又吃亏;坚持做无希望的事。***up to the ~*** 〔美口〕彻底地。**II** ***vt*.** **1.** 触,摸,抚,弄;掌握。**2.** 处理;讨论(问题);对待(人);指挥(军队),统辖。**3.** 〔美〕买卖,经营。**4.** 驯养(马等)。**5.** 〔美〕训练(拳击选手)。~ *sb. roughly* 虐待某人。~ *a subject* 讨论问题。— ***vi*.** **1.** 用手搬运。**2.** 操作;举动。*This car* ~*s easily*. 这车很灵活。*The troops* ~*d well*. 部队军纪很好。***H- with care!*** 小心轻放! ***~ without gloves* [*mittens*]** 严厉对待,毫不留情地对待。**~ bar** 〔常 *pl*.〕(自行车等的)把手。

han·dler [ˈhændlə; ˋhændlɚ] ***n*.** **1.** 处理者,管理者。**2.** (赛马、警犬等的)训练者。**3.** 【自】(信息)处理机。

hand·less [ˈhændlis; ˋhændlɪs] ***a*.** 没有手的;手笨拙的。

han·dling [ˈhændliŋ; ˋhændlɪŋ] ***n*.** **1.** 处理,管理;操纵。**2.** 装卸。~ *equipment* 辅助设备。~ *guy* 搬运索。~ *radius* 工作半径。

hand·sel [ˈhænsəl; ˋhænsl̩] **I** ***n*.** **1.** 贺礼,开张贺礼,新年赠品。**2.** 定钱,保证金。**3.** 第一笔营业收入。**4.** 新上市的东西,初次用[吃]的东西;试样。**II** ***vt*.** (〔英〕***-ll-***) **1.** 给…送贺礼,庆祝…开业[落成]。**2.** 给…付定钱。**3.** 初次吃,第一次试用。

hand·some [ˈhænsəm; ˋhænsəm] ***a*.** **1.** (一般指男子外貌)漂亮的,清秀的,俊美的;(用于女人指体态)优美的,端庄的,温雅的。**2.** 相当大的;(财产等)可观的。**3.** 堂皇的,气派大的,美观的。**4.** 慷慨的,大方的。**5.** 〔美俚〕精巧的,高明的。**6.** 〔古〕便利的,合适的;操纵灵便的。*a* ~ *contribution* 可观的捐款。*a* ~ *fortune* 不小的家产。~ *price* 相当大的价值。~ *treatment* 优待。***H- is that* [*as*] *~ does*.** 〔谚〕品德优美才算真美。**-ness** ***n*.**

hand·some·ly [ˈhænsəmli; ˋhænsəmlɪ] ***ad*.** **1.** 漂亮地,美观地,慷慨地,优厚地。**2.** 【海】慢慢地,当心地,整齐地。***come down ~*** 〔俗〕慷慨解囊,慷慨赠送。

hand·y [ˈhændi; ˋhændɪ] ***a*.** **1.** 手边的,近便的。**2.** 便利的,得心应手的,便于使用的。**3.** 手灵巧的,敏捷的。**4.** (船等)易驾驶的。***as ~ as a pocket in a shirt*** 〔美口〕非常方便。***come in ~*** 迟早有用。**~man** 手巧的人;干杂活的人。**~-talkie, ~-talky** = handie-talkie.

hand·y-dand·y [ˈhændiˌdændi; ˋhændɪ͵dændɪ] ***n*.** (儿童猜对方哪只手握着东西的)猜猜看游戏。

Han·ford [ˈhænfəd; ˋhænfɚd] ***n*.** 汉福德〔美国华盛顿州南部原子能研究重要中心〕。

hang [hæŋ; hæŋ] **I** ***vt*.** (***hung*** [hʌŋ; hʌŋ], **~*ed***) **1.** 悬挂,垂吊 (*to*; *on*; *from*)。**2.** 〔过去式与过去分词为 ~*ed*〕绞死,吊死。**3.** 贴(画等于墙上);裱(壁纸);(用画等)点缀 (*with*)。**4.** 安装(门铃、绞链等)。**5.** 拖延(时日);〔美〕使…悬而不决,搁置。**6.** 〔诅咒语〕…该死,让…见鬼去, *Be ~ed! H- you! You be ~ed!* 〔指人〕该死的家伙! *H- it (all)!* 〔指物〕岂有此理! 真可恶! ~ *oneself* 自缢。*I'll be ~ed if I do so*. 〔口〕我死也不会干那种事。~ *a scythe* 安镰刀把。*Never* ~ *a man twice for one offence*. 〔谚〕打了不罚,罚了不打。*be* ~*ed on the neck* 处以绞刑〔审判书用语〕。~ *the picture on the wall* 把图画挂到墙上。~ *the washing out* 把洗的衣服挂到外面。— ***vi*.** **1.** 悬挂,垂吊。**2.** 被吊死,被绞死。**3.** 倾斜;倚靠;凭依。**4.** 突出;使伸出;迫近 (*over*)。**5.** 附着,缠住。**6.** 摇摆,晃动;徘徊;犹豫不决。**7.** (衣服等)随便披着(等)。**8.** 〔口〕和某人厮混 (*with*)。*The picture was ~ing on the wall*. 图画挂在墙上。*Her hair was ~ing down*. 她的头发披散着。~ ***about*** 徘徊,荡来荡去;缠住不放;在附近逗留。~ ***around*** 【美】= ~ *about*. ~ ***back*** 踌躇不前,退缩。~ ***behind*** 落在后面。~ ***by* [*on*, *upon*] *a thread* [*hair*]** 千钧一发,危在旦夕。~ ***by the eyelids*** 系得不牢,易于落下。~ ***by the wall*** 悬挂墙上不用;束之高阁。~ ***down*** 下垂。~ ***fire*** (枪、炮)发火慢;发射不出;(行动、事态发展)延迟;耽误时间;犹豫不决。~ ***heavy on*** 使劳累,使受苦。~ ***in doubt*** 疑惑不决。~ ***in suspense*** 悬而未决。~ ***in the balance* [*wind*]** 安危未定;成败未决。***H- it all!*** 见鬼! 岂有此理! ~ ***it out*** 〔美〕怠工。~ ***loose*** 保持镇静,放松。~ ***off*** **1.** 放。**2.** 挂断电话。**3.** = hang back. ~ ***on* [*upon*]** **1.** 抱[握]住不放。**2.** 坚持下去。**3.** 赖着不走;继续存在。**4.** 倚,靠。**5.** 不挂断电话。**6.** 渴望。**7.** 有赖于,视…而定。**8.** 专心地听。~ ***on by the eyebrows* [*eyelashes*]** 硬着头皮干下去,自找麻烦。~ ***on sb.'s lips* [*words*]** 听得入神;被某人的口才所迷。~ ***on sb.'s sleeve*** 倚赖某人。~ ***on to*** 紧紧握住,坚持下去 (*I'll ~ on to it until I get another job*. 在未找到另外的工作以前,我要坚持干下去)。~ ***out*** **1.** 把上身伸出(窗外)。**2.** 〔俚〕住 (*Where do you ~ out?* 你住在哪里?)。**3.** 挂出门外[窗外]。**4.** 〔美俚〕闲逛。**5.** 拖延。~ ***out for*** 故意拖延以待良机。~ ***out the laundry* [*wash*]** 〔美俚〕空投伞兵。~ ***out the red flag*** 宣战。~ ***out the white flag*** 求降。~ ***over*** **1.** 接近;挂在…上面。**2.** 突出,伸出。**3.** 迫近,临头,威胁,笼罩。**4.** 被遗留。~ ***round*** 〔美〕= ~ about. ~ ***one on*** 〔俚〕**1.** 向…猛击一拳。**2.** 大醉。~ ***the head* (*down*)** (羞得)低下头。~ ***the jury*** 〔美〕因陪审员意见不一而不能作出判决。~ ***the lip*** 撇嘴〔以表示轻蔑等〕。~ ***to*** 缠住,紧粘着。~ ***together*** **1.** 团结一致,齐心协力。**2.** 前后照应,首尾一致 (*If we don't ~ together, we may fail to do anything*. 如果我们不团结一致,我们做什么事都会失败。*His story does not ~ together*. 他的故事前后矛盾)。~ ***up*** **1.** 挂,吊。**2.** 弃置不问;拖延;中止;挂断电话。**3.** 〔美〕抵押;赊账。~ ***up a mark*** 【体】创新记录。~ ***up one's hat in sb.'s house*** 在别人家里久留不走。~ ***up the numbers*** 宣布比赛(尤指赛马)的结果。~ ***upon*** 靠,挨。(***be***) ***hung on*** 〔口〕对…特别感兴趣。(***be***) ***hung over*** 〔美俚〕因宿醉而感觉不舒服的。(***be***) ***hung up* [*on*]** **1.** (因…而)精神不安的。**2.** 对…上瘾的,迷上…的。**3.** 被滞留。**4.** 受挫折。***let* (*things*) *go ~*** 〔口〕没关系。***let it all ~ out*** 〔美黑人俚〕**1.** 让头发披散。**2.** 无牵挂,无顾忌。**II** ***n*.** **1.** 悬挂的样子。**2.** 〔口〕用法,做法,诀窍。**3.** 〔口〕大意,要点。**4.** (动作的)暂停。*the ~ of a machine* 机器的用法。***get* [*see*] *the ~ of*** 摸清底细,懂得…的用法,知道…的诀窍,理解…。***not care a ~*** 〔口〕毫不在乎。**~bird** ***n*.** 【动】悬巢燕雀。**~dog** **1.** ***n*.** 卑鄙的人。**2.** ***a*.** 卑鄙的,下贱的,羞愧的 (*~dog air* [*look*] 卑

躬屈膝的样子,羞愧畏缩的样子)。~**fire** 迟发,滞火。~**glider** (从悬崖等处滑下的)滑翔风筝,风筝状滑翔机。~**-loose** *a*. 不拘礼节的,随便的,散漫的,无所顾忌的。~**man** 绞刑吏,刽子手。~**nail** (手指上的)倒刺。~**out** 〔俚〕(歹徒等的)聚集处,巢穴;经常去的地方;住处。~**-over** 1. 〔美〕残剩物,遗留物。2. 〔俚〕宿醉〔因饮酒过度引起头痛、恶心等〕。~**tag** (商品上的)使用保养说明标签。~ **time** 跳起后滞留空中的时间,滞空时间。~**-up** 〔俚〕1. 障碍。2. 大难题。3. 苦衷,(个人感情上的)疙瘩。~**wire** 炸弹保险丝。

han·gar [ˈhæŋə; ˋhæŋɚ] *n*. 飞机棚,飞机库。*a* ~ *pilot* 〔美俚〕只会胡吹而根本不会驾驶飞机的人。~ **deck** (航空母舰上的)飞机库甲板。

hang·er [ˈhæŋə; ˋhæŋɚ] *n*. 1. 挂东西的人,糊墙的人。2. 吊[挂]着的东西〔尤指挂在皮带上的短剑〕。3. 挂物的东西;挂钩;【机】吊架,吊轴承。4. 绞杀者,绞刑吏。5. 钩状笔划。6. (旧时水手用的)短刀。7. 〔主英〕陡坡上的丛林。8. 〔美〕(挂在店内的)广告牌。~**-on** [ˈhæŋəˈɔn; ˋhæŋɚˋɑn] *n*. (*pl*. ~**s-on** [ˈhæŋəzˈɔn; ˋhæŋɚzˋɑn])食客;随从。

hang·ing [ˈhæŋiŋ; ˋhæŋɪŋ] **I** *n*. 1. 悬挂,悬吊。2. 吊死,绞刑。3. 〔*pl*.〕悬挂物(如帘子,帷帐,壁纸;工作吊架等)。4. 斜坡,倾斜。**II** *a*. 1. 悬垂的,垂下的;悬挂用的。2. 应绞死的。3. 倾斜的,斜坡的。4. 未完的,未定的。5. 垂头丧气的。*a* ~ *affair* [*matter*] 可能导致绞刑的事。*a* ~ *crime* 死罪。*a* ~ *garden* 空中花园。~ **committee** (绘画展览会的)审查委员会。~ **indention** 【印】除第一行外,余皆缩一字排。~ **paper** 裱糊纸。~ **wall** 【矿】上盘,顶板。

hank [hæŋk; hæŋk] *n*. 1. (线、丝等绕成的)圆环,束,绞。2. 一束[一绞]的长度〔棉线为 840 码,毛线为 560 码〕。3. 【海】纵帆前缘上的帆环。4. 优势,控制。*get* [*have*] *a* ~ *on* [*over*, *upon*] *sb*. 控制某人。~ *for* ~ 两船平排着;〔罕〕平等地,同等地。*in a* ~ 在困难中。

hank·er [ˈhæŋkə; ˋhæŋkɚ] *vi*. 切望,热望;追求(*after*; *for*)。**-ing** *n*. **-ing·ly** *ad*.

han·ky [ˈhæŋki; ˋhæŋkɪ] *n*. 〔口〕手帕。

han·ky-pank [ˈhæŋkiˈpæŋk; ˋhæŋkɪˋpæŋk] *n*. (欢庆场合中的)有奖比赛游戏。

kan·ky-pan·ky [ˈhæŋkiˈpæŋki; ˋhæŋkɪˋpæŋkɪ] *n*. 〔口〕1. 幻术,戏法。2. 欺诈,骗术,花招。3. 毫无意义的言行。*be up to some* ~ 有点鬼鬼祟祟。*play* ~ *with sb*. 欺骗某人。

Han·na [ˈhænə; ˋhænə] *n*. 汉纳〔姓氏〕。

Han·nah [ˈhænə; ˋhænə] *n*. 汉纳〔女子名〕。

Han·ni·bal [ˈhænibəl; ˋhænɪbl̩] *n*. 汉尼拔〔247—183 B.C., 迦太基名将〕。**-i·an** *a*.

Ha·noi [hæˈnɔi; hæˋnɔɪ] *n*. 河内〔越南首都〕。

Han·o·ver, Han·no·ver [ˈhænəvə, Ger. haˈnəuvər; haˋnovɚ, Ger. ˋhænovɚ] *n*. 汉诺威〔德国城市〕。*the House of* ~ (英国的)汉诺威王朝〔1714—1901,自乔治一世至维多利亚女王〕。

Han·o·ve·ri·an [ˌhænəuˈviəriən; ˏhænoˋvɪrɪən] *a*., *n*. (英国)汉诺威 (Hanover) 王室的(成员)。

Hans [hænz; hæns] *n*. 汉斯〔男子名, Johannes 的昵称〕。

han·sa, hanse [ˈhænsə, hæns; ˋhænsə, hæns] *n*. 【史】1. 商业同业公会。2. 商业同业私会会费。**the Hanse** 汉萨同盟〔公元十三至十七世纪北欧城市结成的商业、政治同盟〕。

Han·sard [ˈhænsəd; ˋhænsɚd] *n*. 英国议会记录。

Han·sard·ize [ˈhænsədaiz; ˋhænsɚdaɪz] *vt*. 引证议会记录与(某人)对质。

han·se·at·ic [ˌhænsiˈætik; ˏhænsɪˋætɪk] *a*. 1. 商业同业公会的。2. 〔H-〕汉萨同盟的。*the H- League* 汉萨同盟(= the Hanse)。

han·sel [ˈhænsəl; ˋhænsl] *n*., *v*. (〔英〕**-ll-**) = handsel.

Han·sen [ˈhænsn; hænsn̩] *n*. 汉森〔姓氏〕。~**'s disease** 【医】麻风(= leprosy)。

Han·som [ˈhænsəm; ˋhænsəm] *n*. 汉索姆〔姓氏〕。

han·som [ˈhænsəm; ˋhænsəm] *n*. (车夫驾驶台在后的)单马双轮双座马车。

hant, ha'nt [hænt; hænt] *vt*., *vi*., *n*. 〔美方〕= haunt.

han't [heint; hent] 〔口〕= have [has] not.

Hants. = Hampshire〔英国汉普夏郡〕。

Ha·nu·ka, Ha·nuk·kah, Ha·nuk·ka [ˈhɑːnukɑː; ˋhɑnʊkɑ] *n*. 犹太圣节。

han·u·man [ˈhʌnumɑːn, ˈhɑːn-; ˋhʌnʊmæn, ˋhɑn-] *n*. 1. 瘤猴 (*Presbytis entellus*)〔产于东南亚,瘦小,长尾,食叶〕。2. 〔H-〕哈努曼〔印度神话中的猴神〕。

hap [hæp; hæp] **I** *n*. 1. 〔古〕偶然;机会,幸运。2. 〔常 *pl*.〕意外事件。*good* ~ 幸运。*by good* ~ 侥幸。~*s and mishaps of life* 人生的祸福。**II** *vi*. (**-pp-**) 突然发生,偶然发生。

ha·pax le·go·me·non [ˈheipæks liˈgɔːmənɔn; ˋhɑpæks lɪˋgɑmənɑn] (*pl*. **-na** [-nə; -nə]) 〔Gr.〕只用过一次的字句;罕用语。

hap·chance [ˈhæptʃɑːns; ˋhæptʃæns] *n*. 偶然事件(或情况)。

hap·haz·ard [ˌhæpˈhæzəd; ˏhæpˋhæzɚd] **I** *n*. 偶然性,偶然的事;任意性。**II** *a*., *ad*. 偶然的[地],随意的[地];无计划的[地]。*at* [*by*] ~ 偶然地;任意地。**-ly** *ad*. **-ness** *n*.

haph·ta·ra [ˌhɑːftɑːˈrɑː; ˏhɑftɑˋrɑ] *n*. (*pl*. **-ta·roth** [-ˈrəuθ; -ˋroθ]) 哈夫塔拉〔在犹太教安息日和假日做礼拜时念完《摩西五书》后所念的旧约圣经中的先知预言录〕。

hap·less [ˈhæplis; ˋhæplɪs] *a*. 不幸的,倒霉的。**-ly** *ad*. **-ness** *n*.

hapl(o)- *comb*. *f*. 表示"单","简单": *hapl*oid, *haplo*sis.

hap·log·ra·phy [hæpˈlɔgrəfi; hæpˋlɑgrəfɪ] *n*. 重复字母的漏写〔如把 convivial 漏写为 convial〕。

hap·loid [ˈhæplɔid; ˋhæplɔɪd] **I** *a*. 【生】单元体的,单倍体的。**II** *n*. 单倍体。**-ic** *a*. **-y** *n*.

hap·lol·o·gy [hæpˈlɔlədʒi; hæpˋlɑlədʒɪ] *n*. 重复或类似音节的漏读〔如把 interpretative 读作 interpretive〕。

hap·lont [ˈhæplɔnt; ˋhæplɑnt] *n*. 【生】单元体。

hap·lo·sis [hæpˈləusis; hæpˋlosɪs] *n*. 【生】减半作用。

hap·ly [ˈhæpli; ˋhæplɪ] *ad*. 〔古〕1. 偶然地;侥幸地。2. 或许。

ha'·p'orth [ˈheipəθ; ˋhepɚθ] *n*. 〔英口〕= halfpennyworth.

hap·pen [ˈhæpən; ˋhæpən] *vi*. 1. 发生,〔口〕出现。2. 〔后接不定式〕偶然…,碰巧…(*to do*)。*Do you* ~ *to remember his name*? 你还记得他的名字吗? *If anything should* ~ *to me* ... 万一我有不幸…。*It* (*so*) ~*ed that*... 偶然,…碰巧。*No matter what* [*whatever*] ~*s* 不管发生什么事,不管出现什么情况。*as it* ~*s* 碰巧 (*As it* ~*s*, *I have left the book at home*. 偏巧我把书放在家里了)。*be likely to* ~ 可能要发生。~ *in* 〔美〕偶然到…(来)。~ *in with* 偶然和…碰见。~ *on* [*upon*] 偶然看到[碰到、想到]。~ *what may* 无论发生什么事,不管怎样。

hap·pen·chance, hap·pen·stance [ˈhæpəntʃɑːns, ˈhæpənstəns; ˋhæpəntʃæns, ˋhæpənstəns] *n*. 偶然事件。

hap·pen·ing [ˈhæpəniŋ; ˋhæpənɪŋ] **I** *n*. 〔常 *pl*.〕1. 事件,偶然发生的事。2. 即兴表演;临时的演出〔尤指意在激发观众情绪的滑稽表演〕。**II** *a*. 〔口〕(赶)时髦的。

hap·pi(-coat) [ˈhæpi(kəut); ˋhæpɪ(kot)] *n*. (日常穿

的)宽松外衣。

hap·pi·ly [ˈhæpili; ˋhæpəlɪ] ***ad*.** **1.** 幸运地,幸福地。**2.** 快乐地。**3.** 巧合地,适当地。**4.** 〔古〕偶然。

hap·pi·ness [ˈhæpinis; ˋhæpɪnɪs] ***n*.** **1.** 幸福;〔古〕幸运。**2.** 愉快。**3.** (用语等的)适当。*for the ~ of the greatest number* 为了最大多数人的幸福。

hap·py [ˈhæpi; ˋhæpɪ] ***a*.** **1.** 幸福的,幸运的。**2.** 快乐的,愉快的。**3.** 感到满足的。**4.** 巧妙的,恰当的;可喜的。**5.** 〔口〕有点醉意的,飘飘然的;兴奋的。**6.** 〔常用以构成复合词〕喜欢…的;爱用…的,热衷于…的。*a ~ union* 幸福的结合[婚姻]。*He is as ~ as ~ can be.* 他再幸福没有了。*a ~ choice* 恰当的选择。*a ~ event* 可喜的事。*a ~ idea* 好主意,高见。*a ~ translation* 巧译,妙译。*trigger-~* 动不动爱扳枪机的;好斗的。*power-~* 权迷心窍的。*statistic-~* 热衷于统计数字的。***as ~ as the day is long = as ~ as a clam [king, lark]*** 非常幸福,非常快乐。***be ~ in*** (幸好)有…(*I was once ~ in a son.* 我也有过一个男孩子,可是…)。***be ~ in one's expressions*** 妙语如珠,谈笑风生。***be ~ in one's own degeneration*** 自甘堕落。***be ~ together*** (夫妇)和睦相处。***by a ~ chance*** 恰巧,正巧;顺顺当当。***hit [strike] the ~ mean [medium]*** 采取中庸之道,折衷。~**-go-lucky** ***a*.** 听天由命的,无忧无虑的。~ **hunting ground** (印第安人心目中的)天堂。~ **land** 乐土。~ **pill** 〔口〕镇定药,安定药。

Haps·burg [ˈhæpsbəːg; ˋhæpsbɝg] ***n*.** 哈普斯堡皇室〔奥地利皇室(1276—1918),西班牙皇室(1516—1700),神圣罗马帝国皇室(1438—1806)〕。

hap·ten [ˈhæpten; ˋhæptɛn], **hap·tene** [ˈhæptiːn; ˋhæptin] ***n*.** 【生、化】半抗原。**hap·ten·ic** [hæpˈtenik; hæpˋtɛnɪk] ***a*.**

hap·tic(al) [ˈhæptik(əl); ˋhæptɪk(əl)] ***a*.** 触觉的,与触觉有关的;感触的,能触知的。~ **lens** 眼白镜片〔覆盖眼白部分的隐形眼镜〕。

ha·ra-ki·ri [ˈhærəˈkiri; ˋhærəˋkɪrɪ] ***n*.** 〔Jap.〕切腹自杀。

ha·ram [ˈhɛərəm; ˋhɛrəm] ***n*.** = harem.

ha·rangue [həˈræŋ; həˋræŋ] **I** ***n*.** **1.** (对公众集会作的)长篇大论的演说,慷慨激昂的长篇演说。**2.** 高谈阔论;冗长的说教文章。**3.** 叱责,训斥。**II** ***vt*., *vi*.** (向…)作长篇大论的演说;(向…)高谈阔论。

har·ass [ˈhærəs; ˋhærəs] ***vt*.** **1.** 使烦扰,折磨。**2.** 【军】扰乱,骚扰。*be ~ed by anxiety* 过着焦虑不安的苦日子。*be ~ed with debts* 苦于负债。**-able** ***a*.** **-er** ***n*.** **-ing** ***a*.** **-ingly** ***ad*.**

har·ass·ment [ˈhærəsmənt; ˋhærəsmənt] ***n*.** **1.** 折磨,骚扰。**2.** 折磨人的东西;烦恼,忧虑。

har·bin·ger [ˈhɑːbindʒə; ˋhɑrbɪndʒɚ] **I** ***n*.** **1.** 【史】(王室、军队等)派出打前站的人,先行官。**2.** 通报者,先驱。**3.** 预言者,预兆。*The robin is a ~ of spring.* 知更鸟是春天的报信者。**II** ***vt*.** 为…作先驱;预告,预示。

har·bo(u)r [ˈhɑːbə; ˋhɑrbɚ] **I** ***n*.** **1.** 海港,港口;港湾。**2.** 〔喻〕避难所,藏身处。**3.** 【军】坦克掩蔽场。*an air ~* 航空港。*a ~ barge* 码头驳船。*~ installations* 港口设施。*a ~ pilot* 领港员。*a natural ~* 天然港。*an artificial ~* 人工港。*a ~ of refuge* 避难港。***give ~ to*** 窝藏(犯人)。***in ~*** 停泊中。***make ~*** 入港停泊。**II** ***vt*.** **1.** 隐匿,窝藏(罪犯等)。**2.** 怀抱(恶意)。**3.** 包含,聚藏。*~ malice against sb.* 对某人怀有恶意。— ***vi*.** **1.** 躲藏,潜伏。**2.** 停泊。~**age** ***n*.** 停泊处;避难处。~ **dues** 港务费。~ **master** 港务部长。~ **seal** 【动】斑海豹(*Phoca vitulina*)〔产于美国北大西洋沿岸海中〕。**-less** ***a*.** 无港的,无避难处的。

Har·court [ˈhɑːkət; ˋhɑrkət] ***n*.** 哈科特〔姓氏〕。

hard [hɑːd; hɑrd] **I** ***a*.** **1.** 硬的,坚固的 (*opp*. soft)。**2.** (身体)结实的;(组织等)健全的。**3.** (问题、工作等)困难的,费力的;(人)难对付的 (*opp*. easy)。**4.** 难以忍受的;艰辛的。**5.** 激烈的,猛烈的。**6.** (生活)刻苦的。**7.** 严格的,严厉的。**8.** (人等)冷酷的,(天气)严酷的;(雇主等)刻薄的。**9.** (食物等)粗糙的,难吃的;发酸的。**10.** 【语】发硬音的。**11.** (市价等)稳定的。**12.** 确实的,不容怀疑的。**13.** (钱币)金属制的;(币制)可兑换成金子的。**14.** (水等)含无机盐的。**15.** (酒)烈性的,酒精成分高的。**16.** (声音等)刺耳的;(颜色等)刺目的。**17.** 恶性难改的。**18.** 【军】(飞弹)可从地下发射井发射的;设于地下可防核攻击的。*a ~ bed* 硬板床。*a ~ bargain* 苛刻的交易。*~ common sense* 健全的理智。*a ~ customer* 挑剔的顾客。*~ dealing* 虐待。*~ drinker* 酒量大的人。*~ fact* 铁的事实。*a ~ fight* 恶斗,苦战。*~ food* 粗食 (= ~ fare); 固体食物,马料〔指谷类饲料, *cf*. fodder, mash〕。*a ~ knot* 死结。*~ labour* 苦工,苦役。*a ~ life* 困苦的生活。*~ liquor* 〔美〕烈酒。*a ~ saying* 难于理解的话;难于遵行的格言。*a ~ task* 困难的工作。*~ times* 市面萧条,不景气,艰难时世。*~ winter* 严冬。*~ words* 难于入耳的话。*H- words break no bones.* 〔谚〕直言无害。*~ work* 难苦的工作,苦活。***a ~ case*** **1.** 难处理的事件。**2.** 不堪救药的罪犯。**3.** 〔美〕危重病人。~ ***nut to crack*** 难题。***(as) ~ as a bone [brick]*** 极硬。***(as) ~ as iron*** 坚如铁石,很严厉,很残酷。***(as) ~ as nails*** **1.** 结实,强健。**2.** 冷酷无情。***(as) ~ as the nether millstone*** 铁石心肠。***at ~ edge*** 拚命,认真。***be ~ on [upon] sb.*** 虐待某人;使某人难堪。***be ~ up*** 〔口〕短缺,在急需中 (*be ~ up for money* 手头拮据)。~ ***and fast*** **1.** 严格规定的,刻板的,(规则等)一成不变的。**2.** (船)搁浅无法移动的。***have ~ luck*** 倒霉。***have a ~ time (of it)*** 难受,受苦,遭殃。***in ~ condition*** 身体结实。***learn sth. the ~ way*** 通过困难而学到某事。**II** ***ad*.** **1.** 硬。**2.** 拼命地,努力地。**3.** 猛烈地,重重地。**4.** 困难地,不容易地。**5.** 接近地,立即地。**6.** 〔美口〕非常,极。*try ~* 竭力一试。*think ~* 苦思。*drink ~* 暴饮。***be ~ hit*** (感情等)受到沉重打击,很伤心。***be ~ on [upon]*** 接近,紧跟着 (*be ~ on eighty* 快八十岁。*come in ~ upon sb.'s heels* 紧跟着某人进来)。***be ~ pressed*** 被催逼 (*be ~ pressed for money* 手头很紧。*be ~ pressed for time* 时间很紧)。***be ~ put to it*** 正在为难,陷于窘境。***bear ~ on*** 拼命压迫。***follow ~ after*** 紧紧跟着。***go ~ with sb.*** 使某人为难[受苦]。~ ***by*** 在近旁。***H- aport!*** 【海】左满舵! ***H- astarboard!*** 【海】右满舵! ***H- aweather! = H- up!*** 【海】转舵挡风! ***look [gaze, stare] ~ at*** 死瞪着…。***run sb. ~*** 紧追某人。***take sth. ~*** 对某事耿耿于怀。**III** ***n*.** **1.** 〔英〕硬海滩,登陆处。**2.** 〔英俚〕(囚犯的)强迫苦役。*got two years ~* 被判处两年苦役。~ **back** 精装书,硬书皮的书。~ **bake** 〔英〕杏仁糖。~**-baked** ***a*.** 烤得硬的。~**ball** 棒球。~**-ball squash**硬式壁球。~**-bitten** ***a*.** **1.** 咬起来凶狠的。**2.** 受到战争锻炼的,顽强的。~**board** 硬质纤维板。~**-boiled** ***a*.** **1.** (鸡蛋)煮得老的。**2.** (衣服等)浆硬的,挺括的。**3.** 不动感情的,无情的,强硬的。~**-bound** ***a*.** 硬书皮装订的。~ **cash** **1.** 硬币。**2.** 现金。~ **cheese** 〔英俚〕恶运,倒霉。~ **cider** 〔美〕含酒精的苹果汁。~ **chuck** 【海】粗饼干。~ **coal** 硬煤,无烟煤。~ **copper** 冷加工铜。~ **copy** 清稿;复制件。~**-core** ***a*.** **1.** 硬(果)心的,硬(木)髓的。**2.** (作品)低级色情的。~ **core** **1.** (垫路基等的)碎砖石。**2.** (组织或运动中的)斗志最坚定的核心;铁杆分子。~ **court** 硬地网球场。~**cover** ***a*.** (书籍)精装的,硬书皮的。~ **currency** 硬通货〔在国际市场上可兑换的货币,如美金、英镑等〕(*opp*. soft currency)。~ **disk** 【计】硬盘。~**-drawn** ***a*.** 【机】冷拉的,冷抽的。~ **drug** 〔口〕成瘾毒品,麻醉品〔指一切能使人上瘾的和极有害于身心的毒品,如海洛因或古柯碱〕。~**-earned** ***a*.** 辛辛苦苦得到的;凭血汗挣得的。~**-faced**, ~**-favo(u)red**, ~**-featured** ***a*.** 面貌严厉的,其貌不扬的。~ **facing** 表面淬火,表面硬化。~ **finish** 墙上的油漆。

~**fisted** ***a***. 双手坚硬有力的;吝啬的;强硬的。~**goods** ***n***.〔*pl*.〕经久耐用品〔如汽车、家具等。亦作 ~-goods〕。~**-grained** ***a***. 木理细密的,坚硬的;(性格)固执的。~**hack** 绒毛绣线菊(= steeplebush)。~**-handed** ***a***. 双手牢靠有力的;用高压手段的。~ **hat** **1**. (建筑工人戴的)保护帽。**2**. 建筑工人。**3**. 持保守观点的建筑工程人员。**4**. 真保守假激进的政客,形左实右派。~**head** ***n***. **1**. 精明而讲究实际的人。**2**. 傻瓜。**3**. 头上多刺和多骨头的鱼〔尤指锯鲉、步鱼等〕。~**head sponge** 加勒比海粗纤维海绵〔产于加勒比海地区〕。~**-headed** ***a***. 冷静的;讲究实际的;精明的;顽固的。~**-hearted** ***a***. 无情的,冷酷的。~ **labo(u)r** (囚犯的)强迫苦役。~**-land** ***vi***., ***vt***. (使飞行器)硬着陆。~ **landing**〔喻〕(经济的)硬着陆。~**-line** ***n***., ***a***. 强硬路线(的)(*take a* ~*-line on sth*. 就某事采取强硬路线)。~**-liner** 主张强硬路线的人。~ **lines**〔英〕运气不好。~**-lying money**【英海军】潜艇服役官兵的额外津贴。~ **maple** 糖槭,糖枫 (= sugar maple)。~ **money**〔美〕硬资金,合法政治资金,合法竞选资金。~**-mouthed** ***a***. (马等)难以驾驭的;顽固的,倔强的。~**-nosed** ***a***. **1**. (狗等)嗅觉不灵的。**2**.〔美〕顽固的;丑陋的。**3**. 精明实际的。**4**. 坚持的。~**-of-hearing** ***a***. 耳背,有点聋。~ **oscillation** 强振荡。~ **palate**【解】硬腭。~**pan**〔美〕硬质地层,硬地;坚固的基础;隐藏着的真情 (*get down to the* ~*pan of a question* 把问题彻底弄清楚)。~ **pencil** 硬铅笔。~ **rock** 剧烈摇滚乐。~ **rubber** 硬橡皮,硬质胶。~ **sauce** 甜奶油汁。~ **science** 硬科学,自然科学。~**scrabble** ***a***. 辛苦劳动才能勉强维持生活的。~ **sell** 积极推销。~**-sell** ***a***. 积极推销的。~**-set** ***a***. **1**. 窘迫的。**2**. 安放牢固的。**3**. 坚硬的;坚决的;顽固的。**4**. (鸡蛋)将要孵化的。**5**. (人)空腹的。~ **shadow** 清晰的影子。~**-shell(ed)** ***a***. **1**. 硬壳的。**2**.〔美俚〕坚持己见的,不妥协的,顽固的。~ **shower** 穿透射流,硬射流。~ **site** 地下场,地下设施。~**-spun** ***a***. (纱线的)紧拈的。~**stand** 停机坪;停车场。~**-surface** ***vt***. 在…上铺硬质路面。~ **surfacing** 表面硬化。~ **swearing**〔婉〕赌咒发誓〔指道貌岸然地作伪证〕。~**tack** ***n***. 硬饼干。~**tail** 骡子。~ **tap** 出渣口凝结。~ **ticket** 预定的坐位。~ **top** 金属顶盖式汽车。~**-top** **1**. ***n***. 有硬质路面的地区〔道路〕。**2**. ***vt***. 给…铺硬质路面。~ **tube** 高真空电子管。~**-up** ***a***.〔口〕缺少;急需 (*I'm very* ~*-up just now*. 我现在手头很紧。*be* ~ *-up for sth. to say* 想不出该说什么话)。~**ware**〔集合词〕**1**. 五金器具;金属制品。**2**. (计算机的)硬件;(电子仪器的)零件,部件;(飞弹的)构件;机器;计算机。**3**. 电化教学设备〔指录音机、电唱机、闭路电视等〕。**4**. (军队或警察的)武器装备;〔英俚〕重武器。~**wareman** 五金商人;五金工人。~**-wearing** ***a***. (衣料等)耐穿的。~ **wheat** 硬粒小麦,硬质小麦。~**-wired** ***a***.【计】直接接在计算机上的(线路或元件)。~**-won** 辛苦得来的 (*a* ~*-won victory* 来之不易的胜利)。~**wood** ***n***., ***a***. 硬木(的),硬树木(的)(~*wood trees* 阔叶树〔*cf*. coniferous trees〕)。~**-worked** ***a***. **1**. 累透的。**2**. 陈腐的。~**working** ***a***. 勤勉的,努力工作的。~**-wrought** ***a***. 冷锻的。~ **X-rays** 高透力 X 射线。~ **zone** 硬化区。

hard·en [ˈhɑːdn; ˋhardn] ***vt***. **1**. 使坚固,使变硬。**2**. 使锻炼得坚强;使果断。**3**. 使变冷酷;使顽固。**4**. (把飞弹基地等用水泥等加固或设在地下)使不受爆炸〔热幅射〕之害。*a* ~*ed heart* 冷酷的心。~*(ed) steel* 淬火钢。*a* ~*ed offender* 惯犯。— ***vi***. **1**. 变硬,凝固。**2**. 变强硬;变果断。**3**. 变严厉;变冷酷。**4**. (意见等)坚定;(行情等)看涨。~ ***off*** 使(幼苗)受冷而变得耐寒。**-ed** ***a***. **1**. 变硬的,已定型的。**2**. (飞弹等)有地下发射井的,可从地下发射的。

Hard·en [ˈhɑːdn; ˋhardn̩] ***n***. 哈登〔姓氏〕。

hard·en·a·bil·i·ty [ˌhɑːdənəˈbiliti; ˏhardənəˋbɪlətɪ] ***n***. 可硬化性;可硬化度;【冶】可淬性。

hard·en·er [ˈhɑːdənə; ˋhardənɚ] ***n***. **1**. 锻工;锻件。**2**. 硬化剂。

hard·en·ing [ˈhɑːdəniŋ; ˋhardnɪŋ] ***n***. **1**. 硬化;【冶】淬火。**2**. 硬化剂。*air* ~ 气冷硬化。*case* ~ 表面硬化。~ *by cooling* 冷却硬化。~ *by hammering* 锤击硬化。~ *process* 硬化法。*the* ~ *of arteries* 动脉硬化。~ ***through***【机】淬透。

har·di·hood [ˈhɑːdihud; ˋhardɪhʊd] ***n***. **1**. 大胆;刚毅。**2**. 狂妄,傲慢。**3**. 健壮。

har·di·ly [ˈhɑːdili; ˋhardəlɪ] ***ad***. 大胆地;狂妄自大地。

har·di·ness [ˈhɑːdinis; ˋhardɪnɪs] ***n***. **1**. 强壮,结实;抗性,耐性。**2**. 大胆;勇气;傲慢。*winter* ~ 耐寒性。

Har·ding [ˈhɑːdiŋ; ˋhardɪŋ] ***n***. **1**. 哈丁〔哈定〕〔姓氏〕。**2**. **Warren** ~ 沃伦·哈定〔1865—1923,美国第二十九任总统(1921—1923)〕。

hard·ly [ˈhɑːdli; ˋhardlɪ] ***ad***. **1**. 几乎不,简直不。**2**. 不十分,才,仅。**3**. 严厉地,粗鲁地;苛刻地。**4**. 使劲地,拼命地;辛辛苦苦地。*It's* ~ *true*. 这不像是真的。*He will* ~ *come*. 他不大会来。*I need* ~ *say*. 几乎不必说。*He is* ~ *old enough*. 他稍微年轻了一点。*The battle was* ~ *contested*. 这场仗打得很凶。*live* ~ 日子过得苦。~ *earned* 苦挣来的;〔谑〕便便当当得来的。***deal*** ~ ***with*** 虐待。~ ***any*** 几乎没有。~ ***anybody*** [***anything***, ***anywhere***] 简直没有什么人[什么东西,什么地方](*I gain* ~ *anything*. 我几乎没得到什么)。~ ***ever*** 很少。~ ***...*** ***when*** [***before***] 一…就…,刚…就 (*She had* ~ *reached there when it began to rain*. 她刚到那儿就下雨了)。***think*** [***speak***] ~ ***of*** 把…想得[说得]很坏。

hard·ness [ˈhɑːdnis; ˋhardnɪs] ***n***. **1**. 坚固。**2**. 冷酷无情。**3**. 苛刻。**4**. 困难。**5**. 硬性;硬度。**6**. 飞弹基地防核攻击的能力。*wear* ~ 抗磨力。

hards [hɑːdz; hardz] ***n***.〔*pl*.〕麻屑,毛屑〔*cf*. noil, *flocks and* ~ 纤维屑〔塞缝隙用〕。

hard·ship [ˈhɑːdˌʃip; ˋhardˌʃɪp] ***n***. **1**. 艰难,困苦;辛酸,苦难。**2**. 压制,虐待。*bear* ~ *without complaint* 任劳任怨。*undergo* [*go through*] *all kinds of* ~*s* 备尝辛酸。

har·dy[1] [ˈhɑːdi; ˋhardɪ] ***a***. **1**. 强壮的,能吃苦的,耐劳的。**2**. 大胆的,勇敢的。**3**. 鲁莽的;蛮干的。**4**. (植物)耐寒的。*half* ~【园艺】冬季须防霜雪的。***the*** ~ ***annual*** 耐寒的一年生植物;〔谑〕(议会、报纸)每年提出的老问题。

har·dy[2] [ˈhɑːdi; ˋhardɪ] ***n***. (锻工用的)一种方柄凿。~ *hole* 铁砧插模孔。

Har·dy [ˈhɑːdi; ˋhardɪ] ***n***. **1**. 哈迪〔哈代〕〔姓氏〕。**2**. **Thomas** ~ 汤马斯·哈代〔1840—1928,英国小说家〕。

hare [hɛə; hɛr] **I** ***n***. (*pl*. ~*s*,〔集合词〕~) **1**. 野兔。**2**. 怪人,傻瓜。**3**.〔英俚〕坐车不买票的人。***as mad as a March*** ~ 疯狂得像三月(交尾期)里的野兔。~ ***and hounds*** 兔子与猎犬〔一种儿童游戏,"兔子"在前面撒纸屑跑,"猎犬"在后追逐〕。***First catch your*** ~ (***and then cook him***).〔谚〕先捕兔后烹调;勿谋之过早。***hold*** [***run***] ***with the*** ~ ***and run*** [***hunt***] ***with the hounds*** 两面讨好。***hunt*** [***run***] ***the wrong*** ~ 估计错误,错怪人。***make a*** ~ ***of sb***. 愚弄某人。***start a*** ~ 在讨论中提出枝节问题。**II** ***vi***. 飞跑。~ *away* 逃走,逃跑。~ *off*〔英口〕跑开。~**bell**【植】钓钟柳。~**-brained** ***a***. 轻率的,浮躁的。~**-hearted** ***a***. 胆小的。~**lip** ***n***. 兔唇,豁嘴。

har·em [ˈhɛərem; ˋhɛrəm] ***n***. **1**. (伊斯兰教国家的)闺房,后宫。**2**.〔集合词〕妻妾婢女等的总称。**3**.【动】〔集合词〕(与一只雄兽配偶和聚居的)一群雌兽。

har·i·cot [ˈhærikəu; ˋhɛrɪˏko] ***n***. **1**.〔主英〕扁豆(= bean)。**2**. 浓味羊肉炖蔬菜。

hark [hɑːk; hark] ***vi***.〔主要用于祈使句〕听。*H-* (*ye*)! 听! *H- away* [*off*, *forward*]!〔命令猎犬〕去! —

〔古〕听。~ ***after*** 追随。~ ***back*** (猎狗)循原路重找嗅迹;回到原处,回到本题(*He ~ed back to the subject*. 他回到了本题)。~ ***to*** [***at***]〔口〕听(*Just ~ to* [*at*] *him*! 听他说!)。

ark·en [ˈhɑːkən; ˋharkən] ***vi***. 侧耳倾听(*to*),给予注意。

arl, harle [hɑːl; harl] ***n***. 羽毛上的细毛。

Har·lem [ˈhɑːləm; ˋharləm] ***n***. 哈莱姆〔美国纽约市的一个区,居民大都为黑人〕。**-ite** ***n***. 哈莱姆人。

ar·le·quin [ˈhɑːlikwin; ˋharlıkwın] **I** ***n***. **1**. (英国哑剧或意大利喜剧中)头戴面具和身穿各种颜色衣服的角色。**2**. 丑角;滑稽角色。**3**. 五颜六色。**II** ***a***. 滑稽的,五颜六色的。~ **bug**【动】菜蝽蟓〔一种食白菜等的昆虫〕。~ **snake**【动】珊斑蛇〔美洲的一种珊瑚色的蛇〕。

ar·le·quin·ade [ˌhɑːlikwiˈneid;ˏharlıkwınˋed] ***n***. (哑剧中)丑角出场的一幕,以丑角为主的戏;滑稽表演。

Har·ley [ˈhɑːli; ˋharlı] ***n***. 哈利〔姓氏,男子名〕。~ **Street** [ˈhɑːli striːt; ˋharlı strit] (伦敦的)哈利街〔多名医居住〕。

ar·lot [ˈhɑːlət; ˋharlət] **I** ***n***. 妓女,娼妓。**II** ***a***. 娼妓的,卖淫的。

ar·lot·ry [ˈhɑːlətri; ˋharlətrı] ***n***. **1**. 卖淫。**2**.〔集合词〕妓女。

Har·low [ˈhɑːləu; ˋharlo] ***n***. 哈洛〔男子名〕。

arm [hɑːm; harm] **I** ***n***. 损害,伤害;危害。*no ~ done* 没有人受伤,一切平安无事。*There is no ~ in trying*. 不妨试试。*mean* [*think*] *no ~* 并没有恶意。***come to ~*** 遭不幸,受害。***do sb***. ~ = ***do*** ~ (***to***) ***sb***. 损害某人。***do no*** ~ 无害。***keep out of ~'s way*** 保持安全,避免损伤。***Harm set, ~ get***. = ***Harm watch, ~ catch***.〔谚〕害人终害己。**II** ***vt***. 损害,伤害,危害。

ar·mat·tan [ˌhɑːməˈtæn, hɑːˈmætən; ˏharməˋtæn, harˈmætən] ***n***. (每年11月至次年3月由非洲内陆吹向大西洋海岸的)燥风,哈马丹风。

arm·ful [ˈhɑːmful; ˋharmful] ***a***. 有害的。**-ly** ***ad***. **-ness** ***n***.

arm·less [ˈhɑːmlis; ˋharmlıs] ***a***. **1**. 无害的;没有恶意的。**2**. 没有受到伤害的。(*as*) ~ *as a dove* 温和得像鸽子。*escape* ~ 安全逃脱。**-ly** ***ad***. **-ness** ***n***.

ar·mon·ic [hɑːˈmɔnik; harˋmanık] **I** ***n***. **1**.【乐】泛音;和声。**2**. [*pl*.]【数】谐函数,调和函数。**3**.【物】谐波,谐音。**II** ***a***. **1**. 和睦的,融洽的。**2**.【数】调和的。**3**.【乐】和声的,悦耳的。**4**.【物】谐波的。~ **analysis**【物】傅里叶级数学;【数】调和分〔解〕析,调波分析。~ **function**【数】调和函数。~ **interval**【乐】音程。~ **mean**【数】调和平均(值),调和中项。~ **motion**【物】谐运动。~ **oscillator**【电】谐(波)振(荡)器。~ **progression** [**series**]【数】谐级数,调和级数。~ **tone**【乐】泛音。**-ical** ***a***. **-i·cal·ly** ***ad***.

ar·mon·i·ca [hɑːˈmɔnikə; harˋmanıkə] ***n***. **1**.【乐】口琴(= mouth organ)。**2**. 玻璃键琴(= musical glasses)。**3**. 一种打击乐器。

ar·mon·i·cal [hɑːˈmɔnikəl; harˋmanıkl̩] ***a***. = harmonic.

r·mon·i·con [hɑːˈmɔnikən; harˋmanıkən] ***n***. **1**. harmonica 的单数。**2**. = orchestrion.

r·mon·ics [hɑːˈmɔniks; harˋmanıks] ***n***.【乐】和声学。

r·mo·ni·ous [hɑːˈməunjəs, -niəs; harˋmonıəs] ***a***. **1**. 悦耳的。**2**. 和谐的;融洽的;和睦的。**3**. 调和的,相称的。*a ~ family* 和睦的家庭。**-ly** ***ad***. **-ness** ***n***.

r·mo·nist [ˈhɑːmənist; ˋharmənıst] ***n***. **1**. 和声学家,作曲家;演奏者。**2**. 诗人。**3**. 使和谐协调者,调停者。**4**.【宗】福音书的对照研究者。

r·mo·ni·um [hɑːˈməunjəm; harˋmonıəm] ***n***. 小风琴。

r·mo·ni·za·tion [ˌhɑːmənaiˈzeiʃən; ˏharmənaıˈzeʃən] ***n***. 调和,一致。

har·mo·nize [ˈhɑːmənaiz; ˋharmənˏaız] ***vt***. **1**. 使调和,使一致;使和睦,调停。**2**.【乐】给(曲调等)配和声。— ***vi***. **1**. 调和;融洽(*with*);相称(*with*)。**2**. 成为谐调。~ *in feeling* 感情融洽。**-r** ***n***. 使和谐协调的人。

har·mo·nom·e·ter [ˌhɑːməˈnɔmitə; ˏharməˋnamıtə] ***n***. 和声计,和声表。

har·mo·ny [ˈhɑːməni; ˋharmənı] ***n***. **1**. 调和;融洽;适应。**2**.【乐】谐调,和声(学)。**3**.【宗】四福音对照书。***be in ~ with*** 与…协调一致。***be out of ~ with*** 与…不协调一致。***live in ~*** 和睦相处。

Harms·worth [ˈhɑːmzwə(ː)θ; ˋharmzwəθ] ***n***. 哈姆斯沃斯〔姓氏〕。

har·ness [ˈhɑːnis; ˋharnıs] **I** ***n***. **1**. 马具,挽具。**2**.〔古〕甲胄,铠甲。**3**. 跳伞员、摩托驾驶员的全套衣帽装备。**4**.【纺】综绕;(提花机上的)通丝。**5**.〔美俚〕警察制服;工作装备。***die in ~ = die with ~ on one's back*** 在工作中死去,殉职。***get back into ~*** 重新回去工作。***in double ~*** 已婚的。***in ~*** 做日常工作;受约束。***single ~***〔谑〕光棍生活。***work*** [***run***] ***in double ~*** (两匹马或牛)同时拉车;两人合作;(夫妇)双双工作。**II** ***vt***. **1**. 给…套上马具[轭具];使做固定的工作。**2**. 利用(瀑布、风等),治理。**3**.〔古〕给…穿铠甲。~ *a waterfall* 利用瀑布作动力。~ **bull**, ~ **cop**, ~ **dick**〔美俚〕穿制服的警察,外勤巡警。~ **hitch** 攀踏结〔绳结的一种〕。~ **horse** **1**. 挽马。**2**. (赛马中)拖两轮车比赛的马。~ **race** 挽车赛马〔快马或蹓蹄马拖着单人二轮马车的跑马赛〕。**-er** ***n***. **-less** ***a***. **-like** ***a***.

Har·old [ˈhærəld; ˋhærəld] ***n***. 哈洛德〔男子名〕。

harp [hɑːp; harp] **I** ***n***. **1**. 竖琴。**2**. 竖琴状的东西。**3**. [the H-]【天】天琴座。**4**.〔美俚〕爱尔兰人。***hang one's ~*** [***~s***] ***on the willows*** 乐极生悲。**II** ***vi***. **1**. 弹竖琴。**2**. 唠叨地反复讲(*on*; *upon*)。~ ***on the same string*** 老调重弹。~ ***on one's troubles*** 唠唠叨叨地诉苦。~ **antenna**【无】扇形天线。**-less** ***a***. **-like** ***a***.

harp·er [ˈhɑːpə; ˋharpə] ***n***. 弹竖琴的人,竖琴师。

Har·per [ˈhɑːpə; ˋharpə] ***n***. 哈珀〔姓氏〕。

harp·ings, harp·ins [ˈhɑːpiŋz, -inz; ˋharpıŋz, -ınz] ***n***. *pl*. 船首部外侧腰板;造船用的临时牵条。

harp·ist [ˈhɑːpist; ˋharpıst] ***n***. = harper.

har·poon [hɑːˈpuːn; harˋpun] **I** ***n***. (捕鲸等的)鱼叉,标枪。**II** ***vt***. 用鱼叉叉(鲸鱼)。~ **gun** 捕鲸炮,发射鱼叉的炮。

harp·si·chord [ˈhɑːpsikɔːd; ˋharpsıˏkɔrd] ***n***.【乐】大键琴〔钢琴的前身〕。**-ist** ***n***. 奏大键琴者。

har·py [ˈhɑːpi; ˋharpı] ***n***. **1**. [H-]【希、罗神】鸟身女怪。**2**. 残忍贪婪的人。**3**. 恶妇人。~ **eagle** (中、南美的)角鹰。

har·que·bus [ˈhɑːkwibəs; ˋharkwıbəs] ***n***. (旧时的)火绳枪。

har·ri·dan [ˈhæridən; ˋhærıdən] ***n***. 凶恶的老妇;鬼婆,丑婆。

har·ri·er[1] [ˈhæriə; ˋhærıə] ***n***. **1**. 猎兔狗。**2**. [*pl*.]〔集合词〕打猎队中的猎人和猎狗。**3**. 越野赛跑者。

har·ri·er[2] [ˈhæriə; ˋhærıə] ***n***. **1**. 侵略者,掠夺者;蹂躏者。**2**. 鹞〔一种捕食昆虫和小动物的鹰〕。**3**. [H-](英国生产的)鹞式飞机。

Har·ri·et(t), Har·ri·ot [ˈhæriət; ˋhærıət] ***n***. 哈丽特〔女子名, Henrietta 的异体〕。

Har·ri·man [ˈhærimən; ˋhærımən] ***n***. 哈里曼〔姓氏〕。

Har·(r)ing·ton [ˈhæriŋtən; ˋhærıŋtən] ***n***. 哈灵顿〔姓氏〕。

Har·ris [ˈhæris; ˋhærıs] ***n***. 哈里斯〔姓氏〕。

Har·ri·s(s)on [ˈhærisn; ˋhærısn̩] ***n***. 哈里森〔姓氏〕。

Har·ris tweed [ˈhæris twiːd; ˋhærıs twid] (苏格兰哈利斯地区产的)一种手织呢;哈利斯牌呢。

Har·rod [ˈhærəd; ˋhærəd] ***n***. 哈罗德〔姓氏〕。

Har·ro·vi·an [həˈrəuvjən; həˋrovıən] **I** ***a***. 哈罗 (Harrow) 的,哈罗公学的。II *n*. 哈罗居民;哈罗公学学生〔毕业生〕。

har·row[1] [ˈhærəu; ˋhæro] I *n*. 耙。***under the*** ~ 1. (田等)耙过的。2. 在困苦中,为难。II *vt*. 1. 用耙耙(地)。2. 弄伤,抓伤。3. 使苦恼,折磨。~ (*up*) *a field* 耙地松土。~ (*up*) *one's feelings* 伤感情。— *vi*. (地)被耙松。**-er** *n*.

har·row[2] [ˈhærəu; ˋhæro] *vt*. 〔古〕掠夺,抢劫。**-ment** *n*.

Har·row [ˈhærəu; ˋhæro] *n*. 1. 哈罗〔英国伦敦西北面的一个市镇〕。2. 哈罗公学〔培养英国上层阶级子弟的一所中学 = ~ School〕。

har·row·ing [ˈhærəuiŋ; ˋhæroɪŋ] *a*. 悲惨的,折磨人的。**-ly** *ad*.

har·rumph [həˈrʌmf; həˋrʌmf] I *vi*. 1. 作赫噜声〔清清嗓子的声音,尤指故意大声地清嗓子〕。2. 提抗议;埋怨。II *n*. 清嗓子的动作〔赫噜声〕。

har·ry [ˈhæri; ˋhærɪ] *vt*. (*-ried*; *-ry·ing*) 1. 掠夺,蹂躏。2. 折磨,使苦恼。3. 驱走。— *vi*. 作骚扰性的攻击,掠夺。

Har·ry [ˈhæri; ˋhærɪ] *n*. 1. 哈里〔男子名,Henry 的昵称〕。2. 恶魔,恶鬼〔常说作 old H-〕。3. 胡闹的青年人;伦敦佬〔常略作 'Arry〕。***by the Lord*** ~ 一定。***play old*** ~ ***with*** 使混乱。

harsh [hɑːʃ; hɑrʃ] *a*. 1. 粗糙的;荒芜的,不毛的。2. (表情等)生硬的;(声音)刺耳的;刺目的。3. 严厉的,苛刻的。*a* ~ *climate* 恶劣的气候。*a* ~ *cloth* 粗布。*a* ~ *contrast* 不调和的对照。~ *land* 荒芜的土地。~ *to the taste* 味涩。**-ly** *ad*. **-ness** *n*.

hars·let [ˈhɑːslit; ˋhɑrslɪt] *n*. = haslet.

hart [hɑːt; hɑrt] *n*. (*pl*. ~*s*, 〔集合词〕~) 公鹿〔尤指五岁以上的雄赤鹿〕。*a* ~ *of grease* 〔古〕(正好宰食的)壮鹿。*a* ~ *of ten* 有十枝角的公鹿。

Hart(e) [hɑːt; hɑrt] *n*. 哈特〔姓氏〕。

hart(e)·beest [ˈhɑːt(i)biːst; ˋhɑrt(ɪ)ˏbist] *n*. 【动】(南非)狷羚。

Hart·ford [ˈhɑːtfəd; ˋhɑrtfɚd] *n*. 哈特福德〔美国城市〕。

Hart·mann [ˈhɑːtmən; ˋhɑrtmən] *n*. 哈特曼〔姓氏〕。

harts·horn [ˈhɑːtshɔːn; ˋhɑrtsˏhɔrn] *n*. 1. 鹿角;鹿茸。2. 〔俗〕氨水;阿摩尼亚 (= spirit of ~) 〔因早先用作嗅盐的碳酸铵从鹿角炼取〕。

hart's-tongue [ˈhɑːtstʌŋ; ˋhɑrtsˏtʌŋ] *n*. 【植】1. 荷叶蕨。2. 水龙骨科的一种植物。

har·um-scar·um [ˈhɛərəm ˈskɛərəm; ˋhɛrəm ˋskɛrəm] I *a*. 轻率的,莽撞的。II *ad*. 轻率地,莽撞地。III *n*. 冒失鬼;轻举妄动。

ha·rus·pex [həˈrʌspeks; həˋrʌspɛks] *n*. (*pl*. *-pi·ces* [-pisiːz; -pɪsiz]) (古代罗马根据祭神牺牲的肠进行占卜的)肠卜师。

Harv. = Harvard.

Har·vard [ˈhɑːvəd; ˋhɑrvɚd] *n*. 1. (美国)哈佛大学 (= ~ University)。2. 哈佛大学学生〔毕业生〕。~ **man** 哈佛大学毕业生。

har·vest [ˈhɑːvist; ˋhɑrvɪst] *n*. 1. 收获,收割。2. 收获物;产量,收成。3. 收获期。4. 结果;报酬。*abundant* [*bumper*, *good*, *rich*] ~*s* 丰收。*bad* [*poor*] ~ 歉收。~ *festival* 收获节。*a peak* ~ 最高产量。*reap the* ~ *of one's diligence* 勤有功,勤勉获成果。***make a long*** ~ ***for*** [***about***] ***a little corn*** 小题大做。***owe sb. a day in the*** ~ 受某人的恩惠。II *vt*. 1. 收获(谷物等);在…收割;获得(成果等)。2. 定时杀死(受保护的野生动物)以保持生态平衡。— *vi*. 收获,收割。~ **bug** 【动】恙螨。~ **fly** 〔美〕蝉,秋蝉(= cicada)。~ **home** 1. 收割完毕。2. 庆祝收获完成的节日。3. 收获完成时唱的歌。~ **louse** = ~ bug. ~**-man** 1. 收割庄稼的人;收获季节的帮工。2. 【动】盲蛛。~ **mite** 恙螨,沙蚤(= chigger)。~ **month** 收割月〔九月〕。~ **moon** 秋分前后的满月。~ **mouse** (*pl*. ~ ***mice***) (构巢于谷草中的)欧洲田鼠。~ **tick** = ~ bug.

har·vest·er [ˈhɑːvistə; ˋhɑrvɪstɚ] *n*. 1. 收获者,收割庄稼的人。2. 收割机。~ **thresher** 自动收割脱粒机。

Har·vey [ˈhɑːvi; ˋhɑrvɪ] *n*. 1. 哈维〔姓氏,男子名〕。2. **William** ~ 威廉·哈维〔1578—1657,英国医生,解剖学家、血液循环的发现者〕。

has [强 hæz, 弱 həz, əz, z; 强 hæz, 弱 həz, əz, z] have 的第三人称单数、现在式。

has-been [ˈhæzbin; ˋhæzbɪn] I *n*. 〔口〕曾经时兴的东西;会风流一时的人物。*It is better to be a* ~ *than a never-was*. 〔谚〕宁可昙花一现,不能默默无闻。II *a*. 〔口〕过时的,从前的。

ha·sen·pfef·fer [ˈhɑːzenfefə; ˋhɑzənˏfɛfɚ] *n*. 〔G.〕泡汁炖兔肉。

hash [hæʃ; hæʃ] I *n*. 1. 切碎的食物〔尤指肉丁和洋葱丁〕。2. 拼凑起来的东西;大杂烩。3. 重申,复述,推敲。4. 〔Scot.〕傻瓜。5. 〔美俚〕传闻。6. 〔美俚〕麻醉品。***make a*** ~ ***of*** 〔口〕弄糟。***settle sb.'s*** ~ 使某人服贴;使某人哑口无言;收拾某人。II *vt*. 1. 切细。2. 弄糟。3. 反复推敲。~ ***out*** 〔美口〕长时间讨论后解决。~ ***over*** 〔俚〕重新考虑;详细讨论,长时间讨论。~**head** 〔美俚〕吸毒者。~ **house** 〔美俚〕廉价小餐馆。~**ing** 犬兔追逐游戏〔为世界各地英国侨民所喜爱,游戏时跑在前面的人沿途撒下纸片、粉剂等,大批人尾随其后跟踪追赶〕。~ **mark** 军役袖章,军役袖章上的斜条。~**-slinger** 〔美俚〕(小餐馆的)服务员。~**-up** 〔俚〕改写的作品。

hash·eesh, hash·ish [ˈhæʃiːʃ; ˋhæʃiʃ] *n*. 海吸希〔印度大麻制成的麻醉品〕。

hash·er [ˈhæʃə; ˋhæʃɚ] *n*. 1. 〔美俚〕侍者。2. 厨师,厨师下手。

hash·er·y [ˈhæʃəri; ˋhæʃərɪ] *n*. 〔美俚〕廉价小餐馆。

Has·i·dim [ˈhæsidim, Heb. hɑːˈsiːdim; ˋhæsɪdɪm, Heb. hɑˋsidɪm] *n*. 〔*pl*.〕(*sing*. ***Has·id*** [ˈhæsid, ˈhɑːsid; ˋhæsɪd, ˋhɑsɪd]) 【宗】虔敬派信徒〔犹太神秘主义的一个教派〕。**Ha·sid·ic** [-ˈsidik; -ˋsɪdɪk] *a*. **Has·i·dism** *n*. 【宗】虔敬派。

has·let [ˈheizlit; ˋhezlɪt] *n*. (猪和其他动物的)内脏。

has·n't [ˈhæznt; ˋhæznt] = has not.

hasp [hɑːsp; hæsp] I *n*. 1. 搭扣。2. 【纺】(亚麻或黄麻的)纱绞〔长度为 3,600 码〕。II *vt*. 用搭扣扣上。

has·sel [ˈhæsəl; ˋhæsəl] *n*. = hassle (*n*.)

has·sium [ˈhæsiəm; ˋhæsɪəm] *n*. 【化】𬭶〔第 108 号元素〕。

has·sle [ˈhæsl; ˋhæsl] *n*. 〔口〕激烈争论,争吵。

has·sl·ing [ˈhæsliŋ; ˋhæslɪŋ] *n*. 口角,争吵。

has·sock [ˈhæsək; ˋhæsək] *n*. 1. 蟠团,膝垫。2. 草丛。3. 〔美俚〕(棒球的)垒〔尤指本垒〕。

hast [强 hæst, 弱 həst, əst, st; 强 hæst, 弱 həst, əst, st] 〔诗、古〕have 的第二人称单数现在式〔与 thou 连用〕。

has·ta la vis·ta [ˈɑːstɑː lɑ ˈviːstɑ; ˋɑstɑ lɑ vistɑ] 〔Sp.〕再见! (= See you again!)。

hasta lue·go [ˈɑːstɑː ˈlwegəu; ˋɑstɑ ˋlwɛgo] 〔Sp.〕再见! (= See you later!)。

hasta ma·ña·na [ˈɑːstɑː mɑːˈnjɑːnɑː; ˋɑstɑ mɑˋnjɑnɑ] 〔Sp.〕再见! 明天见! (= See you tomorrow!)。

has·tate [ˈhæsteit; ˋhæstet] *a*. 【植】(叶子)戟状的。

haste [heist; hest] I *n*. 1. 急速,紧迫,仓促。2. 轻率。*Fool's* ~ *is no speed*. 〔谚〕傻瓜紧张,白忙一场。*Marry in* ~ *and repent at leisure*. 〔谚〕草率结婚事后悔恨。*More* ~, *less* [*worse*] *speed*. 〔谚〕欲速则不达。*H- makes waste*. 〔谚〕忙乱易错。***in*** ~ 急忙地;仓促地。***in hot*** ~ 火急。***make*** ~ 赶紧。***make*** ~ ***slowly*** 慢慢快起来,开头别太快。***make*** ~ ***to*** [***and***] (*do sth*.) 赶快(做某事)。II *vi*. 赶紧,匆忙。~ *away* 赶快走掉。— *vt*. 〔古〕使快,催促。

H

has·ten [ˈheisn; ˋhesn] *vt*. 1. 使加紧,催促。2. 促进。— *vi*. 赶紧,赶快。~ *home* 急忙回家。~ *to sb.'s assistance* 赶去救助某人。~ *to the destination* 赶到目的地去。~ *to the scene* 赶到现场。

hast·i·ly [ˈheistili; ˋhestəlɪ] *ad*. 急速地;轻率地,慌忙地。

hast·i·ness [ˈheistinis; ˋhestɪnɪs] *n*. 急速,轻率,慌忙。

Has·tings [ˈheistiŋz; ˋhestɪŋz] *n*. 1. 黑斯廷斯〔姓氏〕。2. 海斯汀斯〔英国地名〕。**Battle of ~** 海斯汀斯战役〔诺曼第的威廉击败英王哈罗德二世的一战〕。

hast·y [ˈheisti; ˋhestɪ] *a*. 1. 急速的。2. 性急的,急躁的。3. 仓促的;轻率的。*a ~ conclusion* 草率的结论。~ **pudding** 〔美〕玉米粥;〔英〕面糊,麦片糊。

hat [hæt; hæt] **I** *n*. 1. 帽子〔一般是指有边的〕,礼帽。2. 红衣主教的红帽;红衣主教的职权[地位]。*bowler ~* 礼帽。*cocked ~* 卷边三角帽;折成三角的信。*gipsy ~* 妇女、儿童戴的宽边帽。*leaf ~* 斗笠。*matinee ~* 看日场戏戴的普通女帽;避免在剧院妨碍别人视线的特制女帽。*red* [*scarlet*] ~ 红衣主教的帽子;红衣主教。*silk* [*stovepipe, tall*] ~ 大礼帽。*His ~ covers his family*. 他是光棍一条。***as black as one's ~*** 纯黑的。***at the drop of a* [*the*] ~** 〔美〕立即,毫不犹豫地。***bad ~*** 〔俚〕坏蛋,卑鄙的人。***be in a* [*the*] ~** 进退两难。***bet one's ~*** 孤注一掷。***black ~*** 〔澳俚〕新来的移民。***by this ~*** 〔口〕我拿一切担保! 千真万确! 毫无疑问。***get into the ~*** 进退两难。***go round with the ~ = make the ~ go round*** 募捐。***hang one's ~ on sb***. 依靠某人。***hang up one's ~ in sb.'s house*** 在别人家里久留不走,长期居住。~ ***in hand*** 卑躬屈节,必恭必敬(*A man's ~ in hand never did him any harm*. 对人恭敬于己无害)。~***s off to sb***. 钦佩某人。***have a brick in one's ~*** 〔俚〕喝醉。***knock into a cocked ~*** 打得不成样子,驳得体无完肤。***I'll bet a ~***. 保证没错。***I'll eat my* [*old Rowley's*] ~**. 我决不,一定不会。***My ~***! 〔俚〕啊呀! 嘿! ***my ~ to a halfpenny! = by this ~***! ***pass* [*send*] *round the ~*** 募捐。***raise* [*take off*] *one's* [*the*] ~ *to*** 向…脱帽致敬。***talk through one's ~*** 〔俚〕说大话,吹牛。***throw* [*have, toss*] *one's ~ in the ring*** 准备加入比赛[竞选、战斗]。***touch one's ~ to*** 碰帽边向…致敬。***under one's ~*** 〔口〕秘密的。**II** *vt*. (*-tt-*) 〔口〕给…戴上帽子。~**band** 帽圈〔指帽边上的一圈丝带〕。~**block** 帽型。~**box** *n*. 帽盒。~**-in-hand** *a*. 对人恭敬的,卑躬的。~ **money** 【海】(货主送给船长的)酬金。~**peg** 供挂帽用的钉。~**pin** *n*. 妇女帽针。~**rack** 1. 帽架。2. 瘦弱的动物。~ **rail** (贴上的)帽挂。~**stand** (可移动的)帽架。~ **tree** 衣帽架。~ **trick** 1. 用帽子变的魔术。2. 巧妙的一着。3. (在板球、足球等运动中)一人进三球或连得三分。

hat·a·ble [ˈheitəbl; ˋhetəbl̩] *a*. = hateable.

hatch[1] [hætʃ; hætʃ] **I** *vt*. 1. 孵化,孵。2. 创造,使发生。3. 图谋,策划。~ *chickens* 孵小鸡。~ *a plot* 搞阴谋。~ *a theory* 创立理论。***Don't count the chickens before they are ~ed***. 〔谚〕蛋尚未孵别数鸡,别太指望没有把握之事。— *vi*. (蛋)孵化;(小鸡)出壳。~ ***out*** 想出计划,结果变成。~ ***up*** 〔美〕发明,设计,计划。*Five chickens ~ed yesterday*. 昨天孵出了五只小鸡。**II** *n*. 1. (小鸡等的)一窝。2. 孵化。~***es, catches, matches and dispatches*** 〔谑〕(报纸上的)出生、订婚、结婚及死亡栏。

hatch[2] [hætʃ; hætʃ] *n*. 1. 【船】入孔,升降孔,舱口;舱口盖。2. (大门上的)便门,小门,短门。3. (水闸的)闸门;鱼栏。*an escape ~* 应急出口。***a booby ~*** 〔美俚〕囚车,监牢;疯人院。***down the ~*** 一饮而尽,干杯。***under ~es*** 1. 【海】受禁闭。2. 在困苦中,受压制。3. 死。~**way** 【海】舱口,升降口。

hatch[3] [hætʃ; hætʃ] **I** *vt*. 在…上画影线。**II** *n*. 影线〔表示阴影的细密平行线条〕。

hatch·el [ˈhætʃəl; ˋhætʃəl] **I** *n*. 【纺】梳麻针排。**II** *vt*. (〔英〕*-ll-*) (用梳麻针排)梳理。

hatch·er [ˈhætʃə; ˋhætʃɚ] *n*. 1. 孵卵的动物。2. 孵卵器。3. 阴谋家。

hatch·er·y [ˈhætʃəri; ˋhætʃərɪ] *n*. 1. (特指鱼和家禽的)孵卵处。2. 大型幼猪养殖场。

hatch·et [ˈhætʃit; ˋhætʃɪt] *n*. 短柄小斧。***bury the ~*** 休战,媾和。***dig* [*take*] *up the ~*** 宣战,开战。***throw* [*fling, sling*] *the ~*** 吹牛。***throw the helves after the ~*** 1. 连受损失。2. 完全放弃。3. 一不做二不休,绝望挣扎。~ **face** 尖脸;面孔瘦削的人。~ **job** 〔口〕人身攻击;恶毒诽谤。~ **man** 〔口〕1. 被雇用的刺客,打手。2. 走卒,走狗。3. 〔美俚〕破坏他人〔尤指竞选人〕名誉的作家[演说者等]。**-try** *n*. 大刀阔斧的削减。

hatch·ing [ˈhætʃiŋ; ˋhætʃɪŋ] *n*. 【机】(制图)晕滃,影线。

hatch·ment [ˈhætʃmənt; ˋhætʃmənt] *n*. (挂在死者门前或墓前的)丧徽。

hate [heit; het] **I** *n*. 怨恨;嫌恶。**II** *vt*. 1. 恨,憎恶。2. 嫌。3. 〔口〕不愿,不喜欢。~ *sb.'s guts* 〔美俚〕恨透某人。~ *the sight of* 讨厌看到。*I ~ troubling* [*to trouble*] *you*. 我真不想打扰你。~ **crime** 出于仇视心理的犯罪行为。~**monger** 煽动仇恨者〔尤指对少数民族煽动仇恨者〕。

hate·a·ble [ˈheitəbl; ˋhetəbl̩] *a*. 可恨的,讨厌的,该受怨恨的。

hate·ful [ˈheitful; ˋhetfʊl] *a*. 可恨的,讨厌的;〔罕〕表示敌意的。**-ly** *ad*. **-ness** *n*.

hate·less [ˈheitlis; ˋhetlɪs] *a*. 不憎恨的;不讨厌的。

hat·er [ˈheitə; ˋhetɚ] *n*. 怀恨者。

hat·ful [ˈhætful; ˋhætfʊl] *n*. 一帽子的容量,许多。

hath [强 hæθ, 弱 həθ, əθ; 强 hæθ, 弱 həθ, əθ] 〔古〕have 的第三人称单数现在式。

Hath·or [ˈhæθɔː; ˋhæθɔr] *n*. (埃及神话中牛头人身的)司爱情及欢乐的女神,爱神。~ **column** 【建】(柱头雕有牛头人身像的)爱神柱。**-ic** *a*. 爱神的;【建】爱神柱的。

hat·less [ˈhætlis; ˋhætlɪs] *a*. 不戴帽子的。

ha·tred [ˈheitrid; ˋhetrɪd] *n*. 仇恨,憎恨,憎恶,敌意,恶意。***have a ~ for* [*of*]** 憎恶…。***in ~ of*** 憎恨。

hat·ter[1] [ˈhætə; ˋhætɚ] *n*. 制[修]帽人;帽商。***as mad as a ~*** 〔口〕疯狂,发狂;大怒〔原为 as mad as an atter〕。

hat·ter[2] [ˈhætə; ˋhætɚ] *n*. 〔澳〕隐居者。

hat·ti [ˈhæti; ˋhætɪ], ***hat·ti·she·rif*** [ˈhætiʃeˈriːf; ˋhætɪʃɛˋrif] *n*. 〔Turk.〕(旧时由土耳其皇帝颁布的不可更改的)敕命。

Hat·tie [ˈhæti; ˋhætɪ] *n*. 哈蒂〔女子名, Harriet(t) 的昵称〕。

hat·ting [ˈhætiŋ; ˋhætɪŋ] *n*. 1. 制帽,制帽法[业]。2. 制帽材料。3. 脱帽礼。

Hat·ty [ˈhæti; ˋhætɪ] *n*. 海蒂〔女子名, Harriet, Harriot 的爱称〕。

hau·ber·geon [ˈhɔːbədʒən; ˋhɔbɚdʒən] *n*. habergeon 的废体。

hau·berk [ˈhɔːbəːk; ˋhɔbɚk] *n*. (中古时代的)锁子甲。

haugh [hɔː, hɑːx, hɑːf; hɔ, hɑx, hɑf] *n*. 〔Scot.〕河边冲积地。

haugh·ty [ˈhɔːti; ˋhɔtɪ] *a*. 1. 傲慢的,骄傲的。2. 〔古〕崇高的,高贵的。**-ti·ly** *ad*. **-ti·ness** *n*.

haul [hɔːl; hɔl] **I** *vt*. 1. (用力)曳,牵,拖。2. 拖运。3. 使降落,降(旗) (*down*)。4. 【海】使(船)改变航向。5. 硬拖,硬拉,把(某人)押交法庭等处盘问[审讯];拘捕。~ *a boat* 拖船。~ *coal* (用车等)装运煤。~ *timber* 拖运木材。— *vi*. 1. 曳,牵,拉 (*at; upon*)。2. (船、风)改变方向。3. 〔喻〕改变主意。~ ***down one's flag* [*colours*]** 屈服,投降。~ ***in*** 拉进。~ ***in with*** 【海】使船靠近。~ ***off*** 1. 改变船的航行以躲避某物。2. 退却,撤退。3. 〔口〕打人前先缩回手臂。~ ***on* [*to, upon*] *the wind***

= ~ *the wind*【海】抢风驶船。~ *over the coals* 申斥,谴责。~ *round*【海】风向逐渐改变;因避危险而迂回航行。~ *up* 1. 船迎风行驶。2. 拖上来。3. 停止。~ *sb*. *up*〔口〕责问某人。**II** *n*. 1. 拖,拉,强曳。2. 拖运;拖运量;拖运路程。3. 一网打得的鱼,捕获物。*long* ~*s by water* 长距离水路运输。*make*〔*get*〕*a fine*〔*good*〕~ 打了一大网鱼;捞了一笔。~ **back** 拉回,拉线。~**ing winch** 绞车,绞盘。

haul·a·bout [ˈhɔːləbaut; ˋhɔləbaʊt] *n*. (供)煤船。

haul·age [ˈhɔːlidʒ; ˋhɔlɪdʒ] *n*. 1. 拖曳;拖运。2. 牵引量;牵引力。3. 拖运费。~ *business* 搬运业。~ *motor* (电)机车。~ *rope* 拖缆。*the road* ~ *industry* 公路货运业。

haul·er [ˈhɔːlə; ˋhɔlɚ] *n*. 〔美〕= haulier.

haul·ier [hɔːljə, -liə; ˋhɔljɚ, -lɪɚ] *n*. 〔英〕1. 拖运者;运输工。2. 货物承运人。3. 拉线。4. 绞车,起重机。

haulm [hɔːm; hɔm] *n*. 1. 麦秸,稻草,豆秸。2. 苫屋顶用的干草。3. (草等的)一枝茎,一秆。

haul·yard [ˈhɔːljed; ˋhɔljɚd] *n*. = halyard.

haunch [hɔːntʃ; hɔntʃ] *n*. 〔常 *pl*.〕1. (人的)腿臀部。2. (动物的)腰腿。3.【建】拱腋,梁腋,柱帽。*squat on one's* ~*es* 蹲着。

haunt [hɔːnt; hɔnt] **I** *vt*. 1. 常去,常到(某地);缠住(某人)。2. (鬼魂等)反复出没于,缠住(某人)。3. (思想等)萦绕;(疾病等)缠(身)。*be* ~*ed by fears* 老是提心吊胆。~ *one*〔*one's memory*〕牵回脑际。*The house is said to be* ~*ed*. 据说这屋有鬼。— *vi*. 1. 经常出没,逗留。2. (鬼魂等)作祟。**II** *n*. 1. 常到的地方;(动物等的)栖息处;(罪犯等的)巢穴。2. 〔方〕幽灵,鬼。*the* ~*s of one's schooldays* 学生时代常去的地方。*a* ~ *of fashion* 讲时髦的地方。*busy* ~*s of men* 人群熙攘的地方。*the* ~*s of criminals* 罪犯的巢穴。*the* ~*s of vice and crime* 罪恶的渊薮。**-er** *n*. 常到的人;常出现的鬼。

haunt·ed [ˈhɔːntid; ˋhɔntɪd] *a*. 1. 闹鬼的,鬼魂经常出没的。2. 反复出现的。3. 令人烦恼的。

haunt·ing [ˈhɔːntiŋ; ˋhɔntɪŋ] *a*. 萦绕心头的,无法甩脱的。*the* ~ *music* 难以忘怀的音乐。**-ly** *ad*.

Haupt·mann [ˈhauptmaːn; ˋhauptmɑn], **Gerhart** 霍普曼〔1862—1946,德国剧作家,小说家,诗人〕。

Hau·sa, Hau·ssa [ˈhausə; ˋhausə] *n*. (*pl*. ~(*s*)) 1. (非洲)豪萨人;〔the ~〕豪萨族。2. 豪萨语。

hau·sen [ˈhauzn, ˈhɔːzn; ˋhauzn̩, ˋhɔzn̩] *n*. 〔G.〕= beluga.

haus·tel·lum [hɔːsˈteləm; hɔsˋtɛləm] *n*. (*pl*. **-tel·la** [-ə; -ə])【动】吸喙〔蝇口器〕。**haus·tel·late** [-it, ˈhɔːstileit; -ɪt, ˋhɔstɪlet] *a*.

haus·to·ri·um [hɔːsˈtɔːriəm; hɔsˋtorɪəm] *n*. (*pl*. **-ri·a** [-ə; -ə])【植】吸器。**haus·to·rial** [-əl; -əl] *a*.

haut·bois [ˈhəubɔi; ˋhobɔɪ] *n*. (*pl*. ~ [ˈhəubɔiz; ˋhobɔɪz]) = hautboy.

haut·boy [ˈhəubɔi; ˋhobɔɪ] *n*. 1.【乐】双簧管(= oboe)。2.【植】麝香草莓。

haute cou·ture [əut kuˈtjuːr; ot kuˋtjur]〔F.〕1. 妇女时装设计师,妇女时装大师设计制作的服装。2. 妇女时装新式样。

haute cui·sine [əut kwiːˈziːn; ˏot kwiˋzin]〔F.〕名厨的烹饪;佳肴,名菜;高级料理。

haute é·cole [ˌəut eiˈkɔːl; ˏot eˋkɔl]〔F.〕1. 高超的骑术,花式骑术。2. 马的特技训练法,高级驯马。

hau·teur [əuˈtəː; hoˋtɝ] *n*. 〔F.〕傲慢。

haut goût [həu ˈguː; ho ˋgu] *n*. 〔F.〕1. 芳香,香味;〔喻〕风味。2. 强烈的气味;调味很浓的菜。3. 臭气。

haut monde [əu ˈmɔ̃ːnd; o ˋmɔ̃nd]〔F.〕上流社会。

Ha·van·a, Ha·van·na(h) [həˈvænə; həˋvænə] *n*. 1. 哈瓦那〔古巴首都〕。2. 古巴烟草;用古巴烟草制成的雪茄烟。

have [强 hæv, 弱 həv, əv, v, (在不定式"to"之前) hæf;强 hæv, 弱 həv, əv, v, (在不定式"to"之前) hæf]〔词形变化〕(1)现在式:(*I*, *you*, *we*, *they*) **have** (*he*, *she*, *it*) **has**, 〔口语略作〕**I've**, **you've**, **we've**, **they've**, **he's**, **she's**, **it's**. (2)过去式:(*I*, *you*, *he*, *she*, *it*, *we*, *they*) **had**, 〔省略形〕**I'd**, **you'd**, **he'd**, **she'd**, **we'd**, **they'd**. (3)否定省略形。**haven't**, **hasn't**, **hadn't**. (4)现在分词: **having**. (5)过去分词: **had**. (6)〔古〕现在式:(*thou*) **hast**, (*he*, *she*, *it*) **hath**;过去式:(*thou*) **hadst**. **I** *vt*. 1. 有,持有,具有,含有。*How much money do you* ~? 你有多少钱? *How many days* ~ *May*? 五月有几天? *I had no news of him*. 我没有他的消息。2. 知道,了解,懂得。*She has your idea*. 她了解你的意思。*He has only a little Latin*. 他只懂一点点拉丁文。*You* ~ *me*, ~ *you not*? 晓得了吗,怎么样?〔出自莎士比亚 *Hamlet*〕。*H- you got*〔*Do you* ~〕*any idea where he lives*? 你知道他住在哪里吗? 3. 吃;喝;吸(烟);洗(澡)。*Will you* ~ *a cigarette*? 抽一支烟吧? ~ *some food* 吃点东西。~ *some water* 喝点水。*What will you* ~? 你要吃什么? ~ *a bath* 洗澡。4. 受,拿,取得。*May I* ~ *this one*? 我能拿这个吗? *She's had three letters from her friend*. 她已经收到朋友的三封来信。~ *a lesson* 受教。5. 接受,忍受,容许〔多用于否定句〕。*I won't* ~ *it*. 我受不了。6. 体验;享受;经受,遭受,碰到。~ *a bad headache* 头痛得厉害。*We had a pleasant holiday*. 我们假日玩得很痛快。7. 使[让、叫]某人做某事〔做某事用不带 to 的不定式来表示〕。*H- him come early*. 让他早点来。8. 使[在]某方面出现某状态〔某状态多用过去分词等结构来表示〕。~ *one's hair cut* (请人)理发。*I had my purse stolen*. 我的钱包被人偷掉了。9. 从事,进行;作(某事)。*Shall we* ~ *a swim*? 我们游泳吗? 10. 表明,说,主张。*as Mr. Jones has it* 据琼斯先生所说。11. 〔和带 to 的不定式连用〕必须,不得不。*Man has to eat*. 人要吃饭。12. 显示,表现。~ *no fear* 不怕。~ *the courage to do sth*. 显示出敢做某事的勇气。13. 〔英俚〕欺骗;〔口〕打败,胜过, *I* ~ *been had*. 我受骗了。*You've no reply to that*; *he has you here*. 你对此一言不答,你在这里是认输了。14. 生育。~ *a baby* 生孩子。★ (*a*) 1. 和 2. 义在否定句与疑问句中,在英国通常不用助动词 do, 用 3. — 8. 义造句时通常用 do; 但有时也可用两种构造而意义不变: *Had you*〔*Did you have*〕*any rain during your journey*? 你路上遇到雨吗? 有时意义稍有不同: *H- you time to do it*? 你(现在)有时间做它吗? *Do you* ~ *much time for your work*? 你工作的时间(经常)很多吗? (*b*) 11. 义在否定句与疑问句中,有时可用 do, 有时可不用 do: *H- you to do this*? (= *Must you do this*?) *Do you* ~ *to do this*? 〔美〕你非做这事不可吗? 〔英〕你经常都得做这事吗? (*c*) have + noun 通常等于同一义的动词: ~ *a dance* = *dance* (跳舞); ~ *a dream* = *dream* (做梦); ~ *a drink* = *drink* (喝)。~ *a smoke* = *smoke* (抽烟)。(*d*) 3. 5. 9. 义在翻译时,须变通运用: ~ *a talk* 谈一谈。~ *a try* 试一试。~ *a class* 上课。~ *a meeting* 开会。~ *a game* 玩一盘。~ *hospitable entertainment* 受到厚待。*I won't* ~ *it*. 我(忍)受不了。~ *a cold* 感冒。~ *a fever* 发烧。**II** *v. aux*. 1. 〔现在完成式〕*I* ~〔*I've*〕*written it*. 我把它写完了。*He has*〔*He's*〕*gone*. 他去了。I ~〔*I've*〕*been there*. 我去过那里。*H- you done it*? 你做完那件事了吗? *Yes*, *I* ~. 是,做完了。*No*, *I haven't*. 不,还没有完。*He has not*〔*hasn't*〕*gone there*. 他还没有到那里去。*Hasn't he gone yet*? 他还没去吗? *No*, *he hasn't*. 是,还没去。2. 〔过去完成式〕*I had*〔*I'd*〕*finished my breakfast when he came*. 他来的时候我已经吃过早饭了。*Had he done it*? 他(那时)已经把那事做好了吗? *Yes*, *he had*. 是的,已经做好了。*No*, *he hadn't*. 不,还没有。3. 〔未来完成式〕*I shall* ~ *read it by the time you turn up* tomorrow morning. 你明早来时我就念完了。4.〔表示假设语气〕If it had not been (= Had it not been) for ...要不是因为[幸而有]…。或 Had I (= If I had) only known it, ... 只要我晓得的话…。5.〔与 got 连用,成 have got, 主英口,意为"有"= have〕I've [haven't] got it. 我[没]有。H- you got any? 你有吗? ★(1)与过去分词结合构成完成式;这时 have, has, had 等通常发弱音。(2)英国用完成式的地方,美国则常单用过去式: I just got here (= I ~ just got here). 我刚到。~ **a bad time** 很倒霉。~ **a bun on** 〔美〕喝醉。~ **a good time** 过得快乐。~ **and hold** 【法】保有,永远领有。~ **at** 袭击;谴责。**H- done**! 停止! ~ **everything one's own way** 样样照自己的意思做;为所欲为。~ **had it** 〔俚〕1. 吃够了苦,受到致命打击。2.(人)已过时。3. 无希望,命已注定。~ **it** 1. 胜利。2.〔口〕被打,挨骂。3. 说,主张。(The ayes [noes] ~ it. 赞成[反对]的占多数。Let him ~ it. 让他倒霉去。Rumour has it that ... 有谣言说…;传闻…。He will ~ it that ... 他坚持说,他硬说…)。~ **it (all) over sb**. 胜过某人。~ **it coming** 〔美口〕活该倒霉。~ **it in for sb**. 〔口〕对某人怀有仇恨,想对某人报仇。~ **it on sb**. 〔美〕比(某人)强,胜过(某人)。~ **it out** 达成谅解;解决掉;得出结果。~ **it out of sb**. 对某人报仇;使某人受罚。~ **it out with sb**. 与某人较量以解决争端;与某人决一雌雄;同某人讲明白。~ **much to do with** 与…很有关系,与…有许多共同之处。~ **nothing for it but** 只得,只好;唯有。~ **nothing to do with** 与…毫无关系,与…并无共同之处。~ **on** 1. 穿着;戴着。2. 有事,有约会;计划做。3.〔口〕欺瞒,骗,使人上钩。~ **one's eye on ...** 注意,注视。~ **one's sleep out** 睡够。~ **only to ... to ...** 只要…就能…(You ~ only to go on and then turn right to find the store. 你只要往前走,再向右拐,就能找到那店)。~ **(got) sb. (stone) cold** 〔俚〕击败某人,控制某人。~ **sb. down** 请某人到乡下作客。~ **sb. in** 1. 请某人来家。2. 叫某人来家干活。~ **sb. on toast** 〔英俚〕骗。~ **sb. up** 1. 请某人到城市作客。2. 对某人起诉,控告某人。~ **sth. back** 收回某物,把某物要回去。~ **sth. in** 屋里备有某物。~ **sth. out** 把某物弄出来(~ a tooth out 拔掉一颗牙)。~ **to do with** 同…有关系。**Let sb. ~ it**. 〔俚〕1. 惩罚某人。2. 和某人讲明自己对他的看法。**III** *n*. 1.〔常 pl.〕〔口〕有产者,有钱人;(天然资源多的)富国。2.〔英俚〕欺骗,诈骗。the ~s and the ~-nots 有钱人和穷人;富国和穷国。

have·lock [ˈhævlɔk; ˋhævlɑk] *n*. (垂在帽子后面保护头颈的)遮阳布。

Have·lo(c)k [ˈhævlɔk; ˋhævlɑk] *n*. 哈夫洛克〔姓氏,男子名〕。

ha·ven [ˈheivən; ˋhevən] **I** *n*. 1. 港口;船舶抛锚处。2. 避难所;安息所。**II** *vt*. 1. 把(船)开进港。2. 使(船)避难,为…提供避难场所,掩护。**-er** *n*. 港务长。**-less** *a*. **-ward** *ad*.

have-not [ˈhævnɔt; ˋhævnɑt] *n*. 〔常 pl.〕穷人;穷国。"have-not" power 缺乏天然资源的强国。

have·n't [ˈhævnt; ˋhævnt] = have not.

ha·ver[1] [ˈheivə; ˋhevɚ] **I** *vi*. 〔主英〕1. 胡说八道,唠叨。2. 犹豫不决,摇摆不定。**II** *n*. 〔常 pl.〕〔主 Scot.〕胡说八道,无聊的话。

ha·ver[2] [ˈhævə; ˋhævɚ] *n*. 野生燕麦。

ha·ver[3] [ˈhɑːvə; ˋhɑvɚ] *n*. (pl. **ha·ver·im** [-ˈveirim; -ˋverɪm]) 伙伴;同事。

hav·er·sack [ˈhævəsæk; ˋhævɚsæk] *n*. 行军[旅行]帆布背包;干粮袋。

hav·il·dar [ˈhævildɑː; ˋhævɪldɑr] *n*. (旧时印度兵的)中士。

hav·ing [ˈhæviŋ; ˋhævɪŋ] *n*. 所有;〔pl.〕所有物,财产。

hav·oc [ˈhævək; ˋhævək] **I** *n*. 1. (自然力、暴动等造成的)大破坏,浩劫;蹂躏,摧残。2. 大混乱,大骚动。**cry ~** 预告灾难将临;命令(军队)掳掠破坏;鼓动暴乱。**make ~ of**, **play [raise] ~ among** = work ~ with 对…大肆破坏;使陷入大混乱。**II** *vt*. (**hav·ocked**; **hav·ock·ing**) 严重破坏,使靡烂。— *vi*. 毁灭。

haw[1] [hɔː; hɔ] *n*. 1.【植】山楂;山楂的果实。2.〔古〕篱;围地;花园;墓地。

haw[2] [hɔː; hɔ] *n*. 1. (马、狗等的)第三眼睑,瞬膜。2.〔常 pl.〕瞬膜炎。

haw[3] [hɔː; hɔ] **I** *n*. 支吾声;呃,嗯〔表示踌躇、疑问等〕。**II** *vi*. 说话支支吾吾,发出呃[嗯]声。hem [hum] and ~ 支支吾吾,闪烁其词;嗯嗯呃呃地说。**III** *int*. 呃!〔话顿住时的发声〕。

haw[4] [hɔː; hɔ] **I** *int*. 〔美〕豁!〔吆喝马等向左转声〕。**II** *vt*. 使(马)向左转。— *vi*. (马等)向左转。

Ha·wai·i [hɑːˈwaiiː; hɑˋwaii] *n*. 夏威夷〔美国州名〕。

Ha·wai·ian [hɑːˈwaiiən; hɑˋwaɪɪən] **I** *a*. 夏威夷的;夏威夷人[语]的。the ~ Islands 夏威夷群岛。**II** *n*. 夏威夷人[语]。~ **guitar** 夏威夷吉他。

haw·finch [ˈhɔːfintʃ; ˋhɔfɪntʃ] *n*.【动】(欧、亚洲的)蜡嘴雀(= grosbeak)。

haw-haw [ˈhɔːˈhɔː; ˋhɔˋhɔ] *int*., *n*., *vi*. 啊啊! 哈哈! 哈哈大笑,哄笑 (= ha-ha)。

hawk[1] [hɔːk; hɔk] **I** *n*. 1. 鹰,隼。2. 贪心汉;凶狠的人;骗子。3. (政治上的)鹰派,主战派。doves and ~s 鸽派和鹰派。Hawks will not pick ~s' eyes out. 〔谚〕同类不相残。**know a ~ from a handsaw [her(o)nshaw]** 还算有判断力,还有点见识。**II** *vi*. 1. 放鹰,用鹰打猎。2. (鹰一样地)袭击,猛扑 (at),(鹰一样地)翱翔,盘旋。— *vt*. (像鹰一样地)捕捉,攫取。~**-eyed** *a*. 眼光敏锐的,(像鹰眼那样)明察秋毫的。~ **monitor** [~**-moth**]【动】天蛾。~**-nosed** *a*. 鹰钩鼻的。~**'s-beard**【植】还阳参属 (Crepis) 植物。~**sbill** 玳瑁。~**weed**【植】山柳菊属 (Hieracium) 植物〔包括桔黄山柳菊 (H. aurantiacum)〕。**-like** *a*.

hawk[2] [hɔːk; hɔk] **I** *vi*. 1. 大声清嗓。2. 咳嗽。— *vt*. 咳出。~ up phlegm 把痰咳出来。**II** *n*. 咳痰声,清嗓声。

hawk[3] [hɔːk; hɔk] *vt*. 1. 叫卖兜售。2. 散布(消息等),传播(谣言等)。

hawk[4] [hɔːk; hɔk] *n*. (泥水工用的带柄方形)灰浆板。

Hawk(e) [hɔːk; hɔk] *n*. 霍克〔姓氏〕。

hawk·er[1] [ˈhɔːkə; ˋhɔkɚ] *n*. 1. 放鹰打猎者。2. 驯鹰者。

hawk·er[2] [ˈhɔːkə; ˋhɔkɚ] *n*. 叫卖的商贩,小贩。No ~s! 小贩禁止入内!

Hawk·eye [ˈhɔːkai; ˋhɔkaɪ] *n*. 〔美〕爱荷华 (Iowa) 州的别名;〔pl.〕爱荷华州人。the ~ State 爱荷华州。

hawk·ing [ˈhɔːkiŋ; ˋhɔkɪŋ] *n*. 养鹰术;放鹰术,放鹰打猎术。

Haw·kins [ˈhɔːkinz; ˋhɔkɪnz] *n*. 霍金斯〔姓氏〕。

hawk·ish [ˈhɔːkiʃ; ˋhɔkɪʃ] *a*. 1. 似鹰的,鹰嘴般的。2. (政治上)有鹰派味道的。

hawk·shaw [ˈhɔːkʃɔː; ˋhɔkˏʃɔ] *n*. 〔口〕侦探,密探。

hawse [hɔːz; hɔz] *n*. 1.【海】锚链孔;有锚链孔的船首部份。2. 船首与锚间的水平距离。3. 双锚停泊时锚链的位置。a clear [an open] ~ 顺畅无结的锚链。a foul ~ 缠结不顺的锚链。~ **bag** 锚链孔塞。~**hole** 锚链孔 (come in through [at] the ~hole 水兵出身)。~**-pipe**【船】锚链筒。

haw·ser [ˈhɔːzə; ˋhɔzɚ] *n*.【海】(供系船、下锚用的)粗绳,大索,钢缆。~ **bend** 单索花结〔绳结的一种〕。~**-laid** *a*. 左捻三根三股索的。

haw·thorn [ˈhɔːθɔːn; ˋhɔˏθɔrn] *n*.【植】山楂。

Haw·thorn(e) [ˈhɔːθɔːn; ˋhɔθɔrn] *n*. 1. 霍索恩[霍桑]〔姓氏〕。2. **Nathaniel ~** 纳·霍桑〔1804—1864,美国小说家〕。

hay[1] [hei; he] **I** *n*. 1. 干草;(喂牲畜的)饲草。2. 成果,酬报。3. 小额款项。4.〔美俚〕床。**between [betwixt] grass and ~ [~ and grass]** (成人与儿童之间的)青少

H

年。*hit the* ～〔美俚〕上床睡觉。*look for a needle in a bundle* [*bottle*] *of* ～ 草捆中找针;大海捞针;徒劳无益。*make* ～ *of* 1. 将…割晒成干草。2. 使混乱,弄乱(头发等)(*of*)。*make* ～ *out of* 使对自己有利。*Make* ～ *while the sun shines*.〔谚〕太阳好,就晒草;乘机行事;抓紧时机。*not* ～〔美俚〕为数可观的一笔钱;相当大的数目。*roll in the* ～〔口〕求爱;调情。**II** *vt*. 1. 割晒(干草)。2. 给…喂干草。3. 使成割制干草的草地。— *vi*. 制成干草;割草晒干。～**box** 干草箱〔保温用〕。～-**burner** *n*. 1.〔俚〕马〔尤指第二流的赛马〕。2. 抽大麻的人。～**cock**〔英〕干草堆,(圆锥形)草堆。～ **fever**【医】花粉热,枯草热。～**field** (牧草)打草场。～**fork** 干草叉。～ **knife** 割草刀。～-**loft** 干草棚,秣棚。～**maker** 1. 翻晒干草的人;干草机。2.〔俚〕猛击一拳。～**making** 1. 翻晒干草。2. 对现有机会的利用。～**mow** 1. 干草堆。2. 干草顶棚。～**rack** 1. 干草饲料槽。2. 干草车的装草架;有装草架的大车。～-**rick**〔英〕= ～stack. ～**ride** *n*.〔美〕乘垫有干草的大车郊游。～**seed** 1. 干草种;干草(尘)屑。2.〔美俚〕乡下佬(*He hasn't got the* ～*seed out of his hair yet*. 他才从乡下出来)。～**seed center** (远离大都市的)农村。～**stack** 干草堆。～**wire** 1. *n*.〔美〕捆干草的铁丝,乱铁丝。2. *a*.〔美俚〕疯狂的;混乱的;杂乱无章的;匆忙拼凑成的(*go* ～*wire* 发疯;出故障,出毛病。*The radio went* ～*wire*. 无线电出了毛病)。

hay[2] [hei; he] *n*. 一种乡村舞蹈。

Hay [hei; he] *n*. 海〔姓氏〕。

hay·bag [ˈheibæg; ˋhebæg] *n*.〔俚〕女人,娘儿们。

Hay·dn [ˈhaidn; ˋhaɪdn̩], **Franz Joseph** 海顿〔1732—1809,奥地利作曲家〕。

Hayes [heiz; hez] *n*. 海斯〔姓氏,男子名〕。

Haynes [heinz; henz] *n*. 海恩斯〔姓氏〕。

Hays [heiz; hez] *n*. 海斯〔姓氏〕。

Hay·ti [ˈheiti; ˋhetɪ] *n*. = Haiti.

hay·ward [ˈheiwəd; ˋheˏwɚd] *n*. (教区、村镇、庄园等的)家畜围篱管理员。

Hay·wood [ˈheiwud; ˋhewud] *n*. 海伍德〔姓氏〕。

ha·zan [ˈhɑːzn, hɑˈzɑːn; ˋhɑzn̩, hɑˋzɑn] *n*. (*pl*. *hazan·im* [-ˈzɑːnim; -ˋzɑnɪm])(犹太人教堂)合唱指挥;领唱者(= hazzan)。

haz·ard [ˈhæzəd; ˋhæzɚd] **I** *n*. 1. 碰巧,机会;偶然的事。2. 孤注一掷,冒险。3. 危险;公害;事故,意外。4. (用骰子玩的)游戏[赌博]。5. (网球场中)可得分的开球;【台球】使球触他球后落入袋中的击法;【高尔夫球】障碍地带。6.〔英方〕马车停车场。*health* ～ 对健康的危害。*a losing* ～(台球戏中)打出的球和他球相撞后落入袋中。*at all* ～*s* 不顾一切危险;务必。*at* [*by*] ～ 1. 在危急中。2. 胡乱地,随便地。*at the* ～ *of* 拼着。*a winning* ～ (台球戏中)打出的球和他球相撞后使他球落入袋中。*be on the* ～ 在危险中,受到威胁。*run the* ～ 冒险,冒险一试。**II** *vt*. 1. 使遭受危险。2. 冒…的危险;冒险一试。～ *a guess* 作无把握的揣测。～ *one's life* 冒生命危险。

Haz·ard [ˈhæzəd; ˋhæzɚd] *n*. 哈泽德〔姓氏〕。

haz·ard·ous [ˈhæzədəs; ˋhæzɚdəs] *a*. 1. 危险的,冒险的。2. 凭运气的。～ *chemicals* 危险的化学品。*a* ～ *climb* 冒险的攀登。-**ly** *ad*. -**ness** *n*.

haze[1] [heiz; hez] **I** *n*. 1. 霾,烟雾,霭;朦胧。2. 疑惑;思想糊涂;暧昧。*in a* ～ 在雾中,渺茫(*with one's minds in a* ～ 糊里糊涂地)。*no* ～ *of doubt* 没有怀疑表现。**II** *vt*. 1. 使雾笼罩,使朦胧。2. 使糊涂。— *vi*. 1. 起雾;变朦胧。2. 变糊涂。-**less** *a*.

haze[2] [heiz; hez] *vt*. 1.【海】罚…做苦工,折磨。2.〔美俚〕欺侮,戏弄(大学新生)。3. 骑马放牧[驱赶]。

ha·zel [ˈheizl; ˋhezl] **I** *n*. 1.【植】榛,榛子,榛实,榛木。2. 淡褐色〔尤指眼睛〕。**II** *a*. 1. 榛树的,榛木制的。2. (眼睛等)淡褐色的。～ **hen** [**grouse**] 松鸡(*Tetrastes bonasia*)〔产于欧洲〕。-**ly** *a*. 1. 榛多的。2. 淡褐色的。

ha·zel·nut [ˈheizlnʌt; ˋhezlnʌt] *n*. 榛子。

Haz·litt [ˈheizlit, ˈhæzlit; ˋhezlɪt, ˋhæzlɪt] *n*. 黑兹利特〔姓氏〕。

ha·zy [ˈheizi; ˋhezɪ] *a*. 1. 多烟雾的,烟雾弥漫的。2. 朦胧的,模糊的。3.〔美俚〕喝醉的。**haz·i·ly** [ˈheizili; ˋhezɪlɪ] *ad*. **haz·iness** [ˈheizinis; ˋhezɪnɪs] *n*.

H.B., **HB** = hard black 硬黑〔表示铅笔芯软硬度的符号〕。

H.B.M. = His [Her] Britannic Majesty('s) 英国皇家的。

HBMS = His [Her] Britannic Majesty's Ship 英国皇家海军舰艇。

H-bomb [ˈeitʃbɔm; ˋetʃˏbɑm] *n*. 氢弹(= hydrogen bomb)。

H.C. = 1. high conductivity 高导电性。2. Holy Communion【宗】圣餐。3. House of Commons〔英〕下(议)院。

H.C.F. = Honorary Chaplain to the Forces〔英〕荣誉随军牧师。

h.c.f. = highest common factor 最大公约数,最大公因子。

HD = 1. Harbor Defense 港口防务。2. heavy-duty 关税重的;重型的;经得起损耗的。

hdbk. = handbook.

hdkf. = handkerchief.

hdqrs. = headquarters.

HDTV = high definition television 高清晰度电视。

HE = high explosive 烈性炸药。

He =【化】元素氦(helium)的符号。

H.E. = 1. His Eminence 阁下〔天主教中对红衣主教的尊称,间接提及时用〕。2. His [Her] Excellency 阁下〔间接提及时的尊称〕。

he[1] [常 hiː, 弱 iː, hi, i; 常 hi, 弱 i, hɪ, ɪ] **I** *pro*. (*pl*. *they*)〔人称代名词,第三人称、单数、男性、主格;所有格为 his, 宾格为 him, 物主代名词为 his〕他,那个男人。*He who* [*that*] …者,…的人。*He would*.〔美〕那家伙就可能那样做;那家伙就是那种人〔含有憎厌的意思〕。*He that talks much errs much*.〔谚〕言多必失。**II** *n*. (*pl*. *hes*, *he's* [hiːz; hiz]) 男人;〔口〕雄,公。*Is it a* ～ *or a she*?(婴孩)是男的还是女的?(动物)是公[雄]的还是母[雌]的? ～-**man** (*pl*. -*men*)〔美口〕健美男子;健壮而充满男性气概的人。

he[2] [hiː; hi] *int*. 嘻!〔常重复作 he! he! 表示嘲笑〕。

he[3] [hei; he] *n*. 希伯来文的第五个字母。

he- *comb*. *f*. 表示"雄","公": *he*-goat.

head [hed; hɛd] *n*. 1. 头,头部,首。2. 头脑,才能;智力,想像力,理解力。3. 前部,上部;顶端,尖突部;船长;(书页等的)天头;(桌位的)首席;弹头。4. 首脑,首长,领导。5. 个人,人数;(牲畜的)匹数,头数。6. 条目,项目,头绪;要点;标题。7. (有头像的)硬币正面(*opp*. tail);(有头像的)邮票。8. (河的)源头;(疮、疖等的)脓头。9. (水站等的)蓄水高度,水位差,水头,落差,压力;势头。10. 海角;岬。11. 头状物体;鹿角;【植】顶梢;谷穗;头状花序;头状叶丛。12. 危机;极点,绝顶;结论。13.〔口〕(宿醉引起的)头痛。14. 酒沫,泡沫;〔英〕(浮在牛乳表面的)奶油。15.〔口〕脑袋,生命;嘴。16.〔俚〕(舰船上的)厕所。17.【矿】水平巷道,煤层中开拓的巷道。18.【机】盖,帽。19.【语】中心成份。20.【乐】音符的符头。21.〔俚〕麻醉药品吸食者;主张种植麻醉药品作物者。*a clear* [*cool*] ～ 明智的[冷静的]头脑。*hot* ～ 急性;急性的人。*level* ～ 头脑清醒的人。*strong* ～ 酒量大的人。*wise* ～ 聪明人;自作聪明的人。*a wooden* ～ 笨蛋,木头人。*Two* ～*s are better than one*.〔谚〕集思广益,三个臭皮匠胜过诸葛亮。*the H-*〔俚〕校长。*twopence per* [*a*] ～ 每客两便士。*20* ～ *of cattle* 二十头牛〔单复数相同〕。*crowned* ～(*s*) 君主,国王,王后。

a deer of the first ～ 初生角的鹿。*the* ～ *of a lake* (河流注入处的)湖口。*scare* ～〔美〕醒目的报纸标题。*Shut your* ～! 住口! **a big ～ and little wit** 脑袋大而智力有限。**above the ～s of** (*an audience*) 深奥得使(听众)不能理解。**addle one's ～** 搞得头昏脑胀,绞尽脑汁。**an old ～ on young shoulders** 少年老成。**at the ～ of** 以…为首,在…的前面。**beat sb.'s ～ off** 打得某人头破血流;使某人焦头烂额。**beat [put, get] sth. out of sb.'s ～** 使某人忘记某事;使某人对某事断念 (*Do get this idea out of your* ～. 抛弃这种念头吧)。**be unable to make ～ or tail of sth.** = *make neither* ～ *nor tail of sth.* **Better be the ～ of an ass than the tail of a horse.** 〔谚〕宁为鸡口,毋为牛后。**break Priscian's ～** 犯语法错误。**bring matters to a ～** 使事态陷于危机。**bury one's ～ in one's hands** 用双手抱头(表示痛苦等)。**bury one's ～ in the sand** 闭眼不看眼前的危险,采取驼鸟政策。**buy sth. over sb.'s ～** 比某人出更高的价格抢购某物。(*down*) **by the ～ 1.**【海】船头比船尾吃水深。**2.**〔俚〕稍醉。**by the ～ and ears = by ～ and shoulders 1.** 粗暴地。**2.**(身材、气度)相当高的 (*taller by the* ～ *and shoulders* (身材)高得多);〔喻〕(能力等)高超得多。**carry [hold] one's ～ high** 趾高气扬。**come into [enter] one's ～** 想起,想到。**come to a ～ 1.**(疮、疖等)化脓。**2.**(时机、事件等)成熟;逼近严重关头,达到顶点。**come under the ～ of** 归入…部,属于…项下。**cost sb. his ～** 断送某人性命。**cut [make] shorter by the ～** 砍头。**drag by (the) ～ and ears 1.** 粗鲁地拖。**2.** 勉强扯进 (*drag sb. out by* ～ *and ears* 蛮横地把某人拖出。*drag the anecdote by the* ～ *and ears into one's conversation* 硬把那件趣闻扯进谈话里)。**draw to a ～** = *come to a* ～. **eat one's ～ off 1.**(家畜等)能吃不能做;(人)好吃懒做。**2.** 失业;无所事事。**fling [throw] oneself at sb.'s ～ [at the ～ of sb.]** (女子)勾引某人,接受某人求婚。**from ～ to foot [heel]** 从头到脚,全身;完全。**gather ～ 1.**(疮、疖等)化脓。**2.**(时机、事情等)成熟。**3.**(风等)增强。**get a ～** 醉得第二天还没有醒酒。**get into one's ～** (酒劲)冲上头。**get [take] it into one's ～** 凭空想到,主观认为,硬想。**get [have] swelled [the big] ～** 自以为了不起。**give a ～**〔口〕使头痛,引起头痛。**give ... his [her, its] ～** 放松缰绳;让某人自由行动。**give one's ～ for the washing** 俯首受辱。**go about with one's ～ in the air** 自高自大,摆架子。**go off one's ～, go out of one's ～** 发疯,发狂。**go to one's [the] ～ 1.** 酒劲冲上头。**2.** 使兴奋;使自高自大。**hang [hide] one's ～** (羞愧得)把头垂下。**hang over sb.'s ～** (危险、灾难)临头。**have a good ～ for** 有…的才能。**have a ～**【医】酒后头痛。**have a (good) ～ on one's shoulders** 有见识;有能力。**have a hard ～** 坚定;头脑顽固。**have a ～ like a sieve** 记忆力很差。**have a long ～** 有远见。**have one's ～ in a tar barrel** 〔美〕陷入困境。**have one's ～ screwed on the right way** 头脑清醒,有判断力。～ **and ears** 全身(陷于) (*in*)。～ **and front** 顶点;本质,要点。～ **and shoulders above** 高出一个头,远远超过。～ **first [foremost] 1.** 头朝下,倒栽葱。**2.** 不顾前后,冒冒失失。～ **of hair** 头发 (*He has a red* ～ *of hair*. 他有一头的红头发)。～ **on** 把船头朝前;迎面地。～ **over ears** 深深地陷入。～ **over heels, heels over ～, Heads I win, (and) tails you lose.** 正面我赢,反面你输〔掷钱币打赌时说,意指无论怎样,我不吃亏〕。～**(s) or tail(s)** 你要正面还是反面?〔掷钱币打赌〕**Heads up!**〔口〕注意! 小心! ～ **to ～** 头对头,交头接耳。**hide one's diminished ～** 失势退隐。**keep one's ～** 镇定,不慌不忙。**keep one's ～ above ground** 活着。**keep [hold] one's ～ above water 1.** 未淹没。**2.** 不负债。**knock ～** 叩头。**knock sb. on [in] the ～** 打某人的头部;杀掉某人,消灭某人。**knock sb.'s ～ off** 轻易胜过某人。**knock their ～s together** 强迫争议双方接触和谈;用武力制止两人争吵。**laugh [run, scream] one's ～ off** 狂笑[奔走,呼叫]不已。**lay [put] ～s together** 一起策划;共同商量。**lie** (*the blame*) **on sb.'s ～** 把(过失等)归罪于某人。**lift (up) one's ～** 振作,欣喜。**lose one's ～ 1.** 被砍头,丧命。**2.** 着慌,不知所措。**loss of ～** 水头抑损,(水)位(抑)损。**make ～ 1.** 前进。**2.** 武装反抗。**make ～ against** 抵抗;制止。**make neither ～ nor tail of** 对某事莫名其妙。**make sb.'s ～ sing** 把某人打得头昏耳鸣。**not right in one's [the] ～** 神经失常。**off (out of) one's ～** 过于兴奋;精神失常。**one's ～ is full of bees** 想入非非,异想天开。**on one's [sb.'s] ～ 1.** 倒立着 (*stand facts on their* ～*s* 颠倒黑白)。**2.**〔口〕易如反掌地 (*can do sth. on one's* ～ 做某事不费吹灰之力)。**3.** 是…的责任 (*Be it on your* ～! 那由你负责!)。**open one's ～**〔美俚〕开口,说。**out of one's ～** 精神错乱。**out of one's own ～** 自己想出来的,独出心裁的。**over ～ and ears in debt [love]** 身负重债[深陷爱情中]。**over sb.'s ～ 1.** 出人头地;被晋升至某人之上。**2.** 使人不能理解。**3.** 不同人商量(而越级告状等)。**put a ～ on sb.** 殴打某人;使某人住口。**put one's ～ in [into] a noose** 自己把头套在绞索中,自投罗网。**put one's ～ into the lion's mouth** 轻入险地,冒大险。**put sth. into [out of] one's ～** 使人想起[忘记]某事。**ram sth. into sb.'s ～** 对某人填鸭式地灌输某事。**raw ～ and bloody bones** 骷髅头和交叉骨[死亡的象征];吓唬小孩的妖怪。**run one's ～ against a wall** 碰壁。**scratch one's ～** 搔头皮,对某事迷惑不解。**screw one's ～ on tight** 保持清醒头脑,精明。**show one's ～** 出现,到场。**soft in the ～** 傻里傻气。**stake one's ～ on** 以生命打赌。**stand on one's ～** 为人古怪。**take sth. into one's ～** 突然想起,心血来潮。**take the ～** 领头,执牛耳。**talk sb.'s ～ off** 啰啰嗦嗦,谈得使人生厌。**turn sb.'s ～** 使某人感到骄傲,使某人头脑发热。**turn sth. over in one's ～** 再三思忖,反复考虑。**trouble one's ～ about sth.** 为某事伤脑筋。**turn ～ over heels** 翻斤斗,颠倒,倒转。**use one's ～** 动脑筋。**wash an ass's ～** 徒劳无益。**weak [touched] in the ～** 脑子笨的。**win by a ～** (赛马时)以一个马头的距离获胜。**work one's ～ off** 苦干,不停地工作。**II *vt*. 1.** 站在…的前头,率领;牵头,打破(记录等)。**2.** 阻拦,妨碍;反抗。**3.** 为(箭等)安头;使构成顶部;在…上加标题。**4.** 把头对着;溯(源);〔美〕使(车、船等)向着某处行驶。**5.** 用头顶(球)。**6.** 砍伐(树等的)顶枝;收割(庄稼);切去(鱼)头〔砍去人头用 behead〕。～ *the list* 名列第一。～ *all records* 打破所有记录。～ *a fish* 切掉鱼头。～ *a nail* 制钉头。— ***vi*. 1.** 前进,出发;驶往 (*for*)。**2.**(果实、麦穗等)成头状物,结实,抽穗。**3.**(疮、疖等)出脓头。**4.**(河流等)发源。**be ～ed for** = ～ *for*. ～ **back 1.** 绕至前方。**2.** 阻止。～ **down** 截去树梢,摘心,掐尖。～ **for** 走向,向…方向前进。～ **into**〔美〕开始,着手。～ **off 1.** 上前拦截(车辆、羊群等),使之转变方向或退回。**2.** 阻止某事;使某人不做某事 (*I* ～*ed him off* [*from*] *making a speech*. 我打断了他演说的念头)。～ **the ball** (踢足球时)顶球。～ **up 1.** 指挥,当主管。**2.** 给…加盖子。**III *a*. 1.** 头的,头部的。**2.** 主要的,首席的。～**ache** 头痛;头痛的事 (*cause [give] a* ～*ache* 叫人头痛)。～**achy *a*.** 头痛的,有头痛病的;使人头痛的。～**band 1.** 头带,束发带。**2.** 印在书页顶端的花饰;嵌在书脊上下两端的布片 (～*band receiver* 头戴式耳机)。～**-block**【矿】井口挡车器;柱帽。～**board** 床头板,床头架。～**-butt *vt*.** 用头顶撞。～ **chair** (牙医诊所、理发店等内的)有头靠的椅子。～**cheese** (猪头、脚、舌等做成的)碎肉冻[香肠]。～ **cold** 伤风(感冒)。～ **count** 人口调查。～ **doctor**〔俚〕精神病医生。～**dress** 头巾,头饰;发式。～ **end** (电视)输入端(指电缆电视系统中共用天线的位置)。～ **fast** 船首系索。～**fish**【动】翻车鲀 (=

H

ocean sunfish)。~**frame**【矿】井架。~ **gate**(运河、水渠的)闸门;总闸。~**gear** 头饰,帽子,安全帽;马首挽具。~**-hunt** 1. *vi*.(原始部落人)割取敌人的头作战利品,猎头;〔美口〕物色人材。2. *vt*.〔美口〕物色(人材)。3. *n*.(原始部落民族的)猎头出征;物色人材,"猎头"活动。~**-hunter** 1. 割取敌人的头作战利品的人。2. 物色人材的人。~**-hunting** 1. 挖角,物色人才。2. (原始部落人)割取人头的习俗。~ **kit**〔美俚〕全套吸毒用具。~ **lamp**(汽车等的)前灯;桅灯;(矿工头上的)照明灯。~**land** 1. 岬。2. 地头,畦界。~**light** 1. = ~lamp. 2. (机翼上的)雷达天线。~ **linesman** 足球赛的巡边员。~**lock**【摔跤】用手臂把对方的头擒住。~**long** *ad*., *a*. 1. 头向前地[的];倒栽葱地[的]。2. 急速地[的]。3. 轻率地[的],鲁莽地[的]。4. 〔古〕险峻地[的](*rush ~long into danger* 鲁莽冒险)。~**man** 1. 首领,酋长。2. 工头,领班,组长。3. 刽子手。~**master**〔英〕校长。~**mistress** 女校长。~ **money** 1. 人头税。2. 旧时按斩首或捕获成绩给与的赏金。3. (移民等的)入境税。~**most** *a*. 最前面的,领头的。~**note** (书的)眉批,顶注;批注。~**office** 总社;总店;总局。~**-on** *a*. 迎头的;(冲突等)正面的。~**-page** 扉页。~**phone** 头戴送受话器,耳机。~**piece** *n*. 1. 胄,盔,帽子,头巾。2. 才智。3. 【印】(书的)扉页;(章节开头的)花饰。4. = ~phone. ~**pin**【体】(九柱戏的)前角柱。***pope's*** ~ 长柄扫帚。~ **pressure** 排出压力。~**quarter** 1. *vi*. 设总部。2. *vt*. 在…设总部;把…放在总部中。~**quarters** *n*.〔*sing*., *pl*.〕1. 指挥部,司令部,大本营。2. 总署;总局;总店。3. 当局。~**race** (水车的)引水槽(*opp*. tailrace)。~ **register**(声音的)高音区。~**rest** (牙医诊所,理发店坐椅的)头靠。~**room** *n*.【建】(门口、水渠等的)净空,净空高度。~**sail** 前帆〔船首斜桅三角帆总称〕。~ **sea** 逆浪,顶头浪。~**set** = ~phone. ~**ship** 首领地位,首领的资格[权威]。~ **shop** 1. 时装店。2. 〔俚〕麻醉毒品店。~**shrinker** 1. 割取敌人头颅使其干缩以作战利品者。2. 〔俚〕精神病医生。~ **smut** 黑穗病。~**spring** 水的源头;根源。~**-stand** 三角顶,三角倒立(杂技)。~ **start** (赛跑起跑时的)让步,抢先。~**stall** 马笼头。~**stock** 车头箱,车床头。~**stone** 1. 墓石。2. 【建】墙基石。~**stream**(大河的)源流。~**strong** *a*. 倔强的,任性的,刚愎的。~**s-up** *a*.〔美〕(做事)有信心并且干得很好的。~ **teacher**〔美俚〕公立中、小学校长。~ **tone** 头腔音〔由头腔发出的共鸣声〕。~ **voice**【音】头声。~**waiter** *n*. 侍者领班。~ **wall**【建】山墙。~**waters**〔*pl*.〕河源,水源。~**way** 1. 前进;进展。2. 【海】航行速度;【矿】进展。3. 【建】净空,净空高度〔由地面至拱顶等的空间〕;【交】(同一路线同一方向上两车之间的)时间间隔。~ **wind** 逆风,顶头风。~**word** 1. 章节前的标题;词目。2. 【语法】复合词的主要部分。~**work** 1. 脑力工作;思维。2. 【建】(拱心石上作成动物头等的)拱顶装饰。3. (足球的)头球技术。~**worker** 脑力劳动者。

head·ed [ˈhedid; ˋhɛdɪd] *a*. 1. 有头的,有标题的;(植物等)结成头的。~ *bolt* 有头螺栓。~ *paragraph* 加有标题的段落。2. 〔常用来组成复合词〕有…头的。*a cool-~ businessman* 头脑冷静的实业家。*a round-~ screw* 圆头螺丝。

head·er [ˈhedə; ˋhɛdɚ] *n*. 1. 制造钉头[工具头]的人[机械]。2. 〔口〕刽子手,断头机;割穗机。3. 【机】通水管,通汽管;集管;(锅炉的)联管箱。4. 【建】露头砖,露头石;半端梁搁栅。5. 〔口〕头朝下一跳[跌落]。6. (足球的)头顶球。*take a ~ off a ladder* 从梯子上倒栽下来。

head·ing [ˈhediŋ; ˋhɛdɪŋ] *n*. 1. 标题,题名;题词,信纸上端所印文字。2. 斩首;(鱼)去头;(植物的)打尖,摘心。3. 【建】露头。4. 【矿】平巷,横坑道。5. 【海、空】(罗盘上指示的)航向;方向;磁向。6. (足球的)用头顶球。7. 〔*pl*.〕【矿】精矿,选矿所得重质部分。8. 【植】抽穗。~ **stage** (植物的)抽穗(期)。

head·less [ˈhedlis; ˋhɛdlɪs] *a*. 1. 无头的;割去头的。2. 无人领导的。3. 无头脑的,愚笨的。

head·line [ˈhedlain; ˋhɛd͵laɪn] **I** *n*. 1. (报刊新闻等的)大字标题;(书籍的)页头标题。2. 〔*pl*.〕新闻广播摘要。*banner ~s* 通栏大字标题。***go into ~s*** 被报纸用大字标题登出。***hit*** [***made***] ***the ~s in the press*** 成为报纸的头条新闻。**II** *vt*. 1. 加标题于。2. 大肆宣传。3. 演出中担任(要角)。~**r** *n*. 1. (报馆的)标题编辑。2. (戏单中用大字写出其姓名的)红角,明星。3. 名人;要事,要闻。

heads·man [ˈhedzmən; ˋhɛdzmən] *n*. 1. 刽子手。2. 捕鲸船指挥。3. 【英矿】运煤工。

heads-up [ˈhedzˈʌp; ˋhɛdzˋʌp] *a*. 〔美口〕机灵的,足智多谋的,随机应变的。

head·y [ˈhedi; ˋhɛdɪ] *a*. 1. 顽固的,任性的;猛烈的。2. 轻率的,鲁莽的。3. (酒等)易使人醉的;易使人兴奋的。4. 〔口〕头脑清楚的。**-i·ly** *ad*. **-i·ness** *n*.

heal [hiːl; hil] *vt*. 1. 医治,治愈(病伤等);使恢复健康。2. 使恢复;使和解。*Time ~s most troubles*. 时间会消除烦恼。~ *the war wounds* 医治战争创伤。— *vi*. (病)痊愈,恢复健康。~ *up* [*over*] (伤口)愈合。~**-all** 万灵药,百宝丹。**-able** *a*. 可治愈的。**-er** *n*. 1. 治疗的人〔尤指试图通过祈祷或信仰治病的人〕。2. 治疗物(*Time is a great ~er*. 〔谚〕时间是治疗感情创伤的良药;时间冲淡一切)。

heal·ing [ˈhiːliŋ; ˋhilɪŋ] **I** *a*. 1. 痊愈中的,恢复健康的。2. 医治用的。*a ~ ointment* 药膏。*the ~ art* 医术。**II** *n*. 治疗(法)。**-ly** *ad*.

health [helθ; hɛlθ] *n*. 1. 健康;健康状态;卫生。2. 昌盛,兴旺;生命力。3. (祝健康的)干杯。*H- is better than wealth*. = *Good ~ is above wealth*. 〔谚〕健康胜于财富。*Here is to your ~!* = *To your ~!* 〔敬酒时用语〕祝您健康! *public ~* 公共卫生。*public ~ work* 保健工作。*a ~ centre* [*station*] 保健站。~ *certificate* 健康证明书。*the board of ~* 卫生局[科]。***broken in ~*** 体弱多病。***drink*** (***to***) ***sb.'s ~*** = ***drink a ~ to sb***. 举杯祝某人健康。***in a delicate state of ~*** 〔婉〕有喜,有孕。***in*** (***good***) ***~*** 健康。***in poor ~*** 不健康。***inquire after sb.'s ~*** 问安,问候。***not ... for one's ~*** 为了物质利益,另有目的(*He is not here for his ~*. 他到这里来另有目的)。***out of ~*** = *in poor ~*. ***propose the ~ of sb***. 提议为某人的健康干杯。***recover*** [***resume***] ***one's ~*** 恢复健康。~ **dollar**〔美〕1. 医疗保健经费。2. 作为公共医疗保健经费征收的税金。~ **food** 保健食品,滋补品。~**-giving** *a*. 增进健康的。~**-guard**〔英〕检疫官。~ **physicist** 保健物理学家,辐射防护物理学家。~ **physics** 保健物理学(一门研究辐射对人体的伤害及其防护的学科)。~ **resort** 休养地。~ **salts**【医】轻泻剂。~ **service** 公共医疗事业。~ **spa** 减肥中心。~ **visitor** 巡回医务人员。

health·ful [ˈhelθful; ˋhɛlθfʊl] *a*. 1. 保健的,有益于健康的。2. 健康的,健全的。**-ly** *ad*. **-ness** *n*.

health·y [ˈhelθi; ˋhɛlθɪ] *a*. 1. 健康的,健壮的;有益于健康的。2. 健全的,卫生的。3. 大量的;旺盛的。*a ~ appearance* [*colour*] 健康的脸色。~ *reading for the young people* 有益青年的读物。**-i·ly** *ad*. **-i·ness** *n*.

Hea·ly [ˈhiːli; ˋhilɪ] *n*. 希利〔姓氏〕。

HEAO = high-energy astronomy observatory 高能天文台(收集天文现象的人造卫星)。

heap [hiːp; hip] **I** *n*. 1. (一)堆,堆积。2. 〔口〕许多,大量。3. 〔美俚〕(破旧)汽车;炼焦堆。*go to ~s of places* 到各处。***a ~ of*** = ***~s of*** 许多的,大量的。***a ~ of time*** 许多时间。***be knocked*** [***struck***] ***all of a ~*** 〔口〕一下子被吓倒;慌作一团。***fall all of a ~*** 咕咚地倒下。***~s of time*** 充裕的时间。***~s of times*** 多次,屡次。***in a ~*** = ***in ~s*** 成山,成堆,累累。***top*** [***bottom***] ***of the ~*** 〔口〕获胜者[失败者]。**II** *vt*. 1. 把…堆成一堆,堆积,堆起(*up*; *together*);积累。2. 大量地给,滥给;拼

H

命添加。**3.** 装满,灌满。*a ~ed spoonful* 满满一调羹。*~ insults on sb.* 对某人百般侮辱。*~ praise upon* 大肆宣扬[颂扬]。*~ titles and honours on a conqueror* 对征服者滥给头衔和勋章。**-ing** *a.* 成堆的。

heaps [hiːps; hips] *ad.* 〔口〕非常,极其。*feel ~ better* 感觉好多了。

hear [hiə; hɪr] (**heard** [həːd; hɝd]) *vt.* **1.** 听,听见,听取。**2.** 得知,闻知,听说。**3.** 注意听,倾听;听(课、歌剧等)。**4.** 【法】审问;听(证人)陈述。**5.** 允许;服从,照准。*I heard a loud noise.* 我听见一声巨响。*I heard that he was ill.* 我听说他有病。*He was heard to groan [groaning].* 人家听见他在呻吟。*They are heard to have come over.* 听说他们已经来了。*~ and examine the reports* (*of*) 听取和审查(…的)报告。*~ a case* 审理案件。*~ a boy's lesson* 检查孩子的功课。— *vi.* **1.** 听,听见,听说。**2.** 得知 (*of*; *about*)。**3.** 〔美〕承认。*So I ~.* 听说就是这样。*You will ~ of [about] this.* 等着瞧吧!〔意指这件事还不算完〕。***H- and tremble!*** 好好听着,好好记住! ***~ from*** 得到…的消息,得到…的信 (*I ~ from her now and then.* 我常常收到她的信)。*H-! H-!* 听哪,听哪! 说得好!〔表示赞成,常用作反语〕。***~ of*** 听到…的事,听到…的话。***~ (more) of*** 关于…的事还未结束。***~ say [tell] (of)*** 听人讲起 (*Have you ever heard tell this matter?* 你听人说起过这件事吗?)。***~ sb. out*** 听某人把话讲完。***make oneself heard*** 把意见等说给人听。***never [not] ~ of [to]*** 〔通常与 will 或 would 同用〕不听从,不愿考虑。**-able** *a.* 听得见的,中听的。

heard [həːd; hɝd] hear 的过去式及过去分词。

hear·er [ˈhiərə; ˋhɪrɚ] *n.* 听的人;旁听者。

hear·ing [ˈhiəriŋ; ˋhɪrɪŋ] *n.* **1.** 听(动作或过程)。**2.** 听力,听觉。**3.** 发言机会。**4.** 审问。**5.** 听得见的范围。**6.** 〔美〕意见听取会。*Her ~ is not very well.* 她耳朵不好。*at the ~ of the news* 听到消息以后。***gain [get] a ~*** 获得发言[申诉]机会。***give sb. a (fair) ~*** 让某人申诉。***hard of ~*** 耳朵不灵。***in sb.'s ~*** 在某人听得见的地方。***out of [beyond] ~*** 在听不见的地方。***within ~*** 在听得见的地方。~ **aid** 助听器。~ **examiner**, ~ **officer** 〔美〕(组织意见听取会的)政府特派调查员。

heark·en [ˈhɑːkən; ˋhɑrkən] *vi.* = harken.

Hearn [həːn; hɝn], **Lafcadio** 赫恩〔1850—1904,美国作家,生于希腊,1894 年后定居日本,取名小泉八云(Koizumi Yakumo)〕。

hear·say [ˈhiəsei; ˋhɪrse] *n.*, *a.* 风闻(的),传闻(的),道听途说(的)。*I speak not from ~.* 我可不是根据传闻这样讲的。~ **evidence** 【法】传闻证据〔指证人根据传说提供的证据〕。~ **rule** 【法】传闻证据否定法。

hearse [həːs; hɝs] **I** *n.* **1.** 灵车。**2.** 〔古〕棺架,棺台。**3.** 【天主】条案形蜡烛排架。**II** *vt.* 用灵车装运;埋葬。

Hearst [həːst; hɝst] *n.* 赫斯特〔姓氏〕。~ **Newspaper Group** (美国)赫斯特报系。

hearst·ling [ˈhəːstliŋ; ˋhɝstlɪŋ] *n.* 〔美口〕赫斯特报系的人。

heart [hɑːt; hɑrt] **I** *n.* **1.** 心脏,心。**2.** 胸,胸部;心胸,心地,心肠,胸怀。**3.** 感情,热情,爱情;灵魂;良心。**4.** 勇气,胆力;勇士。**5.** 精神,气质;心境,心情。**6.** 中心,核心;精华,要点,本质。**7.** 意中人,情人;心爱的人,宝贝儿。**8.** 〔主英〕(土地的)肥沃程度。**9.** 心脏形的东西。**10.** 【牌】红桃,红心;〔*pl.*〕一组红桃花样的纸牌;一种设法不拿到红桃的纸牌游戏。*a broken ~* 心碎,绝望。*abundance of the ~* 感情充沛。*athletic [athlete's] ~* 因运动过度所致的心脏肥大。*a big ~* 胸襟宽度,心胸开阔。*a false ~* 居心险诈,虚伪。*a free ~* 胸怀坦白,无忧无虑。*a hard ~* 冷酷,残忍。*a kind [soft, sympathetic, warm] ~* 好心肠,善良的心。*a light ~* 无忧无虑,快乐。*a single ~* 单纯质朴,一心一意。*a stout ~* 勇敢,果敢。*a ~ of flint [stone]* 铁石心肠。*a ~ of gold = a tender ~* 温柔的心肠,好心肠。*The girl is all ~.* 那姑娘很温柔。*a man of ~* 有感情的人。*one's dear [sweet] ~* 情人。*a true ~* 真正的勇士。*an affair of the ~* 恋爱。*Every ~ knows its own bitterness.* 〔谚〕各人苦恼自己知。*Faint ~ never won fair lady.* 〔谚〕胆怯者赢不到美人。*Nothing is impossible to a willing ~.* 〔谚〕有志者事竟成。*The ~ that once truly loves never forgets.* 〔谚〕真正的爱,其情不渝。*What the ~ thinks the tongue speaks.* 〔谚〕言为心声。*When the ~ is afire, some sparks will fly out at the mouth.* 〔谚〕心里有什么,嘴上藏不住;心直口快。***a change of ~*** **1.** 改变主意。**2.** 变心,变节。**3.** 改邪归正;【宗】改宗,皈依。***a ~ of oak*** 刚强的人,果断的人。***after one's (own) ~*** 符合自己的心意,正中下怀。***at ~*** 在感情深处,内心里。***at the bottom of one's ~*** 内心上。***be enthroned in the ~s*** 念念不忘。***be of good ~*** 心情舒畅。***be sick at ~*** **1.** 苦闷,愁苦,悲观。**2.** 〔婉〕厌恶,恶心。***bless my [your] ~*** 我的天哪! 好家伙! ***break sb.'s ~*** 使某人很伤心,使某人悲痛欲绝。***break the ~ of sth.*** 度过最困难的时刻。***bring sth. home to sb.'s ~*** 〔多用被动结构 be brought 或用 come, go 等〕使某事为某人深知,使某事为某人深受感动。***cross one's ~*** 在胸口画十字〔表示说的是真话〕。***cry [weep] one's ~ out*** 痛哭,哭得死去活来。***cut [touch] sb. to the ~*** 触及某人痛处。***do sb.'s ~ good*** 使某人高兴。***devour one's ~ = eat one's ~ out*** 因伤心而消瘦,忧伤过度。***find it in one's ~ to*** (*do*) 〔常用于否定句中〕意欲(做…),忍心(做…) (*She could not find it in her ~ to leave him.* 她不忍心离开他)。***follow the dictates of one's ~*** 按照自己的爱好。***from one's ~ = from the bottom of one's [the] ~*** 自心底,衷心。***gain [have] sb.'s ~*** 取得某人的欢心,获得某人宠爱。***gather ~*** 鼓起勇气,打起精神。***give ~ to sb.*** 鼓励某人。***give one's ~ to sb.*** 爱上某人。***go to sb.'s ~ [the ~]*** 使某人伤心;说中心病。***go to [get to] the ~ of matter*** 抓住要点。***harden sb.'s ~*** 使某人心肠变硬。***have a ~*** 〔口〕发发慈悲,做做好事。***have a soft [warm] spot in one's ~ for sb.*** 爱上某人。***have sth. at ~*** 把某事放在心上,对某事深切关心。***have no ~*** (*to do sth.*) 不想,无意于。***have one's ~ in*** 专心一意。***have [bring] one's ~ in one's mouth [boots] = one's ~ leaps into one's mouth [throat]*** 吓一大跳。***have one's ~ in one's work*** 专心工作。***have the [one's] ~ in the right place*** 真心实意,好心好意。***have the ~ to do [say]*** 〔常用于否定句中〕有勇气做[说];忍心做[说]。***~ and soul [hand]*** 全心全意地,热心地。***imprint on sb.'s ~*** 铭刻某人心中。***in (good) ~*** **1.** 精神抖擞的,情绪高昂的。**2.** (土地)肥沃的。***in one's ~ (of ~s)*** 在内心深处;秘密地。***in the fullness of one's ~*** 满腔热情地。***in the inmost [secret] recesses of the ~*** 在心坎里。***in the ~ of*** 在…中心。***in the pride of one's ~*** 自豪,得意。***keep a good ~*** 不丧失勇气。***lay one's ~ bare*** 倾吐衷情。***lay sth. to ~*** 把(忠告、责备等)记在心里;,认真考虑。***learn [get, have] sth. by ~*** 熟记。***lie (heavy) at sb.'s ~*** = *weigh upon sb.'s ~.* ***lie near sb.'s ~*** 受到某人的深切关怀。***lose ~*** 沮丧,扫兴。***lose one's ~ to*** 爱上。***make sb.'s ~ bleed*** 使某人非常痛心。***make sb.'s ~ leap*** 使某人大吃一惊。***move [stir, touch] sb.'s ~*** 打动某人的心。***My ~s!*** 【海】勇敢的伙伴们! ***near [nearest] (to) one's ~*** 非常关怀的;重大的,贵重的。***not to have the ~ to do [say] sth.*** 没有勇气做[说];不忍心做[说]。***one's ~ gives a leap*** 吓一跳。***one's ~ is broken*** 心碎,非常伤心。***open [pour out, uncover] one's ~ to sb.*** 向某人倾吐衷情。***out of ~*** **1.** 没精神,没精打采。**2.** (土地)贫瘠的。***pluck up one's ~*** 鼓起勇气,打起精神。***put one's ~ into sth.*** 热心于(某事),一心一意去做(某事)。***put sb.***

out of ～ 使某人失去勇气[心灰意懒]。***read sb.'s*** ～ 看出某人心意。***reverberate*** [***ring***] ***in one's*** ～ 言犹在耳。***search one's*** [***the***] ～ 反省。***set one's*** ～ ***at rest*** [***ease***] 安心,放心。***set one's*** [***sb.'s***] ～ ***on*** (***doing***) ***sth***. 使自己[某人]下决心做某事。***set one's*** [***the***] ～ ***on*** [***upon***] ***sth***. 全神贯注做某事。***speak to the*** ～ 说动人心。***shut one's*** ～ ***to fear*** = ***steal one's*** ～ ***against fear*** 一点不怕;横下心来。***steal sb.'s*** ～ 赢得某人欢心。***take*** ～ = *pluck up one's* ～. ***take*** ～ ***of grace*** 鼓起勇气。***take sth. to*** ～ 对某事痛心,对某事介意。***take sth.*** [***sb.***] ***to one's*** ～ 〔口〕对某事[某人]表示喜爱,喜欢某事[某人]。***take the*** ～ ***out of sb.*** = *tire sb.'s* ～ *out* = put sb. out of ～. ***wear*** [***carry***] ***one's*** ～ ***on*** [***upon***] ***one's sleeve*** 心直口快,过于直率。***wear sb.*** [***sth.***] ***in one's*** ～ 忠于某人[某事]。***weigh upon sb.'s*** ～ 压在某人心上。***win sb.'s*** ～ = *gain sb.'s* ～. ***with a*** ～ ***and a half*** 高兴(做)。***with a heavy*** ～ 心情沉重,闷闷不乐。***with a light*** ～ 高高兴兴,轻松愉快。***with all one's*** ～ = ***with one's whole*** ～ 诚心诚意,真心地。***with half a*** ～ 勉勉强强地,半心半意地。**II** *vt*. 将…记在心中。～ *a warning* 记住警告。～**ache** 心痛;伤心。～ **attack** 心力衰竭,心脏病发作。～**beat** 1. 心跳,心搏。2. 感情。3. 〔喻〕中心,动力。～ **block**【医】心传导阻滞。～('s)-**blood** 生命必需的血液;生命。～**break** 1. *n*. 悲伤,悲痛。2. *vt*. 使心碎。～-**breaking** 令人悲痛的,使人心碎的。～**broken** 悲伤绝望的。～ **burn** 1.【医】胃灼热,心口灼热。2. = ～burning. ～**burning** 不平,不满;妒忌。～ **cherry** 心形樱桃〔甜樱桃的一个变种〕。～ **disease** 心脏病。～ **failure** 心力衰竭;心脏停跳。～**felt** *a*. 深深感觉到的,衷心的。～-**free** *a*. 无拘无束的;无所依恋的。～-**in-(the-)mouth** *a*. 富有刺激性的,令人提心吊胆的。～**land** 心脏地带,中心地带。～-**lung machine** (用于心脏手术的)人工心肺机。～-**man** 接受心脏移植手术者。～-**rending** *a*. 令人悲痛的,令人伤心的。～-**searching** *n*. 内心的反省,对自己感情的检查。～**s-ease**, ～'**s-ease** *n*. 1. 内心平静。2.【植】三色堇。～**sick** *a*. 愁眉苦脸的,闷闷不乐的。～**some** *a*. 1. 精神振作的;令人振奋的。2. 欢乐的,愉快的,活泼的。～**sore** 1. *n*. 悲伤,痛心。2. *a*. 悲伤的,痛心的。～-**stirring** *a*. 振奋人心的。～-**stricken**, ～-**struck** *a*. 痛心的。～**string** *n*. 〔常 *pl*.〕深情,心弦 (*break one's* ～*strings* 使伤心。*pull at* [*touch*] *one's* ～*strings* 打动心弦)。～**throb** 1. 心跳,心悸。2. 〔俚〕〔常 *pl*.〕柔情;感伤;爱人,情人。～-**to**-～ 坦白的,开诚布公的;亲切的。～ **urchin**【动】猬团目 (*Spatangoida*) 动物。～**warming** *a*. 暖人心房的,鼓舞人心的。～-**whole** *a*. 1. 专心一意的;真诚的。2. 勇敢的,不沮丧的。3. 情窦未开的;无所眷恋的。～-**wood**【植】心材。～**worm**【动】犬恶丝虫 (*Dirofilaria immitis*)〔为蚊子所传布,寄生于血液中,尤其在狗、猫等的心脏中〕。

heart·ed [ˈhɑːtid; ˋhartɪd] *a*. 〔常用来构成复合词〕有…心的,心…的。*faint*-～ 心软的。*kind*-～ 仁慈的。*stone*-～ 铁石心肠的。

heart·en [ˈhɑːtn; ˋhartn̩] *vt*. 振作(精神),鼓励,激励 (*up*; *on*)。～*ing news* 令人振奋的消息。— *vi*. 振作起来 (*up*)。

hearth [hɑːθ; harθ] *n*. 1. 壁炉地面。2. 炉边;〔喻〕家庭。3.【冶】(平炉的)炉床;(高炉的)炉膛,炉缸。～ ***and home*** 家园。～**rug** 炉边地毯。～**stone** 1. 炉石;磨石。2. 炉边;家庭。

heart·i·ly [ˈhɑːtili; ˋhartəlɪ] *ad*. 1. 诚恳地,亲切地。2. 热情地,劲头十足地。3. 胃口很好地;(吃、喝)痛快地。4. 完全,非常。*be* ～ *glad* 十分高兴。*eat* ～ 饱餐一顿,吃得津津有味。*set to work* ～ 积极开始工作。*thank sb*. ～ 衷心感谢某人。

heart·i·ness [ˈhɑːtinis; ˋhartɪnɪs] *n*. 诚恳,热心。

heart·less [ˈhɑːtlis; ˋhartlɪs] *a*. 1. 无情的,残酷的。2. 无精打采的。-**ly** *ad*. -**ness** *n*.

heart·y [ˈhɑːti; ˋhartɪ] **I** *a*. 1. 衷心的,诚恳的;恳切的;热诚的。2. 精神饱满的,强健的。3. 营养丰富的;丰盛的;丰饶的。4. 强烈的,猛烈的。5. 胃口好的。*a* ～ *appetite* 好胃口。*a* ～ *welcome* 热情欢迎。***hale and*** ～ (年老而)精神矍烁的。**II** *n*. 1. (英国大学的)运动员。2. 〔古〕朋友,伙伴〔尤指水手〕。*My hearties*!【海】伙伴们! 弟兄们!

heat [hiːt; hit] **I** *n*. 1. 热;热力;热度;热量。2. 体温;发烧。3. (气候的)高温,暑气。4.【冶】熔炼的炉次;装炉量;一炉(钢、铁等)。5. (赛跑等的)一场[盘、轮];预赛,竞赛;一次努力。6. (战斗、争论、演讲等)最激烈的阶段;强烈的感情;愤怒。7. (辣椒等的)辣味。8. (母兽交尾期的)发情。9. 〔美俚〕威逼,压力;警察;(警察对罪犯的)侦察,逼供,穷追。10. 〔美俚〕手枪;炮火,枪弹射击。11. 〔美俚〕喝醉。12. 激情。13. 浓香。*an intense* ～ 酷热。*black* ～ 暗热〔未发光时的热〕。*latent* ～ 潜热。*radiant* ～ 辐射热。*red* ～ 赤热。*sensible* ～【物】显热。*specific* ～【物】比热。*white* ～ 白热〔发光时的热〕;激情。*a* ～ *of steel* 一炉钢。*a dead* ～ 不分胜负的赛跑。*the final* ～ 决赛。*preliminary* ～*s* = *trial* ～*s* 预赛。*prickly* ～ 痱子,汗疣。***a dead*** ～ (竞赛中)并列名次。***at a*** ～ 一口气地,一气呵成。***at*** ～ (母兽等)在交尾期。***at a white*** ～ 白热地,极端激动地。***give sb. the*** ～ 〔美俚〕开枪击毙某人。***have a*** ～ ***on*** 〔美俚〕喝醉酒。***in*** [***on***] ～ = *at* ～. ***in the*** ～ ***of*** 在(辩论等)最激烈的时候。***put the*** ～ ***on sb***. 逼某人干活[付款];使某人为难。***The*** ～'***s on***. 〔美俚〕警察正在穷追罪犯。***turn on the*** ～ 〔美俚〕1. 出死劲干,拼命工作。2. 责备,谴责。3. 激起热情。4. 开枪射击。5. 穷追罪犯。**II** *vt*. 1. 给…加热;使…温暖。2. 使激动,刺激。*a room* ～*ed by stove* 用火炉取暖的房间。— *vi*. 1. 变热;变暖。2. (食物等)发热变质。3. 激动,发怒。*Water* ～*s slowly*. 水是慢慢变热的。～ **barrier** 热障(= thermal barrier)。～ **bump** 热疖子。～ **capacity**【物】热容量。～ **devil** (受热面上方)引起视觉印象摇动的热气。～ **engine** 热力机 (*a* ～ *engine plant* 火电厂)。～ **exchanger** 热交换器。～ **exhaustion** 中暑。～ **flash** (原子爆炸等所产生的)强热。～ **island** 热岛〔城市中由于街道和建筑物密集而特别炎热的区域〕。～**lightning** 闪电〔尤指夏夜无雷声的热闪〕。～**proof** *a*. 耐热的(= ～resistant)。～ **prostration** = ～ exhaustion. ～ **pump** 热泵。～ **rash** 粟粒疹,痱子,汗疹(= miliria)。～ **resisting alloy** 耐热合金。～ **seeker** 热跟踪导弹,红外线自导导弹。～-**set** *vt*. 对(塑料、织物上的皱褶等)进行热定形。～ **sink** 吸热设备,冷源;散热片。～**spot** 1. 雀斑,酒刺。2. 热觉点。～-**stroke** 中暑。～-**treat** *vt*.【冶】对…作热处理。～ **treatment** 热处理。～ **unit** 热(量)单位。～**up** 1. (熔炉、核反应堆、电子线路等的)升温。2. (需求等的)剧增;(局势等的)加剧。～ **value** 发热值。～ **wave** 1. 热浪,热波。2. 热浪期。

heat·ed [ˈhiːtid; ˋhitɪd] *a*. 1. 热的;加热的。2. 激昂的,兴奋的。*a* ～ *argument* 激烈的争论。*the* ～ *term* 〔美〕夏季。-**ly** *ad*. -**ness** *n*.

heat·er [ˈhiːtə; ˋhitɚ] *n*. 1. 加热的人;加热器,散热器;暖房装置。2. 〔美俚〕手枪。3. 〔美俚〕雪茄烟。*gas* ～ 煤气炉。～ **tube** 旁热式电子管。

heath [hiːθ; hiθ] *n*. 1.【植】欧石南属常青灌木;石南。2. 石南丛生的荒野,荒地。*one's native* ～ 出生地,幼年生长的地方。～ **aster**【植】菊科植物〔俗名石南菊,产于北美〕。～ **bell** 欧石南属的花;钓钟柳。～**berry** 岩高兰之类。～**bird**【动】黑松鸡,黑山鸡;(尤指)黑琴鸡。～ **cock** 雄松鸡。～ **family** 杜鹃花科。～ **fowl** = ～-bird. ～ **hen**【动】1. 黑琴鸡(= gray hen)。2. 草原鸡 (*Tympanuchus cupido*)〔产于美国新英格兰,已绝种〕。

hea·then [ˈhiːðən; ˋhiðən] **I** *n*. (*pl*. ～*s*, 〔集合词〕***the***

H

～) 1. (不信基督教、伊斯兰教、犹太教等的)异教徒;多神教信仰者。2. 不信教的人;未开化的人,野蛮人。**II** *a*. 1. 信异教的。2. 不信教的;野蛮的。**-dom** *n*. 异教国;〔集合词〕异教徒;异教的风俗信仰;〔古〕异教。**-ism** *n*. 异教;异教教义,偶像崇拜;野蛮。**-ise, -ize** *vt*., *vi*. (使)信奉异教。**-ry** *n*. 1. = -ism. 2. 异教徒;异教民。

hea·then·ish [ˈhiːðəniʃ; ˋhiðənɪʃ] *a*. 1. 异教的,异教徒的。2. 野蛮的,未开化的。**-ly** *ad*. **-ness** *n*.

heath·er [ˈheðə; ˋhɛðɚ] **I** *n*. 1.【植】石南属植物。2. 石南属植物丛生的荒野。***set the ～ on fire*** 煽起骚动。***take to the ～*** 〔Scot.〕做土匪,落草为寇。**II** *a*. = heathery.

heath·er·y [ˈheðəri; ˋhɛðərɪ] *a*. 1. 石南的;石南丛生的;似石南的。2. 杂色的。～ **mixture**【纺】混色毛纱。～ **tweed**【纺】杂色花呢。**heath·er·i·ness** *n*.

heath·y [ˈhiːθi; ˋhiθɪ] *a*. = heathery.

heat·ing [ˈhiːtiŋ; ˋhitɪŋ] **I** *a*. 1. 加热的;供热的。2. 刺激的。*a ～ drink* 暖身的饮料。*a ～ apparatus* 供暖装置。*～ pipe* 暖气管。*a ～ system* 暖气系统。**II** *n*. 1. 加热;供暖;(建筑物的)暖气装置。2. 白炽,灼热。～ **pad** 电热敷垫。～ **zone** 加热区,加热段。

heat·ron·ic [hiːˈtrɔnik; hiˋtrɑnɪk] *a*.【物】高频(率)电介质加热的。

heaume [həum; hom] *n*. (古代套在头盔上的)连颈重盔,大盔。

heave [hiːv; hiv] **I** *vt*. (～*d* 或 *hove* [həuv; hov]; *heav·ing*) 1. 举,举起。2. 使鼓起,使胀起,挺起(胸部)。3. (吃力地)发出(叹声、呻吟声)。4.〔口〕投掷,扔。5.【海】(用绳)拉起;卷起;使(船)开动。6.【地】使平错,使隆起。*～ a heavy box* 举起一个沉重的箱子。*～ an anchor* 起锚。*～ a brick* 扔砖头。*～ a sigh* 叹息。— *vi*. 1. 举,升起,胀;(浪、地面)起伏。2. 喘息;呕吐。3. 努力,操劳。4.【海】曳,卷 (*at*); (船)开动前进。*～ on the rope* 拉绳子。*heaving waves* 汹涌起伏的波涛。***～ (ship) ahead***【海】收着曳索使(船)前进。***H- away [ho]***! (水手起锚时的呼叫声)用力拉呀! 加劲卷呀! ***～ down*** (使)船倾倒一边以进行清理,维修等。***～ in sight*** (船)进入视野。***～ out*** 1. 将船的龙骨露出水面进行维修。2. 扯起(风帆、旗子等)。***～ the lead***【海】投水砣测水的深度。***～ the sphere***【美棒球】投球。***～ to*** 顶风停船。***～ up*** 1. 起锚。2. 呕吐。**II** *n*. 1. 举起,扛起。2. 胀起,隆起;波动,起伏。3. 呕吐。4.【摔跤】右手勒住对方右肩的摔法。5.【地】平错。6.〔the ～s〕(马的)喘病。*～ of the sea* 海波。

heave-ho [ˈhiːvˈhəu; ˋhivˋho] **I** *n*.〔口〕免职,开除。***get the (old) ～*** 被免职,被开除。***give sb. the (old) ～*** 免某人的职,开除某人。**II** *vi*., *vt*.〔美俚〕用力提起(物品)。

heav·en [ˈhevən; ˋhɛvən] *n*. 1. 天,天空 (*opp*. earth)〔散文通常用 *pl*.〕。2. 天堂,天国,极乐世界,乐园;极快乐的事。3.〔H-〕上帝,神;〔*pl*.〕诸神。*the starry ～s* 星空。*the eye of ～* 太阳。*It's ～ to go angling*. 钓鱼是一大乐事。***By H-***! 老天在上! ***go to ～*** 升天,死。***H- be praised***! = ***Thank H-***! 谢天谢地! ***Good [Gracious, Great] ～s***! 天哪! 哎呀!〔表示惊愕,谴责,非难〕。***～ and earth*** 宇宙,万物;天哪〔惊叫声〕。***H- forbid [forfend]***! 上天不容,绝无此事。***H- (only) knows*** 只有天晓得! 千真万确,向天发誓。***～ of ～s*** = the seventh ～. ***～ on earth*** 人间天堂。***H-'s vengeance is slow but sure***.〔谚〕天网恢恢,疏而不漏。***in ～*** 1. 在天上的;已死的。2.〔用以加强语气〕究竟,到底 (*Where in ～ were you*? 你当时究竟在哪里?)。***move ～ and earth*** 竭尽全力 (*to do*)。***nigger ～***〔美俚〕(戏院等)楼座最高部分。***the seventh ～***【宗】七重天,极乐世界。***The ～ opens***. 下起倾盆大雨。***to ～(s)*** 极度地。***under ～***〔用以加强语气〕究竟,到底。**～-born** *a*. 天生的;天赋的。**～-dust**〔美俚〕可卡因,古柯碱。**～-kissing** *a*. 摩天的,高耸云霄的。**～-reacher** 牧师〔尤指讲道时常常作望天姿势的〕。**～-sent** *a*. 天赐的,极巧的。**～ward** *a*., *ad*. 向天上的[地];向天空的[地]。**～wards** *ad*. 向天上,向天空。

heav·en·li·ness [ˈhevənlinis; ˋhɛvənlɪnɪs] *n*. 神圣,尊严;秀美;十全。

heav·en·ly [ˈhevənli; ˋhɛvənlɪ] **I** *a*. 1. 天的,天空的。2. 神圣的;至上的;天国的。3. 超凡的;超绝的;〔口〕漂亮的;可爱的。*the ～ bodies* 天体。*～ beings [angels]* 天使。*a ～ mind* 虔诚的心。*H- Twins*【天】双子星座。*What ～ peaches*! 多可爱的美人! **II** *ad*. 1. 极,无比的。2. 借天神之力。***The ～ City*** 1. 乐土,天堂。2. 新耶路撒冷。**～-minded** *a*. 虔诚的,圣洁的。

heav·er [ˈhiːvə; ˋhɪvɚ] *n*. 1. 举起[移动]重物的人[工具];举起物。2.【海】(卷起船缆的)杠杆。3. 重量。4.〔美俚〕(棒球的)投手。5. 叉簧;钩键;小铁梃。

heav·i·ly [ˈhevili; ˋhɛvəlɪ] *ad*. 1. 重重地,沉重地。2. 缓慢地;迟钝地。3. 猛烈地,厉害地。4. 沮丧地,灰溜溜地。5. 沉闷地;〔古〕悲伤地。6. 暴虐地。*a ～ wooded area* 树木浓密的地区。*a ～ guarded fortress* 戒备森严的堡垒。*a ～ loaded truck* 重载的卡车。*suffer ～* 受到沉重打击。

heav·i·ness [ˈhevinis; ˋhɛvɪnɪs] *n*. 1. 重,沉重。2. 悲哀,抑郁,痛苦。3. 迟钝,不活泼;疲倦。*～ of movement* 动作的笨拙。～ **quotient** 体重商数(缩写作 HQ)。

heav·ing [ˈhiːviŋ; ˋhivɪŋ] *n*. 举起,拿起,扔去。～ **line**【海】扔到岸上以便将轮船系住的大铁索。**-line bend**【海】丁香结,酒瓶结。

Heav·i·side [ˈhevisaid; ˋhɛvɪˏsaɪd] *n*. 1. 海维赛德〔姓氏〕。2. **Oliver ～** 奥列佛·赫维赛〔1850—1925,英国物理学家〕。

Heav·i·side layer [ˈhevisaid ˈleiə; ˋhɛvɪsaɪd ˋleɚ]【无】海维赛德层,海氏层,E 电离层〔高出地面 100 公里反射电波的大气层,亦作 Kennelly-～ layer〕。

heav·y[1] [ˈhiːvi; ˋhivɪ] *a*. (马)患哮喘病的。

heav·y[2] [ˈhevi; ˋhɛvɪ] **I** *a*. 1. 重的 (*opp*. light),有重量的;重型的;装备重型武器的。2. 大的;大量的,多的;(交通等)拥挤的,稠密的。3. 有力的,沉重的;猛烈的,狂暴的;厉害的,严重的。4. 困难的,繁重的,不易对付的。5. 沉闷的,难忍耐的;悲惨的,忧郁的。6. 迟钝的,笨重的;单调的,乏味的,(文章等)冗长的;(声音等)深沉的。7. (天气)阴沉的;多云的;低压的。8. (食物等)难消化的;(面包等)没发酵好的;(酒等)烈性的。9. 粗的;粗糙的;粗壮的。10. (道路等)难行走的;(土地)难耕作的。11. (眼皮)重垂的;欲睡的,困倦的。12. (剧中角色)庄重的,严肃的;悲剧的。13. (妇女)怀孕的。14. (思想等)深邃的。15.〔美俚〕极好的。16.〔美俚〕老于世故的。*a ～ blow* 沉重的打击。*a ～ bomber* 重型轰炸机。*a ～ brigade* 装备重武器的旅。*～ artillery* 重炮(兵)。*～ industry* 重工业。*a ～ crop* 大丰收。*a ～ drinker* 酒喝得多的人。*a ～ eater* 大肚汉,食量大的人。*a ～ fate* 悲惨的命运。*a ～ fire* 猛烈的炮火。*～ food* 难消化的食物。*a ～ heart* 沉重的心情。*～ money [sugar]* 大笔钱。*a ～ sea* 波涛汹涌的海面。*～ news [tidings]* 噩耗,坏消息。*a ～ road* 泥泞的道路。*a ～ sky* 阴沉的天气。*a ～ sleep* 酣睡。*a ～ smoker* 烟抽得多的人。*a ～ snowfall* 大雪。*～ soil* 难耕的土地。*a ～ style* 枯燥冗长的文体。*a ～ task [work]* 繁重的工作。*a ～ wine* 烈酒。***have a ～ hand*** 笨手笨脚。***～ with child*** 怀孕,大肚子。***～ with fruit*** 果实累累。***～ with sleep*** 睡意正浓。**II** *ad*. = heavily. ★现在多用于复合词或成语。*Time hangs ～ on one's hands*. 时间过得又慢又无聊,度日如年。***lie [sit, weigh] ～ at [on, upon]*** (工作、肠胃等)负担过重。***lie [sit] ～ on one's [the] stomach*** (食物)滞积胃中,不消化。**III** *n*. 1.〔*pl*.〕重物〔尤指重型车辆、重轰炸机、重炮〕。2.【剧】庄重角色,演庄重角色的演员。3. 严肃的报纸。4.〔*pl*.〕

重工业。5.〔*pl*.〕重骑兵队。6.〔美俚〕(影、剧中的)强盗,恶棍。7.〔美俚〕重量级拳击选手。*come the ~ over sb*. 对某人摆架子。*do the* ~〔俚〕自高自大,摆架子。*the Heavies*〔英〕龙骑兵团。~**-armed** *a*. 装备重武器的,重装甲的。~ **bead**〔美〕(五角大楼国防预算中拨款最多的)重点项目。~**-bedded**【地】厚层的。~**-browed** *a*. 眉头紧蹙的。~**-buying** *a*. 大量购入的。~**cake**〔美俚〕一心寻找女生做朋友的男大学生。~ **casting** 大型铸件。~ **click**〔美俚〕(票房收入的)爆满。~ **current** 强电流,大电流。~**-duty** 1. 重载的,重型的;耐用的。2. 关税重的。~**-footed** *a*. 脚步沉重的,笨手笨脚的。~ **fuel** 柴油,重燃(料)油。~**-handed** *a*. 1. 拙劣的。2. 高压的,暴虐的。~**-headed** *a*. 头部大而沉重的;迟钝的。~**-hearted** *a*. 抑郁的;悲伤的。~ **hitter** 大人物,大亨。~ **hour** 忙时。~ **hydrogen**【化】重氢,氘(= deuterium)。~**-laden** *a*. 负重载的;心情沉重的。~ **metal** 1. 重金属。2.〔俚〕巨炮(弹)。3.〔俚〕劲敌。4.〔俚〕伟人。5. 大音量重金属(电子)摇滚乐。~ **(merchant) mill** 大型轧钢厂。~ **oxygen**【化】重氧。~ **repair** 大修。~ **ring**【机】承力环。~**set** *a*. 身体强壮的;身材矮胖的。~**-spar**【化】重晶石。~ **water**【化】重水。~**weight** 1. 身体特重的人。2.【体】重量级拳击[摔跤]运动员〔体重 175 磅以上〕。3.〔美口〕有影响的人,要人。~ **wet**〔英俚〕麦芽酒。

Heb. = Hebrew; Hebrews.

heb·do·mad [ˈhebdəmæd; ˋhɛbdəˏmæd] *n*. 七天,一周;成七的一组。

heb·dom·a·dal [hebˈdɔmədl; hɛbˋdɑmədl̩] *a*. 一周的;每星期的。

heb·dom·a·dar·y [hebˈdɔmədəri; hɛbˋdɑmədərɪ] *a*. = hebdomadal.

He·be [ˈhiːbi; ˋhibɪ] *n*. 1.【希神】青春女神〔在奥林匹斯山替众神斟酒的女神〕。2. 女侍应员,酒吧间的女招待。

he·be·phre·ni·a [ˌhiːbiˈfriːniə; ˏhibɪˋfrinɪə] *n*.【医】青春期痴呆。**he·be·phren·ic** [-ˈfrenik; -ˋfrɛnɪk] *a*.

He·ber [ˈhiːbə; ˋhibɚ] *n*. 希伯〔姓氏〕。

heb·e·tate [ˈhebiteit; ˋhɛbɪtet] I *vt*., *vi*. (使)变迟钝。II *a*. 1. 愚笨的。2.【植】具钝尖头的。

he·bet·ic [hiˈbetik; hɪˋbɛtɪk] *a*. 青春期的,发生于青春期的。

heb·e·tude [ˈhebiˌtjuːd; ˋhɛbɪˏtjud] *n*. 愚钝;感觉迟钝。

He·bra·ic [hi(ː)ˈbreiik; hɪˋbreɪk] *a*. 希伯来人的;希伯来语的。**-i·cal·ly** *ad*.

He·bra·ism [ˈhiːbreiizəm; ˋhibrɪɪzəm] *n*. 1. 希伯来语词[表达方式]。2. 希伯来人的特点[道德,精神,做法等]。3. 希伯来教。

He·bra·ist [ˈhiːbreiist; ˋhibrɪɪst] *n*. 1. 希伯来语语文学家;精通希伯来语的人。2. 希伯来教徒。3. 有希伯来思想道德的人。**-is·tic** *a*.

He·bra·ize [ˈhiːbreiaiz; ˋhibrɪˏaɪz] *vt*., *vi*. (使)希伯来化;(使)成希伯来语。

He·brew [ˈhiːbruː; ˋhibru] I *n*. 1. 希伯来人,〔美〕犹太人。2. 希伯来语。3.〔口〕难听懂的话。*modern* ~ 现在以色列通用的犹太语。*the Epistle to the ~s*【圣】《希伯来人书》。*It's ~ to me*. 那我一点也不懂。II *a*. 1. 希伯来人的。2. 希伯来语的。~**wise** *ad*. 照希伯来文写法自右至左。

Heb·ri·des [ˈhebridiːz; ˋhɛbrəˏdiz] *n*. *pl*. [the ~] 赫布里底群岛〔英国〕。

Hec·a·te [ˈhekəti; ˋhɛkətɪ] *n*.【希神】海克提〔司天地及冥界的女神,后世认为是巫术、魔法女神〕。

hec·a·tomb [ˈhekətəum, -tuːm; ˋhɛkəˏtom, -tum] *n*. 1. (古希腊的)大祭〔尤指一次宰一百头牛的大祭〕。2. 大牺牲,大屠杀。

heck[1] [hek; hɛk] *n*.〔英口〕= hell〔用以加强语气或咒骂〕。*a ~ of a lot of money* 好多好多钱。*What the ~?* (你讲的)什么鬼玩意儿?

heck[2] [hek; hɛk] *n*.〔英方〕(河里阻拦鱼游向的)鱼栏。

heck·le [ˈhekl; ˋhɛkl] I *vt*. 1. 梳理(亚麻等)。2. 质问(当众演说的候选人等)。II *n*. 梳理(= hackle);【纺】针排。

heck·ler [ˈheklə; ˋhɛklɚ] *n*. 质问者。

hec·tare [ˈhektaː, ekˈtaː; ˋhɛkta, ɛkˋtar] *n*. 公顷〔= 100 公亩或 2471 英亩,合 15 市亩〕。

hec·tic [ˈhektik; ˋhɛktɪk] I *a*. 1. (因患肺病等)发烧的,消耗热的;有病态潮红的。2. 患热病的;患肺痨病的。3.〔口〕紧张的,闹哄哄的;兴奋的,狂热的。*a ~ fever* 消耗热。~ *spots* (肺部患者脸颊上的)潮红。*have a ~ time* 非常激动,热闹了一阵。II *n*. 1. 肺病热,消耗热;肺病热患者。2.【医】潮红。**-ti·cal·ly**, **-ly** *ad*. **-ness** *n*.

hecto- *comb*. *f*. 表示"一百":*hecto*graph, *hecto*metre.

hec·to·cot·y·lus [ˌhektəˈkɔtləs; ˏhɛktəˋkɑtləs] *n*. (*pl*. **-y·li** [-ai; -aɪ])【动】化茎腕,交接腕。

hec·tog = hectogram(me).

hec·to·gram(me) [ˈhektəugræm; ˋhɛktoˏgræm] *n*. 百克〔重量单位〕。

hec·to·graph [ˈhektəugraːf; ˋhɛktoˏgræf] I *n*.【印】胶版誊写法。II *vt*. 用胶版誊写法印刷。

hectol. = hectolitre.

hec·to·li·ter, 〔Eng.〕**-tre** [ˈhektəuˌliːtə; ˋhɛktoˏlitɚ] *n*.〔容量单位〕百升,公石(= 1 市石)。

hec·tom. = hectometre.

hec·to·me·tre, 〔Am.〕**-ter** [ˈhektəumiːtə; ˋhɛktoˏmitɚ] *n*.〔长度单位〕百米。

hec·to·new·ton [ˈhektəunjuːtn; ˋhɛktonjutn̩] *n*.【物】〔力的单位〕百牛顿。

hec·tor [ˈhektə; ˋhɛktɚ] I *n*. 威吓者,虚张声势的人。II *vt*., *vi*. 吓唬;欺负;(向…)虚张声势。~ *sb*. *into* [*out of*] 威吓某人做[不做]…。

Hec·tor [ˈhektə; ˋhɛktɚ] *n*. 1. 赫克托〔男子名〕。2. 荷马史诗《伊利亚特》中一勇士名。

hec·to·watt [ˈhektəuwɔt; ˋhɛktowɑt] *n*.〔功率单位〕百瓦。

Hec·u·ba [ˈhekjubə; ˋhɛkjubə] *n*. 海丘巴〔荷马史诗《伊利亚特》中特洛依国王普里安之后〕。

he'd [hiːd; hid] = he had; he would.

hed·dles [ˈhedlz; ˋhɛdlz] I *n*. 〔*pl*.〕【纺】综片,综线,综丝。II *vt*. 使(经线)穿过综眼。

he·der [ˈheidə; ˋhedɚ] *n*. (*pl*. **ha·dar·im** [haːˈdaːrim; haˋdarɪm]) 犹太儿童宗教学校。

hedge [hedʒ; hɛdʒ] I *n*. 1. (用灌木等构成的)树篱,(树枝等编成的)篱笆,(石头、草皮等叠成的)隔墙。2. 障碍物,界限。3. (赌博中的)赌两面,两方下注。4. 模棱两可的话。5. (在交易所中买进现货卖出期货或反之以避免损失的)套头交易。*a dead* ~ 用树枝编成的篱笆,柴垣。*a quickset* ~ 由活树围成的树篱。*a ~ of stones* 石头堆成的围墙。***A ~ between keeps friendship green***. 〔谚〕君子之交淡如水。***be on the*** ~ 耍两面态度,骑墙。***be on the right side of the*** ~ 主意打对了。***come down on the wrong side of the*** ~ 打错了主意。***hang in*** [***on***] ***the*** ~ (诉讼)悬而未决。***make a*** ~ 赌两面。***not grow on every*** ~ 稀少。***over ~ and ditch*** 抄小路。***sit on*** (***both sides of***) ***the*** ~ = *be on the* ~. ***take a sheet off a*** ~ 公然窃取。***the only stick left in one's*** ~ 剩下的唯一办法。II *vt*. 1. 用树篱围住[隔开];围护,防范。2. 设障碍于,妨碍。3. 两方下注以避免(赌博、冒险等的)损失。4. 躲闪,推诿,搪塞。~ *a field* 用树篱围起田地。~ *a question* 对问题避不作答。— *vi*. 1. 作树篱,修树篱。2. 赌两面,(在交易所)做套头交易。3. 躲闪,规避,推诿。4. 做事留后路,说话留余地。~ ***in*** [***round***] ***with*** 用…围住。~ ***off*** 1. 用篱笆隔起来。2. 两面下注。~ ***out*** 用篱笆隔断。III *a*. 1. 树篱的,树篱下的,树篱旁的。2. 偷偷摸摸的,名声不好的;低劣的。~ **bill** 长柄镰。~**-born** *a*. 出身卑贱的。~**hog** *n*. 1.

【动】猬;〔美〕豪猪。2.【军】刺猬弹[反潜用的深水炸弹];铁丝网,环形筑垒阵地。3. 容易发怒的人,难对付的人。4.【植】野毛莨。~**hop** *vi*.〔美〕掠地飞行,极低空飞行,〔俚〕跳栏飞行。~**hopper** 掠地飞行的飞机[驾驶员]。~**hyssop**【植】金黄水八角(*Gratiola aurea*)〔产于美国缅因州到佛罗里达州一带〕。~ **marriage** 1. 秘密结婚。2. 不合法的结婚。~ **priest**〔英〕无知的低级教士。~**-row** 一排栽成树篱的灌木。~ **school** (爱尔兰等地的)露天学校,野外学校,低级学校。~ **sparrow**【动】篱雀。~ **writer** 穷文人,卖文者,寒士。

He·djaz [hiːˈdʒæz; hiˋdʒæz] *n*. = Hejaz.

he·don·ic [hiːˈdɔnik; hiˋdɑnɪk] *a*. 1. 享乐的。2. 享乐主义的,享乐主义者的。**-i·cal·ly** *ad*. **-s** *n*. *pl*.〔用作单数〕1. 享乐主义的学说。2.【心】关于欢乐主义的学说。

he·don·ism [ˈhiːdənizəm; ˋhidənɪzəm] *n*. 享乐主义;【心】欢乐主义。**he·don·ist** *n*. 欢乐主义者,享乐主义者。**he·do·nis·tic** *a*. [-ˈnistik; -ˋnɪstɪk] 欢乐说的,享乐主义的。

-hedral [ˈhiːdrəl; ˋhidrəl] *suf*. 表示"…边的","…面的": poly*hedral*.

-hedron [ˈhiːdrən; ˋhidrən] *suf*. 表示"…边形","…面形": poly*hedron*.

hee·bie-jee·bies [ˈhiːbiˈdʒiːbiz; ˋhibɪˋdʒibɪz] *n*.〔常作 the ~〕〔俚〕神经紧张;颤抖。

heed [hiːd; hid] I *vt*. 注意到,留心。~ *a warning* 注意到警告。— *vi*. 注意,留意。II *n*. 注意,留意。*Take ~ (and you) will surely speed*.〔谚〕谨慎是迅速之本。*give* [*pay*] ~ *to* 注意,留心。*take ~ to* [*of*] 注意,提防。*take no ~ of* 不注意。**-ful** *a*. 注意的,留心的(*of*)。

heed·less [ˈhiːdlis; ˋhidlɪs] *a*. 1. 不注意的,不留心的;不顾…的(*of*)。2. 心不在焉的。**-ly** *ad*. **-ness** *n*.

hee·haw [ˈhiːhɔː; ˋhihɔ] *vi*., *n*. 1. 驴叫(声)。2. 傻笑,大笑。

heel[1] [hiːl; hil] I *vt*.【海】使(船)倾斜。— *vi*. (船)倾侧(*over*)。~ *to port* [*starboard*] 船向左[右]舷倾斜。II *n*. (船的)倾斜(度)。

heel[2] [hiːl; hil] I *n*. 1. 踵,脚后跟。2. [*pl*.](四足动物的)后脚;后脚脚跟;蹄后部。3. (鞋,袜等的)后跟。4. 踵状物[如提琴的弓把,高尔夫球杓头弯曲部,梯子的底脚等]。5.〔美俚〕小偷;卑劣的人,告密者,叛徒;食客,寄生虫。6. [*pl*.]剩余(物),残余(物)。7.〔美俚〕越狱;从作案地点逃跑。*the ~ of Italy* 意大利的东南部。*the iron ~* 铁蹄,专横统治。*wear high ~s* 穿高跟鞋。*at ~ = to ~* 跟在后面。*close at ~* 紧跟着。*at* [*on*, *upon*] *sb.'s ~s* 紧跟着某人。*betake oneself to one's ~s* 溜之大吉。*bring sb. to ~* 使某人跟着来;使某人就范。*clap* [*lay*, *set*] *sb. by the ~s* 给某人钉脚镣,把某人逮捕下狱;制服某人。*come to ~* 服从(规则),跟着(别人转);〔美〕追逐异性;〔喊狗〕跟着来! *cool* [*kick*] *one's ~s* 久等,等得不耐烦。*cop a ~*〔美俚〕逃跑,越狱。*dig in one's ~s = dig one's ~in* 站稳脚步,坚持自己的立场。*down at* (*the*) *~* 1. (鞋)穿掉后跟的。2. (人)不修边幅的,邋里邋遢的。*drag one's ~s* 1. 拖着脚步走。2. 迟缓误事,拖拖拉拉。*follow on* [*upon*] *the ~s of* 紧跟在后面。*follow sb. to ~* 亦步亦趋地追随某人。*get* [*have*] *the ~s of* 赶过,胜过。*H-!* (喊狗声)跟来! *~ and toe* 正常地行走。*~s over head = head over ~s* 1. 头朝下,颠倒。2. 完全地,深深地。*keep to ~! = H-! kick up its ~s* (马)溜腿。*kick up one's ~s* 1.〔俚〕蹦蹦跳跳,狂欢。2. 伸直腿死去,翘辫子。*lay in by the ~s = lay sb.* (*fast*) *by the ~s* 束缚某人手脚;逮捕某人下狱。*make a ~* 踢。*neck and ~s* 全身。*on the ~s of = at sb.'s ~s*. *out at* (*the*) *~s* 袜跟[鞋跟]穿得露出脚跟的;衣衫褴褛的;穷相毕露的。*over head and ~s in love* 一往情深。*raise* [*lift up*] *the ~ against sb*. 凌辱某人。*set one's ~ on* [*upon*] 压制,践踏。*show one's ~ = show a clean pair of ~s = take to one's ~s* 溜掉,逃之夭夭。*take it on ~ and toe*〔美俚〕溜掉。*the ~ of Achilles = Achilles' ~* 致命弱点,要害。*to ~* 追随,紧跟。*tread on sb.'s ~s* 踏着某人的脚迹前进;紧随某人之后。*trip* [*strike*, *throw*] *up sb.'s ~s* 用脚把人绊倒。*turn on one's ~s* 急向后转。*turn up one's ~s* 死,翘辫子。*turn* [*tumble*] *up sb.'s ~s*〔口〕踢倒某人;杀死某人。*under the ~ of* 被蹂躏;受虐待。*with the ~s foremost* [*forward*] 成僵尸。II *vt*. 1. 给(鞋)钉后掌;给(斗鸡)上铁距;【高尔夫球】用杓后跟击(球);(足球)用脚后跟传(球)。2. (用脚后跟)践踏。3. 紧跟,追赶。4. 对…施加压力,催促。5.〔美俚〕供给(钱);提供(武器)。~ *a pair of shoes* 给鞋钉掌。~ *a cigarette butt out* 踩灭烟头。~ *sb. upstairs* 跟着某人上楼。— *vi*. 1. 在后紧跟,快跑。2. 用脚后跟跳舞;(足球)用脚后跟向后传球;【高尔夫球】用杓后跟打球。~ *in*【园艺】在根部培土暂植。~ *out* (足球)用脚后跟向后传球。~**-and-toe** *a*.【体】(步伐)后脚脚尖还未离地前脚脚跟即已着地的(*get on the ~-and-toe*〔美〕赶,加快。*~-and-toe walking*【体】竞走)。~**ball** (鞋匠上光用的)硬蜡和煤烟混合物;(拓碑文的)油烟。~ **bar** 立等可取的修鞋店,(百货商店里)立等可取的修鞋柜台。~**piece** 鞋后跟,踵状物。~**plate** 鞋盘,盘钉〔钉在鞋跟上以护鞋耐磨的铁片〕。~**post** 1. 马房(或牛栏)间隔柱。2. 门柱。~**-tap** 1. 鞋跟皮。2. 杯中残酒(*No ~ taps!* 干杯,一饮而尽)。

heeled [hiːld; hild] *a*. 1. 有鞋后跟的;(斗鸡)带有铁距的。2.〔美俚〕带着手枪的。3.〔美俚〕有钱的。*well ~* 1. (用手枪等)武装齐全的。2. 有充分金钱的。

heel·er [ˈhiːlə; ˋhilɚ] *n*. 1. 绱鞋后跟的人。2. 善踢的斗鸡。3.〔美俚〕唯唯诺诺的小政客。

heel·ing [ˈhiːliŋ; ˋhilɪŋ] *n*. (船的)倾侧。~ *error*【海】倾斜自差。

heel·less [ˈhiːllis; ˋhillɪs] *a*. 没有后跟的。

H.E.F. = high energy fuels 高能燃料。

heft [heft; hɛft] I *n*. 1.〔美、英方〕重量,体重。2.〔喻〕势力,影响。3.〔美口〕大半,大部分。II *vt*. 举起试测…的重量;〔美口、英方〕举起。— *vi*. 重达。*a box ~ing 5 pounds* 重达5磅的箱子。

heft·y [ˈhefti; ˋhɛftɪ] I *a*. 1.〔口〕重的。2.〔口〕强健的,肌肉发达的。3. 异常大的。*a ~ blow* 很重的一击。*a ~ majority* 压倒多数。*a ~ child* 壮大的婴儿。*a ~ book* 一本很重的书。II *n*. 体壮力大的人;〔美拳击〕重量级拳击选手。**-i·ly** *ad*. **heft·i·ness** *n*.

he·gar·i [hiˈgæri, -ˈgɛər-; hiˋgaɪrə, -ˋdʒər-] *n*.【植】谷粒芦粟〔产于苏丹,其茎多汁液,多叶;直穗;粟粒带灰色〕。

He·gel [ˈheigl; ˋhegl], **George Wilhelm Friedrich** 黑格尔〔1770—1831,德国哲学家〕。

He·ge·li·an [heiˈgiːljən; heˋgelɪən] I *a*. 黑格尔哲学的,黑格尔学派的。II *n*. 黑格尔学派哲学家,黑格尔哲学的信徒。

He·ge·li·an·ism [heiˈgiːljənizəm; heˋgelɪənɪzm] *n*. 黑格尔哲学。

heg·e·mon·ic(al) [ˌhi(ː)giˈmɔnik(əl), ˌhedʒi-; ˏhɛdʒəˋmɑnɪk(əl), ˏhɪgɪ-] *a*. 霸权的,统治的。

he·ge·mo·nism [ˌhi(ː)giˈmɔnizəm, ˌhedʒi-; ˏhɛdʒəˋmɑnɪzm, ˏhigɪ-] *n*. 霸权主义。

heg·em·o·nist [ˌhi(ː)giˈmɔnist, ˌhedʒi-; ˏhɛdʒəˋmɑnɪst, ˏhigɪ-] *n*. 霸权主义者。

he·gem·o·ny [hi(ː)ˈgeməni, hiːˈdʒeməni; ˋhɛdʒəˏmonɪ, hiˋgɛmənɪ] *n*. 霸权,霸权主义。

Heg·i·ra [ˈhedʒirə; ˋhɛdʒɪrə] *n*. 1.【宗】(公元622年)穆罕默德由麦加到麦地那的逃亡〔此年即定为伊斯兰教纪元〕。2. [h-]逃亡。

he-goat [ˈhiːgəut; ˋhiˏgot] *n*. 公山羊。*milk a ~ into a*

sieve 徒劳无功，做不会成功的事。

he·gu·men [hiˈgjuːmen; hɪˋgjumen] ***n.***【东正教】修道院长，寺院长。

heh[1] [hei; he] ***n.*** = he[3].

heh[2] [hei; he] ***int.*** 嗨！〔表示惊异、质问〕。

Hei·del·berg [ˈhaidlbəːg; ˋhaɪdl͵bɝg] ***n.*** 海德堡〔德国地名〕。～ **jaw**【人类】史前人的颌骨。～ **man** 海德堡人，欧洲史前人种。

heif·er [ˈhefə; ˋhɛfɚ] ***n.*** **1.** (未生过小牛的)小母牛，母牛。**2.**〔美俚〕女人(尤指年轻姑娘或漂亮妇女)。

heigh [hei; he] ***int.*** 嗨！〔表示注意、质问、鼓舞、高兴等〕。

heigh-ho [ˈheiˈhəu; ˋheˋho] ***int.*** 嗨嗬！〔表示疲劳、丧胆、惊愕、高兴等〕。

height [hait; haɪt] ***n.*** **1.** 高，高度；身高；海拔。**2.**〔常 *pl.*〕高地，山丘。**3.** 高贵，卓越。**4.** 绝顶，顶点；【圣】天。**5.**〔罕〕显贵，高的社会地位。*What's your* ～? 你多高？*I'm five feet in* ～. 我身高五英尺。*the* ～ *above* (*the*) *sea level* 海拔。*in the* ～ *of fashion* 极时髦。*in the* ～ *of summer* 在盛夏。～ *of one's power* 权力的极点。*on the* ～ 高地上的。*the* ～ *of folly* 笨透。***at its*** ～ 正盛，正在绝顶；正起劲。***in*** ～ 以高计。～ ***of land***〔Canad.〕分水界；〔口〕流域。～**-to-paper**【印】铅字标准高度〔在说英语国家是 0.9186 英寸〕。**-ism** ***n.*** 身高歧视〔尤指对矮小男子或高大妇女的歧视〕。**-ist** ***a.*** 身高歧视的。

height·en [ˈhaitn; ˋhaɪtn] ***vt.*** **1.** 升高，增高；提高，加高(*opp.* lower)。**2.** 加强，加深，加剧；增大。**3.** 使高尚；使显著，使突出。**4.** 给(描写、故事)添加细节；给(绘画)加浓色彩。— ***vi.*** **1.** 升高；增加。**2.** (颜色等)变深。

heil [hail; haɪl]〔G.〕**I** ***vt.*** 向…欢呼，向…呼万岁。**II** ***n.*** 嗨！万岁！〔表示欢呼的喊声〕。

hein [ɑːn; ɑn] ***int.***〔F.〕啊！嗯！

Hei·ne [ˈhainə; ˋhaɪnə], **Heinrich** 海因里希·海涅〔1797—1856，德国诗人〕。

hei·nous [ˈheinəs; ˋhenəs] ***a.*** 可恨的，极凶恶的。*a* ～ *crime* 滔天大罪。**-ly** ***ad.*** **-ness** ***n.***

heir [ɛə; ɛr] ***n.*** 后嗣，嗣子(*to*)；继承人。～ *at law*【法】法定继承人。～ *in tail*【法】直系继承人。*legal* [*right*] ～【法】合法继承人。～ *of the* [*one's*] *body* 嫡生子[女]。*the* ～ *to the crown* [*throne*] 王位继承人。*cut off one's* ～ *with a shilling* 用象征性的一先令取消继承者的继承权。～ **apparent** (*pl.* ～***s apparent***)【法】法定继承人，有确定继承权的人。～ **collateral**【法】旁系继承人。～ **presumptive** (*pl.* ～***s presumptive***)【法】假定继承人〔虽有继承权但其继承权可因近亲之出生而消失的人〕。**II** ***vt.*** 继承。

heir·dom [ˈɛədəm; ˋɛrdəm] ***n.*** = heirship.

heir·ess [ˈɛəris; ˋɛrɪs] ***n.*** 嗣女，女继承人。

heir·less [ˈɛəlis; ˋɛrlɪs] ***a.*** 无后嗣的，无继承人的。

heir·loom [ˈɛəluːm; ˋɛrlum] ***n.*** **1.**【法】相传动产〔随不动产转移产权的动产〕。**2.** 祖传宝物，传家宝。

heir·ship [ˈɛəʃip; ˋɛrʃɪp] ***n.*** 继承权；承继，世袭。

heist [haist; haɪst] **I** ***vt.*** **1.**〔方〕举起。**2.**〔美俚〕持凶器行劫，劫夺；偷。**II** ***n.*** 持凶器行劫，劫夺；偷窃。**-er** ***n.*** 持械枪劫者，劫夺者，偷窃者。

Hejaz [hiːˈdʒæz; hiˋdʒæz] ***n.*** 汉志〔阿拉伯西部伊斯兰教国，与 Nejd 合称 Saudi Arabia〕。

He·ji·ra [ˈhedʒirə; hɛˋdʒɪrə, ˋhɛdʒərə] ***n.*** = Hegira.

hek·tare [ˈhektɑː; ˋhɛktɛr] ***n.*** = hectare.

hek·to- = hecto-.

hek·to·gram(me) [ˈhektəgræm; ˋhɛktə͵græm] ***n.*** = hectogram(me).

hek·to·lit·er [ˈhektəlitə; ˋhɛktə͵lɪtɚ] ***n.*** = hectoliter.

hé·las [eiˈlɑːs; eˋlɑs] ***int.***〔F.〕哎呀！哎哟！

held [held; hɛld] hold 的过去式和过去分词。

hel·den·ten·or [ˈheldənteˈnəuə; ˋhɛldəntɛˋnoɚ] ***n.*** 英雄男高音，华格纳歌剧男高音〔指适于演唱歌剧作曲家华格纳 (Wagner) 的歌剧的男高音〕。

Hel·en [ˈhelən; ˋhɛlən] ***n.*** **1.** 海伦〔女子名〕。**2.**【希神】美女海伦〔为斯巴达王 Menelaus 的王后，因她被 Paris 所拐去，引起 Troy 战争〕。

Hel·e·na [ˈhelinə, heˈliːnə; ˋhɛlɪnə, hɛˋlinə] ***n.*** 海伦娜〔女子名〕。

he·li- [ˈheli; ˋhɛlɪ] *comb. f.*〔后接母音〕= helio-: *heli*anthus.

he·li·a·cal [hiːˈlaiəkəl; hɪˋlaɪəkl] ***a.*** 太阳的；与太阳同时升落的。～ ***rising*** [***setting***] (***of a star***)【天】(星的)偕日升[偕日落]。**-ly** ***ad.***

hel·i·am·bu·lance [ˈheliˌæmbjuləns; ˋhɛlɪ͵æmbjʊləns] ***n.*** 救护直升机。

he·li·an·thus [ˌhiːliˈænθəs; ͵hilɪˋænθəs] ***n.***【植】向日葵属植物；〔H-〕向日葵属。

he·li·borne [ˈhelibɔːn; ˋhɛlɪbɔrn] ***a.*** 由直升机运载[输送]的。～ *tactics* 直升机战术。～ *troops* 由直升机运送的部队。

he·li·bus [ˈhelibʌs; ˋhɛlɪ͵bʌs] ***n.*** (作为大都市交通工具的)公共直升机。

hel·i·cal [ˈhelikəl; ˋhɛlɪkl] ***a.*** 螺旋状的，螺旋线的。～ **gear**【机】斜齿轮。**-ly** ***ad.***

hel·i·ces [ˈhelisiːz; ˋhɛlɪ͵siz] helix 的复数。

hel·i·ci·ty [heˈlisiti; hɛˋlɪsətɪ] ***n.***【物】螺旋性。

hel·i·cline [ˈheliklain; ˋhɛlɪ͵klaɪn] ***n.*** 螺旋形坡道。

hel·i·co·gyre [ˈhelikəudʒaiə; ˋhɛlɪkodʒaɪr], **hel·i·co·gyro** [-u; -ʊ] ***n.*** 螺旋桨旋翼直升机。

hel·i·coid [ˈhelikɔid; ˋhɛlɪ͵kɔɪd] **I** ***a.*** 螺状的，螺旋状的。**II** ***n.***【数】螺旋面，螺旋体。**-al** ***a.***

Hel·i·con [ˈhelikən; ˋhɛlɪ͵kən] ***n.*** **1.**【希神】(文艺九女神 Muses 住的)赫利孔山。**2.** 诗思的灵感源泉。**3.**〔h-〕黑里康大号〔一种套在肩上吹的低音大号〕。

hel·i·co·ni·a [ˌheliˈkəuniə; ͵hɛlɪˋkonɪə] ***n.***【植】海里康属 (*Heliconia*) 植物。

Hel·i·co·ni·an [ˌheliˈkəuniən; ͵hɛlɪˋkonɪən] ***a.*** 赫利孔山的。**the** ～ **maids** 文艺九女神(= Muses)。

hel·i·copt [ˈhelikɔpt; ˋhɛlɪkɑpt] ***vt.***, ***vi.*** = helicopter (***vt.***, ***vi.***)。

hel·i·cop·ter [ˈhelikɔptə; ˋhɛlɪ͵kɑptɚ] **I** ***n.*** 直升机。**II** ***vt.*** 用直升机载送。～ *sb. aboard the ship* 用直升机把某人送到船上。— ***vi.*** 乘直升机。～ **carrier** 直升机母舰。**-manship** ***n.*** 驾驶[乘坐]直升机来往。**-ist** ***n.*** 直升机驾驶员。

hel·i·drome [ˈhelidrəum; ˋhɛlɪ͵drom] ***n.*** 直升机机场。

hel·i-home [ˈhelihəum; ˋhɛlɪ͵hom] ***n.*** 直升汽车屋〔直升机与住屋汽车结合而成〕。

hel·i·hop [ˈhelihɔp; ˋhɛlɪhɑp] ***vt.*** (***-hopped***; ***-hopping***) 乘直升机作短程旅行。

helio- [ˈhiːliə; ˋhilɪə] *comb. f.*〔后接辅音〕表示"太阳"：*helio*centric, *helio*graph.

he·li·o·cen·tric [ˌhiːliəuˈsentrik; ͵hilɪoˋsɛntrɪk] ***a.*** 以太阳为中心的；以日心测量的(*opp.* geocentric)。**the** ～ **theory** 地动说，日心说。

he·li·o·cen·tric·ism [ˌhiːliəuˈsentrisizəm; ͵hilɪoˋsɛntrɪsɪzm] ***n.*** 地动说，日心说。

he·li·o·chrome [ˈhiːliəukrəum; ˋhilɪo͵krom] ***n.*** 天然色照片，彩色照片。**he·li·o·chro·mic** ***a.***

he·li·o·chro·my [ˈhiːliəukrəumi; ˋhilɪo͵kromɪ] ***n.*** 天然色照相术，彩色照相术。

he·li·o·gram [ˈhiːliəugræm; ˋhilɪogræm] ***n.*** 回光信号，日光反射信号器发射的信号。

he·li·o·graph [ˈhiːliəugrɑːf; ˋhilɪo͵græf] **I** ***n.*** **1.** 日光反射信号器，回光仪。**2.** 太阳照相机。**3.**【天】日光仪；日光光度计。**4.**【印】日光胶版。**II** ***vt.*** **1.** 用日光反射信号器传达(信号)。**2.** 用太阳照相机拍摄。**-er** ***n.*** 使用回光仪[太阳照相机]的人。

H

he·li·o·gra·phy [ˌhiːliˈɔgrəfi; ˏhilɪˋɑgrəfɪ] ***n*.** **1.** 日光反射信号法。**2.**【印】日光胶版术。**3.**【天】太阳面记述。**he·li·o·graph·ic** [-ˈgræfik; -ˋgræfɪk] ***a*.**

he·li·o·gra·vure [ˈhiːliə*u*grəˈvjuə; ˏhilɪogrəˋvjur] ***n*.**【印】照相凹版(术)。

he·li·o·gy·ro [ˈhiːliə*u*ˌdʒaiərəu; ˋhilɪoˏdʒaɪəro] ***n*.** 直升机。

he·li·ol·a·try [ˌhiːliˈɔlətri; ˏhilɪˋɑlətrɪ] ***n*.** 太阳崇拜。

he·li·ol·o·gy [ˌhiːliˈɔlədʒi; ˏhilɪˋɑlədʒɪ] ***n*.** 太阳研究,太阳学。

he·li·om·e·ter [ˌhiːliˈɔmitə; ˏhilɪˋɑmɪtɚ] ***n*.**【天】量日仪。

He·li·os [ˈhiːliɔs; ˋhilɪɔs] ***n*.**【希神】赫利俄斯〔太阳神〕。

he·li·o·seis·mol·o·gy [ˌhiːliəusaizˈmɔlədʒi; ˏhilɪosaɪzˋmɑlədʒɪ] ***n*.** 太阳地震学〔研究太阳内部地震波活动之学科〕。

he·li·o·scope [ˈhiːliəskəup; ˋhilɪəˏskop] ***n*.** 太阳望远镜;回照器。

he·li·o·sis [ˌhiːliˈəusis; ˏhilɪˋosɪs] ***n*.** (*pl*. ***-ses*** [-siːz; -siz]) **1.**【医】日射病,中暑。**2.**【植】日射病黑斑。

he·li·o·stat [ˈhiːliə*u*stæt; ˋhilɪoˏstæt] ***n*.**【天】定日镜。

he·li·o·tax·is [ˈhiːliə*u*ˈtæksis; ˏhilɪoˋtæksɪs] ***n*.**【生】趋日性。

he·li·o·ther·a·py [ˌhiːliə*u*ˈθerəpi; ˏhilɪoˋθɛrəpɪ] ***n*.**【医】日光疗法。

he·li·o·trope [ˈhelijətrəup; ˋhɛljəˏtrop] ***n*.** **1.**【植】向日性植物;天芥菜属植物。**2.** 天芥菜花的气味[颜色]。**3.** 淡紫色。**4.** 回光仪,日光反射信号。**5.**【地】鸡血石。

he·li·ot·ro·pin(e) [ˌheljəˈtrəupin; hɛljəˋtropɪn] ***n*.**【化】天芥菜精。

he·li·ot·ro·pism [ˌhiːliˈɔtrəpizəm; ˏhilɪˋɑtrəpɪzm] ***n*.**【植】向日性,趋日性。*positive* ～ (茎叶的)向日性。*negative* ～(茎叶的)背日性。

he·li·o·type [ˈhiːliə*u*taip; ˋhilɪoˏtaɪp] ***n*.** 胶版(画)。

he·li·ox [ˈhiːljɔks; ˋhiljɑks] ***n*.** (供深水呼吸用的)氦氧混合剂〔含98%的氦和2%的氧〕。

he·li·o·zo·an [ˌhiːliə*u*ˈzəuən; ˏhiloˋzoən] ***n*.**【动】太阳虫目(*Heliozoa*)动物。**he·li·o·zo·ic** [-ik; -ɪk] ***a*.**

hel·i·pad [ˈhelipæd; ˋhɛlɪˏpæd] ***n*.** = heliport.

hel·i·port [ˈhelipɔːt; ˋhɛlɪˏpɔrt] ***n*.** 直升机场,临时直升机降落点。

hel·i·tank·er [ˈheliˌtæŋkə; ˋhɛlɪˏtæŋkɚ] ***n*.** (装有巨大水箱的)消防直升机。

he·li·um [ˈhiːljəm, -liəm; ˋhilɪəm] ***n*.**【化】氦。～-4 氦4〔氦的最常见同位素〕。

he·lix [ˈhiːliks; ˋhilɪks] ***n*.** (*pl*. ***hel·i·ces*** [ˈhelisiːz; ˋhɛlɪsiz], ～***es*** [ˈhiːliksiz; ˋhilɪksɪz]) **1.** 螺旋线。**2.**【解】耳轮。**3.**【建】螺旋(线)饰。**4.**【动】蜗牛,蜗牛属动物。*normal* ～【机】正交螺旋线。*pancake* ～ 扁平螺旋线圈。

hell [hel; hɛl] **I *n*.** **1.** 地狱,阴间。**2.** 苦境,罪恶之地;极大的痛苦,虐待。**3.** 赌窟。**4.** 恶魔;黑暗势力。**5.** 垃圾箱。**6.** 大混乱,毁坏。**7.** 训斥,咒骂。**8.**〔用以加强语气或咒骂〕胡闹,见鬼。*hungry as* ～ 饿得要命。*living* ～ = *a* ～ *on* [*upon*] *earth* 人间地狱,活地狱。***a*** ～ ***of a*** ... **1.** 极度的;可怕的,糟糕的。**2.** 极好的 (*a* ～ *of a life* 人间地狱。*a* ～ *of a mess* 一塌糊涂。*a* ～ *of an actor* 一个糟糕[出色]的演员)。***all*** ～ ***let loose*** 一团糟。***as*** ～〔口〕很,非常的,极端的;可怕的。***be*** ～ ***for*** 对…极度关心;竭力坚持。***be*** ～ ***on***〔美俚〕对…十分严格;对…十分有害;使…非常痛苦。***beat*** ～ **1.** 令人吃惊。**2.** 超过一切。***blast*** [***knock***] ～ ***out of sb*.** 痛打某人。***catch*** [***get***] ～〔美俚〕挨训斥,受惩罚。***give sb*.** ～ 痛斥某人,狠狠揍某人一顿。***go through*** ～ 赴汤蹈火。***Go to*** ～! 滚蛋! 见鬼去吧! ***have a*** [***the***] ～ ***of a time***〔口〕**1.** 经历一段非常可怕的生活。**2.** 玩得很痛快。***H-***! 见鬼! 混蛋! ～ ***and gone*** 极远的;不可挽回的。～ ***and*** [***or***] ***high water*** 任何困难。***H- breaks loose*.** 喧闹起来,闹得天翻地覆。***the*** ～ ***you say*** 那真叫人吃惊。～ ***to pay*** 痛责,严厉惩罚,后果不堪设想。***in*** ～〔用以加强说气〕究竟,到底 (*What in* ～ *are you doing*? 你究竟在干什么)。***just for the*** ～ ***of it***〔美俚〕就是为了捣乱,只是为了好玩。***like*** ～ **1.**〔俚〕极猛烈,拚命,不顾死活地 (*run like* ～ 拼命跑)。**2.** 哪有这种事,绝不会。***make one's life a*** ～ 过地狱一样的生活。***move*** ～ 想尽办法,无所不用其极。***play*** [***kick up***] ～ ***and Tommy***〔口〕破坏得一塌糊涂;堕落。***play*** ～ ***with*** **1.** 破坏,糟蹋。**2.** 伤害,肃清,消灭。***raise*** ～〔俚〕喧闹,怒斥。***smell*** ～ 受罪,吃苦头。***suffer*** ～ 遭受很大的痛苦。***the*** ～ 见鬼去 (*get the* ～ *out of here* 滚出去!)。***The*** ～ ***of it is*** ...〔美俚〕妙就妙在…;糟就糟在…。***to beat*** ～〔美俚〕〔作副词用〕又快又猛地。***to the*** ～ = *the* ～. ***what the*** ～ **1.**〔用以加强语气或咒骂〕(*What the* ～ *do you want*? 你究竟要什么?) **2.**〔表示无所谓,不在乎〕(*What the* ～, *I may as well go tomorrow instead*. 没什么,我明天去也可以)。

II *vi*. **1.** 放荡地欢闹。**2.** (车辆)急驰。～ ***around*** 混日子;爱出入下等酒吧间。～ **bender** **1.** (北美俄亥俄流域产的)大鲵鱼。**2.**〔美俚〕喧闹的人;鲁莽人。～**-bent** ***a*., *ad*.**〔俚〕固执的[地];拼命的[地],不顾一切的[地]。～**box** 印刷所的坏铅字箱。～**broth**〔古〕巫士行邪术调制的羹汤。～ **buggy**〔军俚〕坦克。～ **camp** 残酷训练营〔日本的一种领导层人员培训班,训练方法严酷而紧张〕。～**cat** 巫婆;泼妇。～**dive** ***vi*.**【空】俯冲轰炸。～**diver** 俯冲轰炸机。～**fire** (惩罚罪人的)地狱火。～**-fired** ***a*., *ad*.** 极度的[地]。～**-for-leather** **1.** ***a*., *ad*.** 拼命的[地],又快又猛的[地]。**2.** ***n*.** 不顾一切,慌忙。～**hole**〔口〕令人厌恶的地方,下流场所。～**hound** (神话中的)地狱看门狗;恶魔,恶鬼一样的人。～**kite** 穷凶极恶的人,残酷的人。～**'s bells** **1.**〔表示惊诧〕喔唷! **2.**〔表示愤慨、不耐烦等〕见鬼! ～ **ship** (对水手进行虐待的)地狱船。**-ward** ***a*., *ad*.** 向着地狱的[地]。**-like** ***a*.**

he'll [hiːl; hil] = he will; he shall.

Hel·las [ˈheləs; ˋhɛləs] ***n*.**〔诗〕希腊。

hel·le·bore [ˈhelibɔː, -bɔə; ˋhɛlɪˏbor, -ˏbɔr] ***n*.** **1.**【植】菟葵;嚏根草属植物。**2.**【药】藜芦。

Hel·lene, Hel·le·ni·an [ˈheliːn, heˈliːniən; ˋhɛlin, hɛˋlinɪən] ***n*.** 古希腊人,希腊人。

Hel·len·ic [heˈliːnik; hɛˋlinɪk] **I *a*.** **1.** 希腊的,希腊人的。**2.** 古希腊文化的;古希腊语的。**II *n*.** (印欧语系之一的)古希腊语。

Hel·len·ism [ˈhelinizəm; ˋhɛlɪnɪzəm] ***n*.** **1.** 希腊语风;古希腊文化。**2.** 对古希腊文化的崇拜。**3.** 古希腊人文主义。**4.** 希腊国民性。

Hel·len·ist [ˈhelinist; ˋhɛlɪnɪst] ***n*.** **1.** 用希腊语的人。**2.** 希腊语言学家;希腊文化研究者[崇拜者]。**3.**【圣】以希腊语为母语的人〔尤指犹太人〕。**4.** 十五世纪在欧洲帮助复兴古典文艺的拜占廷希腊人。

Hel·len·is·tic [ˌheliˈnistik; ˏhɛlɪˋnɪstɪk] ***a*.** **1.** 希腊语言使用者的。**2.** 希腊语言的;希腊语言学家的。**3.** 古希腊建筑式的;古希腊艺术风格的。**-ti·cal·ly *ad*.**

Hel·len·ize [ˈhelinaiz; ˋhɛlənˏaɪz] ***vt*., *vi*.** (使)希腊化。**Hel·leni·za·tion *n*.**

hell·er[1] [ˈhelə; ˋhɛlɚ] ***n*.**〔俚〕= hellion.

hel·ler[2] [ˈhelə; ˋhɛlɚ] ***n*.** **1.** 德国的黄铜币;奥地利的青铜币。**2.** = haler.

hel·ler·i [ˈheləraɪ; ˋhɛləraɪ] ***n*.**【动】剑尾鱼(= swordtail)。

hell·er·y [ˈheləri; ˋhɛlərɪ] ***n*.**〔加拿大俚〕撒野;调皮捣蛋行为。

hell·gram·mite, hell·gra·mite [ˈhelgrəmait; ˋhɛlgrəmaɪt] ***n*.**【动】美洲翅虫(*Corydalis cornuta*)的幼虫。

hel·lion [ˈheliən; ˋhɛlɪən] ***n*.**〔口〕坏人,恶棍;爱恶作剧的人。

hell·ish [ˈheliʃ; ˋhɛlɪʃ] *a*. **1.** 地狱(似)的;魔鬼(似)的,凶恶的。**2.** 〔口〕讨厌的,可憎的。**-ly** *ad*. **-ness** *n*.

hel·lo [ˈheˈləu, heˈləu; ˋhɛˋlo, hɛˋlo] **I** *int*. 喂! 〔用以唤起注意,回答电话或表示问候、惊奇等〕。**II** *vi*., *vt*. (向…)喊一声,"喂"。**III** *n*. 〔表示问候等的声音〕。*Say ~ to your mother*. = *Tell your mother "~" for me*. 代我问候你母亲。*H-! This is Mr. Carter speaking*. (在电话中说)喂! 我是卡特。~ **girl** 〔美口〕女电话接线员。

helm[1] [helm; hɛlm] **I** *n*. **1.** 【船】舵柄;舵轮;舵机。**2.** (国家、企业等的)机要部门,领导。*the clique at the ~ of the war* 战争指导集团。***Down with the ~!*** 转舵背风开! ***ease the ~*** 将舵转回中央位置。***H- alee!*** 转舵背风开! ***put the ~ up*** [***down***] 转舵迎风[背风]。***take the ~ of state*** 掌握政权。***Up with the ~!*** 转舵迎风开! **II** *vt*. 掌(舵);指挥,掌握。

helm[2] [helm; hɛlm] **I** *n*. 头盔。**II** *vt*. 给…戴上头盔。~ **cloud** 〔英方〕(暴风雨时的)盖山乌云。

hel·met [ˈhelmit; ˋhɛlmɪt] **I** *n*. **1.** 头盔;钢盔。**2.** 防护帽;遮阳帽;飞行帽。**3.** 发动机罩。**4.** 盔状花冠[花萼]。**5.** 〔美俚〕警察。*a gas ~* 防毒面具。*a safety ~* (建筑工人等戴的)安全帽。**II** *vt*. 给…戴上头盔。~ **camera** (固定在头盔上的)头盔照像机[摄影机]。**-ed** *a*. **1.** 头盔状的。**2.** 戴头盔的。

Helm·holtz [ˈhelmhəults; ˋhɛlmholts], **H.L.F.von** 冯·赫姆霍尔兹〔1821—1894,德国生理学家及物理学家〕。

hel·minth [ˈhelminθ; ˋhɛlmɪnθ] *n*. 【动】蠕虫,肠虫。

hel·min·thi·a·sis [ˌhelminˈθaiəsis; ˏhɛlmɪnˋθaɪəsɪs] *n*. 【医】蠕虫病,肠虫病。

hel·min·thic [helˈminθik; hɛlˋmɪnθɪk] **I** *a*. **1.** 蠕虫的,肠虫的。**2.** 驱虫的,驱蠕虫的。**II** *n*. 驱虫剂,打蠕虫药。

hel·min·thoid [helˈminθɔid; hɛlˋmɪnθɔɪd] *a*. 肠虫状的,似蠕虫的。

hel·min·thol·o·gy [ˌhelminˈθɔlədʒi; ˏhɛlmɪnˋθɑlədʒɪ] *n*. 蠕虫学。

helms·man [ˈhelmzmən; ˋhɛlmzmən] *n*. (*pl*. ***-men***) 舵手。

he·lo·phyte [ˈheləfait; ˋhɛləfaɪt] *n*. 沼生植物。

Hel·ot [ˈhelət; ˋhɛlət] *n*. **1.** 赫洛特〔古代希腊斯巴达人的奴隶〕。**2.** 〔h-〕奴隶,农奴。

hel·ot·i·sm [ˈhelətizəm; ˋhɛlətɪzəm] *n*. **1.** (古代斯巴达的赫洛特)奴隶制度。**2.** 奴隶身分;奴役现象。**3.** 【生】菌藻共生。

hel·ot·ry [ˈhelətri; ˋhɛlətrɪ] *n*. **1.** 农奴阶级;奴隶制度。**2.** 奴隶地位,农奴地位。

help [help; hɛlp] **I** *vt*. (*~ed*, 〔古〕 ***holp*** [həulp; holp]; *~ed*; 〔古〕 ***holp·en*** [ˈhəulpən; ˋholpən]) **1.** 帮助,援助;救,救济。**2.** 治疗;补救。**3.** 促进,助长。**4.** 〔与 cannot, can 连用〕避免;抑制,阻止;忍耐。**5.** 盛(饭),添(菜),劝(酒)。**6.** 〔婉〕侵吞,窃用。**7.** 〔口〕分配。*God* [*Heaven*] *~s those who ~ themselves*. 〔谚〕天助自助者。*H- me* (*to*) *lift it*. 请帮助我把它抬起来。*So ~ me* (*God*). 〔用于誓语〕愿上帝助我〔因为我在说实话〕;我敢对天发誓。*God ~ him!* 可怜! 可怜虫! *I can't ~ it*. 没有办法。*It can't be ~ed*. = *There is no ~ for it*. 实在没有办法。— *vi*. **1.** 帮助。**2.** 有用,有帮助。**3.** 开饭,上菜。*Don't be longer than you can ~*. 请不要待得太久。*Every little ~s*. 〔谚〕点点滴滴,全有助益。*H-! H-!* 救人啦! ***cannot ~ being*** 不免要成为…。***cannot ~ ... ing*** = 〔美口〕 ***cannot ~ ... but*** (***do***) 不得不…,忍不住要 (*I could not ~ laughing*. 我忍不住不笑)。~ ***a lame dog over a stile*** 帮助人渡过难关。~ ***sb. forward*** [***on***] 搀扶着某人前进;使某人获得进步。~ ***oneself to*** **1.** 自由取食。**2.** 任意占用[取用] (*H- yourself to the cake*. 请随便吃糕饼)。~ ***sb. down*** 把某人搀扶下来。~ ***sb. in*** [***into***] 搀扶某人进入。~ ***sb. off with*** 帮某人脱去。~ ***sb. on with*** 帮某人穿上。~ ***sb. out*** 帮助某人完成工作;补助(费用)。~ ***sb. over*** 帮忙渡过;帮忙越过;帮助打胜。~ ***sb. through*** 帮助某人完成。~ ***sb. to*** **1.** 给某人进食。**2.** 帮助某人得到。~ ***sb. up*** 把某人扶起;扶某人攀登上去。**II** *n*. **1.** 帮助;援助;救济;挽救方法;补救;医治。**2.** 〔单数与不定冠词连用〕助手,帮手,帮忙的人[物]。**3.** 〔口〕(菜的)一份,(酒的)一杯。**4.** 〔美〕佣人,仆人。*a lady ~* 女仆。*a mother's ~* 家庭保姆。*the ~* 女仆,保姆。*There is no ~ for it*. 无法可想。***be of ~*** 有用,有益。***be of much*** [***no***, ***some***] ***~ to sb***. 对某人很有[没有,有些]帮助。***by the ~ of ...*** 得…的帮助。***cry for ~*** 求援;求救。***lay off ~*** 辞退佣人。***with the ~ of*** 在…的帮助下。~**desk** 售后服务部。~**line**(电话局开设的)求助咨询热线。

help·er [ˈhelpə; ˋhɛlpɚ] *n*. **1.** 帮手,助手。**2.** 起救助作用的东西。

help·ful [ˈhelpful; ˋhɛlpfʊl] *a*. 有帮助的,有益的,有用的 (*to*)。**-ly** *ad*. **-ness** *n*.

help·ing [ˈhelpiŋ; ˋhɛlpɪŋ] **I** *a*. 帮助人的,辅助的。*a ~ verb* 助动词。*be ready to give* [*lend*, *reach out*] *a ~ hand* 乐意助人。**II** *n*. **1.** 帮助,支援。**2.** (食物的)一份,一杯。*a second ~* 第二杯。*Have some more ~*. 再来一点。**-ly** *ad*.

help·less [ˈhelplis; ˋhɛlplɪs] *a*. **1.** 无帮助的,未受到帮助的。**2.** 孤弱的,无依无靠的。**3.** 无能的,无用的。***be ~ with mirth*** 笑得打滚,笑破肚皮。**-ly** *ad*. **-ness** *n*.

help·mate, help·meet [ˈhelpmeit, -miːt; ˋhɛlpˏmet, -mit] *n*. **1.** 合作者;良伴,伴侣。**2.** 配偶,妻子[丈夫]。

Hel·sing·fors [ˈhelsiŋfɔːz; ˋhɛlsɪŋfɔrz] *n*. = 〔芬兰〕 Helsinki.

Hel·sin·ki [ˈhelsiŋki; ˋhɛlsɪŋkɪ] *n*. 赫尔辛基〔芬兰首都〕。

hel·ter-skel·ter [ˈheltəˈskeltə; ˋhɛltɚˋskɛltɚ] **I** *ad*. 手忙脚乱地,慌慌张张地,狼狈地,混乱地。**II** *a*. 手忙脚乱的,混乱的。**III** *n*. **1.** 慌张,狼狈。**2.** 乱七八糟的表演。

helve [helv; hɛlv] **I** *n*. (工具的)柄〔尤指斧柄〕。***throw the ~ after the hatchet*** **1.** 〔谚〕赔了夫人又折兵〔接连遭受损失〕。**2.** 全部放弃。**3.** 孤注一掷,一不做二不休。**II** *vt*. 给(斧等)装柄。

Hel·ve·tia [helˈviːʃə; hɛlˋviʃə] *n*. 海尔维希〔瑞士的拉丁语名称〕。

Hel·ve·tian, Hel·vet·ic [helˈviːʃiən, -vetik; hɛlˋviʃɪən, -vɛtɪk] **I** *n*. (古代瑞士)海尔维希族人。**II** *a*. 海尔维希族人的;瑞士(人)的。

hem[1] [hem; hɛm] **I** *n*. (布、衣服的)褶边;折缝。**II** *vt*. (***-mm-***) **1.** 给…缝边;给…镶边。**2.** 围住,关进 (*in*; *about*; *round*)。**3.** 接界。~(***sb.***) ***out*** 排斥,逐出(某人)。— *vi*. 做折边。

hem[2] [hem, hm, mm; hɛm, hm, mm] **I** *int*. 哼! 〔表示踌躇、讽刺、唤起注意或清嗓咳痰时的发声〕。**II** *n*. 哼声;清嗓咳痰声。**III** *vi*. (***-mm-***) 发哼哼声;咳嗽。~ ***and haw*** 〔美〕结结巴巴地说;嗯嗯呃呃〔表示说话时踌躇,或在寻找恰当的字〕。

hem(**a**)**-** *comb. f*. = hemo-.

he·ma·cy·tom·e·ter [ˌhiːməsaiˈtɔmitə, ˌhemə-; ˏhiməsaɪˋtɑmɪtɚ, ˏhɛmə-] *n*. 血球计数器。

he·mag·glu·ti·nate [ˌhiːməˈgluːtineit, ˌhemə-; ˏhiməˋglutɪnet, ˏhɛmə-] *vt*. 【医】使血球凝集。**-na·tion** *n*.

he·mag·glu·ti·nin [ˌhiːməˈgluːtinin, ˌhemə-; ˏhiməˋglutɪnɪn, ˏhɛmə-] *n*. 【医】血球凝集素。

he·mal [ˈhiːməl; himəl] *a*. = haemal.

he·male [ˈhiːˈmeil; ˋhiˋmel] *n*. 〔口〕= he-man.

he-man [ˈhiːmæn; ˋhimæn] **I** *n*. (*pl*. ***-men***) 〔美口〕男子汉。**II** *a*. 男子气的。

hemat- *comb. f*. = hemato-; *hemat*ic.

he·ma·te·in [ˌhiːməˈtiːin, ˌhemə-; ˏhiməˋtiɪn, ˏhɛmə-] *n*. **1.** 【生化】正铁血红素。**2.** 【化】苏木因,氧化苏木精。

he·ma·ther·mal [ˌhiːməˈθəːml, ˌheme-; ˌhiməˋθɚməl, ˌhɛmə-] *a*. 恒温动物的(= homoiothermal)。
he·mat·ic [hiːˈmætik; hiˋmætɪk] *a*. = haematic.
hem·a·tin [ˈhemətin; ˋhɛmətɪn] *n*. = haematin.
hem·a·tin·ic [ˌheməˈtinik; ˌhɛməˋtɪnɪk] **I** *n*.【医】补血剂。**II** *a*. 血红素的,有关血红素的。
hem·a·tite [ˈhemətait; ˋhɛməˌtaɪt] *n*. = haematite.
hemato- *comb.f*. 表示"血": *hemato*ma, *hemato*poiesis.
hem·a·to·blast [ˈhemətəuˌblæst; ˋhɛmətoˌblæst] *n*.【解】血小板,成血细胞。**-blas·tic** [-ˈblæstik; -ˋblæstɪk] *a*.
hem·a·to·cele [ˈhemətəsiːl; ˋhɛmətəsil] *n*. = haematocele.
hem·a·to·crit [ˈhemətəkrit; ˋhɛmətəˌkrɪt] *n*. **1.** 血流比容计,血球容量计。**2.** (用血球容量计测出的)血球密度(= ~ reading)。
hem·a·to·cyte [ˈhemətəsait; ˋhɛmətəˌsaɪt] *n*. = haematocyte.
hem·a·to·gen·e·sis [ˌhemətəuˈdʒenisis; ˌhɛmətoˋdʒɛnəsɪs] *n*. = hematopoiesis. **-to·gen·ic** [-ˈdʒenik; -ˋdʒɛnɪk], **-to·ge·net·ic** [-dʒiˈnetik; -dʒɪˋnɛtɪk] *a*.
hem·a·tog·e·nous [ˌheməˈtɔdʒinəs; ˌhɛməˋtɑdʒənəs] *a*. **1.** 成血的。**2.** (细菌等)由血流所扩散的。
he·ma·tol·o·gy [ˌheməˈtɔlədʒi, ˌhiːmə-; ˌhɛməˋtɑlədʒɪ, himə-] *n*. 血液学。**-log·ic** [-təˈlɔdʒik; -təˋlɑdʒɪk], **-to·log·i·cal** *a*. **he·ma·tol·o·gist** *n*. 血液学家。
he·ma·to·ma [ˌheməˈtəumə; ˌhɛməˋtomə] *n*.【医】血肿(= haematoma)。
he·ma·toph·a·gous [ˌheməˈtɔfəgəs; ˌhɛməˋtɑfəgəs] *a*. 食血为生的,血养的。
hem·a·to·poi·e·sis [ˌhemətəupɔiˈiːsis; ˌhɛmətopɔɪˋisɪs] *n*.【医】血生成。**hem·a·to·poi·et·ic** [-ˈetik; -ˋɛtɪk] *a*.
he·ma·to·ther·mal [ˈhemətəuˌθəːml; ˋhɛmətoˌθɚməl] *a*. 恒温动物的(= homoiothermal)。
he·ma·tox·y·lin [ˌhiːməˈtɔksilin; ˌhiməˋtɑksɪlɪn] *n*. = haematoxylin.
hem·a·to·zo·on [ˌhemətəuˈzəuɔn; ˌhɛmətoˋzoɑn] *n*. (*pl*. **-zo·a** [-ə; -ə]) 血寄生虫。**hem·a·to·zo·ic** [-ik; -ɪk], **hem·a·to·zoal** *a*.
he·ma·tu·re·sis [ˌhiːməˈtjuərisis; ˌhiməˋtjurɪsɪs] *n*.【医】= hematuria.
he·ma·tu·ri·a [ˌhiːməˈtjuriə; ˌhiməˋtjurɪə] *n*.【医】血尿。
heme [hiːm; him] *n*.【生化】原血红素;血质。
hem·el·y·tron, hem·el·y·trum [heˈmelitrɔn, -trʌm; hɛˋmɛlɪtrɑn, -trʌm] *n*. (*pl*. **-tra** [-trə; -trə])【动】半鞘翅〔异翅亚目昆虫的前翅〕。
hem·er·a·lo·pi·a [ˌhemərəˈləupiə; ˌhɛmərəˋlopɪə] *n*. **1.**【医】画盲(症)。**2.** 夜盲(症)(= night blindness)。**hem·er·a·lo·pic** [-ˈlɔpik; -ˋlɑpɪk] *a*.
hemi-, *pref*. 表示"半": *hemi*anopsia, *hemi*cycle.
-hemia *suf*. = -emia.
hem·i·acetal [ˈhemiˌæsətəl; ˋhɛmiˌæsətæl] *n*.【化】半缩醛。
hem·i·a·nop·si·a [ˌhemiəˈnɔpsiə; ˌhɛmɪəˋnɑpsɪə] *n*.【医】偏盲。
he·mic [ˈhiːmik; ˋhimɪk] *a*. 关于血的(= haematic)。
hem·i·chor·date [ˌhemiˈkɔːdeit; ˌhɛmɪˋkɔrdet] **I** *a*. 半索亚门动物的。**II** *n*. 半索亚门动物。
hem·i·cra·ni·a [ˌhemiˈkreiniə; ˌhɛmɪˋkrenɪə] *n*.【医】偏头痛。
hem·i·cy·cle [ˈhemiˌsaikl; ˋhɛmɪˌsaɪkl̩] *n*. **1.** 半圆形。**2.** 半圆形建筑物;半圆形斗技场。
hem·i·dem·i·sem·i·qua·ver [ˌhemiˌdemiˈsemikweivə; ˌhɛmɪˌdɛmɪˋsɛmɪkwevɚ] *n*.〔主英〕【乐】六十四分音符。
hem·i·el·y·tron [ˌhemiˈelitrɔn; ˌhɛmɪˋɛlɪtrɑn] *n*. 半鞘翅(= hemelytron)。
hem·i·glo·bin [ˈhiːmiˌgləubin; ˋhimɪˌglobɪn] *n*.【生化】高铁血红蛋白。
hem·i·he·dral [ˌhemiˈhiːdrəl; ˌhɛmɪˋhidrəl] *a*.【化】(晶体)半面的。~ *form* 半面晶形。
hem·i·hy·drate [ˌhemiˈhaidreit; ˌhɛmɪˋhaɪdret] *n*.【化】半水合物,半水化物。
hem·i·me·tab·o·lous [ˌhemimiˈtæbələs; ˌhɛmɪmɪˋtæbələs] *a*.【动】半变态的(= hemimetabolic)。**-tab·o·lism** *n*.
hem·i·mor·phic [ˌhemiˈmɔːfik; ˌhɛmɪˋmɔrfɪk] *a*.【物】异极的,异极晶形的。
hem·i·mor·phite [ˌhemiˈmɔːfait; ˌhɛmɪˋmɔrfaɪt] *n*.【矿】异极矿。
he·min [ˈhiːmin; ˋhimɪn] *n*.【生化】氯高铁血红素。
Hem·ing [ˈhemiŋ; ˋhɛmɪŋ] *n*. 赫明〔姓氏〕。
Hem·ing·way [ˈhemiŋwei; ˋhɛmɪŋˌwe] *n*. **1.** 海明威〔姓氏〕。**2. Ernest** ~ 欧内斯特·海明威〔1899—1961,美国小说家〕。
hem·i·o·la [ˌhemiˈəulə; ˌhɛmɪˋolə] *n*.【乐】3:2 的比率;五度的;五度音程关系;三倍的(= hemiolia)。
hem·i·par·a·site [ˌhemiˈpærəsait; ˌhɛmɪˋpærəˌsaɪt] *n*. **1.**【动】半寄生虫。**2.**【植】半寄生(植)物。**-par·a·sit·ic** [-ˈsitik; -ˋsɪtɪk] *a*.
hem·i·ple·gia [ˌhemiˈpliːdʒiə; ˌhɛmɪˋplidʒɪə] *n*.【医】半身不遂,偏瘫。
He·mip·te·ra [hiˈmiptərə; hɪˋmɪptərə] *n*.【虫】半翅目。
he·mip·ter·an [hiˈmiptərən; hɪˋmɪptərən] *n*. 半翅目(*Hemiptera*)昆虫〔包括床虱(臭虫)、虱、蚜虫等〕。**he·mip·ter·oid** [-rɔid; -rɔɪd], **he·mip·ter·ous** [-rəs; -rəs] *a*.
hem·i·sphere [ˈhemisfiə; ˋhɛməsˌfɪr] *n*. **1.** (地球或天球的)半球。**2.** 半球地图,半球模型。**3.** 半球上的所有国家[人民]。**4.**【解】大脑半球(= cerebral ~)。**5.** (活动、知识等的)范围,领域。*the Eastern* [*Western*] *H-* 东[西]半球。*Magdeburg* ~*s*【物】马德堡半球〔气压实验用具〕。*a* ~ *of special knowledge* 专业知识的范围。
hem·i·spher·ic(al) [ˌhemiˈsferik(əl); ˌhɛməˋsfɛrɪk(əl)] *a*. 半球的。
hem·i·sphe·roid [hemiˈsfiərɔid; hɛməˋsfɪrɔɪd] *n*. 半球体。
hem·i·stich [ˈhemistik; ˋhɛməstɪk] *n*. (诗的)半句,半行;不完全行。
hem·i·ter·pene [ˌhemiˈtəːpiːn; ˌhɛməˋtɚpin] *n*.【化】半萜。
hem·i·trope [ˈhemitrəup; ˋhɛmɪtrop] **I** *a*.【地】半体双晶的(= hemitropic)。**II** *n*.【地】半体双晶。
hem·line [ˈhemlain; ˋhɛmlaɪn] *n*. **1.** (裙子、衣服等的)底边,贴边。**2.** 上述底边离地的高度。
hem·lock [ˈhemlɔk; ˋhɛmlɑk] *n*. **1.**〔英〕铁杉;毒芹;毒胡萝卜;毒胡萝卜精〔毒药〕。**2.**〔美〕(北美)栂树(= ~ spruce)。~ **parsley** 川芎属植物〔尤指芎䓖〕。
hem·mer[1] [ˈhemə; ˋhɛmɚ] *n*. 哼哼作声的人[机器]。
hem·mer[2] [ˈhemə; ˋhɛmɚ] *n*. **1.** 缝边的人。**2.** (缝纫机的)翻边装置。
hemo- *comb.f*. 表示"血": *hemo*lysin, *hemo*philia.
he·mo·blast [ˈhiːməblæst; ˋhiməˌblæst] *n*. = hematoblast.
he·mo·chro·ma·to·sis [ˌhiːməˌkrəuməˈtəusis; ˌhiməˌkroməˋtosɪs] *n*. 血色素沉着病,血色沉着病。
he·mo·cy·a·nin [ˌhiːməˈsaiənin; ˌhiməˋsaɪənɪn] *n*.【生化】血蓝蛋白。
he·mo·cyte [ˈhiːməsait; ˋhiməˌsaɪt] *n*. 血细胞,血球。
he·mo·cy·tom·e·ter [ˌhiːməusaiˈtɔmitə; ˌhimosaɪˋtɑmɪtɚ] *n*. 血球计数器,血球计。
he·mo·dia [hiˈməudiə; hɪˋmodɪə] *n*.【医】牙敏感。

H

he·mo·di·al·y·sis [ˌhiːməudaiˈælisis; ˏhimodaiˋælɪsɪs] ***n.*** 血渗析,血透析。

he·mo·dy·nam·ics [ˌhiːməudaiˈnæmiks; ˏhimodaɪˋnæmɪks] ***n.***【医】血流动力学。

he·mo·flag·el·late [hiːməuˈflædʒileit; ˏhimoˋflædʒəlet] ***n.***【医】血内鞭毛虫,血鞭虫。

he·mo·glo·bin [ˌhiːməuˈgləubin; ˏhimoˋglobɪn] ***n.***【生化】血红素;血红蛋白(= haemoglobin)。

he·mo·glo·bin·u·ri·a [ˌhiːməˌgləubiˈnjuəriə; ˏhiməˏglobɪˋnjurɪə] ***n.***【医】血红蛋白尿。**he·mo·glo·bin·u·ric** ***a.***

he·moid [ˈhiːmɔid; ˋhimɔɪd] ***a.*** 血状的。

he·mo·lymph [ˈhiːməlimf; ˋhiməlɪmf] ***n.***【医】血淋巴。

he·mo·ly·sin [ˌhiːməˈlaisin; ˏhiməˋlaɪsɪn] ***n.***【医】溶血素(= haemolysin)。

he·mol·y·sis [hiːˈmɔləsis; hiˋmɑləsɪs] ***n.*** (*pl.* ***-ses*** [-siːz; -siz]) 溶血(作用),血球溶解。**he·mo·lyt·ic** [ˌhiːməˈlitik; ˏhiməˋlɪtɪk] ***a.***

he·mo·lyze [ˈhiːməlaiz; ˋhiməlaɪz] ***vi.***, ***vt.*** (***-lyzed***; ***-lyz·ing***) 使溶血,引起(血球)溶解。

he·mo·phile [ˈheməfil, -fail; ˋhɛməfɪl, -faɪl] ***n.*** **1.** 血友病患者。**2.** 嗜血菌。

he·mo·phil·i·a [ˌhiːməˈfiliə; ˏhiməˋfɪlɪə] ***n.***【医】血友病(= haemophilia)。

he·mo·phil·i·ac [ˌhiːməˈfiliæk; ˏhiməˋfɪlɪæk] ***n.*** 血友病患者。

he·mo·phil·ic [ˌhiːməˈfilik; ˏhiməˋfɪlɪk] ***a.*** **1.** 血友病的;患血友病的。**2.** (某些细菌的)嗜血性的。

he·mop·ty·sis [hiˈmɔptisis; hɪˋmɑptɪsɪs] ***n.***【医】咯血。

hem·or·rhage [ˈheməridʒ; ˋhɛmərɪdʒ] **I** ***n.*** **1.**【医】出血(= haemorrhage)。**2.** 〔美俚〕番茄汁。*cerebral* ~ 脑溢血。***have a*** ~〔美俚〕大怒,大发脾气,大为愤慨。**II** ***vi.***【医】出血。

hem·or·rhoid [ˈhemərɔid; ˋhɛməˏrɔɪd] ***n.*** 〔常 *pl.*〕【医】痔(= haemorrhoid)。*internal* [*external*] ~*s* 内[外]痔。

hem·or·rhoid·ec·to·my [ˌhemərɔiˈdektəmi; ˏhɛmərɔɪˋdɛktəmɪ] ***n.*** (*pl.* ***-mies***)【医】痔切除术。

he·mo·sta·sia [ˌhiːməˈsteiʒiə; ˏhiməˋstеʒɪə] ***n.***【医】止血(= haemostasia, hemostasis)。

he·mo·sta·sis [hiˈmɔstəsis; hɪˋmɑstəsɪs] ***n.*** (*pl.* ***-ses*** [-siːz; -siz])【医】**1.** 止血。**2.** 止血法。

he·mo·stat [ˈhiːməstæt; ˋhiməˏstæt] ***n.*** 止血器〔尤指止血钳,止血剂〕。

he·mo·stat·ic [ˌhiːməˈstætik; ˏhiməˋstætɪk] **I** ***a.*** 能够止血的。**II** ***n.*** 止血剂(= haemostatic)。

he·mo·tox·in [ˌhiːməˈtɔksin; ˏhiməˋtɑksɪn] ***n.*** 红血球毒素〔能杀灭红血球的一种毒素〕。**he·mo·tox·ic** [-ˈtɔksik; -ˋtɑksɪk] ***a.***

hemp [hemp; hɛmp] ***n.*** **1.**【植】大麻,大麻纤维。**2.** 纤维,长纤维的植物。**3.** 〔the ~〕由大麻制成的麻醉药(= bhang)。**4.** 〔谑〕绞索。*gambo* ~ 洋麻。*Indian* ~ 黄麻。~ **agrimony** 大麻叶泽兰(*Eupatorium cannabinum*)〔产于欧洲,原用于医药〕。~ **hook** 砍麻刀。~ **nettle**【植】鼬瓣花属(*Galeopis*)植物〔尤指黄鼬瓣花(*Galeopsis tetrahit*),原产欧洲〕。~ **palm** 棕榈。~**seed**【植】大麻子。

hemp·en [ˈhempən; ˋhɛmpən] ***a.*** 大麻(似)的;大麻制的。*a* ~ *collar* 绞首索。

hemp·seed [ˈhempˌsiːd; ˋhɛmpˏsid] ***n.*** **1.** 大麻子(可作鸟食)。**2.** 〔俚〕流氓,无赖;罪大恶极的人。

hem·stitch [ˈhemstitʃ; ˋhɛmˏstɪtʃ] **I** ***n.***【纺】花饰线迹,抽丝线迹,(布边抽丝后做成的)花边;结穗缘饰。**II** ***vt.*** 用抽丝法做(花边),在…上用抽丝法刺绣。

Hen. = Henry.

hen [hen; hɛn] **I** ***n.*** **1.** 母鸡。**2.** 雌禽;雌鱼〔虾、蟹等〕。**3.** 〔俚〕(嘴碎或爱管闲事的)女人,长舌妇。*a* ~ *sparrow* 雌麻雀。*a* ~ *crab* 雌蟹。*a wet* [*an old*] ~〔美俚〕讨厌的人,泼妇。*a* ~ *on* 策划中的阴谋(*There's a* ~ *on.* 其中有阴谋)。***A*** ~ ***is on.*** 有人正策划阴谋。***as mad as a wet*** ~〔美俚〕非常生气。***like a*** ~ ***on a hot girdle*** 像热锅上的蚂蚁,坐立不安;极为难受。***like a*** ~ ***with one chicken*** 大惊小怪,无事忙。***sell one's*** ~***s on a rainy day*** 亏本出售。**II** ***vi.*** (***-nn-***)〔美俚〕(女人)聊天;散播流言蜚语。~**-and-chickens**【植】屋顶长生花。~**-apple**〔俚〕鸡蛋。~ **battery** 备有分隔产卵箱的鸡舍。~ **coop** 鸡窝;〔美俚〕女生宿舍。~**cote** 鸡棚。~ **fruit**〔俚〕鸡蛋。~ **harrier**【动】鸡鹞。~**-hearted** ***a.*** 胆小的。~ **house 1.** 家禽的笼舍。**2.** 〔美俚〕军官俱乐部。~ **party**〔俚〕妇女聚会。~**roost** 鸡窝。~ **track** 潦草难认的字。~**-wife** ***n.*** 养鸡女人。

hen·bane [ˈhenbein; ˋhɛnben] ***n.***【植】天仙子,莨菪(= hyoscyamus)。

hen·bit [ˈhenbit; ˋhɛnbɪt] ***n.***【植】宝盖草(*Lamium amplexicaule*)。

hence [hens; hɛns] **I** ***ad.*** **1.** 〔古〕由是,从此;今后,此后。**2.** 因此,所以,本来〔其后动词常略去不用〕。*five years* ~ 五年之后。*go* [*pass*] ~ 死。*H- with him*! 把他带走! *H-* (*comes*) *the name* ... 因此有…之名。**II** ***int.*** 〔诗〕去。*Hence*! [*Go* ~!] 出去,走开。

hence·forth, hence·for·ward [ˈhensˈfɔːθ; ˈhensˈfɔːwəd; ˌhɛnsˈfɔrθ; ˋhɛnsˋfɔrwəd] ***ad.*** 〔书〕从今以后,今后。

Hench [hentʃ; hɛntʃ] ***n.*** 亨奇〔姓氏〕。

hench·man [ˈhentʃmən; ˋhɛntʃmən] ***n.*** (*pl.* ***-men***) **1.** 亲信,心腹;(政治上的)支持者,仆从,捧场者。**2.** 〔废〕侍从。

hendeca- *comb. f.* 表示"十一": *hendeca*gon.

hen·dec·a·gon [henˈdekəgən; hɛnˋdɛkəgən] ***n.*** 十一角形,十一边形。

hen·dec·a·he·dron [henˌdekəˈhiːdrən; hɛnˏdɛkəˋhidrən] ***n.*** (*pl.* ~***s***, ***-dra*** [-drə; -drə]) 十一角体。**-a·he·dral** ***a.***

hen·dec·a·syl·la·ble [henˌdekəˈsiləbl; hɛnˏdɛkəˋsɪləbl] ***n.*** 十一音节诗句。**-a·syl·lab·ic** [-siˈlæbik; -sɪˋlæbɪk] ***a.***, ***n.***

Hen·der·son [ˈhendəsn; ˋhɛndəsn] ***n.*** 亨德森〔姓氏〕。

hen·di·a·dys [henˈdaiədis; hɛnˋdaɪədɪs] ***n.***【修】重言法,重名法〔用 and 连接两名词以代替一名词及一形容词的修辞法: death and honour (= honourable death). cups and gold (= golden cups)〕。

hen·e·quen, hen·e·quin [ˈhenikin; ˋhɛnɪkɪn] ***n.*** (墨西哥产)黑纳金树;黑纳金树叶的纤维。

Hen·ley [ˈhenli; ˋhɛnlɪ] ***n.*** 亨里〔姓氏〕。

hen·na [ˈhenə; ˋhɛnə] **I** ***n.*** **1.**【植】指甲花,散沫花(*Lawsonia inermis*)。**2.** 散沫花染料〔可染指甲、头发、眼皮〕。**3.** 棕红色。**II** ***a.*** 棕红色的。**III** ***vt.*** 用散沫花染料染(指甲等)。

hen·ner·y [ˈhenəri; ˋhɛnərɪ] ***n.*** 家禽饲养场,养鸡场。

hen·ny [ˈheni; ˋhɛnɪ] ***a.***, ***n.*** 羽毛像母鸡的(雄鸡)。

hen·o·the·ism [ˈhenəθiizəm; ˋhɛnəθɪɪzm] ***n.*** (信仰多神中有一个主神的)单一神教。

hen·peck [ˈhenpek; ˋhɛnˏpɛk] ***vt.*** (妻)管制(丈夫)。

hen·pecked [ˈhenpekt; ˋhɛnˏpɛkt] ***a.*** 〔口〕怕老婆的。

Hen·ri·et·ta [ˌhenriˈetə; ˏhɛnrɪˋɛtə] ***n.*** 亨丽埃塔〔女子名〕。

Hen·ry [ˈhenri; ˋhɛnrɪ] ***n.*** **1.** 亨利〔姓氏,男子名〕。**2.** **O.** ~ 奥·亨利(1862—1901)美国短篇小说家〔真实姓名为 William Sydney Porter〕。

hen·ry [ˈhenri; ˋhɛnrɪ] (*pl.* ***-ries***, ~***s***)【电】亨(利)〔电感单位,略作 H〕。

hent [hent; hɛnt] **I** ***vt.*** (***hent***; ***hent·ing***) 〔古〕**1.** 抓住。**2.** 领悟,理解。**II** ***n.*** 〔古〕**1.** 抓住;领悟,理解。**2.** 理解了的事物;观念;意图。

H

he·or·to·lo·gy [ˌhiːəˈtɔlədʒi; ˌhiəˋtɑlədʒɪ] *n*. 宗教节日学。

HEOS = highly eccentric orbit satellite 高偏心轨道卫星。

hep[1] [hep; hɛp] *n*. 野蔷薇的果实。

hep[2] [hep; hɛp] *a*. 〔美俚〕**1**. 懂得世故的。**2**. 对…熟悉的,对…通晓的,对…有欣赏能力的 (*to*)。*be ～ to movies* 电影通。*put sb*. *～ to* 教某人了解…。～**-cat 1**. 知情人。**2**. 〔美〕爵士音乐[摇摆舞音乐]迷;爵士音乐大师。

hep[3] [hep; hɛp] *int*. 嗬!〔使步伐整齐的口令声〕。

he·par [ˈhiːpɑː; ˋhipɑr] *n*. **1**. 【解】肝。**2**. 肝脏色的物质。

hep·a·rin [ˈhepərin; ˋhɛpərɪn] *n*. 【药】肝素〔一种抗凝血药〕。

hep·a·rin·ize [ˈhepərinaiz; ˋhɛpərɪˏnaɪz] *vt*. 【医】用肝素治疗。

hepat- *comb*. *f*. 表示"肝": *hepat*itis.

hep·a·tec·to·my [ˌhepəˈtektəmi; ˏhɛpəˋtɛktəmɪ] *n*. (*pl*. **-mies**) 【医】肝切除术。

he·pat·ic [hiˈpætik; hɪˋpætɪk] **I** *a*. **1**. 肝的,对肝有影响的。**2**. 肝状的,肝色的。**3**. 欧龙牙草的。*the ～ artery* 肝动脉。**II** *n*. 【植】欧龙牙草。

he·pat·i·ca [hiˈpætikə; hɪˋpætɪkə] *n*. (*pl*. ～*s*, **-cae** [-siː; -si]) 【植】獐耳细辛属植物。

hep·a·ti·tis [ˌhepəˈtaitis; ˏhɛpəˋtaɪtɪs] *n*. 【医】肝炎。*infectious* [*serum*] ～ 传染性[血清]肝炎。

hep·a·ti·za·tion [ˌhepətaiˈzeiʃən; ˏhɛpətaɪˋzeʃən] *n*. 【医】肝样变。

hepato- *comb*. *f*. = hepat: *hepato*sis.

hep·a·to·fla·vin [ˌhepətəuˈfleivin; ˏhɛpətoˋflevɪn] *n*. 【药】核黄素。

hep·a·to·sis [ˌhepəˈtəusis; ˏhɛpəˋtosɪs] *n*. 【医】肝痛,肝病。

Hep·burn [ˈhebəːn; ˋhɛˏbɝn] **1**. 赫伯恩〔姓氏〕。**2**. **James Curtis** ～ 赫伯恩〔1815—1911,美国传教士,医生,语言学家, Hepburn 式日本语罗马字拼法创造人〕。

hep·cat [ˈhepkæt; ˋhɛpˏkæt] *n*. 〔俚〕**1**. 爵士[摇摆舞]音乐迷。**2**. 爵士[摇摆舞]乐队乐师。

He·phaes·tus [hiˈfiːstəs; hɪˋfistəs] *n*. 【希神】赫斐斯塔斯〔火和锻冶之神〕。

Hep·ple·white [ˈheplhwait; ˋhɛplˏhwaɪt] **I** *n*. **1**. 海普怀特〔姓氏〕。**2**. **George** ～ 乔治·海普怀特〔? —1786, 英国家具设计师〕。**II** *a*. 海普怀特式的(家具)〔以纤细轻巧为其特征〕。

hepta- *comb*. *f*. 表示"七": *hepta*d, *hepta*gon.

hep·ta·chord [ˈheptəkɔːd; ˋhɛptəˏkɔrd] *n*. 七弦琴;【乐】七声音阶。

hep·tad [ˈheptæd; ˋhɛptæd] *n*. **1**. 七个,成七的一组,成七的一套。**2**. 【化】七价物,七价元素,七价基。

hep·ta·glot [ˈheptəglɔt; ˋhɛptəglɑt] *a*., *n*. 用七种语言写的(书)。

hep·ta·gon [ˈheptəgən; ˋhɛptəˏgɑn] *n*. 七角形,七边形。**-al** *a*.

hep·ta·hed·ron [ˈheptəˈhedrən; ˋhɛptəˋhɛdrən] *n*. (*pl*. ～*s*, **-dra** [-drə; -drə]) 七面体。**-hed·ral** [-rəl; -rəl] *a*.

hep·tam·er·ous [hepˈtæmərəs; hɛpˋtæmərəs] *a*. 【植】(花)七瓣的(=7-merous)。

hep·tam·e·ter [hepˈtæmitə; hɛpˋtæmɪtɚ] **I** *n*. 七韵步的诗。**II** *a*. 〔诗〕七韵步的。

hep·tane [ˈheptein; ˋhɛpten] *n*. 【化】庚烷。

hep·tar·chy [ˈheptɑːki; ˋhɛptɑrkɪ] *n*. **1**. 〔常 H-〕【英史】(七至八世纪不列颠的盎格鲁和萨克逊人的)七王国。**2**. 七头政治。**3**. 【生】七原型。**-chic**, **-i·cal** *a*.

hep·ta·stich [ˈheptəstik; ˋhɛptəˏstɪk] *n*. 七行诗。

Hep·ta·teuch [ˈheptətjuːk; ˋhɛptəˏtjuk] *n*. 【圣】《旧约全书》的头七卷。

hep·ta·va·lent [ˈheptəˌveilənt; ˋhɛptəˏvelənt] *a*. 【化】七价的。

hep·tode [ˈheptəud; ˋhɛpˏtod] *n*. 【无】七极管。

hep·tose [ˈheptəus; ˋhɛpˏtos] *n*. 【化】庚糖。

heptr =【空】helicopter.

her [常 həː, 弱 əː, hə, ə; 常 hɝ, 弱 ɝ, hə, ə] *pro*. **1**. 〔she 的宾格〕她。**2**. 〔she 的所有格〕她的。**3**. 〔古、诗〕〔作反身代名词用〕= herself. **4**. 〔口〕〔作表语用〕= she. *Give it to ～*. 把这个给她。*I am sorry about ～ leaving*. 我对她的离去很感遗憾。*It's ～, sure enough*. 一定是她。*Her sister sews better than ～*. 她姐姐缝衣服的手艺比她高。*She sat ～ down by the fire*. 她在炉火旁边坐下。～ **indoors** 〔英〕(控制了丈夫的)内当家。

her. = heraldic; heraldry.

He·ra [ˈhiərə; ˋhirə] *n*. 【希神】赫拉〔天后,主神宙斯(Zeus)之妻〕。

Her·a·cles, **Her·a·kles** [ˈherəkliːz; ˋhɛrəkliz] *n*. = Hercules.

Her·a·cli·tus [ˌherəˈklaitəs; ˏhɛrəˋklaɪtəs] *n*. 赫拉克利特〔535? —475 B.C.?, 希腊哲学家〕。

her·ald [ˈherəld; ˋhɛrəld] **I** *n*. **1**. (旧时的)传令官。**2**. (英国中世纪司宗谱纹章的)纹章官。**3**. 通报者;使者;先驱,预兆。*The cuckoo is a ～ of spring*. 杜鹃是春天的先驱。**the Heralds' College** 〔英〕宗谱纹章院。**II** *vt*. **1**. 传达,通告。**2**. 预告,预示…的到来。**3**. 欢呼。*The song of birds ～s the approach of spring*. 百鸟齐鸣报春到。

he·ral·dic [heˈrældik; hɛˋrældɪk] *a*. **1**. 传令官的。**2**. 纹章官的。**3**. 纹章学的。**-di·cal·ly** *ad*.

her·ald·ry [ˈherəldri; ˋhɛrəldrɪ] *n*. **1**. 宗谱纹章官的职位[职权];宗谱记录法。**2**. 纹章学;〔集合词〕纹章,家徽。**3**. 〔诗〕(仪式等的)壮观,豪华。

herb [həːb; hɝb] *n*. **1**. 草,草本植物。**2**. 茎叶可作药品、食品、香料等的植物;香草,药草。**3**. 牧草。*No ～ will cure love*. 〔谚〕相思病无药可医。*the ～ of grace* 芸香。*medicinal ～s* 药草,草药。～ **beer** 草药制的饮料。～ **doctor** 草药医生,土郎中。～ **Paris** 轮药王孙 (*Paris quadrifolia*)〔一种百合科植物〕。～ **Robert** 【植】罗伯特氏老鹳草 (*Geranium robertianum*)。～ **tea**, ～ **water** (草药煎成的)汤药。**-less** *a*. 缺乏草本植物的。

her·ba·ceous [həːˈbeiʃəs; hɝˋbeʃəs] *a*. **1**. 草本的;草质的。**2**. (颜色、纹理、形状等)似绿叶的,叶状的。*a ～ border* (花园沿边)种草本植物的花坛。*a ～ root* [*stem*] 草质根[茎]。

herb·age [ˈhəːbidʒ; ˋhɝbɪdʒ] *n*. **1**. 〔集合词〕草本植物(尤指牧草)。**2**. (草的)茎叶。**3**. 【法】(在他人土地上的)放牧权。

herb·al [ˈhəːbəl; ˋhɝbəl] **I** *a*. 草本植物的,草本植物制的。**II** *n*. **1**. 草药书。**2**. 〔古〕草本志;草本植物志。**3**. 植物标本。**-ist** *n*. **1**. 草本植物学家。**2**. 草药采集人;种草药的人。**3**. 草药商。**4**. 草药医生。

her·bar·i·um [həːˈbeəriəm; hɝˋbɛrɪəm] (*pl*. **-ri·a** [-riə; -rɪə], ～*s*) *n*. **1**. 植物标本集。**2**. 植物标本箱;植物标本室。**3**. 蜡叶标本。

Her·bart [ˈhəːbɑːt; ˋhɝbɑrt] **1**. 赫巴特〔姓氏〕。**2**. **Johann Friedrich** ～ 约翰·弗里德里克·赫巴特〔1776—1841,德国哲学家,教育家〕。

Her·bart·i·an [ˈhəːbɑːtiən; ˋhɝbɑrtɪən] *a*. 赫巴特(学派)的。

Her·bart·i·an·ism [həːˈbɑːtiənizəm; hɝˋbɑrtɪənɪzəm] *n*. 赫巴特的教育说。

herb·ar·y [ˈhəːbəri; ˋhɝbərɪ] *n*. **1**. = herbarium. **2**. 草本植物园,药草园。

Her·bert [ˈhəːbət; ˋhɝbɚt] *n*. 赫伯特〔姓氏,男子名〕。

her·bi·cide [ˈhəːbisaid; ˋhɝbɪˏsaɪd] *n*. 【生化】除莠剂。**-dal** *a*.

H

her·bif·er·ous [həːˈbifərəs; hɝˋbɪfərəs] *a*. 生草的。

her·bi·vore [ˈhəːbivɔː; ˋhɝbɪvɔr] *n*. 〔F.〕食草动物。

her·biv·o·rous [həːˈbivərəs; hɝˋbɪvərəs] *a*. **1**. 吃草的。**2**. 身体粗大而肠子细长的。~ *animals* 食草动物。

her·bo·ri·za·tion [ˌhəːbəraiˈzeiʃən; ˌhɝbəraɪˋzeʃən] *n*. 植物采集,药草收集。

her·bo·rize [ˈhəːbəraiz; ˋhɝbəraɪz] *vi*. 采集植物[药草]。

herb·y [ˈhəːbi; ˋhɝbɪ] *a*. **1**. 草的,草本的。**2**. 草多的,长满草的。

Her·cu·le·an [ˌhəːkjuːˈljən; ˌhɝkjuˋlɪən] *a*. **1**. 【希、罗神】赫尔克里斯的,大力神的。**2**. 力大无比的。**3**. 费力的,非常困难的。*a* ~ *labour* 难巨的劳动。*a* ~ *warrior* 魁梧的战士。

Her·cu·les [ˈhəːkjuliːz; ˋhɝkjəˌliz] *n*. **1**. 【希、罗神】赫尔克里斯,大力神〔主神宙斯之子,力大无比的英雄〕。**2**. 〔h-〕大力士。**3**. 〔the ~〕【天】武仙座, *a regular* ~ 大力士。~ ***'s choice*** 宁可吃苦,不愿享乐。***the Pillars of*** ~ = ~***'s Pillars*** 世界的尽头;直布罗陀海峡两岸的悬岩。~ **beetle** 大金龟子〔南美大甲虫〕。~ **powder** 矿山炸药。~**'s-club** *n*. 【植】**1**. 多刺楤木(*Aralia spinosa*)〔产于美国东部,即土当归属〕。**2**. 美国南部刺椒(*Zanthoxylum clava-herculis*)。

herd[1] [həːd; hɝd] **I** *n*. **1**. 兽群,牛群,猪群。**2**. 〔the ~〕〔蔑〕群众,民众。***ride*** ~ ***on*** **1**. 骑在马上放牧(畜群)。**2**. 监督,管束(*ride* ~ *on the children* 管束小孩子们)。**II** *vt*. 把…赶在一块。— *vi*. 成群,群集(*with*; *together*)。~ **book** 家畜血统记录。~ **instinct** 【心】群居本能。

herd[2] [həːd; hɝd] **I** *n*. 牧人〔通例用作复合词:cow*herd*, shep*herd*, swine*herd*〕。**II** *vt*. 看管(家畜),放牧。

herd·er [ˈhəːdə; ˋhɛdɚ] *n*. **1**. = herdsman. **2**. 〔美俚〕监狱看守。

her·dic [ˈhəːdik; ˋhɝdɪk] *n*. 赫狄克式马车〔由 P. Herdic 发明,为二轮或四轮的低矮马车,座位在两边,门在背后〕。

herd's-grass [ˈhəːdzgrɑːs; ˋhɝdzgrɑs] *n*. **1**. = redtop. **2**. = timothy.

herds·man [ˈhəːdzmən; ˋhɝdzmən] (*pl*. **-men**) *n*. **1**. 〔英〕牧人。**2**. 畜群所有者。**3**. 〔the H-〕【天】牧夫座(= Boötes)。

here [hiə; hɪr] **I** *ad*. **1**. 在这里;到这里;向这里〔*cf*. there〕。**2**. 在这一点上;这时。**3**. 【宗】在这个世界上,在尘世间。**4**. 这里〔用于唤起注意或加强语气,用在名词之后〕。*H- I am*. 我来了,我到了。*H- I come, honey*. 〔美口〕喂。*H- it is*. **1**. 在这里。**2**. 这是给你的。*H-'s sth. for you*. 这一点点东西是送你的。*My friend* ~ *knows it*. 我这里的朋友懂得它。***belong*** ~ 此地人,当地人。~ ***and now*** 就在此时此地。~ ***and there*** 各处;零零落落地。~ ***below*** 在尘世间。***H- goes***! 〔口〕啊,开始吧! 这就动手吧! ~, ***there and everywhere*** 到处。***H- is to you***! = ***H- is to your health***! 祝你健康! 敬您一杯! ~ ***today and gone tomorrow*** 行踪不定,飘忽无常。***H- you*** (***we***) ***are***. 〔口〕**1**. 你(或我们)要的[我的]东西在这里呢。**2**. (你或我们)到了。***look*** [***see***] ~ 〔口〕听我说。***neither*** ~ ***nor there*** 〔口〕与本题无关,没有什么,不中肯。***same*** ~ 〔口〕彼此彼此,我也一样。***this*** ~ [***ere***] ***man*** 〔卑〕= ***this man*** ~ (这儿的)这个人,就是这个人。**II** *n*. 这里;这一点。***from*** ~ 从这里。***in*** ~ 在这里,在这一点上。***near*** ~ 在这附近。***up to*** ~ 到这里。**III** *int*. **1**. 〔唤人注意的话〕喂! **2**. 〔点名时的回答〕到! 有!

here·a·bout(s) [ˈhiərəbaut(s); ˋhɪrəbaʊt(s)] *ad*. 在这附近。

here·af·ter [hiərˈɑːftə; hɪrˋæftɚ] **I** *ad*. **1**. 今后,以后,此后。**2**. 在来世。**II** *n*. **1**. 将来。**2**. 【宗】来世。

here·at [hiərˈæt; hɪrˋæt] *ad*. 〔古〕由是,因此。

here·a·way(s) [ˈhiərəˈwei(z); ˋhɪrəˋwe(z)] *ad*. 在这附近。

here·by [ˈhiəˈbai; ˋhɪrˋbaɪ] *ad*. **1**. 兹,特此;以此〔公文、布告等用语〕。**2**. 〔废〕附近。*Notice is* ~ *given that*... 特此布告。*I* ~ *resign my office*. 特此辞职。

he·re·des [həˈriːdiːz; həˋridiz] *n*. heres 的复数。

he·red·i·ta·bil·i·ty [hiˌreditəˈbility; hɪˌrɛdɪtəˋbɪlətɪ] *n*. = heretability.

he·red·i·ta·ble [həˈreditəbl; həˋrɛdɪtəbl̩] *a*. = heritable.

her·e·dit·a·ment [ˌheriˈditəmənt; ˌhɛrɪˋdɪtəmənt] *n*. **1**. 【法】世袭财产;不动产。**2**. 继承。

he·red·i·tar·i·an [hiˌrediˈtɛəriən; hɪˌrɛdɪˋtɛrɪən] *n*. 遗传论者,信奉遗传说的人。

he·red·i·tar·i·ly [hiˈrediterili; hɪˋrɛdɪtɛrəlɪ] *ad*. 世袭地;遗传地。

he·red·i·tar·y [hiˈreditəri; hɪˋrɛdɪtərɪ] *a*. **1**. 遗传的,遗传性的。**2**. 【法】世袭的。~ *characters* 遗传特征。~ *diseases* 遗传病。*a* ~ *enemy* 世仇。*a* ~ *feud* 宿怨。~ *friendship* 世交。~ *property* 世袭财产。

he·red·i·tism [hiˈreditizəm; həˋrɛdɪtɪzm̩] *n*. 遗传学。

he·red·i·ty [hiˈrediti; hɪˋrɛdətɪ] *n*. **1**. 遗传;遗传性。**2**. 遗传性特征。**3**. 继承;传统。

Her·e·ford [ˈherifəd; ˋhɛrəfɚd] **I** *n*. **1**. (英国)赫勒德郡。**2**. 赫勒福德种牛。**II** *a*. 赫勒福德牛的。

here·from [hiəˈfrɔm; hɪrˋfrɑm] *ad*. 由此。

here·in [ˈhiərˈin; hɪrˋɪn] *ad*. 此中;于此,据此看来。*H- lies the answer*. 答案就在这里。*by the clauses* ~ 根据(本约)所列条款。

here·in·a·bove [ˌhiərinəˈbʌv; ˌhɪrɪnəˋbʌv] *ad*. 在上文。

here·in·af·ter [ˈhiərinˈɑːftə; ˋhɪrɪnˋæftɚ] *ad*. 在下文,以下。~ *called Buyer* 以下统称买方。

here·in·be·fore [ˈhiərinbiˈfɔː; ˌhɪrɪnbɪˋfɔr] *ad*. 在上文,以上。

here·in·be·low [ˈhiərinbiˈləu; ˋhɪrɪnbɪˋlo] *ad*. 在下文。

here·in·to [ˈhiərˈintu; ˋhɪrˋɪntu] *ad*. 到这里面。

here·of [hiərˈɔv; hɪrˋɑv] *ad*. **1**. 关于这个。**2**. 本,此。*upon the receipt* ~ 据此收条。*more* ~ *later* (关于这一点)详见后文。

here·on [hiərˈɔn; hɪrˋɑn] *ad*. = hereupon.

he·res [ˈhiəriːz; ˋhɪriz] *n*. (*pl*. ***he·re·des*** [hiˈriːdiːz; hɪˋridiz]) 【法】继承人。

here's [hiəz; hɪrz] = here is. *Here's to you*! 干杯,祝你成功! 祝你愉快! 〔祝福词〕。

he·re·si·arch [həˈriːziɑːk; həˋrizɪɑrk] *n*. 异教祖师;异教首领。

her·e·sy [ˈherəsi; ˋhɛrəsɪ] *n*. **1**. 异教,异端。**2**. 左道邪说;信奉异端邪说。***be guilty of*** ~ 犯异端邪说罪。***fall into*** ~ 陷入旁门左道。

her·e·tic [ˈherətik; ˋhɛrətɪk] **I** *n*. **1**. 异教徒。**2**. 持非正统见解的人;信奉邪说的人。**II** *a*. = heretical.

he·ret·i·cal [hiˈretikəl; həˋrɛtɪkl̩] *a*. 异教的,异端的。**-ly** *ad*.

here·to [ˈhiəˈtuː; hɪrˋtu] *ad*. 〔古〕到此时;到此地;至此;关于这个。*annexed* ~ 并入于此。

here·to·fore [ˌhiətəˈfɔː; ˌhɪrtəˋfɔr] *ad*. 前此,以前,迄今为止。

here·un·der [hiərˈʌndə; hɪrˋʌndɚ] *ad*. **1**. 在下面,在下(文)。**2**. 依此。*articles enumerated* ~ 下列商品。

here·up·on [ˌhiərəˈpɔn; ˌhɪrəˋpɑn] *ad*. **1**. 于是。**2**. 关于这。

here·with [hiəˈwið; hɪrˋwɪð] *ad*. **1**. 同此,并此〔信中用语〕。**2**. 以此方法。*enclosed* ~ 并此附上。*I am sending you* ~ *a cheque*. 现附上支票壹张。

her·i·ot [ˈheriət; ˋhɛrɪət] *n*. 【英法】租地继承税〔指依据英国封建时代法律规定,佃农死时向地主交纳的钱款或实物〕。

H

her·it·a·ble [ˈheritəbl; ˋhɛrətəbl] *a*. **1.** 被继承的;可继承的。**2.** 被遗传的;可遗传的。**-i·ta·bil·i·ty** *n*. 遗传率;遗传力。**-a·bly** *ad*.

her·it·age [ˈheritidʒ; ˋhɛrətɪdʒ] *n*. **1.** 世袭财产。**2.** (长子)继承权。**3.** 继承物;遗产;传统;文化遗产〔指有历史意义或重大自然生态和考古价值的古建筑、遗迹或自然胜地等〕。**4.** (犹太教圣经中所说的)上帝的选民。

her·i·tance [ˈheritəns; ˋhɛrɪtns] *n*. 〔古〕= inheritance.

her·i·tor [ˈheritə; ˋhɛrətɚ] *n*. (*fem*. **-tress** [-tris; -trɪs]) 继承人。

herl [həːl; hɝl] *n*. **1.** (做假蚊钩的)蚊羽细毛。**2.** 用细羽毛做成的假蚊钩。

Her·man(n) [ˈhəːmən; ˋhɝmən] *n*. 赫尔曼〔男子名〕。

her·maph·ro·dite [həːˈmæfrədait; hɝˋmæfrə͵daɪt] **I** *n*. **1.** 阴阳人,两性人。**2.** 两性体;【动】雌雄同体;【植】雌雄同株。**II** *a*. 具有两性的,具有相反性质的。~ **brig** 【海】双桅帆船。~ **calipers** 【机】**1.** 单边卡钳。**2.** 内外[双用]卡钳。

her·maph·ro·dit·ic(al) [həːmæfrəˈditik(əl); hɝ͵mæfrəˋdɪtɪk(əl)] *a*. 雌雄同体[同株]的;具有相反两种性质的。**-i·cal·ly** *ad*.

her·maph·ro·dit·ism [həːˈmæfrədaitizəm; hɝˋmæfrədaɪ͵tɪzm] *n*. 两性体,雌雄同体[同株]。

her·me·neu·tic(al) [ˌhəːmiˈnjuːtik(əl); ͵hɝmɪnˋjutɪk(əl)] **I** *a*. (圣经)解释(学)的;释经学的。**II** *n*. 〔*pl*.〕释经学;圣经注解学。

HERMES = Heavy Element Radioactive Material Electromagnetic Separator 重放射性同位素电磁分离器。

Her·mes [ˈhəːmiːz; ˋhɝmiz] 【希神】赫耳墨斯〔为众神传信并掌管商业、道路的神〕。*the* ~ *spaceplan* 郝耳墨斯航天飞机〔欧洲太空署正在研制的一种太空穿梭机〕。

her·met·ic(al) [həːˈmetik(əl); hɝˋmɛtɪk(əl)] *a*. **1.** 〔H-〕海尔梅斯神的〔埃及神 Thoth 的希腊名称为 Hermes Trismegistus, 据说为炼丹术始祖〕。**2.** 炼金术的,奥妙的。**3.** 密闭的,密封的。*the H- art* [*philosophy*, *science*] 炼金术。~ **sealing** 【冶】熔解密闭。

her·met·i·cal·ly [həːˈmetikəli; hɝˋmɛtɪkəlɪ] *ad*. 密封地,密闭地;牢牢地。

her·mit [ˈhəːmit; ˋhɝmɪt] *n*. **1.** 隐者,逸士。**2.** (加有葡萄干、核桃、香精的)小甜饼。**3.** 【动】独居性动物。**4.** 【动】(热带森林中的)蜂鸟。*a false* ~ 寄居蟹的一种。*go* ~ 〔美〕过孤独的生活。~ **crab** 【动】寄居蟹。~ **thrush** 【动】北美隐居鹎(*Hylocichla guttata*)。~ **warbler** 【动】森莺(*Dendroica occidentalis*)〔产于北美西部,头部黑黄色,灰背〕。

her·mit·age [ˈhəːmitidʒ; ˋhɝmɪtɪdʒ] *n*. **1.** 隐士住处,茅庐,僻静的住处;修道院。**2.** 隐士生活。**3.** 〔H-〕法国南部产的一种红葡萄酒。**4.** 〔H-〕列宁格勒的一所博物馆。

hern[1] [həːn; hɝn] *n*. 〔英方〕苍鹭(= heron)。

hern[2], **her'n** [həːn; hɝn] *pro*. 〔方〕= hers, her own.

her·ni·a [ˈhəːnjə; ˋhɝnɪə] *n*. (*pl*. ~ *s*, *-ni·ae* [-nii; -nɪɪ]) 【医】疝;突出。

her·ni·al [ˈhəːnjəl; ˋhɝnɪəl] *a*. 疝的。

her·ni·ar·y [ˈhəːnjəri; ˋhɝnɪərɪ] *a*. (治)疝的。

her·ni·ate [ˈhəːnieit; ˋhɝnɪ͵et] *vi*. 【医】形成疝。**-ni·a·tion** *n*.

her·ni·or·rha·phy [ˌhəːniˈɔːrəfi; ͵hɝnɪˋɔrəfɪ] *n*. (*pl*. **-phies**) 【医】疝缝术。

hern·shaw [ˈhəːnʃɔː; ˋhɝnʃɔ] *n*. 〔方〕【动】苍鹭。

he·ro [ˈhiərəu; ˋhɪro] *n*. (*pl*. ~ *es*) **1.** 英雄,豪杰,勇士。**2.** (古代神话中的)神人,半神的勇士。**3.** (小说等的)男主角,男主人翁〔*fem*. heroine〕。~ ***of the quill*** 著名作家,文坛健将。~ ***of the spigot*** 〔谑〕酒鬼。***make a*** ~ ***of*** 赞扬,捧,使英雄化。~ ***sandwich*** "英雄"三明治〔夹着各种冷肉、奶酪和蔬菜的面包卷〕。~ **worship** 英雄崇拜;对个人的盲目崇拜。~**-worship** *vt*. 把…当作英雄崇拜。~**-worship(p)er** 英雄崇拜者。

Her·od [ˈherəd; ˋhɛrəd] *n*. 【圣】(以残暴著称的犹太国王)希律王。**out-Herod** *vt*. (*out-Herod Herod* 比希律王更希律王,比希律王还要残暴。)★ 英语构词法中,在人名前加 out-,除此词外,还有 out-Hitler Hitler (比希特勒还要残暴)等用法。

He·rod·o·tus [hiˈrɔdətəs; hɪˋrɑdətəs] *n*. 希罗多德〔公元前 484? —425?,纪元前 5 世纪希腊历史学家,有历史之父之称〕。

he·ro·ic [hiˈrəuik; hɪˋroɪk] **I** *a*. **1.** 英雄的,勇士的;神人的,超人的。**2.** 英勇的,壮烈的;强大的,崇高的;冒险的;果断的。**3.** (语言)夸张的,高雅的,〔诗〕歌颂英雄的;史诗般的。**4.** (声音)宏大的,(雕像等)大于实物的。**5.** (措施等)冒险的;(药物)剂量大的,猛烈的。~ *conduct* [*deeds*] 英雄行为。*a* ~ *drug* 烈性麻醉品。~ *measures* 冒险的措施。~ *medicine* 烈性的药;剂量大的药。~ *poetry* 英雄诗,史诗。~ *size* [*on a* ~ *scale*] 大于实物的尺寸。***the*** ~ ***age*** 古希腊的"英雄时代"。**II** *n*. **1.** 英雄诗,史诗。**2.** 〔*pl*.〕夸张的言行。**3.** 咬文嚼字,文诌诌。***go into*** ~***s*** 过于夸张。~ **couplet** 英雄偶句诗体〔互相押韵,含有抑扬音步的两行诗。乔叟首先在英诗中采用〕。~ **line**, ~ **metre**, ~ **verse** 英雄诗体。~ **tenor** 英雄男高音,华格纳歌剧男高音。

he·ro·i·cal [hiˈrəuikəl; hɪˋroɪkl] *a*. = heroic (*a*.) **-ly** *ad*.

he·ro·i·com·ic(al) [hiˌrəuiˈkɔmik(əl); hɪ͵roɪˋkɑmɪk(əl)] *a*. (诗、故事等)滑稽史诗体的,壮烈而滑稽的〔一种以史诗体来歌颂卑微或滑稽事物的讽刺性文体〕。

he·ro·i·fy [hiˈrəuifai; hɪˋroəfaɪ] *vt*. 使英雄化。

her·o·in [ˈherəuin; ˋhɛroɪn] *n*. 【药】海洛因,二乙醯吗啡。

her·o·ine [ˈherəuin; ˋhɛroɪn] *n*. **1.** 女英雄。**2.** 烈女,烈妇。**3.** 半神式的女英雄。**4.** (小说等中的)女主角,女主人翁。

her·o·ism [ˈherəuizəm; ˋhɛro͵ɪzəm] *n*. **1.** 英雄气概,英雄行为,英雄品质。**2.** 英雄主义。

her·o·ize [ˈhiərəuaiz; ˋhɪroaɪz] *vt*. 把…英雄化。— *vi*. 以英雄自居。

her·on [ˈherən; ˋhɛrən] *n*. (*pl*. ~(*s*)) 【动】苍鹭。

her·on·ry [ˈherənri; ˋhɛrənrɪ] *n*. 苍鹭的巢穴。

her·ons·bill [ˈherənzbil; ˋhɛrənzbɪl] *n*. 【植】牻牛儿苗属(*Erodium*)植物。

her·pes [ˈhəːpiːz; ˋhɝpiz] *n*. 【医】疱疹。~ **simplex** 【医】单纯疱疹。~ **zoster** 【医】带状疱疹。

her·pet·ic [həːˈpetik; hɝˋpɛtɪk] *a*. 【医】疱疹性的。

her·pe·tol·o·gy [ˌhəːpiˈtɔlədʒi; ͵hɝpɪˋtɑlədʒɪ] *n*. 爬虫学。

Herr [hɛə; hɛr] *n*. (*pl*. ***Her·ren*** [ˈhɛərən; ˋhɛrən]) 〔G.〕**1.** 先生〔与英语 Mr. 相当〕。**2.** 德国绅士。*Meine Herren* 各位(先生),诸位(先生)。

Her·ren·volk [ˈhɛrənfɔlk; ˋhɛrənfolk] *n*. 〔G.〕统治民族。

Her·rick [ˈherik; ˋhɛrɪk] *n*. 赫里克〔姓氏〕。

her·ring [ˈheriŋ; ˋhɛrɪŋ] *n*. (*pl*. ~ *s*, 〔集合词〕~) 鲱鱼,鳍白鱼。*a red* ~ = *kippered* ~ 熏鲱鱼。***as dead as a*** ~ 死得像鲱鱼一样僵硬。***be packed as close as*** ~***s*** 挤得像罐头里的鲱鱼。***draw a red*** ~ ***across the path*** [***track***, ***trail***] 扯些不相关的事转移别人的注意力。***like*** ~***s in a barrel*** 挤在一起。***neither fish, flesh, nor good red*** ~ 非驴非马,不伦不类;不相干的东西。***shotten*** ~ 产过卵的鲱鱼,废物。***the king of the*** ~***s*** 月鱼。~ **gull** 【动】(北大西洋产的)大海鸥。~**-pond** **1.** 海洋。**2.** 〔谑〕北大西洋。

her·ring·bone [ˈheriŋbəun; ˋhɛrɪŋ͵bon] **I** *n*. **1.** 【建】(砖、石头等砌成)鲱骨(式);人字形。**2.** 【纺】海力蒙(衣服),人字呢(衣服)。**II** *a*. 鲱骨状的;人字形的。**III** *vt*. 把…作成人字形,在…上作交叉缝式;在…上作矢尾形(接合)。— *vi*. **1.** 作成人字形;作交叉缝式,作矢尾形接合。**2.** 【滑雪】滑橇尖向外作人字形爬坡。~ **bridging**

人字撑。～ **earth**【电】鱼骨形接地。～ **gear** 人字形齿轮,双螺旋齿轮。～ **pavement**【建】人字式(铺砌)路面。～ **stitch**【纺】人字形缝,缝成人字形的图案。～ **tooth** 人字齿,双螺旋齿。

hers [hə:z; hɝz] *pro*.〔she 的物主代词〕她的,她的东西,她的家属[有关的人]。*Is that his or* ～? 那是他的还是她的? *H- is better than mine*. 她的比我的好。*Give my best wishes to her and* ～. 问候她和她的家人[爱人,朋友等]。*This seems to be a hat of* ～. 这好像是她的帽子。**his and** ～ 丈夫和妻子;男男女女。

Her·schel(l) [ˈhə:ʃəl; ˋhɝʃəl] *n*. **1**. 赫谢尔〔姓氏,男子名〕。**2**. **Sir John William** ～ 小约翰·威廉·赫谢耳〔1792—1871,英国天文学家、哲学家〕。**3**. **Sir William** ～ 老赫谢耳〔1738—1822,英国天文学家小赫谢耳之父,天王星的发现者〕。**4**. 天王星的别名。**5**.【物】赫谢耳〔光源的辐射亮度单位〕。

her·self [hə:ˈself, həˈself; hɝˋsɛlf, həˋsɛlf] *pro*. (*pl*. *themselves*) **1**.〔作反身代词〕她自己。*She ought to be ashamed of* ～. 她应当感到羞愧。*She killed* ～. 她自杀了。**2**.〔加强语气〕她本人,她亲自。*She said it* ～. 她自己说的。*H- an orphan, she understood the situation*. 她本身是个孤儿,理解这情况。**be** [*become*, *come to*] ～ (情绪、健康)处于正常情况(*She is not quite* ～ *today*. 她今天有些反常[不舒服]。*She has come to* ～. 她已复原了,她已恢复正常)。(**all**) **by** ～ 她独自地;她独立地。

Her·sey [ˈhə:si; ˋhɝsɪ] *n*. 赫西〔姓氏〕。

her·story [ˈhə:stəri; ˋhɝstərɪ] *n*. "巾帼"历史〔以女权主义立场解释或撰写的历史〕。

Hert·er [ˈhə:tə; ˋhɝtɚ] *n*. 赫脱〔姓氏〕。

hertz [hə:ts; hɝts] *n*.【电】赫,赫兹〔频率单位;周/秒〕。

Hertz [hə:ts; hɝts], **Hein·rich Ru·dolph**, 赫兹〔1857—1894,德国物理学家〕。

Hertz·i·an [ˈhə:tsiən; ˋhɝtsɪən] *a*. 赫兹的。～ **wave** 赫兹电波〔德国物理学家 H. Hertz 所发现的电磁波〕。

Her·ze·go·vi·na [ˌhɛətsəgəuˈvi:nə; ˏhɛrtsəgoˋvinə] *n*. 黑塞哥维那〔南斯拉夫一地区〕。

he's [常 hi:z; 弱 hiz, iz; 常 hiz, 弱 hɪz, ɪz] = he is; he has.

Hesh·van [heʃˈvɑ:n, ˈheʃvən; hɛʃˋvɑn, ˋhɛʃvən] *n*. 〔Heb.〕犹太历二月。

hes·i·tance, hes·i·tan·cy [ˈhezitəns, -si; ˋhɛzɪtəns, -sɪ] *n*. 踌躇,犹豫(= hesitation)。

hes·i·tant [ˈhezitənt; ˋhɛzɪtənt] *a*. **1**. 踌躇的,犹豫的。**2**. 吞吞吐吐的。**-ly** *ad*.

hes·i·tate [ˈheziteit; ˋhɛzɪˏtet] *vi*. **1**. 犹豫,踌躇;不愿。**2**. 含糊,支吾。**3**. 口吃。～ *about joining the expedition* 他对于是否参加远征队犹豫不决。～ *between fighting and submitting* 或战或降,踌躇不决。～ *to take such a big risk* 不愿冒这样大的险。～ *in speaking* 说话吞吞吐吐。*They* ～*d at nothing to gain their ends*. 他们不惜一切来达到目的。*If there is anything you want, please don't* ～ *to ask me*. 你要是需要什么,请别客气问我要好了。*I don't* ～ *to say that*. 长话短说,开门见山。***He who*** ～***s is lost***.〔谚〕当断不断,必受其患。

hes·i·tat·ing·ly [ˈheziˌteitiŋli; ˋhɛzɪˏtetɪŋlɪ] *ad*. 踌躇地,犹豫地,含糊地。

hes·i·ta·tion [ˌheziˈteiʃən; ˏhɛzɪˋteʃən] *n*. **1**. 踌躇,犹豫。**2**. 含糊。**3**. 口吃。**have no** ～ **in saying** 毫不踌躇地说。**without** ～ 毫不踌躇地,立即。

hes·i·ta·tive [ˈhezitətiv; ˋhɛzɪtətɪv] *a*. 踌躇的。**-ly** *ad*.

Hes·per [ˈhespə; ˋhɛspɚ] *n*.〔诗〕= Hesperus.

Hes·pe·ri·an [hesˈpiəriən; hɛsˋpɪrɪən] **I** *a*.〔诗〕西方的,西方国家的。**II** *n*. 西方国家的人。

Hes·per·ides [hesˈperidi:z; hɛsˋpɛrɪˏdiz] *n*. *pl*. **1**.【希神】看守金苹果乐园的四姊妹。**2**.〔作单数用〕金苹果园。

hes·per·i·din [hesˈperidin; hɛsˋpɛrɪdɪn] *n*.【化】桔皮苷。

hes·per·i·di·um [ˌhespəˈridiəm; ˏhɛspəˋrɪdɪəm] *n*. (*pl*. *-di·a* [-iə; -ɪə]) 柑桔属植物的果实〔如桔或柠檬〕,柑果,柠檬果。

hes·per·or·nis [ˌhespəˈrɔ:nis; ˏhɛspəˋrɔrnɪs] *n*.【古生】黄昏鸟〔美洲大陆产〕。

Hes·per·us [ˈhespərəs; ˋhɛspərəs] *n*.【天】金星,长庚星。

Hess [hes; hɛs] *n*. 赫斯〔姓氏〕。

Hes·se, Hes·sen [ˈhesi, -sn; ˋhɛsɪ, -sn̩] *n*. 黑森〔德国州名〕。

Hes·sian [ˈhesiən; ˋhɛsɪən] **I** *a*. (德国)黑森州的。**II** *n*. **1**. 黑森人。**2**.〔美〕美独立战争时英军中的德国雇佣兵,雇佣兵;为金钱而听人使唤的人;流氓。**3**. [h-] 打包麻布。～ **boots** (黑森士兵穿的)膝前有饰缨的长靴。～ **fly** 麦蝇〔麦的害虫,似蚊〕。

hess·ite [ˈhesait; ˋhɛsaɪt] *n*.【矿】蹄银矿。

hes·so·nite [ˈhesənait; ˋhɛsənaɪt] *n*.【矿】钙铝榴石(= essonite)。

hest [hest; hɛst] *n*.〔古〕= behest.

Hes·ter [ˈhestə; ˋhɛstɚ] *n*. 赫丝特〔女子名, Esther 的异体〕。

hes·ter·nal [hesˈtə:nəl; hɛsˋtɝnəl] *a*. 昨日的;往昔的。

Hes·ti·a [ˈhestiə; ˋhɛstɪə] *n*.【希神】赫斯提〔灶神或炉神〕。

het[1] [het; hɛt] *a*.〔美、英方〕= heated. ～ ***up*** 兴奋,激动,勃然大怒。

het[2], **heth** [het; hɛt] *n*. 希伯来文的第八个字母。

hetae·ra [hiˈtiərə; hɪˋtɪrə] *n*. (*pl*. ***-rae*** [-ri:; -ri]) = hetaira.

he·tae·rism [hiˈtiərizəm; hɪˋtɪrɪzm] *n*. = hetairism.

he·tai·ra [hiˈtaiərə; hɪˋtaɪrə] *n*. (*pl*. ***-rai*** [-rai; -raɪ]) **1**. (古代希腊的)妾;妓女,艺妓。**2**. 依靠美色获取财富、社会地位的女子。**-ric** *a*.

he·tai·rism [hiˈtaiərizəm; hɪˋtaɪrɪzm] *n*. **1**.【考古】(同部族内的)乱婚,杂婚。**2**. 公开蓄妾。

heter(o)- *comb*. *f*. 表示"异","异型","其他"〔元音前用 heter-〕: *hetero*gen.

het·er·o [ˈhetərəu; ˋhɛtəro] **I** *a*.〔美俚〕向异性的,非同性爱的。**II** *n*. 非同性恋者。

het·er·o·aux·in [ˌhetərəuˈɔ:ksin; ˏhɛtəroˋɔksɪn] *n*.【化】吲哚乙酸,异茁长素。

het·er·o·cer·cal [ˌhetərəˈsɔ:kl; ˏhɛtərəˋsɔrkl] *a*.【动】歪尾的〔尤指鲨鱼〕。

het·er·o·charge [ˈhetərəutʃɑ:dʒ; ˋhɛtərotʃɑrdʒ] *n*.【物】混杂电荷。

het·er·o·chro·mat·ic [ˌhetərəukrəuˈmætik; ˏhɛtərokroˋmætɪk] *a*. **1**. 异色的,有异色的;包含不同颜色的;多色的。**2**.【生】异染色质的。

het·er·o·chro·ma·tin [ˌhetərəuˈkrəumətin; ˏhɛtəroˋkromətɪn] *n*.【生】异染色质。

het·er·o·chro·mo·some [ˌhetərəuˈkrəuməsəum; ˏhɛtəroˋkroməsom] *n*.【生】异染色体(= sex chromosome)。

het·er·o·chro·mous [ˌhetərəuˈkrəuməs; ˏhɛtəroˋkroməs] *a*.【生】异色的,不同色的。

het·er·o·clite [ˈhetərəuklait; ˋhɛtəroˏklaɪt] **I** *n*. **1**.【语法】不规则的词〔尤指名词〕。**2**. 违反一般规则的人[事]。**II** *a*. 不规则的,变态的。～ *nouns* [*verbs*] 不规则名词[动词]。

het·er·o·cot·y·lus [ˌhetərəuˈkɔtləs; ˏhɛtəroˋkɑtləs] *n*. (*pl*. *-y·li* [-ai; -aɪ]) = hectocotylus.

het·er·o·cy·cle [ˈhetərəusaikl; ˋhɛtərosaɪkl] *n*.【化】杂环。

het·er·o·cy·clic [ˌhetərəuˈsaiklik; ˏhɛtəroˋsaɪklɪk] *a*.【化】杂环型的。

het·er·o·cyst [ˈhetərəusist; ˋhɛtərosɪst] *n*.【生】异形细

胞。

het·er·o·des·mic [ˌhetərəuˈdesmik; ˌhɛtəroˋdɛsmɪk] ***a***. 【物】杂键的。

het·er·o·dox [ˈhetərəudɔks; ˋhɛtərədɑks] ***a***. **1.** 异端的;异教的。**2.** 违反共认标准的。

het·er·o·dox·y [ˈhetərəudɔksi; ˋhɛtərəˌdɑksɪ] ***n***. (*pl*. **-dox·ies**) **1.** 异端。**2.** 异教;异说。

het·er·o·dyne [ˈhetərəudain; ˋhɛtərəˌdaɪn] **I** ***n***. 【无】外差法,【无】外差法的,成拍的。**II** ***vt***., ***vi***. (使)成拍,(使)致差,(使…)混合。~ **oscillator** 外差振荡器。~ **receiver** 外差式收音机。

het·er·oe·cism [ˌhetəˈriːsizəm; ˌhɛtəˋrisɪzm] ***n***. 【植】转主寄生(现象)。

het·er·o·ga·mete [ˌhetərəugəˈmiːt; ˌhɛtərogəˋmit] ***n***. 【生】异形配子。

het·er·og·a·mous [ˌhətəˈrɔgəməs; ˌhətəˋrɑgəməs] ***a***. **1.** 【生】由异形配子生殖的 (*opp*. isogamous)。**2.** 【植】有异性花的 (*opp*. homogamous)。

het·er·o·gen [ˈhetərəudʒen; ˋhɛtərodʒɛn] ***n***. 【生】异基因。

het·er·o·ge·ne·i·ty [ˌhetərəudʒiˈniːiti; ˌhɛtərodʒəˋniətɪ] ***n***. **1.** 【生】异质性。**2.** 【化】不均匀性。**3.** 【数】不纯一性。

het·er·o·ge·ne·ous [ˈhetərəuˈdʒiːniəs; ˌhɛtəroˋdʒinɪəs] ***a***. **1.** 异种的,异类的。**2.** 异质的,不纯的,成份复杂的 (*opp*. homogeneous)。**3.** 【数】非齐次[性]的,参差的,不纯一的。**4.** 【化】不均匀的,多相的。*a* ~ *light* 杂色光。**-ly** ***ad***.

het·er·o·gen·e·sis [ˌhetərəuˈdʒenisis; ˌhɛtəroˋdʒɛnɪsɪs] ***n***. 【生】异型有性世代交替;突变。

het·er·o·ge·net·ic [ˌhetərəudʒiˈnetik; ˌhɛtərodʒəˋnɛtɪk] ***a***. 【生】异源的。

het·er·og·e·nous [ˌhetəˈrɔdʒinəs; ˌhɛtəˋrɑdʒənəs] ***n***. 【生,医】异源的,异种的,异体的。

het·er·og·o·ny [ˌhetəˈrɔgəni; ˌhɛtəˋrɑgənɪ] ***n***. **1.** 【生】世代交替(= alternation of generations)。**2.** 【植】花柱异长(= heterostyly)。**3.** 形体变异学(= allometry)。**-o·nous** [-nəs; -nəs] ***a***.

het·er·o·graft [ˈhetərəuˈgrɑːft; ˋhɛtəroˌgræft] ***n***. 【医】异质移植物。

het·er·og·ra·phy [ˌhetəˈrɔgrəfi; ˌhɛtəˋrɑgrəfɪ] ***n***. 【语】**1.** 同一字母的不同发音。**2.** 同一词的非标准拼法。

het·er·og·y·nous [ˌhetəˈrɔdʒinəs; ˌhɛtəˋrɑdʒənəs] ***a***. (蜜蜂、蚁等)有生殖和不生殖两种雌性的。

het·er·o·lec·i·thal [ˌhetərəuˈlesiθəl; ˌhɛtəroˋlɛsɪθəl] ***n***. 【生】异卵黄。

het·er·ol·o·gous [ˌhetəˈrɔləgəs; ˌhɛtəˋrɑləgəs] ***a***. **1.** 【生】异素的,异种的。**2.** 【医】异种的,异质的;异要素的。**3.** 不齐的;不等的;不同的。**-o·lo·gy** [-ˈrɔlədʒi; -ˋrɑlədʒɪ] ***n***.

het·er·ol·y·sis [ˌhetəˈrɔlisis; ˌhɛtəˋrɑlɪsɪs] ***n***. 【生化】**1.** 异种溶解。**2.** 异种血解;异族溶解。**-o·lyt·ic** [-əˈlitik; -əˋlɪtɪk] ***a***.

het·er·o·me·tab·o·lism [ˌhetərəumiˈtæbəlizəm; ˌhɛtəromiˋtæbəlɪzm] ***n***. 【动】不全变态。**-o·met·a·bol·ic** [-ˌmetəˈbɔlik; -ˌmɛtəˋbɑlɪk], **-o·me·tab·o·lous** [-miˈtæbələs; -mɪˋtæbələs] ***a***.

het·er·o·mor·phic [ˌhetərəuˈmɔːfik; ˌhɛtəroˋmɔrfɪk] ***a***. **1.** 【生】异形的,异态的;【虫】完全变态的。**2.** 【化】多晶(型)的。**3.** 【物】复形性的。

het·er·o·mor·phism [ˌhetərəuˈmɔːfizəm; ˌhɛtəroˋmɔrfɪzm] ***n***. **1.** 【生】异态性,异态现象。**2.** 【化】多晶(型)现象。**3.** 【物】复形性,复型性。

het·er·o·mor·phy [ˈhetərəuˌmɔːfi; ˋhɛtəroˌmɔrfɪ] ***n***. 【生】异态性,异态现象。

het·er·on·o·mous [ˌhetəˈrɔnəməs; ˌhɛtəˋrɑnəməs] ***a***. **1.** 受外界支配的,他治的,不自治的。**2.** 【生】异律的 (*opp*. autonomous);发展规律不同的,不同于一般形态的,形态互异的。

het·er·on·o·my [ˌhetəˈrɔnəmi; ˌhɛtəˋrɑnəmɪ] ***n***. **1.** 他治,不自治,无自由权[自决权]的状态。**2.** 【生】异律 (*opp*. autonomy)。

het·er·o·nym [ˈhetərənim; ˋhɛtərənɪm] ***n***. **1.** 同形异音异义词〔如读音为 [led; lɛd] 的 lead (铅)和读音为 [liːd; lid] 的 lead (领导)〕。**2.** (两种语言中的)对译同义词。

het·er·on·y·mous [ˌhetəˈrɔniməs; ˌhɛtəˋrɑnɪməs] ***a***. **1.** 同形异音异义词的;同形异音异义词性的。**2.** 不同名称的〔指一对关连词〕。**3.** (视平行线焦点外)影像交叉的。*Son and daughter are* ~. 儿子和女儿是名称不同的一对关连词。**-y·mous·ly** ***ad***.

het·er·op·a·thy [ˌhetəˈrɔpəθi; ˌhɛtəˋrɑpəθɪ] ***n***. 【医】对症疗法;对抗疗法;反应性异常。

het·er·o·phil [ˈhetərəfil; ˋhɛtərəfɪl] ***a***. 【生】(红血球的)嗜异染性的。

het·er·oph·o·bi·a [ˌhetərəuˈfəubiə; ˌhɛtərəˋfobɪə] ***n***. 异性恐怖症。

het·er·oph·o·ny [ˌhetəˈrɔfəni; ˌhɛtəˋrɑfənɪ] ***n***. 【乐】离开同音的声部;(一个声部外所加的)装饰音声部;(非复调的)多声部。

het·er·o·pho·ri·a [ˌhetərəuˈfɔuriə; ˌhɛtəroˋforɪə] ***n***. 【物】隐斜视。

het·er·o·phyl·lous [ˌhetərəuˈfiləs; ˌhɛtəroˋfɪləs] ***a***. 【植】具异形叶的。**-phyl·ly** ***ad***.

het·er·o·phyte [ˈhetərəufait; ˋhɛtərofaɪt] ***n***. 【植】异养植物。**-phyt·ic** [-ˈfitik; -ˋfɪtɪk] ***a***.

het·er·o·plas·ty [ˈhetərəuˌplæsti; ˋhɛtəroˌplæstɪ] ***n***. 【医】异质成形术。**-plas·tic** ***a***.

het·er·o·ploid [ˈhetərəuplɔid; ˋhɛtəroplɔɪd] ***a***. 【生】异倍体的。**-ploi·dy** ***n***.

het·er·o·po·lar [ˌhetərəuˈpəulə; ˌhɛtəroˋpolɚ] ***a***. 【物】异极的。

het·er·o·po·lar·i·ty [ˌhetərəupəuˈlæriti; ˌhɛtəropoˋlærətɪ] ***n***. 【物】异极性。

het·er·op·ter·ous [ˌhetəˈrɔptərəs; ˌhɛtəˋrɑptərəs] ***a***. 【动】**1.** 半翅的;异翅的。**2.** 异翳目的(= hemipterous)。

het·er·o·sex·u·al [ˌhetərəuˈseksjuəl; ˌhɛtəroˋsɛkʃuəl] **I** ***a***. **1.** 异性爱的 (*opp*. homosexual)。**2.** 不同性别的。*a* ~ *flock of ducklings* 一群雌雄夹杂的小鸭。~ *twins* 孪生兄妹,孪生姐弟。**II** ***n***. 异性爱者。

het·er·o·sex·u·al·i·ty [ˌhetərəuˌseksjuˈæliti; ˌhɛtəroˌsɛkʃuˋælətɪ] ***n***. 异性爱。

het·er·o·sis [ˌhetəˈrəusis; ˌhɛtəˋrosɪs] ***n***. 【遗传】杂种优势。**-ot·ic** ***a***.

het·er·o·sphere [ˈhetərəusfiə; ˋhɛtəroˌsfɪr] ***n***. 【气】非均质层。**-o·spher·ic** [-ˈsferik; -ˋsfɛrɪk] ***a***.

het·er·os·po·rous [ˌhetəˈrɔspərəs, ˌhetərəuˈspɔːrəs; ˌhɛtəˋrɑspərəs, ˌhɛtəroˋsporəs] ***a***. 【植】具异形孢子的。

het·er·o·sty·ly [ˈhetərəuˌstaili; ˋhɛtəroˌstaɪlɪ] ***n***. 【植】花柱异长。**-o·sty·lous** ***a***.

het·er·o·tax·i·a, **het·er·o·tax·is**, **het·er·o·tax·y** [ˌhetərəuˈtæksiə, -sis, -si; ˋhɛtəoˌtæksɪə, -sɪs, -sɪ] ***n***. 【医】内脏异位;【地】地层变位。**-o·tac·tic**, **-o·tac·tous**, **-o·tax·ic** ***a***.

het·er·o·thal·lic [ˌhetərəuˈθælik; ˌhɛtəroˋθælɪk] ***a***. 【植】雌雄异株的,异宗配合的。**-thal·lism** ***n***.

het·er·o·tope [ˈhetərəutəup; ˋhɛtərətop] ***n***. 【化】异(原子)序元素;(同量)异序(元)素。

het·er·o·to·pi·a [ˌhetərəuˈtəupiə; ˌhɛtəroˋtopɪə] ***n***. 【医】异位(= heterotopy)。**-o·top·ic** [-əˈtɔpik; -əˋtɑpɪk] ***a***.

het·er·o·troph [ˈhetərəutrɔf; ˋhɛtərətrɑf] ***n***. 【生】异养生物。

het·er·o·troph·ic [ˌhetərəuˈtrɔfik; ˌhɛtərəˋtrɑfɪk] ***a***.

【微】异养的〔指细菌只能从有机物中获得养料,不能从无机物中取得蛋白和醣〕。

het·er·o·tro·phy [ˈhetərəuˌtrɔfi; ˋhɛtərəˏtrɑfɪ] *n*. 【微】异养。

het·er·o·typ·ic [ˌhetərəuˈtipik; ˏhɛtəroˋtɪpɪk] *a*. 【微】异型的(= heterotypical)。

het·er·o·zy·go·sis [ˌhetərəuzaiˈgəusis; ˏhɛtərozaɪˋgosɪs] *n*. 【生】**1.** 杂合现象。**2.** 异型接合性。

het·er·o·zy·gote [ˌhetərəuˈzaigəut; ˏhɛtəroˋzaɪgot] *n*. 【生】异型接合体,异型接合子;杂合体,杂合子。

het·er·o·zy·gous [ˌhetərəuˈzaigəs; ˏhɛtərəˋzaɪgəs] *a*. 【生】杂合的。

het·man [ˈhetmən; ˋhɛtmən] *n*. 〔*pl*.〕**1.** 波兰旧时司令官。**2.** 哥萨克兵的将官。

het·ra·zan [ˈhetrəzæn; ˋhɛtrəzæn] *n*. 【药】海群生。

Het·ty [ˈheti; ˋhɛtɪ] *n*. 海蒂〔女子名, Henrietta 的爱称〕。

heu·land·ite [ˈhjuːləndait; ˋhjuləndaɪt] *n*. 【矿】片沸石。

heu·ris·tic [hjuəˈristik; hjʊˋrɪstɪk] **1.** (教学、研究等)启发(式)的。**2.** (计算机解题)探索法的。~ *method of teaching* 启发式教学法。**-s** *n*. **1.** 启发式教学法,启发式的艺术[应用]。**2.** 【计】直观推断,试探法。**-ally** *ad*.

HEW = (Department of) Health, Education, and Welfare 〔美〕卫生教育和福利部。

hew [hjuː; hju] *vt*. (~*ed*; *hewn* [hjuːn; hjun], ~*ed*) **1.** (用斧等)砍,劈,剁,伐。**2.** 砍倒 (*down*)。**3.** 砍成,切成;剁;砍开,开辟。~ *out a tomb in the rock* 凿岩成墓。— *vi*. **1.** 砍,劈,剁,伐。**2.** 坚持,遵守,恪守 (*to*)。~ ***asunder*** = ~ *to pieces*. ~ ***away*** 砍去,斩去。~ ***one's way*** 开路,辟路;排难前进。~ ***to pieces*** 剁碎。

hew·er [ˈhjuːə; ˋhjuɚ] *n*. 砍伐者;采煤工人。~***s of wood and drawers of water*** 劈柴挑水的人,做苦活的人〔出自圣经〕。

Hew·lett [ˈhjuːlit; ˋhjulɪt] *n*. 休利特〔姓氏〕。

hewn [ˈhjuːn; hjun] **I** hew 的过去分词。**II** *a*. 粗削的。~ **squares** 【林】披方。~ **stone** 粗削石,毛石。~ **timber** 【林】披材。

hex [heks; hɛks] **I** *vt*. 〔美方〕**1.** 施魔法于…。**2.** 给…招来坏运气;使倒霉。**3.** 迷惑。— *vi*. 施魔法。**II** *n*. **1.** 巫婆,术士。**2.** 不吉祥的人[物]。**3.** 魔力。

H

hex(a)- *comb. f*. 表示"六"〔在元音前用 hex-〕: *hexa*d, *hexa*gon.

hex·a·chlo·ro·cy·clo·hex·ane [ˈheksəˌklɔːrəuˌsaikləˈheksein; ˋhɛksəˏkloroˏsaɪkləˋhɛksen] *n*. 【药】六氯环己烷,六六六。

hex·a·chlo·ro·eth·ane [ˌheksəˏklɔːrəuˈeθein; ˏhɛksəˏkloroˋɛθen] *n*. 【化】六氯乙烷(= hexachlorethane)。

hex·a·chlo·ro·phene [ˌheksəˈklɔːrəfiːn; ˏhɛksəˋklorəfin] *n*. 【药】六氯酚〔用于香皂等内作防臭剂〕。

hex·a·chord [ˈheksəkɔːd; ˋhɛksəkord] *n*. 【乐】六声音阶。

hex·ad, hex·ade [ˈheksæd, ˈhekseid; ˋhɛksæd, ˋhɛksed] *n*. **1.** 六;六个;成六的一组。**2.** 【化】六价元素,六价物,六价基。**3.** 【物】六重轴。

hex·a·dec·i·mal [ˌheksəˈdesiməl; ˏhɛksəˋdɛsɪməl] *a*. 十六进制的。

hex·a·em·er·on [ˌheksəˈemərɔn; ˏhɛksəˋɛmərɑn] *n*. **1.** 【圣】"创世"的六天;《创世纪》有关"创世"的六天的记述。**2.** 有关"创世"的论说(= hexahemeron)。

hex·a·gon [ˈheksəgən; ˋhɛksəgən] *n*. 六角形,六边形。**-al** *a*.

hex·a·gram [ˈheksəgræm; ˋhɛksəgræm] *n*. 六线形,六芒星形〔✶〕。

hex·a·hed·ral [ˈheksəˈhedrəl; ˋhɛksəˋhɛdrəl] *a*. 六面体的,有六面体的。

hex·a·he·dron [ˌheksəˈhedrən; ˏhɛksəˋhɛdrən] *n*. (*pl*. ~*s*, *-dra* [-drə; -drə]) 六面体。*a regular* ~ 立方体,正六面体。

hex·a·hem·er·on [ˌheksəˈhemərɔn; ˏhɛksəˋhɛmərɑn] *n*. = hexaemeron.

hex·a·hy·drate [ˌheksəˈhaidreit; ˏhɛksəˋhaɪdret] *n*. 【化】六水合物。

hex·a·hy·dric [ˌheksəˈhaidrik; ˏhɛksəˋhaɪdrɪk] *a*. 【化】六羟的,六元的。*a* ~ *alcohol* 六元醇,六羟基醇。

hex·am·er·ous [hekˈsæmərəs; hɛksˋæmərəs] *a*. (花瓣)有六基数的(= 6-merous)。

hex·am·e·ter [hekˈsæmitə; hɛksˋæmɪtɚ] **I** *n*. 六韵步;六韵步诗体。**II** *a*. = hexametric.

hex·a·meth·yl·ene·tet·ra·mine [ˌheksəˌmeθəliːnˈtetrəmiːn; ˏhɛksəˋmɛθəlintɛtrəmin] *n*. 【化】环六亚甲基四胺,乌洛托品。

hex·a·met·ric [ˌheksəˈmetrik; ˏhɛksəˋmɛtrɪk] *a*. 六韵步的,由六韵步组成的。

hex·a·mine [ˈheksəmiːn; ˋhɛksəˏmin] *n*. 【化】六胺;【药】乌洛托品。

hex·ane [ˈheksein; ˋhɛksen] *n*. 【化】己烷。

hex·ang·u·lar [hekˈsæŋgjulə; hɛkˋsæŋgjulɚ] *a*. 六角的。

hex·a·pla [ˈheksəplə; ˋhɛksəplə] *n*. 用六国语言对译的书。

hex·a·ploid [ˈheksəplɔid; ˋhɛksəplɔɪd] **I** *a*. 【生】有六倍体的。**II** *n*. 【生】六倍体。

hex·a·pod [ˈheksəpɔd; ˋhɛksəˏpɑd] **I** *a*. 有六足的。**II** *n*. 六足动物〔尤指昆虫〕。

Hex·ap·o·da [hekˈsæpədə; hɛkˋsæpədə] *n*. 〔*pl*.〕【动】六足类,昆虫网。

hex·ap·o·dy [hekˈsæpədi; hɛkˋsæpədɪ] *n*. 六韵步诗句。

hex·a·stich [ˈheksəstik; ˋhɛksəˏstɪk] *n*. 六行诗,六节诗。

hex·a·style [ˈheksəstail; ˋhɛksəˏstaɪl] **I** *a*. 【建】有六柱的,六柱式的。**II** *n*. 正面有六柱的建筑物。

hex·a·syl·la·ble [ˈheksəˈsiləbl; ˋhɛksəˋsɪləbl̩] *n*. 六音节(语)。

Hex·a·teuch [ˈheksətjuːk; ˋhɛksəˏtjuk] *n*. 【宗】《旧约全书》的头六卷。

hex·a·va·lent [ˈheksəveilənt; ˋhɛksəˏvelənt] *a*. 【化】有六价的。

hex·en·be·sen [ˈheksənbeizn; ˋhɛksənbezn̩] *n*. 【植】扫帚病,丛枝病(= witches' broom)。

hex·e·rei [ˌheksəˈrai; ˏhɛksəˋraɪ] *n*. 巫术。

hex·ode [ˈheksəud; ˋhɛksod] *n*. 【无】六极管。

hex·one [ˈheksəun; ˋhɛkson] **I** *n*. 【化】异己酮(= methyl isobutyl ketone)。**II** *a*. 由蛋白质水解而成为每一分子中含六个碳原子的有机碱类。

hex·o·san [ˈheksəsæn; ˋhɛksəsæn] *n*. 【化】聚己醣(类)。

hex·ose [ˈheksəus; ˋhɛksos] *n*. 【化】己醣(类)。

hex·yl [ˈheksil; ˋhɛksɪl] *n*. 【化】**1.** 己基。**2.** 六硝炸药,六硝基二苯胺。

hex·yl·res·or·cin·ol [ˌheksilreˈzɔːsinəul; ˏhɛksl̩rɛˋzɔsɪnol] *n*. 【化】己基间苯二酚。

hey [hei; he] *int*. 嗬! 嘿! 〔表示惊愕、喜悦、疑问或唤起注意〕。***Hey for*** ...! …好呀! 〔对某人或某物表示赞美〕。***Hey presto***! 嗬,说变就变! 〔魔术师语〕;嗬,奇怪! ~ **cockalorum** 〔英〕(孩子玩的)跳背游戏。

hey·day[1] [ˈheidei; ˋhede] *int*. 啊呀! 〔表示喜悦,惊异〕。

hey·day[2] [ˈheidei; ˋhede] *n*. **1.** 全盛期。**2.** 〔古〕高兴。*in the* ~ *of youth* 在青春时期,年轻力壮。*in the* ~ *of his vigour* 在他精力最旺盛时期。

Hey·mans [ˈhaimɑːns; ˋhaɪmɑns] *n*. 海曼斯〔姓氏〕。

Hey·ward [ˈheiwəd; ˋhewɚd] *n*. 海沃德〔姓氏〕。

Hey·wood [ˈheiwud; ˋhewʊd] *n*. 海伍德〔姓氏〕。

Hf =【化】hafnium.

hf. = half.

h.f., H.F. = high frequency; height finding; 【印】

heavy face; home forces.
hfbd = half-bound.
HFC = high-frequency current.
hf. cf. = half-calf.
H.G. = High German; His [Her] Grace; 〔英〕Home Guard; Horse Guards.
hg. = hectogram; heliogram; hemoglobin.
Hg =【化】hydrargyrum (汞)(= mercury)。
HGH = human growth hormone 人体生长激素。
hgt. = height.
hgwy = highway.
H.H., HH = His [Her] Highness; His Holiness.
hhd., hhd = hogshead.
HHD = doctor of humanities.
HH(H) = (铅笔) double- (treble-)hard.
H hour [ˈeitʃˌauə; ˋetʃˏaʊr] *n.*【军】1. 预定发起进攻时刻。2. 特定军事行动开始时刻。
HI =【物】hazard index.
H.I. = Hawaiian Islands;【物】high-intensity;〔美〕human interest.
hi [hai; haɪ] *int.* 嗨!〔表示问候或用以唤起注意〕。
HIAA = Health Insurance Association of America 美国健康保险协会。
hi·a·tus [haiˈeitəs; haɪˋetəs] *n.* (*pl.* ~(*es*)) 1. 裂缝,罅隙。2. 脱文;漏字。3.【地】间断。4. 中断,拖宕。5.【逻】(论证的)连锁中断。6.【语音】两个字[音节]中同一元音连续出现时发音的短促停顿〔如 he entered 和 reenter 中的 'e'〕。
Hi·a·wa·tha [haiəˈwɔːθə; ˏhaɪəˋwɑθə] *n.* 哈瓦沙〔美国诗人 Longfellow 的长诗 'The Song of Hiawatha' 中的印第安英雄〕。
hi·ba·chi [hiˈbɑːtʃiː; hiˋbɑtʃi] *n.* (*pl.* ~) (Jap.) (日本)木炭火盆。
hi·ba·ku·sha [hiˈbɑːkuːʃə; hiˋbɑkuʃə] *n.* (Jap.) 原子爆炸余生者〔指 1945 年广岛及长崎原子弹爆炸余生者〕。
hi·ber·nac·u·lum [ˌhaibəˈnækjuləm; ˏhaɪbəˋnækjuləm] *n.* (*pl.* **-u·la** [-lə; -lə]) 1. (植物的)越冬芽。2. (植物的)离体冬芽。3. (动物的)越冬巢;(冬眠动物的)冬眠场所。4. 人工冬眠装置。
hi·ber·nal [haiˈbəːnl; haɪˋbɝnl] *a.* 〔书〕冬天的;寒冷的。~ *annual plants* 越冬一年生植物。
hi·ber·nant [ˈhaibənənt; ˋhaɪbənənt] *a.* (动物)冬眠的。
hi·ber·nate [ˈhaibəneit; ˋhaɪbəˏnet] *vi.* 1. 冬眠;蛰居;越冬。2. 避寒。**-na·tion** *n.*
Hi·ber·ni·a [haiˈbəːnjə; haɪˋbɝnɪə] *n.* 〔诗〕爱尔兰〔拉丁语名〕。**-ni·an** [haiˈbəːnjən; haɪˋbɝnɪən] 1. *a.* 爱尔兰(人)的。2. *n.* 爱尔兰人。
Hi·ber·ni·cism [haiˈbəːnisizəm; haɪˋbɝnɪˏsɪzəm] *n.* 爱尔兰的特点[性格、语言现象、风俗]。
Hi·bis·cus [haiˈbiskəs; haɪˋbɪskəs] *n.*【植】木槿属;(h-)木槿,芙蓉。
hic [hik; hɪk] *int.* 嗝嗝!〔打嗝声,尤指酒醉时的打嗝声〕。II *n.* = hiccup.
hic·cough [ˈhikəp; ˋhɪkəp] *n.*, *vi.*, *vt.* = hiccup.
hic·cup [ˈhikəp; ˋhɪkəp] I *n.* 打嗝,打呃。II *vi.* 打嗝;作打呃声。— *vt.* 打着呃说出 (*out*)。
hic ja·cet [ˈhik ˈdʒeiset; ˋhɪk ˋdʒeset] (L.) 1. …长眠于此〔墓碑语,略作 H.J.〕。2. 碑铭;墓志铭。
hick[1] [hik; hɪk] I *n.* 〔美俚〕乡下佬。II *a.* 〔美俚〕乡下佬(似)的。
hick[2] [hik; hɪk] *vi.* = hiccup (*vi.*).
hick·ey [ˈhiki; ˋhɪkɪ] *n.* (*pl.* ~*s*, *-ies*) 1. 〔口〕器械,小机件,小装置,新玩意儿。2. 弯管器。3. (电气设备的)螺纹接合器。4. 〔口〕疙瘩,粉刺,小脓疱。
Hick·ok [ˈhikɔk; ˋhɪkɑk] *n.* 希科克〔姓氏〕。
hick·o·ry [ˈhikəri; ˋhɪkərɪ] *n.* 1.【植】山核桃属植物。2. 山核桃木;山核桃木手杖[鞭条]。
Hicks [hiks; hɪks] *n.* 希克斯〔姓氏〕。
hid [hid; hɪd] I hide[1]的过去式及过去分词。II *a.* 隐藏的;神秘的。
hi·dal·go [hiˈdælgəu; hiˋdælgo] *n.* (*fem.* **-ga**) 西班牙下级贵族。
hid·den [ˈhidn; ˋhɪdn] I hide[1]的过去分词。II *a.* 隐藏的;秘密的;神秘的。*a* ~ *danger* 隐患。*a* ~ *meaning* 言外之意。*a* ~ *microphone* 窃听器。~ *property* 埋藏的财物,隐财。*a* ~ *traitor* 内奸。~ **agenda** 神秘议程〔指公开的宣言或政策背后隐藏着的其他动机〕;别有用心的动机。~ **tax** 间接税。
hide[1] [haid; haɪd] I *vt.* (**hid** [hid; hɪd]; **hid·den** [ˈhidn; ˋhɪdn], **hid**; **hid·ing**) 1. 藏,隐藏。2. 隐瞒,掩饰;使不知道,向…守秘密 (*from*)。3. 包庇。~ *oneself* 躲藏。~ *one's feelings* 掩饰感情。~ *one's head* [*face*] 把脸藏起来,羞得躲起来。— *vi.* 隐藏,潜伏。~ ***one's light under a bushel*** 不露锋芒。~ ***out*** 〔美〕隐藏,埋伏。~ ***the face*** 转过脸去。~ ***the face from*** 假装不见,转面不顾。~ ***up*** 〔俚〕包庇。II *n.* (对野兽摄影或打猎用的)隐藏处。~**-and-seek** *n.* 捉迷藏。~**away** *n.* 隐蔽所;偏僻的小餐馆。~**out** *n.* 隐藏;躲藏处。
hide[2] [haid; haɪd] I *n.* 1. 兽皮,皮革。2. 〔口〕(人的)皮肤;〔俚〕厚脸皮。*a green* [*raw*] ~ 生皮。***bat*** ~***s*** 〔美俚〕钞票。***dress*** [***tan***] ***sb.'s*** ~ 鞭打某人。***have a thick*** ~ 脸皮厚。***have the*** ~ ***to do sth.*** 厚颜无耻地做某事。~ ***and hair*** 连毛带皮;〔美〕完全。(***neither***) ~ ***nor hair*** 什么也没有;无影踪。***save one's own*** ~ 避免受罚[受害、受伤];保全体肤。***tan sb.'s*** ~ 把某人打一顿。II *vt.* (**hid**; **hid·den**, **hid**; **hid·ing**) 1. 剥(皮)。2. 鞭打。
hide[3] [haid; haɪd] *n.* 〔英〕够养活一家人的土地面积〔约为 60—120 英亩〕。
hide-and-seek [ˈhaidənˈsiːk; ˋhaɪdnˋsik], 〔美〕**hide-and-go-seek** [-ˈgəuˈsiːk; -ˋgoˋsik] *n.* 捉迷藏;蒙混,躲闪。***play*** (***at***) ~ (***with***) (同…)捉迷藏;〔喻〕与躲躲闪闪的人[物]打交道。
hide·a·way [ˈhaidəwei; ˋhaɪdəˏwe] I *n.* 〔口〕1. 隐藏处,隐退的地方。2. 偏僻的小酒吧间[娱乐场所]。II *a.* 隐蔽的,隐藏的。
hide·bound [ˈhaidbaund; ˋhaɪdˏbaʊnd] *a.* 1. 偏狭的,气量狭窄的。2. (动物)因营养不良而瘦骨嶙峋的;(树木)因树皮太紧而影响生长的。3. 墨守成规的;死板的。
hid·e·ous [ˈhidiəs; ˋhɪdɪəs] *a.* 可怕的;骇人听闻的;丑恶的,讨厌的。**-ly** *ad.* **-ness** *n.*
hide·out [ˈhaidaut; ˋhaɪdˏaʊt] *n.* 〔口〕(匪盗等的)巢穴,窝,隐匿处,躲藏处。
hid·ey-hole [ˈhaidihəul; ˋhaɪdɪhol] *n.* = hideaway.
hid·ing[1] [ˈhaidiŋ; ˋhaɪdɪŋ] *n.* 1. 隐匿,躲藏。2. 躲藏处。***be*** [***remain***] ***in*** ~ 躲藏者。***come out of*** ~ 从躲藏处出来。***go into*** ~ 躲藏起来。~**-place** 躲藏处,储藏处。~ **power** (油漆等的)遮盖力,覆盖力,披覆力。
hid·ing[2] [ˈhaidiŋ; ˋhaɪdɪŋ] *n.* 〔口〕鞭打,痛打。***give sb. a good*** ~ 痛打某人。
hi·dro·sis [haiˈdrəusis; hiˋdrosɪs] *n.* 1. 排汗〔尤指大量出汗〕。2.【医】汗病。
hi·drot·ic [haiˈdrɔtik; haɪˋdrɑtɪk] I *a.* 1. 与发汗有关的。2. 使发汗的,促使发汗的。II *n.* 发汗药。
hid·y-hole [ˈhaidihəul; ˋhaɪdɪhol] *n.* = hideaway.
hie [hai; haɪ] (**hied**; ~***ing***, **hy·ing**) *vt.* 使赶紧;催促〔常与反身代词同用〕。*He hied himself to the theatre.* 他赶紧去剧场。— *vi.* 〔诗〕赶往 (*to*)。*Hie thee!* 赶快! *Hie on!* 〔嗾狗〕去!
hi·e·mal [ˈhaiəməl; ˋhaɪəml] *a.* 冬季的;似冬天的,寒冷的。
hi·er·arch [ˈhaiərɑːk; ˋhaɪəˏrɑrk] *n.* 1. 大主教;祭司长。2. 统治集团首领。**-al** *a.*

H

hi·er·ar·chic(al) [ˌhaiəˈrɑːkik(əl); ˏhaɪəˋrɑrkɪk(əl)] ***a*.** **1.** 僧侣统治(集团)的。**2.** 统治集团的。**3.** 等级(制度)的。**-cal·ly** ***ad*.**

hi·er·ar·chism [ˈhaiərɑːkizəm; ˋhaɪərɑrkɪzm] ***n*.** 僧侣政治;僧侣制度。

hi·er·ar·chy [ˈhaiərɑːki; ˋhaɪərɑrkɪ] ***n*.** **1.** 僧侣统治集团,僧侣统治。**2.** 统治集团。**3.** 等级制度。**4.** 【宗】天使团,天使的级别。**5.** 【动、植】(纲、目、科、属等的)分类等级。**6.** 【计】分层,层次。～ *of power* 权力等级。*data* ～【计】数据层次。～ *of memory* 【计】分级存储器系统。

hi·er·at·ic [haiəˈrætik; haɪəˋrætɪk] **I** ***a*.** **1.** 僧侣的,(文字)僧侣所用简体的〔指古埃及僧侣所用的一种简化象形文字〕。**2.** 神圣的。**II** ***n*.** 〔the ～〕= ～ writing 僧侣所用简化文字。

hier(o)- *comb. f.* 表示"神圣的","僧侣的": *hiero*cracy.

hi·er·oc·ra·cy [ˌhaiəˈrɔkrəsi; ˏhaɪəˋrɑkrəsɪ] ***n*.** 僧侣统治;僧侣统治制度。**-o·crat·ic** ***a*.**

hi·er·o·dule [ˈhaiərədjuːl; ˋhaɪərəˏdjul] ***n*.** (古希腊神庙的)圣役〔由奴隶充当〕。

hi·er·o·glyph [ˈhaiərəglif; ˋhaɪərəˏglɪf] ***n*.** **1.** 象形文字,图画文字;秘密文字。**2.** 〔谑〕潦草难解的字。

hi·er·o·glyph·ic [ˌhaiərəˈglifik; ˏhaɪərəˋglɪfɪk] **I** ***a*.** **1.** 象形文字的;用象形文字写成的。**2.** 符号的,有神秘意味的,象征的。**3.** 〔谑〕潦草难解的。**II** ***n*.** **1.** 象形文字。**2.** 〔常 *pl*.〕象形文字绘写法。**3.** 〔常 *pl*.〕难解的符号,潦草难解的文字。

hi·er·o·glyph·i·cal [ˌhaiərəˈglifikəl; ˏhaɪərəˋglɪfɪkəl] ***a*.** = hieroglyphic. **-ly** ***ad*.**

hi·er·ol·a·try [ˌhaiəˈrɔlətri; ˏhaɪəˋrɑlətrɪ] ***n*.** 圣徒[圣物]崇拜(= hagiolatry)。

hi·er·ol·o·gy [ˌhaiəˈrɔlədʒi; ˏhaɪəˋrɑlədʒɪ] ***n*.** **1.** 古埃及象形文字的研究。**2.** (一个民族的)宗教传说,宗教文学,圣典文学。

hi·er·o·phant [ˈhaiərəfænt; ˋhaɪərəˏfænt] ***n*.** **1.** 【宗】(解释秘义的)圣师。**2.** (古代希腊等的)祭司长。

hi·fa·lu·tin [ˌhaifəˈluːtn; ˏhaɪfəˋlutɪn] ***a*.** 夸张的,夸大的(= highfalutin)。

hi-fi [ˈhaiˈfai; ˋhaɪˋfaɪ] **I** ***n*.** **1.** 高保真度(= high fidelity)。**2.** 具有高保真度的收音机[录音机、留声机]。**II** ***a*.** 高保真度的。

Hig·gin·son [ˈhiginsn; ˋhɪgɪnsn] ***n*.** **1.** 希金森〔姓氏〕。**2.** **Thomas Wentworth** ～ 托马斯·温·希金森〔1823—1911,美国作家〕。

hig·gle, hig·gle-hag·gle [ˈhigl, ˈhigl-ˈhægl; ˋhɪgl̩, ˋhɪgl̩-ˋhægl̩] ***vi*.** 讨价还价;讲条件;争执。

hig·gle·dy-pig·gle·dy [ˈhigldiˈpigldi; ˋhɪgl̩dɪˋpɪgl̩dɪ] ***a*., *ad*.** 极紊乱的[地];乱七八糟的[地]。**II** ***n*.** 混乱。

high [hai; haɪ] **I** ***a*.** **1.** 高的〔指物,形容人的身高用 tall〕;高处的;高地的。**2.** 高级的,高等的,高位的,重要的。**3.** 高尚的,崇高的;高贵的。**4.** 昂贵的,奢侈的。**5.** 主要的,严重的,重大的。**6.** 高度的;剧烈的;很大的,非常的;偏激的;极度的,极端的;(色)浓的;高声调的,尖声的。**7.** 高傲的,盛气凌人的。**8.** (精力等)旺盛的;(兴致等)方酣的;(时间、季节)正盛的;恰好到时的。**9.** (食物,尤指肉、野味)有气味的,开始变质的。**10.** 〔美俚〕醉了的,被麻醉品麻醉了的。**11.** 【地】高纬度的,远离赤道的。**12.** 【语音】(舌位)高的。**13.** 【机】(齿轮)以最高速度转动的。*the* ～ *tower* 高塔。*a* ～ *mountain* 高山。*The building is 40 feet* ～. 楼高 40 英尺。～ *feeding* 美食,佳肴。～ *flying* [*flight*] 高空飞行。～ *gear* (汽车)高速挡。～ *latitudes* 高纬度地区。*a* ～ *character* 崇高的人格。*a* ～ *manner* 傲态。～ *cost of living* 高昂的生活费用。*the* ～ *street* 正街,大街〔*cf*. 〔美〕main street〕。*a* ～ *crime* 重大罪行。～ *explosives* 烈性炸药。*a* ～ *voice* 尖嗓门。*a* ～ *folly* 大蠢事。*a* ～ *Tory* 极端的保守党员。～ *noon* 正午;〔喻〕顶峰,尖端。*a* ～ *flavour* 开始变质的味道,馊味。*He is pretty* ～. 他醉得很凶。～ *summer* 盛夏。***get*** ～ ***hat*** = ***wear a*** ～ ***hat***. ***have a*** ～ ***old time*** = ～ ***jinks*** 玩得痛痛快快,过一段极愉快的时间。***have a*** ～ ***opinion of sb*.** 推崇[佩服]某人。***have a*** ～ ***sense of*** (*duty*) 具有高度的(责任)感。～ ***and dry*** **1.** (船)搁浅。**2.** 陷于困境,孤立无援。**3.** (人)落后,过时。～ ***and low*** 各种身份的人,高低贵贱的人。～ ***and mighty*** 地位高的;〔口〕趾高气扬,神气活现。～ ***on*** 热心于,热衷于。～, ***wide and handsome*** 〔美口〕无忧无虑地,充满自信地。***in*** ～ ***favour with*** 非常满意。***in*** ～ ***terms*** 称赞。***of*** ～ ***antiquity*** 老早以前的,远古时候的。***on the*** ～ ***horse*** = ***ride the*** [***a***] ～ ***horse*** 摆架子。***talk in*** ～ ***language*** 说大话,吹牛皮。***wear a*** ～ ***hat*** 〔美〕摆架子。***with a*** ～ ***hand*** 用高压手段。**II** ***n*.** **1.** 高气压;高气压地带。**2.** (纸牌中的)王牌。**3.** 〔美口〕最高水平[记录],高额数字。**4.** 高位,高处;高地。**5.** 〔美〕中学。**6.** 〔the H-〕〔英口〕大街,正街(= High Street, 尤指牛津的大街)。**7.** 〔the ～〕= ～ table. **8.** 〔美〕= ～ school. **9.** (齿轮的)高速度转动。*barometric* ～【气】高气压。*hit an all-time* ～ 创历史上最高纪录。***from*** (***on***) ～ 从天上。～ ***and mighties*** 大人物。***How is that for*** ～? 〔俚〕好不奇怪? ***on*** ～ 在高空;在天上。***the Most High*** 【宗】上帝。**III** ***ad*.** **1.** 高。**2.** 奢侈地。**3.** 高价地。*climb* ～ 登高,上游。*bid* ～ 出高价。*fly* ～ 高飞。*live* ～ 过得奢侈。～ ***and low*** 各处,上上下下 (*search* ～ *and low* 到处搜寻)。***pay*** ～ 付高价。***play*** ～ 大赌;出大牌。***run*** ～ **1.** 潮急,浪大。**2.** 兴奋,激动;(语言)粗暴。**3.** 涨(价)。～**-altitude** ***a*.** 高空的 (*a pilotless* ～*-altitude military reconnaissance plane* 军用无人驾驶高空侦察机。～*-altitude sickness* 高山症)。～ **analysis** 〔作修饰语用〕(肥料)高成份的〔指含有百分之二十以上的植物养料〕。～**-angle** ***a*.** 高射界的;高角的。～ **area** 【天】高气压圈。～ **art** 纯艺术。～**ball** 〔美〕**1.** ***n*.** 掺有苏打水、姜汁酒的威士忌;指示火车全速前进的信号;速度很快的火车。**2.** ***vi*.** 〔俚〕高速前进。～ **barrier** 〔美运〕高栏。～ **beam** 车前灯的远距离光,高光,上方光。～**binder** 〔美俚〕下流政客;骗子;无赖汉,暗杀者。～ **birth** 名门。～**-blooded** ***a*.** 血统纯正的,性质优良的。～ **bloomery** (炼熟铁的)原始高炉。～**blower** 鼻息粗烈的马。～**-blown** ***a*.** 意气扬扬的,自高自大的。～**born** ***a*.** 出身高贵的。～**boy** 〔美〕高脚抽屉柜。～**bred** ***a*.** 出身高贵的,品格高尚的;纯种的,血统纯正的。～ **brass** 优质黄铜。～ **brightness** 最大亮度。～**brow** **1.** ***n*.** 〔美俚〕知识分子;(自以为)有学识的人,有教养的人 (*opp*. lowbrow)。**2.** ***a*.** 〔蔑〕卖弄学问的,自炫博学的。～**-browed** ***a*.** 额头宽大的,有教养的,炫耀学问的。～**browism** ***n*.** 自命不凡,炫耀学问。～ **camp** **1.** (艺术上的)平庸拙劣但时新有趣。**2.** 装腔作势,忸怩作态。～**-capacity** **1.** 爆炸弹头。**2.** 大电容,大容量。～ **chair** 婴儿高脚椅。**H- Church** 【宗】高派教会。～ **churchman** 高派教会教徒。～**class** ***a*.** 高级的。高等的。～ **cockalorum** **1.** 〔美俚〕要人,大老板;自命不凡的人。**2.** 〔英〕(儿童玩的)跳背游戏。～ **colour** 深色。～**-coloured** ***a*.** 深色的;生动的;(脸色)红润的。～ **comedy** 高雅的喜剧。～ **command** 统帅部,最高指挥部;(机关中的)最高领导班子。～ **commissioner** 高级专员〔尤指英联邦各国相互派驻的大使级代表〕。～**-concept** ***a*.** (唱片、小说、电影等因节奏快、情节紧张等)富有刺激性的。**H- Court (of Justice)** 〔英〕高等法院。～ **day** 节日,假日。～**-def** ***a*.** 〔口〕高清晰度的。～**-end** ***a*.** 高档的,高级的。～**-energy particle** 【原】高能粒子。～**-energy physics** 高能物理学。～ **fidelity** **1.** (收音、录音设备等的)高保真度。**2.** 具有高保真度的收音机、录音机或留声机。～**-five** **1.** ***n*.** 举手合掌以示祝贺的手势;庆祝,欢庆。**2.** ***vi*.** 举手合掌表示庆祝。～**flier, -flyer** **1.** 高飞的人[鸟];好高骛远的人。**2.** 极端分子;说大话的人;有手腕的人;极会挥霍的人。**3.** 【英史】(17—18 世纪的)高派教

会人士;保守党员。~-**flown** *a*. **1**. 好高骛远的;高超的。**2**. 夸张的。~**flying** *a*. **1**. 高飞的。**2**. 骄傲的,自命不凡的。~ **frequency**【无】高频(率),高周率〔略作 H. F.〕。~ **furnace** 竖炉。~ **gear** **1**. (汽车等变速器的)高速挡。**2**. 〔口〕全速;全力进行。**H- German** (现为标准德语的)高地德语。~-**grade** *a*. 高级的,优质的,上等的(~-*grade steel* 优质钢)。~ **ground** (辩论、冲突、竞选等中所处的)有利地位,上风(*take the* ~ *ground* 抓住有利的机会)。~ **grown** 长满高大植物的。~-**handed** *a*. 高压的,横暴的(~-*handed measures* 高压手段)。~ **hat** **1**. 高帽。**2**. 〔美〕自大的人;冒充绅士的人。~-**hat** **1**. *n*. 〔俚〕势利鬼,自命不凡的人。**2**. *a*. 骄傲的,势利的;时髦的,贵族派头的。**3**. *vi*., *vt*. (对…)摆架子;盛气凌人地对待(人),冷淡待(人)。~-**hearted** *a*. 勇敢的;果敢的。~-**heeled** *a*. (鞋)高跟的。~ **hurdle** 〔美〕(田径)高栏。~ **iron** 〔俚〕**1**. 铁路干线(轨道)。**2**. 特快火车轨道。~ **jinks** 热闹的玩乐;喧闹。~ **jump** 跳高。~-**keyed** *a*. 感情紧张的;敏感的,兴奋的,高音调的。~-**level** *a*. **1**. 高级官员的,高级官员作出的。**2**. 高级的。~**light** **1**. *vt*. 在…上投上强光;强调,使显著;【美剧】派给;当主角。**2**. *n*. (画中受光最多的)明亮部份;〔常 *pl*.〕(演出等的)精彩场面,精彩节目;(报纸中等)特讯,要闻;要点。~ **liver** 生活奢侈者,挥霍无度者。~-**lows** *n*. *pl*. 有绊皮靴。~-**mettled** *a*. 猛烈的,兴高采烈的。~-**minded** *a*. 品格高尚的;〔古〕高傲的,傲慢的。~-**muckamuck**, ~-**muckety-muck** *n*. 〔美俚〕大人物;神气活现的人。~-**necked** *a*. (衣服)高领的。~ **noon** **1**. 正午。**2**. 全盛时期,顶峰。~-**octane** *a*.【化】辛烷值的。~-**pitched** *a*. **1**. 音调高的,尖声的。**2**. 坡度陡的,(屋顶等)倾斜度大的。**3**. 紧张的;极敏感的。**4**. 高尚的。~ **place** 山顶祭坛〔闪族人早期信奉宗教时进行宗教活动的场所〕。~ **polymer**【化】高分子,高聚物。~-**powered** *a*. 十分强大的;极有权势的;大功率的。~-**precision** *a*. 高精密度的,高准确度的。~-**priced** 高价的,昂贵的。~ **priest** 祭司长〔尤指犹太教的祭司长〕。~-**pressure** **1**. *a*. 高压的;强买强卖的;急迫的,硬干的。**2**. *vt*. 〔口〕强制,逼使,对…施加压力;强行推销。~-**principled** *a*. 原则性高的;操守高洁的。~-**proof** *a*. 酒精含量高的。~ **profile** 高姿态,明确的立场。~-**ranking** *a*. 高级的(*a* ~-*ranking official* 高级官员)。~ **relief** 隆(浮)雕;隆(浮)雕刻品。~-**rise** **1**. *a*. (建筑物)高耸的,多层楼房的。**2**. *n*. 高大建筑物,多层高楼。~ **road** 大路,公路;最容易[美好]的途径(*the* ~*road to ruin* 灭亡之道)。~-**roller** 〔美俚〕肆意挥霍的人;狂赌的人。~-**rolling** *a*. 肆意挥霍的,豪华的。~ **school** 〔美〕中学(*a junior* [*senior*] ~ *school* 初[高]中);〔英〕大学预科。~ **seas** 公海。~ **sign** 暗号。~-**sounding** *a*. 夸大的;动听的;高调的。~-**speed** *a*. 高速的,高速度的(~-*speed photography* 快速照相术。~-*speed steel*【冶】高速钢,锋钢)。~-**spirited** *a*. **1**. 勇敢的,有精神的。**2**. 易激动的;易发怒的,脾气大的。~ **spirits** 高兴,快乐。~-**stepper** **1**. 蹄步高抬的马;有派头的人。**2**. 〔美俚〕生活奢华的人。~ **spot** **1**. 显著点,特点。**2**. 名胜,古迹。~-**strung** *a*. 紧张的,敏感的,易兴奋的。~ **style** 最时髦的服装。~ **table** (英大学餐厅中)校长、导师等的餐桌(俗称 the ~);〔英〕(正式宴会中的)主宾席。~-**tail** *vi*. 迅速撤退,迅速逃走(~-*tail it off with sb*. 同某人一起迅速逃走)。~ **tea** 〔英〕(下午五、六时之间的)正式茶点。~-**tech** *n*. & *a*. 高技术(的),高科技(的)。~ **teens** 十六至十九岁的青少年。~-**temper steel** 激硬化钢。~-**temperature steel** 耐热钢。~-**tension** *a*. 高(电)压(的)。~-**test** **1**. 经过严格试验的;高级的。**2**. (汽油)沸点低的(~-*test gasoline* 高度挥发性汽油)。~ **tide** 高潮。~ **time** **1**. 并不为晚的时候;不早不晚恰当时。**2**. 〔俚〕兴高采烈的时候〔亦作 ~ old time〕。~-**toned** *a*. **1**. 调子高的;〔谑〕崇高的,高尚的;〔讽〕唱高调的。**2**. 〔口〕漂亮的,时髦的;〔口〕优良的,优秀的。~**tops** *n*. 〔复〕高帮运动鞋[旅游鞋]。~ **treason** 叛逆,叛逆罪。~-**up** *n*. 社会地位高的人。~ **water** 高潮;高水位;昌隆。~-**water mark** **1**. 高潮线,满潮标。**2**. 高水位线。**3**. 最高点,绝顶。~ **wine** 酒精成份很高的蒸馏酒。~ **wire** (走钢丝演员表演用的)高空钢丝绳。~-**wire** *a*. 走高空钢丝绳的;危险的。~-**wrought** *a*. 极度紧张的,非常激动地。~-**yield** *a*. 产量很高的;(核武器等)将大量放射性尘埃放入空气的。

high·er [ˈhaiə; ˋhaɪr] *a*. 〔high 的比较级〕较高的;高等的。~ *command*【军】= high command. ~ *criticism* 圣经考证学。~ *education* 高等教育。~ *mathematics* 高等数学。*on a* ~ *plane* 在更高水准上。~-**up** *n*. 〔美口〕领导,上司;要人。

high·est [ˈhaiist; ˋhaɪɪst] **I** *a*. 〔high 的最高级〕最高的。*the* ~ *bidder* (拍卖时)出价最高的人。*the* ~ *good* 至善。*the* ~ *possible price* 最高价格。**II** *n*. 最高者;最高地位。*the H-* 至高无上者,上帝(= the Most High)。*in the* ~【宗】在至高之处的天堂。**III** *ad*. 最高地。

high·fa·lu·tin(g) [ˈhaifəˈluːtin, -tiŋ; ˋhaɪfəˋlutɪn, -tɪŋ] **I** *a*. 夸张的,夸大的。**II** *n*. 夸张的话,大话。

high-jack [ˈhaidʒæk; ˋhaɪˏdʒæk] *vt*. 〔口〕**1**. 抢劫(违禁品等);拦路抢劫(车、人等)。**2**. 劫持(飞机),绑架。**3**. 强逼。

high-jack·er [ˈhaidʒækə; ˋhaɪdʒækɚ] *n*. 抢劫者;劫持飞机者。

high·land [ˈhailənd; ˋhaɪlənd] **I** *n*. **1**. 高地,高原。**2**. 〔the Highlands〕苏格兰高地。**II** *a*. **1**. 高原的。**2**. 〔H-〕苏格兰高地的。~ **fling** 苏格兰高地舞。

high·land·er [ˈhailəndə; ˋhaɪləndɚ] *n*. **1**. 高地人,山地人。**2**. 〔H-〕苏格兰高地人;苏格兰高地联队士兵。

high·ly [ˈhaili; ˋhaɪlɪ] *ad*. **1**. 高,高度地。**2**. 很,非常。**3**. 称赞地。**4**. 高贵地。**5**. 按高额。*a* ~ *gifted actor* 很有天才的演员。*be* ~ *paid* 薪水[工资]高。~ *amusing* 非常有趣的。~ *original* 很有独特性的。*to feel oneself* ~ *flattered* 自觉非常荣幸。***speak*** ~ ***of*** 赞扬,推誉。***think*** ~ ***of*** 尊重。~-**strung** *a*. = high-strung.

high·ness [ˈhainis; ˋhaɪnɪs] *n*. **1**. 高,高度;高位;高价;高尚。**2**. 〔H-〕殿下。*His* [*Her*, *Your*] *H-* 殿下。

hight[1] [hait; haɪt] *a*. 〔古、诗〕所谓…的,被称为…的,名字叫做…的。*a maiden* ~ *Elaine* 名叫埃莱恩的少女。

hight[2] [hait; haɪt] *n*. 〔废〕= height.

high·ty-tigh·ty [ˌhaitiˈtaiti; ˋhaɪtɪˋtaɪtɪ] **I** *a*. **1**. 轻浮的;反复无常的。**2**. 傲慢的,骄傲的。**3**. 易怒的,脾气大的;怒气冲冲的。**II** *n*. **1**. 轻率。**2**. 傲慢。**III** *int*. 哎呀!〔表示傲慢或忿怒〕(= hoity-toity)。

high·way [ˈhaiwei; ˋhaɪˏwe] *n*. **1**. 公路,大路(*opp*. byway)。**2**. 交通干线;正路,直路。**3**. (达到目的的)途径。*a* ~ *to success* 成功之道。*ocean* ~*s* 海洋航路。~ *traffic* 公路交通。~*s and byways* 干道和支路。*the king's* ~ 天下的公路。***go on the*** ~ = ***take*** (***to***) ***the*** ~ 作拦路的强盗。***the silent H-*** 静寂的大路〔指英国泰晤士河〕。~-**man** 拦路强盗,响马。

H.I.H., **HIH** = His [Her] Imperial Highness 殿下〔间接提及时用〕。

hi·jack [ˈhaidʒæk; ˋhaɪˏdʒæk] *vt*. =〔口〕high-jack.

hi·jack·ee [ˌhaidʒæˈkiː; ˏhaɪdʒæˋki] *n*. 劫持事件的受害者;被劫持者。

hi·jack·er [ˈhaidʒækə; ˋhaɪdʒækɚ] *n*. 〔口〕= high-jacker.

hi·jinks [ˈhaiˈdʒiŋks; ˋhaɪˋdʒɪŋks] *n*. = high jinks.

hij·ra(h) [ˈhidʒrə; ˋhɪdʒrə] *n*. = hegira.

hike [haik; haɪk] **I** *vi*. 〔口〕**1**. 步行;作长途徒步旅行,行军;散步。**2**. 飞起,扬起,飘起(*up*)。**3**. 〔美俚〕在高空检修电线。~ *out* 露营。— *vt*. **1**. 拉起,使升起。**2**. 猛提(价格);〔美俚〕涂改(支票以提高票面金额)。**II** *n*. **1**. 徒步旅行;散步;行军。**2**. 提高,增加。*go on* [*take*] *a* ~ 作徒步旅行,去散步。*a pay* ~ *plan* 加薪方案。

hik·er [ˈhaikə; ˋhaɪkɚ] ***n*.** **1.** 徒步旅行者。**2.** 〔美俚〕高空电线检修工。

hi·la [ˈhailə; ˋhaɪlə] hilum 的复数。

HILAC = heavy-ion linear accelerator 重离子直线加速器。

hi·lar [ˈhailə; ˋhaɪlɚ] ***a*.** **1.** 【解】门的;脐的。**2.** 【植】种脐的;(淀粉)脐点的。

hi·lar·i·ous [hiˈlɛəriəs; həˋlɛrɪəs] ***a*.** **1.** 愉快的;热闹的。**2.** 有趣的,妙的。**-ly** ***ad*.** **-ness** ***n*.**

hi·lar·i·ty [hiˈlæriti; hɪˋlærətɪ] ***n*.** 欢乐,高兴;热闹,狂欢。

Hil·a·ry[1] [ˈhiləri; ˋhɪlərɪ] ***n*.** 希勒里〔男子名〕。

Hil·a·ry[2] [ˈhiləri; ˋhɪlərɪ] ***a*.** 圣希勒里节日时候的〔1月13日〕。***the*** ~ ***term*** [***sitting***] **1.** 旧时英国高等法院开庭期〔1月13日—31日〕。**2.** 牛津大学及都柏林大学的春季学期。

Hil·da [ˈhildə; ˋhɪldə] ***n*.** 希尔达〔女子名〕。

Hil·de·brand [ˈhildəbrænd; ˈhɪldəbrænd] ***n*.** 希尔布兰特〔男子名〕(G. = battle sword)。

Hil·de·gard(e) [ˈhildəgaːd; ˋhɪldəgɑrd] ***n*.** 希尔德加德〔女子名〕。

hil·ding [ˈhildiŋ; ˋhɪldɪŋ] **I** ***n*.** 〔古〕卑贱者。**II** ***a*.** 〔古〕卑贱的。

Hill [hil; hɪl] ***n*.** 希尔〔姓氏〕。

hill [hil; hɪl] ***n*.** **1.** 小山〔英国通常指2000英尺以下的山丘〕;〔*pl*.〕丘陵。**2.** 土堆,土墩。**3.** (道路的)斜坡。**4.** 【军】高地。**5.** 〔美〕〔H-〕美国国会(= Capitol H-)。**6.** (植物根部的)土墩,小堆。**7.** 成堆种植的作物。*an artificial* ~ 假山。*H- 305* 三〇五高地。*a* ~ *of corn* 玉米堆。*a potential* ~ 【物】位垒,势垒。***a*** ~ ***of beans*** 〔口〕少量;小事;不值钱的东西。***go over the*** ~ 〔美俚〕越狱;〔军俚〕开小差;偷偷地迅速离开。***go up*** [***down***] ***a*** ~ 上[下]山。~ ***and dale*** (矿山、炭坑等)上[下]坡;坑洼起伏的地方。***over the*** ~ **1.** 渡过难关,渡过危机。**2.** 上了年纪的;走下坡路的。***the gentleman on the*** ~ 〔美〕国会议员。***up*** ~ ***and down dale*** **1.** 上山下坑;到处;彻底,完全。**2.** 猛烈地;坚忍不拔地。**II** ***vt*.** 把…堆成小山;培土于(树木周围)(***up***)。~**billy** ***n*.** 〔美口〕南部山区居民;粗人,乡下人。~**man** ***n*.** 山区居民;印度山地居民。~ **myna** 【动】鹩哥 (*Eulabes religiosa*)〔产于亚洲,能学人语〕。~**side** ***n*.** (小山)山腰,山坡。~ **station** (印度等地的)山中避暑地。~**top** ***n*.** (小山)山顶。

Hill·man [ˈhilmən; ˋhɪlmən] ***n*.** 希尔曼〔姓氏〕。

hil·lo(a) [hiˈləu; hɪˋlo] ***int*., *n*., *v*.** 〔古〕= hollo, holla, halloo.

hill·ock [ˈhilək; ˋhɪlək] ***n*.** 小丘。**-y** [-i; -i] ***a*.**

hill·y [ˈhili; ˋhɪlɪ] ***a*.** **1.** 多小山的;多丘陵的,多斜坡的。**2.** 似小山的;峭峻的。**hill·i·ness** ***n*.**

hilt [hilt; hɪlt] **I** ***n*.** (刀等的)柄,把。*fight* ~ *to* ~ 短兵相接,个对个作战。(***up***) ***to the*** ~ 十分,彻底 (*be proved to the* ~ 被彻底证明)。**II** ***vt*.** 给(刀等)装上把。

Hil·ton [ˈhiltən; ˋhɪltən] ***n*.** 希尔顿〔姓氏〕。

hi·lum [ˈhailəm; ˋhaɪləm] (*pl*. ***-la*** [-lə; -lə]) ***n*.** **1.** 【植】种脐。**2.** (淀粉粒的)脐点。**3.** 【医】门脐(= hilus)。

him [him, 弱 im, əm; hɪm, 弱 ɪm, əm] ***pro*.** **1.** 〔he 的宾格〕他。**2.** 〔口〕〔用作表语〕= he. **3.** 〔古〕〔强势,反身用法〕= himself. *That's* ~. 〔口〕那正是他。**4.** 〔用于 than 之后〕= he. *Him and his wife were sitting by the fire*. 他和他妻子坐在炉火旁边〔现代标准英语须在前面用 He〕。*He sat* ~ *by the fire*. 他在炉火边上坐下来。*His wife is taller than* ~. 他妻子比他高。

H.I.M., HIM = His [Her] Imperial Majesty 陛下〔间接提及时用〕。

Hi·ma·la·ya(s) [ˌhiməˈleiə(z); ˏhɪməˋleə(z)] ***n*.** 喜马拉雅山(脉)。**Hi·ma·la·y·an** [-ən; -ən] ***a*.** 喜马拉雅山脉的。

hi·mat·i·on [hiˈmætiɔn, -ən; hɪˋmætɪɑn, -ən] ***n*.** (*pl*. ***-mat·i·a*** [-ˈmætiə; -ˋmætɪə]) 古希腊人所穿的长方形外衣。

him·bo [ˈhimbəu; ˋhɪmbo] ***n*.** 长相英俊的草包男子。

him·self [himˈself, 弱 im-; hɪmˋsɛlf, 弱 ɪm-] ***pro*.** 〔he 的反身代词或用作加强语气〕(*pl*. ***themselves***) 他自己;他亲自,他本人。**1.** 〔作反身代词〕*He cut* ~. 他割伤了自己。*He gave* ~ *much trouble*. 他自找苦吃。**2.** 〔加强语气〕*He* ~ *says so*. = *He says so* ~. 他本人是这样说的。*I saw him* ~. 我看见他本人了。*H-unhappy, he understood the situation*. 他本人很不幸,所以理解这种情况。**3.** 〔人称代词代用语〕*I can do better than* ~. 我比他本人可以做得更好一些〔在 *better than* 之下为主语〕。*One of the party and* ~ *saw it*. 那群人中的一个人和他本人都看见的。*H- will be there*. 他会亲自去的〔现代标准英语须在前面用 He himself〕。***be*** [***become, come to***] ~ (情绪、健康)处于正常情况(*He is not quite* ~ *today*. 他今天有些反常;他今天不舒服。*He is* ~ *again*. 他复原了,他恢复了正常)。***beside*** ~ 发狂,疯癫。(***all***) ***by*** ~ 独自,独立。***for*** ~ 为自己;自个儿。

hinc·ty [ˈhiŋkti; ˋhɪŋktɪ] ***a*.** 〔美俚〕神气活现的。

Hind. = Hindi; Hindu; Hindustan; Hindustani.

hind[1] [haind; haɪnd] ***a*.** (~***er***; ~(***er***)***most***) 后面的,后边的。★一般用 hinder, 对 fore 说时用 hind. *the* ~ *legs* [*limbs*] (兽的)后腿。~ *wheels* 后轮。***on one's*** ~ ***legs*** 采取坚决或独立的立场。~**brain** 【解】后脑。~**gut** 【解】后肠。~**quarter** ***n*.** (牛、羊、猪等的)后腿肉;~ **quarters** (四腿动物的)两条后腿。

hind[2] [haind; haɪnd] ***n*.** (*pl*. ~***s***, 〔集合词〕~) **1.** (特指3岁以上的)红色雌鹿。**2.** 红鮨鱼。

hind[3] [haind; haɪnd] ***n*.** **1.** 〔古〕雇农;乡下人。**2.** (英格兰北部和苏格兰)有经验的农场工人;农场管理人。

hin·der[1] [ˈhində; ˋhɪndɚ] ***vt*.** 妨害,妨碍;阻止,阻挠。~ *sb. from coming* 阻止某人来。— ***vi*.** 妨害,阻碍。

hind·er[2] [ˈhaində; ˋhaɪndɚ] **I** hind 的比较级。**II** ***a*.** 后面的,后方的。*the* ~ *gate* 后门。*the* ~ *part of a ship* 船的后部。

hind·er·most, hind·most [ˈhaindəməust, ˈhaindməust; ˋhaɪndɚmost, ˋhaɪndmost] **I** hind 的最高级。**II** ***a*.** 最后的。***The devil takes*** [***catches***] ***the*** ~. 〔谚〕迟者遭殃。

Hin·di [ˈhinˈdiː, ˈhindiː; ˋhɪnˋdi, ˋhɪndi] **I** ***a*.** 印度北部的。**II** ***n*.** 印地语。

Hind·ley [ˈhaindli, ˈhindli; ˋhaɪndlɪ, ˋhɪndlɪ] ***n*.** 欣德利〔姓氏〕。

Hin·doo [ˈhinˌduː; ˋhɪnˏdu] = Hindu.

Hin·doo·stan·ee, Hin·doo·sta·ni [hinduˈstæni; hɪnduˋstænɪ] ***a*., *n*.** = Hindustani.

hin·drance [ˈhindrəns; ˋhɪndrəns] ***n*.** **1.** 妨害,障碍。**2.** 起妨碍作用的人[物]。***without let or*** ~ 不受干涉地,通行无阻地;自由地,为所欲为地。

hind·sight [ˈhaindsait; ˋhaɪndsaɪt] ***n*.** **1.** (步枪的)照尺。**2.** (对事件等的)事后聪敏,事后的认识 (*opp*. foresight)。*realize with* ~ 事后才懂得…。***knock*** [***kick***] ***sb.'s*** ~ ***out*** = ***knock*** [***kick***] ***the*** ~ ***off sb.*** 〔美口〕压服某人,使某人畏缩。

Hin·du [ˈhinduː; ˋhɪndu] **I** ***n*.** **1.** 印度人。**2.** 信奉印度教的人。**II** ***a*.** **1.** 印度教的。**2.** 印度人的。**-ism** ***n*.** 印度教。**-ize** [ˈhinduaiz; ˋhɪnduaɪz] ***vt*.** 使改信印度教,使受印度教影响。

Hin·du·stan·i [ˌhinduˈstɑːni; ˏhɪnduˋstɑnɪ] **I** ***n*.** **1.** 兴都斯坦人,印度斯坦人。**2.** 兴都斯坦语,印度斯坦语。**II** ***a*.** **1.** 兴都斯坦的,印度斯坦的。**2.** 兴都斯坦人的,印度斯坦人的。**3.** 兴都斯坦语的,印度斯坦语的。

hinge [hindʒ; hɪndʒ] **I** ***n*.** **1.** 铰链,折叶。**2.** 铰合部,铰。**3.** 枢纽;枢要,中枢,要点;关键,转折点。**4.** (集邮

上粘邮票用的)透明胶水纸。5.〔美俚〕一瞥。*the ~ of the knee* 膝关节。**get** [**take**] **a ~** 看一看。**off the ~s** 1. 铰链脱落;脱节。2. 失常;(精神)错乱。**II** *vt*. 1. 用铰链接合,给(门等)安铰链。2. 使…以(…)为转移[依据]。~ *one's action on* 以…为行动准绳。— *vi*. 1. (门等)装有蝶铰。2. 随着蝶铰转动;〔喻〕看…而定,依…为转移 (*on*; *upon*)。*My acceptance will ~ upon the terms*. 我接受与否将依条件而定。~ **joint** 1.【解】屈戌关节。2.【机】铰链接合。**hinging post** 门柱。**-less** *a*. 无铰链的,不用铰链的。

hinged [hindʒd; hɪndʒd] *a*. 有铰链的,用铰链的。

hin·ny[1] [ˈhini; ˋhɪnɪ] *n*. 駃騠,驴骡〔公马和母驴所生的种间杂种〕。

hin·ny[2], **hin·nie** [ˈhini; ˋhɪnɪ] *n*. 〔Scot.〕宝贝儿(= honey)。

hint [hint; hɪnt] *n*. 1. 暗示。2. 提示,线索。3. 微量,少许,点滴。*a ~ of spice* 一丁点儿香料。*Hints for housewives*. 家庭主妇须知〔作标题或书名〕。**drop** [**give**, **let fall**] **a ~** 给人暗示。**take a ~** 接受别人的暗示,领悟。**II** *vt*. 暗示。*He ~ed vaguely* [*broadly*] *that he might be late*. 他隐约地[明白地]暗示他可能迟来。— *vi*. 暗示 (*at*)。~ *at one's anxiety* 暗示自己很着急。

hin·ter·land [ˈhintəlænd; ˋhɪntɚ͵lænd] *n*. 1. 腹地,内地。2. 〔*pl*.〕穷乡僻壤。3. 可依赖港口供应的内地贸易区;物资供应地区。

hip[1] [hip; hɪp] **I** *n*. 1. 臀部。2.【解】髋,髋部。3.【动】(昆虫的)基节。4.【建】屋脊。5.〔*pl*.〕〔美俚〕不利结局。**catch** [**have**, **get**, **take**] **sb. on the ~** 制服某人,压倒某人。**down in the ~** [**~s**] 马臀骨受伤;垂头丧气,无精打采。**on** [**upon**] **the ~** 〔罕〕处于不利地位。**shoot from the ~** 鲁莽地讲话[行事]。**smite sb. ~ and thigh** 使某人惨败。**sth. on the ~** 〔美谑〕后裤袋中的东西(指扁平的小酒瓶)。**II** *vt*. (**-pp-**) 1. 使(家畜)扭脱股关节;用屁股撞。2.【建】使做成四坡屋顶。~ **bath** 坐浴,半身浴;坐浴浴盆。**~bone** 坐骨,髋骨,无名骨。~ **boot** (消防队员或渔夫所穿)长到大腿的长靴。~ **disease** 股关节症,髋关节症。~ **fire**【军】坐射。~ **gout** 坐骨神经痛。~ **joint**【解】髋关节。~ **roof**【建】四坡屋顶。**~-shooting** *a*. 〔美〕鲁莽行事的;信口开河的。**~-shot** *a*. 髋骨位置不正的;股关节脱节的。

hip[2], **hyp** [hip; hɪp] **I** *n*. 〔口〕病态的忧郁,情绪低沉(= hypochondria)。**II** *vt*. (**-pp-**) 使忧郁。

hip[3] [hip; hɪp] *n*.【植】蔷薇果(= hep[1])。

hip[4] [hip; hɪp] *int*. (集体的)喝采[欢呼]声〔一般仅用于:*Hip! Hip! hurrah!* 嗨! 嗨! 万岁!〕。

hip[5] [hip; hɪp] *a*. 〔美俚〕1. 熟悉内情的,市面灵通的;赶时新的。2. 聪明的,机灵的。3. 〔美〕颓废派的,嬉皮派的。**I'm ~**. 〔美俚〕别噜苏了! 我懂了! ~ **capitalism** 满足"嬉皮"派需要的资本主义工商业。~ **chick** 〔美俚〕熟悉时新东西的女学生。~ **hop** 嬉蹦舞(曲)〔由街头卖艺者表演的一种舞蹈或电子乐曲,所跳多为霹雳舞〕。**~-hugger** *a*. (裤子)紧裹臀部的。**~-huggers** *n*. 〔*pl*.〕紧裹臀部的裤子。

hi·pot [ˈhaipɔt; ˋhaɪpɑt] *n*. 有望迅速飞黄腾达的年轻人;大有潜力[希望]的人〔源自 high potential〕。

hip·parch [ˈhipɑːk; ˋhɪpɑrk] *n*. (古希腊)骑兵司令。

hipped[1] [hipt; hɪpt] *a*. 1. 臀部…的。2. (牲畜等)股关节脱节的。3. (屋顶)有斜脊的。*broad* [*narrow*] ~ 臀部宽[窄]的。*a ~ roof* 四坡屋顶。

hipped[2] [hipt; hɪpt] *a*. 1. 〔英口〕忧郁的;沮丧的。2. 〔美俚〕热衷于…的,迷恋于…的 (*on*)。*feel ~* 觉得郁闷。3. 〔俚〕被激怒的。*be ~ on movies* [*golf*] 电影[高尔夫球]迷。

hip·pi·at·rics [͵hipiˈætriks; ͵hɪpɪˋætrɪks] *n*. *pl*. 〔作单数用〕马医学〔兽医学的一门〕。

hip·pie [ˈhipiː; ˋhɪpɪ] *n*. 〔俚〕嬉皮士,希比派,希皮派〔六十年代美国青年中出现的颓废派青年的称呼。他们对社会怀有某种不满,但以奇装异服、蓄长发、吸毒等来发泄〕。**-dom** *n*. 〔集合词〕嬉皮士世界,颓废派。

hip·pish [ˈhipiʃ; ˋhɪpɪʃ] *a*. 有点忧郁的。

hipp(o)- *comb. f*. 表示"马"〔元音前用 hipp-〕: *hippo*campus.

hip·po [ˈhipəu; ˋhɪpo] *n*. 〔俚〕河马(= hippopotamus)。

hip·po·cam·pus [͵hipəˈkæmpəs; ͵hɪpəˋkæmpəs] *n*. (*pl*. **-pi** [-pai; -paɪ]) 1.【希神】(马头鱼尾的)怪兽。2.【动】海马。3.【解】(脑内的)海马状突起。

hip·pock·et [ˈhipɔkit; ˋhɪpɑkɪt] *a*. 小尺寸的,小规模的。

hip·po·cras [ˈhipəkræs; ˋhɪpəkræs] *n*. (欧洲中世纪的)姜汁补身葡萄酒。

Hip·poc·ra·tes [hiˈpɔkrətiːz; hɪˋpɑkrətiz] 希波克拉底(公元前 460—360?),古希腊的名医,世称医学之父。

Hip·po·crat·ic [͵hipəuˈkrætik; ͵hɪpoˋkrætɪk] *a*. (古希腊医师)希波克拉底的;希波克拉底学派的。

Hip·po·crene [͵hipəuˈkriːni(ː), ˈhipəkriːn; ͵hɪpoˋkrini, ˋhɪpə͵krin] *n*.【希神】赫利孔 (Helicon) 山的灵泉;诗的灵感。

hip·po·drome [ˈhipədrəum; ˋhɪpədrom] *n*. 1. (古希腊、罗马战车和马车的)竞技场,赛马场。2. 马戏场。

hip·po·griff, **hip·po·gryph** [ˈhipəgrif; ˋhɪpəgrɪf] *n*.【希神】半鹰半马的有翅怪兽。

hip·po·pot·a·mus [͵hipəˈpɔtəməs; ͵hɪpəˋpɑtəməs] *n*. (*pl*. **~es**, **-mi** [-mai; -maɪ])【动】河马。

hipps [hips; hɪps] *n*. hip[2]的复数。

hip·py[1] [ˈhipi; ˋhɪpɪ] *n*. = hippie. **-dom** *n*. 美国颓废派,颓废派行为。**-hood** *n*. 美国颓废派身分,颓废派风度。

hip·py[2] [ˈhipi; ˋhɪpɪ] *a*. 臀部大的。

hip·ster [ˈhipstə; ˋhɪpstɚ] *n*. 1. 消息灵通人士,赶时髦的人。2. 机灵的人。3. 美国颓废派成员。4. 爵士音乐迷。

hir·a·ble [ˈhaiərəbl; ˋhaɪrəbl̩] *a*. 能租用的,能雇用的。

hi·ra·gan·a [͵hirəˈgɑːnə; ͵hɪrəˋgɑnə] *n*. 〔Jap.〕(日语字母的草书)平假名。

Hi·ram [ˈhairəm; ˋhaɪrəm] *n*. 海勒姆〔男子名〕。

hir·cine [ˈhəːsain; ˋhɝsaɪn] *a*. 1. 山羊的;像山羊的。2. 羊膻味重的。3. 好色的。

hire [ˈhaiə; haɪr] **I** *n*. 1. 租金;酬金;工钱。2. 租借,雇佣。*motorcars on ~* 〔英〕= *automobiles for ~* 〔美〕出租汽车。*let out* (*sth*.) *on ~* 出租。*pay for the ~ of* 付租费。*work for ~* 做雇佣工作。**for** [**on**] **~** 供租用(*books for ~* 书籍出租)。**II** *vt*. 1. 租用,赁借;雇,雇佣。2. 出租 (*out*)。~ *oneself out as a hack writer* 做雇佣文人。~ *oneself out to* 投靠。~ **on** 找到职业。~ **out** ... (*by the hour*) (按钟头)出租。~ **purchase** [**system**] 〔英〕分期付款销货法。

hire·ling [ˈhaiəliŋ; ˋhaɪrlɪŋ] **I** *a*. 做雇佣工作的。**II** *n*. 1. 佣工;〔蔑〕为钱劳动的人。2. 租用物。

hir·er [ˈhaiərə; ˋhaɪrɚ] *n*. 雇主;租借者。

hir·ing [ˈhaiəriŋ; ˋhaɪrɪŋ] **I** *n*. 雇佣,租赁。**II** *a*. 雇佣的,租赁的。~ **hall** (美国航运业等举办的挨次介绍登记者就业的)职业介绍所,失业工人待雇所。

hi·rise [ˈhairaiz; ˋhaɪraɪz] *n*. = high rise.

Hi·ro·shi·ma [͵hirəˈʃiːmə; hɪrəˋʃimɑ] *n*. 广岛〔日本市、县名〕。

hir·sute [ˈhəːsjuːt; ˋhɝsjut] *a*. (动物达到发情期时)毛多的;有粗毛的;有须的。**-ness** *n*.

hir·su·tu·lous [həːˈsjuːtjələs; hɚˋsjutjələs] *a*. 毛稀少[很短]的。

hir·u·din [ˈhirjudin; ˋhɪrjudɪn] *n*.【生化】水蛭素。

Hir·u·din·e·a [͵hiruˈdiniə; ͵hɪruˋdɪnɪə] *n*. 〔*pl*.〕【动】蛭纲。

hi·ru·di·noid [hiˈruːdnoid; hɪˋrudə͵nɔɪd] *a*. 水蛭的;似水蛭的。

hi·run·dine [hiˈrʌndin, -dain; hɪˋrʌndɪn, -daɪn] I *a*. 燕的;似燕的。II *n*. 燕科鸟。

his [hiz, 弱 iz; hɪz, 弱 ɪz] *pro*. 1. 〔he 的所有格〕他的。2. 〔he 的物主代词〕他的东西。3. 〔古〕〔置于男子名后作所有格〕他的。*in Henry the Fourth* ~ *time* 在亨利四世时代。*This book is* ~, *not mine*. 这本书是他的,不是我的。*himself and* ~ 他(自己)和他的家属。

his(')n [hizn; ˋhɪzn] *pro*. 〔古、方〕= his, his own.

His·pa·ni·a [hisˈpeiniə, -ˈpɑː-; hɪsˋpenɪə, -ˋpɑ-] *n*. 1. 〔诗〕西班牙(= Spain)。2. 古罗马时代西班牙和葡萄牙地区的拉丁名。

His·pan·ic [hisˈpænik; hɪsˋpænɪk] *a*. 1. 西班牙的;西班牙和葡萄牙的。2. 拉丁美洲的。~ *America* 拉丁美洲。

His·pan·i·cism [hisˈpænisizəm; hɪsˋpænɪˏsɪzəm] *n*. (英语上下文中出现的)西班牙语语言现象〔指词、短语等〕。

his·pa·ni·dad [ispaniˈdad; ɪspanɪˋdad] *n*. 〔Sp. 常作 H-〕(在拉丁美洲推行的)西班牙文明至上主义。

his·pa·nism [ˈhispənizəm; ˋhɪspəˏnɪzəm] *n*. 〔常作 H-〕1. = hispanidad. 2. 来源于西班牙语的语言特点。

Hispano- *comb. f*. 表示"西班牙": *Hispano*-Gallican.

His·pa·no-Gal·li·can [ˈhispənə-ˈgælikən; ˋhispənə-ˋgælɪkən] *a*. 西班牙—法国的。

his·pid [ˈhispid; ˋhɪspɪd] *a*. 有鬃的,有刺的,硬毛多的。

hiss [his; hɪs] I *vi*. 1. (鹅、蛇、蒸气等)发嘶嘶声。2. 发嘘嘘声表示反对[鄙视]。*A ball* ~*ed by*. 子弹嘶地一声飞过。~ *for silence* 发嘘声要大家别讲话。— *vt*. 1. 发嘶嘶声表示,嘶嘶地说出。2. 对…发嘘嘘声〔表示反对、鄙视〕,用嘘嘘声轰赶。~ *an actor* 对演员发嘘声。~*sb*. *off* [*away*, *down*] 把某人嘘走。II *n*. 嘘音,嘶嘶的啸声;拖长的 [s] 声。

hist[1] [hist; hɪst] I *int*. 〔古〕嘶嘶! 嘘! 〔促起注意或制止人讲话的发声〕。II *vt*. 向…发嘘声。

hist[2] [hist; hɪst] *n*., *v*. 〔方〕= hoist.

hist. = histology; historian; historical; history.

his·tam·i·nase [hisˈtæmineis, ˈhistəmineis; hɪsˋtæmɪnes] *n*. 【生化】组(织)胺酶。

his·ta·mine [ˈhistəmiːn, -min; ˋhɪstəmin, -mɪn] *n*. 【生化】组(织)胺。**-tamin·ic** [-ˈminik; -ˋmɪnɪk] *a*.

his·ti·dine [ˈhistidiːn, -din; ˋhɪstɪdin, -dɪn] *n*. 【生化】组胺酸。

his·ti·o·cyte [ˈhistiəsait; ˋhɪstɪəsaɪt] *n*. 【生】组织细胞。**-o·cyt·ic** [-ˈsitik; -ˋsitik] *a*.

histo- *comb. f*. 表示"组织": *histo*genesis.

his·to·chem·is·try [ˌhistəuˈkemistri; ˏhɪstoˋkɛmɪstrɪ] *n*. 组织化学。**-ical** [-ikl; -ɪkl̩] *a*. **-i·cal·ly** *ad*.

his·to·gen [ˈhistəudʒən; ˋhɪstodʒən] *n*. 【植】组织元。

his·to·gen·e·sis [ˌhistəuˈdʒenisis; ˏhɪstoˋdʒɛnɪsɪs] *n*. 【生】组织发生。**-ge·net·ic** [-dʒəˈnetik; -dʒəˋnɛtɪk] *a*. **-ge·net·i·cal·ly** *ad*.

his·to·gram [ˈhistəugræm; ˋhɪstoˏgræm] *n*. 【统】(次数)矩形图,直方图。

his·toid [ˈhistɔid; ˋhɪstɔɪd] *a*. 【医】1. 常规组织状的。2. 仅从一种组织发展而来的。

his·tol·o·gy [hisˈtɔlədʒi; hɪsˋtɑlədʒɪ] *n*. 1. 【生】组织学;(生物的)组织机构。2. 研究组织学的论文。

his·tol·y·sis [hisˈtɔlisis; hɪsˋtɑlɪsɪs] *n*. 【生】组织溶解。**-to·lyt·ic** [ˌhistəˈlitik; ˏhɪstəˋlɪtɪk] *a*.

his·tone [ˈhistəun; ˋhɪston] *n*. 【生化】组蛋白。

his·to·pa·thol·o·gy [ˌhistəupəˈθɔlədʒi; ˏhɪstopəˋθɑlədʒɪ] *n*. 组织病理学。

his·to·phys·i·ol·o·gy [ˌhistəuˈfiziˈɔlədʒi; ˏhɪstoˋfɪzɪˋɑlədʒɪ] *n*. 组织生理学。

his·to·plas·mo·sis [ˌhistəuplæzˈməusis; ˏhɪstoplæzˋmosɪs] *n*. 【医】荚膜组织浆菌病。

his·to·ri·an [hisˈtɔːriən; hɪsˋtɔrɪən] *n*. 1. 历史学家。2. 年代史编者,编史家。

his·to·ri·at·ed [hisˈtɔːrieitid; hɪsˋtɔrɪetɪd] *a*. (书页每段开头、每页的边或手稿等)用人[动物]的图像装饰的,有图案的。

his·tor·ic [hisˈtɔrik; hɪsˋtɑrɪk] *a*. 1. 历史上有名的,有历史意义的。2. 历史上的(= historical)。*a*(*n*) ~ *town* 历史名镇。*a*(*n*) ~ *event* 历史事件。*the* ~ [*historical*] *present* 【语法】历史现在时态〔指用现在时态叙述过去的事件,以达到描写生动的目的〕。*a*(*n*) ~ *spot* 史迹,古迹。~ *times* 有史时期 (*opp*. prehistoric times)。

his·tor·i·cal [hisˈtɔrikəl; hɪsˋtɑrɪkəl] *a*. 1. 史学的;有关历史的。2. 历史的,历史上的;过去的。3. 有根据的,真实的,非杜撰的 (*opp*. legendary)。4. 依据历史发展叙述的。5. 历史上著名的〔现在一般用 historic〕。6. 【语法】历史现在时态的。~ *science* 历史学。*the* ~ *method* 历史的方法。~ *studies* 历史研究。*a*(*n*) ~ *novel* 历史小说。*the* ~ *period* 历史阶段。*a*(*n*) ~ *personage* 历史人物。*the* ~ *present* 【语法】= the historic present. *a*(*n*) ~ *treatise* 史论。~ **geography** 历史地理学。~ **linguistics** 历史语言学。~ **school** 历史学派。**-ly** *ad*. 在历史上,从历史观点上说。

his·tor·i·cism [hisˈtɔrisizəm; hɪsˋtɑrɪsɪzəm] *n*. 1. 历史主义。2. 历史发展天定论。3. 对历史传统的崇拜。

his·to·ric·ity [ˌhistəˈrisiti; ˏhɪstəˋrɪsətɪ] *n*. 历史性,真实性。

his·tor·i·cize [hisˈtɔːrisaiz; hɪsˋtɔrəsaɪz] *vt*. 使具历史真实性,赋与…以历史意义。— *vi*. 运用史料。

his·to·ried [ˈhistərid; ˋhɪstərɪd] *a*. 历史上有名的,有历史的,有来由的;作为历史记载的。*a richly* ~ *land* 历史悠久的国家。

his·to·ri·ette [ˌhistɔːriˈet; ˏhɪstorɪˋɛt] *n*. 〔F.〕史话,小史。

his·to·ri·og·ra·pher [ˌhistɔːriˈɔgrəfə; ˏhɪstorɪˋɑgrəfɚ] *n*. 历史家;史官,史料编纂者。

his·to·ri·og·ra·phy [ˌhistɔːriˈɔgrəfi; ˏhɪstorɪˋɑgrəfɪ] *n*. 编史工作,历史编纂学。**-o·gra·phic(al)** *a*.

his·to·ry [ˈhistəri; ˋhɪstərɪ] *n*. 1. 历史,历史学。2. 沿革,来历;(个人的)履历,经历。3. 对过去事件的记载;大事记。4. 对形成未来的进程有影响的事件[思想]。5. 过去的事。6. 历史剧。*a case* ~ 病例,典型例证。*Ancient* [*Medieval*, *Modern*] *H-* 古代[中古、近代]史。*natural* ~ 博物学,自然史。*This sword has a* ~. 这剑有来历。*She has a* ~. 她的身世有难言之隐。*temperature* ~ 温度变化过程。*time* ~ 时间关系曲线图。***be*** ~ 成为历史;完蛋。***H- repeats itself***. 〔谚〕历史往往重演。***make*** ~ 影响历史进程,做名垂青史的大事。

his·to·ther·a·py [ˈhistəuθerəpi; ˋhɪstoθɛrəpɪ] *n*. 【医】组织疗法。

his·tri·on·ic(al) [ˌhistriˈɔnik(əl); ˏhɪstrɪˋɑnɪk(əl)] I *a*. 1. 演员的,戏剧上的;戏剧性的。2. 〔蔑〕像做戏似的,装腔作势的,虚伪的。3. 面部肌肉的。II *n*. 1. 演员。2. 〔*pl*.〕戏剧表演;舞台艺术。3. 〔*pl*.〕戏剧似的言行;装腔作势。~ **muscles** 【解】表情肌。**-i·cal·ly** *ad*.

his·tri·on·i·cism, his·tri·on·ism [ˌhistriˈɔnisizəm, ˈhistriənizəm; ˏhɪstrɪˋɑnɪsɪzəm, ˋhɪstrɪənɪzəm] *n*. 戏剧性,舞台效果。

hit [hit; hɪt] I *vt*. (***hit***; ***hit·ting***) 1. (箭、子弹等)打,打击,命中 (*opp*. miss)。2. 碰撞,使碰撞。3. 偶然碰见,遇见;(搜寻后)找到,发现;想到。4. 袭击,打击,使遭受。5. 抨击,批评;伤…的感情。6. 猜对,说中,戳穿(真相)。7. 适合,投合;要求,请求。8. 达到,完成(指标);〔美俚〕到达,到…去;出现于(报刊等);搜寻(猎踪)。9. 【体】(板球等)得(分);【棒球】打出(安全打)〔打出能使击球者跑到第一垒的一击〕。10. 精确地反映,原样复制。11. 〔美俚〕埋头干;沉溺于。12. 大口大口地吃[喝]。13. 出发,上路。~ *one's head against the door* 头撞在门

H

上。～ *it right* 正中,命中。*You've* ～ *it*. 你猜对了。～ *one's fancy* 正中下怀。*H- the ground*! 卧倒!～ *a likeness* 逼真地复制[绘制]原物。～ *the town* 到达镇上。～ *the job* 〔美俚〕埋头工作。～ *sb. for a loan* 向某人借钱。～ *a new high* (物价等)上涨到新高峰。*The new train can* ～ *100m.p.h.* 新火车时速可达100英里。*The report has* ～ *the papers*. 那篇通讯已经见报。— *vi*. **1.** 打,打击(*at*);命中。**2.** 说中,猜对。**3.** 偶然碰上,碰见(*against*; *on*; *upon*)。**4.** 忽然想起,偶然想到(*on*; *upon*)。**5.** (在内燃机汽缸内)点火。～ *upon a good idea* 灵机一动,忽然想到一个妙主意。*The army* ～ *at dawn*. 军队拂晓时出击。*His head* ～ *against the wall*. 他的头撞到墙上。～ **(...) against** 撞击;把…碰到。～ **at** 批评,嘲笑。～ **for** 〔美〕向…出发。～ **horses together** 齐心协力。～ **it** **1.** 说对;猜对;达到目的。**2.** 〔美〕飞快地走。～ **it off** 性情相投;〔口〕相处得很好(*with*; *together*)。～ **it up** 坚持前进。～ **off** **1.** 〔讽〕逼真地描画,模仿。**2.** 当场作(诗)。**3.** 打掉。**4.** (板球等)得分。**5.** 适合,与…融洽(*with*)。～ **on** [**upon**] 碰见;发现;想出(好办法),想到。～ **on all** [**six**] **cylinders** 汽缸全部点火;〔喻〕拼命工作;性能良好。～ **one's stride** 全力以赴。～ **out** 抨击,猛烈打击(*at*)。～ **sb. below the belt** (拳击)犯规行为,〔喻〕利用不正当手段打击某人,乘某人之危打击他。～ **sb. between the eyes** 使某人有强烈的印象。～ **sb. when he is down** 乘人之危,落井下石。～ **sb. where it hurts** 打中要害,触到某人痛处。～ **the** [**one's**] **books** 〔美俚〕用功。～ **the bottle** 酗酒。～ **the breeze** [**pike**, **trail**] 〔美俚〕旅行;流浪,漂泊。～ **the bull's-eye** 〔美俚〕说到问题的本质。～ **the ceiling** [**roof**] 〔美俚〕勃然大怒。～ **the clock** 〔美〕打上班[下班]记时钟;在上班签到簿上签名。～ **the deck** 〔美俚〕起床工作。～ **the gong** [**pipe**] 〔美俚〕吸鸦片烟。～ **the gow** 〔美俚〕吸食麻醉品。～ **the hay** [**sack**] 〔美俚〕上床睡觉。～ **the headlines** 【美体】出名,成为头条新闻。～ **the high spots** **1.** 上街;上夜总会。**2.** 做事马虎。**3.** 简略介绍。～ **the hustings** 预备竞选的政治活动。～ **the jackpot** 〔美俚〕大获成功,走运。～ **the mark** [**target**] 击中目标,打中要害。～ **the** (**right**) **nail on the head** 命中;中肯。～ **the road** 〔美俚〕上路,出发。～ **the spot** 〔尤指食品,饮料〕提神解乏,使满足。～ **the stands** 上市,开始发售。～ **the tone of society** 善于交际。～ **up** **1.** 催促;加速。**2.** 〔美〕乞求。**3.** (板球等)得(分)。～ **upon a stratagem** 计上心来。**II** *n*. **1.** 打击;命中,击中。**2.** 碰撞。**3.** 演出[尝试]的成功;轰动一时的人物;风行一时的东西。**4.** 批评,讽刺(*at*);俏皮话。**5.** 【棒球】安全打;(棒球等的)得分。**6.** 好运气。**7.** 一剂麻醉毒品,一口大麻烟。**8.** 【计】(对电脑网络某个站点的)一次访问。*a lucky* ～ 偶中,幸中。*a clever* ～ 巧妙的一击;一句巧妙的俏皮话。*His novel was a great* ～. 他的小说大受欢迎。*clear* ～ 【棒球】绝好的安全打,快打。*fair* ～ 好球。～ **or miss** **1.** 不顾胜败地;冒险地。**2.** 漫无目的地。**look to** [**mind**] **one's** ～**s** 抓机会;关心自己的利益。**make a** [**capital**, **great**, **magnificent**, **tremendous**] ～ 博得好评,很受欢迎,很成功。**silent** ～ 〔美〕受欢迎的无声影片。**smash** ～ 〔俚〕成功的演出。～**-and-miss** *a*. 有时打中而有时又打不中的;碰巧的。～**-and-run** *a*. **1.** 闯祸后逃逸的〔通常指汽车司机在造成车祸后逃跑〕。**2.** (打棒球时)打了就跑的,击球跑垒的(*a* ～*-and-run victim* 被已逃跑的汽车压死的人)。～**-and-runner** 闯祸后逃走的汽车司机。～**-com** 一炮打响的情景喜剧。～ **man** 职业凶手。～**-or-miss** *a*. 冒险的;不论成功与否的。～ **parade** (歌曲等的)最流行的一批,流行唱片目录。～**-runner** 〔美〕= ～-and-runner. ～**-skip** = hit-and-run 1. ～ **squad** 恐怖主义者[恐怖分子]集团。

hitch [hitʃ; hɪtʃ] **I** *vi*. **1.** 被挂住,被钩住。**2.** 一颠一簸地移动,跛行,蹒跚。**3.** 〔美俚〕搭便车(= hitchhike)。**4.** 〔口〕和好,协调。**5.** 〔美俚〕结婚(*up*)。*My dress* ～*ed on a nail*. 我的衣服被钉子挂住了。— **vt**. **1.** 拴住,系住,钩住,套住(牛马)。**2.** 急拉,猛拉;扯起;拉进,收进(故事中)。**3.** 〔美俚〕要求搭(车),搭便车去(旅行等)(= hitchhike)。**4.** 〔美俚〕使结婚。～ *a rope over* [*round*] *the bough* 用索子套住树枝。～ *a ride back to school* 搭便车返校。**be** ～**ed** = ～ **oneself** 结婚。～ **horses together** 把马系在一起;〔美〕和好,一致行动。～ **one's waggon to a star** 好高骛远,野心勃勃。～ **up** **1.** 扯起。**2.** (把马等)拴在(车上)。**3.** 〔美俚〕使结婚。**II** *n*. **1.** 系,拴,套,钩。**2.** 起;停止,急止。**3.** 障碍,顿挫。**4.** 【海】索结,结索,索眼。**5.** 〔美军俚〕服役期。**6.** 蹒跚。**7.** 〔美俚〕搭便车旅行。*His three-year* ～ *is not yet completed*. 他的三年兵役还没有满。**without a** ～ 无障碍地,一帆风顺地。～**ing post** 拴马栓。～**hike** **1.** *vi*. 〔美口〕搭乘他人便车旅行。**2.** *vt*. 叫住(过路车等)要求免费搭乘;搭乘便车去(旅行等);获得(免费搭车的)机会。**3.** *n*. 免费搭车。～**hiker** 〔美〕沿途搭乘他人汽车旅行的人。

Hitch·cock [ˈhitʃkɔk; ˋhɪtʃkɑk] *n*. 希契科克〔姓氏〕。

hith·er [ˈhiðə; ˋhɪðɚ] **I** *ad*. 〔古〕向此处。**II** *a*. 这里的,这边的,附近的。～ **and thither** =〔美〕～ **and yon** 到处,向各处,忽东忽西。**on the** ～ **side** (**of** ...) **1.** 在这一边。**2.** (年龄)不到…岁。*on the* ～ *side of sixty* 不到六十岁。

hith·er·most [ˈhiðəməust; ˋhɪðɚmost] *a*. 最近的。

hith·er·to [ˌhiðəˈtuː; ˏhɪðɚˋtu] *ad*. 迄今;到目前为止。

hith·er·ward(s) [ˈhiðəwəd(z); ˋhɪðɚwɚd(z)] *ad*. 〔罕〕= hither *ad*.

Hit·ler [ˈhitlə; ˋhɪtlɚ], **Adolf** 阿道夫·希特勒〔1889—1945,德国纳粹头目〕。

Hit·ler·i·an [hitˈləriən; hɪtˋlɛrɪən] *a*. 希特勒的,希特勒式的,希特勒统治的。

Hit·ler·ism [ˈhitlərizəm; ˋhɪtlərˏɪzəm] *n*. 希特勒主义。

Hit·ler·ite [ˈhitlərait; ˋhɪtlərˏaɪt] **I** *n*. 希特勒主义者,纳粹党徒。**II** *a*. 希特勒主义者的,纳粹党徒的。

hit·ter [ˈhitə; ˋhɪtɚ] *n*. **1.** 打击者,击中者。**2.** 【机】铆钉枪。

Hit·tite [ˈhitait; ˋhɪtaɪt] **I** *n*. **1.** 赫梯人〔小亚细亚东部和叙利亚北部古代部族〕。**2.** 赫梯语。**II** *a*. **1.** 赫梯人的。**2.** 赫梯语的。

HIV = human immunodeficiency virus 人体免疫缺损病毒,艾滋病病毒。

hive [haiv; haɪv] **I** *n*. **1.** 蜂巢,蜂房,蜂箱。**2.** 蜂群。**3.** 蜂巢状物。**4.** 热闹场所;熙攘的人群。*a* ～ *of industry* 繁忙的工厂区。**II** *vt*. **1.** 使(蜂)入蜂箱,贮(蜜)于蜂箱中。**2.** 贮备,积蓄。**3.** 使(人)安居家中。— *vi*. **1.** (蜂)进蜂箱,栖巢中。**2.** 同栖聚居。～ **off** (养蜂)分封;〔喻〕从团体中分出来成为独立的[自治的]部分。～ **nest** 鸟的群栖巢。

hives [haivz; haɪvz] *n*. *pl*. 〔用作 *sing*. 或 *pl*.〕【医】荨麻疹。

hi·ya [ˈhaijə; ˋhaɪjə] *int*. 〔美俚〕你好!(= How are you?)。

H.J., **HJ** = here lies 〔拉丁语 *his jacet* 的略语〕…长眠于此。

HK = **1.** Hong Kong. **2.** House of Keys.

hk. = 【纺】hank.

hl. = hectolitre(s).

H.L., **HL** = House of Lords.

H.L.I. = 【英军】Highland Light Infantry.

hm. = hectometre.

h'm [hm; həm] = hem², hum.

H.M., **HM** = His [Her] Majesty.

H.M.A.S. = His Majesty's Australian Ship 澳大利亚舰船。

HMG = heavy machine gun.

H

HMMWV, Hmmwv [ˈhʌmˌviː; ˋhʌmˏvi] = High Mobility Multipurpose Wheeled Vehicle 高度机动多用途轮式运输卡车〔式样笨拙、色如黄沙,现已取代美军用吉普车〕。

H.M.S. = His [Her] Majesty's Service [Ship] 英国公函[舰船]。

H.M.T. = His Majesty's Trawler 英国拖网船。

Ho =【化】holmium 钬。

H.O., HO = 1. Head Office 总部,总店。2. Home Office (英国)内政部。

ho [həu; ho] *n*. = whore.

ho(a) [həu; ho] *int*. 1. 嗬!〔唤起注意或表示惊讶、满足、喜悦〕。2. 站住!〔止马声〕。***ho! ho! ho!*** 哈!哈!哈!〔嘲笑声〕。***ho! there*** 喂! ***What ho!*** 嗬,什么! (***Westward***) ***ho!***【海】(西)向去啊!

hoa·gy, hoa·gie [ˈhəugi; ˋhogɪ] *n*. (*pl*. ***-gies***) = herosandwich.

hoar [hɔː, hɔə; hɔr, hor] I *a*. 1. (头发)灰白的,白色的。2. 有灰白头发的。3. 〔方〕发霉的。II *n*. 1. 灰白色;白发。2. 白霜(= ~frost)。

hoard [hɔːd; hɔrd] I *n*. 1. 窖藏的财宝,密藏的东西。2. (食品的)贮藏,贮藏物。3. (知识等的)宝库。*a ~ of money* 积蓄。II *vt*. 1. 积蓄;贮藏;囤积 (*up*)。2. 把…隐藏在心中;心怀。~ *gold* 积聚黄金。~ *revenge* 怀恨。— *vi*. 贮藏;囤积。

hoard·er [ˈhɔːdə; ˋhɔrdɚ] *n*. 贮藏者;囤积者。

hoard·ing[1] [ˈhɔːdiŋ; ˋhɔrdɪŋ] *n*. 1. 贮藏;囤积;(货币的)埋藏。2. 〔*pl*.〕贮藏物;囤积物。

hoard·ing[2] [ˈhɔːdiŋ; ˋhordɪŋ] *n*. 1. 〔英〕(空地、修建场所的)临时围篱,板围。2. 广告牌。3. (古代用木头搭在城墙外的)守望台。

hoar·hound [ˈhɔːhaund; ˋhɔrˏhaund] *n*. = horehound.

hoarse [hɔːs; hɔrs] *a*. (嗓子)嘶哑的,沙哑的;刺耳的。*as ~ as a raven* 声音沙哑。*talk oneself ~* 把嗓子说哑。**-ly** *ad*. **-ness** *n*.

hoars·en [ˈhɔːsn; ˋhɔrsn̩] *vt*. 使(嗓子)嘶哑。— *vi*. (嗓子)变嘶哑。

hoarstone [ˈhɔːstəun; ˋhɔrˏston] *n*. 灰色古石;〔英〕(特指史前的)界标石。

H

hoar·y [ˈhɔːri, ˈhɔəri; ˋhɔrɪ, ˋhorɪ] *a*. 1. 灰白的;(因年老)头发变白的,白发的。2. 陈旧的,古老的。3.【植、动】生满灰白毛的。*a ~ head* 须发斑白的头。*the ~ antiquity* 远古。~ *ruins* 古代遗迹。~ **marmot**【动】花白旱獭 (*Marmota caligata*)〔发现于北美洲〕。**hoar·i·ly** *ad*. **hoar·i·ness** *n*.

hoar·y-head·ed [ˈhɔːriˈhedid; ˋhɔrɪˋhɛdɪd] *a*. 白发苍苍的。

ho·at·zin [həuˈætsin; hoˋætsɪn] *n*.【动】(南美产,幼鸟翼上有爪,能攀树的)何爱青鸟 (*Opisthocomus hoazin*),麝雉。

hoax [həuks; hoks] I *n*. 欺骗,愚弄,戏弄;骗术,骗局。II *vt*. 欺骗,戏弄。

hoax·er [ˈhəuksə; ˋhoksɚ] *n*. 欺骗者,戏弄者。

hob[1] [hɔb; hɑb] I *n*. 1. (壁炉一侧的)锅架,开水壶架。2.【机】滚(铣)刀,螺旋铣刀;元阳模;蜗(轮)杆;螺(旋)杆。3. 平头钉。4. 投环戏的标棍;用石头打落棒头钱的游戏。II *vt*. 1. 给…钉平头钉。2.【机】滚铣。

hob[2] [hɔb; hɑb] *n*. 1. 〔英方〕淘气鬼。2. 〔口〕捣乱,恶作剧;破坏。***play*** [***raise***] ~ 1. 恶作剧,捣乱。2. 歪曲 (*with*) (*play ~ with facts* 歪曲事实)。

hob-and-nob [ˈhɔbənˈnɔb; ˋhɑbənˋnɑb] *a*. 亲密的。

Ho·bart [ˈhəubɑːt; ˋhobɑrt] *n*. 1. 霍巴特〔姓氏,男子名〕。2. 霍巴特〔澳大利亚港市〕。

Hobbes [hɔbz; hɑbz] *n*. 1. 霍布斯〔姓氏〕。2. **Thomas ~** 汤马斯·霍布斯〔1588—1679,英国哲学家〕。

Hobbes·i·an [ˈhɔbziən; ˋhɑbzɪən] I *a*. 英国哲学家霍布斯的,霍布斯哲学理论的。II *n*. 霍布斯哲学理论的鼓吹〔追随〕者。

Hob·bism [ˈhɔbizəm; ˋhɑbɪzəm] *n*. 霍布斯的哲学理论。

Hob·bist [ˈhɔbist; ˋhɑbɪst] *a*., *n*. = Hobbesian.

hob·ble [ˈhɔbl; ˋhɑbl̩] I *vi*. 1. 蹒跚,跛行 (*along*; *about*)。2. (说话、行动)疙疙瘩瘩;(诗)不流畅。— *vt*. 1. 使跛行。2. 将(马的)两只脚拴在一起。3. 阻碍。II *n*. 1. 跛行;韵律不全的诗。2. 马的脚绊。3. 〔口、方〕困境。***be in*** [***get into***] ***a*** (***nice***) ~ 陷入进退两难。**~-bush** *n*.【植】桤叶荚蒾 (*Viburnum alnifolium*)。**~ skirt** 膝以下窄狭的裙子。**hob·bling·ly** *ad*.

hob·ble·de·hoy [ˈhɔbldiˈhɔi; ˋhɑbl̩dɪˋhɔɪ] *n*. 青少年;(笨拙的)小伙子。

hob·by[1] [ˈhɔbi; ˋhɑbɪ] *n*. 1. 业余爱好;嗜好,兴趣。2. (小孩玩的)竹马,木马。3. 〔罕〕小马。***mount*** [***ride***] ***a*** [***one's***] ~ (***to death***) 沉溺在业余的嗜好中(不能自拔),反复说[做]自己喜欢做的事(以致令人生厌)。**-ist** *n*. 有业余爱好的人。

hob·by[2] [ˈhɔbi; ˋhɑbɪ] *n*. (用以猎捕小鸟的)小隼。

hob·by·horse [ˈhɔbihɔːs; ˋhɑbɪhɔrs] *n*. 1. 木马,摇马,竹马;玩具马。2. 〔罕〕业余爱好,嗜好。3. 爱反复讲的话题。*Every man has his ~*.〔谚〕人各有所好。***mount*** [***ride***] ***a*** [***one's***] ~ = *mount* [*ride*] *a* [*one's*] *hobby*.

hob·gob·lin [ˈhɔbˌgɔblin; ˋhɑbˏgɑblɪn] *n*. 1. 妖怪,小鬼;淘气鬼。2. 令人厌恶的东西,怪物。

hob·nail [ˈhɔbneil; ˋhɑbnel] I *n*. 1. (钉在靴底上的)平头钉。2. 穿钉有平头钉靴子的人,乡下佬。II *vt*. 在(鞋底等上)钉平头钉。~ **liver**【医】(肝硬变引起的)鞋钉肝,门静脉性肝硬变。**-ed** *a*. (鞋底)钉有平头钉的;土头土脑的。

hob·nob [ˈhɔbnɔb; ˋhɑbˏnɑb] I *vi*. (***-bb-***) 1. 共饮,开怀对饮。2. 恳谈;亲切交往 (*with*; *together*)。II *n*. 聚会,恳谈。III *ad*. 随意地。

ho·bo [ˈhəubəu; ˋhobo] I *n*. (*pl*. ***~(e)s***) 〔美俚〕1. (随季节流动各地的)流动工人。2. (白坐火车到处流浪的)无业游民,流浪汉。~ **belt** 〔美〕加州的香橼栽培区。~ **limited** 〔美俚〕车务员宽待游民的火车。II *vi*. 过流浪生活。**-ism** *n*. 流浪生活。

ho·boe [ˈhəubəu; ˋhobo], **ho·boy** [ˈhəubɔi; ˋhobɔɪ] *n*. = hautboy.

Hob·son [ˈhɔbsn; ˋhɑbsn̩] *n*. 霍布森〔姓氏〕。**~'s choice** 无选择余地〔源自英国 16—17 世纪的租马房经营者汤马斯·霍布森,该马房规定租马的顾客不许挑选〕。

hock[1] [hɔk; hɑk] I *n*. 1.【动】(有蹄类的)跗关节(= ~joint)。2. (猪的)腿肉,肘子。II *vt*. 割断蹄筋使成残废。

hock[2] [hɔk; hɑk] I *n*. 1. 典当,抵押。2. 〔美俚〕监牢。II *vt*. 典当,抵押。***in ~*** 1. 在典当中;借着债。2. 〔美俚〕在坐牢。***out of ~*** 1. 已赎出(典当物)。2. 已不欠债。~ **shop** 〔美俚〕当铺。

hock[3] [hɔk; hɑk] *n*. 〔英〕(德国)莱茵白葡萄酒。

hock·er [ˈhɔkə; ˋhɑkɚ] *n*. 典当者。

hock·ey [ˈhɔki; ˋhɑkɪ] *n*. 曲棍球;曲棍球球棒。*field ~* 曲棍球。*ice ~* 冰上曲棍球,冰球。~ **stick** 曲棍球棒。

Hock·ing [ˈhɔkiŋ; ˋhɑkɪŋ] *n*. 霍金〔姓氏〕。

ho·cum [ˈhəukəm; ˋhokəm] *n*. = hokum.

ho·cus [ˈhəukəs; ˋhokəs] I *n*. 1. 欺骗。2. 蒙汗药酒。II *vt*. (〔英〕***-ss-***) 1. 欺骗。2. 加麻醉剂(在酒中);麻醉。3. 在…中搀假。

ho·cus-po·cus [ˈhəukəsˈpəukəs; ˋhokəsˋpokəs] I *vt*. *vi*. (***-s(s)-***) 〔俚〕哄骗,戏弄。II *n*. 1. (变戏法人转移观众注意力的)咒语[手法]。2. 转移注意力的言语[行动]。3. 欺骗。***play ~*** 玩弄欺骗手法。

hod [hɔd; hɑd] *n*. 1. 灰浆桶,砖泥斗。2. 煤斗。**~ carrier** 泥瓦活小工。

ho·dad, ho·dad·dy [ˈhəudæd, ˈhəuˌdædi; ˋhodæd, ˋhoˏdædɪ] *n*. 常去冲浪海滩假充会冲浪的人,冒牌冲浪运动员。

hod·den, hod·din [ˈhɔdn; ˋhadn̩] **I** *n*. 〔Scot.〕手织粗呢。**II** *a*. 穿着手织粗呢衣服的;土里土气的。~ **gray** [**grey**] 黑白毛交织的手织粗呢。

Ho·dei·da [həuˈdeidə; hoˋdedə] *n*. 荷台达〔阿拉伯也门共和国港市〕。

Hodge[1], **hodge** [hɔdʒ; hadʒ] *n*. 〔英〕乡下人,庄稼汉。

Hodge[2] [hɔdʒ; hadʒ] *n*. 霍奇〔男子名, Roger 的爱称〕。

Hodge·kin [ˈhɔdʒkin; ˋhadʒkın] *n*. 霍奇金〔姓氏〕。~ **'s disease** *n*. 【医】霍奇金病〔淋巴肉芽肿〕。

hodge·podge [ˈhɔdʒpɔdʒ; ˋhadʒˏpadʒ] *n*. = hotchpotch.

Hodg·son [ˈhɔdʒsn; ˋhadʒsn] *n*. 霍奇森〔姓氏〕。

hod·i·er·nal [ˌhɔdiˈəːnl; ˏhadıˋɝnl̩] *a*. 现在的,今天的;今世的。

hod·man [ˈhɔdmən; ˋhadmən] *n*. (*pl*. **-men** [-men; -men]) **1**. 灰泥砖瓦搬运工(= hod carrier),小工,苦工。**2**. 代笔穷文人。

hod·o·graph [ˈhɔdəgrɑːf; ˋhadəgræf] *n*. 【数】速矢端线;【物】速端曲线。

hod·om·e·ter [hɔˈdɔmitə; haˋdamıtɚ] *n*. 车程计,路程计,计距器,轮转计(= odometer)。

hod·o·scope [ˈhɔdəskəup; ˋhadəskop] *n*. 荷多仪;【宇】辐射计数器;【物】测迹仪。

hoe [həu; ho] **I** *n*. 锄头;灰耙。*back* ~ 反向铲,倒铲。*Dutch* ~ 一种锹。*trench* ~ 挖沟机。**II** *vt*., *vi*. 用锄除(草等),用锄(松土等);挖掘。***a hard*** [***tough***] ***row to*** ~ 艰苦生活,困难的工作。***a new row to*** ~ 〔美〕新任务。~ ***a big row*** 〔美〕干大事。~ ***another row*** 〔美〕着手新工作。~ ***one's own row*** 干自己的事,自扫门前雪。~ ***your potatoes*** 〔美〕别管闲事。~**cake** 〔美〕玉米饼。~**down** 〔美俚〕**1**. 一种农村舞。**2**. 喧闹的舞会[宴会]。**3**. 吵闹,争论;闹事,打群架。~ **teeth** 梳形矿耙齿。

hof·fice [ˈhɔfis; ˋhafıs] *n*. 家庭办公室〔利用电脑和电信设备在家办公〕。

Hof·man(n) [ˈhɔfmən; ˋhafmən] *n*. 霍夫曼〔姓氏〕。

Hof·stad·ter [ˈhɔfstætə, ˈhɔfstɑːtə; ˋhafstætɚ, ˋhafstatɚ] *n*. 霍夫施塔特〔姓氏〕。

hog [hɔg; hag] **I** *n*. **1**. 猪〔尤指阉过的,重 120 磅以上的肉用猪〕;阉过的公猪,猪肉;【动】杂食性动物。**2**. 〔口〕贪婪、卑鄙、粗野、龌龊的人。**3**. 〔英方,常拼作 hogg〕尚未剪毛的羊羔;从羊羔身上剪下的毛。**4**. 〔美俚〕火车头。**5**. 【海】扫船底的扫帚。**6**. 【机】弯拱;纸浆桶搅拌器。**7**. 鲁莽的骑[驾]车者。~*-raisers' association* 〔美〕养猪业公会(=〔英〕pigbreeder's association)。***a*** ~ ***in armo(u)r*** 穿漂亮衣服而局促不安的人;动作笨拙的人。***as*** [***like***] ***a*** ~ ***on ice*** 〔美〕(像猪在冰上那样)处境困难。***bring one's*** ~***s to the wrong market*** 〔口〕走错了门路;找不适当的人[场合]提出要求。***drive one's*** ~***s to market*** 〔俚〕大声打鼾。***go*** (***the***) ***whole*** ~ 彻底干,干到底。***live*** [***eat***] ***high on*** [***off***] ***the*** ~ 〔美口〕生活得很阔气,过奢侈的生活。~ ***Latin*** = pig Latin. ~ ***mane*** 剪短的马鬣。***make a*** ~ ***of oneself*** 贪吃,馋嘴。***on the*** ~ 〔美俚〕分文没有。***play the*** ~ 独吞独揽,行为卑鄙。***raise more*** ~***s and less hell*** 〔美〕多干活,少闯祸。**II** *vi*. **1**. (船等像猪背一样)中部拱起。**2**. 〔口〕横冲直撞。**III** *vt*. **1**. 剪短(马鬣等)。**2**. 【海】扫除(船底)。**3**. 使(船底)中部拱曲。**4**. 鲁莽地骑[驾驶](车)。**5**. 【无】扰乱(别人播送)。**6**. 〔美俚〕贪婪地抢夺,抢占(全部或大部);〔美俚〕剽窃(别人的著作等)。~**back** 拱起的背;像猪背一样向上拱起的东西;陡峻的拱地,陡峻的山脊。~ **cholera** 猪霍乱。~ **deer** 豚鹿(= axis)。~**fish** 猪头鱼;鲜红鱼(*Lachnobaimus maximus*)〔产于美国东南沿海〕。~**-killing** 〔美方〕喧闹的聚会。~**leg** 〔美方〕左轮手枪。~**let** 〔美〕小猪。~**man** 养猪人。~**nut** = pignut. ~ **peanut** 【植】同株二型豆(*Amplicarpaea monoica*)〔产于北美洲东部〕。~**pen** 〔美〕猪圈。~ **'s-back** = ~-back. ~**'s fennel** 前胡属植物。~**skin** 猪皮,猪皮做的东西。~ **still** 【化】蒸馏塔。~**wash** **1**. 猪食,泔脚。**2**. 废话;空洞的作品。~ **weed** 猪草〔如美洲豚草〕。~**-wild** *a*. 〔俚〕无约束的,混乱的,过于兴奋而狂乱的。

ho·gan [ˈhəugɔːn; ˋhogɔn] *n*. 印第安人草屋〔多指北美印第安人纳瓦霍 (Navaho) 族用泥和树枝盖的小屋〕。

Ho·garth [ˈhəugɑːθ; ˋhogarθ] *n*. **1**. 霍格斯〔姓氏〕。**2**. **William** ~ 威廉·霍格斯〔1697—1764,英国绘画家和雕刻家〕。

Hog·ben [ˈhɔgbən; ˋhagbən] *n*. 霍格本〔姓氏〕。

Hogg [hɔg; hag] *n*. 霍格〔姓氏〕。

hog·ger·el [ˈhɔgərel; ˋhagərəl] *n*. = hogget **1**.

hog·ger·y [ˈhɔgəri; ˋhagərı] *n*. **1**. 养猪场,猪棚。**2**. 猪群。**3**. 猪一样的举动。

hog·get [ˈhɔgit; ˋhagıt] *n*. **1**. 满一岁的羔羊[小猪,小马]。**2**. = hogshead.

hog·gin [ˈhɔgin; ˋhagın] *n*. (筛过的)夹砂砾石,含砂砾石。

hog·ging [ˈhɔgiŋ; ˋhagıŋ] *n*. 弯曲,扭曲;挠度;凸起。

hog·gish [ˈhɔgiʃ; ˋhagıʃ] *a*. 猪似的;肮脏的;卑鄙的;贪婪的;食量大的。**-ly** *ad*. **-ness** *n*.

hog·ma·nay, -ney [ˈhɔgməˈnei; ˏhagməˋne] *n*. 〔Scot.〕**1**. 大年夜,除夕。**2**. 年夜饭;(给孩子的)年节礼物。

hog·nose [ˈhɔgnəuz; ˋhɔgnoz] *n*. (北美)猪鼻蛇〔又作 ~ snake〕。

hogs·head [ˈhɔgzhed; ˋhagzˏhɛd] *n*. **1**. (容量约 63—140 美制加仑的)大桶。**2**. 液量单位〔52.5 英制加仑 = 198.75 升;63 美制加仑 = 238.5 升〕。

hog·tie [ˈhɔ(ː)gtai; ˋhagˏtaı] *vt*. (**-ti·ed**; **-ty·ing**, **-tie·ing**) **1**. 缚住…的手脚,绑住…的四肢。**2**. 〔口〕使动弹不得〔束住手脚不能进行有效的活动〕。

Ho·hen·zol·lern [ˈhəuəntsələn; ˋhoəntsələn] *n*. **1**. 霍亨索伦王室〔德国普鲁士王室(1701—1918)〕。**2**. 霍亨索伦州〔普鲁士一州名〕。

Ho·ho·kam [ˈhəuˈhəukɑːm; ˋhoˋhokam] *a*. 〔美考古〕霍荷卡姆文化的。~ **culture** 霍荷卡姆文化〔美国西南部 Gila 河流域史前的沙漠文化,该文化有大地洞室、陶器、骨贝装饰品及火葬遗址〕。

ho-hum [ˈhəuˈhʌm; ˋhoˋhʌm] *int*. 喝哼!〔表示无聊、不感兴趣、疲倦等的感叹词〕。

H

hoi(c)k [hɔik; hɔık] *vt*. 〔方〕= hoist.

hoick(s) [hɔik(s); hɔık(s)] *int*. 嗬嚎〔驱赶猎犬声〕。

hoi·den [ˈhɔidn; ˋhɔıdn] *n*. = hoyden.

hoi pol·loi [ˌhɔipəˈlɔi; ˋhɔıpəˋlɔı] 〔Gr.〕**1**. 〔常冠以 the〕民众;群众。**2**. 老百姓,每个人。**3**. 〔美俚〕有钱有势的人,名流。

hoise [hɔiz; hɔız] *vt*. (***hoised***, ***hoist*** [hɔist; hɔıst]; ***hois·ing***) 〔古〕= hoist. ***be hoist with one's own petard*** 〔古〕搬起石头砸自己的脚。

hoist [hɔist; hɔıst] **I** *n*. **1**. 扯起,绞起,升起。**2**. 升举器,起重机,升降机,吊车。**3**. 【海】(帆、旗升起后的)高度;一排信号旗;桅杆中部。**4**. 〔俚〕推,托,举。*air* ~ 气动葫芦,气吊,气压起重机。*carriage* ~ 起重车,卷扬机。*give sb. a* ~ (如爬墙等)把某人往上一推。**II** *vt*. 升,扯起,举起(旗帜等)。— *vi*. 升起来,扯起来。~ ***down*** 扯下。~**hole**, ~**-way** (货物)起卸口;(升降机)通路。

hoist·er [ˈhɔistə; ˋhɔıstɚ] *n*. **1**. 起重机,卷扬机;【矿】提升机,绞车。**2**. 起重机[提升机]的司机。

hoist·ing [ˈhɔistiŋ; ˋhɔıstıŋ] *n*. 起重,提升。~ **cable** 钢丝绳。~ **drum** 绞车滚筒。~ **jack** 千斤顶。

hoi·ty-toi·ty [ˈhɔitiˈtɔiti; ˋhɔıtıˋtɔıtı] **I** *a*. **1**. 轻浮的;反复无常的。**2**. 傲慢的,骄傲的。**3**. 易怒的,脾气大的;怒气冲冲的。**II** *n*. 轻率,傲慢。**III** *int*. 哎呀!〔表示傲慢或忿怒〕。

hoke [həuk; hok] **I** *vt*. (***hoked***; ***hok·ing***) 〔俚〕**1**. 以虚情假意对待;搪塞,敷衍。**2**. 勉强拼凑〔通常与 up 连用〕。**II** *n*. 〔俚〕= hokum. **hok·ey** *a*. 〔俚〕假的,做作的。

ho·k(e)y·po·k(e)y [ˈhəukiˈpəuki; ˋhokıˋpokı] *n*. 〔俚〕

1. (沿街叫卖的)廉价冰淇淋。2. = hocus·pocus.

Hok·kai·do [hɔˈkaidəu; hɑˋkaɪdo] ***n.*** 北海道〔日本〕。

ho·kum [ˈhəukəm; ˋhokəm] ***n.*** 1. 〔俚〕(影剧中)逗人笑或惹人落泪的惯用手法,噱头。2. 欺骗,无聊的话;无聊的主张。

Hol·arc·tic [hɔˈlɑːktik; hɑˋlɑrktɪk] ***a.*** 【动】(大陆动物地区之一)全北区的。

HOLC, holc = Home Owner's Loan Corporation 〔美〕房主贷款公司。

hold[1] [həuld; hold] **I** ***vt.*** (***held*** [held; hɛld]; ***held, hold·en*** [ˈhəuldən; ˋholdən]) 1. (用手、手臂等)拿住,握住,抓住,夹住。2. 有,拥有,保存(财产);掌握,占据,保持(地位等);担任(职务等)。3. 包含,收容;容纳,装着。4. 控制,保持…的状态;支持,托住;压住,止住;吸住(注意等)。5. 〔美〕拘押;扣留;保留;使负(责任等)。6. 怀有,持有(见解等);认为,相信,想;叛决。7. 举行,开(会)。8. 依法占有,用契约约束。9. 【乐】延长(发音)。~ *a pen* 拿钢笔。~ *the baby in one's arms* 抱孩子。*have and* ~ 保有。~ *a pipe between the teeth* 嘴里衔着烟斗。*Lightly won, lightly held.* 〔谚〕得来容易丢失得快。~ *the first position* (*among ...*) 占第一位。*This room can* ~ *fifty people.* 这个房间可以容纳五十人。*The pail* ~*s milk.* 桶内装着牛奶。~ *the door open* 让门开着。~ *oneself in readiness* 准备着。~ *one's breath* 屏息。*H- your hand!* 住手! *H-!* = *H- hand!* 停止。*A fever held him for a week.* 他发烧一个星期了。~ *one to be a fool* 拿人当傻瓜。*I* ~ *it my duty to inform* [*tell*] *you.* 我认为我有责任通知你。*There is no* ~*ing him.* 弄不过他,制不了他。~ *a discussion* 开讨论会。~ *an examination* 举行考试。~ *sb. guilty* 叛定某人有罪。*be held at the station house* 被拘留在警察局。— ***vi.*** 1. 抓着,握着;保持 (*on*; *to*)。2. 持久,耐久;支持得住。3. 继续,继续进行,持续。4. 合用,可适用,(条约等仍然)有效。5. 享有,保有土地[财产、权利等] (*of*; *from*)。6. 停止〔常用于命令式〕。*The rope* ~*s.* 绳子吃得住[不会断]。*Winter still* ~*s.* 冬天还没有过去。*The rule does not* ~ (*good*) *in this case.* 这规则在这种情况下不适用。***be neither to*** ~ ***nor to bind*** 非常激动,无法抑制。***cry*** ~ 命令停止。~ ***a candle to the devil*** 助纣为虐,为虎作伥。~ (***oneself***) ***aloof*** 不接近别人,清高,超然。~ [***keep***] ***at arm's length*** 冷淡待人。~ ***back*** 1. 踌躇,退缩不前。2. 阻止;抑制,压住;扣住 (*from*), 保守秘密,隐瞒。~ ***by*** 赞成(主张);坚持(目的、见解等)。~ (*sb.*) ***captive*** 俘掳,拘捕。~ ***cheap*** 瞧不起,不重视。~ ***dear*** 看重,珍视。~ ***demonstration against*** 举行游行示威反对。~ ***down*** 1. 垂下。2. 压制;牵制;阻止,忍耐;压低(物价等);缩减。3. 〔美口〕维持,保有;保持(职位)。~ ***everything*** [***it***] 〔美口〕停止,等一下。~ ***fast*** [***to***] 坚持。~ ***for*** 适用,适于。~***forth*** 1. 提出;提供;发表(意见)。2. 〔蔑〕滔滔不绝地演说。~ ***from doing sth.*** 忍住不作某事。~ ***good*** [***true***] (***for***) 有效;适用;有理。~ ***hard!*** 〔用于命令式〕停止! 别忙! 等一等! ~ ***in*** 抑制;忍住。~ ***in abhorrence*** [***abomination***] 厌恶,痛恨。~ ***in balance*** 使不稳定,使悬而不决。~ ***... in esteem*** [***honour, regard, respect***] 尊重,尊敬。~ ***in memory*** 记住。~ ***in one's temper*** 忍气吞声。~ ***... in place*** [***position***] 使…保持固定位置。~ [***keep***] ***in play*** 使劳动,使有事做。~ ***in pledge*** 抵押。~ ***in trust*** 保管。~ ***it good*** (***to do***) 以为(做…)是好的。~ ***off*** 1. 使离开,使不接近。2. 抵抗(进攻等)。3. 延缓,拖延 (*The rain still* ~*s off.* 雨还下不来)。~ ***on*** 1. 拉住,抓牢。2. 继续;坚持下去。3. (打电话时)不挂断;〔口〕等一等,停住。4. (交易中)杀价钱。5. (暴风)吹个不停。~ ***on like grim death*** 死不松手。~ ***on one's way*** 不顾干扰地继续前进。~ ***on to*** 盘据,赖着不走。~ (***one's***) ***fire*** 不表示态度。~ ***one's ground*** [***own***] 固守阵地,一步不退,坚持。~ ***one's hand*** [***hands***] 谨慎,留余地。~ ***one's hand high*** 骄傲。~ ***one's horses*** 〔美〕停止,等待 (~ *your horses* 不要忙)。~ ***one's noise*** [***peace, tongue***] 保持沉默。~ ***one's nose*** 用手掩鼻。~ ***out*** 1. 伸出;提出,主张。2. 制止,阻止。3. 支持,维持。4. 不退让,坚持到底。5. 〔美俚〕保留一部份分赃时被隐匿的钱。~ ***out against*** 经受得住,顶得住。~ ***out on sb.*** 不让某人了解情况,隐瞒。~ ***over*** 1. 将…延迟。2. 保存。3. 期满后继续任职;期满后继续占有。4. 加以(恐吓)。5. 胜过,优于。~ ***power over*** 有支配…的权利。~ ***sb. responsible for*** 使某人对…负责。~ ***strike against*** 举行罢工反对。~ ***talks with*** 同…举行会谈。~ ***the bag*** 受害〔详见 bag 条〕。~ ***the fort*** 1. 固守堡垒,打退敌人的进攻。2. 毫不示弱。3. 继续干活。~ ***the rein*** 掌权;执政;支配。~ ***the stage*** 1. 继续活跃在舞台上。2. 引起观众注意。~ ***to*** 赞成,坚持。~ ***together*** (使)团结在一起,(使)结合在一起。~ ***true*** 适用。~ ***up*** 1. 举起;展示;举出(做榜样),揭露出(给人嘲笑)。2. 〔口〕阻止,使停滞,使停顿;〔命令〕停止! 3. 〔美〕拦劫。4. 支持住;持久;忍住。5. 【猎】放慢步子。6. (晴天)继续,〔美〕(雨)停。~ ***up one's hands*** 举起双手表示不抵抗,投降。~ ***up one's head*** 抬着头,打起精神。~ ***up the work*** 停工。~ ***water*** 1. (容器)不漏水。2. (论点)站得住脚,说得有理有据。3. (欲停船时)制住桨。~ ***with*** 赞成,同意;和…抱同一意见。**II** ***n.*** 1. 握住;掌握;保持。2. 支撑点,可攀[踏]的东西;线索,端绪。3. 威力,势力;理解力。4. 容器。5. 监禁,监牢;城砦;避难所。6. 【物】同期,同步。7. 【乐】延长号,延音。8. (拳击、摔跤等中的)擒拿法。9. 保留,预约;关于延迟的通知。10. 〔美〕(飞弹的)延迟倒数,延期发射。(***be***) ***in*** ~***s*** 揪着,扭着。***catch*** [***claw, get, lay, seize, take***] ~ ***of*** 抓住,掌握。***have a*** ~ ***on*** [***over***] 对…有把握[支配力,威力,作用]。***get*** [***have***] ~ ***of the wrong end of the stick*** 完全误解。***keep*** ~ ***of*** [***on***] 握紧。***lay*** ~ ***of*** [***on***] 到手,得到;掌握。***let go*** [***leave, lose***] ~ ***of sth.*** 放松手,放弃。***maintain*** [***relax***] ***its*** ~ ***over ...*** 抓牢[放松]对…的控制。***no*** ~***s barred*** 〔口〕没有清规戒律的约束。***put a*** ~ ***on*** 预约 (*put a* ~ *on a library book* 向图书馆预约借一本书)。~**all** 帆布袋,工具袋。~**back** 1. 妨碍,牵制;障碍物。2. (马车上的)刹车。3. 暂时停顿;暂时被扣下的东西(如工资等)。~**down** (费用等的)缩减。~ **furnace** [**hearth**] 【冶】混合炉,保温炉。~**out** 1. 伸出,延续;提供;坚持;不让步。2. 拖签合同者〔职业运动员对老板讨价还价的举动〕;拒不参加者,拒不达成协议者,坚持不合作者。~**over** 〔口〕1. 残存的人,遗物。2. 任期已满仍然继任的人员。3. 比赛或演出后继续参加的人员。4. 留级的学生。5. 〔俚〕宿醉。~ **up** 1. (交通)堵塞。2. 拦劫,抢劫。3. 〔口〕要高价,敲竹杠。

hold[2] [həuld; hold] ***n.*** 【船】货舱,底层舱。~ *capacity* 货舱容量。*break out the* ~ 开始卸货。*stow the* ~ 装舱。~**man** 舱内装卸工人。

hold·en [ˈhəuldən; ˋholdən] 〔古〕hold 的过去分词。

hold·er [ˈhəuldə; ˋholdɚ] ***n.*** 1. 持(票)人;(土地、权利等的)所有人,货主。2. 烟嘴;(笔)杆。3. 台座,架;夹;储存器。*a* ~ *of an office* 负责人。*a record* ~ 记录保持人。*a share* ~ 股票持有人。*a bit* [*drill*] ~ 【机】钻套。*a cigarette* ~ 烟嘴。*a pen* ~ 笔杆。*a gas* ~ 贮气罐,贮气室。*a lamp* ~ 灯座。*a mirror* ~ 镜架。~**on** ***n.*** (船上的)铆工。

hold·fast [ˈhəuldfɑːst; ˋholdˏfæst] ***n.*** 1. 紧缠,紧握。2. 钩子,钉子,夹钳。3. 【动】吸附器官。4. 【植】固着器。***lose one's*** ~ 放松,控制不住。

hold·ing [ˈhəuldiŋ; ˋholdɪŋ] ***n.*** 1. 把握;支持。2. 持有,享有,所有,财产。3. 〔常 *pl.*〕所有物;保有股份;租借地,保有地;所有权。4. 【体】持球,非法抱人[撞人]。~ *in a business company* 在某公司中的股份。~ **attack** 【军】牵制攻击。~ **company** 控股公司。~ **current** 【电

维持电流。～ **device**【机】夹具。～ **pattern**（飞机在机场上空等待腾出跑道时的）椭圆形盘旋。～ **temperature** 保温温度。～ **time**（电话）占用时间。

hole [həul; hol] **I** *n*. **1**. 洞，穴，孔；（衣服等上的）破洞；伤口；漏洞；窝，坑；水流的深凹处，（河道的）缓流洼。**2**.（兽的）洞穴，窝巢；陋屋，狭小阴暗的地方[房子]；监狱中的隔离牢房。**3**.〔口〕陷阱；绝境。**4**. 缺陷，缺点。**5**.【物】空穴，空子。**6**. 高尔夫球的穴；高尔夫球得分。**7**.〔美〕铁路的支线。**8**. 大型飞弹地下井。**9**.〔美〕小湾，小港。***a ～ in one's coat*** 缺点，瑕疵。***a ～ in the road***〔美口〕村庄。***a poky ～*** 非常闭塞的地方，穷乡僻壤。***a square peg in a round ～*** 不适宜担任某项工作的人〔见 peg 条〕。***every ～ and corner*** 每个角落，到处。***find a ～ to creep out*** 在困境中找出路，寻找脱身之计。***in a devil of a ～*** 处境非常困难。***in a ～*** 陷入绝境，为难。***in the ～***〔口〕经济困难，负债；（在纸牌中）得一负点。***leave a ～ to creep out*** 留后路。***like a rat in a ～*** 像坑中的老鼠一样跑不脱，瓮中之鳖。***make a ～ in*** **1**. 开洞。**2**. 花费过多。***make a ～ in the water*** 跳水自尽。***make ～*** 钻油井。***pick ～s [a ～] in*** 对…吹毛求疵；批评，责备。***pick a ～ in sb.'s coat*** 找某人的岔子。***the nineteenth ～***〔谑〕高尔夫球俱乐部的酒吧间。**II** *vt*. **1**. 穿（孔），打（洞），开（隧道等）；挖（坑等）。**2**. 把…赶入洞中；把（高尔夫球）打入穴中。— *vi*. **1**. 掘洞；钻进洞中。**2**. 把高尔夫球打进穴中。～ ***out*** (***in four***)（四击）将高尔夫球打入穴内。～ ***up*** **1**. 蛰居洞中。**2**. 躲藏。**3**. 安置…在避难处[躲藏处]。**4**. 监禁。～**-and-corner** *a*. 秘密的，偷偷摸摸的。～ **card** 牌面朝下的牌；隐藏的优点。～**-gauge** 内量规，内测微计。～**-in-the-wall**〔英口〕街头取款机。～**-proof** *a*.（衣服等）不会破洞的；（法律等）没有漏洞的。

hole·r [ˈhəulə; ˋholɚ] *n*. **1**. 挖洞者。**2**.（高尔夫球场等）有若干洞穴的场所〔常与数字连用〕。

hole·y [ˈhəuli; ˋholɪ] *a*. 有孔的，多洞的。

hol·i·but [ˈhɔlibət; ˋhɑləbət] *n*. = halibut.

hol·i·day [ˈhɔlədi, ˈhɔlidei; ˋhɑləde] **I** *n*. **1**. 节日，假日，休息日。**2**.〔英 *pl*.〕休假。**3**.〔古〕圣日（= holy day）。***be home for the ～*** 放假回家。***blind man's ～***〔谑〕黄昏。***busman's ～*** 照样做日常工作的休假。***high-days, ～s and bonfire nights***〔谑〕节日，休假日。***make [take] (a week's) ～*** 休假（一星期）。***official ～s*** 法定假日。***on ～*** 在休假中，在度假。***Roman ～*** 以观看别人受苦为乐的娱乐。**II** *a*. 节日的，节日适用的；愉快的，活泼的。～ *clothes* [*attire*]（节日穿的）盛装。～ *mood* [*spirit*] 欢悦的心情。**III** *vi*.〔主英〕度假，休假。～ **English** 一本正经的英语。～**-food** 节日佳肴。～**-maker** 度假者。～ **speeches** [**terms**, **words**] 冠冕堂皇的话，好听的话，奉承话。～ **task**〔英〕学生的假期作业。**-er** *n*. 度假者。

hol·i·days [ˈhɔləˌdeiz; ˋhɑləˏdez] *ad*.〔美〕在假日，每逢假日。

ho·li·er-than-thou [ˈhəuliəðənˈðau; ˋholɪɚðənˋðaʊ] *a*. 假装神圣的；自以为是的。

ho·li·ly [ˈhəulili; ˋholəlɪ] *ad*. 虔诚地；神经地。

ho·li·ness [ˈhəulinis; ˋholɪnɪs] *n*. **1**.【宗】神圣；清净，纯洁。**2**.〔H-〕陛下，宗座〔对罗马教皇等的尊称，常与 His 或 Your 连用〕。

ho·lism [ˈhəulizm; ˋhəulɪzm] *n*.【哲】整体论。**ho·list** *n*. 整体论者。**ho·lis·tic** *a*. **ho·lis·ti·cal·ly** *ad*.

hol·la [ˈhɔlə, hɔˈlɑː; ˋhɑlə, hɑˋlɑ] *int*., *n*., *vi*., *vt*. = hollo(a).

Hol·land [ˈhɔlənd; ˋhɑlənd] *n*. **1**. 荷兰〔正式名称是 *the Netherlands*〕。**2**.〔h-〕〔常 *pl*. 但作 *sing*. 用〕荷兰麻布，洁白亚麻细布，窗帘棉布；〔*pl*.〕荷兰杜松子酒（= ～ gin）。**-er 1**. 荷兰人；荷兰船。**2**.〔h-〕（造纸）打浆机。

hol·lan·daise [ˌhɔlənˈdeiz; ˏhɑlənˋdez] **I** *a*. 荷兰式的。**II** *n*. 蛋黄奶油酸辣酱（= ～ sauce）。

hol·ler [ˈhɔlə; ˋhɑlɚ] **I** *n*. **1**. 呼叫，呼救。**2**.〔美〕盗贼受害人的控诉。**3**.（美国黑人随口哼的）劳动号子。**II** *vt*. 喊出。— *vi*. **1**. 叫喊，大喊大叫。**2**. 诉苦，抱怨。

Holler·ith [ˈhəuləriθ; ˋholərɪθ] *n*.【计】利用凿孔把字母信息在卡片上编码的一种方式〔以美国发明人赫尔曼·霍尔瑞斯（Herman Hollerith, 1860—1929）命名〕。～ **code** 霍尔瑞斯编码。～ **constant** 霍尔瑞斯常数。～ **type machine** 霍尔瑞斯型计算机。

Hol·lis [ˈhɔlis; ˋhɑlɪs] *n*. 霍利斯〔姓氏，男子名〕。

hol·lo(a) [ˈhɔləu; ˋhɑlo] **I** *int*. 喂！**II** *vi*. 喂喂地叫。— *vt*. 向…发"喂"声。**III** *n*. 喂喂地叫声。

hol·low [ˈhɔləu; ˋhɑlo] **I** *vt*. 使成凹形，使成空洞，挖空（*out*）。*river banks ～ed out by rushing water* 被流水掏空的河岸。— *vi*. 变空。**II** *n*. **1**. 凹地，穴，洞坑。**2**. 山谷。*the ～ of the hand* 手心。**III** *a*. **1**. 空的，中空的。**2**. 空虚的，不诚实的，虚伪的。**3**.（声音）瓮塞的，空洞的；沉重的。**4**. 空腹的，饥饿的。～ *cheeks* 凹陷的双颊。～ *eyes* 凹陷的眼睛。～ *pleasures* 空幻的快乐。～ *compliments* 应酬话。*a ～ pretence* 虚伪的借口。～ *promises* 空洞的诺言。～ *race* [*victory*]（因对手弱）没有意思的赛跑[胜利]。～ *square*【军】空方阵。～ *words* 空话。**IV** *ad*.〔口〕完全，彻底。***beat sb.*** (***all***) ～ 打垮某人，把某人打得惨败。～**-drill steel**【冶】空心钻钢。～**-eyed** *a*. 眼睛凹陷的。～**-hearted** *a*. 不真诚的，虚伪的。～ **spar** 红柱石。～**-ware** *n*.〔集合词〕凹形器皿〔尤指凹形银器〕。**-ly** *ad*. **-ness** *n*.

hol·lo·ware [ˈhɔləuˌweə; ˋhɑloˏwer] *n*. = hollowware.

hol·ly [ˈhɔli; ˋhɑlɪ] *n*. **1**.【植】冬青属植物。**2**.（圣诞节时装饰用的）冬青枝。***English ～*** 圣诞树。

Hol·ly [ˈhɔli; ˋhɑlɪ] *n*. 霍莉〔女子名〕。

hol·ly·hock [ˈhɔlihɔk; ˋhɑlɪhɑk] *n*.【植】蜀葵。

Hol·ly·wood [ˈhɔliwud; ˋhɑlɪwʊd] **I** *n*. **1**. 好莱坞〔美国电影业中心〕。**2**. 美国影片。**3**. 美国电影工业，美国电影界。**II** *a*. **1**. 好莱坞（式）的。**2**.〔美俚〕（衣服等）艳丽的，花哨的，（人）做作的。**-ish** *a*. 好莱坞（式）的。**-ize** *vt*. 使好莱坞化。**-er** *n*. 好莱坞地方的人。**-i·an** *a*. **-i·an·a** [-iənə; -ɪənə] *n*. 关于好莱坞生活与历史的书籍、报纸等。

holm [həum; hom] *n*.【植】**1**. 圣栎（= ～oak）。**2**.〔方〕冬青属植物。

Holman [ˈhəulmən; ˋholmən] *n*. 霍尔曼〔姓氏〕。

holm(e) [həum; hom] *n*.〔英方〕**1**. 河边低地。**2**. 河中（或近陆地）的小岛。★英国地名带有 holm(e) 一字的很多：Priest*holm*, Willow *H*-.

Holme(s) [həum(z); hom(z)] *n*. **1**. 霍姆（斯）〔姓氏〕。**2**. **Sherlock** ～ 夏洛克·福尔摩斯〔英国作家柯南道尔（Sir Arthur Conan Doyle）笔下的大侦探〕；〔转义〕名侦探；有解答疑难和推理力的人。**-i·an 1**. *n*. 福尔摩斯迷。**2**. *a*. 福尔摩斯式的。

hol·mi·um [ˈhɔlmiəm; ˋhɑlmɪəm] *n*.【化】钬。

holm·oak [ˈhəumˈəuk; ˋhomˋok] *n*.【植】圣栎。

holo- *comb. f*. 表示"完全"：*holo*gram, *holo*hedral.

hol·o·blas·tic [ˌhɔləuˈblæstik; ˏhɑloˋblæstɪk] *a*.【胚】全裂的〔指某些有小卵黄的卵细胞〕。～ **egg** 全裂卵。

hol·o·caust [ˈhɔləkɔːst; ˋhɑləkɔst] *n*. **1**.（焚烧全兽祭神的）燔祭。**2**. 大屠杀。**3**. 大破裂，浩劫。

Hol·o·cene [ˈhɔləusiːn; ˋhɑləsin] **I** *a*.【地】全新统的，全新世的。**II** *n*.【地】全新世。

ho·lo·crine [ˌhɔləukrin; ˋhɑləkrɪn] *a*.【动】全泌的。

ho·lo·en·zyme [ˌhɔləuˈenzaim; ˏhɑləˋɛnzaɪm] *n*.【生化】全酶。

hol·o·gram [ˈhɔləugræm; ˋhɑləgræm] *n*.【物】全息图，全息照片，综合衍射图。

hol·o·graph [ˈhɔləugrɑːf; ˋhɑləˏgræf] **I** *n*. 亲笔文件[证件]；手书。**II** *a*. 亲笔写的。**III** *vi*. 拍摄全息照片。

hol·o·graph·ic, **hol·o·graph·i·cal** [ˌhɔləuˈgræfik(əl), ˌhəulə-; ˏhɑləˋgræfɪk(l̩)] *a*. **1**. 亲笔写的（=

holograph)。2. 全息照相的,与全息照相有关的。

ho·log·ra·phy [həˈlɔgrəfi; həˋlɑgrəfɪ] *n*. (不用透镜而用激光的)全息照相术;全息学。

hol·o·he·dral [ˌhɔləuˈhiːdrəl; ˏhɑləˋhidrəl] *a*. 【物】全面的;全对称晶形的。

hol·o·he·drism [ˌhɔləuˈhiːdrizəm; ˏhɑləˋhidrɪzəm] *n*. 【物】全对称性。

hol·o·hed·ron [ˌhɔləuˈhedrən; ˏhɑləˋhɛdrən] *n*. 【地】全面体。

hol·o·me·tab·o·lism [ˌhɔləumiˈtæbəlizm; ˏhɑləmɪˋtæbəlɪzm] *n*. 【医】完全变态(= complete metamorphosis)。**hol·ome·tab·o·lous** *a*.

hol·o·mor·phic [ˌhɔləuˈmɔːfik; ˏhɑləˋmɔrfɪk] *a*. 【物】(晶体)对当的。

hol·o·par·a·site [ˌhɔləuˈpærəsait; ˏhɑləˋpærəsaɪt] *n*. 【动】全寄生物。**hol·o·par·a·sit·ic** [-sitik; -sɪtɪk] *a*.

hol·o·phone [ˈhɔləufəun; ˋhɑləfon] *n*. 声音全息记录器。

hol·o·phote [ˈhɔləufəut; ˋhɑləfot] *n*. 全光反射装置,(灯塔等的)全射影。

hol·o·phras·tic [ˌhɔləuˈfræstik; ˏhɑləˋfræstɪk] *a*. 以单词表示全句的,以单词表示片语的〔如命令句 Go!〕。

hol·o·phyt·ic [ˌhɔləuˈfitik; ˏhɑləˋfɪtɪk] *a*. 【生】自养的。

hol·o·plank·ton [ˌhɔləuˈplæŋktən; ˏhɑləˋplæŋktən] *n*. 【动】终生浮游生物,全浮游性生物。

hol·o·scope [ˈhɔləuskəup; ˋhɑləskop] *n*. 全息照相机。**-scop·ic** [ˌhɔləuˈskɔpik; ˏhɑləˋskɑpɪk] *a*. 全面观察的,一览无遗的。

hol·o·thu·ri·an [ˌhɔləuˈθjuəriən; ˏhɑləˋθjurɪən] I *n*. 海参类动物,海参。II *a*. 海参类动物的,海参的。

hol·o·type [ˈhɔləutaip; ˋhɑlətaɪp] *n*. 【分类】1. 全型。2. 完模标本。**hol·o·typ·ic** [-ˈtipik; -ˋtɪpɪk] *a*.

hol·o·zo·ic [ˌhɔləuˈzəuik; ˏhɑləˋzoɪk] *a*. 【生】全动物营养的。

holp [həulp; holp] *v*. 〔古〕help 的过去式。

hol·pen [ˈhəulpən; ˋholpən] *v*. 〔古〕help 的过去分词。

Hol·stein (-Frie·sian) [ˈhɔlstain(ˈfriːʒən); ˋhɑlstaɪn(ˋfriʒən)] *n*. (荷兰)霍尔斯坦种乳牛〔体形大,有黑白斑。原产荷兰 Friesland〕。

H

hol·ster [ˈhəulstə; ˋholstɚ] *n*. 手枪皮套。

holt[1] [həult; holt] *n*. 〔诗〕杂木林;林丘。

holt[2] [həult; holt] *n*. 兽穴〔尤指水獭的巢穴〕。

Holt [həult; holt] *n*. 霍尔特〔姓氏〕。

Hol·tham [ˈhəulθəm; ˋholθəm] *n*. 霍萨姆〔姓氏〕。

ho·lus-bo·lus [ˈhəuləsˈbəuləs; ˋholəsˋboləs] *ad*. 〔口〕一起,一口,一下子。*gulp sth. down* ~ 一口把东西吞下。

ho·ly [ˈhəuli; ˋholɪ] I *a*. 1. 神圣的;神的;供神用的;献身于神的。2. 圣洁的;至善的。3. 虔诚的;崇敬的;宗教的。4. 〔口〕令人生畏的,可怕的;厉害的,非常的。~ *rites* 宗教仪式。~ *ground* 圣地。*a* ~ *place* 灵场。*the* ~ *palace* 圣殿,大殿。*a* ~ *man* 虔诚的信徒。~ *love* 纯真的爱。*a* ~ *terror* 难以对付的家伙,无法无天的小家伙。~ *cow* [*smoke*]! 天哪!〔表示惊讶、强调的感叹语〕。II *n*. 神圣的东西,圣堂。*the Holiest* 至圣者(指上帝或基督)(= the ~ of the holiest)。*the Holy of Holies* 犹太神殿中的至圣所;神圣的地方。**H- Alliance** 【史】(1815—1816 俄、普、奥三国君主订立的)神圣同盟。~ **Ark** 犹太教教堂里保存经文的柜子。**H- Bible** 【宗】圣经。~ **bread** [**loaf**] 圣餐用的面包。**H- City** 圣城〔如耶路撒冷、麦加、罗马〕。**H- Communion** 【宗】圣餐礼。~ **day** 宗教节日。~ **day of obligation** 1. 天主教徒参加弥撒日。2. 天主教的领圣餐日。**H- Father** 【宗】圣父;罗马教皇。**H- Ghost** 【宗】圣灵。**H- Grail** 圣杯〔传说耶稣在最后的晚餐所用的杯〕。~ **hell** 〔口〕臭骂,训斥,严惩。~ **Joe** 〔美俚〕传教师;信徒;〔美口〕(陆军的)随军牧师。**H- Land** 【宗】圣地〔指巴勒斯坦〕。**H- office** (天主教的)宗教法庭。**H- One** 上帝;基督。~ **orders** 圣职,牧师的职位。**H- Roman Empire** 【史】神圣罗马帝国。**H- Saturday** 【宗】耶稣复活节前一周的星期六。**H- Son** 【宗】圣子耶稣。**H- Spirit** = **H- Ghost** 【宗】圣灵。**H- Thursday** 1. 【宗】耶稣升天节。2. 耶稣受难节前一周的星期四。~ **tide** 〔古〕宗教季节;祭祀日;斋期。~ **water** 【天主】圣水;【佛】净水。**H- Week** 复活节前的一周。**H- Writ** 基督教圣经。

ho·ly·stone [ˈhəulistəun; ˋholɪˏston] I *n*. 【海】(磨甲板的)沙石。II *vt*. 用沙石磨(甲板)。

hom·age [ˈhɔmidʒ; ˋhɑmɪdʒ] *n*. 1. 【史】效忠宣誓礼,效忠。2. 顺从,臣服。3. 尊敬。*do* [*pay*] ~ *to* 对…表示敬意;服从。

hom·a·lo·graph·ic [ˌhɔmələˈgræfik; ˏhɑmələˋgræfɪk] *a*. = homolographic.

hom·bre [ˈɔmbre; ˋɔmbre] *n*. 〔Sp.〕人。

hom·burg, Hom·burg [ˈhɔmbəːg; ˋhɑmbɝg] *n*. 翘边帽。

home [həum; hom] I *n*. 1. 家,家庭;家庭生活;〔美〕住宅。2. 本国,故乡;(活动的)中心地,根据地,大本营;(动植物的)栖息地,原产地;(思想等的)发祥地。3. 疗养所;休息所;收容所,养育院(等)。4. 【体】(径赛的)终点;(棒球的)本垒。*the Smith* ~ 〔美〕史密斯的住宅〔=〔英〕Mr. Smith's house〕。*a* ~ *from* ~ 像家一样自在和舒适的地方,旅客之家。*at* ~ 1. 在家;在家接待客人(*She is not at* ~ *today*. 她今日不会客)。2. 在故乡,在本地,在本国(*opp*. abroad)。3. 安适,自在(*be* [*feel*] *at* ~ 觉得安适,无拘束。*Make yourself at* ~. 请随便,别客气)。4. 精通(*in*; *on*; *with*)(*be at* ~ *in French* 法语很好)。*one's long* [*last*, *narrow*] ~ 坟墓。*set for* ~ 向根据地返回。*sit at* ~ 闲居,不活动。II *a*. 1. 家庭的,家乡的,本地的。2. 本国的,本国产的;内地的,国内的。3. 中要害的,严厉的。*the H- Counties* 伦敦附近各郡〔如 Essex, Kent 等〕。*the H- Department* [*office*] 〔英〕内务部。*a happy* ~ *life* 幸福的家庭生活。*the* ~ *market* 国内市场。*H- minister* 内务部长。~ *office* 总机构〔如总公司、总店等〕。~ *question* 中要害的质问。~ *rule* 地方自治。*a* ~ *truth* 使人难堪的事实;逆耳忠言;老生常谈。*be* ~ *free* 遥遥领先,稳操胜券。~ *and dry* 达到目的;安全。III *ad*. 1. 在家,在本国;回家,回国;【棒球】回本垒。2. 全,深,尽量;(议论等)彻底;痛切,切实。*carry* ~ 拿回家。*Is he* ~ *yet*? 他回家了吗? *see sb.* ~ 送某人回家。*He was ordered* ~. 他已奉命回国。*write* ~ *to the government* 写信给本国政府。*bring* ~ *to sb*. 1. 使某人认识,使某人相信(*bring* ~ *to him the importance of industrial modernization* 使他认识工业现代化的重要)。2. 证实某人有某罪(*bring a fraud* ~ *to sb*. 证实某人犯诈骗罪)。*bring oneself* (*come*, *get*) ~ 收回损失;恢复原来地位。*come* ~ 1. 回家,回国。2. 使人沉痛地感到(*Curses* (*like chickens*) *come* ~ *to roost*. 〔谚〕害人终害己)。*drive* ~ 1. 讲明白,使人理解。2. 胜利完成,顺利结束。*drive* [*knock*] *the nail* ~ 把钉子钉牢;〔喻〕坚持到底。*get* ~ 到家,回到;命中。*go* ~ 1. 回家,回国。2. 〔口〕死,回老家,上西天。3. (忠告等)刻骨铭心。*hit* [*strike*] ~ 击中要害;触及痛处。*look at* ~ 扪心自问。*nobody* ~ 疯疯癫癫。*nothing to write* ~ *about* 〔口〕无聊的,平凡的。*press* ~ 极力主张。*push the bolt* ~ 把门闩闩上;关上炮闩。*romp* ~ 赛马时轻易获胜。*row the stroke* ~ 把船桨划到底。*scrape* ~ 费了大劲才达到目的。*swear* ~ 破口大骂。*take* ~ *to oneself* 深刻领会。*thrust a dagger* ~ 全刀刺入。IV *vi*. 1. 回家。2. (动物)回巢穴,回出生地区。3. (飞机)归航,按信号暗示回场;【火箭】(自动)导航,自动寻的。4. 安下家,居住。— *vt*. 1. 把…放在家中,把…送到家中。2. 给…住处。3. 【火箭】使自动寻的。~ *in on* (*target*) (火箭)依靠导航系统自动飞向(目标)。~ **banking** 住家

银行服务〔使家中电脑终端与银行主机相联结而办理各项银行业务〕。~ **base** 1. 根据地;本站。2.【棒球】本垒。~**bird** 深居简出的人。~**body** *n*.(*pl*. -*bod·ies*)家庭至上者;深居简出者,以家庭为生活中心的人。~**born** *a*. 土生土长的。~**bound** *a*. 1. 回家的,回家乡的,回国的;(船)回头开的。2. 不出家门的,闭居在家的。~**boy**〔俚〕同伙。~ **bred** *a*. 家内饲养的;国产的;粗野的。~-**brew** 1. 家里酿的酒〔尤指啤酒〕。2. 当地培育的人[物]。~-**brewed** 1. *a*.(酒)家里酿的。2. *n*. 家内酿的酒。~ **cinema**= ~ theater。~-**coming** *n*. 1. 回老家,回国。2.〔美〕返校节。~ **confinement** [**detention**] 家中监禁[关押]〔指将罪犯拘禁在家中服刑,以电子腕带或脚带等达到随时传呼检查的目的,使罪犯不得擅离拘禁地〕。~ **ec** *n*.〔美国学生用语〕= ~ economics。~ **economics** 持家学,家政学。~-**educate** *vt*. 在家中教育(子女)〔指不送子女上学而让子女在家接受教育〕。~-**farm** 供应大庄园或供自用的农场。~-**felt** *a*. 痛切感到的。~ **freight** 返程运费。~ **front** 1. 大后方。2. 作为一国战争力量组成部分的民用工业。~**girl**〔美俚〕女老乡。~ **grown** *a*.(瓜果、蔬菜等的)本国出产的,当地消费的;土生的。**H- Guard** 英国国民军成员。~ **help** 家务女佣。~ **keeper** 怕出门的人。~**keeping** *a*. 家居不外出的。~ **land** 本国,故国;〔H-〕英国本国。~-**made** *a*. 自己制的,手工的;本国制的。~ **maker** 持家的妇女,主妇。~ **office** 家庭办公室〔参见 hoffice〕。~ **page**【计】主页。~-**owner** (住)房主。~ **plate** = ~ base 2. ~ **range**【生态】巢区〔动物(每日或季节)活动范围〕。~ **room** (学校的)班级会议室〔点名,听报告等的场所〕。~ **rule** 地方自治。~ **run**【棒球】全垒打。~-**sick** *a*. 想家的,患怀乡病的。~ **shopping** 在家购物〔通过家中电脑进行网上购物〕。~**sickness** 思家病,怀乡病。~ **signal** (火车)进站信号。~**spun** 1. *a*. 家里纺的,家里做的;简朴的,粗陋的;朴实的,平凡的,不做作的。2. *n*. 土布;手工纺织呢,手织大衣呢。~-**stead** 1. *n*.(包括附近田地在内的)家宅,宅地;祖传的住宅;〔美、加拿大〕(分给定居移民)居住和耕种的土地。2. *vt*., *vi*.(使)得到[占有]宅地。~-**steader** 1. 占有宅地的人。2. 分得土地的定居移民。~-**stretch** (赛跑)从最后的拐弯到终点间的一段跑道;最后阶段的工作。~ **theater** 家庭影院〔指高保真音响和电视、录像机、影碟机等的组合〕。~-**thrust** 命中的一击;说中要害的批评。~**town** 故乡,家乡。~ **work** 课外习题,家庭作业;家庭工作;(讨论等以前的)准备工作。-**less** *a*. 无家可归的;无饲主的。-**like** *a*. 1. 像家一样舒适、亲切的。2.(饭菜等)简单而有益健康的。-**ward** *a*., *ad*. 向家(的),向家乡(的),向本国(的)。-**wards** *ad*. 向家,向家乡,向本国。

Home [həum, hjuːm; hom, hjum] *n*. 霍姆[休姆]〔姓氏〕。

home·ly [ˈhəumli; ˋhomlɪ] *a*. 1. 家庭的,家常的。2. 朴实的,不做作的。3. 像在家一样的,不拘束的。4.〔美〕不漂亮的,不好看的。*quite a* ~ *sort of body* 极朴实的人。~ *as a mud fence*〔美〕面孔极丑的。**home·li·ness** *n*.

ho·me·o *pref*. 表示"同": *homeo*chromatic.

ho·me·o·chro·ma·tic [ˌhəumiəukrəˈmætik; ˏhomɪəkrəˋmætɪk] *a*.【生】同色的。

ho·me·o·mor·phism [ˌhəumiəuˈmɔːfizm, ˌhɔmiə-ˏhomɪoˋmɔrfɪzəm, ˏhɑmɪə-] *n*.【化】异质同晶(现象)。**ho·me·o·mor·phous** [-fəs; -fəs] *a*.

ho·me·o·path [ˈhəumjəpæθ; ˋhomɪəpæθ] = homoeopath.

ho·me·o·path·ic [ˈhəumiəuˌpæθik; ˏhomɪəˋpæθɪk] *a*. = homoeopathic.

ho·me·op·a·thist [ˌhəumiˈɔpəθist; ˏhomɪˋɑpəθɪst] *n*. = homoeopathist.

ho·me·op·a·thy [ˌhəumiˈɔpəθi; ˏhomɪˋɑpəθɪ] *n*. = homoeopathy.

ho·me·o·sta·sis [ˌhəumiəuˈsteisis; ˏhomɪəˋstesɪs] *n*.【生理】1. 体内平衡,恒定性;稳定状态。2.(社会群体的)自我平衡。**ho·me·o·stat·ic** [-ˈstætik; -ˋstætɪk] *a*.

ho·me·o·ther·mal [ˌhəumiəuˈθəːməl; ˏhomɪəˋθɝməl] *a*. = homoiothermal.

ho·me·o·typ·ic [ˌhəumiəuˈtipik; ˏhomɪəˋtɪpɪk] *a*.【生】同型的;(生殖细胞核的)成熟后第二次分裂的。

ho·mer[1] [ˈhəumə; ˋhomɚ] *n*. 侯马〔1. 希伯来早期的体积量具名,相当于 6¼ 普式耳。2. 希伯来液体量具名,相当于 58 加仑〕。

hom·er[2] [ˈhəumə; ˋhomɚ] I *n*. 1.【棒球】全垒打〔打出可跑完一圈回到本垒的球〕。2. 传书鸽,通信鸽。3.【空】归航信标机,归航台。4. 自动引导飞[导]弹。*a heat-* ~ 有热感应自动引导的飞弹。II *vi*.【棒球】击出全垒打。

Ho·mer[1] [ˈhəumə; ˋhomɚ] *n*. 霍默〔姓氏,男子名〕。

Ho·mer[2] [ˈhəumə; ˋhomɚ] *n*. 荷马〔纪元前 10 世纪前后的希腊盲诗人, *Iliad* 及 *Odyssey* 的作者〕。***H- sometimes nods***.〔谚〕智者千虑,必有一失。

Ho·mer·ic [həuˈmerik; hoˋmɛrɪk] *a*. 1. 荷马的;荷马式的,荷马史诗的。2. 英勇的,巨大的。~ **battle** 英勇的战斗。~ **laughter** 放声大笑〔源出荷马史诗中所写的诸神的大笑〕。~ **verse** 六韵步的诗。

hom·ey [ˈhəumi; ˋhomɪ] *a*.〔美口〕1. 家庭似的,像家里一样安适自在的。2. 温暖的,舒适的。

hom·i·ci·dal [ˌhɔmiˈsaidl; ˏhɑmɪˋsaɪdl] *a*. 杀人的;有杀人癖性的。~ *mania* 杀人狂。

hom·i·cide [ˈhɔmisaid; ˋhɑmɪˏsaɪd] *n*. 1. 杀人(行为),杀人罪。2. 杀人者。*justifiable* ~【法】有正当理由的杀人。

hom·i·let·ic(al) [ˌhɔmiˈletik(əl); ˏhɑmɪˋlɛtɪk(l̩)] *a*. 说教(式)的,布道的;教训性质的。-**i·cal·ly** *ad*.

hom·i·let·ics [ˌhɔmiˈletiks; ˏhɑmɪˋlɛtɪks] *n*.〔*pl*. 用作单数〕说教术,布道术。

hom·i·list [ˈhɔmilist; ˋhɑmɪlɪst] *n*. 说教者,布道者。

hom·i·ly [ˈhɔmili; ˋhɑmɪlɪ] *n*. 1. 布道。2. 使人厌烦的说教。

hom·ing [ˈhəumiŋ; ˋhomɪŋ] I *a*. 1. 回家的,有归还习性的。2.【空】归航的;导航的。II *n*. 归来,(信鸽等的)归还性能;【空】归航,导航;【宇】自动引道。*radar* ~ 雷达自动引导。~ **beacon** 无线电归航信标。~ **device** 导归器。~ **equipment** 自动瞄准[导航]装置,寻的装置。~ **instinct** 归巢本能。~ **missile** 自动寻的飞[导]弹。~ **pigeon** 通信鸽。~ **torpedo** 自动寻的水雷。

hom·i·nid [ˈhɔminid; ˋhɑmɪnɪd] I *n*. 1.【动】人科(*Hominidea*)。2. 原人,原始人类。II *a*. 人科的。

hom·i·nize [ˈhɔminaiz; ˋhɑmɪnaɪz] *vt*. 1. 使(机械等)人性化。2. 利用(世界)为人类服务。-**ni·za·tion** [ˌhɔminaiˈzeiʃən; ˏhɑmɪnaɪˋzeʃən] *n*.

hom·i·noid [ˈhɔminɔid; ˋhɑmɪˏnɔɪd] I *n*.【动】类人猿(*Hominoidea*)。II *a*. 类人猿的;人的;类人的;像人的。

hom·i·ny [ˈhɔmini; ˋhɑmɪnɪ] *n*.〔美〕玉米粥;玉米片。

ho·mo [ˈhəuməu; ˋhomo] *n*., *a*.〔美俚〕= homosexual.

ho·mo [ˈhəuməu; ˋhomo] *n*.(*pl*. ***hom·i·nes*** [ˈhɔminiːz; ˋhɑməniz])〔L.〕人〔学名〕;〔H-〕人类。***H- sapiens*** [ˈseipinz; ˋsepɪnz] 人,智慧人。

homo- *comb*. *f*. 表示"同","似"〔通常用在希腊系语词前(*opp*. hetero-)〕: *homo*centric, *homo*geneous.

ho·mo·cen·tric [ˌhɔməuˈsentrik; ˏhaməˋsɛntrɪk] *a*. 同中心的。

ho·mo·cer·cal [ˌhɔməuˈsəːkl; ˏhaməˋsɝkl̩] *a*.(鱼的)正尾的;等形的。~ **tail**【动】正型尾。

ho·mo·charge [ˈhɔməutʃɑːdʒ; ˋhamətʃardʒ] *n*.【物】纯号电荷。

ho·mo·chro·mat·ic [ˌhɔməkrəuˈmætik; ˏhaməkroˋmætɪk] *a*. 单色的,只有单色的(= homochromous)。

ho·mo·des·mic [ˌhɔməuˈdesmik; ˏhaməˋdɛsmɪk] I *n*.

H

【物】纯键。II *a*.【物】纯键的。

ho·mo·dyne [ˈhɔməudain; ˋhamədaɪn] *n*.【物】零差,零拍。

ho·moe *pref*. = homeo.

ho·moe·cious [ˈhəumjəuʃəs; ˋhomjoʃəs] *a*.(寄生虫的)单种宿主寄生的。

ho·moe·o·path [ˈhəumjəupæθ; ˋhomɪə͵pæθ] *n*.【医】顺势疗法医师。

ho·moe·o·path·ic [ˌhəumjəuˈpæθik; ͵homɪəˋpæθɪk] *a*.【医】顺势疗法的。**-i·cal·ly** *ad*.

ho·moe·op·a·thist [ˌhəumiˈɔpəθist; ͵homɪˋɑpəθɪst] *n*. = homoeopath.

ho·moe·op·a·thy [ˌhəumiˈɔpəθi; ͵homɪˋɑpəθɪ] *n*. 顺势疗法,类似疗法(*opp*. allopathy)。

ho·mo·e·rot·i·cism [ˌhəuməuiˈrɔtisizəm; ͵homoɪˋrɑtɪsɪzəm] *n*. = homosexuality. **ho·mo·e·rot·ic** *a*.

ho·mog·a·my [həˈmɔgəmi; həˋmagəmɪ] *n*. 1.【植】具有同性花;雌雄(蕊)同熟。2.【生】同配生殖(*opp*. heterogamy);同族结婚。**ho·mog·a·mic, ho·mog·a·mous** *a*.

ho·mog·e·nate [həˈmɔdʒineit; həˋmadʒənet] *n*.【医】均浆。

hom·o·ge·ne·i·ty [ˌhɔməudʒeˈniːiti; ͵hamədʒəˋniətɪ] *n*. 1. 同种;同质;同性。2.【数】齐性,均匀;同一性,均衡性,均匀性。

hom·o·ge·ne·ous [ˌhɔməuˈdʒiːnjəs; ͵haməˋdʒinɪəs] *a*. 1. 同种的,同质的,同性的,相似的。2. 纯一的,均质的;均匀的。3.【数】齐性的,齐次的。~ **alloy** 均质合金。~ **light** 单色光。~ **ray** 单色射线。~ **integral equation** 齐次积分方程。**-ly** *ad*. **-ness** *n*.

hom·o·gen·e·sis [ˌhɔməuˈdʒenisis; ͵haməˋdʒenɪsɪs] *n*.【生】纯一生殖。

hom·o·ge·net·ic [ˌhɔməudʒiˈnetik; ͵hamədʒɪˋnetɪk] *a*. = homogenous.

ho·mog·e·nize [həˈmɔdʒənaiz; həˋmadʒə͵naɪz] *vt*. 1. 使均匀。2. 使均质,用高压高速搅拌。~*d milk* 均质牛奶。**hom·oge·ni·za·tion** [həˌmɔdʒənaiˈzeiʃən; hə͵madʒənaɪˋzeʃən] *n*.

ho·mog·e·ni·zer [həˈmɔdʒinaizə; həˋmadʒənaɪzɚ] *n*. 均质器,均化器,高速搅拌器。

ho·mog·e·nous [həˈmɔdʒinəs; həˋmadʒənəs] *a*.【生】同质的〔指因遗传而构造相似的〕;纯系的;同源的。

ho·mog·e·ny [həˈmɔdʒini; həˋmadʒɪnɪ] *n*.【生】同构发生,同源发生。

ho·mog·o·ny [həˈmɔgəni; həˋmagənɪ] *n*. = homostyly. **ho·mogo·nous** [-nəs; -nəs] *a*.

ho·mo·graft [ˈhɔməugrɑːft; ˋhamə͵græft] *n*.【医】同种移植片;自体移植片。

hom·o·graph [ˈhɔməugrɑːf; ˋhamə͵græf] *n*. 同形异义词,同形词〔如 seal 为海豹,又为图章〕。**-ic** *a*.

ho·moi·o·ther·mal [həuˌmɔiəuˈθəːməl; ho͵mɔɪəˋθɝməl] *a*.【动】恒温动物的(= homoiothermic)。

ho·mo·lec·i·thal [ˌhɔməuˈlesiθəl; ͵homəˋlɛsɪθəl] *a*.【动】均卵黄的。

hom·o·log [ˈhɔmələg; ˋhaməlag] *n*. = homologue.

ho·mol·o·gate [hɔˈmɔləgeit; haˋmalə͵get] *vt*. (*-gated*; *-gat·ing*) 1. 赞同,认可。2.【法】正式确认,批准。— *vi*.〔罕〕同意。**ho·mol·o·ga·tion** *n*.

ho·mo·log·i·cal [ˌhɔməˈlɔdʒikəl; ͵haməˋladʒɪkəl] *a*. = homologous. **ho·mo·log·i·cal·ly** *ad*.

ho·mol·o·gize [hɔˈmɔlədʒaiz; həˋmalə͵dʒaɪz] *vt*. 1. 使相应,使一致,使相同。2. 表示与…同系。— *vi*. 同系,同源。

ho·mol·o·gous [hɔˈmɔləgəs; hoˋmaləgəs] *a*. 1. 同源的。2.【生】异体同型的。3.【化】同系列的;同属列的;同周期的。4.【医】同源的。5.【医】= homoplastic. ~ **bodies** 同族体。~ **organs** 同源器官〔如人肺与鱼鳔〕。~ **series**【化】同系列。~ **tissue**【医】同种组织。

hom·o·lo·graph·ic [ˌhɔmələˈgræfik; ͵hamələˋgræfɪk] *a*.【测】等面积的。

hom·o·logue [ˈhɔmələg; ˋhaməlɔg] *n*. 1.【化】同系物。2.【生】(细胞)同源染色体;对应器官。3. 相应物。

ho·mol·o·gy [hɔˈmɔlədʒi; hoˋmalədʒɪ] *n*. 1. 相应,符合;关系相同。2.【化】同系(现象)。3.【生】同源。4.【数】透射;同调。

ho·mo·mor·phism [ˌhɔməˈmɔːfizm; ͵homəˋmɔrfɪzm] *n*. 1. 同形。2.【生】同型性〔指器官或有机体〕。3.【植】同形体[大小]〔如雌蕊和雄蕊〕。4.【动】成幼同型(= homomorphy)。5.【数】同态。**ho·mo·mor·phic, ho·mo·mor·phous** *a*.

hom·o·nym [ˈhɔmənim; ˋhamənɪm] *n*. 1. 同音异义词〔如 bear 与 bare; 广义的 homonym 包括狭义的 homophone 和 homograph〕;同形异义词;同音同形异义词。2. 异人同名。3.【生】异物同名。

hom·o·nym·ic, ho·mon·y·mous [ˌhɔməˈnimik, hɔˈmɔniməs; ͵homəˋnɪmɪk, hoˋmanɪməs] *a*. 同音[同形]异义的;同名的;双关的。

ho·mo·phile [ˈhəuməufail; ˋhoməfaɪl] *n*., *a*. = homosexual.

hom·o·phone [ˈhɔməfəun; ˋhamə͵fon] *n*. 1. 同音字母〔c 与 s, c 与 k 等〕。2. 同音异义词〔狭义的 homophone 相当于狭义的 homonym; 广义的还包含 homograph 一义〕。

hom·o·phon·ic [ˌhɔməˈfɔnik; ͵haməˋfanɪk] *a*. 1.【乐】同音的;同音歌唱的;单旋律歌曲的;单音调乐曲的。2. = homonymous.

ho·moph·o·ny [hɔˈmɔfəni; həˋmafənɪ] *n*. 1.【语】同音异义。2.【乐】同音;齐唱[奏];单旋律歌曲。

ho·mo·plas·tic [ˌhɔməˈplæstik; ͵homəˋplæstɪk] *a*.【生】1. 同型的,相似的。2. 同种的。**-plas·ti·cal·ly** *ad*.

ho·mo-pla·sy [hɔˈmɔplæsi; hoˋmɔplæsɪ] *n*.【生】异体同功。

hom·o·po·lar [ˌhɔməˈpəulə; ͵homəˋpolɚ] *a*.【电】同极的,单极的。~ *generator* 单极发电机。**-i·ty** [-ˈlæriti; -ˋlorətɪ] *n*.

ho·mop·ter·ous [hɔˈmɔptərəs; hoˋmaptərəs] *a*.(昆虫)同翅类的。

ho·mo·sex·u·al [ˌhəuməuˈseksjuəl; ͵homəˋsekʃuəl] I *a*. 同性恋的。II *n*. 同性恋者。

ho·mo·sex·u·al·i·ty [ˌhəuməuˌseksjuˈæliti; ͵homə͵sɛkʃʊˋælətɪ] *n*. 同性恋爱;同性的性行为。

ho·mo·sphere [ˈhɔməsfiə; ˋhaməsfɪr] *n*.【气】均质层。**ho·mo·spher·ic** [-ˈsferik; -ˋsfɛrɪk] *a*.

ho·mos·po·rous [hɔˈmɔspərəs; hoˋmaspərəs] *a*.【植】具同形孢子的;仅产生一种孢子的。

ho·mo·sty·ly [ˈhɔməstaili; ˋhaməstaɪlɪ] *n*.【植】花柱同长。**ho·mo·sty·lous** *a*.

ho·mo·tax·is [ˌhɔməˈtæksis; ͵haməˋtæksɪs] *n*.【地】排列类似。**ho·mo·tax·i·al** [-ˈtæksiəl; -ˋtæksɪəl] *a*.

ho·mo·thal·lic [ˌhɔməˈθælik; ͵homəˋθælɪk] *a*.【动】同宗配合(现象)的。**-thal·lism** *n*.

ho·mo·ther·mal [ˌhɔməˈθəːməl; ͵homəˋθɝməl] *a*. = homoiothermal (= homothermic).

ho·mo·trans·plant [ˌhɔməˈtrænsplɑːnt; ͵homəˋtrænsplant] *n*. = homograft. **-trans·plan·ta·tion** [ˌhɔmətræsplɑːnˈteiʃən; ͵hamətræsplanˋteʃən] *n*.【医】同种移植;自体移植。

hom·o·type [ˈhɔmətaip; ˋhamətaɪp] *n*.【生】同型;等模标本。

ho·mo·zy·go·sis [ˌhɔməzaiˈgəusis; ͵homəzaɪˋgosɪs] *n*.【生】1. 纯质性。2. 纯合基因。**ho·mo·zy·got·ic** [-ˈgɔtik; -ˋgatɪk] *a*.

ho·mo·zy·gote [ˌhɔməˈzaigəut; ͵homəˋzaɪgot] *n*.【生】

H

同型结合子[体],纯合子[体]。**-zy·gous** ***a***.

Homs [həums; hɔms] ***n***. **1.** 胡姆斯〔叙利亚城市〕。**2.** 胡姆斯〔利比亚港市〕。

ho·mun·cule, ho·mun·cle [həu'mʌŋkju:l, -kl; ho-'mʌŋkjul, -kl] ***n***. = homunculus.

ho·mun·cu·lus [həu'mʌŋkjuləs; ho'mʌŋkjələs] ***n***. (*pl*. ***-li*** [-lai; -laɪ]) 矮子,侏儒。

hom·y ['həumi; 'homɪ] ***a***. = homey.

hon [hʌn; hʌn] ***n***. =〔美〕honey.

Hon., hon. = Hono(u)rary; Hono(u)rable.

hon·cho ['hɔ:tʃəu; 'hɔtʃo] ***n***. 〔美俚〕头头,老板。

Hond. = Honduras.

Hon·du·ran [hɔn'djuərən; hɑn'durən] **I** ***a***. 洪都拉斯的;洪都拉斯人的;洪都拉斯文化的。**II** ***n***. 洪都拉斯人。

Hon·du·ras [hɔn'djuərəs; hɑn'durəs] ***n***. 洪都拉斯(宏都拉斯)〔拉丁美洲〕。

hone[1] [həun; hon] **I** ***n***. **1.** 细磨刀石。**2.**【机】磨孔器。**II** ***vt***. **1.** (在细磨刀石上)磨。**2.** 磨孔使放大。

hone[2] [həun; hon] ***vi***. 〔方〕**1.** 咕噜,抱怨。**2.** 渴望。

hon·est ['ɔnist; 'ɑnɪst] ***a***. **1.** 诚实的;正直的,耿直的;坦率的,坦白的,正派的,公正的。**2.** 可敬的,有好名声的。**3.** 〔古〕可靠的,善良的;贞节的。**4.** (金钱)用正当手段获得的。**5.** (酒等)真正的,纯正的。**6.** 朴实的,普通的。*an ~ man* 正直的人。*an ~ woman* 贞节的女人。*an ~ living* 正正派派的生活。*the ~ truth* 原原本本的事实。*~ goods* 真货。*~ food* 普通饭菜。***be ~ with*** 对…说老实话,同…规规矩矩来往。***be quite ~ about it*** 老实说〔常用作插入语〕。***earn*** [***turn***] ***an ~ penny*** 用正当手段挣钱。***H- Injun*** ['indʒən; 'ɪndʒən]! 〔俚〕没错!真的!〔作副词用〕。**H- John** 〔美〕**1.**【军】"诚实的约翰"火箭(一种地对地火箭)。**2.** 〔口〕诚实的人;易受骗的老实人。**~-to-God, ~-to-goodness** ***a***. 真正的,道地的。

hon·est·ly ['ɔnistli; 'ɑnɪstlɪ] ***ad***. 老老实实,正正当当;老实说。

hon·es·ty ['ɔnisti; 'ɑnɪstɪ] ***n***. **1.** 老实;诚实;公正。**2.** 〔古〕贞节;廉耻。**3.**【植】缎花属植物。*H- is the best policy*. 诚实是上策。*~ of purpose* 认真。

hone·wort ['həunˌwə:t; 'honˏwɝt] ***n***. 【植】北柴胡 (*Cryptotaenia canadensis*)〔发现于美国东部〕。

hon·ey ['hʌni; 'hʌnɪ] **I** ***n***. (*pl*. ***~s***, ***honies***) **1.** 蜂蜜;蜜。**2.** 甘美,甜蜜。**3.** 宝贝儿〔称呼用〕;漂亮姑娘;使人非常愉快[满意]的东西。*virgin ~* 生蜜。*my ~* 亲爱的。**II** ***a***. **1.** 蜂蜜似的。**2.** 〔古〕心爱的。**III** ***vt***. (***~ed*** 或 ***hon·ied***; ***-ey·ing***) **1.** 加蜜等使甜。**2.** 说甜言蜜语;奉承。—***vi***. 说甜言蜜语;奉承。***~ up to sb***. 向…灌迷汤。**~ bag** (蜜蜂体中的)蜜囊。**~ bear**【动】蜜熊 (kinkajou) 和懒熊 (sloth bear) 的俗称。**~ bee** 蜜蜂。**~bucket** 〔美俚〕粪桶。**~ bun, ~ bunch** ***n***. 〔口〕宝贝,亲爱的〔多用作亲昵称呼语〕。**~comb 1.** ***n***. 蜜蜂窝;蜂窝状物;【冶】蜂窝状沙眼;(反刍动物的)蜂巢胃。**2.** ***vt***. 使成蜂窝状;渗透进…的各个部分;削弱,把…弄得百孔千疮;破坏(团结等)。**~-cooler** 〔美俚〕(对女子的)奉承;用奉承赢得女子信任的男子。**~ dew 1.** (蚜虫等分泌的)甘汁,蜜露,树蜜。**2.** 甜味烟草。**~ dew melon** 香蜜瓜。**~ eater** 蜜雀 (*Meliphagidae*)〔产于澳大利亚〕。**~fogle** ***vt***. 〔美俚〕用甜言蜜语欺骗。**~ guide** 指蜜鸟 (*Indicatoridae*)〔产于亚非和东印度群岛,据说可引领人、兽找蜂窝,待蜂房被取走后去啄食蜜蜂幼虫〕。**~-lipped** 嘴甜的,甜言蜜语的。**~ locust**【植】美洲皂荚。**~moon 1.** ***n***. 婚后第一月,蜜月,新婚旅行(期间),蜜月旅行。**2.** ***vi***. 度蜜月 (*at*; *in*)。**~mooner** 度蜜月者。**~mouthed** ***a***. = ~lipped. **~ pot** (蜜蚁的)贮蜜囊。**~ sucker 1.** = ~ eater. **2.** 长吻袋貂 (*Tarsipes spenceri*)〔产于澳大利亚〕。**~-suckle**【植】忍冬属。**~sweet** ***a***. 甜如蜜的,极甜的。**~-tongued** ***a***. = ~lipped. **~ wag(g)on** 〔美俚〕**1.** 垃圾车,粪车。**2.** 手提户外马桶。

hon·eyed ['hʌnid; 'hʌnɪd] ***a***. 多蜜的;甜如蜜的。*~ words* 甜言蜜语。

hong [hɔŋ; hɑŋ] ***n***. 〔Chin.〕(中国、日本的)行,商行。

Hong Kong, Hong·kong [hɔŋ'kɔŋ, 'hɔŋ'kɔŋ; hɑŋ'kɑŋ, 'hɑŋ'kɑŋ] 香港。**~ dog** 〔美俚〕(尤指旅行者常患的)腹泻,拉肚子。

hon·ied ['hʌnid; 'hʌnɪd] **I** honey 的过去式和过去分词。**II** ***a***. = honeyed.

hon·ies ['hʌniz; 'hʌnɪz] ***n***. honey 的复数。

honk [hɔŋk; hɑŋk] **I** ***n***. **1.** 雁叫声;类似雁叫声。**2.** 汽车喇叭声。**II** ***vi***. **1.** (雁)叫。**2.** 汽车喇叭响。—***vt***. **1.** 揿喇叭表示。**2.** 〔口〕揿(喇叭)。**~-out** 〔美俚〕失败。

honk·ie, honk·y ['hɔŋki; 'hɑŋkɪ] ***n***. 〔美俚〕(蔑)白人。

honk·y-tonk ['hɔŋkitɔŋk; 'hɑŋkɪtɑŋk] **I** ***n***. 〔美俚〕有舞场的低级酒馆。**II** ***a***. **1.** 低级酒吧的。**2.** (地区)有很多低级酒吧的。

Hon·o·lu·lu [ˌhɔnə'lu:lu:; ˏhɑnə'lulu] ***n***. 火奴鲁鲁(又译檀香山)〔美国港市〕。

hon·or ['ɔnə; 'ɑnɚ] ***n***., ***vt***. 〔美〕= honour.

Ho·nor·a [həu'nɔ:rə; ho'norə] ***n***. 霍诺拉〔女子名(L. = honor),爱称 Nora(h)〕。

hon·or·a·ble ['ɔnərəbl; 'ɑnərəbl] ***n***. 〔美〕= honourable.

hon·o·rar·i·um [ˌɔnə'rɛəriəm; ˏɑnə'rerɪəm] ***n***. (*pl*. ***~s***, ***-rar·i·a*** [-ə; -ə]) 报酬(金),谢礼(金)〔指习惯上或礼貌上不便收取或定出价目的酬金,如润笔、对医师的酬谢等〕。

hon·or·ar·y ['ɔnərəri; 'ɑnərərɪ] **I** ***a***. **1.** 名誉的,名誉上的;义务的。**2.** 荣誉的,光荣的。**3.** (债务等)道义上的,信用的。**4.** 纪念性的。*an ~ degree* 名誉学位。*an ~ member* 名誉会员。*an ~ secretary* 义务秘书〔不领取报酬〕。*an ~ president* 名誉董事长〔没有具体职权〕。*~ debts* (虽无法律强制性但道义上必须偿还的)欠债。*an ~ ode* 赞歌。**II** ***n***. **1.** 名誉团体。**2.** 名誉学位;获名誉学位者。**3.** 〔古〕= honorarium.

Ho·no·ri·a [həu'nɔ:riə; ho'norɪə] ***n***. = Honora.

hon·or·if·ic [ɔnə'rifik; ˏɑnə'rɪfɪk] **I** ***a***. 尊敬的,表示敬意的。*an ~ title* 敬称。**II** ***n***. **1.** 尊称。**2.**【语】敬语〔用于某些东方语言,尤指日语和汉语中所用者,如汉语中的令(郎)、贵(姓)、大(名)等〕。

hon·or·is cau·sa [hɔ'nɔ:ris'kɔ:sə; hɑ'norɪskɔsə] 〔L.〕为名誉起见(= for the sake of honour)。

hon·o(u)r ['ɔnə; 'ɑnɚ] **I** ***n***. **1.** 荣誉,光荣;名誉,面子,体面。**2.** 节操,廉耻,正直;道义;贞操。**3.** 尊敬,敬意。**4.** 高位,高官;[His H-, Your H-] 阁下〔英国主要用于尊称地方法官,美国用于尊称一般法官〕。**5.** 荣典,叙勋;徽章,勋章;〔*pl*.〕敬礼式。**6.** 荣幸,优惠,优待。**7.** 〔*pl*.〕(大学中的)优等成绩;给优等生开设的高级课程;〔英〕优等成绩奖金。**8.** 纸牌中价值最高的牌〔如 A, K, Q, J, 及 10〕。**9.** (高尔夫球的)先打权。**10.** 荣幸〔客套语〕。**11.** 光荣的人,光荣的事〔与不定冠词连用〕。*business ~* 商业信用。*a debt of ~* (无字据的)信用借款。*H- and profit lie not in one sack*. 〔谚〕荣誉和私利,决不在一起。*May I have the ~ of your company at dinner?* 敬备菲酌,恭请光临。*His H- the Judge* 法官阁下。*pass with ~ in mathematics* 数学考试成绩优异。*an ~'s degree* 优等学位。*a sense of ~* 荣誉感,廉耻心。*funeral* [*last*] *~s* 葬礼。*The ~s rest with him*. 集荣誉于一身,他获得很大成功。*military ~s* 军葬礼;军礼。*an affair of ~* 决斗。***a roll of ~*** 阵亡烈士名单。***be on one's ~ to do sth***. = ***be in ~ bound to do sth***., ***be bound in ~ to do sth***. 道义上必须做某事。***come off with ~*** 光荣地完成。***compromise one's ~*** 累及名誉。***do ~ to*** 给…带来荣誉,对…表示敬意。***do the ~s*** (***of the house***) 作主人招待宾客,尽地主之谊。***for*** (***the***) ***~ of***【商】为顾全…的信用起见。***guards of ~*** 仪仗队。***give*** [***pay***] ***~ to*** 向…致

敬。*give one's word of* ～ 用名誉担保。*go in for* ～*s*〔大学用语〕考取优等。*graduate* [*pass*] *with* ～*s* 优等毕业〔考试成绩优等〕。*hold sb. in* ～ 敬重某人。～*bright*〔口〕誓必,一定;以名誉担保。*in* ～ 道义上。*in* ～ *of* 向…表示敬意,为祝贺…,为纪念…。*maid of* ～ 1. 宫女。2.〔美〕女傧相。*make* ～*s to sb.* 向某人致敬。*on* [*upon*] *one's* (*word of*) ～ 以名誉担保。*pledge one's* ～ 用名誉担保。*point of* ～ 有关体面的事。*put sb. on his* ～ 信任某人会重视他的名誉。*save one's* ～ 保全面子。*the code* [*law*] *of* ～ 1. 公认的行为准则。2. 决斗惯例。*the* ～*'s list* 受勋者名单。*the* ～ *of war* 给与战败军队的优待〔如允许其保留武器、旗帜等〕。*with* ～*s easy* 优势均等。**II** *vt.* 1. 尊敬;尊重;给与荣誉,给与…的光荣;以…为荣;向…授勋(*with*);礼遇。2. 接受;【商】承认如期付款,承兑(票据),兑现。～ *a debt in advance* 提前还债。～ *one's promise* 实践诺言。～**-bound** *a.* 为荣誉所不得不做的。～**box**〔美〕诚实报箱(指街头自动售报机)。～**guard** 仪仗队。～**s course** (大学中的)独立研究课程〔通过后即得优等学位〕。**roll** 荣誉名册。～ **system** (学校的)无监考考试制;(监狱的)无看守监禁制。～**s system** (大学的)优等生制度。

hon·o(u)r·a·ble [ˈɔnərəbl; ˋɑnərəbl] *a.* 1. 可敬的,高尚的;正直的,廉洁的;有名誉的,光荣的;体面的。2.〔H-〕阁下〔英国用以尊称阁员、高等法院推事、殖民地行政官、宫中女官、伯爵以下的贵族子弟等;美国用于尊称国会议员及州议员等;略作 Honble, Hon.〕。*an* ～ *discharge* 荣誉退役。*an* ～ *duty* 名誉职位。*an* ～ *mention* 褒奖;表扬。*win* ～ *distinctions* 立下光荣的功劳。*the H- gentleman* [*member*] = *my H- friend* 英国下议员在议场中对其他议员的称呼。*the Most H-* 侯爵、巴斯勋爵、枢密顾问官名字前用的尊称〔略 Most Hon.〕。*the Right H-* 枢密顾问官、伯爵以下贵族、伦敦市长名字前用的尊称〔略 Rt. Hon〕。

hon·o(u)r·a·bly [ˈɔnərəbli; ˋɑnərəblɪ] *ad.* 受尊敬地,体面地;正当地。

hon·o(u)r·if·ic [ˌɔnəˈrifik; ˏɑnəˋrɪfɪk] **I** *a.* 1. 表示尊敬的。2. 敬语的,尊称的。**II** *n.* (尤指东方语中所用的)敬语,尊称。

H

hon·o(u)r(s)·man [ˈɔnə(z)mæn; ˋɑnə(z)mæn] *n.* 大学毕业考试的优等生。

Hon·shu [ˈhɔnʃuː; ˋhɑnʃu] *n.* 本州〔日本〕。

hooch [huːtʃ; hutʃ] *n.*〔美俚〕1. 烈酒。2. 非法酿造和出售的劣酒。

Hood [hud; hʊd] *n.* 胡德〔姓氏〕。

hood[1] [hud; hʊd] **I** *n.* 1. 头巾;(连在外套上的)兜帽。2. (大学制服后以其颜色表示学位及学校的)垂布。3. (马或鹰的)头罩。4. 车盖,车篷;烟囱帽,灯盖;炮塔顶篷;〔美〕(汽车的)引擎罩;打字机的罩子;【海】天窗盖,舱口盖。5.【建】帽盖,出檐。6.【动】羽冠。7. (雷达萤光屏的)遮光板。**II** *vt.* 1. 用头巾包;使(马、鹰等)戴头罩;给…加罩。2. 覆盖,隐蔽。**-less** *a.*

hood[2] [hud; hʊd] *n.*〔美俚〕= hoodlum.

-hood *suf.* 1.〔前接一般名词〕表示"身分","资格":king*hood*. 2.〔前接形容词〕表示境遇,状态,性质:false*hood*. 3.〔前接一般名词〕表示具有特殊性质的集体:neighbour*hood*, priest*hood*.

hood·ed [ˈhudid; ˋhʊdɪd] *a.* 1. 戴头巾的;有头罩的;头兜状的。2. 顶饰羽冠的。3. (眼镜蛇等)颈部因肋骨运动而膨胀的。4. 头部颜色与身体其他部分迥然不同的。～**crow**【动】灰鸦 (*Corvus cornix*)〔产于欧洲,灰背,灰胸,黑头,黑翼,黑尾〕。～ **seal** 冠海豹 (*Cystophora cristata*)〔产于北大西洋,其雄者头部有可膨胀的钩状袋〕。

hood·ette [ˈhuːdet; ˋhudɛt] *n.* 女流氓,女阿飞,女强盗。

hood·lum [ˈhuːdləm; ˋhudləm] *n.*〔美俚〕强盗,流氓,恶棍,阿飞。**-ism** *n.*

hood·man [ˈhudmən; ˋhʊdmən] *n.*〔古〕(捉迷藏游戏中的)蒙眼人。

hood·man-blind [ˈhudmənblaind; ˋhʊdmənˏblaɪnd] *n.*〔古〕捉迷藏(= blindman's buff)。

hoo·doo [ˈhuːduː; ˋhudu] **I** *n.* 1.〔美口〕不吉利的人,不祥之物。2.〔美口〕倒霉,恶运。3. = voodoo (*n*). 4. (因受侵蚀而形成的)一种天然怪岩柱。**II** *vt.* 使遭恶运,使倒霉。

hood·wink [ˈhudwiŋk; ˋhʊdwɪŋk] *vt.* 1. 使(马)带上眼罩。2. 欺瞒,蒙蔽;隐蔽。*Stop your* ～*ing.* 别装了,别装样子。**-a·ble** *a.* **-er** *n.* 欺骗者,骗子。

hoo·ey [ˈhuːi; ˋhuɪ] *n.*, *int.*〔美俚〕胡说,废话。

hoof [huːf; hʊf] **I** *n.* (*pl.* ～*s*,〔罕〕*hooves* [huːvz; huvz]) 1. 蹄;〔谑〕(人的)脚。2. 有蹄类动物。*a cloven* ～ 分趾蹄。*beat* [*pad*] *the* ～ = *be upon the* ～〔俚〕走。～*-and-mouth disease* 出口伤人的臭毛病(= foot-and-mouth disease)。*give sb. the* ～ 叫某人滚蛋。*on the* ～ 1. (牛、马等)活着的,尚未屠宰的。2. 即兴的,临时凑起来的。*see sb.'s* ～ *in* 在…中看出某人势力[影响]。*show the* (*cloven*) ～ (魔鬼)露出爪趾,显出原形。*under the* ～ 被践踏。**II** *vt.* 1. 走。2. 踢;用蹄踏。—*vi.* 1. 走。2. 踢;踏。3. 跳舞。*be* ～*ed* 被踢开;〔口〕被踢脱(差事等)。～ *it*〔美口〕1. 步行。2. 逃走,跑掉。3. 表演跳舞。～ *out* 踢出。～**-and-mouth disease** 口蹄疫 (= foot-and-mouth disease)。～ **beat** 蹄声。～**bound** *a.* 兽蹄因病而感到疼痛紧缩的。～**pad** 蹄垫。～**pick** (剔去蹄下石片等物用的)蹄签。～**print** 蹄印。～**-let** 小蹄。

hoofed [huːft; hʊft] *a.* 有蹄的。

hoof·er [ˈhuːfə; ˋhufɚ] *n.* 1. 步行者。2.〔美俚〕木屐舞[踢跶舞]舞女。3.〔美俚〕黑人。

hoo-ha [ˈhuːˌhɑː, 做感叹词用时 huːˈhɑː; ˋhuˏhɑ, 做感叹词用时 huˋhɑ] **I** *n.*〔主英口〕吵闹,骚乱,骚动。**II** *int.* 呼哈!〔表示吃惊、兴奋等的嘲弄性感叹词〕。

hook [huk; hʊk] **I** *n.* 1. 钩;铁钩;吊钩(= pothook);针钩;镰刀;〔俚〕锚。2. 圈套,陷阱。3. 钩状物;河湾;钩状岬;【动、植】钩状器官;【乐】钩符(ʃ);【拳】肘弯击,钩击;(高尔夫球中的)左曲球。4.〔美俚〕妓女。5.〔美俚〕手,手指。6.〔美俚〕麻醉药〔尤指海洛因〕。*a belt* ～ 皮带扣。*a bill* ～ 钩刀。*a fish* ～ 钓钩。*a telephone* ～ 电话机钩键。*angle with a silver* ～ 行贿。*by* ～ *or* (*by*) *crook* 想方设法,千方百计,不择手段。*drop* [*go, pop, slip*] *off the* ～*s*〔俚〕1. 发狂。2. 死。*get one's* ～*s into*〔美口〕占据,占有;惩罚。*get sb. off the* ～〔美俚〕使某人摆脱危境;解除某人的困难或义务。*get the* ～〔美俚〕被解雇。～, *line, and sinker*〔美俚〕完全地,全部地。*on one's own* ～〔俚〕独力地,独自地。*on the* ～ 1. 陷入圈套;受拘束,难摆脱。2. 拖延。*take* [*sling*] *one's* ～〔俚〕逃亡。*with a* ～ *at the end* 有保留的同意。**II** *vt.* 1. 用钩挂 (*in*; *on*; *up*);用钓钩钓;用钩针织;钩住,钓着。2. (牛)用角尖挑。3. 引(人)上钩,欺骗。4.〔俚〕偷,扒。5.【拳】用肘弯侧击;【高尔夫球】使球向左弯。—*vi.* 1. 弯成钩形;钩住。2. 用角挑。3.【高尔夫球】球向左弯。～ *in* 钩进;钩住。～ *it*〔美俚〕逃走,快跑〔叫人逃走时的警告语〕。～ *Jack*〔美〕偷懒,逃学。～ *on* 钩在一起;用钩子挂;钩上。～ *up* 1. 用钩子钩住;【机】接上。2.【无】〔口〕联播。～ **and eye** 风纪扣。～ **and ladder** 云梯救火车〔有长梯子,拆卸天花板用的钩子及其他设备的救火车〕。～**-bill** 鹦鹉;鹦鹉类的鸟。～ **nose** 1. 钩鼻。2.〔美俚〕犹太人,守财奴。～**-nosed** *a.* 钩鼻的。～**shop**〔美俚〕妓院。～**shot** (篮球)单手勾手投篮。～**-up** *n.* 1.【无】试验线路,电路耦合,接续图。2. 联播电台。3. 联合,同盟。～**-up wire** 架空电线。～ **worm** 钩虫。～ **worm disease** 钩虫病。～ **wrench**【机】钩形板手。**-let** *n.* 小钩子。

hook·(a)h [ˈhukə, -kɑː; ˋhʊkə, -kɑ] *n.* 水烟筒。

hooked [hukt; hʊkt] *a.* 1. 钩状的。2. 有钩的。3. 钩织

成的。4. 〔美俚〕吸毒成瘾的。5. 着迷于…的（*on*）。6. 〔俚〕已婚的。*a* ～ *nose* 钩鼻。*a* ～ *rug* 钩针编织的地毯。**-ness** *n*.

hook·er[1] [ˈhukə; ˋhʊkɚ] *n*. 1. 荷兰双桅渔船。2. 爱尔兰海岸单桅渔船。3. 旧船；废舰。

hook·er[2] [ˈhukə; ˋkʊkɚ] *n*. 1. 【橄榄球】扭夺时的中心选手。2. 〔俚〕引人上钩者；娼妓。3. 一大杯威士忌酒。

hook·er[3] [ˈhukə; ˋhʊkɚ] *n*. 【纺】码布机。

Hook·er [ˈhukə; hʊkɚ] *n*. 胡克〔姓氏〕。

hook·ey [ˈhuki; hʊkɪ] = hooky[2].

hook·y[1] [ˈhuki; ˋhʊkɪ] I *a*. 钩多的；钩状的。II *vt*. 〔美俚〕扒窃。

hook·y[2] [ˈhuki; hʊkɪ] *n*. 〔美俚〕旷课，逃学；逃学者。*play* ～ 逃学。

hoo·li·gan [ˈhu:ligən; ˋhulɪgən] *n*. 〔俚〕阿飞，无赖，小流氓。**-ism** *n*. 无赖行为，流氓习性。

hoop[1] [hu:p; hʊp] *n*. 1. 箍。2. 箍状物；（孩子玩的）铁环。（马戏团供演员穿过的）大铁圈；〔*pl*.〕（旧时衬裙摆用的）裙环；鲸骨圈；戒指。3. （篮球的）篮，篮圈；（槌球戏中的）弓形小门。***go through the*** ～ [～*s*] 受磨炼。***put sb. through the*** ～ 使某人受折磨。***roll one's*** ～ 1. 顺利向前。2. 稳妥办事。3. 〔美俚〕只管自己的事。***trundle a*** ～ ***along*** 滚铁环。—*vt*. 1. 在（桶等）上加箍；用箍围绕。2. 包围；拥抱。～ **iron** （做桶箍的）带钢；铁箍。～**-man** 篮球运动员。～**skirt** 有裙环的女裙。～ **snake** 环箍蛇〔美洲民间传说中尾含在嘴里全身作环状的蛇〕。

hoop[2] [hu:p; hup] I *vi*. 百日咳患者咳嗽时发唬唬声；唬唬地叫。II *n*. 鹄鸣声；（百日咳患者的）呼呼声。**hooping cough** 【医】百日咳。

hoop·er [ˈhu:pə; ˋhupɚ] *n*. 箍桶人。

hoop·la [ˈhu:plɑ:; ˋhuplɑ] *n*. 1. 〔口〕极度兴奋；喧闹。2. 大吹大擂的宣传；大话。3. 投环套物游戏。

hoop·poe [ˈhu:pu:; ˋhupu] *n*. 【动】戴胜科鸟。

hoop·ster [ˈhu:pstə, ˈhup-; ˋhupstɚ, ˋhup-] *n*. 〔美俚〕篮球运动员。

hoo·ray [huˈrei; hʊˋre] *int*., *n*., *vt*., *vi*. = hurrah.

hoos(e)·gow [ˈhu:sgau; ˋhusgaʊ] *n*. 〔美俚〕1. 监狱。2. 警卫室。3. 厕所。

hoosh [hu:ʃ; huʃ] *n*. 〔俚〕一种浓汤。

Hoo·sier [ˈhu:ʒə; ˋhuʒɚ] *n*. 〔美〕印第安纳州人。***the*** ～ ***State*** 印第安纳州的别名。

hoot [hu:t; hut] I *vi*. 1. （表示不满或嘲笑的）唬唬大叫。2. 作猫头鹰叫声。3. 〔英〕（汽笛、汽车喇叭等）嘟嘟，喵喵。—*vt*. 1. 用唬唬声表示（轻蔑、不赞成等）。2. 轰赶。～ ***down*** （把某人）哄下台。～ ***out*** [***away***, ***off***] 轰走。～ ***with laughter*** 狂笑。II *n*. 1. 猫头鹰叫声，汽笛声，汽车喇叭声，表示不满的叫声。2. 极少量。***not care a*** ～[***two*** ～***s***] 毫不在乎。***not worth a*** ～ 毫无价值。～**owl** 【动】角枭〔尤指大枭〕。

hootch [hu:tʃ; hutʃ] *n*. = hooch.

hoot·chy-koot·chy [ˌhu:tʃiˈku:tʃi; ˏhutʃɪˋkutʃɪ] *n*. (*pl*. *-koot·chies*) 胡奇库奇舞〔一种色情的女子舞蹈〕；肚皮舞（= cooch; hootchie-kootchie）。

hoot·en·an·ny [ˈhu:tənæni; ˋhutəˏnænɪ] *n*. 1. 〔方〕（忘记或叫不上名称的）新玩意儿。2. （非正式的）民间歌舞表演会。

hoot·er [ˈhu:tə; ˋhutɚ] *n*. 汽笛。

Hoot·on [ˈhu:tən; ˋhutn] *n*. 胡顿〔姓氏〕。

hoots [hu:ts; huts] *int*. 〔Scot.〕唬！〔表示不满或不赞成〕。

hoove [hu:v; huv] *n*. （动物的）臌胀症。

Hoo·ver[1] [ˈhu:və; ˋhuvɚ] *n*. 1. 胡佛〔姓氏〕。2. **Herbert Clark** 胡佛〔1874—1964，美国第三十一任总统 1929—1933〕。

Hoo·ver[2] [ˈhu:və; ˋhuvɚ] I *n*. 一种真空吸尘器。II *vt*. 用吸尘器扫除。

hooves [hu:vz; huvz] hoof 的复数。

hop[1] [hɔp; hɑp] I *vi*. (*-pp-*) 1. （人）独脚跳，（鸟、蛙等）齐足跳；跳跃；跛行。2. 〔口〕跳舞。3. 〔口〕（飞机）作短途飞行，起飞。4. 〔俚〕（忽然）走掉，走开（*off*）。—*vt*. 1. 跳过；使（球）跳。2. 〔美〕跳上（火车、飞机等）；搭乘。3. 〔口〕飞过；飞越。***be hopping mad*** 〔美口〕气得跳起来，大怒。～ ***it*** 〔口〕赶紧走开。～ ***off*** （飞机）起飞。～ ***on*** [***all over***] 〔俚〕责骂。～ ***the twig*** [***stick***] 〔俚〕1. 逃避债务。2. 忽然死掉。～ ***to it*** 开始作某事。II *n*. 1. 单足跳；弹跳。2. 〔俚〕舞会。3. 飞行；（长距离飞行中的）一段航程。4. 短途旅行；免费搭乘。***catch on the*** ～ 出其不意地，正当其时地；忙乱地。～, ***step*** [***skip***] ***and jump*** 【体】三级跳。***on the*** ～ 〔口〕到处奔忙。～**scotch** 小儿（独脚）跳踢石子的游戏，“造房子”游戏，“踢房子”游戏，“跳方”游戏。～**-toad** 1. 〔儿〕蛤蟆。2. 〔美俚〕痛饮。

hop[2] [hɔp; hɑp] I *n*. 1. 【植】蛇麻草[子]，忽布。2. 〔*pl*.〕（用以使啤酒等带苦味的）蛇麻子。3. 〔美俚〕一种麻醉药〔尤指鸦片〕。4. 瘾君子，有毒瘾的人。***full of*** ～***s*** 〔美俚〕（麻醉品药性未过而）胡说着。II *vt*. (*-pp-*) 1. 在…中加蛇麻子，用蛇麻子加味。2. 用麻醉毒品刺激（*up*）。3. 超额增大（发动机）的功率；超额增大（车辆）发动机的功率。—*vi*. 种蛇麻子，采蛇麻子。***be hopped up*** 〔美俚〕兴奋的；抽鸦片烟抽得昏昏沉沉的，（发动机）被超额加大功率的。～**bind**, ～**bine** 蛇麻草蔓。～ **clover** 黄花苜蓿〔干燥后像忽布〕。～ **field** 蛇麻草田。～ **fiend** 〔美俚〕吸毒鬼。～ **fly** 蛇麻草蚜虫。～ **garden** 蛇麻草园。～**head** 〔美俚〕吸毒鬼。～ **horn beam** 1. 苗榆属（*Ostrya*）植物〔产于北美，尤指美洲铁木（*O. virginiana*）〕。2. 美洲铁木树材。～**joint** 〔美俚〕低级酒店；鸦片馆。～**picker** 采蛇麻草的人；采蛇麻草机。～ **pillow** 蛇麻草做芯子的枕头〔据说可促进睡眠〕。～ **pocket** （可装 168 磅的）蛇麻草袋。～ **pole** 蛇麻草的支柱；细长个子。

Hope [həup; hop] *n*. 霍普〔姓氏，女子名〕。

hope [həup; hop] I *n*. 1. 希望（*opp*. despair）；（有信心的）期望，愿望（*opp*. fear）。2. 寄予希望的人[物]。*cherish* [*entertain*] *the* ～ *that* 抱着…的希望。*live up to the* ～*s of* 不辜负…的期望。*H- deferred maketh the heart sick*. 〔谚〕希望不实现，心碎亦可怜。*H- is a good breakfast, but a bad dinner*. 〔谚〕事前希望真美妙，事情失败成苦恼。*If it were not for* ～, *the heart would break*. 〔谚〕人靠希望而生。*The result exceeds my* ～*s*. 结果出乎我意外。*Where there is life, there is* ～. 〔谚〕有生命就有希望。*He is the* ～ *of his school*. 他是学校的希望。***anchor*** [***lay***, ***pin***, ***set***] ***one's*** ～ ***in*** [***on***] 寄希望于。***beyond*** [***past***] (***all***) ～ 毫无希望，不可挽救。***dash*** [***shatter***] ***sb.'s*** ～***s*** 粉碎某人的希望。***elevate*** [***raise***] ***sb.'s*** ～***s*** 增强某人的信心。***forlorn*** ～ 1. 渺茫的希望，空想。2. 孤注一掷的举动，绝望的事。3. 敢死队。***give up*** (***resign***) ***all*** ～ 放弃一切希望。***in*** ～***s of*** = ***in the*** ～ ***of*** [***that***] 希望着，期待着。***in vain*** ～ 抱着不能实现的希望，幻想地。***lose all*** ～ 失掉一切希望。***one's last*** ～ 最后的希望。***There is a ray of*** ～. 仍有一线希望。***without any*** ～ ***of*** 毫无…的希望。II *vt*. 希望，期待（*that*; *to do*）。～ *to see you soon* 希望能再见到你。*It is* ～*d that* …希望能…，可以指望…。—*vi*. 1. 希望，期望。2. 〔古〕信赖，相信（*in*）。*I* ～ *so*. 但愿如此。*I* ～ *not*. 希望不至如此。*H- for the best, prepare for the worst*. 〔谚〕作最好的打算，作最坏的准备。～ ***against*** ～ 存万一的希望，妄想（*He* ～*s against* ～ *that no one would know the open secret*. 他痴心妄想，但愿谁也不会知道这个公开的秘密）。～ **box** [**chest**] 〔美俚〕女子的嫁妆，装嫁妆的箱子。

hope·ful [ˈhəupful; ˋhopfʊl] I *a*. 1. 有希望的，有前途的。2. 抱着希望的。***a*** ～ ***outlook*** 有希望的前途。***be*** [***feel***] ～ ***of*** [***about***] 对…抱希望[持乐观态度]。II *n*. 有希望成功的人，有希望被选上的人。***a presidential*** ～ 可望当上总统的人。***a young*** ～ 有希望的青年〔常

用为反语〕。-ly *ad*. -ness *n*.

hope·ful·ly [ˈhəupfuli; ˋhopfulɪ] *ad*. 1. 抱有希望地。2. 可以指望(= it is hoped)。

hope·less [ˈhəuplis; ˋhoplɪs] *a*. 没有希望的;绝望的。*a ~ case* 不治之症;绝症病人;不堪造就的人。*~ grief* 绝望的悲伤。-ly *ad*. -ness *n*.

hop·er [ˈhəupə; hopɚ] *n*. 希望者。

Hop·kin(s) [ˈhɔpkin(z); ˋhɑpkɪn(z)] *n*. 霍普金(斯)〔姓氏〕。

Hop·kin·son [ˈhɔpkinsn; ˋhɑpkɪnsn] *n*. 霍普金森〔姓氏〕。

hop·lite [ˈhɔplait; ˋhɑplaɪt] *n*. (古希腊的)装甲步兵。

hop-o'-my-thumb [ˈhɔpəmaiˈθʌm; ˋhɑpəmaɪˋθʌm] *n*. 矮子。

hop·per[1] [ˈhɔpə; ˋhɑpɚ] *n*. 1. 单足跳者;跳虫〔如跳蚤、干酪蛆等〕。2. (磨粉机等的)漏斗,送料斗,加料斗;(卸除垃圾、废土等的)底卸式船[车];贮水槽。3. (钢琴键盘后)抬举小木槌的机件。~ **barge** (船底有漏斗的)垃圾搬运船。~ **car**【铁路】底卸式货车。~**grass**【方】蚱蜢,蝗虫。

hop·per[2] [ˈhɔpə; ˋhɑpɚ] *n*. = hoppicker.

hopping [ˈhɔpiŋ; ˋhɑpɪŋ] *a*. 1. 忙碌的,繁忙的。2. 从一处到另一处的;到处奔忙的。~ *mad* 〔口〕大怒,狂怒。

hop·ple [ˈhɔpl; ˋhɑpl] I *n*. (牛、马等的)脚栓。II *vt*. 1. 把(牛、马等)的双脚拴起来。2. 给(人)带上脚镣;妨碍…的自由。

hop·py [ˈhɔpi; ˋhɑpɪ] *a*. 有蛇麻子味的。

hop·sack·ing [ˈhɔpsækiŋ; ˋhɑpsækɪŋ] *n*.【纺】1. 席纹粗黄麻袋布。2. 板司呢,席纹呢(= hopsack)。

hor. = horizon(tal); horology.

ho·ra [ˈhɔːrə, ˈhəurə; ˋhɔrə, ˋhorə] *n*. 1. 霍拉舞〔罗马尼亚等地一种轻快活泼的民间舞〕。2. 霍拉舞曲。

Hor·ace [ˈhɔrəs; ˋhɑrəs] *n*. 1. 霍勒斯〔男子名〕。2. 贺拉斯〔公元前 65—8 年,罗马诗人,拉丁语原名为 Quintus Horatius Flaccus〕。

Ho·rae [ˈhɔːriː; ˋhori] *n*. 〔*pl*.〕【希神】(掌管季节时序的)季节三女神。

H

ho·ral [ˈhɔːrəl; ˋhorəl] *a*. 1. 每一小时的。2. 时间上的。

ho·ra·ry [ˈhɔːrəri; ˋhorərɪ] *a*. 1. 每小时的。2. 时间上的,表示时间的。3. 持续一小时的。

Ho·ra·tian [həˈreiʃiən; həˋreʃɪən] *a*. (罗马诗人)贺拉斯(Horace)(式)的,贺拉斯的诗歌的;有贺拉斯风格的。

Ho·ra·ti·o [həˈreiʃiəu; həˋreʃɪo] *n*. 霍雷肖〔男子名〕。

horde [hɔːd; hɔrd] I *n*. 1. 蒙古游牧部落。2. 游牧民族;游牧部落。3. 〔蔑〕人群,群。*a ~ of flies* 一大群苍蝇。*a gypsy ~* 吉普赛人部落。*the Golden H-* 金帐汗国。II *vi*. 成群;结成部落而居。

hor·de·o·lum [hɔˈdiːələm; hɔrˋdiələm] *n*. (*pl*. -**la** [-lə; -lə])【医】睑腺炎,麦粒肿。

Hor·deum [ˈhɔːdiəm; ˋhɔrdɪəm] *n*.【植】1. 大麦属。2. 〔h-〕大麦属植物(包括大麦、元麦等)。

hore·hound [ˈhɔːhaund; ˋhɔrˏhaund] *n*. 1. 普通夏至草(*Marrubium vulgare*)。2. 夏至草。3. 夏至流浸膏〔治咳嗽药〕。4. 唇形科植物。

ho·ri·zon [həˈraizn; həˋraɪzn] *n*. 1. 地平;地平线;地平圈。2. 地平仪,水平仪。3.【地】地层,层位。4. 眼界,视界;范围,见识。*apparent ~*【气】视地平。*artificial* [*false*] ~人造地平。*celestial ~*【气】天球地平。*the ~ of knowledge* 知识范围。*radar ~*雷达地平,雷达作用距离。*~ of soil* 土层。*true ~*【气】真地平。*visible ~*【气】可见地平。*Science gives us a new ~*. 科学使我们大开新的眼界。*widen one's ~*开阔眼界。***on the ~*** 在地平线上,刚冒出地平线。

hor·i·zon·tal [ˌhɔriˈzɔntl; ˏhɑrəˋzɑntl] I *a*. 1. 地平的,地平线的。2. 水平的 (*opp*. vertical, perpendicular);卧式的。3. 同一行业的;相同地位的。4.【植】(枝条)平层的。*a ~ axis* 水平轴,横轴。*a ~ bar*【体】单杠。*the ~ line* 地平线,水平线。*a ~ plane* 水平面。*a ~ engine* 卧式发动机。*a ~ rudder*【海、空】水平舵,升降舵。*a ~ range* 广度。*a ~ union* (不同工业内同行业的)跨部门同业工会 (*opp*. vertical union)。~ **proliferation** 核武器拥有国的增加。II *n*. 水平线;水平面;水平物。***out of the ~*** 不成水平的。-ly *ad*. -i·ty *n*. 水平状态[性质位置]。

hor·mone [ˈhɔːməun; ˋhɔrmon] *n*.【生化】荷尔蒙,激素,内分泌。**hor·mo·nal**, **hor·mon·ic** [-ˈmɔnik; -ˋmɑnɪk] *a*.

hor·mon·ol·o·gy [ˌhɔːməˈnɔlədʒi; ˏhɔrməˋnɑlədʒɪ] *n*. 内分泌学。

horn [hɔːn; hɔrn] I *n*. 1. (牛、羊、鹿等动物的)角,触角;(动物头上的)角状羽毛;触须。2. 〔美俚〕鼻子。3. 角质,角质物,角制物;角状物,角状容器。4. (角制)号角;喇叭;(作为管乐器的)号,管。5. 警报器,扬声器,角状扩声器。6. (新月的)钩尖,(铁砧的)尖角,(马鞍的)鞍头。7. 海湾的分叉;河流的支流;岬,海角;半岛;【地】角峰。8.【空】操纵杆。9. 防卫武器;力量;光荣。10. 魔鬼头上的角。11. 〔*pl*.〕其妻与人通奸的人头上所生的角〔譬喻说法,如汉语中的"绿帽子"〕。12. 〔the ~〕〔美俚〕电话。*a fog ~*雾笛。*an English ~*【乐】英国管。*a French ~*【乐】法国号。*a shoe ~*角质鞋拔。*a bull ~*强力扬声器。***a ~ of abundance*** [***plenty***] 丰满角〔希腊神话中主神宙斯所用的山羊角,角中的乳永远倒不完〕;丰裕的象征(= cornucopia)。***blow*** [***toot***] ***one's own ~*** 自吹自擂。***come out at the little end of the ~*** 吹牛失败;说大话没有兑现。***draw*** [***haul***, ***pull***] ***in one's ~s*** 退缩,撤退;克制自己;软化下去。***lift up one's ~*** 趾高气扬;盛气凌人。***lock ~s*** 1. (牛等)用角挑斗。2. 难分难解地搏斗。***lower one's ~*** 卑躬屈膝;降低身分。***on*** [***between***] ***the ~s of a dilemma*** 进退两难。***put*** [***denounce***] ***sb. to the ~***【史】宣布(某人)不受法律保护。***show one's ~s*** 露出凶相。***take a ~*** 喝一杯酒。***take the bull by the ~s*** 不畏艰险。***wind the ~*** 吹号角,吹喇叭;(昆虫)嗡嗡叫,吱吱叫。II *vt*. 1. 在…上装角。2. 把…做成角状。3. (动物)用角抵触[刺挑]。4. 把(牛角)截去;截短(牛角)。5.【船】使(船的框架)与其龙骨成直角。6. (妻)使(丈夫)头上生角(当王八)。~ ***in*** 〔美俚〕闯入,侵入,干涉。III *a*. 角制的,角质的(= horny)。~ **antenna** 喇叭形天线。~**bar** 马车的横木。~**beam**【植】鹅耳枥属树。~**bill**【动】犀鸟科鸟;犀鸟。~**blende**【矿】角闪石。~**book** 1. 角帖书〔纸页上印有文字,其上盖有透明角片的儿童识字书籍〕。2. 初级论文。~ **fly**【动】角蝇(*Haematobia irritans*)〔可咬牛皮肤的一种吸血蝇〕。~-**mad** *a*. 大怒的。~**pipe** 1. 号角〔一种单簧管乐器〕。2. (英国水手跳的)号笛舞;号笛舞曲。~ **pox** 水痘。~**rimmed** *a*. (眼镜)角质架的。~-**rims** 〔俚〕角质边的眼镜。~ **silver** 角银矿(= cerargyrite)。~ **stone**【矿】角岩。~-**swoggle** *vt*. 〔美俚〕欺骗,瞒。~-**tail**【动】树蜂科(*Siricidae*)动物。~**work** 1. 〔集合词〕角制品;角细工。2. (防御用的)角堡。~**worm**【动】天蛾幼虫。

Horn [hɔːn; hɔrn] *n*. 合恩〔南美洲最南端的一岛名〕。***Cape ~*** 合恩角〔智利〕。

Horn·by [ˈhɔːnbi; ˋhɔrnbɪ] *n*. 霍恩比〔姓氏〕。

horned [hɔːnd, ˈhɔːnid; hɔrnd, ˋhɔrnɪd] *a*. 有角的;角状的。*the ~ moon* 〔诗〕半月。~ **bladderwort**【植】角狸藻。~ **grebe**【动】角鸊鷉。~ **lizard** = ~ toad. ~ **owl**【动】枭。~ **pout**【动】角鲶。~ **puffin**【动】角目鸟。~ **toad**【动】角蟾。~ **violet**【植】簇生堇菜。~ **viper**【动】角蝰(*Cerastes cornutus*)〔产于北非〕。

horn·er [ˈhɔːnə; ˋhɔrnɚ] *n*. 1. 制角工人。2. 吹号角者。3. 〔俚〕服海洛因的人。

hor·net [ˈhɔːnit; ˋhɔrnɪt] *n*.【动】大黄蜂。***arouse*** [***stir up***] ***a nest of ~s*** 捅马蜂窝,惹来敌人[反对者]。***arouse*** [***bring***, ***raise***] ***a ~'s nest about one's ears*** 树敌招怨,惹麻烦。

horn·fels [ˈhɔːnfels; ˋhɔrnfɛls] ***n.*** 〔*sing.*, *pl.*〕【矿】角页岩。

horn·ful [ˈhɔːnful; ˋhɔrnfʊl] ***n.*** 满满一角杯。

horn·i·ness [ˈhɔːninis; ˋhɔrnɪnɪs] ***n.*** 角质,硬质。

hor·ni·to [hɔːˈniːtəu; hɔrˋnito] ***n.*** (*pl.* **-tos** [-təuz; -toz])【地】溶岩滴丘。

horn·less [ˈhɔːnlis; ˋhɔrnlɪs] ***a.*** 无角的;无号角的。*a* ~ *sheep* 无角羊。

horn·y [ˈhɔːni; ˋhɔrnɪ] ***a.*** **1.** 角的;角制的。**2.** 角状的,角质的,有角的。**3.** 坚硬如角的;粗硬起老茧的。**4.** 〔美俚〕好色的,猥亵的。**5.** 〔古〕半透明的。*a* ~ *hand* 粗硬的手。*the* ~ *coat* (眼睛的)角膜。~**-handed** ***a.*** 手上长有老茧的。

horol. = horologe; horology.

hor·o·loge [ˈhɔrələdʒ; ˋharəladʒ] ***n.*** 计时仪;钟表,日晷。**-lo·ger** [-ˈrɔlədʒə; -ˋralədʒɚ], **ho·rol·o·gist** [-ˈrɔlədʒist; -ˋralədʒɪst] ***n.*** 钟表制造者;钟表学家;钟表商。**-log·ic(al)** [-ˈlɔdʒik(əl); -ˋladʒɪk(əl)] ***a.*** 钟表的,钟表学的。

hor·o·lo·gi·um [hɔrəˈləudʒiəm; ˌharəˈlodʒɪəm] ***n.*** (*pl.* **-gi·a** [-dʒiə; -dʒɪə]) **1.** = horologe. **2.** 〔the H-〕【天】时钟座。

ho·rol·o·gy [hɔˈrɔlədʒi; kaˋralədʒɪ] ***n.*** **1.** 钟表学;钟表制造术。**2.** 测时法。

hor·o·scope [ˈhɔrəskəup; ˋharəˌskop] ***n.*** **1.** 星占。**2.** 算命天宫图。*cast a* ~ 以占星术算命。**-scop·ic(al)** [-ˈskɔpik(əl); -ˋskapɪk(əl)] ***a.***

ho·ros·co·py [hɔˈrɔskəpi; haˋraskəpɪ] ***n.*** **1.** 星占(占星术算命者所说的人诞生时的)星位,星相。

hor·ren·dous [hɔˈrendəs; haˋrɛndəs] ***a.*** 可怕的。**-ly** ***ad.***

hor·rent [ˈhɔrənt; ˋhɔrənt] **I** ***a.*** 〔诗〕汗毛直竖的,毛骨悚然的。

hor·ri·ble [ˈhɔrəbl, -ribl; ˋhɔrəbl, -rɪbl] ***a.*** **1.** 可怕的,令人毛骨悚然的。**2.** 〔口〕讨厌的,可恶的。*a* ~ *murder* 令人发指的谋杀罪行。~ *weather* 讨厌的天气。**II** ***n.*** 〔常 *pl.*〕衣着古怪的人。**-ness** ***n.*** **hor·ri·bly** ***ad.***

hor·rid [ˈhɔrid; ˋhɔrɪd] ***a.*** (*superl.* ~**est**) **1.** 可怕的。**2.** 〔口〕讨厌的,可恶的。**3.** 〔古〕粗糙的,粗硬的。*What a* ~ *nuisance!* 真讨厌! **-ly** ***ad.*** **-ness** ***n.***

hor·rif·ic [hɔˈrifik; hɔˋrɪfɪk] ***a.*** 可怕的。

hor·ri·fy [ˈhɔrifai; ˋhɔrəˌfaɪ] ***vt.*** **1.** 使恐怖,使毛骨悚然。**2.** 〔口〕使反感,使厌恶。*be horrified at* 一想起…就不寒而栗。*be horrified to hear the news* 听到消息十分惊讶。**-fi·ca·tion** ***n.*** **-ing** ***a.***

hor·rip·i·late [hɔˈripileit; hɔˋrɪpɪˌlet] ***vt.***, ***vi.*** (使)毛发竖立,(使)起鸡皮疙瘩。

hor·rip·i·la·tion [hɔːripiˈleiʃən; haˌrɪpɪˋleʃən] ***n.*** (由于寒冷、恐怖等引起的)毛发竖立;鸡皮疙瘩。

hor·ror [ˈhɔrə; ˋharɚ] ***n.*** **1.** 战栗,恐怖;可怕的事物。**2.** 嫌恶,痛恨。**3.** 讨厌的人[事]。**4.** 〔口〕非常丑恶;糟糕的东西。*He was filled with* ~ *at the sight.* 他看见那种光景就吓得发抖。*the Chamber of H-s* 恐怖陈列室〔原指伦敦 *Tussaud's* 蜡像陈列馆〕。*He is a perfect* ~. 他是一个十分讨厌的家伙。*That coat is a* ~. 〔口〕那件大衣难看透了。***have a*** ~ ***of sth.*** 对某事极厌恶。***the*** ~***s*** 〔口〕战栗,打冷颤〔尤指发酒疯〕。~ **fiction** 恐怖小说。~**-stricken**, ~**-struck** ***a.*** 吓得发抖的,受惊吓的。

hors [hɔː; ɔr] ***ad.***, ***prep.*** 〔F.〕在外,在…之外。~ ***concours*** [kɔ̃ːŋˈkur; kɔŋˋkur] (展览品)不参加竞赛评奖的。~ ***de combat*** [dəˈkɔ̃ːmbaː; dəˋkambɑ] 失却战斗力的。~ ***d'œuvre*** [ˈdəːvr; ˋdoevr] 餐前小吃;〔转义〕无关重要的事。

horse [hɔːs; hɔrs] **I** ***n.*** (*pl.* ~**s**, 〔集合词〕~) **1.** 马〔尤指长大的公马〕,马科动物。**2.** 〔集合词〕骑兵。**3.** 像马的东西,有脚的架子(如衣架、手巾架等);脚搭;(体操用)木马;〔口〕(象棋中的)马。**4.** 〔美俚〕(考试作弊用的)夹带。**5.** 【矿】夹块,夹石;【地】夹层。**6.** 【海】(卷帆时水手的)搭脚索,铁杆。**7.** 〔美俚〕粗汉,笨蛋。**8.** 〔美俚〕碎牛肉。**9.** 〔美俚〕一千美元。**10.** 〔美俚〕恶作剧。**11.** 马力。*hold a* ~ 执住马嘴。*light* ~ 轻骑兵。*A good* ~ *cannot be of a bad colour.* 〔谚〕马好色也正。*A good* ~ *should be seldom spurred.* 〔谚〕好马不宜多加鞭。*a long* ~ 直跳木马。*a side* ~ 横跳木马。*Never swap* [*swop*] ~*s while crossing the stream.* 〔谚〕行到河中别换马。*When two ride on one* ~, *one must sit behind.* 〔谚〕两人同骑一匹马,总有一个坐后头。*You may take a* ~ *to the water, but you cannot make him drink.* 〔谚〕你可带马到水边,却不能强迫它喝水。***a dark*** ~ (赛马中出现的)冷门马;实力难测的竞争者;竞争中出人意料的获胜者。***a*** ~ ***of another*** [***different***] ***colour*** 完全另外一回事。***a*** ~ ***of the same colour*** 那是一回事。***a*** ~ ***on sb.*** 〔俚〕针对某人的恶作剧。***ask a*** ~ ***the question*** 要求马赛跑时拼命。***back the wrong*** ~ (赛马时)下错赌注;支持失败的一方。***be on one's high*** ~ 趾高气扬。***change*** ~ 换马,换班子,调换主持人。***come off one's high*** ~ 放下架子。***eat like a*** ~ 吃得多。***flog a dead*** ~ **1.** 鞭打死马,徒劳。**2.** 企图把已经讨论过并已被搁置的旧事重提。***from the*** ~***'s mouth*** 〔美俚〕(消息等)来自可靠方面。***hitch*** ~ (***together***) = ***put up one's*** ~***s together*** 〔古〕同心协力;情投意合;结婚。***hold one's*** ~ 〔俚〕忍耐,镇静,不冲动。~ ***and foot*** 骑兵和步兵,全军;全力以赴地。~ ***and*** ~ 齐头并进,并驾齐驱。***H-Guards*** 〔英〕近卫骑兵队。***iron*** ~ 〔口〕火车头;自行车;【军】坦克。(***it is***) ***enough to make a*** ~ [***cat***] ***laugh*** 太可笑了。***lock*** [***shut***] ***the barn*** [***stable door***] ***after the*** ~ ***is stolen*** 贼去关门。***look a gift*** ~ ***in the mouth*** 对礼物挑剔。***mount*** [***ride***] ***the high*** ~ 〔口〕趾高气扬,耀武扬威。***on*** ~ ***of ten toes*** = ***on foot's*** ~ 〔谑〕骑两脚马,徒步。***outside of a*** ~ 〔口〕骑在马上。***pay for a dead*** ~ 为死马花钱,花冤枉钱。***play*** ~ **1.** (儿童游戏)骑竹马。**2.** 〔美俚〕胡闹。***play*** ~ ***with sb.*** **1.** 嘲笑某人,愚弄某人。**2.** 无礼对待某人。***play*** ~ ***with sth.*** 〔美俚〕搞乱次序,造成混乱。***proud*** ~ 〔诗〕矫健的马,骏马。***put the cart before the*** ~ 本末倒置。***roll up*** ~ ***and foot*** = ***roll up*** ~, **foot and guns** 使全军覆没。**spur a willing** ~ 鞭打好好干活的马,给以不必要的刺激。***take*** ~ 骑马去;(母马)交尾。***take the*** ~ (母马)受孕。***talk a*** ~***'s hind leg off*** = ***talk the hind leg off a*** ~ 滔滔不绝地谈。***talk*** ~ 说大话,吹牛。***the flying*** [***winged***] ~【希神】(诗神缪斯所骑的)飞马。***the war*** ~ 战马;老兵,老手。***To*** ~! (命令)上马! ***work for a dead*** ~ 从事徒劳的工作。***work like a*** ~ 苦干,实干。**II** ***vt.*** **1.** 给人[车]备马;骑上(马)。**2.** 〔古〕使(某人)平躺放在木马或人背上鞭挞;鞭挞。**3.** 〔口〕猛推。**4.** 【海】虐待。**5.** 〔美〕嘲弄,愚弄。—***vi.*** **1.** 骑马。**2.** 〔美〕作弄人,拿人开玩笑。**3.** 〔卑〕性交。~ ***around*** 〔俚〕起哄,胡闹。**III** ***a.*** **1.** 马的。**2.** 马拉的,骑[套]着马的。**3.** (同类中)大而粗硬的。~**-and-buggy** ***a.*** 〔美〕过时的,老式的。~**back** **1.** ***n.*** 马背;隆起的条状地带。**2.** ***ad.*** 在马背上。~**bean**【植】马蚕豆。~ **block** 骑马墩。~ **box** **1.** 〔英〕(运马用的)有篷货车。**2.** 〔谑〕教堂的条凳席。~**boy** 马夫。~**-breaker** 驯马师。~**car** 〔美〕铁路马车;运马车。~ **chestnut** 七叶树属植物,欧洲七叶树。~ **cloth** (盖在马身上或装饰马用的)马衣,马被。~ **collar** 马颈圈 (*grin through a* ~ *collar* 〔古〕把头从马颈圈伸出来互作鬼脸的游戏;〔喻〕硬充滑稽)。~ **coper**, ~ **couper**, ~ **dealer** 马贩子。~**culture** 〔英〕养马术。~ **doctor** 〔口〕马医,兽医;蹩脚医生。~**-faced** ***a.*** 马脸的;脸长而难看的。~ **feathers** ***n.*** 〔*pl.*〕梦话,胡说八道。~**flesh** **1.** 马肉。**2.** 马〔集合词〕。~**-fly** 虻,马蝇。~**foot** **1.** 【植】款冬。**2.** 【动】鲎。~ **gear** 马具;马力装置。

H

~ **gentian**【植】莛子藨属（*Triosteum*）植物。~**hair** 1. 马毛,马鬃。2. 马毛呢。~ **hide** 1. 马皮。2. 马革。~ **latitudes**〔*pl*.〕【气】回归线无风带。~**laugh** 哄笑,纵声大笑。~**leech** 蚂蝗;贪心汉;榨取者（*daughters of the ~leech* 贪得无厌的人们）。~ **mackerel**【鱼】竹荚鱼;金枪鱼。~**man** 养马的人;骑手,骑师;骑兵。~**manship** 马术。~ **marine** 骑马水兵〔指不存在的东西〕;外行（*Tell it* [*that*] *to the* ~ *marines*! 鬼才会相信!）。~ **master** *n*. 驯马师;租马商。~ **mastership** 御马术。~ **mint** *n*.【植】香蜂草属（*Monarda*）植物〔尤指梦菲薄荷（*M. punctata*）〕。~ **opera**〔美俚〕西部"牛仔"影片[广播剧、电视剧]。~ **pistol** 马枪。~**play** *n*., *vi*. 恶作剧,胡闹。~ **pond** 饮马池;洗马池。~**power**【机】马力。~**pox** 马痘。~ **race** [**racing**] 赛马。~**radish**【植】辣根。~ **rake** 马拉集草机,马拉耧耙。~**'s ass** 傻瓜,脓包。~**sense**〔口〕起码常识。~**-shit** 1. 马粪。2.〔俚〕胡说。~**shoe** 1. *vt*. 给(马)钉掌。2. *n*. 马蹄铁;马蹄形的东西(*a* ~ *shoe magnet* 蹄形磁铁。*a* ~ *shoe nail* 蹄钉。*a* ~ *shoe crab* 鲎)。3. U 形的。~**tail** 1. 马尾。2.【植】木贼属植物。~**-trade** *vi*. 精明地讨价还价。~ **trade** 1. 马的交易。2. 讨价还价后互相让步的交易。~ **trader** 马贩,马商。~**whip** 1. *n*. 马鞭。2. *vt*. 用马鞭鞭打。~ **whispering** 驯马耳语〔欧洲早期的一种驯马术,自 Nicholas Evans 之小说《马语者》(The Horse Whisperer)问世后而重新引人注意〕。~ **woman** 女骑手;女养马人。

horse·less [ˈhɔːslis; ˋhɔrslɪs] *a*. 1. 无马的。2. 无需马的;自动的。*An automobile was formerly called a* ~ *carriage*. 汽车原来被叫做不用马拉的车子。

hors·ey [ˈhɔːsi; ˋhɔrsɪ] *a*. = horsy.

Hors·ley [ˈhɔːsli; ˋhɔrslɪ] *n*. 霍斯利[姓氏]。

hor·som.〔处方〕睡觉时(= at bed time)。

horst [hɔːst; hɔrst] *n*.【地】地垒。

hors·y [ˈhɔːsi; ˋhɔrsɪ] *a*. 1. 马的;马似的。2. 爱马的;爱赛马的;热心改良马匹的。**hors·i·ly** *ad*. **hors·i·ness** *n*.

hort., **hortic.** = horticultural; horticulture.

hor·ta·tion [hɔːˈteiʃən; hɔrˋteʃən] *n*. 劝告;奖励。

hor·ta·tive [ˈhɔːtətiv; ˋhɔrtətɪv] *a*. 劝告性的;忠告性的。**-ly** *ad*.

hor·ta·to·ry [ˈhɔːtətəri; ˋhɔrtəˏtɔrɪ] *a*. = hortative.

Hor·tense [hɔːˈtens; hɔrˋtɛns] *n*. 霍顿斯[女子名](L. = gardener)。

hor·ti·cul·ture [ˈhɔːtikʌltʃə; ˋhɔrtɪkʌltʃɚ] *n*. 园艺(学)。**-tur·al** *a*. 园艺(技术)上的。**-tur·ist** 园艺家。

hor·tus sic·cus [ˈhɔːtəs ˈsikəs; ˋhɔrtəs ˋsɪkəs]〔L.〕1. (压干的)植物标本(集)。2. 一堆枯燥的事实。

ho·san·na [həuˈzænə; hoˋzænə] *n*.【宗】和散那〔赞美上帝的用语〕。

hose [həuz; hoz] **I** *n*. (*pl*. **hose**(*s*),〔古〕***ho·sen*** [ˈhəuzn; ˋhozn]) 1. 长筒袜。2. (旧时男子穿的)紧身裤,短袜。3. 水龙带,软管,胶皮管;蛇管。4. 叶鞘。*half* ~短裤。**II** *vt*. 1. 使穿长筒袜。2. 用胶皮管浇水。3.〔美俚〕向…拍马屁,用甜言蜜语笼络。~ **cart**（消防队的)水管车。~**man** 消防人员。~ **pipe** 水龙软管。~**-tops**〔*pl*.〕无脚部的长筒袜。

Ho·se·a [həuˈziə; hoˋziə] *n*. 1. (纪元前 8 世纪希伯来先知)何西阿。2.《旧约全书》中的《何西阿书》。

Ho·sier [ˈhəuzjə; ˋhoʒɚ] *n*. 霍西尔[姓氏]。

ho·sier [ˈhəuʒə; ˋhoʒɚ] *n*. 经售男袜、内衣和针织品商人,袜商。

ho·sier·y [ˈhəuʒəri; ˋhoʒərɪ] *n*. 1.〔集合词〕男袜;男用针织品。2. 针织品生意;针织厂。

hosp. = hospital.

hos·pice [ˈhɔspis; ˋhɑspɪs] *n*.〔F.〕1. (特指教会、僧侣办的)旅客招待所。2. 救济院,济贫院。

hos·pi·ta·ble [ˈhɔspitəbl; ˋhɑspɪtəbl̩] *a*. 1. 善于招待的,款待周到的;殷勤的,好客的。2. (气候、环境)宜人的,适宜的。3. 易于接受的。*a* ~ *reception* 热情的招待。*a mind* ~ *to new ideas* 善于接受新思想的人。**-ness** *n*. **-bly** *ad*.

hos·pi·tal [ˈhɔspitl; ˋhɑspɪtl̩] *n*. 1. 医院;兽医院。2.〔古〕旅客招待所。3. 慈善收养院。4. (钟表、钢笔等小物件的)修理商店。5. 公立学校〔此意仅作专有名词用,如 Christ's H-〕。*a clearing* ~兵站医院。*a field* ~ 野战医院。*an infectious* ~ 传染病医院。*an isolation* ~ 隔离病院。*lock* ~〔英〕性病医院,花柳病医院。*a lying-in* [*maternity*] ~ 产科医院。*magdalen* ~妓女教养院。*a mental* ~ 精神病医院。***be in*** ~ 住院。***go to*** [***enter***] ~ 入院。***out of*** ~ 出院。***walk the*** ~***s***（医科学生)到医院实习。~ **bed** 医院床〔可以升降活动的床〕。~ **fever** 医院热〔以前在医院里流行的一种斑疹伤寒病〕。~**man**〔美〕海军医务兵。**H- Saturday** [**Sunday**]〔英〕医院募捐的星期六[日]〔星期六在街头募捐,星期日在教堂募捐〕。~ **ship** 医疗船,运送伤病员的船。~ **train** 运送伤病员的列车。**-ist** 院派医师〔病人住院期间替代平时的家庭医师〕。

hos·pi·tal·ism [ˈhɔspitəlizəm; ˋhɑspɪtəlɪzm] *n*. 1. 医院制度。2. 长期住医院给病人带来的不良影响。3. 长期孤儿院生活的不良影响。

hos·pi·tal·i·ty [ˌhɔspiˈtæliti; ˏhɑspɪˋtælətɪ] *n*. 1. (对客人的)亲切招待,款待,〔*pl*.〕殷勤。2. (气候、环境等的)宜人,适宜。*partake of* ~受人款待。

hos·pi·tal·i·za·tion [ˌhɔspitəlaiˈzeiʃən; ˏhɑspɪtəlaɪˋzeʃən] *n*. 1. 住院治疗。2.〔美口〕(保证偿付住院费的)住院保证单(= hospitalization insurance)。

hos·pi·tal·ize [ˈhɔspitəlaiz; ˋhɑspɪtəlˏaɪz] *vt*. 把…送入医院治疗。

hos·pi·tal·(l)er [ˈhɔspitələ; ˋhɑspɪtəlɚ] *n*. 1. 慈善收养院职员。2. 医院牧师。3.〔罕〕就医的人。***Knight H-*** 中世纪在耶路撒冷建立的十字军骑士团救护成员。

host[1] [həust; host] *n*.〔常 H-〕【宗】圣饼,圣餐用面包。

host[2] [həust; host] **I** *n*. 1. 主人（*opp*. guest)。2. (广播、电视的)节目主持人。3. 旅馆老板。4.【生】寄主,宿主。5.【物】晶核,基质。*a* ~ *country* 东道国。***count*** [***reckon***] ***without one's*** ~ 不考虑某些重要因素[未与主要有关人员协商]作计划;无视困难和反对（*You are counting without your* ~. 你是在打如意算盘)。***play*** ~ ***to*** 作东,招待。**II** *vt*. 主办(宴会等);款待。~ **plant**【生植】宿主,寄生。~**-specific** *a*.【生】寄生于特殊宿主上的。

host[3] [həust; host] *n*. 1. 一大群,许多。2.〔古〕军队。3.【计】主机(亦作~ computer)。*a* ~ *of friends* 一大群朋友。*a* ~ *of troubles* 许许多多麻烦。***be a*** ~ ***in one-self*** 能以一当十;一人能做很多人的事。***the*** ~(***s***) ***of heaven*** 1.【宗】天使军。2. 日月星辰。***the Lord*** [***God***] ***of H-s***【圣】万军之主,上帝。

hos·tage [ˈhɔstidʒ; ˋhɑstɪdʒ] *n*. 人质;抵押品。***be held in*** [***as an***] ~被扣作人质。***give*** ~ ***to fortune*** 1. 听天由命。2. 有家室之累。~ ***to fortune*** 随时会失去的人[物]〔尤指妻子、孩子、珍宝〕。**-ship** 充当人质,被抵押状态。

hos·tel [ˈhɔstəl; ˋhɑstl̩] *n*. 1.〔英〕大学宿舍。2.〔美〕(招待徒步旅行青年等的)招待所(= youth ~)。3.〔英古〕旅馆。

hos·teler [ˈhɔstələ; ˋhɑstl̩ɚ] *n*. 1. 招待所管理员;〔古〕旅馆的主人。2. 住招待所的青年旅行者。

hos·tel·ry [ˈhɔstəlri; ˋhɑstl̩rɪ] *n*.〔英古〕旅馆,客栈。

host·ess [ˈhəustis; ˋhostɪs] **I** *n*. 1. 女主人。2. 旅馆女老板。3.〔美〕(餐馆、列车、飞机等的)女服务员,女侍应生。4. (舞厅里的)舞女。*an air-* ~飞机上的女服务员,空中小姐。**II** *vt*. 在…作女主人;作女主人招待。

hos·tile [ˈhɔstail; ˋhɑstɪl] **I** *a*. 1. 敌人的,敌方的。2. 怀有敌意的,敌对的（*to*),不友善的。*a* ~ *army* 敌军。

～*feeling* 敌意。*a* ～ *looks* 显示敌意的面色。*be* ～ *to reform* 反对改革。*assume* [*take*] *a* ～ *attitude* 抱敌对态度。*be* ～ *to* 敌视。～ *operations* 敌对行动。**II** ***n*.** 1.【美史】敌视白人的印第安人。2. 敌对分子。**-ly** ***ad*.**

hos·til·i·ty [hɔsˈtiliti; hɑsˋtɪlətɪ] ***n*.** 1. 敌意,敌视。2. 敌对行为,反抗行为;〔*pl*.〕战争行动;战斗。*feelings of* ～敌意。*an act of* ～敌对行为。*naval hostilities* 海战。*open* [*suspend*] hostilities 开[休]战。*the outbreak of* ～战事的爆发。*the renewal* [*resumption*] *of hostilities* 恢复敌对行动。

hos·tler [ˈɔslə, ˈhɔslə; ˋɑslɚ, ˋhɑslɚ] ***n*.** 1.〔古〕= ostler. 2. 机车[机器]的维修人。

hot [hɔt; hɑt] **I** ***a*.** 1. 热的 (*opp*. cold)。2. (味道)刺激性的,辣的,辛辣的;【猎】野兽的气味强烈的;(色彩)强烈的,给人热感的(如红、黄等)。3. 热烈的,激动的;猛烈的,激烈的;热情的,熟心的;急躁的,发火的。4. 淫秽的;色情的;性欲强的,(动物)正当交尾期的。5. (爵士音乐)节奏快的;〔美俚〕吵闹的,即兴的;兴奋之余自由演奏的。6. 时新的,流行的,热门的;最近的,刚到的,刚做好的;才出锅的,才出炉的,(菜等)热腾腾的;(公债等)才发行的;〔美俚〕刚偷来的;非法得来的;危险的。7. 杰出的,极好的;(选手)强有力的;(演技等)优秀的。8.〔俚〕极走运的;正在颈头上的;竞技状态极佳的。9. (游戏)接近目的物的;差一点就(猜中)的。10. 通高压电的;【原】放射性强的。11. 紧随的,接近的;被通缉的。12.〔俚〕荒诞的,不可信的。*be piping* [*steaming*] ～酷热,闷热。*Strike the iron while it is* ～.〔谚〕趁热打铁,趁机行事。*a* ～ *battle* 激战。～*blush* 红脸。*a* ～ *place in the battle* 激战地。～*words* 激烈话。*a* ～ *argument* 激烈辩论。～*idea*〔美〕极好的主意。*Pepper is* ～. 胡椒是辣的。～*temper* 暴躁的脾气。*a* ～ *scent or trail* 猎物气味强烈或有强烈臭味的路径[打猎用语]。*in* ～ *pursuit* 紧追。*a* ～ *wire* 高压电线。***all* ～ *and bothered*** 〔俚〕骚动中的。***at its*** [***the***] ***hottest*** 在最激烈的一点上。***be* ～ *on sb.'s trail*** 穷追某人。***be* ～ *on*** [***for***] 热中于,热心。***be* ～ *under the collar*** 〔俚〕发怒。***drop sth. like a* ～ *potato*** [***chestnut***]〔口〕急忙扔掉。***get* ～** 1. 变热,发热。2. 激动,发怒。3.〔俚〕使劲干。4. 接近。***get into* ～ *water***〔口〕遭到麻烦,惹来麻烦。***get*** [***catch***] ***it* ～**〔口〕被大骂一顿。***give it to sb.* ～ = *let sb. have it* ～**〔口〕痛骂某人,痛打某人。***go* ～ *and cold*** (***all over***) (因害怕等)感到一阵子热一阵子冷。～***and heavy*** 猛烈;极力,拼命。～ ***and*** ～ (食物)才出锅的,才出炉的。～***and strong*** 猛烈地,激烈地。～***from the press*** 刚印好的。～***off the wire*** 电报[电话]刚刚打来的。***in* ～*blood*** 发怒,激昂。***in* ～*haste*** 火急。***make the place too* ～*for sb.* = *make it too* ～*to hold sb.*** 使某人待不下去。***not so* ～** 不太好,不太杰出。***sizzling* ～** 火烫一样的热;充满愤怒。***the* ～*s***〔美俚〕爱情,性欲。**II** ***vi*.**〔英〕变热;变得激动;骚动起来 (*up*)。 —***vt*.**〔英〕使热 (*up*);刺激,使骚动。**III** ***ad*.** 1. 热;热烈地,猛烈地。2. 愤怒地。3. 趁热。***blow* ～ *and cold*** 无定见,犹豫不决。***come* ～ *on sb.'s heels*** 紧跟某人来。～**air**〔俚〕空话,浮夸的文章。～**-air artist**〔俚〕吹牛大王。～**atom** 热原子(具有放射核的原子)。～**bed** 温床 (*a* ～ *bed of war* 战争的策源地)。～ **blast**【冶】热鼓风。～**blood** 易激动者,轻举妄动者。～**-blooded *a*.** 1. 热血的;易激怒的;血气方刚的;情欲旺盛的。2. (马)英国种的,阿拉伯种的。3. (家畜)良种的。～**box** (火车上的)过热轴承箱。～**-brained *a*.** = hotheaded. ～ **button** 1. (讨论中的)热点;敏感问题;一触苏发的敏感部位。2. (与电视节目主持人联系的)热线按钮。～**cake** 烤饼 (*go* [*sell*] *like* ～ *cakes* (货物)很快地卖光)。～**cell**【原】热室,高放射性物质工作屏蔽室。～**cha** [ˈhɔttʃɑː; ˋhɔttʃɑː]〔美俚〕爵士音乐。～**chair**〔美俚〕电椅。～**chow**〔美口〕热气腾腾的食物。**hot charging**【冶】热装料。～**cockles** 蒙眼猜人游戏。～**cooling** 沸腾冷却。～**corner** 1. (垒球)第三垒。2.〔美俚〕战场[政治]上的关键地方。～ **cross bun** 十字霜糖面包〔尤指基督教四旬斋日所吃者〕。～ **dark matter**【天】热黑体。～ **dog** 1. ***n*.**〔口〕小红肠,热狗,红肠面包;〔美俚〕最佳运动员。2. ***a*.**〔美俚〕极好的。～**dog *vi*., *vt*.** (在作冲浪或滑雪运动时)卖弄(花式动作)。～ **dogging** 吃热狗。～**flash** 绝经期阵发性发热感。～**foot** 1. ***ad*.** 急急忙忙地。2. ***vi*.** 急急忙忙地走。3. ***n*.** 〔*pl*. ～*foots*〕暗中将火柴放在别人鞋中点燃的恶作剧;心灵的刺激,震惊。～ **fusion**【物】热核聚变。～**galvanization** 热镀锌。～ **gas welding** 气焊。～**gospel(l)er** 狂热的清教徒,奋兴派牧师。～**head** 性急的人。～**-headed *a*.** 性急的,鲁莽的。～**house** 1. ***n*.** 温室;陶器干燥室。2. ***a*.** 温室中生长的,人工的,过份纤弱的。3. ***vt*.** 对(儿童)进行温室式教育〔指超前的跳级教育〕。～**iron** 铁水。～**laboratory** 强放射性物质研究实验室。～ **landing** 高速降落。～ **light** 热光,电视广播室中最重要的灯光。～**line** 1. "热线"〔尤指前苏联和美国两国政府首脑间的直接通话线〕。2. 直接联系的途径。3. 电视咨询热线;此种热线广播现场提出的问题。～**link** 1. ***n*.**【计】超文本衔接,热链〔可在短时间内传送大量信息〕。2. ***vt*.**【计】热联,使…作超文本衔接。～ **material** 强放射性物质。～ **money** 1. 赃款;偷来的钱。2. (为牟利)由一国转移至另一国的流动资金。～ **pants**〔美〕(妇女穿在外面的)冬季短裤。～ **pack** 1.【医】热敷。2. (制罐头的)快装法。～**pepper** 1. 辣胡椒。2. 辣胡椒树。～ **pilot**〔美空俚〕优秀的战斗机驾驶员。～ **place**〔美俚〕地狱。～**plane**〔美空俚〕起飞降落极快的飞机。～ **plate** 1. 煤气炉;电炉。2. 餐厅出售的热食。3. 保温盘;烤盘。～ **pot**〔英〕马铃薯炖牛[羊]肉。～ **potato** 难题,棘手的问题。～**-press** 1. ***vt*.** 热压。2. ***n*.** 热压机。～ **pups** = ～ dog. ～ **rod**〔俚〕1. (旧车拆卸改装的)减重高速汽车。2. = ～ rodder. ～ **rodder**〔俚〕减重高速汽车驾驶者。～**rodding** 驾驶减重高速汽车。～**-roll *vt*.**【冶】热轧。～ **seat** 1.〔美俚〕电椅。2. 尴尬处境。～**shoe** 热靴〔摄影机上的闪光灯插座〕。～**-short** 加热就脆的,热脆性的。～ **shortness** 热脆性。～**shot** 1. (运送易腐物品等的)快车,快船,快机。2. 大人物,飞黄腾达的野心家;艺高而自负的人。～ **sketch**〔美俚〕漂亮女人[女学生]。～**spot**〔美俚〕1. 麻烦地点,潜在的危险地区。2. 电椅。3. 低级下流的夜总会。4. 辐射最强处,过热点。～ **spring** 温泉。～ **spur** 1. ***n*.** 性急的人。2. ***a*.** ～**squat**〔美俚〕电椅;被处电刑。～ **strip** 热轧带钢。～**stuff**〔俚〕1. 好手,专家。2. 意志坚强的人。3.脾气暴躁的人;好色的人。4. 大胆的举动,引起轰动的事物。～**tap**【冶】(钢锭的)热帽。～ **tear** 缩裂,热裂。～**-tempered *a*.** 暴躁的,易激怒的。～ **ticket** 热门人物[事件];时尚。～ **war** 热战("冷战"之对)。～ **water** 1. 热水。2. 困境。～**-water bag**, ～**-water bottle** 热水袋。～**-water heating** 暖气设备。～ **well** 温泉。～**-wire** 1. ***a*.**【电】热线式的,热电阻线的。2. ***vt*.** 短路打(火)〔发动汽车时不用车匙,使汽车的电线短路以发动引擎〕。～**wire**〔美俚〕(好)消息。～**-working**【冶】热加工。**-ly *ad*. -ness *n*.**

hotch·pot [ˈhɔtʃˌpɔt; ˋhɑtʃˏpɑt] ***n*.**【法】财产混同〔指将各项产业合并,以便在继承人中平分〕。

hotch·potch [ˈhɔtʃpɔtʃ; ˋhɑtʃˏpɑtʃ] ***n*.** 1. (蔬菜、马铃薯、肉等煮的)浓汤;杂烩。2. 混杂物;杂乱的一堆东西。3. = hotchpot.

Ho·tel [həuˈtel; hoˋtɛl]通讯中代表 h 的词。

ho·tel [həuˈtel; hoˋtɛl] **I** ***n*.** 旅馆,旅社。*a*(*n*) ～ *car*〔美〕带餐车的卧车。*American plan* ～美国式旅馆,膳宿合并计算法。*European plan* ～欧洲式旅馆,膳宿费分别计算。*temperance* ～禁酒旅馆。***His Majesty's* ～**〔谑〕监狱。***the sheriff's* ～**〔俚〕监狱。**II** ***vt*.** 使住旅馆〔通常说～ it〕。～ **car** 带餐室的卧车。～**ing**旅馆式办公室〔指给经常出差,不在公司办公的外勤人员安排的上班

房间，通常不固定，甚至无固定的办公桌〕。~**keeper** 旅店老板。~**-keeping** 旅店业。

hôt·el [əuˈtel; oˋtɛl] ***n***. 〔F.〕官邸；（富人或显要人士的）公馆。~ **de ville** [dəˈviːl; dəˋvil]〔F.〕市政府。~ **Dieu** [djəː; djə]〔F.〕医院。

ho·tel·ier [həuˈteliei; hotəˋlɪr] ***n***. 旅馆老板；旅馆经理。

hot·sy-tot·sy [ˈhɔtsiˈtɔtsi; ˋhɑtsɪˋtɑtsɪ] ***a***. 〔美俚〕好的；壮观的；精彩的。

Hot·ten·tot [ˈhɔtntɔt; ˋhɑtnˏtɑt] ***n***. **1**.（西南非洲）霍屯督族；霍屯督人。**2**. 霍屯督语。

hou·dah [ˈhaudə; ˋhaʊdə] ***n***. = howdah.

Hou·din·i [huːˈdiːni; huˋdinɪ] ***n***. 霍迪尼〔姓氏〕。

hough [hɔk; hɑk] ***n***., ***vt***. 〔英〕= hock[1].

hound [haund; haʊnd] **I** ***n***. **1**. 狗；猎狗，〔英〕〔the ~s〕猎狐的一群猎狗。**2**. 撒纸追逐的"狗兔赛跑"游戏中扮演猎狗的人。**3**.【动】角鲨，星鲨，弓鳍鱼。**4**. 卑鄙的人。**5**.〔构成复合词〕有…迷[瘾]的人。*the ~ of hell = Cerberus*. *an autograph ~* 爱请人在纪念册上签名题字的人。*a jazz ~* 爵士音乐迷。*a publicity ~*〔美俚〕爱在报上露名的人，喜欢自吹自擂的人。***a tea ~*** 〔美俚〕爱交际的人，爱同女人交际的男子；女人腔的男子。***follow*** (***the***) ***~s = ride to ~s*** 骑马纵狗打猎。***hare and ~s*** 撒纸追逐的"狗兔赛跑"游戏。***~s of law*** 缉捕员。***ride before*** [***past***] ***the ~s*** 骑马纵狗打猎；抢光；先下手。**II** ***vt***. **1**. 用猎狗打猎；追逐；迫害。**2**. 唆使，煽动（*on*）；使追逐（*at*）。***be ~ed out of*** 从…中被赶出。~***out*** 挑唆；煽动。

hound² [haund; haʊnd] ***n***. 〔*pl*.〕【船】桅肩。

hound's-tongue [ˈhaundzˈtʌŋ; ˋhaʊndzˏtʌŋ] ***n***.【植】倒提壶属（*Cynoglossum*）植物。

hour [ˈauə; aʊr] ***n***. **1**. 小时，钟头。**2**. 时间，时刻。**3**. 一小时的行程；一小时的工作量。**4**.〔*pl*.〕固定时间〔尤指工作时间〕；课时；【宗】天主教的定时祈祷，祈祷文。**5**. …点钟。**6**. 死期，末日。**7**.（…）时，时代。**8**.〔the ~〕目前，现在。**9**.【天】赤经十五度。**10**.〔H-〕【希神】掌管季节、时序等的女神。*An ~ in the morning is worth two in the evening*.〔谚〕一日之计在于晨。*half an ~ =*〔美〕*a half ~* 半小时。*a quarter of an ~* 一刻钟。*every ~ or two* 每一二小时。*What is the ~?* 现在几点钟了？*The ~ is 11:15*. 十一点一刻了。*school ~'s* 上课时间。*office ~s* 办公时间。*business ~s* 营业时间。*dark ~s* 艰苦的时刻。*The darkest ~ is that before the dawn*.〔谚〕黎明之前天最黑。*golden ~s* 幸福的日子。*The city is two ~s away* [*distant*]. 该城离此两小时路程。*One's ~ has come* [*struck*]. 末日已到，命数已尽。*my boyhood's ~s* 我的童年时代。*The clock struck the ~*. 钟响报时。*combat flying ~*【军】战斗飞行小时。***after ~s*** 办公[营业]时间以后。***at a good ~*** 恰巧，正好，侥幸。***at all ~s*** 随时。***at the eleventh ~*** 在最后时刻，在危急关头。***by the ~*** 按钟点。***for ~s*** (***and ~s***) 好几小时。***for ~s together*** 一连好几小时。***~ after ~*** 一小时又一小时，连续地。***happy ~*** 快乐时光〔晚餐前酒吧或饭店减价供酒时刻〕。***in a good*** [***happy, lucky***] ***~*** 在幸运的时刻。***in an evil*** [***ill***] ***~*** 在不幸的时刻。***in the ~ of need*** 紧急的时候。***keep bad*** [***late***] ***~s*** 迟出迟归，晚起晚睡。***keep good*** [***early, regular***] ***~s*** 早睡早起；早出早归。***make long ~s*** 长时间地工作。***news to this ~*** 〔美〕（无线电广播的）最后消息。***of the ~*** 目前的，现在的，紧急的（*the question of the ~* 目前的问题）。***off ~s*** 业余时间。***on the ~*** 准时地；按整小时地。***out of ~s*** 在上班时间之外。***serve the ~*** 随波逐流；趋炎附势。***the dead ~s*** 半夜三更；夜深人静。***the inevitable ~*** 死期。***the long ~s*** 午夜十一、二点。***the rush ~s*** 交通拥挤时间，高峰时间。***the short ~s*** 午夜以后两、三点。***the small*** [***wee***] ***~s*** 半夜一、二、三点。***the trying ~*** 艰难困苦的时刻。***the unearthly ~*** 太早，早得厉害，早得不像话。***to an ~*** 恰好（*three days to an ~* 恰好三天）。~ **angle**【天】时角。~ **circle**【天】时圈；子午线。~**glass** 沙漏，水漏。~**hand**（钟表的）时针，短针。~ **plate**（钟、表的）字盘。

hou·ri [ˈhuəri; ˋhaʊrɪ] ***n***. **1**. 伊斯兰教天堂中的美女。**2**. 妖艳的美人。

hour·ly [ˈauəli; ˋaʊrlɪ] **I** ***a***. 每小时的，每小时一次的；时时，常常。**II** ***ad***. 每小时一次；时时，随时。

House [haus; haʊs] ***n***. 豪斯〔姓氏〕。

house [haus; haʊs] **I** ***n***. （*pl*. ~s [ˈhauziz; ˋhaʊzɪz]）**1**. 房屋，住宅；住家；一家，一户。**2**. 家，家庭；家务。**3**. 家族；王朝。**4**. 建筑物，馆；商号，社，所，机构；〔美〕旅馆；戏院。**5**.〔集合词〕观众，听众；演出的场次。**6**.（英国式大学）宿舍；全体寄宿生。**7**. 房间，室。**8**.（牲畜、家禽等的）栏，房，棚；（仪器）罩。**9**.（大学等的）校董会（会议）；宗教团体；修道院。**10**.〔the H-〕议会；议院〔特指下院〕；〔集合词〕议员。**11**.〔口〕伦敦证券交易所。**12**.〔美俚〕妓院。**13**.（牛津大学的）基督学院（Christ Church College）。**14**.〔英俚〕救贫院。*An Englishman's ~ is his castle*.〔谚〕英国人的家是他的堡垒，非请不得擅入。*Burn not your ~ to rid it of the mouse*.〔谚〕不要为了驱鼠而焚烧房屋；勿因小失大。*the ~ of David* 大卫王室。*Johnson H-*〔英〕=〔美〕*the Johnson ~* 约翰逊宅。*a business ~* 商店。*H- Full = Full H-*【剧】客满。*a hash ~*〔美〕小饭馆。*a rogue ~*〔口〕监牢。*The ~ rose to its feet*. 全场起立。*The second ~ starts at 9*. 第二场9时开演。*thin ~* 观众稀少。*the White H-*〔美〕白宫。*Name not a halter* [*rope*] *in his ~ that hanged himself*.〔谚〕房里有人吊死，千万别提绳子。***as safe as ~s*** [***a ~***] 十分安全。***be in possession of the H-*** 在议会中发言。***bow down in the H- of Rimmon*** [ˈrimən; ˋrɪmən] 为妥协以达到一致行动而牺牲自己的原则〔源出《圣经》《列王纪》〕。***bring down the ~*** 博得满场喝采。***bring the ~ about one's ears*** 在家中成为众矢之的。(***burn***) ***like a ~ on fire*** 燃烧得又快又猛。***carry the ~*** 博得满场喝采。***clean ~*** **1**. 打扫房屋。**2**. 内部清洗（= ~clean）。***count the ~*** 计算出席人数。***eat sb. out of ~ and home*** 把某人吃穷。***enter the H-*** 当选为议员。***from ~ to ~*** 挨家挨户。***give sb. a lot of ~***〔美俚〕给某人很多鼓励。***~ and home*** 家〔加强语气的说法〕。***~ of assignation*** 妓院。***H- of Burgesses***〔美〕州众议院。~ **of call** **1**. 职业介绍所，待雇所。**2**. 常去的场所〔如酒店等〕。***~ of cards*** 小孩子用纸牌搭成的房子；不牢靠的计划。***H- of Commons***〔英〕众议院，下院。***~ of correction*** 教养院，改造所。***H- of Delegates***〔美〕州参议院。***~ of detention*** 拘留所。***~ of God*** 教堂。***~ of ill fame*** 妓院。***H- of Lords***〔英〕贵族院，上院。***~ of refuge*** 难民收容所；养育院。***H- of Representatives***〔美〕众议院。***iron ~***〔美俚〕监牢。***keep a good ~*** 待客周到。***keep ~*** 料理家务；当家。***keep ~ with*** 和…同住。***keep open ~*** [***doors, table***] 好客，随时欢迎来客。***keep the*** [***one's***] ***~*** 待在家中不外出。***make*** [***keep***] ***a H-***（英下院）使出席议员达法定人数40人。***make sb. free of one's ~*** 让某人自由使用自己的房子。***move ~*** 搬家。***on the ~***〔美俚〕主人开销的，免费的。***play ~*** "做家家"〔儿童假装大人做家务〕。***public ~*** **1**. 公共会堂。**2**.〔英〕酒馆。***put*** [***set***] ***one's ~ in order*** 整理家务；进行必要的改革。***the big house***〔美俚〕（州或联邦的）监狱。***the dark ~***〔婉〕坟墓。***the half-way ~*** **1**. 两市镇间的客店。**2**. 妥协。***the ~ that Jack built*** **1**.〔谑〕重复的故事。**2**.〔俚〕监狱。***the narrow ~*** 坟墓。***the pudding ~***〔俚〕胃，肚子。***the semidetached ~*** 与别家共一道墙的独立住宅。***the third ~***〔美〕"第三院"，国会外的实力派，院外活动集团。**II** [hauz; haʊz] ***vt***. **1**. 供给…房子住[用]；收容，接待，留宿。**2**. 覆蔽，庇护。**3**. 收藏。**4**.【建】嵌入；【海】安置（炮台）；收好（桅木）。**5**. 给（机器、齿轮）装外罩。~ *one's books* 收藏书籍。—***vi***.

1. 住。2. 躲藏(*up*);到达安全处所。~ **agent**〔英〕房地产经纪人。~ **arrest** 本宅软禁〔受软禁者不准离开家〕。~**boat** 可供住家的船,水上住宅;宽敞的游艇。~-**bound** *a*. 因故不能离的;家居不外出的。~**boy** = ~-man. ~**breaker** 为抢劫而侵入他人住宅者;〔英〕拆房屋的人。~**breaking** 为抢劫而侵入住宅;〔英〕拆房屋。~-**broken**, ~**broke** *a*. 1. (猫、狗等)经训练有家居卫生习惯的。2. 有管教的,有礼貌的。~**bug** 臭虫。~ **cat** 家猫;〔美〕老是住在家里的人。~**clean** 1. *vi*. 大扫除;清洗,清理。2. *vt*. 打扫;改革。~**cleaning** 1. 房屋清扫,大扫除。2. 清洗,清理(人员)。~**coat** *n*. 1. 妇女在家穿的宽敞便服。2. = dressing gown. ~ **counsel** 公司的顾问律师。~**detective** 百货公司或旅馆雇佣的私家侦探。~ **dinner** (俱乐部等为会员举办的)晚宴。~ **doctor** 住院医生。~ **dog** 看家狗。~**dress** (家务)女便服。~ **duty** 房捐。~ **famine** 房荒。~**father** 1. 男舍监。2. 一家之父。3. 社团的男性领袖。~ **flag**【海】(商船的)公司旗。~ **flannel** (用作抹布的)粗绒布。~**fly** 家蝇。~-**guest** 在家过夜的来客。~**holder** 户主。~ **hunting** 找房子。~**husband** 家庭主夫。~**keep** *vi*. 〔美口〕自立门户;主持家务。~**keeper** 1. 主妇;女管家。2. 房屋管理人。~**keeping** 1. 家务管理,家政。2. (企业中)房屋的管理(*go* ~ *keeping* 组织家庭)。~**leek**【植】长生草属植物。~**lights** (剧场的)观众席照明灯。~**line**【航】三股左旋扭成的小捆绳子。~**maid** 女仆。~**maid's knee** (因常常跪着劳动而引起的)膝盖骨囊炎。~-**man** *n*. (*pl*. -*men*) 1. 男仆;旅馆勤杂工。2. 保镖。~-**master** 1. 主人,户主,家长。2. 〔英〕(学校宿舍的)舍监。~ **match**〔英〕(学校中的)舍际友谊赛。~**mate** 同住者。~**mistress** 1. 女主人,主妇。2. 女舍监。~ **moss**〔美俚〕在家具下[地板上]积聚的灰尘。~**mother** 照管学生宿舍的女管家。~ **mouse** (*pl*. ~ *mice*) 家鼠。~ **organ** 给职员和顾客看的店刊。~ **party** 招待客人过夜的别墅招待会;享受别墅招待的全体宾客。~ **physician** 住院内科医生。~**phone** (旅馆等不接外线的)内线电话。~**plant** 室内盆栽植物。~-**proud** *a*. 关心家事的;讲究家庭摆设的。~-**raising** 盖房会〔农村中邻里来帮忙盖房子的聚会〕。~**rent** 房租。~-**renter** 租屋的人。~**room** 1. (家内的)卧室;放东西的地方。2. 住宿(*I would not give it* ~ *room*. 屋子窄,我不要那占地方的东西)。~**shoes** 拖鞋。~ **sparrow** = English sparrow. ~**staff** 全体住院医生。~**surgeon** 住院外科医生。~-**to**-~ *a*. 挨户的(*a* ~-*to*-~ *visit* 挨户访问)。~**top** 屋顶(*cry* [*declare*, *preach*, *proclaim*] *sth*. *upon* [*from*] *the* ~-*top*(*s*) 广泛宣扬)。~**wares** *n*. *pl*. 家用器皿〔尤指厨房用具〕。~**warming** 新屋落成宴,暖房酒。~**wife** 1. [ˈhauswaif; ˋhausˌwaɪf] (*pl*. ~*wives*) 主妇。2. [ˈhʌzif; ˋhʌzɪf] (*pl*. ~-*wifes* [ˈhʌzifs; ˋhʌzɪfs], ~-*wives* [ˈhʌzivz; ˋhʌzɪvz]) 针线盒。~**wifely** *a*. 家庭主妇的,主妇似的;节俭的,会当家的。~**wifery** [ˈhausˌw(a)ifəri; ˋhausˏw(a)ɪfərɪ] 家政,家事。~**work** 家务劳动〔烹饪、缝纫等〕。

house·ful [ˈhausful; ˋhausful] *n*. 满屋,一屋子。*a* ~ *of guests* 满屋子客人。

house·hold [ˈhaushəuld; ˋhausˏhold] I *n*. 1. 〔集合词〕全家人;(包含人在内的)家眷,家属,家里人;家庭,户。2. 家务。3. 〔the H-〕〔英〕王室。4. 〔英〕〔*pl*.〕次等面粉。*the king of the* ~ 婴儿。*the number of* ~*s* 户数。***the Imperial*** [***Royal***] ***H***- 1. 皇室,王室。2. 〔集合词〕宫内官。II *a*. 1. 家庭的,家内的,一家的。2. 〔H-〕王室的。3. 家常的,普通的。~ *affairs* 家务。~ *furniture* 家具。~ *expenses* 家庭开支。~ *wares* 家用器具。~**art** 持家艺术。~**effects** 家具,家庭用具。~**gods** (古罗马的)家庭守护神;家庭必需品;传家石。~**franchise** [**suffrage**] 户主选举权。~**management** = ~art. ~**stuff** 〔古〕家具,家产。~ **troops** (王室)近卫队。~**word** 家常话,家喻户晓的用语。

house·hold·er [ˈhausˌhəuldər; ˋhausˏholdɚ] *n*. 1. 占有房子的人,住户。2. 户主。

hou·sel [ˈhauzl; ˋhauzl̩] I *n*. 〔废〕【宗】圣餐;圣餐物〔特指面包〕,圣体(= Eucharist)。II *vt*. 〔废〕对…施圣餐。

house·less [ˈhauslis; ˋhauslɪs] *a*. 1. 无家的。2. 无房屋的。

house·let [ˈhauslit; ˋhauslɪt] *n*. 小房子。

hous·ing¹ [ˈhauziŋ; ˋhauzɪŋ] *n*. 1. 供给住宅。2. 〔集合词〕房屋;住宅。3. 掩护,庇护;避难所。4.【机】壳;套。5.【建】柄穴,炉套。6.【海】桅脚。*bearing* ~ 轴承箱。*fan* ~ 风扇壳。*valve* ~ 阀室。~ *project* 住房建筑计划。*a* ~ *shortage* 房荒。*a* ~ *box*【机】轴箱。***open*** ~ 〔美〕黑人与白人自由混合居住。

hous·ing² [ˈhauziŋ; ˋhauzɪŋ] *n*. 马服;〔常 *pl*.〕马饰,鞍褥。

Hous·man [ˈhausmən; ˋhausmən] *n*. 豪斯曼〔姓氏〕。

Hous·ton [ˈhuːstən, ˈhaustən; ˋhustən] *n*. 豪斯顿〔姓氏〕。

hous·to·ni·a [huːsˈtəuniə; husˋtonɪə] *n*. 【植】北美茜草属(*Rubia*)植物〔开蓝、白或紫花〕。

HOV = high-occupancy vehicle (载客3人以上的)多座客车。

hove [həuv; hov] heave 的过去式及过去分词。

hov·el [ˈhɔvəl; ˋhɑvl̩] *n*. 1. 陋室,放杂物的小房间。2. 茅舍,棚舍。3. 窑的圆锥形外壳。

hov·el(l)·er [ˈhɔvələ; ˋhɑvlɚ] *n*. 无执照的领港员。

Hov·ell [ˈhəuvəl; ˋhovəl] *n*. 霍维尔〔姓氏〕。

hov·er [ˈhɔvə; ˋhɑvɚ] *vi*. 1. 翱翔,盘旋(*about*; *over*)。2. 徘徊(*about*; *near*)。3. 踌躇,彷徨。4. (直升飞机)停悬。—*vt*. 伏窝孵化。II *n*. 翱翔;徘徊。~-**ing act**【国际法】1. 禁止外国船只在领海逗留法。2. 规定三海里领海外的外国船只检查办法的法律。

hov·er·barge [ˈhɔvəbaːdʒ; ˋhɑvɚˏbardʒ] *n*. 大型气垫游艇。

hov·er·craft [ˈhɔvəkraːft; ˋhɑvɚˏkraft] *n*. 水陆两用垫式航行器;气垫船。

hov·er·fer·ry [ˈhɔvəˌferi; ˋhɑvəˏfɛrɪ] *n*. 〔英〕气垫渡船。

hov·er·lin·er [ˈhɔvəˈlainə; ˋhɑvɚˋlaɪnɚ] *n*. 巨型核动力气垫船。

hov·er·plane [ˈhɔvəplein; ˋhɑvɚˏplen] *n*. 〔英〕= helicopter.

hov·er·train [ˈhɔvətrein; ˋhɑvɚˏtren] *n*. 气垫火车。

Ho·vey [ˈhəuvi; ˋhovɪ] *n*. 霍维〔姓氏〕。

how [hau; hau] I *ad*. 1. 怎样,怎么(= in what manner);用什么手段、方法(= by what means)〔疑问副词和连接副词两用〕。*H- does he do it*? 他是怎样做的? *Ask him* ~ *he does it*. 问问他是怎样做的。*H- did it happen*? 事情怎么发生的? *He does not know* ~ *to swim*. 他不知道怎样游泳。2. 情况如何(= in what state)〔指身体健康等状况〕。*H- is she*? 她(身体)怎样? *H- goes it with you*? 你好么? *How are things in your school*? 你们学校的情况怎么样? 3. 价钱多少(= in what price)〔指金钱价值〕。*H- is wheat today*? 今天小麦市价怎样? *Find out* ~ *the exchange is*. 查明汇率多少。4. 几何,多少(= to what extent)〔指数量、程度多少,和形容词或副词连用,用作疑问副词或连接副词〕。*H- many are there*? 有多少? *H- much do you want*? 你要多少? *H- old is he*? 他多大年纪? *I wonder* ~ *old he is*. 不晓得他是几岁。*H- fast are we running now*? 我们现在跑的速度怎么样? *H- often do you go there*? 你多久去那里一次? *H- damaged is the car*? 车子损坏得如何? 5. 以为如何〔多用于征询意见〕。*H- do you like it*? 你觉得它怎么样? 喜欢它吗? *H- would it be to do it tomorrow*? 明天干这件事怎么样? 6. 怎么会,为什么? 〔表现惊异的通俗用法〕。*H- can you talk such nonsense*? 你怎么会这样胡说八道?

H

H- is it that you've come so early? 你怎么来得这么早? *H- happens it that you are late*? 你怎么迟到了? **7.** 怎样(= the way in which)〔关系词〕。*This is ～*. 〔口〕就是这样。*So that's ～ it is*! 原来如此! *I don't see ～*. 〔口〕我看不行。*This is ～ it happened*. 事情就是这样发生的。**8.** = that〔用于间接陈述〕。*I told him ～(= that) I had read in the papers*. 我告诉他我是在报上看见的。**9.** 尽可能(= as best)〔关系词〕。*Do it ～(= as best) you can*. 你尽可能做做看。**10.** 多么〔用作感叹词以修饰形容词、副词或动词〕。*H- absurd*! 多么荒唐! *H- fluently he speaks*! 他说得多流利啊! *H- he snores*! 他的鼾声多大啊! ***all you know ～***〔俚〕尽你所能。***and ～***〔美口〕〔用于加强语气〕当然啰! 那还用说! 可不是! ***Here's ～***! 敬你一杯! 祝你健康! ***H- about ...***? (你以为)…如何? …怎么样? (*H- about going for a walk*? 去散散步怎么样? *How about you let me worry about this*? 你让我来操这份心好不好?) ***H- are you***? **1.** 你身体怎样? **2.** 〔招呼用语〕你好! ***H- come...***? 〔美口〕怎么会的? (*H- come you never visit us anymore*? 你怎么不再来看我们?) ***H- do you do***? 你好! 〔初次见面时用语,对方要用同样的话回答〕。***H- goes it ...***? …的情况怎样? ***H- is that for***? 〔口〕好不…! 多么…! (*H- is that for impudent* [*impudence*]! 多么放肆!) ***H- much***? **1.** (价钱)多少? **2.** 什么? 〔要求对方重讲一遍时用, = 〔英〕What? 〔美〕H-〕。***H- now***? 〔古〕这是怎么回事? 嗳哟! ***H-'s about*** [***for***]? 〔美俚〕= H- about. ***H- so***? 怎么会这样的? 为什么? ***How's that***? **1.** 那是怎么一回事? **2.** 什么? (= How much? **2.**)。**3.** 【板球】(问裁判)击球手出局了吗? ***H- the deuce*** [***devil, dickens, ever, on earth***] ...? 到底怎么回事? ***H- then*** **1.** 这是什么意思? **2.** 后来怎样? 还有什么? **II** ***n***. 方法。*She explained all the ～s and whys of the issue*. 她详尽说明了问题的情况及原由。

how. = howitzer.

How·ard [ˈhau-əd, ˈhauəd; ˋhau-əd, ˋhauəd] ***n***. 霍华德〔姓氏,男子名〕。

how·be·it [hauˈbiːit; haʊˋbiɪt] **I** ***conj***. 〔古〕虽说,虽然。**II** ***ad***. 〔古〕尽管如此;仍然。

how·dah [ˈhaudə; ˋhaʊdə] ***n***. 象轿;驼轿〔驮在象或骆驼背上可供数人乘坐的凉亭状座位〕。

how·die, how·dy [ˈhaudi; ˋhaʊdɪ] ***n***. 〔Scot.〕接生婆,产婆。

how-do-you-do, how-de-do, how-d'ye-do [ˈhaudəjuˈduː, ˈhaudˈduː, ˈhaudiˈduː; ˋhaʊdəjʊˋdu, ˋhaʊdˋdu, ˋhaʊdɪˋdu] ***n***. 〔口〕讨厌、尴尬的局面〔前面常加 fine, pretty, nice 等形容词〕。*Here's a pretty* [*nice*] *～*. 这可太糟了! 这真叫人为难。

how·dy [ˈhaudi; ˋhaʊdɪ] ***int***. 【方】你好! (= How do you do?)

Howe [hau; haʊ] ***n***. 豪〔姓氏〕。***E***. ～ 豪(1819—1867),美国缝纫机发明人。

how·e'er [hauˈɛə; haʊˋɛr] ***ad***., ***conj***. = however.

How·ell(s) [ˈhauəl(z); ˋhaʊəl(z)] ***n***. 豪厄尔(斯)〔姓氏,男子名〕。

how·ev·er [hauˈevə; haʊˋɛvɚ] **I** ***ad***. **1.** 无论如何,不管怎样。**2.** 可是,仍然。**3.** 〔英俚〕究竟。*We have not yet won*; *～, we shall try again*. 我们没有获胜,不过我们还要再试一下。*H- tired you may be, you must do it*. 不管怎样累,你也得做。*We must do something, on ～ humble a scale*. 我们得做点事,不论如何微不足道。*H- did you manage it*? 你究竟怎样处理的? **II** ***conj***. **1.** 不管用什么方法。**2.** 〔古〕虽然。*Arrange your hours ～ you like*. 你爱怎么安排时间就怎么安排。

how·itz·er [ˈhauitsə; ˋhaʊɪtsɚ] ***n***. 榴弹炮。

howl [haul; haʊl] **I** ***vi***. **1.** (狗、狼等)嚎,嗥叫。**2.** (风等)怒号,怒吼。**3.** (人悲痛时的)号叫,哀号,嚎啕大哭。**4.** 狂笑;狂闹,欢闹。*They ～ed with laughter*. 他们高声狂笑。**—** ***vt***. **1.** 吼叫着说出;喝住。**2.** 把…喝下台(*down*; *out*; *away*)。*～ the speaker off the platform* 把演说者轰下台。*～ defiance at the enemy* 吼叫着向敌人挑战。**II** ***n***. **1.** 嚎叫,吠声。**2.** 怒号;叫声。**3.** 狂笑,嚎哭。**4.** 【无】啸声,嗥鸣,颤噪效应。

howl·er [ˈhaulə; ˋhaʊlɚ] ***n***. **1.** 咆哮者;哭叫的人。**2.** 【动】吼猴〔产于南美〕。**3.** 〔口〕愚蠢可笑的错误;大笑话。**4.** 【无】嗥鸣器。*commit a ～* 铸成大错。***come a ～*** 遭到失败。

howl·et [ˈhaulit; ˋhaʊlɪt] ***n***. 〔古、方〕枭(= owlet)。

howl·ing [ˈhauliŋ; ˋhaʊlɪŋ] **I** ***a***. **1.** 咆哮的;嚎叫的。**2.** 荒僻的,凄凉的。**3.** 〔俚〕非常的,极端的。*a ～ lie* 弥天大谎。*a ～ shame* 奇耻大辱。*a ～ success* 巨大的成功。*a ～ swell* 骄横的人。*a ～ wilderness* 野兽咆哮的荒野。**II** ***n***. 【无】啸声,嗥鸣,颤噪效应。*acoustic ～* 音响啸声。*～* **monkey** 【动】吼猴〔发现于中南美,长尾,啼声如吼叫〕。

how·so·ev·er [ˌhausəuˈevə; ˏhaʊsoˋɛvɚ] ***ad***. 无论如何,不管怎样。

how-to [ˈhauˈtuː; ˋhaʊˋtu] ***a***. 〔口〕介绍基础知识的。*a ～ book* 基础知识书,入门书。

hoy[1] [hɔi; hɔɪ] ***int***. 嗬! 喂! 〔唤喊或驱赶家畜等的呼声〕。

hoy[2] [hɔi; hɔɪ] ***n***. 沿海岸航行的短航程独桅小船。

hoy·den [ˈhɔidn; ˋhɔɪdn̩] **I** ***n***. 顽皮姑娘。**II** ***a***. 顽皮姑娘的。

hoy·den·ish [ˈhɔidniʃ; ˋhɔɪdn̩ɪʃ] ***a***. 顽皮女孩似的,带男孩气的。

Hoyle [hɔil; hɔɪl] ***n***. **1.** 霍伊尔〔姓氏〕。**2.** ***Edmond ～*** 埃德蒙·霍伊尔〔1672—1769,英国纸牌戏规则书著者〕。**3.** 霍伊尔所著纸牌游戏书。***according to ～*** **1.** 按照规则的[地]。**2.** 公正的[地]。

Hoyt [hɔit; hɔɪt] ***n***. 霍伊特〔姓氏,男子名〕。

H.P., HP, h.p., hp = **1.** half pay. **2.** horsepower. **3.** high-pressure. **4.** horizontal plane.

H-particle ***n***. 质子。

HPRR = high-performence research reactor 高性率研究反应器。

HPS = handy phone system 【电信】轻便电话系统。

H.Q., h.q., HQs, Hq = Headquarters.

HQ = heaviness quotient 体重商数。

HQMC = 〔美〕Headquarters, Marine Corps.

HR = **1.** homogeneous reactor 均匀反应器。**2.** human resources 人力资源。

H.R. = **1.** 【纺】hank roving 粗纱支数。**2.** Home Rule. **3.** House of Representatives.

hr. = hour(s).

h.r., hr 【棒球】= home run(s).

H-Res = House (of Representatives) Resolution (美国)众议院决议案。

H.R.H., HRH = His [Her] Royal Highness.

hrs. = hours.

Hs 【化】元素𬭶(hassium)的符号。

H.S. = **1.** High School. **2.** 【医】〔L.〕*hora somni* 〔睡眠时〕。

H.S.E. = 〔L.〕*hic sepultus est* (= here lies buried 葬此)。

H.S.H. = His [Her] Serene Highness.

H.T. = **1.** Hawaiian Territory. **2.** heat treat. **3.** high tension.

ht. = **1.** height. **2.** heat.

h.t. = high tenacity.

HTGR = high temperature gas-cooled reactor 高温气冷反应堆。

HTML, html = hypertext markup language 【计】超文本标记语言。

HTTP, http = hypertext transfer protocol 【计】超文本本传

送协议。

HUAC = House Un-American Activities Committee (美国)众议院非美活动调查委员会。

hua·ra·ches [həˈrɑːtʃiːz, Sp. wɑːˈrɑːtʃes; həˋrɑtʃiz, Sp. wɑrˋrɑtʃɛs] ***n. pl.*** 条带鞋帮拖鞋。

hub[1] [hʌb; hʌb] ***n.*** **1.**【机】(轮)毂,旋翼叶毂。**2.** 中心,中枢。**3.** (电器面板上的)电线插孔。**4.**【机】衬套;套壳;中轴壳。*a ~ of industry* [*commerce*] 工业[商业]中心。*the ~ of the universe* 宇宙的中心,世界的中心。***from ~ to tire*** 〔美〕完全,从头到尾。***the H-*** 〔美〕波士顿市的别名。***up to the ~*** 深深陷入,给…完全缠住。**~-cap 1.** (车轮的)毂盖。**2.** 〔美俚〕骄傲自大的人。**~-and-spoke** ***a.*** (机场)毂辐状的,在中心机场周围设有多个相联机场的。

hub[2] [hʌb; hʌb] ***n.*** 〔口〕丈夫〔husband 的缩写〕。

hub·a-hub·a, hub·ba-hub·ba [ˈhʌbəˈhʌbə; ˋhʌbəˋhʌbə] ***int.*** 〔美口〕好极好极! 赞成赞成! 赶快!

Hub·bard [ˈhʌbəd; ˋhʌbəd] ***n.*** 哈伯德〔姓氏〕。

Hub·bard squash [ˈhʌbəd skwɔʃ; ˋhʌbɚd skwɑʃ] 古巴瓜〔一种坚硬的冬季南瓜,瓜皮发绿或发黄,瓜肉呈黄色〕。

Hub·ble [ˈhʌbl; ˋhʌbl] ***n.*** 哈勃〔姓氏〕。~('s) **constant** 【天】哈勃常数〔天文学计量单位,根据哈勃定律计算行星运行速度时使用〕。***the ~*** 哈勃太空望远镜(= ~ Space Telescope)。

hub·ble-bub·ble [ˈhʌblbʌbl; ˋhʌbl͵bʌbl] ***n.*** **1.** 沸腾声。**2.** 吵闹声,骚动。**3.** 水烟筒。

hub·bub [ˈhʌˌbʌb; ˋhʌ͵bʌb], **hub·ba·boo, hub·bu·boo** [ˈhʌbəbuː; ˋhʌbəbu] ***n.*** 吵闹声;喧哗。

hub·by [ˈhʌbi; ˋhʌbɪ] ***n.*** 〔口〕= hub[2].

Hu·bert [ˈhjuːbə(ː)t; ˋhjubɚt] ***n.*** 休伯特〔姓氏〕。

hu·bris [ˈhjuːbris; ˋhjubrɪs] ***n.*** 狂妄自大。**hu·bris·tic** ***a.***

huck·a·back [ˈhʌkəbæk; ˋhʌkə͵bæk] ***n.***【纺】(质地浮松,表面粗糙的棉或亚麻织物,作毛巾用或揩布用的)浮松布。

huck·le [ˈhʌkl; ˋhʌkl] ***n.*** 髋部,臀部,屁股,(羊、鹿的)腰部。**~-backed** ***a.*** 驼背的。**~berry** (*pl.* **-ries**)【植】**1.** 美洲越橘;卵叶越橘。**2.** 美洲越橘子;卵叶越橘子;乌饭树的紫黑浆果。**~bone** 髋骨;(四足兽的)距骨。

huck·ster [ˈhʌkstə; ˋhʌkstɚ] **I** ***n.*** **1.** 叫卖小贩;行商。**2.** 〔美〕代人写广播[电视]商业广告者;大吹大擂推销商品的人。**3.** 唯利是图的人;受雇佣者。*a political ~* 政治贩子。**II** ***vt.*** **1.** 叫卖,零售。**2.** 和…讨价还价。**3.** 吹嘘。*~ one's service* 打零活。**—*vi.*** 讨价还价。

HUD [hʌd; hʌd] ***n.*** 〔美〕房屋及城市发展部〔美国政府于1965年设立的一个部门,全名为 Department of Housing and Urban Development〕。

hud·dle [ˈhʌdl; ˋhʌdl] **I** ***vt.*** **1.** 乱挤,胡乱堆集。**2.** 把…卷作一团 (*into*; *up*; *together*)。**3.** 草率从事 (*up*; *through*);胡乱穿上 (*on*)。**4.** 把…隐藏起来。*~ a job through* 匆匆忙忙地做完一件工作。*~ oneself up* = *be ~d up* 把身体缩成一团。**—*vi.*** **1.** 群集,拥挤 (*together*)。**2.** 卷缩 (*up*)。**3.** 碰头商议。**4.**【橄榄球】赛前球员列队〔等候开球信号〕。*~ over one's duty* 敷衍塞责。*~ together for warmth* 挤在一块取暖。*~ up in a corner* 挤在角落里。**II** ***n.*** **1.** (杂乱的)一团,一堆,一群。**2.** 拥挤,混乱。**3.** 〔美俚〕(秘密)会议;(足球运动员比赛中)碰头商讨战术;【橄榄球】赛前队员列队。*all in a ~* 乱七八糟。*~ upon ~* 成一团,成一堆。***go into a ~ with sb.*** 〔美俚〕同某人秘密商议。***in a ~*** 〔美俚〕在开会。

Hu·di·bras·tic [ˌhjuːdiˈbræstik; ͵hjudɪˋbræstɪk] ***a.*** 〔英国诗人 *Samuel Butler* 讽刺诗〕滑稽式英雄体的;讽刺而滑稽的。

Hud·son [ˈhʌdsn; ˋhʌdsn] ***n.*** **1.** 赫德森〔男子名〕。**2. Henry ~** 亨利·哈得孙〔1576—1611?,英国航海家;美国哈得孙湾(Hudson Bay) 的发现者〕。***the ~ Bay*** 哈得孙湾〔在北美东北部〕。***the ~ River*** 哈得孙河〔美国纽约州的河〕。

Hue, Hué [hjuːˈei; hjuˋe] ***n.*** 顺化〔越南港市〕。

hue[1] [hjuː; hju] ***n.*** **1.** 色,色彩,色调;(意见等的)特色。**2.** 样子,形式。*the ~s of the rainbow* 虹的色彩。*politicians of various ~s* 形形色色的政客。

hue[2] [hjuː; hju] ***n.*** 〔只用于 ~ and cry 短语中〕喊叫声。***a ~ and cry*** **1.** 追捕犯人时的叫声;通缉令。**2.** 大声呼喊;(表示反对的)叫嚷。(*raise a ~ and cry over* [*against*] 对…大喊大叫(表示反对)。*make a ~ and cry* 大嚷大叫起来)。

hueb·ne·rite [ˈhjuːbnərait; ˋhjubnəraɪt] ***n.***【矿】钨锰矿。

hued [hjuːd; hjud] ***a.*** 有某种色调的;有某些种色彩的〔多组成复合词〕。*rosy-~* 玫瑰色的。*dark-~* 黑色的。

huff [hʌf; hʌf] **I** ***vt.*** **1.** 吹胀,提高…的价格。**2.** 吓唬。**3.** 激怒。*~ sb. into silence* 吓得某人不敢讲话。*~ sb. out of the room* 把某人吓出屋外。*~ sb. to pieces* 拼命欺负某人。**—*vi.*** **1.** 吹气,喷气。**2.** 激怒。**3.** 吓唬。**II** ***n.*** 发怒。*in a ~* 怒冲冲地。*get into a ~* 发怒。

huff-duff [ˈhʌfˈdʌf; ˋhʌfˋdʌf] ***n.*** 〔俚〕无线电高频测向仪。

huff·ish [ˈhʌfiʃ; ˋhʌfɪʃ] ***a.*** **1.** 自大的,傲慢的。**2.** 怒冲冲的,不高兴的。**-ly** ***ad.*** **-ness** ***n.***

huff·y [ˈhʌfi; ˋhʌfɪ] ***a.*** (***huff·i·er***; ***-i·est***) = huffish. **huff·i·ly** ***ad.*** **huff·i·ness** ***n.***

hug [hʌg; hʌg] **I** ***vt.*** (**-gg-**) **1.** 紧抱,拥抱,搂抱。**2.** (熊用前腿)抱住。**3.** 抱有,坚持(信仰、偏见等)。**4.** 〔多用反身〕使庆幸,使得意。**5.**【海】靠(海岸)航行;(行人、车辆等)靠近…走。*~ cherished beliefs* 坚持所抱的信念。*The ship was hugging the shore.* 船靠岸航行。***~ oneself on*** [***for***, ***over***] 沾沾自喜,窃喜。**II** ***n.*** **1.** 拥抱。**2.** (熊用前腿的)紧抱。**3.** (摔跤中的)抱住。***give sb. a big ~*** 紧抱住(某人)。**~-me-tight** ***n.*** 〔美〕(女子的)紧身短马甲。

huge [hjuːdʒ; hjudʒ] ***a.*** 巨大的,庞大的,极大的。*a ~ mountain* 大山。***a ~ gate***【美剧】门票的巨大收入。**-ly** ***ad.*** **-ness** ***n.***

huge·ous [ˈhjuːdʒəs; ˋhjudʒəs] ***a.*** 〔谑〕= huge.

hug·ger-mug·ger [ˈhʌgəmʌgə; ˋhʌgɚ͵mʌgɚ] **I** ***n.*** **1.** 混乱。**2.** 〔古〕秘密。**II** ***a.*** **1.** 混乱的。**2.** 秘密的。**III** ***ad.*** **1.** 混乱地。**2.** 秘密地。**IV** ***vt.*** 替…守秘密;压下…不作声张 (*up*)。**—*vi.*** **1.** 胡乱地干。**2.** 秘密行动;密议。

hug·ger·y [ˈhʌgəri; ˋhʌgərɪ] ***n.*** 〔英〕**1.** 律师抢生意的活动。**2.** 高级法院律师要求低级法院律师寄送诉讼事实摘要。

Hug·gins [ˈhʌginz; ˋhʌgɪnz] ***n.*** 哈金斯〔姓氏〕。

Hugh [hjuː; hju] ***n.*** 休〔男子名〕。

Hughes [hjuːz; hjuz] ***n.*** 休斯〔姓氏〕。

Hu·go [ˈhjuːgəu; ˋhjugo] ***n.*** **1.** 雨果〔男子名 Hugh 的异体〕。**2. Victor Mavie ~** 维克多·雨果〔1802—1885,法国小说家,剧作家〕。

Hu·gue·not [ˈhjuːgənɔt; ˋhjugə͵nɑt] ***n.***【史】胡格诺派教徒〔十六、七世纪法国的加尔文派教徒〕。**-ic** ***a.*** **-ism** ***n.*** 胡格诺派的教义。

huh [hʌ; hʌ] ***int.*** 哼! 〔表示轻蔑、吃惊或疑问的感叹词〕。

hui·sa·che [ˈhjuːisɑːtʃi; ˋhjuisɑtʃɪ] ***n.***【植】金合欢 (*Acacia farnesiana*)〔产于德克萨斯和墨西哥〕。

hu·la [ˈhuːlə; ˋhulə], **hu·la-hu·la** [ˈhuːləˈhuːlə; ˋhuləˋhulə] ***n.*** **1.** (波利尼西亚)呼拉圈舞;(夏威夷)草裙舞。**2.** 呼拉圈舞曲,草裙舞曲。**~ hoop** 呼拉圈〔原商标名,一种套在身上游戏用的圈〕。**~ skirt** 草裙。

hulk [hʌlk; hʌlk] **I** ***n.*** **1.** 笨重的大船。**2.** 废船船体;〔*pl.*〕【史】用作监牢等的废船。**3.** 巨大笨重的人[物]。

H

4.(房屋等的)残骸,外壳。II *vi*.〔英方〕1.愈来愈显得巨大(*up*)。2.笨重地移动。**-ing** *a*.庞大的;笨重的。

hulk·y [ˈhʌlki; ˋhʌlkɪ] *a*. =hulking.

Hull[1] [hʌl; hʌl] *n*.赫尔〔姓氏〕。

Hull[2] [hʌl; hʌl] *n*.赫尔〔英国港市〕。

hull[1] [hʌl; hʌl] I *n*.1.(果实等的)外壳;豆荚。2.浆果的花萼。3.薄膜,膜片;被覆物;〔*pl*.〕衣服。II *vt*.脱…的壳,去…的皮。~ **barley** 给大麦去皮。~*ed rice* 糙米。**-er** *n*.脱皮机,脱壳机。

hull[2] [hʌl; hʌl] I *n*.【海】船体,船壳;【空】(水上飞机的)机身;(飞艇的)艇身。~ ***down*** (船)远在只见船桅不见船身的地方;(坦克等)藏在能观察到敌人并能向其射击的隐蔽处。II *vt*.(用鱼雷、炮弹等)打穿(船身)。—*vi*.漂流。

hul·la·ba·loo [ˌhʌləbəˈluː; ˏhʌləbəˋlu] *n*.喧哗,吵闹。***make*** [***raise***] ***a*** ~ 大吵大嚷。

hul·lo(a) [ˈhʌˈləu; ˋhʌˋlo] *int*., *vi*., *vt*. =hello.

hum[1] [hʌm; hʌm] I *vi*.(**-mm-**) 1.(蜜蜂等)嗡嗡叫。2.(在嘴里)咕咕哝哝,磕磕巴巴;哼;哼曲子。3.〔口〕(事业等)变得有生气;忙碌;活跃起来。4.〔俚〕发出恶臭。*My head ~s*.头发昏。—*vt*.1.哼(歌曲)。2.哼歌哄(小孩等)。~ *a child to sleep* 哼着歌哄孩子入睡。~ ***along*** (汽车等)一路发出嗡嗡声前进。~ ***and ha*** [***haw***] (无词可答而)支支吾吾,结结巴巴;〔喻〕踌躇,犹豫。***make things*** ~〔口〕使有活气,使兴旺。II *n*.1.嗡嗡声;哼哼声;嘈杂声。2.〔俚〕恶臭。III *int*.哼!〔表示轻蔑、踌躇、怀疑等〕。

hum[2] [hʌm; hʌm] *n*., *vt*.(**-mm-**)〔口〕欺骗。

hu·man [ˈhjuːmən; ˋhjumən] I *a*.1.人的,人类的(*opp*. divine, animal)。2.凡人皆有的,显示人类特点的。3.有人性的,通人情的。~ *affairs* 人事。*a ~ being* [*creature*] 人。*the ~ race* 人类。*To err is ~*.〔谚〕人皆有过。~ *torpedo* 人控鱼雷。II *n*.〔口、谑〕人;〔the H-〕人类。***less than*** ~ 没人性,不合人道。***more than*** ~ 超人一等。~ **engineering** 1.(特指工业、企业内的)人事管理。2.(专门研究人与机械设备的关系的)人机工程学。~ **equation** 个人倾向;偏见。~ **geography** 人文地理学。~ **nature** 人性。~ **shield** 人(肉)盾(牌)〔以人质或志愿者作为防御袭击使对方投鼠忌器〕。~**ware**【计】人件〔指被视为电脑模拟系统中一个组成部份的人〕。~ **wave** 人潮;(看台上作此起彼伏状的)人浪〔一种啦啦队手法〕;人海战术。**-like** *a*. **-ness** *n*.

hu·mane [hjuːˈmein; hjuˋmen] *a*.1.有人情的,人道的,仁慈的。2.(指学科)高尚的,文雅的。~ *feelings* 慈悲心。*a man of ~ character* 性格温雅的人。~ **killer** 牲口无痛宰杀机。~ **learning** 古典文学。**H- Society** 1.〔英〕拯救溺水者协会。2.慈善协会。3.保护动物协会。~ **studies** 人文学科。**-ly** *ad*. **-ness** *n*.

hu·man·ise [ˈhjuːmənaiz; ˋhjuməˏnaɪz] *vt*., *vi*. =humanize.

hu·man·ism [ˈhjuːmənizəm; ˋhjumənˏɪzəm] *n*.1.人道主义,人本主义,人文主义。2.人文学;〔h- 或 H-〕(文艺复兴期的)古典文学研究。**hu·man·ist** *n*.人性学者;人道主义者,人文主义者,人本主义者;〔h- 或 H-〕(文艺复兴期的)古典文学研究家。**hu·man·is·tic** [ˌhjuːməˈnistik; ˏhjuməˋnɪstɪk] *a*.1.人情的,人性研究的。2.人文学的,人文主义的,人本主义的,人道主义的。

hu·man·i·tar·i·an [hju(ː)ˌmæniˈtɛəriən; hjuˏmænəˋtɛrɪən] I *n*.1.人道主义者。2.慈善家,博爱主义者。II *a*.1.人道主义者的。2.慈善家的;博爱主义者的。**-ism** *n*.1.博爱主义。2.人道主义;人性论。3.【宗】基督凡人论。

hu·man·i·ty [hju(ː)ˈmæniti; hjuˋmænətɪ] *n*.1.人类;(许多)人。2.人性,人情,人道,人性论;〔*pl*.〕人的属性;人类。3.仁爱;博爱;〔*pl*.〕慈善行为。4.文史哲学,人文学。*justice and ~* 仁义。**the humanities** 1.古典文学〔尤指希腊、拉丁文学〕。2.人文学科〔通常包括语言、文学、哲学等〕。

hu·man·ize [ˈhjuːmənaiz; ˋhjuməˏnaɪz] *vt*.1.赋与…人性,使人格化;使适应人体特性。2.使变得博爱仁慈;使通人情。*The milk has been ~d*.这种牛奶业已经过加工,类似人乳。—*vi*.成为人,变得通人情。**hu·man·i·za·tion** *n*.赋与人性,人格化。**-r** *n*.

hu·man·kind [ˈhjuːmənˈkaind; ˋhjumənˏkaɪnd] *n*.人类,人。

hu·man·ly [ˈhjuːmənli; ˋhjumənlɪ] *ad*.1.从人的角度;以人的方法;采用人的手段。2.在人的知识和能力范围内。3.充满人情地。*H- speaking, he cannot recover*.以人力来说,他的病是好不了的。*It is not ~ possible*.这是人力所做不到的[这在人情上是不可能的]。

hu·man·oid [ˈhjuːmənɔid; ˋhjumənɔɪd] I *a*.(形状或举动)近似人的。II *n*.1.类人猿〔尤指无尾猿〕。2.(科学幻想小说中的)星球人。

hu·mate [ˈhjuːmeit; ˋhjumet] *n*.【化】腐植酸盐,腐植酸酯。

hum·ble [ˈhʌmbl; ˋhʌmbl̩] I *a*.1.恭顺的;谦卑的,谦逊的(*opp*. insolent, proud)。2.下贱的(*opp*. noble),(动、植物等)低级的,不值钱的。3.粗陋的;微末的。*a ~ cottage* 寒舍。~ *fare* 粗淡的饮食。*a man of ~ origin* 出身微贱的人。*a ~ occupation* 卑下的职业。***eat ~ pie*** 忍辱含垢,低声下气地道歉。***in my ~ opinion*** 鄙见以为。***your ~ servant*** 〔信末谦恭的自称〕你的恭顺的仆人,晚,职。II *vt*.1.压下(某人的锐气等),使丧失(威信等);贬低。2.使谦卑。~ *sb.'s pride* 压某人的气焰,使某人丢脸。~ *one's enemy* 挫敌人锐气。~ *oneself* 自卑,低声下气。~**bee** *n*.〔英〕=bumblebee. ~ **pie**〔古〕(狩猎后赏给仆从吃的)用鹿内脏做馅的煎饼。~ **plant**【植】含羞草。**-ness** *n*. **hum·bly** *ad*.

Hum·boldt [ˈhʌmbəult; ˋhumbolt] 1. **Baron Friedrich Heinrich Alexander ~ von**, 亚历山大·亨伯特〔1769—1859, 德国博物学家,旅行家及政治家〕。2. **Baron Karl Wilhelm ~ von**, 威廉·亨伯特〔1767—1835, 德国语言学家及外交家,系亚历山大·亨伯特之兄〕。

hum·bug [ˈhʌmbʌg; ˋhʌmˏbʌg] I *n*.1.瞒骗,欺诈。2.谎言,空话,奉承话;用来骗人的东西。3.骗子;吹牛的人。4.〔英〕一种薄荷糖。II *vt*.(**-gg-**) 诈骗,瞒骗。~ *sb. into buying rubbish* 骗人买坏货。~ *sb. out of his money* 诈骗某人钱财。—*vi*.行骗。III *int*.胡说八道! **-ger** *n*.欺骗者,骗子。

hum·bug·ger·y [ˈhʌmbʌgəri; ˋhʌmˏbʌgərɪ] *n*.欺骗,欺诈。

hum·ding·er [hʌmˈdiŋə; ˏhʌmˈdɪŋgɚ] *n*.〔美俚〕非常好的人[物]。

hum·drum [ˈhʌmdrʌm; ˋhʌmˏdrʌm] I *a*.平常的;单调的,无聊的。II *n*.1.单调,无聊。2.无聊的话。3.无聊的人。III *vi*.单调地动作。**-ness** *n*.

Hume [hjuːm; hjum] *n*.1.休姆〔姓氏〕。2. **David** ~ 大卫·休谟〔1711—1776, 苏格兰的史学家,哲学家〕。

hu·mec·tant [hjuːˈmektənt; hjuˋmɛktənt] I *n*.【化】保湿剂〔如甘油〕。II *a*.润湿(剂)的。

hu·mer·al [ˈhjuːmərəl; ˋhjumərəl] I *a*.1.肱骨的,近肱骨的。2.肩的,近肩的。II *n*.(天主教教士做弥撒时用的)披肩(=~ veil)。

hu·me·rus [ˈhjuːmərəs; ˋhjumərəs] *n*.(*pl*. **-ri** [-rai; -raɪ])【解】肱骨。

hu·mic [ˈhjuːmik; ˋhjumɪk] *a*.1.腐植的。2.从腐植质中提取的。~ **acid**【化】腐植酸,黑腐酸。~ **coal**【地】腐植煤。

hu·mid [ˈhjuːmid; ˋhjumɪd] *a*.湿的,湿气重的。**-ly** *ad*. **-ness** *n*.

hu·mid·i·fi·er [hju(ː)ˈmidifaiə; hjuˋmɪdəˏfaɪr] *n*.增湿器,湿润器。

hu·mid·i·fy [hju(:)ˈmidifai; hjuˋmɪdə͵faɪ] *vt*. 使湿润。**hu·mid·i·fi·ca·tion** [hjuːmidifiˈkeiʃən; hju͵mɪudɪfəˋkeʃən] *n*.

hu·mid·i·stat [hjuːˈmidistæt; hjuˋmɪdɪ͵stæt] *n*. 恒湿器,湿度调节器。

hu·mid·i·ty, hu·mid·ness [hju(:)ˈmiditi, -ˈmidnis; hjuˋmɪdətɪ, -ˋmɪdnɪs] *n*. 湿气;【物】湿度。*absolute* ~【物】绝对湿度。*relative* ~【物】相对湿度。

hu·mi·dor [ˈhjuːmidɔː; ˋhjumɪ͵dɔr] *n*. 1. (防止烟草变干的)保润盒;保湿器。2. 装有保湿器的烟草贮藏室。

hu·mi·fy [ˈhjuːmifai; ˋhjumə͵faɪ] *vt*. 使成腐植质。**hu·mi·fi·ca·tion** [ˌhjumifiˈkeiʃən; ͵hjumɪfəˋkeʃən] *n*. **hu·mi·fied** *a*.

hu·mil·i·ate [hju(:)ˈmilieit; hjuˋmɪlɪ͵et] *vt*. 使丢脸,使蒙羞,屈辱,使出丑。*The country was ~d by defeat*. 该国因战败而受辱。~ *oneself* 丢脸,出丑。**hu·mil·i·ating** *a*. 丢脸的,耻辱的,献丑的。**-i·a·tion** [-ˈeiʃən; -ˋeʃən] *n*. 丢脸;蒙羞,屈辱。**hum·il·i·a·tor** *n*. 羞辱者。

hu·mil·i·ty [hju(:)ˈmiliti; hjuˋmɪlətɪ] *n*. 1. 谦恭,谦让。2. [*pl*.]谦让的行为。

HUMINT, hu·mint [ˈhjuːmint; ˋhjumɪnt] = human intelligence 人工情报(指利用间谍搜集情报的业务)。

hu·mi·ture [ˈhjuːmitʃə; ˋhjumɪtʃɚ] *n*. 温湿度[华氏度数与相对湿度之和的一半]。

hum·mel [ˈhʌməl; ˋhʌml] *a*. [Scot.](牛、鹿等)没有角的。

hum·mer [ˈhʌmə; ˋhʌmɚ] *n*. 1. 用鼻哼唱的人;发嗡嗡声的东西。2. = hummingbird. 3. [美俚] = humdinger.

hum·ming [ˈhʌmiŋ; ˋhʌmɪŋ] I *a*. 1. 发嗡嗡声的,哼着唱的。2. [口]忙碌的;活跃的,精力旺盛的;(酒)起泡的;(敲打等)猛烈的。*a ~ knock on the head* 在头上猛敲一下。II *n*. 低唱;哼唱;嗡嗡声,蜂音。~ **bird**【动】蜂鸟,蜂鸟科的鸟。~ **top** 响簧陀螺。

hum·mock [ˈhʌmək; ˋhʌmək] *n*. 1. 小圆丘,圆冈。2. (冰原上的)冰丘;波状地。3. 沼泽中的高地。

hu·mon·gous [hjuːˈmɔŋgəs; hjuˋmɑŋgəs] *a*. 非常庞大的[huge 与 monstrous 之复合语]。

hu·mor [ˈhjuːmə; ˋhjumɚ] [美] = humour.

hu·mor·al [ˈhjuːmərəl; ˋhjumərəl] *a*.【医】体液的。~ *disorders* 体液失调。~ **pathology** 体液病理学。

hu·mor·esque [ˌhjuːməˈresk; ͵hjuməˋrɛsk] *n*.【乐】诙谐曲。

hu·mor·ist [ˈhjuːmərist; ˋhjumərɪst] *n*. [美] = humourist. **-is·tic** *a*.

hu·mor·ous [ˈhjuːmərəs; ˋhjumərəs] *a*. 1. 有幽默感的,诙谐的。2. 可笑的,轻佻的;喜剧的。3. [古]湿性的;体液的。*a ~ writer* 幽默作家。**-ly** *ad*. **-ness** *n*.

hu·mour [ˈhjuːmə; ˋhjumɚ] I *n*. 1. 幽默,诙谐,幽默感。2. 幽默的东西[言词、文章等]。3. (生来的)脾气,性情,气质;(一时的)兴致,心情,情绪。4. (眼球的)玻璃状液体;(旧时生理学所说动物的)体液;(植物的)汁液。5. 古怪的幻想;遐想。5. [*pl*.]有趣的节目。*a sense of ~* 幽默感。*Every man has his ~*. [谚]各人有各人的脾气。*a man of ~* 富有幽默感的人。*a man of sanguine ~* 性情乐观的人。*aqueous* [*vitreous*] ~【解】水样(玻璃状)液。*black ~* 黑色幽默[六十年代美国新兴的一个文学流派]。*dry ~* 绷着脸说的笑话。***in bad ~*** 不高兴。***in good ~*** 高兴。***in no ~ for ...*** 不高兴…,无心…。***in the ~ for*** …高兴…,有意…。***out of ~*** 不高兴。***please sb.'s ~*** 迎合某人。***put sb. in*** [***into***] ***a bad ~*** 使人生气。***the cardinal ~s*** [古]四体液[即 blood, phlegm, choler, melancholy, 据说能决定人的性格]。***when the ~ takes me*** 我高兴的时候。II *vt*. 1. 迎合,迁就,纵容。2. 使自己适应于…;顺着…办;灵活处理[掌握]。*It's not wise to ~ a small child*. 纵容小孩子可不好。*Don't force the lock, you must ~ it*. 别出死力开锁,得试着点儿开。**-ed** *a*. [用于构成复合词]脾气…的。(*good ~ed* 性情好的)。**-ist** *n*. 幽默家,幽默作家;滑稽家,丑角。**-less** *a*. 不幽默的,不滑稽的,无趣味的。**-some** *a*. 幽默滑稽的;古怪的。

hump [hʌmp; hʌmp] I *n*. 1. (驼)峰,(驼子的)驼背,(某些动物背部的)隆肉。2. 小圆丘;[英俚]山脉;海岸凸出部。3.【铁路】驼峰调车场。4. [the H-]驼峰[二次大战时英美飞行员用语,指喜马拉雅山]。5. [英]沮丧,忧郁。6. 危急关头,困难时期,难关。*a camel with two ~s* 双峰骆驼。***get a ~ on*** 1. 赶紧。2. 苦干。***get sb. on the ~*** 使某人大费力气。***get*** [***have***] ***the ~*** 难过。***give sb. the ~*** 使人难过。***hit the ~*** [美俚]越狱;开小差。***live on one's*** (***own***) ~ 自食其力。***on the ~*** 大费精力。***over the ~*** [美俚]工作完成过半,已完成工作中最困难部分;(服苦役等)已渡过一半时间。II *vt*. 1. 使弓起(背);使成驼背。2. [俚]使忧郁。3. [口]使自己努力干[~ oneself]。4. [澳俚]把…背在背上。— *vi*. 1. 隆起。2. 急速移动,飞跑。3. [美俚]努力。~ **back** 1. 驼背,弓背;驼子。2.【动】座头鲸。~ **backed** *a*. 驼背的。

humped [hʌmpt; hʌmpt] *a*. 有隆肉的,驼背的。

humph [hʌmf; hʌmf] I *int*. 哼! [表示怀疑、不满、轻蔑等]。II *vi*. 发"哼"声。III *n*. 哼的一声。

Hum·phr(e)y [ˈhʌmfri; ˋhʌmfrɪ] *n*. 汉弗莱[姓氏,男子名]。

Hump·ty-Dump·ty [ˈhʌmptiˈdʌmpti; ˋhʌmptɪˋdʌmptɪ] *n*. 1. 矮胖子。2. 倒下去就起不来的人;损坏后无法修复的东西。

hump·y[1] [ˈhʌmpi; ˋhʌmpɪ] *a*. 1. 有隆肉的;有驼峰的。2. 隆肉状的;驼峰状的。

hump·y[2] [ˈhʌmpi; ˋhʌmpɪ] *n*. [澳]小棚屋。

hu·mus [ˈhjuːməs; ˋhjuməs] *n*. [L.]腐植质。~ **soil** 腐植土。**-like** *a*.

Humvee, humvee = HMMWV.

Hun., Hung. = Hungarian; Hungary.

Hun [hʌn; hʌn] *n*. 1. 匈奴人,匈奴族。2. [h-][喻]野蛮人,(艺术品等的)任意破坏者。3. [蔑]德国丘八[欧战时用语]。

hunch [hʌntʃ; hʌntʃ] I *n*. 1. 肉峰,隆肉。2. (饼等的)厚片,大块。3. 堆。4. [美口]预感,第六感觉。*have a ~ that ...*, 总觉得…。II *vt*. 1. 弓(背等);使隆起,使成弓状(*up*)。2. 推进。— *vi*. 1. 向前移动。2. 弯成弓状,隆起。~ **back** 驼背;驼子。~ **backed** *a*. 驼背的。

hunch·y [ˈhʌntʃi; ˋhʌntʃɪ] *a*. = humped.

hun·dred [ˈhʌndrəd; ˋhʌndrəd] I *num*. 百,一百个;一百人[物]。*a* [*one*] ~ 一百。*five ~* (*and*) *fifty-four* 五百五十四。*some ~ persons* 约一百人。*two ~* 二百。★伴随数词或数量形容词时复数不加 s;另外, hundred 后有零头时,英语须插用 and,美语常略。II *n*. 1. 一百的记号[100 或 C]。2. [*pl*.]数以百计;许多。3. 一百个一组,一百个人[物]一组。4.【体】百米[码]赛跑;[英]一百镑;[美]一百元;一百岁。5.【英史】郡的分区;[美史]县的分区。*several ~* (*s*) *of persons* 几百人。*nine ~ hours* 上午九点[常写作 0900 hours]。*in nineteen ~* 在一九〇〇年。*in the nineteen ~s* 在二十世纪[即一九〇〇至一九九九年]。*~s of examples* 许多例子。*~s of millions of the working people* 亿万劳动人民。*The old man lived to a ~*. 那位老人活到一百岁。***a cool ~*** [口]百镑巨款;巨款。***a great*** [***long***] ~ 一百二十。***a ~ and one*** 许多(*in a ~ and one ways* 千方百计)。***a*** [***one***] ***~ percent*** 百分之百;全然,完全。***a ~ to one*** 百分之九十九;很有可能地。***by the ~, by ~s*** 数以百计,大批地。***~s and thousands*** 撒在糕饼上做装饰的蜜饯[小糖果]。***~s of*** 好几百,许许多多。***~s of thousands of*** 几十万,无数。***in the ~*** 每百,百分中的。***like a ~ of bricks*** [口]以压倒的势力,来势猛烈地。***ninety-nine out of a ~*** 百分之九十九,几乎全部。

the* (*upper*) *four ～ (美国的)四百家族;名流,上层。**III *a*.** 许多,很多。*I have a* ～ *things to do*. 我有很多事情要做。***not a*** ～ ***miles away*** 〔谑〕离得不怎么远。**H- Days 1.**【法史】(拿破仑再次称帝的)百日天下〔1815年3月20日—6月28日〕。**2.**【美史】(由罗斯福召开的)百日特别国会〔1933年3月9日—6月16日,会上通过多项重要的社会福利法案〕。～**-percent *a*.** 百分之百的;彻底的,十足的。～**-percenter 1.** 极端民族主义分子。**2.** (政治上的)盲从分子;极端分子。～**-percentism** 极端民族主义。～**'s place**【数】百位。**-fold *a*., *ad*., *n*.** 一百倍,一百重。

hun·dredth [ˈhʌndrədθ; ˋhʌndrədθ] ***num*. 1.** 第一百,第一百个,第一百号。**2.** 百分之一。*six* ～*s* 百分之六。**II *a*.** 第一百的,第一百个的。***old H-*** 【宗】《旧约全书》中的《诗篇》第一百篇。

hun·dred·weight [ˈhʌndrədweit; ˋhʌndrədˏwet] ***n*.** 英担〔〔英〕= 112 磅(又叫 long ～);〔美〕= 100 磅(又叫 short～)〕(略 cwt. 或 hwt.)。

hung [hʌŋ; hʌŋ] hang 的过去式及过去分词。

Hung. = Hun.

Hun·gar·i·an [hʌŋˈgɛəriən; hʌŋˋgɛrɪən] **I *a*.** 匈牙利的;匈牙利人的;匈牙利语的。**II *n*. 1.** 匈牙利人。**2.** 匈牙利语。

Hun·ga·ry [ˈhʌŋgəri; ˋhʌŋgərɪ] ***n*.** 匈牙利〔欧洲〕。

hun·ger [ˈhʌŋgə; ˋhʌŋgɚ] **I *n*. 1.** 饥,饥饿。**2.** 食欲。**3.** 渴望,热望 (*for*; *after*)。*H- is the best relish* [*sauce*].〔谚〕饥者易为食。*die from* [*of*] ～饥死。*a* ～ *for learning* 求知欲。～ *after kindness* 渴望得到照顾。**II *vt*.** 使饥饿;使因饥而… (*into*; *out of*)。*try to* ～ *sb*. *into submission* 企图断粮迫使某人屈服。—***vi*. 1.** 饥饿。**2.** 渴望 (*after*; *for*)。～**cure** 饥饿疗法。～ **march** 反饥饿游行。～**marcher** 参加反饥饿游行的人。～ **strike 1. *n*.** 绝食〔尤指狱中的抗议行动〕。**2. *vi*.** 举行绝食抗议,进行绝食斗争。

hun·gri·ly [ˈhʌŋgrili; ˋhʌŋgrəlɪ] ***ad*.** 饥饿似地;渴望地。*go at* [*to*] *it* ～争先恐后地干起来。

hun·gri·ness [ˈhʌŋgrinis; ˋhʌŋgrɪnɪs] ***n*.** 饥饿;渴望;(土地的)贫瘠。

hun·gry [ˈhʌŋgri; ˋhʌŋgrɪ] ***a*. (*-gri·er*; *-gri·est*) 1.** 饥饿的,空腹的;饥饿似的;(工作)引起饥饿的;〔罕〕促进食欲的。**2.** 渴望…的(*for*; *after*)。**3.** (土地)贫瘠的,(土地)不毛的;(年成)饥馑的。**4.** 贫乏的。*be* ～ *for knowledge* 渴望求知。*She was* [*felt*] ～. 她饿了。～ *times* 荒年。*a power-*～ *politician* 有权力欲的政客。*a* ～ *look* 饥色,菜色。***as*** ～ ***as a hawk*** [***hunter*, *wolf***] 非常饥饿。***go*** ～ 挨饿。***the H- Forties***【英史】饥饿的四十年代(1840—1849)。

hunk[1] [hʌŋk; hʌŋk] ***n*.** 〔口〕肉峰;厚片,大片,大块。*a* ～ *of bread and cheese* 一大片干酪面包。～ *of cable* 电缆盘。～*s of iron* 铁块。

hunk[2] [hʌŋk; hʌŋk] ***a*.** = hunky[2].

hunk[3] [hʌŋk; hʌŋk] ***n*.** 〔美俚、贬〕= hunky[1].

hun·ker[1] [ˈhʌŋkə; ˋhʌŋkɚ] ***n*. 1.** 〔H-〕纽约民主党保守派的一员。**2.** 保守派;守旧派。

hun·ker[2] [ˈhʌŋkə; ˋhʌŋkɚ] **I *vi*.** 蹲下。**II *n*.** 〔*pl*.〕臀部,屁股。***on one's*** ～***s*** 蹲下。

hunks [hʌŋks; hʌŋks] ***n*.** (*sing*., *pl*.) 心肠坏的人;贪鄙小人,守财奴,吝啬鬼。

hunk·y[1] [ˈhʌŋki; ˋhʌŋkɪ] ***n*.** (*pl*. ***hunkies***) 〔美俚、贬〕来自中欧或东欧的人〔尤指匈牙利人〕。

hunk·y[2] [ˈhʌŋki; ˋhʌŋkɪ] ***a*.** 〔美俚〕**1.** 很好的,不错的。**2.** 相等的,两相抵消的。**3.** (男子)英俊的,潇洒的。*feel oneself all* ～ 感到已经恢复正常。*get* ～ *with sb*. 同某人不分胜负。

hunk·y-do·ry [ˈhʌŋkiˈdɔːri; ˏhʌŋkɪˋdorɪ] ***a*.** = hunky[2].

Hun·nish [ˈhʌniʃ; ˋhʌnɪʃ] ***a*. 1.** 匈奴的,匈奴似的。**2.** 野蛮的。

Hunt [hʌnt; hʌnt] ***n*.** 亨特〔姓氏〕。

hunt [hʌnt; hʌnt] **I *vt*. 1.** (用狗,马等)追猎,猎取;在…狩猎。**2.** 搜索 (*up*; *out*);追捕,追获。**3.** 驱赶,骚扰,迫害。～ *big game* 猎捕猛兽。～ *ivory* 猎取象牙。～ *the hounds* 用猎犬狩猎。～ *one's horse all winter* 一冬天都骑马狩猎。～ *a county* 在某郡狩猎,搜索某郡的猎物。—***vi*. 1.** 打猎。**2.** (兽类等)猎食。**3.** 探求,搜寻 (*after*; *for*)。**4.**【电】摆动,振荡。**5.** (机器等)不规则地振动。～ *for* [*after*] *a lost book* 找一本丢失的书。～ *high and* ～ *low for sth*. 到处搜寻某物。～ ***and peck*** 看一个键按一个字的打字方法。～ ***counter*** (猎狗)逆着猎物嗅迹追。～ ***down*** 穷追;追捕;搜寻。～ ***for*** [***about***] 追猎;搜寻。～ ***out*** 搜寻出。～ ***up*** 搜索,搜出。**II *n*. 1.** 打猎;打猎队;猎区;猎人会。**2.** 探求,搜索。*a* ～ *ball* 猎人舞会。***be on a*** ～ ***for*** 寻找,找。***have a*** ～ ***for*** 搜求。***still*** ～ 暗中活动。～ **away *n*.** 〔澳〕牧羊犬。～ **box** = ～ing box. ～**-the-slipper** 找拖鞋〔室内游戏〕。

hunt·er [ˈhʌntə; ˋhʌntɚ] ***n*. 1.** 猎人〔英国骑马猎狐兔的人不叫～,叫做 *huntingman*〕;猎狗;猎马;猎食其他动物的野兽。**2.** 〔罕〕探求者,追求者。**3.** (有金属盖保护表面的)猎表,双盖表(= ～ing watch)。***as hungry as a*** ～ 非常饥饿的。～**-gatherer** 采猎者〔指仅仅以采集和渔猎为谋生手段的原始部落人〕。～ **green** 草绿色。～**-killer *a*.** (舰队)为搜寻敌方潜艇而编组的。～**'s moon** 狩猎季节的满月〔即收获季节后的满月〕。

Hunt·er [ˈhʌntə; ˋhʌntɚ] ***n*.** 亨特〔姓氏〕。

hunt·ing [ˈhʌntiŋ; ˋhʌntɪŋ] ***n*. 1.** 打猎,(尤指)狐猎。**2.** 搜索,追寻。**3.**【电】摆动,寄生振荡;(同步电动机的)速度偏差;(自动控制系统的)寻求平衡。*leak* ～【电】泄漏点寻觅,测漏。～ **boot** 猎靴。～ **box** 猎舍。～ **cap** 猎帽。～ **case** 猎用表的表盒。～ **crop** 猎鞭。～ **field**, ～ **ground** 猎场。～ **horn** 猎号。～ **knife** 猎刀。～ **man** 〔英〕猎狐[兔]爱好者。～ **watch** 猎用表。

Hunt·ing·don·shire [ˈhʌntiŋdənʃiə; ˋhʌntɪŋdənʃɪr] ***n*.** 亨廷顿郡〔英国中东部郡名,又名 Huntingdon, Hunts〕.

Hun·ting·ton [ˈhʌntiŋtən; ˋhʌntɪŋtən] ***n*.** 亨廷顿〔姓氏〕。

hunt·ress [ˈhʌntris; ˋhʌntrɪs] ***n*. 1.** 女猎人。**2.** 雌猎马。

hunts·man [ˈhʌntsmən; ˋhʌntsmən] ***n*.** 〔英〕猎人;管猎狗的人。～**-ship *n*.** 打猎术。

hunts·man's-cup [ˈhʌntsmənzˌkʌp; ˋhʌntsmənzˏkʌp] ***n*.** 瓶子草属植物;猪笼草 (= pitcherplant)。

hur·dle [ˈhəːdl; ˋhɝdl̩] **I *n*. 1.** 〔英〕疏篱,树枝编成的篱笆。**2.** 〔*pl*.〕(赛马或赛跑用)栏架,跳栏。**3.**【化】栅格。**4.** 障碍,困难。**5.**【史】(送犯人到刑场的雪橇状)囚笼,囚车。***the high*** [***low***] ～***s***【体】高[低]栏赛跑。**II *vt*. 1.** 用疏篱围住 (*off*)。**2.** 跳过(栏)。**3.** 突破(难关)。—***vi*.** 跳栏;跨越障碍。～ **race** 跳栏赛跑。

hur·dler [ˈhəːdlə; ˋhɝdlɚ] ***n*. 1.** 跳栏运动员。**2.** 编篱笆的人。

hurds [həːdz; hɝdz] ***n*.** 〔*pl*.〕粗亚麻,麻屑,毛屑 (= *hards*)。

hur·dy-gur·dy [ˈhəːdiˈgəːdi; ˋhɝdɪˏgɝdɪ] ***n*.** (*pl*. ***-gurdies***) **1.** 绞弦琴。**2.** 手摇风琴(= barrel organ)。

hurl [həːl; hɝl] **I *n*.** 猛投,猛掷。**II *vt*. 1.** 猛投,猛掷。**2.** 猛推,推翻。**3.** 吐(恶言),激烈地说(出)。～ *threats* [*abuse*] *at sb*. 恶狠狠地威胁[责骂]某人。～ *a spear at* 向(野兽等)投掷标枪。—***vi*. 1.** 猛投,猛掷。**2.** 猛推,猛撞。**3.** 〔美俚〕(垒球中的)投球。～ ***oneself at*** [***upon***] ***the enemy*** 猛攻敌人。～**bat *n*.** (曲棍球的)打球棒。

hurl·er [ˈhəːlə; ˋhɝlɚ] ***n*.** 投掷者;(棒球的)投手。

Hur·ley [ˈhəːli; ˋhɝlɪ] ***n*.** 赫尔利〔姓氏〕。

hurl·ey [ˈhəːli; ˋhɝlɪ] ***n*.** = hurly[1].

hurl·ing [ˈhəːliŋ; ˋhɝlɪŋ] ***n*. 1.** 投掷。**2.** 爱尔兰式棒球。

Hurl·ing·ham [ˈhəːliŋəm; ˋhɝlɪŋəm] ***n*.** 英国马球总会。

hurl·y[1] [ˈhəːli; ˋhɝlɪ] ***n*.** 爱尔兰棒球戏;爱尔兰棒球的球棒。

H

hurl·y²[ˈhəːli; ˋhɚlɪ] ***n*.** 骚乱,喧闹。

hurl·y-burl·y [ˈhəːliˈbəːli; ˋhɚlɪˏbɚlɪ] ***n*.** 骚乱,喧闹。

Hu·ron [ˈhjuərən; ˋhjurən] ***n*.** **1.** (北美易洛魁人中的)休伦族;休伦族人;休伦语。**2.** (北美)休伦湖(= Lake ～)。

Hur·rah, hur·ray [huˈrɑː, huˈrei; huˋrɑ, huˋre] **I *int*.** 万岁! 好哇! *H- for the King*! 国王万岁! **II *n*.** **1.** 欢呼声。**2.** 激动。**3.** 纷争。**III *vi*., *vt*.** (向…)呼万岁,欢呼。**～'s nest** 〔美俚〕大混乱的场所,乱糟糟的东西。

hur·ri·cane [ˈhʌrikən, -kin; ˋhɚɪˏken, -kɪn] ***n*.** **1.** 飓风,十二级风。**2.** 飓风般猛烈的东西;(愤怒或其他感情等的)爆发。**3.** 〔H-〕〔英〕飓风式战斗驱逐机。*a ～ of blows* 一阵猛烈的打击。*a ～ of applause* 暴风雨般的鼓掌。～ **bird** 军舰鸟。～ **deck** 〔美〕(客轮的)最上层甲板,飓风甲板。～ **globe** (灯、烛等的)防风罩。～ **lamp** 防风灯。～ **lantern** 防风灯笼。

hur·ri·coon [ˈhəːrəkuːn; ˋhɚəkun] ***n*.** 侦测飓风汽球。

hur·ried [ˈhʌrid; ˋhɚɪd] ***a*.** 仓促的,慌忙的;草率的。**-ly *ad*. -ness *n*.**

hur·ri·er [ˈhʌriə; ˋhɚɪr] ***n*.** 匆忙的人;催促者。

hur·ry [ˈhʌri; ˋhɚɪ] **I *n*.** **1.** 匆忙;仓促,慌忙。**2.** 〔口〕需要匆忙行动的理由〔用于否定、疑问句中〕。**3.** 混乱,骚动。*Don't go yet — there is no ～.* 别走——不必忙。*Why all this ～?* 为什么这样急匆匆的? *Is there any ～ about it?* 有必要这样匆匆忙忙吗? ***in a ～*** **1.** 匆忙,慌忙。**2.** 急于要;〔口〕愿意地。**3.** 〔口〕容易地,立即(*be in a ～ to leave* 急着要走。*It's not to be understood in a ～.* 这不是一下子就能理解的。*I shall not do it again in a ～.* 我可不乐意再干这事了)。***in no ～*** 不急于…;不愿意;不容易。***no ～*** 不忙,不必着急。***not ... in a ～*** 并不是很快就可…,并不是容易。**II *vt*.** (**-ried**; **-ry·ing**) **1.** 催促,使加快(*up*; *on*; *along*; *away*; *into*; *out*)。**2.** 急派,急忙运去;匆忙移开,匆忙拿走。*He refused to be hurried.* 他不要人催。*soldiers hurried to the front* 急运前线的部队。**—*vi*.** 赶急,赶快,仓促。～ ***along*** 赶快走。～ **away** [**off**] 匆匆离去;使赶快去。～ ***back*** 赶紧折回。～ ***on*** (*with*) 赶紧办理。～ ***over*** 赶快办完。～ ***through*** 匆匆赶完。～ ***up*** 催促,赶紧;赶快,快点(*H- up! You will be late.* 赶快! 你要来不及了。*～-up wagon* 急修车,抢险车)。**～-scurry, ～-skurry** [ˈhʌriˈskʌri; ˋhɚɪˋskʌrɪ] **1.** ***ad*.**, ***a*.** 慌慌张张。**2.** ***n*.** 急躁,慌张。**3.** ***vi*.** 慌忙乱窜,手忙脚乱地干。

Hurst [həːst; hɚst] ***n*.** 赫斯特〔姓氏〕。

hurst [həːst; hɚst] ***n*.** **1.** (海、河的)沙岸。**2.** 有树林的山岗;树林,小丘。

hurt [həːt; hɚt] **I *vt*.** (**hurt**) **1.** 伤害,刺痛。**2.** 使痛心,使伤感情,使不快。**3.** 损害,危害。*Another glass won't ～ you.* 再喝一杯也无妨。*a ～ book* 一本受到损坏的书。*She ～ my feelings.* 她伤了我的感情。**—*vi*.** **1.** 惹起痛苦;伤害,伤痛。**2.** 危害,有害。**3.** 〔方〕需要。*My leg still ～s.* 我的脚还在痛呢。*My shoe is too tight; it ～s.* 我的鞋太紧了,挤脚痛。***feel ～*** 感觉不快。***～ oneself = get ～*** 受伤,负伤。**II *n*.** 伤害;(精神的)苦痛。***do ～ to*** 伤害,损害。

hurt·ful [ˈhəːtful; ˋhɚtfʊl] ***a*.** 有害的,造成伤痛的(*to*)。**-ly *ad*. -ness *n*.**

hur·tle [ˈhəːtl; ˋhɚtl] **I *vi*.** **1.** 猛烈碰撞;发出碰撞声。**2.** 猛烈飞出去,嘘一声射出去。**—*vt*.** **1.** 猛掷,猛射。**2.** 〔古〕猛烈碰撞,使猛烈冲击。～ ***at*** 嘘一声射向;向…猛烈冲击。**II *n*.** 碰撞;碰撞声。

hur·tle·ber·ry [ˈhəːtlberi; ˋhɚtlbɛrɪ] ***n*.** (*pl*. **-ries**) **1.** 越橘,欧洲越橘树;笃斯越橘树;欧洲越橘子;笃斯越橘子(whortleberry)。**2.** = huckleberry.

hurt·less [ˈhəːtlis; ˋhɚtlɪs] ***a*.** 〔古〕无害的;未受伤的。

hus·band [ˈhʌzbənd; ˋhʌzbənd] **I *n*.** **1.** 丈夫(*opp*. wife)。**2.** 〔英〕管家。**3.** 〔古〕节俭的管理人。**4.** 船舶管理人(= ship's ～)。**～'s tea** 〔谑〕丈夫泡的茶〔又淡又冷〕。**II *vt*.** **1.** 节俭地使用[经营]。**2.** 〔古〕耕(地),栽培(植物)。**3.** 〔诗、谑〕使有丈夫;〔罕〕做…的丈夫。**-age** 【海】船舶管理费〔商船船主付与其商务代表的酬金〕。**～-man** 〔古〕庄稼人。**-like *a*.** 善于管理农活的。**-ly *a*.** **1.** 节俭的。**2.** 农夫的,耕作的。**3.** 丈夫的,丈夫般的。

hus·band·ry [ˈhʌzbəndri; ˋhʌzbəndrɪ] ***n*.** **1.** 农业,耕作。**2.** 〔古〕家政;节俭,节约。*animal ～* 畜牧业。*bad ～* 不会当家。*good ～* 会当家。

hush [ʃiː, hʌʃ; hʌʃ] **I *int*.** 嘘! 别响! **II** [hʌʃ; hʌʃ] ***n*.** **1.** 静寂;沉默。**2.** 秘而不宣。*in the ～ of deep night* 深夜静悄悄。**III *vt*.** **1.** 使静下来,使沉默。**2.** 压下…不声张,掩盖。*～ her fears* 使她安静下来不再害怕。*～ the scandal up* 把丑事掩盖住不声张。**—*vi*.** **1.** 静下来,沉默。**2.** 秘而不宣。～ ***up*** 掩盖,秘而不宣。***H- up!*** 别作声! **～boat, ～ ship** 伪装军舰。～ **kit** (用以降低喷气式飞机发动机噪音的)飞机用消音器。～ **money** 封住嘴的贿赂。

hush·a·by [ˈhʌʃəbai; ˋhʌʃəˏbaɪ] **I *int*.** 乖乖睡! **II *vt*.** 哼摇篮曲哄(小儿入睡)。

hush-hush [ˈhʌʃˈhʌʃ; ˋhʌʃˏhʌʃ] **I *a*.** 〔俚〕秘密的,秘而不宣的。*a ～ report* 秘密报告。**II *n*.** 秘密气氛,(政治、战略等方面的)机密。**III *vt*.** 勒令秘而不宣,禁止声张,封锁(新闻)。

husk [hʌsk; hʌsk] **I *n*.** **1.** 外皮,壳,荚;〔美〕玉米包皮;茧衣。**2.** (无用的)外皮,无价值的部分。**3.** 支架。**4.** 牛瘟。**II *vt*.** **1.** 剥去…的外皮,去…的荚。**2.** 用粗嗄声讲(话)。**—*vi*.** 声音变嗄。

husk·ing [ˈhʌskiŋ; ˋhʌskɪŋ] ***n*.** **1.** 〔美〕剥玉米包皮。**2.** 〔美〕农家碾米会〔指邻舍、亲友边碾米边聊天的聚会,又叫 ～-bee〕。*a rice ～ machine* 碾米机。

husk-to·ma·to [ˈhʌsktəˈmɑːtəu; ˋhʌsktəˋmɑto] ***n*.** (*pl*. **-toes**) = groundcherry.

husk·y [ˈhʌski; ˋhʌskɪ] **I *a*.** **1.** 壳的,壳似的;壳多的。**2.** (嗓音)嘎声的,干哑的。**3.** 〔俚〕粗鲁的;结实的,强健的。**II *n*.** 〔口〕强壮结实的人。**-i·ly *ad*. -ness *n*.**

Hus·ky [ˈhʌski; ˋhʌskɪ] ***n*.** **1.** 爱斯基摩人,爱斯基摩语。**2.** 〔h-〕爱斯基摩狗。

hus·sar [huˈzɑː; huˋzɑr] ***n*.** **1.** 轻骑兵。**2.** 十五世纪的匈牙利轻骑兵,轻骑兵〔以制服华丽著称〕。

hus·sif [ˈhʌzif; ˋhʌzɪf] ***n*.** 针线盒(= housewife²)。

Huss·ite [ˈhʌsait; ˋhʌsaɪt] ***n*.** (十五世纪捷克爱国者及宗教改革家)胡斯〔John Huss (1369—1415)〕的拥护者。胡斯运动派成员。**Huss·it·ism *n*.** 胡斯运动;胡斯主义。

hus·sy [ˈhʌsi, ˈhʌzi; ˋhʌsɪ, ˋhʌzɪ] ***n*.** **1.** 轻佻的女子,荡妇。**2.** 鲁莽的女子。

hus·tings [ˈhʌstiŋz; ˋhʌstɪŋz] ***n*.** (*sing*., *pl*.) **1.** 【英史】(1872 年以前)候选人在国会发表竞选演说的讲坛;竞选讲坛。**2.** 选举手续。**3.** 〔英〕地方法院。

hus·tle [ˈhʌsl; ˋhʌsl] **I *vt*.** **1.** 硬挤,乱推,挤进(*into*),挤出(*out of*)。**2.** 硬逼,逼使(*into*)。**3.** 〔口〕使匆匆做成。**4.** 强夺;欺骗。**5.** 强卖;在(某地)竭力推销。*～ sb. into doing sth.* 强使某人作某事。*～ sth. out of the way* 排除障碍物。**—*vi*.** **1.** 乱挤,乱推,挤过去;奔忙。**2.** 〔口〕努力快做。**3.** 骗钱;诱赌;(妓女)拉客。**II *n*.** **1.** 挤;推。**2.** 努力。**3.** 设骗局。***Get a ～ on!*** 快干! 使劲干。

hus·tler [ˈhʌslə; ˋhʌslɚ] ***n*.** **1.** 乱挤乱推者〔尤指扒手同伙〕。**2.** (非法买卖等的)好手;骗子;妓女。**3.** 能干人。

hut [hʌt; hʌt] **I *n*.** **1.** 小屋,茅舍,棚屋。**2.** 【军】临时营房。**3.** 〔美俚〕牢房。**II *vt*., *vi*.** (**-tt-**) (使)住临时营房[小屋]。

hutch [hʌtʃ; hʌtʃ] **I *n*.** **1.** (盛物)箱;橱;碗架。**2.** (动物、家禽的)笼,舍;兔箱。**3.** 〔美方〕(渔夫的)小棚屋。**4.** 【矿】铁车;洗矿槽;跳汰机筛下室;沉积槽底的矿砂。**II *vt*.** **1.** 把…装在箱内。**2.** 【矿】用洗矿槽洗。

hut·ment [ˈhʌtmənt; ˋhʌtmənt] ***n*.** **1.** 【军】设营。**2.** 临

时营房。3. 住临时营房。

Hutt [hʌt; hʌt] ***n***. 赫特〔姓氏〕。

hüt·te [ˈhjutə; ˋhjʊtə] ***n***. 〔G.〕小舍,临时小屋。

hutz·pah [ˈhuːtspə, -pɑː; ˋhutspə, -pɑ] ***n***. = chutzpah.

Hux·ley [ˈhʌksli; ˋhʌksl̩ɪ] ***n***. 1. 赫克斯利〔姓氏〕。2. **Thomas Henry** ~ 汤姆斯·亨利·赫胥黎〔1825—1895,英国生物学家〕。3. **Andrew Fielding** ~ 安德鲁·菲尔丁·赫克斯利〔1918— 英国生理学家。1963 年与 A. L. Hodgkin 和 Sir J. C. Eccles 合得诺贝尔医学奖〕。

huz·za, huz·zah [huˈzɑː; hʊˋzɑ] ***int***., ***n***., ***vi***., ***vt***. = hurrah.

H.V. = high voltage.

hv = heavy.

HVAR = high velocity aircraft rocket 机载高速火箭。

HW = Handford Works 汉福特原子厂。

HWL = 【纺】heat-fast, water-fast, light-fast 耐烫,耐洗,耐晒。

H. W. (M.), HWM, h. w. (m.) = high-water (mark) 高水位线,高潮线。

hwt. = hundredweight (又略作 cwt.).

hwy. = highway.

Hy. = Henry.

hy·a·cinth [ˈhaiəsinθ; ˋhaɪəˏsɪnθ] ***n***. 1.【植】风信子。2. 紫蓝色。3.【矿】红锆石。

hy·a·cin·thine [ˌhaiəˈsinθain; ˏhaɪəˋsɪnθaɪn] ***a***. 1. 似风信子的。2. 紫蓝色的。3. 楚楚可怜的,美丽的。

Hy·a·des, Hy·ads [ˈhaiədiːz, ˋhaiədz; ˋhaɪəˏdiz, ˋhaɪədz] ***n***. 〔*pl*.〕【天】(金牛宫中的)毕(宿)星团。

hy·ae·na [haiˈiːnə; haɪˋinə] ***n***. = hyena.

hy·a·line [ˈhaiəlin; ˋhaɪəlɪn] I ***a***. 1. 玻璃的。2. 〔诗〕透明的,玻璃[水晶]一样的。II ***n***. 1. 透明物;〔诗〕碧空,镜面一样的海。2.【生化】玻黏糖;【解】玻璃质。~ **cartilage**【解】透明软骨。~ **membrane disease** 透明膜(毛根)病。

hy·a·lite [ˈhaiəlait; ˋhaɪəˏlaɪt] ***n***.【矿】玻璃蛋白石。

hy·al(o)- *comb*. *f*. 表示"玻璃(状)的","透明的"〔元音前用 hyal-〕: *hyal*ite, *hyalo*plasm.

hy·a·loid [ˈhaiəlɔid; ˋhaɪəˏlɔɪd] ***a***. 透明的,玻璃状的。~ **membrane**【解】玻璃状体膜。

hy·a·lo·plasm [ˈhaiələˌplæzəm; ˋhaɪələplæzm̩] ***n***.【生】透明质,胞基质。

hy·al·u·ron·ic [ˌhaiəljuˈrɔnik; ˏhaɪəlʊˋrɑnɪk] ***a***. ~ **acid**【生化】玻黏胺糖酸。

hy·al·u·ron·i·dase [ˌhaiəljuˈrɔnideis; ˏhaɪəlʊˋrɑnədes] ***n***.【生化】玻黏胺糖酸酶。

hy·brid [ˈhaibrid; ˋhaɪbrɪd] I ***n***. 1.【生】杂种,杂交种;混血儿。2. (由两种来源的东西组成的)混合物;受过两种不同文化传统教育的人;混合词。3.【化】混成体。4.【无】混合波导联结;等差作用;桥结岔路。II ***a***. 杂种的;混合的;混合语的。*a* ~ *animal* 杂种动物。~ **car**(既有电池发动机又有汽油发动机的)双动力汽车。~ **chip**【计】混合芯片〔指硅基片上涂有一层超导材料的晶片〕。~ **computer** (模拟、数字)混合型计算机。~ **parameter**【数】杂系参数。~ **type**【无】混合型,桥接岔路型,差动式。~ **vigo(u)r**【生】杂种优势。**-ism** ***n***. 1. 杂种,混血,杂交(现象)。2. 混合性,杂种性,混杂作用。

hy·brid·ist [ˈhaibridist; ˋhaɪbrɪdɪst] ***n***. 杂种繁殖者。

hy·brid·i·ty [haiˈbriditi; haɪˋbrɪdətɪ] ***n***. 杂种性。

hy·brid·ize [ˈhaibridaiz; ˋhaɪbrɪdˏaɪz] ***vi***., ***vt***. (使)产生杂种,(使)杂交;(使)混成。**hy·brid·iz·a·ble** ***a***. 能产生杂种的;能杂混的。**hy·brid·iza·tion** ***n***.

hy·bris [ˈhaibris; ˋhaɪbrɪs] ***n***. = hubris.

hyd. = 1. hydraulics. 2. hydrostatics.

hy·da·thode [ˈhaidəθəud; ˋhaɪdəθod] ***n***.【植】排水器〔表皮水分排泄的器官〕。

hy·da·tid [ˈhaidətid; ˋhaɪdətɪd] ***n***.【医】包虫囊。

Hyde [haid; haɪd] ***n***. 海德〔姓氏〕。

Hyde Park [ˈhaidˈpɑːk; ˋhaɪdˋpɑrk] (伦敦的)海德公园。*a* ~ *orator* 街头演说家。

Hy·der·a·bad [ˈhaidərəbɑːd; ˋhaɪdərəˏbæd] ***n***. 海得拉巴〔印度、巴基斯坦的两个同名城市〕。

hydr- *comb*. *f*. 〔用于母音或以 h 开始的词前〕= hydro-.

hydr. = hydraulics.

hy·dra [ˈhaidrə; ˋhaɪdrə] ***n***. (*pl*. ~*s*, ***-drae*** [-driː; -ˋdri]) 1. 〔H-〕【希神】九头蛇〔斩去一头会生出二头〕。2. 难以一下根绝的祸害;大患,不断产生困难的问题。3.【动】水螅,水蛇。4. 〔H-〕【天】长蛇座。~**-headed a.** 1. 多头的,多分支的,多中心的。2. 难根绝的;困难重重的。

hy·drac·id [haiˈdræsid; haɪˋdræsɪd] ***n***.【化】含氢酸。

hy·dra·go·gue [ˈhaidrəgɔg; ˋhaɪdrəˏgɔg] I ***n***.【药】利尿剂,水泻剂。II ***a***. 利尿的,驱水的。

hy·dran·ge·a [haiˈdreindʒiə; haɪˋdrendʒɪə] ***n***. 绣球花属(即八仙花属)的一种植物。

hy·drant [ˈhaidrənt; ˋhaɪdrənt] ***n***. 消防龙头;配水龙头,给水栓,取水管。

hy·dranth [ˈhaidrænθ; ˋhaɪdrænθ] ***n***.【动】水螅体。

hy·drar·gy·rism [haiˈdrɑːdʒirizəm; haɪˋdrɑrdʒərɪzəm] ***n***.【医】汞中毒。

hy·drar·gy·rum [haiˈdrɑːdʒirəm; haɪˋdrɑrdʒərəm] ***n***.【化】汞。

hy·drar·thro·sis [ˌhaidrɑːˈθrəusis; ˏhaɪdrɑrˋθrosɪs] ***n***.【医】关节积水。

hy·drase [ˈhaidreis; ˋhaɪdres] ***n***.【生化】水化酶。

hy·dras·tine [haiˈdræstiːn, -tin; haɪˋdræstin, -tɪn] ***n***.【化】白毛茛碱,(北美)黄连碱。

hy·dras·tis [haiˈdræstis; haɪˋdræstɪs] ***n***.【植】白毛茛。

hy·drate [ˈhaidreit; ˋhaɪdret] I ***n***.【化】水合物。~ *cellulose* 水合纤维素。II ***vt***., ***vi***. (使)成水合物;(使)水合。

hy·drat·ed [ˈhaidreitid; ˋhaɪdretɪd] ***a***.【化】含水的。~ **alumina** 氢氧化铝。

hy·dra·tion [haiˈdreiʃən; haɪˋdreʃən] ***n***.【化】水合(作用)。~ **heat** 水合热。~ **water** 结合水。

hydraul. = hydraulic(s).

hy·drau·lic [haiˈdrɔːlik; haɪˋdrɔlɪk] ***a***. 1. 水力的,液力的;用水发动的。2. 液压的,水压的。3. 水力学的。4.【建】水硬的。~ **bollard** 液压式自动升降隔离桩〔指可阻隔住汽车并可自动升降的交通隔离桩〕。~ **brake** 液压制动机,水力闸;闸式水力测功器。~ **cement** 水硬水泥。~ **crane** 水力起重机。~ **drop** 水力落差。~ **engine** 水力机,水压机,水力发动机。~ **engineering** 水利工程。~ **lift** 水力起重机。~ **lime** 水硬石灰。~ **motor** 水力电动机。~ **press** 水压机。~ **power plant** 水电厂。~ **pump** 水力泵。~ **ram** 水力夯锤,压力扬汲机。~ **test** 水压试验。~ **transport** 1. 水力运输。2. 液压输送。**-li·cal·ly** ***ad***.

hy·drau·li·cian [ˌhaidrɔːˈliʃən; ˏhaɪdrɔˋlɪʃən] ***n***. 水力学家。

hy·drau·lics [haiˈdrɔːliks; haɪˋdrɔlɪks] ***n***. 水力学。

hy·dra·zide [ˈhaidrəzaid; ˋhaɪdrəˏzaɪd] ***n***.【化】醯肼,酰肼。

hy·dra·zine [ˈhaidrəziːn, -zin; ˋhaɪdrəˏzin, -zɪn] ***n***.【化】肼;联氨。

hy·dra·zo·ate [ˌhaidrəˈzəueit; ˏhaɪdrəˋzoet] ***n***.【化】叠氮化物。

hy·dri·a [ˈhaidriə; ˋhaɪdrɪə] ***n***. (*pl*. ***-ae*** [-iː; -i]) 古希腊、古罗马的水罐。

hy·dric [ˈhaidrik; ˋhaɪdrɪk] ***a***.【化】(含)氢的。

-hydric *comb*. *f*. 表示"含酸式氢","含羟基": mono*hydric*.

hy·dride [ˈhaidraid; ˋhaɪdraɪd], **hy·drid** [-rid; -rɪd] ***n***.【化】氢化物。

hy·dro [ˈhaidrəu; ˋhaɪdro] I ***n***. 1. 〔口〕水上飞机(= hydroplane)。2. 〔英俚〕水疗处,接待水疗病人的旅馆(=

hydropathic establishment)。3.〔美口〕水力电;水力发电厂。II *a*. = hydroelectric.

hy·dro- *comb. f*. 表示"水","氢化的","氢的"; *hydro*dynamic, *hydro*carbon.

hy·dro·a·cous·tic [ˈhaidrəuəˈkuːstik; ˏhaɪdroəˋkustɪk] *a*. 液压声能的;水底传音的。

hy·dro·ae·ro·plane [ˈhaidrəuˈɛərəplein; ˏhaɪdrəˋɛrəplen] *n*. = hydroairplane.

hy·dro·air·plane [ˈhaidrəuˈɛəplein; ˏhaɪdrəˋɛrplen] *n*. 水上飞机。

hy·dro·bi·ol·o·gy [ˈhaidrəubaiˈɔlədʒi; ˏhaɪdrəbaɪˋɑlədʒɪ] *n*. 流体生物学。

hy·dro·bomb [ˈhaidrəuˈbɔm; ˋhaɪdrəˏbɑm] *n*. 空投水雷。

hy·dro·bro·mic [ˈhaidrəuˈbrəumik; ˏhaɪdrəˋbromɪk] *a*. ~ **acid**【化】氢溴酸,溴化氢。

hy·dro·car·bon [ˈhaidrəuˈkɑːbən; ˏhaɪdroˋkɑrbən] *n*. 碳氢化合物,烃。

hy·dro·ceph·a·lous, hy·dro·ce·phalic [ˈhaidrəuˈsefələs, ˈhaidrəusiˈfælik; ˏhaɪdrəˋsɛfələs, haɪdrəsɪˋfælɪk] *a*.【医】脑积水的。

hy·dro·ceph·alus [ˈhaidrəuˈsefələs; ˏhaɪdrəˋsɛfələs] *n*.【医】脑积水,水脑。

hy·dro·chlo·ric [ˈhaidrəuˈklɔrik; ˏhaɪdrəˋklorɪk] *a*.【化】氯化氢的。~ **acid** 盐酸,氢氯酸。

hy·dro·chlo·ride [ˈhaidrəuˈklɔraid; ˏhaɪdrəˋkloraɪd] *n*.【化】氢氯化物,盐酸化物,盐酸盐。

hy·dro·cli·mate [ˈhaidrəuˈklaimit; ˏhaɪdrəˋklaɪmɪt] *n*. 水中生物的物理及化学环境〔如水温、酸度等〕。

hy·dro·corti·sone [ˈhaidrəuˈkɔːtisəun; ˏhaɪdroˋkɔrtɪson] *n*.【生化】皮质醇;【药】氢化可的松(= cortisol)。

hy·dro·crack [ˈhaidrəukræk; ˋhaɪdrəˏkræk] *vt*.【化】加氢裂化,氢化裂解。**-er** 氢化裂解器。

hy·dro·cy·an·ic [ˈhaidrəusaiˈænik; ˏhaɪdrosaɪˋænɪk] *a*.【化】氰化氢的。~ **acid** 氢氰酸。

hy·dro·drill [ˈhaidrəudril; ˋhaɪdrodrɪl] **I** *n*. (植物)根部浇注器。**II** *vt*. 用根部浇注器浇注。

hy·dro·dy·nam·ic [ˈhaidrəudaiˈnæmik; ˏhaɪdrodaɪˋnæmɪk] *a*. 1. 水力的;水压的。2. 流体动力学的。

hy·dro·dy·nam·ics [ˈhaidrəudaiˈnæmiks; ˏhaɪdrodaɪˋnæmɪks] *n*. *pl*. 〔用作单数〕流体动力学。

hy·dro·e·lec·tric [ˈhaidrəu-iˈlektrik; ˏhaɪdro-ˋlɛktrɪk] *a*. 水力发电的。*a* ~ *power station* 水力发电站。**-tric·i·ty** *n*.

hy·dro·ex·trac·tor [ˈhaidrəu-iksˈtræktə; ˏhaɪdro-ɪksˋtræktɚ] *n*. 脱水机。

hy·dro·flu·or·ic [ˈhaidrəuflu(ː)ˈɔrik; ˏhaɪdrofluˋɑrɪk] *a*.【化】氟化氢的。~ **acid** 氢氟酸。

hy·dro·foil [ˈhaidrəufɔil; ˋhaɪdroˏfɔɪl] *n*. 1. (水翼船上的)翼。2. 水翼船。

hy·dro·form·ing [ˈhaidrəufɔːmiŋ; ˋhaɪdroˏfɔrmɪŋ] *n*.【化】加氢重整。

hy·dro·gel [ˈhaidrədʒel; ˋhaɪdrədʒɛl] *n*.【化】水凝胶。

hy·dro·gen [ˈhaidridʒən; ˋhaɪdrədʒən] *n*.【化】氢。~ **bomb** 氢弹。~ **bond**【化】氢键。~ **ion**【化】氢离子。~ **oxide** 氧化氢,水。~ **peroxide** 过氧化氢。~ **sulphide** 硫化氢。

hy·dro·gen·ate, hy·dro·gen·ize [haiˈdrɔdʒineit, -naiz; haɪˋdrɑdʒənˏet, -nˏaɪz] *vt*.【化】使氢化,使与氢化合,使还原。**hy·dro·gen·a·tion, hy·dro·gen·i·za·tion** *n*. 加氢(作用)。

hy·dro·gen·i·um [ˌhaidrəuˈdʒiːniəm; ˏhaɪdrəˋdʒɪnɪəm] *n*. 〔化〕金属氢。

hy·dro·gen·ol·y·sis [ˌhaidrəudʒəˈnɔləsis; ˏhaɪdrədʒəˋnɑləsɪs] *n*.【化】氢解作用。

hy·drog·e·nous [haiˈdrɔdʒinəs; haɪˋdrɑdʒɪnəs] *a*.【化】氢的,含氢的。

hy·dro·graph [ˈhaidrəgræf; ˋhaɪdrəˏgræf] *n*. 1. 自记水位计,流量速度计算仪。2. 水文图,水文曲线。

hy·drog·ra·pher [haiˈdrɔgrəfə; haɪˋdrɑˏgrəfɚ] *n*. 水文学家,水文地理学家。

hy·drog·ra·phy [haiˈdrɔgrəfi; haɪˋdrɑgrəfɪ] *n*. 1. 水文学,水文地理学。2. 水道图;水道测量术。**-pher** *n*. 水文学家,水文地理学家。**-phic(al)** *a*. 水路的;水道测量术的。**-phi·cal·y** *ad*.

hy·droid [ˈhaidrɔid; ˋhaɪdrɔɪd] **I** *n*.【动】螅体。**II** *a*. 螅体的,螅状的。

hy·dro·ki·net·ics [ˈhaidrəukaiˈnetiks; haɪdrəkɪˋnɛtɪks] *n*. 流体动力学。

hy·dro·lant [ˈhaidrəlænt; ˋhaɪdrəˏlænt] *n*. (美海军航路局发出的)大西洋航行险情紧急警报。

hy·drol·o·gy [haiˈdrɔlədʒi; haɪˋdrɑlədʒɪ] *n*. 水文学,水理学。

hy·drol·y·sate [haiˈdrɔliseit, -zeit; haɪˋdrɑlɪˏset, -zet] *n*.【化】水解产物(= hydrolyzate)。

hy·drol·y·sis [haiˈdrɔlisis; haɪˋdrɑlɪsɪs] *n*.【化】水解(作用)。

hy·dro·lyte [ˈhaidrəlait; ˋhaɪdrəˏlaɪt] *n*.【化】水解质。

hy·dro·lyt·ic [ˌhaidrəˈlitik; ˏhaɪdrəˋlɪtɪk] *a*.【化】水解的。

hy·dro·lyze [ˈhaidrəlaiz; ˋhaɪdrəˏlaɪz] *vt*., *vi*. (*-lyzed*; *-lyz·ing*) 水解,进行水解。**hy·dro·lyz·a·ble** *a*.

hy·dro·mag·net·ics [ˌhaidrəumægˈnetiks; ˏhaɪdrəmægˋnɛtɪks] *n*. *pl*. 〔作单数用〕磁流体动力学(= magnetohydrodynamics)。**hy·dro·mag·net·ic** *a*.

hy·dro·man [ˈhaidrəmæn; ˋhaɪdrəˏmæn] *n*. 液压操作器,水力控制器。

hy·dro·man·cy [ˈhaidrəumænsi; ˋhaɪdrəˏmænsɪ] *n*. 水卜〔一种以水进行占卜的迷信活动〕。**hy·dro·man·cer** [-sə; -sɚ] *n*. 用水占卜的术士。

hy·dro·ma·ni·a [ˈhaidrəuˈmeinjə; ˋhaɪdrəˋmenɪə] *n*.【医】投水狂,自溺狂。

hy·dro·me·chan·ics [ˈhaidrəumiˈkæniks; ˏhaɪdromɪˋkænɪks] *n*. 流体力学。

hy·dro·me·du·sa [ˈhaidrəumiˈdjuːsə, -ˈduː-; -zə; ˏhaɪdromɪˋdjusə, -ˋdu-; -zə] *n*. (*pl*. *-sae* [-siː; -si]) 水螅水母类。

hy·dro·mel [ˈhaidrəməl; ˋhaɪdrəməl] *n*. 蜂蜜酒〔蜂蜜加水发酵后制成〕。

hy·dro·met·al·lur·gy [ˌhaidrəuˈmetlədʒi; ˏhaɪdrəˋmɛtl̩ɚdʒɪ] *n*. 湿法冶金学[术]。

hy·dro·me·te·or [ˌhaidrəuˈmiːtiə; ˏhaɪdrəˋmitɪɚ] *n*.【气】水汽凝结体。

hy·drom·e·ter [haiˈdrɔmitə; haɪˋdrɑmətɚ] *n*. 液体比重计。

hy·dro·met·ric(al) [ˌhaidrəuˈmetrik(əl); ˏhaɪdrəˋmɛtrɪk(l̩)] *a*. (液体)比重计的;测定比重的。

hy·drom·e·try [haiˈdrɔmitri; haɪˋdrɑmətrɪ] *n*. 液体比重测定(法)。

hy·dro·mor·phic [ˌhaidrəuˈmɔːfik; ˏhaɪdrəˋmɔrfɪk] *a*.【植】具有适于水生的结构特性的。

hy·dro·mo·tor [ˈhaidrəuˈməutə; ˋhaɪdrəˋmotɚ] *n*. 射水发动机,液压马达,油马达。

hy·dro·naut [ˈhaidrəunɔːt; ˋhaɪdrənɔt] *n*.【美海军】深潜器驾驶员。

hy·dro·naut·ics [ˌhaidrəuˈnɔːtiks; ˏhaɪdrəˋnɔtɪks] *n*. 海洋工程学。

hy·dro·ne·phro·sis [ˌhaidrəuniˈfrəusis; ˏhaɪdrənɪˋfrosɪs] *n*.【医】肾盂积水膨出。

hy·dro·ni·um [haiˈdrəuniəm; haɪˋdronɪəm] *n*.【化】水合氢离子(= ~ ion)。

hy·dro·pac [ˈhaidrəpæk; ˋhaɪdrəˏpæk] *n*. (美海军航

路局发出的)太平洋航行险情紧急警报。

hy·dro·path·ic [ˌhaidrəuˈpæθik; ˏhaɪdrəˋpæθɪk] **I** *a*. 水疗法的。*a* ~ *establishment* 水疗处,水疗旅馆。~ *treatment* 水疗法。**II** *n*. 〔口〕水疗处,水疗旅馆。

hy·drop·a·thist [haiˈdrɔpəθist; haɪˋdrɑpəθɪst] *n*. 水疗医生。

hy·drop·a·thy [haiˈdrɔpəθi; haɪˋdrɑpəθɪ] *n*. 【医】水疗法。

hy·dro·phane [ˈhaidrəufein; ˋhaɪdrəˏfen] *n*. 【地】水蛋白石。**hydroph·a·nous** [haiˈdrɔfənəs; haɪˋdrɑfənəs] *a*.

hy·dro·phile [ˈhaidrəufail; ˋhaɪdrəˏfaɪl] *n*. 亲水(性)。

hy·dro·phil·ic [ˌhaidrəuˈfilik; ˏhaɪdrəˋfɪlɪk] *a*. 【化】亲水的。

hy·droph·i·lous [haiˈdrɔfiləs; haɪˋdrɑfɪləs] *a*. **1**. = hydrophytic. **2**. 水媒的。

hy·dro·phobe [ˈhaidrəufəub; ˋhaɪdrəˏfob] *n*. **1**. 【化】疏水物;疏水胶体。**2**. 患恐水病的人[动物]。

hy·dro·pho·bi·a [ˌhaidrəuˈfəubjə; ˏhaɪdrəˋfobɪə] *n*. 【医】恐水病,畏水;狂犬病,瘈咬病。**-bic** *a*. 恐水病的,狂犬病的;患恐水病的。

hy·dro·phone [ˈhaidrəfəun; ˋhaɪdrəfon] *n*. 水听器;水中听音器;水中地震检波器;漏水检查器。

hy·dro·phyte [ˈhaidrəufait; ˋhaɪdrəfaɪt] *n*. 水生植物。

hy·dro·phyt·ic [ˌhaidrəuˈfitik; ˏhaɪdrəˋfɪtɪk] *a*. 【植】水生的。

hy·drop·ic [haiˈdrɔpik; haɪˋdrɑpɪk] *a*. 【医】水肿的,浮肿的。

hy·dro·plane [ˈhaidrəuplein; ˋhaɪdrəˏplen] **I** *n*. **1**. 水上飞机。**2**. 水面滑走快艇。**3**. (潜水艇的)水平舵。**4**. (水上飞机的)水翼。**II** *vi*. **1**. 乘水上飞机。**2**. 作水上滑行。**3**. (汽车车轮)在湿路上打滑,车轮空转。

hy·dro·pneu·mat·ic [ˌhaidrəunjuːˈmætik; ˏhaɪdrənjuˋmætɪk] *a*. 液压气动的。

hy·dro·pneu·mat·ics [ˌhaidrəunjuːˈmætiks; ˏhaɪdrənjuˋmætɪks] *n*. 液压气动学。

hy·dro·po·nic [ˌhaidrəuˈpɔnik; ˏhaɪdrəˋpɑnɪk] *a*. **1**. 溶液培养(学)的;水栽法的。**2**. 溶液培养出来的。

hy·dro·po·nics [ˌhaidrəuˈpɔniks; ˏhaɪdrəˋpɑnɪks] *n*. 溶液栽培法;水栽法〔现在有时指一种为太空飞行员提供新鲜食用植物的方法〕。

hy·drop·o·nist [haiˈdrɔpənist; haɪˋdrɑpənɪst], **hy·dro·pon·i·cist** [ˈhaidrəuˌpɔnisist; ˋhaɪdrəˏpɑnɪsɪst] *n*. 溶液栽培专家。

hy·dro·pow·er [ˈhaidrəupauə; ˋhaɪdroˏpauɚ] *n*. 【电】水力发出的电。

hy·dro·press [ˈhaidrəpres; ˋhaɪdrəˏprɛs] *n*. 液压机。

hy·drop·s(y) [ˈhaidrɔpsi; ˋhaɪdrɑpsɪ] *n*. 【医】积水,水肿(= dropsy)。~ **abdominis** 【医】腹(膜积)水。

hy·dro·qui·none [ˌhaidrəukwiˈnəun; ˏhaɪdrokwɪˋnon] *n*. 【化】氢醌;对苯二酚。

hy·dros. = hydrostatics.

hy·dro·scope [ˈhaidrəuskəup; ˋhaɪdrəˏskop] *n*. **1**. 验湿器;水气计。**2**. 深水望远镜,深水探视仪。**3**. 水力测试器;压力测试器。**-pic** *a*. 吸湿的;湿度计的。

hy·dro-ski [ˈhaidrəuˌskiː; ˋhaɪdroski] *n*. 水橇〔可使飞机在水上或雪地起落的雪橇或水翼〕。

hy·dro·skim·mer [ˈhaidrəuˈskimə; ˋhaɪdrəˋskɪmɚ] *n*. 〔美〕水面滑行艇〔航行于水面上的气垫船〕。

hy·dro·sol [ˈhaidrəˌsɔl, -ˌsɔːl; ˋhaɪdrəˏsɑl, -ˏsol] *n*. 【化】水溶胶。

hy·dro·space [ˈhaidrəˌspeis; ˋhaɪdrəˏspes] *n*. **1**. 大洋水域〔尤指作为科学考查的对象者〕。**2**. 水下空间。

hy·dro·sphere [ˈhaidrəusfiə; ˋhaɪdrəˏsfɪr] *n*. 【气】水界,水圈。

hy·dro·stat [ˈhaidrəustæt; ˋhaɪdrəˏstæt] *n*. 汽锅保险,防爆装置;警水器。

hy·dro·stat·ic(al) [ˌhaidrəuˈstætik(əl); ˏhaɪdrəˋstætɪk(l̩)] *a*. 流体静力(学)的;静水(学)的。~ **balance** 比重器,比重秤。~ **lubricator** 水压滑润器。~ **press** 水压机。~ **pressure** 流体静压,静水压力。

hy·dro·stat·ics [ˌhaidrəuˈstætiks; ˏhaɪdrəˋstætɪks] *n*. 静水力学,流体静力学。

hy·dro·sul·fate, hy·dro·sul·phate [ˌhaidrəuˈsʌlfeit; ˏhaɪdrəˋsʌlfet] *n*. 【化】硫酸氢盐,酸性硫酸盐。

hy·dro·sul·fide, hy·dro·sul·phide [ˌhaidrəuˈsʌlfaid; ˏhaɪdrəˋsʌlfaɪd] *n*. 氢硫化物。

hy·dro·sul·fite, hy·dro·sul·phite [ˌhaidrəuˈsʌlfait; ˏhaɪdrəˋsʌlfaɪt] *n*. 【化】次硫酸盐;(特别指)次硫酸钠。

hy·dro·sul·fu·rous [ˌhaidrəuˈsʌlfurəs; ˏhaɪdrəˋsʌlfʊrəs] *a*. ~ **acid** 【化】次硫酸(= hyposulfurous acid)。

hy·dro·tax·is [ˌhaidrəuˈtæksis; ˏhaɪdrəˋtæksɪs] *n*. 【生】向水性。**hydro·tac·tic** [-ˈtæktik; -ˋtæktɪk] *a*.

hy·dro·ther·a·peu·tic [ˈhaidrəuˌθerəˈpjuːtik; ˋhaɪdroˏθɛrəˋpjutɪk] *a*. 水疗法的。

hy·dro·ther·a·py [ˈhaidrəuˈθerəpi; ˏhaɪdrəˋθɛrəpɪ] *n*. 水疗法。

hy·dro·ther·mal [ˈhaidrəuˈθəːməl; ˏhaɪdrəˋθɝməl] *a*. 热液的,热水(作用)的。~ **deposit** 热液矿床。

hy·dro·tho·rax [ˈhaidrəuˈθɔːræks; ˏhaɪdrəˋθoræks] *n*. 【医】胸膜积水,水胸。

hy·dro·tim·et·er [ˌhaidrəuˈtimitə; ˏhaɪdrəˋtɪmɪtɚ] *n*. 水硬度计。

hy·dro·treat [ˈhaidrəutriːt; ˋhaɪdrotrit] *vt*. 【化】对…作氢化处理。

hy·dro·trop·ism [ˌhaidrəuˈtrɔpizəm; haɪˋdrɑtrəˏpɪzəm] *n*. 【植】向水性。

hy·drous [ˈhaidrəs; ˋhaɪdrəs] *a*. **1**. 【化】水合的,水化的;水状的。**2**. 含水的。

hy·dro·vane [ˈhaidrəuvein; haɪdrəven] *n*. (飞机的)着水板。

hy·drox·ide [haiˈdrɔksaid, -sid; haɪˋdrɑksaɪd, -sɪd] *n*. 【化】氢氧化物。

hy·drox·y [haiˈdrɔksi; haɪˋdrɑksɪ] *a*. 【化】羟(基)的。

hy·drox·yl [haiˈdrɔksil; haɪˋdrɑksɪl] *n*. 【化】羟基。

hy·drox·yl·a·mine [haiˌdrɔksiliˈmiːn, -ˈæmin; haɪˏdrɑksɪlɪˋmin, -ˋæmɪn] *n*. 羟胺,胲。

hy·drox·yl·ate [haiˈdrɔksileit; haɪˋdrɑksɪˏlet] *vt*. (*-at·ed, -at·ing*) 【化】羟化,羟代。**hy·drox·yl·a·tion** *n*.

hy·dro·zin·cite [ˌhaidrəuˈziŋkait; ˏhaɪdrəˋzɪŋkaɪt] *n*. 【矿】水锌矿。

hy·dro·zo·an [ˌhaidrəuˈzəuən; ˏhaɪdrəˋzoən] **I** *a*. 【动】水螅纲的。**II** *n*. 水螅纲动物〔如:水螅、软水母〕。

hy·dyne [ˈhaidain; ˋhaɪdaɪn] *n*. 美国的一种火箭发动燃料。

hy·e·na, hy·ae·na [haiˈiːnə; haɪˋinə] *n*. **1**. 【动】鬣狗。**2**. 残酷的人,贪婪的人,阴险的人。

hy·e·tal [ˈhaiitəl; ˋhaɪɪtl] *a*. 雨的;雨量的。

hyeto- *comb. f*. 表示"雨","下雨": *hyeto*graphy. *hyeto*logy.

hy·e·to·graph [ˈhaiitəugrɑːf; ˋhaɪɪtəˏgræf] *n*. 平均雨量分布图;雨量计。

hy·e·tog·ra·phy [ˌhaiiˈtɔgrəfi; ˏhaɪɪˋtɑgrəfɪ] *n*. 雨量布学;雨量图法。

hy·e·tol·o·gy [ˌhaiiˈtɔlədʒi; ˏhaɪɪˋtɑlədʒɪ] *n*. 降水量学,雨学。

hy·e·tom·e·ter [ˌhaiiˈtɔmitə; ˏhaɪɪˋtɑmɪtɚ] *n*. 雨量表,雨量计。

Hy·fil [ˈhaifil; ˋhaɪfɪl] *n*. 海菲尔〔一种玻璃纤维的商标名〕。

Hy·ge·ia [haiˈdʒi(ː)ə; haɪˋdʒiə] *n*. 【希神】司健康的女神。

hy·ge·ian [haiˈdʒiːən; haɪˋdʒiən] **I** ***a*.** **1.** 健康的，医药卫生的。**2.** 〔H-〕健康女神的。**II** ***n*.** 传授[提倡]卫生术的人。

hy·giene [ˈhaidʒiːn; ˋhaɪdʒin] ***n*.** 卫生学；健康法。*school* ～学校卫生。

hy·gi·en·ic(al) [haiˈdʒiːnik(əl); ˏhaɪˋdʒinɪk(əl)] ***a*.** **1.** 卫生学的。**2.** 卫生的，有益健康的。*a* ～ *laboratory* 卫生实验所。**-i·cal·ly** ***ad*.**

hy·gi·en·ics [haiˈdʒiːniks; haɪˋdʒinɪks] ***n*.** 卫生学，健康法。

hy·gi·en·ist [ˈhaidʒiːnist; ˋhaɪdʒɪnɪst] ***n*.** 卫生学家。

hy·gro- *comb. f.* 表示"湿"，"湿气"：*hygro*meter, *hygro*scopic.

hy·gro·graph [ˈhaigrə*u*grɑːf; ˋhaɪgrəˏgrɑf] ***n*.** 湿度计，湿度自计器。

hy·grol [ˈhaigrɔl; ˋhaɪgrɑl] ***n*.** 【化】胶状汞，汞胶液，胶态汞。

hy·grol·o·gy [haiˈgrɔlədʒi; haɪˋgrɑlədʒɪ] ***n*.** 湿度学。

hy·grom·e·ter [haiˈgrɔmitə; haɪˋgrɑmətɚ] ***n*.** 湿度表。

hy·gro·met·ric [ˌhaigrə*u*ˈmetrik; ˏhaɪgrəˋmɛtrɪk] ***a*.** **1.** 测湿的。**2.** 吸湿性的。

hy·grom·e·try [haiˈgrɔmitri; haɪˋgrɑmətrɪ] ***n*.** 测湿法。

hy·gro·phyte [ˈhaigrəfait; ˋhaɪgrəˏfaɪt] ***n*.** = hydrophyte.

hy·gro·scope [ˈhaigrə*u*skəup; ˋhaɪgrəˏskop] ***n*.** 测湿器。

hy·gro·scop·ic [ˌhaigrə*u*ˈskɔpik; ˏhaɪgrəˋskɑpɪk] ***a*.** **1.** 吸湿的；收湿的。**2.** 湿度器的；可用湿度器计量的。

hy·gro·stat [ˈhaigrə*u*stæt; ˋhaɪgrəˏstæt] ***n*.** 恒湿器，湿度检定箱，测湿计。

hy·gro·ther·mo·graph [ˌhaigrə*u*ˈθəːməgrɑːf, -græf; ˏhaɪgrəˋθɝməˏgrɑf, -ˏgræf] ***n*.** 温湿计。

hy·ing [ˈhaiiŋ; ˋhaɪɪŋ] hie 的另一种现在分词形。

hy·la [ˈhailə; ˋhaɪlə] ***n*.** 【动】**1.** 雨蛙属动物；雨蛙。**2.** 〔H-〕雨蛙属。

hy·le [ˈhaiˌliː; ˋhaɪˏli] ***n*.** 【哲】实质，物质。

hy·lic [ˈhailik; ˋhaɪlɪk] ***n*.** 【哲】实质的，物质的。

hy·loph·a·gous [haiˈlɔfəgəs; haɪˋlɑfəgəs] ***a*.** 食木的〔如某些昆虫〕。

hy·lo·the·ism [ˈhailəˌθiːizəm; ˋhaɪləˏθiɪzm̩] ***n*.** 【哲】物神论，泛神论。

hy·lo·zo·ism [ˌhailəˈzəuizəm; ˏhaɪləˋzoɪzəm̩] ***n*.** 【哲】万物有生论，物活论。

Hy·men [ˈhaimen; ˋhaɪmɛn] ***n*.** **1.** 【希神、罗神】司婚姻之神。**2.** 〔h-〕结婚；婚礼的诗歌。

hy·men [ˈhaimen; ˋhaɪmɛn] ***n*.** 【解】处女膜。

hy·me·ne·al [ˌhaimeˈni(ː)əl; ˏhaɪməˋniəl] **I** ***a*.** 婚姻的。～ *rites* 结婚仪式。**II** ***n*.** **1.** 结婚之歌。**2.** 〔*pl*.〕婚礼，婚姻。

hy·me·no- *comb. f.* 表示"膜"：*hymeno*ptera, *hymeno*pterous.

Hy·me·nom·y·ce·tes [ˈhaiminə*u*maiˈsiːtiz; ˋhaɪmənomaɪˋsitɪz] ***n*.** 【微】伞菌类。

Hy·me·nop·ter·a [ˌhaimiˈnɔptərə; ˏhaɪməˋnɑptərə] ***n*.** 【动】膜翅目。

hy·me·nop·ter·an [ˌhaimiˈnɔptərən; ˏhaɪməˋnɑptərən] **I** ***n*.** 【动】膜翅目昆虫〔包括蜜蜂、胡蜂、蚁类等〕。**II** ***a*.** 膜翅目的（= hymenopterous)。

hymn [him; hɪm] **I** ***n*.** **1.** 【宗】赞美诗，圣歌。**2.** 赞歌。**II** ***vt*., *vi*.** (为…)唱赞歌。～ **book** 赞美诗集。

hym·nal [ˈhimnəl; ˋhɪmnəl] **I** ***n*.** 赞美诗集（= hymnbook)。**II** ***a*.** 赞美诗的；使用赞美诗的。

hym·nar·i·um [himˈneəriəm; hɪmˋnɛrɪəm] ***n*.** (*pl*. ***-nar·i·a*** [-riə; -rɪə])赞美诗集。

hym·nist, hym·no·dist [ˈhimnist, ˈhimnədist; ˋhɪmnɪst, ˋhɪmnədɪst] ***n*.** 赞美诗作者。

hym·no·dy [ˈhimnədi; ˋhɪmnədɪ] ***n*.** **1.** 〔集合词〕赞美诗。**2.** 唱赞美诗。**3.** 写作赞美诗。**4.** 赞美诗研究。

hym·nog·ra·pher [himˈnɔgrəfə; hɪmˋnɑgrəfɚ] ***n*.** = hymnist.

hym·nol·o·gy [himˈnɔlədʒi; hɪmˋnɑlədʒɪ] ***n*.** **1.** 赞美诗学。**2.** 作赞美诗。**3.** 〔集合词〕赞美诗。**hym·no·log·ic** ***a*.**

hy·oid [ˈhaiɔid; ˋhaɪɔɪd] **I** ***a*.** 舌骨的。**II** ***n*.** 【解】舌骨（= the ～ bone)。

hy·o·scine [ˈhaiəsiːn; ˋhaɪəsin] ***n*.** 【化】天仙子碱。

hy·os·cy·a·mine [ˌhaiəˈsaiəmiːn, -min; ˏhaɪəˋsaɪəmin, -mɪn] ***n*.** 【化】天仙子胺。

hy·os·cy·a·mus [ˌhaiəˈsaiəməs; ˏhaɪəˋsaɪəməs] ***n*.** 【植】天仙子，韭沃斯〔一种茄科有毒植物〕。

hyp[1] [hip; hɪp] ***n*.** 【物】亥普〔衰减单位，= 1/10 奈培〕。

hyp[2] [hip; hɪp] ***n*.** 〔古〕= hypochondria.

hyp. = **1.** hypotenuse. **2.** hypothesis. **3.** hypothetical.

hyp- *pref.* = hypo-.

hyp·a·byss·al [ˌhipəˈbisl; ˏhɪpəˋbɪsl̩] ***a*.** 【地】半深成的，浅成的。

hy·pae·thral [hiˈpiːθrəl, hai-; hɪˋpiθrəl, haɪ-] ***a*.** 露天的，无屋顶的〔指古典式建筑和院子〕。

hy·pan·thi·um [hiˈpænθiəm, hai-; hɪˋpænθɪəm, haɪ-] ***n*.** (*pl*. ***-thi·a*** [-ə; -ə])【植】隐头花序。**hy·pan·thi·al** ***a*.**

hy·pal·la·ge [haiˈpælədʒiː; haɪˋpælədʒi] ***n*.** 【修】换置法〔如将 apply water to the wound 说成 apply the wound to water 之类〕。

hype [haip; haɪp] **I** ***vt*.** (***hyped*; *hyp·ing***) **1.** 〔俚〕用药剂刺激，用麻醉剂注射使兴奋〔一般与 *up* 连同〕。**2.** 大肆宣传。**II** ***n*.** 〔美俚〕**1.** 吸毒成瘾的人。**2.** 夸大广告。**3.** 被广泛宣传的人[事]。**4.** 花招，骗局。**-r** ***n*.** 宣传人员。

hyped-up [ˌhaiptˈʌp; ˏhaɪptˋʌp] ***a*.** 〔美俚〕**1.** 人为的；假的，伪造的。**2.** 兴奋的。

hy·per- *pref.* 表示"超出"，"过于"，"极度"：*hyper*sensitive, *hyper*oxide.

hy·per·ac·id [ˌhaipə(ː)ˈræsid; ˏhaɪpɚˋræsɪd] ***a*.** 胃酸过多的。

hy·per·ac·id·i·ty [ˌhaipə(ː)rəˈsiditi; ˏhaɪpərəˋsɪdətɪ] ***a*.** 【医】酸过多，胃酸过多。

hy·per·ac·tive [ˌhaipə(ː)ˈræktiv; ˏhaɪpɚˋæktɪv] ***a*.** 极度活跃的〔尤指活跃得反常的〕。**hy·per·ac·tiv·i·ty** [-ækˈtiviti; -ækˋtɪvətɪ] ***n*.**

hy·per·ae·mi·a [ˌhaipə(ː)ˈriːmiə; ˏhaɪpɚˋimɪə] ***n*.** 【医】充血。**hy·per·ae·mic** ***a*.**

hy·per·aes·the·si·a [ˌhaiperisˈθiːzjə; ˏhaɪpərɛsˋθiʒə] ***n*.** 知觉过敏，感觉过敏。**hy·per·aes·thet·ic** ***a*.**

hy·per·bar·ic [ˌhaipə(ː)ˈbærik; ˏhaɪpɚˋbærɪk] ***a*.** **1.** 超气压的；超比重的。**2.** 超气压处理室的〔指用作处理各种疾病实验的充氧室〕。**hy·per·bar·ism** ***n*.**

hy·per·ba·ton [haiˈpəːbətɔn; haɪˋpɝbətɑn] ***n*.** (*pl*. ～***s***, ***-bata*** [-bətə; -bətə])【修】倒装法〔为加强文义而颠倒词序，一般是主语和述语的次序，例如 Happy is he!〕。

hy·per·bo·la [haiˈpəːbələ; haɪˋpɝbələ] ***n*.** (*pl*. ～***s***, ～***e*** [-liː; -li])【数】双曲线。

hy·per·bo·le [haiˈpəːbəli; haɪˋpɝbəli] ***n*.** 【修】夸张法。

hy·per·bol·ic(al)[1] [ˌhaipə(ː)ˈbɔlik(əl); ˏhaɪpɚˋbɑlɪk(əl)] ***a*.** 【数】双曲线的。**-i·cal·ly** ***ad*.**

hy·per·bol·ic(al)[2] [ˌhaipə(ː)ˈbɔlik(əl); ˏhaɪpɚˋbɑlɪk(əl)] ***a*.** 夸张法的。

hy·per·bo·lism [haiˈpəːbəlizəm; haɪˋpɝbəlɪzəm] ***n*.** **1.** 用夸张法。**2.** 夸张的陈述。

hy·per·bo·lize [haiˈpəːbəlaiz; haɪˋpɝbəˏlaɪz] ***vt*., *vi*.** (***-lized*; *liz·ing***) 对…大肆夸张，夸大。

hy·per·bo·loid [haiˈpəːbəlɔid; haɪˋpɝbəˏlɔɪd] ***n*.** 【数】双曲面。

H

hy·per·bo·re·an [ˌhaipə(ː)bɔːˈriːən; ˏhaɪpɚboˋrɪən] **I** *a*. **1**.〔H-〕【希神】住在北方乐土的。**2**. 极北的;非常寒冷的。**3**. 北国人的。**II** *n*.〔H-〕**1**.【希神】住在北方乐土的人。**2**. 北国人,住在极北方的人。

hy·per·cat·a·lec·tic [ˌhaipə(ː)ˌkætˈlektik; ˏhaɪpɚˏkætˋlɛktɪk] *a*.(诗行的)超音节的〔指在一行诗末音节后尚有的一两个音节〕。

hy·per·charge [ˈhaipətʃɑːdʒ; ˋhaɪpɚtʃɑrdʒ] *vt*. 对…增加压力;加压过重。

hy·per·chlor·hy·dria [ˌhaipəklɔːˈhaidriə; ˏhaɪpɚklorˋhaɪdrɪə, -klɔr-] *n*.【医】胃酸过多(症)。

hy·per·crit·ic [ˌhaipə(ː)ˈkritik; ˏhaɪpɚˋkrɪtɪk] *n*. 苛刻的批评家。

hy·per·crit·i·cal [ˌhaipə(ː)ˈkritikəl; ˏhaɪpɚˋkrɪtɪkḷ] *a*. 吹毛求疵的,过分苛刻的。**-ly** *ad*.

hy·per·crit·i·cism [ˌhaipə(ː)ˈkritisizəm; ˏhaɪpɚˋkrɪtəˏsɪzṃ] *n*. 苛刻的批评。

hy·per·du·li·a [ˌhaipədjuːˈlaiə, -duː-; ˏhaɪpɚdjuˋlaɪə, -du-] *n*.【天主】对圣母的最高崇敬,特殊崇敬。

hy·per·e·las·tic [ˌhaipəriˈlæstik; ˏhaɪpərɪˋlæstɪk] *a*.【物】超弹性的。

hy·per·e·mi·a [ˌhaipə(ː)ˈri(ː)miə; ˏhaɪpɚˋimɪə] *n*. = hyperaemia. **hy·per·e·mic** *a*.

hy·per·es·the·sia [ˌhaiperisˈθiːzjə; ˏhaɪpərɪsˋθiʒə] *n*. = hyperaesthesia. **hy·per·es·thet·ic** *a*.

hy·per·eu·tec·tic [ˌhaipərjuˈtektik; ˏhaɪpərjʊˋtɛktɪk] *a*.【物】高级低共溶体的。

hy·per·eu·tec·toid [ˌhaipərjuˈtektɔid; ˏhaɪpərjʊˋtɛktɔɪd] *n*.【物】高级低共熔体;过共析。~ *steel* 过共析钢。

hy·per·fo·cal distance [ˌhaipə(ː)ˈfəukl; ˏhaɪpɚˋfokḷ]【摄】无穷大焦距。

hy·per·frag·ment [ˌhaipə(ː)ˈfrægmənt; ˏhaɪpɚˋfrægmənt] *n*.【物】含超裂片。

hy·per·gly·ce·mi·a [ˌhaipəglaiˈsiːmiə; ˏhaɪpɚglaɪˋsimɪə] *n*.【医】高血糖。**hy·per·gly·ce·mic** [-mik; -mɪk] *a*.

hy·per·gol [ˈhaipə(ː)gɔl; ˋhaɪpɚgɑl] *n*.【空】自燃式火箭燃料;用自燃料的推进系统。

hy·per·gol·ic [ˌhaipə(ː)ˈgɔlik, -ˈgɔːl-; ˏhaɪpɚˋgɑlɪk, -ˋgɔl-] *a*.(火箭的)自行着火的,自燃的。

hy·per·in·fla·tion [ˌhaipəinfˈleiʃən; ˏhaɪpɚɪnfˋleʃən] *n*. 过度膨胀。

hy·per·in·su·lin·ism [ˌhaipə(ː)ˈinsəlinizm; ˏhaɪpɚˋɪnsəlɪnɪzm] *n*.【医】胰岛机能亢进;胰岛素过多。

hy·per·ker·a·to·sis [ˌhaipə(ː)ˌkerəˈtəusis; ˏhaɪpɚˏkɛrəˋtosɪs] *n*. (*pl*. *-toses* [-siːz; -siz])【医】**1**. 角化过程(症)。**2**. 眼角膜细胞增多。**hy·per·ker·a·tot·ic** [-ˈtɔtik; -ˋtɑtɪk] *a*.

hy·per·ki·ne·sia, hy·per·ki·ne·sis [ˌhaipə(ː)kaiˈniːziə, ˌhaipə(ː)kaiˈniːsis; ˏhaɪpɚkaɪˋniʒɪə, ˏhaɪpɚkaɪˋnɪsɪs] *n*.【医】运动过度。**hy·perki·net·ic** *a*.

hy·per·link [ˈhaipə(ː)liŋk; ˋhaɪpɚlɪŋk] **I** *n*.【计】超文本衔接。**II** *vt*. 将…作超文本衔接。

hy·per·mar·ket [ˌhaipəˈmɑːkit; ˏhaɪpɚˋmɑrkɪt] *n*. 特级市场;巨型超级市场。

hy·per·me·dia [ˈhaipəˌmiːdiə; ˋhaɪpɚˏmidɪə] *n*.(集计算机、录像机、立体声等于一体的教学用)大型传媒装置。

hy·per·me·ter [haiˈpəːmitə; haɪˋpɝmɪtɚ] *n*. 诗体中多余的音节。**-met·ric(al)** [ˌhaipəːˈmetrik(əl); ˏhaɪpɚˋmɛtrɪk(əl)] *a*.

hy·per·me·tro·pi·a [ˌhaipə(ː)miˈtrəupiə; ˏhaɪpɚmɪˋtropɪə] *n*.【医】远视(*opp*. myopia)。**hy·per·me·trop·ic** [-ˈtrɔpik; -ˋtrɑpɪk] *a*.

hy·perm·ne·sia [ˌhaipəmˈniːziə; ˏhaɪpəmˋnizɪə] *n*.【医】记忆增强。

hy·per·no·va [ˈhaipə(ː)ˌnəuvə; ˋhaɪpɚˏnovə] *n*.【天】超新星。

hy·per·on [ˈhaipə(ː)rɔn; ˋhaɪpərɑn] *n*.【物】超子。

hy·per·ope [ˈhaipə(ː)rəup; ˋhaɪpəop] *n*. 远视者。

hy·per·o·pi·a [ˌhaipə(ː)ˈrəupiə; ˏhaɪpəopɪə] *n*. = hypermetropia.

hy·per·os·to·sis [ˌhaipərɔsˈtəusis; ˋhaɪpərɑsˋtosɪs] *n*. (*pl*. *-ses* [-siːz; -siz])【医】骨肥厚。**hy·per·os·tot·ic** [-ˈtɔtik; -ˋtɑtɪk] *a*.

hy·per·ox·i·a [ˌhaipə(ː)ˈrɔksiə; ˏhaɪpɚˋrɑksɪə] *n*.【医】体内氧过剩。

hy·per·ox·ide [ˌhaipə(ː)ˈrɔksaid; ˏhaɪpɚˋrɑksaɪd] *n*.【化】过氧化物。

hy·per·phys·i·cal [ˌhaipə(ː)ˈfizikl; ˏhaɪpɚˋfɪzɪkḷ] *a*. **1**. 超肉体的;超物质的;超自然的。**2**. 与肉体分开的;与物质分开的。**hy·per·phys·i·cal·ly** *ad*.

hy·per·pi·tu·i·ta·rism [ˌhaipəpiˈtjuːətərizm, -ˈtuː-; ˏhaɪpɚpɪˋtjuətəˏrɪzṃ, -ˋtu-] *n*.【医】**1**. 垂体机能亢进。**2**. 由此而引起的巨大发育[巨大畸形]。**hy·per·pi·tu·i·tar·y** [-təriː; -tərɪ] *a*.

hy·per·plane [ˈhaipəplein; ˋhaɪpɚplen] *n*.【数】超平面。

hy·per·pla·si·a [ˌhaipə(ː)ˈpleiʒiə; ˏhaɪpɚˋpleʒɪə] *n*.【医】增生,增殖,数量性肥大。

hy·per·pne·a [ˈhaipəˈniːə, -pəp-; ˏhaɪpɚˋniə, -pɚp-] *n*. 呼吸增强,喘息(= hyperpnoea)。**hy·per·pne·ic** *a*.

hy·per·py·rex·i·a [ˌhaipəpaiˈreksiə; ˏhaɪpɚpaɪˋrɛksɪə] *n*.【医】高烧,体温过高。**hy·per·py·ret·ic** [-ˈretik; -ˋrɛtɪk] *a*.

hy·per·quan·ti·za·tion [ˈhaipə(ː)ˌkwɔntiˈzeiʃən; ˋhaɪpɚˏkwɑntɪˋzeʃən] *n*.【物】超量子化。

hy·per·sen·si·tive [ˌhaipə(ː)ˈsensitiv; ˏhaɪpɚˋsɛnsɪtɪv] *a*. 过敏的,过敏性的。**-ness** *n*.

hy·per·son·ic [ˌhaipə(ː)ˈsɔnik; ˏhaɪpɚˋsɑnɪk] *a*. 高超音速的〔指超音速五倍以上者〕。~ **transport** 超高音速飞机〔缩写作 HST〕。

hy·per·sthene [ˈhaipəːsθiːn; ˋhaɪpɚsθin] *n*.【矿】紫苏辉石。

hy·per·syn·chro·nous [ˌhaipə(ː)ˈsiŋkrənəs; ˏhaɪpɚˋsɪŋkrənəs] *a*.【物】超同步的。

hy·per·ten·sion [ˌhaipəːˈtenʃən; ˋhaɪpɚˋtɛnʃən] *n*. **1**.【医】高血压。**2**. 过度紧张。

hy·per·ten·sive [ˌhaipə(ː)ˈtensiv; ˏhaɪpɚˋtɛnsɪv] **I** *a*. 高血压的。**II** *n*. 高血压患者。

hy·per·text [ˈhaipə(ː)tekst; ˋhaɪpɚtɛkst] *n*.【计】超级存储系统,超文本。

hy·per·therm [ˈhaipə(ː)θəːm; ˋhaɪpɚθɝm] *n*.【医】人工发热器。

hy·per·thy·roid [ˈhaipə(ː)ˈθairɔid; ˏhaɪpɚˋθaɪrɔɪd] **I** *a*. 甲状腺机能亢进的。**II** *n*. 甲状腺机能亢进患者。**-ism** *n*.【医】甲状腺机能亢进。

hy·per·ton·ic [ˌhaipə(ː)ˈtɔnik; ˏhaɪpɚˋtɑnɪk] *a*. **1**.【医】张力亢进的。**2**.【化】高渗性的。**hy·per·to·nic·i·ty** [-təˈnisiti; -təˋnɪsətɪ] *n*.

hy·per·tro·phy [haiˈpəːtrəfi; haɪˋpɝtrəfɪ] **I** *n*. **1**.【医】肥大。**2**. 过度膨胀,过度增大。**II** *vt*., *vi*. (*-phied*; *-phy·ing*) (使)变得异常肥大。**-tro·phied, -troph·ic** *a*.

hy·per·ve·loc·i·ty [ˈhaipə(ː)viˈlɔsiti; ˋhaɪpɚvɪˋlɑsətɪ] *n*. 超高速,特超声速〔指太空飞船或核粒子等的运动速度〕。

hy·per·ven·ti·la·tion [ˌhaipə(ː)ˌventiˈleiʃən; ˏhaɪpɚˏvɛntɪˋleʃən] *n*.【医】换气过度。**hy·per·ven·ti·late** [-ˌeit; -ˏet] *vi*., *vt*.

hy·per·vi·ta·min·o·sis [ˌhaipə(ː)ˌvaitəmiˈnəusis; ˏhaɪpɚˏvaɪtəmɪˋnosɪs] *n*.【医】维生素过多症。

hyp·es·the·si·a [ˌhipisˈθiːʒə; ˏhɪpɪsˋθiʒə] *n*. 感觉减退〔尤指触觉减退〕。**hyp·es·the·sic** [-ˈθiːsik; -ˋθisɪk],

hyp·es·thet·ic [-ˈθetik; -ˋθɛtɪk] *a.*

hy·pe·thral [hiˈpiːθrəl; hɪˋpiθrəl] *a.* = hypaethral.

hy·pha [ˈhaifə; ˋhaɪfə] *n.* (*pl.* **-phae** [-fiː; -fi])【植】菌丝。**-phal** *a.*

hy·phen [ˈhaifən; ˋhaɪfən] I *n.* **1.**【印】连字号〔即"-"〕。**2.** 谈话中音节间的短暂休止。II *vt.* 用连字号连接。

hy·phen·ate [ˈhaifəneit; ˋhaɪfən͵et] I *vt.* **1.** 用连字号连接;把…用连字号移行。**2.** 用连字号写[抄、印]。II *n.*〔美〕归化的美国移民 (= hyphenated American)。

hy·phen·at·ed [ˈhaifəneitid; ˋhaɪfən͵etɪd] *a.* **1.** 用连字号连接的。**2.**〔美〕(公民)归化的;关于归化的美国公民的〔因归化的美国公民常被称为 German-Americans, Irish-Americans 等,原国籍与"美籍"之间用连字号连接,用时含有贬意〕。~ **American** 归化的美国公民。~ **words** (有连字号的)复合词。

hy·phen·a·tion [ˌhaifəˈneiʃən; ͵haɪfəˋneʃən] *n.* **1.** 用连字号的连接。**2.** 连字号。

hyp·na·gog·ic [ˌhipnəuˈgɔdʒik; ͵hɪpnoˋgɑdʒɪk] *a.* **1.** 催眠的,使瞌睡的。**2.** (睡眠)似醒非醒状态的。

hyp·no- *comb. f.* 表示"睡眠","催眠术"〔母音前用 hypn-〕: *hypno*genesis, *hypno*therapy.

hyp·no·a·nal·y·sis [ˌhipnəuəˈnælisis; ͵hɪpnoəˋnælɪsɪs] *n.* 催眠精神分析。

hyp·no·gen·e·sis [ˌhipnəuˈdʒenisis; ͵hɪpnoˋdʒɛnəsɪs] *n.* 催眠。**hyp·no·ge·net·ic** [-dʒeˈnetik; -dʒɛˋnɛtɪk] *a.*

hyp·noid [ˈhipnɔid; ˋhɪpnɔɪd] *a.* 似睡的,似入睡的 (= hypnoidal)。

hyp·nol·o·gy [hipˈnɔlədʒi; hɪpˋnɑlədʒɪ] *n.* 睡眠学,催眠学。

hyp·no·pom·pic [ˌhipnəuˈpɔmpik; ͵hɪpnoˋpɑmpɪk] *a.* 半睡醒状态。

Hyp·nos [ˈhipnɔs; ˋhɪpnɑs] *n.*【希神】睡神。

hyp·no·sis [hipˈnəusis; hɪpˋnosɪs] (*pl.* **-ses** [-siːz; -siz]) *n.* 催眠(状态);催眠术,催眠术研究。

hyp·no·ther·a·py [ˌhipnəuˈθerəpi; ͵hɪpnoˋθɛrəpɪ] *n.*【医】催眠疗法。

hyp·not·ic [hipˈnɔtik; hɪpˋnɑtɪk] I *a.* **1.** 催眠的;有催眠性的。**2.** 易受催眠的;受催眠术影响的。II *n.* **1.** 催眠药。**2.** 在催眠状态中的人;易受催眠的人。**-i·cal·ly** *ad.*

hyp·no·tism [ˈhipnətizəm; ˋhɪpnə͵tɪzəm] *n.* 催眠(术);催眠状态;催眠术研究。

hyp·no·tist [ˈhipnətist; ˋhɪpnətɪst] *n.* 催眠术师。

hyp·no·tize [ˈhipnətaiz; ˋhɪpnə͵taɪz] *vt.* **1.** 对…施催眠术;使入催眠状态。**2.**〔俚〕使着迷,使精神恍惚。**3.** 使着迷。**-tizer** *n.* = hypnotist. **-ti·za·tion** *n.*

hy·po[1] [ˈhaipəu; ˈhaɪpo] *n.*【化】五水合硫代硫酸钠〔hyposulfite of soda 之略,摄影定像用〕,大苏打,海波〔俗称〕。

hy·po[2] [ˈhaipəu; ˋhaɪpo] *n.*〔美口〕**1.** = hypochondria. **2.** = hypochondriac (*n.*).

hy·po[3] [ˈhaipəu; ˋhaɪpo] *n.* **1.** 皮下注射 (= hypodermic injection)。**2.** 刺激。**3.** 吸毒成瘾的人。II *vt.* 给…以刺激。

hy·po- *pref.* 表示 **1.** "在…下"。**2.**【化】"低下","次","亚"〔元音前用 hyp- (*opp.* hyper-)〕: *hypo*glycemia, *hypo*chlorous.

HYPO = high-power water boiler 大功率沸腾式反应堆。

hy·po·blast [ˈhaipəblæst; ˋhaɪpə͵blæst] *n.*【生】内胚层,下胚层;【植】基芽。**-tic** *a.*

hy·po·bran·chi·al [ˌhaipəuˈbræŋkiəl; ͵haɪpoˋbræŋkɪəl] *a.*【动】鳃下的。

hy·po·caust [ˈhaipəkɔːst; ˋhaɪpə͵kɔst] *n.* **1.** (古罗马的)炕。**2.** 罗马式火炕供暖装置。

hy·po·cen·ter, hy·po·cen·tre [ˈhaipəusentə; ˋhaɪposɛntɚ] *n.* (核爆的)震源。

hy·po·chlo·rite [ˌhaipəuˈklɔːrait; ͵haɪpoˋklɔraɪt] *n.*【化】次氯酸盐。

hy·po·chlo·rous [ˌhaipəuˈklɔːrəs; ͵haɪpoˋklɔrəs] *a.*【化】次氯酸的。~ *acid*【化】次氯酸。

hy·po·chon·dri·a [ˌhaipəuˈkɔndriə; ͵haɪpoˋkɑndrɪə] *n.*【医】忧郁症,癔想症,疑病症〔指病态的自拟患病〕。

hy·po·chon·dri·ac [ˌhaipəuˈkɔndriæk; ͵haɪpoˋkɑndrɪæk] I *a.* **1.** 忧郁症的,癔想症的,疑病症的。**2.**【解】季肋部的。II *n.* 忧郁症患者,癔想症患者,疑病症患者。

hy·po·chon·dri·a·cal [ˌhaipəukɔnˈdraiəkəl; ͵haɪpokɑnˋdraɪəkəl] *a.* = hypochondric **1.** **-ly** *ad.*

hy·po·chon·dri·um [ˌhaipəuˈkɔndriəm; ͵haɪpəˋkɑndrɪəm] *n.* (*pl.* **-dri·a** [-ə; -ə]) **1.**【医】忧郁症,癔想症,疑病症。**2.**【解】季肋部。

hy·po·co·ris·tic [ˌhaipəukəˈristik; ͵haɪpokəˈrɪstɪk] *a.*【语】爱称的,表示亲爱的。

hy·po·cot·yl [ˌhaipəˈkɔtl; ͵haɪpəˋkɑtḷ] *n.*【植】(下)胚轴。

hy·poc·ri·sy [hiˈpɔkrəsi; hɪˋpɑkrəsɪ] *n.* 伪善,虚伪。

hyp·o·crite [ˈhipəkrit; ˋhɪpəkrɪt] *n.* 伪善者,虚伪的人。*play the* ~ 装伪君子。

hyp·o·crit·ic(al) [ˌhipəˈkritik(əl); ͵hɪpəˋkrɪtɪk(əl)] *a.* 伪善(者)的,言不由衷的。**-i·cal·ly** *ad.*

hy·po·cy·cloid [ˌhaipəuˈsaiklɔid; ͵haɪpəˋsaɪklɔɪd] *n.*【数】圆内旋轮线,内摆线。

hy·po·derm [ˈhaipədəːm; ͵haɪpəˋdɝm] *n.* **1.** 皮下组织。**2.** = hypoblast.

hy·po·der·mal [ˌhaipəuˈdəːməl; ͵haɪpəˋdɝməl] *a.* **1.**【植】皮下的;【动】真皮的。**2.** 表皮下的。

hy·po·der·mi·a [ˌhaipəuˈdəːmiə; ͵haɪpoˋdɝmɪə] *n.*【医】皮下组织。

hy·po·der·mic [ˌhaipəuˈdəːmik; ͵haɪpoˋdɝmɪk] I *a.* **1.** 皮下的,皮下组织的。**2.** 皮下注射用的。**3.** 刺激性的。II *n.* 皮下注射;皮下注射器。~ **canal** 皮下管。~ **injection** 皮下注射。~ **medication** 皮下注射治疗。~ **needle** 皮下注射针头,安上针头的皮下注射器。~ **syringe** 皮下注射器。**-mi·cal·ly** *ad.*

hy·po·der·mis [ˌhaipəuˈdəːmis; ͵haɪpəˋdɝmɪs] *n.* **1.**【植】下皮;下胚层。**2.**【动】下皮;(昆虫的)真皮。

hy·po·eu·tec·tic [ˌhaipəuju(ː)ˈtektik; ͵haɪpəjuˋtɛktɪk] *a.*【冶】亚共晶的。

hy·po·eu·tec·toid [ˌhaipəuju(ː)ˈtektɔid; ͵haɪpəjuˋtɛktɔɪd] *a.*【冶】亚共析的。~ **steel** 亚共析钢。

hy·po·gas·tric [ˈhaipəuˈgæstrik; ͵haɪpəˋgæstrɪk] *a.* 腹下部的,下腹的。

hy·po·gas·tri·um [ˈhaipəuˈgæstriəm; ͵haɪpəˋgæstrɪəm] *n.* (*pl.* **-tria** [-striə; -strɪə])【解】腹下部,下腹。

hy·po·ge·al [haipəuˈdʒiːəl; ͵haɪpəˋdʒiəl] *a.* **1.** 地中的,起于地中的;地下的。**2.**【植】地下生的〔如花生、松露〕;(尤指)(子叶)留土的。**3.**【动】(打洞、生活、成长于)地下的〔如某些昆虫、动物等〕(= hypogean)。

hy·po·gene [ˈhaipədʒiːn; ˋhaɪpə͵dʒin] *a.*【动】地面下形成的,深成的;上升的。~ **rocks** 深成岩。~ **water** 上升水。

hy·pog·e·nous [haiˈpɔdʒinəs; haɪˋpɑdʒɪnəs] *a.*【植】在下着生的〔如某些蕨类植物叶背面着生的孢子〕。

hy·po·ge·ous [ˌhaipəuˈdʒiːəs; ͵haɪpəˋdʒɪəs] *a.* = hypogeal.

hy·po·glos·sal [ˌhaipəuˈglɔsl; ͵haɪpəˋglɑsḷ] I *a.* 舌下的。II *n.* 舌下神经。

hy·po·gly·ce·mi·a [ˌhaipəuglaiˈsiːmiə; ͵haɪpoglaɪˋsimɪə] *n.*【医】低血糖。

hy·pog·na·thous [haiˈpɔgnəθəs; haɪˋpɑgnəθəs] *a.*【动】下颌突出的,下口式的。

hy·pog·y·nous [haiˈpɔdʒinəs; haɪˋpɑdʒɪnəs] *a.*【植】**1.** (花被、雄蕊)下位的。**2.** 有下位排列部分的。~ **flowers**

下位花。-**ny** [-ni; -ni] ***n***.

hy·poid [ˈhaipɔid; ˋhaɪpɔɪd] **gear**【机】偏轴伞齿轮。

hy·po·ki·ne·sis [ˌhaipəuki'niːsis; ˏhaɪpokɪˋnisɪs] ***n***.【医】运动减退(= hypokinesia)。**hy·poki·net·ic** [-ˈnetik; -ˋnɛtɪk] ***a***.

hy·po·lim·ni·on [ˌhaipəuˈlimniɔn; ˏhaɪpəˋlɪmnɪɑn] ***n***. 深水缺氧层。

hy·po·ma·ni·a [ˌhaipəuˈmeiniə; ˏhaɪpəˋmenɪə] ***n***.【医】轻躁狂。**hypo·man·ic** [-ˈmænik; -ˋmænɪk] ***a***.

hy·po·nas·ty [ˈhaipəˌnæsti; ˋharpəˏnæstɪ] ***n***.【植】偏下性。**hy·ponas·tic** [-ˈnæstik; -ˋnæstɪk] ***a***.

hy·po·ni·trite [ˌhaipəuˈnaitrait; ˏhaɪpəˋnaɪtraɪt] ***n***.【化】连二次硝酸盐。

hy·po·ni·trous [ˌhaipəuˈnaitrəs; ˏhaɪpəˋnaɪtrəs] ***a***. ~ **acid**【化】连二次硝酸。

hy·po·phos·phate [ˌhaipəuˈfɔsfeit; ˏhaɪpəˋfɑsfet] ***n***.【化】连二磷酸盐。

hy·po·phos·phite [ˌhaipəuˈfɔsfait; ˏhaɪpəˋfɑsfaɪt] ***n***.【化】次磷酸盐。

hy·poph·y·sis [haiˈpɔfisis; haɪˋpɑfɪsɪs] ***n***. (*pl*. *-ses* [-siːz; -ˏsiz])【解】垂体。

hy·po·pi·tu·i·ta·rism [ˌhaipəupiˈtju(ː)ətərizm; ˏhaɪpopɪˋtjuətərɪzm] ***n***.【医】1. 垂体机能减退。2. 垂体机能减退症〔如儿童发育减慢,性腺活动减弱等〕。**hy·po·pi·tu·i·tar·y** [-təri; -tərɪ] ***a***.

hy·po·pla·si·a [ˌhaipəuˈpleizjə; ˏhaɪpəˋplezɪə] ***n***. 1.【医】发育不全。2. 细胞灭生(现象)。-**plas·tic** [-ˈplæztik; -ˋplæztɪk] ***a***.

hy·po·py·on [haiˈpəupiɔn; haɪˋpopɪɑn] ***n***.【医】眼前房积脓。

hy·po·scope [ˈhaipəskəup; ˋhaɪpəˌskop] ***n***. 蟹眼式望远镜。

hy·po·sen·si·tize [ˌhaipəuˈsensitaiz; ˏhaɪpəˋsɛnsɪˏtaɪz] ***vt***. (*-tized*; *-tiz·ing*) 使(对抗菌素的)敏感度减退。**hy·po·sen·si·ti·za·tion** ***n***.

hy·po·spray [ˈhaipəusprei; ˋhaɪpoˏspre] ***n***. (不用针头而用压力把药液射入皮下的)无痛皮下喷射器。

hy·pos·ta·sis [haiˈpɔstəsis; haɪˋpɑstəsɪs] ***n***. (*pl*. *-ses* [-siːz; -sɪz]) 1.【哲】本质,实在。2.【宗】三位一体之一,基督人格。3.【医】坠积性充血。4.【化】沉渣,液底沉淀。5.【生】下位。

hy·po·stat·ic(al) [ˌhaipəuˈstætik(əl); ˏhaɪpəˋstætɪk(əl)] ***a***. 1.【哲】本质的,实在的,实体的。2. 沉下的。3. 下位的。~ **union**【宗】基督的位格结合(神人合一)。-**i·cal·ly** ***ad***.

hy·pos·ta·tize [haiˈpɔstətaiz; haɪˋpɑstəˏtaɪz] ***vt***. (*-tized*; *-tiz·ing*) 1.【哲】把…视为实存;使实体化。2. 把个人的存在归于…;使人格化。-**ti·za·tion** [haiˌpɔstətiˈzeiʃən; haɪˏpɑstətɪˋzeʃən] ***n***.

hy·po·style [ˈhaipəustail; ˋhaɪpəstaɪl] **I** ***a***.【建】多柱式建筑的。**II** ***n***. 多柱式建筑。

hy·po·sul·fite, hy·po·sul·phite [ˌhaipəuˈsʌlfait; ˏhaɪpəˋsʌlfaɪt] ***n***.【化】1. 连二亚硫酸盐。2. = hydrosulfite. 3. sodium thiosulfate 的误称。

hy·po·sul·fu·rous [ˌhaipəusʌlˈfjuərəs; ˏhaɪpəsʌlˋfjʊrəs] ***a***. ~ **acid**【化】连二亚硫酸。

hy·po·tax·is [ˌhaipəuˈtæksis; ˏhaɪpəˋtæksɪs] ***n***.【语法】(句法中)从属结构,主从关系〔如主句与从句等〕。**hy·po·tac·tic** [-ˈtæktik; -ˋtæktɪk] ***a***.

hy·po·ten·sion [ˌhaipəuˈtenʃən; ˏhaipəˋtɛnʃən] ***n***.【医】低血压,血压过低。**hy·po·ten·sive** ***a***.

hy·pot·e·nuse [haiˈpɔtinjuːz; haɪˋpɑtnjuz] ***n***.【数】弦,斜边。

hypoth. = 1. hypothesis. 2. hypothetical.

hy·po·thal·a·mus [ˌhaipəuˈθæləməs; ˏhaɪpəˋθæləməs] ***n***. (*pl*. *-mi* [-mai; -maɪ])【医】丘脑下部,下丘脑,下视丘。**hy·po·tha·lam·ic** [-θəˈlæmik; -θəˋlæmɪk] ***a***.

hy·poth·ec [haiˈpɔθek; haɪˋpɑθɛk] ***n***.【法】(不转移财产所有权的)抵押权,担保权。~ **bank** 劝业银行。

hy·poth·e·car·y [haiˈpɔθikeri; haɪˋpɑθɪˏkɛrɪ] ***a***.【法】抵押的;由抵押而获得的。

hy·poth·e·cate [haiˈpɔθikeit; haɪˋpɑθəˏket] ***vt***. (以不转移占有权的方式)抵押(财产)。-**ca·tion** ***n***. 1. 抵押。2. 押船契约;担保契约。3. 对抵押财产的索赔权。-**ca·tor** ***n***.

hy·po·ther·mal [ˌhaipəuˈθəːməl; ˏhaɪpəˋθɝməl] ***a***. 1. 不冷不热的,温热的。2. 体温过低的。3. (某些矿床的)在300℃以上温度下产生的。

hy·po·ther·mi·a [ˌhaipəuˈθəːmiə; ˏhaɪpəˋθɝmɪə] ***n***. 体温过低。

hy·poth·e·sis [haiˈpɔθisis; haɪˋpɑθɪsɪs] ***n***. (*pl*. *-ses* [-siːz; -sɪz]) 1. 假设;假说。2.【逻】前提。

hy·poth·e·size [haiˈpɔθisaiz; haɪˋpɑθəsaɪz] ***vi***., ***vt***. 假设,假定。

hy·po·thet·ic(al) [ˌhaipəuˈθetik(əl); ˏhaɪpəˋθɛtɪk(əl)] ***a***. 1. 假设的。2.【逻】有前提的(*opp*. categorical)。-**cal·ly** ***ad***.

hy·po·thy·roid [ˈhaipəuˈθairɔid; haɪpəˋθaɪrɔɪd] **I** ***a***.【医】甲状腺机能减退的。**II** ***n***.【医】甲状腺机能减退的人。-**ism** ***n***. 甲状腺机能减退。

hy·po·ton·ic [ˌhaipəuˈtɔnik; ˏhaɪpəˋtɑnɪk] ***a***. 1.【医】张力减退的。2.【化】低渗性的。**hy·po·to·nic·i·ty** [-təˈnisiti; -təˋnɪsətɪ] ***n***.

hy·po·xan·thine [ˌhaipəuˈzænθiːn, -θin; ˏhaɪpəˋzænθin, -θɪn] ***n***.【生化】次黄嘌呤。

hy·pox·i·a [haiˈpɔksiə; haɪˋpɑksɪə] ***n***.【医】缺氧症。

hyp·so- *comb*. *f*. 表示"高度":*hypso*meter.

hyp·sog·ra·phy [hipˈsɔgrəfi; hɪpˋsɑgrəfɪ] ***n***. 1. 地形测绘学。2. 等高线法。3. 测高学,测高法。4. 表示不同高度的地形图。

hyp·som·e·ter [hipˈsɔmitə; ˏhɪpˋsɑmɪtɚ] ***n***. 1. 沸点测高计。2. (树木的)三角法测高计。

hyp·som·e·try [hipˈsɔmitri; hɪpˋsɑmɪtrɪ] ***n***. 测高术。**hyp·so·metric** [ˌhipsəuˈmetrik; ˏhɪpsəˋmɛtrɪk] ***a***.

hy·ra·coid [ˈhairəkɔid; ˋhaɪrəkɔɪd] **I** ***n***. = hyrax. **II** ***a***. 蹄兔的。

hy·rax [ˈhaiəræks; ˋhaɪræks] ***n***. (*pl*. *~es*, *-ra·ces* [-rəsiːz; -rəsiz])【动】非洲蹄兔,岩狸。

Hyr·ca·ni·a [həˈkeiniə; həˋkenɪə] ***n***. 赫卡尼亚〔古波斯和马其顿王国的一个省名〕。**Hyr·ca·ni·an** ***a***., ***n***. 赫卡尼亚地方的(人)。

hy·son [ˈhaisn; ˋhaɪsn̩] ***n***. 熙春茶〔中国绿茶的一种〕。

hy·spy [ˈhaispai; ˋhaɪspaɪ] ***n***. (游戏)躲猫,捉迷藏。

hys·sop [ˈhisəp; ˋhɪsəp] ***n***.【植】海索草;海索草属植物。

hys·ter·ec·to·my [ˌhistəˈrektəmi; ˏhɪstəˋrɛktəmɪ] ***n***.【医】子宫切除术。

hys·ter·e·sis [ˌhistəˈriːsis; ˏhɪstəˋrisɪs] ***n***. 1.【物】磁滞。2.【物】滞后现象[作用];迟滞性。3. 平衡阻碍。**hys·ter·et·ic** [-ˈretik; -ˋrɛtɪk] ***a***.

hys·te·ri·a [hisˈtiəriə; hɪsˋtɪrɪə] ***n***. 1.【医】癔病;(特指女人的)歇斯底里。2. 病态的兴奋。

hys·ter·ic [hisˈterik; hɪsˋtɛrɪk] **I** ***a***. 1. 癔病的;歇斯底里的。2. 病态感情[兴奋]式的。**II** ***n***. 歇斯底里患者〔*pl*.〕发歇斯底里;发狂。*go off* (*fall*) *into* ~*s* 发歇斯底里。

hys·ter·i·cal [hisˈterikəl; hɪsˋtɛrɪkl̩] ***a***. 癔病的,歇斯底里的;患癔病的。-**ly** ***ad***.

hys·ter·o- *comb*. *f*. 表示"子宫":*hystero*tomy.

hys·ter·oid, hys·te·roi·dal [ˈhistərɔid, ˌhistəˈrɔidl; ˋhɪstərɔɪd, ˏhɪstəˋrɔɪdl̩] ***a***.【医】癔病似的。

hys·ter·ol·o·gy [ˌhistəˈrɔlədʒi; ˏhɪstəˋrɑlədʒɪ] ***n***.【医】子宫学。

hys·ter·on-prot·e·ron [ˈhistərənˈprɔtərən; ˋhɪstərənˋprɑtərən] ***n***. 〔G.〕1.【修】逆序法;次序倒转〔如 I die

I faint, I fall)。2.【逻】倒逆论法。

hys·ter·ot·o·my [ˌhistəˈrɔtəmi; ˌhɪstəˋrɑtəmɪ] ***n.***【医】子宫切开术。

hys·tri·co·mor·phic [ˌhistrikəˈmɔːfik; ˌhɪstrɪkəˋmɔrfɪk] ***a.***【动】豪猪形啮齿动物(包括豪猪、狼鼠、大耳鼯鼠等)的。

hyte [hait; haɪt] ***a.*** (古、方)疯狂的。

hy·ther·graph [ˈhaiθəgrɑːf; ˋhaɪθəˏgræf] ***n.***【气】温湿图,温度与湿度关系图。

Hz = hertz.

I

I, i [ai; aɪ] (*pl*. ***I's***, ***i's*** [aiz; aɪz]) **1.** 英语字母表第九字母。**2.** 罗马数字 **I**. **3.** **I** 字形的物体,工字形物体。*I-bar* 工字钢,工字条。*I-beam* 工字梁,工字铁条。***dot the i's and cross the t's***. 给字母 i 加点,给字母 t 加短横;点横不丢;一丝不苟;一板一眼地细讲。

I [ai; aɪ] **I** ***pro***. (*pl*. ***we***) (人称代词,第一人称,单数,主格。(*poss. adj*. ***my***; *obj*. ***me***; *poss. pro*. ***mine***)) 我。*It is* ～ 是我(口语也用 It's me)。*It is* ～ *who am to blame*. 应当负责任的是我。*Am* ～ *not* ...? 我难道不是…?(口语通常说作(美) *Ain't* ～? (英) *An't* [*Aren't*] ～?)。*You and* ～. 你和我(英语习惯,除特殊情况外,一般不说 ～ and you [he, she])。**II** ***n***. (*pl*. ～***'s*** 或 ～***s***) **1.** 自我。**2.** 极端自私的人,说话老是"我怎么怎么"的人。**3.** (the ～)【哲】自我意识。*You shouldn't use too many* ～*'s in writing*. 写文章写信时不要老用我怎么怎么的字眼。

I., i. = **1.** island(s). **2.** Idaho. **3.** Independent. **4.** Iowa. **5.** incisor. **6.** interest. **7.** intransitive. **8.** isle(s). **9.**【化】iodine.

-i- *comb. f*. 多用于拉丁语词源的复合词中: curv*i*linear, omn*i*vorous; cune*i*form, Frenchi*f*y.

-i [-ai; -aɪ] 拉丁语系名词的复数词尾: alumn-*i* (< alumn*us*), foc*i* (< foc*us*).

-ia **1.** 拉丁、希腊语名词词尾: hyster*ia*, milit*ia*. **2.** 国名词尾: Austral*ia*. **3.** 希腊、拉丁语名词的复数形: paraphernal*ia*, regal*ia*. **4.** 与人名有关系的花名: dahl*ia*, wistar*ia*. **5.** 动植物分类上的复数形: Cryptomer*ia*.

Ia. = Iowa.

i.a. = (L.) *in absentia* 缺席。

IA = information anxiety (因当代信息过多而感到个人无能为力的)信息焦虑感。

IAAF = International Amateur Athletic Federation 国际业余田径联合会。

IADL = International Association of Democratic Lawyers 国际民主法律工作者协会。

IAEA = International Atomic Energy Agency (联合国)国际原子能总署。

IAF = International Astronautical Federation 国际星际航空联合会。

I·a·go [iːˈɑːgəu; iˋɑgo] ***n***. **1.** 埃古(莎士比亚剧作《奥赛罗》中的反面人物)。**2.** 阴险奸滑的人。

-ial *suf*. 表示"具有…性质的";"属于…的": ceremon*ial*.

LAMAP = International Association of Meteorology and Atmospheric Physics 国际气象和大气物理协会。

i·amb [ˈaiæmb; ˋaɪæmb] ***n***. = iambus.

i·am·bic [aiˈæmbik; aɪˋæmbɪk] **I** ***a***. (英诗)短长格的;抑扬[弱强]格的。**II** ***n***. **1.** 短长格,抑扬格。**2.** (常用复)短长[抑扬]格的诗。

i·am·bus [aiˈæmbəs; aɪˋæmbəs] ***n***. (*pl*. ***-bi*** [-bai; -baɪ], ***-buses***)【韵】短长格,抑扬格。

I·an [iən; ɪən] ***n***. 伊恩(男子名, John 的异体)。

-ian *suf*. = -an: Christ*ian*, reptil*ian*.

-i·an·a *suf*. = -ana.

IAP = international airport 国际机场。

IAR = (美) Institute for Atomic Research.

iar·o·vi·za·tion [ˌjɑːrəvaiˈzeiʃən; ˏjɑrəvaiˋzeʃən] ***n***. = vernalization.

iar·o·vize [ˈjɑːrəvaiz; ˋjɑrəvaɪz] ***vt***. (用人工方法)使(植物)提早开花结实 (= vernalize)。

IARU = International Amateur Radio Union 国际业余无线电爱好者联合会。

IAS = **1.** Institute of Aeronautical Sciences (美)航空科学学院。**2.** indicated airspeed【空】指示空速。

-i·a·sis *suf*. 表示"病","病态": elephant*iasis*.

IATA = International Air Transport Association 国际航空运输协会。

i·at·ric(·al) [iˈætrik(əl), ai-; ɪˋætrɪk(əl), aɪ-] ***a***. 医学的,医疗的,医生的,药物的。

-i·at·rics *comb. f*. 构成名词,表示医学分科: ped*iatrics*.

i·at·ro·chem·is·try [aiˌætrəˈkemistri; aɪˏætrəˋkɛmɪstrɪ] ***n***.【医】医疗化学。

i·at·ro·gen·ic [aiˌætrəˈdʒenik; aɪˏætrəˋdʒɛnɪk] ***a***. 由治疗引起的(尤指由医生的话引起病人的臆测性症候)。

-i·a·try *comb. f*. 构成名词,表示医治法: psych*iatry*.

IAZ = inner artillery zone 高射炮防空禁区。

ib. = (L.) *ibidem*.

I·ba·dan [iˈbædən; ɪˋbædən] ***n***. 伊巴丹(尼日利亚城市)。

IBEC = International Bank for Economic Cooperation 国际经济合作银行。

I·be·ria [aiˈbiəriə; aɪˋbɪrɪə] ***n***. 伊比利亚(西班牙半岛的古名)。

I·be·ri·an [aiˈbiəriən; aɪˋbɪrɪən] **I** ***a***. (包含西班牙、葡萄牙二国在内的)伊比利亚(半岛)的;伊比利亚人的;伊比利亚语的。**II** ***n***. 伊比利亚语。

i·bex [ˈaibeks; ˋaɪbɛks] ***n***. (*pl*. ～***es***, ***ibices*** [ˈibisiːz; ˋɪbɪsiz]) (阿尔卑斯山的)野山羊。

Ib·i·bi·o [ˌibiˈbiːəu; ˏɪbɪˋbio] ***n***. (*pl*. ～(***s***)) **1.** 伊比比欧人(尼日利亚东南部人)。**2.** 伊比比欧语。

ibid. = (L.) *ibidem*.

i·bi·dem [iˈbaidem; ɪˋbaɪdɛm] ***ad***. (L.) 在同书,在同章,在同句,在同处,同上,同前(略 *ib*, *ibid*)。

-i·bil·i·ty *suf*. 表示"可能性": feas*ibility*.

i·bis [ˈaibis; ˋaɪbɪs] ***n***. (*pl*. ～(***es***))【动】鹮,朱鹭;鹮科的涉禽。*the sacred* ～ (古埃及的)灵鸟。

-i·ble *suf*. 表示"可","能","得","堪"(与 -able 同义,但除拉丁系形容词外少用)。divis*ible*, permiss*ible*.

IBM = **1.** intercontinental ballistic missile 洲际弹道飞弹。**2.** International Business Machines Corporation

〔美〕国际商用机器公司。

I·bo [ˈiːbəu; ˋibo] *n*. (*pl*. ~(*s*)) **1**. 伊波人〔尼日利亚东南部的非洲人〕。**2**. 伊波语。

IBRD = International Bank for Reconstruction and Development (联合国)国际复兴(与)开发银行。

Ib·sen [ˈibsen; ˋɪbsn], **Henrik** 亨利·易卜生〔1828—1906,挪威剧作家。以社会问题剧 (*problem play*) 形式对社会作批评、讽刺〕。

Ib·sen·ism [ˈibsənizəm; ˋɪbsənɪzm] *n*. **1**. 挪威戏剧家易卜生提倡的戏剧创作方法。**2**. (提倡演社会问题戏剧的)易卜生主义。

Ib·sen·ist [ˈibsənist; ˋɪbsənɪst] *n*. 易卜生主义者。

Ib·sen·ite [ˈibsənait; ˋɪbsənaɪt] **I** *n*. **1**. 易卜生的崇拜者。**2**. 模仿易卜生的剧作家。**II** *a*. 易卜生的,具有易卜生或其剧作特点的。

IC = **1**. integrated circuit【无】积体[集成]电路。**2**. interior communications 内部通讯联络。

I.C. = *Iesus Christus* (= Jesus Christ); inductance-capacitance; Issued Capital.

i.c. = ionization chamber; between meals【医】(处方)在两餐之间。

i/c = in charge; internal combustion.

-ic[1] *suf*.〔构成形容词〕**1**. 表示"…的","…似的","…性的": bas*ic*, poet*ic*. **2**. 表示"与…有关的": Asiat*ic*, volcan*ic*. **3**. 表示"由…产生的","由…引起的": photograph*ic*, symphon*ic*. **4**. 表示"由…组成的","含有…的": alcohol*ic*, dactyl*ic*. **5**. 表示"原子价较高的"〔指与-ous 结尾的词相比〕: ferr*ic*, sulphur*ic*.

-ic[2] *suf*.〔构成名词〕**1**. 表示"学术","艺术": arithmet*ic*, log*ic*, mus*ic*. **2**. 表示"具有某种性质或特征": class*ic*, crit*ic*. **3**. 表示"呈现出…","受…影响": rust*ic*. **4**. 表示"产生": anaesthet*ic*.

ICA = International Cooperative Alliance (联合国)国际合作社联盟。

-i·cal *suf*. 构成形容词,表示"…的","…似的": chem*ical*. mus*ical*.

-i·cal·ly *suf*. 构成与 -ic, -ical 相应的副词: poet*ically*, com*ically*.

ICAO = International Civil Aviation Organization (联合国)国际民用航空组织。

I·car·i·an [aiˈkeəriən; aɪˋkerɪən] *a*. (像神话中的 Icarus 飞得过高,致使其蜡翼为太阳融化那样)过分冒险的。

ICARUS = intercontinental aerospacecraft range unlimited system 航程无限的洲际宇宙火箭。

Ic·a·rus [ˈaikərəs; ˋaɪkərəs] *n*.【希神】(蜡翼人)伊卡洛斯〔建筑师 Daedalus 之子,以蜡翼飞上天空,但因飞得过高,蜡翼为太阳融化,堕海而死〕。

ICBM = intercontinental ballistic missile 洲际弹道飞弹。

ICC = **1**. International Chamber of Commerce 国际商会。**2**. Interstate Commerce Commission〔美〕州际商务委员会。

ice [ais; aɪs] **I** *n*. **1**. 冰,冰块。**2**.〔英〕雪糕,冰淇淋(= ice cream);〔美〕冰凉饮料[点心]。**3**. 冰状物,糖衣。**4**. (态度)冷淡。**5**.〔俚〕冰毒〔甲基苯丙胺的粉状结晶体,一种易使人上瘾的毒品〕。*eat an* ~ 吃一块雪糕。*two strawberry* ~*s* 两杯冰草莓。*water* ~ 冰糕。***be made of*** ~ 冷若冰霜。***be on*** [***over***] ***thin*** ~ 如履薄冰,处境极为艰险。***break the*** ~ 起头;打破沉闷,开口。***cut no*** [***little***] ~〔美口〕不起作用,无效。***find*** [***get***] ***one's*** ~ ***legs*** 开始学会滑冰。***have one's brains on*** ~〔口〕保持冷静。***on*** ~ **1**.〔美俚〕储备,贮存。**2**. 在监狱中。**3**. 有获胜[成功]的把握。***open*** ~ (不妨碍航行的)散冰。***put ... on*** ~ **1**. 把…暂时搁起,把…遗忘。**2**. 杀死…。**3**. 有把握将…握在手中。***skate on*** [***over***] ***thin*** ~ = ***be on thin ice***. ***straight off the*** ~ 立刻;(食品等)新鲜的。**II** *vt*. **1**. 冰冻;使成冰。**2**. 用冰覆盖,用冰封冻 (*over*)。**3**. 加糖衣(在糖果上)。**4**.〔美俚〕谋杀,凶杀 (*out*)。**5**.〔美俚〕(社交上)忽视,排斥 (*out*)。*The pond was* ~*d over*. 池子给冰封起来了。~ *wine* 冰一冰酒。***be*** ~***d up*** (船)被冰冻结起来了。~ ***the decision*** [***game***]〔美口〕保证胜利。~ ***up*** 用冰填满。— *vi*. 结冰 (*up*; *over*)。~ **age** **1**.【地】冰期;冰河时代。~ **ax(e)** (登山用的)破冰斧。~ **bag** 冰袋〔医用〕。~**berg** **1**. 冰山;流冰。**2**. 不怕冷的人;感情上冷冰冰的人。**3**. 表面上呈现的东西,(事物全貌的)一小部分。~**berg lettuce**【植】冰山形莴苣〔一种卷叶莴苣,叶子不大不小,在顶部紧密地聚成圆形〕。~**blink** (冰原上的)反光。~**boat** 冰上滑行船;破冰船。~**bound** *a*. 被冰封锁着的,被冰封冻着的。~**box** 冰箱;〔美俚〕严寒地带;〔美俚〕单人牢房。~**breaker** **1**. 破冰船;碎冰器。**2**. 基本收费,(出租汽车的)首里收费。~**cap** 冰盖;冰冠。~ **chest** = ~**box** 冰箱,冰库。~ **coating** 敷冰;结冰。~**-cold** *a*. 极冷的,冰冷的。~ **cream** 冰淇淋。~**-cream** *a*. 乳白色的。~**fall** **1**. 冰布〔冰川陡峭部分〕。**2**. 冰崩。~ **field** (两极地方的)冰原。~**floe** (海上)大浮冰。~**foot** (两极地方的)冰壁。~**-free** *a*. 不冻的 (*an* ~*-free port* 不冻港)。~ **glass** 冰花状玻璃。~ **hockey** 冰球,冰上曲棍球。~**-house** 冰室,冰窖;制冰场所;(爱斯基摩人的)冰屋。~**-jam** **1**. 流冰壅塞。**2**. 阻塞,僵局。~**-khana** 冰上汽车比赛。~ **machine** 制冰机。~**man**〔美〕制冰的人;卖冰的人;冰上旅行家;善于在冰上行走的人。~ **milk**〔美〕〔以脱脂乳制作的〕牛奶冻。~ **needle**【气】冰针。~**-out** (水面冰块)融化。~ **pack** 浮冰群;〔美〕冰袋。~ **pantomime** = ~ show. ~**-paper** (制图用)透明纸。~ **pick** (餐桌上用的)碎冰锥。~ **plant**【植】冰叶日中花。~ **rink** 滑冰场。~ **run** 冰橇滑行路。~ **sheet** (长期覆盖着陆地的)大冰原。~ **shelf** 冰棚;(两极地方的)陆缘冰。~ **show** 冰上表演。~ **skate**〔常 *pl*.〕(冰鞋下的)冰刀。~**-skate** *vi*. 溜冰。~ **sucker** 棒冰,冰棍。~**-tray** (冰箱内)制冰块的盘子。~**-up** 全面结冰。~ **water**〔美〕冰水;雪水。~ **yacht** 冰上快艇。

-ice *suf*. 构成名词,表示"状态","性质": just*ice*, serv*ice*.

Ice. = Iceland; Icelandic.

iced [aist; aɪst] *a*. 用冰封着的,加了糖衣的。~ **beer** 冰镇啤酒。~ **jean** 砂洗牛仔裤。~**-water** 冰过的水。

Icel. = Iceland; Icelandic.

Ice·land [ˈaislənd; ˋaɪslənd] *n*. 冰岛〔欧洲〕。~ *moss*【植】(可供食用的)地衣。~ *spar*【矿】冰洲石〔双折射透明方解石〕。

Ice·land·er [ˈaisləndə; ˋaɪsləndɚ] *n*. 冰岛人。

Ice·lan·dic [aisˈlændik; aɪsˋlændɪk] **I** *a*. 冰岛的;冰岛人的;冰岛语的;冰岛文化的。**II** *n*. 冰岛语〔北日耳曼语〕。

ICFTU = International Confederation of Free Trade Unions 国际自由工会联合会。

Ich·a·bod [ˈikəbɔd; ˋɪkəbɑd] *n*. 伊卡博德〔男子名〕。

ich·neu·mon [ikˈnjuːmən; ɪkˋnjumən] *n*.【动】**1**. 獴。**2**. 姬峰 (= ~-fly)。

ich·nite [ˈiknait; ˋɪknaɪt] *n*.【地】化石足迹。

ich·n(o)- *comb. f*. 表示"痕迹","足迹": *ichno*graphy.

ich·no·graph [ˈiknəugrɑːf; ˋɪknoˏgræf] *n*. 平面图。

ich·nog·ra·phy [ikˈnɔgrəfi; ɪkˋnɑgrəfɪ] *n*. 平面图法。**-no·graph·i·c(al)** *a*.

ich·no·lite [ˈiknəlait; ˋɪknəlaɪt] *n*. = ichnite.

ich·nol·o·gy [ikˈnɔlədʒi; ɪkˋnɑlədʒɪ] *n*.【地】化石足迹学,足迹学。**ich·no·log·i·cal** *a*.

i·chor [ˈaikɔː; ˋaɪkɔr] *n*. **1**.【希神】(诸神血管中的)灵液。**2**.【医】腐液,创液,脓水。

i·chor·ous [ˈaikərəs; ˋaɪkərəs] *a*.【医】腐液的,脓水的。

ich·thy·ic [ˈikθiːik; ˋɪkθiɪk] *a*. 鱼的;有鱼的特性的。

ich·thy(o)- *comb. f*. 表示"鱼类的","像鱼的"〔元音前

用 ichthy-]: *ichthyo*logy.
ich·thy·og·ra·phy [ikθi'ɔgrəfi; ˌɪkθɪ'ɑgrəfɪ] *n*. 鱼类志,鱼族学,鱼论。
ich·thy·oid ['ikθiɔid; 'ɪkθɪˌɔɪd] **I** *a*. 像鱼的,鱼状的。**II** *n*. 鱼形脊椎动物。
ich·thy·ol ['ikθiɔl; 'ɪkθɪˌɔl] *n*.【药】鱼石脂,鱼石脂磺酸铵。
ich·thy·ol·a·try [ˌikθi'ɔlətri; ˌɪkθɪ'ɑlətrɪ] *n*. 鱼神崇拜。
ich·thy·o·lite ['ikθiəlait; 'ɪkθɪəˌlaɪt] *n*. 鱼化石。
ich·thy·ol·o·gist [ˌikθi'ɔlədʒist; ˌɪkθɪ'ɑlədʒɪst] *n*. 鱼类学家,鱼学研究者。
ich·thy·ol·o·gy [ˌikθi'ɔlədʒi; ˌɪkθɪ'ɑlədʒɪ] *n*. **1**. 鱼类学。**2**. 鱼类研究。
ich·thy·oph·a·gous [ˌikθi'ɔfəgəs; ˌɪkθɪ'ɑfəgəs] *a*. 食鱼的。
ich·thy·oph·a·gy [ˌikθi'ɔfədʒi; ˌɪkθɪ'ɑfədʒɪ] *n*. 以鱼为食。
ich·thy·or·nis [ikθi'ɔːnis; ɪkθɪ'ɔrnɪs] *n*.【动】鹋。
ich·thy·o·saur ['ikθiəsɔː; 'ɪkθɪəˌsɔr] *n*. (*pl*. *~ia*)【古生】鱼龙。
ich·thy·o·saur·us [ˌikθiə'sɔːrəs; ˌɪkθɪə'sɔrəs] *n*. (*pl*. *~es*) = ichthyosaur.
ich·thy·o·sis [ˌikθi'əusis; ˌɪkθɪ'osɪs] *n*.【医】鱼鳞癣。**ich·thy·otic** *a*.
ICI = Imperial Chemical Industries〔英〕帝国化学工业公司。
-i·cian *suf*. 构成名词,表示"精通者","(专)家","能手": mus*ician*, phys*ician*.
i·ci·cle ['aisikl; 'aɪsɪkl̩] *n*. 冰柱;冷冰冰的人。**-d** *a*.
i·ci·ly ['aisili; 'aɪsɪlɪ] *ad*. 冰似地,冰冷地,冷淡地。
i·ci·ness ['aisinis; 'aɪsɪnɪs] *n*. 冰冷,冰冷的状态。
ic·ing ['aisiŋ; 'aɪsɪŋ] *n*. **1**. (糕点的)糖霜,酥皮。**2**.【空】飞机外身的霜冻。
ICJ = International Court of Justice (联合国)国际法院。
Ickes ['ikis; 'ɪkɪs] *n*. 伊基斯〔姓氏〕。
ick·le[1] ['ikl; 'ɪkl̩] *n*.〔英方〕= icicle.
ick·le[2] ['ikl; 'ɪkl̩] *a*.〔儿〕= little.
ick·y ['iki; 'ɪkɪ] *a*. (*ick·i·er*, *ick·i·est*) **1**. 非常讨厌的。**2**. 黏得难过的。**3**. 太甜的,多愁善感得使人腻烦的。**-i·ly** *ad*. **-i·ness** *n*.
ICM = intercontinental missile 洲际导[飞]弹。
i·con ['aikɔn; 'aɪkɑn] (*pl*. *~s* [-z; -z], *i·co·nes* [-kəniːz; -kəniz]) *n*. **1**. 人像;肖像;画像;雕像;(学术书的)插画。**2**.【宗】圣像。**3**. 偶像,崇拜对象。**4**.【逻】类似记号[表现]。**5**.【计】(电脑)图符,图示影像。**-ize** *vt*. 把…作为偶像,盲目崇拜。
i·con·ic(al) [ai'kɔnik(əl); aɪ'kɑnɪk(əl)] *a*. **1**. 人像的;圣像的;偶像的;偶像般的。**2**. 老一套的,风格固定的。
i·con(o)- *comb*. *f*. 表示"像": *icono*latry.
i·con·o·clasm [ai'kɔnəˌklæzəm; aɪ'kɑnəˌklæzəm] *n*. **1**. 偶像破坏;圣像破坏。**2**. 对传统观念的攻击。
i·con·o·clast [ai'kɔnəklæst; aɪ'kɑnəˌklæst] *n*. **1**. 反对崇拜圣像的人。**2**. 反对崇拜偶像的人。**3**. 攻击传统观念的人。**i·con·o·clas·tic** [aiˌkɔnə'klæstik; aɪˌkɑnə'klæstɪk] *a*. **i·con·o·clas·ti·cal·ly** *ad*.
i·con·o·graph [ai'kɔnəgrɑːf; aɪ'kɑnəˌgræf, -grɑf] *n*. (书刊等的)插图。
i·co·nog·ra·pher [ˌaikɔ'nɔgrəfə; ˌaɪkə'nɑgrəfɚ] *n*. 肖像学者,肖像研究家。
i·co·nog·ra·phy [ˌaikɔ'nɔgrəfi; ˌaɪkə'nɑgrəfɪ] *n*. **1**. 肖像画法。**2**. 肖像学,肖像研究。**3**. 插图,图解。**i·con·o·graph·ic(al)** *a*.
i·co·nol·a·ter [ˌaikɔ'nɔlətə; ˌaɪkə'nɑlətɚ] *n*. 圣像[偶像]崇拜者。
i·co·nol·a·try [ˌaikɔ'nɔlətri; ˌaɪkə'nɑlətrɪ] *n*. 圣像[偶像]崇拜。
i·co·nol·o·gy [ˌaikɔ'nɔlədʒi; ˌaɪkə'nɑlədʒɪ] *n*. **1**.【宗】圣像学;偶像学。**2**. 圣像;偶像(总称)。**3**. 象征性表现;象征主义。**i·con·o·log·i·cal** [aiˌkɔnə'lɔdʒikl; aɪˌkɑnə'lɑdʒɪkl̩] *a*. **i·co·nol·o·gist** *n*.
i·co·nom·e·ter [ˌaikɔ'nɔmitə; ˌaɪkə'nɑmɪtɚ] *n*.【摄】反光镜;【测】测距镜;测影仪;录像器;取景器。
i·con·o·scope [ai'kɔnəskəup; aɪ'kɑnəˌskop] *n*.【物】光电显像管,光电析像管。*image* ~ 移像光电显像管。
i·co·nos·ta·sis [ˌaikɔ'nɔstəsis; ˌaɪkə'nɑstəsɪs] *n*. (*pl*. *-ses* [-ˌsiːz; -ˌsiz]) (东正教)圣障,圣壁。亦作 **i·con·o·stas** [aɪ'kɔnəˌstæs; aɪ'kɑnəˌstæs].
i·co·sa·he·dron ['aikəusə'hedrən; 'aɪkosə'hɛdrən] *n*. (*pl*. *~s* 或 *-ra* [-rə; -rə])【数】二十面体。
ICR = Institute for Cancer Research (美国)癌症研究所。
ICRC = International Committee of the Red Cross 红十字国际委员会。
ICRP = International Commission on Radiological Protection 国际放射性辐射防护委员会。
-ics *suf*. 构成复数型名词。**1**.〔用作单数〕表示"…学","…术": mathemat*ics*, phys*ics*. **2**.〔用作复数〕(a)科学名称加上"my","the","such"等特定的词时: *His mathematics are strong*. (b)表示"行为","活动","体系","性质"的名称时: *Aerobatics take a lot of learning*. **3**. 有若干可单数复数两用者: *Politics is* [*are*] *fascinating*.
I.C.S. = Indian Civil Service; International Correspondence School(s)〔美〕国际函授学校(网)。
I.C.T. = inflammation of connective tissue; Institute of Clay Technology; International Critical Tables.
ic·ter·ic [ik'terik; ɪk'tɛrɪk] *a*.【医】黄疸的。
ic·ter·us ['iktərəs; 'ɪktərəs] *n*. **1**.【医】黄疸。**2**.【植】叶黄病。
ic·tus ['iktəs; 'ɪktəs] *n*. (*pl*. ~(*es*)) **1**. (诗中的)强音,扬音。**2**.【医】暴发病;搏动;冲击。~ *solis* 日射病,中暑(= sunstroke)。
ICU = intensive care unit 特别医疗单位。
I.C.W. = Inter-American Commission of Women; interrupted continuous wave【无】断续等幅波。
i·cy ['aisi; 'aɪsɪ] *a*. (*i·ci·er*; *-ci·est*) **1**. 冰封着的,冰多的。**2**. 冰似的,冰冷的。**3**. 冷淡的,生疏的。*the* ~ *North* 冰天雪地的北方。*an* ~ *welcome* 冷淡的欢迎。*an* ~ *wind* 寒风。
ID = identification 台名识别〔电台或电视台暂时中断广播以宣布台名〕。
ID, I.D. ['aidiː; 'aɪdi] **I** *n*. (*pl*. ***ID's***, ***I.D.'s***) 身分证(= ID card, I.D. card)。**II** 〔ID, Id〕*vt*. **1**. 指认出,识别。**2**. 给(某人)发身份证。*The witness ~ed the suspect*. 证人指认出了嫌犯。
Id. = Idaho.
id. = 〔L.〕*idem*.
I'd [aid; aɪd]〔口〕= I had; I would; I should.
id [id; ɪd] *n*.【生】遗传基质;本能冲动。
I.D. = Infantry Division; inside diameter; Intelligence Department.
-id[1] *suf*. **1**. 表示"…(姑)娘": Dana*id*. **2**. 表示"…流星": Leon*id*【天】狮子座流星。**3**. 用作叙事诗的题名: Aene*id*.
-id[2] *suf*.【动】用作科属动物的名词、形容词: arachn*id*.
-id[3] *suf*. 用以形成原为拉丁语名词的名词: chrysal*id*, pyram*id*.
-id[4] *suf*. 由拉丁语动词、名词作成表示状态的形容词: horr*id*, flu*id*, sol*id*.
-id[5] *suf*.〔美〕= -ide.
I·da ['aidə; 'aɪdə] *n*. 艾达〔女子名〕。
IDA = International Development Association (联合国)国际开发协会。

I

Ida. = Idaho.

-i·dae [iˈdiː; ɪˋdi] *suf*.【动】表示"…科": Fel*idae*.

I·da·ho [ˈaidəhəu; ˋaɪdəho] ***n*.** 爱达荷[美国州名]。

I·da·ho·an [ˈaidəˌhəuən; ˋaɪdəˏhoən] ***a*.** 爱达荷州的。— ***n*.** 爱达荷州人。

-ide *suf*.【化】表示"…化合物": brom*ide*, carb*ide*, ox*ide*.

IDDD = International Direct Distance Dialing 国际直通长途电话。

i·de·a [aiˈdiə; aɪˋdɪə] ***n*. 1.** 主意;念头;思想;计划,打算;意见。**2.** 想像,模糊想法。**3.**【哲】理念,理性概念,观念;【心】表像。**4.**【乐】主题,乐句,音型。*Eastern* [*Western*] *~s* 东方[西方]思想。*the general ~ of an article* 文章大意。*a good ~* 好主意。*a man of ~s* 足智多谋的人。*An ~ struck me*. 我想出了一个主意。*conceive an ~* 起念头。*full of ~s* 主意多。*Such an ~ never occurred to me*. 我从来没有这样想过。*the ~ of such a thing*! 多糊涂的想法! *the young ~* 小孩子的想法。*What is your ~*? 你的意见怎样? *I have no ~ (as to) what you mean*. 我摸不清你的意思。*absolute ~*【哲】绝对观念。*a fixed ~* 固定观念;固执的想法。***an ~ outline of*** [***about***] 关于…的设想。***in ~*** 想像上 (*opp*. in reality)。***put ~s in sb.'s head*** 使某人存奢望,使某人得意忘形。***run a way with the ~*** 不加考虑地附和某种意见,轻率地下结论。***That's the ~***. 〔口〕对了,就是这意思! 这行! 这我同意! ***the big*** [***grand***, ***great***] *~* 〔美〕〔往往表示讽刺〕高见,好主意。***What's the big ~***? 〔美〕有何高见? ***The ~***! 〔口〕什么! 这! 糊涂! 〔表示愤怒、惊异、轻蔑〕。***upon an ~*** 心生一计。***What an ~***! 〔口〕什么话! 多么荒唐! **~man** 谋士。**~phobia** 惧思考症。

i·de·aed, i·de·a'd [aiˈdiəd; aɪˋdɪəd] ***a*.** 有某种看法的,主意多的。

i·de·al [aiˈdiəl; aɪˋdɪəl] **I** ***a*. 1.** 理想的,典型的。**2.** 观念的;想像的;空想的;不切实际的。**3.** 唯心论的;理想主义的。*an ~ place for a holiday* 度假的理想场所。*~ happiness* 想像中的幸福。**II** ***n*.** 理想;典型;模范;空想的事物;【数】理想子环,理想数。*beau ~* 十全十美的理想。***the I- and the Real*** 理想与现实。***That is only an ~***. 那仅仅是空想。**~ point**【数】理想点,假[伪]点。**-ly** ***ad*.**

i·de·a·less [aiˈdiəlis; aɪˋdɪəlɪs] ***a*.** 缺乏理想的,没有主意的。

i·de·al·ism [aiˈdiəlizm; aɪˋdɪəlɪzm] ***n*. 1.** 理想主义。**2.**【哲】唯心论,唯心主义,观念论 (*opp*. materialism)。*historical ~* 历史唯心主义。*objective ~* 客观唯心主义。*subjective ~* 主观唯心主义。

i·de·al·ist [aiˈdiəlist; aɪˋdɪəlɪst] **I** ***n*. 1.** 唯心主义者,唯心论者。**2.** 理论主义者;空想家。**II** ***a*. 1.** 唯心主义的。**2.** 理想主义的;空想家的,唯心论的。*the ~ conception of history* 唯心史观。

i·de·al·is·tic [aiˌdiəˈlistik; aɪˏdɪəˋlɪstɪk] ***a*. 1.** 理想主义者的,空想家的。**2.** 唯心主义者的。**3.** 唯心论的。**-tical·ly** ***ad*.**

i·de·al·i·ty [ˌaidiˈæliti; ˏaɪdɪˋæləti] ***n*.** 理想;空想;想像力。

i·de·al·ize [aiˈdi(ː)əlaiz; aɪˋdi(ɪ)əˏlaɪz] ***vt*.**, ***vi*.** 使理想化,使合于理想。**i·de·al·i·za·tion** ***n*.**

i·de·ate [aiˈdi(ː)eit; aɪˋdi(ɪ)et] **I** ***vt*.** 想像;思考。— ***vi*.** 形成观念。**II** [aiˈdiːit; aɪˋdɪɪt] ***n*.**【哲】与观念相应的客体。

i·de·a·tion [ˌaidiˈeiʃən; ˏaɪdɪˋeʃən] ***n*.** 心理作用,观念作用;观念化。

i·dée fixe [ideˈfiks; ɪdeˋfɪks] 〔F.〕固定的观念;成见。

i·dem [ˈaidem; ˋaɪdem] ***n*.**, ***pro*.**, ***a*.** 〔L.〕同著者;同上,同前〔略 id.〕。~ ***quod*** 同…。

i·den·tic [aiˈdentik; aɪˋdɛntɪk] ***a*. 1.** = identical. **2.** (外交)相同文件的。*an ~ action* 相同行为。*an ~ note* 相同文件[照会]。

i·den·ti·cal [aiˈdentikəl; aɪˋdɛntɪkəl] ***a*.** 同一的;同样的;【数】恒等的 (*with*);【生】同卵的。*on the ~ day* 在同一天。*the ~ person* 同一人。*an ~ conception*【逻】同一概念。*~ twins*【生】同卵双生 (*cf*. fraternal twin)。*~ equation*【数】恒等式,全等式。~ **proposition**【逻】同一命题,同一关系〔主、表语在内涵和外延上一致的命题: *That which is mortal is not immortal*. 凡是会死的就不是永生的〕。**-ly** ***ad*.** 同一;同样。

i·den·ti·fi·a·ble [aiˈdentifaiəbl; aɪˋdɛntɪfaɪəbl̩] ***a*.** 可视为相同的;可证明为同一的。**i·den·ti·fi·a·bly** ***ad*.**

i·den·ti·fi·ca·tion [aiˌdentifiˈkeiʃən; aɪˏdɛntɪfɪˋkeʃən] ***n*. 1.** 认出,识别,鉴定,验明(罪人正身等)。**2.**【心】自居作用。**3.** 身分证。**4.**【数】黏合,同化。*target ~ bomb*【军】目标识别炸弹。~ **card** [**paper**] 身分证。~ **disk** [**tag**] (士兵的)证章。~ **lamp** 标灯。~ **plate** (汽车)牌照。

i·den·ti·fy [aiˈdentifai; aɪˋdɛntəˏfaɪ] ***vt*.** (***-fied***; ***-fy·ing***) **1.** 使等同于…,使成为一致,把…看做一致 (*with*)。**2.** 把…鉴定为同一人[同一物],验明(正身),鉴别,辨认,识别;【生】确定…在分类学上的位置。*~ the payee of a check* 验明支票的取款人。*~ handwriting* 鉴定笔迹。*~ a corpse* 验尸。*~ class status* 划分阶级成分。~ ***oneself with*** 参加到…中去;和…打成一片 (*He identified himself with the masses wherever he went*. 他每到一地,就和那里的群众打成一片)。

I·den·ti·kit [aiˈdentikit; aɪˋdɛntɪkɪt] **I** ***n*.** 〔英〕(由一套有各种类型的眼、鼻、口等透明画组成的)容貌拼具。**II** ***a*.** 〔常 i-〕用容貌拼具拼成的。

i·den·ti·ty [aiˈdentiti; aɪˋdɛntətɪ] ***n*. 1.** 同一,一致;同一性。**2.** 本体;正身;个性。**3.**【逻】同一性。**4.**【数】恒等(式)。*an ~ card* 身份证,居民证。*an ~ disk* [*tag*] (士兵的)证章。*systems suited to its national ~* 符合自己民族特点的制度。*national ~* 民族面貌。*the principle of ~*【逻】同一律。*establish* [*prove*] *one's ~* 证明身份。*mistaken* [*false*] *~* 认错人。*no matter what their ~* 无论什么人。*sink one's ~* 隐瞒历史。~ **crisis**【心】个性转变期〔尤指青春期一段心绪不宁的时间〕。~ **theft** 身份盗窃〔利用从因特网上获取的他人姓名、社会保障号码、住址等信息,冒名申请贷款等的一种犯罪行为〕。

id·e·o·gram, id·e·o·graph [ˈidiəugræm, ˈidiəugrɑːf; ˋɪdɪoˏgræm, ˋɪdɪoˏgrɑf] ***n*. 1.** 会意[表意]文字。**2.** 表意符号(如 5,十,=)。*a Chinese ideograph* 汉字。

id·e·o·graph·ic(al) [idiəuˈgræfik(əl); ˏɪdɪoˋgræfɪk(əl)] ***a*.** 会意的,表意文字的,表意符号的。**-i·cal·ly** ***ad*.**

id·e·og·ra·phy [ˌidiˈɔgrəfi, ˌaid-; ˏɪdɪˋɑgrəfɪ, ˏaɪd-] ***n*.** 会意文字学;表意文字的应用,表意符号的运用。

i·de·o·log·ic(al) [ˌaidiəˈlɔdʒik(əl); ˏaɪdɪəˋlɑdʒɪk(əl)] ***a*.** 思想(体系)上的;意识形态的;空论的。**-i·cal·ly** ***ad*.**

i·de·ol·o·gist [ˌaidiˈɔlədʒist, id-; ˏaɪdɪˋɑlədʒɪst, ɪd-] ***n*.** 理论家;思想家;空想家。

i·de·ol·o·gize [ˌaidiˈɔlədʒaiz; ˏaɪdɪˋɑlədʒaɪz] ***vt*.** (***-giz·ed***, ***-giz·ing***) **1.** 作思想分析。**2.** 改变成某一种思想。

i·de·o·logue [ˈaidiːəulɔg; ˋaɪdioˏlɑg] ***n*.** 〔F.〕思想家,理论家,空想家。

i·de·ol·o·gy [ˌaidiˈɔlədʒi, id-; ˏaɪdɪˋɑlədʒɪ, ɪd-] ***n*. 1.** 观念学。**2.** 思想体系,思想意识。**3.** 观念形态,意识形态,思想方式。**4.** 空想,空论。

i·de·o·mo·tor [ˌaidiəˈməutə, ˈidi-; ˏaɪdɪəˋmotɚ, ˋɪdɪ-] ***a*.**【心】观念运动的。

i·de·o·phone [ˈaidiəfəun, ˈidiə-; ˋaɪdɪəfon, ˋɪdɪə-] ***n*.**【语】摹拟音;像音成份〔许多非洲语言的一种表意法,借助一种重复的声音去创造行为、事物的形象〕。

ides [aidz; aɪdz] ***n*.** 〔*pl*.〕古罗马历 3,5,7,10 每月中的第

15日以及其他各月中的第13日。

id est [id'est; ɪd`ɛst]〔L.〕即,那就是〔= that is (to say),略作 i.e.〕。

id·ge·nus·om·ne [id'dʒi:nəs'ɔmni; ɪd`dʒinəs`ɑmnɪ]〔L.〕= all of that kind.

id·i·o- *comb. f.* 表示"特殊的","特有的","本身的": *idio*morphic.

id·i·o·blast ['idiəˌblæst; `ɪdɪəˏblæst] *n.*【生】异细胞。**-blas·tic** *a.*

id·i·o·chro·mat·ic [ˌidiə*u*krə'mætik; ˏɪdɪokrə`mætɪk] *a.* (矿物等)自色的。

id·i·o·cy ['idiəsi; `ɪdɪəsɪ] *n.* **1.** 白痴。**2.** 极端愚蠢的言行。

id·i·o·e·lec·tric [ˌidiəi'lektrik; ˏɪdɪəɪ`lɛktrɪk] *a.* 非导体的;【物】摩擦生电的。

id·i·o·e·lec·trics [ˌidiəi'lektriks; ˏɪdɪəɪ`lɛktrɪks] *n.* 非导体。

id·i·o·gram ['i:diəgræm; `ɪdɪəˏgræm] *n.*【生】染色体组型,染色体模式图。

id·i·o·graph ['idiəgrɑ:f; `ɪdɪəˏgrɑf] *n.* **1.** 个人特有的署名。**2.** 商标。

id·i·o·graph·ic [ˌidiə'græfik; ˏɪdɪə`græfɪk] *n.* **1.** 个人署名的;商标的。**2.** 具有特点的,独特的,个别的。

id·i·o·lect ['idiə*u*lekt; `ɪdɪolɛkt] *n.*【语】个人习语,个人语型。

id·i·om ['idiəm; `ɪdɪəm] *n.* **1.** 习语,成语。**2.** 惯用语法,某种语言的特性。**3.** 方言,土语。**4.** (某一作家独特的)表现方法;(音乐、美术等的)风格。

id·i·o·mat·ic(al) [ˌidiə'mætik(əl); ˏɪdɪə`mætɪk(əl)] *a.* **1.** 成语的;符合语言习惯的。**2.** 成语丰富的,用很多成语的。**3.** 富有习语性质的。**4.** (某团体或个人)特有的,独特的。**-i·cal·ly** *ad.* **-i·cal·ness, -tic·i·ty** *n.*

id·i·o·mor·phic [ˌidiə'mɔ:fik; ˏɪdɪə`mɔrfɪk] *a.*【矿】自形的,自发的,整形的。

id·i·o·path·i·c [ˌidiə'pæθik; ˏɪdɪə`pæθɪk] *a.*【医】(疾病)特发性的,自发性的。**-i·cal·ly** *ad.*

id·i·op·a·thy [ˌidi'ɔpəθi; ˏɪdɪ`ɑpəθɪ] *n.*【医】特发性的疾病,自发性的疾病。

id·i·o·phone ['idiə*u*fəun; `ɪdɪəˏfon] *n.*【乐】意狄欧风〔一种非膜质的打击乐器〕。

id·i·o·plasm ['idiəplæzəm; `ɪdɪəˏplæzəm] *n.*【生】异胞质。**-matic, -mic** *a.*

id·i·o·syn·cra·sy [ˌidiə'siŋkrəsi; ˏɪdɪə`sɪŋkrəsɪ] *n.* **1.** (人的)特质,特性,个性。**2.** (著者)特有的风格。**3.**【医】特(异反)应性;特异体质,特异素。**-crat·ic** *a.*

id·i·ot ['idiət; `ɪdɪət] *n.* 白痴;〔口〕傻子。~ **board** [**card**]〔俚〕(电视演员的)提词板[牌]。~ **box**〔俚〕电视机。~ **light** (汽车仪表板上的)傻瓜报警灯(当发动机过热或电池需充电时即会闪亮)。~**-proof** *a.* 简单易解的,容易操作的,可靠的 (= foolproof)。

id·i·ot·ic(al) [ˌidi'ɔtik(əl); ˏɪdɪ`ɑtɪk(əl)] *a.* 白痴(一样)的;愚蠢的。**-i·cal·ly** *ad.*

id·i·ot·ism ['idiə*u*tizəm; `ɪdɪotɪzm̩] *n.* **1.** 白痴行为。**2.**〔古〕白痴。**3.**〔废〕= idiom.

IDL = international date line 国际日期变更线,日界线。

i·dle ['aidl; `aɪdl̩] **I** *a.* **1.** 懒惰的,吊儿郎当的。**2.** 空闲的;【机】空转的。**3.** 没用的,无益的,无效的;【物】无功的;无根据的。~ *worms* 懒虫。*I- folks lack no excuses.*〔谚〕懒人不愁无借口。*have one's hands* ~ 空着手,没事。*the* ~ *rich* 有闲阶级。~ *compliment* 应酬话,虚礼。~ *hours* 闲时。*it is* ~ *to say that ...* 说,是没有用的。*an* ~ *dream* 痴心妄想。*an* ~ *rumour* 毫无根据的谣言。***be at an* ~ *end*** 闲着无事,赋闲。***eat* ~*bread*** = ***eat the bread of idleness*** 吃闲饭。***lie* ~** 被搁置;一事不做。***run* ~** (机器)空转。***stand* ~** 袖手旁观。**II** *vt.* 空费,虚度(岁月)。~ ***away one's time*** [***life***] 虚度时光[一生]。— *vi.* 懒,不做事;闲混,闲逛 (*about*);(机器)空转 (*over*)。~ **capacity** 储备容量;备用电器。~ **circuit** 空载电路。~ **current** 无效电流。~ **frequency** 中心频率;未调制的频率。~ **funds** [**money**]【经】游资。~ **motion** 空转。~ **roll** 传动轧辊,随转轧辊。~ **space** 余隙空间。~ **time** 空载时间,停机时间。~ **unit** 闲置设备。~ **wheel**【机】惰轮,空转轮,调紧皮带轮。

i·dle·ness ['aidlnis; `aɪdl̩nɪs] *n.* **1.** 懒惰;坐食。**2.** 赋闲无事,失业。**3.** 无益,无效。*busy* ~ 整天无事忙。*I- is the mother* [*parent, root*] *of all evil* [*sin, vice*].〔谚〕懒惰为万恶之源。*I- rusts the mind.*〔谚〕怠惰使头脑迟钝。***eat the bread of* ~** 坐吃。***live in* ~** 游手好闲。

i·dler ['aidlə; `aɪdlɚ] *n.* **1.** 懒人;游手好闲者。**2.** 不当班的海军士兵。**3.**【机】惰轮,空转轮,调紧皮带轮。**4.**【铁路】空车。

i·dlesse ['aidles; `aɪdlɛs] *n.*〔古、诗〕= idleness.

i·dly ['aidli; `aɪdlɪ] *ad.* 懒惰地;空闲地;无用地。

I·do ['i:dəu; `ido] *n.* 简化世界语〔指1907年在法国发表的世界语改革方案〕。

i·do·crase ['aidə*u*kreis, 'idəu-; `aɪdokres, `ɪdo-] *n.* = vesuvianite 符山石,维苏威石。

i·dol ['aidl; `aɪdl̩] *n.* **1.** 偶像。**2.** 被崇拜的人[物]。**3.**【逻】谬论,谬见。**4.** 幻像;幽灵。***make an* ~ *of sb.*** 崇拜[迷信]某人。

i·do·la [ai'dəulə; aɪ`dolə] *n.* idolum 的复数。

i·dol·a·ter [ai'dɔlətə; aɪ`dɑlətɚ] *n.* 偶像崇拜者;盲目崇拜者。

i·dol·a·tress [ai'dɔlətris; aɪ`dɑlətrɪs] *n.* 偶像的女崇拜者,女盲目崇拜者。

i·dol·a·trize [ai'dɔlətraiz; aɪ`dɑləˏtraɪz] *vt.*, *vi.* (*-trized, -triz·ing*) 盲目崇拜,实行偶像崇拜。

i·dol·a·trous [ai'dɔlətrəs; aɪ`dɑlətrəs] *a.* 崇拜偶像的;盲目崇拜的。**-ly** *ad.* **-ness** *n.*

i·dol·a·try [ai'dɔlətri; aɪ`dɑlətrɪ] *n.* (*pl.* **-tries**) **1.** 偶像崇拜。**2.** 盲目崇拜;过分尊崇。

i·dol·ism ['aidlizəm; `aɪdl̩ɪzm̩] *n.* **1.** = idolatry. **2.**〔古〕谬见;错误推理。

i·dol·ize ['aidəlaiz; `aɪdl̩aɪz] *vt.* 把…当偶像崇拜,盲目崇拜,醉心于。~ *the ancients* 复古。— *vi.* 崇拜偶像。**-i·za·tion** *n.*

i·do·lum [ai'dəuləm; aɪ`doləm] *n.* (*pl.* **-la** [-lə; -lə]) **1.** 幻想,观念。**2.**【逻】谬论,谬见。

i·dyl(l) ['idil, 'aidil; `ɪdɪl, `aɪdɪl] *n.* **1.** 即景诗,田园诗。**2.** (适合田园诗的)民间传说,田园风景。**3.**【乐】田园乐曲,牧歌。

i·dyl·lic [ai'dilik, i'dilik; aɪ`dɪlɪk, ɪ`dɪlɪk] *a.* **1.** 田园诗的,牧歌的。**2.** 质朴宜人的,生动逼真的。

i·dyl(l)·ist ['aidilist; `aɪdɪlɪst] *n.* 田园诗人,田园乐曲[牧歌]作者。

i·dyl(l)·ize ['aidilaiz; `aɪdɪlaɪz] *vt.* 使(生活)成田园诗;使成为牧歌。

I.E. = **1.** Indo-European 印欧语系(的)。**2.** Indian Empire〔旧〕印度帝国。**3.** = industrial engineering 工业工程学。

-ie *suf.* = -y[2] **1.** 表示"小";"小而可爱": beaut*ie*, dear*ie* fair*ie*. **2.** 表示"具有…性质的人(或物)": soft*ie*. **3.** 表示"…职业的人": book*ie*.

i.e. ['ai'i:; `aɪ`i]〔L.〕= *id est* 那就是;即 (= that is to say)。

IEA = International Energy Agency 国际能源机构。

-i·er *suf.* = -eer: brigad*ier*, glaz*ier*.

if [if; ɪf] **I** *conj.* **1.**〔表示条件〕倘若,如果。*If you are tired, we will sit down.* 如果你疲倦了,我们就坐下吧。*Return* ~ *undelivered.* 无法投递,请退回原处。~ *weather permits, ...* 如果天气好的话,…〔常略作 I.W.P.〕。**2.**〔表示假设〕要是,假设。*If I knew, I*

I

would say. 我要知道,我就说了。*If I were a bird, I could fly*. 假使我是只鸟,我就会飞了。*If he had tried, he would have succeeded*. 如果他当初作过尝试,他本来是会成功的。★在书面用语中主语与动词次序颠倒, *if* 即可略去: *Were I in your place*, ... = *If I were in your place*, ...; *Should I find it*, ... = *If I should find it*, ... **3.** 〔表示让步〕虽然,即使。*If he is little, he is strong*. 他年纪虽小,气力倒大。*I will do it* ~ *it kills me*. [*If I die for it*] 我拼命也要干。*His manner*, ~ *patronizing*, *was not unkind*. 他的态度,虽然是以恩人自居,然而并不粗暴。**4.** 〔口〕是否,是不是〔常用于 ask, see, try, doubt, learn, wonder 等词之后〕。*Ask* ~ *he is at home*. 问他在不在家。*I don't know* ~ *he is here*. 我不知道他是不是在这里。**5.** …的时候总是…,一…就。*If I feel any doubt, I ask*. 我一有疑惑就问。**6.** 〔条件句表示愿望、感叹。用过去时态的假设语气〕要是…多好: *If I only knew*! 要是我知道多好!〔可惜不知道〕。***If they had only arrived earlier***! 要是他们当初早点来就好了。***as*** ~ 活像(*as* ~ *he had seen it* 活像他见过似的)。~ ***a day*** [***an inch etc.***] 无论如何应该是…;至少有…(*He is seventy* ~ (*he is*) *a day* (*old*). 他该有七十岁了。*The enemy is 2000 strong* ~ *a man*. 敌人至少有二千人。*I've come three miles* ~ (*I've come*) *a yard*. 我走了该有三英里了)。~ ***and when*** **1.** = if. **2.** = when. ~ ***any*** 即使有也(极少)(*There is little* ~ *any hope*. 希望极少)。~ ***anything*** 甚至可能,或许甚至。~ ***it were not for*** = ~ ***it had not been for*** 若不是…的话。~ ***necessary*** 如有必要。~ ***not*** 要是不,即使不。~ ***only*** **1.** 只要。**2.** 要是…就好(*If only it clears up, we'll go*. 只要天一晴,我们就去。*If only he arrives in time*! 他要是能及时赶到就好了!) ~ ***possible*** 如果可能。~ ***so*** 如果这样。~ ***so be that*** = if. ~ ***you please*** [***will***] **1.** 请。**2.** 〔谑〕如何〔问人意向〕。***What*** (***matters it***) ~ ***I fail***! 失败算什么〔*cf*. what〕。***What*** (***would happen***) ~ ***you should fail***! 你要是失败了怎么办〔那就糟了〕! **II** ***n***. 条件,设想。*Dash these ~s*! 让这一大堆"如果"见鬼去吧! *There is no* ~ *in the case*. 这里没有假定的余地。*Your argument seems to have too many ~s*. 你的论据似乎假设太多。~ **clause** 【语法】条件子句。~ **statement** 计算机用条件语句。

IFC = International Finance Corporation (联合国)国际金融公司。

IFF = identification: friend or foe【军】敌我识别器,敌我识别系统。

if·fy [ˈifi; ˋɪfɪ] ***a***. 〔口〕可怀疑的;不确定的;偶然性的;有条件的。

IFJ = International Federation of Journalists 国际新闻工作者联合会。

I.F.S. = Irish Free State 〔旧〕爱尔兰自由邦。

-i·fy *suf*. = -fy: intens*ify*, solid*ify*.

IG = **1.** Indo-Germanic 印欧语系(的),会印欧语系语言的人。**2.** Inspector General 监察长。

Ig·bo [ˈigbəu; ˋɪgbo] ***n***. = Ibo.

IGD = Inspector General's Department 总监署。

I.G.H.Q. = Industrial Group Headquarters 工业组织管理局〔英国原子能管理局〕。

ig·loo, ig·lu [ˈiglu:; ˋɪglu] ***n***. (*pl*. *~s*) **1.** 爱斯基摩(Eskimo) 人居住的外壳用硬雪块砌成的圆顶小屋。**2.** 圆顶建筑。**3.** 手提透明塑胶保护罩。

ign. **1.** = ignition. **2.** 〔L.〕 unknown.

ig·ne·ous [ˈigniəs; ˋɪgnɪəs] ***a***. **1.** 火的,似火的。**2.** 【地】火成的。~ *magma* 岩浆。~ *rock* 火成岩。

ig·nes·cent [igˈnesnt; ɪgˋnɛsnt] **I** ***a***. **1.** 爆成火焰的。**2.** 碰击而冒火星的。**II** ***n***. 碰击而冒火星的物质。~ *stones* 打火石。

ig·nis fat·u·us [ˈignisˈfætjuəs; ˋɪgnɪsˋfætjuəs] (*pl*. ***ig·nes fat·u·i*** [ˈigni:zˈfætjuai; ˋɪgnizˋfætjuaɪ]) 〔L.〕 **1.** 鬼火,磷火。**2.** 虚幻的希望[目标]。

ig·nit·a·ble, ig·nit·i·ble [igˈnaitəbl; ɪgˋnaɪtəbl] ***a***. 可发火的,易燃的。**-a·bil·i·ty, -nit·i·bil·i·ty** ***n***.

ig·nite [igˈnait; ɪgˋnaɪt] ***vt***. **1.** 点火,点燃;使燃烧。**2.** 使灼热。**3.** 使兴奋,使激动。— ***vi***. 点火,发火,燃烧。

ig·nit·er, ig·nit·or [igˈnaitə; ɪgˋnaɪtɚ] ***n***. **1.** 点火器;传火药,点火剂;点火者。**2.** 引爆装置。

ig·ni·tion [igˈniʃən; ɪgˋnɪʃən] ***n***. **1.** 点火,着火,燃烧;【化】灼热。**2.** 【机】发火装置。~ **charge** 点火药。~ **point**【物】燃点。~ **temperature** 着火温度。

ig·ni·tron [ˈignitrɔn; ɪgˋnɪtrɑn] ***n***. 【无】点火管;引燃管;放电管。

ig·no·ble [igˈnəubl; ɪgˋnobl] ***a***. **1.** 卑鄙的;可耻的,不体面的。**2.** 卑贱的,出身微贱的。**ig·no·bil·i·ty** [ˌignəuˈbiliti; ˏɪgnoˋbɪlətɪ], **-ness** ***n***.

ig·no·bly [igˈnəubli; ɪgˋnoblɪ] ***ad***. 卑贱地;卑鄙地。*be* ~ *born* 出身寒微。

ig·no·min·i·ous [ignəˈminiəs; ˏɪgnəˋmɪnɪəs] ***a***. 可耻的,不光彩的,丢脸的;卑鄙的。*an* ~ *treaty* 屈辱性条约。**-ly** ***ad***. **-ness** ***n***.

ig·no·min·y [ˈignəmini; ˋɪgnəmɪnɪ] ***n***. **1.** 耻辱,污辱,不名誉。**2.** 无耻行为,丑行。

ig·no·ra·mus [ˌignəˈreiməs; ˏɪgnəˋreməs] ***n***. 没有知识的人;愚人。

ig·no·rance [ˈignərəns; ˋɪgnərəns] ***n***. 无知,缺乏教育,愚昧;不知道。*I- of the law excuses no one*. 〔谚〕不懂法律不能作为免罪的口实。*Where* ~ *is bliss, 'tis* (*it is*) *folly to be wise*. 〔谚〕难得糊涂〔该糊涂就得糊涂〕。***from*** ~ 出于无知。***be in*** ~ ***of sth***. 不知某事。***live in a state of*** ~ 浑浑噩噩地生活。***plead*** ~ 声言不知。

ig·no·rant [ˈignərənt; ˋɪgnərənt] ***a***. 无学识的,无知的,愚昧的,由无知引起的。*an* ~ *person* 无知的人。~ *behaviour* 愚蠢行为。***be*** ~ ***of*** 不了解。**-ly** ***ad***.

ig·no·ra·ti·o e·len·chi [ˌignəˈreiʃiəu iˈleŋkai; ˏɪgnəˋreʃɪo ɪˋlɛŋkaɪ] 〔L.〕【逻】用歪曲对方论点的手法驳斥对方。

ig·nore [igˈnɔ:; ɪgˋnɔr] ***vt***. **1.** 忽视,不理,不顾;抹煞(建议)。**2.** 【法】驳回。

ig·no·ro·sphere [ˈignərəuˌsfiə; ˋɪgnərəˏsfɪə(r)] ***n***. 【气】未知层〔在飞机最高飞行高度以上,人类对其所知甚少的大气层最上部〕。

ig·no·tum per ig·no·ti·us [igˈnəutəm pə: igˈnəuʃiəs; ɪgˋnotəm pɚ ɪgˋnoʃɪəs] 〔L.〕 解释得比原来需要解释的事物更难懂,以其昏昏使人昭昭。

Ig·o·rot [ˌi(:)gəˈrəut; i(ɪ)gəˋrot] ***n***. (*pl*. *~s*) (菲律宾)伊哥洛人;伊哥洛语。

i·gua·na [iˈgwɑ:nə; ɪˋgwɑnə] ***n***. 鬣蜥〔西印度、南美所产大蜥蜴〕。

i·guan·o·don [iˈgwɑ:nədɔn; ɪˋgwɑnəˏdɑn] ***n***. 【古生】禽龙〔古代大蜥蜴〕。

IGY = International Geophysical Year 国际地球物理年。

i.h.p. = indicated horsepower 指示马力。

ih·ram [iˈrɑ:m; ɪˋrɑm] ***n***. **1.** 朝圣服〔穆斯林披着到麦加朝圣的双片白布〕。**2.** 穿朝圣服者必须遵守的约法规章。

IHS = Jesus.

IKBS = intelligent knowledge-based system 智能知识库系统〔在某一专业领域具有解决难题和作出决定等功能的电脑系统〕。

Ike [aik; aɪk] ***n***. Isaac 的爱称。

ike [aik; aɪk] ***n***. = iconoscope.

i·ke·ba·na [ˈi:keˈbɑ:nɑ:; ˋikeˋbɑnɑ] ***n***. 〔日〕插花艺术。

i·key [ˈaiki; ˋaɪkɪ] = iky.

i·kon [ˈaikɔn; ˋaɪkɑn] ***n***. = icon.

ik·tas [ˈiktəs; ˋɪktəs] ***n***. 〔美口〕物品,东西;所有物。

i·ky [ˈaiki; ˋaɪkɪ] 〔俚〕 **I** ***a***. 狡猾的,厚颜无耻的,狂妄的。**II** ***n***. **1.** 犹太人;高利贷者。**2.** 当铺。

Il = 【化】illinium (铱)。

il- *pref*.〔用于以字母 l 开始的词之前,表示否定〕: *il*logical.

-il *suf*. = -ile: civ*il*.

i·lang-i·lang [ˈiːlaŋˈiːlaŋ; ˋilaŋˋilaŋ] *n*. **1**. 伊兰伊兰树。**2**. 伊兰伊兰香精。

-ile *suf*. **1**. 作形容词词尾: ag*ile*, fut*ile*. **2**. 作名词词尾: miss*ile*, text*ile*.

il·e·ac, il·e·al [ˈiliæk, ˈiliəl; ˋɪlɪæk, ˋɪlɪəl] *a*. **1**. 回肠的。**2**. 有关回肠的。

il·e·i·tis [ˌiliˈaitis; ˏɪlɪˋaɪtɪs] *n*.【医】回肠炎。

il·e·os·to·my [ˌiliːˈɔstəmi; ˏɪlɪˋastəmɪ] *n*.【医】回肠造口术。

il·e·um [ˈiliəm; ˋɪlɪəm] *n*.【解】回肠。

il·e·us [ˈiliəs; ˋɪlɪəs] *n*.【医】肠梗阻绞痛。

i·lex [ˈaileks; ˋaɪlɛks] *n*. (*pl*. ~***es***)【植】**1**. 圣栎。**2**. 冬青属植物。

il·i·ac [ˈiliæk; ˋɪlɪæk] *a*.【解】肠骨的,髂的。

Il·i·ad [ˈiliəd; ˋɪlɪəd] *n*. **1**. (描写特洛伊战争的英雄史诗)《伊利亚特》。**2**. 荷马式的叙事诗。**3**. 一系列史诗般的战绩。***an*** ~ ***of woes*** 一连串的不幸。

il·i·um [ˈiliəm; ˋɪlɪəm] *n*. (*pl*. ***il·i·a*** [ˈiliə; ˋɪlɪə])【解】肠骨,髂骨。

ilk [ilk; ɪlk] **I** *a*.〔Scot.〕相同的,同一的。**II** *pro*.〔Scot.〕每一。**III** *n*.〔口〕家族,同类。*Hitler and his* ~ 希特勒之流。*liquidate all those not of his* ~ 排斥异己。***of that*** ~同名的,同姓的,同地的;同族的,同类的(*Ross of that* ~ 罗斯地方的罗斯家 (= Ross of Ross))。***that*** ~〔口〕那一家族,那一等级,那一伙。

ill [il; ɪl] **I** *a*. (***worse*** [wəːs; wɝs]; ***worst*** [wəːst; wɝst]) **1**.〔用作表语〕有病的。★英国此义作修饰语时是用 sick. 美国无论作表语或作修饰语通常均用 sick. **2**.〔用作表语〕难过的,不高兴的,不痛快的。**3**.〔用作修饰语〕不健康的,恶劣的,有害的,不幸的。**4**. 困难的,麻烦的。**5**. 拙劣的,笨拙的。*be mentally* ~ 有精神病。*He that is* ~ *to himself will be good to nobody*.〔谚〕不能自爱,焉能爱人。*The sight made me* ~. 这种景象使我难受。*It's an* ~ *wind that blows nobody good*.〔谚〕世上没有对人人都不利的事。*Ill news runs apace*.〔谚〕恶事传千里。~ *deeds* 恶劣行为,坏事。~ *nature* 劣根性。*of* ~ *repute* [*fame*] 名声不好。~ *health* 不健康。~ *fortune* [*luck*] 不幸。~ *will* [*blood*] 怨恨,恶意。~ *breeding* 教养不好。~ *management* 管理不善。*It is* ~ *to be defined*. 很难对它下定义。***be*** ~ ***to please*** 很难讨好。***be*** ~ ***of*** [***with***] (*pneumonia*) 患(肺炎)。***be taken*** ~ 害病。***do sb. an*** ~ ***turn*** 害某人。***fall*** [***get***] ~ 患病,染疾。***meet with*** ~ ***success*** 终于失败。***take in*** ~ ***part*** 误会,动气。**II** *ad*. (***worse***; ***worst***) **1**. 坏,恶劣;拙劣,笨。**2**. 不完全,不充分,几乎不。*behave* ~行为不好。~ *got*, ~ *spent* 悖入悖出。*It* ~ *becomes him to speak so*. 他不应该这样说。*I can* ~ *afford it*. 这我办不到。*use sb*. ~ 残酷地驱使,虐待。*It would go* ~ *with him*. 他要吃亏的。***be*** ~ *accord with* 和…很不相称[不一致]。***be*** ~ ***at ease*** 不安。~ ***off*** 困苦,家境不好。***speak*** ~ ***of*** 说…的坏话。***take sth***. ~ 误会,动气 (*Don't take it* ~ *of him*. 你别为他生气)。***think*** ~ ***of*** 误会。**III** *n*. **1**. 恶,凶;罪恶。**2**.〔*pl*.〕不幸,灾难;病痛。*do* ~ 为害。*the* ~*s of life* 人生的艰难困苦。*bodily* ~*s* 疾病。*the* ~*s that flesh is heir to* 人生不能避免的痛苦,命运的打击。***for good or*** ~ 好歹。***work*** ~ 作恶。~**-adapted** *a*. 不协调的。~**-advised** *a*. 没脑筋的,鲁莽的。~**-affected** *a*. 怀抱不平的,不服气的。~**-being** 病态;不幸;贫穷 (*opp*. well-being)。~**-boding** *a*. 凶兆的,不吉的。~**-bred** *a*. **1**. 无教养的,教养不良的,粗鲁的。**2**. (动物等)劣种的。~**-conditioned** *a*. 情况糟的;心地坏的;病态的。~**-considered** *a*. 考虑欠周的;不适当的;不明智的。~**-defined** *a*. 意思[态度]不明确的;不清楚的;不确定的。~**-disposed** *a*. **1**. 怀敌意的,存心不良的。**2**. 对…不友好的;对…不利的 (*toward*). ~**-effect** 对…产生恶劣影响。~**-equipped** *a*. 装备不良的。~**-fated** *a*. 招致不幸的;注定要倒霉的。~**-favo(u)red** *a*. (容貌)丑的,不漂亮的;使人不快的。~**-fed** 营养不良的。~**-feeling** *n*. 敌意,仇视。~**-fortune** 倒霉。~**-founded** *a*. 无事实根据的;理由不充分的。~**-gotten** *a*. 非法得到的 (~*-gotten gains* 不义之财)。~**-health** 不健康。~**-humo(u)red** *a*. 不高兴的;坏脾气的。~**-judged** *a*. 没有脑筋的,愚昧的,决断失当的。~**-looking** *a*. **1**. 不吸引人的;丑陋的。**2**. 凶相的。~**-mannered** *a*. 没礼貌的,粗鲁的。~**-matched** *a*. = illsorted. ~**-natured** *a*. 怀着恶意的;性情坏的。~**-omened** *a*. 凶兆的,不吉利的。~**-sorted** *a*. 搭配失当的,极不相称的 (*an* ~*-sorted pair* 不相配的一对夫妻)。~**-spent** *a*. 乱花掉的,花钱浪费的。~**-starred** *a*. = ill-fated. ~**-suited** *a*. 不合适的;不适应的。~**-tempered** *a*. = ill-humo(u)red. ~**-timed** *a*. 不合时宜的,不适时的 (*Your remark is* ~*-timed*. 你这话说得不是时候)。~**-treat**, ~**-use** *vt*. 虐待。~**-treatment**, ~ **usage**, ~**-usage** 虐待,滥用,糟塌。~**-wisher** *n*. 幸灾乐祸的人。

Ill. = Illinois.

ill. = **1**. illuminate, illumination. **2**. illustrate, illustration.

I'll [ail; aɪl]〔口〕= I shall; I will.

il·la·tion [iˈleiʃən; ɪˋleʃən] *n*.【逻】**1**. 推论,推理;演绎(法)。**2**. 结论;演绎的结果。

il·la·tive [iˈleitiv; ˋɪletɪv] *a*. **1**. 演绎的,推论的。~ *conjunctions* 推论连接词〔如 *then*, *therefore* 等〕。**-ly** *ad*.

il·laud·a·ble [iˈlɔːdəbl; ɪˋlɔdəbl̩] *a*. 不值得赞美的。

il·le·gal [iˈliːgəl; ɪˋligl̩] *a*. 不法的,非法的。*an* ~ *operation* 堕胎(罪)。**-ly** *ad*.

il·le·gal·i·ty [ˌili(ː)ˈgæliti; ˏɪli(ɪ)ˋgælətɪ] *n*. 违法;犯规;非法行为。

il·le·gal·ize [iˈliːgəlaiz; ɪˋligəlˏaɪz] *vt*. 使非法,宣布…为非法。

il·leg·i·bil·i·ty [iˌledʒiˈbiliti; ɪˏlɛdʒɪˋbɪlətɪ] *n*. 难以辨认;字迹模糊;印刷模糊。

il·leg·i·ble [iˈledʒəbl; ɪˋlɛdʒəbl̩] *a*. 难以辨认的,字迹[印刷]模糊的。

il·leg·i·bly [iˈledʒəbli; ɪˋlɛdʒəblɪ] *ad*. 难以辨认地,字迹[印刷]模糊地。

il·le·git·i·ma·cy [ˌiliˈdʒitiməsi; ˏɪlɪˋdʒɪtɪməsɪ] *n*. **1**. 非法,违法。**2**. 不合理,不合逻辑。**3**. 不符合惯例。**4**. 私生。

il·le·git·i·mate [ˌiliˈdʒitimit; ˏɪlɪˋdʒɪtɪmɪt] **I** *a*. **1**. 非法的,违法的。**2**. 不合理的,不合逻辑的。**3**. 不符合惯例的。**4**. 私生的。**II** *n*. 没有合法身分的人〔指私生子〕。**III** [ˌiliˈdʒitimeit; ˏɪlɪˋdʒɪtɪmet] *vt*. 宣布…为非法。**-ly** *ad*.

il·le·git·i·ma·tion [ˌiliˌdʒitiˈmeiʃən; ˏɪlɪˏdʒɪtəˋmeʃən] *n*. **1**. 认为非法。**2**. 认为[宣布为]私生子。

il·lib·er·al [iˈlibərəl; ɪˋlɪbərəl] *a*. **1**. 缺乏教育的,无教养的。**2**. 吝啬的,气量狭窄的;思想偏狭的。**-ly** *ad*.

il·lib·er·al·i·ty [iˌlibəˈræliti; ɪˏlɪbəˋrælətɪ] *n*. **1**. 缺乏教育,无教养。**2**. 吝啬,气量狭窄,思想偏狭。

il·lic·it [iˈlisit; ɪˋlɪsɪt] *a*. 违法的,违禁的,不正当的。*have* [*maintain*] ~ *relations with a foreign country* 里通外国。~ *intercourse* 私通,通奸。~ *sale* 私卖。**-ly** *ad*. **-ness** *n*.

il·lim·it·a·ble [iˈlimitəbl; ɪˋlɪmɪtəbl̩] *a*. 无限的,广阔无边的,不可计量的。*the* ~ *ocean* 浩渺无边的海洋。**-bil·i·ty**, **-ness** *n*. **-bly** *ad*.

il·lin·i·um [iˈliniəm; ɪˋlɪnɪəm] *n*.【化】铱〔现名 promethium 钷〕。

Il·li·nois [ˌiliˈnɔi(z); ˏɪlɪˋnɔɪ(z)] **I** ***n.*** 伊利诺斯〔美国州名〕。**-an** [-zən; -zən] ***a.*** **-i·an** [-ziən; -zɪən] ***a.*** **Il·li·noi·an** [ˌiliˈnɔiən; ˏɪlɪˋnɔɪən] ***a.*** 伊利诺斯州的;伊利诺斯州人的。**II** ***n.*** 伊利诺斯州人。

il·liq·uid [iˈlikwid; ɪˋlɪkwɪd] ***a.*** **1.** 非现金的;不能立即兑现的。**2.** 无流动资金的。**-di·ty** [-diti; -dətɪ] ***n.***

illit = illiterate.

il·lite [ˈilait; ˋɪlaɪt] ***n.*** 【地】伊利石;伊利水云母。

il·lit·er·a·cy [iˈlitərəsi; ɪˋlɪtərəsɪ] ***n.*** **1.** 失学;未受教育;文盲。**2.** (语言)错误。*wipe out* ~ 扫除文盲。

il·lit·er·ate [iˈlitərit; ɪˋlɪtərɪt] **I** ***a.*** **1.** 不识字的,未受教育的,文盲的。**2.** 缺乏语言[文学]方面知识的。**3.** 语言错误的。*an* ~ *letter* 语言错误百出的信。**II** ***n.*** 失学者,文盲。**-ly** ***ad.*** **-ness** ***n.***

ill·ness [ˈilnis; ˋɪlnɪs] ***n.*** 病,不健康 (*opp.* health)。*suffer from a serious* ~ 害重病;病得很厉害。*triumph over* ~ 战胜疾病; *~es of women* 各种妇女病。

il·log·ic [iˈlɔdʒik; ɪˋlɑdʒɪk] ***n.*** 不合逻辑,缺乏逻辑。

il·log·i·cal [iˈlɔdʒikəl; ɪˋlɑdʒɪkəl] ***a.*** 缺乏逻辑的,不合逻辑的,说不通的,无条理的,无意义的。**-ly** ***ad.*** **-ness** ***n.***

il·log·ical·i·ty [ˈilɔdʒiˈkæliti; ˋɪlɑdʒɪˋkælətɪ] ***n.*** 不合逻辑,矛盾。

il·lo·ty·cin [ˌiləˈtaisin; ˏɪləˋtaɪsɪn] ***n.*** 【药】红霉素〔商品名〕。

illth [ilθ; ɪlθ] ***n.*** = ill-being.

il·lude [iˈluːd; ɪˋlud] ***vt.*** 欺骗;置…于幻觉中。

il·lume [iˈljuːm; ˏɪˋljum] ***vt.*** 〔诗〕照亮;启发。

il·lu·mi·na·ble [iˈljuːminəbl; ɪˋlumɪnəbl̩] ***a.*** 可被照明的。

il·lu·mi·nance [iˈljuːminəns; ɪˋlumɪnəns] ***n.*** 【物】照度,施照度。

il·lu·mi·nant [iˈljuːminənt; ɪˋlumɪnənt] **I** ***a.*** 照明的,发光的。**II** ***n.*** 发光物;照明剂。

il·lu·mi·nate [iˈljuːmineit; ɪˋlumɪˏnet] ***vt.*** **1.** 照亮,照明。**2.** 使光辉灿烂。**3.** 〔英〕装置照明,装饰。**4.** 说明(问题等);启发,启蒙。**5.** (用饰字、饰画)装饰。**6.** 使受辐射照射。— ***vi.*** **1.** 照亮。**2.** 进行辐射照射。

il·lu·mi·nat·ed [iˈljuːmiˌneitid; ɪˋlumɪˏnetɪd] ***a.*** **1.** 照明的;装有照明装饰的;受到启发[启蒙]的;加有彩饰的。**2.** 〔美俚〕喝醉了的。*a well-* ~ *room* 照明良好的房间。*an* ~ *car* 彩车,花车。*an* ~ *manuscript* 金泥写本,彩饰真迹写本。

il·lu·mi·na·ti [ˌiluːmiˈnɑːtiː; ˏɪlumɪˋnɑti] ***n.*** (*pl.*, *sing.* **-na·to** [-təu; -to]) **1.** 自称天才的人们,自认聪明过人的人们。**2.** 〔I-〕光明会〔十八世纪主张自然神论和共和主义的秘密社团〕。**3.** 〔I-〕主张宗教开明的社团。

il·lu·mi·nat·ing [iˈljuːmiˌneitiŋ; ɪˋlumɪˏnetɪŋ] ***a.*** 照亮的,照明的;启发的,说明的。~ *attachments* 照明设备。~ *effect* 照明效果。~ *engineering* 照明工程(学)。~ *flare* (*projectile*)【军】照明弹。

il·lu·mi·na·tion [iˌljuːmiˈneiʃən; ɪˏlumɪˋneʃən] ***n.*** **1.** 照明,光照;照(明)度;〔常用 *pl.*〕灯饰。**2.** 启发,启蒙。**3.** (手写本的)彩饰。*stage* ~ 舞台照明。**il·lu·mi·na·tive** ***a.***

il·lu·mi·na·tor [iˈljuːmineitə; ɪˋlumɪˏnetə] ***n.*** **1.** 照明者。**2.** 发光体,照明装置;灯饰装置。**2.** 启发者。**3.** 装饰书稿的人。

il·lu·mine [iˈljuːmin; ɪˋlumɪn] ***vt.*** 照亮;启发;使发亮。— ***vi.*** 明亮起来。

il·lu·min·ism [iˈluːminizm; ɪˋlumɪnɪzm̩] ***n.*** (历史上的)光明会教义;启蒙主义。**-ist** ***n.***

illus. = illustrated; illustration.

il·lu·sion [iˈluːʒən, iˈljuː-; ɪˋluʒən, ɪˋlju-] ***n.*** **1.** 幻影;幻觉;妄想,幻想;错觉。**2.** (妇女用)透明面纱。*an optical* ~ 视错觉。***be under no*** ~ ***about*** [***as to***] ***sth.*** 对某事不存幻想。**-al**, **-a·ry** ***a.*** **-ism** ***n.*** **1.** 物质世界幻觉说。**2.** 引起错觉的艺术手法。**-ist** ***n.*** 物质世界幻觉论者;幻想家;魔术师。

il·lu·sive [iˈluːsiv; ɪˋlusɪv] ***a.*** 幻影的,幻觉的;错觉上的,迷惑人的。**-ly** ***ad.*** **-ness** ***n.***

il·lu·so·ry [iˈluːsəri; ɪˋlusərɪ] ***a.*** = illusive. **-i·ly** ***ad.***

illust. = illustrated; illustration.

il·lus·trate [ˈiləstreit; ˋɪləstret] ***vt.*** **1.** (用例子、图解等)说明;举例证明。**2.** 加上插图[图解]。*an* ~*d book* [*newspaper*] 有插图的书籍[报纸]。— ***vi.*** 举例。

il·lus·tra·tion [ˌiləsˈtreiʃən; ˏɪləsˋtreʃən] ***n.*** 说明,例证,实例;图解,插画。***in*** ~ ***of*** 作为…的例证。

il·lus·tra·tive [ˈiləstreitiv; ˋɪləstrətɪv] ***a.*** **1.** 说明性质的。**2.** 作为…例证的,能阐释…的 (*of*)。*a simile* ~ *of a subject* 说明问题的比喻。**-ly** ***ad.***

il·lus·tra·tor [ˈiləstreitə; ˋɪləstretə] ***n.*** 说明者;插图画家。

il·lus·tri·ous [iˈlʌstriəs; ɪˋlʌstrɪəs] ***a.*** **1.** 卓越的;杰出的;有名的,著名的。**2.** 辉煌的,灿烂的。~ *accomplishments* 杰出的成就。~ *deeds* 辉煌的事绩。**-ly** ***ad.*** **-ness** ***n.***

il·lu·vi·al [iˈluːviəl; ɪˋluvɪəl] ***a.*** 【地】淀积层的;与淀积层有关的;淀积(作用)的;与淀积(作用)有关的。

il·lu·vi·ate [iˈluːvieit; ɪˋluvɪet] ***vi.*** 【地】经受淀积作用。

il·lu·vi·a·tion [iˌluːviˈeiʃən; ɪˏluvɪˋeʃən] ***n.*** 【地】淀积(作用)。

il·lu·vi·um [iˈluːviəm; ɪˋluvɪəm] ***n.*** (*pl.* *~s*, *-via* [-ə; -ə])【地】淀积层。

il·ly [ˈili; ˋɪlɪ] **I** ***ad.*** 〔口〕坏,恶劣地。*be* ~ *prepared* 准备不充分。**II** ***a.*** = ill.

Il·lyr·i·an [iˈliəriən; ɪˋlɪrɪən] **I** ***a.*** **1.** (古代亚得里亚海东岸地区)伊利里亚的;伊利里亚人的;伊利里亚文化的。**2.** 伊利里亚语〔一般认为属印欧语系〕。**II** ***n.*** 伊利里亚人。

il·men·ite [ˈilminait; ˋɪlmɪnaɪt] ***n.*** 【矿】钛铁矿。

ILO = **1.** International Labo(u)r Organization (联合国)国际劳工组织。**2.** International Labo(u)r Office (联合国)国际劳工局。

I.L.P. = Independent Labour Party. 〔英〕独立工党。

ILS = instrument landing system (航空)仪表着陆系统。

Il·se [ˈilzə; ˋɪlzə] ***n.*** 女名〔*Elizabeth* 的爱称〕。

'im = him.

I.M. = Isle of Man 曼岛[马恩岛]〔英国〕。

I'm [aim; aɪm]〔口〕= I am.

im- *pref.* 用于以 b, m, p 开始的词前。**1.** 表示"向…内";"在…上";"向…": *im*bed, *im*migrate. **2.** 表示"否定": *im*moral, *im*patient.

im·age [ˈimidʒ; ˋɪmɪdʒ] **I** ***n.*** **1.** 像,肖像,画像;偶像。**2.** 影像,图像。**3.** 相像的人(或物);翻版。**4.** 形象,典型。**5.** 形象化的描绘。**6.** 【语】形象化的比喻,象喻。**7.** 【心】概念,意象;心象。*graven* ~ 雕像。~ *frequency* 图像频(率);镜频。*real* ~【物】实像。*television* ~ 电视像。*virtual* ~【物】虚像。*God's* ~ 人体。*He is the* ~ *of his father.* 他活像他父亲。*the spitting* ~ *of* 同…完全一样的人[物]。*speak in ~s* 用比喻讲;说话形象化。*thinking in terms of ~s* 形象思维。**II** ***vt.*** **1.** 作…的像,使…成像。**2.** 反映。**3.** 想像。**4.** 形象地描画;用比喻描写。**5.** 象征。~ **converter**【电】光电变换器;光电图像变换管;图像变换器;显像管。~ **dissector**【电】析像管。**~meister** 形象设计师,形象塑造者。~ **orthicon**【电】超正析(摄)像管,移像正析(摄)像管。**-less** ***a.*** 缺少形象的。

im·age·a·ble [ˈimidʒəbl; ˋɪmɪdʒəbl̩] ***a.*** 可以描摹的。

im·age·ry [ˈimidʒəri; ˋɪmɪdʒərɪ] ***n.*** **1.** 〔集合词〕像,肖像,画像,雕像。**2.** 意象。**3.** 【修】比喻;形象化的描述。

i·mag·i·na·ble [iˈmædʒinəbl; ɪˋmædʒɪnəbl̩] ***a.*** 可以想像得到的。★常与最高级形容词或 *all*, *every*, *no* 等连用,以加强语气。*try every means* ~ 用一切想得

I

出的方法。*the greatest difficulty* ～ 几乎想像不到的困难。*the best thing* ～ 再好没有的东西。**imaginably** *ad*.

i·mag·i·nal [iˈmædʒinəl; ɪˋmædʒɪnəl] *a*. 想像的,有关想像的;【动】成虫的。

i·mag·i·nar·y [iˈmædʒinəri; ɪˋmædʒɪˏnɛrɪ] *a*. 1. 想像中的,假想的(*opp*. actual)。2.【数】虚数的。*an* ～ *enemy* 假想敌人。～ *number* 虚数。～ *root* 虚根。～ *unit* 虚数单位, $\sqrt{-1}$ 符号 *i*. **i·mag·i·na·ri·ly** *ad*. **i·mag·i·na·ri·ness** *n*.

i·mag·i·na·tion [iˌmædʒiˈneiʃən; ɪˏmædʒɪˋneʃən] *n*. 1. 想像,想像力,创造力。2. 妄想;空想。3. 想像出来的事物。*have a good* [*poor*] ～ 想像力好[差];〔谑〕很会[不会]说谎。

i·mag·i·na·tive [iˈmædʒinətiv; ɪˋmædʒɪˏnetɪv] *a*. 想像的;富于想像力的。**-ly** *ad*. **-ness** *n*.

i·mag·ine [iˈmædʒin; ɪˋmædʒɪn] *vt*., *vi*. 1. 想像,设想;猜想,推测。2.〔古〕企图。*Just* ～! 想想看! *I cannot* ～ *who the man is*. 我想不出这个人是谁。*I-yourself* (*to be*) *on a desert island*. 设想你处在一个荒岛上。

im·ag·ism [ˈimədʒizəm; ˋɪmədʒɪzəm] *n*. 意象主义〔一种文学上的流派〕。

im·ag·ist [ˈimədʒist; ˋɪmədʒɪst] **I** *n*. 意象主义者,意象派。**II** *a*. = imagistic.

i·ma·go [iˈmeigəu; ɪˋmego] *n*. (*pl*. ***imagines*** [iˈmeidʒiniːz; ɪˋmedʒɪniz] 或 ~*es*) 1.【动】成虫。2.【心】像,意像。

i·mam, i·maum [iˈmɑːm; ɪˋmɑm] *n*. 1. (伊斯兰教的)阿訇。2.〔I-〕伊玛姆〔伊斯兰教国家元首的称号或指伊斯兰教教长〕。

i·mam·ate [iˈmɑːmeit; ɪˋmɑmet] *n*.【宗】1. 伊斯兰教长国。2. 教长职权。

i·ma·ret [iˈmɑːret; ɪˋmɑrɛt] *n*. (土耳其的)小客店,香客客店。

im·bal·ance [imˈbæləns; ɪmˋbæləns] *n*. 不平衡,失调。

im·balm [imˈbɑːm; ɪmˋbɑm] *vt*. = embalm.

im·be·cile [ˈimbisail, -siːl; ˋɪmbɪsaɪl, -sil] **I** *a*. 低能的;愚笨的。**II** *n*. 低能儿;愚蠢的人。**-ly** *ad*.

im·be·cil·i·ty [ˌimbiˈsiliti; ˏɪmbɪˋsɪlətɪ] *n*. 1. 低能,愚笨。2. 愚蠢的言行。

im·bed [imˈbed; ɪmˋbɛd] *vt*. = embed.

im·bibe [imˈbaib; ɪmˋbaɪb] *vt*. 1. 吸收(养分等),吸进(空气等)。2.〔口〕喝。3. 吸收(思想等)。— *vi*. 喝;吸收,接受。

im·bi·bi·tion [ˌimbiˈbiʃən; ˏɪmbɪˋbɪʃən] *n*. 1.【化】吸液。2. 吸入,吸收。**-al** *a*.

im·bit·ter [imˈbitə; ɪmˋbɪtə] *vt*. 1. 使变苦,加苦味于。2. 使更痛苦;使恶化。3. 使激怒;使怨恨(= embitter)。

im·bod·y [imˈbɔdi; ɪmˋbɑdɪ] *vt*. (*-bod·ied*; *～·ing*) 1. 使肉体化,体现,使具体化。2. 使形体可触知(或可见)。3. 使组成整体。4. 化零为整,拼凑,收录(= embody)。

im·bos·om [imˈbuzəm, -ˈbuːzəm; ɪmˋbuzəm, -ˋbuzəm] *vt*. 1. 把…藏于胸怀内;拥抱;怀抱。2. 围护;包围;遮掩(= embosom)。

im·bow·er [imˈbauə; ɪmˋbauə] *vt*. 用凉亭遮掩(= embower)。

im·bri·cate [ˈimbrikeit; ˋɪmbrɪˏket] **I** *vt*., *vi*. (使)叠盖;(使)成鳞状。**II** [ˈimbrikit; ˋɪmbrɪkɪt] *a*. 1.【动】叠瓦状的;鳞状的。2. 重叠的。

im·bri·ca·tion [ˌimbriˈkeiʃən; ˏɪmbrɪˋkeʃən] *n*. 叠瓦状;鳞甲花样(构造)。**-ca·tive** *a*.

im·bro·gli·o [imˈbrəuliəu; ɪmˋbroljo] (*pl*. ~*s*) *n*. 〔It.〕纷乱,(时局的)纠纷;(戏剧的)复杂情节,思想的混乱,误解,纠葛。

im·brown [imˈbraun; ɪmˋbraʊn] *vt*. 使成褐色(= embrown)。

im·brue [imˈbruː; ɪmˋbru] *vt*. (尤指以血)玷污。～ *one's hands with* [*in*] *blood* 犯杀人罪。**-ment** *n*.

im·brute [imˈbruːt; ɪmˋbrut] *vt*., *vi*. (使)堕落到和禽兽一样,(使)变残忍。

im·bue [imˈbjuː; ɪmˋbju] *vt*. 1. 使吸入(水分等);浸染。2. 使感染,使蒙受;鼓吹;灌注。*He is* ~*d with new ideas*. 他受了新思想的感染。

im·burse [imˈbəːs; ɪmˋbɝs] *vt*. 1. 把…放入钱袋。2. 偿还,付。3. 在经济上支持。

IMCO = Intergovernmental Maritime Consultative Organization (联合国)政府间海事协商组织。

IMF = International Monetary Fund (联合国)国际货币基金组织。

im·id·az·ole [ˌimiˈdæzəul, -əˈzəul; ˏɪmɪˋdæzol, -əˋzol] *n*.【化】咪唑,异吡唑。

im·ide [ˈimaid, -id; ˋɪmaɪd, -ɪd] *n*.【化】吡唑。

im·i·do [ˈimidəu, iˈmiːdəu; ˋɪmɪdo, ɪˋmido] *a*.【化】酰亚胺的;醯亚胺的。

im·ine [ˈimiːn, -in, iˈmiːn; ˋɪmin, -ɪn, ɪˋmin] *n*.【化】亚胺。

im·i·no [ˈiminəu, iˈmiːnəu; ˋɪmɪno, ɪˋmino] *a*.【化】(含)亚胺基的。

imit. = imitation; imitative.

im·i·ta·bil·i·ty [ˌimitəˈbiliti; ˏɪmɪtəˋbɪlətɪ] *n*. 可模仿性。

im·i·ta·ble [ˈimitəbl; ˋɪmɪtəbl] *a*. 可模仿的;值得模仿的。*simple and* ～ *virtues which are within every man's reach* 人人都能办到的简单而值得模仿的美德。

im·i·tate [ˈimiteit; ˋɪmɪˏtet] *vt*. 1. 仿效,模仿;学样;摹拟。2. 仿造;伪造;假充,冒充。～ *the virtues of great and good men* 仿效伟大善良人们的美德。～ *the strokes of model Chinese calligraphy* 临摹字帖的笔法。*Wood is often painted to* ～ *stone*. 木料制品常被人们涂以油漆冒充石料制品。

im·i·ta·tion [ˌimiˈteiʃən; ˏɪmɪˋteʃən] *n*. 1. 模仿,仿效;学习。2. 仿造;仿造品;赝品。3.【生】拟态。～ *leather* 人造革。～ *wool* 人造毛。*Beware of* ~*s*. 谨防假冒。*an* ～ *of marble* 人造大理石。***in*** ～ ***of*** 模仿。～ **milk** 人造牛奶。

im·i·ta·tive [ˈimitətiv; ˋɪməˏtetɪv] *a*. 1. 模仿的,仿效的。2. 爱模仿的。3. 仿制的,伪造的。4.【生】拟态的。***be*** ～ ***of sb***. 仿效某人。～ *arts* 模仿艺术〔指绘画、雕刻〕。～ *music* 拟声音乐。～ *words* 拟声词〔如 *hiss*, *moo*, *tinkle* 之类〕。**-ly** *ad*. **-ness** *n*.

im·i·ta·tor [ˈimiˌteitə; ˋɪməˏtetɚ] *n*. 模仿者;仿造者。

im·mac·u·la·cy [iˈmækjuləsi; ɪˋmækjələsɪ] *n*. 洁净,纯洁;无瑕。

im·mac·u·late [iˈmækjulit; ɪˋmækjəlɪt] *a*. 洁净的,纯洁的;洁白的;〔常谑〕毫无瑕疵的,无缺点的;【生】纯色的,无斑点的。*an* ～ *shirt* 洁白的衬衫。*an* ～ *text* 完全正确的版本。***I- Conception***【宗】(关于圣母玛利亚的)纯洁受胎说,圣灵怀胎说。**-ly** *ad*. **-ness** *n*.

im·mane [iˈmein; ɪˋmen] *a*. 1.〔古〕巨大的;无限的,广大的。2. 残酷的;野蛮的。

im·ma·nen·ce, -nen·cy [ˈimənəns, -si; ˋɪmənəns, -sɪ] *n*. 内在,固有;内在性,固有论。

im·ma·nent [ˈimənənt; ˋɪmənənt] *a*. 1. 内在的,固有的。2. 意识之内的。3.【宗】存在于宇宙万物之内的〔指上帝〕。～ *cause* 内因(*opp*. transcendent cause)。*an* ～ *factor* 内在的因素。**-ly** *ad*.

im·ma·nent·ism [ˈimənəntizm; ˋɪmənəntɪzm] *n*. 1.【哲】内在论,认识固定论。2.【神】上帝无所不在论。

im·ma·nent·ist [ˈimənəntist; ˋɪmənəntɪst] *n*. 内在论者。

Im·man·u·el [iˈmænjuəl; ɪˋmænjʊəl] *n*. 伊曼纽尔〔男子名〕〔Heb. = God with us〕。

I

im·ma·te·ri·al [ˌiməˈtiəriəl; ˌɪməˋtɪrɪəl] *a*. 1. 非物质的,无形的。2. 不重要的,不足取的,琐细的。*It is quite ~ to me*. 那对我无所谓。

im·ma·te·ri·al·ism [ˌiməˈtiəriəlizəm; ˌɪməˋtɪrɪəlˌɪzəm] *n*. 非物质论。

im·ma·te·ri·al·ist [ˌiməˈtiəriəlist; ˌɪməˋtɪrɪəlɪst] *n*. 非物质论者〔英国崇奉贝克莱的主观唯心主义的人〕。

im·ma·te·ri·al·i·ty [ˈiməˌtiəriˈæliti; ˌɪməˌtɪrɪˋælətɪ] *n*. 1. 非物质性,无形物。2. 不重要。

im·ma·te·ri·al·ize [ˌiməˈtiəriəlaiz; ˌɪməˋtɪrɪəˌlaɪz] *vt*. 使无实体,使无形。

im·ma·ture [ˌiməˈtjuə; ˌɪməˋtjur] *a*. 1. 未成熟的。2. 未完成的,不完全的,粗糙的。3.【地】幼年的,未成年的。~ *fruit* 尚未成熟的果实。*an ~ essay* 不成熟的论文。~ *death* 夭折。**-ly** *ad*. **-ness** *n*.

im·ma·tu·ri·ty [ˌiməˈtjuəriti, -ˈtuər-, -ˈtʃuər-; ˌɪməˋtjurətɪ, -tur-, -ˋtʃur-] *n*. 不成熟;生硬;不圆熟;幼稚(= immatureness)。

im·meas·ur·a·ble [iˈmeʒərəbl; ɪˋmɛʒərəbl̩] *a*. 无法计量的;无穷尽的;巨大的,广大的。**-bil·i·ty** *n*. **-bly** *ad*.

im·meas·ur·a·ble·ness [iˈmeʒərəblnis; ɪˋmɛʒərəbl̩nɪs] *n*. 无法计量;无限;广阔无垠。

im·me·di·a·cy [iˈmiːdiəsi; ɪˋmidɪəsɪ] *n*. 直接;直接性;刻不容缓。

im·me·di·ate [iˈmiːdjət; ɪˋmidɪɪt, -dʒət] *a*. 1. 直接的;最接近的。2. 即时的,立即的。3. 当前的,现在的。4. 直觉的。~ *delivery*【商】即交。~ *payment*【商】即付。~ *reply* 立即答覆。~ *shipment*【商】即装。*our ~ plans* 当前计划。*an ~ cause* 直接原因,近因。*in the ~ future* 在最近的将来。~ *information* 第一手消息。*one's ~ neighbour* 紧邻。*one's ~ superior* 顶头上司,上一级领导。~ *perception* 直觉。~ **constituent**【语】直接构成要素。**-ness** *n*.

im·me·di·ate·ly [iˈmiːdjətli; ɪˋmidjətlɪ] **I** *ad*. 1. 马上,立即。2. 直接地,紧密地。~ *in the vicinity* 就在附近。**II** *conj*.〔英〕一…(就…)(= as soon as)。*I told him ~ he came*. 他一来我就告诉他了。

im·med·i·ca·ble [iˈmedikəbl; ɪˋmɛdɪkəbl̩] *a*. 医不好的,无法治疗的。

Im·mel·mann (turn) [ˈimilˌmɑːn, -mən; ˋɪmɪlˌmɑn, -mən]【空】伊麦尔曼式筋斗翻转〔因德国飞行员 M. 伊麦尔曼而得名,飞机作半筋斗翻转后还原〕。

im·me·mo·ri·al [ˌimiˈmɔːriəl; ˌɪməˋmorɪəl] *a*. 无法追忆的;太古的,极古的。*from time ~* 远古以来。**-ly** *ad*.

im·mense [iˈmens; ɪˋmɛns] *a*. 1. 无限的,无穷尽的;巨大的,广大的。2.〔俚〕极好的,极妙的。*an ~ amount* 巨额的。*an ~ ocean* 无边的海洋。*The performance was ~*. 演出很成功。**-ly** *ad*. 无限地,大大地;〔口〕非常,很。**-ness** [iˈmensnis; ɪˋmɛnsnɪs], **-si·ty** [iˈmensiti; ɪˋmɛnsətɪ] *n*. 巨大,广大;无限,无限空间;巨物。

im·men·su·ra·ble [iˈmenʃurəbl; ɪˋmɛnʃurəbl̩] *a*. = immeasurable.

im·merge [iˈməːdʒ; ɪˋmɝdʒ] *vi*. 1. 侵入。2. 专心,埋头。*There is no need to ~ further into this topic*. 不必再钻进这个题目里了。— *vt*.〔古〕= immerse.

im·merse [iˈməːs; ɪˋmɝs] *vt*. 1. 沉浸。2. 给…施浸礼〔基督教中的一种仪式〕。3.〔主要用于 ~ *oneself* 或被动语态〕使埋头,使一心一意地…,卷入,陷入。*be ~d in difficulties* 陷入重重困难中。~ *oneself among the masses* 深入群众中。~ *oneself* [*be ~d*] *in study* 埋头研究。

im·mersed [iˈməːst; ɪˋmɝst] *a*. 1. 浸入的,沉入的。2.【宗】行浸礼的。3.【生】陷入的 4.【植】沉水(生长)的。

im·mers·i·ble [iˈməːsibl; ɪˋmɝsɪbl̩] *a*. (某些电气用品)可置于水中的。

im·mer·sion [iˈməːʃən; ɪˋmɝʃən] *n*. 1. 沉浸,浸没。2.【宗】浸礼。3.【天】掩始。4. 专心。~ *in study* 埋头研究。~ *in thought* 沉思。~ **freezer** 浸液致冷器。~ **heater** 浸没式电热器。~ **lens**【物】浸没透镜。**water ~** 水浸。

im·mesh [iˈmeʃ; ɪˋmɛʃ] *vt*. 网捕;使缠住;使陷入网中(= enmesh)。

im·me·thod·i·cal [ˌimiˈθɔdikəl; ˌɪmɪˋθɑdɪkl̩] *a*. 不规则的,无秩序的,杂乱的。**-ly** *ad*.

im·met·ri·cal [iˈmetrikəl; ɪˋmɛtrɪkəl] *a*. 无韵律的。

im·mie [ˈimiː; ˋɪmi] *n*.〔口〕玛瑙弹球,玻璃弹子。

im·mi·grant [ˈimigrənt; ˋɪmɪgrənt] **I** *a*. (从外国)移来的,移民的,侨民的〔*cf*. emigrant〕。**II** *n*. 1. (来自外国的)移民,侨民。2. 从异地移入的动物[植物]。*European ~s in America*. 住在美国的欧洲侨民。~ **vein**【地】移填矿脉。

im·mi·grate [ˈimigreit; ˋɪmɪˌgret] *vi*. 移居外国,迁移(*opp*. emigrate)。— *vt*. 使移居,移(民)。

im·mi·gra·tion [ˌimiˈgreiʃən; ˌɪmɪˋgreʃən] *n*. 1. 移居;移民入境。2. 移民总称。*the ~ law* 移民法。*an ~ officer* 入境检查员。

im·mi·nence, im·mi·nen·cy [ˈiminəns, -si; ˋɪmɪnəns, -sɪ] *n*. 急迫;迫近的危险[祸患],燃眉之急。

im·mi·nent [ˈiminənt; ˋɪmɪnənt] *a*. 迫切的,危急的,逼近眼前的,临头的。*A storm is ~*. 暴风雨即将来临。**-ly** *ad*.

im·min·gle [iˈmiŋgl; ɪˋmɪŋgl] *vt*., *vi*. (*-gled*, *-gling*) = intermingle.

im·mis·ci·ble [iˈmisəbl; ɪˋmɪsəbl] *a*. 不能混合的,不溶混的。**-bil·i·ty** *n*. **-bly** *ad*.

im·mis·sion [iˈmiʃən; ɪˋmɪʃən] *n*. 注入,注射。

im·mit·i·ga·ble [iˈmitigəbl; ɪˋmɪtɪgəbl̩] *a*. 不能调解的,不能缓和的,不能减轻的。**-bly** *ad*.

im·mix [iˈmiks; ɪmˋmɪks] *vt*., *vi*. 混合,混杂,卷入,搀合。**-ture** [-tʃə; -tʃɚ] *n*.

im·mo·bile [iˈməubail; ɪˋmobaɪl] *a*. 1. 不动的,不机动的,固定的。2. 不变的,静止的。**-bil·i·ty** [ˌiməuˈbiliti; ˌɪmoˋbɪlətɪ] *n*.

im·mo·bi·lize [iˈməubilaiz; ɪˋmobl̩aɪz] *vt*. 1. 使不动,使固定。2. 使(部队、车辆)不能调动。3. 收回(硬币)使不流通。4. (用夹板等)使(肢、关节)不动。**-za·tion** [iˌməubilaiˈzeiʃən; ɪˌmobɪlaɪˋzeʃən] *n*.

im·mod·er·ate [iˈmɔdərit; ɪˋmɑdərɪt] *a*. 无节制的,过度的,过分的(放纵等)。**-ly** *ad*. **-ness** *n*.

im·mod·er·a·tion [iˌmɔdəˈreiʃən; ɪˌmɑdəˋreʃən] *n*. 无节制;放肆,过度,极端。

im·mod·est [iˈmɔdist; ɪˋmɑdɪst] *a*. 1. 不谦虚的,不礼貌的;不正派的;无节制的。2. 莽撞的,卤莽的,不客气的,放肆的。**-ly** *ad*.

im·mod·es·ty [iˈmɔdisti; ɪˋmɑdɪstɪ] *n*. 1. 不谦虚,不礼貌,不正派,无节制。2. 莽撞,卤莽,不客气;放肆。

im·mo·late [ˈiməuleit; ˋɪmoˌlet] *vt*. 1. 宰杀…作祭品。2. 牺牲。3. 杀戮,毁灭。**-la·tion** *n*. **-la·tor** *n*. 被当作祭品的人。

im·mo·ral [iˈmɔrəl; ɪˋmɔrəl] *a*. 1. 不道德的,道德败坏的,邪恶的。2. 不正派的,猥亵的。**-ly** *ad*.

im·mor·al·ist [iˈmɔːrəlist; ɪˋmɔrəlɪst] *n*. 不道德的人〔尤指鼓吹不道德行为者〕。

im·mo·ral·i·ty [ˌiməˈræliti; ˌɪməˋrælətɪ] *n*. 1. 不道德,道德败坏。2. 不道德的行为,伤风败俗的行为。

im·mor·tal [iˈmɔːtl; ɪˋmɔrtl] **I** *a*. 1. 不死的;不灭的。2. 永生的,不朽的。3.〔口〕永久的。4. 神的。**II** *n*. 1. 不死的人[物]。2.〔*pl*.〕(古希腊,罗马神话中的)诸神。3. 不朽的作家。4.〔I-〕法国科学院院士;〔I-s〕古代波斯万人近卫军成员。*the I- Bard* 不朽的诗人〔指莎士比亚〕。*the Forty Immortals* 法国科学院 40 人委员会成员。~ *hand* 必赢的一手牌。**-tal·i·ty** [ˌimɔˈtæliti; ˌɪmɔˋtælətɪ] *n*.

I

im·mor·tal·ize [iˈmɔːtəlaiz; ɪˋmɔrtl̩ˏaɪz] *vt*. 使不朽,使不灭;使传诸永远。**-i·za·tion** *n*.

im·mor·tal·ly [iˈmɔːtəli; ɪˋmɔrtəlɪ] *ad*. 不朽地,永久地;〔口〕非常,很。*be* ～ *green* 万年常青。*be* ～ *glad* 很高兴。

im·mor·telle [ˌimɔːˈtel; ˏɪmɔrˋtɛl] *n*. (坟墓上插用的)灰毛菊、银苞菊等,(花干后色和形状不变的)菊科植物。

im·mo·tile [iˈməutl; ɪˋmotl̩] *a*. 不动的,固定的,不能移动的。

im·mov·a·bil·i·ty [iˌmuːvəˈbiliti; ɪˏmuvəˋbɪlətɪ] *n*. 不动(性),不变(性),固定(性)。

im·mov·a·ble [iˈmuːvəbl; ɪˋmuvəbl] **I** *a*. **1**. 稳定的,固定的。**2**. (精神、决心等)不可动摇的;不屈的;坚定的;冷静的,呆板的。**3**. (节日等)固定不变的;【法】(财产)不动的 (*opp*. movable, personal)。～ *property* 不动产。**II** *n*. 固定不动[不变],〔常用 *pl*.〕【法】不动产。**-bly** *ad*. **-ness** *n*.

im·mune [iˈmjuːn; ɪˋmjun] **I** *a*. **1**. 【医】免疫(性)的。**2**. 有免疫力的,可避免的。**3**. 免除(税等)的。**4**. 不受影响的,无响应的。*be* ～ *against attack* 免受攻击。*be* ～ *from smallpox* 不受天花感染。～ *from taxation* [*taxes*] 免税。**II** *n*. 免疫者。～ **agglutinin** 免疫凝集素。～ **body** = antibody. ～ **serum** 免疫血清。

im·mu·ni·ty [iˈmjuːniti; ɪˋmjunətɪ] *n*. **1**. (税等的)免除 (*from*); 豁免。**2**. 免疫力,免疫性 (*from*)。*acquired* ～后天免疫性。*active* ～自动免疫性。*diplomatic* ～外交豁免权。*the noise* ～【无】抗扰度,抗扰性,抗噪音度。～ **bath** 〔美〕【法】证人起诉豁免权。

im·mu·nize [ˈimju(ː)naiz; ˋɪmjəˏnaɪz] *vt*. 使免疫;使免除 (*against*)。*be* ～*d from disease* 有免疫力。*Vaccination* ～*s people against smallpox*. 种牛痘可以免患天花。**-ni·za·tion** *n*.

im·mu·no·as·say [iˈmjuːnəuˈæsei; ɪˋmjunoˋæse] *n*. 【医】免疫检定法。

im·mu·no·chem·is·try [iˈmjuːnəuˈkemistri; ɪˋmjunoˋkɛmɪstrɪ] 免疫化学。**-chem·i·cal** [-ikl; -ɪkl] *a*.

im·mu·no(-)com·pro·mise [iˈmjuːnəuˈkɔmprəmaiz; ɪˋmjunoˋkɑmprəmaɪz] *vt*. 【生】使…的免疫能力遭损害[削弱]。

im·mu·no·flu·o·res·cence [iˈmjuːnəuˌfluːəˈresəns; ɪˋmjunoˌfluəˋrɛsəns] *n*. 【医】荧光免疫检验法。**-cent** *a*.

im·mu·no·ge·net·ics [iˈmjuːnəudʒiˈnetiks; ɪˋmjunodʒɪˋnɛtɪks] *n*. 〔*pl*.〕〔用作单数〕免疫遗传学。**-net·ic** *a*.

im·mu·no·gen·ic [iˌmjuːnəuˈdʒenik; ɪˏmjunoˋdʒɛnɪk] *a*. 产生免疫性的。**-gen·i·cal·ly** *ad*.

im·mu·no·glob·u·lin [iˈmjuːnəuˈglɔbjulin; ɪˋmjunoˋglɑbjulɪn] *n*. 【生化】免疫球蛋白。

im·mu·nol·o·gy [ˌimjuˈnɔlədʒi; ˏɪmjuˋnɑlədʒɪ] *n*. 【医】免疫学。

im·mu·no·re·ac·tion [iˈmjuːnəuriˈækʃən; ɪˋmjunorɪˋækʃən] *n*. 免疫反应。

im·mu·no·sup·press [ˌimjuːnəusəˈpres; ˏɪmjunosəˋprɛs] *vt*. 抑制(生物体的)对外来物质的免疫反应。— *vi*. 抑制免疫。

im·mu·no·ther·a·py [iˈmjuːnəuˈθerəpi; ɪˋmjunoˋθɛrəpɪ] *n*. 【医】免疫疗法。

im·mure [iˈmjuə; ɪˋmjʊr] *vt*. **1**. 禁闭,监禁。**2**. 〔～ oneself〕使隐居,使足不出户。**3**. 把…镶在墙上,把…埋在墙里。～ *oneself in books* 埋头读书。**-ment** *n*.

im·mu·ta·bil·i·ty [iˌmjuːtəˈbiliti; ɪˏmjutəˋbɪlətɪ] *n*. 不变性,不易性。

im·mu·ta·ble [iˈmjuːtəbl; ɪˋmjutəbl̩] *a*. 不可改变的;永远不变的。**-bly** *ad*. **-ness** *n*.

Im·o·gen [ˈimədʒen; ˋɪmədʒən] *n*. **1**. 伊莫金〔女子名〕。**2**. 莎士比亚作品辛白林 (*Cymbeline*) 中的女主人翁〔贞节的典型〕。

Im·o·gene [ˈimədʒiːn; ˋɪməˏdʒin] *n*. = Imogen **1**.

imp [imp; ɪmp] **I** *n*. **1**. 顽童,小淘气。**2**. 〔口〕小鬼,鬼娃娃。**3**. 〔古〕孩子,后代。**II** *vt*. **1**. 移植羽毛以修补(鹰的翅膀或尾巴)。**2**. 在…上装翅膀。**3**. 加强,增大,补充。

imp. = imperative; imperfect; imperial; implement; imported; imprimatur (= let it be printed); 〔美〕improvement.

Imp. = imperator.

im·pact [ˈimpækt; ˋɪmpækt] **I** *n*. 碰撞;冲击(力);(火箭的)降落[着陆];【军】弹着;影响,效力。*the point of* ～ 弹着点。～ *head* 动压头,动压力值。～ *load* 突加负载。～ *pressure* 动压力,碰撞压力。～ *strength* 冲击韧性;(抗)冲击强度。～ *test* 冲击试验。**II** [imˈpækt; ɪmˋpækt] *vt*. **1**. 装填,填入 (*in*; *into*); 压紧,塞满。**2**. 冲击,碰撞。～ **crater**【地】撞击圆坑,陨石坑。～ **law** 撞击定律。

im·pact·ed [imˈpæktid; ɪmˋpæktɪd] *a*. **1**. 压紧的,嵌入的,嵌塞的,阻生的。**2**. 人口稠密的;十分拥挤的;因人口剧增而使当地公用事业不敷需要的。*an* ～ *area* 人口稠密地区,〔美〕"受冲击区"〔因人口剧增而造成公用事业紧张或不敷需要〕。*an* ～ *tooth* 阻生的牙。

im·pac·tion [imˈpækʃən; ɪmˋpækʃən] *n*. **1**. 装紧,压紧。**2**. 撞击。**3**. 【医】阻生;嵌入,嵌塞。*food* ～食物嵌塞。

im·pair [imˈpeə; ɪmˋpɛr] *vt*. **1**. 损害,损伤。**2**. 减少,削弱。～ *one's health* 损害健康。**-ment** *n*.

im·pa·la [imˈpɑːlə, -ˈpælə; ɪmˋpɑlə, -ˋpælə] *n*. (*pl*. *-la*, *-las*)【动】黑斑羚 (*Aepyceros melampus*)〔产于中非和南非〕。

im·pale [imˈpeil; ɪmˋpel] *vt*. **1**. 刺穿,钉住。**2**. 把…钉在尖桩上处死,把…绑在桩上折磨。**3**. 使无法可想,使绝望;使尴尬。**4**.【纹】把(两个纹章)连扣在一个盾牌上。**5**. 〔罕〕用栅围住。**-ment** *n*.

im·pal·pa·ble [imˈpælpəbl; ɪmˋpælpəbl̩] *a*. **1**. 摸不着的;细微的。**2**. 难以了解的;难以识别的。～ *distinctions of meaning* 意义上的细微区别。**-bil·i·ty** *n*. **-bly** *ad*.

im·pal·u·dism [imˈpæljudizəm; ɪmˋpæljudɪzm] *n*. 【医】疟疾。

im·pa·na·tion [ˌimpəˈneiʃən; ˏɪmpəˋneʃən] *n*. 圣体圣餐合一说。

im·pan·el [imˈpænl; ɪmˋpænl̩] *vt*. = empanel.

im·par·a·dise [imˈpærədais; ɪmˋpærədaɪs] *vt*. **1**. 使登天堂;使无比快乐。**2**. 使成乐园。

im·par·i·ty [imˈpæriti; ɪmˋpærətɪ] *n*. 不等,不匀称;不同,差异。

im·park [imˈpɑːk; ɪmˋpark] *vt*. **1**. 围(鹿等)在园内。**2**. 围(地)作公园[猎苑]。**-ka·tion** [ˌimpɑːˈkeiʃən; ˏɪmparˋkeʃən] *n*.

im·par·lance [imˈpɑːləns; ɪmˋparləns] *n*. **1**. 【法】庭外和解。**2**. 〔废〕商议,讨论;谈判。

im·part [imˈpɑːt; ɪmˋpart] *vt*. **1**. 给予,把…分给,传授 (*to*)。**2**. 告诉,通知 (*to*)。～ *news to sb*. 将消息通知某人。**-ment**, **-ta·tion** *n*.

im·par·tial [imˈpɑːʃəl; ɪmˋparʃəl] *a*. 公平的;无私的,无偏见的。**-i·ty** [ˈimˌpɑːʃiˈæliti; ˋɪmˏparˋʃɪælətɪ] *n*. **-ly** *ad*.

im·part·i·ble [imˈpɑːtibl; ɪmˋpartɪbl̩] *a*. 不能分割的,不可分的。**-bil·i·ty** *n*. **-bly** *ad*.

im·pass·a·ble [imˈpɑːsəbl; ɪmˋpasəbl̩] *a*. **1**. 不可通行的,不可逾越的。～ *roads* 不通行的道路。**2**. 不可流通的。**-bil·i·ty** [-ˈbiliti; -ˋbɪlətɪ] *n*. **-bly** *ad*.

im·passe [æmˈpɑːs, im-; æmˋpas, ɪm-] *n*. **1**. 死路,死胡同。**2**. 绝境;僵局。*reach an* ～ 陷入僵局。

im·pas·si·ble [imˈpæsəbl; ɪmˋpæsəbl̩] *a*. **1**. 不觉疼痛的,麻木的,无感觉的。**2**. 不能伤害的。**3**. 泰然自若的,无动于衷的。**-bil·i·ty** *n*. **-ness** *n*. **-bly** *ad*.

I

im·pas·sion [im'pæʃən; ɪm`pæʃən] *vt*. 激起…的热情,使感动,使感激。**-ed** *a*. 感动的;充满热情的,热烈的(*an ~ed speech* 热烈的发言)。

im·pas·sive [im'pæsiv; ɪm`pæsɪv] *a*. 1. 无感情的,冷淡的。2. 呆钝的。3. 冷静的。4. 无感觉的;无意识的。**-ness**, **-vi·ty** *n*. **-ly** *ad*.

im·paste [im'peist; ɪm`pest] *vt*. 1. 使成糊状。2. 用浆糊封住[粘贴]。3.【绘】涂浓厚色彩于…上。

im·pas·to [im'pɑːstəu; ɪm`pɑsto] *n*. (在画上)厚涂颜料色彩。

im·pa·tience [im'peiʃəns; ɪm`peʃəns] *n*. 1. 不耐烦,急躁。2. 渴望,切望。*He awaited her answer with ~*. 他焦急地等待她的答覆。

im·pa·ti·ens [im'peiʃiˌenz, -ʃənz; ɪm`peʃɪˏɛnz, -ʃənz] *n*.【植】凤仙花属(*Impatiens*)植物。

im·pa·tient [im'peiʃənt; ɪm`peʃənt] *a*. 1. 急躁的,急切的。2. 对…不耐烦,对…忍耐不住(*of*; *with*)。3. 急想,渴望〔后接不定式〕。4.〔古〕不合的,不许的。*be ~ of any interruptions* 对任何干扰都不耐烦。*be ~ with children* 对孩子急躁。*~ for the arrival of May Day* 切望五一节的到来。*be ~ to get about one's business* 急于抓业务。

im·pav·id [im'pævid; ɪm`pævɪd] *a*. 〔古〕无惧的,无畏的。**-ly** *ad*.

im·pawn [im'pɔːn; ɪm`pɔn] *vt*. 1. 典当,抵押。2. 立誓,许诺。

im·pay·a·ble [im'peiəbl; ɪm`peəbl] *a*. 1. 金不换的,极贵重的,无价的。2.〔口〕超越一般限度的;异常的。

im·peach [im'piːtʃ; ɪm`pitʃ] *vt*. 1. 责问,弹劾,检举,告发。2. 责难,指责,不信任,怀疑。*~ sb. with (of) a crime* 控告某人犯罪。*be ~ed for treason* 被告发犯有叛国罪。**-able** *a*. **-ment** *n*.

im·pearl [im'pəːl; ɪm`pɝl] *vt*. 1. 使形成珍珠;使形成珠状物。2. 用珍珠装饰。

im·pec·ca·ble [im'pekəbl; ɪm`pɛkəbl] **I** *a*. 1. 不会做坏事的;不容易做坏事的。2. 无缺点的,无瑕疵的。**II** *n*. 不会作坏事的人;毫无缺点的人。**-bil·i·ty** *n*. **-bly** *ad*.

im·pec·cant [im'pekənt; ɪm`pɛkənt] *a*. 无罪的;无缺点错误的;无咎的。**-can·cy** [-kənsi; -kənsɪ] *n*.

im·pe·cu·ni·ous [ˌimpi'kjuːnjəs; ˏɪmpɪ`kjunjəs] *a*. 没有钱的;贫穷的。**-ni·os·i·ty** [ˌimpiˌkjuːni'ɔsiti; ˏɪmpɪˏkjunɪ`ɑsətɪ], **-ness** *n*. 无钱;贫穷。**-ly** *ad*.

im·ped·ance [im'piːdəns; ɪm`pidəns] *n*.【物】阻抗。*acoustic ~* 声阻抗。

im·pede [im'piːd; ɪm`pid] *vt*. 妨碍,阻碍,阻止:*~ sb.'s progress* 妨碍某人的进步。*The muddy roads ~ our journey*. 我们的旅游被泥泞的道路阻挠了。

im·ped·i·ment [im'pedimənt; ɪm`pɛdɪmənt] *n*. 1. 妨碍,阻碍(*to*);障碍物。2. 法定婚姻的障碍。3.〔*pl*.〕= *impedimenta*。4. 口吃〔又作~ *in speech*〕。***throw ~s in the way*** 阻碍进行。

im·ped·i·men·ta [imˌpedi'mentə; ɪmˏpɛdɪ`mɛntɚ] *n*. 〔*pl*.〕1. 行李。2. 妨碍行进的负重,包袱。3.【军】辎重。

im·ped·i·men·tal [imˌpedi'mentl; ɪmˏpɛdɪ`mɛntl], **im·ped·i·men·ta·ry** [-təri; -tərɪ] *a*. 妨碍的,阻碍的。*causes ~ to success* 阻碍成功的原因。

im·pel [im'pel; ɪm`pɛl] *vt*. (***impelled***; ***impel·ling***) 1. 推动,推进;激励。2. 驱使,迫使,使不得不。*~ sb. to do sth*. 推动某人做某事。*~ling force* 推进力。*What motives ~led him to do so?* 是什么动机促使他这么干? *feel ~led to speak* 觉得不得不说。

im·pel·lent [im'pelənt; ɪm`pɛlənt] *a*. 推动的,推进的,促使的。

im·pel·ler [im'pelə; ɪm`pɛlɚ] *n*. 1. 推进者,推动器。2.【电】转子;转叶片。3.【机】叶轮。*an air ~* 空气叶轮。*an ~ shaft* 叶轮轴。

im·pend [im'pend; ɪm`pɛnd] *vi*. 1. 悬挂,吊(在上头)(*over*)。2. (事件,危险等)逼近;即将临头。*We went indoors because rain ~ed*. 我们进屋里去,因为就要下雨了。**-pend·ence**, **-cy** [-'pendəns, -si; -`pɛndəns, -sɪ] *n*. **-ent** *a*. = impending。

im·pend·ing [im'pendiŋ; ɪm`pɛndɪŋ] *a*. 吊在头上的;逼近的,即将到来的,紧急的。*an ~ danger* 逼在眉睫的危险。

im·pen·e·tra·bil·i·ty [imˌpenitrə'biliti; ɪmˏpɛnɪtrə`bɪlətɪ] *n*. 1. 不可入,不能贯穿;【物】不可入性。2. 不可测知;不可解。3. 无情,冷酷。

im·pen·e·tra·ble [im'penitrəbl; ɪm`pɛnɪtrəbl] *a*. 1. 进不去的;难贯穿的;【物】不可入性的。2. 看不透的,不可测知的,费解的。3. 不动心的,不接受的,顽固的。*~ by a bullet* 子弹打不穿的。*~ darkness* 漆黑。*an ~ mystery* 费解的秘密。*a mind ~ by [to] new ideas* 不接受新思想的顽固头脑。**-ness** *n*. **-bly** *ad*.

im·pen·e·trate [im'penitreit; ɪm`pɛnɪtret] *vt*. 穿,深深戳进;渗透。

im·pen·i·tence [im'penitəns; ɪm`pɛnɪtəns], **im·pen·i·ten·cy** [-si; -sɪ] *n*. 不悔悟;顽固。

im·pen·i·tent [im'penitənt; ɪm`pɛnɪtənt] *a*., *n*. 不悔悟的(人);顽固的(人)。**-ly** *ad*.

imper(at). = imperative.

im·per·a·ti·val [imˌperə'taivəl; ɪmˏpɛrə`taɪvəl] *a*.【语】祈使语气的。

im·per·a·tive [im'perətiv; ɪm`pɛrətɪv] **I** *a*. 1. 命令的,强制的,专横的。2. 不可避免的,绝对必要的,迫切的,紧急的。3.【语】祈使的。*an ~ manner* 专横的态度。*~ mood* 祈使语气。*~ sentence* 祈使句。*It is ~ that we should [it is ~ for us to] act at once*. 我们必须马上行动。*an ~ duty* 紧急任务。*~ necessity* 迫切需要。**II** *n*. 1. 命令;规则;必须做的事。2.【语】祈使语气,祈使语气动词。**-ly** *ad*. **-ness** *n*.

im·pe·ra·tor [impə'rɑːtɔː; ˏɪmpə`rɑtɔr] *n*. 〔L.〕1. (古罗马的)大将军,凯旋将军。2. 皇帝,元首。

im·per·a·to·ri·al [imˌperə'tɔːriəl; ɪmˏpɛrə`tɔrɪəl] *a*. (古罗马)大将军的,皇帝的。**-ly** *ad*.

im·per·cep·ti·ble [ˌimpə'septəbl; ˏɪmpɚ`sɛptəbl] *a*. 1. 感觉不到的,觉察不到的(*to*)。2. 细微的,微妙的。*Color is ~ to the touch*. 颜色是触摸不到的。**-bil·i·ty** [-'biliti; -`bɪlətɪ], **-ness** *n*. **-bly** *ad*.

im·per·cep·tive [ˌimpə'septiv; ˏɪmpɚ`sɛptɪv] *a*. 无知觉的;无知觉力的。**-ness** *n*.

im·per·cip·i·ent [ˌimper'sipiənt; ˏɪmpɛr`sɪpɪənt] *a*. = imperceptive.

im·per·ence ['impərəns; `ɪmpərəns] *n*. = impudence.

imperf. = imperfect; imperforate.

im·per·fect [im'pəːfikt; ɪm`pɝfɪkt] **I** *a*. 1. 不完全的,有缺点的。2. 不完整的,未完成的。3. 法律上不能实施的。4. 减弱的,缩小的。5.【语】未完成体的。*~ combustion* 不完全燃烧。*~ grain* 不饱满的谷粒。*the ~ tense*【语】未完成时。**II** *n*.【语法】未完成体。*~* **fungus** 半知菌,不完全菌类。**-ly** *ad*. **-ness** *n*.

im·per·fect·i·ble [ˌimpə'fektəbl; ˏɪmpɚ`fɛktəbəl] *a*. 不可能完善的。

im·per·fec·tion [ˌimpə'fekʃən; ˏɪmpɚ`fɛkʃən] *n*. 不完全,不足;缺点。

im·per·fec·tive [ˌimpə'fektiv; ˏɪmpɚ`fɛktɪv] **I** *a*.【语法】(俄语等动词的)未完成体的。**II** *n*. 1. 未完成体。2. 未完成体动词。

im·per·fo·rate [im'pəːfərit; ɪm`pɝfərɪt] **I** *a*. 1. 无(气)孔的;不穿孔的。2. (邮票)无齿孔的。3.【解】无孔的,闭锁的。**II** *n*. 无齿孔邮票。

im·pe·ri·a [im'piəriə; ɪm`pɪrɪə] imperium 的复数。

im·pe·ri·al [im'piəriəl; ɪm`pɪrɪəl] **I** *a*. 1. 帝国的,皇帝[皇后]的。2. 合皇帝身分的,庄严的。3.〔英〕〔常 I-〕英帝国(制定)的。4. 超级的,特等的。5. 英国度量衡法定

I

标准的;22×32 英寸的(纸)。*an* ~ *household* 皇室。*an* ~ *envoy* 钦差大臣。*the* ~ *examinations* (封建社会的)科举。~ *politics* 英国政治。~ *preference* 〔英〕国内特惠关税。~ *taxes* 〔英〕国税。*the* ~ *gallon* 英国加仑(=4.546 升)。**II** ***n.*** **1.** 写字纸〔〔英〕22×30 或 32 英寸;〔美〕23×31 英寸〕。**2.** 特等品,特大(号)物品。**3.** 一小绺须〔因拿破仑三世曾留此须而得名〕。**4.** 帝俄时代的金币〔1745 年第一次发行等于 10 卢布;从 1897 年到 1917 年等于 15 卢布〕。**5.** 公共马车顶,放在车顶上的箱子。**6.**【史】神圣罗马皇帝的拥护者。

im·pe·ri·al·ism [im'piəriəlizəm; ɪm`pɪrɪəl͵ɪzəm] ***n.*** 帝国主义。

im·pe·ri·al·ist [im'piəriəlist; ɪm`pɪrɪəlɪst] **I** ***n.*** **1.** 帝国主义者。**2.** 皇帝的支持者;帝制拥护者。**3.** 〔I-〕【史】神圣罗马皇帝的拥护者。**II** ***a.*** 帝国主义的。

im·pe·ri·al·is·tic [imˌpiəriə'listik; ɪm͵pɪrɪə`lɪstɪk] ***a.*** **1.** 帝国主义的,帝国主义者的。**2.** 赞成帝国主义的。**-ti·cal·ly** ***ad.***

im·pe·ri·al·ize [im'piəriəlaiz; ɪm`pɪrɪə͵laɪz] ***vt.*** **1.** 使成帝国。**2.** 使帝国主义化。

im·per·il [im'peril; ɪm`perɪl] ***vt.*** (***im·per·il(l)ed***; ***im·per·il(l)ing***) 危害,使陷于危险。

im·pe·ri·ous [im'piəriəs; ɪm`pɪrɪəs] ***a.*** **1.** 专横的;傲慢的。**2.** 迫切的,紧要的。*an* ~ *manner* 自高自大的样子。~ *need* 紧急的需要。**-ly** ***ad.*** **-ness** ***n.***

im·per·ish·a·ble [im'periʃəbl; ɪm`perɪʃəbl̩] ***a.*** 不灭的,不朽的,永久的。**-bil·i·ty** ***n.*** **-bly** ***ad.***

im·pe·ri·um [im'piəriəm; ɪm`pɪrɪəm] ***n.*** (*pl.* ***-ri·a*** [-riə; -rɪə]) 〔L.〕最高权力;主权;统治权;司法权;裁判权。~ ***in imperio*** 政府中的政府,帝国中的帝国,主权内的主权。

im·per·ma·nence [im'pəːmənəns; ɪm`pɝmənəns], **im·per·ma·nency** [-si; -sɪ] ***n.*** 非永久(性),暂时(性)。

im·per·ma·nent [im'pəːmənənt; ɪm`pɝmənənt] ***a.*** 非永久的,暂时的。

im·per·me·a·ble [im'pəːmjəbl; ɪm`pɝmɪəbl̩] ***a.*** **1.** 不能通过的。**2.** 不能透过的,不可渗透的。*The passage became absolutely* ~. 过道完全不通了。~ *to water* 不透水的。**-bil·i·ty** [imˌpəːmjə'biliti; ɪm͵pɝmjə`bɪlətɪ] ***n.***

im·per·mis·si·ble [ˌimpə'misəbl; ͵ɪmpɚ`mɪsəbl̩] ***a.*** 不允许的,不许可的。**-bil·i·ty** ***n.***

impers. = impersonal.

im·per·scrip·ti·ble [ˌimpə'skriptəbl; ͵ɪmpə`skrɪptəbl̩] ***a.*** 没有文件证明的;非官方的,非正式的。

im·per·son·al [im'pəːsnl; ɪm`pɝsn̩l] **I** ***a.*** **1.** 非个人的,和个人无关的。**2.** 不具人格的;一般性的。**3.**【语法】非人称的。~ *forces* 非人力。*an* ~ *verbs*【语法】非人称动词。~ *pronouns* 非人称代词。**II** ***n.***【语法】非人称动词,非人称代名词。**-i·ty** [imˌpəːsə'næliti; ɪm͵pɝsə`nælətɪ] ***n.*** 与个人无关,非人格性;非人格性的东西。**-ly** ***ad.***

im·per·son·al·ize [im'pəːsnəlaiz; ɪm`pɝsnə͵laɪz] ***vt.*** (***-iz·ed***, ***-iz·ing***) 除去个性;使非人格化,使…不特指。

im·per·son·ate [im'pəːsəneit; ɪm`pɝsə͵net] **I** ***vt.*** **1.** 使人格化,体现。**2.** 模仿,扮演,假冒。**II** ***a.*** 被人格化了的,体现…的。

im·per·son·a·tion [imˌpəːsə'neiʃən; ɪm͵pɝsə`neʃən] ***n.*** 使人格化;体现;扮演;模仿;假冒。

im·per·son·a·tive [im'pəːsəneitiv; ɪm`pɝsə͵netɪv] ***a.*** 扮演的,模仿的。

im·per·son·a·tor [im'pəːsəneitə; ɪm`pɝsə͵netɚ] ***n.*** 扮演者,模仿者。

im·per·son·i·fy [ˌimpə'sɔnifai; ͵ɪmpə`sɑnɪfaɪ] ***v.*** = personify.

im·per·ti·nence [im'pəːtinəns; ɪm`pɝtɪnəns], **im·per·ti·nen·cy** [-si; -sɪ] ***n.*** **1.** 无礼,鲁莽,傲慢。**2.** 不适当,弄错。**3.** 离题,不得要领。**4.** 鲁莽的言行。

im·per·ti·nent [im'pəːtinənt; ɪm`pɝtɪnənt] ***a.*** **1.** 无礼的,鲁莽的,傲慢的。**2.** 不适当的,不恰当的。**3.** 离题的,不得要领的。*an* ~ *youth* 傲慢的青年。*adduce* ~ *facts in support of a theory* 罗列不恰当的事实支持某一学说。**-ly** ***ad.***

im·per·turb·a·ble [ˌimpə(ː)'təːbəbl; ͵ɪmpɚ`tɝbəbl̩] ***a.*** 沉着的,冷静的。**-bil·i·ty** ['impə(ː)ˌtəːbə'biliti; ͵ɪmpɚ͵tɝbə`bɪlətɪ], **-ness** ***n.*** **-bly** ***ad.***

im·per·tur·ba·tion [ˌimpəːtə'beiʃən; ͵ɪmpɝtɚ`beʃən] ***n.*** 沉着,冷静。

im·per·vi·ous [im'pəːvjəs; ɪm`pɝvɪəs] ***a.*** **1.** 不可渗透的,穿不过的,透不过的。**2.** 不受干扰的,不受影响的。**3.** 对(批评等)无动于衷的,不接受的。*an* ~ *desert* 无人能通过的沙漠。*be* ~ *to all reason* 不通情理。**-ly** ***ad.*** **-ness** ***n.***

im·pe·ti·go [ˌimpi'taigəu; ͵ɪmpɪ`taɪgo] ***n.***【医】脓疱病。

im·pe·trate ['impitreit; `ɪmpətret] ***vt.*** (***-trat·ed***, ***-trat·ing***) **1.** 求得。**2.** 〔罕〕恳求,哀求。**-tra·tion** ***n.***

im·pe·tig·i·nous [ˌimpi'tidʒinəs; ͵ɪmpə`tɪdʒənəs] ***a.*** 脓疱病的;如脓疱病的。

im·pet·u·os·i·ty [imˌpetju'ɔsiti; ͵ɪm͵petʃʊ`ɑsətɪ] ***n.*** 激烈,猛烈;急躁;急性病。

im·pet·u·ous [im'petjuəs; ɪm`petʃʊəs] ***a.*** **1.** 激烈的,猛烈的。**2.** 激动的;急躁的;冲动的,轻举妄动的,鲁莽的。*an* ~ *charge* 猛袭。*an* ~ *wind* 狂风。*an* ~ *youth* 急躁的青年。**-ly** ***ad.*** **-ness** ***n.***

im·pe·tus ['impitəs; `ɪmpətəs] ***n.*** **1.** 动量,动力。**2.** 推动,促进。***give*** [***lend***] ***an*** ~ ***to*** 推动,刺激,促进。***with great*** ~用大力。

impf. = imperfect.

imp. gal. = imperial gallon.

im·pi ['impi; `ɪmpɪ] ***n.*** (*pl.* ~*es*, ~*s*) (南非)卡菲尔(*Kaffir*)人的武装部队或其他南方武装部队。

im·pi·e·ty [im'paiəti; ɪm`paɪətɪ] ***n.*** **1.** 不虔诚,不信神。**2.** 不恭敬,不孝。**3.** 不恭敬的言行,邪恶的言行。

imp·ing ['impiŋ; `ɪmpɪŋ] ***n.*** 接枝;接穗。

im·pinge [im'pindʒ; ɪm`pɪndʒ] ***vi.*** **1.** 冲击,撞击(*on*; *upon*; *against*)。**2.** 侵害;侵犯。**3.** (密切)接触。*Rays light* ~ *upon the retina*. 光线射到网膜上。~ *on* [*upon*] *one's authority* 侵犯某人权限。— ***vt.*** (气体等)撞击。**-ment** ***n.***

im·pi·ous ['impiəs; `ɪmpɪəs] ***a.*** **1.** 不信神的,邪恶的。**2.** 不恭敬的,不孝的。**-ly** ***ad.***

imp·ish ['impiʃ; `ɪmpɪʃ] ***a.*** 小鬼似的;顽皮的。**-ly** ***ad.*** **-ness** ***n.***

im·plac·a·ble [im'plækəbl; ɪm`plækəbl̩] ***a.*** **1.** 难宽恕的;难和解的,仇恨深的;毫不留情的。**2.** 不能改变的。*an* ~ *enemy* 死敌。***have an*** ~ ***hatred for ...*** 对…深恶痛绝。**-bil·i·ty** [-'biliti; -`bɪlətɪ], **-ness** ***n.*** **-bly** ***ad.***

im·pla·cen·tal, im·pla·cen·tate [ˌimplə'sentl, -teit; ͵ɪmplə`sɛntl̩, -tet] ***a.*** (哺乳动物)无胎盘的 (= aplacental)。

im·plant [im'plɑːnt; ɪm`plænt] ***vt.*** **I** **1.** 植,栽进。**2.**【医】移植。**3.** 注入,灌输,牢固树立。**II** ['implɑːnt; `ɪmplænt] ***n.*** **1.** 移植片,移植物。**2.**【医】(插入体内治癌症等用的)植入管。

im·plan·ta·tion [ˌimplɑːn'teiʃən; ͵ɪmplæn`teʃən] ***n.*** **1.** 种植。**2.** 插入;灌输,鼓吹。**3.**【医】皮下注射。

im·plau·si·ble [im'plɔːzəbl; ɪm`plɔzəbl̩] ***a.*** 难以置信的,不像有理的。**-bil·i·ty** ***n.*** **-bly** ***ad.***

im·plead [im'pliːd; ɪm`plid] ***vt.*** 控告。— ***vi.*** 起诉。

im·ple·ment ['implimənt; `ɪmpləmənt] **I** ***n.*** 〔常用 *pl.*〕**1.** 工具;器具。**2.** 〔Scot.〕【法】履行(契约等)。*agricultural* [*farm*] ~*s* 农具。*household* ~*s* 家具,日用器具。~*s of warfare* 武器。**II** ***vt.*** **1.** 给…供给器

I

具。2. 执行,履行(契约);落实(政策);贯彻,实施;使生效。3. 把…填满;补充。~ *our foreign policy* 执行外交政策。

im·ple·men·tal [ˌimpliˈmentl; ˏɪmpləˋmentl̩] *a*. 1. 器具的,做器具用的。2. 起作用的,有帮助的。

im·ple·men·ta·tion [ˌimplimenˈteiʃən; ˏɪmpləmenˋteʃən] *n*. 执行,履行;贯彻,落实。

im·ple·tion [imˈpliːʃən; ɪmˋpliʃən] *n*. 满,充满。

im·pli·cate [ˈimplikeit; ˋɪmplɪˏket] I *vt*. 1. 使纠缠,缠绕。2. 令生关系,使牵连。3. 影响〔用于被动语态〕。4. 含有…的意思。*be ~d in* …和…有牵连[有连带关系]。*This confession ~s numerous officials in the bribery scandal*. 这一供认会使许多官员牵连到受贿的丑事中。II [ˈimplikit; ˋɪmplɪkɪt] *n*. 包含[暗指]的东西。

im·pli·ca·tion [ˌimpliˈkeiʃən; ˏɪmplɪˋkeʃən] *n*. 1. 牵连,牵涉,纠缠。2. 含蓄,含意,言外之意。3.【数】蕴涵,蕴含。4. 本质,实质。5.〔常 *pl*.〕推断,结论。**by ~** 含蓄地,用寓意,暗中。*agree by ~* 默契。

im·pli·ca·tive [imˈplikətiv, ˈimplikeitiv; ɪmˋplɪkətɪv, ˋɪmpləˏketɪv] *a*. 1. 含蓄的,意外之意的。2. 牵连的。**-ly** *ad*.

im·plic·it [imˈplisit; ɪmˋplɪsɪt] *a*. 1. 含蓄的,不讲明的。2. 内含的,隐含的 (*opp*. explicit)。3. 绝对的,盲目的。*an ~ agreement* 默契,暗暗同意。*an ~ answer* 含蓄的答覆。~ *obedience* 盲从。~ **confidence in** 盲目相信。~ **differentiation**【数】隐微分法。~ **function**【数】隐函数。**-ly** *ad*.

im·plied [imˈplaid; ɪmˋplaɪd] *a*. 含蓄的,隐含的,不言而喻的,言外的 (*opp*. expressed)。*an ~ consent* 默许。**-ly** [-aidli; -aɪdlɪ] *ad*.

im·plode [imˈpləud; ɪmˋplod] *vi*., *vt*.【物】1. (使)爆聚,(使)内向爆炸;(使)压破。2.【语】用内破裂音发(音)。

im·plore [imˈplɔː; ɪmˋplɔr] *vt*. 恳求,乞求,哀求。~ *sb*. *for sth*. 为某事恳求某人。~ *sb*. *to do sth*. 央求某人做某事。**-ra·tion** [ˌimplɔːˈreiʃən; ˏɪmpləˋreʃən] *n*.

im·plor·ing [imˈplɔːriŋ; ɪmˋplɔrɪŋ] *a*. 恳求的,乞求的,哀求的。**-ly** *ad*.

im·plo·sion [imˈpləuʒən; ɪmˋploʒən] *n*. 1.【物】爆聚,内向爆炸 (*opp*. explosion)。2.【语】内破裂。

im·plo·sive [imˈpləusiv; ɪmˋplosɪv] I *a*. 内破裂形成的。II *n*. 内破裂音。**-ly** *ad*.

im·plu·vi·um [imˈpluːviəm; ɪmˋpluvɪəm] *n*. (*pl*. *-vi·a* [-viə; -vɪə]) (古代罗马房屋院内的)蓄水池。

im·ply [imˈplai; ɪmˋplaɪ] *vt*. (*-plied*; *-ply·ing*) 1. 含蓄,包含;含有…的意思。2. 暗示,暗指。*Silence often implies consent*. 沉默常常表示同意。*Do you realize what his words ~?* 你领会他说话的含意吗? *Do you ~ that ...?* 你的意思是不是说…?

im·po [ˈimpəu; ˋɪmpo] *n*.〔俚〕= imposition, impot.

im·pol·der [imˈpɔldə; ɪmˋpɑldɚ] *vt*. 从海边围垦(土地),把…变成耕地。

im·pol·i·cy [imˈpɔlisi; ɪmˋpɑləsɪ] *n*. 失策,不明智。

im·po·lite [impəˈlait; ɪmpəˋlaɪt] *a*. 没礼貌的,失礼的,粗鲁的。**-ly** *ad*. **-ness** *n*.

im·pol·i·tic [imˈpɔlitik; ɪmˋpɑlətɪk] *a*. 失策的,不得当的,不高明的。**-ly** *ad*.

im·pon·der·a·ble [imˈpɔndərəbl; ɪmˋpɑndərəbl̩] I *a*. 1. 无重量的,极轻的。2. 不可称量的,无法估计的。*be of ~ weight* 重量称不出。II *n*. 1. 无重量的东西,不可量物。2.〔*pl*.〕无法估量的事物[影响、作用]。**-bil·i·ty** [imˌpɔndərəˈbiliti; ɪmˏpɑndərəˋbɪlətɪ], **-ness** *n*. **-bly** *ad*.

im·pone [imˈpəun; ɪmˋpon] *vt*. (*-pon·ed*, *-pon·ing*)〔废〕保证;赌,打赌,作赌注。

im·port [imˈpɔːt, ˈimpɔːt; ɪmˋpɔrt, ˋɪmpɔrt] I *vt*. 1. 输入;进口;引进 (*opp*. export)。2. 意味,表明,说明。3. 对…有重大关系。4.【计】向电脑存储器输入(信息、程序等)。~ *sth*. *from a country* 从某国输入某物。~ *sth*. *into a country* 把某物输入某国。*~ed goods* 进口货。~ *personal feelings into a discussion* 把个人感情带进讨论中。*I should like to know what his action ~s*. 我倒想知道他的行动用意何在。*It ~s us to know*... 知道…对我们有重大关系。*questions that ~ us nearly* 和我们有切身关系的问题。— *vi*. 有(重大)关系。*It ~s little whether we are early or late*. 我们早点迟点没什么关系。II [ˈimpɔːt; ˋɪmpɔrt] *n*. 1. 输入,进口,引进;〔主 *pl*.〕进口货。2. 意义,含义。3. 重要(性)。~ *duties* 进口税。*an ~ surplus* 入超。*an ~ quota* 进口限额。*the ~ of his remarks* 他说话的含意。*a matter of great ~* 大事情。**~/export, ~ and export** *n*., *a*. (电脑上信息、程序等的)输入/输出(的)。

im·port·a·ble [imˈpɔːtəbl; ɪmˋpɔrtəbl̩] *a*. 可进口的。

im·por·tance [imˈpɔːtəns; ɪmˋpɔrtəns] *n*. 1. 重要性。2. 重要地位,显著,有力。3. 骄傲,自大。*a matter of great ~* 重大事情。*a matter of no ~* 无关紧要的事。*a position of ~* 重要地位。*be conscious of one's ~* 自己觉得了不起,自高自大。*speak with an air of ~* 带着傲慢的态度讲话。**attach ~ to** 重视。

im·por·tant [imˈpɔːtənt; ɪmˋpɔrtn̩t] *a*. 1. 重要的,重大的。2. 大量的,许多,大的。3. 优越的,显著的;有权力的。4. 自高自大的。*an ~ figure* [*person*] 要人。*look ~* 了不起似的。**-ly** *ad*.

im·por·ta·tion [ˌimpɔːˈteiʃən; ˏɪmpɔrˋteʃən] *n*. 输入,进口,引进 (*opp*. exportation);进口货,输入品。

im·port·er [imˈpɔːtə; ɪmˋpɔrtɚ] *n*. 进口商,进口者 (*opp*. exporter)。

im·por·tu·nate [imˈpɔːtjunit; ɪmˋpɔrtʃənɪt] *a*. 1. 强求的,缠扰不休的,讨厌的。2. 坚持的,迫切的。**-ly** *ad*.

im·por·tune [imˈpɔːtjuːn; ɪmˋpɔrtʃən] I *vt*. 1. 向…硬要,向…强求,死乞白赖地要求。2. 纠缠。3. (妓女)拉客。~ *sb*. *for sth*. 向某人强求某物。— *vi*. 强求;纠缠不休。II *a*. = importunate. **-ni·ty** [-niti; -nətɪ] *n*.

im·pose [imˈpəuz; ɪmˋpoz] *vt*. 1. 征收(税等),使…负担。2. 强派(工),把…强加给。3. 把(次品等)硬卖给;以…欺骗 (*upon*; *on*)。4.【印】把…拼版,装版。5.〔古〕放置。~ *a tax upon* [*on*] *sb*. 向某人征税。~ *one's opinion upon sb*. 把意见强加于某人。~ *a false article upon* [*on*] *sb*. 拿假货卖给人。~ *hands on sb*.【宗】对某人按手。— *vi*. 1. 利用 (*on*; *upon*)。2. 欺骗 (*on*; *upon*)。3. 施加影响 (*on*; *upon*)。~ *upon sb.'s kindness* 趁人心软。*I am not to be ~d upon*. 我是不会上当的。

im·pos·ing [imˈpəuziŋ; ɪmˋpozɪŋ] *a*. 1. 给人印象深刻的。2. (建筑物等)堂皇的,雄伟的,使人赞叹的。*an ~ appearance* 仪表堂堂。*an ~ building* 壮丽的大楼。*an ~ figure* 大人物,要人。

im·po·si·tion [ˌimpəˈziʃən; ˏɪmpəˋzɪʃən] *n*. 1. 征税,课税;税,负担。2. 强加,强迫接受。3.〔英〕(处罚学生的)惩罚作业〔略:impo, impot〕。4. 欺瞒,哄骗。5.〔罕〕置放,安放;【宗】按手礼。6.【印】拼版,装版。

im·pos·si·bil·i·ty [imˌpɔsəˈbiliti; ɪmˏpɑsəˋbɪlətɪ] *n*. 不可能;不可能的事。

im·pos·si·ble [imˈpɔsəbl; ɪmˋpɑsəbl̩] *a*. 1. 做不到的,不能做的,不可能的。2. 不会有的,不会发生的;不能相信的;〔口〕(帽子等)奇形怪状的。3.〔口〕不能忍受的,讨厌的。*an ~ fellow* 讨厌的家伙。*an ~ event* 不可能发生的事件。*an ~ story* 不能相信的故事。*Nothing is ~ to a willing mind*.〔谚〕天下无难事,只怕有心人。*an ~ task* 不可能的工作。~ **of execution** 无法实行。**next to ~** 几乎是不可能的。**not ~** 并非不可能。**try to do the ~** 想做做不到的事;缘木求鱼。~ **art** 概念"艺术"〔侧重反映艺术家在创作过程中产生的概念的一种"艺术",又称 conceptual art〕。

I

im·pos·si·bly [imˈpɔsəbli; ɪmˋpɑsəblɪ] *ad*. 办不到地，不可能地，无法可想地。*not* ～ 多半，或许。

im·post[1] [ˈimpəust; ˋɪmpost] **I** *n*. **1**. 税，进口税，关税。**2**. 〔俚〕【赛马】强马所负担的重量。**II** *vt*. 〔美〕类分(进口商品，以便征税)。

im·post[2] [ˈimpəust; ɪmpost] *n*. 【建】拱墩，拱基。

im·pos·t(h)ume [imˈpɔstjuːm; ɪmˋpɑstjum] *n*. 〔古〕**1**. 脓肿。**2**. 腐败，道德败坏。

im·pos·tor [imˈpɔstə; imˋpɑstɚ] *n*. 冒名顶替者；骗子。

im·pos·ture [imˈpɔstʃə; ɪmˋpɑstʃɚ] *n*. 冒名顶替；欺骗，诈骗行为，以诈骗为生。

im·pot [ˈimpɔt; ˋɪmpɑt] *n*. **1**. 〔英俚〕= imposition. **2**. impo.

im·po·tence [ˈimpətəns; ˋɪmpətəns], **im·po·ten·cy** [-si; -sɪ] *n*. **1**. 无力，衰弱；无能。**2**. 无效，无法可想。**3**. 【医】阳痿。*We have reduced the enemy to* ～. 我们已经使敌人丧失战斗力。

im·po·tent [ˈimpətənt; ˋɪmpətənt] **I** *a*. **1**. 无力的，虚弱的；软弱无能的，不起作用的。**2**. 【医】阳痿的。*an* ～ *conclusion* 虎头蛇尾。*in* ～ *fury* 干着急。**II** *n*. 虚弱者；阳痿者。**-ly** *ad*.

im·pound [imˈpaund; ɪmˋpaʊnd] *vt*. **1**. (将家畜)关在栏中；拘禁(人等)。**2**. 畜(水等)。**3**. 充公，没收。

im·pov·er·ish [imˈpɔvəriʃ; ɪmˋpɑvərɪʃ] *vt*. **1**. 使穷困。**2**. 使枯竭。*～ed health* 虚弱无力的健康状况。*an ～ed existence* 平淡无味的生存。*～ed rubber* 失去弹性的橡皮。*～ed soil* 贫脊的土壤。**-ment** *n*.

im·pow·er [imˈpauə; ɪmˋpaʊɚ] *vt*. empower 的废体。

im·prac·ti·ca·ble [imˈpræktikəbl; ɪmˋpræktɪkəbl] *a*. **1**. 不能实行的，做不到的，不现实的。**2**. 难对付的，顽梗的(人等)。**3**. 不能用的，不能通行的(道路等)。*an* ～ *scheme* 不能实行的计划。**-bil·i·ty** [-ˈbiliti; -ˋbɪlətɪ], **-ness** *n*. **-bly** *ad*.

im·prac·ti·cal [imˈpræktikəl; ɪmˋpræktɪkl] *a*. **1**. 不实用的，不实际的。**2**. 不能实行的，做不到的。**-ly** *ad*. **-i·ty** [imˌpræktiˈkæliti; ɪmˏpræktɪˋkælətɪ], **-ness** *n*.

im·pre·cate [ˈimprikeit; ˋɪmprɪˏket] *vt*. 咒，诅咒，祈求降(祸)(*upon*)。～ *evil upon sb*. 祈求降祸某人。**-ca·tion** [ˌimpriˈkeiʃən; ˏɪmprɪˋkeʃən] *n*. **-ca·to·ry** *a*.

im·pre·cise [ˌimpriˈsais; ˏɪmprɪˋsaɪz] *a*. 不精确的；不精密的；不确定的；含糊的。**-ly** *ad*. **-sion** [-ˈsiʒən; -ˋsɪʒən] *n*.

im·preg [ˈimpreg; ˋɪmprɛg] *n*. 【建】树脂浸渍木材。

im·preg·na·ble[1] [imˈpregnəbl; ɪmˋprɛgnəbl] *a*. 难攻破的；坚固的，坚定的。*an* ～ *argument* 毫无破绽的议论。*an* ～ *belief* 坚定不移的信念。*an* ～ *bulwark* 坚不可摧的堡垒。～ *virtue* 坚贞不屈的情操。**-bly** *ad*. **-bil·i·ty** [imˌpregnəˈbiliti; ɪmˏprɛgnəˋbɪlətɪ], **-ness** *n*.

im·preg·na·ble[2] [imˈpregnəbl; imˋprɛgnəbl] *a*. 有受精[怀孕]可能的。

im·preg·nate [ˈimpregneit; ˋɪmprɛgnet] **I** *vt*. **1**. 使受精，使怀孕。**2**. 使充满，使饱和(*with*)。**3**. 渗透，灌注，注入(*with*)。*water ～d with salt* 饱含盐的水。**II** [imˈpregnit; ɪmˋprɛgnɪt] *a*. 怀孕的；渗透的；饱和的。**-na·tion** [ˌimpregˈneiʃən; ˏɪmprɛgˋneʃən] *n*. 怀孕，受精；饱和；注入；【矿】围岩中的浸染矿床；【化】渗透。**-tor** *n*. **-to·ry** *a*.

im·pre·sa [imˈpreizə; ɪmˋprezə] *n*. 〔废〕箴言；箴言牌。

im·pre·sa·ri·o [ˌimpreˈsɑːriəu; ˏɪmprɪˋsɑrɪo] *n*. (*pl*. *～s*) 〔It.〕(歌剧团、乐团等的)演出主办人；经理，导演，指挥。

im·pre·scrip·ti·ble [ˌimprisˈkriptibl; ˏɪmprɪˋskrɪptəbl] *a*. 不受法令约束的；不可剥夺的；不可侵犯的。

im·press[1] [imˈpres; ɪmˋprɛs] **I** *vt*. (*～ed* 或〔古〕*im·prest*) **1**. 盖印；在…打上记号。**2**. 使铭记，使记住；使深深感到。**3**. 传递，发送。**4**. 【电】给(线路)加电压。*He did not* ～ *me at all*. 他没有给我留下丝毫印象。*an ～ed current* 外加电流。～ *a mark* (*up*) *on a surface* = ～ *a surface with a mark* 在表面上打记号。*an ～ed stamp* 盖了戳的邮票。～ *an official letter with one's seal* = ～ *one's seal on an official letter* 在公函上盖印。**be favourably** [**unfavourably**] **～ed** 中意[不中意]；得到好的[不好的]印象。**be ～ed by** [**with**] 深感；为…所感动。— *vi*. 引人注意，哗众取宠。**II** *n*. **1**. 盖印；铭刻；印记，记号。**2**. 印象，痕迹；特征。*bear the* ～ *of* 带有…的特征。

im·press[2] [imˈpres; ɪmˋprɛs] *vt*. (*～ed* 或〔古〕*im·prest*) **1**. 强制…服兵役。**2**. 征用。**3**. (在辩论中)引用，利用。**II** [ˈimpres; ˋɪmprɛs] *n*. = impressment.

im·press·i·ble [imˈpresəbl; ɪmˋprɛsəbl] *a*. 可印的，可铭刻的；容易感动的，敏感的。**-bil·i·ty** [imˌpresiˈbiliti; ˏɪmprɛsɪˋbɪlətɪ] *n*. **-bly** *ad*.

im·pres·sion [imˈpreʃən; ɪmˋprɛʃən] *n*. **1**. 印象，感觉；感想，模糊的观念。**2**. 意见，想法。**3**. 影响，效果。**4**. 盖印，印记，压痕。**5**. 【印】印刷，印数，印次，第…版，印刷品；(雕版等的)印图。**6**. (牙齿的)印模。*First ～s are most lasting*. 〔谚〕最初的印象最深刻。*be under the* ～ *that* 有…这样的想法。*give one's ～s of* 陈述自己的意见。*make an* ～ *on sb*. 给某人印象，使某人感动。*make no* ～ *on sb*. 对某人无影响。*a first* ～ *of 200,000 copies* 初版二十万册。*the second* ～ *of the second edition* 再版第二次印刷。

im·pres·sion·a·ble [imˈpreʃənəbl; ɪmˋprɛʃənəbl] *a*. 易感的；敏感的，易受影响的；可以打上记号的；可塑的。**-bil·i·ty** [imˌpreʃənəˈbiliti; ɪmˏprɛʃənəˋbɪlətɪ] *n*.

im·pres·sion·al [imˈpreʃənəl; ɪmˋprɛʃənəl] *a*. 印象的；基于印象的，印象派的。

im·pres·sion·ism [imˈpreʃənizəm; ɪmˋprɛʃənˏɪzəm] *n*. 印象主义，印象派〔十九世纪七十年代兴起的在绘画、文艺方面的一种流派。代表人物绘画方面如西班牙画家毕加索，音乐方面如法国作曲家德彪西〕。

im·pres·sion·ist [imˈpreʃənist; ɪmˋprɛʃənɪst] **I** *n*. **1**. 印象主义者，印象派艺术家。**2**. (专门摹仿名人以取悦观众的)摹仿演员。**II** *a*. 印象主义的，印象派的。

im·pres·sion·is·tic [imˌpreʃəˈnistik; ɪmˏprɛʃənˋɪstɪk] *a*. 印象的，印象主义的，印象派的。**-ti·cal·ly** *ad*.

im·pres·sive [imˈpresiv; ɪmˋprɛsɪv] *a*. 给人深刻印象的，令人难忘的，令人感动的。*an* ～ *ceremony* 给人深刻印象的典礼。**-ly** *ad*. **-ness** *n*.

im·press·ment [imˈpresmənt; ɪmˋprɛsmənt] *n*. 强迫服役；征用，强征。*the* ～ *of soldiers* 强制征兵。

im·pres·sure [imˈpreʃə; ɪmˋprɛʃɚ] 〔古〕= impression.

im·prest[1] [ˈimprest; ˋɪmprɛst] **I** *n*. (政府基金的)预付款；预付公务费。**II** *a*. 【会计】预付的，借支的。

im·prest[2] [imˈprest; ɪmˋprɛst] *v*. 〔古〕impress[1,2] 的过去式和过去分词。

im·pri·ma·tur [ˌimpriˈmeitə; ˏɪmprɪˋmetɚ] *n*. 〔L.〕**1**. (主指天主教的)出版牌照。**2**. (官方审查后的)出版许可。**3**. 认可，批准。

im·pri·mis [imˈpraimis; ɪmˋpraɪmɪs] *ad*. 〔L.〕最初，首先。

im·print [imˈprint; ɪmˋprɪnt] **I** *vt*. **1**. 盖(印)；印刷。**2**. 刻上(记号)，标出(特征)。**3**. 使铭记，使铭感。～ *a letter with a postmark* 信件上盖上邮戳。～ *one's personality on one's writing* 在作品里表现出个性。*ideas forever ～ed on one's mind* 永远铭刻于心。**II** [ˈimprint; ˋɪmprɪnt] *n*. 盖印，刻印；痕迹；特征；印象；(书籍的)版权标记。*the printer's* [*publisher's*] ～ = *the* ～. (书籍版权页上关于出版者、印刷者及发行年月日的)版本说明。

im·print·ing [imˈprintiŋ; ɪmˋprɪntɪŋ] *n*. 【心】铭记〔动物生命早期即起作用的一种学习机制〕。

I

im·pris·on [im'prizn; ɪm`prɪzn] *vt*. 1. 关押,监禁。2. 束缚,限制。**-ment** *n*. 关押,束缚(*be sentenced to one year's imprisonment* 被判一年徒刑)。

im·pro, im·prov ['imprəu(v); `ɪmpro(v)] *n*., *a*. (演员和观众交互进行的)现场即兴表演(的)。

im·prob·a·bil·i·ty [imˌprɔbə'biliti; ɪmˏprɑbə`bɪlətɪ] *n*. 不大可能,不大可能有的事。*Don't worry about such improbabilities as earthquakes*. 不必为像地震这类罕见的事情而担心。

im·prob·a·ble [im'prɔbəbl; ɪm`prɑbəbl̩] *a*. 1. 未必有的,不大可能发生的;罕见的。2.【物】不可几的,非概然的。*an* ～ *story* 不可信的故事。*Rain is* ～. 不像有雨的样子。*It is* ～ *that he will come*. 他不见得会来。**-ably** *ad*. (*not improbably* 或许)。

im·pro·bi·ty [im'prəubiti; ɪm`probətɪ] *n*. 不正直,不诚实;邪恶。

im·promp·tu [im'prɔm*p*tjuː; ɪm`prɑm*p*tju] **I** *ad*., *a*. 即席地[的],临时地[的],无准备地[的]。*an* ～ *speech* 即席演说。*speak* ～即席演讲。**II** *n*. 即席之作;即席演说;即兴演奏。

im·prop·er [im'prɔpə; ɪm`prɑpɚ] *a*. 1. 不适当的,不合适的,非正常的。2. 不正确的,错误的。3. 不道德的;亵渎的,不合礼仪的,下流的。*a remark* ～ *to the occasion* 不合时宜的话。*put sth*. *to an* ～ *use* 误用。～ *language* 无礼的话。*an* ～ *person* 下流的人。～ **fraction**【数】假分数,可约分数。～ **function**【数】非正常函数。～ **integral**【数】广义积分,非正常积分。**-ly** *ad*. **-ness** *n*.

im·pro·pri·ate [im'prəuprieit; ɪm`proprɪˏet] **I** *vt*. 1. 把(教会财产)交俗人保管。2. 把(教会财产)据为己有。**II** [-priit; -prɪɪt] *a*. 变成私人所有的。**-a·tion** [imˌprəupri'eiʃən; ɪmˏproprɪ`eʃən] *n*. **-a·tor** *n*. 保管教会财产的俗人。

im·pro·pri·e·ty [ˌimprə'praiəti; ˏɪmprə`praɪətɪ] *n*. 1. 不适当,不合式;不正当。2. 用词错误。3. 不得体的举止,不正当的行为。

im·prov ['imprəuv; `ɪmprov] = impro.

im·prov·a·ble [im'pruːvəbl; ɪm`pruvəbl̩] *a*. 能改良的,可以改进的。**-bil·i·ty** [imˌpruːvə'biliti; ɪmˏpruvə`bɪlətɪ] *n*. **-bly** *ad*.

im·prove [im'pruːv; ɪm`pruv] *vt*. 1. 改良,改善,增进。2. 利用,活用。3. 增高(土地等的)价值。*The farm tool is not good enough, I am going to* ～ *it*. 这农具不好,我要加以改进。～ *oneself in English* 提高自己的英语水平。～ *the occasion* [*opportunity, shining hour*] 利用机会。～ *every moment* 爱惜每一刻光阴。～ ***away*** [***off***] 想改良反而搞坏。— *vi*. 变好;增加,升值。*The situation is improving*. 情况逐渐好转。*an* ～*d variety* 改良品种。～ ***on*** [***upon***] 改良。

im·prove·ment [im'pruːvmənt; ɪm`pruvmənt] *n*. 1. 改良,改进,增进;进步。2. 利用,活用。3. 〔美〕(增高房屋、土地等价值的)装修,改良措施。4. 更优秀的人,更进步的人。～ *of soil*【农】土壤改良。*This letter is an* ～ *upon* [*on*] *your last*. 这封信比你上次的好。

im·prov·er [im'pruːvə; ɪm`pruvɚ] *n*. 1. 改良者,改进者;改进物。2. 见习生,学徒。

im·prov·i·dence [im'prɔvidəns; ɪm`prɑvədəns] *n*. 目光短浅;不顾将来,不经济,不节约。

im·prov·i·dent [im'prɔvidənt; ɪm`prɑvədənt] *a*. 1. 目光短浅的,不顾将来的。2. 不经济的,不注意节约的。**-ly** *ad*.

im·prov·i·sa·tion [ˌimprəvai'zeiʃən; ˏɪmprəvaɪ`zeʃən] *n*. 1. 即席创作,即席演奏[演唱]。2. 临时凑合的东西,即兴作品。**-al** *a*.

im·prov·i·sa·tor [im'prɔvizeitə; ɪm`prɑvəˏzetɚ] *n*. 即兴诗人,即席演奏[演唱]者。

im·pro·vi·sa·to·re [ˌimprɔˌvizɑ'tɔːre; ɪmprɑˏvɪzə`tor] *n*. 〔It.〕(*pl*. ***-ri*** [-riː; -rɪ]) = improvisator.

im·prov·i·sa·to·ri·al, -to·ry [imˌprɔvizə'tɔːriəl, ˌimprə'vaizətəri; ɪmˏprɑvɪzə`torɪəl, ɪm`prɑvəzəˏtorɪ] *a*. 1. 即席的,即兴的。2. 临时凑合的。

im·prov·i·sa·tri·ce [ˌimprɔˌvizɑ'triːtʃe; ˏɪmprɑˏvɪzə`tritʃɛ] *n*. 〔It.〕(*pl*. ***-ci*** [-tʃiː; -tʃi]) 女即兴诗人,女即席演奏[演唱]者。

im·pro·vise ['imprəvaiz; `ɪmprəˏvaɪz] *vt*. 1. 即席创作,即席演奏[演唱]。2. 临时准备,临时凑成。*an* ～*d makeshift* 临时凑合的办法。*an* ～*d operating room* 临时简易手术室。～ *a bed on a sofa* 把沙发作为临时铺[床]。

im·pro·vis·er ['imprəvaizə; `ɪmprəˏvaɪzɚ] *n*. 即兴诗人,即席演奏[演唱]者。

im·pru·dence [im'pruːdəns; ɪm`prudəns] *n*. 1. 轻率,鲁莽。2. 轻率[鲁莽]的行为[言论]。*commit an* ～犯错误。*have the* ～ *to* 竟然轻率地。

im·pru·dent [im'pruːdənt; ɪm`prudənt] *a*. 轻率的,粗心大意的。**-ly** *ad*.

im·pu·bic [im'pjuːbik; ɪm`pjubɪk] *a*. 未达青春期的,发育未全的,未成熟的。

im·pu·dence ['impjudəns; `ɪmpjədəns] *n*. 1. 厚颜无耻,冒失,无礼。2. 厚颜无耻[冒失、无礼]的言行。*have the* ～ *to do* 竟然厚着脸皮做。*None of your* ～! 别那么不要脸。

im·pu·dent ['impjudənt; `ɪmpjədənt] *a*. 厚颜无耻的,冒失的;无礼的。*an* ～ *young rascal* 蛮横的小流氓。*be* ～ *enough to* (*do*) ... = *so* ～ *as to* (*do*) …竟然无耻到(干、做)。**-ly** *ad*.

im·pu·dic·i·ty [ˌimpju'disiti; ˏɪmpjə`dɪsətɪ] *n*. 无耻;放肆。

im·pugn [im'pjuːn; ɪm`pjun] *vt*. 责难,攻击;指摘(声明、行为、性质等)。**-a·ble** *a*. 可责难的,可攻击的,可反对的。**-ment** *n*.

im·pu·is·sance [im'pju(ː)isns; ɪm`pju(ʊ)ɪsns] *n*. 无能,虚弱,无力。**-is·sant** *a*.

im·pulse ['impʌls; `ɪmpʌls] **I** *n*. 1. 冲动;【物】冲量;推进力;脉冲,【医】冲动,搏动。2. 鼓舞,刺激;一时高兴,兴奋。*a man of* ～感情用事的人。*act from* ～凭一时冲动行事。*be seized with a sudden* ～ *to do sth*. 一时情不自禁地做某事。*feel an irresistible* ～觉得情不自禁。*give an* ～ *to* 刺激,促进。***on the*** ～ ***of the moment*** 由一时高兴。**II** *vt*. 推动。～ **buyer** 一时冲动的买主。～ **buying** (不考虑价格、质量或效用)只凭一时的高兴购物。～ **turbine**【机】冲动式透平。

im·pul·sion [im'pʌlʃən; ɪm`pʌlʃən] *n*. 1. 冲动;推进。2. 刺激,鼓舞。3. 冲力;推动力。

im·pul·sive [im'pʌlsiv; ɪm`pʌlsɪv] *a*. 1. 冲动的;刺激的;被一时感情所驱使的,任性的。2.【物】瞬动的,冲击的。*an* ～ *force* 冲力,推进力。**-ly** *ad*. **-ness** *n*.

im·pu·ni·ty [im'pjuːniti; ɪm`pjunətɪ] *n*. 不受惩罚,无罪;无事,不受损失。***with*** ～不受惩罚地,泰然地。

im·pure [im'pjuə; ɪm`pjʊr] *a*. 1. 不纯的,掺假的。2. 混杂的。3. 不纯洁的,不道德的,下流的。4. (语言)不规范的。*the* ～ *air of towns* 城市里不纯洁的空气。～ *motives* 不纯的动机。～ *language* 下流话。**-ly** *ad*. **-ness** *n*. 不纯 (*impureness acceptor*【无】(半导体中)受主杂质)。

im·pu·ri·ty [im'pjuəriti; ɪm`pjʊrətɪ] *n*. 〔常用 *pl*.〕1. 不纯,不洁。2. 下流,不道德,不贞节,杂质。*impurities in food* 食物中的杂质。*political impurities* 政治渣滓;牛鬼蛇神。

im·put ['imput; `ɪmpʊt] *n*. = input *n*.

im·put·a·ble [im'pjuːtəbl; ɪm`pjutəbl̩] *a*. 可归罪于…的,可归因于…的 (*to*)。*The oversight is not* ～ *to him*. 这一疏忽不能怪他。**-bil·i·ty** [imˌpjuːtə'biliti; ɪmˏpjutə`bɪlətɪ] *n*. **-bly** *ad*.

im·pu·ta·tion [ˌimpju(:)ˈteiʃən; ˏɪmpjʊˋteʃən] *n*. **1.** 归罪,责怪,转嫁罪责。**2.** 毁谤;污名。*cast an ~ on sb.'s character* 诋毁某人人格。

im·put·a·tive [imˈpjuːtətiv; ɪmˋpjutətɪv] *a*. 可归罪的,可责怪的;(罪责)被归于某人的。**-ly** *ad*.

im·pute [imˈpjuːt; ɪmˋpjut] *vt*. 把…归咎于;把…归因于,把…推给;把…转嫁于(*to*)。~ *one's poverty to bad luck* 把贫穷归咎于坏运气。~ *one's failures to one's misfortune* 失败怪命运不好。

impv. = imperative.

in [in; ɪn] **I** *prep*. **1.** 〔表示地点、场所、位置〕在…中,在…内,在…上。*live ~ London* 住在伦敦。~ *the distance* 在远处。~ *the house* 在家中。~ *town* 在城里;〔英〕在伦敦。~ *bed* 在床上,睡着。~ *class* 在上课。~ *the street* [*train*]〔英〕在大街[火车]上。★美国用 on the street [train]。**2.** 〔表示时间〕在…之内,在…之后,过…后;〔美〕…中,…来。~ *the daytime* 在白天。~ (*the*) *spring* 在春天。~ *two months* 在两个月内;过两个月后。~ *those days* 在当时。~ *a few days* 几天以后,几天之内。~ *a moment* [*an instant, a minute*] 立刻,马上。*the coldest day ~ ten years* 十年来最冷的日子。*I haven't seen him ~* [*for*] *years*. 〔美〕我好多年没有见他了。*a man ~ his thirties* 一个三十几岁的男子。**3.** 〔表示状态、情况〕处在…中,在…状态中。*be ~ good health* 健康。~ *haste* 急着,忙着。~ *a circle* 围成圆圈。~ *arms* 武装着。*be ~* (*the*) *fashion* 正流行着,是时髦的。*be ~ liquor* 喝醉了。~ *progress* 在进行中,开始。**4.** 〔表示服装、打扮〕穿着,戴着,带着。*a wolf ~ sheep's skin* 披着羊皮的狼。*a woman ~ white* 穿白衣服的女人。~ *uniform* 穿着制服。~ *spectacles* 戴着眼镜。~ *a top hat* 戴着大礼帽。~ *irons* 带着镣铐。**5.** 〔表示范围、领域、方面〕在…之内,在…方面。~ *my opinion* 我的意见是,据我想。~ *one's power* 在力所能及的范围内,尽力。*Victory is ~ sight*. 胜利在望。*be blind ~ one eye* 瞎了一只眼睛。~ *politics* 在政治方面。*the latest thing ~ loud speakers* 〔口〕最新式的扬声器。~ *all respects* 在各方面。*be strong* [*weak*] ~ *English* 英语很好[不好]。*China is rich ~ products*. 中国物产丰富。*nine ~ ten* 十之八九。*not one ~ ten* 十不得一。*vary ~ colour* [*length, number, size, weight*] 颜色[长度、数目、大小、重量]不一。**6.** 〔表示职业、活动〕从事于,参加着。~ *an amateur play* 参加业余演出。~ *rice* 〔美〕经营米业。~ *trade* 经商。~ *the army* 在军队中(服役)。**7.** 〔表示传达信息的方式或使用的工具、材料等〕以,用。*written ~ pencil* 用铅笔写的。*paint ~ oils* 画油画。*speak* [*talk*] ~ *English* 用英语交谈。~ *a few words* 三言两语,简而言之。*a telegram ~ cipher* 密码电报。*a book ~ cloth* 布面精装书。*have the money ~ gold* 持有的款项是黄金。**8.** 〔表示地位、方式、方法、形式〕用…,以…,按照…,依…,符合于…。~ *this way* 用这个办法。~ *an advisory capacity* 以顾问的身分。~ *this manner* 照这样。~ *foreign style* 照外国式样。*arrange ~ alphabetic order* 按字母顺序排列。*buy ~ instalments* 以分期付款方式购买。*Do everything ~ the interests of the people*. 一切行动都要符合人民利益。**9.** 〔表示目的、原因、动机〕为着…,作为…。~ *pursuit* 追逐。*speak ~ reply* 回答说。~ *honour of his safe return* 为庆祝他的安全归来。*cry out ~ alarm* 吓得叫喊起来。*rejoice ~ one's recovery* 因为病好而高兴。**10.** 〔表示性质、能力〕包含在…之中。*There is some good ~ him*. 他有一些可取的地方。*as far as ~ me lies* 在我能力所及的限度内。*I didn't think he had it ~ him*. 我没有想到他有这个本事。*Sound ~ body, sound ~ mind*. 健全的精神寓于健全的体魄。**11.** 〔表示过程〕在…当儿,在…过程中。*be killed ~ action* 阵亡。*the machine ~ assembling* 在装配中的机器。~ *crossing the river* 在渡河的当儿。**12.** 〔表示同位关系〕在…上,在…身上。*lose a great scholar ~ Dr. X* 失去 X 博士这位大学者。*I have found a friend ~ Juliet*. 我找到了朱丽叶这位朋友。*You made a mistake ~ asking him*. 你求他就错了。**be ~ it** 〔口〕从事,参加在内(*They had a good time, but I was not ~ it*. 他们玩得很高兴,可是我没有参加)。**be ~ it up to the neck** 深陷,沉迷。**~ as** [**so**] **much as** 因为,由于。**~ bad** 〔美〕正在倒霉,关系不好。**~ good** 〔美〕受欢迎,关系好。**~ itself** 本身,实质上。**~ that** 〔古〕因为,由于。**~ twos and threes** 三三两两地。**II** *ad*. **1.** 朝里,向内,在内。*a coat with a furry side ~* 有皮里子的外衣。*Come ~, please*. 请进来。*The horses are ~*. 马(在车上)套着。*When ale is ~, wit is out*. 〔谚〕酒喝多了,智力少了。**2.** 在家。*Is he ~?* 他在家么? *have sb. ~ for dinner* 请某人到家里来吃饭。**3.** 到达,来到;得到。*The train is ~*. 火车到了。*Summer is ~*. 夏天来了。*be a 100 pounds ~* 得到[赚得]100 镑。**4.** 当政,当选,掌握政权。*The Conservatives are ~*. 保守党当政。**5.** 流行,时髦。*Tomatoes are ~*. 番茄上市了。*Those hats are ~*. 那种帽子很流行。**6.** 在狱中。*What offence is Tom ~ for?* 汤姆是因什么罪名坐牢的? **7.** 成功,取胜。*The actor was ~*. 演员获得成功。**8.** 一致。*fall ~ with sb.'s plan* 同某人的计划一致。**9.** (火等)燃烧着;(灯)亮着。*Keep the fire ~*. 让火燃烧着不灭。**10.** 油井正出油。*The well has come ~*. 这口油井出油了。**all ~** 〔美俚〕累极了。**be ~ for** 遭受,不得不受;参加(考试、竞争)。**be ~ for it** 〔口〕**1.** 欲罢不能,骑虎难下。**2.** 难免受罚;深陷困境。**be** [**keep**] **~ with sb.** 跟…亲近;【海】接近…,使接近。**day ~, day out** 一天又一天。**week ~, week out** 一周又一周。**year ~, year out** 年复一年。**have it ~ for sb.** 〔口〕怀恨某人。**~ and ~** 同种交配,近亲交配。**~ and out** 迂曲,作之字形;忽隐忽现,进进出出,里里外外。**In with it!** 把它装进去吧! **In with you!** 〔口〕进去吧。**put a notice ~** 在报上登广告。**III** *a*. **1.** 朝内的,在里面的(*opp*. out)。*an ~ patient* 住院的病人。*the ~ side* 【板球】攻方。**2.** 到站的,抵港的。*an ~ train* 到站列车。**3.** 在朝的,执政的。*the ~ party* 执政党。**4.** 流行的,时髦的。*the ~ thing to do* 流行的事情,时髦的做法。**5.** 赚进的。*be ~ a million dollars* 赚进一百万美元。**IV** *n*. 〔常用 *pl*.〕**1.** 在朝派,执政党,知情者。*the ins and the outs* 执政党与在野党,在朝派和在野派。*know all the ins and outs of a problem* 知道问题的详情。**2.** 【体】(板球或棒球)攻球的一方。*He was bowled before he had been ~ five minutes*. 他攻球未到五分钟便被迫退场了。**3.** 〔美口〕入口;门路。**4.** 〔美俚〕(与大人物的)特殊关系,提携。*enjoy some sort of ~ with the manager* 在一定程度上得到经理的赏识。

in [in; ɪn] *prep*. 〔L.〕= in (*prep*.). ~ ***ab·sen·ti·a*** [æbˈsenʃiə; æbˋsenʃɪə] 缺席,当…不在时。~ ***ae·ter·num*** [iːˈtəːnəm; iˋtɝnəm] 永久,永远。~ ***ar·ti·cu·lo mor·tis*** [ɑːˈtikjuləu ˈmɔːtis; ɑrˋtɪkjulo ˋmɔrtɪs] 临终时。~ ***cam·e·ra*** [ˈkæmərə; ˋkæmərə] 在(法官)私人房间内,秘密;【法】秘密审判。~ ***con·tu·ma·ci·am*** [ˌkɔntjuˈmeiʃiæm; ˏkɑntjʊˋmeʃɪæm] 蔑视法庭。~ ***es·se*** [ˈesi; ˋɛsɪ] 实际存在(*opp*. in posse)。~ ***ex·ten·so*** [iksˈtensəu; ɪksˋtɛnso] 全部,详细,十足。~ ***ex·tre·mis*** [iksˈtriːmis; ɪksˋtrimɪs] 临终时。~ ***fla·grante de·lic·to*** [fləˈgrænti diˈliktəu; fləˋgræntɪ dɪˋlɪkto] 在犯罪当场,在现行中。~ ***for·ma pau·per·is*** [ˈfɔːmə ˈpɔːpəris; ˋfɔmə ˋpɔpərɪs] 作为穷人(免收讼费)。~ ***li·mi·ne*** [ˈlimini; ˋlɪmənɪ] 开头。~ ***lo·co*** [ˈləukəu; ˋloko] 在相当处所,在一定地点。~ ***loco ci·ta·to*** [ˈləukəu saiˈteitəu; ˋloko saɪˋteto] 在前面引文内。~ ***loco pa·ren·tis*** [ˈləukəu pəˈrentis; ˋloko pəˋrɛntɪs] 替代父母,以父母立场。~ ***medi·as res*** [ˈmiːdiæs ˈriːz;

ˋmidiæsˋriz] 在[从]事物中心;从中途(发生的重大事件)(说起)。~ ***me·mo·ri·am*** [mi'mɔːriæm; mɪˋmɔriæm] 为纪念,献给…之灵,祭文,挽诗。~ ***nu·bi·bus*** ['njubibʌs; ˋnjubɪbʌs] 在云中,含糊,不明。~ ***per·pe·tu·um*** [pə'petjuəm; pəˋpetjuəm] 永久。~ ***posse*** ['pɔsi; ˋpɑsɪ] 可能地,潜在的 (*opp*. in esse)。~ ***pro·pri·a per·so·na*** ['prəupriə pə'səunə; ˋproprɪə pəˋsonə] 亲自,自行 (*opp*. by proxy)。~ ***pu·ris nat·u·ral·i·bus*** ['pjuːris nætʃu'rælibʌs; ˋpjurɪs nætʃʊˋrælɪbʌs] 赤裸,全裸。~ ***re*** ['ri; ˋri] 按…的讼诉事件;关于,说到。~ ***si·tu*** ['saitjuː; ˋsaɪtju] 在原来位置,在自然地位。~ ***sta·tu pu·pil·la·ri*** ['steitjuː pjuːpiˋlɑːri; ˋstetju pjupiˋlarɪ] 以被保护人身分;以学徒[学生]身分。~ ***sta·tu quo*** ['steitjuː'kwəu; ˋstetjuˋkwo] 照原样,维持现状。~ ***terro·rem*** [tə'rɔːrem; təˋrɔrɛm] 作为警告。~ ***to·to*** ['təutəu; ˋtoto] 全部,整体。~ ***vit·ro*** ['vaitrəu; ˋvaɪtro] 在(生物)体外;在试管内。

In =【化】indium (铟).

in. = **1**. inch(es). **2**. income.

in-[1] *pref*. 在带有"停止"意义的动词前 = in, on; 在带有"运动"意义的动词前 = into, against, towards. ★ **1**. 在 l 前作 il-; 在 b, m, p 前作 im-; 在 r 前作 ir-: *im*press, *ir*radiate. **2**. 常与古法语中的 en-, em- 并存: *in*quire, *en*quire.

in-[2] *pref*. 无,非。★ 在 l 前作 il-; 在 b, m, p 前作 im-; 在 r 前作 ir-: *il*logical, *im*moral, *ir*rational.

-in[1] *suf*. 表示"属于…的"〔系希腊、拉丁语形容词及其派生名词的词尾〕: ru*in*.

-in[2] *suf*.【化】**1**. = -ine. **2**. 化学制品[药品]等的词尾: aureomyc*in*.

-in[3] *suf*. 〔口、方〕= -ing: go*in* = going.

in-[1] *comb*. *f*. 〔常与名词组成形容词修饰语〕表示"在…之中","正当…"等: in-car 装置于汽车内的;in-career 在职的;in-city 市内的;in-home 家中的;in-process 生产中的;in-state 〔美〕本州的。★ 此种组合的重读音通常落在 in- 上,同时保留原名词的重读音。如 in-city ['in'siti; ˋɪnˋsɪtɪ];但作为 out- 的对应词时,重读音只读在 in- 上,如 in-state students 中的 in-state ['insteit; ˋɪnstet]。

in-[2] *comb*. *f*. 〔常与名词组成名词词组〕表示"最新的","新式的","独有的": in-jargon 流行术语;in-language 现代语言;in-thing 新近流行的东西;in-word 新口头禅。★此种组合的重读音落在 in- 上,如 in-crowd ['inkraud; ˋɪnkraʊd]。

-in *comb*. *f*. 〔置于动词后组成名词〕表示"示威行动","集会"等: sit-in 静坐示威;kneel-in 黑人进入种族隔离教堂参加礼拜;ride-in 黑人乘坐种族隔离汽车;stall-in 故意阻塞交通;smoke-in 争取吸大麻合法化;be-in (颓废派的)社交集会;eat-in 聚餐会;study-in 学习会。

-ina *suf*. **1**. 构成女性名称:Czar*ina*, Georg*ina*. **2**. 构成乐器名称:concert*ina*.

I·na ['ainə; ˋaɪnə] ***n***. 艾娜〔女子名〕。

in·a·bil·i·ty [inə'biliti; ˏɪnəˋbɪlətɪ] ***n***. 无能,无力;无能为力。

in·ac·ces·si·ble [ˌinæk'sesəbl; ˏɪnækˋsɛsəbḷ] ***a***. **1**. 达不到的;进不去的。**2**. 不能见到的;不能接近的。**3**. 得不到的。**-si·bility** ['inækˌsesə'biliti; ˏɪnækˏsɛsəˋbɪlətɪ] ***n***. **-bly** ***ad***.

in·ac·cu·ra·cy [in'ækjurəsi; ɪnˋækjərəsɪ] ***n***. 误差;不精确,不准确,不精确的东西,错误。*avoid the ~ in the use of words* 避免用字不准确。

in·ac·cu·rate [in'ækjurit; ɪnˋækjərɪt] ***a***. 不精密的;不准确的;错误的。**-ly** ***ad***. *an ~ account* 不准确的报表。

in·act. ***a***. =【物】inactive.

in·ac·tion [in'ækʃən; ɪnˋækʃən] ***n***. 不活动;不活跃;怠惰,懒散;迟钝。

in·ac·ti·vate [in'æktiveit; ɪnˋæktɪˏvet] ***vt***. **1**. 使不活动。**2**. 撤销(部队、政府机构等)。**3**.【化】使钝化,减除…的活性;使不旋光。

in·ac·tive [in'æktiv; ɪnˋæktɪv] ***a***. **1**. 不活动的,不活跃的;迟钝的;懒散的。**2**. 没事做的;暂停不用的。**3**.【化】钝性的;【物】不旋光的;无放射性的。**4**.【军】非现役的。**5**.【医】静止性的。*an ~ fleet* 后备舰队。*an ~ machine* 一台停用的机器。*an ~ reserve* 已退役后备队。*~ tuberculosis* 非活动性结核。**-ly** ***ad***. **-ness** ***n***. **-tiv·i·ty** [ˌinæk'tiviti; ˏɪnækˋtɪvətɪ] ***n***.

in·a·dapt·a·ble [ˌinə'dæptəbl; ˏɪnəˋdæptəbḷ] ***a***. **1**. 不能适应的,无适应性的。**2**. 不可改编的。**-bil·i·ty** [ˌinəˌdæptə'biliti; ˏɪnəˏdæptəˋbɪlətɪ], **-a·tion** [ˌinədæp'teiʃən; ˏɪnədæpˋteʃən] ***n***.

in·ad·e·qua·cy [in'ædikwəsi; ɪnˋædɪkwəsɪ] ***n***. (*pl*. **-cies**) **1**. 不充分;不适当。**2**.【医】官能不足,机能不全。*renal* ~肾机能不全。

in·ad·e·quate [in'ædikwit; ɪnˋædɪkwɪt] ***a***. 不适当的;不充足的。*be ~ to do sth*. 不适宜作某件事。*be ~ to (for) a purpose* 不能达到目的。*~ equipment* 不充足的设备。**-ly** ***ad***.

in·ad·mis·si·ble [ˌinəd'misəbl; ˏɪnədˋmɪsəbḷ] ***a***. 不能答应的,不能允许的,难承认的。*~ behavior* 不能允许的行为。**-bili·ty** ['inədˌmisə'biliti; ˏɪnədˏmɪsəˋbɪlətɪ] ***n***. **-bly** ***ad***.

in·ad·vert·ence, in·ad·vert·en·cy [ˌinəd'vəːtəns, -si; ˏɪnədˋvɝtəns, -sɪ] ***n***. 粗心大意,疏忽,错误。*Mistakes proceed from ~*. 错误出自粗心大意。

in·ad·vert·ent [ˌinəd'vəːtənt; ˏɪnədˋvɝtənt] ***a***. **1**. 疏忽的;漫不经心的。**2**. 出于无心的,非故意的,无意中的。**-ly** ***ad***.

in·ad·vis·a·ble [ˌinəd'vaizəbl; ˏɪnədˋvaɪzəbḷ] ***a***. 不可取的,不妥当的;不明智的;不慎重的。**-bili·ty** ***n***.

in·af·fa·ble [in'æfəbl; ɪnˋæfəbl] ***a***. 不和蔼的。

in·al·ien·a·ble [in'eiljənəbl; ɪnˋeljənəbḷ] ***a***. 不可剥夺的;不可分割的;不能转让的。*~ rights* 不可剥夺的权利。*an ~ part of the territory* 不可分割的领土。**-a·bil·i·ty** [inˌeiljənə'biliti; ɪnˏeljənəˋbɪlətɪ] ***n***. **-a·bly** ***ad***.

in·al·ter·a·ble [in'ɔːltərəbl; ɪnˋɔltərəbḷ] ***a***. 不能变更的,不变的。**-bil·i·ty** [inˌɔːltərə'biliti; ɪnˏɔltərəˋbɪlətɪ] ***n***. **-bly** ***ad***.

in·am·o·ra·ta [inˌæmə'rɑːtə; ɪnˏæməˋrɑtə] ***n***. 〔It.〕女爱人,女情人,情妇。

in·am·o·ra·to [inˌæmə'raitəu; ɪnˏæmoˋrɑto] ***n***. 〔It.〕男爱人,男情人。

in-and-in ['inənd'in; ˋɪnəndˋɪn] ***a***., ***ad***. 同种交配的[地],近亲交配的[地]。*~ breeding* 同种[近亲]繁育。

in-and-out ['inənd'aut; ˋɪnəndˋaʊt] ***a***. (证券)短期买卖的。

in·ane [i'nein; ɪˋnen] **I** ***a***. **1**. 空的,空虚的。**2**. 空洞的,无意义的。*make an ~ remark* 言之无物。**II** ***n***. 〔the ~〕空洞无物,无限空间。**-ly** ***ad***.

in·an·i·mate [in'ænimit; ɪnˏænəmɪt] ***a***. **1**. 无生命的,死的。**2**. 无生气的,没精打采的。*an ~ object* 无生物。*~ nature* 无生物界。*an ~ conversation* 沉闷的谈话。**-ly** ***ad***.

in·an·i·ma·tion [inˌæni'meiʃən; ɪnˏænəˋmeʃən] ***n***. 无生命,不活动,不活泼,无生气。

in·a·ni·tion [ˌinə'niʃən; ˏɪnəˋnɪʃən] ***n***. **1**. 无内容,空虚。**2**.【医】营养不足,虚弱。

in·an·i·ty [i'næniti; ɪˋnænətɪ] ***n***. **1**. 空虚,空洞。**2**. 无知,愚妄;〔常 *pl*.〕无聊的话,无聊的事。*irrelevant inanities* 无关痛痒的废话。

in·ap·par·ent [ˌinə'peərənt; ˏɪnəˋpɛrənt] ***a***. 不明显的 (*opp*. apparent)。

in·ap·peas·a·ble [ˌinə'piːzəbl; ˏɪnəˋpizəbḷ] ***a***. 难劝解

的,难说服的,难满足的。

in·ap·pel·la·ble [ˌinəˈpeləbl; ˏɪnəˋpɛləbl̩] *a*. (判决等)不得申诉[上诉]的。

in·ap·pe·tence, -cy [inˈæpitəns, -si; ɪnˋæpɪtəns, -sɪ] *n*. 食欲不振,无胃口;欲望缺乏。

in·ap·pli·ca·ble [inˈæplikəbl; ɪnˋæplɪkəbl] *a*. 不能应用的,不适用的,不合适的。*The principle is ~ to the case*. 这个原则对这件事不适用。**-bil·i·ty** [inˌæplikəˈbiliti; ɪnˏæplɪkəˋbɪlətɪ] *n*. **-bly** *ad*.

in·ap·po·site [inˈæpəzit; ɪnˋæpəzɪt] *a*. 不适合的,不恰当的,不相干的;不对题的。**-ly** *ad*.

in·ap·pre·ci·a·ble [ˌinəˈpriːʃəbl; ˏɪnəˋpriʃəbl̩] *a*. 小得难以觉察的,微不足道的。**-bly** *ad*.

in·ap·pre·ci·a·tion [ˌinəˌpriːʃiˈeiʃən; ˏɪnəˏpriʃɪˋeʃən] *n*. 不正确评价,不欣赏。

in·ap·pre·ci·a·tive [ˌinəˈpriːʃjətiv; ˏɪnəˋpriʃɪetɪv] *a*. 1. 不欣赏…的 (*of*)。2. 评价不正确的,缺乏眼光的。~ *criticism* 妄评。**-ly** *ad*.

in·ap·pre·hen·si·ble [ˌinæpriˈhensəbl; ˏɪnæprɪˋhɛnsəbl̩] *a*. 难了解的,难领会的,不可理解的。

in·ap·pre·hen·sion [ˌinæpriˈhenʃən; ˏɪnæprɪˋhɛnʃən] *n*. 缺乏理解力。

in·ap·pre·hen·sive [ˌinæpriˈhensiv; ˏɪnæprɪˋhɛnsɪv] *a*. 1. 缺乏理解力的。2. 未意识到的;未觉察到危险的。**-ly** *ad*.

in·ap·proach·a·ble [ˌinəˈprəutʃəbl; ˏɪnəˋprotʃəbl̩] *a*. 难接近的;无可比拟的。

in·ap·pro·pri·ate [ˌinəˈprəupriit; ˏɪnəˋpropriɪt] *a*. 不适当的,不相宜的。~ *remarks* 不当的言辞。~ *to the season* 不合时宜。**-ly** *ad*. **-ness** *n*.

in·apt [inˈæpt; ɪnˋæpt] *a*. 1. (对)…不适当的,不合适的 (*for*)。2. 拙劣的,无能的;(在某方面)不熟练的 (*at*)。*an ~ analogy* [*quotation*] 不恰当的比喻[引用]。**-ly** *ad*. **-ness** *n*.

in·apt·i·tude [inˈæptitjuːd; ɪnˋæptətˏjud] *n*. 1. 不适当,不合适。2. 拙笨,无能,不熟练。

in·arch [inˈɑːtʃ; ɪnˋɑrtʃ] *vt*. 【园艺】接枝。

in·arm [inˈɑːm; ɪnˋɑrm] *vt*. 〔诗〕拥抱。

in·ar·tic·u·late [ˌinɑːˈtikjulit; ˏɪnɑrˋtɪkjəlɪt] *a*. 1. 发音不清楚的,口齿不清的。2. 哑口无言的,说不出的,无法言喻的。3. 不会表达内心思想的。4.【动】无关节的。*almost ~ with excitement* 激动得几乎说不出话来。~ *misery* [*pain*] 哑子吃黄连。~ *animals* 无关节动物。**-ly** *ad*. **-ness** *n*.

in ar·ti·cu·lo mor·tis [ˌinɑːˈtikjuːləuˈmɔːtis; ˏɪnɑrˋtɪkjuloˋmɑtɪs] 〔L.〕临终时,弥留之际。

in·ar·ti·fi·cial [ˌinɑːtiˈfiʃəl; ˏɪnɑrtɪˋfɪʃəl] *a*. 1. 非人造的,天然的。2. 单调的,拙劣的,不熟练的。**-ly** *ad*. **-i·ty** *n*.

in·ar·tis·tic(al) [ˌinɑːˈtistik(əl); ˏɪnɑrˋtɪstɪk(l̩)] *a*. 非艺术的,无艺术性的;无艺术修养的。**-ti·cal·ly** *ad*.

in·as·much [ˌinəzˈmʌtʃ; ˏɪnəzˋmʌtʃ] *ad*. 〔与 as 连用,起连接词作用〕因为,由于;〔古〕只要。*Inasmuch as we have no money, it is no good thinking about a holiday*. 因为我们没有钱,所以考虑休假是没有用的。

in·at·ten·tion [ˌinəˈtenʃən; ˏɪnəˋtɛnʃən] *n*. 不注意;漫不经心,疏忽。

in·at·ten·tive [ˌinəˈtentiv; ˏɪnəˋtɛntɪv] *a*. 不注意的;漫不经心的;疏忽的。**-ly** *ad*. **-ness** *n*.

in·au·di·ble [iˈnɔːdəbl; ɪˋnɔdəbl̩] *a*. 听不见的。**-bil·i·ty** [inˌɔːdəˈbiliti; ɪnˏɔdəˋbɪlətɪ] *n*. **-bly** *ad*.

in·au·gu·ral [iˈnɔːgjurəl; ɪˋnɔgjʊrəl] **I** *a*. 就职(仪式)的;开幕的,开始的。*an ~ address* 就职演说;开幕词。*an ~ ceremony* 就职典礼,成立典礼,开幕典礼。*an ~ lecture* (教授)就职讲义。**II** *n*. 〔美〕就职演说,就职典礼。

in·au·gu·rate [iˈnɔːgjureit; ɪˋnɔgjʊˏret] *vt*. 1. 为(新官员、教授等)举行就职典礼。2. 开始;举行(开业、落成、成立等)仪式。3. 创始;开幕,开张。~ *a new era* 开创新纪元。~ *a president* 举行总统就职典礼。*The Export Commodities, Fair was ~d yesterday*. 出口商品交易会昨天开幕了。*the inaugurating general meeting* 成立大会。— *vi*. 致开幕[就职]词。

in·au·gu·ra·tion [iˌnɔːgjuˈreiʃən; ɪˏnɔgjʊˋreʃən] *n*. 就职典礼;〔美〕总统就职典礼;开幕仪式,落成典礼,开通典礼,成立典礼;开张,开始。**I- Day** 美国总统就职日。

in·au·gu·ra·tor [iˈnɔːgjureitə; ɪˋnɔgjʊˏretɚ] *n*. 主持就职仪式者;开创者,创始人。

in·au·gu·ra·to·ry [iˈnɔːgjurətəri; ɪˋnɔgjʊrəˏtorɪ] *a*. = inaugural.

in·aus·pi·cious [ˌinɔːsˈpiʃəs; ˏɪnɔsˋpɪʃəs] *a*. 不吉祥的,不利的。**-ly** *ad*. **-ness** *n*.

in·be·ing [ˈinbiːiŋ; ˋɪnbiɪŋ] *n*. 内在的事物;本质,本性。

in·board [ˈinbɔːd; ˋɪnbɔrd] **I** *a*. 【空】内侧的;【海】船内的,舱内的;靠近船中线的 (*opp*. outboard); 内纵的。~ *cabin* 内侧舱室。~ *profile* 舱内纵剖面图。**II** *ad*. 【海】在船内;在舱内;向内侧。

in·board-out·board [ˈinbɔːdˈautbɔːd; ˋɪnbɔrdˋaʊtbɔrd] **I** *a*. 【船】(小艇的)舷内一舷外动力装置的。**II** *n*. 有舷内一舷外动力装置的小艇。

in·born [ˈinˈbɔːn; ˋɪnˋbɔrn] *a*. 生来的,天赋的,天生的,先天的 (*opp*. acquired)。

in·bound [ˈinbaund; ˋɪnbaʊnd] *a*. (船舶)开回本国的;归航的 (*opp*. outbound);入境的;入站的。

in·bounds [ˈinˈbaundz; ˋɪnˋbaʊndz] *a*. (篮球)从界外掷入界内的。

in·break [ˈinbreik; ˋɪnbrek] *n*. 入侵。

in·breathe [ˈinˈbriːð; ˋɪnˋbrið] *vt*. 吸入;〔喻〕灌输(思想等),启发。

in·bred [ˈinˈbred; ɪnˋbrɛd] *a*. 1. 生来的,先天的。2. 近亲繁殖的。3. 选种产生的。*the ~ line* 近交系。

in·breed [ˈinˈbriːd; ɪnˋbrid] *vt*. (**-bred, -breed·ing**) 1. 〔罕〕使在内部形成[发展]。2.【生】使(动物)近亲繁殖。— *vi*. 1. 进行近亲繁殖。2. (由于社会与文化联系极为局限而)变得文雅过度。

in·breed·ing [ˈinˈbriːdiŋ; ˋɪnˋbridɪŋ] *n*. 1.【生】近亲繁殖,同系交配。2. (知识等)限于狭隘范围。

inc. = inclosure; including; inclusive; income; 〔常 I-〕incorporated 注册; increase.

In·ca [ˈiŋkə; ˋɪŋkə] *n*. 1. 印加人[印卡人]〔南美印第安人的一个部落〕。2. 印加帝国国王(或贵族成员)。**-n** *a*.

in·ca·bloc [ˈiŋkəˌblɔk; ˋɪŋkəˏblɑk] **I** *n*. (手表内的)防震装置。**II** *a*. (手表等)防震的。

in·cal·cu·la·ble [inˈkælkjuləbl; ɪnˋkælkjələbl̩] *a*. 1. 不可胜数的,无数的;极大的。2. 难预测的;靠不住的,无定的。**-bil·i·ty** [inˌkælkjuləˈbiliti; ɪnˏkælkjələˋbɪlətɪ] *n*. **-bly** *ad*.

in·ca·les·cent [ˌinkəˈlesnt; ˏɪnkəˋlɛsn̩t] *a*. 〔罕〕渐热的。**-cence** *n*.

in·can·desce [ˌinkænˈdes; ˏɪnkænˋdɛs] *vt*., *vi*. (使)白热化,(使)遇热发光。

in·can·des·cence, -cy [ˌinkænˈdesns, -si; ˏɪnkænˋdɛsns, -sɪ] *n*. 白炽,白热。

in·can·des·cent [ˌinkænˈdesnt; ˏɪnkænˋdɛsn̩t] *a*. 1. 白热的,白炽的,发白热光的。2. 辉煌的。*an ~ filament* 白热灯丝。~ **lamp** 白炽灯。~ **particle** 发光粒子。~ **sand flow** 【地】热沙流。

in·can·ta·tion [ˌinkænˈteiʃən; ˏɪnkænˋteʃən] *n*. 咒语,咒文,妖术,念咒。

in-cap [ˈinkæp; ˋɪnkæp] *n*. 〔美军俚〕智能麻醉剂〔一种使人失去智能的化学药剂〕。

in·ca·pa·ble [inˈkeipəbl; ɪnˋkepəbl̩] **I** *a*. 1. 无能的,没有用的。2. 不会…的 (*of*)。3.【法】没有资格的。~ *of doing sth*. 无能力做某事。*an ~ officer* 无能的官吏。

~ *of telling a lie* 不会扯谎。*be drunk and* ~烂醉如泥,酩酊大醉。**II** *n*. 没有能力的人。**-bil·i·ty** [inˌkeipəˈbiliti; ɪnˌkepəˋbɪlətɪ] *n*. **-bly** *ad*.

in·ca·pa·cious [ˌinkəˈpeiʃəs; ˌɪnkəˋpeʃəs] *a*. 1. 无能的,无知的;狭小的,容积不大的。2.〔古〕有智力缺陷的。*a silly and* ~ *person* 笨拙无能的人。

in·ca·pac·i·tant [ˌinkəˈpæsitənt; ˌɪnkəˋpæsɪtənt] *n*. = in-cap.

in·ca·pac·i·tate [ˌinkəˈpæsiteit; ˌɪnkəˋpæsɪˌtet] *vt*. 1. 使无能力,使残废。2.【法】使无资格。~ *sb. from singing* 使某人不能歌唱。*be* ~*d from voting* 被剥夺选举权。**-ta·tion** [ˈinkəˌpæsiˈteiʃən; ˋɪnkəˌpæsɪˋteʃən] *n*. **-ta·tor** *n*. = in-cap.

in·ca·pac·i·ty [ˌinkəˈpæsiti; ˌɪnkəˋpæsətɪ] *n*. 1. 无能力。2.【法】无资格;【医】官能不全。~ *for work* [*to work*, *for doing work*] 不能工作。*renal* ~肾功能不全。

In·cap·a·ri·na [inˌkæpəˈriːnə; ɪnˌkæpəˋrinə] *n*. 印加蛋白;高蛋白植物配制食品〔一种棉籽、玉米及高粱面、酵母粉等合制而成。拉美尤用于防止蛋白质缺乏之症〕。

in·cap·su·late [inˈkæpsəleit; ɪnˋkæpsəˌlet] *vt*. (*-lated*, *-lat·ing*) = encapsulate.

in·car·cer·ate [inˈkɑːsəreit; ɪnˋkɑrsəˌret] *vt*. 1. 禁闭,监禁。2.【医】钳闭。**-a·tion** [inˌkɑːsəˈreiʃən; ɪnˌkɑrsəˋreʃən] *n*.

in·car·di·nate [inˈkɑːdineit; ɪnˋkɑrdɪnet] *vt*. (*-nated*, *-nat·ing*) 1.【天主】(使圣职人员)隶属于同一主教管区。2. 提升…为红衣主教。**-na·tion** [inˌkɑːdiˈneiʃən; ɪnˌkɑrdɪˋneʃən] *n*.

in·car·na·dine [inˈkɑːnədain, -din; ɪnˋkɑrnəˌdaɪn, -dɪn] **I** *vt*.【诗】使成肉色[血红色]。**II** *n*., *a*. 肉色(的),淡红色(的);血红色(的)。

in·car·nate [ˈinkɑːneit; ˋɪnkɑrnet] **I** *vt*. 1. 赋予…以形体,使成…的化身。2. 使具体化,体现,实现(理想等)。**II** *a*. [ˈinkɑːnit; ˋɪnkɑrnɪt] 1. 实体化的,成为人形的,化身的。2. 具体化的,体现的。3. 肉色的,红色的,玫瑰红的。*a devil* ~魔鬼的化身。*God* ~神的化身。*Liberty* ~自由的具体表现。

in·car·na·tion [ˌinkɑːˈneiʃən; ˌɪnkɑrˋneʃən] *n*. 肉体化,化身,体现;【医】肉化。*The leading dancer is the* ~ *of grace*. 演主角的舞蹈家简直是美的化身。**-al** *a*.

in·case [inˈkeis; ɪnˋkes] *vt*. = encase.

in·cau·tious [inˈkɔːʃəs; ɪnˋkɔʃəs] *a*. 不慎重的,轻率的;不注意的。**-ly** *ad*. **-ness** *n*.

INCB = International Narcotics Control Board 国际麻醉品管制局。

in·cen·di·a·rism [inˈsendjərizəm; ɪnˋsɛndɪɛˌrɪzəm] *n*. 放火,纵火;挑拨,煽动。

in·cen·di·ar·y [inˈsendjəri; ɪnˋsɛndɪˌɛrɪ] **I** *a*. 1. 放火的,纵火的,燃烧的。2. 煽动性的。*an* ~ *fire* 人放的火。*an* ~ *bomb* [*bullet*] 燃烧弹。*an* ~ *speech* 煽动性的演说。**II** *n*. 1. 纵火者;燃烧弹;易燃物。2. 煽动者。

in·cense[1] [ˈinsens; ˋɪnsɛns] **I** *n*. 1. (焚香时可产生香气的)香,香发出的烟。2. 巴结,奉承。*a stick of* ~ 一根香,一柱香。**burn** [**offer**] ~ **to** 向…烧香,向…献媚。**II** *vt*. 对…烧香,用香熏。— *vi*. 供香,上香。~ **burner** 香炉。~ **cedar**【植】拟肖楠属植物〔产于北美洲西部〕。

in·cense[2] [inˈsens; ɪnˋsɛns] *vt*. 使发怒,激怒。*be* ~*d at sb.'s words* [*conduct*] 对某人的言论[行为]感到愤慨。*be* ~*d against* [*by*, *with*] *sb*. 对…发怒。

in·cen·so·ry [ˈinsensəri; ˋɪnsɛnˌsorɪ] *n*. 有盖香炉。

in·cent [inˈsent; ɪnˋsɛnt] *vt*. 刺激…采取行动;激动。

in·cen·tive [inˈsentiv; ɪnˋsɛntɪv] **I** *a*. 刺激性的,鼓励性质的。~ *pay* (增产)奖金。*be* ~ *to further study* 鼓励进一步研究。**II** *n*. 刺激;鼓励;动机;诱因。*much* ~ (*many* ~*s*) *to work hard* 很多努力工作的动机。~ **wage** (增产)奖励工资。~ **zone** 鼓励性开发区〔多指城市中较萧条的地区,政府对投资该类地区的房地产开发商实行鼓励性政策〕。**-ly** *ad*.

in·cen·tiv·ize, in·cen·tiv·ise [inˈsentivaiz; ɪnˋsɛntɪvaɪz] *vt*. 对…实行物质刺激,以物质刺激鼓励。

in·cept [inˈsept; ɪnˋsɛpt] *vt*. 1. 接受(入会);【生】摄取。2.〔古〕开始。— *vi*. 1. (在英国剑桥大学)取得硕士[博士]学位。2. 就职。

in·cep·tion [inˈsepʃən; ɪnˋsɛpʃən] *n*. 1. 开始,发端。2. (英国剑桥大学)硕士[博士]学位的取得。*at the* (*very*) ~ *of* 在…的开头。

In·cep·ti·sol [inˈseptisɔːl; ɪnˋsɛptɪsɑl] *n*. (美国土壤分类法中的)新开发土,始成土。

in·cep·tive [inˈseptiv; ɪnˋsɛptɪv] **I** *a*. 起头的,开端的;【语法】表示动作开始的。~ *verbs*【语法】开始动词,起动动词。**II** *n*.【语法】表示开始的动词[片语]。**-ly** *ad*.

in·cep·tor [inˈseptə; ɪnˋsɛptɚ] *n*. 1. 开始人,发端者。2. 在英国剑桥大学取得硕士[博士]学位的人。

in·cer·ti·tude [inˈsəːtitjuːd; ɪnˋsɝtɪtjud] *n*. 1. 无把握,不肯定,怀疑。2. 不完全,不稳定。

in·ces·san·cy [inˈsesnsi; ɪnˋsɛsnsɪ] *n*. 持续不断的状态,不间断性。

in·ces·sant [inˈsesnt; ɪnˋsɛsnt] *a*. 不停的,不断的。*a week of* ~ *rains* 连续下了一个星期的雨。**-ly** *ad*. **-ness** *n*.

in·cest [ˈinsest; ˋɪnsɛst] *n*. 乱伦。

in·ces·tu·ous [inˈsestjuəs; ɪnˋsɛstʃʊəs] *a*. 乱伦的;犯乱伦罪的。**-ly** *ad*. **-ness** *n*.

inch[1] [intʃ; ɪntʃ] **I** *n*. 1. 英寸〔旧译时略作 in.〕。2. 少量,少额,少许。3.〔*pl*.〕身长,身段,个子。*an* ~ *of rain* 一英寸的雨量。*Give him an* ~ *and he'll take an ell*.〔谚〕他得寸进尺。*not yield an* ~寸步不让。*an* ~ *of cold steel* 尖刀的一戳。*a man of your* ~*es* 像你一样高的人。**by** ~**es** 一点一点地,渐渐(*die by* ~*es* 渐死,就要死。*kill by* ~*es* 慢慢地折磨死)。**every** ~完全地,彻底地(*He is every* ~ *a local despot* 他彻头彻尾是个土皇帝)。**gather up one's** ~**es** 直站起来。~ **by** ~ = **by** ~**es**. **to an** ~ 丝毫不差地,精密地。**within an** ~ **of** 差点儿,几乎。**within an** ~ **of one's life** 差点儿丧命。**by** ~ **of candle** 通过拍卖。**II** *vt*. 使渐进,使渐动,使一点一点地移动。~ *one's way forward* 慢慢前进。— *vi*. 渐进,一步一步前进。~ *along a ledge on a cliff* 在悬岩的突出部分匍匐而进。

inch[2] [intʃ; ɪntʃ] *n*.〔Scot.〕小岛。

inched [intʃt; ɪntʃt] *a*. 长…英寸的,刻有英寸的。*a 4-*~ *hook* 四英寸长的钩子。

inch·er [ˈintʃə; ˋɪntʃɚ] *n*. 口径[长、直径等]是…英寸的东西。*a six-incher* (口径)六英寸的炮。

inch·meal [ˈintʃmiːl; ˋɪntʃmil] *ad*. 慢慢地,一步一步地,一点一点地。**by** ~ = inchmeal.

in·cho·ate [ˈinkəueit, -kəuit; ˋɪnkoet, -koɪt] *a*. 1. 才开始的;初步的。2. 未完成的,不发达的。**-ly** *ad*. **-ness** *n*.

in·cho·a·tion [ˌinkəuˈeiʃən; ˌɪnkoˋeʃən] *n*. 开始;初期,初步。

in·cho·a·tive [inˈkəuətiv; ɪnˋkoətɪv] **I** *a*. 1. 开始的。2.【语法】表示开始的。**II** *n*.【语法】表示开始的动词[片语]。

inch·worm [ˈintʃwəːm; ˋɪntʃˌwɝm] *n*.【动】尺蠖(虫)。

in·ci·dence [ˈinsidəns; ˋɪnsədəns] *n*. 1. 发生;影响;着落;(税的)负担;影响范围;发生率。2.【空】(机翼)倾角,安装角。3.【数】关联,接合。4.【物】入射,入射角。*the* ~ *of the tax* 税款的负担。*the* ~ *of taxation* 征税的范围。*the* ~ *of disease* 患病的范围。~ *wire* 倾角线。~ *numbers*【数】关联数。*the angle of* ~入射角。*the plane of* ~入射(平)面。

in·ci·dent [ˈinsidənt; ˋɪnsədənt] **I** *n*. 1. (政治性)事故;事变。2. 偶发事件,某事件的附随事件,小事件。3. (剧

情的)枝节,(小说的)插话。4.【法】财产所附带的权利[义务]。**without** ～平安无事。**II** *a*.〔多作表语用〕1.易起的,易有的;附随的。2.【法】附带的(*to*)。3.入射的(*upon*)。*diseases* ～ *to childhood* 幼年容易得的疾病。～(*with one another*)【数】(互相)关联。～ *rays* 入射线。

in·ci·den·tal [ˌinsiˈdentl; ˏɪnsəˋdɛntl] **I** *a*. 1.容易发生的。2.附带的,伴随的,非主要的。3.偶然的。*the dangers* ～ *to a soldier's career* 军人生涯中容易发生的危险。～ *colours* [*images*] 残色〔附带发生的色彩感觉〕。～ *expenses* 杂费。*diseases* ～ *to miners* 矿工易得的疾病。*an* ～ *acquaintance* 萍水相逢的人。*an* ～ *remark* 偶然漏出的话。**II** *n*. 附带事件;〔*pl*.〕杂项,杂费。～ **music**【乐】(剧、影片、诗朗诵等的)配音,配乐。

in·ci·den·tal·ly [ˌinsiˈdentli; ˏɪnsəˋdɛntlɪ] *ad*. 1.附带地,偶然地。2.顺便说一句〔口语中另换话题的用语〕。

in·cin·der·jell [inˈsindədʒel; ɪnˋsɪndədʒɛl] *n*. 凝固汽油〔混有凝固剂的汽油,用以制造燃烧弹等〕。

in·cin·er·ate [inˈsinəreit; ɪnˋsɪnəˏret] *vt*., *vi*. (把…)烧成灰,烧掉,焚化。**-a·tion** *n*. 焚化。**-a·tor** *n*. 焚化者;(垃圾的)焚化炉;火葬炉(*an incinerator ship* 用焚化炉处理垃圾的船只)。

in·cip·i·ent [inˈsipiənt; ɪnˋsɪpɪənt] *a*. 开始的,刚出现的,初期的。*an* ～ *cause* 远因。*an* ～ *disease* 初发的病。*the* ～ *light of day* 曙光。**-ence**, **-en·cy** *n*. **-ly** *ad*.

in·ci·pit [ˈinsipit; ˋɪnsɪpɪt] *n*.〔L.〕(本文自此)开始〔中世纪时抄本开端用语〕。

in·cise [inˈsaiz; ɪnˋsaɪz] *vt*. 1.切入,切开。2.雕刻。

in·cised [inˈsaizd; ɪnˋsaɪzd] *a*. 1.切入的;雕刻的;用锐器切入而做成的。2.(叶子)缺裂的。*an* ～ *leaf* 缺裂的叶子。～ *wound*【医】刀伤,割伤,切伤。

in·ci·sion [inˈsiʒən; ɪnˋsɪʒən] *n*. 1.切入;【医】切开。2.【植】(叶的)缺刻。3.雕刻。

in·ci·sive [inˈsaisiv; ɪnˋsaɪsɪv] *a*. 1.切入的,锐利的。2.尖锐的,深刻的,透彻的。3.【解】切牙的,门牙的。*an* ～ *criticism* 尖锐的批评。*an* ～ *teeth* = incisor. **-ly** *ad*. **-ness** *n*.

in·ci·sor [inˈsaizə; ɪnˋsaɪzɚ] *n*.【解】门齿;切牙(= ～ tooth)。

in·cit·ant [inˈsaitənt; ɪnˋsaɪtənt] **I** *a*. 刺激的,兴奋的。**II** *n*. 1.刺激因素。2.【医】兴奋剂,提神药。

in·ci·ta·tion [ˌinsaiˈteiʃən; ˏɪnsaɪˋteʃən] *n*. 刺激,激励,煽动;刺激物;动机,诱因。

in·cite [inˈsait; ɪnˋsaɪt] *vt*. 1.激励;刺激。2.煽动,唆使。*Insults* ～ *resentment*. 侮辱激起愤恨。～ *a crowd to riot* 煽动群众暴动。

in·cite·ment [inˈsaitmənt; ɪnˋsaɪtmənt] *n*. = incitation.

in·ci·vil·i·ty [ˌinsiˈviliti; ˏɪnsəˋvɪlətɪ] *n*. 1.无礼貌,粗野。2.不礼貌的言行。

in·ci·vism [ˈinsivizəm; ˋɪnsɪvɪzm̩] *n*. 无视公民义务;缺乏爱国心。

incl. = inclosure; including; inclusive.

in-clear·er [ˈinkliərə; ˋɪnklɪrɚ] *n*. 票据交换员。

in-clear·ing [ˈinkliəriŋ; ˋɪnklɪrɪŋ] *n*.〔英〕(票据交换后所收入的)应付票据总额。

in·clem·en·cy [inˈklemənsi; ɪnˋklɛmənsɪ] *n*. 1.(天气的)险恶,凛烈,酷寒。2.冷酷无情。

in·clem·ent [inˈklemənt; ɪnˋklɛmənt] *a*. 1.(天气、气候)险恶的,酷烈的,狂暴的;寒冷的。2.(人)无情的,严酷的。

in·clin·a·ble [inˈklainəbl; ɪnˋklaɪnəbl̩] *a*. 1.倾向于…的,赞成…的。2.可使倾斜的。*be* ～ *to sth*. 倾向于某事。

in·cli·na·tion [ˌinkliˈneiʃən; ˏɪnkləˋneʃən] *n*. 1.倾斜;点头,鞠躬。2.斜坡,倾度;【数】倾角;【天】(轨道的)交角。3.倾向,嗜好。4.爱好的事物。5.体质的倾向;斜角。～ *of an orbit*【天】轨道交角。*express one's consent with an* ～ (*of the head*) 点头表示同意。*an* ～ *to stoutness* 容易发胖的体质。***against one's*** ～违反着本意。***follow one's own*** ～随心所欲。***have an*** ～ ***for*** 爱好,欢喜。**-al** *a*.

in·cline [inˈklain; ɪnˋklaɪn] **I** *vt*. 1.弄斜,使倾斜,使偏向。2.低(头),屈(身)。3.使(某人)倾向于,使(某人)有意思(做某事)〔常用被动态〕。～ *a post against the wall* 把柱子靠墙斜立着。～ *one's ear to sb*. 侧耳倾听某人讲话。～ *one's head in greeting* 低头致意。*His attitude did not* ～ *me to help him*. 他的态度使我不想帮助他。*be* ～*d to go by air* 想要[倾向于]坐飞机去。*Are you* ～*d for a walk*? 你想散步吗? — *vi*. 1.倾斜。2.低头,屈身。3.爱好,赞同。4.易于…,有…的倾向。5.近似。6.【军】侧转前进。～ *toward the speaker to hear more clearly* 斜着身子向发言人靠近,以便听得更清楚些。～ *to traditional way* 喜爱传统的做法。*The leave* ～ *to dark*. 树叶绿得发黑。*purple inclining to red* 近似红色的紫色。*Right* ～! 半面向右转走! **II** *n*. 斜面;坡度。

in·clined [inˈklaind; ɪnˋklaɪnd] *a*. 1.倾斜的;成斜坡的;【数】与线或平面成角的。2.倾向于…的〔同不定式连用〕。～ **plane**【数】斜面。

in·cli·nom·e·ter [ˌinkliˈnɔmitə; ˏɪnkləˋnɑmɪtɚ] *n*. 倾角仪;磁倾计;倾斜仪。

in·close [inˈkləuz; ɪnˋkloz] *vt*. = enclose.

in·clo·sure [inˈkləuʒə; ɪnˋkloʒɚ] *n*. = enclosure.

in·clud·a·ble [inˈkluːdəbl; ɪnˋkludəbl̩] *a*. 可以包括在内的。

in·clude [inˈkluːd; ɪnˋklud] *vt*. (*opp*. exclude) 1.包住,关住。2.包含,包括;算入,计入。*The nutshell* ～*s the kernel*. 果壳裹住果仁。*all charges* ～*d* 包括一切费用[连一切费用在内]。*There were ten present including* [*not including*] *myself*. 连我在内[除我而外]共有十人出席。*The farm* ～*s 160 acres*. 这个农场有160英亩。*He* ～*s everything in his survey*. 他事事调查,巨细无遗。

in·clud·ed [inˈkluːdid; ɪnˋkludɪd] *a*. 1.包入的,包有的,包含的。2.【植】内藏的,不伸出的。

in·clud·i·ble [inˈkluːdəbl; ɪnˋkludəbl̩] *a*. = includable.

in·clu·sion [inˈkluːʒən; ɪnˋkluʒən] *n*. 1.包含,含有。2.参杂;杂质;内涵物。3.【逻】包摄;【医】包涵物;【矿】包体;【冶】夹杂物。～ **body**【医】包涵体。

in·clu·sive [inˈkluːsiv; ɪnˋklusɪv] *a*. (*opp*. exclusive) 1.包围住的,范围广的。2.包括…的;…也算入的(*of*)。3.一切开支包括在内的。4.(语言使用上)不分男女的,(用词上)无男女性别歧视的(如不使用 chairman 而使用 chairperson 等)。*an* ～ *list* 详表。*from Jan. 1st to 31st* ～〔略 incl.〕从1月1日至31日〔1日与31日在内(*cf*.〔美〕Jan. 1st through 31st)〕。*an* ～ *fee* (旅馆)连伙食一切包括在内的费用。*a party of ten*, ～ *of the host* 主客共计十人的聚会。～ *of* 包含。**-ly** *ad*. **-ness** *n*.

in·co·er·ci·ble [ˌinkəuˈəːsəbl; ˏɪnkoˋɝsəbl̩] *a*. 难强制的,不能压制的。

in·cog. [inˈkɔg; ɪnˋkɑg] *a*., *ad*., *n*.〔口〕= incognita, incognito.

in·cog·i·ta·ble [inˈkɔdʒitəbl; ɪnˋkɑdʒɪtəbl̩] *a*.〔罕〕不可想像的;不可思议的;难以置信的。

in·cog·i·tant [inˈkɔdʒitənt; ɪnˋkɑdʒɪtənt] *a*. 没有思虑的;轻率的,不顾及他人的。

in·cog·ni·ta [inˈkɔgnitə; ɪnˋkɑgnɪtə] **I** *n*. (*pl*. ～*s*, *-te* [-tei; -te]) 改用假名的女人;化装出行的女人。**II** *a*. (女人)改用假名的,化装出行的。*She went to Paris* ～. 她化装到巴黎去(了)。

I

in·cog·ni·to [in'kɔgnitəu; ɪn`kɑgnɪto] **I** ***a***., ***ad***. 化装的[地];用假名的[地]。*travel* ~ 微行,微装出游。**II** ***n***. (*pl*. ~*s*, *-ti* [-tiː;-ti]) 微装出游的人;用假名的人。*drop one's* ~ 说出自己的真正身分。

in·cog·ni·za·ble [in'kɔgnizəbl; ɪn`kɑgnɪzəbḷ] ***a***. 不能认识的,不可知。

in·cog·ni·zant [in'kɔgnizənt; ɪn`kɑgnɪzənt] ***a***. 没有认识到的,没意识到的 (*of*)。**-zance** ***n***.

in·co·her·ence [ˌinkəu'hiərəns; ˏɪnko`hɪrəns], **in·co·her·en·cy** [-si; -sɪ] ***n***. 支离破碎;不连贯。*the* ~ *of speech* 语无伦次。

in·co·her·ent [ˌinkəu'hiərənt; ˏɪnko`hɪrənt] ***a***. 支离破碎的,七零八落的,东扯西拉的;不连贯的,前后矛盾的;无条理的,不相干的。**-ly** ***ad***.

in·co·he·sive [ˌinkəu'hiːsiv; ˏɪnko`hisɪv] ***a***. 无凝聚力的;(势力等)易分裂的,散的。

in·com·bus·ti·bil·i·ty ['inkəmˌbʌstə'biliti; ˏɪnkəmˏbʌstə`bɪlətɪ] ***n***. 不燃性。

in·com·bus·ti·ble [ˌinkəm'bʌstəbl; ˏɪnkəm`bʌstəbḷ] **I** ***a***. 不能燃烧的。**II** ***n***. 不燃物。**-bly** ***ad***.

in·come ['inkəm; `ɪnkəm] ***n***. (定期)收入,所得,收益。*an earned* [*unearned*] ~ 劳动[不劳]所得。*draw a large* ~ 收入很多。***live with one's*** ~ 量入为出。~ **account** [**statement**] 损益计算书,收益账。~ **support** 〔英〕(发给穷困失业者的)收入保障金。~ **tax** 所得税。

in·com·er ['inˌkʌmə; `ɪnˏkʌmɚ] ***n***. **1**. 进来者;外来移民;新来者。**2**. 后继者,替手。**3**. 侵入者,闯入者。

in·com·ing ['inˌkʌmiŋ; `ɪnˏkʌmɪŋ] **I** ***n***. (*opp*. outgoing) **1**. 进来,到来。**2**. 〔*pl*.〕收入,岁入。*the* ~ *of spring* 春天的到来。~*s and outgoings* 收支。**II** ***a***. **1**. 进来的,回来的。**2**. 接着来的;继任的。**3**. (利益等)正在产生的,(自然)增殖的。**4**. (居民等)移来的。*the* ~ *mayor* 继任市长。~ *profits* 即将取得的利润。*the* ~ *tide* 涨潮。

in·com·men·su·ra·ble [ˌinkə'menʃərəbl; ˏɪnkə`mɛnʃərəbḷ] **I** ***a***. **1**. 不能按同一标准衡量的,无共同尺度的。**2**. 不能比较的 (*with*); 悬殊的 (*with*)。**3**.【数】不能通约的,无公度的。~ *numbers* 不可通约数。**II** ***n***.【数】无理数;悬殊的东西。**-bil·i·ty** ***n***. **-bly** ***ad***.

in·com·men·su·rate [ˌinkə'menʃərit; ˏɪnkə`mɛnʃərɪt] ***a***. **1**. = incommensurable. **2**. 不相称的,不适当的,不相对应的 (*to*; *with*)。*His abilities are* ~ *to* [*with*] *the task he has been given*. 他的能力同给予他的工作不相适应。**-ly ad.**

I

in·com·mode [inkə'məud; ɪnkə`mod] ***vt***. 使不便,妨碍;打扰,使为难。*One is seriously* ~*d at theatres by ladies' hats*. 戏院中女人的帽子最妨碍人了。

in·com·mo·di·ous [ˌinkə'məudjəs; ˏɪnkə`modjəs] ***a***. **1**. 不舒服的;不方便的。**2**. 小得无回旋余地的。*an* ~ *little bedroom* 一间窄小不堪的卧室。**-ly** ***ad***. **-ness** ***n***.

in·com·mu·ni·ca·ble [ˌinkə'mjuːnikəbl; ˏɪnkə`mjunɪkəbḷ] ***a***. **1**. 不能传达的,无法表达的。**2**. 沉默寡言,孤僻的。**-bil·i·ty** [ˌinkəˌmjuːnikə'biliti; ˏɪnkəˏmjunɪkə`bɪlətɪ], **-ness** ***n***. **-bly** ***ad***.

in·com·mu·ni·ca·do [ˌinkəˌmjuːni'kɑːdəu; ˏɪnkəˏmjunɪ`kɑdo] ***a***. 被禁止接触外界的,(尤指犯人)被单独监禁的。

in·com·mu·ni·ca·tive [ˌinkə'mjuːnikətiv; ˏɪnkə`mjunɪketɪv] ***a***. 不爱说话的,沉默寡言的,不爱交际的。**-ly** ***ad***. **-ness** ***n***.

in·com·mut·a·ble [ˌinkə'mjuːtəbl; ˏɪnkə`mjutəbḷ] ***a***. 不能交换的,不能变换的。**-bil·i·ty** ***n***. **-bly** ***ad***.

in·com·pact [ˌinkəm'pækt; ˏɪnkəm`pækt] ***a***. 不紧密的,松散的;不结实的。**-ly** ***ad***. **-ness** ***n***.

in·com·pa·ra·ble [in'kɔmpərəbl; ɪn`kɑmpərəbḷ] ***a***. 无比的,无双的;不能比较的 (*with*; *to*)。*a woman of* ~ *beauty* 绝代佳人。**-bly** ***ad***.

in·com·pat·i·ble [ˌinkəm'pætəbl; ˏɪnkəm`pætəbḷ] ***a***. **1**. 不相容的,难两立的,矛盾的 (*with*)。**2**.【医】配伍禁忌的。**3**. 不能配合的。*She asked for a divorce because they were utterly* ~. 她请求离婚,因为他们完全合不来。~ *colours* 不调和的色彩。**-bil·i·ty** ['inkəmˌpætə'biliti; ɪnkəmˏpætə`bɪlətɪ] ***n***. **-bly** ***ad***.

in·com·pe·tence, **-ten·cy** [in'kɔmpitəns, -si; ɪn`kɑmpɪtəns, -sɪ] ***n***. **1**. 无能,不熟练。**2**. 不适当,不胜任,不够格。**3**. 法律上无资格。**4**.【医】关闭不全,机能不全。*He lost his job because of* ~. 因为不能胜任,他失掉了(工作)职位。

in·com·pe·tent [in'kɔmpitənt; ɪn`kɑmpɪtənt] **I** ***a***. **1**. 无能的,不熟练的。**2**. 不适当的,不胜任的,不够格的。**3**. 法律上无资格的。*be* ~ *as a teacher* 不适宜当教员。*be* ~ *to teach* [*for teaching*] 不能教书。**II** ***n***. **1**. 无能者。**2**. 不胜任者。**3**. 法律上无资格的人。**-ly** ***ad***.

in·com·plete [ˌinkəm'pliːt; ˏɪnkəm`plit] ***a***. 不完全的,未完成的,不完备的。~ *combustion* 不完全燃烧。~ *reaction*【化】不完全反应。**-ly** ***ad***. **-ness** ***n***.

in·com·ple·tion [ˌinkəm'pliːʃən; ˏɪnkəm`pliʃən] ***n***. 不完全,未完成,不完备。

in·com·pli·ant [ˌinkəm'plaiənt; ˏɪnkəm`plaɪənt] ***a***. 不服从的;不让步的;不柔顺的。**-ance**, **-an·cy** ***n***. **-ly** ***ad***.

in·com·pre·hen·si·ble [ˌinkɔmpri'hensəbl; ˏɪnkɑmprɪ`hɛnsəbḷ] **I** ***a***. **1**. 不能理解的,费解的;莫测高深的。**2**. 〔古〕广大无边的,无限的。**II** ***n***. 无限物,无限者。**-bil·i·ty** ***n***. **-bly** ***ad***.

in·com·pre·hen·sion [inˌkɔmpri'henʃən; ɪnˏkɑmprɪ`hɛnʃən] ***n***. 不了解,缺乏理解。

in·com·pre·hen·sive [inˌkɔmpri'hensiv; ɪnˏkɑmprɪ`hɛnsɪv] ***a***. **1**. 理解不深的,没有理解力的。**2**. 范围狭窄的,包含得很少的。**-ly** ***ad***. **-ness** ***n***.

in·com·press·i·ble [ˌinkəm'presəbl; ˏɪnkəm`prɛsəbḷ] ***a***. 不能压缩的;不易压缩的;坚硬的;不屈的。*an* ~ *fluid* 不可压缩流体。**-bil·i·ty** ['inkəmˌpresə'biliti; `ɪnkəmˏprɛsə`bɪlətɪ] ***n***. 不可压缩性。

in·com·put·a·ble [ˌinkəm'pjuːtəbl; ˏɪnkəm`pjutəbḷ] ***a***. 不能计算的,数不清的。

in·con·ceiv·a·ble [ˌinkən'siːvəbl; ˏɪnkən`sivəbḷ] ***a***. **1**. 不能想像的;不可思议的;不可理解的。**2**. 〔口〕难于相信的,惊人的。**-bil·i·ty** ['inkənˌsiːvə'biliti; ˏɪnkənˏsivə`bɪlətɪ] ***n***. **-bly** ***ad***.

in·con·cin·ni·ty [ˌinkən'siniti; ˏɪnkən`sɪnətɪ] ***n***. 不适合,不协调。**-cin·nous** ***a***.

in·con·clu·sive [ˌinkən'kluːsiv; ˏɪnkən`klusɪv] ***a***. 不确定的;不充分的;不得要领的;不能使人信服的;无确定结果的;无效的。*an* ~ *discussion* 没有结果的讨论。**-ly** ***ad***.

in·con·clu·sive·ness [ˌinkən'kluːsivnis; ˏɪnkən`klusɪvnɪs] ***n***. 不确定,(证据)不充分;(议论)不得要领;不能使人信服;无确定的结果;无效。

in·con·den·si·ble [ˌinkən'densəbl; ˏɪnkən`dɛnsəbḷ] ***a***. 不能凝缩的(= incondensable)。**-bil·i·ty** ***n***.

in·con·dite [in'kɔndit; ɪn`kɑndɪt] ***a***. **1**. (文体)拙劣的,生硬的。**2**. 无礼貌的,粗鲁的。

in·con·form·i·ty [ˌinkən'fɔːmiti; ˏɪnkən`fɔrmətɪ] ***n***. 不一致,不符合 (*to*; *with*)。

in·con·gru·ent [in'kɔŋgruənt, ˌinkən'gruːənt; ɪn`kɑŋgruənt, ˏɪnkən`gruənt] ***a***. 不相合的,不一致的,不适当的,不相称的。**-ence** ***n***. **-ently** ***ad***.

in·con·gru·i·ty [ˌinkɔŋ'gru(ː)iti; ˏɪnkɑŋ`gruətɪ] ***n***. **1**. 不调和,不一致;不相称。**2**. 不协调的事物。

in·con·gru·ous [in'kɔŋgruəs; ɪn`kɑŋgruəs] ***a***. **1**. 不适当的;不适宜的,不合理的。**2**. 不调和的,不相称的,不一致的 (*with*);【数】不等的 (*opp*. congruous)。**-ly** ***ad***. **-ness** ***n***.

in·con·nu [ˌinkə'nuː; ˏɪnkə`nu] ***n***. (*pl*. *-nus*, *-nu*)

【动】白北鲑（*Stenodus mackenziti*）〔产于北美西北和亚洲东北〕。

in·cons·cient [inˈkɔnʃənt; ɪnˋkɑnʃənt] *a*. 无意识的；失去知觉的；漫不经心的。

in·con·sec·u·tive [ˌinkənˈsekjutiv; ˏɪnkənˋsekjʊtɪv] *a*. 不连续的；不连贯的，无顺序的。**-ly** *ad*. **-ness** *n*.

in·con·se·quence [inˈkɔnsikwəns; ɪnˋkɑnsəˏkwɛns] *n*. 1. 不连贯，前后不符，矛盾。2. 不重要。

in·con·se·quent [inˈkɔnsikwənt; ɪnˋkɑnsəˏkwɛnt] *a*. 1. 不合逻辑的，不连贯的，前后不符的；矛盾的。2. 不重要的，无价值的。**-ly** *ad*.

in·con·se·quen·tial [inˌkɔnsiˈkwənʃəl; ɪnˏkɑnsəˋkwɛnʃəl] *a*. 1. 无意义的，不重要的。2. 不连贯的，前后不一的，不合逻辑的。**-i·ty** *n*. **-ly** *ad*.

in·con·sid·er·a·ble [ˌinkənˈsidərəbl; ˏɪnkənˋsɪdərəbl̩] *a*. 不值得考虑的，无足轻重的，些微的。**-bly** *ad*.

in·con·sid·er·ate [ˌinkənˈsidərit; ˏɪnkənˋsɪdərɪt] *a*. 1. 不替别人着想的，不体谅别人的。2. 考虑不周的，粗心的，轻率的。～ *remarks* 轻率的语言。～ *children* 鲁莽的孩子。**-ly** *ad*. **-ness** *n*.

in·con·sid·er·a·tion [ˈinkənˌsidəˈreiʃən; ˏɪnkənˏsɪdəˋreʃən] *n*. 1. 不替别人着想，不会体谅人。2. 考虑不周，粗心，轻率。

in·con·sist·ence [ˌinkənˈsistəns; ˏɪnkənˋsɪstəns], **incon·sist·en·cy** [-si; -sɪ] *n*. 1. 不一致，不协调；前后矛盾，不一贯。2. 不一致的事物，自相矛盾的言行。

in·con·sis·tent [ˌinkənˈsistənt; ˏɪnkənˋsɪstənt] *a*. 1. 不一致的，不调和的（*with*）。2. 前后矛盾的，不合逻辑的。3. 反复无常的。～ **equation**【数】不相容方程，矛盾方程。**-ly** *ad*.

in·con·sol·a·bil·i·ty [ˌinkənˌsəuləˈbiliti; ˏɪnkənˏsoləˋbɪlətɪ] *n*. 无可安慰，无可慰藉（= inconsolableness）。

in·con·sol·a·ble [ˌinkənˈsəuləbl; ˏɪnkənˋsoləbl̩] *a*. 无可安慰的，无可慰藉的。**-bly** *ad*.

in·con·so·nance [inˈkɔnsənəns; ɪnˋkɑnsənəns] *n*. 不调和，不和谐，不一致。

in·con·so·nant [inˈkɔnsənənt; ɪnˋkɑnsənənt] *a*. 不调和的，不和谐的，不一致的（*to*; *with*）。*be* ～ *with* 与…不调和。*be* ～ *to the ear* 刺耳。**-ly ad**.

in·con·spic·u·ous [ˌinkənˈspikjuəs; ˏɪnkənˋspɪkjuəs] *a*. 1. 不显眼的，不引人注意的。2.【植】(花)小而色淡的。**-bly** *ad*. **-ness** *n*.

in·con·stan·cy [inˈkɔnstənsi; ɪnˋkɑnstənsɪ] *n*. 1. 反复无常，易变；无规则。2. 轻浮，无信义。

in·con·stant [inˈkɔnstənt; ɪnˋkɑnstənt] *a*. 1. 反复无常的，易变的；无规则的。2. 轻浮的，无信义的。**-ly** *ad*.

in·con·sum·a·ble [ˌinkənˈsjuːməbl; ˏɪnkənˋsjuməbl̩] *a*. 烧不尽的；用不完的；消耗不了的；【经】非消费性的。**-a·bly** *ad*.

in·con·test·a·bil·i·ty [ˌinkənˌtestəˈbiliti; ˏɪnkənˏtɛstəˋbɪlətɪ] *n*. 不可争，无可争辩。

in·con·test·a·ble [ˌinkənˈtestəbl; ˏɪnkənˋtɛstəbl̩] *a*. 不能争辩的，无怀疑余地的，否定不了的。～ *evidence* 铁证。**-bly** *ad*.

in·con·ti·nence [inˈkɔntinəns; ɪnˋkɑntɪnəns], **in·con·ti·nen·cy** [-si; -sɪ] *n*. 1. 无节制〔尤指纵欲〕；无抑制。2. 不能保持。3.【医】大小便失禁。

in·con·ti·nent[1] [inˈkɔntinənt; ɪnˋkɑntɪnənt] *a*. 1. 无节制的，不能抑制的。2. 不能保持的。3.【医】大小便失禁的。**-ly** *ad*.

in·con·ti·nent[2] [inˈkɔntinənt; ɪnˋkɑntɪnənt] *ad*. 〔古〕立即。**-ly** *ad*.

in·con·trol·la·ble [ˌinkənˈtrəuləbl; ˏɪnkənˋtroləbl̩] *a*. 不能控制的。**-bly** *ad*.

in·con·tro·vert·i·ble [ˌinkɔntrəˈvəːtəbl; ˏɪnkɑntrəˋvɝtəbl̩] *a*. 无可辩驳的，颠扑不破的，不容置疑的。**-bly** *ad*.

in·con·tu·ma·ci·am [ˈinˌkɔntjuːˈmeiʃiæm; ˋɪnˏkɑntjuˋmeʃɪæm]〔L.〕【法】藐视法庭。

in·con·ven·ience [ˌinkənˈviːnjəns; ˏɪnkənˋvinjəns] **I** *n*. 1. 不方便，不自由。2. 为难之处，麻烦的事。*if it is no* ～ *to you* 如果对你方便的话。*put sb. to* ～ 使某人感到不便[为难]。**II** *vt*. 使感不便，使为难，使麻烦。*I hope I do not* ～ *you*. 我希望我不会打扰你。*Do not* ～ *yourself for my sake*. 请不必为我麻烦。

in·con·ven·ient [ˌinkənˈviːnjənt; ˏɪnkənˋvinjənt] *a*. 不方便的，引起不方便的；麻烦的。*if it is not* ～ *to you* 如果你方便的话。**-ly** *ad*.

in·con·vert·i·ble [ˌinkənˈvəːtəbl; ˏɪnkənˋvɝtəbl̩] *a*. 1. 不能变换[转换]的。2. 不能换成硬币的，不能兑换外汇的。～ *notes* [*paper-money*] 不能兑换成硬币的纸币。**-bil·i·ty** [ˌinkənˌvəːtiˈbiliti; ˏɪnkənˏvɝtɪˋbɪlətɪ] *n*. **-bly** *ad*.

in·con·vin·ci·ble [ˌinkənˈvinsəbl; ˏɪnkənˋvɪnsəbl̩] *a*. 不能说服的。**-cibil·i·ty** *n*. **-bly** *ad*.

in·co·or·di·nate [ˌinkəuˈɔːdinit; ˏɪnkoˋɔrdnɪt] *a*. 1. 不配合的。2. 不同格的；不同等的。

in·co·or·di·na·tion [ˌinkəuɔːdiˈneiʃən; ˏɪnkoordɪˋneʃən] *n*. 1. 不配合，不协调。2. 不同格，不同等。

incor(p). = incorporated 注册。

in·cor·po·ra·ble [inˈkɔːpərəbl; ɪnˋkɔrpərəbl̩] *a*. 1. 可以结合的。2. 可合为一体的。3. 可以混合的。4. 可以加入公司、社团的。5. 可以具体化的。

in·cor·po·rate[1] [inˈkɔːpəreit; ɪnˋkɔrpəret] **I** *vt*. 1. 结合，合并，收编。2. 使成为法定组织；〔美〕使成为有限公司；使注册。3. 使混合。4. 使加入。5. 〔罕〕使具体化，体现。*be* ～*d a member of a learned society* 被吸收为学会成员。～ *new ideas into a book* 把新思想收入书内。— *vi*. 1. 合并；混合（*with*）。2. 成为社团，组成公司。*The mill* ～*d with others*. 这家工厂与别家合并了。**II** [-pərit; -pərɪt] *a*. 1. 法定组织的。2. 〔罕〕合并的，结合起来的，具体化了的。

in·cor·po·rate[2] [inˈkɔːpərit; inˋkɔrpərɪt] *a*. 无形(体)的；精神上的，心灵上的。

in·cor·po·rat·ed [inˈkɔːpəreitid; ɪnˋkɔrpəˏretɪd] *a*. 1. 合并的；结合的，联合的。2. 组成法人组织的。

in·cor·po·ra·tion [inˌkɔːpəˈreiʃən; ɪnˏkɔrpəˋreʃən] *n*. 1. 结合，合并，编入。2. 团体，结社，法人，公司。

in·cor·po·ra·tive [inˈkɔːpərətiv, -pəˈreit-; ɪnˋkɔrpərətɪv; -pəˋret-] *a*. 1. 合并的，结合的。2. 成为法人组织的。

in·cor·po·ra·tor [inˈkɔːpəreitə; ɪnˋkɔrpəˏretɚ] *n*. 合并者，社团成员，公司创办人。

in·cor·po·re·al [ˌinkɔːˈpɔːriəl; ˏɪnkɔrˋpɔrɪəl] *a*. 1. 非物质的，精神的；无实体的，无形的。2.【法】无形体的。～ *capital*【经】无形资本。*an* ～ *hereditament*【法】无形遗产。**-ly** *ad*.

in·cor·po·re·i·ty [ˌinkɔːpəˈriːiti; ˏɪnkɔrpəˋriətɪ] *n*. 1. 非物质性；无实体，无形体。2. (*pl*. *-ties*) 无实体物。

in·cor·rect [ˌinkəˈrekt; ˏɪnkəˋrɛkt] *a*. 1. 错误的，不正确的；不妥当的。2. 原稿未经妥善校正的。**-ly** *ad*.

in·cor·rect·ness [inkəˈrektnis; ɪnkəˋrɛktnɪs] *n*. 1. 不正确。2. (尤指)不适当。3. 不真实；不准确；错误；有缺点。

in·cor·ri·gi·bil·i·ty [inˌkɔridʒəˈbiliti; ˏɪnkɑrɪdʒəˋbɪlətɪ] *n*. 难以纠正；不能改正；不能改进；不能改造〔尤指习惯成自然，或指儿童已养成坏习惯难以改正〕（= incorrigibleness）。

in·cor·ri·gi·ble [inˈkɔridʒəbl; ɪnˋkɔrɪdʒəbl̩] **I** *a*. 难以纠正的；不可改造的，不可救药的；固执的，难弄的。**II** *n*. 无可救药的人，不改悔的人。**-bly** *ad*.

in·cor·rupt [ˌinkəˈrʌpt; ˏɪnkəˋrʌpt] *a*. 1. 纯洁的，正直的，廉洁的；不能收买的。2. (版本等)无差错的，无改动的。

I

in·cor·rupt·i·ble [ˌinkəˈrʌptəbl; ˏɪnkəˋrʌptəbl] **I** ***a*.** 1. 不会腐蚀的,不易败坏的。2. 不能收卖的,廉洁的。**II** ***n*.** 不易腐蚀的东西。**-bil·i·ty** ***n*.** **-bly** ***ad*.**

in·cor·rup·tion [ˌinkəˈrʌpʃən; ˏɪnkəˋrʌpʃən] ***n*.** 〔古〕不腐,不朽,廉洁。

incr. = increased; increasing.

in·cras·sate [inˈkræsit; ɪnˋkræsɪt] **I** ***a*.** 【生】增厚的。**II** ***vt*.** 1. 使浓厚。2. 【药】浓缩。**-a·ble** ***a*.**

in·crease [inˈkriːs; ɪnˋkris] **I** ***vt*.** 增加,增大,增多;增强,增进 (*opp*. decrease)。~ *speed* 增加速度。~ *one's pace* 放快脚步。~ *one's efforts* 更加努力。— ***vi*.** 增加;繁殖;〔诗〕(月亮)渐渐变大,渐圆。~ *in number* 数目增加。~ *in power* 权力增大。~ *with years* 逐年增加。**II** [ˈinkriːs; ˋɪnkris] ***n*.** 增加,繁殖;增加量,增大额;〔古〕农产品,作物。*an* [*the*] ~ *of money* 钱数增加。~ *in the population* 人口的增长。***be on the*** ~ 不断增加,正在增加。

in·creas·ing [inˈkriːsiŋ; ɪnˋkrisɪŋ] ***a*.** 增加的,增大的。~ **return**【经】收获递增。

in·creas·ing·ly [inˈkriːsiŋli; ɪnˋkrisɪŋlɪ] ***ad*.** 不断增加地,日益,格外,越来越。*be* ~ *prosperous and strong* 日益繁荣富强。

in·cre·ate [ˌinkriˈeit, ˈinkrieit; ˏɪnkrɪˋet, ˋɪnkrɪet] ***a*.** 非创造出来的〔指神灵之类〕。

in·cred·i·ble [inˈkredəbl; ɪnˋkrɛdəbl̩] ***a*.** 1. 不可相信的。2. 〔口〕不可思议的;惊人的;未必可能的。*with* ~ *speed* 用惊人的速度。**-bil·i·ty** ***n*.** **-bly** ***ad*.**

in·cre·du·li·ty [ˌinkriˈdjuːliti; ˏɪnkrɪˋdjulətɪ] ***n*.** 不相信,怀疑。

in·cred·u·lous [inˈkredjuləs; ɪnˋkrɛdʒələs] ***a*.** 不轻易相信的;表示怀疑的 (*of*; *about*); 奇怪的。*an* ~ *smile* 含有疑意的微笑。**-ly** ***ad*.**

in·cre·mate [ˈinkrimeit; ˋɪnkrɪmet] ***vt*.** 火葬。

in·cre·ment [ˈinkrimənt; ˋɪnkrəmənt] ***n*.** 增额,增值,增长;【数】增量;利润。*unearned* ~【经】自然增值。~ *value duties* 增值税。

in·cre·men·tal [ˌinkriˈmentl; ˏɪnkrɪˋmɛntl̩] ***a*.** 1. 增加的,增大的,增长的。2. 增额的。3. 【数】增量的。

in·cre·men·tal·ism [ˌinkriˈmentlizəm; ˏɪnkrɪˋmɛntl̩ˏɪzəm] ***n*.** (政治和社会改革方面的)渐进主义。

in·cres·cent [inˈkresnt; ɪnˋkrɛsn̩t] ***a*.** 增加的,成长的;〔尤指〕(月的)渐盈的。

in·cre·tion [inˈkriːʃən; ɪnˋkriʃən] ***n*.** 内分泌,内分泌物 (= internal secretion)。**-tion·ar·y**, **-to·ry** ***a*.**

in·crim·i·nate [inˈkrimineit; ɪnˋkrɪmɪˏnet] ***vt*.** 归罪于,使负罪;控告。~ *oneself* 自陷法网。**-na·tion** ***n*.** **-na·tor** ***n*.** **-na·to·ry** ***a*.**

in·croach [inˈkrəutʃ; ɪnˋkrotʃ] ***vt*** = encroach.

in·cross [ˈinkrɔːs; ˋɪnkrɔs] **I** ***n*.** 品种内异系交配体。**II** ***vt*.** = inbreed.

in·crowd [ˈinkraud; ˋɪnkraud] ***n*.** 小圈子,小集团;(小圈子里的)熟人;小集团成员。

in·crust [inˈkrʌst; ɪnˋkrʌst] ***vt*.**, ***vi*.** = encrust.

in·crus·ta·tion [ˌinkrʌsˈteiʃən; ˏɪnkrʌsˋteʃən] ***n*.** 1. 用外皮包覆,结硬壳。2. 硬壳,外皮,外壳,疮痂。3. 渣壳,水锈,水垢。4. 镶嵌;镶嵌物;(建筑物的)表面装饰;镶嵌细工。5. (风俗、习惯等的)逐渐形成。

in·cu·bate [ˈinkjəbeit; ˋɪnkjəbet] ***vi*.** 1. 孵卵;孵化。2. 沉思。3. 【医】(病)潜伏。— ***vt*.** 1. 孵卵;(人工)孵化。2. 保育(早产婴儿)。3. 培养(细菌)。4. 仔细考虑,想(办法),策划。

in·cu·ba·tion [ˌinkjuˈbeiʃən, ˈiŋ-; ˏɪnkjəˋbeʃən, ˏɪŋ-] ***n*.** 1. 孵卵,孵化;培育。2. 策划,图谋,企图。3. 【医】潜伏期。4. 深思熟虑。*artificial* ~ 人工孵化。~ **period** 潜伏期。

in·cu·ba·tion·al [ˌinkjuˈbeiʃənəl, ˌiŋ-; ˏɪnkjəˋbeʃənəl, ˏɪŋ-] ***a*.** 1. 孵卵的,孵化的。2. 【医】潜伏的,潜伏期的。

in·cu·ba·tive [ˈinkjubeitiv; ˋɪnkjəˏbetɪv] ***a*.** 孵卵的;潜伏期的。

in·cu·ba·tor [ˈinkjubeitə; ˋɪnkjəˏbetɚ] ***n*.** 1. 孵卵器;孵卵员。2. 细菌培养器。3. 早产婴儿保育箱。

in·cu·ba·to·ry [inˈkjubeiˌtəri; ˋɪnkjʊbətorɪ] ***a*.** = incubative.

in·cu·bus [ˈiŋkjubʌs; ˋɪŋkjəbʌs] ***n*.** (*pl*. ***-bi*** [-bai; -baɪ], ~***es***) 1. 恶梦,梦魇。2. 沉重的负担,梦魇般的精神压力[压迫者]。

in·cu·des [iŋˈkjuːdiːz; ɪŋˋkjudiz] incus 的复数。

in·cul·cate [ɪnˈkʌlkeit; ɪnˋkʌlket] ***vt*.** 反复灌输;谆谆劝导。**-ca·tion** ***n*.** **-ca·tor** ***n*.**

in·culp·a·ble [inˈkʌlpəbl; ɪnˋkʌlpəbl̩] ***a*.** 无过的;无可责难的;无罪的。

in·cul·pate [ˈinkʌlpeit, inˈkʌl-; ɪnˋkʌlpet, ˋɪnkʌlpet] ***vt*.** 1. 使负罪,控告。2. 连累(某人)受罪。**-to·ry** ***a*.**

in·cul·pa·tion [ˌinkʌlˈpeiʃən; ˏɪnkʌlˋpeʃən] ***n*.** 1. 归罪,控告。2. 连累。

in·cult [inˈkʌlt; ɪnˋkʌlt] ***a*.** 〔罕〕1. 未开垦的。2. 粗野的,粗鲁的。

in·cum·ben·cy [inˈkʌmbənsi; ɪnˋkʌmbənsɪ] ***n*.** 1. (主指牧师的)任职,任期,职权。2. 义务,职责。

in·cum·bent [inˈkʌmbənt; ɪnˋkʌmbənt] **I** ***a*.** 1. 靠在[压在]上面的。2. 有义务的,成为责任的,义不容辞的 (*on*; *upon*)。3. 在职的。4. 弯垂下来的。5. (地层)重叠的,叠覆的,上覆的。*It is* ~ (*up*) *on us to do so*. 这样做是我们义不容辞的责任。**II** ***n*.** 〔英〕教区牧师;〔美国政府或团体、学术机构中〕任职者。

in·cum·ber [inˈkʌmbə; ɪnˋkʌmbɚ] ***vt*.** = encumber.

in·cum·brance [inˈkʌmbrəns; ɪnˋkʌmbrəns] ***n*.** = encumbrance.

in·cu·nab·u·lum [ˌinkjuˈnæbjuləm; ˏɪnkjʊˋnæbjʊləm] ***n*.** (*pl*. ***-la*** [-lə; -lə]) 1. 〔常用复〕初期,黎明期,摇篮时代。2. (特指十六世纪前的)古版本书,古代的作品。**-r** ***a*.**

in·cur [inˈkəː; ɪnˋkɝ] ***vt*.** (***in·curred***; ***in·cur·ring***) 招致,承受,惹起。~ *danger* 遭受危险。~ *hatred* 惹人仇恨。~ *a mountain of debt* 承受巨大债务。

in·cur·a·ble [inˈkjuərəbl; ɪnˋkjʊrəbl̩] **I** ***a*.** 医治不好的,不能矫正的。**II** ***n*.** 〔常 *pl*.〕医不好的病人。*an* ~ *disease* 不治之症。**-bil·i·ty**, **-ness** ***n*.** **-bly** ***ad*.**

in·cu·ri·os·i·ty [inˌkjuəriˈɔsiti; ɪnˏkjʊrɪˋɑsətɪ] ***n*.** 1. 不关心,无好奇心;不爱追根究底。2. 引不起兴趣。

in·cu·ri·ous [inˈkjuəriəs; ɪnˋkjʊrɪəs] ***a*.** 1. 〔古〕不注意的,不关心的;不感兴趣的,不爱追根究底的。2. 〔主要与 not 连用〕乏味的,没兴趣的。*a not* ~ *anecdote* 有趣的逸事。**-ly** ***ad*.**

in·cu·ri·ous·ness [inˈkjuriːəsnis; ɪnˋkjʊriəsnɪs] ***n*.** 无好奇心;无探索意;无兴趣;淡漠。

in·cur·rence [inˈkəːrəns; ɪnˋkɝrəns] ***n*.** 蒙受,招致。

in·cur·rent [inˈkəːrənt; ɪnˋkɝrənt] ***a*.** 流入的〔尤指水流入〕。*the* ~ *canals of sponges* 海绵吸水管。

in·cur·sion [inˈkəːʃən, Am. -ʒən; ɪnˋkɝʃən, -ʒən] ***n*.** 1. 侵入,侵略;袭击。2. (河水等)流入,进入。

in·cur·sive [inˈkəːsiv; ɪnˋkɝsɪv] ***a*.** 攻入的,侵入的,袭击的;流进来的。

in·cur·vate [ˈinkəːveit; ɪnˋkɝvet] **I** ***vt*.**, ***vi*.** (使)弯曲,(使)向心弯曲。**II** ***a*.** 弯曲的,向内弯曲的。**-va·tion** ***n*.**

in·curve[1] [ˈinˈkəːv; ɪnˋkɝv] ***vt*.**, ***vi*.** (使)弯曲,(使)向内弯曲。**-d** ***a*.**

in·curve[2] [inˈkəːv; ɪnˋkɝv] ***n*.** 【棒球】内曲球。

in·cus [ˈiŋkes; ˋɪŋkes] ***n*.** (*pl*. ***-cu·des*** [iŋˈkjuːdiːz; ɪŋˋkjudiz]) 〔L.〕【解】砧骨。

in·cuse [inˈkjuːz; ɪnˋkjuz] **I** ***vt*.** 在(硬币面上)压印。**II** ***a*.** 有压印的,压铸的。**III** ***n*.** (硬币等)压铸;压铸成的花样。

in·cut [ˈinkʌt; ˋɪnkʌt] ***a*.** 1. 插入的。2. 【印】(标题、旁

注等)插入文间的。

Ind [ind; ɪnd]〔古、诗〕= India;〔废〕= the Indies.

in d =〔L.〕*in diēs* (处方用语)每日。

Ind. = **1.** India; Indian. **2.** Indiana.

ind. = **1.** independent. **2.** index. **3.** indicative. **4.** industrial. **5.** indigo.

in·da·ba [inˈdɑːbɑː; ɪnˋdɑbɑ] ***n.*** **1.** (南非本地人的)会议。**2.**〔口〕重要会议。

in·da·mine [ˈindəmiːn, -min; ˋɪndəmin, -mɪn] ***n.***【化】吲达胺。

In·dan·threne [inˈdænθriːn; ɪnˋdænθrin] ***n.*** 阴丹士林染料,标准还原蓝。

in·dan·throne [inˈdænθrəun; ɪnˋdænθron] ***n.***【化】〔阴丹士林的正式名称〕靛蒽醌。

in·debt·ed [inˈdetid; ɪnˋdɛtɪd] ***a.*** **1.** 负债的 (*to*)。**2.** 受过人恩惠的,感激的。*be ~ to sb. for 100 dollars* 欠某人100元。*He was ~ to her for nursing him through pneumonia.* 他感激她护理好他的肺炎。*She is ~ to the library for most of her information.* 她的学识多数是从这个图书馆得来的。*I am ~ to you for kindness.* 谢谢您的好意。**-ness** ***n.***

in·de·cen·cy [inˈdiːsnsi; ɪnˋdisnsɪ] ***n.*** **1.** 粗鄙,猥亵,下流;下流言行。**2.**〔口〕不适当,不合适。

in·de·cent [inˈdiːsnt; ɪnˋdisnt] ***a.*** **1.** 粗鄙的,猥亵的,下流的。**2.**〔口〕不适当的,不合适的。~ *language* 下流话。*leave in ~ haste* 灰溜溜地[很不光彩地]急忙离开。**-ly** ***ad.***

in·de·cid·u·ous [ˌindiˈsidjuəs; ˏɪndɪˋsɪdjuəs] ***a.***【植】常绿的,不落叶的 (*opp.* deciduous)。

in·de·ci·pher·a·ble [ˌindiˈsaifərəbl; ˏɪndɪˋsaɪfrəbl̩] ***a.*** **1.** (密码等)破译不出的。**2.** (字迹等)难辨读的,模糊的,难懂的。

in·de·ci·sion [ˌindiˈsiʒən; ˏɪndɪˋsɪʒən] ***n.*** 不决定,无决断力,优柔寡断,犹豫不决。

in·de·ci·sive [ˌindiˈsaisiv; ˏɪndɪˋsaɪsɪv] ***a.*** **1.** 非决定性的。**2.** 不决定的;无决断力的,优柔寡断的,犹豫不决的。**3.** 不明确的,模糊的。**-ly** ***ad.*** **-ness** ***n.***

indecl. = indeclinable.

in·de·clin·a·ble [ˌindiˈklainəbl; ˏɪndɪˋklaɪnəbl̩] **I** ***a.***【语法】没有格的变化的,没有词尾变化的。**II** ***n.*** 不变词〔名词、代名词、形容词以外的词〕。**in·de·clin·a·bly** ***ad.***

in·de·com·pos·a·ble [ˌindiːkəmˈpəuzəbl; ˏɪndikəmˋpozəbl̩] ***a.*** 不能分解的;难分解的,不腐败的。

in·dec·o·rous [inˈdekərəs; ɪnˋdɛkərəs] ***a.*** 不合礼节的;不正派的;不规矩的;低级趣味的;不体面的。**-ly** ***ad.***

in·dec·o·rous·ness [inˈdekərəsnis; ɪnˋdɛkərəsnɪs] ***n.*** 不合礼节;不正派;不规矩;低级趣味;不体面。

in·de·co·rum [ˌindiˈkɔːrəm; ˏɪndɪˋkɔrəm] ***n.*** **1.** 不合礼节;不正派;不规矩;低级趣味;不体面。**2.** 失礼的言行。

in·deed [inˈdiːd; ɪnˋdid] ***ad.*** **1.** 实际上,真正地。*He is ~ a great man.* 他实在是一个伟人。**2.**〔加强语气〕确实,实在。*I shall be very glad ~.* 那我真太高兴啦。*I-yes! = Yes, ~!* 不错,真的! **3.**〔表示让步〕当然,固然。*There are ~ exceptions.* 当然有例外。**4.**〔表示同意或反语〕真的,真是。*Who is this Mr. James? — Who is he, ~!* 这个詹姆斯先生是谁? ~〔同感〕是谁呀,真的!〔我也不知道的意思〕;〔反〕你问谁? 真是!〔奇怪,你还不知道〕。**5.**〔表示疑问〕当真。*There's a big fire raging. — Indeed?* 起大火了。—真的吗? **6.**〔表示进一层的意思〕甚至。*There are many good people in our school, ~ in the whole society.* 在我们学校里好人很多,其实整个社会都是这样。

indef. = indefinite.

in·de·fat·i·ga·ble [ˌindiˈfætigəbl; ˏɪndɪˋfætɪgəbl̩] ***a.*** 不疲倦的;不屈不挠的。**-bil·i·ty** [ˈindiˌfætigəˈbiliti; ˏɪndɪˏfætɪgəˋbɪlətɪ] ***n.*** **-bly** ***ad.***

in·de·fea·si·ble [ˌindiˈfiːzəbl; ˏɪndɪˋfizəbl̩] ***a.*** 难废除的,不能取消的。**-bil·i·ty** [ˈindiˌfiːzəˈbiliti; ˋɪndɪˏfizəˋbɪlətɪ] ***n.*** **-bly** ***ad.***

in·de·fect·i·ble [ˌindiˈfektəbl; ˏɪndɪˋfɛktəbl] ***a.*** **1.** 不易损坏的,不败的;永存的,不朽的。**2.** 完美的,无缺点的。**-bil·i·ty** [ˈindiˌfektəˈbiliti; ˏɪndɪˏfɛktəˋbɪlətɪ] ***n.*** **-bly** ***ad.***

in·de·fen·si·bil·i·ty [ˌindiˌfensəˈbiliti; ˏɪndɪˏfɛnsəˋbɪlətɪ] ***n.*** **1.** 难防御,难保护。**2.** 难辩解;难辩护;难宽恕。

in·de·fen·si·ble [ˌindiˈfensəbl; ˏɪndɪˋfɛnsəbl̩] ***a.*** **1.** 难防御的,难保护的。**2.** 难辩解的;难辩护的。**3.** 难宽恕的。*an ~ position* 难以防御的阵地。~ *behaviour* 难以宽恕的行为。*an ~ argument* 站不住脚的论点。**-bly** ***ad.***

in·de·fin·a·bil·i·ty [ˌindiˈfainiˈbiliti; ˏɪndɪˋfaɪnɪˋbɪlətɪ] ***n.*** 难限定,难确定;难下定义。

in·de·fin·a·ble [ˌindiˈfainəbl; ˏɪndɪˋfaɪnəbl̩] **I** ***a.*** 难限定的,难确定的;难下定义的。**II** ***n.*** 难以下定义的事物。**-bly ad.**

in·def·i·nite [inˈdefinit; ɪnˋdɛfɪnɪt] ***a.*** (*opp.* definite) **1.** 模糊的,不明确的,不确定的。**2.** 无定限的,无限期的。**3.**【语法】不定的。*a strike of ~ duration* 无限期罢工。*an ~ answer* 含糊其词的回答。*the ~ article* 不定冠词〔*a, an*〕。~ *pronouns* 不定代名词。**4.**【植】(雄蕊)无定数的。***for an ~ time*** 无限期地。***in an ~ manner*** 模模糊糊地,不明确地。~ **integral**【数】不定积分,无定积分。**-ly** ***ad.***

in·def·i·nite·ness [inˈdefənitnis; ɪnˋdɛfənɪtnɪs] ***n.*** **1.** 无定限;〔尤指〕无准限;意思不精确;含糊;轮廓不分明;不明显;无把握;不确定。**2.**【植】(雄蕊的)无定数。**3.**【语法】不定(冠词)。

in·de·his·cent [ˌindiˈhisnt; ˏɪndɪˋhɪsnt] ***a.***【植】不裂的。~ *fruits* 闭果。**-cence** ***n.***

in·de·lib·er·ate [ˌindiˈlibərit; ˏɪndɪˋlɪbərɪt] ***a.*** 未经考虑的,非预谋的,非故意的。

in·del·i·ble [inˈdelibl; ɪnˋdɛlɪbl̩] ***a.*** 不能消除的,擦不掉的;持久的。~ *ink* 去不掉的墨渍。*an ~ pencil* 笔迹难擦掉的铅笔。**-bil·i·ty** [inˌdeliˈbiliti; ɪnˏdɛlɪˋbɪlətɪ] ***n.*** **-bly** ***ad.***

in·del·i·ca·cy [inˈdelikəsi; ɪnˋdɛlɪkəsɪ] ***n.*** **1.** 粗俗,淫猥,下流。**2.** 下流的举动,粗俗的事物。

in·del·i·cate [inˈdelikit; ɪnˋdɛlɪkɪt] ***a.*** **1.** 粗俗的。**2.** 淫猥的,下流的。~ *words* 粗俗的话。**-ly** ***ad.***

in·dem·ni·fi·ca·tion [inˌdemnifiˈkeiʃən; ɪnˏdɛmnəfəˋkeʃən] ***n.*** **1.** 保护,保障。**2.** 赦免。**3.** 赔偿,补偿。

in·dem·ni·fy [inˈdemnifai; ɪnˋdɛmnɪˏfaɪ] ***vt.*** **1.** 保护,保障 (*against*; *from*)。**2.** 赔偿,补偿 (*for*)。**3.** 使免于受罚。~ *sb. from* [*against*] *harm* 保证某人不受损害。~ *sb. for the loss incurred* 赔偿某人所受损失。

in·dem·ni·ty [inˈdemniti; ɪnˋdɛmnətɪ] ***n.*** **1.** 保护,保障。**2.** 损失赔偿,补偿。**3.** 赔偿金;(对战胜国的)赔款。**4.** 免罚,赦免。~ *insurance* 损失补偿保险。*a letter of ~* 赔偿保证书。*a war ~* 战争赔款。

in·de·mon·stra·ble [inˈdemənstrəbl, ˌindiˈmɔns-; ɪnˋdɛmənstrəbl, ˏɪndɪˋmɑns-] ***a.*** 不能证明的;无证明必要的,(道理)自明的。**-bly** ***ad.***

in·dene [ˈindiːn; ˋɪndin] ***n.***【化】茚〔制造合成树脂的原料〕。

in·dent[1] [inˈdent; ɪnˋdɛnt] **I** ***vt.*** **1.** 把…刻成锯齿状,使犬牙交错。**2.** 使弯入,使凹进。**3.** 一式二份[多份]地起草文件[合同等]。**4.**【印】把(每段的首行)缩排二字;【商】用双联订单订货。**5.**【英陆军】征用(物资)。— ***vi.*** 刻上齿痕;首行缩排二字;订约;【英陆军】进行征发;分发双联订单[委托书等]。~ *upon sb. for goods* 向某人订货。**II** ***n.*** **1.** 齿痕,缺刻。**2.** 双联订单;契约;购卖委托书。**3.**〔英〕征用令。**4.**【印】缩排。*order goods by* *means of an* ～ 用订单订货。

in·dent[2] [inˈdent; ɪnˋdɛnt] **I** ***vt*.** 在…上面压凹痕;压印(图案等)。**II** [ˈindent; ˋɪndɛnt] ***n*.** 凹痕。

in·den·ta·tion [ˌindenˈteiʃən; ˏɪndɛnˋteʃən] ***n*.** **1.** 呈锯齿形;缺刻。**2.** 海岸线凹入处。**3.** (印刷或书写中每段首行开端的)空格。**4.** 凹痕。～ *hardness*【物】压痕硬度。

in·dent·ed [inˈdentid; ɪnˋdɛntɪd] ***a*.** **1.** 锯齿状的,犬牙交错的;【印】首行缩排的。**2.** (学徒)有定期契约的。*an* ～ *coastline* 犬牙交错的海岸线。

in·den·tion [inˈdenʃən; ɪnˋdɛnʃən] ***n*.**【印】(行首)缩进;打缺刻;缺刻;凹入,锯齿形。

in·den·ture [inˈdentʃə; ɪnˋdɛntʃɚ] **I** ***n*.** **1.** 合同,契约。**2.**〔*pl*.〕定期服务契约;师徒合同。**3.**【法】(盖有骑缝章的)证书;(商业上的传票等)凭单。**4.** 打缺刻;缺刻;凹凸不平。***take up*** [***be out of***] ***one's*** ～***s*** 服务期满,学徒期满,契约期满。**II** ***vt*.** 立合同决定;用契约束缚(学徒)。

in·de·pend·ence [ˌindiˈpendəns; ˏɪndɪˋpɛndəns] ***n*.** **1.** 独立,自主,自立(*of*; *on*)。**2.** 足够维持闲居生活的收入。**3.** 独立心,自恃心。*national* ～ 民族独立。**I- Day** 美国独立纪念日[7 月 4 日]。

in·de·pend·en·cy [ˌindiˈpendənsi; ˏɪndɪˋpɛndənsɪ] ***n*.** **1.** 独立,自主,自立。**2.** 独立国,独立省。**3.**〔I-〕【宗】独立派运动,公理会教义。

in·de·pend·ent [ˌindiˈpendənt; ˏɪndɪˋpɛndənt] **I** ***a*.** **1.** 独立的,自主的,自治的,有主见的。**2.** 自食其力的,收入足够维持闲居生活的。**3.** 愿意独立的,独立不羁的,自尊心强的。**4.**〔I-〕【宗】独立派的。**5.**【政】无党无派的。**6.** 单独的,不承担义务的,不接受外援的。**7.**【语法】主要的,独立的。**8.**【数】无关的,独立的,无党无派的。*an* ～ *manner* 不愿受约束的样子。*an* ～ *voter* 无党无派选民。*an* ～ *attack*【军】单独进攻。*an* ～ *grocer* 独立经营的杂货商。*an* ～ *clause* (主从复合句中的)主句。*an* ～ *state* 独立国。～ *thinking* 独立思考。*an* ～ *income* 可过富裕生活的收入。***be*** ～ ***of*** **1.** 独立于…之外的,不受…支配的(*be* ～ *of control* 不受控制。*an objective law* ～ *of man's will* 不以人们意志为转移的客观规律)。**2.** 与…无关的,不倚赖…的(*be* ～ *of each other* 互无关系。*be* ～ *of one's parents* 不倚赖父母。*be* ～ *of doctors* 同医生无缘)。**II** ***n*.** **1.** 独立自主的人。**2.** 无党派人士。**3.**【宗】〔I-〕独立派教徒,公理会教徒。～ **counsel**〔美〕独立检查官(*Ms. Lewinsky reached an immunity and cooperation agreement with the Office of the Independent Counsel on July 28, 1998*. 莱温斯基小姐于 1998 年 7 月 28 日和独立检察官办公室达成了一项豁免及合作协议)。～ **functions**【数】独立函数。～ **variable**【数】自变数[量]。～ **tide**【地】独立潮。

in·de·pend·ent·ly [ˌindiˈpendəntli; ˏɪndɪˋpɛndəntlɪ] ***ad*.** 独立地,自主地;自由地,任意地。～ ***of*** 同…无关地,不取决于…地。

in-depth [ˈinˈdepθ; ˋɪnˋdɛpθ] ***a*.** 认真作出的;详细的;深入的;彻底的。*an* ～ *study* 深入的研究。

in·de·scrib·a·ble [ˌindiˈskraibəbl; ˏɪndɪˋskraɪbəbl] **I** ***a*.** **1.** 难于描述的,形容不出的。**2.** 模糊的,不明确的。～ *beauty* 无法形容的美丽。*an* ～ *sensation* 一种莫名其妙的感觉。**II** ***n*.**〔*pl*.〕〔俚〕裤子。**-bil·i·ty** [ˈindisˌkraibəˈbiliti; ˏɪndɪsˏkraɪbəˋbɪlətɪ] ***n*.** **-bly** ***ad*.**

in·de·struct·i·ble [ˌindiˈstrʌktəbl; ˏɪndɪˋstrʌktəbl] ***a*.** 不能破坏的,毁灭不了的;牢不可破的。**-bil·i·ty** [ˈindisˌtrʌktəˈbiliti; ˏɪndɪsˏtrʌktəˋbɪlətɪ] ***n*.** (*the indestructibility of matter* 物质的不灭性)。**-bly** ***ad*.**

in·de·ter·mi·na·ble [ˌindiˈtəːminəbl; ˏɪndɪˋtɝmɪnəbl] ***a*.** **1.** (问题、争执)不能决定的,不能解决的。**2.** 无法确定的,不能查明的。**-bly** ***ad*.**

in·de·ter·mi·na·cy [ˌindiˈtəːminəsi; ˏɪndɪˋtɝmɪnəsɪ] ***n*.** 不确定;不明确;犹豫不决(= indetermination)。～ **principle** = uncertainty principle.

in·de·ter·mi·nate [ˌindiˈtəːminit; ˏɪndɪˋtɝmɪnɪt] ***a*.** **1.** 不确定的,不定的,模糊的。**2.**【语】无确定音值的。**3.**【植】总状的,花被与花苞分隔而未被覆盖着的。**4.** 无结果的,未决定的,仍有疑问的。**5.**【数】不确定的,未定元的。*an* ～ *result* 不明确的结果。*an* ～ *vowel* 含糊母音。*an* ～ *sentence*【法】无定期徒刑。～ *analysis* 不定解析[分析]。*an* ～ *problem*【数】不定问题。～ *cleavage*【动】不定裂,不定形卵裂。**-ly** ***ad*.** **-ness** ***n*.**

in·de·ter·mi·na·tion [indiˌtəːmiˈneiʃən; ˏɪndɪˏtɝmɪˋneʃən] ***n*.** **1.** 不确定,不明确,模糊。**2.** 优柔寡断,犹豫不决。

in·de·ter·min·ism [ˌindiˈtəːminizəm; ˏɪndɪˋtɝmɪnɪzəm] ***n*.** **1.**【哲】非决定论,非定命论,意志自由论。**2.** 难以预测,不可预言。

in·de·ter·min·ist [ˌindiˈtəːminist; ˏɪndɪˋtɝmɪnɪst] **I** ***n*.** 非决定论者。**II** ***a*.** 非决定论的;非决定论者的。

in·dex [ˈindeks; ˋɪndɛks] **I** ***n*.** (*pl*. **-es**, **-di·ces** [-disiːz; -dɪsiz]) **1.** 索引。**2.** 指标,标准,标志。**3.** 示[食]指(=～ finger)。**4.** 指数。**5.**【印】指标,标记,参见号。**6.** (刻度盘上的)指针;【机】(铣床)分度(头)。**7.**〔the I-〕【天主】禁书目录。*card* ～*es* 卡片索引。*Style is an* ～ *of the mind*. 风格是心灵的反映。*the cost of living* ～ 生活费指数。*a price* ～ 物价。*an* ～ *pin* [*plate*] 指度针[盘]。*a fixed* ～ 固定瞄准器。**II** ***vt*.** **1.** 为…加索引;把…编入索引,指明,指出。**2.**〔美口〕按生活指数调整(价格)。— ***vi*.** 加索引。～ **arbitrage**【经】指数套利〔指几乎在同一时间购买和出售股票及相应的期货,利用其差价赚钱〕。～ **crime**〔美〕指数罪案〔联邦调查局每年分类罪案报告中所列的重罪〕。～ **error** 指数误差,指标误差,仪标误差。**I- Expurgatorius**〔L.〕【宗】(书中部分内容应予删节的)禁书目录。～ **fossil**【地】标准化石。～ **head** 分度头,分度器。**I- Librorum Prohibitorum**〔L.〕【宗】绝对禁书目录。～ **number** 指数。～ **of refraction**【物】折射指数。～ **signal** 指引信号,指示信号。**-er** ***n*.** 编索引的人。**-i·cal** ***a*.** **-less** ***a*.** 无索引的。

in·dex·a·tion [ˌindekˈseiʃən; ˏɪndɛkˋseʃən] ***n*.** **1.** 指数的使用。**2.** 指数的编制程序。**3.**【经】指数化〔在通货膨胀时按物价指数自动调整工资、利息等的办法〕。

in·dexed [ˈindekst; ˋɪndɛkst] ***a*.** **1.** 有索引的,编入索引的。**2.** 有(用作书签的)夹书带的。**3.**【计】被变址的。**4.** 与生活、物价指数挂钩的。

In·di·a[1] [ˈindjə, -diə; ˋɪndjə, -dɪə] ***n*.** 印度(亚洲)。～ **cotton** 印度花布。～ **ink** **1.** 墨。**2.** 墨汁。～**man** ***n*.** 印度航线班轮〔早年英国来往于印度和英国之间的商船,尤指英国东印度公司的大型商船〕。～ **paper** **1.** 摹拓纸。**2.** 圣经纸,字典纸。～ **rubber** 橡皮;橡胶;橡胶套鞋。

In·di·a[2] [ˈindiə; ˋɪndɪə] ***n*.** 通信中用以代表字母 i 的词。

In·di·an [ˈindjən, -diən; ˋɪndjən, -dɪən] **I** ***a*.** **1.** 印度的;印度人的;印度文化的。**2.** 西印度群岛的,西印度群岛文化的;印第安人的,印第安文化的。**3.** 玉米做的。**II** ***n*.** **1.** 印度人。**2.** 印第安人(= American ～ 或 Red ～)。**3.** 印第安语。**4.** 过去长期住在印度的欧洲人〔尤指英国人〕。**5.**〔the ～〕【天】印度人座。**6.**〔口〕= ～ corn. ～ **agency** (美国及加拿大的)印第安事务厅。～ **agent** (美国及加拿大的)印第安事务官。～ **bread** **1.** 玉米面包。**2.** = tuckahoe.【体】火棒,瓶状棒。～ **corn**〔英〕玉蜀黍,玉米,苞米。～ **file** 一路纵队。～ **gift**〔口〕送出后企图对方退回的礼物,期待对方还礼的礼物。～ **giver**〔口〕送礼给人以后又索回的人;企图对方还礼而送礼的人。～ **hay**〔美俚〕大麻。～ **hemp** **1.** 磁麻(*Apocynum cannabium*)〔产于美洲。印第安人用其纤维结绳,用其根作药〕。**2.** 大麻(= hemp)。～ **ink** = India ink. ～ **licorice** = jequirity. ～ **mallow**【植】苘麻(*Abutilon theophrasti*)。～ **meal**〔英〕玉米粉。～ **millet** 食用高粱。～ **Mutiny** 印度反英暴动〔1857—1858 年印度士兵反对英国殖民政策的暴动〕。～ **ocean** 印度洋。～ **paintbrush**【植】扁萼花属(*Castilleja*)植物〔尤指红

扁萼花(*C. coccinea*))。~ **pipe** 水晶兰(*Monotropa uniflora*)〔产于北半球〕。~ **pudding** 玉米奶油布丁。~ **red** 1. 印度红〔北美印第安人用以表示战争的涂料〕。2.【化】三氧化铁,氧化正铁。~ **sign** 妖符,不祥的东西〔主用于 ***to have*** (或 ***put***) ***the*** ~ ***sign on*** 短语中〕。~ **states and Agencies** 印度半独立诸邦和管理区。~ **summer** 1. 晚秋的晴暖气候,小阳春。2. 宁静愉快的晚年。~ **Territory** 印第安人保留地〔美国的印第安人居住地区〕。~ **tobacco**【植】路萃利草(祛痰菜)(*Lobelia inflata*)〔一种一年生有毒植物。产于美国东部〕。~ **turnip**【植】印度天南星(*Arisaema triphyllum*)或其根〔也叫 Jack-in-the-pulpit〕。~ **weed** 烟草。~ **wrestling** 1. 扳腕子。2. 拽推比试〔两人右足相抵,右手相握,以强使对方身体失去平衡为止〕。

In·di·an·a [ˌindiˈænə; ˏɪndɪˋænə] ***n.*** 印第安纳〔美国州名〕。

In·di·an·an, In·di·an·i·an [ˌindiˈænən, ˌindiˈæniən; ˏɪndɪˋænən, ˏɪndɪˋænɪən] **I** ***n.*** 印第安纳州人。**II** ***a.*** 印第安纳州的,印第安纳州人的。

In·di·an·ap·o·lis [ˈindiəˈnæpəlis; ˏɪndɪəˋnæpəlɪs] ***n.*** 印第安纳波利斯〔美国城市〕。

In·di·an·ize [ˈindjənaiz, -diə-; ˋɪndjənaɪz, -dɪə-] ***vt.*** 使印度人化,使印度化。**In·di·an·i·za·tion** ***n.***

In·dic [ˈindik; ˋɪndɪk] ***a.*** 1. 印度的。2. 印度—伊朗语族的〔包括印度、巴基斯坦、斯里兰卡过去和现在所讲的多种语言〕。

indic. = indicating; indicative.

in·di·can [ˈindikæn; ˋɪndɪkæn] ***n.***【化】吲哚-3-硫酸。

in·di·cant [ˈindikənt; ˋɪndɪkənt] **I** ***a.*** 指示的。**II** ***n.*** 指示物;【医】病症。

in·di·cate [ˈindikeit; ˋɪndɪket] ***vt.*** 1. 指示,表示;指出。2.【医】表明(症状、原因),需要(治疗方法等);象征,暗示,预示。3. 简单陈述。*Snow ~s the coming of winter.* 下雪表示冬天的到来。~ *assent* (用脸色、动作或态度)表示同意。~**d horse-power**【机】指示马力〔略 i. h. p.〕。~**d power**【机】指示功率。~**d work**【机】指示功。

in·di·ca·tion [ˌindiˈkeiʃən; ˏɪndɪˋkeʃən] ***n.*** 1. 指示,指出,表示。2. 象征,征兆,迹象。3.【医】指示法,适效,指征,适应症。4. 指示器表示的量(或度数)。*There is every ~ (no ~) that we shall have an earthquake.* 所有的[没有]迹象表明,将要发生(一次)地震。

in·dic·a·tive [inˈdikətiv; ɪnˋdɪkətɪv] **I** ***a.*** 1.【语法】陈述的,直陈的。2. 指示…的,表示…的 (*of*)。*the ~ mood* 陈述语气。*Is a high forehead ~ of great mental power?* 前额高表示智慧高吗? **II** ***n.***【语法】陈述语气。**-ly** ***ad.***

in·di·ca·tor [ˈindikeitə; ˋɪndɪketɚ] ***n.*** 1. 指示者;指示物;标识。2.【化】指示剂。3.【机】指示器,示功器。*an ~ card [diagram]* 示功图。*revolution ~* 转速计。*speed ~* 速度计。

in·di·ca·to·ry [inˈdikətəri; ɪnˋdɪkətərɪ] ***a.*** 指示的,表示的 (*of*)。

in·di·ca·trix [ˌindiˈkeitriks; ˏɪndɪˋketrɪks] ***n.*** 1.【数】指标;指示量;指示线,特征曲线。*spherical ~ of scattering* 球面散射指示量。*curvature ~* 曲率指示线。2. 光率体。~ *of optical diaxial crystal* 二轴晶光率体。

in·di·ces [ˈindisiːz; ˋɪndɪsiz] index 的复数。

in·di·ci·a [inˈdiʃiə; ɪnˋdɪʃɪə] ***n.*** indicium 的复数。

in·di·ci·al [inˈdiʃiəl; ɪnˋdɪʃɪəl] ***a.*** 1. 标记的;显示的,指示的。2. 索引的。3. 食指的。

in·di·ci·um [inˈdiʃiəm; ɪnˋdɪʃɪəm] ***n.*** (*pl.* ***in·di·ci·a*** [inˈdiʃiə; ɪnˋdɪʃɪə]) 1. 征候,表示,记号。2.〔美〕(大宗邮件上盖的)邮资总付邮戳。

in·dict [inˈdait; ɪnˋdaɪt] ***vt.***【法】控告,告发,对…起诉。~ *sb. for thief* 控告某人犯有盗窃罪。~ *sb. as a thief* 指控某人为窃贼。*He was ~ed on a charge of thief.* 他因犯盗窃罪被起诉。**-ion** [inˈdikʃən; ɪnˋdɪkʃən] ***n.***

in·dict·a·ble [inˈdaitəbl; ɪnˋdaɪtəbḷ] ***a.*** 可以起诉[告发]的;应起诉的,应告发的。*an ~ offence* 刑事罪。*an ~ offender* 刑事犯。*an offence not ~* 不论罪。

in·dict·ee [ˌindaiˈtiː; ˏɪndaɪˋti] ***n.***【法】被告。

in·dict·er, in·dict·or [inˈdaitə; ɪnˋdaɪtɚ] ***n.***【法】起诉人,原告。

in·dic·tion [inˈdikʃən; ɪnˋdɪkʃən] ***n.*** 1.【罗马史】定额征税法〔罗马皇帝君士坦丁制订的以十五年为一期的征收定额财政税的制度〕。2. 十五年定额税。3. 十五年纪期。4. 十五年纪期中的任何一年。5.〔古〕宣告,公布。

in·dict·ment [inˈdaitmənt; ɪnˋdaɪtmənt] ***n.*** 1. 控告,起诉,告发。2. 诉状,起诉书。*bring in an ~ against sb.* 控告某人。*a bill of ~* 起诉书[状子]。

in·die [ˈindi; ˋɪndɪ] ***n.***〔美俚〕1. 独立经营的电影院[广播电台、电视台]。2. 独立艺术家[团体]。

In·dies [ˈindiz; ˋɪndɪz] ***n.***〔*pl.*〕〔the ~〕东印度群岛 (= the East ~);西印度群岛 (= the West ~)。

in·dif·fer·ence [inˈdifrəns; ɪnˋdɪfrəns], **in·dif·fer·en·cy** [-si; -sɪ] ***n.*** 1. 不关心,不计较,冷淡 (*to; towards*)。2. 不重要,不在乎。3. 中立,中性。4.【语法】任凭关系〔no matter how 或 whatever 等引导的子句所表示的结构〕。*show ~ to personal affairs* 不计较个人的事。*a matter of ~* 无关紧要的事。***with*** ~ 冷淡地,满不在乎地(*face death with supreme ~* 置生死于度外)。

in·dif·fer·ent [inˈdifrənt; ɪnˋdɪfrənt] **I** ***a.*** 1. 漠不关心的,冷淡的,不感兴趣的。2. 公平的,中立的,不偏袒的。3. 平凡的。4. 无关紧要的,无足轻重的,满不在乎的。5.【物】中性的,惰性的。6.【生】未分化的。~ *to hardships and dangers* 置困难危险于度外。*an ~ judge* 铁面无私的法官。*remain ~ in a dispute* 对争论保持中立。*an ~ book* 质量不高的书。*an ~ performance* 水准不高的演出。*meet with ~ success* 获得不大的成功。*be in ~ health* 健康状况不佳。*It is quite ~ to me whether you go or not.* 你去不去,我都无所谓。~ *equilibrium*【物】随遇平衡。*the ~ gas* 惰性气体。*a ~ point* 中性点。**be ~ to** 对…不关心(*be ~ to the sufferings of others* 不关心别人的痛苦)。**II** ***n.*** (对政治、宗教等)冷淡的人。

in·dif·fer·ent·ism [inˈdifərəntizəm; ɪnˋdɪfərəntɪzm] ***n.*** (对宗教的)冷淡主义;冷淡态度;【宗】信教无差别论;冷淡;无差别。**in·dif·fer·ent·ist** ***n.*** 冷淡主义者。

in·dif·fer·ent·ly [inˈdifrəntli; ɪnˋdɪfrəntlɪ] ***ad.*** 1. 不关心地,冷淡地,漫然,漠然。2. 无差别地;无可无不可地;普通地;差得很地〔常同 *but*, *very* 等词连用〕。*look on ~ at a match* 冷淡地参观比赛。*play but ~* 玩得相当糟糕。

in·di·gence, in·di·gen·cy [ˈindidʒəns, -si; ˋɪndɪdʒəns, -sɪ] ***n.*** 贫穷,穷困。

in·di·gene [ˈindidʒiːn; ˋɪndɪdʒin] ***n.*** 当地人;土生的动物[植物]。

in·dig·e·nous [inˈdidʒinəs; ɪnˋdɪdʒɪnəs] ***a.*** 1. 本土的,土生土长的。2. 生来的;为…所固有的 (*to*)。*use ~ raw materials* 就地取材。*an ~ population* 土著居民。*feelings ~ to human beings* 人类固有的感情。**-ly** ***ad.*** **-ness** ***n.***

in·di·gent [ˈindidʒənt; ˋɪndɪdʒənt] ***a.*** 贫困的,贫穷的。**-ly** ***ad.***

in·di·gest·ed [ˌindiˈdʒestid, ˌindaiˈdʒestid; ˏɪndɪˋdʒɛstɪd, ˏɪndaɪˋdʒɛstɪd] ***a.*** 1. 难消化的,不消化的。2. 考虑未成熟的,杂乱的,条理不清的,生硬的。

in·di·gest·i·ble [ˌindiˈdʒestəbl, ˌindaiˈdʒestəbl; ˏɪndɪˋdʒɛstəbḷ, ˏɪndaɪˋdʒɛstəbḷ] ***a.*** 1. 不消化的,难消化的。2. 难理解的,难领略的。**-bil·i·ty** [ˈindiˌdʒestəˈbiliti; ˏɪndɪˏdʒɛstəˋbɪlətɪ] ***n.*** **-bly** ***ad.***

in·di·ges·tion [ˌindiˈdʒestʃən, ˌindaiˈdʒestʃən; ˏɪndɪ-

ˋdʒɛstʃən, ˏɪndaɪˋdʒɛstʃən] **n.** 1. 消化不良,胃弱。2. 杂乱,生硬,难理解。*suffer from* ~ 患消化不良症。*have an attack of* ~ 患消化不良。

in·di·ges·tive [ˌindiˈdʒestiv, ˌindaiˈdʒestiv; ˏɪndɪˋdʒɛstɪv, ˏɪndaɪˋdʒɛstɪv] **a.** 消化不良的,不消化的。

in·dign [inˈdain; ɪnˋdaɪn] **a.** 〔废、诗〕1. 不值得的,无价值的。2. 耻辱的,丢脸的。

in·dig·nant [inˈdignənt; ɪnˋdɪgnənt] **a.** 愤怒的,愤慨的。*be* ~ *at a false accusation* 对诬告愤愤不平。*be* ~ *with a cruel person* 对凶残的人感到愤慨。**-ly** **ad.**

in·dig·na·tion [ˌindigˈneiʃən; ˏɪndɪgˋneʃən] **n.** 愤怒,愤慨,义愤。*arouse the* ~ *of the people* 激起人民的愤怒。*an* ~ *ineeting* 声讨大会。

in·dig·ni·ty [inˈdigniti; ɪnˋdɪgnətɪ] **n.** 轻蔑,侮辱;侮辱的言行。*be subjected to indignities* 受辱。*put an* ~ *upon sb*. [*treat sb. with* ~] 侮辱某人。

in·di·go [ˈindigəu; ˋɪndɪgo] **n.** (*pl*. ~*s*, ~*es*) 1. 靛蓝,靛青;靛蓝类染料。2. 一种深蓝色。3.【植】能产生靛蓝的植物。*the Chinese* ~ 草本靛青。*the Indian* ~木本靛青。*the* ~ *plant* 木蓝。~ **blue** 1. = indigotin. 2. 靛蓝〔光谱七色之一〕。~**blue** **a.** 靛蓝色的。~ **snake**【动】1. 森王靛蛇 (*Drymarchon corais couperi*)〔出现于美国南卡罗来纳到德克萨斯间的低地〕。2. 褐牛蛇(= bull snake)。

in·di·goid [ˈindigɔid; ˋɪndɪgɔɪd] **I** **a.** 靛类的。**II** **n.** 靛类染料。

in·di·go·sol [ˈindigəusɔl; ˋɪndɪgoˏsɑl] **n.**【化】溶靛素(染料)。

in·di·got·ic [ˌindiˈgɔtik; ˏɪndɪˋgɑtɪk] **a.** 靛蓝的,靛青的。

in·dig·o·tin [inˈdigətin; ɪnˋdɪgətɪn] **n.**【化】靛。

in·di·rect [ˌindiˈrekt, -dai-; ˏɪndɪˋrɛkt, -daɪ-] **a.** 1. 间接的,第二手的;迂回的;曲折的。2. 不直截了当的,不坦率的,不诚实的。*an* ~ *answer* 侧面回答。~ *descent* 旁系。~ *fire*【军】间接射击。*an* ~ *route* 迂回的路,绕行的路。*make an* ~ *reference to sb*. 间接提到某人。~ *methods* 不正当的手段。~ **discourse** [**narration**, **speech**] 间接引语。~ **evidence**【法】间接证据。~ **lighting** 间接照明,无影照明。~ **object**【语法】间接受词。~ **passive**【语法】间接被动语态。~ **proof**【逻】间接论证法,归谬法〔反证法的一种,即为了证明原论题的真,而先证明反论题的假〕。~ **tax** 间接税。**-ly** **ad.** **-ness** **n.**

in·di·rec·tion [ˌindiˈrekʃən; ˏɪndɪˋrɛkʃən] **n.** 1. 间接,迂回。2. 不诚实,欺骗。*by* ~ 拐弯抹角地,兜着圈子,间接地。

in·dis·cern·i·ble [ˌindiˈsə:nəbl; ˏɪndɪˋsɝnəbl̩] **a.** 觉察不出的;难辨别的。**-bly** **ad.**

in·dis·cerp·ti·ble [ˌindiˈsə:ptəbl; ˏɪndɪˋsɝptəbl̩] **a.** 不能溶解的,不会溶解的。**-ti·bil·i·ty** [ˈindiˌsə:ptəˈbiliti; ˋɪndɪˏsɝptəˋbɪlətɪ] **n.**

in·dis·ci·pline [inˈdisiplin; ɪnˋdɪsɪplɪn] **n.** 无纪律,缺乏训练。**-plina·ble** **a.** [罕]难驾驭的;训练不好的。

in·dis·creet [ˌindisˈkri:t; ˏɪndɪsˋkrit] **a.** 欠慎重的,轻率的;不得体的。*Is it* ~ *to ask you the reason*? 问问理由可以吗? **-ly** **ad.**

in·dis·crete [ˌindisˈkri:t; ˏɪndɪsˋkrit] **a.** 不分开的;紧凑的。

in·dis·cre·tion [ˌindisˈkreʃən; ˏɪndɪsˋkrɛʃən] **n.** 欠考虑,不慎重,轻率;轻率的言行。*have the* ~ *to do sth*. 居然轻率地做某事。*commit a grave* ~ 生活极不检点〔尤指男女关系〕。

in·dis·crim·i·nate [ˌindisˈkriminit; ˏɪndɪsˋkrɪmɪnɪt] **a.** 1. 不加区别的,不分青红皂白的。2. 任性的,杂乱的。*an* ~ *reader* 乱读书的人。*be* ~ *in making friends* 乱交朋友。*deal out* ~ *blows* 乱打一气。**-ly** **ad.** **-ness** **n.**

in·dis·crim·i·nat·ing [ˈindisˌkrimineitiŋ; ˋɪndɪsˏkrɪmɪnetɪŋ] **a.** 不加区别的,无选择的 (= undiscriminating)。**-ly** **ad.**

in·dis·crim·i·na·tion [ˈindisˌkrimiˈneiʃən; ˋɪndɪsˏkrɪmɪˋneʃən] **n.** 1. 不加区别,无选择,混淆。2. 任意;任性。

in·dis·crim·i·na·tive [ˌindisˈkriminətiv; ˏɪndɪsˋkrɪmɪnətɪv] **a.** 不加区别的。

in·dis·pen·sa·ble [ˌindisˈpensəbl; ˏɪndɪsˋpɛnsəbl] **a.** 1. 不可缺少的,必需的,重要的 (*to*; *for*)。2. 不能撇开的,责无旁贷的。*Air and water are* ~ *to life*. 空气和水是生命所必需的。*an* ~ *obligation* 不可推卸的责任。**-bil·i·ty**, **-ness** **n.** **-bly** **ad.**

in·dis·pose [ˌindisˈpəuz; ˏɪndɪsˋpoz] **vt.** 1. 使厌恶,使不愿。2. 使不适合,使不适当,使不能。3. 使不舒服。*Illness* ~*s a man for enjoyment*. 疾病使人不想娱乐。

in·dis·posed [ˌindisˈpəuzd; ˏɪndɪsˋpozd] **a.** 1. 不舒服的,有病的。2. 厌倦的,不愿的。*I am* ~ *with a cold*. 我因为伤风感到不舒服。*He is* ~ *to go*. 他不愿去。*be* ~ *towards sb*. 讨厌某人。

in·dis·po·si·tion [ˌindispəˈziʃən; ˏɪndɪspəˋzɪʃən] **n.** 1. 不舒服,小病。2. 不想,厌恶。

in·dis·pu·ta·ble [ˌindisˈpju:təbl; ˏɪndɪsˋpjutəbl̩] **a.** 不可争辩的,无可置疑的。**-bil·i·ty**, **-ness** **n.** **-bly** **ad.**

in·dis·sol·u·ble [ˌindiˈsɔljubl; ˏɪndɪˋsɑljəbl̩] **a.** 1. 难溶解的;不能分解的;不能分离的。2. 坚固的;永久不变的。*an* ~ *friendship* 牢不可破的友谊。**-bil·i·ty** **n.** 不溶解性;不分解性;不变性,永久性。**-bly** **ad.**

in·dis·tinct [ˌindisˈtiŋkt; ˏɪndɪsˋtɪŋkt] **a.** 不清楚的,模糊的;朦胧的,不确定的。~ *memories* 模糊的记忆。~ *speech* 暧昧不明的话。**-ly** **ad.** **-ness** **n.**

in·dis·tinc·tion [indisˈtiŋkʃən; ɪndɪsˋtɪŋkʃən] **n.** 不清楚,模糊;不确定,难辨认;同等,同格。

in·dis·tinc·tive [ˌindisˈtiŋktiv; ˏɪndɪsˋtɪŋktɪv] **a.** 不显著的,无特色的;无差别的。**-ly** **ad.**

in·dis·tin·guish·a·ble [ˌindisˈtiŋgwiʃəbl; ˏɪndɪsˋtɪŋgwɪʃəbl̩] **a.** 1. 难区别的,不能辨别的。2. 无特征的。**-bly** **ad.** **-ness** **n.**

in·dis·trib·u·ta·ble [ˌindisˈtribjutəbl; ˏɪndɪsˋtrɪbjutəbl̩] **a.** 不可分配的,不可散布的。

in·dite [inˈdait; ɪnˋdaɪt] **vt.** 〔罕〕著作,写(诗、文等)。~ *a speech* [*poem*] 写演讲稿[诗]。**-ment** **n.** **-r** **n.** 撰述人,作者。

in·di·um [ˈindiəm; ˋɪndɪəm] **n.**【化】铟。

in·di·vert·i·ble [ˌindaiˈvə:təbl; ˏɪndaɪˋvɝtəbl̩] **a.** 不能引开的,难使转向的;难使分心的。**-bly** **ad.**

individ. = individual.

in·di·vid·u·al [ˌindiˈvidjuəl; ˏɪndɪˋvɪdjuəl] **I** **a.** 1. 单一的,个别的,单独的。2. 个人的,个体的。3. 特殊的,特有的,独特的 (*opp*. general, universal)。*give* ~ *attention* [*instruction*] 给予个别注意[教导]。*each* ~ *person* 各个人。*an* ~ *style of speaking* 独特的谈话风格。*a set of* ~ *tea cups* (花色等)各不相同的一套茶杯。**II** **n.** 个人 (*opp*. society, family) 个体,独立单位;〔俚〕人。*a disagreeable* ~讨厌的家伙。*an agreeable* ~ 好人。*a private* ~ 私人,个人。*representative* ~*s* 代表人物。

in·di·vid·u·al·ism [ˌindiˈvidjuəlizəm; ˏɪndɪˋvɪdjuəlɪzəm] **n.** 1. 个人主义,利己主义。2. 个性,独特性。3. 不干涉主义;自由放任主义。

in·di·vid·u·al·ist [ˌindiˈvidjuəlist; ˏɪndɪˋvɪdjuəlɪst] **I** **n.** 个人主义者,利己主义者。**II** **a.** 个人主义的;个人主义者的。*an* ~ *careerist* 个人主义野心家。

in·di·vid·u·al·is·tic [ˌindiˌvidjuəˈlistik; ˏɪndɪˏvɪdjuəˋlɪstɪk] **a.** 个人主义的,个人主义者的。~ *heroism* 个人英雄主义。

in·di·vid·u·al·i·ty [ˌindiˌvidjuˈæliti; ˏɪndɪˏvɪdjuˋælətɪ] *n*. 1. 个体;个人;独立存在。2. 个人的特征,个性。3. 〔*pl*.〕个人的趣味(或嗜好)。*a man of marked* ~ 个性特别的人。

in·di·vid·u·al·ize [ˌindiˈvidjuəlaiz; ˌɪndɪˋvɪdjuəlaɪz] *vt*. 1. 使各不相同,使个体化;使个性化,使有个人特色。2. 一一列举,分别详述。*His peculiar style strongly ~s his work*. 他的特殊文体使他的作品带有显著的个性。**-i·za·tion** [ˌindiˌvidjuəlaiˈzeiʃən; ˏɪndɪˏvɪdjuəlaɪˋzeʃən] *n*.

in·di·vid·u·al·ly [ˌindiˈvidjuəli; ˏɪndɪˋvɪdjuəlɪ] *ad*. 1. 以个人资格。2. 个性上,个别地,各自地,独特地。*traits ~ different* 各不相同的特征。

in·di·vid·u·ate [ˌindiˈvidjueit; ˏɪndɪˋvɪdjʊˏet] *vt*. 使个体化,使具体化,使有个性,使具特色。**-a·tion** *n*. 个性化,个别化。

in·di·vis·i·bil·i·ty [ˈindiˌviziˈbiliti; ˏɪndɪˏvɪzəˋbɪlətɪ] *n*. 不可分性。

in·di·vis·i·ble [ˌindiˈvizəbl; ˏɪndɪˋvɪzəbl̩] I *a*. 1. 不可分割的。2. 【数】除不尽的。II *n*. 不能分割的东西;极微分子,微量。**-bly** *ad*.

In·do- [ˈindəu; ˋɪndo] *comb. f*. 表示"印度";"印度种"。

In·do-Ar·y·an [ˈindəuˈɛəriən, -jən; ˋɪndoˋærɪən, -jən] I *a*. 1. 印度—雅利安族的;印度—雅利安语的。2. = Indic. II *n*. 〔罕〕讲印度语支的一种语言的印度人。

In·do-Chi·na [ˈindəuˈtʃainə; ˋɪndoˋtʃaɪnə] *n*. 印度支那〔亚洲〕。

In·do-Chi·nese [ˈindəu-tʃaiˈniːz; ˋɪndo-tʃaɪˋniz] I *n*. 印度支那人。II *a*. 印度支那的,印度支那人的。

in·do·cile [inˈdəusail; ɪnˋdosaɪl] *a*. 难驯服的,倔强的。

in·do·cil·i·ty [ˌindəuˈsiliti; ˏɪndoˋsɪlətɪ] *n*. 难驯服,倔强。

in·doc·tri·nate [inˈdɔktrineit; ɪnˋdaktrɪˏnet] *vt*. 1. 教训。2. 灌输。~ *sb. with an idea* [*a belief*] 给某人灌输某种思想[信仰]。**-na·tion** [inˌdɔktriˈneiʃən; ɪnˏdaktrɪˋneʃən] *n*.

In·do-Eu·ro·pe·an [ˈindəuˌjuərəˈpiːən; ˏɪndoˏjʊrəˋpiən] I *a*. 印欧语系的。II *n*. 印欧语系;说印欧语系语言的人。

In·do-Ger·man·ic [ˈindəudʒəːˈmænik; ˋɪndodʒɚˋmænɪk] *a*., *n*. = Indo-European.

In·do-Hit·tite [ˈindəuˈhitait; ˋɪndoˋhɪtaɪt] *n*. 1. 印度—赫提语系〔包括印欧语和安纳托利亚语〕。2. 印欧语和赫提语的母语〔赫提语被认为是印欧语系的一个语族〕。

In·do-I·ra·ni·an [ˈindəuiˈreiniən; ˋɪndoɪˋrenɪən] I *a*. 印度—伊朗语族的。II *n*. 印度语和伊朗语的母语。

in·dole [ˈindəul; ˋɪndol] *n*. 【化】吲哚;氮(杂)茚。

in·dole·a·ce·tic [ˈindəuliəˈsiːtik; ˋɪndolɪəˋsitɪk] **acid** 【化】吲哚乙酸,吲哚醋酸。

in·dole·bu·tyr·ic [ˈindəulbjuːˈtirik; ˋɪndolbjuˋtɪrɪk] **acid** 【化】吲哚丁酸。

in·do·lence [ˈindələns; ˋɪndələns] *n*. 1. 懒惰,不积极。2. 【医】不痛,小痛。

in·do·lent [ˈindələnt; ˋɪndələnt] *a*. 1. 懒惰的,不积极的。2. 【医】不痛的,小痛的。*an ~ cyst* 无痛囊肿。**-ly** *ad*.

in·dom·i·ta·ble [inˈdɔmitəbl; ɪnˋdamɪtəbl̩] *a*. 不可屈服的,不屈不挠的;大无畏的;不气馁的。*an ~ spirit* 一往无前的精神,大无畏的精神。*an ~ will* 百折不回的毅力。*an ~ struggle* 不屈不挠的斗争。**-bly** *ad*.

In·do·ne·sia [ˌindəuˈniːzjə; ˏɪndoˋniʃə] *n*. 印度尼西亚〔亚洲〕。

In·do·ne·sian [ˌindəuˈniːʃən, -ʒən; ˏɪndoˋniʃən, -ʒən] I *n*. 印度尼西亚人;印度尼西亚语。II *a*. 印度尼西亚的;印度尼西亚人的;印度尼西亚语的。

in·door [ˈindɔː; ˋɪndɔr] *a*. (*opp*. outdoor) 1. 屋内的,室内的。2. 待在家里的。3. 〔英〕救济院内的。~ *games* 室内游戏。~ *antenna* 室内天线。*an ~ child* 待在家里的孩子。~ *relief* 救济院内的救济品。

in·doors [ˈinˈdɔːz; ˋɪnˋdɔrz] *ad*. 在屋里。*go* ~ 到屋里。*keep* [*stay*] ~ 待在家里,不外出。

in·do·phe·nol [ˌindəuˈfiːnəul, -nɔːl; ˏɪndoˋfinol, -nɔl] *n*. 【纺】靛酚。

in·dor·sa·tion [ˌindɔːˈseiʃən; ˏɪndɔrˋseʃən] *n*. = endorsement.

in·dorse [inˈdɔːs; ɪnˋdɔrs] *vt*. = endorse.

in·dor·see [ˌindɔːˈsiː; ˏɪndɔrˋsi] *n*. = endorsee.

in·dox·yl [inˈdɔksl; ɪnˋdaksl̩] *n*. 【化】吲哚酚。

in·dra [ˈindrə; ˋɪndrə] *n*. 〔印度神话〕因陀罗〔印度神话中印度教的主神、雷神及雨神的人格化〕。

in·draft, in·draught [ˈindrɑːft; ˋɪndrɑft] *n*. 1. 引入,吸入。2. 向内的气流或水流。3. 〔古〕引诱,魅力。

in·du·bi·ta·ble [inˈdjuːbitəbl; ɪnˋdjubɪtəbl̩] *a*. 不容置疑的,明确的。**-bil·i·ty** [inˌdjuːbitəˈbiliti; ɪnˏdjubɪtəˋbɪlətɪ], **-ness** *n*. **-bly** *ad*.

induc. = induction.

in·duce [inˈdjuːs; ɪnˋdjus] *vi*. 1. 劝诱,诱导,敦促。2. 引导,导致。3. 【逻】归纳 (*opp*. deduce)。4. 【电】感应。~ *sb. to do sth*. 劝诱某人做某事。*Nothing shall ~ me to go*. 我怎么都不去。~ *abortion* 人工流产,引产。*weakness ~d by starvation* 因贫困引起的衰弱。*~d current* 感应电流。~ *radioactivity* 感应放射性。*~d velocity* 诱导速度。*inducing current* 施感电流。

in·duce·ment [inˈdjuːsmənt; ɪnˋdjusmənt] *n*. 1. 诱导,劝诱。2. 诱因,动机。3. 【法】提出主张事项前的陈述说明。*have many ~s* [*much ~*] *to do sth*. 很想做某事。

in·duc·er [inˈdjuːsə; ɪnˋdjusɚ] *n*. 1. 诱导者,劝诱者。2. 【化】诱导物。3. 【机】(离心式鼓风机、压缩机泵的)进口段。4. 【电】电感器,诱导体。

in·duct [inˈdʌkt; ɪnˋdʌkt] *vt*. 1. (通过仪式)使就职 (*to*; *into*; *as*)。2. 使正式入会;征调…入伍 (*to*; *into*)。3. 使初步入门,介绍(知识等)。4. 引入,引导。5. 【电】感应,感生。~ *sb. to an office of mayor* 使某人就任市长。~ *sb. into a seat* 引人就座。

in·duct·ance [inˈdʌktəns; ɪnˋdʌktəns] *n*. 【电】电感,感应现象;感应系数;(发动机)进气。~ *bridge* 电感电桥。

in·duct·ee [ˌindʌkˈtiː; ˏɪndʌkˋti] *n*. 就任者;入会者;〔美〕应征(入伍)者。

in·duc·tile [inˈdʌktail; ɪnˋdʌktaɪl] *a*. 1. 没有延性的,不能拉长的。2. 难塑造的,不易弯曲的。3. 不顺从的,难驾驭的。

in·duc·tion [inˈdʌkʃən; ɪnˋdʌkʃən] *n*. 1. 引入,诱发,诱导(作用)。2. 【逻】归纳法,归纳推理 (*opp*. deduction)。3. 就职,就职典礼;入会,入伍。4. 【电】感应,感应现象。5. 〔古〕导言,序幕。6. 首次经验,入门。7. 吸入。*make an ~ from* 由…归纳出来的。*mutual ~* 互感应。*self ~* 自感应。*air ~* 吸气。~ **centre** 征兵中心。~ **coil** 【电】感应线圈,电感线圈。~ **field** 【电】感应磁场,感应电场。~ **furnace** 【冶】感应电炉。~ **heating** 【电】感应加热。~ **motor** 【电】感应电动机,异步电动机。~ **pipe** 进口管。~ **stroke** 【机】吸入冲程。~ **valve** 【机】吸入阀,进气门。**-less** *a*. 无感应的。

in·duc·tive [inˈdʌktiv; ɪnˋdʌktɪv] *a*. 1. 引入的,诱导的 (*to*)。2. 【逻】归纳的,归纳法的 (*opp*. deductive)。3. 【电】感应的,电感的。4. 导论的,绪论的。~ *reasoning* 归纳推理。*an ~ method* 归纳法。*an ~ coil* 有感线圈,电感线圈。*the ~ capacity* 电感容量,电容。~ *coupling* 电感耦合。*the ~ reactance* 【电】感抗。**-ly** *ad*. **-ness** *n*.

in·duc·tiv·i·ty [ˌindʌkˈtiviti; ˏɪndʌkˋtɪvətɪ] *n*. 诱导性;【电】诱导率,感应率,介电常数,电容率。

in·duc·tor [inˈdʌktə; ɪnˋdʌktɚ] *n*. 1. 引导者,授职人。2. 【电】感应器,感应体,感应物,电感线圈,电感器。3. 手摇磁石发电机。4. 【化】诱导物。

in·duc·to·syn [inˈdʌktəsin; ɪnˋdʌktəsɪn] *n*. 【无】感应

I

式传感器。

in·due [in'dju:; ɪn`dju] *vt*. = endue.

in·dulge [in'dʌldʒ; ɪn`dʌldʒ] *vt*. **1.** 纵情,沉迷,沉溺。**2.** 放任,纵容,娇养。**3.** 使满足,使快乐。**4.** 迁就。**5.** 【商】容许延期付款。**6.** 【天主】赦免,恕罪;赋予特权。~ *one's appetite for sweets* 特别爱吃甜食。~ *oneself in smoking* 纵情抽烟。~ *a child* 纵容孩子。~ *the company with a song* 唱歌给大家助兴。*It is sometimes necessary to* ~ *a sick child*. 迁就一个生病的小孩,有时是必要的。— *vi*. **1.** 〔口〕酗酒,嗜酒。**2.** 纵情,沉迷,沉溺。*Will you* ~? 喝一杯吧! ~ *in dreams* 爱空想。

in·dul·gence [in'dʌldʒəns; ɪn`dʌldʒəns] **in·dul·gen·cy** [-si; -sɪ] *n*. **1.** 纵情,沉迷,沉溺。**2.** 放任,纵容,娇养。**3.** 嗜好,着迷的事物。**4.** 恩惠;(天主教的)免罪;赦免。**5.** 【商】付款延期。**6.** 【英史】信教自由。*the Declaration of I-* 【英史】信教自由令。

in·dul·gent [in'dʌldʒənt; ɪn`dʌldʒənt] *a*. 纵容的,放纵的;宽容的,溺爱的。*an* ~ *father* 溺爱的父亲。*be* ~ *to sb*. 对某人宽容。**-ly** *ad*.

in·du·line, in·du·lin ['indjuˌli:n, -lin; `ɪndjuˏlin, -lɪn] *n*. 【纺】引杜林染料;对氮蒽蓝。

in·dult [in'dʌlt; ɪn`dʌlt] *n*. 【天主】罗马教皇的特许。

in·du·na [in'du:nə; ɪn`dunə] *n*. 非洲东南部祖鲁(Zulu)人的族长。

in·du·pli·cate [in'dju:plikit, -'du:-; ɪn`djuplɪkɪt, -`du-] *a*. 【植】(花叶的)内向镊合状的。

in·du·rate ['indjuəreit; `ɪndjʊˏret] **I** *vt*. **1.** 使硬化,使坚硬。**2.** 使无感觉,使无情,使顽固。**3.** 使坚固,使巩固。— *vi*. 变硬;巩固起来。**II** ['indjuərit; `ɪndjʊˏrɪt] *a*. **1.** 硬化的。**2.** 冷酷的。**3.** 顽固的。

in·du·ra·tion [ˌindjuə'reiʃən; ˏɪndjʊ`reʃən] *n*. 硬化;冷酷;顽固。

in·du·ra·tive ['indjuərətiv; `ɪndjʊrətɪv] *a*. 变硬的;无情的。

In·dus ['indəs; `ɪndəs] *n*. 〔the ~〕 **1.** 印度河。**2.** 【天】印第安座。

in·du·si·um [in'dju:ziəm, -'du:-, -ʒi:-; ɪn`djuzɪəm, -`du-, -ʒi-] *n*. (*pl*. **-si·a** [-ə; -ə]) **1.** 【解、动】胚被;幼虫膜。**2.** 【植】柱头下毛圈;囊群盖。**-si·al** [-əl; -əl] *a*.

in·dus·tri·al [in'dʌstriəl; ɪn`dʌstrɪəl] **I** *a*. **1.** 工业的,产业的,实业的。**2.** 工业上用的。**3.** 工业高度发展的。**4.** 从事工业的。**5.** 工人的。**6.** 因勤奋努力而得到的。~ *alcohol* 工业用酒精。~ *diamond* 工业用钻石。~ *arts* 工艺劳作〔美国中小学的一门课程〕。*an* ~ *nation* [*state*] 工业国。*an* ~ *town* 工业城市。*the* ~ *classes* 工人阶级。*an* ~ *reserve army* 工业后备军。~ *workers* 产业工人。~ *training* 职业训练。~ *welfare* 职工福利。*an* ~ *crop* 勤劳而得的收获。**II** *n*. **1.** 产业工人,工业工人。**2.** 工业公司。**3.** 【商】工业股票。~ **archaeology** 工业考古学〔对过去技术发达时代,尤指产业革命后各个阶段的研究〕。~ **disease** 职业病。~ **park** 工业区。~ **relations** 劳资关系。**I- Revolution** (十八世纪六十年代在英国开始的)工业革命,产业革命。~ **school** **1.** 中等工业技术学校。**2.** (“顽劣”青少年被送入改造的)教养学校。~ **store** 员工福利商店。~**-strength** *a*. (产品等)优质的。~ **union** 同一工业内跨行业的职工工会。**-ly** *ad*.

in·dus·tri·al·ism [in'dʌstriəlizəm; ɪn`dʌstrɪəlɪzəm] *n*. 工业[产业]主义。

in·dus·tri·al·ist [in'dʌstriəlist; ɪn`dʌstrɪəlɪst] *n*. 工业主义者;实业家。

in·dus·tri·al·i·za·tion [inˌdʌstriəlai'zeiʃən; ɪnˏdʌstrɪəlaɪ`zeʃən] *n*. 工业化。*intense* ~ 高度工业化。*bring about* ~ 实现工业化。

in·dus·tri·al·ize [in'dʌstriəlaiz; ɪn`dʌstrɪəlaɪz] *vt*., *vi*. (使)工业化。

in·dus·tri·ous [in'dʌstriəs; ɪn`dʌstrɪəs] *a*. 勤恳的,刻苦的。*an* ~ *and simple style of work* 艰苦朴素的工作作风。**-ly** *ad*. **-ness** *n*.

in·dus·try ['indəstri; `ɪndəstrɪ] *n*. **1.** 勤劳,勤奋,刻苦。**2.** 工业,产业,实业,事业。**3.** 〔集合词〕资方。**4.** 有组织的劳动,经常的工作[努力]。*heavy* [*light*] ~ 重[轻]工业。*the automobile* ~ 汽车工业。*the sugar* ~ 制糖业。*the shipping* ~ 航海业。*the broadcasting* ~ 广播事业。*the beauty* ~ 美容业。~**-education marriage** 工教结合。

in·dwell ['in'dwel; ɪn`dwel] *vi*., *vt*. (**in·dwelt** [in'dwelt; ɪn`dwelt] **indwell·ing**) 内在,(使)存在于…之中。

in·dwell·er ['inˌdwelə; `ɪnˏdwɛlɚ] *n*. 内在的精神[力量、原则]。

in·dwell·ing ['in'dweliŋ; ɪn`dwɛlɪŋ] *a*. 存在于内心[灵魂]中的。

-ine *suf*. **1.** 〔构成名词或形容词〕表示“…属的”,“…似的”,“…性质的”: can*ine*, serpent*ine*, mar*ine*. **2.** 〔由科学术语中专有名词构成形容词〕表示“含…的”,“…成的”: alkal*ine*, saturn*ine*. **3.** 〔构成名词〕表示女性的名字[称呼]: hero*ine*. **4.** 〔构成抽象名词〕表示带有技术,处置、行为等抽象意义: discipl*ine*, doctr*ine*. **5.** 〔构成名词〕表示【化】“六节的杂环”,“生物碱”, caffe*ine*. **6.** 构成由意大利语表示小的 *-ino*, *-ina* 转化而来的名词: mandol*ine*, figur*ine*.

in·earth [in'ə:θ; ɪn`ɝθ] *vt*. 〔古〕把…置于土中;埋葬,葬,埋。

in·e·bri·ant [in'i:briənt; ɪn`ibrɪənt] *a*., *n*. = intoxicant.

in·e·bri·ate [i'ni:brieit; ɪ`nibrɪˏet] **I** *vt*. **1.** 使醉;灌醉。**2.** 使兴奋,使发呆。*be* ~*d by success* 因成功而高兴。**II** [i'ni:briit; ɪ`nibrɪɪt] *a*. 喝醉的。**III** *n*. 酒鬼,酒徒。

in·e·bri·a·tion, in·e·bri·e·ty [iˌni:bri'eiʃən, ˌini(:)'braiəti; ɪˏnibrɪ`eʃən, ˏɪnɪ(ɪ)`braɪətɪ] *n*. **1.** 酩酊大醉。**2.** 高兴,如痴如醉。

in·ed·i·ble [in'edibl; ɪn`ɛdɪbl] *a*. 不适于食用的,不能吃的。~ *oil* 非食用油。**-bil·i·ty** [inˌedi'biliti; ɪnˏɛdɪ`bɪlətɪ] *n*.

in·ed·i·ta [in'editə; ɪn`ɛdɪtə] *n*. 〔*pl*.〕未发表的著作。

in·ed·it·ed [in'editid; ɪn`ɛdɪtɪd] *a*. 未经编辑的;未出版的。*an* ~ *document* 不曾发表过的文件。

in·ed·u·ca·ble [in'edjukəbl; ɪn`ɛdjəkəbl] *a*. 不可教育的。

in·ef·fa·ble [in'efəbl; ɪn`ɛfəbl] *a*. **1.** 不可言喻的,不可名状的,说不出的。**2.** 不能说的,应当避讳的。~ *joy* 说不出的高兴。**-bil·i·ty** [ˌiniˌfei'biliti; ˏɪnɪˏfe`bɪlətɪ] *n*. **-bly** *ad*.

in·ef·face·a·ble [ˌini'feisəbl; ˏɪnɪ`fesəbl] *a*. 不能消除的,抹不掉的。*an* ~ *impression* 消灭不了的印象。**-a·bil·i·ty** [ˌiniˌfeisə'biliti; ˏɪnɪˏfesə`bɪlətɪ] *n*. **-bly** *ad*.

in·ef·fec·tive [ˌini'fektiv; ˏɪnɪ`fɛktɪv] *a*. **1.** 无效的,不起作用的。**2.** 不动人的,缺乏艺术性的。**3.** 效率低的,无能的。**-ly** *ad*. **-ness** *n*.

in·ef·fec·tu·al [ˌini'fektjuəl; ˏɪnɪ`fɛktʃəl] *a*. 无效的,不灵验的,徒劳无益的。**-ly** *ad*. **-ness** *n*.

in·ef·fi·ca·cious [ˌinefi'keiʃəs; ˏɪnɛfɪ`keʃəs] *a*. 无效力的,无实效的,疗效不好的。**-ly** *ad*. **-ness** *n*.

in·ef·fi·ca·cy [in'efikəsi; ɪn`ɛfɪkəsɪ] *n*. 无效力,无疗效。

in·ef·fi·cien·cy [ˌini'fiʃənsi; ˏɪnɪ`fɪʃənsɪ] *n*. 无效;无能,不称职。

in·ef·fi·cient [ˌini'fiʃənt; ɪnɪ`fɪʃənt] *a*. 无效力的,无能力的,效能差的,不称职的。**-ly** *ad*.

inel. = inelastic.

in·e·las·tic [ˌini'læstik; ˏɪnɪ`læstɪk] *a*. **1.** 无弹力的,无

伸缩性的。2. 无适应性的,不能变通的,僵硬的,不弯曲的。~ **collision**【物】非弹性碰撞。

in·e·las·tic·i·ty [ˌinilæsˈtisiti;ˏɪnɪlæsˋtɪsətɪ] *n*. 1. 无弹性,无伸缩性。2. 无适应性,不能变通。

in·el·e·gance, -gan·cy [inˈeligəns, -si; ɪnˋɛlɪgəns, -sɪ] *n*. 1. 粗俗,生硬,不雅,不精致。2. 粗俗的东西。

in·el·e·gant [inˈeligənt; ɪnˋɛlɪgənt] *a*. 不雅的;粗俗的,生硬的,粗糙的。**-ly** *ad*.

in·el·i·gi·ble [inˈelidʒəbl; ɪnˋɛlɪdʒəbl̩] I *a*. 不可取的,不合格的,无被选资格的。*be ~ for the position* 无资格任职。II *n*. 不合格的人。**-bil·i·ty** [inˌelidʒəˈbiliti; ɪnˏɛlɪdʒəˋbɪlətɪ] *n*. **-bly** *ad*.

in·el·o·quent [inˈeləkwənt; ɪnˋɛləkwənt] *a*. 不雄辩的,无说服力的;言语不流畅的;无口才的。**-quence** *n*. **-ly** *ad*.

in·e·luc·ta·ble [ˌiniˈlʌktəbl;ˏɪnɪˋlʌktəbl̩] *a*. 难避免的;不可避免的,必然发生的。**-bil·i·ty** [ˌiniˌlʌktəˈbiliti;ˏɪnɪˏlʌktəˋbɪlətɪ] *n*. **-bly** *ad*.

in·el·ud·i·ble [ˌiniˈluːdəbl;ˏɪnɪˋludəbl̩] *a*. 逃脱不了的,躲避不了的。**-bly** *ad*.

in·e·nar·ra·ble [ˌiniˈnærəbl;ˏɪnɪˋnærəbl̩] *a*. 难以描述的,无可名状的。

in·ept [iˈnept; ɪˋnɛpt] *a*. 1. 愚昧的,愚蠢的。2. 不适当的,不适合的。3. 无能的,不称职的。~ *remarks* 不恰当的语言。**-ly** *ad*. **-ness** *n*.

in·ept·i·tude [iˈneptitjuːd; ɪˋnɛptɪtjud] *n*. 不适当;不称职;愚笨;无能。

in·e·qua·ble [inˈekwebl; ɪnˋɛkwɛbl̩] *a*. 不一样的,不均匀的,不公允的。

in·e·qual·i·ty [ˌini(ː)ˈkwɔliti;ˏɪnɪˋkwɑlətɪ] *n*. 1. 不平等,不平均,不平衡,不等量。2. 不相同,互异。3. 变动,变化,高低,起伏。4.【数】不等式;【天】均差。5. (平面等的)不平坦。6. 不胜任。*an ~ of temperature* 温度上的变化。*the ~ of the climate* 气候上的变动。~ *in size* 大小不同。*the ~ between the rich and the poor* 贫富不均。*one's ~ to a task* 不胜任。

in·e·qui·lat·er·al [iniːkwiˈlætərəl; ɪnikwɪˋlætərəl] *a*. 不等边的。*an ~ triangle* 不等边三角形。

in·eq·ui·ta·ble [inˈekwitəbl; ɪnˋɛkwɪtəbl̩] *a*. 不公平的,不公正的,偏私的。**-bly** *ad*.

in·eq·ui·ty [inˈekwiti; ɪnˋɛkwɪtɪ] *n*. 不公平,不公正。

in·e·qui·valve [inˈiːkwəvælv; ɪnˋikwəˏvælv] *a*.【动】(壳的)不等瓣的。

in·e·rad·i·ca·ble [ˌiniˈrædikəbl;ˏɪnɪˋrædɪkəbl̩] *a*. 难以根除的,根深蒂固的。**-bly** *ad*.

in·e·ras·a·ble [ˌiniˈreisəbl;ˏɪnɪˋresəbl̩] *a*. 不能涂抹的,消除不了的。

in·er·ra·ble [inˈerəbl; ɪnˋɛrəbl̩] *a*. 不会错的,绝对正确的。**-bil·ity** [inˌeræˈbiliti; ɪnˏɛræˋbɪlətɪ] *n*. **-bly** *ad*.

in·er·ran·cy [inˈerənsi; ɪnˋɛrənsɪ] *n*. 无错误,绝对正确。

in·er·rant [inˈerənt; ɪnˋɛrənt] *a*. = inerrable.

in·er·rat·ic [ˌiniˈrætik;ˏɪnɪˋrætɪk] *a*. 非反复无常的,有规律的,固定的。~ *stars* 固定的星球。

in·ert [iˈnəːt; ɪˋnɝt] *a*. 1.【物】无自动力的,无活动力的。2.【化】惰性的,非活性的。3. 不活泼的,无生气的;迟钝的。4.【医】无作用的,无效的,中性的。*Stone is an ~ mass of matter.* 石头是一块无生命的物体。~ **gas** 惰性气体。~ **matter** 惰性物质。~ **type**【生】安定型,不活泼型。**-ly** *ad*. **-ness** *n*.

in·er·tia [iˈnəːʃiə; ɪnˋɝʃɪə] *n*. 1.【物】惯性,惰性,惯量。2. 不活动,不活泼,迟钝,惰性。3.【医】无力。*the force of ~* 惯性,惰性。*the law of ~* 惯性定律。*the moment of ~* 转动惯量,惯性矩。~ **governor**【机】惯性调速器。~ **selling** 惯性推销〔把商品寄给并未订货但有可能购买的顾客,如不退货即向其收账〕。**-less** *a*. 无惯性的,无惯量的。

in·er·tial [iˈnəːʃəl; ɪˋnɝʃəl] *a*.【物】惯性的,惯量的。~ **guidance** [**navigation**]【空、海】惯性制导。~ **space** 惯性空间,惯性作用区〔假设有固定座标的地球上空的一部分,用以计算飞弹、太空船等的航道〕。

in·es·cap·a·ble [ˌinisˈkeipəbl;ˏɪnɪsˋkepəbl̩] *a*. 必然发生的,逃避不了的,不可避免的。*an ~ duty* 推卸不了的责任。**-bly** *ad*.

in·es·sen·tial [ˈiniˈsenʃəl;ˏɪnɪˋsɛnʃəl] I *a*. 1. 不重要的,非必需的。2. 无实质的,非物质的。II *n*. 可有可无的东西。**-i·ty** *n*.

in·es·ti·ma·ble [inˈestiməbl; ɪnˋɛstɪməbl̩] *a*. 1. 难以估计的。2. 极贵重的,无价的。*an ~ service* 非常宝贵的贡献。**-bly** *ad*.

in·ev·i·ta·ble [inˈevitəbl; ɪnˋɛvɪtəbl̩] *a*. 1. 不可避免的,不可逃避的;必然的。2. 合情合理的,逼真的。3. 〔口〕照例的,照常的。*the ~ hour* 死期。*with his ~ camera* 照常带着照相机。*the ~* 必然的事情,不可避免的命运。**-bil·ity** [inˌevitəˈbiliti; ɪnˏɛvɪtəˋbɪlətɪ] **-ness** *n*. **-bly** *ad*.

in·ex·act [ˌinigˈzækt;ˏɪnɪgˋzækt] *a*. 1. 不精确的,不准确的。2. 不严格的,不仔细的。**-ly** *ad*. **-ness** *n*.

in·ex·act·i·tude [ˌinigˈzæktitjuːd;ˏɪnɪgˋzæktɪtˏjud] *n*. 不精确,不准确。*a terminological ~* 〔谑〕谎言。

in·ex·cit·a·ble [ˌinikˈsaitəbl;ˏɪnɪkˋsaɪtəbl̩] *a*. 不会激动的,不易感动的,冷静的。

in·ex·cus·a·ble [ˌiniksˈkjuːzəbl;ˏɪnɪksˋkjuzəbl̩] *a*. 1. 无法辩解的。2. 难以原谅的,不可宽恕的。**-bil·i·ty**, **-ness** *n*. **-bly** *ad*.

in·ex·e·cu·ta·ble [inˈeksikjuːtəbl; ɪnˋɛksɪkjutəbl̩] *a*. 不能实行的,难以办到的。

in·ex·er·tion [ˌinigˈzəːʃən;ˏɪnɪgˋzɝʃən] *n*. 不努力;不尽力。

in·ex·haust·i·ble [ˌinigˈzɔːstəbl;ˏɪnɪgˋzɔstəbl̩] *a*. 1. 用不完的,无穷尽的。2. 不知疲倦的,精神好的。**-bil·i·ty** [ˈinigˌzɔːstəˈbiliti; ˋɪnɪgˏzɔstəˋbɪlətɪ] *n*. **-bly** *ad*.

in·ex·haus·tive [ˌinigˈzɔːstiv;ˏɪnɪgˋzɔstɪv] *a*. 1. 〔古〕= inexhaustible. 2. 不详尽的,不彻底的。**-ly** *ad*.

in·ex·ist·ent [ˌinigˈzistənt;ˏɪnɪgˋzɪstənt] *a*. 1. 不存在的,不成立的。2. 〔古〕内在的;固有的,先天的。**-ence** *n*.

in·ex·o·ra·ble [inˈeksərəbl; ɪnˋɛksərəbl̩] *a*. 1. 无情的,铁面无私的。2. 不可动摇的,不屈不挠的。*an ~ law* 不可抗拒的规律。*an ~ struggle* 坚决的斗争。**-bil·i·ty** *n*. **-bly** *ad*.

in·ex·pe·di·ence, -cy [ˌiniksˈpiːdjəns, -si;ˏɪnɪksˋpidjəns, -sɪ] *n*. 不适当;不明智;不得计。

in·ex·pe·di·ent [ˌiniksˈpiːdiənt, -djənt;ˏɪnɪksˋpidɪənt, -djənt] *a*. 不适当的;不明智的;不得计的。**-ly** *ad*.

in·ex·pen·sive [ˌiniksˈpensiv;ˏɪnɪksˋpɛnsɪv] *a*. 花费不多的,廉价的。**-ly** *ad*. **-ness** *n*.

in·ex·pe·ri·ence [ˌiniksˈpiəriəns;ˏɪnɪksˋpɪrɪəns] *n*. 无经验,不熟练。

in·ex·pert [ˌineksˈpəːt;ˏɪnɛksˋpɝt] I *a*. 不熟练的,不老练的,业余的。II *n*. 生手。**-ly** *ad*. **-ness** *n*.

in·ex·pi·a·ble [inˈekspiəbl; ɪnˋɛkspɪəbl̩] *a*. 1. (罪过)不能抵偿的,不能赎的。2. (仇恨等)不能和解的,极深的。**-ness** *n*. **-bly** *ad*.

in·ex·plain·a·ble [ˌiniksˈpleinəbl;ˏɪnɪksˋplenəbl̩] *a*. 不可解释的,难说明的。

in·ex·pli·ca·ble [inˈeksplikəbl; ɪnˋɛksplɪkəbl̩] *a*. 无法说明的,费解的,莫名其妙的。*There are many things which are ~ by science.* 有很多事科学还无法解释。**-bil·i·ty** [inˌeksplikəˈbiliti; ɪnˏɛksplɪkəˋbɪlətɪ] *n*. **-bly** *ad*.

in·ex·plic·it [ˌiniksˈplisit;ˏɪnɪksˋplɪsɪt] *a*. 模糊不清的;含糊的。**-ly** *ad*. **-ness** *n*.

in·ex·plo·sive [ˌiniksˈpləusiv;ˏɪnɪksˋplosɪv] *a*. 不爆炸的,不破裂的。

I

in·ex·press·i·ble [ˌiniksˈpresəbl; ˏɪnɪksˋprɛsəbl̩] **I** ***a.*** 表达不出的,说不出的,难形容的。*a scene of ~ beauty* 难以描绘的美景。**II** ***n.*** 〔*pl.*〕〔古〕裤子。**-bil·i·ty** ***n.*** **-bly** ***ad.***

in·ex·pres·sive [ˌiniksˈpresiv; ˏɪnɪksˋprɛsɪv] ***a.*** **1.** 缺乏表情的;无表情的,无深意的。**2.** 不表白自己的,沉默的。**3.** 〔古〕= inexpressible. *an ~ face* 毫无表情的面孔。**-ly** ***ad.*** **-ness** ***n.***

in·ex·pug·na·ble [ˌiniksˈpʌgnəbl; ˏɪnɪksˋpʌgnəbl̩] ***a.*** 攻不破的,难推翻的;(议论等)确定不移的。*~ hatred* 难解除的仇恨。**-bly** ***ad.***

in·ex·ten·si·ble [ˌiniksˈtensəbl; ˏɪnɪksˋtɛnsəbl̩] ***a.*** 不能扩张的,伸展不了的。

in ex·ten·so [ˌinikˈstensəu; ˏɪnɪkˋstɛnso] 〔L.〕以全文,不加删节地;充分地。

in·ex·tin·guish·a·ble [ˌiniksˈtiŋgwiʃəbl; ˏɪnɪksˋtɪŋgwɪʃəbl̩] ***a.*** 不能消灭的,压制不住的。**-bly** ***ad.***

in·ex·tir·pa·ble [ˌiniksˈtəːpəbl; ˏɪnɪksˋtɝpəbl̩] ***a.*** 不能根除的,不能根绝的。

in·ex·tri·ca·ble [inˈekstrikəbl; ɪnˋɛkstrɪkəbl] ***a.*** **1.** 解不开的。**2.** 纠缠不清的;不能解决的。**3.** 不能解脱的,不能解救的。*an ~ knot* 解不开的结子。*~ confusion* 纠缠不清的混乱。*an ~ maze* 无法解脱的困境。**-bil·i·ty** [inˌekstrikəˈbiliti; ɪnˏɛkstrɪkəˋbɪlətɪ] ***n.*** **-bly** ***ad.***

I·nez [ˈiːnez; ˋinɛz] ***n.*** 伊内兹〔女子名, Agnes 的异体〕。

INF = intermediate(-range) nuclear forces 中程核力量(指中程导弹)。

inf. = **1.** infantry. **2.** infinitive. **3.** information. **4.** 〔L.〕*infra*.

in·fall [inˈfɔːl; ɪnˋfɔl] ***n.*** **1.** 侵入,侵略。**2.** 合流,汇合。**3.** 流入。

in·fal·li·ble [inˈfæləbl; ɪnˋfæləbl̩] **I** ***a.*** **1.** 一贯正确的;不会犯错误的。**2.** 确实可靠的。*an ~ memory* 不会错的记忆。*an ~ remedy* 肯定有效的药方;可靠的补救办法。**II** ***n.*** 一贯正确的人,可靠的事物。**-bil·i·ty** [inˌfæləˈbiliti; ɪnˏfæləˋbɪlətɪ] ***n.*** (*His Infallibility* 罗马教皇〔尊称〕。*papal infallibility*【天主】教皇不谬性[说])。**-bly** ***ad.***

in·fa·mize [ˈinfəmaiz; ˋɪnfəmaɪz] ***vt.*** 使声名狼藉。

in·fa·mous [ˈinfəməs; ˋɪnfəməs] ***a.*** **1.** 名誉极臭的,声名狼藉的。**2.** 伤风败俗的,无耻的,不名誉的。**3.**【法】(因犯重罪)被褫夺公权的;〔美〕被剥夺法律上作证权的。**4.** 很差的,低劣的。*an ~ swindler* 臭名昭著的骗子。*~ behaviour* 丑行。*an ~ crime* 〔英〕丧失廉耻罪;〔美〕(罚作苦役以上的)重罪。*an ~ dinner* 质量极坏的一顿饭。**-ly** ***ad.***

in·fa·my [ˈinfəmi; ˋɪnfəmɪ] ***n.*** **1.** 臭名昭著,声名狼藉。**2.** 出丑,丑行。**3.**【法】(因犯重罪而)丧失公权。*hold sb. up to ~* 使某人出丑。

in·fan·cy [ˈinfənsi; ˋɪnfənsɪ] ***n.*** **1.** 婴儿期,幼时,幼年时代。**2.**【法】未成年。**3.** 初期,摇篮时代,幼年期。*in one's [its] ~* 在摇篮时代。

in·fant [ˈinfənt; ˋɪnfənt] **I** ***n.*** **1.** 婴儿,幼儿〔未满七岁〕。**2.**【法】未成年人〔二十一岁以下〕。**3.** 生手。**II** ***a.*** **1.** 幼儿的;幼小的,幼稚的,初期的。**2.**【法】未成年的。**3.** 婴儿[幼儿]用的。*~ diseases* 小儿病。*~ civilization* 初期文化。*~ fruit* 未熟的水果。*an ~ industry* 新建的工业。*~ food* 幼儿食物。**~s' school** ***n.*** 〔英〕幼儿园。

in·fan·ta [inˈfæntə; ɪnˋfæntə] ***n.*** (西班牙、葡萄牙的)公主(*opp.* infante)〔尤指帝王的长女〕。

in·fan·te [inˈfænti; ɪnˋfæntɪ] ***n.*** (西班牙,葡萄牙的)王子〔尤指帝王的非长子,不能继承王位〕。

in·fan·ti·cid·al [inˌfæntiˈsaidl; ɪnˏfæntɪˋsaɪdl̩] ***a.*** 杀婴儿的;杀幼儿的;杀婴罪的。

in·fan·ti·cide [inˈfæntisaid; ɪnˋfæntɪˏsaɪd] ***n.*** 杀害婴儿;杀婴罪;杀婴犯。

in·fan·tic·i·pate [ˌinfənˈtisipeit; ˏɪnfənˋtɪsɪpet] ***vi.*** 〔主美〕待产。**-tion** ***n.***

in·fan·tile [ˈinfəntail; ˋɪnfənˏtaɪl] ***a.*** **1.** 婴儿的,幼儿的;婴儿期的,幼儿期的。**2.** 适合于婴儿[幼儿]的,幼稚的,孩子气的。**3.** 早期的,初期的。*~ diseases* 小儿病。*~ mortality* 婴儿死亡率。*~ paralysis*【医】婴儿麻痹,小儿麻痹,脊髓灰质炎。

in·fan·ti·lism [inˈfæntilizəm; ɪnˋfæntɪlɪzm] ***n.*** **1.**【医】幼稚型,婴儿型。**2.**【心】幼稚病,幼稚行为。

in·fan·tine [ˈinfəntain, -tin; ˋɪnfənˏtaɪn, -tɪn] ***a.*** 幼稚的;婴儿的;稚气的;孩子的。

in·fan·try [ˈinfəntri; ˋɪnfəntrɪ] ***n.*** **1.** 〔集合词〕步兵。**2.** 步兵团。*~ tactics* 步兵战术。*light ~* 轻步兵。**-man** ***n.*** (*pl.* **-men**) 步兵。

in·farct [inˈfɑːkt; ɪnˋfɑrkt] ***n.***【医】(血管)梗死。

in·farc·tion [inˈfɑːkʃən; ɪnˋfɑrkʃən] ***n.***【医】梗死形成(= infarct)。

in·fare [ˈinˌfɛə; ˋɪnˏfɛr] ***n.*** 〔方〕婚礼招待会,婚宴〔一般于婚礼次日举行〕。

in·fat·u·ate [inˈfætjueit; ɪnˋfætjuet] **I** ***vt.*** **1.** 使冲昏头脑,弄糊涂。**2.** 使迷恋,使错爱。*be ~d with pride* 被骄傲冲昏头脑。*be ~ with sb.* 迷恋某人。**II** ***a.*** = infatuated. **III** ***n.*** 变得昏头昏脑的人;迷恋者。

in·fat·u·at·ed [inˈfætjueitid; ɪnˋfætjuˏetɪd] ***a.*** 变得昏头昏脑的;迷恋着的,跟…打得火热的(*with* a *woman*)。**-ly** ***ad.***

in·fa·tu·a·tion [inˌfætjuˈeiʃən; ɪnˏfætjuˋeʃən] ***n.*** 昏头昏脑,迷惑,迷恋。

in·fea·si·ble [inˈfiːzəbl; ɪnˋfizəbl̩] ***a.*** 不能实行的,办不到的。**-bil·i·ty** [inˌfiːzəˈbiliti; ɪnˏfizəˋbɪlətɪ] ***n.***

in·fect [inˈfekt; ɪnˋfɛkt] ***vt.*** **1.** 传染;散布病毒;侵染。**2.** 使受影响,感染。**3.** (电脑病毒)使(电脑的)存储器[数据]受到感染。*the ~ed area [zone]* 传染病流行区[地带]。*His courage ~ed the followers.* 他的勇气激励了后来人。**be ~ed with** 感染,沾染上。

in·fec·tion [inˈfekʃən; ɪnˋfɛkʃən] ***n.*** **1.** 传染,感染,侵染。**2.** 传染病,染毒物。**3.** 影响;感染。

in·fec·tious [inˈfekʃəs; ɪnˋfɛkʃəs] ***a.*** **1.** 传染的,传染性的。**2.** 易传染的;易感染的。**3.** 有坏影响的,有损害的。*an ~ laugh* 有感染力的一笑。*~ disease* 传染病。*an ~ hospital* 传染病院。*~ water* 带菌水。**~ hepatitis**【医】传染性肝炎。**~ mononucleosis**【医】传染性单核白血球增多。**-ly** ***ad.*** **-ness** ***n.***

in·fec·tive [inˈfektiv; ɪnˋfɛktɪv] ***a.*** **1.** 传染性的,易传染的。**2.** 影响别人的,感染别人的。**-ness** ***n.***

in·fec·tiv·i·ty [ˌinfekˈtiviti; ˏɪnfɛkˋtɪvətɪ] ***n.*** 传染性;易传染性。

in·fe·cund [inˈfekənd, -ˈfiːk-; ɪnˋfɛkənd, -ˋfik-] ***a.*** 不结子的,不妊的;不毛的。**-di·ty** ***n.***

in·fe·li·cif·ic [inˌfiːliˈsifik; ɪnˏfilɪˋsɪfɪk] ***a.*** 引起不幸的。

in·fe·lic·i·tous [ˌinfiˈlisitəs; ˏɪnfɪˋlɪsɪtəs] ***a.*** **1.** 不幸的,不吉的。**2.** 不适当的,不贴切的。*an ~ marriage* 不幸的婚姻。**-ly** ***ad.***

in·fe·lic·i·ty [ˌinfiˈlisiti; ˏɪnfɪˋlɪsətɪ] ***n.*** **1.** 不幸,不吉。**2.** 不适当的事物;不恰当的言行。*There is so much ~ in the world.* 人世间有很多不幸的事。

in·fer [inˈfəː; ɪnˋfɝ] ***vt.*** (***in·ferred***; ***in·fer·ring***) **1.** 推理,推论,推断。**2.** 猜想,臆测。**3.** 表示,意味着,暗示,含有…的意思。*~ a motive from an effect* 从效果推知动机。*What am I to ~ from your remarks?* 你说的话究竟是什么意思呢? *Your silence ~s consent.* 你沉默就是表示同意。— ***vi.*** 作出推论。

in·fer·a·ble [inˈfəːrəbl; ɪnˋfɝəbl̩] ***a.*** 可推断的,可推论的,可推想而知的。

in·fer·ence [ˈinfərəns; ˋɪnfərəns] ***n.*** **1.** 推理,推论;推断,结论,论断;含蓄,含意。**2.** 推断的结果;(逻辑上的)结论。*speak from ~* 推测说。*draw [make] an ~*

from ... 根据…下结论。*the deductive* [*inductive*] ~ 演绎[归纳]推理。

in·fer·en·tial [ˌinfəˈrenʃəl; ˏɪnfəˋrɛnʃəl] ***a*.** 推理的,推论的,推理上的,推论上的。~ *procedure* 推论上的程序。**-ly *ad*.**

in·fe·ri·or [inˈfiəriə; ɪnˋfɪrɪɚ] **I *a*.** (*opp*. superior) **1.** (位置在)下部的,下面的。**2.** (身份)低下的,下级的。**3.** (质量等)低劣的,次的,普通的,差的,劣势的。**4.** 【植】下位的,下生的。**5.** 【解】在下的,在其他器官之下的。**6.** 【军】阶级低的。**7.** 【印】排[抄]在字母下的。**8.** 【天】行星在地球轨道内侧的,在地球与太阳之间的。~ *limit* 【机】下限,最小尺寸。*the* ~ *court* 下级法院。*Woman is* ~ *to man in running*. 妇女跑不过男子。~ *goods* 低档货。*an* ~ *enemy* 劣势敌人。~ *by comparison* 相形见绌。*be* ~ *to sb*. 不及某人。~ *wings* 后翅。*an* ~ *officer* 下级军官。~ *figures* 下附数字〔如 H_2中下附的 2〕。~ *conjunction* 【天】下合。~ *planet* 内行星。**II *n*. 1.** 晚辈,下级(的人);劣者。**2.** 【印】下角码。***be sb.'s* ~ *in*** 在…上不及某人。**-ly *ad*.**

in·fe·ri·or·i·ty [inˌfiəriˈɔriti; ɪnˏfɪrɪˋɑrətɪ] ***n*.** 下位,下部;下级;次级,低级,劣等 (*opp*. superiority)。*have a sense of pride and not of* ~ 有自豪感而不应当有自卑感。~ **complex** [**feelings**] 【心】自卑情结;自卑感〔指心理上的一种病态〕。

in·fer·nal [inˈfəːnl; ɪnˋfɝnḷ] ***a*. 1.** 阴间的,地狱的。**2.** 地狱般的,恶魔似的,穷凶极恶的。**3.** 〔口〕坏透的,可恨的,该死的。~ *regions* 地狱,阴间。*an* ~ *deed* 残暴行为。~ **machine** 【军】定时炸弹,饵雷,诡雷。**-i·ty *n*.**

in·fer·no [inˈfəːnəu; ɪnˋfɝno] ***n*.** (*pl*. ~*s*) **1.** 地狱;阴森恐怖的地方,可怕的东西。**2.** 〔the I-〕《地狱篇》〔但丁所作《神曲》的第一部〕。

in·fe·ro·an·te·ri·or [ˌinfiˌrəuænˈtiəriə; ˏɪnfɪˏroænˋtɪrɪɚ] ***a*.** 下前方的。

in·fer·ra·ble, in·fer·ri·ble [inˈfəːrəbl, -ribl; ɪnˋfɝrəbḷ, -rɪbḷ] ***a*.** = inferable.

in·fer·tile [inˈfəːtail; ɪnˋfɝtaɪl] ***a*. 1.** 不毛的,瘠瘦的,不肥沃的。**2.** 不结果实的,不生育的。**-til·ity** [ˌinfəˈtiliti; ˏɪnfəˋtɪlətɪ] ***n*.**

in·fest [inˈfest; ɪnˋfɛst] ***vt*. 1.** (指老鼠、害虫,盗贼等)大批出没,成群出现。**2.** 在…上寄生,寄生于。*be* ~*ed with pirates* 海盗横行。*warehouses* ~*ed with rats* 老鼠横行的仓库。*fleas* ~*ing cats* 寄生于猫身上的跳蚤。

in·fes·ta·tion [ˌinfesˈteiʃən; ˏɪnfɛsˋteʃən] ***n*. 1.** (老鼠、害虫,盗贼)大批出没,侵扰,蔓延。**2.** (昆虫)传染。

in·feu·da·tion [ˌinfjuˈdeiʃən; ˏɪnfjuˋdeʃən] ***n*.** 赐与封地,采邑授与。

in·fi·del [ˈinfidəl; ˋɪnfɪdəl] **I *a*. 1.** 不信宗教的;异教徒的;不信仰的。**II *n*. 1.** 不信宗教的人。**2.** 异教徒。**-ize *vt*., *vi*.** (使)不信宗教。

in·fi·del·i·ty [ˌinfiˈdeliti; ˏɪnfɪˋdɛlətɪ] ***n*. 1.** 不信神,无宗教信仰。**2.** 不信基督教。**3.** 背信,不忠诚。**4.** (夫妇间的)不忠实,不忠实行为。*conjugal* ~ 私通,不守贞节。

in·field [ˈinfiːld; ˋɪnfild] ***n*. 1.** 宅边田地;可耕地。**2.** (棒球或垒球球场的)内场;内野;全体内野手 (*opp*. outfield)。**3.** 椭圆形跑道内的运动场地。

in·field·er [ˈinfiːldə; ˋɪnfildɚ] ***n*.** (棒球等的)内野手。

in·fight·ing [ˈinfaitiŋ; ˋɪnfaɪtɪŋ] ***n*. 1.** (拳击中的)接近战,贴近对打,近身殴斗。**2.** 混战,乱打。**3.** 暗斗。*deadly* ~ *among the politicians* 政客间的勾心斗角。

in·fil·trate [inˈfiltreit; ɪnˋfɪltret] **I *vt*. 1.** 使渗入,透过 (*through*; *into*);使浸润。**2.** 【军】渗透,通过;侵袭。~ *the tissue with a local anaesthetic* 用局部麻醉剂浸入组织。*an infiltrating column* 渗透纵队。— ***vi*.** 渗入,混进。**II *n*.** 渗入物。

in·fil·tra·tion [ˌinfilˈtreiʃən; ˏɪnfɪlˋtreʃən] ***n*. 1.** 渗入;【医】浸润。**2.** 【军】渗透,通过;渗透活动。**3.** 【化】渗滤。*advance by* ~ 渗透前进。*an* ~ *force* 渗透部队。

in·fil·tra·tor [inˈfiltreitə; ɪnˋfɪlˏtretɚ] ***n*.** 渗入者。

infin. = infinitive.

in·fi·nite [ˈinfinit; ˋɪnfɪnɪt] **I *a*.** (*opp*. finite) **1.** 无限的,无穷的,广大无边的。**2.** 无数的,许许多多的。**3.** 【语法】非限定的,不受人称、数、时态限制的〔如动词不定式、动名词〕。**4.** 【数】无穷(大)的,无尽的。~ *space* 无限空间。*an* ~ *sum of money* 巨额款项。*an* ~ *decimal* 无尽小数。*an* ~ *series* 【数】无穷级数,无限级数。**II *n*. 1.** 无限物。**2.** 【数】无穷(大);无尽。**3.** 〔the ~〕无限,无穷。**4.** 〔the I-〕【宗】造物主,神。***an* ~ *of*** 〔古〕无限的,无限量的。**-ly *ad*. -ness *n*.**

in·fin·i·tes·i·mal [ˌinfiniˈtesiməl; ˏɪnfɪnɪˋtɛsɪmḷ] **I *a*. 1.** 无限小的,无穷小的,极小的,极微的。**2.** 细微末节的。**II *n*.** 【数】无限小,无穷小,微元。~ ***calculus*** 微积分。~ ***geometry*** 微分几何。**-ly *ad*.**

in·fin·i·ti·val [inˌfiniˈtaivəl; ɪnˏfɪnəˋtaɪvḷ] ***a*.** 【语法】不定式的。

in·fin·i·tive [inˈfinitiv; ɪnˋfɪnətɪv] **I *a*.** 【语法】(不受人称、数、时态限制的)动词不定式的。**II *n*.** 【语法】动词不定式〔I can go, I want to go 等中的 go, to go 等〕。~ ***nexus*** 【语】不定式二元语核〔特指 for ... to 这种结构形式〕。

in·fin·i·tude [inˈfinitjuːd; ɪnˋfɪnɪˏtjud] ***n*.** 无限,无穷;无限量,无穷数;无限的范围。*the* ~ *of outer space* 无限的外太空。

in·fin·i·ty [inˈfiniti; ɪnˋfɪnətɪ] ***n*. 1.** = infinitude. **2.** 【数】无穷大〔符号为 ∞〕。**3.** 大量,大宗。*an* ~ *of things* 极多的东西。***at*** ~在无限远的距离上。***to*** ~直到无限。

in·firm [inˈfəːm; ɪnˋfɝm] ***a*.** (~*er*, ~*est*) **1.** 虚弱的,带病的。**2.** 优柔寡断的,懦弱的。**3.** 不巩固的,不牢固的,薄弱的。*be* ~ *with age* 衰老的。~ *of purpose* 意志薄弱的。**-ly *ad*. -ness *n*.**

in·fir·ma·ry [inˈfəːməri; ɪnˋfɝmərɪ] ***n*.** 医院;(学校、工厂等的)医务室;诊所。

in·fir·mi·ty [inˈfəːmiti; ɪnˋfɝmətɪ] ***n*. 1.** 虚弱,衰弱。**2.** 疾病,病症。**3.** 优柔寡断,懦弱;弱点,缺点。*I- often comes with old age*. 虚弱常随年老而来。*infirmities of old age* 老年体弱,老年的病症。

in·fix [inˈfiks; ɪnˋfɪks] **I *vt*. 1.** 把…插入,把…嵌入。**2.** 使深印入(脑海);渗入。**3.** 【语法】插入词腰。*The idea was* ~*ed in students' minds*. 这种概念已经深深地印入学生们的脑海中。**II** [ˈinfiks; ˋɪnfɪks] ***n*.** 【语法】词腰,插入(中缀),中加成分。

in fla·gran·te de·lic·to [ˌinfləˈgræntidiˈliktəu; ˏɪnfləˋgræntɪdɪˋlɪkto] 〔L.〕就在作案时,当场。

in·flame [inˈfleim; ɪnˋflem] ***vt*. 1.** 使燃烧,使炽热。**2.** 激怒;煽动,刺激。**3.** 加剧,使火上加油。**4.** 【医】使红肿,使发炎。*be* ~*d with rage* 激怒。~*d eyes* 红肿的眼睛。*The hills were* ~*d with autumnal tints*. 秋色染山一片红。— ***vi*. 1.** 着火,燃烧。**2.** 激怒。**3.** 发炎。

in·flam·ma·bil·i·ty [inˌflæməˈbiliti; ɪnˏflæməˋbɪlətɪ] ***n*.** 易燃性,可燃性,易激动。

in·flam·ma·ble [inˈflæməbl; ɪnˋflæməbḷ] **I *a*. 1.** 易燃的。**2.** 易激动的,易发怒的。**II *n*.** 可燃物。**-ness *n*. -bly *ad*.**

in·flam·ma·tion [ˌinfləˈmeiʃən; ˏɪnfləˋmeʃən] ***n*. 1.** 着火,发火,燃烧。**2.** 激动。**3.** 【医】红肿,炎症。*the* ~ *of the lungs* 肺炎。

in·flam·ma·to·ry [inˈflæmətəri; ɪnˋflæməˏtorɪ] ***a*. 1.** 刺激性的,煽动性的。**2.** 【医】炎性的,易红肿的。~ *speeches* 煽动性演说。*an* ~ *fever* 炎症热。

in·flat·a·ble [inˈfleitəbl; ɪnˋfletəbḷ] **I *a*.** 可膨胀的。**II *n*.** 可充气物品。

in·flate [inˈfleit; ɪnˋflet] ***vt*.** (*opp*. deflate) **1.** 使膨胀;【机】给…打气。**2.** 使(通货)膨胀,抬高(物价)。**3.** 使骄傲;使得意。~ *the paper currency* 滥发纸币。*be* ~*d*

I

with pride 扬扬得意。— *vi*. 进行充气;膨胀。

in·flat·ed [in'fleitid; ɪn`fletɪd] *a*. 1. 充了气的。2. (语言等)夸张的,言过其实的。3. (通货)恶性膨胀的;(价格)飞涨的,暴涨。4.【植】肿胀的,膨大的。~ *stem* 空心而膨大的茎。*an* ~ *tyre* 充气轮。*an* ~ *style* 夸张的文体。*the* ~ *value of land* 土地的升值。

in·flat·er [in'fleitə; ɪn`fletɚ] *n*. = inflator.

in·fla·tion [in'fleiʃən; ɪn`fleʃən] *n*. (*opp*. deflation) 1. 膨胀。2.【经】通货膨胀;信用膨胀;(物价)暴涨。3. 自负;夸张。4.【工】(气体、空气的)补给,打气,充气,胀气。*runaway* ~ 如脱缰之马的通货膨胀。~ **inlet**【机】充气进口。~ **pressure**【机】充气压力,气胀压力。**-ism** *n*. 通货膨胀政策[现象]。**-ist** 1. *n*. 通货膨胀政策的支持者。2. *a*. 支持通货膨胀政策的。

in·fla·tion·ar·y [in'fleiʃənəri; ɪn`fleʃənərɪ] *a*. 膨胀的;通货膨胀的;由膨胀引起的;由通货膨胀引起的。*the* ~ *policies* 通货膨胀政策。~ **spiral** (通货、物价、工资等的)螺旋形膨胀。

in·flat·or [in'fleitə; ɪn`fletɚ] *n*. 1. 充气者。2. 充气机;打气筒;增压泵。

in·flect [in'flekt; ɪn`flɛkt] *vt*. 1. 使弯曲,使屈折。2.【语】使变音,使转调。3.【语法】使词发生屈折变化。— *vi*.【语法】发生屈折变化。

in·flec·tion [in'flekʃən; ɪn`flɛkʃən] *n*. = inflexion.

in·flec·tive [in'flektiv; ɪn`flɛktɪv] *a*. 1. 屈折的,弯曲的。2.【语】变音的,转调的;【语法】词有屈折变化的。

in·flex·i·ble [in'fleksəbl; ɪn`flɛksəbl̩] *a*. 1. 不可弯曲的。2. 不屈服的,刚直的;坚强的,坚定的。3. 不变的,固定的。*an* ~ *rule* 硬性的规定。*an* ~ *tactics* 呆板的战术。*an* ~ *will* 坚强的意志。**-bil·i·ty** [inˌfleksə'biliti; ɪnˏflɛksə`bɪlətɪ] *n*. **-bly** *ad*.

in·flex·ion [in'flekʃən; ɪn`flɛkʃən] *n*. 1. 弯曲。2. 变音,转调。3.【语法】屈折形式,屈折变化。4.【数】拐折,回折,拐点,回折点。**-less** *a*. 无屈折变化的。

in·flex·ion·al [in'flekʃənəl; ɪn`flɛkʃənl̩] *a*. 1. 弯曲的。2. 抑扬的。3. 有屈折变化的。*an* ~ *language* 有曲折变化的语言。**-ly** *ad*.

in·flict [in'flikt; ɪn`flɪkt] *vt*. 1. 加以(打击等);使受(痛苦、损失等)。2. 处以刑罚,加刑。~ *a wound* (*up*) *on sb*. 使人受伤。~ *heavy casualties* 使蒙受重大伤亡。~ *harm on* 陷害。~ *oneself* [*one's company*] (*up*)*on sb*. 使某人受累,打搅某人。~ *the death penalty upon the murderer* 处杀人犯以死刑。**-a·ble** *a*. **-ion** *n*.

in·flict·er [in'fliktə; ɪn`flɪktɚ] *n*. 加害者,科罚者,处罚者 (= inflictor)。

in-flight ['in'flait; `ɪn`flaɪt] *a*. 飞行中的。~ *movies* 飞机上放映的电影。

in·flo·res·cence [ˌinflɔː'resns; ˏɪnflo`rɛsns] *n*. 1. 开花;开花期。2.【植】花序。3. 花簇;花朵。4. 带附属体的花轴。*the definite* [*indefinite*] ~ 有限[无限]花序。**-cent** *a*.

in·flow ['infləu; `ɪnflo] *n*. 1. 流入,注入。2. 流入物。3. 内流,吸入,吸风。*an* ~ *of bank deposit* 银行存款的增加。

in·flow·ing ['infləuiŋ; `ɪnfloɪŋ] I *a*. 流入的,注入的。II *n*. = inflow.

in·flu·ence ['influəns; `ɪnfluəns] I *n*. 1. 影响,感化(*on*; *upon*)。2. 势力,权势。3. 有影响的人物[事物],有权势的人。4. 感应。*exercise* ~ *on* [*upon*] *sb*. 影响某人,对某人施加影响。*have* ~ *on* [*upon*] *sb*. 对某人有影响。*a man of great* ~ 很有权势的人。*back-stair* ~ 潜在势力,后台势力。*exercise one's* ~ *in sb.'s behalf* 为某人尽力。*have* ~ *over* [*with*] *sb*. 有左右某人的能力。*petticoat* ~ 女性的作用[影响]。*through the* ~ *of* 靠…的力量。*use one's* ~ *for sb*. 为某人尽力[活动]。*within sb.'s sphere of* ~ 在某人势力范围内。*an* ~ *in the politics* 在政界有势力的人。*under the* ~ *of* 1. 受…的影响(*He is under the* ~ *of drink*. 他醉了)。2. 受…的感化。II *vt*. 1. 影响。2. 感化;左右,改变。3.〔婉〕贿赂,运动,收买。4.〔美口〕加(酒)于饮料中。*The weather* ~*s crops*. 天气影响收成。~ *sb*. *for good* 与人为善,使人受良好影响。

in·flu·ent ['influənt; `ɪnfluənt] I *a*. 流入的;能流动的。II *n*. 1. 流入。2. 流入物;流体,液体。3. 支流。4.【生态】一种生物对其他生物的影响。

in·flu·en·tial [ˌinflu'enʃəl; ˏɪnflu`ɛnʃəl] *a*. 1. 有影响的。2. 有势力的,有权力的。~ *action* 感应作用。*an* ~ *man* 有力人物。**-ly** *ad*.

in·flu·en·za [ˌinflu'enzə; ˏɪnflu`ɛnzə] *n*. 1.【医】流行性感冒〔略 flu.〕。2. (马、猪等的)流感。

in·flux ['inflʌks; `ɪnflʌks] *n*. 1. 流入,注入;汇集〔指人或物〕(*opp*. efflux),到来,充斥。2. 注入口,河口。*the* ~ *of foreign goods* 外货充斥。

in·fo ['infəu; `ɪnfo]〔口〕= information. ~**bahn** 信息高速公路。~**mercial**〔口〕商品信息电视片。~**naut**〔口〕信息用户,因特网用户。

in·fold [in'fəuld; ɪn`fold] *vt*. = enfold.

in·form[1] [in'fɔːm; ɪn`fɔrm] *vt*. 1. 告诉,报告,通知〔把某事告某人中,某人为直接受词,某事为 of 的受词〕。2. 使活跃,使充满 (*with*),赋予活力。3.〔罕〕教导。~ *sb*. *of sth*. 把某事告诉某人。*Please* ~ *us how to find his house*. 请告诉我们他的家在哪里。*be rightly* [*wrongly*] ~*ed* 得到正确[错误]的知识[情报]。*be* ~*ed of* 听得,知道。*I beg to* ~ *you that* ..., …特此奉告。~ *oneself of* (由调查中)知道。*Keep sb*. ~*ed of* ... 向人不断报告…。*be well* ~*ed about sth*. (对某事)了如指掌;(对某事)消息灵通。*Breath* ~*s the body*. 呼吸使身体有活力。— *vi*. 告发,密告 (*against*)。~ *against* [*on*] *an agent* 告发一名间谍。

in·form[2] [in'fɔːm; ɪn`fɔrm] *a*.〔古〕不成形的,无形状的。

in-form ['in-'fɔːm; `ɪn-`fɔm] *a*.〔英〕竞技状态良好的。

in·for·mal [in'fɔːməl; ɪn`fɔrml̩] *a*. 1. 非正式的,简略的。2. 不拘礼节[形式]的;口语的。*an* ~ *visit* 非正式访问。~ *proceedings* 简略手续。*an* ~ *style* (日常使用的)语体。**-ly** *ad*.

in·for·mal·i·ty [ˌinfɔː'mæliti; ˏɪnfɔr`mælətɪ] *n*. 1. 非正式;不拘礼节[形式]。2. 变通的行动。

in·form·ant [in'fɔːmənt; ɪn`fɔrmənt] *n*. 1. 通知者,通报者,报告者;密告者。2. (分析当地语音、国语等时的)标准发音者。

in·for·mat·ics [ˌinfə'mætiks; ˏɪnfɚ`mætɪks] *n*.〔*pl*.〕〔用作单数〕信息学。

in·for·ma·tion [ˌinfə'meiʃən; ˏɪnfɚ`meʃən] *n*. 1. 通知,通报,报告。2. 报导,消息,情报。3. 资料,知识,学识。4.【自】信息,数据。5.【法】起诉,告发。*acting on* ~ *received*〔警察作证时用的话〕据报导。*ask for* ~ *about* [*concering*, *on*] *sth*. 打听关于某事的消息。*For fuller* ~, *please contact* .... 欲知详情,请与…联系。~ *concering the enemy* 敌情。*a man of wide* ~ 博学多闻的人。*a mine of* ~ 知识宝库。*official* ~ 官方消息。*pry for* ~ 刺探情报。***firsthand*** ~ 第一手资料。***For Your I- Only*** 仅供参考。***get in*** [***collect***, ***gather***] ~(***up***)***on*** 增加…的知识,搜集…的情报。***lay*** [***lodge***] ~ ***against sb***. 告发某人。~ **bureau** 情报局。~ **desk** 问讯处。~ **engineering** 信息工程学。~ **highway** 信息高速公路。~ **officer** 情报员。~ **science** 1. 情报学。2.【自】信息学。~ ***superhighway*** = ~ highway. ~ **supermarket** 计算机服务中心;自动问讯处。~ **technology** 信息技术〔缩写作 IT〕。~ **theory** 信息论 (= theory of ~)。**-al** *a*.

in·form·a·tive [in'fɔːmətiv; ɪn`fɔrmətɪv] *a*. 提供情报的,报告消息的;增进知识的;有教益的。*an* ~ *book* 资料丰富的书。*an* ~ *talk* 有助益的谈话。**-ly** *ad*. **-ness** *n*.

in·form·a·to·ry [in'fɔːmətəri; ɪn`fɔrmə,torɪ] *a*. = informative.

in·formed [in'fɔːmd; ɪn`fɔrmd] *a*. 有学识的,见闻广的,有情报根据的。*an* ~ *mind* 博学多闻的人。*a well-* ~ *man* 消息灵通的人。*be well-* ~ [*ill-* ~] *as to* ... 深深[不怎么]知道…。~ *public opinion* 明达的舆论。~ *sources* 消息灵通人士。

in·form·er [in'fɔːmə; ɪn`fɔrmɚ] *n*. **1**. 通知者,通报者。**2**. 告密的人,密探。*a common* [*professional*] ~ 专业密探。*turn* ~ *on sb*. 告发某人。

in·fra ['infrə; `ɪnfrə] *ad*. (*opp*. supra) (L.) 在下,在以下。*see* ~ *p*. *40* 参看第40页以下。*vide* ~ 见下,参看下文。~ *dig* = ~ *dignitatem* 降低威严的,有失身份的。

in·fra- *pref*. 表示"在下";"在下部": *infra*structure.

in·fract [in'frækt; ɪn`frækt] *vt*. 〔罕〕破坏法律,违法;背信。**-or** *n*.

in·frac·tion [in'frækʃən; ɪn`frækʃən] *n*. 破坏法律,违法,背信。

in·fra·dyne ['infrədain; `ɪnfrə,daɪn] *n*. 【无】低外差法。

in·fra·hu·man [ˌinfrə'hjuːmən; ,ɪnfrə`hjumən] *a*. **1**. 低于人类的〔尤指类人猿的〕。**2**. 似人类的,类人猿的。

in·fra·lap·sar·i·an [ˌinfrəlæp'sɛəriən, -'sær-; ,ɪnfrəlæp`sɛrɪən, -`sær-] **I** *n*. 堕落而后拯救论者〔加尔文教派的一个分支,说什么上帝等人类堕落之后再来拯救〕。**II** *a*. 堕落而后拯救论的;堕落而后拯救论者的。**-sar·i·an·ism** *n*. 堕落而后拯救论。

in·fran·gi·ble [in'frændʒibl; ɪn`frændʒɪbl] *a*. 不可破的,不能分离的;不能违反的,不可侵犯的。*an* ~ *promise* 不能违反的契约。**-bil·i·ty** [inˌfrændʒi'biliti; ɪn,frændʒɪ`bɪlətɪ], **-ness** *n*. **-bly** *ad*.

in·fra·nics [in'fræniks; ɪn`frænɪks] *n*. 红外线电子学。

in·fra·red ['infrə'red; `ɪnfrə`rɛd] **I** *a*. 【物】红外线的;红外区的;产生红外辐射的;对红外辐射敏感的。*an* ~ *detector* 【军】红外线探测器。~ *maser* 红外激射器。~ *photography* 红外照相术。~ *radiation* 红外辐射。~ *rays* 红外线。*an* ~ *seeker* 红外线寻的制导飞弹(或其弹头)。~ *vidicon* 红外摄像管。**II** *n*. 红外线;红外区。

in·fra·son·ic [ˌinfrə'sɔnik; ,ɪnfrə`sɑnɪk] *a*. 【物】亚声的,次声的〔声频低于人耳所能听到的〕。

in·fra·sound [ˌinfrə'saund; ,ɪnfrə`saʊnd] *n*. 亚声,次声,不可听音。

in·fra·spe·cif·ic [ˌinfrəspi'sifik; ,ɪnfrəspɪ`sɪfɪk] *a*. 同物种的〔如亚种〕。

in·fra·struc·ture [ˌinfrə'strʌktʃə; `ɪnfrə,strʌktʃɚ] *n*. **1**. 基础设施〔尤指社会、国家赖以生存和发展的,如道路、学校、电厂、交通、通讯系统等基本设施〕。**2**. 【军】永久性基地,永久性防御设施。**-tur·al** *a*.

in·fre·quence, -cy [in'friːkwəns, -si; ɪn`frikwəns, -sɪ] *n*. 很少发生,稀罕。

in·fre·quent [in'friːkwənt; ɪn`frikwənt] *a*. 稀罕的,少见的;偶然的。*not* ~ 常常发生的。**-ly** *ad*.

in·fres·sion [in'freʃən; ɪn`frɛʃən] *n*. 【经】膨胀形衰退〔指物价上涨但收入不变甚至削减的状况〕。

in·fringe [in'frindʒ; ɪn`frɪndʒ] *vt*. 破坏(法律等),侵犯(权利等),违反(协议等)。*Be careful not to* ~ *the rights of other people*. 当心不要侵犯别人的权利。— *vi*. 侵犯 (*on*; *upon*)。*Don't* ~ *on* (*upon*) *sb*.*'s privacy*. 不要侵犯某人。**-ment** *n*.

in·fruc·tu·ous [in'frʌktjuəs; ɪn`frʌktjuəs] *a*. **1**. 不结果的,不毛的。**2**. 徒劳的,无效果的。

in·fun·dib·u·la [ˌinfʌn'dibjulə; ,ɪnfʌn`dɪbjulə] *n*. infundibulum 的复数。

in·fun·dib·u·lar [ˌinfʌn'dibjulə; ,ɪnfʌn`dɪbjulɚ], **-late** [-lit; -lɪt] *a*. 【植】**1**. = infundibuliform. **2**. 有漏斗状器官的。

in·fun·dib·u·li·form [ˌinfən'dibjulifɔːm; ,ɪnfən`dɪbjulɪ,fɔrm] *a*. 漏斗状的。~ **corella** 【植】漏斗状花冠。

in·fun·dib·u·lum [ˌinfən'dibjuləm; ,ɪnfən`dɪbjuləm] *n*. (*pl*. **-la** [-lə; -lə]) 【解】漏斗状器官。

in·fu·ri·ate [in'fjuərieit; ɪn`fjʊrɪ,et] **I** *vt*. 激怒,使发怒。**be** ~**d at** 对…极为愤怒。**II** *a*. 狂怒的。**-a·tion** *n*. **-ly** *ad*.

in·fu·ri·at·ing [in'fjuəriˌeitiŋ; ɪn`fjʊrɪ,etɪŋ] *a*. 万分激怒的,令人发怒的。**-ly** *ad*.

in·fus·cate [in'fʌskit, -keit; ɪn`fʌskɪt, -ket] *a*. 烟褐色的〔指昆虫翅〕(= infuscated)。

in·fuse [in'fjuːz; ɪn`fjuz] *vt*. **1**. 注入;灌注,灌输。**2**. 鼓舞,激发;使充满。**3**. 泡(茶);浸渍;泡(药)。~ *the mind* [*sb*.] *with new hope* 用新的希望激励某人。~ *new blood* 注入新鲜血液。~ *tea* 沏茶。

in·fus·er [in'fjuːzə; ɪn`fjuzɚ] *n*. **1**. 鼓吹者。**2**. 注入器;浸渍器,茶壶。

in·fu·si·ble[1] [in'fjuːzəbl; ɪn`fjuzəbl] *a*. 能注入的,能灌输的。

in·fu·si·ble[2] [in'fjuːzəbl; ɪn`fjuzəbl] *a*. 不溶性的,难溶化的。**-bili·ty** [inˌfjuːzə'biliti; ɪn,fjuzə`bɪlətɪ] *n*.

in·fu·sion [in'fjuːʒən; ɪn`fjuʒən] *n*. **1**. 注入;灌输。**2**. 注入物。**3**. 泡制;浸渍。**4**. 浸液;【医】输注。*saline* ~ 盐水输注。~ *of tea* 泡茶,沏茶。*fresh* ~*s* 【医】新鲜浸剂。

in·fu·sion·ism [in'fjuːʒənizəm; ɪn`fjuʒənɪzm] *n*. 【神】灵魂投胎论。**-ist** *n*.

in·fu·sive [in'fjuːsiv; ɪn`fjusɪv] *a*. 趋于灌输的,可灌输的。

In·fu·so·ri·a [ˌinfjuː'zɔːriə; ,ɪnfju`zorɪə] *n*. [*pl*.] 【动】滴虫[纤毛]纲。

in·fu·so·ri·al [ˌinfjuː'sɔːriəl, -'zɔː-; ,ɪnfjʊ`sorɪəl, -`zɔ-] *a*. 滴虫的,含滴虫的,有滴虫特性的。

in·fu·so·ri·an [ˌinfjuː'zɔːriən; ,ɪnfju`zorɪən] **I** *n*. 纤毛虫。**II** *a*. = infusorial.

-ing[1] *suf*. 构成动名词或名词。**1**. 表示"动作": danc*ing*, hunt*ing*. **2**. 表示"职业": bank*ing*, garden*ing*. **3**. 表示"材料": rail*ing*, cloth*ing*. **4**. 表示"动作的结果","产物": paint*ing*, build*ing*. **5**. 表示"动作的对象": sew*ing*, wash*ing*. **6**. 表示"配合": colour*ing*, feather*ing*.

-ing[2] *suf*. 构成现在分词。**1**. 〔用作形容词〕: charm*ing*. **2**. 〔用作介词、副词〕: dur*ing*, notwithstand*ing*. **3**. 〔用作半被动性分词〕: cook*ing* apples.

-ing[3] *suf*. 构成名词。**1**. 加于父名后作子名。Bill*ing* (= son of Bill). **2**. 表示"…类物","…状物","作成物": farth*ing*, geld*ing*.

in·gath·er [in'gæðə; ɪn`gæðɚ] *vt*., *vi*. 〔古〕**1**. 聚集,收集。**2**. 收获,收割。**-ing** ['inˌgæðəriŋ; `ɪn,gæðərɪŋ] *n*.

in·gem·i·nate [in'dʒemineit; ɪn`dʒɛmɪ,net] *vt*. 重申,反复讲。

in·gen·er·ate [in'dʒenərit; ɪn`dʒɛnərɪt] **I** *a*. 〔古〕天生的,固有的。**II** [in'dʒenəreit; ɪn`dʒɛnəret] *vt*. 〔古〕产生于内,产生,生出。

in·gen·ious [in'dʒiːnjəs; ɪn`dʒinjəs] *a*. **1**. 机灵的,足智多谋的,别出心裁的,有独创性的。**2**. 精巧制成的,巧妙的。*an* ~ *mind* 机灵的头脑。*an* ~ *machine* 精巧的机器。**-ly** *ad*. **-ness** *n*.

in·gé·nue [ænʒei'njuː, F. ɛ̃ʒei'njuː; ænʒe`nju, F. ɛ̃ʒe`nju] *n*. (*pl*. ~*s* [-'njuːz; -`njuz]) (F.) 天真的姑娘,扮演天真姑娘的女演员。

in·ge·nu·i·ty [ˌindʒi'njuːiti; ,ɪndʒɪ`njuɪtɪ] *n*. **1**. 机灵,机智,独创性。**2**. 独出心裁,设计新颖;巧妙,精巧。*I- in varying tactics depends on mother wit*. 运用之妙,存乎一心。

in·gen·u·ous [in'dʒenjuəs; ɪn`dʒɛnjuəs] *a*. 直率的,坦白的,老实的;天真的。**-ly** *ad*. **-ness** *n*.

I

in·ger·ence [ˈindʒərəns; ˋɪndʒərəns] *n*. 干涉;侵犯。

In·ger·soll [ˈiŋgəsɔl; ˋɪŋgəsɑl] *n*. 1. 英格索尔〔姓氏〕。2. **Robert Green ～** 罗伯特·格林·英格索尔〔1833—1899,美国法学家,律师,不可知论的倡导者〕。

in·gest [inˈdʒest; ɪnˋdʒɛst] *vt*. 咽下,摄取,吸收。**-i·ble** *a*. 可摄取的。**-ive** *a*. 有关(食物等的)摄取的,供吸收的。**-ion** *n*. 1. 咽下,吸收。2.【机】空气[气体、液体]的吸入。

in·ges·ta [inˈdʒestə; ɪnˋdʒɛstə] *n*. 〔*pl*.〕营养物,食物。

in·gle [ˈiŋgl; ˋɪŋgl] *n*. 〔Scot.〕1. 炉火;火焰。2. 壁炉,火炉。～**-nook** *n*. 〔英〕炉边,壁炉旁的角落。～**side** 炉边,炉旁。

in·glo·ri·ous [inˈglɔːriəs; ɪnˋglɔrɪəs] *a*. 1. 不光彩的,不体面的,可耻的。2. 〔古〕无名的,湮没无闻的。**-ly** *ad*.

in·go·ing [ˈinˌgəuiŋ; ˋɪnˏgoɪŋ] **I** *a*. 1. 进来的,进入的(*opp*. out going)。2. 洞察的,深入的。*the ～ administration* 上台的政府。*an ～ particle* 入射粒子。*an ～ tenant* 新的租户。*an ～ tide* 涨潮。*an ～ writer* 洞察入微的作家。**II** *n*. 1. 进入。2. 〔英〕新租户付给房东的装修费;商号受盘人付出的款子。

in·got [ˈiŋgət; ˋɪŋgət] *n*. 【冶】铸模;铁块,锭。～ *bar* 铸块。～ *dogs* [*tongs*] 锭钳。～ *iron* 锭铁,低碳钢。～ *metal* 金属锭,铸金属。～ *pit* 均热炉。～ *slab* 扁钢锭。

in·graft [inˈgrɑːft; ɪnˋgrɑft] *vt*. = engraft.

in·grain [inˈgrein; ɪnˋgren] **I** *vt*. 1. 【纺】使原纱(或原料)染色。2. 使全部渗透,使根深蒂固(= engrain)。*be deeply ～ed in the mind* 在头脑中根深蒂固。**II** *a*. 1. 由染色原纱[原料]制成的。*an ～ towel* 提花毛巾。2. 遍体渗透的;根深蒂固的。*an ～ criminal* 惯犯。**III** *n*. 1. 原纱[原料]染色;染色原纱织物。2. 固有的品质,本质。

in·grained [inˈgreind, ˈingreind; ɪnˋgrend, ˋɪngrend] *a*. 根深蒂固的。～ *habits* 积习,根深蒂固的偏见。

In·gram(s) [ˈiŋgrəm(z); ˋɪŋgrəm(z)] *n*. 英格拉姆(斯)〔姓氏〕。

in·grate [inˈgreit; ˋɪngret] **I** *n*. 忘恩负义的人。**II** *a*. 〔古〕忘恩的。

in·gra·ti·ate [inˈgreiʃieit; ɪnˋgreʃɪˏet] *vt*. 使迎合,使讨好,使巴结。～ *oneself with sb*., ～ *oneself into sb.'s favour* 讨好某人。**-a·tion** *n*.

in·gra·ti·at·ing [inˈgreiʃieitiŋ; ɪnˋgreʃɪetɪŋ] *a*. 1. 讨好的,迎合的。2. 吸引人的,迷人的。*an ～ smile* 迷人的微笑。**-ly** *ad*.

in·grat·i·tude [inˈgrætitjuːd; ɪnˋgrætɪtjud] *n*. 忘恩负义。～ *to one's parents* 对父母不孝。

in·gra·ves·cence [ˌingrəˈvesns; ˏɪngrəˋvɛsn̩s] *n*. (病势)加重,恶化。

in·gra·ves·cent [ˌingrəˈvesnt; ˏɪngrəˋvɛsn̩t] *a*. (病势)日愈恶化[加重]的。

in·gre·di·ent [inˈgriːdiənt; ɪnˋgridɪənt] *n*. 1. (混合物的)组成部分,成分,要素。2. 【化】拼份,拼料。

in·gress [ˈingres; ˋɪngrɛs] *n*. (*opp*. egress) 1. 进入,入口,进路;进入权;内移。2. 【天】初切。*a means of ～* 入口。～ *of groundwater* 【建】地下水侵入。**-ion** *n*. 进入。

in·gres·sive [inˈgresiv; ɪnˋgrɛsɪv] *a*. 1. 与进入有关的。2. 【语法】动作[情况]的开始的(=inceptive)。

Ing·rid [ˈiŋgrid; ˋɪŋgrɪd] *n*. 英格丽德〔女子名〕。

in-group [ˈin-gruːp; ˋɪn-grup] *n*. 内部集团,自己人集团。

in·grow·ing [ˈinˌgrəuiŋ; ˋɪnˏgroɪŋ] *a*. 向内生长的;(指甲)生进肌肉内的。

in·grown [ˈingrəun; ˋɪngron] *a*. 1. 向内生长的。2. 天生的,生来的。*an ～ toenail* 长入肉内的脚趾甲〔尤指向肉内〕。

in·growth [ˈinˌgrəuθ; ˋɪnˏgroθ] *n*. 1. 向内生长。2. 长进肌肉内的东西。

in·gui·nal [ˈiŋgwinl; ˋɪŋgwɪn̩l] *a*. 【解】腹股沟的。*the ～ canal* 【解】腹股沟管。*the ～ glands* 【解】腹股沟淋巴腺。

in·gulf [inˈgʌlf; ɪnˋgʌlf] *vt*. 吞没,席卷(= engulf)。*battlefields ～ed in smoke and strewn with debris* 浓烟滚滚,瓦砾遍地的战场。**-ment** *n*.

in·gur·gi·tate [inˈgəːdʒiteit; ɪnˋgɝdʒɪˏtet] *vt*., *vi*. 狼吞虎咽,大吃大嚼。**-ta·tion** [inˌgəːdʒiˈteiʃən; ɪnˏgɝdʒɪˋteʃən] *n*.

in·hab·it [inˈhæbit; ɪnˋhæbɪt] *vt*. 居住;栖息。～ *a city* 住在城市。**-a·ble** *a*. 适于居住[栖息]的。**-er** *n*. 居住[栖息]者。

in·hab·it·an·cy [inˈhæbitənsi; ɪnˋhæbɪtənsɪ] *n*. (暂时性的)居住;住处。

in·hab·it·ant [inˈhæbitənt; ɪnˋhæbɪtənt] *n*. 1. 居民,住户,常住居民。2. 栖息的动物。

in·hab·i·ta·tion [inˌhæbiˈteiʃən; ɪnˏhæbɪˋteʃən] *n*. 居住;栖息;住宅,住处。

in·hab·it·ed [inˈhæbitid; ɪnˋhæbɪtɪd] *a*. 有人居住的,有人烟的;住着的;(屋子)在使用(或租用)的。*an ～ island* 有人居住的岛。*be thickly* [*thinly*] ～ 人烟稠密[稀少]的。～ *satellite* 载人卫星。

in·hal·ant [inˈheilənt; ɪnˋhelənt] **I** *a*. 吸入的。**II** *n*. 被吸入的药物或其他东西。

in·ha·la·tion [ˌinhəˈleiʃən; ˏɪnhəˋleʃən] *n*. 吸入;吸入物;吸入剂;吸入法。

in·ha·la·tor [ˈinhəleitə; ˋɪnhəˏletɚ] *n*. 1. 【医】吸入器。2. 口罩呼吸器,防毒面具(= respirator)。

in·hale [inˈheil; ɪnˋhel] *vt*. 1. 吸入。2. 〔美俚〕吃(小餐),喝(咖啡、汤等)。～ *fresh air* 吸入新鲜空气。—*vi*. 吸气。*Inhale! Exhale!* 吸气;呼气! *Do you ～ when you smoke?* 你抽烟时是否把烟深深吸入肺部?

in·hal·er [inˈheilə; ɪnˋhelɚ] *n*. 1. 吸入者;吸入器。2. 【化】吸气器,滤气器。*ether ～* 【医】醚吸入器。

in·har·mon·ic [ˌinhɑːˈmɔnik; ˏɪnhɑrˋmɑnɪk] *a*. 不和谐的,不协调的,冲突的。

in·har·mo·ni·ous [ˌinhɑːˈməunjəs, -niəs; ˏɪnhɑrˋmonjəs, -nɪəs] *a*. 1. 不和谐的,不协调的,嘈杂的。2. 不和睦的,冲突的。**-ly** *ad*. **-ness** *n*.

in·har·mo·ny [inˈhɑːməni; ɪnˋhɑrmənɪ] *n*. 不和谐,不协调,冲突。

in·haul [ˈinˌhɔːl; ˋɪnˏhɔl] *n*. 【海】1. 引索。2. 卷帆索(= inhauler)。

in·here [inˈhiə; ɪnˋhɪr] *vi*. 固有,具有(性质等)(*in*);(权利)属于(人);原有(*in*);含有(意义)。

in·her·ence, -en·cy [inˈhiərəns, -si; ɪnˋhɪrəns, -sɪ] *n*. 内在(性),固有(性),基本属性。

in·her·ent [inˈhiərənt; ɪnˋhɪrənt] *a*. 内在的,固有的,生来的(*in*)。～ *stability* 【空】固有稳定性。*the power ～ in the office of President* 总统一职所具有的权力。*Weight is an ～ quality of matter*. 重量是物质固有的特性。*He has an ～ love of beauty*. 他天生爱美。**-ly** *ad*.

in·her·it [inˈherit; ɪnˋhɛrɪt] *vt*. 1. 继承(传统、遗产、权利等)。2. 经遗传而得(性格、体质等)。*She ～s her mother's looks and her father's temper*. 她继承了母亲的相貌和父亲的脾气。～ *a fortune* 继承财产。—*vi*. 接受遗产;成为继承人。*Astronomy ～s from astrology*. 天文学的前身是占星术。

in·her·it·a·ble [inˈheritəbl; ɪnˋhɛrɪtəb̩l] *a*. 1. 可继承的,有继承权的。2. 可遗传的。**-bil·i·ty** [inˌheritəˈbiliti; ɪnˏhɛrətəˋbɪlətɪ] *n*.

in·her·it·ance [inˈheritəns; ɪnˋhɛrɪtəns] *n*. 1. 继承,承受。2. 遗传;遗传性,遗传质。3. 遗产;继承物,遗赠。4. 天赋。5. 继承权,世袭权。*criss-cross ～* 【生】交叉遗传。*receive sth. by ～* 由继承而获得某物。～ *tax* 〔美〕遗产税,继承税〔英国称 death-duty 或 estate tax〕。

in·her·i·tor [inˈheritə; ɪnˋhɛrɪtɚ] *n*. 继承人;嗣子,后

继者。

in·her·i·tress, in·her·i·trix [in'heritris, -triks; ɪn`herɪtrɪs;-trɪks] *n*. (*pl*. *-tri·ces* [-traisiːz; -traɪsiz]) 女继承人。

in·he·sion [in'hiːʒən; ɪn`hiʒən] *n*. = inherence.

in·hib·it [in'hibit; ɪn`hɪbɪt] *vt*. 1. 抑制,约束。2. 禁止,阻止。3.【宗】使停止教权。~ *wrong desires* 抑制邪念。~ *sb*. *from doing sth*. 禁止某人做某事。

in·hib·it·er, in·hib·i·tor [in'hibitə; ɪn`hɪbɪtɚ] *n*. 禁止者,抑制者;抑制因素〔尤指【化】抑制剂,阻化剂〕。

in·hi·bi·tion [ˌinhi'biʃən; ˏɪnhɪ`bɪʃən] *n*. 1. 禁止,阻止。2.【心】压制,抑制(作用),心障。3.【英法】诉讼停止命令。4.【宗】教权停止命令。5.【化】抑制(作用)。*central* ~【医】中枢抑制。

in·hib·i·to·ry [in'hibitəri; ɪn`hɪbɪˏtorɪ] *a*. 禁止的;抑制的,阻止的。~ *nerve*【生理】抑制神经。

in·ho·mo·ge·ne·i·ty ['inˌhɔməudʒə'niːiti; ˌɪnhɑmədʒə`niətɪ] *n*.【生】不同质,非纯系,不同源。

in·ho·mo·ge·ne·ous [ˌinhəumə'dʒiːniəs, -hɔmə-; ˏɪnhomə`dʒinɪəs, -hɑmə-] *a*. 1.【生】不同质的,非纯系的,不同源的。2. 不均匀的,不纯一的。3.【数】非齐次的。~ *coordinates* 非齐次坐标。

in·hos·pi·ta·ble [in'hɔspitəbl; ɪn`hɑspɪtəbl] *a*. 1. 不好客的,冷淡的,不亲切的。2. 不适于居住的,荒凉的。**-ness** *n*. **-bly** *ad*.

in·hos·pi·tal·i·ty ['inˌhɔspi'tæliti; `ɪnˏhɑspɪ`tælətɪ] *n*. 冷淡,不亲切。

in-house ['inhaus; `ɪnhaʊs] *a*. 由本机构内部产生的,机构内部的。

in·hu·man [in'hjuːmən; ɪn`hjumən] *a*. 1. 非人的,不近人情的。2. 残忍的,野蛮的,无人性的。**-ly** *ad*.

in·hu·mane [ˌinhju(ː)'mein; ˏɪnhjʊ`men] *a*. 不近人情的,薄情的;残忍的,无人道的。**-ly** *ad*.

in·hu·man·i·ty [ˌinhju(ː)'mæniti; ˏɪnhjʊ`mænətɪ] *n*. 1. 无情,残忍,野蛮。2. 残忍行为。

in·hu·ma·tion [ˌinhju(ː)'meiʃən; ˏɪnhjʊ`meʃən] *n*. 埋葬,土葬。

in·hume [in'hjuːm; ɪn`hjum] *vt*. 埋葬,土葬。

in·im·i·cal [i'nimikəl; ɪ`nɪmɪkəl] *a*. 1. 有敌意的,敌视的 (*to*)。2. 不利的,有害的。*nations* ~ *to one another* 互相敌视的国家。*circumstance* ~ *to success* 不利于成功的情况。**-ly** *ad*.

in·im·i·ta·ble [i'nimitəbl; ɪ`nɪmɪtəbl] *a*. 不可仿效的,不可比拟的;无比的,无双的。**-bil·i·ty** [iˌnimitə'biliti; ɪˏnɪmɪtə`bɪlətɪ] *n*. **-bly** *ad*.

in·im·i·ta·ble·ness [i'nimitəblnis; ɪ`nɪmɪtəblnɪs] *n*. 不可仿效,不可比拟,无比,无双。

in·i·on ['iniən; `ɪnɪən] *n*.【解】枕骨隆突。

in·iq·ui·tous [i'nikwitəs; ɪ`nɪkwɪtəs] *a*. 不公正的;不法的,不义的,不公平的,邪恶的。**-ly** *ad*.

in·iq·ui·tous·ness [i'nikwətəsnis; ɪ`nɪkwətəsnɪs] *n*. 不公正;不法;不义;不公平;邪恶。

in·iq·ui·ty [i'nikwiti; ɪ`nɪkwətɪ] *n*. 1. 不公正,不法,不义。2. 不义行为,罪恶,罪过。

init. = initial.

in·i·tial [i'niʃəl; ɪ`nɪʃəl] **I** *a*. 最初的,开始的;原始的;初期的,初发的。*the* ~ *boiling point*【化】初馏点〔第一滴馏物滴下时的温度〕。*the* ~ *cost* [*expenditure*] 开办费。*the* ~ *difficulties* 开始的困难。*the* ~ *issue of a magazine* 杂志的创刊号。*the* ~ *public offering* (股票的)首期上市,初次公开发行。*the* ~ *stage* 初期,开始阶段。*an* ~ *letter* 词首字母。*an* ~ *signature* 仅用姓名词首字母的签名。*an* ~ *word* 词首字母缩略词〔如 NATO〕。**II** *n*. 词首字母,词首大写字母;〔*pl*.〕姓名中的大写字母〔如 John Smith 中的 J. S.〕。**III** *vt*. (*-l(l)ed*, *-l(l)ing*) 在…上记上姓名的词首字母,用词首字母在…上署名;【政】草签,临时签署(条约等)。*an initialled handkerchief* 记有姓名第一字母的手帕。**I- Teaching Alphabet** 初学英语拼音字母〔英国詹姆斯·皮特曼创造的一套拼音字母,计 44 个字,和读音一致,用以教初学者〕。~ **velocity**【物】初速(度)。**-ism** *n*. 词首字母缩略词。**-ly** *ad*. 起初,开始。

i·ni·tial·ize [i'niʃəlaiz; ɪ`nɪʃəlaɪz] *vt*.【计】预置。

in·i·ti·ate [i'niʃieit; ɪ`nɪʃɪˏet] **I** *vt*. 1. 开始,着手;创始,发动;【动】起爆。2. 启发,启蒙,使入门。3. 引进,正式介绍。4. 提议,倡议。~ *a reform* 着手改革。~ *the attack* 开始攻击。~ *pupils into the elements of grammar* 把基本语法教给学生。~ *sb*. *into a secret* 把秘密传授给某人。~ *sb*. *into a club* 正式介绍某人加入俱乐部。*the* ~*d* (集体的)入会者。~ *a constitutional amendment* 提出宪法修正案。**II** [i'niʃiit; ɪ`nɪʃɪɪt] *a*., *n*. 被传授初步知识的(人);新入会的(人)。

in·i·ti·a·tion [iˌniʃi'eiʃən; ɪˏnɪʃɪ`eʃən] *n*. 1. 开始,创始;起爆。2. 教导,指点,启发。3. 正式加入;入会仪式,入党仪式。*vorticity* ~ 涡流的产生。~ **fee**〔美〕入会费。

in·i·ti·a·tive [i'niʃiətiv; ɪ`nɪʃɪətɪv] **I** *a*. 起始的,初步的,创始的。~ *spirit* 主动精神。**II** *n*. 1. 第一步,发端;着手,创始,倡议;主动精神,创始力。2. 〔the ~〕(立法机关对新法案的)动议权;(公民的)创制权。3.【军】(先发制人的)主动性。*subjective* ~ 主观能动性。***have the*** ~ 掌握主动权。***on one's own*** ~ 主动地。***take the*** ~ 带头,采取主动。

in·i·ti·a·tor [i'niʃieitə; ɪ`nɪʃɪˏetɚ] *n*. 1. 开始者,创始者,倡议者。2. 教导者,传授者。3. 引药,引发剂,起爆药。4. 激磁机。*play the role of an* ~ 起带头作用。

in·i·ti·a·to·ry [i'niʃiətəri; ɪ`nɪʃɪəˏtorɪ] *a*. 1. 起始的,发端的,初步的,启蒙的。2. 入会的,入社的,入党的。

in·ject [in'dʒekt; ɪn`dʒɛkt] *vt*. 1. 注入,注射。2. 注满。3. 插入(意见等)。4. 把…射入(轨道)。5.【机】喷射,引射 (*into*)。~ *penicillin into the blood-stream* 把青霉素注入血液。~ *hypodermically* 皮下注射。~ *a remark into the conversation* 插嘴。

in·jec·tion [in'dʒekʃən; ɪn`dʒɛkʃən] *n*. 1. 注射。2. 注射剂,注射液,针药,灌肠(药)。3. 充满,注满。4.【医】充血。5.【机】喷射。6.【宇】(卫星等的)入轨,射入轨道,射入轨道的时间[地点]。*hyperdermic* [*subculaneous*] ~ 皮下注射。*an* ~ *in the buttock* 注射臀部的一针。*fuel* ~ 燃料喷射,注油。~ *pump* 喷射泵,喷油泵。*an* ~ *cylinder* 压射缸。*an* ~ *grid*【电】注频栅极。~ **molding** 喷射造型法,喷射模塑法。~**-molded** *a*. 喷射造型法的,喷射模塑法的。

in·jec·tor [in'dʒektə; ɪn`dʒɛktɚ] *n*. 1. 注射者;注射器,针管。2.【机】喷射器,喷注器,喷雾器,喷头。*an exhaust steam* ~ 排气喷射器。*a spray* ~ 射流式喷嘴。~ **razor** 喷射式刮胡刀。

in·ju·di·cial [ˌindʒu(ː)'diʃəl; ˏɪndʒʊ(u)`dɪʃəl] *a*. 1. 不依照法律形式的,不符合法官身份的。2. = injudicious.

in·ju·di·cious [ˌindʒuː'diʃəs; ˏɪndʒu`dɪʃəs] *a*. 判断欠妥的,不明智的,不慎重的。~ *remarks* 欠考虑的语言。**-ly** *ad*. **-ness** *n*.

In·jun, in·jun ['indʒən; `ɪndʒən] *n*.〔美俚〕印地安人。***get up one's*** ~〔美俚〕发怒。***play one's*** ~ 逃匿。

in·junct [in'dʒʌŋkt; ɪn`dʒʌŋkt] *vt*.〔口〕禁止。

in·junc·tion [in'dʒʌŋkʃən; ɪn`dʒʌŋkʃən] *n*. 命令,责戒;【法】指令,禁令。*lay* ~*s upon* [*on*] *sb*. *to do sth*. 命令某人做某事。

in·junc·tive [in'dʒʌŋktiv; ɪn`dʒʌŋktɪv] *a*. 1. 命令的,训诫的,教训的,指令的。2.【法】禁令的。

in·jur·ant ['indʒurənt; `ɪndʒʊrənt] *n*. 有害的东西。

in·jure ['indʒə; `ɪndʒɚ] *vt*. 1. 损害,毁坏。2. 伤害(感情、自尊心等)。*He* ~*d his left hand in a fire*. 他在火灾中伤了左手。*be badly* ~*d on both legs in a traffic accident* 在车祸中两腿受了重伤。~ *sb*.*'s pride* [*feel-*

I

ings] 伤害别人的自尊心[感情]。

in·jured [ˈindʒəd; ˋɪndʒəd] *a*. 受伤的;受损害的;损伤感情的。*the* ~ 受伤者。~ *looks* 受冤屈的样子。*the* ~ *party* 被害者。*in an* ~ *voice* 用愤怒的声音。*with an* ~ *air* 带着生气的样子。

in·jur·er [ˈindʒərə; ˋɪndʒərɚ] *n*. 毁坏者,加害者,伤害者。

in·ju·ri·ous [inˈdʒuəriəs; ɪnˋdʒʊrɪəs] *a*. 1. 有害的。2. 侮辱的,诽谤的。*a climate* ~ *to health* 有害健康的气候。~ *words* 中伤的言论。

in·ju·ry [ˈindʒəri; ˋɪndʒərɪ] *n*. 1. 损害,毁坏,伤害。2. 伤害的行为。3. 受伤处。*suffer severe injuries* 受重伤。***add insult to*** ~ 伤害之外又加侮辱。***be an*** ~ ***to*** 伤害…,危害…,对…有害。***do sb. an*** ~ = ***do an*** ~ ***to sb.*** 伤害某人。

in·jus·tice [inˈdʒʌstis; ɪnˋdʒʌstɪs] *n*. 1. 不公正,非正义,不公平,权利侵害。2. 不公正的行为。*do sb. an* ~ 使某人受屈,冤枉某人。

ink [iŋk; ɪŋk] I *n*. 1. 墨水;(印刷用的)油墨。2. (乌贼分泌的)墨液。3. 〔俚〕咖啡;廉价酒。*China* [*Chinese*, *India*, *Indian*] ~ 墨,墨汁。*indelible* [*marking*, *permanent*] ~ 不变墨水。*invisible* [*secret*, *sympathetic*] ~ 密写墨水。*printing* ~ 油墨。*writing* ~ 墨水。*as black as* ~ 漆黑的。*sling* ~〔俚〕做职员;当作家;卖文为生。***before the*** ~ ***is dry*** 墨迹未干;立即。***spill printer's*** ~ 付印。II *vt*. 1. 用墨水写;涂油墨;用墨水弄黑,用墨水沾污。2. 〔美〕签名(在…上)。~ *one's fingers* 墨水弄脏手指。~ **in** [**over**] 用墨水描 (~ *in a drawing* 在铅笔底线上用墨水加描)。~ **out** 用墨水涂去。~ **bag** (乌贼的)墨囊。~**-berry** *n*.【植】1. 光滑冬青 (*Ilex glabra*)〔产于北美东部〕。2. 光滑冬青果。3. = pokeweed. ~**-blot test**【心】墨迹测验。~ **bottle** 墨水瓶。~**fish** *n*. 墨鱼,乌贼。~ **holder** 墨水瓶;(自来水笔的)贮墨管。~**horn** (旧时的)角制墨水瓶 (*smell of* ~ *horn* 有学者派头的,学究气的;卖弄学问的)。~ **pad** 印台。~ **pencil** 复写用颜色铅笔。~**pot** 墨水瓶。~ **recorder** 笔写记录器。~ **sac** = ~ bag. ~**-slinger** 〔美〕作家,办事员,记录员。~**-stand** 1. = ~ well. 2. 墨水台。~**stone** 1.【矿】水绿矾。2. 砚。~**-well** (桌上)墨水池。~ **writer** (电报)印字机。**-less** *a*. 没有墨水的,没有墨汁的。

In·ka·tha [iŋˈkɑːtə; ɪŋˋkɑtə] *n*. 因卡塔自由党[南非一黑人政治组织]。

ink·er [ˈiŋkə; ˋɪŋkɚ] *n*.【印】印版上的油墨辊;(电报)印字机。

in·kind [inˈkaind; ɪnˋkaɪnd] *a*. 实物的,非现金的。~ **relief** 救济物资。

ink·i·ness [ˈiŋkinis; ˋɪŋkɪnɪs] *n*. 墨黑,漆黑。

in·kle [ˈiŋkl; ˋɪŋkl̩] *n*. 〔罕〕1. 亚麻带子。2. 编亚麻带子用的线或纱。

ink·ling [ˈiŋkliŋ; ˋɪŋklɪŋ] *n*. 1. 暗示细微的迹象。2. 微微觉得,模糊的想法。*get an* ~ *of* 微微明白。*give an* ~ *of* 给人一些暗示。*have an* ~ *of* 略有所知。

ink·y [ˈiŋki; ˋɪŋkɪ] *a*. (*ink·i·er*; *-i·est*) 涂有墨水的;给墨水弄污的;漆黑的。*an* ~ *handkerchief* 沾了墨水的手帕。~ *darkness* 一片漆黑。~ **cap**【植】墨水盖鬼伞[墨蕈属 (*Coprinus*) 菇类,其顶盖液化成墨汁]。

in·lace [inˈleis; ɪnˋles] *vt*. (*-laced*; *-lac·ing*) = enlace.

in·laid [ˈinˈleid; ˋɪnˋled] I inlay 的过去式和过去分词。II *a*. 镶嵌的,嵌有花样的。*an* ~ *table* 镶嵌花的桌子。~ *work* 镶嵌工艺。

in·land [ˈinlənd; ˋɪnlənd] I *a*. 1. 内地的,内陆的。2. 国内的。*an* ~ *duty* 内地税。~ *navigation* 内河航行。*the* ~ *sea* 内海。*an* ~ *town* 内地城市。~ *commerce* [*trade*] 国内贸易。~ *exchange* 国内汇兑。~ *mails* 〔英〕国内邮件 (=〔美〕domestic mails)。~ *revenue* 〔英〕国内税收 (=〔美〕internal revenue)。~ *telegraph* 国内电报。II [inˈlænd; ɪnˋlænd] *ad*. 在内地;向内地。*go* ~ 到内地去。III [ˈinlənd; ˋɪnlənd] *n*. 内地,国内。

in·land·er [ˈinləndə; ˋɪnləndɚ] *n*. (生长在)内地的人。

in·land·ish [ˈinləndiʃ; ˋɪnləndɪʃ] *a*. 本地的,内地的。

in-law [ˈinlɔː; ˋɪnˏlɔ] *n*. 〔口、常用 *pl*.〕姻亲。

in·lay [ˈinˌlei, inˈl-; ˏɪnˋle, ɪnˋl-] I *vt*. (*-laid* [ˈinˈleid; ˋɪnled]; *-lay·ing*) 1. 镶嵌,镶入;镶(以) (*with*)。2. 用镶嵌物装饰,插入(页、卡片等)。*ivory inlaid with gold* 镶金象牙。II [ˈinlei; ˋɪnle] *n*. 1. 镶嵌物;镶嵌工艺;镶嵌所用材料。2. (作接穗用的)接芽(= ~ graft)。3.【医】嵌体;内置法,嵌入法。**-er** *n*. 镶嵌者。

in·let [ˈinlet; ˋɪnlɛt] I *n*. 1. 进口,入口。2.【电】引入,输入线。3. 水湾,小港。4. 插入物,镶嵌物。*an* ~ *chamber*【机】进气室。~ *and outlet channels* (水库的)进出渠道。~ *eye* 进气孔。*an* ~ *passage*【军】进路。II *vt*. (*inlet*, *inlet·ting*) 1. 引进。2. 嵌入,插入。

in·li·er [ˈinlaiə; ˋɪnlaɪr] *n*.【地】内窗层,内围层,内露层。

in·ly [ˈinli; ˋɪnlɪ] *ad*. 〔诗〕在内;在中心,暗中;从心里。

in·ly·ing [ˈinlaiiŋ; ˋɪnlaɪɪŋ] *a*. 在内的,内部的。

in·mate [ˈinmeit; ˋɪnmet] *n*. 1. 同居人〔尤指同院病人、同狱犯人或住在同一收容所的人〕。2. 居民。*be the* ~ *of* 同住在。*be the* ~ *of sb.'s heart* 留在某人心中。

in·mesh [inˈmeʃ; ɪnˋmɛʃ] *vt*. = enmesh.

in-mi·grant [ˈinˈmaigrənt; ˋɪnˋmaɪgrənt] I *a*. 外地迁来的。II *n*. 外地迁入者;(动物的)引进品种。

in-mi·grate [ˈinˈmaigreit; ˋɪnˋmaɪgret] *vi*. (由外地)移来,迁入。**-tion** *n*.

in·most [ˈinməust; ˋɪnˏmost] *a*. 最内部的;最深入的;秘藏心中的。*one's* ~ *feelings* [*thoughts*] 内心深处的感情[思想]。

inn [in; ɪn] I *n*. 1. 小旅馆,客栈,小饭店,小酒馆。2. 〔古、诗〕住宅,住处。*keep an* ~ 开旅馆。*put up at an* ~ 住客栈。*the Inns of Chancery* 法学院〔原为英国伦敦法学协会管理下的法科学生宿舍〕。*the Inns of Court* 法律协会〔英国伦敦具有授予律师资格权的四个法学团体:*Inner Temple*, *Middle Temple*, *Lincoln's Inn* 及 *Gray's Inn*〕。II *vi*. 住旅馆。~ **holder**, ~**keeper** *n*. 客栈老板,小旅馆老板。

in·nards [ˈinədz; ˋɪnɚdz] *n*. 〔口〕1. 内脏。2. 内部结构,内部机构。

in·nate [ˈineit; ˋɪnet] *a*. 生来的,天生的,先天的,遗传的,固有的。*sb.'s* ~ *courtesy* 某人天生的温文有礼。*an* ~ *defect* 固有的缺点。*an* ~ *gift* 天赋,资质。**-ly** *ad*. **-ness** *n*.

in·ner [ˈinə; ˋɪnɚ] I *a*. (*superl*. ~***most***, ***inmost***) 1. 内部的 (*opp*. outer)。2. 思想的,精神的;内心的,秘密的。*the* ~ *circle* 核心集团。*an* ~ *room* 内室。*I- Temple* (见 inn 条)。*the* ~ *life of man* 人的内心活动,人的精神生活。*an* ~ *meaning* 深意。*one's* ~ *thoughts* 内心深处的思想。~ *world* 内心世界。II *n*. 1. 内部,里面。2. 接近靶心部分,射中接近靶心部分的一发。~ **bar** 〔英〕【法】王室法律顾问(可在法院内庭就座并进行辩护的高级律师)。~ **cabinet** 核心内阁。~ **child** 内心自我。~ **circle** 核心集团。~ **city** 内城区[多为穷人居住,相对于中产阶级居住区与郊区而言]。~**-city** *a*. 内城的;贫民区的。~**-directed** *a*. 有主见的;有自己理想与目标的,不随俗的。~ **flux**【机】内烟道。~ **grid** 1. 控制栅级,控制电极。2. 调制电极。**I- Light**【宗】灵光〔教友派认为是上帝在一个人的灵魂中产生的指引力量〕。~ **man** 1. 灵魂,精神 (*opp*. outer man)。2. 〔谑〕肚子,胃口(*refresh* [*satisfy*] *one's* ~ *man* 吃饱肚子)。~ **part** [**voice**]【乐】中声部。~ **sole** = insole. ~ **space** 1. 思想中的潜意识部分。2. 水下空间,海洋深处。3. 抽象画的质量[深度]。~ **spring mattress** 弹簧垫子。~ **tube** 内胎。**-most** *a*. = inmost.

in·ner·vate [ˈinəːveit, iˈnəː-; ˋɪnɚvet, ɪˋnɚ-] *vt* **1.** 使受神经支配。**2.** 刺激。

in·ner·va·tion [ˌinəːˈveiʃən; ˏɪnɚˋveʃən] *n*. 【解】支配；神经分布；神经兴奋作用[过程]。

in·nerve [iˈnəːv; ɪˋnɚv] *vt*. **1.** 鼓舞。**2.** = innervate.

In·ness [ˈinis; ˋɪnɪs] *n*. **1.** 英尼斯〔姓氏〕。**2. George** ~ 乔治·英尼斯〔1825—1894,美国画家〕。

in·ning [ˈiniŋ; ˋɪnɪŋ] *n*. **1.** 〔单复数相同〕(棒球、板球的)一局,盘,回合。**2.** 海滩荒地的围垦,〔*pl*.〕围垦的土地。**3.** 〔*pl*.〕轮到显身手的机会;任职期间;当权时期。*Our team made 307 runs in its first* ~. 我们队在第一局获307分。***get one's* ~*s*** 碰到好机会,走运。***have a good long* ~*s*** 一直走运;长寿。***have an* ~*s*** 轮到击球;参加某项活动。***have the* ~*(s)*** 当权,执政。

in·no·cence [ˈinəsns; ˋɪnəsns], 〔古〕**in·no·cen·cy** [-si; -sɪ] *n*. **1.** 无罪;清白。**2.** 单纯,天真无邪。**3.** 无知,头脑简单。**4.** 无罪的人,清白无辜的人。**5.** 【医】良性。***assume* [*put on*] *an air of injured* ~** 装出无辜受累的样子。

in·no·cent [ˈinəsnt; ˋɪnəsnt] **I** *a*. **1.** 清白的;无罪的,无辜的。**2.** 〔口〕缺…的,无…的 (*of*)。**3.** 天真无邪的;单纯的。**4.** 头脑简单的,无知的。**5.** 无恶意的,无害的。**6.** 【医】良性的。*be* ~ *of a crime* 无罪。*an* ~ *child* 天真的孩子。*an* ~ *tumour* 良性瘤。*a wall* ~ *of paint* (未抹墙面的)毛墙。**II** *n*. **1.** 无辜的人;天真无邪的人。**2.** 头脑简单的人,笨蛋。***do the* ~** 装糊涂。***massacre* [*slaughter*] *of the* ~*s*** **1.** 屠杀婴儿。**2.** 〔英俚〕(议会趁会期快满而作出的)撤销某些议案的决定。***the* (*Holy*) *Innocents' Day*** 【宗】屠杀无辜婴儿纪念日〔12月28日〕, ~ **passage** (船舶在航行中遇险时)毋需经主权国同意即可在其港口停泊的权利,无害通过(权)。**-ly** *ad*.

in·no·cu·i·ty [ˌinəˈkjuːiti; ˏɪnəˋkjuətɪ] *n*. **1.** 无害,无毒。**2.** 不关痛养,乏味。

in·noc·u·ous [iˈnɔkjuəs; ɪˋnɑkjʊəs] *a*. **1.** 无害的,无毒的。**2.** 无关痛养的,乏味的。*an* ~ *drug* 无毒的药品。~ *generalities* 不关痛养的泛泛之谈。**-ly** *ad*. **-ness** *n*.

in·nom·i·nate [inˈɔminit; ɪˋnɑmɪnɪt] *a*. 无名的;匿名的。~ *bone* 【解】髋骨。

in·no·vate [ˈinəuveit; ˋɪnoˏvet] *vi*. 刷新,革新,改革 (*in*; *on*; *upon*)。— *vt*. 创始。

in·no·va·tion [ˌinəuˈveiʃən; ˏɪnoˋveʃən] *n*. 创新,革新;改革;新设施,新方法,新发明。*technical* ~ 技术革新。*a vitally important* ~ *in industry* 一项具有重大意义的工业上的革新。**-al** *a*. 革新的,富有革新精神的。

in·no·va·tive, in·no·va·tory [ˈinəuveitiv, -təri; ˋɪnoˏvetɪv, -tərɪ] *a*. 革新的,创新的;富有革新精神的。

in·no·va·tor [ˈinəuveitə; ˋɪnoˏvetɚ] *n*. 革新者,改革者。*a technical* ~ 技术革新者。

in·nox·ious [iˈnɔkʃəs; ɪˋnɑkʃəs] *a*. 无害的,无毒的。**-ly** *ad*. **-ness n.**

Inns·bruck [ˈinzbruk; ˋɪnzbrʊk] *n*. 因斯布鲁克〔奥地利东部的城市〕。

in·nu·en·do [ˌinjuˈendəu; ˏɪnjʊˋendo] **I** *n*. (*pl*. ~*es*) **1.** 暗示,讽刺,影射。**2.** 【法】文件中的附注句。*attack by* ~ 旁敲侧击;含沙射影。**II** *vi*. 使用暗讽;【法】加注说明。— *vt*. 用暗讽表现[表达]。

in·nu·mer·a·ble [iˈnjuːmərəbl; ɪˋnjumərəbl] *a*. 无数的,数不清的。**-bly** *ad*.

in·nu·mer·ous [iˈnjuːmərəs; ɪˋnjumərəs] *a*. = innumerable.

in·nu·tri·tion [ˌinjuːˈtriʃən; ˏɪnjuˋtrɪʃən] *n*. 缺乏营养,营养不良。

in·nu·tri·tious, -tive [ˌinjuːˈtriʃəs, -tiv; ˏɪnjuˋtrɪʃəs, -tɪv] *a*. 缺乏营养的;营养不良的。

in·ob·serv·ance [ˌinəbˈzəːvəns; ˏɪnəbˋzɝvəns] *n*. 不留心,玩忽;(对习惯、法律等)不遵守。

in·ob·serv·ant [ˌinəbˈzəːvənt; ˏɪnəbˋzɝvənt] *a*. 不注意的,玩忽的,违反的。

in·oc·u·la·ble [iˈnɔkjuləbl; ɪˋnɑkjələbl] *a*. **1.** 接种的,预防注射的,移植(细菌)的。**2.** 接枝的,接芽的。**3.** 灌输(思想)的。

in·oc·u·lant [iˈnɔkjulənt; ɪˋnɑkjələnt] *n*. = inoculum.

in·oc·u·late [iˈnɔkjuleit; ɪˋnɑkjəˏlet] *vt*. **1.** 【医】给…接种,给…注射预防针,移植(细菌)。**2.** 【植】嫁接;播种。**3.** 注入,灌输(思想)。~ *sb*. *for* [*against*] *smallpox* 给…种痘。*be* ~*d against smallpox* (接受)种痘。~ *sb*. *with new ideas* 给某人灌输新思想。

in·oc·u·la·tion [iˌnɔkjuˈleiʃən; ɪˏnɑkjəˋleʃən] *n*. **1.** 【医】接种;预防注射;(细菌等的)移植。**2.** 感染,灌输(思想等)。**3.** 【植】接枝,接芽;嫁接。**4.** 【医】加孕育剂法。*artificial* ~人工接种。*protective* ~ 预防注射。

in·oc·u·la·tive [iˈnɔkjuleitiv, ɪˋnɑkjəˏletɪv] *a*. 接种的,种痘的。

in·oc·u·la·tor [iˈnɔkjuleitə; ɪˋnɑkjəˏletɚ] *n*. 接种者,注射者;接枝者。

in·oc·u·lum [iˈnɔkjuləm; ɪˋnɑkjələm] *n*. (*pl*. **-u·la**) 接种体,接种物,种菌 (= inoculant)。

in·o·dor·ous [inˈəudərəs; ɪnˋodərəs] *a*. 没有气味的,没有香味的。

in·of·fen·sive [ˌinəˈfensiv; ˏɪnəˋfɛnsɪv] *a*. 无害的;不讨厌的;没有恶意的。**-ly** *ad*. **-ness** *n*.

in·of·fi·cious [inəˈfiʃəs; ɪnəˋfɪʃəs] *a*. **1.** 不尽职责的,无义务观念的,不遵守道义的。**2.** 【法】不履行道德上的义务的〔如无理地剥夺子女或妻子正当的继承权〕。*an* ~ *testament* [*will*] 违反义务观念的遗嘱〔无理剥夺继承人的继承权的遗嘱〕。

in·op·er·a·ble [inˈɔpərəbl; ɪnˋɑpərəbl] *a*. **1.** 【医】不能施行手术的,不宜动手术的。**2.** 不能实行的,行不通的。*an* ~ *cancer* 不宜动手术的癌。

in·op·er·a·tive [inˈɔpərətiv; ɪnˋɑparetɪv] *a*. **1.** 不起作用的。**2.** (法律、规章等)不生效的。**-ness** *n*.

in·o·per·cu·late [ˌinəuˈpəːkjulit; ˏɪnoˋpɝkjəlɪt] *a*. 无囊盖的,无盖的。

in·op·por·tune [inˈɔpətjuːn; ɪnˋɑpɚtjun] *a*. 不合时宜的,不适当的,不凑巧的。*at an* ~ *time* 不合时机。**-ly** *ad*. **-ness** *n*.

in·or·di·nate [iˈnɔːdinit; ɪˋnɔrdɪnɪt] *a*. **1.** 紊乱的,不规则的。**2.** 无限制的,过度的。***keep* ~ *hours*** 过着无规律的生活,熬夜。**-ly** *ad*.

inorg. = inorganic.

in·or·gan·ic [ˌinɔːˈgænik; ˏɪnɔrˋgænɪk] *a*. **1.** 【化】无机的;无机物的。**2.** 无生物的。**3.** 无组织体系的,人造的,无特性的,无活力的。~ *sphere* 【地】无生物界。~ *chemistry* 无机化学。~ *matter* 无机物。**-cal·ly** *ad*.

in·or·gan·i·za·tion [inˌɔːgənaiˈzeiʃən; ɪnˏɔrgənaɪˋzeʃən] *n*. 缺乏组织,无组织;无组织状态。

in·or·nate [ˌinɔːˈneit, inˈɔːnit; ˏɪnɔrˋnet, ɪnˋɔrnɪt] *a*. 不加修饰的;(文体等)朴素的。

in·os·cu·late [iˈnɔskjuleit; ɪˋnɑskjəˏlet] *vi*., *vt*. **1.** (使)(血管等)接合 (*with*);(使纤维等)缠合。**2.** (使)密切结合。**-tion** *n*.

in·o·sine [ˈinəsiːn; ˋɪnəsin] *n*. 【生化】次黄(嘌呤核)苷,肌苷。~ **monophosphate** [ˈmɔnəuˈfɔsfeit; ˋmɑnoˋfɑsfet] 一磷酸肌苷,肌苷酸。

in·o·sin·ic [ˌinəˈsinik; ˏɪnəˋsɪnɪk] *a*. 【生化】次黄(嘌呤核)苷的。~ **acid** 【生化】次黄(嘌呤核)苷酸,肌苷酸。

in·o·si·tol [iˈnəusitəul, -tɔːl; ɪˋnosɪtol, -tɔl] *n*. 【生化】肌醇;环已六醇。

in-pa·tient [ˈinˌpeiʃənt; ˋɪnˏpeʃənt] *n*. 住院病人。

in-per·son [ˌinˈpəːsən; ˏɪnˋpɝsən] *a*. 亲身的;在场的。

in per·so·nam [ˌin pəˈsəunæm; ɪnpɚˋsonæm] 【法】对人〔指判决的对象〕。

in pet·to [iːnˈpetəu; inˋpeto] *ad*. 〔It.〕秘密地,不公开

地〔指教皇指派红衣主教,但尚未提名〕。

in·phase [ˈinfeiz; ˋɪnfez] **a.**【电】(交流)同位相的,同相的。

in·pour·ing [ˈinpɔːriŋ; ˋɪnpɔrɪŋ] **n.**, **a.** 注入(的),倾入(的)。

in·put [ˈinput; ˋɪnpʊt] **I n. 1.**【电】【自】输入;输入端。**2.** 输入电路,输入信号,输入功率[电压]。**3.** 放入物,投入的资金。**II** (***in·put·ted***, ***in·put***; ***in·put·ting***) **vt.**, **vi.** 把(数据等)输入计算机。~**-output analysis**【经】投入—产出分析;输入—输出分析。

in·quest [ˈinkwest; ˋɪnkwɛst] **n. 1.**【法】(有陪审员列席的)审讯;验尸。**2.** 公审庭;陪审团,验尸团。**3.** 判决,调查判决报告。**4.** 查询,调查。*the Great* [*Last*] *I-*【宗】世界末日的大审判。

in·qui·e·tude [inˈkwaiitjuːd; ɪnˋkwaɪɪtˏjud] **n.** 不安,焦虑。

in·qui·line [ˈinkwilain, -lin; ˋɪnkwɪlaɪn, -lɪn] **n.**【动】寄食昆虫,寄食动物。**-lin·ism** [-linizm; -lɪnɪzm] **n.**

in·quire [inˈkwaiə; ɪnˋkwaɪr] **vt. 1.** 打问,打听,问〔向某人打问某事时,某人前用介词 of, 所问某事为直接受词〕。**2.** 调查 (*out*)。**3.**〔古〕质问。~ *a matter of sb.* 向某人打听一件事。~ *of sb. how to proceed with the work* 问某人怎样进行这个工作。~ *of one's friend what one should do* 问朋友自己该怎么办。~ *sb.'s telephone number* 问某人的电话号码。— **vi.** 询问,查问;调查 (*into*)〔问某人某事时,某人前用介词 of, 所问某事前则用 of, about, concerning 等〕。*He ~d of her about her homework.* 他问她家庭作业做得如何。~ *into the deployment of the enemy troop* 调查敌军的兵力布署情况。~ *about trains to London* 打听去伦敦的火车。~ ***after*** 问候(病人等)(*May I ~ after your health?* 你好吗?)。~ ***for* 1.** 询问(行市、商品、地点等)(~ *for a new book* 问问有没有新书)。**2.** 要见 (~ *for the manager* 求见经理)。~ ***into*** 调查;探索。~ ***out*** 问出,查出。

in·quir·er [inˈkwaiərə; ɪnˋkwaɪrɚ] **n.** 询问的人,探究者,调查者。

in·quir·ing [inˈkwaiəriŋ; ɪnˋkwaɪrɪŋ] **a. 1.** 爱追根究底的。**2.** 好奇的。*an ~ look* 诧异的样子。**-ly ad.**

in·quir·y [inˈkwaiəri; ɪnˋkwaɪrɪ] **n. 1.** 询问,质问;追究。**2.** 调查,审查。~ *agency* (工商)调查所,征信所。~ *office* 问讯处,问事处。*hold an official ~* 进行正式调查。*make a searching ~* 追究,探究。*make inquiries* 质问,询问,调查,探访 (*about*; *into*)。*on* [*upon*] ~ 调查之后(的结果)。*make inquiries of sb. about sth.* 向某人询问某事。*hold an ~ into a case* 对一桩案子进行调查。

in·qui·si·tion [ˌinkwiˈziʃən]; ˏɪnkwɪˋzɪʃən] **n. 1.** 调查,审查。**2.**【法】讯问,审理;调查[审查]报告书。**3.**〔the I-〕(中世纪天主教审判异端的)宗教法庭。**4.** (对于被认为是危险分子的)恣意镇压,严厉刑罚。**-al a.**

in·quis·i·tive [inˈkwizitiv; ɪnˋkwɪzɪtɪv] **I a.** 好问人的,好研究的,好盘根究底的,好奇的。**II n.** 好询问的人,爱打听别人事情的人。**-ly ad. -ness n.**

in·quis·i·tor [inˈkwizitə; ɪnˋkwɪzɪtɚ] **n. 1.** 审问者,检查官。**2.**〔I-〕(中世纪天主教的)宗教法庭法官。**3.** 询问器。*the Grand I-* 宗教法庭庭长。*the I- General* (西班牙的)宗教法庭庭长。

in·quis·i·to·ri·al [inˌkwiziˈtɔːriəl; ɪnˏkwɪzɪˋtɔrɪəl] **a. 1.** 审问官(似)的,宗教法官(似)的。**2.** 有关审问的,有关调查的。**3.** 打听别人事情的。**-ly ad.**

in re [inˈriː; ɪnˋri]〔L.〕关于。

in rem [inˈrem; ɪnˋrɛm]【法】对物〔指判决的对象是物或财产〕。

in·road [ˈinrəud; ˋɪnrod] **n. 1.** (突然)袭击,(突然)侵犯 (*upon*; *on*; *into*)。**2.** 损害,侵犯 (*into*; *on*)。*make ~s into a small country* 侵犯一个小国家。*make ~ into sb.'s life* 干预某人的生活。*make ~s* (*up*)*on sb.'s health* 使某人的健康受到损害。

in·rush [ˈinrʌʃ; ˋɪnrʌʃ] **n.** 纤入,闯入;流入。*an ~ of fresh air* 新鲜空气的流入。*the spring ~ of tourists* 旅游者随春天大批涌来。

I.N.S. = International News Service〔美〕〔旧〕国际新闻社。

ins. = **1.** inches. **2.** insulated. **3.** insurance.

in sae·cu·la sae·cu·lo·rum [in ˈsekjulə sekjuˈlɔːrəm; ɪn ˋsɛkjələ sɛkjuˋlɔrəm]〔L.〕永远永远。

in·sal·i·vate [inˈsæliveit; ɪnˋsælɪˏvet] **vt.** (细嚼)把唾液混入(食物)。**-tion** [inˌsæliˈveiʃən; ɪnˏsælɪˋveʃən] **n.**【医】混涎作用,和涎作用。

in·sa·lu·bri·ous [ˌinsəˈljuːbriəs; ˏɪnsəˋljubrɪəs] **a.** (气候、环境等)对身体有害的,不利于健康的。*live in an ~ environment* 在不利于身体健康的环境里生活。

in·sa·lu·bri·ty [ˌinsəˈljubriti; ˏɪnsəˋljʊbrɪtɪ] **n.** 不利于健康,不卫生。

in·sane [inˈsein; ɪnˋsen] **a.** (***-san·er***; ***-est***) **1.** 精神错乱的,精神病的;疯狂的。**2.** 精神病患者的,为疯人开设的。**3.** 非常愚蠢的。*an ~ asylum* [*hospital*] 精神病院,疯人院。*go ~* 发疯。*the ~* 精神病患者,疯子。*a perfectly ~ idea* 极端荒谬的想法。**-ly ad. -ness n.**

in·san·i·tar·y [inˈsænitəri; ɪnˋsænɪtərɪ] **a.** 不卫生的,有害健康的。

in·san·i·ty [inˈsæniti; ɪnˋsænətɪ] **n. 1.** 疯狂,癫狂;精神错乱,精神病。**2.** 非常愚蠢,荒谬。**3.** 蠢事。

in·sa·ti·a·ble [inˈseiʃəbl; ɪnˋseʃəbl] **I a.** 不知足的,贪得无厌的。*an ~ hunger for knowledge* 渴望知识。*be ~ in learning* 学而不厌。**-bil·i·ty** [inˌseiʃjəˈbiliti; ɪnˏseʃjəˋbɪlətɪ], **-ness n. -bly ad.**

in·sa·ti·ate [inˈseiʃiit; ɪnˋseʃɪɪt] **a.** = insatiable. **-ly ad. -ness**, **-ti·e·ty n.**

in·scape [ˈinskeip; ˋɪnskep] **n.** 内在的特性,内在的特质。

in·sce·na·tion [ˌinsiːˈneiʃən; ˏɪnsiˋneʃən] **n. 1.** (戏剧的)舞台演出;舞台布置;舞台调度。**2.** 环境;背景。

in·scribe [inˈskraib; ɪnˋskraɪb] **vt. 1.** 写,记。**2.** 雕,刻。**3.** 登记(姓名,证券等)。**4.** 题献,题赠。**5.** 牢记,铭记。**6.**【数】使(图形)内接。*~d securities* 记名证券。*an ~d stock*〔英〕记名股票[公债]。~ *sb.'s name on a monument* 把某人的名字刻在纪念碑上。~ *one's name in a book* 把名字写在书里面。*This book I ~ to....* 谨将本书献给…。~ *sth. on the memory* 铭记心上。*an ~d circle* 内接圆。**-a·ble a. 1.** 可刻[雕]的。**2.** 可题写的。**-a·ble·ness**, **in·scrib·er n.**

in·scrip·tion [inˈskripʃən; ɪnˋskrɪpʃən] **n. 1.** 记入。**2.** 碑文;铭刻;(赠书上的)题词,署名。**3.** 编入名单,注册;〔英〕(公债等的)登记。*an ~ on a tombstone* 墓志铭,碑文。**-al**, **-tive a.**

in·scroll [inˈskrəul; ɪnˋskrol] **vt.** 把…载于卷册,把…记录下来。

in·scru·ta·ble [inˈskruːtəbl; ɪnˋskrutəbl] **a.** 莫测高深的,不可思议的,费解的。*an ~ smile* 莫名其妙的微笑。**-bil·i·ty** [inˌskruːtəˈbiliti; ɪnˏskrutəˋbɪlətɪ], **-ness n. -bly ad.**

in·seam [ˈinsiːm; ˋɪnsim] **n.** (裤管或衣袖的)内缝;手套毛边内缝。

in·sect [ˈinsekt; ˋɪnsɛkt] **I n. 1.** 虫,昆虫。**2.** 微贱的人,小人。*a destructive ~* 害虫。**II a. 1.** 昆虫的。**2.** 卑劣的。~ *pests* [*vermin*] 虫害。~ *powder* 除虫药粉。~ *wax* 白蜡。

in·sec·tar·i·um [ˌinsekˈtɛəriəm; ˏɪnsɛkˋtɛrɪəm] **n.** (*pl.* ***in·sec·taria*** [ˌinsekˈtɛəriə; ˏɪnsɛkˋtɛrɪə]) 养虫室,昆虫馆。

in·sec·tar·y [ˈinsektəri; ˋɪnsɛktərɪ] **n.** = insectarium.

in·sec·ti·cide [inˈsektisaid; ɪnˋsɛktɪsaɪd] **n.** 杀虫剂。

farm ～ 农业杀虫剂,农药。*spray* ～ 喷射杀虫剂。**-cid·al** ***a*** **.** 除虫的(*insectisidal oil* 杀虫油)。

in·sec·ti·fuge [inˈsektifjuːdʒ; ɪnˋsɛktɪfjudʒ] ***n*** **.** 驱虫剂;除虫药。

in·sec·tile [inˈsektail; ɪnˋsɛktaɪl] ***a*** **. 1.** 虫的;昆虫的,似昆虫的(=insectival)。**2.** 有虫的。

In·sec·tiv·o·ra [ˌinsekˈtivərə; ˏɪnsɛkˋtɪvərə] ***n*** **.** 〔*pl.*〕【动】食虫目。

in·sec·ti·vore [inˈsektivɔː; ɪnˋsɛktɪvɔr] ***n*** **.** 食虫动物[植物]。

in·sec·tiv·o·rous [ˌinsekˈtivərəs; ˏɪnsɛkˋtɪvərəs] ***a*** **.** 以虫类为食的,食虫的。*the* ～ *animals* [*plants*] 食虫动物[植物]。

in·sec·to·cu·tion [inˌsektəˈkjuːʃən; ɪnˏsɛktəˋkjuʃən] ***n*** **.** 通电杀虫。

in·sec·tol·o·gy [ˌinsekˈtɔlədʒi; ˏɪnsɛkˋtɑlədʒɪ] ***n*** **.** 经济昆虫学〔研究昆虫在经济方面对人类所起的作用〕〔*cf.* entomology〕。

in·se·cure [ˌinsiˈkjuə; ˏɪnsɪˋkjʊr] ***a*** **.** (***-cur·er*** ; ***-est***) 不安全的,不牢靠的;(诺言等)靠不住的;(地面、冰等)易坍陷的。*an* ～ *promise* 不可靠的诺言。*an* ～ *investment* 不太保险的投资。**-ly** ***ad*** **.**

in·se·cu·ri·ty [ˌinsiˈkjuəriti; ˏɪnsɪˋkjʊrətɪ] ***n*** **.** 不安全,不牢靠;不安定;易崩坏。*a sense of* ～ 不安全感。

in·sem·i·nate [inˈsemineit; ɪnˋsɛməˏnet] ***vt*** **. 1.** 播(种),栽。**2.** 使受孕,授精。

in·sem·i·na·tion [inˌsemiˈneiʃən; ɪnˏsɛmɪˋneʃən] ***n*** **. 1.** 播种。**2.** 受孕,授精。*artificial* ～ 人工授精。

in·sem·i·na·tor [inˈsemineitə; ɪnˋsɛmɪˏnetɚ] ***n*** **.** 人工授精操作者。

in·sen·sate [inˈsenseit, -sit; ɪnˋsɛnset; -sɪt] ***a*** **. 1.** 无知觉的,无生命的;无感情的。**2.** 残忍的,无情的。**3.** 愚钝的,没有理智的。*mute* ～ *things* 哑然无言的生物。**-ly** ***ad*** **. -ness** ***n*** **.**

in·sen·si·ble [inˈsensəbl; ɪnˋsɛnsəbl] ***a*** **. 1.** 无感觉的,麻木不仁的,昏迷不省的。**2.** 感觉迟钝的,不敏感的。**3.** 不关心的,漫不经心的。**4.** 冷淡的,无情的。**5.** 难看出的,缓慢的。*be* ～ *to* [*of*] *pain* 不感觉疼痛,不感觉痛苦。*be knocked* ～ 被打得人事不省。*fly* ～ 昏过去。*hands* ～ *from cold* 冻得麻木了的手。*be* ～ *of one's danger* 不知道自己面临的危险。*by* ～ *degree* 极慢的。**-bil·i·ty, -ness** ***n*** **. -bly** ***ad*** **.**

in·sen·si·tive [inˈsensitiv; ɪnˋsɛnsətɪv] ***a*** **.** 感觉迟钝的,不敏感的,无感觉的(*to*)。**-ly** ***ad*** **. -ness, -tiv·i·ty** ***n*** **.**

in·sen·ti·ent [inˈsenʃənt; ɪnˋsɛnʃənt] ***a*** **.** 无知觉的,无感觉的;无生命的,无情感的。**-ence, -ti·cy** ***n*** **.**

insep. =inseparable.

in·sep·a·ra·ble [inˈsepərəbl; ɪnˋsɛpərəbl̩] **I** ***a*** **.** 分不开的,不可分离的。～ *friends* 分不开的朋友。*an* ～ *prefix* 【语法】非分离性词首〔dis-, un- 等独立时即无意义〕。**II** ***n*** **.** 〔*pl.*〕不可分的事物;好友。**-bly** ***ad*** **. -bil·i·ty** ***n*** **.**

in·sep·a·ra·ble·ness [inˈsepərəblnis; ɪnˋsɛpərəbl̩nɪs] ***n*** **.** 不可分离(=inseparability)。

in·sep·a·rate [inˈseprit; ɪnˋsɛprɪt] ***a*** **.** 不分开的,不分离的,相连的。

in·sert [inˈsəːt; ɪnˋsɝt] **I** ***vt*** **. 1.** 插进,夹入。**2.** 写进,记入;刊登。**3.** (缝纫中)镶,补。～ *a key in* [*into*] *a lock* 把钥匙插进锁中。～ *a word in a line* 插一个字到行里。～ *an advertisement in a newspaper* 在报上登广告。— ***vi*** **.** 【医】(肌肉)附着。**II** [ˈinsəːt; ˋɪnsɝt] ***n*** **. 1.** 插入物,嵌入物。**2.** 补垫。**3.** 电报头。**4.** 〔*pl.*〕金属型芯,嵌入物。**5.** 插页;【影】插入画面。

in·sert·ed [inˈsəːtid; ɪnˋsɝtɪd] ***a*** **.** 【生】着生的。

in·sert·er [inˈsəːtə; ɪnˋsɝtɚ] ***n*** **.** 插入物,插件。*data* ～ 数据输入器。

in·ser·tion [inˈsəːʃən; ɪnˋsɝʃən] ***n*** **. 1.** 插入;记入;刊登。**2.** 插入物;插入句;插入广告;插锈,补绣。**3.** 【动、植】着生(点)。**4.** 【电】嵌入,介入。**5.** 【医】(肌肉的)附着。*the* ～ *of muscle* 肌附着,肌止端。**-al** ***a*** **.**

in-ser·vice [ˈinˈsəːvis; ˋɪnˈsɝvɪs] ***a*** **.** 在职期间进行的,使用中进行的。

in·ses·so·ri·al [ˌinseˈsɔːriəl; ˏɪnsɛˋsorɪəl] ***a*** **.** (某些鸟的)适于栖止的。

INSET = in-service training 〔英〕(教师的)在职培训。

in·set [inˈset; ɪnˋsɛt] **I** ***vt*** **.** (***in·set***, ***in·set·ted*** ; ***in-set·ting***) 嵌入,插入(插图等)。**II** [ˈinset; ˋɪnsɛt] ***n*** **. 1.** 插入物;插入广告;插页,插图。**2.** 镶边。**3.** 水道;(潮水)流入。

in·sheathe [inˈʃiːð; ɪnˋʃið] ***vt*** **.** (***-sheath·ed***, ***-sheath-ing***) 插入鞘;用鞘覆盖(=ensheathe)。

in·shoot [ˈinʃuːt; ˋɪnʃut] ***n*** **.** 【棒球】内飞球。

in·shore [ˈinˈʃɔː; ˋɪnˈʃɔr] (*opp.* offshore) **I** ***a*** **.** 近海岸的;向陆的。～ *currents* 沿岸流。～ *fishing* [*fishery*] 近海渔业。～ *patrol* 【军】沿海巡逻。*an* ～ *wind* 向陆风。**II** ***ad*** **.** 沿海,靠近海岸。～ *of* 比…靠近海岸。

in·shrine [inˈʃrain; ɪnˋʃraɪn] ***vt*** **.** = enshrine.

in·side [ˈinˈsaid; ˋɪnˈsaɪd] (*opp.* outside) **I** ***n*** **. 1.** 内部,内面。**2.** (道路的)内侧;(跑道的)内道,内圈。**3.** 内容,内心,内情;内幕情报[消息]。**4.** [inˈsaid; ɪnˋsaɪd] (公共马车等的)车内乘客;车内座位。**5.** 期中。**6.** 〔口〕内脏,肠胃。*the* ～ *of the hand* 手心。*the* ～ *of a sidewalk* 人行道内侧。*The CIA from Inside* 《美国中央情报局内幕》。*know the* ～ *of sb.* 了解某人内心。*know the business from* ～ 完全了解这一行业。*the* ～ *of a week* 星期一至星期五。*feel a pain in one's* ～ 感觉肚子痛。**II** [ˈinsaid; ˋɪnsaɪd] ***a*** **. 1.** 里面的,内部的,在屋里的。**2.** 内幕的,秘密的。**3.** 在室内工作的。～ *address* 信纸上的姓名、地址〔信封上姓名地址之对〕。～ *diameter* 内径。～ *facts* 内幕,秘密。～ *information* 内部情报。*For I- Circulation Only* 内部传阅。～ *knowledge* [*story*] 内情,内幕。*an* ～ *man* 内勤人员。**III** [inˈsaid; ɪnˋsaɪd] ***ad*** **.** 在内,在内部,在里面。*There is nothing* ～. 里面什么也没有。**IV** ***prep*** **.** 在…之内,在…里面。*step* ～ *the gate* 跨进门内。*return* ～ *a month* 一月之内回来。～ ***of*** 〔口〕**1.** 在…以内。**2.** (时间上)少于(～ *of a mile* 不到一英里。～ *of a week* 少于一个星期)。～ ***out*** **1.** 从里面翻到外面。**2.** 彻底地(*turn everything* ～ *out* 翻箱倒柜。*know a matter* ～ *out* 对一件事彻底了解)。***on the*** ～ 从里面,在里面(*The door locked on the* ～. 门反锁着)。～ **job** 〔美口〕内部自己人作的案,有内应关系作的案。～ **track 1.** 运动场跑道的内圈。**2.** 有利地位,好机会。

in·sid·er [inˈsaidə; ɪnˋsaɪdɚ] ***n*** **. 1.** 组织或团体内部的人。**2.** 了解内幕者,知内情的人。～ **dealing** 内幕交易〔此种交易能利用了解内情谋利,多指股票交易,亦作～ trading〕。

in·sid·i·ous [inˈsidiəs; ɪnˋsɪdɪəs] ***a*** **. 1.** 阴险的,狡猾的;暗中为害的。**2.** 在不知不觉之间加剧的。*an* ～ *enemy* 阴险的敌人。～ *wiles* 奸计。*the* ～ *approach of age* 不知不觉就老了。**-ly** ***ad*** **. -ness** ***n*** **.**

in·sight [ˈinsait; ˋɪnsaɪt] ***n*** **. 1.** 洞察力;直觉,悟力;眼光;见识。**2.** 【心】顿悟。*a man of deep* ～ 有深远见识的人。*gain* [*have*] *an* ～ *into sb.'s mind* 看透某人心思。

in·sight·ful [ˈinˌsaitful; ˋɪnˏsaɪtful] ***a*** **.** 有见识的,有眼光的;显出洞察力的。

in·sig·ni·a [inˈsigniə; ɪnˋsɪgnɪə] ***n*** **.** (*pl.* ～(*s*); *sing.* ***in·sig·ne*** [-niː; -ni]) **1.** 勋章,国徽。**2.** (权威、尊严、荣誉的)标帜〔如王冠、帝王的宝杖、军人的领章、肩章等〕。*the* ～ *of an order* 勋章。*a red collar* ～ 红领章。

in·sig·nif·i·cance [ˌinsigˈnifikəns; ˏɪnsɪgˋnɪfɪkəns] ***n*** **. 1.** 无意义;不足道;无价值;不重要。**2.** 低微,可鄙。

in·sig·nif·i·can·cy [ˌinsigˈnifikənsi; ˏɪnsɪgˋnɪfɪkənsɪ] ***n*.** 1. = insignificance. 2. 微不足道的人[东西]。

in·sig·nif·i·cant [ˌinsigˈnifikənt; ˏɪnsɪgˋnɪfɪkənt] ***a*.** 1. 无意义的;不足取的;琐碎的;无价值的。2. 小的,低微的,可鄙的。~ *talk* 废话。~ *things* 微不足道的东西。*waste time on* ~ *points* 时间花在琐碎事情上。~ *people* 小人物。~ *town* 小小的城镇。**-ly *ad*.**

in·sin·cere [ˌinsinˈsiə; ˏɪnsɪnˋsɪr] ***a*.** 不诚实的,无诚意的;虚假的,伪善的。**-ly *ad*.**

in·sin·cer·i·ty [ˌinsinˈseriti; ˏɪnsɪnˋsɛrətɪ] ***n*.** 不诚实,无诚意;伪善;不诚实的言行。

in·sin·u·ate [inˈsinjueit; ɪnˋsɪnjʊˏet] ***vt*.** 1. 使潜入,巧妙地进行,慢慢插入 (*into*)。2. 暗讽,暗示。~ *doubts into sb.'s mind* 使某人慢慢产生疑虑。~ *oneself into sb.'s favour* 巧妙地巴结上某人,巧妙地向人献媚求宠。~ *oneself into the crowd* 暗暗地挤进人群。~ *one's doubt of this action* 暗示对于这一行动的怀疑。— ***vi*.** 暗示,含沙射影。~ *that sb. is dishonest* 暗示某人不诚实。**-a·tive, -a·to·ry *a*.**

in·sin·u·at·ing [inˈsinjueitiŋ; ɪnˋsɪnjʊetɪŋ] ***a*.** 1. 暗示(式)的。2. 献媚的,讨好的。*make an* ~ *remark* 暗讽。*speak in an* ~ *voice* 低声下气地说。*an* ~ *smile* 肉麻的微笑。**-ly *ad*.**

in·sin·u·a·tion [inˌsinjuˈeiʃən; ɪnˏsɪnjʊˋeʃən] ***n*.** 慢慢进去;巧妙巴结;暗示。*attack by* ~ 含沙射影地攻击。*make* ~*s* 含沙射影。

in·sin·u·a·tor [inˈsinjueitə; ɪnˋsɪnjʊˏetə] ***n*.** 1. 献媚者。2. 暗示者,暗讽者。

in·sip·id [inˈsipid; ɪnˋsɪpɪd] ***a*.** 1. 没有味道的;不好吃的。2. 乏味的,无风趣的,无生气的。~ *food* 淡而无味的食品。~ *conversation* 枯燥无味的谈话。**-ly *ad*. -ness *n*.**

in·si·pid·i·ty [ˌinsiˈpiditi; ˏɪnsɪˋpɪdətɪ] ***n*.** 无味;枯燥,平淡。

in·sip·i·ence [inˈsipiəns; ɪnˋsɪpɪəns] ***n*.** 〔古〕缺乏才智,愚钝。**-ent *a*.**

in·sist [inˈsist; ɪnˋsɪst] ***vi*.** 1. 硬要,坚持 (*on*; *upon*)。2. 坚决要求,定要。*I will have another glass if you* ~. 你硬要劝我,我只好再喝一杯。*I* ~ *on his innocence*. 我坚认他无罪。*I* ~ *on being present*. 我一定要出席。~ *on a point* 强调一点。*He* ~*s on going with you*. 他坚持要和你一起去。— ***vt*.** 坚决主张;坚决认为;坚决要求 (*that*)。*I* ~ *that he is innocent*. 我坚持认为他是无罪的。*I* ~ *that you shall be present*. 务必请您到场。

in·sist·ence, -ten·cy [inˈsistəns, -si; ɪnˋsɪstəns, -sɪ] ***n*.** 坚持,强调,极力主张。~ (*up*) *on strict obedience* 强调要严格服从。

in·sist·ent [inˈsistənt; ɪnˋsɪstənt] ***a*.** 坚持的,逼人注意的;显眼的,显著的。*an* ~ *demand* 迫切的要求。*an* ~ *rhythm* 动人的旋律。**-ly *ad*.**

in·sist·er [inˈsistə; ɪnˋsɪstɚ] ***n*.** 固执的人,坚持者。

in·si·ti·tious [ˌinsiˈtiʃəs; ˏɪnsɪˋtɪʃəs] ***a*.** (字句等)插入的。

in·snare [inˈsneə; ɪnˋsnɛr] ***vt*.** = ensnare.

in·so·bri·e·ty [ˌinsəuˈbraiəti; ˏɪnsoˋbraɪətɪ] ***n*.** 无节制,饮酒过度,酗酒。

in·so·cia·ble [inˈsəuʃəbl; ɪnˋsoʃəbl̩] ***a*.** 不爱社交的,不会交际的,孤僻的,不讨人喜欢的。**-bil·i·ty *n*. -bly *ad*.**

in·so·far [ˌinsəuˈfɑː, -sə-; ˏɪnsoˋfɑr, -sə-] ***ad*.** 到如此程度〔通常与 as 连用〕。~ *as* 在…限度内,在…的范围内 (*I shall do what I can* ~ *as I am able*. 我力所能及的都要去做。*I- as possible, our examples will be drawn from Chinese*. 在可能范围内,例证均引自汉语)。

in·so·late [ˈinsəuleit; ˋɪnsolet] ***vt*.** 曝晒。

in·so·la·tion [ˌinsəuˈleiʃən; ˏɪnsoˋleʃən] ***n*.** 1. 曝晒。2. 日光浴。3. 【医】中暑,日射病。4. 【气】日射,日射率。

in·sole [ˈinsəul; ˋɪnsol] ***n*.** 鞋内底;鞋垫。

in·so·lence [ˈinsələns; ˋɪnsələns] ***n*.** 1. 傲慢,横蛮。2. 傲慢的态度,侮辱性的言行。

in·so·lent [ˈinsələnt; ˋɪnsələnt] ***a*.** 傲慢的,横蛮无礼的。**-ly *ad*.**

in·sol·u·ble [inˈsɔljubl; ɪnˋsɑljəbl̩] ***a*.** 1. 不能解决的,难解释的。2. 不溶解的,不溶化的。**-bil·i·ty *n*. -bly *ad*.**

in·sol·u·ble·ness [inˈsɔljublnis; ɪnˋsɑljəbl̩nɪs] ***n*.** 1. 难解决;难解释。2. 不溶解,不溶化。

in·solv·a·ble [inˈsɔlvəbl; ɪnˋsɑlvəbl̩] ***a*.** = insoluble.

in·sol·ven·cy [inˈsɔlvənsi; ɪnˋsɑlvənsɪ] ***n*.** 无力偿付债务,破产。

in·sol·vent [inˈsɔlvənt; ɪnˋsɑlvənt] **I *a*.** 无力偿付债务的,破产的。**II *n*.** 无力偿还债务者,破产者。

in·som·ni·a [inˈsɔmniə; ɪnˋsɑmnɪə] ***n*.** 【医】失眠;失眠症。

in·som·ni·ac [inˈsɔmniæk; ɪnˋsɑmnɪæk] **I *a*.** 患失眠症的。**II *n*.** 患失眠症的人。

in·som·ni·ous [inˈsɔmniəs; ɪnˋsɑmnɪəs] ***a*.** 失眠的,患失眠症的。

in·so·much [ˌinsəuˈmʌtʃ; ˏɪnsoˋmʌtʃ] ***ad*.** 1. 到这样的程度,如此地 (*as*; *that*)。*The rain fell in torrents*, ~ *that we were ankle-deep in water*. 大雨滂沱,水深没膝。2. 因为,由于〔与 as 连用 = inasmuch as〕。

in·so·nate [ˈinsəuneit; ˋɪnsonet] ***vt*., *vi*.** (使)受声波(尤指超高频声波)的作用。**-na·tion *n*.**

in·sou·ci·ance [inˈsuːsjəns; ɪnˋsusjəns] ***n*.** 〔F.〕漫不经心,满不在乎。***in·sou·ci·ant a*.** 〔F.〕

in·soul [inˈsəul; ɪnˋsol] ***vt*.** = ensoul.

INSP, insp. = inspect; inspection; inspector.

in·span [inˈspæn; ɪnˋspæn] ***vt*., *vi*.** (***-spanned***; ***-spanning***)〔南非用的英语〕把(牛、马等)套到车上,套(车)。

in·spect [inˈspekt; ɪnˋspɛkt] ***vt*.** 检阅;检查;审查;视察。~ *troops* 阅兵。~ *school* 视察学校。**-a·bil·i·ty *n*. -a·ble *a*. -ing·ly *ad*.**

in·spec·tion [inˈspekʃən; ɪnˋspɛkʃən] ***n*.** 1. 检查,检验;审查。2. 检阅,视察;参观。*bottom* ~ 船底检查。*close* ~ 严格检查。*full* ~ 全船检查。*a house-to-house* ~ 挨户检查。*medical* ~ 检疫;检查身体;卫生检查。~ *arms* 【军】验枪姿势;〔口令用语〕验枪。*an* ~ *door* (军舰上减速器的)窥孔盖。*an* ~ *hole* 【冶】观察孔,检验孔。~ *tools* 【冶】检验工具,控制工具。***for* (*your kind*)** ~ 祈查阅(为感)。***I- declined*!** 谢绝参观。***make an* ~ *of*** 视察(*make an* ~ *of a university* 视察一所大学)。***on the first*** ~ 一看之后。

in·spec·tor [inˈspektə; ɪnˋspɛktɚ] ***n*.** 检查员,监察员,检阅者;视察员。*an* ~ *of ordnance* 【军】军械检验员。*an* ~ *of weights and measures* 度量衡检查员。*an* ~ *of hull* 船身检查员。*a police* ~ 警察巡官。*an* ~ *of schools* = *a school* ~ 督学。~ ***general n*.** 监察长;【美军】检阅总监(*the I- General of the Army* [*Navy*] 美国陆[海]军监察长。*the I- General's Department* 监察署)。**-al, -i·al *a*. -ship *n*.** 检查员[监察员]的地位[职权]。

in·spec·tor·ate [inˈspektərit; ɪnˋspɛktərɪt] ***n*.** 1. 检查员[监察员]的地位[职责]。2. 〔总称〕视察人员,视察团。3. 检查员(监察员等)的管辖区域。

in·spec·to·scope [inˈspektəskəup; ɪnˋspɛktəˏskop] ***n*.** 一种用 X 光透视检查违禁品的器械。

in·spec·tress [inˈspektris; ɪnˋspɛktrɪs] ***n*.** 女检查员,女监察员。

in·sphere [inˈsfiə; ɪnˋsfɪr] ***vt*.** (***-sphered***, ***-spher·ing***) = ensphere.

in·spi·ra·tion [ˌinspəˈreiʃən; ˏɪnspəˋreʃən] ***n*.** 1. 吸气;【机】进气 (*opp*. expiration)。2. 【宗】神的启示;(诗人

的)灵感。3. 鼓舞,激励,感化。4.〔口〕灵机,妙想。5.(上级的)指示,授意,鼓动。*have a sudden* ~ 灵机一动。*draw* [*get*] ~ *from* 从…得到启发。*The poem is a pure* ~. 这首诗纯粹是灵感之作。*the governmental* ~ *of a report* 按政府意旨所作的报告。**-al** *a*. **-ism** *n*. 灵感论,神秘直觉说。**-ist** *n*. 灵感论者。

in·spi·ra·tor [ˈinspəreitə; ˋɪnspə͵retɚ] *n*. 呼吸器;喷汽注水器,注射器。

in·spir·a·to·ry [inˈspaiərətəri; ɪnˋspaɪrə͵torɪ] *a*. 吸气的;吸入的。

in·spire [inˈspaiə; ɪnˋspaɪr] *vt*. 1. 吸,吸气 (*opp*. expire)。2. 注入,灌注。3. 使生灵感,使感悟,使感动。4. 鼓舞,激动,激发。5. 指示,授意。~ *sb*. *with courage* = ~ *courage into sb*. 鼓起某人勇气。~ *a new thought into sb*. 将新思想灌输给某人。— *vi*. 1. 吸入。2. 赋予灵感。

in·spired [inˈspaiəd; ɪnˋspaɪrd] *a*. 1. 受到灵感的。2. 被人授意的,受鼓动的。*an* ~ *poet* 有灵感的诗人。*the* ~ *writings* 圣书。*an* ~ *article* 由别人授意而写成的文章。~ *views* 体现长官意志的意见。

in·spir·ing [inˈspaiəriŋ; ɪnˋspaɪrɪŋ] *a*. 鼓动的,激励的,勇壮的。*an* ~ *sight* 振奋人心的光景。~ *activity* 鼓舞人心的活动。*The music is* ~. 这音乐激动人心。

in·spir·it [inˈspirit; ɪnˋspɪrɪt] *vt*. 振奋,激发,激励。~ *sb*. *to an action* (*to do sth*.) 鼓励某人采取行动(做某事)。**-ing** *a*.

in·spis·sate [inˈspiseit; ɪnˋspɪset] *vt*., *vi*. 1. (使)浓缩,(使)浓厚,(使)强烈。2. (使)(心情)沉重。~ *the gloom of the room atmosphere* 使房子里的空气变得更加阴沉。**-d** *a*. **-tion** *n*. 浓厚化;【化】蒸浓法。**-tor** *n*.【化】蒸浓器。

Inst. = Institute; Institution.

inst. = instant; instrumental.

in·sta·bil·i·ty [ˌinstəˈbiliti; ͵ɪnstəˋbɪlətɪ] *n*. 动摇性,不稳定性;不坚决,反复无常,三心二意。*the* ~ *of human affairs* 人事沧桑。

in·sta·ble [inˈsteibl; ɪnˋstebl̩] *a*. 动摇的,不安定的;不坚定的,易变的;反复无常的 (=unstable)。

in·stal(l) [inˈstɔːl; ɪnˋstɔl] *vt*. (*in·stalled*; *-stal·ling*) 1. 任命,使就(职),把…安插到(*in*)。2. 安置,使坐,使入席。3. 安装(机器),设置。~ *a college president* 任命学院院长。~ *sb*. *in an office* 把某人安插在办公室里。~ *sb*. *in a deck chair* 让某人坐在甲板上的躺椅上。*be* ~*ed in a seat* 在座位上坐定。~ *a heating system* 装设暖气设备。

in·stal·lant [inˈstɔːlənt; ɪnˋstɔlənt] *n*. 任命者。

in·stal·la·tion [ˌinstəːˈleiʃən; ͵ɪnstəˋleʃən] *n*. 1. 就职,就任,就职礼。2. 装置,设备。3. 安装;设置;安置。4. 军事设施。*a heating* ~ 暖气设备。*an* ~ *diagram*【机】装置图。*an ammunition* ~ 弹药补给机关,弹药库。*military* ~*s* 军事设施。

in·stall·er [inˈstɔːlə; ɪnˋstɔlɚ] *n*. 安装者。

in·stal(l)·ment [inˈstɔːlmənt; ɪnˋstɔlmənt] *n*. 1. 分期付款中的每期应付款,摊付金。2. (丛书杂志等的)一部,一期,(小说等)分期连载的一部分。3.〔古〕= installation. *monthly* ~ 每月摊付的款项。*pay by* [*in*] ~*s* 分期付款。*appear in* ~*s* 分期发表[出版]。~ **plan** [**system**]〔美〕分期付款购货法(*buy on the* ~ *plan* 用分期付款办法购买)。

in·stance [ˈinstəns; ˋɪnstəns] **I** *n*. 1. 事例,例证,实例,场合。2. 情况。3. 要求,建议。4.【法】诉讼手续。***in this*** [***your***] ~ 在这种[你的]情况下。***at the*** ~ ***of*** 因…之情,由于…的主张[建议]。*one* ~ *out of many* 许多例子中的一个。*cite* [*give*, *produce*] *an* ~ 举例。*a court of first* ~ 初审庭,预审庭。***in the first*** ~ 最初,首先;在第一审时。***in the last*** ~ 最后,在终审时。***for*** ~例如。**II** *vt*. 举…为例,引以为例,举例证明。

in·stan·cy [ˈinstənsi; ˋɪnstənsɪ] *n*. 1. 紧急,急迫。2. 即时,瞬间。3. 坚持。

in·stant [ˈinstənt; ˋɪnstənt] **I** *a*. 1. 迫切的,紧急的。2. 当月的,本月的〔商业或正式文件中使用,一般略为 inst.〕。3. 立即的,直接的。4. 食物已配制好的。*be in* ~ *need of help* 急需帮助。*the 3rd of this* ~ *June* 这一个六月的三号。*your letter of the 10th* ~ 本月十日尊函。*an* ~ *response* 立即回答。~ *coffee* 速溶咖啡。**II** *n*. 瞬间,时刻,即时。*at that* ~ 在那时候,在那瞬间。*I went that* ~. 我立刻就走了。*this* ~ 立刻,马上。***for an*** ~ 一瞬间(*I couldn't answer for an* ~. 我一时答不上来)。***in an*** ~ 立刻,马上(*I'll be with you in an* ~. 我立刻就来)。***on the*** ~ 立即,即时(*march off on the* ~ 马上出发)。***the*** ~ ***conj***. = as soon as 一…(就)(*The* ~ *we heard the alarm*, *we fell in for action*. 我们一听到警报,就立即集合准备战斗)。~ **lottery**〔美〕即刻对奖的抽彩给奖(彩票上有蜡对号码,购彩票人只须揭去蜡封,即可对奖)。~ **relay** 1. 即时重播〔以录影带录下体育动作,于动作完成后即可用慢动作重播〕。2. 可立时重放的录影。

in·stan·ta·ne [ˌɛ̃ːnstænˈtɑːnei; ͵ɛ̃nstænˋtɑne] *n*. 〔F.〕 1. 快照。2. 简报。

in·stan·ta·ne·ous [ˌinstənˈteinjəs; ͵ɪnstənˋtenjəs] *a*. 即刻的,瞬间的。*an* ~ *bomb* 瞬发炸弹。~ *death* 即刻死去。*an* ~ *effect* 速效。~ *exposure* 自动快速曝光。*an* ~ *photograph* 快照。*an* ~ *response* 即刻的反应。~ *velocity*【物】瞬时速度。**-ly** *ad*. **-ness** *n*.

in·stan·ter [inˈstæntə; ɪnˋstæntɚ] *ad*. 马上,立刻。

in·stan·ti·ate [inˈstænʃieit; ɪnˋstænʃɪ͵et] *vt*. 用具体例证说明。**-a·tion** [inˌstænʃiˈeiʃən; ɪn͵stænʃɪˋeʃən] *n*.

in·stant·ly [ˈinstəntli; ˋɪnstəntlɪ] **I** *ad*. 立即,即刻。**II** *conj*. 一…就。*I telegraphed* ~ *I arrived there*. 我一到了那里就打电报。

in·star[1] [ˈinstɑː; ˋɪnstɑr] *n*. (虫)龄〔幼虫两次蜕皮之间的虫期〕。

in·star[2] [inˈstɑː; ɪnˋstɑr] *vt*. (*-starred*, *-star·ring*) 1. 嵌星,饰以星。2.〔古〕把…摆成星状。

in·state [inˈsteit; ɪnˋstet] *vt*. 任命,使就任;安置,设置。

in sta·tu quo [inˈsteituːˈkwəu; ɪnˋstetuˋkwo]〔L.〕维持现状。

in·stau·ra·tion [ˌinstɔːˈreiʃən; ͵ɪnstɔˋreʃən] *n*. 1. 恢复,修复,更新。2.〔古〕设立,建立。

in·stau·ra·tor [ˈinstɔːreitə; ˋɪnstɔretɚ] *n*. 1. 复兴者,重建者。2. 创立者,设立者。

Inst. C. E. = Institution of Civil Engineers〔英〕土木工程师学会。

in·stead [insˈted; ɪnˋstɛd] *ad*. 代替,顶替。*come another day* ~ 改天再来吧。*Give me this* ~. 请改拿这个给我。~ ***of*** 代替,而不是(*I'll go* ~ *of you*. 我愿代你去。*I gave him advice* ~ *of money*. 我给了他忠告而没有给他钱)。

in·step [ˈinstep; ˋɪnstɛp] *n*. 1. 脚背。2. 盖上脚背的鞋面和袜面部分。3.【动】蹠。

in·sti·gate [ˈinstigeit; ˋɪnstɪ͵get] *vt*. 教唆,煽动,唆使;挑起,发动(战争),策划。~ *sb*. *to do sth*. 唆使某人做某事。~ *a rebellion* 煽动叛乱。~ *a strike* 煽动罢工。**-ga·tor** *n*. 唆使者,煽动者。

in·sti·ga·tion [ˌinstiˈgeiʃən; ͵ɪnstɪˋgeʃən] *n*. 鼓动,煽动;刺激,刺激物。*at* [*by*] *the* ~ *of sb*. 在某人的鼓动下。

in·stil(l) [inˈstil; ɪnˋstɪl] *vt*. 1. 滴注。2. 慢慢灌输。~ *ideas into sb.'s mind* 把思想灌输到某人脑中。

in·stil·la·tion [ˌinstiˈleiʃən; ͵ɪnstɪˋleʃən] *n*. 1. 滴注;【医】滴注法。*rectal* ~【医】直肠滴注法。2. 注入;灌输。3. 滴注物,滴剂,浸润物。

in·stil(l)·ment [inˈstilmənt; ɪnˋstɪlmənt] *n*. 滴注。

in·stinct [ˈinstiŋkt; ˋɪnstɪŋkt] **I** *n*. 1. 本能,才能,直觉。

I

2. 生性,天性,天才。*Suckling is an ~ in mammals*. 哺乳是哺乳动物的本能。*act on* ~ 凭直觉行动。*by* ~ 凭本能,本能地。*Birds learn to fly by* ~. 鸟儿学飞系由于本能。***have an*** ~ ***for*** 生来就有…的本能,有…的才能。II [in'stiŋkt; ɪn`stɪŋkt] ***a***. 充满的(*with*)。*be ~ with life* 充满生气。

in·stinc·tive [in'stiŋktiv; ɪn`stɪŋktɪv] ***a***. 生来的,天生的;本能的;直觉的。**-ly** ***ad***.

in·sti·tute ['institjuːt; `ɪnstə͵tjut] **I** ***n***. **1**. 协会,学会;学院,专科大学;(学院附设的)研究所。**2**. 〔美〕讲习会;(短期)训练班。**3**. 会址,院址,校址,所址。**4**. 原则,规则,惯例。**5**. 〔*pl*.〕(给初学者用的法律、医学等的)浅说,(公认的)基本原理。*an ~ of technology* 理工学院。*a farmers'* ~〔美〕农民讲习所。*a teachers'* ~〔美〕教师训练班。**II** ***vt***. **1**. 设,设立,制定。**2**. 实行,创立,开始。**3**. 任命,【宗】授…以圣职。~ *a government* 组织政府。~ *an inquiry into* 开始调查。~ *an action at law* 提起法律诉讼。~ *a suit against sb*. 对某人提起诉讼。~ *sb. into* [*to*] *a parish* 任命教区牧师。

in·sti·tu·tion [ˌinsti'tjuːʃən; ͵ɪnstə`tjuʃən] ***n***. **1**. 设立,创设,制定。**2**. 惯例,制度,规定。**3**. 学会,协会;院,会,社,馆,所;机关;社会事业机构〔指学校、医院、教会等〕。**4**. 会址,校址,院址,所址。**5**. 【宗】授职;授职礼。**6**. 〔口〕名人,名物。*a public* ~ 公共机关〔指医院、学校〕。*a training ~ for* 训练班。*He is quite an* ~. 他是个很有名的人。

in·sti·tu·tion·al [ˌinsti'tjuːʃənəl; ͵ɪnstə`tjuʃənl̩] ***a***. **1**. 惯例的,规定的,制度上的。**2**. 公共机构的,社会事业性质的〔尤指慈善事业机构〕。**3**. 〔美〕【广告】主要为建立公司产品声誉而创招牌的。*in need of ~ care* 需要慈善事业机构照顾。**-ly** ***ad***.

in·sti·tu·tion·al·ism [ˌinsti'tjuːʃənəlizm; ͵ɪnstə`tjuʃənəlɪzm] ***n***. **1**. 社会事业机构。**2**. 社会慈善机构的救济。**3**. 尊重社会事业和传统制度的政策。

in·sti·tu·tion·al·ize [ˌinsti'tjuːʃənəlaiz; ͵ɪnstə`tjuʃənə͵laɪz] ***vt***. (*-ized*, *-iz·ing*) **1**. 使制度化;使成为习惯;把…看作制度。**2**. 使成惯例;使成为制度;使成为风俗习惯。**3**. 把…送交专门机构治疗[拘留]。**-za·tion** ***n***.

in·sti·tu·tion·ar·y [ˌinsti'tjuːʃəˌnəri; ͵ɪnstə`tjuʃə͵nərɪ] ***a***. **1**. 学会的,协会的,团体的。**2**. 创始的,制定的,规定的(= institutional)。**3**. 【宗】授予圣职的;圣餐制度的。

in·sti·tu·tive ['institjuːtiv; `ɪnstə͵tjutɪv] ***a***. 设立的;(法律等的)制定的;惯例的;制度的;机关的。

in·sti·tu·tor ['institjuːtə; `ɪnstə͵tjutɚ] ***n***. **1**. 设立者,创立者,制定者。**2**. 〔美〕授任圣职者。

Inst. M. E. = Institute of Marine Engineers〔英〕轮机工程师学会。

Inst. N. A. = Institution of Naval Architects〔英〕造船(工程)师学会。

instr. = instructor; instrument; instrumental.

in·struct [in'strʌkt; ɪn`strʌkt] ***vt***. **1**. 教,教授,教导。**2**. 通知,向…提供事实情况。**3**. 命令,指示。~ *sb. in English* 教某人英语。*be ~ed when to start* 得到出发时间的通知。~ *sb. to do sth*. 命令某人做某事。**-i·ble** ***a***.

in·struct·ed [in'strʌktid; ɪn`strʌktɪd] ***a***. **1**. 受教育的。**2**. 被委派的,得到指示的。~ *delegates* 委派的代表。**-ly** ***ad***. **-ness** ***n***.

in·struc·tion [in'strʌkʃən; ɪn`strʌkʃən] ***n***. **1**. 教育,教导。**2**. 教训,教诲。**3**. 〔*pl*.〕指令,训令,指示,细目。*give sb. ~s to do sth*. 命令某人做什么。*an ~ book* 说明书。*maintenance ~s* 维护说明。*operating ~s* 业务[工作]须知,操作规程。***ask for*** ~ 请示。***give ~ in*** 教授。***give ~s to*** 训令。***receive in*** ~ 接受指导。~ **deck**【计】指令卡片组。~ **repertoire** [**set**]【计】指令系统。

in·struc·tion·al [in'strʌkʃənəl; ɪn`strʌkʃənl̩] ***a***. 教授的,教训的,教育的。*for ~ purpose* 用于教育目的。~ **display** 示教显示器。~ **film** 教学影片。~ **television** 教学电视〔缩写为 ITV〕。

in·struc·tive [in'strʌktiv; ɪn`strʌktɪv] ***a***. 有教育意义的,有启发的,有益的。*an ~ film* 科学普及片。~ *lessons* 有益的教训。**-ly** ***ad***. **-ness** ***n***.

in·struc·tor [in'strʌktə; ɪn`strʌktɚ] ***n***. 教导者,教员;〔美〕(大学)讲师。*an ~ in history* 历史教员。*a political* ~ 政治指导员。*an assistant* ~ 助教。**-ship** ***n***. 讲师职位。

in·struc·tress [in'strʌktris; ɪn`strʌktrɪs] ***n***. *fem*. **1**. 〔罕〕女教师。**2**. 女讲师。

in·stru·ment ['instrumənt; `ɪnstrʊmənt] **I** ***n***. **1**. 仪表,仪器〔*cf*. tool, implement〕。**2**. 乐器(= musical ~)。**3**. 【法】证件,证券,文件。**4**. 手段,工具。*airborne ~s* 航空仪表。*all-purpose ~s* 万能仪表。*end ~s* 敏感元件。*nautical ~s* 航海仪器。*optical* ~ 光学仪器。*precision ~s* 精密仪器。*surgical ~s* 外科器械。*stringed ~s* 弦乐器。*wind ~s* 管乐器。*an ~ of credit* 商业证券。*negotiable* ~ 流通票据,可转让证券。*the ~ of ratification* 批准书。*~s of production* 生产工具。*act as sb.'s* ~ 做某人傀儡。*be the ~ of sb.'s death* (误)致某人死亡。**II** ***vt***. **1**. 用仪器装备。**2**. 给乐器编(曲),为管弦乐队编(曲)。**3**. 向…提交法律文件。~ **board** [**panel**] 仪表板。~ **flight** [**flying**]【空】仪表(引导)飞行,盲目[无线电导航]飞行。~ **landing** 盲目[无线电导航]着陆,仪表(引导)降落。

in·stru·men·tal [ˌinstru'mentl; ͵ɪnstrʊ`mɛntl̩] ***a***. **1**. 仪器的,器械的,器具的〔*cf*. vocal〕。**2**. 乐器(上)的,为乐器谱曲的,用乐器演奏的。**3**. 作为手段[工具]的,有帮助的,起作用的。**4**. 【语法】工具格的。~ *drawing* 器械画。~ *errors* 仪器误差,仪表误差。*an ~ ensemble* 器乐重奏曲。~ *music* 器乐。~ *parts* 器乐部。*be ~ to a purpose* 对目的有帮助。~ *in improving the qualities of our products* 有助于提高我们产品的质量。~ **case**【语法】工具格。**-ist** **1**. ***n***. 器乐演奏者;工具主义者。**2**. ***a***. 主张工具主义的,根据工具主义的。

in·stru·men·tal·ism [ˌinstrə'mentlizm; ͵ɪnstrə`mɛntl̩ɪzəm] ***n***. 【哲】工具主义〔实用主义的一种理论〕。

in·stru·men·tal·i·ty [ˌinstrumen'tæliti; ͵ɪnstrʊmɛn`tælətɪ] ***n***. 手段,媒介,工具,帮助。***by*** [***through***] ***the ~ of*** 靠…,借助于…,以…做为手段。

in·stru·men·tal·ly [ˌinstru'mentəli; ͵ɪnstrʊ`mɛntəlɪ] ***ad***. 用仪器地;用乐器地;机械地,间接地。

in·stru·men·ta·tion [ˌinstrumen'teiʃən; ͵ɪnstrʊmɛn`teʃən] ***n***. **1**. 装设仪器;使用仪器;【自】检测仪表;测试设备。**2**. 用乐器演奏谱曲,作曲法〔*cf*. orchestration〕。**3**. 乐曲研究,仪器制造学。**4**. 手段。

in·sub·or·di·nate [insə'bɔːdnit; ͵ɪnsə`bɔrdn̩ɪt] **I** ***a***. **1**. 不服从的,反抗的。**2**. 地位不低[劣]的。**II** ***n***. 不服从的人,反抗者。**-ly** ***ad***.

in·sub·or·di·na·tion ['insəˌbɔːdi'neiʃən; ͵ɪnsə͵bɔrdn̩`eʃən] ***n***. 不服从,反抗。

in·sub·stan·tial [ˌinsəb'stænʃəl; ͵ɪnsəb`stænʃəl] ***a***. 无实体的;不实在的;幻想的;不坚固的;脆弱的。**-ti·al·i·ty** [-ʃiː'æliti, -ʃɪ`ælətɪ] ***n***.

in·suf·fer·a·ble [in'sʌfərəbl; ɪn`sʌfərəbl̩] ***a***. 难忍受的;受不了的。**-bly** ***ad***.

in·suf·fi·cience [ˌinsə'fiʃəns; ͵ɪnsə`fɪʃəns] ***n***. 〔罕〕= insufficiency.

in·suf·fi·cien·cy [ˌinsə'fiʃənsi; ͵ɪnsə`fɪʃənsɪ] ***n***. **1**. 不够,不足,不充分;不适当。**2**. 机能不全〔尤指心阀闭锁不全〕。*the ~ of provisions* 食物不足。*cardiac* ~ 心机能不全。

in·suf·fi·cient [ˌinsə'fiʃənt; ͵ɪnsə`fɪʃənt] ***a***. 不够的,不足的,不充分的;不适当的。**-ly** ***ad***.

in·suf·flate [in'sʌfleit; ɪn`sʌflet] ***vt***. **1**. 吹进,吹上,喷

注。2.【医】把(粉剂、气体等)吹入人体〔尤指肺部〕。3.【宗】对(受洗者)吹气以驱除妖魔〔一种仪式〕。

in·suf·fla·tion [ˌinsəˈfleiʃən; ˌɪnsəˋfleʃən] ***n.*** 吹入,吹上;吹入剂,吹入法。*mouth-to-mouth* ~ 对口吹气法。*oxygen* ~注氧法。

in·suf·fla·tor [ˈinsəfleitə; ˋɪnsəˏfletɚ] ***n.*** 吹入器;吹粉器;(使指纹显出的)指纹吹粉器;吹药器。

in·su·lant [ˈinsələnt; ˋɪnsələnt] ***n.*** 绝缘体;隔音[热]材料。

in·su·lar [ˈinsjulə; ˋɪnsjələ] ***a.*** 1. 海岛的,岛国的,岛形的。2. 岛民的,像岛民的。3. 具有岛民特性的,偏狭的。4. 孤立的,隔绝的,像岛似的。5. 在岛上居住的,位于岛上的。6.【医】岛屿状的,散开的;【解】胰岛的,脑岛的。*an* ~ *climate* 海岛性气候。*an* ~ *fortress* 孤立无援的要塞。

in·su·lar·ism [ˈinsjulərizəm; ˋɪnsjələrɪzm̩] ***n.*** = insularity.

in·su·lar·i·ty [ˌinsjuˈlæriti; ˏɪnsjəˋlærətɪ] ***n.*** 岛国性质;(思想、观点等的)偏狭性。

in·su·late [ˈinsjuleit; ˋɪnsjəˏlet] ***vt.*** 1. 隔离,使孤立。2.【物】使绝缘;使绝热。3. 使成岛。*an* ~*d life* 孤独的生活。~*d body* 被绝缘体。(*an*) ~*d wire*【电】绝缘线。*insulating tape* 胶带。

in·su·la·tor [ˈinsjuleitə; ˋɪnsjəˏletɚ] ***n.*** 1. 隔离者。2. 隔离物,隔振子,隔电子。3.【物】绝缘物,绝缘体,绝缘子;绝热体。*glass* ~ 玻璃绝缘体。*thermal* [*heat*] ~ 热绝缘体。*porcelain* ~ 瓷瓶,瓷绝缘子。

in·su·la·tion [ˌinsjuˈleiʃən; ˏɪnsjəˋleʃən] ***n.*** 1. 隔离,孤立。2.【物】绝缘,绝热。~ *board* 隔音[绝热]板。~ *material* 绝缘材料。~ *resistance*【电】绝缘电阻。*sound* ~ 声绝缘,隔声。*thermal* ~热绝缘,保温层。~ *workshop* 隔热车间。

in·su·lin [ˈinsjulin; ˋɪnsjəlɪn] ***n.***【生化】胰岛素。*bovine* ~ 牛胰岛素。*histone* ~ 组朊胰岛素。*man-made synthetic* ~人工合成胰岛素。*total synthetic crystalline* ~ 完全人工合成结晶胰岛素。~ **shock**【医】胰岛素休克。

in·sult [ˈinsʌlt; ˋɪnsʌlt] **I** ***n.*** 1. 侮辱,凌辱。2.〔古〕攻击,袭击。3. 损害。*enviromental* ~*s* 环境对人体的危害。***add*** ~ ***to injury*** 伤害之外又加侮辱。***offer an*** ~ ***to*** ~侮辱…。***put up with*** [***swallow*** (***down***), ***pocket***, ***take***] ***an*** ~忍受侮辱。***remark or action that*** ~***s*** 侮辱的言行。***sit down under*** ~***s*** 甘受侮辱。**II** [inˈsʌlt; ɪnˋsʌlt] ***vt.*** 侮辱。

in·sult·ing [inˈsʌltiŋ; ɪnˋsʌltɪŋ] ***a.*** 侮辱的,无礼的。*use* ~ *language* 使用侮辱性语言。**-ly** ***ad.***

in·su·per·a·ble [inˈsjuːpərəbl; ɪnˋsjupərəbl] ***a.*** 1. 不能克服的,难以越过的。2. 不可战胜的,无敌的。*an* ~ *barrier* 无法逾越的障碍。~ *heroes* 无敌的英雄。**-bil·i·ty** ***n.*** **-bly** ***ad.***

in·sup·port·a·ble [ˌinsəˈpɔːtəbl; ˏɪnsəˋpɔrtəbl̩] ***a.*** 1. 难堪的,难忍的,不能忍受的。2. 无根据的,无理由的。~ *charges* 无理的指责。**-bly** ***ad.***

in·sup·press·i·ble [ˌinsəˈpresəbl; ˏɪnsəˋprɛsəbl̩] ***a.*** 难制服的,压抑不住的。**-bly** ***ad.***

in·sur·a·bil·i·ty [inˌʃuərəˈbiliti; ɪnˏʃurəˋbɪlətɪ] ***n.*** 可以保险,应当保险。

in·sur·a·ble [inˈʃuərəbl; ɪnˋʃurəbl̩] ***a.*** 可以保险的,应当保险的。~ *interest* 被保险利益。~ *property* 可以接受保险的财产。**-a·bil·i·ty** ***n.***

in·sur·ance [inˈʃuərəns; ɪnˋʃurəns] **I** ***n.*** 1. 安全保障。2. 保险,保险业。3. 保险单〔通称 ~ policy〕。4. 保险费〔通称 premium〕。5. 保险额。*provide* ~ *against floods* 为防洪提供安全措施。*accident* ~ 意外事故保险。*fire* ~ 火灾保险。*labour* ~ 劳动保险。*life* ~ 人寿保险。*marine* ~海上保险,水险。*term* ~ 定期保险。*whole* [*straight*] *life* ~ 终身保险。*an* ~ *agent* 保险代办所,保险经纪人。**II** ***a.***〔美俚〕(篮球赛等)稳胜对方的,胜券在握的。~ **man** 保险推销员。~ **business** 保险(事)业。~ **company** 保险公司。~ **technician** 保险公司技术员[负责审核人寿保险或健康保险投保者的身体状况,以确定保险金支付额大小]。

in·sur·ant [inˈʃuərənt; ɪnˋʃurənt] ***n.*** 被保险人,受保人。

in·sure [inˈʃuə; ɪnˋʃur] ***vt.*** 1. 保险,给…保险。2. 保障,为…提供保证。~ *sb.'s property against fire* 给某人财产保火险。~ *oneself* [*one's life*] *for £5,000* 给某人保寿险五千镑。~ *sth. against loss at sea* 给某物办海上保险。~ *success* 保证成功。— ***vi.*** 投保,承保。~ *against death* 保寿险。*the* ~*d* 被保险人,受保户。*an* ~*d letter* 保价信。

in·sur·er [inˈʃuərə; ɪnˋʃurɚ] ***n.*** 承保人;保险公司。

in·sur·gence [inˈsəːdʒəns; ɪnˋsɝdʒəns] ***n.*** 起义,暴动,叛变行动。

in·sur·gen·cy [inˈsəːdʒənsi; ɪnˋsɝdʒənsɪ] ***n.*** 1. 起义,暴动,叛变行动[性质、状态]。2. = insurgence.

in·sur·gent [inˈsəːdʒənt; ɪnˋsɝdʒənt] **I** ***a.*** 1. 起义的,造反的,暴动的。2. (波涛)汹涌澎湃的。~ *troops* 叛军。**II** ***n.*** 起义者,造反者,暴动者;〔美〕(政党的)反党分子。**-ly** ***ad.***

in·sur·mount·a·bil·i·ty [ˌinsə(ː)ˌmauntəˈbiliti; ˏɪnsɚˏmaʊntəˋbɪlətɪ] ***n.*** 不可克服,难以逾越。

in·sur·mount·a·ble [ˌinsə(ː)ˈmauntəbl; ˏɪnsɚˋmaʊntəbl̩] ***a.*** 不可克服的,难以逾越的。**-bly** ***ad.***

in·sur·rec·tion [ˌinsəˈrekʃən; ˏɪnsəˋrɛkʃən] ***n.*** 起义,叛乱,造反,暴动。*armed* ~ 武装起义。*rise in* ~ 起义,暴动。**-ist** ***n.*** 起义者,叛乱者。

in·sur·rec·tion·al [ˌinsəˈrekʃənəl; ˏɪnsəˋrɛkʃənəl] ***a.*** 起义的,叛乱的。

in·sur·rec·tion·ar·y [ˌinsəˈrekʃənəri; ˏɪnsəˋrɛkʃənərɪ] **I** ***a.*** 起义的,叛乱的。**II** ***n.*** 起义者,叛乱者。

in·sus·cep·ti·ble [ˌinsəˈseptəbl; ˏɪnsəˋsɛptəbl̩] ***a.*** 1. 无感觉的,不受感动的;不易受…影响的(*of*; *to*)。2. 不容许…的。*a mind* ~ *to flattery* 不受奉承的人。*a disease* ~ *of medical treatment* 不能医治的病。*The clause is* ~ *of another interpretation.* 这一条文不能有其他解释。**-bil·i·ty** ***n.*** **-bly** ***ad.***

in·swept [ˈinˌswept; ˋɪnˏswɛpt] ***a.*** (汽车等)前端窄狭的,流线型的。

in't [int; ɪnt]〔古、诗〕= in it.

int. = 1. interjection. 2. intransitive. 3. interest. 4. interim. 5. interior. 6. internal. 7. international. 8. interpreter.

in·tact [inˈtækt; ɪnˋtækt] ***a.***〔作补语用〕未经触动的,未受损的,原封不动的,完整无损的。*keep* [*leave*] *sth.* ~ 使某物保持原样,让某物原封不动。*keep our friendship* ~ 让我们的友谊地久天长。**-ness** ***n.***

in·ta·gliat·ed [inˈtæljeitid; ɪnˋtæljetɪd] ***a.*** 凹雕的。

in·tagl·i·o [inˈtæliəu, -ˈtɑː-; ɪnˋtælɪo, -ˋtɑ-] **I** ***n.*** (*pl.* ~*s*, ***in·tagl·i*** [inˈtɑːljiː; ɪnˋtɑlji]) 凹雕〔*cf.* relief, relievo〕;凹雕玉石〔*cf.* cameo〕。~ *printing* 凹板印刷。**II** ***vt.*** 凹雕。

in·take [ˈin-teik; ˋɪn-tek] ***n.*** 1. 吸入,纳入,收纳。2. 进水口(*opp.* outlet);输入端,(矿井的)进风巷道,通风孔。3. 吸气,进气。4.【医】摄入量,摄取。5. 纳入(数)量,【物】输入能量;【矿】进风量。6.〔英方〕(从沼泽等圈入的)围地,垦地。7. 被收纳的东西,被吸收到团体[组织]里的人。*an* ~ *guide* 吸气导管。~ *of food* 食物摄取。*an* ~ *tower* 进水塔。

in·tan·gi·ble [inˈtændʒəbl; ɪnˋtændʒəbl] **I** ***a.*** 1. 触摸不到的,无实体的,无形的。2. 不可捉摸的,难以确定的,模糊的。~ *value* 无形价值。*an* ~ *asset* 无形财产。~ *ideas* 难以明白的概念。**II** ***n.*** 无形的东西,不可捉摸的东西。**-bil·i·ty** ***n.*** **-bly** ***ad.***

in·tar·si·a [inˈtɑːsiə; ɪnˋtɑrsɪə] ***n.*** 镶嵌细工〔尤指意大

利文艺复兴时代象牙、金属等〕。

in·te·ger [ˈintidʒə; ˋɪntədʒɚ] *n*. 1.【数】整数(*opp*. fraction)。2. 完整的东西,整体。

in·te·ger vi·tae [ˈintidʒə ˈvaitiː; ˋɪntədʒɚ ˋvaɪtɪ] 无过失的,正直的。

in·te·gra·ble [ˈintigrəbl; ˋɪntəgrəbl̩] *a*. 1. 可汇总的,可并合的。2. 可聚合的,可并拢的。3. 可得出总计的。4. 可取消种族隔离的。5.【数】可求积分的。

in·te·gral [ˈintigrəl; ˋɪntəgrəl] I *a*. 1. 完全的;缺一不可的,主要的。2.【数】整的,积分的。*an* ~ *steel plant* 综合钢铁厂。*an* ~ *part of* …的一个主要部分。*an* ~ *whole* 整体。~ *equation* 积分方程。II *n*. 全体,整体;【数】积分。*definite* ~ 定积分。*double* ~ (二)重积分。*indefinite* ~ 不定积分。~ **calculus**【数】积分(学)。**-i·ty** *n*. 完整性。**-ly** *ad*.

in·te·grand [ˈintigrænd; ˋɪntəˏgrænd] *n*.【数】被积函数,被积式。

in·te·grant [ˈintigrənt; ˋɪntəgrənt] I *a*. =integral. *an* ~ *part* (构成)要素。II *n*. 成分,组成部分,要素。

in·te·graph [ˈintigrɑːf; ˋɪntəˏgræf] *n*. 积分仪,积分描图仪,积分曲线仪,积分器。

in·tegrate [ˈintigreit; ˋɪntəˏgret] I *vt*. 1. 使成整体,使并入,使一体化,使结合起来。2. 〔英〕取消(学校的)种族隔离,使(黑人等)不受歧视。3. 表示(面积、温度等的)总和。4.【数】求…的积分。~ *theory with practice* 理论联系实际。~ *the Negroes in this school* 这个学校取消了对黑人的种族歧视。— *vi*. 与…结合起来,成一体(*with*)。*A* ~*s with B*. A 与 B 结合起来,AB 成为一体。II [ˈintigrit; ˋɪntɪgrɪt] *a*. 完整的,完全的。

in·te·grat·ed [ˈintigreitid; ˋɪntəˏgretɪd] *a*. 完整的,完全的。*an* ~ *iron and steel works* 钢铁联合企业。*an* ~ *oil company* 大型石油(联合)公司。~ **circuit**【无】积体[集成]电路,积分电路。~ **circuitry** 集成电路设备;集成电路元件。~ **mill** 全能工厂,综合工厂。~ **school** 兼收白人与黑人子弟的学校。

in·te·gra·tion [ˌintiˈgreiʃən; ˏɪntəˋgreʃən] *n*. 1. 结合;综合;一体化。2.【心】整合(作用)。3.【数】积分(法)(*opp*. differentiation)。4.【经】(产业的)集中。5. 〔美〕取消种族隔离;给以种族上的平等待遇。~ *by parts*【数】部分积分法。

in·te·gra·tion·ism [ˌintiˈgreiʃənizəm; ˏɪntəˋgreʃənɪzəm] *n*. 取消种族隔离主义。**-ist** *n*., *a*. 主张取消种族隔离主义者(的)。

inte·gra·tive [ˈintigreitiv; ˋɪntəˏgretɪv] *a*. 综合的,整[一]体化的;可以并合的;可以结合的;【数】可求积分的。

in·te·gra·tor [ˈintigreitə; ˋɪntəˏgretɚ] *n*. 1. 综合者。2.【数】求积器,积分仪。3.【无】积分电路(=~ circuit)。

in·teg·ri·ty [inˈtegriti; ɪnˋtɛgrətɪ] *n*. 1. 诚实,正直。2. 完全,完整。*a man of* ~ 正直的人。*moral* ~ 骨气,气节。*people of unyielding* ~ 硬汉。*territorial* ~ 领土完整。***in its*** ~完整,原封未动。

in·teg·u·ment [inˈtegjumənt; ɪnˋtɛgjumənt] *n*. 1. (动植物的)覆盖物〔如皮肤,皮膜,壳荚,果皮,珠被等〕。2. 一般覆盖物。**-a·ry** *a*. 外皮的,外皮般的。

in·tel·lect [ˈintilekt; ˋɪntɪlɛkt] *n*. 1. 理智,才智,智力。2. (集合的或个别的)明智者,有才智的人。3. 〔古、俚〕〔*pl*.〕理性。*a man of* ~ 有才智的人。*the* ~(*s*) *of the age* 当代有才智的人士,当代的知识界。

in·tel·lec·tion [ˌintiˈlekʃən; ˏɪntɪˋlɛkʃən] *n*. 理解,智力活动。

in·tel·lec·tive [ˌintiˈlektiv; ˏɪntɪˋlɛktɪv] *a*. 1. 理性的,智力的。2. 有理智的,聪明的。

in·tel·lec·tu·al [ˌintiˈlektjuəl; ˏɪntɪˋlɛktʃʊəl] I *a*. 1. 智力的,理智的。2. 用脑筋的,需智力的。3. 理性的,凭理智行事的,打动别人理智的。*the* ~ *powers* [*faculties*] 智能。*an* ~ *process* 理智作用。*the* ~ *class* 知识分子阶层。~ *employments* [*pursuits*] 脑力工作。II *n*. 知识分子。*highly qualified* ~*s* 高级知识分子。~ **property** 知识产权,智慧产权。**-ism** *n*. 智力活动;【哲】唯理智论。**-ist** *n*. 过分强调智力活动的人;唯理智论者。**-ly** *ad*.

in·tel·lec·tu·al·is·tic [ˌintiˌlektjuəˈlistik; ˏɪntɪˏlɛktjuəˋlɪstɪk] *a*.【哲】唯智论的,唯智主义的。

in·tel·lec·tu·al·i·ty [ˈintiˌlektjuˈæliti; ˋɪntɪˏlɛktjʊˋælətɪ] *n*. 理智,理智性。

in·tel·lec·tu·al·ize [ˌintiˈlektjuəlaiz; ˏɪntɪˋlɛktjʊəlaɪz] *vt*. 赋与理智,使有理智,使理智化。— *vi*. 推理,思考。**-al·i·za·tion** *n*. 理智化。

in·tel·li·gence [inˈtelidʒəns; ɪnˋtɛlɪdʒəns] *n*. 1. 智力,智慧,才智,聪明。2. 通知,消息。3. 情报,谍报,情报机构。4. (导引)信息,(瞄准)信号。5.【宗】〔常 *pl*.〕神,天使。~ *quotient* 智商,智力商数〔略作 I. Q. 心理学家进行智力测验的术语〕。*an* ~ *test* 智力测验。*exchange a look of* ~ 递眼色。*give* ~ *of* 通知。*receive* ~ *of* 接到通知。~ *agent* 情报员。~ *bureau* [*department*] 情报局,情报处。~ *centre* 情报所,情报中心。~ *data* 情报资料。~ *office* 情报处[局];〔美〕职业介绍所。~ *officer* 情报官员。*communications* ~【军】电信侦察。*current* ~【军】动态情报。*the Supreme I-* 上帝。~ **signal**【火箭】信息,信号。

in·tel·li·genc·er [inˈtelidʒənsə; ɪnˋtɛlɪdʒənsɚ] *n*. 1. 报导者,通信员。2. 情报员;间谍。

in·tel·li·gent [inˈtelidʒənt; ɪnˋtɛlɪdʒənt] *a*. 1. 理解力强的,有才智的,聪明的,明智的。2. (电脑等)智能型的。3. (大楼或办公室等)由中央电脑系统控制其设施的。*an* ~ *child* 聪明的孩子。~ *answers to questions* 对问题聪明的答覆。*an* ~ *reader* 聪明的读者。~ **agent**【计】代理人软件程序。~ **knowledge-based system**【计】智能知识库系统〔参见 IKBS 条〕。**-ly** *ad*.

in·tel·li·gen·tial [inˌteliˈdʒenʃəl; ɪnˏtɛlɪˋdʒɛnʃəl] *a*. 1. 智力的,理智的。2. 传送情报的。~ *channels* 情报的渠道。

in·tel·li·gent·si·a [inˌteliˈgentsiə; ɪnˏtɛləˋgɛntsɪə], **in·tel·li·gent·zi·a** [-ˈdʒen-; -ˋdʒɛn-] *n*. 知识分子。*the* ~〔通常为集合词单数〕知识分子,〔总称〕知识界。

in·tel·li·gi·bil·i·ty [inˌtelidʒəˈbiliti; ɪnˏtɛlɪdʒəˋbɪlətɪ] *n*. 1. 可理解性。2. 可理解的事物。

in·tel·li·gi·ble [inˈtelidʒəbl; ɪnˋtɛlɪdʒəbl̩] *a*. 1. 可以理解的,易于了解的,明白的。2.【哲】只能用智力了解的,概念的。~ *speech* 明快的言语。~ *pronunciation* 清晰的发音。*make oneself* ~ 讲得使人了解。**-bly** *ad*.

In·tel·sat [ˈintelsæt; ˋɪntɛlsæt] *n*. 1. 国际电信卫星组织。2. 国际通信卫星。

in·tem·per·ance [inˈtempərəns; ɪnˋtɛmpərəns] *n*. 1. 无节制,放纵;过度,激烈。2. 暴饮,酗酒。

in·tem·per·ate [inˈtemparit; ɪnˋtɛmpərɪt] *a*. 1. 无节制的,放纵的;过度的,激烈的。2. 喝酒过度的,酗酒的。3. (气候等)酷烈的。~ *ambition* 狂妄的野心。~ *language* 狂言。~ *habits* 酒癖。*an* ~ *man* 酒徒。~ *wind* 烈风。*an* ~ *zone* 热[寒]带(*opp*. temperate zone)。~ *weather* 恶劣的天气。**-ly** *ad*.

in·tend [inˈtend; ɪnˋtɛnd] *vt*. 1. 想,打算(*to do*)。2. 企图。3. 打算使…成为。4. 意思是,意指。*I* ~ *to go home*. 我想回家。*I* ~*ed an ode*. 我打算写一首颂歌。*I* ~ *it as a stop-gap*. 我想拿它凑数。*Was this* ~*ed*? 这是故意的吗? *He* ~*s no harm*. 他没有恶意。*The gift was* ~*ed for you*. 这个礼物是要送给你的。*What do you* ~ *by your words*? 你说这些话是什么意思呢?

in·tend·ance [inˈtendəns; ɪnˋtɛndəns] *n*. 1. 监督,管理。2. 行政管理部门。

in·tend·an·cy [inˈtendənsi; ɪnˋtɛndənsɪ] *n*. 1. 监督人[管理人]的职责。2. 监督[管理]人员。3. (殖民主义者在南美的)监督管辖区。

I

in·tend·ant [in'tendənt; ɪn`tɛndənt] ***n*.** 1. 监督人，管理人；经理。2. 【史】(法、西、葡封建王朝的)州长。3. (殖民主义者在南美的)地方行政长官。

in·tend·ed [in'tendid; ɪn`tɛndɪd] **I *a*.** 1. 预期的，打算中的。2. 有意的，故意的。3. 已订婚的。*bring on ～ results* 带来预期的结果。*an ～ insult* 蓄意的侮辱。*one's ～ wife* 未婚妻。**II *n*.** 〔口〕〔加用物主代名词〕已订婚的人。*my ～* 我的未婚妻[夫]。

in·tend·ing [in'tendiŋ; ɪn`tɛndɪŋ] ***a*.** 〔主英〕预期的；未来的；将来的。

in·tend·ment [in'tendmənt; ɪn`tɛndmənt] ***n*.** 1. 〔古〕目的；目标；企图。2. (法律的)含义。

in·ten·er·ate [in'tenəreit; ɪn`tɛnə,ret] ***vt*.** (*-at·ed*; *-at·ing*) 〔罕〕使变柔软。**-a·tion *n*.**

intens. = 1. intensified. 2. intensifier. 3. intensive.

in·tense [in'tens; ɪn`tɛns] ***a*.** (*-tenser*; *-tensest*) 1. 激烈的，强烈的；紧张的。2. 热烈的，热情的，认真的。3. 【摄】(底片)明暗度强的。*an ～ light* 强烈的灯光。～ *cold* 严寒。～ *heat* 酷热。～ *pain* 剧痛。*the ～ sun* 烈日。*an ～ person* 热情认真的人。*an ～ life* 奋发图强的生活。～ *study* 认真的研究。**-ly *ad*. -ness *n*.**

in·ten·si·fi·ca·tion [in,tensifi'keiʃən; ɪn,tɛnsɪfɪ`keʃən] ***n*.** 1. 使强烈，加强，强化。2. 【摄】加厚〔*opp*. reduction〕。

in·ten·si·fi·er [in'tensifaiə; ɪn`tɛnsɪ,faɪr] ***n*.** 1. 【摄】增厚剂；【物】增强剂；【机】增强器。2. 照明装置；【电】增辉电路。*spark ～*【机】火花增强器。

in·ten·si·fy [in'tensifai; ɪn`tɛnsə,faɪ] ***vt*.** (*-fied*; *-fy·ing*) 1. 使强烈，加强；加剧。2. 【摄】加厚(底片阴纹)。— ***vi*.** 强化，变猛烈。

in·ten·sion [in'tenʃən; ɪn`tɛnʃən] ***n*.** 1. 强度，紧张，加强。2. 专心致志，努力。3. 【逻】内包。4. 【数】内涵(*opp*. extension)。5. 【农】集约经营。

in·ten·si·ty [in'tensiti; ɪn`tɛnsɪtɪ] ***n*.** 1. (思想、感情的)强烈，激烈。2. 强度。3. 【摄】(底片的)明暗度。*go mad at the ～ of one's grief* 因为过度悲伤而发疯。～ *of illumination* 照度，光照强度。*bombardment ～* 炮火强度。*current ～* 电流强度。*labour ～* 劳动强度。*luminous ～* 光度。*radiant ～*【物】辐射强度。

in·ten·sive [in'tensiv; ɪn`tɛnsɪv] **I *a*.** 1. 加强的；集中的；深入细致的，彻底的。2. 【语】加强词义的。3. 【农】精耕细作的，集约的。4. 【逻】内包的。5. 【医】渐进的。*an ～ bombardment* 密集炮击。*an ～ study* 彻底的研究。～ *reading* 精读(*opp*. extensive reading 泛读)。～ *adverb* 强义副词〔如 very, awfully, terribly 等〕。～ *agriculture* [*farming*] 细耕农业，集约农业。～ (*and careful*) *cultivation* 精耕细作。**II *n*.** 1. 加强器；加强剂。2. 【语】强义词[词首]。～ **culture** 集约耕作。～ **inoculation** 【医】渐进接种。**-ly *ad*. -ness *n*.**

in·tent [in'tent; ɪn`tɛnt] **I *n*.** 1. 意图；目的。2. 意义，含义。*criminal ～*【法】犯罪意图。*use one's leisure time to good ～* 有益地利用空闲时间。*with good* [*malicious*] *～* 好[恶]意地。*with murderous ～ behind one's smiles* 笑里藏刀。*with ～ to defraud* 存心欺诈。***to all ～s and purposes*** 无论从哪一点来看，事实上，实际上(*The revised edition is to all ～s and purposes a new book*. 修订本简直是本新书。)。**II *a*.** 1. 目不转睛的，集中的；热心的。2. 专心致志的，坚决的。*an ～ look* 凝视。*an ～ person* 热心的人。*be ～ on one's work* 一心一意地工作。**-ly *ad*. -ness *n*.**

in·ten·tion [in'tenʃən; ɪn`tɛnʃən] ***n*.** 1. 意向；意图，目的；打算。2. 〔口〕〔*pl*.〕结婚的意图。3. 意义，意旨。4. 【逻】概念。5. 【医】愈合。*a person of good ～s* 好心人。*by ～* 故意。*have no ～ of doing* 无意做…。*She began to worry that her boy friend's ～s might not be serious*. 她开始担心她的男朋友打算结婚不是认真的。*the ～ of a clause* 条文的意旨。*heal by first ～*【医】第一期愈合。*heal by second ～*【医】第二期愈合。*with good ～s* = *with the best of ～s* 好心好意地，诚心。***with the ～ of*** 打算…，以…为目的。***without ～*** 无意中，不是故意地。

in·ten·tion·al [in'tenʃənəl; ɪn`tɛnʃənl] ***a*.** 有意(识)的，故意的〔*opp*. accidental〕。～ **fallacy** 意图谬误〔新派文学研究的一种文本中心论，认为单纯从作者的主观意图来研究分析作品系一种谬误〕。**-ly *ad*.**

in·ten·tioned [in'tenʃənd; ɪn`tɛnʃənd] ***a*.** 有意的，故意的。★前面常加连字符号(-)与其它词在一起形成复合词：*well-～* 善[好]意的。*maliciously* (*ill*)-～恶意的，蓄意的。

in·ter [in'tə:; ɪn`tɝ] ***vt*.** 埋葬。～ *a dead body into the earth* 把尸首埋起来。

in·ter ['intə; `ɪntə] ***prep*.** 〔L.〕在中间，在内，互相。～ ***alia*** ['intə 'eiliə; `ɪntə `elɪə] 除了别的事物以外，尤其。～ ***nos*** ['nəus; `nos] 莫对别人讲，秘密地。～ ***se*** [-'si:; -`si] 秘密；在同品种之间(交配)。～ ***vivos*** ['vaivəus; `vaɪvos] 【法】在生存者当中。

inter- *comb. f*. 表示"在…中"，"在…间"，"在…内"，"相互"：*inter*act, *inter*city.

in·ter·act[1] [,intər'ækt; ,ɪntər`ækt] ***vi*.** 相互作用，相互影响，互动。**-active *a*.**

in·ter·act[2] ['intərækt; `ɪntərækt] ***n*.** = *entr'acte*.

in·ter·act·ant [,intə'æktənt; ,ɪntə`æktənt] ***n*.** 相互作用物〔尤指化学反应物〕。

in·ter·ac·tion [,intər'ækʃən; ,ɪntər`ækʃən] ***n*.** 1. 相互作用，相互影响，互动。2. 【空】干扰。～ *of electrons*【物】电子的相互作用。*jet-shock ～* 射流-激波干扰。

in·ter·ac·tive [,intə:'æktiv; ,ɪntə`æktɪv] **I *a*.** 相互作用的，相互影响的，互动的。**II *n*.** 交互式视频设备。～ **fiction** 交互式视频小说〔以电脑程序编写，依据指令输出内容〕。～ **toy** (和电影等配套的)交互式玩具。

in·ter·a·li·a [,intə'eiliə; ,ɪntə`elɪə] ***ad*.** 〔L.〕在其他的事物之中；首先，尤其。

in·ter·a·li·os [,intə'eiliəus; ,ɪntə`elɪ,os] 〔L.〕在其余的人中，在其他的人中。

in·ter-Al·lied [,intə(:)rə'laid; ,ɪntərə`laɪd] ***a*.** (第一次大战时)协约国间的。

in·ter-A·mer·i·can [,intərə'merikən; ,ɪntərə`mɛrɪkən] ***a*.** 美洲国家之间的。～ *Development Bank* 泛美开发银行。

in·ter·bang [,intə'bæŋ; ,ɪntə`bæŋ] ***n*.** 问叹号(!?)。

in·ter·blend [,intə(:)'blend; ,ɪntə`blɛnd] ***vt*., *vi*.** (～-*ed*, *-blent*) 混合；相混。

in·ter·bor·ough ['intə(:)'bʌrə; `ɪntə,bɝə] **I *a*.** (各)自治村镇之间的，(各)独立区之间的。**II *n*.** 自治村镇之间的交通工具〔地铁、电车等〕。

in·ter·brain ['intəbrein; `ɪntə,bren] ***n*.** 间脑〔脊椎动物前脑的后部〕(=diencephalon)。

in·ter·breed [,intə'bri:d; ,ɪntə`brid] ***vt*., *vi*.** = hybridize.

in·ter·ca·lar·y [in'tə:kələri; ɪn`tɝkələrɪ] ***a*.** 1. (历法)闰的。2. 插入的，添加的，夹层的。*an ～ day* 闰日(二月二十九日)。*an ～ month* 闰月。*an ～ year* 闰年(二月)。*an ～ plate* 加插板。～ *strata*【地】夹层。

in·ter·ca·late [in'tə:kəleit; ɪn`tɝkə,let] ***vt*.** 1. 设置(闰日[闰月]等)。2. 插入；添加。**-la·tion *n*.**

in·ter·cede [,intə(:)'si:d; ,ɪntə`sid] ***vi*.** 1. 调停，调解。2. 代为请求，说情。～ *with the teacher for sb*. 为某人向老师说情。

in·ter·cel·lu·lar [,intə(:)'seljulə; ,ɪntə`sɛljulə] ***a*.** 【生】(细)胞间的。～ *space* 胞间隙。～ *substance* 胞间质。

in·ter·cept [,intə(:)'sept; ,ɪntə`sɛpt] **I *vt*.** 1. 拦截，截击(敌军)，截断(光、热、水等)，阻止，中止。2. 窃听，侦听。3. 交切，相交，交叉。4. 【数】(在两点或两线间)截取。～

a messenger 阻拦信使。～ *a forward pass* 阻止前进。**II** ***n*.** **1.** 拦截,截击。**2.** 窃听,侦听。**3.**【数】截距,截断。～ *heading*【军】截击航向。*an* ～ *mission*【军】截击任务。*an* ～ *officer*【军】截击军官。*an* ～ *station*【军】侦听台。～ *of a line* [*plane*] 线[面]的截距。**-tive** ***a*.**

in·ter·cept·er, in·ter·cep·tor [ˌintə(:)ˈseptə; ˏɪntə-ˋsɛptə-] ***n*.** **1.** 拦截者,阻止者。**2.**【空】遮断器;阻止器;扰流板。**3.**【军】截击机,拦击机;拦截器;拦截导弹。**4.** 截击机雷达台,窃听器。～ *plate* 翼缝扰流板。

in·ter·cep·tion [ˌintə(:)ˈsepʃən; ˏɪntə-ˋsɛpʃən] ***n*.** **1.** 拦截;截击;遮断,阻止;截取。**2.** 窃听,侦听;【空】雷达侦察。*long-range* ～【空】远距离雷达侦察。*blind* ～【空】(用仪表)盲目拦截。*ground-controlled* ～【军】地面控制截击(设备)。

in·ter·ces·sion [ˌintəˈseʃən; ˏɪntə-ˋsɛʃən] ***n*.** **1.** 调解,说情。**2.**【宗】代人祈祷。***make an*** ～ ***to A for B*** 向某甲为某乙说情。***through sb.'s*** ～经某人调解。**-al** ***a*.**

in·ter·ces·sor [ˌintəˈsesə; ˏɪntə-ˋsɛsə-] ***n*.** **1.** 调解者,说情者。**2.**【宗】代理主教。

in·ter·ces·so·ry [ˌintəˈsesəri; ˏɪntə-ˋsɛsərɪ] ***a*.** 调解的,说情的;代人祈祷的。

in·ter·change [ˌintə(:)ˈtʃeindʒ; ˏɪntə-ˋtʃendʒ] **I** ***vt*.** **1.** 交换,互换。**2.** 交替(位置等)。**3.** 使更叠发生;轮流进行。～ *civilites* 相互问候。～ *gifts* 互赠礼品。～ *cares with pleasures* 有苦有乐。～ *labour and repose* 劳逸兼顾。～ *letters* 互通信件。～ *opinions* [*views*] 交换意见。— ***vi*.** 交替发生;交换位置。**II** [ˈintə(:)ˈtʃeindʒ; ˋɪntətʃendʒ] ***n*.** **1.** 交换,交替。**2.**【建】互通式立体交叉,道路立体枢纽。*an* ～ *of personnel* 人事更叠。

in·ter·change·a·ble [ˌintə(:)ˈtʃeindʒəbl; ˏɪntə-ˋtʃendʒəbl̩] ***a*.** 可交换的,可更替的;可互换的。**-bil·i·ty, -ness** ***n*.** **-bly** ***ad*.**

in·ter·cit·y [ˌintəˈsiti; ˏɪntəˋsɪtɪ] ***a*.** 城市间的,市际的。*an* ～ *bus* 市际公共汽车。

in·ter·class [ˈintə(:)ˈklɑːs; ˋɪntə-ˋklæs] ***a*.** 年级之间的。*an* ～ *basketball tournament* 年级之间进行的篮球赛。

in·ter·clav·i·cle [ˌintəˈklævikl; ˏɪntə-ˋklævɪkl̩] ***n*.** 【解】锁间骨;(龟的)锁间骨甲。**-vic·ular** [-kləˈvikjulə; -kləˋvɪkjʊlə-] ***a*.**

in·ter·col·lege [ˌintəˈkɔlidʒ; ˏɪntə-ˋkɑlɪdʒ] ***a*.** = intercollegiate.

in·ter·col·le·gi·ate [ˌintə(:)kəˈliːdʒiit; ˏɪntə-kəˋlidʒɪɪt] ***a*.** 大学[学院]间的。*an* ～ *regatta* 院际[校际]船赛。

in·ter·co·lo·ni·al [ˌintə(:)kəˈləunjəl; ˏɪntə-kəˋlonɪəl] ***a*.** 殖民地间的。

in·ter·co·lum·nar [ˌintə(:)kəˈlʌmnə; ˏɪntə-kəˋlʌmnə-] ***a*.**【建】柱间的。

in·ter·co·lum·ni·a·tion [ˈintə(:)kəˌlʌmniˈeiʃən; ˏɪntə-kəˏlʌmnɪˋeʃən] ***n*.**【建】分柱法。

in·ter·com [ˈintə(:)kɔm; ˋɪntə-kɑm] ***n*.** (军舰、飞机等内的)通讯装置,内部通讯联络系统。

in·ter·com·mu·nal [ˌintəˈkɔmjunl; ˏɪntəˋkɑmjʊnl̩] ***a*.** 社团之间的,社会团体间所共有的。

in·ter·com·mu·ni·cate [ˌintə(:)kəˈmjuːnikeit; ˏɪntə-kəˋmjunɪˏket] ***vi*.** 互通;互相联系,互相通信。*intercommunicating rooms* 互通的房间。*intercommunicating set* 内部互通电话机。

in·ter·com·mu·ni·ca·tion [ˌintə(:)kəˌmjuːniˈkeiʃən; ˏɪntə-kəˏmjunɪˋkeʃən] ***n*.** 互相联系,互相通信;内部通信联络。

in·ter·com·mun·ion [ˌintə(:)kəˈmjuːnjən; ˏɪntə-kəˋmjunɪən] ***n*.** **1.**【宗】各教派间共同举行的圣餐。**2.** 各教派之间的思想感情交流。

in·ter·com·mu·ni·ty [ˌintə(:)kəˈmjuːniti; ˏɪntə-kəˋmjunətɪ] **I** ***n*.** 公用,共有,共同参加。**II** ***a*.** 共同体间的,共通性。

in·ter·con·nect [ˌintə(:)kəˈnekt; ˏɪntə-kəˋnɛkt] ***vt*.**, ***vi*.** (使)互相联系。*be closely* ～ *ed* 相互紧密地联系在一起。

in·ter·con·nec·tion [ˌintə(:)kəˈnekʃən; ˏɪntə-kəˋnɛkʃən] ***n*.** 相互联系。

in·ter·con·ti·nen·tal [ˌintəˌkɔntiˈnentl; ˏɪntə-ˏkɑntɪˋnɛntl̩] ***a*.** 洲际的;(飞机、火箭飞弹等的)可跨洲飞行的。*an* ～ (*ballistic*) *missile* 洲际(弹道)飞弹。*an* ～ *ballistic rocket* 洲际弹道火箭。

in·ter·con·ver·sion [ˌintə(:)kənˈvəːʃən; ˏɪntə-kənˋvɝʃən] ***n*.**【化】互变(现象)。

in·ter·con·ver·ti·ble [ˌintə(:)kənˈvəːtəbl; ˏɪntə-kənˋvɝtəbl̩] ***a*.** 可互相转换的。**-bil·i·ty** ***n*.** **-bly** ***ad*.**

in·ter·cool·er [ˌintə(:)ˈkuːlə; ˏɪntəˋkulə] ***n*.**【机】中间冷却器。

in·ter·cos·tal [ˌintə(:)ˈkɔstl; ˏɪntə-ˋkɑstl̩] **I** ***a*.** **1.**【解】肋间的。**2.**【植】生于叶脉间的。～ *muscles* 肋间肌。～ *nerves* 肋间神经。**II** ***n*.**【解】肋间肌。**-ly** ***ad*.**

in·ter·course [ˈintə(:)kɔːs; ˋɪntə-kɔrs] ***n*.** **1.** 交际,来往;相互关系。**2.** 精神上的交换,神交,灵交。**3.**【生】交合。*commercial* [*trade*] ～通商,商业关系。*diplomatic* ～外交来往。*friendly* ～友好往来,交际。*social* ～社交。*have* [*hold*] ～ *with sb.* 和某人交际。*illicit* ～私通。*sexual* ～性交。

in·ter·crop [ˌintəˈkrɔp; ˏɪntə-ˋkrɑp] **I** ***vt*.**, ***vi*.** (***-cropped***, ***-crop·ping***) 间作,间种。**II** [ˈintəkrɔp; ˋɪntə-krɑp] ***n*.** 间种作物。

in·ter·cross [ˌintə(:)ˈkrɔs; ˏɪntə-ˋkrɔs] **I** ***vt*.**, ***vi*.** **1.** (使)交叉。**2.** (使)杂交。**II** ***n*.** 异种交配;杂种。

in·ter·crys·tal·line [ˌintə(:)ˈkristəlain; ˏɪntə-ˋkrɪstəˏlaɪn] ***a*.** 晶粒间的。～ *fracture*【地】晶间破裂。～ **recrystallization** 晶间再结晶。～ *rupture*【物】(晶)粒间断裂。

in·ter·cul·tur·al [ˌintə(:)ˈkʌltʃərəl; ˏɪntə-ˋkʌltʃərəl] ***a*.** 在不同文化的人们中间的。

in·ter·cur·rent [ˌintə(:)ˈkʌrənt; ˏɪntə-ˋkʌənt] ***a*.** **1.** 在过程中发生的,介入的。**2.**【医】间发的;介入的;并发的。*an* ～ *disease* 间发病。**-ly** ***ad*.**

in·ter·de·nom·i·na·tion·al [ˌintədiˌnɔmiˈneiˌʃənl; ˏɪntə-dɪˏnɑmɪˋneʃənl] ***a*.**【宗】在各教派之间的;各教派共有的;涉及不同教派的。

in·ter·den·tal [ˌintə(:)ˈdentl; ˏɪntə-ˋdɛntl̩] ***a*.** **1.** 齿间的。**2.**【语言】齿间音的,舌齿音的〔如[θ]〕。～ **splint**【医】齿间夹板。

in·ter·de·part·men·tal [ˌintə(:)diˌpɑːtˈmentl; ˏɪntə-dɪˏpɑrtˋmɛntl̩] ***a*.** 部门之间的。**-ly** ***ad*.**

in·ter·de·pend [ˌintə(:)diˈpend; ˏɪntə-dɪˋpɛnd] ***vi*.** 互相依赖,互相依存。

in·ter·de·pend·ence, in·ter·de·pend·en·cy [ˌintə(:)-diˈpendəns, -si; ˏɪntə-dɪˋpɛndəns, -sɪ] ***n*.** 互相依赖,互相依存。

in·ter·de·pend·ent [ˌintə(:)diˈpendənt; ˏɪntə-dɪˋpɛndənt] ***a*.** 互相依赖的,互相依存的。**-ly** ***ad*.**

in·ter·dict [ˌintə(:)ˈdikt; ˏɪntə-ˋdɪkt] **I** ***vt*.** **1.** 禁止,制止。**2.**【军】闭锁,阻断(敌人通路)。**3.**【宗】停止教权。～ *sb. from doing sth.* 禁止某人做某事。～ *sth. to sb.* 禁止某人使用某物。**II** [ˈintə(:)dikt; ˋɪntə-ˏdɪkt] ***n*.** **1.** 禁止,制止。**2.** 禁令。**3.**【宗】停止教权的命令。*lay a town under an* ～ 停止某一城市的宗教活动。**-tor** ***n*.** 禁止者。

in·ter·dic·tion [ˌintə(:)ˈdikʃən; ˏɪntə-ˋdɪkʃən] ***n*.** **1.** 禁止;制止。**2.**【军】闭锁,阻断。*a barrage of* ～ 封锁火力。～ *fire* 远距离拦阻射击。**-to·ry** ***a*.**

in·ter·dig·i·tate [ˌintə(:)ˈdidʒiteit; ˏɪntə-ˋdɪdʒɪtet] ***vt*.** 两手手指交叉锁住。

in·ter·dis·ci·pli·nar·y [ˌintə(:)ˈdisiplinəri; ˏɪntə-ˋdɪsɪplˏnɛrɪ] ***a*.** 涉及两种以上训练的;涉及两门以上学科的。*an* ～ *approach to cultural history* 有关文化史的多方面探讨。

in·ter·do·min·ion [ˌintədəˈminjən; ˏɪntədə`mɪnjən] ***a.*** 英联邦自治领之间的。

in·ter·est [ˈintrist, ˈintərist; `ɪntrɪst, `ɪntərɪst] **I *n.* 1.** 利害关系,利害;〔常 *pl.*〕利益。**2.** 趣味;感兴趣的事。**3.** 兴趣,关注;爱好。**4.** 重要性;势力;影响。**5.** 利息;利率。**6.** 权利;股份,所有权;事业;财产。**7.** 行业。*the public ~s* 公众利益。*It is to your ~ to give up smoking.* 戒烟对你有好处。*know one's own ~s* 很精明,会打算。*look after one's own ~s* 照顾自己利益。*take the ~s of the whole into account* 顾全大局。*vested ~s* 既得利益。*feel* [*have, take*] *an ~ in sth.* 对某事感兴趣。*feel* [*have, take*] *no ~ in sth.* 对某事不感兴趣。*it is of ~ to note that* 值得注意的是;饶有兴趣的是。*place of ~* 名胜。*a matter of considerable ~*相当重要的事。*a matter of little ~* 不大重要的事。*have ~ with sb.* 对某人产生影响。*lose one's ~ with sb.* 对某人失去影响。*through ~* 通过别人的援引。*annual ~* 年利。*daily ~*日息。*compound ~*复利。*simple ~*单利。*buy an ~ in* 作…的股东,买…的股票。*the business ~*商业界。*the landed ~*地主。*the money ~*金融业者。*the shipping ~*航运界。***in the ~(s) of*** 为了…的利益,为了。***lose ~*** 不再感兴趣,不再引起兴趣。***make ~ with sb.*** (从利害关系出发)施加影响于某人。***take (an) ~ in*** 对…感兴趣。***sink one's own ~s*** 不考虑自己的利益。***with ~* 1.** 带着兴趣(*hear it with ~* 津津有味地听)。**2.** 附利息;加重(*return a blow with ~* 加重还击)。**3.** 通过某种关系(*obtain a position with ~* 通过某种关系取得职位)。**II *vt.*** 使发生兴趣,使开心,使注意;使生关系,使有份儿。*be ~ed in sth.* 对某事有兴趣。*Can I ~ you in a game of golf?* 你有兴趣和我打高尔夫球吗? *~ oneself in an enterprise* 为某项事业奔走。*~ sb. in an enterprise* 使某人加入某项事业。*the person ~ed* 关系人。**~-free *a.*** 无息的 (*an ~-free loan* 无息贷款)。~ **group** 利益集团。

in·ter·est·ed [ˈintristid; `ɪntrɪstɪd] ***a.* 1.** 对…感兴趣的,有趣睐的 (*in*)。**2.** 有关系的,有份儿的,有利害关系的。**3.** 为私利打算的,偏私的。*be ~ in music* 爱好音乐。*~ spectators* 感兴趣的观众。*with an ~ look* 带着感兴趣的样子。*the ~ parties* 有关的当事人。*the person ~*关系人。*~ motives* 不纯洁的动机。*~ witness* 偏心的证人。**-ly *ad.* -ness *n.***

in·ter·est·ing [ˈintristiŋ; `ɪntrɪstɪŋ] ***a.*** 引起兴趣的,有趣的。*in an ~ condition* [*situation*]〔英〕有孕,有喜。*~ conversation* 有兴趣的谈话。**-ly *ad.***

in·ter·face [ˈintə(ː)ˌfeis; `ɪntəˏfes] **I *n.*** 分界面,两个独立体系的相交处。**II *vt.*** (**-*faced, -fac·ing***) 把界面缝合。— ***vi.*** 交流,交谈。

in·ter·fa·cial [ˌintə(ː)ˈfeiʃəl; ˏɪntə`feʃəl] ***a.* 1.** 界面的,面际的。**2.** 界面角的。~ **angle**【地】面交角。~ **tension**【物】面际张力。

in·ter·faith [ˈintə(ː)ˌfeiθ; `ɪntəˏfeθ] ***a.*** 在信仰不同的人之间的,涉及各种信仰者的。

in·ter·fere [ˌintəˈfiə; ˏɪntə`fɪr] ***vi.* 1.** (利害、要求等)抵触,冲突 (*with*)。**2.** 干涉,干预;调停,排解。**3.** 妨碍,打扰。**4.** 有害于。**5.**【物】干扰。**6.** (马等行走、奔跑时)一脚碰在另一脚上。**7.** (橄榄球赛中)阻挡,犯规撞人。**8.**【法】对发明专利权提起诉讼。*interests interfering with each other* 互相冲突的利害关系。*~ in private concerns* 干涉他人私事。*Don't ~ with him.* 别打扰他。*I shall go tomorrow, if nothing ~s.* 如果没有妨碍,我明天就走。*Sedentary habits often ~ with health.* 长坐不动的习惯往往有害于身体。

in·ter·fer·ence [ˌintəˈfiərəns; ˏɪntə`fɪrəns] ***n.* 1.** 冲突,抵触。**2.** 干涉,干预。**3.** 妨碍,打扰,阻碍物。**4.**【物】干扰;干涉。*linguistic ~*本族语对外语学习的干扰。*stop ~ from outside* 制止外来干涉。***run ~ for*** (橄榄球赛中)保护(带球者)以防对方抢球。~ **colours** 干涉色。~ **wave** 干涉波。

in·ter·fe·ren·tial [ˌintəfəˈrenʃəl; ˏɪntəfə`renʃəl] ***a.***【物】干涉的,干扰的。

in·ter·fer·ing [ˌintəˈfiəriŋ; ˏɪntə`fɪrɪŋ] ***a.*** 干涉的,多管闲事的;互相冲突的;干扰的。

in·ter·fer·om·e·ter [ˌintəfiˈrɔmitə; ˏɪntəfɪ`rɑmətə] ***n.***【物】干涉仪,干扰计。**-met·ric** [-fiərəˈmetrik; -fɪrə`metrɪk] ***a.* -e·try *n.***

in·ter·fer·on [ˌintə(ː)ˈfiərɔn; ˏɪntə`fɪrɑn] ***n.***【生化】干扰素。

in·ter·fer·tile [ˌintəˈfəːtail; ˏɪntə`fɜtaɪl] ***a.*** 可混种繁殖的,可杂交的。**-til·i·ty** [-fəˈtiliti; -fə`tɪlətɪ] ***n.***

in·ter·file [ˌintəˈfail; ˏɪntə`faɪl] ***vt.*** 将…归档,把…合并为一宗档案;使归入系列。

in·ter·flow [ˌintə(ː)ˈfləu; ˏɪntə`flo] **I *vi.*** 合流,互通。**II** [ˈintə(ː)fləu; `ɪntəflo] ***n.*** 合流,互通。*the ~ of commodities between the urban and rural areas* 城乡之间的商品交流。

in·ter·flu·ent [inˈtəːfluənt; ɪn`tɜfluənt] ***a.*** 交流的,流在中间的。

in·ter·fluve [ˈintə(ː)fluːv; `ɪntəˏfluv] ***n.***【地】河间地;江河分水区。

in·ter·fold [ˌintəˈfəuld; ˏɪntə`fold] ***vt., vi.*** 折叠。

in·ter·fuse [ˌintə(ː)ˈfjuːz; ˏɪntə`fjuz] ***vt.*** 使渗入;使混入;混合,使充满。— ***vi.*** 混合,融合。

in·ter·fu·sion [ˌintə(ː)ˈfju(ː)ʒən; ˏɪntə`fjuʒən] ***n.*** 渗入;混合,融合。

in·ter·ga·lac·tic [ˌintəgəˈlæktik; ˏɪntəgə`læktɪk] ***a.***【天】存在于星系际的,发生于星系际的。~ *space* 星系际空间。

in·ter·gen·er·a·tion·al [ˌintə(ː)ˌdʒenəˈreiʃənl; ˏɪntəˏdʒenə`reʃənl] ***a.*** 存在于两代[数代]人之间的。

in·ter·gla·cial [ˌintəˈgleisjəl; ˏɪntə`glesɪəl] ***n., a.***【地】间冰期(的)。

in·ter·grade [ˌintə(ː)ˈgreid; ˏɪntə`gred] **I *vi.*** (**-*grad·ed; -grad·ing***) 渐次变形,逐渐融合。**II** [ˈintəˌgred; `ɪntəˏgred] ***n.*** 间渡。**-da·tion** [-greiˈdeiʃən; -gre`deʃən] ***n.***

in·ter·group [ˈintə(ː)ˈgruːp; `ɪntə`grup] ***a.*** 集团之间的,涉及集团之间的〔尤指不同种族之间的〕。

in·ter·growth [ˈintə(ː)grəuθ; `ɪntəˏgroθ] ***n.***【物】共生,交互生长。

in·ter·im [ˈintərim; `ɪntərɪm] **I *n.* 1.** 暂时,临时。**2.** 临时协定。**3.** [the I-]【史】(宗教改革时的)临时敕令。*in the ~*在间歇的当儿,在过渡期间。**II *a.*** 临时的,暂时的,期中的。*an ~ dividend* (未决算前的)期中股利。*an ~ government* 过渡政府。*an ~ council* 临时议会。*an ~ report* 中期报告,临时性报告。*an ~ trial* 临时试验;期中试验。*an ~ certificate* 临时证件。

in·te·ri·or [inˈtiəriə; ɪn`tɪrɪə] **I *a.* 1.** 内的;内部的;室内的 (*opp.* exterior)。**2.** 内地的。**3.** 国内的〔*opp.* foreign〕。**4.** 内面的,内心的,秘密的。*~ guards*【军】内卫兵。*operate on ~ lines*【军】内线作战。*an ~ city* 内城。*~ trade* 国内贸易。*an ~ cabinet* 秘密内阁。**II *n.* 1.** 内部,内景。**2.** 内地。**3.** 内务,内政。**4.** 内心,本性。*the ~ of a house* 室内。*travel in the ~*内地旅行。*the U.S. Department of the I-* 美国内政部〔英国为 Home office〕。*the Minister of the I-* (法德意等国的)内政部长。*the Secretary of the I-*〔美〕内政部长。~ **angle**【数】内角。~ **decoration 1.** 室内装饰,室内摆设。**2.** 室内装饰术,室内装饰业。~ **decorator** 室内装饰家[工人,师傅]。**-ly *ad.***

in·te·ri·or·ize [inˈtiəriəraiz; ɪn`tɪrɪərˏaɪz] ***vt.*** (**-*iz·ed, -iz·ing***) 使(观念、道德标准等)深入内心。**-i·za·tion** [inˌtiːriəraiˈzeiʃən; ɪnˏtɪrɪəraɪ`zeʃən] ***n.***

interj. = interjection.

in·ter·ja·cent [ˌintə(:)ˈdʒeisənt; ˏɪntɚˋdʒesənt] ***a***. 处在中间的。

in·ter·ject [ˌintə(:)ˈdʒekt; ˏɪntɚˋdʒɛkt] ***vt***. 突然插入,插话,插嘴说。~ *a question* 突然插入问题。

in·ter·jec·tion [ˌintə(:)ˈdʒekʃən; ˏɪntɚˋdʒɛkʃən] ***n***. **1**. 突然的叫声,感叹。**2**.【语法】感叹词〔如 oh, ah, alas 等〕。**3**. 插入,插入物。

in·ter·jec·tion·al [ˌintə(:)ˈdʒekʃənl; ˏɪntɚˋdʒɛkʃənl̩] ***a***. 叫声的,感难的;感叹词的;插入的,插入语的。**-ly** ***ad***.

in·ter·jec·tor [ˌintə(:)ˈdʒektə; ˏɪntɚˋdʒɛktɚ] ***n***. 插入者,插入物。

in·ter·jec·to·ry [ˌintə(:)ˈdʒektəri; ˏɪntɚˋdʒɛktorɪ] ***a***. = interjectional.

in·ter·lace [ˌintə(:)ˈleis; ˏɪntɚˋles] ***vt***. 使交织,使组合,使交错 (*with*)。~*d branches* 交错的树枝。*be* ~*d with another thing* 与另一事物交织在一起。~*d scanning*【电视】飞跃扫描,隔行扫描。— ***vi***. 交织,交错,夹杂。*interlacing arches*【建】交叉拱门。

in·ter·lace·ment [ˌintəˈleismənt; ˏɪntɚˋlesmənt] ***n***. 组合,交加,交杂,交织。

in·ter·lam·i·nate [ˌintəˈlæmineit; ˏɪntɚˋlæmɪnet] ***vt***. (***-nat·ed***; ***-nating***) **1**. 插于薄片间。**2**. 置于交错薄片间。**-na·tion** ***n***.

in·ter·lard [ˌintə(:)ˈlɑːd; ˏɪntɚˋlɑrd] ***vt***. **1**. 以肥肉等加于(待煮的食物)。**2**. 使混杂,在…中插入不相干的东西。~ *one's speech with foreign words* 在讲话中夹杂外国词儿。**-ment** ***n***.

in·ter·lay [ˌintəˈlei; ˏɪntɚˋle] ***vt***. (***-laid*** [-leid; -led]; ***-lay·ing***) 置于其中。

in·ter·lay·er [ˈintə(:)ˌleiə; ˋɪntɚˏleɚ] ***n***.【建】夹层,间层;【物】界层,隔层。

in·ter·leaf [ˈintəˌliːf; ˋɪntɚˏlif] **I** ***n***. (*pl*. ***-leaves***) **1**. 中间层,夹层。**2**. 夹入书页中的空白纸。**3**. 夹页上印[写]的东西。**II** ***vt***. = interleave.

in·ter·leave [ˌintə(:)ˈliːv; ˏɪntɚˋliv] ***vt***. **1**. 使隔行;使交织;交替,交插。**2**. 在…插入空白纸;在(书页)间装订衬纸。**3**.【电视】隔行(扫描)。

in·ter·line, in·ter·line·ate [ˌintə(:)ˈlain, ˌintə(:)ˈliniːeit; ˏɪntˋlaɪn, ˏɪntɚˋlɪniet] ***vt***. **1**. 写在…的行间,印在…的行间。**2**. 隔行书写,隔行印刷。**3**. 在(衣服)面子和里子之间加内衬。~ *notes on pages* 在版面的行间加上注释。~ *a translation in a text* 在正文的行间插入译文。*a proof* ~*d with corrections* 在行间加有修改的校样。~ *a garment with an inner lining* 衣服里面加上内衬。**-a·tion** ***n***.

in·ter·lin·e·ar [ˌintə(:)ˈliniə; ˏɪntɚˋlɪnɪɚ] ***a***. **1**. 写在[印在]行间的。**2**. 一本书用不同的文字隔行对照印出的。~ *notes* 行间注释。*a Latin text with an* ~ *translation* 一本逐行对照翻译的拉丁原文书。**-ly** ***ad***.

In·ter·lin·gua [ˌintəˈliŋgwə; ˏɪntɚˋlɪŋgwə] ***n***. 拉丁国际语〔以拉丁语所派生的语言为主创造的一种文字,便于国际上使用,尤其在科技方面〕。

in·ter·lin·ing [ˈintəˈlainiŋ; ˋɪntɚˋlaɪnɪŋ] ***n***. **1**. 衣服衬里。**2**. 衣服里衬布料。

in·ter·link [ˌintə(:)ˈliŋk; ˏɪntɚˋlɪŋk] **I** ***vt***. 把…互相联系起来。**II** ***n***. 连环。

in·ter·lock [ˌintə(:)ˈlɔk; ˏɪntɚˋlɑk] **I** ***vt***., ***vi***. (使)连结,(使)连锁。~*ing branches* 交错的树枝。~*ing device* 连锁装置。~*ing director* 兼任经理。~*ing directorate* 连锁董事会〔董事会中有几个成员由某几个人共同兼任以便使企业经营协调,统一控制〕。~*ing signal* 连锁信号。**II** ***n***. 连结,连锁,连锁装置。

in·ter·lo·cu·tion [ˌintə(:)ləuˈkjuːʃən; ˏɪntɚləˋkjuʃən] ***n***. 对话,会话,交谈。

in·ter·loc·u·tor [ˌintə(:)ˈlɔkjutə; ˏɪntɚˋlɑkjətɚ] ***n***. (*fem*. ***-tress***, ***-trice***, ***-trix***) **1**. 对话者,参加交谈的人。**2**. 美国滑稽戏中由白人扮演黑人和引人发笑的配角。

in·ter·loc·u·to·ry [ˌintə(:)ˈlɔkjutəri; ˏɪntɚˋlɑkjəˏtorɪ] ***a***. **1**. 对话的,对话体的;插在对话中的。**2**. 插入的,插话的。**3**.【法】(判决等)在诉讼期间宣告的,非最后的。~ *wit* 对话中插入机智话[打趣话]。*an* ~ *divorce decree* 宣布离婚判决书。

in·ter·lope [ˌintə(:)ˈləup; ˏɪntɚˋlop] ***vi***. **1**. 侵犯他人权利。**2**. 闯入,干涉。**3**. 无执照营业。

in·ter·lop·er [ˈintə(:)ləupə; ˏɪntɚˋlopɚ] ***n***. (为营利而)干涉他人事务者,无执照营业者。

in·ter·lude [ˈintə(:)luːd, -ljuːd; ˋɪntɚlud, -ljud] ***n***. **1**. 幕间;幕间插入的戏。**2**. 插曲;【乐】间句。**3**. 穿插,间歇;穿插事件。~*s of bright weather* 间隔的晴朗天气。*a forest with* ~*s of open meadow* 夹有空旷草地的森林。

in·ter·lu·nar [ˌintəˈluːnə; ˏɪntɚˋlunɚ] ***a***.【天】无月期的〔指残月后与新月前之间看不见月亮的四天〕。

in·ter·knit [ˌintəˈnit; ˏɪntɚˋnɪt] ***vt***., ***vi***. (***-knit·ted***, ***-knit***; ***-knitting***) 编合,交缠,缠结。

in·ter·mar·riage [ˌintə(:)ˈmæridʒ; ˏɪntɚˋmærɪdʒ] ***n***. **1**. 异族[不同宗教、不同人种间的]通婚。**2**. 近族[近亲]通婚。

in·ter·mar·ry [ˌintə(:)ˈmæri; ˏɪntɚˋmærɪ] ***vi***. **1**. (同种族、家族、宗教、阶级间)内部通婚。**2**. 近族通婚。**3**.【法】结婚。

in·ter·med·dle [ˌintə(:)ˈmedl; ˏɪntɚˋmɛdl̩] ***vi***. 干涉(他人事情),管闲事,多嘴 (*in*; *with*)。**-r** ***n***.

in·ter·me·dia [ˌintə(:)ˈmiːdjə; ˏɪntɚˋmidɪə] intermedium 的复数。

in·ter·me·di·ar·y [ˌintə(:)ˈmiːdjəri; ˏɪntɚˋmidɪˏɛrɪ] **I** ***a***. **1**. 中间的,居间的。**2**. 中间人的;媒介的,调解人的。**II** ***n***. **1**. 中间人,调解人。**2**. 媒介,媒介物;手段,工具。**3**. 中间形态,中间阶段。~ *business* 牙行,掮客。*through the* ~ *of* 经…的手。

in·ter·me·di·ate [ˌintə(:)ˈmiːdjət; ˏɪntɚˋmidɪət] **I** ***a***. 中间的,居间的。*the* ~ *class* (船的)特别三等。*an* ~ *compound* 中间化合物;中间体。**II** ***n***. 中间物;中间分子,中间人;【化】中间体;期中考试;中间试验。**III** ***vi***. 起调解作用;起媒介作用 (*between*)。~ *culture* 补植。~ *elements* 中间分子。~ **frequency**【无】中频。~ *forces* 中间力量。~ **host**【生】中间宿主。~**-range** [**medium-range**] **ballistic missile** 中程弹道飞弹〔略 IRBM〕。~ **zone**【军】中间阵地[地带]。**-ly** ***ad***. 在中间。**-ness**, **-di·a·cy** ***n***. 调解。

in·ter·me·di·a·tion [ˌintə(:)ˌmiːdiˈeiʃən; ˏɪntɚˏmidɪˋeʃən] ***n***. 调解。

in·ter·me·di·a·tor [ˌintə(:)ˈmiːdjətə; ˏɪntɚˋmidɪˏetɚ] ***n***. 中间人,调解人。

in·ter·me·din [ˌintəˈmiːdn; ˏɪntɚˋmidn̩] ***n***.【医】(垂体)中叶激素。

in·ter·me·di·um [ˌintə(:)ˈmiːdiəm; ˏɪntɚˋmidɪəm] ***n***. (*pl*. ***-dia***, ~***s***) 中间体,媒介物。

in·ter·ment [inˈtəːmənt; ɪnˋtɝmənt] ***n***. 埋葬,葬礼。

in·ter·me·tal·lic [ˌintə(:)miˈtælik; ˏɪntɚmɪˋtælɪk] ***a***. 金属间的,金属间化合的。

in·ter·mez·zo [ˌintə(:)ˈmetzəu; ˏɪntɚˋmɛtzo] ***n***. (*pl*. ~***s*** [-z, -z], ***-mez·zi*** [-ˈmetzi; -ˋmɛtzɪ]) 幕间演出;【乐】间奏曲。

in·ter·mi·gra·tion [ˌintə(:)maiˈgreiʃən; ˏɪntɚmaɪˋgreʃən] ***n***. 相互迁移。

in·ter·mi·na·ble [inˈtəːminəbl; ɪnˋtɝmɪnəbl̩] ***a***. 无限的,无止境的;冗长的。*the I-* 无限的实在。**-ness** ***n***. **-bly** ***ad***.

in·ter·min·gle [ˌintə(:)ˈmiŋgl; ˏɪntɚˋmɪŋgl̩] ***vt***. 使搀和,使混合 (*with*)。~ *one thing with another* 把一种东西和另一种东西搀和起来。— ***vi***. (与…)混合 (*with*)。~ *with sth*. 和某种东西混合起来。

in·ter·mis·sion [ˌintə(:)ˈmiʃən; ˏɪntɚˋmɪʃən] ***n***. 中止,

中断,间歇;(学校的)课间休息〔*cf*.〔英〕recess, break〕;(戏剧的)幕间休息〔*cf*.〔英〕interval〕。**without** ~ 不停地,不间断地。**-mis·sive** ***a***.

in·ter·mit [ˌintə(:)ˈmit;ˌɪntɚˋmɪt] ***vi***. (**-*tt*-**) 一时停止,(发烧、疼痛等)中止,间断,(脉搏等)间歇。*The fever ~s*. 一会儿发烧,一会儿不发烧。— ***vt***. 使间断,使中断。~ *one's efforts* 暂停努力。

in·ter·mit·tence [ˌintə(:)ˈmitəns;ˌɪntɚˋmɪtn̩s] ***n***. 中断,间断;间歇性,周期性。

in·ter·mit·tent [ˌintə(:)ˈmitənt;ˌɪntɚˋmɪtənt] **I** ***a***. 间断的,断断续续的,周期性的。*an ~ discharge* 间歇放电。~ *fever*【医】间歇热。~ *fighting* 打打停停的战斗。~ *jet* 脉动式喷气发动机。~ *noise* 断断续续的闹声。~ *oiling*【机】间歇油润。~ *reaction*【化】间歇反应。*an ~ spring* 间歇泉。*the ~ yield*【农】隔年收获。**II** ***n***.【医】= intermittent fever. **-ly** ***ad***.

in·ter·mix [ˌintə(:)ˈmiks;ˌɪntɚˋmɪks] ***vt***., ***vi***. (使)混杂;(使)混合。*Coal seams ~ed with iron ore*. 煤层和铁矿混杂在一起。

in·ter·mix·ture [ˌintə(:)ˈmikstʃə;ˌɪntɚˋmɪkstʃɚ] ***n***. 混合;混合物。

in·ter·mo·lec·u·lar [ˌintə(:)məˈlekjulə; ˋɪntɚməˋlɛkjələ] ***n***. 分子间的。

in·ter·mon·tane [ˌintəˈmɔntein;ˌɪntɚˋmɑnten] ***a***. 山的,山间的。*an ~ lake* 山间湖。

in·ter·mun·dane [ˌintəˈmʌndein;ˌɪntɚˋmʌnden] ***a***. 星际的,天体之间的。

in·tern[1] [inˈtəːn; ɪnˋtɝn] **I** ***vt***. 拘禁(俘虏等);扣留(船只等)。*These soldiers were ~ed in a neutral country until the war was over*. 这些士兵被拘留在一个中立国,直到战争结束。**II** [ˈintəːn; ˋɪntɝn] ***n***. = internee.

in·tern[2] [ˈintəːn; ˋɪntɝn] **I** ***n***. = interne. **II** ***vi***. 做实习医生。

in·ter·nal [inˈtəːnl; ɪnˋtɝnl̩] **I** ***a***. **1**. 内的,内部的(*opp*. external)。**2**. 国内的,内政的。**3**. 体内的,内服的。**4**. 内在的,本质上的,固有的。**5**. 主观的,内心的,精神的。~ *organs* 内脏。*the ~ parts of the body* 身体的内部。~ *resistance*【物】内阻力,内电阻。~ *structure* 内部构造。~ *debts* 内债。~ *navigation* 内河航行。~ *trade* 国内贸易。~ *revenue* 国内税收。*an ~ trouble* 内乱。*an ~ war* 内战。~ *remedies* 内服药。~ *bleeding* 内出血。~ *injuries* 内伤。~ *secretion* 内分泌。*for ~ use* 内用(药)。~ *evidence* 内证。~ *monologue* 内心独白。~ *peace* 内心的平静。*the ~ world* 主观世界。**II** ***n***. **1**. 〔*pl*.〕内脏,内部器官。**2**. 本质,本性。~ **carotid artery** 颈内动脉。~ **ear** 内耳。~ **gauge** 塞规。~ **medicine** 内科学。~ **respiration**【生】内呼吸;组织呼吸。~ **rhyme** (诗歌中的)词间韵,行间韵。**-ly** ***ad***.

in·ter·nal-com·bus·tion [inˈtəːnl-kəmˈbʌstʃən; ɪnˋtɝnl̩-kəmˋbʌstʃən] ***a***.【机】内燃的。~ *engine* 内燃机。

in·ter·nal·i·ty [ˌintə(:)ˈnæliti;ˌɪntɚˋnælətɪ] ***n***. 内在,内在性。

in·ter·nal·ize [inˈtəːnəlaiz; ɪnˋtɝnl̩ˌaɪz] ***vt***. (***-ized***; ***-iz·ing***) 使变成内部的;使…成为个人品性的一部分〔尤指把他人的态度,想法等变成自己的思想方式〕。**-i·za·tion** ***n***. 内在化。

in·ter·nat. = international.

in·ter·na·tion·al [ˌintə(:)ˈnæʃənəl;ˌɪntɚˋnæʃənl] **I** ***a***. 国际(上)的,国际间的;世界的;〔I-〕国际劳工联盟的;〔I-〕国际信号的。*an ~ conference* 国际会议。*an ~ court* 国际法庭。~ *games* [*matches*] 国际运动比赛。*an ~ official record*【体】世界公认最高纪录。~ *copyright* 国际著作权。*an ~ treaty* 国际条约。~ *waters* 国际航路,公海。*the I- Working Men's Association* 国际劳工联盟〔普通单称 International〕。*hoist an ~ "B"* 悬挂国际信号旗 B。**II** ***n***. **1**. 国际运动比赛参加者。**2**. 取得一国国籍而长期侨居他国的人。**3**. 〔I-〕国际劳工联盟;跨国工会。**I- Bank for Reconstruction and Development** (联合国)国际复兴开发银行。~ **candle**【物】国际烛光。**I- Chamber of Commerce** 国际商会。~ **date line** 日界线,国际日期变更线(= date line)。**I- Development Association** (联合国)国际开发协会。**I- Finance Corporation** (联合国)国际金融公司。**I- Geophysical Year** 国际地球物理年。**I- Monetary Fund** (联合国)国际货币基金组织。~ **law** 国际法。~ **private law** 国际私法。**I- Phonetic Alphabet** 国际音标。~ **pitch** 音乐会的音高标准〔较通常标准略高〕。~ **unit(s)** (测定维生素成份、效果等的)国际单位。**-ly** ***ad***.

in·ter·na·tion·al·ism [ˌintə(:)ˈnæʃənəlizəm;ˌɪntɚˋnæʃənl̩ɪzəm] ***n***. 国际主义(*opp*. nationalism);国际性。

in·ter·na·tion·al·ist [ˌintə(:)ˈnæʃənəlist;ˌɪntɚˋnæʃənl̩ˌɪst] **I** ***n***. 国际主义者;国际法学家;〔美〕国际派。**II** ***a***. 国际主义的。**-ic** ***a***. 国际主义的。

in·ter·na·tion·al·i·za·tion [intəˌnæʃənəlaiˈzeiʃən;ˌɪntɚˌnæʃənələˋzeʃən] ***n***. 国际化;国际共管。

in·ter·na·tion·al·ize [ˌintə(:)ˈnæʃənəlaiz;ˌɪntɚˋnæʃənl̩ˌaɪz] ***vt***. 使国际化;把…置于国际共管之下。

in·ter·naut [ˌintəˈnɔːt;ˌɪntɚˋnɔt] ***n***.【计】因特网用户。

in·terne [ˈintəːn; ˋɪntɝn] ***n***. 〔美〕实习医生。

in·ter·ne·cine [ˌintə(:)ˈniːsain;ˌɪntɚˋnisaɪn] ***a***. **1**. 自相残杀的,两败俱伤的;血腥的。**2**. (集团内部)互相冲突的。~ *war* 大血战。

in·tern·ee [ˌintəːˈni;ˌɪntɝˋni] ***n***. (战争时期的)被扣留者;【军】拘留民,拘留犯。

In·ter·net [ˈintənet;ˋɪntənɛt] ***n***.【计】因特网,国际互联网。

in·ter·net [ˈintənet;ˋɪntənɛt] ***n***.【计】互联网。**-ize vt**. 使因特网化。

in·ter·neu·ron [ˌintəˈnjuərən, -ˈnuər-;ˌɪntɚˋnjurɑn, -ˋnʊər-] ***n***.【解】中间神经元(= internuncial neuron)。

in·ter·nist [ˈintənist, -ˈtəː-; ˋɪntənɪst, -ˋtɝ-] ***n***. 内科医生(*opp*. surgeon)。

in·tern·ment [inˈtəːnmənt; ɪnˋtɝnmənt] ***n***. 拘留;收容。***an ~ camp***〔英〕俘虏收容所〔美 detention camp〕。

in·ter·node [ˈintəˌnəud; ˋɪntɚˌnod] ***n***. **1**.【动、解】神经节间[结间]。**2**.【植】节间。**-nod·al** ***a***.

in·ter nos [ˈintə(:)ˈnəus; ˋɪntɚˋnos] 〔L.〕只限于咱俩之间〔不得外传〕(= between ourselves)。*I don't believe in his sincerity; but this is ~*. 我看他没有什么诚意;不过,这一点是不能对外人讲的。

in·tern·ship [ˈintəːnʃip; ˋɪntɝnˌʃɪp] ***n***. **1**. 实习医生的职务。**2**. 实习医生的实习期。

in·ter·nun·cial [ˌintə(:)ˈnʌnʃəl;ˌɪntɚˋnʌnʃəl] ***a***. 在中间的,联系的。~ **neuron**【解】中间神经元(= interneuron)。

in·ter·nun·ci·o [ˌintə(:)ˈnʌnʃiəu;ˌɪntɚˋnʌnʃɪˌo] ***n***. (*pl*. *~s*) **1**. 信使,使节,中间人。**2**. 罗马教皇的公使代表。

in·ter·o·ce·an·ic [ˈintə(:)rˌəuʃiˈænik; ˋɪntərˌoʃɪˋænɪk] ***a***. 海洋间的。

in·ter·o·cep·tor [ˌintərəuˈseptə;ˌɪntəroˋsɛptɚ] ***n***. 内感受器,内受(纳)器。**-tive** ***a***. ~ **endings** 内受器末梢。

in·ter·of·fice [ˌintəˈɔːfis, -ˈɔf-;ˌɪntɚˋɔfɪs, -ˋɑf-] ***a***. 本机关办公室之间的。

in·ter·os·cu·late [ˌintəˈɔskjuleit;ˌɪntɚˋɑskjəˌlet] ***vi***. (***-lated***; ***-lating***) **1**. 相互关系,互相接触。**2**.【生】具有共同性。**in·ter·os·cu·lant** [-lənt; -lənt] ***a***. **-la·tion** ***n***.

in·ter·page [ˌintə(:)ˈpeidʒ;ˌɪntɚˋpedʒ] ***vt***. 把…印入[插入]书页间。

in·ter·pel·lant [ˌintəːˈpelənt;ˌɪntɚˋpɛlənt] ***a***. 质问的。

in·ter·pel·late [ˌintəːˈpeleit;ˌɪntɚˋpɛlet] ***vt***. (在议会中

就政府政策等向有关人)质问。**-la·tion** *n*. **-la·tor** *n*.

in·ter·pen·e·trate [ˌintə(:)ˈpenitreit; ˌɪntɚˋpenɪˌtret] *vt*. 贯通;渗透。— *vi*. 互相贯通,互相渗透。**-tra·tion** *n*. 互相贯通;【建】交截细工。**-tra·tive** *a*.

in·ter·per·son·al [ˌintəˈpəːsənl; ˌɪntɚˋpɝsənl] *a*. 1. 人与人之间的。~ *relationships* 人与人之间的关系。~ *skills* 人际交往技巧。2. 人与人之间的关系的,涉及人与人之间的关系的。**-ly** *ad*.

in·ter·phase [ˈintə(:)feiz; ˋɪntɚˌfez] *n*. 【动】(细胞的)分裂期间。

in·ter·phone [ˈintə(:)fəun; ˋɪntɚˌfon] *n*. (办公室等)内部电话,内部通讯装置;对讲(电话)机;内线自动电话机。

in·ter·plan·e·tar·y [ˌintə(:)ˈplænitəri; ˌɪntɚˋplænəˌtɛrɪ] *a*. 星际间的,行星际的。~ *navigation* 星际导航。~ *travel* 星际航行。

in·ter·plant [ˌintə(:)ˈplɑːnt; ˌɪntɚˋplænt] *vt*. 1. 【农】间作,套种。2. 在…间插栽幼树。

in·ter·play [ˈintə(:)ˈplei; ˋɪntɚˋple] I *n*. 相互作用;相互影响。*the* ~ *of light and shadow* 光影交错。II *vi*. 相互作用,相互影响。

in·ter·plead [ˌintə(:)ˈpliːd; ˌɪntɚˋplid] *vi*. (*-plead·ed*, *-plead*, *-pled*; *-plead·ing*) 【法】(提出债权要求者)互相诉讼。**-er** *n*. 互相诉讼,互相诉讼者。

In·ter·pol [ˈintə(:)pəul; ˋɪntɚpol] *n*. 国际刑警组织〔全称:International Criminal Police Organization〕。

in·ter·po·late [inˈtəːpəuleit; ɪnˋtɝpoˌlet] *vt*., *vi*. 1. 窜改(文稿)。2. 增添,插入。3. 【数】插值,内插,内推。**-la·tion** [inˌtəːpəuˈleiʃən; ɪnˌtɝpoˋleʃən] *n*. 1. 窜改。2. 插入,插入物。3. 【数】插值法,内插法,内推法。**-la·tor** *n*. 窜改者,插入者。

in·ter·pol·y·mer [ˈintə(:)ˈpɔlimə; ˋɪntɚˋpɑlɪmɚ] *n*. 【化】互聚物,共聚物。**-po·lym·er·i·za·tion** *n*. 共聚作用。

in·ter·pos·al [ˌintə(:)ˈpəuzl; ˌɪntɚˋpozl̩] *n*. = interposition.

in·ter·pose [ˌintə(:)ˈpəuz; ˌɪntɚˋpoz] *vt*. 1. 放入,插入。2. 提出(异议)。3. 【影】使一镜头迅速替换(另一镜头)。~ *oneself* 插手,干预。~ *one's authority* 利用自己职权干涉。— *vi*. 1. 插进来,干预。2. 调解。3. 插嘴。

in·ter·po·si·tion [inˌtəːpəˈziʃən; ˌɪntɚpəˋzɪʃən] *n*. 1. 插入;干涉;调停;提出异议。2. 插入物。

in·ter·pret [inˈtəːprit; ɪnˋtɝprɪt] *vt*. 1. 说明,解释。2. 翻译,口译。3. 把…理解为,把…看作。4. (根据自己的诠解)演奏,表演。~ *a dream* 圆梦。~ *sb.'s laughter as an insult* 把某人的笑声看作是耻辱。— *vi*. 解释;口译。**-a·ble** *a*. 可以解释的。

in·ter·pre·ta·tion [inˌtəːpriˈteiʃən; ɪnˌtɝprɪˋteʃən] *n*. 1. 解释,说明。2. 翻译。3. 表演,演奏。*put a favourable* ~ *on* 对…作有利的解释。*signal* ~ 信号解释。*What is the* ~ *of this poem*? 这首诗的译文是什么意思?

in·ter·pre·ta·tive [inˈtəːprəteitiv; ɪnˋtɝprəˌtetɪv] *a*. = interpretive. **-ly** *ad*.

in·ter·pret·er [inˈtəːpritə; ɪnˋtɝprɪtɚ] *n*. (*fem*. *-pret-ress*) 1. 解释者;判断者;译员;口译者。2. 【军】情报判读员。3. 【自】翻译器;翻译程序。**-ship** 翻译人员的职务〔身分〕。

in·ter·pre·tive [inˈtəːpritiv; ɪnˋtɝprɪtɪv] *a*. 解释的;翻译的;说明的。**-ly** *ad*.

in·ter·ra·cial [ˌintə(:)ˈreiʃəl; ˌɪntɚˋreʃəl] *a*. 不同人种间的;不同种族间的(= interrace)。

in·ter·ra·di·al [ˌintə(:)ˈreidiəl; ˌɪntɚˋrediəl] *a*. 射线间的;半径之间的。**-ly** *ad*.

in·ter·reg·num [ˌintə(:)ˈregnəm; ˌɪntɚˋrɛgnəm] *n*. (*pl*. ~*s*, *-na* [-nə; -nə]) 1. (旧王死后新王尚未登基的)空位期;(政治改组期间的)政权空白期。2. 间歇,中断。

in·ter·re·late [ˌintə(:)riˈleit; ˌɪntɚrɪˋlet] *vt*., *vi*. (*-lat-ed*, *-lat·ing*) (使)相互联系。**-lat·ed** *a*. **-lat·ed·ness** *n*.

in·ter·re·la·tion [ˈintə(:)riˈleiʃən; ˌɪntɚrɪˋleʃən] *n*. 相互关系,相互联系(性)。**-ship** *n*. 相互关系。

in·ter·rex [ˈintəˌreks; ˈɪntɚˌrɛks] *n*. (*pl*. *in·ter-reges* [-ˌriːdʒiːz; -ˌridʒiz]) 摄政王。

in·ter·rog. = interrogation, interrogative.

in·ter·ro·gate [inˈterəgeit; ɪnˋtɛrəˌget] *vt*. 询问,质问,审问。~ *a prisoner* 审问囚犯。— *vi*. 提出问题。

in·ter·ro·ga·tion [inˌterəˈgeiʃən; ɪnˌtɛrəˋgeʃən] *n*. 1. 讯问,质问,审问。2. 【语法】疑问句。3. 问号〔?〕。*an* ~ *mark* [*point*, *note*] 【语法】疑问号。

in·ter·rog·a·tive [ˌintəˈrɔgətiv; ˌɪntəˋrɑgətɪv] I *a*. 讯问性的,表示疑问的;质问的。*an* ~ *adverb* 疑问副词。*an* ~ *pronoun* 疑问代词。II *n*. 疑问词。**-ly** *ad*.

in·ter·ro·ga·tor [inˈterəgeitə; ɪnˋtɛrəˌgetɚ] *n*. 1. 讯问者,质问者,审问者。2. 【无】询问器,问答机。*airborne* ~ 飞机用讯问器。*low-power* ~ 低功率询问器。

in·ter·rog·a·to·ry [ˌintəˈrɔgətəri; ˌɪntəˋrɑgəˌtorɪ] I *a*. 表示疑问的,讯问的,质问的。*an* ~ *tone* 质问的口气。*the* ~ *method* (*of teaching*) 问答式(教学法)。II *n*. 1. 疑问,讯问,质问,审问;〔*pl*.〕【法】书面质问。2. 表示询问的符号[信号]。**-to·ri·ly** *ad*.

in·ter·rupt [ˌintəˈrʌpt; ˌɪntəˋrʌpt] *vt*. 1. 阻止;妨碍;遮断。2. 打断(别人的话等);中断;打搅。3. 截断。~ *a view* 遮住视线。*Don't* ~ *me*. 别打搅我。*He* ~*ed college to serve in the army*. 他中断大学的学业到军队服役。~ *sb. in his work* 打搅某人工作。*May I* ~ *you to comment on that last remark*? 对不起,刚才这句话是什么意思请讲讲。~ *an electric current* 截断电流。— *vi*. 打扰,(别人谈话时)插嘴。

in·ter·rupt·ed [ˌintəˈrʌptid; ˌɪntəˋrʌptɪd] *a*. 被遮断的,被阻止的,不通的,中断的。~ *screw* 断纹螺丝。**-ly** *ad*.

in·ter·rupt·er, **in·ter·rupt·or** [ˌintəˈrʌptə; ˌɪntəˋrʌptɚ] *n*. 1. 打断者,阻碍者,障碍物。2. 【电】断续器,断流器。*an* ~ *gear* 【机】断续齿轮。*a periodic* ~【电】周期性断续器。*a primary* ~【电】原电路断续器。

in·ter·rup·tion [ˌintəˈrʌpʃən; ˌɪntəˋrʌpʃən] *n*. 1. 打断;中断;停止。2. 断绝,断路。3. 插话,打岔。4. 障碍物,遮断物。5. 中断期,休止期。~ *of communication* 交通中断。*service* ~业务中断。*without* ~无间断,继续。*alternating current* ~交流电流断路。

in·ter·rup·tive, **in·ter·rup·to·ry** [ˌintəˈrʌptiv, ˌintəˈrʌptəri; ˌɪntəˋrʌptɪv, ˌɪntəˋrʌptərɪ] *a*. 1. 遮断的,中断的,阻碍的。2. 打断的,打扰的。

in·ter·scho·las·tic [ˌintəskəˈlæstik; ˌɪntɚskəˋlæstɪk] *a*. 学校之间的。~ *athletics* (中等学校的)校际比赛。

in·ter·sect [ˌintə(:)ˈsekt; ˌɪntɚˋsɛkt] *vt*. 横断,横切,和…相交。*The line AB* ~*s the line CD at E*. 直线 AB 与直线 CD 相交于 E 点上。— *vi*. 相交,交叉。*The lines AB and CD* ~ *at E*. 直线 AB 与直线 CD 相交于 E 点上。

in·ter·sec·tion [ˌintə(:)ˈsekʃən; ˌɪntɚˋsɛkʃən] *n*. 1. 横断,横切;交叉,相交。2. 【数】交集。3. 交点,交叉线,十字路口。4. 逻辑乘法。

in·ter·sec·tion·al [ˌintə(:)ˈsekʃənl; ˌɪntɚˋsɛkʃənl̩] *a*. 1. 交点的;形成交点的。2. 地区之间的。~ *football games* 区际足球赛。

in·ter·serv·ice [ˌintə(:)ˈsəːvis; ˌɪntɚˋsɝvɪs] *a*. 【军】军种间的。

in·ter·sex [ˈintəseks; ˋɪntɚˌsɛks] *n*. 1. 【生】(中)间性,雌雄间体。2. 不分性别。

in·ter·sex·u·al [ˌintəˈseksjuəl; ˌɪntɚˋsɛksjuəl] *a*. 1. 两性之间的。2. 具有雌雄特征的。3. 不分性别的,男女平等的。~ *rivalry* 间性对抗。

in·ter·sol·u·bil·i·ty [ˌintəˌsɔljuˈbiliti; ˌɪntɚˌsɑljə-

I

ˋbɪlətɪ] *n*.【化】互溶性,互溶度。

in·ter·space [ˈintə(:)ˈspeis; ˋɪntəˋspes] **I** *n*. 1. 空间,空隙〔指场所、时间〕,间隙。2. 星际。**II** [ˌintəˈspeis; ˏɪntə-ˋspes] *vt*. (*-spaced*; *-spac·ing*) 1. 在…之间留出空间。2. 在…之间填补空间。

in·ter·spe·cif·ic [ˌintə(:)spiˈsifik; ˏɪntəspɪˋsɪfɪk] *a*.【生】(异)种间的。

in·ter·sperse [ˌintə(:)ˈspəːs; ˏɪntəˋspəs] *vt*. 1. 散布;散置(*between*; *among*)。2. 点缀,装饰。~ *peach trees among the willows* 桃柳相间。~ *a book with pictures* 使书图文并茂。

in·ter·sper·sion [ˌintə(:)ˈspəːʃən; ˏɪntəˋspəʃən] *n*. 散布,散置;点缀,装饰。

in·ter·sput·nik [ˌintəˈsputnik; ˏɪntəˋsputnɪk] *n*. 前苏联全球卫星通讯系统。

in·ter·sta·di·al [ˌintə(:)ˈsteidiəl; ˏɪntəˋstedɪəl] *n*.【地】间冰段。

in·ter·stage [ˌintə(:)ˈsteidʒ; ˏɪntəˋstedʒ] *a*. 级间的,级际的。~ **coupling**【无】级间耦合。

in·ter·state [ˌintə(:)ˈsteit; ˏɪntəˋstet] *a*. 〔美〕各州间的,州际的。**I- Commerce Commission** 〔美〕州际商务委员会。

in·ter·stel·lar [ˈintə(:)ˈstelə; ˏɪntəˋstɛlə] *a*.【天】星际的。~ *aeronautics* 星际航行。~ *space* 星际空间。

in·ter·stice [inˈtəːstis; ɪnˋtəstɪs] *n*. 间隙,空隙,裂缝。

in·ter·sti·tial [ˌintə(:)ˈstiʃəl; ˏɪntəˋstɪʃəl] **I** *a*. 1. 裂缝间的;空隙的;在裂缝间的。2.【解】细胞(组织)间隙的,间质的。3.【物】填隙的。~ *cells* 间质细胞。~ *tissue* 间质组织。~ *alloy* 填隙式合金。~ *structure* 填隙式结构。**II** *n*.【物】填隙,填隙子。~ **cell-stimulating hormone**【生】(促)间质细胞激素。(= luteinizing hormone) **-ly** *ad*.

in·ter·text [ˈintətekst; ˋɪntətɛkst] *n*. (有赖于其他文本起作用的)互文文本。

in·ter·tex·ture [ˌintə(:)ˈtekstʃə; ˏɪntəˋtɛkstʃə] *n*. 交织,交织物。

in·ter·tid·al [ˌintə(:)ˈtaidl; ˏɪntəˋtaɪdl̩] *a*. 潮间(地)带的。

in·ter·till [ˌintə(:)ˈtil; ˏɪntəˋtɪl] *vt*. 1. 中耕。2. 在作物的畦行间耕作。*~ed crops* 中耕作物。**-age** *n*. 中耕;间作。

in·ter·trib·al [ˌintə(:)ˈtraibl; ˏɪntəˋtraɪbl̩] *a*. 部落间的。

in·ter·trop·i·cal [ˌintə(:)ˈtrɔpikl; ˏɪntəˋtrɑpɪkl̩] *a*. 南北回归线之间的,夏至与冬至线之间的。

in·ter·twine [ˌintə(:)ˈtwain; ˏɪntəˋtwaɪn] *vt*., *vi*. (使)缠结,(使)缠绕在一起。

in·ter·twist [ˌintə(:)ˈtwist; ˏɪntəˋtwɪst] *vt*., *vi*. 捻合;缠结。

in·ter·u·ni·ver·si·ty [ˈintə(:)ˌjuːniˈvəːsiti; ˏɪntəˏjunɪˋvəsətɪ] *a*. 大学间的。*an* ~ *match* 大学校际比赛。

in·ter·ur·ban [ˌintə(:)ˈəːbən; ˏɪntəˋəbən] **I** *a*. 城市间的。*an* ~ *bus* 市际公共汽车。*an* ~ *railway* 城市之间的铁路。**II** *n*. 城市间的交通路线[车辆]。

in·ter·val [ˈintəvəl; ˋɪntəvəl] *n*. 1. (空间方面的)间隔;空隙。2. (时间方面的)间隔,间歇;工间休息,幕间休息。3.【军】(各小队间的)间隔。4.【乐】音程。5.【数】区间。6. 〔美〕= intervale. *an* ~ *of five metres* 相隔五米。*after a year's* ~ 隔一年后。*I-* —*10 Min*. 休息十分钟〔常用于演出节目单中〕。*in the ~s of business* 在工作空隙时间。*There is a two hour's* ~ *to the next train*. 下一班火车还要过两个小时。**at ~s** 时时;处处;偶尔。**at ~s of** 每隔…〔就时间、场所说〕。**at long ~s** 间或。**at regular ~s** 每隔一定时间[距离]。**at short ~** 常常。**in the ~s** 不一会儿,不久。**lucid ~** 1. 狂人神志清醒的时候。2. 阴天太阳偶然出现的时候。3. 在暴风雨似的事件中平静的时期;生活平静的时刻。

in·ter·vale [ˈintə(:)veil; ˋɪntəvel] *n*. 〔美〕(丘陵间的)低地,平地;(适于耕作的)河滩地。

in·ter·val·(l)ic [ˌintə(:)ˈvælik; ˏɪntəˋvælɪk] *a*. 1. 间隔的,间歇的,幕间的,工间的。2. 悬殊的。3.【乐】音程的。

in·ter·var·si·ty [intə(:)ˈvɑːsəti; ɪntəˋvɑrsətɪ] *a*. 〔英〕= interuniversity.

in·ter·vene [ˌintə(:)ˈviːn; ˏɪntəˋvin] *vi*. 1. 插进,介入〔介于时间或空间当中〕。2. 调停。3. 干预,干涉。4.【法】(第三者为保护个人权利)参加诉讼。~ *between two objects* 夹在两件东西当中。*the years that* ~(*d*) 其中有几年。*I shall come if nothing ~s*. 如果没有别的事,我就来。~ *in a dispute* 调停争端。~ *between two people quarrelling* 在两个争吵者之间进行调解。~ *in the internal affairs of other countries* 干涉他国内政。**-r**, **-ven·or** *n*. 干涉者,介入者,调停者。

in·ter·ven·ient [ˌintəˈviːnjənt; ˏɪntəˋvinɪənt] **I** *a*. 干预的;介入的,调解的。**II** *n*. 干涉者;调解人;插入物。

in·ter·ven·tion [ˌintə(:)ˈvenʃən; ˏɪntəˋvɛnʃən] *n*. 1. 插进,介入。2. 调解,排解。3. 干涉,干预,妨碍。*armed* ~ = ~ *by arms* 武装干涉。

in·ter·ven·tion·ist [ˌintə(:)ˈvenʃənist; ˏɪntəˋvɛnʃənɪst] **I** *n*. 内政干涉者,武装干涉者,主张在国际事务中进行干涉的人。**II** *a*. 1. 干涉的,干涉者的。2. 进行干涉的,主张进行干涉的。**-tion·ism** *n*. 干涉主义。

in·ter·ver·te·bral [ˌintə(:)ˈvəːtibrəl; ˏɪntəˋvətɪbrəl] *a*. 椎骨间的。~ **disk**【解】椎间盘。**-ly** *ad*.

in·ter·view [ˈintəvjuː; ˋɪntəˏvju] **I** *n*. 1. 接见;会见;会谈;协商。2. (记者的)访问;访问记。3. 口头审查。*have* [*hold*] *an* ~ *with sb*. 会见某人。*give* [*grant*] *an* ~ *to sb*. 接见某人。*job* ~ 对申请工作者的口头审查。**II** *vt*. 接见;会见;(记者)访问。**-ee** *n*. 被会见者;被接见者;被采访者。**-er** *n*. 会见者;接见者;采访者。

in·ter vi·vos [ˌintə(:)ˈviːvəus; ˋɪntəˋvivos] *ad*. 〔L.〕在生存者之间。

in·ter·vo·cal·ic [ˌintə(:)vəuˈkælik; ˏɪntəvoˋkælɪk] *a*.【语】两母音间的〔指子音〕。

in·ter·volve [ˌintə(:)ˈvɔlv; ˏɪntəˋvɑlv] *vt*., *vi*. 卷进;缠绕;(使)互卷;(使)互相盘绕。

in·ter-war [ˈintə(:)ˈwɔː; ˋɪntəˏwɔr] *a*. 两次战争之间的。

in·ter·weave [ˌintə(:)ˈwiːv; ˏɪntəˋwiv] *vt*. (*-wove* [-ˈwəuv; -ˋwov], *~d*; *-wov·en* [-ˈwəuvən; -ˋwovən], *~d*; *-weav·ing*) 使交织,织进;使交错编织;使紧密结合,使混杂。~ *truth with fiction* 真伪混杂。— *vi*. 交织,混杂。

in·ter·wind [ˌintə(:)ˈwaind; ˏɪntəˋwaɪnd] *vt*., *vi*. (*-wound* [-ˈwəund; -ˋwond]) (使)互相盘绕,(使)互卷。

in·ter·zon·al [ˌintə(:)ˈzəunəl; ˏɪntəˋzonl̩] *a*. 地带之间的。

in·tes·ta·cy [inˈtestəsi; ɪnˋtɛstəsɪ] *n*. 无遗嘱,无遗嘱死亡。

in·tes·tate [inˈtesteit; ɪnˋtɛstet] **I** *a*. 没有留下遗嘱的;不能根据遗嘱处理的。*die* ~没有遗嘱就死了。**II** *n*. 无遗嘱死亡者。

in·tes·ti·nal [inˈtestinl; ɪnˋtɛstɪnl̩] *a*. 1. 内部的;生活在内部的。2. 肠的;在肠内的。*the* ~ *canal* 肠腔,肠。~ *catarrh*【医】肠炎。~ **fortitude** 持久力;勇气。**-ly** *ad*.

in·tes·tine [inˈtestin; ɪnˋtɛstɪn] **I** *a*. 内部的;国内的。~ *war* 内战。**II** *n*. 〔常 *pl*.〕【解】肠。*the large* [*small*] ~大[小]肠。

in·thral(l) [inˈθrɔːl; ɪnˋθrɔl] *vt*. (*-thral·led*; *-thral·ling*) 迷惑,迷,擒,俘虏,〔罕〕使做奴隶,奴役(= enthral(l))。

in·throne [inˈθrəun; ɪnˋθron] *vt*. = enthrone.

in·ti·ma [ˈintimə; ˋɪntɪmə] ***n*.** (*pl*. ***-mae*** [-miː; -mi], ***-mas***)【解】内膜。

in·ti·ma·cy [ˈintiməsi; ˋɪntɪməsɪ] ***n*.** **1.** 亲密,亲近,友好。**2.** 〔婉〕私通,亲热。**3.** 〔*pl*.〕亲昵行为。*be on terms of* ～亲密。

in·ti·mate¹ [ˈintimit; ˋɪntəmɪt] **I** ***a*.** **1.** 亲密的,亲近的;密切的。**2.** 直接的,完全的,详细的。**3.** 内部的,内心深处的,本质的。**4.** 个人的,私人的。**5.** 私通的。*an* ～ *friend* 亲密的朋友。*be on* ～ *terms with sb*. 同某人关系密切。*an* ～ *knowledge of life* 熟悉生活。*one's* ～ *feelings* 心内感觉。～ *reflections* 内省。*the* ～ *structure of matter* 物质的内部结构。*one's* ～ *affairs* 私事。*an* ～ *diary* 私人日记。*be* ～ *with a woman* 同某妇人有不正当的性关系。**II** ***n*.** 亲密的朋友,知己。**-ness** ***n*.**

in·ti·mate² [ˈintimeit; ˋɪntə͵met] ***vt*.** **1.** 宣布,通知,通告,明白表示。**2.** 暗示,提示。～ *one's approval of a plan* 表明同意某项计划。**-ly** ***ad*.**

in·ti·ma·tion [ˌintiˈmeiʃən; ͵ɪntəˋmeʃən] ***n*.** **1.** 告知,通知,通告。**2.**【法】正式宣告,正式宣布。**3.** 暗示,提示。

in·time [ænˈtiːm; ænˋtim] ***a*.** 〔F.〕亲切的(= intimate)。

in·tim·i·date [inˈtimideit; ɪnˋtɪmə͵det] ***vt*.** **1.** 恫吓,恐吓。**2.** 威逼某人做某事(*into*)。*This cannot* ～ *us*. 这吓不倒我们。～ *sb*. *into doing sth*. 胁迫某人做某事。**-da·tor** ***n*.** **-da·to·ry** ***a*.**

in·tim·i·da·tion [inˌtimiˈdeiʃən; ɪn͵tɪməˋdeʃən] ***n*.** 威胁,恐吓。*surrender to* ～ 屈服于威胁。*atomic* ～原子恫吓。

in·ti·mist [ˈintimist; ˋɪntəmɪst] **I** ***a*.** 描绘内心思想和感情的。**II** ***n*.** 描绘内心的作家[画家]。

in·tim·i·ty [inˈtimiti; ɪnˋtɪmətɪ] ***n*.** **1.** 秘密,亲密。**2.** 本质,本性。

in·tinc·tion [inˈtiŋkʃən; ɪnˋtɪŋkʃən] ***n*.**【宗】(圣餐的)面包浸酒。〔系一种宗教浸礼仪式。把圣餐的面包浸入酒中,然后分给参加受圣餐的每人两片〕。

in·tine [ˈintiːn, -tain; ˋɪntin, -taɪn] ***n*.** = endospore.

in·ti·tle [inˈtaitl; ɪnˋtaɪtl̩] ***vt*.** (***-tled***, ***-tling***) = entitle.

in·tit·ule [inˈtitjuːl; ɪnˋtɪtjul] ***vt*.** 给(法令等)命名,加标题于…。

Intl. = International.

in·to [元音前读 ˈintu, 句尾主读 ˈintuː, 辅音前读 ˈintə; ˋɪntʊ, ˋɪntu, ˋɪntə] ***prep*.** **1.** 〔表示动向〕向内,到…里。*go* ～ *a room* 走进屋里。*come* ～ *the garden* 来到园里。*look* ～ *the box* 看箱子里头。*peer* ～ *the darkness* 探望暗处。*throw sth*. ～ *the fire* 把某物扔进火里。*get* ～ *trouble* 遇到麻烦。*inquire* ～ *a matter* 对某事进行调查。**2.** 〔表示时间〕进入[继续]到。*look* ～ *the future* 展望未来。*pass out of childhood* ～ *manhood* 从童年进入成年。*work far* [*well*] ～ *the night* 工作到深夜。**3.** 〔表示变化状态、结果〕转入,变成,聚成,迫使(*opp*. out of)。*turn water* ～ *ice* 使水变成冰。*translate English* ～ *Chinese* 把英语翻译成汉语。*burst* ～ *tears* 突然哭起来。*collect them* ～ *heaps* 把他们聚集起来。*be flogged* ～ *submission* 被迫屈服。**4.** 〔表示撞击〕。*bumper* ～ *a door* 撞在门上。*run* ～ *a tree* 碰[撞]在树上。**5.** 〔表示从事工作、活动等〕。*enter* ～ *dictionary making* 从事词典编纂工作。*go* ～ *teaching* 投入教学工作。**6.**【数】乘〔a×b 读作 a ～ b= a multiplied by b〕;除〔a÷b 读作 b ～ a = a divided by b〕。**7.** 〔方〕= in. *He fought* ～ *the Revolution*. 〔美〕他参加过独立战争。**8.** 〔美俚〕深深卷入于;对…有很大兴趣。*He and his wife are both* ～ *art*. 他和他太太都迷恋艺术。**9.** 〔美俚〕欠…的债。***be*** ～ ***sb*. *for sth*.** 为某物欠了某人的债。

in·toed [ˈintəud; ˋɪntod] ***a*.** 脚趾向内弯曲的。

in·tol·er·a·bil·i·ty [inˌtɔləraˈbiliti; ɪn͵tɑlərəˋbɪlətɪ] ***n*.** 不堪;难忍;难受(= intolerableness)。

in·tol·er·a·ble [inˈtɔlərəbl; ɪnˋtɑlərəbl̩] ***a*.** 不堪的;难忍的;难受的。**-bly** ***ad*.**

in·tol·er·ance [inˈtɔlərəns; ɪnˋtɑlərəns] ***n*.** **1.** 不容纳异说[意见、信仰],偏狭;固执。**2.**【医】不耐(性)〔对某些药物的过敏反应〕。

in·tol·er·ant [inˈtɔlərənt; ɪnˋtɑlərənt] **I** ***a*.** 偏狭的,气量狭窄的;忍受不住的,不耐…的。～ *of* 不能容忍的,不耐…的。*plants* ～ *of shade* 不耐阴的植物。*be* ～ *of great heat* 不耐高温。**II** ***n*.** 不容忍的人;偏狭的人。**-ly** ***ad*.**

in·tomb [inˈtuːm; ɪnˋtum] ***vt*.** = entomb.

in·to·nate [ˈintəuneit; ˋɪnto͵net] ***vt*.**, ***vi*.** = intone.

in·to·na·tion [ˌintəuˈneiʃən; ͵ɪntoˋneʃən] ***n*.** **1.** 音的抑扬。**2.** 语调,声调。*a falling* [*rising*] ～降[升]调。**3.**【乐】发声,转调。**4.**【宗】吟诵,咏唱;(圣歌等的)起始句。～ **pattern**【语】调型。**-al** ***a*.**

in·tone [inˈtəun; ɪnˋton] ***vt*.** **1.** 吟诵,咏唱(圣歌、祷文等)。**2.** 唱(圣歌等的)起始唱句。**3.** 给…一种特殊音调。— ***vi*.** **1.** 吟诵,咏唱。**2.** 发出拖长的声音。**-r** ***n*.** 吟诵者,咏唱者。

in·tor·sion [inˈtɔːʃən; ɪnˋtɔrʃən] ***n*.** **1.**【植】(茎的)螺旋形盘绕,弯曲,绕缠。**2.**【医】内扭转,内扭。

in·tort [inˈtɔːt; ɪnˋtɔrt] ***vt*.** 〔罕〕〔常用于过去分词〕向内扭结。

in to·to [inˈtəutəu; ɪnˋtoto] ***ad*.** 〔L.〕完满地,完全地,总的看来,总共地。

In·tour·ist [ˈintuərist; ˋɪnturɪst] ***n*.** 前苏联国际旅行社。

in·tox·i·cant [inˈtɔksikənt; ɪnˋtɑksɪkənt] **I** ***n*.** 麻醉品;〔尤指〕酒精饮料。**II** ***a*.** 使醉的,麻醉的,沉醉的。

in·tox·i·cate [inˈtɔksikeit; ɪnˋtɑksɪ͵ket] ***vt*.** **1.** 使醉。**2.** 使陶醉。**3.** 使中毒。*become* ～*d from wine* 喝醉了酒。*be* ～*d by* [*with*] *one's success* 陶醉于自己的成就。*be* ～*d with joy* 欣喜若狂。**-ca·tion** ***n*.**

in·tox·i·cat·ing [inˌtɔksiˈkeitiŋ; ɪn͵tɑksɪˋketɪŋ] ***a*.** **1.** 醉人的。*an* ～ *beverade* 酒类。**2.** 令人陶醉的。**-ly** ***ad*.**

intr. = intransitive.

in·tra- *comb*. *f*. 表示"内","在内","内部"〔主用于学术用语〕: *intra*cellular, *intra*mural, *intra*venous.

in·tra·cel·lu·lar [ˌintrəˈseljulə; ͵ɪntrəˋseljələ˞] ***a*.** 细胞内的;发生于个体细胞内的。

in·tra·cit·y [ˌintrəˈsiti; ͵ɪntrəˋsɪtɪ] ***a*.** 市内的。

in·trac·ta·ble [inˈtræktəbl; ɪnˋtræktəbl̩] ***a*.** **1.** 倔强的,难处理的。**2.** 难操作的,难加工的。**3.** 难治疗的;难对付的。*an* ～ *child* 难管教的孩子。*an* ～ *metal* 难加工的金属。～ *pain* 难消除的疼痛。**-bil·i·ty**, **-bleness** ***n*.** **-bly** ***ad*.**

in·tra·cu·ta·ne·ous [ˌintrəkjuːˈteiniəs; ͵ɪntrəkjuˋtenɪəs] **test**【医】皮内试验。

in·tra·da [inˈtrɑːdə; ɪnˋtrɑdə] ***n*.**【乐】前奏,引子。

in·tra·der·mal [ˌintrəˈdəːml; ͵ɪntrəˋdə˞ml̩] ***a*.** 皮内的;皮层内的。

in·tra·dos [inˈtreidɔs; ɪnˋtredɑs] ***n*.**【建】拱腹(线)。

in·tra·mo·lec·u·lar [ˌintrəməˈlekjulə; ͵ɪntrəməˋlɛkjələ˞] ***a*.** 作用于分子内的;存在于分子间的;发生于分子内的。**-ly** ***ad*.**

in·tra·mu·ral [ˌintrəˈmjuərəl; ͵ɪntrəˋmjʊrəl] ***a*.** **1.** 城墙内的;城市内的;建筑物内的;大学内的。**2.**【解】(器官)壁内的。*an* ～ *railway* 市内铁路。～ *sports* 校内运动。～ *strife* 内部倾轧。**-ly** ***ad*.**

in·tra·mus·cu·lar [ˌintrəˈmʌskjulə; ͵ɪntrəˋmʌskjələ˞] ***a*.** 位于肌肉的;肌内的。～ **injection**【医】肌肉注射。**-ly** ***ad*.**

in·tra·net [ˈintrənet; ˋɪntrənɛt] ***n*.**【计】内联网。

intrans. = intransitive.

in·tran·si·gence [inˈtrænsidʒəns; ɪnˋtrænsɪdʒəns] ***n*.** 拒绝调解,不让步,不妥协(= intransigency)。

in·tran·si·gent [in'trænsidʒənt; ɪn`trænsɪdʒənt] **I** *a*. 拒绝调解的,不让步的,不妥协的。**II** *n*. 不妥协的人〔尤指政治上的〕。**-gent·ly** *ad*.

in·tran·si·tive [in'trænsitiv; ɪn`trænsɪtɪv] **I** *a*.【语法】不及物的。*an* ~ *verb*【语法】不及物动词。**II** *n*.【语法】不及物动词。**-ly** *ad*.

in·trant ['intrənt; `ɪntrənt] *n*. = entrant.

in·tra·psy·chic [ˌintrə'saikik; ˏɪntrə`saɪkɪk] *a*. 存在于头脑中的;存在于灵魂中的,出现于头脑[灵魂]中的(= intrapsychical)。**-chi·cal·ly** *ad*.

in·tra·spe·cif·ic [ˌintrəspi'sifik; ˏɪntrəspɪ`sɪfɪk] *a*.【动】种内的。

in·tra·state [ˌintrə'steit; ˏɪntrə`stet] *a*. 州内的〔尤指美国的一州内的〕。

in·tra·tel·lu·ric [ˌintrəte'ljuərik; ˏɪntrəte`ljʊrɪk] *a*. **1**. 地内形成的,位于地内的;出现于地内的。**2**. 尚处于地下岩浆期的。

in·tra·u·ter·ine [ˌintrə'ju:tərin; ˏɪntrə`jutərɪn] *a*. 子宫内的。~ (**conceptive**) **device** 子宫内安放的避孕环〔缩写为 IUD〕。

in·trav·a·sa·tion [inˌtrævə'seiʃən; ɪnˏtrævə`seʃən] *n*.【医】内沉,内渗,进入血管或淋巴管的异物。

in·tra·ve·hi·cle [ˌintrə'vi:ikl; ˏɪntrə`viɪkl̩] *a*. 太空飞行器内的。

in·tra·ve·nous [ˌintrə'vi:nəs; ˏɪntrə`vinəs] *a*.【医】静脉内的,静脉注射的。~ *drip* 静脉滴注。~ *injection* 静脉注射。**-ly** *ad*.

in·tra·zon·al [ˌintrə'zəunl; ɪntrə`zonl̩] *a*.【植】隐域的。

in·treat [in'tri:t; ɪn`trit] *vt*., *vi*. = entreat 的古变体。

in·trench [in'trentʃ; ɪn`trentʃ] *vt*., *vi*. = entrench.

in·trep·id [in'trepid; ɪn`trɛpɪd] *a*. 刚毅的,勇猛的,无敌的,无畏的。**-id·i·ty**, **-ness** *n*. **-ly** *ad*.

Int. Rev. = Internal Revenue.〔英〕国内税收。

in·tri·ca·cy ['intrikəsi; `ɪntrɪkəsɪ] *n*. **1**. 纷乱,错综,复杂。**2**.〔*pl*.〕错综复杂的事物。

in·tri·cate ['intrikit; `ɪntrɪkɪt] *a*. **1**. 缠结的,错综的,复杂的。**2**. 精致的。*an* ~ *piece of machinery* 复杂的机器。*an* ~ *plot* 情节复杂。*an* ~ *problem* 复杂的问题。**-ly** *ad*. **-ness** *n*.

in·tri·g(u)ant ['intrigənt; `ɪntrəgənt] *n*. 阴谋者;奸夫。

in·tri·g(u)ante [ˌintri'gænt; ˏɪntrə`gænt] *n*. 女阴谋者,淫妇。

in·trigue [in'tri:g; ɪn`trig] **I** *n*. **1**. 阴谋,密谋;诡计。**2**. 私通;勾结。**3**. (戏剧、小说等的)纠葛,伏线。*political* ~*s* 政治阴谋。**II** *vi*. **1**. 计划阴谋,密谋(*against*)。**2**. 私通(*with*)。~ *against one's friends* 阴谋陷害朋友。~ *with a woman* 同某女人私通。— *vt*. **1**. 用诡计取得;〔古〕哄骗。**2**.〔新闻用语〕使发生兴趣,使着迷,使好奇。*The news* ~*d all of us*. 这新闻引起了大家的兴趣。

in·trigu·er [in'tri:gə; ɪn`trigɚ] *n*. 阴谋家;私通者。

in·trigu·ing [in'tri:giŋ; ɪn`trigɪŋ] *a*. **1**. 阴谋的;与阴谋有关的。**2**. 引起兴趣的,有魅力的。*an* ~ *smile* 动人的微笑。*a most* ~ *piece of news* 最引人兴趣的消息。**-ly** *ad*.

in·trin·sic [in'trinsik; ɪn`trɪnsɪk] *a*. (*opp*. extrinsic) **1**. 内在的;本来的;真正的,实在的。**2**.【解】内部的,体内的。~ *energy*【物】内能。~ *qualities* 本质。~ *value* 实价,内在的价值。~ **factor**【生化】内因子〔使胃吸收维生素 B_{12}的胃液〕。

in·trin·si·cal [in'trinsikəl; ɪn`trɪnsɪkəl] *a*. = intrinsic. **-ly** *ad*. **-ness** *n*.

int·ro- *comb*. *f*. 表示"在内","向内": *intro*spect; *intro*vert.

introd; intro. = introduction; introductory.

in·tro·duce [ˌintrə'dju:s; ˏɪntrə`djus] *vt*. **1**. 引导,带领。**2**. 介绍。**3**. 使开始经验[体验]。**4**. 推广,采用,引进。**5**. 提出(议案等)。**6**. 以…作为文章、讲话的开头。**7**. 插入。**8**. 开始。~ *a guest into the parlour* 领客人进客厅。*Allow me to* ~ *Dr. Li* (*to you*). 请允许我(向你)介绍这位李大夫。~ *a freshman to campus life* 向新生介绍校内生活。~ *oneself* 自我介绍。~ *a person to town life* 让某人开始城市生活。~ *a new fashion* 采用新式样。*Space science has* ~*d many new words*. 太空科学采用许多新词汇。~ *a bill into Congress* 向大会提出提案。~ *a motion* 提出动议。~ *a humorous note in a speech* 先讲几句幽默话作为演讲的开场白。~ *a subject with a short preface* 用短序开始讨论一个问题。~ *an electric wire into a conduct* 把电线插入导管内。~ *a probe into a wound* 把探针插进伤口里。~ *a talk with an anecdote* 在正式讲演之前先讲一则轶事。**in·troduc·i·ble** *a*.

in·tro·duc·er [ˌintrə'dju:sə; ˏɪntrə`djusɚ] *n*. 介绍人,推荐人;引进者;提出者;导引器。

in·tro·duc·tion [ˌintrə'dʌkʃən; ˏɪntrə`dʌkʃən] *n*. **1**. 引导;传入。**2**. 介绍。**3**. 推广,采用;引进。**4**. (育种)引种。**5**. 序,导言,绪言;【乐】前奏,序奏。**6**. 初步,入门(书),概论。*The word is a recent* ~. 这个词是新传来的词。*a letter of* ~ 介绍信。~ *of better strains of seeds* 良种的采用。*An I- to Chemistry*《化学入门》。

in·tro·duc·tive [ˌintrə'dʌktiv; ˏɪntrə`dʌktɪv] *a*. = introductory.

in·tro·duc·to·ry [ˌintrə'dʌktəri; ˏɪntrə`dʌktorɪ] *a*. 介绍的;导言的,绪言的;预备的。~ *address* 介绍辞;开会辞。~ *note* 按语。~ *remarks* 绪言,开场白。**-ri·ly** *ad*. **-ri·ness** *n*.

in·tro·gres·sion [ˌintrə'greʃən; ˏɪntrə`grɛʃən] *n*.【生】基因渗入。**-sive** [-'gresiv; -`grɛsɪv] *a*.

in·tro·it [in'trəuit, 'introit; ɪn`troɪt, `ɪntrɔɪt] *n*.【天主】祭文〔祭司在主持祭祀时所唱的赞美诗等〕;【英国国教】圣餐仪式前所唱的歌。

in·tro·ject [ˌintrə'dʒekt; ˏɪntrə`dʒɛkt] *vt*.【医】〔精神分析学方面的用词〕吸取,摄取。**-tion** *n*.

in·tro·mis·sion [ˌintrəu'miʃən; ˏɪntro`mɪʃən] *n*. **1**. 送入,插入。**2**. 允许进入,进入。

in·tro·mit [ˌintrəu'mit; ˏɪntro`mɪt] *vt*. (**-mit·ted**; **-mitting**) **1**. 送入,插入。**2**. 允许进入,进入。**-mit·tent** *a*.

in·trorse [in'trɔ:s; ɪn`trɔrs] *a*.【植】内向的。~ **anther** 向心的花药(*opp*. extrorse)。**-ly** *ad*.

in·tro·spect [ˌintrəu'spekt; ˏɪntro`spɛkt] *vt*., *vi*. 对思想感情等进行反省。

in·tro·spec·tion [ˌintrəu'spekʃən; ˏɪntro`spɛkʃən] *n*. 内省,反省。**-ist** **1**. *a*. 内省的,反省的。**2**. *n*. 内省者,反省者。

in·tro·spec·tive [ˌintrəu'spektiv; ˏɪntro`spɛktɪv] *a*. 内省的,反省的。**-ly** *ad*. **-ness** *n*.

in·tro·ver·si·ble [ˌintrəu'və:səbl; ˏɪntro`vɝsəbl̩] *a*. 可向内翻的,可向内弯的。

in·tro·ver·sion [ˌintrəu'və:ʃən; ˏɪntro`vɝʃən] *n*. **1**. 内曲,内翻。**2**. 内向,反省。**3**.【心】内倾,内向性(*opp*. extroversion)。

in·tro·ver·sive [ˌintrəu'və:siv; ˏɪntro`vɝsɪv] *a*. **1**. 内曲的,内翻的。**2**. 内向的,内省的。**3**.【心】内倾的。

in·tro·vert [ˌintrəu'və:t; ˏɪntro`vɝt] **I** *vt*. **1**. 使内翻,使向内弯。**2**. 使(思想)内向,使内省。**3**.【动】使(器官)向里翻。~ *sth*. *inward* 使某物向里弯。~ *one's attention upon oneself* 使注意力内向。— *vi*. 进行内省;成为内弯的。**II** ['intrəvə:t; `ɪntrəˏvɝt] *n*. **1**.【心】内向型性格的人。**2**. 内弯[内翻]的东西。**III** *a*. = introverted (*opp*. extrovert).

in·tro·vert·ed [ˌintrəu'və:tid; ˏɪntrə`vɝtɪd] *a*. 有内向特征的;有内向性格的;内弯性的,内翻的。

in·tro·ver·tive [ˌintrəu'və:tiv; ˏɪntro`vɝtɪv] *a*. = introversive.

in·trude [inˈtruːd; ɪnˋtrud] *vt*. **1**. 硬把自己挤进(*into*)；把观点等强加于他人。**2**.【地】使浸入其他地层。～ *oneself into a meeting* 闯进会场。～ *one's opinions upon sb*. 把自己的意见强加于人。～ *liquid magma into solid rocks* 把糊浆灌到岩层中去。～*d rocks*【地】侵入岩。— *vi*. 闯进(*upon*)；打扰,入侵。～ *upon sb.'s privacy* 闯入某人的私室。*I hope I am not intruding*. 我希望我不致打扰你。

in·trud·er [inˈtruːdə; ɪnˋtrudɚ] *n*. **1**. 闯入者,侵入者；爱管闲事的人,好干涉的人。**2**. 夜盗；【空】轰炸机。

in·tru·sion [inˈtruːʒən; ɪnˋtruʒən] *n*. **1**. 闯入,侵入；干涉,打扰,妨碍。**2**.【地】侵入；侵入岩(浆)。

in·tru·sive [inˈtruːsiv; ɪnˋtrusɪv] *a*. (*opp*. extrusive) **1**. 闯进的；侵入的。**2**.【地】侵入岩形成的。*the* ～ *sound*【语音】插入音。～ *body*【地】侵入岩体。～ *rocks*【地】侵入岩。**-ly** *ad*. **-ness** *n*.

in·trust [inˈtrʌst; ɪnˋtrʌst] *vt*. = entrust.

in·tu·bate [ˈintjubeit; ˋɪntjʊbet] *vt*.【医】把管子插进(喉头等)。

in·tu·ba·tion [ˌintjuˈbeiʃən; ˏɪntjʊˋbeʃən] *n*.【医】插管,插管法。

in·tu·it [inˈtju(ː)it; ˏɪnˋtjʊɪt] *vt*., *vi*. 直观,由直觉知道。**-a·ble** *a*.

in·tu·i·tion [ˌintju(ː)ˈiʃən; ˏɪntjʊˋɪʃən] *n*. 直感,直觉知识,直感事物。**-ist 1**. *n*. 直观论者,直觉主义者。**2**. *a*. 直观论的,直觉主义的。

in·tu·i·tion·al [ˌintju(ː)ˈiʃənl; ˏɪntjʊˋɪʃənḷ] *a*. 直觉的；直观的。**-ist** *n*., *a*. = intuitionist.

in·tu·i·tion·al·ism [ˌintjuːˈiʃənəlizəm; ˏɪntjuˋɪʃənḷɪzm] *n*. = intuitionism.

in·tu·i·tion·ism [ˌintjuːˈiʃənizəm; ˏɪntjuˋɪʃənɪzəm] *n*.【哲】直观主义,直观论。

in·tu·i·tive [inˈtju(ː)itiv; ɪnˋtjuɪtɪv] *a*. 直觉的；直观的。*an* ～ *truth* 直观真理。**-ly** *ad*. **-ness**, **-tiv·ism** *n*. 直观论；直觉主义。**-tiv·ist** *n*., *a*. = intuitionist.

in·tu·mesce [ˌintju(ː)ˈmes; ˏɪntjuˋmɛs] *vi*. 膨胀,肿起；扩大。

in·tu·mes·cence [ˌintju(ː)ˈmesns; ˏɪntjuˋmɛsns] *n*. **1**. 膨胀；肿大；扩大。**2**. 肿胀物。**3**. (油漆等遇热时的)泡沸。

in·tu·mes·cent [ˌintju(ː)ˈmesnt; ˏɪntjuˋmɛsnt] *a*. **1**. 膨胀的；肿起的；扩大的。**2**. (油漆等遇热时)泡沸的。

in·turned [ˈintəːnd; ˋɪntɚnd] *a*. **1**. 向内弯的。**2**. 性格内向的；自我中心的。

in·tus·sus·cept [ˌintəssəˈsept; ˏɪntəssəˋsɛpt] *vt*. **1**. 摄吸营养。**2**. 吸取,接收。**3**. 使肠子套叠。**4**. 使反折。

in·tus·sus·cep·tion [intəsəˈsepʃən; ˏɪntəsəˋsɛpʃən] *n*. **1**. (营养的)摄取；(思想等的)吸收,接受。**2**.【生】内填,内滋。**3**. 缩入；反折；【医】肠套叠。

in·twine [inˈtwain; ɪnˋtwaɪn] *vt*., *vi*. = entwine.

in·twist [inˈtwist; ɪnˋtwɪst] *vt*. = entwist.

in·u·lase [ˈinjuleis; ˋɪnjəles] *n*.【化】菊粉酶。

in·u·lin [ˈinjulin; ˋɪnjəlɪn] *n*.【化】菊粉。

in·unc·tion [inˈʌŋkʃən; ɪnˋʌŋkʃən] *n*. **1**. 涂油。**2**.【医】涂擦,涂擦法。**3**. 软膏；〔*pl*.〕涂擦剂。

in·un·dant [inˈʌndənt; ɪnˋʌndənt] *a*. 涨溢的,泛滥的。

in·un·date [ˈinəndeit; ˋɪnənˏdet] *vt*. 淹没,泛滥；使充满。*be* ～*d with water* 充满了水。*a place* ～*d with visitors* 参观者络绎不绝的地方。**-da·tion** *n*. 洪水,泛滥。**-da·tor** *n*. **-da·to·ry** *a*.

in·ur·bane [ˌinəːˈbein; ˏɪnɚˋben] *a*. 粗野的,不礼貌的,粗鄙的。**-ban·i·ty** *n*.

in·ure [iˈnjuə; ɪˋnjʊr] *vt*. 〔常用被动语态〕使习惯于；锻炼。*be* ～*d to cold* 使身体耐寒。～ *oneself to hardship* 使自己能吃苦耐劳。— *vi*.【法】生效,适用；有助于。～ *to the prosperity and welfare of the nation* 有利于全国国民的繁荣与福利。**-ment** *n*.

in·urn [inˈəːn; ɪnˋɝn] *vt*. 把(骨灰)装入瓮内；埋葬。～ *ashes of the dead into an urn* 把骨灰放入缸内。

in u·ter·o [inˈjuːtərəu; ɪnˋjutəro] *ad*. 〔L.〕在子宫内,未诞生,在诞生前,在未来。

in·u·tile [inˈjuːtil; ɪnˋjutɪl] *a*. 无益的,没有用的。**-ly** *ad*.

in·u·til·i·ty [ˌinjuˈtiləti; ˏɪnjʊˋtɪlətɪ] *n*. **1**. 无益,无用。**2**. 无用的人,废物。*talk inutilities* 说废话。

inv. = **1**. invented; inventor. **2**. invoice.

in va·cu·o [in ˈvækjuːəu; ɪnˋvækjʊˏo] *ad*. 〔L.〕在空处,在真空中。

in·vade [inˈveid; ɪnˋved] *vt*. **1**. 侵入,侵略(他国),侵犯(权利)。**2**. 蜂拥而入,挤满。**3**. 打扰。**4**. (疾病、声音等)袭来,侵袭。*The town was* ～*d by a crowd of tourists*. 这个城市涌进了一群游客。～ *sb.'s privacy* 打扰某人。*a body* ～*d by disease* 受到疾病侵入的身体。— *vi*. 进行侵略。

in·vad·er [inˈveidə; ɪnˋvedɚ] *n*. 侵略者；侵入者；侵犯者；侵入物。

in·vag·i·nate [inˈvædʒineit; ɪnˋvædʒɪˏnet] *vt*. **1**. 摄吸,吸取。**2**. 使内陷；把…收入鞘内；使(管、器官等)内缩；使反折(= intussuscept)。— *vi*. 反折；入鞘；凹入。

in·vag·i·na·tion [inˌvædʒiˈneiʃən; ɪnˏvædʒɪˋneʃən] *n*. **1**. 内陷；入鞘；反折。**2**. 反折处；内陷[入鞘]部分。**3**.【医】肠套叠。

in·va·lid[1] [ˈinvəlid; ˋɪnvəlɪd] **I** *a*. **1**. 有病的,病弱的,伤残的。**2**. 病人用的。～ *soldiers* 伤兵。*an* ～ *chair* 病人用椅。*an* ～ *diet* 病号菜饭。**II** *n*. 病人,病弱者,病号,伤病军人。*a resort of* ～*s* 伤病员疗养地。**III** [ˌinvəˈliːd; ˏɪnvəˋlid] *vt*. **1**. 使病弱；使伤残。**2**. 把…作为伤病员处理。*be* ～*ed for life* 成终身病人。*be* ～*ed home* 被作为伤病员送回家。*be* ～*ed out of the army* 因伤病而奉命退伍。— *vi*. **1**. 失去健康。**2**. 因伤病而退伍。

in·val·id[2] [inˈvælid; ɪnˋvælɪd] *a*. **1**. 无用的；不能成立的。**2**.【法】无效的,作废的。～ *arguments* 站不住脚的论点。～ *cheques* 无效的支票。～ *claims* 无效的要求。～ *contracts* 无效的契约。*declare a marriage* ～ 宣布结婚无效。**-ly** *ad*.

in·val·i·date [inˈvælideit; ɪnˋvælɪˏdet] *vt*. 使无效,使失效。

in·val·i·da·tion [inˌvæliˈdeiʃən; ɪnˏvælɪˋdeʃən] *n*. 无效,失效。

in·va·lid·ism [ˈinvəlidizəm; ˋɪnvəlɪdˏɪzəm] *n*. 病弱,虚弱,伤残。

in·va·lid·i·ty [ˌinvəˈliditi; ˏɪnvəˋlɪdətɪ] *n*. **1**. 无效力。**2**. (因病残而)丧失工作能力。

in·val·u·a·ble [inˈvæljuəbl; ɪnˋvæljʊəbḷ] *a*. 无法估价的,无价的；非常贵重的。*an* ～ *treasure* 无价之宝。**-bly** *ad*. **-ness** *n*.

in·var [inˈvɑː; ɪnˋvɑr] *n*.【冶】因钢,因瓦(铁镍)合金,不胀钢,恒范钢。

in·var·i·a·ble [inˈvɛəriəbl; ɪnˋvɛrɪəbl] **I** *a*. 无变化的；不变的；一律的。**II** *n*.【数】不变量,常数。**-bil·i·ty**, **-ness** *n*. 不变性。**-bly** *ad*. 不变地；永恒地；常常。

in·var·i·ant [inˈvɛəriənt; ɪnˋvɛrɪənt] **I** *a*. 不变的,无变度的；一定的,恒定的。**II** *n*.【数】不变式；不变量。**-i·ance** *n*.

in·va·sion [inˈveiʒən; ɪnˋveʒən] *n*. **1**. 侵入,侵略。**2**. 侵害,侵犯。**3**.【医】发病,发作。*an* ～ *of locust* 蝗虫的侵袭。*cultural* ～ 文化侵略。*an* ～ *of disease* 疾病的侵入。*make an* ～ *upon* 侵入,袭击。～ *of sb.'s privacy* 非法干预某人的私事。

in·va·sive [inˈveisiv; ɪnˋvesɪv] *a*. 侵略性的,侵害的；侵袭的。**-ness** *n*. 侵略性,侵袭性。

in·vec·tive [inˈvektiv; ɪnˋvɛktɪv] **I** *a*. 诽谤的,责骂的。**II** *n*. 〔*pl*.〕骂人的话。*a stream of coarse* ～*s* 一连串

下流的骂人话。*utter ~s against sb*. 痛骂某人。**-ly** *ad*. **-ness** *n*.

in·veigh [in'vei; ɪn`ve] *vi*. 痛骂,猛烈攻击(*against*)。~ *against bureaucracy* 指责官僚主义。

in·veigh·er [in'veiə; ɪn`veɚ] *n*. 咒骂者,攻击者。

in·vei·gle [in'vi:gl, -'vei-; ɪn`vigl, -`ve-] *vt*. 诱惑,诱骗,诱陷。~ *sb. into* (*doing*) *sth*. 诱骗某人做某事。~ *sb. out of sth*. 〔口〕骗取某人东西。**-ment** *n*.

in·vei·gler [in'vi:glə, -'vei-; ɪn`viglə, -`ve-] *n*. 诱骗者,诱陷者,诱惑者。

in·ve·nit [in'veinit; ɪn`venɪt] *v*. (*pl*. ***in·ve·ne·runt*** [ˌinvi'niərənt; ˏɪnvɪ`nɪərənt]) 〔L.〕〔第三人称单数〕(某某)作,创制。

in·vent [in'vent; ɪn`vɛnt] *vt*. **1**. 发明,创作,创造。**2**. 捏造,虚构。*Morse ~ed the telegraph*. 摩尔斯发明电报。~ *an excuse* 捏造借口。**-er**, **-or** *n*. 发明者,创造者。

in·ven·tion [in'venʃən; ɪn`vɛnʃən] *n*. **1**. 发明,创造。**2**. 新发明,发明的东西。**3**. 创造力,发明才能。**4**. 捏造,虚构。**5**. 〔古〕发现。**6**. 【乐】创意曲。*Necessity is the mother of ~*. 〔谚〕需要是发明之母。*make an ~* 发明;杜撰。*a registered ~* 注过册的新发明。

in·ven·tive [in'ventiv; ɪn`vɛntɪv] *a*. 发明创造的,有发明能力的,能独出心裁的,有创造力的。~ *powers* 发明创造的能力。**-ness** *n*. 有发明创造能力;独创性;独创能力。**-ly** *ad*.

in·ven·to·ry ['invəntri; `ɪnvəntrɪ] **I** *n*. **1**. (财产等的)清单,报表;(商品的)目录。**2**. 盘存,存货。*an aircraft ~*【军】编制内飞机总数。*physical ~*【商】实地盘存。~ *control* (计算机的)编目控制。~ *liquidating*【商】减少存货。*make* [*take*, *draw up*] *an ~ of* 编制…的目录,开列…的清单。**II** *vt*. 编制(商品等的)目录,开清单,盘存。**-to·ri·al** [-'tɔriəl; -`tɔrɪəl] *a*. **-to·ri·al·ly** *ad*.

in·ve·rac·i·ty [ˌinvə'ræsiti; ˏɪnvə`ræsətɪ] *n*. **1**. 不诚实;虚伪。**2**. (*pl*. ***-ties***) 谎言,欺骗。

in·ver·ness [ˌinvə'nes; ˏɪnvɚ`nɛs] *n*. 长披风,带护肩的斗篷(= I- ['invənes; `ɪnvənɛs] cape [cloak, coat])。

in·verse [in'və:s; ɪn`vɝs] **I** *a*. 相反的;逆的;翻转的,倒转的。*an ~ network* 倒置(电)网络。~ *time* 逆时,反时。*an ~ transistor* 换接晶体管。**II** *n*. 反面;反量,倒数。*be an ~ measure of a number of* 是同…成反比。'*Evil*' *is the ~ of* '*good*'. "恶"是"善"的反面。**III** *vt*. 使倒转,使成反面。~ **function**【数】反逆函数。~ **proportion**【数】反比例。~ **ratio**【数】反比,逆比。

in·verse·ly [in'və:sli; ɪn`vɝslɪ] *ad*. 相反地。~ *as the square of* 与…的平方成反比。~ *proportional to* 成反比。

in·ver·sion [in'və:ʃən; ɪn`vɝʃən] *n*. **1**. 倒转,反转,逆转;倒置,转换。**2**. 倒置物,颠倒现象。**3**.【语法】倒装法,语序倒置法;(语言的)卷舌。**4**.【数】反演。**5**.【乐】(和音、主题等的)转回。**6**.【化】转化。**7**.【机】(四杆机构的)机架变化。**8**.【医】内翻。**9**.【精神病学】同性恋。**10**.【气】逆温,逆增。**11**.【生】(染色体的)倒位。**12**.【电】(直流电转成交流电的)换流;【自】反相。~ *of relief*【地】地形倒置。~ *point* 转化点。~ *hybrid* 倒位杂种。*the ~ layer* 逆温层。

in·ver·sive [in'və:siv; ɪn`vɝsɪv] *a*. 反向的,倒转的。

in·vert [in'və:t; ɪn`vɝt] **I** *vt*. **1**. 翻过来,(上下、前后)倒置,反转。**2**.【乐】转回。**3**.【化】转化。~ *a glass* 把茶杯扣起来。**II** ['invə:t; `ɪnvɝt] *n*. **1**.【建】仰拱。**2**. 性欲颠倒的人。**3**. 颠倒了的事物。**III** ['invə:t; `ɪnvɝt] *a*.【生化】转化的。~ *sugar* 转化糖。

in·vert·ase [in'və:teis; ɪn`vɝtes] *n*.【生化】转化酶,蔗糖酶。

in·ver·te·brate [in'və:tibrit; ɪn`vɝtɪbrɪt] **I** *a*. **1**.【动】无脊骨的,无脊椎的。**2**. 无骨气的,软弱无能的。**II** *n*. **1**. 无脊椎动物。**2**. 没骨气的人。

in·vert·ed [in'və:tid; ɪn`vɝtɪd] *a*. 反转的;倒转的;倒置的;(电压)反接的。~ *arch*【建】仰拱。~ *blockade* 空中封锁。~ *engine*【机】倒缸发动机。~ *flight*【军】倒飞。~ **comma** 引号(= quotation mark)。~ **mordent**【乐】逆波音。

in·vert·er [in'və:tə; ɪn`vɝtɚ] *n*.【电】**1**. 换流器;倒相器,倒换器。**2**. 变换电路。**3**. 反相旋转换流器。

in·vert·i·ble [in'və:tibl; ɪn`vɝtɪbl] *a*. **1**. 可颠倒的,可反转的。**2**.【化】可转化的。

in·vest [in'vest; ɪn`vɛst] *vt*. **1**. 使穿;使带(勋章等)。**2**. 授与,赋予。**3**. 使带有(某种性质等)。**4**.【军】包围。**5**. 投资,投入(时间、精力等)。~ *sb. with a decoration* 给某人戴上奖章。~ *sb. with full power* 把全权授与某人。~ *sb. in an office* 任命某人担任某职务。*be ~ed with mystery* 使带有神秘色彩。*The enemy ~ed the city*. 敌人包围了那个城市。~ *money in stocks* 投资购买股票。~*ed capital* 投入资本。— *vi*. **1**. 投资(*in*)。~ *heavily in sth*. 对某事大量投资。**2**. 〔口〕买进(*in*)。~ *in a hat* 买帽子。

in·ves·ti·gate [in'vestigeit; ɪn`vɛstɪˏget] *vt*. 研究,调查;审查。*Scientists ~ the nature*. 科学家研究自然。~ *a murder* 审查杀人案件。— *vi*. 研究,调查。~ *into an affair* 调查一件事情。

in·ves·ti·ga·tion [inˌvesti'geiʃən; ɪnˏvɛstɪ`geʃən] *n*. **1**. 研究,调查;审查。**2**. 研究论文,调查报告。*make an ~ on* [*of*, *into*] *sth*. 对某事进行调查研究。*The matter is under ~*. 这事正在调查中。

in·ves·ti·ga·tive, **in·ves·ti·ga·to·ry** [in'vestigeitiv, -gətəri; ɪn`vɛstɪˏgetɪv, -gətorɪ] *a*. 研究的,调查的,爱调查研究的。

in·ves·ti·ga·tor [in'vestigeitə; ɪn`vɛstɪgetɚ] *n*. 研究者,调查者,侦查员。

in·ves·ti·tive [in'vestitiv; ɪn`vɛstətɪv] *a*. **1**. 投资的,有投资能力的,有投资可能的。**2**. 授权[任命]的。

in·ves·ti·ture [in'vestitʃə; ɪn`vɛstɪtʃɚ] *n*. **1**. 〔英〕授职(仪式);授权。**2**. (性格等的)赋予。**3**. 服装,装饰。**4**. (封建时代的)封地仪式。

in·vest·ment [in'vestmənt; ɪn`vɛstmənt] *n*. **1**. 投资;投资额;(时间、资本等的)投入;投入资金的东西。**2**. 授职(仪式);授权。**3**. 包围,封锁。**4**. 覆盖。*make an ~ in* 投资。~ **bank** 投资银行。~ **fund** 投资信托,投资公司〔投资于证券者〕。~ **company** [**trust**] 投资信托公司。~ **letter stock** 投资信股;未登记股票(= letter stock)。

in·ves·tor [in'vestə; ɪn`vɛstɚ] *n*. **1**. 投资者。**2**. 授权者。**3**. 包围者,围攻者。

in·vet·er·a·cy [in'vetərəsi; ɪn`vɛtərəsɪ] *n*. (成见、仇恨、习惯等的)根深蒂固。

in·vet·er·ate [in'vetərit; ɪn`vɛtərɪt] *a*. 根深蒂固的,长期形成的,积重难返的。*an ~ conservative* 顽固不化的保守派。*an ~ disease* 宿疾,老毛病。*an ~ enemy* 不共戴天的仇敌。*an ~ habit* 积习。*an ~ smoker* 烟瘾很大的人。**-ly** *ad*.

in·vid·i·ous [in'vidiəs; ɪn`vɪdɪəs] *a*. **1**. 引起反感的,令人厌恶的。**2**. 招嫉妒的,招猜忌的。~ *remarks* 不中听的话。~ *distinctions* 使人反感的差别。~ *position* 招人猜忌的地位。**-ly** *ad*. **-ness** *n*.

in·vig·i·late [in'vidʒileit; ɪn`vɪdʒɪˏlet] *vi*. 〔英〕监考;〔罕〕监视。**-la·tion** *n*. **-la·tor** *n*.

in·vig·or·ate [in'vigəreit; ɪn`vɪgəˏret] *vt*. 提神,使强壮;鼓舞,激励。~ *the national spirit* 振奋民族精神。

in·vig·or·at·ing, **-a·tive** [in'vigəreitiŋ, -tiv; ɪn`vɪgəˏretɪŋ, -tɪv] *a*. 提神的,爽快的,令人鼓舞的。*an ~ climate* 令人心旷神怡的气候。~ *news* 鼓舞人心的消息。

in·vig·or·a·tion [inˌvigə'reiʃən; ɪnˏvɪgə`reʃən] *n*. 增益精力;滋补;鼓舞。

in·vig·or·a·tor [in'vigəreitə; ɪn`vɪgəˏretɚ] *n*. 激励

者；补药。

in·vin·ci·bil·i·ty [inˌvinsiˈbiliti; ɪnˏvɪnsɪˋbɪlətɪ] ***n.*** 无敌。

in·vin·ci·ble [inˈvinsəbl; ɪnˋvɪnsəbl] ***a.*** 无敌的；战无不胜的。*an* ～ *army* 常胜军。～ *ignorance* 无法可想的愚蠢。**-ci·ble·ness** ***n.*** = invincibility. **-bly** ***ad.***

in vi·no ve·ri·tas [in ˈviːnəu ˈveritæs, -ˈvainəu-; ɪnˋvino ˋvɛrɪtæs, -ˋvaɪno-] [L.] 酒醉吐真言。

in·vi·o·la·bil·i·ty [inˌvaiələˈbiliti; ɪnˏvaɪələˋbɪlətɪ] ***n.*** 不可侵犯，神圣；不可违背。

in·vi·o·la·ble [inˈvaiələbl; ɪnˋvaɪələbl] ***a.*** 神圣的，不可侵犯的；不可违背的。*an* ～ *promise* 不可违背的诺言。*an* ～ *heavens* 不可违背的上苍。**-bly** ***ad.***

in·vi·o·late [inˈvaiəlit; ɪnˋvaɪəˏlɪt], **-d** [-leitid; -letɪd] ***a.*** 不受侵犯的；神圣的，无污点的。*keep one's faith* ～ 坚持信仰。**-vio·la·cy, -ness** ***n.*** **-ly** ***ad.***

in·vis·cid [inˈvisid; ɪnˋvɪsɪd] ***a.*** 非黏滞性的；无韧性的；不能展延的。

in·visi·ble [inˈvizəbl; ɪnˋvɪzəbl] **I** ***a.*** **1.** 看不见的，无形的。**2.** 不显眼的，微小得看不出的。**3.** 不露面的，谢绝来客的。**4.** 未列在公开账目上的，统计表上看不出的。～ *cap* (传说中的)隐身帽。～ *spectrum* 【物】不可见光谱。～ *mending* 织补。～ *to the naked eye* 肉眼看不见。*keep oneself* ～ *in his room* 躲在屋内不露面。～ *assets* 账外资产。**II** ***n.*** 看不见的人[物]。〔the ～〕【宗】幽冥世界，冥界；〔the I-〕神，上帝。**I- Empire** 无形帝国〔美国三 K 党活动初期的别称〕。～ **export** 无形输出。～ **green** 深绿。～ **import** 无形输入。～ **ink** 密写墨水〔经热气或药品作用方显字迹的墨水〕。～ **supply** (农家未出售的)余粮总量。～ **transactions** 无形交易〔指非具体商品的交易，如航运、保险、旅游等〕。**-bil·i·ty, -ness** ***n.*** **-bly** ***ad.***

in·vi·ta·tion [ˌinviˈteiʃən; ˏɪnvɪˋteʃən] ***n.*** **1.** 招待，邀请；请帖。**2.** 吸引，诱惑。*accept* [*decline*] *an* ～接受[谢绝]邀请。*admission by* ～ *only* 凭柬入场。*an* ～ *tournament* 邀请赛。*at the* ～ *of sb.* 应某人邀请。*The* ～*s are out.* 请帖已发出。

in·vi·ta·tion·al [ˌinviˈteiʃənl; ˏɪnvɪˋteʃənl] ***a.*** 邀请的，应邀参加的。*an* ～ *art exhibit* 一件应邀参加展出的美术作品。

in·vi·ta·to·ry [inˈvaitətəri; ɪnˋvaɪtəˏtorɪ] ***a.*** 邀请的，招待的。

in·vite [inˈvait; ɪnˋvaɪt] **I** ***vt.*** **1.** 招待；邀请。**2.** 请求，征求。**3.** 引起，吸引。*an* ～*d guests* 来宾。*be* ～*d out* 应邀，被邀请。～ *sb. in* 邀请某人到家里。～ *oneself* 不请自到。～ *sb. to consider* 请求某人考虑。*Questions are* ～*d.* 欢迎提问题。～ *tenders* 招(人投)标。～ *war* 引起战争。*Every scene* ～*s the ravished eye.* 场场引人入胜。**II** [ˈinvait; ˋɪnvaɪt] ***n.*** 〔口〕招待，邀请。**-e** ***n.*** 被招待者，被邀请者。**-r** ***n.*** 招待者，邀请者。

in·vit·ing [inˈvaitiŋ; ɪnˋvaɪtɪŋ] ***a.*** 引人注目的，吸引人的。**-ly** ***ad.*** **-ness** ***n.***

in vitro [inˈvaitrəu; inˋvaɪtro] ***n.*** 〔L.〕在试管内。～ **fertilization** 试管受精，体外受精。

in vi·vo [in ˈviːvəu; ɪnˋvivo] [L.] 在活微生物中出现的。

in·vo·cate [ˈinvəukeit; ˋɪnvoˏket] ***vt., vi.*** 〔罕〕祷求，祈求，祈灵。

in·vo·ca·tion [ˌinvəuˈkeiʃən; ˏɪnvoˋkeʃən] ***n.*** **1.** 祈祷；祈求。**2.** 召唤魔鬼，符咒，咒语。**3.** (法权的)行使，(法规、条文等的)援引；发动。

in·vo·ca·tion·al [ˌinvəuˈkeiʃənl; ˏɪnvoˋkeʃənl] ***a.*** 祈求的；祈祷的，恳求的。

in·voc·a·to·ry [inˈvɔkətəri; ɪnˋvɑkəˏtorɪ] ***a.*** 祈祷的，恳求的。

in·voice [ˈinvɔis; ˋɪnvɔɪs] **I** ***n.*** **1.** 【商】发票，装货清单。**2.** 货物的托运。～ *specification* 发票明细单。*receive a large* ～ *of goods* 接受大宗商品的托运。**II** ***vt., vi.*** 开(…的)发票，开(…的)清单。～ **book** ***n.*** 进货簿；发票存根。

in·voke [inˈvəuk; ɪnˋvok] ***vt.*** **1.** 祈求(神灵)保佑，乞灵于，用符咒召唤。**2.** 恳求，乞求。**3.** 行使(法权等)，实行。**4.** 援引(法规、条文等)。**5.** 引起，产生。～ *evil spirits* 召唤恶魔。～ *the power of the law* 请求依法支持。～ *sb.'s help* 恳求某人帮助。～ *economic sanctions* 实行经济制裁。～ *the veto in the meeting* 在会议中行使否决权。～ *an article of the U.N. Charter* 援引《联合国宪章》条文。～ *new problems* 引起一些新问题。**-r** ***n.*** 祈求者。

in·vol·u·cel [inˈvɔljusel; ɪnˋvɑljusɛl] ***n.*** 【植】小总苞，小叶苞。**-cel·late** ***a.***

in·vo·lu·crate [ˈinvəluːkrit, -kreit; ˋɪnvəˏlukrɪt, -kret] ***a.*** 【植】有总苞的；有花被的；有蒴苞的。

in·vo·lu·cre [ˈinvəluːkə; ˋɪnvəˏlukɚ] ***n.*** **1.** 【解】外皮，包膜。**2.** 【植】花被，蒴包，总苞。

in·vo·lu·crum [ˌinvəˈluːkrəm; ˏɪnvəˋlukrəm] ***n.*** = involucre (*pl.* ***involucra*** [ˌinvəˈluːkrə; ˏɪnvəˋlukrə]). **-lu·cral** ***a.***

in·vol·un·tar·y [inˈvɔləntəri; ɪnˋvɑlənˏtərɪ] ***a.*** **1.** 无意识的，不自觉的。**2.** 非故意的，偶然的。**3.** 非自愿的，不随意的(*opp.* voluntary)。*Sneezing is* ～. 打喷嚏是不自觉的。*an* ～ *confession* 不打自招的供状。～ *homicide* 【法】过失杀人(罪)。～ *muscles* 【解】不随意肌。**-tar·i·ly** ***ad.*** **-tari·ness** ***n.***

in·vo·lute [ˈinvəluːt; ˋɪnvəˏlut] **I** ***a.*** **1.** 纷乱的，错综复杂的。**2.** 【植】内卷的。**3.** 内旋的；螺状的。～ *teeth* [*gear*] 【机】渐开线齿轮。**II** ***n.*** 【数】渐伸线，渐开线，切展线。**III** [ˌinvəˈluːt; ˏɪnvəˋlut] ***vi.*** **1.** 内卷，卷起。**2.** 恢复原状。**3.** 消失，消散。

in·vo·lu·tion [ˌinvəˈluːʃən; ˏɪnvəˋluʃən] ***n.*** **1.** 卷入，纠缠；错综复杂。**2.** 【数】乘方。**3.** 【生】退化；内转(*opp.* evolution)。**4.** 【医】萎缩，退化，复旧。**5.** 复杂的句型。*senile* ～老年性退化。

in·volve [inˈvɔlv; ɪnˋvɑlv] ***vt.*** **1.** 包缠，卷缠。**2.** 拖累，连累，使陷入，使卷入(漩涡)。**3.** 包围，围住，笼罩(*in*; *with*)。**4.** 包括，涉及，引起，包含；含有…的意义。**5.** 〔主用被动式〕使埋头，使专注。**6.** 【数】把某数字乘方。*be* ～*d in trouble* 陷入烦恼。*Clouds* ～ *the mountain top.* 云雾笼罩山头。*The real meaning of his remark is* ～*d in ambiguity.* 他这句话的真正意思很难捉摸。～ *much difficulty* 带有许多困难。*This* ～*s an increase of the national debt.* 这样就难免使国债增加。*be* ～*d in working out a plan* 专心一意地制定计划。～ *a number to the fifth power* 把某数字五乘方。***become*** ～***d in*** 卷入，陷入。***be*** ～***d in*** 被包入；被卷入漩涡，被连累(*be* ～*d in war* 被卷入战争漩涡。*be* ～*d in debt* 债台高筑。*be* ～*d in disaster* 陷入不幸)。***get*** ～***d with*** 给…缠住。

in·volved [inˈvɔlvd; ɪnˋvɑlvd] ***a.*** **1.** 卷入的，陷入的。**2.** (财政上)困难的。**3.** 复杂的；混乱的，晦涩的。**4.** 有关的，所包含的。～ *phraseology* 晦涩的措词。*an* ～ *sentence* 复杂的句子。*all governments* ～ 各有关政府。*the various academic questions* ～涉及到的各种学术问题。

in·volve·ment [inˈvɔlvment; ɪnˋvɑlvmənt] ***n.*** **1.** 包缠，缠绕；包含，含有。**2.** 牵连的事务，复杂的情况。**3.** 财政困难。

invt. = inventory.

in·vul·ner·a·ble [inˈvʌlnərəbl; ɪnˋvʌlnərəbl] ***a.*** **1.** 不会受伤害的，刀枪不入的。**2.** 无可辩驳的。～ *arguments* 无懈可击的[攻不破的]论点。**-bil·i·ty** ***n.*** **-bly** ***ad.***

in·ward [ˈinwəd; ˋɪnwɚd] (*opp.* outward) **I** ***a.*** **1.** 内面的，内部的；向内的。**2.** 内地的。**3.** 内心上的，亲密的，

I

熟悉的。4.(声音)低沉的,暗自说着的。5. 本来的,本质上的。6.【商】进口的,输入的,引进的。~ *correspondence* 来信。*an* ~ *curve* 内弯。*the* ~ *organs of the body* 身体内部的器官。*an* ~ *voyage* 归航。~ *Asia* 亚洲的腹地。~ *happiness* 内心的喜悦。~ *struggle* 内心的斗争[挣扎]。~ *nature of a thing* 事物的本质。*speak in an* ~ *voice* 说话的声音低沉。~ *charges* 入港费。*an* ~ *entry* 进口申请书。*an* ~ *manifest* 进口货清单。~ *processing* 运进加工。**II** *n*. 1.(物体的)内部;内心。2.〔*pl*. 常例作 [ˈinwədz; ˋɪnwɚdz]〕〔口〕内脏,(作食品的)肠,胃。*a pain in the* ~*s* 肚子痛。3.〔*pl*.〕〔英〕进口税,进口货。**III** *ad*. 1. 向内,向内心。~ *bound*【海】向内行驶。*slope* ~ 向内倾斜。2. 向着内心,进入心灵。**-ly** *ad*. 1. 在内,在内部;内里,向内,向中心(*bleed* ~*ly* 内出血)。2. 在心灵深处;思想上;精神上(~*ly resentful* 内心不满的)。3. 暗自地(*speak* ~*ly* 自言自语)。**-ness** *n*. 1. 真相,真意;本性;本质。2. 心性,灵性。3. 思想感情的深度,诚挚。

in·wards [ˈinwədz; ˋɪnwɚdz] *ad*. = inward (*ad*.).

in·weave [inˈwiːv; ɪnˋwiv] *vt*. (*-wove* [-wəuv; -ˋwov], *-weaved*; *-woven* [-ˈwəuvn; -ˋwovn], *-wove*, *-weaven* [-wiːvn;-wivn̩]; *-weav·ing*) 使织入,使交织。

in·win·ter [ˈinwintə; ˋɪnwɪntɚ] *vt*. 护饲(羊群等)在室内过冬。

in·wrap [inˈræp; ɪnˋræp] *vt*. = enwrap.

in·wreathe [inˈriːð; ɪnˋrið] *vt*. = enwreathe.

in·wrought [ˈinˈrɔːt; ˋɪnˋrɔt] *a*. 1. 织有(花纹)的,绣有…的,嵌有…的(*with*)。2. 纺织品中织入花纹的,加花纹的(*in*; *on*)。3. 与…紧密配合的。*skirts* ~ *with patterns* 织有图案的裙子。

I·o [ˈaiəu; ˋaɪo] *n*. 1.【希神】爱莪〔主神宙斯的情人,后为宙斯之妻 Hera 施法变为母牛〕。2.【天】木星的第二卫星。

Io =【化】ionium 放射性元素钍-230 的符号。

I/O = Input/Output【自】输入/输出。

IOC = International Olympic Committee 国际奥林匹克委员会。

IOCS = input-output control system 输入-输出控制系统。

i·od- *comb.f*. 表示"碘": *iod*ate.

i·o·date [ˈaiədeit; ˋaɪəˏdet] **I** *vt*. 用碘处理;向…加碘。**II** *n*.【化】碘酸盐。**-da·tion** *n*.

i·od·ic [aiˈɔdik; aɪˋɑdɪk] *a*. 碘的;含碘的;五价碘的。~ **acid** 碘酸。

i·o·dide, i·o·did [ˈaiədaid, -did; ˋaɪəˏdaɪd, -dɪd] *n*. 碘化物。~ *of potassium* 碘化钾。

i·o·di·nate [ˈaiədineit; ˋaɪədɪˏnet] *vt*. (*-nat·ed*; *nat·ing*)【化】碘化;用碘处理。**-na·tion** *n*.

i·o·dine, -din [ˈaiədiːn, -din; ˋaɪəˏdin, -dɪn] *n*. 1.【化】碘。2.〔口〕碘酊。*an* ~ *number* 碘值。~ *preparation* 碘剂。*tincture of* ~【药】碘酊。

i·o·dism [ˈaiədizm; ˋaɪədɪzm̩] *n*.【医】碘中毒。

i·o·dize [ˈaiədaiz; ˋaɪəˏdaɪz] *vt*. 用碘[碘化物]处理;使含碘。~*d salt* 加碘食盐〔加有少量的碘化钠或碘化钾〕。

i·o·do- *pref*. = iod-.

i·o·do·form [aiˈɔdəfɔːm; aɪˋɑdəˏfɔrm] *n*.【化】碘仿,三碘甲烷。

I·o·dol [ˈaiədəul; ˋaɪədol] *n*. 碘末防腐剂〔商标名,碘的黄色晶状粉末,用作消毒剂〕。

i·o·dom·e·try [ˌaiəˈdɔmitri; ˏaɪəˋdɑmətrɪ] *n*.【化】碘量滴定法。**-tric** [-dəuˈmetrik; -doˋmɛtrɪk] *a*.

i·o·do·pro·tein [ˌaiədəuˈprəutin, -prəutiːin; ˏaɪədoˋprotɪn, -protiɪn] *n*.【化】碘蛋白。

i·o·dop·sin [aiəˈdɔpsin; aɪəˋdɑpsɪn] *n*. 视蓝紫质,视青紫素。

i·o·dous [aiˈəudəs, ˈaiədəs; aɪˋodəs, ˋaɪədəs] *a*. 亚碘的。

I. of W. = Isle of Wight〔英〕怀特岛。

IOJ = International Organization of Journalists 国际新闻工作者协会。

i·o·lite [ˈaiəˌlait; ˋaɪəˏlaɪt] *n*. = cordierite.

IOM = Isle of Man 马恩岛〔英国〕。

I·o moth [ˈaiəu mɔθ; ˋaɪo mɑθ]【动】大蚕蛾(*Automeris io*)〔产于北美,后翅上有眼状斑,其幼虫的毛有毒,能螯人〕。

i·on [ˈaiən, ˈaiɔn; ˋaɪən, ˋaɪɑn] *n*.【物】离子。*positive* [*negative*] ~正[负]离子。~ **engine** 离子发动机。~ **exchange** 离子交换(作用)。~ **exchange resin** 离子交换树脂。~ **exclusion** 离子排斥。~ **implantation** 离子注入技术〔制造半导体的一个程序〕。~ **rocket** 离子火箭。

-ion *suf*.〔构成名词〕。1. 表示行为的过程,结果。2. 表示状态[情况]。translat*ion*, condemnat*ion*, fus*ion*, conscript*ion*, correct*ion*.

I·o·ni·a [aiˈəuniə; aɪˋonɪə] *n*. 爱奥尼亚〔位于小亚细亚西岸,包括爱琴海的岛屿。公元前十一世纪曾为古希腊工商业和文化中心之一〕。

I·o·ni·an [aiˈəunjən, -niən; aɪˋonɪən, -njən] **I** *a*. 爱奥尼亚(人)的;【建】爱奥尼亚式的。**II** *n*. 爱奥尼亚人,爱奥尼亚语。*the* ~ *mode*【乐】爱奥尼亚音阶法。~ **Islands** 爱奥尼亚岛屿〔小亚细亚西岸〕。~ **Sea**〔希〕爱奥尼亚海。

I·on·ic [aiˈɔnik; aɪˋɑnɪk] **I** *a*. 爱奥尼亚的,爱奥尼亚人的;爱奥尼亚音步的;【建】爱奥尼亚式的。~ *capital* 爱奥尼亚式的柱顶。**II** *n*. 爱奥尼亚语;〔i-〕【印】一种粗字面铅字。~ **dialect** 爱奥尼亚方言。~ **foot** 爱奥尼亚音步。

i·on·ic [aiˈɔnik; aɪˋɑnɪk] *a*. 离子的。~ *bond* [*link*]【化】离子键。**-i·ty** *n*. 离子性,电离度。

i·o·ni·um [aiˈəuniəm; aɪˋonɪəm] *n*.【化】钍-230〔天然存在的放射性元素,钍的同位素〕。

i·on·i·za·tion [ˌaiənaiˈzeiʃən; ˏaɪənaɪˋzeʃən] *n*.【物】电离(作用);离子化。~ *by impact* [*light*] 碰撞[光感]电离。~ *constant* 电离常数。*an* ~ *gauge* 电离压力[真空]计。~ *layer* 电离层。*photo* ~ 光致电离。~ **chamber** 电离室。

i·on·iz·a·bil·i·ty [ˌaiənaizəˈbiliti; ˏaɪənaɪzəˋbɪlətɪ] *n*. 电离度。

i·on·ize [ˈaiənaiz; ˋaɪəˏnaɪz] *vt*. (使)电离,使电离成离子。— *vi*. 电离。**-r** *n*. 电离剂[器]。

i·on·o·gen [aiˈɔnədʒən; aɪˋɑnədʒən] *n*. 电离质,电离物;可离子化的基团。**-gent·ic** [-ˈdʒentik; -ˋdʒɛntɪk] *a*.

i·on·o·me·ter [aiˈəunəmiːtə; aɪˋonəmitɚ] *n*. 1. 离子计,离子测定仪。2. 射线强度计。

I·o·none [ˈaiənəun; ˋaɪəˏnon] *n*.【化】"紫罗(兰)酮"〔商标名〕;〔i-〕紫罗(兰)酮〔制香水的一种原料〕。

i·on·o·phone [aiˈɔnəfəun; aɪˋɑnəˏfon] *n*.【无】离子扬声器。

i·on·o·pho·re·sis [ˌaiənəˈfɔrəsis; ˏaɪənəˋfɔrəsɪs] *n*.【化】电离电泳作用。

I·on·o·sonde [aiˈɔnəsɔnd; aɪˋɑnəˏsɑnd] *n*.【无】电离层探测器。

i·on·o·sphere [aiˈɔnəsfiə; aɪˋɑnəsˏfɪr] *n*.【物】电离层(= ionized layer)。**-spher·ic** *a*. (= ~ layer). ~ **wave** 游离层波。

IOS = International Organization for Standardization (联合国)国际标准化组织。

i·o·ta [aiˈəutə; aɪˋotə] *n*. 1. 希腊语的第九个字母〔即 I, ι = i〕。2. 微小,一点。*have not an* ~ *of* 没有一点儿…。*not change by an* ~ 丝毫不变。

i·o·ta·cism [aiˈəutəsizəm; aɪˋotəsɪzəm] *n*. 1. 过多使用"i"字母〔希腊字母 iota〕。2. 对其他母音加 [iː] 音的倾向〔尤其希腊语如此〕。

I

IOU, I.O.U. [ˈaiəuˈjuː; ˋaɪoˋju] *n*. 借据〔由 I owe you. 的读音缩略转义而成〕。
-iour *suf*. 表示"…的人"：pav*iour*, sav*iour*.
-ious *suf*. 表示"具有…特质的","充满…的"：delic*ious*, fur*ious*, prec*ious*, prodig*ious*, relig*ious*.
I.O.W. = Isle of Wight〔英〕怀特岛。
I·o·wa [ˈaiəwə; ˋaɪəwə] *n*. 爱荷华〔美国的州名〕。**-wan** **1.** *a*. 爱荷华州的,爱荷华州人的。**2.** *n*. 爱荷华州人。
IP = **1.** initial point 起点。**2.** Internet Protocol【计】网际协议。
IPA = **1.** International Phonetic Association 国际语音学协会。**2.** International Phonetic Alphabet 国际音标。
ip·e·cac, ip·e·cac·u·an·ha [ˈipikæk, ˌipiˌkækjuˈænə; ˋɪpɪˏkæk, ˏɪpɪˏkækjuˋænə] *n*. **1.**【植】吐根。**2.** 吐根的茎和根;吐根制剂。
Iph·i·ge·ni·a [iˌfidʒiˈnaiə; ɪˏfɪdʒɪˋnaɪə] *n*.【希神】(迈锡尼王阿伽门农的女儿)伊芙琴尼亚。
IPI = International Press Institute 国际新闻学会。
IPO = initial public offering【经】(股票的)首次公开上市。
ip·o·moe·a [ˌipəˈmiːə, ˌaipəˈmiːə; ˏɪpəˋmɪə, ˏaɪpəˋmiə] *n*. **1.**【植】番薯属(*Ipomoea*)植物。**2.** 番薯。甘薯、蕹菜等。
IPPF = International Planned Parenthood Federation 国际计划生育联合会。
IPR = intellectual property rights 知识库权,智慧库权。
I.P.R. = Institute of Pacific Relations〔美〕太平洋学会。
ips, i.p.s. = inches per second 每秒英寸[…英寸/秒]。
ip·se dix·it [ˈipsi ˈdiksit; ˋɪpsɪ ˋdɪksɪt] (*pl*. ***ip·se dix·its***)〔L.〕武断的话;亲口所述(= he himself said it)。
ip·si·lat·er·al [ˌipsiˈlætərəl; ˏɪpsɪˋlætərəl] *a*. (身体的)同一侧的;影响身体的同一侧的。**-ly** *ad*.
ip·sis·si·ma ver·ba [ipˈsisimə ˈvəːbə; ɪpˋsɪsɪmə ˋvɝbə]〔L.〕作者的原话(= the very word)。
ip·so fac·to [ˈipsəu ˈfæktəu; ˋɪpsoˋfækto]〔L.〕照那个事实,根据事实本身。
ip·so ju·re [ˈipsəu ˈdʒuəriː; ˋɪpsoˋdʒuri]〔L.〕根据法律本身,依法律。
IPU = Inter-Parliamentary Union 各国议会联盟。
IPY = International Polar Year 国际极年。
IQ, I.Q. = intelligence quotient 智商,智力商数〔心理学家进行智力测验的术语〕。
i.q. =〔L.〕*idem quod* 同…(= the same as)。
IR = infrared.
Ir = iridium【化】元素铱的符号。
Ir. = Ireland; Irish.
ir- [iə; ɪr] *pref*.〔用于以 r 开始的字前面〕。**1.** 表示"不","非",如：*ir*replaceable, *ir*responsible, *ir*respective. **2.** 表示"进入"、"在内",如：*ir*regation, *ir*ruption.
I·ra [ˈaiərə; ˋaɪrə] *n*. 艾拉〔男子名〕。
IRA, I.R.A. = Irish Republican Army 爱尔兰共和军。
i·ra·cund [ˈairəkʌnd; ˋaɪrəkʌnd] *a*.〔古〕易怒的;暴躁的。**-di·ty** *n*.
i·ra·de [iˈrɑːdi; ɪˋrɑdɪ] *n*. **1.** (穆斯林)教徒的统治者的法令[教令]。**2.**【史】土耳其皇帝的敕令。
I·rak [iˈrɑːk; ɪˋrɑk] *n*. = Iraq.
I·ra·ki [iˈrɑːki; ɪˋrɑkɪ] *n*., *a*. = Iraqi.
I·ran [iˈrɑːn; ɪˋrɑn] *n*. 伊朗〔亚洲〕。
Iran. = Iranian.
IRANAIR = Iranian Airways 伊朗航空公司。
I·ra·ni·an [iˈreinjən; ɪˋrenɪən] **I** *a*. 伊朗的,伊朗人的,印欧语系的〔包括波斯语、普什图语、阿韦斯塔语、库尔德斯坦语等〕。**II** *n*. 伊朗人;伊朗语系。
Iraq [iˈrɑːk; ɪˋrɑk] *n*. 伊拉克〔亚洲〕。
I·ra·qi [iˈrɑːki; ɪˋrɑkɪ] **I** *n*. (*pl*. ～*s*) 伊拉克(*Iraq*)人;伊拉克人讲的阿拉伯语。**II** *a*. 伊拉克的;伊拉克人的;伊拉克人讲的阿拉伯语的。
i·ras·ci·ble [iˈræsibl; ɪˋræsɪbl] *a*. 易怒的,性情暴躁的。**-bil·i·ty, -ble·ness** *n*. **-bly** *ad*.
i·ra·ser [iˈreisə; ɪˋresɚ] = infra-red amplification by stimulated emission of radiation 红外线雷射器;红外线雷射。
i·rate [aiˈreit; ˋaɪret] *a*. 愤怒的,发怒的,激怒的。**-ly** *ad*. **-ness** *n*.
I.R.B. = Irish Republican Brotherhood 爱尔兰共和兄弟会。
IRBM = intermediate range ballistic missile 中程弹道飞弹。
IRC = **1.** International Red Cross 国际红十字会。**2.** Internet Relay Chat【计】英特网中继聊天。
ir·dome [ˈiədəum; ˋɪədom] *n*.【物】可通过红外线的整流罩,红外穹门。
ire [ˈaiə; ˋaɪr] *n*.〔诗〕怒火,忿怒。**-ful·ness** *n*.
Ire. = Ireland.
ire·ful [ˈaiəful; ˋaɪrfʊl] *a*.〔诗〕发怒的,忿怒的。**-ly** *ad*.
Ire·land [ˈaiələnd; ˋaɪrlənd] *n*. 爱尔兰。
I·rene [aiˈriːni, ˈairiːn; aɪˋrinɪ, aɪˋrin] *n*. **1.** 艾琳〔女子名〕。**2.**【希神】和平的女神。
i·ren·ic(al) [aiˈrenik(əl); aɪˋrɛnɪk(əl)] *a*. 促进和平的,和平的,爱好和平的。～ *means* 和平的手段。**-i·cal·ly** *ad*.
i·ren·i·con [aiˈreniˌkən; aɪˋrɛnɪkən] *n*. = eirenicon.
i·ren·ics [aiˈreniks, aiˈriːniks; aɪˋrɛnɪks, aɪˋrinɪks] *n*.〔作单数用〕(基督教各教派)和睦相处论〔促进基督教各派在神学观点的分歧上和平相处的主张或做法〕;和平相处神学。
I·re·ton [ˈaiətn; ˋaɪrtn] *n*. 艾尔顿〔姓氏〕。
Ir·i·an [ˌiəriˈɑːn; ˏɪrɪˋɑn] 伊里安〔"新几内亚"的印尼语名称〕。
i·rid [ˈairid; ˋaɪrɪd] *n*.【植】鸢尾科植物。
i·ri·da·ceous [ˌairiˈdeiʃəs; ˏaɪrɪˋdeʃəs] *a*.【植】鸢尾科的。
ir·i·dec·to·my [ˌiəriˈdektəmi, ˌaiəri-; ˏɪrɪˋdɛktəmɪ, ˏaɪrɪ-] *n*. 〔*pl*. **-mies** [-miːz; -miz]〕【医】虹膜切除术。
ir·i·des [ˈiəriˌdiːz, ˈaiəri-; ˋɪrɪˏdiz, ˋaɪrɪ-] iris 的复数。
ir·i·des·cence [ˌiriˈdesns; ˏɪrɪˋdɛsns] *n*. **1.**【气】虹彩。**2.** 彩虹色。
ir·i·des·cent [ˌiriˈdesnt; ˏɪrəˋdɛsnt] *a*. **1.**【气】虹彩的。**2.** 彩虹色的。**3.**【纺】闪光的,闪色的。～ *cloud* 虹彩云。～ *fabric* 闪光织物,闪色织物。**-ly** *ad*.
i·rid·ic [iˈridik, ai-; ɪˋrɪdɪk, aɪ-] *a*. **1.** 铱的;含铱的。**2.** 含四价铱化合物的。**3.** 虹膜的。
i·rid·i·um [aiˈridiəm; aɪˋrɪdɪəm] *n*.【化】铱。
ir·i·dos·mine [ˌiəriˈdɔzmin, ˌaiəri-, -ˈdɔsmiːn; ˏɪrɪˋdɑzmɪn, ˏaɪrɪ-, -ˋdɑsmin] *n*.【矿】铱锇矿(= iridosmium)。
I·ris [ˈaiəris; ˋaɪrɪs] *n*. **1.** 艾丽斯〔女子名〕。**2.**【希神】(为诸神报信的)彩虹女神。
i·ris [ˈaiəris; ˋaɪrɪs] *n*. (*pl*. **-es**; ***i·ri·des*** [ˈaiəridiːz; ˋaɪrɪdiz]) **1.**【解】(眼球的)虹膜。**2.** 虹;虹状物;虹彩,彩虹色。**3.**【物】膜片,可变光阑,(照相机的)光圈(= ～diaphragm)。**4.**【植】鸢尾属植物,鸢尾,蝴蝶花。**5.**【矿】彩虹色石英。～ **diaphragm**【摄】光圈。～**-in**【电视】圈入;【电影】淡入。～**-out**【电视】圈出;【电影】淡出。
i·ris·at·ed [ˈaiəriseitid; ˋaɪrɪsetɪd] *a*. 虹彩的,彩虹色的。
i·ris·a·tion [ˌairiˈseiʃən; ˏaɪrɪˋseʃən] *n*.【气】虹彩。
i·rised [ˈaiərist; ˋaɪrɪst] *a*. 彩虹色的。
I·rish [ˈaiəriʃ; ˋaɪrɪʃ] **I** *a*. 爱尔兰的;爱尔兰人的;爱尔兰语的。*too* (*bloody*) ～! 当然! **II** *n*. **1.** 爱尔兰语。**2.**〔*the* ～〕爱尔兰人。**3.**〔口〕怒火。*get one's* ～ *up*〔美〕发怒,大发脾气。～ **bridge** (横过路面的)石砌明水沟。～ **bull** 自相矛盾的说法。～ **coffee** 爱尔兰咖啡〔咖啡加

威士忌和奶油的饮料〕。～ **daisy**【植】蒲公英。～ **diamond** 水晶。～ **Free State** (1922—1937)爱尔兰自由邦。～ **Gaelic** 爱尔兰居尔特语。～ **hurricane**〔俚〕海上风平浪静时细雨蒙蒙。～**man** *n*. (*pl*. ～**men**) 爱尔兰人。～**man's dinner**〔美〕绝食。～**man's promotion** [**rise**] 明升暗降。～**man's sidewalk**〔美〕人行道。～**marathon**【美体】接力赛跑。～ **moss**【植】角叉菜。～ **nightingale**〔俚〕男高音歌唱者。～ **point** (**lace**) 爱尔兰手工花边。～ **potato**〔美〕马铃薯〔又叫 white potato, 即普通的白马铃薯,同 sweet potato 区别而言〕。～ **setter** 黑褐色长毛猎狗。～ **stew** 马铃薯洋葱煮羊肉。～ **terrier** 爱尔兰㹴。～ **welcome**〔俚〕欢迎随时光临的邀请。～ **wolfhound** 爱尔兰大猎狗。～**-woman** *n*. (*pl*. ～**women**) 爱尔兰妇女。**-ism** *n*. 爱尔兰习语,爱尔兰风土人情。**-ry** *n*. 1.〔集合词〕爱尔兰人。2. 爱尔兰人性格。

I·rish·ize [ˈaiəriʃaiz; ˋaɪrɪʃ͵aɪz] *vt*. 使爱尔兰化,使具有爱尔兰风格。

i·ri·tis [aiəˈraitis; aɪˋraɪtɪs] *n*.【医】虹膜炎。

irk [əːk; ɝk] *vt*.〔书〕使苦恼,使厌倦。*It ～s me to lie*. 我讨厌说假话。

irk·some [ˈəːksəm; ˋɝksəm] *a*. 讨厌的,令人厌倦的,使人厌烦的。**-ly** *ad*. **-ness** *n*.

Ir·kutsk [əːˈkutsk, iəˈkutsk; ɝˋkʊtsk, ɪrˋkʊtsk] *n*. 伊尔库次克(俄罗斯城市)。

IRMA = individual retirement mortgage account 个人退休抵押[按揭]账号〔指退休者以房产作抵押而每月获得一定数量的贷款〕。

IRO = International Refugee Organization 国际难民组织。

i·ron [ˈaiən; ˋaɪɚn] **I** *n*. 1. 铁。2. 铁器,铁制品;小刀,尖刀;熨斗,烙铁。3.〔俚〕(牛羊身上打的)烙印。4. 脚镣,手铐;马镫。5. (高尔夫球)铁头球棒。6.〔俚〕手枪,小枪。7. 铁剂,含铁补药。8. 铁色。9. (坚忍不拔的)毅力,意志。10.〔俚〕机器;机械设备〔相对于人员(personnel)而言〕。11.〔俚〕电脑硬件(= computer hardware)。*cast* ～ 铸铁。*pig* ～ 生铁。*scrap* ～ 废铁。*wrought* ～ 熟铁,锻铁。*Strike while the* ～ *is hot*.〔谚〕趁热打铁。*an electric* ～ 电熨斗。*an electric soldering* ～ 电烙铁。*fire* ～*s* 炉子的生火用具。*a smoothing* ～ 熨斗。*put sb. in* ～*s* 给某人系上脚镣手铐。*a barking* [*shooting*] ～ 手枪。*a man of* ～ 铁汉,意志坚强的人;铁面无私的人。～ *or gold* 毅力或金钱。*muscles of* ～ 非常结实的肌肉。*rule with a rod of* ～ 用高压手段统治。*as hard as* ～ 铁一样坚硬。*fresh from* (*off*) *the* ～*s* 崭新的;刚从学校出来的。*have* (*too*) *many* ～*s in the fire* 揽在手里的事过多。*in* ～*s* 带着脚镣手铐;【海】帆船掉不过头来。*the* ～ *hand in the velvet glove* 面善心狠。*put all* ～*s* [*every* ～] *in the fire* 使用一切手段[方法]。*pump* ～ (在健身房内)练举重。**II** *a*. 1. 铁的,铁制的。2. 铁似的,坚强的,顽强的;巩固的;坚忍不拔的。3. 严格的;冷酷无情的。～ *dross* [*dust*, *filings*] 铁屑。*an* ～ *constitution* 健壮的体格。*an* ～ *will* 坚强的意志。**III** *vt*. 1. 烫(衣服等)。2. 给…上脚镣手铐。3. 给…装铁具。— *vi*. 1. 烫衣服。2. (衣服等)被烫平。～ *out* 1. 烫平;用铁滚轧平。2.〔美〕使和解,调停。3. 压平(物价)。4.〔美俚〕杀掉。5. 消除 (～ *out misunderstandings* 消除误解)。～ **age** 1.〔神话〕黑铁时代。2. (人类的)颓废时期,末世。*the I- Age*【考古】铁器时代。～**bark** *n*.【植】1. 桉树属 (*Encalyptus*) 植物。2. 桉树属木材。～**bound** *a*. 1. 包铁的。2. 坚硬的;严厉的。3. 岩石围绕的,险阻的。～ **butt**〔口〕厚脸皮。*I- Chancellor*【史】铁血宰相〔指德国首相俾士麦〕。～ **channel** 槽钢。～**clad** 1. *a*. 装甲的〔现在多用 *armoured*〕;〔美〕严格的,无可推诿的(誓约等)(*an* ～*clad note*〔口〕有担保的期票。*an* ～*clad proof* 铁证)。2. *n*. 装甲舰。～ **curtain** 铁幕。～ **fisted** *a*. 吝啬的;残忍的。～ **foundry** 翻砂厂,铸铁厂,铸铁车间。～ **glance**【矿】镜铁矿。～**-gray**, ～**-grey** *a*. 铁灰色,灰白色。～**hand** 严厉的手段,严刑峻法。～**handed** *a*. 铁腕的,严厉的,用高压手段的。～ **hat**〔美俚〕礼帽。～**-hearted** *a*. 无情的,铁石心肠的。～ **horse**〔口〕火车头,机车。～ **house**〔美俚〕监狱。～ **lung** 铁肺〔人工呼吸器〕。**I-maiden** 铁女〔旧刑具名〕。～ **man** 1. 钢铁工人;〔美俚〕体力坚强的运动选手,铁汉。2.〔美俚〕银元。～**-master** 铁工厂老板。～ **melting furnace**【冶】化铁炉,熔铁炉。～**monger**〔英〕铁器商,五金商。～**mongery**〔英〕铁器类,五金制品类;铁器店,五金店。～**mo(u)ld** 1. *n*. (布等上的)铁锈迹;墨水斑点。2. *vt*., *vi*. (使)弄上锈迹[墨水迹];(使)生锈。～ **ore** 铁矿。～ **pony**〔美俚〕摩托车。～**-pumper**〔美俚〕举重者。～ **pyrite** 黄铁矿(= pyrite)。～ **rations**【军】(非有命令不得食用的)应急干粮。～ **rice bowl**〔中〕铁饭碗〔指收入与就业永远有保障而不受工作勤懒和业绩大小的影响〕。～ **rule** 苛政。～**rust** 铁锈。～ **sand** 铁砂。～**side** 1. 勇敢果断的人。2.〔I-〕〔常 *pl*.〕【英史】克伦威尔铁甲军。3.〔常 *pl*.〕铁甲舰。～**smith** 铁匠,锻工。～**stone** 1.【矿】铁石,含铁矿石,菱铁矿。2. (英国产)坚硬的白色瓷器〔又名 ～stone china〕。～**ware** 铁器,五金制品。～**-weed**【植】斑鸠菊属 (*Vernonia*) 植物。～**wire** 铁丝。～**wood**〔美〕木质坚硬的树;坚质木材(*a black* ～*wood* 野橄榄树)。～**work** 1. 铁工。2. 铁制品。3. (建筑物、船舶等的)铁制部分。～**worker** 1. 钢铁工人,铁器工人。2. 铁桥构架工。～**works** *n*.〔*sing*., *pl*.〕钢铁厂。

i·ron·er [ˈaiənə; ˋaɪɚnɚ] *n*. 1. 熨衣工。2. 轧布机;研光机;碾压机。

i·ron·ic(al) [aiəˈrɔnik(əl); aɪˋrɑnɪk(əl)] *a*. 1. 冷嘲的,反语的;讽刺的。2. 令人啼笑皆非的。～ *remarks* 冷言冷语。*an* ～ *smile* 冷笑。**-i·cal·ly** *ad*.

i·ron·ing [ˈaiəniŋ; ˋaɪɚnɪŋ] *n*. 1. 熨烫。2.〔集合词〕要烫的衣服;烫过的衣服。～ **board** [**table**] 熨衣台。

i·ron·ist [ˈaiərənist; ˋaɪrənɪst] *n*. 讽刺家,冷嘲者。

I·ron·side [ˈaiənsaid; ˋaɪɚn͵saɪd] *n*. 艾恩赛德〔姓氏〕。

i·ro·ny[1] [ˈaiərəni; ˋaɪrənɪ] *n*. 1. 反语;讽刺,讥讽。2.【修】反语法。*the* ～ *of fate* [*circumstances*] 命运的嘲弄。*Socratic* ～ 苏格拉底式的佯装无知法。

i·ron·y[2] [ˈaiəni; ˋaɪɚnɪ] *a*. 铁的;铁似的;含铁的。

Ir·o·quoi·an [͵irəˈkwɔiən; ͵ɪrəˋkwɔɪən] **I** *a*. 易洛魁语系的。**II** *n*. 1. 易洛魁人〔北美的一个印第安部族〕。2. 易洛魁语。

Ir·o·quois [ˈirəkwɔi, -kwɔiz; ˋɪrəkwɔɪ, -kwɔɪz] **I** *n*. 易洛魁人。**II** *a*. 易洛魁族的,易洛魁人的。

ir·ra·di·ance, ir·ra·di·an·cy [iˈreidiəns, -si; ɪˋredɪəns, -sɪ] *n*. 1. 发光;射出光线。2. 光辉,灿烂。3. 启示。4.【物】辐照度。

ir·ra·di·ant [iˈreidiənt; ɪˋredɪənt] *a*. 发光的;光辉的,灿烂的。

ir·ra·di·ate [iˈreidieit; ɪˋredɪ͵et] **I** *vt*. 1. 照耀;发光。2. 使明白,启发,阐明。3. 放射,扩散,送出。4. 用 X 射线,紫外线或日光等照射;【物】辐照。*a face* ～*d by* [*with*] *a smile* 喜气洋洋的脸。～ *the mind* 启发心窍。～ *a subject* 摆清问题。～ *energy* 发送出能量。～*d foods* 紫外线食品〔受紫外线照射使含有丙种维他命的食品〕。— *vi*. 发光,变得光辉灿烂。**II** *a*. 有放射力的,发光的。**ir·ra·di·a·tive** *a*. **ir·ra·di·a·tor** *n*.【物】辐射器。

ir·ra·di·a·tion [i͵reidiˈeiʃən; ɪ͵redɪˋeʃən] *n*. 1. 照耀;发光。2. 阐明,启发。3.【物】光渗,照光,辐照。4.【医】照射。5. 扩散。～ *damage* 辐射损伤。～ *sickness*【医】辐射病。～ *of excitation*【医】兴奋扩散。

ir·ra·di·ca·ble [iˈrædikəbl; ɪˋrædɪkəbḷ] *a*. 无法根除的。

ir·ra·tion·al [iˈræʃənəl; ɪˋræʃənəl] **I** *a*. 1. 无理性的。2. 不合理的;荒谬的。3.【数】无理的。～ *conduct* 荒唐

的行为。*an* ～ *expression* 无理式。*an* ～ *equation*【数】无理方程式。*an* ～ *function* 无理函数。*an* ～ *number* 无理数。**II** *n*. **1**. 无理性的生物。**2**. 无理数。**-ly** *ad*. **-ness** *n*.

ir·ra·tion·al·ism [iˈræʃənəlizəm; ɪˋræʃənəl͵ɪzəm] *n*.【哲】**1**. 非理性思想,不合理性的信仰[行为]。**2**. 非(反)理性主义。**ir·ra·tion·al·ist** *n*.

ir·ra·tion·al·i·ty [i͵ræʃəˈnæliti; ɪ͵ræʃəˋnælətɪ] *n*. **1**. 非理性;不合理。**2**. 不合理的事。

ir·ra·tion·al·ize [iˈræʃənəlaiz; ɪˋræʃənəl͵aɪz] *vt*. 使无理性;使不合理。

Ir·ra·wad·dy [͵irəˈwɔdi; ͵ɪrəˋwɑdɪ] *n*. 伊洛瓦底江〔缅甸〕。

ir·re·al·iz·a·ble [iˈriəlaizəbl; ɪˋrɪəlaɪzəbl] *a*. **1**. 不能实现的,不能达到的。**2**. 不能兑成现金的。

ir·re·claim·a·ble [͵iriˈkleiməbl; ͵ɪrɪˋkleməbl] *a*. 不能恢复的,不能取回的;不能开垦的;不能矫正的。**-bly** *ad*.

ir·rec·og·niz·a·ble [iˈrekəgnaizəbl; ɪˋrɛkəg͵naɪzəbl] *a*. 不能认识的,不能辨认的;不能承认的。

ir·rec·on·cil·a·ble [iˈrekənsailəbl; ɪˋrɛkən͵saɪləbl] **I** *a*. **1**. 不能和解的。**2**. 不可调和的 (*to*; *with*)。*be* ～ *to* [*with*] *sb*. 同某人势不两立。～ *enemies* 死敌。～ *as fire and water* 如水火不相容。**II** *n*. 不能和解的人;(政治上的)死硬派;〔*pl*.〕不能调和的思想[信仰等]。**-bil·i·ty** *n*. **-bly** *ad*.

ir·re·cov·er·a·ble [͵iriˈkʌvərəbl; ͵ɪrɪˋkʌvərəbl] *a*. 不能恢复的;不能挽回的;医治不好的;不能收回的(贷款等)。～ *losses* 无法弥补的损失。**-bly** *ad*.

ir·re·cu·sa·ble [͵iriˈkjuːzəbl; ͵ɪrɪˋkjuzəbl] *a*. 回绝不了的,不可抛弃的,不可拒绝的。**-bly** *ad*.

ir·re·deem·a·ble [͵iriˈdiːməbl; ͵ɪrɪˋdiməbl] **I** *a*. **1**. 不能赎回的。**2**. (公债、纸币等)不能偿还的;不能兑成现金的。**3**. 难矫正的;不能恢复[医治、补救]的。～ *banknote* 不兑现纸币。**II** *n*. 定期偿还公债〔指到期之前不能偿还〕。**-bly** *ad*.

ir·re·den·ta [͵iriˈdentə; ͵ɪrɪˋdɛntə] *n*. (根据历史或居民的种族)应属甲国而被乙国统治的地区。

ir·re·den·tism [͵iriˈdentizəm; ͵ɪrɪˋdɛntɪzəm] *n*. 领土收复主义,民族统一主义。

ir·re·den·tist [͵iriˈdentist; ͵ɪrɪˋdɛntɪst] **I** *n*. (十九世纪意大利的)领土收复主义者,民族统一主义者。**II** *a*. **1**. 领土收复主义的,民族统一主义的。**2**. 住在收复地区的;关于有待收复地区居民的。

I

ir·re·duc·i·ble [͵iriˈdjuːsəbl; ͵ɪrɪˋdjusəbl] *a*. **1**. 不能降低[削减]的。**2**.【医】难回复的,难复位的。**3**.【数】不能化简的,不能约的,既约的。～ *equation* 不可约方程。～ *fraction* 既约分数。～ *minimum* 最小值。**-bil·i·ty** *n*. **-bly** *ad*.

ir·re·flex·ive [͵iriˈfleksiv; ͵ɪrɪˋflɛksɪv] *a*.【物】漫反射的,反自反的。～ *relation*【逻】反(非)自反关系。

ir·ref·ra·ga·ble [iˈrefrəgəbl; ɪˋrɛfrəgəbl] *a*. 不能驳倒的,不可争辩的,不能否认的。**-bil·i·ty** *n*. **-bly** *ad*.

ir·re·fran·gi·ble [͵iriˈfrændʒibl; ͵ɪrɪˋfrændʒɪbl] *a*. **1**. 不能违犯的。**2**.【光】不可折射的。**-bly** *ad*.

ir·ref·u·ta·ble [iˈrefjutəbl; ɪˋrɛfjʊtəbl] *a*. 无可辩驳的,不能反驳的,驳不倒的。*an* ～ *fact* 无可辩驳的事实。**-bil·i·ty** *n*. **-bly** *ad*.

irreg. = irregular; irregularly.

ir·re·gard·less [͵iriˈgɑːdlis; ͵ɪrɪˋgɑrdlɪs] *a*., *ad*.〔非正式用语〕= regardless.

ir·reg·u·lar [iˈregjulə; ɪˋrɛgjələ] **I** *a*. **1**. 不规则的,无规律的。**2**. 非正规的;非正式的;法律上无效的。**3**. 不合常规的,不正当的。**4**. 不整齐的;参差不一的。**5**.【语法】不规律变化的。**6**.〔美〕(商品)等外的,有小缺陷的。*be* ～ *in one's attendance* 不时缺席。*an* ～ *curve* 不规则曲线;曲线板。*an* ～ *liner* 不定期航船。～ *menstruation* 月经不调。*an* ～ *physician* 无照开业的内科医生。～ *troops* 非正规军。～ *conduct* 不正当的行为。*an* ～ *coast line* 曲折的海岸线。～ *teeth* 不整齐的牙齿。～ *verbs* 不规则动词。*slightly* ～ *shirts* 略有缺陷的衬衫。**II** *n*. **1**. 非正规的人[物]。**2**.〔常 *pl*.〕非正规兵。**3**.〔美〕〔常 *pl*.〕等外品。**-ly** *ad*.

ir·reg·u·lar·i·ty [i͵regjuˈlæriti; ɪ͵rɛgjʊˋlærətɪ] *n*. **1**. 不规则,无规律。**2**. 非正则,非正式。**3**. 不正规的事物,违法乱纪,非法行为。**4**. 不整齐,参差不一。**5**.【语法】不规则变化。**6**. 例外。～ *of attendance* 有时缺席。*internal* ～【物】内在紊乱。*operating* ～ 工作事故。

ir·rel·a·tive [iˈrelətiv; ɪˋrɛlətɪv] *a*. (与…)无关系的 (*to*); 不相干的。**-ly** *ad*.

ir·rel·e·vance, ir·rel·e·van·cy [iˈrelivəns, -si; ɪˋrɛlɪvəns, -sɪ] *n*. **1**. 不恰当;无关系;不相干,不对题。**2**. 缺乏时代性。

ir·rel·e·vant [iˈrelivənt; ɪˋrɛlɪvənt] *a*. **1**. 不恰当的;(与…)无关系的;不相干的 (*to*), 不对题的。**2**. 缺乏时代性的,落后于潮流的。*What he said is* ～ *to the matter*. 他所说的和事实本身毫无关系。**-ly** *ad*.

ir·re·liev·a·ble [͵iriˈliːvəbl; ͵ɪrɪˋlivəbl] *a*. 不能解决的;不治的;不能减轻的;不可刻成浮雕的。

ir·re·li·gion [͵iriˈlidʒən; ͵ɪrəˋlɪdʒən] *n*. 无宗教;轻视宗教,无宗教信仰,反对宗教。**-ist** *n*. 无宗教信仰者,反对宗教者。

ir·re·li·gious [͵iriˈlidʒəs; ͵ɪrəˋlɪdʒəs] *a*. **1**. 无宗教的,不信[敌视]宗教的。**2**. 违反宗教的,亵渎的,不敬神的。**-ly** *ad*.

ir·rem·e·a·ble [iˈremiəbl, -ˈriːmi-; ɪˋrɛmɪəbl, -ˋrimɪ-] *a*.〔古〕一去不复返的,有去无回的。

ir·re·me·di·a·ble [͵iriˈmiːdiəbl; ͵ɪrəˋmidɪəbl] *a*. **1**. 医治不好的。**2**. 不可挽回的,不可弥补的,难改正的。*an* ～ *disease* 不治之症。～ *faults* 无可挽救的过失。**-bleness** *n*. **-bly** *ad*.

ir·re·mis·si·ble [͵iriˈmisibl; ͵ɪrəˋmɪsɪbl] *a*. **1**. 不能原谅的,不可宽恕的。**2**. 不能避免的,必须承担的。**-bly** *ad*.

ir·re·mov·a·ble [iriˈmuːvəbl; ͵ɪrəˋmuvəbl] *a*. **1**. 不能移动的;不能清除的。**2**. 不能罢免的,不能撤职的。**-bil·i·ty** *n*. **-bly** *ad*.

ir·rep·a·ra·ble [iˈrepərəbl; ɪˋrɛpərəbl] *a*. 不能修补的;不能恢复的,不能挽回的,不能弥补的。*an* ～ *loss* 无可弥补的损失。**-ness** *n*. **-bly** *ad*.

ir·re·peal·a·ble [͵iriˈpiːləbl; ͵ɪrəˋpiləbl] *a*. **1**. 执行(决议)的,维护(法令)的。**2**. 不能放弃的,无法否定的。

ir·re·place·a·ble [͵iriˈpleisəbl; ͵ɪrəˋplesəbl] *a*. **1**. 不能恢复原状的。**2**. 不能替代的,失掉了就无法弥补的。

ir·re·plev·i·a·ble [͵iriˈpleviəbl; ͵ɪrəˋplɛvɪəbl] *a*.【法】不准保释的;(物件)被扣押的;不能收回的。

ir·re·press·i·ble [͵iriˈpresəbl; ͵ɪrəˋprɛsəbl] **I** *a*. 压制不住的,约束不了的。**II** *n*. 控制不住的人。**-bil·i·ty** *n*. **-bly** *ad*.

ir·re·proach·a·ble [͵iriˈprəutʃəbl; ͵ɪrəˋprotʃəbl] *a*. 无可指摘的,无缺点的,无过失的。**-bil·i·ty** *n*. **-bly** *ad*.

ir·re·sist·i·ble [͵iriˈzistəbl; ͵ɪrəˋzɪstəbl] *a*. **1**. 不可抗拒的,压制不了的,非常坚强的。**2**. 具有非常的魅力的。*an* ～ *force*【法】不可抗力。*She saw an* ～ *skirt in the store window*. 她看见商店的橱窗里有一条叫人着迷的裙子。**-bil·i·ty** *n*. **-bly** *ad*.

ir·res·o·lu·ble [iˈrezəljubl; ɪˋrɛzəljubl] *a*. 不可分解的;不能溶化的,不能解决的。

ir·res·o·lute [iˈrezəljuːt; ɪˋrɛzə͵ljut] *a*. 无决断的,犹豫不决的,优柔寡断的,踌躇不定的;动摇的。**-ly** *ad*. **-ness** *n*.

ir·res·o·lu·tion [ˈi͵rezəˈljuːʃən; ˋɪ͵rɛzəˋljuʃən] *n*. 无决断,优柔寡断;无定见。

ir·re·solv·a·ble [͵iriˈzɔlvəbl; ͵ɪrɪˋzɑlvəbl] *a*. **1**. 不能分解的,不能分离的。**2**. 不能解决的。

·re·spec·tive [ˌiris'pektiv; ˏɪrɪs`pɛktɪv] *a*. 不顾[不考虑,不同](…)的 (*of*)。~ *of a person* 不顾某人。~ *of the consequences* 不顾后果。~ *of age* 不同年龄大小。~ *as to whether … or …* 不同其是否…。**-ly** *ad*.

·re·spir·a·ble [ˌiris'paiərəbl; ˏɪrɪs`paɪrəbḷ] *a*. 不适于呼吸的。

·re·spon·si·ble [ˌiris'pɔnsəbl; ˏɪrɪ`spɑnsəbḷ] **I** *a*. **1**. 不承担责任的,不需负责任的。**2**. 无责任感的;不负责任的;不可靠的。*It is very ~ of him not to answer my letter*. 不回复我的信是他太不负责任。**II** *n*. 不承担责任的人,无责任心的人。**-bil·i·ty, -ness** *n*. **-bly** *ad*.

·re·spon·sive [ˌiris'pɔnsiv; ˏɪrɪs`pɑnsɪv] *a*. **1**. 不回答的。**2**. 没有反应的 (*to*)。**-ly** *ad*. **-ness** *n*.

·re·ten·tion [ˌiri'tenʃən; ˏɪrə`tenʃən] *n*. **1**. 不能保持,无把持力。**2**.【医】(小便的)失禁。

·re·ten·tive [ˌiri'tentiv; ˏɪrə`tentɪv] *a*. 不能保持的,无保持力的;不能保留的。

·re·trace·a·ble [ˌiri'treisəbl; ˏɪrə`tresəbḷ] *a*. 难查出的,不能探索的,无法描绘的。**-bly** *ad*.

·re·triev·a·ble [ˌiri'triːvəbl; ˏɪrə`trivəbḷ] *a*. 不能弥补的,不能挽救的,不能恢复的。*an ~ loss* 无可弥补的损失。**-bil·i·ty** *n*. **-bly** *ad*.

·rev·er·ence [i'revərəns; ɪ`rɛvərəns] *n*. **1**. 不虔诚;不尊敬。**2**. 无礼;傲慢。**3**. 不敬的行为[言语]。*be held in ~* 丢丑。*They did ~s to the teachers*. 他们对老师很不尊敬。

·rev·er·ent [i'revərənt; ɪ`revərənt] *a*. **1**. 不虔诚的;不尊敬的。**2**. 无礼的。**-ly** *ad*.

·rev·er·en·tial [ˌirevə'renʃəl; ˏɪrevə`renʃəl] *a*. = irreverent.

·re·vers·i·ble [ˌiri'vəːsəbl, -sibl; ˏɪrə`vɝsəbḷ] *a*. **1**. 不可逆的,不能翻转的,不能倒置的,不能倒退的。**2**.【法】不能取消的,不能改变的。~ *cycle*【机】不可逆循环。~ *process*【物】不可逆过程。~ *reaction*【化】不可逆反应。*the ~ decisions of the court* 不可撤消的法院判决。**-bil·i·ty** *n*. 不可逆性。**-bly** *ad*.

·rev·o·ca·ble [i'revəkəbl; ɪ`revəkəbl] *a*. **1**. 不能取消的,不可废止的。**2**. 不能改变的;不能挽回的。~ *letter of credit* 不可撤销信用证。*make an ~ decision* 做出不可变更的决定。*speak ~ words* 讲了决定性的言语。**-a·bil·i·ty, -ness** *n*. **-bly** *ad*.

·ri·den·ta [ˌiri'dentə; ˏɪrə`dɛntə] *n*. = irredenta.

·ri·ga·ble ['irigəbl; `ɪrɪgəbḷ] *a*. 可灌溉的。

·ri·gate ['irigeit; `ɪrəˏget] *vt*. **1**. 灌溉。**2**.【医】冲洗(伤口)。**3**. 滋润,使清新。*a land ~d by many streams* 有不少河流灌溉的土地。~ *the desert* 灌溉荒地。—*vi*. **1**. 进行灌溉。**2**. 〔美俚〕饮酒过度。

·ri·ga·tion [ˌiri'geiʃən; ˏɪrə`geʃən] *n*. **1**. 灌溉;水利。**2**.【医】冲洗(法),〔*pl*.〕冲注洗剂。*bring the farmland under ~* 使农田水利化。*an ~ canal* [*channel*] 灌溉渠。*an ~ project* 灌溉计划。**-al** *a*. **-ist** *n*. 灌溉者,水利专家。

·ri·ga·tor ['irigeitə; `ɪrəgetɚ] *n*. **1**.【农】灌溉者;灌溉设备[用具]。**2**.【医】冲洗器。

·rig·u·ous [i'rigjuːəs; ɪ`rɪgjuəs] *a*. 〔古〕**1**. 潮湿的,水分充分的。**2**. 灌溉的。

·ri·ta·ble ['iritəbl; `ɪrətəbl] *a*. **1**. 易怒的,急躁的。**2**.【医】易激动的,过敏性的。**-bil·i·ty** [-'biliti; -`bɪlətɪ], **-ness** *n*. **-bly** *ad*.

·ri·tant ['iritənt; `ɪrətənt] **I** *a*. 刺激的,有刺激性的;引起发炎的。~ *gas*【军】刺激性毒气。**II** *n*. 刺激,刺激品,刺激剂。

·ri·tate ['iriteit; `ɪrətet] *vt*. **1**. 激怒,使发怒,使急躁。**2**. 刺激,使兴奋。**3**. 使不舒服,使发炎,使疼痛。—*vi*. 起使人不愉快的影响[效果]。

·ri·tat·ed [ˌiri'teitid; ˏɪrə`tetɪd] *a*. **1**. 被激怒的,生了气的。**2**. (皮肤等)变粗的;发红的;因刺激而发炎的。*be ~ at* [*by, against, with*] 因…而发怒[着急]。

ir·ri·tat·ing ['iriˌteitiŋ; `ɪrəˏtetɪŋ] *a*. **1**. 惹人生气的,使人不愉快的。**2**.【医】起刺激作用的。*He brought us many ~ news*. 他带给我们许多令人沮丧的消息。**-ly** *ad*.

ir·ri·ta·tion [ˌiri'teiʃən; ˏɪrɪ`teʃən] *n*. **1**. 激怒,愤怒,生气,焦躁。**2**.【医】刺激,兴奋,疼痛,发炎。**3**. 刺激物。*mechanical ~* 机械性刺激。

ir·ri·ta·tive ['iriteitiv; `ɪrəˏtetɪv] *a*. 使人发怒的,使人不快的;刺激性的。

ir·ro·ta·tion·al [ˌirəu'teiʃənl; ˏɪro`teʃənḷ] *a*.【物】无旋的。~ *motion* 无旋运动。

ir·rupt [i'rʌpt; ɪ`rʌpt] *vi*. **1**. 突然侵入,突然闯入 (*into*),猛然发作。**2**.【生态】(动物的)激增繁殖。**-tion** *n*. **-tive** *a*.

IRSC = International Radium Standard Commission 国际镭标准委员会。

IR seeker = infrared seeker 红外搜索器。

ir·tron ['əːtrɔn; `ɝtrɑn] *n*.【天】类星星系,红外光射电源。

Ir·vin ['əːvin; `ɝvɪn] *n*. 欧文〔姓氏,男子名〕。

Ir·ving ['əːviŋ; `ɝvɪŋ] *n*. **1**. 欧文〔姓氏,男子名〕。**2**. **Washington** ~华盛顿·欧文〔1783—1859,美国作家〕。

Ir·win ['əːwin; `ɝwɪn] *n*. 欧文〔姓氏,男子名〕。

is [强 iz, 弱(在浊音后)z,(在清音后)s; ɪz, z, s] be 的第三人称,单数,现在时,陈述语气。

is. = island; isle.

ISA = individual savings account 〔英〕个人储蓄账户。

Isa. = Isaiah.

I.S.A. = International standard atmosphere 国际标准大气(压)。

I·saac ['aizək; `aɪzək] *n*. **1**. 艾萨克〔男子名〕。**2**.【圣】以撒〔希伯来族长,犹太人的始祖亚伯拉罕和撒拉所生的独生子〕。

Is·a·bel ['izəbel; `ɪzəbɛl] *n*. 伊莎贝尔〔女子名, Isabelle, Isabella 的异体〕。

Is·a·bel·la [ˌizə'belə; ˏɪzə`bɛlə] *n*. 伊莎贝拉〔女子名, Bella 的爱称〕。

is·a·bel·line [ˌizə'belin; ˏɪzə`belɪn] *a*. 灰黄色的。

is·a·cous·tic [ˌaisə'kuːstik; ˏaɪsə`kustɪk] *a*.【物】等音强的;与等音强有关的。

i·sa·go·ge ['aisəˌgəudʒi; ˏaɪsə`godʒɪ] *n*. (对研究一门科学的)序言,概论。**-gog·ic** [-'gɔdʒik; -`gɑdʒɪk] *a*.

I·sa·iah [ai'zaiə; aɪ`zaɪə] *n*. **1**. (公元前七、八世纪希伯来大预言家)以赛亚。**2**.【圣】(《圣经·旧约》中的)《以赛亚书》。**3**. 艾赛亚〔男子名〕。

i·sal·lo·bar [ai'sæləbɑː; aɪ`sæləˏbɑr] *n*.【气】等变压线。**-ic** *a*. (~*ic chart* 等变压图)。

i·sa·tin ['aisətin; `aɪsətɪn] *n*.【纺】靛红,2,3-吲哚二酮。

ISBN = International Standard Book Number 国际标准书号。

ISC = **1**. International Sericultural Commission 国际蚕丝业委员会。**2**. International Space Congress 国际宇宙空间大会。

Is·car·i·ot [is'kæriət; ɪs`kerɪət]【宗】**1**. 以色加略人〔指出卖耶稣的犹大〕。**2**. 叛徒。

is·ch(a)e·mi·a [is'kiːmiə; ɪs`kimɪə] *n*.【医】局部缺血,局部贫血。**-mic** *a*.

is·chi·ad·ic, -at·ic [ˌiski'ædik, -'ætik; ˏɪskɪ`ædɪk, -`ætɪk] *a*. **1**.【解】臀部的,坐骨(神经)的。**2**.【动】坐节的;(昆虫的)侧板的。

is·chi·um ['iskiəm; `ɪskɪəm] *n*. (*pl*. *is·chi·a* ['iskiə; `ɪskɪə]) **1**.【解】坐骨。**2**.【动】坐节;(昆虫的)侧板。

ISDN = Integrated Subscriber Digital Network【电信】综合业务数字网〔俗称"一线通",指以现代数字技术在标准通话线上兼作通话和数据服务〕。

-ise[1] *suf*. 构成名词,表示"状态","性质"〔*cf*. -ice〕:

I

exercise, franchise.

-ise[2] *suf*. = -ize.

-ish[1] *suf*. 构成形容词,表示 1."…的","…民族的","…语的":English, heathenish. 2."…似的","…气的","患…的":fiendish, foolish, feverish. 3."…一样的":childish, monkish. 4."微…的":coldish. 5.〔口〕"左右":4:30ish 四点半左右,come at tenish next Monday 下星期一十点左右来,I'll call on you dinnerish. 我大约在吃饭前后来找你。

-ish[2] *suf*. 构成动词:abolish, finish, punish.

Ish·er·wood [ˈiʃə(:)wud; ˋɪʃɚwud] *n*. 伊舍伍德〔姓氏〕。

Ish·ma·el [ˈiʃmeiəl; ˋɪʃmɪəl] *n*. 1.【圣】(亚伯拉罕的庶子)以实玛丽。2. 被社会唾弃的人。

Ish·ma·el·ite [ˈiʃmiəlait; ˋɪʃmɪəlˏaɪt] *n*. 1.【圣】以实玛利的后裔。2. 被社会唾弃的人。**-it·ish** *a*.

i·sin·glass [ˈaiziŋglɑːs; ˋaɪzɪŋˏglæs] *n*. 1. 鱼胶。2.【地】白云母薄片。

I·sis [ˈaisis; ˋaɪsɪs] *n*.【埃神】爱希丝〔司生育与繁殖的女神〕。

isl. (*pl*. *isls*) = island; isle.

Is·lam [ˈizlɑːm, -læm, -ləm; ˋɪzlɑm, -læm, -ləm] *n*. 1. 伊斯兰教,回教。2.〔集合词〕伊斯兰教信徒,穆斯林。3. 伊斯兰教国家,伊斯兰世界。

Is·lam·a·bad [isˈlɑːməbɑːd; ɪsˋlɑməbɑd] *n*. 伊斯兰堡〔巴基斯坦首都〕。

Is·lam·ic, Is·lam·it·ic [izˈlæmik, ˌizləˈmitik; ɪzˋlæmɪk, ˏɪzləˋmɪtɪk] *a*. 伊斯兰教的,穆斯林的。

Is·lam·ism [ˈizləmizəm; ˋɪzləmɪzəm] *n*. 伊斯兰教教义〔习俗〕;回教。

Is·lam·ite [ˈizləmait; ˋɪzləmˏaɪt] *n*. 伊斯兰教徒,穆斯林。

Is·lam·ize [ˈisləmaiz, ˈiz-; ˋɪsləmˏaɪz, ˋɪz-] *vt*., *vi*. (*-iz·ed*, *-iz·ing*) 使皈依伊斯兰教,使改信伊斯兰教。**-i·za·tion** *n*.

is·land [ˈailənd; ˋaɪlənd] **I** *n*. 1. 岛,岛屿。2. 岛状物;孤立的地区;孤立的组织。3.【船】航空母舰或船只的上层建筑〔如舰桥、舰台等〕。4.〔美〕大草原中的森林地带。5. (街道中的)交通安全岛,让车地点;路岛(= traffic safety island)。6.【解】岛;脑岛;胰岛。7. (喷气式飞机中的)导管固定部。*a floating* ~ 浮岛。~ *territories* 属岛。*an* ~ *of resistance*【军】孤立支撑点。*a pedestrian* ~ (交叉口处的)行人安全岛。*a safety* [*street*] ~ (路中)安全岛。*blood* ~ 血岛。*~s of Langerhans*【医】胰岛。***Islands of the Blessed*** [***Blest***]【希神】极乐岛,福人岛。**II** *a*. 岛的,岛国的。*an* ~ *empire* 岛国。**III** *vt*. 1. 使成岛状。2. 使孤立。3. 像岛屿一样分布。*a prairie ~ed with grooves* 树丛像岛屿分布着的大草原。~**-hopping** *n*.【军】越岛作战。~ **hopping strategy**【军】越岛作战战术。~ **platform** (火车站上的)岛式站台。~ **universe** 岛宇宙〔以前 external galaxy 的称呼〕。**-less** *a*. 无岛屿的。

is·land·er [ˈailəndə; ˋaɪləndɚ] *n*. 岛民;岛上居民。

isle [ail; aɪl] **I** *n*. (小)岛。★在诗或散文中通常作地名用,如 Isle of Wight, British Isles 等。**II** *vt*. 使成岛;使隔离。— *vi*. 住在岛上。**Isles of the Blessed** = Islands of the Blessed.

is·let [ˈailit; ˋaɪlɪt] *n*. 1. 小岛;岛状地带,孤立地点。2.【解】胰岛。*~s of Langerhans* = islands of Langerhans.

Isls., **isls.** = islands.

ism [ˈizəm; ˋɪzəm] *n*. 主义,学说,制度。*an age of ~s* 主义、学说多的时代。*various ~s of modern literature and art* 当代文艺的各种流派。

-ism [-izəm; -ɪzəm] *suf*. 构成抽象名词,表示:1."主义","学说","信仰","制度":marxism, atomism. 2."行为","行动":criticism, vandalism. 3."状态":barbarism. 4."特征","特性":colloquialism. 5."病态"alcoholism.

Is·ma·i·li·a [ˌizmaiˈliːə; ˏɪzmaɪˋlɪə] *n*. 伊斯梅利亚〔埃及城市〕。

Is·ma·il·i·an [ˌismeiˈiliən; ˏɪsmeˋɪlɪən] *n*. (穆斯林)伊斯迈里派教徒。

is·n't [ˈiznt; ˋɪznt] 〔口〕= is not.

I.S.O. = Imperial Service Order〔英〕帝国服役勋章。

i·so- *comb*. *f*. 构成科技性质的名词或形容词。1. 表"等","同":isocheim, isochore, isochronism, isomorphic, isotope. 2. 表示"同分异构","异构"。

i·so·a·cet·y·lene [ˌaisəuəˈsetiliːn; ˏaɪsoəˋsɛtɪlin] *n*.【化】异乙炔。

i·so·ag·glu·ti·na·tion [ˌaisəuəˌgluːtəˈneiʃən; aɪsoˏglutəˋneʃən] *n*. 同种凝集反应,同族凝集现象。

i·so·ag·glu·ti·na·tive [ˌaisəuəˈgluːtiˌneitiv; ˏaɪsoˋglutɪˏnetɪv] *a*. 同种凝集的,同族凝集的。

i·so·ag·glu·ti·nin [ˌaisəuəˈgluːtinin; ˏaɪsoəˋgluˏtənɪn] *n*. 同种凝集素,同族凝集素。

i·so·an·ti·bod·y [ˌaisəuˈæntibɔdi; ˏaɪsoˋæntɪbɑdɪ] *n*. (*pl*. ***-bodies***)【医】异抗体,同族抗体。

i·so·an·ti·gen [ˌaisəuˈæntidʒən; ˏaɪsoˋæntɪdʒən] *n*.【医】异抗原,同种抗原。

i·so·bar [ˈaisəubɑː; ˋaɪsobɑr] *n*. 1.【气】等压线。2.【化】同量异位素。

i·so·bar·ic [ˌaisəuˈbærik; ˏaɪsoˋbærɪk] *a*. 1.【气】等压线的。2.【化】同量异位的。~ *line* 等压线。~ *surface* 等压面。~ *nucleus* 同量异位核。~ *spin* 同位旋。

i·so·bath [ˈaisəuˌbɑːθ; ˋaɪsoˏbæθ] *n*. 等(水)深线。

i·so·bu·tyl·ene [ˌaisəuˈbjuːtiliːn; ˏaɪsoˋbjutəlin] *n*.【化】异丁烯(= isobutene)。

i·so·cheim [ˈaisəuˌkaim; ˋaɪsoˏkaɪm] *n*.【气】等冬温线。**-al** *a*.

i·so·chor, i·so·chore [ˈaisəuˌkɔː; ˋaɪsoˏkɔr] *n*.【物】等体积线,等容线。~ ***of reaction***【物】反应与温热关系。**-ic** *a*.

i·so·chro·mat·ic [ˌaisəukrəuˈmætik; ˏaɪsokroˋmætɪk] *a*.【物】等色的,单色的,一色的;【摄】正色的。

i·soch·ro·nal, -nic, -nous [aiˈsɔkrənl, -nik, -nəs; aɪˋsɑkrənl, -nɪk, -nəs] *a*. 1. 等时的。2. 发生于相等间隔时间内的。~ *oscillation* 等时振荡。**-ly** *ad*. **-nism** *n*.【物】等时性。

i·soch·ro·nize [aiuˈsɔkrəˌnaiz; aɪˋsɑkrəˏnaɪz] *vt*. (*-nized*, *-niz·ing*) 使等时,使发生在相等间隔时间内。

i·soch·ro·ous [aiˈsɔkrəuəs; aɪˋsɑkroəs] *a*. 等色的,同色的。

i·so·cli·nal, i·so·clin·ic [ˌaisəuˈklainl, -ˈklinik; ˏaɪsoˋklaɪnl, -ˋklɪnɪk] **I** *a*. 等倾斜的,等斜的。~ *fault*【地】等斜断层。~ *valley*【地】等斜谷。~ *line on a map* 地图上的等斜线。**II** *n*.【物】等磁倾线,等倾线。**-ly** *ad*.

i·soc·ra·cy [aiˈsɔkrəsi; aɪˋsɑkrəsɪ] *n*. (*pl*. ***-cies***) 平等参政权,平等参政权制度。

i·so·cy·a·nate [ˌaisəuˈsaiəneit; ˏaɪsoˋsaɪəˏnet] *n*.【化】异氰酸盐。

i·so·cy·a·nine [ˌaisəuˈsaiəniːn, -nin; ˏaɪsoˋsaɪənin, -nɪn] *n*.【纺】异花青。

i·so·cy·clic [ˌaisəuˈsaiklik, -ˈsiklik; ˏaɪsoˋsaɪklɪk, -ˋsɪklɪk] *a*.【化】等节环(型)的,同素的,〔尤指〕碳环的(= carbocyclic)。

i·so·di·a·met·ric [ˌaisəuˌdaiəˈmetrik; ˏaɪsoˏdaɪəˋmɛtrɪk] *a*. 等直径的,等轴的。

i·so·di·a·phere [ˌaisəuˈdaiəfiə; ˏaɪsoˋdaɪəfɪr] *n*.【物】等超额中子核素。

i·so·di·mor·phism [ˌaisəudaiˈmɔːfizm; ˏaɪsodaɪˋmɔrfɪzm] *n*.【化】同二晶(现象)。**-phous** [-fəs; -fəs] *a*.

i·so·dose [ˈaisəuˌdəus; ˋaɪsoˏdos] *a*.【物】等剂量的,

剂量线的。

i·so·dy·nam·ic [ˌaisəudaiˈnæmik; ˏaɪsodaɪˋnæmɪk] *a*. 【物】等力的;等能的。~ *line*【物】等(磁)力线。

i·so·e·lec·tric [ˌaisəuiˈlektrik; ˏaɪsoɪˋlɛktrɪk] *a*. 【物】等电位的,零电位差的。~ *point*【物】等电离点。

i·so·e·lec·tron·ic [ˌaisəuilekˈtrɔnik; ˏaɪsoɪlɛkˋtrɑnɪk] *a*. 等电子的。**-i·cal·ly** *ad*.

i·so·eu·gen·ol [ˌaisəuˈjuːdʒinɔl; aɪsoˋjudʒɪnɑl] *n*. 【化】异丁子香酚。

i·so·ga·mete [ˌaisəuˈgæmit, -gəˈmiːt; ˏaɪsoˋgæmɪt, -gəˋmit] *n*. 【生】同形配子。**-met·ic** [-ˈmetik; -ˋmɛtɪk] *a*.

i·sog·a·my [aiˈsɔgəmi; aɪˋsɑgəmɪ] *n*. 【生】同配生殖。**-mous** [-məs; -məs] *a*.

i·so·gen·e·sis [ˌaisəuˈdʒenisis; ˏaɪsoˋdʒɛnɪsɪs] *n*. 【生】同源。

i·sog·e·nous [aiˈsɔdʒənəs; aɪˋsɑdʒənəs] *a*. 【生】有同源的。**-ly** *ad*.

i·sog·e·ny [aiˈsɔdʒəni; aɪˋsɑdʒənɪ] *n*. 【生】同源。

i·so·ge·o·therm [ˌaisəuˈdʒiəθəːm; ˏaɪsoˋdʒɪəˏθɝm] *n*. 等地温线。**-al** *a*.

i·so·gloss [ˈaisəuglɔs; ˋaɪsoˏglɑs] *n*. 【语】1. 同言线,同语线,等语线,(方言地图上的)同言线。2. 某特定地区的语言特点。

i·so·gon [ˈaisəugɔn; ˋaɪsoˏgɑn] *n*. 1. 等角多角形。2. 【气】同风向线。3. 【物】等(磁)偏线。

i·sog·o·nal [aiˈsɔgənl; aɪˋsɑgənḷ] *a*. 【数】等角的。~ *transformation* 等角变换。

i·so·gon·ic [ˌaisəuˈgɔnik; ˏaɪsoˋgɑnɪk] I *a*. 1. 等偏角的。2. 【物】等偏角的;等(磁)偏的;等偏线的。II *n*. 等(磁)偏线。

i·sog·o·ny [aiˈsɔgəni; aɪˋsɑgənɪ] *n*. (生物体各部的)对称发育。

i·so·gram [ˈaisəugræm; ˋaɪsogræm] *n*. 【气】等值线(图)。

i·so·graph [ˈaisəugrɑːf; ˋaɪsogræf] *n*. 1. 【空】等线图。2. 【自】(解微分方程用的)求根仪。**-ic** *a*.

i·so·gyre [ˈaisəudʒaiə; ˋaɪsodʒaɪr] *n*. 【物】同消色线。

i·so·he·dral [ˌaisəuˈhiːdrəl; ˏaɪsoˋhidrəl] *a*. 【物】等面的。

i·so·hel [ˈaisəuhel; ˋaɪsoˏhɛl] *n*. (地图上的)等日照线。

i·so·hy·dric [ˌaisəuˈhaidrik; ˏaɪsoˋhaɪdrɪk] *a*. 【化】等氢离子的。~ *solutions* 等氢离子溶液。

i·so·hy·et [ˌaisəuˈhaiət; ˏaɪsoˋhaɪət] *n*. 【气】等雨量线。**-al** *a*.

i·so·lan·tite [ˌaisəuˈlæntait; ˏaɪsoˋlæntaɪt] *n*. 【无】爱索兰太特〔陶瓷高频绝缘材料,状如滑石〕。

i·so·late [ˈaisəleit; ˋaɪsəˏlet] I *vt*. 1. 隔离,使孤立。2. 【电】绝缘。3. 【化】使离析。4. 【微】使(细菌)分离;使与种群隔离。*an* ~*d patient* 被隔离的病人。~ *oneself from all society* 隐居。II *n*. 【微】分离菌;隔离种群。~**d point**【数】孤立点,孤点。

i·so·la·tion [ˌaisəuˈleiʃən; ˏaɪsoˋleʃən] I *n*. 1. 隔离,分离;孤立,单独。2. 封锁交通。3. 【电】绝缘。4. 【化】离析(作用)。*fight in* ~ 孤军作战。II *a*. 孤立主义的,孤立主义者的。~ **hospital** 隔离医院。*an* ~ *booth* 隔音室。~ **ward** 隔离病室。**-ism** *n*. 孤立主义。**-ist** *n*. 孤立主义者,孤立派。

i·so·la·tor [ˈaisəleitə; ˋaɪsəˏletɚ] *n*. 1. 隔离者,隔离物;孤立者。2. 【电】绝缘体(= insulator)。

i·so·lead [ˈaisəuliːd; ˋaɪsoˏlid] *n*. 【军】等提前量曲线(= ~ curve)。

i·so·lette [ˌaisəˈlet; ˏaɪsəˋlɛt] *n*. 〔(F.) isolette, 商标名〕不足月婴儿人工抚育器。

i·so·leu·cine [ˌaisəuˈluːsiːn, -sin; ˏaɪsoˋlusin, -sɪn] *n*. 【化】异亮胺酸。

i·so·line [ˈaisəulain; ˋaɪsoˏlaɪn] *n*. = isogram.

i·sol·o·gous [aiˈsɔləgəs; aɪˋsɑləgəs] *a*. 【化】同构异素的。**-logue**, **-log** [-səˌlɔːg, -ˌlɔg; -səˏlɔg, -ˏlɑg] *n*.

i·so·mag·net·ic [ˌaisəumægˈnetik; ˏaɪsomægˋnɛtɪk] I *a*. 1. 等磁的。2. 等磁力点的。~ *lines on a map* 地图上的等磁线。II *n*. 等磁线。

i·so·mer [ˈaisəumə; ˋaɪsomɚ] *n*. 【化】同分异构体;【物】同质异构素。~ *of nucleus* 原子核的同质异构素。*an optical* ~旋光异构体。

i·so·mer·ic(al) [ˌaisəuˈmerik(əl); ˏaɪsoˋmɛrɪk(əl)] *a*. 【化】同分异构的,同质异能的。~ *change* 异构变化。*an* ~ *nucleus* 同质异构核。**-cal·ly** *ad*.

i·som·er·ism [aiˈsɔmərizəm; aɪˋsɑmərɪzəm] *n*. 同分异构性;同质异构性。*core* ~ 原子核心同质异构性。

i·som·er·i·za·tion [aiˌsɔməraiˈzeiʃən; aɪˏsɑməraɪˋzeʃən] *n*. 【化】异构化(作用)。

i·som·er·ous [aiˈsɔmərəs; aɪˋsɑmərəs] *a*. 1. 等分数的。2. 【植】等基数的;【动】(昆虫)等跗节的。3. 【化】= isomeric.

i·so·met·ric [ˌaisəuˈmetrik; ˏaɪsoˋmɛtrɪk] I *a*. 1. 【化、物】等轴的;立方的;等轴晶的。2. 等体积的,等容积的。3. 等比例的;等角的,等距离的;等径的。~ *system*【物】立方系,立方晶系。~ *drawing* 等角图;等距画法。~ *projection* 等角投影。II *n*. 等容线(= ~ line)。~ **exercise** 静力锻炼肌肉运动〔如以手推墙等〕。

i·so·met·ri·cal [ˌaisəuˈmetrikəl; ˏaɪsoˋmɛtrɪkəl] *a*. = isometric (*a*.). **-ly** *ad*.

i·so·met·rics [ˌaisəuˈmetriks; ˏaɪsoˋmɛtrɪks] *n*. 【体】静力锻炼法〔*cf*. isometric exercise〕。

i·so·me·tro·pi·a [ˌaisəumiˈtrəupiə; ˏaɪsomɪˋtropɪə] *n*. 【医】(两眼的)折光相等。

i·som·e·try [aiˈsɔmitri; aɪˋsɑmɪtrɪ] *n*. 1. 度量相等。2. 【地】等高。

i·so·morph [ˈaisəumɔːf; ˋaɪsomɔrf] *n*. 【生】同态体,(类质)同晶型体。

i·so·mor·phic [ˌaisəuˈmɔːfik; ˏaɪsoˋmɔrfɪk] *a*. 1. 同晶型的。2. 【生化】同形的,同态的(= isomorphous)。

i·so·mor·phism [ˌaisəuˈmɔːfizəm; ˏaɪsoˋmɔrfɪzm] *n*. 1. 【生】同态性,同形性,同态现象。2. 【化】(类质)同晶型(现象)。3. 【数】同构。

i·so·mor·phous [ˌaisəuˈmɔːfəs; ˏaɪsoˋmɔrfəs] *a*. 【物、化】同晶的,同晶型性,同态的,类质同像的,类质同晶型的。~ *crystal* 同形晶体。~ *pair* 同形偶。~ *replacement* 同形置换。~ *substitution* 同型替换。

i·so·ni·a·zid [ˌaisəuˈnaiəzid; ˏaɪsoˋnaɪəzɪd] *n*. 【药】异烟肼,雷米封〔肺结核药〕。

i·son·o·my [aiˈsɔnəmi; aɪˋsɑnəmɪ] *n*. 法律平等;权利平等;特权平等。

i·so·oc·tane [ˌaisəuˈɔktein; ˏaɪsoˋɑkten] *n*. 异辛烷。

i·so·path·ic [ˌaisəuˈpæθik; ˏaɪsoˋpæθɪk] *a*. 【医】同源疗法的。

i·sop·a·thy [aiˈsɔpəθi; aɪˋsɑpəθɪ] *n*. 同源疗法。

i·so·phane, **-phene** [ˈaisəufein, -fiːn; ˋaɪsofen, -fin] *n*. 【气】(植物生长阶段中)同时开花线,同时线;等物候线。

i·so·phyl·lous [ˌaisəuˈfiləs; ˏaɪsoˋfɪləs] *a*. 等叶的。

i·so·phyl·ly [ˈaisəuˌfli; ˋaɪsoˏflɪ] *n*. 【植】等叶式。

i·so·pi·es·tic [ˌaisəupaiˈestik; ˏaɪsopaɪˋɛstɪk] I *a*. 示等压的。II *n*. 等压线(= isobar)。

i·so·pleth [ˈaisəupleθ; ˋaɪsoˏplɛθ] *n*. 【气】等值线。

i·so·pod [ˈaisəpɔd; ˋaɪsəˏpɑd] I *n*. 等足目 (*Isopoda*) 动物。II *a*. 等足目动物的 (= isopodan)。

i·so·prax·ism [ˌaisəuˈpræksizəm; ˏaɪsoˋpræksɪzm] *n*.

i·so·pre·na·line [ˌaisəuˈprenəli(ː)n; ˏaɪsoˋprɛnəlin] *n*. 【药】异丙基肾上腺素。

i·so·prene [ˈaisəupriːn; ˋaɪsoˏprin] *n*. 【化】异戊间二烯。

i·so·pro·pyl [ˌaisəuˈprəupil; ˏaɪsoˋpropɪl] *n*. 【化】异丙

I

基。

i·sop·te·rous [ai'sɔptərəs; aɪ`sɑptərəs] ***a*.**【动】(昆虫)等翅目的。

i·so·pulse ['aisəupʌls; `aɪsopʌls] ***n*.**【无】衡定脉冲。

i·sos·ce·les [ai'sɔsili:z; aɪ`sɑsl͵iz] ***a*.**【数】(三角形)等腰的,等边的。*an* ~ *triangle* 等腰三角形。

i·sos·cope ['aisəuskəup; `aɪsos͵kop] ***n*.**【自】同位素探伤仪。

i·so·seis·mal, i·so·seis·mic [͵aisəu'saizməl, -mik; ͵aɪso`saɪzməl, -mɪk] **I *a*. 1.** 等震的。**2.** 等震线的。**II *n*.** 等震线。

is·os·mot·ic [͵aisɔs'mɔtik; ͵aɪsɑs`mɑtɪk] ***a*.** = isotonic.

i·so·spon·dy·lous [͵aisəu'spɔndiləs; ͵aɪso`spɑndɪləs] ***a*.**【动】等椎类鱼的,与等椎类(鱼)有关的。

i·so·spore ['aisəuspɔ:; `aɪso͵spɔr] ***n*.**【生】同形孢子。

i·so·spo·rous [͵aisəu'spɔ:rəs; ͵aɪso`spɔrəs] ***a*.** 孢子同型的(= homosporous)。

i·so·spo·ry ['aisəu͵spɔ:ri; `aɪso͵spɔrɪ] ***n*.**【生】孢子同型。

i·sos·ta·sy [ai'sɔstəsi; aɪ`sɑstəsɪ] ***n*. 1.** 压力均衡。**2.**【地】地壳均衡。*the theory of* ~ 地壳均衡说。

i·so·stat·ic [͵aisəu'stætik; ͵aɪso`stætɪk] ***a*.** 均衡的。~ *compensation*【地】均衡补偿。

i·so·ste·mo·ny [͵aisəu'sti:məni; ͵aɪso`stimənɪ] ***n*.**【植】同基数雄蕊式。**-nous *a*.**

i·so·there ['aisəu͵θiə; `aɪso͵θɪr] ***n*.**【气】等夏温线。**-er·al** [ai'sɔθirəl; aɪ`sɑθɪrəl] ***a*.**

i·so·therm ['aisəuθə:m; `aɪso͵θɝm] ***n*.**【气】等温线,恒温线。

i·so·ther·mal [͵aisəu'θə:məl; ͵aɪso`θɝml] **I *a*.** 等温的,等温线的。~ *atmosphere* 等温大气。**II *n*.** 等温线,恒温线。*a reduced* ~ 对比等温线。

i·so·tone ['aisəutəun; `aɪso͵ton] ***n*. 1.**【物】等中子(异位)数;【化】同中子异荷素。**2.** 等渗性,等压性,等张性。

i·so·ton·ic [͵aisəu'tɔnik; ͵aɪso`tɑnɪk] ***a*. 1.**【化】等中子异位的。**2.** 等张的,等渗压的。~ *concentration*【化】等渗[等压]浓度。~ *muscle*【医】等张肌。**-i·cal·ly *ad*. -nic·i·ty** [-'nisiti; -nɪsətɪ] ***n*.**

i·so·tope ['aisəutəup; `aɪsotop] ***n*.**【化、物】同位素。

i·so·top·ic [͵aisəu'tɔpik; ͵aɪso`tɑpɪk] ***a*.** 同位素的。~ *abundance ratio* 同位素丰度比。~ *spin* 同位旋。**-al·ly *ad*.**

i·sot·o·py [ai'sɔtəpi; aɪ`sɑtəpɪ] ***n*. 1.**【数】合伦。**2.**【物、化】同位素学。

i·so·tron ['aisəutrɔn; `aɪso͵trɑn] ***n*.**【物】同位素分析器。

i·so·trope ['aisəuətrəup; `aɪso͵trop] ***n*.**【物】均质,各向同性,各向同性晶体。

i·so·trop·ic, i·sot·ro·pous [͵aisəu'trɔpik, ai'sɔtrəpəs; ͵aɪso`trɑpɪk, aɪ`sɑtrəpəs] ***a*.** 各向同性的。~ *scattering* 各向同性散射。

i·sot·rop·ism [ai'sɔtrəpizəm; aɪ`sɑtrəpɪzəm] ***n*.**【物】各向同性(现象)。

i·sot·ro·py [ai'sɔtrəpi; aɪ`sɑtrəpɪ] ***n*.** 各向同性(现象),无向性,均质性。

i·so·type ['aisəutaip; `aɪsotaɪp] ***n*. 1.** 等型〔适应于不同地区生活的动物[植物]〕。**2.** 反映统计数字的象征性图表。

ISP = Internet service provider【计】因特网服务提供者。

I-spy ['ai'spai; `aɪ`spaɪ] ***n*. 1.** 捉迷藏。**2.** 一种文字游戏。

Isr. = Israel.

Is·ra·el ['izreiəl; `ɪzreəl] ***n*. 1.** 以色列〔亚洲〕。**2.**〔总称〕以色列人,犹太人;〔喻〕【宗】上帝的选民。

Is·rae·li [iz'reili; ɪz`relɪ] **I *n*.** 以色列人,犹太人。**II *a*.** 以色列的,犹太的;以色列人的,犹太人的。

Is·ra·el·ite ['izriəlait; `ɪzrɪəl͵aɪt] **I *n*. 1.** 古以色列人;犹太人。**2.**【宗】上帝的选民。**II *a*.** 古以色列(人)的,犹太(人)的。

Is·ra·el·it·ic [͵izriə'litic; ͵ɪzrɪə`lɪtɪk], **Is·ra·el·it·is**[h] ['izriəlaitiʃ; `ɪzrɪəlaɪtɪʃ] ***a*.** 以色列人的,犹太人的。

Is·sei ['i:s'sei; `is`se] ***n*.** (*pl*. **~s**) 第一代移居美国的日本人。

is·su·a·ble ['iʃu(:)əbl; `ɪʃuəbl] ***a*. 1.** 可发表的;可发行的。**2.** 可争辩的,可辩论的;可辩护的。**-bly *ad*.**

is·su·ance ['iʃu(:)əns; `ɪʃuəns] ***n*. 1.** 发行,颁布。**2.** 配给。

is·su·ant ['iʃu(:)ənt; `ɪʃuənt] ***a*. 1.**〔罕〕发表的;发行的。**2.**【纹】只能见上部的。*a lion* ~ 半身狮子。

is·sue ['iʃu:; `ɪʃu] **I *n*. 1.** 出口;河口。**2.** 结果,结局;成绩。**3.** 收获,收益。**4.** 颁布,发行;发行额;发行物。**5.** 流出,(血、水等的)涌出;【病】出血,流脓。**6.**【法】子孙,子女。**7.** 论点;争论问题;商讨;【法】争点,争端。*bring sth. to a successful* ~ 使某事圆满结束。*decide the* ~ *of the battle* 决定战役胜败。*a bank of* ~ 发行银行。*a new* ~(纸币等的)新发行;(书报等的)新版;(军需品等的)新发给。*items of* ~(军队的)补给品。*monetary* ~ 货币放行。*the* ~ *of an order* 命令的颁布。*the latest* ~ 最近一期报刊。*an* ~ *of blood* = *a bloody* ~ 出血,流血。*die without* ~死后无子无孙。*a major* ~ *of principle* 大是大非的问题。*a minor* [*side*] ~ 枝节问题。*debate an* ~ 讨论问题。*distinguish right from wrong on* ~*s of major importance* 分清大是大非。*the burning* ~ *of the day* 燃眉之急的问题。***at*** ~不一致,不相容;【法】在争论中;待裁决的(*be at* ~ *with sb*. 与某人意见不一致。*point at* ~ 争点)。***bring an*** ~ ***to a close*** 把问题解决。***face the*** ~正视事实,认真对待事实。***force an*** ~ 强迫对方表示态度。***in*** ~ 在争论中。***in the*** ~ 结局,到头来。~ ***of fact*** 事实上的争点。~ ***of law*** 法律上的争点。***join*** ~ (***with***) 对…持异议,和…争持;【法】诉讼双方一同提出争持焦点请求裁决。***make an*** ~ ***of sth*.** 把某事当作问题,反对…。***put to the*** ~ 使对问题便于作出决定。***raise a new*** ~ 提出新论点。***ride off on a side*** ~专谈枝节问题。***take*** ~ ***with sb*.** 反对某人,同某人争执。**II *vi*. 1.** 出,流出,涌出,发出。**2.** 生,起;得…结果。**3.** (报刊等的)发行,发布。**4.** 提出抗议,进行辩护。**5.**【法】传代,传下。*The students* ~*d out into the streets*. 学生涌到街上。*Blood* ~*d from the cut*. 血从伤口流出。*smoke issuing from a chimney* 从烟囱里涌出的烟。*The oversight* ~*d in heavy losses*. 疏忽造成重大损失。~ *forth* [*out*] 出来,跳出,迸出。~ *from* 生自…,是…的子孙。— ***vt*. 1.** 使流出,放出。**2.** 发行(邮票等);发布(命令);发行(书刊);出版。**3.** 发给,配给。~ *an order* 发布命令。~ *ammunition to troops* 发弹药给军队。~ **advocacy** 议题述评〔一种需耗费巨资的广告手段〕。~ **positioning**【政】对竞选问题的表态。

is·sue·less ['isju:lis; `ɪsjulɪs] ***a*. 1.** 无子女的。**2.** 无结果的。*an* ~ *effort* 徒劳。**3.** 无可争辩的。

is·su·er ['isju(:)ə; `ɪsjuə] ***n*.** 发行者,出版者。

-ist[1] *suf*. 构成名词,表示 **1.** 动作的实践者:antagon*ist*, tour*ist*. **2.** "…主义者",信仰者:athe*ist*, imperial*ist*, social*ist*. **3.** "专业人员":pian*ist*, botan*ist*, dent*ist*, flor*ist*.

-ist[2] *suf*. 构成形容词,表示"具有…特性的":dilettant*ist*.

Is·tan·bul [͵istæn'bu:l; ͵ɪstæn`bul] ***n*.** 伊斯坦布尔〔旧称君士坦丁堡〕。

Isth., isth. = isthums.

isth·mi·an ['isθmiən; `ɪsθmɪən] **I *a*. 1.** 地峡的。**2.**〔I-〕希腊科林斯(Corinth)地峡的;巴拿马地峡的。*the I- Canal* 巴拿马运河。**II *n*.** 地峡地带居民。***I- Games*** 科林斯地峡运动大会〔古希腊四大竞技之一,其盛大仅次于 *Olympic Games*〕。

isth·mus ['isməs, 'isθməs; `ɪsməs, `ɪsθməs] ***n*.** (*pl*. ~*es*) **1.** 地峡,地颈,土腰。**2.**〔the I-〕(巴拿马)地峡;(苏

伊士)地峡。3.【解】峡,器官峡,管峡。~ *of thyroid* 甲状腺峡。

is·tic [ˈistik; ˋɪstɪk], **-is·ti·cal** [-tikəl, -tɪkəl] *suf*. 构成形容词,如:real*istic*, art*istic*.

is·tle [ˈistli; ˋɪstlɪ] ***n***. 龙舌兰纤维〔从中、南美出产的龙舌兰科植物提制而成,用以制绳索、网、篮等编制物〕。

ISV = International Scientific Vocabulary 国际通用科技词汇。

it[1] [it; ɪt] ***n***.〔英口〕意大利苦艾酒。

it[2] [it; ɪt] **I** ***pro***. (*sing*. *nom*. ***it***; *obj*. ***it***; *poss*. ***its***; *pl*. *nom*. ***they***; *obj*. ***them***; *poss*. ***their***) 它,这。**1**.〔指已说过的东西,指无生命的东西,也可指不分性别的幼儿、动物〕。*Is this the peony? No,* ~ *is the tree-peony*. 这是芍药吗? 不,这是牡丹。*He took a stone and threw* ~. 他拾起一块石头,把它扔了出去。*The child lost its way*. 这孩子迷路了。**2**.〔指心中记着或成为问题的人物、事情和行为〕。*Go and see who* ~ *is*. 去看看是谁? *It's me*.〔口〕是我(=It is I.)。*Oh, it's you!* 哦,是你呀! *It's the girls having their rehearsal*. 是女同学在排戏。*It's the wind shaking the window*. 是风刮得窗户响。**3**.〔用作无人称动词的主语,或表示天气、时日、距离、状态、情况、事体、温度、问候语等〕。*It rains*. 下雨了。*It is cold*. 天冷。*It is a long way to the sea*. 离海很远。*It is five minutes' walk*. 要走五分钟。*Is* ~ *well with you?* 你身体好吗? *We had a splendid time of* ~. 那时候我们真快乐。*There* ~ *is, do what you like*. 好罢,你高兴怎样就怎样办。*run for* ~ 逃走。**4**.〔预用 it 代表其后所说的事实上的主语[受词]〕。*It is right to do so*. 这样做是对的。*It is no use trying*. 试也无用。*It is certain that we shall succeed*. 我们是一定会成功的。*It is a nuisance, this delay*. 这样拖延,实在是讨厌。*I don't think* ~ *worth-while taking such trouble*. 我想不值得费这么大的事了。**5**.〔作先行代词,用于表示强调的句型中〕。*It is the factory that we have been wanting to visit*. 这就是我们一直想访问的工厂。*It was here that I first met him*. 这就是我初次与他见面的地方。*It is I that am fortunate*. 幸运的是我〔句中动词应和 I 的人称数相一致〕。**6**.〔用于作及物动词用的名词之后作受词〕。*cab* ~ 坐车去。*foot* ~ 走。*lord* ~ 摆架子。*queen* ~ 扮演女王;玩女王派头。**7**.〔口语中用作某种动词的含糊的受词〕。*as ill luck will have* ~ 偏偏不巧。*fight* ~ *out* 打到底。*get with* ~ 振作精神。*Go* ~ *while you are young*. 趁你还年轻就努力干罢。*have* ~ *one's own way I have done* ~我搞糟了。*Keep at* ~. 坚持下去! ***as*** ~ ***is*** [***was***] 事实上,既然如此(*As* ~ *is, we can hardly get to the station by 6 o'clock*. 事实上,我们六点钟以前是很难赶到车站的。)。***as*** ~ ***were*** 似乎,可以说是(*This book give, as* ~ *were, a picture of the evil old society*. 这本书可以说是罪恶的旧社会的一幅图景)。**II** ***n***. **1**.〔俚〕绝妙的人;理想的东西;登峰造极。*In a lilac sun bonnet she was* ~. 她戴着一顶紫色遮阳帽,漂亮极了。*For barefaced lying you are really* ~. 以无耻造谣而论,你真算得上天下第一。★作此义解时,通常写作斜体并加重发音。**2**.〔口〕性的魅力。*have* ~ 有性感。**3**.〔美俚〕傻瓜,笨蛋。**4**.(瞎子摸鱼游戏中的)瞎子。**5**.〔俚〕讨厌的人。*He is a perfectly* ~. 他太讨厌了。**6**.〔常作 I-〕自大的人,自负者。**7**.〔英口〕= *Italian vermouth*.

It., Ital. = **1**. *Ital*ian. **2**. *Ital*ic. **3**. *Ital*y.

ITA = Independent Television Authority.〔英〕独立电视局。

it·a·col·u·mite [ˌitəˈkɔljumait; ˏɪtəˋkɑljəˏmaɪt] ***n***.【地】(淤积岩层中的)晶莹小颗砂石。

it·a·con·ic [ˌitəˈkɔnik; ˏɪtəˋkɑnɪk] **acid**【化】亚甲基丁二酸,衣康酸,乌头二酸。

I·tal·ia [iˈtɑːljɑː; ɪˋtɑljɑ] ***n***.〔It.〕意大利(=Italy)。

I·tal·ian [iˈtæljən; ɪˋtæljən] **I** ***a***. 意大利的;意大利人的;意大利语的;意大利文化的。**II** ***n***. 意大利人;意大利语。~ **cloth**【纺】意大利棉毛呢,(英国制)黑色直贡呢。~ **East Africa** 意大利从前的东非殖民地。~ **hand** **1**. 暗中干预,不露痕迹的操纵。**2**. = ~ handwriting. ~ **handwriting** 意大利字体〔现今英法意所通行的书写体〕〔*cf*. Gothic〕。~ **iron** 圆筒形烫斗〔用以烫皱花边〕。~ **sonnet** = petrarchan sonnet. ~ **warehouse** 意大利杂货店。~ **warehouseman** 意大利杂货商。

I·tal·ian·ate [iˈtæljəneit; ɪˋtæljənˏet] **I** ***a***. 意大利形式[外貌,风格]的。**II** ***vt***. 使意大利化(= Italianize)。

I·tal·ian·ism [iˈtæljənizəm; ɪˋtæljənɪzm] ***n***. 意大利式;意大利精神[气质];意大利腔;意大利语调;对意大利特色的爱好。

I·tal·ian·ize [iˈtæljənaiz; ɪˋtæljənˏaɪz] ***vt***., ***vi***. 意大利化。

I·tal·ic [iˈtælik; ɪˋtælɪk] **I** ***a***. **1**.【印】意大利字体的,斜体的。**2**.〔I-〕古代意大利(人)的,意大利语族的。~ *type* 斜体活字。**II** ***n***. **1**.〔主 *pl*.〕斜体字〔*cf*. Roman〕。**2**.〔I-〕意大利语族。*in* ~*s* 用斜体。*I quote the passage; the* ~*s are mine*. 我引用这一节,着重点是我加上的。

i·tal·i·cise, -cize [iˈtælisaiz; ɪˋtælɪˏsaɪz] ***vt***. 用斜体字印刷;在字下划线表示(排斜体)。**-ci·za·tion** [iˌtælisaiˈzeiʃən; ɪˏtælɪsaɪˋzeʃən] ***n***.

I·tal·i·cism [iˈtælisizəm; ɪˋtælɪsɪzəm] ***n***. = Italianism.

I·tal·i·ot, I·tal·i·ote [iˈtæliət, iˈtæliəut; ɪˋtælɪət, ɪˋtælɪˏot] **I** ***n***.【史】意大利南部古希腊殖民地居民。**II** ***a***. 意大利南部古希腊殖民地的。

It·a·ly [ˈitəli; ˋɪtlɪ] ***n***. 意大利〔欧洲〕。

ITC = Infantry Training Centre 步兵训练中心。

itch [itʃ; ɪtʃ] **I** ***n***. **1**. 痒; [the ~]【医】疥癣。**2**. 热望,渴望。*have an* ~ *for*... 心里很想…。*the barber's* ~ 须癣。*the grocer's* ~ 脓疱性湿疹。**II** ***vi***. **1**. 痒,发痒。**2**. 渴望,极想。*I scratched him where he* ~*ed*. 我搔他的痒处。~ *for a try* 跃跃欲试。*My fingers* ~ *to box his ears*. 我手痒,很想打他的耳光。~ **mite**【动】疥癣虫,痒螨。

itch·ing [ˈitʃiŋ; ˋɪtʃɪŋ] ***a***. **1**. 痒的。**2**. 渴望着的,焦急着的。*be* ~ *to do sth*. 渴望做某事。***have an*** ~ ***palm***〔口〕贪财。***have an*** ~ ***ear*** 想听闲话。

itch·y [ˈitʃi; ˋɪtʃɪ] ***a***. (***itch·i·er***; ***-i·est***) 生疥癣的,发痒的;渴想中的。**itch·i·ness** ***n***.

-ite *suf*. 构成名词,表示 **1**. "…的居民","…的后代","…分子","…党员","…主义者": Israel*ite*, Trotsky*ite*. **2**.〔学术用语〕(a)岩石、矿物的名称: dolom*ite*, haemat*ite*. (b)化石名称: ammon*ite*, trilob*ite*. (c)盐类名称: selen*ite*, sulf*ite*. (d)炸药名称: cord*ite*, dynam*ite*. (e)商标名称: ebon*ite*, vulcan*ite*.

i·tem [ˈaitəm, ˈaitem; ˋaɪtəm; ˋaɪtɛm] **I** ***n***. **1**. 条,条款,项目,品目,细目。**2**. (新闻的)一条,一则;(戏剧的)节目。*business* ~营业项目。~ *by* ~ 逐条。*end* ~*s* 成品。*local* ~*s* 地方新闻。**II** ***ad***.〔逐条列举时开头用〕又,同上。~ **pricing** (对出售商品的)逐件标价〔多指当局颁布的硬性规定〕。~ **veto** 提案部分项目否决权〔美国某些州州长的职权之一〕。

i·tem·ize [ˈaitəmaiz; ˋaɪtəmaɪz] ***vt***.〔美〕分条开列,详细列举。~ *a bill* 分别开账。*an* ~*d account* 细账。

it·er·ance, it·er·an·cy [ˈitərəns, -si; ˋɪtərəns, -sɪ] ***n***. 反复,重复,重复申说。

it·er·ate [ˈitəreit; ˋɪtəret] ***vt***. **1**. 反复,重复,重复地说。**2**. 叠代。**-a·tion** [ˌitəˈreiʃən; ˏɪtəˋreʃən] ***n***. **1**. 反复,重复地说。**2**. 叠代法,叠演。**-a·tive** ***a***. 反复的,重复的;叠代的,叠接的。

Ith·a·ca [ˈiθəkə; ˋɪθəkə] ***n***. **1**. 伊萨卡岛〔爱奥尼亚群岛之一,位于希腊西部爱奥尼亚海中,为希腊神话中

Ulysses 的故乡〕。2. 伊萨卡城镇〔美国〕。**-a·can** *a*.

ith·er [ˈiðə; ˋɪðə] *a*., *pro*. 〔Scot.〕= other; either.

I·thu·ri·el [iˈθjuəriəl; ɪˋθjʊrɪəl] *n*. (Milton 著《失乐园》中的)负责搜捕魔鬼的天使。~**'s spear** 验证真伪的可靠物。

itin. = itinerant; itinerary.

i·tin·er·a(n)·cy [iˈtinərə(n)si, aiˈt-; ɪˋtɪnərə(n)sɪ, aɪˋt-] *n*. 1. 巡回。2. 流动团体[组织]。3. 牧师轮流巡回制度。

i·tin·er·ant [iˈtinərənt; ɪˋtɪnərənt] **I** *a*. 巡回的,流动的。**II** *n*. 巡回者〔如巡回传教士;巡回法官;行商〕。~ *peddlers* 行商。*an* ~ *judge* 巡回法官。*an* ~ *library* 流动图书馆。

i·tin·er·ar·y [aiˈtinərəri, iˈt-; aɪˋtɪnəˏrərɪ, ɪˋt-] **I** *n*. 1. 旅行指南。2. 旅行日记。3. 旅行日程。4. 旅程,路线。**II** *a*. 巡回的,流动的;旅行的;旅行途中的,巡回中的。*an* ~ *map* 路线图。*an* ~ *pillar* [*column*] 路标。

i·tin·er·ate [iˈtinəreit, aiˈt-; ɪˋtɪnəret, aɪˋt-] *vi*. 巡回,巡游;巡回裁判。*an itinerating library* 流动图书馆。**-a·tion** *n*. = itineracy.

-i·tion *suf*. 构成名词,表示"动作","状态":defin*ition*, exped*ition*.

-i·tious *suf*. 构成形容词:amb*itious*, exped*itious*.

-i·tis *suf*. 表示"炎(症)":bronch*itis*, gastr*itis*.

-i·tive *suf*. 构成形容词及名词:appos*itive*, pun*itive*.

it'll [ˈitl; ˋɪtl̩] = it will; it shall.

ITO = International Trade Organization 国际贸易组织。

-i·tous *suf*. 构成形容词 = calam*itous*, felic*itous*.

its [its; ɪts] *pro*. 〔it 的所有格〕它的,其。*the plan and* ~ *realization* 计划及其实施。

it's [its; ɪts] 1. = it is. 2. = it has.

it·self [itˈself; ɪtˋsɛlf] *pro*. (*pl*. ***themselves***) 1. 它自己,它本身〔作为反身代词〕。*The dog is stretching* ~. 这条狗在伸懒腰。*The baby tripped and hurt* ~. 这娃娃摔倒跌伤了。2. 自身,本身〔也用以加强语气〕。*At last the house* ~ *fell down*. 房子终于自己倒了。*Doing is* ~ *learning*. 做本身就是学习。*Even the well* ~ *was empty*. 甚至连井也是空的。***by*** ~ 单独地,孤零零地;独立的。***in*** ~实质上,本身。***of*** ~ 自行,自然而然的。

it·sy·bit·sy [ˈitsiˈbitsi; ˋɪtsɪˋbɪtsɪ] *a*. 〔口〕1. 极小的,纤小的。2. 浮华而不实用的。

ITT = International Telephone and Telegraph Corporation 〔美〕国际电话电报公司。

ITTF = International Table Tennis Federation 国际乒乓球联合会。

it·ty-bit·ty [ˈitiˈbiti; ˋɪtɪˋbɪtɪ] *a*. 〔口〕不大点儿〔摹仿儿语〕(= itsybitsy)。

ITU = International Telecommunication Union (联合国)国际电信联盟。

ITV = 1. industrial television 工业电视。2. instructional television 教学电视。3. Independent Television 〔英〕独立电视公司〔英国商业电视网〕。

-ity *suf*. 构成抽象名词,表示"性质","状态","程度":calam*ity*, pur*ity*, solubil*ity*.

IU, I.U. = international unit(s)【生、药】国际单位。

IUCD = IUD.

I.U.D. = intrauterine device 子宫内(避孕)器具。

-i·um *suf*. 构成名词 1. 表示化学元素的拉丁名字:sod*ium*, ion*ium*. 2. 表示正离子:ammon*ium*, carbon*ium*.

IUPAC = International Union of Pure and Applied Chemistry 国际纯理论和应用化学联合会。

IUPAP = International Union of Pure and Applied Physics 国际纯理论和应用物理联合会。

IUS = International Union of Students 国际学生联合会。

I.V. = initial velocity 初速度。

i.v. = increase value 增值。

I·van [ˈaivən; ˋaɪvən] *n*. 1. 伊凡〔男子名, John 的体〕。2. 伊凡三世〔1440—1505, 世称俄国大公, 在位期1462—1505〕。3. 伊凡四世〔1530—1584, 世称伊凡雷帝1547—1548 年在位的俄国第一个沙皇〕。

IVBA = International Volleyball Association 国际排球合会。

I've [aiv; aɪv] = I have.

-ive *suf*. 构成形容词,表示 1. "…的","与…有关的","有…性质的":nat*ive*, substant*ive*. 2. "倾向于…活的":amus*ive*, creat*ive*.

Ives [aivz; aɪvz] *n*. 1. 艾凡斯〔男子名〕。2. Charles Edward ~ 查理·爱德华·艾凡斯〔1874—1954, 美国作家〕。3. James M. ~ 詹姆斯·姆·艾凡斯〔1824—1895, 国印刷术创始人之一〕。

IVF = in vitro fertilization【医】试管受精。

i·vied [ˈaivid; ˋaɪvɪd] *a*. 常春藤覆盖着的。

i·vo·ry [ˈaivəri; ˋaɪvərɪ] **I** *n*. 1. 象牙;(河马、独角鱼的牙齿。*artificial* ~人造象牙。*fossil* ~古代巨象的牙化石。2. 象牙色,乳白色。3. 〔*pl*.〕象牙雕制品,仿牙制品。4. 牙质(= dental ~)。5. 厚光纸。6. 〔常 *pl*〕〔俚〕牙齿;骰子;撞球;弹子;钢琴键。***show one's ivori*** 龇牙咧嘴。***solid*** ~〔美俚〕头脑迟钝的人。***wash one ivories*** 〔口〕喝酒。**II** *a*. 1. 象牙制成的,似象牙的。象牙色的,乳白色的。~ **black** 象牙墨〔象牙烧制的黑颜料〕。~**-billed woodpecker** 蓝黑色的白尖嘴啄木鸟 ~**-dome** *n*. 〔俚〕笨蛋。~ **nut** 象牙椰子,植物象牙(vegetable ~)。~ **palm** 象牙椰子树。~ **paper** (艺术用的)带象牙光泽的厚光纸。~ **tower** 象牙之塔。~**towered** *a*. 关在象牙之塔内的。~ **white**, ~ **yellow** 白色。~**-white** *a*. 乳白色的。

Ivory Coast [ˈaivəriˈkəust; ˋaɪvərɪˋkost] 象牙海岸〔洲〕。

i·vy [ˈaivi; ˋaɪvɪ] **I** *n*. 【植】常春藤属。*the English* ~春藤。*the Boston* ~【植】爬山虎。*the ground* ~常春芥,连钱草。**II** *a*. 1. 学院的,学究式的。2. 纯理论的,象的;无实用意义的。**III** *vt*. 用常春藤点缀[覆盖],使满常春藤。~ **butter-cup** 常春藤毛茛。**I- League** 1. (国东北部八个名牌大学的)常春藤联合会(由 Brow Columbia, Cornell, Dartmouth, Harvard, Princeton the U. of Pennsylvania 和 Yale 大学所组成)。2. 属该组织的名牌大学或其师生。3. 名牌大学派头。~**leaved** *a*. 常春藤(叶)的。~**-leaved crowfoot** 常春藤茛。

I.W. = interrupted wave; Isle of Wight;【化】isotop weight.

I-way = information highway 〔口语叫法〕。

i·wis [iˈwis; ɪˋwɪs] *ad*. 〔古〕当然;确实地。

IWS = International Wool Secretariat 国际羊毛书记处。

I.W.T. = Inland Water Transport 〔英〕内河航运。

I.W.W., IWW = Industrial Workers of the Wor 〔美〕世界产业工人组织。

IX = ion exchange 离子交换。

-ix *suf*. -or 型阳性名词的阴性型后词尾:execut*rix*.

ix·i·a [ˈiksiə; ˋɪksɪə] *n*. 【植】1. 鸢尾属。2. 加州藜芦

Ix·i·on [ikˈsaiən; ɪkˋsaɪən] *n*. 【希神】伊克塞翁〔帖撒国王〕。~**'s wheel** 地府旋轮〔Ixion 因为向赫拉(Hera求爱,受神惩罚,被绑在永远旋转的地狱车轮上〕。

ix·tle [ˈikstli, ˈis-; ˋɪkstlɪ, ˋɪs-] *n*. = istle.

I·yar [iːˈjɑː, ˈiːjɑː; ɪˋjɑr, ˋijɑr] *n*. 〔Heb.〕(犹太历)八月

-i·za·tion *comb. f*. 构成与 -ize 型动词相应的名词civil*ization*, organ*ization*.

-ize *suf*. 1. 构成及物动词,表示(a)"使成为","使变成""使…化":civil*ize*, national*ize*. (b)"使变成…状","生…":crystall*ize*, hypothes*ize*. (c)像…似地从事动,"照…法处理":calvan*ize*, bowdler*ize*. (d)"作…理","使…渗透","使与…结合":dramat*ize*, iod*ize* oxid*ize*. 2. 构成不及物动词,表示"成为","变成","

化”：apostat*ize*，sympath*ize*．★-ize 与 -ise 英美尚无一定用法，但美语中多用 -ize。下列数语则英美均用 -ise：advertise，comprise，devise，revise，surprise．

·**mir** [iz'miə; ɪz`mɪə] ***n*.** 伊兹密尔〔即士麦那(Smyrna)，土耳其海港〕。

Iz·ves·ti·a [iz'vestjə; ɪz`vɛstjə] ***n*.**《消息报》。

iz·zard ['izəd; `ɪzə·d] ***n*.**〔古、方〕字母 z。*from A to* ～ 自始至终，彻底地。

iz·zat ['izət; `ɪzət] ***n*.**〔Ind.〕名誉，荣誉；自尊心；自大。

J

j [dʒei; dʒe] (*pl*. ***J's*, *j's*, *Js*, *js*** [dʒeiz; dʒez]) **1.** 英语字母表第十字母。★J，j 原为 I，i 的异体字母，17 世纪才开始确定 j 为子音字母，i 为母音字母。**2.** 第十。**3.**【数】与 y 轴平行的单位矢量。**4.** J 字形物体[记号]〔如 J 字形螺钉或 J 字形钩等〕。**5.** J 字母在语音上通常发的塞擦音[dʒ]。**6.**【数】虚数 $\sqrt{-1}$。*a J* (*-pen*) 宽尖钢笔尖。***a*. 1.** J 或 j 的。**2.** J 形的。**3.** 第十的。

. = **1.** Journal. **2.** Judge. **3.** Justice.

.**j.** = **1.**【牌】Jack. **2.**【物】joule 焦耳。

ı [jaː; ja] ***ad*.** (G.) = yes.

ı. = January.

.**A.**，**JA** = **1.** Joint Account (数人)共有的(银行存款等)账户。**2.** Judge Advocate 军法官；军法检察官。**3.** Joint Agent 联合代理人。

ı·**al goat** ['dʒeiəlgəut, 'jaːl-; `dʒeəlgot, `jal-]【动】(埃塞俄比亚，上埃及等地产的)长角野山羊。

ıb [dʒæb; dʒæb] **I *vt*.** (*-bb-*) **1.** 刺，戳。**2.** 捅；猛碰。～ *one's elbow into sb.'s side* 用胳膊肘猛碰别人的腰部。～ *a wild hog with a spear* = ～ *a spear into a wild hog* 用长矛猛刺野猪。— ***vi*.** 刺，戳，刺进(*into*)；猛击(*at*)。～ ***a right***〔美拳击〕挥右拳猛击。～ ***a vein***〔美俚〕进行麻醉品注射。**II *n*.**〔口〕**1.** 猛戳，刺进；【军】连续戳。**2.** 猛碰；【拳】短促有力的戳击。**3.**〔美俚〕皮下注射。*receive a* ～ *in the arm*〔口〕在臂上打一针[接种]。～***-off n*.**〔美俚〕麻醉药的皮下注射；注射麻醉药后发生的作用。

a·bal·pur [ˌdʒʌbəl'puə; ˏdʒʌbəl`pʊr] ***n*.** 贾巴尔普尔〔印度中央邦的城市〕。

ab·ber ['dʒæbə; `dʒæbə·] **I *n*. 1.** 急促不清的话。**2.** 无意义的话；莫名其妙的话。**II *vi*. 1.** 急急忙忙地说。**2.** 闲聊。**3.** (猿猴等)吱吱喳喳地叫。— ***vt*.** 急促不清地说。**-er *n*.** 说话莫名其妙的人，说话荒唐的人。

ab·ber·wock·y ['dʒæbəwɔki; `dʒæbə·ˏwɑkɪ] **I *n*.** 无聊的话[文章]。**II *a*.** 莫名其妙的。

ab·i·ru ['dʒæbiruː; `dʒæbəˏru] ***n*.**【动】**1.** (美国南部和南美的)林鹳(= wood ibis)。**2.** 非洲凹嘴鹳(= *Ephippiorhynchus senegalensis*)。

ab·o·ran·di [ˌdʒæbə'rændi; ˏdʒæbə`rændɪ] ***n*.** 毛果芸香(= *Pilocarpus jaborandi*)〔产于南美，是芸香科植物的叶干，内含生物碱〕。

a·bot [ʒæ'bəu, F. ʒabo; ʒæ`bo, F. ʒabo] ***n*. 1.** 镶在女服胸前的皱褶花边，胸饰。**2.** 十八世纪男子穿的衬衫领子前的皱褶花边。

AC = Joint Aircraft Committee 飞机制造联合委员会。

.**A.C.** = Junior Association of Commerce 青年商会。

ac. = Jacob; Jacobus.

a·cal [haː'kaːl; ha`kal] ***n*.** (*pl*. ***-ca·les*** [-'kaːleis; -`kales]，～***s***) (墨西哥和西南美的)木桩小茅屋〔用木桩涂泥作墙的茅屋〕。

ac·a·mar ['dʒækəmaː; `dʒækəmar] ***n*.**【动】鹟䴕〔产于中南美，为食鱼鸟〕。

ja·ca·na, ja·ca·na [ˌʒaːsə'naː; ˏʒasə`na] ***n*.**【动】水雉〔产于热带和亚热带〕。

jac·a·ran·da [ˌdʒækə'rændə; ˏdʒækə`rændə] ***n*.**【植】兰花楹属(*Jacaranda*)植物。

j'accuse [ʒə'kuːz; ʒə`kuz] (F.) **1.** 我控诉。**2.** 强烈控诉，强烈谴责。

jac·inth ['dʒæsinθ; `dʒæsɪnθ] ***n*. 1.**【矿】红锆石；橘红色的宝石。**2.** 橘红色。

jack[1] [dʒæk; dʒæk] **I *n*. 1.**〔常 J-〕杰克〔男子名，也作 John 的俗称或昵称〕。**2.**〔J-〕普通人，男子，家伙，小伙子。**3.** 水手，水兵，海员(= Jack Tar)。**4.** 伐木工；杂役，打杂工。**5.** (烤肉等用的)铁叉旋转器；脱鞋器。**6.**〔J〕(纸牌中的)杰克〔在国王(King)和王后(Queen)之下〕。**7.** 赢得的大量赌注。**8.**【机】起重器；千斤顶；(支柱等)支撑物。**9.**【电】插座，插口；塞孔；弹簧开关。**10.**【机】传动装置；动力油缸。**11.** (标、国籍的)船首旗，公司旗。**12.** 公驴；幼雄鲑鱼；寒鸦。**13.**〔美〕长耳大野兔(= jack rabbit)。**14.** (滚球游戏中作靶子的)小白木球；(抛石游戏中所用的)小石块[金属片]。**15.**〔美〕(夜间打猎或捕鱼用的)篝灯。**16.**〔美俚〕金钱。**17.** 苹果酒；白兰地酒。**18.**【矿】打眼机；安全防风灯罩。**19.**【矿】闪锌矿。**20.** 屈体跳水法。**21.** (时钟的)钟锤。**22.**〔英俚〕票面为 50 英镑的纸币。*automobile* ～ 汽车千斤顶。*bridging* ～【电】并联塞孔，桥接塞孔。*cheap J-* 小贩。*hydraulic* ～ 液压千斤顶。*oil* ～ 油压千斤顶。*ratchet* ～ 棘轮起重器。*screw* ～ 螺旋撑杆；螺旋千斤顶。*tripod* ～ 三脚起重器。***A good J- makes a good Gill*** [***Jill***].〔谚〕夫善使妻贤。***All shall be well, J- shall have Gill*** [***Jill***].〔谚〕有情人皆成眷属。***All work and no play makes J- a dull boy*.**〔谚〕用功不玩耍，弄得孩子会变傻。***before you can*** [***could***] ***say J- Robinson*** 转瞬间，突然，说时迟那时快。***climb like a steeple*** ～ 善于爬山。***Every J- shall have his Gill*** [***Jill***].〔谚〕人必有偶。***J- among the maids*** 讨好妇女的男子。***every man*** ～，***every*** ～ ***one*** [***man***] 人人，每个人。***J- and Gill*** [***Jill***] 少年和姑娘；男人和女人。***J- at a pinch*** 临时拉来帮忙的人。***J- in the water***〔俚〕码头脚夫。***J- Johnson***【军】重型炮弹。***J- of all trades*** 什么事都能干的人，万能博士，三脚猫。***J- of all trades and master of none*.** 行行皆通，样样稀松。***J- of*** [***on***] ***both sides*** 骑墙派。***J- of straw* 1.** 稻草人。**2.** 无资产者。**3.** 寄生者。***make one's*** ～ **1.** 达到目的。**2.** 赚大钱。***not a*** ～ 一个也不。***the Union J-*** 英国国旗。**II *a*.** (动物)雄的，公的。**III *vi*.** 用篝灯打猎[捕鱼]。— ***vt*. 1.** (用起重器)起，举，扛。**2.** 增加，抬高(物价等)。**3.** 放弃。停止(工作、计划等)。**4.** 申诉，责备，规劝(*up*)。**5.** 夜间用篝灯捕(鱼)[猎(兽)]。**6.**〔美俚〕拔(枪等)(*out*)。— ***vt*.** 持枪抢劫(汽车等)。～(*up*) *a car* 把汽车顶起。～(*up*) *expenditure* 增加开支。***be*** ～***ed up***〔口〕败事，完蛋，筋疲力尽。**Jack-a-dandy *n*.**

花花公子。**Jack-a-Lent** (*pl*. *Jack-a-Lents*) *n*. 1. 四旬斋期游戏中被击的小玩偶。2. 小人物。~**-ass** 1. 公驴。2. 笨蛋,傻瓜。~**assery** 愚蠢的行为。~**bean**【植】洋刀豆(*caravalia ensifornis*)〔产于美国南部,作饲料用,籽可食〕。~**boots** *n*. *pl*. 过膝的长统靴。~**fish** *n*. 鱼〔土名儿,尤指白斑狗鱼(*Esor lucius*)〕。~ **engine** 辅助发动机。**Jack Frost**〔霜寒的拟人化名称〕霜精,严寒。~**fruit** *n*.【植】1. 波罗蜜树〔产于东印度〕。2. 波罗蜜树果实。3. 波罗蜜树木材。~**hammer** *n*. 轻型凿岩机;风镐,气锤。~ **Horner** 自负的小孩子。**Jack-in-office** *n*. (*pl*. *Jacks-in-office*) 自命不凡的小官吏,作威作福的芝麻官,摆官架子的人。~**-in-the-box** *n*. (*pl* ~*-in-the-boxes*, ~*s-in-the-box*) 1. (打开盖子即有玩偶跳起的)玩偶匣。2. (能放出多种玩意的)盒子焰火。3.【机】差动齿轮[装置]。**Jack-in-the-Green** *n*. (*pl*. *Jack-in-the-Creens*, *Jacks-in-the-Green*) 花屋中的人〔西俗五月一日用冬青和鲜花扎成小屋,人居其中上街游行〕。~**-in-the-pulpit** *n*.【植】天南星。**Jack Ketch**〔英〕绞刑吏。~**knife** 1. *n*. 大折刀;屈体跳水法。2. *vt*. 用大折刀切。3. *vi*. (跳水等时)屈体。~ **ladder**【船】木踏板绳梯。~**lamp** 安全灯。~**leg** *a*., *n*. 1. 技术不高明的(人);外行的(人)。2. 不诚实的(人);不择手段的(人)。3. 权宜之计的(行动)。~**light** 1.【猎】*n*. (用以引诱鱼或猎物的)篝火。2. *vt*. 用篝火[灯]引猎(兽类);用篝火等诱捕(鱼类)。~**-o'-lantern** 1. 磷火。2. 行踪不定的人。3. 使人迷惑的事物。4.〔美〕南瓜灯。~ **pine**【植】短叶松(*Pinus banksiana*)〔产于加拿大和美国北部,针叶短而成对排列〕。~ **plane**【机】粗刨,大刨。~ **post**【机】轴柱。~**pot** *n*. 1.【牌】(要有一对杰克以上的好牌才能开局下注的)赌注。2. 积累的赌注。3.〔古〕(彩票等的)头奖;(可在任何冒险事业中取得的)最大成功。4.〔美〕困境(*hit the* ~*pot*〔俚〕赢得大笔赌注;获得极大成功,运气非常好)。~ **pudding**〔古〕丑角。~ **rabbit**【动】(北美)长耳大野兔。~ **rafter**【建】小椽。~**screw**【机】螺旋起重器。~**shaft** *n*. 中间轴,副轴,驱动半轴。~ **snipe**【动】小鹬。~ **Sprat** 矮子,侏儒。~ **staff** 舰首旗杆。~**stay** 1.【机】撑杆。2.【船】天幕边索;支索;(汽艇用)分隔索。~ **tar**, **J- Tar** 水手;水兵。~ **towel** 环状毛巾(= roller towel)。~**-up** *n*. 1.〔美口〕增加,上涨。2. (海上钻探石油用的)自升式钻塔。

jack[2] [dʒæk; dʒæk] *n*. 1. (中世纪步兵护身的)无袖皮上衣。2.〔古〕装酒的皮罐。

jack[3] [dʒæk; dʒæk] *n*. 1. (东南亚等地产的)面包树。2. 面包树果实。

jack- [dʒæk; dʒæk] *comb*. *f*.〔构成名词〕1. 表示"雄性",如: *jack*ass 公驴。2. 表示"大",如: *jack*boot 长统靴。3. 表示"男孩或人",与连字号"-"组合在一起,如 *jack*-in-the-box 玩偶匣〔打开盖子即有玩偶跳起〕。

J

jack·al ['dʒækɔːl; ˋdʒækɔl] I *n*. 1.【动】胡狼。2. 爪牙,走狗。3. 骗子,诈骗者。~ ***from*** [***of***] ***the same lair*** 一丘之貉。***play the*** ~ ***to the tiger*** 为虎作伥。II *vi*. 作爪牙,当走狗(*for*)。

jack·a·napes ['dʒækəneips; ˋdʒækə͵neps] *n*. 1.〔古〕驯服的猴子。2. 傲慢无礼而又专横的人。3. 顽劣孩子。

jack·a·roo, jack·e·roo [ˌdʒækə'ruː;͵dʒækəˋru] *n*.〔澳俚〕(牧场的)新牧童。

jack·daw ['dʒækdɔː; ˋdʒæk͵dɔ] *n*. 1.【动】穴鸟,寒鸦(*Corvus monedula*)〔产于欧洲的一种类似乌鸦的黑鸟〕。2. = grackle. ~ ***in peacock's feathers*** 乌鸦披着孔雀毛;鸦学彩凤。

jack·et ['dʒækit; ˋdʒækɪt] I *n*. 1. 短上衣,外套。2. 包书纸,护封;公文套;唱片套;弹壳。3. (动物的)皮毛;(马铃薯等的)皮。4.【机】盒,罩,套,外壳。5. (软木)救生衣。*cylinder* ~汽缸套。*life* (*-saving*) ~救生衣。*potatoes boiled in their* ~*s* 连皮煮的马铃薯。***dust*** [***lace***, ***swinge***, ***thrash***, ***trim***] ***sb.'s*** ~殴打某人。***Pull down your*** ~!〔口〕安静些。***send in one's*** ~ 辞职不干。***warm sb.'s*** ~惩罚某人,辱骂某人。II *vt*. 给…穿短上衣;给…盖上罩子[套子等];给…包上护封 2.〔口〕打。*a steam* ~*ed kettle* 双重蒸煮锅。~ **cr** 连皮一块儿炸的土豆[马铃薯]片,带皮炸土豆片。

jack·et·ing ['dʒækitiŋ; ˋdʒækɪtɪŋ] *n*. 1.【机】套。〔口〕殴打,鞭打。

jack·ing ['dʒækiŋ; ˋdʒækɪŋ] *n*. 1.【纺】(走锭纺纱机的)走车牵伸;叠层轧光揉布工艺。2. 用篝灯打猎[捕鱼]。

jacks [dʒæks; dʒæks] *n*.〔作单数用〕抛石游戏。

jack·smelt ['dʒæksmelt; ˋdʒæk͵smɛlt] *n*.【动】似银鱼(*Atherinopsis californiensis*)〔产于太平洋〕。

Jack·son[1] ['dʒæksn; ˋdʒæksn] *n*. 杰克逊〔地名:1. 美密西西比州的首府。2. 美国密执安州南部的城市。3. 国田纳西州城市〕。

Jack·son[2] ['dʒæksn; ˋdʒæksn] *n*. 杰克逊〔姓氏,男名〕。1. Andrew ~安德鲁·杰克逊〔1767—1845,美国军,于1829—1837任美国第七任总统〕。2. **Helen Mar Hunt** ~海伦·玛丽安·亨特·杰克逊〔1830—1885,本 Fiske,美国女小说家〕。3. **Robert Houghwout** ~罗特·霍伍特·杰克逊〔1892—1954,美国法学家〕。

Jack·so·ni·an [dʒæk'səuniən; dʒækˋsonɪən] I *a*. (国第七任总统)杰克逊的;与杰克逊有关的,杰克逊政的,与杰克逊政策有关的。II *n*. 杰克逊的追随者。

jack·stone ['dʒækstəun; ˋdʒæk͵ston] *n*. 1. 抓子游戏子儿。2. [*pl*.]〔动词用单数〕= jacks.

jack·straw ['dʒækstrɔː; ˋdʒæk͵strɔ] *n*. 1. 稻草人(straw man)。2. (抽杆游戏用的)细木杆[塑料杆等]。

jack·y ['dʒæki; ˋdʒækɪ] *n*. 1. = Jack Tar. 2.〔英〕杜子酒。

Ja·cob ['dʒeikəb; ˋdʒekəb] *n*. 雅各〔《圣经》中人名,有几个,其中一个是犹太人的祖先之一,即以色列;另一是耶稣的门徒〕。~**'s ladder** 1.【圣】(雅各在梦中见的)天使上下的天梯。2.【海】(有木或铁制踏板的)绳梯 3.【植】花葱。4. (吊桶的)循环链。~**'s staff** 1. 香客杖 2. (测量器的)支架;测高器;测距器。~**'stears**【植】苡。

Jac·o·be·an [ˌdʒækə'bi(ː)ən; ͵dʒækəˋbiən] I *a*. 1. 国詹姆士一世的,詹姆士一世时代(1603—1625)的。黑橡木色的(家具)。II *n*. 1. 詹姆士一世时代的作家[人、外交家等]。2. = Jacobite. ~ ***determinant***【数】数行列式。

Jac·o·bin ['dʒækəbin; ˋdʒækəbɪn] *n*. 1.【宗】多明我派修道士。2.【史】(1789年法国革命时代的)雅各宾党〔因其俱乐部会址设在巴黎雅各宾修道院而得名〕。3. 进民主派成员。4. [j-]【动】毛领鸽。**-ic(al)** *a*. 雅各宾(人)的。**-ism** *n*. 雅各宾主义;激进民主主义。

Jac·o·bite ['dʒækəbait; ˋdʒækə͵baɪt] *n*. 1. 英王詹姆二世退位以后的拥戴者,要求詹姆士二世的后裔继承位者。2. 美国小说家亨利·詹姆士 (Henry James) 的拜者。**-bit·ic**, **-bit·i·cal** *a*.

ja·co·bus [dʒə'kəubəs; dʒəˋkobəs] *n*. 英国詹姆士一时代铸制的金币〔约合20先令〕(= unite)。

jac·o·net ['dʒækənit; ˋdʒækə͵nɛt] *n*. 1. 白色薄棉布医用防水细纱布。2. 一面轧光的染色棉布。

jac·quard [dʒə'kɑːd; dʒəˋkɑrd] *n*.〔常作 J-〕1.【纺】提花机(= ~ loom)。2. 提花织物(= ~ weave)。**J- loom** 提花机〔法国人 Jacquard (1752—1834)发明的织布机〕

Jac·que·line ['dʒækliːn; ˋdʒæklin] *n*. 杰奎琳〔女子名〕

Jac·que·ric [ʒæk'riː, F. ʒakri; ʒækˋri, F. ʒakrɪ] *n* [F.] 1. (1358年法国的)札克雷农民起义。2. [j-]农民起义。

jacta est alea ['dʒæktə est'eiljə; ˋdʒæktə estˋelɪə] [L.] 骰子已经掷出〔凯撒(Caesar)越过卢比孔(Rubicon)河与庞培(Pompey)决战时讲的话〕;木已成舟,事已决定。

jac·ta·tion [dʒæk'teiʃən; dʒækˋteʃən] *n*. 1. 吹嘘,夸。2.【医】辗转不安。

jac·ti·ta·tion [ˌdʒækti'teiʃən; ͵dʒæktɪˋteʃən] *n*. 1

【医】辗转不安;四肢或肌肉的抽动。2.〔古〕自夸,自吹。3.【法】诈称(为某人的配偶)。~ *of marriage* 冒称配偶罪。

jac·u·late [ˈdʒækjuleit; ˋdʒækjəˏlet] *vt*., *vi*. 投掷。**-lation** *n*.

jade[1] [dʒeid; dʒed] **I** *n*. 1. 玉,翡翠。2. 翡翠色。**II** *a*. 1. 玉制的。2. 翡翠色的。~ **green** 绿玉色。~ **plant** 乔木状青锁龙(*Crassula arborescens*)〔产于南非和亚洲〕。**Jade Squad**〔美〕翡翠侦缉队〔纽约市警察局一个专门打击亚裔犯罪集团的部门〕。~**stone** 硬玉。

jade[2] [dʒeid; dʒed] **I** *n*. 1. 劣马,驽马,老马,疲备不堪的马。2.〔贬〕荡妇,女流氓。3.〔谑〕女人。**II** *vt*., *vi*. (使)疲倦;(使)疲惫不堪,(使)精疲力尽。

jad·ed [ˈdʒeidid; ˋdʒedɪd] *a*. 1. 精疲力竭的。2. (因过饱或过多)腻烦的。*a* ~ *appetite* 败坏的胃口。**-ly** *ad*. **-ness** *n*.

jade·ite [ˈdʒeidait; ˋdʒedaɪt] *n*. 硬玉,翡翠。

jad·ish [ˈdʒeidiʃ; ˋdʒedɪʃ] *a*. 1. 精疲力竭的,疲倦的。2. 差的;破旧的。

j'adoube [ʒɑːˈduːb; ʒɑˋdub] 〔F.〕我把棋子摆摆正〔下棋的人用手碰到并不想移动的棋子时向对方打招呼的话 = I adjust〕。

jae·ger[1] [ˈjeigə; ˋjegɚ] *n*. (纯毛织)雅茄呢;雅茄呢做的服装。

jae·ger[2] [ˈjeigə; ˋjegɚ] *n*. 1.【动】贼鸥。2. 猎人,穿猎人服装的保镖。3.〔主 J-〕(旧德国或奥地利军队中的)狙击兵。

Jaf·fa [ˈdʒæfə; ˋdʒæfə] *n*. 雅法〔巴勒斯坦西部港口〕。~ **orange** 雅法橙。

Jaff·na [ˈdʒæfnə; ˋdʒæfnə] *n*. 贾夫纳〔斯里兰卡的港口〕。

jag[1] [dʒæg; dʒæg] **I** *n*. 1.〔古〕织品上的 V 字形凹口〔尖裂缝〕。2. 锯齿形缺口的突出部。*a* ~ *of rock* 一块突出的岩石。**II** *vt*. (**-gg-**) 1. 在…上刻 V 形凹口。2. 把…撕成锯齿状,把…切得参差不齐。3. 在(衣服)上开叉〔穿饰孔〕。*a jagged rent in cloth* 一块布上撕成锯齿状的裂口。— *vi*. 1. 刺,戳。2. 颠簸地移动。

jag[2] [dʒæg; dʒæg] *n*. 1.〔方〕(马的)一驮之量。2.〔美俚〕狂饮,酒席。3.〔口〕(感情等的)突发(时期),一阵。*have a* ~ *on* 酩酊大醉。*a crying* ~ 大哭一阵。*a laughing* ~ 一阵大笑。

Jag [dʒæg; dʒæg] *n*.〔口〕美洲豹牌小汽车(= Jaguar)。

J.A.G. = Judge Advocate General〔美〕军法处长。

Jag·an·nath [ˈdʒʌgəˌnɑːt, -nɔːt; ˋdʒʌgəˏnɑt, -nɔt] *n*. = Juggernaut.

JAGD = Judge Advocate General's Department〔美〕军法署。

jä·ger [ˈjeigə; ˋjegɚ] *n*. = jaeger[2].

jag·ged [ˈdʒægid; ˋdʒægɪd] *a*. 锯齿状的,有缺口的,参差不齐的,粗糙的,凸凹不平的。*a* ~ *rock* 巉岩。**-ly** *ad*. **-ness** *n*.

jag·ger·y [ˈdʒægəri; ˋdʒægərɪ] *n*. 棕榈糖;粗糖。

jag·gy [ˈdʒægi, ˋdʒægɪ] *a*. (**-gi·er**; **-gi·est**) = jagged.

jag·uar [ˈdʒægwɑː; ˋdʒægwɑr] *n*.【动】美洲豹。

jag·ua·run·di [ˌdʒægwəˈrʌndi; ˏdʒægwəˋrʌndɪ] *n*. 小豹猫〔产于美洲的热带和亚热带,短腿长尾细身子,毛呈灰色〕。

Jah [dʒɑː; dʒɑ] **Jah·ve(h)**, **Jah·we(h)** [ˈjɑːvei; ˋjɑve] *n*. = Jehovah.

jai a·lai [ˈhailai, ˌhaiəˈlai; ˋhaɪlaɪ, ˏhaɪəˋlaɪ] *n*. 〔Sp.〕回力球〔一种与手球相似的球类活动,流行于拉丁美洲〕。

jail [dʒeil; dʒel]〔美〕*n*., *vt*. = gaol. ~**bait** 1. 与其有性行为即构成强奸罪的未成年女子。2. 性感女郎。3. 任何会为之下狱的诱惑。~**bird** 囚犯,惯犯。~**-break** 越狱。~ **delivery** 1. 劫狱,用暴力释放囚犯。2. 把囚犯带去法庭受审出空监狱。~ **glass** 塑料玻璃〔以热塑性塑料制成,常用于监狱、精神病院等场所〕。~**house** 监狱。

jail·er, jail·or [ˈdʒeilə; ˋdʒelɚ] *n*. 监狱看守(= gaoler)。

jail·er·ess [ˈdʒeləris; ˋdʒɛlərɪs] *n*. 监狱女看守。

Jain [dʒain; dʒaɪn], **Jai·na** [ˈdʒainə; ˋdʒaɪnə] **I** *a*. (印度的)耆那教的,耆那教徒(式)的。**II** *n*. 耆那教教徒。

Jain·ism [ˈdʒainizəm; ˋdʒaɪnɪzəm] *n*. 耆那教〔印度非婆罗门教的一派,其教义与佛教有些相同,主张苦行与戒杀〕。

Ja·kar·ta [dʒəˈkɑːtə; dʒəˋkɑrtə] *n*. 雅加达(= Djakarta)〔印度尼西亚首都〕。

jake[1] [dʒeik; dʒek] *n*.〔贬〕粗鲁的乡下人,家伙。

jake[2] [dʒeik; dʒek] *a*.〔美俚〕对的,好的,令人满意的。*Everything is* ~ *with me*. 万事如意。

jake[3], **jakey** [dʒeik, ˈdʒeiki; dʒek, ˋdʒekɪ] *n*.〔俚〕牙买加姜汁酒〔在禁酒时代作为饮料〕。~ **leg** 由于饮酒而引起的麻痹症。

jakes [dʒeiks; dʒeks] *n*.〔古、方〕屋外厕所,茅坑。

JAL = Japan Air Lines 日本航空公司。

jal·ap [ˈdʒæləp; ˋdʒæləp] *n*.【植】1. 药喇叭〔球根牵牛〕。2. 药喇叭的根制做的泻药。

jal·a·pin [ˈdʒæləpin; ˋdʒæləpɪŋ] *n*.【化】紫茉莉苷。

Ja·lis·co [hɑːˈliskə; hɑˋlɪskə] *n*. 哈利斯科〔墨西哥太平洋岸的州,首府为瓜达拉哈拉〕。

ja·lop·(p)y [dʒəˈlɔpi; dʒəˋlɑpɪ] *n*.〔美俚〕1. 破旧的汽车〔飞机〕。2. 车辆。

jal·ou·sie [ˈʒælu(ː)ziː; ˋʒæluzi] *n*.【建】百叶窗。

jam[1] [dʒæm; dʒæm] **I** *n*. 1. 拥挤,阻塞。2. (机器等因拥塞)轧住,停顿。3.【无】干扰,失真。4.〔美口〕困境,窘境;和警察等口角。5.〔美俚〕一举手之劳的事情。*a* ~ *of logs in a river* 挤满一河的木材。*a traffic* ~ 交通拥挤,交通阻塞。***be in*** [***get into***] ***a*** ~ 处于[陷入]困境。**II** *vt*. (**-mm-**) 1. (把…)挤进,塞进。2. 使(机器等)轧住,使卡住,使塞满。3. 轧伤,压碎。4.【无】干扰。5. 使(通道等)堵塞。~ *one's clothes into a suitcase* 把衣服塞进箱子里。*The bus was* ~*med full*. 公共汽车挤得很满。*The driver* ~*s the brakes on*. 司机煞住车。*a ship* ~*med in ice* 被夹在冰里的船。— *vi*. 1. 塞满,拥挤;挤进。2. 楔紧;(机器等)轧住不动。3.〔美俚〕改奏即兴爵士音乐活跃空气,参加爵士音乐演奏会。4. (在一个集体中)拼命工作,玩命干。5.【无】干扰。*The gearing* ~*med*. 齿轮装置卡住。~ *into the lift* 挤进电梯。*The brakes* ~*med*. 刹车失灵了。~ **nut**【机】锁紧螺母,防松螺母。~ **-packed** *a*. 包装扎实的,塞紧的,挤得水泄不通的。~ **session**〔美俚〕爵士音乐即席演奏会;一群演奏者为自己举行的非正式演奏会。~ **welding**【机】对接焊。

jam[2] [dʒæm; dʒæm] **I** *n*. 1. 果酱。2.〔俚〕奢侈;酒席,好菜。*real* ~〔俚〕美好的东西,好菜,使人痛快的事。**II** *vt*. (**-mm-**) 1. 给…涂上果酱。2. 制成果酱。*jamming sugar* 果酱用糖。~ **tomorrow** 可望而不可得的好事。

Jam. = Jamaica; James.

Ja·mai·ca [dʒəˈmeikə; dʒəˋmekə] *n*. 牙买加〔拉丁美洲国家,英联邦的成员,首都金斯顿〕。~ **rum** 牙买加甜酒。

Ja·mai·can [dʒəˈmeikən; dʒəˋmekən] **I** *a*. 牙买加的,牙买加人的。**II** *n*. 牙买加人。

jamb(e) [dʒæm; dʒæm] *n*. 1.【建】门窗侧壁;侧柱;〔*pl*.〕壁炉两旁的墙。2.【矿】矿柱;矿脉中的土石层。

jam·ba·lay·a [ˌdʒʌmbəˈlaiə; ˏdʒʌmbəˋlaɪə] *n*. 1.〔大米与虾米、牡蛎、火腿、鸡肉等烹调而成的〕什锦饭。2. 杂烩,混合物。

jam·beau [ˈdʒæmbəu; ˋdʒæmbo] *n*. (*pl*. **-beaux** [-bəuz; -boz]) (中世纪的)胫甲〔护胫铠甲〕。

jam·bo·ree [ˌdʒæmbəˈriː; ˏdʒæmbəˋri] *n*.〔口〕1. 大喝大闹;大型娱乐会,庆祝会。2. 大集会;全国[国际]的童子军大会。3. 有多种娱乐的节目单。

James [dʒeimz; dʒemz] *n*. 1. 詹姆斯〔姓氏,男子名〕。2. (《圣经》中的)《雅各书》。

J

Jame·son [ˈdʒeimsn, ˈdʒimsn; ˋdʒemsn̩, ˋdʒɪmsn̩] ***n.*** 詹姆森〔姓氏〕。

James·town [ˈdʒeimztaun; ˋdʒemzˏtaʊn] ***n.*** 詹姆斯敦〔1. 圣赫勒拿岛首府。2. 1607年英国在美洲建立的第一个殖民地居地,在维吉尼亚州詹姆士河的河口处。3. 美国纽约西南部的城市〕。

jam·mer [ˈdʒæmə; ˋdʒæmɚ] ***n.*** 1.【无】干扰发射机,干扰发射台。2.【机】U型钢丝芯撑,簧丝芯撑。

jam·ming [ˈdʒæmiŋ; ˋdʒæmɪŋ] ***n.***【无】1. 收报时的干扰;人为干扰。2. 扰乱台,干扰台。3. 抑制。*spot* ～局部干扰。～ **intensity** 干扰强度。

Jam·mu [ˈdʒʌmuː; ˋdʒʌmu] ***n.*** 查谟〔城市,位于亚洲查谟和克什米尔的西南〕。

Jam·mu and Kash·mir [ˈdʒʌmuː ən kæʃˈmiə; ˋdʒʌmu ən kæʃˋmɪr] ***n.*** 查谟和克什米尔〔在亚洲,一部分属于印度,一部分属于巴基斯坦〕。

jam·my [ˈdʒæmi; ˋdʒæmɪ] ***a.*** 1. 粘上果酱的。2.〔英〕使人愉快的,适意的。

jam-pack [ˈdʒæmˈpæk; ˋdʒæmˋpæk] ***vt.*** 塞满,挤满,充满。～ *the basket with all kinds of fruit* 用各种水果把篮子装满。*Vacationists ～ed the trains.* 火车里装满了休假的人。

jams [dʒæmz; dʒæmz] ***n.***〔*pl.*〕1.〔口〕睡衣裤。2. 睡裤式游泳裤。

Jam·shed·pur [dʒʌmʃedˈpuə; dʒʌmʃɛdˋpʊr] ***n.*** 贾姆谢普尔〔印度的钢铁工业城市,位于东北部的比哈尔邦〕。

Jan. = January.

Ja-na·ta [dʒəˈnɑːtə; dʒəˋnɑtə] ***n.*** 人民党〔印度的主要政党之一〕。

Ja·ná·ček [ˈdʒænəʃek; ˋdʒænəʃɛk], **Leoš** 利奥斯·杰纳谢克〔1854—1928,捷克作曲家〕。

Jane [dʒein; dʒen] ***n.*** 1. 珍〔女子名,Joan(n)的异体〕。2.〔蔑、美俚〕姑娘,女学生。*a G.I.* ～女兵。～ ***Doe*** 〔美〕法律诉讼中隐匿真名的女方。

Jan·eite [ˈdʒeinait; ˋdʒenaɪt] ***n.*** 英国小说家珍·奥斯汀(Jane Austin)的崇拜者。

Ja·net [ˈdʒænit; ˋdʒænɪt] ***n.*** 珍妮特〔女子名,Jane的昵称〕。

jan·gle [ˈdʒæŋgl; ˋdʒæŋgl̩] **I** ***vi.*** 1. (铃等)发出刺耳的声音。2.〔英俚〕说长道短,散布流言蜚语。3.〔古〕吵架,争论。— ***vt.*** 1. 乱摇铃使发出刺耳声。2. 吵吵闹闹地讲。3. 使…心烦意乱。*The whine of the motors ～d her nerves.* 马达的轰鸣吵得她心烦意乱。**II** ***n.*** 1. 吵闹,口角。2. 刺耳的声音。3. 空谈。

Jan·is·sary [ˈdʒænisəri; ˋdʒænəˏsɛrɪ] ***n.*** = Janizary.

jan·i·tor [ˈdʒænitə; ˋdʒænətɚ] ***n.*** (*fem.* ***-tress***) 1. 看门人,守门人。2. 照管一座房屋或办公室的工人。**-i·al** ***a.***

J

Jan·i·zar·y [ˈdʒænizəri; ˋdʒænəˏzɛrɪ] ***n.*** 1.【史】14—19世纪土耳其苏丹的近卫步兵。2. 土耳其士兵。3.〔喻〕亲信,拥护者;亲信部队的成员。

jank [dʒæŋk; dʒæŋk] ***vi.***〔美军俚〕(为躲避地面高射炮火而)同时改变飞行方向和高度,闪避。

jan·nock [ˈdʒænək; ˋdʒænək] ***a.***〔英方〕老实的;诚实的;真心的,爽直的。

Jan·u·ar·y [ˈdʒænjuəri; ˋdʒænjuɛrɪ] ***n.*** 一月。*in* ～在一月里。*on* ～*10* 一月十日。*on the evening of* ～ *15* 一月十五日晚。～ **effect**【商】元月效应〔指股票持有者往往在年底抛出,使股价下跌,到来年一月又多购进,使股市行情迅速回升〕。

Ja·nus [ˈdʒeinəs; ˋdʒenəs] ***n.***【罗神】看守门户的两面神。**～-faced** ***a.*** 脸朝两面的;虚伪的,口是心非的。

Jap [dʒæp; dʒæp] ***a.***, ***n.***〔常贬〕= 1. Japan. 2. Japanese.

Ja·pan [dʒəˈpæn; dʒəˋpæn] ***n.*** 日本,日本国〔亚洲〕。*the* ～ *Current* 日本海流,黑潮。*the Sea of* ～ 日本海。～ **allspice** 腊梅。～ **cedar**【植】柳杉。～ **china** 日本产瓷器。～ **clover**【植】鸡眼草(*Lespedeza striata*)〔美国西南部种植作为干饲料〕。～ **cypress** 扁柏。～ **earth** 日本阿仙药染料。～ **ink** 墨。～ **medlar** 枇杷。～ **wax** 日本蜡。

ja·pan [dʒəˈpæn; dʒəˋpæn] **I** ***n.*** 1. 日本漆;亮漆。2. 日本式漆器。3. 日本式物品〔如日本瓷器、日本丝等〕。～ *black* 黑漆。**II** ***vt.*** (***-nn-***) 1. 给…涂漆。2. 使平滑光亮。*japanned leather* (黑色)漆皮。**III** ***a.*** 1. 日本漆器的,具有日本漆器特征的。2. 涂了日本漆的。～ **cabinet** 漆饰五屉柜。～ **ware** 漆器。

Jap·a·nese [ˌdʒæpəˈniːz; ˏdʒæpəˋniz] **I** ***a.*** 1. 日本的;日本人的。2. 日语的。**II** ***n.*** (*sing.*, *pl.*) 1. 日本人。2. 日语。*a* ～ 一个日本人。*the* ～〔集合词〕日本人。～ **andromeda**【植】马醉木(*Pieris japonica*)〔一种常绿植物〕。～ **(flowering) cherry**〔植〕日本樱花。～ **iris**【植】花菖蒲(*Iris kaempferi*)。～ **ivy** 耙山虎(= Boston ivy)。～ **lantern** 灯笼(= Chinese lantern)。～ **oyster**【动】日本长蛎(*Ostrea gigas*)。～ **persimmon** 1.【植】亚洲柿树(*Diospyros kaki*)。2. 柿子。～ **plum** 李(*Prunus salicina*)〔原产于中国〕。～ **quince**【植】1. 贴梗海棠树(*Chaenomeles lagenaria*)。2. 贴梗海棠。～ **rose** 蔷薇;〔俚〕山茶。～ **spurge**【植】富贵草(*Pachysandra terminalis*)〔一种种于草坪的常绿草〕。～ **tissue** 薄纸。

Jap·a·nesque [ˌdʒæpəˈnesk; ˏdʒæpəˋnɛsk] ***a.*** 日本式的。

Ja·pan·ism [dʒəˈpænizəm; dʒəˋpænɪzm] ***n.*** 1. 日本精神[性格]。2. 日本迷。3. 日语语法。4. 日本研究。

Jap·a·ni·za·tion [ˌdʒæpənaiˈzeiʃən; ˏdʒæpənaɪˋzeʃən] ***n.*** 日本化。

Jap·a·nize [ˈdʒæpənaiz; ˋdʒæpəˏnaɪz] ***vt.*** 使日本化,使成日本式。

ja·pan·ner [dʒəˈpænə; dʒəˋpænɚ] ***n.*** (油)漆工。

Japano- *comb. f.* 义为"日本": *Japano*phile.

Jap·a·nol·o·gy [ˌdʒæpəˈnɔlədʒi; ˏdʒæpəˋnɑlədʒɪ] ***n.*** 日本学,日本事物的研究。**-nol·o·gist** ***n.*** 研究日本的学者,日本学专家。

Jap·a·no·phile [ˈdʒæpənə*u*fail; ˋdʒæpənəˏfaɪl] ***n.*** 亲日派,亲日分子。

Ja·pan·o·phobe [dʒəˈpænə*u*fəub; dʒəˋpænəˏfob] ***n.*** 憎恶日本的人。

Jap·a·no·pho·bi·a [dʒæpənəuˈfəubiə; dʒæpənəˋfobɪə] ***n.*** 憎恶日本,恐日病。

jape [dʒeip; dʒep] **I** ***vi.*** 说笑话,戏谑,嘲弄。— ***vt.***〔罕〕开…的玩笑,嘲弄。**II** ***n.*** 1. 笑话,笑柄。2. 嘲弄;愚弄。

Ja·pheth [ˈdʒeifeθ; ˋdʒefɪθ] ***n.***【圣】雅弗〔挪亚(Noah)三个儿子中的幼子〕。

Ja·phet·ic [dʒeiˈfetik; dʒeˋfɛtɪk] ***a.*** 1. 雅弗(Japheth)的。2. 印欧(Indo-European)的〔旧称〕。

Ja·pon·ic [dʒəˈpɔnik; dʒəˋpɑnɪk] ***a.*** 1. 日本的;日本人的;日本特有的。2. 日语的。

ja·pon·i·ca [dʒəˈpɔnikə; dʒəˋpɑnɪkə] ***n.***【植】日本榅桲,日本山茶。

Ja·ques [ˈdʒeikwiz; ˋdʒekwɪz] ***n.*** 詹奎兹〔莎士比亚所著剧本《如愿》(As You Like It)中的犬儒学派哲学家〕。

jar[1] [dʒɑː; dʒɑr] **I** ***vi.*** (***-rr-***) 1. 发出刺耳的声音,轧轧作响。2. 给人烦躁[痛苦]的感觉,刺激(*on*);(发出刺耳声地)撞击(*on*; *upon*; *against*)。3. 震动,震荡(不和谐地)反响,回荡。4. (意见、行动等)不一致,冲突,激烈争吵(*with*)。～ *on sb.* 给某人不快之感。～ *on sb.'s nerves* [*ear*] 刺激某人神经[耳朵]。*Their opinions* ～ *with ours.* 他们的意见和我们不一致。*It* ～*s with the surroundings.* 同周围环境不调和。— ***vt.*** 1. 使震动,使摇动。2. 使发出刺耳的声音。3. 给…不愉快的感觉;刺激神经等。*He was badly* ～*red by the blow.* 这个打击使他的神经受到很大的刺激。*The wind* ～*red the whole house.* 风吹得全屋轧轧地响。**II** ***n.*** 1. 刺耳的声音,轧轧声。2. 剧烈的震动。3. (精神上、肉体上)受到的

刺激[打击]。4. 冲突;不和,口角,争执。5.(节奏等)突然中止。*a hit of a* ～〔俚〕意外的震动。*family* ～*s* 家庭口角。*get a* ～ 受刺激。*be at a* ～在争执中。

jar[2][dʒɑː; dʒɑr] ***n*.** 1.(圆柱形、大口的)罐子,坛子,瓶子。2. 一罐[坛、瓶]的量。3.【电】电瓶,蓄电池壳。4.【电】加耳〔电容量单位,=1/900 微法〕。*a bell* ～钟罩。*a* ～ *of oil* 一罐油。*two* ～*s of honey* 两坛蜂蜜。*accumulator* ～蓄电池容器。*battery* ～蓄电池壳,蓄电池容器,电池槽,电瓶。*Vacuum* ～真空瓶,真空干燥器。

jar[3][dʒɑː; dʒɑr] ***n*.**〔古〕旋转。★今仅用于短语(*up*) *on the* [*a*] ～(门)半开着,微开着。

jar·di·niere [ˌʒɑːdiˈnjeə; ˏʒardnˋɪr] ***n*.**〔F.〕1. 花盆架;(装饰用的)花盆,花瓶。2. 花果叶花纹。3. 肉食的配头〔由几种蔬菜分别切开煮熟制成〕;炒素。

jar·gon[1][ˈdʒɑːgən; ˋdʒargən] **I *n*.** 1. 行话;黑话,隐语。2. 难懂的话,莫名其妙的话。3. 南腔北调的混合语〔如 Pidgin English, lingua franca 等〕。4. 奇特粗俗的语言[方言],土话。5.(鸟等)叽叽喳喳的叫声。*critics'* ～ 评论家的专用语。*law* ～法律界行话。**II *vi*., *vt*.** = jargonize. **-ic, -is·tic *a*.**

jar·gon[2], **jar·goon** [ˈdʒɑːgɑːn, dʒɑːˈguːn; ˋdʒargɑn, dʒarˋgun] ***n*.** 晶体锆灰色,非晶体锆黑色。

jar·go·nel(l)e [ˌdʒɑːgəˈnel; ˏdʒargəˋnel] ***n*.**(法国)早熟种黄梨。

jar·gon·ize [ˈdʒɑːgənaiz; ˋdʒargənˏaɪz] ***vi*.** 1. 讲难懂的话[行话、隐语、黑话]。2. 用行话[黑话等]写文章。— ***vt*.** 1. 用难懂的话[行话、隐语、黑话]讲或写。2. 使成为难懂的话。

jarl [jɑːl; jarl] ***n*.**【史】古代北欧的首领,贵族。

jar·o·vize [ˈjɑːrəvaiz; ˋjarəˏvaɪz] ***vt*.** 使春化;使加速开花结果(= vernalize)。**-vi·za·tion *n*.** 春化作用,春化处理。

jar·rah [ˈdʒærə; ˋdʒærə] ***n*.** 红柳桉树(*Eucalyptus marginata*)〔产于澳大利亚,红心,木质坚硬〕。

jar·ring [ˈdʒɑːriŋ; ˋdʒarɪŋ] **I *a*.** 1. 刺耳的。2. 不和谐的。**II *n*.** 1. 刺耳声。2. 振动。3. 冲突,倾轧,争执。**-ly *ad*.**

jar·v(e)y [ˈdʒɑːvi; ˋdʒarvɪ] ***n*.** 1.〔英口〕出租马车车夫。2.(爱尔兰的)轻便二轮马车车夫。

Jar·vis [ˈdʒɑːvis; ˋdʒarvɪs] ***n*.** 贾维斯〔男子名〕。

JAS = Journal of the Aeronautical Science〔美〕《航空科学学报》〔期刊名称〕。

Jas. = James.

ja·sey [ˈdʒeizi; ˋdʒezɪ] ***n*.**〔英口〕假发〔尤指毛线做的假发〕。

jas·min(e) [ˈdʒæsmin; ˋdʒæsmɪn] ***n*.** 1.【植】素馨;茉莉。2. 类似素馨的植物〔如栀子等〕。3. 素馨[茉莉]香水。4. 淡黄色。*the American* ～圆叶茑萝。*the Arabian* ～茉莉。*the winter* (*flowering*) ～迎春(花)。

Ja·son [ˈdʒeisn; ˋdʒesn] ***n*.** 1. 贾森〔男子名〕。2.【希神】伊阿宋〔忒萨利亚王子,曾率领一支勇敢的队伍乘 Argo 号船到海外寻找金羊毛,在 Medea 的帮助下,终于成功〕。

Jas·per [ˈdʒæspə; ˋdʒæspɚ] ***n*.** 贾斯珀〔男子名〕。

jas·per [ˈdʒæspə; ˋdʒæspɚ] ***n*.** 1.【矿】碧玉。2. 墨绿色。3.【圣】宝石。

Jas·pers [ˈjɑːspəs; ˋjæspɚs] ***n*.** Karl ～ 卡尔·雅斯帕尔斯〔1883—1969,德国哲学家〕。

jas·pil·ite, jas·pi·lyte [ˈdʒæspəlait; ˋdʒæspəˏlaɪt] ***n*.**【矿】(含有赤铁矿类似碧玉的)矽[硅]质岩石。

jas·sid [ˈdʒæsid; ˋdʒæsɪd] ***n*.**【植】浮尘子科(*Jassidae*)动物。

jato, JATO [ˈdʒeitəu; ˋdʒeto] = jet-assisted takeoff【空】1. 助飞。2. 助飞器,起飞加速器。～ *unit* 助飞装置,起飞加速装置。*reverse* ～反向助飞器,喷气煞车。

jaun·dice [ˈdʒɔːndis; ˋdʒɔndɪs] **I *n*.** 1.【医】黄疸;黄疸症〔如肝炎〕。2. 妒忌,猜忌;偏见。**II *vt*.** (***-diced***; ***-dic·ing***) 1. 使产生黄疸。2. 使妒忌,使猜忌,使成偏见。

jaun·diced [ˈdʒɔːndist; ˋdʒɔndɪst] ***a*.** 1. 害黄疸病的。2. 有偏见的,有猜忌心的,嫉妒心重的。*take a* ～ *view of sth*. 用持有偏见的眼光来看待某事。

jaunt [dʒɔːnt; dʒɔnt] **I *vi*.** 作短途游览。～*ing car*(爱尔兰的)轻快二轮马车。**II *n*.** 短途游览。

jaun·ty [ˈdʒɔːnti; ˋdʒɔntɪ] **I *a*.** 1.〔古〕斯文的。2. 时髦的,时兴的。3. 快活的,轻快的,活泼的;洋洋得意的;满怀信心的。**II *n*.**〔英俚〕舰船纠察队长,运输船纠察长。**-ti·ly *ad*. -ti·ness *n*.**

Jav. = Java(nese).

Ja·va [ˈdʒɑːvə; ˋdʒɑvə] ***n*.** 1. 爪哇〔印度尼西亚的大岛,面积 130,510 平方公里〕。2. 爪哇咖啡。3.〔俚〕〔常 j-〕咖啡。4. 爪哇鸡。5.【计】Java 语言〔源自 Java coffee,电脑编程专家据说都喜欢饮用此种咖啡〕。～ **canvas** 刺绣(用)十字布。～ **cotton** 木棉。～ **man** 爪哇猿人。～ **Sea** 爪哇海〔太平洋的一部分〕。～ **sparrow** 文鸟。

Ja·van [ˈdʒɑːvən; ˋdʒɑvən] ***a*., *n*.** = Javanese.

Jav·a·nese [ˌdʒævəˈniːz; ˏdʒævəˋniz] **I *a*.** 1. 爪哇的,爪哇人的。2. 爪哇语的。**II *n*.**〔*sing*., *pl*.〕1. 爪哇人。2. 爪哇语。

jav·e·lin [ˈdʒævlin; ˋdʒævlɪn] ***n*.** 标枪,投枪。～ **formation**【军】(轰炸机的)标枪队形。～ **throw(ing)**【体】掷标枪。～ **thrower** 标枪投手。

jav·e·li·na [ˌhɑːviˈliːnə; ˏhævɪˋlinə] ***n*.**〔美〕西貒,野猪(= peccary)。

jaw [dʒɔː; dʒɔ] **I *n*.** 1. 颌,颚。2.〔*pl*.〕上下颌,口部,口腔。3.〔*pl*.〕(峡谷、通路等的)狭口,咽喉。4.【机】爪,虎钳牙;叉头,〔*pl*.〕夹片。5.〔*pl*.〕危险境遇。6.〔口〕嚼舌头,说废话;讲道,训人。*the lower* [*upper*] ～下[上]颌。*the* ～*s of danger* 险境。*be snatched from the* ～*s of death* 从死亡的绝境中被抢救出来。*get into* [*out of*] *the* ～*s of death* 陷入[逃脱]险境。***be all*** ～ 刺刺不休,一篇空话。***Hold your*** ～! 住嘴! 别唠叨了! ***Jaws of life*** 救生叉〔一种剪刀状液压机械,其叉头可强行分开堆积物或举托起重物,多用于地震救生等场所〕。***lantern*** ～尖瘦的嘴脸。***sb.'s*** ～ ***drops*** 某人惊讶得目瞪口呆。***wag one's*** [***the***] ～(*s*) 喋喋不休。**II *vt*.**〔俚〕向…唠叨;唠唠叨叨地训斥。— ***vi*.**〔俚〕唠叨;唠唠叨叨地责备。～ **breaker** 1.〔口〕难发音的字。2.〔美俚〕一种圆的硬糖。3.【矿】颚形碎石[矿]机。～**-breaking *a*.** 极难发音的。～ **crusher** 颚式破碎机,虎口碎矿机。～ **plate** 腭板,颌板。

jaw·bone [ˈdʒɔːˈbəun; ˋdʒɔˋbon] **I *n*.** 1. 腭骨,颌骨,牙床骨。2.〔美俚〕借贷;借到的款子。3.〔美俚〕(财务上的)信用。**II *vi*.**〔美俚〕1. 耐心地讲道理以达到赊买[借贷等]目的。2. 赊卖给人;借贷给人。— ***vt*.**〔美俚〕1. 赊买,借到。2. 利用职权企图压服(某人),利用权势对…施加压力。**III *ad*.**〔美俚〕凭信用地。*buy* ～赊买;分期付款购买。

jaw-jaw [ˈdʒɔːˈdʒɔː; ˋdʒɔˋdʒɔ]〔英俚〕**I *vi*.** 喋喋不休;进行冗长而乏味的讨论。**II *n*.** 长谈;冗长而无结果的讨论。

jay [dʒei; dʒe] ***n*.** 1.【动】樫鸟。2.〔口〕爱唠叨的傻瓜。3.〔美俚〕花花公子;乡下佬;呆汉,容易受骗的人。4. 中蓝色。5.〔美俚〕大麻卷烟。***scalp sb. for a*** ～ 愚弄某人。～**bird *n*.**【动】樫鸟〔～的方言变体〕。

Jay [dʒei; dʒe] ***n*.** 1. 杰伊〔姓氏,男子名〕。2. John ～约翰·杰伊〔1745—1829,美国政治家和法学家〕。

jay·cee [ˈdʒeiˈsiː; ˋdʒeˋsi] ***n*.**〔美〕1. 国际青年会(Junior Chamber, International)会员。2. 美国青年会(United States Jaycee)会员〔源出 J. C. 二字母的发音〕。

jay·gee [ˈdʒeiˈdʒiː; ˋdʒeˋdʒi] ***n*.**〔美〕海军中尉。

jay·hawk·er [ˈdʒeiˌhɔːkə; ˋdʒeˏhɔkɚ] ***n*.** 1.〔美俚〕(南北战争时期)废除农奴派的游击队员。2. 强盗;袭击者,掠夺者。3.〔口〕[J-]堪萨斯州人。*the J- State*〔美〕堪萨

J

斯州。

jay·hawk·ing [ˈdʒeihɔːkiŋ; ˋdʒeˏhɔkɪŋ] ***n*.** 〔美俚〕盗窃；掠夺。

jay·vee [ˈdʒeiˈviː; ˋdʒeˋvi] ***n*.** 〔美〕大学运动队二队(或其成员)〔源出 junior versity 开首二字母 j 和 v 的发音〕。

jay·walk [ˈdʒeiˌwɔːk; ˋdʒeˏwɔk] ***vi*.** 〔美口〕(不遵守交通规则)乱穿马路。*No ~ing!* 不要乱穿马路! **-er *n*.** 乱穿马路的人。

jazz [dʒæz; dʒæz] **I *n*. 1.** 爵士音乐，爵士舞(曲)。**2.** 〔美俚〕爵士音乐风格〔刺激、兴奋、活泼、放纵〕；活泼放纵。**3.** 浮华而不实的行为；陈腔滥调的废话。**II *a*. 1.** 爵士音乐的。**2.** 不调和的；(色彩等)花哨恶俗的。*a ~ garden* 有舞池的咖啡馆。*a ~ hound* 舞迷。**III *vt*. 1.** 把…奏成爵士音乐。**2.** 在…中加入爵士音乐风味；使有刺激性，使活泼 (*up*)。**3.** 〔美俚〕加快…的速度。— ***vi*. 1.** 奏爵士乐；跳爵士舞。**2.** 游荡 (*around*)。~**ballet** 爵士芭蕾舞。~ **band** 爵士乐队。~ **buff** 爵士音乐迷。~**-funk** 爵士乡土乐。~**man** (*pl*. **-men**) 爵士音乐演奏者。~ **music** 爵士音乐。**-ist *n*.** 爵士音乐爱好者。**-y *a*. 1.** 有爵士音乐特征的。**2.** 〔美俚〕活泼放纵的。**-i·ly *ad*. -i·ness *n*.**

J.B. = John Bull.

J.C. = **1.** Jesus Christ. **2.** Julius Caesar. **3.** jurisconsult.

J.C.B. = 〔L.〕*Juris Civilis Baccalaureus* 民法学士(= Bachelor of Civil Law)。

J.C.D., JCD = **1.** 〔L.〕*Juris Canonici Doctor* 教会法博士 (= Doctor of Canon Law)。**2.** 〔L.〕*Juris Civilis Doctor* 民法学博士 (= Doctor of Civil Law)。

J.C.R. = Junior Combination Room; Junior Common Room 〔英〕大学三年级学生公共休息室。

JCS = Joint Chiefs of Staff 〔美〕参谋长联席会议。

jct. = junction.

JD = **1.** 〔L.〕*Jurum Doctor* 法学博士 (= Doctor of Laws)。**2.** juvenile delinquency (or delinquent) 少年罪犯。

Je. = June.

jeal·ous [ˈdʒeləs; ˋdʒɛləs] ***a*. 1.** 妒忌心重的，吃醋的；出于妒忌的。**2.** 猜疑的，留意提防的。**3.** 爱惜的，注意的，戒备的。**4.** 【宗】〔罕〕(上帝)要求绝对忠实和崇敬的。*a ~ wife* 一个爱妒忌的妻子。*be ~ of sb.'s fame* 妒忌某人的名声。*a ~ guardian* 谨慎的保护人。*with ~ care* 小心翼翼。*a citizen ~ of* [*for*] *his rights* 珍惜自己权利的公民。*a ~ rage* 怨愤。~ **glass** 不透明玻璃。**-ly *ad*. -ness *n*.**

jeal·ous·y [ˈdʒeləsi; ˋdʒɛləsɪ] ***n*. 1.** 妒忌，猜忌。**2.** 小心提防，谨慎戒备。

Jean [dʒiːn; dʒin] ***n*.** 吉恩〔**1.** 男子名，John 的异体。**2.** 女子名，Joanna 的异体〕。

jean [dʒein; dʒen] ***n*. 1.** 【纺】三页细斜纹布。**2.** 〔*pl*.〕(三页细斜纹蓝布做的)工作服，工装裤。*blue jeans* 牛仔裤，牛仔装。~**swear** 便服工装裤。

Jeanne [dʒiːn; dʒin] ***n*.** 珍妮〔女子名，Joan(n)的异体〕。

Jean·(n)ette [dʒiˈnet; dʒɪˋnɛt] ***n*.** 珍妮特〔女子名，Jeanne 的昵称〕。

Jeans [dʒiːnz; dʒinz] ***n*. 1.** 琼斯〔姓氏〕。**2. Sir James (Hopwood)** ~ 詹姆士·琼斯〔1877—1946，英国数学家，物理学家，天文学家〕。

jeans·wear [ˈdʒiːzwɛə; ˋdʒizwɛr] ***n*.** 〔总称〕(各式)牛仔裤，牛仔装。

Jeb(b) [dʒeb; dʒɛb] ***n*.** 杰布〔姓氏〕。

je·bel [ˈdʒebl; ˋdʒɛbḷ] ***n*.** 〔Ar.〕山，高山〔时常作阿拉伯地方名字用〕。*J- Druze* (*Druse*) (叙利亚的)德鲁兹山。

jee [dʒiː; dʒi] **I *int*., *n*.** 驾!〔驭马用语"向右走!"，"向前走!"之意〕**II *vt*., *vi*.** (***jeed***; ***jee·ing***) (使马)向前[右]走(= gee)。

jeep [dʒiːp; dʒip] **I *n*. 1.** 吉普车；小型越野汽车。**2.** 【军】小型护航航空母舰(= ~ carrier)。**3.** 有线电视系统。**4** 新兵。**5.** 轻型侦察机。*TV ~* (实况转播的)电视车。**I *vi*.** 坐吉普车旅行。— ***vt*.** 用吉普车运输。

jee·pers [ˈdʒiːpəz; ˋdʒipɚz] ***int*.** 天呀!〔表示惊讶、强调等的适度感叹词〕。

jeer[1] [dʒiə; dʒɪr] **I *n*.** 嘲笑，戏弄。**II *vi*., *vt*.** 嘲笑，戏弄 (*at*)。**-ing·ly *ad*.**

jeer[2] [dʒiə; dʒɪr] ***n*.** 〔常 *pl*.〕【海】升降帆的滑车索。

jeer·er [ˈdʒiərə; ˋdʒɪrɚ] ***n*.** 嘲笑者，戏弄者。***J-s must be content to taste of their own broth*.** 〔谚〕嘲笑人者必被人笑。

Jeff [dʒef; dʒɛf] ***n*.** Jeffrey 的爱称。

Jef·fers [ˈdʒefəz; ˋdʒɛfɚz] ***n*. 1.** 杰佛斯〔姓氏〕。**2. John Robinson** ~ 约翰·鲁滨逊·杰佛斯〔1887—1962，美国诗人〕。

Jef·fer·son [ˈdʒefəsn; ˋdʒɛfɚsn] ***n*. 1.** 杰弗逊〔姓氏〕。**2. Thomas** ~ 汤姆斯·杰斐逊〔1743—1826，美国政治家，第三任总统，独立宣言的起草人〕。~ **City** 杰斐逊城〔美国密苏里州的首府〕。~ **Day** 杰斐逊诞辰纪念节〔4月 13 日，在美国某些州为法定假日〕。**-so·ni·an** [ˌdʒefəˈsəuniən; ˏdʒɛfɚˋsonɪən] **1. *a*.** 杰斐逊特性的；杰斐逊思想的，杰斐逊民主的。**2. *n*.** 杰斐逊追随者。**-so·ni·an·ism *n*.** 杰斐逊主义。

Jeff·rey(s) [ˈdʒefri(z); ˋdʒɛfrɪ(z)] ***n*.** 杰弗里(斯)〔姓氏，男子名，Jeff 为其昵称〕。

je·had [dʒiˈhɑːd; dʒɪˋhɑd] ***n*.** = jihad.

Je·ho·vah [dʒiˈhəuvə; dʒɪˋhovə] ***n*.** 【宗】(对上帝的称呼)耶和华。

Je·ho·vist [dʒiˈhəuvist; dʒɪˋhovɪst] ***n*.** = Yahwist.

Je·hu [ˈdʒiːhjuː; ˋdʒihju] ***n*. 1.** 【圣】耶和〔以色列国王，相传为莽撞的御车者。**2.** 〔j-〕〔俚〕出租马车车夫；出租汽车司机。**3.** 〔谑〕莽撞的车夫[司机]。***drive like*** ~〔美口〕开飞车。

je·june [dʒiˈdʒuːn; dʒɪˋdʒun] ***a*. 1.** 缺乏营养的；(土地等)贫瘠的。**2.** (内容等)空洞的；枯燥无味的。**3.** 幼稚的，不成熟的。*a ~ diet* 缺乏营养的食物。*a ~ narrative* 枯燥无味的叙述。*a ~ behavior toward others* 孩子气的待人态度。**-ly *ad*. -ness *n*.**

je·ju·nec·to·my [ˌdʒidʒuːˈnektəmi; ˏdʒɪdʒuˋnɛktəmɪ] ***n*.** (*pl*. ***-mies***) 【医】空肠切除术。

je·ju·num [dʒiˈdʒuːnəm; dʒɪˋdʒunəm] ***n*.** (*pl*. ***-na*** [-nə; -nə]) 【解】空肠。

Je·kyll [ˈdʒiːkil, ˈdʒekil; ˋdʒikɪl, ˋdʒɛkɪl] ***n*.** 杰基尔〔姓氏〕。

Je·kyll and Hyde [ˈdʒekil ənd ˈhaid; ˋdʒɛkɪl ənd ˋhaɪd] 有两种面目的人，具双重人格的人〔原为英国小说家斯蒂文生故事中的一个人物，他服用自配的药物，使自己时而变恶，时而变善〕。*lead a Jekyll and Hyde existence* 过双重人格的生活。

jell [dʒel; dʒɛl] **I *vi*.** 〔美口〕**1.** 凝成胶状，结冻。**2.** (意见、计划等)定形，具体化，变明确。— ***vt*. 1.** 使成胶状，使结冻。**2.** 使定形，使具体化，使明确。*plans that haven't ~ed yet* 没有定形的计划。**II *n*.** 果子冻；肉冻；胶状物。

jel·la·ba [dʒeˈlɑːbɑː; dʒɛˋlæbɑ] ***n*.** = djellaba.

jel·lied [ˈdʒelid; ˋdʒɛlɪd] ***a*. 1.** 成胶状的，胶黏的，胶质的。**2.** 外涂胶状物的。**3.** 拌有果子冻的。~ **gasolene** 胶凝汽油，凝气油剂。

jel·li·fy [ˈdʒelifai; ˋdʒɛləˏfaɪ] ***vt*., *vi*. 1.** (使)成胶状。**2.** (使)变松懈，(使)变软弱。**-fi·ca·tion *n*.** 胶凝；冻结；凝结。

Jell-O [ˈdʒeləu; ˋdʒɛlo] ***n*.** 〔美〕(商标名)吉露牌果子冻〔作甜食吃〕；〔j-〕果子冻。

jel·ly [ˈdʒeli; ˋdʒɛlɪ] **I *n*. 1.** (透明)冻(胶)，胶状物。**2.** 果子冻，肉冻。**3.** 畏惧，优柔寡断。**4.** 〔美俚〕不费力的事，不花钱得来的东西。***beat sb. to*** [***into***] ***a*** ~ 痛打某人。**II *vt*.** (***-lied***; ***-ly·ing***) **1.** 使成胶质；使冻。**2.**

J

在…上加胶冻物。— *vi*. 1. 结冻,凝结,成胶状。2. 〔美俚〕闲逛聊天。~ **baby** = ~ bean. ~**-bag** 做果酱时滤果汁用的袋。~ **bean** *n*. 豆形胶质软糖。~**fish** 1.【动】水母,海蜇。2. 〔美俚〕无骨气的人;优柔寡断的人。~ **graph** 胶版。~ **roll** *n*. 涂果子冻的薄卷饼。

jem·a·dar [ˈdʒemədɑː; ˋdʒemədɑr] *n*. 〔Ind.〕1. 印度军队中的尉官。2. 印度警官。3. 仆人头目。4. 〔印度用的英语〕〔口〕打扫工。

jem·my [ˈdʒemi; ˋdʒɛmɪ] *n*. 1. = jimmy. 2. 〔英〕羊头肉。

Je·na [ˈjeinə; ˋjenə] *n*. 耶拿〔德国城市〕。

je ne sais quoi [ʒə nə ˌseiˈkwɑː; ʒə nə ˏseˋkwa] 〔F.〕1. 难以描绘和表达的东西[事件]。2. 我不知道是什么(= I do not know what)。

Jen·ghiz Khan, Jen·ghis Khan [ˈdʒengisˈkɑːn; ˋdʒɛngɪsˋkɑn] 成吉思汗〔1162—1227, 大蒙古国创造者, 即元太祖〕(= Genghis Khan)。

Jen·kin(s) [ˈdʒenkin(z); ˋdʒɛnkɪn(z)] *n*. 詹金(斯)〔姓氏〕。

Jen·ner(s) [ˈdʒenə(z); ˋdʒɛnɚ(z)] *n*. 1. 詹纳(斯)〔姓氏〕。2. **Edward** ~爱德华·詹纳〔1749—1823, 英国医生,种痘法的首创人〕。3. **William** ~威廉·詹纳〔1815—1898,英国医生〕。

jen·net [ˈdʒenit; ˋdʒɛnɪt] *n*. 1. 一种西班牙产的小马。2. 母驴。

Jen·ni·fer [ˈdʒenifə; ˋdʒɛnəfɚ] *n*. 詹妮弗〔女子名〕。

Jen·nings [ˈdʒeniŋz; ˋdʒɛnɪŋz] *n*. 詹宁斯〔姓氏〕。

Jen·ny [ˈdʒeni; ˋdʒɛnɪ] *n*. 詹妮〔女子名〕。

Jen·ny [ˈdʒeni; ˋdʒɛnɪ] *n*. 1.【机】移动起重机,移动吊车。2.【纺】(同时可织几条线的)旧式纺纱机。3. 雌鸟;母驴;某些雌性动物。~ **ass** 母驴。~ **wren** 雌鹪鹩〔俗名"巧妇鸟"〕。

jeop·ard [ˈdʒepəd; ˋdʒɛpɚd] *vt*. 〔美〕= jeopardize.

jeop·ard·ize, jeop·ard·ise [ˈdʒepədaiz; ˋdʒɛpɚˏdaɪz] *vt*. 使受危险[危害],危及。~ *one's life* 冒生命危险。

jeop·ard·y [ˈdʒepədi; ˋdʒɛpɚdɪ] *n*. 1. 危难,危险。2.【法】有罪受刑的可能性。3. 刑事案件中被告的处境。*be in ~ of one's life* 处于生命危险中。*guarantee against double ~* 对同一罪犯不受双重审判的保障。

je·quir·i·ty [dʒiˈkwiəriti; dʒɪˋkwɪrətɪ] *n*. (*pl*. *-ties*)【植】1. 相思豆,红豆(= ~ bean)。2. 相思子(= *Abrus precatorius*)。

Jer. = Jeremiah; Jeremy; Jerome; Jersey.

jer·bo·a [dʒəːˈbəuə; dʒɚˋboə] *n*.【动】跳鼠〔后腿特长〕。

jer·e·mi·ad [ˌdʒeriˈmaiəd; ˏdʒɛrɪˋmaɪəd] *n*. 哀诉;哀史,悲哀的故事。

jer·e·mi·ah [ˌdʒeriˈmaiə; ˏdʒɛrɪˋmaɪə] *n*. 1. 杰里迈亚〔男子名, Jerry 为其昵称; Jeremy 的异体〕。2.【宗】耶利米〔公元前六、七世纪时希伯来的大预言家〕。3.【宗】(《圣经·旧约》中的)《耶利米书》。4. 对于前途抱悲观主义的人。

Jer·e·my [ˈdʒerimi; ˋdʒɛrəmɪ] *n*. 杰里米〔男子名〕。

Jer·i·cho [ˈdʒerikəu; ˋdʒɛrɪko] *n*. 1. 耶利哥〔死海以北的古城〕。2. 〔口〕非常遥远的地方。***from ~ to June*** 非常遥远地。***Go to ~!*** 滚蛋! ***stay [tarry] in ~ until one's beard is grown*** 静待时机。

jerk[1] [dʒəːk; dʒɚk] **I** *n*. 1. 急促而猛烈的动作;猛地一拉[一推、一扭、一扔等]。2.【医】(因反射动作引起的)肌肉痉挛。3. [*pl*.](因受感动引起的)四肢或脸部的抽搐。4.【体】举重的挺举。5. 〔美俚〕笨蛋,傻瓜;微不足道的人。*a knee ~*膝跳(反射)。*physical ~s* 〔口〕体操。***get a ~ on*** 卖力干,赶紧干。***in a ~*** 立刻,马上。***pull with a ~*** 猛地一扯。***put a ~ to [into] it*** 使劲干,努力干。**II** *vt*. 1. 猛拉,猛推,猛撞,猛扭。2. 急促说出,突然说出。3. 〔俚〕在冷饮店里供应(苏打水、冰淇淋等)。~ *a fish out of the water* 猛地从水里拉出一条鱼。— *vi*. 1. 急拉,猛推,猛撞。2. 颠簸地行进。3. 痉挛。*The door ~ed open*. 门突然开了。~ ***chin music*** 多嘴。~ ***out one's words*** 脱口说出。

jerk[2] [dʒəːk; dʒɚk] *vt*. 把(牛肉)切成薄片晒干。*~ed beef* 牛肉干。**II** *n*. = jerky[2].

jer·kin [ˈdʒəːkin; ˋdʒɚkɪn] *n*. 1. (十六、十七世纪时)一种无袖紧身皮茄克;短上衣。2. 女用背心。

jerk·wa·ter [ˈdʒəːkwɔːtə; ˋdʒɚkˏwɔtə] **I** *n*. 〔美〕铁路专用支线。**II** *a*. 1. 铁路专用支线上的。2. 〔口〕不重要的,微小的,乡下的。*a ~ town* 铁路上的小镇。*a ~ train* 慢车。*a ~ person* 无足轻重的人。

jer·ky[1] [ˈdʒəːki; ˋdʒɚkɪ] *a*. (***jerk·i·er***; ***-i·est***) 1. 急拉的;急跳的;急动的。2. 痉挛性的。3. 颠簸的,不平稳的。4. 愚蠢的,笨拙的。5. 拗口的,佶屈聱牙的。*a ~ vehicle* 颠簸的破车辆。*a ~ mind* 疯子。**-i·ly** *ad*. **-i·ness** *n*.

jer·ky[2] [ˈdʒəːki; ˋdʒɚkɪ] *n*. 肉片干,牛肉干。

jer·o·bo·am [ˌdʒerəˈbəuəm; ˏdʒɛrəˋboəm] *n*. 大酒杯〔尤指盛香槟酒的酒杯〕。

Je·rome [dʒəˈrəum; dʒəˋrom] *n*. 杰罗姆〔姓氏,男子名, Jerry 为其昵称〕。

jer·que [dʒəːk; dʒɚk] *vt*. 〔英〕检查(船中有无私货)。**-r** *n*. 船舶检查员,水上稽查员。

jer·ri·can [ˈdʒerikæn; ˋdʒɛrɪˏkæn] *n*. = jerrycan.

Jer·(r)old, Jer·ald [ˈdʒerəld; ˋdʒɛrəld] *n*. 杰罗尔德〔男子名, Gerald 的异体〕。

jer·ry[1] [ˈdʒeri; ˋdʒɛrɪ] *a*. 草率了事的,偷工减料的,马虎应付的。~**-build** *vt*. 偷工减料地建造。~ **builder** *n*. 偷工减料的营造商。~ **building** 偷工减料的建筑工程。~**-built** *a*. 偷工减料地建造的,用贱料草草建成的。~ **can** 五加仑的大汽油[水]罐(= jerrican)。

jer·ry[2] [ˈdʒeri; ˋdʒɛrɪ] *n*. 〔英俚〕夜壶,尿罐。

Jer·ry [ˈdʒeri; ˋdʒɛrɪ] *n*. 1. 杰丽〔女子名, Geraldine 的昵称〕。2. 〔英俚〕德国兵,德国人。

jer·ry·man·der [ˈdʒeriˌmændə; ˋdʒɛrɪˏmændɚ] *v*., *n*. = gerrymander.

Jer·sey [ˈdʒəːzi; ˋdʒɚzɪ] *n*. 泽西岛〔英吉利海峡中最大的岛〕。~ **barrier** (公路上的)防碰撞护栏〔混凝土锥形路障,用以分割对面驶来的车辆之车道〕。~ **City** 泽西城〔美国新泽西州东北部的海港城市〕。

jer·sey [ˈdʒəːzi; ˋdʒɚzɪ] *n*. (*pl*. *~s*) 1. 〔J-〕泽西种乳牛。2.【纺】平针织物。3. 针织紧身内衣;卫生衫,运动衫。

Je·ru·sa·lem [dʒeˈruːsələm; dʒeˋrusələm] *n*. 耶路撒冷〔巴勒斯坦古城,犹太教、基督教和伊斯兰教的圣地〕。*The New ~* 天堂,乐园。~ **artichoke** 1.【植】北美菊芋(洋姜)(*Helianthus tuberosus*)。2. 洋姜。~ **cherry**【植】冬珊瑚(*Solanum pseudo-capsicum*),毛叶冬珊瑚(*Solanum capsicastrum*)。~ **cricket**【动】耶路撒冷蟋蟀〔产于美国西部干燥地区〕。~ **oak**【植】总状花藜(*Chenopodium botrys*)〔产于美国北部和加拿大〕。~ **thorn**【植】1. 扁叶轴木(*Parkinsonia aculeata*)〔产于美洲热带地区〕。2. 滨枣,刺马甲子(= christ's thorn)。

Jer·vis [ˈdʒɑːvis, ˈdʒəːvis; ˋdʒɑvɪs, ˋdʒɚvɪs] *n*. 杰维斯〔姓氏〕。

Jes. = Jesus.

Jes·per·sen [ˈjespəsn, ˈdʒes-; ˋjɛspəsn, ˋdʒɛs-], **Otto** ~ 奥托·叶[杰]斯帕森〔1860—1943, 丹麦语言学家,尤以英语见长〕。

jess [dʒes; dʒɛs] **I** *n*. 猎鹰的脚带。**II** *vt*. 给(鹰)系上脚带。

jes·sa·mine [ˈdʒesəmin; ˋdʒɛsəmɪn] *n*. = jasmin(e).

Jes·se [ˈdʒesi; ˋdʒɛsɪ] *n*. 1. 杰西〔男子名, Jess 为其昵称〕。2.【宗】耶西〔以色列王大卫的父亲之名〕。~ **tree**【宗】耶稣的家谱。~ **window** 书有耶稣家谱的玻璃窗。

jes·se, jes·sie, jes·sy [ˈdʒesi; ˋdʒɛsɪ] *n*. 〔美俚〕辱骂;殴打。***catch ~*** 〔美俚〕受责骂;被殴打。***give sb. ~*** 〔美俚〕痛责某人;殴打某人。

J

Jes·si·ca [ˈdʒesikə; ˋdʒɛsɪkə] ***n.*** 洁西卡〔女子名〕。

Jes·sie [ˈdʒesi; ˋdʒɛsɪ] ***n.*** 洁西〔女子名〕。

jest [dʒest; dʒɛst] **I** ***n.*** **1.** 玩笑,笑话,俏皮话。**2.** 戏谑,诙谐;打趣。**3.** 笑柄。***Better lose a ～ than a friend*** 〔谚〕宁肯少说笑话,决不得罪朋友。***be a standing ～*** 经常被嘲笑的对象。***break*** [***drop***] ***a ～*** 说笑话。***in ～*** 开玩笑地(*speak half in ～, half in earnest* 半真半假地讲)。***～ing apart*** 〔作插入语用〕说正经的。***make a ～ of sb.*** 愚弄某人。**II** ***vi.*** **1.** 取笑,嘲弄(*at*)。**2.** 开玩笑,打趣(*with*)。*Please don't ～ with me.* 请别和我开玩笑。*～ at sb.* 嘲笑某人。— ***vt.*** 对…开玩笑,嘲笑。**～book** ***n.*** 笑话书。**-ful** ***a.***

jest·er [ˈdʒestə; ˋdʒɛstɚ] ***n.*** **1.** 爱说笑话的人。**2.** 小丑,(中世纪的)弄臣。

jest·ing [ˈdʒestiŋ; ˋdʒɛstɪŋ] **I** ***n.*** 笑话;滑稽,诙谐。**II** ***a.*** 开玩笑的,爱说笑话的,滑稽的。**-ly** ***ad.***

Je·su [ˈdʒiːzjuː; ˋdʒizju] ***n.*** 〔古〕= Jesus〔尤用于呼格〕。

Jes·u·it [ˈdʒez*j*uit; ˋdʒɛz*j*ʊɪt] ***n.*** **1.** 【天主】耶稣会会士。**2.** 阴险的人,虚伪狡诈的人。*the ～s* 耶稣会。***～s'*** [***～'s***] ***bark*** 【植】金鸡纳树皮,金鸡纳皮。**-ic(al)** ***a.*** **-i·cal·ly** ***ad.***

Jes·u·it·ism [ˈdʒezjuitizəm; ˋdʒɛzʊɪtɪzəm] ***n.*** **1.** 耶稣会的教义。**2.** 〔j-〕狡猾,阴险。

Jes·u·it·ize [ˈdʒezjuitaiz; ˋdʒɛzʊɪt͵aɪz] ***vt*** (***-ized, -iz·ing***) **1.** 使成为耶稣会会员。**2.** 使变狡猾,使变阴险。

Jes·u·it·ry [ˈdʒez*j*uitri; ˋdʒɛz*j*ʊɪtrɪ] ***n.*** = Jesuitism.

Je·sus [ˈdʒiːzəs; ˋdʒizəs] **I** ***n.*** **1.** 杰西〔男子名〕。**2.** 【宗】耶稣〔基督教的创始人〕。*the society of ～* (天主教的)耶稣会。***knock the ～ out of sb.*** 把某人打得昏头昏脑。**II** ***int.*** 天哪! 岂有此理!〔表示怀疑、不满、失望、惊恐、痛苦,甚至辱骂,有时也说 ～ Christ!〕。～ **Christ** 耶稣基督。

JET = Joint European Torus 欧洲联合核变实验装置。

jet[1] [dʒet; dʒɛt] **I** ***n.*** **1.** 【矿】煤玉,黑色大理石。**2.** 乌黑发亮的颜色。**II** ***a.*** **1.** 煤玉制的,黑色大理石制的。**2.** 乌黑发亮的。*her ～ hair* 她那一头乌油油的秀发。**～-black** ***a.*** 乌黑发亮的,黑玉色的。**jet·ted** ***a.*** 用黑玉装饰的。

jet[2] [dʒet; dʒɛt] ***n.*** **1.** 喷射,喷出;【物】喷注,气流;射流。**2.** 喷口,喷嘴;喷射器。**3.** 【空】喷气式发动机;喷气[喷射]式飞机。**4.** 喷出物;〔喻〕喷流式的涌出物。*an electron ～* 电子束,电子流。*a plasma ～* 等离子流。*a nozzle ～* 汽嘴。*travel by ～* 乘喷气式飞机旅行。*talk in a ～* 滔滔不绝地谈话。*a ～ of water sent up by a fountain* 喷泉中喷出的水束。***at a single ～*** 一想就懂。***at the first ～*** 由于一时的冲动。**II** ***vt.*** (**-tt-**) **1.** 喷射出(水流等)。**2.** 用喷气式飞机载送。— ***vi.*** **1.** 喷射。**2.** 乘坐喷气式飞机。**3.** 飞速移动。**III** ***a.*** **1.** 喷气式(发动机)推进的。**2.** 用喷气式飞机的。**3.** 迅速的,飞快的。**～airplane** = ～plane. ～ **blower** 【机】喷气鼓风机。**～boat** 喷气快艇。～ **burner** 喷射口,火口。～ **engine** 喷气发动机,空气喷气发动机。**～foil** 〔主英〕喷气式水翼船。～ **generator** 【物】喷注发生器,液哨(超音波发生器)。～ **lag** (乘喷气式飞机高速飞行引起的)生理节奏失调;(连续几次航行后的)疲累;时差感;飞行时差反应。**～liner** 喷气客机〔尤指班机〕。**～plane** 喷气式飞机。**～port** 喷气式飞机机场。**～powered** 喷气动力的。**～-propelled** ***a.*** 喷气发动机推动的,喷射推进式的。**～-propeller** 喷气式推进器,喷气式螺旋桨。～ **propulsion** 【空】喷气推进。～ **pump** 【机】喷射泵。～ **set** 喷气机旅行界〔乘喷气客机到处旅行的富翁阶层〕。～ **setter** 乘喷气飞机到处旅行的富人。**～-ski** **1.** ***n.*** (以动力驱动、有水橇形扁平龙骨的)喷气式滑橇。**2.** ***vi.*** 作喷气式滑水运动。～ **stream** **1.** 急流,喷流。**2.** 【空】喷射气流,喷流。～ **vane** 喷气导流控制片,燃气舵。

jet·bead [ˈdʒebiːd; ˋdʒɛbid] ***n.*** 【植】鸡麻属〔灌木,花为四瓣,呈白色;果似小珠,发亮而呈黑色〕。

je·té [ʒəˈtei; ʒəˋte] ***n.*** 〔F.〕(芭蕾舞)越步。

je·ton [ˈdʒetn; ˋdʒɛtn] ***n.*** (公用电话等的)自动计费器。

jet·sam [ˈdʒetsəm; ˋdʒɛtsəm] ***n.*** **1.** 船舶遇难时投弃的货物[船上的装备]。**2.** 沉入海底或冲上岸的废弃货物[设备]。**3.** 废弃的东西。**flotsam and ～** **1.** 飘浮海面或冲到岸上的船只残骸或其货物。**2.** 流离失所者,流浪者,被毁掉的人。**3.** 零碎物,无价值的东西。

jet·ti·son [ˈdʒetisn; ˋdʒɛtɪsn] **I** ***n.*** **1.** (紧急情况下的)投弃货物。**2.** 抛弃,放弃。**II** ***vt.*** **1.** (在紧急情况下)向海中投弃(货物等)。**2.** 扔弃(累赘物品)。**3.** (飞机等在飞行时)投弃(炸药、辅助装备、燃料等)。

jet·ty[1] [ˈdʒeti; ˋdʒɛtɪ] ***a.*** **1.** 煤玉似的。**2.** 乌黑发亮的。

jet·ty[2] [ˈdʒeti; ˋdʒɛtɪ] **I** ***n.*** (*pl.* ***-ties***) **1.** 防波堤。**2.** 码头。**3.** 【建】建筑物的突出部。**II** ***vi.*** (***-tied; -ty·ing***) 突出,伸出。

jeu [ʒəː; ʒɛ] ***n.*** (*pl.* ***jeux*** [ʒəː(z); ʒɛ(z)]) 〔F.〕 **1.** 游戏,娱乐。**2.** 【乐】演奏。～ ***de mots*** [F. ˈʒəːdəˈməu; ʒɛdəˋmo] 双关话,俏皮话。～ ***d'es·prit*** [F. ˈʒəːdesˈpriː; ˋʒɛdɛsˋpri] 机智的话,妙语。

jeune fille [F. ʒœnˈfiːjə; ʒœnˋfijə]〔F.〕年轻女子,小姐。

jeune pre·mier [F. ʒœn prəˈmje; ʒœn prəˋmjɛ]〔F.〕扮演少年主角的男演员。

jeu·nesse do·rée [F. ʒœnɛs dɔre; ʒœˋnɛs doˋrɛ]〔F.〕阔少爷,花花公子。

jeux [ʒəː(z); ʒɛ] jeu 的复数。

Jev·ons [ˈdʒevənz; ˋdʒɛvənz] ***n.*** **1.** 杰文斯〔姓氏〕。**2.** William Stanley ～ 威廉·斯坦利·杰文斯〔1835—1882,英国经济学家和逻辑学家〕。

Jew [dʒuː; dʒu] **I** ***n.*** **1.** 犹太人,犹太教徒。**2.** 〔贬〕高利贷者;守财奴;奸商。*an unbelieving ～* 疑心重的人。*the wondering ～* 流浪的犹太人,流浪者。(***as***) ***rich as a ～*** 大财主。***go to the ～s*** 〔俚〕向高利贷者借钱。***Tell that to the ～s.*** 鬼相信那种话。***worth a ～'s eye*** 〔古〕极为贵重。**II** ***vt.*** 〔j-〕 **1.** 〔俚〕欺骗。**2.** 〔口〕杀价购买(*down*)。**～-baiter** 迫害犹太人者。**～-baiting** 迫害犹太人。**-dom** **1.** 〔集合词〕犹太人;犹太人的世界。**2.** 犹太教。

jew·el [ˈdʒuːəl; ˋdʒuəl] **I** ***n.*** **1.** 宝石,宝玉。**2.** 宝石饰物,镶有宝石的装饰品。**3.** 贵重的人[物]。**4.** 手表中的宝石轴承。*a ～ of a boy* 宝贝孩子。**II** ***vt.*** (***jewel(l)ed; jewel(l)ing***) **1.** 用宝石装饰。**2.** 把宝石轴承镶进(手表中)。**～weed** 【植】(北美产)凤仙花属(*Impatiens*)植物。**-like** ***a.***

Jew·el(l) [ˈdʒuːəl; ˋdʒuəl] ***n.*** 朱厄尔〔女子名〕。

jew·el·(l)er [ˈdʒuːələ; ˋdʒuələ˞] ***n.*** 宝石匠;宝石商,珠宝商。**～'s bar** 贵金属工艺品的坯子。

jew·el·lery, jew·el·ry [ˈdʒuːəlri; ˋdʒuəlrɪ] ***n.*** **1.** 珠宝类。**2.** 珠宝饰物。

Jew·ess [ˈdʒuːis; ˋdʒuɪs] ***n.*** 犹太妇女。

Jew·ett [ˈdʒuːit; ˋdʒuɪt] ***n.*** **1.** 朱伊特〔姓氏〕。**2.** **Sarah Orne** ～萨拉·奥恩·朱伊特〔1849—1909,美国女小说家〕。

jew·fish [ˈdʒuːˌfiʃ; ˋdʒu͵fɪʃ] ***n.*** (*pl.* ～(***es***)) 【鱼】暖海鱼属〔如大海鲈(*Stereolepis gigas*)或石斑鱼(*Epinephelus itajara*)〕。

Jew·ish [ˈdʒu(ː)iʃ; ˋdʒuɪʃ] **I** ***a.*** 犹太人的;犹太人似的,犹太人作风的。*the ～ calendar* 犹太历〔希伯来人用的阴阳合历〕。**II** ***n.*** = Yiddish. **-ly** ***ad.*** **-ness** ***n.***

Jew·ry [ˈdʒuəri; ˋdʒurɪ] ***n.*** **1.** 〔集合词〕犹太人;犹太民族。**2.** 犹太人居住区域。

Jew's-ear [ˈdʒuːziə; ˋdʒuz͵ɪr] ***n.*** 【植】黑木耳。

Jew's-harp, Jews'-harp [ˈdʒuːzhɑːp; ˋdʒuz͵hɑrp] ***n.*** (咬在牙齿上用手弹的)口拨琴。

Jez·e·bel [ˈdʒezəbl; ˋdʒɛzəbl] ***n.*** **1.** 耶西别〔古代以色列国王亚哈的妻子,残忍淫荡〕。**2.** 〔j-〕无耻放荡的女人,胭脂虎。

J

jg, j.g. =【美海军】junior grade.

JHS = 1.〔希〕*Jesus Hominum Salvator*【宗】耶稣救世主。2. Junior High School〔美〕初级中学。

jiao [dʒau; dʒaʊ] *n.*〔Chin.〕(中国辅币单位)角。

jib[1] [dʒib; dʒɪb] *n.* 1.【机】吊车臂,挺杆,绞辘;人字起重机的桁。2.【矿】截盘。～ **crane** 摇臂吊车,旋臂吊车。～ **door** (与墙同样高矮和同样颜色的)隐门。

jib[2] [dʒib; dʒɪb] I *n.*【海】船首三角帆。*cut off sb.'s* ～ 打断他人谈话。*the cut of one's* ～相貌,仪表。II *vt.* (*-bb-*) 使(帆、桁等)从一边转到另一边。— *vi.* 船帆等从一边转到另一边。～ **boom**【海】第二斜桅。～**-headed** *a.* 刀刃成三角帆形的;【海】三角的〔指纵帆〕。

jib[3] [dʒib; dʒɪb] *vi.* (*-bb-*) 1.(马等)退缩,横跑,后退。2.(人)踌躇不前。～ *at* 对…表示踌躇,讨厌 (～ *at hard work* 不愿做艰苦的工作)。

jib·ba(h) [ˈdʒibə; ˋdʒɪbə] *n.* (穆斯林男子穿的)长布袍。

jib·ber [ˈdʒibə; ˋdʒɪbɚ] *n.* 后退的马;踌躇不前的人。

jibe[1] [dʒaib; dʒaɪb] *vi.* (帆)从一舷转至他舷。— *vt.* 使调换方向,使改变航道。

jibe[2] [dʒaib; dʒaɪb] *n.*, *vt.*, *vi.* 嘲笑,嘲弄。**-r** *n.* 嘲笑者,嘲弄者。

jibe[3] [dʒaib; dʒaɪb] *vi.*〔美口〕与…一致;符合 (*with*)。*accounts that don't* ～ 与实际开支不符的账目。

JIC = 1. Joint Intelligence Committee〔美〕联合情报委员会。2. joint intelligence center〔美〕联合情报中心。

Jid·da(h) [ˈdʒidə; ˋdʒɪdə] *n.* 吉达〔沙特阿拉伯红海沿岸的海港城市〕。

jiff, jif·fy [dʒif, ˈdʒifi; dʒɪf, ˋdʒɪfɪ] *n.*〔口〕一会儿。*in a* ～马上,立刻。*wait* (*half*) *a* ～ 稍等一下。

jig [dʒig; dʒɪg] I *n.* 1. 捷格舞〔一种轻松快速的三拍子舞〕;捷格舞曲;快步舞(曲)。2.(诱饵在水中上下跳动的)冰下鱼钩。3.【矿】筛选机,跳汰机;跳汰选矿法。4.【机】夹具;钻模;装配架;模具,规尺,样板。5.【无】衰减波群。*an assembly* ～ 装配架。*reaming* ～铰孔夹具。*in* ～ *time* 马上,极快地。*on the* ～ 战战兢兢地。*The* ～ *is over* [*up*]〔俚〕一切都完了。*The whistle* ～*s to a milestone.* 对牛弹琴。II *vt.*, *vi.* (*-gg-*) 1. 跳(捷格舞);(使)跳跃。2.(使)(上下前后急剧)跳动。3. 用特种钓鱼钩钓(鱼)。4.【矿】筛(矿)。5.【机】用夹具加工(工件等)。～ **borer** 钻模镗床,坐标镗床。～ **plate** 夹具模;钻板模。～ **point** 基点。～ **welding** 焊接夹具。～ **washer** 跳汰洗矿机。

jig·ger[1] [ˈdʒigə; ˋdʒɪgɚ] *n.* 1. 开跳汰机的工人;【矿】筛矿器,跳汰机。2. 跳捷格舞的人。3.【机】小滑车,盘车,辘轳。4.【海】补助帆;一种小帆船。5.〔俚〕小巧复杂的东西,小玩意。6.【无】减幅振荡变压器;可变耦合变压器。7.〔美〕(混合饮料用的 $1\frac{1}{2}$ 盎司)量杯;一量杯的酒。8.【高尔夫球】小头铁球棒。～ **mast** (四桅船的)后桅;(小艇的)船尾小桅。

jig·ger[2] [ˈdʒigə; ˋdʒɪgɚ] *n.* =chigoe, chigger.

jig·gered [ˈdʒigəd; ˋdʒɪgɚd] *a.*〔口〕'damned'的委婉语。*Well, I'm* ～! 不会吧! *I'll be* ～ *if ....* 哪有…的事。

jig·ger·y-pok·er·y [ˈdʒigəriˈpəukəri; ˋdʒɪgərɪˋpokərɪ] *n.*〔口〕阴谋,诡计;欺骗;秘密活动;诈骗。

jig·gle [ˈdʒigl; ˋdʒɪgl̩] I *vt.*, *vi.* (使)轻轻摇晃[跳动]。II *n.*〔美〕轻轻的摇晃[跳动]。

jig·gly [ˈdʒigli; ˋdʒɪglɪ] *a.* 1. 摇晃的,不稳定的。2.〔美俚〕有性挑逗意味的。

jig·saw [ˈdʒigsɔː; ˋdʒɪgsɔ] I *n.*〔美〕锯曲线机,钢丝锯,竖锯。*a war of* ～ *pattern*【军】犬牙交错的战争态势。II *vt.* (*-sawed*; *-sawed*, *-sawn*) 1. 用锯曲线机锯。2. 使互相交错搭接。～ **puzzle** (玩具)益智分合板,拼板玩具。

ji·had [dʒiˈhɑːd; dʒɪˋhɑd] *n.* 1.【宗】穆斯林的护教战争,圣战;宗教讨伐。2. 维护信仰[主义、政策等]的运动 (*for*);反对某项主义[政策、学说、信仰等]的运动 (*against*)。*a* ～ *against a new doctrine* 反对新教义的运动。

Jill [dʒil; dʒɪl] *n.* = Gill (*opp. Jack*). 1. 吉尔〔女子名〕。2.〔罕〕少女,妇女〔尤指情人〕。

jil·lion [ˈdʒiljən; ˋdʒɪljən] *n.*〔美俚〕巨量。

jilt [dʒilt; dʒɪlt] I *n.* 任意遗弃情人的女子。II *vt.* (女子)任意遗弃(情人)。

jil·tee [dʒilˈtiː; dʒɪlˋti] *n.*〔美〕被遗弃的人。

Jim [dʒim; dʒɪm] *n.* 吉姆〔男子名, James 的略称或昵称〕。

jim·ber·jawed [ˈdʒimbədʒɔːd; ˋdʒɪmbɚˏdʒɔd] *a.* 下颌突出的。

Jim Crow [ˈdʒimˈkrəu; ˋdʒɪmˋkro]〔美〕1.〔贬〕黑人。2. 对黑人的种族歧视(= Jim Crowism)。3.〔j- c-〕【机】弯轨机。*the Jim Crow car* 黑人专用火车(或电车)。

Jim-Crow, jim-crow [ˈdʒimˈkrəu; ˋdʒɪmˋkro] I *a.* 1.〔贬〕黑人的。2. 歧视黑人的。3. 黑人专用的。*a Jim-Crow school* 黑人专用学校。*Jim-Crow Law* 歧视黑人的法律。II *vt.* 歧视(黑人)。

jim-dan·dy [ˈdʒimˈdændi; ˋdʒɪmˋdændɪ] I *n.*〔口〕出色人物,优秀人物;讨人喜欢的东西。II *a.*〔口〕优秀的,头等的,非常讨人喜欢的。

jim·jams [ˈdʒimdʒæmz; ˋdʒɪmˏdʒæmz] *n. pl.*〔俚〕1.(因酒精中毒引起的)震颤性谵妄。2.〔常与 the 连用〕极度紧张不安。

Jim·mie [ˈdʒimi; ˋdʒɪmɪ] *n.* =Jimmy.

Jim·my [ˈdʒimi; ˋdʒɪmɪ] *n.* 吉米〔男子名, James 的昵称〕。

jim·my [ˈdʒimi; ˋdʒɪmɪ] I *n.* 1.〔美〕(盗贼用的)撬门棍。2.【机】短撬棍。3. 煤车。II *vt.* (*-mied*; *-my·ing*)(用撬棍)撬,撬开。*The burglar jimmied a window.* 盗贼撬开了一扇窗。

jim·son weed [ˈdʒimsnwiːd; ˋdʒɪmsnˏwid]【植】曼陀罗〔一年生的有毒草本植物,叶带臭味,花似喇叭,呈黄色或淡紫色,果有刺〕。

jin[1] [dʒin; dʒɪn] *n.* =jinni.

jin[2] [dʒin; dʒɪn] *n.*〔Chin.〕(市)斤(=0.5 公斤)。

jing·bang [ˈdʒiŋˈbæŋ; ˋdʒɪŋˋbæŋ] *n.*〔俚〕团体;群众;许多。*the whole* ～ 全体,统统。

jin·gle [ˈdʒiŋgəl; ˋdʒɪŋgl̩] I *n.* 1.(小铃,钱币等的)叮当声;发叮当声的东西。2. 诗的简单韵律;韵律简单的字句[音节]。3.(爱尔兰或澳洲的)二轮有顶马车。II *vt.*, *vi.* 1.(使)叮当响。2.(使)(诗句和音乐等)具有简单而又引人注意的韵律[节奏]。*The bells* ～*d.* 铃声叮当。～ *the keys* 把钥匙弄得叮零当郎直响。～ **bell** 1. 门铃;装在雪撬上的铃铛。2.(通知船速的)信号铃。～ **jangle** 1. *n.* 叮当声;〔美俚〕钱。2. *vi.* 发出叮当声。**jin·gly** *a.* 叮当响的;简单押韵的。

jin·gled [ˈdʒiŋgld; ˋdʒɪŋgl̩d] *a.*〔美俚〕喝醉的。

jin·go[1] [ˈdʒiŋgəu; ˋdʒɪŋgo] *n.* (*pl.* ～*es*) 侵略主义者,沙文主义者,武力外交政策论者。**-ism** *n.* 侵略主义,沙文主义,武力外交政策。**-ist** *n.* 侵略主义者,沙文主义者。

jin·go[2] [ˈdʒiŋgəu; ˋdʒɪŋgo] *int.* **by** (**the living**) ～啊呀!天哪!〔表示快乐、惊异或加强语气〕。

jin·go·is·tic [ˌdʒiŋgəuˈistik; ˏdʒɪŋgoˋɪstɪk] *a.* 侵略主义的,侵略分子的。**-cal·ly** *ad.*

jink [dʒiŋk; dʒɪŋk] I *vi.* 1. 闪开,急忙避开,急转。2.〔俚〕(飞机)颠簸飞行〔躲避高射炮火等〕。— *vt.* 避开,躲开。II *n.* 1. 闪开,急忙回避。2.〔*pl.*〕喧闹的游戏。*give the* ～*s* 巧妙避开。*high* ～*s* 大吵大闹的嬉戏。

jinn [dʒin; dʒɪn] *n.* *jinni* 的复数〔一般把此词当作单数,并加了一个复数形式 *jinns*〕。

jin·nee, jin·ni [dʒiˈniː; dʒɪˋni] *n.* (*pl.* **jinn**) (伊斯兰教中的)神灵。

jin·rik·(i)·sha, jin·rick·sha [dʒinˈrikʃə; dʒɪnˋrɪkʃə], **jin·rick·shaw** [dʒinˈrikʃɔː; dʒɪnˋrɪkʃɔ] *n.* 人力车,黄包车。

JINS =juvenile(s) in need of supervision〔美〕需要管教

的青少年,不良青少年。

jinx [dʒiŋks; dʒɪŋks] **I** ***n***. 〔美口〕**1.** 不吉祥的人[物]。**2.** 倒霉,坏运气。*a* ~ *day* 不吉利的日子。***break*** [***smash***] ***the*** ~(运动比赛)连败之后转向胜利。**II** ***vt***. 使倒霉;破坏。

ji·pi·ja·pa [ˌhiːpiːˈhɑːpə; ˌhipiˋhɑpə] ***n***.【植】**1.** 巴拿马草 (*Carludovica palmata*)〔产于中南美,叶子可编草帽〕。**2.** 巴拿马干草。**3.** 巴拿马帽(= Panama hat)。

JIS = Japanese Industrial Standard 日本工业规格,日本工业标准。

jism [ˈdʒizəm; dʒɪzm] ***n***. 〔俚〕精力,力量,元气。

JIT = just-in-time【商】及时盘存调节法〔指及时盘点库存,以便按照销售状况来调节产量〕。

jit·ney [ˈdʒitni; ˋdʒɪtnɪ] **I** ***n***. **1.** 〔美俚〕五分硬币,镍币。**2.** (票价低廉的)小型公共汽车,收费低廉的公共汽车。**3.** 便宜货,次等品。**II** ***vt***., ***vi***. 乘坐公共汽车(去)。~ **bag** 〔美俚〕手提小皮包。~ **circuit** 〔美〕郊区的廉价戏。~ **dance** 〔美〕费用低廉的公共舞会。

jit·ter [ˈdʒitə; ˋdʒɪtɚ] **I** ***vi***. 〔口〕紧张不安,烦燥不安;战战兢兢,颤抖。**II** ***n***. 〔*pl*.〕〔美俚〕极度的紧张不安。*have the* ~*s* 极度紧张不安;战战兢兢。

jit·ter·bug [ˈdʒitəbʌg; ˋdʒɪtɚˌbʌg] **I** ***n***. **1.** 神经紧张不安的人。**2.** 吉特巴舞[随爵士音乐节拍跳的快速舞]。**3.** 跳吉特巴舞的人。**4.** 爵士舞曲迷。**II** ***vi***. (***-gg-***) 跳吉特巴舞。

jit·ter·y [ˈdʒitəri; ˋdʒɪtərɪ] ***a***. 〔美俚〕神经极度紧张不安的。

jiu·jit·su, jiu·jut·su [dʒjuːˈdʒitsuː; dʒjuˋdʒɪtsu] 〔Jap.〕 ***n***. = jujitsu.

Ji·va·ro [ˈhiːvɑːrəu; ˋhivɑro] ***n***. **1.** (*pl*. ~(*s*)) 黑瓦洛人〔厄瓜多尔南部和秘鲁北部的一个印第安部族的成员〕。**2.** 黑瓦洛语。

jive [dʒaiv; dʒaɪv] **I** ***n***. **1.** (节奏快速、活泼的)爵士音乐。**2.** 爵士音乐中的专业术语;吸毒者等用的黑话。**3.** 〔美俚〕花言巧语;蠢话,废话。**II** ***vi***. **1.** 奏爵士乐。**2.** 〔美俚〕用花言巧语欺骗;干无益的蠢事。— ***vt***. **1.** 奏(爵士乐);随着爵士音乐跳(舞)。**2.** 欺骗,取笑。~**-ass** 〔美俚〕爱嬉闹的人;骗子;装腔作势的人。

JJ. = Judges; Justices.

JL = Journal; July.

Jn = June; junior; Junction.

Jno. [dʒɔn; dʒɑn] = John.

Jo [dʒəu; dʒo] ***n***. 乔〔Joseph, Josephine 的简称〕。

Jo. = Joel; John; Joseph; Josephine.

jo [dʒəu; dʒo] ***n***. (*pl* ~***es***) 〔Scot.〕情人。

joad [dʒəud; dʒod] ***n***. 〔美〕(随农业季节而劳动的)流动工人。

Joan(n) [dʒəun; dʒon] ***n***. 琼〔女子名〕。

Jo·an·na [dʒəuˈænə; dʒoˋænə] ***n***. 乔安娜〔女子名,Joan 的异体〕。

Job [dʒəub; dʒob] ***n***. **1.** 乔布〔男子名〕。**2.** 约伯〔《圣经》中的人物,以忍艰耐劳著称〕。**3.** 《旧约圣经》中的《约伯记》(= the book of ~)。*the patience of* ~极度的忍耐。*It would try the patience of* ~. 那就太气人了。~**'s comforter** 增加别人痛苦的安慰者,对别人的悲痛假安慰真刺激的人。~**'s dock** 医院。~**'s news** 噩耗,坏消息。~**'s post** 传恶耗者,报讯者。~**'s pound** 监狱。~**'s tears**【植】**1.** 〔作单数用〕川谷,菩提子 (*Coix lacryma-jobi*)〔一种热带草本植物,果实可作念珠,仁籽可食〕。**2.** 川谷米珠。

job[1] [dʒɔb; dʒɑb] **I** ***n***. **1.** 工作,活计。**2.** 零活,散工,包工。**3.** 任务,职责,作用。**4.** 加工的物品[原料];结果;产品。**5.** 〔美口〕职业,职位,地位。**6.** 犯罪的行为,〔尤指偷盗〕;损人的事;假公济私的事,贪污行为。**7.** 〔口〕事件,情况,事情。**8.** 〔口〕费力的事。**9.** 〔俚〕人,女人。**10.** 〔口〕汽车。*make a thorough* ~ *of it* 把这件事做彻底。*a man paid by the* ~ 计件工。*odd* ~*s* 零活,杂务。*It is your* ~ *to be on time*. 你有责任按时来。*This is a put-up* ~. 〔俚〕这是骗局,这是阴谋。*a queer* ~ 蹊跷。*a fat* ~ 肥缺。*be out of a* ~失业。*look out for a* ~ 找工作。*have a* ~ *as a typist* 担任打字员的职务。*His poem is a superb* ~. 他的诗是一部出色的作品。*The theft must have been an inside* ~. 这一窃案一定是内部人干的。*a good* ~舒服的工作。*a bad* ~吃力不讨好的事。*have a hard* ~ *to do sth*. 做某事很吃力。*It was a real* ~ *to talk over that noise*. 要压过那样的吵闹声讲话真费劲。*a straight* ~(没有拖车的)载重汽车。***by the*** ~ 包做,计件。***do a*** ~ ***on sb***. 〔俚〕整垮某人,损毁某人。***do sb.'s*** ~ ***for him***, ***do the*** ~ ***for sb***. **1.** 代某人做事。**2.** 〔俚〕送掉某人的命(*This will do his* [*the*] ~ *for him*. 这会送掉他的命)。~***s for the boys*** 〔口〕酬劳支持自己的人的肥缺职位,美差。***just the*** ~ 恰好要的东西。***keen of a*** ~〔口〕很想工作。***lie down on the*** ~敷衍了事。***make a good*** ~ ***of*** 办好;处理好。***make the best of a bad*** ~设法收拾残局;尽量减少损失。***nose a*** ~ ***in everything*** 到处看到有利可图。***on the*** ~〔俚〕(努力)工作者。***put up a*** ~ ***on sb***. 〔美〕捉弄某人,欺骗某人。**II** ***vi***. (***-bb-***) **1.** 作零工,作包工,打杂。**2.** 假公济私,营私舞弊。**3.** 做股票经纪。— ***vt***. **1.** 承包,分包(工程等);(临时)雇用。**2.** 临时租用,出租(车,马等)。**3.** 代客买卖(股票等);批发(商品等)。**4.** 用假公济私的手腕处理。**5.** 〔美俚〕除掉,搞垮。**6.** 〔美俚〕欺骗,欺诈。~ *sb. out of his money* 骗走某人的钱。*a jobbing house* 〔美〕批发庄。~ ***about*** 做散工。~ ***sb. into a post*** 用营私舞弊的手段使某人就任,卖官鬻爵。~ ***off*** 赚钱卖出;非法处分。~ ***out*** 把巨大的工作分包出去。~ **action** (警察等的)临时性罢工示威。~ **analysis** 企业工种分析学〔研究各工种的操作、劳动条件、工人技术水准等〕。~ **bank** 职业库〔由政府主办、使用电脑统筹资料以安排就业的机构〕。~ **case**【印】铅字盒。~ **commuting** 远途往返上班活动。~ **control block**【计】作业控制块;作业控制分程序。**J- Corps** 就业团(计划)〔美国政府为无业青年搞的就业训练计划〕。~ **holder** **1.** 有职业者。**2.** 〔美〕公务员。~ **hopping** 为求经济利益而改行,跳厂,跳槽。~ **hunter** 〔美〕找事的人,求职者。~ **library**【计】作业库。~ **lot** **1.** (货物的)搭配花色批发。**2.** 随便搭配花色批发〔尤指货质低劣者〕。~ **master** 出租车[马]的人。~ **printer** 承印零星印件的印刷商。~ **printing** 零星小商品印刷〔如印刷信封上端的文字、传单、请帖等〕。~**-splitting** 一工分做制〔把全日工改为两个半日工的办法〕。~ **work** **1.** 包工;散工。**2.** 零件印刷。

job[2] [dʒɔb; dʒɑb] ***n***., ***vt***., ***vi***. 〔方〕= jab.

jo·ba·tion [dʒəuˈbeiʃən; dʒoˋbeʃən] ***n***. 〔口〕冗长的训诫,谴责。

job·ber [ˈdʒɔbə; ˋdʒɑbɚ] ***n***. **1.** 散工,零工,包工。**2.** 〔英〕租车人,租马人。**3.** 〔英〕股票经纪人。**4.** 假公济私的人。**5.** 批发商。

joe·ber·nowl [ˈdʒɔbəˌnəul; ˋdʒɑbɚˌnol] **I** ***n***. 〔口〕笨蛋,蠢汉。**II** ***a***. 愚蠢的。

job·ber·y [ˈdʒɔbəri; ˋdʒɑbərɪ] ***n***. 假公济私;徇私舞弊。

job·less [ˈdʒɔblis; ˋdʒɑblɪs] ***a***. **1.** 无职业的;失业的。**2.** 与失业有关的。*the* ~ 失业者。**-ness** ***n***.

JOBS = job opportunities and basic skills 就业与技能工程(培训)。

Jo·cas·ta [dʒəuˈkæstə; dʒoˋkæstə] ***n***.【希神】裘娥卡斯达〔因命运捉弄,竟成为其子伊狄帕斯之妻,发觉后即自尽身死〕。

Jock [dʒɔk; dʒɑk] ***n***. 〔英〕〔军俚〕苏格兰(尤指高地)的士兵。

jock[1] [dʒɔk; dʒɑk] ***n***. **1.** = jockey (***n***.). **2.** 爱好者,…迷。*a computer* ~ 电脑迷。

jock[2] [dʒɔk; dʒɑk] ***n***. = jockstrap.

jock·ey [ˈdʒɔki; ˋdʒɑkɪ] **I** ***n***. **1.** 职业赛马骑师。**2.** 〔古〕

J

马商。**3.** 驾驶员;(机器等的)操作者。**4.**〔英〕小伙子,下属,帮手。**5.** 薄膜。**6.**【机】连接装置。**II** *vt*.(*-eyed*; *-ey·ing*) **1.** 骑(马)参加比赛;驾驶(汽车等);操作(机器)。**2.** 欺骗,欺诈。**3.** 移动。~ *sb. into doing sth.* 骗某人做某事。~ *sb. into a trap* 诱骗某人落入圈套。~ *sb. out of sth.* 诈取某人某物。— *vi*. **1.** 当职业赛马骑师。**2.** 运用手段谋利。~ ***for position*** **1.** (赛马时)挤其他骑师以占有利位置。**2.** 运用手段谋利。~ **cap** (有尖帽舌的)赛马骑师帽。**J- Club** **1.** (英国的)赛马总会。**2.**〔j- c-〕赛马俱乐部。~ **pulley**【机】导轮。~ **rollers** 张力辊。

jock·o [ˈdʒɔkəu; ˋdʒako] ***n***.【动】黑猩猩。

jock·strap [ˈdʒɔkstræp; ˋdʒakˏstræp] ***n***. **1.** 下体护身〔男运动员的弹性织物〕。**2.**〔俚〕运动员〔贬称,亦作 jock〕。

jo·cose [dʒəˈkəus; dʒəˋkos] ***a***. 开玩笑的,诙谐的,滑稽的。**-ly** ***ad***. **-ness** ***n***.

jo·cos·i·ty [dʒəuˈkɔsiti; dʒoˋkasətɪ] ***n***. **1.** 滑稽,诙谐,戏谑。**2.**〔*pl*.〕诙谐的言行。

joc·u·lar [ˈdʒɔkjulə; ˋdʒakjələ˞] ***a***. **1.** 诙谐的,滑稽的,好开玩笑的。**2.** 打趣的,寻乐的。**-ly** ***ad***.

joc·u·lar·i·ty [ˌdʒɔkjuˈlæriti; ˏdʒakjəˋlærətɪ] ***n***. **1.** 滑稽,诙谐。**2.** 滑稽的言行。

joc·und [ˈdʒɔkənd; ˋdʒakənd] ***a***. 欢乐的,快活的。**-ly** ***ad***.

jo·cun·di·ty [dʒəuˈkʌnditi; dʒoˋkʌndətɪ] ***n***. **1.** 欢乐,快活。**2.**〔*pl*.〕欢乐[快活]的言行。

Jodh·pur [dʒɔdˈpuə; dʒodˋpur] ***n***. 乔德普尔〔印度贾拉斯坦邦的城市〕。

jodh·pur [ˈdʒɑːdpə; ˋdʒadpə˞] ***n***. **1.**〔*pl*.〕骑马裤。**2.** 短马靴。

Joe [dʒəu; dʒo] **I** ***n***. **1.** 乔〔男子名,Joseph 的昵称〕。**2.**〔美口〕〔j-〕〔对不相识者的称呼〕家伙。**3.** 美国兵〔=G. I. Joe〕。**4.** =Joe Miller. **5.**〔j-〕〔英俚〕四便士的银币。**6.**〔j-〕〔Scot.〕情人=jo. **7.**〔j-〕〔美俚〕咖啡。***a good*** ~〔美〕讨人喜欢的家伙。~ **Miller** 滑稽书,笑话集;陈套滑稽。*I don't see the J- Miller of it*. 我觉得这没有什么逗乐的。***Not for*** ~!〔俚〕决不干,决不是! **II** ***a***.〔美俚〕知内情的。***get*** ~ ***to sth***. 了解某事内情。***put sb***. ~使某人得知内情。~ **Blow** [**Doakes**] 老百姓。~ **college**〔美口〕男大学生。

Jo·el [ˈdʒəuel; ˋdʒoɛl] ***n***. **1.** 约珥〔男子名〕。**2.** 约珥〔古代希伯来预言者〕。**3.** (《旧约圣经》中的)《约珥书》。

joe-pye weed [ˌdʒəuˈpai-wiːd; ˏdʒoˋpaɪ-wid] ***n***.〔美〕紫花,紫菀草。

jo·ey [ˈdʒəui; ˋdʒoɪ] ***n***. **1.**〔澳〕小袋鼠;小动物。**2.**〔英俚〕三便士硬币。

jog[1] [dʒɔg; dʒag] **I** ***vt***.(*-gg-*) **1.** 轻推,轻撞;轻摇。**2.** 唤起(记忆),提醒。**3.** 使(马)缓步前进。**4.**【印】使(纸张)整齐,把(纸张)垛齐。~ *sb. with one's elbow to get his attention* 用肘轻推某人以引起他的注意。~ *sb.'s memoy* 唤起某人注意。— ***vi***. **1.** 颠簸地移动。**2.** 磨磨蹭蹭地走。**3.** 缓慢而平稳地进行。**4.** 熬时间。**5.** (为健身而进行)慢跑。*The bus* ~*ged along*. 那辆公共汽车上下颠簸地行驶。~ *a few miles on horseback* 骑马慢慢地走几英里。*Matters* ~ *along*. 事情按部就班地进行。*We must* ~ *along* [*on*] *somehow*. 我们得一步步干下去。*Time keeps* ~*ging on*. 时间不断地消磨掉。**II** ***n***. **1.** 轻推;轻摇,轻撞。**2.** 慢步,缓行。~**ging pants** 慢跑运动裤。~**ging shoe** 慢跑运动鞋。~ **trot** **1.** 慢步,缓行。**2.** 单调的进程,常规。

jog[2] [dʒɔg; dʒag] **I** ***n***. **1.**〔美〕(线、面上的)参差不齐,凹凸不平。**2.** 突然的转向。**II** ***vi***.(*-gg-*) **1.** 凹进,凸出。**2.** 突然转向。

jog·gle[1] [ˈdʒɔgl; ˋdʒagl̩] **I** ***vt***., ***vi***. 轻轻摇动。**II** ***n***. 轻轻颠摇。

jog·gle[2] [ˈdʒɔgl; ˋdʒagl̩] **I** ***n***.【建】齿合扣;接榫。**II** ***vt***. 啮合;榫接。~ **joint** 啮合接;肘接;榫接。

Jog·ja·kar·ta [ˌdʒɔgjəˈkɑːtɑ; ˏdʒagjəˋkartɑ] ***n***. 日惹〔印度尼西亚城市,或称 Djojakarta〕。

Jo·han·nes [dʒəuˈhænis; dʒoˋhænɪs] ***n***. 约翰尼斯〔男子名,John 的别称〕。

jo·han·nes [dʒəuˈhæniz; dʒoˋhænɪz] ***n***.(*pl*. ***~nes***) 葡萄牙十八、十九世纪的金币。

Jo·han·nes·burg [dʒəuˈhænisbəːg; dʒoˋhænɪsˏbɝg] ***n***. 约翰内斯堡〔南非(阿扎尼亚)城市〕。

Jo·han·nis·ber·ger [dʒəuˈhɑːnisbəːgə; dʒəˋhænɪsˏbɝgə˞] ***n***.(德国 Johannisberg 产)高级白葡萄酒。

John [dʒɔn; dʒan] ***n***. **1.** 约翰〔男子名〕;使徒约翰〔耶稣十二门徒之一〕;(新约《圣经》中的)《约翰福音》。**2.**〔美俚〕〔j-〕盥洗室,〔j-〕厕所。**3.**〔俚〕〔j-〕男子〔尤指容易受骗的人〕。**4.**〔美俚〕〔j-〕嫖客。~ **Barleycorn** 粮食酒,啤酒〔拟人化的称呼〕。~ **Bull** 约翰牛〔英国或英国人的绰号〕。~ **Bullism** 英国人的品质[性格、精神]。~ **Chinaman**〔贬〕典型中国人。~ **Citizen** 普通人,老百姓。~ **Company**〔口〕【史】东印度公司。~ **Doe**【法】在不动产收回诉讼中对不知真实姓名的当事人的称呼(*opp*. Richard Roe)。~ **Dory**【动】海鲂。~ **Hancock**〔美俚〕亲笔签名。~ **Henry** **1.** 美国歌谣中的传奇式英雄。**2.** 亲笔签名。~**-o'-Groat's** (**-House**) 苏格兰的最北端(*from* ~*-o'-Groat's to Land's End* 英国全国)。~ **Q. Public**, ~ **Q.**, ~ **Q. Citizen**〔美〕普通人,一般群众。~ **the Apostle**【宗】使徒约翰〔耶稣最爱的弟子〕。~ **the Baptist**【宗】施洗礼的约翰。

john [dʒɔn; dʒan] ***n***.〔美俚〕**1.** 厕所(尤指男用厕所)。**2.** 嫖客。**3.** (尤指受骗的)男人,家伙。**4.** 警察;侦探。**5.** 新兵。

john·boat [ˈdʒɔnbəut; ˋdʒanˏbot] ***n***.(一种在内河行驶的)平底小船。

John·ny, John·nie [ˈdʒɔni; ˋdʒanɪ] ***n***. **1.** 强尼〔男子名,John 的昵称〕。**2.**〔美俚〕=John. **3.**〔口〕〔j-〕家伙;纨袴子弟。**4.**〔j-〕(住院病人穿的)短袖无领罩衫。**johnny-cake**〔美〕玉米饼;〔澳〕麦面饼。~**-come-lately**〔美〕新来者,生手,暴发户。~ **Crapaud**, ~**Crapeau**〔口〕法国人。~**-jump-up**【植】美洲紫罗兰;〔美〕野生三色紫罗兰。~ **Newcome** [**Raw**] 生手,新兵。~ **One-Note**〔美口〕看问题片面的人,死脑筋。~**-on-the-spot**〔口〕**1.** ***n***. 召之即来者。**2.** ***a***. 召之即来的。~ **Reb**【美史】联邦士兵〔拟人化称呼〕。~ **Trots**〔用作 *sing*.〕〔美俚〕腹泻,拉肚子。

Johns [dʒɔnz; dʒanz] ***n***. 约翰斯〔姓氏〕。

John·son [ˈdʒɔnsn; ˋdʒansn] ***n***. **1.** 约翰逊〔姓氏〕。**2. Samuel** ~塞缪尔·约翰逊〔1709—1784,英国文学家,词典编纂家〕。~ **grass**【植】阿拉伯高粱(*Sorghum halepense*)〔产于美国南部,作牧草、饲料用〕。~ **noise**【无】约翰逊噪声,热(激)噪声。

John·son·ese [ˌdʒɔnsəˈniːz; ˏdʒansn̩ˋiz] ***n***. 塞缪尔·约翰逊的文体[文风]。

John·so·ni·an [dʒɔnˈsəunjən, -niən; dʒanˋsonɪən] ***a***. 约翰逊 (Samuel Johnson) (风格)的;矫揉造作的,夸张的。

Johns·ton [ˈdʒɔnstən, ˈdʒɔnsn; ˋdʒanstən, ˋdʒansn̩] ***n***. 约翰斯顿〔姓氏〕。

Jo·hore [dʒəuˈhɔː; dʒoˋhor] ***n***. 柔佛〔马来西亚之一州〕。

Jo·hore Bah·ru [dʒəuˈhɔː ˈbɑːruː; dʒoˋhor ˋbaru] ***n***. 新山〔柔佛邦的首府,在新加坡对面〕。

joie de vi·vre [F. ʒwɑdˈviːvr; ʒwadəˋvivr]〔F.〕生活之欢乐,尽情享受生活之乐趣。

join [dʒɔin; dʒɔɪn] **I** ***vt***. **1.** 接合,连接,使结合。**2.** 参加,加入,作(团体等的)成员;和(某人)作伴。**3.** 回(原岗位),归(队)。**4.** 联合;使结交,使联姻。**5.** 会合,合流。**6.**〔口〕毗连,接近。~ *two points by a straight line* 用直线把两点连起来。*J- us in a walk*. 和我们一起走走。~ *battle* 参战。~ *the army* 参军。~ *the Party* 入党。~ *sb. in the discussion* 同某人一起讨论。~ *one's*

J

ship 回到船上。*The brook* ~*s the river*. 小川同河流汇合。*His house* ~*s mine*. 他的家就在我家的隔壁。— *vi*. 1. 结合,联合(*with*; *to*)。2. 参加,加入(*in*; *with*)。3. 毗连,接近。*My mother* ~*s with me in congratulating you*. 我的母亲跟我一道向你祝贺。*In this point I* ~ *with you*. 这一点我跟你一致。~ *in a conversation* 参加谈话。~ ***forces with*** 1. 军队会师。2. 同…合作,同…联合。~ ***hands with*** 1. 同…联合。2. 同…合伙开店。3. 同…做夫妻。~ ***issue***【法】共同起诉;进行辩论。~ [***take***] ***issue with sb. on sth.*** 就某事与某人争论。~ ***the colours*** 服兵役。~ ***the*** (***great*** 或 ***silent***) ***majority*** 死。~ ***up***〔口〕1. 参军,入伍。2. 联合起来。**II** ***n***. 1. 连接;结合。2. 接合处,接合点,接合线,接合面。*You can hardly see the* ~ *in the coat*. 你几乎看不出那件外衣的接缝。~**d-up** ***a***.〔口〕成熟的;老练的。

join·der [ˈdʒɔində; ˋdʒɔɪndɚ] ***n***. 1. 连接;接合;汇合;联合。2.【法】联合诉讼;原告或被告的联合,共同诉讼;对另一方提出的争论之点的接受。

join·er [ˈdʒɔinə; ˋdʒɔɪnɚ] ***n***. 1. 结合者;结合物。2. 细木工,小木匠。3.〔美口〕加入许多俱乐部和社团的人。

join·er·y [ˈdʒɔinəri; ˋdʒɔɪnərɪ] ***n***. 1. 细木工技术[行业]。2. 细木工的制作物。

join·ing [ˈdʒɔiniŋ; ˋdʒɔɪnɪŋ] ***n***. 连接,结合;接缝。~***-up in parallel***【电】并接。~***-up in series***【电】串接。

joint [dʒɔint; dʒɔɪnt] **I** ***n***. 1. 接合,榫接合处,接合点。2.【解】关节。3.【植】节。4.【电】接头。5.【建】接缝。6. (硬皮书面的)折合线;两条钢轨的连接物。7.【地】节理。8. (用来烤食的)大块肉;带骨的腿肉。9.〔美俚〕下流场所〔指赌窟,小酒店等〕,热闹场所。10.〔美俚〕(大麻叶烟的)吸用场所,吸毒窝;大麻叶烟。*air-tight* ~【机】气密接合。*ball and socket* ~ 球窝关节。*Charcot's* ~夏柯氏关节〔脊髓痨性关节病〕。*expansion* ~伸缩(接)缝。*finger* ~手指关节。*knee* ~ 膝关节。*rivet* ~【机】铆(钉接)合。*water-tight* ~【机】水密结合。*an eating* ~〔美俚〕小饭馆。*a hop* ~〔美俚〕鸦片烟馆。***out of*** ~ 1. 脱节,脱榫,脱臼。2. 纷乱。3. 不协调。4. 不满。***put sb.'s nose out of*** ~ 使某人丢脸;推翻某人的计划。***put one's foot*** [***arm***, ***knees***] ***out of*** ~使足[臂、膝]脱臼。***the*** ~ ***in sb.'s armour*** 要害,致命的弱点。**II** ***a***. 1. 连接的,结合的。2. 联合的,共同的;同时的。3. 合办的,共有的。4. 连带的。*a* ~ *association* 联合会。~ *authors* 合著者。*a* ~ *communiqué* 联合公报。*a* ~ *declaration* [*statement*] 联合声明。~ *exercise* [*manoeuvre*] 联合演习。~ *owners* 有共同所有权的物主。*a* ~ *pipe* 接合管。*a* ~ *property* 共有的财产。*a* ~ *protest* 共同抗议。*during their* ~ *lives*〔法律用语〕当他们都活着的时候。*in our* ~ *names* 连名。*a* ~ *state-private enterprise* 公私合营企业。~ *responsibility* [*liability*] 连带责任。**III** ***vt***. 1. 使在接口处连接,接合。2. 使有接头。3. 从接口处分开,自关节处切断;把(肉)切成带骨的大块。4.【建】用油灰涂(接缝)。5. 焊接。— ***vi***. 1. 贴合。2.【植】生节;长关节。~ **account** (银行存款等的)联合账户。~ **action** 1. 联合行动[战斗]。2.【法】共同诉讼。~**-chair**【建】接轨垫板。**J- Chiefs of Staff**〔美〕国防部参谋长联席会议。~ **committee** (议会两院或几个组织的)联合委员会。~ **pin** 连接销。~ **resolution** (议会两院的)共同决议。~ **return** 夫妇合报的所得税申报书。~ **session** [**convention**] (议会两院的)联席会议。~ **stock** 合股。~**-stock company** [**corporation**] 股份公司。~ **venture** 合资(企业)。~**-weed**【植】海滨假蓼(*Polygonella articulata*)。~**-worm**【动】禾节虫,禾茎广肩小蜂。

joint·ed [dʒɔintid; ˋdʒɔɪntɪd] ***a***. 有接缝的;有节的,有关节的。

joint·er [ˈdʒɔintə; ˋdʒɔɪntɚ] ***n***. 1. 接合人;接合物;接合器。2. (泥工用的)抹子。3. (木工用的)长刨。4.【农】三角犁。

joint·ing [ˈdʒɔintiŋ; ˋdʒɔɪntɪŋ] ***n***. 1. 焊接;连接;接合。2. 填料,垫料封泥。~ *rule* (石工用的)长标尺,接榫规。

joint·less [ˈdʒɔintlis; ˋdʒɔɪntlɪs] ***a***. 无接缝的;无关节的。

joint·ly [ˈdʒɔintli; ˋdʒɔɪntlɪ] ***ad***. 联合地,连带地,共同地。~ *and severally* [*separately*] *liable* 连带和单独负责。

joint·ress [ˈdʒɔintris; ˋdʒɔɪntrɪs] ***n***.【法】享有寡妇产权的妇女。

join·ture [ˈdʒɔintʃə; ˋdʒɔɪntʃɚ] **I** ***n***. 1.【法】(丈夫生前指定的)由妻子继承的遗产;寡妇所得财产。2.〔罕〕连接,接合,接合处。**II** ***vt***. 指定身后由(妻子)继承财产;使(妻子)继承遗产。

joist [dʒɔist; dʒɔɪst] **I** ***n***.【建】1. 搁栅;小梁;(地板等的)托梁。2. 工字钢(= ~ steel)。**II** ***vt***. 为…架搁栅;为…装托梁。~ **ceiling** 搁栅平顶。~ **shears** 型钢剪切机。~ **steel** 工字钢,梁钢。

joke [dʒəuk; dʒok] **I** ***n***. 1. 笑话,戏谑,诙谐。2. 笑柄,笑料。3. 容易的事,易如反掌的事。4. 不足取的东西;无实质性价值的东西;空话。*A* ~ *never gains an enemy but often loses a friend*.〔谚〕戏谑永远不能化敌为友,反而常常失去朋友。*carry* [*push*] *the* ~ *too far* 玩笑开得太过分了。*It is all a* ~. 这完全是笑话。*It is no* ~. 可不是开玩笑的事。*for a* ~ 当作笑话,开玩笑。*say sth. in a* ~是开玩笑说的。*be* [*become*] *the standing* ~ *of the company* 成了朋友间的笑柄。*That test was a* ~. 那个测验太容易了。*turn everything into a* ~ 把任何事情都当儿戏。***a practical*** ~恶作剧。***be but a*** ~只不过开开玩笑,完全是句空话。***crack*** [***cut***, ***make***] ***a*** ~ 说笑话。***have one's*** ~开玩笑。***joking apart*** [***aside***]〔口〕且别开玩笑;言归正传。***make a*** ~ ***about sb.*** [***sth.***] 拿某人[某事]开玩笑。***play a*** ~ ***on sb.*** 取笑某人,欺骗某人。***put the*** ~ ***on sb.***〔美〕开某人玩笑。***The*** ~ ***is on him.*** 玩笑开在他身上了,结果他当了傻瓜。**II** ***vi***. 说笑话;开玩笑。*Now you must be joking*. 你是说笑罢。— ***vt***. 1. 和…开玩笑,取笑,愚弄。2. 以说笑话取得(赏赐等)。~**book** 幽默小说。

jok·er [ˈdʒəukə; ˋdʒokɚ] ***n***. 1. 滑稽角色,诙谐者。2.〔俚〕人,家伙,东西。3.〔J-〕【牌】百搭〔可代替任何一张牌或作王牌〕。4.〔美〕非法酒店;非法酒吧。5.〔美〕(为使法案失效而插入的)伏笔。6. 隐蔽的障碍[挫折];没有预料到的因素。

joke·ster [ˈdʒəukstə; ˋdʒokstɚ] ***n***.〔美口〕好开玩笑的人,爱逗乐的人。

jok·ing [ˈdʒəukiŋ; ˋdʒokɪŋ] ***a***. 开玩笑的。*This is no* ~ *matter*. 这不是开玩笑的事。**-ly** ***ad***.

jo·kul, jökull [ˈjəukul; ˋjokʊl] ***n***. (冰岛终年积雪的)雪山。

jo·ky [ˈdʒəuki; ˋdʒokɪ] ***a***. 爱开玩笑的。

jol·li·fi·ca·tion [ˌdʒɔlifiˈkeiʃən; ˏdʒɑləfəˋkeʃən] ***n***. 欢乐,欢宴,(节日)庆祝。

jol·li·fy [ˈdʒɔlifai; ˋdʒɑləˏfaɪ] ***vt***. (***-fied***; ***-fy·ing***)〔口〕使欢乐,使高兴。— ***vi***. 寻欢,作乐〔尤指喝酒〕。

jol·li·ness [ˈdʒɔlinis; ˋdʒɑlɪnɪs] ***n***. 愉快,高兴。

jol·li·ly [ˈdʒɔlili; ˋdʒɑləlɪ] ***ad***. 愉快地,高兴地。

jol·li·ty [ˈdʒɔliti; ˋdʒɑlɪtɪ] ***n***. 欢乐;欢庆;欢宴。

jol·lop [ˈdʒɔləp; ˋdʒɑləp] ***n***.〔俚〕1. 药;泻药。2. 烈酒。3.〔美〕(食物的)一大份。

jol·ly [ˈdʒɔli; ˋdʒɑlɪ] **I** ***a***. 1. 愉快的,快活的,有趣的,兴高采烈的。2.〔口〕极愉快的,令人高兴的。3.〔口〕大大的。4. 微醉的。*a* ~ *companion* 有趣的伙伴。*as* ~ *as a sandboy* 兴高采烈。*We're having* ~ *weather*. 天气宜人。*a* ~ *fool* 大傻瓜。*What a* ~ *mess I am in!* 这个事情真糟。*the* ~ *god* 酒神。***a*** ~ ***dog about town***〔俚〕快活的游人。***grow*** ~(因喝醉而)高兴。**II** ***ad***.〔英口〕非常,很。*a* ~ *good fellow* 大好人。*all* ~

fine 好极了。*be so* ～ *green* 非常天真。*have a* ～ *bad time of it* 糟透了。*It is a* ～ *good job that you came*.〔口〕你来了真好极了。*I'll be* ～ *glad to help you*. 我很高兴帮助你。*take* ～ *good care* 特别当心。*You will* ～ *well have to do sth*. 你非得去做某事。**III** *n*. **1**. 寻欢作乐。**2**.〔美〕奉承,逢迎。**3**. =～ boat. **4**.〔英俚〕皇家陆战队兵士;水兵。**4**.〔俚〕老年阔佬,老富豪。***a tame*** ～民兵,义勇兵。***get one's jollies*** 作乐。**IV** *vt*. (*-lied*; *-ly·ing*) **1**.〔口〕(用哄、捧等方式)使高兴,使愉快(*along*; *up*)。**2**. 开…的玩笑,戏弄。— *vi*. 开玩笑。～ *with sb*. 同某人开玩笑。～ **boat** (附属于大船上的)单座艇。～ **fellow 1**. 快活人;有趣的伙伴。**2**. 酒徒。**3**.〔俚〕贼。**J- Roger** (饰有白色骷髅等的)海盗[黑]旗。～**-up 1**.〔俚〕非正式的舞会,跳舞。**2**.〔俚〕酒宴;豪饮。

jolt [dʒəult; dʒolt] **I** *vt*. **1**. 使颠簸,摇晃。**2**. (拳击中)猛击(对手)。**3**. 使吃惊,使慌乱;使(精神)受刺激。**4**. (粗暴地)突然干涉。— *vi*. (车辆等)颠簸;摇晃。**II** *n*. **1**. (车辆的)摇晃,颠簸。**2**. 突然的猛击〔尤指拳击〕;一击。**3**. 震惊,引起震惊的事情。**4**. 意外的挫折。**5**.〔美俚〕(麻醉药的)注射。**6**. 少量(可提神的东西)。*With a tremendous* ～ *the car started*. 汽车狠狠摇晃一下才起动了。*The news gave me quite a* ～. 这消息使我大吃一惊。*pour a* ～ *of whisky* 倒一点威士忌提提神。***pass a*** ～ 猛然一击。～**-waggon** *n*.〔美方〕农家牛车。**-ingly** *ad*.

jolt·er·head [ˈdʒəultəhed; ˋdʒoltəˏhɛd] *n*. 大傻瓜。

jolt·y [ˈdʒəulti; ˋdʒoltɪ] *a*. 摇晃的,颠簸的。

Jon [dʒɔn; dʒon] *n*. 乔恩〔男子名,Jonah 和 Jonathan 的略称〕。

Jon(a). = Jonathan.

Jo·nah [ˈdʒəunə; ˋdʒonə] *n*. **1**. 乔纳〔男子名〕。**2**. 约拿〔《圣经》中希伯来的预言者〕。**3**. 带来不幸的人,灾星,(为避免带来不幸而)被牺牲的人。**4**. (《旧约圣经》中的)《约拿书》。**5**.〔美俚〕爵士音乐迷。～**'s gourd 1**. 蓖麻。**2**. 朝生暮死的东西。～ **trip** 不幸的航程;不成功的计划。**-esque** *a*.

Jo·nas [ˈdʒəunəs; ˋdʒonəs] *n*. = Jonah.

Jon·a·than [ˈdʒɔnəθən; ˋdʒɑnəθən] *n*. **1**. 乔纳森〔男子名,Jon 为其昵称〕。**2**. 典型的美国人〔亦作 Brother ～〕。**3**.〔美〕一种红皮的晚秋苹果。**4**. 约拿单〔《圣经》中索尔 (Saul) 的长子,大卫 (David) 的好朋友〕。

Jones [dʒəunz; dʒonz] *n*. 琼斯〔姓氏〕。

jon·gleur [ʒɔːŋˈgləː, ʒɔŋ-; ˋdʒɑŋglə] *n*.〔F.〕中世纪法国和英国的游吟诗人。

jon·quil [ˈdʒɔŋkwil; ˋdʒɑŋkwɪl] *n*.【植】(水仙属)长寿花。～ *colour* 淡黄色。

Jon·son [ˈdʒɔnsn; ˋdʒɑnsn] *n*. 琼森〔姓氏〕。

Jor·dan[1] [ˈdʒɔːdn; ˋdʒɔrdn̩] *n*. 乔丹〔姓氏〕。

Jor·dan[2] [ˈdʒɔːdən; ˋdʒɔrdən] *n*. **1**. 约旦〔亚洲〕。**2**. 〔the ～〕约旦河。～ **almond 1**. 杏仁〔大量用于糖果中〕。**2**. 彩色糖衣杏仁。**-ian** *a*. 约旦的。

jor·dan [ˈdʒɔːdn; ˋdʒɔrdn̩] *n*.〔废〕便壶,尿罐(= chamber pot)。

jor·na·da [hɔrˈnɑːdə; hɔrˋnɑdə] *n*.〔Sp.〕**1**. 一天的旅程。**2**. (美南部、墨西哥的)荒漠地带。

jo·rum [ˈdʒɔːrəm; ˋdʒorəm] *n*. 大杯;一满杯(量)。

Jos. = Joseph; Josiah.

Jo·seph [ˈdʒəuzif; ˋdʒozəf] *n*. **1**. 约瑟夫〔男子名〕。**2**. 约瑟〔《圣经》中人物,一指雅各 (Jacob) 的第十一个儿子;一指马利亚 (Mary) 之夫〕。**3**. 正派男子,讨厌女人的男子。**3**.〔j-〕十八世纪妇女骑马时穿的大氅。～***'s coat*** 【植】苋菜 (*Amaranthus tricolor*)。

Jo·se·phine [ˈdʒəuzifiːn; ˋdʒozəˏfin] *n*. 约瑟芬〔女子名〕。

Josh [dʒɔʃ; dʒɑʃ] *n*. 乔希〔男子名,Joshua 的昵称〕。

josh [dʒɔʃ; dʒɑʃ] **I** *n*.〔美俚〕揶揄,嘲笑,戏弄。**II** *vt*., *vi*.〔美俚〕(无恶意地)戏弄,哄骗,(和…)开玩笑。**-er** *n*. 开玩笑的人,戏弄者。

Josh·u·a [ˈdʒɔʃwə; ˋdʒɑʃuə] *n*. **1**. 乔舒亚〔男子名〕。**2**. 约书亚〔《圣经》中人物,古代以色列人首领摩西的继承者〕。**2**.《约书亚书》〔旧约《圣经》中的一卷〕。～ **tree** 【植】短叶丝兰(= *Yucca brevifolia*)〔产于美国西南部〕。

jos·kin [ˈdʒɔskin; ˋdʒɑskɪn] *n*.〔俚〕乡巴佬,笨人。

joss [dʒɔs; dʒɑs] *n*. (中国的)神像,菩萨。～ **house** *n*. (中国的)寺,庙;神龛。～ **paper** (中国祭祀用的)钱纸,锡箔。～ **stick** (中国祭神用的)香。

joss·er [ˈdʒɔsə; ˋdʒɑsə] *n*. **1**.〔澳〕牧师。**2**.〔英〕家伙;傻子。

jos·tle [ˈdʒɔsl; ˋdʒɑsl̩] **I** *vt*. **1**. (用肘)推,挤,撞;贴近。**2**. 惹,刺激,使激动。**3**. 与…竞争,与…争夺。*He* ～*d his way through a crowd*. 他从人群中挤过去。～ *sb*. *away* [*from*, *out of*] 把某人推开。*Many cars lay jostling each other at the parking lot*. 许多汽车在停车场上紧紧挨着。*The thought* ～*d her complacency*. 这种想法使她不安。— *vi*. **1**. 拥挤,推撞;贴近。**2**. 竞争,争夺。～ *against sb*. 推撞某人。*The crowd* ～*d into the theater*. 人群挤进了戏院。～ ***with each other*** 互相倾轧。～ ***with sb***. ***for sth***. 同某人争抢某物。**II** *n*. 拥挤,推撞。**-r** *n*. 推撞者;〔美〕扒手。

jot [dʒɔt; dʒɑt] **I** *n*. **1**. (字母的)一点,一划。**2**.〔通例用否定结构〕一点儿,少量。*not care a* ～ *about* ... 对…毫不在乎。*not one* ～ *or little* 一丝一毫也不〔有时亦作 not a ～〕。**II** *vt*. (*-tt-*) 匆匆记下 (*down*)。～ *down ones license number* 匆匆记下某人的执照号。

jo·ta [ˈhəutə; ˋhotə] *n*. (西班牙)阿拉贡双人舞。

jot·ter [ˈdʒɔtə; ˋdʒɑtə] *n*. **1**. 匆匆记下某事的人。**2**. (作备忘录用的)小笔记本,小本子。

jot·ting [ˈdʒɔtiŋ; ˋdʒɑtɪŋ] *n*. 简短的笔记,略记。

Jo·tun(n) [ˈjɔːtun; ˋjɔtun] *n*. (北欧神话中)巨人族的一员。～**-heim** [-heim; -hem] 巨人之家。

Joule [dʒuːl, dʒəul; dʒul, dʒol] *n*. **1**. 朱尔〔姓氏〕。**2**. **James P**. ～焦耳〔1818—1889,英国物理学家〕。

joule [dʒaul; dʒuːl; dʒaul, dʒul] *n*.【物】焦耳〔能量和功的单位〕。

jounce [dʒauns; dʒauns] **I** *vi*. (车辆等)摇晃,震动,颠簸。— *vt*. 使震动,使摇晃,使颠簸。**II** *n*. 震动,摇晃;颠簸。

jouncy [ˈdʒaunsi; ˋdʒaunsɪ] *a*. 摇晃的,颠簸的。

jour. = journal; journalist; journeyman.

jour de fête [F. ʒur də fɛt; ʒur də fɛt]〔F.〕节日。

jour·nal [ˈdʒəːnl; ˋdʒɝnl̩] *n*. **1**. 日记,日志。【海】航海日记。**2**.【会计】分类账,日记账。**3**. 日报;定期刊物,杂志。**4**.〔the Journals〕(立法机关、委员会等的)议事录。**5**.【机】轴颈。*a monthly* ～月刊。*thrust* ～【机】止推轴颈。*yellow* ～黄色新闻。～ **box** 【机】轴颈箱。

jour·nal·ese [ˌdʒəːnəˈliːz; ˏdʒɝnlˋiz] *n*. (草率、低劣的)新闻笔调。

jour·nal·ism [ˈdʒəːnəlizəm; ˋdʒɝnlˏɪzəm] *n*. **1**. 新闻工作,新闻写作,新闻编辑,报刊出版;新闻出版界。**2**.〔集合词〕报刊,报刊文章;(有别于学术专著的)报刊通俗文章。**3**. 新闻学。*yellow* ～ = yellow journal.

jour·nal·ist [ˈdʒəːnəlist; ˋdʒɝnlɪst] *n*. **1**. 新闻工作者,报刊编辑,报刊撰稿人,记者;报刊经营者。**2**. 记日记的人。*yellow* ～黄色记者。**-is·tic** *a*. **-is·ti·cal·ly** *ad*.

jour·nal·ize [ˈdʒəːnəlaiz; ˋdʒɝnlˏaɪz] *vt*. 把…记入日记[日记账、日志]。— *vi*. **1**. 记日记。**2**. 记日记账。**3**. 从事报刊工作[事业]。

jour·ney [ˈdʒəːni; ˋdʒɝnɪ] *n*. **1**. (通常指陆上的)旅行〔*cf*. voyage〕;路程,旅程。**2**. 历程;道路。*a two days'* ～两天的路程。*A pleasant* ～ *to you*! = *I wish you a good* [*happy*] ～! 祝你一路顺风。*life's* ～人生的历程。*the* ～ *to success* 成功之道。***be*** (***away***) ***on a*** ～ 在旅行中(不在家)。***break one's*** [***the***] ～ ***at***... 在…中

J

途下车。***cheat the*** ～消磨旅途的寂寞。***get to one's ～'s end*** 到目的地。***go*** [***start, set out***] ***on a long*** ～出发作长途旅行。***go on one's last*** ～死。***make*** [***take, undertake***] ***a*** ～旅行。**II** ***vi***. 旅行。～ *by land* 陆上旅行。～ *on foot* 徒步旅行。**-man** (*pl*. **-men**, *fem*. **-wo·man**) **1.** (由学徒工升成的)工匠。**2.** 雇工, 短工, 计日工。**3.** (工厂)技工。**4.** 被雇者。**-work** 短工, 散工; 临时的工作。

jour·no [ˈdʒəːnəu; ˋdʒɝno] ***n***. 〔英俚〕新闻记者。

joust [dʒaust; dʒaʊst] **I** ***n***. **1.** (骑士等的)马上枪术比武。**2.** 〔*pl*.〕比赛。**3.** 斗争。**II** ***vi***. **1.** 骑马进行枪术比武。**2.** 参加比赛。

Jove [dʒəuv; dʒov] ***n***. **1.** 【罗神】= Jupiter. **2.** 〔诗〕木星。***by*** ～! 〔英〕哎哟! 天哪! 好家伙!

jo·vi·al [ˈdʒəuvjəl, -viəl; ˋdʒovjəl, -vɪəl] ***a***. **1.** 〔J-〕【罗神】主神朱庇特的(= jovian)。**2.** 〔J-〕【天】木星的。**3.** 快活的, 高兴的, 愉快的。**-ly** ***ad***.

jo·vi·al·i·ty [ˌdʒəuviˈæliti; ˏdʒovɪˋælətɪ] ***n***. **1.** 快活, 高兴, 愉快。**2.** 〔*pl*.〕愉快的话, 快活的行为。

Jo·vi·an [ˈdʒəuviən; ˋdʒovɪən] ***a***. **1.** 【罗神】主神朱庇特(Jupiter)的; 朱庇特似的。**2.** 雄伟的, 威风凛凛的。**3.** 【天】木星的。

Jow·ett [ˈdʒauit, ˈdʒəuit; ˋdʒaʊɪt, ˋdʒoɪt] ***n***. **1.** 乔伊特〔姓氏〕。**2. Benjamin** ～班杰明·乔伊特〔1817—1893, 英国古典学者, 柏拉图著作翻译家〕。

jowl [dʒaul; dʒaʊl] ***n***. **1.** 颌; 颌骨; 下颌; 下巴。**2.** 颊; 猪的颊肉。**3.** (牛、禽类的)喉袋, 垂肉; (鸟的)嗉囊。**4.** 鱼头及头边部分。***cheek by*** [***with***] ～亲热; 和…靠近。

Joy [dʒɔi; dʒɔɪ] ***n***. 乔伊〔女子名〕。

joy [dʒɔi; dʒɔɪ] **I** ***n***. **1.** 快乐, 高兴。**2.** 乐事, 乐趣。**3.** 喜庆, 欢乐。**4.** 最大的幸福。*be filled with* [*be full of*] ～*s* 非常高兴。*I wish* [*give*] *you* ～ *of your success*. 我祝贺你的成功, 恭喜恭喜。*in* ～快活, 高兴。*jump* [*leap*] *for* ～欢喜得跳起来, 欢欣鼓舞。*shouts of* ～欢呼。*sing and dance for* [*with*] ～高兴得载歌载舞。*to one's great* ～使人特别高兴的是。*share* ～*s and sorrows of life* 同甘共苦。*There was great* ～ *in the city*. 城内一片欢腾。*Joys shared with others are more enjoyed*. 〔谚〕与众同乐, 其乐无穷。**II** ***vi***. 欢欣, 高兴。～ *in sb.'s success* 为某人的成功而高兴。— ***vt***. 〔诗〕使高兴, 享受。～**bells** ***n***. 〔*pl*.〕(教堂中通报喜庆事件的)报喜钟, 庆祝钟。～**-firing** 以开枪表示欢庆, 开枪庆祝。～**house** 〔美俚〕妓院。～**-juice** 〔美俚〕酒。～**pop** ***vi***. 〔美俚〕逢场作戏地吸毒。～**-powder** 〔美俚〕吗啡。～ **ride** 〔口〕驾车兜风〔尤指偷车以高速胡乱行驶〕。～**rider** 驾车兜风的人。～**riding** 驾车兜风。～**-smoke** 逢场作戏的吸毒。～ **stick** 〔俚〕飞机操纵杆; 操纵方向的装置。

joy·ance [ˈdʒɔiəns; ˋdʒɔɪəns] ***n***. 〔古〕快乐, 喜悦。

Joyce [ˈdʒɔis; ˋdʒɔɪs] ***n***. 乔伊斯〔姓氏, 女子名〕。

J

joy·ful [ˈdʒɔif*u*l; ˋdʒɔɪfəl] ***a***. **1.** 快乐的, 快活的, 高兴的。**2.** 令人开心的, 使人喜悦的。*a* ～ *countenance* 喜笑颜开。*a* ～ *event* 喜事。～ *tidings* 喜讯。**-ly** ***ad***. **-ness** ***n***.

joy·less [ˈdʒɔilis; ˋdʒɔɪlɪs] ***a***. 不愉快的, 不高兴的。**-ly** ***ad***. **-ness** ***n***.

joy·ous [ˈdʒɔiəs; ˋdʒɔɪəs] ***a***. = joyful. **-ly** ***ad***. **-ness** ***n***.

J.P. = Justice of the Peace 兼理一般司法事务的地方官, 治安官。

Jp. = jet propulsion 喷气推进。

JPL = Jet Propulsion Laboratory 〔美〕喷气推进实验所。

Jr., jr. = **1.** journal. **2.** junior.

J.S. = **1.** judgment Summons 〔英〕判决债务传票。**2.** judicial separation 法院判决的夫妇分居。

JSF = joint strike fighter 【军】联合攻击战斗机。

JST = Japan Standard Time 日本标准时间。

Jt.-ed. = Joint-editor 合编者(之一)。

ju·ba [ˈdʒuːbə; ˋdʒubə] ***n***. (美国黑人的)朱巴舞〔以手帕等加强舞蹈节奏〕。

jub·bah [ˈdʒubə; ˋdʒʊbə] ***n***. 〔Ar.〕裾巴〔穆斯林男女均穿的宽敞外衣〕。

ju·be [ˈdʒuːbi; ˋdʒubɪ] ***n***. 【建】(教堂的)圣坛隔栏; 圣殿屏廊。

ju·ber·ous [ˈdʒuːbərəs; ˋdʒubərəs] ***a***. 〔美方〕怀疑的, 犹豫的。

ju·bi·lance, -cy [ˈdʒuːbiləns, -si; ˋdʒubɪləns, -sɪ] ***n***. 欢呼, 兴高采烈, 喜气洋洋。

ju·bi·lant [ˈdʒuːbilənt; ˋdʒubɪlənt] ***a***. 欢呼的; 喜气洋洋的, 欢欣鼓舞的。**-ly** ***ad***.

ju·bi·la·rian [ˌdʒuːbiˈlɛəriən; ˏdʒubɪˋlɛrɪən] ***n***. 五十周年纪念的庆祝者。

ju·bi·la·te [ˈdʒuːbileit; ˋdʒubɪlˏet] ***vi***. 欢呼, 欢欣。

Ju·bi·la·te [ˌdʒuːbiˈlɑːti; ˏdʒubəˋlɑtɪ] ***n***. **1.** 【宗】复活节后的第三个星期日。**2.** 《旧约圣经》中的《诗篇》第一百篇(的乐曲)〔即 the Old Hundred(th)〕。

ju·bi·la·tion [ˌdʒuːbiˈleiʃən; ˏdʒubɪˋleʃən] ***n***. 欢呼; 喜悦; 庆祝(胜利)。

ju·bi·lee [ˈdʒuːbiliː; ˋdʒublˏi] ***n***. **1.** 〔J-〕(古代犹太)五十年节〔每五十年举行一次庆祝解放和复兴的节日〕。**2.** (天主教的)大赦年。**3.** (结婚等)五十周年纪念; 二十五周年纪念。**4.** 欢乐的节日。**5.** 欢乐。**6.** 〔美〕(歌唱未来幸福时日的)黑人民歌。*the silver* ～二十五周年纪念。*the golden* ～ 五十周年纪念。*the diamond* ～ 六十周年纪念。*The Diamond J-* 英国维多利亚女王统治六十周年纪念(一八九七年)。*We had a big* ～ *to celebrate the victory*. 我们举行盛大的纪念以祝贺胜利。*They abandoned themselves to* ～ 他们沉醉在狂欢之中。～ **port** 1897 年英国女皇维多利亚即位六十周年纪念时酿造的葡萄酒。～**singer** 唱黑人民歌的美国黑人歌手。～ **song** 〔美〕黑人民谣, 黑人灵歌。

ju·che [ˈtʃuːtʃei; ˋtʃutʃe] ***n***. 〔Kor.〕自主。

Jud. = Judges; Judgment; judicial; Judith.

Ju·dae·a, Ju·de·a [dʒuːˈdiːə; dʒuˋdiə] ***n***. 犹地阿〔古代罗马统治下的巴勒斯坦南部地区〕。

Ju·dae·o-, Ju·de·o- [dʒuːˈdiəu; dʒuˋdɪo] ***comb. f***. 表示"犹太的"如: *Judaeo*phile.

Ju·dae·o·phile [dʒuːˈdiəufail; dʒuˋdɪəfaɪl] ***a***. 对犹太人亲善的。

Ju·dah [ˈdʒuːdə; ˋdʒudə] ***n***. **1.** 朱达〔男子名〕。**2.** 犹太〔《旧约圣经》中犹太人十二列祖之一〕。**3.** 巴勒斯坦南部古王国。

Ju·da·ic(al) [dʒu(ː)ˈdeiik(əl); dʒuˋdeɪk(ɪ)] ***a***. **1.** 犹太人的; 犹太民族的; 犹太文化的。**2.** 犹太教的。

Ju·da·ism· [ˈdʒuːdeiizəm; ˋdʒudɪɪzəm] ***n***. **1.** 〔宗〕犹太教。**2.** 对犹太风俗[仪式等]的遵奉。**3.** 犹太人的文化、社会和宗教信仰。**4.** 全体犹太人。

Ju·da·ist [ˈdʒuːdeiist; ˋdʒudɪɪst] ***n***. 犹太教信徒; 尊崇犹太风俗的人。

Ju·da·ize, Ju·da·ise [ˈdʒuːde*i*aiz; ˋdʒudɪˏaɪz] ***vt***. 使犹太化; 使信仰犹太教。— ***vi***. 犹太化, 信奉犹太教。**-z[s]a·tion** ***n***. **-z[s]er** ***n***.

Ju·das [ˈdʒuːdəs; ˋdʒudəs] ***n***. **1.** 犹大〔耶稣的门徒, 出卖耶稣者〕。**2.** (伪装亲善的)叛徒。**3.** 〔j-〕(门、墙上的)监视孔, 窥视孔 (= ～ window)。～**colo(u)r** (胡须等的)红色。～**-colo(u)red** ***a***. 红色的。～ **kiss** 假亲热, 口蜜腹剑, 阴险的背叛。～ **tree** 【植】紫荆 (cercis 的俗称)。

Judd [dʒʌd; dʒʌd] ***n***. 贾德〔姓氏〕。

jud·der [ˈdʒʌdə; ˋdʒʌdɚ] **I** ***vi***. 摇动; 振动; 颤动。**II** ***n***. 颤抖, 震动声。

Jude [dʒuːd; dʒud] ***n***. **1.** 裘德〔男子名〕。**2.** 《犹大书》〔《圣经·新约》中的篇名〕。

Ju·den·het·ze [ˈjuːdənhetsə; ˋjudənˏhɛtsə] ***n***. 〔G.〕迫害犹太人(= Jewbaiting)。

Judg. = Judges.

judge [dʒʌdʒ; dʒʌdʒ] **I** ***n***. **1.** 审判员, 法官, 推事。**2.** 〔J-〕

最高审判者〔指神、上帝〕。**3.**（纠纷等的）评判者；（比赛等的）裁判员。**4.** 鉴定人，鉴赏家。**5.**【史】士师〔犹太所罗国王以前的统治者〕。**6.**〔J-〕〔*pl*.〕（《旧约圣经》中的）《士师记》（= the Book of Judges）。*an associate* ～，*a side* ～ 陪审员。*an examining* [*preliminary*] ～ 第一审判员。*as grave* [*sober*] *as a* ～ 像法官那样庄重，非常严肃。*act as* ～ *at the race* 在赛跑中担任裁判员。*a good* ～ *of horses* 善于识马的人。*He is no* ～ *in such matters*. 他对这些事是外行。***be no*** ～ ***of*** 不能鉴定。**II** ***vi***. **1.** 判决；审理；审判。**2.** 裁判；评定；裁决。**3.** 监定；识别；评价。**4.** 断定，认为。**5.**〔古〕批评，指责。～ *works of art* 评价艺术品。*It was* ～*d better to set out at once*. 认为立刻出发比较好。—***vi***. **1.** 下判断，作出裁判。**2.** 作评价。～ *by* [*from*] *appearances* 由外观上判断。*judging from the fact* 由事实上推测。～ *between two combatants* 在两个竞技者之间裁决胜负。**J- Advocate** 总军法官；军法检查官。**J- Advocate General** 军法署署长。**J- Advocate General's Department** 军法署，军法处。～**-made** 由法官[判决]创造的（*the* ～*-made law*【法】判例法）。

judg(e)·mat·ic(al) [dʒʌdʒˈmætik(əl); dʒʌdʒˋmætɪk-(!)] ***a***.〔口〕眼光敏锐的，考虑周到的，明智的。**-i·cal·ly *ad***.

judg(e)·ment [ˈdʒʌdʒmənt; ˋdʒʌdʒmənt] ***n***. **1.** 审判，裁判，判决。**2.** 由判决所确定的债务；确定债务的判决书。**3.** 鉴定，评价，判断。**4.** 判断力，见识；精明。**5.** 意见，看法；批评，指责。**6.** 公正，正义〔《圣经》中用语〕。**7.**〔J-〕【宗】上帝的最后审判（日）（= the Last J- 或 J-Day）。**8.** 天罚，报应。*a* ～ *against the plaintiff* 裁定原告败诉的判决。*a* ～ *for the plaintiff* 裁定原告胜诉的判决。*a* ～ *of acquittal* 无罪的宣判。*a* ～ *of conviction* 有罪的宣判。*sit in* ～ *on a case* 审判一件案子。*a* ～ *creditor* 判决确定的债权人。*a* ～ *debt* 判决确定的债务。*an error of* ～ 判断错误。*form a* ～ *upon facts* 根据事实作出判断。*a man of sound* ～判断力健全的人。*a man without* ～无判断力的人。*disturb the* ～令人迷惑。*exercise* [*use*] *one's* ～运用判断力。*show good* ～判断力强。*in my personal* ～根据我个人的见解。*on one's own* ～按照自己的意见，独断。*private* ～一己之见〔特指宗教上不同传统的见解〕。*It is a* ～ *on you for getting up late*. 这是你睡懒觉的报应。***Daniel come to*** ～. 好一个丹尼尔，好公正的清官〔现在一般用作讽刺语〕。***give*** [***pass***, ***render***] ～ (***up***) ***on sb***. 对某人下判决，定案。～ ***by default***【法】缺席判决。***to the best of one's*** ～根据本人认识所及。**J- Day**【宗】上帝的最后审判（日）（= the Last J-）。～ **debt** 经法院裁定的债务。～ **reserved**【法】审讯后延缓判决。～ **seat** **1.** 裁判员席。**2.** 法院。

judge·ship [ˈdʒʌdʒɪʃip; ˋdʒʌdʒˏʃɪp] ***n***. 法官地位；法官职权；法官任期。

ju·di·ca·ble [ˈdʒu:dikəbl; ˋdʒudɪkəbl̩] ***a***. **1.** 可裁判的；可审判的。**2.** 应受审判的。

ju·di·ca·tive [ˈdʒu:dikətiv; ˋdʒudɪˏketɪv] ***a***. 审判的，判决的；司法的；法院裁决的。

ju·di·ca·to·ry [ˈdʒu:dikətəri; ˋdʒudɪkəˏtorɪ] **I *a***. 审判的，司法的。**II *n***. 法院；审判制度。

ju·di·ca·ture [ˈdʒu:dikətʃə; ˋdʒudɪkətʃɚ] ***n***. **1.** 司法。**2.** 司法权。**3.** 审判员的职权[职务、地位]。**4.** 审判制度。**5.** 审判员，法院。*the Supreme Court of J-*〔英〕最高法院。

ju·di·cial [dʒu(:)ˈdiʃəl; dʒuˋdɪʃəl] ***a***. **1.** 司法的，审判上的。**2.** 审判员的；法官的；法院的；法院判决的[规定的]。**3.** 法官似的，符合法官身分的。**4.** 考虑周到的；慎重的；公平的，公正的。**5.**【宗】上帝审判的。～ *affairs* 司法。*a* ～ *assembly* 审判大会。*the* ～ *bench*〔集合词〕法官。～ *circles* = *the* ～ *world* 司法界。*the* ～ *departments* 司法部门。*the J- Department* (*Office*) 司法部。～ *gravity* 像审判员那样严肃。*a* ～ *pestilence* 天降瘟疫。*a biography* ～ *in purpose* 一本批判性的传记。*a man with a* ～ *mind* 内心公正的人。～ *functions* 司法职能。～ **chemistry** 法医化学。～ **murder** 合法但不公正的死刑判决。～ **police** 法警。～ **power** 司法权。～ **precedent** 判例。～ **proceedings** 审判程序；诉讼手续（*take* ～ *proceedings against sb*. 对某人起诉）。～ **sale** 法院判决的拍卖。～ **separation** 法院判决的夫妇分居。**-ly *ad***.

ju·di·ci·ar·y [dʒu(:)ˈdiʃiəri; dʒuˋdɪʃɪərɪ] **I *a***. 法院的，审判员的；司法的。～ *proceedings* 审判程序。**II *n***. **1.** 司法部。**2.**〔集合词〕审判员。**3.** 法院系统，法院制度。

ju·di·cious [dʒu(:)ˈdiʃəs; dʒuˋdɪʃəs] ***a***. 有见识的，明智的；合机宜的；审慎的。**-ly *ad***. **-ness *n***.

Ju·dith [ˈdʒu:diθ; ˋdʒudɪθ] ***n***. 朱迪丝〔女子名〕。

ju·do [ˈdʒu:dəu; ˋdʒudo] ***n***. (*pl*. ～(*s*))〔Jap.〕日本柔术，日本柔道〔日本的一种摔跤运动〕。

ju·do·ka [ˈdʒu:dəukɑ:; ˋdʒudokɑ] ***n***.（日本）柔术家，柔道家。

Jud·son [ˈdʒʌdsn; ˋdʒʌdsn̩] ***n***. 贾德森〔姓氏，男子名〕。

Ju·dy [ˈdʒu:di; ˋdʒudɪ] ***n***. 朱迪 **1.**〔女子名〕。**2.** 英国木偶戏《笨拙与朱迪》（Punch and Judy）中的男主角（Punch）之妻。

jug[1] [dʒʌg; dʒʌg] **I *n***. **1.**（有把手、小口、用以盛水或酒等的）大壶，罐，盂；陶制啤酒壶。**2.** 罐中物，壶中物。**3.**〔俚〕监牢。**4.**〔美俚〕银行，保险箱。**5.**〔俚〕一瓶威士忌酒。**II *vt***. **1.** 将（兔肉等）炖煨〔通常用过去分词〕。**2.** 把…装进壶[罐]中。**3.**〔俚〕关押，监禁。*jugged hare* 用土锅炖的野兔肉。～ **band**〔美〕瓶罐乐队〔以口琴、卡苏为乐器，以敲打瓶、罐、搓板、水桶等加强节奏效果的小民乐队或小爵士乐队〕。～**-handled *a***. **1.** 不匀称的。**2.** 单方面的；片面的。

jug[2] [dʒʌg; dʒʌg] **I *n***.（特指夜莺等的）叫声。**II *vi***. 模仿夜莺等啭鸣，发出夜莺般的鸣声。

ju·gal [ˈdʒu:gəl; ˋdʒugəl] ***a***. **1.**【解】颧骨的。**2.** 面颊的。～ **bone** 颧骨。

ju·gate [ˈdʒu:geit; ˋdʒuget] ***a***.【生】（鳞翅目昆虫）具翅轭的。

jug·ful [ˈdʒʌgful; ˋdʒʌgˏful] ***n***. **1.** 满壶，满罐。**2.** 非常多。*not by a* ～〔俚〕一点也不，决不。

Jug·ger·naut [ˈdʒʌgənɔ:t; ˋdʒʌgɚˏnɔt] ***n***. **1.**【印度教】讫里什那（Krishna）神像；〔喻〕世界的主宰。**2.**〔常用 j-〕可怕的，不可抗拒的力量。**3.**〔常用 j-〕使人盲目崇拜和牺牲的事物（= ～ car）。～ **car** 讫里什那神车〔据说讫里什那为 Vishnu 的化身，每年都用车载此神像举行巡行仪式，许多人相信被神像车辗死即可升天，因而不惜投身车下〕。

jug·gins [ˈdʒʌginz; ˋdʒʌgɪnz] ***n***.〔俚〕傻瓜。

jug·gle [ˈdʒʌgl; ˋdʒʌgl] **I *vi***. **1.**（用球、小刀、盘子等）玩杂耍；变戏法。**2.** 耍花招。**3.** 歪曲，窜改；欺骗（*with*）。～ *with balls* 耍球。～ *with history* 歪曲历史。～ *with sb*. 耍弄某人。～ *with words* 玩文字游戏。—***vt***. 耍（球、小刀、盘子等）；耍弄。**2.** 用戏法变出；欺骗，诈取。**3.** 歪曲，窜改，颠倒（事实等）。**4.** 对…抓[握]不住[牢]。～ *a fan into a bird* 把扇子变成鸟。～ *money out of sb*. = ～ *sb*. *out of his money* 骗取某人的钱。～ *sb*. *into doing sth*. 骗某人做某事。～ *sth*. *away* 耍花招骗取某物。～ *black and white* 混淆黑白。～ *the figures* 窜改数字。**II *n***. **1.** 变戏法，玩杂耍，魔术。**2.** 耍花招，欺诈，欺骗。

jug·gler [ˈdʒʌglə; ˋdʒʌglɚ] ***n***. **1.** 玩杂耍的人；魔术师。**2.** 骗子。*a* ～ *with words* 诡辩家。

jug·gler·y [ˈdʒʌgləri; ˋdʒʌglərɪ] ***n***. **1.** 魔术。**2.** 花招，把戏。**3.** 欺诈，欺骗。

jug·head [ˈdʒʌghed; ˋdʒʌgˏhɛd] ***n***.〔美俚〕笨蛋，傻瓜。

Ju·go-Slav, Ju·go·slav [ˈju:gəuˈslɑ:v; ˋjugoˋslɑv] **I *a***. 南斯拉夫（人）的（= Yugoslav）。**II *n***. 南斯拉夫人。

Ju·go·sla·vi·a, Ju·go·sla·vi·a [ˈjuːgəuˈslɑːvjə; ˋjugo-ˋslɑvɪə] ***n*.** 南斯拉夫(= Yugoslavia)。

Ju·go·sla·vi·an [ˈjuːgəuˈslɑːvjən; ˋjugoˋslɑvɪən] **I *n*.** 南斯拉夫人(= Yugoslavian)。**II *a*.** 南斯拉夫的；南斯拉夫人的。

jug·u·lar [ˈdʒʌgjulə; ˋdʒʌgjələ˞] **I *a*. 1.**【解】喉的，颈的；颈静脉的。**2.** (鱼)喉部有腹鳍的；(鳍)在喉部的。**II *n*.**【解】颈静脉。*the ~ vein* 颈静脉。

jug·u·late [ˈdʒʌgjuleit; ˋdʒʌgjəˏlet] ***vt*. 1.** 割断…的喉咙；扼杀，勒死。**2.**【医】(采用极端措施)阻止(病的)恶化。

ju·gum [ˈdʒuːgəm; ˋdʒugəm] ***n*.** (*pl*. **-ga** [-gə; -gə], ~**s**)【生】腕锁；(翅)轭。

juice [dʒuːs; dʒus] **I *n*. 1.** (菜蔬、果实、植物等的)汁、液、浆。**2.**〔*pl*.〕体液。**3.** 精，精髓，精力。**4.**〔美俚〕电，电流，汽油，液体燃料，硝化甘油。**5.**〔俚〕酒〔尤指威士忌酒〕，冷饮。**6.** (舞台等的)照明员，灯光员。**7.**〔俚〕非法之财，油水；高利；薪水，收入。**8.** 高利贷款。**9.**〔俚〕权势，地位。*fruit ~* 果子汁。*grape ~* 葡萄汁。*meat ~* 肉汁。*the ~s* 体液。*duodenal ~(s)* 十二指肠液。*gastric ~(s)* 胃液。*the ~ of life* 生命的活力，元气。*~d rehearsal* 电视节目预演。***full of ~*** 充满活力；盛气凌人。***give her ~***〔美俚〕**1.** 设法使事情进行顺利。**2.** 开快(汽车的)速度。***stew in one's own ~*** 自作自受。***tread*** [***step***] ***on the ~*** 加速，促进。**II *vt*. 1.**〔口〕从…中榨汁。**2.** 在…中加汁。**3.**〔美俚〕使触电死亡；以电刑处决(死囚等)。~ *a cow* 挤牛奶。~ ***up*** 使有精力，使活跃。~ **box** 盛放果汁的小纸盒。~ **dealer**〔俚〕放印子钱的人。**J-'s-harp** 口拨琴(= Jew's-harp)。~ **head**〔美俚〕酒鬼。~ **joint**〔美俚〕**1.** 果汁摊。**2.** 酒吧间，夜总会。**3.** (禁酒法废止前的)秘密酒馆。~ **peddler**〔美口〕电力公司。**-less *a*.** 无汁的。

juic·er [ˈdʒuːsə; ˋdʒusə˞] ***n*. 1.** 榨汁器。**2.**〔美俚〕一贯酗酒的人。**3.**〔美俚〕(舞台等的)照明员，灯光员。

juic·y [ˈdʒuːsi; ˋdʒusɪ] ***a*. 1.** 多汁的。**2.** (天气)多雨的，阴湿的。**3.**〔口〕有趣的，津津有味的；刺激性强的。**4.** (色调)鲜润的，绚烂的。**5.** 油水多的，报酬多的。**6.** 有力的，活力充沛的。**7.** 微醉的。*a ~ contract* 有利可图的合同。*a ~ pear* 汁水多的梨。*a ~ road* 道路泥泞。*a ~ bit of gossip about sb*. 关于某人的有声有色的小道消息。*a ~ kick* 猛踢。**-i·ly *ad*. -i·ness *n*.**

ju·jit·su [dʒuːˈdʒitsuː; dʒuˋdʒɪtsu] ***n*.**〔Jap.〕柔术，柔道〔日本的一种拳术和摔跤术〕。~ **politics** 柔道政治〔指竞选时针锋相对，对批评报之以猛烈的反批评等〕。

ju·ju [ˈdʒuːdʒuː; ˋdʒudʒu] ***n*. 1.** 物神〔西非某些部族用语〕。**2.** 符咒；魔力。

ju·jube [ˈdʒuːdʒu(ː)b; ˋdʒudʒub] ***n*. 1.**【植】枣子；枣树；枣属植物；枣酱。**2.** 枣味[枣状]胶糖。

ju·jut·su [dʒuːˈdʒutsuː, -ˈdʒʌt-; dʒuˋdʒʊtsu, -ˋdʒʌt-] ***n*.**〔Jap.〕= jujitsu.

J

juke [dʒuːk; dʒuk] ***vt*.** (美式橄榄球赛中)用假动作诱使(对方球员)离位。

juke·box, juke box [ˈdʒuːkbɔks; ˋdʒukˏbɑks] ***n*. 1.**〔美口〕(在酒吧间、餐馆等投入硬币就自动演唱的)自动电唱机。**2.**〔美口〕(电脑的)自动光盘只读存储器，光盘自动交换(存储)器。

juke joint [ˈdʒuːk dʒɔint; ˋdʒuk dʒɔɪnt] ***n*.**〔美〕备有自动电唱机的小餐馆或小舞厅。

Jul. = July.

ju·lep [ˈdʒuːlep; ˋdʒulɪp] ***n*. 1.** (服药用的)糖水；药制饮料。**2.** 威士忌[白兰地]酒加糖和薄荷的冷饮。**3.** 含香草的冷饮。

Jules [dʒuːlz; dʒulz] ***n*.** 朱尔斯〔男子名，Julius 的异体〕。

Jul·ia [ˈdʒuːljə; ˋdʒuljə] ***n*.** 朱莉亚〔女子名〕。

Jul·ian [ˈdʒuːljən, -liən; ˋdʒuljən, -lɪən] **I *n*.** 朱利安〔男子名〕。**II *a*.** (古罗马独裁者)儒略·凯撒(*Julius Caesar*)的。~ ***calendar*** 儒略历〔即当前用的阳历〕。

Ju·li·an·a [ˌdʒuːliˈɑːnə; ˏdʒulɪˋænə] ***n*.** 朱莉安娜〔女子名〕。

ju·li·enne [ˌdʒuːliˈen; ˏdʒulɪˋɛn] **I *n*.**〔F.〕菜丝汤。**II *a*.** (将蔬菜)切成丝的。*green beans ~* 青豆丝。*~ potatoes* 洋芋[马铃薯]丝。

Ju·li·et [ˈdʒuːliət, -liət; ˋdʒuljət, -lɪət] ***n*. 1.** 朱丽叶〔女子名〕。**2.** 莎士比亚悲剧《罗米欧与朱丽叶》中的女主角。~ **cap** 朱丽叶女帽〔带在后脑的帽子，常作新娘婚礼服的一部分〕。

Ju·li·ett [ˈdʒuːliet; ˋdʒulɪˏɛt] 通讯中用以代表字母 j 的词。

Jul·ius [ˈdʒuːliəs; ˋdʒuljəs] ***n*.** 朱利叶斯〔男子名〕。

Ju·ly [dʒu(ː)ˈlai; dʒuˋlaɪ] ***n*.** 七月〔略作 Jul., Jl., Jy.〕。

Ju·ma·da [dʒuˈmɑːdə; dʒuˋmɑdɑ] ***n*.**〔Ar.〕回历年中的五月或六月。

jum·bal [ˈdʒʌmbəl; ˋdʒʌmbl̩] ***n*.** = jumble.

jum·ble[1] [ˈdʒʌmbl; ˋdʒʌmbl̩] ***n*.** 环形甜薄饼。

jum·ble[2] [ˈdʒʌmbl; ˋdʒʌmbl̩] **I *vt*.** 搞乱，使混杂(*up*; *together*)。— ***vt*.** 搞乱，混杂乱成一团。**II *n*. 1.** 混乱，杂乱；混乱的一堆。**2.**〔英〕旧杂品义卖；旧杂货义卖品。~ **sale** 旧杂货拍卖。~ **shop**〔英〕廉价杂品店。

jum·bly [ˈdʒʌmbli; ˋdʒʌmblɪ] ***a*.** 混乱的，乱七八糟的。

jum·bo [ˈdʒʌmbəu; ˋdʒʌmbo]〔口〕**I *n*.** (*pl*. ~**s**) **1.** 体大而笨拙的人[动物、物件]；大型喷气式客机；庞然大物。**2.**〔J-〕(伦敦动物园的)大象。**3.** 大受欢迎的人。**4.** 钻车；移动式钻机台；高炉渣口冷却器。**II *a*.** 巨大的，特大的。~ *jet* 大型喷气式客机。

jum·buck [ˈdʒʌmbʌk; ˋdʒʌmbʌk] ***n*.**〔澳〕羊。

jump [dʒʌmp; dʒʌmp] **I *vi*. 1.** 跳，跳跃，跳起；弹跳，跳动。**2.** (用降落伞从飞机里)跳出。**3.** 猛烈地移动；积极行动，奔忙，活跃。**4.** 跳过，越过；越级提升。**5.** (物价等)猛增，暴涨。**6.** (结论)匆匆作出；(话题、主张等)突然改变。**7.** 随随便便，(注意力等)无目的地转移；(工作等)任意更动。**8.** 欣然接受(*at*)，急切投入(*in*; *into*)。**9.** 一致，符合。**10.** (电影中的映像)歪跳，颠倒。**11.** (桥牌中的)跳级叫牌。~ *from seat* 从座位上跳起来。~ *to one's feet* (由坐着)一跃而起。~ *for* [*with*] *joy* 欢跃。~ *at once* 立即行动。*The whole town is ~ing*. 全镇一片活跃。~ *over a page or two* 跳过一两页。*Gold Shares ~ed yesterday*. 昨天黄金股票猛涨。*The steel output is ~ing*. 钢产量正在猛增。~ *at* [*to*] *a conclusion* 匆匆作出结论，轻率断定。~ *from one topic to another* 从一个话题跳到另一个话题。~ *from job to job* 盲目地调换工作。~ *to another employment* 另有高就。~ *at the job* 抢着接受任务。~ *at the chance* 急切地抓住机会。*Good* [*Great*] *wits will ~ together*.〔谚〕智者所见略同。*Her opinions ~ with mine*. 她的意见和我一致。*His tastes and his means do not ~ together*. 他的爱好跟他的收入不相称。— ***vt*. 1.** 跳过，越过。**2.** 使跳跃，使颤动。**3.** 使惊起。**4.** 跳上，跳下，搭上。**5.** 突然离开(轨道等)，擅离(职守)。**6.** 使(物价等)猛涨；使(人)连升职位[级别]。**7.** (报刊中)把(文章一部分)转入他页。**8.**【电】跨接，跳线。**9.**【地】把(岩石)冲击打眼。**10.**〔口〕猛攻，叱责。**11.** (打桥牌时)跳级叫高。**12.** (赛跑、开车)抢在…前出发；抢先于…。**13.**〔俚〕(因欠债等)逃离，逃亡。**14.** 非法侵占(采矿权等)。**15.** (在煎锅中)摇动着煎煮。**16.**〔美〕交换(工作等)；交流(经验等)。~ *a section* 跳过一节。~ *a fence* 跳过篱笆。~ *a baby up and down on one's knees* 把孩子抱在膝上上下颠动。~ *a horse across a ditch* 纵马跃过小沟。~ *sb. out of chair* 使某人吃惊得从椅子上跳起。~ *a bus* 跳上公共汽车。*The train ~ed the rail* [*track*]. 火车出轨了。~ *ship* 离职弃船。~ *town* 逃离城市。*They ~ their prices to offset heavy expenditures*. 他们提高物价来抵消庞大的开支。*The college ~ed him from instructor to full professor*. 大学突然把他从讲师提升为

正教授。～ *the green light* 抢绿灯〔在红灯转换以前把车开过去〕。～ *a claim* 霸占土地[矿权等]。***be ～ed into doing sth.*** 被骗去做某事。～ ***down sb.'s throat*** 〔口〕驳得某人哑口无言,问住。～ ***in the lake*** 〔口〕离开不再讨厌。～ ***in with both feet*** 全力以赴。～ ***like parched peas*** 横蹦乱跳。～ ***off*** **1.**【军】突然出动攻击。**2.** 开始。～ ***on*** [***all over***] **1.** 严词责备。**2.** 突然袭击。～ (***one's***) ***bail*** 在保释后逃亡。～ ***out of one's skin*** 惊喜若狂,大吃一惊。～ ***sb. out*** 叱责某人。～ ***the broom*** 结婚。～ ***over the broomstick*** 姘居。～ ***the gun*** 〔美〕仓促行动;【体】未开号令声偷跑。～ ***the queue*** 插队,不按次序排队。***J- to it!*** 〔俚〕赶快! ～ ***up and down*** 跳上跳下。**II *n*. 1.** 跳跃;跳跃运动;一跳的距离;(需要跳越的)障碍。**2.** 惊跳;〔the ～s〕震颤;心神不定。**3.** (物价等的)暴涨,猛增。**4.** (系列的)中断;矿脉的断层;急转。**5.** (航空途中的)短程。**6.** (起步、出发时)抢先。**7.**【印】〔口〕(报刊文章的)转页,转版。**8.**【自】跳变,转移。**9.** 〔俚〕(爵士音乐等的)急奏。**10.**【建】大放脚的梯级。**11.** 跳伞。**12.** (象棋中)吃对方子的一着。**13.** 〔the ～s〕〔俚〕强效可卡因。*the broad* [*long*] ～跳远。*the high* ～ 跳高。*the pole* ～撑杆跳。*give sb. a* ～使某人吓一跳。*The prices take a* ～. 物价暴涨。*at a* ～一跃。*on one's last* ～ *from New York to San Francisco* 从纽约到旧金山的航空途中最后一段路程。*a forced* ～被迫跳伞。***at a full*** ～全速。***be all of a*** ～胆战心惊。***get*** [***have***] ***the*** ～ ***on*** 抢在…之前行动。***keep the enemy on the*** ～ 使敌人疲于奔命。***on the*** ～〔口〕来回奔忙;在忙碌中。***on the keen*** ～赶快。**III *a*.** (爵士音乐中)急拍子的。*a* ～ *tune* 急奏曲。～ **area** (降落伞的)降落地。～ **ball** (篮球的)跳球。～ **cut(s)** (影片)跳剖。～**ed-up** ***a*. 1.** 暴发的,刚发财的。**2.** 自大的;无耻的。～ **function**【数】跃变函数。～ **hook**【体】(篮球的)钩手跳投。～ **if not** (计算机中的)条件转移。～ **instruction**【计】转移指令,跳越指令。～**-off *n*.** (赛跑或进攻的)开始。～ **pass** (篮球、橄榄球)跳起传球。～**-rope** 跳绳(运动)。～ **seat**(轿车等前后座之间的)折叠式小座位。～ **shot** (篮球)跳起投篮。～**-start *vt*. 1.** 强力启动。**2.** 使充满生机。～ **suit 1.** 跳伞服;修车技工工作服。**2.** 妇女连身裤紧身便服。～ **wire**【电】跨接线。**-a·ble *a*.**

jump·er[1] [ˈdʒʌmpə; ˋdʒʌmpɚ] ***n*. 1.** 跳跃者;跳跃的选手;跳伞者;(送货车上)递送包件的人。**2.** 跳虫〔如蚤等〕;经过训练能跳越障碍的马。**3.**【电】跳线,跨接线。**4.** 长凿子,(钟表的)棘爪,制轮爪,掣子。**5.** (儿童)雪橇。**6.** (船的)桅间牵索。**7.**【地】冲击钻杆;跳动器械。～ **stay** (船的)横牵索。

jump·er[2] [ˈdʒʌmpə; ˋdʒʌmpɚ] ***n*. 1.** 工作服。**2.** (妇女穿的)无袖连衣裙[布拉吉];〔英〕妇女的宽上衣。**3.** 〔*pl*.〕(孩童的)连衫裤。

jump·ing [ˈdʒʌmpiŋ; ˋdʒʌmpɪŋ] **I *n*.** 跳动,跃变。**II *a*.** 跳跃的,用于跳跃的。～ **bean** 跳豆〔墨西哥灯台草的种子,因寄生幼虫,故能跳动,也称 Mexican ～ bean〕。～**-disease**【医】痉跳病。～ **jack** (用线牵动的)娃娃玩具。～ **mouse**【动】北美林跳鼠。～ **net** 救生网〔用于接救从楼上跳下来的人〕。～**-off** (铁路等的)中间小站。～**-off place 1.** 偏僻的地方。**2.** 旅行的终点,下车处。**3.** 山穷水尽的地步。**4.** 起点,出发站。～ **pole** (撑竿跳用的)撑竿。～ **sheet** 〔英〕(失火时接住从楼上跳下的人用的)接跳布。～ **trace routine**【计】转移跟踪程序。

jump·y [ˈdʒʌmpi; ˋdʒʌmpɪ] ***a*.** (***-i·er***; ***-i·est***) **1.** 跳跃的,急剧变化的。**2.** 心惊肉跳的,神经质的。**-i·ly *ad*. -i·ness *n*.**

Jun. = **1.** June. **2.** Junior.

Junc, junc. =junction.

jun·co [ˈdʒʌŋkəu; ˋdʒʌŋko] ***n*.** (*pl*. ～*s*)【动】雪鹀。

junc·tion [ˈdʒʌŋkʃən; ˋdʒʌŋkʃən] ***n*. 1.** 接合,连接,连络。**2.** 接合点,交叉点,(河流的)汇合处,(铁道的)联轨点。**3.**【电】中继线。**4.**【物】接头,结。*We effected a* ～ *of our two armies*. 我们使自己的两支军队会师了。*make a* ～ 取得联络,连接起来。～ **box** 接线盒,套管;连轴器。～ **diode** 面结型二极管。～ **efficiency** 中继效率。～ **group** 中继电阻,中继线群。～ **laser** 面结型雷射器。～ **line** [**rail**] 联轨线。～ **service** 短程通信。～ **station** 联轨站,枢纽站,换车站。～ **transistor** 接合(式)电晶体。

junc·ture [ˈdʒʌŋktʃə; ˋdʒʌŋktʃɚ] ***n*. 1.** 结合,连结,接缝,接合点;交界。**2.** 时机,关头。**3.**【语】连音。*an important* ～ *in a man's career* 人生历程中的重要关键。*at this* ～ 在这个时候。*in the present critical* ～ *of things* 在目前这一危急关头下。

June [dʒuːn; dʒun] ***n*. 1.** 琼〔女子名〕。**2.** 六月〔略作 Jun., Je.〕。～ **beetle** [**bug**] (美国北部的)六月甲虫;(美国南部的)无花果虫。

Ju·neau [ˈdʒuːnəu; ˋdʒuno] ***n*.** 朱诺〔美国阿拉斯加州的首府〕。

june·ber·ry [ˈdʒuːnberi; ˋdʒun͵bɛrɪ] ***n*.** (*pl*. ***-ries***)【植】**1.** 唐棣属 (*Amelanchier*) 植物。**2.** 唐棣属植物的果实。

jun·gle [ˈdʒʌŋgl; ˋdʒʌŋgl] ***n*. 1.** (热带的)丛林,密林,莽丛。**2.** 〔the J-〕〔俚〕(伦敦证券交易所内的)西非洲矿业股票市场;西非洲矿业股票交易人。**3.** 〔美俚〕(无业游民的)露营地,集合处;城市中人口稠密的居民区[工业区]。**4.** 一堆混乱的东西;错综复杂的事。**5.** 为生存而残酷斗争的地方。～ *warfare* 丛林战。～ **fever** 丛林热〔指一名黑人男子想与白人妇女发生性关系的强烈欲望〕。～ **fowl** 原鸡〔东印度的野鸡,雄的称 ～ cock, 雌的称～ hen〕。**J- Gym** 一种儿童攀爬器具(包括杆、梯子等)的商标名称;〔j- gym〕儿童攀爬器具。～ **justice** 弱肉强食;私刑。～ **law** 弱肉强食原则。

jun·gli [ˈdʒʌŋgli; ˋdʒʌŋglɪ] **I *n*.** 印度丛林居民。**II *a*. 1.** 住在印度丛林地带的。**2.** 印度丛林居民。**3.** 土头土脑的,粗野的。

jun·gly [ˈdʒʌŋgli; ˋdʒʌŋglɪ] ***a*. 1.** 丛林的,丛林地带的。**2.** 像丛林的;丛林地带居民的。

jun·ior [ˈdʒuːnjə; ˋdʒunjɚ] **I *a*. 1.** 较年幼的,较年小的 (*opp*. senior)〔常略为 Jr. 或 Jun., 加在姓名之后,指兄弟二人中的弟弟或由于父子同名在儿子姓名后加上 J-〕。**2.** 资历较浅的;日期较后的。**3.** 由青少年组成的,专为青少年准备的。**4.** (美国四年制大学或中学中的)三年级的;低年级的。*be* ～ *to sb*. 比某人年少。*John Smith*, J- [Jn., Jun.] 小约翰·史密斯。*Smith* ～ 指同级中较幼的史密斯。～ *members of the staff* 年资较低的职工。*a* ～ *partner* 地位较低的伙伴。～ *readers* 青少年读物。*the* ～ *class* 三年级。**II *n*. 1.** 年少者。**2.** 低班生;等级较低者;晚辈。**3.** (美国四年制大学或中学的)三年级生。**4.** 少女衣服尺寸。*He is my* ～ *by three years*. = *He is three years my* ～. = *He is three years* ～ *to me*. 他比我小三岁。～ **college 1.** 〔美〕初级大学〔指一二年制大学〕。**2.** 〔美俚〕监狱。～ **high school** 〔美〕初级中学。**J- League** 〔美〕女青年会〔多为有闲妇女组成,开展慈善活动等〕。～ **miss 1.** (十三至十五、六岁的)少女。**2.** 苗条妇女和少女的衣服尺寸。～ **school** 〔美〕小学。～ **varsity** (大学院校的)体育代表队二队。

jun·ior·i·ty [ˌdʒuːniˈɔriti; dʒunɪˋɑrətɪ] ***n*. 1.** 年少,较年幼者的身份。**2.** 晚辈[下级]的身份[处境]。

ju·ni·per [ˈdʒuːnipə; ˋdʒunəpɚ] ***n*.**【植】桧属植物,红松。*the* ～ *tamarisk* 华北柽柳〔又名三春柳或红柳〕。*the Chinese* ～桧。*the common* ～欧洲刺柏。

junk[1] [dʒʌŋk; dʒʌŋk] **I *n*. 1.** (肉等的)大块,厚片。**2.** (填缝隙用的)旧绳絮。**3.** 〔古〕(船上用的)腌牛肉。**4.** 〔口〕零碎废物〔烂铁、旧罐等〕;废物堆。**5.** 〔俚〕麻醉品,毒品〔鸦片、海洛因等〕。**6.** 便宜货,假货;废话,哄骗。**7.** 抹香鲸头部的脂肪组织。*a* ～ *of mutton* 一大块羊肉。**II *vt*. 1.** 把…当作废物丢掉。**2.** 把…分成块。～ **bond** 不值钱的债券,垃圾债券。～ **bottle** 深色厚玻璃瓶。～

J

dealer 废品商,废旧船具商人。~ **fax** (传真机从外界收到的)大批宣传性传真件,垃圾传真件(如广告等)。~ **food** (热量高而营养价值低的)劣等食品。~ **heap** 〔美俚〕破旧汽车。~ **jewelry** 〔口〕不值钱的服饰珠宝。~ **mail** 垃圾邮件,三等邮件〔指大量邮寄的广告、宣传品、通知单、征求意见单,征求订户单〕。~ **man** 旧货商,废品商。~ **market** 废旧货市场。~ **price** 赔本价钱。~ **shop** 废品店;旧船具店。~ **yard** 废品清理场;破旧汽车堆积场。

junk[2] [dʒʌŋk; dʒʌŋk] ***n*.** (中国的)平底帆船,舢板船。*a motorized* ~机帆船。~ **man** 帆船船工。

junk[3] [dʒʌŋk; dʒʌŋk] ***n*.** 毒品〔尤指海洛因〕。

Jun·ker [ˈjuŋkə; ˋjuŋkɚ] ***n*.** 〔G.〕**1.** 容克〔音译;意为普鲁士地主贵族之子〕;德国贵族地主。**2.** 专制的德国军官。**3.** 容克地主的特性[政策等]。**-dom, -ism** ***n*.** 容克地主的精神。

jun·ker [ˈdʒʌŋkə; ˋdʒʌŋkɚ] ***n*.** 〔美俚〕**1.** 吸毒者。**2.** 破旧得不能使用的汽车。

jun·ket [ˈdʒʌŋkit; ˋdʒʌŋkɪt] **I** ***n*.** **1.** 冻奶食品;乳酥。**2.** 宴会,欢聚;〔美〕野餐。**3.** 游览;(以视察为名)利用公费的旅行。**II** ***vi*.** **1.** 设宴请客,举行野餐。**2.** 旅游,游山玩水;用公费旅行。— ***vt*.** 宴请,设宴招待。

junk·ie, junk·y [ˈdʒʌŋki; ˋdʒʌŋkɪ] ***n*.** (*pl*. ***junk·ies***) **1.** 〔俚〕吸毒者〔尤指吸食海洛因者〕。**2.** 〔口〕爱好者,…迷。

Ju·no [ˈdʒuːnəu; ˋdʒuno] ***n*.** **1.** 【罗神】(主神朱庇特的妻子)朱诺;天后;司婚姻的女神。**2.** 气派高贵的美人。

Ju·no·esque [ˌdʒuːnəuˈesk; ˏdʒunoˋesk] ***a*.** (妇女)像朱诺般雍容华贵的。

jun·ta [ˈdʒʌntə; ˋdʒʌntə] ***n*.** (*pl*. *~s*) 〔Sp.〕**1.** 执政团〔指革命或政变后控制政府的政治集团;秘密团体〕。**2.** (西班牙、拉丁美洲、意大利等国的)立法[行政等]机构。**3.** 秘密政治集团,小集团;派系。*a military* ~ 发动政变后上台的军政府。

jun·to [ˈdʒʌntəu; ˋdʒʌnto] ***n*.** (*pl*. *~s*) = junta 3.

Ju·pi·ter [ˈdʒuːpitə; ˋdʒupɪtɚ] ***n*.** **1.** 【罗神】(主神)朱庇特。**2.** 【天】木星。**3.** 〔美〕一种中程弹道飞弹的名字。***by*** ~! 〔古〕哎哟! 天哪! 好家伙! ~ **Fulgur** [**Fulminator**] 雷神。~ **Pluvius** 雨神。

ju·pon [ˈdʒuːpɔn, dʒuːˈpɔn; ˋdʒupɑn, dʒuˋpɑn] ***n*.** 铠甲罩衣,铠甲衬衣。

Ju·ra [ˈdʒuərə; ˋdʒurə] ***n*.** 【地】侏罗纪,侏罗系(= Jurassic period [system])。

ju·ra [ˈdʒuərə, ˈjuːrə; ˋdʒurə, jurə] ***n*.** 〔L.〕*jus*[1]的复数。

ju·ral [ˈdʒuərəl; ˋdʒurəl] ***a*.** **1.** 法制的;法律上的。**2.** 关于权利义务的。**-ly** ***ad*.**

ju·rant [ˈdʒuərənt; ˋdʒurənt] ***a*.** 【法】立誓的;宣誓的。

Ju·ras·sic [dʒuəˈræsik; dʒuˋræsɪk] **I** ***a*.** **1.** 【地】侏罗纪[系]的。**2.** 〔口〕古老的,历史悠久的。**II** ***n*.** 【地】侏罗纪[系](= ~ period [system])。

ju·rat[1] [ˈdʒuəræt; ˋdʒuræt] ***n*.** **1.** (Chinque Ports 地方的)市政长官。**2.** (Channel Islands 地方的)名誉法官。

ju·rat[2] [ˈdʒuəræt; ˋdʒuræt] ***n*.** 【法】宣誓证明文件(或说明书)〔说明宣誓时的时间、地点和在场人的文件,作为宣誓书附件〕。

ju·ra·to·ry [ˈdʒuərətəri; ˋdʒurəˏtorɪ] ***a*.** 【法】宣誓的;以誓言表达的。

***Jur. D*.** = 〔L.〕*Juris Doctor* (= Doctor of Law).

ju·rel [huːˈrel; huˋrel] ***n*.** 【动】鲹。

ju·rid·i·c(al) [dʒuəˈridik(əl); dʒuˋrɪdɪk(l̩)] ***a*.** **1.** 审判上的,司法上的;法院的。**2.** 法律上的,合法的。~ **association** 社团法人。~ **days** 法院开庭日。~ **person** 法人。**-cal·ly** ***ad*.**

ju·ris·con·sult [ˈdʒuəriskənˌsʌlt; ˋdʒurɪskənˏsʌlt] ***n*.** = jurist.

ju·ris·dic·tion [ˌdʒuərisˈdikʃən; ˏdʒurɪsˋdɪkʃən] ***n*.** **1.** 裁判权;司法;司法权。**2.** 管辖权;管辖范围;权限。***be under the*** ~ ***of sb*.** 在某人管辖[权限]之下。***exercise*** [***have***] ~ ***over sb*.** 对某人有裁判权。**-al** ***a*.**

jurisp. = jurisprudence.

ju·ris·pru·dence [ˌdʒuərisˈpruːdəns; ˏdʒurɪsˋprudəns] ***n*.** **1.** 法学,法理学。**2.** 法学的分支〔如民法、刑法、行政法等〕。**3.** 法律体系。**4.** (民法中的)法院审判规程,判决录。*medical* ~ 法医学。

ju·ris·pru·dent [ˌdʒuərisˈpruːdənt; ˏdʒurɪsˋprudənt] **I** ***a*.** 精通法律的。**II** ***n*.** 法律学家。**-den·tial** ***a*.** **-dential·ly** ***ad*.**

ju·rist [ˈdʒuərist; ˋdʒurɪst] ***n*.** **1.** 法理学家;法律著述家。**2.** 法科学生。**3.** 法律专家;法官;律师。

ju·ris·tic(al) [dʒuəˈristik(əl); dʒuˋrɪstɪk(l̩)] ***a*.** **1.** 法律的,法律上的;法学的。**2.** 法学家的;法理学的。*a* ~ *act* 法律行为。*a* ~ *fact* 法律承认的事实。~ *theory* 法律理论。**-ti·cal·ly** ***ad*.**

ju·ror [ˈdʒuərə; ˋdʒurɚ] ***n*.** **1.** 陪审员;(展览会、竞赛等的)评审委员,评奖人。**2.** (表示忠诚等的)宣誓人。*a grand* ~大陪审委员团中的一员;大陪审员。

ju·ry[1] [ˈdʒuəri; ˋdʒurɪ] ***n*.** 【法】**1.** 陪审团。**2.** (展览会、竞赛等的)全体评审员,评奖人。**3.** 舆论的裁决。*common* [*petty*, *trial*] ~【法】普通陪审团,小陪审团。*coroner's* ~【法】验尸陪审团。*grand* ~【法】大陪审团。*packed* ~〔口〕被买通的陪审团。*special* ~【法】特别陪审团。***hang the*** ~ 〔美〕(律师等通过不正当手段施加影响)使陪审团由于意见分歧而无法作出决定。~ **box** 陪审席。~**-fixer** 〔美俚〕收买[胁迫]陪审员的人。~ **-man** 陪审员。~**-woman** 女陪审员。

ju·ry[2] [ˈdʒuəri; ˋdʒurɪ] ***a*.** 【海】(船上)应急用的,暂时的。*a* ~ *anchor* 应急锚。~ *repairs* 临时应急的修理。~ **mast** 【海】应急桅杆。~**-rigged** ***a*.** 【海】临时配备的。~ **rudder** 【海】应急舵。~ **strut** 应急支柱。

jus[1] [dʒʌs; dʒʌs] ***n*.** (*pl*. ***jur·a*** [ˈdʒuərə; ˋdʒurə]) 〔L.〕**1.** 法;法律,法律制度。**2.** 法律的原则;法律保证的权力[权利]。~ ***ad rem*** 对物权。~ ***canonicum*** (宗教改革前的)教堂法,寺院法(= canon law)。~ ***civile*** 民法。~ ***criminale*** 刑法。~ ***gentium*** **1.** 古罗马侨民法。**2.** 国际法(= international law)。~ ***in re*** 物权。~ ***natural*** [***naturale***] 自然法。~ ***sanguinis*** 血统主义〔以父母国籍决定子女国籍的规定〕。~ ***scriptum*** 成文法。~ ***soli*** 出生地主义〔以出生地决定国籍的规定〕。

jus[2] [F. ʒy; ʒy] ***n*.** 〔F.〕汁液;肉汁,浆汁。*roast beef au* ~有汁烤牛肉〔菜单用语〕。

jus, just = justice.

jus·sive [ˈdʒʌsiv; ˋdʒʌsɪv] **I** ***a*.** 【语法】表示命令的。**II** ***n*.** 【语法】表示命令的词[格、语气等]。

just[1] [dʒʌst; dʒʌst] **I** ***a*.** **1.** 公正的,正值的;公平的,正义的。**2.** 恰当的;适当的;应得的。**3.** 正当的,合法的。**4.** 合理的,有充分根据的。**5.** 精确的,正确的。*a* ~ *man* 正直的人。*a* ~ *decision* 公正的裁决。*a* ~ *price* 公平的价格。*a* ~ *punishment* 应受的惩罚。*a* ~ *praise* 应得的赞扬。*a* ~ *claim* [*title*] 正当的要求[权利]。*a* ~ *opinion* 合理的意见。~ *suspicions* 有理由的怀疑。~ *weights* 精确的砝码。*a* ~ *balance of colours* 色彩协调。*a* ~ *report* 真实的报导,正确的报告。**II** ***ad*.** **1.** 正好,恰好,正要。**2.** 刚才,方才,刚刚。**3.** 只不过;仅仅。**4.** 差一点,好不容易。**5.** 〔口〕真正,实在,非常。**6.** 请,试着…看! 〔用于祈使语气中〕。**7.** 直接,就。*It is* ~ *six (o'clock)*. 现在正好六点钟。*It is* ~ *on six (o'clock)*. 马上就要六点钟了。*I was* ~ *going when he came in*. 他进来时我正要走。*This is* ~ *the point*. 问题就在这里。*We* ~ *missed the train*. 我们正好没有赶上火车。*He has* ~ *come*. 他才来。*He is only* ~ *of age*. 他刚刚成年。*She is not* ~ *a singer*. 她不仅是一位歌唱家。~ *a taste* 只是尝了尝。*I'm* ~ *teasing you*. 我只不过给你闹着玩。~ *east of the church* 就在

教堂的东面。～ *there* 就在那里。*I* ～ *managed to get there in time*. 我好不容易才及时赶到那里。*I only* ～ *caught the last bus*. 我刚好赶上末班公共汽车。*Every one was so happy that time* ～ *flew*. 人人都很快活，所以日子像飞一样地过得极快。*Do you like beer*? — *Don't I*, ～! 你爱喝啤酒吗? —不爱?! 爱喝极啦! *Did he cry*? — *Didn't he*, ～! 他哭吗? —不哭! 哭得很厉害呢! ～ *splendid*! 好极了。*J- look at this picture*. 看一看这幅画吧。*J- shut the door, will you*? 关一关门,好吗? *J- fancy* [*think of*] *the terrible result*. 想想那种可怕的后果吧! *J- come in*. 请进来吧。～ **about** 正是…附近,几乎。～ **after** 在…之后就。～ **as** 1. 正像。2. 正在…的时候。～*-as-good articles* 代用品。～ ***as it is*** [***they were***] 恰好如此,照原样。～ **as...**, **so** …正像…一样,…也。～ ***as you please*** 随您的意。～ ***in time*** 恰巧,正好赶上。***J-*** (***like***) ***my luck***! 啊呀,又是倒霉! ～ ***now*** 刚才;正在。～ **so** 正要那样。～ ***the same*** 完全一样。～ ***the thing*** 适合的东西,很合用。～ ***then*** 正在那时。～ ***the opposite*** [***reverse***], ～ ***the other way about*** 恰恰相反。***not*** ～ ... ***but*** 不仅…而且…。***only*** ～ ***enough*** 勉强过得去。～**-in-time**【商】及时盘存调节法〔参见 JIT 条〕。**-ly** *ad*. **-ness** *n*.

just[2] [dʒʌst; dʒʌst] *n*., *vi*. =joust.

jus·te-mi·lieu [F. ʒystəmiˈljø; ʒystmɪˋljø] *n*. 〔F.〕中庸之道(=golden mean)。

jus·tice [ˈdʒʌstis; ˋdʒʌstɪs] *n*. 1. 正义,公道;公正,公平。2. 正确;妥当,确实。3. 正当(理由),合法。4. 审判,司法。5. 审判员,法官,(治安)推事;〔英〕高等法院法官;〔美〕最高法院法官。6. 〔J-〕正义女神。*have a sense of* ～有正义感。*deny sb*. ～对某人不公平。*social* ～社会正义。*treat sb*. [*sth*.] *with* ～秉公对待某人[某事]。*Both sides have some* ～ *in their claims*. 双方的要求都有些理由。*examine* [*inquire*] *the* ～ *of a complaint* 审查控诉是否正当。*administer* ～ 执法,行使审判职权。*a court of* ～法院。*the Department of J-* 〔美〕司法部。*the* ～*s* (全体)法官。*Mr*. *J- X* 〔美〕某某法官先生。*Lord J- X* 〔英〕某某法官阁下。***bring sb***. ***to*** ～把某人缉拿归案,依法处分某人。***do*** ～ ***to*** 1. 公平评判;公平对待(*To do him* ～, *we must say that he is honest*. 说句公道话,他是诚实的)。2. 酷肖,极像,逼真(*The photograph has done you* ～. 这张照片很像你本人)。3. 欣赏,大吃,饱食(*do* ～ *to a meal* 饱餐一顿)。***do oneself*** ～充分发挥自己的本领。***in*** ～ ***to sb***. 为了对某人公平起见。***poetic***(***al***) ～(只有在小说、诗歌中才能见到而在现实生活中却很难遇到的)理想的赏罚严明。***temper*** ～ ***with mercy*** 宽严相济;恩威并施。**J- of the Peace** 治安推事。**Justice's** ～执法不当的审判〔讽刺治安推事往往以一己之见代替法律〕。

jus·tice·ship [ˈdʒʌstisʃip; ˋdʒʌstɪsˏʃɪp] *n*. 法官[治安推事]的身份[资格、地位、职务]。

jus·ti·ci·a·ble [dʒʌsˈtiʃiəbl; dʒʌsˋtɪʃɪəbl̩] *a*. 可交法院审判的。

jus·ti·ci·ar [dʒʌsˈtiʃiɑː; dʒʌsˈtɪʃɪɚ] *n*. 1.【英史】(从十一世纪诺曼第人入侵直到十三世纪金雀花王朝初期的)首席政法官。2. 高等法院法官。

jus·ti·ci·ar·y [dʒʌsˈtiʃiəri; dʒʌsˋtɪʃɪˏɛrɪ] I *n*. 1. =justiciar. 2. 法官的裁判权。II *a*. 司法上的,法官职务上的。

jus·ti·fi·a·ble [ˈdʒʌstifaiəbl; ˋdʒʌstəˏfaɪəbl̩] *a*. 1. 可证明为有理的,正当的,无可非议的。2. 情有可原的,可辩护的。～ *abortion* 正当堕胎〔因怀孕将危及母亲健康者〕。～ *homicide* 有正当理由的杀人〔因为自卫或是阻止暴行〕。***be*** (***seem***) ***hardly*** ～说不过去。***be the least*** ～最要不得的,最不应该的。**-bil·i·ty** *n*. **-bly** *ad*.

jus·ti·fi·ca·tion [ˌdʒʌstifiˈkeiʃən; ˏdʒʌstəfəˋkeʃən] *n*. 1. 认为正当,证明为正当;正当的理由,辩护,辩明。2. 无咎,无过失;【神学】释罪〔由于理所当然,犯罪可不受谴责〕。4.【印】(活字的)整理,装版。*in* ～ *of one's behavior* 为自己的行为辩护。*attack sb*. *without* ～毫无理由攻击某人。*for sb*.'*s* ～为了证明某人无咎。*What's your* ～ *for being so late*? 你来得这样迟有何理由? ～ ***by faith***【神学】因为信仰耶稣而可释罪。

jus·ti·fi·ca·tive, **jus·ti·fi·ca·tory** [ˈdʒʌstifikeitiv, -təri; ˋdʒʌstəfəˏketɪv, -torɪ] *a*. 认为正当的;辩护性的,辩解的。

jus·ti·fi·er [ˈdʒʌstifaiə; ˋdʒʌstəˏfaɪɚ] *n*. 1. 辩解者;证明者;释罪者。2.【印】整版工人。3.【印】空铅,隔条。

jus·ti·fy [ˈdʒʌstifai; ˋdʒʌstəˏfaɪ] *vt*. (***-fied***; ***-fy·ing***) 1. 证明…有道理,为…辩护。2. 为…提供法律根据,宣誓证明(自己)有财力作保。3.【神学】对…释罪。4.【印】整(版),装(版),调整(铅字)的间隔使全行排满。*designs that are economically justified* 经济上合算的设计。*I hope I am justified in saying that*... 我以为我可以说…。～ *oneself for one's conduct* 证明自己的行为是正当的。— *vi*. 1.【法】提出充分法律证据,证明合法。2. 证明自己财力上有资格作保证人[保释人]。3.【印】整版,装版;(铅字)各行长度正合适。

Jus·tin [ˈdʒʌstin; ˋdʒʌstɪn] *n*. 贾斯廷〔男子名〕。

Jus·ti·na [dʒəsˈtiːnə, -tai-; dʒʌsˋtinə, -taɪ-] *n*. 贾斯廷娜〔女子名〕。

jus·tle [ˈdʒʌsl; ˋdʒʌsl̩] *v*., *n*. =jostle.

Jus·tus [ˈdʒʌstəs; ˋdʒʌstəs] *n*. 贾斯特斯〔男子名〕。

jut [dʒʌt; dʒʌt] I *vi*. (*-tt-*) 突出;伸出 (*out*; *forth*; *up*)。— *vt*. 使突出;使伸出。II *n*. 1. 突出;伸出。2. 突出部分,伸出部分。

Juta [ˈdʒuːtə; ˋdʒutə] *n*. 朱塔〔姓氏〕。

jute [dʒuːt; dʒut] *n*.【植】1. 黄麻属植物,黄麻;长蒴黄麻。2. 黄麻纤维。*Chinese* ～苘麻,青麻。

Jute [dʒuːt; dʒut] *n*. 朱特人〔古代居住在北欧日德兰半岛的日耳曼人一部落集团〕;〔*pl*.〕朱特族。

jut·ty [ˈdʒʌti; ˋdʒʌtɪ] *n*. (*pl*. ***-ties***) =jetty.

juv. =juvenile.

ju·ve·nes·cence [ˌdʒuːviˈnesns; ˏdʒuvəˋnesns] *n*. 1. 返老还童,变年轻。2. 少年时期,从婴儿时期向青年时期的过渡。

ju·ve·nes·cent [ˌdʒuːviˈnesnt; ˏdʒuvəˋnɛsnt] *a*. 1. 返老还童的,变年轻的。2. 年轻的,从婴儿时期向青年时期过渡的。

ju·ven·ile [ˈdʒuːvinail; ˋdʒuvənaɪl] I *a*. 1. 青少年的,年少的。2. 适于青少年的,供青少年用的。3. 幼稚的。*a* ～ *adult* 将成年的少年。～ *books* 少年读物。～ *literature* 儿童文学。～ *behaviour* 幼稚的行为。II *n*. 1. 青少年。2. 少年读物。3. 演少年的演员。4. 羽毛未丰的鸟,雏鸟;(供竞赛用的)两岁的马。～ **court** 少年法庭。～ **delinquency** 少年犯罪。～ **delinquent** 少年罪犯。～ **hormone** (昆虫)返幼激素。～ **lead** 1. 青少年扮演的主角。2. 扮演青少年的主角演员。～ **officer** 主管少年犯罪的警官。

ju·ve·nil·i·a [ˌdʒuːviˈniliə; ˏdʒuvɪˋnɪlɪə] *n*. 1. (某作家、画家等)青少年时代的作品(集)。2. 少年文艺读物。

ju·ve·nil·i·ty [ˌdʒuːviˈniliti; ˏdʒuvəˋnɪlətɪ] *n*. 1. 年少,年幼。2. 幼稚,幼稚的言行[思想等]。3. 〔集合词〕少年人。

ju·ve·nil·i·za·tion [dʒuːˌviniliˈzeiʃən; dʒuˏvɪnɪlɪˋzeʃən] *n*.【生】保幼化〔尤指以保幼激素,使昆虫的发育和成熟受到阻碍,系一种病虫害防治法〕。

ju·ve·noc·ra·cy [ˌdʒuːviːˈnɔkrəsi; ˏdʒuviˋnɑkrəsɪ] *n*. 青年统治〔指由年轻人管理国家〕。

ju·vie, **ju·vey** [ˈdʒuːvi; ˋdʒuvɪ] *n*. 〔美俚〕1. 少年罪犯,失足青少年。2. 少年罪犯教养所。

jux·ta- *comb*. *f*. 表示"次","近","并": *juxta*position.

jux·ta·pose [ˈdʒʌkstəpəuz; ˏdʒʌkstəˋpoz] *vt*. 使并置,使并列。

jux·ta·po·si·tion [ˌdʒʌkstəpəˈziʃən; ˏdʒʌkstəpəˋzɪʃən]

n. 并置,并列。
JV =1. junior varsity. 2. joint venture.
jwlr. =jewel(l)er.
J.X. =〔L.〕*Jesus Christus* (=Jesus Christ)耶稣基督。
Jy. =July.

K

K, k [kei; ke] (*pl*. ***Ks***, ***K's***; ***ks***, ***k's*** [keiz; kez]) **1.** 英语字母表第十一字母。**2.** K字形物体[记号]。**3.** 一个序列中的第十一〔若J略去则为第十〕。**4.**【数】与Z轴平行的单位矢量。**5.**【化】元素钾(Potassium)的符号〔由拉丁名 Kalium 而来〕。**6.**〔K〕【气】积云(cumulus)的符号。**7.**〔K〕【数】常数(constant)的符号。**8.** 代表数字"千"(10^3)。*a salary of $ 14K* = a salary of $ 14,000 一万四千美元的薪金。**9.** 千〔电子计算机的存储单位,相当于1024二进位组或1000字符〕。*a computer memory of* 64k 存储量为64k的计算机。**10.** K形的。**11.** 第十一的〔若J略去,则为第十的〕。**K-series** (光谱线的)K系列。**K-shell** K层,K电子层,K壳层。
K., k. = **1.**【电】capacity. **2.** karat, carat. **3.**【物】Kelvin. **4.** kilo. **5.** kilogram(me). **6.** king. **7.** knight. **8.**【海】knot. **9.** kope(c)k(s). **10.** krona, kronor. **11.** krone, kroner, kronen.
K-a corps〔美〕为送信、看门、打斗而训练的一群警犬。
KA, ka =kiloampere.
ka [kɑː; kɑ] *n*.〔Egy.〕【宗】(古埃及人或偶像的)灵魂,鬼魂,阴魂。
ka. =kathode, cathode.
Kaa·ba [ˈkɑːbə; ˋkɑbə] *n*. =Caaba.
kab [kæb; kæb] *n*. 开普(=cab)〔古希伯来粮食等干物的量具名,相当于二夸脱〕。
kab·(b)a·la [ˈkæbələ, kəˈbɑːlə; ˋkæbələ, kəˋbɑlə] *n*. =cab(b)ala.
ka·bob [kəˈbɔb; kəˋbɑb] *n*. =kebab.
ka·boo·dle [keˈbuːdl; keˋbudl] *n*. = caboodle.
ka·bu·ki [ˌkɑːbuːˈki; ˌkɑbuˋkɪ] *n*.〔Jap.〕歌舞伎〔创始于17世纪的日本传统剧种〕。
Ka·bul [ˈkɔːbul; ˋkɑbʊl] *n*. 喀布尔〔阿富汗首都〕。
Ka·byle [kəˈbail; kəˋbaɪl] *n*. **1.** 卡拜尔人〔北非阿尔及利亚或突尼斯的柏柏尔族之一〕。**2.** 卡拜尔语。
kad·dish [ˈkɑːdiʃ; ˋkɑdɪʃ] *n*.【犹】珈底什〔每日作礼拜时或为死者祈祷时唱的赞美诗〕。
ka·di [ˈkɑːdi; ˋkɑdɪ] *n*. =cadi.
kaf [kɑːf, kɔːf; kæf, kɔf] *n*.〔Heb.〕希伯来语的第十一个字母"כ, ך"〔相当于英语的 k〕。
kaf·fee·klatsch [ˈkɑːfeiˌklɑːtʃ, ˈkɔːfiːˌklætʃ; ˋkɑfeˏklætʃ, ˋkɔfiˏklætʃ] *n*.〔美〕咖啡会〔一种非正式聚会,如家庭妇女白天聚在一起边喝咖啡边聊天。亦作 kaffee klatsch〕。
Kaf·(f)ir [ˈkæfə; ˋkæfɚ] *n*. **1.** 异教徒〔阿拉伯人对不信伊斯兰教的人的蔑称〕。**2.** (南非洲说班图语的)卡菲尔人;卡菲尔语。**3.**〔*pl*.〕〔英〕南非洲矿山股票。**4.**〔k-〕一种高粱(=~ corn)。
kaf·fi·yeh [ˈkɑːfiːjə; kɑˋfijə] *n*. 阿拉伯人的头巾。
kaf·tan [ˈkæftən; ˋkæftən] *n*. =caftan.
ka·go [ˈkɑːgəu; ˋkɑgo] *n*.〔Jap.〕日本轿子。
Ka·go·shi·ma [ˌkɑːgəˈʃiːmə; ˏkɑgoˋʃimɑ] *n*. 鹿儿岛〔日本港市〕。
kai·ak [ˈkaiæk; ˋkaɪæk] *n*. =kayak.
kail [keil; kel] *n*. =kale.
kail·yard [ˈkeiljɑːd; ˋkeljard] *n*. =kaleyard.
kai·nite [ˈkain(a)it; ˋkaɪnaɪt, ˋkeəˏnaɪt] *n*.【矿】钾盐镁矾。
kai·ser [ˈkaizə; ˋkaɪzɚ] *n*. **1.** 德国皇帝。**2.**〔K-〕神圣罗马帝国的皇帝。**3.**〔K-〕第一次世界大战前德国和奥国的皇帝。**4.**〔K-〕行使绝对权威的人;独裁者。**-dom** *n*. 皇帝的地位[权力、统治区]。**-ism** *n*. 独裁政治。
kai·ser·in [ˈkaizərin; ˋkaɪzərɪn] *n*. (德国等的)皇后。
kai·zen [ˈkaizen;ˋkaɪzen] *n*.〔Jap.〕改进,改善〔指企业通过听取工人意见和分析研究等方法不断改善经营管理〕。
ka·ka [ˈkɑːkə; ˋkɑkə] *n*. (新西兰产的)卡卡鹦鹉。
ka·ka·po [ˌkɑːkəˈpəu; ˏkɑkəˋpo] *n*. (*pl*. ~*s*)【动】鸮鹉(*Strigops habroptilus*)〔新西兰的一种鹦鹉〕。
ka·ke·mo·no [ˌkækiˈməunəu; ˏkækɪˋmono] *n*. (*pl*. ~*s*)〔Jap.〕(挂在墙上的)字画,条幅。
ka·ki [ˈkɑːki; ˋkɑkɪ] *n*. (*pl*. ***-kis***)〔Jap.〕**1.** 亚洲柿树。**2.** 柿子(=Japanese persimmon)。
ka·kis·toc·ra·cy [ˌkækiˈstɔkrəsi; ˏkækəˋstɑkrəsɪ] *n*. 坏人政府,恶人政治。
kal. =kalends; calends.
ka·la-a·zar [ˌkɑːlɑːɑːˈzɑː; ˏkɑlɑ·ɑˋzɑr] *n*.【医】黑热病。
Kal·an·cho·e [ˌkælənˈkəui; ˏkælənˋkoɪ] *n*.【植】高凉菜属。
kale [keil; kel] *n*. **1.**【植】羽衣甘蓝。**2.**〔Scot.〕青菜,蔬菜;菜汤。**3.**〔美俚〕钞票,钱(= ~ seed)。~**yard** *n*.〔Scot.〕菜园。~**yard school** 菜园派〔19世纪末叶用苏格兰方言描写生活的一派作家〕。
ka·lei·do·phone [kəˈlaidəfəun; kəˋlaɪdəˏfon] *n*.【物】发音体振动显像仪。
ka·lei·do·scope [kəˈlaidəskəup; kəˋlaɪdəˏskop] *n*. **1.** 万花筒。**2.** 万花筒般千变万化的情景。*the ~ of life* 变化莫测的人生。
ka·lei·do·scop·ic(al) [kəˌlaidəˈskɔpik(əl); kəˏlaɪdəˋskɑpɪk(l)] *a*. 万花筒(一样)的,千变万化的。**-i·cal·ly** *ad*.
kal·ends [ˈkæləndz; ˋkæləndz] *n*.〔*pl*.〕=calends.
Ka·le·va·la [ˌkɑːləˈvɑːlɑː; ˏkɑlɪˋvɑlɑ] *n*.《英雄的国土》〔芬兰史诗名,由 Elias Lönnrot 根据民间传说编写,1835年初版〕。
kal·ian [kɑːlˈjɑːn; kɑlˋjɑn] *n*. 伊朗的水烟筒。
ka·lif, ka·liph [ˈkælif; ˋkælɪf] *n*. =caliph.
Ka·li·man·tan [ˌkɑːliˈmɑːntɑːn; ˏkɑlɪˋmɑntɑn] *n*. 加里曼丹〔旧称婆罗洲(Borneo),为亚洲一大岛,构成印尼的四个省〕。
ka·li·um [ˈkeiliəm; ˋkelɪəm] *n*.【化】钾(=potassium)。
kal·mi·a [ˈkælmiə; ˋkælmɪə] *n*. 山月桂属(*Kalmia*)

植物〔北美的一种长绿灌木,如山月桂〕。

Kal·much, Kal·muk [ˈkælmʌk; ˋkælmʌk] ***n.*** **1.** 卡尔美克人〔高加索东北部和新疆北部的蒙古族人〕。**2.** 卡尔美克语(=Kalmyk)。

ka·long [ˈkɑːlɔŋ, ˈkæ-; ˋkɑlɑŋ, ˋkæ-] ***n.***【动】狐蝙蝠〔以果实为食,产于马来群岛的一种大蝙蝠〕。

kal·pa [ˈkælpə; ˋkælpə] ***n.***〔Sans.〕【宗】劫〔根据印度教的宇宙论,宇宙从创始到毁灭的一个周期,约四十三亿二千万年〕。

kal·pak [ˈkælpæk; ˋkælpæk] ***n.*** 羊皮帽,黑毡帽(=calpace, calpack)。

kal·so·mine [ˈkælsəmain; ˋkælsəmaɪn] ***n.***, ***vt.*** =calcimine.

ka·ma·la [kəˈmeilə, ˈkæmələ; kəˋmelə, ˋkæmələ] ***n.***〔Sans.〕**1.**【植】粗糠柴(*Mallotus philippinensis*)〔东印度一种树〕。**2.** 咖马拉〔粗糠柴蒴果腺毛制成的轻细粉末,用作红色染料和驱虫药〕。

Kam·chat·ka [kæmˈtʃætkə; kæmˋtʃætkə] ***n.*** 堪察加半岛〔位于鄂霍次克海和白令海之间〕。

kame [keim; kem] ***n.***(冰川溶化时淤积起来的含有砾子的)小沙丘。

ka·me·rad [ˌkæməˈrɑːt; ˏkæməˋrɑt] **I** ***int.*** 伙计!〔第一次世界大战时,德国兵表示投降时的用语〕。**II** ***vi.*** 投降。

Ka·mi [ˈkɑːmi; kɑmɪ] ***n.***(*sing.*, *pl.*)〔Jap.〕神。

ka·mi·ka·ze [ˌkɑːmiˈkɑːzi; ˏkɑmɪˋkɑzɪ] ***n.***〔Jap.〕**1.**〔K-〕(第二次世界大战末期日本空军中驾驶满载炸弹之飞机作自杀性攻击的)神风(突击)队队员。**2.** 神风队所使用的飞机。

Kam·pa·la [kɑːmˈpɑːlə; kɑmˋpɑlə] ***n.*** 坎帕拉〔乌干达首都〕。

kam·pong [ˈkɑːmpɔːŋ; ˋkɑmpɑŋ] ***n.***〔Ma.〕(马来亚的)小村庄;茅屋群。

kamp·tu·li·con [kæm*p*ˈtjuːlikən; kæmpˋtjulɪkən] ***n.*** 橡皮地毯。

Kam·pu·che·a [kɑːmˈpuːtʃiə; kɑmˋputʃɪə] ***n.*** 柬埔寨〔亚洲〕(=Cambodia). **-n** ***a.*** & ***n.***

kam·seen, kam·sin [kæmˈsiːn; kæmˋsin] ***n.*** =Khamseen, Khamsin.

Kan., Kans. =Kansas.

ka·na [ˈkɑːnə; ˋkɑnə] ***n.***(*pl.* ~*s*)〔Jap.〕假名〔日语字母,由汉字简化而成〕。

Ka·na·ga·wa [kəˈnɑːgəwə; kəˋnɑgəwə] ***n.*** 神奈川〔日本县名〕。

Ka·nak·a [ˈkænəkə; ˋkænəkə] ***n.***(夏威夷及南洋群岛的)卡内加人。

ka·na·my·cin [ˌkænəˈmaisin; ˏkænəˋmaɪsɪn] ***n.***【药】卡那霉素。

Ka·na·rese [ˌkɑːnəˈriːz; ˏkɑnəˋriz] **I** ***a.***(印度)卡纳拉(Kanara)地区的;卡纳拉人的;卡纳拉语的。**II** ***n.***(*pl.* ~)**1.** 卡纳拉人。**2.** =Kannada.

Ka·na·za·wa [kəˈnɑːzəwə; kəˋnɑzəwə] ***n.*** 金泽〔日本港市〕。

Kan·da·har [ˌkændəˈhɑː; ˏkændəˋhɑr] ***n.*** 坎大哈〔阿富汗城市〕。

Kan·dy [ˈkændi; ˋkændɪ] ***n.*** 康提〔斯里兰卡城市〕。

Kane [kein; ken] ***n.*** 凯恩〔姓氏〕。

kang [kɑːŋ; kɑŋ] ***n.***〔Chin.〕炕。

kan·ga·roo [ˌkæŋgəˈruː; ˏkæŋgəˋru] ***n.***(*pl.* ~*s*; 集合词 ~)【动】大袋鼠。~ **care** 袋鼠护理法〔将早产婴儿长时间紧贴地抱在胸前,以肌肤相亲代替烘箱的一种护理方法〕。~ **closure**(英国议会下院的)限制议事法跳议法,抽议法〔规定议会或委员会主席有权决定几个修正案中何者应进行辩论,何者予以搁置〕。~ **court**〔美口〕(非法的或不按法律程序的)非正规法庭;(囚犯在狱中举行的)模拟法庭。~ **rat** 鼷〔大洋洲产,也称 rat ~〕,美洲有袋啮齿类动物。

kan·ji [ˈkændʒiː; ˋkændʒi] ***n.***(*pl.* ~(*s*))〔Jap.〕日本汉字。

Kan·na·da [ˈkɑːnədə; ˋkɑnədə] ***n.*** 卡纳达语〔印度迈索尔邦及其附近印度南部地区讲的一种主要的德拉维德语〕。

Ka·no [ˈkɑːnəu; ˋkɑno] ***n.*** 卡诺〔尼日利亚城市〕。

ka·noon [kɑːˈnuːn; kɑˋnun] ***n.***(波斯和阿拉伯五六十根弦的)齐特拉琴。

Kan·pur [kɑːnˈpuə; kɑnˋpʊr] ***n.*** 坎普尔〔印度北方邦的城市〕。

Kans. =Kansas.

kan·san [ˈkænzən; ˋkænzən] **I** ***a.***(美国)堪萨斯州的;堪萨斯州人的。**II** ***n.*** 堪萨斯州人。

Kan·sas [ˈkænzəs; ˋkænzəs] ***n.*** 堪萨斯〔美国州名〕。

Kant [kænt; kænt], **Immanuel** 伊曼纽尔·康德〔1724—1804,德国哲学家〕。

kan·tar [kɑːnˈtɑː; kɑnˋtɑ] ***n.*** 坎塔尔〔伊斯兰国家的重量单位,从 100 磅到 700 磅不等〕。

Kant·i·an [ˈkæntiən, -tjən; ˋkæntɪən, -tjən] **I** ***a.*** 康德的;康德哲学的。**II** ***n.*** 康德学派的人,康德主义者。**-ism** ***n.*** =Kantism.

Kant·ism [ˈkæntizəm; ˋkæntɪzəm] ***n.*** 康德哲学,康德主义。

Kant·ist [ˈkæntist; ˋkæntɪst] ***n.*** 康德派哲学家,康德主义者。

Ka·nu·ri [kɑːˈnuəri; kɑˋnʊrɪ] ***n.*** **1.**(*pl.* ~(*s*))卡努里人〔尼日利亚西北部及其附近地区的穆斯林〕。**2.** 卡努里语〔卡努里人讲的尼罗—撒哈拉语〕。

kao·liang [ˌkauˈliæŋ; ˏkaʊˋlɪæŋ] ***n.***〔Chin.〕高粱(=sorghum)。

ka·o·lin(e) [ˈkeiəlin; ˋkeəlɪn] ***n.*** 高岭土,瓷土(=china clay)。

ka·o·lin·ite [ˈkeiəlinait; ˋkeəlɪˏnaɪt] ***n.***【矿】高岭石。

ka·o·lin·ize [ˈkeiəlinaiz; ˋkeəlɪnˏaɪz] ***vt.*** 使高岭土化。

ka·on [ˈkeiɔn; ˋkeɑn] ***n.***【物】K 介子。

Ka·pell·meis·ter [kæˈpelmaistə; kæˋpɛlˏmaɪstɚ] ***n.***(*sing.*, *pl.*)〔G.〕〔蔑〕合唱团(管弦乐队的)指挥。~ **music** 一般性的音乐,没有创造性的音乐。

kaph [kɑːf, kɔːf; kɑf, kɔf] ***n.*** =kaf.

ka·pok [ˈkeipɔk; ˋkepɑk] ***n.*** 木棉。

kap·pa [ˈkæpə; ˋkæpə] ***n.*** **1.** 希腊语的第十个字母"K, k"。**2.**(遗传学上的)卡巴粒。

ka·put [kəˈput; kəˋpʊt] ***a.***〔俚〕(仅作表语用)**1.** 坏了的,过时了的。**2.** 完蛋了的,彻底失败了的。

Ka·ra·chi [kəˈrɑːtʃi; kəˋrɑtʃɪ] ***n.*** 卡拉奇〔巴基斯坦港市〕。

Kar·a·ite [ˈkeərəait; ˋkɛrəˏaɪt] ***n.***【犹】圣经派信徒〔该派于八世纪成立于中东,不接受犹太法学博士的教义或犹太法典,只信仰圣经〕。**Kar·a·ism** ***n.***【犹】圣经派教义。

Ka·ra-Kal·pak [kɑːˌrɑːkɑːlˈpɑːk; kɑˏrakɑlˋpak] ***n.*** **1.** 卡拉卡巴克人〔乌兹别克的土耳其族人〕。**2.** 卡拉卡巴克语。

kar·a·kul [ˈkærəkəl; ˋkærəkəl] ***n.*** **1.** 中亚卡拉库尔羊。**2.** 宽尾羊羔皮〔用此意时一般拼为 caracul〕。

ka·ra·o·ke [ˌkærəˈəuki; ˏkærəˋokɪ] ***n.***〔Jap.〕卡拉 OK(演唱)。~ **bars** 卡拉 OK 歌厅。~ **cabs**(车上装有音响,可供乘客唱歌的)卡拉 OK 出租车。

kar·at [ˈkærət; ˋkærət] ***n.*** =carat.

ka·ra·te [kəˈrɑːti; kəˋrɑtɪ] ***n.***〔Jap.〕空手道〔一种徒手自卫拳术,源自日本冲绳岛〕。

Ka·re·li·an [kəˈriːliən, -ˈriːljən; kəˋrilɪən, -ˋriljən] **I** ***a.*** **1.** 卡累利阿的;卡累利阿人的。**II** ***n.*** **1.** 卡累利阿人〔属芬兰族,居于卡累利阿和芬兰东部〕。**2.** 卡累利阿语〔卡累利阿人讲的芬兰语〕。

Ka·ren [ˈkɑːren, Am. kəˈrən; ˋkærən, ˋkɑrən] ***n.*** **1.** 克伦〔女子名〕。**2.**(缅甸的)克伦人;克伦语。

K

Karl [kɑːl; karl] *n*. 卡尔〔男子名,Charles 的异体〕。

Kar·lo·vy Var·y [ˈkɑːləviˈvɑːri; ˋkarləviˋvarɪ] 卡罗维发利〔捷克西部城市〕。

kar·ma [ˈkɑːmə; ˋkarmə] *n*. 〔Sans.〕 **1.**【宗】羯磨〔梵文译音〕,业〔决定来世命运的所作所为〕。**2.** 因果报应,因缘。

ka·ro·shi [kæˈrəuʃi; kæˋroʃɪ] *n*. 〔Jap.〕过劳死〔因工作长期过度劳累致死,亦作～ syndrome〕。

ka·ross [kəˈrɔs; kəˈrɑs] *n*. (南非用兽皮制的)披肩;皮褥;皮毯。

ka(r)·roo [kəˈruː; kəˋru] *n*. (*pl*. ～***s***) **1.** 南非干燥台地。**2.**【地】无水亚黏土草原。

karst [kɑːst; karst] *n*.【地】喀斯特,岩溶。～ **cave** 岩溶洞。

kart [kɑːt; kart] *n*. **1.** 小型汽车;小型车子。**2.** 微型赛车。

kar·tell [kɑːˈtel; karˋtɛl] *n*. = cartel.

kar·y·o- [ˈkæriəu; ˋkærɪo] *comb. f.* 表示"核": *karyo*gamy, *karyo*lysis.

kar·y·og·a·my [ˌkæriˈɔgəmi; ˏkærɪˋɑgəmɪ] *n*【生】核配(合)。

kar·y·o·ki·ne·sis [ˌkæriəukaiˈniːsis; ˏkærɪəkaɪˋnisɪs] *n*.【生】有丝分裂;核分裂。

kar·y·o·lymph [ˈkæriəlimf; ˋkærɪəˏlɪmf] *n*.【生】核液。

kar·y·ol·y·sis [ˌkæriˈɔlisis; ˏkærɪˋɑləsɪs] *n*.【生】核溶解。**-y·o·lit·ic** *a*.

kar·y·om·i·to·sis [ˌkæriəuˈmaitəusis; ˏkærɪoˋmaɪtosɪs] *n*.【生】(细胞核的)有丝分裂。

kar·y·on [ˈkæriən; ˋkærɪən] *n*.【生】细胞核,核。

kar·y·o·plasm [ˈkæriəuplæzəm; ˋkærɪəˏplæzəm] *n*.【生】核质,核浆。

kar·y·o·some [ˈkæriəsəum; ˋkærɪəˏsom] *n*.【生】染色质核仁,核粒。

kar·y·o·tin [ˌkæriˈəutin; ˏkærɪˋotɪn] *n*.【生】染色质,染色体,染色粒(= chromatin)。

kar·y·o·type [ˈkæriətaip; ˋkærɪəˏtaɪp] *n*.【生】染色体组型。**-typic** [-tipik; -tɪpɪk], **-typical** *a*.

kar·zy, kar·zey [kɑːzi; karzɪ] *n*. 〔俚〕厕所;抽水马桶。

kas·bah [ˈkɑːzbɑː; ˋkazbɑ] *n*. = casbah.

ka·sha [ˈkɑːʃə; ˋkɑʃə] *n*. 荞麦粥;麦粥。

ka·sher [ˈkɑːʃə; ˋkɑʃɚ] = kosher.

Kash·mir [kæʃˈmiə, ˈkæʃˈmiə; kæʃˋmɪr] *n*. 克什米尔。

Kash·mir·i [kæʃˈmiəri; kæʃˋmɪrɪ] *n*. **1.** 克什米尔语。**2.** (*pl*. ～(***s***)) 克什米尔人。

Kash·mir·i·an [kæʃˈmiriən; kæʃˋmɪrɪən] **I** *a*. 克什米尔的,克什米尔人的,克什米尔语的。**II** *n*. 克什米尔人。

kash·rut(h) [kɑːʃˈruːt, ˈkɑːʃrut; kɑʃˋrut, ˋkɑʃrʊt] *n*. (犹太教)饮食教规。

Ka·shu·bi·an [kæˈʃjuːbiən; kæˋʃjubɪən] *n*. 卡舒比语〔波兰北部所说的一种近似波兰语的西斯拉夫方言〕。

ka·so·lite [ˈkæsəlait; ˋkæsəˏlaɪt] *n*.【矿】矽[硅]铅铀矿。

kat [kɑːt; kat] *n*. = khat.

Ka·tab·a·sis [kəˈtæbəsis; kəˋtæbəsɪs] *n*. **1.**【希腊史】"大败退"〔据希腊历史学家色诺芬 (Xenophone)所写《希腊远征波斯记》(*the Anabasis*) 记载,追随波斯王塞鲁士(Cyrus)的希腊雇用军战败后大举向海边撤退,史称"大败退"〕。**2.** 〔k-〕 (*pl*. ***-ses*** [-siːz; -siz]) (军队的)撤退。

kat·a·bat·ic [ˌkætəˈbætik; ˏkætəˋbætɪk] *a*. (风等)下降的,下吹的 (*opp*. anabatic)。～ **wind**【气】下降风,下吹风。

ka·tab·o·lism [kəˈtæbəlizəm; kəˋtæbəlɪzəm] *n*.【生】分解代谢〔catabolism 的异体〕。

ka·ta·ka·na [ˈkætəˈkɑːnə; ˏkætəˋkanə] *n*. 〔Jap.〕(日语字母楷书)片假名。

Ka·tan·ga [kəˈtæŋgə; kəˋtæŋgə] *n*. 加丹加〔扎伊尔沙巴地区(Shaba)的旧名〕。

Ka·ta·ther·mom·e·ter [ˌkætəθəˈmɔmitə; ˏkætəθəˋmamɪtɚ] *n*. 冷却温度表,冷却率温度表。

Kate [keit; ket] *n*. 凯特〔女子名,Catherine 的昵称〕。

ka·tha·rev·ou·sa [ˌkɑːθɑːˈrevuːsɑ; ˏkaθɑˋrevusa] *n*. (符合古希腊语用法的)现代希腊语;地道希腊语。

Kath·ar·ine, Kath·er·ine, Kath·ryn [ˈkæθərin; ˋkæθrɪn] *n*. 凯瑟琳〔女子名,Kitty 为其昵称,Catherine 的异体〕。

ka·thar·sis [keˈθɑːsis; kɛˋθasɪs] *n*. = catharsis.

Kath·leen [ˈkæθliːn; ˋkæθlin] *n*. 凯瑟琳〔女子名,Catherine 的异体〕。

kath·ode [ˈkæθəud; ˋkæθod] *n*. = cathode.

kat·i·on [ˈkætaiən; ˋkætaɪən] *n*. = cation.

Kat·man·du [ˌkɑːtmɑːnˈduː; ˏkatmanˋdu] *n*. 加德满都〔尼泊尔首都〕。

ka·ty·did [ˈkeitidid; ˋketɪˏdɪd] *n*. 蝈蝈儿,纺织娘(= catydid)。

katz·en·jam·mer [ˌkætsənˈdʒæmə; ˏkatsənˋjamɚ] *n*. **1.** 喧闹。**2.** 坐立不安;沮丧。**3.** 剧烈的头痛〔尤指因宿醉引起者〕。

Kauf·man(n) [ˈkɔːfmən; ˋkɔfmən], **Angelica**, 安吉利卡·考夫曼〔1741—1807,瑞士女画家〕。

kau·ri [ˈkauriː; ˋkaʊri] *n*. 〔Maori〕【植】**1.** 南方贝壳杉 (*Agathis australis*)〔产于纽西兰〕。**2.** 南方贝壳杉木。**3.** 贝壳松脂,栲树脂。

ka·va [ˈkɑːvə; ˋkavə] *n*. **1.** 卡瓦胡椒 (*Piper methysticum*) (= ～ pepper)。**2.** 卡瓦酒(= kavakava)。

ka·vass [kəˈvæs; kəˋvæs] *n*. **1.** (土耳其显贵的)卫士。**2.** (土耳其的)武装警察。

kay·ak [ˈkaiæk; ˋkaɪæk] *n*. **1.** 爱斯基摩独木舟〔一种独人的小划子,木船体外面裹以海豹皮〕。**2.** (用帆布或塑料制的)小划子。

Kay(e) [kei; ke] *n*. 凯〔女子名,Catherine 的昵称〕。

kay·o [ˈkeiˈəu; ˋkeˋo] **I** *n*. (*pl*. ～***s***) 〔美俚〕【拳】击倒(= K.O., knock-out)。**II** *vt*. 〔美俚〕【拳】击倒。**-ed** *a*. 被拳击倒的。

ka·za·chok [kɑːzɑːˈtʃɔːk; kazaˋtʃɔk] *n*. (*pl*. ***-zach·ki*** [-zɑːtʃˈkiː; -zatʃˋki]) = kazatsky.

Ka·zak(h) [kɑːˈzɑːk; kaˋzak] *n*. 哈萨克人;哈萨克族。

Ka·zak(h)·stan [ˌkɑːzɑːkˈstɑːn; ˏkazakˋstan] *n*. 哈萨克斯坦〔亚洲国名〕。

Ka·zan [kəˈzɑːn; kəˋzan] *n*. 喀山〔鞑靼首府〕。

ka·zat·sky, ka·zat·ski [kəˈzɑːtski; kəˋzatskɪ] *n*. (*pl*. ***-skies***) 〔Russ.〕(由一名男演员独舞的)哥萨克舞(= kazatska)。

ka·zoo [kəˈzuː; kəˋzu] *n*. 小笛〔一种玩具乐器〕。

KB = King's bishop (国际象棋中与"王"同列配置的)象。

K.B. = **1.** King's Bench 英国高等法院。**2.** Knight Bachelor 英国古代最低级爵士。

K-ball·ing [ˈkeiˌbɔːliŋ; ˋkeˏbɔlɪŋ] *n*. 〔美俚〕飞机零件的拆用。

k·bar [ˈkeibɑː; ˋkebar] *n*. 千巴〔气压或声压单位〕(= kilobar)。

K.B.E. = Knight Commander of the British Empire 〔英〕不列颠帝国高级勋位爵士。

K.C., KC = **1.** King's Counsel 英国王室法律顾问。**2.** Knight Commander 英国(第二等的)高级爵士。**3.** Knight(s) of Columbus 〔美〕(天主教)慈善会(成员)。**4.** King's College 〔英〕皇家学院。

kc. = kilocycle(s).

kcal. =【物】kilocalorie(s).

K.C.B. = Knight Commander of the Bath 〔英〕巴斯高级勋位爵士。

K.C.I.E. = Knight Commander of the Indian Empire

〔英〕印度帝国高级勋位爵士。

K.C.M.G. = Knight Commander of St. Michael and St. George〔英〕圣迈克尔和圣乔治高级勋位爵士。

K.C.S.I. = Knight Commander of the Star of India〔英〕印度星级勋位高级爵士。

K.C.V.O. = Knight Commander of the Royal Victorian Order〔英〕皇室维多利亚勋章高级爵士。

K.D., k.d. = knocked down【商】拆开的,卸开的,分解的。

K.E. = kinetic energy【物】动能。

ke·a [ˈkeiə; ˋkeə] *n*.【动】(新西兰产的)食肉鹦鹉。

Kean(e) [kiːn kin] **Edmund** 埃德蒙·基恩〔1787—1833, 英国男演员〕。

Keats [kiːts; kits], **John** 约翰·济慈〔1795—1821, 英国诗人〕。

ke·bab [kəˈbɑːb; kəˋbɑb] *n*. 1.〔常 *pl*.〕烤腌(羊)肉串。2.(肉串上的)肉块。

keb·bok, keb·bock [ˈkebɔk; ˋkɛbɑk] *n*.〔Scot.〕干酪, 乳酪。

Ke·ble [ˈkiːbl; ˋkibḷ], **John** 约翰·基布尔〔1792—1866, 英国公理会牧师和诗人, 牛津运动的创始人〕。

Kech·ua [ˈketʃwaː; ˋkɛtʃwɑ] *n*. = quechua. **kech·uan** *a*., *n*.

Ke·chu·ma·ran [ˈketʃuməˈraːn; ˋkɛtʃuməˋrɑn] *n*. = quechumaran.

keck [kek; kɛk] *vi*. 1. 作呕, 恶心。2. 表示[感觉]厌恶 (*at*)。3.(鸟)咯咯地叫。

keck·le [ˈkekl; ˋkɛkḷ] *vi*., *n*. = cackle.

ked·dah [ˈkedə; ˋkɛdɑ] *n*. 捕象陷阱。

kedge [kedʒ; kɛdʒ] I *n*. 小锚(又称 kedge-anchor)。II *vt*., *vi*. 1. 抛锚移(船)。2.(使)船跟着锚抛去的方向移动。

ked·ger·ee [ˌkedʒəˈriː; ˏkɛdʒəˋri] *n*.(印度的)鸡蛋葱豆饭;欧洲用鱼和米、蛋作的食品。

ke·ef [kiːˈef; kiˋɛf] *n*. 1.(吸毒后产生的)迷糊状态。2.(有上述作用的)麻醉品。

keek [kiːk; kik] *vi*.〔Scot., 英方〕偷看, 窥视; 侦察。

keel[1] [kiːl; kil] I *n*. 1.(船等的)龙骨。2.〔诗〕船。3.(动物的)龙骨脊, 脊棱;(植物的)龙骨瓣。*false* ~【船】副龙骨, 保险龙骨。**on an even** ~ 1. 船首船尾在同一水平上的[地], 平稳的[地]。2. 稳定的[地]。3. 均衡的[地]。4. 神志清楚的[地]。II *vt*. 1. 给(船等)装龙骨。2. 把(船)等翻过来(以便修理), 使(船)倾覆。3.〔诗〕以龙骨破(浪)前进。— *vi*.(船等)翻身, 倾覆。~ **over** 1. 翻身, 倾覆, 颠倒。2.〔口〕突然昏倒。~**blocks** *n*.【船】龙骨墩。~**boat** *n*. 内河运货船。~**haul** *vt*. 1. 把(某人)用绳子缚在船底拖曳(作为惩罚)。2. 严厉斥责。~ **line** *n*.【船】首尾线, 龙骨线。~ **piece** 龙骨件材。~ **surface** 飞机垂直安定的翼面。

keel[2] [kiːl; kil] *n*. 1.(运煤的)平底船〔尤指运煤的驳船〕。2. 一驳船的煤。3.〔英〕煤的重量单位(=21.2 长吨)。

keel[3] [kiːl; kil] *n*.(给木材等做记号的)红色颜料, 代赭石。

keel·age [ˈkiːlidʒ; ˋkilɪdʒ] *n*.〔英〕入港税, 停泊税。

ke(e)·lson [ˈkelsən; ˋkɛlsən] *n*.【船】内龙骨。

keen[1] [kiːn; kin] *a*. 1. 锐利的, 锋利的 (*opp*. dull)(言语等)刺人的。2. 敏锐的, 敏捷的。3. 厉害的, 强烈的, 激烈的。4. 泼辣的, 热心的, 渴望的。5.〔美俚〕漂亮的; 愉快的; 极好的。*a razor with a* ~ *edge* 刀口锋利的剃刀。*a* ~ *scent* 刺鼻的气味。*be* ~ *of hearing* [*sight*] 听觉[视觉]敏锐。~ *eyes* 锐眼。*a* ~ *intelligence* 聪慧过人。*a* ~ *observer* 敏锐的观察者。*a* ~ *critic* 尖锐的批评家。*a* ~ *north wind* 凛烈的北风。*a* ~ *sense of justice* 强烈的正义感。*a* ~ *appetite* 强烈的食欲。~ *desire* 强烈的欲望。*a* ~ *golfer* 热爱高尔夫球的人。*be* ~ *on stamp collecting* 喜欢集邮。~ *prices* 极低廉的价格。**be dead** ~ **on sth**.〔口〕非常喜爱。**be** ~ **about** 喜爱, 着迷。**be** ~ **on**〔口〕喜爱, 渴望。**be** ~ **to** 非常想(*I am* ~ *to go to the cinema*. 我非常想去看电影)。(**as**) ~ **as mustard** 极热心的。~ **eyed** *a*. 目光尖锐的。**-ly** *ad*. **-ness** *n*.

keen[2] [kiːn; kin] I *n*.〔爱尔兰〕号哭, 恸哭;(号哭着唱出的)挽歌。II *vt*., *vi*. 为安慰(死者)而号哭, 恸哭。

keen·er [ˈkiːnə; ˋkinɚ] *n*.〔爱尔兰〕哭丧者〔尤指以哭号为职业的人〕。

keep [kiːp; kip] I *vt*. (**kept** [kept; kɛpt]) 1. 拿着, 保持; 保存, 保留; 保管, 把守(门等); 保守(秘密等)。2. 保护, 防护, 防守。3. 履行; 遵守。4. 庆祝, 过(节), 过(年), 举行(仪式)。5. 抚养; 雇用。6. 饲养。7. 备有, 经售。8. 经营, 开设, 管理。9. 继续沿着…走。10. 整理, 料理。11. 记住; 记载, 记入。12. 挽留, 留住; 拘留。13. 使…保持着(某种状态)〔用此义时在受词后加补语〕。14. 制止, 防止, 妨碍; 隐瞒。15. 留在(房屋等)内; 保持在(座位等)上不动。~ *a stick in one's hand* 手里拿着一根棍子。*You may* ~ *the magazine as your own*. 你把那本杂志当作自己的东西留下来好啦(不必还)。*The bank* ~*s money for people*. 银行替人保管存款。~ *a fortress* [*town*] *against the enemy* 防守要塞[城市]抵御敌人。*Who* ~*s the goal*? 谁守球门? ~ *a promise* 守约。~ *the rules* 守规则。~ *early hours* 早睡早起。~ *late hours* 晚睡晚起。~ *a secret* 守秘密。~ *one's word* 履行诺言; 说话算话。~ *one's birthday* 做生日, 祝寿。~ *Chinese New Year* 过春节。*have a wife and family to* ~ 要养家。~ *chickens* 养鸡。~ *a motorcar* 自备汽车。*Do you* ~ *postcards here*? 你们这里有明信片吗? ~ *a school* 办学校。~ (*a*) *shop* 开店。~ *the middle of the road* 一直沿着路中间前进。~ *house* 管理家务。~ *a fact in mind* 心里记住一件事。~ *accounts* [*books*] 记账。~ *a diary* 记日记。*What* ~*s him here, I wonder*? 我不知道他待在这里干什么? *I won't* ~ *you long*. 我不会耽搁你很久。~ *sb*. *in custody* 扣留某人。~ *a razor sharp* 使剃刀经常锋利。*Cold bath* ~*s me in good health*. 冷水浴使我健康。~ *the window open* 把窗子开着。~ *the tears from one's eyes* 忍住眼泪。*He* ~*s nothing from me*. 他什么事都不瞒我。~ *a child away from the fire* 让孩子离火远一点。~ *sb*. *from hurting himself* 提防某人受伤。*Illness kept me from coming yesterday*. 我昨天因病没有来。~ *one's bed* 卧床不起。~ *the house* 足不出户。— *vi*. 1. 继续, 保持, 维持。2.〔口〕逗留; 住在; 呆。3.〔口〕(店等)开着,(学校)上课。4. 继续不断〔用此义时常接动词 -ing〕。5.(食物等)保持不坏。6. 拖, 搁。7. 保持某种路线[方向、活动]。*K- dry*! 切勿受潮。*K- silent*! 别作声, 保持肃静。*Where do you* ~? 〔尤指剑桥大学〕你住在哪里? *School* ~*s till four o'clock*. 学校上课到四点钟。*K- smiling*. 别悲观, 常常笑笑吧。*The baby kept crying all night*. 婴儿哭了一夜。*These fish will* ~ *overnight*. 这些鱼过夜不会坏。*The matter will* ~ *until tomorrow*. 问题拖到明天再讲。*Traffic* ~*s to the right*. 车辆等靠右边走。~ *check on* 检查, 监督。~ **a firm** [**tight**] **hand** [**rein**] **on sb**. 紧紧地控制某人。~ **at** 1. 纠缠 (*They kept at me with their appeals for subscriptions*. 他们硬要我捐款)。2. 坚持地做。~ **at it**〔口〕使劲, 加油干。~ **away** 不挨近, 避开, 离开。~ **back** 1. 退缩。2. 隐瞒。3. 阻止。4. 留住。~ **bad** [**good**] **company** 跟坏[好]人交往。~ **dark** 保守秘密, 不泄密。~ **down** 1. 压住; 镇压, 压服。2.【印】用小活字排印。3. 缩减。4. 保留(食物等)。5. 一直坐着, 一直睡着。~ **from** 1. 避开(~ *from talking* 避而不谈)。2. 禁止(~ *sb*. *from smoking* 禁止某人抽烟)。3. 隐瞒 (~ *sth*. (*back*) *from sb*. 对某人隐瞒某事)。4. 抑制 (*He couldn't* ~ *from crying*. 他禁不住哭了)。~ **hold of** 抓住不放。~ **in** 1. 扣留, 下课后罚学生留校。2. 压住, 控制。3.【印】排紧。4. 让(火)烧着。5. 闭门不

K

出。~ ***in with sb***. 与某人友好相处。~ ***it up***〔口〕加紧做;坚持做下去。~ ***off*** 1. 防止,不让接近,避开(敌人等)。2. 不接近(*K- off the grass*.(牌告)勿踏草地)。~ ***on*** 1. 穿[戴]着不脱。2. 继续(*doing*)(~ *on blowing one's nose* 一直在擤鼻子)。★ *on ... -ing* 表示动作的反复。~ *...-ing* 表示状态的继续。~ ***on at*** 1. 继续干。2. 纠缠。3. 责骂不休。~ ***one's bones green*** 不衰老。~ ***one's head*** 不激动,保持冷静。~ ***oneself to oneself*** 不与人往来,不交际,离群索居。~ ***out*** 1. 把…关在门外,不使入内(*Danger*. *K- out*. 危险。切勿入内)。2. 阻止,挡住(~ *out sunlight* 遮住阳光)。3.【印】疏排。4. 不参加,不卷入。~ ***out of*** 置身于…之外(= *out of sb.'s affair* 不过问某人的事)。~ ***sb. shady***〔美口〕蒙蔽某人,不让某人了解事实真相。~ ***sb. underfoot*** 控制某人。~ to 坚持,遵守,不违背(*K- to every promise you have made*. 一切诺言都必须坚守不渝。*K- to your task till you've finished*. 坚持工作,直到做完为止)。~ ***sb. advised*** [***conversant***, ***posted***] ***on sth***. 使某人了解某事。~ ***sb. busy*** 不让某人闲着。~ ***sb. going*** 1. 用金钱帮助某人。2. 维持某人生活。~ ***sb. going in sth***. 供给某人以某物。~ ***to oneself*** 1. ***vi***. 不交际,不与人往来。2. ***vt***. 保守秘密。~ ***under*** 压住,控制(*The firemen managed to* ~ *the fire under*. 火势总算被救火员控制住了)。~ ***up*** 1. 支持,维持;保持。2. 继续,持续;停歇。3. 不为(病等)所屈,能支持。4.【印】用大写正体排印。~ ***up with*** [***on***] 跟上(人、时势等),不落后(~ *up with the situation* 跟上形势)。**II** ***n***. 1. 保持,保养;管理。2. 生活资料,衣食;饲料。3.【史】中世纪城堡的最牢固的部分,城堡的高楼;堡垒;要塞,坚固据点。4. 监牢,监狱。*be worth one's* ~值得保存[饲养]。*earn one's* ~挣生活费。*the castle* ~城堡的高楼。***for*** ~***s***〔口〕1. 分胜负(*play for* ~*s* 有输赢的游戏)。2.〔口〕永远地(*settle the controversy for* ~*s* 一劳永逸地解决这一纠纷。*The fight is on for* ~*s*. 斗争永远不断。*You may have the book for* ~*s*. 这本书你拿去好了,不必归还)。***in bad*** [***low***] ~ 保存得不好。***in good*** [***high***] ~ 保存得好。

keep·er [ˈkiːpə; ˋkipɚ] ***n***. 1. 看守人;看护人;猎场看守人;动物园的饲养员。2. 管理人,保管人〔英国常用作官职名〕。3.(商店客栈等的)所有者,经营者。4. 衔铁,永磁衔铁。5.【机】保位物;止动螺帽,锁紧螺母;夹子,夹头,卡箍。6. 履行者,遵守者;记录员。7. 耐藏的水果[蔬菜]。*a park* ~〔美〕运动场管理员;〔英〕猎场管理员。*a shop* ~店主。~ *of magnet* 保磁用衔铁。*oil* ~油承。*a* ~ *of his words* 说话算数的人。*a good* [*bad*] ~耐藏的[不耐藏的]物品。*the K- of the Exchange and Mint*〔英〕造币局局长。*the K- of the King's Conscience*(作国王国务上行为负责人的)大法官。*the K- of the Privy Seal*〔英〕御玺官。*the Lord K-*(*of the Great Seal*)〔英〕国玺官。**-less** ***a***. **-ship** ***n***.

keep·ing [ˈkiːpiŋ; ˋkipɪŋ] **I** ***n***. 1. 保持,保有,保留;〔*pl*.〕保留物。2. 管理,看守,保管。3. 供养,饲养。4. 一致;协调。*This stamp is worth* (*the*) ~. 这枚邮票值得保存。*in safe* ~ 保管得好。*The papers are in my* ~. 文件由我在保管。*the* ~ *of one's family* 抚养全家。*loose* ~ 散放饲养。***in*** ~ ***with*** 和…一致,与…协调。***out of*** ~ ***with*** 和…不一致,与…不协调。**II** ***a***. 1. 适于贮藏的。2. 坚贞的。~ *apples* 耐贮藏的苹果。*a* ~ *husband* 忠实的丈夫。~ **room**〔美〕起居室,内客厅。

keep·sake [ˈkiːpseik; ˋkipˏsek] ***n***. 纪念品;(精装)纪念本。

kee-rect [ˈkiːrekt; ˋkirekt] ***a***.〔美俚〕正确的;完全对头的。

kees·hond [ˈkeisˌhɔnd; ˋkesˏhand] ***n***. 荷兰狮毛狗。

kees·ter [ˈkiːstə; ˋkistɚ] ***n***. = keister.

keet [kiːt; kit] ***n***.【动】珍珠幼鸟。

kef [kef, keif; kɛf, kef] ***n***. = keef.

kef·fi·yeh [kəˈfiːə; kəˋfiə] ***n***. = kaffiyeh.

keg [keg; kɛg] ***n***. 1. 小桶〔容量通常少于10加仑〕。2. 桶〔钉子的重量单位 = 100磅〕。

keis·ter, kees·ter [ˈkiːstə; ˋkistɚ] ***n***.〔俚〕1. 手提皮箱,小提包,挎包。2. 屁股。3.〔扒手用语〕后裤袋。

Keith [kiːθ; kiθ] ***n***. 基斯〔姓氏,男子名〕。~**'s mum** 基思妈妈〔指心地善良而思想平庸的一般中年妇女〕。

keg·ler, kegel·(l)er [ˈkeg(ə)lə; ˋkɛg(ə)lɚ] ***n***.(板球等的)击球员。

keit·lo·a [ˈkaitləuə, ˈkeit-; ˋkaɪtˏloə, ˋket-] ***n***.【动】轻犀(*keitloa*)〔南非所产的两角犀〕。

Ke·lao [ˈkəˈlau; ˋkeˋlaʊ] ***n***. 仡佬族;仡佬族人。

Kel·land [ˈkelənd; ˋkɛlənd] ***n***. 凯兰〔姓氏〕。

Kel·ler [ˈkelə; ˋkɛlɚ] ***n***. 1. 凯勒〔姓氏〕。2. **Helen Adams** ~海伦·凯勒〔1880—1968,美国盲哑女作家〕。

Kel·l(e)y [ˈkeli; ˋkɛlɪ] ***n***. 凯利〔姓氏,男子名〕。

Kel·logg [ˈkelɔg; ˋkɛlɔg] ***n***. 凯洛格〔姓氏〕。

kel·ly, Kel·ly [ˈkeli; ˋkɛlɪ] **green**(浓厚的)黄绿色。

ke·loid [ˈkiːlɔid; ˋkilɔɪd] ***n***.【医】瘢痕瘤,瘢痕疙瘩。

kelp [kelp; kɛlp] ***n***. 1. 巨藻;海草,大型褐藻。2. 海草灰〔从中可提取碘〕。

kel·pie, kel·py [ˈkelpi; ˋkɛlpɪ] ***n***.〔Scot.〕(传说中能诱人自溺的)马形水怪。

kel·son [ˈkelsn; ˋkɛlsn̩] ***n***.【船】内龙骨。

Kelt [kelt; kɛlt] ***n***. = Celt.

kelt [kelt; kɛlt] ***n***.(产卵后的)鲑鱼[鳟鱼]。

kel·ter [ˈkeltə; ˋkɛltɚ] ***n***. = kilter.

Kelt·ic [ˈkeltik; ˋkɛltɪk] ***a***., ***n***. = Celtic.

Kel·vin [ˈkelvin; ˋkɛlvɪn] ***n***. 1. 凯尔文〔男子名〕。2. **Lord William Thomson** ~ 威廉·汤姆逊·凯尔文〔1824—1907,英国物理学家〕。~ **effect**【无】集肤效应。~ **scale**【物】开氏温标。

Ke·mal·ism [kəˈmɑːlizəm; kəˋmɑlɪzm̩] ***n***. 基马尔主义〔土耳其共和国第一任总统 Kemal (1881—1938)所提倡的政治主张。基马尔旧译凯末尔〕。

Ke·mal·ist [kəˈmɑːlist; kəˋmɑlɪst] **I** ***n***. 基马尔主义者。**II** ***a***. 基马尔主义的,基马尔式的。

Kem·ble [ˈkembl; ˋkɛmbl̩] ***n***. 肯布尔〔姓氏,男子名〕。

kemp [kemp; kɛmp] **I** ***n***. 1.〔英方〕(在收割庄稼竞赛时所获的)冠军。2. 粗羊毛。**II** ***vi***.(在收割庄稼时)争取冠军。

kempt [kempt; kɛmpt] ***a***. 干净的,整洁的,收拾得干净利落的。

Ken. = Kentucky.

ken[1] [ken; kɛn] **I** ***n***. 1. 眼界,视野;景象。2. 知识范围,见地。*beyond* [*out of*, *outside*] *one's* ~在知识范围之外。*in one's* ~ 在知识范围之内。**II** ***vt***., ***vi***.(~***ned*** [-d; -d], ***kent*** [kent; kɛnt]; ***ken·ning***) 1.〔Scot.〕认识;知道。2.〔古〕看出。

ken[2] [ken; kɛn] ***n***.〔俚〕(盗贼等的)巢穴,窝。

ke·naf [kəˈnæf; kəˋnæf] ***n***. 1. 洋麻,槿麻(*Hibiscus cannabinus*)〔亚洲热带植物,似黄麻〕。2. 洋麻[槿麻]纤维。

kench [kentʃ; kɛntʃ] ***n***.(腌制鱼或皮革的)长方形大腌箱。

Ken·dal (green) [ˈkendl; ˋkɛndl̩] ***n***. 1.(英国)肯达尔绿色粗呢。2. 肯达尔绿。

Ken·dall [ˈkendl; ˋkɛndl̩] ***n***. 肯德尔〔姓氏,男子名〕。

Ken·nan [ˈkenən; ˋkɛnən] ***n***. 凯南〔姓氏〕。

Ken·ne·dy [ˈkenidi; ˋkɛnədɪ] ***n***. 肯尼迪〔姓氏〕。~ **Round**〔常用 K- round〕肯尼迪回合〔美国总统肯尼迪1962年发起的对西欧共同市场之间的谈判,目的是打破六国关税壁垒以扩大美国出口〕。

ken·nel[1] [ˈkenl; ˋkɛnl̩] **I** ***n***. 1. 狗窝;〔*pl*.〕养狗场。2.(狐等栖身的)洞。3. 一群猎狗,一群野兽。4. 鄙陋的小矮房,陋室。*go to* ~(狐等)藏到洞中。**II** ***vt***., ***vi***.

K

(〔英〕-*ll*-) 1. (使)住在狗窝内;(使)待在窝内;(使)钻进狗窝。2. (使)(人)住进陋室。

ken·nel[2] [ˈkenl; ˋkɛnl] *n*. 阴沟,路旁的下水道。

Ken·nel·ly [ˈkenəli; ˋkɛnəlɪ] *n*. 肯内利〔姓氏〕。

Ken·nel·ly-Heav·i·side layer [ˈkenəliˈhevisaidˈleə; ˋkɛnəlɪˋhɛvɪˏsaɪdˋleɚ]【无】肯涅利—海维赛层,E 电离层(=E-layer)。

Ken·neth [ˈkeniθ; ˋkɛnɪθ] *n*. 肯尼思〔男子名〕。

ken·ning [ˈkeniŋ; ˋkɛnɪŋ] *n*. 1. 〔Scot.〕知道,认识。2. 微量;痕迹。2. 〔古、诗〕隐喻表达法〔一般用复合词作比喻,如以 "whale-path"(鲸路)喻"大海","oar-steed"(划马)喻"船"〕。

Ken·ny [ˈkeni; ˋkɛnɪ] *n*. 肯尼〔姓氏〕。**K- method** [**treatment**] 肯尼疗法〔早期用热裹和锻炼身体治疗小儿麻痹症的方法,为澳大利亚护士伊丽莎白·肯尼所创〕。

ke·no [ˈkiːnəu; ˋkino] *n*. (*pl*. ~*s*) 叠纸牌赌博。

ke·no·sis [kiˈnəusis; kɪˋnosɪs] *n*.【神】(基督的)对神性的放弃。**ke·not·ic** [-ˈnɔtik; -ˋnɑtɪk] *a*.

ken·o·tron [ˈkenətrɔn; ˋkɛnəˏtrɑn] *n*.【无】高压整流二极管。~ **rectifier** 二极管整流器。

kens·peck·le [ˈkenspekl; ˋkɛnˏspɛkl̩] *a*. 明显的,容易发现的,引人注意的。

Kent[1] [kent; kɛnt] *n*. 肯特〔姓氏,男子名〕。

Kent[2] [kent; kɛnt] *n*. 肯特郡〔英格兰东南端〕。

kent [kent; kɛnt] *v*. ken[1]的过去式及过去分词。

Kent·ish [ˈkentiʃ; ˋkɛntɪʃ] *a*. 英国肯特郡的。~ **fire** (观[听]众表示不耐烦或抗议时)长时间有节奏的鼓掌。~ **man** 麦特威(Medway)河以西的肯特人,西肯特人〔*cf*. man of Kent 东肯特人〕。~ **rag** 肯特郡产坚硬砂质石灰岩。

kent·ledge [ˈkentlidʒ; ˋkɛntlɪdʒ] *n*.【船】压载用的生铁。

Ken·tuck·i·an [kenˈtʌkiən; kɛnˋtʌkɪən] I *a*. 肯塔基州的,肯塔基州人的。II *n*. 肯塔基州人。

Ken·tuck·y [kenˈtʌki; kənˋtʌkɪ] *n*. 肯塔基〔美国州名〕。~ **coffee tree**【植】加拿大皂荚 (*Gymnocladus dioica*)〔产于美国东部,籽可作咖啡代用品〕。

Ken·ya [ˈkiːnjə, ˈkenjə; ˋkinjə, ˋkɛnjə] *n*. 肯尼亚〔非洲〕。**-n** 1. *a*. 肯尼亚的,肯尼亚人的。2. *n*. 肯尼亚人。

Ken·yon [ˈkenjən; ˋkɛnjən] *n*. 凯尼恩〔姓氏〕。

ke·os [ˈkeiɔs; ˋkiɑs] = kea.

ke·pi [ˈkeipiː, ˈkepiː; ˋkepi, ˋkɛpɪ] *n*. (有平圆顶及水平帽沿的)法国军帽。

Kep·ler [ˈkeplə; ˋkɛplɚ], **Johann** 约翰·开普勒〔1571—1630,德国天文学家,物理学家〕。~**'s laws** 行星运动三定律。**-ian** *a*. J. 开普勒的。

Kep·pel [ˈkepəl; ˋkɛpəl] *n*. 凯珀尔〔姓氏〕。

Keprom = keyed-access erasable programmable read-only memory【计】键控存取可擦可编程序只读存储器〔含有保护程序的电子锁设置〕。

kept [kept; kɛpt] I keep 的过去式及过去分词。II *a*. 被收买的,受人供养的;受人控制的。*the* ~ *press* 御用报纸。*a* ~ *woman* 情妇,外室。

ker- [kəː; kɚ]〔象声词〕*comb*. *f*. 表示强烈的抨击,撞击声,如: *ker*plunk(击水的砰声)。

Ker·a·la [ˈkerələ; ˋkɛrələ] *n*. 喀拉拉〔印度邦名〕。

ke·ram·ic [kiˈræmik; kɪˋræmɪk] *a*. = ceramic.

ke·ram·ics [kiˈræmiks; kɪˋræmɪks] *n*. = ceramics.

ker·a·tec·to·my [ˌkerəˈtektəmi; ˏkɛrəˋtɛktəmɪ] *n*. (*pl*. -*mies*)【医】角膜切除术。

ker·a·tin [ˈkerətin; ˋkɛrətɪn] *n*.【生化】角蛋白,角朊。

ker·a·ti·tis [ˌkerəˈtaitis; ˏkɛrəˋtaɪtɪs] *n*.【医】角膜炎。

ker·a·t(o)- *comb*. *f*. 表示"角","角质": *kerato*plasty.

ker·a·tog·e·nous [ˌkerəˈtɔdʒənəs; ˏkɛrəˋtɑdʒənəs] *a*.【解】引起角质组织生长的。

ker·a·toid [ˈkerəˌtɔid; ˋkɛrəˏtɔɪd] *a*. 角状的;角质的。

ker·a·to·plas·ty [ˈkerətəuˌplæsti; ˋkɛrətəˏplæstɪ] *n*. (*pl*. -*ties*)【医】角膜成形术。

ker·a·tose [ˈkerətəus; ˋkɛrəˏtos] I *a*. 角质的。II *n*. 角质物。

ker·a·to·sis [ˌkerəˈtəusis; ˏkɛrəˋtosɪs] *n*. (*pl*. -*ses* [-siːz, -siz])【医】1. 皮肤的角质生长〔如疣〕。2. 角化症。

ker·a·tot·o·my [ˌkerəˈtɔtəmi; ˏkɛrəˋtɑtəmɪ] *n*. (*pl*. -*mies*)【医】角膜切开术。

kerb [kəːb; kɚb] *n*. 〔英〕1. (街道的)路边镶边石。2. 井栏(=curb)。*on the* ~场外交易,交易所收场后的买卖。~ **crawl** *vi*. 〔英〕(驾驶汽车者为寻找娼妓)沿路边缓慢行驶。~ **drill** (行人横穿马路演习的)简便规章。~ **market** 场外证券市场。~ **stone** 〔英〕= **curbstone**. ~ **weight** (无人无货的汽车)空载重量。

ker·chief [ˈkəːtʃif; ˋkɚtʃɪf] *n*. (*pl*. ~*s*, -*chieves*) 1. (妇女的)头巾;围巾。2. 〔诗〕手巾,手帕。**-ed** *a*. 包着头巾的,围着围巾的。

Ke·res [ˈkerəs; ˋkɛrəs] *n*. (*sing*., *pl*.) 1. 克勒斯人〔新墨西哥的七个印第安人村庄的居民〕。2. 克勒斯语(=Keresan)。

kerf [kəːf; kɚf] I *n*. 1. (斧、锯等的)劈痕,截口;【机】(气割的)切缝。2. 切割下之物。II *vt*. 在(木材等)上锯切口。

ker·fuf·fle [kə(ː)ˈfəfəl; kɚˋfʌfəl] *n*. 混乱,骚动,动乱。

ker·mes [ˈkəːmi(ː)z; ˋkɚmiz] *n*. 1. 虫胭脂,胭脂虫粉。2. (胭脂虫寄生的)胭脂虫栎 (~ oak)。3.【矿】硫氧锑矿。

ker·mess, ker·mis [ˈkəːmes, ˈkəːmis; ˋkɚmɛs, ˋkɚmɪs] *n*. 1. (荷兰、比利时等国的)露天集市;露天狂欢。2. 〔美〕热闹的义卖集市〔游艺〕。

Ker·mit [ˈkəːmit; ˋkɚmɪt] *n*. 克米特〔姓氏,男子名〕。

Kern [kəːn; kɚn] *n*. 1. 克恩〔姓氏〕。2. **Jerome** ~ 杰罗姆·克恩〔1885—1945,美国作曲家〕。

kern[1] [kəːn; kɚn]〔英方〕I *vt*., *vi*. 结(果实)。II *n*. (果实的)核;仁;颗粒。~ **oscillation**【物】核振荡。

kern[2], **kerne** [kəːn; kɚn] *n*. 1. (古爱尔兰的)轻步兵。2. 爱尔兰农夫,乡下人。

ker·nel [ˈkəːnl; ˋkɚnl] I *n*. 1. (果实的)核,仁。2. 谷粒,麦粒。3. 内核,核心,要点。4.【原】(原子)核。5.【数】(积分方程的)影响函数核。6.【机】模芯。7.【电】(带电导体中)零磁场强度线。*the* ~ *of the question* 问题的核心,问题的要点。II *vt*. (-*l*(*l*)-) 把…包在核内。~ **sentence**【语法】(生成语法中的)核心句。**-(l)ed** *a*. 有核[仁]的。

ker·nic·ter·us [kəːˈniktərəs; kɚˋnɪktərəs] *n*.【医】核黄疸。

kern·ite [ˈkəːnait; ˋkɚnˏaɪt] *n*.【地】四水硼砂。

ker·o·gen [ˈkerədʒən; ˋkɛrədʒən] *n*.【矿】油母质,油原。~ **shale** 油页岩。

ker·o·sene, ker·o·sine [ˈkerəsiːn; ˋkɛrəˏsin] *n*. 煤油,火油(=~ oil)。*a* ~ *lamp* 〔美〕煤油灯。

ker·plunk [kəːˈplʌŋk; kɚˋplʌŋk] *ad*. (击水的)扑通声。

Kerr [kɑː, kəː; kɛr, kɚ] *n*. 克尔〔姓氏〕。

ker·ri·a [ˈkeriə; ˋkɛrɪə] *n*.【植】棣棠属 (*kerria*) 植物〔尤指棣棠花 (*grria japonica*)〕。

Ker·ry [ˈkeri; ˋkɛrɪ] *n*. 克里〔男子名〕。

ker·sey [ˈkəːzi; ˋkɚzɪ] *n*. (英国)克瑟手织窄面斜纹呢;〔*pl*.〕克瑟斜纹呢织品。

ker·sey·mere [ˈkəːzimiə; ˋkɚzɪmɪr] *n*. 斜纹细毛料,开士米毛料(= cassimere)。

ke·ryg·ma [kəˈrigmə; kəˋrɪgmə] *n*.【宗】1. 宣讲福音。2. 宣讲中强调福音的要旨。**ker·yg·mat·ic** [ˌkerigˈmætik; ˏkɛrɪgˋmætɪk] *a*.

kes·trel [ˈkestrəl; ˋkɛstrəl] *n*.【动】茶隼。

ket·a·mine [ˈketəmiːn; ˋkɛtəmin] *n*.【药】克他命,氯胺酮〔一种快速麻醉剂〕。

ketch [ketʃ; kɛtʃ] *n*.【海】双桅船。

ketch·up [ˈketʃəp; ˋkɛtʃəp] *n*. 番茄沙司,番茄酱。

K

ke·tene [ˈkiːtiːn; ˋkitin] ***n.***【化】1. 乙烯酮。2. 烯酮。

ket(o)- *comb. f.* 表示"酮": *ket*one, *keto*genic.

ke·to·gen·e·sis [ˌkiːtəuˈdʒenisis; ˏkitoˋdʒɛnəsɪs] ***n.***【化】生酮作用。**ke·to·gen·ic** ***a.***

ke·tol [ˈkiːtəul, -tɔːl; ˋkitol, -tɔl] ***n.***【化】酮醇。

ke·tone [ˈkiːtəun; ˋkiton] ***n.***【化】酮。~ **body**【化】酮体。**keton·ic** ***a.***

ke·to·ne·mi·a [ˌkiːtəuˈniːmiə; ˏkitoˋnimɪə] ***n.***【医】酮血症。

ke·to·nu·ri·a [ˌkiːtəuˈnjuəriə; ˏkitoˋnjʊrɪə] ***n.***【医】酮尿。

ke·tose [ˈkiːtəus; ˋkitos] ***n.*** 酮醣。

ke·to·sis [kiˈtəusis; kɪˋtosɪs] ***n.***【医】酮病。

ke·to·ster·oid [ˌkiːtəuˈstiərɔid; ˏkitoˋstɪrɔɪd] ***n.*** 酮类固醇。

Ket·ter·ing [ˈketəriŋ; ˋkɛtərɪŋ] ***n.*** 凯特灵〔姓氏〕。

ket·tle [ˈketl; ˋkɛtl] ***n.*** 1. (烧水用的)水壶,水锅。2. 小汽锅。3.【地】锅穴(= ~ hole)。*A watched ~ never boils.*〔谚〕看着的水壶永不开〔性急也无用〕。***a (pretty) ~ of fish*** 1. 困境,窘境,尴尬的境地。2. 要处理的事情。~ **holder** ***n.*** (锅把的)布套。

ket·tle·drum [ˈketldrʌm; ˋkɛtḷdrʌm] ***n.*** (打击乐器中的)铜鼓。**-mer** ***n.*** 击鼓人。

kev, Kev [kev; kev] ***n.*** (*sing.*, *pl.*) 千电子伏特。

kev·el [ˈkevəl; ˋkɛvəl] ***n.***【海】缆耳,盘绳栓。★小型的称作 cleat。

Kew(Gardens) [kjuː; kju] ***n.*** 伦敦西郊国立植物园。

kew·pie [ˈkjuːpiː; ˋkjupi] ***n.*** (有手有鬈发的圆脸蛋)洋娃娃。

Kew·pie doll [ˈkjuːpiː dɔl; ˋkjupi ˋdɑl] 丘比洋娃娃〔商标名〕。

key[1] [kiː; ki] **I** ***n.*** 1. 钥匙。2. 要害,关口,要冲。3. 关键,线索,秘诀;解法。4. (外国书的)直译本,图例,题解,图解,解释。5.【乐】调,主音调;(思想、表现等的)基调,调子。6. (上钟表发条等的)钥匙;【机】楔,栓,销子。7.【电】电键,电钥。8.【建】板条间灰泥,初涂,拱顶石,冠石。9.〔常 *pl.*〕(钢琴等的)键,(打字机的)键盘。10.〔*pl.*〕精神权威〔尤指教皇权〕。11.【植】翅果。*false* [*skeleton*] ~配制的钥匙。*master* ~万能钥匙。*turn the* ~ 转动钥匙;开锁。*Aden, the ~ to the Middle East* 亚丁—中东的咽喉。*a ~ to one's success* 成功的秘诀。*the ~ to a riddle* 谜底。*the ~ to the code* 电码索引。*a high* [*low*] ~高昂[低沉]的调子。*all in the same* ~千篇一律。*a chromatic* ~钢琴等的黑键。*a natural* ~钢琴等的白键。***get*** [***have***] ***the ~ of the street*** 被关在屋外;流浪街头。***hold the ~s of*** 支配,控制。***in a minor ~*** 用低调;带着阴郁的情绪。***lay*** [***put***] ***the ~ under the door*** 闭门而去。***the golden*** [***silver***] ~贿金。***the House of Keys*** 英国马恩岛 (Isle of Man) 的下院。***the king's*** [***queen's***] ***~s*** 警察破门捕人时所用的器具。***the power of the ~s*** 教皇的权威。***under lock and ~*** 郑重保管。**II** ***vt.*** 1. 锁上;插上(栓等) (*in*; *on*)。2.【乐】调整…的调子,给…调音。3.【建】用拱顶石装饰 (*in*)。4. 键控,发(报)。5. 为…提供解决的线索[答案]。6. 用动植物特征分类表鉴定(生物标本)。7. 使(绘画等)具有某种色调[色彩]。~ *a piano* 调整钢琴的音调。~ *the strings* 调弦。— ***vi.*** 使用钥匙。~ ***off*** [***out***]【电】切断。~ ***on***【电】接通。~ ***up*** 1. 使升调门;使紧张,鼓舞。2. 提出(要求等)。**III** ***a.*** 1. 主要的。2.〔口〕极好的,顶呱呱的。*the ~ industries* 主要工业,基本工业。*a ~ man* 要人,核心人物〔*cf.* ~ man〕。*a ~ point* 要点。*a ~ position* 据点;要职。~ **atom**【物】钥原子。~ **bed**【地】标准层。~ **board** 1. ***n.*** (钢琴、打字机等的)键盘;挂钥匙的板;键盘式电子乐器。2. ***vi.*** 操作键盘字排字机。3. ***vt.*** 向(自动键盘)进料,操纵(自动开关)。~ **cabinet** 电话控制盒。~ **club** 钥匙俱乐部〔西方私人夜总会,成员自带钥匙〕。~ **colour** 基本色。~ **diagram** 概略原理图,解说图。~ **drawing** 解释图;索引图。~ **-frame**〔电〕键架。~ **fruit**【植】翅果〔如枫树、榆树等果实〕。~ **groove** 链槽。~**hole** 1. ***n.*** 锁眼;栓孔;钥匙孔(*listen at* [*spy through*] *the ~ hole* 由锁眼里面偷听[看])。2. ***a.*** 透露内情的(*a ~ hole reporter* 报导内幕的记者)。~ **industry** 国家基本工业〔如钢铁、煤矿工业等〕。~ **instruction**【计】引导指令。~**light** 主灯光,基本灯光。~**lock** 遥控锁〔例如在车外亦可锁上汽车的车窗和车门〕。~**man** 要人,骨干分子,中心人物。~ **metal** (有色金属)母合金。~ **modulation** 键控调制。~ **money** (房地产经纪人索取的)额外小费,顶费,挖费。~**note** 1. ***n.***【乐】主调音,基音;主旨,要旨,基调(*give the ~note to* 决定…的主要方针。*strike* (*sound*) *the ~ note of* 揣摩[试探]…的主要动向)。2. ***vt.***〔美〕在(会议等场合)发表施政方针;给…定下基调。~ **noter** ***n.*** 定基调的人,作主要讲话的人。~**pad** (操作电脑或其他仪器等的)键盘,键板。~ **pattern** 卍字花纹。~**phone** 按钮式电话机〔比拨号式先进〕。~ **punch** 键控穿孔器。~ **ring** 钥匙圈。~ **seat** = ~way. ~ **sender** 电键发送器。~**sending** 电键选择[拨号]。~ **signature**【乐】调号。~ **source** 密码索引,密码本。~**stone** 1.【键】拱顶石,冠石,塞缝石。2.【无】梯形失真(光栅)。3. 要旨,根本原理。~**stroke**【计】击键。~**way** ***n.***【机】键槽,销座;锁槽。~ **well** 关键井;基准井;基准钻孔;注入井,加压油井,控制井。

key[2] [kiː; ki] ***n.*** 礁,暗礁(= cay, quay)。

keyed [kiːd; kid] ***a.*** 1. 带键的〔如键盘乐器〕。2.【建】用拱顶石加固的。3. 定调的;调子…的〔常用以构成复合词〕。4. 使调子和谐一致的。~**-up** ***a.*** 激动的。

key·er [ˈkiːə; ˋkiɚ] ***n.*** 1.【无】电键器;键控器;调制器;控制器。2. 定时器,计时器。

Keyes [kiːz, kaiz; kiz, kaɪz] ***n.*** 凯斯〔姓氏〕。

Keynes [keinz; kenz] ***n.*** 1. 凯恩斯〔姓氏〕。2. **John Maynard** ~约翰·梅纳德·凯恩斯〔1883—1946, 英国经济学家和作家〕。

Keynes·i·an [ˈkeinziən; ˋkenzɪən] **I** ***a.*** 凯恩斯理论的;符合凯恩斯理论的。**II** ***n.*** 凯恩斯主义者。**-an·ism** ***n.***

Key·stone [ˈkiːstəun; ˋkiˏston] ***a.*** 吉斯通式的〔指类似吉斯通电影公司拍的庸俗喜剧无声片,如描绘一群愚蠢无能的警察(Keystone Kops)疯狂追捕的场面〕。**K- State** 宾夕法尼亚州的诨名。

K.G. = Knight of the Garter〔英〕嘉德勋爵士。

kg. = 1. keg(s). 2. kilogram(me)(s).

K.G.B., KGB =〔Russ.〕Komitet Gosudarstvennoi Bezopasnosti (= Committee of State Security)克格勃〔前苏联国家安全委员会〕。

kg-m = kilogram-meter, 公斤-米,千克-米。

Kgs. = Kings (O.T.)〔《旧约全书》中的《列王纪》〕。

Kha·ba·rovsk [kʌˈbaːrəfsk; kʌˋbarəfsk] ***n.*** 哈巴罗夫斯克〔即伯力,俄罗斯城市〕。

kha·di [ˈkaːdi; ˋkadi] ***n.*** 印度土布(= khaddar)。

khaf [haːf, hɔːf; haf, hɔf] ***n.*** 希伯来语第十一个字母 (*kaf*) 的变体。

kha·ki [ˈkaːki; ˋkakɪ] **I** ***a.*** 1. 土黄色的。2. 卡其布的。**II** ***n.*** (*pl.* ~***s***) 1. 卡其布。2. 土黄色。3.〔*pl.*〕卡其布军服,卡其布裤子。***be in*** ~是军人。***get into*** ~参军,入伍。~ **election**〔英〕利用紧张局势博取多数人投票的选举。

kha·lif(a) [kaːˈliːf(ə); kaˋlifə] ***n.*** = caliph.

kha·li·fat(e) [ˈkaːlifæt; ˋkalɪˏfæt] ***n.*** = caliphate.

Khal·khas [ˈkælkəz; ˋkælkəz] ***n.*** 柯尔克孜族;柯尔克孜族人。

kham·sin [ˈkæmsin, kæmˈsiːn; ˋkæmsɪn kæmˋsin] ***n.*** 喀新风〔埃及的一种干热南风〕。

khan[1] [kaːn, kæn; kan, kæn] ***n.***【史】可汗〔古代土耳其、鞑靼、蒙古、突厥各族最高统治者的尊称〕。2. 汗〔古代中亚,阿富汗等国统治者和官吏的尊称〕。

K

khan[2][kaːn, kæn; kɑn, kæn] ***n.*** (土耳其等地供旅行者停宿的)简陋驿店,商栈。

khan·ate[ˈkaːneit, ˈkæn-; ˋkɑnet, ˋkæn-] ***n.*** 可汗的领土,汗国。

khaph [hɑːf, hɔːf; hɑf, hɔf] ***n.*** = khaf.

kha·pra beetle [ˈkaːprə; ˋkɑprə]【动】谷斑皮蠹(*Trogoderma granarium*)〔伤害谷物的一种毁灭性害虫,原生于南亚和东南亚〕。

Khar·kov [ˈkaːkɔf; ˋkɑrkɔf] ***n.*** 哈尔科夫〔乌克兰城市〕。

Khar·t(o)um [kaːˈtuːm; kɑrˋtum] ***n.*** 喀土穆〔苏丹首都〕。

khat [kaːt; kɑt] ***n.*** 阿拉伯茶(*Catha edulis*)〔产于非洲和阿拉伯,鲜叶可嚼或泡茶〕。

khed·ah [ˈkedə; ˋkɛdə] ***n.*** 捕象陷阱(= keddah)。

khe·dive [kəˈdiv; kəˋdɪv] ***n.*** 埃及总督〔1867—1914年土耳其驻埃及代表的尊称〕。

khet, kheth [hɛ; hɛt] ***n.*** = het.

khi [kai; kaɪ] ***n.*** = chi〔希腊语字母表第22字母〕。

Khmer [kəˈmɛə; kəˋmɛr] ***n.*** **1.** 高棉人。**2.** 高棉语。~ **Rouge** 红色高棉〔70年代柬埔寨国内的一支政治和武装力量〕。

Khoi·san [ˈkɔisaːn; ˋkɔɪsɑn] ***n.*** (南非)克瓦桑语族〔包括霍屯督语(*Hottentot*)和布希曼语(*Bushman*)〕。

Kho·mei·ni [hɔˈmeini; hɑˋmenɪ] ***n.*** 霍梅尼〔全名为Ayatollah Ruhollah ~, 1902—1989, 伊朗政治和宗教领袖〕。

Khond [kɔnd; kɔnd] ***n.*** 孔德人〔印度中东部德拉维德各部落的居民〕。

Khor·ram·shahr [ˌkɔːrəmˈʃɑː; ˏkɔrəmˋʃɑr] ***n.*** 霍拉姆沙赫尔〔伊朗港市〕。

Kho·war [ˈkəuwaː; ˋkowɑr] ***n.*** 高瓦尔语〔巴基斯坦西北部使用的一种印度—伊朗语〕。

Khrush·chev [kruːʃˈtʃɔːf; kruʃˋtʃɔf], **N. S.** 赫鲁晓夫〔1894—1971, 曾任前苏联部长会议主席(1958—1964)〕。

khud [kʌd; kʌd] ***n.*** 〔Hind.〕悬崖,绝壁;峡谷。*a ~ stick* 爬山杖。

khus·khus [ˈkʌskəs; ˋkʌskəs] ***n.*** (印度)须芒草茎〔可做扇子〕(= cuscus)。

kHz = kilohertz.

Ki. = Kings.

KIA = killed in action 阵亡。

ki·ang [kiːˈæŋ; kiˋæŋ] ***n.*** (内蒙古、西藏的)骞驴(*Equus kiang*)。

kib·ble[1][ˈkibl; ˋkɪbl] ***n.*** (凿井用的)铁吊桶。

kib·ble[2][ˈkibl; ˋkɪbl] **I** ***vt.*** 把…磨成粗粒;把…压成碎块。~*d biscuits* 压碎的饼干。**II** ***n.*** (磨成粗粒[压成碎块]的食物[狗食等]。

kib·butz [kiˈbuːts, -ˈbuts; kɪˋbuts, -ˋbuts] ***n.*** (*pl.* ***-butzim*** [ˌkiːbuˈtsiːm; ˏkibuˋtsim]) (以色列)集居区〔尤指集体农场〕。

kib·butz·nik [kiˈbuːtsnik; kɪˋbutsnɪk] ***n.*** (以色列)集居区居民;集体农场农民。

kibe [kaib; kaɪb] ***n.*** 〔古〕冻疮〔尤指脚后跟的冻疮〕。***gall*** [***tread on***] ***sb.'s*** ~***s*** 触及某人痛处,伤害某人感情。

ki·bit·ka [kiˈbitkə; kɪˋbɪtkə] ***n.*** 〔Russ.〕**1.** (鞑靼人的)圆顶帐篷。**2.** (俄国)有篷顶的乡下雪车。

kib·itz [ˈkibits; ˋkɪbɪts] ***vi.*** 〔口〕(牌戏旁观者等)多嘴,乱出主意;多管闲事。— ***vt.*** (看牌戏等时)对(牌戏等)乱出主意。~ *a card game* 看玩纸牌时乱出主意。

kib·itz·er [ˈkibitsə; ˋkɪbɪtsɚ] ***n.*** (观看牌戏等时)乱出主意的人,多管闲事的人。

kib·lah [ˈkiblaː; ˋkɪblɑ] ***n.*** 〔Ar.〕穆斯林朝觐的方向〔即朝着麦加殿堂的方向〕。

ki·bosh [ˈkaibɔʃ; ˋkaɪbɑʃ] ***n.*** 〔俚〕胡说。***put the ~ on*** 使彻底失败,挫败,制服(*Another such injury will put the ~ on his athletic career.* 再受一次这样的伤,就会使他的运动事业告吹)。

kick[1][kik; kɪk] **I** ***vt.*** **1.** 踢。**2.**【机】朝…反冲,(枪炮等)向…后坐。**3.**〔美俚〕拒绝(求婚者);申斥;解雇。**4.** 戒除(毒瘾)。**5.** (足球)踢球(得分)。**6.** 使(汽车)加速。~ *the ball back* 把球踢回去。~ *the car into higher gear* 给汽车挂快档。*The gun ~ed his shoulders.* 枪因后坐力的作用撞着他的肩膀。~ *goal* 踢进一球得分。— ***vi.*** **1.** 踢。**2.** (枪炮等)后坐;【机】反冲;(仪表指针)急冲,突跳。**3.**〔口〕反对,反抗;发牢骚。**4.**【板球】反跃(*up*)。**5.**〔俚〕死。*That horse ~s.* 那匹马老爱踢。~ ***about*** = ~ *around*. ~ ***against*** [***at***] 向…踢;反对,反抗,拒绝(~ *against* [*at*] *harsh treatment* 对虐待表示抗议)。~ ***around***〔口〕**1.** 仗势欺人。**2.** 到处流浪;经常改变行业。**3.** 从各个角度考虑[调查、讨论等]。**4.** 海阔天空地随便聊。~ ***back*** **1.** 踢回;反冲;〔口〕突然退缩。**2.**〔美俚〕退赔(赃物)。**3.** 交付(租金、佣金、酬金等)。~ ***in*** **1.** 破门而入。**2.**〔俚〕死。**3.**〔美〕捐(款),捐助;清还。~ ***off*** **1.** 踢脱(鞋等)。**2.** (足球)中线开球;开始(某种活动)。**3.**〔俚〕翘辫子,死。~ ***oneself*** 严厉自责。~ ***out*** **1.** 踢出。**2.** 踢足球出界。**3.**〔口〕逐出,解雇,开除。~ ***sb. downstairs*** 把某人踢下楼;撵走,赶出。~ ***sb. upstairs*** 把某人踢上楼;明升暗降。~ ***the bucket***〔俚〕翘辫子,死去。~ ***the clouds*** [***wind***] 被绞死。~ ***up*** 踢起(灰尘);引起(骚动)。~ ***up a dust*** [***fuss, row, shindy, shine***]〔俚〕引起骚扰。~ ***up its heels*** (马)溜腿。~ ***up one's heels*** **1.** 高兴得跳起来。**2.** 活跃一阵。**3.**〔俚〕翘辫子,死去。**II** ***n.*** **1.** 踢;踢伤。**2.** 反冲;反应力;反击力;(枪炮等的)后坐力;(赛跑等的)冲刺力。**3.**〔口〕反对,拒绝;牢骚。**4.** 踢足球;踢足球的人。**5.**〔口〕(酒等的)刺激;极度的兴奋[快感]。**6.**〔英俚〕六便士硬币。**7.**〔俚〕戏闹;猛烈出击。**8.**〔俚〕提高。**9.**〔the ~〕〔俚〕解雇,撤职。*a death-bed* [*dying, last*] ~垂死挣扎。*give a ~ at* 踢一下。*The bruise was caused by a ~.* 这伤痕是脚踢的。*I have no ~ against that.* 我对于那一点并无异议。*a bad ~*足球踢得糟的人。*a good ~*踢足球的好手。*get a big ~ out of ...*〔美俚〕从…得到极大的快感[愉快]。*a whiskey with lots of ~ in it* 劲儿很足的威士忌酒。*There is not much ~ in the cocktail.* 这种鸡尾酒没有多少劲儿。*two and a ~* 二先令六便士。*a demand for a salary ~*要求增加工资。*have no ~ left*〔口〕无力反抗,无反击力。***a ~ in one's gallop***〔俚〕异想天开。***a ~ in the pants*** [***teeth***] 意想不到的挫折。***get the ~***〔俚〕被解雇,***give sb. the ~***免某人职,解雇某人。(***get***) ***more ~s than halfpence*** 未受优待反遭虐待,很费力气而很少获利,得不偿失。***on a ~***〔美俚〕正在迷恋。***off a ~***不再迷恋。~**-ass**〔美俚〕**I** ***a.*** 粗暴的;强大的。**II** ***n.*** 精力,活力。~**-back** **1.**〔口〕强烈的反应。**2.**〔俚〕佣金[酬金、回扣等]的支付。**3.** 佣金,酬金,回扣。~**ball** 儿童垒足球〔垒球规则的足球游戏〕。~**boxing** 脚踢式拳击〔泰国等流行的一种允许用光脚踢对方的一种拳击〕。~**-it centre** (美国)戒毒中心。~**-off** ***n.*** **1.** (足球)开球。**2.** (战役或运动等)开始;首回。~**on** (自动寻线机)跳出。~**out** ***n.*** **1.** (足球中的)踢球出界。**2.**〔口〕撵走;撤职,解雇。~ **pad**〔美俚〕解除麻醉毒瘾的场所。~ **pleat** 运动褶裙。~ **sorter**〔口〕振辐分析器,选分仪。~**stand** 自行车或摩托车支架;撑脚架。~**-start** ***vt.*** 强力启动;为…提供最初推动力。~ **starter** (摩托车等的)反冲式起动器。~ **transformer** 脉冲变压器。~ **turn** 活动[转动]撑架。~ **up**〔口〕骚乱;吵闹,鼓噪。

kick[2][kik; kɪk] ***n.*** (玻璃瓶等的)凹底。

Kick·a·poo [ˈkikəˌpuː; ˋkɪkəˏpu] ***n.*** (*pl.* ~(*s*)) **1.** 克卡普人〔墨西哥印第安人部落的人〕。**2.** 克卡普语。

kick·er [ˈkikə; ˋkɪkɚ] ***n.*** **1.** 踢人者。**2.** 爱踢的马。**3.**〔口〕爱唱反调的人,发牢骚者。**4.** (枪炮中的)送弹装置。**5.**【宇】喷射器;抛掷器。**6.**〔俚〕未料到的困难;隐藏的

难点。**7.**〔俚〕出乎意料的结局;突然的转折。**8.**〔俚〕(游艇等艇身之外的)辅助发动机。

kick·shaw [ˈkikʃɔː; ˋkɪk͵ʃɔ] ***n*. 1.** 佳肴;特别讲究的菜。**2.** 华而不实的小玩意儿。

kid[1] [kid; kɪd] **I *n*. 1.** 小山羊;小羚羊。**2.** 小山羊皮;(食用)小山羊肉;〔*pl*.〕小山羊皮手套[皮鞋]。**3.**〔口〕孩子,少年,儿童。**II *a*. 1.** 小山羊皮制的。**2.** 较幼的。*my ~ brother* (*sister*) 我的小弟弟(妹妹)。*a ~ prof* 〔美俚〕年轻教授[讲师]。*the ~ lay* 抢夺[偷]外出购物的儿童的钱〔盗贼用语〕。**III *vi*., *vt*.** (**-*dd*-**) (山羊、羚羊等)产(小羊)。~ **divorce** (法律上)子女与父母脱离关系。~**-glove(d)** ***a*.** 温和的;过分讲究的;考虑周到的(*~-glove(d) methods* 软的手段)。~ **gloves** 羔皮手套(*handle with ~ gloves* 〔口〕小心而巧妙地处理[对待];作圆通处理)。~ **skin** 羊羔皮〔制鞋、手套用〕。~**(s') stuff**〔俚〕适合于孩子的东西;极简单容易的东西。~**ware** (电脑的)儿童软件〔一般供 6–10 岁儿童使用的教育和游戏软件〕。

kid[2] [kid; kɪd] **I *n*.** 嘲弄;欺骗。**II *vt*.** (**-*dd*-**) **1.** 欺骗;愚弄。**2.** 取笑,戏弄。*It's the truth; I wouldn't ~ you*. 这是真的,我不骗你。— ***vi*.** 戏弄,取闹 (*around*)。*No kidding*. 别开玩笑。

kid[3] [kid; kɪd] ***n*.** (水手盛食物的)小木桶。

Kidd [kid; kɪd] ***n*.** 基德〔姓氏〕。

Kid·der·min·ster [ˈkidəminstə; ˋkɪdə͵mɪnstɚ] ***n*.** (英国基德明斯特市所产两面花纹颜色相反的)双面提花地毯。

kid·die [ˈkidi; ˋkɪdɪ] ***n*.** = kiddy.

kid·dle [ˈkidl; ˋkɪdl] ***n*.** 鱼梁;鱼簖〔捕鱼的一种工具〕。

kid·dush [kiˈduːʃ, ˈkiduʃ; kɪˋduʃ, ˋkɪdʊʃ] ***n*.**【犹】吉都什〔节日和安息日(星期六)前夕举行的祝福仪式〕。

kid·dy, [ˈkidi; ˋkɪdɪ] ***n*.** (*pl*. **-*dies***)〔口〕小家伙,小孩〔kid 的昵称〕。~ **car** 小孩玩的三轮脚踏车。

kid·nap [ˈkidnæp; ˋkɪdnæp] ***vt*.** (〔英〕**-*pp*-**)诱拐(小孩等);绑架。

kid·nap·ee [ˈkidnæpi; ˋkɪdnæpɪ] ***n*.**〔美〕被绑架的人,肉票。

kid·nap·per [ˈkidnæpə; ˋkɪdnæpɚ] ***n*.** 拐子;绑架者。

kid·ney [ˈkidni; ˋkɪdnɪ] ***n*. 1.**【解】肾。**2.** (动物的)腰子〔供食用〕。**3.** 脾气,性格。*a man of that ~*那一种脾气的人。*a man of the right ~*脾气好的人。*artificial ~*人工肾。~ **basin** 腰盘。~ **beans** 菜豆;肾形豆。~**-buster**〔美俚〕**1.** 崎岖不平的路。**2.** 颠簸得非常厉害的卡车。~ **machine** = artificial ~. ~ **ore** 肾状矿石。~ **potato** 卵形马铃薯。~**-shaped *a*.** 肾形的。~ **stone**【医】肾结石。

kid·ol·o·gy [kiˈdɔlədʒi; kɪˋdɑlədʒɪ] ***n*. 1.** 儿童心理学。**2.**〔英口〕笑料,笑柄。

kid·ult [ˈkidʌlt; ˋkɪdʌlt] ***a*.** (电视节目等)同时适合儿童和成年人口味的。

kid·vid [ˈkidvid; ˋkɪdvɪd] ***n*.**〔美口〕儿童电视节目。

kief [kiːf; kif] ***n*.** = keef.

kiel·ba·sa [kiːlˈbaːsə; kilˋbɑsə] ***n*.** (*pl*. **-*si*** [-siː; -si], **~*s***) 〔Pol.〕波兰熏肠。

K

Kiel [kiːl; kil] ***n*.** 基尔〔德国港市〕。~ **Canal** 基尔运河。

kier [kiə; kɪr] ***n*.** (漂白、染色用的)煮布锅。

kie·sel·guhr, kie·sel·gur [ˈkiːzlguə; ˋkizl̩͵gʊr] ***n*.**【地】矽[硅]藻土。

kie·ser·ite [ˈkiːzərait; ˋkizə͵raɪt] ***n*.**【地】硫镁矾,水镁矾。

Ki·ev [ˈkiːev; kiˋɛv] ***n*.** 基辅〔乌克兰城市〕。

kif [kif; kɪf] ***n*.** = kef.

Ki·ga·li [kiˈgɑːli; kiˋgɑlɪ] ***n*.** 基加利〔卢安达首都〕。

kike [kaik; kaɪk] ***n***〔俚、蔑〕犹太人。

Ki·kon·go [kiːˈkɔŋgəu; kiˋkɑŋgo] ***n*. 1.** 刚果人〔即班图人〕。**2.** 刚果语〔即班图语〕。

Ki·ku·yu [kiˈkuːjuː; kɪˋkuju] ***n*. 1.** (*pl*. ~(*s*)) 吉库尤人〔肯尼亚从事农业生产者〕。**2.** 吉库尤语〔吉库尤人讲的班图语〕。

kil. = kilometre(s).

kil·der·kin [ˈkildəkin; ˋkɪldɚkɪn] ***n*. 1.** 基德尔钦〔英国旧容量单位,等于 16—18 加仑,即 1/2 桶(barrel)〕。**2.** (装液体等的)小桶。

kil·erg [ˈkiləːg; ˋkɪl͵ɝg] ***n*.**【物】千尔格〔功的单位〕。

Kil·i·man·ja·ro [ˈkilimənˈdʒɑːrəu; ˋkɪlɪmənˋdʒɑro], **Mount** 吉力马扎罗山〔非洲最高峰,高 19,321 英尺〕。

kill[1] [kil; kɪl] **I *vt*. 1.** 杀死,弄死;屠宰,屠杀。**2.** 扼杀,毁掉。**3.** 消磨(时间)。**4.** 中和;抵消。**5.** 否决(议案等);(断然)拒绝(申请等)。**6.** 涂掉,删去。**7.** (网球等的)杀(球)。**8.**〔口〕使着迷,使感到有趣。**9.** 煞住,使停住,使(机器等)停止运转;切断(电流)。**10.** 耗尽;喝光,吃光。**11.** 使(声音)降低[消失]。**12.** 使筋疲力尽,喝光。*be ~-ed in action* 阵亡,战死沙场。*The frost ~ed the seedings*. 严霜把幼苗冻坏了。*~ sb.'s appetite* 使某人倒胃口。*The news ~ed their hopes*. 这消息使他们的希望破灭。*~ time* 消磨时间。*The wallpaper ~s the furniture*. 家具给糊墙纸衬得不好看了。*~ a bill* 否决议案。*~ a petition* 毅然拒绝申请。*The editor ~ed the local item*. 编辑把地方新闻删去了。*The funny play nearly ~ed me*. 这个有趣的剧儿乎把我笑死了。*~ a live circuit* 截断通电电路。*~ an engine* 使发动机停火。*~ one's hunger* 充饥。*~ the pain* 止痛。*They ~-ed a bottle of wine*. 他们把一瓶酒喝完了。— ***vi*. 1.** 杀,杀害;被杀死。**2.** (植物等)被弄死;(家畜等)适于屠宰。**3.** 产生不可抗拒的效果。*Thou shalt not ~*. (摩西十诫中)不可杀人。*These flowers ~ easily*. 这些花很容易枯死。*The ox ~s well*. 牛的出肉率高。***be dressed*** [***got up***] ***to ~*** 着意打扮以求迷人。~ ***down*** 杀死;冻死。~ ***off*** [***out***] 杀光,消灭。~ ***oneself to***〔接不定式〕〔美口〕费九牛二虎之力去(…)。~ ***or cure*** 孤注一掷,好歹(*I'll try it, ~ or cure*. 不论吉凶祸福,我都要试一试)。~ ***two birds with one stone***〔谚〕一石二鸟,一举两得。~ ***with kindness*** 爱之适以害之,宠坏。***to ~***〔俚〕过分地,过度地(*dance to ~*拼命地跳舞)。**II *n*. 1.** 杀死,杀伤。**2.** (被打死的)猎获物。**3.** (网球等的)杀球。**4.** 被击毁的敌机[敌舰、敌潜艇等]。*mass ~ weapons* 大规模杀伤性武器。*a plentiful ~*丰富的猎获物。***be in at the ~* 1.** 猎物被杀时在场。**2.** 事情结尾时在场。~**-devil 1.** 假饵。**2.**〔方〕一种甜酒;劣质廉价饮料。~**joy *n*. 1.** 扫兴的人[物]。**2.** 令人扫兴的,煞风景的。~ **shot**【体】扣杀。~**time *n*.** 用来消磨时间的事,消遣。

kill[2] [kil; kɪl] ***n*.**〔美方〕水路,小河〔常用作地名:Schuyl*kill*, Cats*kill*〕。

kill·deer [ˈkildiə; ˋkɪldɪr] ***n*.** (*pl*. ~(*s*))【动】双胸斑沙鸻(*Charadrius vociferus*)〔北美所产的一种小鸟,叫声又高又尖〕。

killed [kild; kɪld] ***a*. 1.** 被杀死的;被屠宰的。**2.**【冶】镇静的。**3.**【化】饱和了的。**4.** 断开的。**5.** (疫苗等)不再有传染力的。~ *lines* 断线。~ **lime** 消石灰,失效石灰。~ **steel** 优质钢,镇静钢。

kil·ler [ˈkilə; ˋkɪlɚ] ***n*. 1.** 杀人者,凶手。**2.** 逆戟鲸(= ~whale)。**3.** 杀死…的药剂[东西],宰杀的器具。**4.**〔口〕迷人的人[物]。**5.**【无】限制器,抑制器,瞄准器。**5.** 待屠宰的牲畜。*a humane ~*使动物无痛苦的屠宰机。*a submarine ~*防潜舰艇。*a weed ~*除草药。*a noise ~*噪声抑制器。*a robot ~*雷达自动瞄准器。*a spot ~*亮点消除器,余辉消除器。*That flowered hat is a real ~*. 那顶花帽真漂亮。~ **bee** 杀人蜂〔一种凶悍伤人的非洲蜜蜂〕。~ **boat** 捕鲸船。~**-diller**〔俚〕突出的人(或事物);不平常的人(或事物)。~ **instinct** 嗜杀本能。~ **satellite** 拦截卫星。~ **technology** 科技杀手〔指一旦推出即压倒本领域其它一切技术的新科技手段〕。

kil·lick [ˈkilik; ˋkɪlɪk] ***n*. 1.** 小锚,石锚。**2.** 做锚用的石块。

kil·li·fish [ˈkilifiʃ; ˋkɪlɪfɪʃ] *n*. (*pl*. ~(*es*))【动】鳉科(*Cyprinodontidae*)鱼,底鳉。

kill·ing [ˈkiliŋ; ˋkɪlɪŋ] **I** *a*. **1**. 致死的。**2**. 使人疲乏的。**3**.〔口〕吸引人的,迷人的。**4**.〔口〕滑稽的。*a ~ disease* 致命的病。*a ~ work* 令人精疲力竭的工作。*a ~ caricature* 笑死人的漫画。**II** *n*. **1**. 杀害,屠杀。**2**. (一次行猎的)猎获品。**3**. (交易等)赚的一笔大钱;突然获得的大成功。*make a ~ on silk deal* 做丝绸生意赚大钱。**-ly** *ad*.〔口〕吸引人地,迷人地。

kil·lock [ˈkilək; ˋkɪlək] *n*. = killick.

Kil·mer [ˈkilmə; ˋkɪlmɚ] *n*. 基尔默〔姓氏〕。

kiln [kiln; kɪln] **I** *n*. 窑。**II** *vt*. 在窑里烧制[烘干]。~-**dry** *vt*. 在窑内烘干。~ **man** *n*. 烧窑工人。

kil·o- *comb.f*. 表示"千": *kilo*watt.

Ki·lo [ˈkiːləu; ˋkɪlo] *n*. 通讯中用以代表字母 k 的词。

ki·lo [ˈkiːləu; ˋkɪlo] *n*. **1**. 公斤,千克(= kilogram)。**2**. 公里千米(= kilometer)。~ **bomb**【军】轻燃烧弹,重一公斤的燃烧弹。

ki·lo [ˈkiːləu; ˋkɪlo] (*pl*. ~*s*) *n*. = kilogramme, kilometre, kilolitre. &c.

kil·o·am·pere [ˈkiləuˌæmpɛə; ˋkɪloˏæmpɪr] *n*. 千安培。

kil·o·bar [ˈkiləuˌbɑː; ˋkɪləˏbɑr] *n*. 千巴〔汽压单位〕。

kil·o·byte [ˈkiləuˌbait; ˋkɪloˏbaɪt] *n*.【计】千字节〔电脑信息单位, =1000 字节〕。

kil·o·cal·o·rie [ˈkiləuˌkæləriː; ˋkɪləˏkæləri] *n*. 大卡,千卡〔热量单位〕。

kil·o·cu·rie [ˈkiləuˌkjuəri; ˋkɪləˏkjurɪ] *n*.【原】千居里,放射性强度单位〕。

kil·o·cy·cle [ˈkiləuˌsaikl; ˋkɪləˏsaɪkl̩] *n*.【无】千周,千赫(兹)。

kil·o-e·lec·tron-volt [ˈkiləuiˈlektrənˈvəult; ˋkɪloɪˋlɛktrɑnˋvolt] *n*.【原】千电子伏特。

kil·o·gram(me) [ˈkiləugræm; ˋkɪləˏgræm] *n*. 公斤,千克。

kil·o·gram-me·tre, 〔美〕**kil·o·gram-me·ter** [ˈkiləgræmˈmiːtə; ˋkɪləˏgræmˋmitɚ] *n*.【物】公斤米,千克米〔功的单位〕。

kil·o·hertz [ˈkiləuˌhəːts; ˋkɪləˏhɝts] *n*. (*pl*. **-hertz**) 千赫。

kil·o·li·ter, 〔英〕**kil·o·li·tre** [ˈkiləuliːtə; ˋkɪləlitɚ] *n*. 千升。

kil·o·me·ter, 〔英〕**kil·o·li·tre** [ˈkiləuˌmiːtə; ˋkɪləˏmitɚ] *n*. 千米,公里。**-met·ric**, **-ri·cal** *a*.

kil·o·par·sec [ˈkiləuˌpɑːˌsek; ˋkɪləˏpɑrˏsɛk] *n*.【天】千秒差距。

kil·o·stere [ˈkiləuˌstiə; ˋkɪləˏstɪr] *n*. 千立方米。

kil·o·ton [ˈkiləuˌtʌn; ˋkɪləˏtʌn] *n*. 千吨〔核爆力单位〕。

kil·o·var [ˈkiləuvɑː; ˋkɪləˏvɑr] *n*.【电】千乏,无效千伏安。

kil·o·volt [ˈkiləuvəult; ˋkɪləˏvolt] *n*.【电】千伏(特)。

kil·o·volt-am·pere [ˈkiləuˌvəultˈæmpɛə; ˋkɪləˏvoltˋæmpɪr] *n*. 千伏(特)安(培)。

kil·o·watt [ˈkiləuwɔt; ˋkɪləˏwɑt] *n*.【电】千瓦(特)。~-**hour**【电】千瓦(特)(小)时,略作 K.W.H.〕。~-**meter** 千瓦计,电力计。

Kil·pat·rick [kilˈpætrik; kɪlˋpætrɪk] *n*. 基尔帕特里克〔姓氏〕。

kilt [kilt; kɪlt] **I** *n*. **1**. (苏格兰高地男子穿的)褶叠短裙,〔通常用格子呢制做〕。**2**. (妇女和儿童穿的)苏格兰式短裙。**II** *vt*.〔Scot.〕**1**. 卷起,撩起(裙等)(*up*)。**2**. 使(衣服)有直褶。

kil·ter [ˈkiltə; ˋkɪltɚ] *n*.〔美俚〕(身心等的)良好状态。*in* ~情形好,舒服。*out of* ~情形不好,不舒服。

kilt·ie [ˈkilti; ˋkɪltɪ] *n*. (*pl*. ~*s*) 穿苏格兰高地短裙的人[兵]。

kim·ber·lite [ˈkimbəlait; ˋkɪmbɚˏlaɪt] *n*.【地】角砾云橄岩,金伯利岩。

kim·chi [ˈkimtʃiː; ˋkɪmtʃi] *n*.〔Kor.〕朝鲜泡菜。

ki·mo·no [kiˈməunəu; kɪˋmono] *n*. (*pl*. ~*s*)〔Jap.〕**1**. 和服。**2**. 和服式女晨衣。

kin [kin; kɪn] **I** *n*. **1**.〔集合词〕亲属,亲戚。**2**. 亲属关系。**3**. 家族,门第。**4**. 性质相似的东西;地位[职业]相近的人。*What ~ is he to you*? 他和你是什么关系? *He comes of good ~*. 他出身好。*We are near of ~*. 我们是近亲。**II** *a*. **1**. 有亲属关系的。**2**. 同类的,同质的。*He is ~ to me*. 他是我的亲属。*We are ~*. 我们是亲属。**be ~ to 1**. 是…的亲戚。**2**. 类似,近于。***count ~ with***〔Scot.〕**1**. 和…算亲属关系,和…是近亲。**2**. 和…比血统[门第]。***more ~ than kind*** 亲戚不亲。***near of ~*** 近亲。***next of ~***【法】最近的亲族。***of ~*** 有亲属关系(*They are not of ~*. 他们没有亲属关系)。**-less** *a*. 无家属[亲属]关系的。**-ship** *n*. 家属[亲属]关系;像家属[亲属]的密切关系。

-kin *suf*. 表示"小": lamb*kin*, prince*kin*.

kin- *comb.f*. = *kine*.

kin·aes·the·si·a [ˌkinisˈθiːʒə; ˏkɪnɪsˋθiʒə] *n*.【心】动觉(= kinesthesia, kinaesthesis)。**kin·aes·thet·ic** [-ˈθetik; -ˋθɛtɪk] *a*.

ki·nase [ˈkaineis, ˈkineis; ˋkaɪnes, ˋkɪnes] *n*.【生化】激酶。

kin·chin [ˈkintʃin; ˋkɪntʃən] *n*.〔俚〕小孩〔盗贼隐语〕。*the ~ lay*〔盗贼俚〕抢[偷]外出购物小孩的钱。

kind[1] [kaind; kaɪnd] *a*. **1**. 厚道的,仁慈的,仁爱的;和蔼的。**2**. 亲切的。**3**.〔古〕相爱的,充满柔情的。**4**. 容易处理的;(毛)柔软的;(矿石)易采的。*be ~ to* 对…厚道。*be so kind as to* (*do*) = *be ~ enough to* (*do*) 请…。*It is very ~ of you*. 谢谢你的好意。*It is very ~ of you to come*. 难得你来。*He has a ~ word for everybody*. 他对任何人说话都很恳切。*Your ~ attention will oblige*. 请您费心,拜托拜托。*Give my ~ regards to....* 请代我向…问好。*with ~ regards* 祝好,致敬礼〔信尾用语〕。*stone ~ for dressing* 容易加工的石头。

kind[2] [kaind; kaɪnd] *n*. **1**. 种;类;属;〔贬〕帮,伙。**2**. 性质,本质。**3**. 实物,商品;同样的东西。**4**.〔古〕天性;家族,世系。**5**.〔古〕方式,方法。**6**.【宗】圣餐用品,圣礼〔指面包及葡萄酒〕。*that ~ of bread* 那一种面包。*the human ~* 人类。*the cat ~* 猫属。*many different ~s of things* [*stamps*] 许多不同种类的东西[邮票]。*He is not the ~ of person to lie*. 他不是那种说谎的人。*Hitler and his ~* 希特勒之流。*differ in ~, not merely in degree* 不仅程度不同,性质也不同。*act after one's ~* 按自己的一套作法办理。***a ~ of* 1**. 一种,一类(*He is a ~ of fool*. 他是一种傻瓜。*a ~ of gentleman* 绅士一类的家伙)。**2**. 几分;稍稍(*have a ~ of feeling that ...* 有点感觉到…)。***all ~s of*** 各种各样的。***in a ~*** 有几分,在某种程度上。***in ~* 1**. 用实物(*pay in ~* 用实物缴纳)。**2**. 以同样的方法(回敬)(*be repaid in ~ for one's rudeness* 以无礼回报无礼)。**3**. 性质上(*differ in ~* 性质上不同)。~ ***of***〔口〕有点儿;有几分(*I ~ of thought he would come*. 我有点儿感到他要来)。★ ~ of 常被说作 kind o', kind a' [ˈkaində; ˋkaɪndə], kinder [ˈkaində; ˋkaɪndɚ], 主要在形容词前,有时在动词前用作副词: *That's ~ o' good*. 那个还好。*He acted kinder ugly*. 他干得有点儿丢脸。*He ~ o'* [*kinder*] *laughed*. 他有点儿要笑。***nothing of the ~*** 毫不相似,决不是那样(*I shall do nothing of the ~*. 我决不做这种事)。***of a ~* 1**. 同一种类的(*Things of a ~ come together*. 物以类聚)。**2**. 徒有其名的;蹩脚的(*coffee of a ~* 徒有其名的咖啡)。***something of the ~*** 那一类的东西。***these ~ of men = men of this ~***〔口〕这样的人。***the worst ~***〔美口〕极其,非常(*He loves this picture the worst ~*. 他极爱这张画)。

kind·a [ˈkaində; ˋkaɪndə] 〔口〕= kind of.

kin·der·gar·ten [ˈkindəˌgɑːtn; ˋkɪndəˏgɑrtn̩] ***n.*** 幼儿园;幼稚园。**-er** = kinder·gart·ner **1.** 幼稚园老师[保育员]。**2.** 幼稚园的儿童。

kind-heart·ed [ˈkaindˈhɑːtid; ˋkaɪndˋhɑrtɪd] ***a.*** 厚道的,仁慈的,富于同情心的。**-ly** ***ad.*** **-ness** ***n.***

kin·dle [ˈkindl; ˋkɪndl̩] ***vt.*** **1.** 点燃,照耀。**2.** 煽动,鼓舞,激发。～ *an audience* 煽动听众。～ *sb. with* [*to*] *passion* 激发某人的感情。— ***vi.*** **1.** 着火,烧起来。**2.** 发亮,照耀。**3.** 兴奋,激动。*Her eyes ～d with excitement.* 她兴奋得两眼闪闪发光。

kin·dling [ˈkindliŋ; ˋkɪndlɪŋ] ***n.*** **1.** 点火,燃烧。**2.** 〔常 *pl.*〕引火物;〔美〕引火柴(= ～ *wood*)。*His wagon was smashed into ～ wood.* 他的货车撞得稀烂。～ **point** 着火点,燃点。～ **temperature** 着火温度。

kind·ly [ˈkaindli; ˋkaɪndlɪ] **I** ***a.*** **1.** 厚道的,亲切的;有同情心的,体贴的。**2.** (气候等)温和的,宜人的;适于…的。**3.** 〔古〕自然的,天然的,天性的。**4.** 土生土长的。*a ～ heart* 慈悲心肠。*a ～ weather* 宜人的气候。～ *soil for crops* 适于耕作的土地。*the ～ fruits of the earth* 土地上生长的丰富果实。**II** ***ad.*** **1.** 厚道地,亲切地;有同情心地,体贴地。**2.** 诚恳地,衷心地。**3.** 请〔客套语〕。**4.** 自然地,容易地。*be ～ treated* 受到亲切接待。*Thank you ～.* 衷心地感谢你。*K- refrain from smoking.* 请勿吸烟。***take*** (***sth.***) ～ **1.** 善意地解释(事物)。**2.** 诚恳地接受(忠告等)。***take ～ to*** 自然而然地爱上了。**-li·ly** ***ad.*** **-liness** ***n.***

kind·ness [ˈkaindnis; ˋkaɪndnɪs] ***n.*** **1.** 厚道,亲切。**2.** 友好的态度[行为],好意。*out of ～* 出于好意。*Will you do me a ～?* 你能帮我一下忙吗?

kin·dred [ˈkindrid; ˋkɪndrɪd] **I** ***n.*** **1.** 宗族。**2.** 亲属[亲戚]关系;血缘关系。**3.** 〔集合词〕亲属;血缘族〔遗传学用语〕。**4.** 类似,同质 (*with*)。*claim ～ with sb.* 声称与某人有亲戚关系。**II** ***a.*** **1.** 亲属的;亲戚的;宗族的。**2.** 类似的,同种的,同源的,同性质的。～ *languages* 同源的语言。～ *tribes* 同族的部落。

kine[1] [kain; kaɪn] ***n.*** 〔*pl.*〕〔古〕母牛;牛。

kine[2] [ˈkini; ˋkɪnɪ] ***n.*** = kinescope.

kine- *comb. f.* 表示"运动": *kine*matic, *kine*tic.

kin·e·ma [ˈkinimə; ˋkɪnəmə] ***n.*** 〔英〕= cinema.

ki·ne·mat·ic(al) [ˌkainiˈmætik(əl); ˏkɪnəˋmætɪk(l̩)] ***a.*** 【物】运动学(上)的。～ **design** 机动设计。**-i·cal·ly** ***ad.***

ki·ne·mat·ics [ˌkainiˈmætiks; ˏkɪnəˋmætɪks] ***n.*** 【物】运动学。

kin·e·mat·o·graph [ˌkainiˈmætəgrɑːf; ˏkɪnəˋmætəˏgræf] ***n.***, ***vt.***, ***vi.*** = cinematograph. **-y** ***n.*** **-ic** ***a.***

ki·ne·mo·me·ter [ˌkainiˈmɔmitə; ˏkɪnəˋmɑmɪtə] ***n.*** 〔物〕流速计[表];感应式转速表,灵敏转速计。

kin·e·photo [ˈkainifəutə; ˋkɪnəˏfotə] ***n.*** 映像管录影;屏幕录影。～ *equipment* 屏幕录影设备。

kin·e·scope [ˈkiniskəup, ˈkaini-; ˋkɪnɪsˏkop, ˋkaɪnɪ-] **I** ***n.*** **1.** (电视)映像管。**2.** 映像管录影,电视屏幕纪录片。**II** ***vt.*** 拍摄(电视节目)的屏幕纪录片。*colour ～* 彩色映像管。～ **grid** 映像管控制栅极。～ **recorder** 屏幕录影机[录影装置]。～ **recording** 屏幕录影。

ki·ne·si·at·rics [kaiˌniːsiˈætriks; kaɪˏnisɪˋætrɪks] ***n.*** *pl.* 〔用作单数〕【医】运动疗法。

ki·ne·sics [kiˈniːsiks, kai-; kɪˋnisɪks, kaɪ-] ***n.*** *pl.* 〔用作单数〕人体动作学,举止神态学〔研究姿势、表情等非语言的人体动作与人际沟通的关系的一种科学〕。**ki·ne·sic** [-ˈnesik; -ˋnɛsɪk] ***a.***

ki·ne·si·ol·o·gy [kaiˌniːsiˈɔlədʒi, ki-; kaɪnisɪˋɑlədʒɪ, kɪ-] ***n.*** 【医】人体运动学。

-kinesis *comb. f.* 表示"运动": karyo*kinesis*.

ki·ne·si·the·ra·py [kaiˌniːsiˈθerəpi; kaɪˏnisɪˋθɛrəpɪ] ***n.*** 【医】运动疗法。

kin·es·the·si·a, kin·es·the·sis [ˌkainisˈθiːʒə, -sis; ˏkaɪnɪsˋθiʒə, -sɪs] ***n.*** 【医】运动觉。**kin·es·thet·ic** [-ˈθetik; -ˋθɛtɪk] ***a.***

ki·net·ic [kaiˈnetik; kaɪˋnɛtɪk] ***a.*** **1.** 【物】动力(学)的,运动的。**2.** 活动的,活跃的,能动的,有力的。～ *friction* 动摩擦。*the ～ molecular theory* 分子运动论。～ *theory of heat* [*gases*] 热[气态]运动论。*a man of ～ energy* [*force*] 精力充沛的人。～ **art** 动态艺术〔指部分设计成动态并配以音响、照明等的雕塑艺术〕。～ **energy** 动能。～ **friction** 动摩擦。

ki·net·ics [kaiˈnetiks; kaɪˋnɛtɪks] ***n.*** *pl.* 〔用作单数〕动力学。

ki·net·in [ˈkainətin; ˋkaɪnətɪn] ***n.*** 【植】激动素。

kinet·o- *comb. f.* 表示"运动": *kineto*graph, *kineto*scope.

ki·ne·to·graph [kaiˈniːtəgrɑːf; kaɪˋnitəˏgræf] ***n.*** (早期的)活动电影摄影机。**-er** ***n.*** **-ic** ***a.***

ki·ne·to·phone [kaiˈniːtəˌfəun, kiˈniː-; kaɪˋnitəˏfon, kɪˋni-] ***n.*** (早期的)有声电影机。

ki·net·o·plast [kiˈniːtəˌplæst; kɪˋnitəˏplæst] ***n.*** 【医】动基体。

ki·ne·to·scope [kaiˈniːtəskəup; kaɪˋnitəˏskop] ***n.*** (早期的)活动电影放映机。

kin·folk(s) [ˈkinfəuk(s); ˋkɪnˏfok(s)] ***n.*** 〔*pl.*〕亲戚,亲属(= kinsfolk)。

king [kiŋ; kɪŋ] **I** ***n.*** **1.** 王,国王,君主 (*opp.* subject);(部落的)首领,魁首。**2.** (某界)巨子,…大王。**3.** 王一样的东西。**4.** (纸牌中的)老 K(国王);(国际象棋的)王;(西洋跳棋的)王棋。**5.** 〔K-〕【宗】上帝,耶稣。**6.** (水果、植物等中)最上等品。**7.** 〔The K-s〕(《旧约圣经》中的)《列王纪》。*the K- of England* 英国国王。*a ～ of the Indians* 印第安人的首领。*an oil ～* 石油大王。*a pirate ～* 海盗头目。*a fur ～* 毛皮巨商。*a railway ～* 铁路大王。*the ～ of beasts* 百兽之王。*the ～ of birds* 鸟王〔指鹰〕。*K- of day* 太阳。～ *of fish* 鲸。*the ～ of gases* 芥气。*the ～ of metals* 金。*the ～ of middles* 〔美〕【拳】中量级拳击选手。*the ～ of the jungle* 虎。*the ～ of the countryside* 土皇帝。*the ～ of the sea* 〔谑〕鲱鱼。*the ～ of pears* 上等品种的梨。*tragedy ～* 在悲剧中扮演主角的男演员。***a K- Log*** 有名无实的君王,放任而无权的君王。***a ～ of shreds and patches*** 专事抄袭的小文人。***a K- stork*** 暴君。***go up K- Street*** 〔澳〕破产。***Kings go mad and the people suffer for it.*** 〔谚〕国王发狂,百姓遭殃。***Kings have long arms*** [***hands***]. 〔谚〕国王手长,百姓理短。***more royalist than the ～*** 比国王还国王。***The K- can do no wrong.*** 〔谚〕国王不会犯错误〔指国王无权,实权在内阁〕。***turn King's*** [***Queen's***, ***State's***] ***evidence*** 供出对同犯不利的证据。**II** ***vi.*** **1.** 做国王。**2.** 统治。— ***vt.*** 立…为王。～ ***it*** 做国王,统治;称王称霸 (*over*)。**K- at** [**of**] **Arms** 英国主管纹章的长官。～**bird** 【动】极乐鸟。～**bolt** 【机】中心立轴;(汽车转向关节)主销;大螺丝。**K- Charles's spaniel** 黑褐色长耳小狗。～ **cobra** 眼镜蛇,眼镜王蛇 (*Naja hannah*)。～ **crab** 鲎(= horseshoe crab)。～**craft** 统治者的统治权术。～**cup** 【植】鳞茎毛茛;驴蹄草。～ **fish** **1.** 食用大棘鳍。**2.** 〔美口〕头子,首领。～**fish·er** 翠鸟,鸡,鱼狗。**K- James Version** = Authorized Version. **K- Lear** **1.** 《李尔王》〔莎士比亚悲剧名〕。**2.** 该剧的主角李尔王〔传说中的英国国王〕。～**maker** ***n.*** **1.** 〔谑〕(总统竞选时)候选人手下的竞选工作人员;左右候选人选择的重要人物。**2.** 国王拥立者。**K- of Bliss** [**Glory, Heaven**] 神,基督。**K- of Kings** 神,上帝。**K- of the Castle** (小儿游戏中的)山寨大王。～ **oscillator** 主振荡器。～**pin** **1.** (滚球)中柱。**2.** 〔口〕首要人物,中心人物,领袖。**3.** = ～bolt. ～**post** 【建】人字架上的中柱,中柱,桁架中柱;【船】吊杆柱。～**-post truss** 【建】单柱桁架。～ **salmon** 大鳞大麻哈鱼。～**-size(d)** ***a.*** **1.** 特大

K

的,特长的。2. 不寻常的。~ **snake**【动】王蛇(*Lampropeltis getulus*)〔产于美国南部〕。~**truss**【建】有中柱的桁架,单柱桁架。~**wood** 1. (巴西)西阿拉黄檀木。2. 西阿拉黄檀树(*Dalbergia cearensis*)。**King's Bench** 英国高等法院。**King's blue** = cobalt blue【矿】钴蓝。**King's colour** 英军的团旗。**King's [Queen's] Council** 英国王室法律顾问。**King's [Queen's] English** 标准英语。**King's [Queen's] evidence**【法】刑事案件的揭发证词〔通常由同案犯提供〕。**King's evil** 瘰疬〔旧时认为此病经国王一触即可痊愈的迷信〕。**King's head**〔俚〕邮票。**King's highway** 1. 水陆交通干线。2. 行为的大道,正道。**king's picture [portrait]**〔英俚〕钱。**King's pipe** 伦敦船坞内的焚毁炉。**King's silver** 纯银。**King's weather** 适合庆典时的晴朗天气。**King's yellow** = orpiment 雌黄。**-less** *a*. 无国王的;无政府状态的。**-let** 1. 小王,小国的王。2.【动】戴菊鸟。**-like** *a*. 国王似的。**-ling** 小王。**-ship** *n*. 1. 王位;王权;王尊。2. 国王统治;君主政体。3. 陛下〔有时用作对君主的称谓,前面加 his〕。

king·dom [ˈkiŋdəm; ˋkɪŋdəm] *n*. 1. 王国。2.〔K-〕【宗】天国,神政。3. 领域。4. 界〔指自然三界之一〕。*the United K-* (大不列颠与北爱尔兰)联合王国。*the ~ of God [heaven]* 天国。*the ~ of science* 科学领域。*The mind is the ~ of thought*. 头脑是思想的王国。*the animal [vegetable, mineral]* ~动[植、矿]物界。***come into one's*** ~〔俚〕发迹,因继承财产而成为富翁,飞黄腾达,获得权力。~ ***come***〔口〕来世,天国(*go to ~ come* 死。*send sb. to ~ come* 送某人上西天)。

King·lake [ˈkiŋleik; ˋkɪŋlek] *n*. 金莱克〔姓氏〕。

king·ly [ˈkiŋli; ˋkɪŋlɪ] **I** *a*. 1. 国王的;君主地位的。2. 国王似的;适合国王身份的。3. 君主政体的。*the ~ power* 王权。*a ~ crown* 王冠。*a ~ bearing* 君王的风度。**II** *ad*. 国王似地。**-li·ness** *n*.

Kings·ton [ˈkiŋstən; ˋkɪŋstən] *n*. 1. 金斯敦〔牙买加首都〕。2. 金斯敦〔诺福克岛首府〕。3. 金斯敦〔圣文森特首府〕。

kink [kiŋk; kɪŋk] **I** *n*. 1. (线、绳、索、头发等的)纽结,绞缠。2. 乖僻,偏执;怪想法,狂念。3. 奇方妙法。4. (背、颈等处的)痉挛,抽筋。5. (计划的设想或机器设计等方面的)缺陷。**II** *vt*., *vi*. (使)纠结,(使)绞缠。~**-cough** *n*.【医】百日咳。

kin·ka·jou [ˈkiŋkədʒuː; ˋkɪŋkədʒu] *n*.【动】(中、南美产的)蜜熊。

kin·kle [ˈkiŋkl; ˋkɪŋkl̩] **I** *n*. 1. (头发等的)卷曲;小纽结。2.〔喻〕模糊的暗示。**II** *vt*., *vi*. (使)卷曲,(使)纽结。**-d** *a*. 卷曲的,有小纽结的。

kink·y [ˈkiŋki; ˋkɪŋkɪ] *a*. 1. 绞缠的;(头发)卷曲的。2.〔俚〕不正当的。3.〔英〕性情乖僻的,古怪的。~ *thread* 绞缠的线。~**-haired** *a*. 卷发的。

kin·ni·ki·nic(k) [ˌkinikiˈnik; ˏkɪnɪkəˋnɪk] *n*. (北美印第安人用树叶和树皮制成的)烟草代用品。

ki·no[1] [ˈkiːnəu; ˋkino] *n*. (*pl*. ~**s**) 桉树胶(= ~ gum)。

ki·no[2] [ˈkiːnəu; ˋkino] *n*. (*pl*. ~**s**) 电影院(= cinematograph)。

Kin·sey [ˈkinzi; ˋkɪnzɪ] *n*. 金西〔姓氏〕。

kins·folk [ˈkinzfəuk; ˋkɪnzˏfok] *n*.〔*pl*.〕〔集合词〕家属;亲戚;亲属〔亦作 ~s〕。

Kin·sha·sa [kinˈʃɑːsə; kɪnˋʃɑsə] *n*. 金沙萨〔刚果(金)首都〕。

kin·ship [ˈkinʃip; ˋkɪnʃɪp] *n*. 亲属关系,亲戚关系。

kins·man [ˈkinzmən; ˋkɪnzmən] *n*. (*pl*. **-men**) 男亲属。

kins·wom·an [ˈkinzˌwumən; ˋkɪnzˏwʊmən] *n*. (*pl*. **-wom·en** [-ˌwimin; -ˏwɪmən]) 女亲属。

kin·tal [ˈkintl; ˋkɪntl] *n*. = quintal.

ki·osk [kiˈɔsk; kɪˋɑsk] *n*. 1. (土耳其和波斯式的)凉亭,亭子。2. (车站、广场等处的)书报摊,音乐台,广告亭,公共电话亭。

Kio·to [kiˈəutəu; kiˋoto] *n*. = Kyoto 京都〔日本〕。

Ki·o·wa [ˈkaiəuwɑː, -əwə; ˋkaɪowɑ, -əwə] *n*. 1. (*pl*. ~(*s*)) 凯欧瓦人〔美国俄克拉荷马州印第安人〕。2. 凯欧瓦语。

kip[1] [kip; kɪp] *n*. (没有鞣制过的)生幼兽皮[小牛皮、羔羊皮]。

kip[2] [kip; kɪp] **I** *n*.〔俚〕旅店,客栈;床。**II** *vi*.〔俚〕1. 睡觉;住客栈。2. 逃学。

kip[3] [kip; kɪp] *n*. (*pl*. ~(*s*))〔老挝货币单位〕基普。

kip[4] [kip; kɪp] *n*. 基普〔重量单位,相当于 1,000 磅〕。

Kip·ling [ˈkipliŋ; ˋkɪplɪŋ] *n*. 1. 基普林〔姓氏〕。2. **Rudyard** ~ 拉迪亚德·基普林〔1865—1936,英国作家,诗人〕。

kip·per [ˈkipə; ˋkɪpɚ] **I** *n*. 1. (产卵期或产卵后的)雄鲑[鳟鱼]。2. 熏[腌]鲑鱼[鳟鱼]。3.〔俚〕人,家伙。**II** *vt*. 腌制[熏制、晒干](鲑、鲱等鱼)。

Kir·by [ˈkəːbi; ˋkɝbɪ] *n*. 柯比〔姓氏,男子名〕。

Kir·(g)hiz [ˈkəːgiz; ˋkɝgɪz] *n*. (*pl*. ~(*es*)) 1. 吉尔吉斯人。2. 吉尔吉斯语。

Kir·(g)hi·zia [kəːˈgiːziə; kɚˋgizɪə] *n*. 吉尔吉斯。**-n** *a*.

ki·ri [ˈkiri; ˋkɪrɪ] *n*.〔Jap.〕(日本)泡桐树。

kirk [kəːk; kɝk] *n*.〔Scot.〕教会。~**man** 1. 苏格兰教会的信徒。2.〔Scot.〕教士,教徒。~**-session** 苏格兰教会基层理事会。

kir·mess [ˈkəːmis; ˋkɝmɪs] *n*. kermess, kermis 的变体。

kirn [kəːn, kiən; kɝn, kɪrn] *n*.〔Scot., 英方〕1. 收获节。2. 收获完毕的最后一捆。

kirsch·was·ser [ˈkiəʃvɑːsə; ˋkɪrʃˏvɑsɚ] *n*.〔G.〕樱桃酒。

kir·tle [ˈkəːtl; ˋkɝtl̩] *n*. 1. 女长袍;外裙。2.〔古〕男外衣。

Ki·san·ga·ni [ˌkiːsənˈgɑːniː; ˏkisənˋgɑni] *n*. 基桑加尼〔刚果(金)城市〕。

Ki·shi·nev [ˈkiʃinef; ˋkɪʃəˏnɛf] *n*. 基什尼奥夫〔摩尔达维亚城市〕。

kish·ke [ˈkiʃkə; ˋkɪʃkə] *n*. = derma (= kishka)。

Kis·lev [ˈkislef; ˋkɪslɛf] *n*.〔Heb.〕(犹太历)三月。

kis·met [ˈkismet; ˋkɪsmɛt] *n*.〔Turk.〕〔常 K-〕命运,天命〔亦作 kismat〕。

kiss [kis; kɪs] **I** *n*. 1. 吻。2.〔诗〕(微风等的)轻拂,轻触,轻抚。3.【撞球】球与球的接触。4. 蛋白小甜饼;小糖果。5.〔儿〕(奶、茶等上浮的)泡泡。*give a ~* 接个吻。*snatch [steal] a* ~偷吻。***blow [throw] a ~ at [to] sb***. 向某人飞吻(= ~ ***one's hand to sb***.)。***Judas*** ~阴险的背叛,口蜜腹剑。**II** *vt*. 1. 吻。2.〔诗〕(微风等)轻拂,轻触,轻抚。~ *the baby on the cheek* = ~ *the baby's cheek* 吻婴儿的颊。~ *sb. goodby(e)* 吻别某人。~ *sth. goodby(e)* 无可奈何地失掉[去掉]某物。*The breeze ~ed the face*. 轻风拂面。— *vi*. 1. 接吻。2. 轻触,轻抚。3.【撞球】(球与球的)接触。~ *and be friends* 接吻复归于好。*make glasses* ~碰杯。~ ***away*** 1. 吻掉(眼泪等)。2. 为女人花费金钱。~ ***hand [the hand]*** 吻(国王的)手〔一种正式的致意或大臣等就任时的仪式〕。~ ***off***〔俚〕拒绝;(无理地)把…解雇,开除。~ ***one's hand to sb***. 向某人飞吻。~ ***the Bible [the Book]*** 吻《圣经》宣誓。~ ***the canvas [resin]***〔美俚〕(在职业性拳击中)被击倒。~ ***the dust*** 1. 屈服。2. 被杀。~ ***the ground*** 1. 俯伏在地。2. 受辱。~ ***the hare's foot*** 迟到。~ ***the post*** 吃闭门羹。~ ***the rod*** 受罚。~***up to (sb.)*** 拍(某人的)马屁。~**-and-tell** 详细描述个人隐私的。~**-ass**〔美俚〕1. 马屁精,谄媚者。2. 奉承拍马。~**-in-the-ring** *n*. (男女青年围成环状而相互追逐的)追吻游戏。~**-me-quick** *n*. 1. 垂于额前的卷发。2. (戴在头部后的)小罩帽。3.【植】野生三色紫罗兰[虎耳草]。~ **of death** 表面上友好实际上坑害人的行为。~ **of life**

(口对口的)人工呼吸;起死回生的措施。～**off** *n*.〔俚〕(特指粗暴无理的)解雇;开除。

kiss·er [ˈkisə; ˋkɪsɚ] *n*. **1**. 接吻者。**2**.〔俚〕嘴;嘴唇;脸,面孔。

kiss·ing [ˈkisiŋ; ˋkɪsɪŋ] *a*. **1**. 接吻的。**2**. 轻触的,轻抚的。**3**. 关系亲密的。*be on* ～ *term with* ... 同…交情不错。～ **bug 1**. 咬嘴唇;面孔等的害虫〔如锥鼻虫〕。**2**. 好接吻的人,想接吻的愿望(*She's got the* ～ *bug*. 她有想接吻的意思)。～ **cousin** [**kin**] **1**. 可以互行接吻礼的亲戚。**2**.〔俚〕关系融洽的人,可以相容的事。～ **crust** (烘烤时面包与面包接触处形成的)面包软壳。～ **gate** 〔英方〕(只能通过一人的)小门。

Kis·sin·ger [ˈkisəndʒə; ˋkɪsɪndʒɚ] *n*. 基辛格〔姓氏〕。

kiss·y [ˈkisi; ˋkɪsɪ] *a*.〔口〕想要接吻的。

kist[1] [kist; kɪst] *n*.〔Scot., 英方〕箱子;盒;柜子。

kist[2] [kist; kɪst] *n*. = cist.

kit[1] [kit; kɪt] **I** *n*. **1**.〔方〕木桶;(盛鱼、奶油等的)小桶。**2**. 成套工具[用具、物件、器材、设备];整套配件。**3**.【军】士兵的个人装备。**4**. 工具箱;工具袋;用具包;(旅行等的)行装。**5**.〔口〕全部;一群(人);一套东西。*shoemaker's* ～一套鞋匠用具。～ *inspection*【军】装备检查。*a travel* ～一套旅行用物件。*a riding* ～骑马的行装。*a tropical* ～用于热带地区的装备。*a first aid* ～急救药箱。*a spare parts* ～备用零件箱。*a tool* ～工具箱。(***the whole***) ～ ***and boodle*** [***caboodle***] 全部人马[全套东西]。**II** *vt*. (*-tt-*) 装备。～ **bag 1**. 长形帆布用具袋。**2**.【军】(士兵个人的)长形帆布装备袋。

kit[2] [kit; kɪt] *n*. (从前跳舞教师用的)小提琴。

kit[3], **kitt** [kit; kɪt] *n*. **1**. 小猫(= kitten)。**2**. 小狐;软毛小动物;软毛小动物的毛皮。

Ki·ta·kyu·shu [ˈkiːtɑːˈkjuːʃuː; ˋkitɑˋkjuʃu] *n*. 北九州〔日本港市〕。

Kit-Cat [ˈkitkæt; ˋkɪtkæt] *n*. **1**. 十八世纪英国辉格党人俱乐部的成员。**2**. [kit-cat] 小于半身但包括双手的画像(=～ portrait)。～ **Club**【英史】在詹姆士二世时辉格党的政治家们建立的俱乐部。

kitch·en [ˈkitʃin; ˋkɪtʃɪn] **I** *n*. **1**. 厨房,灶间。**2**.〔集合词〕炊事人员。**3**. (便于携带的)全套炊具。*an army field* ～军用野外炊具。**II** *a*. **1**. 厨房的。**2**. 在厨房工作的。**3**. (语言)粗俗的,不雅的。*a* ～ *help* 厨房帮手。～ **cabinet 1**. 厨柜。**2**. (=常用 K- C-)美国第七任总统杰克逊的)私人顾问团;政府首脑的私人顾问团[参谋团、智囊团]。～ **garden** 菜园。～ **maid** 帮厨女工。～ **match** 用于点煤气炉的粗头火柴。～ **midden**【考古】贝冢,贝丘。～ **physic** 滋补身体的食物;美味。～ **police 1**. 帮厨的士兵。**2**. (犯过失士兵的)帮厨勤务。～ **sink 1**. *n*. 厨房中的洗涤盆[水池];搬不动的东西;乱七八糟的东西;〔喻〕(绘画、戏剧等中)极端现实主义的东西(*everything but the* ～ *sink* 可以想像到的一切)。**2**. *a*. (剧本等)表现西方现代生活中肮脏情景的。～ **stuff 1**. 供烹饪用的食物〔尤指菜蔬〕。**2**. 厨房的下脚〔尤指从锅上弄下的油垢〕。～ **unit**〔英〕(兼做洗涤盆、厨柜的)一套厨房设备。～**ware** 厨房用具。

K

kitch·en·er [ˈkitʃinə; ˋkɪtʃɪnɚ] *n*. **1**. 厨师,厨房总管。**2**.〔英〕(烧饭用的)铁炉。

kitch·en·ette [ˌkitʃiˈnet; ˏkɪtʃɪˋnɛt] *n*. 小厨房。

kite [kait; kaɪt] **I** *n*. **1**.【动】鸢。**2**. 骗子;流氓,光棍。**3**. 风筝。**4**. 轻型飞机;风筝式飞机;〔美俚〕飞机。**5**. [*pl*.]【海】(微风时使用的)最高的轻帆。**6**.【商】抵用票据,空头支票。**7**.〔美俚〕信。***draw in a*** ～ 收风筝。***fly*** [***send up***] ***a*** ～ **1**. 放风筝。**2**. 试探舆论。**3**. 开空头支票。**4**.〔美〕(从狱中)非法寄出信件;(为告贷或求助而)寄航空信。***fly one's own*** ～图谋私利。***go fly a*** ～〔美俚〕滚开。***higher than a*** ～〔美俚〕**1**. 极高。**2**. 大醉。**II** *vi*.〔口〕**1**. (像风筝一样)上升,飞起。**2**.【商】用空头支票骗钱。— *vt*. **1**. 使(物价等)上涨。**2**.【商】用空头支票骗(人)。～**-airship** 系留气艇。～ **balloon** [**sausage**] (用于军事观测)圆柱形系留气球。～ **camera** 俯瞰图照相机。～**-flying**〔美〕(以事后便于否认的方式)胡乱发布政治新闻〔旨在试探舆论〕。～ **mark** (英国标准化协会的)规格说明标志。

kith [kiθ; kɪθ] *n*. **1**. 亲属。**2**.〔古〕朋友,相识,邻居。～ ***and kin*** 亲属;朋友。

kithe [kaið; kaɪð] *vt*., *vi*. (*kithed*, *kith·ing*)〔Scot., 英方〕**1**. 以行动表示,证明。**2**.〔废〕以语言表示,宣布,公布。

kit·kat [ˈkitkæt; ˋkɪtkæt] *n*. = kit-cat.

ki·tool [kiˈtuːl; kɪˋtul] *n*. = kittul.

kitsch [kitʃ; kɪtʃ] *n*. [G.] 迎合低级趣味的拙劣作品。**-y** *a*.

kit·ten [ˈkitn; ˋkɪtn] **I** *n*. **1**. 小猫。**2**. 小的哺乳动物。**3**. 顽皮姑娘。***have*** (***a litter of***) ～***s***〔口〕发怒;烦恼;兴奋。**II** *vi*., *vt*. (猫)产(仔)。～**ball**〔美〕垒球。

kit·ten·ish [ˈkitniʃ; ˋkɪtnɪʃ] *a*. **1**. 小猫似的;嬉耍的,活蹦乱跳的。**2**. 忸怩作态的。**-ly** *ad*. **-ness** *n*.

kit·ti·wake [ˈkitiweik; ˋkɪtɪˏwek] *n*.【动】三趾鸥;海鸥。

kit·tle [ˈkitl; ˋkɪtl̩] **I** *a*.〔Scot.〕**1**. 烦躁的,容易激动的。**2**. 敏捷的,灵巧的。**3**. 多变的,无常的。**4**. 难应付的,难驾驭的。～ *cattle* 难驾驭的牛;难对付的人[事]。**II** *vt*. **1**. 逗(人)笑;使快活。**2**. 使困惑,使为难。

Kit·tredge [ˈkitridʒ; ˋkɪtrɪdʒ] *n*. 基特里奇〔姓氏〕。

kit·tul [kiˈtuːl; kɪˋtul] *n*. (东印度的)棕榈[棕树]。

Kit·ty [ˈkiti; ˋkɪtɪ] *n*. 基蒂〔女子名, Catherine 的昵称〕。

kit·ty[1] [ˈkiti; ˋkɪtɪ] *n*.〔儿〕小猫。

kit·ty[2] [ˈkiti; ˋkɪtɪ] *n*. **1**. (纸牌戏中的)全部赌注。**2**. (从每人赌注中抽出的)头钱。**3**.〔口〕凑集的金钱[物品];共同的资金〔尤指小额集存的储蓄〕。

kit·ty-cor·nered [ˈkitiˌkɔːnəd; ˋkɪtɪˏkɔrnɚd] *a*., *ad*. = cater-cornered.

Ki·tu·ba [kiːˈtuːbə; kɪˋtubə] *n*. 吉土巴语〔刚果河下游及其支流一带所讲的商业语言,由刚果语、凌加拉语(*lingala*)和法语混合而成〕。

Kit·we [ˈkiːtwei; ˋkitwe] *n*. 基特伟〔赞比亚城市〕。

ki·va [ˈkiːvə; ˋkivə] *n*. 基瓦〔美国印第安人举行宗教仪式、开会、工作、休息等用的大圆屋〕。

ki·wi [ˈkiːwiː; ˋkiwi] *n*. **1**.【动】鹬鸵,几维〔纽西兰产的一种不能飞行的鸟〕。**2**.〔军俚〕不飞行的空军军官,地勤军官。**3**. [K-]〔口〕纽西兰人。

KKK, **K.K.K.** = Ku Klux Klan〔美〕三 K 党。

KKt = King's Knight (国际象棋中与"王"并列配置的)马。

kl. = kilolitre(s).

Kla·math [ˈklæməθ; ˋklæməθ] *n*. (*pl*. ～(*s*)) **1**. 克拉马斯人〔美国俄勒冈州南部的北美印第安人〕。**2**. 克拉马斯语。

Klan [klæn; klæn] *n*.〔美〕**1**. = Ku Klux Klan. **2**. 三 K 党分部。～**s·man** *n*. (*pl*. *-men*) 三 K 党党员。

klatch, **klatsch** [klætʃ, klætʃ] *n*. (非正式的)聚会,谈话会。

Klaus [klaus klaʊs] *n*. 克劳斯〔男子名〕。

klax·on [ˈklæksn; klæksn̩] *n*. 电警笛;电喇叭;高音汽笛。

Klee·nex [ˈkliːneks; ˋklinɛks] *n*. **1**. "克里奈克斯"〔一种用作面巾纸的薄页纸商标名〕。**2**.〔有时用 k-〕一张面巾纸。

kleig [kliːg; klig] *n*. = klieg.

klepht [kleft; klɛft] *n*. **1**. (十五世纪希腊被土耳其并吞后上山坚持斗争的)希腊爱国者。**2**. (希腊等地的)山贼。

klep·to·ma·ni·a [ˌkleptəuˈmeiniə; ˏklɛptəˋmenɪə] *n*. 偷盗癖。

klep·to·ma·ni·ac [ˌkleptəuˈmeiniæk, ˏklɛptəˋmenɪæk] *n*. 有偷盗癖的人。

klep·to·scope [ˈkleptəuskəup; ˋklɛptəˏskop] *n*.【军】潜望镜。

klieg [kliːg; klig] *n*. ~ **eyes** (由于强烈光线的照射而引起的)眼结膜炎。~ **light** (摄电影用)溢光灯,强烈弧光灯。

Kline [klain; klaɪn] **test**【医】克氏梅毒试法。

klip·das [ˈklipdæs; ˋklɪp͵dæs] *n*. 〔S. Afr.〕野兔,兔蹄。

klip·spring·er [ˈklipˌspriŋə; ˋklɪp͵sprɪŋɚ] *n*. (*pl*. *-ers*, *-er*) 山羚 (*Oreotragus oreotragus*)〔产于东非和南非〕。

klong [klɔːŋ; klɑŋ] *n*. 〔Thai.〕(泰国的)运河,水道。

kloof [kluːf; kluf] *n*. 〔南非〕深谷,峡谷。

kludge, kluge [kluːdʒ; kludʒ] *n*.【计】异机种系统,用勉强凑合的元件配套而成的计算机。

klutz [klʌts; klʌts] *n*. 〔美俚〕粗笨的人,木头人,傻瓜;不善交际的人。

klys·tron [ˈklaistrən; ˋklaɪstrən] *n*.【电】速(度)调(制)(电子)管,调(制)速(度)管。~ **oscillator** 速调管振荡器。

km. = **1**. kilometre(s). **2**. kingdom.

K(-)mart [ˈkeimɑːt; ˋkemɑrt] *a*. 廉价的,朴实无华的。

KMT = Kuomintang.

kn., **kn** = knot.

knack [næk; næk] *n*. **1**. 诀窍,窍门;(练习而得的)技巧;妙法。**2**. 需要技巧的工作。**3**. 花巧,花样。**4**. (言语、行为等的)习惯,癖。**5**. 玩具,小玩意。***have one's own ~ in*** 对…有独到之处。***There's a ~ in it***. 这里面有窍门。

knack·er [ˈnækə; ˋnækɚ] *n*. **1**. 收买和屠宰废马的人;收买老病家畜[家畜尸体]的人。**2**. 收买废屋[废船]的人。**3**. 〔方〕老病无用的家畜〔尤指马〕。***go to the ~s*** (马)被屠宰。**-y** *n*. 〔英〕废马屠宰场;家畜尸体处理场。

knack·wurst [ˈnɑːkˌwəːst, G. ˈknɑːkˌvuəʃt; ˋnæk͵wɝst, G. ˋknæk͵vurst] *n*. 熏腊肠。

knack·y [ˈnæki; ˋnækɪ] *a*. 巧妙的;机灵的。

knag [næg; næg] *n*. **1**. 木节,木瘤。**2**. (挂物用的)木钉。

knag·gy [ˈnægi; ˋnægɪ] *a*. 节多的;疙瘩多的。

knap[1] [næp; næp] **I** *vt*. (*-pp-*)〔方〕**1**. 敲打,碰撞,打(火石等)。**2**. 打碎;砸碎(石头等)。**3**. 猛咬;啃。**4**. 喋喋不休地讲,闲聊。**II** *n*. 〔方〕猛击;敲。

knap[2] [næp; næp] *n*. 〔方〕小山的顶;小山。

knap·per [ˈnæpə; ˋnæpɚ] *n*. 敲碎(石头等)的人;破碎器;碎石槌。

knap·sack [ˈnæpsæk; ˋnæp͵sæk] *n*. (军用或旅行用)背包。

knap·weed [ˈnæpwiːd; ˋnæp͵wid] *n*.【植】矢车菊属植物。

knar [nɑː; nɑr] *n*. 木瘤,木节。

knave [neiv; nev] *n*. **1**. 流氓,无赖。**2**. 〔古〕仆人。**3**. (纸牌中的)杰克 (*Jack*)。~ [**rogue**] **in grain** 大坏蛋,无赖透顶的人。~ **of hearts** **1**. 讨好女人的人。**2**. (纸牌中的)红心杰克。

knav·er·y [ˈneivəri; ˋnevərɪ] *n*. 流氓行为;无赖行为;诈骗;恶作剧。

knav·ish [ˈneiviʃ; ˋnevɪʃ] *a*. 无赖的;骗人的;奸诈的。**-ly** *ad*. **-ness** *n*.

knead [niːd; nid] *vt*. **1**. 揉,捏(面粉、陶土等);捏做(面包、陶器等)。**2**. 按摩(肌肉等)。**3**. 陶冶(性情);锻炼(性格)。~ *and shape one's children to one's thought* 按照自己的思想培养塑造子女。— *vi*. 揉,捏。

knee [niː; ni] *n*. **1**. 膝,膝盖,膝头,膝关节。**2**. (长裤、长袜等的)膝部。**3**. (马、犬等的)腕骨;(鸟类的)胫骨。**4**. 膝状物;【机】弯头(管),膝(形)杆;架合角铁;(铣床的)升降台;【建】扶手弯头,曲材;(木船用的)肋材。**5**. 曲线的弯曲处。**6**. (用膝的)碰击。*at one's mother's ~s* 在母亲膝下,幼小时候。***bend*** [***bow***] ***the ~ before*** [***to***] ***sb***. 向某人屈膝,屈服于。***bow the ~ to Baal*** 崇拜偶像。***bring sb. to his ~s*** 迫使某人屈服。***draw up the ~s*** 伸直膝盖。***drop*** (***on***)***to one's ~s*** 跪下。***fall on a ~*** 屈下一膝。***fall on one's ~s*** 跪下。***get ~ to ~ with sb***. 同某人促膝谈心。***give*** [***offer***] ***a ~ to sb***. (在拳击中)当助手;支持,帮忙。***go down on one's ~s*** 跪下。***gone at the ~s*** 〔俚〕(马)衰老。***go on one's ~s*** 跪着,卑躬屈膝地。***on bended ~s*** 屈膝跪着。***on the ~s of the gods*** 人力所不及的;尚未可定[知]的。***rise on the ~s*** 站起来。**II** *vt*. (~*d*; ***knee·ing***) **1**. 用膝盖碰。**2**. 用弯头[弯管]接合。**3**. 〔口〕使(裤子的)膝部凸出。~ **action**【机】膝(形)杆动作;膝(形)杆作用 (~ *action suspension*【机】独立悬挂)。~ **and column** (铣床的)升降台。~ **brace**【机】隅撑,角撑。~ **breeches** 短裤。~**cap** **1**.【解】髌,膝盖骨。**2**. 护膝。~**-deep** *a*. 深到膝的,没膝的;深陷在…中的 (*in*)。~**-high** *a*. 高到膝盖的 (~*-high to a duck* [*grasshopper*, *mosquito*] 很小的,微不足道的,无聊的)。~**-hole** (写字台等)容纳膝部的地方 (*a ~-hole desk* 左右有抽屉的写字台)。~ **iron** 隅铁。~ **jerk**【医】膝反射(= patellar reflex)。~**-jerk** *vi*. *& vt*.(对…)作出本能反应。~ **joint** **1**.【解】膝关节。**2**.【机】弯头接合,肘接,臂接。~ **pad** 护膝。~**-pan**【解】髌;膝盖骨。~ **piece** 膝甲〔护膝铠甲〕。~ **pipe** 曲管。~ **point** (曲线)弯曲点。~ **roof** 覆斜屋顶。~**-sprung** *a*. (马由于屈肌腱的收缩)把膝向前弯的。~ **swell** (风琴的)膝板,增音器。~ **tool** 膝形刀。~ **voltage** (曲线)膝处电压。

kneel [niːl; nil] **I** *vi*. (***knelt*** [nelt; nɛlt], 或 *~ed*) 跪下,跪着 (*before*; *to*, *down*)。**II** *n*. 跪的动作[姿态] ~**ing bus** 下跪式公共汽车〔能将车体降低到与路缘齐平,使乘客不需跨越即可上车〕。**-ing·ly** *ad*.

kneel·er [ˈniːlə; ˋnilɚ] *n*. **1**. 跪垫。**2**. 跪台。**3**. 跪拜的人。

kneel-in [ˈniːlin; ˋnil͵ɪn] *n*. 〔美〕祈祷示威〔黑人进入白人教堂参加礼拜以示对种族隔离政策的抗议〕。

knell [nel; nɛl] **I** *n*. **1**. 钟声,丧钟声。**2**. 凶兆 (*of*)。**II** *vt*. 〔古〕**1**. 敲丧钟。**2**. 敲丧钟报丧。— *vi*. **1**. 敲丧钟,发丧钟声。**2**. 发出不吉利的声音。***sound*** [***toll***] ***the death ~ for*** [***of***] ***sth***. [***sb***.] 给某物[人]敲丧钟,宣告某物[人]死亡。

knelt [nelt; nɛlt] kneel 的过去式及过去分词。

Knes·set [ˈkneset; ˋknɛset] *n*. (以色列)议会。

knew [njuː; nju] know 的过去式。

Knick·er·bock·er [ˈnikəbɔkə; ˋnɪkɚ͵bɑkɚ] *n*. **1**. (最初到美国纽约的)荷兰移民的子孙;荷兰籍纽约人;纽约人。**2**. 〔k-〕〔*pl*.〕(在膝下扎起的)灯笼裤。

knick·ers [ˈnikəz; ˋnɪkɚz] *n*. 〔*pl*.〕**1**. 〔口〕knickerbockers. **2**. (女用)扎口短裤。

knick·knack [ˈniknæk; ˋnɪk͵næk] *n*. 小家具;小玩意;小摆设;小装饰品。

knick·knack·er·y [ˈnikˌnækəri; ˋnɪk͵nækərɪ] *n*. 〔集合词〕小家具类;小玩具类;小摆设类;小装饰品类。

knife [naif; naɪf] **I** *n*. (*pl*. ***knives*** [naivz; naɪvz]) **1**. 小刀;餐刀;菜刀。**2**. 〔诗〕短刀,匕首。**3**.【机】(切断器的)刃部;(机器上的)刀具[刀片]。**4**. 〔the ~〕【外】手术刀。*a folding ~* 折刀。*a ~ and fork* (吃西餐用的)一副刀叉。*a pocket ~* (可折合的)小刀。*a table ~* 餐刀。***before you can*** [***could***] ***say ~*** 〔口〕说时迟那时快;一眨眼;突然。***cut like a ~*** (风等)冷得刺骨。***get*** [***have***] ***a*** [***one's***] ***~ into sb***. 对某人报复,猛烈攻击某人,同某人过不去。***go*** [***pass***] ***under the ~*** 〔口〕动外科手术,开刀。***have a horror of the ~*** 怕动外科手术。***play a good ~ and fork*** 吃得津津有味;饱餐一顿。***sharpen one's ~ for sb***. 准备惩罚[攻击]某人。***That one could cut it with a ~***…十分明显的,非常压抑的。***under the ~*** 〔口〕动外科手术。***war to the ~*** 血战,鏖战。**II** *vt*. **1**. 拿小刀切;拿尖刀戳。**2**. 〔口〕秘密打击,用阴险手段击败,背叛。**3**. 刀切似地穿过。**4**. 用括刀涂(颜料等)。— *vi*. (刀似地)劈开,穿过。~ **board** **1**. 磨刀板。**2**.【史】公共马车顶上的长座位。~ **edge** **1**. 刀口,刀

刃。2. 锋利的边缘。3. (门框、舱门等的)刃形边缘。4. 【机】(天平等的)刃形支承。~**-edged** 锋利的,锐利的。~ **grinder** 1. 磨刀工人。2. 磨刀装置;磨刀石;砂轮。~ **machine** 磨刀机。~ **money** (中国古时的)刀币。~ **rest** (餐)刀架。~**smith** 小刀匠。~ **switch**【电】刀形开关,闸刀开关。

knife·point [ˈnaifpɔint; ˋnaɪf͵pɔɪnt] ***n.*** 刀尖。***at*** ~在(刀尖)威胁下。

knight [nait; naɪt] ***n.*** 1. (欧洲中世纪的)骑士;武士,勇士〔尤指打仗或比武时作贵妇人侍从或斗士的人〕。2. (古罗马的)骑士〔奴隶主集团中的一个阶层的成员〕;(古希腊雅典的)第二等级公民。3. 〔英〕爵士〔得用 Sir 的称号,其夫人可称为 Dame, 民间称为 Lady〕。4.【英史】郡选议员。5. (政治、社交、慈善团体的)会员,社员,团员;某一事业[主义等]的忠诚拥护者。6. 〔谑〕专家,大家。7. (国际象棋中的)马。~ *of fortune* 〔婉〕冒险家。~ *of the brush* 美术家,画家。~ *of the cleaver* 〔谑〕肉商。~ *of the cue* 打撞球的。~ *of the green cloth* 爱玩牌的人,牌迷,赌徒。~ *of the hammer* 打铁工人,铁匠。~ *of the lady* 妇女的保护人;情夫。~ *of the pen* [*pencil*, *quill*] 文人,要笔杆的。~ *of the pestle* (*and mortar*) 药剂师。~ *of the post*【英史】以作假见证为职业的人。~ *of the road* 1. 拦路贼。2. 无业游民。3. 流动推销员。~ *of the Round Table* (亚瑟王的)圆桌骑士。~ *of the Rueful* [*Woeful*] *Countenance* 愁颜骑士〔指唐·吉诃德〕。~ *of the whip* 〔谑〕马车夫。~ *of the whipping-post* 〔谑〕骗子。*K- without Fear and without Reproach* 见义勇为的骑士。*Knights of Columbus*【天主】哥伦布骑士团〔罗马天主教的一个所谓"国际互助慈善"团体名,成立于 1882 年〕。*Knights of Labour*【美史】(1869 年成立的秘密工会)劳动骑士团。*Knights of Pythias* 派西亚斯骑士团〔"所谓互助慈善"团体名,成立于 1864 年,派西亚斯,公元前四世纪希腊哲学家〕。*Queen's* ~(国际象棋中)和"王后"同列配置的"马"。**II** ***vt.*** 把…封为骑士[爵士]。~**age** 骑士,爵士;骑士[爵士]名录;骑士[爵士]的地位。~ **bachelor** 英国古代最低级爵士。~ **commander** 英国第二等高级爵士。~**-errant** ***n.*** (*pl.* ~*s-errant*) 1. (中世纪的)游侠骑士。2. 侠客,好汉。~**-errantry** 骑士风度;侠义行为。~**-head** ***n.*** (船首斜桅的)支撑杆。~**hood** 1. 骑士[爵士]资格[地位、身份]。2. 骑士精神,骑士道,侠义。3. 骑士,爵士。**K- Hospitaler** (1096—1099 前后的)十字军救护团团员。~**('s) service**【史】以服兵役为条件对土地享有的占有权。**K- Templar** (*pl.* ***Knights Templars***) 1. 圣殿骑士团骑士〔十二世纪侵略性的十字军参加者以"保护圣墓"名义而建立的军事宗教团体的成员〕。2. (共济会中一个宗派)"互助慈善"团的成员。**-ly** 1. ***a.*** 骑士[爵士](般)的;侠义的;由骑士[爵士]组成的。2. ***ad.*** 骑士般地,侠义地。

knish [keˈniʃ; kɛˋnɪʃ] ***n.*** 克尼什烙薄面卷〔一种肉(干酪)馅烤[煎]薄面卷〕。

knit [nit; nɪt] **I** ***vt.*** (***knit·ted*** 或 ***knit***; ***knit·ting***) 1. 编织,编结;针织;把(毛线等)织成(衣服)。2. 使皱起,使皱紧。3. 拼合(碎片等),粘合;接合(折骨等)。4. (由于共同利益等)使(家族等)联合。5. 使(论点等)紧密,使(文章等)紧凑〔多用过去分词〕。~ *wool into stockings* 织毛线袜。~ *stocking out of wool* 用毛线织袜。~ *timbers* 拼接木材。*Mortar* ~*s bricks together*. 灰泥把砖粘合在一起。*be* ~ *together by common interests* [*marriage*] 因共同利益[婚姻关系]而结合起来。~ *one's brows* 皱眉。*a closely* ~ *argument* 严密的论点。*a well-*~ *frame* 结实的体格。— ***vi.*** 1. 编织,编结,针织。2. (折骨等)接合,结合。3. (眉头)皱起,皱紧。4. (植物)生长,结果实;(蜂)蜂拥,成群。*She often knits while reading*. 她看书的时候常编织东西。*The broken bones* ~ (*together*). 折骨接合起来了。*Her brows* ~ *in thought*. 她皱眉深思。~ ***in*** 编入,织进。~ ***up*** 1. 编织成,织补。2. 结束(议论等)。3. 结合。**II** ***n.*** 1. 编织,针织;编结。2. 编织品,编织衣物。~ *goods* 编织品,针织品,卫生衣类。*a* ~ *goods mill* 针织厂。~**-wear** ***n.*** 针织品(*woollen* ~*wear* 羊毛织物)。

knit·ter [ˈnitə; ˋnɪtɚ] ***n.*** 1. 编织者,编织工人。2. 针织机,编织机。

knit·ting [ˈnitiŋ; ˋnɪtɪŋ] ***n.*** 1. 编织,针织。2. 编织物;针织品。3. 接合,结合;联合。***attend*** [***mind***, ***get down to***, ***stick close to***, ***tend to***] ***one's*** ~各人自扫门前雪。~ **machine** 编织机,针织机。~ **needle** 织针,毛衣针。

knives [naivz; naɪvz] ***n.*** knife 的复数。

knob [nɔb; nɑb] ***n.*** 1. 疖,瘤,疙瘩;〔俚〕头。2. 球形突出物;(树干等的)节;(棒等的)圆顶。3. 门拗,门把,拉手,球形捏手。4.【机】旋钮,按钮,调节器。5. (旗竿、桅杆上的)雕球饰,顶华。6. (砂糖等的)团粒,团块。7. 〔美〕圆丘;〔*pl.*〕丘陵地带。***with*** ~***s on*** 〔俚〕尤其突出地,更加。**II** ***vt.*** (***-bb-***) 1. 使有球形突出物;在…上生疖(长瘤)。2. 给(门等)装球形捏手。3. (琢石时)将(多余石块)敲掉。— ***vi.*** 鼓起,突出。~ **insulator**【电】瓷柱。~**-kerrie** (旧时南非本地人用作武器的)圆头棍。~ **lock** 一种弹簧锁。

knob·ble [ˈnɔbl; ˋnɑbl̩] ***n.*** 疖子,瘤子,疙瘩。

knob·bly [ˈnɔbli; ˋnɑblɪ] ***a.*** = knobby.

knob·by [ˈnɔbi; ˋnɑbɪ] ***a.*** 1. 疖多的。2. 疙瘩多的。3. 小圆丘多的。4. 〔美俚〕(服装等)时髦的,流行的,漂亮的。5. 小球形的。6. (问题等)棘手的,使人困惑的。**knob·biness** ***n.***

knob·stick [ˈnɔbstik; ˋnɑbstɪk] ***n.*** 1. = knobkerrie. 2. 〔英〕罢工时上工的工人,工贼。

knock [nɔk; nɑk] **I** ***vt.*** 1. 敲,打,击;敲掉,去掉。2. 使碰撞;撞倒;凿打(洞等)。3. 〔英俚〕使震惊,给…强烈印象。4. 〔美口〕找…岔子,对…挑剔,糟蹋。~ *one's head against the door* 以头撞门,头撞到门上。~ *the wall down* 把墙拆除。~ *a hole in a wall* 在墙上凿一洞。~ *in a nail* 敲进一枚钉子。*What* ~*s me most is his ignorance*. 使我大吃一惊的是他的无知。— ***vi.*** 1. 敲,打,击 (*at*; *on*)。2. 碰,撞。3. (机器发生毛病)发出爆击声。4. 〔美俚〕找岔子,说坏话。5. 奔忙,忙乱。*Who is* ~*ing*? 谁在敲门? ~ *into sb*. 撞在某人身上。~ ***about*** [***around***] 1. 接连敲打;乱打,乱敲。2. 殴打,虐待,(浪等)冲打(船只)。3. 〔口〕流浪,漂游,到处漫游。~ ***against*** 1. 碰撞;同…冲突。2. 偶然遇见。~ ***at*** 敲(门、窗等)(~ *at an open door* 多此一举。~ *at the wrong door* 找错了门路)。~ ***away*** 敲下,敲掉。~ ***back*** 〔俚〕一口喝掉。~ ***civ***(***v***)***ies into shape*** 〔美〕训练新兵。~ ***down*** 1. 打倒,撞倒。2. (拍卖时)敲槌卖出。3. 〔俚〕请求(~ *sb. down for a song* 要求某人唱歌)。4. 〔俚〕使减价。5. 打败,驳倒。6. 拆除;拆卸(~ *down a machine* 拆卸机器)。7. 〔俚〕获得(收入、薪金等),揩油,贪污。8. 〔美俚〕介绍。~ ***for a loop*** [***goal***] 〔美俚〕1. 猛击,打昏;用酒灌醉。2. 破坏。3. 使人吃惊。~ ***for admittance*** 敲门求见。~ ***head*** 叩头。~ ***home*** (把钉子等)敲牢,钉到头;彻底打击。~ ***in*** [***into***] 打进,敲进,(英大学)迟到后敲门进去。~ (***sb.***) ***into a cocked hat*** 1. 把(某人)的计划破坏。2. 把(某人)打得鼻青脸肿。3. 把(某人)驳得体无完肤。4. 超越,胜过(某人)。~ ***sb. into the middle of next week*** 打败,痛击(某人)。~ ***it off*** 〔美俚〕住口! 别再吵了! ~ ***off*** 1. 敲落,敲掉,把…击倒 (~ *sb. off his feet* 把某人打倒在地)。2. 中止(工作) (~ *off* (*work*) *for lunch at noon* 正午停工吃午饭)。3. 即席作(诗文等)(~ *off a few lines* 匆匆写上几句)。4. 减低(价格),减少(速度)(~ *off ten per cent for cash* 如付现金可减价一成)。5. 〔美俚〕杀死;压倒。~ (***sb.***) ***on the head*** 1. 把(某人)打昏过去,打死。2. 破坏(某人的计划等)。~ ***oneself out*** 把自己弄得筋疲力竭。~ ***out*** 1. 打出,敲出。2. 敲空(~ *out a pipe* 敲出烟斗中的烟灰)。3. (拳击中)彻底打倒,使屈服 (~ *out*

K

an enemy plane 打落一架敌机)。4. 使失去效能,使无用;破坏。5. 急速做好,匆匆拟出(计划等)(~ *out an idea* 匆匆想出个主意)。6. 【无】脱模。~ **over** 〔俚〕1. 弄倒,打翻。2. 屈服;死。3. 〔美〕(警察)袭击,逮捕,搜查。~ ***over a drink*** 〔美俚〕喝杯酒。~ ***sb.'s head off*** 轻易胜过某人。~ ***the bottom*** [***stuffing tar***] ***out of*** 敲掉(箱子等的)底;打破(规则等),推翻(学说等),彻底弄明白。~ ***the breath out of sb.'s body*** 使某人大吃一惊。~ ***the spots off*** [***out of***] ***sb***. 1. 痛打某人,痛击某人。2. 大大超过某人。~ ***together*** 1. 使碰撞;颤抖着相碰(*K- their heads together* 让他们的头撞一撞〔有时指以武力强制两个打架的人停手〕)。2. 拼凑;赶造,赶建。~ ***to pieces*** 1. 打碎。2. 推翻(论点)。~ ***under*** (向…)投降(*to*)。~ ***up*** 1. 敲起,叫起(熟睡中的人)。2. (在板球赛中)很快得分。3. 〔英口〕(使)筋疲力尽。4. 赶做,赶造,赶安排(~ *up a meal* 匆匆做好一顿饭。~ *up a hen-house* 赶搭起一个鸡窝)。5. (装订)弄齐(纸)边。6. 〔美俚〕使受孕。~ ***up against*** = ~ ***against***. **II** ***n***. 1. 敲,打击;(狠狠)一击;敲门(声)。2. 不幸;挫折;艰苦;困苦。3. (机器等发出的)爆(击)声,爆击。4. 〔美俚〕吹毛求疵,找碴儿。5. 〔英俚〕(板球赛中的)盘,局,回合。6. 【无】敲击信号。7. 〔英俚〕拍卖时互相勾结压价的商人集团,有压价人捣鬼的拍卖。*a* ~ *at* [*on*] *the door* 敲门声。*a* ~ *on the head* 头上捱了一拳。*a* ~*test engine* 测爆机。*The engine is* ~*ing badly*. 引擎的爆击声响得厉害。*stand* [*take*] *the* ~*s* 忍受指摘。***get the*** ~ 〔口〕1. 被辞退,被解雇。2. 喝醉。***talk the*** ~ 〔俚〕1. 经济上受到沉重打击;拮据,手头紧。2. 喝醉。~**about** 1. ***a***. 吵闹的,喧嚣的;〔口〕流浪的;(衣服)结实的。2. ***n***. 武打戏的表演[演员];结实的东西;狠斗;,流浪汉;快帆船。~**-down** 1. ***a***. 击倒的;压倒的;能拆开的,折叠式的;(拍卖)价格最低的。2. ***n***. 打倒;打倒的一击;〔俚〕强烈的酒;互殴,乱斗;可拆散的东西;〔美俚〕介绍;降低。~**-down(-and)-drag-out** ***a***. (拳击中)打倒而被拖出的,你死我活的,残酷无情的。~**ed-down** ***a***. (家具等)未装配的。~**-knee** 【医】膝内翻症;〔*pl*.〕内翻膝。~**-kneed** ***a***. 膝内翻的。~ **meter** 爆震计。~**out** 1. ***a***. 拳击猛烈的,打倒的;在拍卖时互相串通用廉价买得的;使昏迷的(~*out drops* 〔俚〕(放在饮料中的)迷药;蒙汗药);引人注目的,轰动一时的。2. ***n***. (拳击)把对手打倒的一击,打倒;彻底的击败;(拍卖时)互相串通的压价收买;〔俚〕轰动一时的东西,引人注目的人。~ **rating** 爆击率。~**-reducer** 【化】抗震剂。~ **wurst** = knackwurst.

knock·er [ˈnɔkə; ˋnɑkɚ] ***n***. 1. 敲门人,来访者。2. 门扣,门环。3. 〔口〕吹毛求疵的人;顽固的悲观主义评论家。***up to the*** ~〔俚〕1. 完全地,十分地(*be ready up to the* ~作好了充分准备)。2. 健康正常(*do not feel up to the* ~感觉身体不够好)。~**-up** ***n***. 〔英〕喊醒工人起来工作的人。

knoll[1] [nəul; nol] ***n***. 圆丘,土墩。

knoll[2] [nəul; nol] ***n***., ***vt***., ***vi***. 〔英方,古〕= knell.

knop [nɔp; nɑp] ***n***. 1. (门上的)圆形把手;扣子,拉手。2. 【建】蕾形饰,顶华。3. (树干等的)节,花芽。

knot [nɔt; nɑt] **I** ***n***. 1. 结,绳结,结节;(装饰用的)花结,蝴蝶结。2. (婚姻等的)结合。3. (树木或木材上的)节疤;(人或动物身上的)硬块,节,瘤。4. 一小群,一小队,一小簇。5. 紧缩,收缩;紧缩感。6. 难事,难题,麻烦事;(问题的)要点;(戏剧、小说的)情节的症结。7. 【海】节(=浬/小时),浬,海里。8. (工人扛物用的)垫肩,头垫(=Porter's ~)。*a figure-of-eight* ~"8"字结,*a fool's* [*granny's*] *knot* 打得不牢固的结。*a reef* ~平结,方结。*a true lover's* [*true-love*] ~(象征忠贞爱情的)同心结,鸳鸯结。*make* [*tie*] *a* ~ *in a rope* 把绳子打个结。*loosen* [*undo, untie*] *a* ~把结解开。*the marriage* [*nuptial*] ~婚姻[夫妇]关系。*stand about in* ~*s* 三五成群地站着。*the* ~ *of the matter* 问题的症结。*His stomach was all in* ~*s*. 他的胃收缩成一团。*a matter full of legal* ~*s* 充满法律纠葛的事。*a* ~ *in a gland* 【医】腺瘤,腺疖。*She can do* [*make, steam*] *35* ~*s*. 那艘船时速 35 海里。*a shoulder* ~肩章。***a Gordian*** ~ 1. 难解的结;难办的事;棘手的问题。2. (问题或故事情节等的)焦点,关键。***at the rate of*** ~***s*** 〔口〕非常快,迅速。***cut the*** (***Gordian***) ~快刀斩乱麻。***get into*** ~ ***s*** 困惑不解。***seek a*** ~ ***in a rush*** [***bulrush***] 想平地起风波。***tie in*** ~***s*** 〔口〕使人迷惑不解,使人糊涂不堪。***tie oneself*** (***up***) ***in***(***to***) ~***s*** 陷入苦境。**II** ***vt***. (*-tt-*) 1. 把…打结;把…连结;捆扎,包扎。2. 使密切结合。3. 使纠结。4. 皱(眉)。5. 打结成(缝)。~ *a parcel safely* 把小包扎紧。— ***vi***. 1. 打结,成结,作花结。2. 纠集,纠缠。3. 形成硬块。4. 打结成缝。~**grass** ***n***. 【植】两耳草;软花属植物。~**hole** ***n***. (木板或树上的)节孔。~**root** ***n***. 【植】甘露子,草石蚕。**-less** ***a***. 无结的。**-like** ***a***. 似结的。

knot·ted [ˈnɔtid; ˋnɑtɪd] ***a***. 1. 打结的。2. 全是结子的。3. 纠缠的;错综复杂的。4. 费解的,令人困惑的;棘手的。

knot·ter [ˈnɔtə; ˋnɑtɚ] ***n***. 1. 打结的人[物]。2. 解结的人[物]。

knot·ting [ˈnɔtiŋ; ˋnɑtɪŋ] ***n***. 结形花边。

knot·ty [ˈnɔti; ˋnɑtɪ] ***a***. 1. 有节的,有结的;节疤多的。2. 纠纷的,棘手的。*a* ~ *rope* 多结的绳子。*a* ~ *passage* 难懂的一段文字。~ **pine** 多结松木〔供内部装饰和做某些家具用〕。**-ti·ly** ***ad***. **-ti·ness** ***n***.

knot·work [ˈnɔtwəːk; ˋnɑtˏwɝk] ***n***. 缕饰;编结工艺。

knout [naut; naʊt] **I** ***n***. 皮鞭〔沙俄所用刑具〕;〔the ~〕笞刑。**II** ***vt***. 鞭打,对…处笞刑。

know [nəu; no] ***v***. (***knew*** [njuː; nju]; ***known*** [nəun; non]) **I** ***vt***. 1. 知道;了解,懂得。2. 相识,认识;结识。3. 能区别,能分辨,能识别。4. 熟悉,精通,记牢。5. 体验,尝受;经历。6. 〔古〕与(女性)发生性关系。~ *the facts* 知道[了解]事实。*Do you* ~ *English*? 你懂英语吗? ~ *for certain that* ... 确实知道。*the importance of* ~*ing oneself* 知己的重要性,自知之明的重要性。*Do you* ~ *how to play chess*? 你会下棋吗? *The man has gone and nobody* ~*s where*. 谁也不知道那个人到哪里去了。*Who* ~*s if it may be so*? 也许是这样的。(*as*) *you* ~, *don't you* ~〔用作插入语〕你也知道,你是知道的。*We all knew him to be honest*. 我们都以为他是老实的。*I never* ~ *such a man*. 我从来不认识这样一个人。*I* ~ *him to speak to*. 我不深知他,只是见面打打招呼罢了。*I* ~ *of him, but I do not* ~ *him personally*. 我知道他,但不认识他。*I knew him at once*. 我立刻认出他来。*I knew him for an American*. 我看出他是个美国人。*I would* ~ *her even in a crowd*. 就是在人群中,我也能认出她来。~ *right from wrong* 分辨是非。*He doesn't* ~ *a friend from an enemy*. 他不分敌友。*I don't* ~ *him from Adam*. 我简直不晓得他是谁。~ *one's lines by heart* 背熟自己的台词。*I have told you I don't* ~ *how many times not to touch it*. 我对你说不要碰它,不知多少次了。~ *sb. by name* 只知道某人的名字;能说出某人的名字。~ *sb. by sight* 同某人只是面熟。~ *truth through practice* 通过实践认识真理。*He has known better days*. 他过过好日子。*He never knew fear*. 他从来不知道害怕。*His wrath knew no bounds*. 他怒不可遏。— ***vi***. 知道,了解,懂得。*Do you* ~ *of that matter*? —*Yes, I* ~. 你知道那件事吗? —我知道。*The best method I* ~ *of*. 我所知道的最好的方法。*I* ~ *of its being so*. 我知道是如此的。***all one*** ~***s*** 〔口〕力所能及的一切;尽全力(地)(*He will do all he* ~*s*. 他会拼命干的)。***before you*** ~ ***where you are*** 〔口〕立即,马上。***don't I*** ~ ***it*** 〔口〕就算我知道〔表示无可奈何的同意〕。***for all*** [***aught***] ***I*** ~就我所知(*For all I* ~, *the matter may have been settled*. 据我所知,这事也许早解决了)。***God***

K

[*Goodness*, *Heaven*, *Lord*, *the Lord*] *knows*! 天晓得! 谁知道! (*God* ~*s that it is true*. 这绝对是真的。*God* [*Heaven*] ~*s where he fled*. 谁知道他跑到哪里去了。*He is always busy with God knows what*. 谁知道他整天在忙啥东西)。*I* ~ *what*. 我有一个新的想法[建议]。***I knew it***. 我早知道那件事要发生。***I want to*** **~**.〔美口〕哎呀,啧〔表示惊讶等〕。***I wouldn't*** **~**.〔美〕我不知道。~ ***a thing or two***, ~ ***black from white***, ~ ***chalk from cheese***, ~ ***how many beans make five***, ~ ***one's way about***, ~ ***what's what*** 精明,有经验,有判断力,明事理,洞悉世态人情。~ ***about*** [***of***]... 知道关于…的情况。~ ***all the answers***〔口〕1. 聪明伶俐。2. 自称无所不知的人,知识里手。~ ***better*** (***than that***, ***than to do***) 明白事理(而不致于…)(*I* ~ *better than to do such a thing*. 我决不会蠢到去干那样的事)。~ ***one's goods*** [***onions***, ***stuff***]〔美〕精通某事[某问题],有充分的专门知识。~ ***one's business*** 精通自己干的一行。~ ***one's own mind*** 有自己的想法,果断。~ ***the time of day*** 消息灵通;能见机行事。~ ***what one is about*** 一切能应付裕如。***To*** **~** ***everything is to*** **~** ***nothing***.〔谚〕样样都懂,样样不通。***What do you*** **~**?〔口〕真想不到。***What do you*** **~** ***about this*** [***that***]?〔口〕你看怪不怪? 真没有想到。***Who*** **~*s***?〔口〕怎么知道呢? 说不定。***You never*** **~** ***what you can do till you try***.〔谚〕下手尝试,才知自己有几分本事。**II** ***n***.〔口〕知晓,知情〔仅用于成语〕。***be in the*** **~**了解内情。***not in the*** **~**不明真相。***those in the*** **~**〔口〕消息灵通人士。**~-all, ~-it-all** 1. ***n***.〔口〕自称无所不知的人,知识里手;〔反〕万事通。2. ***a***. 自称无所不知的,万事通的。**~-how** ***n***.〔口〕专门技能,知识,窍门(*the* ~*-how of atomic bomb* 制造原子弹的技术)。**~bot** 智能机器人〔由knowledge和robot二字拼缀而成,多指电脑的智能软件〕。**~-nothing** ***n***. 1. 无知的人。2. 不可知论者。3.【美史】(十九世纪反对外来移民、天主教等的)一种秘密党派成员。**~-nothingism** ***n***. 1. 不可知论;(对一切事物均答不知的)不知道主义、一问三不知。2.〔k-〕【美史】(十九世纪反对外来移民等的)秘密党派的排外主义。

know·a·ble [ˈnəuəbl; ˋnoəbl] **I** ***a***. 可知的,可认识的;易知的。**II** ***n***.〔常 *pl*.〕知道的事。~*s and unknowables* 知道的和不知道的事。**-bil·i·ty** ***n***. 可知性。

know·ing [ˈnəuiŋ; ˋnoɪŋ] **I** ***a***. 1. 知道的,有知识的;有见识的。2. 机敏的,机警的,聪明的。3. 老练的,世故的,狡猾的。4. 故意的,成心的。5. 心照不宣的,会意的。6. 自以为无所不知的。7.〔口〕时髦的,漂亮的。*a* ~ *scholar* 饱学之士。*a* ~ *dog* 机警的狗。*a* ~ *look* 会意的一瞥。*the* ~ *one* 万事通,自以为无所不知的人。**II** ***n***. 知道;认识。***There is no*** **~...** 无法知道(*There is no* ~ *when he will come*. 无法知道他什么时候来)。**-ly** ***ad***. 1. 故意地。2. 会意地。3. 老练地。**-ness** ***n***.

knowl·edge [ˈnɔlidʒ; ˋnɑlɪdʒ] ***n***. 1. 知识;学识,学问。2. 了解,理解;消息。3. 认识。4.〔古〕学科。5.〔古〕性关系。*book* ~书本知识。*K- is power*.〔谚〕知识就是力量。*practical* ~实际的知识。*secondhand* ~第二手知识,传授来的知识。*working* ~ *of French* 法语知识学到能应用的地步。*I have no* ~ *of London*. 我对伦敦毫无所知。*It is within your* ~ *that* ... 这是你所知道的。*The* ~ *of our victory caused great joy*. 我们获得胜利的消息传来,万众欢腾。*perceptual* ~感性认识。*logical* [*rational*] ~理性认识。*the theory of* ~【哲】认识论。*branches of* ~学科。*carnal* ~性经验;【法】性关系。***come to sb.'s*** **~**被某人知道。***common*** [***general***] **~**众所周知,常识。***grow out of*** (***sb.'s***) **~**被忘掉了。***have some*** [***a general***, ***a thorough***] **~** ***of*** 懂得一点,懂得一个大概,精通。***not to my*** **~**我知道并不是那样。***out of all*** **~**(变得)认不出来,无法辨认。***to my*** **~**据我知道。***to sb.'s certain*** **~**据某人确知。***to the best of my*** **~**据我所知,就我所知而论(= *so far as I know*)。***Too much*** **~** ***makes the head bald***.〔谚〕知识太多老得快。***without sb.'s*** **~** 不通知某人,背着某人。**~-box** ***n***. 1.〔俚〕头。2.〔美俚〕校舍。~ **economy** 知识经济。~ **industry** 知识产业。~ **factory**〔美〕学校〔尤指高等院校〕;教育机构。**~-intensive** ***a***. 知识密集型的。~ **worker** 知识工人〔指专业技术人员〕。

knowl·edge·a·ble [ˈnɔlidʒəbl; ˋnɑlɪdʒəbl] ***a***.〔口〕有知识的;精明的。*a* ~ *question* 有见地的问题。*a* ~ *student* 有头脑的学生。

known [nəun; non] I know 的过去分词。**II** ***a***. 大家知道的;知名的;已知的。*a nationally* ~ *writer* 全国知名的作家。***be it*** **~** ***that***... 特此通告。***be*** **~** ***as*** = ***be*** **~** ***by the name of***... 通称,叫做。***be*** **~** ***for***... 因…而著名。***be*** **~** ***to***... 为…所知。***make*** **~**发表,公布。***make oneself*** **~** ***to sb***. 向某人作自我介绍。***make sth***. **~** ***to sb***. 向某人公布某事。~ **number**【数】已知数。~ **quantity** 1.【数】已知量。2.〔口〕名人;人们熟知的东西。

Knox [nɔks; nɑks] ***n***. 诺克斯〔姓氏〕。

Knt. = knight.

knuck·le [ˈnʌkl; ˋnʌkl] **I** ***n***. 1. 指关节,指节。2.〔通常 *pl*.〕铜指节套(= ~ duster, 又称 brass ~s)。3. (小牛、猪等的)膝关节,脚圈;肘,蹄。4.【机】钩爪,关节;铰结,肘形接;【船】船尾棱缘;【建】(屋顶等的)脊。*a coupler* ~车钩关节。*a universal joint* ~【机】万向接头关节。***get a rap on*** [***over***] ***the*** **~*s*** 挨骂,受申斥。***give sb. a rap on*** [***over***] ***the*** **~*s*** 责骂某人,申斥某人。***near the*** **~**〔口〕(笑话等)近似猥亵的,接近诲淫的。**II** ***vt***. 用指关节打[压,碰,擦]。— ***vi***. (儿童弹玻璃弹子时)以指关节贴地 (*down*)。~ **down** 1. 开始认真工作;干劲十足地干(~ *down for an hour and finish* 认真干一个小时把…干完)。2. (向…)投降 (*to*) (= ~ under)。~ ***under to sb***.〔口〕(向某人)认输,屈服。~ **ball**【棒球】指节球,指关节球〔把指尖叩在球面上投的球,也叫 knuckler〕。~ **bone** ***n***. 1. 指关节骨;(牛羊等的)跖骨。2.〔*pl*.〕用跖骨玩的游戏;(小牛等的)肘骨肉。**~-duster** 指关节保护套〔套在四指关节上的铜套,握拳时铜套向外,作打人的武器〕。**~head**〔口〕傻瓜,笨蛋。**~joint** 1. 骨关节。2.【机】铰结,肘形接。~ **pin** 关节销。~ **tooth** 圆顶齿。

knuck·ler [ˈnuklə; ˋnʌklɚ] ***n***. = knuckle ball.

Knud·sen [ˈnuːdsən; ˋnudsən] **effect**【物】努特生效应。

knurl [nəːl; nɝl] **I** ***n***. 1. (树木等的)硬节,瘤。2. 小的隆起物;金属表面上的小粒;(硬币边上的)小凸边压花;【机】压花,滚花。3. (打字机上使滚筒转动的)圆形按钮[旋钮]。4.〔Scot.〕矮小结实的人。**II** ***vt***. 在(硬币等的)边上)作小凸边;【机】在…上滚花。**-ing** ***n***.【机】滚花。**-y** ***a***. 多节的;滚花的。

knurr, knur [nəː; nɝ] ***n***. 1. (树木等的)节疤。2.〔英〕木球〔球戏用〕。

knut [nʌt; nʌt] ***n***.〔谑〕纨袴子弟,花花公子(= nut)。

K.O., k.o. = knock-out.

ko·a [ˈkəuə; ˋkoə] ***n***.〔Haw.〕【植】寇阿相思树 (*Acacia koa*)〔产于夏威夷,为建筑和家具用材,树皮可用于鞣皮〕。

ko·a·la [kəuˈɑːlə; koˋɑlə] ***n***.【动】考拉〔大洋洲无尾熊〕。

ko·ban [ˈkəuˈbɑːn; ˋkoˋbɑn] ***n***.〔Jap.〕(日本的)警察分局,派出所。

ko·an [kəun; kon] ***n***.【佛】心印,以心传心〔佛教禅宗沉思中的重要一环,以一种简短而不合逻辑的问题,使思想脱离理性的范畴〕。

kob [kɔb; kɑb] ***n***.【动】非洲水羚 (*Kobus kob*)〔产于东南非〕。

Ko·be [ˈkəubi; ˋkobɪ] ***n***. 神户〔日本城市〕。

Ko·ben·havn [ˌkəːbənˈhaun; ˏkɝbənˋhaʊn] 哥本哈根〔丹麦文写法〕。

K

kob·old [ˈkɔbəuld; ˋkɑbold] ***n.***【德神】帮助做家务的小精灵;(矿山等的)地下精灵。

Koch [G. kɔːx; kɔx], **Robert** 罗伯特·柯霍〔1843—1910,德国细菌学家,医学家,结核菌、霍乱菌发现者〕。

ko·dak [ˈkəudæk; ˋkodæk] **I** ***n.*** **1.** 手提照相机。**2.**〔K-〕〔美〕柯达〔柯达公司的照相机和照相材料的商标名〕。**3.** 小型照相机拍的照片。**II** ***vi.***, ***vt.*** 用手提照相机拍(照片)。~ **moment** 留下了美好记忆的时刻。

ko·di·ak bear [ˈkəudiːˌæk; ˋkodiˏæk]【动】科迪亚克棕熊(*Ursus middendorffi*)〔产于科迪亚克岛及其邻近地区,体重可达 1,500 磅〕。

ko·el [ˈkəuəl; ˋkoəl] ***n.*** 鬼布谷〔产于印度、东印度群岛及澳大利亚的一种类似杜鹃的鸟〕。

Koest·ler [ˈkestlə; ˋkɛstlɚ] ***n.*** 凯斯特勒〔姓氏〕。

K. of C. = Knight(s) of Columbus〔美〕(天主教)慈善会(成员)。

Koh·i·noor, Koh-i-noor [ˈkəuinuə; ˋkoɪˏnʊr] ***n.*** **1.** 皇冠钻石〔英国皇冠上一颗重 108 克拉的印度产大钻石〕。**2.**〔k-〕出类拔萃的东西。

kohl [kəul; kol] ***n.*** (阿拉伯妇女涂眼圈的)眼圈墨。

kohl·ra·bi [ˈkəulˈrɑːbi; ˋkolˋrɑbɪ] ***n.***【植】球茎甘蓝。

koi·ne [kɔiˈnei, ˈkɔinei, -niː; kɔɪˋne, ˋkɔɪne, -ni] ***n.***〔K-〕**1.** 柯因内语〔希腊罗马时代东地中海等希腊语国家的共同语〕。**2.** 共同语。

ko·ji [ˈkəudʒi; ˋkodʒɪ] ***n.***【微】(日本)曲。

ko·kan·ee [kəuˈkæniː; koˋkæni] ***n.*** (*pl.* ***-ees***, ***-ee***) 红大麻花鱼(*Oncorhynchus nerka kennerlyi*)〔产于美国西北部〕。

kok-sa·ghyz, kok-sa·gyz [ˈkəuksæˈgiːz; ˋkoksæˋgiz] ***n.***【植】橡胶草,青胶蒲公英(*Taraxacum kok-saghyz*)〔俄罗斯的一种蒲公英,从其根部可提炼橡胶〕。

ko·la [ˈkəulə; ˋkolə] ***n.*** = cola. ~ **nut** (非洲)可拉果。

ko·lin·sky [kəuˈlinski; kəˋlɪnskɪ] ***n.*** 亚洲貂,西伯利亚貂。~ **skins** 元皮。

Kol·khoz [kɔlˈhɔz; kəlˋkɔz] ***n.***〔Russ.〕(前苏联的)集体农庄。

Köln [G. kœln; kɝln] ***n.*** 科隆〔德国城市〕。

ko·lo [ˈkəuləu; ˋkolo] ***n.*** (*pl.* ~***s***) 科洛舞〔塞尔维亚的一种民间舞蹈〕。

Kom·in·tern [ˈkɔmintəːn; ˋkɑmɪnˏtɝn] ***n.*** = Comintern.

kom·man·da·tu·ra [kəˌmændəˈturə; kəˏmændəˋtʊrə] ***n.*** 军事管制总部〔尤指第二次世界大战后苏联等国在欧洲城市所设的此类机构〕。

Ko·mo·do dragon [kəˈməudəu ˈdrægən; kəˋmodo-ˋdrægən] ***n.***【动】科莫多巨蜥(*Varanus komodoensis*)〔产于印尼科莫多岛,全长 9 英尺,当今地球上最长的蜥蜴〕。

Kom·so·molsk [ˌkɔmsəˈmɔlsk; ˏkɑmsəˋmɑlsk] ***n.*** 共青城〔俄罗斯城市〕。

Kon·go [ˈkɔŋgəu; ˋkɑŋgo] ***n.*** (*pl.* ~(***s***)) **1.** (安哥拉和刚果的)班图人。**2.** 班图语。

ko·nim·e·ter [kəuˈnimitə; koˋnɪmətɚ] ***n.*** 尘度计,计尘器〔测量空气浮尘量用〕。

kon·i·ol·o·gy [ˌkəuniˈɔlədʒi; ˏkoniˋɑlədʒɪ] ***n.*** 空气中的灰尘;微尘学。

kon·i·scope [ˈkɔniskəup; ˋkɑnɪˏskop] ***n.*** 检尘器。

kon·zern [G. kɔnˈtseən; kɑnˋtsɛrn] ***n.***〔G.〕【经】康采恩。

koo·doo [ˈkuːduː; ˋkudu] ***n.*** (*pl.* ~(***s***)) (南非产)条纹羚羊(= kudu)。

kook [kuːk; kuk] ***n.***〔美俚〕傻子;怪人;狂人。

kook·a·bur·ra [ˈkukəbəːrə; ˋkukəbɝrə] ***n.***【动】笑鸿(*Dacelo gigas*)〔一种澳大利亚翠鸟〕。

kook·y, kook·ie [ˈkuːki; ˋkukɪ] ***a.***〔美俚〕傻的,古怪的;发狂的。**kook·i·ness** ***n.***

Koord [kəːd, kuəd; kɝd, kʊrd] ***n.*** = Kurd.

koosh [kuːʃ; kuʃ]〔美俚〕***vt.*** 拒绝聘用(求职者等)。

Koo·te·nay [ˈkuːtnei; ˋkutne] ***n.*** = Kutenai.

kop [kɔːp; kɑp] ***n.***〔南非〕山,山岳。

kop. = kope(c)k.

ko·pe(c)k [ˈkəupek; ˋkopɛk] ***n.***〔俄罗斯辅币名〕戈比〔100 戈比 = 1 卢布〕。

koph [kɔːf; kɔf] ***n.*** 希伯来语第十九个字母。

kop·je, kop·pie [ˈkɔpi; ˋkɑpɪ] ***n.*** (南非的)小山,丘陵。

kor [kɔː; kɔr] ***n.*** 固尔〔希伯来早期量具名,作固体量具相当于 6$\frac{1}{4}$ 普式耳;作液体量具相当于 58 加仑〕(= homer)。

Ko·ran [kɔˈrɑːn; koˋrɑn] ***n.*** (伊斯兰教)《古兰经》,《可兰经》。**-ic** ***a.***

Kor·do·fan·i·an [ˌkɔːdəˈfæniən; ˏkɔrdəˋfænɪən] ***n.*** 科尔多凡语〔非洲语言中的刚果—科尔多凡语系的一个语族,有五个语支〕。

Ko·re·a [kəˈriə, kɔ(ː)ˈriə; kəˋriə, koˋriə] ***n.*** 朝鲜;韩国。*the Democratic People's Republic of* ~朝鲜民主主义人民共和国。*the Republic of* ~大韩民国。

Ko·re·an [kəˈriən; kəˋriən] **I** ***a.*** 朝鲜的,韩国的;朝鲜族的;朝鲜话的。**II** ***n.*** 朝鲜人,韩国人;朝鲜族;朝鲜话。

Korn·berg [ˈkɔːnbəg; ˋkɔrnbɝg] ***n.*** 科恩伯格〔姓氏〕。

Kor·sa·koff's psychosis [**syndrome**] [ˈkɔːsəˌkɔːfs; ˋkɔrsəˏkɔfs]【医】柯萨可夫氏精神病〔由于酒精中毒,维生素缺乏等引起的精神病,表现为多发性神经炎、失去记忆和不辨方向等〕。

ko·ru·na [ˈkəuruːnɑː; ˋkɔrunɑ] ***n.*** (*pl.* ~***s***, ***ko·run***) **1.** 克朗〔捷克货币名称,等于 100 赫勒(*Haller*)〕。**2.** 克朗币〔硬币〕。

kos [kəus; kos] ***n.*** (*pl.* ***kos***) 科斯〔印度的长度名,长度由 1.5—3 英里,各地不一〕。

ko·sher [ˈkəuːʃə; ˋkoʃɚ] **I** ***a.*** **1.**【犹】(按犹太教食规)清洁可食的;供应清洁可食食物的。**2.** 按犹太教传统食谱烹调的。**3.**〔俚〕可以的;正当的;正确的。**II** ***n.*** **1.** 按犹太教食规清洁可食的食品。**2.**〔口〕合法的卫生食品,犹太教食品。**III** ***vt.*** 使(食物)清洁可食。

ko·to [ˈkəuˈtəu; ˋkoˋto] ***n.*** (*pl.* ~***s***)〔Jap.〕(日本的)十三弦古筝。

ko(w)·tow [ˈkəuˈtau; ˋkoˋtau] **I** ***n.***〔Chin.〕叩头,磕头。**II** ***vi.*** **1.** 叩头,磕头。**2.** 拍马屁;奉承(*to*)。

kot·wal [ˈkɔtwɑːl; ˋkotwɑl] ***n.***〔Hind.〕(印度的)警察局长;行政长官。

kot·wa·li [ˈkəutwɑːli; ˋkotwɑlɪ] ***n.***〔Hind.〕(印度的)警察局。

kou·miss [ˈkuːmis; ˋkumɪs] ***n.*** **1.** (中亚地区牧民用马乳或骆驼乳做的)乳酒。**2.** (欧美人的)牛奶酒。

Kour·bash [ˈkuəbæʃ; ˋkʊrbæʃ] ***n.*** = Kurbash.

KP, K.P. = kitchen police.

Kp = king's pawn (国际象棋中"王"前面的)兵。

KR = king's rook (国际象棋中与"王"同列配置的)车。

Kr =【化】krypton 元素氪的符号。

kr =【物】kiloroentgen.

kr. = **1.** krona. **2.** krone.

kraal [krɑːl; krɑl] **I** ***n.*** **1.** (南非当地居民有栅栏防护的)村庄;村中居民。**2.** (南非的)羊栏,牛栏。**II** ***vt.*** 把(家畜)关进栏内。

kraft [krɑːft; kræft] ***n.*** 牛皮纸(= ~ paper)。

krait [krait; kraɪt] ***n.***〔Hind.〕(产于南亚和东南亚的)孟加拉毒蛇。

kra·ken [ˈkrɑːkən; ˋkrɑkən] ***n.*** (相传常在挪威海中出现的)海怪。

Kra·ków [ˈkrækau, Pol. ˈkrɑːkuːf; ˋkrækau, ˋkrɑkuf] ***n.*** 克拉科夫〔波兰城市〕。

kra·ter [ˈkreitə, ˈkrɑː-; ˋkretɚ, ˋkrɑɚ] ***n.*** 搀和器〔古希腊把酒和水搀和在一起的一种双柄大口罐〕。

K ra·tion [ˈkei ˈræʃən; ˋke ˋræʃən] (美军三包一天分,内有肉、饼干、香肠等的)K 种口粮袋,应急口粮。

K

Krebs [krebz; krɛbz] ***n.*** 克雷布斯〔姓氏〕。

Kreis·ler [ˈkraislə; ˋkraɪslɚ] ***n.*** 克赖斯勒〔姓氏〕。

krem·lin [ˈkremlin; ˋkrɛmlɪn] **I** ***n.*** 〔Russ.〕 **1.** (俄国的)城堡。**2.** 〔the K-〕(莫斯科的)克里姆林宫,俄罗斯政府。**II** ***a.*** 〔K-〕克里姆林宫的;俄罗斯政府的。

Krem·lin·ol·o·gy [ˈkremlinˈɔlədʒi; ˏkrɛmlɪnˋɑlədʒɪ] ***n.*** 〔口〕(西方国家的)苏联政策研究。**-ol·o·gist** ***n.*** 苏联政策研究专家。

kre·o·sote [ˈkriəsəut; ˋkriəˏsot] ***n.*** = creosote.

krep·lach [ˈkreplɑːk, -lək; ˋkrɛplæk, -lək] ***n.*** 〔*pl.*〕三角馄饨。

kreut·zer, ***kreu·zer*** [ˈkrɔitsə; ˋkrɔɪtsɚ] ***n.*** 〔G.〕克娄泽〔13 世纪至 19 世纪中叶德国和奥地利通行的一种铜币〕。

Krieg·ie [ˈkriːgi; ˋkrigɪ] ***n.*** 〔G.〕战俘。

krieg·spiel [ˈkriːgspiːl; ˋkrigspil] ***n.*** 〔G.〕(用作盘上战术指挥训练的)军棋游戏。

krill [kril; krɪl] ***n.*** (*pl.* ***krill***)【动】磷虾。

krim·mer [ˈkrimə; ˋkrɪmɚ] ***n.*** 克里米亚黑(灰)色羊羔皮。

kris [kris; krɪs] ***n.*** 马来西亚人的波纹刀刃短剑(= crease, creese)。

Krish·na [ˈkriʃnə; ˋkrɪʃnə] ***n.***【印度神】(象征丰收和幸福的)牧牛神讫里什那。**-ism** ***n.*** 牧牛神崇拜。

Kriss Krin·gle [ˈkris ˈkriŋgl; ˋkrɪs ˋkrɪŋgl̩]【宗】= Santa Claus.

Kroll [krəul; krol] ***n.*** 克罗尔〔姓氏〕。

kro·na [ˈkrəunə; ˋkronə] ***n.*** **1.** (*pl.* ***-nor*** [-nɔː; -nɔr]) (瑞典的货币单位)克朗。**2.** (*pl.* ***-nur*** [-nə; -nɚ]) (冰岛的货币单位)克朗。

kro·ne[1] [ˈkrəune; ˋkronɛ] ***n.*** (*pl.* ***-r*** [-nɛə; -nɛr]) (丹麦、挪威的货币单位)克朗。

kro·ne[2] [ˈkrəunə; ˋkronə] ***n.*** (*pl.* ***-nen*** [-nən; -nən]) **1.** 旧德国金币。**2.** 旧奥国银币。

Kron·s(h)tadt [ˈkrɔnʃtæt; ˋkrɑnsˏtæt] ***n.*** 喀琅施塔得〔俄罗斯港市〕。

Kroo, Kru [kruː; kru] **I** ***n.*** 克鲁人〔利比里亚沿海岸具有熟练技术的黑种人水手〕。**II** ***a.*** 克鲁人的。

Kroo·boy [ˈkruːbɔi; ˋkrubɔɪ] ***n.*** 克鲁人。

Kroo·man [ˈkruːmən; ˋkrumən] ***n.*** (*pl.* ***-men***) = Krooboy.

Kro·pot·kin [krəuˈpɔːtkin; krəˋpɑtkɪn], **Prince Pëtr Aleksyeevich** 克鲁泡特金〔1842—1921,俄国地理学家,无政府主义者〕。

K.R.R. = King's Royal Rifles〔英〕皇家步枪队。

Kru [kruː; kru] ***n.*** = Kroo.

krul·ler [ˈkrʌlə; ˋkrʌlɚ] ***n.*** = cruller.

krumm·horn, krum·horn [ˈkrumhɔːn, ˈkrʌm-; ˋkrʊmˏhɔrn, ˋkrʌm-] ***n.*** 变号〔一种古双簧乐器〕。

Krupp [krʌp; krʌp], **Alfred** 克鲁伯〔1812—1887,德国军火制造商〕。

Krutch [kruːtʃ; krutʃ] ***n.*** 克鲁奇〔姓氏〕。

kryp·tol [ˈkriptɔl; ˋkrɪptɑl] ***n.*** 粒状碳〔电极粒状物〕,碳棒;矽[硅]碳棒。

kryp·ton [ˈkriptɔn; ˋkrɪptɑn] ***n.***【化】氪。

kry·tron [ˈkritrɔn; ˋkrɪtrɑn] ***n.*** 氪电子高速计时装置〔多用于核爆炸监控,由 krypton 和 electronic 二词拼缀成〕。

Ks. = Kansas.

Kshat·ri·ya [ˈkʃætriə; ˋkʃætrɪə] ***n.*** 刹帝利〔印度四大封建种姓的第二种姓(武士或贵族)〕。

Kt = knight (国际象棋中的)马。

kt = karat 开〔黄金成色单位〕。

kts = knots per hour 节(海里/小时)〔复数〕。

Kua·la Lum·pur [ˈkwɑːlə ˈlumpuə; ˋkwɑlə ˋlʊmpur] 吉隆坡〔马来西亚首都〕。

Ku·blai Khan [ˈkuːblai ˈkɑːn; ˋkublaɪ ˋkɑn] ***n.*** 忽必烈〔1216? -1294,元世祖,中国元朝皇帝,成吉思汗之孙〕。

ku·chen [ˈkuːkən, -hən; ˋkukən, -hən] ***n.*** 〔G.〕糕点〔德国早餐点心〕。

Ku·ching [ˈkuːtʃiŋ; ˋkutʃɪŋ] ***n.*** 古晋〔马来西亚港市〕。

ku·dos [ˈkjuːdɔs; ˋkjudɑs] ***n.*** 〔口〕名誉,光荣,荣誉。

ku·du [ˈkuːduː; ˋkudu] ***n.*** (*pl.* ~(***s***)) = koodoo.

kud·zu [ˈkudzuː; ˋkʊdzu] ***n.***【植】(产于中国和日本的)葛(*Pueraria thunbergiana*)。

Ku·fic [ˈkjuːfik, ˈkuː-; ˋkjufɪk, ˋku-] ***a.*** 古阿拉伯字母表〔使用于巴比伦南部地区〕(= Cufic)。

Kui·by·shev [ˈkwibiʃev; ˋkuɪbɪʃɛv] ***n.*** 古比雪夫〔俄罗斯城市〕。

Ku Klux [ˈkjuːˈklʌks, kuː-; ˋkjuˏklʌks, ku-] **1.** Ku Klux Klan 之略。**2.** (用私刑迫害黑人和进步工人的美国恐怖组织)三 K 党党徒(= Ku Kluxer)。

Ku Klux·er [ˈkjuː ˈklʌksə; ˋkju ˋklʌksɚ] ***n.*** 三 K 党成员。

Ku Klux Klan [ˈkjuː klʌksˈklæn; ˋkjuˏklʌksˋklæn] ***n.*** 三 K 党。

Ku Klux·ism [ˈkjuː ˈklʌksizəm ˋkju ˋklʌksɪzəm] 三 K 党主义。

kuk·ri [ˈkukri; ˋkukrɪ] ***n.*** (印度廓尔喀人用的)曲刀。

ku·lak [kuːˈlɑːk; kuˋlɑk] ***n.*** (*pl.* ***kulaki*** [ˈkuːlɑːki; ˋkulakɪ]) 〔Russ.〕富农。

Kul·tur [kulˈtuə; kulˋtʊr] ***n.*** 〔G.〕**1.** 文明,文化〔与英语 culture 相当〕。**2.** 〔讽〕德国文化〔指沙文主义、军国主义、恐怖主义等〕。**3.** 德国纳粹分子等统治下的社会组织[制度]。

kul·tur·kampf [kulˈtuːəkɑːmpf; kulˋturkɑmpf] ***n.*** 〔G.〕(1873—1887 年罗马天主教会和德国政府之间围绕教育和教职任命权进行的)文化斗争。

Ku·ma·mo·to [ˈkuːməˈməutəu; ˋkuməˋmoto] ***n.*** 熊本〔日本城市〕。

ku·mis(s) [ˈkuːmis; ˋkumɪs] ***n.*** = koumiss.

küm·mel [ˈkuməl; ˋkɪməl] ***n.*** 〔G.〕茴香甜酒。

kum·mer·bund [ˈkʌməbʌnd; ˋkʌmɚˏbʌnd] ***n.*** 腰围,腹带,腹套(= cummerbund)。

kum·quat [ˈkʌmkwɔt; ˋkʌmkwɑt] ***n.***【植】金钱桔(= cumquat)。

kung fu [ˈkuŋˈfuː; ˋkʊŋˋfu] **I** ***n.*** 〔中〕功夫〔指中国武术的徒手格斗术〕。**II** ***vt.*** 用功夫击打(对手)。

kunz·ite [ˈkuntsait; ˋkʊntˏsaɪt] ***n.***【地】紫锂辉石。

Kuo·min·tang [ˈkwəuminˈtæŋ; ˋkwomɪnˋtæŋ] ***n.*** 〔Chin.〕〔the ~〕(中国)国民党。

Kur·bash [ˈkuəbæʃ; ˋkurbæʃ] **I** ***n.*** (旧时土耳其、埃及用作抽打犯人的)皮鞭。**II** ***vt.*** 鞭笞。

Kurd [kəːd, kɚd] ***n.*** 库尔德人〔主要居住在伊朗库尔德斯坦和高加索南部的穆斯林游牧民族〕。

Kurd·ish [ˈkəːdiʃ, ˈkuə-; ˋkɚdɪʃ, ˋkʊrdɪʃ] **I** ***a.*** 库尔德人的;库尔德语的;库尔德文化的。**II** ***n.*** 库尔德语。

Ku·ril(e) Islands [kuˈriːl ˈailəndz; ˋkʊril ˋaɪləndz] 千岛群岛。

Kur·o·shi·o [kuˈrəu[illegible]əu; kʊˋroʃio] ***n.*** (从台湾东面的菲律宾海流向日本[illegible])暖流(= Japan current)。

kur·ra·jong [ˈkərədʒɔːŋ; ˋkɚrədʒɔŋ, -dʒɔŋ] ***n.***【植】异叶瓶木(*Brachychiton populneum*)〔澳大利亚树名,其枝根可以织撒和席〕。

kur·saal [ˈkuəzɑːl; ˋkurˏzɑl] ***n.*** 〔G.〕(德国温泉、海水浴场等处的)娱乐馆。

Kurt [kəːt, kuət; kɚt, kurt] ***n.*** 库尔特〔男子名,Conrad 的昵称〕。

kurt(o)- *pref.* 表示"鼓起","凸出":*kurto*sis.

kur·to·sis [kəːˈtəusis; kɚˋtosɪs] ***n.***【统】峭度。~ *of frequency curve* 频率曲线峰态。

ku·ru [ˈkuːru; ˋkuru] ***n.***【医】苦鲁病〔发现于新几内亚东部高原的一种中枢神经系统退化症〕。

ku·rus [kuˈruːʃ; kʊˋruʃ] ***n.*** (*pl.* ***ku·rus***) 库鲁〔土耳其货币名,等于 1/100 土镑,亦称里拉〕。

Kusch [kuʃ; kʊʃ] ***n.*** 库施〔姓氏〕。

K

Ku·te·nai, Ku·te·nay [ˈkuːtnei; ˋkutne] ***n*. 1.** 库特内人〔居住美国蒙大拿和爱达荷两州以及加拿大哥伦比亚省的印第安人〕。**2.** 库特内语。

Ku·wait [kuˈweit; kʊˋwet] ***n*. 1.** 科威特〔亚洲〕。**2.** 科威特〔科威特首都〕。

Ku·wai·ti [kuˈweiti, kəˈwaiti; kʊˋwetɪ, kəˋwaɪtɪ] **I *a*.** 科威特的；科威特人的。**II *n*.** 科威特人。

kv. = kilovolt(s).

KVA, KVa, kva = kilovolt-ampere 千伏安。

kvas(s) [kvɑːs; kvɑs] ***n*.** 〔Russ.〕葛瓦斯〔一种类似啤酒的清凉饮料〕。

kvell [kvel; kvɛl] ***vi*.** 〔美俚〕吹牛；扬扬得意。

kvetch [kvetʃ; kvɛtʃ] 〔美俚〕**I *n*.** 老是抱怨的人；老是找岔子的人。**II *vi*.** 抱怨；找岔子。

kw. = kilowatt(s).

Kwa [kwɑː; kwɑ] ***n*.** 克瓦语〔非洲西部和北部讲的尼日尔-刚果语族的一个语支〕。

kwa·cha [ˈkwɑːtʃɑː; ˋkwɑtʃɑ] ***n*.** (*pl*. ***kwa·cha***) 克瓦查〔赞比亚和马拉维的货币名称〕。

Kwa·ki·u·tl [ˌkwɑːkiːˈuːtl; ˏkwɑkiˋutl] ***n*. 1.** 夸丘特尔人〔加拿大不列颠哥伦比亚省的一个印第安人部落的居民〕。**2.** 夸丘特尔语。

kwa·shi·or·kor [ˌkwɑːʃiːˈɔːkɔə; ˏkwɑʃiˋɔrkɔr] ***n*.** 夸休可尔症，红发儿症〔由于婴儿断奶后食物中严重缺乏蛋白质，所引起的一种营养不良，症状如矮小、水肿、腹部突出、皮肤及毛发呈红色、肝病等〕。

kwh., KWH, K. W. H., kw-h, kw-hr = kilowatt-hour 千瓦小时。

KWIC = key word in context【计】上下文关键字，前后文关键字。

KWOC = key word out of context【计】上下文外关键字，前后文外关键字。

ky. = Kentucky.

ky·ack [ˈkaiæk; ˋkaɪæk] ***n*.** (美国西部挂在鞍子两边的)皮包[帆布包]。

ky·ak [ˈkaiæk; ˋkaɪæk] ***n*.** = kayak.

ky·a·nite [ˈkaiənait; ˋkaɪəˏnaɪt] ***n*.** = cyanite.

ky·an·ize [ˈkaiənaiz; ˋkaɪənˏaɪz] ***vt*.** 给(木材)注入升汞，用升汞溶液(给木材)防腐。

kyat [kjɑːt; kjɑt] ***n*.** 元〔缅甸货币名，等于 100 分 (*pyas*)〕。

Kyd [kid; kɪd] ***n*.** 基德〔姓氏〕。

kyle [kail; kaɪl] ***n*.** 海峡。

ky·lin [ˈkɑilin, ˈkiːlin; ˋkaɪlɪn, ˋkilɪn] ***n*.** 〔Chin.〕【动】麒麟〔雄的谓之麒，雌的谓之麟〕。

ky·lix [ˈkailiks, ˈkiliks; ˋkaɪlɪks, ˋkɪlɪks] ***n*.** (*pl*. ***ky·li·kes*** [-kiːz; -kiz]) 双柄杯〔古希腊用的大口酒杯〕。

ky·lo(e) [ˈkailəu; ˋkaɪlo] ***n*.**【动】(苏格兰高地产)长角牛犊。

ky·mo·gram [ˈkaiməugræm; ˋkaɪməˏgræm] ***n*.**【医】记波图。

ky·mo·graph [ˈkaiməugrɑːf; ˋkaɪməˏgrɑf, -ˏgræf] ***n*.**【医】记波器，描波器。**-ic *a*.**

ky·mo·gra·phy [kaiˈmɔgrəfi; kaɪˋmɑgrəfɪ] ***n*.** 记波照相术，记波法。

Kym·ric [ˈkimrik; ˋkɪmrɪk] ***a*., *n*.** = Cymric = Welsh.

Kym·ry, Kym·ri [ˈkimri, ˈkimriː; ˋkɪmrɪ, ˋkɪmri] ***n*.** (*pl*. ***-ry, -ri, -ries***) = Cymry.

Kyo·to [kiˈəutəu; ˋkjoto] ***n*.** 京都〔日本城市〕。

ky·pho- *pref*. 表示"向前弯曲"：*kypho*scoliosis, *kypho*sis.

ky·pho·sco·li·o·sis [ˈkaifəuˌskəliˈəusis; ˏkaɪfoˏskalɪˋosɪs] ***n*.**【医】脊柱后侧凸。

ky·pho·sis [kaiˈfəusis; kaɪˋfosɪs] ***n*.**【医】脊柱后凸，驼背。**kyphot·ic** [kaiˈfɔtik; kaɪˋfɑtɪk] ***a*.**

kyr·gyz·stan [kiəˈgizstæn; kɪrˋgɪstæn] ***n*.** 吉尔吉斯斯坦〔中亚国名〕。

Kyr·i·e e·le·i·son [ˈkiriˌei iˈleisəun; ˋkɪrɪˏeɪəˋleəsn] 〔Gr.〕【宗】恳求主怜悯我们〔希腊正教和天主教用作弥撒的起始语；英国圣公会用作对十诫的回答语〕。

kyte [kait; kaɪt] ***n*.** 〔Scot.〕胃，肚子。*fill one's* ～ 饱腹。

Kyu·shu [ˈkjuːˈʃuː; ˋkjuʃu] ***n*.** 九州〔日本〕。

L

L, l [el; ɛl] (*pl*. ***L's, l's*** [elz, ɛlz]) **1.** 英语字母表第十二字母。**2.** L形物，【机】L字管；L形建筑物。**3.** 第 11〔连J计算时为第 12〕。**4.**〔the L〕〔美口〕elevated railroad 高架铁路 (*ride on the L* 坐高架电车。*an L station* 高架铁路车站)。**5.** (罗马数字的)50〔*LV* = 55. *LXIV* = 64. *CXL* = 140〕。**6.**〔L.〕【物】潜热 (latent heat) 的符号。***the three L's***【海】三L〔指 lead (测铅)的用法，latitude (纬度)的知识，及严密的 look-out (守望)〕。**L-beam, L-iron** 不等边角钢。**L-cathode** 金属多孔阴极，L型阴极。**L-square** 直角板。

L, £ = [L.] *libra* (= pound)。

L., l. = 1. lady. **2.** lake. **3.** lambert. **4.** land. **5.** large. **6.** Latin. **7.** latitude. **8.** law. **9.** league. **10.** left. **11.** ledger. **12.** length. **13.** liberal. **14.**〔L.〕*libra* (*e*). **15.** licentiate. **16.** light. **17.** line. **18.** link. **19.** lira, lire. **20.** litre(s). **21.** lodge. **22.** lord. **23.** lost. **24.** low. **25.** lumen.

L.A. = **1.** Law Agent 法律代理人。**2.** Legislative Assembly〔美〕州的两院制议会。**3.** Library Association〔英〕图书馆协会。**4.** Local Agent (房地产保险公司)驻地方代理人。

La =【化】lanthanum.

La. = Louisiana.

la[1] [lɑː; lɑ] ***n*.**【乐】长音阶全音阶的第六音，A 音的唱名。

la[2] [lɔː, lɑː; lɔ, lɑ] ***int*.**〔古、方〕啊呀！看哪！〔用以加强语气或表示惊愕〕。～ *me*!〔俚〕啊呀！

LA = light [low] alcohol 轻[低]度酒精饮料〔如啤酒、葡萄酒等〕。

LAA, L.A.A. = light antiaircraft 轻型高射炮；轻型高射炮兵。

laa·ger [ˈlɑːgə; ˋlɑgə] **I *n*. 1.** (用货车等围成的)野营。**2.**【军】车阵；(用各种车辆围成的)临时防御阵地；装甲车停车处。**II *vi*. 1.** 围成车阵。**2.** 驻扎在车阵内。— ***vt*.** 把(车辆等)围成车阵[临时阵地]。

lab. [læb; læb] *n.* 〔口〕= 1. labo(u)r. 2. laboratory.

Lab. [læb; læb] = 1. Labour Advisory Board 劳工咨询委员会。2. Laborite 工党党员。3. Labrador 拉布拉多半岛〔加拿大〕。

lab·a·rum [ˈlæbərəm; ˋlæbərəm] (*pl.* ***lab·a·ra*** [-rə; -rə]) *n.* 拉伯兰旗〔1. 罗马帝国后期的军旗。2. (罗马天主教的)教旗〕。

lab·da·num [ˈlæbdənəm; ˋlæbdənəm] *n.* 【化】劳丹脂,半日花脂〔作香料用〕。

lab·e·fac·tion [ˌlæbiˈfækʃən; ˏlæbɪˋfækʃən] *n.* 动摇;衰弱;朽败;崩溃,覆灭。

la·bel [ˈleibl; ˋlebl] **I** *n.* 1. 纸条,贴条,标签,签条。2. 称号,绰号。3. 标记,符号。4. (字典中用的)说明性略语。5. (有胶水的)邮票[印花税票]。6.【建】披水石。7. 〔古〕布条,带子;封文件的丝带。*attach a ~ on ...* 在…上加标签。*union ~* 〔美〕(证明产品确是工会会员制成或销售的)工会标签。*acquire the ~ of* 得了…的绰号。**II** *vt.* (〔英〕*-ll-*) 1. 贴标签于,用签条标明。2. 把…叫做,把…列为。3. (用放射性同位素)使(元素或原子)示踪;(用示踪原子)使(化合物等)示踪。*~ a trunk for Paris* 给箱子贴上运往巴黎的标签。*The bottle is ~(l)ed "Poison".* 瓶上标明"有毒"。*~ sb. (as) a turncoat* 把某人叫做叛徒。

la·belled [ˈleibld; ˋlebld] *a.* 加有标记的;示踪的。~ **atom** 示踪原子。

la·bel·lum [ləˈbeləm; ləˋbɛləm] *n.* (*pl.* ***la·bel·la*** [ləˈbelə; ləˋbɛlə])【植】唇瓣。

la·bi·a [ˈleibiə; ˋlebɪə] *n.* labium 的复数。~ **majora** [məˈdʒaurə; məˋdʒorə]【解】大阴唇。~ **minora** [miˈnɔːrə; mɪˋnorə]【解】小阴唇。

la·bi·al [ˈleibiəl; ˋlebɪəl] **I** *a.* 1. 嘴唇的,唇状的。2.【语】唇音的。**II** *n.* 1. 风琴管。2. 唇音〔[b][p][m]等〕。**-ism** *n.* 唇音的特征,发唇音的倾向,好发唇音。**-i·ty** *n.* **-ly** *ad.*

la·bi·al·ize [ˈleibiəlaiz; ˋlebɪəˏlaɪz] *vt.* 1. 用唇发音。2. 使唇音化。**-i·za·tion** [ˌleibiəlaiˈzeiʃən; ˏlebɪəlaɪˋzeʃən] *n.*

la·bi·ate [ˈleibieit; ˋlebɪet] **I** *a.* 1. 唇形的。2.【植】唇形科的。3.【动】有唇形物的。**II** *n.*【植】唇形科植物。~ **corolla** 唇形花冠。

la·bile [ˈleibail; ˋlebaɪl] *a.* 1. 易变化的;【物、化】不稳定的。2.【电】滑动的,不安定的。~ **gene**【生】易变基因。~ **oscillator** 易变振荡器。~ **shower** 晶霰。~ **state**【化】不稳定态,易变态。

la·bi·o- *comb. f.* 表示"唇的";"唇和…的": *labio*dental.

la·bi·o·den·tal [ˌleibiəuˈdentl; ˏlebɪoˋdɛntəl] **I** *a.*【语音】用唇齿发音的。**II** *n.* 唇齿音〔[f]、[v]等〕。

la·bi·o·na·sal [ˌleibiəuˈneizl; ˏlebɪoˋnezl] **I** *a.*【语音】唇鼻音的〔如 m〕。**II** *n.* 唇鼻音。

la·bi·o·ve·lar [ˌleibiəuˈviːlə; ˏlebɪoˋvilɚ] **I** *a.*【语音】唇软颚音的〔如 w〕。**II** *n.* 唇软颚音。

la·bi·um [ˈleibiəm; ˋlebɪəm] *n.* (*pl.* ***-bi·a*** [-biə; -bɪə]) 1. 〔*pl.*〕【解】唇;阴唇。2.【动】(无脊椎动物的)唇状部分;(昆虫的)下唇。3.【植】(唇形花冠的)下唇瓣。

la·bor [ˈleibə; ˋlebɚ] *n.*, *v.* 〔美〕= labour. **L- Day** 美国劳工节〔九月的第一个星期一,相当于欧洲的 May Day〕。**L- Department** 〔美〕劳动部。

lab·o·ra·to·ri·al [ˌlæbərəˈtɔːriəl; ˏlæbərəˋtorɪəl] *a.* 实验(室)的。**-ly** *ad.*

la·bo·ra·to·ry [ləˈbɔrətəri, ˈlæbərətəri; ˋlæbərətorɪ, ˋlæbrəˏtorɪ] *n.* 1. 实验室,化验室,研究室。2. 炉房。3. 化学工厂;药厂。4. 实验课。*a chemical ~* 化学实验室。*an express ~* 快速化验室。*a hygienic ~* 卫生试验所。~ *rats* 实验用鼠。~ *sole* 炉底,炉床。~ **course** 实验学科。~ **school** 为学生实习而设的大学实验学校。

la·bo(u)red [ˈleibəd; ˋlebəd] *a.* 费力做成的;费力的,吃力的。

la·bo·ri·ous [ləˈbɔːriəs; ləˋborɪəs] *a.* 1. 费力的,麻烦的。2. 勤勉的。3. (文体的)不流畅的。*a ~ task* 吃力的工作[任务]。**-ly** *ad.* **-ness** *n.*

la·bor·ite [ˈleibərait; ˋlebəˏraɪt] *n.* 1. 工党党员或支持者。2. 〔L-〕英国工党党员;工党支持者 (= Labourite)。

la·bour [ˈleibə; ˋlebɚ] **I** *n.* 1. 劳动。2. 努力,苦干。3. 工作;活计。4. 工人 (*opp.* capital; management);〔集合词〕劳工,工人阶级,体力劳动者 (*opp.* professional)。5. 〔L-〕(英国或英联邦成员国的)工党。6. 〔*pl.*〕世事,俗务。7. 分娩,临产阵痛。8.【海】船只的剧烈摇动。*forced ~* 强迫劳动。*free ~*【史】自由民的劳动;美国未加入工会者的劳动。*hard ~* 劳役,苦役。*mental ~* 脑力劳动。*manual* [*physical*] ~ 体力劳动。~*-consuming processes* 重体力劳动作业。*cheap ~* 廉价劳动力。~ *and capital* 劳资双方。*skilled ~* 熟练劳动。*surplus ~*【经】剩余劳动。*the Minister of L- and National Service* 〔英〕劳工大臣。*the Ministry of L- and National Service* 〔英〕劳工部。*unskilled ~* 不熟练工人。*the L- vote* 支持工党的选票。*His ~s are over.* 他的一生结束了。*a woman in ~* 临产的妇女。*difficult ~* 难产。*natural ~* 顺产。~ *of love* 不取报酬自愿承担的工作,义务劳动,社会工作。~ *of Sisyphus* = *Sisyphean ~* 沉重而无结果的工作。*lost ~* = ~ *lost* 徒劳。~ *leader* 工会领袖。(*the*) *L- Leader* 工党领袖。~ *of Hercules* = *Herculean ~*(*s*) 需要极大努力的工作。

II *vi.* 1. 工作;劳动。2. 努力(争取) (*for*);出力。3. 分娩;产前阵痛。4. (船只)剧烈摇动;颠簸;困难地前进。~ *at a task* 埋头工作;辛苦地干。~ *after wealth* 忙于赚钱。~ *for bread* 挣饭吃。~ *at a problem* 绞尽脑汁地做一道难题。*I ~ed to understand him.* 我努力想了解他。*The wheels ~ed in the sand.* 车轮在沙中空转(无法前进)。*The ship ~ed in the heavy seas.* 船在大海中吃力地前进。— *vt.* 1. 使劳动;出力做。2. 详细论述。3. 使疲倦;麻烦。4. 〔古〕耕种。5. 开(矿)。*I'll not ~ the point.* 这一点我就不详细谈了。~ *the reader with unnecessary detail* 以不必要的细节来困惑读者。~ ***for breath*** 觉得呼吸困难。~ ***on*** [***along***] ***the way*** 勉强前进。~ ***one's way*** 克服困难前进。~ ***under*** 在…下耗费精力[感到困难]。~ ***under a delusion*** 想错,误解。**L- Bureau** 劳动局。~ **camp** 1. (对犯人实行强制劳动的)劳动营。2. 流动工人营地。~ **content**【经】(商品成本中的)加工费。~ **cost** 人工成本。~ **court** 劳资争议法庭。**L- Day** (五一国际)劳动节。~ **dispute** 劳资争议。~ **exchange** 1. 物物平等交换,产品交换。2. 职业介绍所;〔英〕劳工介绍所。~ **force** 劳动力。~ **insurance** 劳动保险。~**-intensive** *a.* 劳动密集型的。~ **market** 劳动市场。~ **movement** 工人运动。~ **organization** 工人组织。~ **pains** 产前阵痛。~ **relations** 劳资关系。~**-saving** *a.* 省力的,减轻劳动的。~ **turn over** (工人雇入、解雇、转业等变动的)工人移动率。~ **union** 工会。

la·boured [ˈleibəd; ˋlebəd] *a.* = labored.

la·bo(u)r·er [ˈleibərə; ˋlebərɚ] *n.* 工人;劳工,劳动者。*a free ~* 自由劳动者。*a hired farm ~* 雇农。*a long-term ~* 长工。*a seasonal ~* 短工。

la·bo(u)r·ing [ˈleibəriŋ; ˋlebərɪŋ] *a.* 1. 劳动的。2. 费力的,辛苦的。3. (船)剧烈颠簸的。*a ~ man* 工人,劳动者。***take the ~ oar*** 担任最困难的工作。**-ly** *ad.*

la·bo(u)r·ism [ˈleibərizəm; ˋlebərɪzm] *n.* 工党[工会]的主义[政策]。

la·bo(u)r·ist [ˈleibərist; ˋlebərɪst] *n.* 〔英〕= Labo(u)rite.

la·bo(u)r·some [ˈleibəsəm; ˋlebəsəm] *a.* 吃力的。

la·bra [ˈleibrə, ˈlæbrə; ˋlebrə, ˋlæbrə] *n.* labrum 的复数。

L

Lab·ra·dor [ˈlæbrədɔː; ˋlæbrədɔr] ***n***. 拉布拉多〔北美哈德逊湾与大西洋间的半岛〕。~ **current** (加拿大)拉布拉多(冷)洋流〔从巴芬 (Baffin) 海湾经拉布拉多和纽芬兰流入墨西哥湾流的北极寒流〕。~ **retriever** 拉布拉多猎犬〔能衔回猎物的猎犬〕。

lab·ra·dor·ite [ˈlæbrədɔːrait; ˋlæbrədɔrˏaɪt] ***n***.【地】富拉玄武岩;拉长石。

la·bret [ˈleibret; ˋlebrɛt] ***n***. (某些原始民族用的)嘴唇装饰物〔指介壳、骨片等〕。

lab·roid [ˈlæbrɔid, ˈleibrɔid; ˋlæbrɔɪd, ˋlebrɔɪd] **I** ***a***.【动】咽颌亚目 (*Pharyngognathi*)〔包括隆头鱼科和鹦嘴鱼科〕的。**II** ***n***. 咽颌亚目的鱼。

la·brum [ˈleibrəm; ˋlebrəm] ***n***. (*pl*. ***-bra*** [-brə; -brə])【动】上唇,外唇。

la·bur·num [ləˈbəːnəm; ləˋbɝnəm] ***n***.【植】金链花;金链花属[毒豆属]植物。

lab·y·rinth [ˈlæbərinθ; ˋlæbəˏrɪnθ] ***n***. **1**. 迷宫,曲径。**2**. (事件等的)错综复杂,纠纷;曲折;难事。**3**.【解】(内耳的)迷路。*bony* ~ 骨迷路。*membranous* ~ 膜迷路。

lab·y·rin·thi·an [ˌlæbəˈrinθiən; ˏlæbəˋrɪnθɪən], **lab·y·rin·thic** [-ik -ɪk], **lab·y·rin·thine** [-ain; -aɪn] ***a***. **1**. 迷宫的,迷宫似的。**2**. 曲折的,错综复杂的。

lac[1] [læk; læk] ***n***.【化】虫胶,紫胶,虫脂。~ **insect**【动】紫胶虫。

lac[2] [læk; læk] = lakh.

L.A.C., LAC = **1**. leading aircraft(s)man〔英〕空军二等兵。**2**. London Athletic Club〔英〕伦敦田径俱乐部。

lac·co·lite, lac·co·lith [ˈlækəlait, ˈlækəliθ; ˋlækəˏlaɪt, ˋlækəlɪθ] ***n***.【地】岩盖。~ **mountain** 岩盖山。

lace [leis; les] **I** ***n***. **1**. (鞋)带子,系带。**2**. 花边,饰边;饰带,丝带,缎带;辫带。**3**. (带有装饰图案的)精细网织品,透孔织品。**4**. (加在咖啡或食物中的)少量烈性酒。*shoe* ~*s* 鞋带。*a dress trimmed with* ~*s* 有花边的服装。*gold* ~ (外交官、海军等的服装所饰的)金边。**II** ***vt***. **1**. 结(鞋)带,用带子系紧。**2**. 在…上穿带子;交织,刺绣。**3**. 镶花边于,加条纹于。**4**.〔口〕鞭打。**5**. 给…搀酒;搀合,混合。~ *one's waist in* 用带束腰。*be tight-*~*d* 腰束得太紧。*coffee* ~*d with brandy* 加白兰地的咖啡。— ***vi***. **1**. 结带子;用带子系紧。**2**.〔口〕打,鞭打。*These boots* ~. 这靴子是结带的。~ ***into***〔口〕打,鞭打;斥骂。~ ***sb.'s coat*** [***jacket***]〔俚〕鞭打某人。~ ***up*** 用带子束[结]紧。~ **boots** 穿带长统靴。~**-curtain** ***a***. **1**. 矫饰的。**2**. 模仿中产阶级的,极想成为中产阶级的。~ **frame** 花边制造机。~ **glass** 有花边状图案的玻璃器皿。~**man** 花边商人。~ **paper** 花边纸。~ **pillow** 编织花边时放在膝上的垫子。~**-ups**〔口〕缚带的鞋子[袜子]。~**wing**【动】脉翅目昆虫。~ **work**【纺】网眼针织物,花边针织物。**-less** ***a***. 没有带子的,不镶花边的。**-like** ***a***. 带子般的,花边状的。

laced [leist; lest] ***a***. **1**. 有带子的;结带子的。**2**. 镶着花边的。**3**. (花)有彩色条纹的。**4**. (咖啡等)加有酒的。

Lac·e·dae·mo·ni·an [ˌlæsidiˈməunjən, -niən; ˏlæsɪdɪˋmonɪən, -nɪən] **I** ***a***. **1**. 古代斯巴达的,古代斯巴达人的,古代斯巴达文化的。**2**. 语言简洁的。**II** ***n***. 古代斯巴达人。

lac·er·a·ble [ˈlæsərəbl; ˋlæsərəbl̩] ***a***. 划得破的,容易撕碎的。

lac·er·ate [ˈlæsəreit; ˋlæsəˏret] **I** ***vt***. **1**. 撕碎,划破,割裂(软组织等)。**2**. 使痛心,使苦恼。**II** [ˈlæsərit; ˋlæsərɪt] ***a***. **1**. 撕碎了的,划破了的。**2**.【植】(叶子等)撕裂状的。**3**. 精神深受创伤的;悲痛的。**-ly** ***ad***.

lac·er·a·tion [ˌlæsəˈreiʃən; ˏlæsəˋreʃən] ***n***. **1**. 撕裂,划破。**2**. 伤口,裂口。**3**. 痛苦,悲痛,苦恼。**-a·tive** ***a***.

La·cer·ta [ləˈsəːtə; ləˋsɝtə] ***n***.【天】蝎虎(星)座。

la·cer·til·i·an [ˌlæsəˈtiliən; ˏlæsəˋtɪlɪən] ***a***., ***n***.【动】= saurian.

lach·es [ˈleitʃiz; ˋletʃɪz] ***n***.【法】懈怠,玩忽职守。

Lach·e·sis [ˈlæksis; ˋlæksɪs] ***n***.【希神】命运三女神之一。

Lach·ry·ma Chris·ti [ˈlækrəmə ˈkristi; ˋlækrəmə ˋkrɪstɪ] ***n***. (意大利产)浓烈甘美的红葡萄酒〔原意为基督的泪〕。

lach·ry·mal [ˈlækriməl; ˋlækrəml̩] **I** ***a***. 泪的;满是泪水的;泌泪的。**II** ***n***.〔*pl*.〕泪腺。~ **canal**【解】泪管。~ **gland**【解】泪腺。~ **sac**【解】泪囊。

lach·ry·ma·tion [ˌlækriˈmeiʃən; ˏlækrɪˋmeʃən] ***n***. 流泪。

lach·ry·ma·tor [ˈlækriˌmeitə; ˋlækrɪˏmetɚ] ***n***. 催泪剂,催泪物,(尤指)催泪毒气。

lach·ry·ma·to·ry [ˈlækrimətɔːri; ˋlækrɪmətorɪ] **I** ***a***. 泪的;催泪的。**II** ***n***. 泪壶〔古罗马人墓中发现的细颈小瓶,据说是送葬人接眼泪的小壶〕。~ **gas**【军】催泪毒气。~ **shell** [**bomb**]【军】催泪弹。

lach·ry·mose [ˈlækriməus; ˋlækrɪˏmos] ***a***. **1**. 落泪的;爱流泪的。**2**. 催泪的,悲哀的。**-ly** ***ad***.

lac·i·ly [ˈleisili; ˋlesəlɪ] ***ad***. 花边状[式]地,带状[式]地。

lac·i·ness [ˈleisinis; ˋlsɪnɪs] ***n***. 带状;花边状。

lac·ing [ˈleisiŋ; ˋlesɪŋ] ***n***. **1**. 结带;镶花边;编丝。**2**. 衣服系带,鞋带;花边;【电】花线。**3**. (咖啡等中加用的)调味酒。**4**. (花瓣、羽毛等上的)条纹。**5**.〔口〕鞭打,殴打;【拳】猛击。

la·cin·i·ate [ləˈsiniit; ləˋsɪnɪɪt] ***a***. **1**. 有穗的,有穗边的。**2**.【植】条裂的,锯齿状的。

lack [læk; læk] **I** ***vi***. 缺乏,不够,不足〔主要用现在分词形式 lacking〕。*Money is* ~*ing*. 钱不够。*Nothing is* ~*ing for your comfort*. 你的舒适设备,应有尽有了。— ***vt***. **1**. 缺乏,不够,不足。**2**. 需要。*The vote* ~*s five of being a majority*. 得票数差五票不足多数。*It* ~*s 10 minutes of seven*. 现在是七点差十分。*That fellow* ~*s common sense*. 那家伙缺乏理智。*What do you* ~? 你要买点什么?〔旧时小贩叫卖声〕。★下列例句中的 lacking 可作介词看待: Lacking (without) any better idea, adopt mine. 没有更好的主意,就采用我的主意吧。**II** ***n***. **1**. 缺乏,不足。**2**. 缺少的东西,需要的东西。*the* ~ *of sleep* 睡眠不足。***for*** [***by***, ***from***, ***through***] ~ ***of*** 因缺乏…,因无…。***have no*** ~ ***of*** 不(缺)乏。

lack·a·dai·si·cal [ˌlækəˈdeizikəl; ˏlækəˋdezɪkəl] ***a***. **1**. 若有所思的,感伤的。**2**. 装腔作势的。**3**. 无精打采的,懒洋洋的。**-ly** ***ad***. **-ness** ***n***.

lack·a·day [ˈlækədei; ˋlækəˏde] ***int***.〔古〕悲哉! 哀哉!

lack·er [ˈlækə; ˋlækɚ] ***n***., ***vt***. = lacquer.

lack·ey [ˈlæki; ˋlækɪ] **I** ***n***. (*pl*. ~*s*) **1**. (穿制服的)仆人,仆从。**2**. 走狗。**II** ***vt***. **1**. 侍候,服侍。**2**. 奉承,谄媚。

lack·lus·tre, 〔美〕**-ter** [ˈlækˌlʌstə; ˋlækˏlʌstɚ] **I** ***a***. **1**. (眼睛等)没有光泽的。**2**. 毫无生气的。**II** ***n***. **1**. 无光泽。**2**. 缺乏生气。

La·comb [ləˈkəum; ləˋkom] ***n***. **1**. 勒科姆种〔加拿大勒科姆实验站培养的一种白猪〕。**2**.〔常 l-〕勒科姆白猪。

la·con·ic(al) [ləˈkɔnik(əl); ləˋkɑnɪk(əl)] ***a***. (文章、说话等)简洁的,简短的;精练的。**-i·cal·ly** ***ad***.

la·con·i·cism, lac·o·nism [ləˈkɔnisizəm, ˈlækənizəm; ləˋkɑnəsɪzəm, ˋlækənɪzəm] ***n***. **1**. (语句的)简短,简洁,精练。**2**. 精练的语句;警句。

lac·quer [ˈlækə; ˋlækɚ] **I** ***n***. **1**. (涂在金属上的)漆。**2**. 真漆;(中国、日本等地产的)天然漆。**3**. 硝基漆,清喷漆。**4**. 漆器。**II** ***vt***. 在…上涂漆。~ **plant** [**tree**] 漆树。~**ware** 漆器。

lac·quer·er [ˈlækərə; ˋlækərɚ] ***n***. 漆工。

lac·quer·ing [ˈlækəriŋ; ˋlækərɪŋ] ***n***. **1**. 上漆。**2**. 漆涂层。

lac·quey [ˈlæki; ˋlækɪ] ***n***., ***vt***. = lackey.

lac·ri·mal [ˈlækriməl; ˋlækrɪml̩] ***a***., ***n***. = lachrymal.

lac·ri·ma·tion [ˌlækriˈmeiʃən; ˏlækrəˋmeʃən] ***n***. = lachrymation.

lac·ri·ma·tor [ˈlækrimeitə; ˋlækrəmetɚ] ***n***. = lachrymator.

lac·ri·ma·to·ry [ˈlækrimətɔːri; ˋlækrəmə,torɪ] ***a***., ***n***. = lachrymatory.

lac·ri·mose [ˈlækriməus; ˋlækrəmos] ***a***. = lachrymose.

la·crosse [ləˈkrɔs; ləˋkrɑs] ***n***. 曲棍网兜球(运动)〔曲棍上附有一网兜,把球兜着设法投入对方球门中〕。

lact- *comb*. *f*. 〔用于元音前〕= lacto-.

lac·tam [ˈlæktæm; ˋlæktæm] ***n***. 【化】内醯胺,内酰胺。

lac·ta·ry [ˈlæktəri; ˋlæktərɪ] ***a***. 〔古〕乳的;产乳白浆汁的。

lac·tase [ˈlækteis; ˋlæktes] ***n***. 【生化】乳糖酶。

lac·tate [ˈlækteit; ˋlæktet] **I** ***vi***. **1**. 出奶,分泌乳汁。**2**. 喂奶,授乳。**II** ***n***. 【化】乳酸盐。*calcium* ~ 乳酸钙。

lac·ta·tion [lækˈteiʃən; lækˋteʃən] ***n***. **1**. 乳汁的分泌。**2**. 授乳,哺乳。**3**. 授乳期。

lac·te·al [ˈlæktiəl; ˋlæktɪəl] **I** ***a***. **1**. 乳的,乳汁的;乳状的。**2**. 含有乳状液的,输送乳状液的。**3**. 乳糜管的。*the* ~ *gland* 【解】乳线。**II** ***n***. 〔*pl*.〕【解】乳糜管(= ~ vessels)。**-ly** ***ad***.

lac·tes·cence [lækˈtesəns; lækˋtɛsəns] ***n***. **1**. 乳汁状,乳汁色。**2**. 乳汁的形成。**3**. 【植】乳汁的分泌。

lac·tes·cent [lækˈtesnt; lækˋtɛsənt] ***a***. **1**. 成为乳汁状的。**2**. 产乳汁的。**3**. 【植】分泌乳汁的。

lac·ti- *comb*. *f*. = lacto-.

lac·tic [ˈlæktik; ˋlæktɪk] ***a***. 乳的;乳汁的;得自乳汁的。~ **acid** 【化】乳酸。~ **fermentation** 【微】乳酸发酵。

lac·tif·er·ous [lækˈtifərəs; lækˋtɪfərəs] ***a***. **1**. 输送乳汁的;产生乳汁的。**2**. 【植】分泌乳状汁的。*the* ~ *duct* 【解】输乳管。

lac·to- *comb*. *f*. 表示"乳";"乳酸";"乳糖"〔母音前用 lact-〕: *lacto*bacillus.

lac·to·ba·cil·lus [ˌlæktəubəˈsiləs; ˏlæktobəˋsɪləs] ***n***. (*pl*. *-cil·li* [-ai; -aɪ]) 【微】乳杆菌,乳酸杆菌。

lac·to·fla·vin [ˌlæktəuˈfleivin; ˏlæktoˋflevɪn] ***n***. 【生化】核黄素(= riboflavin)。

lac·to·gen·ic [ˌlæktəˈdʒenik; ˏlæktəˋdʒɛnɪk] ***a***. 催乳的,刺激乳腺分泌的。~ **hormone** 催乳激素。

lac·tom·e·ter [lækˈtɔmitə; lækˋtɑmətɚ] ***n***. 乳比重计,乳汁计。

lac·tone [ˈlæktəun; ˋlækton] ***n***. 【化】内酯。

lac·to·prene [ˈlæktəpriːn; ˋlæktəprin] ***n***. 【化】聚酯橡胶,乳胶〔人造橡胶〕。

lac·to·pro·te·in [ˌlæktəuˈprəutiːn, -prəutiːin; ˏlæktəˋprotin, -protiɪn] ***n***. 【生化】乳蛋白(质)。

lac·tose [ˈlæktəus; ˋlæktos] ***n***. 【化】乳糖。

la·cu·na [ləˈkjuːnə; ləˋkjunə] ***n***. (*pl*. **-s**, ***-nae*** [-niː; -ni]) ***n***. **1**. 空隙;(知识面等的)空白;(文章中等的)脱漏,缺文。**2**. 【解】腔隙,陷窝。**3**. 【植】(孢粉)空隙,腔隙。**4**. 【地】缺失(地层);洼地。*air* ~ 气隙。*blood* ~ 血(腔)隙。

la·cu·nar [ləˈkjuːnə; ləˋkjunɚ] **I** ***a***. 有花格平顶的(= lacunal)。**II** ***n***. (*pl*. ~*s*, ***lac·u·nar·i·a*** [ˌlækjuˈneriə; ˏlækjəˋnɛrɪə]) 【建】**1**. 花格平顶。**2**. 花格平顶的凹板。

la·cu·nose [ləˈkjuːnəus; ləˋkjunos] ***a***. **1**. 多孔的,多空隙的。**2**. 多空白的;脱漏多的。

La·cus [ˈlækəs; ˋlekəs] ***n***. 【天】(月面上的)湖。

la·cus·tri·an [ləˈkʌstriən; ləˋkʌstrɪən] **I** ***a***. = lacustrine. **II** ***n***. (尤指史前时代的)湖上居民。

la·cus·trine [ləˈkʌstrain; ləˋkʌstrɪn] ***a***. **1**. 湖泊的。**2**. 生活[栖息]在湖上[中]的。**3**. 【地】湖中形成的。~ *dwellings* (史前)湖上村落。*the* ~ *age* (史前)湖上生活时代。~ *fishes* 湖鱼。~ *plants* 湖沼植物。~ *deposits* 【地】湖成冲积物。*a* ~ *plain* 【地】湖成平原。~ *soil* 【地】湖积土。

lac·y [ˈleisi; ˋlesɪ] ***a***. (***lac·i·er***; ***-i·est***) **1**. 有花边的,有带子的。**2**. 花边状的,带子状的。**-i·ly** ***ad***. **-i·ness** ***n***.

lad [læd; læd] ***n***. **1**. 少年,小伙子。**2**. 〔俚〕情人。**3**. 〔口〕伙伴,老朋友。**4**. 〔英〕管赛马房的马夫。**5**. 〔俚〕放荡鬼。*a* ~ *in his teens* 十几岁的小伙子。*my* ~*s* (表示亲密的称呼)哥儿们,弟兄们。*one of the* ~*s* 〔口〕自己人。*He's a bit of a* ~. 那家伙有点儿放荡。

lad·a·num [ˈlædənəm; ˋlædənəm] ***n***. 〔L.〕= labdanum.

lad·der [ˈlædə; ˋlædɚ] **I** ***n***. **1**. 梯子。**2**. 梯状物;〔喻〕(进身的)阶梯,成功的手段。**3**. 〔英〕(袜子抽丝而形成的)梯形裂缝(= ~-like hole)。*a Jack* ~ 【船】木踏板绳梯。*a scaling* ~ 云梯。*climb a rung of the social* ~ 社会地位增高。~ *of success* 发迹的阶梯。***climb up the*** ~ 往上爬,官运亨通。***get one's foot on the*** ~ 开始,着手。***get up*** [***mount***] ***a*** ~ **1**. 上梯。**2**. 〔俚〕被处绞刑,被吊死。***He who would climb the*** ~ ***must begin at the bottom***. 〔谚〕千里之行始于足下。***Jacob's*** ~ **1**. 【圣】天梯。**2**. 〔口〕陡梯。**3**. 【海】绳梯,软梯。**4**. 从乌云中照射出来的一道太阳光。**5**. 【植】花葱。***kick away*** [***down***, ***over***] ***the*** ~ ***by which one rose*** 过河拆桥。***see through a*** ~ 看出显而易见的东西。**II** ***vi***. **1**. 〔英〕(袜子)抽丝。**2**. 成名,走红。~ *to the top of one's profession* 爬到本行业的最高峰。— ***vt***. **1**. 用梯子爬(墙等)。**2**. 在…架设梯子。**3**. 使(袜子)发生抽丝现象。~ *a wall* 用梯子爬墙。~ *a water tower* 在水塔上架梯子。~**-back** ***a***. (椅子等)背部有梯式靠背的。~ **company** 云梯救火队。~**proof** ***a***. 〔英〕(袜子等)不抽丝的。~ **stitch** 梯形(图案)刺绣法。~ **truck** 云梯救火车。**-less** ***a***. **-like** ***a***.

lad·die [ˈlædi; ˋlædɪ] ***n***. 〔主 Scot.〕少年,年青人;小伙子;〔俚〕老兄。

lade [leid; led] ***vt***. (***lad·ed***; ***lad·ed***, ***lad·en*** [ˈleidn; ˋledn̩]) **1**. 装载,把…装到[装进](车、船内);使担负〔主用 *p*.*p*.〕。**2**. 汲出(船水)。**3**. 塞满,把…压倒。~ *a ship with cargo* 把货物装载于船上。~ *water out of a boat* 从船里戽出水。— ***vi***. **1**. 装货。**2**. 汲取液体。

Lade·fo·ged [ˈlædifəugid; ˋlædɪfogɪd] ***n***. 拉迪福吉德〔姓氏〕。

lad·en[1] [ˈleidn; ˋledn̩] **I** lade 的过去分词。**II** ***a***. **1**. 装着货的;结满果实的。**2**. 有精神负担的,心情沉重的,苦恼的。*trees* ~ *with fruit* 果实累累的树。*camels laden with bundles of silk* 载着一捆捆丝的骆驼。*a heart* ~ *with sorrow* 忧心忡忡。

lad·en[2] [ˈleidn; ˋledn̩] ***vt***., ***vi***. = lade.

la-di-da [ˈlɑːdiˈdɑː; ˏlɑdɪˋdɑ] **I** ***a***. 〔口〕装腔作势的;装模作样的;故作文雅的。**II** ***n***. 〔口〕**1**. 装腔作势的人;装模作样的人;故作文雅的人。**2**. 装腔作势;矫揉造作。**III** ***int***. 太不像样!〔表示对装腔作势,浮华作风的嘲笑〕。

la·di·fy [ˈleidifai; ˋledɪfaɪ] ***vt***. **1**. 使成为贵妇人;把…称为夫人;把…看作贵妇人。**2**. 使适合贵妇人的身分〔口味〕。**ladi·fied** ***a***. 有贵妇人风度的。

La·din [ləˈdiːn; ləˋdin] ***n***. **1**. 拉登语〔瑞士东部格劳宾登和奥地利西部蒂罗尔的一种方言〕。**2**. 说拉登语的人。

lad·ing [ˈleidiŋ; ˋledɪŋ] ***n***. **1**. 装载;汲取。**2**. 船货,货物。**3**. 重量,压力。*a bill of* ~ 装货凭单;提(货)单。

La·di·no [ləˈdiːnəu; ləˋdino] ***n***. **1**. 拉地诺语〔土耳其和一些其他地中海国家的西班牙犹太人讲的一种西班牙方言〕。**2**. (*pl*. **-nos**) 〔拉美〕混血儿。

la·dle [ˈleidl; ˋledl̩] **I** ***n***. **1**. 长柄杓子。**2**. 【机】铸杓;铸桶;铁[钢]水包。**II** ***vt***. **1**. (用杓子)舀,戽。**2**. 〔口〕给与,赠送。~ ***in*** 舀进;混入,掺入。~ ***out*** 舀出;端出;提供。

la·dle·ful [ˈleidlful; ˋledl̩ˏfʊl] ***n***. 一满杓。

La·do·ga [ˈlɑːdəgə; ˋlɑdogə] ***n***. (俄罗斯西北部的)拉多加湖。

la·drone [ləˈdrəun; ləˋdron] ***n***. 强盗〔西班牙语地区用语〕。

la·dy [ˈleidi; ˋledɪ] ***n***. **1**. 贵妇;淑女。**2**. 〔L-〕夫人,小姐

L

〔英国拥有某些爵位的贵族妻女的尊称〕。**3.**〔常 *pl*.〕女士(们)〔用作称呼语〕。**4.** 女主人〔仅用于 ~ of the house 一语〕;太太,小姐〔仆人对主妇的称呼〕。**5.** 情妇;妻子;未婚妻。**6.**〔*pl*. 用作 *sing*.〕女厕所〔= ladies' room〕。**7.**〔用作修饰语〕女性。**8.**〔L-〕【宗】圣母。**9.**〔L-〕女王。*Ladies and gentlemen*! 女士们,先生们! *a ~ aviator* 女飞行家。*a ~ doctor* 女医生。*a ~ dog*〔谑〕母狗。*be not quite a ~* 不大像个贵妇人。*extra* [*walking*] ~ 跑龙套的女演员。*fancy ~* **1.** 情妇。**2.** 妓女。*fine ~* **1.** 上流妇女。**2.** 硬装作贵妇人的女子。*Ladies first*!〔口〕(男子让路时说的)女士们请先走! *Our L-* 圣母马利亚(= the Virgin Mary)。*Our Sovereign ~*〔古,诗〕女王。*the first ~* (*of the land*)〔美〕总统[元首]夫人。*the leading ~* 担任女主角的女演员。*the old ~* 老妇人;〔俚〕母亲;妻子。*one's good ~* 妻子;老婆。*the Old L- in* [*of*] *Threadneedle Street* 英格兰银行〔别称〕。*young ~* **1.** (未出嫁的)青年女子。**2.**〔口〕爱人。**ladies' gallery** (英国下议院的)妇女旁听席。**ladies' man** = ~'s man. **ladies' room** 公共女厕所,女盥洗室。**ladies' tresses** = ~'s tresses. ~ **beetle** = ~**bird** = ~**bug**【动】瓢虫。**L- Bountiful** 慷慨的女慈善家〔英国剧作家法夸尔喜剧《纨绔子弟的计谋》中的人物名〕。~ **chair** 两人用手交叉搭成的座架〔抬运伤员用〕。~ **chapel** 大教堂内的圣母堂。**L- Day**【宗】**1.** 报喜节(3月25日)。**2.**〔英〕春季结账日(3月25日)。~**finger**〔美〕**1.** 指形糕饼。**2.**〔*pl*.〕【美拳】拳头。~-**fish** *n*. (*pl*. ~*fish*, ~*fishes*)【动】海鲢 (*Elops saurus*)〔产于热带海洋〕。~**help**〔英〕(作为家属待遇的)女帮工。~**hood** **1.** 贵妇的身分[品格]。**2.**〔集合词〕太太们,小姐们。~-**in-waiting** (皇后或公主的)亲随,宫廷女侍。~-**killer** 专门勾引女子的人。~**kin** 小女孩;〔爱〕小姐。~**like** *a*. **1.** 贵妇人似的;优雅的,温柔的。**2.** (男子)带女人腔调的。~**love** 情妇。**L- Mayoress**〔英〕伦敦市长夫人。~ **of easy virtue** 放荡的女子;淫妇,妓女。~ **of letters**〔谑〕女文学家。~ **of one's heart** 意中人。~ **of pleasure** 妓女。~ **of the bedchamber**〔英〕宫廷女侍。~ **of the evening** 妓女。~ **of the frying pan**〔谑〕女厨子。~**'s companion** 女用手提包;针线包。~**'s maid** 侍女。~**'s man** 喜欢在妇女中厮混献殷勤的男子。~**'s slipper**【植】欧洲杓兰;杓兰属植物。~**'s-smock**【植】**1.** 草地碎米荠,酢浆草。**2.** 布谷鸟剪秋罗;〔美〕石芥花。~ **'s-thumb**【植】春蓼 (*Polygonum persicaria*)〔一种一年生植物〕。~**'s tresses**【植】绶草属 (*Spiranthes*)。~ **'s-wind** 软风,微风。~**ship** **1.** 夫人[贵妇]的身份[品格]。**2.**〔常 L-〕〔英〕夫人,小姐〔对有 Lady 头衔的妇女的尊称〕(*your* [*her*] *Ladyship* 太太,小姐)。

la·dy·fy [ˈleidifai; ˋledəfaɪ] *vt*. = ladify.

La·e [ˈlɑːei; ˋlɑe] *n*. 莱城〔新几内亚首都〕。

lae·o·trop·ic [ˈliːətrɔpik; ˋliətrɑpɪk] *a*. 左转的〔如螺纹和腹足纲的软体动物〕。

lae·vo- *comb*. *f*. = levo-.

La Fa·yette [ˌlɑːfaiˈet; ˏlæfɪ(j)ˋɛt] *n*. **1.** 拉法埃脱〔男子名〕。**2. Marquis de ~** 马奎斯·德·拉法埃脱〔1757—1834 法国将军,政治家。美国独立战争时,曾率领法军援助美军〕。

La Fon·tain [lɑːfɔnˈtein; lɑfɔnˋten] *n*. **Jean de** 拉封登〔1621—1695 法国诗人,寓言作家〕。

LAFTA = Latin-American Free Trade Association 拉丁美洲自由贸易协会。

lag[1] [læg; læg] **I** *vi*. (-*gg*-) **1.** 延迟,逗留,落后;慢条斯理地走。**2.** 未充分发展。**3.**【电】滞后。**4.** 慢慢地减少,变弱,松懈。~ *behind* 落后。~ *in phase*【电】相位滞后。*Interests ~s in such matters*. 对这类事的兴趣慢慢地减少了。—*vt*. **1.** 落后于;【电】滞后于。**2.**〔废〕使落后。*Japan ~s U.S.A. in developing computer technology*. 日本在发展电脑技术方面落后于美国。**II** *n*. **1.** 迟延;减速;滞后,落后,逗留。**2.** (两件事之间)相隔的时间。**3.** (牲畜等的)落后者,掉队者。*go forward without ~* 毫不延迟地进行。*the ~ of the tide* 迟潮时间。*a time ~* 时间滞差,时滞。*a time ~ of two months* 迟两个月的时间。**III** *a*. **1.** 迟的,慢的。**2.** 最后的。

lag[2] [læg; læg] **I** *n*. **1.** 桶板。**2.** (锅炉等的)外套,防护套;(纺织)纹板。**II** *vt*. (-*gg*-) 给…加上外套。~ **bolt** [**screw**] 方头木螺钉,方头尖螺丝。

lag[3] [læg; læg] **I** *vt*. (-*gg*-)〔俚〕**1.** 把…关进牢里;把(犯人等)押送去做苦役。**2.**〔英俚〕逮捕。**II** *n*.〔俚〕**1.** 囚犯;前科犯。**2.** 服刑期间,苦役期间。*an old ~* 惯犯。

lag·an [ˈlægən; ˋlægən], **lag·end** [ˈlægənd; ˋlægənd] *n*.【法】(海船发生事故时)系以浮标投入海中的货物。

lag b'O·mer [ˌlɑːg ˈbəumə; ˋlɑg ˏbomɚ] 犹太八月节〔犹太历8月18日〕。

la·ger [ˈlɑːgə; ˋlɑgɚ] *n*. 贮藏啤酒〔一种淡啤酒,酿成后贮藏数月,澄清后饮用,又作 ~ beer〕。

lag·gard [ˈlægəd; ˋlægɚd] **I** *a*. 迟缓的,落后的。**II** *n*. **1.** 迟钝的人,慢吞吞的人。**2.** 市价落后有价证券。**-ly** *ad*.

lag·ger[1] [ˈlægə; ˋlægɚ] *n*. **1.** 落伍者,落后者;落后的事物。**2.** 停滞的经济指数。

lag·ger[2] [ˈlægə; ˋlægɚ] *n*.〔俚〕囚犯,惯犯。

lag·ging[1] [ˈlægiŋ; ˋlægɪŋ] **I** *n*. 落后,迟延。**II** *a*. 慢的,落后的。~ **circuit** 滞后电路。~ **device**【电】滞相装置。~ **edge**【电】(脉冲的)下降边。**-ly** *ad*.

lag·ging[2] [ˈlægiŋ; ˋlægɪŋ] *n*. **1.** (锅炉等的)外套,防护套,罩壳。**2.** 加套;横板;护壁板。**3.**【建】套板;横档板;支拱板条。

la·gniappe, la·gnappe [lænˈjæp; lænˋjæp] *n*.〔美〕(送给顾客的)小赠品。

lag·o·morph [ˈlægəmɔːf; ˋlægəˏmɔrf] *n*.【动】兔形目 (*Lagomorpha*)〔兔、野兔等〕。**-ic** *a*.

la·goon, la·gune [ləˈguːn; ləˋgun] *n*. 环礁湖;咸水湖;潟湖。

La·gos [ˈleigɔs; ˋlɑgəs] *n*. 拉各斯〔尼日利亚首都〕。

La Gua·i·ra [Sp. lɑˈgwairɑ; lɑˋgwaɪrɑ] *n*. 拉瓜伊拉〔委内瑞拉港市〕。

lah-di-dah, lah-de-dah [ˈlɑːdiˈdɑː; ˋlɑdɪˋdɑ] = la-di-da.

La·hore [ləˈhɔː; ləˋhor] *n*. 拉合尔〔巴基斯坦城市〕。

LAI =〔It.〕*Linee Aeree Italiane* 意大利航空公司。

la·ic [ˈleiik; ˋleɪk] **I** *a*. **1.** 俗人的〔与僧侣相对而言〕。**2.** 外行的(= laical)。**II** *n*. 俗人;外行人。

la·i·cize [ˈleiisaiz; ˋleəˏsaɪz] *vt*. **1.** 使还俗;使世俗化;将(公职等)交给俗人去办。**2.** 将(公职等)让外行担任。**la·i·ci·za·tion** [ˌleiisaiˈzeiʃən; ˏleɪsaɪˋzeʃən] *n*.

la·i·cism [ˈleiisizəm; ˋleəsɪzəm] *n*. 政权还俗主义〔反对教权主义,限制教会的政治权力和影响的政策和原则〕。

laid [leid; led] lay[1] 的过去式和过去分词。~ *out*〔美俚〕负伤的;昏过去的,昏厥的;喝醉的。~-**back** *a*. 松弛的;自在的;从容不迫的。~ **paper** 直纹纸;条纹纸。

laigh [leih; leh] *a*., *ad*.〔Scot.〕低的,低矮的。

lain [lein; len] lie[1] 的过去分词。

lair[1] [lɛə; lɛr] **I** *n*. **1.** 兽窝,兽穴,兽窟。**2.**〔英〕(送家畜到市场时路上给家畜休息用的)围栏。**3.** (人的)休息处,常去处;躲藏处。〔Scot.〕墓地;〔古〕床。*the pirate's ~* 海盗的巢穴。**II** *vi*. (兽)进窝,在洞穴里睡。—*vt*. **1.** 把(兽等)赶进窝里;把(家畜等)关进围栏里。**2.** 把…作为洞穴;给…设洞穴。

lair[2] [lɛə; lɛr] **I** *n*.〔Scot.〕泥潭,泥沼。**II** *vt*. 使陷入泥潭。—*vi*. (在泥水中)打滚。

Laird [lɛəd; lɛrd] *n*. 莱尔德〔姓氏〕。

laird [lɛəd; lɛrd] *n*.〔Scot.〕地主。**-ly** *ad*. **-ship** *n*.

lais·ser-faire, lais·sez-faire [ˈleiseiˈfɛə; ˏlɛseˋfɛr] **I** *n*.〔F.〕放任,不干涉主义;自由放任〔尤指政府对工商业的政策〕。**II** *a*. 放任(主义)的。~ *capitalism* 自由资本主义。

Lais·ser-al·ler, lais·sez-al·ler [ˈleiseizælei; lɛseɑ-

L

ˋle] *n*.〔F.〕自由,放任。

Lais·ser-pas·ser, ***lais·sez-pas·ser*** [ˈleiseipæˈsei; lɛˋsepɑˋse] *n*.〔F.〕通行证,护照。

la·i·ty [ˈleiiti; ˋleətɪ] *n*.〔集合词〕**1**. (与教士、僧侣等相对的)俗人。**2**. (与专家相对的)外行。

La·ius [ˈlaijəs; ˋlaɪəs] *n*.【希神】(被儿子伊狄帕斯杀死的底比斯国王)拉伊俄斯。

Lake [leik; lek] *n*. 莱克〔姓氏〕。

lake[1] [leik; lek] *n*. **1**. 湖;(公园等中的)池塘,小湖。**2**. (贮油等的)池。*The Great L-* 大西洋。*The Great L-s* 北美洲五大湖。*the L-s* (英国北部的)湖泊地区。***Go jump in the ~!*** 〔美俚〕别来麻烦! 滚开! 不要吵! **L- Country, L- District** = the Lakes. ~ **dweller** (尤指史前的)湖上居民。~ **dwelling** (尤指史前时代建造在木桩上的)湖上桩屋。~ **front** 湖边平地。~ **let** 小湖。**L- Poets, L- School** 湖畔派〔十八世纪末十九世纪初以华滋华斯为首的一种浪漫主义诗歌流派〕。**L- State** 大湖州〔美国密执安州的别称〕。**L- Success** 成功湖〔在纽约近郊,1952年以前为联合国秘书处所在地〕。~ **trout**【动】灰红点鲑(*Salvelinus namaycush*)〔产于北美洲深水湖中〕。

lake[2] [leik; lek] *n*. **1**.【化】色淀;沉淀染料。**2**. 胭脂红。~ **colour** 色淀染料。~ **oil** 琥珀油。

lake[3] [leik; lek] *vi*. 血球溶解。—*vt*. 使(血液)发生血球溶解。

lak·er [ˈleikə; ˋlekɚ] *n*. **1**. 湖鱼〔尤指鳟鱼〕。**2**. 湖船〔尤指北美洲五大湖上的船〕。

lakh [lɑːk; læk] *n*.〔Ind.〕**1**. 十万(特指十万卢比)。**2**. 巨额,无数。

lak·y[1] [ˈleiki; ˋlekɪ] *a*. **1**. 湖的;湖水的。**2**. 多湖的。**3**. 湖状的。

lak·y[2] [ˈleiki; ˋlekɪ] *a*. 胭脂红色的。

lak·y[3] [ˈleiki; ˋlekɪ] *a*.【医】(血液中)部分红血球已崩坏的,泄色的。

lall [læl; læl] *vi*.【语音】**1**. [l] 发音不正确。**2**. 将[r]音读成[l]音。**lal·la·tion** [læˈleiʃən; læˋleʃən] *n*.

Lal·lan [ˈlælən; ˋlælən] **I** *a*.〔Scot.〕苏格兰东南部低地的。**II** *n*. ①苏格兰东南部低地。②苏格兰东南部低地方言(= Lallans)。

L'Al·le·gro [læˈleigrəu; læˋlegro] 快活人〔原为弥尔顿一首诗的题目〕。

Lam. = Lamentations【圣】《哀歌》。

lam[1] [læm; læm] *vi*., *vt*. (*-mm-*)〔俚〕(用棍子等)打,鞭打,笞责(*out*; *into*)。

lam[2] [læm; læm] *vi*. (*-mm-*), *n*.〔美俚〕逃走,潜逃。***on the*** ~ 在潜逃中(*a convict on the* ~ 在逃犯)。***take it on the*** ~ 潜逃,远走高飞。

la·ma[1] [ˈlɑːmə; ˋlɑmə] *n*. (中国西藏、蒙古的佛教僧侣)喇嘛。

la·ma[2] [ˈlɑːmə; ˋlɑmə] *n*.【动】= llama.

La·ma·ism [ˈlɑːməizəm; ˋlɑməɪzəm] *n*. 喇嘛教。

La·ma·ist [ˈlɑːməist; ˋlɑməɪst] **I** *n*. 喇嘛教徒。**II** *a*. = Lamaistic.

La·ma·is·tic [ˌlɑːməˈistik; ˏlɑməˋɪstɪk] *a*. **1**. 喇嘛教徒的。**2**. 喇嘛教的;与喇嘛教有关的。

La·mar [ləˈmɑː; ləˋmɑr] *n*. 拉马尔〔姓氏,男子名〕。

La·marck [ləˈmɑːk; ləˋmɑrk], **Jean Baptiste Pierre Antoine de Monet, Chevalier de** 拉马克〔1744—1829,法国博物学家,进化论者〕。**-i·an** **1**. *a*. 拉马克学说的。**2**. *n*. 拉马克学派的人。**-ism** *n*. 拉马克的进化论〔学说〕。

la·ma·ser·y [ˈlɑːməsəri; ˋlɑməˏserɪ] *n*. 喇嘛庙。

lam·as·ter [ˈlæməstə; ˋlæməstɚ] *n*.〔美俚〕= lamister.

Lamb [læm; læm] *n*. **1**. 拉姆〔姓氏〕。**2**. **Charles** ~ 查尔斯·兰姆〔1775—1834,英国散文家,批评家〕。

lamb [læm; læm] **I** *n*. **1**. 羔羊,小羊;小羚羊。**2**. 羔羊肉;羔羊皮。**3**. 像羔羊般柔弱[温和、天真烂漫]的人。**4**. 〔俚〕容易上当的人〔尤指在证券交易方面〕。**5**. 好宝宝,小乖乖〔对孩子的爱称〕。**6**.〔the L-〕【宗】耶稣。*my* ~ 好宝宝。***a fox*** [***wolf***] ***in*** **~*'s skin*** 伪君子,伪善者。***as well be hanged*** [***hung***] ***for a sheep as*** (***for***) ***a*** ~ 一不做二不休。***like a*** ~ **1**. 驯顺地,乖乖地。**2**. 天真烂漫地;容易上当地。***the*** ~ ***of God*** 神的羔羊,耶稣。**II** *vt*. **1**. 生(小羊)。**2**. 照顾(产期母羊)。*vi*. 生小羊。~**kill** = sheep laurel. ~**kin** 小羊羔;小家伙,小鬼〔有时用作对儿童的爱称〕。~**like** *a*. **1**. 羔羊似的,怯弱的,温和的。**2**. 天真烂漫的。~**skin** **1**. 羔羊皮〔尤指带羊毛的〕。**2**.羔皮革,羊皮纸。**3**.仿羔羊皮织物;纬面缎纹绒布。~**'s-quarters**【植】藜(*Chenopodium album*)〔一种一年生草本植物,嫩叶可食用〕。~**'s wool** 羔毛〔极柔软的高级羊毛〕;加糖水苹果丁的甜啤酒。

lam·ba·da [læmˈbɑːdə; læmˋbɑdə] *n*. 伦巴达舞(曲)〔源自巴西的一种色情舞〕。

lam·bast(e) [læmˈbeist; læmˋbest] *vt*. **1**.〔俚〕鞭打,狠揍。**2**. 严厉申斥。

lamb·da [ˈlæmdə; ˋlæmdə] *n*. **1**. 希腊语第十一个字母〔Λ, λ 与英语字母 L 相当〕。**2**. 微升〔百万分之一升〕。**3**. λ 粒子(= ~ particle)。~ **hyperon** λ 超子。~ **point**【物】λ 点。

lamb·da·cism [ˈlæmdəsizəm; ˋlæmdəsɪzm̩] *n*. **1**. L 字使用过多。**2**. = lallation.

lamb·doid [ˈlæmdɔid; ˋlæmdɔɪd] *a*. **1**. 希腊语第十一个字母(Λ)的。**2**.【解】(枕骨和顶骨间的骨缝)人字形的。

lam·ben·cy [ˈlæmbənsi; ˋlæmbənsɪ] *n*. **1**. (光、火焰等的)轻轻摇曳,微微闪耀。**2**. 柔光。**3**. (诙谐等的)巧妙。

lam·bent [ˈlæmbənt; ˋlæmbənt] *a*. **1**. (火焰等)在燃烧中,轻轻摇曳的,闪烁的。**2**. (眼睛等)微亮的;发柔光的。**3**. (诙谐等)巧妙的。**-ly** *ad*.

Lam·bert [ˈlæmbə(ː)t; ˋlæmbɚt] *n*. **1**. 兰伯特〔姓氏〕。**2**.【物】朗伯〔亮度单位〕。

Lam·beth [ˈlæmbəθ; ˋlæmbɪθ] *n*. **1**. 伦敦朗伯斯区。**2**. 伦敦坎特伯雷大主教宫邸(= ~ Palace);该宫邸所在地。**3**. 坎特伯雷大主教的地位[职位]。

lam·bre·quin [ˈlæmb(r)əkin; ˋlæmb(r)əˏkɪn] *n*. **1**. (门窗等上部的)垂饰;(橱柜的)帘幕。**2**. (瓷器边缘上的)扇形彩色图案。**3**. (中世纪骑士铁盔上的)饰罩,覆巾。

lame[1] [leim; lem] **I** *a*. (***lam·er***, ***lam·est***) **1**. 跛的,瘸的,残废的。**2**. 僵痛的。**3**. 有缺点的;(论据等)站不住脚的;不中用的。**4**. (诗)不合韵律的。*be* ~ *of* [*in*] *one leg* 跛一条腿的。*go* ~ 变成瘸子。*walk* ~ 跛行,一瘸一拐地走。*a* ~ *excuse* 站不住脚的辩解。*a* ~ *imitation* 低劣的仿制品。~ *verses* 蹩脚的诗。***help a*** ~ ***dog over a stile*** 帮助人渡过难关。**II** *vt*. **1**. 使跛,使残废,把…弄残废。**2**. 使不中用。*be* ~*d for life* 终身残废。— *vi*. 跛行。**III** *n*. **1**. 古板守旧的人;落后分子。**2**. 消息不灵的人,不知情况[内情]的人。~**brain**〔口〕蠢人,笨蛋,傻瓜。~**brained** *a*. 蠢,笨,傻。~ **duck** **1**. 残废者,不中用的人[物]。**2**.〔美〕(任期快满未再当选而暂时留守的)即将去职的官员[议员]。**3**.〔美〕不能再竞选连任的总统。**4**. 无力履行财政债务的股票投机者。**-ly** *ad*. **-ness** *n*.

lame[2] [leim; lem] *n*. **1**. (金属)薄板,薄片。**2**.〔*pl*.〕(古代护身甲上的)重叠金属片。

la·mé [lɑːˈmei; læˋme] *n*.〔F.〕金银线织物。

la·med [ˈlɑːmid; ˋlɑmɪd] *n*. 希伯来语第十二个字母。

la·mel·la [ləˈmelə; ləˋmɛlə] *n*. (*pl*. *-lae* [-iː; -i], *~s*) **1**. 薄片,薄层,薄板,薄结构。**2**.【解】同心板骨;【动】鳃瓣,壳层;【植】菌褶;栉片。**-r** *a*. 片状的;层状的。**-ly** *ad*.

lam·el·late [ˈlæməleit, ləˈmeleit; ˋlæməˏlet, ləˋmɛlet] *a*. **1**. 包含薄片层的,排成薄片层形的,似薄片层的。**2**. = lamelliform.

la·mel·li·branch [ləˈmelibræŋk; ləˋmɛlɪbræŋk] **I** *n*.【动】瓣鳃网(*Pelecypoda*)软体动物〔如蛤、蠔等〕。**II** *a*. 瓣鳃网的(= lamellibranchiate)。

L

la·mel·li·corn [lə'melikɔːn; lə`mɛlə,kɔrn] **I** ***a***.【动】1. 鳃角的。2. 鳃角类(甲虫)的〔包括小金虫和蟑螂等〕。**II** ***n***. 鳃角类甲虫。

la·mel·li·form [lə'melifɔːm; lə`mɛləfɔrm] ***a***. 薄片形的,薄片状的,片状的,鳞状的,鳃状的。

la·mel·li·ros·tral [ləˌmeli'rɔstrəl; lə,mɛlə`rɑstrəl] ***a***.【动】扁嘴类的〔如野鸭、鹅等水禽〕(= lamellirostrate)。

la·mel·lose [lə'meləus, 'læmələus; lə`mɛlos, `læməlos] ***a***. = lamellate. **-los·i·ty** [-'lɔsiti; -`lɑsətɪ] ***n***.

la·ment [lə'ment; lə`mɛnt] **I** ***n***. 1. 恸哭,哀悼,悲叹。2. 哀歌,挽歌,悼词。**II** ***vi***. 悲叹,哀悼。～ *for a friend over his death* 哀悼朋友的故去。— ***vt***. 1. 哀悼,痛惜。2. 悲叹。～ *the death of a hero* 为英雄逝世而哀悼。～ *one's folly* 悔恨自己的愚笨。*We ～ed his absence*. 我们对他的缺席深感遗憾。

lam·en·ta·ble ['læməntəbl; `læməntəbl̩] ***a***. 1. 可悲的,可叹的。2. 哀伤的,悲哀的。3. (作品,制作物等)质量低的;不像样的。**-bly** ***ad***.

lam·en·ta·tion [ˌlæmen'teiʃən; ,læmən`teʃən] ***n***. 1. 悲叹;哀悼;痛哭。2. [L-s] (旧约《圣经》中的)《哀歌》。

la·ment·ed [lə'mentid; lə`mɛntɪd] ***a***. 被哀悼的。***the late*** ～ 死者(特指亡夫)。**-ly** ***ad***.

la·ment·ing [lə'mentiŋ; lə`mɛntɪŋ] ***a***. 悲伤的,悲哀的。**-ly** ***ad***.

la·mi·a ['leimiə; `lemɪə] ***n***. (*pl*. *～s*, *-ae* [-miiː; -mɪi]) 1.【希罗神】半人半蛇吸血女怪。2. 妖妇。

lam·i·na ['læminə; `læmənə] ***n***. (*pl*. ***-nae*** [-niː; -ni], *～s*) 1. (金属或动物组织的)薄片,片层,薄层,叠层,层状体。2.【植】叶片。**-l**, **-ry** ***a***. = laminar.

lam·i·na·ble ['læminəbl; `læmɪnəbl̩] ***a***. 可辗薄的,可切成薄片(层)的。

lam·i·nar ['læmənər; `læmɪnɚ] ***a***. 由薄片或层状体组成的,薄片状的;层状的。～ *flow*【物】片流,层流。

lam·i·nate ['læmineit; `læmə,net] **I** ***vt***. 1. 把(金属等)辗压成薄板。2. 把…切[分]成薄片。3. 用薄片叠成。4. 用薄板覆盖。5. 黏合(薄片)。—***vi***. 变[分]成薄板[薄片]。**II** ['læminit; `læmɪnɪt] ***n***. 薄片制品;层压板。**III** ['læminit; `læmɪnɪt] ***a***. = laminated.

lam·i·nat·ed ['læmineitid; `læmə,netɪd] ***a***. 由薄片叠成的;层状的。～ **chain** 分片链。～ **coal** 页煤。～ **core**【电】叠片铁心。～ **plastics**【化】层压塑料。～ **wood** 层积木,胶合板。

lam·i·na·tion [ˌlæmi'neiʃən; ,læmə`neʃən] ***n***. 1. 层压;叠合。2.【电】叠片,铁心片。3. 叠片结构;层压结构。4.【地】纹理。5. = lamina.

lam·i·nec·to·my [ˌlæmi'nektəmi; ,læmɪ`nɛktəmɪ] ***n***. (*pl*. ***-mies***)【医】椎板切除术。

lam·i·ni·tis [ˌlæmi'naitis; ,læmə`naɪtɪs] ***n***.【兽医】蹄叶炎。

lam·ish ['leimiʃ; `lemɪʃ] ***a***. 1. 有点瘸的。2. 不怎么完善的。

lam·is·ter ['læmistə; `læmɪstɚ] ***n***. 〔美俚〕= lamster.

Lam·mas (Day) ['læməs; `læməs] ***n***. 八月一日收获节。***at later*** [***latter***] ～ 决不会再有的〔因为一年只一个8月1日〕。

lam·mer·gei·er, **lam·er·gey·er** ['læməgaiə; `læmɚ-gaɪr] ***n***.【动】髭兀鹰 (*Gypaetus barbatus*)〔产于欧亚的一种大鹰〕。

lamp [læmp; læmp] **I** ***n***. 1. 灯。2. 灯泡。3. 电子管。4. (智慧等的)明灯;思想的指导。5. 〔诗〕(明亮的)天体〔日、月、星〕。6. 〔*pl*.〕〔俚〕眼睛,炬火。*an amber* ～ (表示交通危险而悬挂的)黄色信号灯。*an amplifying* ～【电】放大管。*an arc* ～ 弧光灯。*a blackout* ～ 防空灯。*a crater* ～ 凹孔放电管;点源录影灯。*a daylight* ～ 日光灯。*a dim* ～ 磨砂灯泡。*a discharge* ～ 放电灯,放电管。*an electric* ～ 电灯。*a kino* ～ 映像管。*an oil* (〔美〕*kerosene*) ～ 煤油灯。*an ultraviolet* ～ 紫外线灯。～ *of heaven* 发亮的天体〔日、月、星〕。～ *of Phaebus* 太阳。*Aladdin's* ～ 阿拉丁的神灯,如意灯。***hand*** [***pass***] ***on the*** ～ 助长知识的发达[文化的进步]〔出自古希腊的火炬接力赛跑〕。***rub the*** ～ 很容易地实现自己的计划〔像摩擦阿拉丁神灯一般〕。***smell of the*** ～ 带有(在灯下)苦心构思的痕迹。**II** ***vt***. 1. 〔诗〕照亮。2. 〔美俚〕看,看到。～**black** 1. 灯黑色,灯烟色。2. 油烟。～ **bulb** 电灯泡。～ **burner** 灯口。～ **chimney** (煤油灯用)玻璃灯罩。～ **holder** (插电灯泡的)灯座。～**-hour**【电】灯时。～**house** (仪器上的)光源。～ **light** 灯火,灯光。～**lighter** (已往街灯的)点灯者 (*like a* ～*lighter* 很快地,迅速地)。～**post** 灯杆,路灯柱。～**shade** 灯罩 ～**shell**【动】酸浆介〔一种带壳的海内蠕形动物〕。～**stand** 灯柱。～**wick** 灯心。**-less** ***a***.

lam·pa·de·pho·ri·a [ˌlæmpədi'fɔːriə; ,læmpədɪ`fɔrɪə] ***n***. (古希腊的)火炬接力赛跑 (= lampadedromy)。

lam·pas[1] ['læmpəs; `læmpəs] ***n***.【兽医】腭嵴红肿 (= lampers)。

lam·pas[2] ['læmpəs; `læmpəs] ***n***. 〔F.〕彩花细锦缎〔全丝、全棉或丝棉交织〕。

lam·pi·on ['læmpiən, `læmpɪən] ***n***. (马车上装饰用)彩色小油灯。

lam·poon [læm'puːn; læm`pun] **I** ***n***. 讽刺文[诗]。**II** ***vt***. 写讽刺诗[文]讽刺。**-er**, **-ist** ***n***. 讽刺作家。

lam·prey ['læmpri; `læmprɪ] ***n***.【动】七鳃鳗,八目鳗。

lam·pro·phyre ['læmprəfaiə; `læmprəfaɪr] ***n***.【地】煌斑岩。

Lamp·son ['læm*p*sn; `læmsn] ***n***. 兰普森〔姓氏〕。

lam·ster ['læmstə; `læmstɚ] ***n***. 〔美俚〕潜逃者,逃亡者;逃犯,逃兵。

Lan, lan [læn; læn] = local area network【计】局部地区网络。

la·na·i [lɑː'nɑːi; lɑ`nɑɪ] ***n***. (上有顶棚的)夏威夷式阳台,晒台。

la·nate ['leineit; `lenet] ***a***.【植、动】绵状的;具绵状毛的;面上有细绒[细毛]的。

Lan·ca·shire ['læŋkəʃiə; `læŋkəʃɪr] ***n***. 兰开夏〔英国郡名〕。

Lan·cas·ter ['læŋkəstə; `læŋkəstɚ] ***n***. 1. 兰开斯特〔英、美城市〕。2.【英史】兰开斯特王朝〔1399—1461〕。

Lan·cas·tri·an [læŋ'kæstriən; læŋ`kæstrɪən] **I** ***a***. 1. 兰开夏郡的。2. 兰开斯特城的。3.【英史】兰开斯特王朝的。**II** ***n***. 1. 兰开夏郡人。2. 兰开斯特城的居民。3.【英史】(尤指玫瑰战争中)拥护兰开斯特王朝的人。

Lance [lɑːns; læns] ***n***. 兰斯〔男子名, Lancelot 的昵称〕。

lance [lɑːns, -æ-; læns, -æ-] **I** ***n***. 1. 标枪,长矛。2. 〔*pl*.〕枪骑兵,持长矛骑马的战士。3. 矛状器具;捕鲸枪;【军】撞杆〔旧时装填大炮弹药的杆〕。4.【医】柳叶刀,双刃小刀。*oxygen* ～ 氧气切割枪,氧气切割嘴。***break a*** ～ ***with sb***. 和某人比赛[争论]。**II** ***vt***. 1. 用矛刺穿。2.【医】用柳叶刀割开。3. 投,掷。— ***vi***. 急速前进。～ **corporal** (英国陆军中代理下士而薪俸并不增加的)一等兵。～ **fish**【动】= launce. ～ **sergeant**【英军】代理中士〔由下士暂时代理的中士〕。

lance·let ['lɑːnsəlit; `lænslɪt] ***n***.【动】蛞蝓鱼,文昌鱼。

Lan·ce·lot ['lɑːnsələt; `lænsələt] ***n***. 兰斯洛特〔1. 男子名。2. 亚瑟王 (*King Arthur*) 故事中圆桌骑士之一〕。

lan·ce·o·lar ['lænsiələ; `lænsɪəlɚ], **lan·ce·o·lat·e(d)** ['lɑːnsiəlit(id); `lænsɪəlɪt(ɪd)] ***a***. 1. 矛尖状的。2.【植】(叶)披针形的。

lanc·er ['lɑːnsə; `lɑnsɚ] ***n***. 1. 持标枪的人。2. 枪骑兵。3. 〔*pl*.〕特种四人对舞 (quadrille) (舞曲)。

lan·cet ['lɑːnsit, læn-; `lænsɪt, læn-] ***n***. 1.【医】柳叶刀;刺血针;口针。2.【建】矛尖状装饰;尖拱 (= ～ arch);尖头窗 (= ～ window)。

lan·cet·ed ['lɑːnsitid; `lænsətɪd] ***a***.【建】矛尖状装饰的;有尖拱的;有尖头窗的。

L

lan·ci·form [ˈlænsifɔːm; ˋlɑnsəˏfɔrm] *a*. 矛(尖)状的;标枪状的。

lan·ci·nate [ˈlænsiˈneit; ˋlænsənet] *vt*. (*-nat·ed*; *-nat·ing*) 刺;扎;撕裂〔现除医学外罕用〕。*a ~ pain* 刀绞般的疼痛。**lan·ci·na·tion** [ˌlænsiˈneiʃən; ˏlænsəˋneʃən] *n*.

Lancs. = Lancashire.

land [lænd; lænd] **I** *n*. **1.** 陆地,地面。**2.** 土地,田地;农田;〔*pl*.〕所有地,地产。**3.** 国土,国,国家;领土;地方;(…的)世界;地带,境界。**4.** 台阶。**5.** 采掘段。**6.** (枪炮的)阳堂线。**7.** 〔美口〕老天爷! (= Lord)。**8.** (刀刃的)厚度,刃棱面;(纹间)表面。**9.** 平台。*a ~ campaign* [*warfare*] 陆战。*go by ~* 从陆路去。*arable ~* 适于耕作的土地。*open barren ~* 开荒。*coal ~* 煤田。*green ~* 牧场。*~ reclamation* 开垦荒地。*waste ~* 荒地。*work* [*go*] *on the ~* 务农。*Do you have much ~ in France?* 你在法国有很多地皮么? *own houses and ~s* 拥有房地产。*come home from foreign ~s* 从外国归来。*from all ~s* 来自各国。*home* [*native*] *~* 祖国。*throughout the ~* 全国各地。*in the ~ of dreams* 在梦乡。*in the ~ of the living* 在人世,在现世。*Back to the ~!* 回故乡去! (文学上)回到田园生活! *back ~s* 穷乡僻壤。**bad ~s** **1.** 易受侵蚀、不堪耕作的干旱土地。**2.** 〔B- L-〕美国西部这类荒地。*the ~ of cakes* 糕饼国〔指苏格兰〕。*the L- of Flowers* 花卉之乡〔美〕〔佛罗里达州的别名〕。*the ~* [*L-*] *of Nod* 睡乡。*the ~ of Promise* [*Covenant*]【圣】应许的乐土〔指上帝应许赐给亚伯拉罕子孙的迦南乐土〕。*the ~ of stars and stripes* 星条旗之国〔指美国〕。*the ~ of the bone-dry free* 〔讽〕没有喝酒自由的国家〔指实施禁酒法时期的美国〕。*the ~ of the golden fleece* 金羊毛之国〔澳大利亚的别号〕。*the ~ of the leal* 天堂。*the ~ of the Rose* 玫瑰之国〔指英国〕。***clear ~*** 清除土地上的树木等(以备耕种)。***clear the ~*** (船只)离岸出海。***close with the ~*** 接近陆地。***Dixie L-*** **1.**【史】美国南方实行奴隶所有制的各州。**2.** 美国南方各州。***good ~*** 〔美口〕天啊! 好家伙! 糟糕! ***how the ~ lies*** **1.**【海】在什么方位? **2.** 形势如何? 情况如何 (*find out how the ~ lies* 摸清情况)。***~ flowing with milk and honey***【圣】乳与蜜成河的国土;富裕的福地。***L- ho!*** 看到陆地啦!〔海员在航海中发现陆地时的欣喜喊声。〕***lay*** [***shut in***] ***the ~***【海】远出海中不见陆地。***lie along*** [***keep in with***] ***the ~*** 沿岸航行。***make*** (***the***) ***~*** 看见陆地,到岸。***My L-!*** = good ~! ***no man's ~*** **1.**【史】无主地。**2.**【军】无人地带,真空地带。***on ~*** 在陆地上。***see ~*** **1.** 看到陆地。**2.** 行将达到目的。***see how the ~ lies*** 观察形势。***set*** (***the***) ***~*** 测陆地的方向。***sight the ~*** = *make* (*the*) *~*. ***the ~ of the living*** 人世,现世。***the lay*** [***lie***] ***of the ~*** **1.**【海】海岸的方向,陆地的位置。**2.** 事物的情况 ***touch*** [***reach***] ***~*** (从海上)逃到陆上;〔喻〕得到稳固的立足点。

II *vt*. **1.** 使上陆,使登岸;使(飞机)着陆,使降陆。**2.** 自船[飞机]上卸下;将(捕到的鱼等)拉上岸[船]。**3.** 使到达,把…送到。**4.** 〔口〕捞到,获得。**5.** 打。**6.** 使处于。**7.** (骑师)使(马)进入决胜点(跑得第一名)。*The pilot ~-ed the aeroplane*. 驾驶员使飞机着陆。*The ship ~ed its passengers*. 船让旅客登岸。*The detective ~ed the criminal*. 侦探捕获了罪犯。*~ a prize* 得奖。*This ~-ed me in great difficulties*. 这使我非常为难了。*be nicely ~ed* 〔反语〕一筹莫展,毫无办法。*~ a man with coat that doesn't fit* 给人穿不合身的上衣。— *vi*. **1.** 上岸,登陆 (*at*); (飞机)着陆。**2.**【无】接地。**3.** 到达。**4.** 陷入。**5.** (马)跑得第一名。**6.** (罪犯等)落网。*The passengers ~ed*. 旅客都已上岸。*The thief ~ed in jail*. 罪犯被捕入狱。**~ on** 〔俚〕申斥,批评。**~ *on one's*** [***both***] ***feet*** 逢凶化吉。**~ agency** 〔英〕地产管理(处);〔美〕土地买卖代办所。**~ agent** 〔英〕地产经理人,土地管理人;〔美〕地产经纪人。**~-air** *a*.【军】**1.** 地对空的。**2.** 陆空联合的。**~ bank** 〔美〕(专营地产抵押业务的)地产银行。**~-based** *a*. 在陆地上有基地的,岸基的。**~ breeze** 陆风〔自陆地吹向海上的微风〕。**~ carriage** 陆运。**~ casing**【机】下套管。**~ clearance**【机】周刃隙角。**~ contract** 房地产转让分期付款契约。**~ crab** 陆栖蟹。**~fall** **1.** 远洋航行后初见陆地,接近陆地 (*make a bad ~fall* 未按预计时间靠岸。*make a good ~-fall* 按预计时间靠岸)。**2.**【空】着陆。**3.** 地崩。**4.** 土地所有权的突然获得。**~fill** **1.** 垃圾填埋洼地,垃圾填筑地。**2.** 把…埋入垃圾填筑地。**~ force(s)** 陆军。**~form** 地形。**~ girl** 〔英〕(战时代替男子作农业劳动的)青年农民妇女。**~grabber** **1.** 霸占土地者。**2.** 〔爱〕驱逐佃户而收买[承租]其土地的人。**~-grant** *a*. 被拨给土地的〔指美国获得政府拨给土地的大学,条件是必须开授有关农业和机械技术课程〕。**~ grant** [美](为建设铁路或给大学的)拨赠土地。**~holder** **1.** 土地所有者。**2.** 土地租用人。**~-hunger** 土地占有欲。**~-jobber** 地产投机商;地皮掮客。**~lady** **1.** (旅馆等的)女店主。**2.** 女地主,女房东。**~ law** 土地法。**~ line** 陆上通讯[运输]线。**~ locked** *a*. **1.** (湖等)被陆地包围着的) (*a ~ locked country* 内陆国家)。**2.**【动】(鲑等)生活在与海洋隔绝的淡水中的。**~lord** **1.** 地主 (*the ~lord class* 地主阶级。*the despotic ~lord* 恶霸地主)。**2.** (旅馆等的)店主;房东。**~ lordism** 地主所有制。**~lubber** **1.** 没有出过海的;不习惯海上生活的人。**2.** 外行水手。**~mark** **1.** 界标。**2.**【海】陆标。**3.** (一生中或历史上的)突出事件;划时期的事件。**4.** (有特殊历史价值或艺术价值的)地面文物;受保护的文物建筑。**~mass** 大陆块,大片陆地。**~ measure** **1.** 地积制。**2.** 地积单位[如英亩、公顷等]。**~ mine** **1.** 地雷。**2.** 第二次世界大战中用降落伞投下的薄壳炸弹。**~(-)mobile** *a*. (导弹等装在火车或卡车上)地面上移动的。**L- of the Midnight Sun** 午夜太阳国〔指挪威〕。**L- of the Rising Sun** 日出之国〔指日本国〕。**~ office** 土地管理局〔处理和登记国家的土地买卖事宜〕。**~-office business** 〔口〕兴旺的生意,买卖兴隆。**~ owner** 土地拥有者;地主。**~ownership** 土地拥有者的身分[地位]。**~ owning** *a*., *n*. 拥有土地的(人)。**~ patent** 土地证。**~ plaster** 石膏肥料。**~-poor** *a*. 有地无钱的〔指拥有大量土地、但因土地税高和产量低而缺现款者〕。**~ power** **1.** 陆军(实力)。**2.** 陆军强国。**~rail** = corncrake. **~ reform** 土地改革。**~rover** 轻便汽车〔英制工农业用吉普车型〕。**~ scurvy**【医】紫癜。**~'s end** **1.** (一国或一地的)末端地区。**2.** 〔L- End〕美国最西端小村。**~ service** 陆军兵役。**~ shark** **1.** (专骗登陆水手的)码头骗子。**2.** 抢土地者。**~side** **1.** (向旅客开放的)机场公共场所。**2.** 犁侧板,耕沟壁。**~skip** 〔废〕landscape 的变体。**~slide** 〔主美〕**1.** = landslip. **2.** 〔美〕(选举的)大胜利;压倒的优胜 (*the momentum of a ~slide* 排山倒海之势)。**~slip** 〔英〕山崩;崩塌;塌方。**~ swell** (海岸附近的)巨浪。**~ tax** 土地税。**~ tie**【建】着地拉杆。**~ waiter** 海关人员。**~wash** **1.** 波浪对海岸的冲击。**2.** 高潮线。**~ way** *n*. 陆路;陆路交通。**~ wind** = ~ breeze. **~worker** 农夫。**~(-)yacht** 大型轿车;大型旅宿汽车。

lan·dau [ˈlændɔː; ˋlændɔ] *n*. **1.** 双排座后活顶小客车,双排座敞篷轿车。**2.** 双排座开合[脱卸]式顶篷四轮马车,活顶四轮马车。**~let**, **~lette** 小型车顶折叠式马车。

land·ed [ˈlændid; ˋlændɪd] *a*. **1.** 有土地的,地主方面的。**2.** 土地的;地产的,不动产的。**3.** (运到)陆地上的;上了岸的。*the ~ classes* 地主阶级。*the ~ interest* 地主方面的利益。*a ~ estate* = *~ property* 地产。*newly ~ fish* 刚刚卸到岸上的鱼。

lan·der [ˈlændə; ˋlændɚ] *n*. **1.**【矿】司罐工人,把钩工人。**2.** (太空飞行)着陆器,着陆舱。**3.** (输送金属用的)斜槽。

L. & G. = loss and gain 损益。

L

land·grave [ˈlændgreiv; ˋlændˏgrev] *n*. 1. 伯爵领主〔中世纪德国拥有土地的伯爵〕。2. 某些德国王公的称号。**-gra·vi·ate** [-ˈgreiviit; -ˋgreviɪt] *n*. 伯爵领主的职位[权力,领地]。**-gra·vine** [-grəˌviːn; -grəˏvin] *n*. 女伯爵领主;伯爵领主夫人。

land·ing [ˈlændiŋ; ˋlændɪŋ] *n*. 1. 登陆;着陆,降落;下车。2. 登陆处;(飞机)着陆地;码头;(车站的)月台。3. 【建】楼梯平台;梯台;【林】集材场,贮木场;【矿】装卸台。4. 【无】(电子的)沉陷,沉淀。*make* [*effect*] *a* ~ 登陆;着陆。*make a forced* ~ 强迫降落,迫降。*make a safe* ~ 安全降落。*make a soft* ~ 软着陆。***Happy*** ~! 祝旅途平安〔送行者向上飞机的人告别语〕。~ **account** 【商】起货报告。~ **book** 【商】起货清单。~ **certificate** 〔美〕登陆证。~ **charges** 〔*pl*.〕起货费。~ **craft** 登陆艇。~ **field** [**ground**] 着陆地,飞机场。~ **force** 登陆部队,陆战队。~ **gear** 【空】起落装置,起落架。~ **net** (用以抄取上钩的鱼的)抄网。~ **party** 登陆(分遣)队。~ **place** 登陆处,码头;着陆地。~ **run** 降落滑行距离。~ **ship** 登陆舰。~**-ship-tank** 登陆舰〔略作 L. S. T.〕. ~ **skid** 【空】起落橇。~ **speed** (最低)着陆速度。~ **stage** 趸船,栈桥。~ **station** 【空】降落站。~ **strip** 1. (飞机场的)起落跑道。2. 可着陆地区。~ **T**, ~ **tee** 【空】(指示飞机着陆的) T 形着陆标志, T 字布。~ **wire** = antilift wire. ~**waiter** = landwaiter.

länd·ler [ˈlentlə; ˋlɛntlɚ] *n*. 1. 兰德勒舞〔奥地利农村的一种民间舞蹈,慢节奏,三拍子〕。2. 兰德勒舞曲。

land·less [ˈlændlis; ˋlændlɪs] *a*. 无土地的;无不动产的;无陆地的。

land·oc·ra·cy [lændˈɔkrəsi; lændˋɑkrəsɪ] *n*. 〔谑〕大地主阶级。**land·o·crat** 地主阶级分子。

Lan·don [ˈlændən; ˋlændən] *n*. 兰登〔姓氏〕。

Lan·dor [ˈlændɔː; ˋlændɚ] *n*. 1. 兰道〔姓氏〕。2. **Walter Savage** ~ 沃尔特·萨维奇·兰道〔1775—1864,英国散文家,诗人〕。

Land·sat [ˈlændˌsæt; ˋlændˏsæt] *n*. (由美国政府发射的)地球资源卫星。

land·scape [ˈlænd*s*keip; ˋlænskep] **I** *n*. 1. 风景,景致。2. 山水画,风景画,风景摄影。3. 【地】景观,地形。4. 眼界,前景展望。*a* ~ *of snow* 雪景。*a* ~ *in oil* 风景油画。**II** *vt*. 美化(自然环境等)。— *vi*. 1. 做自然环境美化工作。2. 做庭园设计师。~ **architect** 环境美化专家。~ **architecture** 园林建筑学。~ **gardener** 园艺美化家。~ **gardening** 造园法。~ **painter** 风景画家,山水画家。~ **painting** 风景画(法)。

land·scap·ist [ˈlænd*ˌ*skeipist; ˋlænskepɪst] *n*. 1. 风景画家。2. 庭园设计师。

Land·seer [ˈlænsiə; ˋlændsɪr] *n*. 兰西尔〔姓氏〕。

lands·man [ˈlændzmən; ˋlændzmən] *n*. (*pl*. **-men** [-mən; -mən]) 1. 陆居人;未出过海的人;(无经验的)新水手。2. 本国人,同胞。

land·sturm [ˈlɑːndʃturm; ˋlɑndˏʃturm] *n*. 1. 〔G.〕(战时)全国总动员〔宣布征召六十岁以下全部男子〕。2. 战时后备军。

land·ward [ˈlændwəd; ˋlændwɚd] **I** *ad*. 向陆地 (= landwards)。**II** *a*. 面向陆地的。~ *wind* 海风。

land·wehr [G. ˈlɑːntveə; ˋlɑntˏver] *n*. 〔G.〕(受过训练的)后备役人员。

Lane [lein; len] *n*. 莱恩〔姓氏,男子名〕。

lane [lein; len] *n*. 1. 小路,小巷。2. (行列间的)通路。3. 航道;空中走廊;规定的单向行车道。4. 【体】跑道。5. 〔the L-〕(伦敦的剧院区)特鲁利街 (= Drury Lane)。*a blind* ~ 死路,死胡同。*the inside* [*outside*] ~ 内[外]车道。***It is a long*** ~ ***that has no turning***. 〔谚〕路必有弯;山穷水尽还有路。***the red*** ~ 喉咙。~ **route** 外洋航线 (= ocean ~)。

lang. = language.

lang·bein·ite [ˈlæŋbainait; ˋlæŋbaɪnaɪt] *n*. 【化】无水钾镁矾。

Lange [ˈlæŋə; ˋlɑŋə] *n*. 兰格〔姓氏〕。

Lang·land [ˈlæŋlənd; ˋlæŋlənd] *n*. 1. 兰兰〔姓氏〕。2. **William** ~ 威廉·兰兰〔1332? —1400,英国诗人〕。

lang·lauf [ˈlɑːŋˌlauf; ˋlɑŋˏlaʊf] *n*. 〔G.〕越野滑雪。**-er** 越野滑雪者。

Lang·ley [ˈlæŋli; ˋlæŋlɪ] *n*. 1. 兰利〔姓氏〕。2. **Samuel Pierpont** ~ 塞缪尔·皮尔庞特·兰利〔1834—1906,美国天文学家,物理学家和航空学先驱者〕。

lang·ley [ˈlæŋli; ˋlæŋlɪ] *n*. (*pl*. ~**s**)【物】兰〔能通量单位〕。

Lang·muir [ˈlæŋmjuə; ˋlæŋmjʊr] *n*. 兰米尔〔姓氏〕。

Lan·go·bard [ˈlæŋgəuˈbɑːd; ˋlæŋgoˋbɑrd] *n*. (意大利北部)伦巴第人。**-ic** 1. *a*. 伦巴第的;伦巴第语的;伦巴第文化的。2. *n*. 伦巴第语。

lan·gouste [lɑːŋˈguːst; lɑŋˋgust] *n*. 〔F.〕【动】龙虾 (= spiny lobster)。

lang·syne [ˈlæŋˈsain; ˋlæŋˋsaɪn] *ad*., *n*. 〔Scot.〕很久以前;往昔。

Lang·ton [ˈlæŋtən; ˋlæŋtən] *n*. 兰顿〔姓氏〕。

lan·guage [ˈlæŋgwidʒ; ˋlæŋgwɪdʒ] *n*. 1. 语言;(某民族,某国的)国语;语调,措词。2. (谈话者或作者所使用的)言语,语风,文风,文体。3. 专门用语,术语。4. (动物的)叫声;(动作,手势等所表示的)表意语。5. 【自】机器代码 (= machine ~)。6. 〔俚〕粗话,骂人的话;坏话。7. 态度,立场。8. 〔古〕民族;某国国民。*a common* ~ 共同的语言。*a dead* ~ 死语言。*a foreign* ~ 外国语。*a living* ~ 活语言。*long* ~ (与符号语言相对的)通用语言。*oral* [*spoken*] ~ 口语。*the Chinese* ~ 汉语。*written* ~ 书面语。*high* ~ 夸张的言词。*in his own* ~ 按他自己的说法。*with a great command* [*an easy flow*] *of* ~ 口若悬河。*legal* ~ 法律用语。*medical* ~ 医学用语。*parliamentary* ~ 议会辞令;有礼貌的话。*the* ~ *of diplomacy* 外交辞令。*the* ~ *of the science* 科学用语。*finger* [*gesture*, *sign*] ~ 手势语。*the* ~ *of flowers* 花语〔如以 lily 象征纯洁等〕。*the* ~ *of the eyes* 目语,眉目传情。*billing gate* ~ = ~ *of the fish-market* 下流的粗话。*in strong* ~ 用激烈的下流话。*use* (*bad* [*foul*, *warm*]) ~ *to sb*. 谩骂某人。***in fourteen*** ~***s*** 〔美俚〕非常。***speak the same*** ~ 说共同的语言,信仰和观点相同。~ **arts** (中小学的)语言艺术学科。~ **planning** 语言规划〔如制订和实施语言规范化方案等〕。~ **master** 语言教师。

langue d'oc [ˌlɑːŋgəˈdɔk; lɑ̃gˋdɔk] *n*. 〔F.〕1. 中世纪法国南部方言。2. 现代的普罗旺斯语 (= modern Provençal)。

langue d'o·ï l [ˌlɑːŋgəˈdɔil; lɑ̃gˋdɔɪl] *n*. 〔F.〕1. 中世纪法国北部方言。2. 现代法语 (= modern French)。

lan·guet, **lan·guette** [ˈlæŋgwit; ˋlæŋgwɛt] *n*. 小舌,舌状物;起舌状作用的东西。

lan·guid [ˈlæŋgwid; ˋlæŋgwɪd] *a*. 1. 疲倦的。2. (天气)阴沉的;(市面等)不兴旺的,萧条的。3. 无精打采的,不活泼的;不高兴的,不情愿的。4. 缓慢的。**-ly** *ad*. **-ness** *n*.

lan·guish [ˈlæŋgwiʃ; ˋlæŋgwɪʃ] **I** *vi*. 1. 衰弱,疲倦。2. (草木等)凋萎。3. 烦恼;焦思,渴望 (*for*)。4. 憔悴;潦倒。5. (兴趣等)减弱,减少。6. 作出楚楚动人的伤感之态[倦态等]。*My interest in the subject has greatly* ~*ed*. 我对这一问题的兴趣大大减退了。*All business* ~*es*. 百业萧条。*The leaves* ~*ed in the drought*. 天旱使树叶枯萎。~ *for home* 因为思家而憔悴。~ *for years in a dungeon* 长年苦尝铁窗风味。**II** *n*. 1. 憔悴。2. 惹人怜爱的感伤模样[倦态等];脉脉含情。**-er** *n*. **-ment** *n*.

lan·guish·ing [ˈlæŋgwiʃiŋ; ˋlæŋgwɪʃɪŋ] *a*. 1. 衰弱下去的。2. 焦思的,忧郁的。3. (疾病等)长期拖延的。4. 故作感伤[倦态]而引人怜爱的;脉脉含情的。**-ly** *ad*.

L

lan·guor [ˈlæŋɡə; ˋlæŋɡɚ] ***n*.** **1.** (温暖气候等引起的)疲倦;倦怠。**2.** 意气消沉;郁闷。**3.** 〔常 *pl*.〕柔情。**-ous** ***a*.** **-ous·ly** ***ad*.**

lan·gur [ˌlʌŋˈɡuə; lʌŋˋgur] ***n*.** 【动】龄猴 (*Presbytis*)〔东南亚一种长尾猴〕。

lan·iard [ˈlænjəd; ˋlænjɚd] ***n*.** = lanyard.

la·ni·ar·y [ˈlæniəri; ˋlenɪˏɛrɪ] **I** ***a*.** 【解】(牙)适于扯裂东西的;(犬)牙的。**II** ***n*.** 【解】短刀形犬牙。

La·nier [ləˈniə; ləˋnɪr] ***n*.** 拉尼尔〔姓氏〕。

la·nif·er·ous, la·nig·er·ous [ləˈnifərəs, ləˈnidʒərəs; ləˋnɪfərəs, ləˋnɪdʒərəs] ***a*.** 有细毛的,羊毛状的。

lan·i·tal [ˈlænitæl, -təl; ˋlænɪtæl, -təl] ***n*.** 人造羊毛。

lank [læŋk; læŋk] ***a*.** **1.** 瘦的,细长的。**2.** (草等)长而柔软的。**3.** (头发)长而无卷曲的。**-ly** ***ad*.** **-ness** ***n*.**

Lan·kes·ter [ˈlæŋkistə; ˋlæŋkəstɚ] ***n*.** 兰基斯特〔姓氏〕。

lank·y [ˈlæŋki; ˋlæŋkɪ] ***a*.** (***lank·i·er***; ***-i·est***) 瘦长的,细长的。**-i·ly** ***ad*.** **-i·ness** ***n*.**

lan·ner [ˈlænə; ˋlænɚ] ***n*.** 【动】南非隼(尤指狩猎用的这种雌鹰)。

lan·ner·et [ˌlænəˈriːt; ˏlænəˋrɛt] ***n*.** 【动】南非雄隼。

Lan·ny [ˈlæni; ˋlænɪ] ***n*.** 兰尼〔男子名, Lawrence 的昵称〕。

lan·o·lin(e) [ˈlænəli(ː)n; ˋlænəlɪn] ***n*.** 羊毛脂。

la·nose [ˈleinəus; ˋlenos] ***a*.** = lanate.

Lan·sing [ˈlænsiŋ; ˋlænsɪŋ] ***n*.** 兰辛〔姓氏〕。

lans·que·net [ˈlænskənet; ˋlænskəˏnɛt] ***n*.** **1.** (16—17世纪德国的)雇佣兵。**2.** 兰斯克内特牌戏〔源出德国的一种纸牌赌博〕。

lan·ta·na [lænˈteinə, -ˈtɑː-; lænˋtenə, -ˋtɑ-] ***n*.** 【植】马缨丹属 (*Lantana*)〔生长于美洲热带和亚热带〕。

lan·tern [ˈlæntən; ˋlæntɚn] **I** ***n*.** **1.** 提灯,灯笼;街灯。**2.** 幻灯 (= magic ～)。**3.** (灯塔的)灯火室。**4.** 【建】天窗灯笼式屋顶。**5.** 【机】油环,套环。*a Chinese* ～ 灯笼。*a dark* ～ (仅一孔漏光的)暗灯。*a* ～ *procession* 提灯游行。*a signal* ～ 信号灯。*The Feast of L-s* (中国的)上元节,灯节,元宵节。*Lantern-and-candle light!* 小心火烛〔伦敦更夫的呼声〕。*the parish* ～ 〔方〕月亮。**II** ***vt*.** **1.** 供给…以灯火;给…配上提灯。**2.** 把…吊死在街灯柱上。～ *a lighthouse* 给灯塔点上灯火。～ *a fishing boat* 给渔船配上提灯。～**-and-candle man** 伦敦更夫。～ **fish** 【动】灯笼鱼。～ **fly** 【动】白蜡虫。～ **jaw** 突出的下巴。～**-jawed** ***a*.** 下巴突出的,双颊深陷的。～ **pinion** [**wheel**] 灯笼式小齿轮。～ **ring** (泵的)套环。～ **slide** 幻灯片。～ **tree** 【植】红白合木 (*Crinodendron hookerianum*)〔智利产的一种树,美国南部有时用该树作装饰品〕。

lan·tha·nid(e) [ˈlænθəˌnid, -ˌnaid; ˋlænθəˏnɪd, -ˏnaɪd] ***n*.** 【化】镧化物,镧族元素。～ **series** 【化】镧系〔即稀土元素〕。

lan·tha·num [ˈlænθənəm; ˋlænθənəm] ***n*.** 【化】镧。

lant·horn [ˈlæntən; ˋlæntɚn] ***n*.** 〔废〕lantern 的变体。

Lan·tian man ***n*.** 【人类】蓝田(猿)人。

la·nu·go [ləˈnjuːɡəu, -ˈnuː-; ləˋnjugo, -ˋnu-] ***n*.** (婴儿的)胎毛;(昆虫身上的)细毛;柔毛。**la·nu·gi·nous** [-dʒinəus; -dʒɪnəs], **la·nu·gi·nose** [-dʒinəs; -dʒəˏnos] ***a*.**

lan·yard [ˈlænjəd; ˋlænjɚd] ***n*.** **1.** 【军】(发射火炮等用的)牵索,拉火绳。**2.** (船上系物用的)短绳。**3.** (挂在水手脖子上的)系刀绳,小绳。**4.** 勋带。

Lao [lau, ˈlɑːəu; laʊ, ˋlɑo] ***a*.**, ***n*.** (*pl*. ～(*s*)) Laotian.

La·oc·o·ön [leiˈɔkəuɔn; leˋɑkəwɑn] ***n*.** **1.** 【希神】拉奥孔〔特洛伊的祭师,因警告特洛伊人不要中木马计而触怒天神,连同其二子被巨蟒缠死〕。**2.** (表现拉奥孔父子垂死时与巨蟒奋勇搏斗的)拉奥孔雕像。**3.** 英勇搏斗者。

La·od·i·ce·an [ˌleiəudiˈsiən; leˏɑdɪˋsɪən] ***a*.**, ***n*.** (对政治、宗教等)不热心的(人),冷淡的(人)。

La·os [lauz; laʊz] ***n*.** 老挝〔亚洲〕。

La·o·tian [leiˈəuʃən; leˋoʃən] **I** ***a*.** 老挝的;老挝人的;老挝文化的。**II** ***n*.** **1.** 老挝人,寮人。**2.** 老挝语。

lap[1] [læp; læp] **I** ***n*.** **1.** 膝;〔喻〕怀抱,境遇。**2.** (衣服的)下摆,裙兜,衣兜。**3.** 〔诗〕(山间的)凹地,山坳;(书等的)面。**4.** 养育所,休息处。**5.** 〔古〕耳朵。**6.** 【体】(跑道的)一圈;一段行程;工作阶段。**7.** 重叠部分,重叠量;【机】余面。**8.** 【建】(瓦的)互搭,搭接。**9.** (滚筒上绳索的)一圈;【纺】棉卷,毛卷。**10.** 掌管,范围。*have a baby on one's* ～ 把孩子放在膝上。*hold a child in* [*on*] *one's* ～ 把孩子抱在膝上。***drop*** [***dump***] ***the whole thing in*** [***into***] ***sb.'s*** ～ 把事情都推在某人身上。***Everything falls into sb.'s*** ～. (某人)事事顺利。(***be*** [***lie***]) ***in the*** ～ ***of the gods*** 在神的掌握之中,结果尚难预料。***in Fortune's*** ～ = ***in the*** ～ ***of Fortune*** 走运,运气好。***in nature's*** ～ 在大自然的怀抱里。***in the*** ～ ***of future*** 未来的事情,尚在未知之数。***in the*** ～ ***of luxury*** 极尽奢华。***sit in the*** ～ ***of*** 倒在…怀抱里。***throw oneself into the*** ～ ***of*** 投入…的怀抱,投靠。**II** ***vt*.** (***lapped*** [læpt; læpt]; ***lap·ping*** [ˈlæpiŋ; ˋlæpɪŋ]) **1.** 包围,包住。**2.** 折叠,重叠,搭叠。**3.** 把…抱在膝上;把…爱护地怀抱着。**4.** 【纺】使(经过栉梳的棉花)成卷。**5.** 赛跑时比(某人)领先…圈;跑完(全程的)。～ *oneself in a blanket* 用毯子裹住身体。*She was* ～*ped in luxury*. 她生活奢侈。～ *a wrist in a bandage* 用纱布包住手腕。～ *the course* 跑完全程。～ *roofslates* 迭盖石板瓦。—***vi*.** **1.** 被包住,围起。**2.** 部分重叠,搭接;并排。**3.** 伸出,突出,露出。**4.** 跑完全程。*Joy* ～*ped over her*. 她沉浸于欢乐中。～ ***over*** 重叠。(*His reign* ～*s over into the sixteenth century*. 他的统治延至十六世纪)。～ **belt** (汽车座位上系在腰部的)安全带。～ **board** ***n*.** 膝板〔放在膝上当桌子用的平板〕。～ **dissolve** 〔电影、电视〕叠化〔一个镜头未完,另一个镜头重叠出现,然后原镜头逐渐消逝的摄影手法〕。～ **dog** 叭儿狗。～ **joint**, ～**-joint**, ～**ped joint** 搭接(处)。～**-joint flange** 松套法兰。～ **robe** 围毯,膝毯〔坐车、坐雪橇和看户外运动等盖在膝上使下身保暖的毯子〕。～**stone** 皮匠放在膝上的垫石[铁]。～**-strap** (飞机乘客系在腰部的)安全带。～ **time** 【体】跑一圈的时间。～**top** ***a*.** (电脑)微型便携式的。～**ful** ***a*.** 一满兜。

lap[2] [læp; læp] **I** ***n*.** **1.** 舔;舔一次的分量;一舔。**2.** (波浪的)拍打声。**3.** 〔俚〕淡饮料。***take a*** ～ ***at*** 舔一下。**II** ***vt*.** (***-pp-***) **1.** 舔,舔食。**2.** 拼命吃[喝]。**3.** 爱听(奉承话)。**4.** (波浪)拍打。*Cats* ～ *water*. 猫舔水。*The sea* ～*s the base of the cliff*. 海浪拍打悬崖的底部。—***vi*.** **1.** 舔,舔食。**2.** (波浪)拍打。～ ***up*** [***down***] **1.** (贪婪地)舔光,喝干。**2.** 欣然接受;热切倾听。～ **pool** 小型健身游泳池。

lap[3] [læp; læp] **I** ***n*.** (磨宝石等的)磨盘,研磨机。**II** ***vt*.**, ***vi*.** (***-pp-***) 用磨盘磨;研磨,磨光。

lap·a·rot·o·my [ˌlæpəˈrɔtəmi; ˏlæpəˋrɛktəmɪ] ***n*.** 【医】剖腹术。

La Paz [lɑː ˈpæz; lɑˋpɑs] 拉巴斯〔玻利维亚首都,政府所在地,法定首都是苏克雷 (Sucre)〕。

la·pel [ləˈpel; ləˋpɛl] ***n*.** 〔主 *pl*.〕(西服上衣的)翻领。～ **mike** 〔口〕(挂在翻领上的)佩带式话筒。

lap·i·cide [ˈlæpisaid; ˋlæpəsaɪd] ***n*.** 石工。

lap·i·dar·i·an [ˌlæpiˈdɛəriən; ˏlæpəˋdɛrɪən] ***a*.** = lapidary ***a*.**

lap·i·dar·ist [ˈlæpiˈdɛərist; ˋlæpəˏdɛrɪst] ***n*.**, ***a*.** = lapidary.

lap·i·dar·y [ˈlæpidəri; ˋlæpəˏdɛrɪ] **I** ***n*.** **1.** 玉石[宝石]工。**2.** 玉石[宝石]工艺。**3.** 玉石[宝石]鉴赏家;宝石商。**II** ***a*.** **1.** 玉石[宝石]雕刻的;与玉石雕刻有关的。**2.** 铭刻在石上的。**3.** (文字等)有碑铭风格的,简洁优雅的。～ **inscriptions** 碑文。～ **style** 【修】碑文体。

lap·i·date [ˈlæpideit; ˋlæpəˏdet] ***vt*.** 〔古〕用石头投掷,

L

用石头砸死。

lap·i·da·tion [ˌlæpiˈdeiʃən; ˏlæpəˋdeʃən] ***n*.** **1.** 投石击毙刑。**2.** 投掷乱石。

la·pid·i·fy [ləˈpidifai; ləˋpɪdɪˏfaɪ] ***vt*.**, ***vi*.** 〔古〕(使)变成石头。**-dif·ic(al)** ***a*.** **-i·fi·ca·tion** [-ˌpidifiˈkeiʃən; -ˏpɪdəfɪˋkeʃən] ***n*.**

la·pil·li [ləˈpilai; ləˋpɪlaɪ] ***n*.** lapillus 的复数。

la·pil·lus [ləˈpiləs; ləˋpɪləs] ***n*.** (*pl*. ***la·pil·li*** [-lai; -laɪ])【地】火山砾。

lap·in [ˈlæpin; F. laˋpɛ̃; ˋlæpɪn] ***n*.** 〔F.〕兔;兔的毛皮。

lap·is laz·u·li [ˌlæpisˈlæzjulai; ˋlæpɪsˋlæzjəlaɪ] 〔L.〕 **1.**【地】天青石,青金石。**2.** 天青石色。

La·place [lɑːˈplɑːs; laˋplas], **Pierre Simon, Marquis de** 拉普拉斯〔1749—1827,法国天文学家、数学家〕。

Lap·land [ˈlæplænd; ˋlæpˏlænd] ***n*.** 拉普兰〔北欧地名,包括挪威、瑞典、芬兰北部及俄罗斯西北部科拉(Kola)半岛的一个地区〕。

Lap·land·er [ˈlæplændə; ˋlæpˏlændɚ] ***n*.** 拉普(兰)人。

La Pla·ta [ləˈplɑːtə; ləˋplɑtə] 拉普拉塔〔阿根廷港市〕。

Lapp [læp; læp] ***n*.** **1.** (分布在挪威、瑞典、芬兰和俄罗斯北部的)拉普(兰)人。**2.** 拉普(兰)语。

lap·pet [ˈlæpit; ˋlæpɪt] ***n*.** **1.** (衣、帽等的)垂片,垂襞;垂饰。**2.** 耳垂,(火鸡等颈部的)垂肉。**3.** = lapel.

Lap·pic, Lap·pish [ˈlæpik, ˈlæpiʃ; ˋlæpɪk, ˋlæpɪʃ] **I** ***a*.** 拉普兰的,拉普兰人的。**II** ***n*.** 拉普兰语。

lapse [læps; læps] **I** ***n*.** **1.** 时间的消逝[推移,间隔]。**2.** 缓流。**3.** 错失,过失,小错。**4.** 行为失检,偏离正道;堕落。**5.** 废除;【法】(权利等的)丧失,消失。**6.** (气温,气压等的)骤降,下降。**7.**【物】垂直梯度。*after a ～ of five years* 事隔五年之后。*～ of time* 时光的流逝,一段时间。*with the ～ of time* 随着时间的过去。*the ～ of a stream* 溪水的缓流。*a ～ of attention* 一时疏忽。*a ～ of memory* 记错。*a ～ of the pen* 笔误。*a ～ of the tongue* 失言。*a ～ into crime* 犯罪。*a moral ～* 道德败坏。*a ～ from respectability* 有失体面。*a ～ from virtue* 堕落;违背道德的行为。**II** ***vi*.** **1.** (时间)悄悄流逝(*away*)。**2.** 退步(*away*; *back*);堕落;犯罪,陷入,堕入。**3.**【法】(权利、任期等)终止,失效;【法】转归(*to*)。**4.** 塌陷。*～ backward* 落后。*～ into ruin* 塌陷成一片废墟。*～ into vice* 陷入罪恶活动,变坏。*～ from good manners* 行为渐渐变坏。*The conversation ～d.* 谈话停止了。*The tenure of the office has ～d.* 任期届满。— ***vt*.** 使失效,废止。～ **a policy** 废止一项政策。～ **rate**【气】(与高度成比例的)气温直减率,递减率。

lap·sus [ˈlæpsəs; ˋlæpsəs] ***n*.** 〔L.〕(*pl*. ～ [-sjuːs; -sjus]) 失误;错误;差错。～ ***ca·la·mi*** [ˈkæləmai; ˋkæləˏmaɪ] 笔误,写错。～ ***lin·guae*** [ˈliŋgwai; ˋlɪŋgwɪ] 失言;口误。～ ***me·mo·riae*** [meˈmɔːrii; mɛˋmɔrɪɪ] 记错。

La·pu·ta [ləˈpjuːtə; ləˋpjutə] ***n*.** 飞鸟,拉普他岛〔英国作家江奈生·斯威夫特(Jonathan Swift)所著《格列佛游记》中的一个飞岛,岛上居民多幻想而不务实际〕。

La·pu·tan [ləˈpjuːtən; ləˋpjutən] **I** ***n*.** 飞岛居民,拉普他岛人。**II** ***a*.** 拉普他人的,拉普他人似的;不切实际的,异想天开的,荒诞不经的。

lap·wing [ˈlæpwiŋ; ˋlæpˏwɪŋ] ***n*.**【动】凤头麦鸡,田凫。

la·que·us [ˈlekwiəs; ˋlɛkwɪrs] ***n*.**【解】蹄系,绾带(= lemni-scus)。

lar [lɑː; lɑr] ***n*.** (*pl*. *～es* [ˈlɛəriːz; ˋlɛriz], *～s*) **1.** 〔常 *pl*.〕(古罗马人崇拜的)家神,护家神。**2.** (*pl*. *～s*)【动】(马来群岛的)白掌猿(= ～ ***gibbon***)。

lar·board [ˈlɑːbəd; ˋlɑrbɚd] **I** ***n*.**【海】左舷〔为避免与 starboard (右舷)混淆,现一般用 port 一词代替〕。**II** ***a*.** 左舷方面的。**III** ***ad*.** 朝左舷方面。

lar·ce·ner, lar·ce·nist [ˈlɑːsinə, ˈlɑːsinist; ˋlɑrsṇɚ, ˋlɑrsnɪst] ***n*.** 盗窃犯,窃贼,侵占犯。

lar·ce·nous [ˈlɑːsinəs; ˋlɑrsənəs] ***a*.** **1.** 偷窃的;构成偷窃[侵占]罪的。**2.** 犯偷窃[侵占]罪的。**-ly** ***ad*.**

lar·ce·ny [ˈlɑːsni; ˋlɑrsnɪ] ***n*.**【法】窃盗罪,非法侵占他人财产。

larch [lɑːtʃ; lɑrtʃ] ***n*.** **1.**【植】落叶松属。**2.** 落叶松木材。

lard [lɑːd; lɑrd] **I** ***n*.** 猪油。**II** ***vt*.** **1.** 在…涂上猪油。**2.** 嵌(腌肥肉片)到(牛肉、鸡肉)中。**3.** 润色(文章等),点缀(谈话等)。～ *a boned chicken* 用腌肉片塞填去骨鸡。～ *one's conversation with Latin words* 在会话中引用拉丁语。～ **beetle**【动】火腿皮蠹。～**-bucket** 〔美俚〕胖子。～ **fruit**【植】猪油果(也称油渣果、油瓜)。～ **head** 〔美俚〕蠢人。～ **like** ***a*.**

lar·da·ceous [lɑːˈdeiʃəs; lɑrˋdeʃəs] ***a*.** **1.** 猪油(似)的。**2.**【医】豚脂样的,含淀粉样蛋白的。

lard·er [ˈlɑːdə; ˋlɑrdɚ] ***n*.** **1.** 藏肉所,食品库。**2.** 家中贮存的食品。

Lard·ner [ˈlɑːdnə; ˋlɑrdnɚ] ***n*.** 拉德纳〔姓氏〕。

lar·do [ˈlɑːdəu; ˋlado] ***n*.** 薰肉。

lar·don [ˈlɑːdən; ˋlɑrdən], **lar·doon** [lɑːˈduːn; lɑrˋdun] ***n*.** (烹调前嵌在肉中的)肥咸肉[腊肉]片。

lard·y [ˈlɑːdi; ˋlɑrdɪ] ***a*.** (***lard·i·er***; ***lard·i·est***) **1.** 含猪油的;脂肪多的,肥的。**2.** 猪油似的,涂猪油的。～**-dardy** ***a*.** 〔英俚〕装模作样的;怪模怪样的;装得娇弱无力的。

la·res [ˈlɛəriːz; ˋlɛriz] ***n*.** lar 的复数。～ ***and penates*** **1.** (古罗马人崇拜)护家神。**2.** 家珍,家宝。

lar·gac·til [lɑːˈgæktil; lɑrˋgæktɪl] ***n*.**【药】氯普马嗪(= chlorpromazine)。

lar·gan·do [lɑːˈgɑːndəu; lɑrˋgɑndo] ***a*.**, ***ad*.** 〔It.〕= allargando.

large [lɑːdʒ; lɑrdʒ] **I** ***a*.** **1.** (体积,空间,数量,规模等)大的,巨大的;(权限等)广泛的。**2.** (心胸)宽广的,度量大的;(眼界等)开阔的,(见识等)广博的。**3.** (艺术风格等)奔放的,气魄宏大的;夸张的。**4.**【海】顺风的。*a ～ calibre gun* 大口径炮。*a ～ garden* 大花园。*a ～ room* 大房间。*～ and small sizes* 大小尺寸。*be ～ of limbs* 大手大脚。*a ～ family* 多子女的家庭。*a ～ number* 大批(= ～numbers)。*a ～ population* 人口众多。*a ～ farmer* 富农。*a ～ merchant* 巨商。*have a ～ discretion* 有广泛的决定权。*～ powers* 大权。*～ units* 大兵团。*a ～ heart* 宽宏大量。*a man of ～ views* 见识广博的人。*～ tolerance* 胸怀广大。★ large 在口语中不像 big 那样常用,也不像 great 那样含有“伟大”,“壮大”的意义。***as ～ as life*** **1.** 和原物一样大小。**2.** 〔谑〕亲自,千真万确(*There he was as ～ as life.* 他本人就在那里)。**II** ***n*.** 大〔仅用于下列习语〕。***at ～*** **1.** 自由,随便;拉杂地,零乱地。(*He scatters imputations at ～.* 他乱讲坏话)。**2.** 未被捕,逍遥自在(*Is the prisoner still at ～?* 犯人还未归案么?)。**3.** 全体;普遍;一般(*the people at ～* 一般人民)。**4.** 充分,详细(*talk at ～* 详细讲)。**5.** 未决定(*leave the matter at ～* 让事件无着落)。**6.** 无固定职位[任所]的(*a gentleman at ～* 无职宫廷官吏;〔谑〕无一定职业的人。*an ambassador at ～* 〔美〕无任所大使)。**7.** 〔美〕(非某一选区而是)全州选出的(*a Congressman at ～* 州选议员)。**8.** 笼统地(*arrangements made at ～* 笼统作出的安排)。***in (the) ～*** **1.** 大规模地。**2.** 一般地。**III** ***ad*.** **1.** 大,大大地。**2.** 详细地。**3.** 夸大地。**4.**【海】顺风地(*sail ～* 顺风航行)。***by and ～*** 从全体看来。***talk ～*** 吹牛,说大话。～ **calorie** 大卡,千卡。～**-cap** 〔美口〕大盘股〔市场资本总额在50亿美元以上的股票〕。～**-eyed** ***a*.** **1.** 大眼的。**2.** 大针孔的。**3.** 睁大眼睛的。～**-handed** ***a*.** 大手大脚的;大方的,慷慨的。～**-hearted** ***a*.** 慷慨的,富于同情心的,正直的。～**-minded** ***a*.** 气量大的;宽宏大量的;思想开通的。～**mouth (black) bass**【动】大口黑鲈。～**-scale** ***a*.** **1.** (地图等的)大比例的。**2.** 大规模的;大面积的;巨型的(*～-scale business operations* 大规模的经营)。～**-tonnage product** 大量产品。

large·ly [ˈlɑːdʒli; ˋlɑrdʒlɪ] *ad*. **1.** 大量地。**2.** 主要地。**3.** 慷慨地。*build* ~ 大兴土木。*His failure is* ~ *due to timidity*. 他的失败主要是由于胆小。*give* ~ 慨然捐助。

large·ness [ˈlɑːdʒnis; ˋlɑrdʒnɪs] *n*. **1.** 巨大;广大。**2.** 伟大。**3.** 慷慨。**4.** 广博。*have* ~ *of mind* 思想开通,襟怀坦白。

lar·gess(e) [ˈlɑːdʒes, ˈlɑːdʒis; ˋlɑrdʒɪs, ˋlɑrdʒɪs] *n*. **1.** 慷慨地赏赐[援助];赏赐物。**2.** 〔古〕慷慨。**3.** 本性。***cry*** ~ 讨赏钱。

lar·ghet·to [lɑːˈgetəu; lɑrˋgɛto] **I** *a*., *ad*. 〔It.〕【乐】稍缓慢,稍宽广。**II** *n*. 【乐】小广板。

larg·ish [ˈlɑːdʒiʃ; ˋlɑrdʒɪʃ] *a*. 稍大的。

lar·go [ˈlɑːgəu; ˋlɑrgo] **I** *a*., *ad*. 〔It.〕【乐】缓慢,宽广。**II** *n*. 【乐】广板。

lar·i·at [ˈlæriət; ˋlærɪət] *n*., *vt*. 〔美〕= lasso.

lar·ine [ˈlærin, -rain; ˋlærɪn, -raɪn] *a*. 【动】**1.** 鸥科的,鸥亚科的。**2.** 鸥的;似鸥的。

lark[1] [lɑːk; lɑrk] **I** *n*. 【动】云雀;百灵科鸣禽。*a meadow* ~ 〔美〕像寒鸦的小鸟。***as cheerful*** [***gay, happy***] ***as a*** ~ 非常快乐。***If the sky falls, we shall catch*** ~***s***. 〔谚〕天塌了正好捉云雀,杞忧无益。***rise*** [***be up***] ***with the*** ~ 早起。**II** *vi*. 捉云雀。

lark[2] [lɑːk; lɑrk] **I** *n*. 〔口〕嬉戏,戏谑,玩笑,玩乐。*What a* ~! 真有趣! ***be up to sb.'s*** ~***s*** 在开某人的玩笑。***for a*** ~ 当作玩笑。***have a*** ~ ***with sb***. = ***have*** ~***s with sb***. 开某人玩笑。**II** *vi*. **1.** 嬉戏,闹着玩。**2.** 骑马越野。***Stop*** ~***ing about***! 别开玩笑了! —*vt*. **1.** 取笑,愚弄。**2.** 骑(马)越野;骑马跳越。

Lar·kin [ˈlɑːkin; ˋlɑrkɪn] *n*. 拉金〔男子名〕。

lark·spur [ˈlɑːkspəː; ˋlɑrkˏspɝ] *n*. 【植】飞燕草。

lark·y [ˈlɑːki; ˋlɑrkɪ] *a*. (***lark·i·er***; ***lark·i·est***) 爱耍闹的;嬉戏的。

larn [lɑːn; lɑrn] *vt*., *vi*. 〔俚,谑〕= learn.

lar·ri·gan [ˈlærigən; ˋlærɪgən] *n*. 〔美〕(伐木工人穿的)长统鹿皮靴。

lar·ri·kin [ˈlærikin; ˋlærəˏkɪn] **I** *n*. 〔澳俚〕恶棍,无赖。**II** *a*. 吵闹的。

lar·rup [ˈlærəp; ˋlærəp] **I** *vt*. **1.** 〔方〕打,鞭打。**2.** 彻底击败。—*vi*. 垂着头懒散地走。**II** *n*. 一击。

Lar·ry [ˈlæri; ˋlærɪ] *n*. 拉里〔男子名, Lawrence 的昵称〕。

lar·va [ˈlɑːvə; ˋlɑrvə] *n*. (*pl*. ***-s***, ***-vae*** [-viː; -vi]) **1.** 【动】幼虫;幼体。**2.** 〔废〕鬼,妖怪。

lar·val [ˈlɑːvəl; ˋlɑrvl] *a*. 【动】幼虫的;幼体的;幼虫期的;幼虫形的,幼体形的。

lar·vi·cide [ˈlɑːvisaid; ˋlɑrvɪˏsaɪd] *n*. 杀幼虫剂。**-vi·cid·al** *a*.

la·ryn·gal [ləˈriŋgəl; ləˋrɪŋgəl] **I** *a*. 【语音】喉音的。**II** *n*. 喉音。

la·ryn·ge·al [ˌlærinˈdʒiːəl, ləˈrindʒiəl; ləˋrɪndʒɪəl, ˏlærɪnˋdʒiəl] **I** *a*. **1.** 【解】喉的。**2.** 【医】侵犯喉头的;医喉的。**3.** 【语音】喉音的。**II** *n*. 【语音】喉音。**-ly** *ad*.

la·ryn·ges [ləˈrindʒiːz; ləˋrɪndʒiz] *n*. larynx 的复数。

lar·yn·gic [ləˈrindʒik; ləˋrɪndʒɪk] *a*. = laryngeal.

lar·yn·gi·tis [ˌlærinˈdʒaitis; ˏlærɪnˋdʒaɪtɪs] *n*. 【医】喉炎。

lar·yn·g(o)- *comb. f*. 表示"喉的","喉部和…的": *laryng*itis, *laryngo*scope.

lar·yn·gol·o·gy [ˌlæriŋˈgɔlədʒi; ˏlærɪŋˋgɑlədʒɪ] *n*. 【医】喉科学。**laryn·go·log·i·cal** [ləˈriŋgəˈlɔdʒikl; ləˋrɪŋgəˋlɑdʒɪkl] *a*. **lar·yn·gol·o·gist** *n*. 喉科医师。

la·ryn·go·pha·ryn·ge·al [ləˌriŋgəufəˈrindʒiəl, -dʒəl; ləˏrɪŋgofəˋrɪndʒɪəl, -dʒəl] *a*. 咽喉的。

la·ryn·go·phone [ləˈriŋgəfəun; ləˋrɪŋgəˏfon] *n*. 喉头送话器。

la·ryn·go·scope [ləˈriŋgəskəup; ləˋrɪŋgəˏskop] *n*. 【医】喉镜。

lar·yn·got·o·my [ˌlæriŋˈgɔtəmi; ˏlærɪŋˋgɑtəmɪ] *n*. 【医】喉切开术。

lar·ynx [ˈlæriŋks; ˋlærɪŋks] *n*. (*pl*. ***~es***, ***la·ryn·ges*** [ləˈrindʒiːz; ləˋrɪndʒiz]) 【解】喉。

la·sa·gna [ləˈzɑːnjə; ləˋzɑnjə] *n*. 【烹】烤宽面条〔上浇肉末番茄汁〕(= lasagne)。

las·car [ˈlæskə; ˋlæskə] *n*. **1.** (旧时欧洲轮船上的)印度水手。**2.** (旧时英国陆军中的)印度炮兵。

las·civ·i·ous [ləˈsiviəs; ləˋsɪvɪəs] *a*. **1.** 淫荡的,好色的。**2.** 色情的,猥亵的。**-ly** *ad*. **-ness** *n*.

lase [leiz; lez] *vi*. (***lased***; ***las·ing***) 发射[放射,产生]激光,使产生镭射。

la·se·con [ˈleisəkɔn; ˋlesəkɑn] *n*. 激光射光转换器。

la·ser [ˈleizə; ˋlezə] *n*. 镭射激光,受激发射光,激光;莱塞;激光器,光激射器 (= light amplification by stimulated emission of radiation)〔由以上各词首字母组成的缩略词〕。a ~ *space-to-ground voice link* 镭射空对地通话联系。*glass* ~ 玻璃镭射器。~ **bomb** 【军】**1.** *n*. 镭射制导炸弹。**2.** *vt*. 以镭射炸弹轰击。~ **bounce** 镭射反射。~ **cane** (盲人用的)镭射手杖〔可发射红外激光发现障碍物〕。~ **fusion** 镭射聚变,激光聚变〔由激光器的光能辐射脉冲引发的核聚变〕。~**disk** (激)光盘〔亦作 ~disc〕。~ **gun** 镭射枪;【计】激光笔。~ **memory** 激光存储器〔以扫描激光束来检索信息〕。~**-print** *vt*. 激光打印。~ **printer** 激光打印机。~ **scanner** 激光扫描仪。~ **tracking** 镭射跟踪。**-ing** = lasing.

lash[1] [læʃ; læʃ] **I** *n*. **1.** 鞭打,鞭挞,抽打;〔the ~〕鞭笞刑。**2.** 鞭子(尤指鞭子上的皮条)。**3.** (波浪等的)冲击,(雨水等的)击打。**4.** 讽刺;严厉的谴责。**5.** (狗等的)摇尾。**6.** 眼睫毛。**7.** 【机】(轮齿等的)隙,余隙,空隙。*the* ~ *of storm* 风暴的冲击。*back* ~ 【机】齿隙。*work under the whip* ~ 在鞭笞下工作,被强迫劳动。***under the*** ~ 受体刑;遭痛骂。**II** *vt*. **1.** 打,鞭打。**2.** (波浪等)冲击;急打。**3.** 激起,煽动。**4.** 骂,讽刺,挖苦;严厉谴责。**5.** (狗等)愤激地摇(尾巴)。*The waves* ~ *the shore*. 波浪冲击海岸。~ *sb. into a fury* 激得某人大怒。—*vi*. **1.** 鞭打。**2.** (风、波浪等)冲打。**3.** 讽刺;痛骂。**4.** (马等)踢 (*out*)。~ *back at* 猛烈反击。***come*** ~ ***down*** (雨)下得很大。~ ***down the silverware*** 【美体】稳拿银杯〔尤指在帆船竞赛中〕。~ ***out*** **1.** 猛打;(马)乱踢。**2.** 大骂,抨击。**3.** 大量生产[印制]。

lash[2] [læʃ; læʃ] *vt*. 用绳[链等]捆绑。~***-up*** 〔口〕**1.** 应急办法,应急物。**2.** 安排,布置。

lash·er [ˈlæʃə; ˋlæʃə] *n*. **1.** 鞭打者;责骂者。**2.** 〔英方〕拦河坝,堰;从堰上泄出的水;(堰下容纳泄出水的)蓄水池。

lash·ing [ˈlæʃiŋ; ˋlæʃɪŋ] *n*. **1.** 鞭打;非难,申斥。**2.** 〔*pl*.〕捆绑。**3.** 捆绑用的绳子。**4.** 〔英方〕许多,大量 (*of*)。

Lash·io [ˈlɑːʃjəu; ˋlɑʃjo] *n*. 腊戌〔缅甸城市〕。

lash·kar [ˈlæʃkɑː; ˋlʌʃkə] *n*. = lascar.

las·ing [ˈleisiŋ; ˋlesɪŋ] **I** *n*. 镭射[激光]作用。**II** *a*. 产生镭射[激光]的。

Las·ki [ˈlæski; ˋlæskɪ] *n*. 拉斯基〔姓氏〕。

Las Pal·mas [lɑːsˈpɑːlməs; lɑsˋpɑlmɑs] 拉斯帕尔马斯〔加那利岛上一港口〕。

L-as·par·a·gi·nase [ˌelæspəˈrædʒəneis; ˏelæspəˋrædʒənes] *n*. 【药】左旋天冬醋胺酸酶〔用于阻断白血病等癌细胞生长〕。

lass [læs; læs] *n*. **1.** 少女,小姑娘 (*opp*. lad)。**2.** 情人。**3.** 〔Scot.〕使女。

Las·salle [ləˈsæl; lɑˋsɑl], **Ferdinand** 拉萨尔〔1825—1864,德国工人运动中机会主义派别的首领〕。

Las·salle·an [ləˈsæliən; ləˋsælɪən] *n*. 拉萨尔派成员。*the* ~*s* 拉萨尔派〔十九世纪六十至七十年代德国工人运动中的机会主义派别〕。**-ism** *n*. 拉萨尔主义。

las·sie [ˈlæsi; ˋlæsɪ] *n*. 〔Scot.〕 **1.** 少女,小姑娘。**2.** 情人。

las·si·tude [ˈlæsitjuːd; ˋlæsəˏtjud] *n*. **1.** 疲倦,疲乏。**2.** 厌倦,无精打采。

las·so [ˈlæsəu; ˋlæso] **I** *n*. (*pl*. ~(*e*)*s*) (一端有活结;用以捕捉牛马等的)套索。**II** *vt*. 用套索捕捉。**-er** *n*. 使用套索的人。

last[1] [lɑːst; læst] **I** *a*. (*opp*. first) **1.** 最后的,末尾的;最后剩下的。*We will defend our motherland to the ~ drop of our blood*. 我们愿为保卫祖国流尽最后一滴血。*for the ~ time* 最后一次。*~ but one* [*two*] 倒数第二[三]。*the ~ spurt* 最后的努力。*the ~ train* 末班火车。**2.** 临终的。*in one's ~ moments* 临死时。**3.** 紧接前面的,刚过去的。*in the ~ few months* 在最近几个月。*~ month* [*week*] 上月[星期]。*the month* [*week*] *before ~* 上上个月[星期]。*in January ~* 刚过去的一月。*on Sunday ~* 刚过去的星期天。*~ night* 昨晚。*this day ~ year* 去年今日。**4.** 最近的,最新流行的,最时髦的。*the ~ thing in hats* 最时髦的帽子。**5.** 最上的。*a paper of the ~ importance* 极端重要的文件。**6.** 最糟糕的,最坏的。*the ~ crime* 最恶劣的罪行。**7.** 决定性的,结论性的,权威性的。*He has said the ~ word on the matter*. 他对于这一问题提出了决定性意见。*the ~ explanation* 结论性的解释。**8.** 极少可能的;最不适当的。*He is the ~ man to do it*. 他决不会干那件事。*That is the ~ thing to try*. 那种事不值得去试。*the ~ man I expected to see* 我决没有料想会见面的人。*the ~ man I want to see* 我最不想见的人。*The ~ thing they want is ...* 他们最不乐意的事是…。**9.** 〔加强语气用〕每一的。*every ~ square inch of good land* 每一平方英寸的良田。*Tell me every ~ word*. 把每句话一五一十告诉我。*The lecture won't start until every ~ person is seated*. 直到每一个人就座以后,演讲才开始。**10.** 最低的。*the ~ boy in the class* 班上倒数第一的男孩。*the ~ prize* 最低的奖赏。★ last 和 latest 的区别:(1)表现连续事物的'最末'事物时,一般用 last: *the last number of the Spectator* 《旁观者》(周刊)的最后一期。(2)表现尚未完结的连续事物时,一般用 latest 或 last: *the latest* [*last*] *installment of the story* 本期连载小说。***put the ~ hand to*** 完成。***the ~ great change*** 长眠,死。***the ~ cry*** 最新流行品。***the ~ days*** [***times***] (人的)临终;世界的末日。***the ~*** (***news***) ***I heard...*** 据最近的消息。***to the ~ man*** 到最后一人。**II** *ad*. **1.** 最后。*L- came the students* 最后来的是学生。*Who spoke ~?* 谁最后讲的话? **2.** 上一次,最近一次。*I ~ met him in London*. 我最近一次在伦敦遇见他。*Since I saw you ~*. 自上次见你之后。**3.** 最后一点,总起来说。*and ~, I'd like to consider the economic aspects* 最后我想考虑一下经济方面的情况。*~* ***but not least*** 最后但不是最不重要的一点。*~* ***of all*** 最后。**III** *n*. **1.** 最后,临终。*from first to ~* 自始至终。*I was at his bedside at the very ~*. 一直到他临终我都守在他的床边。*the night before ~* 前夜。**2.** 最近的人[物]。*as I said in my ~* 像我在前函中说的。*I received your ~ in June*. 我在六月收到你最后一封信。*The ~ out will please shut the door*. 最后出去的人请关门。**3.** 动作[行为]的最后一次。*look one's ~ at* 朝…看最后一次。**4.** 〔美〕末尾。*the ~ of the week* 周末。*the ~ of the month* 月底〔不一定是最后一天〕。***at ~*** 终于 (*At ~, man has reached the moon*. 人类终于到达了月球)。***at long ~*** 好容易才。***breathe*** [***gasp***] ***one's ~*** 断气,死。***hear the ~ of*** 最后听到。***see the ~ of*** 最后一次看见。***the ~ of pea-time*** 〔美〕最后阶段,终点。***the ~ of the mohicans*** "最后的莫希干人"〔原为美国作家 J.M. Coope 所著小说的名称,指某种衰亡没落人物最后的残存者〕。***to*** [***till***] ***the ~*** 直到最后,至死,(军队)苦战到最后一兵一卒 (*hold on to the ~* 坚持到底)。~ **day** 【宗】最后审判日,世界末日。~ **ditch** 最后一道防线;最后的依靠[手段] (*fight to the ~ ditch* 打到底)。~**-ditch** *a*. 拼死抵抗的,无后退余地的,最后挣扎的 (*~-ditch struggle* 拼死斗争)。~ **hurrah** (事业快完结时的)最后一搏,最后的努力[尝试]。**L- Judg(e)ment** 【宗】 **1.** (世界末日时上帝对人类的)最后审判。**2.** (上帝对人类的)最后审判日。~**-minute** *a*. 最后一分钟的,紧急关头的。~ **name** 姓。~ **quarter** 下弦(月)。~ **rites** 【宗】 **1.** (为死者举行的)最后仪式。**2.** 为临终者举行的圣礼。~ **sleep** 长眠,死。~ **straw** 使人不能忍受的最后一击;使人不支而垮下的因素。**L- Supper** 【宗】(耶稣被害前夕和十二门徒共进的)最后晚餐。~ **word** **1.** (起裁决性作用的)最后一句话;定论;最后决定权。**2.** 完美的事物。**3.** 〔口〕最新式样;最先进的品种。

last[2] [lɑːst; lɑst] **I** *vi*. 继续;持久,耐久,经久。*The storm will not ~ long*. 暴风雨不会持续很久。*if my health ~s* 如果我的健康许可。*Our money will ~ till we get home*. 我们的钱足够到家了。*The festival ~ed two weeks*. 节日持续了两星期。*This cloth ~s well*. 这种布很耐穿。*This cloth will not ~ long*. 这布不经穿。— *vt*. 够用,使得以维持;经受住。*This watch will ~ me a lifetime*. 这只表够我用一辈子。~ ***out*** 支持到底,维持到最后 (*Will this coal ~ out the winter?* 这点煤能够烧一冬吗?)。**II** *n*. 持久力,精力。

last[3] [lɑːst; lɑst] **I** *n*. 鞋楦头。**II** *vt*. 用鞋楦头来调整。***stick to one's ~*** 安分守己,不管闲事 (*Let the cobbler stick to his ~*. 让人人各守本分)。

last[4] [lɑːst; lɑst] *n*. 拉〔英国重量及容量单位,约 4000 磅〕。*a ~ of wool* 1 拉羊毛 (= 4368 磅)。*a ~ of corn* 1 拉麦 (= 80 蒲式耳)。

Las·tex [ˈlæsteks; ˋlæstɛks] *n*. 橡皮线,松紧线〔商标名〕。

last·ing [ˈlɑːstiŋ; ˋlæstɪŋ] **I** *a*. 耐久的,持久的。*a ~ peace* 持久的和平。**II** *n*. **1.** 耐久。**2.** 斜纹织物。**-ly** *ad*. **-ness** *n*.

last·ly [ˈlɑːstli; ˋlæstlɪ] *ad*. 最后;终于。*L-, I must point out that ...* 最后,我必须指出…。

Las Vegas [lɑːsˈveigəs; lɑsˋvegəs] *n*. 拉斯维加斯〔美国城市,以赌博闻名,俗称"大西洋赌城"〕。

Lat. = Latin.

lat. = latitude.

lat [lɑːt; lɑt] *n*. (*pl*. ***lats, la·ti***) (拉脱维亚的货币单位)拉特。

La·ta·ki·a [ˌlætəˈkiː(ː)ə; ˏlætəˋkiə] *n*. **1.** 拉塔基亚〔叙利亚港市〕 **2.** (拉塔基亚附近产的)一种上等烟草 (= ~ tobacco)。

latch[1] [lætʃ; lætʃ] **I** *n*. **1.** 闩,插销。**2.** 碰锁,弹簧锁。**3.** 【机】档器,击子,活门。*guard ~* 保护锁键。*The door is on the ~*. 门上了闩。***off the ~*** 活栓开着。***on the ~*** 活栓扣着。**II** *vt*., *vi*. 用碰锁锁上(门等),用插销扣上(门等)。*Will the door ~?* 门锁得上么? ~ **key** (住所大门)弹簧锁钥匙 (*win one's ~key* 取得出入大门的钥匙,可以自由进出[行动])。~ **key child** 父母为双职工的孩子。~**key voter** 〔蔑〕住在旅馆里的选民。~ **lock** 弹簧锁。~**string** (由门外拉开活栓锁的)栓锁带 (*draw in the ~string for* 〔美〕不许自由出入。*hang out the ~string for* 允许自由出入)。

latch[2] [lætʃ; lætʃ] *vi*. 获得;抓住;占有;理解 (*on to*)。

latch·et [ˈlætʃit; ˋlætʃɪt] *n*. 〔古〕鞋带。

late [leit; let] **I** *a*. (***later, latter; latest, last***) **1.** 迟,晚。**2.** 晚期的,后期的。**3.** 晚近的,新近的,近时的。**4.** 已去世的,已故的。**5.** 前任的;卸任不久的。*a ~ comer* 迟到者。*be two minutes too ~ for the train* 来晚了两分钟没有赶上火车。*be ~ for school* [*work*] 小学[上班]迟到。*be ~ from school* [*an office*] 迟迟从学校[办公室]回来。*a ~ customer* 晚来顾客。*a ~ dinner* 晚上的正餐。*a ~ marriage* 晚婚。*a ~ worker* 通常工作很晚的人。*at a ~ hour* 在很晚的时候。*in*

L

one's ～ *years* 晚年。*in the* ～ *afternoon* 傍晚。*in the* ～ *seventies* 七十年代后期。*in the* ～ *20th century* 二十世纪末叶。～ *crops* 晚熟作物。～ *spring* 暮春。*one's* ～ *residence* 故居。*the* ～ *belligerents* 前不久的交战国。*the* ～ *earthquake* 最近的地震。*my* ～ *husband* (寡妇用语) 亡夫。*the* ～ *Professor Li* 已故的李教授。*the* ～ *prime minister* 前总理[首相]。**keep** ～ **hours** 迟睡迟起。**of** ～ 近来。**of** ～ **years** 近年来。**II** *ad*. **1.** 迟;过迟,来不及。**2.** 晚;到深夜。**3.** 以前是,原先是。**4.** 不久前;最近。*as* ～ *as 1945* 近在 1945 年。*Better* ～ *than never*. 〔谚〕迟做总比不做好。*come* ～ 来迟。*It is never too* ～ *to learn*. 〔谚〕活到老,学到老。*ripen* ～ 晚熟。*early and* ～ 从早到晚。*early or* ～ = sooner or later. ～ *in 1960's* 在二十世纪六十年代后期。*work* ～ *into the night* 工作到深夜。*his own room*, ～ *his uncle's* 他自己的屋子,以前是他叔父住的。*Mr. Smith*, ～ *of London* 最近住在伦敦的史密斯先生。*I saw her as* ～ *as yesterday*. 直到昨天我还看见过她。**sit up** ～ 深夜不睡。～ **fee** (英国邮局在规定时间之后投递邮件所收的)过时补加费。～ **gate** 后闸门。**L- Greek** (二世纪至六世纪用的)后期希腊语。**L- Latin** (二世纪至六世纪用的)后期拉丁语。～**-model** *a*. 新型的。**-ness** *n*.

lat·ed [ˈleitid; ˋletɪd] *a*. 〔诗〕迟来的,姗姗来迟的,迟到的。

la·teen [ləˈtiːn; læˋtin] **I** *a*. (地中海上帆船用的)三角帆的。**II** *n*. 三角帆 (= ～ sail); 三角帆船。～**-rigged** *a*. 装有三角帆的。

late·ly [ˈleitli; ˋletlɪ] *ad*. 近来,最近。★英国口语中的否定句,疑问句多用 lately, 肯定句则用其他说法。*I haven't seen him* ～ . *Have you seen him* ～? *I saw him recently* [*a short time ago*].

lat·en [ˈleitn; ˋletn̩] *vi*., *vt*. (使)变迟,(使)晚生长。

la·ten·cy [ˈleitənsi; ˋletn̩sɪ] *n*. **1.** 隐伏,潜伏,潜在。**2.** 潜伏物,潜在因素。

La Tène [lɑːˈten; lɑˋtɛn] 【考古】拉特尼文化〔公元前约 600 年到公元约 100 年间存在于中欧的一种铁器时代文化,特征为武器及用具上附有铜、金、釉彩等装饰〕。

la·tent [ˈleitənt; ˋletn̩t] **I** *a*. 存在但看不见的;潜伏的;潜在的。**II** *n*. 隐约的指印,潜指印。～ **ambiguity** 【法】潜在含糊性〔指法律文件文字本身清楚,但由于外在证据而使其产生一种以上含义〕。～ **bud** 【植】潜伏芽,休眠芽。～ **deed** 【法】秘密保存二十年以上的证件。～ **force** 潜力。～ **heat** 【物】潜热。～ **image** 【摄】(底片上已拍摄,但尚未显影的)潜像[影]。～ **period** 【医】潜伏期。～ **root** 【数】潜伏〔本征,特征〕根。**-ly** *ad*.

lat·er [ˈleitə; ˋletɚ] **I** *a*. (late 的比较级)更[较]迟的;更后的。**II** *ad*. 在后,过后。*I will see you* ～ . = *See you* ～ . 再见。*no* ～ *than* 不迟于。～ **on** 过后,以后。**sooner or** ～ 早晚,迟早(总有一天)。

lat·er·ad [ˈlætəˈræd; ˋlætəræd] *ad*. 【解】向侧面地。

lat·er·al [ˈlætərəl; ˋlætərəl] **I** *a*. **1.** 横的,侧面的,旁边的;横向的。**2.** 【语音】边音的,旁流的,(舌)边的。～ *buds* 生在侧面的蓓蕾,旁蕾。*a* ～ *branch* (*of a family*) 旁系(亲属)。～ *pressure* 【物】旁压力。*a* ～ *root* 侧根。*a* ～ *view* 侧面图。**II** *n*. **1.** 侧部的东西,侧向生长的东西。**2.** 【电】支线。**3.** 横材。**4.** 【矿】走向平巷;【建】横向排水沟。**5.** 【语音】边音,旁流音。～ **action** 【军】侧翼推进。～ **coordinate** 横坐标。～ **guidance** 俯仰制导,相控盲目降落装置。～ **inversion** 图像水平装置。～ **line** 【动】(鱼及两栖类的)侧线(感官)。**-ly** *ad*.

lat·e·ral·i·ty [ˌlætəˈræliti; ˏlætəˋrælɪtɪ] *n*. 对一个侧面的偏重〔如惯用右手〕;偏向一侧状态。

lat·er·al·ize [ˈlætərəˏlaiz; ˋlætərəˏlaɪz] *vt*. 使向侧面。

Lat·er·an [ˈlætərən; ˋlætərən] *n*. **1.** (罗马的)拉特兰大教堂。**2.** 拉特兰官。

lat·er·ite [ˈlætərait; ˋlætəˏraɪt] *n*. 【地】红土,砖红壤,铁矾土。

lat·er·i·za·tion [ˌlætəriˈzeiʃən; ˏlætərəˋzeʃən] *n*. 【地】红土化作用。**lat·er·ize** [-əraiz; -əraɪz] *vt*. (**-iz·ed**, **-iz·ing**) 使红土化。

lat·est [ˈleitist; ˋletɪst] *a*. (late 的最高级)最迟的,最后的;最近的,最新的。*the* ～ *fashion* 最新式样。*the* ～ *news* 最后消息。*the* ～ *thing* 新奇的东西,最新发明品。**at** (**the**) ～ 至迟。

la·tex [ˈleiteks; ˋletɛks] *n*. (*pl*. **～es**, **lat·i·ces** [ˈlætisiːz; ˋlætəsiz]) 【植】橡浆,乳液,树乳,胶乳。

lath [lɑːθ; læθ] **I** *n*. (*pl*. **～s** [lɑːθs; lɑθs]) 【建】板条,板桩。*a* ～*-and-plaster shed* (木架)板条,灰面屋。*a* ～ *painted to look like iron* 虚张声势的胆小鬼。*a* ～ *cutter* 割板机。*a measuring* ～ 测量标竿。**as thin as a** ～ 骨瘦如柴。**II** *vt*. 给…钉板条;用板条覆盖[衬里]。～ **house** 【园艺】遮光育苗室。

lathe [leið; leð] **I** *n*. 【机】车床,镟床 (= turning-～)。*an automatic* ～ 自动车床。*an automatic turret* ～ 自动六角车床。*a boring* ～ 镗床。*a drill* ～ 钻孔车床。*a programme-controlled vertical* ～ 程序控制立式车床。*a screw-cutting* ～ 旋螺丝车床。*a tool-maker* ～ 工具车床。*a universal* ～ 万能车床。*a vertical* ～ 立式车床。*a* ～ *turner* 车工。*a* ～ *dog* 车床夹头。**II** *vt*. 用车床加工。

la·thee, **la·thi** [ˈlɑːti; ˋlɑtɪ] *n*. (印度人作武器的)铁箍棒。

lath·er[1] [ˈlɑːðə; ˋlæðɚ] **I** *n*. **1.** 肥皂泡,泡沫。**2.** (马等的)汗沫。**3.** 〔喻〕激动,焦躁。*make a* ～ *on sb.'s face* 在某人脸上涂肥皂沫。**be** (**all**) **in a** ～ 满身是汗;〔口〕激动。**A good** ～ **is half a shave**. 〔谚〕好的基础是成功的一半。**II** *vi*. **1.** 涂肥皂沫;发泡沫。**2.** (马)流汗。— *vt*. **1.** 在…上涂肥皂沫。**2.** 使某人焦急[紧张] (*up*)。**3.** 〔俚〕狠狠地打。～ *one's face before shaving* 刮脸前先在脸上涂上肥皂沫。

lath·er[2] [ˈlɑːðə; ˋlɑðɚ] *n*. 钉板条工人。

lath·er·y [ˈlæðəri; ˋlæðərɪ] *a*. 泡沫造成的;泡沫覆盖的;起泡沫的。

lath·ing [ˈlɑːθiŋ; ˋlæθɪŋ] *n*. **1.** 钉板条。**2.** 〔集合词〕板条。

lath·y [ˈlɑːθi; ˋlæθɪ] *a*. (**lath·i·er**; **-i·est**) 板条似的;狭长的。

lati- *comb*. *f*. 表示"宽的","阔的": *lati*tude.

lat·i·ces [ˈlætisiːz; ˋlætəˏsiz] *n*. latex 的复数。

lat·i·cif·er·ous [ˌlætiˈsifərəs; ˏlætəˋsɪfərəs] *a*. 产生橡浆[乳液]的,含有橡浆的;分泌橡浆的。

lat·i·fun·di·um [ˌlætiˈfʌndiəm; ˏlætəˋfʌndɪəm] *n*. (*pl*. **-dia** [-diə; -dɪə]) 大庄园,大领地,大地产。

lat·i·mer·i·a [ˌlætiˈmiəriə; ˏlætɪˋmɪrɪə] *n*. 【动】矛尾鱼 (*Latimeria chalumnae*)〔产于南非东海岸,特别是莫桑比克海峡〕。

Lat·in [ˈlætin; ˋlætɪn] **I** *a*. **1.** 拉丁的;拉丁语的;拉丁人的。**2.** 天主教的。*the* ～ *peoples* 拉丁民族。**II** *n*. **1.** 拉丁语,拉丁字母表。**2.** 拉丁人(尤指拉丁美洲人);古罗马人。**3.** 罗马天主教徒。*Old* ～ (公元前 75 年以前的)古代拉丁语。*Classical* ～ (公元前 75 年至公元 175 年间的)古典拉丁语。*Late* ～ (公元 175—600 年的)后期拉丁语。*Medieval* [*Middle*] ～ (约公元 600—1500 年的)中世纪拉丁语。*Modern* [*New*] ～ (公元 1500 年以后的)近代拉丁语。*Low* [*Vulgar*] ～ (公元 175 年前后)民间拉丁语,俗拉丁语。*dog monk's* ～ 不纯正的[半通不通的]拉丁语。*thieves'* ～ 盗贼用黑话。～ **America** 拉丁美洲。～ **American** 拉丁美洲人。～ **Church** (以拉丁语作礼拜仪式的)罗马天主教。～ **cross** 纵长十字。～ **Quarter** (巴黎的)拉丁区。～ **rite** 【宗】罗马天主教的礼拜仪式。～ **school**, ～ **grammar school** (以拉丁语及希腊语为主科的)拉丁(文法)学校。～ **square** 【统】拉丁方。

Lat·in·ate [ˈlætineit; ˋlætənet] *a*. 拉丁语的;从拉丁语派生的;近似拉丁语的(= Latinic)。

la·ti·ne [ləˈtainiː; ləˋtaıni] ***ad***. 〔L.〕在拉丁语内,用拉丁文写。

Lat·in·ism [ˈlætinizəm; ˋlætn͵ızəm] *n*. **1**. 拉丁语风,拉丁语[词、成语等]。**2**. 拉丁性质。

Lat·in·ist [ˈlætinist; ˋlætnıst] *n*. 拉丁语学家;罗马文化研究家。

La·tin·i·ty [ləˈtiniti, læ-; læˋtınətı, læ-] *n*. **1**. 拉丁语的使用[写作]。**2**. 拉丁语风。**3**. 拉丁语法。

Lat·in·ize [ˈlætinaiz; ˋlætn͵aız] *vt*. **1**. 把…译成拉丁语。**2**. 使拉丁化。**3**. 使(信条、教义)罗马天主教化,使符合天主教的仪式[习惯等]。**4**. 使有拉丁语特征。— *vi*. **1**. 有拉丁语特征。**2**. 有天主教影响的表现。**-i·za·tion** *n*.

La·ti·no [læˈtiːnəu, lə-; laˋtino, lə-] *n*. (*pl*. ~*s*) 拉丁美洲人。

lat·ish [ˈleitiʃ; ˋletıʃ] *a*., *ad*. 稍迟的[地],稍晚的[地]。

lat·i·tude [ˈlætitjuːd; ˋlætə͵tjud] *n*. **1**. 纬度 (*opp*. longitude)。**2**. 【天】黄纬。**3**. 〔*pl*.〕(以纬度而论的)地区,地方,地域。**4**. (见解、思想、行动的)自由。**5**. 〔罕〕范围,活动余地;〔罕〕宽度。**6**. 【摄】胶片曝光时间的有效范围[伸缩限度]。*high* [*low*] ~*s* 高[低]纬度地方,离赤道远[近]的地方。*thirty degrees north* [*south*] ~ 北[南]纬三十度。***be allowed some*** ~ 被允许有若干自由。***out of one's*** ~ 越出自己的本行[知识]以外 (*He is out of his* ~. 他在干外行事)。***understand sth. in its proper*** ~ 充分理解某事。

lat·i·tu·di·nal [͵lætiˈtjuːdinl; ͵lætəˋtjudənl̩] *a*. 纬度的。

lat·i·tu·di·nar·i·an [͵læti͵tjuːdiˈnɛəriən; ͵lætə͵tjudn̩ˋɛrıən] **I** *a*. 自由主义的,放任主义的;放纵的;不拘泥于教义的。**II** *n*. 自由主义者;不拘泥于教条的人。**-ism** *n*. (宗教信仰上的)自由主义。

lat·ke [ˈlɑːtki; ˋlɑtkı] *n*. (*pl*. ~*s*) 马铃薯饼〔特指用生马铃薯磨碎制成〕。

la·tri·a [ləˈtraiə; ləˋtraıə] *n*. 【天主】专对天主的礼拜。

la·trine [ləˈtriːn; ləˋtrin] *n*. 作成沟形或坑形的厕所,公共厕所。

-la·try *comb. f*. 表示"崇拜": ido*latry*, Mario*latry*.

lat·ten, lat·tin [ˈlætən, ˈlætin; ˋlætn, ˋlætın] *n*. **1**. 金属薄板,镀锡铁片。**2**. 黄铜片,类似黄铜的合金片。

lat·ter [ˈlætə; ˋlætɚ] *a*. **1**. 后面的,末了的,末尾的 (*opp*. first)。**2**. 〔the ~〕(二者中)后者的,〔用作 *pro*.〕后者 (*opp*. the former)。**3**. 近来的,晚近的。**4**. 〔古〕最后的,末期的。*the* ~ *half of the month* [*year*] 下半月[年]。*Of the two the* ~ *is better than the former*. 二者中后者比前者好。*in these* ~ *days* 近来,现今。*one's* ~ *end* 某人的结局,死。~**-day** *a*. 近来的,晚近的;现代的。**-ly** *ad*. 〔罕〕近代,后来。

lat·ter·most [ˈlætəməust; ˋlætɚ͵most] *a*. (排列在)最后的。

lat·tice [ˈlætis; ˋlætıs] **I** *n*. **1**. 格子。**2**. 【物】点阵;网络。**3**. 【建】格构。*crystal* ~ 晶体;【物】点阵,晶格。*a* ~ *frame* 格子框架。**II** *vt*. **1**. 把…制成格子状。**2**. 用格子覆盖[装饰]。~ **bridge** 格构桥。~ **girder** 格构大梁,花格大梁。~ **network** X 形(电)网络。~ **points** 格点,网点。~ **tower** 【无】(支持天线的)格架塔。~ **window** 格子窗。~**-work** *n*. **1**. 格子。**2**. 格子细工,格子花样。

lat·ticed [ˈlætist; ˋlætıst] *a*. 制成格子的;装有格子的。*a* ~ *door* [*window*] 装格子的门[窗]。

lat·ti·ci·nio [͵lætiˈtʃiːnjəu; ͵lætıˋtʃinıo] *n*. 〔It.〕不透明乳白玻璃〔常以线条形式构成玻璃器皿上的装饰〕。

Lat·ti·more [ˈlætimɔː; ˋlætə͵mor] *n*. 拉铁摩尔〔姓氏〕。

Lat·vi·a [ˈlætviə; ˋlætvıə] *n*. 拉脱维亚〔波罗的海一国家名〕。**-n I** *a*. **1**. 拉脱维亚(人)的。**2**. 拉脱维亚语的。**II** *n*. **1**. 拉脱维亚人。**2**. 拉脱维亚语。

la·uan [ləˈwɑːn; ləˋwɑn] *n*. 【植】(菲律宾产的)柳安树;柳安木料。

laud [lɔːd; lɔd] **I** *vt*. 赞美,称赞。~ *sb. to the skies* 对某人备加赞颂。**II** *n*. **1**. 赞美,称赞。**2**. 〔*pl*.〕赞美歌;松歌,颂乐。

laud·a·ble [ˈlɔːdəbl; ˋlɔdəbl̩] *a*. 值得称赞的。~ *feats* 可称颂的功绩[杰出事迹]。**-a·bil·i·ty** [͵lɔːdəˈbiliti; ͵lɔdəˋbılətı] *n*.

laud·a·num [ˈlɔdnəm; ˋlɔ̣dənəm] *n*. 【药】鸦片酊。

lau·da·tion [lɔːˈdeiʃən; lɔˋdeʃən] *n*. 赞美,称赞。

laud·a·tive [ˈlɔːdətiv; ˋlɔdətıv], **-to·ry** [-təri; -tərı] *a*. 赞美的,称赞的。

laugh [lɑːf; læf] **I** *n*. **1**. 笑,笑声。**2**. 令人发笑的事。**3**. 嘲笑,取乐;〔*pl*.〕玩笑,逗乐。*He gave a loud* ~. 他大笑一声。*She laughed a hearty* ~. 她放声大笑。*The joke raised a* ~. 这笑话引起一阵大笑。*sardonic* ~ 狞笑,冷笑。*What a* ~ *to say that*! 说出那种话来真可笑! *give sb. the* ~ *for his folly* 因为某人的愚蠢行为而嘲笑他。*beat sb. for* ~*s* 打某人一顿取乐。***break into a*** ~ 突然笑起来。***get*** [***have***] ***the*** ~ ***at*** [***of, on***] ***sb***. 反过来笑某人,轮到某人受嘲笑。***have a good*** [***hearty***] ~ 笑得痛快。***have the*** ~ ***on one's side*** = ***get*** [***have***] ***the*** ~ ***at*** [***of, on***] ***sb***. ***holy*** ~ 狂笑,神经质的大笑。***with a*** ~ 笑着,一笑。**II** *vi*. **1**. 大笑;发笑。**2**. (自然物等)呈现令人欢快的形态。*Green pines* ~ *in the breeze*. 青松迎风欢笑。*The hill* ~*s with verdure*. 山上一片青葱,欣欣向荣。— *vt*. **1**. 以笑表示。**2**. 笑得使…。*He* ~*ed his dissent*. 他笑着表示不同意。~ *a reply* 以笑作答。~ *oneself to death* 笑得要死。~ *sb. out of his belief* 笑得某人失去信心。***burst out*** ~***-ing*** 放声大笑。***He*** ~***s best who*** ~***s last***. 〔谚〕最后笑的人笑得最好。***He who*** ~***s at crooked men should need walk very straight***. 〔谚〕要笑别人驼背,自己就要挺起胸膛走路。***It is enough to make a cat*** [***horse***] ~. 太可笑了。***L- and grow fat***. 〔谚〕心宽体胖。***L-, and the world will*** ~ ***with you***. 〔谚〕你如果乐观,世界将陪着欢笑。~ ***at*** **1**. 因…而发笑 (~ *at a joke* 听了笑话而发笑)。**2**. 嘲笑 (We ~*ed at his fancy*. 我们嘲笑他异想天开)。**3**. 付之一笑,不以为意 (~ *at difficulties* 对困难一笑置之)。~ ***away*** **1**. 付之一笑,笑着不理。**2**. 笑着消磨(时间) (~ *away all one's apprehensions* 对自己的一切忧虑付之一笑)。~ ***down*** 用笑声来打断[拒绝]。~ ***in*** [***up***] ***one's sleeve*** 暗暗发笑,窃笑。~ ***in sb.'s face*** 当面嘲笑某人。~ ***off*** **1**. 一笑置之。**2**. 以笑来排除(怒气、窘境等) (~ *off sb.'s suspicions* 以嬉笑排除某人的疑心)。~ ***oneself into convulsions*** [***fits***] 笑破肚皮。~ ***on the wrong side of one's mouth*** [***face***] 笑脸变成哭脸,由得意变成失意。~ ***out*** 哄笑。~ ***out one's consent*** 含笑表示同意。~ ***out of court*** 付之一笑。~ ***over*** 笑着谈论。(~ *over a letter* 笑着谈论一封信)。~ **track** 笑声声带〔多指预先录制好观众笑声插入电视节目中〕。

laugh·a·ble [ˈlɑːfəbl; ˋlæfəbl̩] *a*. 可笑的,有趣的。

laugh·a·bly [ˈlɑːfəbli; ˋlæfəbl̩ı] *ad*. 可笑。*look* ~ *archaic* 样子古老得可笑。

laugh·ing [ˈlɑːfiŋ; ˋlæfıŋ] **I** *a*. **1**. 笑的,笑着的,笑着似的。**2**. 可笑的。*This is no* ~ *matter*. 这可不是什么好笑的事。**II** *n*. 笑。*hold one's* ~ 忍住笑。~ **gas** 【化】笑气。~ **hyena** 【动】笑猿,斑猿。~ **jackass** 【动】笑鸪。~**-stock** 笑柄 (*make a* ~*-stock of oneself* 丢人,出洋相)。**-ly** *ad*.

laugh·ter [ˈlɑːftə; ˋlæftɚ] *n*. **1**. 笑,笑声。**2**. 〔古〕好笑的事。**3**. 〔美俚〕力量悬殊得可笑的体育比赛。***burst into*** ~ 放声大笑。***die with*** ~ 笑得要死。***Homeric*** ~ 宏亮[健康]的笑声〔原指荷马史诗中天上诸神的大笑声〕。***roar with*** ~ 哄堂大笑。

Laugh·ton [ˈlɔːtn; ˋlɔtn̩] *n*. 劳顿〔姓氏〕。

launce [lɔːns, læns, lɑːns; lɔns, læns, lɑns] *n*. 【动】玉

筋鱼（ = sand eel）。

launch[1][lɔːntʃ, lɑːntʃ; lɔntʃ, lɑntʃ] **I** ***vt*.** **1.** 使（船）下水。～ *a ship from a shipyard* 使船从船坞下水。**2.** 发射；投出；提出，发出。**3.**（把孩子等）送出；使独立谋生。**4.** 开办，创办；发动，发起；开展。～ *a man-made* [*an artificial*] *satellite* 发射人造卫星。～ *an airplane* 使飞机起飞。～ *a spear* 投矛。～ *a torpedo* 发射鱼雷。～ *into space a sputnik-ship* 向太空发射人造卫星。～ *one's child in* [*into*] *the world* 把子女送到社会上。～ *sb. in* [*into*] *business* 使某人进入商界。～ *a new enterprise* 创办新企业。～ *a fierce attack* 开始猛攻。～ *a mass movement* 开展群众运动。～ *a campaign of abuse* 开始互骂。～ *threats against sb.* 对某人发出威胁。— ***vi*.** **1.** 起飞，下水。**2.** 投入。**3.** 开始，着手进行。*A bird* ～*ed off.* 鸟飞走了。～ *into a strong rebuke* 激烈斥责。～ *on one's study* 开始学习。～ *upon the production of cars* 开始生产汽车。～ **out** **1.** 船下水。**2.** 出航（～ *out on a journey* 首途旅行）。**3.** 开始（～ *out in a new scheme* 开始新的计划）。**4.** 挥霍。～ ***out into*** **1.** 乘船出海；投身…（界）。**2.** 开始，着手。**3.** 挥霍（～ *out into extravagance* 大肆挥霍）。**II** ***n*.** 发射，下水。～ *of a new liner* 新（定期）客轮［班机］下水［首航］。～ **airplane** 火箭运载机。～ **pad**（火箭等的）发射台。～ **vehicle** 运载火箭；活动发射装置。～ **window** 发射时限〔指条件适合发射太空船的一段时期〕。

launch[2][lɔːntʃ, lɑːntʃ; lɔntʃ, lɑntʃ] ***n*.** 汽艇，游艇。*a motor* ～ 摩托艇。

launch·er [lɔːntʃə, lɑːntʃə; ˋlɔntʃɚ, lɑntʃɚ] ***n*.** **1.** 弹射器；弹弓；石弩。**2.**（安装在步枪上的）手榴弹发射器。**3.**（飞弹、太空飞船等的）发射装置。

launch·ing [ˈlɔːntʃiŋ, ˈlɑːntʃiŋ; ˋlɔntʃɪŋ, ˋlɑntʃɪŋ] ***n*.** **1.** 发射。**2.** 起飞；（船等）下水；下水典礼。**3.** 开办。*battery* ～（飞弹的）齐射。*zero-length* ～（火箭）原地发射，垂直发射。～ **pad** = launch pad. ～ **site** 发射场，发射场的全部设备。～ **tube**（水雷等的）发射管。～ **ways**（船的）下水滑道。

laun·der [ˈlɔːndə, ˈlɑːndə; ˋlɔndɚ, ˋlɑndɚ] **I** ***vt*.** **1.** 洗（衣等）。**2.**（洗后）烫（衣等）。**3.**〔美俚〕贪污，侵吞；（把款项等）非法转移〔如秘密通过外国银行汇到国外等〕，洗（黑钱）。**4.** 粉饰，消除…的污点。— ***vi*.** **1.** 洗烫衣物。**2.** 经洗；耐烫。*This fabric* ～*s well.* 这种织品经洗耐用。**II** ***n*.**【矿】槽洗机，流槽。**-a·bil·i·ty** ***n*.** **-a·ble** ***a*.** **-er** ***n*.** **-ing** ***n*.** **1.**（衣物等的）洗涤，洗熨。**2.**（来路可疑钱财的）污迹洗刷。**3.**〔俚〕掩饰。

Laun·der·ette [ˌlɔːndəˈret, ˌlɑːn-; ˏlɔndəˋret, ˏlɑn-] ***n*.**〔美〕自动洗衣店的招牌；〔l-〕自动洗衣店〔设有由顾客自行操作的自动洗衣机〕。

laun·dress [ˈlɔːndris, ˈlɑːndris; ˋlɔndrɪs, ˋlɑndrɪs] ***n*.** 洗烫衣物的女工。

Laun·dro·mat [ˈlɑːndrəˌmæt, ˈlɔːn-; ˋlɔndrəmæt, ˋlɔn-] ***n*.**〔美〕自动洗衣店的招牌；〔l-〕自动洗衣店。

laun·dry [ˈlɔːndri; ˋlɔndrɪ] ***n*.** **1.** 洗衣。**2.** 洗衣房，洗衣店。**3.** 要洗的东西，洗好的东西。**4.**（国外的）洗黑钱处。***hang out the*** ～〔军俚〕空投伞兵。～ **list** **1.** 交付洗衣店的待洗衣服清单。**2.**〔喻〕一大张清单［名单，项目单等］。～ **machine** 洗衣机。～**-man** 洗衣工人。～**woman**（*pl.* **-wom·en**）= laundress.

Lau·ra [ˈlɔːrə; ˋlɔrə] ***n*.** 劳拉〔姓氏〕。

Lau·ra·sia [lɔːˈreiʒə, -ʃə; lɔˋreʒə, -ʃə] ***n*.**【地】劳亚古大陆〔被认为是古代曾存在的大陆名，包括北美洲和欧亚大陆，约在古生代末期分离开来〕。

lau·re·ate [ˈlɔːriit; ˋlɔrɪɪt] **I** ***a*.** **1.** 戴桂冠的。**2.** 有戴桂冠资格的，卓越的。**3.**（桂冠）用月桂树造的。**II** ***n*.** **1.** 戴桂冠的人。**2.**〔L-〕桂冠诗人（ = Poet L-）。**3.** 奖金［荣誉］获得者。**III** ***vt*.** **1.** 使戴桂冠，授以荣誉。**2.** 授以桂冠诗人的称号。～**ship** 桂冠诗人的称号［身份］。

lau·re·a·tion [ˌlɔːriˈeiʃən; ˏlɔrɪˋeʃən] ***n*.** 授以桂冠［荣誉］。

Lau·rel [ˈlɔrəl; ˋlɔrəl] ***n*.** 劳雷尔〔女子名〕。

lau·rel [ˈlɔrəl; ˋlɔrəl] **I** ***n*.** **1.**【植】月桂树，月桂树叶，月桂属植物。**2.**（表示荣誉的）桂冠；〔*pl.*〕光荣，荣誉；【美体】（比赛的）胜利。***look to one's*** ～***s*** 小心保持荣誉。***rest on one's*** ～***s*** 安于已得名誉，安于小成，吃老本。***win*** [***gain***, ***reap***] ***one's*** ～***s*** 博得名声。**II** ***vt*.**（**-l(l)-**）**1.** 使戴桂冠。**2.** 给以荣誉。

lau·rel(l)ed [ˈlɔrəld; ˋlɔrəld] ***a*.** 戴桂冠的；获得荣誉的。

Lau·rence [ˈlɔrəns; ˋlɔrəns] ***n*.** 劳伦斯〔姓氏，男子名〕。

Lau·ren·ti·an [ˈlɔːrenʃiən; lɔˋrɛnʃən] ***a*.**, ***n*.** **1.**【地质】劳伦系（的）。**2.**（加拿大等 St. Lawrence 河附近的）劳伦系岩石层。

lau·ric acid [ˈlɔːrik æsid; ˋlɔrɪk æsɪd]【化】月桂酸；十二（烷）酸。

Lau·rie [ˈlɔ(ː)ri; ˋlɔrɪ] ***n*.** 劳丽〔女子名，Laura 的昵称〕。

lau·rus·ti·nus [ˌlɔrəsˈtainəs; ˏlɔrəsˋtaɪnəs] ***n*.**【植】（南欧产）一种高大的常绿灌木（ = laurestinus）。

lau·ryl alcohol [ˈlɔːril ˈælkəhɔl; ˋlɔrɪl ˋælkəhɑl]【化】十二（烷）醇。

Lau·sanne [ləuˈzæn; loˋzæn] ***n*.** 洛桑〔瑞士城市〕。

lav [læv; læv] ***n*.**〔美口〕盥洗室（ = lavatory）。

la·va [ˈlɑːvə; ˋlɑvə] ***n*.**【地】熔岩；火山岩；〔*pl.*〕火山岩层。*aqueous* ～ 泥流岩。

la·va·bo [ləˈveibəu; ləˋvebo] ***n*.**（*pl.* ～*es*, ～*s*）**1.**【宗】洗手礼。**2.** 行洗手礼时用《诗篇》。**3.** 洗手礼手巾［水盘］。**4.** 洗手所；〔*pl.*〕盥洗室。

lav·age [læˈvɑːʒ, ˈlævidʒ; ˋlævɪʒ, ˋlævɪdʒ] ***n*.**【医】灌洗；洗出法；洗胃；灌肠。

la·va-la·va [ˈlɑːvəˈlɑːvə; ˋlɑvɑˋlɑvɑ] ***n*.**〔Samoan〕（南太平洋岛屿特别是萨摩亚群岛居民穿的）花腰布；短裙。

lav·a·liere, **lav·a·lier** [ˌlɑːvəˈliə, ˈlævə-; ˏlævəˋlɪr, ˋlævə-] ***n*.** **1.** 项链上的垂饰（ = *lavallière*）。**2.**（挂在脖子上或上衣等处的）微型话筒。

la·va·tion [læˈveiʃən; læˋveʃən] ***n*.**【医】= lavage.

lav·a·to·ry [ˈlævəˌtəri; ˋlævəˏtorɪ] ***n*.** **1.** 盥洗室；厕所。**2.** 洗脸盆；【宗】洗礼盆。

lave[1][leiv; lev] ***vt*.**, ***vi*.**〔诗〕洗；（波浪）冲刷（河岸）。

lave[2][leiv; lev] ***n*.**〔Scot.〕遗留物，剩余物。

lave·ment [ˈleivmənt; ˋlevmənt] ***n*.**【医】灌洗；洗出法。

lav·en·der [ˈlævində; ˋlævəndɚ] **I** ***n*.** **1.**【植】熏衣草。**2.** 熏衣草的花［叶、茎］。**3.** 淡紫色。***lay*** (***up***) ***in*** ～ **1.** 小心保存（以备日后使用）。**2.** 送进当铺。**3.** 禁闭，关进监狱。**II** ***a*.** **1.** 熏衣草的。**2.** 淡紫色的。**III** ***vt*.** 夹熏衣草（在衣间），用熏衣草熏香。～ **water** 熏衣草香水。

la·ver[1][ˈleivə; ˋlevɚ] ***n*.** **1.**〔古〕盥洗用具（如盆等）。**2.**（犹太教祭司用的）铜质洗涤盆。**3.**【宗】洗礼盘；洗礼水。

la·ver[2][ˈleivə; ˋlevɚ] ***n*.** **1.**【植】紫菜属的一种，甘紫菜。**2.**【植】石莼属的一种。

lav·er·ock [ˈlævərək; ˋlævərək] ***n*.**〔Scot.〕云雀。

lav·ish [ˈlæviʃ; ˋlævɪʃ] **I** ***vt*.** 大量地乱用，浪费；挥霍；滥花；慷慨地给与。～ *care upon one's children* 溺爱儿女。～ *money on sth.* 在某事上乱花钱。～ *praises on sb.* 乱捧某人。**II** ***a*.** **1.** 过分大方的，慷慨的；大量的。**2.** 过于丰富的，过度的，浪费的。*be* ～ *of money* 用钱大手大脚的。～ *hospitality* 过于好客。**-ly** ***ad*.** **-ment**, **-ness** ***n*.**

La·voi·sier [ˌlɑːvwɑˈzjei; ˏlɑˏvwɑˋzje], **A. L.** 拉瓦锡〔1743—1794，法国化学家，氧发现者〕。

Law [lɔː; lɔ] ***n*.** 劳〔姓氏〕。

law[1][lɔː; lɔ] **I** ***n*.** **1.** 法律，法令；法典。**2.** 法学；诉讼；司法界；律师（界），律师职务。**3.**（事物或科学的）法则，规律；定律，定理。**4.**（生活中或各种娱乐游戏的）惯例；规则；（宗教）戒律。**5.**（行猎时给与所猎猎物，比赛时给与弱方的）宽让时间［距离］。**6.**〔美俚〕〔the ～〕司法人员；警察；监狱看守。*abide by the* ～ 守法。*break the* ～ 犯

L

法。*contract* ～ 契约法。*deal with sb. according to* ～ 依法处理某人。*domestic* ～ 国家法。*Draconian* ～*s* 古雅典执政官德拉科的法律,〔喻〕严峻的法律。*private* ～ (处理私人关系,私人财产等的)私法。*the blue-sky* ～〔美〕无信用股票取缔法。*maintain* ～ *and order* 维持法律和秩序。*be learned in the* ～ 精通法学。*read* [*study*] ～ 学法律。*follow* [*practice*] ～ 做律师 (= go in for ～)。*the* ～ *of the land* 国法。*go to* ～ *against sb.* 跟某人打官司。*a* ～ *of nature* (= *a natural* ～) 自然规律。*the jungle* ～ 丛林的法则,弱肉强食原则。*the L- of Nature* [*Reason*] 天理。*Where they saw chance, we see* ～. 从他们过去所看到的偶然性中,我们发现了规律。*Boyle's* ～【物】波义耳定理。～ *of conservation of energy* 能量守恒定律。～ *of mass action* 质量作用律;分量作用定律。～ *of motion* 运动三定律。～ *of parity* 宇称定律。～ *of relativity* 相对论。～ *of social development* 社会发展规律。～ *of the unity of opposites* 对立统一规律。～ *of universal gravitation* 万有引力定律。～ *of zero or unity*【统】零一律。*Ohm's* ～【电】欧姆定律。*the* ～ *of painting* 绘画法。*the* ～*s of the chase* 狩猎规则。*blue* ～*s* 清教徒式的严酷法律。*club* ～ 暴力[大棒]政治;俱乐部规章。～ *of honour* 行为法则;决斗惯例。***a*** [***the***] ～ ***of the Medes and Persians*** 不可更改的法律。***be a*** ～ ***to*** [***unto***] ***oneself*** 照自己的意思去做,独断独行。***be at*** ～ 在诉讼[审判]中。***be bad*** ～ 违背法律。***be beyond the*** ～ 在法律范围以外。***be bred to the*** ～ 被训练成律师[法官]。***be good*** ～ 符合法律。***be outside the*** ～ 不合法。***be within the*** ～ 合法。***contend at*** ～ 诉讼,打官司。***give*** (***the***) ～ ***to sb.*** 对某人发号施令。***go to*** ～ ***with sb.*** = ***have*** [***take***] ***the*** ～ ***of sb.*** 控告某人。***lay down the*** ～ 发号施令。***strain*** [***stretch***] ***the*** ～ 枉法,曲解法律。***take the*** ～ ***into one's own hands*** (= have the ～ in one's own hands) 随意处罚,滥用法律。**II** ***vi.***, ***vt.*** 〔俚〕起诉,控告。～**-abiding** ***a.*** 守法的。～**-book** 法律学课本;法律学书籍,法典。～ **breaker** 违法分子,犯法者。～**breaking** 违法,犯法;违法的。～**-court** 法庭。～ **French** 诺曼底法语。～ **giver** 立法者,法典制定人。～**-giving** **1.** ***n.*** 立法,制定法典。**2.** ***a.*** 立法的。～**-hand** (英国旧时)写法律文件的一种书法。**L- Lord** 〔亦作 l- l-〕〔英〕上院执掌司法的议院。～ **maker** 立法人;协助制定法律者〔尤指立法委员〕。～**making** 立法;协助制定法律。～**man** (*pl.* ***-men***) 执法者〔尤指美国联邦法院执行官、司法官、警察等〕。～ **merchant** 商业惯例,商法。～**monger** 讼棍。～ **office** 〔美〕法律事务所。～ **officer** 司法官;检察长[次长]。**L- of Moses** = mosaic ～. ～ **of nations** = international ～. ～ **of parsimony**【哲】最经济规律。～ **stationer** **1.** 法律书籍商。**2.** 法律文件代书人。～ **suit** 诉讼(案件) (*bring in* [*enter*] *a* ～ *suit against sb.* 对某人起诉)。～ **term** **1.** 法律用语。**2.** 法庭开庭期。

law[2] [lɔ:; lɔ] ***int.*** 〔英俚〕天哪! 嗳呀!

Lawes [lɔ:z; lɔz] ***n.*** 劳斯〔姓氏〕。

law·ful [ˈlɔ:fəl; ˋlɔfəl] ***a.*** 合法的;法定的;守法的。*a* ～ *act* 合法行为。*a* ～ *age* = ～ *years* 法定年龄,成年。～ *goods*【法】中立国船只装载的货物。*a* ～ *day* (法院)开庭日;(法律上规定的)营业日。**-ly** ***ad.*** **-ness** ***n.***

lawk(s) [lɔ:k(s); lɔk(s)] ***int.*** 〔俚,Lord 的讹用〕嗳呀! 糟了!

law·less [ˈlɔ:lis; ˋlɔlɪs] ***a.*** **1.** 无法律的,不能实施法律的。**2.** 不法的,违法的,无法无天的。*a* ～ *man* 不法之徒。～ *passions* 无法控制的情欲。～ *practices* 违法行为。

lawn[1] [lɔ:n; lɔn] ***n.*** **1.** 上等细麻布。**2.** 英国国教主教的职位。～ **sleeves** **1.** 上等细(麻)布袖。**2.** 主教的职位。

lawn[2] [lɔ:n; lɔn] ***n.*** **1.** 草地,草坪,草场。**2.** 〔诗〕林间空地。～ **bowling** 草地滚球戏。～ **dart** 草地(扔)飞镖(游戏)。～ **mower** 割草机,割草人。～ **party** 〔美〕草坪招待会,露天招待会。～ **ten·nis** 草地网球。

lawn·y[1] [ˈlɔ:ni; ˋlɔnɪ] ***a.*** 细麻布做的,细麻布一样的。

lawn·y[2] [ˈlɔ:ni; ˋlɔnɪ] ***a.*** 草地(多)的;草地一样的。

Law·rence [ˈlɔrəns; ˋlɔrəns] ***n.*** **1.** 劳伦斯〔姓氏〕。**2. E. O.** ～ 劳伦斯〔1901—1958,美国物理学家,回旋加速器的发明人〕。**3. David Herbert** ～ 戴维·赫伯特·劳伦斯〔1885—1930,英国小说家〕。

law·ren·ci·um [lɔ:ˈrensiəm, lɑ:-; lɔˋrɛnsɪəm, lɑ-] ***n.*** 【化】铹。

laws [lɔ:z; lɔz] ***int.*** = law[2].

law·yer [ˈlɔ:jə; ˋlɔjɚ] ***n.*** **1.** 律师。**2.** 法律家。***a forecastle*** ～〔美俚〕经常爱争论[抱怨、议论]的人。***a good*** ～ 懂法律的人。***a Jack-leg*** ～〔美〕讼棍。***a philadelphia*** ～〔美〕很精明的人;狡猾的人。**a poor** ～ 不懂法律的人。***enough to puzzle a philadelphia*** ～〔美〕太错综复杂使人难于弄明白的。***He is no*** ～. 他不懂法律。

Law·son [ˈlɔ:sn; ˋlɔsn] ***n.*** 劳森〔姓氏〕。

lax[1] [læks; læks] **I** ***a.*** **1.** (肠)宽松的,易通便的,腹泻的。**2.** 松弛的;质地松的。**3.** 不严格的,马虎的;不精密的;含糊的。**4.**【植】(花簇)疏松的。**5.**【乐】弛缓的,不紧张的 (*opp.* tense)。**6.**【语音】(母音)松弛的。～ *morals* 行为放荡。～ *discipline* 松懈的纪律。～ *vowels*【语音】松母音。**II** ***n.*** 泻肚,下痢。**-ly** ***ad.*** **-ness** ***n.***

lax[2] [læks; læks] ***n.***【动】(挪威、瑞典的)鲑。

lax·a·tion [lækˈseiʃən; lækˋseʃən] ***n.*** **1.** 松弛,弛缓。**2.**【医】轻泻。

lax·a·tive [ˈlæksətiv; ˋlæksətɪv] **I** ***a.*** **1.** 通大便的;有轻度腹泻的。**2.** 放松的;放肆的。**II** ***n.***【药】轻泻剂。**-ly** ***ad.*** **-ness** ***n.***

lax·i·ty [ˈlæksiti; ˋlæksətɪ] ***n.*** **1.** 轻泻(性)。**2.** 松弛。**3.** (纺织品等的)疏松。**4.** 粗心,疏忽。

lay[1] [lei; le] **I** ***vt.*** (***laid*** [leid; led]; ***lay·ing***) **1.** 放,搁,摆。～ *oneself down* 躺下。**2.** 安排;预备;布置。～ *a fire* 准备生火。～ *an ambush* 设下埋伏。～ *a snare* [*trap*] 设下陷阱。～ *mines* 布雷,埋雷。～ *the table for breakfast* 摆食具预备开早饭。**3.** 铺设;敷设;砌砖。～ *a pavement* 铺装路面。～ *a railroad track* 铺铁路轨道。～ *the foundations of* 奠定…的基础。**4.** 产卵,生蛋。～ *eggs* 下蛋,产卵。**5.** 涂布,涂覆。～ *a wall with paint* 用油漆涂墙。～ *plaster on the wall* 在墙上涂灰泥。**6.** 使负担;抽税,加处罚。～ *a burden on sb.* 把负担加在某人身上。～ *duties on imports* 对进口货抽税。**7.** 打倒。～ *sb. low* 打败某人。*The storm laid the crops.* 暴风吹倒了庄稼。**8.** 镇压,使静下来。*A city is laid in the dust* [*in ashes, in ruins*]. 全城化为灰烬[废墟]。*water the street to* ～ *the dust* 街上洒水压灰尘。**9.** 归罪,嫁祸。～ *the blame on sb.* 责怪某人。～ *a fault to sb.'s charge* [*at sb.'s door*] 归咎于某人。**10.** 想出,拟定。～ *one's plans* 拟定计划。**11.** 提出,提示;申述(主张等)。～ *claim to sth.* 对某物提出所有权要求。～ *an indictment* 提起公诉。～ *the question before a committee* 把问题提交委员会。**12.** 规定(损害数量)。～ *the damage at £100.* 确定损失为一百英镑。**13.** 打赌,下赌注。～ *a* [*bet*] *wager* 下赌注。*I* ～ *five dollars he will not come.* 我赌五块钱他不会来。**14.** (将故事等的场面)放在(某地)。*The scene of the tale is laid in London.* 故事发生在伦敦。**15.** 埋,葬;平息;消除;平服。～ *sb.'s doubts* 打消某人的疑虑。**16.** 使处于某种状态[地位]。～ *bare a scheme* 揭露阴谋。～ *sb. under* (*an*) *obligation* (*to*) 使某人对…承担义务。**17.** 打,砍。～ *one's axe to the tree* 用斧头砍树。**18.** (扭)绞;搓;编。～ *a hedge* 把树枝编成树篱。～ (*up*) *a rope* 搓绳。**19.**【军】瞄准(炮)。— ***vi.*** **1.** 生蛋。*The hens don't* ～ *in this cold weather.* 这样冷的天气鸡不生蛋。**2.** 打赌,保证。～ *on a horse race* 赌跑马。**3.** 准备 (*for*)。**4.**【海】就位。～ *aft* 到船尾就位。**5.** 拼命干。*The sailors laid to their oars.* 水手们用力划桨。

~ *a* (*one's*) *course* **1.** (船朝某一方向)直驶。**2.** 制订计划。~ *a ship aboard* 把船紧逼敌船(以便越舷进攻)。~ *about* **1.** 向四面八方攻击,奋战。**2.** 努力奋斗,尽全力。**3.** 作准备。~ *aside* **1.** 留起,保存,贮蓄。**2.** 搁开,放在一边,留出(~ *aside a day for golf* 打一天高尔夫球)。**3.** 放弃,丢弃(*He was laid aside six months by an accident*. 他因事故已停止工作六个月了)。~ *asleep* 埋葬;使一命呜呼。~ *at* 对准…打过去,攻击。~ *away* **1.** 保存,留起,贮蓄。**2.** 〔美〕埋葬。~ *back* **1.** 使向后。**2.** 放回,送回。**3.** 放松,不紧张。~ *before* 拿出,提出。~ *by* **1.** = ~ aside. **2.** 【海】 = ~ to. ~ *down* **1.** 放下。**2.** 铺设(铁路),建造(船等)。**3.** 拟定(计划等)。**4.** 贮藏(酒等)。**5.** 确定,规定。**6.** 扔弃,放弃(*The enemy laid down their arms*. 敌人放下武器投降。~ *down one's life for the country* 为国牺牲。~ *down one's commission* 辞职)。**7.** 支付;下赌注。**8.** 在(田里)栽(~ *down a field in grass* 在田里栽牧草)。**9.** 写下,记下,画下。~ *eyes on* 看见,发现。~ *fast* (*by the heels*) 拘束;监禁。~ *field to field* 不断地增加所有地[财产]。~ *for* 准备(占领;攻击等);埋伏着等待。~ *great store upon* 重视。~ *hands on* **1.** 抓住,逮住。**2.** 得到,找到。**3.** 袭击,伤害。**4.** 行按手礼。~ *hands on oneself* 自杀。~ *heavy odds that* 坚决主张,确实声明。~ *in* **1.** 贮藏。**2.** 〔俚〕吃。**3.** 修剪(树篱等)。~ *in for* 申请;设法购买;企图获得。~ (*an*) *information against* 告发。~ *into* 〔俚〕痛打;痛斥。~ *it on* (*thick*) 〔俚〕 = ~ *it on with a trowel* 〔俚〕乱夸赞,乱恭维。~ *off* **1.** 暂时解雇;〔美〕解雇,辞退(= 〔英〕 stand off)。**2.** 停止(工作等);〔美〕休息,休养。**3.** 区分,划分(土地)。**4.** 【海】(使)离开(海岸、他船);【船】放大样。**5.** 〔美〕脱(衣服)。~ *off your lid* 〔美〕不要自大,别摆架子。~ *on* **1.** 加给。**2.** 袭击,攻击。**3.** 安装(*Is gas laid on?* 安装煤气了吗?)。**3.** 抽、征(税等)。**4.** 涂(颜料等)。**5.** 使(狗)跟踪追赶(猎物)。**6.** 下,发(命令);挥鞭等。~ *one's account with* 把…算在里头;指望,期待。~ *one's bones* 被埋葬,死。~ *one's cards on the table* 〔美〕摊牌,把一切都说出来。~ *oneself open to* 暴露在,蒙受(~ *oneself open to suspicion* 遭受嫌疑)。~ *oneself out* 煞费苦心,竭力(*They laid themselves out to entertain us*. 他们为了款待我们煞费苦心)。~ *oneself out for* 作准备,决心。~ *one's hopes on* 指望,期待。~ *one's plans* 准备,布置。~ *open* **1.** 切开,割开。**2.** 揭开;暴露;揭穿。~ *out* **1.** 消费,使用;投资。**2.** 展开,铺开(以便使用);暴露出来。**3.** 布置,安排,设计(花园等)。**4.** 准备入殓安葬。**5.** 〔俚〕打倒,〔美俚〕打昏。~ *over* **1.** = overlay. **2.** 〔美俚〕展期,延期。**3.** 中途下车。**4.** 胜过,力量超过。~ *to* **1.** 【海】把船停下;船顶着风停止。**2.** 把(功、过)归于。**3.** 努力干。**4.** 打。~ *to heart* 非常挂心,铭记在心。~ (*sb.*) *to rest* [*sleep*] **1.** 使睡,使休息。**2.** 埋葬,葬。~ *together* 聚集,聚拢;比较。~ (*sb.*) *under restraint* 拘束某人。~ *up* **1.** 贮蓄。**2.** 留着不用;搁置。**3.** 使卧床不起。**4.** 将船只拆卸进坞。~ *upon* 〔古〕勒索。~ *violent hands on sb.* 对某人下毒手,杀某人。~ *wait for* 埋伏着等待。~ *waste* 破坏,使荒废。

II *n*. **1.** 位置;方向;地理形势。*the* ~ [*lie*] *of the land* 地形;形势,局势,事态。**2.** 绳索的股数[拧法];(裁剪)铺放。**3.** 分红,分配渔获品。**4.** 方针,计划;〔俚〕工作,职业,生意。*start a new* ~ 开始新的工作。**5.** 〔美〕代价,价格。*sell sth. at a good* ~ 以高价售出。**6.** 层,隐蔽处。**7.** 下蛋。*be in full* [*good*] ~ (经常地,正常地)下蛋。*on the* ~ (黑话)(小偷、扒手等)下手,作案。*the kid* [*kinchin*] ~ (黑话)偷窃[抢夺]出外购物的儿童的财物。~ **about** 〔主英口〕游手好闲,二流子,无业游民。~ **away plan** 逐月付款的累积购买法。~**-by** **1.** (河道中的)泊[错]船处。**2.** 铁路侧线,旁轨。**3.** (公路上的)停[错]车处。**4.** 【农】(作物种植中的)最后一遍田间操作。~ **day** 【海】(租船契约所允许的)装卸货物日期,停泊日数〔过期应缴纳延期费〕。~ **figure** **1.** 人体活动模型。**2.** 傀儡般的人物。~ **off** **1.** 解雇。**2.** (临时)解雇期。**3.** 关闭;停歇。**4.** 停止活动[比赛]时期。~ **out** **1.** 布局;设计;安排;陈设。**2.** 版面编排。**3.** 一套器具[工具、衣服等]。**4.** 〔美口〕事态,情况。**5.** 〔美〕地形,坐落〔指建筑物及四周环境〕。~ **over** *n*. 中途的短暂停留。~ **shaft** 【机】副轴、中间轴、水平轴。~ **stall** 〔英〕垃圾堆。~ **up** (篮球)上篮,切入篮〔篮下跳起单手投篮〕。

lay[2] [lei; le] *a*. **1.** 一般信徒的,俗人的,凡俗的(*opp*. clerical)。**2.** 无经验的,外行(人)的(*opp*. professional)。**3.** 【纸牌】非主牌的,普通牌的。~ **analyst** 非专业的心理分析学家。~ **brother** (在修道院内干勤杂工的)俗人修士。~**man** **1.** 俗人;平信徒。**2.** 门外汉,外行。~**person** = ~man. ~ **reader** **1.** 【宗】(圣公会主持礼拜的)俗人司仪。**2.** 外行[非专业人员]的读者,一般读者。

lay[3] [lei; le] *n*. **1.** 民歌,民谣;短诗。**2.** 歌曲;曲调;音乐的旋律;鸟的啼啭。

lay[4] [lei; le] lie[1] 的过去式。

Lay·ard [lɛəd; lɛrd] *n*. 莱亚德〔姓氏〕。

lay·er [ˈleiə; ˋleɚ] **I** *n*. **1.** 放置者,铺设者,计划者。**2.** 【赛马】(一般)赌客。**3.** 产卵的鸡。**4.** 【军】瞄准手。**5.** 层;阶层;地层;涂层。**6.** 【植】压条,倒伏庄稼。**7.** 敷设轨。**8.** 垫片,层板,夹层,膜。*a brick* ~ 砌砖者。*a mine* ~ 布雷舰艇。*a bad* [*good*] ~ 生蛋少[多]的鸡。*a* ~ *of rock* 一层岩石。*boundary* ~ 边层。*carburized* ~ 渗炭层。*turberlent* ~ 紊流附面层。~*s and backers* (赛马等的)赌客。**II** *vt*. **1.** 分层砌。**2.** 用压条法繁殖。—*vi*. 庄稼倒伏。~ **cake** 〔美〕多层奶油蛋糕。~**age** 【植】压条。**-ing** *n*. 分层套穿式时装。

lay·ette [leiˈet; leˋɛt] *n*. 〔F.〕婴儿的全套用品〔如衣服、被褥、洗涤用具等〕。

lay·ing [ˈleiiŋ; ˋleɪŋ] *n*. **1.** 布置;层积;铺设。**2.** (炮的)瞄准。**3.** 搓绳;搓绳法。**4.** 最初所涂底层。**5.** 产卵期;产卵数;一次孵的蛋。*the* ~ *on of hands* 【宗】按手礼。

la·zar [ˈlæzə, ˈlei-; ˋlezɚ, ˋle-] *n*. 恶疾病人〔尤指麻疯病人〕。~ **house** 麻疯医院。**-like** *a*.

laz·a·ret, laz·a·ret·to [ˌlæzəˈret, -ˈretəu; ˏlæzəˋrɛt, -ˋrɛto] *n*. (*pl*. ~*s*) **1.** 传染病医院(特指麻疯医院)。**2.** 检疫所;检疫船。**3.** 【海】(近船尾的)贮藏室。

Laz·a·rus [ˈlæzərəs; ˋlæzərəs] *n*. **1.** 【圣】浑身生疮的拉撒路。**2.** 〔常作 l-〕麻疯乞丐;穷人。~ *and Dives* 穷人和富人。

laze [leiz; lez] **I** *vt*., *vi*. 偷懒;混日子。~ *away one's life* 混过一辈子。~ *time away* 蹉跎岁月。**II** *n*. **1.** 懒散。**2.** 混过去的时间。

la·zi·ly [ˈleizili; ˋlezɪlɪ] *ad*. 偷懒地,懒洋洋地,吊儿郎当地。

la·zi·ness [ˈleizinis; ˋlezɪnɪs] *n*. 懒惰;偷懒。

laz·u·li [ˈlæzjulai; ˋlæzjʊˏlaɪ] *n*. = lapis lazuli. **-ne** *a*.

laz·u·lite [ˈlæzjuˌlait; ˋlæzjʊˏlaɪt] *n*. 【地】天蓝石。**laz·u·lit·ic** [ˌlæzjuˈlitik; ˏlæzjuˋlɪtɪk] *a*.

laz·u·rite [ˈlæzjuˌrait; ˋlæzjʊˏraɪt] *n*. 【地】天青石,青金石。

la·zy [ˈleizi; ˋlezɪ] *a*. (*-zi·er*; *-zi·est*) **1.** 懒惰的,没精打采的。**2.** 慢吞吞的。**3.** 令人懒散的。*a* ~ *boy* [*beggar, dog*] 〔口〕懒鬼。*a* ~ *stream* 缓流。*a hot*, ~ *summer* 夏日炎炎正好眠。~ **back** 马车座位的靠背。~**bed** 〔英〕马铃薯培植床。~**bones**, ~**boots** 〔口〕懒骨头。~ **eight** 【空】8 字形飞行法。~ **eye** (**blindness**) 【医】(一目)弱视(= amblyopia)。~ **guy** 【船】吊杆稳索。~ **jack** 【机】屈伸起重机。**L- susan** (餐桌上便于自取食物的)旋转盘。~ **tongs** 【机】(用以钳取远处东西的)惰钳,伸缩钳。**-ish** *a*. 懒散的,懒洋洋的。

laz·za·ro·ne [ˌlæzəˈrəuni; ˏlæzəˋrone] *n*. 〔It.〕(*pl*. *-ro·ni* [-niː; -ni]) (意大利拿不勒斯街头的)以行乞和

L

做杂工度日的流浪者。
LB, L. B. = 〔L.〕*Literarum Baccalaureus* 文学士 (= Bachelor of Letters 或 Bachelor of Literature)。
lb. = 〔L.〕*libra(e)* (= pound(s)) 磅。
lb. ap. = pound, apothecaries 药衡磅。
lb. av. = pound, avoirdupois 常衡磅。
lb. in. = pound-inch 磅-英寸。
LBO = leveraged buyout.
lbs. = 〔L.〕*librae* 磅 (= pounds)。
lb. t. = pound troy. 金衡磅。
LC = **1.** Library of Congress 〔美〕国会图书馆。**2.** landing craft 登陆艇。**3.** left centre (舞台的)中心部左方。
L. C. = **1.** Lord Chancellor 〔英〕大法官。**2.** Lower Canada 下加拿大〔魁北克省的旧称〕。
l. c. = **1.** lower case【印】小写字母盘。**2.** 〔L.〕*loco citato* 在前面引文中。
L / C, l / c = letter of credit【商】信用状。
L. C. C. = London County Council 〔英〕伦敦郡议会。
LCD = Liquid crystal diode [display]【无】液晶二极管, 液晶显示器。
LCI = Landing Craft, Infantry 〔美〕步兵登陆艇。
L. C. J. = Lord Chief Justice 〔英〕高等法院院长。
L. C. L. = less-than-carload (铁路运输中的)零担的。
L. C. M., LCM = lowest (or least) common multiple【数】最小公倍数。
LCP = **1.** landing craft, personnel 人员登陆艇。**2.** liquid-crystal polymer 液晶聚合物。
LCT = landing craft, tank 坦克登陆艇。
LD = **1.** lethal dose【医】致死剂[药]量。**2.** line of departure【军】进攻出发线。**3.** long distance 长途电话通讯;长途电话局(或交换机);长途话务员。**4.** learning-disabled 学习不能的,失去学习能力的。
L. D. = **1.** Lady Day【宗】报喜节。**2.** Doctor of Letters 文学博士。**3.** Low Dutch 低地荷兰语。**4.** 〔L.〕*Laus Deo* (= Praise be to God)【宗】荣誉属于上帝。**5.** left door 左(侧)门。**6.** London Docks 〔英〕伦敦船坞。
Ld. = **1.** Limited. **2.** Lord.
ldg. = loading.
L-do·pa [elˈdəupə; ɛlˋdopə] ***n.***【药】左旋多巴〔 = levodopa 治帕金森综合症〕。
Ldp., Lp. = Ladyship; Lordship.
Ldry = Laundry.
L. D. Tel. = long-distance telephone 长途电话。
LE = **1.** low explosive 低级炸药。**2.** labo(u)r exchange 实物交换,产品交换;职业介绍所;〔主英〕(劳工部的)劳工介绍所。
-le *suf.* 附在动词之后,表示"动作的小幅度重复": hobb*le*, pratt*le*, wigg*le*.
lea[1] [liː; li] ***n.*** 〔主诗〕草地,牧场。
lea[2] [liː; li] ***n.***【纺】缕,小绞〔棉纱长 120 码;麻纱长 300 码;毛纱长 80 码〕。
leach [liːtʃ; litʃ] **I** ***n.*** **1.** 沥滤。**2.** (采灰汁用的)滤灰,灰汁;滤汁。**3.** 沥滤器,滤灰槽。**II** ***vt.,* *vi.*** 滤,用水漂;溶化,溶解。**-able** ***a.***
leach·y [ˈliːtʃi; ˋlitʃɪ] ***a.*** (土壤)有气孔的;能渗透的。
Lea·cock [ˈliːkɔk; ˋliˏkɑk] ***n.*** 利科克〔姓氏〕。
lead[1] [led; lɛd] **I** ***n.*** **1.** 铅,铅制品。**2.**【海】测铅,测深锤,水砣。**3.** 〔*pl.*〕(铺屋顶的)铅皮;铅皮屋顶;【印】插铅,铅条。**4.** 铅笔心。**5.** 子弹,枪弹。*white* ~ 铅白,碱式碳酸铅。*work* ~ (鼓风炉产含银)粗铅。*yellow* ~ 铅黄,氧化铅。*an ounce of* ~ 一颗子弹。***arm the*** ~ 注兽脂入测深锤底部凹处〔以便黏起泥沙而了解海底情况〕。***as dull as*** ~ 色泽像铅一样灰暗的;非常鲁钝的。***cast*** [***heave***] ***the*** ~【海】用水砣[测锤]测深。***get the*** ~ 饮弹,中弹。***pump*** ~ ***into sb.*** 〔口〕向某人扫射。***swing the*** ~ 〔军俚〕装病,偷懒。**II** ***vt.*** **1.** 用铅覆盖,塞铅。**2.** 用铅条固定住。~*ed glass* 铅条玻璃。**3.** 加铅[铅的化合物]于。~*gasoline* 加铅汽油,乙基化汽油。**4.**【印】排空铅,(在行间)插铅条。— ***vi.*** **1.** 用水砣[测锤]测深。**2.** 被铅覆盖;被铅塞住。~ **acetate**【化】醋酸铅;乙酸铅。~ **arsenate**【化】砷酸铅;砷酸气铅。~ **colic**【医】铅毒疝。~**-covered** ***a.*** 镀铅的,铅包的。~**-free** ***a.*** 无铅的。~ **glass** 铅玻璃。~ **hardening** 铅浴淬火。~ **line**【海】测锤绳。~ **pencil** 铅笔。~**-pipe** [**cinch**] 〔美俚〕 **1.** 轻而易举的事。**2.** 肯定的事情。~ **poisoning**【医】铅中毒。~ **swinging** 〔英俚〕偷懒;逃避工作。~ **tetraethyl** 四乙铅 (= tetraethyl ~)。~ **wool** [**yarn**]【建】(接铅管用的)铅毛。~**work** 铅衬;铅制品。~**works** 制铅工厂,铅矿熔炼厂。**-less** ***a.***
lead[2] [liːd; lid] **I** ***vt.*** (*led* [led; lɛd]) **1.** 领导,引导,带领。**2.** 搀,牵。**3.** 领头,压倒,占首位,居第一;【体】领先。**4.** 率领,指挥,领导,主持。**5.** 引导某人做某事;诱使某人做某事〔接不定式〕。**6.** 过某种生活[日子]。**7.** 使…过某种生活。**8.** 超前瞄准射击(飞机,飞鸟等)。**9.**【拳击】先向对手打一拳。**10.**【牌】先出牌。~ *sb. by the nose* 牵着某人的鼻子走。~ *a horse by the bridle* 牵着马的缰绳。*He* ~*s his class in English.* 英语方面他在全班数第一。~ *a happy* [*miserable*] *life* 过幸福[悲惨]生活。~ *sb. a dog's life* 使某人过着受折磨的日子。~ *a case* (律师)主持一个案件。~ *a campaign* 指挥一场战役。~ *an army* 带领一支军队。~ *a fashion* 开风气。~ *the procession* 走在仪仗队前头。~ *the choir* 指挥合唱队。~ *the singing* 领唱。~ *the way* 引路,领路。~ *sb. astray* 把某人引入歧途。~ *sb. into a trap* 引某人落入圈套。*What led you to think so?* 是什么使得你这样想的呢? *Chance led him to London.* 偶然的机会导致他到伦敦来。*The pipes* ~ *the water into the fields.* 这些管道把水引到田里。*This path will* ~ *you to the station.* 你走这条路可以到火车站。— ***vi.*** **1.** 向导,引导。~ *in the charge* 冲锋在前。**2.** (道路等)通到。**3.** 导致;引起 (*to*)。**4.** 领先,打头,居首位。**5.**【牌】(先)出牌。*All roads* ~ *to Rome.* 〔谚〕条条道路通罗马。*This road* ~*s to the river.* 这条路通往河边。*Oxford led by two lengths.* 牛津队在赛艇中占先两艘艇身。*Who* ~*s?* 谁先出牌。~ ***away*** 带走;引诱,诱入。~ ***back*** **1.** 带回。**2.** 按搭档所出花色出牌。~ ***for the prosecution*** (律师)主持诉讼。~ ***nowhere*** 不会有什么结果。~ ***off*** **1.** 开始,开头,牵头 (~ *off the debate* 领头辩论)。**2.** 领走 (*The students were led off the school by the teacher.* 老师带着学生离开了学校)。~ ***on*** **1.** 引领…继续前进。**2.** 引诱,诱使。~ ***out*** 开始,领头,领舞伴(离开座位)起舞。~ ***out of*** 直通。~ ***to*** 通向,导致。~ ***up to*** 渐渐诱入,把话题渐渐引到…;【牌】设法引出。**II** ***n.*** **1.** 领导,指导;指导地位,首位;榜样。**2.** 领先,优势;领先的程度[距离、时间等]。**3.** 领先者;领唱者;主角。**4.** (新闻等的)导言,引子,按语;在前的重要消息。**5.** 管道;导线;【矿】矿脉。**6.**【乐】序曲,前奏。**7.** 线索,提示,暗示。**8.** 拳击的第一拳;牌戏中先出的牌,出牌权。**9.** 牵引带〔如牵狗的带〕。*take the* ~ *in* 领导,带头,居首位。*With him in the* ~, *all the others followed suit.* 在他带动下,别的人也都跟上来了。*follow the* ~ *of sb.* 跟着某人走,效法某人。*give sb. a* ~ **1.** 带头,以身作则。**2.** 给某人提示。*gain* [*have*] *the* ~ *in a race* 在赛跑中领先。*have a* ~ *of ten metres over the other runners* 比其他赛跑的人领先十米。*hold a safe* ~ 遥遥领先。*The story starts off with a* ~. 故事用一段引子开始。*play the* ~ *in a film* 在一部影片中担任主角。*the juvenile* ~ 青年主角。*phase* ~ 相位超前。*a hot* ~ 很好的线索。*provide* ~*s for further research* 为进一步的研究提供了线索。***have a long*** ~ ***on*** 遥遥领先。***return the*** ~【牌】跟牌,(在下一轮)出搭档者所出花色的牌。**III** ***a.*** **1.** 领头的,领先的。**2.** 最重要的,头条的,以显著地位刊载的。*a* ~ *bomber*

领队轰炸机。*a* ~ *horse* 带头[领先]的马。*a* ~ *editorial* 主要[头版]社论。*a* ~ *headline* 头条标题。~ **angle** 超前角,导前角。~**-in** 1.【无】引入线〔英国也叫 down-~〕。2. 介绍,开场白。~ **network** 超前网络;强制四端网络。~ **number** 导数。~ **off** 开始,开端;打出的头一拳;先发球者。~ **screw** 导螺杆,丝杆。~ **time** (制造业)投产准备阶段。~**-up** 导致物。**-a·ble** *a*. 能被领导的;能被指挥的。

lead·en [ˈledn; ˋlɛdn] *a*. 1. 铅制的,铅质的。2. 铅灰色的。3. 沉重的,沉闷的。4. 钝的;质量差的;低廉的。~ *sky* 铅灰色的天空。*a* ~ *pipe* 铅管。~ *limbs* 沉重无力的手脚。~ *rules* 麻烦的规则。*a* ~ *sword* 钝刀。~**-eyed** 眼睛无光的。~**-foot·ed** *a*. 缓慢的,慢条斯理的。

Lead·en·hall [ˈlednhɔːl; ˋlɛdnhɔl] *n*. 伦敦肉类市场。

lead·er [ˈliːdə; ˋlidɚ] *n*. 1. 领导(人),领袖,首领,首长。2. 乐队指挥;领唱者;首席小提琴手;第一女高音。3. 主要辩护人,首席律师。4. (报刊的)社论。5. 向导船,先头舰;领机;先导马。6.【机】导杆,导管;【建】水落管;排水沟;引线,导火线;【矿】露头,导脉;【机】主轮。7.【植】主干,顶枝。8.【印】指引线。9.【影】(叙事)字幕。10.【商】吸引客人的特价品。11.【数】首项,领项。12.【解】腱,筋。13.【经】主要指数[指标](= leading indicator)。*the* ~ *of the Opposition* (资本主义国家的)在野党[反对党]领袖。*a destroyer* ~【军】驱逐领舰。*a* ~ *plane*【空】长机。***a blind*** ~ ***of the blind*** 盲人领盲人。***community*** ~ 社会活动家。***floor*** ~〔美〕政党的国会领袖。***follow my*** ~ (一种儿童游戏)学领袖。~ ***of praise*** 〔Scot.〕教堂唱诗班的领导人。~**less** *a*. 无领袖的,无领导的。~**mill** 精整轧机。~ **writer** 社论作者;〔英〕社论委员〔美国叫做 editorial writer〕。

lead·er·ette [ˌliːdəˈret; ˌlidəˋrɛt] *n*. (报纸等的)短评;(新闻纪事等前的)编者按语。

lead·er·ship [ˈliːdəʃip; ˋlidɚʃɪp] *n*. 1. 领导,指导。2. 领导人员。3. 领导能力,领导权。*collective* ~ 集体领导。*the* ~ *and the led* 领导者与被领导者。

lead·ing[1] [ˈlediŋ; ˋlɛdɪŋ] *n*. 1. 铅制覆盖物。2. 空铅,铅条,铅皮。*the* ~ *of a stained-glass window* 有色玻璃窗的铅框。

lead·ing[2] [ˈliːdiŋ; ˋlidɪŋ] I *n*. 1. 领导,指导。2. 引导。*a man of light and* ~ 权威,大家,有真才实学的人。~ *of water to arid lands* 把水引到旱地去。II *a*. 1. 指导的,领导的。*a* ~ *cadre* 领导干部。2. 主要的;主导的;扮演主角的;第一位的。*the* ~ *topics of the hour* 当前最主要的话题。*a* ~ *part* 主角。*a* ~ *lady* [*man*] 演主角的女[男]演员。~ **aircraftman** 〔英〕空军上等兵。~ **article** 1.〔英〕社论。2.【商】(吸引顾客的)特价品。~ **business** 主要角色。~ **case**【法】典型案件。~ **coefficient**【数】首项系数。~ **current**【电】超前电流。~ **edge** (飞机翼的)前缘。~**-edge** *a*. (技术上)领先的,尖端的,前沿的。~ **fossil**【地】标准化石。~ **light** (社会团体中)有影响的人物。~ **motive** 1. 主要动机。2.【乐】主导主题,主导旋律。~ **note** = ~ tone. ~ **question**【法】诱导性的提问。~ **rein** 驾驭马的缰绳。~ **seaman** 〔英〕海军一等水兵。~ **staff** 附在牛鼻环上的棒头。~ **strings** [*pl*.] (带幼儿学走路的)引带;〔喻〕指导,管教 (*be in* ~ *strings* 不能独立;还在学步;为他人所操纵)。~ **tone**【乐】导音。~ **wind** 顺风。

lead·plant [ˈledˌplɑːnt; ˋlɛdˏplænt] *n*. 〔美〕【植】灰毛紫穗槐 (*Amorpha canescens*)。

leads·man [ˈledzmən; ˋlɛdzmən] *n*. (*pl*. **-men** [-men; -mɛn])【海】测铅手,测深员。~**'s platform** 测深台。

lead·wort [ˈledˌwəːt; ˋlɛdˏwɝt] *n*.【植】白花丹属 (*Plumbago*)〔尤指欧洲蓝茉莉 (*P. europaea*)〕。

lead·y [ˈledi; ˋlɛdɪ] *a*. 似铅的;铅制的。

leaf[1] [liːf; lif] I *n*. (*pl*. **leaves**) 1. 叶;〔集合词〕叶子;茶叶,烟叶。2. 花瓣。3. (书刊等的)一张(两面)。4. 金属薄片,箔。5.【建】叶饰。6. (门等的)页扇。7. (可折叠的)活动桌面;(办公桌等的)桌盖。8. (飞机的)天窗。9. (步枪的)瞄准尺;【机】小轮齿。10.〔英方〕帽边。11. (汽车等片弹簧的)簧片。*shed leaves* (树)落叶。*a rose* ~ 一片玫瑰花花瓣。***come into*** ~ 长叶,发芽。***in*** ~ 生叶子的,叶茂盛的。***leaves without figs*** 空谈,口惠而实不至。***take a*** ~ ***out of sb.'s book*** 模仿某人。***the fall of the*** ~ 落叶时;秋天。***turn over a new*** ~ 翻开新的一页;革面洗心,过新生活。II *vi*. 1. 生叶,长叶。2.〔美〕翻书页。*The trees are beginning to* ~ *out*. 树木正在开始长叶。~ *through a book* 把书翻阅一遍。— *vt*. 翻…的书页。~ **blade** 嫩叶;叶片。~ **bridge** 跳桥。~ **bud** 叶芽。~**-cast** 落叶病。~ **fat** (猪)板油。~ **hopper**【动】叶蝉。~ **insect**【动】蝓。~ **lard** (板油炼出的)上等猪油。~ **miner**【动】潜叶虫〔其幼虫生存于叶脉和叶茎内〕。~ **mo(u)ld**【农】腐叶堆[土];叶霉病。~**(-)peeper** (外出观赏秋季黄叶等的)赏秋游客。~ **rust** (谷类等的)叶锈病。~ **spot**【植】叶斑。~ **spring** 弹簧板[片]。~ **stalk**【植】叶柄。~ **valve** 簧片阀。**-ed** *a*. 有叶的。**-less** *a*. 无叶的。

leaf[2] [liːf; lif] *n*. 〔英军俚〕休假。

leaf·age [ˈliːfidʒ; ˋlifɪdʒ] *n*. 〔集合词〕(树)叶;叶丛;叶饰。

leaf·let [ˈliːflit; ˋliflɪt] I *n*. 1. 小叶,嫩叶。2. 复叶的一片。3. 叶状器官。4. 传单;广告,仿单,散叶印刷品。II *vt*. 向…散发传单。~ *a rally* 在群众大会上散发传单。**-eer** 散发传单的人。

leaf·y [ˈliːfi; ˋlifɪ] *a*. (***leaf·i·er***; ***-i·est***) 1. 叶多的,叶茂盛的。2. 叶状的,叶子覆盖着的。3. 阔叶的,叶子做成的。*the* ~ *month of June* 树叶茂盛的六月。*a* ~ *plant* 阔叶植物。*a* ~ *shade* 树荫。

league[1] [liːg; lig] I *n*. 1. 同盟,联盟,盟约。2. 社团,联合会,竞赛联合会。3. (蒙古的)盟。4. 种类,类型。*the L- of Nations* (1914—1946 年的)国际联盟。***the L-*** 〔史〕神圣同盟(= the Holy L-)。***be in*** ~ 联合[团结]起来干某事[反对某人](*to do*; *against sb*.)。***be in the*** ~ ***of*** 与…是同类型的人〔常用否定结构〕(*He just* [*simply*] *isn't in your* ~. 他和你根本不是同类型的人)。***in*** ~ ***with*** 与…同盟[联合、有好感];同…勾结[沆瀣一气](*She may have been in* ~ *with the thieves*. 她可能同盗窃犯勾结)。II *vt*., *vi*. (使)结盟;(使)联合[团结]。*They were* ~*d together by a tacit treaty*. 他们根据默契关系联合起来了。*The nations* ~*d together to stop the war*. 这些国家结成联盟来制止战争。~**-match** 联赛。~ **table** 〔英〕对照表,比较表。

league[2] [liːg; lig] *n*. 里格〔长度名;在英美约为三英里或三海里〕。

lea·guer[1] [ˈliːgə; ˋligɚ] *n*. 结盟者,盟员;同盟者[国]。

lea·guer[2] [ˈliːgə; ˋligɚ] I *n*. 〔古〕围攻;围攻部队[阵营]。II *vt*. 〔古〕包围。

leak [liːk; lik] I *n*. 1. 漏洞,漏罅,裂缝。2. 漏;漏水,漏气,漏出,渗漏;泄漏。3. 漏出物;【电】漏电,漏泄电阻。4. 〔俚〕撒尿。*a* ~ *detector* 检漏气。*a* ~ *in the boiler* 锅炉的裂缝。*A small* ~ *will sink a great ship*. 〔谚〕小患不治成大灾。*spring* [*start*] *a* ~ 出漏洞,生漏缝。*stop* [*plug*] *a* ~ 塞漏洞。*officially inspired* ~*s* 官方故意透露的消息。*do* [*have*, *take*] *a* ~ 〔俚〕撒尿。II *vi*., *vt*. 1. (使)漏,(使)渗。2. (使)漏出,使泄漏。*The roof* ~*s*. 屋顶漏水。~ ***off*** 漏泄。~ ***out*** 漏出;泄漏。~ **hunting** 检漏,测漏。~**-proof** *a*. 不漏的,密闭的。

leak·age [ˈliːkidʒ; ˋlikɪdʒ] *n*. 1. 漏,漏出。2. 泄露。3. 漏出物,漏出量。4.【商】漏损率;漏损量。*cause a* ~ 引起渗漏。*a* ~ *of information* 走漏消息。~ **conductor** 线路闭雷器。~ **current**【电】漏泄电流。~ **test** 密封性试验。

Lea·key [ˈliːki; ˋlikɪ] *n*. 利基〔姓氏〕。

L

leak·y [ˈliːki; ˋlikɪ] *a*. (*leak·i·er*; *-i·est*) 1. 漏的,有漏洞的。2. 〔口〕容易泄漏秘密的。3. 小便失禁的。*a* ~ *person* [*vessel*] 不守秘密的人。**-i·ness** *n*.

leal [liːl; lil] *a*. 〔Scot.〕〔诗〕忠实的;诚实的。*the land of the* ~ 天国。

lean[1] [liːn; lin] I *vi*. (~*ed* [liːnd; lind], 〔英〕 *leant* [lent; lɛnt]) 1. 倾斜,倾侧;躬屈,弯斜。2. 倚靠;依靠,依赖。3. (思想等)倾向;偏向;偏袒。*The pillar* ~*s to the north*. 柱子朝北倾斜。~ *against the wall* 倚墙。~ *on a stick* 拄着手杖。~ *on the table* 倚靠在桌子上。~ *on* [*upon*] *sb*. *for support* 靠某人支持。~ *backward* 向后仰。~ *forward* 探过身去。~ *out of the window* 身子探出窗外。~ *over a book* 低头看书。*I rather* ~ *to* [*toward*] *your view*. 我倒比较倾向你的见解。— *vt*. 1. 使倾斜。2. 使…倚靠。~ ***off*** 〔口〕停止倚靠〔主要用命令式〕。~ **on** [**upon**] 1. 靠在。2. 倚赖。3. 【军】据险(固守) (*The enemy* ~*ed upon the river*. 敌人据河而守)。~ **over backward** 〔口〕(为纠正偏向而)采取极端相反的态度,矫枉过正。~ ***to one side*** 倾向一方。II *n*. 倾斜;偏差。*a wall with a slight* ~ 稍微有点倾斜的墙。~**-to** 1. *n*. 单坡屋顶的小房子,披屋。2. *a*. 【建】单坡的。**-ing** 倾斜,倾向。

lean[2] [liːn; lin] I *a*. 1. 瘦的,瘠瘦的。2. 贫乏的,贫弱的(才能等);枯燥无味的(文章等)。3. 瘠薄的,不毛的。4. 没收成的。5. 利益少的,不合算的。6. 营养少的,脂肪少的,瘦的(肉)。*as* ~ *as a rake* 骨瘦如柴。~ *coal* 【矿】贫煤。*a* ~ *year* 凶年。~ *work* 没有利益的工作。*a* ~ *diet* 粗食。II *n*. 瘦肉。**-ly** *ad*. **-ness** *n*.

lean·ing [ˈliːniŋ; ˋlinɪŋ] I *a*. 倾斜的。*the L- Tower of Pisa* 比萨斜塔。II *n*. 倾斜;倾向。

leant [lent; lɛnt] lean[1]的过去式和过去分词的异体词。

leap [liːp; lip] I *vi*. (***leapt*** [lept; lɛpt], ***leaped*** [liːpt; lipt]) 〔现在除成语外,普通用 jump〕。1. 跳跃,跃起;跳越;迅速行动。2. (胸部等)跳动。3. 交尾。~ *for* [*with*] *joy* 雀跃。~ *on a horse* 跳上马。~ *over a fence* 跳过篱笆。*Look before you* ~. 〔谚〕三思而后行。*My heart* ~*s up when I behold the rainbow in the sky*. 我一看到天空的虹,我的心就扑通地跳。*one's heart* ~*s into one's mouth* (因惊恐)心剧烈跳动。~ *at a chance* [*an opportunity*] 抓住机会。~ *from one topic to another* 从一个话题跳到另一个话题。~ *to conclusions* 匆匆作出结论。~ *to the eye* 涌现在眼前,历历在目。— *vt*. 1. 跳过,跳越。~ *a wall* 跳墙。2. 使跳过。~ *a horse over a fence* 使马跳过篱笆。~ ***at*** 扑向;跳起来[急切地]接受,抢着抓住 (~ *at a proposal* 欣然接受提议)。~ ***out of one's skin*** 得意忘形。II *n*. 1. 跳跃;飞跃,跃进;跳跃的高度[距离]。2. 交尾。*take a* ~ *over an obstacle* 越过障碍物。*a* ~ *of seven metres* 七米的跃距。***a*** ~ ***in the dark*** 1. 冒险的行动,轻举妄动。2. 死。***by*** ~***s and bounds*** 飞跃地,突飞猛进地。***in one*** ~ 一跃。***reach at a single*** ~ 一蹴而就。***with a*** ~ (收入等)突然增加等。***with*** ~***s and bounds*** 有飞跃的发展;飞跃地,迅速地。~ **day** 闰日〔指2月29日〕。~**-frog** 1. *n*. 跳背游戏;蛙跳(游戏)。2. *vi*. 作蛙跳动作;(车辆等)忽前忽后地行进。3. *vt*. 闪过;越过,跃过;【军】使两支部队交互跃进;互相增进。~ **frogging tactics** 蛙跳战术。~ **second** 闰秒〔以原子钟测时每年需加上或减去的一秒钟〕。~ **year** 闰年。

leap·er [ˈliːpə; ˋlipɚ] *n*. 跳跃者。

leapt [lept; lɛpt] leap 的过去式及过去分词。

Lear [liə; lɪr] *n*. 1. 利尔〔姓氏〕。2. *Britain* 岛的传说中的王;莎士比亚的剧作《李尔王》中的主人翁。

learn [ləːn; lɝn] *vt*. (***learned*** [ləːnd; lɝnd], ***learnt*** [ləːnt; lɛnt]) 1. 学,学到,学会;习得。2. 记住。3. 听到,知道,弄清楚,了解到。4. 〔俚〕教。~ *English* 学英语。~ (*how to*) *ride* 学骑马。~ *the lines of a play* 背台词。*I* ~ *it from* [*of*] *him*. 我是从他那里听来的。~ *the news of* ... 接到…的消息。*This will* ~ *you to keep out of mischief*. 这将教训你不要再捣蛋了。— *vi*. 1. 学,学会。2. 听到,知道,认识到。~ *fast* 学得快。~ *like a parrot* 鹦鹉学舌般地背诵。*I* ~*ed of his death only yesterday*. 我昨天才听说他去世。***I am*** [***have***] ***yet to*** ~ ***the truth***. 我还不知道真相呢〔带怀疑对方的口气〕。***It is*** ~***ed that*** ... 据悉。~ ***by*** [***from***] ***experience*** = ~ ***to one's cost*** 学乖。~ ***by heart*** 记住。~ ***by rote*** 死记,机械地学会。***Soon*** ~***t, soon forgotten***. 〔谚〕学得快,忘得快〔强记容易忘却〕。***We regret to*** ~ ***that*** .... (函电等习用语)惊悉…。**-a·ble** *a*.

learn·ed [ˈləːnid; ˋlɝnɪd] *a*. 1. 有学问的;博学的;精通某门学问的;〔英〕精通法律的。2. 学术上的;学问上的;需要经过学习研究的;有(高深)学问的。*a* ~ *man* 学者。*the* ~ 学者〔总称〕。*my* ~ *friend* [*brother*] 〔英〕阁下〔律师在下议院或法庭上对同事的敬称〕。*a* ~ *periodical* 学术期刊。*a* ~ *society* 学会。*the* ~ *profession* 需要学问的职业〔尤指律师、医生、牧师等职业〕。~ *skills* 学到的技术。*a* ~ *language* 学术语言〔尤指拉丁语〕。*a* ~ *word* 高深[学者使用]的词;学来的词。***be*** ~ ***in the law*** 精通法律。~ **helplessness** 习得性束手无策感〔因长期依赖社会福利或政府救济生活而产生的缺乏去独立谋生的自信〕。**-ly** *ad*.

learn·er [ˈləːnə; ˋlɝnɚ] *n*. 学习者;初学者。*an advanced* ~ 程度较高的学习者;进修者。

learn·ing [ˈləːniŋ; ˋlɝnɪŋ] *n*. 学,学习;学问,学识;专门知识。*good at* ~ 善于学习。*a man of* ~ 学者。***New*** ~ 新学问,新科学〔尤指十六世纪在英国传播的宗教改革学说及用希伯来文及希腊文对于《圣经》的考证研究〕。~ **disability** 【医】学习不能〔因神经系统有缺陷而致使学习能力有障碍〕。

learnt [ləːnt; lɝnt] learn 的过去式及过去分词。

lease[1] [liːs; lis] I *vt*. 1. 出租(土地)。2. 租借(土地)。II *n*. 1. 租契,租约。2. 租借权。3. 租借物。4. 租借期限。***a*** ~ ***of life*** 寿命。***a perpetual*** ~ 永久租借权。***give sb. a new*** ~ ***of life*** 使某人重新振作起来。***hold on*** [***by***] ~ 租借。***put out to*** ~ 出租。(***take***) ***a new*** ~ ***of life*** 得庆更生。***take on*** ~ 租借。

lease[2] [liːs; lis] I *n*. 【纺】分经,分绞。II *vt*. 使分经,使分绞。~**-back** 回租〔出售产业同时长期租用该产的作法,也称 sale and ~-back〕。~**hold** 1. *a*. 租来的,借来的。2. *n*. 租得物;租借期 (*a life* ~*hold* 租借地终身保有权)。~**hold·er** 租借人。~**-lend**, **L--Lend** *n*., *a*., *vt*. = lend-lease. **leas·a·ble** *a*. **-less** *a*. **-r** *n*.

leash [liːʃ; liʃ] I *n*. 1. (系狗的)皮带,皮条。2. (打猎用语)三只(狗、兔等);成三的一组。3. (织机筘上经线穿过的)综束,综把,吊环。4. 束缚,控制。*a* ~ *of hounds* (拴在一起的)三只狗。*a* ~ *of days* 一连三天。***hold*** [***have***] ***in*** ~ 用皮带系住(狗);束缚,控制。***slip the*** ~ 猎狗挣脱皮带;摆脱束缚。***strain at the*** ~ 猎狗想挣脱皮带;努力争取自由。II *vt*. 1. 用皮带系上。2. 束缚,控制。

leas·ing [ˈliːziŋ; ˋlizɪŋ] *n*. 〔古〕虚言,谎话。

least [liːst; list] I *a*. (little 的最高级,比较级为 less 或 lesser) 1. 最小的,最少的 (*opp*. most)。2. 最不重要的,地位最低的。3. 〔美方〕年纪最小的;(动、植物)最小种类的。*the* ~ *distance* 最小的距离。*the* ~ *number* 最小数。*the* ~ *squares* 【数】最小平方,最小二乘方。*the last but not the* ~ 最后的但并非最不重要的。*sb.'s* ~ *one* 某人最小的孩子。II *ad*. 最小,最少。*the* ~ *angry man* 丝毫没有脾气的人。*Young people are the* ~ *conservative*. 青年人最不保守。~ ***of all*** 尤其是,最不 (*I like that* ~ *of all*. 我最不爱那个)。***not the*** ~ 1. (最小的)一点…也没有 (*There is not the* ~ *wind today*. 今天一点风也没有)。2. 〔强调 not〕不少,非常,很 (*There's not the* ~ *danger*. 危险可不少呢)。

III ***n*.** 最小，最少，最少量，最小限度。*Of two evils, the ～ should be taken.* 两害相权取其轻。*That's the ～ of my anxieties.* 那是我最不担心的。***at*** (***the***) ～ 至少，起码(*The trip will take three days at ～.* 这一趟旅行最少得走三天)。***at the very*** ～〔用以加强语气〕= at (the) ～. ***in the*** ～ 一点，丝毫。***not in the*** ～ 一点也不(*I am not in the ～ afraid of it.* 那我一点也不怕)。***The ～ said, the soonest mended*** = Least said, soonest mended; The ～ said the better.〔谚〕话越少越好。***to say the*** ～ (***of it***) 至少可以这样说，退一步讲。～ **common denominator**【数】最小公分母。～ **common multiple**【数】最小公倍数。～**ways**〔方〕，～**-wise**〔口〕***ad*.** 至少，无论如何。～**-worst** ***a*.** 别无(更佳)选择下的那种选择的，没有(更好)办法的办法的，差中最优的。

leat [liːt; lit] ***n*.**〔英方〕磨坊专用水渠。

leath·er [ˈleðə; ˋlɛðɚ] **I** ***n*. 1.** 皮，皮革。**2.** 革制品；〔美口〕皮鞋；皮带；〔俚〕(板球、足球等用的)球，撞球棒的头；〔*pl.*〕(骑马用)皮短裤，皮绑腿；〔美俚〕皮包，皮夹子。**3.**〔俚〕皮肤。**4.** 狗耳的下垂部分。**5.**〔the ～〕〔美俚〕拳击中的一击。*American* ～〔英〕油布，漆布；人造革。*enamel* ～ 漆皮。*heavy* ～ 原革。*imitation* ～ 漆布。*patent* ～ 漆皮。*mountain* ～ 石棉。***hell-bent for*** ～ 非常快，极快。***lose*** ～〔俚〕擦破皮肤。(***There is***) ***nothing like*** ～.〔谚〕自夸自赞〔相传一皮匠认为护城利器莫过于皮革，故云〕。**II** ***vt*.** 制成皮；蒙上皮，钉皮；〔口〕(用皮带等)抽打。**III** ***a*.** 皮革的，皮革制的。～ **and prunella** 衣着外表的差异；无关紧要的事情。～**back**【动】棱皮龟(*Dermochelys coriacea*)〔它的体重可达 1—200 磅，是龟中最大者〕。～**board** (做鞋底用的)再生革。～**-bound** ***a*.** 皮面精装的。～**cloth** 漆布，油布。～**-head 1.**〔俚〕笨蛋。**2.**〔美俚〕守夜人，巡警。**3.**〔L-〕美国宾夕法尼亚州人。～**-hunting**〔俚〕(板球的)防守。～**jack·et 1.**【动】无腹鳍刺鲀。**2.**〔英〕长脚蝇的蛆。～**neck**〔美俚〕海军陆战队士兵。～ **welting** 鞣革。～**wood**【植】沼泽革木(*Dirca palustris*)〔产于北美〕。

leath·er·et(te) [ˌleðəˈret; ˏlɛðəˋrɛt] ***n*.** 人造革。

leath·ern [ˈleðəːn; ˋlɛðɚn] ***a*.** 皮革的，似皮革的；革制的，革质的。

leath·er·oid [ˈleðəˌrɔid; ˋlɛðəˏrɔɪd] ***n*. 1.** 勒塞洛伊德〔一种绝缘纸皮的商标名〕。**2.** 人造革，绝缘纸皮；薄钢纸。

leath·er·y [ˈleðəri; ˋlɛðərɪ] ***a*. 1.** 似革的，革质的。**2.** 强韧的。

leave[1] [liːv; liv] **I** ***vt*.** (***left*** [left; lɛft]; ***leav·ing***) **1.** 离开，脱离；退出；辞去；遗弃；放弃，停止(某事)。**2.** 剩下；遗留；留下；遗赠。**3.** 听任；让某人做某事；留置不动。**4.** 交付；委托。**5.** 使…处于某种状态〔后接分词等〕。**6.** 使…成某状态而离去。**7.** (从旁)走过去〔经过，通过〕。～ *Japan for France* 离日赴法。～ *medicine for art* 放弃医学改学艺术。～ *school* 离校〔指毕业或退学〕。*Winter will ～ us soon.* 冬天即将过去。～ *a card on sb.* 留名片给某人。～ *a deep impression on our minds* 在我们心里留下了深刻的印象。～ *her at home* 把她留在家里。～ *no room* [*scope*] *for doubt* 不容置疑。*Six from seven ～s one.* 七减六剩一。*To be left till called for.* (邮件等)留局待领。*Nothing was left to accident.* 没有一件事是靠运气的。*L- him go.* 让他走吧。*L- him to do as he likes.* 某人爱做什么，就让他做什么。～ *sth. undone* 放着某事不做。～ *the work until tomorrow* 把工作留到明天去做。*He left a widow and two children.* 他死时留下遗孀和两个孩子。*He left her £ 500.* 他遗给她五百镑。*I left my book in the car.* 我把书丢在汽车里了。～ *a sum in the bank* 存款在银行里。～ *sb. in charge of the matter* 委托某人负责办理此事。～ *sb. sth.* (～ sth. with sb.) 把某物交给某人。*L- this* (*up*) *to me.* 把这事交给我。～ *the door open* 让门开着。*Nothing was left undone.* 要做的都做了。*I left my father quite well an hour ago.* 一小时前我离开父亲时，他还是好好的。～ *the park on the left* 靠公园左手走过去。— ***vi*. 1.** 离去；走掉；动身，出发。**2.**〔古〕停止。*It's time for us to ～.* = It's time we leave. 我们该走了。*I am leaving for London tomorrow.* 我明天动身到伦敦去。***be*** (***nicely***) ***left*** 被骗，上当。***be well left*** 得大量遗产。***get left* 1.** 被遗弃。**2.** 被打败。～ ***about*** 把东西丢下不管。～ ***alone*** 丢下不管，不理会(*L- him alone.* 别管他。*L- alone the books.* 别动书)。～ ***behind* 1.** 遗留(*He has left a sweet memory behind.* 他留芳百世)。**2.** 留下(～ *one's book* 忘记把书带去)。**3.** 追过，超过(*I left him far behind.* 我把他远远丢在后面)。～ ***go*** [***loose***] ***of sth.***〔口〕松手放掉(某物)；放弃(某物)。～ [***loose***] ***hold of*** 放手，松手。～ ***in the air*** 搁置，使悬而不决。～ ***it at that*** [***as it is***]〔俚〕就那么好了。～ ***much to be desired*** 还有待改进。～ ***no means untried*** 用尽方法。～ ***nothing to be desired*** 完美无缺。～ ***off* 1.** 戒除，停止(*begin where one's father left off* 继承父业)。**2.** 不再穿，不再用。～ ***sb. cold*** [***cool***] 使人扫兴。～ ***oneself wide open***〔美〕暴露在打击之下。～ ***out* 1.** 省去，删去。**2.** 遗漏。**3.** 不考虑；没有考虑。**4.**〔美〕离开。**5.** 忘记；忽视。～ ***out of account*** [***consideration***] 不去注意，置之度外。～ ***over* 1.** 留下，剩下。**2.** 展期，延期。～ ***severely alone*** 尽量不干涉，不发生关系，敬而远之。～ ***sb.*** (***out***) ***in the cold***〔口〕不睬某人。～ ***sb. the bag to hold*** 把麻烦事推给某人。～ ***sb. to himself*** [***to his own devices, to sink or swim***] 听其自然，让他自生自灭。～ ***sb. unmoved*** 对某人毫无影响。～ ***sth. as it is*** 听其自然。～ ***the track***〔美〕出轨。～ ***undone*** (应作的事)不去做。～ ***unpaid*** (应付款项)不付。～ ***well*** [***enough***] ***alone*** = let well [enough] alone. ～ ***word*** 留言。**II** ***n*.**【撞球】(前一人击球后)遗留下来的球的位置。**-r** ***n*.** 离开的人〔常指学校的毕业生〕。

leave[2] [liːv; liv] ***n*. 1.** 许可，同意。**2.** 告假，休假；假期。*I beg ～ to inform you of it.* 特此奉告。*I take ～ to consider the matter settled.* 请原谅我认为这件事已经解决。*a ～ of absence* 准假〔一般指时间较长的假〕；假期；休假。*a ticket of ～* 假释许可证。*break* [*overstay*] *one's ～* 超过假期。*go home on ～* 请假回家。*sick ～* 病假。***by*** [***with***] ***your*** ～〔口〕请原谅，对不起。***get one's*** ～ 被免职。***have*** [***go on***] ～ 请准假。～ ***off*** 休假许可。～ ***out*** 外出许可。***neither with your ～ nor by your*** ～ 不管你喜欢不喜欢，不管你怎么讲。***on*** ～ 请假中，在休假。***refuse ～ to*** 拒不允许。***take French*** ～ 不告而别，溜之大吉。***take ～ of one's senses*** 发狂。***without*** ～ 擅自。***without a 'by*** [***with***] ***your ～'***〔俚〕未经许可地，擅自。～**breaker** 超假的人。

leave[3] [liːv; liv] ***vi*.** (植物)生叶，长叶。

leaved [liːvd; livd] ***a*.** 有…叶的，…叶的〔构成复合词〕。*a broad-～ tree* 阔叶树。*a four-～ clover* 四枚叶子的三叶草。*a two-～ screen* 二折屏风。

leav·en [ˈlevn; ˋlɛvən] **I** ***n*. 1.** 酵母，曲，发酵剂。**2.** 潜在作用，影响力。**3.** 气味，色调。*the old ～* (难革除的)旧习气，陋习，陋规。**II** ***vt*.** 使发酵；发生影响；使带…气味。

leaves [liːvz; livz] ***n*.** leaf 的复数。

leav·ing [ˈliːviŋ; ˋlivɪŋ] ***n*. 1.**〔*pl.*〕剩余物，残余。**2.** 剩余。*the ～s of meals* 剩余的饭菜。

leave-tak·ing [ˈliːvˌteikiŋ; ˋlivˏtekɪŋ] ***n*. 1.** 告辞，告别。**2.** 告别辞。*His ～ was brief.* 他的告别辞很简短。

leav·y [ˈliːvi; ˋlivɪ] ***a*.** leafy 的古体。

Leb·a·nese [ˌlebəˈniːz; ˏlɛbəˋniz] **I** ***a*.** 黎巴嫩的，黎巴嫩人的。**II** ***n*.** 黎巴嫩人。

Leb·a·non [ˈlebənən; ˋlɛbənən] ***n*.** 黎巴嫩〔西南亚国家〕。

Le·bens·raum [ˈleibənsˌraum; ˋlebənsˏraum] ***n.*** 生存空间〔德国法西斯作向外侵略借口的反理论〕。

Leb·ku·chen [ˈleibˌkuːhən; ˋlebˏkuhən] ***n.*** 蜜饯果饼〔一种德国式糕饼〕。

lech [letʃ; lɛtʃ] **I *vi.*** 〔俚〕好色;贪求 (*for*; *after*)。**II *n.*** 〔俚〕**1.** 淫欲,色欲。**2.** 淫棍,色鬼。

lech·er [ˈletʃə; ˋlɛtʃɚ] ***n.*** 淫棍,好色的人。

lech·er·ous [ˈletʃərəs; ˋlɛtʃərəs] ***a.*** **1.** 好色的,淫荡的。**2.** 色情的,挑逗性的。

lech·er·y [ˈletʃəri; ˋlɛtʃərɪ] ***n.*** 色欲;好色,淫荡。

lec·i·thin [ˈlesiθin; ˋlɛsəθɪn] ***n.*** 【生化】卵磷脂。

lec·i·thin·ase [ˈlesiθiˌneis; ləˋsɪθənes] ***n.*** 【生化】卵磷脂酶。

lec·tern [ˈlektə(ː)n; ˋlɛktɚn] ***n.*** **1.** (教堂中的)读经台。**2.** (演讲台上的)小台架。

lec·tion [ˈlekʃən; ˋlɛkʃən] ***n.*** **1.** (礼拜时)诵读的经文。**2.** (同一著作不同版本的)异文。

lec·tion·ar·y [ˈlekʃənəri; ˋlɛkʃənˏɛrɪ] ***n.*** 【宗】(为全年礼拜时诵读用的)经文选。

lec·tor [ˈlektə; ˋlɛktə] ***n.*** **1.** 【宗】(教堂做礼拜时的)读经人。**2.** 【天主】读经人〔四个最低等级中的第三等级。其他三个等级:一.祭司助手。二.被摩人。三.看门人〕。**3.** 讲师。

lec·ture [ˈlektʃə; ˋlɛktʃɚ] **I *n.*** **1.** 讲义,讲演,讲话 (*on*)。**2.** 教训,训斥。*attend a* ~ 听报告;上课。*deliver* [*give*] *a* ~ 讲课,讲演。*a curtain* ~ 枕边训话,妻子私下对丈夫的责备。*read sb. a* ~ 教训某人一顿。**II *vi.*** 讲授,讲演。~ *on chemistry* 讲授化学。— ***vt.*** **1.** 向…演讲,给…讲课。**2.** 训导,训斥。~ **room** 讲堂。~**ship** **1.** 讲师的职位[资格、身分]。**2.** (大学的)讲座。~ **theater** [**theatre**] 阶式讲堂。~ **tour** 演讲[讲学]旅行。

lec·tur·er [ˈlektʃərə; ˋlɛktʃərɚ] ***n.*** **1.** 演讲者。**2.** (大学、学院中的)讲师;训导者。

LED = **1.** large electronic display 大电子显示器。**2.** light emitting diode 光发射二极管。

led [led; lɛd] lead[2]的过去式及过去分词。***a.*** 受指导的,受控制的;被牵着走的。*a* ~ *captain* 善于拍马的人。*a* ~ *farm* 〔Scot.〕主人远居他地的农庄。*a* ~ *horse* 备用马。***be* ~ *by the nose*** 受别人支配,被人操纵,仰人鼻息。

Le·da [ˈliːdə; ˋlidə] ***n.*** 【希神】勒达〔斯巴达王后,与化为天鹅的宙斯交接而生了引起特洛伊战争的海伦〕。

le·der·ho·sen [ˈleidəˌhəuzən; ˋledɚˏhozn] ***n.*** (阿尔卑斯山民的)皮短裤。

ledg. = ledger.

ledge [ledʒ; lɛdʒ] ***n.*** **1.** 壁架。**2.** 【地】(岩石突出的)岩架;岩礁;暗礁。**3.** 【矿】矿脉。**-d *a.*** 有壁架的;有突出物的;有暗礁的。

ledg·er [ˈledʒə; ˋlɛdʒɚ] ***n.*** **1.** 总账,分类账,底账。**2.** (墓坟的)台石。**3.** 【建】(脚手架)横木,卧材。**4.** 底饵。~ **bait** 底饵[固定鱼饵]。~ **blade** 【纺】剪毛机上的固定刀片。~ **board** **1.** 托梁横木;板条。**2.** (栅栏的)横顶板;栏杆的扶手。~ **line** **1.** 【乐】加线。**2.** 附有底饵的钓丝。~ **tackle** 能使钓饵沉于水底的鱼具。

Lee [liː; li] ***n.*** **1.** 李〔姓氏,男子名,女子名〕。**2.** **Robert Edward** ~ 罗伯特·爱德华·李〔1807—1870,美国南北战争时南军总司令〕。

lee [liː; li] **I *n.*** **1.** 保护,庇护。**2.** 【海】下风,背风面 (*opp.* windward, weather side)。**3.** 庇护所;避风处。**4.** 【地】背冰川面。***on*** [***under***] ***the*** ~ 在背风处。**II *a.*** 背风的。*the* ~ *side* 蔽面,背风面。~ **board** 【船】边的横漂抵板。~ **shore** 下风岸;〔喻〕危险的境地 (*on a* ~ *shore* 在困难[危险]中)。~ **tide** 背风潮。

leech[1] [liːtʃ; litʃ] **I *n.*** **1.** 【动】水蛭,蚂蝗,(特指)医用蛭。**2.** 榨取他人脂膏者,吸血鬼,重利盘剥者,高利贷。**3.** 〔古〕医师。***stick to sth.*** [***sb.***] ***like a*** ~ 钉住[缠住]不放。**II *vt.*** **1.** 用水蛭吸血。**2.** 榨取干净,吸尽血汗。~ *sb. white* 把某人的精力[钱财等]榨取干净。~ **craft** 〔古〕医术。

leech[2] ***n.*** 【船】帆的纵缘。

Leeds [liːdz; lidz] ***n.*** 利兹〔英国城市〕。

leek [liːk; lik] ***n.*** 【植】青蒜,韭葱。***eat*** [***swallow***] ***the*** ~ 忍受耻辱。***not worth a*** ~ 毫无价值。

leer[1] [liə; lɪr] **I *n.*** 斜瞅,睨视,横目。**II *vi.***, ***vt.*** (愤恨、轻蔑地)斜眼瞅,瞟 (*at*; *upon*)。

leer[2] [liə; lɪr] ***n.*** 【化】(玻璃的)退火炉。

leer·y [ˈliəri; ˋlɪrɪ] ***a.*** (*leer·i·er*; *-i·est*) 〔口〕**1.** 机警的,狡猾的。**2.** 对…怀有戒心 (*of*)。*a* ~ *old bird* 老滑头。

lees [liːz; liz] ***n.*** 〔*pl.*〕(葡萄酒等的)渣滓;沉积物;残渣。*drain* [*drink*] *a cup to the* ~ **1.** 喝干。**2.** 备尝辛酸。*the* ~ *of life* 残年。*There are* ~ *to every wine.* 〔谚〕有酒就有酒渣。

leet[1] [liːt; lit] ***n.*** 【英史】(封建领主设的)民事法庭或该法庭的管辖范围。

leet[2] [liːt; lit] ***n.*** 〔Scot.〕候选人名单。*a short* ~ 最后一选的候选人名单。

Lee Tsung-dao [ˈliːdzuŋˈdau; ˋlidzʊŋˋdaʊ] ***n.*** 李政道 (1926— ,华裔美国物理学家,因发现违反宇称守恒定律现象,对粒子物理学理论作出重大贡献,与杨振宁共获1957年诺贝尔物理学奖)。

Leeu·wen·hoek [ˈleivənˌhuːk; ˋlevənˏhuk], **A. van** ~ 雷文霍克〔1632—1723,荷兰博物学家,显微镜创制者〕。

lee·ward [ˈliːwəd, ˈluːed; ˋliwɚd, ˋluɚd] **I *a.*** 【海】下风的,在下风处的。**II *ad.*** 在下风,向下风。**III *n.*** 下风,背风面。**-most *a.*** 〔古〕最下风的。**-ly *a.*** 易向下风漂流的。

Lee·ward Islands [ˈliːwəd; ˋliwɚd] ***n.*** 背风群岛〔西印度小安的列斯群岛的北部〕。

lee·way [ˈliːwei; ˋliˏwe] ***n.*** **1.** 【海】风压〔船在行进中被冲向下风〕;风压差;风压角〔进路与航路间的角〕;【空】偏流〔因风力造成飞行上的偏差〕。**2.** 时间的损失,落后。**3.** 〔口〕灵活性;余裕,余地。***have*** ~ 有回旋余地;〔口〕有充裕时间。***have much*** [***a great deal of***] ~ ***to make up*** 要花大力才能赶上。***leave some*** ~ 留有余地。***make*** ~ **1.** 漂离航道。**2.** 离开预定航道。***make up*** (***for***) ~ **1.** 赶上;弥补(损失)。**2.** 摆脱困难。***retain a certain*** ~ 保持相当的灵活性。

left[1] [left; lɛft] leave 的过去式及过去分词。~ *on base* 【棒球】(攻守换班时)留在垒上。

left[2] [left; lɛft] **I *a.*** **1.** 左的,左边的,左侧的。**2.** 左翼的;〔L-〕左派的。***have two*** ~ ***hands*** 非常笨拙。~ **field** 【棒球】左外野。**II *ad.*** 向左;在左边。*Eyes* ~! 向左看齐! *L- dress*! 向左看齐! *L- face* [*turn*]! 向左转! *L- wheel* 左转弯走! **III *n.*** **1.** 左,左面,左侧;〔美〕(船的)左弦。**2.** 〔常作 L-〕(议长席左侧的)议员;急进党,左派;(哲学、宗教的)革新派,急进派。**3.** 【军】左翼;【棒球】左外野。*on the* ~ *of* 在…的左面。*Keep to the* ~! 靠左边走! ***over the*** ~ (***shoulder***) 倒过来说,恰恰相反。~ **field** 〔美口〕活动中心以外的地区[范围],局外人圈子。~**-hand *a.*** **1.** 左手的,左边的;用左手的。**2.** 勉强的,不合理的 (*a* ~*-hand marriage* 门户不相当的婚姻)。**3.** 非法的。~**-handed *a.*** **1.** 用左手的。**2.** 惯用左手的。**3.** 笨拙的。**4.** 可疑的,暧昧的;不诚实的;居心叵测的 (*a* ~*-handed compliment* 假恭维)。**5.** 门户不相当的,地位不相称的(婚姻)。**6.** 〔古〕不吉利的。**7.** 向左旋转的,反时针的 (*a* ~*-handed screw* 左转螺丝)。**IV *ad.*** 用左手。*write* ~*-handed* 用左手写字。~**-hander** **1.** 左撇子,用左手的人。**2.** (在拳击中)用左手的一击;意外的打击。~ **heart** 心左半侧〔包括左心室和左心房,向肺部以外的全身输送血液〕。~**-leaning *a.*** 左倾的。~**-minded *a.*** 〔美〕古怪的。~**most *a.*** 最左的,极左的。~ **wing** (政党等的)左翼。~**-wing *a.*** 左翼的,急进

L

的。～**-winger** 左派。

left·ism [ˈleftizəm; ˋlɛftɪzm̩] ***n.*** 〔有时 L-〕左派观点[主张、运动]。

left·ist [ˈleftist; ˋlɛftɪst] **I** ***a.*** 〔L-〕左派的。**II** ***n.*** 左派的人。

left-lug·gage [ˈleftˈlʌgidʒ; ˋlɛftˋlʌgɪdʒ] ***n.*** 寄存行李。*a ～ office* 行李寄存处。

left-off [ˈleftˈɔ(:)f; ˋlɛftˋɔf] ***a.*** (衣服等)弃置不用的,脱下不穿的。

left·o·ver [ˈleftˌəuvə; ˋlɛftˏovɚ] **I** ***n.*** 剩余物〔如剩菜〕。**II** ***a.*** 剩余的;未用完的;吃剩的。

left·ward(s) [ˈleftwəd(z); ˋlɛftwɚd(z)] **I** ***a.*** 左面的,左侧的。**II** ***ad.*** 向左面,在左方。

left·y [ˈlefti; ˋlɛftɪ] **I** ***n.*** 〔俚〕**1.** 左撇子,用左手的人。**2.** 左派的人,左倾的人。**II** ***a.***, ***ad.*** = ～-handed.

leg [leg; lɛg] **I** ***n.*** **1.** 腿;(猪、羊等)供食用的腿。**2.** (桌椅等的)腿脚;支架;支柱;支管。**3.** 三角形底部以外的侧边。**4.** (裤子等的)腿部;袜统;靴统;脚管。**5.** 假腿。**6.** 〔英俚〕骗子。**7.** (板球中)击球员左后方场地。**8.** 【海】抢风直驶的一段航程;旅程的一段。**9.** 〔古〕后脚一弯的行礼,屈膝礼。**10.** 喷道。**11.** 【电】引线,支线;多相变压器的铁心柱;(多相系统的)相。**12.** (牌戏等上下两局中的)一局,一盘。**13.** 〔～s〕持久力;(尤指影片)持续的轰动效应。*a ～ of the law* 警察;律师;执法人员。*as fast as one's ～s could carry one* 开足马力,拼命跑。*be all ～s (and wings)* **1.** 又瘦又长,长手长脚。**2.** 【海】樯又多又高。*be off one's ～s* 跌倒;站不住;(因走路、站立或工作过久而)筋疲力尽。*be run off one's ～s* 破产。*change the ～* (马)改换步调。*dance sb. off his ～s* 使某人跳舞跳得筋疲力尽。*fall on* [*upon*] *one's ～s* [*feet*] 跌下但未跌倒;侥幸度过困境。*feel* [*find*] *one's ～s* **1.** (婴儿)开始能行走[站起]。**2.** 对自己的能力开始有了自信心。*find* [*get*] *one's ice ～* 学会滑冰。*get a ～ in* 〔口〕得到…的信任。*get one's ～ over the traces* 〔美〕违反党或组织的利益。*get* [*set*] *sb. on his ～s* **1.** 使某人恢复健康。**2.** 使某人经济自主。*get up on one's hind ～s* 〔口〕气势汹汹,盛气凌人。*give sb. a ～ up* **1.** 扶人上马。**2.** 帮助某人渡过困难。*hang a ～* 裹足不前;犹豫不决。*have a bone in one's ～* 不善行走,难于行走。*have (got) by the ～* 〔美〕使处于困难地位。*have ～s* 走得快;出名出得快;有忍耐力。*have not a ～ to stand on* (言论等)没有根据;站不住脚。*have one's ～ over the harrows* 不受管制,拒绝服从。*have* [*put, stretch*] *one's ～s* [*feet*] *under sb.'s mahogany* 受某人款待〔指请吃饭〕。*have the ～s of* 比…跑得快。*in high ～* 非常高兴。*keep one's ～s* 立定脚跟;不跌倒。*keep on* [*upon*] *one's ～s* 一直站着。*～ and ～* 双方得分相等,平分秋色。*～ before wicket* (板球)击球员违反规则用腿截球。*lose one's ～s* 〔俚〕喝得东倒西歪,喝醉。*make a ～* 〔古〕弯膝行礼,打千儿。*on* [*upon*] *one's ～s* **1.** 站着〔尤指演说时〕。**2.** 病后能下床走动。**3.** 发达的,富裕的。*on* [*upon*] *one's last ～s* 奄奄一息;快要结束。*pull sb.'s ～* 〔口〕愚弄某人,嘲弄某人。*put* [*set*] *one's best ～ first* [*foremost, forward*] 〔口〕全力以赴。*run off one's ～s* 累得精疲力尽,疲于奔命。*run sb. off his ～s* 使某人筋疲力尽。*shake a ～* **1.** 〔口〕跳舞。**2.** 〔美俚〕赶紧。*shake a loose* [*free*] *～* 过放荡生活,放荡。*show a ～* 〔口〕起床。*show ～* 〔美俚〕逃跑。*stand on one's own ～s* 不依赖他人,自立。*stretch one's ～s* 散步,遛遛腿。*stretch one's ～s according to the coverlet* 适应环境,量入为出。*take to one's ～s* 逃走,溜之大吉。*talk the hind ～ off a donkey* [*horse*] 唠叨不休。*try it on the other ～* 〔俚〕使用另一办法[最后一着]。*walk* [*trot*] *sb. off his ～s* 使人走累。

II ***vi.*** (**-gg-**) **1.** 〔口〕走,徒步走;跑。**2.** (为…)奔走,卖力 (*for*)。**3.** 用腿抵住运河隧洞壁推船通过。— ***vt.*** 用腿抵壁把船推过运河隧洞。～ *it* 走着去;跑;逃走 (*Leg it as fast as you can.* 快快跑吧!)。～ **art** 曲线美照片;裸体照片。～ **bail** 〔谑〕逃走 (*give ～ bail* 逃跑,越狱)。～**-bye** 【板球】(投手投球击中击球员身体的)得分。～**-guard** (运动员的)护腿。～**iron** **1.** ***n.*** 脚镣。**2.** ***vt.*** 用脚镣锁住。～**man** **1.** 〔美〕采访记者。**2.** (机关办公室的)外勤,跑腿人。～**-of-mutton** ***a.*** 羊腿状的〔尤指羊腿状衣袖或三角状帆〕。～**-pull** 欺骗;恶作剧,嘲弄。～**-rest** (病人等用的)脚凳。～**room** (轿车或剧院等座位的)放脚处。～ **show** 大腿戏。～**work** 〔口〕跑外工作,外勤,跑腿儿活;新闻采访工作。**-less** ***a.*** 无腿的。**-like** ***a.***

leg. = **1.** legal. **2.** legate. **3.** legato. **4.** legislature.

leg·a·cy [ˈlegəsi; ˈlɛgəsɪ] **I** ***n.*** **1.** 【法】(动产的)遗赠;遗产。**2.** 传代物;传统,遗教。*inherit a ～* 继承遗产。*a ～ of hatred* [*ill-will*] 宿恨,世仇。*a rotten ～* 烂摊子。**II** ***a.*** 【计】(电脑软件因使用时间太长而)老化的。～**-hunter** 为争得遗产而钻营奉承的人。

le·gal [ˈliːgəl; ˋlig!] **I** ***a.*** **1.** 法律(上)的。**2.** 法定的,合法的,正当的。**3.** 【宗】按照摩西律法的。*one's ～ status* 合法地位。*the ～ profession* 律师业。*a ～ adviser* 法律顾问。*a ～ fare* 法定运费。**II** ***n.*** **1.** 法定权利。**2.** 依法必须登报的声明。**3.** 〔*pl.*〕储蓄银行[信托公司]可以用来投资的证券。～ **cap** 律师公文纸〔$8\frac{1}{2}$英寸宽,13(或14)英寸长,带边纸的白纸〕。～ **holiday** 法定假日。～ **limit** (汽车等的)法定速限。～ **list** (储蓄银行等的)合法投资。～ **person** 法人。～ **remedy** 法律的制裁。～ **reserve** (银行等的)法定准备金。～ **separation** (夫妻的)合法分居。～ **tender** 合法货币〔指可以用来偿债而债主必须接受的货币〕。

le·gal·ese [ˌliːgəˈliːz; ˏligəˋliz] ***n.*** 晦涩的公文,法律用语。

le·gal·ism [ˈliːgəlizəm; ˋligəlɪzm̩] ***n.*** **1.** 墨守法规,条文主义;文牍主义。**2.** 【宗】信奉律法〔与信奉福音相对〕。

le·gal·ist [ˈliːgəlist; ˋligəlɪst] ***n.*** **1.** 墨守法规者,条文主义者;法律学家。**2.** 【宗】律法主义者。**-ic** ***a.*** **-i·cal·ly** ***ad.***

le·gal·i·ty [li(ː)ˈgæliti; lɪˋgælətɪ] ***n.*** **1.** 合法性;法律性。**2.** 守法主义。**3.** 【宗】墨守律法。**4.** 〔*pl.*〕法律上的义务。

le·gal·i·za·tion [ˌliːgəlaiˈzeiʃən; ˏlig!əˋzeʃən] ***n.*** 合法化;批准;法律上认可。

le·gal·ize [ˈliːgəlaiz; ˋlig!aɪz] ***vt.*** 法律认可,使合法,合法化。

le·gate[1] [liˈgeit; ˋlɛgɪt] ***vt.*** 作为遗产让与,遗赠。*give and ～* 作为遗产让与。

leg·ate[2] [ˈlegit; ˋlɛgɪt] ***n.*** **1.** 罗马教皇的使节。**2.** 使节,国使。～**ship** 使节的职权[任期]。

leg·a·tee [ˌlegəˈtiː; ˏlɛgəˋti] ***n.*** 【法】遗产承受人,受遗赠人。

leg·a·tine [ˈlegətain; ˋlɛgətɪn] ***a.*** **1.** 教皇使节的;国使的。**2.** 国使职权规定的。

le·ga·tion [liˈgeiʃən; lɪˋgeʃən] ***n.*** **1.** 使节的派遣;使节所负的使命。**2.** 公使馆;公使馆全体人员。**3.** 使节的职位[职权]。

le·ga·to [leˈgɑːtəu; lɪˋgɑto] ***a.***, ***ad.*** 〔It.〕【乐】连奏。

le·ga·tor [liˈgeitə; lɪˋgetɚ] ***n.*** **1.** 遗赠人。**2.** 立遗嘱人。

leg·end [ˈledʒənd; ˋlɛdʒənd] ***n.*** **1.** 传说;神话。**2.** 伟人传。**3.** (奖章、纪念牌等的)铭文,题跋。**4.** 地图的图例,插图的说明。**5.** 〔the L-〕【宗】圣徒故事集 (= the Golden L-)。

leg·end·ar·y [ˈledʒəndəri; ˋlɛdʒəndˏɛrɪ] **I** ***a.*** 传说(中)的;传奇(中)的,传说[传奇]似的。**II** ***n.*** **1.** 传说集;【宗】圣统传。**2.** 传说编纂者。

leg·end·ry [ˈledʒəndri; ˋlɛdʒəndrɪ] ***n.*** 传说;传奇文学。

leg·er·de·main [ˈledʒədəˈmein; ˋlɛdʒɚdɪˋmen] ***n.*** (变)戏法;骗术;花招。

leg·er line [ˈledʒə; ˋlɛdʒɚ] 【乐】加线〔五线谱的上加线或下加线〕。

le·ges [ˈliːdʒiːz, ˈleigeis; ˋlidʒiz, ˋleges] ***n.*** 〔L.〕 lex 的

L

复数。

leg·ged [ˈlegid, legd; ˋlɛgɪd, lɛgd] *a*. **1**.〔用作构词成分〕:有腿的。**2**. 有…腿的。*a long-~ man* 腿长的人。*a four-~ animal* 四足动物。

leg·ger [ˈlegə; ˋlɛgɚ] *n*. **1**. = legman. **2**. 用腿抵住运河隧洞壁把船推过去的人。**3**. 织袜统机;织袜统工人。**4**.(屠宰场等处)加工腿肉的工人。

leg·ging [ˈlegiŋ; ˋlɛgɪŋ] *n*.〔主 *pl*.〕绑腿;(幼儿用的)细腿毛线裤。

leg·go [ˈlegəu; ˋlɛgo] *int*.〔英俚〕放开! (= let go)。

leg·gy [ˈlegi; ˋlɛgɪ] *a*. (*-gi·er*; *-gi·est*) **1**. (特指小孩、小马等)腿细长的,细腿的。**2**.【植】茎长的。**3**. 露腿的。

Leg·horn [ˈlegˈhɔːn; ˋlɛgˋhɔrn] *n*. **1**. 来亨〔意大利地名〕。**2**.〔或 l-〕[leˈgɔːn; ˋlɛgɚn] 来亨鸡。**3**.〔l-〕[ˈleghɔːn; ˋlɛghɔrn] 意大利麦杆缏,意大利麦缏草帽 (= ~ hat)。

leg·i·ble [ˈledʒəbl; ˋlɛdʒəbl̩] *a*. 容易辨认的,易读的(笔迹),(字迹)清楚的。**-bil·i·ty** *n*. **-ness** *n*. **-bly** *ad*.

le·gion [ˈliːdʒən; ˋlidʒən] *n*. **1**. 古罗马军团〔约有三千至六千步兵,辅以骑兵〕。**2**. 军团,大批部队。**3**. 众多,大批,无数。**4**.〔L-〕= American L-, Foreign L- 等的简称。*a ~ of followers* 大批追随者。*Their name is Legion* [*legion*]. 他们很多。*the American* [*British*] ~ 美国[英国]军团〔退伍军人组织〕。**L- of Hono(u)r** 法国勋级会荣誉军团〔1802 年拿破仑为表彰有功勋者而成立的荣誉团体名〕。**L- of merit** 军功勋章〔美国政府向本国或外国军人颁发的勋章〕。

le·gion·ar·y [ˈliːdʒənəri; ˋlidʒən͵ɛrɪ] **I** *a*. **1**. (古罗马)军团的;军队的。**2**. 退伍军人协会的。**3**. 很多的。**II** *n*. **1**. 古罗马军团的兵。**2**. 退伍军人协会会员。~ **ant** 行军蚁〔美国热带一种成群结队吞食其前进路上的昆虫和动物的蚂蚁 = army ant〕。

le·gion·aire [ˌliːdʒəˈnɛə; ͵lidʒəˋnɛr] *n*. **1**. 军团的一员。**2**.〔常 L-〕美国军团(美国退伍军人组织)成员。**3**. 外籍军团〔由外国人组成的军队中(如过去法国在北非的殖民军中的外籍军团)〕的一员。

Legis. = **1**. legislation. **2**. legislature.

leg·is·late [ˈledʒisˌleit; ˋlɛdʒɪs͵let] *vi*. 制定法律,立法。— *vt*.〔美〕依法律…。~ *sb. out of an office*〔美〕按法定手续免某人的职。

leg·is·la·tion [ˌledʒisˈleiʃən; ͵lɛdʒɪsˋleʃən] *n*. **1**. 立法。**2**.〔集合词〕法规。**3**. 立法机构的审议事项。***paternal*** ~ 家长式的(限制公民自由的)繁琐立法。

leg·is·la·tive [ˈledʒisˌleitiv; ˋlɛdʒɪs͵letɪv] **I** *a*. 立法的;有立法权的;立法部门的 (*cf*. administrative, executive, judicial)。*a ~ bill* 法案。*the ~ body* 立法机关。~ *power* 立法权。*the L- Bureau* 法制局。**II** *n*. 立法权;立法机关。~ **assembly**〔常作 L- Assembly〕**1**. 美国各州的两院制议会。**2**. 两院制议会的下院。**3**. 一院制立法议会。~ **council**〔常作 L- Council〕**1**. 英国议会的上院。**2**. (英国殖民地或美国领地的)一院制议会。**3**. 美国州议会的常设委员会。

leg·is·la·tor [ˈledʒisˌleitə; ˋlɛdʒɪs͵letɚ] *n*. 立法者;议员;立法机关成员,立法委员。**-ial** *a*. **-ship** *n*.

leg·is·la·ture [ˈledʒisˌleitʃə; ˋlɛdʒɪs͵letʃɚ] *n*. 立法机关,立法部,议会;〔美〕(特指)州议会。

le·gist [ˈliːdʒist; ˋlidʒɪst] *n*. 法律学家。

le·git [ləˈdʒit; ləˋdʒɪt]〔美俚〕**I** *a*. **1**. 合法的,守法的。**2**. (戏剧、剧院等)正统的。**II** *n*. 正统剧;正统剧院。***on the*** ~ 正当的;在合法范围之内。

le·git·i·ma·cy [liˈdʒitiməsi; lɪˋdʒɪtəməsɪ] *n*. **1**. 合法性;正统性。**2**. 嫡系;嫡出;正统。

le·git·i·mate [liˈdʒitimit; lɪˋdʒɪtəmɪt] *a*. **1**. 合法的,正常的,正当的。**2**. 正统的。**3**. 嫡系的,嫡出的。**4**. (感情等)真实的。*a ~ claim* 正当要求。*a ~ inference* 合理的推断。~ *drama* 正统戏。**II** [-meit; -met] *vt*. **1**. 使合法;认为正当;认为正统。**2**. 承认(庶子)为嫡出。**-ly** *ad*. **-ma·tion** [-ˈmeiʃən; -ˋmeʃən] *n*.

le·git·i·ma·tize [liˈdʒitiməˈtaiz; lɪˋdʒɪtəmətaɪz] *vt*. (*-tiz·ed*, *-tiz·ing*) = legitimize.

le·git·i·mism [liˈdʒitimizəm; lɪˋdʒɪtəmɪzm̩] *n*. 正统主义。

le·git·i·mist [liˈdʒitimist; lɪˋdʒɪtəmɪst] **I** *n*. 正统王朝拥护者。**II** *a*. 正统王朝拥护者的。

le·git·i·mize [liˈdʒitiˌmaiz; lɪˋdʒɪtə͵maɪz] *vt*. (*-mized*, *-miz·ing*) **1**. 使合法化,宣布合法化;〔尤指〕使合法;予以法律保障[地位];官方[正式]认可;授予…权力,(对非婚生子)给予合法地位。**2**. 证明…有理。**-za·tion** *n*.

le·gong [ˈleigɔːŋ; ˋlegɔŋ] *n*.〔Balinese〕黎弓舞〔印度巴厘的一种传统女子双人舞〕。

leg·ume [ˈlegjuːm; ˋlɛgjum] *n*.【植】**1**. 豆科植物。**2**. 豆荚。**3**. (食用)豆。*~s bacteria* 根瘤细菌。

le·gu·men [liˈgjuːmən; lɪˋgjumən] *n*. (*pl*. ***legumina*** [-minə]) = legume.

le·gu·min [liˈgjuːmin; lɪˋgjumɪn] *n*.【生化】豆球朊,豆球蛋白。

le·gu·mi·nous [leˈgjuːminəs; lɪˋgjumənəs] *a*.【植】**1**. 荚的,有荚的;生豆的。**2**. 豆科的。~ *crops* 豆科作物。~ *plants* 豆科植物。

Le Ha·vre [ləˈhɑːvr; ləˋhɑvr] 勒阿弗尔〔法国港市〕。

Leh·mann [ˈleimən, lemən] *n*. 莱曼〔姓氏〕。

le·hu·a [leiˈhuːɑː; lɪˋhuɑ] *n*.【植】夏威夷桃金娘树;这种树的木材或花。

lei[1] [ˈleii; ˋleɪ] *n*. (*pl*. *~s*) (夏威夷人戴在颈上的)花环。

lei[2] [lei; le] *n*. leu 的复数。

Leib·nitz [ˈlaibnits; ˋlaɪbnɪts], **Gottfried Wilhelm von** 莱布尼茨〔1646—1716,德国哲学家、数学家〕。

Lei·ca [ˈlaikə; ˋlaɪkə] *n*.【摄】莱卡照相机〔商标名〕。

Leices·ter [ˈlestə; ˋlɛstɚ] *n*. **1**. 莱斯特〔英国城市〕。**2**. 莱斯特郡〔英国郡名〕(= ~ shire). **3**. 莱斯特羊 (= ~ sheep)。

Leigh [liː; li] *n*. 利〔姓氏,男子名〕。

Leigh·ton [ˈleitn; ˋletn̩] *n*. 莱顿〔姓氏〕。

Le(i)·la [ˈliːlə; ˋlilə] *n*. 莉拉〔女子名〕。

Leip·zig [ˈlaipzig; ˋlaɪpsɪg] *n*. 来比锡〔德国城市〕。

leish·man·i·a·sis [ˌliʃməˈnaiəsis; ͵lɪʃməˋnaɪəsɪs] *n*.【医】利什曼(原虫寄生)病;(尤指)黑热病。

leis·ter [ˈliːstə; ˋlistɚ] **I** *n*. (三齿)鱼叉。**II** *vt*. 叉鱼。

leis·ure [ˈleʒə, Am. ˈliːʒə; ˋlɛʒɚ, ˋliʒɚ] *n*. **1**. 空闲,闲暇。**2**. 悠闲,安逸。*wait sb.'s ~* 等到病人有空时。*a life of ~* 悠闲的生活。***at*** ~ **1**. 在闲暇中,有空〔常作表语〕。**2**. 从容不迫地〔常作副词〕。**3**. 失业〔作定语或表语〕。***at one's*** ~ 有空时,方便时 (*Drop in to see me at your ~*. 有空时请到我这里来)。**II** *a*. 闲暇的,有空的,有闲的(阶级等)。~ **suit** 休闲装。**-less** *a*. 无空闲的。

lei·sured [ˈleʒəd, Am. ˈliːʒəd; ˋlieɚd, ˋliʒɚd] *a*. 有闲空的;悠闲自在的。*the ~ classes* 有闲阶级。

lei·sure·ly [ˈleʒəli, Am. ˈliːʒəli; ˋliʒɚlɪ] **I** *a*. 从容不迫的,悠闲的。**II** *ad*. 从容不迫地,慢慢地,悠然,悠闲地。*work ~* 悠闲地工作。**-ness** *n*.

Leith [liːθ; liθ] *n*. 利斯〔姓氏〕。

leit·mo·tif, ***leit·mo·tiv*** [ˈlaitməuˌtiːf; ˋlaɪtmo͵tif] *n*.【乐】**1**. 主导旋律,主导主题。**2**. 中心思想[主题]。

lek [lek; lɛk] *n*. 列克〔阿尔巴尼亚货币名,等于 100 昆塔 (*quintar*)〕。

Le·land [ˈliːlənd; ˋlilənd] *n*. 利兰〔姓氏,男子名〕。

LEM = **1**. lunar excursion module 登月舱,月球探测飞船。**2**. laser energy monitor 雷射[激光]能量监控器。

Lem·an [ˈlemən; ˋlɛmən] *n*. 莱曼〔姓氏〕。

le·man [ˈlemən; ˋlɛmən] *n*.〔古〕爱人,情人,奸夫,情妇。

lem·ma[1] [ˈlemə; ˋlɛmə] *n*. (*pl*. *~ta* [-tə, -tə], *~s*) **1**.【逻、数】(辅)助定理,引(定)理,预备定理。**2**. (诗等的)主题,题目。**3**. (词典的)词目。**4**. (图画等上的)题词。

lem·ma[2] [ˈleme; ˋlɛmɛ] *n*.【植】(禾本科小穗的)外稃。

lem·ming [ˈlemiŋ; ˋlɛmɪŋ] *n*.【动】(北极的)旅鼠。

lem·nis·cus [lemˈniskəs; lɛmˋnɪskəs] *n*. (*pl*. *-nis·ci* [-ˌniszai; -ˏnɪsaɪ])【解】丘系,蹄系。

lem·on [ˈlemən; ˋlɛmən] **I** *n*. **1.** 柠檬;柠檬树。**2.** = lemon yellow. **3.**〔美俚〕无聊的人[物],没有价值的东西,叫人失望的人[物]。***hand sb. a*** ~〔口〕欺骗某人,把不值钱的东西卖给某人。***The answer's a*** ~.〔俚〕你这个(可笑的)建议,无法回答[理解]。**II** *a*. 柠檬的,柠檬味的;柠檬色[黄]的,柠檬制的。~ **balm**【植】蜜蜂花(*melissa officinalis*)〔一种叶带香味的多年生薄荷,可用作食物和药物的香料〕。~ **butter** (**sauce**) **1.** 柠檬黄[奶]油。**2.** 柠檬黄[奶]油汁。~ **day lily**【植】金针菜。~ **drop** 柠檬硬糖。~ **kali** 柠檬汽水。~ **law** 次品[劣货]补偿法〔规定商家须为购买了次品或劣货的顾客提供补偿的法律〕。~ **squash**〔英〕鲜柠檬苏打水。~ **squeezer** 柠檬压榨器。~ **tart**(常作老年富翁情妇的)金发女郎,高级妓女。~ **yellow** 柠檬色[黄],柠檬黄颜料。**-ish, -like** *a*.

lem·on·ade [ˌleməˈneid; ˏlɛmənˋed] *n*. 柠檬汽水。

lem·on·y [ˈleməni; ˋlɛmənɪ] *a*. 柠檬的,有柠檬香味的。

lem·pi·ra [lemˈpiːrɑː; lɛmˋpirə] *n*. (*pl*. *-ras*) 伦皮拉〔洪都拉斯货币名〕。

le·mur [ˈliːmə; ˋlimɚ] *n*.【动】狐猿。

Le·na [ˈliːnə; ˋlinə] *n*. **1.** 莉娜〔女子名, Helena 的昵称〕。**2.** (俄罗斯和俄罗斯联邦)勒拿河。

lend [lend; lɛnd] **I** *vt*. (*lent* [lent; lɛnt]) **1.** 借给,贷与,出借 (*opp*. borrow). **2.** 借助,提供。**3.** 使(自己)适合。**4.** 添加。~ *money at interest* 取息贷款。*This fact ~s probability to the story*. 从这个事实看来,这个故事好像是真的。— *vi*. 贷款。~ ***a*** (***helping***) ***hand with*** [***in***] 帮助,帮忙。~ ***assistance*** [***aid***] ***to*** 帮助。~ ***itself to*** 对…有用[适合]。***L- me your ears***. 请听我说吧。~ ***one's countenance to*** 赞成;支持。~ ***one's name to*** 让人用自己的名义。~ ***one's turn*** 让位子。~ ***oneself to*** 给…卖命。~ ***out*** 借出(书等)。~ ***sb. a box on the ear*** 打某人一记耳光。**II** *n*. (短期)贷款。*take a ~ of*〔英俚〕通融一下。**-a·ble** *a*.

lend·er [ˈlendə; ˋlɛndɚ] *n*. 出借人,贷方;贷款者。

lend·ing [ˈlendiŋ; ˋlɛndɪŋ] **I** *n*. **1.** 借给,贷与。**2.** 借出物,贷出物;租借物;附属物;〔*pl*.〕借来的衣服。**II** *a*. 贷出的。~ **library 1.** 收费图书馆。**2.**〔英〕公共图书馆;图书馆的借书处。~ **stock**【商】抵押品。

lend-lease [ˈlendˈliːs; ˋlɛndˋlis] **I** *vt*. 根据租借法案供给。**II** *a*. **1.** 由租借法批准的。**2.** 批准租借法的。**III** *n*. 平等租借交换。*the Lend-Lease Act* (1941 年美国制订的)租借法。

length [leŋθ; lɛŋθ] *n*. **1.** 长,长度,长短。**2.** (时间的)长短,期间。**3.** (赛艇的)一艇的长度;一马的长度。**4.** 程度,范围。**5.**【板球】球程;投至适当距离的球。**6.**【语】音长。**7.** 一段,一节。*a dress ~, a ~ of cloth* 一段料。*a ~ of pipe* [*tubing*] 一节管子。*The boat won by three ~s*. 这只艇以三艇长之差得胜。*a* (*good*) *~ ball* 球程准确的球。***at arm's*** ~ 在手臂伸得到的地方,疏远 (*keep sb. at arm's ~* 不与接近,敬而远之)。***at full*** ~ **1.** 冗长地;充分地,详细地 (*give all the facts at full ~* 提供详细的材料)。**2.** 全身平伸地 (*lie at full ~* 挺直身体躺着)。***at great*** ~ 冗长地,啰啰唆唆地。***at*** ~ **1.** 最后,终于,好容易才。**2.** 充分地,详细地 (*speak at great ~* 详细讲了好久)。***at some*** ~ 相当详尽地。***cannot see beyond the ~ of one's nose*** 鼠目寸光。***draw out to a great*** ~ 拖得很久,占去很长时间。***fall*** [***measure***] ***all one's*** ~ 直挺挺地倒下。***find*** [***get, have, know***] ***the ~ of sb.'s foot*** 了解某人的弱点。***go*** (***to***) ***all ~s*** [***any ~***] = ***go to great ~s*** 什么事都做得出;不遗余力。***go*** (***to***) ***the ~ of*** (***doing***) 甚至于,不惜。***go the whole ~ of it*** 彻底干;干到底。~ ***of*** (***sb.'s***) ***days*** [***life***] 某人的寿命。***measure one's*** (***own***) ~ 跌倒在地。***of some*** ~ 相当长。***over*** [***through***] ***the ~ and breadth of*** 到处,四面八方。***work at arm's*** ~ 在不利的条件下工作。

length·en [ˈleŋθən; ˋlɛŋθən] *vt*. 延长,伸长,拉长。~ *a vowel*【语音】拖长母音音长。— *vi*. 变长;延伸;转为 (*into*). *Summer ~s* (*out*) *into autumn*. 夏去秋来。*The days are ~ing*. 白天长起来了。*The shadows ~*. 天色渐黑;年纪渐老;死期已近。~ **out** 过分延长。

length·ways [ˈleŋθˌweiz; ˋlɛŋkθˏwez] *ad*. 纵长地。

length·wise [ˈleŋθˌwaiz; ˋlɛŋkθˏwaɪz] *ad*. , *a*. 纵长地[的]。

length·y [ˈleŋθi; ˋlɛŋkθɪ] *a*. (*length·i·er*; *-i·est*) **1.** 过长的,漫长的。**2.** 冗长的,啰唆的(演说、文章等)。**-i·ly** *ad*. **-i·ness** *n*.

le·ni·ence, -en·cy [ˈliːniəns, -si; ˋlinɪəns, -sɪ] *n*. **1.** 宽大,宽厚,怜悯。**2.** 宽大的行为。*a policy of ~* 宽大政策。*excessive ~* 宽大无边。

le·ni·ent [ˈliːnjənt; ˋlinɪənt] *a*. **1.** 宽大的,宽厚的,怜悯的。**2.**〔古〕减轻痛苦的,缓解的。**-ly** *ad*.

Len·in·grad [ˈleningræd, -grɑːd; ˋlɛnɪngræd, -grɑd] *n*. 列宁格勒〔前苏联大城市,1991 年后改名为 St. Petersburg〕。

le·nis [ˈliːnis, ˈlei-; ˋlinɪs, ˋle-] **I** *a*.【语音】弱(辅音)的〔发音时肌肉松弛,如浊连续音〕。**II** *n*. 弱辅音。

len·i·tive [ˈlenitiv; ˋlɛnətɪv] **I** *a*. 有缓和作用的,止痛的。**II** *n*.【药】止痛剂,缓和剂。

len·i·ty [ˈleniti; ˋlɛnətɪ] *n*. **1.** 宽大;慈悲。**2.** 宽大的处理。

le·no [ˈliːnəu; ˋlino] *n*.【纺】**1.** 纱罗织法〔经纱双股扭织〕。**2.** 纱罗织物,通花布。

lens [lenz; lɛnz] *n*. (*pl*. *~es*) **1.** 透镜;一组透镜。**2.**【解】(眼球的)晶体。**3.**【摄】(照相机的)镜头。**4.** 凸透镜状物件;汽车的灯玻璃。**5.**【矿】透镜状油矿;扁豆状矿体。**6.** 隐形眼镜(= contact ~)。*a concave* [*convex*] ~ 凹面[凸面]镜。*an electron ~* 电子透镜。*a biconcave* [*biconvex*] ~ 双凹[双凸]面透镜。*the power of a ~* 透镜的焦强。~ **louse**〔美影俚〕抢镜头的人。~**man** (*pl*. *-men*)〔美口〕摄影师。~ **shyness**〔美影俚〕新演员在摄影机前的畏怯心理,怯场。~ **turret** (摄影机或电视机上的)透镜旋转台。

lent [lent; lɛnt] lend 的过去式及过去分词。

Lent [lent; lɛnt] *n*. **1.** (基督教的)四旬斋,大斋期〔指复活节前的四十天〕。**2.**〔*pl*.〕〔英〕(剑桥大学)春季赛艇会。~ **lily 1.**〔英〕= daffodil. **2.** = Madonna lily. ~ **term**〔英〕春季学期。

-lent *suf*. 表示"充满…的";"富于…的";"以…为特征的": pesti*lent*, vio*lent*.

len·ta·men·te [ˌlentəˈmentei; ˏlɛntəˋmɛntə] *ad*.【乐】缓慢地。

len·tan·do [lenˈtɑːndəu; lɛnˋtɑndo] *ad*. , *a*.【乐】渐慢。

Lent·en [ˈlentn; ˋlɛntən] *a*. **1.** 四旬斋的;大斋期的。**2.** 四旬斋时举行的;适合于四旬斋的;简朴的,简陋的;没有肉食的;严肃的。~ *clothing* 朴素的衣服。*a ~ face* 阴沉的脸。~ *fare* 斋,素菜。*a ~ pie* 无肉斋饼。

len·tic [ˈlentik; ˋlɛntɪk] *a*.【生态】静水的;生活于静水(如湖泊、池塘等)中的。

len·ti·cel [ˈlentisəl; ˋlɛntəˏsɛl] *n*.【植】皮孔。**len·ti·cel·late** [ˌlentiˈselit; ˏlɛntəˋsɛlet] *a*.

len·tic·u·lar [lenˈtikjulə; lɛnˋtɪkjəlɚ] *a*. **1.** 双凸透镜状的。**2.** 透镜的。**3.** (眼球的)晶(状)体的。**4.**【地】透镜状的,扁豆状的。**5.**【摄】凹凸式(胶片)的。~ *film* (电影的)凹凸式胶片。~ *sand*【地】透镜状地层。

len·tic·u·late [lenˈtikjuˌleit; lɛnˋtɪkjəˏlet] *vt*. (*-lated*, *-lat·ing*) 使成为凹凸式胶片〔加上特殊滤色器可摄出带自然色的照片〕。**len·tic·u·la·tion** *n*.

L

len·tic·u·lated [len'tikjuleitid; lɛn`tɪkjuə,letɪd] ***a.*** = lenticular.

len·ti·form ['lentiˌfɔːm; `lɛntə,fɔrm] ***a.*** = lenticular.

len·tig·i·nous [len'tidʒinəs; lɛn`tɪdʒənəs] ***a.*** **1.** 雀斑的,斑点的。**2.** 长雀斑的,长斑点的 (= lentiginose)。

len·ti·go [len'taigəu; lɛn`taɪgo] ***n.*** (*pl.* ***len·tig·i·nes*** [len'tidʒiˌniːz; lɛn`tɪdʒə,niz]) 斑点,【医】雀斑。

len·til ['lentil; `lɛntɪl] ***n.***【植】小扁豆(属)。

len·tisk ['lentisk; `lɛntɪsk] ***n.***【植】乳香黄连木。

len·tis·si·mo [len'tisiˌməu; lɛn`tɪsə,mo] ***a.***, ***ad.***【乐】非常缓慢。

len·ti·tude ['lentitjuːd; `lɛntətjud] ***n.***〔古〕缓慢;懒散。

len·to ['lentəu; `lɛnto] ***ad.***, ***a.***〔It.〕【乐】徐缓地[的];柔和地[的]。

len·toid ['lentɔid; `lɛntɔɪd] ***a.*** 透镜状的。

l'en·voi, l'en·voy ['lenvɔi; `lɛnvɔɪ] ***n.***〔F.〕(诗、文的)结束语,尾声。

LEO【物】= **1.** low enrichment ordinary water reactor 低浓缩普通水反应堆。**2.** low earth orbit【宇航】近地轨道。

Le·o ['li(ː)əu; `lio] ***n.*** **1.** 利奥〔男子名〕。**2.**【天】狮子座;狮子宫。~ **minor**【天】小狮(星)座。

Le·on ['li(ː)ən; `liən] ***n.*** 利昂〔男子名, Leo 的异体〕。

Lé·ón ['leiən; le`ɔn] ***n.*** **1.** 〔西班牙西北部城市〕。**2.** 莱昂〔墨西哥中部城市〕。**3.** 莱昂〔尼加拉瓜西部城市〕。

Le·o·na [liː'əunə; li`onə] ***n.*** 利昂娜〔女子名〕。

Leon·ard ['lenəd; `lɛnəd] ***n.*** 伦纳德〔姓氏,男子名〕。

Leo·nar·do da Vin·ci [ˌliːə'nɑːdəudə'vintʃi; ,liə`nɑrdodə`vɪntʃɪ] ***n.*** 达·芬奇〔1452—1519 意大利文艺复兴时期伟大画家、雕刻家、建筑学家〕。

Le·o·nar·desque [ˌliːənɑː'desk; ,liənɑr`dɛsk] ***a.*** (意大利画家)(达)芬奇式[风格]的。

le·one [liː'əun; li`on] ***n.*** 利昂〔塞拉利昂货币名,等于 100 分(cents)〕。

Le·o·nid ['li(ː)ənid; `liənɪd] ***n.*** (*pl.* ***~s***, ***~es*** [-iːz; -iz])【天】狮子座流星。

le·o·nine ['liːənain; `liə,naɪn] ***a.*** **1.** 狮子(似)的。**2.** 雄壮的;勇猛的。

Le·o·nor·a [ˌli(ː)ə'nɔːrə; ,liə`norə] ***n.*** 利奥诺拉〔女子名, Eleanor 的异体〕。

LEP = large electron-positron collider【物】大型正负电子对撞机。

leop·ard ['lepəd; `lɛpəd] ***n.***【动】豹。*an American* ~ 美洲豹(= jaguar)。*a hunting* ~ 猎豹(= cheetah)。*a snow* ~ 雪豹(= ounce²)。*Can the* ~ *change his spots*? 本性难移。~ **spot** 豹斑〔常指一方在另一方地域内的分散据点,在地图上标示不同,状如豹斑〕。

leop·ard·ess ['lepədis; `lɛpədɪs] ***n.***【动】母豹。

le·o·tard ['liːəˌtɑːd; `liətɑrd] ***n.*** (杂技和舞蹈演员等穿的)高领长袖紧身衣;紧身衣。

lep·er ['lepə; `lɛpə] ***n.*** **1.** 麻疯病人。**2.** 别人避之唯恐不及的人。~ **colony** (孤岛等的)麻疯病人隔离区。~ **house** 麻疯病人收容所。

lep·i·do- [li'pidəu; lɪ`pɪdo] *comb. f.* 表示"鳞": *lepidopterous.*

le·pid·o·cro·cite [ˌlepidəu'krəusait; ,lɛpɪdo`krosaɪt] ***n.***【矿】纤铁矿。

le·pid·o·lite [li'pidəˌlait, 'lepidəˌlait; lə`pɪdə,laɪt] ***n.***【矿】锂云母。

Lep·i·dop·ter·a [ˌlepi'dɔptərə; ,lɛpɪ`dɑptərə] ***n.*** 〔*pl.*〕【动】鳞翅目(昆虫),蝶类。

lep·i·dop·ter·al [ˌlepi'dɔptərəl; ,lɛpə`dɑptərəl] ***a.***【动】鳞翅目(昆虫)的,蝶类的。

lep·i·dop·ter·an [ˌlepi'dɔptərən; ,lɛpə`dɑptərən] ***n.***【动】鳞翅目 (*Lepidoptera*) 昆虫〔包括蝶和蛾〕。

lep·i·dop·ter·ist [ˌlepi'dɔptərist; ,lɛpə`dɑptərɪst] ***n.*** 鳞翅目昆虫学家。

lep·i·dop·ter·ous [ˌlepi'dɔptərəs; ,lɛpə`dɑptərəs] ***a.*** = lepidopteral.

lep·i·do·si·ren [ˌlepidəu'sairən; ,lɛpɪdə`saɪrən] ***n.***【动】美洲肺鱼 (*Lepidosiren paradoxa*)〔产于南美沼泽等死水中〕。

lep·i·do·sis [ˌlepi'dəusis; ,lɛpə`dosɪs] ***n.*** (*pl.* ***lepidoses*** [ˌlepi'dəusiːz; ,lɛpə`dosiz]) 动物鳞片的排列和特质。

lep·i·dote ['lepiˌdəut; `lɛpɪdot] ***a.***【生】有鳞片的。

lep·o·rid ['lepərid; `lɛpərɪd] **I** ***n.*** (*pl.* ***le·por·i·dae*** [li'pɔːriˌdiː; lɪ`pɔrɪ,di])【动】兔科 (*Leporidae*)。**II** ***a.*** 兔科的。

lep·o·rine ['lepəˌrain, -rin; `lɛpə,raɪ, -rɪn] ***a.*** 野兔的;如野兔的。

lep·re·chaun ['leprəˌkɔːn, -ˌkɑːn; `lɛprə,kɔn, -,kɑn] ***n.*** (爱尔兰传说中帮主妇做事的勤奋的)小精灵。

lep·ro·sa·ri·um [ˌleprə'seəriəm; ,lɛprə`sɛrɪəm] ***n.*** (*pl.* ***-ri·ums***, ***-ri·a*** [-ə; -`sɛrɪə]) 麻疯病院;麻疯病人隔离区[收容所]。

lep·rose ['leprəus; `lɛpros] ***a.***【生】多鳞的;鳞状的。

lep·ro·sy ['leprəsi; `lɛprəsɪ] ***n.*** **1.**【医】麻疯病。**2.** 极坏的作用,有危害性的事物。*moral* ~ 道德败坏。

lep·rous ['leprəs; `lɛprəs] ***a.*** **1.** 麻疯的;似麻疯的;患麻疯的。**2.** 不洁净的,丑恶的。**3.** 鳞状的,有鳞被的。**-ly** ***ad.*** **-ness** ***n.***

lep·to- ['leptə; `lɛptə] *comb. f.* 表示"小","细","薄": *lepto*cephalic.

lep·to·ce·phal·ic [ˌleptəusi'fælik; ,lɛptosə`fælɪk] ***a.*** 头盖骨狭小的。

lep·to·ceph·a·lus [ˌleptə'sefələs; ,lɛptə`sɛfələs] ***n.*** (*pl.* ***-li*** [-lai; -laɪ])【动】叶状幼体。

lep·to·dac·tyl [ˌleptəu'dæktil; ,lɛptə`dæktl̩] ***a.***, ***n.***【动】脚趾细长的(禽类或兽类)。

lep·to·dac·ty·lous [ˌleptə'dæktləs; ,lɛptə`dæktɪləs] ***a.*** 有细长趾的〔如某些鸟类〕。

lep·ton[1] ['leptən; `lɛptɑn] ***n.*** (*pl.* ***lep·ta*** [-tə; -tə]) **1.** 雷普塔〔古希腊小硬币名〕。**2.** 雷普塔〔希腊现行货币名,等于一德拉克马 (*drachma*) 的 1/100〕。

lep·ton[2] ['leptɔn; `lɛptɑn] ***n.***【物】轻粒子,轻子。~ *number* 轻子数。**-ic** ***a.***

lep·to·some ['leptəsəum; `lɛptə,som] **I** ***n.*** 体格细长的人,瘦弱型的人。**II** ***a.*** 体格细长的,瘦弱型的。

lep·to·spire ['leptəˌspaiə; `lɛptə,spaɪr] ***n.***【医】钩端螺旋体。

lep·to·spi·ro·sis [ˌleptəuspai'rəusis; ,lɛptospaɪ`rosɪs] ***n.***【医】钩端螺旋体病。**lep·to·spi·ral** [-'spairəl; -`spaɪrəl] ***a.***

Ler·mon·tov ['ljermɔntəf; `ljermʌntɔf] **Mikhail Yurevich** 莱蒙托夫〔1814—1841 俄国诗人,小说家〕。

le roi le veut [lə'rwɑːlə'vəː; lə`rwɑlə`və]〔F.〕国王对此同意。

le roi s'avisera [lə'rwɑːsɑː'viːzərɑː; lə`rwɑsɑ`vizərɑ]〔F.〕国王将加考虑〔委婉的拒否用语〕。

Les·bi·an ['lezbiən, -bjən; `lɛzbɪən, -bjən] **I** ***a.*** **1.** (古希腊)勒斯波斯岛 (Lesbos) 的。**2.** 女性同性恋的。~ **love** (女性间的)同性恋。**II** ***n.*** **1.** 勒斯波斯岛的居民。**2.** 搞同性恋的女子。**-ism** ***n.*** 女性间的同性恋关系[行为]。

lèse-ma·jes·té ['leiz'mæʒestei; ,lez,ma,ʒɛs`te] ***n.*** 〔F.〕 = lese majesty.

lese maj·es·ty ['liːz'mædʒisti; `liz`mædʒɪstɪ] ***n.***【法】欺君罪,叛逆罪。

le·sion ['liːʒən; `liʒən] **I** ***n.*** **1.** 损害,损伤。**2.**【医】(机体、器官等的)损害。*focal* ~ 病灶损害。*periodontal* ~ 牙周损害。**II** ***vt.*** 损害,对…造成损伤[损害]。

Les·ley, Les·lie ['lezli, 'lesli; `lɛzlɪ, `lɛslɪ] ***n.*** 莱斯莉〔女子名〕。

Les·lie ['lezli, 'lisli; `lɛzlɪ, `lɪslɪ] ***n.*** 莱斯利〔姓氏,男子

名)。

Le·sot·ho [ləˈsəuthəu; ləˋsotho] *n*. 莱索托〔非洲〕。

les·pe·de·za [ˌlespiˈdiːzə; ˏlɛspəˋdizə] *n*.【植】胡枝子属(*Lespedeza*)〔一年生或多年生植物,用以改良土壤和作为牲畜饲料〕。

less [les; lɛs] **I** *a*.〔little 的比较级之一〕**1.** 更小的,较小的,更少的,较少的。**2.** 较次的,较劣的,较不重要的;身分较低的。*find* ~ *difficulty with one's work* 觉得工作困难较少。*Your shadow hasn't grown any* ~. 你一点也没有瘦。*an article of* ~ *weight* 更轻的东西。*Eat more vegetable and* ~ *meat*. 多吃蔬菜少吃肉。*He spends* ~ *time at work than at play*. 他工作上的时间比游玩时间少。~ *but better* 少而精。*L- noise, please!* 请静一点。*More haste,* ~ *speed*.〔谚〕欲速则不达。*try to make* ~ *mistakes* 尽量少犯错误。*an article of* ~ *value* 更不值钱的东西。*a matter of* ~ *importance* 次要的事情。*James the L-* 副手杰姆斯,打下手的杰姆斯。★ 表示数量意义时, fewer 比 less 普通: *Fewer people study Latin today than formerly*. 现在学拉丁文的人比从前少了。***far*** ~ 远不及。***little*** ~ 少一点。***little*** ~ ***than*** 相差无几。***more or*** ~ 多少,或多或少,若干。***no*** ~ ***than*** **1.** 正好…,至少…,有…那么多(*He has no* ~ *than three daughters*. 他有三个女儿之多)。**2.** 原来就是,…那样的(*He was no* ~ (*a person*) *than the mayor*. 他原来就是市长)。***nothing*** ~ ***than*** = no ~ than (*We expected nothing* ~ *than an attack*. 受攻击是预料到的)。

II *ad*. **1.** 较少,更少。**2.** 没有…那样。*be* ~ *known* 不大著名。*He is* ~ *fat than he was*. 他不及过去胖了。*The heat has grown* ~ *intense*. 没有先前那样热了。*Eat* ~, *drink* ~ *and sleep more*. 少吃少喝多睡觉。*Speak* ~ *and listen more*. 少讲多听。***no*** ~ ***... than*** 不下于,和…同样(*He is no* ~ *clever than his brother*. 他跟他兄弟一样聪明)。***none the*** ~ = ***not the*** ~ = ***no*** ~ 仍旧,依然(*He has faults, but I like him none the* ~. = *I like him none the* ~ *for his faults*. = *He has faults; none the less, I like him*. 他有缺点,但我仍旧喜欢他)。***not*** ~ ***than*** 不少于;至少(*Each party shall consist of not* ~ *than ten*. 每组至少由十人组成)。***not*** ~ ***... than*** 在…方面不下于(*The pupil was not* ~ *famous than his master*. 学生同老师齐名)。***nothing*** ~ ***than*** 完全一样(*He is nothing* ~ *than a thief*. 他简直是个贼)。***sth.*** ~ ***than*** 较…少几分。***still*** [***even, much***] ~〔附在否定句后〕更不用说,何况(*We fear no death, still* ~ *difficulties*. 我们死都不怕,何况困难)。

III *prep*. 少掉;不足;减去。*a year* ~ *three days* 一年差三天。*Five* ~ *three leaves two*. 五减三剩二。

IV *n*. 较少,更小。*expect to see* ~ *of sb*. 不想多见某人。*He is* ~ *of a fool than he looks*. 他不像看上去那样笨。*He will not take* ~. 他不肯少拿〔坚持要那么多〕。*in* ~ *than a year* 在不到一年的时间里。*L- of your nonsense*. 少说废话。*L- than twenty of them remain now*. 他们剩下的现在还不到二十人。***any the*** ~ 更少一点,更小一些(*He did not work any the* ~ *for his illness*. 他虽有病在身,工作却没有少做)。***in*** ~ ***than no time*** 立刻,马上。***nothing*** ~ ***than*** 同样,正好是,恰恰是。~**-than-carload** *a*. (铁路运输中的)零担的 ~**-than-truckload** *a*. 卡车零担的。

-less *suf*.〔附在名词或动词之后〕**1.** 构成形容词,表示"无","缺","没有": end*less*, home*less*, leaf*less*. **2.** 构成副词,表示"不": doubt*less*.

les·see [leˈsiː; lɛˋsi] *n*.【法】承租人,租户。

less·en [ˈlesn; ˋlɛsn] *vt*. **1.** 缩小,减少;减轻。**2.** 贬低;轻视,看不起。— *vi*. 变小,变少,减少。

less·er [ˈlesə; ˋlɛsɚ] *a*.〔little 的比较级之一〕**1.** 更小的,更少的;较小的。**2.**【乐】= minor. *a* ~ *nation* 小国。*a* ~ *power* 弱国。**L- Bear**【天】小熊座。~ **panda**【动】小熊猫(*Ailurus fulgens*)。

Le·ssing [ˈlesiŋ; ˋlɛsɪŋ] **Gotthold Ephraim** 莱辛〔1729—1781 德国诗人,批评家〕。

les·son [ˈlesn; ˋlɛsn] **I** *n*. **1.** 功课。**2.** 一节课,(教科书中的)一课。**3.**〔*pl*.〕课程。**4.** 教训,训诫;惩戒。**5.**【宗】日课。*hear sb. his* ~ 听人温习功课。*L- Three* 第 3 课。*give* ~*s in music* 教音乐。*object* ~ 实物教学;明显的实例。***be a*** ~ ***to*** 对…是一个教训。***give a*** ~ ***to sb.*** = ***give sb. a lesson*** 教训某人,申斥某人。***learn one's*** ~ 得到教训。***read sb. a*** ~ 教训某人一顿。***take*** [***have***] ~***s in English from sb.*** 跟某人学英语。**II** *vt*. **1.** 教课。**2.** 教训,训斥。

les·sor [leˈsɔː; ˋlɛsɔr] *n*.【法】出租人。

lest [lest; lɛst] *conj*. **1.** 唯恐,免得〔引出副词子句〕。**2.**〔用在 fear, afraid 等词的后面,引出名词子句〕= that. *He fled* ~ *he* (*should*) *be arrested*. 他唯恐被捕于是就逃跑了。*I was afraid* ~ *he should come too late*. 我怕他来得太迟。

Les·ter [ˈlestə; ˋlɛstɚ] *n*. 莱斯特〔姓氏,男子名〕。

let[1] [let; lɛt] (*let*; *let·ting*) *vt*. **1.** 容许,让,听任;使得。**2.** 假设,假定。**3.** 出借,出租。**4.** 使流出;泄漏,放出;让通过。**5.** (把工作等)让人承包,承办。*Don't* ~ *this happen again*. 别让这种事情再发生了。*L- me try*. 让我试一下。*L- nobody lag behind*. 别让任何人落后。*L- them do their worst*. 让他们尽量作恶吧! *L- us* [*Let's*] *go at once*. 我们马上走吧! *L-* ∠*ABC be an angle of ninety degrees*. 假设 ∠ABC 为直角。*He* ~ *it be known that ....* 他对人说…。*L- him do it*. 让他去做吧。~ *sb. through* 让某人通过。*Please* ~ *me know*. 请告诉我。*We* ~ *him go*. 我们放他走了。~ (*out*) *a sigh* 叹一口气。*The water is* ~ *into the tank*. 让水流入水箱。*This pair of boots* ~ (*in*) *water*. 这只靴子漏水。*House* [*Room*] *to L-*. 房屋[房间]招租。~ *one's house* 出租房屋。— *vi*. 租出,被人借用中。*The house* ~*s for 100 dollars a month*. 这所房子月租一百元。*The room* ~*s well*. 这个房间价高[不易租出]。~ ***alone*** **1.** 不理,不管,放任(*L- him alone to do it*. 任他自己去做罢)。**2.** 更不用说(*I can't speak French,* ~ *alone Russian*. 我连法语也不会讲,更不用说俄语了。*He knows Latin and Greek,* ~ *alone English*. 他懂拉丁文和希腊语,英语更不在话下)。~ ***be*** 不管,听任(*L- her be*. 别打扰她)。~ ***blood***【医】放血,流血。~ ***by*** 让人过去(*L- me by, please*. 借光,让让路)。~ ***down*** **1.** 放落,放下(~ *down the blinds* 放下百叶窗)。**2.** 抛弃,使失望(~ *him down* 使他失望)。**3.** 损坏威信,丢面子,搞臭。~ ***drive at ...*** 向…打出,向…投掷。~ ***fall*** [***drop, slip***] **1.** 落下,倒下。**2.** 不当心泄漏,无意中说出。**3.**【数】画(垂线等)。~ ***fly*** **1.** 发射,投射。**2.** 骂。~ ***fly at*** 发射,射出。***L- George do it***.〔美俚〕让别人干吧。~ ***go*** **1.** 放开;释放。**2.** 发射。**3.** 放任不管。**4.** 拳打,辱骂。**5.** 辞退。~ ***go hang*** 放任,不管。~ ***in*** **1.** 放入(~ *in some fresh air* 打开门窗透透新鲜空气。~ *sb. in* 让某人进来)。**2.** 插入,嵌入。**3.**〔俚〕欺骗。**4.** 使受损失,陷入…。~ ***in on***〔美〕告诉,告知。~ ***into*** **1.** 放进。**2.** 嵌进。**3.** 告诉,告知(~ *sb. into a secret* 告诉某人秘密)。**4.**〔俚〕打击,殴打;责骂。~ ***it go at that*** 谈论到此为止。~ ***loose*** 放掉,释放;放任。***L- me see***. 让我想想看。~ ***off*** **1.** 放(枪,花炮等);说出(俏皮话等)。**2.** 宽恕,从轻处理(~ *sb. off lightly* 从轻发落)。**3.** 漏出,放出(水、瓦斯等)。**4.** 免除(约束、工作、责任等)。~ ***on***〔口〕**1.** 泄密。**2.** 假装。~ ***oneself go*** 尽情(做某事);忘乎所以。~ ***out*** **1.** 放出。**2.** 泄漏。**3.** 放宽,放大,放长。**4.** 出租(车、马等)。**5.**〔美口〕放学;散场。**6.** 打,踢,骂(*at*)。**7.**〔美俚〕解雇。~ ***pass*** 不追究,原谅,宽恕。~ ***ride*** 不管,放任自流。~ ***slide***〔美〕不关心,放过。~ ***slip*** **1.** 解开,放

L

走。2. 无意中说出。3. 错过(机会等)。~ *sb*. *down easily* [*gently*] 给某人留面子〔不加深究〕。~ *sb*. *have it* 〔美俚〕殴打某人,让某人吃苦头。~ *things go hang* = ~ *things slide* 随它去,不管它,听其自然。~ *up* 〔口〕停止,中止;(风雨等)减弱。~ *up on* 〔口〕宽大对待。~ *us say* 比方说,假定说。~ *well* [*enough*] *alone* (已经够好了)就让它去,不要画蛇添足。**II** *n*. 〔英口〕出租;租出的房屋。*get a* ~ *for the room* 为这房间找到租户。

let[2] [let; lɛt] **I** *vt*. (*let·ed*, *let*; *let·ting*) 〔古〕阻碍,防害。**II** *n*. 1. 〔古〕障碍,阻碍。2. (网球等)球触网。*without* ~ *or hindrance* 毫无障碍。

-let *suf*. 1. 表示"小"。ring*let*, stream*let*. 2. 表示"在…上佩带的饰品":ank*let*, arm*let*.

Le·ta [ˈliːtə; ˋlitə] *n*. 莉塔〔女子名〕。

letch [letʃ; lɛtʃ] *vi*., *n*. = lech.

let·down [ˈletˌdaun; ˋlɛtˏdaʊn] *n*. 1. 〔美〕(速度,努力等的)下降,减少。2. 松劲。3. 〔口〕失望,令人失望的事物。

le·thal [ˈliːθəl; ˋliθəl] **I** *a*. 致死的,致命的,杀伤性的;〔美〕外援以提供武器形式进行的,提供军援的。*a* ~ *chamber* 煤气屠杀室。*a* ~ *dose* 致死剂量〔略 LD〕。~ *gas* 致死性毒气。~ *weapons* 凶器。~ *military aid* 提供武器的军援〔non-~ aid 则仅提供食品衣物、医疗援助等〕。**II** *n*. = ~ gene. ~ **gene** 致死基因,致死因子,致死因素〔也称 ~ factor〕。**-i·ty** *n*. 致死性,杀伤力;致死率。**-ly** *ad*.

le·thar·gic(al) [leˈθɑːdʒik(əl); lɪˋθɑrdʒɪk(əl)] *a*. 1. 昏睡(状态)的,嗜眠的,瞌睡的。2. 催人昏睡的。**-gi·cal·ly** *ad*.

leth·ar·gize [ˈleθəˌdʒaiz; ˋlɛθɚˏdʒaɪz] *vt*. (*-giz·ed*, *-giz·ing*) 使昏睡;使没精打采。

leth·ar·gy [ˈleθədʒi; ˋlɛθɚdʒɪ] *n*. 1. 嗜眠症。2. 没精打采;懒散,呆滞;无生气。

Le·the [ˈliːθi(ː); ˋliθi] *n*. 1. 【希神】忘河〔人饮其水,就忘却过去〕。2. 〔l-〕忘却。**le·the·an** [liˈθiːən; liˋθiən] *a*. 1. 忘河的。2. 使人忘却过去的。

Le·ti·tia [liˈtiʃiə; lɪˋtɪʃɪə] *n*. 利蒂希娅〔女子名〕。

l'é·toile du nord [leiˈtwɑːldjuːˈnɔː; leˋtwɑldjuˋnɔr] 〔F.〕北极星。

let's [lets; lɛts] = let us.

Lett [let; lɛt] *n*. 1. 列特人〔波罗的海东岸,尤其是拉脱维亚的一个民族〕。2. 列特语。

let·ted [ˈletid; ˋlɛtɪd] 1. 〔废〕let[1]的过去式和过去分词。2. let[2]的过去式和过去分词的异体。

let·ter[1] [ˈletə; ˋlɛtɚ] *n*. 出租人。

let·ter[2] [ˈletə; ˋlɛtɚ] **I** *n*. 1. 字母,文字。2. 【印】活字,铅字。3. 书信。4. 〔*pl*.〕文学,学问;〔*pl*.〕读写初步知识。5. 〔常 *pl*.〕证书,许可证。6. 字面(意义),形式。7. 〔美〕运动服上的字母标志。*teach a child his* ~*s* 教孩子识字。*black* ~ 古代英国哥特式黑体字。*white* ~ 罗马体活字。*a man of* ~*s* 文人。*art and* ~*s* 文学艺术。*the commonwealth* [*republic*] *of* ~*s* 文坛。*the profession of* ~*s* 著作界。*in* ~ *and in spirit* 形式与精神皆在,在形式和内容上。*the* ~ *of the law* 法律条文,法律字面上的意义。***be slow at one's*** **~*s*** 读书进步慢。***by*** ~ 以书信形式 (*inform sb*. *by* ~ 写信通知某人)。***call*** **~*s*** 呼号。***drop*** ~ 〔美〕托人由一地带到另一地付邮的信件。~ ***worship*** 拘泥字句。***night*** ~ 夜间无线电报。***to the*** ~ 1. 严格按照字句,彻头彻尾,不折不扣。2. 详细知道;了如指掌。***win one's*** ~ 当上运动选手。**II** *vt*. 写[刻,印]上文字[字母],标上字母分类;加标题。— *vi*. 1. 写上字母。2. 【美体】当上选手。~ **balance** (邮局中称信的)信秤。~ **board** 【印】铅字盘。~ **bomb** 邮件爆炸物,书信炸弹。~ **book** 书信发文簿。~**-bound** *a*. 拘泥字句的。~ **box** 信筒;信箱。~**boxing** (电影、电视等的)宽银幕式,宽屏幕式。~ **card** 〔英〕邮简。~ **carrier** 邮递员。~ **case** (携带用)文件夹。~ **drop** 投信口。~**form** 1. 字母形式〔尤指字母的设计、发展中所呈现的形状〕。2. 信笺。~ **founder** 铸铅字的人。~**gram** 书信电报〔较普通电报为慢〕(*a day* ~ *gram* 昼间书信电报〔当天送达〕。*a night* ~ *gram* 夜间书信电报〔次日送达〕)。~ **head** 笺头〔印在信纸上端的人名或商行的名称、地址等〕。2. 印有上述笺头的信笺。~ **lock** 字码锁。~**man** 〔美〕(得奖的)运动员。~ **missive** 传达上级命令、任命、许可、邀请的函件。~ [~**s**] **of marque** [**and reprisal**] 武装私人船舶捕押敌船的许可证。~**-paper** 信纸,信笺。~**-perfect** *a*. 1. 【剧】台词记得很熟的。2. (文件、校样等)完全正确的。~**-press** 【印】1. 〔主英〕有插图的书中正文。2. 活版印刷。~ **set** 【印】1. 文字版面的胶印。2. 书信复写器。~ **sheet** 邮简。~**s of administration** 【法】遗产管理委任状。~**s of business** (英国国王发出的)召开教会高级人士会议通知书。~**s of credence** (= ~s credential) (外交)国书。~**s of recall** (外交)召回使节的公文。~**s patent** 专利特许证。~**s testamentary** 【法】遗嘱执行状〔法院向遗嘱执行人发的证书〕。~**-weight** 1. 镇纸,纸压。2. = ~ balance. ~ **writer** 1. 写信者;书信代书人。2. 尺牍。3. 书信复写器。

let·tered [ˈletəd; ˋlɛtɚd] *a*. 1. 识字的,有文化的。2. 有学问的。3. 有文字的,印有字母的。

let·ter·er [ˈletərə; ˋlɛtərɚ] *n*. 字母[文字]刻写人。

let·ter·ing [ˈletəriŋ; ˋlɛtərɪŋ] *n*. 1. 手写字,印刷字,雕刻字。2. 写字,印字,刻字。

Let·tic [ˈletik; ˋlɛtɪk] *a*., *n*. = Lettish.

Let·tish [ˈletiʃ; ˋlɛtɪʃ] **I** *a*. 列特人的;列特语的。**II** *n*. 列特人,列特语。

Let·tre de ca·chet [letr də kɑːˈʃei; ˋlɛtr də kaˋʃe] (*pl*. *let·tres de cachet*) 〔F.〕密信;〔尤指〕(法国革命前国王不通过法律手续发出的)秘密逮捕令。

let·tuce [ˈletis; ˋlɛtɪs] *n*. 1. 【植】莴苣。2. 〔美俚〕钞票。

let·up [ˈletˌʌp; ˋlɛtˏʌp] *n*. 〔美口〕停止,中止;休息。*He jaws with no* ~. 他没完没了地讲。*It rained without* ~. 雨下个不停。

le·u [ˈleu; ˋlɛʊ] *n*. (*pl*. *lei* [lei; le]) (罗马尼亚的货币单位)列伊。

leu·c(o)- *comb*. *f*. 表示"白色";"无色":*leuco*cyte, *leuco*rrh(o)ea.

leu·c(a)e·mi·a [ljuːˈsiːmiə; luˋsimɪə] *n*. = leuk(a)emia.

leu·cine [ˈluːsiːn, -sin; ˋlusin, -sɪn] *n*. 【化】白胺[氨]酸。

leu·cite [ˈluːsait; ˋlusaɪt] *n*. 【地】白榴石。

leu·co·cyte [ˈljuːkəˌsait; ˋljukəˏsaɪt] *n*. = leukocyte.

leu·co·cy·th(a)e·mi·a [ˌljuːkəusaiˈθiːmiə; ˏlukosaɪˋθimɪə] *n*. = leuk(a)emia.

leu·co·cy·tosis [ˌljuːkəsaiˈtəusis; ˏlukosaɪˋtosɪs] *n*. = leukocytosis.

leu·co·my·cin [ˈljuːkəˌmaisin; ˋljukəˏmaɪsɪn] *n*. 【药】白霉素。

leu·co·plast(id) [ˈljuːkəuplæst(id); ˋljukəplæst(ɪd)] *n*. 【植】白色体,白色粒。

leu·cor·rh(o)e·a [ˌljuːkəˈriːə; ˏljukəˋriə] *n*. = leukorrhea.

leu·cot·o·my [ljuˈkɔtəmi; luˋkɑtəmɪ] *n*. 【医】脑白质切除术。

leu·k(a)e·mi·a [ljuːˈkiːmiə; ljəˋkimɪə] *n*. 【医】白血病。**leu·ke·mic** [-mik; -mɪk] 1. *a*. 白血病的。2. *n*. 白血病患者。**leu·ke·moid** [-mɔid; -mɔɪd] *a*.

leuk(o)- *comb*. *f*. = leuc(o)-.

leu·ko·cyte [ˈlukəˌsait; ˋlukəˏsaɪt] *n*. 白血球,白血细胞。**leu·ko·cyt·ic** *a*. **leu·ko·cyt·oid** *a*.

leu·ko·cy·to·blast [ˌljuːkəˈsaitˌblæst; ˏlukəˋsaɪtˏblæst] *n*. 白血球细胞形成核。**-ic** [-ˈblæstik; -ˋblæstɪk] *a*.

leu·ko·cy·to·sis [ˌljuːkəsaiˈtəusis; ˏlukəsaɪˋtosɪs] *n*. 【医】白血球增多。**leu·ko·cy·tot·ic** [-ˈtɔtik; -ˋtɑtɪk] *a*.

L

leu·ko·der·ma [ˌljuːkəˈdəːmə; ˏlukəˋdɚmə] *n*.【医】角斑;角白膜斑。

leu·ko·dys·tro·phy [ˌljuːkəˈdistrəfi; ˏlukəˋdɪstrəfɪ] *n*.【医】脑白质营养不良。

leu·ko·pe·ni·a [ˌljuːkəˈpiːniə; ˏlukəˋpinɪə] *n*.【医】白血球减少。**leu·ko·pe·nic** *a*.

leu·ko·poi·e·sis [ˌljuːkəpɔiˈiːsis; ˏlukəpɔɪˋisɪs] *n*.【医】白血球生成。**leu·ko·poi·etic** [-ˈetik; -ˋɛtɪk] *a*.

leu·kor·rhe·a [ˌljuːkəˈriːə; ˏlukəˋriə] *n*.【医】白带过多。**-l** *a*.

leu·ko·sis [ljuːˈkəusis; ljuˋkosɪs] *n*. = leuk(a)emia.

LEV = low emission vehicle 低排放量汽车。

lev [lɛf; lɛf] *n*. (*pl*. **le·va** [ˈlevə; ˋlɛvə]) 列弗〔保加利亚货币名,等于 100 斯托丁基 (*stotinki*)〕.

Lev. = Leviticus.

Le·val·loi·si·an [ˌlevəˈlɔiziən; ˏlɛvəˋlɔɪzɪən] *a*. 列瓦洛期文化的〔指旧石器时代中期文化。列瓦洛是法国地名,该地出土的文物特点为片状工具〕。

Le·vant [liˈvænt, lə-; ləˋvænt, lə-] *n*. **1**. 地中海东部沿岸诸国和岛屿〔包括叙利亚、黎巴嫩、巴勒斯坦等〕。**2**. = ~ morocco. **3**. 〔l-〕地中海上的强烈东风。~ **morocco** (装订书籍用的)优质山羊鞣皮。**-ine** *a*., *n*. 地中海东部沿岸诸国和岛屿的(人)。

le·vant [liˈvænt; ləˋvænt] *vi*. 〔英〕躲债逃匿。

le·vant·er[1] [liˈvæntə; ləˋvæntɚ] *n*. **1**. (地中海上的)强烈东风。**2**. 〔L-〕地中海东部沿岸诸国和岛屿的人。

le·vant·er[2] [liˈvæntə; lɪˋvæntɚ] *n*. 〔英〕逃亡者;躲债逃匿的人。

le·va·tor [liˈveitə; ləˋvetɚ] *n*. (*pl*. **lev·a·to·res** [ˌlevəˈtɔːriːz; ˏlɛvəˋtɔriz], **le·va·tors**) **1**.【解】提肌。**2**.【医】脑骨碎片镊子。

lev·ee[1] [ˈlevi; ˋlɛvɪ] *n*. **1**. (国王等起床后的)接见。**2**. 〔英〕(国王专对男臣举行的)早朝,接见;(法国宫廷的)早朝。**3**. 〔美〕总统招待会。**4**. 专为某人举行的招待会。

lev·ee[2] [ˈlevi; ləˋvɪ] **I** *n*. **1**. 〔美〕(河中泥沙形成的)冲积堤。**2**. 天然堤。**3**. 码头。**II** *vt*. 筑堤。

lev·el [ˈlevl; ˋlɛvl̩] **I** *n*. **1**. 水平仪,水准仪;水准测量。**2**. 水平线,水平面;水平状态;平面,平地。**3**. 水平,水准;水位;标准;高度;层次;级;等级。**4**.【物】能级,电平;【矿】主平巷。*4000 metres above sea* ~ 海拔四千米。*the* ~ *of the sea* = (the) sea ~. (标准)海面。*the rise and fall of water* ~ 水位的升降。*a normal blood-sugar* ~ 正常血糖量标准。*above* [*below*] *the general* ~ 在一般水准以上[以下]。*at eye* ~ 齐眼睛那么高。*high* ~ *bombing* 高空轰炸。*the ground* ~【物】基级。*at the grass-roots* ~ 在基层。*social* ~*s* 社会地位。*the government at all* ~*s* 各级政府机关。*top-* ~ *talks* 最高级会谈。*the* ~ *of a gun* 瞄准线。*the* ~ *of vision* 视线。*take a* ~ 作水准测量。*a dead* ~ 平面,平地;单调;【矿】空层,备用层。***bring sb. to his*** ~ 打掉某人的傲气。***find*** [***seek***] ***one's*** (***own***) ~ 找到相称的位置(*Water tries to find its* ~. 水往低处流)。~ ***to*** ~ ***administration*** 分级管理。***land on the street*** ~〔美口〕失业。***on a*** ~ ***with sb***. 和某人同一水准;和某人同等(地位)。***on the deal*** ~〔美口〕极正直的,极诚实的。***on the*** ~〔美口〕**1**. 公平地,公正地。**2**. 老实说,实实在在 (*On the* ~ *I am awfully disappointed*. 老实说我完全失望)。***rise to higher*** ~ 水平提高。

II *a*. (~***er***; ~***est***; 〔英〕~***ler***; ~***lest***) **1**. 水平的,平坦的。**2**. 同高度的;程度[水准,级别]相同的;【电】等位的;【乐】平调的。**3**. 平稳的;冷静的。**4**. 平直的。**5**. 均匀的,平均分布的;保持一定水平[状态]的;恒定的。~ *ground* 平地。*make a surface* ~ 使表面变平。*a* ~ *race* 势均力敌的赛跑。*sing* [*speak*] *in* ~ *tones* 用平板的声音唱[说]。*keep a* ~ *head in a crisis* 在危险时刻保持冷静的头脑。*give sb. a* ~ *look* 平直地看某人一眼。*keep a workshop at a* ~ *temperature* 保持车间恒温。***be*** ~ ***with sb***. 跟某人相齐;跟某人同等。***do one's*** ~ ***best***〔口〕竭尽全力。

III *ad*. **1**. 水平地,平坦地。**2**. 准确,一直。**3**. 和…成水平,同样高。**4**. 和…不分优劣,势均力敌地。*The missile went* ~ *to its mark*. 火箭准确打中目标。*fill a basin* ~ *with the brim* 把盆装满到盆边。*draw* ~ *with sb*. 同某人拉平。

IV *vt*. (**-l**(***l***)**-**) **1**. 使成水平;使平坦;弄平;平整。**2**. 使同等;拉平;废除。**3**. 推倒,夷平。**4**. 对准,瞄准。**5**. 测定高度。**6**. 使(声音、色调等)平板。~ *down the ground* 铲平地面。~ *up the ground* 填平地面。~ *a speech to the capacity of the audience* 按听众水平演讲。~ *all social distinctions* 消除一切社会差别。~ *a gun at the enemy* 把枪瞄准敌人。~ *a satire against sb*. 针对某人进行讽刺。— *vi*. **1**. 用武器瞄准;对准 (*at*)。**2**. 用水平仪测量高度。**3**.【空】(着陆时)水平飞行。**4**. 拉平。**5**. 坦率地对待。*I'll* ~ *with you*. 我将对你开诚布公。~ *the enemy stronghold in the dust* = ~ *the enemy stronghold to* [*with*] *the ground* 把敌人的堡垒夷平。~ ***off*** **1**. 弄平,整平。**2**. 达到同一水准;(物价等)稳定。**3**. (飞机降落前)水平飞行。~ ***up*** [***down***] 提高[降低]成同一水准,提高[降低]成一样,扯平,平整。~ **crossing** 〔英〕(道路)平面交叉点,道口,岔口。~ **curve** = contour line. ~ **compensator** 分层补偿器。~ **control** (信号)电平调整,级位控制。~ **flight** 水平飞行。~ **funding** 定额拨款〔一个财政年度或一定时期内预算拨款保持不变的财务政策〕。~ **gauge** 水平仪;水位计。~ **headed** *a*. 稳健的,头脑冷静的。~ **indicator** 液面指示器;电平指示器。~ **meter** 电平表,电平测量器。~ **of significance**【统】有效(位)水平 (= significance ~)。~**-peg** *vi*. 〔英〕保持平衡,保持均势。~ **pressure** 扯平压力。

lev·el(**l**)**·er** [ˈlevələ; ˋlɛvl̩ɚ] *n*. **1**. 把事物弄平[使事物相等,消除差别]的人[物]。**2**. 水准测量员;校平器,(钢板)矫平机。**3**. 平等主义者。**4**. 〔L-〕(英国十七世纪的)平均主义者。

lev·el·(**l**)**ing** [ˈlevəliŋ; ˋlɛvl̩ɪŋ] *n*. 测平,校平;平整(土地);水准测量。*a* ~ *instrument* [*mechanism*] 水准仪。*a* ~ *machine* (道路)整平机;【冶】钢板矫平机。~ **pole** [**rod, staff**] 水准(标)尺。

Le·ver[1] [ˈliːvə; ˋlivɚ] *n*. 利弗〔姓氏〕。

le·ver[2] [ˈliːvə, Am. ˈlevə; ˋlivɚ, ˋlɛvɚ] **I** *n*. **1**. 杆,杠。*a ball* ~ 浮球杆。*a brake* ~ 闸杆。*a control* ~ 控制杆。*a throttle* ~ 节流杆。*a timing* ~ 定时杆。**2**. 手段。*Pity is a* ~ *for quickening love*. 怜悯是加速爱情的手段。**II** *vt*., *vi*. 用杠杆撬动;撬开 (*along*; *up*). *control* ~ 用杆操纵。

le·ver·age [ˈliːvəridʒ; ˋlɛvərɪdʒ] **I** *n*. **1**. 杠杆作用。**2**. 杠杆装置;杠杆机构。**3**. 臂比,杠杆率;扭转力矩。**4**. 达到目的的手段;势力;影响。**II** *vt*. **1**. 对…施加影响[运用权力]。**2**. 为…提供杠杆装置。**3**. 以"杠杆收购法"投资于(某个基金)。~**d buyout**【经】杠杆收购〔一小批投资者借巨款收购下一家公司,再以该公司收益还债〕。

lev·er·et [ˈlevərit; ˋlɛvərɪt] *n*. 一岁的小兔。

lev·i·a·ble [ˈleviəbl; ˋlɛvɪəbl̩] *a*. 可征收的(税等),得课税的(货物等)。

le·vi·a·than [liˈvaiəθən; lɪˋvaɪəθən] *n*. **1**. 〔L-〕(《圣经》中象征邪恶的)海中怪兽。**2**. 大船;巨型远洋舰;大海兽;庞然大物。**3**. 势力大的人,大人物。**4**. 〔L-〕《利维坦》〔英国十七世纪著作家霍布斯论国家组织的著作〕;权力集中的(君主)国家。

lev·i·er [ˈleviə; ˋlɛvɪə] *n*. 强征人(尤指征税人)。

lev·i·gate [ˈlevigeit; ˋlɛvəˏget] *vt*. **1**. 粉碎,弄成粉;弄成糊。**2**. 磨光,磨细。**3**. 澄清,洗净;洗矿。**-ga·tion** [ˌleviˈgeiʃən; ˏlɛvɪˋgeɪʃən] *n*.

lev·in [ˈlevin; ˋlɛvɪn] *n*. 〔古〕电光。

Le·vi's [ˈliːvaiz; ˋlivaɪz] *n*. 〔*pl*.〕牛仔裤〔商标名,写作

levis〕。

lev·i·tate [ˈleviteit; ˋlɛvə͵tet] *vt.*, *vi.* (使)轻轻浮起, (使)飘浮空中。**-ta·tion** [ˌleviˈteiʃən; ͵lɛvəˋteʃən] *n.* 悬浮,漂浮,浮置。

Le·vite [ˈliːvait; ˋlivaɪt] *n.* **1.**【圣】利未人,利未人的子孙。**2.**〔俚〕犹太人。

Le·vit·ic(al) [liˈvitik(əl); ləˋvɪtɪk(əl)] *a.* 利未人的,利未族的。

lev·i·ty [ˈleviti; ˋlɛvətɪ] *n.* **1.** 轻率,轻浮,轻薄。**2.** 变化无常。**3.**〔罕〕轻。

le·vo- *comb. f.* 表示"向左的,左旋的": *levo*glucose, *levo*rotation.

le·vo·do·pa [ˌlevəuˈdəupə; ͵lɛvoˋdopə] *n.*【药】= L-dopa.

le·vo·glu·cose [ˌliːvəuˈgluːkəus; ͵livoˋglukos] *n.*【化】左旋葡萄糖。

le·vo·gy·rate [ˌliːvəuˈdʒaireit; ͵livoˋdʒaɪret] *a.* = levorotatory, levogyrous.

le·vo·ro·ta·tion [ˌliːvəurəuˈteiʃən; ͵livoroˋteʃən] *n.*【物】左旋。

le·vo·ro·ta·to·ry [liːvəuˈrəutəˌtɔːri; ͵livoˋrotə͵torɪ] *a.* **1.** 左旋的,反时针方向转动的。**2.** 使偏正光面,向左方旋转的〔如某些水晶等物〕。

lev·u·lin [ˈlevjulin; ˋlɛvjəlɪn] *n.*【化】多缩[聚]左旋糖。

lev·u·lose [ˈlevjuˌləus; ˋlɛvjə͵los] *n.*【化】左旋糖,果糖。

Lev·y [ˈliːvi, ˈlevi; ˋlivɪ, ˋlɛvɪ] *n.* 利维〔姓氏〕。

lev·y [ˈlevi; ˋlɛvɪ] **I** *vt.* (*lev·ied*; *lev·y·ing*) **1.** 征收;索取。**2.** 征集,征用。**3.** (动员)发动战争。**4.**【法】扣押,索取。~ *a fine* [*tax*] *on sb.* 向某人征收罚金[税款]。~ *a ransom on sb.* 向某人索取赎金。~ *troops* 征集军队。~ *war against* [*upon*] ... 对…开战。— *vi.* **1.** 征税;抽款。**2.** 扣押财产。~ ***blackmail upon*** 讹诈,敲诈。~ ***on*** 扣押。**II** *n.* **1.** 征税,派款,征收额。**2.** 召集,征集,募集,征募兵额。*a capital* ~ 资本课税。*a* ~ *in kind* 征用实物。*green levies and veteran soldiers* 新兵和老兵。~ *en masse* 〔F.〕= ~ in mass (战时)全民总动员。

lewd [luːd; lud] *a.* **1.** 好色的,淫猥的。**2.**〔古〕粗野的,卑鄙的,邪恶的。**-ly** *ad.* **-ness** *n.*

Lew·es [ˈlu(ː)is; ˋljuɪs] *n.* 路易斯〔姓氏〕。

Lew·is [ˈlu(ː)is; ˋljuɪs] *n.* **1.** 路易斯〔姓氏,男子名, Louis 的异体〕。**2.** **Sinclair** ~ 辛克莱·路易斯〔1885—1951 美国作家,获 1930 年诺贝尔文学奖〕。

lew·is [ˈlu(ː)is; ˋljuɪs], **lew·is·son** [ˈluːisən; ˋluɪsən] *n.*【机】起重爪;吊楔;地脚螺栓。

lew·is·ite [ˈluːiˌsait; ˋluɪsaɪt] *n.*【化】路易斯式毒气。

lex [leks; lɛks] *n.* (*pl.* ***leges*** [ˈliːdʒiːz; ˋlidʒiz]) 〔L.〕法律。~ ***loci*** [ˈləusai; ˋlosaɪ] 地方法律。~ ***non scripta*** [nɔnˈskriptə; nɑnˋskrɪptə] 不成文法。~ ***scripta*** 成文法。~ ***talionis*** [ˌtæliˈəunis; ͵tæliˋonɪs] 同害惩罚法〔以其人之道还治其人的办法〕。

lex. [leks; lɛks] = lexicon.

lex·eme [ˈleksiːm; ˋlɛksim] *n.*【语】词素,词位,辞汇单位。**lex·em·ic** [-ˈsiːmik; -ˋsimɪk] *a.*

lex·i·cal [ˈleksikəl; ˋlɛksɪkl̩] *a.* **1.** 辞汇的。**2.** 辞典编纂上的。**-ly** *ad.*

lexicog. = **1.** lexicographer. **2.** lexicography.

lex·i·cog·ra·pher [ˌleksiˈkɔgrəfə; ͵lɛksəˋkɑgrəfɚ] *n.* 辞典编纂者。

lex·i·co·graph·i·cal [ˌleksikəˈgræfikəl; ͵lɛksəkəˋgræfɪkəl] *a.* 辞典编纂上的。~ ***order*** 字母次序。

lex·i·cog·ra·phy [ˌleksiˈkɔgrəfi; ͵lɛksəˋkɑgrəfɪ] *n.* 辞典编纂(法),辞典学。

lex·i·col·o·gy [ˌleksiˈkɔlədʒi; ͵lɛksɪˋkɑlədʒɪ] *n.*【语】辞汇学。**lex·ico·log·i·cal** [-kəˈlɔdʒikl; -kəˋlɑdʒɪkl̩] *a.* **lex·i·col·o·gist** *n.*

lex·i·con [ˈleksikən; ˋlɛksɪkən] *n.* **1.** (尤指希腊语、希伯来语或拉丁语的)辞典。**2.** 特殊辞汇,专门辞汇。

lex·ig·ram [ˈleksigræm; ˋlɛksɪgræm] *n.*【语】词符〔用来代表词的任何符号〕。

lex·ig·ra·phy [lekˈsigrəfi; lɛkˋsɪgrəfɪ] *n.* (以一个符号代表一个词的)符合文字。

lex·is [ˈleksəs; ˋlɛksəs] (*pl.* ***lex·es***) *n.* 辞,辞汇。

ley [lei; le] *n.* 牧草地。

Ley·den [ˈleidn, ˈlaidn; ˋledn̩, ˋlaɪdn̩] *n.* 莱顿〔荷兰城市〕。~ ***jar*** [**bottle, vial**]【物】(在 Leyden 发明的)莱顿电瓶。

lez [lez; lɛz] *n.*〔美俚〕女同性恋者〔常带贬意, = lesbian〕。

leze majesty [liːz; liz] = lese majesty.

LF = low frequency【无】低频。

L / F = ledger folio 分类账页。

lf = left fielder (棒球)左外野[场](手)。

l.f. = light face【印】细体铅字。

l.f.c. = low-frequency current 低频电流。

L.F.TK = light fast tank 轻型快速坦克。

L.G. = **1.** Life Guards〔英〕近卫(骑兵)团。**2.** Low German 低地德语。

l / g = grams per litre 克 / 升。

L.G.O.C. = London General Omnibus Company〔英〕伦敦通用公共汽车公司。

l.h. = left hand【乐】左手。

L.H.A. = Lord High Admiral〔英旧〕海军大臣。

L.H.D. = *Litterarum Humaniorum Doctor* (= Doctor of Humane letters) 希腊,拉丁古典文学博士。

L.H.T. = Lord High Treasurer〔英旧〕财政大臣。

L.I. = **1.** Long Island 长岛。**2.** Light Infantry 轻步兵。**3.**【物】low-intensity 低强度的。

Li =【化】lithium. **li.** = link.

li [liː; li] *n.* (*pl.* ~)〔Chin.〕(中国里程单位)里。

li·a·bil·ity [ˌlaiəˈbiliti; ͵laɪəˋbɪlətɪ] *n.* **1.** 责任,义务。**2.**〔*pl.*〕负债,债务 (*opp.* assets). **3.** 倾向;易于…的倾向[性质]。**4.** 不利条件。*hold no* ~ *for damages* 不负赔偿责任。*limited* [*unlimited*] ~ 有限[无限]责任。~ *for military service* 有服兵役义务。*assets and liabilities* 资产与负债。*meet one's liabilities* 偿还债务。~ *to disease* 弱不禁风。~ *to error* 容易犯错误。*Poor handwriting is a* ~ *in getting a job.* 拙劣的书法是求职的不利条件。

li·a·ble [ˈlaiəbl; ˋlaɪəbl] *a.* **1.** (对…)应负(法律)责任的,有义务的。**2.** 应受的,应服从的。**3.** 有…倾向的,易…的,易陷于…的,易害…的;〔口〕大概,多半,很可能。*be* ~ *for a debt* = *be* ~ *to pay a debt* 有偿还债务责任。*be* ~ *to the law* 应服从法律。*be* ~ *to the penalty* 该受罚。*be* ~ *to tax* 应付税。*be* ~ *to catch cold* 容易伤风。*Difficulties are* ~ *to occur* 容易出问题。*He is* ~ *to fits of temper* 他动不动就发脾气。*He is* ~ *to come today.* 他今天很可能会来。

li·aise [liːˈeiz; lɪˋez] *vi.* (*-ais·ed*, *-ais·ing*)〔主英口〕与…建立联系,连络 (*with*)。

li·ai·son [li(ː)ˈeizɑːn, -zn; ͵lieˋzɔ̃, -zn] *n.* 〔F.〕**1.**【语】连音〔指法语中词尾的无声子音与后面一词的词头母音连结所成的发音;英语中指 r 与后面一词的词头母音连结所成的发音〕。**2.**【烹】加浓料〔使汤等浓厚用的鸡蛋等物〕。**3.** 私通。**4.**【军】联络。~ *officer* 联络官。

li·a·na [liˈɑːnə; lɪˋɑnə], **li·ane** [liˈɑːn; lɪˋɑn] *n.*【植】藤本植物,蔓生植物。~ **rubber** 藤胶。

liang [ljɑːŋ; ljɑŋ] *n.*〔Chin.〕(中国衡量单位)两。

li·ar [ˈlaiə; ˋlaɪɚ] *n.* 说谎的人。*Show me a* ~, *and I will show you a thief.*〔谚〕说谎是偷窃的开始。

Li·as [ˈlaiəs; ˋlaɪəs] *n.*【地】**1.** 里阿斯统(早侏罗世)。**2.**〔l-〕蓝色石灰岩。**Li·as·sic** [laiˈæsik; laɪˋæsɪk] *a.*

lib. = **1.** liberal. **2.** library; librarian. **3.**〔L.〕*liber* (= book). **4.**〔L.〕*libra* (= pound)。

L

lib [lib; lɪb] ***n.*** 〔口〕解放(=liberation)。Women's Lib 妇女解放(运动)。

li·ba·tion [laiˈbeiʃən; laɪˋbeʃən] ***n.*** **1.** (倒酒在地上祭神的)奠酒;祭奠用的酒。**2.** 〔谑〕饮酒,酒。

Lib·by [ˈlibi; ˋlɪbɪ] ***n.*** **1.** 莉比〔女子名, Elizabeth 的昵称〕。**2.** 利比〔姓氏〕。

li·bel [ˈlaibəl; ˋlaɪbl] **I** ***n.*** **1.** 诽谤文;【宗】诽谤的诉状。**2.**【法】诽谤,诽谤罪。**3.** 侮辱,对人不公平。*sue sb. for* ～ 控告某人犯诽谤罪。*The greater the truth, the greater* [*worse*] *the* ～. 〔谚〕事情越真实,诽谤越厉害〔相当于"道高一尺,魔高一丈"〕。*This photograph is a* ～ *on her*. 这张照片简直是诽谤〔把她照得太难看了〕。**II** ***vt.*** (〔英〕***-ll-***) **1.** 污蔑,诽谤。**2.**【法】发表诽谤…的文件;进行文字诽谤。**3.**【海事和教会法】提出书面控告;控诉。**4.** 对…作不好看的描画;对…不够公平。— ***vi.*** 诽谤。

li·bel(l)·ant [ˈlaibələnt; ˋlaɪbələnt] ***n.*** **1.** 诽谤者。**2.** (向海事或宗教裁判所起诉的)控告人。

li·bel(l)·ee [ˌlaibəˈliː; ˏlaɪbəˋli] ***n.*** **1.** 被诽谤者。**2.** (在海事或宗教裁判所中的)被控告者。

li·bel(l)·er, li·bel(l)·ist [ˈlaibələ, -list; ˋlaɪbələ˞, -lɪst] ***n.*** 诽谤者。

li·bel(l)·ous [ˈlaibələs; ˋlaɪbələs] ***a.*** **1.** 诽谤的。**2.** 爱中伤的。**-ly** ***ad.***

li·ber [ˈlaibə, ˈliːbɛə; ˋlaɪbə˞, ˋlibɛr] ***n.*** (*pl.* ***li·bri*** [ˈlaibrai, ˈliːbriː; ˋlaɪbraɪ]) 〔L.〕书册;簿册〔尤指契据登记簿〕。

lib·er·al [ˈlibərəl; ˋlɪbərəl] **I** ***a.*** **1.** 自由人的;不受束缚的。**2.** 大方的;慷慨的。**3.** 心胸宽大的,思想开明的;公正的,没有偏见的。**4.** 丰富的,充足的。**5.** 自由的,不拘泥于字义的,广泛的(解释等)。**6.** 自由主义的;〔L-〕自由党的。*He is* ～ *of* [*with*] *his money*. 他用钱大方。*a* ～ *table* 丰盛的饭菜。～ *ideas* 开明的思想。*a* ～ *translation* 意译。**II** ***n.*** **1.** 思想开明的人。**2.** 自由主义者。**3.** 〔L-〕自由党党员,支持自由党的人。～ **arts** 文科〔原意为自由人应具有的学识〕。～ **education** 文科教育〔相对于职业教育,专门技术教育而言,原意为自由人应受的教育〕。～**-minded** ***a.*** 气量宽宏的;思想解放的。**L-Party** 〔英〕自由党。**L- Unionist** 〔英〕自由统一党员。**-ly** ***ad.*** **-ness** ***n.***

lib·er·al·ism [ˈlibərəlizəm; ˋlɪbərəlˏɪzəm] ***n.*** 自由主义。**lib·er·al·ist** ***n.***, ***a.*** 自由主义者(的)。**lib·er·al·is·tic** [ˌlibərəˈlistik; ˏlɪbərəˋlɪstɪk] ***a.*** 自由主义的。

lib·er·al·i·ty [ˌlibəˈræliti; ˏlɪbəˋrælətɪ] ***n.*** **1.** 思想开明;气量大;公平;豪爽,磊落。**2.** 大方,慷慨;礼物。**3.** 丰富,丰满。

lib·er·al·ize [ˈlibərəlaiz; ˋlɪbərəlˏaɪz] ***vt.*** **1.** 使自由化;使自由主义化。**2.** 放宽限制。**3.** 解除官方控制。**-ization** ***n.***

lib·er·ate [ˈlibəreit; ˋlɪbəˏret] ***vt.*** **1.** 解放,释放;解除;使脱离。**2.**【化】释出,放出;【物】使(力)起作用。**3.** 〔俚〕偷,劫掠〔尤指对于被打败的敌人〕。～ *the mind from prejudice* 解除心中偏见。*John* ～*d two cameras*. 约翰缴获了两个照相机。**-d** 被解放了的 (*the* ～*d area* 解放区)。

lib·er·a·tion [ˌlibəˈreiʃən; ˏlɪbəˋreʃən] ***n.*** **1.** 释放,解放。**2.** 〔化〕释出,放出,析出(作用)。*the* ～ *of heat* 放热。**-ism** ***n.*** 政教分立主义。**-ist** **1.** ***n.*** (妇女)解放组织的成员;政教分立主义者。**2.** ***a.*** 解放组织成员的;政教分立主义者的。

lib·er·a·tor [ˈlibəˌreitə; ˋlɪbəˏretə˞] ***n.*** 解放者,释放者。

Li·ber·i·a [laiˈbiəriə; laɪˋbɪrɪə] ***n.*** 利比里亚〔非洲〕。

Li·ber·i·an [laiˈbiəriən; laɪˋbɪrɪən] **I** ***a.*** 利比里亚的;利比里亚人的;利比里亚文化的。**II** ***n.*** 利比里亚人。

lib·er·tar·i·an [ˌlibəˈtɛəriən; ˏlɪbə˞ˋtɛrɪən] **I** ***n.*** **1.** (思想或行动等的)自由论者。**2.**【哲】自由意志论者。**II** ***a.*** 自由的;自由论者的;自由意志论者的。**-ism** ***n.*** 自由意志论。

li·ber·té, é·ga·li·té, fra·ter·ni·té [liberˈtei egaːliˈtei frɑterniˈte; lɪbɛrˋte ɛgalɪˋte frɑtɛrnɪˋteɪ] 〔F.〕自由、平等、博爱〔法国一七八九年资产阶级革命的口号〕。

li·ber·ti·ci·dal [liˌbəːtiˈsaidl; lɪˏbə˞təˋsaɪdl] ***a.*** 扼杀自由的。

li·ber·ti·cide [liˈbəːtisaid; lɪˋbə˞təˏsaɪd] **I** ***n.*** **1.** 扼杀自由。**2.** 扼杀自由者。**II** ***a.*** = liberticidal.

lib·er·tine [ˈlibə(ː)tain, -tiːn; ˋlɪbə˞ˏtin] **I** ***n.*** **1.** 浪子,放荡的人。**2.**【宗】自由思想家。**3.** 古罗马获得自由的奴隶。**II** ***a.*** 放荡的;自由思想的。*a chartered* ～ 〔谑〕天下公认的浪子。

lib·er·tin·ism [ˈlibətinizəm; ˋlɪbə˞tɪnɪzəm] ***n.*** **1.** 放荡,放纵。**2.**【宗】自由思想。

lib·er·ty [ˈlibəti; ˋlɪbə˞tɪ] ***n.*** **1.** 自由(权)。**2.** 解放,释放。**3.** 〔*pl.*〕特许权;特权〔自治权,选举权,参政权等〕。**4.** 〔英〕自由地区,特许区域;(管)辖区;(某种)范围。**5.** 放肆,无礼,不客气;冒昧,擅自行动。**6.**【哲】意志自由。**7.**【海】(短时间)上岸许可〔较长时间为 leave〕。～ *of action* 行动的自由。～ *of choice* 选择的自由。～ *of conscience* (= religious ～) 宗教[信仰]自由。*natural* ～ 天赋自由权。*Give me* ～, *or give me death*. 不自由,毋宁死。*the liberties of the city of London* 伦敦市的特权。～ *of a prison* 犯人放风地段。*be guilty of a* ～ 放肆无礼。*Excuse my liberties*. 请原谅我的冒昧。～ *in one's translation* 翻译不够忠实。*You may have the* ～ *of this room*. 你可以随时使用这个房间。***at*** ～ **1.** 自由,随意 (*at* ～ *to air one's views* 可以自由发表意见)。**2.** (人、东西)闲着 (*I am very busy now, but I'll be at* ～ *presently*. 我现在很忙,不久就有空了)。***get one's*** ～ 获得自由,得到释放。***set sb. at*** ～ 释放某人;恢复某人的自由。***take liberties with*** **1.** 跟…无礼;调戏(妇女) (*Don't take liberties with a stranger*. 别同陌生的人无礼)。**2.** 损害(*take liberties with one's health* 糟蹋身体)。**3.** 歪曲,任意改变 (*take liberties with a text* 任意更改原文。*take liberties with grammar* 不顾语法规则)。***take the*** ～ ***of doing*** [***to do***] 冒昧行事。**L- Bell** "自由钟"〔美国费城独立厅的大钟,1776 年 7 月 4 日鸣该钟宣布美国独立;1835 年破损〕。～ **cap** = cap of liberty. ～ **hall** 便厅〔指客人可以在此自由自在、不拘礼节的房间〕。～ **man** 〔英〕获准上岸的水手。～ **pass**【军】外出许可,外出许可证。**L-Ship** "自由轮"〔美国第二次世界大战期间大量建造的一种万吨商船〕。

li·bid·i·nal [liˈbidnəl; lɪˋbɪdənəl] ***a.*** libido 的,性欲的。**-ly** ***ad.***

li·bid·i·nous [liˈbidinəs; lɪˋbɪdənəs] ***a.*** 好色的,淫荡的。**-ly** ***ad.*** **-ness** ***n.***

li·bi·do [liˈbaidəu; lɪˋbaɪdo] ***n.*** 性的本能,性欲;【心】"利比多"〔弗洛伊德心理分析学说中的精神动力,实际即是性的本能〕。

Li·bra [ˈlaibrə; ˋlaɪbrə] ***n.*** 〔L.〕【天】天平座;天平宫。

li·bra [ˈlaibrə; ˋlaɪbrə] ***n.*** 〔L.〕 (*pl.* ***-brae*** [-briː; -bri]) **1.** 磅〔略 lb〕。**2.** [ˈliːbrɑ; ˋlibrɑ] 镑〔略 £〕。

li·braire [liˈbrɛə; lɪˋbrɛr] ***n.*** 〔F.〕书店;〔古〕图书馆。

li·brar·i·an [laiˈbrɛəriən; laɪˋbrɛrɪən] ***n.*** **1.** 图书馆长,图书管理员。**2.** 图书馆管理学专家。～**ship** 图书馆长[图书管理学专家]的职位[资格]。

li·brar·y [ˈlaibrəri; ˋlaɪˏbrɛrɪ] ***n.*** **1.** 图书馆,图库;藏书楼;藏书。**2.** 丛书,文库。*a circulating* ～ 流动图书馆。*a free* ～ 免费图书馆。*reference* ～ (书不外借的)参考图书馆。*have a* ～ *of 5000 volumes* 藏书五千册。*Everyman's L-* 〔英〕人人文库[丛书]。***a walking*** ～ 活字典,博学家。～ **edition** 图书馆版〔开本较大,较坚固的布面精装本〕。**L- of Congress** 国会图书馆〔美国于 1800 年建立的国家图书馆〕。～ **science** 图书馆学。～ **steps** 图

L

书馆用(可折叠的)小梯。

li·brate [ˈlaibreit; ˋlaɪbret] *vi*. **1.** 摆动。**2.** 保持平衡。

li·bra·tion [laiˈbreiʃən; laɪˋbreʃən] *n*. **1.** 振动,摆动;平衡。**2.**【天】天平动。*optical* ~ 光学天平动。~ *of the moon* 月球的天平动。

li·bra·to·ry [ˈlaibrətəri; ˋlaɪbrətorɪ] *a*. 摆动的,振动的;保持平衡的。

li·bret·tist [liˈbretist; lɪˋbrɛtɪst] *n*. (歌剧的)脚本作者。

li·bret·to [liˈbretəu; lɪˋbrɛto] *n*. (*pl*. ~*s*, *-ti* [-tiː; -ti]) 歌剧脚本。

Li·bre·ville [ˌliːbrəˈviːl; ˏlibrəˋvil] *n*. 利伯维尔〔加蓬首都〕。

li·bri [ˈlaibrai; ˋlaɪbraɪ] *n*. liber 的复数。

li·bri·form [ˈlaibrəˌfɔːm; ˋlaɪbrɪˏfɔrm] *a*.【植】韧型的。

Lib·ri·um [ˈlibriəm; ˋlɪbrɪəm] *n*. 〔或 l-〕【药】利眠宁 (= chlordiazepoxide)。

Lib·y·a [ˈlibiə; ˋlɪbɪə] *n*. 利比亚〔非洲〕。

Lib·y·an [ˈlibjən, -biən; ˋlɪbjən, -bɪən] **I** *a*. 利比亚的;利比亚人的。**II** *n*. 利比亚人。

lice [lais; laɪs] *n*. louse 的复数。

li·ce·i·ty [laiˈsiːəti; laɪˋsiətɪ] *n*. 合法。

li·cence, li·cense [ˈlaisəns; ˋlaɪsns] **I** *n*. **1.** 许可,特许;许可证,特许证,执照。**2.** 放纵,放肆;(文艺、美术、音乐等的)奔放,不羁,破格。*a* ~ *to sell spirits* 出售酒类许可证。*give full* ~ *to do sth*. 授权放手做某事。*Have I your* ~ *to remove the fence*? 你让我拆除这篱笆吗? *a* ~ *to practise medicine* 行医执照。*apply for a driving* ~ 申请驾驶执照。*grant a marriage* ~ 颁发结婚证书。*special* ~ (坎特伯雷大主教所发)结婚特别许可证。*The invading troops displayed the most unbridled* ~. 入侵军队胡作非为到了极点。**under** ~ 领有执照。**II** *vt*. 批准,许可;发许可证[执照]。~ ***sb. to practise as a doctor*** 批准某人作开业医生。~ **fee** 牌照费。~ **plate** [**tag**] (汽车等的)牌照。

li·cenced, li·censed [ˈlaisənst; ˋlaɪsnst] *a*. 得到许可的,领有执照的;公认的。*a* ~ *house* 有执照的酒店[妓院]。~ *premises* 特准卖酒的店家[地区]。*a* ~ *satirist* 公认的讽刺家。

li·cen·cee, -see [ˌlaisənˈsiː; ˏlaɪsnˋsi] *n*. 被许可的人,领有执照[许可证]的人;特许酒店。

li·cen·cer, li·cen·ser, li·cen·sor [ˈlaisənsə; ˋlaɪsənsɚ] *n*. 认可者,发许可证[执照]者。*a* ~ *of plays* [*films, the press*] 剧本[电影、出版物]检查官。

li·cen·sure [ˈlaisənʃə, -ˌsuə; ˋlaɪsnʃə, -sur] *n*. 许可证的发给〔如营业执照等〕。

li·cen·ti·ate [laiˈsenʃiit; laɪˋsɛnʃɪɪt] *n*. **1.** 硕士。**2.** (大学或学会等认可的)有开业资格的人。**3.** 无牧师资格而被允许传道的人。

li·cen·tious [laiˈsenʃəs; laɪˋsɛnʃəs] *a*. **1.** 放肆的,放荡的,淫荡的。**2.** 〔罕〕不顾规则的,破格的(文体等)。**-ly** *ad*. **-ness** *n*.

li·cet [ˈlaiset; ˋlaɪsɛt] 〔L.〕(那是)准许[合法]的。

lich [litʃ; lɪtʃ] *n*. 〔Scot. 英方〕死尸,尸体。

li·chee [ˈliːˌtʃiː; ˋliˏtʃi] *n*. = litchi.

li·chen [ˈlaikən; ˋlaɪkɪn] **I** *n*. **1.**【植】地衣。**2.**【医】苔癣。**II** *vt*. 使生满地衣。

li·chened [ˈlaikend; ˋlaɪkɪnd] *a*. 生着[盖满]地衣的。

li·chen·in [ˈlaikənin; ˋlaɪkənɪn] *n*.【化】地衣淀粉。

li·chen·ol·o·gy [ˌlaikəˈnɔlədʒi; ˏlaɪkəˋnɑlədʒɪ] *n*.【植】地衣学。

li·chen·ous [ˈlaikinəs; ˋlaɪkɪnəs] *a*. **1.** 生满地衣的。**2.** 苔癣病的。

lich·gate [ˈlitʃgeit; ˋlɪtʃget] *n*. 〔英〕有屋顶的公墓入口〔可暂时停放棺材等待主持牧师等到来〕。

licht [likt; lɪkt] *a*., *ad*., *n*., *vi*., *vt*. 〔Scot.〕light 的异体。

Li·ci·an [ˈliʃiən; ˋlɪʃɪən] **I** *a*. 利西亚的;利西亚人的;利西亚语的。〔利西亚,西南亚细亚地中海的古国〕。**II** *n*. **1.** 利西亚人。**2.** 利西亚语。

lic·it [ˈlisit; ˋlɪsɪt] *a*. 合法的,正当的。**-ly** *ad*.

lick [lik; lɪk] **I** *vt*. **1.** 舔;舔吃。**2.** (波浪、火焰等)触及,蔓延,吞没,掠过。**3.** 〔口〕鞭打;打败,胜过。~ *a saucer clean* 把碟子舔干净。*The flames* ~*ed up everything there*. 火焰吞没了那里的一切。*I cannot* ~ *a fault out of him*. 我无论怎样打都改不了他的缺点。*That man deserves to be well* ~*ed*. 那个人应当被人狠狠揍一顿。*This* ~*s me*. 我弄不清楚这是怎么回事。— *vi*. **1.** 像舔东西一样蔓延;(波浪)轻轻拍打。**2.** 胜过,赢得,高速行进。*go off as hard as one can* ~ 赶快跑走。~ **(*all*) *creation*** = ~ ***everything*** 〔俚〕胜过一切;无可比拟。~ ***into shape*** 使像样;教养;锻炼。~ ***off*** [***away***] 舔吃;舔尽。~ ***one's lips*** [***chops***] 切盼,馋涎欲滴。~ ***sb.'s boots*** [***feet, shoes, spittle***] 巴结某人,奉承某人。~ ***the dust*** 被杀;屈服。~ ***up*** 舔光;(火焰)烧光。**II** *n*. **1.** 舔,一舔。**2.** 一舔的量,少量,些许。**3.** 〔美〕野兽跑去舐盐的盐渍地 (= salt lick)。**4.** 〔俚〕重打,痛殴。**5.** 〔口〕速度,速力。**6.** 〔俚〕轮到的机会。**7.** 〔美俚〕(即兴插入的)爵士音乐装饰乐句。*put on a* ~ *of paint* 涂上一层薄漆。*big* ~*s* 〔美、澳〕费力的工作。*at a great* ~ = (*at*) *full* ~ 急忙。***give a*** ~ ***and a promise*** (把工作)马马虎虎做好〔约定以后再去完成〕。***give sb. a*** ~ ***with the rough side of one's tongue*** 对某人出言粗鲁,出恶言伤害某人。***put in best*** [***big, solid***] ~***s*** 尽最大努力,苦干。~**-spit(tle)** 马屁精,奉承者。

lick·er·ish [ˈlikəriʃ; ˋlɪkərɪʃ] *a*. **1.** 讲究吃的;贪吃的;狼吞虎咽的。**2.** 渴望的。**3.** 好色的,淫荡的。**-ly** *ad*. **-ness** *n*.

lick·e·ty-split [ˈlikətiˈsplit; ˋlɪkətɪˋsplɪt] *ad*. 〔口〕极为迅速地。

lick·ing [ˈlikiŋ; ˋlɪkɪŋ] *n*. **1.** 舔。**2.** 〔口〕狠狠的一顿打;〔俚〕惨败。***get a good*** ~ 被痛打。***give sb. a good*** ~ 痛打某人。***take the*** ~ 遭惨败。

Lick Ob·ser·va·to·ry 李克天文台〔美国加利福尼亚州汉密尔顿山顶上〕。

lic·o·rice [ˈlikəris; ˋlɪkərɪs] *n*. = liquorice.

lic·tor [ˈliktə; ˋlɪktɚ] *n*. (古罗马的)执法吏〔肩荷象征刑法的束棒,在行政长官前面喝道,并执行捕捉人犯等事的小吏〕。

lid [lid; lɪd] **I** *n*. **1.** 盖子;〔美俚〕帽子。**2.** 眼睑 (= eyelid)。**3.**【动】= operculum. **4.** 制止,取缔。**5.** 〔美俚〕一小包大麻烟〔约一盎司〕。*clamp* [*clap*] *a* ~ *on gambling* 取缔赌博。***blow one's*** ~ 发脾气,勃然大怒。***blow the*** ~ ***off sth***. 揭盖子,把丑事公开出来。***flip one's*** ~ 〔美俚〕**1.** 大发脾气。**2.** 失去理智。**3.** 放声狂笑。***keep down the*** ~ = ***keep the*** ~ ***on*** 隐瞒罪恶。***put the*** ~ ***on*** **1.** 〔英俚〕结束。**2.** 〔美俚〕禁止,取缔。**3.** 胜过一切,冠绝。***sit on the*** ~ 压制;镇压。***take the*** ~ ***off*** 揭盖子,揭露丑事。***the*** ~ ***is on*** 事情完蛋了,无话可说了。***with the*** ~ ***off*** 开着盖儿;使丑事暴露于众。**II** *vt*. (*-dd-*) 给装盖子,盖盖子。

li·dar [ˈlaidə; ˋlaɪdɚ] *n*. **1.** 雷射[激光]雷达。**2.** 雷射[激光]定位器。**3.** 光探测和测距。

lid·ded [ˈlidid; ˋlɪdɪd] *a*. **1.** 有盖子的,盖着的。**2.** 长着…眼睑的;眼睑呈…状的。*with heavy-*~ *eyes* 眼皮重垂着。

Lid·del(l) [ˈlidl, liˈdel; ˋlɪdl, lɪˋdɛl] *n*. 利德尔〔姓氏〕。

lid·less [ˈlidlis; ˋlɪdlɪs] *a*. **1.** 无盖的。**2.** 无眼睑的。**3.** 〔诗〕(眼睛)睁着的;注视的。

Li·do [ˈliːdəu; ˋlido] *n*. **1.** 丽都〔意大利威尼斯附近一个小岛,为著名的游乐地〕。**2.** 〔l-〕海滨浴场;(露天)游泳池〔尤指远洋客轮上的〕。

lie[1] [lai; laɪ] **I** *vi*. (*lay* [lei; le]; *lain* [lein; len]; *lying*) **1.** 躺,横卧〔过去分词不常用, *I have lain down* 可改作 *I have been lying down*〕. ~ *face downward*

俯卧。～ *in bed* 睡觉。～ *on a bed* 躺在床上。～ *on one's back* 仰卧。～ *on one's side* 侧卧。**2.**〔常带表语〕(静止不动地)呆着。～ *idle* 不活动;(资金)呆滞。～ *motionless* 呆着不动。～ *sick* 卧病。**3.**(东西)被平放。*Let it* ～. 让它在那里(别动)。*Snow* ～*s thick on the fields*. 田野里铺着厚厚一层雪。*The book* ～*s open on the table*. 那本书摊在桌上。*The land* ～*s waste*. 土地荒废了。**4.** 东西被存放。*the fund lying at the bank* 存在银行的基金。**5.** 被埋葬。～ *in the cemetery* 葬在公墓。**6.** 在,位于。*Japan* ～*s* (*to the*) *east of China*. 日本位于中国以东。*The house* ～*s high*. 这房子坐落在高处。**7.**(抽象事物)存在,在于,有(…关系)。*How* ～*s the land*? 情况如何。*The choice* ～*s between death and dishonour*. 在死亡与受辱之间任择其一。*The difficulty* ～*s here*. 困难就在这里。**8.**(风景等)展现,伸展。*A bright future* ～*s ahead*. 前途光明。*the landscape lying before us* 在我们面前展现的风景。*The path* ～*s along the coast*. 路线沿着海岸展开。**9.**(船只)停泊;(部队)驻扎;(猎鸟等)蹲着。～ *at anchor* (抛锚)停泊着。**10.** 处于某种状态。*Don't leave your books lying about*. 别把你的书四处乱扔。*His plans* ～ *hidden*. 他的计划还不清楚。*How do they* ～ *to each other*? 他们之间的关系怎样? **11.**【法】成立,可受理。*The appeal does not* ～. 控诉不成立。***as far as in me*** ～***s*** 尽我的力量。～ ***about*** 散在。～ ***against*** 靠在。～ ***along*** 躺成大字形,尽量伸直手脚;【海】因侧风歪朝一边。～ ***along the land*** [***shore***] 沿岸航行。～ ***at sb.'s door*** (责任)在某人。～ ***at one's heart*** …挂在心上;老是思慕着。～ ***at the mercy of*** 处在…操纵之下,被…支配着。～ ***back*** 向后靠。～ ***by*** **1.** 躺在…边上。**2.** 近在手边,由…保管着。**3.** 放在一旁,没有使用。**4.** 休息。**5.**【海】= ～ to. ～ [***keep***] ***close*** 躲着,挤在一块。～ ***dead*** 〔美〕躲着,隐藏着。～ ***doggo*** 〔口〕隐伏不动。～ ***down*** **1.** 躺下。**2.**〔口〕躺在睡椅上休息(～ *down on the job* 不干活,磨洋工)。**3.** 屈服;盲从(*take it lying down* 俯首贴耳地屈服)。～ ***down under*** 甘受(侮辱等)。～ ***heavy*** [***hard***] (***up***) ***on*** 压迫,使痛苦。～ ***in*** **1.**(分娩后)坐月子。**2.**(原因、本质等)在于,存在于(*The case* ～*s in a nutshell*. 这件事情用一句话就可以说明了)。～ ***in sb.*** **1.** 集中在,全在(*All their hopes* ～ *in him*. 他们的希望全在他身上)。**2.** 依…而定,系于;…能做得到。～ ***in the way*** 妨害,阻碍。～ ***in wait for*** 埋伏着等待。～ ***low*** **1.** 伏卧。**2.** 隐蔽,不露声色。**3.** 死。**4.** 受屈辱。～ ***off*** **1.**(船)稍微离开(陆地或他船)。**2.**〔俚〕(赛跑中)初跑时控制速度。**3.** 暂时停止工作,歇一歇。～ ***on*** [***upon***] **1.** 落在…的肩上(*It* ～ *on us to lick illiteracy*. 扫除文盲是我们的责任)。**2.** 依赖(～ *on the result* 要看结果如何)。**3.** 成为…的负担,压迫(～ *heavy on one's conscience* 良心非常难受。～ *heavy on one's stomach* (食物)滞积胃中)。～ ***open*** 开着,暴露着。～ ***over*** **1.** 事情暂时搁置,缓办(*Let the matter* ～ *over until next month*. 把这个问题留到下月再解决吧)。**2.**(支票等)过期未付。～ ***to*** (船)顶风停住;集中全力在…(*The crew lay to their oars*. 船员拼命划桨)。～ ***under*** 蒙受,遭到。～ ***up*** **1.** 卧床;病倒(不能出门)。**2.** 退隐。**3.**(船)入坞。～ ***with*** **1.** 和…发生性关系。**2.**(责任、义务、决定权等)在于…(*It* ～*s with you to decide*. 该由你决定)。**II** ***n*.** **1.** 位置,状态。**2.** 巢,穴,窝。**3.**(高尔夫球的)球位。**4.**〔英口〕躺;休息。*go and have a* ～ 去躺一下。～**-abed** 睡懒觉的人。～**-down** **1.** 小睡,小憩。**2.**(在大街等)卧地抗议示威。～**-in** **1.**〔口〕睡懒觉。**2.** 卧地示威。

lie[2] [lai; laɪ] **I** ***n*.** **1.** 谎言,谎话。**2.** 虚伪,欺诈;假相。*L-s have short legs*.〔谚〕谎言终究要败露。*act a* ～ (用实际行动)骗人。*a black* ～ 用心险恶的谎话。*a white* ～ 无恶意的谎话。*His promise was a big* ～. 他的诺言是个大欺骗。*worship a* ～ 盲目崇拜错误的事物。*He would not take the* ～. 他不服气别人说他撒谎。***a*** ～ (***made***) ***out of*** (***the***) ***whole cloth*** = ***a*** ～ ***with a latchet*** 说得天花乱坠的谎话。***give sb. the*** ～ 指责某人说谎。***give the*** ～ ***to*** 当面拆穿…的谎话;证明虚伪,和…相矛盾。***live a*** ～ 过欺骗人的生活。***nail a*** ～ ***to the counter*** 揭穿弄虚作假[谎言]。***swap*** ～***s*** 〔美口〕讲空话,闲谈,胡扯。***the big*** ～ **1.** 弥天大谎。**2.** 编造谎言并大肆宣传的骗人手段。**II** ***vi*.**, ***vt*.** (***lied***; ***lying***) 说谎;欺骗;迷惑。～ *oneself out of trouble* 聊以自慰。～ *sb. into doing sth*. 骗某人去做某事。～ *sb. out of his money* 骗某人钱财。～ ***away*** 骗取(名誉等),骗去。～ ***in one's teeth*** [***throat***] 〔古〕无耻地瞪着眼[当面]撒谎。～ ***like a gas-meter*** 乱撒谎。～ **detector** 〔美〕测谎器。

Lieb·frau·milch [ˈliːbfrauˌmilk, G. ˈliːpfrauˌmilkh; ˋlibfraʊˏmɪlk, ˋlipfrəʊˏmɪkh] ***n*.** 〔G.〕圣母酒〔一种莱茵区白葡萄酒〕。

Lie·big [ˈliːbig; ˋlɪbɪg], **J. Baron von** 李比希〔1803—1873,德国化学家〕。

Liech·ten·stein [ˈliktənˌstain; ˋlɪktənˏstaɪn] ***n*.** 列支敦士登〔欧洲〕。

lied [liːd; lid] ***n*.** (*pl*. ***lied·er*** [-ə; -ɚ]) 〔G.〕歌曲,浪漫曲〔主要指十九世纪德国的浪漫曲〕。

Lie·der·kranz [ˈliːdəˌkrɑːnts; ˋlidɚˏkrɑnts] ***n*.** 〔G.〕**1.**【商标】歌王干酪。**2.** 男声合唱团。**3.** 一组歌曲。

lief [liːf; lif] **I** ***ad*.** 欣然,乐意地。～ ***or loath*** 不管愿不愿意。***would*** [〔古〕***had***] ***as*** ～ ... (*as*) 宁…(不…);(与其…)不如…(*I would* [*had*] *as* ～ *go there as anywhere*. 我宁愿到那里也不到别处)。***would*** [***had***] ***liefer*** ... ***than*** ... 宁…不…,与其…不如…(*I would liefer die than surrender*. 我宁愿死也不投降)。**II** ***a*.** 〔古〕**1.** 乐意的,情愿的。**2.** 亲爱的。

Li·ège [liˈeiʒ; lɪˋeʒ] ***n*.** 列日〔比利时城市〕。

liege [liːdʒ; lidʒ] **I** ***n*.** **1.** 君主,王侯。**2.**〔the ～s〕臣民,家臣。**II** ***a*.** **1.** 君主的,至上的。**2.** 臣民的;君臣关系的。*my* ～! (称呼)陛下! *a* ～ *lord* 君主。～ *subjects* 臣民。**3.** 忠诚的。**-man** **1.** 臣民。**2.** 忠实的部下。

li·en[1] [ˈli(ː)ən; liən] ***n*.**【法】扣押权,留置权。***have a*** ～ ***on*** 对…有留置权。***have a prior*** ～ ***on*** 对…有先取权。

li·en[2] [ˈlaien; ˋlaɪən] ***n*.** [L.]【解】脾(= spleen)。**-al** ***a*.**【医】脾炎的。

li·e·ni·tis [ˌlaiəˈnaitis; ˏlaɪəˋnaɪtɪs] ***n*.**【医】脾炎。

li·er [ˈlaiə; ˋlaɪɚ] ***n*.** 躺卧者。

li·erne [liːˈəːn; lɪˋɝn] ***n*.**【建】枝肋。

lieu [ljuː; lu] ***n*.** 处所。***in*** ～ ***of*** 代,代替。

Lieut. = Lieutenant.

Lieut. Col. = Lieutenant Colonel〔英〕陆军[海军陆战队]中校;〔美〕陆军[空军、海军陆战队]中校。

Lieut. Comdr. = Lieutenant Commander〔英、美〕海军少校。

Lieut. Gen. = Lieutenant General〔英〕陆军[海军陆战队]中将;〔美〕陆军[空军、海军陆战队]中将。

Lieut. Gov. = Lieutenant Governor (省或地区的)代理总督,副总督;〔美〕副州长。

lieu·ten·an·cy [〔英陆军〕lefˈtenənsi, 〔英海军〕ləˈt-, 〔美〕ljuːˈt-; lɛfˋtɛnənsɪ, ləˋt-, ljuˋt-] ***n*.** 陆军中尉[海军上尉等]的职位[任期]。

lieu·ten·ant [〔英陆军〕lefˈtenənt; lɛfˋtɛnənt; 〔英海军〕ləˈt-; ləˋt-; 〔美〕ljuːˈt-; ljuˋt-] ***n*.** **1.** 副官。**2.**〔英〕陆军中尉,海军上尉。**3.**〔美〕海军上尉。*deputy* ～〔英〕副郡长。*a first* ～〔美〕陆军[空军]中尉,海军中尉。*a second* ～〔中、美〕陆军[空军]少尉;〔英〕陆军少尉〔空军少尉叫 *pilot officer*〕。*a* ～ *of junior grade*〔美〕海军中尉。*a sub-* ～〔英〕海军中尉。*an acting sub-* ～〔英〕海军少尉。～ **colonel** 陆军中校。～ **commander** 海军少校。～ **general** 陆军中将。～ **governor**〔英〕代理总督,

L

副总督;〔美〕代理州长,副州长。

lieve [liːv; liv] **ad.**, **a.** = lief.

life [laif; laɪf] **n.** (*pl.* **lives** [laivz;laɪvz]) **1.** 生命,性命。**2.** 一生;寿命;【原】(亚原子粒子的)生命期;使用期限,耐久性。**3.** 人生,人事;世间,尘世。**4.** 生计,生活。**5.** 传记。**6.** 〔集合词〕生物。**7.** 实物;原物(大小)。**8.** 生命力;精神,生气;弹性;精华,主要力量。**9.** 被保险者。**10.** 无期徒刑。*Many lives were lost*. 死了不少人。*sacrifice* [*give*, *lay down*] *one's ~ for the country* 为国牺牲。*There is no ~ on the moon*. 月球上没有生命。*the average ~ of a nation* 一国人口的平均寿命。*the ~ of an artificial satellite* 人造卫星的寿命。*the ~ of the present Government* 现内阁的寿命。*While there is ~ there is hope*. 〔谚〕一息尚存,希望不灭;留得青山在,不怕没柴烧。*a ~ of struggle* 战斗的一生。*a matter of ~ and death* 生死攸关的事情。*devote one's whole ~ to the study of science* 一辈子献身于研究科学。*high* [*low*] *~* 上层[下层]生活。*lead* [*live*] *a happy ~* 过幸福生活。*political ~* 政治生涯。*struggle for ~* 生存竞争。*way of ~* 生活方式。*begin ~ as a worker* 工人出身。*enter upon ~* 踏进社会。*get on in ~* 立身处世。*see much of ~* 见过不少世面。*see nothing of ~* 没见过世面。*The L- of Plato* 《柏拉图传》。*animal ~* 动物。*bird ~* 鸟类。*forest ~* 林中生物。*insect ~* 昆虫。*plant ~* 植物。*a ~ class* 人体写生课。*a still ~* 静物画。*as large as ~* 像实物那样大。*The portrait is drawn from* (*the*) *~*. 这幅像是写生的。*The portrait is drawn to the ~*. 这幅像画得惟妙惟肖。*full of ~* 生气勃勃。*add* [*give*] *~ to an article* 增加文章的生气。*the ~ of the society* 社会的中心人物。*The batsman was given a ~*. 击球员获得新机会。*a bad ~* 估计活不到平均寿命的人。*a good ~* 估计会超过平均寿命的人。*my dear ~* 我的命根子。*If found guilty, he will get ~*. 如果证实有罪,他将被判处无期徒刑。*the ~ of a bow* 弓的弹力。***a future ~*** 【宗】来生。***all one's ~*** 一辈子,毕生,终生。***anything for a ~*** 只要能安宁,什么都行。***as much as one's ~ is worth*** 〔口〕性命攸关。***attempt the ~ of sb.*** 企图弄死某人。***be settled in ~*** 生活得到安顿。***Bless my ~*** = Bless me. ***bother*** [***harass***, ***nag***, ***plague***, ***worry***] ***the ~ out of sb.*** 跟某人纠缠不休。***breathe*** [***infuse***] (***a***) ***new ~ into*** = give new ~ to 给予生气,赋予生机。***bring to ~*** 使苏醒,使复活。***carry*** [***take***] ***one's ~ in one's hands*** 手里提着脑袋过日子,过冒险生活。***choke the ~ out of sb.*** 把某人闷死。***come to ~*** 苏醒过来。***depart*** (***from***) ***this ~*** 离开人间,逝世。***escape with bare ~*** 仅以身免,死里逃生。***escape with ~ and limb*** 仅以身免,死里逃生。***eternal ~*** 【宗】永生。***expectation of ~*** (= 〔美〕 ***~ expectancy***) 估计寿命。***fight for dear ~*** 死拼,作殊死战。***flee*** [***run***] ***for dear*** [***one's***] ***~*** 拼命跑走。***for ~*** **1.** 终身。**2.** 为逃[保]命。***for one's ~*** = ***for dear*** [***very***] ***~*** **1.** 为逃[保]命。**2.** 拼命。***for the ~ of me*** 即使要我的命,无论如何(也不…等)。***from*** (***the***) ***~*** 从原物,用原物做范本。***get a chance in ~*** 得到出头[发迹]的机会。***have*** [***get***] ***a ~*** 过着[过上]正常的和丰富多彩的生活。***have the time of one's ~*** 〔俚〕过着一生中最快乐的时期。***How's ~*** 〔口〕你近来生活好么? ***I'll bet my ~*** 我敢打赌。***in ~*** **1.** 生前,活着的时候 (*late in ~* 在晚年)。**2.** 完全,全然 (*anything in ~* (无论)什么都。*nothing in ~* 绝没有,毫不)。***insure one's ~*** 保人寿险。***lay down one's ~*** 抛弃生命,牺牲生命。***lead a fast ~*** 过放荡的生活。***lead sb. a dog's ~*** 使某人过悲惨的生活。***lead*** [***live***] ***a double ~*** 过双重人格的生活,搞两面派。***~ for ~*** 以命偿命。***lose one's ~*** 死。***make one's own ~*** 自己谋生。***not on your ~*** 〔口〕绝不,绝不可能。***on my ~*** = upon my ~. ***pawn one's ~*** 以生命保证。***raise*** [***recall***] ***to ~*** 使苏醒,使复活。***ride for dear ~*** 拼命奔驰。***safe in ~ and limb*** 安全无恙。***see ~*** **1.** 交游广。**2.** 见世面。***seek the ~ of*** = attempt the ~ of. ***sell one's ~ dearly*** 奋勇杀敌,负伤阵亡。***small ~*** (肖像)比真人略小的尺寸。***take*** [***get***] ***a new*** [***fresh***] ***lease of ~*** 死里逃生。***take one's*** (***own***) ***~*** 自杀。***take one's ~ in both hands and eat it*** 过惊涛骇浪的冒险生活。***take sb.'s ~*** 干掉某人。***the ~ of Riley*** 〔美俚〕放纵的生活。***the ~ of the party*** 社交场合中的中心人物。***the ~ of the world to come*** = ***the other*** [***future***] ***~*** 来世。***this ~*** 现世。***to the ~*** 大小和实物一样,逼真。***true to ~*** 逼真,栩栩如生。***upon*** [***'pon***] ***my ~*** 拼着这条命,誓必。**~-and-death**, **~-or-death** **a.** 生死攸关的,极重要的。**~ annuity** 终身年金。**~ assurance** 〔英〕 = ~ insurance. **~ belt** 救生带。**~blood** **1.** 〔诗〕生命必需的血液,鲜血;〔喻〕生命线,命脉;力量的泉源。**2.** 嘴唇[眼睑]的痉挛。**~boat** 救生艇。**~ boat ethics** 救生艇伦理〔指处于紧急情况下的权宜之计,此时往往不能完全考虑人道主义诉求〕。**~ buoy** 救生圈。**Life Card** 生命卡,激光缩微病历卡。**~ cycle** 【生】**1.** 生活周期,生活史。**2.** 与上述类似的周期,生命周期。**~ estate** 非世袭的终身财产。**~ expectancy** 预期寿命。**~-force** 生命力。**~-giving** **a.** **1.** 给与生命的。**2.** 提神的。**~ guard** **1.** 〔*Life-Guards*〕〔英〕近卫骑兵旅。**2.** 近卫兵。**3.** (机器上的)排障器。**4.** 〔美〕(游泳场的)救生员 (= ~ savers)。**~ history** **1.** 【生】生活史。**2.** 人生历程。**~ insurance** 〔美〕人寿保险。**~ interest** 终身财产所有权。**~ jacket** 救生衣。**~-kiss** 口对口人工呼吸。**~-line** **1.** 救生索;(潜水员的)通报绳。**2.** 命脉,生命线。**~-long** **a.** 终身的,毕生的,一生的。**~manship** 虚张声势以达到目的的手法。**~ member** 终身会员。**~ net** (消防队用的)救生网。**~-office** 人寿保险业;人寿保险公司办事处。**~ peer** 一代贵族。**~ peerage** 一代贵族的爵位。**~ preserver** **1.** 救生用具;浮衣。**2.** 〔英〕护身用具〔手枪、带刀手杖、棍棒等〕。**~ raft** 救生筏。**~saver** **1.** 救命的人。**2.** 〔美〕救生员。**3.** 〔俚〕应急的东西。**~saving** **1.** **a.** 救生的。**2.** **n.** 救生〔尤指救护溺水者免于溺毙〕。**~ science** 〔常 *pl.*〕生命科学〔所指包括生物学、医学、人类学、社会学〕。**~-size(d)** **a.** 同原物[自身]一样大的。**~span** = ~time. **~-spring** 生命的源泉。**~-strings** 〔*pl.*〕生命线。**~ style** 生活作风,生活方式;【商】迎合消费者生活方式的经销概念。**~-support system** (宇航员或危急病人等的)生命维持系统。**~ table** = mortality table. **~time** **1.** 一生,终生。**2.** 【原】寿命。**~-work** 毕生事业;一生中最重要的工作。**~ zone** 生物带。**-like** **a.** 逼真的,栩栩如生的。

life·less [ˈlaiflis; ˋlaɪflɪs] **a.** **1.** 无生命的;〔尤指〕从未有过生命的。**2.** 无生气的。**3.** 已死的。**4.** 无生物的。**5.** 呆板的,单调沉闷的;不活跃的。***a ~ planet*** 无生物行星。**-ly** **ad.** **-ness** **n.**

lif·er [ˈlaifə; ˋlaɪfɚ] **n.** **1.** 无期徒刑。**2.** 无期徒刑犯。**3.** 职业军人。

lift [lift; lɪft] **I** **vt.** **1.** 举起,使升起,提起,抬起;提高;提升。**2.** 使高尚;鼓舞。**3.** 运送,搬运;空运 (= airlift). **4.** 偷窃;偷去;抄袭,剽窃。**5.** 起出,拔起;掘出;拔营。**6.** (把板球等)向高空击去。**7.** 〔美〕清偿;赎出,赎取(典押物)。**8.** 解除,撤除,撤消。*~ that parcel down the shelf* 把那包东西从架上拿下来。*~ weights* 举重。*Mount Qomolungma ~s its cone into the clouds*. 珠穆朗玛峰顶高耸入云。*~ the tariff* 〔美〕提高税率。*His wallet was ~ed*. 他的皮夹子被人扒走了。*~ a passage from the book* 从书中剽窃一段文字。*~ a mortgage* 偿付抵押债款。*~ the ban on* 解除对…的禁令。*~ the curfew* 撤消宵禁。— **vi.** **1.** 被提高,升起。**2.** 消散。**3.** 水涨船高,(船)乘浪升高。**4.** (地面)隆起。**5.** 耸立。*The window will not ~*. (往上提起的)窗子开不开。*The fog ~*. 雾消散。**~ off** 【空】起飞。~

one's hat (把帽子从头上拿起一下)脱帽致敬。～ ***sb.'s face*** 用美容术伸平面皱,为某人整容。～ ***up*** 提起来,上升。～ ***up a cry*** 高声大叫。～ ***up one's*** [***the***] ***eyes*** [***face***] 仰望,注视;祈祷。～ ***up one's*** [***the***] ***feet*** 快去援救。～(***up***) ***one's*** [***the***] ***hand*** 1. (举手)起誓。2. 祈祷。～(***up***) ***one's*** [***the***] ***hand against*** 反叛,攻击,压制。～ ***up one's head*** 抬头;(因自信,得意等)昂起头来;狂喜。～ ***up one's*** [***the***] ***heel*** 不以礼相待。～ ***up with pride*** 得意扬扬。**II** ***n***. 1. 举起;抬高;提升,搬起。2. 高昂的姿态。3. 情绪昂扬,精神振奋。4. (一次)举重量,起重量;【矿】(一次)采掘量。5.【机】扬力,(水泵)扬程;【空】升力,浮力。6.〔英〕电梯;吊车;升降机(=〔美〕elevator)。7. 起重机;千斤顶。8. 鞋后跟皮的一层。9. 土地的隆起,小丘。10. (雾等的)消散。11. 帮助,帮忙,照顾。*a* ～ *in cost* 费用[成本]提高。*walk with the proud* ～ *of one's head* 昂首阔步。*a* ～ *of sheet steel* 一次吊起的钢板。***give sb. a*** ～ 给某人以鼓励;帮某人的忙;在半路上让某人搭自己的车;扶某人上车。***a dead*** ～ (不用起重机等机械)用人力硬搬;〔喻〕费力的艰巨任务。～**back** 斜车顶开启式小轿车〔车顶倾斜并可向上开启的轿车〕。～ **boy**〔英〕= ～man. ～ **bridge** 升降吊桥。～ **cable**, ～ **wire**【空】升力线,升力索。～**-drag ratio**【空】升阻比,(空)气动(力)性能。～ **hammer** 落锤。～ **irrigation** 抽水灌溉。～**man** ***n***.〔英〕开电梯的工人。～**off**【空】保险伞下降;(飞机、飞弹等的)起飞;发射(时刻),起离(时刻),初动。～ **pump**【机】扬水泵,提升泵。～**-slab**【建】吊板法,楼板顶升法〔一种吊装预制板的建筑方法〕。～ **truck** 起重机车[车辆];自动装卸车。

lift·er [ˈliftə; ˋlɪftɚ] ***n***. 1. 起重者。2. 升降机,起重机。3. 推料机。4. 升降杆,推杆。5. 电磁铁的衔铁。6. ～ **winch** 起重绞车。

lift·ing [ˈliftiŋ; ˋlɪftɪŋ] ***n***. 举起;吊起;上升。～ **area** 升力面积。～ **body**【空】太空和高空飞行两用机〔可重返大气层并自行着陆〕。～ **gear** 起重机。～ **jack** 千斤顶;起重吊车。～ **pins** 推杆;造型机顶杆。～ **ring** 提圈。～ **screw** 螺旋起重机;升力螺旋桨。

lig [lig; lɪg] ***n***.〔英俚〕供人闲逛的时髦场所,灯红酒绿的地方。

lig·a·ment [ˈligəmənt; ˋlɪgəmənt] ***n***. (*pl*. ～***s***, ～***a*** [-mentə; -mɛntə]) 1. 系带。2.【解】带,韧带。

lig·a·men·tal, -tar·y, -tous [ˌligəˈmentl, -ˈmentəri, -ˈmentəs; ˏlɪgəˋmentl, -ˋmentərɪ, -ˋmɛntəs] ***a***. 带状者,韧带(似)的。

li·gan [ˈlaigən; ˋlaɪgən] ***n***. = lagan.

lig·and [ˈligənd, ˈlaigənd; ˋlɪgənd, ˋlaɪgənd] ***n***.【化】配合基[体],向心配合(价)体。

lig·ase [ˈligˌeis; ˋlɪgˏes] ***n***.【生】联结酶。

li·gate [ˈlaigeit; ˋlaɪget] ***vt***. 绑扎;【医】结扎(血管等)。

li·ga·tion [laiˈgeiʃən; laɪˋgeʃən] ***n***. 1. 绑扎。2.【医】结扎;缚法;结扎线,缚线。

lig·a·ture [ˈligətʃuə; ˋlɪgəˏtʃʊr] **I** ***n***. 1. 绑扎,结扎。2. 带子;绷带;【医】结扎线;缚线。3. 连系物。4.【印】连字〔如 æ, fi 等〕;连字符号(-),连字弧线。5.【乐】连结线,连音。**II** ***vt***. 绑扎,结扎。

li·geance [ˈlaidʒəns, Am. ˈli-; ˋlaɪdʒəns, ˋlɪ-] ***n***. 效忠;忠心〔如臣对君,人民对政府等〕。

li·ger [ˈlaigə; ˋlaɪgɚ] ***n***. (雄狮和雌虎生的)狮虎。

light[1] [lait; laɪt] **I** ***n***. 1. 光,光线;光明,亮光(*opp*. darkness). *Hang the picture in a good* ～. 把那幅画挂在能看清楚的地方。2. 发光体,光源;灯,信号灯;灯塔;天体。*a blackout* ～ 防空灯。*ancient* ～*s* 保护光线不受挡住的权利。*the greater* ～ 太阳。*the lesser* ～ 月亮。3.〔俚〕(舞台的)脚光。*before the* ～*s* 在舞台上;登台演出。4. 日光;白昼;黎明。*Let's leave before the* ～ *fails*. 我们要在天黑以前离开。*L- is breaking*. 天已破晓。*The attack was on at the first* ～. 天一亮,进攻就开始了。5. 窗;天窗;取光孔;(温室的)玻璃屋顶[墙壁];【法】光线不受(邻居)阻碍权。*a room with* ～*s on three sides* 三方都有光线进来的房间。6. 明白,显露;启发,说明;教化。*new* ～*s on a question* 说明问题的新线索。7. 见解,见识;眼光。*see sb. in a new* ～ 用新眼光看待某人。8. 光;〔诗〕视力;眼神;〔*pl*.〕〔俚〕眼睛。9. 名家,权威;明星。*the guiding* [*shining*] ～ 显赫人物。*the leading* ～*s of diplomacy* 外交界头面人物。*the literary* ～*s of the day* 当代文豪。10.【宗】荣光,福祉。*the inner* ～ 灵光。11. (绘画中的)明亮部分,投光部分。～ *and shade* (a) 明暗。(b)强烈的对比。*the high* ～ *of a picture* 画的强光部份。12. 火花,点火物。*a box of* ～*s*〔英〕一盒火柴。*put a* ～ *to the fire* 点火。*strike a* ～ 擦火柴。*Will you give me a* ～? 借个火儿。13.【法】采光权(= ancient ～s)。14.〔*pl*.〕智能。*do one's best according to one's* ～*s* 尽力而为。***A*** ～ ***breaks in upon sb***. 某人恍然大悟。***be*** [***go***] ***out like*** ～〔美俚〕(a)醉得不省人事。(b)被打昏;昏睡。***between the*** ～***s*** 在黄昏时。***between two*** ～***s*** 在夜里;乘黑夜。***bring to*** ～ 暴露,揭露。***by the*** ～ ***of nature*** 本能地,自然而然地。***cast*** [***shed, show, throw, turn***] ***light on*** [***upon***] ***sth***. 阐明。***come to*** ～ 显露,出现。***expose sth. to the*** ～ ***of day*** 把某事暴露在光天化日之下。***fast*** ～ 耐光。***get in sb.'s*** ～ 挡人光线,妨碍人。***get out of the*** ～ 不妨碍。***give a*** [***the***] ***green*** ～ 开绿灯,准许前进。***give*** ～ ***on*** [***upon***] 使…明白,使明显。***in a good*** [***bad***] ～ 在看得清楚[不清楚]的地方。***in*** ～ 被光线照着。***in the*** ～ ***of*** 1. 以…的模样。2. 按照,根据。3. 当作…(*view his conduct in the* ～ *of a crime* 把他的行为当作犯罪看)。～ ***at the end of tunnel*** 隧道尽头的光明,出头之日。～ ***of one's eye*** [***eyes***] 心爱的人,掌上明珠。～ ***of sb.'s countenance***〔谑〕照顾,恩惠,好意。***man of*** ～ ***and leading*** 权威,大家。***place*** [***put***] ***in the clearest*** ～ 阐述得非常清楚。***place*** [***put***] ***sb***. [***sth***.] ***in a different*** ～ 对某人[某事]另有一种看法。***place*** [***put***] ***sb***. [***sth***.] ***in a false*** ～ 使人误解某人[某事];把某人[某事]说得面目全非。***place*** [***put***] ***sb***. [***sth***.] ***in a favourable*** ～ 把某人[某事]说得特别好。***put out*** [***quench***] ***sb.'s*** ～ 杀死某人,送某人归天。***put out the*** ～ 熄灯。***see a*** [***the***] ***red*** ～ 觉察到危险。***see*** ～ 理会。***see*** [***view***] ***sth. in a different*** ～ 从另一种观点来看某事。***see sth. in its true*** ～ 对某事有正确的见解。***see sth. in the same*** ～ 对某事有同样的看法。***see the*** ～ (***of day***) 1. (人)出生,出世。2. 领悟。***set*** ～ ***to*** 点火。***shut one's*** ～ ***off*** 死。***stand*** [***be***] ***in one's own*** ～ 1. 背光。2. 损害自己的利益。***stand*** [***be***] ***in sb.'s*** ～ 1. 挡住某人的光线。2. 妨碍某人前程。***switch*** [***turn***] ***off the*** ～***s*** 关电灯。***switch*** [***turn***] ***on the*** ～***s*** 开电灯。***white*** ～ 1. 白昼的光。2. 公正的判断。

II ***vt***. (***light·ed*** [ˈlaitid; ˋlaɪtɪd], ***lit*** [lit; lɪt]) 1. 点火,点燃。～ *a cigarette* 点着香烟。2. 照亮,照耀。3. 使发光,光润,使春风满面。4. 用灯照亮道路。～ *sb. to bed* 点灯带人去睡。— ***vi***. 1. 点火,点着(火)。*He fished out a cigarette and lit up*. 他摸出一支烟来点着了。2. 变亮;(眼睛)发亮,满面春风。～ ***into*** 攻击;责备。～ ***out for***〔美口〕逃往。～ ***up*** 1. 点火,点灯;弄亮,照亮;点香烟。2. 变快活;有喜色。

III ***a***. (*opp*. dark) 1. 发光的,明亮的。*It's beginning to get* ～. 天亮了。2. 浅色的,淡色的。*a* ～ *blue* 浅蓝色。～ **adaptation** 光适应。～ **blues** 剑桥大学的选手、啦啦队。～ **buoy**【海】灯浮标。～ **due** [**duty**] 灯塔税。～ **echo**【天】光反射〔由超新星爆炸所引起〕。～ **evening** 薄暮。～ **fast** ***a***. 耐光的〔尤指颜色〕。～**-fastness** 耐光。～**house** 灯塔。～**house tube**【无】灯塔管。～ **meter** 曝光表,照度计。～ **pollution** (街灯、广告、玻璃墙等发出眩目强光所造成的)光污染。～ **pen**【电】光笔。～**proof** ***a***. 不透光的。～ **quantum**【物】= photon. ～**ship** 灯船,灯塔船。～ **show** (伴随摇摆舞音乐暗示迷幻效果的)

光影闪烁表演。~**s out 1.** 熄灯号(铃)。**2.** 就寝时间。~**-struck** ***a***.【摄】漏过光的。~**tight** ***a***. 防光的,不透光的。~ **tracer** 曳光弹。~ **trap 1.** 蛾灯,光捕虫器。**2.** 暗室进出口的避光装置。~**wave**【物】光波。~**wood** 易燃的木头;轻材,多脂材。~**-year**【天】光年。

light[2] [lait; laɪt] **I** ***a***. (*opp*. heavy) **1.** 轻的。*as ~ as a feather* 轻如鸿毛。~ *industry* 轻工业。**2.** 少量的,轻微的,微弱的。~ *applause* 微弱的掌声。*a ~ frost* 微霜。~ *losses* 轻微的损失。*a ~ meal* 吃得不多的一餐饭。*a ~ mistake* 小错。*a ~ rain* 小雨。*a ~ sleep* 微睡。**3.** 容易消化的,清淡的。~ *beer* 淡啤酒。~ *food* 清淡的食物。*a ~ soup* 清汤。**4.** 无积载的,装货少的。~ *traffic* 轻量交通。*the ~ watermark* 船不装货时的吃水线。**5.** 轻快的;轻装的;轻便的。*a ~ bomber* 轻轰炸机。*a ~ car* 轻便汽车。*a ~ cruiser* 轻巡洋舰。*a ~ machine-gun* 轻机关枪。*300 ~ cavalry* [*horse*] 三百轻骑兵。**6.** 容易的,轻松的。~ *illness* 轻病。~ *punishment* 不重的惩罚。~ *work* 轻活。**7.** 噪音柔和的。**8.** 分量不足的。*a ~ coin* 分量不足的钱币。*give ~ weight* 克扣分量。**9.** 轻松愉快的。*a ~ heart* 轻松愉快的心情。*be ~ of heart* 心情轻松愉快。~ *literature* 轻松文学。~ *music* 轻音乐。~ *reading* 轻松读物。**10.** 轻率的,轻浮的,轻薄的。*a ~ woman* 轻佻的妇女。*as ~ as a butterfly* 轻佻,轻率。~ *conduct* 轻浮的举动。~ *opinions* 轻率的意见。*person of ~ character* 轻薄的人。~*est word* 毫无意义的话。**11.** 松脆的,易碎的,疏松的。*a ~ cake* 松软的蛋糕。~ *sand* 松砂。~ *soil* 轻质土,砂土。**12.** 易醒的。*a ~ sleeper* 睡得不沉的人。**13.**【建】精巧的,优美的。~ *architecture* 精巧的建筑。**14.**【语音】弱音的。*a ~ syllable* 弱音音节。**15.** 不重要的,琐碎的。~ *conversation* 随便闲聊。**16.** 晕眩的。*He was a bit ~ after the illness*. 病后他有点头晕。**17.** 轻快的,灵巧的。*be ~ on one's feet* 脚步轻快。*have a ~ hand* 手灵巧。~ *movement* 轻快的行动。**18.** 人手不足的,缺少人员的。***~ in hand*** (马等)容易驾驭的,(人)容易相处的。***~ in the head* 1.** 头晕,眼花。**2.** 头脑简单,愚蠢。***L- gains make heavy purses***. 〔谚〕因小失大。***~ of belief*** = ~ of ear 耳朵软,轻信。***~ of fingers*** 手脚不干净,有偷窃癖。***make ~ of*** 轻视,小看。(*make ~ of the danger* 不把危险放在心上). ***set ~ by*** 轻视。***sit ~ on*** (工作等)对…负担不重 (*Her years sit ~ on her*. 她年事虽长,但不见老。)

II ***ad***. 轻地,轻快地;轻装地。*L- come, ~ go*. = Lightly come, lightly go. *sleep ~* 睡得不熟。*travel ~* 轻装旅行。~ **air** 软风〔一级风〕。~**-armed** ***a***.【军】轻武器装备的。~ **artillery** 轻型火炮,轻炮兵。~ **bob** 〔英〕轻步兵。~ **bread** (美国南部)用酵母发酵的白面包。~ **breeze** 轻风〔二级风〕。~ **chain**【生】轻(多肽)链。~**-duty** ***a***. (机器等)轻型的;可用轻型机械做成的。~ **engine** 不挂列车的机车。~**er-than-air** (航空器等)轻于空气的。~**face** ***n***., ***a***.【印】白体活字(的)。~**-fingered** ***a***. **1.** 手指灵巧的。**2.** 有窃盗癖的 (*a ~-fingered gentleman* 〔谑〕扒手). ~**-footed** ***a***. 走路轻快的;轻盈的 (= 〔诗〕~foot). ~**-footedly** 走路轻快地。~**-footedness** 走路轻快。~**-handed** ***a***. **1.** 手上没有什么[多少]东西的。**2.** 人手不足的。**3.** 手巧的,手法高明的。~**headed** ***a***. **1.** 头昏眼花的。**2.** 轻率的;轻浮的。~**hearted** ***a***. 无忧无虑的,心情愉快[轻松]的。~ **heavyweight** (拳击等的)轻重量级运动员〔体重为 161—175 磅〕。~**-heeled** 〔古〕**1.** 步子轻快的。**2.** 放纵的,淫荡的。~ **horse**, ~**horseman** 轻骑兵。~ **housekeeping** 轻的家务活。~**-minded** ***a***. 不严肃的,轻浮的。~**-o'-love** (*pl*. ***~-o'-loves***) 荡妇。~ **opera** 轻歌剧。~**plane** 轻型飞机〔尤指私人小飞机〕。~ **rail** 轻轨〔指有轨电车等轻型车辆的铁轨〕。~**-skirts** 〔作单数用〕轻浮的妇女。~ **verse** (幽默讽刺的)打油诗。~ **water**【原】普通水〔与重水相对而言〕。~**weight 1.** ***n***. 标准重量以下的人[动物];轻量级选手;不重要的人;不够坚强的人,不能胜任的人。**2.** ***a***. 轻量的;平均重量以下的;不重要的。

light[3] [lait; laɪt] ***vi***. (***lit*** [lit; lɪt] 或 ***~ed***) **1.** 〔古〕下马,下车;停落。**2.** 鸟歇在树上。**3.** 偶然遇见;偶然得到。**4.** 〔方〕突然发生。*The bird lit on a branch*. 小鸟歇在枝头。—***vt***.【海】拉起(绳索等),移动(风帆等)。~ ***into*** 〔美俚〕责备,攻击,骂。~ (***up***) ***on*** 偶尔碰见,发现。~ ***on one's feet*** [***legs***] 双脚落地;幸免;侥幸成功。~ ***out*** 〔美俚〕逃走,溜掉。

light·en[1] [ˈlaitn; ˋlaɪtn] ***vt***. **1.** 照亮,点亮;点火。**2.** 弄明白,启发。**3.** 使春风满面,使(眼睛)发亮。**4.** 使(绘画)色调轻柔明朗。— ***vi***. **1.** 发亮,变亮。**2.** 打闪。*A full moon ~ed our path*. 一轮明月照亮了我们的道路。*It thundered and ~ed*. 雷电交作。

light·en[2] [ˈlaitn; ˋlaɪtn̩] ***vt***. **1.** 减轻(负担);缓和,减少。**2.** 使轻松,使高兴。—***vi***. 变轻,变轻松,舒畅起来。~ *a ship of her cargo* 减轻船载。

light·er[1] [ˈlaitə; ˋlaɪtɚ] ***n***. **1.** 点火者;点火器。**2.** 打火机;引燃器。*spark ~* 点火器。

light·er[2] [ˈlaitə; ˋlaɪtɚ] **I** ***n***. 驳船。**II** ***vt***. 用驳船运。

light·er·age [ˈlaitəridʒ; ˋlaɪtərɪdʒ] ***n***. **1.** 驳运费。**2.** 驳船运送[装卸]。**3.** 驳运船。

light·er·man [ˈlaitəmən; ˋlaɪtɚmən] ***n***. (*pl*. ***-men***) 驳船工人。

light·ing [ˈlaitiŋ; ˋlaɪtɪŋ] ***n***. **1.** 照明;照明设备;舞台灯光。**2.** 点火,发火。**3.** (画中的)明暗分布。~**-up time** 行驶车辆的规定开灯时间。

light·ish [ˈlaitiʃ; ˋlaɪtɪʃ] ***a***. **1.** (颜色)稍淡的。**2.** 重量稍差的;载货少的。

light·less [ˈlaitlis; ˋlaɪtlɪs] ***a***. **1.** 无光的,暗的。**2.** 不发光的。

light·ly [ˈlaitli; ˋlaɪtlɪ] ***ad***. **1.** 轻轻地。**2.** 轻易地,容易地,不费力地;轻捷地。**3.** 泰然自若地;淡然地;清淡地。**4.** 轻率地。**5.** 轻松地,轻快地;愉快地。**6.** 轻蔑地。*He wears his seventy years ~*. 他简直看不出有七十岁。*get off ~* 轻易逃脱。*L- come, ~ go*. 〔谚〕悖入悖出,来得容易去得快。*take bad news ~* 对坏消息不以为意。*behave ~* 轻举妄动。*Don't take it ~* 不可等闲视之。*give up sth. ~* 轻易放弃某物。*leap ~ over a ditch* 轻轻跳过小沟。*think ~ of sb.'s achievements* 轻视某人的成绩。*punish ~* 从轻处罚。~ *cooked* 烹调得很清淡。

light·ness[1] [ˈlaitnis; ˋlaɪtnɪs] ***n***. **1.** 轻。**2.** 敏捷,机敏。**3.** 精巧,优美。**4.** 轻率;轻浮。**5.** 愉快,轻松。**6.** 清淡;易消化。

light·ness[2] [ˈlaitnis; ˋlaɪtnɪs] ***n***. **1.** 明亮,光亮度。**2.** (色调的)清淡。

light·ning [ˈlaitniŋ; ˋlaɪtnɪŋ] **I** ***n***. **1.** 闪电,电光。**2.** 意外的幸运。**3.** 〔美俚〕劣等威士忌酒。*chain* [*forked*] ~ 叉状闪电。*heat* [*summer*] ~ (夏季的)无声闪电,热闪。*sheet ~* 片状闪电。*The ~ has struck a house*. 雷电击倒了一座房子。*chained ~* 〔美俚〕下等酒。*forty-rod ~* 〔美俚〕下等烈性酒。***a ~ before death*** 回光返照。***a ~ attack*** 突然袭击,闪电袭击。***at*** [***like***, ***with***] (***greased***) ~ 闪电似的,风驰电掣地,一眨眼。**II** ***vi***. 闪电。~ **arrester** 避雷针。~ **beetle** [**bug**] 〔美〕萤火虫。~ **conductor** 避雷导线。~ **rod 1.** 避雷针。**2.** 喷气式战斗机。~ **strike 1.** 雷击。**2.** 闪电式罢工。~ **war** 闪击战。

lights [laits; laɪts] ***n***. *pl*. (供食用的)兽类肺脏。

light·some[1] [ˈlaitsəm; ˋlaɪtsəm] ***a***. **1.** 轻快的,敏捷的。**2.** 愉快的;无忧无虑的。**3.** 轻薄的;轻浮的。**-ly** ***ad***. **-ness** ***n***.

light·some[2] [ˈlaitsəm; ˋlaɪtsəm] ***a***. **1.** 发光的。**2.** 明亮的;光亮的。

lign·al·oes [laiˈnæləuz, lig-; ˏlaɪnˋæloz, lɪg-] ***n***. 沉香

木。

lig·ne·ous [ˈligniəs, -njəs; ˋlɪgnɪəs, -njəs] ***a.*** 木的,木质的;木头似的。

lig·n(i)- *comb.f.* 表示"木":*ligni*fy.

lig·ni·fy [ˈligniˌfai; ˋlɪgnə͵faɪ] ***vt.*** (***-fi·ed, -fy·ing***) 使…木质化,木质化,变为木。**-fi·ca·tion** [ˌlignifiˈkeiʃən; ͵lɪgnəfɪˋkeʃən] ***n.***

lig·nin [ˈlignin; ˋlɪgnɪn] ***n.***【化】木质素。

lig·nite [ˈlignait; ˋlɪgnaɪt] ***n.***【矿】褐煤(= brown coal)。

lig·no- *comb.f.* = lign(i).

lig·no·caine [ˈlignəˌkein; ˋlɪgnə͵kən] ***n.***【药】利多卡因,赛鲁卡因〔又称 lidocaine, xylocaine, 局部麻醉及抗心律紊乱药〕。

lig·no·cel·lu·lose [ˌlignəuˈseljuləus; ͵lɪgnoˋsɛljə͵los] ***n.***【化】木质纤维素。**lig·no·cel·lu·los·ic** [-ˈləusik; -ˋlosɪk] ***a.***

lig·nose [ˈligəus; ˋlɪgnos] ***n.*** **1.** = liguin. **2.** 含有硝酸甘油和木质纤维的炸药。

lig·num vi·tae [ˈlignəmˈvaitiː; ˋlɪgnəmˋvaɪti] **1.** = guaiacum. **2.** 愈创树的特硬木材〔商业上的俗称〕。

lig·ro·in(e) [ˈligrəuin; ˋlɪgroɪn] ***n.***【化】挥发油,轻石油,石油醚,粗汽油,里格若英(= benzine)。

lig·u·la [ˈligjulə; ˋlɪgjʊlə] ***n.*** (*pl.* ***-lae*** [-ˌliː; -li], ***-las***)【动】(昆虫的)唇舌。

lig·u·late [ˈligjulit; ˋlɪgjʊ͵lɪt] ***a.***【植】舌状的;有叶舌的。~ *corolla* 舌状花冠。

lig·ule [ˈligjuːl; ˋlɪgjul] ***n.***【植】叶舌,舌状;舌状花冠。

lik·a·ble [ˈlaikəbl; ˋlaɪkəbl̩] ***a.*** 可爱的,讨人喜欢的;亲切的,和蔼的。**-ness** ***n.***

like[1] [laik; laɪk] **I** ***vt.*** **1.** 喜欢,爱好。*He ~s vegetables.* 他喜欢蔬菜。*I ~ apples better than pears.* 苹果和梨比较起来,我更爱吃苹果。**2.** 希望,想要,喜欢,愿意做某事〔后接不定式或动名词〕。*I should much ~ to come.* 我很想来。*He doesn't ~ to smoke [smoking].* 他不喜欢吸烟。**3.** 希望[欢迎]某人做某事〔后接带 to 的不定式,在美国口语中可接 for ... 加带 to 的不定式结构〕。*I ~ people to tell the truth.* 我希望人们说实话。*I ~ for him to come soon.* 我欢迎他马上来。**4.** 使某人感到适宜[惬意]。*Lobster doesn't ~ me.* (吃)龙虾对我的健康不合适。**5.** 对某事物有某种感觉[观感]。*How do you ~ this poem?* 你觉得这首诗怎么样? *I ~ your imprudence.* 我看你就是脸皮厚。— ***vi.*** **1.** 喜欢,愿意,希望。**2.** 〔方〕赞同。*Do as you ~.* 你喜欢怎么做就怎么做。*You may take as you ~.* 你可以任意拿。***if you ~*** 如果你喜欢的话(*You may come if you ~.* 高兴的话请过来。*I am shy if you ~.* 〔重读 shy〕(如果你要那么说)就算我怕见人吧〔但实际并不怕见人〕;〔重读 I〕那就说我怕见人吧〔但不能说别人也这样〕)。***I ~ that!*** 你倒说得出!说得倒好! ***~ it or not*** 〔插入语〕不管你喜欢不喜欢。**II** ***n.*** 〔*pl.*〕嗜好。*one's ~s and dislikes* 好恶,爱憎。

like[2] [laik; laɪk] **I** ***a.*** (***more ~, most ~***; 〔诗〕***lik·er, lik·est***) **1.** 相像的,相似的,类似的;同类的,同样的,同等的。~ *figure*【几】相似形。~ *terms*【数】同类项。*two men of ~ pursuits and tastes* 志趣相同的两个人。*I cannot cite a ~ instance.* 我一时举不出类似的例子。*in ~ manner* (用)同样(方式)。*on this and ~ occasions* 在这种场合和类似的场合。**2.** 相似,类似〔用作表语〕。*The two sisters are very ~.* 这姐妹俩非常相像。*Things which seem to be ~ may be different.* 看来相同的东西实际可能不同。**3.** 〔方、古〕可能,大概〔用作表语〕。*'Tis ~ that he's gone mad.* 他大概是疯了。*It is ~ we shall see him no more.* 恐怕不会再见到他了。*It's ~ to happen again.* 说不定又要来一下。**4.** 〔古〕简直,几乎要。*I am ~ to cry whenever I think of my love.* 我每想到自己的情史,简直要痛哭起来。***L- father, ~ son.*** 有其父必有其子〔文中前一 like 为关连词,后一 like 为指示词〕。

II ***prep.*** **1.** 像…那样,和…一样。*a thing ~ that* 像那样的东西。*swim ~ a fish* 像鱼那样游泳。*Don't talk ~ that.* 讲话不要像那个样子。**2.** (表面、外观、内容等)与…相似。*Your necklace is just ~ mine.* 你的项链和我的项链很相似。*The wind in the trees made a sound so much ~ the sea.* 林中风声响动,和海水声极其相似。**3.** 能表明…特征。*It is ~ him to forget our appointment.* 把我们的约会忘掉,这正是他的行径。**4.** 有…征候;有…希望[姿态]。*It doesn't look ~ rain.* 不像要下雨的样子。*The snow looks ~ lasting.* 这场雪看样子要继续下的。*You sound ~ a professor.* 您讲话很有教授风度。**5.** 想要做某事〔前面通常用动词 feel, 后面用名词或动名词形式〕*I feel ~ a ride in my new sports car.* 我想乘坐我新买的赛跑汽车行驶一趟。*I didn't feel ~ going out for dinner.* (当时)我不想到外面去吃饭。**6.** 〔非规范用法〕诸如…等,像…等等〔 = as, such as〕。*There are numerous hobbies you might enjoy, ~ photography or painting.* 大家可以享用的文娱活动有许许多多,如摄影和绘画等等。***~ a book*** 详细地;准确地;严谨地(*He speaks ~ a book.* 他讲话用词严谨。*I can read his mind ~ a book.* 我对他的心事了如指掌)。***~ anything*** 非常,极其;…得不成样子(*The maid wanted ~ anything to try on her mistress's clothes.* 这位女仆很想把女主人的衣服穿起来试试看)。***~ nothing on earth*** 世间稀有的。***nothing ~*** **1.** 没有什么比…更…〔nothing 用作名词〕(*There is nothing ~ a cold drink of water when one is thirsty.* 渴的时候什么东西也比不上一杯凉水)。**2.** 丝毫〔哪方面〕都不像…那样…(*It was nothing ~ what we expected.* 事情一点也不像原来所期望的那样)。***nothing ~ [near] as [so] ... as*** 远远不像…那样…(*This is nothing ~ as good as that.* 这个远远不如那个那样好)。***something ~*** **1.** 几乎,差不多,有几分像。**2.** 大约。**3.** 了不起的…;像样的…(*It looks something ~ this.* 看来跟这个差不多。*It cost us something ~ $ 1,000.* 我们在这方面约花了一千美元。*He is something ~ an orator.* 他是一位了不起的讲演家)。★ 根据现代多数辞典对词性划分的情况,本辞典关于 like 一词的条目,凡词后带有宾语的均作为介词处理,用作名词的修饰语或作表语用的则均作形容词处理。

III ***ad.*** **1.** 像…,和…一样地。**2.** 〔口〕多半,恐怕。**3.** 〔口〕似乎,宛如,简直。*I thought ~ you.* 我想的和你一样。(***as***) ***~ as not*** 〔口〕大概,十之八九(*He will come, as ~ as not.* 他多半会来)。***~ anything [blazes, crazy, fun, mad, one o'clock, the devil]*** 〔俚〕极,非常,猛烈地(*be brave ~ anything* 勇敢非常)。*very ~ = ~ enough* 多半是的,很可能如此。

IV ***conj.*** 〔美口〕好像,如同。*I cannot do it ~ you do.* 我不能做得像你那样。*Now swing your bat ~ I do.* 来,照我的样子挥动球棒。

V ***n.*** **1.** 相似的人[物];同样的人[物]。**2.**【高尔夫球】分数相同的一击。*Hitler and his ~* 希特勒之流。*I shall never do the ~ again.* 我决不再那样搞了。*We shall never see his ~ again.* 我们再也看不到他那样的人了。***and such [the] ~*** = or the ~ 等等,诸如此类。***L- attracts [draws to] ~.*** 〔谚〕物以类聚。***L- cures ~.*** 〔谚〕以毒攻毒。***L- for ~.*** 以牙还牙。***L- knows ~.*** 〔谚〕英雄识英雄。***Requite [return] ~ for ~.*** 一报还一报,即以其人之道还治其人之身。***the ~ of it*** 那一类的东西。***the ~s of me*** 〔口〕像我这样(不行)的人。***the ~s of you*** 〔俚〕像你这样了不起的人。**-minded** ***a.*** 有同样思想的,志同道合的。

-like *suf.* 〔附在名词之后,构成形容词或副词〕表示"…一样","像…":lily*like*, woman*like*.

like·a·ble [ˈlaikəbl; ˋlaɪkəbl̩] ***a.*** = likable.

L

like·li·hood, like·li·ness [ˈlaiklihud, -nis; ˋlaɪklɪˏhʊd, -nɪs] ***n.*** **1.** 可能(性)。**2.** 【数、统】似然,似真。**3.** 〔古〕希望,前途。*There is no ~ of his coming again.* 他不见得会再来了。*a young man of great ~* 很有前途的青年。***in all ~*** 十之八九,多半。

like·ly [ˈlaikli; ˋlaɪklɪ] **I** ***a.*** (***more ~, most ~, like·li·er; -li·est***) **1.** 很可能的。**2.** 很像真事的,像是可信的,好像可靠的。**3.** 适当的,恰好的;有希望的。**4.** 〔方〕漂亮的,吸引人的。*be ~ of success* 可能成功。*He is not ~ to come = It is not ~ (that) he will come.* 他不见得来。*Such a case is possible, but not ~.* 这种情况是可能的,但不见得会发生。*his most ~ halting place* 他很可能会停歇的地方。*It is ~ they will win.* 他们很可能要赢。*It is ~ to be cold there.* 那里可能很冷。*It is ~ to rain.* 像要下雨。*That's a ~ story!* 说得倒像! 像煞有介事! *a ~ house* 适当的房子。*a ~ spot to build on* 有希望[适合]大兴土木的地方。*a ~ young man* 有前途[希望]的青年。**II** ***ad.*** 〔英国常加 *very*; *most*〕多半,大概,有可能。*I shall most [very] ~ see you again.* 我一定能再见到你。***as ~ as not*** (= mostly [very] ~) 很可能,说不定 (*He'll forget all about it as ~ as not.* 他说不定[很可能]会把这件事情忘得一干二净)。~ ***enough*** 恐怕,也许。

lik·en [ˈlaikən; ˋlaɪkən] ***vt.*** **1.** 比作 (*to*)。**2.** 〔罕〕使像,弄得像…。

like·ness [ˈlaiknis; ˋlaɪknɪs] ***n.*** **1.** 相似,类似 (*between*; *to*)。**2.** 像,肖像,画像。**3.** 外表,表面现象。*a bad ~* 不很像的肖像。*a flattering ~* 比本人还要好看的像。*a good ~* 很像的肖像。*a living ~* 栩栩如生的肖像。***in the ~ of*** 貌似,假装 (*an enemy in the ~ of a friend* 伪装成朋友的仇敌)。***take sb.'s ~*** 给某人画像[照像]。

like·wise [ˈlaikwaiz; ˋlaɪkˏwaɪz] ***ad.*** **1.** 同样地,一样地。**2.** 也,而且。

li·kin [ˈliːkiːn; ˋliˋkin] ***n.*** 〔Chin.〕(十九世纪中叶至二十世纪三十年代的中国货物过境税)厘金。

lik·ing [ˈlaikiŋ; ˋlaɪkɪŋ] ***n.*** 兴趣,嗜好。***be to sb.'s ~*** 合某人的意,合某人的胃口。***have a ~ for*** 喜欢。***on (the) ~*** 实习的;试用的。***take a ~ to [for]*** 开始喜欢…,爱上…。

li·kud [liːˈkuːd; liˋkud] ***n.*** 利库德集团〔以色列一政党,1973 年成立〕。

li·ku·ta [liˈkuːtɑː; liˋkutɑ] ***n.*** (*pl.* ***ma·ku·ta*** [mɑː-; mɑ-]) 里库塔〔萨伊货币名,等于 1/100 萨伊〕。

li·lac [ˈlailək; ˋlaɪlək] **I** ***n.*** **1.** 【植】丁香花属;丁香花,紫丁香。**2.** 淡紫色。**II** ***a.*** 淡紫色的。

lil·i·a·ceous [ˌliliˈeiʃəs; ˏlɪlɪˋeʃəs] ***a.*** 【植】百合科的。

lil·ied [ˈlilid; ˋlɪlɪd] ***a.*** **1.** 多百合花的;百合花覆盖的。**2.** 〔诗〕百合花似的;洁白的。

Lil·ien·thal [ˈliliənθɔːl; ˋlɪlɪənˏtɑl] ***n.*** 利连索尔〔姓氏〕。

Lil·(l)i·an [ˈliliən; ˋlɪlɪən] ***n.*** 莉莲〔女子名, Elizabeth 的昵称〕。

lil·li·bul·le·ro [ˈlilibəˈliərəu; ˋlɪlɪbəˋlɪro] ***n.*** **1.** 英国勒里不利罗〔1688 年政变时流行的一首讽刺爱尔兰天主教歌曲的部分叠句〕。**2.** 上述歌曲。

Lil·li·put [ˈliliˌpʌt; ˋlɪləˏpʌt] ***n.*** (英国作家 Swift 作小说《格列佛游记》中的)小人国。

Lil·li·pu·tian [ˌliliˈpjuːʃiən, -ʃjən; ˏlɪləˋpjuʃən; -ʃjən] **I** ***a.*** **1.** 小人国的;小人国人的。**2.** 矮小的;卑陋的,心胸狭窄的。**II** ***n.*** **1.** 小人国人。**2.** 〔l-〕小人,矮子。

Lil·on·gwe [ˈliləŋkwi; ˋlɪləŋkwɪ] ***n.*** 利隆圭〔马拉维首都〕。

lilt [lilt; lɪlt] **I** ***vi.***, ***vt.*** **1.** 欢唱,快活地唱。**2.** 轻快地跳动。**II** ***n.*** **1.** 轻快的歌曲。**2.** (诗等的)韵律;节。**3.** 轻快的动作。

Lil·y [ˈlili; ˋlɪlɪ] ***n.*** 莉莉〔女子名〕。

lil·y [ˈlili; ˋlɪlɪ] **I** ***n.*** **1.** 【植】百合属;百合,百合花。**2.** 纯白的东西;纯洁的人;〔常 *pl.*〕洁白美丽的颜色。**3.** 〔常 *pl.*〕= fleur-de-lis. **4.** 〔美俚〕女人腔调的男人。***gild [paint] the ~*** 在百合花上镀金[擦粉],画蛇添足。***lilies and roses*** 美观。***the ~ of the valley*** (*pl.* ***lilies of the valley***)【植】欧铃兰 (*Convallaria majalis*)。**II** ***a.*** 百合(花)的;洁白的;纯洁的。~ **iron** 头上装有倒钩的鱼叉。~**-livered** ***a.*** 胆怯的;胆小的〔词出莎士比亚悲剧《麦克佩斯》〕。~ **pad** 浮在水面上的睡莲叶子。~**-white** **1.** ***a.*** 纯白的;〔美〕纯白种运动派的。**2.** ***n.*** 〔美〕排斥黑人的纯白种运动派成员。

lim. = limit.

Li·ma[1] [ˈliːmə; ˋlimə] ***n.*** 利马〔秘鲁首都〕。~ **bean** (美洲)利马豆,白扁豆。

Li·ma[2] [ˈlimə; ˋlɪmə] 通讯中用以代表字母 l 的词。

lim·a·cine [ˈliməˌsain, ˈlai-; ˋlɪməˏsaɪn, ˋlaɪ-] ***a.*** 蛞蝓的,似蛞蝓的 (= limaciform)。

li·man [liˈmɑːn; lɪˋmɑn] ***n.*** 河口,江河入海处的港湾。

limb[1] [lim; lɪm] **I** ***n.*** **1.** 肢,手足;翼,翅膀。**2.** 大树枝。**3.** 分支;突出物;(河的)支流。**4.** (句中的)子句。**5.** 骨干;爪牙。**6.** 顽童。~ *of the devil [hell]* = ~ *of satan, the devil's [fiend's]* ~ (坏人的)爪牙;顽童。~ *of the bar [law]* 警察,律师。***out on a ~*** 〔口〕处于危险境地。***pull [tear] sb. ~ from ~*** 撕裂某人肢体。***rest one's tired ~s*** 使疲倦的四肢休息。**II** ***vt.*** **1.** 割断…的四肢,肢解。**2.** 砍树枝。**-less** ***a.*** 无肢的;无翼的;无枝叉的。

limb[2] [lim; lɪm] ***n.*** **1.** (日、月等天体的)边缘。**2.** (四分仪等的)分度弧。**3.** 【植】瓣片;萼檐;冠檐。

lim·bate [ˈlimbeit; ˋlɪmbet] ***a.*** 边缘明显的〔如颜色与主体不同〕。

lim·bec(k) [ˈlimˌbek; ˋlɪmˏbɛk] ***n.*** 〔古〕= alembic.

limbed [limd; lɪmd] ***a.*** 〔常用以构成复合词〕有…肢[分枝,翼]的。*long-~* 有长肢[枝、翼]的。*short-~* 有短肢[枝、翼]的。

lim·ber[1] [ˈlimbə; ˋlɪmbɚ] **I** ***a.*** **1.** 柔软的;可塑的;易弯曲的。**2.** 轻快的,敏捷的。~ *terms* 可变通的条件。**II** ***vt.*** 使柔软。— ***vi.*** 柔和一下身体,(比赛前)做做预备运动 (*up*)。

lim·ber[2] [ˈlimbə; ˋlɪmbɚ] **I** ***n.*** (炮车的)拖车。**II** ***vt.***, ***vi.*** 把炮系在拖车上。

lim·bers [ˈlimbəz; ˋlɪmbɚz] ***n.*** 〔*pl.*〕(船底龙骨两侧的)污水道,污水孔。

lim·bo[1] [ˈlimbəu; ˋlɪmbo] ***n.*** (*pl.* ~***s***) **1.** 【宗】地狱的外缘〔善良的非基督徒或未受洗礼者的灵魂归宿处〕。**2.** 监牢,拘禁。**3.** 丢弃废物的地方;易被疏忽的地方。**4.** 中间过渡状态[地带]。

lim·bo[2] [ˈlimbəu; ˋlɪmbo] ***n.*** 林勃舞〔西印度群岛一种特技舞蹈〕。

Lim·burg·er [ˈlimbəːgə; ˋlɪmbɚgɚ] ***n.*** (比利时)林堡干酪。

lim·bus [ˈlimbəs; ˋlɪmbəs] ***n.*** (*pl.* ***-bi*** [-bai; -baɪ]) (色差较大的)明显边缘。

lime[1] [laim; laɪm] **I** ***n.*** **1.** 石灰。**2.** 黏鸟胶。*caustic [quick, unslaked] ~* 生石灰。*slaked [slack] ~* 熟石灰。~ *and water* 石灰水。~ *process* 灰退法〔用石灰去皮革上的毛〕。~ *soil* 钙质土。**II** ***vt.*** **1.** 用石灰处理;撒石灰;浸在石灰水中。**2.** 涂黏鸟胶,用黏鸟胶捕捉;诱陷。~ **burner** 烧石灰工人。~ **glass** 钙玻璃。~ **kiln** 石灰窑。~ **light** **1.** (旧时用燃烧石灰的办法照明舞台的)石灰光,灰光灯;舞台照明,聚光灯;舞台上照明部分。**2.** 众人注目的中心 (*be fond of the ~light* 爱引人注意,爱出风头。*come into [take] the ~light* 变成人们注意的中心。*in the ~light* 引人注目。*a tendency to seek ~light* 风头主义)。*throw ~ light on* 阐明,使真相毕露;把光集中在…;使显著,使成注目中心。~ **pit** 石灰石坑,石灰窑。~ **stone** (石)灰岩。~ **sulfur [sulphur]** 石(灰)硫(黄)混合杀虫剂。~ **twig** **1.** 涂有黏鸟胶的树

L

枝。2. 罗网,陷阱。~**water** 石灰水。

lime[2][laim; laɪm] ***n***. 【植】椴属;欧椴。

lime[3][laim; laɪm] ***n***. 【植】酸橙。~ **juice** 酸橙汁。~ **juicer**〔俚〕1. 英国佬;英国水兵。2. 英国船。

lime·ade [ˈlaimˈeid; ˋlaɪmˋed] ***n***. 酸橙汁,柠檬水。

li·men [ˈlaimen; ˋlaɪmɛn] ***n***. 【心】阈限。

lim·er·ick [ˈlimərik; ˋlɪmərɪk] ***n***. (按 aabba 押韵的)五行打油诗。

li·mes [ˈlaimi:z; ˋlaɪmiz] ***n***. (*pl*. ***limites*** [ˈlimiti:z; ˋlɪmɪtiz]) 境界。

Lim·ey [ˈlaimi; ˋlaɪmɪ] ***n***. = lime-juicer.

li·mic·o·line [laiˈmikəˌlain, -lin; laɪˋmɪkəˏlaɪn, -lɪn] ***a***. 【动】栖居岸边的〔尤指涉禽类〕。

li·mic·o·lous [laiˈmikələs; laɪˋmɪkələs] ***a***. 【动】生活于泥中的。

lim·i·nal [ˈliminl; ˋlɪmɪnḷ] ***a***. 【心】阈限的。

lim·it [ˈlimit; ˋlɪmɪt] **I *n***. **1**. 界限,界线;边界。**2**. 极限,限度;限制。**3**. 〔*pl*.〕范围,范域。**4**. 限价;限额;赌注限额;猎物限额。*place ~s on the number of men* 限制人数。*set a ~ to* ... 对…加以限制。*the danger ~* 危险线;极点。*reach the ~ of one's patience* 忍无可忍了。~ *value*【数】极限值。*the age ~ for enlistment* 入伍的年龄限制。*There is a ~ to everything*. 凡事都有限度。*be the ~*太过分,叫人无法容忍。***go beyond*** [***over***] ***the ~***超过限度。***go the ~***运动赛完全局[全场]。***go to any ~***竭尽全力。***off ~s***〔美〕(军人)禁入地区(*Off ~s to all unauthorized personnel*. 闲人免进)。***on ~s***〔美〕(军人)活动地区。***reach the ~ of one's resources*** 山穷水尽。***the inferior ~*** **1**. 最迟的限期。**2**. 最小的限额。***the ~***〔口〕使人无法容忍的人[物],到了绝顶的事物。***the ~ man*** 在赛跑时受最大让步的运动员。***the superior ~*** **1**. 最早的限期。**2**. 最大的限额。***That's the ~ .*** 这算到头了,不能再容忍了。***to the*** (***utmost***) ~ 到极点(*strain oneself to the ~*竭尽全力)。***within ~s*** 适当地,在一定范围之内。***within the city ~s*** 在市内。***within the ~s of*** 在…的范围之内。***without ~*** 无限制地,无限地。**II *vt***. **1**. 限制,限定。**2**. 减少。~ *the number to fifty* 把数目限制到五十。~ *the expenses* 节省开支。~ **cycle** 极限循环〔指周而复始的活动方式,如心跳、海浪拍岸等〕。**-a·ble *a***.

lim·i·tar·y [ˈlimitəri; ˋlɪmɪtərɪ] ***a***. 有限制的;受到限制的。

lim·i·ta·tion [ˌlimiˈteiʃən; ˏlɪməˋteʃən] ***n***. **1**. 限制。**2**. 界限;极限;限度;局限性;限制因素。**3**. 【法】(诉讼)时效,有效期限。*a ~ on imports* 进口限制。*an arms ~* 军备限制。*Each man has his ~s*. 人各有所不能。*know one's own ~s* 有自知之明。*owing to the ~ of space* 限于篇幅。

lim·i·ta·tive [ˈlimiteitiv; ˋlɪmətetɪv] ***a***. 限定的,有限制的。

lim·it·ed [ˈlimitid; ˋlɪmɪtɪd] **I *a***. **1**. 有限的,有限制的;【政】(君主权力)受宪法限制的。**2**. 〔美〕乘客名额有限制的,速度快的,停站少的。**3**. 智力[能力等]有限的。*a ~ war* 有限战争。~ *number* 少数。*a ~ express* (*train*) 特别快(车)。*a ~ mail* (定额)特别邮车。*They possess a rather ~ intelligence*. 他们的知识面相当狭窄。~ *monarchy* 君主立宪政体,有限君主制。**II *n***. 高级快车。~ (**liability**) **company**〔英〕股份有限公司〔用在公司名字之后时,作 Limited, 或略作 Ltd. 美国叫 incorporated company〕。~ **policy** 有限制的保险证书。~ **service**【军】(人员)不适合担任战斗任务;(装备,器材)不适用于战区。**-ly *ad***. **-ness *n***.

lim·it·er [ˈlimitə; ˋlɪmətɚ] ***n***. **1**. 限制物。**2**. 限制器,限动器,限幅器。*speed ~*限速器。

lim·it·ing [ˈlimitiŋ; ˋlɪmətɪŋ] ***a***. 限制(性)的,有限制力的,起限定作用的〔不涉及性质的各种定语如: several, four 等〕。~ **factor** 限制因素〔对有机物的生活或对人口数量、分布起限制作用的客观环境〕。~ **quantity** 影响量。

lim·it·less [ˈlimitlis; ˋlɪmɪtlɪs] ***a***. 无界限的,无限制的;无限期的;一望无际的。

lim·i·trophe [ˈlimitrəuf; ˋlɪməˏtrof] ***a***. 位于边界上的,边界接壤的。*two ~ countries* 相邻的两国。

li·miv·o·rous [laiˈmivərəs; laɪˋmɪvərəs] ***a***. 【动】食泥的〔如蚯蚓〕。

lim·mer [ˈlimə; ˋlɪmɚ] ***n***. 〔英俚〕流氓,恶棍;不正经的女人。

limn [lim; lɪm] ***vt***. **1**. 描画;勾划。**2**. 描写;生动地叙述。

limn·er [ˈlimnə; ˋlɪmɚ] ***n***. 画师,画匠,描述者。

lim·net·ic [limˈnetik; lɪmˋnɛtɪk] ***a***. 【生】生活于湖沼的。

lim·nol·o·gy [limˈnɔlədʒi; lɪmˋnɑlədʒɪ] ***n***. 湖沼学。

li·mo [ˈliməu; ˋlɪmo] ***n***. 〔口〕= limousine.

lim·o·nene [ˈliməˈni:n; ˋlɪməˏnin] ***n***. 【化】苧烯。

li·mo·nite [ˈlaiməˌnait; ˋlaɪməˏnaɪt] ***n***. 【矿】褐铁矿。

lim·ou·sine [ˈlimu(:)zi:n; ˏlɪmuˋzin] ***n***. 轿车;大型高级轿车;接送旅客的交通车。~ **liberal**〔美讽〕大轿车自由主义者〔指富有的自由主义者〕。

limp[1][limp; lɪmp] **I *vi***. **1**. 一瘸一拐地走。**2**. 慢腾腾地进行。**3**. (诗)韵律[抑扬]紊乱。**II *n***. **1**. 跛行。**2**. 挣扎着慢慢前进。**3**. (诗的)韵律紊乱。**-ing·ly *ad***. 一瘸一拐地。

limp[2][limp; lɪmp] ***a***. **1**. 柔软的。**2**. 易曲的。**3**. 柔弱的,无生气的。**4**. (装订)软面的。~ *as a doll* [*rag*] 无精打采的。**-ly *ad***. **-ness *n***.

lim·pet [ˈlimpit; ˋlɪmpɪt] ***n***. **1**. 【动】蝛,帽贝。**2**. 牢牢抱住某物〔官职等〕不舍的人;恋栈者。**3**. 水下爆破弹(= ~ mine). ***stick like a ~*** 纠缠不休。

lim·pid [ˈlimpid; ˋlɪmpɪd] ***a***. **1**. 清澈的,透明的。**2**. 明朗的,清晰的。**3**. 平静的,无忧无虑的。**-pid·i·ty** [-ˈpɪdətɪ; -ˋpɪdətɪ] ***n***. **-ly *ad***. **-ness *n***.

limp·kin [ˈlimpkin; ˋlɪmpkɪn] ***n***. 【动】秧鸡(*Aramus vociferus*)〔产于美国弗罗里达州与西印度群岛〕。

limp·sy, limp·sey [ˈlimpsi; ˋlɪmpsɪ] ***a***. (***-si·er; -si·est***)〔方〕软弱无力的。

lim·u·lus [ˈlimjuləs; ˋlɪmjələs] ***n***. (*pl*. ***-li*** [-ˌlai; -ˏlaɪ])【动】鲎(= horseshoe crab)。

lim·y [ˈlaimi; ˋlaɪmɪ] ***a***. (***lim·i·er; -i·est***) **1**. 含石灰的,石灰质的;石灰似的。**2**. 涂有黏鸟胶的;黏的。**-i·ness *n***.

lin. = **1**. lineal. **2**. linear.

lin·a·ble [ˈlainəbl; ˋlaɪnəbḷ] ***a***. 可作线状排列的;能划线的。

lin·ac [ˈlainæk; ˋlɪnæk] ***n***. 【物】linear accelerator.

lin·age [ˈlainidʒ; ˋlaɪnɪdʒ] ***n***. **1**. (原稿等的)行数。**2**. (稿费的)行数计酬法。

lin·al·o·ol [liˈnæləuˌɔl; lɪˋnæloˏɔl] ***n***. 【化】里哪[芫荽]醇,沉香(萜)醇。

linch·pin [ˈlintʃˌpin; ˋlɪntʃˏpɪn] ***n***. **1**. 车辖,制轮楔。**2**. 关键。*the ~ upon which success or failure depends* 成败的关键。

Lin·coln [ˈliŋkən; ˋlɪŋkən] ***n***. **1**. 林肯〔姓氏,男子名〕。**2**. **Abraham ~** 林肯〔1809—1865,美国第十六任总统,1862年颁布奴隶解放令〕。**3**. 〔美〕林肯牌大轿车〔福特汽车厂产的名牌豪华汽车〕。~ **green**【纺】林肯绿呢。~**'s Inn** (英国四法学协会之一的)林肯法学会。

Lin·coln·i·an [liŋˈkəuniən; ˏlɪŋkoˋnɪən] ***a***. 美国林肯总统的,关于林肯总统的。

lin·co·my·cin [ˌliŋkəˈmaisən; lɪŋkəˋmaɪsən] ***n***. 【药】林可霉素〔链霉素的一种〕。

Lin·da, Lyn·da [ˈlində; ˋlɪndə] ***n***. 琳达〔女子名〕。

lin·dane [ˈlinˌdein; ˋlɪnˏden] ***n***. 【化】六氯化苯,林丹。

Lind·bergh [ˈlindbə:g; ˋlɪnbɝg] ***n***. 林德伯格〔姓氏〕。

lin·den [ˈlindən; ˋlɪndən] ***n***. 【植】欧椴;美洲椴;菩提树。

Lind·say [ˈlindzi; ˋlɪnzɪ] ***n***. 林赛〔姓氏〕。

L

line[1] [lain; laɪn] **I** ***n*.** **1.** 线;绳索;钓丝;测深度用绳,卷尺。*a fishing* ~ 钓鱼线。*be clever with rod and* ~ 会钓鱼。*hang the clothes on the* ~ 把衣服挂在绳子上。**2.** (诗文的)一行;短信;〔*pl*.〕短诗;〔*pl*.〕罚课〔罚学生抄写拉丁诗百行等〕。*just a* ~ *to tell you that* ... 迳启者。**3.** 路线,铁路线;航线;交通线;铁轨。*a belt* ~ 环行线电车路;环行铁路。*a blockade* ~ 封锁线。*an air* ~ 航空线。*a* ~ *of supply*【军】补给线。*the down* [*up*] ~ 火车的下[上]行线。*the main* ~ *of a railway* 铁道干线。**4.** 排,行列;【陆军】两列横队;整列的战舰;阵形。*attack in* ~ 横队进攻。*draw up in* [*form into*] ~ 排成二列横队。*the* ~ *abreast* [*ahead*] 航队横[纵]列。**5.** (英陆军的)正规军;(美军的)战斗部队;前线部队。**6.** 条纹;皱纹;掌纹。*a face covered with deep* ~*s of care* 满面愁容。**7.** 家系,血统,朝代;门第。*a direct* ~ 直系。*relations in the female* ~ 母系亲属。**8.** 界线。*a dividing* ~ 分界线。*go* [*step*] *over the* ~ 越界;超越限度。**9.** 方面,范围;擅长,专门;行业。*It is not in my* ~ *to interfere*. 干涉不是我干的。*Cards are not in my* ~. 打牌不是我的拿手[嗜好]。*Geology is his particular* ~. 地质学是他的专长。*What* ~ (*of business*) *are you in*? 你从事的是哪门行业? *I am in the farm side* ~. 我经营的是农村副业。**10.** (商品的)种类,存货。*a full* ~ *of winter wear* 各种冬装,一应俱全。*the best-selling* ~ *in scarf* 最畅销的一种围巾。**11.** 形状,外形,轮廓。*have good* ~*s in one's face* 面孔的轮廓很好。**12.** 方针,路线,方法。*guiding* ~ 方针。**13.** 〔*pl*.〕【剧】台词。*memorize one's* ~*s* 记诵台词。**14.** 〔*pl*.〕结婚证书 (= marriage ~s)。**15.**【数】线,直线;【无】扫描线 (= scanning ~);【乐】乐谱的线;〔*pl*.〕【船】船体线图。*a curved* ~ 曲线。*a straight* ~ 直线。*an undulating* ~波状线。~ *of centres* 连心线。*ruled* ~*s* 格子线。**16.** *the* ~ 赤道。**17.** 情报,迹象,消息。*give sb. a* ~ *on sth*. 对某人透露一点有关某事的情况。*try to get* [*have*] *a* ~ *on sth*. 想打听到某事。**18.** (长度单位)十二分之一英寸。**19.** 缰绳。**20.** 金属线;电线;线路;管;管道作业线。*Hold the* ~, *please*. (电话)请等一等。*L- busy*. (电话)〔美〕占线,有人在打〔英国说 Number engaged〕. *an extension* ~ (电话)分机。*a main* ~ (电话)中继线。*a sewage* ~ 下水管道,污水管道。*a telegraph* ~ 电报线路。*an assembly* ~ 装配线。*a production* ~ 生产线。**21.** 战线,前线。*fight behind the enemy* ~*s* 在敌后作战。*the first* ~ *of defence* 第一道防线。**22.** 〔*pl*.〕(英军的)一排营帐。*inspect the* ~*s* 巡视营房。**23.** 命运,运气。*Hard* ~*s*! 倒霉! ***all along the*** ~ 在全线,在每一点上;到处。***be in*** ~ **1.** 成直线,排成一行。**2.** 有希望。**3.** 符合,依照。***be in one's*** ~ **1.** 擅长。**2.** 合胃口。***be out of one's*** ~ **1.** 不擅长。**2.** 不合胃口。***below the*** ~ 在水准以下。***bring*** [***get***] ***into*** ~ 使成一排;使一致;使合作 (*with*). ***by*** (***rule and***) ~ = ***by*** ~ ***and level*** 准确地,精密地;正确地。***come*** [***fall***] ***into*** ~ **1.** 排齐。**2.** 一致,协力,合作 (*with*). ***cross the*** ~ (船)通过赤道〔通常举行庆祝〕。***down the*** ~ **1.** 往市中心去。**2.** 完全地 (*back sb. down the* ~ 完全支持某人)。***draw a*** ~***.between*** ... 区别清楚。***draw the*** [***a***] ~ 划界线 (*One must draw the* ~ *somewhere* 忍耐也有个限度。*know when* [*where*] *to draw a* ~ 不越轨,知道分寸)。***draw up in*** [***into***] ~ 排队。***drop*** [***send***] ***a*** ~ [***a few*** ~***s***] 写封短信。***form into*** ~ 排成一行。***give sb***. ~ ***enough*** 先纵后擒〔原意为鱼吞饵后暂将钓丝放长,然后钓起〕。***go up the*** ~ 到前线去。***have sb. on a*** ~ **1.** 愚弄某人,跟某人开玩笑。**2.** 操纵某人。***hew to the*** ~ 循规蹈矩,服从纪律。***hit the*** ~ 〔美〕**1.** (橄榄球赛中)带球冲过对方防线。**2.** 勇敢果断地行事。***hold the*** ~ **1.** (打电话时)等着不挂断。**2.** 坚持下去。***in a*** ~ 成一行,排队。***in*** ~ ***for*** 〔美〕即将得到,取得胜算。***in*** ~ ***with*** 和…成一直线;〔美〕和…一致,符合。***keep to*** [***take***] ***one's own*** ~ 干自己的本行;坚持自己的原则。***lay*** [***put***] ***it on the*** ~ **1.** 付钱。**2.** 坦率地说,提供证据。~ ***upon*** ~ 得一进二地,一步接一步地(推进)。***muff one's*** ~***s***【剧】接不上台词。***no hard and fast*** ~ ***can be drawn between*** ... ***and***.... …和…是不能截然分开的。***on a*** ~ 同等的,同等地。***on the*** ~ **1.** (挂)在不高不低的地方。**2.** 模棱两可。**3.** 立即,马上。**4.** 处于危险状态。**5.** 沦为妓女。***on the same*** ~ 以同样方式。***on this*** ~ 按此方针。***out of*** ~ **1.** 不成一直线。**2.** 不一致,不协调。***ride the*** ~〔美〕骑马赶回离群的牧畜。***shoot a*** ~〔俚〕吹牛,说大话。***sign on the dotted*** ~***s*** 在虚线上署名;全部接受。***take a strong*** ~ 干得起劲;采取强硬手段。***take the air*** ~ 走直线,走最短的路。***the bread*** ~ 失业者领取免费面包的长蛇阵。***the*** ~ ***of beauty*** 美的线条,S形线条。***the*** ~ ***of conduct*** 行为的准确。***the*** ~ ***of duty*** 值勤,公务 (*be wounded in the* ~ *of duty* 因公负伤)。***throw a good*** ~ 会钓鱼。***toe the*** ~ **1.** 准备起跑。**2.** 服从纪律。***under the*** ~ 在赤道上。

II ***vt*.** **1.** 画线,画轮廓;用线划分。**2.** 起皱纹。*a face* ~*d with age* 因年老起了皱纹的脸。**3.** 排成一行;沿…排列。*a road* ~*d with trees* 两旁种着树的路。*People* ~ *the streets to welcome*. 人们夹道欢迎。**4.** (给演员)勾脸。**5.** 派工作 (*to*). —***vi*.** 排齐,排队。~ ***off*** 用线划开。~ ***out*** **1.** 标出,划线标明。~ *out the route on the map* 在地图上把路线标示出来。**2.** 把…排成行;【植】列植。**3.** 用线条标明…需要删去。**4.** 迅速移动。*The plane* ~*d out east*. 飞机向东直飞而去。**5.** 放声高唱。*He* ~*d out a few songs upon request*. 他在大家请求之下唱了几首歌。~ ***through*** 划掉,(一笔)勾销。~ ***up*** 整顿(机械等);排成一列;使(兵士)排齐;整顿阵容。~ **backer** (橄榄球)前锋。~ **chief** 机场外场保养组组长。~ **crosser** **1.** 工贼。**2.** 越出行为规范者;失礼者。~ **dance** ***n*. & *vi*.** 排成一行(的)肩并肩跳舞。~ **drawing** 线条画〔如钢笔画、铅笔画等〕。~ **drive**【棒球】平直球,直球。~ **engine** 直列式发动机。~ **engraving** 线雕;线雕画。~ **firing**【军】横队射击。~**-haul** ***n*.** 长途运输。~ **lamp** 呼叫灯,号灯。~ **loop** 电话回路。~ **man** **1.** 护路工,养路工。**2.**【电】线务员,线路工人。**3.**【军】架线兵。**4.** (橄榄球)前锋。**5.**【测】执线人。~ **men's climber** 脚扣〔电工上电杆时套在鞋上的钩状物〕。~ **of battle** (军队或军舰的)战列,战斗队形。~ **of beauty** 美的线条。~ **of conduct** 行为的准则。~ **of credit** (银行对某客户的)贷款最高限额。~ **officer** 前线军官。~ **of scrimmage** (橄榄球假想的)前锋抢球线。~ **of sight** **1.** 视线,瞄准线〔也叫 ~ of vision〕。**2.**【无、电视】视线〔发射天线至地平线之间的直线距离〕。~**-of-sight** ***a*.** 视线的,瞄准线的。~**-of-sight reception** 视距信号接收。~ **production** 流水作业。~ **radio** 有线载波通信。~ **selector** 终接器,寻线器。~ **shaft** 总轴,天轴,机轴,动力轴。~ **shafting** 传动轴系。~ **shooter** 吹牛的人。~ **shooting** 吹牛。~**sman** **1.**【电】线务员,线路工人。**2.** 护路工,养路工。**3.** (球类比赛中的)巡边员。**4.**〔英〕正规军陆军士兵,列兵。~ **speed** 线速度。~ **squall**【气】线飑。~ **tape** 卷尺。~**-to-ground** **1.** 线路对地的。**2.** 线路接地。~ **unit** 接线盒。~**-up** **1.** 一排人〔尤指排队受检查的嫌疑犯〕。**2.** (抱有相同兴趣或宗旨的)一组人;(用途相同的)一批东西。**3.** (比赛时)球员的阵容。

line[2] [lain; laɪn] ***vt*.** **1.** 镶(衣服)里子;裱褙;衬里。**2.** 填塞。~ *a coat with fur* 用皮子给大衣衬里。*a study* ~*d with books* (四壁)摆满书的书房。~ ***one's pocket***(***s***) [***purse***]〔口〕填塞私囊,中饱。~ ***the inside***〔俚〕填肚皮,吃饱。

line[3] [lain; laɪn] ***vt*.** 交尾。

lin·e·age[1] [ˈliniidʒ; ˋlɪnɪɪdʒ] ***n*.** 血统,世系,门第。

lin·e·age[2] [ˈlainidʒ; ˋlaɪnɪdʒ] ***n*.** = linage.

L

lin·e·al [ˈliniəl; ˋlɪnɪəl] *a*. 1. 直系的,正统的。2. 嫡系的,世袭的;祖先传来的。3. 世系的,属同一世系的。4. 线的,线状的;用线的。5. = linear. 6. 战斗部队的。*a ~ ascendant* [*descendant*] 直系尊属后裔,子孙。**-ly** *ad*.

lin·e·a·ment [ˈliniəmənt; ˋlɪnɪəmənt] *n*. 〔常 *pl*.〕面貌;轮廓;特征。

lin·e·ar [ˈliniə; ˋlɪnɪə] *a*. 1. 线的,直线的。2. 长度的。3.【数】一次的,线性的。4.【动、植】线状的;细长的。5. 由线条组成的,以线条为主的,强调线条的。~ *amplification* 直线放大。*a ~ equation* 一次方程式。*a ~ leaf* 线形叶。~ *arts* 线条艺术。~ **accelerator**【物】直线性加速器。~ **algebra**【数】线性代数。~ **distortion**【无】线性失真。~ **measure** 1. 测量长度。2. 长度单位制〔尤指 12 英寸 = 1 英尺等单位制〕。~ **perspective** 直线透视。~ **programming**【数】线性规划。~ **thinking**【心】线性思维〔一种由因推果,再推论到下一个原因等的直线型思维方式〕。

lin·e·ar·i·ty [ˌliniˈæriti; ˏlɪnɪˋærətɪ] *n*. 线性,直线性。

lin·e·ar·ize [ˈliniəˌraiz; ˋlɪnɪəˏraɪz] *vt*. (*-iz·ed*, *-iz·ing*) 直线[线性]化。**-i·za·tion** [ˌliniəraiˈzeiʃən; ˏlɪnɪəraɪˋzeʃən] *n*. 线性化。

lin·e·ate [ˈliniːit, -niˌeit; ˋlɪnɪɪt, -nɪˏet] *a*. 有线的;标线的;有条纹的。

lin·e·a·tion [ˌliniˈeiʃən; ˏlɪnɪˋeʃən] *n*. 1. 画线,标线。2. 轮廓。3. 一列线。

lin·en [ˈlinin; ˋlɪnɪn] I *n*. 1. 亚麻布,亚麻线。2. 〔*pl*.〕亚麻布类;〔集合词〕亚麻布制品[衬衫、被单等]。3. = ~ paper. ***shoot one's ~*** (放下手)露出袖口。***wash one's dirty ~ in public*** [***at home***] 家丑外扬[不外扬]。II *a*. 亚麻的,亚麻布制的;亚麻色的。~ **closet** (放床单、桌布等的)亚麻织品衣橱。~ **draper** 〔英〕亚麻布制品商。~ **paper** 布纹纸。

lin·en·ette [ˌliniˈnet; ˏlɪnɪˋnɛt] *n*.【纺】充亚麻织物。

lin·e·o·late [ˈliniəˌleit; ˋlɪnɪəˏlet] *a*.【生】有细条纹的。

lin·er[1] [ˈlainə; ˋlaɪnə] *n*. 1. (固定航线的)定期班;班机。2. 画线者。3. 画线的工具。4. (棒球中的)直球,平球。

lin·er[2] [ˈlainə; ˋlaɪnə] *n*. 1. 制衬里[衬垫等]的人;装衬里[衬垫等]的人。2. 衬里;【机】衬垫,套圈,衬套。*a bearing ~* 轴瓦。

line·y [ˈlaini; ˋlaɪnɪ] *a*. (*lin·i·er*, *lin·i·est*) = liny.

ling[1] [liŋ; lɪŋ] *n*.【动】鳕科鱼;长身鳕鱼。

ling[2] [liŋ; lɪŋ] *n*.【植】石南。

-ling *suf*. 1. 附在名词后构成名词,表示"小","不重要","低劣":duck*ling*, prince*ling*. 2. 附在名词、形容词、副词后构成名词,表示"…的人[物]":dar*ling*, nurs*ling*, shalve*ling*, under*ling*. 3. 〔古、方〕附在名词或形容词后构成副词,表示"方向","状态":dark*ling*, flat*ling*, side*ling*.

linga, lingam [ˈliŋgə, ˈliŋgəm; ˋlɪŋgə, ˋlɪŋgəm] *n*. 1.【宗】男性生殖器像〔印度为湿婆神 Siva〕。2. 〔梵语语法〕男性。

Lin·ga·la [liŋˈgɑːlə; lɪŋˋgɑlə] *n*. 林格拉语〔刚果西部使用的一种混合班图语〕。

ling·cod [ˈliŋˌkɔd; ˋlɪŋˏkɑd] *n*. (*pl*. *-cod*, *-cods*)【动】蛇齿单线鱼〔北太平洋中的一种大鱼〕。

lin·ger [ˈliŋgə; ˋlɪŋgə] *vi*. 逗留;徘徊;拖延。— *vt*. 挨过,拖延(时间)。~ ***on a subject*** 踌躇考虑;絮絮不休地说一件事。~ ***out one's life*** 苟延残喘。~ ***over one's work*** 磨洋工。

L

lin·ge·rie [ˌlænʒəˈriː, ˈlæn-; ˏlænʒəˋri, ˋlæn-] *n*. 〔F.〕亚麻布制品〔妇女、小孩的内衣,睡衣之类〕。

lin·ger·ing [ˈliŋgəriŋ; ˋlɪŋgərɪŋ] *a*. 逡巡的,拖延的;踌躇的。*a ~ disease* 缠绵不愈的病。*cast a ~ look behind* 踌躇地回头一看。**-ly** *ad*.

lin·go [ˈliŋgəu; ˋlɪŋgo] *n*. (*pl*. *~es*) 〔蔑〕听不懂的话〔指外国话、术语等〕;隐语。

ling·on·ber·ry [ˈliŋənˌberi; ˋlɪŋənˏbɛrɪ] *n*. (*pl*. *-ries*) = cowberry.

lingu- *comb*. *f*. 表示"舌","语言":*lingu*ist, *lingu*late.

lin·gua [ˈliŋgwə; ˋlɪŋgwə] *n*. (*pl*. *-guae* [-gwiː; -gwi]) 1. 舌;下咽头。2. 语言。~ **franca** 1. 佛兰卡语〔意大利、法兰西、阿拉伯、希腊、西班牙等国语言的混合语。通行于地中海各港〕。2. (国际商业上通用的)混合语。

lin·gual [ˈliŋgwəl; ˋlɪŋgwəl] I *a*. 1. 舌的,舌状的,舌旁的。2.【语音】舌音的。3. = linguistic. II *n*. 舌音;舌音字母〔t, d, l, n, s 等〕。**-ly** *ad*.

Lin·gua·phone [ˈliŋgwəfəun; ˋlɪŋgwəˏfon] *n*.【商标名】灵格风〔英国一家把各国语言教材灌制成唱片和录音带的制造商的商标名称〕。*the ~ English course* 灵格风英语教程。*the ~ method* 灵格风教授法。

lingui- *comb*. *f*. = lingu-.

lin·gui·form [ˈliŋgwifɔːm; ˋlɪŋgwɪˏfɔrm] *a*. 舌形的,舌状的。

lin·gui·ne [liŋˈgwiːniː; lɪŋˋgwini] *n*. 宽面条。

lin·guist [ˈliŋgwist; ˋlɪŋgwɪst] *n*. 1. 语言学家。2. 通多种外国语的人。

lin·guis·tic(al) [liŋˈgwistik(əl); lɪŋˋgwɪstɪk(əl)] *a*. 语言的;语言学的。~ **atlas** 方言地图,语言地图。~ **form** 语言形态〔如词素、单词、单语、句子等〕。~ **geographer** 语言地理学家。~ **geography** 语言地理学。~ **stock** 1. 基础语,母语〔母语及其所衍生出来的亲属语言和亲属方言〕。2. 讲上述语言或方言的本地人。

lin·guis·ti·cian [ˌliŋgwisˈtiʃən; ˏlɪŋgwɪsˋtɪʃən] *n*. 语言学家。

lin·guis·tics [liŋˈgwistiks; lɪŋˋgwɪstɪks] *n*. 语言学。*comparative ~* 比较语言学。*general ~* 一般语言学。

lin·gu·late [ˈliŋgjuleit; ˋlɪŋgjʊˏlet] *a*. 舌形的,舌状的。

linguo- *comb*. *f*. = lingu-.

lin·hay [ˈlini; lɪnɪ] *n*. 〔方〕= linn(e)y.

lin·i·ment [ˈlinimənt; ˋlɪnɪmənt] *n*.【药】搽剂,擦剂。

linin [ˈlainin; ˋlaɪnɪn] *n*.【生】核丝。

lin·ing [ˈlainiŋ; ˋlaɪnɪŋ] *n*. 1. (衣服等的)衬里,里子;衬料。2. 〔古〕内容。3. 装衬里[衬套等]。4.【机】衬,衬套,套筒,衬垫;(汽机的)气套。5.【建】隔板。

link[1] [liŋk; lɪŋk] I *n*. 1. 环;链环。2. (编织物的)链圈。3. (链状物中的)一节;(多节香肠等的)一节;单节小香肠。4. 承前启后的人[物];环节,联系。5.【机】连杆,滑环,链节。6.【化】键,键合;【计】链接,衔接。7. (测量用长度单位)令〔= 7.92 英寸〕。8. 〔*pl*.〕(衬衫袖口的)链扣(= cuff ~s). 9.【无】通讯线路;网络节;固定接线。10.【电】熔丝。11. 〔*pl*.〕〔方〕河道弯曲处。*draw ~* 牵引连杆。*drive ~* 传动杆。*all-round ~s, radio relay ~* 无线电中继线路。*One ~ broken, the whole chain is broken*. 〔谚〕一环断,全链断。*The chain is no stronger than its weakest ~*. = *The strength of a chain is its weakest ~*. 〔谚〕一环软弱,全链不强。***the missing ~*** 短缺的环节;全部推论[材料]中还不能衔接之处;设想存在于人类与类人猿之间的过渡生物;联系;环接;握(手),搭(手臂)。II *vi*. 连结;联合。— *vt*.【计】链接,衔接。~ ***up with*** 和…同盟,和…提携;结亲。~ **lever** 提环杆。~**man** 1.【橄榄球、足球等】(中锋与后卫间的)联络员。2. (广播、电视辩论节目中的)调停员。3. 中间人,中介。~**-motion**【机】连杆运动。~ **mounting** 插环。~ **receiver**【无、讯】中继接收机,接力接收机。~ **rod** (副)连杆。~**s-and-~s machine** 双反面针织机,回复机。~**up** 连结,联合,会合。~ **verb** = linking verb. ~**work** 1. 环节联结物〔如链条〕。2.【机】联动齿轮系统,联动装置,链系。

link[2] [liŋk; lɪŋk] *n*. 火把,火炬。~**boy**, ~**man** 拿火炬的人。

Link trainer [ˌliŋkˈtreinə; ˏlɪŋkˋtrenə] *n*. 林克式地上飞行练习装置。

link·age [ˈliŋkidʒ; ˋlɪŋkɪdʒ] *n*. 1. 联系;连锁;联动;连接。2.【化】键合。3. 链系,联动装置。4.【电】耦合;磁链;匝连。*the brake* ~ 制动联动装置。*a strategy of* ~ 关联战略〔在国际谈判中故意把两个或更多个问题拉扯到一起,借以向对方施加压力〕。

link·ing [ˈliŋkiŋ, ˋlɪŋkɪŋ] *n*. 耦合,结合,咬合;联系;连接。~**-up ship** 联络舰。~**-up station** 中继电台。~ **verb** 联系动词〔其后可接用作表语的一些动词,如 be, get, seem, become 等〕。

Link·la·ter [ˈliŋkˌleitə; ˋlɪŋkˏletɚ] *n*. 林克莱特〔姓氏〕。

links [liŋks; lɪŋks] *n*.〔*pl*.〕1.〔Scot.〕(海边高低起伏的)砂丘。2.〔亦可用作单数说作 a links〕高尔夫球场。~**land** = links 1. ~**man**〔美〕打高尔夫球的人。

linn [lin; lɪn] *n*.〔Scot.〕1. 瀑布;瀑布下的水潭。2. 溪谷,绝壁。

Linn. = 1. Linnaeus. 2. Linnean.

Lin·n(a)e·an [liˈni(ː)ən; lɪˋniən] *a*.【生】瑞典博物学家林奈的;按照林奈命名法的。

Lin·nae·us [liˈni(ː)əs; lɪˋniəs], **Carolus** 林奈〔1707—1778,瑞典博物学家,瑞典原名为 Karl von Linné〕。

lin·net [ˈlinit; ˋlɪnɪt] *n*.【动】朱顶雀,红雀。

lin·n(e)y [ˈlini; ˋlɪnɪ] *n*.〔英方〕农家棚屋。

lino. = linotype.

li·no [ˈlainəu; ˋlaɪno] *n*. = linoleum. ~**cut** *n*. 1. 亚麻油毡浮雕(版)。2. 油毡浮雕的印刷图样。

li·no·le·ate [liˈnəuliˌeit; lɪˋnolɪˏet] *n*.【化】亚油酸盐(或酯)。

lin·o·le·ic acid [ˌlinəˈliːik; ˏlɪnəˋliɪk] 亚油酸。

lin·o·le·nate [ˌlinəˈliːneit; ˏlɪnəˋlinet] *n*.【化】亚麻酸盐(或酯)。

lin·o·le·nic acid [ˌlinəˈliːnik; ˏlɪnəˋlinɪk]【化】亚麻酸。

li·no·le·um [liˈnəuljəm; lɪˋnolɪəm] *n*. 亚麻油(地)毡,漆布。

lin·o·type [ˈlainəˌtaip; ˋlaɪnəˏtaɪp] I *n*. 1. 行型活字铸造机[排版机]。2. 行型活字;行型活字印刷品。II *vi*. 操纵行型活字铸造机。— *vt*. 用行型活字铸造机排版。

lin·sang [ˈliŋsæŋ; ˋlɪŋsæŋ] *n*.【动】林狸〔产于澳大利亚等地〕。

lin·seed [ˈlinsiːd; ˋlɪnˏsid] *n*. 亚麻子[仁]。~ **cake** 亚麻子饼。~ **meal** 亚麻子饼粉。~ **oil** 亚麻子[仁]油。

lin·sey(-wool·sey) [ˈlinziˈwulzi; ˋlɪnzɪˋwʊlzɪ] *n*. 1.【纺】亚麻羊毛交织物。2. 混杂物;梦话,胡话。

lin·stock [ˈlinstɔk; ˋlɪnstɑk] *n*. (古时放炮用的)火绳杆。

lint [lint; lɪnt] *n*. 1. 皮棉 (= ~ cotton)。2. (作绷带用的)软麻布。3. 棉绒。~ **art** 棉绒(装饰)艺术。

lin·tel [ˈlintl; ˋlɪntl̩] *n*.【建】楣;壁炉横梁。

lint·er [ˈlintə; ˋlɪntɚ] *n*. 1. 剥绒机。2.〔*pl*.〕棉籽绒,棉短绒。

lint·white [ˈlintˌwait; ˋlɪntˏwaɪt] *n*. = linnet.

lin·y [ˈlaini; ˋlaɪnɪ] *a*. (*lin·i·er*; *-i·est*) 1. 像一根线的;细弱的。2. 由线条构成的;多线条的,多纹路的,多皱纹的。

li·on [ˈlaiən; ˋlaɪən] *n*. 1. 狮子。2. 勇猛的人,慓悍的人。3. 名流,名人。4.〔*pl*.〕名胜〔过去参观伦敦的人必去看伦敦塔的狮子〕。5.〔L-〕【天】狮子座;狮子宫;【徽】狮印;狮子纹章。*A* ~ *at home, a mouse abroad*.〔谚〕在家像狮子,出外成老鼠。*The* ~ *is not so fierce as he is painted*.〔谚〕传闻往往失实。***a*** ~ ***in the way*** [***path***] 途中的障碍,拦路虎。***as bold*** [***brave***] ***as a*** ~ 勇猛如狮。~ ***and unicorn*** (捧英国皇室徽章的)狮子和独角兽。***make a*** ~ ***of sb***. 使某人红极一时。***put*** [***run***] ***one's head into the*** ~***'s mouth*** 轻入险境,冒险。***see the*** ~***s***〔英〕游览名胜。***show sb. the*** ~***s***〔英〕带领某人游览名胜。***the*** (***old***) ***British L-*** 英国的别称。***the*** ~***'s share*** 最大最好的份额〔语出《伊索寓言》〕。***the*** ~***'s skin*** 表面的威武。***twist the*** ~***'s tail*** (尤指美国记者)说英国坏话。~**heart** 1. 勇士。2.〔L-〕英王理查一世。~**hearted** *a*. 勇猛的,大胆的。~**-hunter** *n*. 1. 猎狮者。2. 专事巴结社会名流的人。~**hood**, ~**ship** 社会名流的地位。**-like** *a*.

li·on·cel [ˈlaiənˌsel; ˋlaɪənˏsɛl] *n*. 幼狮;小狮子。

Li·o·nel [ˈlaiənl; ˋlaɪənl̩] *n*. 莱昂内尔〔男子名〕。

li·on·ess [ˈlaiənis; ˋlaɪənɪs] *n*. 母狮。

li·on·et [laiənit; ˋlaɪənɪt] *n*. 小狮子。

li·on·ism [ˈlaiənizəm; ˋlaɪənɪzəm] *n*. 1. 专事巴结名流的行为。2.【医】(麻疯病者后期的)狮面症状。

li·on·ize [ˈlaiənaiz; ˋlaɪənˏaɪz] *vt*. 1. 捧人,捧为名流。2.〔英〕游览名胜;导游名胜。— *vi*. 1. 巴结名流。2.〔英〕游览名胜。**-r** *n*. 专事巴结名流的人。**-iz·a·tion** *n*.

L.I.P. = life insurance policy 人寿保险单。

lip [lip; lɪp] I *n*. 1. 嘴唇。2. 唇状物;(杯、壶等的)口,边;【植】唇瓣;(管乐器的)管唇。3.〔俚〕无理[礼]的回答;冒昧的话,无礼。4.〔美〕律师。5.〔~s〕【计】(人工智能电脑的)每秒逻辑推理次数。*an upper* ~ 上唇。*an under* [*a lower*] ~ 下唇。*be as close as the* ~*s are to the teeth* = *be closely related as* ~*s and teeth* 唇齿相依。*I heard it from his* ~*s*. 我听他亲口讲的。*She never opened her* ~*s*. 她从来不开口。*Don't give me any* ~! 别讲这种荒唐话! 不要这么无礼! *None of your* ~!〔俚〕别放肆! ***be steeped to the*** ~***s in*** 深陷…之中。***bite one's*** ~ (为压制感情)咬紧嘴唇。***button up one's*** ~〔美俚〕住嘴,保守秘密。***carry*** [***have***, ***keep***] ***a stiff upper*** ~ 倔强,固执;坚持下去。***curl the*** [***one's***] ~ 撇嘴〔表示轻蔑或讨厌〕。***escape*** [***pass***] ***sb.'s*** ~***s*** (话)无意中说漏嘴。***from the*** ~***s outward*** 不假思索地;敷衍地。***hang on sb.'s*** ~***s*** 被某人的话迷住,听得入神。***hang one's*** ~ 沮丧。***lick*** [***smack***] ***one's*** ~***s*** (馋得)舐嘴唇;垂涎三尺。***make*** (***up***) ***a*** ~ (因不平、生气等而)撅嘴。***on sb.'s*** ~***s*** (话)就在嘴边。***on the*** ~***s of*** 1. 在…中间流传。2. 出诸…之口,挂在…嘴上。***part with dry*** ~***s*** 没有接吻即分手。***pass one's*** ~***s*** 1. 被某人吃掉[喝完]。2. 被某人冲口说出。***put*** [***lay***] ***one's finger to one's*** ~***s*** 把手指搁在嘴唇上〔叫人沉默时的手势〕。***read sb.'s*** ~***s*** 揣摩某人的口气。***refuse toopen one's*** ~***s*** 拒不开口。***rush to one's*** ~***s*** (话)一齐涌到嘴边。***seal sb.'s*** ~***s*** 封住某人嘴巴,禁止某人说话。***shoot out one's*** ~***s*** 蔑视地撅嘴。***Zip your*** ~***s***!〔美俚〕闭嘴! II *vt*. (*-pp-*) 1. 用嘴唇接触;〔诗〕吻。2. (波浪)冲刷(海岸)。3. 轻轻地说;〔俚〕唱;〔美俚〕吹奏。4. 把高尔夫球打到穴边而未进去。— *vi*. 1. (吹奏管乐器时)用嘴唇。2. (水)潺潺地响。III *a*. 1. 唇的。2. 口头上的。3. 唇音的。~ *consonants* 唇子音。*a* ~ *comfort* 空口安慰。~**-deep** *a*. 口头上的;无诚意的。~ **language** (聋哑者用嘴唇形状表示语声的)唇话,视话。~ **microphone** (戴在讲话人嘴唇上的)唇式传声器。~**print** 唇印〔嘴唇留下的印痕,据说人各不同〕。~**-read** *vt*., *vi*. (~***-read*** [-red; -rɛd]; ~***-reading***) 观唇辨意〔如聋哑人根据讲话者的唇动去理解其意〕。~**-reader** 善于观唇辨意的人〔如聋哑者〕。~**salve** 1. 润唇(防裂)油膏。2. 拍马屁,奉承。~ **service** 空口答应[应酬话],口惠。~**speaker** 擅长用嘴唇动作和聋哑人交谈的人。~**stick** 口红,唇膏。~**-synch** *vt*., *vi*., *n*. 对口形〔使口的动作与录音讲话等的声音一致,如电影配音等〕。~**-worship** 口是心非的崇拜。

li·pase [ˈlaipeis, ˈlipeis; ˋlaɪpes, ˋlɪpes] *n*.【化】脂(肪)酶。

lip·id [ˈlipid, ˈlaipid; ˋlɪpɪd; ˋlaɪpɪd] *n*.【化】脂类 (= lipide)。

lip·(o)- *comb. f*. 表示"脂肪的": *lipo*lysis, *lipo*tropic.

lip·o·fill·ing [ˌlipəˈfiliŋ; ˏlɪpəˋfɪlɪŋ] *n*.【医】脂肪植入法〔做手术向体内植入脂肪以整容〕。

li·pog·ra·phy [liˈpɔgrəfi; lɪˋpɑgrəfɪ] *n*. (书写时)字母或词的脱漏,漏写。

li·poid [ˈlipɔid, ˈlaipɔid; ˋlɪpɔɪd, ˋlaɪpɔɪd] I *a*.【生化、

L

化】类脂的(= lipoidal)。**II** ***n.*** 类脂物,类脂化合物。

li·pol·y·sis [liˈpɔlisis; lɪˋpɑləsɪs] ***n.*** 脂解(作用)。**lip·o·lyt·ic** [ˈlipəˈlitik; ˏlɪpəˋlɪtɪk] ***a.***

li·po·ma [liˈpəumə, lai-; lɪˋpomə, laɪ-] ***n.*** (*pl.* ***-po·ma·ta*** [-tə; -tə], ***-po·mas***)【医】脂肪瘤。**-tous** ***a.***

lip·o·phil·ic [ˌlipəˈfilik; ˏlɪpəˋfɪlɪk] ***a.*** 亲脂的;嗜肥的。

lip·o·pro·tein [ˌlipəˈprəutiːn, -ˈprəutiːin; ˏlɪpəˋprotin, -ˋprotiɪn] ***n.***【生】脂蛋白。

lip·o·suc·tion [ˌlipəˈsʌkʃən; ˏlɪpəˋsʌkʃən] ***n.***【医】脂肪抽吸法〔一种整容外科手术,切开皮肤以真空泵吸出多余的皮下脂肪〕。

lip·o·trop·ic [ˌlipəˈtrɔpik; ˏlɪpəˋtrɑpɪk] ***a.***【生化】抗脂(肪)的,减少脂肪积聚的。**li·pot·ro·pism** [liˈpɔtrəpizm; lɪˋpɑtrəpɪzm] ***n.***

lipped [lipt; lɪpt] ***a.*** **1.** 有唇的〔常作复合词,如 tight-~ 嘴唇紧闭的;嘴紧的〕。**2.** 有嘴的(壶、杯等)。**3.**【植】= labiate.

lip·pen [ˈlipn; ˋlɪpən] ***n.***, ***vt.***, ***vi.*** 〔主 Scot.〕信任;信托。

lip·per [ˈlipə; ˋlɪpɚ] ***n.***【海】**1.** 涟漪;细浪。**2.** 浪花,水花。

lip·ping [ˈlipiŋ; ˋlɪpɪŋ] ***n.*** **1.**【解】(骨的)唇形变。**2.** (吹管乐器时的)嘴形,唇形。

Lip(p)·man(n) [ˈlipmən; ˋlɪpmən] ***n.*** 李普曼〔姓氏〕。

lip·py [ˈlipi; ˋlɪpɪ] ***a.*** (***-pi·er***; ***-pi·est***) 〔俚〕无礼的;傲慢的。**lip·pi·ness** ***n.***

Lip·ton [ˈliptən; ˋlɪptən] ***n.*** 利普顿〔姓氏〕。

liq. = **1.** liquid. **2.** liquor.

liq·uate [liˈkweit; ˋlaɪkwet] ***vt.***【冶】熔解,熔析。**li·qua·tion** ***n.***

liq·ue·fa·cient [ˌlikwəˈfeiʃənt; ˏlɪkwəˋfeʃənt] **I** ***a.*** 液化的;使成为液体的;促使液化的。**II** ***n.*** 液化素,解凝剂。

liq·ue·fac·tion [ˌlikwiˈfækʃən; ˏlɪkwɪˋfækʃən] ***n.*** 液化(作用)。

liq·ue·fi·er [ˈlikwiˌfaiə; ˋlɪkwɪˏfaɪr] ***n.*** **1.** 液化器。**2.** 液化器操作工。

liq·ue·fy [ˈlikwifai; ˋlɪkwəˏfaɪ] ***vt.***, ***vi.*** (使)液化。**liq·ue·fi·a·ble** ***a.***

li·ques·cent [liˈkwesnt; lɪˋkwɛsnt] ***a.*** 可液化的,融解的。**li·ques·cence** ***n.***

li·queur [liˈkjuə; lɪˋkjʊr] **I** ***n.*** **1.** (饭后饮用的)甜露酒。**2.** (饮甜露酒的)小酒杯(= ~ glass)。**II** ***vt.*** 用甜露酒调味。

liq·uid [ˈlikwid; ˋlɪkwɪd] **I** ***n.*** **1.** 液体。**2.**【语】流音〔如[l],[r]〕。**II** ***a.*** **1.** 液体的,液态的,流动的。**2.** 清澄的,透明的。**3.** 易变的,不稳定的。**4.** 流畅的,流利的;柔和的,清脆的。**5.**【语】流音的。**6.**【经】流动的,易变为现金的。*a ~ sky* 明朗的天空。*~ opinions* 易变[多变]的意见。~ **air** 液态空气。~ **assets**【商】流动资产。~ *capital* 流动资本。~ **crystal** 液晶(体)。~ **diet[food]** 流质食物。~ **fire** 液体燃烧剂。~**-measure** ***n.*** **1.** 液量单位〔如 gill, pint, quart, gallon 等; *cf.* dry-measure〕。**2.** 液体测量器。~ **oxygen** 液态氧。~ **phase**【物】液相。~ **state**【物】液态。**-ly** ***ad.*** **-ness** ***n.***

liq·uid·am·bar [ˈlikwidˌæmbə; ˋlɪkwɪdˏæmbɚ] ***n.*** **1.**【植】胶皮糖香树(*Liquidambar styraciflua*)〔产于亚洲和北美〕。**2.** 胶皮糖香液。

liq·ui·date [ˈlikwideit; ˋlɪkwɪˏdet] ***vt.*** **1.** 清理,清算(破产的公司等);了结;清偿(债务等)。**2.** 除掉,消灭,杀掉;结束。**3.** (拿证券、资产等)换成现款。— ***vi.*** 清算;破产。

liq·ui·da·tion [ˌlikwiˈdeiʃən; ˏlɪkwɪˋdeʃən] ***n.*** **1.** (公司等的)清理,清算;(债务的)清偿,了结;(资产等的)变现。**2.** 清除,消灭;取消,杀掉。***go into*** ~ (公司等)破产,停业清理。~ **sale** 停业清理大拍卖。

liq·ui·da·tion·ism [ˌlikwiˈdeiʃənizəm; ˏlɪkwɪˋdeʃənɪzəm] ***n.*** 取消主义。**-tion·ist** ***n.***, ***a.*** 取消主义者[的]。

liq·ui·da·tor [ˈlikwideitə; ˋlɪkwɪˏdetɚ] ***n.*** 清算人。

liq·uid·i·ty [liˈkwiditi; lɪˋkwɪdətɪ] ***n.*** **1.** 液性。**2.** 流动性,流畅。

liq·uid·ize [ˈlikwidaiz; ˋlɪkwəˏdaɪz] ***vt.*** 使成液体,使液化。

liq·ui·fy [ˈlikwifai; ˋlɪkwəˏfaɪ] ***vt.***, ***vi.*** = liquefy.

liq·uor [ˈlikə; ˋlɪkɚ] **I** ***n.*** **1.** 液,液体。**2.**【药】溶液;液剂。**3.** 煮汁,煎汁。**4.** (特指蒸馏制成的)酒。*meat ~* 肉汁。*~ traffic* 酒的非法买卖。*malt ~* 啤[麦]酒类〔*ale, beer, porter* 等〕。*spirituous ~* 烧酒;烈性酒。*vinous ~* 葡萄酒。***be fond of ~*** 喜欢喝酒。***be in ~ = be (the) worse for ~*** 喝醉。***carry one's ~ like a gentleman*** 毫无醉意。***take [have] a ~ [~-up]*** 〔俚〕喝酒提神。***under the influence of ~*** 有点醉,微醉。**II** ***vt.***, ***vi.*** 泡溶;浸在液体中;上油(在鞋子等上);〔俚〕喝酒(*up*)。~ **head** 醉汉。

liq·uo·rice [ˈlikəris; ˋlɪkərɪs] ***n.***【植】甘草属,甘草。~ **stick** 〔美俚〕单簧管。

li·quor·ish[1] [ˈlikəriʃ; ˋlɪkərɪʃ] ***a.*** **1.** = lickerish. **2.** 嗜酒的。**-ly** ***ad.*** **-ness** ***n.***

li·quor·ish[2] [ˈlikəriʃ; ˋlɪkərɪʃ] ***n.*** = liquorice.

li·ra [ˈliərə; ˋlɪrə] ***n.*** (*pl.* ***lir·e*** [-ri; -rɪ], ~***s***) (意大利货币单位)里拉。

lir·i·pipe [ˈliəriˌpaip; ˈlɪrəˏpaɪp] ***n.*** (教士服等的)长披巾,长披肩。

Li·sa [ˈliːzə, ˈlaizə; ˋlizə, ˋlaɪzə] ***n.*** 莉莎〔女子名,Elizabeth 的昵称〕。

Lis·bon [ˈlizbən; ˋlɪzbən] ***n.*** 里斯本〔葡萄牙首都〕。

lisle [lail; laɪl] ***n.*** **1.** (法国 Lisle 出产的坚牢的)莱尔棉线。**2.** 莱尔线织物。

lisp [lisp; lɪsp] **I** ***vi.***, ***vt.*** **1.** 咬着舌头发音〔如将 s, sh [ʃ], z 等音读作 the [θ, ð]〕。**2.** (孩子似地)口齿不清地说。*She ~s.* 她说话口齿不清。**II** ***n.*** **1.** 咬舌头,口齿不清。**2.** 咬舌头发出的声音;(树叶、流水等的)沙沙声。

lis·pen·dens [lisˈpendenz; lɪsˋpɛndɛnz] ***n.*** 〔L.〕【法】未决的诉讼,悬案。

lisp·ing·ly [ˈlispiŋli; ˋlɪspɪŋlɪ] ***ad.*** 咬着舌头地,口齿不清地。

lis·som [ˈlisəm; ˋlɪsəm] ***a.*** **1.** 柔软的。**2.** 轻快的,灵活的,敏捷的。**-ly** ***ad.*** **-ness** ***n.***

list[1] [list; lɪst] **I** ***n.*** **1.** 清单,目录,表,一览表;名单。**2.** (交易所中)全部上市证券。**3.** = ~price. *an active ~* 现役军人名册。*a black ~* 黑名单。*a casualty ~* 伤亡名单。*an export ~* 出口商品清单[目录]。*a packing ~* 装箱单。*a reading ~* 阅读书目。*a reserved ~* 后备役军人名单。*a retired ~* 复员军人名单。*a shopping ~* 购物清单。***be struck off the ~*** 被除名。***close the ~*** 截止征募。***draw up [out] a ~*** 造表。***head [lead] the ~*** 名列第一。***make a ~*** = draw up a ~. ***on the ~*** 在名册中。***on the sick ~*** 害着病。***pass first on the ~*** 以第一名通过考试。***stand first on the ~*** 居首位;名列前茅。**II** ***vt.*** **1.** 登记;记入目录中,记入表中,列入名单[簿]中。**2.** 征募,列入军籍。— ***vi.*** **1.** 入伍。**2.** 列入价目表。*~ed securities*【美商】上市证券。~**price** (商品)目录价格,价目单上定价〔出售时根据不同情况打折扣或增加各种附加费用〕。

list[2] [list; lɪst] **I** ***n.*** **1.** 布边,布头,布条。**2.** 狭条;(木板上截下的)木条。**3.** 田埂。**4.**【建】边饰;扁带饰。**5.** 〔*pl.*〕(中世纪竞技场的)围栏,栅栏;竞技场,运动场;竞争场所。**6.** (马背中央等处的)深色条纹。***enter the ~s against*** 向…挑战;应战;出战。**II** ***vt.*** **1.** 给…装布边。**2.** 把(布条等)拼成一块。**3.** 从木板上截下边条。**4.** 犁地。

list[3] [list; lɪst] ***vt.***, ***vi.*** 〔诗〕听,倾听。

list[4] [list; lɪst] ***vt.***, ***vi.*** (***listed***, 〔古〕***list***; ***listed***; *3rd sing.* ***list***, ***listeth***) 中…的意,称…的心;希望,想(*to*

L

do). *He did as him* ～. 他按他自己的意思做了。

list[5] [list; lɪst] **I** *vi*., *vt*.(船等)倾斜。**II** *n*. 倾斜(性)。*That ship has a* ～ *to port* [*a port* ～]. 那条船向左倾斜。

list·el [ˈlistl; ˋlɪstl̩] *n*.【建】扁带饰。

lis·ten [ˈlisn; ˋlɪsn̩] **I** *vi*. 1. 听。2. 听从,服从 (*to*)。3. 听上去,听起来。～ *with strained ears* 竖起耳朵听。*L- to me*. 听我说。*We* ～*ed but we heard nothing*. 我们听着,但什么也没听见。～ *to reason* 服从道理。～ *to temptation* 甘受诱惑。*It doesn't* ～ *reasonable*. 〔美口〕这听上去并不适当。～ **for** 倾耳听,等着听 (～ *for an answer* 候覆)。～ **in** 1. 收听,监听。2. 偷听,窃听。**II** *n*. 听,倾听。*Please have a* ～ *to this*. 请听听这个吧。**on the** ～ 注意地听着。

lis·ten·er [ˈlisnə; ˋlɪsnɚ] *n*. 1. 听者;收听者。2.〔俚〕耳朵。～**-in** (*pl*. **-in**) 1. 收听者。2. 监听者;偷听者。**-ship** 听众(人数)。

lis·ten·ing [ˈlisniŋ; ˋlɪsnɪŋ] **I** *n*. 倾听。**II** *a*. 1. 收听的,留心的,注意的。2. 助听的。～ **button** 耳塞助听器。～ **gear** 听音器。～**-in** 收听无线电。～**-in device**【军】潜听装置。～**-in line** 监听线;听话线。～ **post**【军】听音哨;(一般的)情报监听处。～ **station**【军】雷达[无线电]侦察接收站;监听站。

Lis·ter [ˈlistə; ˋlɪstɚ] *n*. 李斯德〔Joseph, 1827—1912, 英国外科医生〕。**-ism**【医】李斯德消毒法。**-ize** *vt*.【医】施行李斯德消毒法。

lis·ter[1] [ˈlistə; ˋlɪstɚ] *n*. (农机)双壁开沟犁。

list·er[2] [ˈlistə; ˋlɪstɚ] *n*. 造表人,编目人。

lis·ter·ine [ˈlistəriːn; ˋlɪstərɪn] *n*. 防腐溶液。

list·ing [ˈlistiŋ; ˋlɪstɪŋ] *n*. 1. 造表,编目。2. 表册上的项目〔如房地产中间人关于待售房产的记载〕。3. 表册。

list·less [ˈlistlis; ˋlɪstlɪs] *a*. 冷淡的;懒洋洋的,无精打采的,倦怠的。**-ly** *ad*. **-ness** *n*.

list·serv [ˈlistsəːv; ˋlɪstsɝv] *n*.【计】专题通信服务〔因特网上的邮件自动分发系统〕。**-r**【计】专题通信服务器程序。

lit [lit; lɪt] light 的过去式及过去分词。*a*. 1. 照亮的,点着的。2.〔美俚〕喝醉了的,被毒品麻醉了的。*be* ～ *up* 〔俚〕喝醉了;被毒品麻醉了。

lit. = 1. literally. 2. literary. 3. literature. 4. litre.

lit·a·ny [ˈlitəni; ˋlɪtn̩ɪ] *n*. 1.【宗】启应祷文。2. (枯燥、重复的)连续不断的说明〔叙述〕。*the L-* (英国教会《公祷文》中的)启应析文。

Lit. B., **Lit B** = Litt. B.

li·tchi [ˈliːtʃi; ˋlitʃɪ] *n*.【植】荔枝树;荔枝。

lit-crit [ˈlitˈkrit; ˋlɪtˋkrɪt] *n*. 文学批评,文学评论。

Lit. D., **Litt. D.** =〔L.〕Lit(t)erarum Doctor (= Doctor of Literature) 文学博士。

-lite *comb. f*. 表示"石","矿物","岩石","化石": chryso*lite*, hya*lite*, oo*lite*.

li·te·pen·den·te [ˈlaitiːpenˈdentiː; ˋlaɪtipenˋdɛnti]〔L.〕在审理中。

li·ter [ˈliːtə; ˋlitɚ] *n*.〔美〕= litre.

lit·er·a·cy [ˈlitərəsi; ˋlɪtərəsɪ] *n*. 识字,能读能写;有学问 (*opp*. illiteracy). *a* ～ *campaign* 扫盲运动。*a* ～ *class* 扫盲班。

lit·erae hu·ma·ni·o·res [ˈlitəriː hjuˌmeiniˈɔːriːz; ˋlɪtəri hjuˏmænɪˋoriz]〔L.〕1. 人文学科。2. 希腊罗马古典语文研究。

lit·er·al [ˈlitərəl; ˋlɪtərəl] **I** *a*. 1. 文字的,文字上的。2. 字面上的,逐字逐句的。3. 没有夸张的,朴实的,原原本本的。4. 呆板的,平庸的,乏味的。5. 字母的,用字母代表的。*the* ～ *arithmetic* 代数学。*a* ～ *translation* 逐字逐句直译。*a* ～ *interpretation* 字面解释。*the* ～ *truth* 原原本本的实情。**II** *n*.【印】错排,文字上的错误。***in the*** ～ ***sense of the word*** 照字面的意思;实在,真正 (*In the* ～ *sense of the word*, *I heard nothing*. 我听实在是没有听到〔但可能看到过〕)。～ **contract**【法】成文契约,书面契约。**-i·ty** [-ˈræliti; -ˋrælətɪ] 直译;实际;精确。**-ness** *n*.

lit·er·al·ism [ˈlitərəlizəm; ˋlɪtərəlˏɪzm] *n*. 拘泥字义[文字];直译;【美】写实主义。**-ist** *n*. 拘泥字义[文字]者;直译者;直写主义者。

lit·er·al·ize [ˈlitərəˌlaiz; ˋlɪtərəˏlaɪz] *vt*. (**-iz·ed**, **-iz·ing**) 1. 照字面解释。2. 对…逐字逐句翻译。**-za·tion** *n*.

lit·er·al·ly [ˈlitərəli; ˋlɪtərəlɪ] *ad*. 1. 照字义;逐字地。2. 确实,真正,完全。3. 差不多,简直。*The city was* ～ *destroyed*. 城市差不多全毁了。*In the race he* ～ "*flew*" *round the track*. 他在赛跑中简直像飞似地绕着跑道跑。

lit·er·a·ri·ly [ˈlitərərili; ˋlɪtərərɪlɪ] *ad*. 文学上,学问上,学术上。

lit·er·ar·i·ness [ˈlitərərinis; ˋlɪtərərɪnɪs] *n*. 文学性,文艺性。

lit·er·ary [ˈlitərəri; ˋlɪtəˏrɛrɪ] *a*. 1. 文学的,文学上的。2. 通文学的;喜欢文学的;以写作为职业的。3. 书本上的;书面语的。～ *columns* (报纸等的)文艺栏。*a* ～ *image* 文学形象。～ *works* [*writings*] 文学作品。*a* ～ *executor* 遗稿保管人。*a* ～ *man* 文学家,学者,作家。～ *property* 著作权,版权。～ *pursuits* 文字生涯。*quite a* ～ *person* 擅长文学的人。～ *style* 书面体。

lit·er·ate [ˈlitərit; ˋlɪtərɪt] **I** *a*. 1. 有学问的,有文化的;能写能读的 (*opp*. illiterate). 2. 精通文学的;会写作的。**II** *n*. 识字的人;有学问的人。**-ly** *ad*.

lit·er·a·ti [ˌlitəˈrɑːtiː, -ˈreitai; ˏlɪtəˋrɑtɪ, -ˋretaɪ] *n*. 〔*pl*.〕(*sing*. **-tus** [-təs; -təs])〔L.〕文学家;文人学士。

lit·e·ra·tim [ˌlitəˈreitim; ˏlɪtəˋretɪm] *ad*.〔L.〕逐字地,按照原文。

lit·er·a·tion [ˌlitəˈreiʃən; ˏlɪtəˋreʃən] *n*. 用字母代表声音或词。

lit·er·a·tor [ˈlitəˌreitə; ˋlɪtəˏretɚ] *n*. 文人;作家。

lit·er·a·ture [ˈlitəritʃə; ˋlɪtərətʃɚ] *n*. 1. 文学,文学作品。2. 文献。3. 文学研究;著作业,著作。4.〔口〕(广告、宣传用的)印刷品。5. (为乐器演奏用的)一组乐曲。6.〔古〕学识,学问。*English* ～英国文学。*light* ～大众[通俗]文学。*polite* ～纯文学。*mathematical* ～数学文献。*a person of infinite* ～学识广博的人。

lit·e·ra·tus [ˌlitəˈrɑːtəs; ˏlɪtəˋretəs] *n*.〔L.〕literati 的单数。

lith- *comb. f*. = litho-.

-lith *comb. f*. 1. 表示"石","人造石": aero*lith*, grano*lith*, mega*lith*. 2. 表示"结石": uro*lith*. 3. 表示"矿石","岩石": licco*lith*.

Lith. = Lithuania(n).

lith., **litho.**, **lithog.** = lithograph(y)。

lith·arge [ˈliθɑːdʒ, liˈθɑːdʒ; ˋlɪθɑrdʒ, lɪˋθɑrdʒ] *n*.【化】1. 密陀僧,一氧化铅。2. 正方铅矿。

lithe [laið; laɪð] *a*. 1. 柔软的。2. 敏捷的,轻快的。**-ly** *ad*. **-ness** *n*. **-some** *a*. = lithe.

lith·i·a [ˈliθiə; ˋlɪθɪə] *n*. 1.【化】氧化锂。2.【医】结石病。～ **water** 锂盐矿水。

lith·i·as·is [liˈθaiəsis; lɪˋθaɪəsɪs] *n*.【医】结石病。*renal* ～肾结石。

lith·ic [ˈliθik; ˋlɪθɪk] *a*. 1. 石的。2.【化】锂的。3.【医】结石的。

lith·i·um [ˈliθiəm; ˋlɪθɪəm] *n*.【化】锂。

lith·o- *comb. f*. 表示"石","岩石","结石": *litho*graph, *litho*phere.

lith·o·graph [ˈliθəgrɑːf; ˋlɪθəˏgræf] **I** *n*.【印】石[平]版,石[平]版画。**II** *vt*. 石印,用平版印刷。

li·thog·ra·pher [liˈθɔgrəfə; lɪˋθɑgrəfə] *n*. 石印[平版印刷]工人。

lith·o·graph·ic [ˌliθəˈgræfik; ˏlɪθəˋgræfɪk] *a*. **1.** 平版画的;石印的,平版印刷品的。**2.** 平版印刷(术)的。**-i·cal·ly** *ad*.

li·thog·ra·phy [liˈθɔgrəfi; lɪˋθɑgrəfɪ] *n*. 石印[平版印刷]术;平版印刷品。

lith·oid, -al [ˈliθɔid, -l; ˋlɪθɔɪd, -l] *a*. 石质的,石状的。

li·thol·o·gy [liˈθɔlədʒi; lɪˋθɑlədʒɪ] *n*. **1.**【地】岩性学;岩性。**2.**【医】结石学。**-log·ic(al)** *a*. **-log·i·cal·ly** *ad*.

lith·o·marge [ˈliθəˈmɑːdʒ; ˋlɪθəˋmɑrdʒ] *n*.【地】密高岭土。

lith·o·me·te·or [ˌliθəˈmiːtiə; ˏlɪθəˋmitɪə] *n*.【气】大气尘粒。

lith·on·trip·tic [ˌliθənˈtriptik; ˏlɪθənˋtrɪptɪk] **I** *a*.【医】溶结石的;碎结石的。**II** *n*.【药】溶石药,碎石药。

lith·o·phyte [ˈliθəˌfait; ˋlɪθəˏfaɪt] *n*.【植】岩表植物〔如地衣〕,石生植物。**-o·phyt·ic** [-ˈfitik; -ˋfɪtɪk] *a*.

lith·o·pone [ˈliθəˌpəun; ˋlɪθəˏpon] *n*. 锌钡白。

lith·o·print [ˈliθə*u* print; ˋlɪθəˏprɪnt] *vt*. 用照相胶印法印刷。

lith·o·sphere [ˈliθəˌsfiə; ˋlɪθəˏsfɪr] *n*.【地】岩石圈,陆界。

li·thot·o·my [liˈθɔtəmi; lɪˋθɑtəmɪ] *n*.【医】膀胱切开取石术,膀胱石切除术。**-tom·ic, -tom·i·cal** [ˌliθəˈtɔmikl; lɪθəˋtɑmɪkl] *a*. **li·thot·o·mist** *n*. (膀胱)切石专家。**-o·mize** *vt*. 做膀胱切石手术。

li·thot·ri·ty [liˈθɔtriti; lɪˋθɑtrɪtɪ] *n*.【医】碎石术。

Lith·u·a·ni·a [ˌliθju(ː)ˈeinjə, -niə; ˏlɪθjʊˋenɪə, -nɪə] *n*. 立陶宛〔欧洲〕。

Lith·u·a·ni·an [ˌliθju(ː)ˈeiniən; ˏlɪθjʊˋenɪən] **I** *a*. 立陶宛的,立陶宛人[语]的。**II** *n*. 立陶宛人;立陶宛语。

lit·i·ga·ble [ˈlitigəbl; ˋlɪtɪgəbl̩] *a*.【法】可诉讼的。

lit·i·gant [ˈlitigənt; ˋlɪtəgənt] **I** *a*. 有关诉讼的。*the parties* ~诉讼当事人。**II** *n*. 诉讼当事人。

lit·i·gate [ˈlitigeit; ˋlɪtəˏget] *vt*., *vi*. 诉诸法律,打官司;争论。

lit·i·ga·tion [ˌlitiˈgeiʃən; ˏlɪtəˋgeʃən] *n*. 诉讼,起诉。

li·ti·gious [liˈtidʒəs; lɪˋtɪdʒɪəs] *a*. **1.** 好诉讼的,爱打官司的;爱争论的。**2.** 可诉讼的,可争论的。**-ly** *ad*. **-ness** *n*.

lit·mus [ˈlitməs; ˋlɪtməs] *n*.【化】石蕊。~ **paper**【化】石蕊试纸。~ **test** 石蕊试验;〔喻〕简单而具有决定性的试验。**-less** *a*. 中性的。

li·to·tes [ˈlaitəutiːz; ˋlaɪtəˏtiz] *n*.【语】曲意法,间接表达法,反语法〔如将 little 用作 not, rather 用作 very much indeed; 又如用 no small 代 great, not bad 代 very good〕。

li·tre [ˈliːtə; ˋlitɚ] *n*. (容量单位)升。

Lit·sea [ˈlitsiə; ˋlɪtsɪə] *n*.【植】(樟科中的)木姜子属。

Litt.B. =〔L.〕*Literarum Baccalaureus* (=Bachelor of Letters 或 Bachelor of Literature) 文学士。

Litt. D. =〔L.〕*Literarum Doctor* (=Doctor of Letters 或 Doctor of Literature) 文学博士。

lit·ten [ˈlitn; ˋlɪtn̩] *a*. 〔古〕点燃的。

lit·ter [ˈlitə; ˋlɪtɚ] **I** *n*. **1.** 担架,舁床;轿舆。**2.** (兽类睡眠用的)褥草,垫圈。**3.** 枯枝层,落叶层。**4.** 七零八碎的东西,杂乱。**5.** (猪等)同胎生下的小崽。~ *bearers* 担架兵。*a* ~ *of little pigs* 一窝小猪。~ *of weeds* 枯草层。**be in** ~ (狗、猪等)临产。**in a** ~ (房间等)乱七八糟,杂乱。**II** *vt*. **1.** 铺褥草。**2.** 乱丢(东西)。**3.** 弄乱(房间等) (*with*). **4.** (猪等)产仔。— *vi*. **1.** (家畜等)产仔。**2.** 乱丢东西,乱丢废物〔垃圾等〕。~ **bag** 废物袋〔如在汽车中置备,供丢弃废物〕。~**-bin** 废物箱。~**bug** 公共场所乱扔废纸废物的人。~**pick** 垃圾大清除行动。~ **stream** 垃圾流〔指废弃物泛滥成灾〕。

lit·ter·ae hu·mani·o·res [ˈlitəriː hjuˌmeiniˈɔːriːz; ˋlɪtəri hjʊˏmenɪˋoriz] = literae humaniores.

lit·té·ra·teur [ˌliterəˈtəː; ˏlɪtərəˋtɝ] *n*. 〔F.〕文学家;文人。

lit·ter·i·ness [ˈlitərinis; ˋlɪtərɪnɪs] *n*. 杂乱。

lit·ter·y [ˈlitəri; ˋlɪtərɪ] *a*. **1.** 褥草的;满是稻草的。**2.** 杂乱的;不整洁的。

Lit·tle [ˈlitl; ˋlɪtl] *n*. 利特尔〔姓氏〕。

lit·tle [ˈlitl; ˋlɪtl] **I** *a*. (*less* 或 *lesser*; *least*; 〔俚、方〕*-tler*; *-tlest*) ★ less, lesser, least 通例是与 more, most 相对应的用语,表示数量、程度方面的小,亦可代替表示形体小的。smaller, smallest. 又: little 除"小"的意义之外,还含有可怜、轻蔑等的感情。习惯上只说 great and little, big and little, great and small, large and small, 不说 large and little, big and small. **1.** (*opp*. big) 小,小的;年轻的,年纪小的,可爱的。*a* ~ *dog* 小狗。*a* ~ *drop* [*a* ~ *glass*] *of whisky* 一小滴[一小杯]威士忌酒。*the* ~ *Smiths* 斯密士(家)的孩子们。*my* ~ *man* [*woman*] 小弟弟[姑娘]。*a nice* ~ *thing* 可爱的小家伙。*our* ~ *life* 我辈短促的生命〔人生如寄之意〕。**2.** (*opp*. great) 孩子似的,孩子气的;琐碎的,小的,吝啬的,心地狭窄的。*L- things amuse* ~ *minds*. 小孩欢喜小东西。*sb.'s* ~ *game* 孩子似的[可笑的]举动[手法]。*a* ~ *thing* 小事。*a* ~ *mind* [*soul*] 狭小的气量。**3.** 〔表示数量等的否定用法,无冠词〕(*opp*. much) 只有少许[一点点],没有多少。*There is but* ~ *hope*. 没有多少希望。*I have* ~ *hope, if any*. = *I have* ~ *or no hope*. 简直没有希望。**4.** 〔表示数量等的肯定用法,加冠词〕〔*cf*. *a few*〕有一点。*There is a* ~ *hope*. 有一点希望。*a* ~ *time* [*while*] *ago* 片刻之前,刚才。*I will go a* ~ *way with you*. 我陪你走一段路。*A* ~ *care would have prevented it*. 稍微当心一点,这种事情就不会发生。★有时纯属礼貌上的形式,无表示微少的意义,只作 some 的代用语。例: *Let me give you a* ~ *mutton*. 让我给你(一点)羊肉。*May I have a* ~ *money*? 给我(点)钱好吗? *A* ~ *more* [*less*] *sugar, please*. 请给我多[少]来一点糖。*only a* ~ *wine* 只一点点酒。*I gave him the* ~ *money that I had*. = *I gave him what* ~ *money I had*. 我把所有的一点点钱统统给了他。**but** ~ 只一点点 (*I have but* ~ *money*. 我只有一点点钱)。**go but a** ~ **way to** 差得远,不够。**make** ~ **of** **1.** 不重视,轻视,不以为意。**2.** 难了解,不领会。~ **ones** 孩子们〔加用 our, her 等〕。~ **or no** 简直没有,几乎没有。**no** ~ (=not a ~)不少,很多。**very** ~ 很少;一点也没有 (*He has very* ~ *sense*. 他没有常识。*He takes very* ~ *trouble about his work*. 他做事一点也不用心)。

II *n*. **1.** 〔肯定用法,表示程度、数量的〕小,少。*Every* ~ *helps*. 〔谚〕点点滴滴都起作用。*know a* ~ *of everything* 什么都懂一点。*the* ~不重要[无足轻重]的人。*A* ~ *is better than none*. 聊胜于无。**2.** 〔否定用法,无冠词〕一点点,少许,些许。*He has seen* ~ *of life*. 他不懂世故。*L- remains to be said*. 简直没有什么可以讲了。*I got but* [*very, rather*] ~ *out of it*. 我简直没有从这当中得着什么。**a** ~ **at a time** 每次少许。**after a** ~ 过了一会儿。**by** ~ **and** ~ = ~ **by** ~ 一点一点地,慢慢地,逐渐地。**for a** ~ 一会儿,不久。**from** ~ **up** 〔美〕从幼年起。**in** ~ 小规模的,小型的。~ **or nothing** = ~ **if anything** 简直没有,几乎没有。**not a** ~ 不少,相当多。**quite a** ~ 〔美口〕大量,许多,丰富。**the** ~ = **what** ~ 仅有的一点 (*He did the* ~ *that* [*what* ~] *he could*. 他尽到了他仅有的微力)。

III *ad*. **1.** 〔肯定用法,加冠词 a〕一点,稍,略。*I speak English a* ~. 我稍能说一点英语。*Wait a* ~. 等一下。*He is a* ~ *better today*. 他今天好一点了。**2.** 〔否定用法,无冠词〕毫不,一点也不;几乎不,简直不〔主要和 know, imagine, dream, think, guess 等词连用〕。~ *known writers* 不大出名的作家,无名作家。*He* ~ *knows*. 他不知道。~ **better** [**less**] **than** 和…一样,和…没有差别,半斤八两。~ **more than** 和…一样[无差

别]。~ ***short of*** 简直是,几乎。***set*** ~ ***by*** 轻视。***think*** ~ ***of*** 不重视,不在乎。**L- Bear**【天】= Ursa minor. ~**-ease**【史】使人立卧不得的牢笼。~ **finger** 小指(*twist* [*wrap*] *around one's* ~ *finger*. 轻而易举地控制[施影响于]他人)。**L- Fox**【天】= Vulpecula. ~ **go**〔英〕(剑桥大学)学士学位的小考[预考]。~ **hours** 1. 夜半一二点钟。2.〔L- Hours〕(天主教的)日间例行祷告课〔即晨祷,三时课,午祷,九时课等〕。~ **Joe**〔美俚〕骰子中的四点。~ **leaf**【植】小叶病。**L- League** 少年棒球协会。**L- Leaguer** 少年棒球协会会员。~ **magazine** 小杂志〔一种刊登试验性文艺作品的非商业性而且发行有限的小杂志〕。~ **Mary**〔口〕肚子。~ **neck**【动】小颈蛤贝〔产于美国,通常生吃,也叫 ~ neck clam〕。~ **office** (天主教的)小礼拜。~ **people** (民间迷信中的)小精灵。**L- Rhody** 美国罗得岛州的别称。**L- Rock** (美国)小石城。**L- Russian** 小俄罗斯人〔乌克兰人的旧称〕。~ **slam**【桥牌】小满贯。~ **theatre** 1. (大学或艺术团体等实验演出用的)小剧场。2. 小剧场演出的戏剧。~ **woman** 1. 懂事的小女孩。2.〔美俚〕妻子。

lit·tle·ness [ˈlitlnis; ˋlɪtl̩nɪs] ***n***. 1. 小。2. 少量,些许。3. 褊狭,吝啬,卑鄙。

Lit·tle·ton [ˈlitltən; ˋlɪtl̩tən] ***n***. 利特尔顿〔姓氏〕。

lit·tlish [ˈlitliʃ; ˋlɪtlɪʃ] ***a***. 有点儿小的。

lit·to·ral [ˈlitərəl; ˋlɪtərəl] **I *a***. 海滨的;沿岸的;沿海的(*opp*. pelagic);【生】栖息在沿岸浅海中的。~ *fauna* 沿岸动物区系。*the* ~ *province* 沿海省份[地区]。**II *n***. 沿(海)岸地区。**-ly *ad***.

li·tur·gic(al) [liˈtəːdʒik(əl); lɪˋtɝdʒɪkl̩] ***a***. 礼拜仪式的。**-cal·ly *ad***. 按照礼拜仪式的。

lit·ur·gist [ˈlitədʒist; ˋlɪtədʒɪst] ***n***. 1. 使用(或主张使用)礼拜仪式者。2. 礼拜仪式方面的权威。

lit·ur·gy [ˈlitə(ː)dʒi; ˋlɪtɚdʒɪ] ***n***. 1. 礼拜仪式。2.〔the L-〕(英国教会的)《公祷文》;(希腊正教的)圣餐仪式。

litz wire [ˈlits ˌwaiə; ˋlɪts ˏwaɪr]【电】编织线,绞合线。

liv·a·bil·i·ty [ˌlivəˈbiliti; ˏlɪvəˋbɪlətɪ] ***n***. 1. (家禽、牲畜等的)存活率。2. 适于居住。

liv·a·ble [ˈlivəbl; ˋlɪvəbl] ***a***. 1. (房子、气候等)可以[适合]居住的。2. (生活条件,工作条件等)有生活价值的。3. (人)易于相处的,能与之共同生活的。**-ness *n***.

live[1] [liv; lɪv] ***vi***. 1. 生存;活着〔现常用 be alive 或 be living〕。2. 生活,过日子,过活;做人,处世。3. 居住。4. 生活得很愉快、高兴;在生活中得到享受。5. 一直活到;(事物)继续发展[存在];(船等)度过危险。6. (人物形像等)栩栩如生,生动如真;留在别人的记忆中。*L- and let* ~.〔谚〕自己活也让别人活。*He* ~*s what he teaches*. 他言行如一。*He* ~*s* [*is living*] *in France*. 他住在法国。~ *under the same roof* 住在一幢房子里。*She* ~*d and died a virgin*. 她终身没有结婚。*I have* ~*d today*. 我今天过得很高兴。*L- and learn*.〔谚〕活到老,学到老。~ *to be a hundred* 活到一百岁。*The ship* ~*d in the storm*. 这船没有在风浪中沉没。*make a historical character* ~把历史人物描写得非常生动。*His memory* ~*s*. 他活在人的心中。— ***vt***. 1. 过(…的生活);度过。2. (在自己的生活中)表现,实行,实践。(***as sure***) ***as I*** ~ 的的确确 (*He is dead, as I* ~. 他确实死了)。***He*** ~***s long that*** ~***s well***.〔谚〕活得好就是活得久。~ ***a double life*** 过双重(人格)生活。~ ***a lie*** 过虚伪的生活。~ ***above*** [***beyond***] ***one's income*** [***means***] 生活和收入不相称,入不敷出。~ ***by*** 1. 靠…为生 (~ *by one's hands* 自食其力。~ *by one's fingers' ends* 靠手艺过活)。2. 住在…附近。~ ***by oneself*** 独居。~ ***carefully*** 俭省地[有节制地]过日子。~ ***down*** 靠以后的行为洗清污名等。~ ***down to*** (*sb.'s expectation*) 辜负(某人的期望等)。~ ***from hand to mouth*** 做一天吃一天地过日子。~ ***hard*** 过困俭生活。~ ***in*** 1. 住进。2. (雇员)住在东家 (*opp*. ~ out)。~ ***in ease*** 过得逍遥自在。~ ***in*** [***within***] ***oneself*** 孤独地生活。~ ***in the past*** 靠着缅怀往昔过日子〔意味着目前生活不如意等〕。~ ***it up***〔俚〕狂欢;纵情作乐。~ ***off*** 1. 住在…之外。2. 以…为生。~ ***on*** [***upon***] 1. 以…为主食 (~ *on rice* 以米为主食)。2. 靠…生活 (~ *on sixpence a day* 每天花六便士维持生活)。3. 继续活着。~ ***on forever*** 万古长青。~ ***on the cross***〔俚〕以偷窃为生;行为不正。~ ***out*** 1. (雇员等)外宿,住在外面。2. 活过,多活(一定期间) (~ *out another month* 又多活一个月)。~ ***rough*** 过苦日子。~ ***single*** 过独身生活。~ ***through*** 度过 (~ *through an economical crisis* 度过经济危机)。~ ***to oneself*** 过孤独的生活。~ ***up to*** 量…过日子;实行(主义等);生活得无愧于,配得上,够得上;达到预期标准 (~ *up to expectations* 终于取得预期的东西[事业的成功等])。~ ***well*** 1. 过有道德的生活。2. 过优裕生活。~ ***with sb***. 1. 和某人同居。2. 寄住在某人处 (~ *with sb. in peace* 和某人和平共处)。***where sb***. ~***s***〔美俚〕某人的要害 (*The word goes right where I* ~. 这话正刺中我的要害)。~**-forever** 景天属植物。~**-in** 1. ***a***. 和他人未婚同居的。2. ***n***. 未婚同居的对象。

live[2] [laiv; laɪv] **I *a***. 1. 活的,有生命的 (*opp*. dead)。*a* ~ *fish* 活鱼。*a* ~ *fence* 树篱。2.〔谑〕〔常接在 real 之后〕真的,活生生的。*a real* ~ *mountain* 真正的山。*There's a real* ~ *burglar under my bed*! 我床下面真有一个窃贼。3. 活泼的,有精神的,生气勃勃的。*a* ~ *man* 精力旺盛的人。~ *eyes* 炯炯有神的眼睛。*the* ~ *murmur of a summer's day* 夏天的虫声。4. 目前大家感觉兴趣的,当前的。*a* ~ *issue* [*question*] 尚在争论中的问题。5. (机器等)能开动的;传动的;动力发动的。*a* ~ *axle* 传动轴。6. 燃烧着的。~ *coals* 燃烧着的炭。*a* ~ *hatred* 盛怒。7. 装着炸药的实弹,有作用,充电的。*a* ~ *bomb* 未爆炸的炸弹。~ *shell shooting* 实弹射击。8. 未使用过的;(岩石等)未采掘的;原状的。~ *feathers* 由活鸟身上拔下来的羽毛。*a* ~ *match* 没擦过的火柴。9. 正在使用着的;(球等)正在玩的。*a* ~ *machine* 可以使用的机器。*a* ~ *runway* 现用跑道。10. (稿子等)尚未排版的。11. (空气)清新的;(颜色)鲜艳的。~ *air* 空气新鲜。12. (参加)实况播送的。*It was a* ~ *broadcast, not a recording*. 那是实况转播,不是录音。**II *ad***. 在(表演)现场,从(表演)现场,实况地。*The trial was broadcast* ~ *from the courtroom*. 审判情况是从审判室实况转播的。~ **account**【商】流水账。~ **bait** (钓鱼用的)活饵。~**-box** 放在河中使鱼虾保持新鲜的箩筐[栅栏]。~ **centre**【机】活顶尖,活顶针。~ **firing** 实际发射。~ **graphite** 含铀块石墨。~ **load**【机】动(力)负载,活载荷;工作负载,有效负载。~ **lode** 可采矿脉。~ **oak**【植】1. 栎属〔尤指弗吉尼亚栎 (*Quercus virginiana*)〕。2. =Encina (木叶栎)。3. 栎木。~ **parking** 司机等候在车内的车辆停放。~ **pick-up**【电视】实况录像;播送室内实况广播。~ **quartz** 含矿石英。~ **room** 交混回响室。~ **steam** 新汽〔直接从锅炉出来的高压蒸汽,与"废气"相对而言〕。~ **steam valve** 进气阀。~**stock *n***. 家畜,牲畜 (*a* ~*stock farming* 畜牧)。~ **studio** 具有较好音响装置的播音室。~ **time** 实况转播时间。~ **ware**【计】活件〔指电脑操作员、编程员、系统分析员等〕。~ **wire** 1. 通电的电线。2. 生龙活虎般的人。

live·a·ble [ˈlivəbl; ˋlɪvəbl] ***a***. =livable.

-lived [-livd, -ˈlaivd; -lɪvd, -ˋlaɪvd] *comb. f*. 表示"寿命…的";"生活…的": *long*-lived, *short*-lived.

live·li·hood [ˈlaivlihud; ˋlaɪvlɪˏhʊd] ***n***. 生活,生计。*means of* ~生活资料。***earn*** [***get, gain, make***] ***a*** ~ 谋生。***earn an honest*** ~ 规规矩矩地挣钱生活。***pick up a scanty*** ~ 过苦日子。

live·li·ly [ˈlaivlili; ˋlaɪvlɪlɪ] ***ad***. 活泼地,生气勃勃地;快活地,热闹地;生动地,鲜明地。

live·li·ness [ˈlaivlinis; ˋlaɪvlɪnɪs] ***n***. 活泼,快活,热闹,

L

繁华;生动,鲜明;强烈。*a certain* ～〔军俚〕猛烈的炮火。

live·long [ˈlivˌlɔŋ; ˋlɪvˏlɔŋ] *a*. 漫长的;整个的;完全的。*the* ～ *day* 一整天。*the* ～ *night* 漫漫长夜。

live·ly [ˈlaivli; ˋlaɪvlɪ] **I** *a*. **1**. 活泼的,精神旺盛的,充满生气的;愉快的,活跃的。**2**. (舞蹈等)轻快的;(球等)弹性好的。**3**. (船)行驶轻快的,驾驶灵便的。**4**. (色彩等)鲜明的,强烈的。**5**. (描写等)逼真的,生动的。**6**. (感情等)强烈的,热烈的。**7**. 振奋的,提神的。**8**. 〔谑〕惊心动魄的,使人提心吊胆的。*a* ～ *description* 生动的描写。*a* ～ *imagination* 丰富的想像力。*a* ～ *discussion* 热烈的讨论,激烈的辩论。*a* ～ *sense of gratitude* 深厚的谢意。*make it* [*things*] ～ *for sb*. 使某人紧张[为难]。***as*** ～ ***as a grip*** 非常快活。***have a*** ～ ***time*** 大为慌乱[活跃]一阵(*The enemy had a* ～ *time during the battle*. 敌人在战火中大为慌乱)。***take a*** ～ ***interest in*** 对…抱有强烈兴趣。**II** *ad*. 生气勃勃地,精力充沛地;活生生地;鲜明地。

liv·en [ˈlaivən; ˋlaɪvən] *vt*., *vi*. (使)活跃起来,(使)愉快;变得愉快;振奋起来〔常与 up 连用〕。**-er** *n*.

liv·er[1] [ˈlivə; ˋlɪvɚ] *n*. **1**. 【解】肝脏。**2**. (食用)肝。**3**. 赤褐色。*a hot* ～热情。*a lily* [*white*] ～怯懦,胆小。～ *oil* (鱼)肝油。～ **wing** **1**. (煮熟的鸡的)右膀。**2**. 〔谑〕(人的)右膀。～ **colour** 肝色,赤褐色。～ **complaint** 肝病。～ **extract** 【药】肝浸膏,肝精。～ **fluke** 【医】肝吸虫。～ **leaf** 【植】獐耳细辛属;地钱(= hepatica)。～ **spot** (皮肤上的)雀斑,褐黄斑。～**wort** 【植】欧龙牙草。～**wurst** 【烹】(肝泥灌制的)肝肠。

liv·er[2] [ˈlivə; ˋlɪvɚ] *n*. 生活者;居住者。*a clean* ～洁身自好的人。*a close* ～吝啬的人,守财奴。*an evil* ～ = *a fast* [*loose*] ～浪子,放荡的人。*a free* [*high*] ～考究享受[吃喝玩乐]的人;生活奢侈的人。*a good* ～品德好的人;考究饮食的人;〔方〕生活优裕的人。*a hearty* ～贪吃的人。*the longest* ～【法】活得最久的受益人。

liv·er·ied [ˈlivərid; ˋlɪvərɪd] *a*. 穿特殊制服的,穿号衣的。

liv·er·ish [ˈlivəriʃ; ˋlɪvərɪʃ] *a*. **1**. 肝色的。**2**. 有肝病的。**3**. 脾气坏的,易怒的。

Liv·er·pool [ˈlivəpuːl; ˋlɪvɚˏpul] *n*. 利物浦〔英国港市〕。

Liv·er·pud·li·an [ˌlivəˈpʌdliən; ˏlɪvəˋpʌdlɪən] *a*., *n*. 利物浦的(人)。

liv·er·y[1] [ˈlivəri; ˋlɪvərɪ] *a*. **1**. 像肝的。**2**. 有肝病征状的。

liv·er·y[2] [ˈlivəri; ˋlɪvərɪ] *n*. **1**. (侍从、仆人穿的)特别制服,号衣。**2**. 伦敦各种行会会员的制服;伦敦同业工会会员。**3**. 〔古〕侍从,仆从。**4**. 〔诗〕鸟等的服装、装束。**5**. (马的)日粮;(人的)口粮,配给粮食。**6**. =～ stable. (马的)马房。**7**. 【法】财富所有权的让渡(批准书)。**8**. 各种车辆出租行。*the* ～ *of spring* 春天的服装。*the* ～ *of grief* [*woe*] 丧服。～ *and bait* 马的口粮。***at*** ～ (马)付饲料[或费用]托人代养(着)(*keep a horse at* ～ 领饲料代人养马;付饲料托人养马;出租马)。***in*** ～ 穿着制服。***out of*** ～ 不穿制服,穿着便衣。***sue*** (***for***) ***one's*** ～ (继承人)向法院申诉要求让渡财产。***take up one's*** ～ 入同业公会。***the*** ～ ***of sb.'s opinion*** 借用某人的意见。～ **coach** 出租马车。～ **company** 伦敦市同业公会〔因从前同业会员穿规定制服〕。～**man** **1**. (伦敦的)同业公会会员。**2**. 出租马车的人。**3**. 〔古〕(穿特殊制服的)侍从,仆从。～ **stable** (出租车马的)马车行,马房。

lives [laivz; laɪvz] *n*. life 的复数。

liv·id [ˈlivid; ˋlɪvɪd] *a*. **1**. 铅色的,青灰色的。**2**. (被打伤而呈现)青黑色的。**3**. 〔英口〕怒冲冲的。*a face* ～ *with rage* 气得发青的脸。*a* ～ *face* 苍白的脸,死灰色的脸。*a* ～ *hue* 带青色。～ *hatred* 刻骨之恨。**-ly** *ad*. **-ness** *n*.

li·vid·i·ty [liˈviditi; lɪˋvɪdətɪ] *n*. 铅色,青灰色;(被打伤而呈现的)青黑色。

liv·ing [ˈliviŋ; ˋlɪvɪŋ] **I** *a*. **1**. 活着的,生存着的;有生命的;在活动中[起作用]的;在使用中的。**2**. 活泼的,生动的;生气勃勃的,旺盛的;强烈的,猛烈的。**3**. 天然的,自然状态的;未开采过的。**4**. 栩栩如生的,逼真的。**5**. (维持)生活的;(适于)居住的。**6**. 〔口〕(加强语气词) = very. **7**. 生活的,维持生活的。～ *beings* 生物。*the greatest* ～ *poet* 现在活着的第一流诗人。～ *coals* 燃烧着的煤块。*a* ～ *language* 活的语言。～ *water* 活水。*a* ～ *faith* 强烈的信仰。*a* ～ *gale* 烈风。*a* ～ *rock* 天然岩石。*He is the* ～ *image of his father*. 他活像他的父亲。～ *conditions* 生活条件。*the* ～ *area* 适于居住的地方。*scare the* ～ *daylights out of sb*. 把某人吓得半死。～ *likeness* 逼真的画像。～ *picture* (由活人扮演的)活画。～ *pledge* 资产抵押。*the* ～生者,现存者。*the* ～ *theatre* 舞台剧〔与电影及电视相对而言〕。***within*** ～ ***memory*** 在世人记忆中的。**II** *n*. **1**. 生活;生计;生存。**2**. 〔英〕教士的俸禄。**3**. 〔古〕财产。*high* ～奢华的生活。*good* ～讲究(吃喝)的生活。*plain* ～ *and high thinking* 生活朴素思想高超。*the art of* ～生活的艺术。*the cost of* ～生活费用。*the standard of* ～生活水准。***earn*** [***get***, ***make***] ***one's*** ～ 谋生。***in the land of the*** ～ 活着的,现存的。***make a good*** ～ 过安乐生活。**L- Buddha** (喇嘛教的)活佛。～ **death** 活受罪〔指生活境遇〕;活地狱。～**-in** (被雇者)住在东家,供住。～ **movie** (使观众如同身历其境的)环形剧场立体电影。～**-out** (被雇者)住在外面,不供住。～ **room** **1**. 起居室。**2**. = ～ space. ～ **space** **1**. 生存空间。**2**. (房屋的)可居住面积。～ **unit** (公寓)套房。～ **wage** 生活工资。～ **will** 要求在病入膏肓无可救药时,不必用人工方法勉强延长生命的书面声明。**-ly** *ad*. **-ness** *n*.

Liv·ing·ston [ˈliviŋstən; ˋlɪvɪŋstən] *n*. 利文斯顿〔姓氏〕。

Liv·ing·stone [ˈliviŋstən; ˋlɪvɪŋstən] *n*. 利文斯通〔姓氏〕。

li·vre [ˈlivə, F. liːvr; ˋlɪvɚ, livr] *n*. 里弗尔〔法国十九世纪前货币名,原相当于一磅银子,后为法郎所代替〕。

l.i.w. = lost in weight 重量不足[损耗]。

lix·iv·i·ate [likˈsiviˌeit; lɪkˋsɪvɪˏet] *vt*. (**-at·ed**, **-at·ing**) = leach. **-i·a·tion** *n*.

lix·iv·i·um [likˈsiviəm; lɪkˋsɪvɪəm] *n*. (*pl*. **-i·ums**, **-i·a** [-ə;-ə])【化】浸滤液,灰汁;硷汁。

liz·ard [ˈlizəd; ˋlɪzɚd] *n*. **1**. 【动】蜥蜴。**2**. 一种家养的杂色金丝雀。**3**. 〔L-〕〔美〕阿拉巴马州的别号;〔Lizards〕阿拉巴马州人。*a house* ～守宫,壁虎。～**fish** 【动】歧须鮠科(*synodontidae*)的鱼。

Liz·zie [ˈlizi; ˋlɪzɪ] *n*. 莉齐〔女子名,Elizabeth 的昵称〕。

liz·zie [ˈlizi; ˋlɪzɪ] *n*. 〔美俚〕廉价的破旧汽车;早期的福特牌汽车。*a* ～ *label* 〔美俚〕汽车上的标记;旧汽车的标记。*a* ～ *stiff* 〔美俚〕坐破旧汽车到处移动的流动工人[流浪者]。

L.J. = Lord Justice 〔英〕上诉法院法官。

Lju·blja·na [ˈljuːbljɑːnɑː; ˋljubljɑnɑ] *n*. 卢布尔雅那〔前南斯拉夫城市〕。

LL. = **1**. Late Latin 后期拉丁语。**2**. Low Latin (公元二世纪的)民间拉丁语,俗拉丁语。

ll. = lines.

'll = will, shall (如 she'll, I'll 等)。

lla·ma [ˈlɑːmə; ˋlɑmə] *n*. 【动】美洲驼,无峰驼。

lla·no [ˈlɑːnəu; ˋlɑno] *n*. (*pl*. ～**s**) 南美洲的大草原。

LL. B., **LLB** = 〔L.〕 *Legum Baccalaureus* (= Bachelor of Laws) 法学士。

LL. D., **LLD** = 〔L.〕 *Legum Doctor* (= Doctor of Laws) 法学博士。

Llew·el·lyn [lu(ː)ˈwelin; luˋɛlɪn] *n*. 卢埃林〔男子名〕。

LL.JJ. = Lords Justices 〔英〕上诉法院法官(复数)。

L

L(l)oyd [lɔid; lɔɪd] *n*. 劳埃德〔男子名〕。

Lloyd's [lɔidz; lɔɪdz] *n*. (伦敦经营海上保险及船舶检查注册的)劳埃德商船协会。***A1 at*** ~ **1.** (在劳埃德商船协会注册的)第一级(船)。**2.** 最好的,第一流的。~ **list** 劳埃德协会海报。~ **Register** 劳埃德船舶年鉴(= ~ Register of British and Foreign Shipping)。

L.L.T. = London Landed Terms 伦敦起卸货条例。

LM 1.【宇】= lunar module 登月舱。**2.** = low middling〔美〕七级白棉。

lm =【物】lumen.

LMF = liquid metal fuel 液态金属燃料。

LMG = light machine gun 轻机枪。

L.M.S. 1. London Missionary Society【宗】伦敦传教会。**2.** London Mathematical Society〔英〕伦敦数学学会。

LMT = local mean time 地方平均时。

L.N.E.R. = London North-Eastern Railway〔英〕伦敦东北铁路。

LNG = liquefied natural gas 液化天然气。

lo [ləu; lo] *int*.〔古〕看哪! 瞧! *Lo and behold*! 嗳哟,你瞧!〔叙述惊人的事情前的用语。〕

loach [ləutʃ; lotʃ] *n*.【动】泥鳅。

load [ləud; lod] **I** *n*. **1.** 装载,担子;负担;工作(负荷)量。**2.** (车船等的)装载量;一驮,一车,一飞机。**3.**【电、机】(机械等的)负载(量),负荷(量);发电量。**4.** 充填,装药,装弹。**5.**〔*pl*.〕许多,大量,一大堆。**6.**〔俚〕使人喝醉的量。**7.**【生】(不利)负荷〔指有害基因的存在〕。*a* ~ *of care* 精神负担。*a* ~ *of debt* 债务的负担。*be ever ready to bear a heavy* ~ *on one's shoulders* 勇于挑重担。*a cart* ~ *of furniture* 一货车家具。*a* ~ *of hay* 一堆干草。*We have to make three ~s of the cargo*. 我们得把货物分成三批装运。*genetic* ~【生】遗传负荷〔指有害基因的存在〕。*the breaking* ~ 最大载荷。*the capacity* ~ 满载。*the dead* [*static*] ~ 恒载,静(荷)载,自重。*the live* [*moving*, *mobile*] ~ 活负载,动荷载。*the peak* ~ 最大负载,峰负载 *the permissible* ~ 容许负载。*the rated* ~ 额定载荷。*the safe* ~ 安全负载。*the working* ~ 资用负载。*~s of friends* 大批朋友。*~s of time* 充裕的时间。*a teaching* ~ *of twenty hours a week* 每星期二十小时的教学任务。***be a*** ~ ***off one's mind*** 如释负重。***get a*** ~ ***of***〔美俚〕仔细听;注意看。***have a*** ~ ***on***〔美俚〕喝醉。***lay not all the*** ~ ***on the lame horse***〔谚〕别把担子都放在跛马身上;别把希望完全寄托在不中用的人身上。***take a*** ~ ***off one's feet***〔美俚〕坐下休息。***take a*** ~ ***off sb.'s mind*** 解除某人思想负担,使某人放心。**II** *vt*. **1.** 把货装到(船、车等)上;装(货)。**2.** 装满,使负担。**3.** 把子弹装到(枪里);把胶卷装入(照相机)。**4.** 用铅加重(骰子、手杖等);用低劣物质等搀入。**5.** (人寿保险)加收额外保险费。~ *cargo into the hold* 把货装进船舱。*a heart ~ed with care* 心事重重。*a table ~ed with delicacies* 摆满佳肴的桌子。*air ~ed with carbon* 充满碳气的空气。~ *one's stomach with food* 吃得太多。~ *sb. with praise* 极力称赞某人。*I am ~ed*. 我的枪已上好子弹。~ *a camera with film* 给照相机装胶卷。*This wine has been ~ed*. 这种酒是搀了水的。— *vi*. **1.** (在枪里)装弹药;装料。**2.** (车、船等)装货;上船,上车。*Load*!【军】装子弹! *The ship is ~ing for London*. 这船正装货运往伦敦。*They ~ed into the boat*. 他们上船了。***be ~ed down with***〔美〕= ***be ~ed up with*** 装着…,存有(某种股票等)。~ ***down*** 装载甚重。***~ed for bear***〔俚〕**1.** 有充分准备。**2.** 生气;准备打架。~ ***the dice against sb***. 对某人使用加重骰子;使用不正当手段占人便宜。~ **displacement**【海】满载排水量。~ **draught**, ~ **draft**【海】满载吃水。~ **factor**【电】负载因数,负载系数。~ **line** 满载吃水线。~ **shedding** (为防电站超载而实行的)分区停电。~ **water line** = ~ line.

load·age [ˈləudidʒ; ˋlodɪdʒ] *n*. 装载量。

load·ed [ˈləudid; ˋlodɪd] *a*. **1.** 载重的;有负荷的,装着货的,有含意的。**2.** 装子弹的;灌过铅的;搀有杂质的;加有填料的。**3.**〔美俚〕喝醉了的。**4.**〔美俚〕富有的,钱很多的。**5.** 吃饱了的。*a* ~ *question* 另有意义的问题。~ *cane* 铅头杖。~ *dice* (容易掷出六点的)铅心骰子。~ *rubber* 填料橡胶。~ *wine* 搀过的酒。*a* ~ *stomach* 吃得很饱的肚子。

load·er [ˈləudə; ˋlodɚ] *n*. 装货的人;载货设备;装弹机;装填者,(尤指跟猎人)装弹药的人。

load·ing [ˈləudiŋ; ˋlodɪŋ] *n*. **1.** 装货。**2.** 装载量;重量;载荷;(船只等的)货载。**3.** 填充物,填料。**4.** 额外人寿保险。~ *and unloading* 装卸。~ *charges* 装货费。~ *days* 装货期限。~ **coil**【电】加感线圈。~ **waveguide**【无】加载波导。

loadsa- *comb. f*. = load of〔口〕大量:*~money* 巨额财富。*~space* 大量的空间。

load·star [ˈləudstɑ:; ˋlod͵stɑr] *n*. **1.**【天】北极星。**2.** 目标;指导原则。

load·stone [ˈləudstəun; ˋlod͵ston] *n*. **1.** 天然磁石。**2.** 吸引人的东西。

loaf[1] [ləuf; lof] *n*. (*pl*. ***loaves***) **1.** 一个面包〔通常重1,2,4磅〕。**2.** 面包形糖块(= sugar ~);面包形菜肴、食品等〔如一个菜心〕。**3.**〔英口〕脑袋。*Half a* ~ *is better than no bread*.〔谚〕半个面包比没有面包好。*The* ~ *has risen in price*. 面包涨价了。*a white* ~ (高级)白面包。*a brown* ~ 黑面包。*a* ~ *of cheese* 长方形大块干酪。*Use your* ~! 用脑袋想想! ***loaves and fishes*** 私利;眼前的利益;不很正当的利益,油水。

loaf[2] [ləuf; lof] **I** *vi*., *vt*. 混日子;游荡。~ ***away*** 虚度(*Don't* ~ *away your time*. 别虚度光阴)。~ ***on***〔美〕在某人处做食客。~ ***on a job*** 干活磨磨蹭蹭。~ ***through life*** 游荡一辈子。**II** *n*. 混日子。***have a*** ~ 游手好闲。***on the*** ~ 在游荡,混日子。

loaf·er [ˈləufə; ˋlofɚ] *n*. **1.** 游手好闲的人,二流子,无业游民。**2.** 平底便鞋,懒人鞋。~ *way* 二流子习气。**-ish** *a*.

loam [ləum; lom] **I** *n*. **1.** 肥土,沃土;壤土。**2.** (制砖等的)黏砂土。**II** *vt*. 用肥土填[覆盖]。

loam·y [ˈləumi; ˋlomɪ] *a*. (*-i·er*; *-i·est*) 肥土似的,含肥土的。

loan[1] [ləun; lon] **I** *n*. **1.** 出借,借出,贷。**2.** 借出物;资金;公债,贷款。**3.** 外来语(= ~ word);外来风俗习惯。*Will you favour me with* [*May I have*] *the* ~ *of this book*? 我可以把你的这本书借用一下么? *domestic* [*foreign*] ~ 内[外]债。*public* [*government*] ~ 公债。~ *for consumption* 消费贷款。***ask for the*** ~ ***of*** 请求借用…。***have the*** ~ ***of*** 借。~ ***on personal guarantee*** 保证贷款。~ ***on personal security*** 信用贷款。~ ***on security*** 担保贷款。***on*** ~ 出借;借。**II** *vt*., *vi*.〔美〕借贷,借出(*out*)。~ **collection** 借用展品〔为举行展览而借用的画、古董等〕。~ **holder** 债券持有人;(押款的)受押人。~ **myth** 外来神话。~ **note** 借据。~ **office** 贷款处;当铺;公债募集处。~ **shark**〔口〕高利贷者。~ **shift** 已经部分同化的外来词〔例:smearcase 原词是 *schmierkäse*〔G.〕〕。~ **syndicate** 借款财团。~ **translation** 仿造语(= calque)。~**word** 外来语。

loan[2] [ləun; lon], **loan·ing** [ˈləuniŋ; ˋlonɪŋ] *n*.〔Scot.〕**1.** 小路。**2.** 挤牛奶的场地。

loan·a·ble [ˈləunəbl; ˋlonəbl] *a*. 可借出的。

loan·ee [ləuˈni:; lonˋi] *n*. 借入者,债务人。

loan·er [ˈləunə; ˋlonɚ] *n*. **1.** 出借者,租出者。**2.** 借用物〔汽车、无线电、打字机等〕,出租物。

loath [ləuθ; loθ] *a*. 厌恶,讨厌,不愿(*to do*; *that*)。(*be*) ~ ***for him to go*** 不愿意他去。***nothing*** ~ 很愿意,很高兴。

loathe [ləuð; loð] *vt*., *vi*. 讨厌,厌恶;〔口〕不欢喜。~

the sight of food 看见吃的东西就恶心。

loath·ful [ˈləuðful; ˋloðfəl] ***a***.〔罕〕= loathsome.

loath·ing [ˈləuðiŋ; ˋloðɪŋ] ***n***. 厌恶,憎恨。

loath·li·ness [ˈləuðlinis; ˋloðlɪnɪs] ***n***. 厌恶。

loath·ly [ˈləuðli; ˋloθlɪ] ***a***. **1.**〔古〕= loathsome. **2.** 不愿意地。

loath·some [ˈləuðsəm, ˈləuθ-; ˋloðsəm, ˋloθ-] ***a***. 令人讨厌的;可厌的;叫人恶心的。**-ly** ***ad***. **-ness** ***n***.

loath·y [ˈləuði; ˋloðɪ] ***a***. = loathsome.

loaved [ləuvd; lovd] ***a***.〔英〕(卷心菜等)结成球的。

loaves [ləuvz; lovz] ***n***. loaf 的复数。

lob[1] [lɔb; lɑb] **I** ***vi***. (**-bb-**) **1.** 慢慢地走[跑、动] (*along*)。**2.**【网球】吊高球;【板球】扔得慢而低。— ***vt***. **1.** 吊高球。**2.**〔古〕使垂下。**II** ***n***. **1.** 笨重的人,傻大个儿。**2.**【网球】高球;【板球】下手球。

lob[2] [lɔb; lɑb] ***n***. = lugworm.

lo·bar [ˈləubə; ˋlobɚ] ***a***.【医】(肺)叶的;【植】浅裂片的。~ *pneumonia* 大叶肺炎。

lo·bate, lo·bat·ed [ˈləubeit, -id; ˋlobet, -ɪd] ***a***.【植】有裂片的;分裂的;【动】有叶状膜的,有蹼的。

lo·ba·tion [lə*u*ˈbeiʃən; loˋbeʃən] ***n***. 叶状;形成叶状;叶片。

lob·by [ˈlɔbi; ˋlɑbɪ] **I** ***n***. **1.** 门廊,门厅,过厅。**2.** (英国下院的)会客室,休息室;(表决时分别投票的)投票厅 (= division ~)。**3.**〔美〕(出入议院休息室用收买等手段左右法案的)院外活动集团。**II** ***vi***., ***vt***. (***-bied***; ***-by·ing***) **1.**〔美〕(在会议室中)运动议员,收买议员;运动通过议案。**2.** 暗中运动。~ **man** (戏院、剧场等的)收票员。**-ing, -ism** ***n***.〔美〕(国会的)院外活动;游说,疏通。**-er, -ist** ***n***. 院外活动集团的成员;进行疏通的人,说客。

lobe [ləub; lob] ***n***. **1.** 耳垂。**2.**【植】裂片;圆裂片;滚裂片。**3.**【无】波瓣,瓣。**4.**【解】(肺、脑、肝等的)叶。**5.**【机】凸角。**6.** (气球的)舵囊,气袋。~ **chamber** 翼室。

lo·bec·to·my [lə*u*ˈbektəmi; loˋbektəmɪ] ***n***.【医】叶[肝、脑、肺或甲状腺的一叶]切除术。

lobed [ləubd; lobd] ***a***. **1.** = lobate. **2.**【植】浅裂的;圆裂的;分裂的。

lo·be·li·a [ləuˈbiːljə; loˋbiljə] ***n***.【植】半边莲。

lo·be·line [ˈləubiˌliːn, -lin; ˋlobəlin, -lɪn] ***n***.【药】洛贝林〔呼吸中枢兴奋药〕,山梗菜硷,山梗烷醇酮。

Lo·bi·to [lə*u*ˈbiːtəu; loˋbito] ***n***. 洛比托〔安哥拉港市〕。

lob·lol·ly [ˈlɔblɔli; ˋlɑblɑlɪ] ***n***. **1.** 稠麦片粥。**2.**〔方〕泥坑。**3.** 粗人;乡下人。**4.** 火炬松;火炬松木 (= ~ pine)。~ **boy** [**man**] 打杂的帮工;军医助手,看护兵。

lo·bo [ˈləubəu; ˋlobo] ***n***.【动】(美国西部产)大灰狼。

lo·bot·o·mized [ləuˈbɔtəˈmaizd; loˋbɑtəˏmaɪzd] ***a***. 迟钝的〔好像是切除了前额脑叶似的〕。

lo·bot·o·my [ləuˈbɔtəmi; loˋbɑtəmɪ] ***n***. = leucotomy.

lob·scouse [ˈlɔbˌskaus; ˋlɑbˏskaus] ***n***. 肉、菜、硬饼干混烹的一种海员饮食。

lob·ster [ˈlɔbstə; ˋlɑbstɚ] ***n***. **1.** 大螯虾;大螯虾肉。**2.** 龙虾(= spiny [spini; spɪnɪ]);龙虾肉。**3.**〔蔑〕英国兵。**4.** 笨人,傻子;容易受骗的人。***red as a*** ~ 虾一样红的(脸等)。~**-eyed** ***a***. 眼睛凸出的。~ **pot** [**trap**] 捕虾篓。~ **shift** [**trick**]〔美口〕(报馆人员的)夜班采访;夜班。~ **tail 1.** 甲壳类动物的尾巴。**2.** 甲壳类动物的尾肉。~ **thermidor**【烹】蘑菇龙虾。

lob·u·lar [ˈlɔbjulə; ˋlɑbjulɚ] ***a***. 有小裂片的,有小叶的;小裂片[小叶]状的。

lob·ule [ˈlɔbjuːl; ˋlɑbjul] ***n***. **1.**【植】小裂片;腹片。**2.**【解】小叶。

lob·worm [ˈlɔbˌwəːm; ˋlɑbˏwɚm] ***n***. = lugworm.

loc. = **1.** location. **2.** local.

lo·cal [ˈləukəl; ˋlokḷ] **I** ***a***. **1.** 地方的,当地的,本地的。**2.** 局部的。**3.** 乡土的,狭隘的,片面的。**4.**【邮】本市的,本地的;【铁路】区间的。**5.**【数】轨迹的。*a* ~ *adverb* 表示地点的副词(如 here, there 等)。*a* ~ *custom* 地方习惯。*a* ~ *name* 地名。~ *news* 本地新闻。*a* ~ *station* 地方电台。~ *anaesthesia* 局部麻醉。*a* ~ *point of view* 偏狭的见解。~ **colour** (文艺作品的)乡土色彩,地方色彩。~ **court** 地方法院。~ **examinations**〔英〕地方考试。~ **exchange** 市内电话局。~ **government** 地方政府;地方自治。~ **option** [**veto**] 当地居民抉择权。~ **oscillation**【物】本机振荡。~ **preacher**【宗】被允许在当地讲道的教友。~ **strain** 局部应变。~ **stress**【物】局部应力。~ **time**【无】地方时。~ **war** [**operations**] 局部战争。**II** ***n***. **1.** (报纸上的)本地新闻。**2.** 本地居民;本地律师;本地教士;本地医生。**3.** 慢车。**4.** 工会支部。**5.**〔英〕= ~ examination(s). **6.**〔*pl*.〕本地球队。**7.**〔英口〕本地酒店,附近的小酒店[馆]。**8.** 在一定地区使用的邮票。

lo·cale [ləuˈkɑːl; loˋkæl] ***n***. (事故等发生的)现场,地点,场所。***in whatever*** **~*s*** 在任何场合下。

lo·cal·ism [ˈləukəlizəm; ˋlokḷˏɪzəm] ***n***. **1.** 地方风俗。**2.** 土话,方言,土音。**3.** 乡土观念,地方主义;地方性。**4.** 思想闭塞,心胸狭隘。

lo·cal·i·ty [ləuˈkæliti; loˋkælətɪ] ***n***. 地点,位置,场所,方向;地区;(植物的)产地;环境。*a description of* ~关于地点的记载。*one's bump* [*sense*] *of* ~对于场所的记忆力。*the* ~ *of a crime* 犯罪地点。

lo·cal·iz·a·ble [ˈləukəlaizəbl; ˋlokḷaɪzəbḷ] ***a***. 能地方化的,可以定域的。**-a·bi·li·ty**【物】可局限性,可定域性。

lo·cal·i·za·tion [ˌləukəlaiˈzeiʃən; ˏlokḷaɪˋzeʃən] ***n***. **1.** 定位,定域。**2.** 局限。**3.** 地方化。*fault* ~探伤;障碍部位测定。

lo·cal·ize, lo·cal·ise [ˈləukəˌlaiz; ˋlokḷˏaɪz] ***vt***. **1.** 使局限于某一地方[局部];使(军队)分驻各地。**2.** 定位,定域。**3.** 地方化,添地方色彩。**4.** 集中(注意等)(*upon*)。**5.** 找出(部位、原因、地点等)。**6.**〔美〕写本地新闻。— ***vi***. 局限,集中。

lo·cal·iz·er [ˈləukəˌlaizə; ˋlokḷˏaɪzɚ] ***n***.【海】定位器,定位信标。

lo·cal·ly [ˈləukəli; ˋlokəlɪ] ***ad***. **1.** 在地方上。**2.** 局部地,在局部上。**3.** 在本地。

Lo·car·no [ləuˈkɑːnəu; loˋkɑrno] ***n***. 洛迦诺〔瑞士城市〕。

lo·cate [lə*u*ˈkeit; loˋket] ***vt***. **1.**〔美〕设置在…,确定…的位置;位于,在〔用被动语态〕。**2.** 住(在某处)。**3.** 说出来源;找出,探出(痛处等)。**4.**【法】出租(土地等)。**5.**〔美〕设计,计划。— ***vi***.〔美口〕居住,住下来。

lo·cat·er [ˈləukeitə; loˋketɚ] ***n***.〔英〕= locator.

lo·ca·tion [ləuˈkeiʃən; loˋkeʃən] ***n***. **1.** 定位;【铁路】定线,〔美〕测量,设计。**2.** 位置,场所,地点。**3.** 拍摄外景;外景拍摄地。**4.** (房屋,土地等的)出租。**5.** 非洲土著居住的城郊。*a* ~ *beacon* 定位标灯。*fault* ~障碍点测定。*be on* ~正在拍外景。*a good* ~ *for* 定…的好地方。

loc·a·tive [ˈlɔkətiv; ˋlɑkətɪv] **I** ***a***.【语法】表示位置的。**II** ***n***.【语法】位置格 (= ~ case);位置格的词。

lo·ca·tor [ˈləukeitə; ˋloketɚ] ***n***. **1.** 定位器;探测器;无线电定位器,雷达。**2.** 勘定地界者。*an echo* ~回声[回波]勘定器。*a fault* ~探伤仪,故障探测器。

loc. cit. =〔L.〕*loco citato* 在上述引文中。

loch [lɔk, lɔx; lɑk, lɑx] ***n***.〔Scot.〕**1.** 滨海湖。**2.** 海湾。

lo·chi·a [ˈləukiə, lɔˈkiə; ˋlokɪə, lɑˋkɪə] ***n***.【医】恶露,产褥排泄。

lo·ci [ˈləusai; ˋlosaɪ] ***n***. locus 的复数。

lock[1] [lɔk; lɑk] **I** ***n***. **1.** 锁,闩,栓。**2.** (运河等的)船闸。**3.** 制轮楔。**4.**【机】气闸,气塞,锁气室。**5.**【军】枪机。**6.** 锁住,固定。**7.**〔俚〕拘留所。**8.**〔英〕性病医院 (= ~hospital). **9.**【自】同步。**10.** 结合,固着。**11.** (摔跤的)揪扭。**12.** 煞车。*off the* ~未锁。*on the* ~锁着。*trick*

～(对字的)密码锁。～ *the stable door after the horse has been stolen* 贼走关门。**be at [on, upon] the ～** 〔方〕在窘困中。**～, stock and barrel** 全部;完全。**under ～ and key** 锁着,妥为保藏。**II** *vt*. **1**. 锁,锁上。**2**. 收藏起来,秘藏。**3**. 抱紧,挽住;揪扭。**4**. (使资本等)固定。**5**. 使固定。**6**. 用水闸止住;使通过水闸(*up*; *down*). **7**. 卡住,塞住。**8**. 将曲面印版装在轮转印刷机滚筒上。*～ a secret in one's heart* 严守秘密。*be ～ed in a fight* 打得难分难解。*be ～ed in contemplation* 陷入沉思。*The ship was ～ed fast in ice*. 这条船被冰封住。*The gears are ～ed*. 齿轮卡住了。— *vi*. **1**. 锁住。**2**. 紧闭,不动。**3**. 抱住,揪扭,嵌进。**4**. (船)通过水闸;造水闸。～ **away** 锁起来。～ **down** 让船开出水闸。～ ***horns*** 争论(*over*)。～ **in** [**into**] 关起来;锁在里面。～ **in synchronism** 进入同步。～ **on** 用雷达波束自动跟踪(目标)。～ **oneself in** 把自己关在里面,闭门谢客。～ **out 1**. 关在外面。**2**. (资本家)封闭工厂。～ **up 1**. 上锁,锁住。**2**. 监禁。**3**. 收藏(文件等)。**4**. 固定(资本)。～**-away** 〔英〕长期证[债]券。～ **bolt**【机】锁紧螺栓。～**-chain** 锁车轮链条。～**down** 〔美〕单独关押。～**fast** *a*. 〔Scot.〕锁牢的。～ **gate** 闸门。～**-in** 〔美〕**1**. 关进。**2**. 占领并封锁建筑物的示威行动。～**jaw**【医】牙关紧闭症,咀嚼肌痉挛;破伤风。～**-keeper** 闸门管理员。～**master** (运河)船闸看管人。～**nut**【机】**1**. 防松螺帽。**2**. 对开螺帽(= ～ nut)。～**-on 1**. (雷达的)自动跟踪。**2**. (潜艇等之间)密封通道的接通。～**out 1**. 锁定,闭锁。**2**. 停工,闭厂〔厂主对付罢工的一种方法〕。**3**. 排定教员;将学生关在课室外。**4**.【海】(水下舷窗的)锁定;封锁。～ **sman** = ～-keeper. ～**smith** 锁匠。～ **step** 连锁步伐〔队列行进时步伐完全一致;固定不变的方式[安排]〕。～**-stitch** 双线连锁缝纫法。～**up 1**. 锁,闭,锁住。**2**. (学校等晚上的)关门时间。**3**. 拘留所,监狱。**4**. 资本的固定,固定资本。**-less** *a*. 无锁的;无船闸的。

lock[2] [lɔk; lɑk] *n*. **1**. 一绺卷发;〔*pl*.〕头发。**2**. (干草、羊毛等的)小量,一把,一撮。

lock·age [ˈlɔkidʒ; ˋlɑkɪdʒ] *n*. **1**. 水闸结构(材料)。**2**. 水闸通行税。**3**. (水闸中的)水位高度。**4**. 水闸通过。

Locke [lɔk; lɑk] *n*. **1**. 洛克〔姓氏〕。**2**. **John** ～洛克〔1632—1704,英国哲学家〕。

Lock·er [ˈlɔkə; ˋlɑkɚ] *n*. 洛克〔姓氏〕。

lock·er [ˈlɔkə; ˋlɑkɚ] *n*. **1**. 上锁的人;(英国海关的)仓库管理人。**2**. (公共更衣室等中可锁起来的)小橱,抽屉,小室。**3**. 冷藏间。**4**. (船上的)橱柜,库房。**5**. (车轮上的)锁具,锁扣装置。*a shot* ～【海】弹药库。*a chain* ～ 锚链舱。***Davy Jone's*** ～ 海底;水手的坟墓(*be in* [*go to*] *David Jone's* ～葬身海底)。***not a shot in the*** ～ 身上没有一文钱。～ **paper** 冷藏包装纸。～ **room** (体育馆、游泳池、工厂等的)更衣室。

lock·et [ˈlɔkit; ˋlɑkɪt] *n*. (挂在表链等下面装相片等用的)小金盒。

Lock·hart [ˈlɔkət, ˈlɔkhaːt; ˋlɑkhart, ˋlɑkɚt] *n*. 洛克哈特〔姓氏〕。

Lock·i·an [ˈlɔkiən; ˋlɑkɪən] *a*. (英国)洛克(Locke)(哲学)的,洛克学派的。

lo·co[1] [ˈləukəu; ˋloko] **I** *n*. **1**. = ～ weed. **2**. = ～ disease. **3**. 患疯草病的动物。**4**. 疯子。**II** *a*. 〔俚〕发疯的,精神错乱的。**III** *vt*. **1**. 用疯草毒害。**2**. 〔俚〕使发疯,使发狂。～ **disease**【医】疯草病〔马、牛、羊食疯草后引起的一种神经病〕。～ **weed** 疯草〔黄芪属(*Astragalus*)和棘豆属(*Oxytropis*)植物,产于北美洲西部,牛、羊、马食之引起疯草病〕。**-ed** *a*. **1**. (动物)患疯草病的。**2**. (人)发疯的,发狂的。**-ism** *n*. = ～ disease.

lo·co[2] [ˈləukəu; ˋloko] *n*. 〔美俚〕火车头,机车(locomotive 的缩写)。

lo·co- *comb*. *f*. 表示"从一处到另一处": *loco*motion.

lo·co ci·ta·to [ˈləukəu siˈteitəu; ˋloko saɪˋteto] 〔L.〕在上述引用文中〔略作 loc. cit. 或 l.c.〕。

lo·co·fo·co [ˌləukəuˈfəukəu; ˏlokoˋfoko] *n*. 〔美〕**1**. 摩擦火柴;摩擦点火的雪茄。**2**. 〔L-〕1835 年纽约民主党激进派(成员);〔废〕民主党人。

lo·co·mo·bile [ˌləukəˈməubi(ː)l; ˏlokəˋmobɪl, -bil] **I** *n*. 自动机车。**II** *a*. 自动推进的。

lo·co·mote [ˌləukəˈməut; ˏlokəˋmot] *vi*. 移动;走动;行进。

lo·co·mo·tion [ˌləukəˈməuʃən; ˏlokəˋmoʃən] *n*. **1**. 运动,移动,位移;运动力,移动力,运转力。**2**. 旅行。

lo·co·mo·tive [ˌləukəˈməutiv; ˏlokəˋmotɪv] **I** *n*. **1**. 火车头,机车。**2**. 〔*pl*.〕〔俚〕脚。**3**. 能行动的动物。**4**. 节奏逐渐快起来的集体欢呼。*Use your ～s!* 走呀! **II** *a*. **1**. 运动的,运转的,移动的。**2**. 有运动力的,起推动作用的。**3**. 机动的。**4**. 〔谑〕旅行的;爱旅行的。*a ～ person* 〔谑〕常常旅行的人。*in these ～ days* 在当今旅行方便的时代中。～ **engine** 机车,火车头。～ **engineering** 机车工程。～ **faculty** [**power**] 运动能力,移动力。～ **oil** 汽缸油。～ **organs** 脚。～ **tender** 煤水车。

lo·co·mo·tor [ˌləukəˈməutə; ˏlokəˋmotɚ] **I** *a*. 运动的,移动的,运动器官的。～ *ataxia* [*ataxy*]【医】运动失调病,脊髓痨。**II** [ˈləukəməutə; ˋlokəˏmotɚ] *n*. 有运动力的人[物];移动发动机。

lo·co·mo·to·ry [ˌləukəˈməutəri; ˏlokəˋmotərɪ] *a*. = locomotor.

loc·u·lar [ˈlɔkjulə; ˋlɑkjulɚ] *a*.【生】有细胞的;有小室的。

loc·u·late [ˈlɔkjulit, -leit; ˋlɑkjəlet, -let] *a*. = locular.

loc·u·li·ci·dal [ˌlɔkjuliˈsaidl; ˏlɑkjələˋsaɪdəl] *a*.【植】室背[胞间]开裂的。

loc·u·lus [ˈlɔkjuləs; ˋlɑkjələs] *n*. (*pl*. **-li** [-laɪ; -ˏlai])【动、植】小腔;小室〔如子房、花药等〕;子囊腔(= locule)。

lo·cum [ˈləukəm; ˋlokəm] *n*. 〔口〕= locum tenens.

lo·cum te·nens [ˈləukəm ˈtiːnenz; ˋlokəm ˋtinenz] (*pl*. ～ *tenentes*) 代理牧师;代理医师。

lo·cus [ˈləukəs; ˈlokəs] *n*. (*pl*. ***lo·ci*** [ˈləusai; ˋlosaɪ]) **1**. 场所,地点,所在地。**2**.【数】轨迹。**3**.【生】基因座。**4**. (书籍、文献等中的某一)文句,章节,段落。

locus ci·ta·tus [ˈləukəs siˈteitəs; ˋlokəs sɪˋtetəs] 〔L.〕引述的文句[章节]等。

lo·cus clas·si·cus [ˈləukəs ˈklæsikəs; ˋlokəsˋklæsɪkəs] 〔L.〕常受人引用的文句[章节]。

lo·cus in quo [ˈləukəs inˈkwəu; ˋlokəs ɪnˋkwo] 〔L.〕现场,当场。

lo·cus si·gil·li [ˈləukəs siˈdʒilai; ˋlokəs sɪˋdʒɪlaɪ] 盖印处,签名盖章处〔略 L. S.〕。

locus stan·di [ˈləukəsˈstændai; ˋloˏkəsˋstændaɪ] (公认的)正式地位;参加权;(可到法院[议会]中为某一问题争辩的)陈述权。

lo·cust [ˈləukəst; ˋlokəst] *n*. **1**. 蝗虫;蚱蜢。**2**. 〔美〕蝉。**3**. 破坏者;贪吃的人。**4**.【植】洋槐;刺槐,洋槐[刺槐]的木材。**5**.【植】角豆树。**6**. 〔美俚〕警棍。*oriental migratory* ～东亚飞蝗。～ **bean**【植】角豆。～ **tree**【植】刺槐。

lo·cu·tion [ləuˈkjuːʃən; loˋkjuʃən] *n*. **1**. 特别的说话方式;语风;语法。**2**. 惯用语,成语,短语。

L.O.D. = Little Oxford Dictionary《小牛津辞典》。

lode [ləud; lod] *n*. **1**. 矿脉;丰富的蕴藏。**2**. 〔英方〕水路,(沼泽的)排水沟。**3**. 天然磁石(= loadstone)。

lo·den [ˈləudn; ˋlodn] *a*.【纺】**1**. 罗登(缩绒厚)呢〔全毛或与驼毛交织,能防水〕。**2**. 罗登(缩绒厚)呢色〔深橄榄色〕。

lode·star [ˈləudˌstaː; ˋlodˏstar] *n*. = loadstar.

lode·stone [ˈləudˌstəun; ˋlodˏston] *n*. = loadstone.

Lodge [lɔdʒ; lɑdʒ] *n*. 洛奇〔姓氏〕。

lodge [lɔdʒ; lɑdʒ] **I** *n*. **1**. (森林、猎场等的)看守小屋;(学校、工厂等的)门房,传达室。**2**. 〔古〕小屋,草屋;(北美印第安人的)小屋,帐篷;其中的居住者。**3**. (海狸、獭等的)巢穴,窝。**4**. (共济会、秘密结社、工会等的)支部会员们;支部会员聚会处;支部。5.〔美〕大学生联谊会,大学女生联谊会。6.〔英〕(剑桥大学)院长住宅。7.(游览区的)小旅馆。*the grand* ~(共济会等支部的)干事;理事。**II** *vi*. 1. 暂住,寄宿。2.(箭、枪等)竖立;(子弹等)停留,进入。3.(庄稼等)倒伏。4. 猎物逃入丛中。~ *at an inn* 住旅馆。~ *with sb*. 寄住某人家中。*A bullet ~d in his thigh*. 子弹打进他的大腿里。— *vt*. 1. 留宿,使住宿。2. 存放,寄存。3. 把(子弹等)打入,射进,打在。4.(风)吹倒,使倒伏。5. 提出(报告、抗议等)。6. 授与。7.(将猎物)赶进巢穴。*The hotel is well* [*ill*]-*~d* 这旅馆设备好[不好]。~ *money in a bank* [*with a person*] 把钱存在银行里[寄存在某人处]。~ *a protest against sb*. 向人提出抗议。~ *a complaint against sb*. *with the authorities concerned* 向有关当局对某人提出控诉。~ *information against* 告密。~ *power in* [*with*, *in the hands of*] *sb*. 把权力交给某人。

lodg·er [ˈlɔdʒə; ˋlɑdʒɚ] *n*. 寄宿者,房客。*take in ~s* 接受房客[寄宿者]。

lodg(e)·ment [ˈlɔdʒmənt; ˋlɑdʒmənt] *n*. 1. 住处,寄宿处;立足点。2.【军】占领;占领后的紧急防御工事;据点。3.(担保品等的)交存,寄存;存款,贮蓄;贮存。4. 提出。5. 沉积(物);沉积处。*a ~ area* 滩点占领区;空降作战初期占领区。*the ~ of a protest* 抗议的提出。*a ~ of dirt inside the radio* 收音机内的积尘。***effect*** [***find***, ***make***] ***a*** ~ 1. 占领阵地,获得据点。2. 占牢固的地位。3. 征服人心。

lodg·ing [ˈlɔdʒiŋ; ˋlɑdʒɪŋ] *n*. 1. 住宿,寄宿。2. 住处,寄宿处。3.〔*pl*.〕出租的房间,公寓。4. 存放处。5.(庄稼等)倒伏。*ask for a night's* ~ 借宿一晚。*board and ~* 膳宿,包吃包住。*dry* ~ 不供伙食的寄宿。***take up one's ~s*** 决定住处,投宿。~**-house** 公寓(*a common ~-house*〔英〕包住不包吃的公寓)。

lod·i·cule [ˈlɔdiˌkjuːl; ˋlɑdɪˏkjul] *n*.【植】浆片,鳞片。

Lódź, Lodz [luːʒ; ludʒ] *n*. 罗兹〔波兰城市〕。

lo·ess [ˈləuis; ˋlo·ɪs] *n*.【地】黄土。~**-child**, ~**-doll** 黄土结核,沙姜(石)。**-al**, **-i·al**, **-ic** *a*.

Loe·we [ˈləui; ˋloɪ] *n*. 洛伊〔姓氏〕。

L of C = Lines of Communication 交通线。

lo-fi [ˈləufai; ˋloˏfaɪ] *a*. 保真度不高的,非保真的;灵敏度不高的。

LOFT = low frequency radio telescope 低频射电[无线电]望远镜。

loft [lɔ(ː)ft; lɔft] **I** *n*. 1.(屋顶下的)顶楼,阁楼。2.(堆干草等用的)厩楼。3.(讲堂、教堂等的)楼厢。4.〔美〕(仓库、商业建筑物等的)顶层。5. 鸽房;鸽群。6.【高尔夫球】打高球;(高尔夫球棒端的)高击斜面。*a fixed* [*mobile*] ~固定[移动]鸽房。**II** *vt*. 1. 贮存在阁楼上;加造阁楼。2. 放(鸽子)进鸽房,在鸽房里养鸽子。3.(把高尔夫球)高打出去。4. 把…向(空间)发射。5. 跳过(障碍物)。— *vi*.【高尔夫球】打高球。

loft·er [ˈlɔ(ː)ftə; ˋlɔftɚ] *n*.【高尔夫球】(打高球用的)高击棒。

loft·ing [ˈlɔftiŋ; ˋlɑftɪŋ] *n*. 1. 放样;理论模线的绘制。2.【军】上仰轰炸〔投弹后飞机迅速爬升以避免受震波影响〕。~ **iron** = lofter.

lofts·man [ˈlɔftsmən; ˋlɑftsmən] *n*. (*pl*. ***-men***)(造船或造飞机的)放样员。*a mould* ~放样工人。

loft·y [ˈlɔ(ː)fti; ˋlɔftɪ] *a*. (***loft·i·er***, ***-i·est***) 1. 极高的,巍峨的。2. 高尚的,崇高的。3. 骄傲的,傲慢的。*a ~ mountain* 高山。~ *aims* 崇高的目的。~ *contempt* [*disdain*] 藐视。*speak in a ~ strain* 说大话。**-i·ly** *ad*. **-i·ness** *n*.

log[1] [lɔg; lɔg] **I** *n*. 1. 原木,圆木,干材。2. 测程仪,计程仪。3. 航海日志,(飞行员用的)航行日志;旅行日记。4.〔英〕裁缝店日工的工作时间表。5.【机】记录表。*clear ~* 干材。*heave* [*throw*] *the ~* 用测程仪测船速。*sail by the ~* 靠测程仪测船位航行。*a rough ~* 航海日志草稿。*a smooth ~* 誊清的航海日志。*a performance ~*(机器等的)运转情况记录(簿)。*a well ~* 钻井记录。***as easy as falling*** [***rolling***] ***off a ~***〔美〕极容易。***in the ~*** 未经斧削过的。***keep the ~ rolling***〔美〕使工作高速度地进行下去。***Roll my ~ and I'll roll yours***〔谚〕互相帮忙;互相吹嘘。***sleep like a ~*** 睡得很死。***split the ~***〔美〕分析,解释。**II** *vt*. (***-gg-***) 1.(把树)砍倒。2. 锯成圆材;拖(木头)。3. 把…记入航海[飞行]日志;把…输入电子计算机(*in*)。4. 航行;飞行;以…的时速飞行[航行]。5. 给(船体、机翼等)的线形图[轮廓线]放样。— *vi*. 采伐树木。~ ***in***[***off***]【计】开始[停止]使用电脑工作,进入[退出]电脑工作系统。~**book** = ~(*n*.) 3. ~ **cabin**(用圆木搭建的)小木屋。~ **chip**【海】(测程仪的)测程板。~**jam** 1. 浮木阻塞。2. 工作障碍。~ **line**【海】测程仪线。~ **reel**【海】测程仪线路车。~**wood** 1.【植】洋苏木树(*Haematoxylon campechianum*)〔产于中美和西印度群岛,枝带刺,开小黄花〕。2. 洋苏木木料[染料]。

log[2] [lɔg; lɑg] *n*. = logarithm.

log[3] [lɔg; lɑg] **I** *vt*. (***-gg-***) 向…提供补给品。**II** *n*. 补给品的发放,补给品发放的日子。

LOG, log = logarithum.

log. = logic.

Lo·gan [ˈləugən; ˋlogən] *n*. 洛根〔姓氏,男子名〕。

log·an [ˈlɔgən; ˋlogən] *n*. 摇石(= ~ stone)。

lo·gan·ber·ry [ˈləugənbəri; ˋlogənˏbɛrɪ] *n*.【植】罗甘莓〔blackberry 和 raspberry 的杂交种〕。

lo·ga·ni·a [ləuˈgeiniə; loˋgenɪə] *a*.【植】马钱科(*Loganiaceae*)的。

log·a·oe·dic [ˌlɔːgəˈiːdik, ˌlɔg-; ˋlɔgəˋidɪk, ˏlɑg-] **I** *a*.(扬抑格和扬抑抑格交混或抑扬格和抑抑扬格交混的)混合音步诗律的。**II** *n*. 混合音步诗。

log·a·rithm [ˈlɔgəriθəm; ˋlɔgəˏrɪðəm] *n*.【数】对数。*common ~s* 常用对数。*general ~s* 普通对数。*natural ~* 自然对数。*the table of ~s* 对数表。

log·a·rith·mic [ˌləugəˈriθmik, -iðm-; ˏlɔgəˋrɪθmɪk, -ɪðm-] *a*. 对数的。~ *function* 对数函数。*a ~ scale* 计算尺。~ *series* 对数级数。*the ~ table* 对数表。**-cal·ly** [-kəlɪ] *ad*. 用对数。

loge [ləuʒ; loʒ] *n*. [F.] 1. 小屋,摊棚。2.(剧场中的)包厢,前座。3.(房间等)隔开的一小块地方。

log·ged [lɔgd; lɑgd] *a*. 1. 在水中泡重了的(圆木)。2. 低湿的,浸透的(土地)。

log·ger [ˈlɔgə; ˋlɑgɚ] *n*. 1. 伐木工,锯木工。2. 圆木装载机;圆材拖车。3.【物,机】测井仪;(参数自动分析)记录器。

log·ger·head [ˈlɔgəhed; ˋlɔgɚˏhɛd] *n*. 1. 笨人,傻子。2. 捕鲸船船尾圆柱。3. 铁球棒。4.【动】= ~shrike. 5.【动】= ~turtle. ***at ~s with sb***. 和某人相争,同某人不和。***fall*** [***get***, ***go***] ***to ~s*** 争吵起来。~**shrike**【动】�

log·gi·a [ˈlɔdʒə, ˈlɔdʒiə; ˋlɑdʒɪə, ˋlɑdʒə] *n*. (*pl*. ~*s*, ***log·gi·e*** [ˈlɔddʒei; ˋlɑddʒe])【建】凉廊。

log·ging [ˈlɔgiŋ; ˋlɔgɪŋ] *n*. 1. 伐木事业;伐木量。2. 载入值班簿[航行日志];记录;存入。3. 记下调谐位置。4.【地】录井,测井。~ *clearing* 集材。*a ~ railway* 森林(运送木材)铁路。

log·gy [ˈlɔgi; ˋlɑgɪ] *a*. = logy.

log·i·a [ˈlɔgiə; ˋlɑgɪə] *n*. 〔*pl*.〕(*sing*. ***logion***)(宗教家的)名言集;[L-](《圣经》上所无的)耶稣语录。

log·ic [ˈlɔdʒik; ˋlɑdʒɪk] *n*. 1. 逻辑,理论学。2. 推理[方法];逻辑性,条理性。3. 威力,压力,强制(力)。*deductive* [*inductive*] ~演绎[归纳]逻辑。*dialectical ~* 辩证逻辑。*formal ~* 形式逻辑。*a gangster ~* 强盗逻辑,恶徒的歪理[言行]。*mathematical ~* 数理逻辑。*pure ~* 纯粹逻辑。*He is not governed by ~*. 他没有逻辑

L

性。*That is not* ～. 那不合逻辑。*the irresistible* ～ *of facts* 事实的不可抗拒的威力。*the* ～ *of events* [*war*] 事件[战争]的强制力。*His* ～ *is shaky*. 他的推理站不住脚。**chop** ～ 诡辩。～ **bomb**【计】逻辑炸弹〔指隐藏在电脑程序中的病毒〕。～ **core**【自、数】逻辑磁心。

-logic, -logical *suf*. 〔构成与 -logy 结尾的名词相应的形容词〕表示"…学的":bio*logical*, philo*logical*.

log·i·cal [ˈlɔdʒikəl; ˋlɑdʒɪkl] *a*. **1.** 逻辑的,逻辑上的;逻辑学上的。**2.** 合乎逻辑的。**3.** 逻辑上必然的。～ *constants* 逻辑常词[常项]。～ *necessity* 逻辑的必然性。*a* ～ *argument* 条件分明的论证。*a* ～ *process* 合理的程序,合乎逻辑的[必然的]过程。*the* ～ *result* 必然的结果。～ **empiricism** 逻辑经验主义。**-ly** *ad*. **-ness** *n*. ～ **positivism** 逻辑实证主义。

log·i·cal·i·ty [ˌlɔdʒiˈkæliti; ˏlɑdʒɪˋkælətɪ] *n*. 逻辑性。

lo·gi·cian [ləuˈdʒiʃən; loˋdʒɪʃən] *n*. 逻辑学家,论理学家。

lo·gie [ˈləugi; ˋlogɪ] *n*. (演戏用的)假珠宝。

log·i·on [ˈlɔgiɔn; ˋlɑgɪɑn] *n*. logia 的单数。

-logist *suf*. 表示"某一学科的专家,学者,研究者":antho*logist*, bio*logist*.

lo·gis·tic [ləuˈdʒistik; loˋdʒɪstɪk] **I** *n*. **1.**【逻、数】逻辑斯蒂,符号[数理]逻辑;计算术。**2.**【军】后勤(学)。**II** *a*.【军】后勤学的;后勤的 (=logistical). **-al·ly** *ad*.

lo·gis·tics [ləuˈdʒistiks; loˋdʒɪstɪks] *n*.【军】后勤学;后方勤务。*a* ～ *base* 后勤基地。～ *department* 后勤部。

log·nor·mal [ˈlɔgˈnɔːməl; ˋlɑgˋnɔːməl] *a*.【数】对数正态的。**-mal·i·ty** [ˌlɔgnɔˈmæliti; ˏlɑgnɑˋmælətɪ] *n*. **-ly** *ad*.

log·o- *comb. f*. 表示"词","语":*logo*gram, *logo*graph.

lo·go [ˈlɔgəu; ˋlɑgo] *n*. =logotype.

log·o·gram [ˈlɔgəugræm; ˋlɑgəˏgræm] *n*. **1.** 语标,词符〔如用 $ 表示 dollar 之类〕;略字〔如用 s. 表示 shilling 之类〕。**2.** 速记符号。**-mat·ic** *a*.

log·o·graph [ˈlɔgəugrɑːf; lɑgəˏgræf] *n*. **1.** =logogram. **2.** =logotype.

log·o·griph [ˈlɔgəgrif; ˋlɔgəgrɪf] *n*. 字谜〔如字母移位,回文,换音变词等游戏〕。

lo·gom·a·chy [lɔˈgɔməki; ləˋgɑməkɪ] *n*. **1.** 对言语[文词]的争执;口角;舌战。**2.**〔美〕字谜游戏。

lo·gom·e·ter [lɔˈgɔmitə; lɑˋgɑmɪtɚ] *n*. **1.**【电】电流比(率)计;比率表。**2.** 对数计算尺。

log·or·rhe·a [ˌlɔgəˈriːə; ˏlɔgəˋriə] *n*.【医】多言癖。

Log·os [ˈlɔgɔs; ˋlɑgɑs] *n*. **1.**【哲】逻各斯,理性;理念。**2.**【神】(三位一体的第二位)基督或上帝的话,道。

log·o·type [ˈlɔgə*u*taip; ˋlɑgəˏtaɪp] *n*. **1.**【印】成语铅字,连合活字。**2.** (广告等用的)标识[语句]。

log·roll [ˈlɔgrəul; ˋlɔgˏrol] *vi*.〔美〕**1.** 互相帮助(滚木头)。**2.** 互相捧场。**3.** 做水上踩滚木游戏。— *vt*. 互投赞成票促使提案通过。

log·roll·ing [ˈlɔgrəuliŋ; ˋlɔgˏrolɪŋ] *n*.〔美〕**1.** 滚木头,搬运木材。**2.** 支援,互助,合作。**3.** 互相吹嘘。**4.** 水上踩滚木游戏。

-logue *suf*. **1.** 表示"谈话","写作":dia*log*(*ue*), cata*log*(*ue*). **2.** 表示"学者","专家":sino*logue*.

lo·gy [ˈləugi; ˋlogɪ] *a*. (*-gi·er*; *-gi·est*)〔美〕**1.** 举动迟钝的,笨的。**2.** 弹性不足的。

-lo·gy *suf*. **1.** 表示"…学","…论":philo*logy*. **2.** 表示"语","词":tauto*logy*.

loid [lɔid; lɔɪd] *n*.〔俚〕撬锁塑料片〔小偷用来拨开弹簧锁舌的〕。

loin [lɔin; lɔɪn] *n*. **1.**〔*pl*.〕【解】腰;耻骨区;生殖器官。**2.** (牛、羊等的)腰肉。***a fruit*** [***child***] ***of one's*** ～***s*** 自己生的孩子。***be sprung from sb.'s*** ～ 是某人所生。***gird up one's*** ～***s*** 束紧腰带,准备行动。～**-cloth** 腰带。

loir [ˈlɔiə; lɔɪr] *n*.【动】(欧洲产)大睡鼠。

Loire [lwɑːr; lwɑr] *n*. 罗亚河〔法国第一大河〕。

Lo·is [ˈlə*u*is; ˋloɪs] *n*. 洛伊丝〔女子名〕。

loi·ter [ˈlɔitə; ˋlɔɪtɚ] *vi*., *vt*. 游手好闲,闲逛;耽搁;混日子;混掉(时间)(*away*)。

loi·ter·er [ˈlɔitərə; ˋlɔɪtərɚ] *n*. 闲混的人,混日子的人。

loi·ter·ing·ly [ˈlɔitəriŋli; ˋlɔɪtərɪŋlɪ] *ad*. 游手好闲地,懒散地,吊儿郎当地。

Lo·ki [ˈləuki; ˋlokɪ] *n*.【北欧神】洛基〔不断制造纠纷、祸害的神〕。

LOL = laughing out loud【计】大笑。

loll [lɔl; lɑl] *vi*. **1.** 懒洋洋地躺[靠];闲荡。**2.** (头等)下垂。**3.** (舌头等)伸出 (*out*)。～ *against a wall* 懒散地靠在墙上。～ *in a chair* 懒洋洋地靠在椅子上。～ *about the streets* 在街上闲荡。— *vt*. **1.** 垂下;伸出。(*out*). **2.** (把头、手脚等)懒洋洋地靠着。**3.** 吊儿郎当地混日子。(*away*). **-ingly** *ad*.

lol·la·pa·loo·sa, lol·la·pa·loo·za [ˌlɔləpəˈluːzə; ˏlɑləpəˋluzə] *n*.〔美俚〕非常出色的人[物]。

Lol·lard [ˈlɔləd; ˋlɑlɚd] *n*.【英宗史】(十四世纪的)威克利夫 (John Wyclif) 派教徒。**Lol·lard·ism, Lol·lard·ry** *n*. 威克利夫主义。

lol·li·pop [ˈlɔliˌpɔp; ˋlɑlɪˏpɑp] *n*.〔常 *pl*.〕**1.**〔英俚〕钱。**2.** 棒棒糖;糖果。**3.**〔英〕拦车棒〔一根长棍上钉有一个大圆牌,用来在过街处拦阻车辆通过,让小学生放学时安全走过街道〕。**4.** 棒棒糖工具〔在建筑物上加盖数层后呈棒棒糖状〕。

lol·lop [ˈlɔləp; ˋlɑləp] *vi*. **1.** 跳跳蹦蹦地走。**2.** = loll, lounge.

lol·ly [ˈlɔli; ˋlɑlɪ] *n*. (*pl*. ***-lies***)〔英方〕**1.** 钱。**2.** 硬糖果。

lol·ly·gag [ˈlɔliˌgæg; ˋlɑlɪˏgæg] *vi*. (***-gag·ged***, ***-gag·ging***)〔美口〕浪费时间;闲游浪荡。

lol·ly·pop [ˈlɔlipɔp; ˋlɑlɪˏpɑp] *n*. =lollipop.

Lom·bard [ˈlɔmbəd, ˈlʌmbəd; ˋlɑmbɚd, ˋlʌmbard] **I** *n*. **1.**【史】伦巴族人〔日耳曼民族之一〕;伦巴族人后裔。**2.** (意大利的)伦巴第人。**3.** 从事金融业的伦巴第人;放债者,银行家。**4.** 〔l-〕银行,当铺。**5.** 〔l-〕〔俚〕愚蠢的富人,有钱的傻瓜。**II** *a*. =Lombardic. ～ **loan** 英格兰银行给商业银行的证券抵押贷款。～ **Street** 伦巴第人街,伦敦的银行街;金融市场,金融界;伦敦的金融中心。

Lom·bar·dia [ˌlɔmbəˈdiə; ˏlɑmbɚˋdɪə] *n*. =Lombardy.

Lom·bar·dic [lɔmˈbɑːdik; lɑmˋbardɪk] **I** *a*. 伦巴第族的;伦巴第(人)的;伦巴第式的。**II** *n*. 伦巴第草写体。

Lom·bar·dy [ˈlɔmbədi; ˋlɑmbɚdɪ] *n*. 伦巴第〔意大利一地区〕。

Lom·bro·si·an [lɔmˈbrəuziən, lɑmˋbroʒən] *a*. 隆布洛索犯罪学理论的〔隆布洛索是意大利的犯罪学家,他的学派认为犯罪者是明显的隔代遗传类型〕。

Lo·mé [ləuˈmei; ˏloˋme] *n*. 洛美〔多哥首都〕。

lo·ment [ˈləument; ˋlomɛnt] *n*.【植】节荚。(= lomentum). **-a·ceous** [-mənˈteiʃəs; -mənˋteʃəs] *a*.

lon., long. = longitude.

Lon·don [ˈlʌndən; ˋlʌndən] *n*. **1.** 伦敦〔姓氏〕。**2.** 伦敦〔英国首都〕。*the Greater* ～大伦敦〔包括市区及郊区〕。～**ivy** 伦敦的烟雾。～ **particular**〔口〕伦敦特有的大雾。～ **pride** 虎耳草属植物的一种。～ **smoke** 暗灰色。**-er** 伦敦人。**-ism** 伦敦式;伦敦腔。**-ize** *vt*. 使成伦敦式,使伦敦化。

Lon·don·der·ry [ˌlʌndənˈderi; ˏlʌndənˋdɛrɪ] *n*. 伦敦德里〔英国港市〕。

lone [ləun; lon] *a*. **1.** 寂寞的。**2.** 无人烟的,人迹稀少的;孤寂的。**3.**〔谑〕独身的,寡居的。**4.** 孤独的;无伴的。*a* ～ *flight* 单独飞行。*the L- Star State* 德克萨斯州〔别称〕。～ **hand** **1.** 独行其是的人。**2.** (牌戏中的)头家。～ **wolf** =loner.

lone·ly [ˈləunli; ˋlonlɪ] *a*. (*-li·er*; *-li·est*) **1.** 寂寞的。**2.** 幽静的;孤独的,孤单的。**3.** 荒凉的,人迹稀少的。**-liness** *n*.

lon·er [ˈləunə; ˋlonɚ] ***n*.** 〔口〕独来独往的人,性格孤癖的人。

lone·some [ˈlənsəm; ˋlonsəm] **I** ***a*. 1.** 幽静的;寂寞的,孤独的。**2.** 凄凉的,人迹稀少的。*feel* ~ 寂寞。**II** ***n*.** 自己(一人)。***by*** [***on***] ***one's*** ~ 独自地;单独地;靠自己的力量。**-ly** ***ad*.**

Long [lɔŋ; lɔŋ] ***n*.** 朗〔姓氏〕。

long[1] [lɔŋ; lɔŋ] ***vi*.** 渴想,极想,渴望 (*for*,〔古〕*after*; *to do*)。

long[2] [lɔŋ; lɔŋ] **I** ***a*.** (~***er*** [ˈlɔŋgə; ˋlɔŋgɚ]; ~***est*** [ˈlɔŋgist; ˋlɔŋgɪst]) **1.** 长,长的。*a* ~ *way* 远距离。*a* ~ *way off* 离得很远。*It is five feet* ~. 这有五英尺长。**2.** 个子高的。*a* ~ *man* 高个子的人。**3.** 长久的,长期的。*a* ~ *friendship* 长期的友谊。*a* ~ *memory* 长久不忘的好记性。*a* ~ *note* 远期票据。*It will be* ~ *before we know the truth*. 很久以后真相才会大白。*It will not be* ~ *before we know the truth*. 不久真相就会大白。*Now we shan't be* ~!〔口〕这回就好啦! **4.** 冗长的,拖长的。*Don't be* ~ *about it*! 别慢吞吞的。*She is* ~ *in coming*. 她姗姗来迟。**5.** …以上,足足。*three* ~ *hours* 足足三小时。*a* ~ *mile* 一英里以上。**6.** 达到远方的。*have a* ~ *arm* (为了扩张势力)把手伸到老远。*take a* ~ *view of the matter* 从长远考虑这事。**7.** 〔诗〕长音的,重读的;【语音】长音(节)的。**8.**【商】行情看涨的,做多头的。*be on the* ~ *side of the market*. 做多头。**9.** 长于…的。*be* ~ *on understanding* 理解力强。**10.** 众多的,充足的,大的。*Corn is in* ~ *supply*. 谷物供应充足。*fetch* ~ *prices* 售得高价。*have a* ~ *family* 有很多子女。*read a* ~ *list of books* 读很多书。***as broad as it is*** ~ 反正都一样。***as*** ~ ***as*** **1.** 长达…,达…之久 (*as* ~ *as five years* 长达五年之久)。**2.** = so long as. ***as*** ~ ***as one's arms*** 极长。***at*** (***the***) ~***est*** 至多。***be*** ~ ***in ... ing*** 很不容易… (*Spring is* ~ *in coming*. 春天好不容易才来)。***before*** (***very***) ~ 不(需很)久。***by a*** ~ ***chalk*** [***shot***, ***way***] = ***by*** ~ ***chalks*** 〔口〕在很大程度上,远远,…得多。***make a*** ~ ***arm*** 把手伸得老远。***make a*** ~ ***guess*** 作大致估计。***not by a*** ~ ***chalk*** [***shot***] 绝不;差得远。***one's*** ~ ***home*** 坟墓 (*go to one's* ~ *home* 死)。

II ***ad*. 1.** 长久;久已。*The opportunity was not* ~ (*in*) *coming*. 机会不久就来了。*He will not be* ~ *for this world*. 他活不了多久了。*I have* ~ *been meaning to write*. 我早就想写信了。*It was* ~ *before he recovered*. 他的病好久才痊愈。**2.** 始终。*all day* [*night*] ~整天[夜]。*all one's life* ~一辈子。**3.** 遥远地。*a* ~*-travelled person* 曾到远处旅行的人。***any*** ~***er*** 〔用于否定〕(不)再 (*I shall not wait* (*any*) ~*er*. 我不再等了)。***how*** ~? 多久 (*How* ~ *have you been here*? 你来了多少时候?)。~ ***after*** 很久之后。~ ***ago*** [***since***] 老早[以前]。~ ***before*** 老早以前。***no*** ~***er*** 已不,不再。***So*** ~〔口〕再见! ***so*** ~ ***as*** 只要 (*Stay so* ~ *as you like*. 只要你喜欢尽管待在这儿好啦)。

III ***n*. 1.** 长期间。*It will not take* ~. 这不需要很多时间。**2.** 〔the L-〕= ~ vacation. **3.** 〔*pl*.〕【商】看涨的人,做多头的人。(*opp*. shorts). **4.**【语音】长母音;长音节;长子音。**5.** (服装的)长尺寸;〔*pl*.〕长裤。***for*** ~ 长久 ~***s and shorts*** **1.** 诗〔尤指古希腊的和古拉丁的〕。**2.**【建】长短砌合。***the*** ~ ***and the short of it is that...*** 要点,梗概,总之。~**-ago 1.** ***a*.** 从前的,往时的。**2.** ***n*.** 〔the ~〕往时,古昔。~**-awaited** ***a*.** 期待已久的。**L-Beach** (美国)长滩。~ **beard** 〔口〕老人,长者。~**-bill** 长嘴的鸟(尤指沙锥鸟,鹬)。~ **boat** (放在大船上的最大的)大艇。~**bow** 大弓 (*draw* [*pull*] *the* ~*-bow* 吹牛)。~**-cherished** ***a*.** 长期渴望的。~**cloth** 细棉布。~**-clothes** 〔*pl*.〕襁褓。~**-dated** ***a*.** 远期的。~**-day** ***a*. 1.** 工作日长的。**2.**【植】长日照的。~**-distance** ***a*. 1.** 长途的,长距离的 (*a* ~*-distance bomber* 远程轰炸机)。**2.** 长途电话的。~ **distance 1.** 长途电话通讯。**2.** 长途电话交换局[交换机];长途话务员。~ **division**【数】长除法。~ **dozen** 十三个。~**-drawn** (**-out**) ***a*.** 拉长的 (~*-drawn sigh* 长叹)。~**-eared** ***a*. 1.** 有长耳朵的。**2.** 驴子似的;笨的。~ **face** 不愉快的脸色。~ **field**【板球】离击球员最远的外场。~ **green** 〔美俚〕钞票。~ **hair** 〔美口〕**1.** 知识分子(气味)的〔尤指爱好古典音乐的〕(= ~haired)。**2.** ***n*.** 知识分子〔尤指爱好古典音乐的〕。**3.** ***n*.** = hippie. ~**hand** 普通写法 (*opp*. shorthand). ~ **head** 长头人。~ **headed** ***a*. 1.** 头颅长的。**2.** 聪明的,有远见的。~ **hop** 长途飞行。~**-horn 1.** 〔美〕长角牛。**2.** 德克萨斯州人〔绰号〕。**3.** (探测飞机的)测音器。~**-horned beetles**【动】天牛科 (*Cerambycidae*)甲虫。~**-horned grasshopper**【动】长角螽斯。~ **hours** 夜晚十一、二点钟,午夜 (*opp*. small hours)。~ **house** (美洲易洛魁人和其他印地安部落的)议事厅。~ **hundred** 一百二十;一百多。~ **hundredweight** 长担,英担〔等于 112 磅〕。**L- Island** (纽约附近的)长岛。~ **johns** 〔口〕长内衣裤。~ **jump** 跳远。~ **leaf pine**【植】长叶松 (*Pinus palustris*)〔产于美国南部,木质硬而沉,经济价值很高〕。~**-legged** ***a*.** 长腿的。~**-lived** ***a*.** 长寿的。~ **measure** = linear measure. ~ **moss** = Spanish moss. ~**-nine** 〔美〕廉价雪茄烟。~ **off**【板球】掷球员在左后方的守场员。~**-on**【板球】掷球员右后方的守场员。**L- Parliament**【英史】长期议会〔1640 年 11 月 3 日开幕,1653 年被克伦威尔驱散,1659 年重开,1660 年解散〕。~ **pig** 食人生番嘴里的牺牲品。~ **play** 慢转唱片,密纹唱片。~**-playing** ***a*.** (唱片的)慢转的〔33⅓转速〕。~**-playing record** 慢转密纹唱片。~ **primer** 五号与六号间的铅字。~**-range** ***a*.** 远程的;长期的 (*a* ~*-range fire* 远程射击。*a* ~*-range missile* 远程飞弹。*a* ~*-range research* 深入的研究)。~ **robe** 律师服装。~**-run** ***a*.** 长远的。~ **shillings** 〔口〕优厚的工资。~**shore** ***a*.** 沿岸工作的。~**shoreman** 码头搬运工人;近海渔民;〔口〕海滨零杂工人。~**-short story** 较长的短篇小说,中篇小说。~ **shot** 没有希望当选的候选人。~**-sighted** ***a*. 1.** 眼力好的;有眼光的,有先见之明的。**2.** 远视的。~**some** ***a*.** 〔方〕漫长的;过长的;冗长的。~**spur**【动】铁爪鹀〔产于北极地带及北美大平原〕。~**standing** ***a*.** 长期间的,长年累月的 (a ~*-standing policy* 传统政策)。~**stop** 〔英〕用来抑制[阻挡,阻止]的人或物。~**-suffering 1.** ***a*.** 能忍耐的,坚忍的。**2.** 坚忍。~ **suit 1.**【牌戏】(手上的牌中)张数多的那一花色。**2.** 长处,胜过别人的东西。~**-term** ***a*. 1.** 长期的;时间持续很长的。**2.** (资本、借贷等的)涉及较长期限的〔半年以上〕。~**-term memory** 【计】长期存储器〔由永久储存的信息构成的存储器部份〕。~**-tested** ***a*.** 久经考验的。~**time** ***a*.** 长期的。~**-timer 1.** 在某地住过很久的人;长期从事某项工作的人。**2.** 长期徒刑犯。**L- Tom** 远程大炮。~ **ton** 长吨〔英制等于 2240 磅〕。~**-tongued** ***a*.** 长舌的,话多的,饶舌的。~ **vacation 1.** 大学暑假。**2.** 法院夏季休庭。~ **wave**【无】长波。~**-wave** ***a*.** 长波的。~**ways**, ~**wise** ***ad*.** = lengthwise. ~**-winded** ***a*. 1.** 气长的。**2.** 喋喋不休的,冗长的。**-ly** ***ad*.** **-ness** ***n*.**

-long *suf*. 表示"向","在":end*long*, side*long*.

lon·gae·val [lɔnˈdʒiːvəl; lɑnˋdʒivəl] ***a*.** = langeval.

lon·gan [ˈlɔŋgən; ˋlɑŋgən] ***n*. 1.**【植】龙眼。**2.** 龙眼(指果实),桂圆。

lon·ga·nim·i·ty [ˌlɔŋgəˈnimiti; ˏlɑŋgəˋnɪmətɪ] ***n*.** 忍受(伤痛);坚忍,忍耐。

longe [lʌndʒ; lʌndʒ] **I** ***n*. 1.** 练马长绳。**2.** 使用练马绳练马。**II** ***vt*.** (***longed***; ***longe·ing***, ***long·ing***) 用练马绳训练马的各种步态。

lon·ge·ron [ˈlɔndʒərən; ˋlɑndʒərən] ***n*.** 〔常 *pl*.〕【空】(飞机的)纵梁,大梁。

lon·ge·val [lɔnˈdʒiːvəl; lɑnˋdʒivəl] ***a*** 〔罕〕长寿的。

lon·gev·i·ty [lɔnˈdʒeviti; lɑnˋdʒɛvətɪ] ***n*. 1.** 长寿。**2.**

长期供职,资历。~ **pay**〔美〕年资附加工资。

lon·ge·vous [lɔnˈdʒiːvəs; lanˋdʒivəs] ***a.*** 【罕】长寿的。

Long·fel·low [ˈlɔŋˌfeləu; ˋlaŋˏfɛlo] ***n.*** **1.** 朗费罗〔姓氏〕。**2. Henry Wadsworth** ~ 亨利·沃兹沃思·朗费罗〔1807—1882,美国著名诗人〕。

lon·gi·corn [ˈlɔndʒiˌkɔːn; ˋlandʒəˏkɔrn] ***a.*** 有长角的;具长触角的〔如某些甲虫〕。

long·ies [ˈlɔːŋiːz; ˋlɔŋiz] ***n.*** 〔*pl.*〕〔美口〕= long johns.

long·ing [ˈlɔŋiŋ; ˋlɔŋɪŋ] **I** ***n.*** 渴望,热望 (*for*)。**II** ***a.*** 渴望的。**-ly** ***ad.***

long·ish [ˈlɔŋiʃ; ˋlɔŋɪʃ] ***a.*** 稍长的,略长的。

lon·gi·tude [ˈlɔndʒitjuːd; ˋlandʒəˏtjud] ***n.*** **1.** 经度,经线〔*cf.* latitude〕。**2.** 【天】黄经。*the meridian of ~* 黄经圈。**3.** 〔谑〕长,长度。

lon·gi·tu·di·nal [ˌlɔndʒiˈtjuːdinl; ˏlandʒəˋtjudnl] ***a.*** **1.** 经度的,经线的。**2.** 纵的,纵向的。~ *mass* 【物】纵质量。*a ~ section* 纵剖面。**-ly** ***ad.***

Long·man [ˈlɔŋmən; ˋlaŋmən] ***n.*** 朗曼〔姓氏〕。

Lon·go·bard [ˈlɔŋgəuˌbaːd; ˋlaŋgoˏbard] ***n.*** (*pl.* ***-bards***, ***Lon·go·bar·di*** [-ˈbaːdi; -ˋbardɪ]) = Lombard ***n.*** **-ic** ***a.***

Long·street [ˈlɔŋstriːt; ˋlaŋstrit] ***n.*** 朗斯特里特〔姓氏〕。

longue ha·leine [F. lõg alɛn; ˋlɔŋgæˋlen] 〔F.〕长期努力。*a work of* [*de*] *longue haleine* 需要长期努力的工作[著作]。

lon·guette [lɔːŋˈget; lɔŋˈget] ***n.*** (长及小腿肚的)长裙,长连衫裙。

lon·gueur [lɔŋˈgəː; lɔŋˈgɝ] ***n.*** 〔F.〕(小说、乐曲等的)冗长而枯燥无味的部分。

lon·i·ce·ra [ləuˈnisərə; loˋnɪsərə] ***n.*** 【植】〔L-〕忍冬属;忍冬;金银花。~ *distillate* 金银花露。

Lons·dale [ˈlɔnzdeil; ˋlanzdel] ***n.*** 朗斯代尔〔姓氏〕。

loo[1] [luː; lu] ***n.*** 一种纸牌赌博。

loo[2] [luː; lu] ***n.*** 〔英口〕便所。

loo·by [ˈluːbi; ˋlubɪ] ***n.*** 笨人,蠢汉。

Loo·choo (Islands) [ˈluːˈtʃuː; ˋluˋtʃu] ***n.*** 琉球 (= Ryukyu Islands)。

Loo·choo·an [ˈluːˈtʃuːən; ˋluˋtʃuən] **I** ***a.*** 琉球的;琉球人的。**II** ***n.*** 琉球人。

loo·ey, loo·ie [ˈluːi; ˋluɪ] ***n.*** 〔美军俚〕中[少]尉。

loo·fa(h) [ˈluːfə; ˋlufa] ***n.*** = luffa.

look [luk; lʊk] **I** ***vi.*** **1.** 看,注视,盯 (*at*)。*Look!* 你瞧!看哪! *We ~ed but saw nothing.* 我们看是在看,可是什么也没有看见。**2.** 〔带有表语〕显得,好像。~ *sick* 显得有病的样子。*He does not ~ his age.* 他看上去不像是有这个年纪的人。*He ~s very tired.* 他好像很疲倦。*He ~s every inch a worker.* 他没有一处不像工人。*It ~s as though we should have a storm.* 好像要有暴风雨。*It ~s like rain.* 看来要下雨。~ *happy* 喜形于色。**3.** 留心,注意;弄清,查明。*L- (to it) that they do not escape.* 当心别让他们逃跑了。*L- if it is right.* 查查对不对。**4.** (房屋等)朝着,面向;(事实、情况等)倾向…,倾向…。*The house ~s (to the) south.* 这房子朝南。*Conditions ~ toward war.* 局势趋向战争。**5.** 预期。*I did not ~ to meet you here.* 我没有想到在这里遇见你。— ***vt.*** **1.** 用眼色表示,用态度表示。*He ~ed his consent* [*thanks*]. 他用眼睛表示了同意[谢意]。**2.** 瞧,注视,打量。~ *sb. into silence* 瞪着某人不敢作声。~ *sb. full in the face* 盯着某人的面孔细看。~ *sb. out of countenance* 瞧得人局促不安。~ *sb. up and down* 上上下下打量某人。~ ***about*** (***one***) 四下里看;观察形势;戒备,警戒;计划行动。~ ***about for*** 四下寻找。~ ***after*** **1.** 回头看;目送。**2.** 寻求,渴望。**3.** 注意,照管,照应,看守。~ ***ahead*** 考虑未来,预先做好准备。***L- ahead, Sir!*** 【海】看前面。~ ***alive*** 当心;快些! ~ ***around*** 〔美〕= ~ *round*. ~ ***as if*** 看起来好像,似乎,好像。~ ***at*** **1.** 看,查看 (*The girl is pretty to ~ at.* 这个姑娘好看)。**2.** 考虑,着眼于 (~ *at problems all-sidedly* 全面地看问题)。~ ***away*** 把脸转过去,看别的地方。~ ***back*** **1.** 回头看;回顾;追想 (*to*; *upon*)。**2.** (对事业等)不起劲。***L- before you leap.*** 〔谚〕三思而后行。~ ***beyond the grave*** 考虑身后事。~ ***big*** 洋洋自得,盛气凌人。~ ***black*** 脸色凶恶,形势恶劣。~ ***blue*** (人)无能;灰溜溜的,颓丧。~ ***death*** 杀气腾腾。~ ***death in the face*** 不顾死活。~ ***down*** **1.** 看下面,俯视。**2.** 蔑视,看不起 (*on*; *upon*)。**3.** 跌价。~ ***for*** **1.** 寻找。**2.** 期待,渴望。~ ***forward to*** 盼望,期待 (~ *forward to a prosperous old age* 盼望一个富裕的晚年。~ *forward to seeing you again* 期望重见你们)。***L- here!*** 喂,注意! ~ ***ill*** **1.** 看上去有病,看来不漂亮。**2.** (事情)很糟。~ ***in*** **1.** 看看,一瞥 (*at sth*)。**2.** 顺便访问 (*on sb.*)。~ ***into*** **1.** 窥视。**2.** 调查;过问。~ ***like ...*** 好像;像要 (*The place ~s like rabbits.* 这地方好像有兔子)。~ ***off*** 把眼睛转开。~ ***on*** **1.** 看做 (*as*)。**2.** 旁观,观看 (~ *on the bright* [*dark*] *side* 看光明[黑暗]的一面)。**3.** 面向 (*to*)。~ ***on with sb.*** 和某人同看一本书。~ ***one's age*** 和年龄相称。~ ***oneself*** 和平常一样,不改常态 (~ *quite oneself again* 完全恢复(健康)了)。~ ***out*** **1.** 注意,警惕。**2.** 期待 (*for*)。**3.** 看外头;展望 (*on*; *over*)。**4.** 找出,挑选,寻找。~ ***over*** **1.** 过目,大致看一看。**2.** 检验,调查,查究。**3.** 放过,宽待。~ ***round*** **1.** 掉头看,环顾,到处寻找。**2.** 仔细考虑,察看。~ ***sharp*** 非常留心(看);赶快。~ ***through*** **1.** 透过(玻璃等)看。**2.** 看穿,看破。**3.** 彻底调查;从头看完,通读一遍。~ ***to*** **1.** 注意;照料,照应。**2.** 依赖,指望 (~ *to sb. for help* 指望某人帮助)。**3.** 〔美〕倾向…,以…为目的,企图。~ ***to be*** 〔美〕像… (*It ~ed to be about eight feet tall.* 看上去有八英尺高)。~ ***to it that*** 注意,留心。~ ***toward(s)*** **1.** 〔口〕为…干杯。**2.** 〔美〕倾向…,趋向,取…的方向,指向。~ ***up*** **1.** 向上看。**2.** (物价等)上涨,(市面等)兴旺。**3.** (在辞典中)查找,查出。**4.** 访问,看望。**5.** 尊敬 (*to*)。~ ***upon*** = ~ *on*. ~ ***well*** **1.** 像很健康;看上去漂亮。**2.** (事情)顺利。***L- you!*** 注意! ***to ~ at sb.*** [***sth.***] 〔常作插入语〕据某人[某事]的外表下判断。**II** ***n.*** **1.** 〔常 *pl.*〕容貌,相貌,面貌。*Don't judge a man by his ~s.* 不要凭外表判断人。*good ~s* 好相貌。*lose one's ~s* (女子)容颜衰老。*the ~ of his face* 他的面貌。**2.** 脸色。**3.** 样子,外表。*a kind ~* 温和的样子。*an amused ~ in sb.'s eyes* 某人眼中暗地感到有趣[可笑]的神色。*a serious ~* 严肃的脸色。*I don't like the ~ of him.* 我不喜欢他那个样子。*the ~ of the sky* 天色。**3.** 一看,一瞥。*give sb. a ~* 看某人一眼。*give sb. a dirty ~* 瞪某人一眼。*steal a ~* 偷看一眼。***cast a ~ at*** 瞥一眼。***have*** [***take***] ***a*** (***good***) ***~ at*** (仔细)看一看。***have a ~ of*** 像,仿佛。***in good ~s*** 样子很健康。***take on a new ~*** 具有新气象。***take on an ugly ~*** 情况不佳。***upon the ~*** 在寻找中。***wither sb. with a ~*** 〔谑〕看得某人惶恐不安。**~-ahead** ***a.*** 有预见力的,有预见性的。**~-alike** 〔美俚〕面貌很相似的人。**~-in** **1.** 一瞥。**2.** 短暂的访问;走马看花 (*give sb. a ~-in* 顺便访问某人)。**3.** (在比赛中)获胜的希望 (*have a ~-in* 有可能取胜)。**4.** 【足球】迅速传球(给以对角线方向跑向球场中部的球员)。**~-over** 粗略的一看。**~-see** 〔俚〕走马看花;调查;视察旅行。~ **through** 透视,监听。**~up** 查找;【自】检查。**-ism** 容貌歧视。

look·er [ˈlukə; ˋlʊkɚ] ***n.*** **1.** 观看者;〔英〕检查员。**2.** 外貌漂亮的人。*~s on TV* 电视观众。*cloth ~s* 织物检查员。*a good ~* 俊男,美女。*a handsome ~* 美男子。**~-in** ***n.*** (*pl.* ***~s-in***) 看电视的人。

look·er-on [ˈlukərˈɔn; ˏlʊkɚˋan] ***n.*** (*pl.* ***look·ers-on*** [ˈlukəzˈɔn; ˏlʊkɚzˋan]) 旁观者;观察者;观看者。*Lookers-on see most of the game.* 〔谚〕旁观者清。

look·ing-glass [ˈlukiŋglaːs; ˋlʊkɪŋˏglæs] **I** ***n.*** 镜子;窥镜。**II** ***a.*** 完全相反的,颠倒的,悖理的。*a ~ world* 是

L

非颠倒的世界。～ **chemistry**【化】镜像化学〔参见 mirror-image chemistry〕。

look·ing-in *n*. (在家)观看电视。

look·out [ˈlukaut; ˋlʊkˏaʊt] *n*. **1.** 守望,看守,警戒。**2.** 守望者,看守者。**3.** 瞭望台,监视哨。**4.** 远景,前途。**5.** 某人应做的事;任务,职守;警戒。*keep* [*take*] *a sharp* ～ *for* 小心提防,注意戒备。*on the* ～ *for* 注意,警惕。*an antiaircraft* ～对空监视哨。*a* ～ *post* [*sentry*] 监视哨。*a* ～ *tower* 瞭望塔。*a bad* ～ *for sb*. 对某人来说并不美妙的前景。*That is his own* ～. 那是他自己的事。

loo·loo [ˈluːluː; ˋlulu] *n*. = lulu.

loom[1] [luːm; lum] *n*. **1.** 织布机;织布法;织布业。**2.** 桨柄,橹柄。**3.**【空】翼肋腹部。*a hand* ～手工织机。*a power* ～动力织机。

loom[2] [luːm; lum] **I** *vi*. 朦胧出现;(危险、忧虑等)阴森森地逼近。*A ship* ～*ed* (*up*) *through the fog*. 一只船在雾中隐隐出现。*Trifles* ～ *large to an anxious mind*. 顾虑多的人,草木皆兵。**II** *n*. 朦胧出现的形像;巨大的幻影。

loom[3] [luːm; lum] *n*. **1.** = loon[2]. **2.** = guillemot.

loon[1] [luːn; lun] **I.** *n*. **1.** 懒人;废物;蠢汉。**2.** 疯子,狂人。**3.**〔Scot.〕男孩,小伙子。**4.**〔Scot.〕情妇;妓女。**II.** *vi*.〔英俚〕游手好闲,闲荡。～ **pants**〔英〕游荡裤〔一种喇叭裤〕。

loon[2] [luːn; lun] *n*. **1.**【动】鹏鹛 (*Gavia immer*)。**2.** (捕鱼的)潜鸟。*common* ～白嘴潜鸟。

loon·ey, loon·y [ˈluːni; ˋlunɪ] **I** *a*. (*loon·i·er*, *loon·i·est*)〔俚〕笨拙的;疯狂的。**II** *n*. (*pl*. *loonies*) 疯子;傻瓜。～ **bin**〔俚〕精神病院,疯人院。

loop [luːp; lup] **I** *n*. **1.** (用线、带等打成的)圈,环,匝,框,环孔,线圈;【医】(常 the ～)宫内避孕环。**2.** 环状物,搭环,拎环。**3.** (铁路上的)让车道,环道。**4.**【无】回路,回线,波腹,环形天线。**5.**【数】自变;【计】循环;(程序中)一群指令的重复。**6.**【空】翻圈飞行,翻筋斗;【溜冰】(单脚)打圈儿。**7.**〔美〕闹市区;〔the L-〕芝加哥的商业区。*a safety* ～ 保险圈。*a wire* ～钢丝套圈。***knock*** [***throw***] ***for a*** ～〔美俚〕**1.** 使神志不清;打昏,使醉倒。**2.** 给人极好的印象。**3.** 出色地通过[做成]。***on the*** ～〔美〕在匆匆旅行中。***out of the*** ～ 在圈内人物之外的,不在…圈子内的。**II** *vt*. **1.** 使(绳等)成圈,打成圈;【电】把导线连成回路。**2.** 用圈围住;(用环)箍住。(*up*; *back*). **3.** 使作成环状运动;【空】翻筋斗。— *vi*. **1.** 打环,成圈。**2.**【空】翻筋斗。**3.** (像尺蠖似的)伸屈前进。～ ***the loop***【空】翻筋斗;(骑自行车等)兜圈子。～ **aerial** [**antenna**]【无】环形天线。～**hole** **1.** (堡垒的)枪眼;窥孔。**2.** 逃路;〔尤指〕(用来摆脱义务、不遵守法律、不履行合同等的)遁词,借口,(契约中的)漏洞;欺骗性圈套。～ **knot** 环结〔绳结的一种〕。～ **line** 环线,圈线。～ **stitch**【纺】连环针脚。～**-the-**～ **1.** (在疾驰或迅速转动中利用离心力使乘坐者在一段路程上头部朝下的娱乐装置)翻筋斗列车。**2.**【空】翻筋斗飞行。

looped [luːpt; lupt] *a*. **1.** 有圈[环]的;成圈[环]的。**2.**〔美〕酩酊大醉的。

loop·er [ˈluːpə; ˋlupɚ] *n*. **1.**【动】尺蠖。**2.**【纺】套口机;缝袜头机;弯纱轮。**3.** 打环的人,打环装置。**4.** (驾飞机)翻筋斗的人。

loop·y [ˈluːpi; ˋlupɪ] *a*. (*loop·i·er*; *loop·i·est*) **1.** 多环的,一圈一圈的。**2.**〔俚〕神经错乱的;呆头呆脑的。

loose [luːs; lus] **I** *a*. (*loos·er*, *loos·est*) **1.** 松的,宽的,松散的。*a cloth of* ～ *texture* 稀松(不紧实的)织物。～ *clothing* 宽大的衣服。*a* ～ *knot* 松的结。**2.** 松开的,没加束缚的,自由的。*a* ～ *criminal* 在逃罪犯。*a horse* ～ *of its tether* 没有系住的马。*the* ～ *end of a string* 绳子松开的一端。**3.** 模糊的,不确切的,不严谨的。*a* ～ *style* 不简练的文体。*a* ～ *thinker* 思想不严密的人。*a* ～ *translation* 不严密的译文。**4.** 散漫的,荒淫的,放荡的。*a* ～ *fish* 浪子。*a* ～ *woman* 放荡的女子。*have a* ～ *tongue* 惯于随口乱讲。*lead a* ～ *life* 过放荡生活。～ *conduct* 放纵。*lordly, luxurious,* ～ *and idle life* 骄奢淫逸的生活。**5.** 松动的。*have* ～ *bowels* 拉肚子。*a* ～ *tooth* 松动的牙齿。**6.** 散放的,散装的。～ *cash* [*change, coins*] 零钱。～ *mushroom* 散装蘑菇。**7.** 自由的,无拘束的。～ *capital* [*funds*] 游资。*a* ～ *hour* 闲暇时间。**8.** 疏松的。**9.**【化】游离的。**10.** (色、染料等)易退色的。*a* ～ *dye* 容易退色的染料。**11.**【医】咳出痰的。*a* ～ *cough* 咳嗽带痰。**12.** 队形散开的。*in* ～ *order*【军】散开的队形。*a* ～ *game* [*play*]【橄榄球】不互相扭夺的比赛。***at a*** ～ ***end*** 没有着落;没有工作[职业];未确定解决。***break*** ～ 逃出,迸发出。***cast*** ～ 解开(绳索等);放出(鹰、犬等)。***come*** [***get***] ～ 解开,松开。***cut*** ～ **1.** 使脱离拘束。**2.**〔口〕狂欢。**3.** 逃脱,摆脱 (*cut* ～ *from old habits* 革除旧习惯。*cut* ～ *from old ties* 割断老关系)。***have a screw*** ～ **1.** 螺丝钉松了。**2.** (精神等)有点失常[不对头]。***let*** [***turn***] ～ 放走,释放。***let*** ～ ***one's anger*** 发怒,暴躁起来。***set*** ～ 放走。***shake oneself*** ～ 把身体摆脱。***There is a screw*** ～ ***somewhere***. 这里面有点不对头[有点问题]。***with a*** ～ ***rein*** 放松缰绳;放任。**II** *ad*. = loosely. ***hold*** ～ ***to sth***. 对…漠不关心。**III** *vt*. **1.** 解(结等);弄松;放松;放掉。**2.** 放(枪、箭)(*off*)。～ *hold* (*of*) 松手,放任。— *vi*. **1.** 变松,松开,松弛。**2.** 放射,开枪。**3.**〔主英〕放学。**4.** 解缆,开船。**IV** *n*. 解放;放任,发射。***be on the*** ～〔口〕**1.** 无拘束;散漫;逍遥法外。**2.** 放荡;纵情游乐。***give*** (***a***) ～ ***to one's feelings*** [***fancy***] 放纵感情。～**-bodied** *a*. (衣服等)宽大的。～**-box**〔英〕放饲场,放饲马房。～ **cannon** 喜欢放横炮的人,我行我素者,不受控制的人。～**-fitting** *a*. 配上去稍大的。～**-flowing** *a*. 缓缓流着的,轻轻飘着的。～**-jointed** *a*. **1.** (接头)松动的。**2.** 吊儿郎当的,随意行动的。～**-leaf** *a*. 活叶(式)的。～**-limbed** *a*. 手脚灵活的 (*a* ～*-limbed dancer* 舞姿轻盈的舞蹈演员)。～**-minded** *a*. 思想散漫的。～ **pulley** [**wheel**]【机】游滑轮。～ **smut**【农】(谷类)散黑穗病。～**-tongued** *a*. 嘴松的,言语随便的;信口开河的;饶舌的;唠叨的。**-ly** *ad*. **-ness** *n*.

loos·en [ˈluːsn; ˋlusn] *vt*. **1.** 放松。**2.** 使(纪律)松弛。**3.**【医】通大便;使咳出痰来。— *vi*. 变松,宽松,松散。*By degrees her tongue was* ～*ed*. 她的话渐渐多起来了。～ ***up***〔美口〕**1.** 宽松,宽舒。**2.** 信口开河。**3.** 慷慨解囊。

loose·strife [ˈluːsstraif; ˋlusˏstraɪf] *n*.【植】排草属植物(尤指黄连花);千屈菜属植物(尤指千屈菜)。

loot[1] [luːt; lut] **I** *n*. **1.** 掠夺物;战利品。**2.** (官吏的)赃物,非法收入。**3.** 抢劫,掠夺。**4.**〔俚〕金钱。**II** *vt*., *vi*. 劫掠(都市);洗劫;抢劫;强夺;(官吏)贪污。

loot[2] [luːt; lut] *n*.〔美俚〕= lieutenant.

loot·er [ˈluːtə; ˋlutɚ] *n*. 掠夺者,抢劫者,强夺者。

lop[1] [lɔp; lɑp] **I** *vt*., *vi*. (*-pp-*) **1.** 伐,砍;修剪(树枝)(*off*; *away*)。**2.** 砍(头),斩断(手等)(*off*, *away*)。**3.** 割裂,删除。**II** *n*. **1.** 除枝,修剪。**2.** 剪下的树枝,小枝。

lop[2] [lɔp; lɑp] **I** *vt*. (*-pp-*) (兔子把耳朵)垂下来,耷拉下来。— *vi*. **1.** 低垂,垂挂。**2.** 懒洋洋地躺着[靠着];懒洋洋地走动[行动],吊儿郎当地闲混 (*about*)。**3.** 一跳一跳地走动。*A rabbit* ～*ped among cabbages*. 一只兔子在白菜之间一跳一跳钻来钻去。**II** *n*. 垂耳兔。**III** *a*. 垂下的。～ *ears* 垂下的耳朵。～**-ear** 垂耳,垂耳兔。～**-eared** *a*. 垂耳的。～**per** 修剪树木的工人,修剪树木的长柄剪刀。～**ping** 修剪;〔常 *pl*.〕修剪下来的树枝。

lop[3] [lɔp; lɑp] **I** *vi*. (*-pp-*) (水面)起小波。**II** *n*. 小波。

lope [ləup; lop] **I** *vi*., *vt*. (使马等)大步跳跃着慢跑,(兔等)跳着飞奔。**II** *n*. 大步慢跑;飞奔。

lo·pho·branch [ˈləufəˌbræŋk, ˈlɔfə-; ˋlofəˏbræŋk, ˋlɑfə-] **I** *a*.【动】总鳃类的〔包括海龙亚科和海龙科〕。**II**

n. 总鳃类的鱼。

lo·pho·phore [ˈləufəˌfɔː, lɔfə-; ˋlofəˏfɔr, lɑfə-] *n*.【动】触(手)冠,总担;纤毛环。

lop·py [ˈlɔpi; ˋlɑpɪ] *a*. (*-pi·er*, *-pi·est*) 散垂的,下垂的。

lop·sid·ed [ˈlɔpˈsaidid; ˋlɑpˋsaɪdɪd] *a*. 倾向一面的;不平衡的,不匀称的,偏重的。*a* ~ *spill*【美棒球】一面倒的大败。**-ly** *ad*. **-ness** *n*.

***loq*.** = loquitur.

lo·qua·cious [ləuˈkweiʃəs; loˋkweʃəs] *a*. 1. 多嘴的,多话的。2. (鸟)啁啾不休的;(水)潺潺不息的。**-ly** *ad*. **-ness** *n*.

lo·quac·i·ty [ləuˈkwæsiti; loˋkwæsətɪ] *n*. 多嘴;喋喋不休;吵闹,喧噪。

lo·quat [ˈləukwɔt; ˋlokwɑt] *n*.【植】枇杷树;枇杷。

loq·ui·tur [ˈlɔkwitə; ˋlɑkwətɚ] *vi*. 〔L.〕〔略 loq.〕他[她]说。

lor [lɔː; lɔr] *int*. 〔英俚〕天啊! 上帝! (= Lord.)

Lo·ra [ˈləurə; ˋlorə] *n*. 洛拉〔女子名, Laura 的异体〕。

lor·al [ˈlɔːrəl; ˋlorəl] *a*. (鸟类,爬虫类,鱼类的)眼端的。

lor·an [ˈlɔːrən; ˋloræn] *n*. 劳兰〔远航仪〕,长途航海用雷达设备;远距离无线电导航系统〔long-range navigation 的缩略, *cf*. shoran〕。

lor·cha [ˈlɔːtʃə; ˋlɔrtʃə] *n*. 西式中国三桅帆船。

lord [lɔːd; lɔrd] **I** *n*. 1. 君主。2. 封建主,领主;贵族;地主。3. 〔英〕勋爵〔对某些贵族或高级官员的尊称〕。4. 主〔指上帝,基督〕。5. 主人,所有者。6. (某一方面的)巨头。7. 〔口〕老爷;丈夫。8.【占星】首座星。*our sovereign* ~ *the King* 国王陛下。*the* ~ *of the manor* 庄园领主。*the* ~ *of the soil* 地主,领主〔的尊称〕。*the Lords* 英国上议院全体议员。*Civil L-* 海军部文官委员。*First L- of the Admiralty* (英国)海军大臣。*First Sea L-* (英国)海军部第一次官。*the House of Lords* 英国上议院。*the L- Mayor of London* 伦敦市长。*L-, how they laughed!* 天哪,他们笑成那个样子了! *a cotton* ~棉花大王。*the press* ~*s* 新闻界巨头。*a* ~ *of few acres* 小地主,小土地所有者。***as drunk as a*** ~ 酩酊大醉。***by the L- Harry!*** 见鬼,岂有此理! ***be*** ~ ***of*** 领有;拥有。***in the year of our L-*** ... 在公元…年。***live like a*** ~ 过奢华的生活。~ ***and master*** 1. 丈夫,一家之主。2. 东家,主人。***L- bless me*** [***my soul***]! = ***L- have mercy!*** 老天爷! 啊呀! 老天保佑! (***the***) ***L- knows!*** 天晓得! 谁知道! ***L- love you*** [***your heart***]〔俚〕哎呀! 真是! ***New*** ~***s, new laws***. 〔谚〕新官上任三把火。***paper*** ~〔Scot.〕由于担任某种职务而得到勋爵称号的人。***swear like a*** ~ 乱骂,叱责。***take it as easy as a L- Mayor***〔俚〕满不在乎。***the*** ~***s of creation*** 万物之灵,人类;〔谑〕男人们。***the*** ~***s of the harvest*** 1. 农场主,收获的所有者。2. 收割作物的带头人。***treat sb. like a*** ~ 对待某人像王公一般,非常阔绰地款待某人。**II** *vi*. 作威作福。— *vt*. 使成贵族;加贵族封号。***will not be*** ~***ed over*** 不许别人作威作福。~ ***it over***... 称王道霸;作威作福。**L- Bishop** 主教〔正式的称呼〕。**L- Chamberlain** (*of the Household*)〔英〕宫务大臣。**L- Chief Justice (of England)** (英国)首席法官。**L- (God)! = Good L-!** ~ **chancellor** (英国)大法官〔兼任上议院议长〕。**L- High Steward of England** 1. 英国皇家总管大臣。2. 贵族法庭审判长。**L- High Treasure** (英国)财务大臣。**L- Justice Clerk**〔Scot.〕高等法院副院长。**L- Justice General** 高等法院院长。**L- of Host**【宗】耶和华,上帝。**L- of misrule** (中古英国圣诞节饮宴和游戏的)司仪。(**the**) ~ **paramount** 君主。**L- President (of the Council)** (英国)枢密大臣。(**the**) ~ **Provost** (爱丁堡等都市的市长)。**Lord's day**【宗】主日;星期日。**L- speaker** (英国)上议院议长。**Lord's Prayer**【宗】主祷文。~**s spiritual**〔英〕上议员主教议员。**Lord's Supper**【宗】1. 最后的晚餐 (= Last Supper)。2. 圣餐式;圣餐。**Lord's table**【宗】祭坛,圣餐台。~**s temporal**〔英〕上议院贵族议员。**-less** *a*. 无君主的;无丈夫的。

lord·ing [ˈlɔːdiŋ; ˋlɔrdɪŋ] *n*. 〔废〕1. = lordling. 2. 大人,老爷〔称呼语,通常用复数〕。

lord·ling [ˈlɔːdliŋ; ˋlɔrdlɪŋ] *n*. 〔蔑〕小贵族,小老爷。

lord·ly [ˈlɔːdli; ˋlɔrdlɪ] **I** *a*. (*-li·er*; *-li·est*) 1. 贵族(似)的,有气派的。2. 傲慢的。***in*** ~ ***way*** 气派十足地。**II** *ad*. 贵族似地,气派十足地;傲慢地。**-li·ness** *n*.

lor·do·sis [lɔːˈdəusis; lɔrˋdosɪs] *n*.【动】脊柱前凸。**lor·dot·ic** [-ˈdɔtik; -ˋdɑtɪk] *a*.

Lord's [lɔːdz; lɔrdz] *n*. 伦敦大板球场〔即 Marylebone 板球俱乐部总部 = Lord's Cricket Ground〕。

lords-and-la·dies [ˈlɔːdzənˈleidiz; ˋlɔrdzənˋledɪz] *n*.【植】1. 斑叶阿若母 (*Arum maculatum*)。2. 天南星 (*Arisaema triphyllum*).

lord·ship [ˈlɔːdʃip; ˋlɔrdʃɪp] *n*. 1. 贵族[领主]的身分。2. 领主的统治权。3. 贵族的领地。4. 〔英〕〔常作 L-〕阁下。*your* [*his*] ~爵爷〔对贵族及某些高级官员的尊称,常戏谑地用于常人或动物〕。

lore[1] [lɔː, lɔə; lɔr, lor] *n*. 1. (特殊的)学问,(专门的)知识;博学。2. 口头传说。3. 〔古〕传授。*doctors'* ~祖传医学。*folk* ~民间文学。*herbal* ~本草学。*the* ~ *of the Egyptians* 古代埃及人的知识。

lore[2] [lɔː; lɔr] *n*.【动】(鸟的眼与啄之间,爬虫及鱼的眼与鼻之间的)眼端,眼光。

Lor·e·lei [ˈlɔːrəlai; ˋlɔrəˏlaɪ] *n*. 罗利勒〔德国传说中一个以美色和歌声迷惑船夫使船遭难的女妖〕。

Lo·ren·zo [lɔˈrenzəu; ləˋrɛnzo] *n*. 洛伦佐〔男子名〕。

Lo·ret·ta [ləˈretə; ləˋrɛtə] *n*. 洛蕾塔〔女子名〕。

lor·gnette [lɔːˈnjet; lɔrnˋjɛt] *n*. 〔F.〕长柄眼镜;(附有长柄的)观剧用望远镜。

lor·gnon [lɔːˈnjɔ̃; lɔrˋnjɔ̃] *n*. 1. 单眼镜或双眼镜〔如夹鼻眼镜〕。2. = lorgnette.

lo·ri·ca [ləˈraikə; ləˋraɪkə] *n*. (*pl*. **-cae** [-siː; -si]) 1. 古罗马胸甲。2.【动】兜甲。**-i·cate** [ˈlɔːriˌkeit, lɑri-; ˋlɔrəˏket, lɑrɪ-], **-i·cat·ed** *a*.

lor·i·keet [ˈlɔːriˌkiːt; ˋlɔrɪˏkit] *n*.【动】青绿色小鹦鹉。

lo·ris [ˈlɔːris; ˋlorɪs] *n*. (*pl*. **loris**)【动】懒猴属;懒猴 (*Loris gracilis*); 蜂猴 (*Nycticebus tardigradus*)。

lorn [lɔːn; lɔrn] *a*. 〔诗、谑〕被遗弃的,孤单的;荒凉的。**-ness** *n*.

Lor·na [ˈlɔːnə; ˋlɔrnə] *n*. 洛娜〔女子名〕。

Lor·raine [lɔˈrein; lɑˋren] *n*. 洛林〔法国东北部地名〕。

lor·ry [ˈlɔri; ˋlurɪ] *n*. 1. 〔英〕运货汽车,卡车 (= 〔美〕truck). 2. 平板四轮运货马车。3. (矿山,铁路的)手车;矿车;推料车。~**-hop**, ~**-jump** *vi*. 〔俚〕(不出钱)搭乘卡车旅行。

lo·ry [ˈlɔːri; ˋlɔrɪ] *n*.【动】猩猩鹦鹉。

LOS = 1. line of scrimmage 散兵线。2. line of sight 视线,瞄准线。3. lunar orbiter spacecraft 月球轨道太空船。

Los [lɔːs; lɔs] *n*. 〔美口〕Los Angeles 的简称。

los·a·ble [ˈluːzəbl; ˋluzəbl̩] *a*. 容易丢失的,能输掉的。**-ness** *n*.

Los Al·a·mos [lɔsˈæləməus; lɔsˋæləmos] 洛斯阿拉莫斯〔美国城市〕。

Los An·gel·es [lɔsˈændʒələs, -liːz; lɔsˋændʒələs, -liz] 洛杉矶〔美国城市〕。

lose [luːz; luz] *vt*. (*lost* [lɔst; lɔst]; *los·ing*) 1. 丢失,丧失。~ *one's balance* 失去平衡,跌倒。~ *one's head* 被斩首;被搞糊涂。~ *one's life* 丢了性命。*The doctor* ~*s his patient*. 医生没有治好病人;病人另找医生了。2. 迷失,使迷路,使迷惑。~ *oneself* [*be lost*] *in the woods* 在森林中迷路。~ *one's way* 迷路。3. 白费,浪费。~ *no time in beginning work* 立即开始工作。*There is no love lost between the two*. (a)〔废〕他们彼此相爱。(b) 他们并不相爱。*There's not a moment to*

~. 一分钟也不能浪费。**4.** 错过。~ *an opportunity* 错过机会。~ *one's train* 没赶上火车。**5.** 看漏,听漏,逸失,放跑。*I did not* ~ *a word of his speech*. 他的演说我没有听漏一个字。~ *the thread of an argument* 抓不住论据的线索。**6.** 输掉;使失败。~ *a battle* 战败。~ *a game* 输一局。*The motion was lost by a majority of two*. 动议以两票之差被否决了。**7.** 〔主用被动语态〕灭亡,杀死,破坏,湮没。*be lost to all sense of shame* 恬不知耻。*The ship was lost with all hands*. 那艘船和船上所有的人一齐沉没了。**8.** 忘记。~ *one's French* 法语都忘光了。**9.** 摆脱,脱离。~ *one's cold* 伤风好了。~ *one's fear* 解除忧虑。**10.** 使失去。*Reckless driving may* ~ *you even your life*. 乱开车甚至会送掉你的命。*Such behaviour lost him our trust*. 他这种行为使我们不再信任他了。— *vi*. **1.** 亏本,蚀本;受损失。*I don't want you to* ~ *by me*. 我不愿让你为我受损失。**2.** 失败;输 (*opp*. win). **3.** (钟、表等)走慢。*Does your watch gain or* ~? 你的表走得快,还是走得慢? **4.** 衰弱。*The invalid is losing*. 病人在逐渐衰弱。~ ***in beauty*** (人老)色衰。~ ***one's labour*** [***pains***] 白费气力。~ ***one's temper*** 发怒。~ ***out*** 〔美口〕失败,输掉。~ ***the battle*** [***day***, ***field***] 战败。~ ***the scent of*** 失去嗅迹,失去猎物的踪迹。

lo·sel [ˈləuzl, ˈluː-; ˋlozl, ˋlu-] **I** ***n***. 〔古、方〕没有价值的人;无用的人。**II** ***a***. 〔古、方〕没有价值的;无用的。

los·er [ˈluːzə; ˋluzɚ] ***n***. **1.** 损失者;损失物;失败者;输者。**2.** 〔美〕被判过徒刑的罪犯。**3.** 〔英〕= losing hazard. *a good* [*bad*] ~输了不生气[生气]的人,输了不在乎[反应不好]的人。*a three-time* ~服过三次徒刑的罪犯。*Losers are always in the wrong*. 〔谚〕胜者为王,败者为寇。*You shall not be the* ~ *by it*. 不会让你因此吃亏的。***come off a*** ~ 损失;亏损;输;失败。

los·ing [ˈluːziŋ; ˋluzɪŋ] **I** ***a***. 亏本的;看来要输的;失败的。*a* ~ *game* 无胜利希望的比赛。**II** ***n***. 失败。〔*pl*.〕(尤指投机等的)损失。~ **hazard** 【撞球】击球未能使之落袋,自己的球反而落袋,因此受到罚分。

loss [lɔs; lɔs] ***n***. **1.** 丧失;丢失,遗失。**2.** 减损,损失,亏损(额);损耗;减少,下降。**3.** 失败;输掉。**4.** 错过;浪费。**5.** 损毁;【军】伤亡;〔*pl*.〕伤亡及被俘人数。~ *of sight* 失明。*copper* ~【电】铜耗。*core* [*iron*] ~【电】铁耗。*a dead* ~净亏,纯损。*an idling* ~空转损耗。*a total* ~总损失。*His death is a great* ~ *to the country*. 他的死是国家的大损失。*profit and* ~盈亏。*suffer heavy* ~*es* 遭受重大损失。~ *of pressure* 压力下降。~ *in weight* 重量[体重]减少。~ *of weight* 失重。*the* ~ *of a war* 战败。~ *of opportunity* 错过机会。***at a*** ~ **1.** 无办法,为难 (*I am at a* ~ *what to do*. 我就是不知道怎样办才好)。**2.** (猎犬)失去猎物嗅迹。**3.** 亏本地 (*sell sth*. *at a* ~赔本卖出某物)。***cut a*** [***the***] ~ 赶紧脱手以免多受损失。***for a*** ~ 处于苦恼中 (*throw them for a* ~ 使他们苦恼)。***make a*** ~ 亏损。***without*** (***any***) ~ ***of time*** 即刻,马上。~ **leader** 为招揽顾客而亏本出售的货物。~ **list** 【军】伤亡名单。~**maker** 亏本企业。~**making *a***. (显然)亏本的。~ **ratio** 损害率〔保险公司在某一时期中支付的赔偿费在收入保险费中所占比率〕。

lost [lɔst; lɔst] **I** ***v***. lose 的过去式及过去分词。**II** ***a***. **1.** 失去了的;丢失了的;错过的,放过的。**2.** 输掉的;失败的;打败了的。**3.** 浪费了的,白费的。**4.** 不知所措的,为难的。**5.** 遭难的;死去了的。**6.** 迷路的;入迷的,忘我的,忘乎所以的。**7.** 被忘却的;失传的。*a* ~ *advertisement* 遗失广告。(*the*) *Lost and Found* 失物招领处。*a* ~ *battle* 败仗。*cry out* ~ *and terrible words*. 喊出绝望和可怕的话。~ *labour* 徒劳。*a* ~ *opportunity* 错过的机会。*a* ~ *prize* 没有争取到的奖品。~ *time* 浪费掉的时间。*A soldier was* ~ *in him*. 他可惜没有成为战士。*a* ~ *child* 迷路的孩子。*feel* ~不知所措。*a* ~ *ship* 沉没了的船。*a man* ~ *in thought* 想得出神的人。*a* ~ *art* 失传的艺术。*a* ~ *city* 湮没无闻的城市。***be*** ~ ***on*** [***upon***] 对…不起作用 (*My kindness is* ~ *upon him*. 我对他好也没用)。***be*** ~ ***to*** 感觉不到…;不再来,已不可能 (*be* ~ *to sight* 看不见了。*be* ~ *to shame* 恬不知耻。*Hope was never* ~ *to him*. 他从来没有绝望过)。***Get*** ~! 〔美俚〕走开! 别打扰我! ***give sb***. ***up for*** ~ 认为某人已死,认为某人不可救药。~ ***in astonishment*** [***wonder***] 惊异万分。~ ***of wits*** 无能的,老迈昏庸的。***What's*** ~ ***is*** ~. 〔谚〕失者不可复得。~ **cause** 已告失败[必将失败]的事业[运动]。~ **generation** 迷惘的一代〔指第一次世界大战前后走投无路的一代美国青年〕。~ **motion** 【机】空动。~ **river** 【地】干河,隐入河。~ **souls** 永坠地狱的灵魂;堕落的人。~ **tribes** 失去的部落〔组成古代以色列王国的十个部落,公元前722年作为俘虏被带到亚述〕。

lot [lɔt; lɑt] **I** ***n***. **1.** 运气,命运。*His* ~ *has been a hard one*. 他命运不好。**2.** (抽)签,(拈)阄。*be chosen by* ~通过抽签被选中。*decide by* ~抽签决定。*The* ~ *came to* [*fell upon*] *him*. 他中签了。*draw* ~抽签。**3.** (货物等)一堆,一批,一分。*a new* ~ *of hats* 一批新帽子。*sell by* [*in*] ~*s* 分批出售。**4.** 一块地皮。*an open* [*a vacant*] ~空地。*a parking* ~停车处。*house and* ~房屋与宅地。**5.** 〔口〕家伙,人。*a bad* ~坏蛋。*a sorry* ~一批糟糕的家伙。**6.** 〔英〕税。*scot and* ~(英国从前的)市民税。**7.** 〔美〕电影摄影场,马戏场。**8.** 〔口〕大量,许多;非常,相当;〔the ~〕全部,一切。~*s* [*a* ~] *of people* 许多人。~*s and* ~*s* (*of*) 许许多多。*A* ~ *you care*! 〔讽〕你太费心思啦。*I like him quite a* ~. 我非常喜欢他。*Thanks a* ~. 多谢。*Get away, the whole* ~ *of you*! 你们统统走开。*That is the* (*whole*) ~. 整个就是这些了。***a good*** [***great***] ~大量,很多。***a job*** ~ **1.** 整批买卖的杂货。**2.** 杂乱的一伙[一堆]。***an odd*** ~ 不成整数的一批货色;不满一百股的零星股票。***a round*** ~ (热门股票的)一百股或其倍数;(冷门股票的)十股或其倍数。***cast*** [***throw***] ***in one's*** ~ ***with*** 和…同命运。***cast*** ~***s*** 掷骰子决定。***It falls to sb***.***'s*** ~. = ***The*** ~ ***falls to sb***. 命该,命中注定。***jump across*** ~***s*** 〔美〕从原野中横穿过去;抄小路走。~ ***production*** 成批生产。***the*** ~ ***is cast*** 选择已经作出。**II** ***vt***. **1.** 划分(土地等);分批;分堆(出售商品) (*out*). **2.** 拈阄分给。— ***vi***. 抽签。~ ***on*** [***upon***] 〔美俚〕指望,倚赖,期待。

lo·ta(h) [ˈləutə; ˋlotə] ***n***. 〔Hind.〕铜制小水壶〔常为球形〕。

loth [ləuθ; loθ] ***a***. = loath.

Lo·tha·ri·o [ləuˈθɑːriəu; loˋθɛrɪ,o] ***n***. (*pl*. ~*s*) 专事勾引妇女的浪子。

lo·tic [ˈləutik; ˋlotɪk] ***a***. 【生态】激流的;生活于水流[急湍]中的。

lo·tion [ˈləuʃən; ˋloʃən] ***n***. **1.** 【药】洗液,洗剂。**2.** 洗涤。

lo·tos [ˈləutəs; ˋlotəs] ***n***. = lotus.

lot·ta [ˈlɔtə; ˋlɑtə] 〔美俚〕= a lot of.

lot·ter·y [ˈlɔtəri; ˋlɑtərɪ] ***n***. **1.** 抽彩给奖法,打彩票。**2.** 不可靠的事。*a* ~ *ticket* 彩票,奖券。*a great* ~虚无飘渺的事。

Lot·tie [ˈlɔti; ˋlɑtɪ] ***n***. **1.** 洛蒂〔女子名〕。**2.** Charlotte 的别名。

lot·to [ˈlɔtəu; ˋlɑto] ***n***. 落托数卡牌戏〔玩者数人各执一数码卡片,卡上记有数码三行,每行五个数字。主持人负责从专用的小圆盘中抽摇数码签。玩者数码卡的数字与签码上的数字相同时,可将卡上的数字消去,最先消完者获胜〕。

lo·tus [ˈləutəs; ˋlotəs] ***n***. **1.** 【希神】忘忧树;(吃后就忘记一切、流连忘返的)忘忧果。**2.** 【植】莲属;白睡莲;百脉根属。**3.** 【建】荷花饰,莲饰。*Indian* ~藕莲。~**-eater** 【希神】吃了上述忘忧果而忘记一切、流连忘返的人;〔喻〕醉生梦死,不负责任、贪图安乐的人。**-eating 1.** ***n***. 醉生梦死但图安乐的行为。2. *a*. 贪图安乐的。～ **land** 安乐乡;安逸。～ **position** (瑜伽派的)盘腿打坐。

louche [luːʃ; luʃ] *a*. 品德有问题的;声名狼藉的。

loud [laud; laʊd] **I** *a*. 1. 响亮的,大声的 (*opp*. quiet, soft). 2. 高声吵闹的,喧噪的。3. 强调的,坚持的,热心的。4. 〔口〕怪臭的,难闻的。5. 〔口〕(衣服、颜色等)过分鲜艳的,俗气的;(行为等)粗俗的。*a* ～ *voice* 大声。*a* ～ *denial* 断然的否认。*be* ～ *in demands* 啰啰嗦嗦地要求。*be* ～ *in one's praise* 极力称赞。**II** *ad*. 大声,高声。*laugh* ～ *and long* 大声笑个不停。*Speak* ～*er*! 说大声一点。～**-hailer** 手提式电子扩音器;强力扩声器;低音大喇叭。(= bullhorn). ～**-looking** *a*. 〔美〕过分鲜艳的,花哨俗气的。～ **mouth** 吵闹的人,大声说话的人。～**mouthed** *a*. 嘶叫的;吵嚷的。～**-speaker** 扬声器,喇叭。～**-spoken** *a*. 大声说的。**-ish** *a*. 稍响亮的。**-ly** *ad*. 1. 高声地,大声地。2. 扎眼地,花哨地。**-ness** *n*. 1. 高声,大声。2. 喧闹。3. 鲜艳夺目,华美;俗气。4. 【物】响度,音量。

loud·en [ˈlaudn; ˋlaʊdn̩] *vt*., *vi*. (使声音)变响亮[更响亮]。

Lough [lʌf; lʌf] *n*. 洛夫〔姓氏〕。

lough [lɔk; lɑk] *n*. 〔Ir.〕1. 湖泊。2. 海湾。

Louie [ˈlu(:)i; ˋlʊɪ] *n*. 路易〔男子名,Louis 的异体〕。

Lou·is [ˈlu(:)i, ˈlu(:)is; ˋlʊɪ, ˋlʊɪs] *n*. 路易斯〔男子名〕。

Lou·i·sa [lu(:)ˈiːzə; luˋizə] *n*. 路易莎〔女子名〕。

lou·is d'or [ˈluːiˈdɔː; ˏlʊɪˋdɔr] *n*. 〔F.〕金路易〔旧时法国金币,值 20 法郎〕。

Lou·ise [lu(:)ˈiːz; luˋiz] *n*. 路易丝〔女子名〕。

Lou·i·si·an·a [lu(:)ˌiːziˈænə; lʊɪzɪˋænə] *n*. 路易斯安那〔美国州名〕。

Lou·i·si·an·an [lu(:)ˌiːziˈænən; ˏlʊɪzɪˋænən] **Lou·i·si·an·i·an** [-niən; ˏlʊɪzɪˋænɪən] **I** *a*. 路易斯安那州的,路易斯安那州人的。**II** *n*. 路易斯安那州人。

Lou·is·ville [ˈlu(:)ivil; ˋlʊɪsvɪl] *n*. 路易斯维尔〔美国城市〕。

lounge [laundʒ; laʊndʒ] **I** *n*. 1. 闲荡,闲逛,漫步。2. 懒洋洋的步调[姿势]。3. (旅馆等的)散步场;休息室,娱乐室。4. (一端有一靠枕,但没有靠背的)长沙发,躺椅。**II** *vi*., *vt*. 1. 闲荡,闲逛 (*about*)。2. 懒洋洋地靠[躺] (*on a sofa*). 3. 吊儿郎当地混日子 (*away*). ～ **car** 〔美〕沙发[软席]车厢。～ **lizard** 〔美俚〕1. 常在旅馆休息等处闲混,追求逸乐的寄生虫。2. 爱同妇女厮混的男子;以陪伴妇女跳舞等为生的男子。～ **music** 休闲音乐。～ **suit** 〔主英〕西装便服〔以别于各种礼服〕。**loung·ingly** *ad*.

loung·er [ˈlaundʒə; ˋlaʊndʒɚ] *n*. 闲逛的人;吊儿郎当的人,懒人。

loup [laup, ləup, luːp; laʊp, lop, lup] *vi*., *vt*., *n*. 〔Scot.〕跳跃。

loupe [luːp; lup] *n*. 寸镜〔珠宝店、表店等使用的高倍放大镜〕。

loup-ga·rou [lugɑˈru; lugɑˋru] *n*. (*pl*. ***loups-ga·rous*** [lugɑˈru; lʊgɑˋru]) 【神话】变成狼的人,狼人;〔泛指〕大而残忍的狼(= werewolf)。

lour [ˈlauə; laʊr] **I** *vi*. 1. 皱眉头,怒目而视 (*at*; *on*; *upon*). 2. (天空等)阴起来,变坏;(云、雪等)就要来似的。**II** *n*. 1. 不高兴的面容,愁眉不展的脸色。2. 恶劣的天色。

Lou·ren·co Mar·ques [ləuˈrensəuˈmɑːks; loˋrɛnsoˋmɑrkɛs] *n*. 洛伦索马贵斯〔莫桑比克城市〕。

lour·ing [ˈlauəriŋ; ˋlaʊrɪŋ] *a*. 1. 不高兴的。2. 恶劣的;阴沉的。～ *looks* 不高兴的面容。～ *sky* 阴云密布的天空。**-ly** *ad*.

lour·y [ˈlauəri; ˋlaʊrɪ] *a*. = lowery.

louse [laus; laʊs] **I** *n*. (*pl*. ***lice*** [lais; laɪs]) 1. 虱。2. (附于动、植物上的)小虫;寄生虫。3. (*pl*. ***louse***) 〔美俚〕不受欢迎的人,卑鄙的人。**II** *vt*. 捉虱子,除虱子。～ ***around*** 〔美俚〕游荡,闲混。～ ***up*** 〔美俚〕变坏;弄糟;毁坏。～**-borne** *a*. 【医】虱传播的。～**-cage**, ～**-case** *n*. 〔美俚〕1. 帽子。2. (火车的)守车。3. (伐木工的)山中小屋。～**-trap** 〔美俚〕绒线围肚。～**wort** 【植】马先蒿属。(*Pedicularis*) 植物。

lous·y [ˈlauzi; ˋlaʊzɪ] *a*. (***lous·i·er***; ***-i·est***) 1. 尽是虱子的,多虱的。2. 糟糕的;不清洁的。3. 讨厌的,卑鄙的。4. 〔美俚〕富有的,有很多…的。5. 【纺】(丝)茸毛的。*be* ～ *with money* 有许多钱。**-i·ly** *ad*. **-i·ness** *n*.

lout[1] [laut; laʊt] **I** *n*. 蠢人,丑角般人物。**II** *vt*. 愚弄;嘲弄,把…当作蠢人。

lout[2] [laut; laʊt] *vi*. 1. 鞠躬。2. 屈服。

lout·ish [ˈlautiʃ; ˋlaʊtɪʃ] *a*. 粗野的,不知礼貌的。**-ly** *ad*.

lou·ver, **lou·vre** [ˈluːvə; ˋluvɚ] *n*. 1. 【建】固定百叶窗;〔*pl*.〕百叶窗板(= ～ board). 2. (通风用的)天窗,烟窗。3. (汽车的)散热孔,放气孔,放气窗;(有褶缝的)发动机盖。～ **shutter** 活百叶窗。～ **window** 固定百叶窗。

Lou·vre [luːvr; ˋluvɚ] *n*. (巴黎的)卢浮宫〔现为世界著名美术博物馆之一〕。

LOV = low-occupancy vehicle 载客量低的车辆。

lov·a·ble [ˈlʌvəbl; ˋlʌvəbl̩] *a*. 可爱的。**-a·bil·i·ty** [ˌlʌvəˈbiliti; ˏlʌvəˋbɪlətɪ], **-a·ble·ness** *n*. **-a·bly** *ad*.

lov·age [ˈlʌvidʒ; ˋlʌvɪdʒ] *n*. 【植】1. (用作调味香料等的)拉维纪草。2. 女贞属植物。

lov·at [ˈlʌvət; ˋlʌvət] *n*. (苏格兰呢常用的)绿中透蓝灰色的混合色。

love [lʌv; lʌv] **I** *n*. 1. 爱,热爱,爱戴。*give* [*send*] *one's* ～ *to sb*. 向某人致意,问候某人。*mutual* ～互相爱慕。*show great* ～ *to* [*towards*] *one's comrades* 热爱同志。～ *of one's country* 热爱祖国。2. 爱好;所爱的东西。*have a* ～ *for* [*of*] *sports* 爱好体育运动。3. (两性间的)恋爱;爱情。*one-sided* ～单相思,单恋。4. 性关系。5. 爱人〔尤指女性,意中人〕。6. 〔L-〕爱的化身,爱神 (= Cupid). 7. 〔口〕可爱的人;可爱的东西。*He is an old* ～. 他是个愉快的人。*It's a* ～, *isn't it*? 真可爱啊,不是么? *What a* ～ *of a dog*! 这狗多可爱! *What* ～*s of teacups*! 这些茶杯真好! 8. 爱人,宝贝。*My* ～ 亲爱的;宝宝〔对爱人、孩子的称呼〕。9. 【体】零分。～ *all* 双方零分,打成零比零。～ *five* = *five* ～ 5 比 0。***a labour of*** ～ 爱做的事,不取报酬而自愿做的事。***be in*** ～ ***with*** 热爱,迷恋。***be out of*** ～ ***with*** 不喜欢,讨厌。***fall in*** ～ ***with*** 爱上。***fall out of*** ～ ***with*** 不再爱,爱情中断。***Faults are thick where*** ～ ***is thin***. 爱情淡薄时,样样都不顺眼。***for*** ～ 1. 由于高兴。2. 不要钱,免费。3. (玩牌等)不用钱赌输赢。***for*** ～ ***or money*** 无论出任何代价,无论如何。***for the*** ～ ***of*** 为着,为了。***for the*** ～ ***of Heaven*** [***Mike***] 千万,看在老天爷面上。***for*** (***the***) ～ ***of*** (***the***) ***game*** 为了兴趣,不是有所贪图而是为了爱好。***L- and cough cannot be hid***. 〔谚〕爱情像咳嗽,压不住。～ ***at first sight*** 一见钟情。***L- cannot be forced***. 〔谚〕爱情不能强求。～ ***in a cottage*** 糟糠夫妻。***L- is blind***. 〔谚〕恋爱是盲目的。***L- is neither bought nor sold***. 〔谚〕爱情不能买卖。***L- is the mother of*** ～. 〔谚〕情生情,爱生爱〔爱是互相的〕。***L- lives in cottages as well as in courts***. 〔谚〕爱情不分贫富。***make*** ～ ***to sb***. 向某人调情[求爱]。***No herb will cure*** ～. 〔谚〕相思病无药可治。***One*** ～ ***drives out another***. 〔谚〕新的爱情来,旧的爱情去。***play for*** ～ (指打牌不是赌钱而只是)打着玩玩。**II** *vt*. 1. 爱,热爱;爱戴。～ *our motherland* 热爱祖国。2. (两性间)爱慕。3. 赞美,称赞。4. 有…的倾向 (*to do*); 〔口〕欢喜,爱好 (*to do*). *a plant that* ～*s shade* 一种喜阴的植物。*Will you come*? *I should* ～ *to*. 你打算来么? 我希望能来。— ***vi***. 爱。***L- me***, ～ ***my dog***. 〔谚〕爱屋及乌。～ **affair** 1. 恋爱事件;风流韵事。2. 强烈爱好。～ **apple** 番茄。～ **beads** 情爱珠〔六、七十年代西方嬉皮士所带象

征情爱的彩色珠串〕。~**bird** 相思鸟〔鹦鹉类〕。~ **child** (*pl*. ~-*ren*) 私生子。~-**crossed** *a*. 在爱情中不走运的。~ **feast** 1. = agape[2]. 2. 聚餐会;恳亲会。~ **game** (网球等的)败方得零分的比赛,一方全胜的比赛。~-**grass**【植】画眉草。~ **handles**〔俚〕腰间赘肉。~-**in** (嬉皮士等的)友爱大聚会。~-**in-a-mist** = ~-**in-a-puzzle**【植】黑种草。~-**in-idleness**【植】三色堇。~ **knot** 相思结,同心结。~ **letter** 情书。~-**lies-bleeding**【植】鸡冠花,(苋科)老枪谷,千穗谷。~ **life**〔口〕(一生中的)恋爱经历。~**lock** (女人的)娇发;耳边曲垂发绺(伊丽莎白一世和詹姆斯一世时廷臣的一种发式。~**lorn** *a*. 失恋的,害相思病的,苦恋的。~-**making** 调情,谈情说爱,求爱;性交。~ **match** 出自爱情的婚姻。~-**nest**〔美俚〕爱情的窝巢〔新婚家庭,爱人幽会处〕。~ **philter**〔**philtre, potion**〕媚药〔据信能使人对某人发生爱情〕。~ **seat** 鸳鸯椅。~ **set**【网球】败方得零分的一盘比赛。~**sick** *a*. 害相思病的。~**sickness** 相思病。~ **song** 情歌,恋歌。~ **story** 恋爱小说,爱情故事。~**struck** *a*. 在爱情中神魂颠倒的。~ **token** 爱情纪念品。

love·a·ble [ˈlʌvəbl; ˋlʌvəbl̩] *a*. = lovable. **-a·bil·i·ty**, **-ness** *n*. **-a·bly** *ad*.

Love·lace [ˈlʌvleis; ˋlʌvˏles] *n*. 薄情寡义的浪荡子,登徒子〔原为 Richardson 小说 *Clarissa Harlowe* 中人物的名字〕。

love·less [ˈlʌvlis; ˋlʌvlɪs] *a*. 没有爱情的;得不到爱情的。**-ly** *ad*. **-ness** *n*.

Lov·ell [ˈlʌvəl; ˋlʌvəl] *n*. 洛弗尔〔姓氏〕。

love·ly [ˈlʌvli; ˋlʌvlɪ] **I** *a*. (**-*li·er***; **-*li·est***) **1**. 可爱的,美丽的。**2**.〔口〕快乐的,愉快的。**3**. 高尚的,纯洁的。**II** *n*.〔口〕**1**. 美女。**2**. 漂亮的东西。**-li·ly** *ad*. **-li·ness** *n*.

Lov·er [ˈlʌvə; ˋlʌvɚ] *n*. 洛弗〔姓氏〕。

lov·er [ˈlʌvə; ˋlʌvɚ] *n*. **1**. 情人,爱人,情夫。**2**.〔*pl*.〕相爱的男女。**3**. 嗜好者,爱好者。*a pair of ~s = two ~s* 一对情侣。**-less** *a*. 没有情人的。**-like** *a*. 情人般的。**-ly** *a*., *ad*.

love·some [ˈlʌvsəm; ˋlʌvsəm] *a*.〔古、方〕可爱的。

lov·ey-dov·ey [ˈlʌviˈdʌvi; ˋlʌvɪˋdʌvɪ] *a*.〔俚〕过分亲爱的;多情的。

lov·ing [ˈlʌviŋ; ˋlʌvɪŋ] *a*. 爱的,有爱情的,钟情的,忠实的。*Our ~ subjects*〔英〕我的忠实臣民〔诏敕用语〕。*Your ~ friend* 你的好友〔信末用语〕。~ **cup** 1. 爱杯〔有数个把手以便轮饮的大酒杯〕。2. 纪念杯,奖杯。~-**kindness** 慈爱。**-ly** *ad*. 慈爱地,仁慈地,亲切地(*Yours lovingly = Lovingly yours* 你的亲爱的〔信末用语〕)。**-ness** *n*.

low[1] [ləu; lo] (-*er*, -*est*) (*opp*. high) **I** *a*. **1**. 低的;浅的,矮的。~ *flight* 低飞。*a ~ temperature* 低温。~ *tide* [*water*] 低潮。*The glass is ~*. 水银柱降低了。*The water is ~*. 水浅了。**2**. 卑下的;低等的,地位低的。*a ~ fellow* 下流人。*a man of ~ birth* [*origin*] 出身低微的人。~ *forms of life* 下等动物。**3**. 粗野的,无教养的,下流的。*a ~ style of writing* 粗俗的文体。~ *tastes* 低级趣味。~ *tricks* 卑鄙手段。**4**. (价值等)低廉的,低下的;(数量)少的。~ *cost* 低成本。*sell at a ~ price* 廉价出售。*a ~ opinion of* 对…评价不高。**5**. 消沉的,虚弱的;无精神的。*be ~ in spirits = be in ~ spirits* 无精打采。*feel ~* 情绪低落。*in a ~ state of health* 健康状态不佳。**6**. 倒下的,已死的,埋葬了的。*The great man is ~*. 那个伟人已经去世。**7**. (饮食等)粗劣的,没有营养的。*a ~ diet* 简陋的食物。**8**. 近年的;时期较近的。*an event of a ~er date* 近期发生的事件。*relics of ~ antiquity* 近古代的遗物。**9**. 低调的,低音的,(发音时)舌位放低的。*a ~ vowel* 低母音。*speak in a ~ voice* 低声说话。**10**.〔L-〕【宗】(英国)低教派的,低教会的。**11**. 低速的。*a ~ gear*【机】低速挡。**12**.〔英〕低年级的。**13**.【气】气压低的。*a ~ area* 低气压区域。~ *cloud ceiling* 低云幕。**14**. 不足的,快枯竭的,缺钱的。*be ~ in* (*one's*) *pocket* 口袋里无钱。*be ~ on ammunition* 军火供应不足。~ *morale* 士气沮丧。**15**. (衣服)低领的,袒胸露颈的。*a ~ dress* 低领衣,袒胸衣〔妇女夜礼服〕。

II *ad*. **1**. 低;低矮;在低处;往下地。*located ~ on the slope of a hill*. 位处山坡低处。*bow ~* 深深地鞠躬。*hit ~* 朝下部打。*The candles are burning ~*. 蜡烛快点完〔已很短〕。*The sands are running ~*. 沙漏里的沙愈来愈低,时间快完;寿命将尽。**2**. 地位低下地,卑下地,卑劣地。*fall ~* 堕落。**3**. 价格〔价值〕低;程度〔能力〕低。*buy sth. ~* 廉价买得某物。**4**. 低声地,以低音调。*I cannot get* (*down*) *so ~*. 我不能发那么低的声音。*talk ~* 小声谈话。**5**. 收入低;生活水平低。*live ~* 过穷苦日子。**6**. 晚近。*I find it as ~ as the 18th century*. 我发现近在 18 世纪也有。***bring ~*** 使减少;使跌落;使恶化。***lay ~*** 打倒,砍倒(树木);杀死;埋。***lie ~*** **1**. 蹲着,倒地不起,死。**2**.〔口〕隐匿;潜伏。***play it ~*** (***down***) ***upon*** 卑鄙地对待,歧视。***run ~*** 减少。

III *n*. **1**. (汽车等的)低速;低速齿轮。*put it in ~* 放第一挡〔低速挡〕。**2**. 低气压区。**3**.〔常 *pl*.〕低地。**4**. (竞赛的)最低分数;得分最低的人;最小王牌。~-**alloy** *a*.【冶】低合金的。~-**angle** *a*.【军】小俯冲角的(~-*angle bombing* 小俯冲角轰炸)。~ **beam** 车头短焦距光。~ **blow** 1.【拳击】打击腰部以下部位〔犯规动作〕。2. 卑劣的行动;卑劣的进击。~**born** *a*. 出身低微的。~-**boy**〔美〕矮屉柜。~**bred** *a*. 1. 出身低微的。2. 没有教养的,粗鲁的。~**brow** *a*., *n*.〔美口〕文化程度低的(人),教养不高的(人)(*opp*. high-brow). ~-**browed** *a*. 前额低的;(建筑物)入口处低的。~**cal** *a*.〔口〕(食物)低卡路里的。~ **camp** 低级的矫揉做作〔指文艺活动中不自觉地使用夸张陈腐等表现手段,以别于自觉地使用 (high camp)〕。2. 阴暗的。~ **carbon**【冶】低碳的。**L- Church**〔英〕低教会派。**L- -Church** *a*. 低教会派的。**L- Churchman** (*pl*. -*men*) 低教会派成员(或信徒)。~ **comedy** 滑稽戏,滑稽杂耍。~-**cost** *a*. 低价出售的;低价买得到的。**L- Countries** 低地国〔荷兰、比利时和卢森堡〕。~-**down** *a*. 1. 非常低的。2. 下贱的,卑鄙的。~-**down** *n*.〔俚〕真相,内幕(*get the ~down on* 得知…的内幕)~-**duty** *a*. 小功率的,轻型的,不重要的。~-**end** *a*. 低档次的,低级的,低价位的。~ **emission vehicle** 低排放量汽车。~ **frequency**【物】低频(率)。~ **gear** 低排挡,低速齿轮。**L- German** 1. (德国北部的方言)低地德语。2. 西日耳曼语支。~-**grade** *a*. 1. 低等的,品质低劣的。2. 低度的(*a ~-grade fever* 低烧)。~-**key(ed)** *a*. 低强度的;低调的;放低的,有节制的。**L- Latin** 俗拉丁语。~ **latitude** 低纬度。~-**level** 低水平的,低级别的。~**life** 1. 社会地位低微的人。2.〔美俚〕卑鄙的人。~-**lived** *a*. 生活水平低的;卑劣的。~-**lying** *a*. 低下的;低地的,低洼的;低低的(~-*lying hills* 低低的群山。~-*lying land* 低洼地)。**L- mass** (无烧香、奏乐等的)小弥撒(= Private mass). ~-**minded** *a*. 低级的;下流的。~-**necked** *a*. 露出胸部的;开领低的;露出颈和胸的〔指妇女衣服等,也叫 ~-neck〕. ~-**pitched** *a*. 低调的,低音的;(屋顶)倾斜缓的(*opp*. high-pitched). ~-**pressure** *a*. 1. 低压的。2. 轻松的。~ **profile** 不引人注目的形象,隐蔽不露的活动;低姿态的活动。~-**priced** *a*. 廉价的,索价不高的。~-**proof** *a*. (酒的)烈度低的,含酒精成分低的。~ **relief** 半浮雕,浅浮雕(= bas-relief). ~-**rise** 1. *a*. 楼层不多的,低层的。2. *n*. 低层楼房。~ **seam**【矿】薄煤层。~-**spirited** *a*. 没有精神的,意气消沉的。~ **silhouette** = ~ profile. **L- Sunday** 复活节后第一个星期日。~ **tea**〔美〕简单的晚餐(*opp*. high tea). ~-**tension** *a*. 低压的;带低压的;低压操作的。~-**test** *a*. (汽油的)高温气化的〔指低级汽油〕。~ **tide** 1. 潮水的低潮;低潮时间。2. 最低点。~ **water** 低水位,低潮(*at ~ water* 处于低潮。*in ~*

water 手头拮据)。~**-water mark** 1. 低潮线,低水位标志。2. 最低点。**-ness** *n*.

low[2] [ləu; lo] **I** *vi*., *vt*. (牛)哞哞地叫;哞哞地;(牛叫似地)说(*forth*). **II** *n*. 牛叫声,哞。

Low·ell [ˈləuəl; ˋloəl] *n*. 洛厄尔[姓氏,男子名]。

low·er[1] [ˈləuə; ˋloɚ] **I** *a*. [low 的比较级] 1. 较低的。2. 下级的,低级的。~ *animals* 下等动物。3. 南部的。*in* ~ *Manhattan* 在曼哈顿南部。4. 早期的。[L-]【地】早期的。*L- Permain* 二叠纪早期。5. 下游的。*the* ~ *Nile Valley*. 尼罗河下游区。6. [英]低年级的。*a* ~ *boy* [英]低年级男生。*a* ~ *school* 初级小学。~ **bound** 【数】下界,低界。~ **case**【印】小写字母盘。~**-case** 1. *a*. 小写的。2. *n*. 小写字母。3. *vt*. 用小写字母排印。~ **class** 下层社会。~ **classman** [美](学校的)低年级生[一二年级生]。~ **criticism** 对照《圣经》原文的校勘。~ **deck** 1. 下甲板。2. [*pl*.][英]海军士兵;舰上的低级军官和水手。**L- Empire**【史】东罗马帝国。~ **fungus**【生】低等真菌[如黏菌]。**L- House** [常用 ~ home]下院,众议院。~ **limit** 下限,最小限度。~ **regions** 1. = ~ world. 2. [谑]地下室;佣人住房,下房。~ **world** 1. 【宗】阴间,黄泉 (= nether world). 2. 尘世;大地,地球。**II** *vt*. 1. 放下,放低,降下。~ *a flag* 降旗。~ *the aim of a gun* 把枪瞄得低一些。2. 减价。~ *the price* 减低价格。3. 减弱;降低。*A cold has ~ed his resistance*. 伤风削弱了他的抵抗力。~ *one's sights* 降低抱负。~ *one's voice* 放低声音。4. [俚]吞下,咽下。5. 贬低。*That remark ~ed him in my opinion*. 那句话降低了他在我观感上的身价。— *vi*. 1. 降落,降低,减弱。2. 放下小艇;降下帆篷。~ ***oneself*** 降低自己的身份。~ [***strike***] ***one's*** [***the***] ***colours*** [***flag***] 屈服,投降;降低要求,退让,让步。

low·er[2] [ˈlauə; ˋlauɚ] *vi*., *n*. = lour.

low·er·ing[1] [ˈləuəriŋ; ˋloərɪŋ] *a*. 1. (天气)阴霾的,昏暗的,恶劣的。2. 不高兴的,愁眉苦脸的。**-ly** *ad*.

low·er·ing[2] [ˈləuəriŋ; ˋlauərɪŋ] **I** *a*. 1. 卑劣的。2. 体力减弱的。**II** *n*. 低下;减损。

low·er·most [ˈləuəˌməust; ˋloɚˏmost] *a*. 最下的,最低的。

low·er·y [ˈləuəri; ˋlaurɪ] *a*. 阴霾的,昏暗的;阴沉的。

Lowes [ləuz; loz] *n*. 洛斯[姓氏]。

low·est [ˈləuist; ˋloɪst] *a*. [low 的最高级]最下的,最低的;最小的;最便宜的。***at the*** ~ 至少,至低。~ **common denominator** 1. = least common denominator. 2. 为广大群众接受、理解的事物。~ **common multiple** = least common multiple.

low·ing [ˈləuiŋ; ˋloɪŋ] *n*. 牛叫声。

low·ish [ˈləuiʃ; ˋloɪʃ] *a*. 有点儿低的;较便宜的;小声的。

low·land [ˈləulənd, -ˈlænd; ˋloˏlənd, -lænd] **I** *n*. 低地。**II** *a*. 低地的;在低地里的;从低地来的。**the Lowlands** 苏格兰低地。**low·land·er** *n*. 低地人。**Low-land·er** *n*. 苏格兰低地人。

low·ly [ˈləuli; ˋlolɪ] **I** *a*. (*-li·er*; *-li·est*) 1. 地位低的;卑下的;低级的。2. 普通的,平凡的。3. 谦恭的。**II** *ad*. 1. 卑下地,低下地。2. 谦恭地,客气地。3. 低声地,不响亮地。**low·li·ness** *n*.

Lowndes [laundz; laundz] *n*. 朗兹[姓氏]。

lox[1] [lɔks; lɑks] *n*. 液态氧 (= *li*quid *ox*ygen)。

lox[2] [lɔks; lɑks] *n*. 熏鲑鱼,熏马哈鱼。

lox·o·drome [ˈlɔksədrəum; ˏlɑksəˋdrom] *n*. 1.【海】斜航;斜驶线。2.【天】恒向线。

lox·o·drom·ic(al) [ˌlɔksəˈdrɔmik(əl); ˏlɑksəˋdrɑmɪk(l̩)] *a*.【海】斜航的。**-drom·ics**, **-od·romy** [lɔkˈsɔdrəmi; lɑkˋsɑdrəmɪ] *n*.【海】斜航法。

loy·al [ˈlɔiəl; ˋlɔɪəl] **I** *a*. 忠诚的;忠实的。*be* ~ *to a cause* 忠于事业。~ *conduct* 正直的行为。**II** *n*. [常 *pl*.] 忠实信徒。**-ism** *n*. 效忠,忠诚。**-ist** *n*. 1. 效忠者[尤指效忠于旧政权者]。2. [常用 L-] (美国革命时期的)亲英分子。3. [L-] (西班牙内战时)拥护共和国政府者。**-ly** *ad*. **-ness** *n*.

loy·al·ize [ˈlɔiəlaiz; ˋlɔɪəlaɪz] *vt*. 使忠诚;使效忠。

loy·al·ty [ˈlɔiəlti; ˋlɔɪəltɪ] *n*. 忠诚;忠心。~ card 忠诚卡[商店发给顾客记录其每次购物价款的以便给予不同折扣优惠的身份卡]。

loz·enge [ˈlɔzindʒ; ˋlɑzɪndʒ] *n*. 1. 菱形。~ ***effect*** [***motive***] 菱形花纹。2. 菱形物;菱形玻璃;(宝石的)菱形面。3.【徽】菱形盾[用于寡妇、未婚女子、死者的纹章中]。4.【药】锭剂,糖锭。*cough* ~*s* 止咳糖。

LP, L.P., l.p. = 1. low pressure 低压;低气压。2. long primer【印】十点铅字。3. long playing 密纹的;密纹唱片 (= ~ record). 4. large paper 大开本。5. Labour Party [英]工党。6. large post 大开信纸。

LPM, lpm = lines per minute 每分钟行数。

L'pool = Liverpool.

L.P.S., LPS = 1. Lord Privy Seal [英]掌玺大臣。2. London Press Service 英国新闻处。

L.P.T.B. = London Passenger Transport Board [英旧]伦敦客运局。

lq. = liquid.

LR = liquid rocket 液体燃料火箭。

Lr = lawrencium【化】铹。

LRCS = League of Red Cross Societies 红十字会协会。

LRL = Lunar receiving laboratory 月球收集物研究室[密封无菌,用于研究从月球上收集来的样品]。

LRPA = long-range patrol aircraft 远程巡逻飞机。

LRR = long-range radar 远程雷达。

LRV = 1. lunar roving vehicle 月上爬行车。2. light rail vehicle 轻型有轨电车。

LS = 1. landing ship 登陆舰。2. Licentiate in Surgery 有资格开业的外科医生。3. [L.] *Locus Sigilli* 盖印处。

LSD = lysergic acid diethylamide 麦角酸二乙基酰胺[一种麻醉药物]。

L.S.D. = Lightermen, Stevedores and Dockers [英]驳船、搬运和码头工人。

l.s.d., £.s.d. = [L.] *librae*, *solidi*, *denarii* (= pounds, shillings and pence) 镑,先令和便士;[口]金钱。

LSI = 1. large-scale integration 大规模集成(电路)。2. launch success indicator 发射成功指示器。

L.S.O. = London Symphony Orchestra. [英]伦敦交响乐团。

LSS = landing ship, support 支援登陆舰。

LST = landing ship, tank 坦克登陆舰。

L.S.T. = Local Standard Time【天】地方标准时。

LSU = landing ship, utility 通用登陆舰。

L.S.W.R. = London and South-Western Railway [英]伦敦西南铁路。

Lt. = Lieutenant.

L.T.A. = London Teachers' Association [英]伦敦教师协会。

Lt. Col. = Lieutenant Colonel [英]陆军[海军陆战队]中校;[美]陆军[空军、海军陆战队]中校。

Lt. Comdr. = Lieutenant Commander [英、美]海军少校。

Ltd. = Limited [常用于股份有限公司的名称后]。

Lt. Gen. = Lieutenant General [英]陆军[海军陆战队]中将;[美]陆军[空军、海军陆战队]中将。

Lt. Gov. = Lieutenant Governor (省或地区的)代理总督,副总督;(美)副州长。

Lt Inf = Light Infantry 轻步兵。

L.T.L. = less-than-truckload 卡车零担的。

l.tn. = long ton.

Lu = 1. Louisa. 2. Louise. 3.【化】lutecium.

Lu·an·da [luːˈɑːndə; luˋændə] *n*. 罗安达[安哥拉首都]。

Lu·ang Pra·bang [ˈluɑːŋ prɑːˈbɑːŋ; ˋlwɑŋ prɑˋbɑŋ] 琅勃

拉邦〔老挝城市〕。

lu·au [luːˈau, ˈluːau; luˋaʊ, ˋluaʊ] ***n*.** **1.** 〔Haw.〕夏威夷宴会〔一般有娱乐节目〕。**2.** 〔美〕〔喻〕(意外的)财源。

Lu·ba [ˈluːbɑː; ˋlubɑ] ***n*.** **1.** (*pl*. *-bas*, *-ba*) 卢巴人〔刚果南部农民〕。**2.** 卢巴语。

lub·ber [ˈlʌbə; ˋlʌbɚ] **I** ***n*.** **1.** 傻大个子,笨大汉。**2.** 无经验的水手。**II** ***a*.** 大而笨拙的。~ *grasshopper*【动】钝蝗(*Romalea microptera*)〔产于美国东南部〕。~-**land** (想像中)极舒适的地方。~ **('s) hole**【海】桅楼升降口。~**('s) line** [**mark**, **point**]【海】船首基线。~ **world** = ~-land.

lub·ber·ly [ˈlʌbəli; ˋlʌbɚlɪ] **I** ***a*.** 粗笨的,笨拙的。**II** ***ad*.** 粗笨地,拙劣地。**-li·ness** ***n*.**

lube [luːb; lub] ***n*.** **1.** 润滑油 (= ~ oil). **2.** 润滑,涂油 (=lubrication)。

Lub·lin [ˈluːblin; ˋlublɪn] ***n*.** 卢布林〔波兰城市〕。

lu·bri·ca·ble [ˈluːbrikəbl, ˈljuː-; ˋlubrɪkəbl̩, ˋlju-] ***a*.** 可以涂油的;可弄润滑的。

lu·bri·cant [ˈluːbrikənt; ˋlubrɪkənt] **I** ***a*.** (使)润滑的。~ *oil* 润滑油。**II** ***n*.** **1.** 润滑剂,润滑油。**2.** 能减少摩擦的东西。**3.** 〔美俚〕奶油,黄油。

lu·bri·cate [ˈluːbrikeit; ˋlubrɪˏket] ***vt*.** **1.**【机】涂油,上油;使润滑。**2.** 〔俚〕(为了使事情进行顺利些等目的)劝酒;行贿,收买。— ***vi*.** **1.** 起润滑作用,充当润滑剂。**2.** 〔美俚〕喝一杯。**lubricating oil** 润滑油。**-d** 〔美俚〕喝醉了的。

lu·bri·ca·tion [ˌluːbriˈkeiʃən; ˏlubrɪˋkeʃən] ***n*.** 润滑,油润,上油;润滑作用。~ *groove* 油槽。*ring* ~油环润滑法。

lu·bri·ca·tor [ˈluːbrikeitə; ˋlubrɪˏketɚ] ***n*.** **1.** 润滑剂;注油器。**2.** 加润滑剂的人,注油人。

lu·bri·cious [luːˈbriʃəs; luˋbrɪʃəs] ***a*.** = lubricous.

lu·bric·i·ty [ljuːˈbrisiti; luˋbrɪsətɪ] ***n*.** **1.** 光滑,滑润性,润滑能力。**2.** 难捉摸;动摇,不稳定。**3.** 狡猾。**4.** 淫荡。

lu·bri·cous [ˈluːbrikəs; ˋlubrɪkəs] ***a*.** **1.** 滑润的,光滑的。**2.** 难捉摸的;动摇的,不稳定的。**3.** 淫荡的。

lu·bri·to·rium [luːbriˈtɔːriəm; lubrɪˋtɔrɪəm] ***n*.** 〔美〕(汽车)加油站。

Lu·bum·ba·shi [ˌluːbuːmˈbɑːʃiː; ˏlubumˋbɑʃi] ***n*.** 卢本巴希〔扎伊尔城市〕。

lu·carne [ˈljuːkɑːn; luˋkɑn] ***n*.**【建】老虎窗,屋顶窗。

Lu·cas [ˈluːkəs; ˋlukəs] ***n*.** 卢卡斯〔姓氏〕。

Luce [ljuːs; ljus] ***n*.** 卢斯〔姓氏〕。

luce [lus; lus] ***n*.**【动】白斑狗鱼(*Esox lucius*).

lu·cen·cy [ˈljuːsnsi; ˋljusnsɪ] ***n*.** **1.** 发亮。**2.** 透明。

lu·cent [ˈljuːsnt; ˋlusnt] ***a*.** **1.** 发亮的。**2.** 透明的。

Lu·cern(e) [ljuːˈsəːn; ljuˋsɝn] ***n*.** 卢塞恩〔瑞士城市〕。

lu·cern(e) [luːˈsəːn; luˋsɝn] ***n*.** 〔主英〕【植】首蓿(=〔美〕alfalfa)。

lu·ces [ˈluːsiːz; ˋlusiz] ***n*.** lux 的复数异体。

Lu·cia [ˈluːsjə; ˋluʃə] ***n*.** 露西娅〔女子名〕。

Lu·cian [ˈluːsjən; ˋluʃən] ***n*.** 卢西恩〔男子名〕。

lu·cid [ˈluːsid; ˋlusɪd] ***a*.** **1.** 清澈的,透明的。**2.** 清楚的;明白的。**3.** 神志清醒的。**4.** 光辉的,明亮的。**5.**【天】肉眼可见的;【植、动】光滑的。~ *streams* 清澈的河流。*a* ~ *mind* 清楚的头脑。*a* ~ *interval* (精神病患者的)神志清醒时候;(暴风雨,扰乱等的)暂时平静的一段时间。~ **dream** 清醒梦〔做梦时尚保持某种自我意识〕。**-ly** ***ad*.** **-ness** ***n*.**

lu·cid·i·ty [luːˈsiditi; luˋsɪdətɪ] ***n*.** **1.** 清澄,透明。**2.** 清楚,明白。**3.** 神志清醒。**4.** 洞察力。

Lu·ci·fer [ˈluːsifə; ˏlusəˋfɚ] ***n*.** **1.** 金星,晓星。**2.** 魔鬼,恶魔〔Satan 的别名〕。*as proud as* ~非常傲慢。**3.** 〔l-〕摩擦火柴,安全火柴 (= ~ match).

lu·cif·er·ase [ljuːˈsifəˌreis; ljuˋsɪfəres] ***n*.**【生化】萤光(素)酶。

lu·cif·er·in [luˈsifəˌrin; luˋsɪfərɪn] ***n*.**【化】萤光素。

lu·cif·er·ous [luːˈsifərəs; luˋsɪfərəs] ***a*.** **1.** 发光的,发亮的。**2.** 聪明的;有洞察力的。

Lu·ci·na [luːˈsainə; luˋsaɪnə] ***n*.**【罗神】司生育的女神。

lu·cite [ˈluːsait; ˋlusaɪt] ***n*.**【商标】(有机玻璃)留西特,【化】2-甲基丙烯酸,合成萤光树脂。

luck [lʌk; lʌk] **I** ***n*.** **1.** 运气,造化。**2.** 幸运,侥幸。**3.** 〔古〕带来幸运的东西。*good* ~幸运。*Good* ~ *to you*! 祝你成功;一路平安。*have bad* [*hard*, *ill*, *tough*] ~ 不幸,倒霉。*Bad* ~ *to you*! 你这该死的! *The* ~ *is in favour of me*. 运气来了,走运了。*The* ~ *turns against me*. 运气变坏了,倒霉了。*Just* [*It is just*] *my* ~. 唉,又是倒霉! *He has had the* ~ *to succeed*. 他侥幸成功了。***as good* ~ *would have it*** 幸亏,侥幸。***as ill* ~ *would have it*** 不幸。***as* ~ *would have it*** 碰巧;碰得不巧〔意思究竟是幸还是不幸,要根据上下文决定〕。***be down on one's*** ~〔口〕倒霉。***be in*** ~ 交好运。***be in*** ~***'s way*** 走运。***be off one's*** ~ = ***be out of*** ~ 运气不好。***by*** (***good***) ~ 侥幸,幸亏。***came to*** ~ 走起运来。***crowd*** [***press***, ***push***, ***stretch***] ***one's*** ~〔美俚〕过分依靠自己的好运气;碰到好运后指望侥幸再得到好运。***for*** ~ 祝福,祈求好运。***have no*** ~ 运气不好。***have the*** ~ ***to*** 幸而,侥幸。***play in*** [***to***] ***big*** ~〔美〕走运,得意。***play*** (***in***, ***to***) ***hard*** ~〔美〕倒霉,不走运。***ride one's*** ~ 指望运气。***rough*** ~ 倒霉。***the devil's own*** ~ **1.** 〔口〕莫名其妙的好运气。**2.** 〔讽〕非常倒霉。***try one's*** ~ 碰运气。***wish sb. all the*** ~ ***in the world*** 祝某人一切顺利。***worse*** ~ 不幸,不巧,偏巧。**II** ***vi*.** 侥幸成功,靠运气行事 (*into*; *on*; *onto*; *out*; *through*). *Don't expect to* ~ *through without an effort*. 别指望不经过努力就能侥幸成功。~ **money** [**penny**]〔英〕吉利钱〔常指旧时出售牲口的人为求吉利,在成交后还给买主的一小笔钱〕。

luck·less [ˈlʌklis; ˋlʌklɪs] ***a*.** 不幸的,运气坏的,倒霉的。**-ly** ***ad*.** **-ness** ***n*.**

luck·y [ˈlʌki; ˋlʌkɪ] **I** ***a*.** (***luck·i·er***; ***-i·est***) **1.** 运气好的,侥幸的。**2.** 兆头好的,吉祥的。**3.** 〔俚〕难得的,碰巧的;顺便的。**4.** 很恰当的,*a* ~ *guess* [*hit*, *shot*] 侥幸猜中,碰上。*L- bargee* [*beggar*, *devil*, *dog*, *rascal*] 幸运儿。*touch* ~交好运。*a* ~ *day* 好日子,吉日;很顺利的一天。**II** ***n*.** 〔俚〕逃亡。***cut*** [***make***] ***one's*** ~ 逃走。~ **bag** **1.** 摸彩袋。**2.** (军舰上的)失物箱。~ **dip** 摸彩袋。~ **strike** 好运气。**luck·i·ly** ***ad*.** **luck·i·ness** ***n*.**

lu·cra·tive [ˈluːkrətiv, ljuː-; ˋlukrətɪv, lju-] ***a*.** **1.** 有利的,赚钱的,合算的。**2.**【军】值得作为目标的。*a* ~ *investment* 有利的投资。*a* ~ *target* 可获战果的攻击目标。**-ly** ***ad*.** **-ness** ***n*.**

lu·cre [ˈluːkə; ˋlukɚ] ***n*.** 利益,赚头;金钱。*filthy* ~不义之财,肮脏钱。

Lu·cre·tia [luːˈkriːʃjə; luˋkriʃɪə] ***n*.** **1.** 卢克丽霞〔女子名〕。**2.** 罗马传说中的贞妇,贞节的模范。

Lu·cre·ti·us [luːˈkriːʃiəs; luˋkriʃəs] ***n*.** **1.** 卢克莱修〔男子名〕。**2.** **Carus** ~ 卢克莱修〔99? —55B.C. 罗马哲学家、诗人〕。

lu·cu·brate [ˈljuːkju(ː)ˌbreit; ˋljukjʊˏbret] ***vi*.** **1.** (在灯下)刻苦钻研;苦思冥想。**2.** 学究式地写作;详细论述。

lu·cu·bra·tion [ˌljuːkju(ː)ˈbreiʃən; ˏljukjʊˋbreʃən] ***n*.** **1.** (在灯下)刻苦钻研;苦思冥想。**2.** 苦心孤诣之作。**3.** 〔常作复数〕〔谑〕学究气的作品。

lu·cu·bra·tor [ˈljuːkju(ː)ˌbreitə; ˋljukjʊˏbretɚ] ***n*.** 刻苦钻研者;学究式的写作者。

lu·cu·lent [ˈljuːkjulənt; ˋljukjʊlənt] ***a*.** **1.** 明亮的,清澈的,透明的。**2.** 明白的,明显的。**-ly** ***ad*.**

Lu·cul·lus [luːˈkʌləs; luˋkʌləs] ***n*.** 卢库勒斯〔古罗马将军兼执政官,以巨富和举办豪华大宴著名〕。**-cul·lan** [-ən; -ən], **-cul·li·an** [-iən; -ɪən], **-cul·le·an** [ˌlukəˈliən; ˏlukəˋliən] ***a*.**

L

Lu·cy [ˈluːsi; ˋlusɪ] *n*. 露西〔姓氏,女子名〕。～ **stoner** 主张女子结婚后用自己姓名者〔因美国女权主义者露西·斯通 (Lucy Stone, 1818—1893)而得名〕。

Lud [lʌd; lʌd] *n*. 〔英〕 = Lord. *My* ～ [miˈlʌd; mɪˋlʌd] = My Lord.

Ludd·ism [ˈlʌdizm; ˋlʌdɪzm̩] *n*. = Ludditism.

Ludd·ite [ˈlʌdait; ˋlʌdaɪt] *n*. **1.** 鲁德分子〔英国 1811 年—1816 年以捣毁纺织机械为手段,抗议资本家降低工资和解雇工人的团体的成员〕。**2.** 〔l-〕强烈反对提高机械化和自动化者。

Ludd·it·ism [ˈlʌdəˌtizəm; ˋlʌdəˏtɪzm̩] *n*. 强烈反对在任何方面提高机械化和自动化。

lu·dic [ˈluːdik; ˋludɪk] *a*. 游戏的。

lu·di·crous [ˈluːdikrəs; ˋludɪkrəs] *a*. 可笑的;荒唐的。**-ly** *ad*. **-ness** *n*.

Lud·wig [ˈlʌdwig; ˋlʌdwɪg] *n*. 路德维格〔男子名, Louis 的异体〕。

lu·es [ˈluːiːz; ˋluiz] *n*. 〔L.〕 **1.** 疫病,传染病。**2.** 梅毒 (= ～ venerea). ～ ***Boswelliana*** [ˌbɔzweliˈɑːnə; ˏbɑzwelɪˋanə] 巴斯威尔 (Boswell)式的夸大〔指过分美化所描述的对象〕。

lu·et·ic [lju(ː)ˈetic; ljuˋɛtɪc] *a*. 梅毒的;疫病的,传染病的。**-ally** *ad*.

Luf·be·ry cir·cle [ˈlʌfbəri ˈsəːkl; ˋlʌfbərɪtˋsɝkl̩] 【军】(空战中飞机组成圆圈状队形,各机互相掩护的)卢氏圆圈队形。

luff [lʌf; lʌf] *n*. 【海】 **1.** 抢风行驶,贴风行驶。**2.** 船首两舷的弯曲部;纵帆的前缘。**3.** (货物在起重时的)起落摆动。**II** *vi*., *vt*. 抢风行驶;(帆船竞赛)驶出(对方)上风。***L- her = L- the helm*** 〔对舵手下达的命令〕转航向风! ～ ***up*** 船侧受风而行。

luf·fa [ˈlʌfə; ˋlʌfə] *n*. **1.** 【植】丝瓜 (= dish-cloth gourd). **2.** 丝瓜筋[络]。

luft·mensch [ˈluftˌmenʃ; ˋlʊftˏmɛnʃ] *n*. (*pl*. ***-mensch-en*** [-ˌmenʃən; -ˏmɛnʃən]) (G.) 空想家,不切实际的人,不脚踏实地的人。

Luft·waf·fe [G. ˈluftvɑfə; ˋlʊftˏvɑfə] *n*. 〔G.〕(第二次世界大战中的)纳粹德国空军。

lug[1] [lʌg; lʌg] *n*. = lugworm.

lug[2] [lʌg; lʌg] *n*. = lugsail.

lug[3] [lʌg; lʌg] **I** *n*. **1.** 用力拉,被拖的东西。**2.** 懒人。**3.** 〔*pl*.〕〔美俚〕摆架子,装腔作势。**4.** 〔美俚〕勒索,敲诈(到的钱财)。***pile*** [***put***] ***on*** ～***s*** 〔美俚〕摆架子。***put the*** ～ ***on*** 向…敲诈[勒索]。**II** *vt*., *vi*. (***-gg-***) **1.** 使劲拉,用力拖 (*about*; *along*; *at*); 硬拉走 (*along*). **2.** 〔口〕引出(无关系的话等) (*in*; *into*). **3.** 拖动,沉重地挪动。

lug[4] [lʌg; lʌg] *n*. **1.** 〔Scot.〕耳朵。**2.** 耳状物(如柄、把手等)。**3.** 【机】突起,凸出部,突缘;【电】焊片,接线片。**4.** (马具上的)皮环;衔套。**5.** 〔俚〕笨家伙。

Luge [luːʒ; luʒ] **I** *n*. (竞赛用单人或双人)平底雪橇。**II** *vi*. (***-luged***, ***-luge·ing***) 雪橇竞赛。

Lu·ger [ˈluːgə; ˋlugɚ] **I** *n*. 〔G.〕鲁格尔〔德国造半自动手枪的商标名〕。**II** *n*. 〔常用 l-〕鲁格尔手枪。

lug·gage [ˈlʌgidʒ; ˋlʌgɪdʒ] *n*. **1.** 〔英〕行李,随身行李 (=〔美〕 baggage). **2.** 〔美〕提包,皮箱。**3.** 红褐色。*check one's* ～寄存行李,打行李票。*hand* ～手提行李。*excess* ～超重行李。*personal* ～随身行李,小件行李。*registered* ～托运行李。～**-carrier** *n*. (自行车等的)载物架。～**-rack** (火车等的)行李架。～ **van** 〔英〕行李车 (=〔美〕 baggage car).

lug·ger [ˈlʌgə; ˋlʌgɚ] *n*. 斜桁横帆小船。

lug·gie [ˈlʌgi; ˋlʌgɪ] *n*. 〔Scot.〕带耳状拎环的木桶。

lug·sail [ˈlʌgseil, -sl; ˋlʌgˏsel, -sl̩] *n*. 【船】斜桁横帆,斜桁四角帆。

lu·gu·bri·ous [luːˈgjuːbriəs; luˋgjubrɪəs] *a*. (像是过分做作而显得可笑的)忧伤的,悲痛的;阴郁的,如丧考妣的。**-ly** *ad*. **-ness** *n*.

lug·worm [ˈlʌgˌwəːm; ˋlʌgˏwɝm] *n*. 【动】沙蠋〔可作钓饵用〕。

Luke [luːk; luk] *n*. 卢克〔男子名,基督教《圣经》中译为"路加"〕。

luke·warm [ˈljuːkwɔːm; ˋljukˋwɔrm] *a*. **1.** 微温的。**2.** 不热心的,冷淡的,不起劲的。**-ly** *ad*. **-ness** *n*.

lull [lʌl; lʌl] **I** *n*. **1.** 间歇,暂停。**2.** 催眠的东西〔尤指催眠曲〕。*a* ～ *in the storm* 风暴的暂息。*a bombing* ～ 暂时停炸。**II** *vt*. **1.** 使安静。**2.** 哄骗。**3.** 镇静,缓和。～ *a baby to sleep* 哄小孩睡觉。～ *sb. into a false sense of security* 骗某人使产生虚假的安全感。～ *sb.'s suspicions* 消除某人的猜疑。— *vi*. 变平静。**-ing·ly** *ad*. 催人入睡的。

lull·a·by [ˈlʌləbai; ˋlʌləˏbaɪ] **I** *n*. **1.** 催眠曲,摇篮曲。**2.** 轻柔的声音(如微风吹拂声,潺潺流水声)。**II** *vt*. 唱摇篮曲催眠。

Lulu [ˈluːluː; ˋlulu] *n*. Louisa, Louise 的爱称。

lu·lu [ˈluːluː; ˋlulu] **I** *n*. 〔美俚〕 **1.** 突出的人物[事情]〔如漂亮的少女;难学的功课〕。**2.** 特种津贴开支项目。*a* ～ *of a mistake* 明显的错误,大错误。**II** *a*. 极好的;第一流的。

lum [lʌm; lʌm] *n*. 〔Scot. 英方〕烟筒。

lum·ba·go [lʌmˈbeigəu; lʌmˋbego] *n*. (*pl*. ～*s*) 【医】腰痛,腰部风湿痛,腰肌痛。**lum·ba·gi·nous** [-dʒinəs; -dʒɪnəs] *ad*.

lum·bar [ˈlʌmbə; ˋlʌmbɚ] **I** *a*. 腰(部)的。**II** *n*. 【解】腰动脉;腰神经;腰椎。

lum·ber[1] [ˈlʌmbə; ˋlʌmbɚ] **I** *n*. 〔美〕 **1.** 木材,木料,方料;〔英〕原木。**2.** 破烂东西,碎屑,废物。*clear* ～上等木材。*the L- State* 〔美〕缅因州的别号。**II** *vt*. **1.** 杂乱地堆积,把烂东西堆满(房屋)。**2.** 阻碍。(*up*). **3.** 采伐(木材)。— *vi*. **1.** 阻塞。**2.** 〔美〕采伐木材,拖运木材。～**jack 1.** 伐木工人。**2.** 短夹克衫。～ **jacket** 伐木者穿的夹克衫。～**man** 伐木者;集材者〔尤指监工、经理人等〕;木材商;木材运输船。～**mill** 制材厂,锯木厂。～ **room** 杂物房。～**yard** 木材堆置场。**-er** *n*. **-less** *a*. **-ly** *ad*.

lum·ber[2] [ˈlʌmbə; ˋlʌmbɚ] **I** *vi*. 笨重地移动;隆隆地行进。*a* ～*ing cart* 隆隆响着走的车。**II** *n*. 隆隆声。

lum·ber·ing [ˈlʌmbəriŋ; ˋlʌmbərɪŋ] **I** *n*. **1.** 伐木业。**II** *a*. **1.** 笨重的。**2.** 动作迟缓步子沉重的。**3.** 笨拙的;表达不流畅的。

lum·ber·some [ˈlʌmbəsəm; ˋlʌmbɚsəm] *a*. 麻烦的;笨重的。

lum·bri·ca·lis [ˌlʌmbriˈkeilis; ˏlʌmbrəˋkelɪs] *n*. (*pl*. ***-ca·les*** [-liːz; -liz]) 【解】蚓(状)肌 (= lumbraical)。

lum·bri·coid [ˈlʌmbriˌkɔid; ˋlʌmbrəˏkɔɪd] *a*. 蚯蚓状的,类似蚯蚓的。

lu·men [ˈljuːmin; ˋljumɪn] *n*. (*pl*. ***-mi·na*** [-minə; -mɪnə]) **1.** 【物】流明〔光通量单位〕。**2.** 【解】(管)腔。

lu·mi·naire [ˌljuːmiˈnɛə; ˏljumɪˋner] *n*. 【物】泛光灯[发光、照明]设备;光源。

lu·min·al [ˈljuminæl; ˋljʊmənəl] *n*. 【药】鲁米那〔一种镇静剂〕。

lu·mi·nance [ˈljuːminəns; ˋljumɪnəns] *n*. **1.** 发光,光亮。**2.** 亮度,耀度,照度,发光率[密度]。

lu·mi·nant [ˈljuːminənt; ˋljumɪnənt] **I** *a*. 发光的。**II** *n*. 发光体。

lu·mi·nar flow [ˈljuːminər fləu; ˋljumɪnər flo] 【物】片流。

lu·mi·nar·y [ˈljuːminəri; ˋljuməˏnerɪ] *n*. **1.** 天体。**2.** 发光体。**3.** (学识等方面的)杰出人物;名人。*the great* ～太阳。

lu·mine [ˈljuːmin; ˋljumɪn] *vt*. = illumine.

lu·mi·nesce [ˌljuːmiˈnes; ˏljumɪˋnɛs] *vi*. (***-nesc·ed***, ***-nesc·ing***) 发(冷)光;变明亮。

lu·mi·nes·cence [ˌljuːmiˈnesns; ˏljuməˋnɛsns] *n*. 【物】

L

发光,发萤[冷、磷]光。**-nes·cent** [-ˈnesnt; -ˋnɛsnt] *a*.

lu·mi·nif·er·ous [ˌljuːmiˈnifərəs; ˏljuməˋnɪfərəs] *a*. 发光的,发萤[冷]光的;传光的。

lu·mi·nom·e·ter [ˌljuːmiˈnɔmitə; ˏljuməˋnɑmətɚ] *n*.【物】照度计。

lu·mi·no·phor(e) [ˈljuːminəfɔː; ˋljumənəfɔr] *n*.【物】发光体[团]。

lu·mi·nos·i·ty [ˌljuːmiˈnɔsiti; ˏljuməˋnɑsətɪ] *n*. 1. 光明,光辉。2.【物】发光度;(辐射能的)发光效率。3. 发光物,发光体;辉点。4.【原】(射束中的)加速粒子数密度。

lu·mi·nous [ˈljuːminəs; ˋljumənəs] *a*. 1. 发光的;明亮的;照耀着的;辉耀的。2. 明白易懂的;有启发性的。3. 明快的,爽朗的。4. 光明的,灿烂的。*a* ~ *body* 发光体。*a* ~ *compass* 夜光罗盘。~ *paint* 发光漆。*a square* ~ *with sunlight* 阳光普照的广场。*full of* ~ *ideas* 富有启发性意义的。*His prose is simple and* ~. 他的散文简明易懂。*a* ~ *smile* 爽朗的微笑。*the* ~ *future* 光辉前途。~ **energy**【物】光能。~ **flux**【物】光束,光通量。~ **intensity**【物】发光强度。**-ly** *ad*. **-ness** *n*.

lum·me [ˈlʌmi; ˋlʌmɪ] *int*.〔英俚〕哎呀! 啊! 噢!〔用以加强语气或表示惊讶、赞同等;= Lord love me!〕

lum·mox [ˈlʌməks; ˋlʌməks] *n*.〔美口〕笨拙的人,笨蛋。

lum·my [ˈlʌmi; ˋlʌmɪ] I *int*.〔英〕= lumme. II *a*.〔英俚〕头等的。

lump[1] [lʌmp; lʌmp] I *n*. 1. 块,团。2. 疱,肿瘤,疖子。3.〔俚、方〕一大堆,许多。4.〔口〕笨蛋;矮胖子。5.〔*pl*.〕〔美俚〕责打;指责;应得的惩罚。*a* ~ *of sugar* 一块(方)糖。***all of a*** ~ 结成一团;肿成一个球似的。***a*** ~ ***in one's*** [***the***] ***throat*** (由于悲痛要哭)喉咙哽住。***a*** ~ ***of avarice*** [***selfishness***] 道地的贪婪鬼[自私自利者]。***a*** ~ ***of clay*** [***earth***] 1. 一块泥土。2.【圣】人;无情的人。***by*** [***in***] ***the*** ~ 1. 大批地,成群地。2. 总共。***get*** [***take***] ***one's*** ~ 咎由自取地挨打骂。***in a*** [***one***] ~ 一次全部地。***on a*** ~ ***sum basis*** 按照一次总付的办法。***take by*** [***in***] ***the*** ~ 1. 大批地拿。2. 总括起来。II *vt*. 1. 使成块,使成团;集总;总括;一起处理;总括起来说(*together*; *with*; *in with*; *under*). 2. 笨重地移动。3. 把所有的赌注都下在…上(*on*). ~ *the expense* 把开销混在一起计算。~ *dough* 把面粉揉成团。~*ed capacity*【物】集总电容。~*ed parameter*【物】集总参数。— *vi*. 1. 成块,成团。2. 肿胀成瘤。3. 笨重地行走(*along*); 一屁股坐下(*down*). ~ ***together*** 总计。~ **sugar** 成块的糖;糖块,方糖。~ **sum** (一次结清的)总额。~ **work** 总包的工作,包干工作。

lump[2] [lʌmp; lʌmp] *vt*.〔口〕忍耐,忍受。*If you don't like it*, (*you may*) ~ *it*. 不高兴也得忍耐。

lump[3] [lʌmp; lʌmp] *n*. = ~fish. ~**fish** (*pl*. *-fish*, *-fishes*)【动】圆鳍鱼科(*Cyclopteridae*)〔尤指圆鳍鱼(*Cyclopterus lumpus*)〕. ~ **sucker** = ~fish.

lump·ec·to·my [lʌmˈpektəmiː; lʌmˋpɛktəmi] *n*.【医】乳房瘤切除术。

lump·en [ˈlʌmpən, Am. ˈlumpən; ˋlʌmpən, ˋlumpən] *a*. 1. (从本阶级中)游离出来的;分化出来的。2. 粗鲁的,愚蠢的,落后的。

lump·er [ˈlʌmpə; ˋlʌmpɚ] *n*. 1. 码头装卸工人。2. 小包工头,小承包商。3.【生】堆合分类者。

lump·ing [ˈlʌmpiŋ; ˋlʌmpɪŋ] *a*.〔口〕沉重的,大的;很多的。*a* ~ *great helping of pudding* 很大的一份布丁。~ *weight* 很大的重量。

lump·ish [ˈlʌmpiʃ; ˋlʌmpɪʃ] *a*. 1. 块状的;多团块的。2. 笨重的;笨拙的,迟钝的;矮胖的。3. 沉闷的,学究式的,令人讨厌的。

lump·y [ˈlʌmpi; ˋlʌmpɪ] *a*. (***lump·i·er***, ***lump·i·est***) 1. 多团块的;结成块的。2. 满是疙瘩的;粗糙的。3. 波浪起伏的。4. 愚钝的;呆头呆脑的。5.〔英俚〕醉醺醺的。~ **jaw**【医】放线菌病(= actinomycosis). **lump·i·ly** *ad*. **lump·i·ness** *n*.

Lu·na [ˈljuːnə; ˋljunə] *n*. 1.【罗神】月神;月亮。2.〔l-〕〔炼金术用语〕银。〔l-〕~ **moth**【虫】月形天蚕蛾(*Tropaealuna*)的蛾。

lu·na·cy [ˈljuːnəsi; ˋljunəsɪ] *n*. 1. 疯癫,精神错乱。2. 蠢笨的行为,疯狂的行为。

lu·nar [ˈljuːnə; ˋljunɚ] *a*. 1. 月的,月球上的;按月球的运转而测定的。2. 似月的;新月形的,半月形的。3. (光)苍白的,微弱的。4. 银的,含银的。~ **bone**【解】半月状骨。~ **calendar** 阴历。~ **caustic**【化】硝酸银。~ **distance** 月距〔月与太阳或星之间的角距〕。~ **eclipse** 月蚀。~ **mansions**【天】二十八宿。~ **mass**【天】月球质量〔用作天文质量单位〕。~ (**excursion**) **module**【宇】登月舱。~ **month** 太阴月〔约 29½ 日〕。~ **naut** 登月太空人。(**the**) **L- New Year** 阴历新年,春节。~ **observation** 太阴观测。~ **orbit** 绕月轨道。~ **politics** 空论,不切实际的问题。~ **probe** 月球探测。~ **rainbow** 月虹,月夜的虹。~ **rover** [**roving vehicle**] 月上爬行器。~ **scape** 月貌。~ **year** 太阴年〔约 354 日 8 小时〕。

lu·nar·i·an [luːˈnɛəriən; luˋnɛrɪən] *n*. 1. (遐想的)月球居民,月球人。2. 月球研究者。

lu·nate [ˈljuːnit; ˋljunet] *a*. 新月形的,半月形的。

lu·na·tic [ˈljuːnətik; ˋljunətɪk] I *a*. 1. 疯癫的,精神错乱的。2. 疯狂的;极端愚蠢的。3. 为收容精神病人而设的。II *n*. 1. 精神病人,疯子。2. 狂人,怪人,愚人。~ **asylum** 疯人院,精神病院〔现在常称 mental home 或 mental institution〕. ~ **fringe** 极端分子,极端主义者。

lu·na·tion [ljuːˈneiʃən; ljuˋneʃən] *n*. 太阴月(= lunar month).

lunch [lʌntʃ; lʌntʃ] I *n*. 1. 午餐;(两餐之间)便餐,点心。2. 作午餐[便餐]用的食物;〔美〕便餐。*a* ~ *party* 午餐会。II *vi*., *vt*. 吃午餐[便餐];供给午餐[便餐]。~ **box**〔口〕便携式电脑。~**-bucket** *a*.〔美〕"饭盒"阶层的,蓝领阶层的,工人阶级的。~ **counter**〔美〕(餐馆的)便餐柜台;便餐馆。~**-hooks**〔美俚〕1. 手;手指。2. 牙齿。3. 非难,恶评。~ **room** 便餐馆,小吃馆。~**time** 午餐时间。~**time abortion**〔口〕饭间打胎〔指以真空吸引术实行人工流产,用时极短〕。

lunch·eon [ˈlʌntʃən; ˋlʌntʃən] *n*. 1. 午餐,午宴,午餐会。2. 两餐之间吃的一点食物。~ **meat** 午餐肉。

lunch·eon·ette [ˌlʌntʃəˈnet; ˏlʌntʃəˋnɛt] *n*.〔美〕小餐馆。

lun·che·te·ri·a [ˌlʌntʃiˈtiəriə; ˏlʌntʃɪˋtɪrɪə] *n*. 简易自助餐馆。

lune[1] [ljuːn; ljun] *n*. 半月形,弓形,月牙形;新月形物;月亮。~ *of a sphere*【数】球面二角形。

lune[2] [ljuːn; ljun] *n*. 拴鹰隼的皮带。

lunes [ljuːnz; ljunz] *n*. *pl*. 精神病的发作。

lu·nette [ljuːˈnet; ljuˋnɛt] *n*. 1. 半月形(物)。2.【筑城】眼镜堡〔具有两个正面和两个侧面的突出工事〕;【军】(炮车等上的)牵引环。3.【建】弧面窗;弦月窗。4.〔*pl*.〕潜水游泳时的护目。5. 玻璃表面。6. 断头台上的断头孔。

lung [lʌŋ; lʌŋ] *n*. 1. 肺脏,肺。2. (无脊椎动物的)呼吸器官。3.【医】辅助呼吸的装置。4.〔*pl*.〕〔英〕可供呼吸新鲜空气的地方。*an iron* ~【医】铁肺,人工呼吸器。***at the top of one's*** ~***s*** 用最高嗓子。***have good*** ~***s*** 声音大。***the*** ~***s of London*** 伦敦市内的肺〔指公园等绿化空旷地方〕。***try one's*** ~***s*** 使尽嗓子叫。~**-duster**, ~**-fogger**〔美俚〕香烟。~**fish** (***-fish***, ***-fishes***)【动】肺鱼。~ **irritant** 窒息性毒剂。~ **power** 发声力;肺力。~ **sac** 肺囊。~ **wort**【植】疗肺草属(*Pulmonaria*);肺衣,地衣。

lunge[1] [lʌndʒ; lʌndʒ] I *n*. 1. (刀剑的)刺,戳。2. 突出;突进;猛冲。II *vi*. (用剑等)刺,戳;猛向前冲(*at*; *out*).— *vt*. 刺,推。

lunge[2] [lʌndʒ; lʌndʒ] I *n*. 1. 练马索。2. 圆形练马场。II *vt*. 在练马场或用练马索练(马)。

lunged [lʌŋd; lʌŋd] *a*. 肺似的,有肺的。*deep-* ~ 声音洪

L

亮的。*one-* ～单肺的。

lung·er [ˈlʌŋə; ˋlʌŋɚ] *n*. 〔美俚〕肺病病人。

lun·gi [ˈluŋgi; ˋluŋgi] *n*. (印度人用的)腰布;头巾。

lu·ni·form [ˈluːnifɔːm; ˋlunɪfɔrm] *a*. 新月形的。

Lu·nik [ˈljuːnik; ˋljunɪk] *n*. 月球卫星。

lu·ni·log·i·cal [ˌljuːnəˈlɔdʒəkəl; ˏljunəˋlɑdʒəkəl] *a*. 研究月球的〔尤指研究月球的地质〕。

lu·ni·so·lar [ljuːniˈsəulə; ˏljuniˋsolɚ] *a*. 月与日的;由于月日的引力的。*the* ～ *calendar* 阴阳历。～ *cycle* [*period*] 太阴太阳周期。～ *precession* 【天】日月岁差。

lu·ni·tid·al [ˈljuːniˈtaidl; ˋljuniˋtaɪdl] *a*. 【天】月潮的。～ **interval** 【天】月潮间隔。

lun·ker [ˈlʌŋkə; ˋlʌŋkɚ] *n*. 同类中特大者(尤指大鱼)。

lunk·head [ˈlʌŋkhed; ˋlʌŋkˏhɛd] *n*. 〔美俚〕笨人,傻瓜。

Lu·no·khod [ˌljuːnəˈhɔːt; ˏljunəˋhɔt] *n*. 〔Russ.〕月上步行者。

lunt [lʌnt, lunt; lʌnt, lunt] **I** *n*. 〔Scot.〕**1**. 慢燃火柴;火炬。**2**. 烟。**II** *vt*., *vi*. 〔Scot.〕点燃;冒烟。

lu·nu·la [ˈljuːnjulə; ˋljunjulə] *n*. (*pl*. *-lae* [-liː; -ˏli]) 新月形的,新月状表记〔如甲弧影〕(= lunule). **-r** *a*.

lu·nu·late [ˈljuːnjulit, -leit; ˋljunjulet, -ˏlet] *a*. **1**. 新月形的。**2**. 有新月形标记的 (= lunulated).

lu·nule [ˈljuːnjuːl; ˋljunjul] *n*. 半月状的东西[记号];甲弧影。

lun·y [ˈluːni; ˋlunɪ] *n*. (*pl*. *lun·ies*), *a*. (*lun·i·er*, *lun·i·est*) = looney, loony.

Lu·per·ca·li·a [ˌljuːpəˈkeiliə, -ˈkæljə; ˏljupəˋkeilɪə, -ˋkæljə] *n*. *pl*. 古罗马牧神节〔二月十五日〕(= *Lupercal n*. *sing*.) **Lu·per·ca·li·an** *a*.

lu·pin, lu·pine[1] [ˈljuːpin; ˋljupɪn] *n*. 【植】白羽扇豆。

lu·pine[2] [ˈljuːpain; ˋljupaɪn] *a*. 狼(似)的;凶恶的;贪婪的。

lu·pous [ˈljuːpəs; ˋljupəs] *a*. 【医】狼疮的。

lu·pu·lin [ˈljuːpjulin; ˋljupjulɪn] *n*. 【化】蛇麻腺,忽布素。

lu·pus [ˈljuːpəs; ˋljupəs] *n*. **1**. 【医】狼疮。**2**. 〔L-〕【天】豺狼座。～ **erythematosus** [ˌerəθeməˈtəusəs; ˏɛrəθeməˋtosəs] 【医】红斑狼疮。～ **vulgaris** [ˈvʌlgeəris; ˋvʌlgɛrɪs] 【医】红斑样寻常狼疮。

LUR = London Underground Railway 伦敦地下铁道。

lur [luə; lur] *n*. S 形铜号〔史前期的乐器,尤指北欧地区的〕。

lurch[1] [ləːtʃ; lɝtʃ] **I** *n*. **1**. (船忽然发生的)倾侧。**2**. (醉汉的)东歪西倒,蹒跚。**3**. 〔美〕倾向,癖好。**II** *vi*. **1**. (船)突然倾侧。**2**. 东歪西倒,蹒跚。～ *toward* 歪向。～ *against a post* 歪靠在木柱上。

lurch[2] [ləːtʃ; lɝtʃ] *n*. (某些牌戏中)大败,惨败;〔喻〕极狼狈的处境,困境。*leave sb*. *in the* ～ 在某人危难时舍弃不顾。

lurch[3] [ləːtʃ; lɝtʃ] **I** *vi*. 〔英方〕(偷偷摸摸地)徘徊,逡巡;偷偷地躲藏在某处,埋伏。— *vt*. 〔古〕欺骗。**II** *n*. 〔古〕潜行,徘徊,逡巡;潜伏,埋伏。

lurch·er [ˈləːtʃə; ˋlɝtʃɚ] *n*. **1**. 〔古〕小偷。**2**. 奸细;间谍。**3**. (偷猎者所用的)杂种猎狗。

lur·dan(e) [ˈləːdn; ˋlɝdn] **I** *n*. 〔古〕懒散无能的人。**II** *a*. 〔古〕懒散无能的。

lure [ljuə; ljur] **I** *n*. **1**. 鹰师系在绳上用以诱回猎鹰的彩色羽毛。**2**. 引诱剂,诱惑品,诱饵。**3**. 诱惑,魅力。**II** *vt*. **1**. 用诱物把(鹰)诱回。**2**. 引诱,诱惑 (*away*; *into*; *on*) ～ *the enemy in deep* 诱敌深入。

Lur·ex [ˈluəreks; ˋlurɛks] *n*. **1**. 一种塑料皮铝线的商标名称。**2**. 〔l-〕塑料皮铝线,铝丝织物。

lu·rid [ˈljuərid; ˋlurɪd] *a*. **1**. 青的,苍白的。**2**. (天空、风景、电光等)可怕的,阴惨的,惊人的。**3**. (夕阳等)血红的,红得像火一样的。**4**. 过分渲染的;(画的颜色等)刺目的,俗气的。*a* ～ *story* [*scene*] 悲惨的故事[景象]。*cast* [*throw*] *a* ～ *light on* 使显得凄惨,说得可怕。**-ly** *ad*. **-ness** *n*.

lurk [ləːk; lɝk] **I** *vi*. **1**. 潜伏,埋伏 (*about*; *in*; *under*). **2**. 潜藏,潜在。**3**. 偷偷地行动,鬼鬼祟祟地活动 (*about*; *along*; *out*). **4**. 【计】(在新闻组中)潜身漫游〔只读而不写〕。～*ing place* 潜伏处,隐藏处。**II** *n*. **1**. 潜伏,潜在,潜行。**2**. 〔英俚〕欺骗,欺诈。*on the* ～ 暗中窥视,偷偷侦察。**-er** *n*. 潜伏者,偷偷侦察的人。**-ingly** *ad*. 偷偷地,暗暗地。

Lu·sa·ka [luːˈsɑːkə; luˋsɑkə] *n*. 卢萨卡(色加)〔赞比亚首都〕。

Lu·sa·tian [luːˈseiʃən; luˋseʃən] *n*., *a*. = Sorbian.

lus·cious [ˈlʌʃəs; ˋlʌʃəs] *a*. **1**. 甘美的,芬芳的。**2**. 过分的香甜的,令人腻味的。**3**. 形容过甚的,俗恶的。**4**. 引起官能欲望的;肉欲的;诱惑性的,色情的。**-ly** *ad*. **-ness** *n*.

lush[1] [lʌʃ; lʌʃ] *a*. **1**. 多汁的;味美的,芬芳的。**2**. 青葱的;草木茂盛的。**3**. 丰富的,豪华的。**4**. 繁荣的,有利的。**5**. 〔口〕(过分)花哨的。**-ly** *ad*. **-ness** *n*.

lush[2] [lʌʃ; lʌʃ] 〔俚〕**I** *n*. **1**. 酒。**2**. 醉汉。**II** *vt*., *vi*. (使)喝醉。～**-roller**, ～**-worker** 〔美俚〕摸醉汉口袋的扒手。**-ed** *a*. 〔俚〕喝醉了的。

lush·er [ˈlʌʃə; ˋlʌʃɚ] *n*. 〔美俚〕醉汉,酒鬼。

LUSI = lunar surface inspection 月球表面考察。

Lu·si·ta·ni·a [ˌluːsiˈteiniə; ˏlusiˋtenɪə] *n*. **1**. 路西塔尼亚〔古罗马的一个省名,为今葡萄牙的大部和西班牙西部地区〕。**2**. "路西塔尼亚号"〔1915 年 5 月 7 日被德国潜艇在爱尔兰附近海域击沉的一艘英国豪华轮〕。

lust [lʌst; lʌst] **I** *n*. **1**. 欲望,贪欲。**2**. 渴望,热烈追求。**3**. 肉欲,色情。**II** *vi*. **1**. 渴望,贪求 (*after*; *for*). **2**. 好色。

lus·ter[1] [ˈlʌstə; ˋlʌstɚ] *n*. 好色的人,荒淫的人。

lus·ter[2] [ˈlʌstə; ˋlʌstɚ] *n*. = lustre[1-2].

lust·ful [ˈlʌstful; ˋlʌstfəl] *a*. **1**. 多欲的;贪心的。**2**. 好色的,淫荡的。**3**. 〔古〕强壮的。**-ly** *ad*. **-ness** *n*.

lust·i·hood [ˈlʌstihud; ˋlʌstɪˏhud] *n*. 〔古〕精力充沛;强壮。

lust·i·ly [ˈlʌstili; ˋlʌstəlɪ] *ad*. 强有力地;活泼地;拼命地,起劲地。

lust·i·ness [ˈlʌstinis; ˋlʌstɪnɪs] *n*. 活泼;精力充沛。

lus·tra [ˈlʌstrə; ˋlʌstrə] lustrum 的复数。

lus·tral [ˈlʌstrəl; ˋlʌstrəl] *a*. **1**. 除邪的;去垢的;净化的。～ *water* 净水。**2**. 〔古〕每五年的;延续五年的。

lus·trate [ˈlʌstreit; ˋlʌstret] *vt*. (*-trat·ed*, *-trat·ing*) 祓除。**-tration** [-ˈtreiʃən; -ˋtreʃən] *n*.

lus·tre[1] [ˈlʌstə; ˋlʌstɚ] *n*. **1**. 光泽;光彩;光辉。**2**. 光荣,荣誉。**3**. 〔主英〕光面呢绒[绸缎]。**4**. 釉,光瓷器皿(= ～ware)。**5**. 分枝烛台,(吊挂式)分枝灯架。*add* ～ *to* 给…增光。*shed* [*throw*] ～ *on* 使…有光辉。～**ware** 光瓷器皿。**-less** *a*. 无光泽的,无光彩的。

lus·tre[2] [ˈlʌstə; ˋlʌstɚ] *n*. = lustrum.

lus·trine [ˈlʌstrin; ˋlʌstrɪn] *n*. 〔英〕(作衣里用的)光亮绸,羽纱;全丝光亮塔夫绸。

lus·tring [ˈlʌstriŋ; ˋlʌstrɪŋ] *n*. 【纺】**1**. 光亮绸,羽纱;加光丝带。**2**. (纱布等的)加光整理过程。

lus·trous [ˈlʌstrəs; ˋlʌstrəs] *a*. **1**. 有光泽的;有光彩的。**2**. 光辉的;灿烂的;显赫的。**-ly** *ad*. **-ness** *n*.

lus·trum [ˈlʌstrəm; ˋlʌstrəm] *n*. (*pl*. ～*s*, *lus·tra* [ˈlʌstrə; ˋlʌstrə]) **1**. (古罗马每五年普查人口后举行的)大祓;(古罗马的)人口普查。**2**. 五年时间。

lust·y [ˈlʌsti; ˋlʌstɪ] *a*. (*lust·i·er*; *-i·est*) **1**. 强壮的;有精神的,活泼的。**2**. 丰盛的,吃得极饱的。

lu·sus na·tu·rae [ˈljuːsəs nəˈtjuəriː; ˋljusəs nəˋtjuri] 〔L.〕大自然的玩笑[恶作剧];自然界中的畸形物;天然畸形,畸形的人[动植物];反常现象。

lut·a·nist [ˈluːtənist; ˋlutnɪst] *n*. 古琵琶演奏者。

lute[1] [ljuːt; ljut] **I** *n*. (14—17 世纪时用的)古琵琶。

L

play the ~ to a cow 对牛弹琴。*a rift within the ~* 不和〔疯癫〕的前兆。**II** *vi.*, *vt.* 演奏古琵琶。

lute[2] [ljuːt; ljut] **I** *n.* **1.** 封泥。**2.** 封闭器。**II** *vt.* 用封泥封闭。

lu·te·al [ˈluːtiəl; ˋlutiəl] *a.*【生化】(属于)黄体的。

lu·te·ci·um [luːˈtiːʃiəm, -siəm; luˋtiʃɪəm, -sɪəm] *n.* = lutetium 的旧名。

lu·te·in [ˈluːtiin; ˋlutɪɪn] *n.*【生化】**1.** 叶黄素。**2.** 黄体制剂。

lu·te·in·ize [ˈluːtiːinaiz; ˋlutɪənˏaɪz] *vt.* (*-iz·ed*, *-iz·ing*)【生化】刺激黄体分离。— *vi.* 使成为黄体部分。*luteinizing hormone* 黄体发生(激)素。**-i·za·tion** *n.*

lu·te·nist [ˈluːtnist; ˋlutənɪst] *n.* lutanist 的异体。

lute·o·lin [ˈluːtiəlin; ˋlutɪolɪn] *n.*【化】藤黄菌素。

lu·te·ous [ˈluːtiəs; ˋlutɪəs] *a.* 深橘黄色的。

lute·string [ˈluːtistriŋ; ˋlutˏstrɪŋ] *n.* = lustring.

Lu·te·tia [luːˈtiːʃə; luˋtiʃə] *n.* 鲁特西亚〔巴黎的古代名称〕。

Lu·te·tian [ljuːˈtiːʃən; ljuˋtiʃən] *a.* 巴黎的。

lu·te·ti·um [luːˈtiːʃiəm; luˋtiʃɪəm] *n.*【化】镥。

Luth. = Lutheran.

Lu·ther [ˈluːθə; ˋluθɚ] *n.* **1.** 卢瑟〔姓氏,男子名〕。**2.** Martin ~ 马丁·路德〔1483—1546,德国宗教改革家〕。

Lu·ther·an [ˈljuːθərən; ˋljuθərən] **I** *a.* 马丁·路德的;路德教(派)的。*the ~ Church* 路德教〔信义会、路德会等的总称〕。**II** *n.* 路德教教徒;马丁·路德的信徒。**-ism** = **Lu·therism** 路德教(教义)。

lu·thern [ˈluːθən; ˋluðɚn] *n.* 老虎天窗,屋顶窗。

lu·thi·er [ˈluːtiə; ˋlutɪr] *n.* 弦乐器工匠。

lut·ing [ˈluːtiŋ; ˋlutɪŋ] *n.* = lute.

lut·ist [ˈluːtist; ˋlutɪst] *n.* **1.** = lutanist. **2.** 古琵琶工匠。

luv·vie, luv·vy [ˈlʌvi; ˋlʌvɪ] *n.* 〔英,口〕亲爱的〔用作称呼〕。

Lu·wi·an [ˈluːiən; ˋluɪən] **I** *n.* 卢威语〔小亚细亚地区的一个语种,已消亡〕。**II** *a.* 卢威语的。(= Luvian).

lux [lʌks; lʌks] *n.* (*pl.* ***luxes*** [ˈlʌksiz; ˋlʌksɪz], ***luces*** [ˈluːsiːz; ˋlusiz])【物】勒克司〔照明单位〕。

Lux. = Luxemburg.

lux·ate [ˈlʌkseit; ˋlʌkset] *vt.*【医】使脱骱;使脱位;使离线。**lux·a·tion** *n.*

luxe [luks, lʌks; lʊks, lʌks] *n.* 〔F.〕上等,华美;奢侈,豪华。*articles de ~* 奢侈品。*édition de ~* 精装本。*train de ~* 特等车。

Lux·em·b(o)urg [ˈluksəmˌbəːg; ˋlʌksəmˏbɝg] *n.* **1.** 卢森堡〔欧洲〕。**2.** 卢森堡〔卢森堡首都〕。

lux·me·ter [ˈlʌksˌmitə; ˋlʌksˏmɪtə] *n.*【物】照度计,勒克司计。

lux·on [ˈlʌksɔn; ˋlʌksɑn] *n.*【物】光子。

lux·u·ri·ance, -an·cy [lʌgˈzjuəriəns, -si; lʌgˋʒʊrɪəns, -sɪ] *n.* **1.** 繁茂,丰富,多产。**2.** 华美,奢华。

lux·u·ri·ant [lʌgˈzjuəriənt; lʌgˋʒʊrɪənt] *a.* **1.** 繁茂的;多产的;丰富的。**2.** 华美的,绚烂的;奢华的。**-ly** *ad.*

lux·u·ri·ate [lʌgˈzjuərieit; lʌgˋʒʊrɪet] *vi.* **1.** 繁茂。**2.** 生活奢华,沉迷(在…)(*in*; *on*);享受。*~ in sunshine* 尽情享受日光。

lux·u·ri·ous [lʌgˈzjuəriəs; lʌgˋʒʊrɪəs] *a.* **1.** 豪华的,奢侈的。**2.** 非常舒适的。**3.** 精美而昂贵的。**4.** 词藻华丽的。*a ~ table* 奢侈的饭菜〔筵席〕。**-ly** *ad.* **-ness** *n.*

lux·u·ry [ˈlʌkʃəri; ˋlʌkʃərɪ] **I** *n.* **1.** 奢侈,豪华。**2.** 奢侈品;美食,美衣。**3.** 乐趣,享受。*the ~ of a good book* 好书的乐趣〔享受〕。*What a ~ it is to be alone!* 单独一人多舒服。***be lapped in ~*** 穷奢极欲。***live in ~*** 生活奢华。**II** *a.* 奢华的,豪华的。*a ~ hotel* 豪华的旅馆。~ **consumption**【农】(作物对土壤中的氮或钾硷的)过度吸收。

Lu·zon [luːˈzɔn; luˋzɑn] *n.* 吕宋(岛)〔菲律宾〕。

LV = **1.** legal volt【电】法定伏特。**2.** low voltage【电】低压。**3.** landing vehicle 登陆车辆。**4.** launch vehicle 活动发射装置;运载火箭。

lv. = leave(s).

LVI = landing vessel, infantry 步兵登陆舰。

Lvov [lvɔf; lvɔf] *n.* 利沃夫〔乌克兰城市〕。

LVT = landing vessel, tank 坦克登陆舰。

LW = **1.** left wing 左翼。**2.** long wave 长波。**3.** low water 低水位;低潮。

Lw = lawrencium【化】铹。

LWM = low water mark 低潮标记。

lx = lux.

-ly[1] *suf.* 加在形容词或分词之后,构成副词,表示"方式","状态","时间","地点","程序","程度","方向","方面"等。bold*ly*, great*ly* smiling*ly*, unexpected*ly*; economical*ly*, scientifical*ly*. ★以 -le 结尾的词,则应略去 -e 后再加 -y: feeb*ly* nob*ly*.

-ly[2] *suf.* 加在名词之后,构成形容词。**1.** 表示"像…的";"有…性质的": king*ly*, man*ly*. scholar*ly*. **2.** 表示"反复发生的","每一特定时期发生一次的","以…为周期的", hour*ly*, dai*ly*, week*ly*, month*ly*, year*ly*.

Ly·all·pur [ˈliːəpur; ˋliəpʊr] *n.* 莱亚尔普尔〔巴基斯坦城市〕。

ly·ard, ly·art [ˈlaiəd, ˈlaiət; ˋlaɪɚd, ˋlaɪɚt] *a.* 〔Scot.〕带灰白色条纹的,灰白色的。

ly·can·thrope [ˈlaikənθrəup, laiˈkænθrəup; ˋlaɪkənˏθrop, laɪˋkænˏθrop] *n.* **1.**【医】变狼狂患者。**2.** = werewolf.

ly·can·thro·py [laiˈkænθrəpi; laɪˋkænθrəpɪ] *n.* **1.** (女巫)化为狼的妖术。**2.**【医】变狼狂〔自以为已变成狼的精神病〕。

ly·cée [ˈliːsei; liˋse] *n.* 〔F.〕(法国公立)高级中学,大学预科。

ly·ce·um [laiˈsi(ː)əm; laɪˋsiəm] *n.* **1.** 学园,学会;〔美〕文艺团体;文化(教育)宫。**2.** 〔L-〕(亚里斯多德讲学的)莱森学园;亚里斯多德派的哲学。**3.** 〔L-〕(伦敦的)莱森戏院。**4.** = *lycée*.

ly·chee [ˈliːtʃiː; ˋlitʃi] *n.* = litchi.

lych-gate [ˈlitʃgeit; ˋlɪtʃˏget] *n.* = lichgate.

lych·nis [ˈliknis; ˋlɪknɪs] *n.*【植】剪秋罗属。

ly·co·pod [ˈlaikəpɔd; ˋlaɪkəpɑd] *n.*【植】**1.** 石松属。**2.** = lycopodium. **3.** = club moss.

ly·co·po·di·um [ˌlaikəˈpəudiəm; ˏlaɪkəˋpodɪəm] *n.* **1.**【植】石松科植物。**2.** 石松粉。

lydd·ite [ˈlidait; ˋlɪdaɪt] *n.* 苦味酸〔立德〕炸药。

Lyd·gate [ˈlidgeit; ˋlɪdget] *n.* 利德盖特〔姓氏〕。

Lyd·i·a [ˈlidiə; ˋlɪdɪə] *n.* **1.** 莉迪亚〔女子名〕。**2.**【史】吕底亚〔小亚细亚一古国〕。

Lyd·i·an [ˈlidiən, -djən; ˋlɪdɪən, -djən] **I** *a.* **1.** 吕底亚的;吕底亚人的;吕底亚语的。**2.** 柔婉的,柔媚的;欢乐的;肉感的。*~ airs* 哀曲,柔婉的音乐,靡靡之音。**II** *n.* 吕底亚人;吕底亚语。*~ stone* 试金石。

lye [lai; laɪ] *n.* 灰汁;硷液。

Ly·ell [ˈlaiəl; ˋlaɪəl] *n.* **1.** 莱尔〔姓氏〕。**2.** **Sir Charles ~** 查尔兹·莱尔〔1797—1875,英国地质学家〕。

ly·gus bug [ˈlaigəs; ˋləɪgəs]【动】盲属昆虫〔其中的很多种危害植物〕。

ly·ing[1] [ˈlaiiŋ; ˋlaɪɪŋ] lie[2]的现在分词。**I** *a.* 说谎的,虚妄的,虚伪的。*a ~ rumour* 谣传,谎言。**II** *n.* 说谎,谎话,虚伪。**-ly** *ad.*

ly·ing[2] [ˈlaiiŋ; ˋlaɪɪŋ] lie[1]的现在分词。**I** *a.* 卧着的,躺着的。**II** *n.* 横卧;横卧处。~ ***down*** 躺倒认输;不作反抗;~***-in-state*** 著名人物的遗体公开陈列告别仪式(*~-in-state hall* 遗体告别礼堂)。~***-in-the-road death*** 交通事故死亡。

ly·ing-in [ˈlaiiŋˈin; ˋlaɪɪŋˋɪn] **I** *n.* 产期;分娩。**II** *a.* 分娩的;产科的;产期的。*a ~ hospital* 产院,产科医院。

L

a ～ *physician* 产科医生。
lyke-wake [ˈlaikweik; ˋlaɪkwek] ***n***. 〔Scot.〕夜间守尸。
Lyle [lail; laɪl] ***n***. 莱尔〔姓氏,男子名〕。
Lyl·y [ˈlili; ˋlɪlɪ] ***n***. 利利〔姓氏〕。
Ly·man [ˈlaimən; ˋlaɪmən] ***n***. 莱曼〔姓氏,男子名〕。
Lym·pa·ny [ˈlimpəni; ˋlɪmpənɪ] ***n***. 林帕尼〔姓氏〕。
lymph [limf; lɪmf] ***n***. **1**. 清泉。**2**.【解】淋巴(液)。**3**.【医】(淋巴液状)浆,苗。*vaccine* ～ 菌苗,疫苗。～ **node**【解】淋巴结[腺]。
lym·phad·e·ni·tis [limˌfædiˈnaitis; lɪmˏfædɪˋnaɪtɪs] ***n***.【医】淋巴腺炎。
lym·phan·gi·al [limˈfændʒiəl; lɪmˋfændʒɪəl] ***a***.【解】淋巴管的。
lym·phan·gio·gram [limˈfændʒiəgræm; lɪmˋfændʒɪəˏgræm] ***n***.【医】= lymphogram.
lym·phan·gi·og·ra·phy [limˌfændʒiˈɔgrəfi; lɪmˋfændʒɪˋɑgrəfɪ] ***n***.【医】= lymphography. **lymphangiographic *a***.
lym·phan·gi·tis [ˌlimfænˈdʒaitis; ˏlɪmfænˋdʒaɪtɪs] ***n***.【医】淋巴管炎。
lym·phat·ic [limˈfætik; lɪmˋfætɪk] **I *a***. **1**.【医】淋巴的,含淋巴的。**2**. 淋巴质的;淋巴腺的;淋巴腺疾病引起的。**3**. 软弱的;苍白的;迟钝的。*a* ～ *gland* 淋巴腺。*a* ～ *vessel* 淋巴管。**II *n***.【解】淋巴腺,淋巴管;黏液质〔旧时生理学所说人四种气质之一〕。**-i·cal·ly *ad***.
lym·pho·blast [ˈlimfəblæst; ˋlɪmfəˏblæst] ***n***.【医】成淋巴细胞,淋巴母细胞。
lym·pho·cyte [ˈlimfəsait; ˋlɪmfəˏsaɪt] ***n***.【医】淋巴细胞,淋巴球。**lym·pho·cyt·ic** [-ˈsitik; -ˋsɪtɪk] ***a***.
lym·pho·cy·to·sis [ˌlimfəsaiˈtəusis; ˏlɪmfosaɪˋtosɪs] ***n***.【医】淋巴球增多。**lym·pho·cy·tot·ic** [-ˈtɔtik; -ˋtɑtɪk] ***a***.
lym·pho·gram [ˈlimfəˌgræm; ˋlɪmfəˏgræm] ***n***.【医】淋巴系造影照片。
lym·pho·gran·u·lo·ma [ˌlimfəˌgrænjuˈləumə; ˏlɪmfəˏgrænjʊˋlomə] ***n***. (*pl*. ***-mas***, ***-ma·ta*** [-mətə; -mətə]【医】淋巴肉芽肿。**-tous *a***.
lym·phog·ra·phy [limˈfɔgrəfi; lɪmˋfɑgrəfɪ] ***n***.【医】淋巴系造影术。**-pho·graph·ic *a***.
lymph·oid [ˈlimfɔid; ˋlɪmfɔɪd] ***a***. 淋巴(腺)样的;淋巴腺组织(样)的。
lym·pho·ma [limˈfəumə; lɪmˋfomə] ***n***. (*pl*. ～***s***, ***-ta***)【医】淋巴(组织)瘤。
lym·pho·poi·e·sis [ˌlimfəupɔiˈiːsis; ˏlɪmfopɔɪˋisɪs] ***n***.【医】淋巴细胞增殖。
lym·pho·sar·co·ma [ˌlimfəusɑːˈkəumə; ˏlɪmfosɑrˋkomə] ***n***.【医】淋巴肉瘤。**-lous *a***.
lym·phous [ˈlimfəs; ˋlɪmfəs] ***a***. 淋巴的,淋巴性的,含淋巴的。
lyn·ce·an [linˈsi(ː)ən; lɪnˋsiən] ***a***. **1**. 山猫(似)的;猞猁狲似的。**2**. 山猫眼似的,眼光锐利的。
Lynch [lintʃ; lɪntʃ] ***n***. 林奇〔姓氏〕。
lynch [lintʃ; lɪntʃ] **I *n***. 私刑。**II *vt***. 私刑处死;〔古〕私刑拷打。～ **law *n***. 私刑〔非法杀害〕。**-er *n***. 施私刑者。**-ing** 私刑。
lynch·pin [ˈlintʃpin; ˋlɪntʃpɪn] ***n***. = linchpin.
Lynd [lind; lɪnd] ***n***. 林德〔姓氏〕。
Lynn [lin; lɪn] ***n***. 林恩〔姓氏,男子名,女子名〕。
lynx [liŋks; lɪŋks] ***n***. (*pl*. ～***es***,〔集合词〕～) **1**.【动】猞猁狲,山猫。**2**. 猞猁狲皮,山猫皮。**3**.〔L-〕【天】天猫座。～**-eyed *a***. 眼光锐利的。
Ly·on [ˈlaiən; ˋlaɪən] ***n***. 苏格兰司章的长官〔又叫 ～ King of Arms〕.
ly·on·naise [ˌlaiəˈneiz; ˏlaɪəˋnez] ***a***.【烹】加洋葱(丝)的。
Ly·on(s) [ˈlaiən(z); ˋlaɪən(z)] ***n***. 莱昂(斯)〔姓氏〕。
Ly·ons [ˈlaiənz; ˋlaɪənz] ***n***. 里昂〔法国城市〕。
ly·o·phil·ic [ˌlaiəˈfilik; laɪəˋfɪlɪk] ***a***.【化】亲液的(= lyophile).
ly·oph·i·lize [laiˈɔfilaiz; laɪˋɑfɪˏlaɪz] ***vt***. (***-liz·ed***, ***-liz·ing***) 冻干〔尤指生物产品〕。**-r** 冻干机。**-i·li·zation *n***.
ly·o·pho·bic [ˌlaiəˈfəubik; ˏlaɪəˋfobɪk] ***a***.【化】疏液的。
Ly·ra [ˈlaiərə; ˋlaɪrə] ***n***.【天】天琴座。
ly·rate [ˈlaiərit; ˋlaɪret] ***a***. 竖琴状的。
lyre [ˈlaiə; laɪr] ***n***. **1**. 古希腊七弦竖琴。**2**.〔the ～〕抒情诗。**3**.〔L-〕【天】= Lyra. **4**. (乐队用的)乐谱架。～ **bird**【动】琴鸟。
lyr·ic [ˈlirik; ˋlɪrɪk] **I *n***. **1**. 抒情诗;抒情作品。**2**.〔*pl*.〕民歌中的词句。**II *a***. **1**. 希腊竖琴的。**2**. 可用希腊竖琴伴奏的。**3**. 抒情的,抒情诗的。**4**. 感情用事的;感情冲动的。*a* ～ *poet* 抒情诗人。～ *poetry* 抒情诗。*the* ～ *drama* 歌剧。*explode with* ～ *wrath* 勃然大怒。
lyr·i·cal [ˈlirikəl; ˋlɪrɪkl̩] ***a***. = lyric (***a***.). *become* ～ 感情冲动起来。**-ly *ad***. **-ness *n***.
lyr·i·cism [ˈlirisizəm; ˋlɪrəsɪzm̩] ***n***. **1**. 抒情诗性质,抒情性;抒情诗体;抒情语句。**2**. 感情冲动;情绪高涨[激昂]。
lyr·i·cist [ˈlirisist; ˋlɪrɪsɪst] ***n***. 抒情诗人。
ly·ri·form [ˈlaiərifɔːm; ˋlaɪrəfɔrm] ***a***. 竖琴状的。
lyr·ism [ˈlaiərizəm; ˋlaɪrɪzəm] ***n***. **1**. 弹奏竖琴。**2**. [ˈliərizəm; ˋlɪrɪzəm] = lyricism.
lyr·ist [ˈlaiərist, ˈlirist; ˋlaɪrɪst, ˋlɪrɪst] ***n***. **1**. 竖琴演奏者。**2**. [ˈlirist; ˋlɪrɪst] 抒情诗人。
lyse [lais; laɪs] ***vt***., ***vi***. (***lysed***, ***lys·ing***)【生化,医】细胞溶解;病状渐退。
Ly·sen·ko·ism [laiˈseŋkəuizəm; laɪˋseŋkoɪzəm] ***n***. 李森科学派[学说]。
ly·ser·gic acid [laiˈsəːdʒik æsid; laɪˋsɝdʒɪk æsɪd]【化】麦角酸。
ly·sim·e·ter [laiˈsimitə; laɪˋsɪmətɚ] ***n***.【化】渗水计,溶度(估定)计。**-met·ric *a***.
ly·sin [ˈlaisn; ˋlaɪsɪn] ***n***.【生化】细胞溶素。
ly·sine [ˈlaisiːn; ˋlaɪsin] ***n***.【生化】赖胺酸。
ly·sis [ˈlaisis; ˋlaɪsɪs] ***n***. (*pl*. ***ly·ses*** [ˈlaisiːz; ˋlaɪsiz]) **1**.【生化】细胞[细菌]溶解。**2**.【医】(病的)渐退,消散;松解术。
ly·so·cline [ˈlaisəklain; ˏlaɪsəˋklaɪn] ***n***.【海】(海水中的)分解水层。
ly·so·gen·e·sis [ˌlaisəˈdʒenisis; ˏlaɪsəˋdʒɛnɪsɪs] ***n***.【微】溶源性,溶菌作用的产生。
ly·sol [ˈlaisɔl; ˋlaɪsɑl] ***n***.【药】(消毒防腐剂)来沙尔;【化】煤酚皂溶液,杂酚皂液。
ly·so·some [ˈlaisəsəum; ˋlaɪsəˏsom] ***n***.【生】溶(酶)体。**-somal *a***.
ly·so·staph·in [ˌlaisəˈstæfən; ˏlaɪsəˋstæfən] ***n***.【生化】溶葡萄球菌酶。
ly·so·zyme [ˈlaisəzaim; ˋlaɪsəˏzaɪm] ***n***.【生化】溶菌酶。
lyt·ic [ˈlitik; ˋlɪtɪk] ***a***. **1**. (细胞)溶素的。**2**. 溶解的;促使溶解的。**3**.【医】松解的,渐退的。
lyt·ta [ˈlitə; ˋlɪtə] ***n***. (*pl*. ***-tae*** [-tiː; -ti]) (犬等舌下的)纵行蠕虫状纽带。
Lyt·ton [ˈlitn; ˋlɪtn̩] ***n***. **1**. 利顿〔姓氏〕。**2**. **Edward George Earle ～ Bulwer-, 1st Baron Lytton** 第一代利顿男爵〔1803—1873,英国小说家,剧作家,政治家,著有小说《庞培城的末日》等〕。**3**. **Edward Robert Bulwer-Lytton, 1st Earle Lytton** 第一代利顿伯爵〔1831—1891,英国政治家,诗人,笔名为 Owen Meredith, 系第一代利顿男爵之子〕。

M

M, m [em; ɛm] (*pl*. ***M's, m's*** [emz; ɛmz]) **1.** 英语字母表第十三字母。**2.** M 形状的东西;【印】= em. **3.** M (罗马数字) 1,000. MCML = 1950. $\bar{M}$ = 1,000,000.

M., m. = **1.** majesty. **2.** male. **3.** mark(s). **4.** married. **5.** masculine. **6.** medicine. **7.** medium. **8.** 〔L.〕 *meridies* (= noon); *A. M.* [*a. m.*] 午前,上午。**9.** metre(s). **10.** middle. **11.** mile(s). **12.** minim. **13.** minute(s). **14.** month. **15.** morning. **16.** mountain. **17.** modulus. **18.**【物】mass. **19.** Marshal. **20.** Master. **21.** Medieval. **22.** Monday. **23.** 〔F.〕 *Monsieur*. **24.** mega-. **25.** mole. **26.** Marquis. **27.** motor. **28.** meridian. **29.** muscle.

M' = Mac, Mc 马克,米克,麦克〔苏格兰人和爱尔兰人姓氏附有 Mac 的略称,如 M'Donald 麦克唐纳〕。

M.A., MA = **1.** Master of Arts 文科硕士。**2.** military academy 陆军军官学校;军事学院。

Ma = **1.** Minnesota. **2.**【化】元素钨 (masurium)的符号。

ma [mɑː; mɑ] ***n***. 〔儿口〕妈〔mamma 之略〕。~ ***and pa*** 〔美〕夫妻店,家庭经营的小店铺。

ma'am ***n***. 〔madam 的缩写〕 **1.** [mæm, mɑːm; mæm, mɑm] 〔英〕夫人;女士〔对王族贵夫人的尊称〕。**2.** [məm, m; məm, m] 〔口〕太太;小姐〔女仆等对主妇的称呼〕 ★现在仅用于句中或句尾。~ **school** 乡村或小镇女教师办的小学校(= dame school)。

Maas [mɑːz; mɑz] ***n***. 马斯〔姓氏〕。

Maas·tricht [ˈmɑːstrihəːt; ˋmɑstrɪhɝt] ***n***. 马斯特里赫特〔荷兰一城市〕。~ **Treaty** 马(斯特里赫特条)约〔1992 年欧盟于此地签订的旨在实现欧洲一体化的条约〕。

Maat [məˈɑːt; məˋɑt] ***n***.【埃神】真理正义之神。

Mab [mæb; mæb] ***n***. 梅布〔女子名〕。

Ma·bel [ˈmeibəl; ˋmebl] ***n***. 梅布尔〔女子名〕。

Mac [mæk; mæk] ***n***. **1.** 麦克〔男子名, *cf*. Mac-〕。**2.** 〔俚〕(称呼用)老兄,老弟,伙计。

mac [mæk; mæk] ***n***. 〔口〕= mackintosh.

Mac- *pref*. 〔后接苏格兰或爱尔兰人名〕= son of 〔略 Mc, Mᶜ, M'; 相当于 Welsh 的 Ap-, Irish 的 O', English 的 -son, -s, Norman 的 Fitz-〕: *Mac*donald, *Mac*Donald; *Mᶜ*Donald; *M'*Donald.

ma·ca·bre, ma·ca·ber [məˈkɑːbr, -bə; məˋkabɚ, -brə] ***a***. 以死亡为主题的;可怕的,阴惨的。***dance*** ~ 死的舞蹈 (= dance of death)。

ma·ca·co [məˈkeikəu; məˋkeko] ***n***. (*pl*. ~***s***)【动】狐猴。

mac·ad·am [məˈkædəm; məˋkædəm] ***n***. **1.** 碎石(路);碎石路面。**2.** 〔M-〕麦克亚当〔姓氏〕。

mac·a·dam·i·a nut [ˌmækəˈdeimiə; ˏmækəˋdemɪə] 【植】澳洲坚果。

mac·ad·am·ize [məˈkædəmaiz; məˋkædəmˏaɪz] ***vt***. 筑(碎石路);用碎石铺(路)。**-zation** [məˌkædəmaiˈzeiʃən; məˏkædəmaɪˋzeʃən] ***n***. 碎石铺路法。

Ma·cao [məˈkau; məˋkaʊ] ***n***. 澳门〔中国东南一海岛〕。

ma·caque [məˈkɑːk; məˋkɑk] ***n***.【动】猕猴;短尾猴。

mac·a·ro·ni [ˌmækəˈrəuni; ˏmækəˋronɪ] ***n***. (*pl*. ~***s***, ~***es***) **1.** 意大利通心面条,通心粉。**2.** (18 世纪伦敦装模作样学欧洲大陆派头的)时髦男子;(泛指)花花公子。~ **cheese** 干酪烤通心面条。~ **wheat** 硬质小麦(= durum wheat)。

mac·a·ron·ic [ˌmækəˈrɔnik; ˏmækəˋrɑnɪk] **I** ***a***. 混淆的;(混合现代语和拉丁语尾的)混合体的。**II** ***n***. 〔*pl*.〕两种语言混合写成的诗文。

mac·a·room [ˌmækəˈruːn; ˏmækəˋrun] ***n***. 蛋白杏仁小甜饼(干)。

Mac·Ar·thur [məˈkɑːθə, mkˈɑːθə; məkˋɑrθɚ, mkˋɑrθɚ] ***n***. 麦克阿瑟〔姓氏〕。

ma·cas·sar [məˈkæsə; məˋkæsɚ] ***n***. 望加锡油〔一种植物性发油,又叫 ~ oil〕。

Ma·cau·lay [məˈkɔːli; məˋkɔlɪ] ***n***. **1.** 麦考利〔姓氏〕。**2.** **Thomas Babington** ~ 汤马斯·巴宾顿·麦考莱〔1800—1859,英国历史学家、作家、政治家〕。

ma·caw[1] [məˈkɔː; məˋkɔ] ***n***.【鸟】金刚鹦鹉,鹁鹦。

ma·caw[2] [məˈkɔː; məˋkɔ] ***n***.【植】美国棕榈 (= macaw palm, macaw tree)。

Mac·beth [məkˈbeθ; məkˋbɛθ] ***n***. 麦克佩斯〔莎士比亚所作悲剧之一的主人翁〕。

Macc. = **Mac·ca·bees** [ˈmækəbiːz; ˋmækəˏbiz] ***n***. 马卡比父子〔曾拯救叙利亚犹太人脱离希腊王暴政 (175—164 B.C.)的犹太人〕;马卡比家族。

Mac·ca·be·an [ˌmækəˈbiːən; ˏmækəˋbiən] ***a***. 马卡比父子[家族]的。

mac·ca·boy, mac·ca·baw [ˈmækəbɔi, -bɔː; ˋmækəˏbɔɪ, -bɔ] ***n***. 马可巴鼻烟。

Mac·Cra·cken [məˈkrækən; məˋkrækən] ***n***. 麦克拉肯〔姓氏〕。

Mac·Don·ald [məkˈdɔnəld; məkˋdɑnəld] ***n***. 麦克唐纳〔姓氏〕。

Mac·Don·nell [ˌmækdəˈnel; ˏmækdəˋnɛl] ***n***. 麦克唐奈〔姓氏〕。

Mac·Dow·ell [məkˈdauəl; məkˋdaʊəl] ***n***. 麦克道尔〔姓氏〕。

mace[1] [meis; mes] ***n***. **1.** 钉头槌〔中古武器〕。**2.** (作为市长、大学校长等职权表征的)权标,权杖;〔the M-〕(英国下院议长的)职杖;执权标者 (= macebearer)。**3.**【撞球】(从前用来击 bagatelle 球的)平头杆。~**bearer** 执权杖者。

mace[2] [meis; mes] ***n***. 豆蔻香料〔肉豆蔻种子的干皮〕;肉豆蔻(树)。

Mace [meis; mes] **I** ***n***. 梅斯毒气〔一种暂时伤害性压缩液态毒气〕。**II** ***vt***. 用梅斯毒气向…攻击。

Maced. = Macedonia(n).

mac·é·doine [ˌmæseˈdwɑːn; ˏmæseˋdwɑn] ***n***. 〔F.〕 **1.** 拌蔬菜;拌水果沙拉;蔬菜水果混合开胃菜。**2.** 混杂物。

Mac·e·do·nia [ˌmæsiˈdəunjə; ˏmæsəˋdonɪə] ***n***. **1.** 马其顿〔巴尔干半岛中部一国〕。**2.** (巴尔干半岛中南部的)马其顿地区。**-do·ni·an** [ˌmæsiˈdəunjən, -niən; ˏmæsəˋdonjən, -niən] ***a***., ***n***. 马其顿的;马其顿人[语]〔略 Maced.〕。

Mac·e·don·ic [ˌmæsiˈdɔnik, ˏmæsəˋdɑnɪk] ***a***. = Macedonian.

mac·er [ˈmeisə; ˋmesɚ] ***n***. **1.** 执权杖者(= macebearer). 2. 〔Scot.〕法院官吏。

mac·er·ate [ˈmæsəreit; ˋmæsəˏret] *vt*. 1. 使浸软,浸渍,浸解。2. 使瘦,使饿瘦,折磨,虐待。— *vi*. 浸软,饿瘦。

mac·er·a·ter, mac·er·a·tor [ˈmæsəreitə; ˋmæsəˏretɚ] *n*. 1. 浸渍者;浸解者。2. 纸浆制造机。

mac·er·a·tion [ˌmæsəˈreiʃən; ˏmæsəˋreʃən] *n*. 1. 绝食饿瘦。2.【化】浸软;浸渍(作用);离析,浸解。

Mach [mɑːk, G. mak; mɑk, mək] *n*.【物】马赫〔超高速单位,马赫数,= ~ number〕。~**meter** 马赫计。~ **wave** (原子弹爆炸时的)冲击波,马赫波。

mach. = machine; machinery; machinist.

mache [ˈmɑːʃei; ˋmɑʃe] *n*.【化】马谢〔空气或液体中所含氡的浓度单位〕。

ma·che·te [mɑːˈtʃeiti; mɑˋtʃetɪ] *n*. 1. (中、南美人用的)大砍刀。2. 葡萄牙四弦小吉他琴。

Mach·i·a·vel [ˌmækiəˈvel; ˏmækɪəˋvɛl] *n*. = Machiavellian.

Mach·i·a·vel·li [ˌmækiəˈveli; ˏmækɪəˋvɛlɪ] *n*. 尼科洛·马基雅维里〔1469—1527,意大利政治家及历史学家,主张为达目的利用权术,不择手段〕。

Mach·i·a·vel(l)ian [ˌmækiəˈveliən; ˏmækɪəˋvɛlɪən] **I** *a*. 马基雅维里式的;阴谋的;不择手段的。**II** *n*. 马基雅维里式的政治人物,不择手段的阴谋家。**-vel·lism** *n*. 马基雅维里主义;阴谋诡计。**-vel·list** *n*.

ma·chic·o·late [mæˈtʃikəuleit; məˋtʃɪkoˏlet] *vt*. 在…上开堞眼[枪眼]。**-d** *a*. 有堞眼的,有枪眼的。**-la·tion** *n*. [mæˌtʃikəˈleiʃən; məˏtʃɪkəˋleʃən]

ma·chi·co·lis [ˌmɑːʃiˈkuːli; ˏmɑʃɪˋkulɪ] *n*.【军】突堞;凸堞枪眼[堞眼]。

machin. = machinery.

ma·chin·a·ble [məˈʃiːnəbl; məˋʃinəbl] *a*. 可用机器制造[加工]的。**-a·bil·i·ty** [məˌʃiːnəˈbiliti; məˏʃinəˋbɪlətɪ] *n*. (可)切削性;机制性。

mach·i·nate [ˈmækineit; ˋmækəˏnet] *vt*., *vi*. 策划,阴谋。**-na·tion** [ˌmækiˈneiʃən; ˏmækəˋneʃən] *n*. 策划,阴谋,诡计。**-na·tor** *n*. 阴谋家。

ma·chine [məˈʃiːn; məˋʃin] **I** *n*. 1. 机(器),机械;机关,机构。2. 印刷机器;缝纫机;打字机;汽车;自行车;三轮车;飞机;〔美俚〕救火机。3. 机械地工作的人[机构],机械似的人。4. 〔美〕(政党的)领导机关[核心小集团];干部,党员。5.【美海】轮机中士。6. (诗、小说或剧本中所安排的)超自然的力量[人物]。*a mowing* ~割草机。*a reaping* ~收割机。~ *cotton* 机制线,轴线。~ *oil* 机油[机器润滑油]。~ *printing* 机器印染。**II** *vt*. 用机器制造;用电动机器缝纫[印刷];用机械加工。~ **bolt** 机制螺栓。~**-building** 机器制造(工业)。~ **carbine** 冲锋枪,卡宾枪。~ **gun** 机关枪。~**-gun** *vt*. 用机(关)枪扫射。~**-hour** 一台机器在一小时内的工作量。~ **intelligence** 机器智能,人工智能 (= artificial intelligence)。~ **language**【自】机器语言,计算机语言。~**-made** *a*. 机制的(*opp*. hand-made)。~**-man** 机器工人;(特指)印刷工人。~ **pistol** 自动手枪。~**-readable** *a*. 可直接为计算机使用的。~ **rifle** 自动步枪。~ **screw** 机(器)螺钉。~**-sewed** *a*. 机器缝的。~ **shop** 〔美〕金工车间;机械工厂。~**-smashing** *n*. 捣毁机器。~ **time** 1. = ~-hour. 2. 计算机时间〔完成一个运算项目时间〕。~ **tool** 机床,工作母机。~**-tooled** *a*. 经机床加工而成的;全靠机器的。~ **translation** 机器翻译〔由计算机将一种语言译成另一种语言〕。~**-wool** 再生毛。~ **work** 机械工作;(用以增强文学作品戏剧效果的)布局,设计。

ma·chin·er·y [məˈʃiːnəri; məˋʃinərɪ] *n*. 1. 〔集合词〕机器,机械;机件;(机器的)运转部分。2. (政府等的)机关,组织,机构。3. (小说、戏剧等的)情节,设计〔特指为增强效果而安排的超自然的人物或事件〕。4. 工具,手段,方法。*state* ~国家机器。

ma·chin·ist [məˈʃiːnist; məˋʃinɪst] *n*. 机械师;机工;钳床;[机床]技工〔尤指缝纫车工〕;〔美〕(政党的)干部。~**'s mate**【美海军】轮机军士长。

ma·chis·mo [mɑːˈtʃiːzməu; mɑˋtʃizmo] *n*. 〔Sp.〕男子(雄武)气概。

ma·cho [ˈmɑːtʃəu; ˋmɑtʃo] **I** *n*. 〔Sp.〕(*pl*. ***-chos*** [-tʃəus;-tʃos]) 健壮男子。**II** *a*. 雄壮的;雄武的;有胆量的。

ma·chree [məˈkriː, məˈhriː; məˋkri, məˋhri] *n*. 心肝,宝贝儿〔英-爱尔兰亲昵语〕。*mother* ~我的好妈妈。

Ma·chu Pic·chu [ˈmɑːtʃuːˈpiːktʃuː; ˋmɑtʃuˋpiktʃu] 玛丘匹克丘〔秘鲁中南部古印坎城遗迹〕(= Machupicchu)。

mac·in·tosh [ˈmækintɔʃ; ˋmækɪnˏtɑʃ] *n*. = mackintosh.

Mac(k) [mæk; mæk] *n*. 麦克〔男子名〕。

Mac·kay(e) [məˈkai; məˋkaɪ] *n*. 麦凯〔姓氏〕。

mack·er·el [ˈmækrəl; ˋmækərəl] *n*. (*pl*. ~*s*, 〔集合词〕~)【鱼】鲐鱼〔又叫鲭鱼〕;马鲛鱼。~ **gale** [**breeze**] 鲭风〔适于捕鲭的较强的风〕。~ **sky** 鱼鳞天〔有卷积云的天空〕。

mack·i·naw [ˈmækinɔː; ˋmækəˏnɔ] *n*. 〔美〕(双排钮方格纹)厚呢短大衣。**M- blanket** (美国西部人用的)方格厚毛毯。**M- boat** (美国大湖中的)平底船。**M- coat** = mackinaw。

Mack·in·tosh [ˈmækintɔʃ; ˋmækɪnˏtɑʃ] *n*. 1. 麦金托什〔姓氏〕。2. 〔m-〕防水胶布;胶布雨衣。

mack·le [ˈmækl; ˋmækl] **I** *n*.【印】1. 墨污;污点;污斑。2. 模糊印张。**II** *vt*., *vi*.【印】印刷模糊;重叠印刷;使模糊。

Ma·claren [məˈklærən; məˋklærən] *n*. 麦克拉伦〔姓氏〕。

ma·cle [ˈmækl, ˋmækl̩] *n*. (钻石的)双晶;短空晶石;(矿物的)黑斑。

Ma·clean(e) [məˈklein; məˋklen] *n*. 麦克莱恩〔姓氏〕。

Mac·Leish [məkˈliːʃ; məkˋliʃ] *n*. 麦克利什〔姓氏〕。

Mac·Leod [məˈklaud; məˋklaud] *n*. 1. 麦克劳德〔姓氏〕。2. **John James Richard** ~ 约翰·詹姆斯·理查德·麦克劳德〔1876—1935,苏格兰生理学家,获 1923 年诺贝尔医药奖〕。

Mac·Mil·lan, Mac·mil·lan [məkˈmilən; məkˋmɪlən] *n*. 麦克米伦〔姓氏〕。

ma·con·o·chie [məˈkɔnəki; məˋkɑnəkɪ] *n*. 军用罐头烩菜肉;罐头食品。

Mac·Pher·son [məkˈfəːsn; məkˋfɝsn̩] *n*. 麦克弗森〔姓氏〕。

macr- *comb*. *f*. (后接元音) = macro-.

mac·ra·mé [məˈkrɑːmi; ˋmækrəˏme] *n*. (家具装饰用的)流苏,结节,花边(= ~ lace)。

Mac·rea·dy [məˈkriːdi; məˋkridɪ] *n*. 麦克里迪〔姓氏〕。

mac·ro [ˈmækrəu; ˋmækro] **I** *a*. 1. 巨大的;极厚的;特别突出的。2. 大量使用的。**II** *n*.【自】宏指令〔macroinstruction 的缩写〕。

macro- *comb*. *f*. 大,巨,宏,长,粗 (*opp*. micro-): *macro*engineering 宏观工程(学)。

ma·cro·bi·an [məkˈrəubiən; mækˋrobɪən] **I** *a*. 长命的,长寿的。**II** *n*. 长寿者〔尤指百岁以上的〕。

mac·ro·bi·o·sis [ˌmækrəubaiˈəusis; ˏmækrəbaɪˋosɪs] *n*. 长命,长寿。

mac·ro·bi·ot·ic [ˌmækrəubaiˈɔtik; ˏmækrəbaɪˋɑtɪk] *a*. 能促进长寿的;长命的,长寿的。

mac·ro·bi·ot·ics [ˌmækrəubaiˈɔtiks; ˏmækrəbaɪˋɑtɪks] *n*. 〔作单数用〕长寿术〔以特殊饮食延年益寿术〕。

mac·ro·brew [ˈmækrəbruː; ˋmækrobru] *n*. 宏酿啤酒〔大批量生产的啤酒〕。

mac·ro·ceph·a·lous, mac·ro·ce·phal·ic [ˌmækrəuˈsefələs, -siˈfælik; ˏmækroˋsɛfələs, -sɪˋfælɪk] *a*.【医】大头的,长头的。

mac·ro·ceph·a·ly [ˌmækrəuˈsefəli; ˏmækroˋsɛfəlɪ] *n*.

【医】巨颅,巨头(*opp*. microcephaly)。

mac·ro·chem·is·try [ˌmækrəuˈkemistri; ˏmækro-ˋkemɪstrɪ] *n*. (不用显微镜、不作微量分析的)常量化学。

mac·ro·cli·mate [ˈmækrəuˌklaimət; ˋmækroˏklaɪmɪt] *n*.【气】大气候。**-matic** [-klaiˈmætik; -klaɪˋmætɪk] *a*.

mac·ro·cosm [ˈmækrəkɔzəm; ˋmækrəˏkɑzəm] *n*. **1.**【物】(大)宇宙,宏观世界 (*opp*. microcosm)。**2.** 全域,(大的)整体。**-ic** *a*.

mac·ro·cosmos [ˈmækrəkɔzəm; ˋmækrəˏkɑzmɑs] *n*. = macrocosm.

mac·ro·cyst [ˈmækrəsist; ˋmækrəsɪst] *n*.【医】大囊肿。

mac·ro·cyte [ˈmækrəsait; ˋmækrəˏsaɪt] *n*.【医】(恶性贫血的)大红细胞;巨红血球。**-cyt·ic** [-ˌsitik; -ˋsɪtɪk] *a*.

mac·ro·dont [ˈmækrədɔnt; ˋmækrəˏdɑnt] *a*.【医】巨牙的。

mac·ro·eco·nom·ics [ˌmækrəuˌiːkəˈnɔmiks; ˏmækro-ˏikəˋnɑmɪks] *n*. [用作 *sing*.] 大[宏观]经济学[研究经济体系中起作用的各种因素或经济部门之间的相互关系]。

mac·ro·ev·o·lu·tion [ˌmækrəuˌevəˈluːʃən; ˏmækro-ˏɛvəˋluʃən] *n*.【动】大幅演化,种外演化[指涉及新品种、新生物的出现的大规模和长时间的演化]。

ma·cro·ga·mete [ˌmækrəuˈgæmiːt, -gəˈmiːt; ˏmækro-ˋgæmit, -gəˋmit] *n*.【医】大配子。

mac·ro·graph [ˈmækrəgrɑːf, -græf; ˋmækrəˏgrɑf, -græf] *n*.【物】(实物大小或大于实物的)宏观图(*opp*. micrograph); 肉眼图。

ma·crog·ra·phy [məˈkrɔgrəfi; məˋkrɑgrəfɪ] *n*. 肉眼检查;【医】写字过大症。

mac·ro·in·struc·tion [ˌmækrəuinˈstrʌkʃən; ˏmæk-roɪnˋstrʌkʃən] *n*.【自】宏指令。

mac·ro·lev·el [ˈmækrəˌlevl; ˋmækrəˏlɛvḷ] *a*. 宏观(水平)的。

mac·ro·mere [ˈmækrəmiə; ˋmækrəmɪr] *n*.【医】(细胞分裂的)大(分)裂球。

ma·crom·e·ter [məˈkrɔmitə; məˋkrɑmɪtɚ] *n*. 测远器。

mac·ro·mol·e·cule [ˌmækrəuˈmɔlikjuːl; ˏmækro-ˋmɑləˏkjul] *n*.【化】巨分子,高分子(= macromole)。**-lar** *a*.

ma·cron [ˈmækrɔn; ˋmækrɑn] *n*. 长音符(-)[例:ā, ī, ū]。

mac·ro·nu·cle·us [ˌmækrəuˈnuːkliəs; ˏmækro-ˋnuklɪəs] *n*.【生】(原生动物细胞的)巨核,大核。**-cle·ar** *a*.

mac·ro·nu·tri·ent [ˌmækrəuˈnjuːtriənt; mækro-ˋnjutrɪənt] *n*. (植物所需的)大量化学养料[如碳]。

mac·ro·phage [ˈmækrəfeidʒ; ˋmækrəfedʒ] *n*.【生】巨噬细胞。

mac·ro·phys·ics [ˌmækrəuˈfiziks; ˏmækrəˋfɪzɪks] *n*. 宏观物理学[研究可直接地、单独地观察和测量的物体的物理学]。

mac·rop·ter·ous [mæˈkrɔptərəs; mæˋkrɑptərəs] *a*.【动】有大翅的;有大鳍的。

mac·ro·scop·ic, -i·cal [ˌmækrəuˈskɔpik, -ikəl; ˏmækrəˋskɑpɪk, -ɪkəl] *a*.【物】肉眼可见的;宏观的,粗视的,粗显的。

mac·ro·spo·ran·gi·um [ˌmækrəuspəˈrændʒiəm; ˏmækrəspəˋrændʒɪəm] *n*. (*pl*. **-gi·a** [-ə; -ə])【生】大孢子囊 (= megasporangium)。

mac·ro·spore [ˈmækrəspɔː; ˋmækrəˏspor] *n*.【植】大孢子。

mac·ro·struc·ture [ˌmækrəuˈstrʌktʃə; ˏmækro-ˋstrʌktʃɚ] *n*.【物】宏观结构。

mac·ro·vi·rus [ˌmækrəuˈvaiərəs; ˏmækroˋvaɪrəs] *n*.【计】宏病毒。

ma·cru·ran [məˈkruərən; məˋkrurən] *n*.【动】十足甲壳类[包括虾、蟹]。**-cru·rous, -cru·ral, -cru·roid** *a*.

mac·u·la [ˈmækjulə; ˋmækjulə] *n*. (*pl*. **-lae** [-liː; -li]) (太阳的)黑点;(矿石的)斑点,瑕疵;(皮肤上的)痣,(色)斑。

mac·u·lar [ˈmækjulə; ˋmækjulɚ] *a*. 有斑点的;有污点的。

mac·u·late [ˈmækjuleit; ˋmækjʊˏlet] **I** *vt*. 弄脏,玷污。**II** [-lit; -lɪt] *a*. = macular.

mac·u·la·tion [ˌmækjuˈleiʃən; ˏmækjuˋleʃən] *n*. 斑点,污点;【生】斑纹;玷污。

mac·ule [ˈmækjuːl; ˋmækjul] *n*. 点,斑;疱;(尤指)痣;太阳的黑点(= macula)。

mac·u·lu·te·a [mækˈluːtiə; mækˋlutɪə] *n*.【解】黄斑。

ma·cum·ba [məˈkumbə; məˋkumbə] *n*. 马康巴教[伏都教与基督教的某些教义相结合的巴西的一种宗教]。

Mad., Madm. = Madam.

MAD [读作 mæd; mæd] = mutual assured destruction【军】相互确保摧毁[指每一方在遭受对方核攻击时都有反击对方而造成两败俱伤的能力]。

mad [mæd; mæd] **I** *a*. (~**der**; ~**dest**) **1.** 狂,发狂的,疯狂的;(狗等)患狂犬病的。**2.** 凶猛的,狂暴的;鲁莽的,糊涂的。**3.** 狂热的,入迷的。**4.** [口]愤怒的,生气的(*at*; *about*)。**5.** 非常高兴的,极快活的。*He was very* ~. [美]他非常生气。*a* ~ *torrent* 激流。**be** ~ **about** [**after**; **for**; **on**] 急切地想,发狂似地想;迷于,迷着…。**be** ~ **at** 对…发怒 (*I was rather* ~ *at missing my train*. 我没赶上火车,气极了)。**be** ~ **with joy** 狂喜。**drive** [**send**] **sb**. ~使(人)发狂。**go** ~ 发狂。**have a** ~ **time** 欢闹一场。**hopping** ~ [口]气得直跳;怒不可遏。**like** ~ [口]迅速地,猛烈地。~ **as a March hare** [**as a hatter**] (像春兔一样)疯狂的。~ **as a wet hen** [美]非常生气。**run** ~ = **go** ~. **run** ~ **after something** 给…迷住,狂爱…。**II** *vt*., *vi*. (*p*., *p.p*. **madded**) [罕] = madden. ~ **apple** 茄子。~**brained** *a*. 莽撞的;奔放的;狂热的。~**cap 1.** *n*. 狂妄的人,鲁莽的人。**2.** *a*. 鲁莽的,荒唐的 (~*cap pranks* 胡作妄为的恶作剧;胡闹)。~ **cow disease**【兽医】疯牛病[牛染上此病,其肉食之对人体有害]。~**-doctor** 精神病医生。~**-dog** *vt*. [俚]像疯狗一样恶狠狠地盯着看(人)。~**-house** 精神病院、疯人院、混乱、吵闹的场所;[美空俚]驾驶室。~**man** 疯子;[美卡车司机语] = highjacker. ~ **minute** [军口](一分钟 12—15 发的)猛烈射击。~ **money** [美]女人身边带的钱,女人藏着以备急需的一点钱,女人的私财。~**woman** 女狂人,女疯子。**-ly** *ad*. 疯狂地,疯狂似地;莽撞地,狂热地;粗野地;狂怒地;愚蠢地;极端地。**-ness** *n*. 癫狂;狂乱,狂暴;疯狂,狂热。

Mad·a·gas·car [ˌmædəˈgæskə; ˏmædəˋgæskɚ] *n*. **1.** 马达加斯加[非洲,马尔加什共和国的简称]。**2.** 马达加斯加岛[非洲]。

mad·am [ˈmædəm; ˋmædəm] *n*. (*pl*. ~**s**, 或 ***mesdames*** [ˈmeidæm; ˋmedæm]) **1.** 夫人,太太,女士[对妇女的尊称,以前代替 Mrs. 用于姓前称呼长辈的妇女;在其他字句之后,口语常略作 ma'am, mam, 俚语略作 marm, mum, m'm 或 m. 例: yes, ma'am; no, ma'am; [俚] yes, 'm, no, 'm; thank you, ma'am]。**2.** (家庭)主妇。**3.** [口]喜欢差使别人的女子。**4.** 妓院鸨母。*This way please*, ~. 这边请,女士[接待用语,复数借用 ladies]。(*Dear*) *M-* (亲爱的)女士[书信中对不熟识女子的称呼,可兼指已婚或未婚]。

mad·ame [ˈmædəm, maːˈdaːm; ˋmædəm, mɑˋdɑm] *n*. (*pl*. ***mesdames*** [ˈmeidæm; meˋdɑm] 或 ~**s**) [F.] **1.** 太太[对已婚妇女的法国式称呼];夫人[用于妇人姓前或称号前的法国式尊称];女歌唱家、艺术家相互间的称号。**2.** [美俚]妓院老板娘,老鸨。***M- Tussaud's*** [təˈsəuz, -ˈsɔːdz; təˋsoz, -ˋsɔdz] (伦敦的)塔梭滋夫人蜡像陈列馆。

mad·a·ro·sis [ˌmædəˈrəusis; ˏmædəˋrosɪs] ***n***. 【医】睫毛脱落;眉毛脱落。

mad·den [ˈmædn; ˋmædn̩] ***vt***. 使发狂;使大怒。— ***vi***. 〔罕〕发狂。

mad·den·ing [ˈmædniŋ; ˋmædnɪŋ] ***a***. 使人发狂的;使人气极的。**-ly** ***ad***.

mad·der [ˈmædə; mædɚ] ***n***. 【植】茜草属植物茜草根;【纺】茜草染料;鲜红色。

mad·ding [ˈmædiŋ; ˋmædɪŋ] ***a***. **1.** 发狂的,癫狂的,疯狂的。**2.** 使人狂怒的。*set the world* ~使举世若狂。

mad·dish [ˈmædiʃ; ˋmædɪʃ] ***a***. 微狂的。

made [meid; med] make 的过去式及过去分词。***a***. **1.** …制的,(人工)做成的;拼成的。**2.** 体格…的。**3.** 保证成功的。**4.** 虚构的。*foreign*-~ [*ready*-~] *clothes* 外国做的[现成的]衣服。~ *land* [*ground*] 填筑地。*a* ~ *story* 编造出来的故事。*He is* ~ *of money*. 他很有钱。*a* ~ *dish* 杂烩。*well*-~体格好的。*a* ~ *man* 成功者。***be*** ~ ***from*** 由…制成的。***be*** ~ ***of*** …制的,用…制成的。~ ***up of*** 由…组成。~**-to-order** ***a***. 定制的;合身的。~**-up** ***a***. **1.** 制成的;拼好版的。**2.** 虚构的,捏造的;做作的。**3.** 化了妆[装]的。**4.** 决定了的;坚定的 (*a made-up tie* 预制固定式的领结。*made-up lips* 涂了口红的嘴唇)。

Ma·dei·ra [məˈdiərə; məˋdɪrə] ***n***. **1.** 马德拉(群)岛〔在非洲西北部大西洋中〕。**2.** 〔常 m-〕(马德拉岛产的)白葡萄酒;马德拉蛋糕(= ~ cake)。**3.** 〔Rio ~〕马代拉河〔巴西〕。

Ma·de·leine [ˈmædəlin, ˈmædəlein; ˋmædəlɪn, ˋmædlen] ***n***. **1.** 马德琳〔女子名〕。**2.** 〔m-〕重油杯糕。

Mad·e·le·ni·an [ˌmædiˈliːniən; ˏmædɪˋlinɪən] ***a***. = Magdalenian.

Mad·e·line [ˈmædəlin, ˈmædəlain; ˋmædəlɪn, ˋmædəlaɪn] ***n***. 马德琳〔女子名〕。

ma·de·moi·selle [ˌmædəməˈzel; ˏmædəməˋzɛl] ***n***. 〔F.〕(*pl*. ***mes·de·moi·selles*** [ˌmeidmwɑˈzel, ˌmeidəmˈzel; ˏmedmwɑˋzel, ˏmedəmˋzɛl]) 小姐〔用于未婚女子姓名前的法国式敬称,与英语 Miss 相当,单数略为 Mlle.,复数略为 Mlles.〕;〔英〕法国女(家庭)教师。

Madge [mædʒ; mædʒ] ***n***. 玛奇〔女子名, Margaret 的昵称〕。

ma·di·a [ˈmeidiə; ˋmedɪə] ***n***. 【植】智利向日葵。~**-oil** 智利葵子油〔橄榄油的代用品,渣作饲料〕。

Mad·i·son[1] [ˈmædisn; ˋmædəsn̩] ***n***. **1.** 墨迪逊〔姓氏〕。**2. James** ~詹姆斯·墨迪逊〔1751—1836,美国第四任总统〕。

Mad·i·son[2] [ˈmædisn; ˋmædəsn] ***n***. 麦迪逊〔美国城市〕。~ **Avenue** 麦迪逊大街〔美国纽约市的一条街,美国广告业中心〕。

Madm. = Madam.

Ma·don·na [məˈdɔnə; məˋdɑnə] ***n***. **1.** 【宗】圣母(玛利亚);圣母画像[雕像]。**2.** 〔m-〕〔It.〕= madam. ~ **lily** 白百合花。

Ma·dras [məˈdrɑːs; məˋdræs] ***n***. **1.** 马德拉斯〔印度港市〕。**2.** 〔m-〕马德拉斯狭条衬衫布。

ma·dre [ˈmɑːdre; ˋmɑdrɛ] ***n***. 〔Sp.〕母亲。

mad·re·pore [ˌmædriˈpɔː; ˋmædrɪˏpor] ***n***. 【动】石珊瑚,石蚕〔珊瑚的一种〕。

mad·re·por·ite [ˈmædriˌpɔːrait; ˋmædrəpəˏraɪt] ***n***. 【动】(棘皮动物体中,海水进入脉管系统的)筛板,穿孔板。

Ma·drid [məˈdrid; məˋdrɪd] ***n***. 马德里〔西班牙的首都〕。**-drile·ni·an** [mædriˈliːniən; mædrɪˋlinɪən] **I** ***a***. 马德里的。**II** ***n***. 马德里人。

mad·ri·gal [ˈmɑːdrigəl; ˋmɑdrɪgəl] ***n***. 情歌;小曲;【乐】牧歌。

Ma·dri·le·ña [mɑːdriˈlenjɑː; mɑdrɪˋlenjɑ] ***n***. (*pl*. ~***s***) 〔Sp.〕马德里(Madrid) 女人。

ma·dri·lène [ˌmædriˈlen, F. mɑdriːˈlɛn; ˏmædrɪˋlɛn, F. mɑdriˋlɛn] ***n***. 〔F.〕马德里番茄肉汤。

Ma·dri·le·ño [mɑːdriˈleinjəu; mɑdrɪˋlenjo] ***n***. (*pl*. ~***s***) 〔Sp.〕马德里(男)人。

ma·du·ro [məˈduərəu; məˋdʊro] ***a***., ***n***. 〔Sp.〕浓烈的(雪茄烟)。

mad·wort [ˈmædwəːt; ˋmædˏwɝt] ***n***. 【植】**1.** 庭荠属植物。**2.** 香雪球 (= alyssum)。

mae [mei; me] ***a***., ***n***., ***ad***. 〔Scot.〕more 的变体。

Mae·ce·nas [mi(ː)ˈsiːnæs; mɪˋsinəs] ***n***. 文学、艺术的赞助者〔原为维吉尔(Virgil)及霍拉斯(Horace)的保护者〕。

Mael·strom [ˈmeilstrəum; ˋmelstrəm] ***n***. 挪威西海岸的大漩涡;〔m-〕大漩流;大祸乱,灾害。

mae·nad [ˈmiːnæd; ˋminæd] ***n***. **1.** = bacchante. **2.** 激动异常的女人;疯狂的女人。**-ic** [miˈnædik; mɪˋnædɪk] ***a***.

ma·es·to·so [ˌmɑːesˈtəuzəu, -səu; ˏmɑɛsˋtoso, -so] ***a***., ***ad***. 〔It.〕【乐】庄严的[地],雄伟的[地]。

ma·es·tro [mɑːˈestrəu; ˋmaɪestro] ***n***. (*pl*. ~***s***, ***-tri*** [-triː; -trɪ]; *fem*. ***-tra*** [-trə;-trə]) 〔It.〕艺术大师〔大作曲家,名指挥等〕;〔美俚〕[ˈmaistrəu; ˋmaɪstro] 乐队指挥[领班];(球队等的)领队。

Mae·ter·linck [ˈmeitəliŋk; ˋmetɚˏlɪŋk], **Maurice** 梅特林克〔1862—1949,比利时剧作家,诗人,获 1911 年诺贝尔文学奖〕。

Mae West [ˈmeiˈwest; ˋmeˋwest] 〔军俚〕(飞行员穿的)海上救生衣〔源为美国一电影女明星名〕。

maf·fick [ˈmæfik; ˋmæfɪk] ***vi***. 〔英口〕狂欢庆祝,狂喜。

Ma·fi·a, Maf·fi·a [ˈmɑːfiə; ˋmɑfɪˏɑ] ***n***. 〔It.〕**1.** 〔m-〕(西西里的)民众对法律和政府的敌视;反政府秘密组织。**2.** (意大利,美国等的)反社会黑帮,黑手党。

maf·ic [ˈmæfik; ˋmæfɪk] ***a***. 【地】(火成岩的)镁铁质。

Ma·fi·o·si [ˌmɑːfiˈəusi; ˏmɑfɪˋosɪ] ***n***. *pl*. (*sing*. ***-so*** [-səu;-so]) 〔It.〕**1.** 反政府秘密组织成员;社会黑帮分子。**2.** 〔m-〕黑手党成员。

MAG = military advisory group 军事顾问团。

mag[1] [mæg; mæg] ***n***. 〔英俚〕半便士。

mag[2] [mæg; mæg] ***n***. = magneto. *a* ~*-generator* 永磁发电机;(手摇)磁石发电机。

mag. = **1.** magazine. **2.** magnetic; magnetism. **3.** magneto. **4.** magnitude.

mag·a·zine [ˌmægəˈziːn; ˏmægəˋzin] ***n***. **1.** 杂志;期刊〔原义"知识的宝库"〕。**2.** 弹药库,仓库;(连发枪的)弹仓,弹匣,弹盘。**3.** (自动加煤炉的)燃料储存仓。**4.** 【摄】底片[胶卷]盒。**5.** 资源地,宝库。*an expense* ~临时弹药库。~ **gun** [**rifle**] 连发枪。~ **stove** 自动加煤炉。

mag·a·log [ˈmægəlɔg; ˋmægəlɑg] ***n***. 杂志商品目录。

Mag·da·len, Mag·da·le·ne [ˈmægdəlin, ˈmægdəliːn; ˋmægdəˏlɪn, ˋmægdəˏlin] ***n***. **1.** 马格德琳〔女子名〕。**2.** 〔the ~〕【圣】抹大拉的马利亚〔原为妓女,后改恶向善,见《路加福音》〕。**3.** [m-]从良的妓女;〔英〕济良所,妓女收容所 (= ~ home)。

Magdalen [ˈmɔːdlin; ˋmɔdlɪn] **College** 英国牛津大学莫德林学院。

Mag·da·le·ni·an [ˌmægdəˈliːnjen; ˏmægdəˋlinɪən] ***a***., ***n***. 【考古】马格德林(期)〔欧洲旧石器时代的最后期〕。

mage [meidʒ; medʒ] ***n***. 〔古〕魔法师;魔术家;学者。

Ma·gel·lan [məˈgelən, -ˈdʒelən; məˋdʒɛlən, -ˋdʒɛlən], **Ferdinand** 麦哲伦〔1480? —1521,葡萄牙航海家〕。

Mag·el·lan·ic [mægəˈlænik, mædʒə-; ˏmægəˋlænɪk, mædʒə-] ***a***. 麦哲伦的;麦哲伦发现的。~ **clouds** 【天】麦哲伦云〔南半球所见空中的星云〕。

Ma·gen Da·vid [mɑːˈgein dɑːˈviːd, ˈmɔːgən ˈdɔːvid; mɑˋgen dɑˋvid, ˋmɔgən, ˋdɔvɪd] 〔Heb.〕大卫之星;六角星〔犹太教和以色列的标志;由一正一倒的两个等边三角形套在一起组成〕(= Star of David)。

ma·gen·ta [mə'dʒentə; mə`dʒɛntə] **I** ***n***. 红色苯胺染料;(碱性)品红;洋红。**II** ***a***. 品红色的。

Mag·gie ['mægi; `mægɪ] ***n***. 玛吉〔女子名〕

mag·got ['mægət; `mægət] ***n***. **1**. (尤指干酪蝇的)蛆。**2**. 空想,狂想,奇想。***have a ~ in one's head*** [***brain***] 想入非非,异想天开。***when the ~ bites*** 有兴致的时候。

mag·got·y ['mægəti; `mægətɪ] ***a***. **1**. 多蛆的。**2**. 胡思乱想的,想入非非的。

mag·hem·ite [mæg'hemait; mæg`hɛmaɪt] ***n***. 【矿】磁赤铁矿。

Ma·gi ['meidʒai; `medʒaɪ] ***n***. ***pl***. (***sing***. ***Magus***) **1**. 【圣】〔the (three) ~〕(由东方来朝拜初生基督的)三贤人。**2**. 古波斯祆教僧侣阶级。

Ma·gi·an ['meidʒiən; `medʒɪən] **I** ***a***. 古波斯祆教僧侣的。**II** ***n***. 古波斯祆教僧侣;祆教徒;魔法师,魔术家。

Ma·gi·an·ism ['meidʒiənizəm; `medʒɪənɪzm̩] ***n***. (古波斯的)祆教。

mag·ic ['mædʒik; `mædʒɪk] **I** ***a***. 魔术的,巫术的,幻术的,不可思议的,有奇异魔力的。~ *words* 咒语。*a ~ wand* 魔杖。~ *beauty* 妖艳无比的美丽。**II** ***n***. 魔法,巫术,幻术,妖术;魔术,戏法;不可思议的魔力。*black* [*white*] ~驱使恶魔[天神]的魔术。*natural* ~(不借助神力的)奇术。***as*** (***if***) ***by*** ~ 像使用魔术般。***like*** ~ 不可思议地快;立刻,马上。~ **bullet** 魔弹〔指能消灭病菌、病毒、癌细胞等而又不会伤害宿主的药,如六〇六等〕。~ **cookie**【计】魔饼;"神奇甜饼"〔网站用以追踪访问者的一类代码〕。~ **cube** 魔方〔玩具〕。~ **hand** (核反应堆等操作时用的)机械手,人造手。~ **lantern** 幻灯。~ **nucleus**【原】幻核。~ **square** 纵横图,幻方〔一大方框分成井字形的小方框,小方框中的数字纵向相加或横向相加,其和相等〕。

mag·i·cal ['mædʒikəl; `mædʒɪkl̩] ***a***. = magic. **-ly** ***ad***.

ma·gi·cian [mə'dʒiʃən; mə`dʒɪʃən] ***n***. 魔法师,妖道,术士;魔术家,变戏法的人。

ma·gilp [mə'gilp; mə`gɪlp] ***n***. (油画调色用)溶油(= megilp)。

Maginot Line ['mæʒinəu; `mæʒə,no] 马其诺防线〔第二次世界大战前法国在德法边境所建造〕。

mag·is·te·ri·al [,mædʒis'tiərəl; ,mædʒɪs`tɪrɪəl] ***a***. **1**. 长官(一样)的。**2**. 教师的;师长作风的;严正的,有权威的。**3**. 横暴的,傲慢的。**4**. 公平的,公正的(人等)。**5**. 硕士的。

mag·is·tra·cy ['mædʒistrəsi; `mædʒɪstrəsɪ] ***n***. 长官的职务[职权、职位、任期等];〔集合词〕地方行政官;地方行政官的管辖区。

ma·gis·tral [mə'dʒistrəl; `mædʒɪstrəl] ***a***. 教师的,主人的;按医师处方的;〔罕〕有权威的,独断的。*the ~ staff* (学校的)全体教职员。

mag·is·trate ['mædʒistrit, -treit; `mædʒɪs,tret, -trɪt] ***n***. (行政兼司法的)长官[地方长官、市长等];治安法庭法官。*the Chief* [*First*] *M-* 君主,元首,总统。*a civil* [*judicial*] ~行政[司法]官。*a Police M-* 违警罪法庭法官。**-ship** magistrate 的职务[地位、任期]。

Mag·le·mo·si·an [,mægli'məuziən; ,mæglɪ`mozɪən] ***a***. (中石器时代中期欧洲北部)马格来莫斯文化的。

mag(-)lev ['mæg,lev; `mæg,lɛv] ***n***. 磁浮火车〔指高速列车悬浮于磁场上方的超导磁体上〕。

mag·ma ['mægmə; `mægmə] ***n***. (***pl***. ~***ta*** [-tə; -tə], ~***s***) (矿物,有机物等的)稀糊状混合物;【地】岩浆;稠液;【药】乳浆剂。

magn. = **1**. magnetism. **2**. magneto.

Mag·na C(h)ar·ta ['mægnə'kɑːtə; `mægnə`kɑrtə] **1**. 【英史】大宪章。**2**. (一般)保障公民权利、自由的法令。

mag·na cum lau·de ['mɑːgnɑːkum'laude, 'mægnə-; `mɑgnɑkum`laudɛ, `mægnə-] 〔L.〕优异成绩(毕业)〔表彰高等院校毕业生用语〕。

Mag·na est ve·ri·tas, et prae·va·le·bit ['mægnə est 'veritəs et priː'vælibit; `mægnə ɛst`vɛrɪtəs ɛt pri`vælɪbɪt] 〔L.〕真理伟大,终必胜利。

mag·na·li·um [mæg'neiljəm; mæg`nelɪəm] ***n***. 【冶】镁铝合金。

mag·na·nim·i·ty [,mægnə'nimiti; ,mægnə`nɪmətɪ] ***n***. 宽仁,雅量,高尚;宽宏大量的行为;高尚的行为。

mag·nan·i·mous [mæg'næniməs; mæg`nænəməs] ***a***. 气量大的,高尚的。**-ly** ***ad***.

mag·nate ['mægneit; `mægnet] ***n***. 大资本家,巨头,富豪;权贵;…大王。*an oil* ~煤油大王。*a territorial* ~大地主。*the financial ~s* 金融巨头。

mag·ne·sia [mæg'niːʃə; mæg`niʃə] ***n***. 【化】氧化镁;【矿】镁氧;〔口〕碳酸镁[泻盐]。*carbonate of* ~ = ~ *alba* 碳酸镁。~ *brick* 镁砖。~ *cement* 镁氧水泥。~ *mica* 黑云母。~ *spar* 菱镁矿。*sulphate of* ~硫酸镁,泻盐。

mag·ne·sian [mæg'niːʃən; mæg`niʃən] ***a***. 镁的;(含)氧化镁的。~ *limestone* 白云石,含镁石灰岩。

mag·ne·site ['mægnisait; `mægnə,saɪt] ***n***. 【矿】菱镁矿;【化】碳酸镁。

mag·ne·si·um [mæg'niːziəm; mæg`nizɪəm] ***n***. 【化】镁。~ *alloy* 镁合金。~ *bomb* 镁燃烧弹。~ *flare* 镁光照明弹。~ *light*【摄】镁光灯。

mag·net ['mægnit; `mægnɪt] ***n***. **1**. 磁体;磁石;磁铁。**2**. 有吸引力的东西[人]。*a bar* ~条形磁铁[体]。*a horseshoe* ~ 马蹄形磁铁。*a ~ school* 重点学校,名校,有吸引力的学校。*a natural* ~天然磁。

mag·net·ic [mæg'netik; mæg`nɛtɪk] ***a***. **1**. 磁(性)的;(可)磁化的。**2**. 吸引人心的;有魅力的。**3**. 催眠术的。~ **amplifier**【无】磁放大器。~ **attraction** 磁吸引。~ **axis** 磁轴。~ **bearing** 磁针方位。~ **bottle**【物】磁瓶。~ **bubble**【计】磁泡〔以极高速度穿过集成电路的微小圆形磁畴,每一个磁泡代表一个单位的二进制信息〕。~ **clutch** 磁力离合器。~ **compass** 磁罗盘。~ **core** 磁心。~ **course** 磁航向,磁罗盘航向。~ **declination** [**deviation**]【物】磁差,磁偏;偏差;磁偏角。~ **detector**【无】磁性检波器。~ **elements** 地磁要素。~ **equator**【天】磁赤道(= aclinic line)。~ **field** 磁场。~ **flux** 磁通量。~ **force** 磁力。~ **hysteresis** 磁滞。~ **induction**【物】磁感应;磁感应强度(又作 ~ flux density)。~ **ink** 磁性墨水。~ **iron** 磁铁。~**-levitation train** 磁浮火车〔参见 mag(-)lev 条〕。~ **meridian**【天】磁子午线。~ **mine** 磁(性水)雷。~ **moment** 磁矩。~ **needle** 磁针,指南针。~ **north** 磁北。~ **permeability** 导磁系数,导磁性。~ **pickup**【无】电磁式拾波[音]器;变磁阻拾音器。~ **pole** 磁极。~ **recorder** 磁录音机;磁记录器;(电视)录影机。~ **recording**【无】磁录音。~ **reluctance** 磁阻。~ **resonance imaging**【医】(核)磁共振成像〔一种检查人体内部组织的方法〕。~ **storm** 磁暴。~ **tape** 磁带。~ **wire** 磁线,磁导线,磁性钢丝;录音钢丝。

mag·net·ics [mæg'netiks; mæg`nɛtɪks] ***n***. 磁学;磁性元件。

mag·net·ism ['mægnitizəm; `mægnə,tɪzəm] ***n***. **1**. 磁(性),磁力;磁学。**2**. (人格、道德等的)吸引力,魅力;催眠术。*animal* ~动物磁性说。*terrestrial* ~地磁;地磁学。

mag·net·ist ['mægnitist; `mægnɪtɪst] ***n***. 磁学家;催眠术家。

mag·ne·tite ['mægnitait; `mægnə,taɪt] ***n***. 【矿】磁铁矿。

mag·net·i·za·tion [,mægnitai'zeiʃən; ,mægnətaɪ`zeʃən] ***n***. 磁化(强度);起磁。

mag·net·ize ['mægnitaiz; `mægnə,taɪz] ***vt***. **1**. 使磁化,使生磁性;使有磁力。**2**. 吸引,感动。**3**. 催眠。— ***vi***. 受磁。**-r** ***n***. 磁化器。

mag·ne·to [mæg'niːtəu; mæg`nito] ***n***. (***pl***. ~***s***) 磁电机;永磁发电机〔magneto-electric machine 或 magneto-dynamo 之略〕;磁石式,永磁式。~ *generator*

永磁电机。～ *system* 永磁(电话)式。

magneto- *comb. f.* = magnetic. ～some 磁体。～therapy 磁疗法。

mag·ne·to·bell [mæg'niːtəubel; mæg`nitobɛl] ***n.*** 磁石电铃。

mag·ne·to·elas·tic·i·ty [mæg'niːtəu ˌelæs'tisiti; mæg`nitoˏɛlæs`tɪsətɪ] ***n.***【物】磁致弹性。

mag·ne·to·e·lec·tric [mæg'niːtəui'lektrik; mægnitoɪ`lɛktrɪk] ***a.***【物】磁电的。

mag·ne·to·e·lec·tric·i·ty [mæg'niːtəuiˌlek'trisiti; mæg`nitoɪˏlɛk`trɪsətɪ] ***n.*** 磁电。

mag·ne·to·gas·dy·nam·ics [mæg'niːtəuˌgæsdai'næmiks; mæg`nitoˏgæsdaɪ`næmɪks] ***n.*** 磁性气体动力学。

mag·ne·to·graph [mæg'niːtəugrɑːf, -græf; mæg`nitəˏgrɑf, -græf] ***n.*** 地磁强度记录仪。

mag·ne·to·hy·dro·dy·nam·ics [mæg'niːtəuˌhaidrəudai'næmiks; mæg`nitoˏhaɪdrədaɪ`næmɪks] ***n.*** *pl.*〔动词用单数〕磁流体动力学。**-ic** ***a.***

mag·ne·tom·e·ter [ˌmægni'tɔmitə; ˏmægnə`tɑmətɚ] ***n.*** 磁强计;地磁仪。

mag·ne·to·mo·tive [mægˌniːtəu'məutiv; mægˏnitə`motɪv] ***a.*** 起磁的,生磁流之力的。

mag·ne·ton ['mægnitɔn; `mægnəˏtɑn] ***n.*** 磁子。

mag·ne·to·phone [mæg'niːtəufəun; mæg`nitofon] ***n.*** 磁带录音机[器]。

mag·ne·tor ['mægnitə; `mægnɪtɚ] ***n.*** 磁电机。

mag·ne·to·re·sist·ance [mægˌniːtəuri'zistəns; mægˏnitorɪ`zɪstəns] ***n.***【物】磁致电阻。**-sistive** ***a.***

mag·ne·to·scope [mæg'niːtəuskəup; mæg`nitəˏskop] ***n.*** 验磁器。

mag·ne·to·sphere [mæg'niːtəusfiə; mæg`nitəsfɪr] ***n.***【天】磁层。**-sphe·ric** [-'sfiərik, -'sfeərik; -`sfɛrɪk, -`sfɛərɪk] ***a.***

mag·ne·to·stric·tion [mægˌniːtəu'strikʃən; mægˏnitə`strɪkʃən] ***n.***【物】磁致伸缩;磁力控制。

mag·ne·to·tel·e·phone [mæg'niːtəu'telifəun; mæg`nito`tɛlɪˏfon] ***n.*** 永磁电话。

mag·ne·tron ['mægnitrɔn; `mægnəˏtrɑn] ***n.***【无】磁控(电子)管。*rising-sun* ～旭日型磁控管。

magni- *comb. f.* 大 (*opp.* micro-)。

mag·nif·ic, mag·nif·i·cal [mæg'nifik, -ikəl; mæg`nɪfɪk, -ɪkəl] ***a.***〔古〕庄严的,崇高的,壮丽的,宏伟的,堂皇的;豪言壮语的。

Mag·nif·i·cat [mæg'nifikæt; mæg`nɪfɪˏkæt] ***n.*** (晚祷时唱的)圣母马利亚赞美歌;〔m-〕颂歌,赞美歌。***sing ～ at matins*** 夏裘冬葛,做事不合时宜〔早祷唱晚祷颂歌〕。

mag·ni·fi·ca·tion [ˌmægnifi'keiʃən; ˏmægnəfə`keʃən] ***n.*** 放大,扩大;夸张;称赞;【光】放大率[倍数]。

mag·nif·i·cence [mæg'nifisns; mæg`nɪfəsns] ***n.*** 宏大,庄严,壮丽,堂皇,豪华。

mag·nif·i·cent [mæg'nifisnt; mæg`nɪfəsnt] ***a.*** 宏大的,庄严的,堂皇的;(衣服、装饰等)华丽的;极其动人的;(体型)优美的,健壮的;〔口〕顶呱呱的。**-ly** ***ad.***

mag·nif·i·co [mæg'nifikəu; mæg`nɪfəˏko] ***n.*** (*pl.* ～*-es*) (古时)威尼斯共和国的贵族;要人,权贵。

mag·ni·fier ['mægnifaiə; `mægnəˏfaɪɚ] ***n.*** 放大者,扩大者,放大镜,放大器。

mag·ni·fy ['mægnifai; `mægnəˏfaɪ] ***vt.*** (*-fied*) **1.** (凸镜等)扩大,放大,映大。**2.** 夸张,夸大;〔古〕推崇,夸奖;赞美;〔罕〕增大。～ ***oneself*** 自大,自夸。～ ***oneself against*** ... 尊己抑人。～**ing glass** 放大镜。～**ing power** 放大率。

mag·nil·o·quence [mæg'niləkwəns; mæg`nɪləkwəns] ***n.*** (文风、语言等)华而不实;大话;虚夸。

mag·nil·o·quent [mæg'niləkwənt; mæg`nɪləkwənt] ***a.*** 华而不实的,夸张的,夸大的,吹牛的。**-ly** ***ad.***

mag·ni·tude ['mægnitjuːd; `mægnəˏtjud] ***n.*** 广大,巨大;伟大,重大,重要性;大小;积;量;【数】量值;【天】(恒星的)等,等级,光度。～ *equation*【天】星等差。～ *of eclipse*【天】食分。*of the first* ～(星的光度)(第)一等的;最大的;最重要的(人物等)。

mag·no·li·a [mæg'nəuljə; mæg`nolɪə] ***n.***【植】木兰。**M- State**〔美〕密西西比州的别名。

mag·non ['mægnɔn; `mægnɑn] ***n.***【物】磁振子。

mag·num ['mægnəm; `mægnəm] ***n.*** **1.** (两夸脱容量的)大酒瓶,一大酒瓶。**2.**〔M-〕马格南左轮(手枪)(= ～ revolver)。～ **bonum** ['bəunəm; `bonəm] 大黄李;大马铃薯。

mag·num o·pus ['mægnəm'əupəs; `mægnəm `opəs]〔L.〕个人的重大事业;(文学、艺术上的)大作,杰作,巨著。

Mag·nus effect ['mægnəs i'fekt; `mægnəs ɪ`fɛkt]【物】马格努斯效应。

mag·nus hitch ['mægnəs hitʃ; `mægnəs hɪtʃ]【海】三重结〔一种绳结〕。

mag·ot ['mægət, mɑ'gəu; `mægət, mɑ`go] ***n.*** **1.** (中国及日本的瓷制或象牙制的、装在瓶盖等上作捏手的)奇形偶像。**2.**【动】北非产无尾猿 (= Barbary ape)。

mag·pie ['mægpai; `mægˏpaɪ] ***n.*** **1.**【鸟】鹊。**2.** 碎嘴子,爱说话的人。**3.**〔俚〕半便士。**4.** 靶子自外数第二圈,打中自外数第二圈的一枪〔打中这一圈时,用黑白旗打信号,故名〕。**5.** (花边的)黑白花纹。

M. Agr. = Master of Agriculture 农科硕士。

mags·man ['mægzmən; `mægzmən] ***n.*** **1.** 杂志撰稿人。**2.**〔俚〕骗子。

mag·uey ['mægwei; `mægwe] ***n.***【植】龙舌兰;〔美〕牧童用的索子(= maguey rope)。～ *hemp* 剑麻。

ma·gus ['meigəs; `megəs] ***n.*** (*pl.* ***magi*** ['meidʒai; `medʒaɪ]) **1.** 古波斯僧,袄教僧。**2.** (古代的)魔术家,占星家。

Mag·yar ['mægjɑː; `mægjɑr] **I** ***n.*** (匈牙利的)马札尔人;马札尔语,匈牙利语。**II** ***a.*** 马札尔人的,马札尔[匈牙利]语的。～ (*blouse*) (袖子和其他部分连成一块的)马札尔衫。

Ma·gyar·or·szág ['mɔdjɑːɔːsɑːg; `mɑdjarˏɔrsɑg] ***n.*** "匈牙利"的匈语名称。

ma·ha·ra·ja(h) [ˌmɑːhə'rɑːdʒə; ˏmɑhə`rɑdʒə] ***n.*** 大君〔印度土邦主〕。

ma·ha·ra·ni, -nee [ˌmɑːhə'rɑːniː; mɑhə`rɑni] ***n.*** 大君妃〔印度土邦主的妻〕;女土邦主,女大君。

ma·hat·ma [mə'hætmə; mə`hætmə] ***n.***〔Sans.〕(密教的)大善知识;大圣,圣雄;圣贤;伟人。

Ma·ha·ya·na [ˌməhɑː'jɑːnə; ˏmɑhə`jɑnə] ***n.***〔Sans.〕【佛】大乘,摩诃衍。

Mah·di ['mɑːdi(ː); `mɑdi] ***n.*** (*pl.* ～***s***) (伊斯兰教)救世主。

Mah·dism ['mɑːdizəm; `mɑdɪzm̩] ***n.*** (伊斯兰教)救世主降临说。

Ma·hi·can [mə'hiːkən; mə`hikən] **I** ***n.*** **1.** 马希坎部落〔美国阿尔衮琴印第安人的一个部落,主要居于哈得逊河上游流域〕。**2.** 马希坎人。**3.** 莫希坎人 (= Mohegan)。**II** ***a.*** 马希坎人的。

mah-jong(g) ['mɑː'dʒɔŋ; mɑ`dʒɔŋ] ***n.***〔汉〕麻将牌,麻雀牌。

mahl·stick ['mɔːlstik; `mɑlˏstɪk] ***n.*** = maulstick.

ma·hog·a·ny [mə'hɔgəni; mə`hɑgənɪ] ***n.***【植】桃花心木;红木,赤褐色;〔口〕食桌;餐桌;蜜味杜松子酒。*the Chinese* ～香椿。***be under the*** ～ 醉倒在食桌下。***put*** [***stretch***] ***one's legs under sb.'s*** ～受人款待;作某人的食客。***with one's knees under the*** ～就席,坐席。

Ma·hom·e·dan, Ma·hom·et·an [mə'hɔmidən, mə'hɔmitən; mə`hɑmɪdən, mə`hɑmətən] ***a.***, ***n.*** = Mohammedan.

Ma·hom·et [mə'hɔmit; mə`hɑmɪt] *n*. = Mohammed.

Ma·hom·et·an·ism [mə'hɔmitənizəm; mə`hɑmətənɪzm] *n*. = Mohammedanism.

ma·ho·ni·a [mə'həuniə; mə`honɪə] *n*.【植】十大功劳属植物。

Ma·hound [mə'haund, -'huːnd; mə`haʊnd, -`hund] *n*. 1.〔古〕= Mohammed. 2.〔Scot.〕魔鬼。

ma·hout [mə'haut; mə`haʊt] *n*. 驭象人,象夫。

Mah·rat·ta [mə'rɑːtə; mə`rætə] *n*. (西印度)马哈拉特邦人,马拉他人。

Mah·rat·ti, Mah·ra·ti, Ma·ra·thi [mə'rɑːti; mə`rætɪ] *n*. (印度的)马拉他语。

mah·seer ['mɑːsiə; `mɑsɪr] *n*. 马西亚鱼〔印度的一种河鱼〕。

mah·zor [mɑːh'zɔː, 'mɑːhzə; mɑh`zɔr, `mɑhzɚ] *n*. (*pl*. *-zors*, Heb. *-zor·im* [-'zɔːrim; -`zɔrɪm]) 犹太祷告书〔内有各节日的礼拜仪式〕。

maid [meid; med] *n*. 1. 处女,未婚女子,闺女;〔诗〕少女,姑娘。2. 婢,侍女,女仆。*an old* ~老处女。*a lady's* ~侍女。*a* ~ *in waiting* = *a* ~ *of honour*. *a* ~ *of all work* 什么活儿都干的女仆。*a* ~ *of hono(u)r* 1.〔英〕英国女王[王后,公主]的(未婚)女侍从官。2.〔美〕(主要)女傧相。3. 杏仁柠檬蛋糊饼。

mai·dan [mai'dɑːn; maɪ`dɑn] *n*.〔印度英语〕练兵场,操场;(用作市场或散步场的)空地,广场。

maid·en ['meidn; `medn] I *n*.〔古〕1. 处女,未婚女子,闺女,少女。2.【英史】苏格兰的一种断头台。3. = ~ over. II *a*.〔通常只用作修饰语〕1. 处女的,少女的;未婚的。2. 纯洁的,清净的。3. 初次的,还未用过[经历过等]的;(巡回法庭)无案件的。*a* ~ *aunt* 独身姑母。*a* ~ *lady* 未婚女人。*a* ~ *speech* (议员等的)首次演说。*a* ~ *voyage* 处女航。*a* ~ *battle* 初次战斗。~ *soil* 处女地,未垦地。*a* ~ *assize* 没有刑事案件的巡回法庭。*a* ~ *castle* [*fortress*] 从未陷落过的城寨。*a* ~ *flight* 初次飞行。*a* ~ *horse* 从未跑赢过的马。*one's* ~ *name* 女子的娘家姓氏。*a* ~ *race* 全由未跑赢过的马参加的赛马。*a* ~ *sword* 新刀,尚未染过血的剑。~ **hair**【植】掌叶铁线蕨;铁线蕨。~ **hair tree**【植】银杏树,公孙树,白果树。~**head** 1.〔古〕= maidhood, ~-hood. 2.【解】处女膜。~**hood** 处女性,处女时期。~ **over**【板球】未得分的投球。

maid·en·ish ['meidniʃ; `mednɪʃ] *a*. 处女的,处女似的;老处女似的。

maid·en·like ['meidnlaik; `mednˌlaɪk] *a*. 处女似的;柔和的,羞涩的,羞答答的。

maid·en·li·ness ['meidnlinis; `mednlɪnɪs] *n*. 处女态;羞涩,柔和,娇羞。

maid·en·ly ['meidnli; `mednlɪ] *a*. 处女似的,少女似的;谨慎的,柔和的,娇羞的。

maid·ish ['meidiʃ; `medɪʃ] *a*. 少女(一样)的;老处女的。

maid·ser·vant ['meidsəːvənt; `medˌsɚvənt] *n*. 女仆。

ma·ieu·tic, -ti·cal [mei'juːtik(l); me`jutɪkl] *a*. 1. (苏格拉底用语)"产婆术"。2. 产科学的,助产学的。

mai·gre ['meigə; `megɚ] *a*. 素的,吃斋的。*The doctor advised me to live* ~(= *on* ~ *food*). 医生嘱咐我吃素。

mai·hem ['meihem; `mehɛm] *n*.【法】1. 残害人的肢体[器官]的罪。2. 蓄意损害,有意识挑起的暴行(= mayhem)。

mail[1] [meil; mel] I *n*. 锁子甲;铠甲;(动物的)锁子状甲壳。II *vt*. 使穿锁子甲。~**-clad** *a*. 穿着锁子甲的。

mail[2] [meil; mel] I *n*. 1. 邮政;邮袋;〔the ~〕〔美〕(一批)邮件,邮件的一次发送[收集]〔英国限指寄到国外的邮件,一般邮件用 the post〕。2. 邮件运输工具〔邮船、邮车等〕。3. 邮务员,邮递员。4.〔*pl*.〕〔美〕邮递;邮政(制度)。5.〔古〕袋,旅行包,行囊。*an ordinary* [*a surface*] ~平信;陆上(或海上)邮递。*the Indian* ~〔英〕寄往印度的邮件。*air* ~航空(邮件)。*Is there any* ~ *for me?*〔美〕我有信吗? *by* ~〔美〕邮(寄)(=〔英〕by post)。II *vt*.〔美〕把(邮件)投入邮箱;邮寄。~ *a letter* 寄信。~**bag**〔美〕邮袋。~**boat** 邮船。~ **bomb** 1. 邮件炸弹〔藏在邮件或邮包中的炸弹,拆开即炸〕。2.【计】爆炸性电子函件,电子邮件炸弹〔向某一网址发送数量庞大的电子邮件使其电脑无法工作〕。3. *vt*.【计】向…发送电子邮件炸弹。~**box** 邮箱。~ **car** (铁路)邮车。~ **carrier** 邮递员。~ **cart** 邮车;(手推)婴儿车。~ **catcher** 邮包装卸器〔火车行进中将邮包装上或卸下邮车的装置〕。~ **chute** (可使大楼上层邮件自动落入楼下邮箱内的)邮件滑送槽。~ **clerk**〔美〕邮局办事员;(机关、企业中)邮件管理员。~ **coach** 邮政车,邮车。~ **cover**〔美〕邮检制度。~ **day** 邮件截止日。~ **drop** 1. 邮筒;邮筒槽口。2. 秘密通信地址。~**man**〔美〕邮递员。~ **matter** 邮件。~ **order** 函购,邮购(*a* ~*-order house* 邮售商行)。~**out** 邮递广告传单。~ **plane** 邮(政飞)机。~ **train** 邮(政列)车。

mail·a·ble ['meiləbl; `meləbl] *a*. 能邮寄的。

mailed [meild; meld] *a*. 披着锁子甲的,装甲的;【动】被甲的。*the* ~ *fist* 武力,铁腕。

Mail·er ['meilə; `melɚ] *n*. 梅勒〔姓氏〕。

mail·er ['meilə; `melɚ] *n*. 1. 邮寄者。2. 邮件打戳、分类、称重机。3. 邮寄品的容器。4. 邮船。5. 附在信件中的广告印刷品。

mail·ing ['meiliŋ; `melɪŋ] *n*. 邮寄;邮寄品;邮寄者一次寄发的一批邮件。*a* ~ *list* 通信[发送]名单。*a* ~ *machine* = mailer 2. *a* ~ *table* 邮件分理台。*a* ~ *tube* 邮寄纸筒〔寄印刷品或易碎品用〕。~ **shot**〔英〕邮购目录。

Mail·lard ['meiləd; `melɚd] *n*. 梅勒德〔姓氏〕。

mail·lot [mɑː'jəu; mɑ`jo]〔F.〕1. (体操运动员)紧身衣。2. 整件女游泳衣。

maim [meim; mem] *vt*. 残害;使残废;使负重伤。

maimed [meimd; memd] *a*. 负重伤的,伤残的。

main [mein; men] I *a*. 1. 主要的,主,全,总。2. 充分的,尽量的;全力的,有力的。*the* ~ *clause* 主要子句,主句。*a* ~ *event* =〔俚〕*a* ~ *go* 主要比赛。*the* ~ *fleet* 主力舰队。~ *operations* 主力战。*the* ~ *pipe* 总管(道)。*a* ~ *squeeze*〔美俚〕中心人物,首脑,大老板。*the* ~ *line*〔英〕(铁路)干线;〔美〕主血管;【电话】中继线。***by*** ~ ***force*** [***strength***] 全力;全靠武力[力量]。~ ***chance*** 获利良机(*have an eye for the* ~ *chance* 注意抓住谋取私利的良机)。***with*** ~ ***strength*** 用全力。II *n*. 1. 体力,气力;力〔仅用于 with might and ~中〕;主要部分,要点〔仅用于 *for* [*in*] *the* ~中〕;2.〔诗〕大海,大洋;〔古〕本土(= mainland)。3. (自来水、煤气等的)总管;干线,干管。4.【海】= mainmast; mainsail. *water from the* ~自来水。*a water* ~自来水总管。*a supply* ~自来水总管;馈电干线。***for*** [***in***] ***the*** ~ 大体上,大致,大抵。***turn on the*** ~〔俚〕哭出来。***with*** (***all one's***) ***might and*** ~ 尽全力。III *vt*.〔美俚〕把(海洛因等)注射进静脉。~**-beam**【海】全船面。~ **body**【军】主力,本队;(文件的)正文。~ **boom**【船】主帆桁。~ **brace**【海】大桅转桁索(*splice the* ~ *brace*〔海俚〕拿酒给船员喝;痛饮)。~ **centre** 中枢。~ **course** = mainsail; 主要课程;主菜。~ **deck**【船】主甲板;(两层甲板时的)上甲板,正甲板;(三层甲板时的)中甲板。~ **drag**〔美俚〕(城市、村镇的)主街,大街。~ **frame** (大型计算机的)主机;主机机架。~ **hatch**【船】主舱口;中部舱口。~ **hold**【船】中部船舱。~**land** 大陆,本土〔对岛屿、半岛而言〕。~**line** 主线,(铁路)干线,正线;〔美俚〕主血管;对主血管的海洛因注射。~**mast**【船】大桅,主桅。~ **plane**〔英军〕机翼;主翼。~ **prise**【法】对罪犯按期出庭的保证。~ **royal**【海】大桅最高第二帆。~**sail**【船】(横帆船 main yard 上、纵帆船 main gaff 上的)大帆,主帆。 ~-

sheet 主帆索。~**spring** 主发条;主要原因,主要动机。~-**stay**【船】大桅主索;中坚,台柱;靠山,主要的生活来源(*Agriculture is the ~stay of a country*. 农为国本)。~ **stem** = ~**stream** *n*. 主流;主要倾向;(事物的)极富于生命力的部分。~**top** *n*.【船】大桅楼(*~top gallant-mast*【海】大二接桅。~ *top-mast*【海】大一接桅。~ *top-plane*【空】上主翼。~*topsail*【海】大一接帆)。~ **yard**【船】大桅下桁。

Maine [mein; men] *n*. **1**. 缅因〔美国州名〕。**2**. 梅恩〔姓氏〕。

main·ly [ˈmeinli; ˋmenlɪ] *ad*. 主要;大概;大抵。

mai·no(u)r [ˈmeinə; ˋmenə] *n*.【法】赃品。

Main Street [ˈmein striːt; ˋmenˏstrit] *n*. **1**. (小城镇的)主街,大街。**2**. 〔美〕乡镇中的实利主义阶层;乡镇典型居民的态度、意见。

main·tain [meinˈtein; menˋten] *vt*. **1**. 保持;维持;继续。**2**. 坚持,维护。**3**. 供养,扶养。**4**. 维修,保养。**5**. (坚决)主张;强调。~ *discipline* 维持纪律。~ *peace and order* 维持治安。~ *one's ground* (*against*) (对…)站稳[坚持]自己立场。~ *oneself* 自立。

main·tain·a·ble [meinˈteinəbl; menˋtenəbl] *a*. 可保持的,可维持的;可供养的;可维修的;可坚持的,可主张的。

main·te·nance [ˈmeintinəns; ˋmentənəns] *n*. **1**. 保持,维持,保养;保管,保存,维护,维修;继续;支持的手段。**2**. 坚持;主张;拥护,支持。**3**. 扶养,供给;生活,生计。**4**.【法】对诉讼一方的非法援助;依法应负的对他人的赡养义务。*cost of* ~维持费。*preventive* ~预防性维修[检修]。*separate* ~(给妻子的)分居津贴。~ *of membership*〔美〕工会会员资格保留条款。~ *of possession* 占有,保有,保全。~ *of way*【铁道】护路。**M- Command**【英军】保管[维修]总队。~ **drug** 维持药〔合法给予吸毒者的麻醉品,其剂量足以维持戒毒药效而又可防止产生脱瘾病症〕。~ **man** 维修工。~ **work** 维修工作。

Mainz [maints; maɪnts] *n*. 美因茨〔德国城市〕。

mair [mεə; mεr] *a*. 〔Scot.〕更多的;更大的;更好的;更高的;另外的;其余的(= more)。

mair·ie [meˈriː; meˋri] *n*. 〔F.〕市府大楼;县区的行政大楼。

Mai·sie [ˈmeizi; ˋmezɪ] *n*. 梅齐〔女子名,Margaret 的昵称〕。

mai·son de san·té [mezɔ̃ də sɑ̃te; ˏmeˋzɔ̃ də sɑ̃ˋte] 〔F.〕私立医院;疗养院。

mai·son·(n)ette [ˌmeizəˈnet; ˏmezəˋεt] *n*. 小住宅;(二层楼的)公寓房子;〔英〕分别出租的房间。

maist [meist; mest] *a*. 〔Scot.〕最多的,最大的,最高的;大概的;大多数的(=most)。

Mait·land [ˈmeitlənd; ˋmetlənd] *n*. 梅特兰〔姓氏〕。

maî·tre [ˈmeitrə; ˋmεtrə] *n*. 〔F.〕= master 1. ~ ***d'hôtel*** [dəuˈtel; doˋtεl] 旅馆主人;管家,总管;饭店服务员总管;(加)奶油柠檬(调味)酱。

maize [meiz; mez] *n*. **1**. 〔英〕【植】玉蜀黍,玉米。★美国、加拿大叫 corn。**2**. 玉米色。*the* ~ *country*〔美〕穷乡僻壤。~ *oil* 玉米油。

mai·ze·na [meiˈziːnə; meˋzinə] *n*. 〔英〕玉米粉。

Maj. = Major.

ma·jes·tic, **ma·jest·i·cal** [məˈdʒestik, -tikəl; məˋdʒεstɪk, -tɪkəl] *a*. 有威严的,庄严的,堂堂的,威风凛凛的。**-i·cal·ly** *ad*.

maj·es·ty [ˈmædʒisti; ˋmædʒɪstɪ] *n*. **1**. 威严,威风;尊严,庄严。**2**. 主权,统治权;帝位;[M-]陛下[尊称]。**3**. 光轮中的耶稣[圣母、上帝]圣像。*His Britannic M-* 英国国王陛下〔略 H. B. M.〕。*His* [*Her*] *Imperial M-* 皇帝[皇后]陛下〔略 H. I. M. 或 H. M.〕。*Their* (*Imperial*) *Majesties* 皇帝皇后两陛下〔略号 T. (I.) M.〕。*Your M-* 陛下〔直接对话时的尊称〕。*His Majesty's guests*〔俚〕囚犯。*His Majesty's hotel*〔谑〕监狱。*His Satanic M-*〔谑〕魔王。

Maj. Gen. = Major General〔英〕陆军(或海军陆战队)少将;〔美〕陆军(或空军、海军陆战队)少将。

Maj·lis [mædʒˈlis; mædʒˋlɪs] *n*. 伊朗(或伊拉克)的议会。

ma·jol·i·ca [məˈjɔlikə, -ˈdʒɔl-; məˋjɑlɪkə, -ˋdʒɑl-] *n*. 马略尔卡陶器〔16 世纪意大利产的装饰用陶器〕;马略尔卡陶器的现代仿制品。

ma·jor[1] [ˈmeidʒə; ˋmedʒə] **I** *a*. (*opp*. minor) **1**. 较大的;较多的;较优的;主要的;第一流的;较大范围的。**2**. 成年的;〔英〕(学校中同姓同学中的)年长的。**3**.【逻】大(前提);【乐】大调的,大音阶的。*a* ~ *angle* 优角。a ~ *axis*【数】长轴(线)。*the* ~ *vote* 多数票。*the* ~ *industries* 主要工业。*Brown* ~年纪较大的布朗。*a* ~ *combat* 主力战。*a* ~ *engagement* 大战,会战。~ *operations* 大规模作战。*a* ~ *overhaul* 大修。*the* ~ *part* 过半,大部,多数。**II** *n*. **1**. 成年人。**2**.【逻】大名词;大前提。**3**.【乐】大调;大音阶。**4**.〔美〕专修科目;专科生。**III** *vi*.〔美口〕主修,专攻〔*cf*. minor〕。~ *in history* 主修历史。~ **league**〔美〕棒球联合总会(即"全国棒球联合会"或"全美职业棒球联合会")〔*cf*. minor league〕。~ **mode**【乐】大调调式。~ **offensive** 主攻,大规模进攻。~ **order** 高级圣职〔**1**.【天主】司祭;助祭;副助祭。**2**. (其他一些基督教派的)主教;牧师;助祭〕。~ **premise**【逻】大前提。~ **scale**【乐】大音阶。~ **sceptre**【美体】全国锦标。~ **seminary**【天主】祭司神学院。~ **seventh**【乐】大七度。~ **suit** (桥牌中"黑桃"或"红桃"的)一手高记分值同花。~ **term**【逻】大名辞;【数】大词,大项。~ **tone**【乐】大全音。~ **upset**【美体】大败。

ma·jor[2] [ˈmeidʒə; ˋmedʒə] *n*. 〔苏、美等〕陆军[空军]少校;〔英〕陆军少校〔空军少校叫 squadron leader〕;【军俚】= sergeant major;【军】…长。*a drum* ~(军队)鼓手长。~ **general**〔英〕陆军[海军陆战队]少将;〔美〕陆军[空军、海军陆战队]少将。**-ship** *n*. 陆军少校的职位。

ma·jor-do·mo [ˈmeidʒəˈdəuməu; ˋmedʒəˋdomo] *n*. **1**. (意大利、西班牙王室的)管家;〔谑〕大管家。**2**.〔美〕(南部农牧场的)监管人;(New Mexico 州的)灌溉管理员。

ma·jor·ette [ˌmeidʒəˈret; ˏmedʒəˋrεt] *n*. 军乐队女领队,军乐队女指挥的简称(= drum majorette)。

ma·jor·i·tar·i·an [məˌdʒɔriˈtεəriən; məˏdʒɑrɪˋtεrɪən] **I** *n*. 多数主义者。**II** *a*. 多数主义的。**-ism** *n*. 多数主义。

ma·jor·i·ty [məˈdʒɔriti; məˋdʒɔrətɪ] *n*. **1**. 大多数,过半数,大部分。**2**. (选举)(多于对方全体票数的)多得票数 (*cf*. plurality)。★例如:A 得 120 票,B 得 70 票,C 得 30 票时,A 的 majority 是 20 票,A 的 plurality 则是 50 票。**3**. 陆军少校的职位,少校级。**4**. 成年;法定年龄。*The minority is subordinate to the* ~. 少数服从多数。*attain* [*reach*] *one's* ~达到成年。*the* ~ *opinion* 多数人的意见。***be in the* ~ *by*** ... 仅多…票。***by a* ~ *of*** 多得…票(当选)。***join*** [***go over to***, ***pass over to***] ***the*** ~ 死去。***the silent*** ~ 沉默的大多数,沉默的群体〔指政治上不愿公开表态但却抱有一定看法的大多数民众〕。~ **leader** (议会中)多数党领袖。~ **rule** 多数裁定原则。

Ma·jun·ga [məˈdʒʌŋgə; məˋdʒʌŋgə] *n*. 马任加〔马达加斯加港市〕。

ma·jus·cule [ˈmædʒəskjuːl, Am. məˈdʒʌskjuːl; mæˋdʒəskjul, ˋmædʒʌskjul] **I** *n*. (*pl*. ~*s*, *-culae* [-kjuliː; -kjʊli]) 大字体;大写字母。**II** *a*. 大字体的,大写的。

make [meik; mek] **I** *vt*. (*made* [meid; med]) **1**. (a) 做,作,造,制造,做成,造成,建设;创作,著作,拟,起草;制定,设置;征收。*I am not made that way*. 我生性不是那样。~ *enemies* 树敌。(b)准备,预备,布置,整理;训练,养乖(狗)。~ *a bed* 准备床铺,铺床。~ *tea* 泡茶,沏茶。~ *the cards* 洗牌。*M- hay while the sun shines*. 趁晴晒草;〔转义〕勿失良机,利用合适的时机。

(c)构成。*Oxygen and hydrogen ~ water*. 氧和氢构成水。*Cold tea ~s excellent drink in summer*. 凉茶是夏天的好饮料。*The country is made up of meadow and marsh*. 那地区全是草地和沼泽。(d)行,实行;定,签订,缔结。~ *a bow* 鞠躬。~ *a journey* 旅行。~ *a contract* 定契约。(e)述,说,提出,(赛艇)划得好。~ *a joke* 说笑话;开玩笑。~ *a speech* [〔美〕 *an address*] 演说。(f)得,获得;挣,赚;【牌】赢;(东西)能卖…;【体】得分。~ *money* 挣钱,赚钱。~ *a reputation* 博得名声。~ *a trick* (玩牌)赢一墩牌。*The picture ~s a good price*. 这画卖得好价钱。(g)走,行,进行;【海】开始看见;〔俚〕赶得上…,赶上。(*a train*) ~ *ten miles a day*. 一日走十英里。(h)计算,算定,估计;以为,认为,看做;抱有;思想[考虑、推测]…。*What time do you ~ it* = *What do you ~ the time*? 你看(现在)几点钟了? *He is not such an ass* [*a goose*] *as they ~ him*. 他并没有像大家想像的那样笨。(i)成为;等于;总计。*Two and two ~ four*. 2加2得[等于]4。(j)设计,发明;决定;【商】定(价钱)。(k)【电】开,通(电流)(*opp*. break). (l)发生,使发生,成为…的原因。~ *a difference*, *mark*; ~ *peace*, *trouble*, *work*, 等等〔见各该名词〕。(m)吃。~ *a good dinner* [*meal*] 吃饱一顿好餐。(n)行动得像…。~ *a fool of oneself* 丢丑,使自己成为笑柄。(o)翻译。(p)偷。(q)〔美口〕发现,知道,认识;成为…的会员,在…里得到一个地位;使(异性等)着迷。*He made the team*. 他成了队员。**2.** 〔make + 宾语 + 补语〕使…成为(某种人或物);使某人的处境或某事的状况如何。~ *him a soldier* 使他成为军人。~ *her happy* 使她幸福。**3.** 〔make + 宾语 + 不带 to 的不定式。但在被动语态结构中则用带 to 的不定式〕使(…)…,强迫…(做某事)。~ *him understand* [*laugh*] 使他了解[笑]。~ *the grass grow* 使草生长。*He was made to go*. 他是被迫去的。**4.** 〔make + 宾语 + 过去分词〕使(…)…,使(别人)…。*Too much wine ~s men drunk*. 饮酒过多使人醉。~ *oneself understood* 使人了解自己的意思。*What ~s him honoured*? 什么使他受人尊敬? **5.** 〔make + 间接宾语 + 直接宾语〕做…给…。*I made him a new suit*. 我做了一套新的衣服给他。*She will ~ him a good wife*. 她会成为他的好妻子[贤内助]。**6.** 〔make + 名词常等于与该名词同义的动词〕:~ *haste* = hasten. ~ (*an*) *answer* = answer. ~ (*an*) *appointment* = appoint.

— ***vi*.** **1.** 前进,向…去 (*for*); 预备去,将去。**2.** 开始 (*to do something*); 行动得(像…); 似乎要。*He ~s as if he would escape*. 他装作要逃走的样子。*He made to strike me*. 他要动手打我。**3.** (潮)满,涨;(潮水)开始涨。*The tide is making fast*. 潮水在急涨。*Water was making in the hold*. 舱里的水越来越多。**4.** 有效验 (*for*; *against*; *with*)。**5.** 指向,趋向,指示;朝某方向前进。*All the evidence ~s in the same direction*. 所有的证据都指向同一个方向。**6.** 在进行中。**7.** 被制造;被处理。*Bolts are making in this shop*. 这个工厂正在制造螺栓。**8.** 〔宾语省略,后接形容词,表示某种状态、方式〕:~ *ready* 作好准备。~ *bold* 冒昧,敢于。**9.** 进行中,将完成。~ ***a break*** 〔美俚〕做错,出丑,失言;打断谈话;企图越狱;(*with*) 与…断绝关系。~ ***a dead set*** 不屈不挠地干;拼命攻击。~ ***a getaway*** 〔美俚〕逃亡,逃掉。~ ***a go*** 〔美俚〕成功,得到。~ ***a killing*** 〔美俚〕赚大钱,发大财。~ ***a place*** 〔美口〕闯入某处抢东西。~ ***a play for*** 〔美口〕百般勾引,使出浑身解数迷惑,拿出所有本领求得。~ ***a touch*** 〔美俚〕向人讨钱。~ ***after*** 〔古〕追赶;跟随。~ ***against*** 和…冲突;不利于…,妨碍 (*opp*. ~ for)。~ ***and break*** 接通和切断(电路)。~ ***as if*** = ~ ***as though*** 假装,装着。~ ***at*** 向…前进;袭击,攻击;扑向 (*The tiger made at the men*. 老虎向人们扑了过来)。~ ***away*** (急急)离去,逃走,逃亡。~ ***away with*** **1.** 带走,拿走,偷;杀死;毁弃,减掉 (~ *away with oneself* 自杀)。**2.** (把钱)花光,用光;浪费;吃掉。~ ***back*** 回来,归。~ ***believe*** 假装。~ ***bold*** [***free***] **1.** 冒昧,请允许我 (*I ~ bold to give you a piece of advice*. 我不揣冒昧,贡献您一点意见)。**2.** 对某人放肆无礼,任意[擅自]处理某事 (*with*) (*In his article he ~s free with facts*. 他在文章里以随便的态度对待事实)。**3.** 随便使用。~ ***colours*** 【海】(早晨八时)升船旗。~ ***contact*** 接通电流;接触。~ ***dead*** 【电】切断。~ (*sth*.) ***do*** = ~ ***do with*** (*sth*.) 用(某物)设法应付。~ ***down*** 清算;改小,准备。~ ***for*** (*opp*. ~ against) **1.** 有利于;对…有益;倾向于。**2.** 拥护,支持。**3.** 向…前进;袭击。~ (*sth*.) ***from*** 用…做材料[样子]制造 (*Wine is made from grapes*. 葡萄酒是用葡萄酿造的) 〔*cf*. ~ of〕。~ ***harbour*** 入港,到埠。~ ***hey-hey*** [hei-hei; he-he] 〔美俚〕胡闹,瞎闹。~ ***him step*** 【美体】使对方尽量奋斗。~ ***in*** 到…去,进入;干涉;参加。~ ***into*** 制成,做成;使转变为。~ ***it*** 赶到;办成功;规定时间;〔美俚〕性交。~ ***it good upon*** (*sb*.) 凭威力使(某人)接受自己的话。~ ***it hot for*** 使受不了,使为难;拼命攻击。~ ***it one's business to do*** 把…当作自己的任务去干。~ ***it pay*** 使合算。~ ***it so*** 【海】命令打钟。~ ***it up*** 和解,讲和 (*with*)。~ ***it up to*** 偿,赎。~ ***of*** **1.** 用(木材等)造(船等)〔指制成品保有原材料形状者,否则用 ~ from〕; 养成,训练成 (~ *a teacher of one's son* 把孩子培养成教师)。**2.** 了解;认为 (*can ~ nothing of it* 弄不明白。*I ~ nothing of it*. 我认为那没有什么了不起)。~ ***off*** 去,急忙跑掉[离开],逃走,逃亡。~ ***off with*** 拐走,拐跑,偷去,拿走。~ ***one*** (***of the party***) 加入团体。~ ***one's living*** 谋生;得到生活费。~ ***one's own life*** 决定生活方向。~ ***oneself*** 自学。~ ***oneself strange*** 假装生客,假装吃惊。~ ***oneself understood*** 使了解自己意思。~ ***or mar*** [***break***] 使(计划等)(完全)成功或(完全)失败。~ ***out*** **1.** 理解,领悟;发现,看出 (*I could not ~ out what the police wanted*. 我不明白警察要的是什么。*I ~ out a ship in the distance*. 我看见远处有一条船)。**2.** 起草,拟,填写,开列 (~ *out a list* 开清单)。**3.** 证明,说得像,说成,说是 (*He ~s me out a fool*. 他把我说成一个傻瓜)。**4.** 成就,完成。**5.** 消磨(时光)。**6.** 〔美口〕设法周转,东拼西凑的过日子;扩大,伸张 (*He ~s out to keep out of debt*. 他东拼西凑总算是没有背债。*How are things making out*? 事情进展得怎样?)。~ ***out a good case*** 自圆其说。~ ***out of*** **1.** 用…制做… 〔*cf*. ~ of〕。**2.** 理解;了解。~ ***over*** 让,转让,移交;改造,改制(特指衣服等)(~ *over a coat* 把一件外套翻新)。~ ***record*** 创造新纪录。~ ***straight shoot*** 〔美口〕走最近的路,采取最直接的方法。~ ***sure*** 尽力做到,保证;深信,有把握。~ ***sure of*** 弄清楚,查明无误 (*M- sure of your facts before you write the article*. 先弄明白事实,然后再写文章)。~ ***the air blue*** 〔美〕骂街,满口下流话。~ ***the bull's eye*** (射击)中的;得显著胜利。~ ***the queer*** 〔美俚〕伪造货币。~ ***through with*** 完成。~ ***time*** 急往,急匆匆地去。~ ***towards*** 向…前进。~ ***up*** **1.** 补,弥补,补给,补充,补足 (*for*) (*Each ~ up what the other lacks*. 互通有无。~ *up* (*for*) *a loss* 弥补损失。~ *up for lost time* 补回损失的时间)。**2.** 修理;制作;装配。**3.** (由种种要素)组成,合成;调配成。**4.** 作成,起草,编辑,编纂。**5.** 打扮;【剧】化装。**6.** 定,决定;签订;调解,排解(争吵、纠纷等) (*shake hands and ~ it up* 握手言归于好)。**7.** 决算,清算。**8.** 包,收拾。**9.** 做,缝。**10.** 捏造。**11.** 争论。**12.** 【印】拼版,整版;(印刷品的)编排;【铁道】调配(车辆)(~ *up a train of cars* 调配一列车)。~ ***up to*** 接近;巴结;向女人求爱;补偿,赔还(某人)。~ ***up with*** 和…讲和[和解]。~ ***with*** 做动作;做出;使用;提供。

II *n*. **1.** 构造,组织。**2.** 脾性,性格,天性。**3.** 体格;形状;样式,样子;种类,品质。**4.** 制造,制法;产量。**5.** 【电】(电路的)接通。*a man of his ~* 像他那种性格的人。*What ~ of car is this*? 这是什么厂出品的汽车?

home [foreign] ～本国[外国]制。things of Japanese ～日本制品。～ **and break**【电】通断开关。～ **and mend**〔英〕【海】闲暇时候。**on the** ～〔口〕在构成[增长、改进]中;拼命弄钱,拼命吸引异性注意,想尽办法巴结;野心勃勃的,努力向上的;机警的,不落空的。～ **bate**〔罕〕挑斗的人,挑唆吵架的人。～**-believe** 1. *n*. 假装,假托;假装的人。2. *a*. 假装的。～**fast** 系船浮子,拴船柱;系船桩。～**-game** 嘲笑的对象;笑柄。～**over** 彻底改变,大翻新,改头换面。～**-peace** = peacemaker. ～**shift** 1. *n*. 将就,凑合,一时之计,权宜之计,临时手段 (*use an empty box as a ～shift for a table* 以空箱当饭桌凑合使用)。2. *a*. 暂时的,一时的。～**-sport** = make-game. ～**-up** 1. (演员的)装扮,打扮,化装;化装用具;化妆品。2. 组织,构造,结构。3. 体格;性格;【印】版面;垫版;拼版 (*elements in one's ～-up* 特征)。4. 假装,虚构。5.〔美〕补考,补充,补偿。～**weight** 补足重量的东西;填料;(尤指)小蜡烛;没有价值的人[东西];不重要的议论。～**-work** 为使工作者不闲散而分派的工作。

mak·er [ˈmeikə; ˋmekɚ] *n*. 1. 制造者,制作人,制造商;创造者;出票人。2.〔our, his, the M-〕造物主,上帝。3.〔古〕诗人。4.【电】接合器。*the policy ～s* 决定政策的人,决策者。**go to [meet] one's M-** 死。～**-up** (*pl*. ～***s-up***)【印】拼版工人;〔英〕制品装配工;服装工人。

mak·ing [ˈmeikiŋ; ˋmekɪŋ] *n*. 1. 制作(物),制造(物),生产;一次制造量;发展[发达]过程;成功的原因[手段];组织;〔常 *pl*.〕原料,材料。2.〔口〕〔*pl*.〕利益,赚头,所得。3.〔*pl*.〕素质,要素。4.〔*pl*.〕〔美口〕(自卷自抽的)卷烟材料[纸和烟]。5. (煤矿中挖出来的)粉煤。*the ～s of a good garden* 一个美好的花园的条件。**be the ～ of** 成为…的基础,保证…的成功 (*His failure has been the ～ of him*. 他的失败成了他成功的原因)。**have the ～s of** 具有…的素质。**in** ～ 制造中,建设中。**in the** ～ 酝酿中的,在发展过程中的;未完成的。～**-up price**〔美〕(股票的)核定价格。

-making *suf*.〔口〕使人…的:sick- [shy-] ～.

Mak·kah [ˈmækə; ˋmækə] *n*. 麦加〔阿拉伯语 Mecca,为伊斯兰教圣城〕。

Ma·ku·a [mɑːˈkuːɑː; mɑˋkuɑ] *n*. 1. (*pl*. ～(***s***)) 马库阿人〔莫桑比克北部和附近的坦噶尼喀人〕。2. 马库阿语。

ma·ku·ta [mɑːˈkuːtɑː; mɑˋkutɑ] *n*. likuta (里库塔〔扎伊尔的货币名〕)的复数。

mal [mɑːl; mɑl] *n*.〔F.〕= sickness. ～ ***de mer*** [ˈmɛə; ˋmɛr]晕船。～ ***du pays*** [djuˈpei; djuˋpe]怀乡病。

mal- *comb. f*. 1. = bad, badly (*opp*. bene-): *mal*treat; *mal*development 发育不良。2. = not, un-: *mal*content. 3. = imperfect, deficient: *mal*formation.

Ma·la·bo [ˈmɑːlɑːbəu; ˋmɑlɑbo] *n*. 马拉博〔赤道几内亚首都〕。

Ma·lac·ca [məˈlækə; məˋlækə] *n*. 1. 马六甲〔马来西亚港市〕。2.【史】满喇加国。*the Strait of* ～马六甲海峡〔亚洲〕。～ **cane** (用棕榈树干制成的)马六甲手杖。

mal·a·chite [ˈmæləkait; ˋmælə͵kaɪt] *n*.【矿】孔雀石。

mal·a·co·derm [ˈmæləkədəːm; ˋmæləkədɚm] *n*.【动】软皮动物,(尤指)海葵 (sea anemone)。

mal·a·col·o·gy [ˌmæləˈkɔlədʒi; ͵mæləˋkɑlədʒɪ] *n*. 软体动物学。

mal·a·cos·tra·can [ˌmæləˈkɔstrəkən; ͵mæləˋkɑstrəkən] *a*.【动】软甲亚纲 (Malacostraca) 的 (= malacostracous)。**-tra·cous** [-kəs; -kəs] *n*. 软甲亚纲动物。

mal·ad·dress [ˌmæləˈdres; ͵mæləˋdrɛs] *n*. 粗鲁,拙笨,笨。

mal·ad·just·ed [ˈmæləˈdʒʌstid; ͵mæləˋdʒʌstɪd] *a*. 精神失调的;【心】不能适应环境的;顺应不良的。

mal·ad·jus·tive [ˈmæləˈdʒʌstiv; ͵mæləˋdʒʌstɪv] *a*. 引起失调的。

mal·ad·just·ment [ˈmæləˈdʒʌstmənt; ͵mæləˋdʒʌstmənt] *n*. 1. 调节不善,调理不善;失调。2. 不适应;【心】顺应不良。

mal·ad·min·is·ter [ˈmælədˈministə; ͵mælədˋmɪnəstɚ] *vt*. 胡乱处理,瞎搞,胡搞(公共事务)。**-tration** *n*. 恶政,乱政;(公务、公事的)处理不善,管理不善,紊乱。

mal·a·droit [ˈmæləˈdrɔit; ͵mæləˋdrɔɪt] *a*. 笨拙的,拙劣的,愚钝的。**-ly** *ad*. **-ness** *n*.

mal·a·dy [ˈmælədi; ˋmælədɪ] *n*. 1. 毛病,疾病;(社会的)弊端,弊病;歪风。2. (葡萄酒的)酸腐。

ma·la fi·de [ˈmeilə ˈfaidi; ˋmeləˋfaɪdɪ] *ad*., *a*.〔L.〕不守信义地[的];恶意地[的];不诚实地[的],狡猾地[的] (*opp*. bona fide)。

ma·la fi·des [ˈmeilə ˈfaidi; ˋmeləˋfaɪdi] *n*.〔L.〕不诚实,恶意。

Mal·a·ga [ˈmæləgə; ˋmæləgə] *n*. 1. 马拉加〔西班牙南部省名及其首府名〕。2. 马拉加白葡萄酒。

Mal·a·gas·y [ˌmæləˈgæsi; ͵mæləˋgæsɪ] **I** *a*. 马尔加什人[语]的,马达加斯加岛的。**II** *n*. (*pl*. ～, ***-sies***) 马尔加什共和国〔非洲〕;马尔加什人[语];马达加斯加岛人。

mal·a·gue·na [ˈmæləˈgeinjə, -ˈgweinə; ˋmæləˋgenjə, -ˋgwenə] *n*. (西班牙)马拉加民歌;马拉加民间曲调;马拉加民间舞蹈。

ma·laise [mæˈleiz; mæˋlez] *n*.〔F.〕不舒服;小病,微恙;精神欠爽。

mal·a·mute [ˈmæləmjuːt; ˋmɑlə͵mjut] *n*. 阿拉斯加雪橇狗 (= Alaskan ～)。

Ma·lan [ˈmælən; ˋmælən] *n*. 马伦〔姓氏〕。

mal·an·ders [ˈmæləndəz; ˋmæləndəz] *n*.〔*pl*.〕【兽医】膝皲。

mal·a·pert [ˈmæləpəːt; ˋmælə͵pɝt] *a*., *n*.〔古〕没礼貌的(人);脸皮厚的(人)。

mal·a·prop, mal·a·pro·pi·an [ˈmæləprɔp, ˌmæləˈprɔpiən; ˋmælə͵prɑp, ͵mæləˋprɔpɪən] *a*. 滑稽地错用语词的,文字弄错的,可笑的。

mal·a·prop·ism [ˈmæləprɔpizəm; ˋmæləprɑp͵ɪzəm] *n*. 语词的滑稽误用〔如将 loquacity 误为 locality, instinctive 误为 insentive 之类〕;被误用得可笑的词。

mal·ap·ro·pos [ˌmælˈæprəpəu, Am. ˌmælæprəˈpəu; ͵mælˋæprəpo, ͵mælæprəˋpo] **I** *a*.〔常用作表语〕不合时宜的;不适当的。**II** *ad*. 不凑巧。**III** *n*. 不适当的言行。

ma·lar [ˈmeilə; ˋmelɚ] *n*., *a*. 颧骨(的),颊(的)。

ma·lar·i·a [məˈlɛəriə; məˋlɛrɪə] *n*.〔古〕瘴气;【医】疟疾。**-i·al, -i·an, -i·ous** *a*.

ma·lar·i·al·ist [məˈlɛəriəlist; məˋlɛrɪəlɪst] *n*. 疟疾专家。

mal·ate [ˈmæleit, ˈmeileit; ˋmælet, ˋmelet] *n*.【化】苹果酸,苹果酸盐(或酯)。

mal·a·thi·on [ˌmæləˈθaiɔn; ͵mæləˋθaɪɑn] *n*. 马拉硫磷,马拉息昂,马拉松〔一种有机磷杀虫剂〕。

Ma·la·wi [mɑːˈlɑːwi; mɑˋlɑwɪ] *n*. 马拉维〔非洲,旧称尼亚萨兰〕。

Ma·lay [məˈlei; məˋle] **I** *n*. 马来人[语];【动】马来鸡 (= ～ fowl)。**II** *a*. 马来(半岛)的;马来人[语]的。～ **Archipelago [Peninsula]** 马来群岛[半岛]。～ **fowl** 马来鸡。

Ma·lay·a [məˈleiə; məˋleə] *n*. 马来亚;马来半岛。

Mal·a·ya·lam [ˌmæliˈɑːləm; ͵mæləˋjɑləm] *n*. (印度西南海岸 Malabar 的)德拉维族 (Dravidian)语。

Ma·lay·an [məˈleiən; məˋleən] *a*., *n*. = Malay.

Ma·lay·o-Pol·y·ne·sian [məˌleiəuˌpɔliˈniːʒən, -ʃən; mə͵leo͵pɑlɪˋniʒən, -ʃən] **I** *a*. 马来—玻里尼西亚语系的;南岛语系的。**II** *n*. 马来—玻里尼西亚语;南岛语。

Ma·lay·sia [məˈleiʒə; məˋleʒə] *n*. 马来西亚〔亚洲〕;= Malay Archipelago 马来群岛。**-n I** *a*. 马来西亚的;马

来西亚人的。**II** ***n*.** 马来西亚人。

Mal·colm [ˌmælkəm; ˋmælkəm] ***n*.** 马尔科姆〔姓氏,男子名〕。

mal·con·for·ma·tion [ˈmælkɔnfɔːˈmeiʃən; ˏmælkɑnfɔrˋmeʃən] ***n*.** 难看,丑。

mal·con·tent [ˈmælkəntent; ˋmælkənˏtɛnt] **I** ***a*.** (尤指对政府)抱怨的,不满的。**II** ***n*.** 不满者;不满。

mal de mer [mɑːldəˈmer; mɑldəˋmɛr] 〔法〕晕船。

Mal·dive [ˈmɔːldaiv, ˈmældaiv; ˋmɔldaɪv, ˋmældaɪv] ***n*.** 马尔代夫〔亚洲〕。**-div·i·an** **1.** ***a*.** 马尔代夫的。**2.** ***n*.** 马尔代夫人;马尔代夫语。

Male [ˈmɑːlei; ˋmɑle] ***n*.** 马累[马律]〔马尔代夫首都〕。

male [meil; mel] **I** ***a*.** (*opp*. female) 男、公、雄;男性的;阳性的,【植】雄性的,仅有雄蕊的;全是男人的。*the* ~ *choir* 男声合唱队。*a* ~ *flower* 雄花。*a* ~ *chauvinist pig* (常缩作 MCP)歧视妇女的人;大男子主义者。~ **bonding** 男人之间的情谊;男人小圈子。**II** ***n*.** 男,男子,男性;雄性动物;【植】雄性植物;【自】插入式配件。~ **fern**【植】绵马。~ **hormone** 雄性激素。~ **screw** 阳螺旋,柱螺纹。~ **tank** (装有轻炮、机枪的)重战车。

male- *comb*. *f*. (*opp*. bene-) = evil, ill.

malease [mæˈliːz; mæˋliz] ***n*.** = malaise.

mal·e·dict [ˈmælidikt; ˋmæləˏdɪkt] **I** ***a*.** 〔古〕被诅咒的;可恶的,讨厌的。**II** ***vt*.** 〔古〕诅咒,咒骂。

mal·e·dic·tion [ˌmæliˈdikʃən; ˏmæləˋdɪkʃən] ***n*.** **1.** 诅咒,诬蔑。**2.** 诽谤 (*opp*. benediction)。***utter a*** ~ 诅咒。

mal·e·fac·tion [ˌmæliˈfækʃən; ˏmæləˋfækʃən] ***n*.** 犯罪行为,坏事;罪恶。

mal·e·fac·tor [ˈmælifæktə; ˋmæləˏfæktɚ] ***n*.** (*opp*. benefactor) 犯罪分子;作恶者;坏人。

ma·lef·ic [məˈlefik; məˋlɛfɪk] **I** ***a*.** 有害的,邪恶的。**II** ***n*.** 【占星】凶星。

ma·lef·i·cence [məˈlefisns; məˋlɛfəsn̩s] ***n*.** 邪恶的行径,坏事;毒害;邪恶性。

ma·lef·i·cent [məˈlefisnt; məˋlɛfəsn̩t] ***a*.** 犯罪的,做坏事的;有害的 (*to*); 邪恶的。

ma·le·ic [məˈliːik; məˋliɪk] ***a*.** ~ **acid**【化】马来酸,顺丁烯二酸。~ **hydrazide**【化】马来醯[酰]肼。

mal·e·mute [ˈmælimjuːt; ˋmælɪmjut] ***n*.** = malamute.

mal·en·ten·du [malɑ̃ːnˈtɑ̃ːndy; malɑ̃tɑ̃ˋdy] **I** ***a*.** 〔F.〕误解的,误会的。**II** ***n*.** 误解,误会。

ma·lev·o·lence [məˈlevələns; məˋlɛvələns] ***n*.** 恶意,坏心肠,黑心,恶毒,狠毒的行为。

ma·lev·o·lent [məˈlevələnt; məˋlɛvələnt] ***a*.** 有恶意的,心肠坏的,恶毒的,幸灾乐祸的 (*opp*. benevolent)。**-ly** ***ad*.**

mal·fea·sance [mælˈfiːzəns; ˏmælˋfizn̩s] ***n*.** 【法】坏事;(尤指官吏的)非法行为,渎职(罪)。

mal·fea·sant [mælˈfiːzənt; ˏmælˋfizn̩t] **I** ***a*.** 胡作非为的,做坏事的。**II** ***n*.** 犯罪者。

mal·for·ma·tion [ˌmælfɔːˈmeiʃən; ˏmælfɔrˋmeʃən] ***n*.** 畸形(性);畸形物,畸形体。

mal·formed [ˈmælˈfɔːmd; mælˋfɔrmd] ***a*.** 畸形的;残缺的。

mal·func·tion [mælˈfʌŋkʃən; mælˋfʌŋkʃən] ***n*.** 失灵;机能失常;故障;事故。*guidance* ~【空】制导设备失灵。

Mal·gache [mælˈgæʃ; mælˋgæʃ] Malagasy 的法语拼写形式。

mal·gré lui [malˈgreˈlui; malˋgreˋlʊɪ] 〔F.〕非出于本意地,情不自禁地。

Ma·li [ˈmɑːliː; ˋmɑli] ***n*.** 马里〔非洲〕。

ma·lic ac·id [ˈmeilik ˈæsid; ˋmelɪkˋæsɪd] 【化】苹果酸,羟基丁二酸。

mal·ice [ˈmælis; ˋmælɪs] ***n*.** 恶意,恶感,恶念,毒心;怨恨,【法】预谋。~ *prepense* [*aforethought*] (杀人的)预谋。***bear*** ~ ***to*** [***towards***] 对…怀恨。***stand mute of*** ~【法】对被控罪名拒不答辩。

ma·li·cious [məˈliʃəs; məˋlɪʃəs] ***a*.** 有恶意的,存心不良的,有敌意的;蓄意的;预谋的。~ *mischief* 蓄意破坏他人财产的行为。***make*** ~ ***remarks*** 骂。**-ly** ***ad*.** **-ness** ***n*.**

ma·lign [məˈlain; məˋlaɪn] **I** ***a*.** (*opp*. benign) 有害的,邪恶的;恶性的(疾病等);〔罕〕有恶意的,恶毒的。*a* ~ *influence* 坏影响。**II** ***vt*.** 诬蔑,诽谤,中伤。*His face ~s him*. 他相貌不好人好。**-er** ***n*.** 诬蔑者。**-ly** ***ad*.** 有害地;恶意地。

ma·lig·nance, ma·lig·nan·cy [məˈlignəns, -si; məˋlɪgnəns, -sɪ] ***n*.** (极端的)恶意;恶毒的行为;不吉,凶;【医】恶性;恶性肿瘤。

ma·lig·nant [məˈlignənt; məˋlɪgnənt] **I** ***a*.** **1.** 有恶意的;恶毒的。**2.** 恶性的(疾病等)(*opp*. benignant)。**3.** 有害的;邪恶的;不吉利的。**4.**【英史】保王党的。**II** ***n*.** 怀恶意的人;【英史】保王党党员。~ *cholera* 恶性霍乱。**-ly** ***ad*.**

ma·lig·ni·ty [məˈligniti; məˋlɪgnətɪ] ***n*.** 恶意,敌意,毒心;怨恨;【医】(病的)恶性。

ma·li·hi·ni [ˌmæliˈhiːni; ˏmælɪˋhinɪ] ***n*.** 〔Haw.〕新到夏威夷的人;夏威夷人中的外来者。

ma·lines [məˈliːn; F. maˈlin; məˋlin, maˋlɪn] ***n*.** **1.** 梅克林花边 (= Machlin lace)。**2.** 马林丝纱罗〔女服或面纱用的一种细丝网〕。

ma·lin·ger [məˈliŋgə; məˋlɪŋgɚ] ***vi*.** (士兵为逃避勤务)装病。**-er** ***n*.**

ma·lin·ger·y [məˈliŋgəri; məˋlɪŋgərɪ] ***n*.** 假病。

Ma·lin·ke [məliŋˈkei; məlɪŋˋke] ***n*.** **1.** (*pl*. ***-kes***, ***-ke***) (非洲西岸)马林凯人。**2.** 马林凯语。

ma·lism [ˈmeilizəm; ˋmelɪzəm] ***n*.** 世恶说。

mal·i·son [ˈmælizn, -sn; ˋmæləzn̩, -sn̩] ***n*.** 〔古〕诅咒,咒骂,诽谤 (*opp*. benison)。

mal·kin [ˈmɔːkin; ˋmɔkɪn] ***n*.** 〔废、英方〕**1.** 懒婆娘。**2.** 拖布。**3.** 稻草人。**4.** 野兔。**5.** 猫。

mall[1] [mɔːl; mɔl] ***n*.** = maul.

mall[2] [mɔːl; mɔl] ***n*.** **1.** 林荫路,林荫散步场。**2.** 铁圈球(场)(= pall-mall)。**3.** 铁圈球槌。**4.**〔美〕购物中心,商场。**The M-** [mæl; mæl] 伦敦 St. James 公园的林荫路。~ **intercept** 〔美〕(商场为听取顾客意见而进行的)顾客购物动向调查。~ **rat** 〔美〕成天泡商场的人。~**-walk** 商场散步。

mal·lard [ˈmæləd; ˋmælɚd] ***n*.** (*pl*. ~(*s*)) 〔集合词〕【鸟】雄野鸭,绿头鸭,凫;野鸭肉。

mal·le·a·bil·i·ty [ˌmæliəˈbiliti; ˏmælɪəˋbɪlətɪ] ***n*.** (金属的)可锻性,展性;柔顺性,顺从。

mal·le·a·ble [ˈmæliəbl; ˋmælɪəbl̩] ***a*.** 可锻的,可锤薄的,有延展性的,韧性的;柔顺的;顺从的。~ **iron** 韧铁。~ **castiron** 韧性铸铁,可锻铸铁。

mal·lee [ˈmæli; ˋmælɪ] ***n*.** (南澳洲产)小桉树。

mal·lein [ˈmæliin; ˋmælɪɪn] ***n*.** 【医】(接种诊断用)马鼻疽杆菌。

mal·le·muck [ˈmælimʌk; ˋmælɪmʌk] ***n*.** 【鸟】海洋鸟〔海燕、信天翁等〕。

mal·le·o·lar [məˈliːələ; məˋliəlɚ] ***a*.** 踝的。

mal·le·o·lus [məˈliːələs; məˋliələs] ***n*.** 【解】踝;【植】压条。

mal·let [ˈmælit; ˋmælɪt] ***n*.** 木槌,槌,(打马球等用的)球棍,【解】锤骨;(*pl*.)【美体】马球。

mal·le·us [ˈmæliəs; ˋmælɪəs] ***n*.** (*pl*. ***-lei*** [-liai; -lɪˏaɪ]) 【解】锤骨 (= hammer);〔M-〕【动】擅木贝属;(马)鼻疽。

mal·low [ˈmæləu; ˋmælo] ***n*.** 【植】锦葵属。*Indian* ~ 苘麻;青麻。~ **rose**【植】= **rose** ~ 木槿属植物(尤指草芙蓉)。

malm [mɑːm; mɑm] ***n*.** 泥灰岩,柔软的白垩岩;白垩土;钙质砂土;黏土和白垩的混合物;白垩砖。

malm·sey [ˈmɑːmzi; ˋmɑmzɪ] ***n*.** (希腊)醇香白葡萄酒。

mal·nour·ished [mælˈnʌriʃt; mælˋnɝɪʃt] *a*. 营养不良的。

mal·nu·tri·tion [ˈmælnjuːˈtriʃən; ˏmælnjuˋtrɪʃən] *n*. 营养不良。

mal·oc·clu·sion [ˌmæləˈkluʒən; ˏmæləˋkluʒən] *n*. 【医】(上下牙齿的)错位咬合。

ma·lo·dor·ant [mæˈləudərənt; mælˋodərənt] *a*., *n*. 恶臭的;恶臭物。

mal·o·dor·ous [mæˈləudərəs; mælˋodərəs] *a*. 有恶臭的。**-ly** *ad*. **-ness** *n*.

mal·o·do(u) [ˌmæˈləudə; ˏmæˋlodə] *n*. 恶臭,臭气。

Ma·lone [mæˈləun; məˋlon] *n*. 马隆〔姓氏〕。

ma·lon·ic [məˈlɔnik, -ˈləunik; məˋlɑnɪk, -ˋlonɪk] *a*. ～ **acid**【化】丙二酸。

Mal·o·ry [ˈmæləri; ˋmælərɪ] *n*. 马洛里〔姓氏〕。

Mal·pigh·i·an [mælˈpigiən; mɑlˋpigɪən] *a*. 【解】马尔丕基氏的。～ **bodies** [**capsules, corpuscles**] 肾小体;马尔丕基氏体。～ **layer**【生】生发层。～ **tubules**【生】马尔丕基氏管。

mal·po·si·tion [ˌmælpəˈziʃən; ˏmælpəˋzɪʃən] *n*. 位置不正;【产科】错位;胎位不正。

mal·prac·tice [ˈmælˈpræktis; mælˋpræktɪs] *n*. 1.【医】疗法失当,滥治。2. 玩忽职守,渎职;歪风,恶癖;【法】违法行为。～*s hindering the construction of key projects* 破坏重点建设的歪风。

malt [mɔːlt; mɔlt] **I** *n*. 麦芽;麦芽酒,啤酒;麦乳精。**II** *a*. 麦芽的;含麦芽的;麦芽制的。**III** *vt*. 1. 使成麦芽。2. 用麦芽制造[处理]。— *vi*. 1. (麦粒)发芽。2. 制麦芽。3.〔俚〕喝啤酒。～*ed milk* 麦乳精(奶)。～ **dust** 麦芽糖。～ **extract** 麦芽膏;麦精。～**horse** 磨麦芽的马;笨人。～**house** 麦芽作坊;麦芽贮藏所。～ **kiln** 麦芽干燥窑。～ **liquor** 啤酒。～**man** 麦芽制造人。～ **sugar** 麦芽糖。～**worm**〔古〕大酒鬼。

Mal·ta [ˈmɔːltə; ˋmɔltə] *n*. (地中海中的)马耳他〔欧洲〕。～ **fever** 马耳他热〔一种热病〕。

malt·ase [ˈmɔːlteis; ˋmɔltes] *n*. 【生化】麦芽糖酶。

Mal·tese [ˈmɔːlˈtiːz; mɔlˋtiz] **I** *a*. 马耳他岛(人)的。～ **cat** 马耳他猫〔蓝灰色家猫〕。**II** *n*. 〔*sing*., *pl*.〕马耳他岛人[语]。～ **cross** 1. 马耳他十字架。2.【植】皱叶剪秋罗。

mal·tha [ˈmælθə; ˋmælθə] *n*. 软沥青。

Mal·thus [ˈmælθəs; ˋmælθəs] *n*. 1. 马尔萨斯〔姓氏〕。2. **Thomas Robert** ～ 马尔萨斯〔1766—1834,英国经济学家〕。

Mal·thu·si·an [mælˈθjuːzjən; mælˋθjuzɪən] **I** *a*. 马尔萨斯的;马尔萨斯人口论的。**II** *n*. 马尔萨斯人口论者。**-ism** *n*. 马尔萨斯人口论;马尔萨斯主义。

malt·ing [ˈmɔːltiŋ; ˋmɔltɪŋ] *n*. 麦芽制造(法)。

malt·ose [ˈmɔːltəus; ˋmɔltos] *n*. 【化】麦芽糖。

mal·treat [mælˈtriːt; mælˋtrit] *vt*. 虐待;乱用。**-ment** *n*.

malt·ster [ˈmɔːltstə; ˋmɔltˏstɚ] *n*. 麦芽制造人。

malt·y [ˈmɔːlti; ˋmɔltɪ] **I** *a*. 1. 麦芽的,含麦芽的,用麦芽做的,像麦芽的。2.〔俚〕喝醉了的。**II** *n*.〔美〕啤酒。

Maltz [mɔːlts; mɔlts] *n*. 莫尔兹〔姓氏〕。

mal·va·ceous [mælˈveiʃəs; mælˋveʃəs] *a*. 【植】锦葵属的。

mal·va·si·a [ˌmælvəˈsiːə; ˏmælvəˋsiə] *n*. 1. (希腊)莫瓦西亚白葡萄酒。2. 酿莫瓦西亚白葡萄酒的葡萄。**-n** *a*.

mal·ver·sa·tion [ˌmælvəːˈseiʃən; ˏmælvɚˋseʃən] *n*. (公务员的)违法行为;贪污,受贿;盗用公款。

mal·voi·sie [ˈmælvɔizi; ˋmælvɔɪzɪ] *n*. = malmsey.

mam, ma·ma [mæm, məˈmɑː; mæm, məˋmɑ] *n*. = mamma.

mam·ba [ˈmɑːmbə; ˋmɑmbə] *n*. 树眼镜蛇属的蛇〔尤指非洲树蛇〕。

mam·bo [ˈmɑːmbəu; ˋmɑmbo] **I** *n*. 1. 曼波乐曲〔源出古巴黑人,4/4 拍,第二拍第四拍为强拍〕。2. 曼波交际舞。**II** *vi*. 跳曼波舞。

mam·e·lon [ˈmæmilən; ˋmæmɪlən] *n*. 圆丘。

Mam·e·luke [ˈmæmiluːk; ˋmæməˏluk] *n*. 1.【史】马穆鲁克〔中世纪埃及的一个军事统治阶层的成员〕。2.〔m-〕奴隶,奴隶兵。

Mamie [ˈmeimi; ˋmemɪ] *n*. 梅米〔女子名, Margaret 的昵称〕。

ma·mil·la [mæˈmilə; mæˋmɪlə] = mammilla.

mam·il·late(d) [ˈmæmileit(id); ˋmæmɪlˏet(ɪd)] *a*. = mammillate(d).

Mam·luk [ˈmæmluːk; ˋmæmluk] *n*. = Mameluke.

mam·ma[1] [məˈmɑː; ˋmɑmə] *n*.〔儿〕妈妈。*a* ～*'s baby*〔美俚〕漂亮的女学生。

mam·ma[2] [ˈmæmə; ˋmæmə] *n*. (*pl*. **-mae** [ˈmæmiː; ˋmæmi]) (哺乳动物的)乳房。

mam·mal [ˈmæməl; ˋmæml] *n*. 哺乳纲动物。

Mam·ma·lia [mæˈmeiljə; mæˋmelɪə] *n*. 〔*pl*.〕【动】哺乳纲。

mam·ma·li·an [mæˈmeiljən; mæˋmelɪən] *n*., *a*. 哺乳动物(的)。

mam·ma·lif·er·ous [ˌmæməˈlifərəs; ˏmæməˋlɪfərəs] *a*. 【地】含有哺乳动物遗骸的。

mam·mal·o·gy [mæˈmælədʒi; mæˋmælədʒɪ] *n*. 哺乳动物学。

mam·ma·ry [ˈmæməri; ˋmæmərɪ] *a*. 【解】乳房的;胸的。～ *cancer* 乳癌。～ *gland* 乳腺。

mam·mec·to·my [məˈmektəmi; məˋmɛktəmɪ] *n*. = mastectomy.

mam·mee, mam·mey [mæˈmiː, mæˈmei; mæˋmi, mæˋme] *n*. 【植】(美洲热带地方的)曼密树;曼密果。

mam·met [ˈmæmit; ˋmæmɪt] *n*. 1. 偶像。2.〔英方〕玩偶;傀儡(= maumet)。

mam·mif·er·ous [mæˈmifərəs; mæˋmɪfərəs] *a*. 有乳房的,哺乳动物的。

mam·mi·form [ˈmæmifɔːm; ˋmæmɪˏfɔrm] *a*. 乳房状的。

mam·mil·la [mæˈmilə; mæˋmɪlə] *n*. (*pl*. **-lae** [-liː; -li])【解】乳头;乳头状构造;疣。

mam·mil·lar·y [ˈmæmiləri; ˋmæməˏlɛrɪ] *a*. 乳头的;乳头似的;有乳房状突起的。

mam·mil·late [ˈmæmileit; ˋmæmɪˏlet] *a*. 1. 有乳头的。2. 乳头状的。**-la·tion** [-ˈleiʃən; -ˋleʃən] *n*.

mam·mil·li·form [məˈmilifɔːm; məˋmɪlɪfɔrm] *a*. 乳头状的。

mam·mock [ˈmæmək; ˋmæmək] **I** *n*.〔古、方〕碎片,碎屑。**II** *vt*.〔古、方〕使成碎片,把…撕成碎片。

mam·mo·gen [ˈmæmədʒən; ˋmæmədʒən] *n*. 乳腺发育激素。

mam·mo·gen·ic [ˌmæməˈdʒenik; ˏmæməˋdʒɛnɪk] *a*. 促进乳房发育的。

mam·mog·ra·phy [məˈmɔgrəfi; mæˋmɑgrəfɪ] *n*. 【医】早期胸部肿瘤 X 射线透视法。

mam·mon [ˈmæmən; ˋmæmən] *n*. (作为偶像或罪恶根源看的)财富,金钱;〔M-〕财神。

mam·mon·ism [ˈmæmənizəm; ˋmæmənɪzm] *n*. 拜金主义。

mam·mon·ist [ˈmæmənist; ˋmæmənɪst], **mam·mon·ite** [ˈmæmənait; ˋmæməˏnaɪt] *n*. 拜金主义者。

mam·moth [ˈmæməθ; ˋmæməθ] **I** *n*. 1. 猛犸(象)〔古生代的巨象〕。2. 巨物,庞然大物。**II** *a*. 巨大的。**M- Cave** (美国 Kentucky 州的)大钟乳洞。～ **tree** 大树。

mam·my [ˈmæmi; ˋmæmɪ] *n*.〔儿〕妈;〔美南部〕黑人保姆。

man [mæn; mæn] **I** *n*. (*pl*. **men** [men; mɛn]) 1.〔无冠词、单数〕人,人类;【生】人科。2. 男人;大人,成年男子;男子汉,大丈夫;要人,名人;〔冠词用 the; my; your

等]人,对手。**3.**〔古〕家臣,从者,部下,仆人,〔主 *pl.*〕雇员,工人;〔*pl.*〕水兵,士兵(*opp.* officers)。**4.** 丈夫;〔方〕情人。**5.**(大学的)学生;(某某大学)出身的人。**6.**〔亲爱、轻蔑、焦急意义的称呼〕你,喂。**7.**(象棋)棋子。**8.**〔用作不定代词〕人,谁。**9.**〔the M-〕〔美俚〕警察;〔黑人俚〕白人。*M- is mortal.* 人都是会死的。*a ~ of all work* 多面手,万能先生。*What a piece of work is a ~!* 人啊真是一个杰作! *You don't give a ~ a chance.* 你不给人家一个机会呀。*Be a ~!* 拿出大丈夫气概来。*Let any ~ come, I am his ~.* 谁来都好,我来对付。*I know my ~.* 我知道对手(是怎样一个人)。*Come, ~, we've no time to lose.* 喂,来呀,时间不早啦。*officers and men* 官兵。*Hurry up, ~ (alive)!* 赶快,喂! *Nonsense, ~!* 胡说! ★ 美国商业中对顾客称 gentleman 和 lady, 对自己店员称 man 和 woman. ***a ~ about town*** 出入于娱乐、社交等场所的男子;花天酒地中鬼混的人;〔英〕(伦敦的)高等游民。***a ~ among men*** 男子汉中的男子汉,特出的人物。***a ~ and a brother*** 同胞兄弟,亲兄弟。***a ~ of …***(某处)生长的人(*a ~ of Shanghai* 上海人)。***a ~ of the people*** 人民的儿子。***as a ~*** 一致地;作为一个男子;就人的观点而论。***as men go*** 就一般人而论。***as one [a] ~*** 异口同声,团结一致地。***be one's own ~*** 独立自主,有自己的自由;精力充沛。***best ~*** 男傧相 ***be the whole ~ at*** 专心…。***between ~ and ~*** 像男子汉对男子汉;两人中私下讲。***John Tamson's ~*** 怕老婆的男人。***like a ~*** 男子汉似的,有丈夫气。***little ~***〔谑、爱〕小鬼,小家伙。***make (sb.) a ~ = make a ~ of (sb.)*** 使成大人,使能处事成人(*His father's death has made a ~ of him.* 他父亲死后,他就变得像个大人了)。***M- alive!*** 什么! 是怎么回事!〔表示惊讶、抗议〕。***~ and boy*** 从儿童时代以来,从小到大。***~ and wife*** 夫妇。***~ for ~*** 以一个人比一个人。***~ Friday*** 忠仆。***~ hour*** 工时。***~ in the moon*** 月中人;空想人物,虚构人物。***~ in the oak*** 鬼,妖怪。***~ of God*** 牧师,教士;预言者。***~ of his hands*** 手巧的人,有手艺的人;武艺家。***~ of his word*** 守约的人,可靠的人。***~ of honour*** 有信义的人,君子。***~ of letters*** 作家,学者,编辑,文人。***~ of men*** 特出[优秀]人物。***~ of parts*** 才子。***~ of resources*** 足智多谋的人。***M- of Sorrows*** 耶稣基督。***~ of straw*** 稻草人;假想的敌人;场面人物;虚构人物;没钱的人。***~ of the world*** 通世故的人;上层社交界人物;俗人。***~ on horseback***(权势高出政府之上的)军阀,军事领袖;军事独裁者。***~ on the firing line***【美棒球】投手。***~ to ~ = ~ for ~. mistake one's ~*** 看错对方(是怎样一个人)。***My ~!*** 喂!〔对下面人的称呼〕。***new ~***(新加入某一社会集团的)新人。***old ~*** **1.** 老前辈,老朋友。**2.** 船长;工头。**3.** 父亲,丈夫。***play the ~*** 显示男子汉气概。***the dead ~*** 冗员。***the forgotten ~*** 被遗忘的人。***the inner ~*** 精神,灵魂;〔谑〕胃,肚子。***the ~ in [on] the street***〔口〕普通人,一般人(*opp.* expert)。***(all) to a ~*** 到最后一人;全部;满场一致(*They were killed to a ~.* 他们全部被杀了)。

II *vt.* (*manned*; *man·ning*) **1.** 给…配置兵[人]员,配置船员(在船上)。**2.** 使人就(职位等);操纵;养乖(鹰等)。**3.** 使拿出丈夫气概,使鼓起勇气(*oneself*)。*~ the ship* 配置船员;使人上船。*~ the side = ~ the yards* 举行上船礼。*~ the guns* 就位,准备开炮。***~ it out*** 硬着骨头干到底,有男子汉气魄。***~ up***(给矿业、农业等)补充人力。~**-at-arms** (*pl. men-*)(中世纪)兵士;重骑兵。~ **bender**【美体】摔跤选手。~**-child** (*pl. men-children*) 男孩;儿子。~**-eater** 食人者,食人虎,食人鲨鱼,咬人的马。~**-engine**【采】井内载人升降机。~**-god** (*pl. men-gods*) 神人。~**handle** *vt.* 用人力推动[开动];〔口〕虐待,粗暴地对待。~ **handler**【美体】摔跤选手。~**-hater** 愤世嫉俗的人;讨厌男人的女人。~**-haul** *vt.* 用人力拖拉。~**hole** 人孔,(阴沟的)检修孔;【铁路】避孔。~**-hour** 工时,一人一小时的工作量。~ **jack** 个人(*every ~ jack* 人人,每人)。~**-killer** 杀人的人[物];〔美〕杀人监[工作繁重,规则严厉的监狱];不让人接近的烈马。~**-made** *a.* 人工的,人造的。~ **midwife** (*pl. men midwives*)〔罕〕产科医生。~**-milliner** (*pl. men-milliners*) 女衣帽商〔男性〕;无事忙(的男子)。~**-month** 人工月〔一个人工作的一个月〕。~**-of-war** (*pl. men-of-war*) 军舰(主指从前木造的兵舰)。~**-of-war bird** 军舰鸟(= frigate bird)。~**-portable** *a.* 一个人能搬动的。~**power** 人力;【机】人力〔功率单位,= 1/10 马力〕;有效人员总数。~**-rate** *vt.* 对(火箭等)作安全评定〔证实火箭或宇宙[太空]飞船能安全进行载人飞行〕。~**-rope**【海】(作扶手的)舷梯索。~**servant** (*pl. menservants*) 男仆。~**-size(d)** *a.*〔美口〕大人尺寸的;数目[分量]极大的;适合[需要]男子(担当)的;吃力的,困难的。~**slaughter** 杀人,(尤指)【法】过失杀人(罪)。~**slayer** 杀人的人,凶手。**manning table**〔美〕战斗部署表。~**-time** (*pl. men-times*) *n.* 人次。~**-to-~** *a.* **1.** 坦率的。**2.**(球赛中)人钉人的。~**trap** **1.** *n.* (*-traps, men-traps*)【英史】(从前捕捉侵入领土内的人用的)捕人机[陷阱];危险场所[东西];诱惑人的场所[赌场等]。**2.** *vt.* (*p., p.p. -trapped*) 在…布置捕人机。~**way**【矿】人行巷道。~**-year** 一人在一年内完成的工作量。**-less** *a.* 没有人[男人]的;〔古〕卑鄙的,残忍的。**-let**〔美〕矮小的人;不足道的人。**-like** *a.* 像人的;像男人的,有大丈夫气概的;男人似的,(女人)胜过男人的。**-wise** *ad.* 以男人的本分;像男子汉那样地。

-man *comb. f.* (*pl.* **-men**) **1.**〔职业〕…人:post*man*, dust*man*, clergy*men*. **2.**〔籍贯〕…国人,…居民:Eng-lish*man*, country*man*. **3.** …船:*man*-of-war, merchant*man*, India*man*.

Man. = Manhattan; Manila; Manitoba.

ma·na [ˈmɑːnɑː; ˋmɑnɑ] *n.* 神力,超自然力。

man·a·cle [ˈmænəkl; ˋmænəkl] **I** *n.*〔常 *pl.*〕手铐;束缚,拘束。**II** *vt.* 给…上手铐;束缚。

man·age[1] [ˈmænidʒ; ˋmænɪdʒ] *vt.* **1.** 办理,处置,处理;支配,管理;经营。**2.**(用手)使用,驾驭,操纵,开动;训练(马)。**3.**〔主要和 can; be able to 连用〕处理,办,做;〔口〕对付;吃。**4.** 设法…;弄得…;〔反语〕好不容易地把…。*~ the affairs of a nation* 处理国家事务。*~ cattle* 管理家畜。*~ a motor-car* 开汽车。*I cannot ~ it alone.* 我一个人办不了。*Can you ~ another slice?* 能再吃一片吗? *So you ~d it after all.* 结果你还是弄成功了。*Did you ~ it?* 你们做到了没有? *He ~d (= was foolish enough) to make a mess of it.* 他真不错,把事情弄得糟透了。— ***vi.*** 处理,办理;应付,对付,敷衍(过去)。*I shall ~ with the tools I have.* 我要用现有的工具设法对付。***~ on one's income*** 按收入过日子。***~ to be in time*** 设法及时。***~ to make both ends meet*** 设法使收支平衡。***~ without …*** 在没有…下敷衍过去。~**d care**〔美〕有管理的保健医疗〔费用受到控制,每一次的诊断费和医疗费都由保险公司分别支付,而不是无限额地最后总结账〕。~**d currency** 管理通货。

man·age[2] [ˈmænidʒ; ˋmænɪdʒ] *n.* **1.**〔古〕练马。**2.** 调教过的马的动作和步调。**3.** 骑马学校,马术练习所(= manège)。

man·age·a·ble [ˈmænidʒəbl; ˋmænɪdʒəbl] *a.* 易处理的,易办的;易管理的;可以设法的;易驾驭的,乖,温顺的。**-bly** *ad.* **-ness** *n.*

man·age·ment [ˈmænidʒmənt; ˋmænɪdʒmənt] *n.* **1.** 办理,处理;管理,经营;经营力,经营手腕。**2.** 安排;妥善对待。**3.**〔the ~〕〔集合词〕(工商企业)管理部门;董事会;厂方,资方。*one man ~* 一长制。*the ~ of economy* 经济管理。*land ~* 土地规划。

man·ag·er [ˈmænidʒə; ˋmænɪdʒɚ] *n.* **1.** 处理者;经理(人),管理人;经营者。**2.** 干事,理事,【剧】舞台监督,导演;〔*pl.*〕(英议会)两院协议会委员;〔英〕【法】财务管理

人。3.〔美〕(政党等的)领袖。4. 策士,干才,干练的人。*a stage* ～舞台监督。*a good* [*bad*] ～会[不会]理财的人,(尤指)会[不会]当家的主妇。

man·ag·er·ess [ˈmænidʒəres; ˋmænɪdʒərɪs] *n*.〔英〕女经理,女管理人。

man·ag·e·ri·al [ˌmænəˈdʒiəriəl; ˏmænəˋdʒɪrɪəl] *a*. 经理的,管理人的;处理[管理]上的。

man·ag·er·ship [ˈmænidʒəʃip; ˋmænɪdʒəˏʃɪp] *n*. 经理[管理人]身分[职位、任期、权力]。

man·ag·ing [ˈmænidʒiŋ; ˋmænɪdʒɪŋ] I *a*. 1. 处理的,管理的;首脑的。2. 善于处理的,善经营的。3. 爱管闲事的,爱自己操持的(女人等)。4. 节俭的;吝啬的。*a* ～ *director* 总经理;常务董事;社长。*a* ～ *partner* 执行业务的合伙人。II *n*. 处理,管理。

Ma·na·gua [məˈnɑːgwə; məˋnɑgwə] *n*. 马那瓜[马拿瓜]〔尼加拉瓜首都〕。

man·a·kin [ˈmænəkin; ˋmænəkɪn] *n*. 1. 美洲小艳羽鸟。2. = manikin.

Ma·na·ma [mæˈnæmə; mæˋnæmə] *n*. 麦纳玛〔巴林首都〕。

ma·ña·na [mɑːˈnjɑːnɑː; mɑˋnjɑnɑ] *n*., *ad*.〔Sp.〕明天;(在)不确定的将来。

man·a·tee [mænəˈtiː; ˏmænəˋti] *n*.【动】海牛。

Man·ches·ter [ˈmæntʃistə; ˋmænˏtʃɛstə] *n*. 曼彻斯特〔英国城市〕;纺织工业中心。～ ***department*** (商店的)棉织品部。～ ***goods*** 棉布类。***The*** ～ ***Guardian*** 曼彻斯特卫报。～ ***terrier*** 曼彻斯特㹴。

Man·ches·ter·ism [ˈmæntʃistərizəm; ˋmæntʃɪstərɪzəm] *n*. 自由贸易主义。

man·chet [ˈmæntʃit; ˋmæntʃɛt] *n*.〔古、英方〕1. 精粉面包。2. 精粉面包卷;精粉小面包。

Man·chu [mænˈtʃuː; mænˋtʃu] I *a*. 满族的;满族人的;满族语的。II *n*. 满族人;满族的通古斯语。

Man·chu·ria [mænˈtʃuəriə; mænˋtʃʊrɪə] *n*. 满洲〔中国东北的旧称〕。

Man·chur·i·an [mænˈtʃuəriən; mænˋtʃʊrɪən] *a*., *n*. 满族的;满族人(的)。～ **ash**【植】水曲柳。～ **elm** 青榆。～ **fir** 辽东冷杉。

man·ci·ple [ˈmænsipl; ˋmænsəpl̩] *n*. (大学或修道院等的)伙食承办人。

Man·cu·ni·an [mænˈkuːnjən; mænˋkjunɪən] *a*., *n*. (英国)曼彻斯特 (Manchester)的(人);曼彻斯特公立学校的(人)。

-man·cy *comb. f*. 卜,占:geomancy.

M&A = mergers and acquisitions【商】合并与收购。

man·da·la [ˈmʌndələ; ˋmændələ] *n*.【佛、印度教】曼达拿,曼陀罗,曼荼罗〔宣传平等周遍十法界的宗教思想〕。

Man·da·lay [ˌmændəˈlei; ˋmændəˏle] *n*. 曼德勒[瓦城]〔缅甸城市〕。

man·da·mus [mænˈdeimes; mænˋdeməs] *n*.【法】(致下级法院的)训令。

Man·dan [ˈmændæn; ˋmændæn] *n*. 1. (*pl*. ～(*s*)) 曼丹人〔居于美国北达科他州的平原印第安人〕。2. 曼丹语。

man·da·rin[1] [ˈmændərin; ˋmændərɪn] *n*. 1. (中国清朝的)官吏;[M-]中国官话 (= ～ language)〔普通话的旧称〕。2.〔谑〕达官,要人;守旧的政党领袖。3. 穿中国古代官服的玩偶。～ **dialect** 中国官话〔中国北京或北方方言的旧称〕。～ **duck**【鸟】鸳鸯。～ **fish** 桂鱼,鳜。～ **porcelain** 绘有中国古代官吏图像的瓷瓶。

man·da·rin[2], **man·da·rine** [ˈmændəriːn, ˈmændərin; ˋmændərin, ˋmændərɪn] *n*. 中国柑橘(树) (= ～ orange);柑橘酒;橙黄色(染料)。

man·da·tar·y [ˈmændətəri; ˋmændəˏtɛrɪ] *n*.【法】受任者,受托者,被委托人;代理人;受托管理国。

man·date [ˈmændeit; ˋmændet] I *n*. 1. 命令,训令;指令。2.〔美〕(执行判决的)命令,指令;上级法院[官员]对下级法院[官员]的训令。3. (选民对选出的代表、议会等的)授权。4.【法】财产委托;(国际上的)委托管理。5.【商】支付命令;雇佣契约。II *vt*. 委托管理。*a* ～*d territory* 托管地。

man·da·tor [ˈmændeitə; mænˋdetə] *n*. 命令者,委托者。

man·da·to·ry [ˈmændətəri; ˋmændəˏtorɪ] I *a*. 命令的,训令的;委任的,委托的 (*upon*);〔美〕强迫的,义务性质的。～ *administration* [*rule*] 委托管理。*a* ～ *power* 受托管理国。II *n*. = mandatary.

Man·de [ˈmɑːndei; ˋmɑnde] I *n*. 1. (*pl*. ～(*s*)) 曼丁哥人〔西非黑人,包括马林凯人等〕。2. 曼丁哥语。II *a*. 曼丁哥人的;曼丁哥语的。

Man·de·an [mænˈdiən; mænˋdɪən] I *n*. 1. 曼德恩人〔诺斯替(Gnostic)教派信徒,今伊拉克尚有其后裔〕。2. 曼德恩语。II *a*. 1. 曼德恩人的;曼德恩学说的。2. 曼德恩的。

Man·der [ˈmɑːndə; ˋmɑndə] *n*. 曼德〔姓氏〕。

man·di·ble [ˈmændibl; ˋmændəbl] *n*.【解】下颚骨;颚,(特指)下颚;【鸟】嘴的上部[下部];【虫】上颚;(蝇的)口钩。

man·dib·u·lar [mænˈdibjulə; mænˋdɪbjələ] *a*. 颚的,像颚的。

man·dib·u·late [mænˈdibjuːlit; ˋmænˋdɪbjulɪt] I *a*.【动】具颚的。II *n*. 具颚昆虫。

Man·din·go [mænˈdiŋgəu; mænˋdɪŋgo] *n*. 曼丁哥人〔西非洲黑人民族之一〕;曼丁哥语。

man·do·la, **man·do·ra** [ˈmændələ, -rə; mænˋdolə, -rə] *n*.〔It.〕【乐】中曼陀林(琴)。

man·do·lin, **man·do·line** [ˈmændəlin, ˌmændəˈliːn; ˋmændl̩ˏɪn, ˏmændl̩ˋin] *n*.【乐】曼陀林(琴),瓢琴。

man·drag·o·ra, **man·drake** [mænˈdrægərə; mænˋdrægərə] *n*. 1.【植】曼德拉草〔根可作麻醉剂〕。2.〔mandrake〕〔美〕(= May apple) 盾叶鬼臼。

man·drel, **man·dril** [ˈmændril; ˋmændrəl] *n*.【机】轴胎,心轴,紧轴;【冶】(铸造用的)圆形心轴;(采矿用的)鹤嘴锄,铁镐。*built-up* ～组合心轴。*press* ～压进心轴。*taper shank* ～锥柄心轴。

man·drill [ˈmændril; ˋmændrɪl] *n*.【动】(西非洲的)狒狒,大猴。

man·du·cate [ˈmændjukeit; ˋmændʒuˏket] *vt*.〔罕〕嚼,咀嚼,吃,狼吞虎咽地吃。

man·du·ca·tion [ˌmændjuˈkeiʃən; ˏmændʒuˋkeʃən] *n*. 咀嚼。

man·du·ca·to·ry [mænˈdjuːkətəri; mænˋdʒukəˏtorɪ] *a*. 咀嚼的,适于咀嚼的。

mane [mein; men] *n*. (马、狮子等的)鬃毛;(人的)长头发。***make neither*** ～ ***nor tail of*** 完全不懂…。

maned [meind; mend] *a*. 有鬃毛的。

ma·nège [mæˈneiʒ; mæˋnɛʒ] *n*.〔F.〕= manage[2].

ma·nes, **M-** [ˈmeiniːz; ˋmeniz] *n*.〔*pl*.〕1.〔古罗马〕(祖先等的)灵;灵魂;阴间诸神。2.〔M-〕波斯预言家(= Mani)。

ma·neu·ver [məˈnuːvə; məˋnuvə] *n*., *v*.〔美〕= manoeuvre.

mane·y [ˈmeini; ˋmenɪ] *a*. 鬃毛似的。

Man·fred [ˈmænfred; ˋmænfrɛd] *n*. 曼弗雷德〔男子名〕。

man·ful [ˈmænful; ˋmænfəl] *a*. 有男子汉气魄的;雄伟的;刚勇的;果断的。**-ly** *ad*. **-ness** *n*.

man·ga [ˈmɑːŋgɑː; ˋmɑŋgɑ] *n*.〔Jap.〕漫画。

man·ga·bey [ˈmæŋgəbei; ˋmæŋgəbe] *n*.【动】白眉猴属动物。

man·ga·nate [ˈmæŋgəneit; ˋmæŋgəˏnet] *n*.【化】锰酸盐。

man·ga·nese [ˌmæŋgəˈniːz, ˈmæŋgəniːz; ˏmæŋgəˋnis, ˋmæŋgəˏnis] *n*.【化】锰。*black* ～氧化锰。～ *ocher* 黑

赭石。～ *spar*【矿】菱锰矿。～ *steel* 锰钢。

man·gan·ic [mæŋˈgænik; mænˋgænɪk] *a*.(似)锰的;三价锰的;六价锰的。～ *acid* 锰酸。

man·ga·nin [ˈmæŋgənin; ˋmæŋgənɪn] *n*. 锰铜;锰镍铜齐。

man·ga·nite [ˈmæŋgənait; ˋmæŋgə͵naɪt] *n*.【矿】水锰矿;【化】亚锰酸盐。

man·ga·nous [ˈmæŋgənəs; ˋmæŋgənəs] *a*.【化】亚锰的,二价锰的,锰似的,含锰的。～ *acid* 亚锰酸。

mange [meindʒ; mendʒ] *n*. **1**.(牛、狗等的)疥癣,癞疮。**2**. 皮肤不洁。

man·gel(-wur·zel) [ˈmæŋgl(ˈwəːzl); ˋmæŋgl̩(ˋwɚzl̩)] *n*.〔英〕【植】饲料甜菜。

man·ger [ˈmeindʒə; ˋmendʒɚ] *n*. **1**. 秣桶,马[牛]槽。**2**.【海】船首挡水板。***dog in the*** ～ 占着茅坑不拉屎。

man·gi·ly [ˈmeindʒili; ˋmendʒɪlɪ] *ad*. = mangy.

man·gle[1] [ˈmæŋgl; ˋmæŋgl̩] *vt*. **1**. 乱切,乱砍,割碎,弄伤。**2**. 破坏,弄糟,损坏;(因发音拙劣等)使话听不懂。*a* ～ *corpse* 被砍得血肉模糊的尸体。～ *a piece of music* (因演奏技巧拙劣)糟踏了一个乐曲。**-r** *n*. 乱砍…的人;绞肉机。

man·gle[2] [ˈmæŋgl; ˋmæŋgl̩] **I** *n*. 轧布机;轧板机;研光机;碾压机;轧液机。**II** *vt*. 用轧布机研光。**-r** *n*.(布等的)研光机;(橡胶的)压延机;绞肉机;榨甘蔗机;轧机操作者。

man·go [ˈmæŋgəu; ˋmæŋgo] *n*.(*pl*. ～(*e*)*s*) 芒果;芒果树。～ **fish**【动】印度四指马鲅, ～ **trick** (印度魔术)现结芒果。

man·gold(-wur·zel) [ˈmæŋgəld(ˈwəːzl); ˋmæŋgəld-(wɚzl̩)] *n*. = mangel(-wurzel).

man·go·nel [ˈmæŋgənel; ˋmæŋgə͵nɛl] *n*. 古代军用射[抛]石机。

man·go·steen [ˈmæŋgəustiːn; ˋmæŋgə͵stin] *n*. 倒捻子(树)。

man·grove [ˈmæŋgrəuv; ˋmæŋgrov] *n*.【植】(热带沿海生长的)红树(林),栲树(林)。～ **cuckoo**【鸟】(西印度群岛的)郭公鸟的一种。

man·gy [ˈmeindʒi; ˋmendʒɪ] *a*. 生满疥癣的,尽是癞疮的;污秽的,肮脏的;〔口〕卑劣的。

Man·hat·tan [mænˈhætən; mænˋhætn̩] *n*. 曼哈顿[美国纽约市中心];曼哈顿商业区;〔m-〕曼哈顿鸡尾酒。～ **District** 第二次世界大战中美国原子弹研究总部。～ **Project** 第二次世界大战中美国原子弹研究计划。**-ize** *vt*. 使(城市)曼哈顿化[指将城市建成布满高层建筑的做法]。

Man·hat·tan·ese [mænˈhætəniːz; mænˋhætn̩͵iz] **I** *a*. 纽约的。**II** *n*. 纽约人;纽约话;纽约时髦话。**-tan·ite** *n*.〔美俚〕纽约人。

man·hood [ˈmænhud; ˋmænhʊd] *n*. 人的状态;(男性)大人,成人;刚毅,丈夫气;〔集合词〕(成年)男子。*the whole* ～ *of the country* 全国男子。*a perfect* ～完人,君子。***arrive at*** ～ 成年。***in the prime of*** ～ 壮年,盛年。

ma·ni·a [ˈmeinjə, -niə; ˋmenjə, ͵-nɪə] *n*.【医】狂躁,癫狂;狂热,狂慕,狂爱;…狂,…热,…癖。*a* ～ *for* [*the* ～ *of*] *dancing* 跳舞狂。*the football* ～足球狂。

-mania *comb. f*. **1**. 特种习癖:klepto*mania*, megalo*mania*. **2**. 狂热的嗜好:biblio*mania*, mono*mania*. **3**. 赞美,醉心:Anglo*mania*.

ma·ni·ac[1] [ˈmeiniæk; ˋmenɪ͵æk] **I** *a*. 躁狂的;疯狂的;狂热的。**II** *n*. 躁狂者;疯子。**-a·cal·ly** *ad*.

ma·ni·ac[2] [ˈmeiniæk; ˋmenɪ͵æk] *n*. 一种高速电子数字计算机〔*m*athematical *a*nalyzer, *n*umerical *i*ntegrator *a*nd *c*omputer 的首字母缩合词〕。

-maniac *comb. f*. **1**. 表示"…狂[迷、癖]的":biblio*maniac*. **2**. 表示"…狂[迷、癖]者":biblio*maniac*.

ma·ni·a·cal [məˈnaiəkəl; məˋnaɪəkl̩] *a*. = maniac. **-ly** *ad*.

ma·nic [ˈmeinik, ˈmænik; ˋmenɪk, ˋmænɪk] **I** *a*.【医】躁狂的。**II** *n*. 躁狂者。～**-depressive** *a*.(由两种症候交替发生所致的)躁狂抑郁症的。

Man·i·chae·an, Man·i·che·an [͵mæniˈkiːən; ͵mænəˋkiən] *n*., *a*. 摩尼教(的);摩尼教徒(的)。

Man·i·ch(a)e·ism [ˈmænikiːizəm; ˋmænə͵kiɪzəm] *n*.(伊朗的)摩尼教,明暗教;明暗[善恶]对立说。

Man·i·chee [ˈmænikiː; ˋmænəki] *n*. 摩尼教徒。

man·i·cure [ˈmænikjuə; ˋmænɪ͵kjʊr] **I** *n*. 修指甲(术)。**II** *vt*. **1**. 为…修指甲,修…的指甲。**2**. 修剪,修平。～ *parlour* 指甲美化室。

man·i·cur·ist [ˈmænikjuərist; ˋmænɪ͵kjʊrɪst] *n*. 指甲美化师。

man·i·fest [ˈmænifest; ˋmænə͵fɛst] **I** *a*. 明白的,明显的。**II** *vt*. **1**. 指明,表明;明白表示。**2**. 证明;使了解。**3**. 把…记在货单上。**4**.〔～ oneself〕(鬼、征候等)出现。— *vi*. **1**.(鬼等)出现。**2**. 表明(政治上的)意见,发表宣言。～ ***itself*** 显出,现出。**III** *n*.【商】(船长交海关的)船货清单。～ **destiny** 天定命运论,命定扩张说[19 世纪鼓吹美国对外侵略扩张为天命所定的一种理论]。**-ly** *ad*.

man·i·fes·ta·tion [͵mænifesˈteiʃən; ͵mænəfɛsˋteʃən] *n*. **1**. 表现,表示;显现。**2**. 发表政见,政治示威;公开声明。**3**.【心】神秘现象的具体化。

man·i·fes·to [͵mæniˈfestəu; ͵mænəˋfɛsto] **I** *n*.(*pl*. ～(*e*)*s*) 宣言,声明;告示,布告。**II** *vi*.〔罕〕发表宣言[声明]。

man·i·fold [ˈmænifəuld; ˋmænə͵fold] **I** *a*. **1**. 许多的;种种的,多样的,多方面的,五花八门。**2**. 由许多部分形成的。*maintains* ～ *links with* 和…有千丝万缕的关系。**II** *n*. **1**. 复写本。**2**.【机】歧管,集合管;复式接头。**3**.【数】簇,流形。～ **paper** 打字纸。～ **writer** 复写器。**III** *vt*., *vi*.(用复写器等)复写,复印。

man·i·hot [ˈmænihɔt; ˋmænɪhɑt] *n*. 木薯 (= cassava).

man·i·kin [ˈmænikin; ˋmænəkɪn] *n*. **1**. 矮人,侏儒;(画家等用的)木制模特儿,人体模型;人体解剖模型。**2**. = mannequin. **3**. = manakin. *a* ～ *girl* 服装模特儿。

Ma·nil(l)·a [məˈnilə; məˋnɪlə] *n*. 马尼拉[菲律宾首都]。

ma·nil·(l)a [məˈnilə; məˋnɪlə] *n*. 吕宋(雪茄)烟;马尼拉麻;马尼拉纸。～ **hemp** 马尼拉麻。～ **nut** 落花生。～ **paper** 马尼拉纸。～ **rope** 吕宋绳,白棕绳。

man·i·oc [ˈmæniɔk; ˋmænɪ͵ɑk] *n*. = cassava.

man·i·ple [ˈmænipl; ˋmænəpl̩] *n*. **1**. 天主教神父左臂上佩的饰带。**2**.(古罗马军团的)步兵支队。

ma·nip·u·lar [məˈnipjulə; məˋnɪpjələ] **I** *a*. **1**.(古罗马军队的)支队的。**2**. 操作的;操纵的;手术的;应付的。**II** *n*. 支队的士兵。

ma·nip·u·late [məˈnipjuleit; məˋnɪpjə͵let] *vt*. **1**.(有技巧地)使用,开动(机械等);巧妙地处理(问题等);摆布,巧妙地操纵(人等)。**2**. 窜改(账目等)。**3**. 操纵(市价、市场),控制。～ *a convention* 操纵会议。～ *voters* 收买投票人。— *vi*. 巧妙地处理,巧妙地使用。

ma·nip·u·la·tion [məˌnipjuˈleiʃən; mə͵nɪpjʊˋleʃən] *n*. **1**.(熟练的)操作;操作法;手法。**2**.(市场等的)操纵,控制。**3**.(外科)手技,手法。*conjoined* ～双手操作法。*remote* ～远距离操作,遥控。**-tive, -to·ry** *a*.

ma·nip·u·la·tor [məˈnipjuleitə; məˋnɪpju͵letɚ] *n*. **1**. 用手处理[操作]的人;巧于处理的人。**2**. 操纵者;控制器。**3**. 窜改者。**4**. 运动器具;【摄】板架,保板器。

man·i·to, man·i·tou, man·i·tu [ˈmænitəu, -tuː; ˋmænə͵to, -tu] *n*.(*pl*. ～*s*)(北美 Algonquian 人信奉的)自然神。

man·kind [mænˈkaind; mænˋkaɪnd] *n*. **1**. 人类,人。**2**. [ˈmænkaind; ˋmænkaɪnd] 男性,男子(*opp*. womankind)。

man·li·ness [ˈmænlinis; ˋmænlɪnɪs] *n*. 男子气,雄伟,勇敢,刚毅,大胆。

man·ly [ˈmænli; ˋmænlɪ] *a*. **1**. 有男子汉气魄的;雄赳赳的;大胆的,勇敢的;果断的,刚毅的。**2**. 适合男子的。**3**. 男子似的,(女人)胜过男子的。

Mann [mæn; mæn] *n*. 曼〔姓氏〕。

man·na [ˈmænə; ˋmænə] *n*. **1**. 【圣】吗哪(《圣经》所说古以色列人漂泊荒野时上帝所赐的食物);神粮;美味;不期而获的东西;振奋精神的东西。**2**. 【医】(作缓泻剂用的)甘露,木蜜。~ *in sorts* [*tears*] 下[上]等木蜜。**~-ash** 【植】欧洲白蜡树。**~-croup** 粗小麦粉。

Mann Act [mæn; mæn] 麦恩法案〔美国1910年6月在国会通过的一项法案,禁止州与州之间贩运妇女作不道德的勾当〕。

man·ned [mænd; mænd] *a*. 载人的;由人操纵的。*a* ~ *spaceship* 载人宇宙[太空]船。

man·ne·quin [ˈmænikin; ˋmænəkɪn] *n*. 服装模特儿〔服装店雇用的以穿时装供展览为职业的妇女〕;(橱窗里的)服装模型。

man·ner [ˈmænə; ˋmænɚ] *n*. **1**. 方法,做法。**2**. 态度,样子,举止;〔*pl*.〕礼貌,规矩。**3**. 〔*pl*.〕风俗,习惯,惯例,生活方式。**4**. (艺术、文学的)风格手法,样式,体;癖。**5**. 种类。*houses built in the Chinese* ~中国式住宅。*What* ~ *of man is he*? 他是怎样一个人? *the grand* ~高尚的态度。*Where are your* ~*s*? 规矩呢? 你还有没有礼貌? *good* ~*s* 有礼貌。*bad* ~*s* 没礼貌。***after the*** ~ ***of*** 仿效,学…的样;…式的。***after this*** ~ 照这样,像这样。***all*** ~ ***of*** 种种,各色各样的(人、东西等等)。***by all*** ~ ***of means*** = *by all means*. ***by no*** ~ ***of means*** 决不,一点也不。***develop a*** ~ ***of one's own*** 独创一派,自成一家。***have no*** ~ ***of*** (*right*) 毫无(权利)。***have no*** ~***s*** 不懂礼貌,没规矩。***in a*** ~ 在某种意义上;多少,有点。***in a*** ~ ***of speaking*** 不妨说;说起来。***in an all-round*** ~ 全面。***in like*** ~ 同样地。***in the*** ~ 在现行中,当场。***in the*** ~ ***of*** 照…的式样。***in this*** ~ 如此,照这样。***in what*** ~ 怎么样。***make*** [***do***] ***one's*** ~***s*** 行礼。***no*** ~ ***of*** 一点没有。***to the*** ~ ***born*** 生来的;生来适于某种地位[职业]的;生在那种习惯中的。***with the*** ~ = ***in the*** ~.

man·nered [ˈmænəd; ˋmænɚd] *a*. 〔和形容词或副词连用〕举止…的,(文体)墨守旧风格的,矫揉造作的。*well-*~ 有礼貌的。*ill-*~ 没礼貌的,撒野的。*a* ~ *style of writing* 矫揉造作的文体。

man·ner·ism [ˈmænərizəm; ˋmænəˏrɪzəm] *n*. **1**. (尤指文艺上的)守旧,作风守旧;矫揉造作的风格。**2**. 怪癖;(特指演员说话、动作等的)习气。

man·ner·ist [ˈmænərist; ˋmænərɪst] *n*. 作风守旧的人;风格特别的作家[艺术家];矫揉造作者;有怪癖的人。

man·ner·less [ˈmænəlis; ˋmænɚlɪs] *a*. 不懂礼貌的,没规矩的。

man·ner·ly [ˈmænəli; ˋmænɚlɪ] *a*., *ad*. 有礼貌的[地],谦恭的[地],殷勤的[地]。**-li·ness** *n*.

Mann·heim [ˈmænhaim; ˋmænhaɪm] *n*. 曼海姆〔德国城市〕。

man·ni·kin [ˈmænikin; ˋmænəkɪn] *n*. = manikin.

Man·ning [ˈmæniŋ; ˋmænɪŋ] *n*. 曼宁〔姓氏〕。

man·nish [ˈmæniʃ; ˋmænɪʃ] *a*. (女人)男子似的;(孩子)大人似的;适合男子的。*What a* ~ *way to thread a needle*! 穿针线真像男人一样地笨。**-ly** *ad*. **-ness** *n*.

man·nite [ˈmænait; ˋmænaɪt] *n*. 甘露糖醇(= mannitol)。**-nit·ic** [məˈnitik; məˋnɪtɪk] *a*.

man·ni·tol [ˈmænitəul, -tɔːl; ˋmænəˏtol, -ˏtɑl] *n*. 【化】甘露糖醇。

ma·noeu·ver·a·ble [məˈnuːvrəbl; məˋnuvrəbl̩] *a*. **1**. 机动的;可调动的。**2**. 操纵灵敏的。

ma·noeu·vre [məˈnuːvə; məˋnuvɚ] **I** *n*. **1**. 【军】(军队、兵舰的)机动,调动,部署;〔*pl*.〕军事演习。**2**. 策略;策动;谋略,巧计,诡计,花招,伎俩,手法。*anti-air-raid* ~ [*drill*] 防空演习。*a political* ~政治花招。*This* ~ *of his is a diabolical conspiracy*. 他这一手是个居心叵测的大阴谋。**II** *vi*. (*-vred*, *-vered*; *-vring*, *-vering*) 演习;调动,部署;用计,耍花招。— *vt*. 使演习;调动;用策略使…,用计使…。*a manoeuvering aircraft* 特技飞机。~ *the enemy into* [*out of*] *a position* 用计谋使敌军进入[撤出]某一阵地。

ma·nom·e·ter [məˈnɔmitə; məˋnɑmətɚ] *n*. 【物】流体或气体压力计,测压器;【医】血压计。

man·o·met·ric [ˌmænəˈmetrik; ˏmænəˋmɛtrɪk] *a*. 流体压力计的,用测压器测的。~ *flames* 【物】感压焰。*a* ~ *thermometer* 压差温度计。

ma non trop·po [mɑːnɔnˈtrɔpəu; mɑnɑnˋtrɑpo] 〔It.〕【乐】但不可过度。

man·or [ˈmænə; ˋmænɚ] *n*. **1**. 〔英〕(封建时代由贵族管辖的)采邑,领地;(现今贵族的、包括贵族邸第在内的)庄园。**2**. 〔美〕永久租借地。*a capital* ~直属领地。*the lord of the* ~ 庄园领主。~ **house**, ~ **seat** 庄园主的住宅。

ma·no·ri·al [məˈnɔːriəl; məˋnɔrɪəl] *a*. 庄园[采邑]的。*a* ~ *lord* 领主。*a* ~ *slave* 农奴。**-ly** *ad*.

man·nose [ˈmænəus; ˋmænos] *n*. 【化】甘露糖。

man·o·stat [ˈmænəustæt; ˋmænoˏstæt] *n*. 【物】稳压器,恒压器。

man·qué [F. mɑ̃ˈke; mɑ̃ˋke] *a*. 〔F.〕(*fem*. ***-quée***) 〔用于名词后〕没有成功的。*a poet* ~失意落魄的诗人。

man·sard [ˈmænsɑːd; ˋmænsɑrd] *n*. (法国建筑家 Mansard 设计的)覆斜屋顶〔*cf*. gambrel roof〕;(覆斜屋顶的)屋顶室,阁楼。

manse [mæns; mæns] *n*. 牧师住宅〔尤指长老教会〕;〔古〕房主住宅。

Mans·field [ˈmænsfiːld; ˋmænzˏfild] *n*. 曼斯菲尔德〔姓氏〕。

man·sion [ˈmænʃən; ˋmænʃən] *n*. **1**. 宅第,公馆。**2**. 〔*pl*.〕〔英〕大楼,公寓〔美国叫 apartment house〕。**3**. (大楼中的)一套房间。**4**. 【天】宫,宿。*lunar* ~*s* 【天】二十八宿。~ **house** (领主或地主的)邸宅,公馆;〔the M- House〕伦敦市长官邸。

Man·son [ˈmænsn; ˋmænsn] *n*. 曼森〔姓氏〕。

man·sue·tude [ˈmænswitjuːd; ˋmænswɪˏtjud] *n*. 〔古、罕〕柔顺,温和。

man·ta [ˈmæntə, Sp. ˈmɑːntɑː; ˋmæntə, ˋmɑntɑ] *n*. **1**. 粗布,粗棉织品,粗布围巾,粗皮披肩。**2**. 马毯,马衣。**3**. 【动】鸢魟;灰色鲸;鮟鱇,琵琶鱼,章鱼,乌贼。

man·teau [ˈmæntəu; ˋmænto] *n*. (*pl*. ~*s*, ***manteaux*** [-z; -z]) 〔F.〕斗篷,披风〔尤指女用〕。

man·tel [ˈmæntl; ˋmæntl] *n*. **1**. 壁炉面饰;炉额。**2**. 壁炉架。★英国 **1**. 义说作 ~piece, **2**. 义说作~shelf; 美国 **1**. 义常说作~, **2**. 义常说作 ~piece. **~board** 壁炉架。**~piece** 壁炉面饰,壁炉台。**~shelf** (*pl*. ***-shelves***) 壁炉架。**~tree** 壁炉楣;壁炉面饰。

man·tel·et [ˈmæntəlit; ˋmæntəlɪt] *n*. **1**. (女用)小斗篷。**2**. 【军】弹盾;移动雉堞;着弹观察所。

man·tel·let·ta [ˌmæntəˈletə; ˏmæntəˋlɛtə] *n*. (红衣主教等穿的)无袖法衣。

man·tic [ˈmæntik; ˋmæntɪk] *a*. 占卜的;预言的。

man·til·la [mænˈtilə; mænˋtɪlə] *n*. (女用)小披风;(西班牙女人用的)薄头纱;大面纱。

man·tis [ˈmæntis; ˋmæntɪs] *n*. (*pl*. ~*es*; ***man·tes*** [ˈmæntiːz; ˋmæntiz]) 【虫】螳螂。*a praying* ~合掌螳螂。~ *shrimp* 口脚类动物(= stomatopod)。

man·tis·sa [mænˈtisə; mænˋtɪsə] *n*. 【数】假数,(对数的)尾数。

man·tle [ˈmæntl; ˋmæntl] **I** *n*. **1**. 披风,罩衣。**2**. 一层(被覆)幕,盖罩。**3**. (煤气灯)纱罩;【解】外表;【动】套膜;

(鸟的)翕;【机】(水车的)槽;(高炉的)环梁壳;【地】地幔。**4.**【徽】徽章背景和周围的彩饰。**5.** 继承标帜,衣钵。**6.** = mantel. ***One's ~ falls on*** [***descends to***] ***another***. 衣钵传给别人,精神影响别人。***take the ~*** (***and ring***) (寡妇)誓不再嫁。**II** ***vt***. 披上斗篷;覆,包;隐蔽。— ***vi***. (液体表面)结皮;(酒、汽水等)盖满泡沫;覆;(鸟)展开翅膀;展开,扩展;(脸)涨红。~ ***with roses*** (两颊)涨满桃红色。~ **cavity** 套腔。~ **plume**【地】地幔涌流〔地幔中熔融物质的巨大上升流〕。~ **rock** 风化层,土被,表皮岩。

mant·let [ˈmæntlit; ˋmæntlɛt] ***n***. = mantelet 2.

man·tling [ˈmæntliŋ; ˋmæntlɪŋ] ***n***. 斗篷料;徽章彩饰;壁炉面饰。

Man·toux test [mænˈtuː, ˈmæntuː; mænˋtu, ˋmæntu]【医】曼透氏试法〔检查肺结核〕。

man·tra [ˈmʌntrə, ˈmæn-; ˋmʌntrə, ˋmæn-] ***n***. 颂歌,圣歌;咒语〔尤指四吠陀经典内作为咒文或祷告唱念者〕。

man·tu·a [ˈmæntjuə; ˋmæntʃʊə] ***n***. **1.** (17—18世纪流行的)宽松女大衣。**2.** = mantle.

man(u)- *pref*. 表示"手的,手工的"。

man·u·al [ˈmænjuəl; ˋmænjʊəl] **I** ***a***. **1.** 手的,手作的,手工的,用手操作的;便于手头应用的。**2.**【法】现有的。~ *labour* 手工劳动。*a ~ worker* 体力劳动者。*the ~ alphabet* (聋哑人用的)手语字母。*a ~ fire-engine* 手压灭火机。~ *training* (学校的)手工学科〔特指木工〕。~ *exercises* 刀枪操练。*a sign ~*签名,亲笔署名。**II** ***n***. **1.** 手册;说明书;便览;指南,宝鉴;教本;(中世纪的)祈祷书。**2.**【军】刀枪操练。**3.**【乐】键盘。**4.** 手压灭火机。*a school ~*教科书。*the service ~*维修守则,使用细则。**-ly** ***ad***. 用手;亲自,实际。

ma·nu·bri·um [məˈnuːbriːəm, -njuː-; məˋnubrɪəm, -nju-] ***n***. (*pl*. ***-bria*** [-ə; -ə], ***-bri·ums***) **1.** 柄式结构;柄状突起;柄状体。**2.** (尤指)【动】(腔肠动物的)垂管;(昆虫的)前腹片;前胸骨;前腹板。

man·u·code [ˈmænjukəud; ˋmænjʊˏkod] ***n***. 极乐鸟类。

Man·u·el [ˈmænjuel; ˋmænjʊɛl] ***n***. 曼纽尔〔男子名,Em(m)anuel 的异体〕。

manuf. = manufactory; manufacture(d); manufacturer.

man·u·fac·to·ry [ˌmænjuˈfæktəri; ˏmænjəˋfæktərɪ] ***n***. 制造厂;工厂。

man·u·fac·ture [ˌmænjuˈfæktʃə; ˏmænjəˋfæktʃɚ] **I** ***vt***. **1.** (成批)生产,制造。**2.** 捏造,虚构,粗制滥造(文学作品等)。— ***vi***. 从事制造。**II** ***n***. **1.** (成批的)制造,(特种)工业,工厂。**2.** 制造品,产品;〔蔑〕(文学上的)滥作。*a thing of home* [*foreign*] ~本国[外国]制品。*the steel ~*制钢工业。*silk ~s* 丝织品。

man·u·fac·tur·er [ˌmænjuˈfæktʃərə; ˏmænjəˋfæktʃərɚ] ***n***. 制造商,厂主,制造厂。

man·u·fac·tur·ing [ˌmænjuˈfæktʃəriŋ; ˏmænjəˋfæktʃərɪŋ] ***a***. 制造的,从事工业的。*a ~ town* 工业城市。*a ~ district* 工业区。*the ~ industry* 制造业。

ma·nul [ˈmeinul; ˋmenʊl] ***n***. (西藏、蒙古的)小野猫。

man·u·mis·sion [ˌmænjuˈmiʃən; ˏmænjəˋmɪʃən] ***n***. (农奴、奴隶的)解放;解放证。

man·u·mit [ˌmænjuˈmit; ˏmænjəˋmɪt] ***vt***.【史】解放(农奴或奴隶)。

man·u·mit·ter [ˌmænjuˈmitə; ˏmænjəˋmɪtɚ] ***n***. 解放者。

man·u·mo·tor [ˌmænjuˈməutə; ˏmænjəˋmotɚ] ***n***. 手推车。

ma·nure [məˈnjuə; məˋnjʊr] **I** ***n***. 肥料。*artificial ~*人造肥料。*nitrogenous ~*氮肥。*barn yard* [*farmyard*] ~厩[堆]肥。*green ~*绿肥。*a ~ spreader* 施肥机。**II** ***vt***. 施肥于…。

ma·nus [ˈmeinəs; ˋmenəs] ***n***. (*pl*. ***ma·nus***) **1.** (四肢动物的)手,前掌。**2.** (罗马法律)夫权。

man·u·script [ˈmænjuskript; ˋmænjəˏskrɪpt] **I** ***a***. 手写的,手抄的。**II** ***n***. 抄本;(著者的)原稿〔略:MS.;〔*pl*.〕MSS.〕; 手写(*opp*. print)。*The work is still in ~*. 那本著作仍旧没有印刷〔原稿未动〕。

man·ward [ˈmænwəd; ˋmænwɚd] ***ad***., ***a***. 面向人类(的),关于人(的)。

man·wise [ˈmænwaiz; ˋmænˏwaɪz] ***ad***. 以男人的本分,像男子汉那样。

Manx [mæŋks; mæŋks] **I** ***a***. 英国曼(Man)岛的;曼岛人[语]的。**II** ***n***. 曼岛人[语];〔集合词〕(无尾)曼岛猫〔又作~ cat〕。

Manx·man [ˈmæŋksmən; ˋmæŋksmən] ***n***. (*pl*. ***-men***) 曼(Man)岛人[男人]。~**woman** 曼岛女人。

man·y [ˈmeni; ˋmɛnɪ] **I** ***a***. (***more***; ***most***) (*opp*. few; *cf*. much) 许多的,多数的,很多的,多。★ 1. 在口语中,尤其是在英国口语中,除用作肯定句的主词或接用于 too, so, as, how 之后以外,带有否定、疑问、条件意义: M- people think so. Did you see ~ people? 2. 在其他肯定句中常作 a lot of, a (large) number of, a great [good] many 等的代用语。3. 文语中通例是以单数用作倒装句法中的表语: Many's the time (= often) I've seen him do it.

II ***pro***. 许多人[物]。*M- of us were tired*. 我们当中的许多人都疲倦了。*I have a few, but not ~*. 我有一点儿,可是不多。

III ***n***. **1.** 多数人[东西]。*There are a good ~ of them*. 那样的人很多[那种东西很多]。*A great ~ stayed away*. 很多人没来。**2.** 〔the ~〕大多数人,一般人,群众。***a good*** [***great***] ~很多的,非常多的。***as ~*** 和…一样多(的);同数(的) (*He made six mistakes in as ~ lines*. 六行里就错了六处)。***as ~ again*** 再同样多的,加倍的。***as ~ as ...*** **1.** 多少…多少,…的都… (*Take as ~ as you want*. 你要多少就拿多少。*They admit as ~ as come*. 来多少就可以进去多少)。**2.** 整整的〔一般指数目而言〕(*He has been working at his book as ~ as five years*. 他的书已经整整写了五年了)。***as*** [***like***] ***so ~*** **1.** 像许多人一样(*He failed like so ~ before him*. 像他前面的许多人一样,他失败了)。**2.** 同数的,和…一样多的(= as ~)。***be one too ~*** 多余的东西,碍手碍脚的东西。***be*** (***one***) ***too ~ for*** 比某人高明,胜过某人;为某人所不能理解 (*He is* (*one*) *too ~ for me*. 我弄他不赢,我拿他没办法)。***how ~*** 多少,几何 (*How ~ boys are there?* 有多少男孩?)。***~ a*** [***an***] 〔诗、古〕许许多多,很多(*~ a day* 多日〔语气较强于 *~days*〕)。***~ a*** [〔古〕***an***] ***one*** 许许多多人。***M- a pickle makes a muckle***. 积少成多,集腋成裘。~ (***and ~***) ***a time*** = ~ ***a time and oft*** 〔诗、古〕= ***on ~ occasions*** = ~ ***times*** 多次,不知多少次。***not ~*** 〔俚〕少许的,些少的。***not so ~ as*** 没那么多,少于。***so ~*** 那么多的,同数的 (*in so ~ words* 露骨地(说)。*So ~ men, so ~ minds*. 〔谚〕十人十心。*There are so ~ mistakes that I can not count them*. 错误多得数不清)。~**-fold** ***ad***. 许多倍地。~**-headed** ***a***. 多头的。~**-minded** ***a***. 三心二意的。~**plies** 〔*sing*., *pl*.〕重瓣胃〔反刍类的第三胃(= omasum)〕。~**-sided** ***a***.【几】多边的;多方面的,多才多艺的,兴趣广泛的。~**-stage** ***a***. 多段的,多级的;多串联的。~**wheres** ***ad***. 在许多地方。

many- *comb. f*. = many.

man·za·na [mɑːnˈzɑːnə; manˋzanə] ***n***. (中南美的)面积单位〔1至2英亩〕。

man·za·ni·ta [ˌmænzəˈniːtə; ˏmænzəˋnitə] ***n***.【植】熊果属植物。

Ma·o·ri [ˈmɑːri, ˈmauri; ˋmarɪ, ˋmaʊrɪ] **I** ***n***. (*pl*. ~***s***) (新西兰的)毛利人;毛利语。**II** ***a***. 毛利人[语]的。

MAP = Military Aid Program〔美〕军事援助计划。

map [mæp; mæp] **I** ***n***. **1.** 地图;天体图;图。**2.** 〔美俚〕脸,面孔。**3.** 〔美俚〕(染色体上基因排列的)遗传图。***off***

the ～〔口〕不重要的；消失的；过时的；陈腐的。*on the* ～〔口〕存在的；重要的；有名的，占显著地位的，起主要作用的。*put oneself on the* ～ 发生，发现；使自己出名，出人头地。*put sb.*［*sth.*］*on the* ～ 使某人［某事］出名。*wipe off the* ～ 把…消灭掉。**II** *vt*. **1**. 测绘，为…绘制地图；勘测，制订。**2**.〔美俚〕测定(染色体中基因的)位置。～ **out** 规划，安排。～ **board** 图板。～**like** *a*. 像地图的。～ **measurer** 量图仪，地图里程计算器。～ **mounter** 裱地图的人。～ **scale** 地图比例尺。

ma·ple [ˈmeipl; ˋmepl] *n*.【植】槭，枫；枫木；槭糖浆味，淡棕色；〔*pl*.〕【美体】篮球场的地板。*hard* ～硬木。*Japanese* ～鸡爪枫。～*s five*【美体】篮球队。～ **leaf** 枫叶〔Canada 的国徽〕。～ **sugar** 槭糖。～ **syrup** 槭糖浆；槭树汁。

map·per, map·pist [ˈmæpə, -pist; ˋmæpə˞, -pɪst] *n*. 制图者；绘图人。

map·ping [ˈmæpiŋ; ˋmæpɪŋ] *n*.【数】映像，映射。

Ma·pu·to [mæˈputə; mæˋputə] *n*. 马普托(马布多)〔莫桑比克首都〕。

ma·quette [mɑːˈket; mɑˋket] *n*. (雕塑、建筑等设计的)小模型。

ma·quil·a·do·ra [məˌkiləˈdɔːrə; məˏkɪləˋdorə] *n*. 〔Span.〕墨西哥美资工厂〔由美国人开办，招收墨西哥人为劳工〕。

ma·quil·lage [ˌmækiːˈjɑːʒ; ˏmækiˋjɑʒ] *n*.〔F.〕化妆品。

Ma·quis [ˈmɑːki; ˏmɑˋkɪ] *n*. (*pl*. **-quis** [-ˈkiːz; -ˋkiz] 马基〔第二次世界大战中抗击纳粹的法国地下组织成员〕。

mar [mɑː; mɑr] **I** *vt*. 毁损，弄坏，弄糟。*make*［*mend*］*or* ～ 完全成功或彻底失败。**II** *n*. 损伤，毁损，障碍。

Mar. = March.

mar. = **1**. married. **2**. maritime.

Mara [ˈmɑːrə; ˋmɑrə] *n*. 玛拉〔女子名，Mary 的异体〕。

mar·a·bou, mar·a·bout [ˈmærəbuː, -buːt; ˋmærəˏbu, -but] *n*.【鸟】(非洲)大鹳；秃鹳；鹳毛；【纺】马拉布生丝；单丝经缎。

Mar·a·bout [ˈmærəbuːt; ˋmærəbut] *n*. 伊斯兰教托钵僧或隐士；伊斯兰教隐士的坟墓或圣祠。

mar·aca [məˈrɑːkə; məˋrɑkə] *n*. (南美等处跳舞乐队用的)响葫芦。

Mar·a·cai·bo [ˌmærəˈkaibəu; ˏmærəˋkaɪbo] *n*. 马拉开波〔委内瑞拉港市〕。

mar·ag·ing steels [ˈmɑːreidʒiŋ; ˋmɑredʒɪŋ] 马氏体钢〔具有极高强度的镍铁合金，从马丁散体钢中以不淬火的方法弭散硬化而成〕。

mar·a·nath·a [ˌmærəˈnɑːθə; ˏmærəˋnæθə] *n*. 咒诅话。

mar·a·schi·no [ˌmærəsˈkiːnəu; ˏmærəˋskino] *n*. (*pl*. ～*s*)〔It.〕野樱桃酒。～ *cherries* 野樱桃酒味糖水樱桃。

mar·as·mus [məˈræzməs; məˋræzməs] *n*.【医】消瘦，衰弱。**maras·mic** *a*.

Ma·ra·tha [məˈrɑːtə; məˋrɑtə] *n*. (西印度)马拉地族人。

Ma·ra·thi [məˈrɑːtiː; məˋrɑti] *n*. 马拉地语。

mar·a·thon [ˈmærəθən; ˋmærəˏθɑn] **I** *n*. 马拉松长跑〔正式路程是 26 英里 385 码(＝42.195 公里)，又名 ～ race〕；长距离赛跑；(各种)持久比赛。**II** *a*. (比赛等)需要极大持久力的。**III** *vi*. 参加持久比赛。**-er** *n*. 参加持久比赛的人。

mar·a·tho·ni·an [ˌmærəˈθəuniən; ˏmærəˋθonɪən] **I** *n*. 马拉松赛跑选手。**II** *a*. 马拉松的。

ma·raud [məˈrɔːd; məˋrɔd] **I** *vi*., *vt*. 掠夺，抢劫，劫掠(*on*; *upon*)。**II** *n*.〔罕〕劫掠。～*ing hordes* 盗匪。

ma·raud·er [məˈrɔːdə; məˋrɔdə˞] *n*. 掠夺者，抢劫者。

mar·a·ve·di [ˌmæreˈveidi; ˏmærəˋvedɪ] *n*. (*pl*. ～*dis*) 马勒威迪〔西班牙的古铜币〕。

mar·ble [ˈmɑːbl; ˋmɑrbl] **I** *n*. **1**. 大理石；〔*pl*.〕大理石雕刻品。**2**. (小儿游戏用)弹子；〔*pl*.〕弹子戏。**3**.〔*pl*.〕〔俚〕理智；常识。*as hard*［*cold*］*as* ～ 大理石一样坚硬［冰冷］的，冷酷无情的。*Elgin* [ˈelgin; ˋɛlgɪn] ～*s* 不列颠博物馆所藏希腊帕特嫩神庙(*Parthenon*)的大理石雕刻。*M- Arch* (伦敦海德公园东北入口的)大理石拱门。**II** *a*. **1**. 大理石(似)的；有大理石纹彩的。**2**. 无情的，冷酷的；纯白的。～ *paper* 云纹纸。～ *dust* 云石粉。～ *soap* 斑纹皂。*a* ～ *brow* 白眉毛。～ *cake* 大理石纹奶油蛋糕。**III** *vt*. 把(纸、书边、肥皂等)做成大理石花纹形状；〔罕〕把…弄得像大理石一样的白。～**-edged** *a*. (精装书)云纹边的。～**-hearted** *a*. 铁石心肠的，无情的，冷酷的；麻木的。

mar·ble·ize [ˈmɑːblaiz; ˋmɑrblˏaɪz] *vt*. 弄成大理石花纹。

mar·bling [ˈmɑːbliŋ; ˋmɑrblɪŋ] *n*. **1**. 大理石纹着附术，大理石纹加工法。**2**. 大理石纹状。

mar·bly [ˈmɑːbli; ˋmɑrblɪ] *a*. 大理石似的；含大理石的；冒充大理石的；冷酷的，冷淡的。

marc [mɑːk; mɑrk] *n*. (葡萄等的)榨渣，果渣，苹果［葡萄］渣酿制的白兰地酒。

mar·can·do [mɑːˈkɑːndəu; mɑrˋkɑndo] *a*., *ad*. 〔It.〕【乐】清晰的［地］。

mar·ca·site [ˈmɑːkəsait; ˋmɑrkəˏsaɪt] *n*.【矿】白铁矿；用作饰品的白铁矿石。

mar·cel [mɑːˈsel; mɑrˋsɛl] **I** *n*. 波浪卷发〔又叫 ～ wave〕。**II** *vt*. 使(头发)烫成波浪形。**-cel·ler** [-ə; -ə˞] *n*. 烫发师。

mar·cel·la [mɑːˈselə; mɑrˋsɛlə] *n*. 凸纹布。

mar·ces·cent [mɑːˈsesnt; mɑrˋsɛsnt] *a*.【植】凋存的，凋而不落的。**-cence** *n*.

March[1] [mɑːtʃ; mɑrtʃ] *n*. 马奇〔姓氏〕。

March[2] [mɑːtʃ; mɑrtʃ] *n*. 三月〔略作 Mar.〕。*in* ～在三月。～ *comes in like a lion and goes out like a lamb*.〔谚〕三月天气来如猛狮，去如绵羊。～ **brown** (钓鱼用的)拟饵；蜉蝣。～ **hare** 交尾期的野兔(*mad as a* ～ *hare* 发情若狂)。

march[1] [mɑːtʃ; mɑrtʃ] **I** *n*. **1**. 行进；进军，行军；【军】进军行程，推进里程；步调。**2**. 艰苦的长途旅行。**3**. 进展，发展。**4**.【乐】进行曲。*a line of* ～ 行军路线。*a forced* ～ 强行军，兼程行军。*a hunger* ～(失业者的)饥饿游行。(*a*) *quick*［*slow*］～快［慢］步走。*double* ～跑步。*the* ～ *of events* 事件的进展。*a dead* ～送葬曲。*a* ～ *column* 行军纵队。*a* ～ *formation* 行军队形。～ *order* 行军次序；行军命令。～ *table* 行军计划表。～*es immune from enemy interference* 旅次行军。～*es subject to hostile interference* 战备行军。*be on*［*in*］*the* ～ 进行中。*steal a* ～ (*up*) *on* 偷袭(敌人)；越过；偷偷抢在某人之前。**II** *vt*. 使前进，使行军，使进军；拖走，拖去。— *vi*. **1**. 进，进行，进军，推进。**2**. 脚步沉重地走。**3**. (事件等)发展，进展。～ *against the enemy* 向敌方推进。～ *at ease* 常步前进。～ *into* 长驱直入。～ *off* 出发；使走，带走(～ *a man off*［*away*］*to gaol* 把人带到牢里)。～ *on* 继续前进；使前进，逼进，向…推进。～ *past* (检阅时)分列前进。～**-in** *n*. **1**. (军队)进入(攻占的城市等)。**2**. (运动员的)进场。～**ing order** 军装。～**ing orders** 开拔令。～**-past** (检阅时的)分列式。

march[2] [mɑːtʃ; mɑrtʃ] **I** *n*.【史】边界，边境；〔常 *pl*.〕(特指英格兰和苏格兰或威尔斯的)接界地区。*riding the* ～*es*【史】(都市等的)境界检查。**II** *vi*. 毗连，邻接(*upon*; *with*)。

March. = Marchioness.

marche funèbre [marʃ fynɛːbr; marʃ fynɛbr] *n*.〔F.〕送葬曲，衰悼曲。

Mär·chen [ˈmɛːrçən; ˋmɛrxən] *n*.〔G.〕童话，民间传说。

march·er[1][ˈmɑːtʃə; ˋmɑtʃɚ] ***n***. 行军者,游行者。

march·er[2][ˈmɑːtʃə; ˋmartʃɚ] ***n***. **1.** 边疆居民。**2.**〔英〕边境防务长官。

mar·che·se [mɑːˈkeze; marˋkeze] ***n***. (*pl*. ***-che·si*** [-ziː; -zi]) (意大利的)侯爵。

mar·che·sa [mɑːˈkezɑː; marˋkezɑ] ***n***. (*pl*. ***-che·se*** [-ze; -zi]) (意大利的)女侯爵;(意大利的)侯爵夫人。

mar·chion·ess [ˈmɑːʃənis; ˋmarʃənɪs] ***n***. 侯爵夫人,侯爵未亡人〔也用作称号〕;女侯爵。

march·pane [ˈmɑːtʃpein; ˋmartʃˏpen] ***n***. 杏仁糖霜;杏仁糖(= marzipan)。

Mar·cia [ˈmɑːʃə; ˋmarʃə] ***n***. 玛西雅〔女子名〕。

Mar·cion·ism [ˈmɑːʃənizəm; ˋmarʃənɪzəm] ***n***.【宗史】马西翁教派〔公元 2—3 世纪兴起的一个基督教派,其教义摈弃《旧约》和《新约》的大部〕。**-cion·ite** [-nait; -naɪt] ***n***.

Mar·co·ni [mɑːˈkəuni; marˋkonɪ], **Guglielmo** ～ 马可尼〔1874—1937,意大利无线电报发明者〕。**I**〔m-〕***n***. 无线电报。**II**〔m-〕***vi***., ***vt***. 打无线电报。

mar·co·ni·gram [mɑːˈkəunigræm; marˋkonɪˏgræm] ***n***. (马可尼式)无线电报。**-co·ni·graph** [-grɑːf; -graf] ***n***. (马可尼式)无线电报机。

Marconi rig【海】马可尼帆(= Bermuda rig)。

Mar·co Po·lo [ˈmɑːkəu ˈpəuləu; ˋmarko ˋpolo] 马可波罗〔1254? —1324,意大利旅行家〕。

Mar·cus [ˈmɑːkəs; ˋmarkəs] ***n***. 马库斯〔男子名〕。

Mar·di gras [ˈmɑːdiːˈgrɑː; ˋmardɪˋgrɑ]〔F.〕基督教四旬斋(Lent)开始的前一天〔意为"滴油的星期二",西方的狂欢节之一〕。

Mar·duk [ˈmɑːduk; ˋmarduk] ***n***. 马杜克〔古代巴比伦人的主神〕。

mare [mɛə; mɛr] ***n***. 牝马,母马;母驴。***go on shanks'*** ～ 走着去。***a grey*** ～ 比丈夫能干的女人[妻子]。***Money makes the*** ～ (***to***) ***go***. 有钱能使鬼推磨。***The grey*** ～ ***is the better horse***. 女人[妻子]当家;牝鸡司晨。***Whose*** ～***'s dead***? 怎么啦? ***win the*** ～ ***or lose the halter*** 孤注一掷。～**'s nest** 一场空的发现;骗人的东西;一团糟的地方[情况]。～**'s tail**【气】马尾云;【植】杉叶藻。

ma·re [ˈmɛəri; ˋmɛrɪ] ***n***.〔L.〕海;【天】(月亮,火星表面的)海(指阴暗区)。～ ***clau·sum*** [ˈklɔːsəm; ˋklɔsəm] 领海 (= closed sea)。～ ***lib·e·rum*** [ˈlibərəm; ˋlɪbərəm]公海(= open sea)。～ ***nos·trum*** [ˈnɔstrəm; ˋnɑstrəm] 我们的海〔地中海的罗马名〕;属于一国或由两国或多国协议共同使用的可通航水域。

Ma·ré·chal Niel [ˈmɑːʃəl niːl; ˋmarʃəl nil] ***n***.〔F.〕【植】尼尔元帅黄蔷薇。

ma·rem·ma [məˈremə; məˋremə] ***n***. (*pl*. ***-me*** [-miː; -mi]) 瘴气多的滨海沼泽地〔尤指意大利西部的滨海区域〕。

mar·eo·graph [ˈmæriəgrɑːf; ˋmærɪəˏgraf] ***n***. 自记测潮仪。

marg. = margin; marginal.

Mar·ga·ret [ˈmɑːgərit; ˋmargrɪt] ***n***. 玛格丽特〔女子名,Madge, May 的昵称〕。

mar·gar·ic [mɑːˈgærik; marˋgærɪk] ***a***.【化】十七酸的,真珠酸的。～ **acid** 十七酸,真珠酸。

mar·ga·rin(e) [ˌmɑːdʒəˈriːn, ˈmɑːgərin; ˏmardʒəˋrin; ˋmargərɪn] ***n***. 人造奶油,植物奶油。

mar·ga·rite [ˈmɑːgərait; ˋmargəraɪt] ***n***. **1.** 珍珠云母。**2.** 珠状晶体物质。**3.**〔废〕珍珠。

mar·gay [ˈmɑːgei; ˋmarge] ***n***.【动】(南美)虎猫。

marge[1][mɑːdʒ; mardʒ] ***n***.〔诗〕边缘。

marge[2][mɑːdʒ; mardʒ] ***n***.〔英口〕= margarine.

mar·gent [ˈmɑːdʒənt; ˋmardʒənt] ***n***.〔古〕边缘;(书的)旁注。

Mar·ger·y [ˈmɑːdʒəri; ˋmardʒərɪ] ***n***. 玛洁里〔女子名,Margaret 的异体〕。

Mar·gie [ˈmɑːdʒi; ˋmardʒɪ] ***n***. 玛吉〔女子名,Margaret 的昵称〕。

mar·gin [ˈmɑːdʒin; ˋmardʒɪn] **I** ***n***. **1.** 边缘;边缘部分;范围,限界;【军】图廓。**2.** (版心外)空白;栏外,栏外注解。**3.**【商】原价和卖价之差,赚头;【股】保证金,垫头,储备。**4.** 余裕,余地,余额。**5.** 差数;幅度。*the* ～ *of cultivation* 耕种界限。*the* ～ *of safety* 安全限度。*the overload* ～过载定额。*the narrow* ～ *of profit* 微利。*go near the* ～(道德上)接近危险地步。*safety* ～【物】安全系数。**II** ***vt***. 给…镶边;在…加旁注;【股】为…付保险金。

mar·gin·al [ˈmɑːdʒinəl; ˋmardʒɪnl] ***a***. **1.** 边的,边缘的;记在栏外的,旁注的;限界的,边际的。**2.** 收入仅敷支出的。～ *land* 瘠薄的土地,不毛之地。*a* ～ *lake*【地】冰前湖。～ *notes* 旁注。～ *profits* 限界利润,边际利润。～ *subsistence* 起码的生活。～ *utility* (*theory*)【经】边际效用(价值说)。**-ize** ***vt***. 忽略,忽视,排斥;使边缘化,使处于次要地位。

mar·gi·na·lia [ˌmɑːdʒiˈneiljə; ˏmardʒəˋnelɪə] ***n***.〔*pl*.〕旁注;次要的东西。

mar·gin·al·ly [ˈmɑːdʒinəli; ˋmardʒɪnəlɪ] ***ad***. 在边上,边沿地。

mar·gin·at·e(d) [ˈmɑːdʒineit(id); ˋmardʒənet(ɪd)] ***a***. 有边的,有边缘的。

Mar·got [ˈmɑːgəu; ˋmargo] ***n***. 玛戈〔女子名,Margaret 的昵称〕。

mar·gra·vate, mar·gra·vi·ate [ˈmɑːgrəveit, mɑːˈgreivieit; ˏmarˋgreˏvet, ˏmarˋgrevɪet] ***n***. (罗马帝国或德国的)侯爵封地;边省总督管领地。

mar·grave [ˈmɑːgreiv; ˋmargrev] ***n***.【史】(德国边境省份的)总督;(德国的)侯爵。

mar·gra·vine [ˈmɑːgrəviːn; ˋmargrəˏvin] ***n***. margrave 的夫人[未亡人]。

Mar·gue·rite [ˌmɑːgəˈriːt; ˏmargəˋrit] ***n***. 玛格丽特〔女子名,Margaret 的异体〕。

mar·gue·rite [ˌmɑːgəˈriːt; ˏmargəˋrɪt] ***n***.【植】木茼蒿;雏菊;延命菊属植物。

Ma·ri·a [məˈraiə, məˈriə; məˋraɪə, məˋriə] ***n***. 玛丽亚〔女子名,Mary 的异体〕。*a black* ～囚车。

ma·ri·a·chi [ˈmɑːriːˈɑːtʃi; ˏmariˋɑtʃɪ] ***n***. (*pl*. ***-chis*** [-z; -z]) **1.** 墨西哥流浪乐队艺人。**2.** 墨西哥流浪乐队。**3.** 墨西哥乐队演奏的乐曲。

ma·ri·age à la mode [ˈmæriɑːʒ ɑː lɑː məud; maˋrjaʒ a la mod]〔F.〕(基于私利的上流社会)时式结婚。

ma·ri·age de con·science [ˈmæriɑːʒ də kõsjɑ̃s; maˋrjaʒ də kõsjɑ̃s]〔F.〕常婚。

ma·ri·age de con·ve·nance [ˈmæriɑːʒ də ˋkõvənɑ̃ːns; maˋrjaʒ də kõvˋnɑ̃s]〔F.〕基于利益关系的婚姻;权宜婚姻。

Ma·ri·an[1][ˈmɛəriən; ˋmɛrɪən] **I** ***a***. 圣母玛利亚的;(英国及苏格兰的)玛利一世女王的。**II** ***n***. 追随(苏格兰女王)玛利一世的保皇派成员。

Mar·i·an[2][ˈmɛəriən, ˈmæriən; ˋmɛrɪən, ˋmærɪən] ***n***. 玛丽安〔女子名,Mariana 的异体〕。

Ma·ri·an·a [ˌmɛəriˈænə; ˏmɛrɪˋænə] ***n***. 玛丽安娜〔女子名,Mary 的异体〕。

Ma·ri·an·a Islands, Ma·ri·an·as [ˌmɛəriˈænə ˈailəndz, ˈmɛəriˈænəz; ˏmɛrɪˋænə ˋaɪləndz, ˏmɛrɪˋænəz] 马里亚纳群岛〔西太平洋〕。

Ma·ria·na·o [Sp. ˌmariaˈnao; ˏmarjɑˋnao] ***n***. 马里亚瑙〔古巴城市〕。

Ma·rie [ˈmɑːri(ː), məˈriː; ˋmari, məˋri] ***n***. 玛丽〔女子名,Mary 的异体〕。

Mar·i·et·ta [mɛəriˈetə; ˏmɛrɪˋɛtə] ***n***. 玛丽埃塔〔女子名,Maria 的昵称〕。

mar·i·gold [ˈmærigəuld; ˋmærəˏgold] ***n***.【植】金盏花;万寿菊。～ **window**【建】车轮窗,菊花窗。

M

ma·ri·jua·na, ma·ri·hua·na [ˌmɑːriˈhwɑːnɑː; ˏmɑrɪˋhwɑnə] *n*. 1. 野生烟草。2. (印度)大麻;大麻干叶〔混在香烟里抽,有麻醉作用〕。*a ~ cigarette* 大麻烟卷。

ma·rim·ba [məˈrimbə; məˋrɪmbə] *n*. (中非和南美的)原始木琴;现代经过改良的原始木琴。

ma·ri·na [məˈriːnə; məˋrinə] *n*. 1. 小游艇船坞。2. 〔M-〕玛丽娜[女子名]。

mar·i·nade [ˌmæriˈneid; ˏmærəˋned] **I** *n*. (用酒、醋、香料等配合成的)腌泡汁;在腌泡汁里泡的肉[鱼]。**II** [ˈmærineid; ˋmærɪned] *vt*. = marinate.

mar·i·nate [ˈmærineit; ˋmærəˏnet] *vt*. 用腌泡汁泡。

ma·rine [məˈriːn; məˋrin] **I** *a*. 海的,海上的;海事的,海运的;海军的;生在海中的,海产的。*a ~ barometer* 船用晴雨计。*M- Law* 海事法[海商法]。*a ~ cable* 海底电线。*the M- Corps* 〔美〕海军陆战队。*the ~ court* 海事法庭。*a ~ store* 旧船具店。*~ stores* 〔英〕船具,船舶用品;旧船具类商品。*~ soap* 船用肥皂,海水皂。*a ~ engine* 轮机。*~ insurance* 海上保险。*a ~ policy* 海上保险单。*~ products* 海产物,水产物。**II** *n*. 1. 海军陆战队士兵[军官];(军舰的)地勤海军。2. 海事,海运业;(欧洲大陆各国的)海军(部);船舶,舰队;海画,海景。3. 〔俚〕空瓶;新水兵。*blue* [*red*] *~s* 海军陆战队炮[步]兵。*the mercantile* [*commercial*] *~*(一国的)商船(队)。*the ~ belt* 领海。*a* (*dead*) *~*空瓶。***Tell that to the ~s*** [***horse-~s***]! = ***That will do for the ~s***! 〔口〕谁信你那一套! 我才不受你的骗呢!。

mar·i·ner [ˈmærinə; ˋmærənɚ] *n*. 水手,船员。*a master ~*(商船或渔船的)船长。*~'s card* 海图。*~'s needle* [*compass*] 罗盘针;航海罗盘。

ma·ri·nism [məˈriːnizəm; məˋrinɪzəm] *n*. (意大利诗人马利诺 (Marino)式的)极讲究技巧的文体。

Mar·i·ol·a·try [ˌmɛəriˈɔlətri; ˏmɛrɪˋɑlətrɪ] *n*. (迷信式的)圣母玛利亚崇拜〔攻击者用语〕。

Mar·i·ol·o·gy [ˌmɛəriˈɔlədʒi; ˏmɛrɪˋɑlədʒɪ] *n*. 圣母玛利亚论[研究]。

Mar·i·on [ˈmɛəriən, ˈmæriən; ˋmɛrɪən, ˋmærɪən] *n*. 1. 玛丽恩〔女子名,Mary 的昵称〕。2. 马里恩〔姓氏,男子名〕。

mar·i·o·nette [ˌmæriəˈnet; ˏmærɪəˋnɛt] *n*. (木偶戏用的)牵线木偶。

Mar·i·po·sa lily [**tulip**] [ˌmɑːriˈpəuzə, -sə; ˏmærəˋpozə, -sə] 【植】1. 蝴蝶百合〔产于北美西部,开白、红、黄、紫色的花朵〕。2. 蝴蝶百合花。

Ma·ri·sat [ˈmærəˌsæt; ˋmærəˏsæt] *n*. 〔美〕海上通信卫星。

mar·ish [ˈmæriʃ; ˋmærɪʃ] *n*., *a*. 〔诗〕沼泽(的)。

Ma·rist [ˈmɛərist; ˋmɛrɪst] *n*. (天主教的)玛利亚会会员。

ma·ri·tal [ˈmæritl; ˋmærətl] *a*. 丈夫的;婚姻的。*~ obligations* 丈夫(对妻子)的义务。*~* **rape**【律】婚内强奸〔指丈夫违背妻子意愿以粗暴手段强行与之发生性行为〕。

ma·ri·tal·ly [ˈmæritəli; ˋmæˋrətəlɪ] *ad*. 作为丈夫;婚姻上作为夫妇;像结了婚似地。

ma·rit·ic·ide [məˈritisaid; məˋrɪtɪsaɪd] *n*. 杀夫[妻]的人[行为]。

mar·i·time [ˈmæritaim; ˋmærəˏtaɪm] *a*. 海的,海上的;海事的,海运的;沿海的;生在沿海地带的。*~ association* 海事协会。*~ climate* 海洋性气候。*M- Customs Administration* (中国的)海关总署。*The M- Exchange* (纽约的)海运交易所。*a ~ power* 海洋国家;海运国。*M- Provinces* (加拿大的)沿海各省。

mar·jo·ram [ˈmɑːdʒərəm; ˋmɑrdʒərəm] *n*. 【植】茉乔栾那属;牛至属。

Mar·jo·rie, Mar·jo·ry [ˈmɑːdʒəri; ˋmɑrdʒərɪ] *n*. 玛乔里〔女子名,Margery 的异体〕。

Mark[1], **Marc** [mɑːk; mɑrk] *n*. 马克〔男子名,Marcus 的异体〕。

Mark[2] [mɑːk; mɑrk] *n*. 【宗】(基督教《圣经》中的篇名)《马可福音》;《马可福音》的作者马可。

mark[1] [mɑːk; mɑrk] **I** *n*. 1. 印,记号,符号,标记;标志,指标;十字押〔文盲的签名〕。2. 靶子;标识;目标。3. 迹,痕迹;斑点。4. 特征,特质,特性。5. (考试等的)分数。6. 显著,高贵,卓越;荣誉,名声。7. 界限,限度;限界线;〔the ~〕标准。8. 【海】测标;(船舶)载重线标志;【橄榄球】有踢球权利者用脚在地上画的印,脚跟印 (= heel-~);【体】起步线;【拳】心窝。9. 【史】中世纪日尔曼民族的村落公社。10. 【美军】(武器的)型号。11. 〔古〕境界,边境。12. 〔美〕嗜好;老好人,易受欺骗的人;施钱[食品]给无业游民的场所。*a trade ~*商标。*a price ~*(商品上的)标价牌。*full ~s* 满分,一百分。*get 80 ~s for English* 英语得 80 分。*On your ~s*!【体】各就各位! *a bad ~*一(项)过(失);污点。*a good ~*一(项)功(劳);优点;操行良好的标记;良好的声誉或信用。*an easy* [*a soft*] *~*易受骗的人,冤大头。***bear*** [***show***] ***~s of ...*** 有…的痕迹。***below the ~***在标准以下。***beside*** [***wide of***] ***the ~***不中肯;不切合,不恰当。***beyond the ~***过度,过分。***Bless the ~***! = *Save the ~*! ***cut the ~***(箭)在靶前落下。***fall*** [***come***] ***short of the ~***不到标准,不合格。***get off the ~***【体】起步,出发;开始(工作等)。***go wide of the ~*** 没打中,离目标太远;离题太远。***God bless the ~***! = *Save the ~*! ***have a ~ on*** 喜欢,爱好。***hit the ~*** 打中目标,中靶;(发言)中肯;达到目的。***make one's ~*** 出名。***~ of mouth*** (表示马龄的)门齿凹〔6 岁左右从下齿起开始无凹〕。***miss the ~*** 未中的;不成功,失败。***of ~*** 知名的,杰出的 (*a man of ~*名人,要人。*a man of no ~*普通人)。***on the ~*** 〔美〕作比赛[起步]准备的。***over*** [***under***] ***the ~***估计过高[低]。***overshoot the ~***过度。***Save the ~***! 1. 不要见怪;不客气地说〔常用作插入语〕。2. 天哪! 这还了得!〔表示惊愕、嘲笑、讽刺的话〕。***shoot*** [***answer***] ***wide of the ~*** 离目标很远;答非所问。***short of the ~*** 没有达到标准。***take one's ~ amiss*** 失算,失策。***toe the ~*** (赛跑时)用脚尖踏在起步线上;守规则;负责任。***up to the ~*** 达到标准,过得去;美满;健康;舒适 (*I am not up to the ~*. 我身体不舒服;能力不够)。***within the ~*** 合乎标准;过得去。**II** *vt*. 1. 加记号于,加符号于,作记号于,记上,标记上,记录。2. 给…记分数;表示…的位置;【猎】记清(禽兽逃匿处);(球赛)钉住。3. 指示,使注意。4. 〔诗〕注目,注意;想。5. 【商】给…标价。6. 定…的界限,区分,区划。7. 〔通常用被动式〕使有特色,污点[伤痕,斑点等]。8. 设计,计划;(命运)注定;【军】指定。*M- me* [*my words*]. 注意听。— *vi* 1. 注意,想。2. 【橄榄球】作脚跟印。3. 记分数。4. (马的门齿凹)表示年龄。*~* ***down*** 记下;减价;【猎】记清(禽兽逃往处)。*~* ***off*** (用线条、符号等)划分,区分 (*~ off spheres of influence* 划分势力范围)。*~* ***out*** 指示,划定,划出;拟订(计划),设计;注意;选拔;消去 (*~ out a lawn for tennis* 划定网球场)。*~* ***out for*** 选定[决定]给与…(*be ~ed out for promotion* 已选定…给与提升)〔通常 *p.p.*〕。*~* ***papers*** 批卷子,给考试卷子打分数。*~* ***time*** 【军】踏步;踌躇,犹豫不决。*~* ***up*** 涨价;记上,加上,赊账。*~* ***with a white stone*** 当作喜庆[吉利]的事件记下。**~down** 标低售价;标低的金额。*~* **up** 标高售价;标高的金额;(加在商品成本上以决定售价)的金额;〔美〕(对法案所作的)最后审订。

mark[2] [mɑːk; mɑrk] *n*. 1. 马克〔德国货币〕。2. (英国以前的)马克〔相当于旧制 13 先令 4 便士〕。3. (中世纪欧洲大陆的)金[银]马克〔通常为 8 盎司〕。

marked [mɑːkt; mɑrkt] *a*. 1. 有记号的,加印记的。2. 受监视[注意]的。3. 显著的,著名的,(差别等)明显的。*a ~ cheque* 【商】保证兑现的支票。*a ~ man* 嫌疑分子;〔美〕累犯;名气不好的人;有异常才能的人。*a ~ difference* 显著的差别。*~ coldness* 故意的冷淡。**-ly** *ad*. **-ness** *n*.

mark·er [ˈmɑːkə; ˋmarkɚ] ***n*. 1.** 作记号的人;打分数的人;记分器;划线器;指示器;【无】指点标;(撞球等的)记分员。**2.**【军】标靶兵;标兵;标竿;旗标;书签;〔美〕纪念标,纪念碑;里程碑。**3.** (校中专职)点名先生;经常给学生记分数的先生;监猎人。**4.**【英军】(轰炸用)照明弹。**5.**〔美〕遗传标记,基因标记。*a* ～ *light* 标灯。*a ground* ～地面照明弹。***not a*** ～ ***to*** [***on***]〔美〕不能和…相比,远远配不上。

mar·ket [ˈmɑːkit; ˋmarkɪt] **I** ***n*. 1.** (尤指牲畜和食品的)集市;市场;菜市,菜场。**2.** 需要,销路;推销地区。**3.** 市价;行情,市面,市况。**4.**〔美〕食品店;〔英〕【法】公共市场设置权。*a cotton* [*stock*] ～棉花[股票]市场。*There is no* ～ *for that class of goods here*. 那一类货物这里不需要[无销路]。*The* ～ *rose* [*fell*] 行情俏拔[疲落]。*a sick* ～萧条的市面。*a swimming* ～ 兴旺的市面。*The* ～ *is dull*. 市面呆滞。***at the*** ～照市价。***be on the long side of the*** ～把持物品或证券以待涨价时出卖;做多头,买进期货。***bring one's eggs*** [***hogs, goods***] ***to the wrong*** [***a bad***] ～失策,失算,失误。***bring to*** ～= ***put*** [***place***] ***on the*** ～出售。***bull the*** ～(多头)大量抢购,买涨,哄买。***come into the*** ～上市。***corner the*** ～囤积居奇,大量买进股票[商品]使价格上涨。***engross*** [***forestall***] ***the*** ～垄断市场。***feed to*** ～ 为出售而养肥(家畜等)。***find a*** ～ 找着销路。***go badly to*** ～买[卖]吃亏。***go to*** ～ 上市场买东西;〔口〕筹办,企图。***hold the*** ～ 垄断市场,囤积居奇。***in*** ～ 在买卖中。***in the*** ～拿去卖;正要出售。***in the*** ～ ***for*** (某人)想买,要买。***lose one's*** ～放过(买卖)良机。***make a*** ～【股】在交易所中故意买卖某企业股票,制造兴旺气象;煽动市面。***make a*** [***one's***] ～ ***of*** 利用,利用…赚钱,把…当做摇钱树。***make one's*** ～ 出售存货。***mar another's*** [***one's***] ～搞垮别人[自己]买卖。***mend one's*** ～ 改进买卖情况。***overrun one's*** ～ 因不肯脱手失去出售时机。***overstand one's*** ～ 讨价过高失去出售良机。***play the*** ～〔美〕做投机买卖。***raid the*** ～〔口〕使行情发生波动。***raise the*** ～ ***upon***〔口〕向…要高价。***rig the*** ～〔口〕操纵市场;捣乱市价。**II** ***vi*.** 在市场买卖,作买卖,卖,买。— ***vt*.** 在市场上出售;把…拿到市场去卖。～ **bell** (报告开市的)市场钟。～ **cross** (中世纪市场上的)市场十字架。～ **day** 定期集市日。～ **garden** 商品菜园(= truck-garden)。～ **gardener** 商品菜园经营者。～ **letter**〔美〕商情报告单。～(-)**maker**【商】(股市上的)旺市制造者。～(-)**making** 制造股市旺市。～ **overt** 公开市场。～ **place** 市场;商业中心地。～ **price** 市场价格;时价,市价。～ **rate** 市价,行情。～ **research** 市场调研〔研究市场某些具体商品供求关系〕。～ **town** 特准按期举行集市的小镇。～ **value** (商品的)市场价值,市价。

mar·ket·able [ˈmɑːkitəbl; ˋmarkɪtəbl̩] ***a*. 1.** 可销售的;适销的;有销路的。**2.** 市场买卖的。～ *value* 市场价值。**-a·bil·i·ty** ***n*.**

mar·ket·eer [ˌmɑːkiˈtiə; ˏmarkɪˋtɪr] ***n*.** 市场商人。

mar·ket·er [ˈmɑːkitə; ˋmarkɪtɚ] ***n*.**〔美〕在市场中买卖的人。

mar·ket·ing [ˈmɑːkitiŋ; ˋmarkɪtɪŋ] ***n*. 1.** 商品销售业务。**2.** 商品自生产者转移到消费者手中的一系列有关机能。**3.**〔集合词〕市场购买的货品;适合市场上销售的货品。**4.** 市场学。***go*** [***do one's***] ～上市场买[卖]东西去。～ **research** 销售调查。～ **station** 商业基地。

Mark·ham [ˈmɑːkəm; ˋmarkəm] ***n*.** 马卡姆〔姓氏〕。

mar·khor [ˈmɑːkɔː; ˋmarkɔr] ***n*.** (阿富汗至印度一带山区的)捻角山羊。

mark·ing [ˈmɑːkiŋ; ˋmarkɪŋ] **I** ***n*. 1.** 作记号;记分;记号,印记,点;(尤指鸟兽的皮、羽毛等的)斑纹,条纹。**2.**【商】(支票的)认付。**II** ***a*.** 赋与特征的,使显眼的。～ **board** (比赛时用的)记分牌;(股票交易所的)行情揭示牌。～ **gauge** (木工用的)线准;划线规。～ **ink** (在待洗衣服等上作记号用的)不退色墨水;打印墨水。～ **iron** 烙印铁。

mark·ka [ˈmɑːkkɑː; ˋmarkkɑ] ***n*.** (*pl*. **-kaa** [-kɑː; -kɑ]) 马克〔芬兰货币单位,等于 100 盆尼 (penni)〕。

mark·man [ˈmɑːkmən; ˋmarkmən] ***n*.**〔废〕= marksman.

marks·man [ˈmɑːksmən; ˋmarksmən] ***n*.** (*pl*. **-men**) 打靶能手;狙击手;神枪手;【美军】二等射手;轻兵器射手的最低等级。**-ship** ***n*.** 射击术,枪法,弓术。

Mark Tap·ley [ˈmɑːkˈtæpli; ˋmarkˋtæplɪ] 极快活的人〔出自 Dickens 所作小说 Martin Chuzzlewit〕。

Mark Twain [ˈmɑːk ˈtwein; ˋmarkˋtwen] 马克·吐温〔美国作家 Samuel Langhorne Clemens (1835—1910) 的笔名〕。

marl[1] [mɑːl; marl] **I** ***n*.**【地】泥灰岩灰泥〔肥料用〕;泥灰砖;〔诗〕泥土。***burning*** ～ 焦热地狱的磨难〔出自英国诗人 Milton 的 Paradise Lost〕。**II** ***vt*.** 在…撒泥灰土,用泥灰土施肥。

marl[2] [mɑːl; marl] ***vt*.**【海】用细绳缠(大缆等)。

mar·la·ceous [mɑːˈleiʃəs; marˋleʃəs] ***a*.** 泥灰质的;像泥灰岩的。

Marl·bor·ough [ˈmɔːlbərə, ˈmɑːl-; ˋmɔrlbərə, ˋmarl-] ***n*.** 马尔伯勒〔姓氏〕。

Marl·bor·ough House [ˈmɔːlbərə ˈhaus; ˋmɔrlbərə ˋhaʊs] 英国王储的伦敦宫殿,东宫。

Mar·lene [ˈmɑːliːn, mɑːˈliːn; ˋmarlin, marˋlin] ***n*.** 马琳〔女子名〕。

Mar·lin [ˈmɑːlin; ˋmarlɪn] ***n*.** 马林〔男子名〕。

mar·lin [ˈmɑːlin; ˋmarlɪn] ***n*.**【鱼】(sailfish, spearfish 类的)大马林鱼。

mar·line [ˈmɑːlin; ˋmarlɪn] ***n*.**【海】小绳,细索;油麻绳,左捻双股绳。～**-spike**【船】穿索针;解索针,解缆钻。

marl·ite [ˈmɑːlait; ˋmarlaɪt] ***n*.** 抗风化的泥灰岩。

Mar·low(e) [ˈmɑːləu; ˋmarlo] ***n*. 1.** 马洛〔姓氏〕。**2. Christopher** ～克里斯托弗·马娄〔1564—1593,英国诗人、剧作家〕。

marl-pit [ˈmɑːlpit; ˋmarlpɪt] ***n*.** 泥灰岩采掘场。

marl·stone [ˈmɑːlstəun; ˋmarlston] ***n*.**【地】泥灰质岩,泥灰石。

marl·y [ˈmɑːli; ˋmarlɪ] ***a*.** (***marl·i·er***; ***-i·est***) 似泥灰土的,泥灰质的;泥灰土多的,土地肥沃的。

marm [mɑːm; marm] ***n*.**〔俚〕= ma'am.

Mar·ma·duke [ˈmɑːmədjuːk; ˋmarməˏdjuk] ***n*.** 马默杜克〔男子名〕。

mar·ma·lade [ˈmɑːməleid; ˋmarməled] ***n*.** (带果皮的)橘子[柠檬]果酱。～ **tree**【植】美国榄 (Calocarpum sapota)〔产于美洲热带地区〕。

Mar·ma·ra [ˈmɑːmərə; ˋmarmərə] ***n*.** *Sea of* ～ (通黑海的)马尔马拉海。

mar·ma·tite [ˈmɑːmətait; ˋmarmətaɪt] ***n*.**【矿】铁闪锌矿。

mar·mite [ˈmɑːmait; ˋmarˏmaɪt] ***n*. 1.** 砂锅。**2.**〔俚〕壶形炸弹。**3.** 曲精〔专卖品名〕;【化】酸制酵母。

mar·mo·lite [ˈmɑːməlait; ˋmarməˏlaɪt] ***n*.**【矿】白蛇纹石[岩]。

Mar·mo·ra [ˈmɑːmərə; ˋmarmərə] ***n*.** = Marmara.

mar·mo·re·an, mar·mo·re·al [mɑːˈmɔːriən, -riəl; marˋmorɪən, -rɪəl] ***a*.**〔诗〕大理石(似)的;似大理石雕像的;滑腻的,白的;大理石制的。

mar·mo·set [ˈmɑːməzet; ˋmarməˏzɛt] ***n*.**【动】(厚毛如绒的南美)狨猴。

mar·mot [ˈmɑːmət; ˋmarmət] ***n*.**【动】土拨鼠,旱獭;玛摩游泳帽。

mar·o·cain [ˈmærəkein; ˋmærəˏken] ***n*.**【纺】马罗坎平纹绉。

Mar·o·nite [ˈmærənait; ˋmærəˏnaɪt] ***n*.** 马龙教徒〔黎巴嫩的希腊教派〕。

ma·roon[1] [məˈruːn; məˋrun] **I** ***n*. 1.** 避居西印度群岛及

圭亚那山中的黑人〔原为逃亡黑奴〕。**2.** 被放逐到孤岛的人。**II** ***vt.*** 把…放逐到孤岛;(因洪水等)使孤立。*~ed on roofs* 被(洪水)围困在屋顶上。— ***vi.*** **1.**〔美〕带着帐篷旅行[野营]。**2.** 闲荡;吊儿郎当地过日子。

ma·roon[2] [mə'ruːn; mə`run] **I** ***a.*** 酱紫色的,褐红色的。**II** ***n.*** 酱紫色,褐红色;纸炮烟火[玩具]。

ma·roon·er [mə'ruːnə; mə`runə] ***n.*** 海盗;被流放到孤岛上的人;脱逃的奴隶;〔美〕野营旅行者。

mar·plot ['mɑːplɔt; `mar͵plɑt] ***n.*** 好管闲事而破坏了计划[事业]的人;害人精。

mar·que [mɑːk; mɑrk] ***n.*** **1.** (海上的)捕拿外国[敌方]船只的特许证;有捕拿特许证的船。**2.** 商品(尤指汽车等)的型号[式样]。*letters of ~* (*and reprisal*) (海上)捕拿特许证。

mar·quee [mɑː'kiː; mɑr`ki] ***n.*** 大帐幕;〔美〕(戏院教堂等入口的)门罩;〔英〕马戏团帐幕的正面入口。

Mar·que·san [mɑː'keizn, -'keisn; mɑr`kezən, -`kesn̩] **I** ***n.*** **1.** (大洋洲)马克萨斯人。**2.** 马克萨斯语。**II** ***a.*** **1.** 马克萨斯群岛的;马克萨斯人的。**2.** 马克萨斯的。

mar·quess ['mɑːkwis; `mɑrkwɪs] ***n.***〔英〕= marquis. **M- of Queensbury Rules** 昆斯伯里拳击基本规则〔现代拳术的基本规则,规定所用的手套和分回合等〕。

mar·que·try, mar·que·te·rie ['mɑːkitri; `mɑrkətrɪ] ***n.*** 镶嵌工艺,镶木细工。

mar·quis ['mɑːkwis; `mɑrkwɪs] (*fem.* ***mar·chioness*** ['mɑːʃənis; `mɑrʃənɪs]) ***n.*** **1.** 侯爵;公爵长子的尊称。**2.**〔M-〕马奎斯〔姓氏〕。

mar·quis·ate ['mɑːkwizit; `mɑrkwɪzɪt] ***n.*** 侯爵的身分[地位];侯爵领地。

mar·quise [mɑː'kiːz; mɑr`kiz] ***n.***〔F.〕**1.** (英国以外的)侯爵夫人。**2.** 拼镶成[切割成]两头尖的椭圆形宝石;镶有这种形状宝石(或数颗这种形座)的戒指。**3.**〔古〕帐幕,帐篷。

mar·qui·sette [ˌmɑːki'zet; ˏmɑrkɪ`zɛt] ***n.*** (作窗帘等用的)亮绸;薄纱罗。

mar·quois scale ['mɑːkwɔiz 'skeil; `mɑrkwɔɪz `skel]【测】平行线尺。

Mar·ra·kech, Mar·ra·kesh [mə'rækeʃ; mə`rɑkɛʃ] ***n.*** 马拉喀什〔摩洛哥城市〕。

mar·ram ['mærəm; `mærəm] ***n.***【植】滨草〔生在海边的禾本科植物,又作~ grass〕。

Mar·ra·no [mə'rɑːnəu; mə`rɑno] ***n.*** (*pl.* ***-nos***) 被迫改信基督教的犹太人〔在西班牙宗教法庭上,为了免被处死或迫害,被迫表示信仰基督教实则仍秘密信犹太教的犹太人〕。

mar·riage ['mæridʒ; `mærɪdʒ] ***n.*** **1.** 结婚,婚姻;婚礼;结婚生活,夫妇关系。**2.** 密切结合。**3.**【牌】同花 king 和 queen 的配合。*a common-law* [*a Scotch*] *~* 自由结婚,自由同居。*a civil ~* (不举行宗教仪式的)登记结婚。*a communal* [*group*] *~* 杂婚;群交共婚制。*his* [*her*] *uncle by ~* 夫系[妻系]的叔伯辈姻亲。*the ~ of true minds* 真心实意的结合。*~ of convenience* 基于利害关系的婚姻,权宜婚姻。***give*** [*sb.*] ***in ~*** 把某人嫁出。***take sb. in ~*** 娶某人。~ **articles** [**contract**] (规定财产权等的)结婚契约。~ **bed** **1.** 婚床。**2.** 房事。~ **broker** 媒人。~ **ceremony** 婚礼。~ **encounter**〔美〕婚姻关系恳谈会〔数对夫妻于周末座谈交换意见,以促进双方感情〕。~ **favours** 婚礼花束[缎带花结]。~ **lines**〔英〕结婚证明书。~ **portion** 妆奁,嫁赀。~ **service** (在教会中举行的)婚礼。~ **settlement** 夫妇财产契约。

mar·riage·able ['mæridʒəbl; `mærɪdʒəbl] ***a.*** 可以结婚的;已到结婚年龄的。*a girl of ~ age* 已到结婚年龄的姑娘。**-a·bil·i·ty** ***n.***

mar·ried ['mærid; `mærɪd] **I** ***a.*** 已婚的 (*opp.* single);夫妇的;紧密结合着的;〔美俚〕两手带了手铐的。*a ~ man* 已婚男子,有配偶的男人。*a newly ~ couple* 一对新婚夫妇。*~ love* 夫妇的爱。**II** ***n.*** (*pl.* *~s*) 已婚的人。

mar·rier ['mæriə; `mærɪə] ***n.*** 结婚者;为男女双方举行结婚仪式的牧师[官员]。

mar·ron·nier [mærɔ'nje; mærɔ`njɛ] ***n.***〔F.〕【植】七叶树。

mar·rons gla·cés ['mærɔn 'glɑːsei; ma`rɔ̃ gla`se]〔*pl.*〕〔F.〕蜜饯[糖衣]栗子。

mar·row[1] ['mærəu; `mæro] ***n.*** **1.**【解】髓,骨髓。**2.** 精髓,精华;实质。**3.** 滋养品。**4.** 生气,活力。**5.**〔英〕食用葫芦。***the ~ of the land*** 国力。***to the ~*** (***of one's bones***) 透骨;彻底的 (*be frozen to the ~* 寒冷彻骨。*He is an aristocrat to the very ~ of his bones.* 他是一个道道地地的贵族)。

mar·row[2] ['mærəu; `mæro] ***n.***〔Scot.〕〔方〕朋友;配偶;敌手;对手;长得一模一样的人物(*of*)。

mar·row·bone ['mærəubəun; `mæro͵bon] ***n.*** 髓骨;(食髓的)胫部牛肉;〔*pl.*〕〔谑〕膝;〔*pl.*〕= crossbones. *Bring him to his ~s!* 揍他! *get* [*go*] *down on one's ~s* 〔谑〕跪下。*ride in the ~ coach* [*stage*] 骑两脚马去,走着去。

mar·row·fat, mar·row pea ['mærəufæt, 'mærəupiː; `mærofæt, `mæropi] ***n.*** 大(粒品种)豌豆。

mar·row squash ['mærəu skwɔʃ; `mæro skwɑʃ]【植】西葫芦〔一种皮硬而光滑的椭圆形瓜〕。

mar·row·y ['mærəui; `mærəwɪ] ***a.*** **1.** 骨髓多的。**2.** 强壮的;丰富的。**3.** (文章)简洁有力的。

Mar·rue·cos [ˌmɑː'wekəus; ˏmɑr`wɛkos] 摩洛哥的西班牙语名称。

mar·ry[1] ['mæri; `mærɪ] ***vt.*** **1.** 结婚;娶;嫁。**2.** 使结婚〔用被动语态〕;把…嫁出;使娶媳,使成家。**3.** (牧师)主持结婚礼;证婚。**4.** 使结合;【海】把(绳子的两头)编在一起,捻成一条。*He married his daughter to a farmer.* 他把他的女儿嫁给一个农民。*a ditty married to a beautiful air* 小调配上优美的乐曲。— ***vi.*** 结婚。***get married*** 结婚。~ ***a fortune*** 和有钱人结婚。~ ***beneath one*** 和身分低的人结婚。~ ***into the purple*** 与显贵联姻。~ ***off*** 嫁出。~ ***over a broomstick*** 同居。~ ***up*** 使成夫妇[未婚夫妻]。~ ***with the left hand*** 和身分低微的人结婚。

mar·ry[2] ['mæri; `mærɪ] ***int.***〔古〕哎呀! 哟! 真! 真是!〔表示惊愕、轻蔑、愤怒等〕。*M- come up!* 哎唷! 这怎么啦!

Mars [mɑːz; mɑrz] ***n.*** **1.**【天】火星。**2.**【罗神】玛尔斯,战神,军神;战争;骁勇的人。

Mar·sa·la [mɑː'sɑːlə; mɑr`sɑlɑ] ***n.***〔It.〕(西西里岛的)马沙拉白葡萄酒。

Mar·seil·laise [mɑːsə'leiz; ˏmɑrsl̩`ɛz] ***n.*** 马赛曲〔法国国歌〕。

Mar·seilles [mɑː'seilz; mɑr`selz] ***n.*** 马赛〔法国港市〕。

mar·seilles [mɑː'seilz; mɑr`selz] ***n.*** 提花马赛布。

mar·sel·la [mɑː'selə; mɑr`sɛlə] ***n.*** = marcella.

marsh [mɑːʃ; mɑrʃ] ***n.*** 沼地,沼泽,湿地。~ **gas** 沼气,甲烷。~ **hawk** 鸡鹞 (*Circus cyaneus*)〔产于美洲,筑巢于地上,捕鼠、蛙、蛇等为食〕。~ **hen**【动】秧鸡。~ **mallow**【植】药蜀葵;果汁软糖。~ **marigold**【植】立金花;驴蹄草。~**-ore** 沼铁矿。

Mar·shal ['mɑːʃəl; `mɑrʃəl] ***n.*** 马歇尔〔男子名〕。

mar·shal ['mɑːʃəl; `mɑrʃəl] **I** ***n.*** **1.** (法国等的)陆军元帅〔英国则称 Field-M-〕。**2.**〔英〕空军元帅(= M- of the Air)。**3.** 宪兵主任[司令官](= provost-~)。**4.** (英国宫廷的)典礼官;(集会的)司仪。**5.**〔英〕纹章局长。(= Earl M-)。**6.**〔英〕(流动法庭的)法官的秘书。**7.**〔英〕大学学监的随员。**8.**〔美〕联邦法院的执行官;市执法官;市警察局长。*a field ~*〔英〕陆军元帅。*the M- of the Royal Air Force*〔英〕空军元帅。*an Air Chief M-*〔英〕空军上将。*an air ~*〔英〕空军中将。*the ~ of France* 法国陆军元帅。**II** (〔英〕***-ll-***) ***vt.*** **1.** 使排

列;〔喻〕安排;整顿,整理;【徽】配列(纹章在盾等上);【法】(整理破产、分配遗产时)决定分派次序。**2.** 带,领,引导。～ *a person into his place* 引某人入座。— ***vi***. 排列,集合。*a marshalling yard* (车站内)货车编组[调车]场。

mar·shal·cy, mar·shal·ship [ˈmɑːʃəlsi, -ʃip; ˋmɑrʃəlsɪ, -ʃɪp] ***n***. marshal 的职位[权力]。

Mar·shall Islands [ˈmɑːʃəl ˈailəndz; ˋmɑrʃəl ˋaɪləndz] 马绍尔群岛[西太平洋]。

Mar·shal·sea [ˈmɑːʃəlˌsiː; ˋmɑrʃəlˏsi] **1.** (在皇室司法官控制下的)英国法庭〔于 1849 年废除〕。**2.** 马夏尔西监狱〔伦敦萨斯瓦克关禁债务人的监狱,已于 1842 年废除〕。

marsh·y [ˈmɑːʃi; ˋmɑrʃɪ] ***a***. (***marsh·i·er***; ***-i·est***) (多)沼地的;沼泽似的;生在沼泽的。**-i·ness** ***n***.

Mar·so·khod [ˌmɑːsəˈhɔːt; ˏmɑrsəˋhɔt] ***n***. 〔Russ.〕(前苏联科学家设计的)火星探索飞行器。

Mar·ston [ˈmɑːstən; ˋmɑrstən] ***n***. 马斯顿〔姓氏〕。

mar·su·pi·al [mɑːˈsjuːpjəl; mɑrˋsjupɪəl] **I** ***a***. 【动】有袋(目)的;袋(状)的。**II** ***n***. 有袋动物。～ **frog** 背上有卵袋的南美袋蛙。

mar·su·pi·um [mɑːˈsjuːpjəm; mɑrˋsjupɪəm] ***n***. (*pl*. ***marsupia*** [-piə; -pɪə]) 【动】袋,育儿袋;卵袋。

mart [mɑːt; mɑrt] ***n***. **1.** 〔诗、古〕市场。**2.** 商业中心地。**3.** 拍卖场。

Mart. = Martial.

mar·ta·gon [ˈmɑːtəgən; ˋmɑrtəgən] ***n***. 【植】头巾百合 (*Lilium martagon*) 〔开白、紫花朵〕。

mar·tel [ˈmɑːtel; ˋmɑrtɛl] ***n***. 【史】战槌;槌。

mar·tel·lo tow·er [mɑːˈteləu ˈtauə; mɑrˈtɛlo ˋtaʊr] 【筑城】(防御海岸的)石造圆形小炮塔。

mar·ten [ˈmɑːtin; ˋmɑrtɪn] ***n***. (*pl*. ～***s***, 〔集合词〕～) 【动】貂;貂皮。

mar·tens·ite [ˈmɑːtnzait; ˋmɑrtnˏzaɪt] ***n***. 马丁体〔显微镜下所见的炼钢的针状组织〕。**-sit·ic** [-tənˈzitik; -tənˋzɪtɪk] ***a***.

Mar·tha [ˈmɑːθə; ˋmɑrθə] ***n***. 玛莎〔女子名〕。

mar·tial [ˈmɑːʃəl; ˋmɑrʃəl] ***a***. **1.** 战争的,战时的;勇武的,尚武的,好战的;像军人的;军事的,陆海军的 (*opp*. civil)。**2.** 〔M-〕战神玛尔斯(Mars)的;【天】火星的。*a court*-～ 军事法庭。～ *music* 军乐。～ *spirit* 士气。～ **art** 技击。～ **law** 戒严令;军事管制法;军法,军令。**-ly** ***ad***. 勇敢地,勇武地,好战地。

mar·tial·ism [ˈmɑːʃəlizm; ˋmɑrʃəlɪzm] ***n***. 尚武精神;士气。

mar·tial·ize [ˈmɑːʃəlaiz; ˋmɑrʃəlˏaɪz] ***vt***. 使配合战争;使军事化;使整军经武;激励士气。

Mar·ti·an [ˈmɑːʃjən; ˋmɑrʃɪən] **I** ***n***. (假想的)火星人。**II** ***a***. 战神的;火星的;(假想的)火星人的。

Mar·tin [ˈmɑːtin; ˋmɑrtɪn] ***n***. 马丁〔姓氏,男子名〕。***St***. ～***'s day*** 圣马丁节(= Martinmas)。***St***. ～***'s summer*** 〔英〕小阳春〔11 月 11 日圣马丁节前后暖和时期〕。～ **furnace** 【冶】平炉,马丁炉。

mar·tin [ˈmɑːtin; ˋmɑrtɪn] ***n***. 岩燕。*a house* ～ 欧洲家燕。*a sand* [*bank*] ～ 灰沙燕。

Mar·ti·neau [ˈmɑːtinəu; ˏmɑrtɪˋno] ***n***. 马蒂诺〔姓氏〕。

mar·ti·net [ˌmɑːtiˈnet; ˏmɑrtnˋɛt] ***n***. 〔主蔑〕(训练上)纪律严肃的人〔尤指陆海军军纪官〕;严格的人。**-ism** [-izəm; -ɪzəm] ***n***. 严格的训练;严格。

mar·tin·gal(e) [ˈmɑːtiŋgeil; ˋmɑrtnˏgel] ***n***. 马颔缰;鞅;【船】第二斜桅的下方支索;输后加倍下注的赌法。

mar·ti·ni[1] [mɑːˈtiːni; mɑrˋtinɪ] ***n***. 马蒂尼枪〔从前英国陆军的步枪,又名 the Martini Henry rifle〕。

mar·ti·ni[2] (cock·tail) [mɑːˈtiːni ˈkɔkteil; mɑrˋtinɪ ˋkɑkˏtel] ***n***. 马丁尼鸡尾酒〔艾酒、杜松子酒等混合酒〕。

Mar·ti·nique [ˌmɑːtiˈniːk; ˏmɑrtnˋik] ***n***. 马提尼克(岛)〔拉丁美洲〕。

Mar·tin·mas [ˈmɑːtinməs; ˋmɑrtɪnməs] ***n***. 圣马丁节〔11 月 11 日〕。

mart·let [ˈmɑːtlit; ˋmɑrtlɪt] ***n***. **1.** 欧洲燕。**2.** 〔诗〕= martin. **3.** 【徽】无足鸟〔分家后第四子的徽章〕。

mar·tyr [ˈmɑːtə; ˋmɑrtɚ] **I** ***n***. **1.** 殉教者;殉道者;烈士,殉难者,牺牲者 (*to*)。**2.** (因病等)长期受痛苦的人 (*to*)。*a* ～ *to a cause* 义士。***be a*** ～ ***to*** 害着…病;受着…的折磨。***die a*** ～ ***to one's principle*** 为主义而牺牲。***make a*** ～ ***of*** 牺牲,折磨。***make a*** ～ ***of oneself*** 装出牺牲者[殉教者]姿态博取信誉。**II** ***vt***. (对坚持某种主义或信仰的人进行)杀害;迫害,折磨。**-dom** ***n***. 殉教;殉道,殉难;殉节;赴义;苦恼,痛苦。

mar·tyr·ize [ˈmɑːtəraiz; ˋmɑrtəˏraɪz] ***vt***. 使殉难,把…作牺牲;折磨。

martyro- *comb. f*. 表示"烈士";"殉教者": *martyrology*.

mar·tyr·ol·o·gy [ˌmɑːtəˈrɔlədʒi; ˏmɑrtəˋrɑlədʒɪ] ***n***. 殉教史;殉教者列传。

mar·tyr·y [ˈmɑːtəri; ˋmɑrtərɪ] ***n***. 为纪念殉教者而建立的圣祠;表明殉教者殉难地点或圣骨置放处的建立物。

MARV = manoeuvring re-entry vehicle【军】机动重返大气层运载工具〔重返大气层时可通过操纵改变其飞行方向,以避开对方防御性导弹的拦截〕。

Mar·va [ˈmɑːvə; ˋmɑrvə] ***n***. 玛瓦〔女子名〕。

mar·vel [ˈmɑːvəl; ˋmɑrvl] **I** ***n***. **1.** 惊奇的东西;可惊叹的人物,(…方面)的非凡人物,奇才。**2.** 〔古〕惊愕,惊叹。*He is a perfect* ～. 〔口〕他真是个奇人。*The* ～ *is that* ... 奇异的是…。*The less* ～ *if* ... 如果…便不稀奇。*Use lessens* ～, *it is said*. 俗话说,多见不怪[少见多怪]。**II** ***vi***. (〔Eng.〕***-ll-***)〔古〕**1.** 惊叹,惊异 (*at*; *that*)。— ***vt***. 对…觉得奇怪,诧异(*how*; *why*; *if*; *what*)。★词义强于 wonder. ～**-of-Peru** ***n***. 【植】紫茉莉,胭脂花。

Mar·vell [ˈmɑːvəl; ˋmɑrvəl] ***n***. 马维尔〔姓氏〕。

mar·vel·ous, mar·vel·lous [ˈmɑːviləs; ˋmɑrvləs] **I** ***a***. 奇异的,不可思议的,奇怪的;〔口〕妙极的;了不起的。**II** ***n***. 〔the ～〕怪事。**-ly** ***ad***. **-ness** ***n***.

mar·vie, mar·vy [ˈmɑːvi; ˋmɑrvɪ] ***int***. 〔美俚〕妙极了(= marvelous)。

Mar·vin [ˈmɑːvin; ˋmɑrvɪn] ***n***. 马文〔姓氏,男子名〕。

Marx·i·an [ˈmɑːksjən; ˋmɑrksɪən] ***a***., ***n***. = Marxist.

Marx·ism [ˈmɑːksizəm; ˋmɑrksɪzm] ***n***. 马克思主义。～*-Leninism* 马克思列宁主义,马列主义。

Marx·ist [ˈmɑːksist; ˋmɑrksɪst] **I** ***n***. 马克思主义者。**II** ***a***. 马克思主义的。

Ma·ry [ˈmɛəri; ˋmɛrɪ] ***n***. **1.** 玛丽〔女子名〕。**2.** 【圣】圣母玛利亚〔耶稣的母亲〕。～ **Jane** 〔美俚〕大麻(= marijuana)。～ **Janes** 玛丽·简女鞋〔商标名,一种低跟皮鞋〕。

Mar·y·ann [ˌmɛəriˈæn; ˏmɛrɪˋæn] ***n***. 玛丽安〔女子名〕。

Mar·y·land [ˈmɛərilænd; ˋmɛrɪlənd] ***n***. 马里兰〔美国州名〕。

Mar·y·mass [ˈmɛəriməs; ˋmɛrɪməs] ***n***. 圣母玛利亚节;(尤指)报喜节〔普通叫 Lady Day〕;〔Scot.〕圣母升天节。

mar·zi·pan [ˌmɑːziˈpæn; ˋmɑrzəˏpæn] ***n***. = marchpane. ～**layer** 〔英〕杏仁蛋白层〔指股票公司中地位仅次于合伙人的经营管理人员〕。

MAS = Malaysian Airline System 马来西亚航空公司。

-mas *suf*. 节,节日: Christ*mas*.

mas., **masc.** = masculine.

Ma·sai [mɑːˈsai; mɑˋsaɪ] ***n***. **1.** (*pl*. ～(*s*)) 马萨伊人〔肯尼亚和坦噶尼喀牧民〕。**2.** 马萨伊语。

mas·ca·ra [mæsˈkɑːrə; mæsˋkærə] ***n***. (染)睫毛油。

mas·cle [ˈmæskl; ˋmæskl] ***n***. **1.** (13 世纪铠甲的)菱形钢铠片。**2.** 【徽】中空菱形纹。

mas·con [ˈmæskɔn; ˋmæskɑn] ***n***. 【地】(月表下的)质量密集,质量高度密聚。

mas·cot [ˈmæskət; ˋmæskət] ***n***. 福神;吉人;吉祥物[物品、动物等]。

M

mas·cu·line [ˈmɑːskjulin; ˋmæskjəlɪn] (*opp*. feminine) **I** *a*. **1.**【语】阳性的。**2.** 男(性)的,雄的。**3.** 男子气概的;有力的;勇敢的;雄赳赳的。**4.** (女子)有男子气的。**II** *n*.【语】阳性;阳性词;男性的东西;男子;男孩。～ **ending**〔诗〕(用于行末音节上的)重音行末。～ **gender**【语】阳性。～ **rhyme**〔诗〕(最后一音有重音节处才押韵的)阳韵。**-ly** *ad*. **-ness**, **-linity** [-liniti; -ˋlɪnətɪ] *n*. 丈夫气,刚毅。

mas·cu·lin·ize [ˈmæskjuliˌnaiz; ˋmæskjəlɪnˏaɪz] *vt*. (*-ized*; *-iz·ing*) 使男子化〔尤指使(女人)具有男子特征〕。**-za·tion** *n*.

mase [meiz; mez] *vi*. 激射;产生和放大微波。

Mase·field [ˈmeisfiːld; ˋmesˏfild] *n*. 梅斯菲尔德〔姓氏〕。

ma·ser [ˈmeizə; ˋmezɚ] *n*.〔缩〕(*m*icrowave *a*mplification by *s*timulated *e*mission of *r*adiation) 脉泽,微波激射;微波激射器;受激辐射微波放大器。

Ma·se·ru [ˈmæzəruː; ˋmæzəru] *n*. 马塞卢〔莱索托首都〕。

mash[1] [mæʃ; mæʃ] **I** *n*. 麦芽浆〔啤酒原料〕;(喂牛马的)面粉[米糠]浆;捣成糊状的东西;马铃薯(等捣烂的)泥;乱糟糟的一团。*sausage and* ～〔俚〕香肠马铃薯泥。***all to* (*a*) ～** …得极烂,稀烂。**II** *vt*. 磨碎,捣烂。～ **tub** (做)麦芽汁(的)桶。

mash[2] [mæʃ; mæʃ]〔俚〕**I** *vt*. 向…调情;诱惑。**II** *n*. 使人着迷的人,情人。***be ～ed on*** 恋着,爱着。***make a ～ on***〔美俚〕使爱上,使看中。***make one's ～*** 使人神魂颠倒,使人着迷。

mash·er[1] [ˈmæʃə; ˋmæʃɚ] *n*. 捣碎机[器];捣碎者;制麦芽浆的工人。

mash·er[2] [ˈmæʃə; ˋmæʃɚ] *n*.〔俚〕调戏女性的人。

Mash·had [mɑːʃˈhɑːd; mɑʃˋhɑd] *n*. 马什哈德〔即 Meshed 迈谢德〕〔伊朗城市〕。

mash·ie [mæʃi; ˋmæʃɪ] *n*.【高尔夫球】铁头短球棒。

mash·y [ˈmæʃi; ˋmæʃɪ] *a*. (***mash·i·er***; ***-i·est***) 磨碎的,稀烂的。

mas·jid [ˈmʌsdʒid; ˋmʌsdʒɪd] *n*. 伊斯兰教寺院。

mask [mɑːsk, Am. -æ-; mɑsk, -æ-] **I** *n*. **1.** 假面具,伪装,掩蔽物;面罩;防毒面具(= gas mask);【物】掩模;(劈剑,棒球等用)护面;(用蜡等从死人面部模制成的)蜡模遗容(= deathmask)。**2.** 口实;掩饰。**3.** 假面跳舞会;戴假面者;假面戏。**4.** (纪念打猎的)狐头,狐面。**5.** (筑城)遮障,掩蔽角面堡;【印】蒙片;【摄】蔽光框。**6.**【计】时标,时间标志。*a flu* ～ 防感冒戴的口罩;卫生口罩。***assume* [*put on*, *wear*] *the* ～** 戴假面具,掩盖真面目。***drop* [*pull off*, *throw off*] *the* ～** 摘下假面具;现出本来面目。***under the* ～ *of*** 假托,在…假面具下。**II** *vt*. **1.** 在(脸)上戴假面具;化装。**2.** 蒙蔽,遮蔽,隐,覆;【军】掩蔽,隐蔽(兵力、炮位);掩护;(因逼近敌方)妨碍(友军)炮火射程;【印】(制版时)用蒙片修正(底片色调);【摄】用蔽光框修改(照相的大小、形状等)。— *vi*. 戴假面具;化装;参加化装舞会。*We could not fire, as we were ～ed by our first line*. 第一线挡住,我们无法射击。

mas·ka·longe, **mas·ka·nonge** [ˈmæskələndʒ, -ˈnɔndʒ; ˋmæskəˏlɑndʒ, -ˏnɑndʒ] *n*. = maskinonge.

masked [mɑːskt; mæskt] *a*. 戴假面具的,蒙着脸的;化装的;(感情等)隐蔽着的,遮蔽着的;【医】潜伏的,不明的;【植】假面状的。*a* ～ *ball* 化装跳舞会。*a* ～ *battery* 掩蔽炮台。*a* ～ *fever*【医】潜热。*a* ～ *pupa*【动】隐蛹。

Mas·ke·lyne [ˈmæskilain; ˋmæskɪlaɪn] *n*. **1.** 马斯基林〔人名〕。**2.** N. ～ 尼·马斯基林〔1732—1811,英国天文学家,航海历的发明者。〕

mask·er [ˈmɑːskə; ˋmæskɚ] *n*. 戴假面具的人;参加假面舞会的人;演假面具者。

mask·ing [ˈmɑːskiŋ; ˋmæskɪŋ] *n*. 伪装;化装;掩蔽;掩模。～ **tape**【印】不透光胶纸〔一般是深红色,在涂玻璃底版时用来遮盖和保护版边〕。

mas·ki·nonge [ˈmæskinɔndʒ; ˋmæskəˏnɑndʒ] *n*. 大梭鱼。

mas·lin [ˈmæzlin; ˋmæzlɪn] *n*.〔英〕(小麦和裸麦等的)混合粉,混合粉面包;谷类和豆类间种的庄稼;混合物。

mas·och·ism [ˈmæzəkizəm; ˋmæzəˏkɪzəm] *n*. **1.**【心】(色情)受虐狂 (*opp*. sadism)。**2.** 自我虐待,以苦为乐的精神。**-ist** *n*. **-is·tic** *a*.

Ma·son [ˈmeisn; ˋmesn̩] *n*. **1.** 梅森〔姓氏,男子名〕。**2.** ～**jar** 梅森食瓶〔一种大口玻璃瓶,有螺旋盖子,供家庭贮藏食品用〕。

ma·son [ˈmeisn; ˋmesn̩] **I** *n*. 石匠;(中世纪的)工匠工会会员;〔M-〕共济会(会员)。**II** *vt*. 用石或砖修建。～ **bee**【虫】石蜂〔一种孤栖蜜蜂,用黏土、沙子、泥做巢〕。

Ma·son-Dix·on Line [ˈmeisnˈdiksn lain; ˋmesn̩ˋdɪksn̩ laɪn]〔美〕梅逊-狄克逊分界线〔Pennsylvania 和 Maryland 州间的界线,此线延伸为后来区分美国南部和北部的标志〕。

ma·son·ic [məˈsɔnik; məˋsɑnɪk] *a*. **1.** (中世纪)石匠工会的。**2.**〔M-〕共济会(成员)的。

Ma·son·ite [ˈmeisənait; ˋmesn̩ˏaɪt] *n*. 梅斯奈纤维板,夹布胶木板〔商标名〕。*m- process* 湿式纤维板制造法。

ma·son·ry [ˈmeisnri; ˋmesnrɪ] *n*. **1.** 石工技术;石工行业;石造建筑。**2.** 〔M-〕共济会制度[纲领、仪式];〔集合词〕共济会成员。

Ma·so·ra, **Ma·so·rah** [məˈsɔːrə; məˋsorə] *n*. 玛索拉〔**1.** 犹太人的希伯来文本圣经教义。**2.** 体现此教义的圣经批注〕。

Mas·o·rete, **Mas·o·rite** [ˈmæsəriːt, -rait; ˋmæsərit, -raɪt] *n*. 玛索拉的编纂者。**-ret·ic** [-ˈretik; -ˋretɪk] *a*.

masque [mɑːsk, mæsk; mɑsk, mæsk] *n*. (中世纪流行的)假面戏剧;假面戏剧本;化装舞会。

mas·quer [ˈmɑːskə; ˋmæskɚ] *n*. = masker.

mas·quer·ade [ˌmæskəˈreid, mɑːs-; ˏmæskəˋred, mɑs-] **I** *n*. 假面[化装]舞会[聚会];假面戏;化装舞会上穿的服装;伪装;假托;掩饰。**II** *vi*. 参加化装舞会;化装;冒充,假托;假装。

mas·quer·ad·er [ˌmæskəˈreidə; ˏmæskəˋredɚ] *n*. 化装跳舞者;假装者,冒充者;戴假面具者。

Mass. = Massachusetts.

mass[1] [mæs; mæs] **I** *n*. **1.** 块,堆,团。**2.** 群众,集团;〔the ～es〕群众;民众。**3.** 大量;大宗;众多;〔the ～〕大部分,大半;主体;总体。**4.**【物】质量。**5.**【军】集团纵队,密集队形。**6.**【矿】体。*a* ～ *of earth* 一大块泥土。*a* ～ *of letters* 一大堆信件。*The ～es have boundless creative power*. 人民群众有无限的创造力。*a* ～ *of manoeuvre* 实施机动集团。*proper* ～ 静质量。*the ～es* 群众,大众。***be* ～ *of*** 一团…,全身…,遍体…(*He is a* ～ *of bruises*. 他遍体鳞伤)。***from the ～es, to the ～es*** 从群众中来,到群众中去。***in the* ～** 整个儿地;总体上,合计。***the* (*great*) ～ *of...*** …的大部分。***to be at one with the ～es*** 同群众打成一片。**II** *vt*. 使成一团;集中(力量等);【军】使密集。— *vi*. 集中,聚集。*～ed body*【军】密集部队。*～ed formation*【军】密集队形。～ **action**【物】质量作用;浓度作用。～ **attack**【军】集中攻击。～ **balance** 质量平衡。～ **bargaining** 团体会谈。～ **breeding** 大量繁殖;大批饲养。～ **communication** 大众传播〔指报刊、广播、电视的宣传〕。～ **cult** (通过商业化的广播、电视节目等传播的)大众文化。～ **defect**【物】质量亏损。～ **flights**【空】大机群飞行,编队飞行。～ **game** 集体竞赛。～ **media** 大众传播媒介〔指报纸、杂志、广播和电视,大众传播工具〕。～ **meeting** (尤指政治性质的)大会,群众大会。～ **motion**【物】整体运动。～ **noun**【语】物质名词。～ **number**【物、化】(原子)质量数。～ **outbreak**【虫】(瘟疫、虫害等)突然蔓延;大规模流行。～**-produce** *vt*. 大量生产。～**-production** 大量

[成批]生产。～ **psychology** 群众心理。～ **society** 大众社会;广大群众。～ **spectrograph** 质谱仪。～ **spectrometer** 质谱测定器。～ **suggestion** 群众煽动。～ **tactics** 密集战术。

Mass, mass[2] [mæs, mɑːs; mæs, mɑs] ***n*.** 弥撒;弥撒的仪式[祷告、音乐];弥撒曲。*a high* [*solemn*] ～ (有烧香、奏乐等的)大弥撒。*a low* [*private*] ～ (无烧香、奏乐的)小弥撒。***by the*** ～ 一定,的确。***say*** [***read***] ～ 作弥撒,念经。～**-bell** 弥撒钟。～**-book** (天主教的)弥撒经。

mas·sa [ˈmæsə; ˋmæsə] ***n*.** 〔美方〕= master.

Mas·sa·chu·setts [ˌmæsəˈtʃuːsits; ˏmæsəˋtʃusɪts] ***n*.** 马萨诸塞〔旧译麻省,美国州名〕。

mas·sa·cre [ˈmæsəkə; ˋmæsəkɚ] **I** ***n*.** 大屠杀,残杀;(牲畜的)成批屠宰。**II** ***vt*.** **1.** 屠杀;残杀。**2.** 乱切,乱砍。**3.** 损害;弄糟。

mas·sage [ˈmæsɑːʒ; məˋsɑʒ] **I** ***n*.** **1.** 按摩(术),推拿(法)。**2.**【计】(数据等的)窜改。**II** ***vt*.** **1.** 按摩,推拿。**2.**【计】(电子计算机)处理,分理;窜改(数据)。**3.** 精心培植(人事关系)。**-ger, -sagist** ***n*.** 按摩师。

Mas·sa·wa, Mas·sa·ua [mɑːˈsɑːwɑː; məˋsɑwə] ***n*.** 马萨瓦〔埃塞俄比亚港市〕。

mass·cult [ˈmæskʌlt; ˋmæskʌlt] ***a*.** 〔美口〕大众文化的。

mas·sé [mæˈsei; mæˋse] ***n*.** 〔F.〕【撞球】挫杆。

mas·se·ter [mæˈsiːtə; mæˋsetɚ] ***n*.**【解】咬肌。**-ic** ***a*.**

mas·seur [mæˈsəː; mæˋsɝ] ***n*.** (*pl*. ～***s*** [-z; -z]) 男按摩师。

mas·seuse [mæˈsəːz; mæˋsɝz] ***n*.** (*pl*. ～***s*** [-iz; -ɪz]) 女按摩师。

mas·si·cot [ˈmæsikɔt; ˋmæsɪˏkɑt] ***n*.**【化】铅黄,黄丹,天然一氧化铅。

mas·sif [ˈmæsiːf; ˋmæsif] ***n*.** 〔F.〕【地】丛山,山岳;地块,断层块。

Mas·sine [ˈmæˈsiːn; ˋmæˋsin] ***n*.** 马辛〔姓氏〕。

mass·i·ness [ˈmæsinis; ˋmæsɪnɪs] ***n*.** 〔古〕大而重,厚重,巨大(= massiveness)。

mas·sive [ˈmæsiv; ˋmæsɪv] ***a*.** **1.** 大的,重的。**2.** 魁伟的;结实的;实心的。**3.** 大规模的;大量的。**4.** (容貌、精神等)有力的,坚定的;【心】宽大的。**5.**【地】块状的,大块的。**6.**【矿】均匀构造的,非晶质的。a ～ *forehead* 宽大的前额。～ *mountains* 块状丛山。*a* ～ *deposit* 块状矿床。

Mas·son [ˈmæsn; ˋmæsn] ***n*.** 马森〔姓氏〕。

mass·y [ˈmæsi; ˋmæsɪ] ***a*.** (***mass·i·er***; ***-i·est***) **1.** 〔诗〕= massive. **2.**【物】有质量的。

mast[1] [mɑːst; mæst] **I** ***n*.** 桅;柱,竿,天线杆,天线塔;(停飞船的)栓柱。★三桅船从船头起依次为 foremast 前桅, mainmast 大桅,主桅, mizzenmast 后桅。桅上有接桅时从下而上依次为 lower mast 下桅, top mast 中桅, topgallant mast 上桅, royal mast 顶桅。***after*** [***before***] ***the*** ～ 作为普通水手。***at the*** ～ 在上甲板大桅下〔水手集合处〕。***spend a*** ～ 桅竿被折断。**II** ***vt*.**【船】给…装桅竿;扯(帆)。～**head** **1.** ***n*.** 桅顶,〔特指〕下桅桅顶;桅顶瞭望人;〔美〕报头栏;报头;(书刊的)版权页。**2.** ***vt*.** 挂(旗等)在桅顶;(罚水手)使爬上桅顶。～**-house** 桅竿制造厂。

mast[2] [mɑːst; mæst] ***n*.** 榉、槲、栗等的果实〔可作猪饲料〕。～ **cell**【生】肥大细胞。

mas·ta·ba [ˈmæstəbə; ˋmæstəbə] ***n*.**【考古】(古代埃及的)石室坟墓,石椁。

mas·tec·to·my [mæsˈtektəmi; mæsˋtɛktəmɪ] ***n*.** (*pl*. ***-mies***)【医】乳房切除术;乳腺摘除术。

-mas·ted [ˈmɑːstid; ˋmæstɪd] ***a*.** 有桅的;…桅的: *a three-* ～ *schooner* 三桅帆船。

mas·ter [ˈmɑːstə; ˋmæstɚ] **I** ***n*.** **1.** 主人;雇主,老板(*opp*. servant);船长;船主;家长;校长。**2.** 〔常无冠词〕善能[长于、精通]…的人;胜者,征服者。**3.** 〔英〕教师,老师,先生(= school-master);师傅。**4.** 〔the M-〕【圣】基督,主。**5.** 能手,名家,大师,〔特指〕名画家;名家作品;大家,名人。**6.** 〔M-〕〔用在人名前作称呼〕少爷〔M- Tom, M- Smith〕。**7.** 〔M-〕〔Scot.〕子爵[男爵]的长子,大少爷〔the M- of Ballantrae〕。**8.** 〔M-〕硕士〔Doctor 和 Bachelor 间的学位〕。**9.** (Oxford, Cambridge 大学的)学生宿舍主任;【法】助理法官;(英国皇室的)御马长官,宴务局长(等)。**10.** 原版录音片,主盘〔即唱片的负片〕。～ *and man* 主人和仆人。*Like* ～, *like man*. 有其主必有其仆。*the* ～ *of the house* 户主。*a language* ～ 语文老师。*the passed M-* 前任会长[主任]。*a passed* ～ (世所公认的)名家。*a* ～ *of oratory* 演说家。*M- of Arts* 文科硕士。*M- of Science* 理科硕士。*a M- in the schools* 硕士初试主考员。*the* ～ *of ceremonies* (宫廷中的)典礼官;(会场中的)司仪。***be*** ～ ***in one's own house*** 不受别人干涉。***be*** ～ ***of*** 所有;通,精通;能自由处理。***be*** ～ ***of oneself*** 自制。***be*** ～ ***of a situation*** 控制局面。***be one's own*** ～ 能独立自主,不受别人牵制。***make oneself*** ～ ***of*** 熟练,精通,能自由控制[掌握]。***the old*** ～***s*** 画坛大师(的作品)。**II** ***a*.** 主要的;为首的;优秀的。*a* ～ *clock* (调整其他电钟的)母钟,标准钟。*a* ～ *mason* 手艺高超的石匠师傅。*a* ～ *builder* 建筑承包人;建筑家。*a* ～ *hand* 能手。*a* ～ *mind* 伟人,杰出人物。*a* ～ *station*【电】主控台。*a* ～ *stroke* (丰功)伟绩;妙举,大成功。*a* ～ *switch* 总开关。**III** ***vt*.** **1.** 作…的主人,控制,统治。**2.** 制服,征服;压制(情欲);养乖,养训(动物)。**3.** 熟练,精通。**4.** 晾干(染料等)。～ *one's temper* 压制着脾气,忍着气。～ *English* 精通英文。～ *a subject thoroughly* 完全掌握某门学问。～**-at-arms** (*pl*. ***mas·ters-at-arms***) 〔英〕【海】纠察长。～**dom** ***n*.** 控制(权、力)。～ **general** 〔英陆军〕(军需局、军械局的)局长。～**hood** = mastership. ～ **key** **1.** 万能钥匙。**2.** (解决困难、争论等的)难题解决法;关键。**3.**【电】总电键。～**mariner** 船长。～ **mechanic** 熟练技工(尤指工长)。～**mind** **1.** ***vt*.** 〔英〕策划,暗中指挥。**2.** ***n*.** 出谋划策的人;具有极大才智的人。～**-piece**, ～**work** 杰作,名作。～ **plan** 总计划。～ **sergeant** 〔美军〕军士长。～**ship** 硕士学位;校长职位;精通,练达;控制;胜利。～**-singer** = Meistersinger.

-mas·ter [-ˈmɑːstə; -ˋmɑstɚ] *comb*. *f*. 有…桅船的: *a four-* ～ 四桅船。

mas·ter·ful [ˈmɑːstəful; ˋmæstɚfəl] ***a*.** **1.** 主人派头的;专横的,傲慢的。**2.** 巧妙的;熟练的;名家的。

mas·ter·ly [ˈmɑːstəli; ˋmæstɚlɪ] **I** ***a*.** 巧妙的,熟练的;名家的;〔古〕= masterful. **II** ***ad*.** …到家,巧妙地。

mas·ter·y [ˈmɑːstəri; ˋmæstərɪ] ***n*.** 控制;控制权;统治力;胜利,制服;首位,优势;精通,熟练。*the* ～ *of the seas* 制海权。*Gain* ～ *by striking first*. 先发制人而占上风〔*cf*. strike〕。***gain*** [***get, obtain***] ***the*** ～ ***of*** 控制;精通,善能。***strive for*** ～ 争雌雄。

mas·tic [ˈmæstik; ˋmæstɪk] ***n*.** (用作亮漆原料、香料等的)乳香(脂);乳香树;涂料;胶黏剂;乳香酒〔加有乳香的葡萄酒〕;淡黄色。

mas·ti·ca·ble [ˈmæstikəbl; ˋmæstɪkəbl] ***a*.** 可咀嚼的;可撕捏的。**-bil·i·ty** [ˌmæstikəˈbiliti; ˏmæstɪkəˋbɪlətɪ] ***n*.**

mas·ti·cate [ˈmæstikeit; ˋmæstəˏket] ***vt*.** 嚼,咀嚼;撕捏;素炼〔指将橡胶揉成浆状〕。

mas·ti·ca·tion [ˌmæstiˈkeiʃən; ˏmæstəˋkeʃən] ***n*.** 咀嚼(作用);【化】撕捏(作用);捏和(作用);(橡胶)素炼。

mas·ti·ca·tor [ˈmæstikeitə; ˋmæstəˏketɚ] ***n*.** 咀嚼者[器官];碎肉器;割碎机;撕捏机;素炼机;割碎机等操作者;〔*pl*.〕〔谑〕牙齿。

mas·ti·ca·to·ry [ˈmæstikeitəri; ˋmæstəkəˏtorɪ] **I** ***a*.** 咀嚼的,咀嚼器官的;适于咀嚼的;撕捏的。**II** ***n*.** (用以促进唾液分泌的)咀嚼物〔橡皮糖、烟草等〕。

mas·tiff [ˈmæstif; ˋmæstɪf] ***n*.** 一种滑皮短腰大看家狗。

mas·ti·goph·o·ran [ˌmæstəˈgɔfərən; ˏmæstəˋgɑfərən] **I**

M

n.【动】鞭毛虫(*Mastigophora*)动物。**II** *a*. 鞭毛虫的。**-rous** [-rəs; -rəs] *a*.

mas·ti·tis [mæsˈtaitis; mæsˋtaɪtɪs] *n*.【医】乳房炎,乳腺炎。

mast·less[1] [ˈmaːstlis; ˋmæstlɪs] *a*. 无桅的。

mast·less[2] [ˈmaːstlis; ˋmæstlɪs] *a*. 不结果实的。

mas·to·car·ci·no·ma [ˌmæstəukaːsiˈnəumə; ˏmæsto-ˏkarsɪˋnomə] *n*.【医】乳癌。

mas·to·don [ˈmæstədɔn; ˋmæstəˏdɑn] *n*.【古生】(第三纪的)柱牙象;庞然大物;大人物;〔美拳〕重量级拳击家。

mas·to·don·tic [ˌmæstəˈdɔntik; ˏmæstəˋdɑntɪk] *a*. 柱牙象的;巨大的。

mas·toid [ˈmæstɔid; ˋmæstɔɪd] **I** *a*. 乳头状的,乳房状的。**II** *n*.【解】(耳后的)乳突(骨);〔俚〕(= mastoiditis)。

mas·toid·ec·to·my [ˌmæstɔiˈdektəmi; ˏmæstɔɪd-ˋɛktəmɪ] *n*. (*pl*. **-mies**)【医】乳突切除术。

mas·toid·i·tis [ˌmæstɔiˈdaitis; ˏmæstɔɪdˋaɪtɪs] *n*.【医】乳突(骨)炎。

mas·tur·bate [ˈmæstəbeit; ˋmæstɚˏbet] *vi*., *vt*. (**-bated**; **-bat·ing**) (对…)行手淫。**-ba·tion** [-ˈbeiʃən; -ˋbeʃən] *n*. **-ba·tor** *n*. **-ba·tor·y** [-bətəri; -bətorɪ] *a*.

ma·su·ri·um [məˈsjuəriəm; məˋsurɪəm] *n*. 钨〔元素 technetium 锝的旧名〕。

masut [məˈzuːt; məˋzut] *n*. = mazut.

MAT = Master of Arts in Teaching 教育硕士。

mat[1] [mæt; mæt] **I** *n*. **1**. 席子;蹭鞋垫(= doormat);(体操等用的)垫子;(花瓶等的)垫子;〔美〕(照片、画等的)垫纸。**2**. (装糖及咖啡等的)蒲包;一包的量。**3**.【海】防擦垫。**4**. (毛、杂草等的)丛,簇。**5**.【印】铸印版用的纸型。***leave*** (*a person*) ***on the*** ~ 不接待客人。***on the*** ~【军俚】被拖到长官面前,被处罚;〔美〕被责备,受调查。**II** *vt*. 在…上铺席子,给…盖席子;编织;〔主用 *p*.*p*.〕使缠结。*matted hair* 乱蓬蓬的头发。— *vi*. 缠结。~-**man** 摔跤手。

mat[2] [mæt; mæt] **I** *a*. 无光泽的;闷光的;表面粗糙的。**II** *n*. (毛玻璃等的)消光(面);消光器;(绘画等的)衬底纸;(相框的)闷光金边。**III** *vt*. 使(画面等)不现光泽,使成闷光;给(画)配闷光金边;使(金属玻璃等)褪光。

mat. [mæt; mæt] *n*. 〔Am.〕= matinee.

Mat·a·be·le [ˌmætəˈbiːli; ˏmætəˋbilɪ] *n*. (*pl*. ~(**s**)) 马塔比黑人〔1837 年被荷兰殖民者后裔布尔人从德兰士瓦无理驱逐至罗德西亚的祖鲁人〕。

Ma·ta·di [məˈtaːdi; məˋtadɪ] *n*. 马塔迪〔刚果(金)港市〕。

mat·a·dor [ˈmætədɔː; ˋmætəˏdɔr] *n*. **1**.【斗牛】斗牛士。**2**.【牌戏】一种王牌。

match[1] [mætʃ; mætʃ] *n*. (一根)火柴;〔古〕(从前大炮发火用的)火绳,导火线。*light* [*strike*] *a* ~ 擦火柴。*a safety* ~ 安全火柴。*a lucifer* ~ 黄磷火柴。~**book** 纸夹火柴。~**box** 火柴盒。~**lock** (旧时的)火绳枪。~-**maker** 火柴制造人[厂]。~**safe** = ~box. ~**stick** 火柴杆。~**wood** **1**. 制火柴杆的木料。**2**. 碎片(*make* ~-*wood of sth*. = *reduce sth*. *to* ~*wood* 把某物弄粉碎)。

match[2] [mætʃ; mætʃ] **I** *n*. **1**. 比赛,竞赛。**2**. 对手,敌手;伙伴,(很相配的)一对,一副。**3**. 一对中的一方。**4**. 婚姻;配偶。**5**.【机】假型,配比;【电】匹配。*Have you a* ~ *for this ribbon*? 有没有和这一样的丝带? *We shall never see his* ~. 他那样的人恐怕不会有第二个了。*They are right* ~*es*. 他们正是好配偶。***be a*** ~ ***for*** 可以和…相匹敌;是某人的对手,和…很相配[协调]。***be more than a*** ~ ***for*** 胜过,强过(*He is more than a* ~ *for me*. 他比我强)。***be no*** ~ ***for*** 敌不过;不是…对手。***find*** [***meet***] ***one's*** ~ 遇到对手,棋逢敌手(*He never met his* ~. 他从来没有败过)。***make a good*** ~ 找到好对象。***make a*** ~ 作媒。***make a*** ~ ***of it*** 结婚。***play a*** ~ 比赛。***play off a*** ~ (平局后)再赛以决胜负。**II** *vt*. **1**. 使对抗,使较量;敌得过。**2**. 和…相配[相称]。**3**. 使相配,使成对,使相称。**4**. 使结婚。**5**. (掷钱币等)以作决定。*a* ~*ed plate method* 双层造型法。*No one can* ~ *him*. 没有人敌得过他。~ *a colour* 配一种颜色。*Can you* ~ *me this silk*? 你能替我配一段这样的绸子吗? ~ *strides* 〔美运〕赛跑。— *vi*. 相称,相适合,相配;结合(成为夫妇)。*Let beggars* ~ *with beggars*. 龙配龙,凤配凤,癞驴配破磨。*with everything to* ~ 连同一套附属品。~ **ball** = match point. ~ **board**【木工】(一边榫头、另一边榫眼、可互相嵌合的)假型板。~**boarding** 铺假型板。~**joint** 合榫,企口接合。~-**maker** 媒人;好作媒的人;运动比赛组织者。~**mark** **1**.【机】配合记号。**2**. *vt*. 加配合记号于…。~-**play** **1**. 赛球〔如网球比赛等〕。**2**.【高尔夫】以通盘由球座打入穴中所得的分数计分的比赛。~ **point**【体】决胜点,争取胜利所必需的最后一分。

match·a·ble [ˈmætʃəbl; ˋmætʃəbl̩] *a*. 能匹敌的,敌得过的;对等的;相配的。~ ***to none*** = matchless.

matchet(te) [mæˈtʃet; mæˋtʃɛt] *n*. = machete.

match·less [ˈmætʃlis; ˋmætʃlɪs] *a*. 无敌的,无比的。

mate[1] [meit; met] **I** *n*. **1**. (工人间的)伙伴,同事;老兄,老弟〔工人、水手间的亲密称呼〕。**2**. 配偶〔男女任何一方〕;动物之偶(尤指鸟类);(一对中的)一只;配对物。**3**.【海】(商船的)大副;驾驶员;【海军】〔美〕二级准尉的助手〔相当于军士级别〕;【医】(军医等的)助手。*the chief* [*first*] ~ (船长之下的)大副。*a boatswain's* ~ 水手长的助手。*a surgeon's* ~ 军医助手。***go*** ~***s with*** 与…合伙,和…成为伙伴。**II** *vt*., *vi*. (使)成伙伴,(使)成配偶(*with*),(使)(鸟等)匹配,(使)交配(*with*);(使)紧密配合。

mate[2] [meit; met] *n*., *vt*.【象棋】逼将;将军;将死。***give*** ~ ***to*** 将军,将死(对方的王)。***fool's*** ~ 走动两步棋就出现的败局。

ma·te[3], **ma·té** [ˈmætei; ˋmæte] *n*. (用冬青类巴拉圭茶树叶制成的)马黛茶;马黛茶叶[树];(用吸管吸的)马黛茶壶。

ma·te·las·sé [ˈmætləˈsei, F. mɑtlɑˈse; ˋmætləˋse, mɑtlɑˋsɛ] **I** *a*. 马特拉斯的;提花的。**II** *n*. 马特拉斯〔一种提花凸纹双层织物,布面起绗缝垫褥形状〕。

ma·te·lot [ˈmætləu; ˏmatˋlo] *n*. 〔F.〕〔俚〕水手。

mat·e·lote [ˈmætələt; ˋmætəˏlot], ***mat·e·lotte*** [-lɑt; -ˏlɑt] *n*. 〔F.〕**1**.【烹】酒、葱等调料汁炖鱼。**2**. 马塔洛水手舞。

ma·ter [ˈmeitə; ˋmetɚ] *n*. (*pl*. ***ma·tres*** [ˈmeitriz; ˋmetrɪz]) 〔英〕〔学生俚〕母亲(= mother)。

ma·ter dol·o·ro·sa [ˈmeitəˌdəuləˈrəusə; ˋmetɚˏdolə-ˋrosə] *n*. 〔L.〕悲伤的母亲;〔M- D-〕悲伤的圣母玛利亚像。

ma·ter·fa·mil·i·as [ˈmeitəfəˈmiliæs; ˏmetɚfəˋmɪlɪ-ˏæs] *n*. 〔L.〕主妇。

ma·te·ri·al [məˈtiəriəl; məˋtɪrɪəl] **I** *a*. **1**. 物质的(*opp*. spiritual)。**2**. 身体上的,肉体上的;物欲的,追求实利的;卑俗的。**3**. 有形的,实体的;物质性的。**4**. 重要的,实质性的,必需的。**5**.【逻、哲】实质上的,实体上的,内容上的(*opp*. formal);【法】本质的。*the* ~ *universe* 物质世界。~ *civilization* 物质文明。~ *comforts* 使物质生活舒适的东西〔食品、衣服等〕。~ *pleasure* 肉体的快乐。~ *point*【理】质点。*a* ~ *being* 有形物。~ *property* 有形财产。*a very* ~ *difference* 重大的差别。*a point* ~ *to one's argument* 论证要点。~ *element* 要素。***be*** ~ ***to*** 对于…重要。***in*** ~ ***form*** 用具体的形式。**II** *n*. 材料,原料;(军用)物资;织物,料子;资料;题材;素材;〔*pl*.〕必需品,用具;设备;品质;人材,人物。*building* ~(*s*) 建筑材料。*raw* ~(*s*) 原(材)料。*condemned* ~(*s*) 报废器材。~ *for a novel*

M

小说素材。*writing* ~*s* 笔墨纸类,文具。~ **noun**【语】物质名词。~**s-intensive** *a*.(商品等)材料密集型的,需耗费大量原材料的。

ma·te·ri·al·ism [məˈtiəriəlizəm; məˋtɪrɪəl͵ɪzəm] *n*.【哲】唯物主义;唯物论;实利主义;【美】写实主义。*dialectic(al)* ~ 辩证唯物主义。*historical* ~ 历史唯物主义。

ma·te·ri·al·ist [məˈtiəriəlist; məˋtɪrɪəlɪst] **I** *n*. 唯物主义者;实利主义者。**II** *a*. 唯物主义的;唯物主义者的。~ *dialectics* 唯物辩证法。

ma·te·ri·a·lis·tic [məˌtiəriəˈlistik; mə͵tɪrɪəˋlɪstɪk] *a*. 唯物主义的;唯物主义者的;物质主义的;物质主义者的。~ *interpretation* [*conception*] *of history* 唯物史观。

ma·te·ri·a·lis·ti·cal·ly [məˌtiəriəˈlistikəli; mə͵tɪrɪəlˋɪstɪkəlɪ] *ad*. 在唯物论上,就唯物主义的观点来看。

ma·te·ri·al·i·ty [məˌtiəriˈæliti; mə͵tɪrɪˋælətɪ] *n*. 物质性;实体性,有形(物)(*opp*. spirituality);【法】重要性;实质性,[*pl*.]物质,实体。

ma·te·ri·al·ize [məˈtiəriəlaiz; məˋtɪrɪəlaɪz] *vt*. 赋与…以形体,使具体化;使物质化;实现;使(鬼魂等)现形。—*vi*. 具体化,体现;(希望、计划等)实现,成为事实。~ *one's ideas* 实现自己的理想。**-i·za·tion** *n*. 物质化(作用)。

ma·te·ri·al·ly [məˈtiəriəli; məˋtɪrɪəlɪ] *ad*. 物质上,有形地(*opp*. spiritually);【哲、逻】实质上;显著地,大大地;相当地。

ma·te·ri·a med·i·ca [məˈtiəriə ˈmedikə; məˋtɪrɪə ˋmɛdɪkə] [L.][总称]药物;药物学;药物学论著。

ma·té·ri·el [məˌtiəriˈel; mə͵tɪrɪˋɛl] *n*. [F.]物资;装备;(军队、团体等的)设备,设施;作战物资;物力;武器(*opp*. personel)。

ma·ter·nal [məˈtəːnl; məˋtɝnl] *a*. **1.** 母亲的;像母亲的,母性的。**2.** 母方的,母系的;[谑]自己母亲的。~ *love* 母爱。~ *impression* 胎教,母亲印痕。*one's* ~ *grandfather* 外祖父。*one's* ~ *uncle* 舅父。~ *mortality rate* 产妇死亡率。**-ism** *n*. 纵容,溺爱。**-ly** *ad*.

ma·ter·ni·ty [məˈtəːniti; məˋtɝnətɪ] **I** *n*. 母性;母道;怀孕;产科医院。**II** *a*. 产妇用的。~ **bag** (教区送给贫民的)接生包。~ **benefit** 产期津贴。~ **centre** 孕妇顾问处。~ **clinic** 妇女保健站。~ **hospital** 产科医院。~ **leave** 产假。~ **nurse** 助产士;产科护士。~ **ward** (医院里的)产科病房。

mate·y [ˈmeiti; ˋmetɪ] *a*. [口]易接近的;易为人亲近的。

math [mæθ; mæθ] *n*. **1.** [口] = mathematics. **2.** [英方]割草。

math. = mathematical; mathematician; mathematics.

math·e·mat·i·cal [ˌmæθiˈmætikəl; ͵mæθəˋmætɪkl] *a*. 数学(上)的,数理的;严正的,精确的。~ *instruments* 制图仪器。~ *logic* 数理逻辑(= symbolic logic)。~ **biology** 数理生物学。**-ly** *ad*.

math·e·ma·ti·cian [ˌmæθiməˈtiʃən; ͵mæθəməˋtɪʃən] *n*. 数学家。

math·e·mat·ics [ˌmæθiˈmætiks; ͵mæθəˋmætɪks] *n*. 数学。★通常作单数用,带有"计算能力"意义时,作复数用,如:*His* ~ *are not good*. 他不长于计算。*applied* [*mixed*] ~ 应用数学。*pure* ~ 纯数学。

Math·er [ˈmeiðə, ˈmæðə; ˋmeðɚ, ˋmæðɚ] *n*. 马瑟[姓氏]。

maths [mæθs; mæθs] *n*. [英] = mathematics.

ma·ti·co [məˈtiːkəu; məˋtiko] *n*. [Sp.]【植】狭叶胡椒树;(可作止血剂用的)狭叶胡椒树树叶。

Ma·til·da [məˈtildə; məˋtɪldə] *n*. 马蒂尔达[女子名]。

mat·in [ˈmætin; ˋmætɪn] **I** *n*. **1.** [*pl*.]【英国国教】早课,晨祷;早课时刻;【天主】(夜半或黎明的)祷告时刻。**2.** [*sing*., *pl*.][诗](鸟的)朝鸣,晨歌。**II** *a*. 黎明的,早晨的;早课的,晨祷的。

mat·in·al [ˈmætinl; ˋmætɪnl] *a*. = matin (*a*.)

mat·i·née [ˈmætinei; ͵mætnˋe] *n*. [F.](戏剧、音乐会等的)日戏,日场;日间的社交集会;(女人早晨穿的)便装。*a* ~ *doll* 穿得漂漂亮亮去看日戏的女人。*the* ~ *hat* 日戏女帽。*a* ~ *idol* 风流小生,(西方影剧界)受到女观众崇拜的男演员。

mat·ing [ˈmeitiŋ; ˋmetɪŋ] *n*.【生】交配。

mat·jes herring [ˈmɑːtjəsheriŋ; ˋmɑtjəshɛrɪŋ] 糟青鱼。

mat·lo(w) [ˈmætləu; mætlo] *n*. [英俚] = matelot.

mat·rass [ˈmætrəs; ˋmætrəs] *n*.【化】(旧时蒸馏用的)长颈卵形瓶。

matri- *comb*. *f*. 母: *matri*arch.

ma·tri·arch [ˈmeitriɑːk; ˋmetrɪ͵ɑrk] *n*. 女家长,女族长;[通例、谑]家长[族长]的妻子。

ma·tri·ar·chal, ma·tri·ar·chic [ˌmeitriˈɑːkəl, -kik; ͵metrɪˋɑrkəl, -kɪk] *a*. 女家长[族长]的;母权的,母系(继承)的。

ma·tri·ar·ch·y [ˈmeitriɑːki; ˋmetrɪ͵ɑrkɪ] *n*. 女家长[族长]制,母权制。

ma·tric [məˈtrik; məˋtrɪk] *n*. [matriculation 之略]大学入学考试。

ma·tri·ces [ˈmeitrisiːz; ˋmetrɪ͵siz] *n*. matrix 的复数。

ma·tri·cid·al [ˌmeitriˈsaidəl; ͵metrəˋsaɪdl] *a*. 杀母的。

ma·tri·cide [ˈmeitrisaid; ˋmetrə͵saɪd] *n*. 杀母(罪);杀母者。

ma·tric·u·lant [məˈtrikjulənt; məˋtrɪkjələnt] *n*. 大学投考人;被录取的新生。

ma·tric·u·late [məˈtrikjuleit; məˋtrɪkjə͵let] **I** *vt*. 准许入(大)学;录取。—*vi*. 被录取;注册入学。**II** [-lit; -lɪt] *n*. 被许入学者。

ma·tric·u·la·tion [məˌtrikjuˈleiʃən; mə͵trɪkjəˋleʃən] *n*. 录取入学;入学礼;(大学)入学考试。

ma·tri·lin·e·al [ˌmætriˈliniəl; ͵mætrɪˋlɪnɪəl] *a*. 母系的。**-ly** *ad*.

mat·ri·mo·ni·al [ˌmætriˈməunjəl, -niəl; ͵mætrəˋmonɪəl, -njəl] *a*. 婚姻的;夫妇的。*a* ~ *advertisement* 征婚广告。**-ly** *ad*.

mat·ri·mo·ny [ˈmætriməni; ˋmætrə͵monɪ] *n*. **1.** 结婚,婚姻;婚姻生活;夫妇关系。**2.** 抽对子[一种纸牌戏]。~ **vine**【植】宁夏枸杞。

ma·trix [ˈmeitriks; ˋmetrɪks] *n*. (*pl*. ***ma·trices*** [ˈmeitrisiːz; ˋmetrɪsiz] 或~***es***) **1.**【解】子宫;母体;发源地,策源地,摇篮;【生】衬质细胞;间质;基质;母质。**2.**【矿】母岩;脉石;【冶】基体;【地】脉石;填质;杂矿石。**3.** [ˈmætriks; ˋmætrɪks]【印】字模;型版,纸型;铸型,阴模。**4.**【阵】(矩)阵,方阵;母式;【物】间架;【无】矩阵变换电路。**5.**【染】原色[红黄蓝白黑五种]。*the* ~ *of a nail*【解】指甲床。~ **algebra**【数】矩阵代数。~ **sentence**【语法】基句,母句。

ma·tron [ˈmeitrən; ˋmetrən] *n*. **1.** (年龄相当大的、有声望的)妇女,主妇;保姆;(学校等的)女主任;女舍监;护士长;(妇女组织等的)女会长;女主席;总干事。**2.** 母种畜。*a police* ~ (女监狱的)女管理员;女看守。*a* ~ *of honour* [美](新娘的已婚)主伴娘。

ma·tron·age [ˈmeitrənidʒ; ˋmetrənɪdʒ] *n*. 主妇等的身分[职责];[集合词]主妇们,保姆们。

ma·tron·ize [ˈmeitrəˌnaiz; ˋmetrən͵aɪz] *vt*. (***-ized***; ***-iz·ing***) **1.** 使显出主妇的派头。**2.** 陪伴,伴随。

ma·tron·like, ma·tron·ly [ˈmeitrənlaik, -trənli; ˋmetrən͵laɪk, -trənlɪ] *a*. 主妇似的,管家婆似的;保姆似的;有威严的,严肃的;安详的;沉着的。

ma·tron·ship [ˈmeitrənʃip; ˋmetrən͵ʃɪp] *n*. 主妇等的身分[地位、任务]。

mat·ro·nym·ic [ˌmætrəˈnimik; ͵mætrəˋnɪmɪk] *a*. 取自母名的;母名的。

M.A.T.S. = Military Air Transport Service [美]军事空运局。

Matt [mæt; mæt] *n*. 马特[男子名, Matthew 的昵称]。

Matt. = Matthew, Matthias.

matt, matte [mæt; mæt] ***a.***, ***n.***, ***vt.*** = mat².

mat·ta·more [ˈmætəmɔː; ˋmætəˏmor] ***n.*** 〔罕〕地下室(仓库)。

matte [mæt; mæt] **I** ***n.*** 【冶】锍,冰铜。**II** ***vt.*** 使(硫化铜矿等)成为冰铜。

mat·ted [ˈmætid; ˋmætɪd] ***a.*** **1.** 铺着席子的。**2.** 编织的,编织成席的。**3.** (杂草等)遍地丛生的,乱蓬蓬的。~ *hair* 乱蓬蓬的头发。

mat·ter [ˈmætə; ˋmætɚ] **I** ***n.*** **1.** 物质 (*opp*. spirit, mind);物体。**2.**【逻】命题的本质;【哲】内容 (*opp*. form);(书籍、演说等的)内容、主旨(*opp*. manner, style)。**3.** 材料,要素,成分。**4.** 原因,根据,理由。**5.** 物品,物件;邮件。**6.** 事,事情,事件;〔*pl*.〕〔代名词性质的用法〕事态,情形,情况。**7.** 重大事件,重要事故;麻烦,毛病。**8.** (议论、讨论等的)问题。**9.**【医】脓;【印】原稿;排版。*animal* [*vegetable*, *mineral*] ~ 动物[植物、矿物]质。*solid* [*liquid*, *gaseous*] ~ 固[液、气]体。*coloring* ~ 色素。*printed* ~ 印刷品。*postal* ~ 邮件。*M-s are different*. 情形有所不同。*How have ~s stood*? 一向情况怎样? *What's the ~ with you*? 你怎么啦? 出了什么事? 〔对不平、不幸等说〕。*Nothing is the ~* (*with me*). (我)没什么。*It won't ~*. 那也不要紧。*It is no laughing ~*. 这可不是开玩笑的事。*a ~ of political power* 政权问题。***a ~ for*** [***of***] ***complaint*** 令人抱怨的事。***a ~ in dispute*** [***question***] 争执中的问题。***a ~ in hand*** 当前的问题,眼前的问题。***a ~ of*** **1.** …的问题 (*a ~ of life and death* 生死攸关的问题。*a ~ of habit* 习惯问题)。**2.** 大约;…左右 (*for a ~ of 30 years* 约三十年)。***a ~ of course*** 理所当然的(事情)〔*cf*. ~-of-course〕。***a ~ of fact*** **1.** 事实,事实问题〔*cf*. ~-of-fact〕。**2.**【法】按证据来判定可靠与否的陈述。***a ~ of opinion*** 有争论余地的问题。***a ~ of record*** 法院有案可查的案件。***as a ~ of fact*** 事实上,其实。***as ~s stand*** = ***as the ~ stands*** 照目前状况。***carry ~s with a high hand*** 处事专横。***for that ~*** = ***for the ~ of that*** 讲到那件事;关于那一点。***in the ~ of*** 关于…;就…而论。***no ~*** 没事儿,不要紧(*It is no ~*. = *It makes no ~*. 那不算一回事;那不要紧)。***no ~ how*** [***what***, ***when***, ***which***, ***who***, ***where…***] 不管怎样[什么,什么时候,哪一个,谁,什么地方](*No ~ what he says, don't go*. 不管他怎么讲都不要去。*It is not true, no ~ who may say so*. 不管谁那样讲都不是真的)。***on certain specialized ~s*** 就某些专业方面。***take ~s easy*** [***seriously***] 轻视[重视]问题。***take up a ~ with*** 和…交涉。***to make ~s worse*** 尤其糟糕的是。***What is the ~ with…***? 怎么啦? 出了什么事? 出了什么毛病? 〔谑〕…有什么不好? ***What's the ~***? 怎么一回事? 出了什么事? ***What ~***? = ***No ~***. 那有什么要紧? 不要紧。**II** ***vi.*** **1.** 要紧,重要,有重大关系。★主要用于否定句、疑问句。**2.** 化脓,出脓。*It does not ~* (*if…*). (即使…也)不要紧。*What does it ~*? 那有什么要紧? **~-of-course** ***a.*** 当然的,不用说的。**~-of-fact** ***a.*** 事实上的,实际上的,如实的,实事求是的;平凡的,乏味的。

Mat·thew [ˈmæθjuː; ˋmæθju] ***n.*** **1.** 马修〔男子名〕。**2.**【宗】马太〔耶稣十二门徒之一〕;(基督教《圣经》中的)《马太福音》。

Mat·thews [ˈmæθjuːz; ˋmæθjuz] ***n.*** 马修斯〔姓氏〕。

Mat·thi·as [məˈθaiəs; məˋθaɪəs] ***n.*** **1.** 马赛厄斯〔男子名〕。**2.**【圣】马提亚〔代替 Judas Iscariot 成为基督十二门徒之一〕。

mat·ting [ˈmætiŋ; ˋmætɪŋ] ***n.*** = mat¹, mat².

mat·tins [ˈmætnz; ˋmætnz] ***n.*** = matins.

mat·tock [ˈmætək; ˋmætək] ***n.*** 鹤嘴锄;掘根耜。

mat·toid [ˈmætɔid; ˋmætɔɪd] ***n.*** 半疯子;奇人,怪人。

mat·tress [ˈmætris; ˋmætrɪs] ***n.*** **1.** (床用)垫子。**2.**【土木】(护岸)木排,枝篱。*a spring* [*straw*] ~ 弹簧[草]垫子。

Mat·ty [ˈmæti; ˋmætɪ] ***n.*** 马蒂〔Martha, Mathilda 的昵称〕。

mat·u·rate [ˈmætjureit; ˋmætʃʊˏret] ***vi.***, ***vt.***【医】(使)化脓;(使)成熟。

mat·u·ra·tion [ˌmætjuˈreiʃən; ˏmætʃʊˋreʃən] ***n.***【医】化脓;(果实等的)成熟;(才能等的)圆熟;(化学纤维的)老化。

mat·u·ra·tive [məˈtjuərətiv; məˋtjʊrətɪv] ***a.***, ***n.***【医】促使化脓的;化脓药。

ma·ture [məˈtjuə; məˋtjʊr] **I** ***a.*** (***-tur·er***; ***-tur·est***) **1.** (有机体)熟的,成熟的;(精神、智力)圆熟的,发育完全的。**2.** (葡萄酒等)酿成的。**3.** 成年人的;【地】壮年的。**4.** 仔细考虑过的,慎重的;贤明的。**5.** (票据等)已到期的。*the ~ age* [*years*] (能辨是非的)成熟年龄。*a ~ plan* 慎重的计划。**II** ***vt.*** 使熟;使成熟;完成;慎重拟定(计划等)。— ***vi.*** 熟,成熟;(票据等)到期。*Wine and judgement ~ with age*. 酒陈味醇,人老识深。**-ly** ***ad.*** **-ness** ***n.***

Ma·turin [ˈmætjurin; ˋmætjʊrɪn] ***n.*** 马丘林〔姓氏〕。

ma·tu·ri·ty [məˈtjuəriti; məˋtjʊrətɪ] ***n.*** 成熟(度),完成;(票据等的)到期;【医】化脓;【地】壮年;壮年期。***come to ~*** 成熟。***on*** [***at***] ***~*** 满期,到期。

ma·tu·ti·nal [ˌmætju(ː)ˈtainl; məˋtjutɪnl] ***a.*** 清晨的,拂晓的;早。**-ly** ***ad.***

mat·zo [ˈmɑːtsəu; ˋmɑtso] ***n.*** (*pl*. ***mat·zot***, ***mat·zoth*** [-tsəut, -tsəuθ; -tsot, -tsoθ]) 犹太逾越节薄饼〔逾越节期间犹太人所吃的一种扁而薄的硬面饼〕(= matsah)。

mat·y¹ [ˈmæti, ˈmeiti; ˋmætɪ, ˋmetɪ] ***n.*** 〔印〕男仆。

ma·ty² [ˈmeiti; ˋmetɪ] ***a.*** = matey.

maud [mɔːd; mɔd] ***n.*** (苏格兰牧羊人穿的)柳条灰呢;柳条灰呢旅行毯。

Maud(e) [mɔːd; mɔd] ***n.*** 莫德〔女子名〕。

maud·lin [ˈmɔːdlin; ˋmɔdlɪn] **I** ***a.*** 易哭的,易感伤的;喝醉了就哭的。**II** ***n.*** 脆弱的感情。

Maugham [mɔːm; mɔm] ***n.*** 莫姆〔姓氏〕。

mau·gre, mau·ger [ˈmɔːgə; ˋmɔgɚ] ***prep.*** 〔英古〕不管,不顾,虽。

mau·kin [ˈmɔːkin; ˋmɔkɪn] ***n.*** **1.** 懒婆娘。**2.** 拖布。**3.** 稻草人。**4.** 野兔。**5.** 猫(= malkin)。

maul [mɔl; mɔl] **I** ***n.*** 大木槌。~ *and wedges* 〔美〕樵夫用的各种工具;全部。**II** ***vt.*** **1.** 打伤;打破,抓破,刺破;虐待,粗暴地对待,粗笨的处理。**2.** 严厉批评。**3.** 〔美〕用楔和大槌劈开。*badly ~ed* 焦头烂额。*Stop ~ing the cat*. 别虐待猫。

maul·er [ˈmɔːlə; ˋmɔlɚ] ***n.*** 使用木槌的人;粗暴对待别人的人;〔美俚〕拳头;拳击家。

maul·ey, maul·ie [ˈmɔːli; ˋmɔlɪ] ***n.*** 〔俚〕手,拳头。

maul·stick [ˈmɔːlstik; ˋmɔlˏstɪk] ***n.*** (画家描绘细线时支持右手用的)腕杖。

Mau Mau [ˈmauˌmau; ˋmaʊˏmaʊ] (*pl*. ***Mau Mau***, ***Mau Maus***) "茅茅"〔肯尼亚 1951 年出现的反对英国殖民统治的爱国武装组织名称〕。

mau-mau [ˈmauˌmau; ˋmaʊˏmaʊ] ***vt.*** 〔美俚〕恐吓。

mau·met [ˈmɔːmit; ˋmɔmɪt] ***n.*** **1.** 〔废〕偶像。**2.** 〔英方〕玩偶,傀儡。

maun [mɔːn; mɔn] ***v. aux.*** 〔Scot.〕= must¹ (***v. aux.***)

Mau·na Ke·a [ˈmaunəˈkeiə; ˋmaʊnəˋkeə] ***n.*** 莫纳克亚山〔夏威夷岛的死火山,太平洋上最高山,4,183 米〕。

Mau·na Lo·a [ˈmaunə ˈləuə; ˋmaʊnə ˋloə] ***n.*** 莫纳罗亚山〔夏威夷岛的活火山〕。

maund [mɔːnd; mɔnd] ***n.*** 印度、土耳其、伊朗等国大小不等的衡量名〔尤指折合 82.28 磅的印度重量单位〕。

maun·der [ˈmɔːndə; ˋmɔndɚ] ***vi.*** **1.** 〔英方〕唠唠叨叨地讲,咕哝。**2.** 徘徊;闲逛;没精打采地做事 (*along*;

about)。**-er** ***n.***

maun·dy [ˈmɔːndi; ˋmɔndɪ] ***n.*** **1.**【宗】濯足礼。**2.**〔英〕(在濯足节举办的)贫民抚恤金的赐与。～ *money*〔英〕贫民抚恤金。**M- Thursday** 濯足节〔复活节前的星期四〕。

Maur·a [ˈmɔːrə; ˋmɔrə] ***n.*** 莫拉〔女子名〕(Ir. = Mary)。

Mau·rice [ˈmɔris; ˋmɔrɪs] ***n.*** 莫里斯〔姓氏,男子名〕(L. = Moorish, dark-coloured)。

Mau·ri·ta·ni·a [ˌmɔ(ː)riˈteinjə; ˏmɔrɪˋtenɪə] ***n.*** 毛里塔尼亚(茅利塔尼亚)〔非洲〕。

Mau·ri·ti·us [məˈriʃəs; mɔˋrɪʃɪəs] ***n.*** 毛里求斯(毛里斯)〔非洲〕。

Mau·ser [ˈmauzə; ˋmaʊzɚ] ***n.***〔商标名〕毛瑟枪〔又作 Mauser rifle〕。

mau·so·le·um [ˌmɔːsəˈliəm; ˏmɔsəˋlɪəm] ***n.*** (*pl.* ～*s*, ***-le·a*** [-ˈliːə; -ˋliə]) **1.**〔M-〕(小亚细亚七大奇迹之一的)卡里亚(Caria)王陵(350 B.C.)。**2.** 陵庙,陵。**3.** 大而阴森的房屋[房间]。**mau·so·le·an** [ˌmɔːsəˈliən; ˏmɔsəˋlɪən] ***a.***

mau·vais quart d'heure [ˈməuveizkɑːˈdəː; ˏmoˋvɛˏkarˋdɝ]〔F.〕不愉快的一刻工夫。

mau·vais su·jet [ˈməuveiz ˈsuːʒei; ˏmoˋvɛˋsuʒe]〔F.〕废物,没出息的人,饭桶;无赖。

mau·vaise honte [ˈməuveizˈɔ̃ːnt; ˏmoˋvɛzˋɔ̃t]〔F.〕抱歉;不好意思,羞涩;假谦虚。

mauve [məuv; mov] **I** ***n.*** 苯胺紫(染料);红紫色。**II** ***a.*** 红紫色的。

ma·var [ˈmævɑː; ˋmævɑr]〔缩〕***n.*** (*m*ixer *a*mplification by *v*ariable *r*eactance 的首字母缩略词)脉伐〔可变电抗混频放大〕;低噪声微波放大器。

ma·ven [ˈmevən; ˋmɛvən] ***n.*** 专家。

mav·er·ick [ˈmævərik; ˋmævrɪk] **I** ***n.***〔美西部〕无畜主烙印的小动物〔多指离开母牛而迷失的小牛〕;〔口〕(团体中)闹独立性的人;持异见者;无党无派的政治家。**II** ***vi.*** 迷路,迷失。

Ma·vis [ˈmeivis; ˋmevɪs] ***n.*** 梅维斯〔女子名〕。

ma·vis [ˈmeivis; ˋmevɪs] ***n.***〔Scot.〕〔诗〕【鸟】善鸣画眉。

ma·vour·neen, ma·vour·nin [məˈvuəniːn; məˋvʊrnin] ***n.***, ***int.***〔Ir.〕(对女人说)我的亲爱的(!)。

maw [mɔː; mɔ] ***n.*** 动物的胃;反刍动物的第四胃;(动物、鱼类等的)喉咙;食管;口部;〔谑〕人胃,肚子。**～-bound** ***a.*** (牲畜)便秘的。**～-worm** ***n.*** 线虫;伪君子。

maw·kin [ˈmɔːkin; ˋmɔkɪn] ***n.*** = malkin.

mawk·ish [ˈmɔːkiʃ; ˋmɔkɪʃ] ***a.*** **1.** 叫人作呕的;讨厌的;不好吃的,无味的。**2.** 易流泪的,易感伤的。**-ly** ***ad.*** **-ness** ***n.***

maw·seed [ˈmɔːsiːd; ˋmɔsid] ***n.*** 罂粟子。

Maw·son [ˈmɔːsn; ˋmɔsn̩] ***n.*** 莫森〔姓氏〕。

Max [mæks; mæks] ***n.*** 马克斯〔男子名, Maximilian 的昵称〕。

max [mæks; mæks] **I** ***n.*** = maximum. *to the* ～ 最大限度地,彻底地。**II** ***vt.*** & ***vi.*** 〔～ out〕(使)绞尽脑汁;(使)竭尽全力。

maxi [ˈmæksi; ˋmæksɪ] ***n.*** **1.** = maxiskirt. **2.** 长大衣。

maxi- *pref.* 表示"特别长的","特大的"。

max·il·la [mækˈsilə; mæksˋɪlə] ***n.*** (*pl.* ***-lae*** [-liː; -li])【解】颌骨;上颌;【动】下颌肢,小颚,下颚。**-ry** ***a.***【解】上颌(骨)的。***n.*** 上颌骨。

max·il·li·ped [mækˈsiliˌped; mækˋsɪlɪˏpɛd] ***n.***【动】(甲壳类的)颚足;(昆虫的)颚肢。

Max·im [ˈmæksim; ˋmæksɪm] ***n.*** 马克沁机关枪〔一种老式机枪〕(= ～ gun)。

max·im [ˈmæksim; ˋmæksɪm] ***n.*** 格言,箴言;谚语;原理,主义;(行为的)准则。

max·i·ma [ˈmæksimə; ˋmæksəmə] ***n.*** maximum 的复数。

max·i·mal [ˈmæksiməl; ˋmæksəməl] ***a.*** 极为可能的;最大的;最高的;最全的。**-ly** ***ad.***

max·i·mal·ist [ˈmæksiməlist; ˋmæksəməlɪst] ***n.*** 最高纲领主义者 (*opp.* minimalist)。

Max·i·mil·i·an [ˌmæksiˈmiljən; ˏmæksəˋmɪlɪən] ***n.*** 马克西米利安〔男子名,其昵称为 Max.〕。

max·im·ite [ˈmæksiˌmait; ˋmæksəˏmaɪt] ***n.*** 马克沁炸药〔一种用于穿甲弹的高爆力炸药〕。

max·i·mize [ˈmæksimaiz; ˋmæksəˏmaɪz] ***vt.*** 使…增加[扩大、加强]到最大限度;充分重视;找出…的最高值(*opp.* minimize)。— ***vi.***【神】尽量广义地解释(教义等)。**-za·tion** ***n.***

max·i·mum [ˈmæksiməm; ˋmæksəməm] **I** ***n.*** (*pl.* ～*s*, ***-ma*** [-mə; -mə]) 极点,最大,最高,最高额,最大值;最高点;最大限度;【数】极大(值)(*opp.* minimum)。*The excitement was at its* ～. 兴奋到极点。**II** ***a.*** 最大的,最高的,顶点的,最多的。～ *draught* [*draft*]【海】最大吃水深度。～ *obscuration*【天】蚀甚。*a* ～ *range* 最大射程。*a* ～ *thermometer* 最高温度计。

Max·ine [mækˈsiːn; mækˋsin] ***n.*** 马克辛〔女子名〕。

max·i-se·ries [ˌmæksiˈsiəriːz; ˏmæksɪˋsɪəriz] ***n.*** 长篇电视连续剧。

max·i·skirt [ˈmæksiˌskəːt; ˋmæksɪˏskɝt] ***n.*** 长及脚踝的长裙。

Max·well [ˈmækswəl; ˋmækswɛl] ***n.*** 马克斯韦尔〔姓氏,男子名〕。

max·well [ˈmækswel; ˋmækswɛl] ***n.*** 麦(克斯韦)〔磁通量单位〕。*M- field equations* 麦克斯韦(电磁)场方程(式)。

May[1] [mei; me] ***n.*** 梅〔姓氏,女子名, Mary 的昵称〕。

May[2] [mei; me] **I** ***n.*** **1.** 五月。**2.**〔英〕五朔节的庆祝活动。**3.**〔诗〕青春。**4.**〔m-〕〔英〕山楂属植物。**5.**〔*pl.*〕(Cambridge 大学的)五月考试;五月赛艇。*the queen of* (*the*) ～ = *May queen.* **II** ***vi.*** 庆祝五朔节;采五月花。～ **apple**【美植】鬼臼〔五月结黄色卵形果实〕,鬼臼果。～ **beetle**, ～ **bug**【虫】鳃角金龟科吃植物叶片的甲虫(如跳甲)。**～-blob** 驴蹄草。～ **bush** 山楂。～ **Day** 五一劳动节;五朔节。**～day** 无线电话中呼救信号。～ **dew** 五月(一日的)朝露。**～fair** 五月墟市,伦敦海德公园东面的贵族住宅区;伦敦上层社交界。**～flower 1.**〔m-〕五月开放的花;〔英〕山楂;〔美〕岩梨。**2.**〔the M- Flower〕"五月花号"〔1620 年把清教徒由英国运到美国的船〕。**～fly 1.**【虫】蜉蝣。**2.**【虫】飞蝼蛄。**3.** (钓鱼用的)人造飞蝼蛄[蜉蝣]。～ **games** 五月节的游戏;嬉戏,闹玩。**～-grass** 复活节钟草。**～pole** (花和彩条装饰的)五月柱〔少年男女于五朔节围绕跳民间舞〕。～ **queen** 五月女王〔在五朔节游戏中扮女王的少女〕。**～thorn** = hawthorn. **～tide**, **～time** 五月(的季节)。**m- tree**【植】英国山楂。**～weed**【植】母菊属;臭甘菊(= dog fennel)。～ **Week**〔Cambridge 大学〕五月赛艇周〔五月底到六月初〕。～ **wine** 五月酒〔一种用车叶草、菠萝和柑橘片调味的白酒制作的混合酒〕。

may[1] [mei; me] *aux.* ***v.*** (*neg.* ～ ***not***, ***mayn't*** [meint; ment]; *p.* ***might*** [mait; maɪt], *neg.* ***might not***, ***mightn't*** [ˈmeitnt; ˋmaɪtnt]) ★无不定式、分词、动名词等;第三人称现在时单数也不加 s;常后接不带 to 的不定式。**1.** (a)〔表示可能性,否定形用～ not〕或许,也许,可能,也未可知,也说不定。***He*** ～ [～ *not*] *go.* 他也许[不]去。*Who knows but it* ～ *be true?* 说不定是真的。*She* ～ *be idle for aught I know.* 她或许闲着也说不定。(b) (～ + have done, have been) 也许…了,也许是…。*He* ～ *have done so.* 他也许那样做了。**2.**〔表示许可,或用于请求许可,否定式用 must not〕可,可以。*M- I come and see you?* 我可以来看你吗? *M- I smoke here?* — *Yes, you* ～ (*smoke*). *No, you must not.* 可以在这里抽烟吗? ——可以(抽)。不可以(抽)。〔～ not 语气较弱: You ～ not smoke here. 这儿最好不抽烟〕。**3.**〔表示有充分理由,常与 well 连用,否定式

用 cannot〕(完全)能,(满)可以,不妨。*You ~ call him a scholar, but you cannot call him a genius.* 你可以说他是学者,但不能说他是天才。*You ~ well say so.* 你完全可以这样说。**4.**〔用在表示目的的状语从句中〕(使…)可以;为…;(以便)能。*We work hard (so) that we ~ succeed.* 我们为想成功拼命工作。**5.**〔用在表示让步的状语从句中〕不管,无论,尽管。*whoever ~ say so = no matter who ~ say so* 无论谁那么说。*Come what ~, I will try it.* 无论发生什么,我要试它一试。**6.**〔表示祈求、愿望、诅咒〕愿。*May you live long!* 或 *Long ~ you live!* 祝君长寿! *M- you succeed!* 祝你成功!〔主词和动词位置常颠倒〕。**7.**〔在疑问句中表示不确定〕会;究竟;不知道是(谁,什么,为什么…)〔多和 ask, think, wonder, doubt 等动词连用〕。*Who ~ you be?* 不知道你是哪一位啊? **8.**〔=can〕能,可以。*One ~ see that at a glance.* 那是一眼就看得清的。*He who runs ~ read.* 可以边跑边读(明白简易到极点)。**9.**〔用在表示可能的名词性从句中〕*It is possible that he ~ come tomorrow.* 他也许明天会来。**10.**〔书〕〔用在表示要求、希望等的名词性从句中〕能够,会。*I hope he ~ succeed.* 希望他会成功〔*cf.* might〕。**as best one ~** 极力设法,尽最大努力。**as the case ~ be** 依情形,看情况。**be that as it ~** 虽然;就算是这样。**~ as well ...** 最好…,还是…好(*You ~ as well begin at once.* 你最好立刻开始。*You ~ as well go.* 你还是去好〔其后 as not 的意义变得极弱而被省略〕)。(**it**) **~ be** 多半。**that ~ well be** 这事很可能是有的。

may² [mei; me] ***n.***〔诗〕少女,姑娘。

Ma·ya [ˈmɑːjə; ˋmɑjə] ***n.*** 玛雅人〔中美洲的印第安人,在美洲被西方发现前已有高度文化〕;玛雅语。**Mayan** ***a., n.*** 玛雅人〔语〕的,玛雅人〔语〕。

ma·ya [ˈmɑːjə; ˋmɑjə] ***n.***〔Sans.〕幻影;虚妄。

may·be [ˈmeibi; ˋmebɪ] ***ad.*** 大概,多半,或许。*And I don't mean ~ (either).*〔美俚〕我可不是说了不算的〔往往是恐吓话〕。

May·er(s) [ˈmeiə(z), mɛə(z); ˋmeə(z), mɛr(z)] ***n.*** 迈耶(斯)〔姓氏〕。

may·est [ˈmeiist, meist; ˋmeɪst, mest] may 的古体〔may 的第二人称单数现在时陈述语气与 thou 合用〕。

may·hap [ˈmeihæp; ˋme͵hæp] ***ad.***〔古〕= perhaps.

may·hem [ˈmeihem; ˋmehɛm] ***n.***【法】残害人的肢体〔器官〕罪〔泛指故意的损害或暴力行为〕;〔美〕【拳击】打倒。

May·ing [ˈmeiiŋ; ˋmeɪŋ] ***n.*** 五朔节的庆祝(活动);五朔节采花活动。*go (a-) maying* 举行五朔节;去采五月花。

May·nard [ˈmeinəd; ˋmenɚd] ***n.*** 梅纳德〔男子名〕。

mayn't [meint; ment]〔口〕= may not.

may·on·naise [͵meiəˈneiz; ͵meəˋnez] ***n.***〔F.〕蛋黄酱,蛋黄汁;搀〔浇〕蛋黄酱的食物(鱼、肉、菜等)。

may·or [ˈmɛə; ˋmeɚ] ***n.*** 市长。*a Lord M-* (伦敦及其他大都市的)市长。*The Lord M-'s Day* 伦敦市长就职日。*the M- of the Palace*【法史】(法兰克王国的)大宰相。**-al** [ˈmɛərəl; ˋmeərəl] ***a.*** **-al·ty** [ˈmɛərəlti; ˋmeərəltɪ], **-ship** ***n.*** 市长的职位〔任期〕。

may·or·ess [ˈmɛəris; ˋmeərɪs] ***n.*** 市长夫人;女市长。

mayst [meist; mest] ***v.***〔古〕= mayest.

maz·ard [ˈmæzəd; ˋmæzɚd] ***n.* 1.** 野樱。**2.**〔废〕头;脸。

maz·a·rine [͵mæzəˈriːn; ͵mæzəˋrin] **I** ***a.*** 深蓝色的。**II** ***n.*** 深蓝色;深蓝色衣服〔衣料〕;(穿深蓝色长袍的)伦敦市政会成员。*the ~ robe* (伦敦市政会成员所穿的)深蓝色长袍。

Maz·da [ˈmæzdə; ˋmæzdə] ***n.*** (拜火教的)创造主;麦芝达牌电灯泡。

Maz·da·ism, Maz·de·ism [ˈmæzdəizəm; ˋmæzdəɪzm] ***n.*** (古波斯的)拜火教(= Zeroastrianism)。

maze [meiz; mez] **I** ***n.*** 迷津,迷宫,迷魂阵;困惑,为难。**II** ***vt.***〔多用 *p.p.*〕使困惑,使为难,迷惑。

maz·el tov, maz·el·tov, maz·zel·tov [ˈmɑːzl͵təuv, -͵tɔːv; ˋmɑzl͵tov, -͵tɔv]〔希伯来语〕祝你走运〔祝贺语〕。

ma·zer [ˈmeizə; ˋmezɚ] ***n.*** (木制或金属的)大杯,大盏。

ma·zu·ma [məˈzuːmə; məˋzumə] ***n.***〔美俚〕钱。

ma·zur·ka [məˈzəːkə, -ˈzuəkə; məˋzɝkə, -ˋzurkə] ***n.*** 玛祖卡舞〔轻快活泼的波兰舞〕;玛祖卡舞曲。

ma·zut [məˈzuːt; məˋzut] ***n.*** 重油;黑油。

ma·zy [ˈmeizi; ˋmezɪ] ***a.*** (***-zi·er; -zi·est***)(迷津一样)弯曲回绕的;纠缠不清的,混乱的;为难的;困惑的。**-i·ly** ***ad.*** **-i·ness** ***n.***

maz·zard [ˈmæzəd; ˋmæzɚd] ***n.*** 欧洲甜樱桃树;欧洲甜樱桃(= sweet cherry)。

M.B., MB =〔L.〕**1.** *Medicinae Baccalaureus* 医学士(= Bachelor of Medicine)。**2.** *Musicae Baccalaureus* 音乐学士(= Bachelor of Music)。**3.** Memorandum book 备忘录,记事录。

M.B.A. = Master of Business Administration 工商业管理硕士。

Mba·ba·ne [mbɑːˈbɑːn; mbɑˋbɑn] ***n.*** 姆巴巴纳〔斯威士兰首都〕。

M.B.E., MBE = Member (of the Order) of the British Empire〔英〕帝国勋章获得者。

MBO = management by object 目标管理法。

MBS = Mutual Broadcasting System〔美〕相互广播公司。

Mbun·du [mˈbuːnduː; mˋbundu] ***n.* 1.** (*pl.* ~(*s*)) 姆邦杜人〔安哥拉中西部讲班图语的人〕。**2.** 姆邦杜语。

M.C., MC = **1.** master of ceremonies 典礼官;司仪。**2.** medical corps 医疗队。**3.** Member of Congress 国会议员。**4.** Military Cross〔英〕军功十字勋章。**5.** margin-(al) credit 限界信贷,边际信用。

mc = **1.** machine. **2.** megacycle. **3.** millicurie 毫居里(放射单位)。

Mc- *comb. f.* 意为"麦当劳式的":*Mc*Job 低薪又无前途的工作〔如洗盘子、做餐厅服务等〕

M.C.C. = Marylebone Cricket Club〔英〕马里列博恩板球俱乐部。

Mc·Car·thy [məˈkɑːθi; məˋkɑrθɪ] ***n.*** 麦卡锡〔姓氏〕。

Mc·Car·thy·ism [məˈkɑːθiːizəm; məˋkɑrθɪɪzəm] ***n.*** 麦卡锡主义〔源自美国议员麦卡锡的政治活动〕。

Mc·Car·thy·ite [məˈkɑːθiait; məˋkɑθɪaɪt] ***n.*** 麦卡锡主义分子。

Mc·Clel·lan [məˈklelən; məˋklɛlən] ***n.*** 麦克莱伦〔姓氏〕。

Mc·Clure [məˈkluə; məˋklʊr] ***n.*** 麦克卢尔〔姓氏〕。

Mc·Cor·mack [məˈkɔːmək; məˋkɔrmək] ***n.* 1.** 麦考马克〔姓氏〕。

Mc·Cor·mick [məˈkɔːmik; məˋkɔrmɪk] ***n.* 1.** 麦考密克〔姓氏〕。**2.** C.H. ~ 麦考密克〔1809—1884,美国收割机发明者〕。

Mc·Coy [məˈkɔi; məˋkɔɪ] **I** ***n.*** 麦科伊〔姓氏,用于美俚短语〕。*the real ~* 真正的〔出色的〕人〔东西〕。**II** ***a.*** 真正的。

Mc·Do·nald [məkˈdɔnəld; məkˋdɑnəld] ***n.*** 麦克唐纳〔姓氏〕。

Mc·Dowell [məkˈdauəl; məkˋdaʊəl] ***n.*** 麦克道尔〔姓氏〕。

Mc·Fee [məkˈfiː; məkˋfi] ***n.*** 麦克菲〔姓氏〕。

M.Ch. =〔L.〕*Magister Chirurgiae* (= Master of Surgery)外科硕士。

Mc·In·tosh [ˈmækin͵tɔʃ; ˋmækɪn͵tɑʃ] ***n.* 1.** 麦金托什苹果〔美国人麦金托什培育的一种晚熟的红苹果〕(= McIntosh Red)。**2.** 麦金托什〔姓氏〕。

Mc·In·tyre [ˈmækintaiə; ˋmækɪntaɪə] ***n.*** 麦金太尔〔姓氏〕。

Mc·Ken·na [məˈkenə; məˋkɛnə] ***n.*** 麦肯纳〔姓氏〕。

Mc·Kin·ley [məˈkinli; məˋkɪnlɪ] ***n*.** 麦金利〔姓氏〕。
M.C.L. = Master of Civil Law 民法硕士。
Mc·Mil·lan [məkˈmilən; məkˋmɪlən] ***n*.** 麦克米伦〔姓氏〕。
Mc·Na·ma·ra [ˌmæknəˈmɑːrə; ˋmæknəˏmærə] ***n*.** 麦克纳马拉〔姓氏〕。
MCS = **1.** Master of Commercial Science 商学硕士。**2.** Master of Computer Science 计算机学硕士。**3.** Missile Control System 导弹控制系统。
M.D., MD = **1.** 〔L.〕*Medicine Doctor* 医学博士(= *Doctor of Medicine*)。**2.** medical department 医务部。**3.** mentally deficient 精神上有缺陷的。**4.** maximum demand 最大负荷;最大需要(量)。
M/D, m/d = **1.** memorandum of deposit 存款单,送款单。**2.** month's date [months after date] 发票后…月。
MD = minidisc 迷你镭射唱片,微型激光唱片。
Md = mendelevium【化】钔。
Md. = Maryland.
MDAP = Mutual Defense Assistance Program〔美〕共同防御援助计划。
M-Day [ˈemdei; ˋɛmde] ***n*.**【军】= Mobilization day 动员日。*the* ~ *plan* 动员计划。
Mdlle. = 〔F.〕*Mademoiselle* 小姐。
Mdm. = Madam 夫人,女士。
Mdme. = 〔F.〕*Madame* 夫人,女士。
mdnt = midnight 午夜。
M.D.S. = Master of Dental Surgery 牙(外)科硕士。
MDC = more developed country 较发达国家。
mdse; mdse. = merchandise 商品,货物(总称)。
M.E., ME = **1.** Mechanical Engineer 机械工程师。**2.** Military Engineer 工程兵;军事工程师。**3.** Mining Engineer 采矿工程师。**4.** Middle English 中古英语。**5.** Methodist Episcopal (基督教)卫理公会主教派的。
ME = marriage encounter.
Me = methyl【化】甲基。
Me. = Maine.
m.e. = most excellent 最杰出的。
me [miː, mi; mi, mɪ] ***pro*.** **1.** 〔I 的宾格〕我〔把我,对我,给我等〕。**2.** 〔口〕〔用作表语 = I〕。It's ~ 〔口〕是我(= It is I)。**3.** 〔口〕〔用于 than 后面, = I〕。*She's stronger than* ~. 她比我坚强。**4.** 〔古、诗〕我自己(= myself)。*I will lay* ~ *down and sleep*. 我要躺下睡了。**5.** 〔用在感叹句中〕*Ah* ~! 哎呀! 噫! *Dear* ~! 〔诗〕唷! 哎哟! 哎呀! *Woe is* ~! 〔诗〕可怜! 哀哉。★此外特别是在伊莉莎白王朝时代只用来加强语调,如: *Where goeth* ~ *this track*? 这条小道究竟通到哪里? *He ate* ~ *a pound of beef*. 他吃了我一磅牛肉。*I built* ~ *a house*. 〔美俚〕我盖了所房子〔这里的 me 是冗语〕。~ ***and you both*** 〔美俚〕关于这点我赞成你。***take it from*** ~ 〔俚〕我的话千真万确。
me·a cul·pa [ˈmiːəˈkʌlpə, ˈmeiɑːˈkulpɑː; ˋmiəˋkʌlpə, ˋmeɑˋkulpɑ] 〔L.〕(这是)我的过失! 是我不对! 怪我!
mead[1] [miːd; mid] ***n*.** 〔诗〕= meadow.
mead[2] [miːd; mid] ***n*.** 蜂蜜酒。
Mead(e) [miːd; mid] ***n*.** 米德〔姓氏〕。
mead·ow [ˈmedəu; ˋmɛdo] ***n*.** (特指割制干草用的)草地,草原;(河边)低草地。*a floating* ~ 易涝牧场。~ *ore* 冶铁矿。~ *soil* 草甸土。~ **beauty**【植】瑞克希阿属(拟)(*Rhexia*)植物。~ **bright** 驴蹄草。~ **clover**【植】红苜蓿。~ **fescue**【植】牛尾草。~ **foxtail**【植】草原看麦娘〔狗尾草等〕。~ **lark**【鸟】(美国)野百灵鸟类。~ **lily** (= Canada lily)【植】加拿大百合。~ **mouse** (= field mouse) 野鼠,田鼠。~ **mushroom** 洋蘑菇。~ **pine**【植】问荆。~ **rue**【植】唐松草属植物。~ **saffron**【植】秋水仙。~**sweet**【植】笑靥花;珍珠花;麻叶绣球。
mead·ow·y [ˈmedəui; ˋmɛdoɪ] ***a*.** 草原(似)的;有草地的;牧场多的。

mea·gre, mea·ger [ˈmiːgə; ˋmigɚ] ***a*.** (人、动物等)瘦的;(土地)不毛的;粗陋的,贫弱的;思想贫乏的;枯燥的(作品等)。*a* ~ *person* 瘦人。**-ly *ad*.** 瘦;粗陋。**-ness *n*.**
meal[1] [miːl; mil] **I *n*.** 餐,饭,一餐,一顿(饭),一客(饭);进餐(时间);〔英〕一次挤奶量。*a square* [*light*] ~ 盛[便]餐。*at* ~*s* 在吃饭时。*between* ~*s* 在两餐之间。*during the* ~ 在吃饭时候。*have* [*take*] *a* ~ 进餐,吃饭。***make a*** [***hearty***] ~ ***of*** 饱餐一顿…。~***s on wheels*** 上门福利餐〔每日给老人或病残人送饭上门的服务〕。**II *vi*.** 进餐,吃饭。~ **pack** 餐包〔包装在盘中的速冻食物,加热后即可食〕。~**ticket *n*.** **1.** 饭票。**2.** 〔美俚〕供给吃饭〔生活费〕的人;施舍的人;老好人,易被欺骗的人,傻子。**3.** 赖以为生的东西〔指手艺、才能、双手等〕。~**time *n*.** 吃饭时间。
meal[2] [miːl; mil] **I *n*.** (小麦以外的谷、豆等没有筛过的)粗粉;(种子、油饼等的)碎粉;〔美〕玉米碴子;〔Scot., Ir.〕燕麦片。~ **worm**【虫】粉虫。**II *vt*.** 碾碎。
meal·er [ˈmiːlə; ˋmilɚ] ***n*.** 〔美俚〕住在一处而在另一处吃饭的房客。
meal·ie [ˈmiːli; ˋmilɪ] ***n*.** 〔*pl*.〕玉米。
meal·i·ness [ˈmiːlinis; ˋmilɪnɪs] ***n*.** 粉状,粉性;撒粉状;婉转柔和的话;甜言蜜语。
meal·y [ˈmiːli; ˋmilɪ] ***a*.** (***meal·i·er***; ***-i·est***) **1.** 粉状的;粉质的;富含淀粉的;(翅等)有粉的;(脸色等)苍白的;(马)毛色有白花的。**2.** 〔口〕说话委婉的;甜言蜜语的。~**-bug**【虫】水蜡虫,粉虫〔葡萄害虫〕。~**-mouthed *a*.** 转弯抹角说的;油嘴滑舌的,会说话的。
mean[1] [miːn; min] (***meant*** [ment; mɛnt]) ***vt*.** **1.** 意,有…的意思,意思是…。**2.** 意指,用…意思说;意味着,就是。**3.** (用语言、绘画等)表示意思,表示。**4.** 预定,计划,图谋;〔作被动用〕企图表现。**5.** 预定(人或东西)作某种用途,弄成…;暗指着说。*What does this word* ~? 这个字是什么意思? *I* ~ *what I say*. 我是说的正经话〔不是开玩笑〕;我是说到就要做到的;我讲的话是算数的。*I meant it for* [*as*] *a joke*. 我是说着玩的。*You don't* ~ *to say so*! 不会吧! 你是开玩笑吧! *I* ~ *that you are a liar*. 我说你是个撒谎的。*What do you* ~ *by that*? 你做的[说的]那是什么意思? *What do you* ~ *by 'passion'*? 你所说的 passion 是什么意思? *What do you* ~ *to do*? 你打算做什么? *I* ~ *you to go*. 我打算叫[请]你去。*I did not* ~ *to deceive you*. 我并没有打算欺骗你。*My father* ~*s me to be a worker*. 我父亲打算叫我成为一个工人。*He was meant for* [*to be*] *a soldier*. 他生来是要成为一个军人的;他父母是要把他培养成一个军人的。*This portrait is meant for me*. 这张肖像是要给我的。— ***vi*.** **1.** 用意。**2.** 具有意义。***and to*** ~ ***it*** 说到做到。~ ***a great deal*** [***much***] 意味深长;重要。~ ***business*** 认真;算数的。~ ***mischief*** 有恶意,有坏心眼儿;有凶兆。~ ***well*** [***ill***] ***by*** [***to, toward***] 对…有好意[恶意]。
mean[2] [miːn; min] ***a*.** **1.** 下贱的,卑劣的;(身份)低微的,卑贱的;卑鄙的;自私的。**2.** 下等的,劣等的;普通的,中等的,平庸的。**3.** 汗颜的,难看的;吝啬的,小气的。**4.** 〔美俚〕害羞的,觉得不好意思的;(马)脾气坏的;讨厌的,麻烦的;没精神的,不大舒服的;〔美俚〕老练的,巧妙的;极好的;可爱的;非常愉快的。*people of* ~ *birth* 出身低微的人。*a* ~ *cottage* 简陋的乡下房子。***be*** ~ ***about*** [***over***] 在…方面很小气[吝啬]。***feel*** ~ 〔美俚〕觉得不好意思,害臊。***have a*** ~ ***opinion of*** 蔑视,轻视,瞧不起 (*He has a* ~ *opinion of himself*. 他很自卑)。***no*** ~ 相当的,不差的,很好的(*of no* ~ *ability* 很有才能)。***of*** ~ ***understanding*** 理解力差的,笨的。***the great and the*** ~ 贵贱上下。
mean[3] [miːn; min] **I *a*.** 中间的;中庸的;平均的;中等的;中项的。*the* ~ *deviation*【统】平均差。*the* ~ *distance* 平均距离。*a* ~ *proportional*【数】比例中项。

the ～ (*solar*) *time* [*day*]【天】平(太阳)时[日]。*the* ～ *sun*【天】平太阳。*the* ～ *temperature* 平均温度。*the* ～ *velocity* 平均速度。**for the ～ time** 在此期间,暂时。**in the ～ time** = *in the meantime*. ～ **line** 等分线。～ **sea level** 平均海平面,海拔〔略 MSL, m.s.l.〕。**II** *n*. **1.** (两端的)中央,中部,中间;【数】平均(数、值),中数;【逻】(三段论的)中项;中名辞,媒辞(= ～ term);【伦】中庸;【乐】中音部。**2.** 〔*pl*.〕〔常作单数看待〕方法,手段,工具;媒介。**3.** 〔*pl*.〕〔常作单数看待〕财产,资力,资产,收入。～*s of production* 生产资料;生产手段。*an arithmetic* [*a geometric*] ～ 等差[等比]中项。*the* ～*-square deviation*【统】均方差。*There is a* ～ *in all things*. 凡事都有一定限度。*a* ～*s to an end* 达到目的的手段。*a man of* ～*s* 资本家,财主。**by all** (**manner of**) ～**s 1.** 必定,务必;千方百计;不惜一切。**2.** 〔回答〕好的,当然当然。**by any ～s** 无论如何;以一切可能的手段。**by fair ～s or foul** 千方百计地,不择手段地。**by ～s of** 用,以,依靠。**by no** (**manner of**) ～**s** 决不,无论如何也不,丝毫不,一点也不;并没有(*He is by no* ～*s a pleasant man to deal with*. 他决不是一个好打交道的爽快人)。**by some ～s** (**or other**) 设法;用某种办法。**by what ～s** 怎么;用什么办法。**live beyond** [**within**] **one's ～s** 不按照[按照]收入过日子。**～s of living** 生活手段。♣**～s test** 〔英〕(发放失业救济金前举行的)生活状况调查。**using every possible ～s** 千方百计。

me·an·der [miˈændə; mɪˋændɚ] **I** *n*. **1.** 〔*pl*.〕河曲,蜿曲,弯曲;曲曲折折的路。**2.** 漫步,散步;〔常 *pl*.〕迂回旅行。**3.** 漫谈;闲聊。**4.**【建】回纹波形饰。**II** *vi*. **1.** 曲曲折折地流。**2.** 没目的地散步 (*along*);聊天,漫谈。～ **line**【测】折测线。

me·an·der·ing [miˈændəriŋ; mɪˋændrɪŋ] **I** *n*. **1.** 曲折的路。**2.** 聊天,漫谈。**II** *a*. 曲折的;弯弯曲曲的;散步;聊天的。**-ly** *ad*.

me·an·drine [miˈændri(ː)n; mɪˋændri(ɪ)n] *a*. 〔罕〕弯弯曲曲的;(珊瑚表面)蟠曲的。

mean·ie, mean·y [ˈmiːni; ˋminɪ] *n*. (*pl*. **mean·ies**) 〔口〕小气的人;自私的人;残暴的人。

mean·ing [ˈmiːniŋ; ˋminɪŋ] **I** *n*. **1.** 意思,意义;词义。**2.** 〔古〕主意,企图,目的。**3.**【逻】内涵;外延。**II** *a*. 有意思的,意味深长的;有所企图的。*a literal* ～ 字面意义,字义。**full of ～** 意味深长的。**ill-～** 恶意。**well-～** 善意。**with ～** 有意思的。**-ful** *a*. 意味深长的。**-less** *a*. 无意义的,没意思的。**-ly** *ad*. 有意思地,故意地。

mean·ly [ˈmiːnli; ˋminlɪ] *ad*. 下贱地,卑劣地;卑鄙地;汗颜地;小气地,吝啬地。*think* ～ *of* 藐视,看不起。

mean·ness [ˈmiːnnis; ˋminnɪs] *n*. 下贱,卑劣,卑鄙;粗野;劣等,粗恶;吝啬,小气。

mean-spir·it·ed [ˈmiːnˈspiritid; ˋminˋspɪrətɪd] *a*. 卑劣的。

meant [ment; mɛnt] mean 的过去式及过去分词。

mean·time, mean·while [ˈmiːnˈtaim, ˈmiːn*h*wail; ˋmin͵taɪm, ˋmɪn͵*h*waɪl] **I** *ad*. 其间,在那当中,一会儿的工夫;到那个时候以前,一方面,同时。**II** *n*. 中间,当中时间。**in the meantime** [**meanwhile**] 在这期间,这时。

mea·sled [ˈmiːzld; ˋmizḷd] *a*. 患麻疹的,出着疹子的。

mea·sles [ˈmiːzlz; ˋmizḷz] *n*. *pl*. **1.**【医】〔作单数用〕麻疹;疹子(*M- is decidedly infectious*. 麻疹肯定是有传染性的);〔美俚〕梅毒;〔作复数用〕麻疹的红斑点(*The* ～ *begin to turn pale on the face*. 脸上疹子颜色开始转淡)。**2.** 〔作单数用〕【兽医】(牛、猪的)囊虫病。**3.** 〔作复数用〕【摄】斑点。*false* [*French*, *German*, *hybrid*] ～ 风疹。

mea·sly [ˈmiːzli; ˋmizlɪ] *a*. (**-sli·er**; **-sli·est**) **1.** 麻疹(似)的,出着疹子;有囊虫病的;含绦虫的。**2.** 〔俚〕没用的,没价值的;卑鄙的,下贱的,使人看不起的;微不足道的;少[小]得可怜的。

meas·ur·a·ble [ˈmeʒərəbl; ˋmɛʒərəbḷ] *a*. 可量的,可测量的,相当的,适当的。**come within a ～ distance of** 临,逼近,接近。**-bly** *ad*. 到可以测定的程度,多少;适当;到某种程度。**-bil·i·ty, -ness** *n*.

meas·ure [ˈmeʒə; ˋmɛʒɚ] **I** *n*. **1.** 尺寸,尺度,量,分量;【数】测度;度量法;计量单位。**2.** 量具,量器。**3.** (衡量)标准,准绳;程度;限度,界限,范围;过度,分寸;本分,份儿。**4.**【数】约数。**5.**【韵】韵律;【乐】拍子,调子;小节;(慢而庄重的)舞蹈;〔古〕跳舞,舞蹈。**6.** 〔常 *pl*.〕手段,措施,策略,步骤,方法,办法。**7.** 法案,议案,方案。**8.**【印】行宽;页宽;〔*pl*.〕【地】层组;地层。*angular* ～ 角度。*circular* ～ 弧度。*apothecaries'* ～ 药衡制(容积单位)。*cubic* ～ 体积。*dry* [*liquid*] ～ 干[液]量。*linear* ～ = *long* ～ 长度。*solid* ～ 容积。～ *of capacity* 容量。*square* [*superficial*] ～ 面积。*yard* ～ 码尺。*weights and* ～*s* 权度,度量衡。*a* ～ *or so of grain* 一两斤粮食。*a common* ～ 公约数。*the greatest common* ～ 最大公约数〔略作 G.C.M.〕。*hygienic* ～ 卫生措施。*coal* ～*s* 煤层。**adopt ～s** 采取措施,处置。**beyond** [**above, out of**] ～ 无可估量,过分,极度。**by ～** 按大小;论升;按尺寸。**drink a ～** 喝一点儿。**give full** [**good**] ～ 给足分量。**give short ～** 少给分量。**give** [**show**] **the ～ of** 成为…的标准,表示…的程度(*This book shows the* ～ *of the author's intelligence*. 由这本书可看出作者的智慧水准)。**have sb.'s ～ to an inch** 看穿[看透]某人。**in** (**a**) **great** [**large**] ～ 很,大半,大部分。**in a ～** = **in some ～** 有几分,多少,稍稍。**keep** [**observe**] ～(**s**) 守中庸之道。**keep ～s with** 宽大对待。**know no ～** 没有边际,没有止境。**～ for ～** 报复,以牙还牙。**～s to an end** 达到目的的手段。**set ～s to** 限制。**take ～s** = *adopt* ～*s*. **take ～ of** 测定。**take one's ～** = **take the ～ of ...** 量某人的尺寸;打量某人。**take the ～ of sb.'s foot** 看穿某人的根底[能力]。**to fill up the ～ of** 使(不幸等)越过能忍受的程度;更糟糕的是。**to ～** 照尺寸;按拍子,合调子。**tread a ～** 〔古〕跳舞。**use hard ～s** 虐待,用残暴手段。**within ～** 适度地,适可地。**without ～** 非常,过度。

II *vt*. **1.** 量,计量,测量(大小、容量、尺寸等)。**2.** 打量,估量,判断(人物、力量)。**3.** 比较,比赛,较量(*with*)。**4.** 区分(*off*);分派(*out*)。**5.** 使均衡,使相称,调整。**6.** 〔诗〕通过,去,走,遍历。～ *sb. for new clothes* 为某人量尺寸做新衣。～ *one's strength with another* 和人赛力。～ *one's desires by* [*to*] *one's fortune* 使欲望同财力相适合。— *vi*. **1.** 量尺寸。**2.** 有…长[宽、高等]。*The room* ～*s 20 feet across*. 房间宽 20 英尺。～ **an opponent**【美体】打败对方。～ **another's corn by one's own bushel** 照自己标准去判断别人;以己度人。～ **back** 后退。～ **off** 区分,区划。～ **oneself with** 和…比赛。～ **one's length** 卧倒地上。～ **out** 分给(一定份量)。～ **strides**【美体】赛跑。～ **swords with** (在决斗前)和人比剑的长短;拿剑和…相斗;和…相争。～ **thrice and cut once** 三思而后行。～ **up** 〔美〕合标准,合格。～ **up to** [**with**] 〔美〕符合,达到(希望等)。～ (*sb*.) **with one's eye** 上上下下打量(人)。

meas·ured [ˈmeʒəd; ˋmɛʒɚd] *a*. **1.** 量过的,合标准的;适度的。**2.** 慎重的,仔细想[考虑]过的(话等)。**3.** 整齐的(步调等)。**speak in ～ terms** 考虑着说,谨慎小心地说。**-ly** *ad*.

meas·ure·less [ˈmeʒəlis; ˋmɛʒɚlɪs] *a*. 无可估量的,无限的,非常的。

meas·ure·ment [ˈmeʒəmənt; ˋmɛʒɚmənt] *n*. **1.** 测量,计量,量度。**2.** 份量,尺寸,大小,宽度,厚度,深度(等)。**3.** 测量法。～ *goods* (按体积、容积计算的)体积货物。

meas·ur·ing [ˈmeʒəriŋ; ˋmɛʒrɪŋ] *n*., *a*. 测量(的),测量用(的)。*remote* ～ 遥测。～ **chain** 测链。～ **glass**

[**cup**] 量(液)杯。~ **line** 测线,测绳。~ **tape** 卷尺。~ **worm**【虫】尺蠖。

meat [miːt; mit] *n*. **1.** (食用)肉。**2.** 〔古〕食物;〔古〕餐。**3.** (蛋、贝、果子等的)肉;(蟹、虾等的)肉。**4.** (书的)内容,实质。*butcher's* ~ 家畜的肉。*white* [*light*] ~ 白肉〔指鸡等禽类胸脯肉〕。*red* ~ 红肉〔指牛肉、羊肉等〕。*dark* ~ 黑肉〔指烧不白的鸡(腿)肉〕。*green* ~ 青菜,蔬菜。*inside* ~ 可吃的内脏。*One man's* ~ *is another man's poison*. 利于甲者未必利于乙。***after*** ~, ***mustard*** 饭后上芥末,〔转义〕雨后送伞。***as full*** (*of errors*) ***as an egg is of*** ~ (头脑等)充满了(错误);尽是(错误)。***be at*** ~ 正在吃饭。***be*** ~ ***and drink to*** 对(某人)是无上的乐趣。***be*** ~ ***for sb.'s master*** 太好。~ ***and potatoes*** 〔美俚〕重点,基础。***sit at*** ~ 就席。~-**and-potatoes** *a*. 〔美俚〕重要的,基本的。~**ball** **1.** 肉丸。**2.** 〔俚〕笨蛋;令人讨厌的人。~ **chopper**, ~ **grinder** 绞肉机,碎肉机。~-**eating** *a*. 吃肉的。~ **fly**【虫】肉蝇。~ **head** 〔俚〕笨蛋。~ **hooks** 〔*pl*.〕〔美俚〕拳头;手。~ **maggot** 肉蝇的幼虫,蛆。~**man** 卖肉佬;屠夫。~ **market** 〔美〕肉店。~-**packing** 肉类工业〔包括屠宰、加工、包装、批发等〕。~ **pie** 肉馅饼。~ **safe** (防猫鼠等的)橱柜,菜柜,金属纱罩。~ **screen** (烤肉用的)热反射板。~**space**【计】物质世界〔相对于网上虚拟世界而言〕。~ **tea** (有肉食冷盘等的下午)正式茶点小餐。~-**ware**【计】肉件〔指设计和操作电脑的工程技术人员,亦作 wetware〕。~**works** 屠宰场;肉品加工厂。

me·a·tus [mi(ː)ˈeitəs; mɪˋetəs] *n*. (*pl*. ~*es*, ~) 〔L.〕【解】道,管。*the urethral* ~ 尿道。

meat·y [ˈmiːti; ˋmitɪ] *a*. (***meat·i·er***; ***-i·est***) 肉(似)的;多肉的;滋养的;内容丰富的;有力的。~ *cotton* (杂质少的)纯净棉。

mec., **mech.** = mechanic.

Mec·ca [ˈmekə; ˋmɛkə] *n*. **1.** 麦加〔沙特阿拉伯,希贾兹首府〕。**2.** 〔常作 m-〕朝拜的地方,圣地;仰慕的目标;发祥地,发源地。**-n** *n*., *a*. 麦加人(的)。

Mec·ca·no [məˈkɑːnəu; məˋkɑno] *n*. (儿童)钢件结构玩具〔商标名〕。

mech. = mechanical; mechanics.

me·chan- *comb*. *f*. 机械: *mechan*ism.

me·chan·ic [miˈkænik; məˋkænɪk] **I** *n*. **1.** 机工;技工;机械地工作的人。**2.** 〔*pl*.〕= mechanics. **3.** 〔美俚〕专开保险箱的盗贼;玩牌(等赌具)时专门弄虚做假的人。*a radio* ~ 无线电技工。**II** *a*. 〔古〕= mechanical. ~'**s lien** 技工留置权〔建筑施工中的工资和费用的扣押权〕。

me·chan·i·cal [miˈkænikəl; məˋkænɪkl] *a*. **1.** 机械的;机械制的。**2.** 机械学的,力学的;物理上的(*opp*. chemical)。**3.** 机工的,技工的;自动的;机械(地工作)的,无意识的;勉强的。**4.**【哲】机械论的。**5.** 〔古〕粗野的。*a* ~ *brake* 机力制动器。*a* ~ *stoker* (自动)加煤机。~ *labour* 体力劳动。~ *equivalent of heat*【物】热功当量。~ *drawing* 机械制图。~ *energy* 机械能。~ *movement* 机械运动。~ *power* 机械功率。~ *resistance*【物】力阻。~ *tissue*【植】机械组织。*the* ~ *transport*【英陆军】汽车运输队〔略 M.T.〕。~ **astronomy** 天体力学。~ **bank** 玩具储蓄箱。~ **engineer** 机械工程师。~ **engineering** 机械工程。**-ly** *ad*. 机械地;无意识地;用机械。**-ness** *n*. 机械性,自动。

me·chan·i·cal·ism [miˈkænikəlizəm; mɪˋkænɪkəlˏɪzm] *n*. **1.**【哲】机械论。**2.** 机械行动。

me·chan·i·cal·ist [miˈkænikəlist; mɪˋkænɪkəlɪst] *n*. 机械论者。

mech·a·ni·cian [ˌmekəˈniʃən; ˏmɛkəˋnɪʃən] *n*. 技师;机械学家;技工。

me·chan·ics [miˈkæniks; məˋkænɪks] *n*. *pl*. **1.** 〔作单数用〕力学〔*cf*. statics; kinetics; kinematics〕;机械学。**2.** 〔作复数用〕结构;构成法;技巧。*quantum* ~ 量子力学。

mech·a·nism [ˈmekənizəm; ˋmɛkəˏnɪzəm] *n*. **1.** (机械)结构;机械装置[作用];(故事的)结构。**2.**【哲】机械论(*opp*. vitalism)。**3.**【文艺】手法;技巧;途径〔*cf*. style, expression〕。**4.** (自然现象等的)作用过程;【化】历程。**5.**【生】机制,机能;【乐】机理。【心】作用机理。*preset* ~ 程序机构。*early development* ~【遗传】初期发育规律。*migration* ~【生】迁移机能。~ *of hearing* 听的机能。~ *of action*【生化】作用动力。~ *of polymerization*【化纤】聚合历程。

mech·a·nist [ˈmekənist; ˋmɛkəˏnɪst] *n*. **1.** 〔罕〕= mechanician. **2.**【哲】机械论者。

mech·a·nis·tic [ˌmekəˈnistik; ˏmɛkəˋnɪstɪk] *a*. **1.** 机械论的;依据机械论的。**2.** 机械学的;力学的;机械概念的。**-ti·cal·ly** *ad*.

mech·a·nize [ˈmekənaiz; ˋmɛkəˏnaɪz] *vt*. 使机械化;用机械装备;用机械操作。*a* ~*d unit* = *a* ~*d force* 机械化部队。**-za·tion** [ˌmekənaiˈzeiʃən; ˏmɛkənəˋzeʃən] *n*. (军队等的)机械化;机能化。

mech·an·o- *comb*. *f*. = mechan-.

mech·an·o·ther·a·py [ˌmekənəuˈθerəpi; ˏmɛkənoˋθɛrəpɪ] *n*.【医】机械[力学]疗法。

mech·a·tron·ics [ˌmekəˈtrɔniks; ˏmɛkəˋtrɑnɪks] *n*. 机械电子学。

Mech·lin [ˈmeklin; ˋmɛklɪn] *n*. 梅克林花边〔比利时 Mechlin 城产,又作 ~ lace〕。

Mechs [meks; mɛks] *n*. 〔美俚〕= mechanized force 机械化部队。

me·co·nic [miˈkɔnik; mɪˋkɑnɪk] *a*. ~ **acid**【化】袂康酸〔得自鸦片中〕。

me·co·ni·um [miˈkəuniəm; məˋkonɪəm] *n*.【医】胎粪,胎尿;蛹便;〔废〕鸦片。

me·cop·ter·an [miˈkɔptərən; mɪˋkɑptərən] *n*.【动】长翅目(*Mecoptera*)昆虫。**-ter·ous** [-əs; -əs] *a*.

M.ED., **MED** = 〔美〕Master of Education 教育学硕士。

med. = **1.** medical; medicine. **2.** medieval. **3.** medium.

Med [med; mɛd] *n*. 〔美俚〕地中海。

med·al [ˈmedl; ˋmɛdl̩] **I** *n*. 奖章;徽章;勋章;纪念章;证章。a ~ *of honor* 〔美〕荣誉勋章。*a prize* ~ 奖章[牌]。*a* ~ *bar* 〔美〕胜利纪念章。*a war* ~ 从军纪念章。**II** *vt*. 授予…奖章。***M- for Merit*** 〔美〕功绩奖章〔对有特殊功绩的非军事人员所发的军事奖章〕。***M- of Freedom*** 〔美〕自由勋章〔1963 年前对在战争中有特殊贡献的非军事人员发的军事勋章,1963 年后,有贡献的军事人员也可获得〕。***the reverse*** (***side***) ***of the*** ~ 问题的另一方面。~ ***play***【高尔夫球】按全盘击数计分的比赛。~**ed**, **medalled** *a*. 受奖章的;带徽章的。

med·al·et [ˈmedlet; ˋmɛdlɛt] *n*. 小奖章[徽章]。

me·dal·lic [miˈdælik; məˋdælɪk] *a*. **1.** (像)奖章[徽章]的。**2.** 奖章上显示的。

me·dal·lion [miˈdæljən; mɪˋdæljən] *n*. **1.** 大奖章,大徽章。**2.** (肖像等的)圆形浮雕;团花图样。**3.** 〔美俚〕出租汽车经营牌照;有牌照的出租汽车。~ *carpet* 团花毯。

med·al(l)·ist [ˈmedəlist; ˋmɛdl̩ɪst] *n*. 得奖章者;奖章雕刻家;奖章搜集家。*a gold* ~ 金质奖章获得者。

Me·dan [meˈdɑːn; meˋdɑn] *n*. 棉兰〔印度尼西亚城市〕。

med·dle [ˈmedl; ˋmɛdl̩] *vi*. **1.** 弄,摸弄,用手玩弄;参与,发生关系(*with*)。**2.** 干涉,插手,多事(*with*; *in*)。*Don't* ~ *with the clock*. 不要弄钟。***neither make nor*** ~ 〔口〕不干涉。

med·dl·er [ˈmedlə; ˋmɛdlɚ] *n*. 多事者,好管闲事者;干涉者。

med·dle·some [ˈmedlsəm; ˋmɛdl̩səm] *a*. 爱管闲事的。**-ness** *n*.

Mede [miːd; mid] *n*. (伊朗西北部 Media 地方的)米堤亚人。***the law of the*** ~***s and Persians*** 不可改的制度

M

[习惯]。

Me·de·a [miˈdiə; mɪˋdɪə] ***n.*** 【希神】美狄亚〔科尔喀斯国王之女,以巫术著称,曾帮助伊阿宋取得金羊毛〕。

Me·del·lin [ˌmedeˈjiːn; ˏmɛdɛˋjin] ***n.*** 麦德林〔哥伦比亚城市〕。

med·e·vac [ˈmedəvæk; ˋmɛdəvæk] **I** ***n.*** 〔美口〕救伤直升机。**II** ***vt.*** 用救伤直升机运送(伤员)。

me·di- *comb.f.* 表示"中间的": *medi*eval.

me·di·a[1] [ˈmediə, Am. ˈmiːdiə; ˋmɛdɪə, ˋmidɪə] ***n.*** (*pl.* ***-di·ae*** [-diiː; -dɪi]) **1.** 〔L.〕【语】带声破裂子音;(带声)不送气破裂音([b][d][g])。**2.**【解】血管的中膜;【虫】中脉。**3.** 〔M-〕伊朗西北部的古王国。

me·di·a[2] [ˈmiːdjə; ˋmidɪə] ***n.*** **1.** medium 的复数。**2.** 〔用作 *sing.*〕媒体,传播媒介〔指报刊、广播、电视等〕。~ **event** 重大新闻事件〔为促使新闻媒介予以广泛报道而安排的宣传活动〕。~ **hack** 写低级通俗新闻的记者,三流记者。~**crat** 媒体巨头。

me·di·a·cy [ˈmiːdiəsi; ˋmidɪəsɪ] ***n.*** 介在,媒介;灵媒。

me·di·ad [ˈmiːdiæd; ˋmidɪˏæd] ***ad.*** 【生】中向,中央向。

me·di·ae·val [ˌmediˈiːvəl; ˏmidɪˋivl] ***a.*** 中世纪的;中古(式)的;中世(风)的。**M- Greek** 中世纪希腊语。**M-Latin** 中世纪拉丁语。**-ly** ***ad.*** 成中古式,依中古精神。

med·i·ae·val·ism [ˌmediˈiːvəlizəm; ˏmɛdɪˋivəlɪzəm] ***n.*** **1.** 中世纪精神,中世纪信仰;中世纪风俗。**2.** 热中于中世纪信仰[习惯、风俗等];欣赏中世纪特征的信仰[风俗等];中世纪遗风。

med·i·ae·val·ist [ˌmediˈiːvəlist; ˏmɛdɪˋivəlɪst] ***n.*** 中世纪史[文艺]研究家;中世纪风俗[信仰]爱好者。

med·i·ae·val·ize [ˌmediˈiːvəlaiz; ˏmidɪˋivəlˏaɪz] ***vt.*** 使成中古式,使符合中世纪习惯[理想等]。

me·di·al [ˈmiːdjəl; ˋmidɪəl] ***a.*** 中间的,中央的,中部的;平均的;普通的,中常的。*a* ~ *consonant* 【语】(在词中的)中间子音。~ *temperature* 平均温度,中位温度。*the* ~ *section* 【数】中外比分割,黄金分割。**-ly** ***ad.***

me·di·an [ˈmiːdjən; ˋmidɪən] **I** ***a.*** **1.** 中央的,中间的。**2.**【数】中线的,中(位)数的,中值的。**3.**【语】(舌)边音的;舌边中间开放的。*the* ~ *line* 中线。*the* ~ *artery* (*vein*) 中动[静]脉。*the* ~ *section* 正中切面[切片]。*the* ~ *point* 【数】重心。**II** ***n.*** 【解】中动脉;中静脉;正中神经;【数】中线;中(位)数,中值。**-ly** ***ad.***

me·di·ant [ˈmiːdjənt; ˋmidɪənt] ***n.*** 【乐】中音〔音阶的第三音〕。

me·di·as·ti·num [ˌmiːdiæsˈtainəm; ˏmidɪæsˋtaɪnəm] ***n.*** (*pl.* ***-na*** [-nə; -nə]) 【解】(胸腔)纵隔。

me·di·ate [ˈmiːdiit, -djət; ˋmidɪˏet, -dɪət] **I** ***a.*** **1.** 〔罕〕中间的。**2.** 要靠媒介的;间接的。~ *inference* 间接推理。**II** [ˈmiːdieit; ˋmidɪet] ***vt.*** 调停,调解;传达(思想等)。— ***vi.*** 调解,斡旋,作中人仲裁 (*between*); 处在中间,介于。**-ly** ***ad.*** 在中间,居中;间接。

me·di·a·tion [ˌmiːdiˈeiʃən; ˏmidɪˋeʃən] ***n.*** 调解,调停,仲裁;【天】中天。

me·di·a·ti·za·tion [ˌmiːdiətaiˈzeiʃən; ˏmidɪətaɪˋzeʃən] ***n.*** 并吞。

me·di·a·tive [ˈmiːdieitiv; ˋmidɪˏetɪv] ***a.*** 调停的,调解的。

me·di·a·tize [ˈmiːdiətaiz; ˋmidɪəˏtaɪz] ***vt.*** **1.** (大国)并吞(小国);【史】(保留旧君主名义上的主权而)合并(其国)。**2.** 使处于中间[附属]地位。— ***vi.*** 进行调解;【史】成为神圣罗马帝国的间接属国。

me·di·a·tor [ˈmiːdieitə; ˋmidɪˏetɚ] ***n.*** 调解人,斡旋者,中人;〔the M-〕【宗】耶稣基督;【化】【生】介体。

me·di·a·to·ri·al, me·di·a·tory [ˌmiːdiəˈtɔːriəl, -təri; ˏmidɪəˋtorɪəl, -ˏtorɪ] ***a.*** 调解的。

me·di·a·tress [ˈmiːdieitris; ˋmidɪˏetrɪs] ***n.*** 女调解人。

me·di·a·trix [ˌmiːdiˈeitriks; ˏmidɪˋetrɪks] ***n.*** (*pl.* ***-tri-ces*** [-ˈeitraisiːz; -ˋetrɪsiz]) = mediatress.

med·ic[1] [ˈmedik; ˋmɛdɪk] ***n.*** 〔美俚〕医生;【美军】军医助手;医学生。

med·ic[2] [ˈmedik; ˋmɛdɪk] ***n.*** 苜蓿属植物。

med·i·ca·ble [ˈmedikəbl; ˋmɛdɪkəbḷ] ***a.*** 可医治的,医得好的。

Med·i·aid [ˈmediˌeid; ˋmɛdɪˏed] ***n.*** 〔美〕医疗补贴计划。

Med·i·caid [ˈmedikeid; ˋmɛdɪked] ***n.*** 〔亦 m-〕〔美〕公共医疗补助制。

med·i·cal [ˈmedikəl; ˋmɛdɪkl] **I** ***a.*** **1.** 医学的,医术的;医疗的;医师的。**2.** 医药的。**3.** 内科的(*opp.* surgical)。~ *jurisprudence* 法医学。*a* ~ *man* [*practitioner*] 医生,开业医生〔包括 physician, surgeon 等〕。*a* ~ *officer* 军医,医官。*the* ~ *art* 医术。*a* ~ *certificate* 健康证明书,诊断书。*the* ~ *department* 医务部。~ *science* 医学。*a* ~ *examination* 体格检查。*a* ~ *examiner* 法医;验尸员;体检医生。*a* ~ *orderly* 看护兵。*free* ~ *care* 公费医疗。~ *troops* 卫生队。***under* ~ *treatment*** 在治疗中。**II** ***n.*** 〔口〕医科学生;医生;体格检查。**-ly** ***ad.*** 医学上;用医药[医术、医学]。

me·dic·a·ment [meˈdikəmənt; məˋdɪkəmənt] ***n.*** 药物,药剂。

Med·i·care [ˈmediˌkeə; ˋmɛdɪˏkɛr] ***n.*** 〔亦 m-〕〔美,加〕国家医疗照顾制〔对老年病人的某些医疗费和住院费由国家负担的制度〕。

med·i·cas·ter [ˈmedikæstə; ˋmɛdɪˏkæstɚ] ***n.*** 江湖医生;庸医。

med·i·cate [ˈmedikeit; ˋmɛdɪˏket] ***vt.*** 用药治疗;在…中加入药品。*a* ~*d bath* 药浴。~*d soap* 药皂。

med·i·ca·tion [ˌmediˈkeiʃən; ˏmɛdɪˋkeʃən] ***n.*** **1.** 药物疗法;加入药物;药物处理。**2.** 药物;药剂。

med·i·ca·tive [ˈmedikətiv; ˋmɛdəˏketɪv] ***a.*** 有药效的,可医治的;加有药品的。

Med·i·ce·an [ˌmediˈtʃiːən; ˋmɛdɪˋtʃiən] ***a.*** (中世纪意大利佛罗伦斯)美第奇(Medici)家族的。

med·i·chair [ˈmeditʃɛə; ˋmɛdɪˏtʃɛr] ***n.*** 医疗椅〔装有电子传感器,能测知人的生理活动状况〕。

med·i·cide [ˈmedisaid; ˋmɛdɪsaɪd] ***n.*** 医药辅助自杀。

me·dic·i·na·ble [meˈdisinəbl; məˋdɪsṇəbḷ] ***a.*** = medicinal.

me·dic·i·nal [meˈdisinəl; mɛˋdɪsṇl] ***a.*** 医学的,医药的,药用的;医疗的,治病的。*a* ~ *herb* 药草。~ *preparations* (内服或外用)药剂,药膏。**-ly** ***ad.***

med·i·cine [ˈmedsin, -disin; ˋmɛdəsn, -dɪsn] **I** ***n.*** **1.** 医药;(尤指)内服药。**2.** 医学,医术;内科(治疗)(*opp.* surgery)。**3.** 有功效的东西;良药。**4.** (北美印第安人的)咒术,魔术。**5.** 〔俚〕酒。**6.** 〔美俚〕情报。*patent* ~*s* 专卖药;成药。*a good* ~ *for cold* 感冒良药。*practise* ~ 开业行医。***no*** ~ 〔美俚〕与事无关的情报。***take*** ~ 吃药。***take one's*** ~ 吃苦药;受到惩罚;忍气吞声做应做的事;〔俚〕喝酒。***the virtue of*** ~ 药的功效。**II** ***vt.*** 〔古〕使…吃药,下药。~ **ball** (锻炼身体用的)实心软皮球。~ **chest** 药箱,药柜。~ **dance** 驱病舞;巫术舞。~ **man** (原始人的)巫医;〔美俚〕医生。~ **show** 走江湖卖膏药。

med·i·co [ˈmedikəu; ˋmɛdɪko] ***n.*** (*pl.* ~***s***) 〔谑〕医生;医科学生。

med·i·co- *comb.f.* = medical.

med·i·co·bo·tan·i·cal [ˈmedikəuˈbətænikəl; ˋmɛdɪkobəˋtænɪkəl] ***a.*** 药用植物学的。

med·i·co·le·gal [ˈmedikəuˈliːgəl; ˋmɛdɪkoˋligəl] ***a.*** 法医学的。

me·di·e·val [ˌmediˈiːvəl; ˏmidɪˋivl] ***a.*** = mediaeval.

med·i·gap [ˈmedigæp; ˋmɛdɪgæp] ***n.*** 补充性医疗保险〔私人健康保险之一种,以辅助政府医疗保险之不足〕。

Me·di·na [meˈdiːnə; məˋdinə] ***n.*** 麦地那〔伊斯兰教圣地之一,位于沙特阿拉伯西北部〕。

me·di·o [ˈmiːdiəu; ˋmidɪo] ***n.*** 〔美俚〕五分镍币。

me·di·o·cre [ˈmiːdiəukə; ˋmidɪˏokɚ] ***a.*** 普普通通的,

中等的,平庸的;〔蔑〕劣等的,无价值的。

me·di·oc·rity [ˌmiːdiˈɔkriti; ˏmidɪˋɑkrətɪ] ***n*.** 普通,平凡;平庸;平平常常的才能;平凡的人。

Medit. = Mediterranean (Sea)。

med·i·tate [ˈmediteit; ˋmɛdəˏtet] ***vi*.** 深思;沉思,冥想;反省 (*on*; *upon*)。— ***vt*.** 考虑;企图;策划,计划。~ *revenge* 企图复仇。~ *the Muse* 构想诗句。**-tation** ***n*.** 熟虑;(特指宗教上的)默想;〔*pl*.〕冥想录 (*religious meditations* 坐禅)。**-ta·tive** ***a*.** 默想的,冥想的。**-tator** ***n*.** 默想者,冥想家;计划者。

Med·i·ter·ra·nean [ˌmeditəˈreinjən; ˏmɛdətəˋrenɪən] **I** ***n*.** **1.** 地中海(= ~ Sea)。**2.** 地中海地区的居民。**3.** 地中海沿岸的高加索人。*the* ~ *race* 地中海沿岸的高加索人种。**II** ***a*.** **1.** 地中海(地区)的。**2.** 地中海沿岸的高加索人的。**3.** 〔m-〕陆地包围着的;〔军〕离海岸远的。~ **climate** 地中海气候。~ **fever**【医】地中海热,波状热。~ **fruit fly** 地中海果蝇〔一种危害水果的双翅蝇类〕。

me·di·um [ˈmiːdjəm; ˋmidɪəm] **I** ***n*.** (*pl*. **-dia** [-diə, -djə; -dɪə, -djə]) **1.** 媒介物;传导体;媒质,基质,介质,介体;中间物;环境、生活情形。**2.** 手段,方法;媒介;〔常作 *pl*.〕宣传工具;传播媒介〔指报刊、广播、电视等〕。**3.** 中间,中庸;【数】中数,平均;【逻】中名辞;【生】培养基,培养液;颜料溶解液。**4.** 女巫,降神者。**5.**【剧】(射火灯灯前的)隔板。**6.** (纸张的)中号尺寸;〔*pl*.〕中型轰炸机。*mass media* 大众传播媒介;宣传工具。*the happy* ~ 中庸。*the circulating* ~ = *the* ~ *of circulation* 通货。**II** ***a*.** 中等的,中级的,普通的;平均的。~ *quality* (中级)物品。*a* ~ *bowler*【板球】(速球与缓球之间的)中球投球员。***by*** [***through***] ***the*** **~** ***of*** 通过,以…为媒介。~ ***of advertisement*** 广告媒介〔指报刊等〕。~ ***of exchange*** 交换媒介;货币;支票。~ **frequency**【电】中频。~ **shot**【摄】中景。~ **steel** 中硬钢。~ **wave**【无】中波。~**-sized** ***a*.** 中等大的。

me·di·um·is·tic [ˌmiːdjəˈmistik; ˏmidɪəˋmɪstɪk] ***a*.** 巫术的。

me·di·us [ˈmiːdiəs; ˋmidɪəs] ***n*.** = mediant.

med·lar [ˈmedlə; ˋmɛdlɚ] ***n*.**【植】欧楂。*the Japan(ese)* ~ 枇杷。*the* ~*-bush* 卵圆叶唐棣。

med·ley [ˈmedli; ˋmɛdlɪ] **I** ***n*.** **1.** 混合,混杂,乌合之众。**2.** 杂录;集成歌(曲);杂色布;【美体】混合径赛;混合径赛参加者。**3.** 〔古〕混战。*a* ~ *of races* 杂族共聚。**II** ***a*.** 混合的,混杂的。~ **race** [**relay**] **1.** 混合接力赛跑。**2.** 各段不同游泳式的游泳赛。

Mé·doc [ˈmedɔk; ˋmedɑk] ***n*.** (法国 Médoc 地方的)红葡萄酒。

Med·res·co [ˈmedreskəu; ˋmɛdresko] ***n*.** 助听器〔商标名〕。

me·dul·la [meˈdʌlə; mɪˋdʌlə] ***n*.** (*pl*. **-lae** [-liː; -li]) 〔L.〕**1.**【解】骨髓;脊髓;延髓;髓(质);(特指心脏的)中心;(神经纤维的)髓鞘。**2.**【植】木髓。**3.**【微】菌髓。~ ***ob·lon·ga·ta*** [ˌɔblɔŋˈgɑtə; ˏɑblɑŋˋgɑtə] 延髓。~ ***spi·na·lis*** [ˈspainəlis; ˋspaɪnəlɪs] 脊髓。

me·dul·lar·y [meˈdʌləri; mɛˋdʌlərɪ] ***a*.** ~ **ray**【解、植】髓(射)线。~ **sheath**【解、植】髓鞘。

med·ul·lat·ed [ˈmedəleitid; ˋmɛdəˏletɪd] ***a*.** **1.** 具髓的;具髓质的。**2.** 有髓的。

me·dul·li·tis [ˌmedəˈlaitis; ˏmɛdəˋlaɪtɪs] ***n*.**【医】骨髓炎。

Me·du·sa [miˈdjuːzə; məˋdjusə] ***n*.**【希神】美杜莎,蛇发女怪。**-like** ***a*.** 像蛇发女怪的,令人恐怖的。

me·du·sa [miˈdjuːzə; məˋdjusə] ***n*.** (*pl*. **~s**, **-sae** [-siː, -ziː; -si, -zi])【动】水母(体),水母的;水母体的;伞盖体的。

me·du·soid [miˈdjuːsɔid; məˋdjusɔɪd] **I** ***a*.** 类水母体的。**II** ***n*.** 类水母体。

meed [miːd; mid] ***n*.** 〔诗〕报酬;奖赏,赏与;称赞,足够的份儿,值得接受的东西(*of*)。*one's* ~ *of praise* 应有的称赞。

meek [miːk; mik] ***a*.** 温顺的,柔和的;虚心的;卑躬屈节的 (*opp*. self-assertive);逆来顺受的;善忍的。***as*** **~** ***as a lamb*** [***a maid***, ***Moses***] 非常柔和,非常温顺。~**-eyed** ***a*.** 眼光柔和的。**-ly** ***ad*.** 温顺,柔和;卑躬屈节地。**-ness** ***n*.** 温顺,柔和;卑躬屈节。

meer·kat [ˈmiəkæt; ˋmɪrkæt] ***n*.** **1.** (南非)海岛猫鼬,蒙哥。**2.** 〔废〕猴子。

meer·schaum [ˈmiəʃəm; ˋmɪrʃəm] ***n*.** **1.**【矿】海泡石。**2.** 海泡石烟斗。

meet[1] [miːt; mit] **I** ***vt*.** (***met*** [met; mɛt]) **1.** 遇见,碰上,擦过,相遇。**2.** 迎接,出迎;会见,见面;面谈。**3.** 认识,初次会见。**4.** 面临;抵抗,和…会战,答覆,反驳。**5.** 满足,迎合。**6.** 如期偿付;偿还;践约。**7.** (路、河流等)相合,交叉;和…接触;与…碰撞。*I must go to the station to* ~ *my friend*. 我该到车站去接朋友了。*I'm very glad to* ~ *you*. 会见你很高兴;久仰,久仰。*I have arranged to* ~ *him at the hotel at six o'clock*. 我已约好六点钟在旅馆同他会见。*More is meant than* ~*s the ear*. (话中)意义比听到的更多;大有言外之意。~ *the eyes* 被看到。*M- Mr. Brown* 〔美〕这位是布朗先生。~ *the requirements of students and laymen* 满足学生和一般人的要求。~ *expenses* 偿付开支。~ *a bill* 支付到期的票据。*The buses* ~ *all trains*. 公共汽车联系着所有(到站)列车。~ *objections* 反驳反对意见。—***vi*.** **1.** 相会,相遇;会合。**2.** (线的两端)相合;相交,相连接。**3.** 见面;聚会;集会,开会。**4.** (品质)兼备,共存 (*in*)。**5.** 合意,和解。**6.** 会战。*Political integrity and ability* ~ *in her*. 她德才兼备。*This belt won't* ~ *round my waist*. 这个腰带不够长。~ *in battle* 兵戎相见,战场周旋。***be met by*** 遇着。***make both ends*** **~** 使收支相抵;量入为出。~ (*sb*.) ***halfway*** 和人妥协[相让];迁就某人。~ ***one's end*** [***fate***, ***death***] 死(~ *one's fate calmly* 从容死去)。~ ***one's engagements*** 践约,履行契约;偿还。~ ***one's liabilities*** 偿还债务。~ ***sb.'s eye*** 和某人的目光相遇;回看某人。~ ***the case*** 适合,合用。~ ***together*** 集合,会合。~ ***trouble halfway*** 自寻烦恼,杞人忧天。~ ***up with*** 〔美方〕遇着,碰见。~ ***with*** 遇见,碰见;遭遇,经验;偶然发现;达到,〔美〕符合。**II** ***n*.** **1.** 集合,会;赛会。**2.** 集合者;集合地点。**3.** 〔英〕(打猎竞赛等)出发前的集合。**4.**【数】(直线或平面的)交点,交线;交(集)。*an athletic* ~ 运动会。*an air* ~ 〔美〕航空大会。~**-and-greet** 见面会。

meet[2] [miːt; mit] ***a*.** 〔古〕适当的,适合的,相称的 (*for*; *to do*; *to be done*; *that*)。*It's* ~ *that we should help each other*. 我们应当互相帮助。**-ly** ***ad*.** **-ness** ***n*.**

meet·ing [ˈmiːtiŋ; ˋmitɪŋ] ***n*.** **1.** 会合,集合;会见;会议,(特殊的)大会,集会,会;会众。**2.** 决斗;会战;遭遇。**3.** 〔M-〕(Quaker 教徒的)礼拜会。**4.** (河川的)合流点,连接点。*an on-the-spot* ~ 现场会议。*a basket-* ~ 郊游会。*a farewell* [*welcome*] ~ 欢送[欢迎]会。*a general* [*ordinary*] ~ 大[例]会。*a social* ~ 联欢会,同乐会。***break up*** [***dissolve***] ***a*** **~** 解散会议,闭会。***call a*** **~** 召集大会。***hold a*** **~** 开会。~ ***engagement*** 遭遇战。***speak in*** **~** 〔美〕发表意见。~ ***of minds*** 意见一致。~**house** 〔美〕〔英蔑〕教堂,礼拜堂;〔英〕非国教徒的礼拜堂。~ **place** 会场。

M.E.F. = Middle East Forces 〔英〕驻中东(武装)部队。

meg [meg; mɛg] ***n*.**【计】兆字节(= megabyte)。

meg(a)- *comb. f*. **1.** 大。**2.** 兆,百万。

meg·a [ˈmegə; ˋmɛgə] ***a*.** **1.** 〔口〕宏大的。**2.** 〔口〕精彩的。~**debt** 巨大债务。~**dink** 〔口〕金融巨头。~**flops**【计】每秒百万次浮点连算。~**hit** 极成功的产品[作品等]。~**merger** 巨型合并,强强联合。~**plex** (含多幢分支建筑物的)巨型建筑;巨型影院。~**star** 超级明星。~**-trend** 大趋势。

meg·a·buck [ˈmegəbʌk; ˋmɛgəˏbʌk] ***n*.** 〔俚〕一百万美

元。

meg·a·byte [ˈmegəˌbait; ˋmɛgə͵baɪt] *n*. 【计】兆字节。

meg·a·ce·phal·ic, meg·a·ceph·a·lous [ˌmegəsəˈfælik, -ˈsefələs; ͵mɛgəsəˋfælɪk, -ˋsɛfələs] *a*. 巨头的。

meg·a·cy·cle [ˈmegəˌsaikl; ˋmɛgə͵saɪkl] *n*. 【无】兆周。

meg·a·death [ˈmegəˌdeθ; ˋmɛgə͵dɛθ] *n*. 百万人死亡〔搞核讹诈者用以计算核爆炸杀伤力的所谓计算单位〕。

meg·a·dyne [ˈmegədain; ˋmɛgə͵daɪn] *n*. 【物】兆达(因)。

meg·a·erg [ˈmegəˌəːg; ˋmɛgə͵ɝg] *n*. 【物】兆尔格。

meg·a·far·ad [ˌmegəˈfærəd; ͵mɛgəˋfærəd] *n*. 【电】兆法(拉)。

meg·a·fog [ˈmegəfɔg; ˋmɛgəfɑg] *n*. 雾信号器。

meg·a·game [ˌmegəˈgeim; ͵mɛgəˋgem] *n*. 大赛。

meg·a·ga·mete [ˌmegəˈgæmit, -gæˈmiːt; ͵mɛgəˋgæmɪt, -gæˋmit] *n*. 【医】大配子(= macrogamete)。

meg·a·hertz [ˈmegəˌhəːts; ˋmɛgə͵hɝts] *n*. (*pl*. ～)【物】兆赫(兹)。

meg·a·lith [ˈmegəliθ; ˋmɛgə͵lɪθ] *n*. (史前建筑遗存的)巨石;巨碑。

meg·a·lith·ic [ˌmegəˈliθik; ͵mɛgəˋlɪθɪk] *a*. 巨石的。

megalo- *comb*. *f*. 大,巨大。

meg·a·lo·blast [ˈmegələ*u*blaːst; ˋmɛgəlo͵blæst] *n*. 【医】巨成红血细胞,巨胚红血球。**-ic** [ˌmegələ*u*ˈblæstik; ͵mɛgəloˋblæstɪk] *a*. (*megaloblastic anaemia* 有核巨红血球性贫血)。

meg·a·lo·car·di·a [ˌmegələuˈkaːdiə; ͵mɛgəloˋkardɪə] *n*. 【医】心肥大。

meg·a·lo·ceph·a·ly [ˌmegələ*u*ˈsefəli; ͵mɛgəloˋsɛfəlɪ] *n*. 异常大的头。**-ce·phal·ic** [-seˈfælik; -seˋfælɪk] *a*. 头部异常巨大的。

meg·a·lo·ma·ni·a [ˈmegələ*u*ˈmeinjə; ͵mɛgələˋmenɪə] *n*. 自大狂;妄自尊大;【医】夸大妄想狂。

meg·a·lo·ma·ni·ac [ˌmegələ*u*ˈmeiniæk; ͵mɛgələˋmenɪ͵æk] *n*., *a*. 妄自尊大的(人);患夸大狂的(人)。**-manic** [ˈmegələ*u*ˈmænik; ˋmɛgələˋmænɪk] *a*.

meg·a·lop·o·lis [ˌmegəˈlɔpəlis; ͵mɛgəˋlɑpəlɪs] *n*. 特大城市。**-pol·i·tan** [-ləˈpɔlitən; -loˋpɑlətn̩] *a*., *n*.

meg·a·lops [ˈmegəˌlɔps; ˋmɛgə͵lɑps] *n*. (*pl*. *-losp*, *-lop·ses*)(蟹)大眼幼体期。**-lop·ic** *a*.

meg·a·lo·sau·rus [ˌmegələˈsɔːrəs; ͵mɛgələˋsɔrəs] *n*. 【古生】斑龙。

mega·parsec [ˌmegəˈpaːsek; ͵mɛgəˋparsɛk] *n*. 【天】百万秒差距。

meg·a·phone [ˈmegəfəun; ˋmɛgə͵fon] I *n*. 扩音器;喇叭筒,喊话筒;传声筒。II *vt*., *vi*. 用喇叭筒喊话;广泛宣传。

meg·a·pod [ˈmegəˌpɔd; ˋmɛgə͵pɑd] I *a*. 大足的。II *n*. = megapode.

meg·a·pode [ˈmegəˌpəud; ˋmɛgə͵pod] *n*. 【动】营冢鸟〔产于澳大利亚和东印度群岛〕。

meg·a·scope [ˈmegəskəup; ˋmɛgə͵skop] *n*. 【物】(放大不透明物体的)放大幻灯。**-scop·ic** [-ˈskɔpik; -ˋskɑpɪk] *a*. 肉眼可见的,宏观的;粗视的;放大幻灯的;被扩大的。

meg·a·spo·ran·gi·um [ˌmegəspəˈrændʒiəm; ͵mɛgəspəˋrændʒɪəm] *n*. (*pl*. *-gi·a* [-ə; -ə])【植】大孢子囊。

meg·a·spore [ˈmegəspɔː; ˋmɛgə͵spor] *n*. 【植】大孢子。**-sporic** [-ˈspɔːrik; -ˋsporɪk] *a*.

meg·a·spo·ro·phyll [ˌmegəˈspɔːrəfil; ͵mɛgəˋsporəfɪl] *n*. 【植】大孢子叶。

me·gasse [miˈgæs; məˋgæs] *n*. (尤指甘蔗的)榨渣。

meg·a·tan·ker [ˌmegəˈtæŋkə; ͵mɛgəˋtæŋkɚ] *n*. 1. 百万吨级油轮,超级油轮。2. 兆,百万〔量度单位〕。

meg·a·there [ˈmegəθiə; ˋmɛgə͵θɪr] *n*. 【动】大懒兽〔一种古生物〕。

Meg·a·the·ri·um [ˌmegəˈθiəriəm; ͵mɛgəˋθɪrɪəm] *n*. 【古生】大懒兽科。

meg·a·ton [ˈmegəˌtʌn; ˋmɛgə͵tʌn] *n*. 1. 百万吨。2. 百万吨级〔核爆力计算单位〕。**-ic** [ˌmegəˈtʌnik; ͵mɛgəˋtʌnɪk] *a*.

meg·a·tron [ˈmegətrʌn; ˋmɛgə͵trʌn] *n*. 【无】塔形(电子)管。

meg·a·volt [ˈmegəvəult; ˋmɛgə͵volt] *n*. 【电】兆伏(特),百万伏特。

meg·a·watt [ˈmegəwɔt; ˋmɛgə͵wɑt] *n*. 【电】兆瓦(特)。

meg·ger [ˈmegə; ˋmɛgɚ] *n*. 【电】高阻表,兆欧表,摇表,迈格表。

me·gil·lah [məˈgilə; məˋgɪlə] *n*. 【俚】1. 颇费唇舌的解释;说来话长的故事。2. 复杂事情。

me·gilp [məˈgilp; məˋgɪlp] *n*. (油画用)溶油剂。

meg·ohm [ˈmegəum; ˋmɛg͵om] *n*. 【电】兆欧(姆)。

me·grim[1] [ˈmiːgrim; ˋmigrɪm] *n*. 1. 【医】周期性偏头痛。2. 〔*pl*.〕忧郁。3. 【兽医】眩晕〔马脑充血〕。4. 空想,幻想;怪念头。

me·grim[2] [ˈmiːgrim; ˋmigrɪm] *n*. (一种)鲽鱼。

Mei·ji [ˈmeidʒiː; ˋmedʒɪ] *n*. 〔Jap.〕明治〔明治天皇年号〕。

mein·ie, mein·y [ˈmeini; ˋmenɪ] *n*. 1. 【废】(封建的)家臣;随从;门客;家族;家户。2. 〔Scot.〕群众;大众。

Mein Kampf [main ˈkaːmpf; ͵maɪn ˋkamf] 〔G.〕《我的奋斗》〔希特勒所写宣扬其法西斯主义的书〕。

mei·o·bar [ˈmaiəbaː; ˋmaɪəbar] *n*. 【气】低压区等压线;低压区。

mei·o·sis [maiˈəusis; maɪˋosɪs] *n*. (*pl*. *-ses* [-siːz; -siz]) 1. 【生】减数分裂,成熟分裂。2. 【修】间接肯定法,曲言法(= litotes)〔例:not a few regrets〕。

Meis·ter·sing·er [ˈmaistəˌsiŋə; ˋmaɪstɚ͵sɪŋɚ] *n*. (*sing*., *pl*.) 〔G.〕(14—16 世纪德国的)职工歌手;职工诗歌协会会员。

meit·ner·i·um [ˈmaitnəriəm; ˋmaɪtnərɪəm] *n*. 【化】鿏〔第 109 号元素〕。

Mek·ka [ˈmekə; ˋmɛkə] = Mecca.

me·kom·e·ter [miːˈkɔmitə; miˋkɑmɪtɚ] *n*. (枪炮的)测距器。

Me·kong [ˈmeiˈkɔŋ; ˋmeˋkɑŋ] *n*. 湄公河。

mel [mel; mɛl] *n*. 蜂蜜〔尤指药用蜜〕。

mel·a·mine [ˈmeləmiːn; ˋmɛləmin] *n*. 【化】三聚氰(酰)胺,蜜胺。～ **resin** 【化】蜜胺树脂;三聚氰酰胺树脂。

mel·an- *comb*. *f*. 1. 表示"黑": *melan*ian. 2. 表示"黑素": *melan*otic.

mel·an·cho·li·a [ˌmelənˈkəuljə; ͵mɛlənˋkolɪə] *n*. 【医】忧郁病。**-cho·li·ac** *a*., *n*. 患忧郁病的(人)。

mel·an·chol·ic [ˌmelənˈkɔlik; ͵mɛlənˋkɑlɪk] I *a*. 忧郁(症)的;使人抑郁的;神经质的。II *n*. 忧郁病患者。

mel·an·chol·y [ˈmelənkəli; ˋmɛlən͵kɑlɪ] I *n*. 1. 忧郁;忧郁症。2. 愁思,沉思。II *a*. 1. 忧郁的;令人伤感的;意气消沉的。2. 沉思默想的。

Mel·a·ne·sia [ˌmeləˈniːzjə; ͵mɛləˋniʒə] *n*. 美拉尼西亚〔西南太平洋的岛群〕。

Mel·a·ne·si·an [ˌmeləˈniːzjən, -ziən, -ʒiən; ͵mɛləˋniʒən, -zɪən, -ʒən] *n*., *a*. (大洋洲中部)美拉尼西亚人[语](的)。

mé·lange [meiˈlɑ̃ːnʒ; meˋlɑ̃ʒ] *n*. 〔F.〕1. 混合物,什锦,杂烩;(文学)杂记,杂集。2. 【纺】混色毛纱;混色效应;混条机。

me·la·ni·an [miˈleiniən; məˋlenɪən] *a*. 1. 〔常作 M-〕【人种】黑发黑肤的,黑色人种的。2. 黑色素的。

me·lan·ic [məˈlænik; məˋlænɪk] *a*. 1. 【动】黑变病的;有黑变病特征的。2. 黑色素过多的。

mel·a·nin [ˈmelənin; ˋmɛlənɪn] *n*. 【医】黑(色)素。

mel·a·nism [ˈmelənizəm; ˋmɛlənɪzm̩] *n*. 【医】黑色素过多;黑素沉着症;【生】黑化;暗化。

mel·a·nite [ˈmeləˌnait; ˋmɛlənaɪt] *n*. 【地】黑榴石。

mel·a·nize [ˈmelənaiz; ˋmɛlə͵naɪz] *vt*. (*-nized*, *-niz-*

M

ing) 1. 黑化。2. 使…变黑,使成黑色。

mel·a·no- *comb.f.* = melan-.

Mel·a·noch·ro·i [ˌmeləˈnɔkrəuai;ˏmɛləˋnɑkroˏaɪ] *n.* 【人种】淡黑白色人种〔高加索人种中头发浓黑肤色淡白的种族〕。

mel·a·no·cyte [ˈmelənəuˈsait, məˈlænə-; ˋmɛlənoˏsaɪt, məˋlænə-] *n.* 【医】黑素细胞。

mel·a·noid [ˈmelənɔid; ˋmɛləˏnɔɪd] *a.* 1. 【生化】染黑的,暗黑的。2. 【医】黑变病的;黑变病状的。

mel·a·no·ma [ˌmeləˈnəumə; ˏmɛləˋnomə] *n.* (*pl.* **-mas**, **-ma·ta** [-mətə; -mətə]) 【医】黑瘤。

me·la·no·sis [ˌmeləˈnəusis;ˏmɛləˋnosɪs] *n.* 【医】色素浸润,黑变病。

mel·a·no·tic [ˌmeləˈnɔtik;ˏmɛləˋnɑtɪk] *a.* 以黑色素为特征的;(患)黑变病的。

mel·a·nous [ˈmelənəs; ˋmɛlənəs] *a.* 黑肤黑发的。

mel·a·phyre [ˈmeləˌfaiə; ˋmɛləˏfaɪr] *n.* 〔废〕【地】暗斑岩。

mel·a·stome [ˈmeləˌstəum; ˋmɛləˏstom] *a.* 【植】野牡丹科植物的。

Mel·ba [ˈmelbə; ˋmɛlbə] *n.* 梅尔巴〔女子名〕。

melba toast [ˈmelbə təust; ˋmɛlbə tost] (烘烤得很脆的)薄片面包干。

Mel·bourne [ˈmelbən; ˋmɛlbɚn] *n.* 墨尔本〔即新金山,澳大利亚港市〕。

Mel·chers [ˈmeltʃəz; ˋmɛltʃɚz] *n.* 梅尔彻斯〔姓氏〕。

Mel·chior [ˈmelkiɔː; ˋmɛlkɪɔr] *n.* 梅尔基奥尔〔姓氏〕。

Mel·chite, Mel·kite [ˈmelkait; ˋmɛlkaɪt] *n.* (埃及、以色列和叙利亚行拜占廷仪式的)阿拉伯语天主教徒。

meld [meld; mɛld] *vt.*, *vi.* 〔美〕吞没;合并。

mê·lée [ˈmelei; ˋmele] *n.* 〔F.〕互殴,乱斗,混战;激烈的论战;混乱的人群[一堆]。

mel·ic [ˈmelik; ˋmɛlɪk] *a.* 1. 歌的;诗的〔尤指成诗节的希腊诗〕。2. 抒情的;抒情诗的;拟加以咏唱的。

mel·i·lot [ˈmeliˌlɔt; ˋmɛlɪˏlɑt] *n.* 草木犀属植物(= sweet clover)。

mel·i·nite [ˈmelinait; ˋmɛlɪˏnaɪt] *n.* 麦宁炸药〔含有苦味酸的猛烈炸药〕。

mel·io·rate [ˈmiːljəreit; ˋmiljəˏret] *vt.*, *vi.* = ameliorate. **-ra·tion** *n.* 土壤改良(= amelioration)。**-ra·tive** *a.* = ameliorative. **-rat·or, -rat·er** *n.* = ameliorator. ★英国多通用 ameliorate 等。

mel·io·rism [ˈmiːljərizəm; ˋmiljərɪzm̩] *n.* 世界向善论;社会改善论。

mel·ior·i·ty [miːˈljɔriti; milˋjɑrətɪ] *n.* 改善,进步;卓越,优越性。

me·lis·ma [məˈlizmə; məˋlɪzmə] *n.* (*pl.* **-ma·ta** [-mətə; -mətə], **-mas**) 【乐】装饰音。**-ma·tic** [ˈmelizˈmætik; ˋmɛlɪzˋmætɪk] *a.*

me·lis·sa [miˈlisə; məˋlɪsə] *n.* 【植】蜜蜂花〔薄荷属〕。

me·li·te·mi·a [meliˈtiːmiə; mɛlɪˋtimɪə] *n.* 【医】糖血症。

mell [mel; mɛl] *vt.*, *vi.* 〔英方〕1. 混合;加入。2. 弄,摸弄;参与;干涉。

mel·lay [ˈmelei; ˋmɛle] *n.* 〔古〕= mêlée.

mel·ler [ˈmelə; ˋmɛlɚ] *n.* 〔美俚〕= melodrama.

mel·lif·er·ous [meˈlifərəs; məˋlɪfərəs] *a.* 产蜜的;带蜜的;甜的。

mel·lif·lu·ence [meˈlifluəns; məˋlɪfluəns] *n.* (声音、言词的)甜美;流畅;迷人。

mel·lif·lu·ent, mel·lif·lu·ous [meˈlifluənt, -əs; məˋlɪfluənt, -əs] *a.* 〔古〕(话、声音等)甘美的,甜蜜的,流畅的。*a ~ speech* 甜言蜜语。**-ly** *ad.*

mel·lit·ic [meˈlitik; mɛˋlɪtɪk] *a.* ~ *acid* 【化】苯六(羧)酸,苯六甲酸。

Mel·lon [ˈmelən; ˋmɛlən] *n.* 梅隆〔姓氏〕。

mel·lo·phone [ˈmeləfəun; ˋmɛləˏfon] *n.* 一种类似中音萨克号的圆形铜管乐器〔在乐队中常代替法国号〕。

mel·lo·tron [ˈmelətrɔn; ˋmɛlətrɑn] *n.* 电子琴。

mel·low [ˈmeləu; ˋmɛlo] **I** *a.* (**~er**; **~est**) 1. 甘美多汁的,(瓜、果等)成熟的;(酒)芳醇的。2. (土壤等)肥沃的。3. (人格、思想等)老练的,完美的。4. (音、色、光等)柔美的,圆润的,丰美的。5. 〔口〕高兴的,愉快的;温和的;有点醉的。~ *age* 成熟的年龄。**II** *vt.* 1. 使柔和;使芳醇。2. 使成熟,使丰美。— *vi.* 1. 变柔和;变芳醇。2. 成熟;变得丰美[柔和]。**-ly** *ad.* **-ness** *n.*

mel·low·y [ˈmeləui; ˋmɛloɪ] *a.* = mellow.

melo [ˈmeləu; ˋmɛlo] *n.* 〔美俚〕= melodrama.

me·lo·de·on, me·lo·dion, me·lo·dium [miˈləudiən; məˋlodɪən] *n.* 小型脚踏风琴〔一种谐音手风琴〕。

me·lo·di·a [məˈləudiə; məˋlodɪə] *n.* 【乐】八尺风琴音栓。

me·lod·ic [meˈlɔdik; məˋlɑdɪk] *a.* 旋律的;调子美妙的。

me·lod·i·ca [miˈlɔdikə; məˋlɑdɪkə] *n.* 口风琴。

me·lod·ics [miˈlɔdiks; mɪˋlɑdɪks] *n.* 旋律学。

me·lo·di·ous [miˈləudjəs; məˋlodɪəs] *a.* (有)旋律的,旋律优美的,音调悦耳的。**-ly** *ad.* **-ness** *n.*

mel·o·dist [ˈmelədist; ˋmɛlədɪst] *n.* 歌唱家;(作曲旋律优美的)作曲家。

mel·o·dize [ˈmelədaiz; ˋmɛləˏdaɪz] *vt.* 使有优美的旋律,使悦耳动听;把…谱成乐曲。— *vi.* 作曲,谱曲;产生旋律。

mel·o·dra·ma, mel·o·drame [ˈmelədrɑːmə, -ˈləud-; ˋmɛləˏdrɑmə, -dræmə] *n.* 情节剧,传奇剧;戏剧性的事件[行为];〔古〕乐剧。

mel·o·dra·mat·ic [ˌmeləudrəˈmætik;ˏmɛlədrəˋmætɪk] *a.* 情节剧作风的;戏剧似的;感情夸张的;惊人的;轰动的。**-i·cal·ly** *ad.*

mel·o·dra·mat·ics [ˌmeləudrəˈmætiks; ˏmɛlədrəˋmætɪks] *n.* 〔*pl.*〕感情夸张的[情节剧似的、轰动的]行为。

mel·o·dram·a·tist [ˌmeləuˈdræmətist; ˏmɛləˋdræmətɪst] *n.* 情节剧作者。

mel·o·dram·a·tize [ˌmeləuˈdræmətaiz; ˏmɛləˋdræməˏtaɪz] *vt.* 使具有情节剧特点;把(小说等)改写成情节剧。

mel·o·dy [ˈmelədi; ˋmɛlədɪ] *n.* 1. 甜蜜的音乐,好听[和谐]的调子;好听的声音;歌曲;适合唱歌的诗。2. 【乐】旋律,曲调;主调。~ *of one's utterance* 讲话的抑扬顿挫。

mel·o·lon·thid [ˌmeləˈlɔnθid; ˏmɛləˋlɑnθɪd] *n.* 【动】鳃角金龟〔一种食植物根的昆虫〕。

mel·o·ma·ni·a [ˌmeləˈmeinjə; ˏmɛləˋmenɪə] *n.* 音乐狂。**-ic** *a.*

mel·on [ˈmelən; ˋmɛlən] *n.* 1. 【植】甜瓜。2. 〔美俚〕额外红利;横财。*water* ~ 西瓜。*musk* ~ = *oriental* ~ 香瓜,甜瓜。***cut a*** ~ 〔俚〕分配额外红利;分红;分肥。***cut the*** ~ 〔俚〕瓜分利益。**~-cutting** 〔美俚〕分红;分肥。~ **tree** 【植】番柧树。

Mel·pom·e·ne [melˈpɔminiː; mɛlˋpɑməˏni] *n.* 【希神】掌管悲剧的女神。

melt [melt; mɛlt] *vi.* (**~ed**; **~ed**, ***mol·ten*** [ˈməutən; ˋmotn]) 1. 融化;熔化;液解。2. 逐渐消散[消失、变淡]。3. (心等)变软,生怜悯的心情;(决心等)软化。4. 溶合,逐渐转化成。5. (云等)变成雨。6. (音乐、声音等)变得柔润。7. 〔口〕感到热极。*I am simply ~ing (with heat).* 〔口〕热死了,热得要命。*Clouds ~ed away.* 云变成雨了。— *vt.* 1. 使融化[熔化、溶解]。2. 使软化,使感动。3. 使消散[消失]。4. 浪费;〔英俚〕(把支票等)兑现。*Heat will ~ iron.* 热度可使铁熔化。~ ***away*** 融掉;消失;(钱)渐渐花光;(使)着迷,弄得恍恍惚惚 (*The snow soon ~ed away.* 雪不久就化了)。~ ***down*** 熔化,销毁(货币等);〔俚、谑〕变卖财产。~ ***into*** 熔成…,化为;消散于…;因心软而…,感动得(~ *into air* 化为云烟,消失。~ *into distance* 消失在远方。~ *into*

M

tears 心变软而哭起来)。～ ***like wax*** 像蜡一样融化。～ **down** 1. 熔化了的金属,溶化物;熔[溶]解量;熔炉的一次装料。2. 熔解;【原】(核反应堆芯棒的)突然局部熔解;〔喻〕无法控制的突发性灾难;(股票的)暴跌;(利润的)剧降;(某个体系的)崩溃。

melt·age [ˈmeltidʒ; ˋmɛltɪdʒ] ***n***. 1. 熔化。2. 熔化物;熔化量。

melt·ing [ˈmeltiŋ; ˋmɛltɪŋ] ***a***. 1. 融[熔]化的。2. 心软的,受感动的,易感动的。3. 使人感动的,使人感伤的,温柔的,动人的。*a ～ mood* 感伤的心情。～ **point** 熔点。～ **pot** 坩埚,熔化锅;各种族融合之国〔通常指美国〕(*go into the ～ pot* 被改造;(心等)变软;软化。*put* [*cast*] *into the ～ pot* 重作,改造)。

mel·ton [ˈmeltən; ˋmɛltn] **I** ***n***. (英国)麦尔顿呢〔又作 M- Cloth〕。**II** ***a***. 麦尔顿呢做的。

Mel·va [ˈmelvə; ˋmɛlvə] ***n***. 梅尔瓦〔女子名〕。

Mel·ville [ˈmelvil; ˋmɛlvɪl] ***n***. 梅尔维尔〔姓氏,男子名〕。

Mel·vin, Mel·vyn [ˈmelvin; ˋmɛlvɪn] ***n***. 梅尔文〔姓氏,男子名〕。

mem. = 1. member. 2. memento. 3. memoir. 4. memorandum. 5. memorial.

mem·ber [ˈmembə; ˋmɛmbɚ] ***n***. 1. (团体的)一分子,成员;会员;社员;议员;委员。2. 政党支部。3. 手足,肢体;身体各部,(人及动物的)器官。4. 各部,部分。5.【语法】分句;成分。6.【数】元,分子,(方程的)端边;【逻】推论的命题;【机】构件,部件;【化】节,(环中)原子数。*a League ～* 团员。*a Party ～* 党员。*a M- of Congress* 〔美〕国会议员〔略作 M.C.〕。*a M- of Parliament* 〔英〕下院议员〔略作 M.P.,〔*pl*.〕M.P.s 或 MM.P.〕。*a ～ of a family* 家庭的一分子。*a ～ as of right* 当然会员。*a full* [*probationary*] *～* 正式[非正式]会员。*the unruly ～* 难于控制的器官〔指舌头〕。*a driven* [*driving*] *～*【机】从动[主动]构件。～ *bank* 〔美〕(联邦准备银行的)会员银行。**-ship** ***n***. 会员[委员]的身份[地位、资格];会籍;会员人数;会员全体(*Party membership* 全体党员;党籍)。

(-)membered [ˈmembəd; ˋmɛmbɚd] *comb. f*. …手足的;有…肢体的;有…会员的: *large-～* 手足巨大的。

mem·bra·na·ceous [ˌmembrəˈneiʃəs; ˏmɛmbrəˋneʃəs] ***a***. = membranous.

mem·brane [ˈmembrein; ˋmɛmbren] ***n***. 1.【解、生】(薄)膜,隔膜。2.〔古〕(古文件的)(一页)羊皮纸。*the mucous ～* 黏膜。～ **bone**【解】膜[成]骨。～ **labyrinth**【解】膜迷路。**-bra·neous** [-niəs; -nɪəs], **-bra·nous** [-nəs; nəs] ***a***. 膜(状)的,膜质的;隔膜的。

mem·brum vi·ri·le [ˈmembrəm viˈraili; ˋmɛmbrəm vɪˋraɪlɪ] 〔L.〕阴茎(= penis)。

me·men·to [meˈmentəu; mɪˋmɛnto] ***n***. (*pl*. ～*s*, ～*es*) 纪念品;令人回忆的东西;令人警惕的东西;〔谑〕记忆;做梦似的心境。

me·men·to mo·ri [meˈmentəu ˈmɔːrai; mɪˋmɛnto ˋmoraɪ] 〔L.〕死的警告,死的象征[骷髅等]。

mem·o [ˈmeməu; ˋmɛmo] ***n***. 〔口〕= memorandum.

mem·oir [ˈmemwɑː; ˋmɛmwɑr] ***n***. 1. 传记,实录;〔*pl*.〕回忆录,自传。2. 研究报告,论文;〔*pl*.〕…学会纪要,…学会论文集。3.〔罕〕(外交上的)备忘录。

mé·moire [memˈwɑː; mɛmˋwɑr] ***n***. 〔F.〕(外交上的)备忘录。

mem·o·ra·bil·i·a [ˌmemərəˈbiliə; ˏmɛmərəˋbɪlɪə] ***n***. *pl*. (*sing*. ***-rab·i·le*** [-ˈræbili; -ˋræbəli]) 〔L.〕值得记忆的事情,应记录下来的地方[东西];(重大事件的)记录;(伟大人物的)言行录。

mem·o·ra·ble [ˈmemərəbl; ˋmɛmərəbl] ***a***. 可记忆的,不可忘记的,难忘的;重大的,著名的。**-bly** ***ad***., **-bil·i·ty** [ˌmemərəˈbiliti; ˏmɛmərəˋbɪlətɪ] ***n***.

mem·o·ran·dum [ˌmeməˈrændəm; ˏmɛməˋrændəm] ***n***. (*pl*. ～*s*, 亦作 ***-da*** [-də; -də]) 〔L.〕1. 记录。2.【外交】照会,备忘录。3.【商】便笺[函];(按一定格式印好的)通知书;寄售物品通知书。4.【法】(契约等条文的)节略;摘要;会章,(公司)规章。*send a thing on ～* 拿东西寄售。*the ～ of an association* 〔英〕(公司、协会的)成立简章。*the ～ of complaint*【法】抗告状。～ **book** 备忘录。

mem·o·ri·al [miˈmɔːriəl; məˋmɔrɪəl] **I** ***a***. 纪念的;记忆的;追悼的。**II** ***n***. 1. 纪念物,纪念品;纪念日;纪念馆;纪念碑;纪念仪式。2.〔常 *pl*.〕记录,备忘录;年代记,编年史。3. (提交议会等的)建议书;(外交上的)备忘录。4. 请愿书;抗议书。5.〔美口〕纪念死者的慈善捐款。*a ～ festival* 纪念节。*a ～ service* 追悼会;追思礼拜。**M- Day** 〔美〕= Decoration Day (美国)阵亡将士纪念日〔原定为5月30日,现为5月份最后一个星期一〕。

me·mo·ri·al·ist [miˈmɔːriəlist; məˋmorɪəlɪst] ***n***. 1. 建议[请愿]书起草人[署名人];建议[请愿]者。2. 回忆录[传记]作者。

me·mo·ri·al·ize, me·mo·ri·al·ise [miˈmɔːriəlaiz; məˋmorɪəlˏaɪz] ***vt***. 1. 向…请愿[建议];上条陈。2. 纪念。**-iz·er** ***n***. **-i·za·tion** ***n***.

me·mo·ri·a tech·ni·ca [miˈmɔːriə ˈteknikə; məˋmɔrɪə ˋtɛknəkə] 〔L.〕记忆术,记忆加强法。

me·mor·i·ter [miˈmɔritə; məˋmɑrətɚ] **I** ***ad***. 〔L.〕凭记忆。**II** ***a***. 暗记的。

mem·o·rize, mem·o·rise [ˈmeməraiz; ˋmɛməˏraɪz] ***vt***. 1. 记忆,暗记。2.〔罕〕记录。3.【自】存储。**-riz·er** ***n***. **-ri·za·tion** ***n***.

mem·o·ry [ˈmeməri; ˋmɛmərɪ] ***n***. 1. 记忆;记忆力;【自】存储器;信息存储方式;存储量。2. 回忆。3. 纪念。4. 死后的名声,遗芳。5. 追想得起的年限[范围]。*artificial ～* 记忆法。*retentive ～* 良好的记忆力。*a translation ～* (电子计算机的)译码存储器。*Keep your ～ active*. 好好记住,不要忘记。*It is but a ～*. 那不过是往事而已。***bear*** [***have, keep***] ***in ～*** 记着,没有忘记。***beyond*** [***within***] ***the ～ of man*** [***men***] 在有史以前[以来]。***cherish the ～ of*** (*sb*.) 怀念(某人)。***come to one's ～*** 想起,忆及,苏醒。***commit to ～*** 记住。***from ～*** 凭记忆。***have a good*** [***bad, poor, short***] ***～*** 记性好[坏]。***have no ～ of*** 完全忘记。***If my ～ serves me***. 如果我的记性不错。***in ～ of*** 纪念…。***of blessed*** [***famous, happy, glorious***] ***～*** 故〔加在已死王公名上的颂词〕(*King Charles of blessed ～* 已故查理王)。***slip sb.'s ～*** 被某人一时忘记。***to the best of one's ～*** 就记忆所及。***to the ～ of*** 献给…〔著者书前纪念性题词〕。***within living ～*** 现在还被人记着。～ **bank**【自】存储体,记忆体。～ **drum**【自】存储磁鼓〔电子计算机存储装置上记录资料的磁带或磁道组〕。～ **recovery**【医】记忆恢复术。～ **switch**【计】(需由电脉冲关闭的)存储开关。～ **trace**【生化】记忆痕〔脑部吸收或记忆资料时产生的化学变化〕。

Mem·phis [ˈmemfis; ˋmɛmfɪs] ***n***. 1. 孟菲斯〔古埃及城市〕。2. 孟菲斯〔美国城市〕。

mem·sa·hib [ˈmemˌsɑːib, -ˈsɑːb; ˋmɛmˏsaɪb, -ˋsɑb] ***n***. 〔Ind.〕夫人;太太〔从前印度人对欧洲妇女的尊称〕。

men [men; mɛn] ***n***. man 的复数。

men·ace [ˈmenəs; ˋmɛnɪs] **I** ***vt***. 吓,恐吓,胁迫;使有危险(*with*)。*My plan is ～d with failure*. 我的计划有失败的危险。— ***vi***. 进行威胁。**II** ***n***. 胁迫,威吓;威胁,危险。**-r** ***n***. 威胁者,恐吓者。**menacing** ***a***. 威胁的,险恶的。

men·ac·ing·ly [ˈmenəsiŋli; ˋmɛnɪsɪŋlɪ] ***ad***. 威胁地,恐吓着;险恶,逼近。

me·nad [ˈmiːnæd; ˋminæd] ***n***. = maenad.

men·a·di·one [ˌmenəˈdaiəun; ˏmenəˋdaɪon] ***n***. 【化、药】甲萘醌,维生素 K_3。

mé·nage [meˈnɑːʒ; meˋnɑʒ] ***n***. 〔F.〕家庭;家务(管理),

家政。

mé·nage *à trois* [menɑːʒɑ ˈtrwɑ; menɑʒɑ ˋtrwɑ]〔F.〕三人姘居〔夫妇和其一的姘头共同生活〕。

mé·nag·er·ie [miˈnædʒəri; məˋnædʒərɪ] *n*.〔F.〕动物园;供展览的一批动物。

men·ar·che [miˈnɑːki; məˋnɑrkɪ] *n*. 月经初期。

Men·cken [ˈmeŋkin, ˈmeŋkən; ˋmɛŋkɪn, ˋmɛŋkən] *n*. 门肯〔姓氏〕。

mend [mend; mɛnd] **I** *vt*. **1**. 修补,修理;织补,缝补。**2**. 改正,纠正;改进,改善;订正,改订。**3**. 加强;加快;加(火);增加…的引诱力[魔力、力量]。**4**. 治愈,使恢复健康。~ *a road* 修路。~ *a fire* 加(柴、炭给)火。~ *one's ways* 改正(不良)行为。~ *one's pace* 加快脚步。— *vi*. (事态过错、毛病等)变好,好转,改好,改善;痊愈。*It is never too late to* ~. 改过不嫌迟;过则勿惮改。***Least said, soonest ~ed***. 话少易正,少说为妙。~ ***matters*** [***the matter***] 改善情况。~ ***or end*** 要么改进要么停办;不改则废。***on the ~ing hand*** = ***on the*** ~. **II** *n*. 改进;修理;修理部份;痊愈。***on the*** ~ (病)将好;(情况)在好转。**-a·ble** *a*. 可修补的,可改善的,可改正的。

men·da·cious [menˈdeiʃəs; mɛnˋdeʃəs] *a*. 虚假的;捏造的;爱扯谎的。**-ly** *ad*.

men·dac·i·ty [menˈdæsiti; mɛnˋdæsətɪ] *n*. 虚假,谎话;捏造;撒谎;撒谎癖。

Men·del [ˈmendl; ˋmɛndəl], **Gregor Johann** 孟德尔〔1822—1884,奥地利遗传学家〕。~*'s Law* 孟德尔定律。

Men·de·ley·ev [ˌmendəˈleief; ˏmɛndəˋleef], **D.I.** 门捷列夫〔1834—1907,俄国化学家〕。~*'s Law*【化】门捷列夫定律,化学元素周期律。

men·de·le·vi·um [ˌmendəˈleviəm; ˏmɛndəˋlivɪəm] *n*.【化】钔。

Men·de·lian [menˈdiːljən; mɛnˋdilɪən] *a*., *n*. 孟德尔(定律)的;孟德尔学派的人。

Men·del·ism, Men·de·li·an·ism [ˈmendəlizəm, -ˈdiːliənizəm; ˋmɛndəlɪzəm, -ˋdilɪənɪzm] *n*.【生】孟德尔遗传学说;孟德尔主义。

Men·dels·sohn [ˈmendlsn; ˋmɛndlsn] *n*. **1**. 孟德尔森〔姓氏〕。**2**. ~**-Bartholdy, Felix** 孟德尔森〔1809—1847,德国作曲家〕。

mend·er [ˈmendə; ˋmɛndɚ] *n*. 修理者,改正者,修正者。

men·di·can·cy [ˈmendikənsi; ˋmɛndɪkənsɪ] *n*. 乞讨生活;行乞。

men·di·cant [ˈmendikənt; ˋmɛndɪkənt] **I** *a*. 行乞的,乞食的。**II** *n*. 乞丐,托钵僧。*a* ~ *friar* 托钵僧。~ *orders* 托钵僧团。

men·dic·i·ty [menˈdisiti; mɛnˋdɪsətɪ] *n*. = mendicancy.

mend·ing [ˈmendiŋ; ˋmɛndɪŋ] *n*. **1**. 织补,缝补;修理。**2**. 织补物。

men·folk(s) [ˈmenfəuk; ˋmɛnˏfok] *n*.〔口〕(家里或社会的)男人们。

M. Eng. = Master of Engineering 工程(学)硕士。

men·ha·den [menˈheidn; mɛnˋhedn] *n*.〔*sing*., *pl*.〕【鱼】(作肥料或炼油用的)鲱鱼,步鱼。

men·hir [ˈmenhiə; ˋmɛnhɪr] *n*.【考古】巨石,糙石巨柱〔史前遗物〕。

me·ni·al [ˈmiːnjəl; ˋminɪəl] **I** *a*. 奴性的,卑下的;奴仆的,仆人的。**II** *n*. 奴仆;卑下[奴性]的人。**-ly** *ad*. 奴仆似地,奴颜婢膝地。

Mé·nière's syndrome [**disease**] [meiˈnjeəz; meˋnjɛəz]【医】美尼尔氏症〔内耳功能失调,症状是晕眩、呕吐、耳鸣等〕。

me·nin·ges [miˈnindʒiːz; məˋnɪndʒiz] *n*. *pl*. (*sing*. ***me·ninx*** [ˈmiːniŋks; ˋminɪŋks])【解】脑[脊]膜。**-geal** [-dʒiəl; -dʒɪəl] *a*.

men·in·gi·tis [ˌmeninˈdʒaitis; ˏmɛnɪnˋdʒaɪtɪs] *n*.【医】脑膜炎。**-git·ic** *a*.

me·nin·go·cele [məˈniŋgəsiːl; məˋnɪŋgəsil] *n*.【医】脑(脊)膜突出。

me·nin·go·coc·cus [məniŋgəuˈkɔkəs; məˏnɪŋgəˋkɑkəs] *n*. (*pl*. ***-coc·ci*** [-ˈkɔksai; -ˋkɑksaɪ]) 脑膜炎双球菌。**-coc·cal** [-ˈkɔkl; -ˋkɑkl], **-coc·cic** [-ˈkɔksik; -ˋkɑksɪk] *a*.

me·ninx [ˈmiːniŋks; ˋminɪŋks] *n*. meninges 的单数。

me·nis·cus [miˈniskəs; məˋnɪskəs] *n*. (*pl*. *~es*, *-ci* [-sai; -saɪ]) 新月形(物);【物】凹凸透镜;【物】(由毛细管现象形成的)管内液面的凹[凸]面〔水呈凹形,水银呈凸形〕;【解】半月板。

me·no [ˈmenəu; ˋmeno] *ad*.〔It.〕【乐】更少,较少。

men-of-war [ˈmenəvˈwɔː; mɛnəvˋwɔr] *n*. man-of-war 的复数。

men·ol·o·gy [miˈnɔlədʒi; mɪˋnɑlədʒɪ] *n*. **1**. 月志。**2**.【希腊教】圣徒节日历;诸圣略传。

Me·nom·i·ni [məˈnɔmini; məˋnɑmɪnɪ] *n*. **1**. (*pl*. *-nis*, *-ni*) 梅诺米尼人〔原居于美国密执安,现居威斯康辛州的一支印第安人〕。**2**. 梅诺米尼语(= Menominee)。

me·no mos·so [ˈmeinəu ˈmɔsəu; ˋmeno ˋmoso]〔It.〕【乐】稍慢。

men·o·pause [ˈmenəpɔːz; ˋmɛnəˏpɔz] *n*.【医】停经;经绝(期)〔45—50 岁间〕。

men·o·rah [məˈnəurə, -ˈnɔːrə; məˋnorə, -ˋnɔrə] *n*. 大烛台,分枝烛台〔尤指犹太教七分枝烛台或犹太圣节用九分枝烛台〕。

men·or·rha·gia [ˌmenəˈreidʒiə; ˏmɛnəˋredʒɪə] *n*.【医】月经过多。

mens [menz; mɛnz] *n*. [L.] 心,精神。~ ***conscia recti*** [ˈmenz ˈkɔnʃiəˈrektai; ˋmɛnz ˋkɑnʃɪəˋrɛktaɪ] 坦然的心,自问无愧的心。~ ***sana in corpore sano*** [menz ˈseinə in ˈkɔːpəri ˈseinəu; mɛnz ˋsenə ɪn ˋkɔrpəri ˋseno] 有健全的身体才有健全的精神;健全的精神寓于健全的身体。

Men·sa [ˈmensə; ˋmɛnsə]【天】山案(星)座。

men·sal[1] [ˈmensəl; ˋmɛnsəl] *a*. 饭桌上(用)的。

men·sal[2] [ˈmensəl; ˋmɛnsəl] *a*. 每月的。

men·ses [ˈmensiːz; ˋmɛnsiz] *n*. *pl*. 月经。

Men·she·vik [ˈmenʃəvik; ˋmɛnʃəvɪk] **I** *n*.〔Russ.〕(*pl*. *~s*, ***-vi·ki*** [-viːki; -vikɪ]) 孟什维克,少数派。**II** *a*. 孟什维克的。

Men·she·vism [ˈmenʃivizəm; ˋmɛnʃɪvɪzəm] *n*. 孟什维主义。

Men·she·vist [ˈmenʃivist; ˋmɛnʃɪvɪst] **I** *n*. 孟什维主义者。**II** *a*. 孟什维主义的。

men·stru·al [ˈmenstruəl; ˋmɛnstruəl] *a*. **1**.【天】每月(一回)的。**2**. 月经的。~ **flow** 月经。~ **disorder** 月经不调。~ **extraction**【医】月经浸出法〔排空子宫以终止妊娠的一种方法〕。

men·stru·ate [ˈmenstrueit; ˋmɛnstruˏet] *vi*. 来月经,行经。

men·stru·a·tion [ˌmenstruˈeiʃən; ˏmɛnstruˋeʃən] *n*. 月经;月经期间。*irregular* ~ 月经不调。

men·stru·ous [ˈmenstruəs; ˋmɛnstruəs] *a*. (有)月经的;行经的。

men·stru·um [ˈmenstruəm; ˋmɛnstruəm] (*pl*. *~s*, ***-tru·a*** [-struə; -struə]) *n*. 溶媒,溶剂。

men·sur·a·ble [ˈmenʃurəbl; ˋmɛnʃurəbl] *a*. **1**. 可度量的,可测量的。**2**.【乐】定量的;有固定节奏的。**-bil·i·ty** *n*. 可测性。

men·su·ral [ˈmenʃurəl; ˋmɛnʃurəl] *a*. **1**. 关于度量的;量的。**2**.【乐】有定律的。

men·su·ra·tion [ˌmensjuəˈreiʃən; ˏmɛnʃəˋreʃən] *n*. 测定,测量;【数】测定法,求积法;【物】量法。

mens·wear [ˈmenzˌweə; ˋmɛnzˏwɛr] *n*. 男人服装;男子

M

服饰用品(= men's wear)。

-ment *suf*. 前接动词[〔罕〕形容词]以形成表示动作、结果、状态等的名词，例：atone*ment*；employ*ment*；achieve*ment*.

men·tal[1] [ˈmentl; ˋmɛntl̩] **I** *a*. **1.** 内心的；精神的，思想的；心理的 (*opp*. corporal)。**2.** 智慧的，智[脑]力的。**3.** 闷在心里的，暗自思考的。**4.** 〔口〕精神病的；意志薄弱的，愚笨的。*a* ～ *worker* 脑力劳动者。～ *disorder* [*derangement*] 精神错乱。～ *culture* 精神修养。～ *age* 智力年龄。～ *deficiency* 智力缺陷。～ *faculties* 智力，智能。*a* ～ *test* 智力测验。～ *reservation* 内心保留〔对某事有看法但不说出来〕。～ *arithmetic* 心算。*a* ～ *home* 精神病院。*a* ～ *case* [*patient*] 精神病患者。*a* ～ *specialist* 精神病专科医生。**II** *n*. 〔口〕精神病；精神病患者。***make a* ～ *note of*** 记住。～ **healing** 【医】心理治疗，精神治疗。～ **retardation** 智力缺陷，精神薄弱，智力迟钝。～ **telepathy** 心电感应。**-ly** *ad*. 在心里，精神上，智力上。

men·tal[2] [ˈmentl; ˋmɛntl̩] *a*. 【解】颚的，颏的。

men·tal·ism [ˈmentlizəm; ˋmɛntl̩ɪzəm] *n*. 【哲，心】心灵主义。**-tal·is·tic** *a*. **-is·ti·cal·ly** *ad*.

men·tal·ist [ˈmentlist; ˋmɛntl̩ɪst] *n*. **1.** 【哲、心】心灵主义者。**2.** 具有心灵感应能力者(自称可洞察他人心思或把自己思想传给他人的人)。

men·tal·i·ty [menˈtæliti; mɛnˋtælətɪ] *n*. 脑力，智力；精神；心理，意识；思想。

men·ta·tion [menˈteiʃən; mɛnˋteʃən] *n*. 精神[心理]作用；心理活动；思想。

Men·tha [ˈmenθə; ˋmɛnθə] *n*. 【植】薄荷属。

men·tha·ceous [menˈθeiʃəs; mɛnˋθeʃəs] *a*. 【植】薄荷科的，唇形科的。

men·thene [ˈmenθiːn; ˋmɛnθin] *n*. 【化】萜烯。

men·thol [ˈmenθɔl; ˋmɛnθol] *n*. 【化】薄荷醇，萜醇。*a* ～ *pencil* 薄荷锭。

men·tho·lat·ed [ˈmenθəleitid; ˋmɛnθəˏletɪd] *a*. 【化】薄荷醇的；薄荷醇处理的；薄荷醇浸的。

men·tion [ˈmenʃən; ˋmɛnʃən] **I** *vt*. **1.** 说起，讲到，谈到，提到，写到；记载。**2.** 提述；提名表扬。*Don't* ～ *it*. 不要客气，哪儿的话。***not to*** ～… 不用说，更不必说。**(*not*) *worth* ～*ing*** (不)值得一说[一提]。***without*** ～**-*ing*** 更不必说了。**II** *n*. 说到，提及；提述；提名表扬。*an honourable* ～ 表扬。***at the* ～ *of*** 当说到…，一说到…。***make* ～ *of*** 说到，写到，提到 (*He made no* ～ *of it*. 他没有提到那件事。*M- was made of it*. 曾提到那件事)。***make no* ～ *of*** 不提，不谈；不写。**-a·ble** *a*. 可以提起的；值得一提的。

(-)men·tioned *comb*. *f*. 说到的，提到的：*above-*～ 上述。*before-*～ 前述。

men·tor [ˈmentɔː; ˋmɛntɚ] **I** *n*. **1.** 辅导教师；指导人；(美国足球)教练。**2.** 〔M-〕曼托尔〔希腊史诗《奥德赛》中奥德修斯的忠诚朋友，奥德修斯之子的良师〕。**II** *vt*. 指导，做…的良师。

men·u [ˈmenjuː; ˋmɛnju] *n*. (*pl*. ～*s*) **1.** 菜单。**2.** 餐，饭菜；菜肴。*We had an admirable* ～. 我们吃了一顿美餐。

Men·u·hin [ˈmenjuin, ˈmenu*h*in; ˋmɛnjuɪn, ˋmɛnu*h*ɪn] *n*. 梅纽因〔姓氏〕。

MEO = medium earth orbit 【宇航】中间地球轨道〔介于近地轨道和远地轨道之间〕。

me·ow [mjuː, mjau; mju, mɪˋau] **I** *vi*. **1.** (猫)咪咪地叫。**2.** 吐恶言毒语；〔美俚〕发牢骚。**II** *n*. **1.** 猫叫声。**2.** 怨言。

me·per·i·dine [məˈperidiːn; məˋpɛrədin] *n*. 【药】哌替啶〔用作镇静剂和止痛药〕。

Me·ph·is·to·phe·le·an, -li·an [ˌmefistəˈfiːliən, -ljən; ˏmɛfɪstəˋfilɪən, -ljən] *a*. 靡菲斯特 (Mephistopheles) (似)的；狡猾刻毒的；恶魔般的。

Meph·is·toph·e·les [ˌmefisˈtɔfiliːz; ˏmɛfəˋstɑfəˏliz] *n*. 靡菲斯特〔歌德 (Goethe) 所作《浮士德》中的恶魔〕；魔鬼般的人；狡猾刻毒的人。

me·phit·ic, me·phit·i·cal [meˈfitik(əl); mɛˋfɪtɪk(əl)] *a*. 有毒的；有恶臭的；毒气的。*mephitic air* 二氧化碳气。

me·phi·tis [meˈfaitis; mɛˋfaɪtɪs] *n*. 臭气；毒气；恶臭。

me·pro·ba·mate [məˈprəubəmeit; məˋprobəmet] *n*. 【药】安宁，氨甲丙二酯〔商品名称为眠尔通〕。

meq. = milliequivalent.

mer. = meridian; meridional.

mer·bro·min [məˈbrəumin; mɚˋbromɪn] *n*. 汞溴红，红汞。

merc [məːk; mɝk] *n*. 〔口〕外国雇佣兵 (= mercenary)。

mer·can·tile [ˈməːkəntail; ˋmɝkənˏtaɪl] *a*. **1.** 商人的，贸易的，商业的。**2.** 【经】重商主义的。*a* ～ *paper* 商业票据。*a* ～ *firm* 商店。*the* ～ *law* 商法。*the* ～ *marine* (全国)商船；(一国的)商船船员。*the* ～ *system* [*doctrine*, *theory*] 重商制度[主义]。

mer·can·til·ism [ˈməːkəntailizəm; ˋmɝkənˏtaɪlɪzəm] *n*. **1.** 重商主义。**2.** 商人性格；商业本位；商业理论[活动]；商用术语。

mer·can·til·ist [ˈməːkəntailist; ˋmɝkənˏtaɪlɪst] *n*. 重商主义者。

mer·cap·tan [məˈkæptæn; mɚˋkæptæn] *n*. 【化】硫醇。

mer·cap·tide [məˈkæptaid; mɚˋkæptaɪd] *n*. 【化】硫醇盐。

mer·cap·to [məˈkæptəu; mɚˋkæpto] *a*. 【化】巯基，氢硫基。

Mer·ca·tor [məˈkeitɔː; mɚˋketɚ], **G.** 麦卡托〔1512—1594，佛兰德 (Flanders) 的地理学家，(地图)制图学家〕。～**'s chart** 麦卡托地图。～**'s projection** 麦卡托投影图法。

Mer·ce·des [ˈməːsidiːz; ˋmɝsɪdiz] *n*. 默西迪丝〔女子名〕。

mer·ce·na·ry [ˈməːsinəri; ˋmɝsn̩ˏɛrɪ] **I** *a*. 图利的，为了金钱工作的；被雇佣的。～ *attitude* 雇佣观念。**II** *n*. (外国的)雇佣兵(= ～ troops)。

mer·cer [ˈməːsə; ˋmɝsɚ] *n*. 〔英〕布商，(尤指)绸缎商人。

mer·cer·i·za·tion [ˌməːsəraiˈzeiʃən; ˏmɝsəraɪˋzeʃən] *n*. 碱液处理，丝光处理[工艺]；碱化，浸碱作用。

mer·cer·ize [ˈməːsəraiz; ˋmɝsəˏraɪz] *vt*. 对…施行碱液处理[丝光处理]。～*d cotton* 府绸，丝光棉布。

mer·cer·y [ˈməːsəri; ˋmɝsərɪ] *n*. 〔英〕**1.** 绸布店；绸布业。**2.** 绸布类货物。

mer·chan·dise [ˈməːtʃəndaiz; ˋmɝtʃənˏdaɪz] **I** *n*. 〔集合词〕商品，货；〔古〕商业。*general* ～ 杂货。*the M-Marks Act* 〔英〕商标法。**II** *vi*. 〔美〕做买卖；做生意。— *vt*. 〔美〕买卖；推销。**-dis·er** *n*. 商人。

mer·chant [ˈməːtʃənt; ˋmɝtʃənt] **I** *n*. **1.** 商人；〔英〕批发商；(尤指)贸易商。**2.** 〔美〕零售商〔英国仅用于 *a coal* ～，*a wine* ～〕。**3.** 〔蔑〕家伙，人。**4.** …狂。*a speed* ～ 乱用高速开汽车的人。*a* ～ *of death* 死亡商人〔指军火制造商〕。**II** *a*. 商人的；商业的。*the* ～ *marine* [*service*] (全国)商船；(一国)商船船员。*a* ～ *ship* [*vessel*] 商船。*a* ～ *bank* 〔英〕证券银行；〔美〕投资银行。*a* ～ *captain* (商船的)船长；船主。*a* ～ *prince* 豪商。*the M- Queen* (意大利的)威尼斯市。*a* ～ *seaman* (商船的)船员。*the M- Shipping Act* 〔英〕商船条例。*a* ～ *tailor* 兼售衣料的裁缝店。**-able** *a*. 可买卖的，有销路的。**-like** *a*. 像商人的。**-man** (*pl*. **-men**) 货船，商船；〔古〕商人。

Mer·cia [ˈməːʃə; ˋmɝʃə] *n*. 莫西亚〔原英格兰中部和南部的一个盎格鲁—撒克逊王国〕。

Mer·cian [ˈməːʃən; ˋmɝʃɪən] **I** *a*. 莫西亚的；莫西亚人的；莫西亚方言的。**II** *n*. **1.** 莫西亚人。**2.** 莫西亚古英语方言。**3.** 〔偶指〕(由莫西亚方言演变而来的)中世纪英语方言。

mer·ci·ful [ˈməːsifu l; ˋmɝsɪfəl] ***a*.** 仁慈的,温和的;(情形)良好的,顺利的;(处罚)宽大的。**-ly** ***ad*.** **-ness** ***n*.**

mer·ci·less [ˈməːsilis; ˋmɝsɪlɪs] ***a*.** 冷酷无情的,狠心的,残忍的。~ *blows* 无情打击。**-ly** ***ad*.** **-ness** ***n*.**

mer·cu·rate [ˈməːkjureit; ˋmɝkjəˏret] **I** ***vt*.** 【化】使汞化,用汞处理。**II** ***n*.** 汞化产物。

mer·cu·ri·al [məːˈkjuəriəl; mɝˋkjʊrɪəl] **I** ***a*.** **1.** 〔M-〕墨丘利 (Mercury) 神的;【天】水星的。**2.** 轻松的,活泼的;有机智的;三心二意的。**3.** 雄辩的;狡诈的;贼性的。**4.** 水银的,含水银的,汞的。~ *gaiety* 活泼开朗。~ *exchange rates* 变动不定的兑换率。*a* ~ *barometer* 水银气压计。*a* ~ *column* 水银柱。*a* ~ *gauge* [*barometer*] 水银气压计。~ *ointment* 含汞药膏。~ *poisoning* 水银[汞]中毒。~ *treatment* 水银疗法。**II** ***n*.** 水银剂,汞制剂。**-ly** ***ad*.** **-ism** ***n*.** 水银[汞]中毒。

mer·cu·ri·al·i·ty [ˌməːkjuəriˈæliti;ˏmɝkjʊrɪˋælətɪ] ***n*.** 敏捷,活泼;易变,三心二意;多机智。

mer·cu·ri·al·ize [məːˈkjuəriəlaiz; mɝˋkjʊrɪəˏlaɪz] ***vt*.** **1.** 用水银处理;【医】对…施行汞剂疗法。**2.** 使活泼[轻松、敏捷、愉快]。

Mer·cu·ri·an [məːˈkjuəriən; mɝˋkjʊrɪən] ***a*.** 水星的;墨丘利 (Mercury) 神的。

mer·cu·ric [məːˈkjuərik; mɝˋkjʊrɪk] ***a*.** 水银的,含水银的;【化】汞的;含二价汞的。~ **chloride** 氯化汞,升汞。~ **oxide** 【化】氧化汞;一氧化汞;三仙丹。

mer·cu·rize [ˈməːkjuraiz; ˋmɝkjʊraɪz] ***vt*.** 【化】= mercurate.

Mer·cu·ro·chrome [məˈkjuərəkrəum; mɝˋkjʊrəˏkrom] ***n*.** **1.** 【药】汞溴红,红汞〔局部抗菌药〕。**2.** 〔m-〕红药水〔汞溴红的水溶液〕。

mer·cu·rous [ˈməːkjurəs; mɝˋkjʊrəs] ***a*.** 【化】亚汞的;含一价汞的。~ *chloride* 氯化亚汞,甘汞。

mer·cu·ry [ˈməːkjuri; ˋmɝkjərɪ] ***n*.** **1.** 【化】汞,水银。**2.** 水银柱;水银剂;温度表;晴雨表。**3.** 活气,活泼;精神,元气。**4.** 〔M-〕【罗神】墨丘利〔诸神的使神;工匠、盗贼等的保护神〕;【天】水星。**5.** 〔谑〕使者;〔M-〕信使;报导者〔常用作报纸、杂志名〕。**6.** 【美体】赛跑家,径赛选手。**7.** 【植】山靛。*The* ~ *is rising*. 温度正在上升;市况正在好转;情绪好起来,高兴起来。*He has no* ~ *in him*. 他没有精神。~ **air pump** 汞(汽)泵〔排气用〕。~ **arc** 【电】汞弧。~**-arc lamp** 水银弧光灯。~ **barometer** [**thermometer**] 水银晴雨[温度]表。~ **chloride** **1.** 氯化汞;升汞 (= mercuric chloride)。**2.** 甘汞;氯化亚汞 (= calomel)。~**-vapour lamp** 水银灯。~**-vapour rectifier** 汞汽[水银]整流器。

mer·cy [ˈməːsi; ˋmɝsɪ] ***n*.** **1.** 仁慈;怜悯;宽恕;恩惠。**2.** 幸运;侥幸;〔美口〕感谢。*the heart of the Goddess of Mercy* 菩萨心肠。*Mercy*! = *Mercy* (*up*) *on us*! 啊呀! 我的天哪! *That is a* ~. 那真是幸运。***at the*** ~ ***of*** 完全受…支配,任由…摆布,在…掌握中。***for*** ~ = ***for*** ~***'s sake***! 请大发慈悲! 请可怜可怜! 求求您! ***have*** ~ (***up***) ***on*** = ***show*** ~ ***to*** 可怜…,怜悯。***leave to the tender mercies of*** 〔反〕任由…摆布,使吃…的苦头 (*He was left to the tender mercies of the landlord*. 他大受地主的虐待)。***What a*** ~ ***that***...! 幸好,幸亏(*What a* ~ [*It is a* ~] *that you did not go*! 幸亏你没去)。***without*** ~ 狠着心肠,毫不容情地,残忍地。~ **killing** 减少痛苦的处决;无痛苦致死术。(= euthanasia)。~ **seat** 【宗】约柜上的金板;上帝的御座。

mere[1] [miə; mɪr] ***a*.** **1.** 单单的,只,不过。**2.** 全然的;纯粹的。*a* ~ *child* 仅仅是个孩子。*a* ~ *pretext* 不过(是)托辞〔口实〕。*That is the merest folly*. 那真糊涂透了。*of* ~ *motion* 【法】自动的。

mere[2] [miə; mɪr] ***n*.** 〔诗、方〕池沼。

mere[3] [miə; mɪr] ***n*.** 〔英〕边境(线)。

Mer·e·dith [ˈmeridiθ; ˋmɛrədɪθ] ***n*.** 梅雷迪思〔男子名〕。

mere·ly [ˈmiəli; ˋmɪrlɪ] ***ad*.** 单;只;纯粹;全然。~ *a matter of form* 完全是一个形式问题。***not*** ~ ... ***but also*** 不仅…而且 (*She was not* ~ *beautiful, but* (*also*) *talented*. 她不仅长得美,而且有才干)。

mer·en·gue [məˈreŋgei; məˋrɛŋge] ***n*.** **1.** 梅伦格舞〔海地和多米尼加的一种交际舞〕。**2.** 梅伦格舞曲。

mer·e·tri·cious [ˌmeriˈtriʃəs; ˏmɛrəˋtrɪʃəs] ***a*.** **1.** 〔古〕娼妓(一样)的。**2.** (装饰、文体等)耀眼的;俗不可耐的,俗气的。**3.** (论据等)虚夸的。**-ly** ***ad*.**

mer·e·trix [ˈmeritriks; ˋmɛrɪtrɪks] ***n*.** (*pl*. **meretrices** [-traisiːz; -traɪsiz]) 娼妓。

mer·gan·ser [məːˈgænsə; mɝˋgænsɚ] ***n*.** (*pl*. ~*s*, 〔集合词〕~)【鸟】秋沙鸭。

merge [məːdʒ; mɝdʒ] ***vt*.** 吞没,吸收;使消失(在…中) (*in*; *into*);【法】合并(公司等)使并入,使结合,融合 (*into*; *with*)。*All fear was* ~*d in curiosity*. 在好奇心驱使下忘了一切恐怖。— ***vi*.** 被吞没,被吸收,收入,消没在;合并,并入。*The twilight* ~*d into darkness*. 薄暮已消失在黑暗之中。~ *with the masses* 同群众打成一片。

mer·gee [ˈməːdʒiː; ˋmɝdʒi] ***n*.** 合并的一方。

mer·ged [məːdʒd; mɝdʒd] ***a*.** 〔美俚〕结了婚的。

mer·gence [ˈməːdʒəns; ˋmɝdʒəns] ***n*.** 没入,消失;合并,结合,融合。

merg·er [ˈməːdʒə; ˋmɝdʒɚ] ***n*.** (企业等的)合并,并吞;结合;合并者(= mergence);【法】托拉斯(= trust)。**-ite** ***n*.** 赞成合并的人。

me·rid·i·an [məˈridiən; məˋrɪdɪən] **I** ***n*.** **1.** 【天】子午圈[线];正午。**2.** 顶点,绝顶;全盛期。*the prime* [*first*] ~ 本初子午线,格林尼治子午线。*the* ~ *of life* 壮年。**II** ***a*.** 子午圈的;正午的;顶点的,绝顶的;全盛时期的。***be calculated to*** [***for***] ***the*** ~ ***of*** 为了适合…的兴趣[能力、习惯等]。~ **altitude** 中天高度。~ **passage** [**transit**] 中天。~ **sun** 正午的太阳。

me·rid·io·nal [məˈridiənl; məˋrɪdɪənl] **I** ***a*.** **1.** 子午圈[线]的;最高的,全盛的。**2.** 南欧(人)的,法国南部人的;南方的。**II** ***n*.** 南欧人,(尤指)法国南部人。

me·ringue [məˈræŋ; məˋræŋ] ***n*.** **1.** (覆盖在糕、饼上烤熟的)蛋白糖霜。**2.** (盛冰淇淋、水果的)蛋白酥皮筒[卷];蛋白甜饼。

me·ri·no [məˈriːnəu; məˋrino] ***n*.** (*pl*. ~*s*) (原产西班牙的)美利奴绵羊;美利奴羊毛;美利奴呢(衣);美利奴绒线。

mer·i·stem [ˈmeristem; ˋmɛrɪˏstɛm] ***n*.** 【植】分生组织。

mer·it [ˈmerit; ˋmɛrɪt] **I** ***n*.** **1.** 价值;美点,长处,优点。**2.** 〔常 *pl*.〕功劳,功绩,功勋,成就;良好的品质[事实、行为];(学校里的)记功分[罚分之对]。**3.** 〔常 *pl*.〕功过,功罪。**4.** 〔*pl*.〕【法】法律意义[根据];是非曲直。*a man of* ~ 有长处的人,有功劳的人。*a certificate of* ~ 奖状。*His teacher gave him ten* ~*s*. 老师给他记了十个功分。*the* ~*s and demerits of* …的优点和缺点;…的功过[得失]。***according to one's*** ~***s*** 按价值,按资质。***make a*** ~ ***of*** = ***take*** ~ ***to oneself for*** 把…当做自己的功劳宣传,自夸…是自己的功劳。***on one's own*** ~***s*** 靠实力,靠真价。***on the*** ~***s of the case*** 按事件的是非曲直。***the order of*** [***for***] ***M-*** 〔英〕殊勋勋章。**II** ***vt*.** 有…的价值,值得…;应受;因功而得。~ *reward* 应该受奖。~ **roll** 成绩表,赏罚表。~ **system** (量才录用或提升的)人才制度。

mer·i·toc·ra·cy [ˌmeriˈtɔkrəsi;ˏmɛrəˋtɑkrəsɪ] ***n*.** **1.** 学术界名流。**2.** 英才教育。**3.** 能人统治。**-crat** ***n*.** 能人统治集团的一员。**-crat·ic** ***a*.**

mer·i·to·ri·ous [ˌmeriˈtɔːriəs; ˏmɛrəˋtorɪəs] ***a*.** 有功勋的,有功劳的;有价值的;可称赞的;值得奖励的。*a* ~ *service medal* 勋绩奖章。**-ly** ***ad*.** 可赞美。**-ness** ***n*.**

merl(e) [məːl; mɝl] ***n*.** 〔Scot.〕【鸟】〔古〕= blackbird.

Mer·lin, Mer·lyn [ˈməːlin; ˋmɝlɪn] *n*. 1. 默林〔男子名〕。2. 亚瑟王 (King Arthur)〔传说中的预言家,魔术师〕。3. 〔m-〕【鸟】欧洲鸽鹰,灰背隼。

mer·lon [ˈməːlən; ˋmɝlən] *n*. (筑城)城齿。

mer·maid [ˈməːmeid; ˋmɝˏmed] *n*. (传说中的)美人鱼;美人鱼徽章;〔美〕女游泳健将。

mer·man [ˈməːmæn; ˋmɝˏmæn] *n*. (传说中的)雄性人鱼;〔美〕男子游泳健将。

mero- *comb.f*. 一部分;部分的。

mer·o·blast [ˈmerəblæst; ˋmɛrəˏblæst] *n*. 【生】不全裂卵。

mer·o·blas·tic [ˌmerəˈblæstik; ˏmɛrəˋblæstɪk] *a*. 【遗传】不全裂卵的。**-al·ly** *ad*.

mer·o·crine [ˈmerəkrin, -krain, -kriːn; ˋmɛrəkrɪn, -kraɪn, -krin] *a*. 局泌的,局部分泌腺的。

me·rog·o·ny [məˈrɔgəni; məˋrɑgənɪ] *n*. 【生】无核卵发育,卵片发育。

mer·o·hed·ral [ˌmerəˈhedrəl; ˏmɛrəˋhɛdrəl] *a*. (水晶)缺面体的。

mer·o·mor·phic [ˌmerəˈmɔːfik; ˏmɛrəˋmɔrfɪk] *a*. 【数】半纯的,有理型的,逊纯的。

mer·o·plank·ton [ˌmerəˈplæŋktən; ˏmɛrəˋplæŋktən] *n*. 【动】季节浮游生物。

-merous *suf*. 【植】分成许多部分的: penta*merous* = 5-merous. 五基数的。

mer·o·zo·ite [ˌmerəˈzəuait; ˏmɛrəˋzoaɪt] *n*. 【生】裂殖子,裂体性芽胞。

mer·ri·ly [ˈmerili; ˋmɛrɪlɪ] *ad*. 快乐地,愉快地,高兴地。

Mer·ri·mac [ˈmeriˌmæk; ˋmɛrɪˏmæk] *n*. 1. 梅里麦克〔美国南北战争时南部联邦的一艘装甲舰名〕。2. 美国梅里麦克河(= Merrimack)。

mer·ri·ment [ˈmerimənt; ˋmɛrɪmənt] *n*. 欢乐。

mer·ri·ness [ˈmerinis; ˋmɛrɪnɪs] *n*. 愉快,快活。

Mer·ritt [ˈmerit; ˋmɛrɪt] *n*. 梅里特〔姓氏,男子名〕。

Mer·ry [ˈmeri; ˋmɛrɪ] *n*. 梅丽〔女子名〕。

mer·ry [ˈmeri; ˋmɛrɪ] *a*. (*-ri·er*; *-ri·est*) 1. 愉快的,快活的;有趣的;生动的;轻快的,激烈的。2. 〔口〕微醉的。***as ~ as a cricket*** [***a grig***, ***a lark***] 非常快活。***make ~*** 作乐,宴乐,逗乐。***make ~ over*** 嘲弄,挖苦。***~ men*** (已往骑士或土匪首领的)随从,侍从。***~ men of May*** 落潮时的危险潮流。**~-andrew** 丑角,滑稽演员;笨人。**~ dancers** 北极光。**~-go-down** 〔口〕强烈的啤酒。**~-go-round** 旋转木马;走马灯;使人忙得团团转的事务;〔口〕蛛网式道路;〔美俚〕(对决定事项或接见客人的)故意拖延 (*get the ~-go-round* 〔美俚〕苦等,久等)。**~make** *vi*. 〔古〕快快活活玩,欢乐。**~making** 欢乐;喝酒作乐,狂欢。**~-run-round** 〔美〕= merry-go-round. **~thought** (鸟胸的)叉骨(= wishbone)。

mersh [məːʃ; mɝʃ] *a*. 〔俚〕唯利是图的,牟取暴利的。

Mer·ton [ˈməːtn; ˋmɝtn̩] *n*. 默顿〔姓氏〕。

Mer·vin [ˈməːvin; ˋmɝvɪn] *n*. 默文〔男子名, Marvin 的异体〕。

me·sa [ˈmeisə; ˋmesə] *n*. 1. 〔美〕台地,方山。2. 【无】台式晶体管。

mé·sal·liance [meiˈzæliəns; meˋzæliɛns] *n*. 〔F.〕和身份低的人缔结的婚姻。

mes·arch [ˈmezɑːk, mes-; ˋmɛzɑk, mɛs-] *a*. 1. 【植】中始式的。2. 【生态】中生演替的。

mes·cal [mesˈkæl; mɛsˋkæl] *n*. 1. (墨西哥人爱喝的)龙舌兰酒。2. (其汁能制酒的)龙舌兰。3. 【植】球顶仙人鞭〔其球状茎头叫~ button〕。

mes·ca·line [ˌmeskəliːn, -lin; ˋmɛskəlin, -lɪn] *n*. 【化】墨斯卡灵〔一种生物碱,用做幻觉剂〕。

mes·dames [meiˈdæm; meˋdɑm] 〔F.〕 *madame* 的复数。

mes·de·moi·selles [ˌmeidəmwɑːˈzel; ˏmɛdmwaˋzɛl] 〔F.〕 *mademoiselle* 的复数。

me·seems [mi(ː)ˈsiːmz; miˋsimz] *vi*. (*p*. ***-seemed***) 〔古〕据我想,我以为。

mes·em·bri·an·the·mum [miˌzembriˈænθiməm; mɛsˏɛmbrɪˋænθɪməm] *n*. 【植】松叶菊;日中花。

mes·en·ceph·a·lon [ˌmesenˈsefəlɔn; ˏmɛsɛnˋsɛfəˏlɑn] *n*. 【解】中脑。

me·sen·chy·ma [miˈzeŋkimə; mɛsˋɛŋkəmə] *n*. = mesenchyme.

mes·en·chyme [ˈmesəŋkaim, ˈmez-; ˋmɛsɛŋkaɪm, ˋmɛz-] *n*. 【遗传】间(充)质。**-chy·mal** [mezˈeŋkaiməl, mez-; mɛzˋɛŋkaɪməl, mɛz-] *a*.

mes·en·ter·i·tis [ˌmezentiˈraitis, mes-; ˏmɛsɛntəˋraɪtɪs, mɛz-] *n*. 【医】肠系膜炎。

mes·en·ter·on [meˈzentərɔn, mes-; mɛsˋɛntərɑn, mɛs-] *n*. (*pl*. *-ter·a* [-ə;-ə]) 中肠(= midgut)。**-ic** *a*.

mes·en·te·ry [ˈmesəntəri; ˋmɛsn̩ˏtɛrɪ] *n*. 【解】肠系膜,隔膜。

mesh [meʃ; mɛʃ] **I** *n*. 1. 网眼;筛孔;〔*pl*.〕网,网状物,网络;网丝;铜纱;〔*pl*.〕法网。2. 【机】(齿轮的)啮合。*a 60 ~ screen* (每英寸有)60 孔的筛子。*a net with half-inch ~es* 半英寸孔的网。**II** *vt*. 1. 用网捕;使缠住。2. 【机】(使)咬合,钩住 (*with*)。3. 编[织]网;使成网状。*~ a net* 编网。— *vi*. 1. 被网住,落网。2. 紧密配合;【机】互相啮合 (*with*)。***be caught in ~es of the law*** 陷入法网。***be in ~*** (齿轮)互相咬住。~ **knot** 单索花(= sheet bend)。~**work** 网状物,网。

Mesh·ed [ˈmeʃed, Am, məˈʃed; ˋmɛʃɛd, məˋʃɛd] *n*. 麦什德(即 Mashhad 马什哈德)〔伊朗城市〕。

me·shu·ga, me·shug·ga, me·shu·gah [məˈʃugə; məˋʃʊgə] *a*. 〔俚〕疯狂的,发狂的,精神病的。

me·si·al [ˈmiːzjəl, ˈmezjəl; ˋmizɪəl, ˋmɛzɪəl] *a*. 中央的,中间的,中部的 (*opp*. lateral)。*the ~ plane* (动物体的)正中面。

me·sic [ˈmezik, ˈmes-, ˈmiːzik, -sik; ˋmɛzɪk, ˋmɛs-, ˋmizɪk, -sɪk] *a*. 1. 【植】需中湿水分的。2. 【生态】中湿的。3. 【物】介子的;与介子有关的。

me·sit·y·lene [miˈsitəliːn; məˋsɪtəlin] *n*. 【化】莱。

mes·jid [ˈmesdʒid; ˋmɛsdʒɪd] *n*. 伊斯兰教寺院(= masjid)。

mes·mer·ic [mezˈmerik; mɛsˋmɛrɪk] *a*. 催眠(术)的;使人迷惑的;难以抗拒的。**-i·cal·ly** *ad*.

mes·mer·ism [ˈmezmərizəm; ˋmɛsməˏrɪzəm] *n*. 催眠术;催眠状态;催眠力;难以抗拒的魅力。**-mer·ist** *n*. 催眠术师。

mes·mer·i·za·tion [ˌmezməraiˈzeiʃən; ˋmɛsməraɪˋzeʃən] *n*. 施催眠术;催眠状态。

mes·mer·ize [ˈmezməraiz; ˋmɛsməˏraɪz] *vt*. 给…施行催眠术;迷惑;感化。**-r** *n*. 催眠者。

mesn·al·ty [ˈmiːnəlti; ˋminəltɪ] *n*. 1. (英国古代)中层领主的土地。2. 中层领主的(身份)。

mesne [miːn; min] *a*. 【法】中间的。*the ~ process* (诉讼的)中间手续[程序]。*the ~ profits* 中间收益。~ **lord** 中层封建领主。

mes·o- *comb.f*. 中央,中间,中,适: *meso*economic 中介经济的。

mes·o·ben·thos [ˌmesəuˈbenθɔs, ˌmez-; ˏmɛsəˋbɛnθɑs, ˏmɛz-] *n*. 深海生物。

mes·o·blast [ˈmesəublɑːst; ˋmɛsəˏblæst] *n*. 【生】= mesoderm.

mes·o·carp [ˈmesəkɑːp; ˋmɛsəˏkɑrp] *n*. 【植】中果皮。

mes·o·ce·phal·ic [ˌmesəusiˈfælik, ˌmez-; ˏmɛsosəˋfælɪk, ˏmɛz-] *a*. 【解】中等头型的;头颅指数在 76—80.9之间的头颅的(= mesocephalous)。**-ceph·a·ly** [-ˈsefəli; -ˋsɛfəlɪ] *n*.

meso·chro·ic [ˌmesəuˈkrəuik, ˌmez-; ˏmɛsoˋkroɪk, ˌmɛz-] *a*. 肤色在深浅之间的。

M

mes·o·cra·ni·al [ˌmesəuˈkreiniəl, ˌmez-; ˏmɛso-ˋkrenɪəl, ˏmɛz-] *a*. 具中颅的〔颅指数在 76—80.9 之间〕(= mesocranic)。**-cra·ny** [-ˌkreini; -ˏkrenɪ] *n*.

mes·o·crat·ic [ˌmesəuˈkrætik, ˌmez-; ˏmɛsəˋkrætɪk, ˏmɛz-] *a*.【矿】中色的;包含 30—60%的矿物的。

mes·o·derm [ˈmesədə:m; ˋmɛsəˏdɝm] *n*.【生】中胚层。

mes·o·gas·tri·um [ˌmesəuˈgæstriəm, ˌmez-; ˏmɛsə-ˋgæstrɪəm, ˏmɛz-] *n*. (*pl*. **-tri·a** [-ə; -ə])【解】1. 胃系膜。2. 中腹部。**-gas·tric** *a*.

mes·o·gle·a, mes·o·gloe·s [ˌmesəuˈgliə, ˌmez-; ˏmɛsə-ˋglɪə, ˏmɛz-] *n*.【解】中胶层。**-gle·al, -gloe·al** *a*.

mes·o·lim·ni·on [ˌmesəuˈlimniən, ˌmez-; ˏmɛsə-ˋlɪmnɪən, ˏmɛz-] *n*. 温水层(= thermocline)。

Mes·o·lith·ic [ˌmesəuˈliθik, ˌmez-; ˏmɛsəˋlɪθɪk, ˏmɛz-] *a*. 中石器时代的。

me·som·er·ism [miˈsɔmərizəm; mɪˋsɑmərɪzəm] *n*. 1.【化】中介(现象);稳[缓]变异构(现象)。2.【无】共振。

mes·on [ˈmesɔn, ˈmi:s-; ˋmɛsɑn, ˋmis-] *n*. 1.【物】介子,重电子。2.【动】正中面。~ **factory** 介子工厂〔能产生强烈介子射线以探索原子核的粒子加速器〕。**-ic** *a*.

mes·o·neph·ros [ˌmesəuˈnefrɔs, ˌmez-; ˏmɛsəˋnɛfrɑs, ˏmɛz-] *n*.【解】中肾。**-neph·ric** *a*.

mes·o·ni·um [miˈsəunjəm; mɪˋsonɪəm] *n*.【物】介子素。

mes·o·pause [ˈmesəˌpɔ:z, ˈmez-; ˋmɛsəˏpɔz, ˋmɛz-] *n*.【气】中间层顶。

mes·o·pe·lag·ic [ˌmesəupəˈlædʒik; ˏmɛsəpəˋlædʒɪk] *a*. 海洋中层的〔深约 650—3000 英尺〕。

mes·o·phyll [ˈmesəfil; ˋmɛsəˏfɪl] *n*.【植】叶肉,含绿组织,中形叶。

mes·o·phyl·lic [ˌmesəuˈfilik, ˌmez-; ˏmɛsəˋfɪlɪk, ˏmɛz-] *a*.【植】叶肉的(= mesophyllous)。

mes·o·phyte [ˈmesəfait, ˈmez-; ˋmɛsəfaɪt, ˋmɛz-] *n*.【植】(在中等湿度下生长的)中生植物;中生代植物。**-phyt·ic** [-ˈfitik; -ˋfɪtɪk] *a*.

mes·o·plasm [ˈmesəuplæzəm; ˋmɛsəˏplæzəm] *n*.【生】中胚层质。

mes·o·plast [ˈmesəuplɑ:st; ˋmɛsəˏplæst] *n*.【生】细胞核。

Mes·o·po·ta·mia [ˌmesəpəˈteimjə, -miə; ˏmɛsəpə-ˋtemjə, -mɪə] *n*. 美索不达米亚〔小亚细亚 Tigris 和 Euphrates 两河流域间的古王国,现今伊拉克所在地〕。**-mian** *a*., *n*. 美索不达米亚的;美索不达米亚人(的)。

mes·o·some [ˈmesəsʌm; ˋmɛsəˏsʌm] *n*.【生】中间体,细胞膜中层。

mes·o·sphere [ˈmesəsfiə; ˋmɛzəˏsfɪə] *n*.【气】中圈,中层,散逸层。

mes·o·the·li·al [ˌmesəuˈθi:liəl, ˌmez-; ˏmɛsəˋθilɪəl, ˏmɛz-] *a*.【解】间皮的。

mes·o·the·li·o·ma [ˌmesəuˌθi:liˈəumə, ˌmez-; ˏmɛsə-ˏθilɪˋomə, ˏmɛz-] *n*.【医】间皮瘤。

mes·o·the·li·um [ˌmesəuˈθi:liəm, ˌmez-; ˏmɛsəˋθilɪəm, ˏmɛz-] *n*. (*pl*. **-li·a** [-ə; -ə])【解】间皮。

mes·o·tho·rac·ic [ˌmesəuθɔ:ˈræsik, ˌmez-; ˏmɛsəθɔ-ˋræsɪk, ˏmɛz-] *a*.【动】(昆虫的)中胸的。

mes·o·tho·rax [ˌmesəuˈθɔ:ræks, ˏmɛz-; ˏmɛsəˋθoræks, ˏmɛz-] *n*.【虫】中胸。

mes·o·tho·ri·um [ˌmesəuˈθɔ:riəm, ˌmez-; ˏmɛsə-ˋθorɪəm, ˏmɛz-] *n*. 1. 新钍。2. 新钍-I〔镭同位素 Ra^{228}〕。3. 新钍-II〔锕同位素 Ac^{228}〕。

mes·o·tron [ˈmesətrɔn; ˋmɛsəˏtrɑn] *n*. = meson.

mes·o·tro·phy [ˈmesəˌtrɔfi; ˋmɛsəˏtrɑfɪ] *n*.【微】半自养,中间营养。

Mes·o·zo·a [ˌmesəuˈzəuə, ˌmez-; ˏmɛsəˋzoə, ˏmɛz-] *n*. 〔*pl*.〕【动】中间动物〔原生动物与腔肠动物中间的一种动物〕。

Mes·o·zo·ic [ˌmesəuˈzəuik, ˌmez-; ˏmɛsəˋzoɪk, ˏmɛz-] *n*., *a*.【地】中生代(的),中生代岩石(的)。

mes·quite, mes·quit [mesˈki:t, ˈmeski:t; mɛsˋkit, ˋmɛskit] *n*.【植】1. 牧豆树属植物。2. 螺丝豆〔牧豆树属植物的豆荚〕;螺丝豆树(= screwbean)。

mess [mes; mɛs] I *n*. 1. (尤指流体的)食品;(给猎狗等吃的)混合饲料。2. 混乱,纷乱;大杂烩;肮脏,污秽。3. 过失,错误;困境。4. (尤指海陆军的)伙食团;集体用膳人员;〔无冠词〕会餐,聚餐;食堂;(普通的)餐,膳食,伙食。5. (鱼的)一网;〔英方、美〕一次挤得的牛奶。6. 〔美俚〕笨人,邋遢鬼。*a complete* ~ 一团糟。*the army's supplies and* ~ 军队的给养和伙食。***be at*** ~ 在食堂吃饭。***get into a*** ~ 陷入困境;犯错误。***go to*** ~ 去食堂吃饭。***in a*** ~ 1. 肮脏,尽是泥。2. 混乱,紊乱。3. 困难。***lose the number of one's*** ~ 死,被杀死。***make a*** ~ ***of*** 把…弄糟[弄坏]。***make a*** ~ ***of it*** 把事情搞得一团糟。***a*** ~ ***of pottage*** 付出巨大代价得到的物质享受;眼前小利。II *vt*. 1. 弄脏;搞乱,弄糟。2. 〔古〕为…配给食物;给…供膳。3. 妨碍;干扰。4. 粗暴对待[处理]。— *vi*. 1. 供膳。2. 集体用膳。3. 搞乱。4. 瞎摆弄;干涉。~ ***about*** 磨洋工;闲荡。~ ***around*** 〔美俚〕浪费时间;混(日子);乱管闲事。~ ***up*** 〔美俚〕陷入困境;弄糟(计划等);粗暴处理。~ **deck**【海】住舱甲板〔船员吃饭处〕。~ **gear** 〔美〕吃饭用具〔刀、叉和匙子〕。~ **hall** 〔美〕食堂。~ **jacket** 短制服〔紧身短上衣,公共场所服务人员的制服或军便服〕。~ **kit**【军】野战食具(= ~ gear)。~**mate** 〔主水手语〕同吃饭的伙伴。~ **rack** 食橱。~ **table** (船内的)共同餐桌。~**tin** (军用)饭盒。~**-up** 〔口〕混乱。

mes·sage [ˈmesidʒ; ˋmɛsɪdʒ] I *n*. 1. 通信;口信;问候;祝词;讯,消息,情报,电报,通报;【物】信息;【生】遗传密码单位〔表明氨基酸合成某种蛋白质时的排列顺序〕。2. 〔美〕(总统的)咨文。3. 启示;教训,(预言者的)神示;要旨;寓言。4. (使者接受的)任务,使命。5. 广告词句。*an oral* [*a verbal*] ~ 口信。*a wireless* ~ 无线电报。*a* ~ *to the nation* 告国人书。*a congratulatory* ~ 贺电,贺辞,献词。*a* ~ *centre* 通讯社;收发室。*a New Year* ~ 新年祝贺。~ *rate* (电话的)计次价目。*State of the Unions M-* 〔美〕国情咨文。***go on*** [***do***] ***a*** ~ 出外为人办事。***leave a*** ~ 留话。~ ***of greetings*** 贺电,贺信;祝词。***send a person on a*** ~ 派人出去。II *vt*. 通知,通告;发信号告知。

mes·sa·line [ˌmesəˈli:n; ˏmɛsəˋlin] *n*. 美色林全丝软缎。

mes·sei·gneurs [ˌmeseˈnjə:z; ˏmɛsenˋjɝz] *n*. 〔F.〕 monseigneur 的复数。

mes·sen·ger [ˈmesindʒə; ˋmɛsndʒɚ] *n*. 1. 使者,送信人,邮递员,信差;【军】通信兵,传令兵。2. 前驱;先驱者。3. 顺着风筝线送到天空的纸片。4.【海】大轮索;传递(重索的)细索;引绳。5.【生】信使〔一种传递遗传信息的化学物质〕。*a corbie* ~ 一去不回的送信人;回得很晚的使者〔源出基督教《圣经》的《创世纪》〕。*Dawn is the* ~ *of day*. 黎明是白昼的先驱。*a King's* [*Queen's*] ~ 〔英〕送公文的差役。~ **call** 传呼(电话)。~ **RNA**【生】信使核糖核酸。~ **service**【军】传令勤务。

Mes·si·ah [miˈsaiə; məˋsaɪə] *n*. 1. 〔the ~〕弥赛亚〔犹太人所期待的救世主〕。2.【基督教】救世主,基督。3. 〔m-〕(人民、国家等所期待的)救星,解放者。**mes·si·an·ic** [ˌmesiˈænik; ˏmɛsɪˋænɪk] *a*. 救世主的;以救世主自居的。

Mes·sias [məˈsaiəs; məˋsaɪəs] *n*. 〔m-〕(人民、国家等所期待的)救星;解放者(= Messiah)。

mes·sieurs [ˈmesəz; ˋmɛsɚz] *n*. 〔*pl*.〕〔F.〕 monsieur 的复数〔略作 Messrs.〕。

Mes·si·na [meˈsi:nə; məˋsinə] *n*. 墨西拿。***the Strait of*** ~ (意大利与西西里岛间的)墨西拿海峡。

Messrs. [ˈmesəz; ˋmɛsɚz] = Messieurs.

mes·suage [ˈmeswidʒ; ˋmɛswɪdʒ] *n*.【法】宅院。

mess·y [ˈmesi; ˋmɛsɪ] *a*. (***mess·i·er***; ***-i·est***) 污秽的,肮脏的。*a* ~ *job* 脏活;难搞的工作。

mes·ti·zo [mes'tiːzəu; mɛs`tizo] ***n***. 混血人〔尤指印第安人与白人的混血人〕。

MET = Middle Europe Time 中欧时间。

met [met; mɛt] meet 的过去式及过去分词。

met. = **1**. metaphor. **2**. metaphysics. **3**. meteorological. **4**. metropolitan.

met(a)-, meth- *pref*. 后;间,中;同;变;亚;元(等)。★元音前用 met-;辅音前用 meta-; 送气音(aspirate)前用 meth-.

me·tab·a·sis [me'tæbəsis; mə`tæbəsɪs] ***n***. (*pl*. ***-ses*** [-siːz; -siz]) **1**.【医】变症,转移;病状转变。**2**.【修】主题[题材]转移。

met·a·bol·ic [ˌmetə'bɔlik; ˏmɛtə`bɑlɪk] ***a***. **1**. 变化的,变形的。**2**.【生】新陈代谢的,代谢作用的。~ **nucleus** 静止核。~ **stage** 代谢期。~ **water**【生】代谢水。

me·tab·o·lism, me·tab·o·ly [me'tæbəlizəm, me'tæbəli; mə`tæbḷɪzəm, mɛ`tæbəlɪ] ***n***.【生】新陈代谢,代谢作用。

me·tab·o·lite [mi'tæbəlait; mɪ`tæbəˏlaɪt] ***n***.【生化】代谢物。

me·tab·o·lize [mə'tæbəlaiz; mə`tæbḷˏaɪz] ***vt***., ***vi***. (***-lized***; ***-liz·ing***) (使发生)代谢变化。**-liz·a·ble** ***a***.

me·tab·o·lous [ˌmə'tæbələs; mə`tæbələs] ***a***.【生】变态的;变质的;变形的。

met·a·car·pus [ˌmetə'kɑːpəs; ˏmɛtə`kɑrpəs] ***n***. (*pl*. ***-pi*** [-pai; -paɪ])【解】掌,(尤指)掌骨。**-car·pal** ***a***.

met·a·cen·tre, [Am.] **met·a·cen·ter** ['metəˌsentə; `mɛtəˏsɛntɚ] ***n***. (浮力的)定倾中心。**-tric** ***a***.

met·a·chem·is·try [ˌmetə'kemistri; ˏmɛtə`kɛmɪstrɪ] ***n***. 原子结构化学;超级化学。

met·a·chro·ma·tism [ˌmetə'krəumətizəm; ˏmɛtə`kromətɪzm] ***n***.【医】变色(反应)。

met·a·chro·sis [ˌmetə'krəusis; ˏmɛtə`krosɪs] ***n***.【动】变色(机能)。

met·a·gal·ax·y ['metəˌgæləksi; ˏmɛtə`gæləksɪ] ***n***.【天】总星系,宇宙。**-lac·tic** [ˌmetəgə'læktik; ˏmɛtəgə`læktɪk] ***a***.

met·age ['miːtidʒ; `mitɪdʒ] ***n***. 容量[重量]的官方检定;(容量、重量)检定费。

met·a·gen·e·sis [ˌmetə'dʒenisis; ˏmɛtə`dʒɛnəsɪs] ***n***.【生】(有性生殖与无性生殖)世代交替。**-gen·et·ic** [ˌmetədʒi'netik; ˏmɛtədʒə`nɛtɪk] ***a***.

me·tag·na·thous [mə'tægnəθəs; mə`tægnəθəs] ***a***. **1**. (交喙鸟等)下颚骨尖交叉的。**2**. 交嘴的。**-na·thism** ***n***.

met·al ['metl; `mɛtl] **I** ***n***. **1**. 金属;金属制品;金属合金。**2**.【化】金属元素;(*opp*. alloy);金属性。**3**.【徽】金色;银色。**4**.【海】(全舰)炮数;(一次发出的)炮火力。**5**. 铸铁熔液;熔解玻璃。**6**. (铺路的)碎石料〔通常叫 road ~〕。**7**. [*pl*.]〔英〕铁轨。**8**. 成色,成分;勇气;气质;根性。**9**.【印】活字金;排好活字的版。**10**.〔英〕〔总称〕【军】坦克,装甲车。**11**.〔口〕重金属电子摇滚乐(= heavy ~)。*base* ~*s* 贱金属〔铜、铁、铅等〕;基底金属;碱金属。*heavy* ~*s* 重金属;〔总称〕重型坦克[装甲车];重炮;巨弹;强敌。*light* ~*s* 轻金属。*noble* [*perfect*, *precious*] ~*s* 贵金属。*He is of true* ~. 他是一个真正有勇气的人。***run off*** [***leave***] ***the*** ~***s*** (火车)出轨。**II** ***vt***. ([英] ***-ll-***)用金属包;用碎石铺(路面)。*a* ~*ed road* 碎石路。~ **ceramic** 金属陶瓷。~ **head** 〔俚〕重金属摇滚乐迷。~ **lath** 金属网,钢丝网。~ **master** [**negative**] 录声主盘。~ **positive** 第一模盘。~**ware** 金属器皿〔如厨房用具等〕。

metal(l). = metallurgical; metallurgy.

met·al·de·hyde [mi'tældəhaid; mɪ`tældəˏhaɪd] ***n***.【化】介乙醛;低聚乙醛。

met·a·lin·guis·tics [ˌmetəliŋ'gwistiks; ˏmɛtəlɪŋ`gwɪstɪks] ***n***. 〔作单数用〕语言文化因素学〔研究语言和文化的其他因素之间的关系〕。

met·al·ize ['metəlaiz; `mɛtḷˏaɪz] ***vt***. = metallize.

me·tal·lic [mi'tælik; mə`tælɪk] ***a***. 金属的;金属性的,金属质的;金属制的。~ *currency* 金属硬币,硬币。~ *lustre* 金属光泽。~ *prints* 金属粉印花布。*a* ~ *pile* 伏打电池。~ *soap*【化】金属皂。*the* ~ *standard*【经】金银本位。**-li·cal·ly** ***ad***.

met·al·lide ['metəlaid; `mɛtəˏlaɪd] ***vt***. 电解电镀。

met·al·lid·ing ['metəlaidiŋ; `mɛtəˏlaɪdɪŋ] ***n***. 电解电镀法。

met·al·lif·er·ous [ˌmetə'lifərəs; ˏmɛtḷ`ɪfərəs] ***a***. 产金属的;含金属的。~ *mines* 金属矿山。

met·al·line ['metlin, -ain; `mɛtḷɪn, -ˏaɪn] ***a***. **1**. 似金属的;金属质的;含金属的。**2**. 含金属盐的。

met·al·list, met·al·ist ['metlist; `mɛtḷɪst] ***n***. **1**. 金属工。**2**. 主张使用硬币者。

met·al·lize ['metəlaiz; `mɛtḷˏaɪz] ***vt***. **1**. 用金属(或金属化合物)处理;使金属化。**2**. 使(橡皮)硬化。**3**. 喷镀金属(粉)于;使导体化。**-za·tion** [ˌmetəlai'zeiʃən; ˏmɛtəlaɪ`zeʃən] ***n***. 敷金属(法);金属喷镀(法)。

met·al·lo·graph [mi'tæləgrɑːf, -græf; mɪ`tæləˏgrɑf, -græf] ***n***. **1**. (装有照相机的)金相显微镜。**2**. (金属表面的)显微照片;射线[电子]显微照片。

met·al·log·ra·phy [ˌmetə'lɔgrəfi; ˏmɛtḷ`ɑgrəfɪ] ***n***. 金相学。

met·al·loid ['metəlɔid; `mɛtlˏɔɪd] **I** ***a***. 似金属的。**II** ***n***. 非金属;类金属,准金属。

met·al·lo·scope [mi'tæləuskəup; mɪ`tæloˏskop] ***n***. 金相显微镜。

met·al·lur·gic, met·al·lur·gi·cal [ˌmetə'ləːdʒik, -dʒikəl; ˏmɛtə`lɝdʒɪk, -dʒɪkəl] ***a***. 冶金(学)的;冶金术的。~ *coal* 冶金煤,炼焦煤。~ *coke* 冶金焦炭。~ *industry* 冶金工业。**-gi·cal·ly** ***ad***.

met·al·lur·gist [me'tælədʒist; mɛ`tælɚdʒɪst] ***n***. 冶金学家。

met·al·lur·gy [me'tæləˌdʒi; mɛ`tælɚˏdʒɪ] ***n***. 冶金;冶金学;冶金术。

met·al·work ['metlwəːk; `mɛtḷˏwɝk] ***n***. 金属制品[制造]。**-er** ***n***. 金属制造工。**-ing** 金属制造;金属加工。

met·a·math·e·mat·ics [ˌmetəˌmæθi'mætiks; ˏmɛtəˏmæθə`mætɪks] ***n***. [作单数用]数理哲学。

met·a·mer ['metəmə; `mɛtəmɚ] ***n***.【化】位变异构体;【植】单体;【物】条件等色。

met·a·mere ['metəmiə; `mɛtəˏmɪr] ***n***. **1**. = metamer. **2**.【动】体节,分裂片。

met·a·mer·ic [ˌmetə'merik; ˏmɛtə`mɛrɪk] ***a***. **1**.【化】位变异构的。**2**.【动】分节的。**-i·cal·ly** ***ad***.

me·tam·er·ism [me'tæmərizəm; mɪ`tæmərɪzm] ***n***. **1**.【化】位变异构(现象);同分异构性。**2**.【动】体节分裂,分节(现象)。**3**.【物】条件配色。

met·a·mor·phic [ˌmetə'mɔːfik; ˏmɛtə`mɔrfɪk] ***a***. **1**. 变化的,变形的;改变结构的。**2**.【地】变成的,变性的,变质的。~ *rock* 变质岩。

met·a·mor·phism [ˌmetə'mɔːfizəm; ˏmɛtə`mɔrfɪzm] ***n***. **1**.【地】变质(作用)。**2**. 变态,变形,变化。

met·a·mor·phose [ˌmetə'mɔːfəuz; ˏmɛtə`mɔrfoz] ***vt***. 使变形[质];使变成(*to*; *into*)。*a* ~*d leaf* 变态叶。— ***vi***. 变形;变质。

met·a·mor·pho·sis [ˌmetə'mɔːfəsis; ˏmɛtə`mɔrfəsɪs] ***n***. (*pl*. ***-ses*** [-siːz; -siz]) 变形,变状;(一般)变质;【生】变态。

met·a·neph·ros [ˌmetə'nefrəs; ˏmɛtə`nɛfrɑs] ***n***. (*pl*. ***-roi*** [-rɔi; -rɔɪ])【解】后肾。**-neph·ric** ***a***.

met·aph. = metaphor(ical); metaphysical; metaphysics.

met·a·phase ['metəfeiz; `mɛtəˏfez] ***n***.【生】中期〔细胞分裂的一个时期〕。

Met·a·phen ['metəfen; `mɛtəˏfɛn] ***n***. 袂塔酚〔一种防腐

剂商标名〕。

met·a·phor [ˈmetəfə; ˋmɛtəfɚ] ***n.*** 【修】隐喻,暗喻〔the curtain of night 之类〕;(某种概念、品质或情况等的)象征。

met·a·phor·i·cal [ˌmetəˈfɔrikəl; ˏmɛtəˋfɔrɪkl] ***a.*** 隐喻的。**-ly** ***ad.*** 用隐喻;用比喻。

met·a·phos·phate [ˌmetəˈfɔsfeit; ˏmɛtəˋfɑsfet] ***n.*** 偏磷酸盐。

met·a·phos·phor·ic [ˌmetəfɔsˈfɔːrik; ˏmɛtefɑsˋfɔrɪk] ***a.*** ～ **acid** 偏磷酸,二缩原磷酸。

met·a·phrase [ˈmetəfreiz; ˋmɛtəˏfrez] **I** ***vt.*** **1.** 逐字翻译,直译〔*cf.* paraphrase〕。**2.** 修改…的词句。**3.**〔古〕以诗体翻译。**II** ***n.*** **1.** 直译,逐字逐句的翻译。**2.**〔古〕诗体翻译。

met·a·phrast [ˈmetəˌfræst; ˋmɛtəˏfræst] ***n.*** 改写者〔如将散文改写为诗的人〕。

met·a·phras·tic [ˌmetəˈfræstik; ˏmɛtəˋfræstɪk] ***a.*** 直译的。

met·a·phys·ic [ˌmetəˈfizik; ˏmɛtəˋfɪzɪk] **I** ***n.*** 形而上学;玄学;玄学体系。**II** ***a.*** = metaphysical.

met·a·phys·i·cal [ˌmetəˈfizikəl; ˏmɛtəˋfɪzɪkl] ***a.*** **1.** 形而上学的;玄学的。**2.** 超自然的;先验的,超感觉的。**3.** 玄奥的;抽象的;穿凿入微的,过分细腻的。**-ly** ***ad.***

met·a·phy·si·cian, met·a·phys·i·cist [ˌmetəfiˈziʃən, -ˈfizist; ˏmɛtəfəˋzɪʃən, -ˋfɪzɪst] ***n.*** 形而上学的;玄学家。

met·a·phys·i·cize [ˌmetəˈfizisaiz; ˏmɛtəˋfɪzɪˏsaɪz] ***vi.*** 形而上学地思维[研究、讲、写等]。

met·a·phys·ics [ˌmetəˈfiziks; ˏmɛtəˋfɪzɪks] ***n.***〔作单数用〕形而上学,玄学(*opp.* dialectics);纯抽象的空论;空谈。

met·a·pla·sia [ˌmetəˈpleiʒə; ˏmɛtəˋpleʒə] ***n.*** **1.**【生】组织转化。**2.** 组织变形〔如软骨的骨化〕。**-plas·tic** [-ˈplæstik; -ˋplæstɪk] ***a.***

met·a·plasm [ˈmetəplæzəm; ˋmetəplæzm̩] ***n.***【语】词形变化;【生】后成质〔*cf.* protoplasm〕。

met·a·pol·i·ti·cian [ˌmetəˌpɔliˈtiʃən; ˏmɛtəˏpɑlɪˋtɪʃən] ***n.***〔常蔑〕形而上学政治学家。

met·a·pol·i·tics [ˌmetəˈpɔlitiks; ˏmɛtəˋpɑləˏtɪks] ***n.***〔常蔑〕形而上学政治学。**-lit·i·cal** ***a.***

met·a-po·si·tion [ˌmetəpəˈziʃən; ˏmɛtəpəˋzɪʃən] ***n.***【化】间位。

met·a·pro·tein [ˌmetəˈprəutiːn; ˏmɛtəˋprotin] ***n.***【生化】变性蛋白。

met·a·psy·chol·o·gy [ˌmetəsaiˈkɔlədʒi; ˏmɛtəsaɪˋkɑlədʒɪ] ***n.*** 心理玄学。

met·a·scope [ˈmetəskəup; ˋmɛtəˏskop] ***n.***【物】**1.** 红外线指示器。**2.**(借投射红外线能在荧光屏上看见黑暗中物体的一种)红外线望远镜。

met·a·se·quoi·a [ˈmetəsiˈkwɔiə; ˋmɛtəsɪˋkwɔɪə] ***n.***【植】水杉。

met·a·sil·i·cate [ˌmetəˈsilikit; ˏmɛtəˋsɪlɪˏket] ***n.***【化】硅酸盐。

met·a·so·ma·tism [ˌmetəˈsəumətizm; ˏmɛtəˋsomətɪzm] ***n.***【地】交代(作用);交代变质(作用)。**-mat·ic** [-səuˈmætik; -soˋmætɪk] ***a.***

met·a·so·ma·to·sis [ˌmetəˌsəuməˈtəusis; ˏmɛtəˏsoməˋtosɪs] ***n.*** = metasomatism.

met·a·some [ˈmetəsəum; ˋmɛtəˏsom] ***n.***【地】代替矿物,交代矿物;新成体。

met·a·sta·ble [ˌmetəˈsteibl; ˏmɛtəˋstebl̩] ***a.***【化】亚稳的,准稳的。～ **atom** 准稳原子。**-bil·i·ty** [-ˈbiliti; -ˋbɪlətɪ] ***n.*** 准稳度。

me·tas·ta·sis [meˈtæstəsis; məˋtæstəsɪs] ***n.*** (*pl.* ***-ses*** [-siːz; -siz]) **1.**【医】(病毒)转移。**2.**【生】新陈代谢。**3.**【地】同质蜕变。**4.**【修】(话题)急转,(主题)急变。**5.**〔罕〕变形,变态。**-stat·ic** ***a.***

me·tas·ta·size [məˈtæstəˌsaiz; məˋtæstəˏsaɪz] ***vi.*** (***-sized***; ***-siz·ing***)【医】(癌等向身体其他部位)转移。

met·a·tar·sal [ˌmetəˈtɑːsəl; ˏmɛtəˋtɑrsəl] ***n.***, ***a.*** 跖骨(的)。

met·a·tar·sus [ˌmetəˈtɑːsəs; ˏmɛtəˋtɑrsəs] ***n.*** (*pl.* ***-si*** [-sai; -saɪ])【解】跖骨;【虫】跗基节;【鸟】跗跖。

me·tath·e·sis [meˈtæθəsis; məˋtæθəsɪs] ***n.*** (*pl.* ***-ses*** [-siːz; -siz]) **1.**【语】换位(作用);换位构成的词。**2.**【医】病变移位法。**3.**【化】复分解,置换(作用);易位(作用)。**-thet·i·cal** ***a.***

met·a·tho·rax [ˌmetəˈθɔːræks; ˏmɛtəˋθoræks] ***n.***【虫】后胸。

me·tat·ro·phy [miˈtætrəfi; mɪˋtætrəfɪ] ***n.*** **1.**(菌类等的)寄生吸食;后生营养。**2.**【医】营养障碍,营养异常。

met·a·xy·lem [ˌmetəˈzailem; ˏmɛtəˋzaɪlɛm] ***n.***【植】后生木质部。

mé·ta·yage [ˈmeteijɑːʒ; meteˋjɑʒ] ***n.***〔F.〕分益佃耕制。

mé·ta·yer [miˈteiə; mɪˋteɪr] ***n.***〔F.〕分益佃农。

met·a·zo·an [ˌmetəˈzəuən; ˏmɛtəˋzoən] ***n.***, ***a.***【动】后生动物(的)。

Met·calfe [ˈmetkɑːf; ˋmɛtkɑf] ***n.*** 梅特卡夫〔姓氏〕。

Metch·ni·koff [ˈmetʃnikɔf; ˋmɛtʃnɪˏkɔf] **Elie.** 梅奇尼可夫〔1845—1916,俄国生物学家、细菌学家〕。

Met Co = meteorological company〔美〕气象连。

mete[1] [miːt; mit] ***vt.*** **1.**〔诗〕量,测量。**2.** 评定(功过);派定;分给。～ *out rewards* 给予报酬。

mete[2] [miːt; mit] ***n.*** 境界,界石。～*s and bounds*【法】边界,分界。

met·em·pir·ics [ˌmetemˈpiriks; ˏmɛtɛmˋpɪrɪks], **met·em·pir·i·cism** [ˌmetemˈpirisizəm; ˏmɛtɛmˋpɪrɪsɪzəm] ***n.***【哲】先验主义,先验论。**-pir·i·cal** ***a.*** (*opp.* empirical)。

met·em·pir·i·cist [ˌmetemˈpirisist; ˏmɛtɛmˋpɪrɪsɪst] ***n.*** 先验论者。

met·em·psy·cho·sis [ˌmetempsiˈkəusis; ˏmɛtəmsaɪˋkosɪs] ***n.*** (*pl.* ***-ses*** [-siːz; -siz])【宗】(灵魂的)轮回,转生。

met·en·ceph·a·lon [ˌmetenˈsefəˌlɔn; ˏmɛtɛnˋsɛfəˏlɑn] ***n.*** (*pl.* ***-la*** [-lə; -lə])【解】后脑。**-phal·ic** [-səˈfælik; -səˋfælɪk] ***a.***

me·te·or [ˈmiːtjə; ˋmitɪɚ] ***n.*** **1.** 流星。**2.**(流星的)曳光;昙花一现的东西。**3.**〔古、罕〕大气现象。～ **burst** 流星(尾迹)爆发〔会产生电离粒子,其辐射强度骤增〕。

me·te·or. = meteorology.

me·te·or·ic [ˌmiːtiˈɔrik; ˏmitɪˋɔrɪk] ***a.*** **1.** 大气的;气象上的;流星的,陨星的。**2.** 流星似的;使人眼花缭乱的;闪烁的;昙花一现的,迅速的。～ *iron* 陨铁。*a* ～ *shower* 流星雨。*a* ～ *stone* 陨石。*the* ～ *theory of nebula* 星昙流星说。*water* ～ 天落水,大气水。*a* ～ *career* 昙花一现的生涯。

me·te·or·ite, me·te·or·o·lite [ˈmiːtjərait, -tiə-; ˋmitɪərˏaɪt, -tɪə-] ***n.*** 陨星;陨石;陨铁。

me·te·or·it·ic [ˌmiːtiəˈritik; ˏmitɪəˋrɪtɪk] ***a.***【地】陨石的。

me·te·or·it·ics [ˌmiːtjəˈritiks; ˏmitɪəˋrɪtɪks] ***n.*** *pl.*〔用作 *sing.* 或 *pl.*〕陨星学,流星学。

me·te·or·o·graph [ˌmiːtiˈɔːrəgrɑːf, -græf; ˏmitɪˋɔrəˏgrɑf, -ˏgræf] ***n.*** 气象计。**-graph·ic** ***a.***

me·te·or·oid [ˈmiːtjərɔid; ˋmitɪərˏɔɪd] ***n.*** 流星体,陨星体。**-al** ***a.***

me·te·or·o·log·ic, -i·cal [ˌmiːtjərəˈlɔdʒik(əl); ˏmitɪərəˋlɑdʒɪk(əl)] ***a.*** 气象的,气象学(上)的。*a* ～ *code* 气象符号。*a* ～ *observatory* 气象台。*the M- Office*〔英〕气象台。*a* ～ *report* 天气预报。*a* ～ *station* 气象(观测)站。**-ly** ***ad.***

me·te·or·ol·o·gist [ˌmiːtjəˈrɔlədʒist; ˏmitɪəˋrɑlədʒɪst] ***n.*** 气象学家。

me·te·or·ol·o·gy [ˌmiːtjəˈrɔlədʒi; ˏmitɪəˋrɑlədʒɪ] ***n.*** 气象学;(某一地区的)气象(状态)。

me·ter[1] [ˈmiːtə; ˋmitɚ] **I** ***n.*** **1.** 测量仪表,计量器;计,表。**2.** 计量人;计量官。*a dry* [*wet*] ~ 干[湿]式煤气表。*an electric* ~ 电表。*a gas* ~ 气量计;煤气表。*a water* ~ (自来)水表。***The*** ~ ***is running.*** 出租车收费表在不停地走;〔喻〕开支越来越大;后果越来越严重。**II** ***vt.*** 用表计算[测量、记录]。~ **maid** 处理违犯交通规则〔如停车超时,乱过马路等〕的女警察。~**ed mail** 收费邮件〔以现金代邮票的邮件,收费数目用戳子盖在信封上〕。

me·ter[2] [ˈmiːtə; ˋmitɚ] ***n.*** 〔美〕= metre.

-meter *suf.* **1.** …计,…表: baro*meter*, thermo*meter*; pedo*meter*; gas*ometer*, speedo*meter*. **2.** 〔美〕米: kilo*meter*. **3.** 【韵】音步: hexa*meter*.

me·ter·age [ˈmiːtəridʒ; ˋmitərɪdʒ] ***n.*** 量度,测度;用度费用。

met·e·strus [metˈiːstrəs; mɛtˋistrəs] ***n.*** 【动】动情后期。

mete-wand, mete-yard [ˈmiːtwənd, ˈmiːtjɑːd; ˋmitwɑnd, ˋmitjɑrd] ***n.*** 〔英〕评价的标准。

meth- = met(a)-.

Meth. = Methodist.

meth [meθ; mɛθ] ***n.*** 〔美俚〕甲安非他明〔一种兴奋剂 = methamphetamine〕。

meth·ac·ry·late [meθˈækrəleit; mɛˋθækrəˏlet] ***n.*** 异丁烯酸盐[酯],甲基丙烯酸盐[酯]。~ **resin** 异丁烯酸酯树脂,甲基丙烯酸酯树脂。

meth·a·cryl·ic acid [ˌmeθəˈkrilik; ˏmɛθəˋkrɪlɪk] 异丁烯酸;甲基丙烯酸。

meth·a·done [ˈmeθədəun; ˋmɛθəˏdon] ***n.*** 【药】美沙酮〔一种镇痛药〕。

meth·ane [ˈmeθein; ˋmɛθen] ***n.*** 【化】甲烷,沼气。~ **series** 【化】甲烷系。

meth·a·nol [ˈmeθənɔl, -nəul; ˋmɛθənol, -nol] ***n.*** 【化】甲醇,木醇。

Meth·e·drine [ˈmeθidriːn; ˋmɛθədrɪn] ***n.*** **1.** 盐酸脱氧麻黄碱的商标。**2.** 〔m-〕盐酸脱氧麻黄碱〔用做解除忧郁、疲劳的药物〕。

me·theg·lin [miˈθeglin; məˋθɛglɪn] ***n.*** 蜂蜜酒。

met·he·mo·glo·bin [metˈhiːməˌgləubin, -ˈhemə-; mɛtˋhiməˏglobɪn, -ˋhɛmə-] ***n.*** 【生化】正铁血红蛋白。

me·the·na·mine [məˈθiːnəmiːn, -min; mɛˋθinəmin, -mɪn] ***n.*** 亚甲四胺,乌洛托品〔用于橡胶、药品、炸药的制造〕。

me·thinks [miˈθiŋks; mɪˋθɪŋks] (*p.* ***methought***) ***vi.*** 〔无人称动词〕〔古〕我想,据我看来(= it seems to me)。

me·thi·o·nine [meˈθaiəniːn; mɛˋθaɪəˏnin] ***n.*** 【生化】蛋氨酸,甲硫氨酸。

metho-, meth- *comb. f.* 甲基: *metho*xide.

meth·od [ˈmeθəd; ˋmɛθəd] ***n.*** **1.** 方法,方式;顺序。**2.** (思想、言谈上的)条理,规律,秩序。**3.** 【生】分类法。**4.** 〔M-〕【剧】融入法〔指演员完全融入角色的精湛演技〕。*a scientific* ~ 科学方法。*the zero* [*null*] ~ 衡消法。*the oral* ~ 口授法。*a man of* ~ 有条有理的人。*There's* ~ *in his madness.* 他虽似疯狂其实颇有理性。*work with* ~ 照手续[规矩]办事。

me·thod·ic, me·thod·i·cal [miˈθɔdik, -ikəl; məˋθɑdɪk, -ɪkəl] ***a.*** 有次序的,有组织的;有计划的,有条不紊的,有一定方式的。**-i·cal·ly** ***ad.*** **-i·cal·ness** ***n.***

Meth·od·ism [ˈmeθədizəm; ˋmɛθədˏɪzəm] ***n.*** **1.** 【宗】卫理公会派(教义、仪式)。**2.** 〔m-〕严守法则;墨守成规。

Meth·od·ist [ˈmeθədist; ˋmɛθədɪst] **I** ***n.*** **1.** 【宗】卫理公会教徒。**2.** 〔m-〕〔蔑〕在宗教上极严格的人。**3.** 〔m-〕方法论者;【生】分类学家。**II** ***a.*** = Methodistical.

Meth·o·dis·tic, Meth·o·dis·ti·cal [ˌmeθəˈdistik, -tikəl; ˏmɛθədˋɪstɪk, -tɪkəl] ***a.*** **1.** 卫理公会派的。**2.** 〔m-〕有次序的,循规蹈矩的,一丝不苟的,严格的。

meth·od·ize [ˈmeθədaiz; ˋmɛθəˏdaɪz] ***vt.*** 为…定次序[规矩,方式等],使(工作等)有条理,给…分门类。

meth·od·ol·o·gist [ˌmeθəˈdɔlədʒist; ˏmɛθədˋɑlədʒɪst] ***n.*** 方法学家。

meth·od·ol·o·gy [ˌmeθəˈdɔlədʒi; ˏmɛθədˋɑlədʒɪ] ***n.*** 方法学,方法论;研究法;【生】分类法。**-log·i·cal** [ˌmeθədəˈlɔdʒikəl; ˏmɛθədəˋlɑdʒɪkəl] ***a.***

meth·o·trex·ate [ˌmeθəˈtrekseit; ˏmɛθəˋtrɛkset] ***n.*** 【药】甲胺喋呤〔用以治白血病和肿瘤〕。

me·thought [miˈθɔːt; mɪˋθɔt] methinks 的过去式。

meth·ox·ide [meˈθɔksaid; mɛθˋɑksaɪd] ***n.*** 甲醇盐;甲氧基金属;甲氧化物(= methylate)。

meth·ox·y·chlor [məˈθɔksiklɔː; məˋθɑksɪˏklɔr] ***n.*** 【化】甲氧氯;甲氧滴滴涕〔杀蚊蝇剂〕。

Me·thu·se·lah [miˈθjuːzələ; məˋθjuzələ] ***n.*** **1.** 麦修彻拉〔《圣经》中的长寿者〕。**2.** 〔m-〕大酒瓶〔容量为 6.5 夸脱〕。

meth·yl [ˈmeθil, ˈmiːθail; ˋmɛθɪl, ˋmiθəl] ***n.*** 【化】甲基。~ **acetate** 醋酸甲酯。~ **alcohol** 甲醇,木醇。~ **benzene** 甲苯(= toluene)。~ **blue** 甲基蓝。~ **bromide** 甲基溴,溴(代)甲烷。~ **chloride** 甲基氯,氯(代)甲烷。~ **violet** 龙胆紫(= gentian violet)。

meth·yl·al [ˌmeθiˈlæl, ˈmeθilæl; ˏmɛθəˋlæl, ˋmɛθəlæl] ***n.*** 【化】甲缩醛,甲醛缩二甲醇〔用做溶剂、麻醉剂〕。

meth·yl·a·mine [ˌmeθiləˈmiːn, -ˈlæmiːn; ˏmɛθələˋmin, -ˋlæmin] ***n.*** 【化】甲胺。

meth·yl·ate [ˈmeθileit; ˋmɛθəˏlet] **I** ***vt.*** 使甲基化,向…导入甲基[加入甲醇]。**II** ***n.*** 甲基化产物;甲醇金属。~**d spirit(s)** 甲基化酒精,用甲醇变性的酒精。

meth·yl·ene [ˈmeθiliːn; ˋmɛθəlin] ***n.*** 【化】甲叉,甲撑,亚甲(基)。~ **blue** 【化】(碱性)亚甲蓝。

me·thyl·ic [miˈθilik; mɪˋθɪlɪk] ***a.*** 甲基的,得自甲基的,含甲基的。

me·tic·u·lous [miˈtikjuləs; məˋtɪkjələs] ***a.*** **1.** 过分注意琐事的,小心翼翼的,胆小的。**2.** 细致的,明察秋毫的。~ *cares* 无微不至的关怀。*careful and* ~ *calculation* 精打细算。**-ly** ***ad.***

mé·tier [ˈmeitjei; ˋmetje] ***n.*** 〔F.〕职业,生意,工作;专长(尤指得心应手的工作)。

mé·tis [meiˈtiːs; meˋtis] ***n.*** 〔F.〕(*fem.* ***mé·tisse*** [meiˈtiːs; meˋtis]) (尤指加拿大的)白种人和印第安人的混血人;〔美〕黑白混血人;【动】杂种。

me·tol [ˈmiːtɔl; ˋmitol] ***n.*** 甲胺酚,甲氨基酚;密妥耳〔显像药〕。

me·ton. = metonymy.

Me·ton·ic [meˈtɔnik; məˋtɑnɪk] ***a.*** (公元前五世纪雅典天文学家)梅通 (Meton) 的,梅通发现的。*the* ~ *cycle* 梅通周期。

met·o·nym [ˈmetənim; ˋmɛtənɪm] ***n.*** 换喻词,转喻词。

me·ton·y·my [miˈtɔnimi; mɪˋtɑnəmɪ] ***n.*** 【修】换喻,转喻〔如用 crown 表 king, 用 sword 表 war〕。**-nym·ic, -i·cal** ***a.***

me-too [ˈmiːˈtuː; ˋmiˋtu] **I** ***a.*** 〔美口〕行仿效计策的;持仿效态度的(尤指政客仿效其政敌的策略的态度)。**II** ***vt.*** 〔美口〕模仿,同意(对方的政见等)。**-ism** ***n.***

met·ope [ˈmetəup; ˋmɛtop] ***n.*** 【建】排档间饰。

me·top·ic [miˈtɔpik; mɪˋtɑpɪk] ***a.*** 【解】额的;前面的。

met·o·pon [ˈmetəpɔn; ˋmɛtəˏpɑn] ***n.*** 【药】米托本,甲二氢吗啡酮〔一种麻醉镇痛剂〕。

met·o·pos·copy [ˌmetəˈpɔskəpi; ˏmɛtəˋpɑskəpɪ] ***n.*** 相学,观相术;骨相学。

Met. R. = Metropolitan Railway 〔英〕首都地下铁道。

me·tral·gi·a [miˈtrældʒiə; mɪˋtrældʒɪə] ***n.*** 【医】子宫痛。

Met·ra·zol [ˈmetrəzɔl; ˋmɛtrəˏzol] ***n.*** 【药】伸戊四唑,五甲烯四氮唑〔一种中枢神经系统刺激剂〕。

me·tre[1] [ˈmiːtə; ˋmitɚ] ***n.*** 【韵】韵律;格律;(诗的)音步形

式;【乐】拍子。

me·tre² [ˈmiːtə; ˋmitə] *n.* 米。*a running* ～ 直线米。～**bridge** 滑线电桥。

me·tre-kil·o·gram(me)-sec·ond [ˈmiːtəˈkiləgræm-ˈsekənd; ˋmitəˏkɪləgræmˋsɛkənd] *a.* 米公斤秒制。

met·ric [ˈmetrik; ˋmɛtrɪk] *a.* **1.** 公制的,米制的;十进制的;习惯于用公制的。**2.** 度量的。～ *space* 距离空间。*a* ～ *ton* 公吨(=1000公斤)。*the* ～ *system* 米制,公制。～ **count**【纺】公制支数。～ **hundredweight** 公担〔等于50公斤的一种衡制〕。～ **mile**【体】一千五百米。～ **space** 度量空间。

met·ri·cal [ˈmetrikəl; ˋmɛtrɪkl] *a.* **1.** 韵律的,格律的;诗的。**2.** 测[度]量(用)的。～ *compositions* 韵文,诗。*a* ～ *romance* 韵文小说。～ *geometry* 测量几何。**-ly** *ad.*

me·tri·cian, met·rist [miˈtriʃən, ˈmetrist; mɛˋtrɪʃən, ˋmɛtrɪst] *n.* 韵文作者;精于韵律者;韵律学家。

met·rics [ˈmetriks; ˋmɛtrɪks] *n.* 韵律学,诗作法。

met·ri·fy [ˈmetrifai; ˋmɛtrɪˏfaɪ] *vt.*, *vi.* (*-fied*; *-fying*) **1.** (使)采用十进制。**2.** 用韵律写;(把…)写成诗;改(散文)成诗。**-fic·a·tion** [ˌmetrifiˈkeiʃən; ˏmɛtrɪfɪˋkeʃən] *n.* 采用十进制。

me·tri·tis [miˈtraitis; mɪˋtraɪtɪs] *n.*【医】子宫炎。

Met·ro [ˈmetrəu; ˋmɛtro] **I** *n.*〔英〕**1.** = the Metropolitan Railway. **2.** 地下铁道。**3.**〔m-〕大都市地方政府。**II** *a.*〔m-〕大都市的。

Met·ro·lin·er [ˈmetrəlainə; ˋmɛtrəlaɪnə] *n.* (行驶于华盛顿与纽约之间的)快速火车。

me·tro·log·i·cal [ˌmetrəˈlɔdʒikəl; ˏmɛtrəˋlɑdʒɪkl] *a.* 计量学的。

me·trol·o·gist [miˈtrɔlədʒist; mɪˋtrɑlədʒɪst] *n.* 计量学家;度量衡工作者。

me·trol·o·gy [miˈtrɔlədʒi; mɪˋtrɑlədʒɪ] *n.* 计量学[制];度量衡学[制]。

me·tro·ma·ni·a [ˌmetrəˈmeinjə; ˏmɛtrəˋmenɪə] *n.* 作诗狂。

met·ro·nome [ˈmetrənəum; ˋmɛtrəˏnom] *n.*【乐】节拍器。*repeat like a* ～ 机械地重复。

met·ro·nom·ic [ˌmetrəˈnɔmik; ˏmɛtrəˋnɑmɪk] *a.* 节拍器的;像节拍器的。

me·tro·nym·ic [ˌmiːtrəˈnimik, ˌme-; ˏmitrəˋnɪmɪk, ˏmɛ-] *a.* 来自母亲(或女系祖先)的姓名的(*opp.* patronymic)。*a* ～ *family* 母姓家庭。～ *tribes* 母姓部落。

me·tron·ymy [meˈtrɔnimi; mɛˋtrɑnəmɪ] *n.*【社】母姓制。

me·trop·lex [ˈmetrəpleks; ˋmɛtrəplɛks] *n.* 大都会区。

me·trop·o·lis [miˈtrɔpəlis; məˋtrɑplɪs] *n.* **1.** 首都。**2.**【宗】大主教区。**3.** (产业、艺术等的)中心;主要都市,都会。**4.**【希腊史】殖民地的母国。**5.**【生】种属中心地。*the M-*〔英〕伦敦。*a* ～ *of commerce* 商业中心。

met·ro·pol·i·tan [ˌmetrəˈpɔlitən; ˏmɛtrəˋpɑlətən] **I** *a.* **1.** 首都的;主要城市的。**2.** 大主教教区的。**3.** 宗主国的。*the* ～ *district* 首都行政区。*the M- Railway*〔英〕伦敦地下铁道。*the* ～ *state* 宗主国。*the* ～ (*bishop*) 大主教。**II** *n.* 大城市人;有大城市气派的人;大主教。

met·ro·pol·i·tan·ize [ˌmetrəˈpɔlitənaiz; ˏmɛtrəˋpɑlɪtəˏnaɪz] *vt.* (*-ized*; *-iz·ing*) 使大都会化;使具有大都会特点。**-tan·ism** *n.* 大都会主义;大都会生活的特点;大都会对其居民的影响。**-tani·za·tion** [ˌmetrəˌpɔlitəˈnaizeiʃən; ˏmɛtrəˏpɑlɪtəˋnaɪzeʃən] *n.*

me·tror·rha·gi·a [ˌmiːtrəˈreidʒiə; ˏmitrəˋredʒɪə] *n.*【医】子宫出血,血崩症。

-metry *suf.* …测定法[术],…测定学: geo*metry*.

met·tle [ˈmetl; ˋmɛtl] *n.* 气质,脾性,性格;勇气;精神,气概。*a man of* ～ 有气概的人。**be** (**up**) **on one's** ～ 奋发,鼓起勇气。**put** [**set**] **sb. to** [**on, upon**] **his** ～ 激励[鼓励]某人。

met·tled, met·tle·some [ˈmetld, ˈmetlsəm; ˋmɛtld, ˋmɛtlsəm] *a.* 有精神的,精神饱满的,勇敢的,威风凛凛的。**-ly** *ad.*

Metz [mets; mɛts] *n.* 梅斯〔法国城市〕。

me·um [ˈmiːəm; ˋmiəm] *pro.*〔L.〕我的东西。～ ***et tu·um*** [etˈtjuːəm; ɛtˋtjuəm] 我的和你的(= mine and thine);人我之别;各自所有权。

meu·nière [muˈnjeə; muˋnjɛr] *a.*〔F.〕黄油炸鱼的〔鱼沾上面粉;用黄油炸后撒上柠檬汁和芥末〕。

MEV, Mev, mev, m.e.v. = million electron volts 兆电子伏(特),百万电子伏(特)。

MEW = microwave early warning【军】微波预先警报。

M.E.W. = Ministry of Economic Warfare〔英旧〕经济作战部。

mew¹ [mjuː; mju] **I** *n.* 咪咪〔猫叫声〕。**II** *vi.* (猫、海鸟等)咪咪地叫。

mew² [mjuː; mju] *n.*【鸟】海鸥〔通常叫 sea-mew〕。

mew³ [mjuː; mju] **I** *n.* **1.** (换羽时用的)鹰笼。**2.** (催肥鸡等用的)育肥笼。**3.** 换羽。**4.**〔*pl.*〕〔英〕〔作单数用〕(设有马车房的)马店。**II** *vt.* 把(鹰)关在笼里;关起,藏起(*up*)。

mew⁴ [mjuː; mju] *vt.*, *vi.*〔古〕(使)(鹰等)换羽;(使)(鹿)换角。

mewl [mjuːl; mjul] **I** *n.* (婴儿等的)低哭声。**II** *vi.* 低声哭泣;(猫)咪咪地叫。

Mex. = Mexican; Mexico.

Mex·i·can [ˈmeksikən; ˋmɛksɪkən] **I** *n.* **1.** 墨西哥人。**2.**〔美方〕有墨西哥人和印第安人血统的人。**3.** (印第安语系中的)一种阿茨蒂克(Aztec)语。**II** *a.* 墨西哥(人)的。～ **bean beetle**【动】墨西哥瓢虫。～ **hairless** (**dog**) 墨西哥秃狗〔除头上有一片毛和尾端有毛之外全身无毛〕。～ **wave** 墨西哥人潮,人浪〔人群依次起立再坐下,形成波浪式人潮,始创者为1986年世界杯足球赛在墨西哥举行时的当地观众〕。

Mex·i·co [ˈmeksikəu; ˋmɛksɪˏko] *n.* **1.** 墨西哥〔拉丁美洲〕。**2.** 墨西哥〔墨西哥州名〕。**3.** 墨西哥城〔墨西哥首都〕(= ～ City)。

Mey·er [ˈmaiə; ˋmaɪə] *n.* 迈耶〔姓氏〕。

Mey·er·hof [ˈmaiəhɔːf; ˋmaɪəˏhɔf], **O.** 梅尔霍夫〔1884—1951,德国生理学家〕。

mez·ca·line [ˈmezkəliːn; ˋmɛzkəˏlin] *n.* 墨斯卡灵〔一种幻觉剂 = mescaline〕。

me·ze·re·um [məˈziəriəm; məˋzɪrɪəm] **I** *n.* **1.**【植】欧亚瑞香。**2.** 欧亚瑞香皮。**II** *a.* 瑞香料的(= mezereon)。

me·zu·za [məˈzuzə, -ˈzuː-; məˋzuzə, -ˋzu-] *n.* (*pl.* **-zot(h)** [-zəut; -zot], **-za(h)s**)【犹】门柱圣卷〔犹太家庭挂于门柱之上的小羊皮纸圣经卷〕。

mez·za·nine [ˈmezəniːn; ˋmɛzənin] *n.* (底楼与二楼之间的)夹层(楼面);(戏院的)楼厅包厢;(舞台下的)底层。

mez·zo [ˈmedzəu; ˋmɛdzo] *a.*, *ad.*〔It.〕【乐】中,适中,半。～ ***forte***【乐】中强,不很响。～ ***piano***【乐】中弱,不很轻。～***-soprano***【乐】女中音;女中音歌手。

mez·zo-ri·lie·vo [ˈmedzəuriljˈeivəu; ˏmɛdzoriljˋevo] *n.*〔It.〕(*pl.* ***mez·zi-ri·lie·vi***) 半凸雕。

mez·zo·tint [ˈmedzəutint; ˋmɛdzətɪnt] **I** *n.* 镂刻凹板(作品);制成镂刻凹版,印刷法[印刷品]。**II** *vt.* 把…制成镂刻凹版。

MF = **1.**〔常作 mf〕medium frequency【无】中频。**2.**〔It.〕〔常作 mf〕*mezzo forte*【乐】不很响,中强。**3.** machine finish [mill finish] 机械光滑度〔印书纸或封面纸由研光机研出的光滑程度〕。**4.** Middle French 中世纪法语。**5.** middling fair〔美〕一级棉。

mf. = **1.** microfarad. **2.** millifarad. **3.** manufacture.

mfd. = manufactured.

mfg. = manufacturing.
MFN = most favo(u)red nation 最惠国。
MFR = manufacturer.
mfr. = manufacturer.
mfs. = manufactures.
M.F.V. = motor fleet vessel 海军内燃机船。
MG = machine gun 机枪。
Mg = magnesium【化】镁。
mg. = milligram(me)(s).
M.G.C. = Machine Gun Corps 机枪队。
MGM = Metro-Goldwin-Mayer 美国米高梅影片公司。
Mgr. = **1**. manager. **2**.〔F.〕*Monseigneur*. **3**.〔It.〕*Monsignor(e)*.
M.H.G. = Middle High German 中世纪高地德语。
mho [məu; mo] ***n***.〔Ohm 的倒写〕【电】姆(欧)。
M.H.R. = Member of the House of Representatives〔美〕众议院议员。
MI = **1**. military intelligence 军事情报;军事情报工作;军事情报部门。**2**. medical inspection 检疫。**3**. malleable iron【冶】可展铁,锻铁。
Mi = Mississippi 密西西比。
mi [miː; mi] ***n***.〔It.〕【乐】全音阶第三音。
mi. = mile.
MIA = missing in action【军】战斗失踪人员。
Mi·am·i [maiˈæmi; maɪˋæmɪ] (*pl*. ~(***s***)) ***n***. **1**. 迈阿密〔美国港市〕。**2**. 迈阿米人〔美国印第安人的一支〕。
mi·aow, mi·aou [mi(ː)ˈau; mɪˋaʊ] **I** ***n***. 喵〔猫叫声〕。**II** ***vi***. 喵喵地叫。
mi·as·ma [miˈæzmə; maɪˋæzmə] ***n***. (*pl*. ~***s***, ~***ta*** [-tə; -tə]) (腐败有机物发散的)毒气,(尤指)瘴气;有害的气氛[影响]。
mi·as·mal, mi·as·mat·ic, mi·as·mic [miˈæzməl, miəzˈmætik, miˈæzmik; mɪˋæzməl, mɪəzˋmætɪk, mɪˋæzmɪk] ***a***. 毒气的,瘴气的。*miasmic fever* 疟疾。
mi·au(l) [mi(ː)ˈau, mjau; mɪˋaʊ, mjaʊ] ***vi***. = miaow.
MIB = master of international business 国际工商硕士。
mi·ca [ˈmaikə; ˋmaɪkə] ***n***.【矿】云母。
mi·ca·ceous [maiˈkeiʃəs; maɪˋkeʃəs] ***a***. **1**. 云母(似)的;含云母的。**2**. 分层的;有光彩的。
Mi·cah [ˈmaikə; ˋmaɪkə] ***n***. **1**. 迈卡〔男子名〕。**2**. 弥迦〔公元前八世纪的希伯来先知〕;《圣经·旧约》中的篇名《弥迦书》。
mi·ca·schist, mi·ca·slate [ˈmaikəsist, -sleit; ˋmaɪkəsɪst, -slet] ***n***.【地】云母片岩。
Mi·caw·ber·ism [miˈkɔːbərizəm; meˋkɔbərɪzm] ***n***. 幻想突然走运的乐天主义〔出自 Dickens 所著小说 David Copperfield 中人物 Micawber〕。
M.I.C.E. = Member of the Institute of Civil Engineers〔英〕土木工程师学会会员。
mice [mais; maɪs] ***n***. mouse 的复数。
mi·cel·la [maiˈselə; maɪˋsɛlə] ***n***. (*pl*. ***-lae*** [-liː; -li]) = micell(e).
mi·celle [maiˈsel, mi-; maɪˋsɛl, mɪ-] ***n***. **1**.【生】分子团。**2**.【化】胶束;胶态离子;细胞束;胶粒。**-cel·lar** ***a***.
Mich. = Michael; Michaelmas; Michigan.
Mi·chael [ˈmaikl; ˋmaɪkl] ***n***. **1**. 迈克尔〔男子名〕。**2**. 米迦勒〔天使长〕。*the Order of St*. ~ *and St*. *George* 圣米迦勒与圣乔治勋章〔英国文官勋章之一〕。
Mich·ael·mas [ˈmiklməs; ˋmɪklməs] ***n***. 米迦勒节〔9月29日,英国四大结账日 (Quarter days) 之一〕。~ **daisy**【植】紫苑。~ **goose** 米迦勒节吃的鹅。
Mi·chel(le) [miːˈʃel; miˋʃɛl] ***n***. 米歇尔〔女子名〕。
Mi·chel·an·ge·lo [ˌmaikəˈlændʒiləu; ˌmaɪklˋændʒəˌlo], **Buonarrotti** 米开朗基罗〔1475—1564,意大利雕刻家、画家、建筑家、诗人〕。
Mi·chel·son [ˈmitʃəlsn, ˈmikəlsn; ˋmɪtʃəlsn̩, ˋmɪkəlsn̩] ***n***. 米歇尔森〔姓氏〕。
Mich·el·son [ˈmitʃəlsn, ˈmaikəlsən; ˋmɪtʃəlsn̩, ˋmaɪkəlsn̩], **Albert Abraham** 米切尔森〔1852—1931,美国物理学家〕。
Mi·che·ner [ˈmitʃinə; ˋmɪtʃɪnɚ] ***n***. 米歇纳〔姓氏〕。
Mich·i·gan [ˈmiʃigən; ˋmɪʃəgən] ***n***. **1**. 密歇根[密执安]〔美国州名〕。**2**. 密歇根[密执安]湖〔美国〕(= Lake ~)。
mich·ing [ˈmitʃiŋ; ˋmɪtʃɪŋ] ***a***.〔方〕隐藏着的。
Mick [mik; mɪk] ***n***.〔美俚、蔑〕爱尔兰人。
Mick·ey [ˈmiki; ˋmɪkɪ] ***n***. 米基〔男子名, Michael 的昵称〕。
mick·ey[1] [ˈmiki; ˋmɪkɪ] ***n***.〔加拿大俚〕十三两装的威士忌酒。
mick·ey[2] [ˈmiki; ˋmɪkɪ] ***n***.〔英俚〕精神;骄傲,傲慢;自夸。★主要用于下述短语中: take the ~ 取笑;嘲弄。take the ~ out of 杀某人的威风。
Mick·ey (Finn), mick·ey (finn) [ˈmiki ˈfin; ˋmɪkɪ ˋfɪn]〔美俚〕混有麻醉药[泻药]的酒。
Mick·ey Mouse [ˈmiki maus; ˋmɪkɪ ˋmaʊs] **I** ***n***. **1**. 米老鼠〔美国卡通片中的主角〕。**2**.〔英空口〕分掷炸弹的装置。**3**.〔美军俚〕多余或无关重要的东西。**4**.〔美学俚〕简单容易的学院课程。**II** ***a***. **1**.〔美俚〕幼稚的,过于简单的;不重要的,与实际无关的。**2**.〔美俚〕(伴舞音乐)陈旧乏味的。
mick·le [ˈmikl; ˋmɪkl] **I** ***a***.〔Scot.〕〔古〕大的;许多的。**II** ***n***. 大量,多量。*Many a little* [*pickle*] *makes a* ~. = *Every little makes a* ~ [*muckle*]. 积少成多。
Mick·y [ˈmiki; ˋmɪkɪ] ***n***. 米基〔男子名, Michael 的昵称〕。
Mic·mac [ˈmikmæk; ˋmɪkmæk] ***n***. **1**. (*pl*. ***-macs***, ***-mac***) 密克马克人〔纽芬兰和加拿大沿海各省的一支印第安人〕。**2**. 密克马克语。
mi·cra [ˈmaikrə; ˋmaɪkrə] ***n***. micron 的复数。
mi·cri·fy [ˈmaikrifai; ˋmaɪkrəˏfaɪ] ***vt***. (***-fied***; ***-fying***) 使变小,使无足轻重。
micro- [ˈmaikrəu; ˋmaɪkro] *comb*. *f*. **1**. 小,微: *micro*cosm. **2**. 扩大: *micro*phone. **3**. 显微镜的: *micro*örganism. **4**. 微(=100 万分之一): *micro*ampere 微安(培)。*micro*farad 微法(拉)。*micromicro*farad 微微法。*micro*mho 微姆(欧)。*micro*volt 微伏(特)。
mi·cro [ˈmaikrəu; ˋmaɪkro] ***n***., ***a***.〔美口〕**1**. 微型电脑(的)。**2**. 特超短裙(的)。
mi·cro·al·loy [ˈmaikrəuˈælɔi; ˏmaɪkroˋælɔɪ] ***n***. 微合金。~ *diffused transistor* 微合金型扩散晶体管。
mi·cro·am·pere [ˈmaikrəuˈæmpεə; ˏmaɪkroˋæmpɪr] ***n***.【电】微安(培)。
mi·cro·a·nal·y·sis [ˈmaikrəuəˈnælisis; ˏmaɪkroəˋnæləsɪs] ***n***.【化】微量分析。**-an·a·lyst** [-ˈænlist; -ˋænlɪst] ***n***.
mi·cro·bak·ing [ˈmaikrəuˈbeikiŋ; ˋmaɪkroˋbekɪŋ] ***n***. 用微波炉烘烤食物。
mi·cro·bal·ance [ˈmaikrəuˈbæləns; ˏmaɪkroˋbæləns] ***n***. 微量天平。
mi·cro·bar [ˈmaikrəubɑː; ˋmaɪkrobɑr] ***n***. 微巴〔压力单位〕。
mi·cro·bar·o·graph [ˈmaikrəuˈbærəgræf; ˏmaɪkroˋbærəˏgræf] ***n***.【气】微(气)压计
mi·crobe [ˈmaikrəub; ˋmaɪkrob] ***n***. 微生物;(尤指引起疾病的)细菌。
mi·cro·bi·al, mi·cro·bian, mi·cro·bic [maiˈkrəubiəl, -biən, -bik; maɪˋkrobɪəl, -bɪən, -bɪk] ***a***. 微生物的,细菌的,因细菌而起的。
mi·cro·bi·cide [maiˈkrəubisaid; maɪˋkrobəˏsaɪd] ***n***.【化】杀微生物剂(= bactericide)。**-cidal** ***a***.
mi·cro·bi·ol·o·gy [ˌmaikrəubaiˈɔlədʒi; ˏmaɪkrobaɪˋɑlədʒɪ] ***n***. 微生物学。
mi·cro·bi·o·ta [ˈmaikrəuˈbaiəutə; ˏmaɪkroˋbaɪotə] ***n***.

微生物群。

mi·cro·bi·ot·ic [ˈmaikrəubaiˈɔtik; ˋmaɪkrobaɪˋɑtɪk] *a*. 微生物群的。

mi·cro·brew [ˈmaikrəubruː; ˋmaɪkrobru] *n*. (现酿现卖的)微酿啤酒。

mi·cro·bus [ˈmaikrəubʌs; ˋmaɪkro͵bʌs] *n*. 〔美〕微型公共汽车。

mi·cro·ca·lip·ers [ˈmaikrəuˈkælipəz; ͵maɪkroˋkælɪpɚz] *n*. 【机】千分尺;测微器。

mi·cro·card [ˈmaikrəukɑːd; ˋmaɪkro͵kɑrd] *n*. 缩微卡〔每张可缩印印刷物二百页以上;供以后放大阅读〕。

mi·cro·ceph·a·lous [ˈmaikrəuˈsefələs; ͵maɪkroˋsɛfələs] *a*. 头异常小的。

mi·cro·chem·is·try [ˈmaikrəuˈkemistri; ͵maɪkroˋkɛmɪstrɪ] *n*. 微量化学。

mi·cro·chip [ˈmaikrəutʃip; ˋmaɪkro͵tʃɪp] *n*. 〔美口〕微型集成电路片;微晶片。**-ping**【计】微型芯片跟踪〔指在动物体内塞入集成电路片以跟踪其行迹而进行监控〕。

mi·cro·chro·nom·eter [ˈmaikrəukrəˈnɔmitə; ͵maɪkrokrəˋnɑmɪtɚ] *n*. 分秒表,瞬时计。

mi·cro·cir·cuit [ˈmaikrəuˈsəːkit; ͵maɪkroˋsɝkɪt] *n*. 【无】微型电路。**-cuit·ry** *n*. 微型电路技术。

mi·cro·cli·mate [ˈmaikrəuˈklaimit; ͵maɪkroˋklaɪmɪt] *n*. 小气候。**-matic** *a*.

mi·cro·cli·ma·tol·o·gy [ˌmaikrəuˌklaiməˈtɔlədʒi; ͵maɪkro͵klaɪməˋtɑlədʒɪ] *n*. (微)小气候学。**-gist** *n*. 小气候学者。

mi·cro·cline [ˈmaikrəuklain; ˋmaɪkrə͵klaɪn] *n*. 【地】微斜长石。

mi·cro·coc·cus [ˌmaikrəuˈkɔkəs; ͵maɪkrəˋkɑkəs] *n*. (*pl*. *-coc·ci* [-ˈkɔksai; -ˋkɔksaɪ]) 小球菌,球状细菌。

mi·cro·com·put·er [ˈmaikrəukəmˈpjuːtə; ˋmaɪkrəkəm͵pjutɚ] *n*. 微型电子计算机。

mi·cro·cook [ˈmaikrəukuk; ˋmaɪkrokʊk] *vt*. **1.** 用微波炉烹调(食物)。**2.** 〔俚〕用超级电脑高速处理(数据等)。

mi·cro·co·py [ˈmaikrəuˈkɔpi; ˋmaɪkrə͵kɑpɪ] *n*. (用缩微胶卷摄制成的)缩微(复制)本,缩微副本。

mi·cro·cosm [ˈmaikrəukɔzəm; ˋmaɪkrə͵kɑzəm] *n*. **1.** 微观世界[宇宙](*opp*. macrocosm), (为宇宙缩影的)人;人类社会。**2.** 缩影。*Each day is a ~ of all life*. 一天是一生的缩影。

mi·cro·cos·mic, mi·cro·cos·mi·cal [ˈmaikrəuˈkɔzmik, -mikəl; ͵maɪkrəˋkɑzmɪk, -mɪkəl] *a*. (像)微观世界的。~ *salt*【化】小天地盐〔四水合磷酸氢铵钠的别名〕。

mi·cro·crith [ˈmaikrəukriθ; ˋmaɪkro͵krɪθ] *n*. 【化】(作为单位的)氢原子量。

mi·cro·crys·tal·line [ˌmaikrəuˈkristəlain, -lin; ͵maɪkroˋkrɪstəlaɪn, -lɪn] *a*. 【化】微晶(质)的。

mi·cro·cyte [ˈmaikrəusait; ˋmaɪkrə͵saɪt] *n*. 【医】小红血球。**-cyt·ic** [-ˈsitik; -ˋsɪtɪk] *a*.

mi·cro·dont [ˈmaikrəudɔnt; ˋmaɪkrə͵dɑnt] *a*. 有小牙的(= microdontous)。**-ism** *n*.

mi·cro·dot [ˈmaikrəudɔt; ˋmaɪkrə͵dɑt] *n*. 【摄】微点拷贝,微点照片〔进行间谍活动等拍摄文件等用〕。

mi·cro·e·lec·tron·ics [ˈmaikrəuilekˈtrɔniks; ͵maɪkroɪlɛkˋtrɑnɪks] *n*. 〔作单数用〕微电子学,超小型电子工学。**-tronic** *a*.

mi·cro·el·e·ment [ˈmaikrəuˈelimənt; ˋmaɪkro͵ɛləmənt] *n*. **1.** 【化】微量元素。**2.** 微型元件。

mi·cro·en·cap·su·lat [ˌmaikrəuinˈkæpsəleit, -sju-; ͵maɪkroɪnˋkæpsəlet, -sju-] *vt*. 把(微粒药物、液滴的)用胶囊封闭。**-su·la·tion** *n*.

mi·cro·en·vi·ron·ment [ˈmaikrəuinˈvaiərəment; ͵maɪkroɪnˋvaɪrəmənt] *n*. 【生】(动植物生长的)微(小)环境。

mi·cro·ev·o·lu·tion [ˌmaikrəuˌevəˈljuːʃən; ͵maɪkro͵ɛvəˋljuʃən] *n*. 【生】微进化,种内进化。

mi·cro·fac·tion [ˈmaikrəuˈfækʃən; ͵maɪkroˋfækʃən] *n*. 小宗派,小集团。

mi·cro·far·ad [ˈmaikrəˈfærəd, -əd; ͵maɪkroˋfærəd, -əd] *n*. 【电】微法(拉)〔电容单位〕。

mi·cro·fiche [ˈmaikrəufiːʃ; ˋmaɪkrə͵fiʃ] *n*. 缩微胶片。

mi·cro·film [ˈmaikrəufilm; ˋmaɪkrə͵fɪlm] **I** *n*. (印刷品等的)缩微胶卷;缩微照片。**II** *vt*. 用缩微法摄制(印刷品等)。— *vi*. 摄制缩微胶卷。**-er** *n*. 缩微摄影机。

mi·cro·form [ˈmaikrəufɔːm; ˋmaɪkrə͵fɔrm] **I** *n*. (文件等的)缩微过程;〔集合词〕缩微印刷品。**II** *vt*. 把…复制在缩微材料上。

mi·cro·ga·mete [ˈmaikrəuˈgæmiːt; ͵maɪkroˋgæmit] *n*. 【生】小配子。

mi·cro·gram [ˈmaikrəugræm; ˋmaɪkro͵græm] *n*. **1.** 微克(重量单位,符号为 μg)(= microgramme)。**2.** 显微照片;微写器。

mi·cro·graph [ˈmaikrəugrɑːf, -græf; ˋmaɪkrə͵grɑf, -græf] *n*. 微写器;【物】微动扩大测定器;显微(镜)制图[照相、照片]。

mi·crog·ra·phy [maiˈkrɔgrəfi; maɪˋkrɑgrəfɪ] *n*. **1.** 显微(镜)照相(检查),显微照相术。**2.** 【医】字体过小症。

mi·cro·groove [ˈmaikrəugruːv; ˋmaɪkrə͵gruv] *n*. (唱片的)密纹。~ *recording* 密纹录声。

mi·crohm [ˈmaikrəum; ˋmaɪkrom] *n*. 【电】微欧(姆)。

mi·cro·lite [ˈmaikrəulait; ˋmaɪkro͵laɪt] *n*. **1.** 【物】微晶。**2.** 【矿】细晶石,钽烧绿石。

mi·cro·lith [ˈmaikrəuliθ; ˋmaɪkro͵lɪθ] *n*. (中石器时代的)细小石器。

mi·cro·li·tre, mi·cro·li·ter [ˈmaikrəuˈliːtə; ˋmaɪkro͵litɚ] *n*. 微升(千分之一毫升)。

mi·crol·o·gy [maiˈkrɔlədʒi; maɪˋkrɑlədʒɪ] *n*. **1.** 显微学。**2.** 留心琐事,剖析毫末。

mi·cro·mech·an·ism [ˈmaikrəuˈmekənizəm; ͵maɪkroˋmɛkənɪzəm] *n*. 【物】微观机构。

mi·cro·mere [ˈmaikrəumiə; ˋmaɪkro͵mɪr] *n*. 小(分)裂球,小裂细胞。

mi·cro·me·rit·ics [ˈmaikrəuˈmiritiks; ˋmaɪkroˋmɪrɪtɪks] *n*. 微晶(粒)学;微尘学。

mi·cro·me·te·or·ite [ˈmaikrəuˈmiːtiərait; ͵maɪkroˋmitɪə͵raɪt] *n*. 【地】微陨星,陨石微粒。

mi·cro·me·te·or·oid [ˈmaikrəuˈmiːtiərɔid; ͵maɪkroˋmitɪə͵rɔɪd] *n*. 【天】微流星体。

mi·cro·me·te·or·ol·o·gy [ˌmaikrəuˌmiːtiəˈrɔlədʒi; ͵maɪkro͵mitɪəˋrɑlədʒɪ] *n*. 微气象学。**-gist** *n*.

mi·crom·e·ter [maiˈkrɔmitə; maɪˋkrɑmətɚ] *n*. 【机】测微计,千分尺;【天】测距器。~ **calliper** [**gauge**] 千分卡尺,螺旋测径器。~**screw**【机】测微螺旋。~ **sight** 测微瞄准器。

mi·crom·e·try [maiˈkrɔmitri; maɪˋkrɑmətrɪ] *n*. 测微术,测微法。

mi·cro·mi·cron [ˈmaikrəuˈmaikrɔn; ͵maɪkroˋmaɪkrɑn] *n*. 微微米[10^{-12} 米]。

mi·cro·min·i [ˈmaikrəuˈmini; ͵maɪkroˋmɪnɪ] *n*. 超超短裙,超迷你裙。

mi·cro·min·i·a·ture [ˈmaikrəuˈminiətʃə, -ˈminitʃə; ͵maɪkroˋmɪnɪətʃɚ, -ˋmɪnɪtʃɚ] *a*. (电子元件,线路等)超小型的,微型的;使用超小型电子元件(线路)的;使用微型电子元件(线路)的。

mi·cro·mi·ni·a·tur·i·za·tion [ˈmaikrəuˌminjətʃəraiˈzeiʃən; ͵maɪkro͵mɪnɪətʃərəˋzeʃən] *n*. 超小型化,微型化生产。

mi·cro·min·i·a·tur·ize [ˌmaikrəuˈminiətʃəraiz; ͵maɪkroˋmɪnɪətʃər͵aɪz] *vt*. (*-ized*; *-iz·ing*) 使超小型化,使微型化。

mi·cro·mod·ule [ˈmaikrəuˈmɔdjuːl; ͵maɪkroˋmɑdjul] *n*. 【无】微型组件,超小型器件。

M

mi·cro·mon·ey [ˈmaikrəuˈmʌni; ˋmaɪkroˋmʌnɪ] ***n.*** 网络微量收费〔电脑因特网上收取的少量货币,亦作 micropayment 或 micropricing〕。

mi·cro·mo·tor [ˈmaikrəuˈməutə; ˏmaɪkroˋmotɚ] ***n.*** 【电】微电机。

mi·cron [ˈmaikrɔn; ˋmaɪkrɑn] ***n.*** (*pl.* ~s, *-cra* [-krə; -krə]) 微米〔100 万分之一米,符号 μ〕。

Mi·cro·ne·sia [ˈmaikrəuˈniːzjə; ˏmaɪkroˋniʒə] ***n.*** 密克罗尼西亚〔西太平洋的岛屿〕。

Mi·cro·ne·sian [ˈmaikrəˈniːzjən, -ʃən; ˏmaɪkrəˋniʒən, -ʃən] ***a.***, ***n.*** 密克罗尼西亚(人、语)的;密克罗尼西亚人(语)。

mi·cron·ize [ˈmaikrənaiz; ˋmaɪkroˏnaɪz] ***vt.*** (*-ized*; *-iz·ing*) 使成为(直径小到几微米的)粒子。

mi·cro·nu·cle·us [ˈmaikrəuˈnjuːkliəs, -ˈnuː-; ˏmaɪkroˋnjuklɪəs, -ˋnu-] ***n.*** 【生】小核。**-clear** ***a.***

mi·cro·nu·tri·ent [ˈmaikrəuˈnjuːtriənt, -ˈnuː-; ˏmaɪkroˋnjutrɪənt, -ˋnu-] ***n.*** 微量营养素。

mi·cro·or·gan·ism [ˈmaikrəuˈɔːgənizəm; ˏmaɪkroˋɔrgənˏɪzəm] ***n.*** 微生物。

mi·cro·pac·er [ˈmaikrəuˈpeisə; ˋmaɪkroˋpesɚ] ***n.*** 【商标】微电脑跑鞋〔鞋舌上装有微电脑,使显示器上亮出跑过的距离、时间,步速等〕。

mi·cro·par·a·site [ˈmaikrəuˈpærəsait; ˏmaɪkroˋpærəˏsaɪt] ***n.*** 【生】微寄生物。**-sit·ic** [-ˈsitik; -ˋsɪtɪk] ***a.***

mi·cro·phone [ˈmaikrəufəun; ˋmaɪkrəˏfon] ***n.*** 话筒,传声器,麦克风〔略 mike〕。~ *capsule* (电话)炭精盒。**-phon·ic** ***a.***

mi·cro·phon·ics [ˈmaikrəuˈfɔniks; ˏmaɪkrəˋfɑnɪks] ***n.*** 〔用作单数〕【无】颤噪效应,颤噪声。

mi·cro·pho·to·graph [ˈmaikrəuˈfəutəgrɑːf; ˏmaɪkrəˋfotəgræf] ***n.*** 显微照相(片),缩微照片,缩微放大照片。

mi·cro·pho·tog·ra·phy [ˈmaikrəufəˈtɔgrəfi; ˏmaɪkrəfəˋtɑgrəfɪ] ***n.*** 显微[缩微]照相术。

mi·cro·phyte [ˈmaikrəufait; ˋmaɪkrəˏfaɪt] ***n.*** 微小植物,微生物,细菌。

mi·cro·porous [ˈmaikrəuˈpɔːrəs; ˏmaɪkroˋporəs] ***a.*** 多微孔的,微孔性的。

mi·cro·print [ˈmaikrəuˌprint; ˋmaɪkrəˏprɪnt] ***n.*** (文件等的)缩微印刷品。

mi·cro·probe [ˈmaikrəuprəub; ˋmaɪkrəˏprob] ***n.*** 微探针〔一种使用细聚焦电子束的仪器〕。

mi·cro·pro·ces·sor [ˈmaikrəuˈprəusesə; ˋmaɪkroˋprosɛsɚ] ***n.*** 【计】微处理器。

mi·cro·pyle [ˈmaikrəpail; ˋmaɪkroˏpaɪl] ***n.*** **1.** 【植】珠孔;卵孔。**2.** 【动】卵(膜)孔。**-py·lar** [-ˈpailə; -ˋpaɪlɚ] ***a.***

mi·cro·py·rom·e·ter [ˌmaikrəupaiˈrɔmitə; ˏmaɪkropaɪˋrɑmətɚ] ***n.*** 精测高温计。

mi·cro·ra·di·o·graph [ˌmaikrəuˈreidiəugrɑːf, -græf; ˏmaɪkroˋredɪəˏgræf, -grɑf] ***n.*** X 射线显微相片。**-graph·ic, -i·cal** ***a.*** **-gra·phy** [-ˌreidiˈɔgrəfi; -ˏredɪˋɑgrəfɪ] ***n.***

mi·cro·read·er [ˈmaikrəuˌriːdə; ˋmaɪkroˏridɚ] ***n.*** 显微阅读器。

mi·cros. = microscopy.

mi·cro·scope [ˈmaikrəuskəup; ˋmaɪkrəˏskop] ***n.*** 显微镜。*a binocular* ~ 双目显微镜。*an electron* ~ 电子显微镜。*a field ion emission* ~ (比电子显微镜效率大 5—10 倍的)场致离子投影显微镜。*a reading* ~ 读数显微镜。*a solar* ~ 日光显微镜。

mi·cro·scop·ic, mi·cro·scop·i·cal [ˌmaikrəuˈskɔpik, -ikəl; ˏmaɪkrəˋskɑpɪk, -ɪkəl] ***a.*** **1.** (像)显微镜的。**2.** 用显微镜可见的;微观的;极微的(*opp.* macroscopic)。*a ~ examination* 显微镜检查。*a ~ organism* 微生物。**-i·cal·ly** ***ad.*** **1.** 用显微镜。**2.** 极微。

mi·cros·co·pist [maiˈkrɔskəpist; maɪˋkrɑskəpɪst] ***n.*** 会用显微镜的人。

mi·cros·co·py [maiˈkrɔskəpi; maɪˋkrɑskəpɪ] ***n.*** 显微镜学;显微镜使用术。

mi·cro·se·cond [ˈmaikrəuˈsekənd; ˏmaɪkroˋsɛkənd] ***n.*** 微秒〔百万分之一秒〕。

micro-sec·tion [ˈmaikrəuˈsekʃən; ˏmaɪkroˋsɛkʃən] ***n.*** (显微镜检查用的)薄切片,(显微)磨片。

mi·cro·seism [ˈmaikrəsaizəm; ˋmaɪkrəsaɪzm̩] ***n.*** 【地】微震,脉动。**-seis·mic, -seis·mi·cal** ***a.***

mi·cro·seis·mo·graph [ˌmaikrəuˈsaizməgrɑːf; ˏmaɪkrəˋsaɪzməˏgræf] ***n.*** 微震计,微动计。

mi·cro·seis·mol·o·gy [ˈmaikrəusaizˈmɔlədʒi; ˏmaɪkrəˏsaɪzˋmɑlədʒɪ] ***n.*** 【地】微震学。

mi·cro·seis·mom·e·ter [ˌmaikrəusaizˈmɔmitə; ˏmaɪkrəsaɪzˋmɑmətɚ] ***n.*** 微震计。

mi·cro·serf [ˈmaikrəusəːf; ˋmaɪkrosɚf] ***n.*** 网虫,网奴〔指沉迷于电脑网络的人〕。

mi·cro-slide [ˈmaikrəuslaid; ˋmaɪkrəˏslaɪd] ***n.*** (显微镜的)载玻片。

mi·cro·some [ˈmaikrəusəum; ˋmaɪkrəˏsom] ***n.*** 【生】微粒体,微体。

mi·cro·sphere [ˈmaikrəusfiə; ˋmaɪkrəˏsfɪr] ***n.*** 【动】中心球,缩小球体。

mi·cro·spo·ran·gi·um [ˌmaikrəuspəˈrændʒiəm; ˏmaɪkrəspəˋrændʒɪəm] ***n.*** (*pl.* *-gi·a* [-ə; -ə]) 【植】小孢子囊。

mi·cro·spore [ˈmaikrəuspɔː; ˋmaɪkrəˏspor] ***n.*** 【植】小孢子;(显花植物的)花粉粒。

mi·cro·spo·ro·phyll [ˈmaikrəuˈspɔːrəfil; ˏmaɪkrəˋsporəfɪl] ***n.*** 【植】小芽胞叶。

mi·cro·stom·a·tous [ˈmaikrəuˈstɔmətəs, -ˈstəumə-; ˏmaɪkrəˋstɑmətəs, -ˋstomə-] ***a.*** 有小口的(= microstomous)。

mi·cro·struc·ture [ˈmaikrəuˈstrʌktʃə; ˋmaɪkroˏstrʌktʃɚ] ***n.*** 显微结构,微观结构〔如金属或合金放在显微镜下所看到的结构〕。

mi·cro·sur·ger·y [ˈmaikrəuˈsəːdʒəri; ˏmaɪkroˋsɝdʒərɪ] ***n.*** 显微外科手术。

mi·cro·syn [ˈmaikrəusin; ˋmaɪkrosɪn] ***n.*** 微动同步器;微动协调器;精密自动同步机。

mi·cro·tome [ˈmaikrəutəum; ˋmaɪkrəˏtom] ***n.*** (显微)切片机[刀]。

mi·crot·o·my [maiˈkrɔtəmi; maɪˋkrɑtəmɪ] ***n.*** 【医】切片法。**-mist** ***n.*** 制作切片专家。

mi·cro·tone [ˈmaikrəutəun; ˋmaɪkrəˏton] ***n.*** 【音】微分音。

mi·cro·tron [ˈmaikrəutrɔn; ˋmaɪkrəˏtrɑn] ***n.*** 电子回旋加速器。

mi·cro·tron·ics [ˌmaikrəuˈtrɔniks; ˏmaɪkrəˋtrɑnɪks] 〔*pl.*〕***n.*** 〔用作 *sing.*〕【无】微(型)电子学。

mi·cro·waves [ˈmaikrəuweivz; ˋmaɪkrəˏwevz] ***n.*** 〔*pl.*〕微波,超短波。~ **oven** 微波炉〔用以烧烤食品〕。

mi·cro·zyme [ˈmaikrəuzaim; ˋmaɪkrəˏzaɪm] ***n.*** 酵母菌。

mic·tu·rate [ˈmiktʃureit; ˋmɪktʃəˏret] ***vt.***, ***vi.*** (使)排尿(= urinate)。

mic·tu·ri·tion [ˌmiktjuəˈriʃən; ˏmɪktʃəˋrɪʃən] ***n.*** 【医】排尿。

mid[1] [mid; mɪd] ***a.*** (*superl.* ***midmost*** [ˈmidməust; ˋmɪdmost]) **1.** 中央的,中部的,中间的〔常构成复合词〕。**2.** 【语】央母音的,半开母音的。*from ~ May to ~ September* 从五月中旬到九月中旬。***in ~ air*** [***mid-air***] 在半空中。***in ~ career*** [***course***] 在中途。**~day** ***n.***, ***a.*** 正午(的),日中(的)(*~day flower* 松叶菊)。**~heaven** 中空;中天;【天】子午圈。**~iron** 【高尔夫球】(在 cleek 与 mashie 之间的)中铁头棒。**~land** ***n.***, ***a.*** 内地(的);中部地方(的);被陆地包围着的;〔M-〕英国中

M

部地方(的方言);美国中部及东部一些州(的方言)(*the Midlands* 英国中西部诸郡〔伯明翰四周〕)。~**most** *a*. (= middlemost). ~**night** *n*., *a*. 午夜(的);漆黑(的)(*the* ~ *night sun* (极圈内盛夏或隆冬出现的)夜半的[子夜的]太阳。*burn the* ~*night oil* 用功到深夜,开夜车)。~**noon**〔罕〕中午,正午。~**-off**【板球】投球员左侧的外场守场员(的位置)。~**-on**【板球】在投球员右侧的外场守场员(的位置)。~**point** 中点;中心点;近中心点。~**rib**【植】叶的中脉。~**-sea** 外海,外洋。~**section** 中部。~**ship** 船身中部。~**shipman**〔英〕海军军官候补生〔俗称 *middy*, 因值班时常在舰中央〕;〔美〕海军学校学生。~**shipmite**〔谑〕= midshipman. ~**ships** *ad*., *n*.【海】(在)船的中央;(在)船身中部。~**-shot**【摄】中景。~**stream** 中流。~**summer** 盛夏,仲夏;夏至〔6月21日〕前后(*the* ~*summer daisy* 法国菊。*the Midsummer Day* 施洗约翰节〔6月24日,英国四结账日之一〕。*the* ~*summer madness* 大疯狂)。~**-week** 一周的当中;(教友派的)星期三。~**winter** 仲冬,冬至。~**year**〔口〕在学年中期举行的考试;〔*pl*.〕学年中期考试时期。

mid[2], **'mid** [mid; mɪd] *prep*.〔诗〕= amid.

mid. = **1**. middle. **2**. midnight. **3**. midshipman.

MIDAS = **1**. Missile Defense Alarm System (美国空军)导[飞]弹防御警报系统。**2**. missile defence alarm satellite 导[飞]弹防御警报卫星。

Mi·das [ˈmaidəs; ˋmaɪdəs] *n*. **1**.【希神】迈达斯〔弗利治亚 (Phrygia) 国王。相传贪财,求神赐给点物成金的法术〕。**2**. 大富豪。

mid·brain [ˈmidˌbrein; ˋmɪdˏbren] *n*. 中脑(= mesencephalon)。

mid·cult [ˈmidˈkʌlt; ˋmɪdˏkʌlt] *n*.〔美口〕中产阶级文化。

mid·den [ˈmidn; ˋmɪdn̩] *n*.〔方〕粪堆;【考古】贝冢(= kitchen ~)。

mid·dle [ˈmidl; ˋmɪdl] **I** *n*. **1**. 中央,正中;中间,中部;中途。**2**. 人体的中部,腰部。**3**. 中间物,媒介物;中人,中间人,调解人;中间派。**4**.【逻】中名词,媒辞;【语】(希腊语动词的)中间态;【数】中项(= ~ term)。**5**.〔常 *pl*.〕(报纸等的)文学性短文,中间读物;【商】中级(货)品。**6**.【板球】防守中柱(~ stump)的球棍拿法。**7**.【足球】从左右翼将球传到锋线中央,中央传球。**8**.【美拳】中量级拳击选手。***in the*** ~ ***of*** 正在…当中;在…的中途;在…的中央;在…的中部。***knock*** [***send***] ***sb. into the*** ~ ***of next week*** 把(某人)打昏过去。**II** *a*. **1**. 中央的,正中的,中间的。**2**. 中等的,中级的。**3**.〔M-〕(英语等)中古的。~ **age** 中年,壮年〔约35—55岁间或40—60岁间〕。~**-aged** *a*. 中年的。**M- Ages** 中世纪。**M- America** **1**. 中美洲。**2**. 美国中产阶级社会(有时尤指美国中西部中产阶级)。~ **article**〔英〕(周刊杂志等的)文学性随笔,中间读物〔因排在政治论文与新书评介的中间〕。**M- Atlantic States** 美国大西洋中部各州〔即纽约州、新泽西和宾夕法尼亚〕。~ **breaker** *n*. 双壁开沟犁。~ **brow** **1**. *n*.〔口〕中产阶级趣味(或观点)的人。**2**. *a*.〔口〕中产阶级趣味[观点]的〔常当轻蔑或取笑词用〕。~ **class** 中产阶级,中间阶层。~**-class** *a*. 中间阶级的;〔罕〕品质中等的。~ **course** [**way**] 中庸,中道。~ **distance** [**ground**]【绘】(前景和背景间的)中景;中距离。~ **dress** 水手服装式运动衣。~ **ear**【解】中耳。~ **earth**〔诗〕地球〔因在天国和地狱之间〕。**M- East** 中东〔地中海东岸至印度地区,通常包括 Near East 在内〕。**M- Empire**【史】埃及中王国。**M- English** 中世纪英语〔略 M.E.〕。~ **finger** 中指。**M- French** 中世纪法语〔指14—16世纪的法语〕。**M- Greek** 中世纪希腊语(= Medieval Greek)。~ **ground** 中间立场,中立。~ **height** 中等身材;半山腰。**M- High German** 中世纪高地德语。**M- Irish** 中世纪爱尔兰语。~ **life** **1**. = middle age. **2**. 中等生活。**M- Low German** 中世纪低地德语。~**man** 掮客,中间人。~ **manager** 中层经理〔负责执行具体任务而不参与全局性的决策〕。~**most** *a*. 正中的。~**-of-the-road** 中间路线。~**-of-the-roader** 中间派,中间人物[势力]。~ **piece**〔美〕马甲。~ **scenee** 中年期〔40—65岁〕。~ **school** 中学校。~**-sized** 中等尺寸的,中号的。**M- States**〔美〕中部诸州。~ **stick** 中尺〔36英寸半〕。~ **term**【逻】中名词;【数】中项。~ **tooth** 主牙。~**ware**【计】中件〔执行控制程序和应用程序之间的中间任务之软件〕。~ **watch**【海】夜半值班〔午夜零时到四时〕。~**weight** **1**. *a*.【拳、摔跤】中量级(的)。**2**. *n*. 中量级拳击[摔跤等]选手〔147—160磅(66—72公斤)〕。**M- West**〔美〕中西部(各州)。**M- Western** 中西部(各州)的。**M- Westerner** 中西部(各州)的人。

Mid·dle·ton [ˈmidltən; ˋmɪdltən] *n*. 米德尔顿〔姓氏〕。

mid·dling [ˈmidliŋ; ˋmɪdlɪŋ] **I** *a*. 中等的,普通的;第二流的;不好不坏的。*I feel only* ~. 我精神还好。**II** *ad*. 中等,相当。~ *good* 相当好的。**III** *n*.〔常 *pl*.〕中级品;(小麦的)粗粉;〔美〕标准[中等]棉花;中纱。

mid·dor·sal [ˈmidˈdɔːsəl; ˋmɪdˋdɔrsəl] *a*.【解】背部中央的。

mid·dy [ˈmidi; ˋmɪdɪ] *n*. **1**.〔口〕= midshipman. **2**. (妇女、小孩穿的)水手式服装(= ~ blouse)。

Mid·gard [ˈmidgɑːd; ˋmɪdˏgɑrd] *n*.【北欧神】尘世,凡间〔*cf*. Asgard〕。

midge [midʒ; mɪdʒ] *n*. **1**. (蚊、蚋等)小虫;蠓;极小的鱼。**2**. 小个子;侏儒。*a wheat* ~ 小麦吸浆虫。

midg·et [ˈmidʒit; ˋmɪdʒɪt] *n*. **1**. 小个子(的人);侏儒。**2**.〔加拿大〕蚋。**3**. 小照片(又叫~photograph)。**4**. (同类事物中)极小者。*a* ~ *submarine* 小型[袖珍]潜艇。*a* ~ *tractor* 微型拖拉机。

mid·gut [ˈmidˌgʌt; ˋmɪdˏgʌt] *n*.【解】中肠。

Mi·di [miˈdi; mɪˋdɪ] *n*.〔F.〕米迪〔法国南部〕。

MIDI [ˈmidi; ˋmɪdɪ] *n*. = musical instrument digital interface【计】音乐设备数字界面〔指将电子乐器、合成器和电脑接通〕。

mi·di [ˈmidi; ˋmɪdɪ] *n*.〔美〕(一种长及腿肚子的)半长裙[衣]。

mid·i·nette [ˌmiːdiːˈnet; ˏmidiˋnet] *n*.〔F.〕〔俚〕(巴黎的)女店员。

mid·leg [ˈmidleg; ˋmɪdˏlɛg] **I** *n*. **1**. 中足。**2**. (昆虫的)中对足。**II** *ad*. 向中足。

mid·line [ˈmidlain; ˋmɪdˏlaɪn] *n*. 中线。

mid·rash [ˈmidˌrɑːʃ; ˋmɪdˏrɑʃ] *n*. (*pl*. ***mid·rash·im*** [midˈrɑːʃim; mɪdˋrɑʃɪm], ***mid·rash·oth*** [-ʃəut; -ʃot]) (从犹太人被巴比伦俘虏奴役时期开始到公元1200年间所作的)犹太法学博士的圣经注释。**the M-** 上述注释的总称。**-ic** *a*.

mid·riff [ˈmidrif; ˋmɪdrɪf] **I** *n*. **1**.【解】横膈膜。**2**.〔美俚〕肚子,下腹部。**3**. (女子的)露腰上衣。**II** *a*. 腰线露在外的。

midst[1] [midst; mɪdst] **I** *n*. 中,中间,中央。★现在只用在如下成语中。***from*** [***out of***] ***the*** ~ ***of ...*** 从…当中。***in our*** [***your***] ~ 在我们[你们]中间。***in the*** ~ ***of us*** 在我们当中。***in*** [***into***] ***the*** ~ ***of*** 在[向]…当中。**II** *ad*. 在中间,在中央。***first***, ~, ***and last*** 始终一贯,彻头彻尾。

midst[2], **'midst** [midst, mitst; mɪdst, mɪtst] *prep*.〔诗〕= amidst.

mid-Vic·to·ri·an [ˌmidvikˈtɔːriən; ˏmɪdvɪkˋtorɪən] **I** *a*.〔英〕**1**. 维多利亚王朝中期(1850—1890)的;维多利亚中期文化[道德、艺术]的。**2**. 旧式的,一本正经的;操行严谨的;沉闷的。**II** *n*. **1**. 维多利亚王朝中期时代的人。**2**. 具有维多利亚时代中期思想观点举止的人。

mid·way [ˈmidwei; ˋmɪdwe] **I** *n*. **1**. 中途,半路。**2**.〔美〕(展览会等的)商场,娱乐场。**II** [ˈmidˈwei; ˋmɪdˋwe] *a*. 中途的。*a* ~ *station* 错车站。**III** *ad*. 在中途,在半路。

Mid·way Islands [ˈmidwei ˈailəndz; ˋmɪdwe ˋaɪləndz] *n*. 中途岛。

Mid·west [ˈmidˈwest; ˋmɪdˋwɛst] *n*. 〔美〕= Middle West. **-ern** *a*., **-ern·er** *n*.

mid·wife [ˈmidwaif; ˋmɪdˏwaɪf] **I** *n*. (*pl*. *-wives*) 助产士,接生员〔婆〕。**II** *vt*. 为…接生;〔喻〕协助…的产生。

mid·wife·ry [ˈmidwifəri; ˋmɪdˏwaɪfərɪ] *n*. 助产术,产科学。

M.I.E.E. = Member of the Institute of Electrical Engineers〔英〕电机工程师协会会员。

mien [miːn; min] *n*. 风采,态度,样子。

miff [mif; mɪf] **I** *n*. 〔口〕小争执;生气。**II** *vt*., *vi*. 〔口〕(使)发脾气,(使)生气。***be* ~*ed with*** [***at***] 生…的气。***get*** [***have, take***] ***a*** ~ 生气。***in a*** ~ 生着气。

miffed [mifd; mɪfd] *a*. 〔美口〕生气的,发怒的,恼火。*I was ~ when they laughed at my new wig*. 每当他们嘲笑我的新假发,我就感到恼火。

MIG [mig; mɪg] *n*. 米格式飞机。

mig·gle [ˈmigl; ˋmɪgl] *n*. 〔方〕**1**. (小孩玩的)玻璃弹珠。**2**. 〔*pl*.〕弹珠戏。

might[1] [mait; maɪt] *v*. *aux*. may 的过去式。**1**. 〔在陈述句中,为 may 的过去式,表示一般的可能性〕可能,会。*No one but a king or prince ~ build a castle*. 除了国王或公国君主外,那时什么人都不能修建城堡。*I said that it ~ rain*. 我说过可能会下雨。**2**. 〔表示不太确实的可能性〕也许,或许。*I'm afraid it ~ rain tonight*. 我看今晚恐怕要下雨。*Who ~ the man be*? 这个人会是谁呢? *Did you see that car nearly hit me? I ~ have been killed*. 那辆汽车几乎撞着我,你看见了吗? 要是撞上,我也许就完蛋了。**3**. 〔表示许可,在疑问和建议时比 may 更委婉和礼貌〕可以。*I asked him if I ~ leave*. 我问他可不可以离开。"*M- I come in*?" "*Yes, you may*." "我可不可以进来?" "可以,请。" *M- I suggest a stroll after lunch*? 午饭后是不是可以去散步? **4**. 〔表示愿望、祝愿、请求、嘱咐和轻微的责备〕请,愿,…就好了;该;还是…好。*I hoped you ~ succeed*. 我原是希望你成功的。*I wish I ~ help you*. 我能帮助你就好了。*You ~ post this letter for me*. 请代我把这封信寄一下。*O! ~ I see him just once more*! 唉! 我能再见他一次就好了! *You ~ write more frequently*. 你该经常写信才是。*You ~ at least offer to help*! 你至少该帮帮忙。*You ~ as well go*. 你还是去好。*No one will eat this food; it ~ just as well be thrown away*. 这东西没人吃,不如扔掉好。**5**. 〔在条件句中,主句或从句的叙述含有推测或假设意味〕如能〔从句中〕;便会;说不定会〔主句中〕。*I would go if I ~*. 如我能去我就去。*You ~ believe me if you read it*. 你读一读,便会相信我了。*If you had tried a little harder, you ~ have succeeded*. 当初你如果再努力一下,说不定你会成功的。*We lost the football match, but we ~ well have won if one of our players hadn't been hurt*. 这场足球比赛我们输了,可是如果我们的一位运动员不受伤的话〔事实上受了伤〕,那我们说不定会踢赢的。**6**. 〔在 that ... might 结构中,表示目的〕为了。*He studied hard that he ~ serve the country well*. 为了很好地为祖国服务,他会刻苦钻研。*She turned away so that no one ~ see that her eyes were filled with tears*. 为了不让人看出她泪水盈眶,她把脸背过去了。**7**. 〔用于从句中,表示让步〕虽然,尽管,无论。*Whatever ~ happen, he was determined to do it*. 无论发生什么,他决心去干。*You ~ think you're very clever, but that doesn't give you the right to order me about*. 尽管你认为自己非常聪明,但这决不是说你有随意摆弄我的权利。~**-have-been** *n*. 本来或许可以发生的事情;本来或许可以有所成就的人。

might[2] [mait; maɪt] *n*. **1**. (身体或精神的)力,力气。**2**. 权力;势力;兵力。**3**. 智力,才干,能力。***by*** ~ 用武力。***with ~ and main*** = ***with all one's*** ~ 尽全力,拚命。

might·i·ly [ˈmaitili; ˋmaɪtl̩ɪ] *ad*. **1**. 强烈地,猛烈地,有力地。**2**. 〔口〕非常,极。

might·i·ness [ˈmaitinis; ˋmaɪtɪnɪs] *n*. **1**. 强大,有力;伟大。**2**. 高位,高官。**3**. 〔古〕〔M-〕阁下〔对高官贵人的尊称: His M-〕。*his high* ~ 〔反〕尊贵的阁下〔指高傲的人〕。

mightn't [ˈmaitnt; ˋmaɪtnt] = might not.

might·y [ˈmaiti; ˋmaɪtɪ] **I** *a*. (***might·i·er***; ***-i·est***) **1**. 强大的,有力的;伟大的;刚毅的。**2**. 巨大的,非凡的。**3**. 〔口〕大的,非常的。*a ~ hit* 极其轰动的作品〔事物、人物〕。*a ~ wind* 猛烈的风,大风。~ *works* 奇迹。***high and*** ~ 趾高气扬,神气活现。***make a ~ bother*** 搞出大麻烦。**II** *ad*. 〔方、美口〕非常,很,大。*a ~ good thing* 非常好的事情。*It is ~ easy*. 容易透顶。

mig·ma·tite [ˈmigmətait; ˋmɪgməˏtaɪt] *n*. 【地】混合岩。

mi·gnon [ˈmi(ː)njɔn; ˋmɪnjɑn] **I** *a*. 〔F.〕娇小玲珑的,可爱的。**II** *n*. 可爱的孩子。

mi·gnon·ette [ˌminjəˈnet; ˏmɪnjənˋɛt] *n*. 【植】**1**. 木犀草。**2**. 灰绿色。**3**. 法国细丝花边。~ **tree**【植】散沫花,指甲花。~ **wood**【植】菱叶海桐花。

mi·graine [ˈmaigrein, ˈmiː-; ˋmaɪgren] *n*. 〔F.〕【医】周期性偏头痛。

mi·grant [ˈmaigrənt; ˋmaɪgrənt] **I** *a*. = migratory. **II** *n*. 候鸟;移栖动物;移居者〔*cf*. emigrant, immigrant〕。

mi·grate [maiˈgreit, ˈmaigreit; maɪˋgret, ˋmaɪgret] *vi*. 迁移;移居,(尤指)移居海外;(鸟的)定期移栖;(鱼的)洄游;【化、物】移动,徙动。

mi·gra·tion [maiˈgreiʃən; maɪˋgreʃən] *n*. **1**. 移住,迁移;移动;徙动。**2**. (鸟)移栖,迁徙;(鱼)洄游;(植物)侵移。**3**. 移住者群,移栖群。**4**.【化、物】原子移动;电离子的移动。

mi·gra·tor [maiˈgreitə; ˋmaɪgretɚ] *n*. 移居者;候鸟。

mi·gra·to·ry [ˈmaigrətəri; ˋmaɪgrəˏtorɪ] *a*. 移栖的,移居的;移动的;游牧的;漂泊的。*a ~ bird* 候鸟。

mih·rab [ˈmiːrɔb; ˋmirɑb] *n*. (清真寺院面向麦加的那道墙内的)壁龛。

M.I.J. = Member of the Institute of Journalists〔英〕新闻工作者学会会员。

mi·ka·do [miˈkɑːdəu; məˋkɑdo] *n*. 〔常作 M-〕日本天皇〔西洋人对日本天皇的称呼〕。

Mike [maik; maɪk] *n*. 迈克〔男子名, Michael 的昵称〕。

mike[1] [maik; maɪk] *vi*., *n*. 〔俚〕偷懒,鬼混,怠工。***on the*** ~ 偷懒,吊儿郎当地。

mike[2] [maik; maɪk] *n*. 〔microphone 之略〕〔口〕话筒;送话器,微音器。~ **fright** 话筒前的胆怯。

mi·kron [ˈmaikrɔn; ˋmaɪkrɑn] *n*. 〔G.〕= micron.

mil [mil; mɪl] *n*. **1**.【电】密耳(千分之一英寸)。**2**.【军】密位〔= 1/6400 周角〕。**3**. = milliliter.

mil. = **1**. mileage. **2**. military. **3**. militia. **4**. million.

mi·la·di, mi·la·dy [miˈleidi; mɪˋledɪ] *n*. (*pl*. ***-dies***) **1**. 夫人,太太〔欧洲大陆人对英国贵妇的称呼〕;英国贵妇人。**2**. 非常时髦的女人,上流女人。

mil·age [ˈmailidʒ; ˋmaɪlɪdʒ] *n*. = mileage.

Mi·lan, Mi·la·no [miˈlæn, It. miˈlɑːno; mɪˋlæn, mɪˋlɑno] *n*. **1**. 米兰〔意大利城市〕。**2**. 〔m-〕米兰草帽。

Mi·la·nese [ˌmiləˈniːz; ˏmɪlənˋiz] **I** *n*. 〔*sing*., *pl*.〕米兰人。**II** *a*. 米兰人的。*the M-* 旧米兰公国领地。

milch [miltʃ; mɪltʃ] *a*. 有奶的,生乳的,挤奶用的。*a ~ cow* 乳牛;〔口〕财源;摇钱树。*treat sb. as a ~ cow* 把某人当作摇钱树。

mild [maild; maɪld] *a*. **1**. 温和的,温厚的,温良的,柔和的,静淑的。**2**. (处罚等)宽大的;(病等)轻微的;适当的。**3**. 不苦的,适口的。**4**.【冶】低碳的,软的。~ *base* 弱碱。*a ~ cigar* 味淡的雪茄烟。*a ~ case* 轻症。~

M

steel 软钢。～ *weather* 温暖的天气。**as ～ as a lamb** [*a dove, May, milk*] 非常温和的。**be ～ in disposition** 性格温柔。**be ～ of manner** 态度温和。**draw it ～** 说[做]得适度,不夸张。

mild·en [ˈmaildn; ˋmaɪldən] *vt., vi.* (使)温和;(使)变暖和;(使)和缓。

mil·dew [ˈmildjuː; ˋmɪl͵dju] **I** *n.* **1.** 霉。**2.**【植】霉病。*the powdery* ～ 白粉菌;白粉病。**II** *vt., vi.* (使)发霉。

mil·dewed, mil·dew·y [ˈmildjuːd, -i; ˋmɪl͵djud, -ɪ] *a.* **1.** 发了霉的,发霉臭的。**2.** 陈腐的。

mild·ly [ˈmaildli; ˋmaɪldlɪ] *ad.* **1.** 温和地,柔和地。**2.** 适度地。**put it ～** 说得婉转些。

mild·ness [ˈmaildnis; ˋmaɪldnɪs] *n.* 温和;柔和。

Mil·dred [ˈmildrid; ˋmɪldrɪd] *n.* 米尔德丽德〔女子名〕。

mile [mail; maɪl] *n.* **1.** 英里,哩(＝1609米)。**2.** 一英里赛跑。*He was ～s and ～s my superior.* 他比我强得多。*the international nautical* [*air*] ～ 国际海[空]里(＝1852米)。*a nautical* [*geographical*] ～ 海里,浬(〔英〕＝6080英尺〔英国又叫 *admiralty* ～〕,〔美〕＝6080.27英尺)。*the statute* ～ 法定英里〔5280英尺〕。*the three ～s limit* [*belt, zone*] 领海三英里。**be ～s easier** 容易得多。**It stands** [**sticks**] **a ～.** 〔俚〕十分明白,显而易见。**not a hundred ～s from** [**off**] 离…不远,差不多。～**post** 里程标。～**stone 1.** 里程碑;里程标。**2.** (一生中或历史上的)划时代事件。

mile·age, mil·age [ˈmailidʒ; ˋmaɪlɪdʒ] *n.* **1.** 英里数,里程。**2.** (按英里计算的)运费。**3.** 〔美〕(公务员出差时)按英里支付的旅费。**4.** 汽车消耗一加仑汽油所行的平均里程。**5.** 好处,利润。*traffic* ～【交】周转量。

mil·er [ˈmailə; ˋmaɪlɚ] *n.* 〔口〕作一英里赛跑的运动员[马];一英里赛跑。

Miles, Myles [mailz; maɪlz] *n.* 迈尔斯〔男子名〕。

mi·les glo·ri·o·sus [ˈmailiːz ˌglɔːriˈəusəs, ˈmiːleis-; ˋmaɪliz͵glɔrɪˋosəs, ˋmiles-] 〔L.〕骄兵〔尤指古典喜剧中爱自吹自擂的士兵角色〕。

Mi·le·sian [maiˈliːziən, -zjən; maɪˋliʒɪən, -zjən] **I** *n.* 爱尔兰人。**II** *a.* 爱尔兰的。

mil·foil [ˈmilfɔil; ˋmɪl͵fɔɪl] *n.* 【植】蓍草[芪草];小二仙草。

Mil·ford [ˈmilfəd; ˋmɪlfəd] *n.* 米尔福德〔姓氏,男子名〕。

mil·i·a·ri·a [ˌmiliˈɛəriə; ͵mɪlɪˋɛrɪə] *n.* 粟疹,(热)痱子,汗疹。

mil·i·ar·y [ˈmiliəri; ˋmɪlɪ͵ɛrɪ] *a.* 粟粒状的;【医】粟疹的。～ *fever* 粟疹(热)。

mi·lieu [ˈmiːljəː; miˋljɚ] *n.* 〔F.〕周围,(社会)环境;背景。

milit. ＝ military.

mil·i·tan·cy [ˈmilitənsi; ˋmɪlətənsɪ] *n.* **1.** 交战状态;好战。**2.** 战斗精神;战斗性。

mil·i·tant [ˈmilitənt; ˋmɪlətənt] **I** *a.* **1.** 战斗中的,交战中的。**2.** 斗志昂扬的,富于战斗性的。**3.** 好战的。*a ～ task* 战斗任务。*always ～ in struggle* 斗志昂扬。**II** *n.* 富有战斗精神的人,斗士。**-ly** *ad.*

mil·i·ta·rism [ˈmilitərizəm; ˋmɪlətərɪzəm] *n.* **1.** 黩武主义,军国主义(*opp.* pacifism);黩武政治。**2.** 尚武(精神)。

mil·i·ta·rist [ˈmilitərist; ˋmɪlətərɪst] *n.* **1.** 军国主义者,军阀。**2.** 军事专家。**-ic** *a.*

mil·i·ta·rize [ˈmilitəraiz; ˋmɪlətə͵raɪz] *vt.* **1.** 使军事化;武装。**2.** 使军国主义化;使好战。**-za·tion** *n.*

mil·i·tar·y [ˈmilitəri; ˋmɪlə͵tɛrɪ] **I** *a.* **1.** (*opp.* civil) 军人的,军队的。**2.** 陆军的。**3.** 军事的,军用的。**4.** 好战的,战斗性的。**5.** 〔军俚〕不好的,讨厌的。*a ～ academy* [*institute, school*] 陆军军官学校;军事学院。*a ～ adviser* 军事顾问。*a ～ aeronautical school* 军事航空学校。*a ～ aeroplane* 军用机。～ *affairs* 军事,军务。～ *age* 兵役年龄。～ *arts* 军事艺术。*a ～ band* 军乐队。～ *circles* 军界。*a ～ commentator* 军事评论家。*a ～ correspondent* 随军记者。～ *courtesy* 陆军礼节,军礼。～ *discipline* 军纪。～ *drill* 军事训练。～ *expenditures* [*expenses*] 军费。～ *fever* 伤寒症。～ *history* 战史。*a ～ hospital* 陆军医院。～ *intelligence* 军事情报;军事情报工作[部门]。～ *law* 军法。*a ～ man* 军人。～ *operation* 作战;军事行动。～ *organization* 军制,陆军编制。～ *pits* 散兵坑。*the ～ police* 宪兵(队)。～ *prestige* 武威。～ *regulations* 军事法规。*a ～ review* 阅兵式。～ *science* 军事科学。～ *secrets* 军事机密。～ *service* 兵役。～ *merits* 军功,武功。～ *stores* 军需品。*the ～ top* (兵舰的)战斗桅楼。～ *training* 军事训练。**II** *n.* 〔集合词〕军队;军人;〔the ～〕军方。**call in the ～** 借军队的力量。～-**industrial complex** 军工联合体〔军事权力机构与军事物资工业的联合,被认为是操纵美国经济与对外路线的强大势力集团〕。**-tar·i·ly** *ad.* 在军事上,从军事角度。

mil·i·tate [ˈmiliteit; ˋmɪlə͵tet] *vi.* **1.** 发生影响,起作用。**2.** 〔废、罕〕服兵役,战斗,争,冲突 (*against*)。*Ill health ～d against his chance of success.* 身体不好误了他成功立业的机会。～ *in favor of* 便于,有助于,促进。

mi·li·tia [miˈliʃə; məˋlɪʃə] *n.* 民兵;〔英〕国民军。～-**man** (男)民兵。

mil·i·um [ˈmiliəm; ˋmɪlɪəm] *n.* (*pl.* **-i·a** [-ə; -ə]) 【医】粟粒疹。

milk [milk; mɪlk] **I** *n.* **1.** 乳,奶;牛奶。**2.** 乳状物;乳状液;【药】乳剂。**3.** 〔废〕鱼子。**4.** 【赛马】不正当利益。**5.** 〔美俚〕雪。**6.** 【物】子同位素。*as white as ～* 牛奶一样白,纯白。*a ～ diet* 牛奶餐,乳饵。*condensed* [*Swiss*] ～ 炼乳。*separated ～, skimmed ～* 脱脂乳。*whole ～* 全脂乳。*a powder(ed) ～* 奶粉。*blue ～* 搀水牛奶(＝ watered ～);(因细菌)变青的牛奶。*acidophilus ～* 酸牛奶。*Bristol ～* 布里斯托尔酒。～ *of lime* 石灰乳。～ *of magnesia* 镁乳(泻药)。～ *of sulphur* 硫黄乳。**in ～** 在授乳期的(*a cow in ～* 乳牛)。～ **and honey** 乳和蜜(般的享受);丰饶,繁荣。～ **and roses** 白中泛红的脸色。～ **and water** 搀水的牛奶;无味的谈话[讲义];过分的感伤(*cf.* ～-and-water)。～ **for babes** (读物、教理等)适合儿童的东西,初步的东西(*opp.* strong meat)。～ **of human kindness** 自然而然的人情;同情心。***M- Route*** 〔美俚〕奶路〔商人向华盛顿各政府机关做买卖的门道〕。～ **route** 〔美空俚〕短距离航线;美大陆横断航线给油机。**spilt ～** 不可挽回的事情(*It's* [*There's*] *no good* [*use*] *crying over spilt ～.* 无法挽回的事哭也无益)。

II *vt.* **1.** 挤…的奶;挤(奶)。**2.** 〔卑〕榨取,剥削,鱼肉(他人)。**3.** 抽取(树液);拔(蛇毒等的)毒。**4.** 〔俚〕套出消息;(自电线)偷听(电报电话)。— *vi.* **1.** 出奶,挤奶。**2.** (天气)变阴 (*up*)。*The cows are ～ing well this season.* 这一季乳牛出奶很旺。～ **the audience**【美剧】为想博得喝采过分卖力。～ **the bull** [**ram**] 缘木求鱼,做没希望的事情。～ **the market** [**street**] 〔美俚〕操纵股票市场从中渔利。～ **abscess**【医】乳房脓疮,奶疮。～-**and-water** *a.* 无味的,无力的;动辄感伤的。～ **bar** 奶品柜台,奶品店。～ **crust** (婴儿头上、脸上的)小泡湿疹;乳痂。～**fish** 遮目鱼。～ **fever** (产妇的)产褥热。～-**float** 〔英〕送奶车。～ **glass** 乳白色玻璃。～ **leg**【医】产妇股白肿病。～-**livered** *a.* ＝ white-livered. ～ **maid** 挤奶女工。～ **man** 卖[送]牛乳的人;挤牛乳的人。～ **pudding** 牛奶布丁。～ **punch** 牛奶和酒等的混合甜饮料。～ **ranch** 〔美〕奶品农场。～ **round**(大公司在大学内进行的)校园巡回招聘。～ **run** 〔美空俚〕(清晨执行来回轰炸[侦察]任务的)定期飞行;容易执行的常规飞行任务。～**shake** 泡沫牛奶(牛奶和冰淇淋等的混合饮料)。

~sickness (牛、马等牲口的)震颤病;(因食病牛牛奶或牛肉而引起的)乳毒病。~snake 乳蛇(一种北美无毒游蛇)。~sop 懦夫,没骨气的人。~sopism 怯懦。~-stage (农作物的)乳熟期;灌浆。~sugar 乳糖。~toast 牛奶吐司(热奶泡烤面包片)。~tooth【解】乳齿。~-vetch【植】黄芪[黄耆]属;紫云英。~-walk 送乳区域。~weed【植】马利筋。~-white *a*. 乳白的。~wood〔口〕(热带产)乳树。~wort〔口〕【植】远志属。

milk·er [ˈmilkə; ˋmɪlkɚ] ***n***. **1**. 挤奶人;挤奶器。**2**. 乳牛。**3**.【物】子同位素发生器。

milk·i·ness [ˈmilkinis; ˋmɪlkɪnɪs] ***n***. **1**. (液体的)乳状(性);浊白色;乳白色。**2**. 柔弱;温顺。

milk·shed [ˈmilkˌʃed; ˋmɪlkˏʃɛd] ***n***. 供应城市牛奶的牛奶场区。

milk·y [ˈmilki; ˋmɪlkɪ] ***a***. (***milk·i·er***; ***-i·est***) **1**. (颜色或组织)像牛奶的,乳白色的;浑浊的;柔弱的。**2**. (食品)加了牛奶的;(植物)分泌乳汁的。~ ***in the filbert***〔美〕神经错乱的;疯狂的;笨的。**M- Way**【天】银河。

Mill [mil; mɪl] ***n***. **1**. 米尔〔姓氏〕。**2**. **James** ~ 詹姆斯·米尔〔1773—1836,英国经济学家〕。**3**. **John Stuart** ~ 约翰·斯图亚特·米尔〔1800—1873,英国逻辑学、经济学家〕。

mill[1] [mil; mɪl] **I** ***n***. **1**. 风力[水力、汽力]磨粉机,风磨,水磨,水碾(等);磨坊,面粉厂。**2**. 厂,工场。**3**. (咖啡、胡椒等的)粉碎器,碾碎器;(水果的)压榨机;铸币机;【冶】轧钢机;(矿石等的)研磨机;截断机。**4**.【机】铣床;铣刀。**5**.〔俚〕拳赛;互殴;可随意加入的比赛。**6**.〔美俚〕拷问;监狱。**7**. 打字机。**8**.〔美俚〕机车;马达。**9**. 缓慢前进的过程。*Much water runs by the ~ that the miller knows not of*. 见远不见近。*No ~, no meal*. 不磨面,没饭吃。*a paper ~* 造纸厂。*a bar ~* 小型轧钢厂。*a coffee ~* 咖啡研磨机。*a stamp ~* 捣碎机。*a wash ~* 淘泥机。*Bristol ~* 卡(片)纸板。*gin ~* 小酒店。***draw water to*** (***one's***) ~ 为自己打算。***go*** [***put***] ***through the*** ~ (使)饱尝辛酸,(使)身经磨炼。**II** ***vt***. **1**. 磨碎,碾碎;锯(木材);【机】磨;铣。**2**. 粉碎。**3**. 辗(或滚)压(金属);砑(布)使紧密;轧花边(在纸币上)。**4**. 搅拌;使…起泡。**5**.〔俚〕拿拳头打。— ***vi***. **1**. 使用水车[制粉机等]。**2**.〔俚〕用拳头殴斗。**3**. (家畜)成群兜圈子;(鲸鱼)突然兜转方向。~**board** 书皮纸板。~**cake** 亚麻子饼;油饼。~ **construction**【建】工厂建筑;耐火构造。~**dam** (水磨用的)水闸[贮水池]。~ **hand** 磨坊工人,制粉工人;(尤指)纺纱工人。~**-in** ***n***. 环行示威〔示威者团团转地游行,造成交通阻塞的示威行动〕。~ **man** 轧钢工,滚轧工人。~**pond**, ~**pool** 水磨用贮水池。~**-race** ***n***. **1**. (推动水车的)水流。**2**. (水车用)水沟。~**-run 1**. = ~race. **2**. (用碾磨测定矿质的)一定量矿砂。**3**. 锯木厂可售出的木材产量。**4**. 普通产品;〔喻〕平庸普通的人;平凡的东西。~**-run** ***a***. **1**. 刚从机器中生产出来的;未经检验的;未分等级的。**2**. 一般的,普通的。~**-stone** 磨石;粉碎器;重担 (*between the upper and the nether ~ stones* 陷在苦境。*hard as the nether ~-stone* 残酷。~*stone grit*【地】磨石硬沙岩。*see* [*look*] *through* [*into*, *far into*] *a ~stone* 感觉(尤指眼光)十分锐利。*weep ~stones*〔口〕决不哭;毫不伤心)。~ **stream** = mill race. ~ **tail** (水磨的)排水沟。~ **wheel** 水车(的轮子)。~ **work** 水磨(厂)机械;水磨机械的安装[设计];构件加工(~*work plant* 加工工厂)。~**wright** 水磨匠,水磨设计人;机械安装工人。

mill[2] [mil; mɪl] ***n***.〔美〕密尔〔一美元的千分之一〕。

mil·lage [ˈmilidʒ; ˋmɪlɪdʒ] ***n***. 按每美元值抽若干密尔(千分之一美元)的税。

Mil·lais [ˈmilei; mɪˋle] ***n***. 米莱〔姓氏〕。

Mil·lard [ˈmiləd, ˈmilɑːd; ˋmɪləd, ˋmɪlɑrd] ***n***. 米勒德〔姓氏,男子名〕。

Mil·lay [miˈlei; mɪˋle] ***n***. 米莱〔姓氏〕。

milled [mild; mɪld] ***a***. **1**. 碾碎的,碾磨过的;粉碎的;铣过的。**2**. (硬币的)边缘弄高并轧花边的。

mille·fleurs [ˌmiːlˈfləː; milˋflɚ] ***a***. (挂毯图案的)万花斑驳的。

mil·le·nar·i·an [ˌmiliˈnɛəriən; ˏmɪləˋnɛrɪən] **I** ***a***. **1**. 一千年的。**2**.【基督教】一千年至福的。**3**. (相信)太平盛世(会到来)的。**II** ***n***. 相信一千年至福说的人。**-ism** ***n***. 一千年至福说。

mil·le·nar·y [ˈmilineri; ˋmɪləˏnɛrɪ] **I** ***a***. **1**. 一千年的。**2**. 一千年至福的;信奉一千年至福说的。**II** ***n***. **1**. 一千年(期间);千周年纪念。**2**. 信奉一千年至福说的人。

mil·len·ni·al [miˈleniəl; məˋlɛnɪəl] ***a***. **1**. 一千年的。**2**. 一千年至福的。***The Millennial Generation*** 千年一代〔指1981年以后出生的一代人,到新千年到来时正好成年〕。**-ism** ***n***. = millenarianism.

mil·len·ni·um [miˈleniəm; məˋlɛnɪəm] ***n***. (*pl*. ~*s*, ***-ni·a*** [-niə; -nɪə]) **1**. 一千年(间);千周年纪念。**2**. 一千年至福。**3**. (幻想中的)黄金时代,太平盛世。~ **bug**【计】(电脑)千年虫〔电脑跨入2000年时可能产生的程序问题,亦作 ~ bomb, ~ glitch 或 y2k〕。

mil·le·ped, **mil·le·pede** [ˈmiliped, -piːd; ˋmɪləˏpɛd, -ˏpid] ***n***.【动】马陆;千足虫。

mil·le·pore [ˈmilipɔː; ˋmɪlɪˏpor] ***n***. 千窝珊瑚,千孔虫。

Mil·ler [ˈmilə; ˋmɪlɚ] ***n***. 米勒〔姓氏〕。

mill·er [ˈmilə; ˋmɪlɚ] ***n***. **1**. 磨坊主,面粉厂主;工厂经营人。**2**. 铣床;铣工。**3**. 碾磨机工人。**4**. 粉翅蛾。**5**.〔卑〕拳击家。*Too much water drowned the ~*. 过犹不及。~***'s-thumb*** 杜父鱼;杜父鸟。

mill·er·ite [ˈmilərait; ˋmɪlɚˏaɪt] ***n***.【矿】针镍矿。

mil·les·i·mal [miˈlesiməl; mɪˋlɛsəməl] **I** ***a***. 千分之一的。**II** ***n***. 千分之一。

mil·let [ˈmilit; ˋmɪlɪt] ***n***. **1**.【植】小米,粟。**2**. 狗尾草属植物。*African ~* 稷,龙爪稗。*German* [*Hungarian*] *~ = small foxtail ~* 粟,小米。*hog* [*bread*] *~* 黍,糜。*Indian ~ = great ~* 高粱。*Italian ~* 粟。*~ grass* 粟草。

milli- *comb*. *f*. (表示)"毫","千分之一"。

mil·li·am·pere [ˌmiliˈæmpɛə; ˏmɪlɪˋæmpɪr] ***n***. 毫安(培)。

mil·liard [ˈmiljɑːd; ˋmɪljɚd] ***n***.〔英〕十亿,十万万(=〔美〕billion)。

mil·li·ar·y [ˈmiliˌɛəri; ˋmɪlɪˏɛrɪ] **I** ***a***. 古罗马里的;千步尺的。**II** ***n***. (*pl*. ***-ar·ies***) 古罗马里程碑。

mil·li·bar [ˈmilibɑː; ˋmɪlɪˏbɑr] ***n***.【气】毫巴〔气压的单位=1/1000 bar〕。

Mil·li·cent [ˈmilisnt; ˋmɪləsnt] ***n***. 米莉森特〔女子名〕。

mil·li·cron [ˈmilikrɔn; ˋmɪlɪkrɑn] ***n***. = millimicron.

mil·li·cu·rie [ˈmiliˌkjuri; ˋmɪləˏkjʊrɪ] ***n***.【物】毫居(里)〔1/1000居里〕。

Mil·lie [ˈmili; ˋmɪlɪ] ***n***. 米莉〔女子名,Mildred 的昵称〕。

mil·lieme [miːˈljem; miˋljɛm] ***n***. 米利姆〔埃及、苏丹和利比亚的货币名称,等于1/1000镑〕。

mil·lier [miːˈljei; miˋlje] ***n***.〔F.〕法吨(=1000公斤)。

mil·li·far·ad [ˈmiliˌfærəd, -əd; ˋmɪlɪˏfæræd, -əd] ***n***.【电】毫法(拉)〔千分之一法拉,电容单位〕。

mil·li·gal [ˈmiliˌgæl; ˋmɪlɪˏgæl] ***n***.【物】毫伽〔重力加速度单位〕。

mil·li·gram(me) [ˈmiligræm; ˋmɪlɚˏgræm] ***n***. 毫克〔千分之一克〕。

mil·li·hen·ry [ˈmiliˌhenri; ˋmɪlɪˏhɛnrɪ] ***n***.【电】毫亨(利)〔电感单位〕。

Mil·li·kan [ˈmilikən; ˋmɪləkən] ***n***. 米利肯〔姓氏〕。

mil·li·li·tre, **mil·li·li·ter** [ˈmililiːtə; ˋmɪləˏlitɚ] ***n***. 毫升〔千分之一升〕。

mil·lime [ˈmiliːm, -im; ˋmɪlim, -ɪm] ***n***. 米利姆〔突尼斯货币和硬币名称,等于1/1000第纳尔〕。

mil·li·me·tre, **mil·li·me·ter** [ˈmiliˌmiːtə; ˋmɪləˏmitɚ] ***n***. 毫米〔千分之一米〕。

mil·li·mi·cron [ˈmiliˌmaikrɔn; ˋmɪlɪˏmaɪkrɑn] ***n***. (*pl*. ***-cra*** [-krə; -krə]) 毫微米〔千分之一微米〕。

mil·li·mi·cro·se·cond [ˈmiliˌmaikrəuˈsekənd; ˋmɪlɪˏmaɪkroˋsɛkənd] ***n***. 毫微秒。

mil·line [ˈmilˈlain; ˋmɪlˋlaɪn] ***n***. **1**. 百万行〔广告的计算单位,即用 5½ 点字体登一栏(长 1/14 英寸)印出于百万份的刊物上〕。**2**. 登"百万行"广告的费用。

mil·li·ner [ˈmilinə; ˋmɪlənɚ] ***n***. **1**. 女帽头饰商〔通例指女性〕。**2**. 〔废〕杂货商〔卖意大利 Milan 地方产花边、帽子、针、缎带等杂货的商人,通常指男性〕。*a man-*～ 为小事忙忙碌碌的人。

mil·li·ner·y [ˈmilinəri; ˋmɪləˏnɛrɪ] ***n***. 女帽类;女帽商。

mill·ing [ˈmiliŋ; ˋmɪlɪŋ] ***n***. **1**. 磨;制粉;碾碎。**2**.【机】铣;铣削法;铣出的齿边。**3**. 轧货币的花边,轧出的花边;浆洗。**4**. 〔俚〕拳击;殴打。**5**. 考验,磨炼。**6**. 〔美〕(家畜)成群兜圆圈。**7**. 旋转犁。**8**.【矿】选矿。**9**.【纺】缩绒,缩呢,毡合。～ **machine** 铣床;缩绒机,缩绒呢。～ **tool** [**cutter**] 铣刀。

mil·li·nor·mal [ˈmiliˈnɔːməl; ˋmɪlɪˋnɔrməl] ***a***.【化】毫规度的,毫克当量的。

mil·lion [ˈmiljən; ˋmɪljən] **I** ***num***. 百万;百万个(人或物)。★复数形式为～(s), 如 five ～(s). **II** ***n***. **1**. 〔*pl*.〕无数,许许多多。**2**. 百万元;百万(镑、美元、法郎)。*The force of habit in* ～*s and tens of* ～*s is a most formidable force*. 千百万人的习惯势力是最可怕的势力。～***s upon*** ～***s of the masses*** 千千万万的群众。***the*** ～ 群众。

mil·lion·aire, 〔*fem*.〕 **mil·lion·air·ess** [ˌmiljəˈnɛə, -ris; ˏmɪljənˋɛr, -rɪs] ***n***. 百万富翁,大富翁,富豪。

mil·lion·ette [ˌmiljəˈnet; ˏmɪljəˋnɛt] ***n***. 小百万富翁,小富豪。

mil·lion·fold [ˈmiljənfəuld; ˋmɪljənˏfold] ***a***., ***ad***. 百万倍的[地];成百万倍。

mil·lionth [ˈmiljənθ; ˋmɪljənθ] ***num***. 第一百万(个);百万分之一(的)。

mil·li·pede, **mil·li·ped** [ˈmilipiːd, -ped; ˋmɪləpid, -pɛd] ***n***. = millepede.

mil·li·rad [ˈmiliˌræd; ˋmɪləˏræd] ***n***. 毫拉(德)〔千分之一拉德,辐射剂量单位〕。

mil·li·sec·ond [ˈmiliˌsekənd; ˋmɪləˏsɛkənd] ***n***. 毫秒。

mil·li·volt [ˈmiliˌvəult; ˋmɪləˏvolt] ***n***.【电】毫伏(特)。

mil·li·watt [ˈmiliwɔt; ˋmɪləˏwɑt] ***n***.【电】毫瓦(特)。

Mills bomb [ˈmilzˈbɔm; ˋmɪlzˋbɑm] ***n***. 卵形手榴弹。

Milne [mil, miln; mɪl, mɪln] ***n***. 米尔恩〔姓氏〕。

Milner [ˈmilnə; mɪlnɚ] ***n***. 米尔纳〔姓氏〕。

mi·lo [ˈmailəu; ˋmaɪlo] ***n***. **1**. 白(或黄)穗芦粟。**2**. 〔M-〕迈洛〔男子名〕。

mi·lor(d) [miˈlɔː(d); mɪˋlɔr(d)] ***n***. 先生,老板(= my lord)〔法国人对英国绅士的称呼〕。

milque·toast [ˈmilktəust; ˋmɪlkˏtost] ***n***. 〔美俚〕意志薄弱的人,没勇气的人。**-ish** ***a***.

mil·reis [ˈmilreis; ˋmɪlˏres] ***n***. (*sing*., *pl*.) **1**. (从前的)葡萄牙金币。**2**. 巴西货币单位(=1,000 reis)。

MILSAT = military satellite 军事卫星。

milt [milt; mɪlt] **I** ***n***. **1**.【解】脾脏。**2**. 鱼精液。**II** ***a***. 产卵期雄鱼的。**III** ***vt***. 使(鱼卵)受精。

milt·er [ˈmiltə; ˋmɪltɚ] ***n***. **1**. 射精期的雄鱼。**2**. 鱼精液。

Mil·ton [ˈmiltən; ˋmɪltn̩] ***n***. **1**. 米尔顿〔姓氏,男子名〕。**2**. **John** ～ 约翰·密尔顿〔1608—1674,英国诗人, *Paradise Lost* 的作者〕。

Mil·to·ni·an, **Mil·ton·ic** [milˈtəuniən, -tɔnik; mɪlˋtonɪən, -tɑnɪk] ***a***. **1**. (英国诗人)密尔顿的,密尔顿诗风的。**2**. 雄浑的,(文体等)庄严的。

Mil·wau·kee [milˈwɔːki(ː); mɪlˋwɔkɪ] ***n***. 密尔沃基〔美国城市〕。

mim [mim; mɪm] ***a***. 〔英方〕故作恬静的;假装羞怯的;假作端庄的。

mime [maim; maɪm] **I** ***n***. **1**. (古希腊、罗马的)笑剧;摹拟表演。**2**. 丑角,小丑;哑剧演员。**II** ***vi***. 作摹拟表演,演滑稽角色〔通常为哑剧〕。

M.I.Mech.E. = Member of the Institution of Mechanical Engineers〔英〕机械工程师学会会员。

mim·e·o [ˈmimiə; ˋmɪmɪə] **I** ***n***. 〔美口〕油印品。**II** ***vt***. 用油印机油印。

mim·e·o·graph [ˈmimiəgrɑːf; ˋmɪmɪəˏgræf] **I** ***n***. (商标名)滚筒油印机;油印品。**II** ***vt***. 用滚筒油印机印刷,油印。

mi·me·sis [maiˈmiːsis, mi-; maɪˋmisɪs, mɪ-] ***n***. **1**. 模仿,摹拟。**2**.【生】拟态。

mi·met·ic [miˈmetik, mai-; mɪˋmɛtɪk, maɪ-] ***a***. **1**. 模仿的,摹拟的,巧于模仿的。**2**.【生】拟态的;【病】拟似的;【矿】类似的。**3**.【语】拟声的。～ *gestures* 模仿性的姿态。*a* ～ *crystal*【矿】拟晶,似晶。**-i·cal·ly** ***ad***.

mim·e·tism [ˈmimitizəm; ˋmɪmɪtɪzm̩] ***n***.【生】拟态;【心】模仿性。

mim·ic [ˈmimik; ˋmɪmɪk] **I** ***a***. **1**. 模仿的,摹拟的,假的。**2**.【生】拟态的。*a* ～ *battle* 模拟战。*a* ～ *gene*【生】同效基因。～ *tears* 假哭,假流泪。**II** ***n***. **1**. 巧于模仿的人;摹拟笑剧的演员,丑角。**2**. 仿造物,模写物。**III** ***vt***. (***mimicked***; ***mimicking***) **1**. 学样;学样取笑;摹拟;模写;活像…。**2**.【生】拟形,拟色。～ **board** 模拟板〔以图解方式和灯显示一个复杂系统的板或屏幕〕。**-al** ***a***.

mim·ick·er [ˈmimikə; ˋmɪmɪkɚ] ***n***. 学人样的人,模仿者。

mim·ic·ry [ˈmimikri; ˋmɪmɪkrɪ] ***n***. **1**. 模仿;摹拟;学样;模写;仿造品。**2**.【生】拟态。

mim·in·y-pim·i·ny [ˈmiminiˈpimini; ˋmɪmənɪˋpɪmənɪ] ***a***. = niminypiminy.

M.I.M.M. = Member of the Institution of Mining and Metallurgy〔英〕采矿及冶金学会会员。

mi·mo·sa [miˈməuzə; mɪˋmozə] ***n***.【植】含羞草。

Min. = **1**. Minister. **2**. Ministry.

min. = **1**. mineralogy. **2**. minim. **3**. minimum. **4**. mining. **5**. minor. **6**. minute.

mi·na[1] [ˈmainə; ˋmaɪnə] ***n***. (*pl*. ***-nae*** [-niː; -ni], ～***s***) 古希腊等地的货币单位和重量单位〔约等于 100 drachma〕。

mi·na[2] ***n***. = myna.

min·a·ble, **mine·a·ble** [ˈmainəbl; ˋmaɪnəbl̩] ***a***. 可采掘的,可采矿的。

mi·na·cious, **min·a·to·ry** [miˈneiʃəs, ˈminətəri; mɪˋneʃəs, ˋmɪnəˏtorɪ] ***a***. 威吓的,威胁性的。

mi·nac·i·ty [miˈnæsiti; mɪˋnæsətɪ] ***n***. 威吓。

mi·nar [miˈnɑː; mɪˋnɑr] ***n***. **1**. 灯塔。**2**. 小塔,望楼。

min·a·ret [ˈminəret; ˏmɪnəˋrɛt] ***n***. (清真寺院的)尖塔。

mince [mins; mɪns] **I** ***vt***. **1**. 切碎,剁碎,斩细,绞碎(肉等)。**2**. 婉转地说,半吞半吐地说。— ***vi***. **1**. (用小步子)装腔作势地走。**2**. 装腔作势地讲。***not*** ～ ***matters*** [***one's words***] 直说,坦白地说,不吞吞吐吐。**II** ***n***. 肉末(= ～d meat)。～ **meat** (加有葡萄干、苹果、糖、牛板油、香料等的做馅用的)百果馅;肉末(*make* ～ *meat of* 把…剁成肉末,粉碎,彻底击败;歼灭)。～**-pie** ***n***. 百果馅饼。〔*pl*.〕〔美俚〕眼睛。

minc·er [ˈminsə; ˋmɪnsɚ] ***n***. **1**. 绞肉机。**2**. 装腔作势的人。**3**. 走路忸怩作态的人。

minc·ing [ˈminsiŋ; ˋmɪnsɪŋ] ***a***. **1**. (说话、举动)装腔作势的,装模作样的。**2**. 剁碎用的。**-ly** ***ad***.

mind [maind; maɪnd] **I** ***n***. **1**. 心,精神(*opp*. body);心力,知,智力,智慧(*opp*. heart)。**2**. 愿望,目的;意向,意志,决心;见解,意见。**3**. 记忆,记性,记忆力;回想。**4**. 心胸,头脑;人。**5**.【宗】追思弥撒;【基督】〔M-〕上帝;神道。*Nothing in the world is difficult for one who sets his* ～ *to it*. 世上无难事,只怕有心人。*a frame* [*state*]

M

of ～ (一种)心境,心情;精神状态。*the Greek* ～ 希腊精神。*the public* ～ 公众意见,舆论。*Out of sight, out of* ～. 眼不见,心不想;离久情疏。*a turn* [*cast*] *of* ～ 心地,癖性,脾气。*It has gone* [*passed*] *out of my* ～. 这事我已经记不起了。*I awoke to my full* ～. 我醒过来了[神志清醒了]。*a scientific* ～ 科学头脑。*the great* ～(*s*) *of the time* 当代有才智的人(们)。*the master* ～ 卓绝伟才。***absence of*** ～ 心不在焉。***after one's*** ～ 合…的心意。***a month's*** ～ 人死后一月举行的追思弥撒;〔英〕爱好。***apply*** [***bend***] ***the*** ～ ***to*** 专心…,把精神灌注在…,一心一意…。***bear*** [***have, keep***] ***in*** ～ 记住,记在心里(*Bear what I say in* ～. 别忘记我的话)。***be in two*** [***several***] ～***s*** 犹豫不决,三心两意,心里摇动 (*about*)。***be of a*** [***one***] ～ 意见一致,抱同样的看法。***be of your*** ～ 同你意见一致。***blow one's*** ～〔美俚〕经历迷幻感,极度刺激。***bring*** [***call***] ***to one's*** ～ 想起。***change*** [***alter***] ***one's*** ～ 改变想法[主意],变卦。***come to*** [***into***] ***one's*** ～ 想起。***dawn on one's*** ～ 开始明白。***disclose*** [***say, speak, tell***] ***one's*** ～ 直率表明意见,说明心事。***give*** (*sb.*) ***a bit*** [***piece***] ***of one's*** ～ 直率说给(某人)听,当面责骂。***give one's*** (***whole***) ～ ***to*** 一心一意地…,专心…。***go out of one's*** ～ 被忘却;发狂。***have a great*** [***good***] ～ ***to*** 非常想…,极有意…。***have a*** ～ ***of one's own*** 自有定见。***have a*** ～ ***to*** (*do*) 想,有意。***have half a*** ～ ***to*** (*do*) 有几分想…。***have in*** ～ 记住;考虑;想,打算,企图。***have no*** [***little***] ～ ***to*** (*do*) 一点儿也[简直]不想…。***have*** (*something*) (***up***) ***on one's*** ～ 把…挂在心上,担心着,惦念着。***in*** [***to***] ***my*** ～ 我以为…,我认为…。***in sound*** [***one's right***] ～ 精神无异状,神志清醒(*He cannot be in his right* ～. 他一定是疯了)。***keep an open*** ～ 不抱成见;虚心。***keep*** [***have, set***] ***one's*** ～ ***on*** 注意,留意;专心。***keep one's own*** ～ 有决断;自有主意。***let*** (*sb.*) ***know one's*** ～ 不客气地对人提意见。***lose one's*** ～ 发狂。***make up one's*** ～ 决心 (*to do*)。***of a*** [***one, the same***] ～ 意见一致;看法相同。***of sound*** ～ 神志清醒。***off one's*** ～ 丢开不再想;忘怀,置诸脑后(*That is off my* ～. 那我已经忘了)。***one's*** ～***'s eye*** = ***the*** ～***'s eye***. ***open one's*** ～ ***to*** 告诉意见[心思]给…。***out of one's*** ～ 在发疯;忘记。***pass*** [***go***] ***out of*** ～ 被忘却。***presence of*** ～ 沉着,镇定。***put*** [***keep***] ***sb. in*** ～ ***of*** 使(某人)想起…;提醒某人。***read another's*** ～ 看出别人的心思。***rush upon one's*** ～ 突然想起。***set one's*** ～ ***at rest*** [***ease***] 安心。***set one's*** ～ ***upon*** 专心于。***speak one's*** ～ ***out*** 把心里话说出来。***take one's*** ～ ***off*** 丢开不再想。***tell sb. one's*** ～ 把心意告诉给某人;坦率对某人提意见。***the*** ～***'s eye*** 心眼,想像。***time out of*** ～ 太古时代;从太古。***to one's*** ～ 个人认为;合意。***turn one's*** ～ ***to*** 注意。***weigh on one's*** ～ 挂在心上;担心。***uppermost in one's*** ～ 在某人头脑里占第一位,成为某人注意的中心。***with ... in*** ～ 把…搁在心上。

II ***vt*.** **1.** 注意,留心,当心;〔命令〕留心。**2.** 照应,照料。**3.**〔否定、疑问、条件句〕对…不高兴,反对。**4.**〔Scot.〕〔古〕记着。**5.**〔罕〕使想起。*M- your own business*. 别管闲事。*M- your head*. 当心你的头。*M- your eye!*〔俚〕当心! 留神! *M- what you are about*. 当心点;别胡闹呀。*M- you come early*. 记住一定早点来呀。*M- what I tell you*. 记住我的话。*Never* ～ (*about*) *the expense!* 花多花少请你别在意。*Never* ～ *him!* 别管他。*I should not* ～ *a glass of beer*. 有一杯啤酒喝也好〔真想喝〕。*M- you'll slip!* 当心! 别滑倒啦。*I don't* ～ *a bit*. 我一点也不在意。— ***vi*.** **1.** 注意,留心,当心。**2.** 反对,不高兴。**3.** 挂在心上,记住,牵挂,担心。*Never* ～! 不要紧! 没什么! ***I don't*** ～ (*doing sth.*), ***but I do*** ～ (*... ing*). 我不在乎[不计较]…,我就怕…。***if you don't*** ～ ... 要是你不反对,要是你不介意。～ ***one's P's and Q's*** 言行谨慎,谨言慎行。～ ***out!***〔俚〕当心! 让开! ～ ***that...*** 留心…,一定…。～ ***you*** 你听着〔表示让步或提出条件的插句〕(*But I have no objection,* ～ *you*. 不过,你听着,我并不反对)。***Would*** [***do***] ***you*** ～ (*doing sth.*)? …可以吗? 你不反对…么? 对不起,请你…(*Would you* ～ *shutting the door?* 对不起,请你把门关上好吗?)。～ **blind** ***a*.** 茫然的,头脑一片空白的。～**-blow** ***vt*.**〔美俚〕使产生幻觉,使经历迷幻感,极度刺激。～**-blower** ***n*.** **1.** 迷幻剂。**2.** 吸毒者(尤指吸服迷幻剂者)。**3.** 迷幻的感受。**4.** 动人心弦[引起幻觉]的东西。～**-blowing** ***a*.** 动人心弦的,(麻醉品等)引起幻觉的。～ **cure,** ～ **healing** 精神疗法。～ **mapping** 心理测定。～ **reader** 自称能知他人心事的人。～ **reading** 测心术。～**-set** 思维定式,不易改变的思想倾向,僵化的心态。～ **stuff**【哲】精神素材。～**'s eye** 想像。～ **virus**【计】心灵病毒〔网上发布的可能导致收看者行为失控的不良文化信息〕。

Min·da·na·o [ˌmindɑːˈnau; ˏmɪndəˋnɑo] ***n*.** 棉兰老(岛);明达瑙(岛)〔菲律宾〕。

mind·ed [ˈmaindid; ˋmaɪndɪd] ***a*.** **1.** 有意志的〔用作修饰语〕。**2.** 想…的〔用作表语,与不定式连用〕。**3.** 有…之心的,有…精神的,热心…的,关心…的〔构成复合词〕。*He is* ～ *to do so*. 他是想这样干的。*small-* ～ 气量小的。*low-* ～ 卑鄙的。*feeble-* ～ 低能的;意志薄弱的。*air-* ～ 热心航空的。

mind·er [ˈmaində; ˋmaɪndɚ] ***n*.** (家畜、机器、幼儿等的)看管人。

mind·ful [ˈmaindful; ˋmaɪndfəl] ***a*.** 〔通例用作表语〕注意…的,留心…的;不忘…的 (*of*) (*opp*. forgetful)。**-ly** ***ad*.**, **-ness** ***n*.**

mind·less [ˈmaindlis; ˋmaɪndlɪs] ***a*.** **1.** 不注意的,不留心的;无心的;无意识的。**2.** 愚钝的。**-ly** ***ad*.**, **-ness** ***n*.**

Min·do·ro [minˈdɔːrəu; mɪnˋdoro] ***n*.** (菲律宾中部的)民都洛。

mine[1] [main; maɪn] ***pro*.** **1.**〔I 的物主代词〕我的(东西),我的家属,我的亲戚。*The book is* ～. 这本书是我的。*He was kind to me and* ～. 他对我和我的家属都好。*That is no business of* ～. 那不关我的事情。*The game is* ～. (比赛的结果)是我赢了。**2.**〔古、诗〕我的(= my): (a) 用在头一个字母是元音或 h 的名词前: ～ *eye*, ～ *heart*. (b)用在名词后: *lady* ～.

mine[2] [main; maɪn] **I** ***n*.** **1.** 矿,矿山,矿井;【矿】铁矿。**2.** 资源;(知识、资料等的)源泉,宝库。**3.**【军】坑道;地雷坑。**4.** 地雷(= land ～);水雷;火箭炮弹。**5.**【动】(昆虫的)潜道。*a coal* ～ 煤矿。*a gold* ～ 金矿。*the* ～*s* 矿业。*a* ～ *of information* 知识的宝库。*an acoustic* [*a sonic*] ～ 音响引爆水雷,感音水雷。*a floating* [*drifting, surface-*] ～ 漂流水雷。*a magnetic* ～ 磁性水雷。*a submarine contact* ～ 海中触发水雷。***charge a*** ～ 装填地雷。***lay a*** ～ 布置地雷[水雷];推翻(*for*)。***spring a*** ～ ***on*** (*sb.*) 冷不防袭击(某人)。***strike a*** ～ 触雷。***work a*** ～ 办矿,开矿。**II** ***vt*.** **1.** 开(矿),采(矿)采掘;打(矿井),挖(矿道)。**2.** 在…中[下]敷设地雷[水雷];发射(火箭炮弹);(用雷)炸毁,爆破。**3.** 用阴谋暗害,破坏。～*oil shale* 开采油页岩。— ***vi*.** **1.** 开矿,采矿;挖坑道。**2.** 布雷。～ **barrage** 雷幕。～ **belt** 雷带。～ **captain** 矿工头。～ **chamber** 雷室。～ **clearance** 扫雷,排雷。～ **detector** 探雷器。～ **dragging** 水雷扫除工作。～ **dredger** 扫雷艇。～ **field** 矿区;【军】布雷区[场]。～ **hunter**【军】扫雷艇。～ **layer** 布雷舰艇(= mine-laying vessel)。**a** ～**-laying squad** 布雷队。～**-laying submarine** 布雷潜水艇。～ **planter** 布雷船;布雷兵。～**-prop** 矿柱,坑木。～**-run** 原矿。～**sweeper** 扫雷舰[器]。～**-sweeping** 海上扫雷(工作)。～ **thrower** 掷雷筒。～ **vessel** 水雷舰。～ **warfare** 地雷战;水雷战。～**-water**【矿】矿水,井下水。～**-worker**〔主美〕矿工。

Mi·nen(wer·fer) [ˈmiːnən(veəfə); ˋmɪnən(vɛrfɚ)] ***n*.**

〔G.〕德式迫击炮。

min·er [ˈmainə; ˋmaɪnɚ] ***n*.** **1.** 矿工;地雷工兵;采矿机。**2.** 〔*pl*.〕〔美商〕矿业股。**coal ~** 采煤工人。**~'s disease** 矿工病。**~'s friend** 达维 (Davy) 式安全灯。**~'s phthisis** 【医】矽肺;矿工痨病;炭末入肺病。

min·er·ag·ra·phy [ˌminəˈrægrəfi; ˏmɪnəˋrægrəfɪ] ***n*.** 【矿】矿相学。

min·er·al. = mineralogy.

min·er·al [ˈminərəl; ˋmɪnərəl] **I** ***n*.** **1.** 矿物;〔口〕矿石;【化】无机物。**2.** 〔英〕〔*pl*.〕= ~ water. **II** ***a*.** 矿物(性)的;含矿物的;无机的。*the ~ kingdom* 矿物界。**~ detector** 【无】矿石[晶体]检波器。**~ fertilizer** 无机肥料。**~ jelly** 矿冻,矿物冻。**~ oil** 矿物油。**~ rights** 开矿权。**~ spring** 矿泉。**~ tar** 软沥青(= maltha)。**~ vein** 矿脉。**~ water** 矿泉(水),矿质水。**~ wax** 地蜡,石蜡(= ozokerite)。**~ wool** 矿渣绒。

min·er·al·ize [ˈminərəlaiz; ˋmɪnərəlˏaɪz] ***vt*.** 使矿物化,使矿化;使含矿物。— ***vi*.** 探矿;促进矿化。**-i·zation** [ˌminərəlaiˈzeiʃən; ˏmɪnərələˋzeʃən] ***n*.** 【地】矿化(作用);成矿作用。**-r** ***n*.** **1.** 【化】造矿元素;【地】矿化因素。**2.** 探矿者,采矿者。

min·er·a·log·i·cal [ˌminərəˈlɔdʒikəl; ˏmɪnərəˋlɑdʒɪkl̩] ***a*.** 矿物学(上)的。

min·er·al·o·gist [ˌminəˈrælədʒist; ˏmɪnɚˋrælədʒɪst] ***n*.** 矿物学家。

min·er·al·o·gy [ˌminəˈrælədʒi; ˏmɪnɚˋrælədʒɪ] ***n*.** 矿物学。

min·er·al·oid [ˈminərəlɔid; ˋmɪnərəˏlɔɪd] ***n*.** 类矿物,似矿物,准矿物。

Mi·ner·va [miˈnəːvə; məˋnɝvə] ***n*.** 【罗神】米诺瓦〔司智慧、学问、战争等的女神〕。

mi·ne·stro·ne [ˌminiˈstrəuni; ˏmɪnəˋstronɪ] ***n*.** 〔It.〕意大利浓菜汤。

min·e·ver [ˈminivə; ˋmɪnəvɚ] ***n*.** (中世纪贵族用作里子或装饰用的)白毛皮。

min·gle [ˈmiŋgl; ˋmɪŋgl̩] ***vt*.** 使相混,使混合。*with ~d feelings* 悲喜交集地。— ***vi*.** **1.** 混合 (*with*)。**2.** 混在一起;参加,加入 (*among*; *in*);交际 (*with*)。*~ in* [*with*] *the crowd* 混入人群。*They ~ very little in society*. 他们很少交际。**~-mangle** 混合。

min·gy [ˈmindʒi; ˋmɪndʒɪ] ***a*.** 〔英口〕卑鄙的;吝啬的,小气的。

min·i [ˈmini; ˋmɪnɪ] ***n*.** **1.** 同类中的极小者。**2.** 超短裙,迷你裙(= miniskirt)。**3.** 微型汽车(= minicar)。**~-course** 简明课程。**~disk** **1.** 迷你镭射唱片,微型激光唱片。**2.** 【计】小型软盘。**~ hub** 小型中转航空港。**~-minded** ***a*.** 没有头脑的,愚蠢的。**~planet** 小行星。

min·i·ate [ˈminieit; ˋmɪnɪˏet] ***vt*.** **1.** 在…上涂朱红。**2.** 用彩色文字装饰(抄本)。

min·i·a·ture [ˈminjətʃə; ˋmɪnɪətʃɚ] **I** ***n*.** **1.** (中世纪抄本上的)彩饰画;(象牙等上的)微小画像,纤细画(术);缩图,缩模;小型器件。**2.** 【影】模型布景,模型舞台装置。**II** ***a*.** 小型的,缩小的;小规模的。*a ~ camera* 小型照相机。*a ~ car* 微型汽车。*a ~ war* 小规模战争。***in ~*** 小型的,小规模的,缩图的;用纤细画法画成的。**III** ***vt*.** **1.** 使成小型。**2.** 把…画成纤细图,缩写。

min·i·a·tur·ist [ˈminjətʃərist; ˋmɪnɪətʃərɪst] ***n*.** 纤画家,微图画家。

min·i·a·tur·ize [ˈminiətʃəraiz; ˋmɪnɪətʃəraɪz] ***vt*.** 使微型化。**-i·za·tion** [ˌminiətʃəraiˈzeiʃən; ˏmɪnɪətʃərəˋzeʃən] ***n*.**

min·i·boom [ˈminibuːm; ˋmɪnɪˏbum] ***n*.** 短暂繁荣。

min·i·bus [ˈminibʌs; ˋmɪnɪˏbʌs] ***n*.** 微型公共汽车。

min·i·cab [ˈminikæb; ˋmɪnɪkæb] ***n*.** 微型出租汽车。

min·i·cam [ˈminikæm; ˋmɪnɪˏkæm] ***n*.** = miniature camera.

min·i·cri·sis [ˈminikraisis; ˋmɪnɪˏkraɪsɪs] ***n*.** 短暂危机。

Min·i·é [ˈminiː, ˈminiːei; ˋmɪni, ˋmɪnɪˏe] **ball** 锥形来福枪弹。

min·i·fy [ˈminifai; ˋmɪnəˏfaɪ] ***vt*.** 弄小(少),使缩小;削减;轻视。

min·i·kin [ˈminikin; ˋmɪnɪkɪn] **I** ***n*.** 微小的东西;小扣针;小人,小动物;【印】最小铅字。**II** ***a*.** 微小的,纤小的;矫揉造作的。

min·im [ˈminim; ˋmɪnɪm] ***n*.** **1.** 微物,一滴,一点点,一丝丝;〔蔑〕极矮小的人。**2.** (药剂用)量滴〔液量最小单位,英制 = 0.0592 毫升,美制 = 0.0616 毫升〕。**3.** 一画,一笔(尤指 m, n 等字母中自上至下的一笔)。**4.** 【乐】半音符。

min·i·ma [ˈminimə; ˋmɪnəmə] ***n*.** minimum 复数的异体。

min·i·mal [ˈminiməl; ˋmɪnɪml̩] **I** ***a*.** **1.** 最小的,极微的,最低(限度)的。**2.** 最简单派艺术的。**II** ***n*.** 最简单派艺术作品〔抽象艺术的一种〕。**~ art** 最简单派艺术。

min·i·mal·ist [ˈminiməlist; ˋmɪnɪməlɪst] ***n*.** (政治上的)最低纲领派(*opp*. maximalist);最简单派艺术家。

min·i·mize [ˈminimaiz; ˋmɪnəˏmaɪz] ***vt*.** **1.** 使减到最少,按最小限度估计。**2.** 轻视。**-za·tion** [ˌminimaiˈzeiʃən; ˏmɪnəmaɪˋzeʃən] ***n*.**

min·i·miz·er [ˈminimaizə; ˋmɪnəˏmaɪzɚ] ***n*.** 把事情估计得过低的人,轻视(哲学难题等)的人。

min·i·mum [ˈminiməm; ˋmɪnəməm] **I** ***n*.** (*pl*. *~s*, ***-ma*** [-mə; -mə]) 最小,最低,最少限度;【数】极小(值)。*the irreducible ~* 无法减少的最小限度。*The thermometer reached the ~ for the year*. 寒暑表降到当年最低度数。**II** ***a*.** 最少的,最小的,最低的。*the ~ value* 【数】极小值。**~ range** 最小射程。**~ thermometer** 最低温度计。**~ wage** (法定)最低工资。

min·i·mus [ˈminiməs; ˋmɪnɪməs] ***a*.** 〔英〕(学校里同姓同学)年纪最轻的。★琼斯三弟兄依年龄大小称为 Jones major, Jones minor, Jones ~.

min·ing [ˈmainiŋ; ˋmaɪnɪŋ] **I** ***n*.** **1.** 采矿,采矿业,矿业。**2.** 敷设地雷[水雷]。**II** ***a*.** 开矿的,采矿的。*a ~ engineer* 采矿工程师。*~ engineering* 采矿工程(学)。*the ~ industry* 采矿工业。

min·ion [ˈminjən; ˋmɪnjən] ***n*.** **1.** 〔贬〕宠儿,宠臣,宠物。**2.** 走狗,奴才。**3.** 〔称呼〕顽皮姑娘。**4.** (七点大小的)小活字。**5.** 僚属。*a ~ of fortune* 〔蔑〕幸运的宠儿。*the ~s of the law* 〔蔑〕狱吏;警察。

min·is·cule [ˈminiskjuːl; ˋmɪnɪskjul] **I** ***n*.** (= minuscule) **1.** (中世纪古抄本的)小书写体。**2.** 小书写体字母。**3.** 小字。**II** ***a*.** **1.** 小书写体的;小书写体字母的;小字的。**2.** 极小的,微小的,细微的。

min·ish [ˈminiʃ; ˋmɪnɪʃ] ***vt*.** 〔古〕减少,缩小。

min·i·skirt [ˈminiˌskəːt; ˋmɪnɪˏskɝt] ***n*.** 超短裙,迷你裙。

min·is·ter [ˈministə; ˋmɪnɪstɚ] **I** ***n*.** **1.** 部长;阁员,大臣;〔*pl*.〕政府。**2.** 公使;外交使节。**3.** 【宗】牧师;〔英〕非国教派牧师。★英国国教派牧师叫 vicar, rector, curate. **4.** 〔罕〕代理人。**5.** 仆人,侍从,臣下。*the Prime M-* 内阁总理,首相。*the M- for* [*of*] *Foreign Affairs* 外交部长。*the M- of Defense* 国防部长。*the Council of Ministers* (苏联等国的)部长会议。*the ~ plenipotentiary* 全权公使。**II** ***vi*.** **1.** 做牧师;侍奉;伺候,服侍。**2.** 尽力,出力,帮助;对…有帮助,有贡献 (*to*)。*a ~ing angel* 救星。*~ to a person's vanity* 满足某人的虚荣心。*~ to a sick man's wants* 照顾病人需要。— ***vt*.** 〔古〕**1.** 供给。**2.** 举行(祭祀)。

min·is·te·ri·al [ˌminisˈtiəriəl; ˏmɪnəsˋtɪrɪəl] ***a*.** **1.** 部长[牧师、公使等]的。**2.** 代理的;辅助的,附属的(*opp*. directing);有帮助的,有贡献的。**3.** 行政(上)的(*opp*. judicial)。*the ~ party* 〔英〕政府党。*the ~ benches* (英国议会下院)政府党(席)(*opp*. opposition

M

benches)。**-ist** ***n***.〔英〕内阁支持者。**-ly** ***ad***. 作为部长[大臣、牧师]。

min·is·trant [ˈministrənt; ˋmɪnɪstrənt] **I** ***a***. 服务的,侍奉的,辅佐的。**II** ***n***. 侍奉者,辅助者。

min·is·tra·tion [ˌminisˈtreiʃən; ˏmɪnəˋstreʃən] ***n***. **1**. 行宗教仪式;(特指牧师的)职务;服务。**2**. 救助,救济。

min·is·tra·tive [ˈministrətiv; ˋmɪnɪstrətɪv] ***a***. = ministrant.

min·is·try [ˈministri; ˋmɪnɪstrɪ] ***n***. **1**. 服务,侍奉。**2**. 牧师的职务;〔集合词〕牧师。**3**. 部长的任务[职务、任期]。**4**.〔常作 M-〕〔英〕内阁;〔英〕(政府的)部(=〔美〕department)。**5**. 公使团。*The M- has resigned*. 内阁辞职了。*the M- of Foreign Affairs* 外交部。

mini·sub [ˈminisʌb; ˋmɪnɪˏsʌb] ***n***. 小型潜水艇。

Min·i·tel [ˈminitəl; ˋmɪnɪtəl] ***n***. (法国的)公共信息网络终端〔法国的电脑电视终端,一种讯息传视系统〕。

mini·track [ˈminitræk; ˋmɪnɪˏtræk] ***n***. 人造卫星[火箭]的电子跟踪系统。

min·i·tube [ˈminitjuːb; ˋmɪnɪˏtjub] ***n***. 小型[袖珍]电视机。

mini·type [ˈminitaip; ˋmɪnɪˏtaɪp] ***n***. 微型,小型。

min·i·um [ˈminiəm; ˋmɪnɪəm] ***n***. 朱红色,【化】铅丹,红铅,四氧化三铅。

min·i·ver [ˈminivə; ˋmɪnəvɚ] ***n***. = minever.

mink [miŋk; mɪŋk] ***n***. **1**.【动】水貂。**2**. 貂皮。

Minn. = Minnesota.

Min·na [ˈminə; ˋmɪnə] ***n***. 明娜〔女子名〕。

Min·ne·ap·o·lis [ˌminiˈæpəlis; ˏmɪnɪˋæpl̩ɪs] ***n***. 明尼阿波利斯〔美国城市〕。

min·ne·sing·er [ˈminiˌsiŋə; ˋmɪnɪˏsɪŋɚ] ***n***.〔G.〕(德国中世纪的)吟游诗人。

Min·ne·so·ta [ˌminiˈsəutə; ˏmɪnɪˋsotə] ***n***. 明尼苏达〔美国州名〕。

Min·nie [ˈmini; ˋmɪnɪ] ***n***. 明妮〔女子名,Mary 的昵称〕。

min·nie [ˈmini; ˋmɪnɪ] ***n***.〔军俚〕= Minenwerfer.

min·now [ˈminəu; ˋmɪno] ***n***.【鱼】鲹鱼;小鱼,杂鱼。***a Triton among*** [***of***] ***the*** **~*s*** 鸡群一鹤。***throw out a*** **~** ***to catch a whale*** 弃小引大。

Mi·no·an [miˈnəuən; mɪˋnoən] ***a***. (公元前 2800—1100 年前后以克里特 (Crete) 岛为中心发达起来的)米诺斯文化的。

Mi·nol [ˈmainɔl; ˋmaɪnɑl] ***n***.【海军】(比 T.N.T. 约强 50%的)猛烈炸药。

mi·nor [ˈmainə; ˋmaɪnɚ] **I** ***a***. (*opp*. major) **1**. 较小的,少数的,小…。**2**. 不重要的,二三流的,较次的。**3**. 未成年的;〔英〕(在两个同姓学生中)年纪较小的,小…。**4**.【乐】小调的,小音阶的。**5**.〔美〕(大学中)次要学科的。*a* ~ *fault* 轻微过失。*a* ~ *injury* 轻伤。*a* ~ *matter* 小事。*a* ~ *arc*【数】小弧,劣弧。***in a*** **~** ***key*** 用小调;用小音阶;小声闷气的(谈话等)。**II** ***n***. **1**.【法】未成年者。**2**.【数】子式;【逻】小名词,小前提;【乐】小调,小音阶。**3**.〔M-〕【天主】方济各派修道士。**4**. (美大学)副科,选修科;【橄榄球】在对方球门后将球打落;〔*pl*.〕= ~ leagues. **III** ***vi***. (美大学)兼修,把…选作副科 (*in*)。**M- Leagues**〔美〕Major League 以下的美国职业棒球队。~ **mode**【乐】小调调式。~ **order**【天主】四个低级圣职人员之一。~ **planet**【天】小行星。~ **premise**【逻】小前提。~ **scale**【乐】小调,小音阶。~ **seminary**【天主】初级神学院。~ **term**【逻】小名词。

Mi·nor·ca [miˈnɔːkə; mɪˋnɔrkə] ***n***. **1**. 米诺卡岛〔西地中海〕。**2**.〔m-〕米诺卡鸡(= ~ fowl)。

Mi·nor·ite [ˈmainərait; ˋmaɪnəˏraɪt] ***n***. = Franciscan.

mi·nor·i·ty [maiˈnɔriti, mi-; məˋnɔrətɪ, mɪ-] ***n***. (*opp*. majority) **1**.【法】未成年(时期)。**2**. 少数;少数党;较少票数;少数民族。*The* ~ *is subordinate to the majority*. 少数服从多数。

Mi·nos [ˈmainɔs; ˋmaɪnəs] ***n***.【希神】迈诺斯〔克里特岛的王,死后做阴间法官〕。

Mi·not [ˈmainət; ˋmaɪnət] ***n***. 迈诺特〔姓氏〕。

Min·o·taur [ˈmainətɔː; ˋmɪnəˏtɔr] ***n***.【希神】人身牛头怪物。

Min. Plen. = Minister Plenipotentiary 全权公使。

MINS [minz; mɪnz] ***n***.〔美〕= minor(s) in need of supervision 需要管教的未成年人。

Minsk [minsk; mɪnsk] ***n***. 明斯克〔白俄罗斯城市〕。

min·ster [ˈminstə; ˋmɪnstɚ] ***n***. 修道院附属礼拜堂;大教堂。

min·strel [ˈminstrəl; ˋmɪnstrəl] ***n***. **1**. (中世的)吟游诗人。**2**.〔诗〕诗人,乐人,歌手,音乐家。**3**. 旅行音乐师;〔*pl*.〕(常由白人扮演的)化装黑人乐队(= negro [Christy] ~s)。~ *show* 化装黑人乐队的演出。

min·strel·sy [ˈminstrəlsi; ˋmɪnstrəlsɪ] ***n***. **1**. 吟游诗人的诗(歌);弹琴,吟唱。**2**.〔集合词〕吟游诗人;诗歌集。**3**.〔诗〕(鸟的)歌;诗歌。

mint[1] [mint; mɪnt] ***n***.【植】薄荷。***pay tithe of*** **~** (***and anise***) ***and cummin*** 放弃大事守小节〔出自《圣经》马太福音第 23 章第 23 节〕。~ **oil** 薄荷油。~ **sauce** 薄荷卤汁〔吃烤小羊肉拌用〕;〔英俚〕钱。

mint[2] [mint; mɪnt] **I** ***n***. **1**. 造币厂。**2**. 巨额。**3**. 富源。*a* ~ *of money* 大量金钱,巨额财富。*a* ~ *of trouble* 千辛万苦。~ *drops*〔美俚〕钱。**II** ***a***. 崭新的,完美的;新造的。***in*** **~** ***state*** [***condition***] (书籍、邮票等)崭新的,刚印好的。**III** ***vt***. **1**. 铸造(货币)。**2**. 创造(新词,新句等)。~ **mark** (币面)刻印。~ **master** 造币厂长。~ **weight** (货币的)标准重量。**-er** ***n***. 造币厂工人,造币者。

mint[3] [mint; mɪnt] **I** ***vt***.〔主 Scot.〕**1**. 打算,准备(做某事)〔与不定式连用〕。**2**. 试图,尝试〔后接名词〕。**3**. 把矛头指向某人[事],打击某人。*They* ~ *to leave tomorrow*. 他们准备明天走。~ *another stroke* 试图再次打击。— ***vi***. **1**. 装腔做势,磨蹭 (*at*)。**2**. 渴求 (*at*)。**3**. 暗示,表示 (*at*)。*Don't* ~ *at it, do it*. 别磨蹭,说干就干。*They cannot understand what we* ~ *at, unless we speak it out*. 我们不讲明,他们不会了解我们的意思。**II** ***n***. 尝试。*Make a* ~ *at*. 试试看。

mint·age [ˈmintidʒ; ˋmɪntɪdʒ] ***n***. **1**. 铸造钱币;造币权;造币费。**2**. 造币材料。**3**. (货币等的)刻印。**4**.〔总称〕硬币。

min·u·end [ˈminjuend; ˋmɪnjʊˏɛnd] ***n***.【数】被减数 (*opp*. subtrahend)。

min·u·et [ˌminjuˈet; ˏmɪnjʊˋɛt] ***n***. (17 世纪兴起的三拍子)小步舞(曲)。

mi·nus [ˈmainəs; ˋmaɪnəs] **I** ***a***. (*opp*. plus) 负(的),减的;零下的。*a* ~ *sign* 负号,减号。*a* ~ *quantity* 负数,负量。~ *charge*【电】负电荷。~ *electricity* 阴电,负电。~ *material* 次品。*The temperature is* ~ *twenty degrees*. 温度是零下二十度。**II** ***prep***. 没有…的;丢掉,失去;减(去);少掉。*Seven* ~ *four is three*. 七减四等于三。*a purse* ~ *its contents* 空钱袋。*He came back* ~ *an arm*. 他失去了一只胳膊回来了。*He was* ~ *fifty dollars*. 他花了五十块钱。**III** ***n***. 负数,负量;负号,减号;差少,欠缺,损失。

mi·nus·cule [miˈnʌskjuːl; mɪˋnʌskjul] ***n***. = miniscule.

min·ute[1] [ˈminit; ˋmɪnɪt] **I** ***n***. **1**. 分〔一小时或一度的 1/60〕。**2**. 一会儿工夫;一瞬间,刹那。**3**. 备忘录,笔记;〔*pl*.〕(会议)记录。*Wait a* ~. 等一下。*five* ~*s to* [*pass*] *six* 六点差[过]五分。***in a few*** **~*s*** 几分钟工夫就,立刻。***in a*** **~** 马上,即刻。***make a*** **~** ***of*** 记录,记下。***the*** **~** (***that***) 一…(就)〔作连词用,引出时间状语从句〕(*I knew him the* ~ *I saw him*. 我一见他就认出了他)。***this*** **~** 现在就,即刻。***to the*** **~** 一分不差,正,恰好(*He appears at five o'clock to the* ~. 他正巧五点钟来到)。***up to the*** **~** 最新的。**II** ***vt***. **1**. 精确地测定…的时间。**2**. 记录,记下 (*down*)。~ **bell** 分钟〔报丧

或举行丧礼时每分钟鸣钟一次〕。～ **book** (会议)记录簿,记事簿。～ **glass** 计时沙漏。～ **gun** 分炮〔为高级军官举行葬礼或船舶遇难时每分钟发一次的号炮〕。～ **hand** (钟表的)分针,长针。～**man**【美史】(独立战争期间的)后备民兵。～ **mark** 分的符号。～ **steak** 快熟薄肉排。～**-to-minute broadcasting** 实况广播。

mi·nute[2] [maiˈnjuːt; məˋnjut] ***a***. **1**. 微小的,细小的;琐碎的;极少的。**2**. 详细的,精密的。～ *descriptions* 细致的描写[记述,说明]。*a* ～ *observer* 细心的观察者。**-ly** ***ad***. **-ness** ***n***.

min·ute·ly [ˈminitli; ˋmɪnɪtlɪ] ***ad***., ***a***. **1**. 每分钟(的)。**2**. 时常发生(的)。

mi·nu·ti·ae [maiˈnjuːʃiiː; mɪˋnjuʃɪ͵i] ***n***. 〔*pl*.〕细节,细目;小节,琐事。

minx [miŋks; mɪŋks] ***n***. 疯姑娘,顽皮姑娘。

min·yan [minˈjɑːn, ˈminjən; mɪnˋjɑn, ˋmɪnjən] ***n***. (*pl*. ***min·ya·nim*** [-jɑːˈniːm; -jɑˋnim], ～*s*) 〔Heb.〕【犹】祈祷班〔由十名十三岁以上男子组成〕。

Mi·o·cene [ˈmaiəsiːn; ˋmaɪə͵sin] ***n***., ***a***. 【地】第三纪中新统(的),第三纪中新世(的)。

mi·o·sis [ˈmaiəusis; maɪˋosɪs] ***n***. 【医】瞳孔缩小。

MIP = **1**. marine insurance policy 海运保险单。**2**. 〔常作 m.i.p.〕mean indicated pressure 平均指示压力。

MIPS [mips; mɪps] = million instructions per second 【计】百万指令/秒,每秒钟执行一百万条指令。

Miq·ue·lon Is. [ˌmikəˈlɔn; ͵mɪkəˋlɑn] ***n***. 密克隆岛。

mir [miə; mir] ***n***. 〔Russ.〕米尔(沙俄时代的一种村社组织)。

Mi·ra·bel [ˈmirəbel; ˋmɪrəbɛl] ***n***. 米拉贝尔〔女子名〕。

mir·a·belle [ˈmiərəˌbel, ˌmiərəˈbel; ˋmɪrə͵bɛl, ͵mɪrəˋbɛl] ***n***. 【植】**1**. 布拉斯李树〔产于欧洲〕。**2**. 布拉斯李子。**3**. 布拉斯白兰地。

mi·ra·bi·le dic·tu [maiˈræbiliː ˈdiktjuː; maɪˋræbɪli ˋdɪktu] 〔L.〕说也奇怪。

mi·rab·i·le vi·su [miˈræbili ˈvaisju; mɪˋræbɪlɪ ˋvaɪsjʊ] 〔L.〕光怪陆离的。

mi·ra·bi·li·a [ˌmiərəˈbiliə; ͵mɪrəˋbɪlɪə] ***n***. 〔*pl*.〕〔L.〕奇事;奇迹。

mi·rab·i·lite [miˈræbilait; mɪˋræbɪlaɪt] ***n***. 【化】芒硝。

mir·a·cle [ˈmirəkl; ˋmɪrəkl] ***n***. **1**. 奇迹;奇事,奇人。**2**. 奇迹剧。***to a*** ～ 奇迹般地;不可思议地。***work*** ～***s*** 创造奇迹。～ **fruit** 奇迹果〔一种核浆果,食后可使接着吃的东西带甜味〕。～ **play** (中世纪基督教)奇迹剧。

mi·rac·u·lous [miˈrækjuləs; məˋrækjələs] ***a***. **1**. 奇迹般的,不可思议的,令人惊叹的;非凡的。**2**. (能够)创造奇迹的。**-ly** ***ad***. **-ness** ***n***.

mir·a·dor [ˌmirəˈdɔː; ͵mɪrəˋdor] ***n***. 〔Sp.〕(可供眺望的)角塔;窗户;阳台。

mi·rage [ˈmirɑːʒ; məˋrɑʒ] ***n***. 海市蜃楼,蜃景;幻想,妄想。

Mi·ran·da [miˈrændə; mɪˋrændə] ***n***. 米兰达〔女子名〕。

mir·bane [ˈməːbein; ˋmɝben] ***n***. 【化】硝基苯;密斑油。

mire [ˈmaiə; maɪr] **I** ***n***. **1**. 泥沼;淤泥;矿泥。**2**. 〔罕〕沾污,污辱;污物。***drag*** (*sb*.) ***through the*** ～ 使丢丑,侮辱,搞臭。***find*** [***stick***] ***oneself in the*** ～弄得一筹莫展,束手无策,陷进泥坑里。**II** ***vt***. **1**. 使溅满泥泞;使陷进泥坑里。**2**. 使进退不得;使为难。— ***vi***. **1**. 弄得浑身是泥,陷入泥坑。**2**. 进退不得,一筹莫展。*She ～d her car and had to go for help*. 她开的车陷入泥泞中,不得不请人帮助。

Mir·i·am [ˈmiriəm; ˋmɪrɪəm] ***n***. 米丽亚姆〔女子名,Mary 的异体〕。

mir·i·ness [ˈmaiərinis; ˋmaɪrɪnɪs] ***n***. 泥泞。

mirk [məːk; mɝk] ***n***., ***a***. = murk.

mirk·y [ˈməːki; ˋmɝkɪ] ***a***. = murky.

mir·ror [ˈmirə; ˋmɪrɚ] **I** ***n***. **1**. 镜;反射镜。**2**. 反映;借鉴;榜样。*a concave* [*convex*] ～ 凹[凸]镜。*an electron* ～ 电子反射镜。*the* ～ *of fashion* 流行事物的代表。*a* ～ *of the times* 时代的反映。***done with*** ～***s*** 〔美俚〕用诡计弄成功的;神秘莫测地完成的。***hold the*** ～ ***up to nature*** 反映自然。**II** ***vt***. 映,反射;反映。～ **image**【物】镜像;镜中人;镜中物。～ **writing** ***n***. 倒写。

mirth [məːθ; mɝθ] ***n***. 欢乐;欢笑。

mirth·ful [ˈməːθful; ˋmɝθfəl] ***a***. 欢乐的,高兴的;欢笑的。**-ly** ***ad***. 快快乐乐,高高兴兴。**-ness** ***n***.

mirth·less [ˈməːθlis; ˋmɝθlɪs] ***a***. 不快乐的,悲伤的;郁闷的。**-ly** ***ad***. **-ness** ***n***.

MIRV = multiple independently targeted reentry vehicle【军】多弹头分导重返大气层运载工具。～ *missile* 分导式多弹头导[飞]弹。

mir·y [ˈmaiəri; ˋmaɪrɪ] ***a***. (***mir·i·er***; ***-i·est***) 泥泞的,泥深的;沾满泥的;脏的。**mir·i·ness** ***n***.

mir·za [ˈməːzə; ˋmɝzə] ***n***. 〔波斯〕加在皇族姓名下的尊称;冠于学者、官吏姓名前的敬称。

MIS = management information system【计】管理信息系统〔即办公室电脑管理系统〕。

mis-[1] *pref*. 错,错误的;坏,不利的。★在动词和形容词前起副词作用,在动名词和名词前具有形容词的意味,在已有坏义的字前时,通常属古语,表示加强意义;*mis*dread, *mis*doubt.

mis-[2] *comb*. *f*. 〔用于母音前〕= miso-.

mis·ad·ven·ture [ˈmisədˈventʃə; ͵mɪsədˋvɛntʃɚ] ***n***. 意外事故,不幸,灾难,横祸。***by*** ～ 因意外事故;因过失。***homicide*** [***death***] ***by*** ～【法】过失杀害,误杀。

mis·ad·vice [ˌmisədˈvais; ͵mɪsədˋvaɪs] ***n***. 错误的劝告,馊主意。

mis·ad·vise [ˈmisədˈvaiz; ͵mɪsədˋvaɪz] ***vt***. 给…出馊主意;错误地劝告。

mis·aimed [misˈeimd; ͵mɪsˋemd] ***a***. 看错了的;打错了主意的。

mis·al·li·ance [ˌmisəˈlaiəns; ͵mɪsəˋlaɪəns] ***n***. 不适当的配合;不相称的结合[婚配]。

mis·al·ly [ˌmisəˈlai; ͵mɪsəˋlaɪ] ***vt***. (***-lied***; ***-ly·ing***) 不适当地结合[配合];错配。

mis·an·dry [ˈmisændri; ˋmɪ͵sændrɪ] ***n***. (女子)嫌恶男子。

mis·an·thrope, mis·an·thro·pist [ˈmizənθrəup, miˈzænθrəpist; ˋmɪsən͵θrop, mɪˋzænθrəpɪst] ***n***. 厌恶人类者,厌世者(*opp*. philanthropist)。

mis·an·throp·ic, mis·an·throp·i·cal [ˌmizənˈθrɔpik, -ikəl; ͵mɪsənˋθrɑpɪk, -ɪkəl] ***a***. 厌恶人类(者)的,厌世(者)的。

mis·an·thro·pize [miˈzænθrəpaiz, miˈsæn-; mɪˋzænθrə͵paɪz, mɪˋsæn-] ***vi***. 厌恶人类,厌世。

mis·an·thro·py [miˈzænθrəpi; mɪsˋænθrəpɪ] ***n***. 厌恶人类,厌世,愤世嫉俗。

mis·ap·ply [ˈmisəˈplai; ͵mɪsəˋplaɪ] ***vt***. 误用,错用,滥用。**-plica·tion** ***n***., **-plied** ***a***. 被误用了的。

mis·ap·pre·hend [ˈmisˌæpriˈhend; ͵mɪsæprɪˋhɛnd] ***vt***. 误解,误会。**-hen·sion** ***n***., **-hen·sive** ***a***. 易误会的。

mis·ap·pro·pri·ate [ˌmisəˈprəuprieit; ͵mɪsəˋproprɪ͵et] ***vt***. 乱用;挪用(别人的钱);私吞;【法】侵占,霸占。**-a·tion** ***n***.

mis·ar·range [ˈmisəˈreindʒ; ͵mɪsəˋrendʒ] ***vt***. **1**. 排错。**2**. 安排不当。

mis·ar·range·ment [ˌmisəˈreindʒmənt; ͵mɪsəˋrendʒmənt] ***n***. 误排,错列,排错,错乱次序。

mis·be·come [ˈmisbiˈkʌm; ͵mɪsbɪˋkʌm] ***vt***. (***-be·came*** [-biˈkeim; -bɪˋkem], ***-be·come*** [-biˈkʌm; -bəˋkʌm]) 不合,不适合,不配。**-coming** ***a***.

mis·be·got·ten, mis·be·got [ˈmisbiˌgɔtn, -gɔt; ͵mɪsbɪˋgɑtn̩, -gɑt] ***a***. 私生的;非法产生的;起源不光彩的。

mis·be·have [ˈmisbiˈheiv; ͵mɪsbɪˋhev] ***vt***. 使行为不当(～ *oneself*)。— ***vi***. **1**. 做坏事,行为不当,不规矩,作

弊。2. 行为失常。-d a.

mis·be·havio(u)r [ˈmisbiˈheivjə; ˏmɪsbiˋhevjɚ] n. 不规矩(行为),品行不良。

mis·be·lief [ˈmisbiˈliːf; ˏmɪsbəˋlif] n. 误信,谬见;信奉邪教;信仰错误。

mis·be·lieve [ˈmisbiˈliːv; ˏmɪsbəˋliv] vi. 误信,信邪说,信仰邪教。— vt. 不信。-liev·er 异教徒;误信者,信邪说者。-liev·ing a. 异端的,信仰邪教的。

mis·be·seem [ˈmisbiˈsiːm; ˏmɪsbəˋsim] vt. = misbecome.

mis·birth [ˈmisˈbəːθ; mɪsˋbɝθ] n. = miscarriage 2.

mis·brand [ˈmisˈbrænd; mɪsˋbrænd] vt. 1. 把…打错了标记[烙印]。2. 把…贴上假标记[商标]。

misc. = miscellaneous; miscellany.

mis·cal·cu·late [ˈmisˈkælkjuleit; mɪsˋkælkjəˏlet] vt., vi. 算错,估错,错认。-lation n.

mis·call [ˈmisˈkɔːl; mɪsˋkɔl] vt. 叫错,错称;〔英方〕谩骂某人。

mis·car·riage [misˈkæridʒ; mɪsˋkærɪdʒ] n. 1. 失策,失败。2. 流产,早产。3. (信件等的)误投,误送。~ *of one's plans* 计划失败。*a ~ of justice* 误判(案);审判不公(案件)。

mis·car·ry [misˈkæri; mɪsˋkærɪ] vi. 1. 失策,失败。2. 流产;早产。3. (信等)被误投[误送]。

mis·cast [ˈmisˈkɑːst, -ˈkæst; mɪsˋkɑst, -ˋkæst] vt. (*-cast*; *-cast·ing*) 1. 使做不相称的事;使(演员)扮演不相称的角色。2. 对(戏剧)作不适当的角色分配。

mis·ce·ge·na·tion [ˌmisidʒiˈneiʃən; ˏmɪsɪdʒəˋneʃən] n. 人种混杂;混血。

mis·cel·la·ne·a [ˌmisiˈleiniə; ˏmɪsəˋlenɪə] n. 〔pl.〕杂集;杂录,杂记。

mis·cel·la·ne·ous [ˌmisiˈleinjəs, -niəs; ˏmɪslˋenjəs, -nɪəs] a. 各种各样的,五花八门的,混杂的;多方面的。~ *business* 杂务。~ *goods* 杂货。*a ~ writer* 多面手作家,多才多艺的作家。

mis·cel·la·ny [miˈseləni; ˋmɪslˏenɪ] n. 1. 〔pl.〕杂集,杂录,杂记。2. 混合物,杂物。-nist n. 杂文[杂记]作家。

mis·chance [misˈtʃɑːns; mɪsˋtʃæns] n. 不幸,灾难,横祸;故障。**by ~** 不幸,不巧。

mis·chief [ˈmistʃif; ˋmɪstʃɪf] n. (pl. ~s) 1. (物质上的)损害,灾害,灾祸,危害;(身体、机器等的)毛病,故障。2. (精神上的)毒害,坏影响。3. 造成损害的人;祸根。4. 顽皮,淘气;〔口〕顽皮孩子,淘气精;〔口〕= devil. *There is carelessness, but no ~.* 粗心大意是有的,恶意倒没有。*One ~ comes on the neck of another.* 祸不单行。*a regular little ~* 十分淘气的孩子。*What the ~ (= the devil) do you want?* 你究竟要什么? **cause ~** 引起灾祸。**do ~** 造成损害。**do sb. a ~** 〔口〕使某人受到损害;打伤某人,使某人受伤;杀死某人。**go [get] into ~** 玩起鬼把戏来,淘气起来。**keep out of ~** 不胡闹。**make ~ between** 使双方不和,离间。**mean ~** 怀恶意。**out of (pure) ~** 闹着玩儿。**play the ~ with** 弄坏…的身体[健康],加害;弄坏(机器等),使发生毛病;把…弄得一塌糊涂(*The wind has played the ~ with my papers.* 风把我的文件吹得乱七八糟)。**The ~ (of it) is that ....** 麻烦的是,伤脑筋的是…。**up to ~** 要胡闹[捣蛋],在玩鬼把戏(*The children are up to ~.* 小孩子们想胡闹)。**~-maker** 离间者。**~-making** n., a. 离间(的);离间手段。**~-monger** 离间者。

mis·chie·vous [ˈmistʃivəs; ˋmɪstʃɪvəs] a. 1. 为害的,有害的;爱玩鬼把戏的。2. 顽皮的,淘气的;有点带恶意的。*a ~ glance* 恶意的一瞥。-ly ad. -ness n.

mis·ci·bil·i·ty [ˌmisiˈbiliti; ˏmɪsəˋbɪlətɪ] n. 1. 可混性,混和性;溶混性。2. 混和法。

mis·ci·ble [ˈmisibl; ˋmɪsəbl] a. 可溶和的,易混合的(*with*)。~ *oil* 混合油剂。

mis·code [ˈmiskəud; ˋmɪskod] vt. 【自】错编〔提供错误的遗传密码〕。

mis·col·our [misˈkʌlə; mɪsˋkʌlɚ] vt. 1. 把…着错色粉。2. 对…作歪曲叙述;颠倒黑白。

mis·con·ceive [ˈmiskənˈsiːv; ˏmɪskənˋsiv] vt. 误解。— vi. 有错误看法(*of*)。

mis·con·cep·tion [ˈmiskənˈsepʃən; ˏmɪskənˋsɛpʃən] n. 误解,错觉,看法错误。

mis·con·duct [misˈkɔndʌkt; mɪsˋkɑndʌkt] I n. 1. 行为不正,不规矩;(尤指官吏等的)胡作非为,渎职。2. 通奸。3. 办错,处置失当。*commit ~ with* 和…通奸。II [miskənˈdʌkt; mɪsˋkəndʌkt] vt. 1. 办错,处理…失当。2. 〔~ oneself〕不规矩;与…通奸(*with*)。

mis·con·struc·tion [ˈmiskənsˈtrʌkʃən; ˏmɪskənˋstrʌkʃən] n. 误解,误会;解释错误,曲解;(房屋)盖错。

mis·con·strue [ˈmiskənˈstruː; ˏmɪskənˋstru] vt. 误会,误解;曲解。

mis·count [ˈmisˈkaunt; mɪsˋkaunt] vt., vi., n. 算错;(尤指投票数的)点错,计数误差,计算误差。

mis·cre·ant [ˈmiskriənt; ˋmɪskrɪənt] I a. 1. 邪恶的,恶劣的。2. 〔古〕异端的。II n. 1. 恶棍,歹人。2. 邪教徒;不信教的人。

mis·cre·ate [ˈmiskriˈeit; ˏmɪskrɪˋet] vt., vi. 误造,误创,误作。

mis·cre·at·ed [ˈmiskriˈeitid; ˏmɪskrɪˋetɪd] a. 畸形的;丑怪的。

mis·cue [ˈmisˈkjuː; mɪsˋkju] n., vi. 【撞球】弹子棒打滑;【剧】错过提示;反应不及时。

mis·date [ˈmisˈdeit; mɪsˋdet] I vt. 写错[弄错](日期)。II n. 错写的日期[年代]。

mis·deal [ˈmisˈdiːl; mɪsˋdil] I n. 【牌】发错牌。II (*mis·dealt* [-ˈdelt; -ˋdɛlt]) vi., vt. 发错(牌)。

mis·deal·er [misˈdiːlə; mɪsˋdilɚ] n. 【牌】发错牌者。

mis·deal·ing [ˈmisˈdiːliŋ; mɪsˋdilɪŋ] n. 做错,不正当行为。

mis·deed [ˈmisˈdiːd; mɪsˋdid] n. 恶劣行为;罪行。

mis·de·mean [ˌmisdiˈmiːn; ˏmɪsdɪˋmin] vt., vi. 〔罕〕= misbehave.

mis·de·mean·ant [ˌmisdiˈmiːnənt; ˏmɪsdɪˋminənt] n. 行为不端[不规矩]的人;【法】轻罪犯人。

mis·de·mean·o(u)r [ˌmisdiˈmiːnə; ˏmɪsdɪˋminɚ] n. (一般的)不正当的行为,恶劣的品行;坏事;【法】轻罪。*commit a ~* 犯轻罪。*a high ~* 【法】重罪。

mis·de·scrip·tion [ˈmisdisˈkripʃən; ˏmɪsdɪˋskrɪpʃən] n. 不完全的记述,(特指契约中要点项目的)误记。

mis·dial [ˈmisdaiəl; ˋmɪsdaɪəl] vt. 拨错(电话号码)。

mis·di·rect [ˈmisdiˈrekt; ˏmɪsdəˋrɛkt] vt. 1. 指导[指挥]错误。2. 写错(信封)。3. 指错(地点、方向)给…。4. (法官对陪审员)指示错误。5. 瞄错,打歪;用错(精力、才能等)。

mis·do [misˈduː; mɪsˋdu] vt. (*-did*; *-done*; *-do·ing*) 错办。— vi. 〔废〕干坏事,作恶。

mis·do·ing [ˈmisˈdu(ː)iŋ; mɪsˋduɪŋ] n. 坏事,恶行。

mis·doubt [misˈdaut; mɪsˋdaut] I vt. 〔古〕怀疑;挂念,担心(*that*)。II n. 〔古〕怀疑;悬念。

mise [miːz, maiz; miz, maɪz] n. 1. 【史】协定。2. 赌注。3. 【法】权利令状上的争论点。

mis·ease [misˈiːz; mɪsˋiz] n. 1. 〔古〕不安;苦恼。2. 〔废〕贫穷。

mis·ed·u·ca·tion [ˈmisˌedjuːˈkeiʃən; ˋmɪsˏɛdjuˋkeʃən] n. 错误教育。

mis·em·ploy [ˌmisemˈplɔi; ˏmɪsɪmˋplɔɪ] vt. 误用,滥用。-ment n.

mise en scène [ˈmiːzɑːnˈsein; ˋmizɑ̃nˋsen] 〔F.〕1. 舞台演出的调度。2. 舞台的布景道具。3. 导演。4. 自然[社会]环境。

mi·ser[1] [ˈmaizə; ˋmaɪzɚ] n. 吝啬的人,小气鬼,守财奴;

〔古〕可怜的人。

mi·ser² [ˈmaizə; ˋmaɪzɚ] *n*. (矿山、凿井用)钻孔机,凿井机;【矿】管形提泥钻头。

mis·er·a·ble [ˈmizərəbl; ˋmɪzərəbl] **I** *a*. **1**. 不幸的,痛苦的,可怜的,(生活)悲惨的,(消息)使人伤心的;(肉体上)受折磨的。**2**. 卑劣的,不要脸的,可耻的。**3**. 简陋的,(饮食)粗陋的;破烂的,肮脏的;糟糕的;缺乏的;不充足的。*a* ~ *cold* 重感冒。~ *with hunger and cold* 饥寒交迫。*a* ~ *scoundrel* 无耻之徒。**II** *n*. 不幸的人;穷困不堪的人。

mis·er·a·bly [ˈmizərəbli; ˋmɪzərəblɪ] *ad*. **1**. 不幸地,可怜地,悲惨地;糟糕地;卑劣地。**2**. 非常,极,大大地(*fail* ~)。

Mis·e·re·re [ˌmizəˈriəri; ˏmɪzəˋrɛrɪ] *n*. **1**. (拉丁语译《圣经》的)第51篇赞美歌。**2**. 〔m-〕哀求,乞怜;【建】= misericord(e)1.

mis·er·i·cord(e) [miˈzerikɔːd; mɪˋzɛrɪˏkɔrd] *n*. **1**. (教堂中装在折椅上以便起立时支持身体用的)椅背突板。**2**. (修道院中的)斋堂。**3**. 短剑。

mi·ser·li·ness [ˈmaizəlinis; ˋmaɪzɚlɪnɪs] *n*. 吝啬。

mi·ser·ly [ˈmaizəli; ˋmaɪzɚlɪ] *a*. 吝啬的;小气的。

mis·er·y [ˈmizəri; ˋmɪzərɪ] *n*. 苦难,不幸;苦痛,疼痛;惨状,悲惨的境遇;贫穷。*M- loves company*. 同病相怜。~ **index**【经】贫困指数,经济不景气指数〔通货膨胀率加失业率〕。

mis·es·teem [ˌmisəˈstiːm; ˏmɪsəˋstim] **I** *vt*. 对…不能正确评价;误估…的价值。**II** *n*. 缺乏适当的估价。

mis·es·ti·mate [misˈestiˌmeit; mɪsˋɛstəˏmet] **I** *vt*. 误算,误估。**II** *n*. [-mit; -mɪt] 错误的估计。**-ma·tion** *n*.

mis·fea·sance [misˈfiːzəns; mɪsˋfizəns] *n*. 犯罪,违法;【法】不法行为,滥用职权。

mis·file [ˈmisˈfail; mɪsˋfaɪl] *vt*. 把(文件等)归错档案。

mis·fire [ˈmisˈfaiə; mɪsˋfaɪr] **I** *n*. (枪等的)不发火,射不出;(内燃机的)不着火。**II** *vi*. 不发火,打不出;不着火,开动不起来;不奏效,不中要害。*~d points* 不得要领的[不中肯的]论点。

mis·fit [ˈmisfit; ˋmɪsˏfɪt] **I** *n*. 不适合;不合身的衣着;不容易适应环境的人。**II** *vt*., *vi*. **1**. (对…)不合适;(衣服等)对…不合身。**2**.【物】错合。*This coat ~s me*. 这件上衣对我不合身。

mis·for·tune [misˈfɔːtʃən; mɪsˋfɔrtʃən] *n*. **1**. 背运,倒霉,不幸;灾难,灾祸。**2**. 私生子;生私生子。*M- might be a blessing in disguise*. 塞翁失马,安知非福。*M-s tell us what fortune is*. 不经灾难不知福。*M-s never come singly* [*alone*]. = *One* ~ *rides upon another's back*. 祸不单行。*by* ~ 不幸。*have the* ~ *to* (*do*) 不幸(而)。

mis·give [misˈgiv; mɪsˋgɪv] *vt*. (*mis·gave* [-ˈgeiv; -ˋgev]; *mis·giv·en* [-ˈgivn; -ˋgɪvn]) 使疑惑[害怕、焦心、忧虑等]起来。*His heart misgave him*. 他疑惑[害怕、担心]起来了。

mis·giv·ing [misˈgiviŋ; mɪsˋgɪvɪŋ] *n*. 〔否定以外通常用 *pl*.〕疑惑,忧虑,担心,不安。*full of* ~(*s*) 满心疑惑,十分不安。

mis·got·ten [ˈmisˈgɔtn; mɪsˋgɑtn̩] *a*. **1**. 以不正当手段取得的。**2**. = misbegotton. ~ **treasure** 不义之财。

mis·gov·ern [ˈmisˈgʌvən; mɪsˋgʌvɚn] *vt*. 对(政务等)管理不当。**-ment** *n*. 错误的行政管理。

mis·growth [ˈmisˈgrəuθ; mɪsˋgroθ] *n*. 异常发育。

mis·guide [ˈmisˈgaid; mɪsˋgaɪd] *vt*. 〔主用 *p*. *p*.〕指导错误;带错方向;使误入歧途。**-guid·ance** *n*. 错误的指导。

mis·guid·ed [ˈmisˈgaidid; mɪsˋgaɪdɪd] *a*. 被指导错误的,被带错的,搞错的;误入歧途的。**-ly** *ad*. **-ness** *n*.

mis·han·dle [ˈmisˈhændl; mɪsˋhændl] *vt*. **1**. 用错;瞎弄,乱弄。**2**. 粗暴对待,虐待。**3**. 办错;胡乱处置。

mi·shan·ter [miˈʃæntə; mɪˋʃæntɚ] *n*. 〔Scot.〕不幸,灾祸,灾难。

mis·hap [ˈmishæp, misˈhæp; ˋmɪsˏhæp, mɪsˋhæp] *n*. 不幸的事,灾难。*the haps and ~s of life* 人生祸福。*without* ~ 平安无事。

mis·hear [ˈmisˈhiə; mɪsˋhɪr] *vt*., *vi*. (*-heard* [-ˈhəːd; -ˋhɝd]) 听错。

mis·hit [ˈmisˈhit; mɪsˋhɪt] **I** *n*. 打歪。**II** [misˈhit; mɪsˋhɪt] *vt*. 把…打歪。

mish·mash [ˈmiʃmæʃ; ˋmɪʃˏmæʃ] *n*. 混杂物;杂烩。

Mish·na, Mish·nah [miʃˈnɑː, ˈmiʃnə; mɪʃˋnɑ, ˋmɪʃnə] *n*. (*pl*. *Mish·na·yot* [ˌmiʃnɑːˈjəut; ˏmɪʃnɑˋjot]) **1**. 犹太教法典的第一部分。**2**. 犹太教法典的第一部分的注释。**3**. 著名犹太法学博士的教义。**Mish·na·ic** *a*.

mis·in·form [ˈmisinˈfɔːm; ˏmɪsɪnˋfɔrm] *vt*. 误传,传错,报错。**-for·ma·tion** *n*. 误传,误报,错误的消息。

mis·in·form·ant [ˌmisinˈfɔːmənt; ˏmɪsɪnˋfɔrmənt] *n*. 误报者,提供不正确消息者,误传者(= misinformer)。

mis·in·ter·pret [ˈmisinˈtəːprit; ˏmɪsɪnˋtɝprɪt] *vt*. 曲解,误释,误译。**-pre·ta·tion** *n*. **-pre·ter** [ˌmisinˈtəːpritə; ˏmɪsɪnˋtɝprɪtɚ] *n*. 误译者;误解者,误释者。

mis·join·der [ˌmisˈdʒɔində; ˏmɪsˋdʒɔɪndɚ] *n*.【法】诉讼当事人的不当的联合。

mis·judge [ˈmisˈdʒʌdʒ; mɪsˋdʒʌdʒ] *vt*., *vi*. **1**. 判断错,看错。**2**. 低估,轻视。**-ment**, **-judg·ment** *n*.

Mis·kolc [ˈmiʃkəults; ˋmɪʃkolts] *n*. 米什科尔茨〔匈牙利城市〕。

mis·la·bel [misˈleibl; mɪsˋlebl̩] *vt*., *vi*. (*-beled*, *-belled*; *-bel·ing*, *-bel·ling*) (在…上)误贴标签。

mis·land [misˈlænd; mɪsˋlænd] *vt*.【海】弄错(起卸港),卸错(船货)。

mis·lay [misˈlei; mɪsˋle] (*mis·laid* [-ˈleid; -ˋled]) *vt*. 把(东西)误放;搁忘;丢失。

mis·lead [misˈliːd; mɪsˋlid] (*mis·led* [-ˈled; -ˋlɛd]) *vt*. 把…带错路;把…引入歧途;使迷惑[误解];哄骗。

mis·lead·ing [misˈliːdiŋ; mɪsˋlidɪŋ] *a*. 引入歧途的;使人误解的,晦涩的;骗人的;使人迷惑的。**-ly** *ad*.

mis·like [misˈlaik; mɪsˋlaɪk] *vt*. 〔古、方〕嫌,厌恶。

mis·man·age [ˌmisˈmænidʒ; mɪsˋmænɪdʒ] *vt*. 把…办错,对…管理不当,对…处理失当。**-ment** *n*.

mis·mar·riage [ˌmisˈmæridʒ; mɪsˋmærɪdʒ] *n*. 不相配的婚姻。

mis·match [ˈmisˈmætʃ; mɪsˋmætʃ] **I** *vt*. 配错,使不适当地配合。**II** *n*. 错配;不适当的婚姻。

mis·mate [misˈmeit; mɪsˋmet] *vt*., *vi*. (使)配合不当;(使)配偶[结婚]不当;(使)配合拙劣。

mis·name [ˈmisˈneim; mɪsˋnem] *vt*. 叫错(名字);误称。

mis·no·mer [ˈmisˈnəumə; mɪsˋnomɚ] *n*. 误称;使用不当的名称;用词不当。

mis·o- *comb*. *f*. 嫌,厌(*opp*. philo-): *miso*capnic.

mis·o·cap·nic [misɔˈkæpnik; mɪsɑˋkæpnɪk] *a*. 厌恶香烟的。**-nist** *n*. 厌恶香烟的人。

mi·soc·y·ny [miˈsɔsini; mɪˋsɑsənɪ] *n*. 厌犬症。**-nist** *n*. 讨厌狗的人。

mi·sog·a·my [miˈsɔgəmi; mɪˋsɑgəmɪ] *n*. 厌恶结婚;厌婚症。**-mist** *n*. 厌恶结婚的人。

mi·sog·y·nic [ˌmaisəˈdʒinik, ˌmi-; ˏmaɪsəˋdʒɪnɪk, mɪ-] *a*. 厌恶女人的。

mi·sog·y·ny [maiˈsɔdʒini, miˈs-; maɪˋsɑdʒɪnɪ, mɪˋs-] *n*. 厌恶女人;厌女症[癖]。**-nist** *n*. 厌恶女人的人。

mi·sol·o·gy [miˈsɔlədʒi; mɪˋsɑlədʒɪ] *n*. 厌恶理论[说理]。**-gist** *n*. 厌恶理论的人。

mis·o·math [miˈsɔmæθ; mɪˋsɑmæθ] *n*. 厌恶数学的人。

mis·o·ne·ism [ˌmisəuˈniːizəm; ˏmɪsəˋniɪzm̩] *n*. 厌新(症),守旧主义。

mis·o·pe·dia [ˌmisəuˈpiːdiə; ˏmɪsoˋpidɪə] *n*. 嫌子女症。**-dist** *n*. 嫌子女症患者。

mis·o·pho·bia [ˌmisəuˈfəubiə; mɪsəˋfobɪə] *n*.【医】极

端的洁癖;不洁恐怖。

mis·o·po·lem·i·cal [ˌmisəupəuˈlemikəl; ˏmɪsəpoˋlɛmɪkəl] ***a*.** 厌恶战争的。

mis·per·ceive [ˌmispəˈsiːv; ˏmɪspəˋsiv] ***vt*.** 误解,错误感觉。**-per·cep·tion** ***n*.**

mis·pick·el [ˈmispikəl; ˋmɪsˏpɪkḷ] ***n*.**【矿】毒砂,砷黄铁矿。

mis·place [ˈmisˈpleis; mɪsˋples] ***vt*.** **1.** 把…放错地方;〔口〕忘记把…放在什么地方。**2.** 爱[信]错(人)〔多用被动语态〕。**-ment** ***n*.** 误放。

mis·play [ˈmisˈplei; mɪsˋple] **I** ***n*.** 〔美〕(球类运动)动作错误,失误;误演,误奏。**II** ***vt*.** (打球时)使(球)失误;打错(牌)。

mis·plead [ˌmisˈpliːd; ˏmɪsˋplid] ***vt*., *vi*.** (***-pled***; ***-pleading***) (为…)不正确地辩护。

mis·plead·ing [ˌmisˈpliːdiŋ; mɪsˋplidɪŋ] ***n*.**【法】(辩护时所作的)不正确的申述[疏漏]。

mis·print [misˈprint; mɪsˋprɪnt] ***n*., *vt*.**【印】印错,误印。

mis·prise [misˈpraiz; mɪsˋpraɪz] ***vt*.** = misprize.

mis·pri·sion[1] [misˈpriʒən; mɪsˋprɪʒən] ***n*.** **1.** (特指公职人员的)玩忽职守,渎职。**2.**【法】知情不报;隐匿犯人。**3.** (反对政府、法院等的)煽动行为。**4.** 误解,搞错。~ *of felony* 隐匿重罪。

mis·pri·sion[2] [misˈpriʒən; mɪsˋprɪʒən] ***n*.** 〔英古〕蔑视,轻视。

mis·prize [misˈpraiz; mɪsˋpraɪz] ***vt*.** 蔑视,轻视,看不起。

mis·pro·nounce [ˈmisprəˈnauns; ˏmɪsprəˋnauns] ***vi*., *vt*.** 读错(发音)。

mis·pro·nun·ci·a·tion [ˈmisprəˌnʌnsiˈeiʃən; ˏmɪsprəˏnʌnsɪˋeʃən] ***n*.** 错误的发音。

mis·quote [ˈmisˈkwəut; mɪsˋkwot] ***vt*.** 引错,误引(文字、语句)。**-ta·tion** [-kwəuˈteiʃən; -kwoˋteʃən] ***n*.**

mis·read [misˈriːd; mɪsˋrid] ***vt*.** (***-read*** [-red; -rɛd]) 读错,解释错…的意思。

mis·reck·on [ˌmisˈrekən; ˏmɪsˋrɛkən] ***vt*.** 误算。

mis·re·mem·ber [ˌmisriˈmembə; ˏmɪsrɪˋmɛmbɚ] ***vt*., *vi*.** **1.** 记错。**2.** 〔方〕忘记。

mis·re·port [ˌmisriˈpɔːt; ˏmɪsrɪˋport] **I** ***vt*.** 误报;谎报。**II** ***n*.** 误报;谎报。

mis·rep·re·sent [ˈmisˌrepriˈzent; ˏmɪsrɛprɪˋzɛnt] ***vt*.** **1.** 传错,误传;曲解;诬告,把…颠倒黑白。**2.** 不尽职[不正当地]代表。**-er** ***n*.** 传达错误的人;不尽职[不正当]的代表。**-ta·tion** ***n*.** **1.** 错误的传达。**2.**【法】虚伪的陈述,诈称。

mis·rule [ˈmisˈruːl; mɪsˋrul] **I** ***n*.** **1.** 不正确的[作风恶劣的]行政管理,虐政,苛政。**2.** 无秩序,紊乱。**II** ***vt*.** 管错;作风恶劣地管理。

miss[1] [mis; mɪs] ***n*.** (*pl*. ~***es***) **1.** 〔M-〕…小姐。★ **1.** 有两个以上未婚罗滨逊姐妹时,姐姐通常加在姓前叫 M- Robinson,妹妹加在姓及洗礼名前叫 M- Joan (Robinson);姐妹一起叫 the M- Robinsons 或〔古〕the Misses Robinson. **2.** 〔*pl*.〕的 misses 发音与 Mrs. [ˈmisiz; ˋmɪsɪz] 相同,也有发音作 [ˈmisiz; ˋmɪsɪz] 的。**2.** 〔谑、蔑〕姑娘,(特指)小女学生。**3.** 〔对女佣人,女店员的称呼〕小姐。**4.** 〔古〕情妇。*a saucy* ~ 莽撞的姑娘。

miss[2] [mis; mɪs] **I** ***vt*.** **1.** 把(看准的东西)失去,让…跑掉,没打中;没猜中;没到手,没拿到,没抓到,没达到;没赶上(车子等);没看到,看漏;漏掉;失落;达不到…的标准,够不上,不够。**2.** 不守(约),不尽(义务);缺;发觉没有[不在]。**3.** 因…没有[不在]而感觉寂寞[不方便];惦念。**4.** 缺席,旷工。**5.** 逃却,免去,躲避。~ *one's aim* 没打中。~ *one's hold* 放掉,放跑(已经抓住了的东西)。~ *an opportunity* 失去机会。~ *a catch*【板球】漏接。*He* ~*ed the bank*. 他跳不过河而落水了。*I* ~*ed him in a crowd*. 我在人群中把他挤丢了。~ *the train* 没赶上火车。*It* ~*es being a great picture*. 这算不了一幅名画。*I shall* ~ *you very much*. 你不在我就寂寞了。*He barely* ~*ed being killed*. 他几乎送了命。*He hasn't* ~*ed a day's work in years*. 他多年来一天也未旷工。— ***vi*.** **1.** 打不中,打歪;失败。**2.** 不见;得不着,没…着 (*of*; *in*)。~ ***fire*** (枪炮)打不响;(俏皮话等)不好笑;得不到预想的效果。~ ***one's dinner*** 吐饭。~ ***one's step*** [***footing***] 失脚,踩滑。~ ***one's tip*** 出岔子;失败,没达到目的。~ ***one's way*** 迷路。~ ***stays*** (船)抢风失败。~ ***the bus*** 〔口〕失去好机会。~ ***the*** [***one's***] ***mark*** 没打中目标;认错目标;失败;不恰当。~ ***the point*** 不懂(俏皮话等的)妙处。**II** ***n*.** **1.** 得不着,寻不着;猜错,不中;失败。**2.** 故意逃避;逃脱。**3.** 〔俚〕没有了…的寂寞。*A* ~ *is as good as a mile*. 小失败也是失败[差之毫厘失之千里]。*It's hit or* ~. 不计成败,好歹一试,孤注一掷。*She feels the* ~ *of her children*. 她感到没了孩子的寂寞。***give a*** ~【撞球】故意打一个空球;避免,避开;不碰动。***give sb*. *a*** ~ 假装没有看见某人,故意避开某人。***give it a*** ~ 〔美俚〕跳过去;略去,省去。***near*** ~ 虽不命中但近得足够毁坏目标。

Miss. = Mississippi.

mis·sa [ˈmisə; ˋmɪsə] ***n*.**【天主】弥撒(= Mass)。

mis·sal [ˈmisəl; ˋmɪsḷ] ***n*.**【天主】弥撒书;祷告书。

mis·say [misˈsei; mɪsˋse] ***vt*., *vi*.** (***-said*** [-ˈsaid; -ˋsaɪd]; ***-say·ing***) 〔主古〕**1.** 误信,失言。**2.** 说(…的)坏话,诬蔑,谩骂,毁谤。

mis·sel(thrush) [ˈmizəl; ˋmɪsḷ] ***n*.**【鸟】大鸫。

mis·send [ˈmisˈsend; mɪsˋsɛnd] ***vt*.** (***-sent*** [-ˈsent; -ˋsɛnt]) 送错(邮件等)。

mis·sense [ˈmisˌsens; ˋmɪsˏsɛns] ***n*.**【生】误义〔包括一个或一个以上密码子转变的遗传突变〕。

mis·shape [misˈʃeip; mɪsˋʃep] ***vt*.** 弄丑,使残废;使破相。**mis·sha·pen** ***a*.** 残废的,畸形的;破相的,丑陋的。

mis·sile [ˈmisail, Am. ˈmisəl; ˋmɪsaɪl, ˋmɪsəl] ***n*.** 投射器;飞射器[箭、炮弹等],射弹,飞弹;导弹。*an air-to-air* (*guided*) ~ 空对空飞弹,机载飞弹。*an atom-tipped* ~ 原子弹头飞弹。*a homing* ~ 自动寻的飞弹。*an intercontinental ballistic* ~ 洲际弹道导弹〔略 I.C.B.M.〕。*an infrared homing* ~ 红外线寻的导弹,红外线自动导引导弹。*a staged* ~ 多级导弹。*a development* ~ 试验导弹。**-man** ***n*.** 导弹制造者[设计者];火箭发射手,导弹操作手;导弹专家。**-ry** ***n*.** 导弹技术;导弹〔总称〕。

miss·ing [ˈmisiŋ; ˋmɪsɪŋ] ***a*.** 失去的,不见了的,下落不明的,失踪的。*killed*, *wounded*, *or* ~ 死伤或失踪者。*the* ~ *link* (体系中)缺少的一环;【动】类人猿与人类之间的假想过渡动物。*There is a page* ~. 缺少一页。

mis·sion [ˈmiʃən; ˋmɪʃən] **I** ***n*.** **1.** 派遣;国家代表团的派遣;代表团;使团;(伊斯兰教的)朝觐团;特使;〔美〕驻外使节,大[公]使馆。**2.** 使命,任务;天职;【军】战斗任务;飞行任务。**3.** 传道,传教;(特指到国外的)传道团体[本部、根据地];传道区;传道期间;传道权;传道馆;传道会;贫民救济会。*an economic* ~ 经济代表团。*the* ~ *at Japan* 驻日本大使馆。*a diplomatic* ~ 外交使团。*be sent on a* ~ 是带有使命派出去的。*It seems to be his* ~ *to help others*. 他的天职好像就是帮助别人。**II** ***vt*.** **1.** 给…交代任务;派遣;把任务交给。**2.** 向…传教。~ **control**【宇航】太空飞行指挥中心。~ **creep** 任务蠕变〔指违反本人意愿的任务范围加大,这种增加往往是在不知不觉中发生的〕。

mis·sion·ar·y [ˈmiʃənəri; ˋmɪʃənˏɛrɪ] **I** ***a*.** 传教(士)的。**II** ***n*.** 传教士;(某某主义的)宣传者。

mis·sion·er [ˈmiʃənə; ˋmɪʃənɚ] ***n*.** (教区)传教士(= missionary)。

mis·sion·ize [ˈmiʃənaiz; ˋmɪʃənˏaɪz] ***vt*.** 向…传教;对…宣传…主义;使…皈依自己的宗教信仰。— ***vi*.** 进行传道。

mis·sis [ˈmisiz; ˋmɪsɪz] ***n*.** **1.** 〔用于已婚妇女姓前〕…夫

人〔普通写作 Mrs.〕。**2.**〔口、爱称〕太太〔仆人对女主人的称呼〕;(自己或别人的)太太,妻子,夫人。*How's your* ～? 你的夫人好吗?

miss·ish [ˈmisiʃ; ˋmɪsɪʃ] ***a.*** 小姑娘似的,女学生似的;小姐般一本正经的。

Mis·sis·sip·pi [ˌmisiˈsipi; ˏmɪsəˋsɪpɪ] ***n.*** **1.** 密西西比〔美国州名〕。**2.**〔the ～〕密西西比河〔美国〕。

mis·sive [ˈmisiv; ˋmɪsɪv] **I** ***a.***〔古〕已经送出去的,指令的。**II** ***n.*** 公文;书信。

Mis·sour·i [miˈzuəri; məˋzurɪ] ***n.*** **1.** 密苏里〔美国州名〕。**2.**〔the ～〕密苏里河〔美国〕。***from*** ～〔美俚〕怀疑的,不轻易相信的(*I'm from* ～. 我要见到确实证据才相信)。

mis·speak [misˈspiːk; mɪsˋspik] ***vt.***, ***vi.*** (*-spoke* [-ˈspəuk; -ˋspok]; *-spoken* [-ˈspəukən; -ˋspokən]; *-speak·ing*) 误言,失言。

mis·spell [ˈmisˈspel; mɪsˋspɛl] ***vt.*** (*-spelled* [-ˈspelt; -ˋspɛlt], *-spelt*) 拼错。**-ing** ***n.*** 拼写错误。

mis·spend [ˈmisˈspend; mɪsˋspɛnd] ***vt.*** (*-spent* [-t; -t]) 浪费,虚度。*a misspent youth* 浪费了的青春。

mis·state [ˈmisˈsteit; mɪsˋstet] ***vt.*** 错说;虚称;谎报。**-ment** ***n.*** 误言。

mis·step [ˈmisˈstep; mɪsˋstɛp] ***n.*** 失足;失策,错误。

mis·sus [ˈmisəz; ˋmɪsəz] ***n.***〔口、方〕= missis.

miss·y [ˈmisi; ˋmɪsɪ] ***n.***〔口、爱称〕小姑娘;小姐。

mist [mist; mɪst] **I** ***n.*** **1.** 雾。★ mist 较 fog 淡,较 haze 浓。**2.** (眼睛的)迷糊,朦胧。**3.** 起蒙蔽作用的东西。*Scotch* ～ (苏格兰山区特多的)浓雾;雾雨。***cast*** [***throw***] ***a*** ～ ***before sb.'s eyes*** 蒙蔽[迷糊]某人。***in a*** ～ 迷惑着,心里徬徨着。**II** ***vt.*** 给雾蒙住;使朦胧,使模糊,使迷糊。— ***vi.***〔主词用 it〕下雾。

mis·tak·a·ble [misˈteikəbl; məˋstekəbl̩] ***a.*** 易错的,易误会的。

mis·take [misˈteik; məˋstek] **I** ***vt.***, ***vi.*** (***mis·took*** [-ˈtuk; -ˋtʊk]; ***mis·taken*** [-ˈteikən; -ˋtekən]) 弄错;误会,想错;看错;误解。*He mistook that stick for a snake.* 他把那根棍子错看成蛇了。*She has mistaken me.* 她误会了我的话了。**II** ***n.*** 错误,过失,事故;想错,看错;误会,误解。*There is no mistaking.* 没错。*There is no* ～ *about it.* 那是确实无误的。***and no*** ～〔口〕(加强以上所述)确确实实(*They have come to grief and no* ～. 他们确确实实失败了)。***by*** ～ 因错误。***make a*** ～ 犯错误,做错,想错。

mis·tak·en [misˈteikən; məˋstekən] **I** mistake 的过去分词。**II** ***a.*** 错误的;想错了的;看错了的;误解了的,误会了的。*You are* ～. 你(弄)错了。～ ***identity*** 认错人。**-ly** ***ad.*** 错,误。

mis·taught [ˈmisˈtɔːt; mɪsˋtɔt] ***a.*** 被教错的。

mis·ter [ˈmistə; ˋmɪstɚ] **I** ***n.*** **1.**〔通常作 Mr.〕先生〔男子姓名前或职称前: *Mr. Smith*, *Mr. Henry Smith*, *Mr. President*〕。**2.**〔口〕先生〔招呼不知姓名的人〕。**3.** 老百姓,平民。**4.** 丈夫。*Look here*, ～! 喂,先生! ***be he prince or mere*** ～ 不管他是王子还是平民。***a plain*** ～ 普通人。**II** ***vt.*** 称…先生。*Don't* ～ *me.* 不要叫我先生。**M- Charley** [**Charlie**]〔美黑人俚〕白人。

mis·ter·y [ˈmistəri; ˋmɪstərɪ] ***n.*** = mystery[2].

mist·flow·er [ˈmistˌflauə; ˋmɪstˏflauɚ] ***n.***【植】雾花泽兰〔产于美洲东部〕。

mist·ful [ˈmistful; ˋmɪstful] ***a.*** = misty.

mis·think [misˈθiŋk; mɪsˋθɪŋk] ***vi.*** (*-thought* [-ˈθɔːt; -ˋθɔt]; *-think·ing*)〔古〕想错了。— ***vt.***〔古〕对…有坏的看法。

mist·i·ly [ˈmistili; ˋmɪstəlɪ] ***ad.*** 雾深地;朦胧地,迷迷糊糊地。

mis·time [ˈmisˈtaim; mɪsˋtaɪm] ***vt.*** **1.** 使(言行等)不合时宜。**2.** 搞错…的时间。**3.** 打错(拍子)。～*d remarks* 不合时宜的话。

mist·i·ness [ˈmistinis; ˋmɪstɪnɪs] ***n.*** 薄雾状;朦胧;模糊,不明了。

mis·tle·toe [ˈmisltəu; ˋmɪsl̩ˏto] ***n.***【植】槲寄生〔其小枝常用作圣诞节的装饰〕。*giant* ～*s*【植】桑寄生。～ **fig**【植】黄榕。～ **honeysuckle**【植】五室忍冬。～ **thrush** 槲鸫(= mistle thrush)。

mis·told [misˈtəuld; mɪsˋtold] ***ad.*** 被传错,被误报。

mis·took [misˈtuk; mɪsˋtʊk] mistake 的过去式。

mis·tral [ˈmistrəl; ˋmɪsˋtrəl] ***n.*** (法国地中海沿岸一带的)干燥寒冷的北风。

mis·trans·late [ˈmistrænsˈleit; ˏmɪstrænsˋlet] ***vt.*** 译错。**-la·tion** [-ʃən; -ʃən] ***n.*** 误译。

mis·treat [misˈtriːt; mɪsˋtrit] ***vt.*** 虐待。**-ment** ***n.***

mis·tress [ˈmistris; ˋmɪstrɪs] ***n.*** **1.** (*opp.* master) 女主人,主妇;老板娘;女…的名家[能手]。**2.**〔M-〕〔古〕…夫人;…小姐。★现只用缩写 Mrs. [ˈmisiz; ˋmɪsɪz] 放在夫姓前,如 *Mrs. Jones*, *Mrs. Henry Jones*, *Mrs. Henry*(*Jones*); 法律文件等中写作 *Mrs. Mary Jones*. 17 世纪以前写作 Mistress. **3.**〔英〕女教师。**4.** 情妇;〔诗〕情人,爱人〔指女子〕。*The moon, the* ～ *of the night.* 月亮,夜的女王。*a French* ～ 法语女教师。***be one's own*** ～ 自己(女子)作得了主。***be*** ～ ***of...*** 占有着…。***be*** ～ ***of the situation*** 能控制局面。***be*** ～ ***of the world*** 称霸世界。***M- of the Adriatic*** = Venice. ***M- of the Robes***〔英〕女王的女侍长。***M- of the seas*** 海上霸主〔旧指英帝国〕。***M- of the World*** 世界霸主〔罗马帝国的别称〕。**-ship** ***n.*** mistress 的身份。

mis·tri·al [ˈmisˈtraiəl; mɪsˋtraɪəl] ***n.***【法】**1.** (因手续错误形成的)无效审判。**2.**〔口〕(因陪审员意见不一的)未决审判。

mis·trust [ˈmisˈtrʌst; mɪsˋtrʌst] ***n.***, ***v.*** 疑心,疑惑,不相信。**-er** ***n.*** 疑心者。**-ing·ly** ***ad.***

mis·trust·ful [ˈmisˈtrʌstful; mɪsˋtrʌstfl̩] ***a.*** 多疑的,不相信的 (*of*)。**-ly** ***ad.***

mist·y [ˈmisti; ˋmɪstɪ] ***a.*** (***mist·i·er***; ***-i·est***) **1.** 有薄雾的;朦胧的。**2.** (思想等)不清的,模糊的。**3.** (眼睛)泪汪汪的。**4.** 无知识的,蒙昧的。**-i·ly** ***ad.*** **-i·ness** ***n.***

mis·un·der·stand [ˈmisʌndəˈstænd; ˋmɪsʌndɚˋstænd] (***mis·stood*** [-ˈstud; -ˏstʊd]) ***vt.*** 误会,误解;曲解。**-ing** ***n.*** 误会,误解;不和,隔阂;争执。

mis·us·age [ˈmisˈjuːzidʒ; mɪsˋjusɪdʒ] ***n.*** **1.** (字句等的)误用。**2.** 虐待。

mis·use [ˈmisˈjuːz; mɪsˋjuz] **I** ***vt.*** 错用(字句等);滥用;虐待。**II** [-ˈjuːs; -ˋjus] ***n.*** 误用,滥用。

mis·us·er [ˈmisˈjuːzə; mɪsˋjuzɚ] ***n.*** 误用者,虐待者;【法】滥用者。

mis·val·ue [ˌmisˈvæljuː; mɪsˋvælju] ***vt.*** 误估,低估。

mis·word [misˈwəːd; mɪsˋwɝd] ***vt.*** 措词不当。

mis·write [misˈrait; mɪsˋraɪt] ***vt.*** (*-wrote* [-ˈrəut; -ˋrot]; *-writ·ten* [-ˈritən; -ˋrɪtən]; *-writ·ing*) 误写,错写。

MIT = Massachusetts Institute of Technology〔美〕马萨诸塞理工学院,麻省理工学院。

Mitch·ell [ˈmitʃəl; ˋmɪtʃəl] ***n.*** 米歇尔〔姓氏,男子名〕。

mite[1] [mait; maɪt] ***n.*** **1.** 极小的东西。**2.** (从前 *Flanders* 通用的)小铜币;小钱;〔英俚〕= half a farthing. **3.** 小孩子。**4.**〔口〕一点点;少而难得的捐助,一臂之力。***a*** ～ ***of a*** (*child* etc.) 小得可怜的(孩子等)。***contribute one's*** ～ ***to*** 为…尽微力。***not a*** ～ 一点也不…。***offer a*** ～ ***of comfort*** 仅能用心里话安慰。***the widow's*** ～ 寡妇的一文钱〔少而可贵的捐助〕。

mite[2] [mait; maɪt] ***n.*** 小虫;螨类,干酪蛆。*a red* ～ 红蜘蛛。*a* ～ *on an elephant* 大小悬殊。～ *of grape* 葡萄毛毡病。

mi·ter [ˈmaitə; ˋmaɪtɚ] ***n.***, ***vt.*** = mitre.

Mit·ford [ˈmitfəd; ˋmɪtfɚd] ***n.*** 米特福德〔姓氏〕。

Mith·ra·i·cism, **Mith·ra·ism** [miθˈreiisizəm,

ˈmiθreiizəm; mɪθˋreɪsɪzm, ˋmɪθreɪzm] *n*. (古波斯的)太阳神崇拜。

Mith·ra·ist [ˈmiθrəist; ˋmɪθrəɪst] *n*. (古波斯的)崇拜太阳神者。

Mith·ras [ˈmiθrəs; ˋmɪθræs] *n*. (波斯的)太阳神。

mith·ri·date [ˈmiθrideit; ˋmɪθrɪˏdet] *n*. 万应解毒药〔一种早先被认为是一切毒药的解毒剂的药剂〕。

mith·rid·a·tize [miθˈridətaiz; ˋmɪθrəˏdetaɪz] *vt*. (常服小量毒药)使有人工耐毒作用。

mit·i·cide [ˈmaitisaid; ˋmaɪtəˏsaɪd] *n*. 杀螨剂。

mit·i·gate [ˈmitigeit; ˋmɪtəˏget] *vt*., *vi*. 镇静,缓和;减轻。*to mitigate the flood* 分洪。**-tion** *n*. 镇静,缓和;减轻。**-tive** 1. *a*. 缓和性的。2. *n*. 缓和剂。**-tor** *n*. 缓和者;缓和剂。**-to·ry** *a*. = mitigative.

mi·to·chon·dri·a [ˌmaitəˈkɔndriə; ˏmaɪtəˋkɑndrɪə] *n*. 〔*pl*.〕(*sing*. **-drion** [-driɔn; -drɪɔn])【生】粒线体。

mi·to·sis [miˈtəusis; mɪˋtosɪs] *n*. (*pl*. **-ses** [-siːz; -siz])【生】有丝分裂,丝状核分裂。

mi·tot·ic [miˈtɔtik; mɪˋtɑtɪk] *a*. 【生】有丝分裂的。

mi·trail·leur [ˌmitraiˈəː, F. mitrɑˈjœːr; ˏmɪtraɪˋɝ, mɪtrɑˋjœr] *n*. 〔F.〕机枪手。

mi·trail·leuse [ˌmitraiˈəːz; ˏmɪtraɪˋɝz] *n*. 〔F.〕机关枪。

mi·tral [ˈmaitrəl; ˋmaɪtrəl] I *a*. 僧帽瓣状的,主教冠(状)的。~ *stenosis* 僧帽瓣硬化。~ *valve* 僧帽瓣。II *n*. 【解】(心脏的)僧帽瓣,二尖瓣(= ~ valve)。

mi·tre [ˈmaitə; ˋmaɪtɚ] I *n*. 1. 主教冠;僧帽;主教等的职位〔职权〕。2. 【木工】斜接;斜角缝;斜榫;斜角尺。II *vt*. 1. 给与…以主教冠;升任某人为主教(等)。2. 使斜接。*a ~ joint* 斜削接头,斜面接合,斜角联接。*a mitring machine* 【印】斜切机。~ **box** 辅锯箱,夹背锯箱。~ **gear** 等径伞齿轮。~ **wheels** 〔*pl*.〕正角斜齿轮。

mi·tred [ˈmaitəd; ˋmaɪtɚd] *a*. 1. 戴着主教冠的;担任了主教的。2. 有斜面接合的。

mitt [mit; mɪt] I *n*. 1. = mitten. 2. 〔俚〕手,掌;拳头;〔美俚〕无手人;〔美俚〕逮捕;〔*pl*.〕手铐;〔美俚〕看手相的(= ~reader)。II *vt*. 〔美俚〕和…握手。***give sb. the frozen ~*** 极端冷对某人。***tip sb.'s ~*** 〔美〕泄露某人的企图。

mit·ten [ˈmitn; ˋmɪtn] *n*. 1. (仅拇指分开的)两指手套;(女用)露指长手套。2. 〔*pl*.〕〔美俚〕拳击手套,棒球手套;手。***get the ~*** (向女人求爱)遭到拒绝;被解雇,被撵走。***give (sb.) the ~*** (女人)拒绝求爱,给碰钉子;解雇,撵走。***handle without ~s*** 不客气地处置,无情对待。~ **sport** 〔美俚〕拳击。

mit·ti·mus [ˈmitiməs; ˋmɪtəməs] *n*. 〔口〕解雇通知,免职,解雇;【法】徒刑执行令,下狱状;法院转移案卷的命令。***get one's ~*** 被免职,被解雇。

mity [ˈmaiti; ˋmaɪtɪ] *a*. 多螨的。

mitz·vah, mits·vah [mitsˈvɑː, ˈmitsvə; mɪtsˋvɑ, ˋmɪtsvə] *n*. (*pl*. **mitzvoth** [-ˈvəut; -ˋvot], **mitzvahs**)【犹太教】1. 诫命。2. 奉行神命。

mix [miks; mɪks] I *vt*. (~**ed**, 〔古〕***mixt*** [mikst; mɪkst]) 1. 混,混合,搀合;混合起来做。2. 使结合;使结交,使交往。3. 使(动物)杂交。4. 混淆,混同(无形物)(*with*)。5. (给…)配制;调制。~ *a salad* 拌沙拉。~ *wine with water* = ~ *water in wine* 用水搀酒。— *vi*. 1. 混,相混合,相溶合 (*in*; *with*)。2. 结合,结交,交往 (*with*);亲密地来往,合得来。3. 变成杂种。4. 有牵连,参与 (*in*)。5. 〔美俚〕参加殴斗[比赛](= ~ it)。*They do not ~ well*. 他们不大合得来。***be [get] ~ed up in [with]*** 加入(流氓组织等),参与(坏事)。~ ***in society*** 出入社交界。~ ***it up*** 〔俚〕做骗人的比赛[假比赛];通同作弊。~ ***up*** 调匀,拌匀;混淆,混同;使结交坏朋友;【拳击】猛烈互击。II *n*. 混合;〔口〕混杂,混乱;〔美俚〕打架;比赛。

mix·a·ble [ˈmiksəbl; ˋmɪksəbl] *a*. 可混的;可混合的;可混杂的。

mixed [mikst; mɪkst] *a*. 1. 混成的,混合的。2. 混杂的,各式各样的。3. 男女混合(成)的;各阶层混合成的。4. 〔英〕男女同校的。5. 〔口〕头脑混乱的;喝醉了的 (*up*)。~ *biscuits* 什锦饼干。~ *motives* 不纯洁的动机。*a ~ train* (客、货)混合列车。*a ~ number* 【数】带分数。*a ~ chorus* 混声合唱(团)。*a ~ vowel* (中)央母音。***have ~ feelings*** 悲[惊]喜交集。~ **bag** 混杂;(尤指)杂七杂八混在一起的东西[人]等。~ **bud** 【植】混合芽。~ **doubles** 【球赛】(每队一男一女的)混合双打。~ **foursome** 〔美〕由两对男女举行的高尔夫球比赛。~ **grades** 异级混合物,(石油产品的)不同类混合物。~**-handed** *a*. 左右手(各有正常)分工的〔和"左撇子"相对而言〕。~ **marriage** 异族[教]通婚。~ **media** 1. 艺术的混合效应法〔如表演、彩色灯光、录音带等多种手段的混合运用〕。2. 混合画法〔如在一幅作品上采用水彩和蜡笔〕。~**-up** *a*. 混乱的;迷惑的。**-ness** *n*. 混合,混成;混杂。

mix·en [ˈmiksn; ˋmɪksn] *n*. 〔古、方〕粪堆。

mix·er [ˈmiksə; ˋmɪksɚ] *n*. 1. 混合者。2. 混合[搅拌]器;【冶】混铁炉;混频器;【无】混频管。3. 〔原美、口〕交际家;交谊会;【无】录音师。*a good [bad] ~* 会[不会]交际的人。

mix·ing [ˈmiksiŋ; ˋmɪksɪŋ] *n*. 混合;【影】录音;【无】混频。

mix·ol·o·gist [mikˈsɔlədʒist; mɪkˋsɑlədʒɪst] *n*. 〔美俚〕酒吧侍者,酒吧间配酒者。

mix·o·lyd·i·an [ˌmiksəˈlidiən; ˏmɪksəˋlɪdɪən] *a*. 【乐】1. 混合里第亚调式。2. 中世纪教堂音乐调式〔相当于带小七度的现代大调式〕。

mixt [mikst; mɪkst] mix 的异体过去式和过去分词。

mixt. = mixture.

Mix·tec [ˈmiːstek; ˋmistɛk] *n*. 1. (*pl*. **-tecs**, **-tec**) 米斯特克人〔墨西哥瓦哈卡、盖雷罗和普埃布拉州的一支印第安人〕。2. 米斯特坎语。

Mix·tec·an [miːsˈtekən; misˋtɛkən] *n*. 米斯特坎语〔墨西哥四个印第安语族之一〕。

mix·ture [ˈmikstʃə; ˋmɪkstʃɚ] *n*. 1. 混合,混杂;混合状态。2. 混合物;混合体;(内燃机等用的)混合气;【医】混合剂,药水;混合烟草〔又叫 smoking ~〕。3. 【织】麻花织品;优缺点均有的人。*a ~ of grief and comfort* 悲喜交集(的感情)。***the ~ as before*** 照处方笺配药;〔口〕处理办法如前。***with a ~ of*** 夹有,加有,带有。~ **ratio** 混合比。~ **strength** 混合浓度。

mix-up [ˈmiksʌp; ˋmɪksˏʌp] *n*. 〔口〕混乱;混战;混合物;迷惑。

Mi·zar [ˈmaizɑː; ˋmaɪzɑr] *n*. 【天】开阳,北斗六〔大熊(星)座〕。

miz·zen, miz·en [ˈmizn; ˋmɪzn] *n*. 【船】后桅〔又叫 mizzenmast〕;后帆;最后部的纵帆〔又叫 mizzen sail〕。~**mast** 【船】(三桅船上的)后桅。~ **rigging** 后桅索具。~ **sail** 后桅帆。~**top** 【船】后桅楼。~**yard** 【船】后桅横桁。

miz·zle[1] [ˈmizl; ˋmɪzl] *vi*., *n*. 〔英〕(下)毛毛雨,蒙蒙雨,细雨。*It ~s*. 下毛毛雨了。

miz·zle[2] [ˈmizl; ˋmɪzl] *vi*. 〔英俚〕逃亡,逃走;撤走。

miz·zle[3] [ˈmizl; ˋmɪzl] *vt*. 〔方〕使糊涂,使迷惑。

miz·zly [ˈmizli; ˋmɪzlɪ] *a*. 下着毛毛雨的,蒙蒙雨的。

MK, mk. = markka.

MKS = metre-kilogram(me)-second system 米-千克-秒单位制。

mks. = marks.

mkt. = market.

ML = 1. Master of Laws 法学硕士。2. minelayer 布雷舰艇。3. motor launch 摩托艇;汽艇。4. muzzle-loading 前装式的,前膛的。5. Licentiate in Medicine 有资格开业的医生。6. Licentiate in Midwifery 有资格开业

的助产士。

ml. = millilitre(s).

M.L.A. = **1.** Modern Language Association〔英〕现代语言学会。**2.** Member of the Legislative Assembly 立法议会议员;立宪(制宪)议会议员。

MLD = median lethal dose【医】半数致死量。

M.L.D. = minimum lethal dose【医】最小致死量。

MLG = Middle Low German 中世纪低地德语。

Mlle. =〔F.〕*Mademoiselle*.

Mlles. =〔F.〕*Mesdemoiselles*.

M.L.N.S. = Ministry of Labour and National Service〔英旧〕劳工及国民义务兵役部。

MLR = **1.** main line of resistance〔美〕防御主阵地前沿。**2.** minimum lending rate 最低贷款利率〔英格兰银行的官方利率,相当于美联储的贴现率〕。

M.L.S. = Master of Library Science 图书馆学硕士。

MM. =〔F.〕*Messieurs*.

M.M. = **1.** Military Medal〔英〕军功章。**2.** Ministry of Munitions 军需部。**3.** Machinist's Mate【美海】机械军士。**4.** mercantile marine 商船(总称)。**5.**〔L.〕mutatis mutandis 作相应的变更,作必要的修改。

mm, mm. = **1.** millimetre. **2.**〔L.〕*millia*.

Mme. =〔F.〕*Madame*.

Mmes. =〔F.〕*Mesdames*.

MMRBM = mobile medium-range ballistic missile 机动中程弹道导[飞]弹。

M.Mus., M Mus = Master of music 音乐硕士。

MN = magnetic north 磁北。

Mn = manganese【化】锰。

mne·mon [ˈniːˌmɔn; ˋniˏmɑn] ***n.*** 记忆单位〔理论上储存于脑中的最小信息单位〕。

mne·mon·ic [niːˈmɔnik; niˋmɑnɪk] ***a.*** 记忆的;记忆术的;增进记忆的。*a ~ system* 记忆法。*~ rhymes* (帮助记忆的)顺口溜(等)。**-s** [-s; -s] ***n.*** 记忆法[术]。

Mne·mos·y·ne [*m*ni(ː)ˈmɔziniː; *m*nɪˋmɑsəni] ***n.***【希神】记忆女神。

mne·mo·tech·ny [ˈniːməutekni; ˋnimətɛknɪ] ***n.*** = mnemonics.

M.O., MO, m.o. = **1.** money order 汇票;邮政汇票。**2.** mail order 函购,邮购。**3.** medical officer 军医;军医主任。**4.** mass observation 民意调查。

Mo = **1.** Monday. **2.** molybdenum【化】钼。

Mo. = Missouri 密苏里〔美国州名〕。

mo [məu; mo] ***n.***〔俚、谑〕= moment. *Wait half a ~.* 请等一等。

mo. = month; monthly.

-mo *suf.* (纸张的)开: 16 mo = sixteen*mo* 十六开〔略作16°〕, 12mo = duodeci*mo* 十二开〔略作12°〕。

mo·a [ˈməuə; ˋmoə] ***n.***【鸟】恐鸟〔现已灭绝〕。

Mo·ab·ite [ˈməuəbait; ˋmoəbˏaɪt] **I** ***n.*** (*fem.* ***-it·ess*** [-ˌbaitis; ˋmoəˏbaɪtɪs]) **1.** (死海东部和南部古国)古莫阿布人。**2.** 古莫阿布语〔已消亡〕。**II** ***a.*** 古莫阿布的,古莫阿布人的(= Moabitish)。

moan [məun; mon] **I** ***vi.***, ***vt.*** 呻吟,哼;〔古、诗〕悲叹,哭。**II** ***n.*** 呻吟声;(波浪、风等的)号,啸,萧萧声;悲叹声,呜咽声;〔诗〕悲叹。***make (one's) ~***〔古〕悲诉,诉委曲。**-ing·ly** ***ad.***

moan·ful [ˈməunf*u*l; ˋmonfəl] ***a.*** 呻吟的,悲叹的;忧伤的。**-ly** ***ad.***

moat [məut; mot] **I** ***n.***【筑城】(城)壕;护城河。**II** ***vt.*** 挖壕围绕。

mob [mɔb; mɑb] **I** ***n.***〔集合词〕**1.**〔蔑〕暴民,暴徒;观众,民众,乌合之众。**2.**〔俚〕(盗贼等的)一党,一伙。**3.**〔美俚〕匪帮,匪党;一群罪犯;观众。*a ~ of rioters* 一伙暴徒。*the swell ~* 穿得很讲究的扒手或骗子。**II** ***vt.*** (**-bb-**) 群众袭击,成群暴动,聚众滋扰;成群欢呼。*The returning soldiers were mobbed in the streets.* 归来的士兵们在街上受到了群众的欢呼。*~ it* 聚众滋扰。— ***vi.*** 乱挤。*~ forward* 向前乱挤。~ **law** 暴民的法律;私刑。~ **psychology** 群众心理。~ **scene**【影】群众场面。

mob. = mobile.

mob·bish [ˈmɔbiʃ; ˋmɑbɪʃ] ***a.*** 暴徒似的,骚扰的,暴乱的,无纪律的。

mob·cap [ˈmɔbkæp; ˋmɑbˏkæp] ***n.*** (于18世纪和19世纪初流行的室内)头巾式女帽。

mo·bile [ˈməubail, -bil; ˋmoˏbaɪl, -bɪl] **I** ***a.*** **1.** 活动的,运动的;可动的。**2.** 易变的;易感动的;易变通的,灵活的,反复无常的。**3.** 机动的,流动的;装在车上的;用车辆运输的。**4.** 运动物体的,活动装置的。**II** ***n.*** **1.** 可动物,可动装置;(现代抽象派艺术)动的雕塑。**2.**〔美口〕汽车;(特指)蒸汽汽车。**3.**〔口〕移动电话(= ~ phone)。**4.**〔古〕= mob. *a ~ floodlight* 活动探照灯。*~ features* 富有表情的面貌。*a ~ mind* 多变的心思。*~ troops* [*units*] 快速部队。*a ~ drama group* 巡回剧团。~ **home** 活动住房〔由大型拖车改装而成多少可长期在某处停放的住房〕。~ **phone** 移动电话,手机。~ **unit** 活动专门设备车〔如广播宣传车、巡回爱克斯光检查车、电视摄影汽车、救护车等〕。~ **warfare**【军】运动战。

mo·bil·i·ty[1] [məuˈbiliti; moˋbɪlətɪ] ***n.*** **1.** 可动性,活动性,能动性。**2.** 灵活性,可变动性。**3.**【物】动性,迁移率;【化】淌度;【军】运动性,机动性。*the ionic ~* 离子迁移率[淌度]。

mob·il·i·ty[2] [mɔˈbiliti; mɑˋbɪlətɪ] ***n.*** 群众。*~ and nobility*〔谑〕老百姓和贵族。

mo·bi·liz·a·ble [ˈməubilaizəbl; ˋmobəˏlaɪzəbl̩] ***a.*** 可动员的。

mo·bi·li·za·tion [ˌməubilaiˈzeiʃən; ˏmobl̩əˋzeʃən] ***n.*** **1.** 动员;流通,应用。**2.**【法】不动产的动产化;【地】活动作用。*~ orders*【军】动员令。*national ~* 国民总动员。*the ~ of financial resources* 财力的动用。

mo·bi·lize [ˈməubilaiz; ˋmobl̩ˏaɪz] ***vt.*** **1.** 发动,调动;使可动。**2.** 使流通;使(不动产)变成动产。*~ the masses* 发动群众。— ***vi.*** 动员(起来)。

mob·oc·ra·cy [mɔˈbɔkrəsi; mɑbˋɑkrəsɪ] ***n.*** **1.** 暴徒统治;暴民政治。**2.** 作为统治者的暴民。

mob·o·crat [ˈmɔbəkræt; ˋmɑbəˏkræt] ***n.*** 暴民领袖;支持暴民政治的人;惑众取宠的政治家。

MOBS = Multiple Orbit Bombardment System 多弹头轰炸系统。

mobs·man [ˈmɔbzmən; ˋmɑbzmən] ***n.***〔口〕**1.** 暴民中的一个成员。**2.** 服装漂亮的扒手。

mob·ster [ˈmɔbstə; ˋmɑbstɚ] ***n.***〔俚〕暴徒,匪徒,歹徒。

mo·camp [ˈməukæmp; ˋmokæmp] ***n.*** 旅馆式营地,旅行营地。

moc·ca·sin [ˈmɔkəsin; ˋmɑkəsn] ***n.*** (北美印地安人等穿的)鹿皮靴;硬底软(拖)鞋;(南美)有毒水蛇;噬鱼蛇。~ **flower**【植】老虎七,鬼督邮,杓兰。

Mo·cha [ˈməukə; ˋmokə] ***n.*** 穆哈〔阿拉伯也门共和国西南一海港〕。

mo·cha [ˈməukə; ˋmokə] **I** ***n.*** **1.** (原指阿拉伯产的)摩加咖啡〔又叫 Mocha coffee〕;上等咖啡;〔口〕任何咖啡。**2.** 摩加皮〔阿拉伯山羊的鞣皮,做手套用〕。**3.** 摩加(调味)香料〔用咖啡(或与巧克力混合)制成的调味浸剂〕。**II** ***a.*** **1.** 加有摩加香料的。**2.** 一种深褐色的。~ **stone**【矿】苔纹玛瑙。

mock [mɔk; mɑk] **I** ***vt.*** **1.** 嘲笑,挖苦。**2.** 学样子嘲弄;模拟。**3.** 骗,引诱,钓。**4.** 使徒劳;使失望。**5.** 使无效,挫败;无视。*be ~ed with false hopes* 被空幻的希望欺骗了。*The river ~ed all their efforts to cross.* 他们作了一切努力还是没能渡过这条河。— ***vi.*** 嘲弄,愚弄(*at*)。*~ up* 制作大模型。**II** ***n.***〔古〕= mockery. ***make a ~ of*** = make a mockery of. **III** ***a.***〔用作 Attrib.〕假的;虚幻的;模拟的。*a ~ battle* 模拟战,演

习。~ *lead* = ~ *ore* 闪锌矿。*a* ~ *trial* 模拟裁判。*a* ~ *moon* 幻月〔月晕的光轮〕。~ *modesty* 假谦虚,假客气。~ **auction** 1. = Dutch auction. 2. (使用囮子的)骗人拍卖。~ **duck** 充鸭〔做成鸭形的羊肩肉〕。~-**heroic** *a*., *n*. 嘲弄[滑稽]地模仿英雄风格的(作品、诗歌)。~-**majesty** 虚张声势,空架子。~ **orange**【植】山梅花;桑橙;葡萄牙桂樱,像橙子的葫芦。~ **plane** 假挪威槭。~ **soup**, ~ **turtle soup** 充海龟汤的小牛头汤。~ **strawberry** 蛇莓。~-**up** 1. (教学实验用的)实物大模型(飞机、大炮、机械等)。2.【军】伪装工事。

mock·er [ˈmɔkə; ˋmɑkɚ] *n*. 嘲笑者;学人样嘲弄人的人;【鸟】= mockingbird.

mock·er·y [ˈmɔkəri; ˋmɑkərɪ] *n*. 1. 愚弄,嘲笑,挖苦。2. 笑柄。3. 学样,冒牌,(拙劣的)模仿。4. 恶劣[可鄙]的事例。5. 徒劳。*They went through the* ~ *of a trial*. 他们遭受了不公正的审判。***hold*** (*sb*., *sth*.) ***up to*** ~ 拿某人[某事]寻开心,玩弄…。***make a*** ~ ***of*** 嘲笑,戏弄,以某人作为笑柄。

mock·ing·bird [ˈmɔkiŋbəːd; ˋmɑkɪŋˏbɝd] *n*.【鸟】模仿鸟〔产于北美南部及西印度群岛〕。

mock·ing·ly [ˈmɔkiŋli; ˋmɑkɪŋlɪ] *ad*. 嘲笑地,愚弄地。

mock·ing-stock [ˈmɔkiŋsˈtɔk; ˋmɑkɪŋsˋtɑk] *n*. 笑柄。

mod [mɔd; mɑd] I *n*.〔亦 M-〕〔英〕现代派分子,时髦派分子〔英国六十年代的嬉皮士〕。II *a*.〔亦 M-〕现代派分子的;有现代派分子的特点的。

mod. = 1. moderate. 2. modern. 3. modulus.

mod·a·cryl·ic [ˌmɔdəˈkrilik; ˏmɑdəˋkrɪlɪk] *a*.【化】变性聚丙烯腈的。

mo·dal [ˈməudl; ˋmodl] *a*. 1. 方式上的,形态上的;【哲】(对本质、内容说的)形式(上)的。2.【语法】语气(mood)的;表示情态(manner)的。3.【逻】程式的;【乐】调式的;【法】规定执行[应用]方式的;【统计】众数的。*a* ~ *legacy* 指定用途的遗产。~ *auxiliary* 情态助动词(*can*, *may*, *might*, *must*, *should*, *would* 等)。-**ly** *ad*.

mo·dal·i·ty [məuˈdæliti; moˋdælətɪ] *n*. 形态,样式,方式;【数】模态;【逻】程式;感觉道〔如视觉道〕;物理疗法。

mode [məud; mod] *n*. 1. 法,样,方法,方式。2. 模,型;样式,体裁,款式;习惯。3. 风尚;〔the ~〕流行,时髦。4.【语法】= mood. 5.【乐】(古希腊的)旋法调,(近代的)调式。6.【逻】程式,样式,论式;【统计】众数。***all the*** ~ 非常流行。***become the*** ~ 流行起来。***in*** ~ 正流行,新式。***out of*** ~ 不流行,老式。~-**locked** *a*. 锁模的(指雷射器调整了光相位,能产生极短暂脉冲的)。

Mod E, Mod. E. = Modern English 现代英语。

mod·el [ˈmɔdl; ˋmɑdl] I *n*. 1. 模型,雏型;原型;设计图;模范;(画家、雕刻家的)模特儿;样板。2. 典型,模范。3. (女服装店雇用的)时装模特儿。4. 样式,型。5.〔口〕极相似的人[东西]。II *a*. 模型的,模范的。*a clay* ~【雕】黏土原型。*a working* ~ 机器的运转模型。*a* ~ *shot*【摄】模型镜头。*a* ~ *aeroplane* 模型飞机。*a* ~ *test* 典型试验。*The boy is the perfect* ~ *of his father*. 这孩子活像他父亲。***after*** [***on***] ***the*** ~ ***of*** 仿效…,拿…当做模范。***stand*** ~ 做模特儿。III (〔英〕-*ll*-) *vt*. 1. 作…的模型[雏型]。2. (依照模型)制作,仿造,建造(*after*; *on*; *upon*)。3. 设计,仿照,拿…做模范。— *vi*. 做模型;做模特儿。*delicately* ~*ed features* 清秀的面貌。~ *a garden after the manner of Kew* 仿照(伦敦) Kew 植物园设计的花园。~ ***oneself up*** (***on***) ***sb***. 仿效某人。

mod·el·ler, mod·el·er [ˈmɔdlə; ˋmɑdl̩ɚ] *n*. 模型(尤指塑像)作者;造型者。

mod·el·ling, mod·el·ing [ˈmɔdliŋ; ˋmɑdlɪŋ] *n*. 制造模型的方法,造型(术);塑像术;【美】立体感(表现法);模特儿职业。*the* ~ *of one's features* 某人脸部的形象。

mo·dem [ˈməudem; ˋmodɛm] I *n*.【无】调制解调器。II *vt*.【计】通过调制解调器向…发送电子邮件。— *vi*. 用调制解调器联通。

mod·e·na [ˈmɔdinə; ˋmɑdɪnə] *n*. 深紫色。

mod·er [ˈməudə; ˋmodɚ] *n*.【自】脉冲编码装置。

mod·er·ate [ˈmɔdərit; ˋmɑdərɪt] I *a*. 有节制的,温和的,稳健的;中庸的;中等的;适度的;普通的;〔美俚〕(人等)慢吞吞的,迟钝的;【物】慢化的,减速的。*a* ~ *breeze* 和风,四级风。*a* ~ *gale* 疾风,七级风。~ *prices* 公道的价格。~ *terms* 适度的条件[代价]。II *n*. 稳健的人,温和主义者。III [ˈmɔdəreit; ˋmɑdəˏret] *vt*. 使和缓,使减轻;节制,节约;调节;【物】慢化,减速。— *vi*. 变和缓;变稳定;做调人,做会场司仪,主持(会议)。***exercise a moderating influence on*** 对…起缓和作用。-**ly** *ad*. 适度,适中,普通。-**ness** *n*.

mod·er·a·tion [ˌmɔdəˈreiʃən; ˏmɑdəˋreʃən] *n*. 1. 缓和,减轻;节制;温和,中庸,适度,中等。2. 稳定,镇定;【物】慢化,延时,减速(作用)。3.〔*pl*.〕(牛津大学)B.A. 学位的第一次考试〔略 mods.〕。~ *in eating and drinking* 节制饮食。***in*** ~ 适中地。

mod·er·a·tism [ˈmɔdərətizəm; ˋmɑdərətɪzm] *n*. (政治、宗教上的)稳健[温和、中庸]主义。-**list** *n*. 稳健主义者。

mod·e·ra·to [ˌmɔdəˈrɑːtəu; ˏmɑdəˋrɑto] *ad*., *a*.〔It.〕【乐】中速地(的),有节制地(的),中板,用中板。*allegro* ~ 中快板。

mod·er·a·tor [ˈmɔdəreitə; ˋmɑdəˏretɚ] *n*. 1. 仲裁者,调解者。2. (牛津大学 B.A. 学位第一次考试的)主考员;(剑桥大学数学优等考试的)监考员。3.〔美〕主席,议长;审判者;【宗】长老会会议主席。4.【物】(原子堆中的)减速剂,慢化剂;【化】阻滞剂,缓和剂。-**ship** *n*. moderator 的职位[任期]。

mod·ern [ˈmɔdən; ˋmɑdɚn] I *a*. 现代的;近代的;现代式[化]的,时新的,新派的,时髦的,摩登的。II *n*. 现代人;近代人;新思想家,现代派人物;【印】近代铅字字体。~ *history* 近代史。~ *languages* 近代语言,现代语言。*a* ~ *army* 现代化部队。~ *automatic weapons* 现代自动武器。~ *dance* 现代舞蹈〔西方近代舞蹈〕。*M- English* 近代英语〔略 Mod. E.〕。*M- Hebrew* 现代希伯来语〔尤指近代以色列语〕。~ *school* [*side*]〔英〕近代学科分部。~ *times* 现代。*the M- Athens* 现代雅典,〔〔英〕爱丁堡,〔美〕波士顿的别名〕。*the M- Babylon* 现代巴比伦〔伦敦市的别名〕。-**ly** *ad*. -**ness** *n*.

mod·ern·ism [ˈmɔdənizəm; ˋmɑdɚnˏɪzəm] *n*. 1. 现代词语;现代习惯,现代用法。2. 现代思潮;现代风尚,现代标准。3.【宗】现代主义(19 世纪末 20 世纪初天主教会内部的一种神学思潮)。

mod·ern·ist [ˈmɔdə(ː)nist; ˋmɑdɚnɪst] *n*. 现代主义者。

mod·ern·is·tic [mɔdəˈnistik; mɑdɚˋnɪstɪk] *a*. 现代派的,现代作风的;现代主义(者)的。

mo·der·ni·ty [mɔˈdəːniti; mɑˋdɝnətɪ] *n*. (*opp*. antiquity) 现代性,新式,现代作风;〔*pl*.〕现代事物。

mod·ern·i·za·tion [ˌmɔdənaiˈzeiʃən; ˏmɑdɚnəˋzeʃən] *n*. 1. 现代化。2. 现代化的事物[版本等]。*achieve* ~ *of science and technology* 实现科学技术的现代化。*produce* ~*s of Shakespeare's plays* 出版莎士比亚剧作的现代化版本。

mod·ern·ize [ˈmɔdə(ː)naiz; ˋmɑdɚnˏaɪz] *vt*., *vi*. 使现代化;近代[现代]化;用现代化方法。

mod·est [ˈmɔdist; ˋmɑdɪst] *a*. 谨慎的,谦虚的,客气的;羞怯的;(尤指妇女)端庄的;优雅的,淑静的,贞节的;有节制的,适度的,适中的;不大的。***Be*** ~ 要谦虚。-**ly** *ad*.

mod·es·ty [ˈmɔdisti; ˋmɑdəstɪ] *n*. 谨慎,谦虚,虚心;(尤指妇女的)端庄,淑静;节制,中肯;朴实;羞怯。*M- helps one to go forward*. 虚心使人进步。

modi [ˈməudai; ˋmodaɪ] *n*. modus 的复数。

mod·i·cum [ˈmɔdikəm; ˋmɑdɪkəm] *n*.〔常用 *sing*.〕一点点,少量。*a* ~ *of sleep* 小睡。

mod·i·fi·a·ble [ˈmɔdifaiəbl; ˋmɑdə͵faɪəbl] *a*. 1. 可修改的,可改变的。2. 可缓和的,可减轻的。3.【语】可修饰的。-**bil·i·ty** *n*.

mod·i·fi·ca·tion [ˌmɔdifiˈkeiʃən; ͵mɑdəfəˋkeʃən] *n*. 变更,更改,修正;改良,改进;缓和;修改;减轻;限制;【生】诱发变异,变态,变体,变型;【语法】修饰;(用变音符号的)母音改变。

mod·i·fi·ca·tor [ˈmɔdifikeitə; ˋmɑdɪfə͵ketɚ] *n*. 1. 更改者;修改者。2.【语法】修饰语。

mod·i·fi·ca·to·ry [ˈmɔdifiˈkeitəri; ˋmadəfə͵ketərɪ] *a*. 修正的;更改的;调整的;缓和的,减轻的;【语法】修饰的。

mod·i·fi·er [ˈmɔdifaiə; ˋmɑdə͵faɪɚ] *n*. 修改者;更改者;【橡胶】改良剂,调节剂;【语法】修饰语。

mod·i·fy [ˈmɔdifai; ˋmɑdə͵faɪ] *vt*. 变更;修改;减轻,缓和,调节;限制;【哲】规定,限定;【语法】修饰;(用变音符号)改变(母音)。～ *one's demands* 减低要求。～ *the terms of the contract* 变更契约条款。*modified wool* 变性羊毛。

mo·dil·lion [məuˈdiljən; məˋdɪljən] *n*.【建】托饰。

mo·di·o·lus [məuˈdaiələs; moˋdaɪələs] *n*. (*pl*. **-o·li** [-lai; -laɪ])【解】蜗轴。

mod·ish [ˈməudiʃ; ˋmodɪʃ] *a*. (古)流行的,时髦的。-**ly** *ad*. -**ness** *n*.

mod·iste [məuˈdiːst; moˋdist] *n*. (F.)(专做妇女衣、帽的)女裁缝。

MODS = manned orbital development station【宇】载人轨道研究站。

mods (英) = moderations 3.

mod·u·la·bil·i·ty [ˌmɔdjuləˈbiliti; ͵mɑdjələˋbɪlətɪ] *n*.【无】调制能力,调制本领。

mod·u·lar [ˈmɔdjulə; ˋmɑdʒʊlɚ] *a*. 1.【数】模的,模数的,系数的。2. 组件的,制成标准尺寸的。

mod·u·lar·i·ty [ˌmɔdjuˈlæriti; ͵mɑdjəˋlærətɪ] *n*.【自】积木性,模块性(指应用模块组装电子计算机等)。

mod·u·late [ˈmɔdjuleit; ˋmɑdʒə͵let] *vt*. 1. 调节,调整(声音等)。2. 缓和,减轻。3.【无】使改变周波数,调制;【乐】使转调,使变调。— *vi*. 1.【乐】变调,转调;【无】调制。2. (美俚)通过民用波段无线电台讲话。

mod·u·la·tion [ˌmɔdjuˈleiʃən; ͵mɑdʒəˋleʃən] *n*. 调整,调节;(声调的)抑扬,变化;【乐】转调,变调;【无】调制。*amplitude* ～ 振幅调制,调幅。*frequency* ～ 频率调制,调频。*over*～ 过(度)调(制)。

mod·u·la·tor [ˈmɔdjuleitə; ˋmɑdʒə͵letɚ] *n*. 调整者,调节者;【无】调制者,调节器。

mod·ule [ˈmɔdjuːl; ˋmɑdʒul] *n*. 1. 测量流水等的单位(1秒100升)。2.【建】圆柱下部半径度。3.【物】模,系数,模数,模量。4.【无】微型组件;组件;模块。5. (太空船上各个独立的)舱。

mod·u·lo [ˈmɔdjuləu; ˋmɑdjʊlo] *prep*.【数】对…模。

mod·u·lus [ˈmɔdjuləs; ˋmɑdjələs] *n*. (*pl*. **-li** [-lai; -laɪ])【数、物】模数,模量;系数。*a* ～ *of elasticity* 弹性模量。

mo·dus [ˈməudəs; ˋmodəs] *n*. (*pl*. ***mo·di*** [-dai; -daɪ], ～***es***) (L.)法,方法,方式。～ ***operandi*** [ɔpəˈrændai; ͵ɑpəˋrændaɪ] 运用法,做法操纵法。～ ***vivendi*** [viˈvendai; vɪˋvendaɪ] 生活方法,生活态度;(争执双方之间的)暂时协定;权宜之计,妥协。

Moe·so-Goth, Moe·so·goth [ˈmiːsəuˌgɔθ; ˋmiso͵gɑθ] *a*. 密西哥德人(公元三世纪古罗马密西亚省的哥德族人)。

Moe·so-Goth·ic, Moe·so·goth·ic [ˌmiːsəuˈgɔθik; ͵misoˋgɑθɪk] *a*. 密西哥德人的;密西哥德语的。

M of E = Maintenance of equipment 设备维修(保养)。

mo·fette, mof·fette [məuˈfet; moˋfɛt] *n*.【地】碳酸喷气孔。

mo·fus·sil [məuˈfʌsil; məˋfʌsl̩] *n*. (Hind.)乡下,乡村。

M of W = Maintenance of way【铁路】养路,线路养护。

mog [mɔg; mɑg] *vi*. (***mogged***; ***mog·ging***) (方) 1. 重步稳步前进。2. 撤退,撤营;离开,移去。

Mo·ga·di·shu, Mo·ga·di·scio [ˌmɔgəˈdiʃuː, ˌmɔgəˈdiʃiəu; ͵mɑgəˋdɪʃu, mɑgəˋdɪʃɪo] *n*. 摩加迪沙(索马里首都)。

mo·gi·la·lia [mɔdʒiˈleiliə; ͵mɑdʒɪˋlelɪə] *n*.【医】口吃;发音困难症。

Mo·gul [məuˈgʌl, ˈməugʌl; moˋgʌl, ˋmogʌl] *n*. 1. (16世纪征服并统治印度的)莫卧儿人(尤指历史上的)蒙古人。2. (m-)(美)富豪,权贵,贵族,专制君主;大人物;货车,火车头。*a high* ～ (美)贵族,大官。*the Great* [*Grand*] ～ 印度莫卧儿帝国的皇帝。

mo·gul [ˈməugl; ˋmogl̩] *n*.【滑雪】滑雪道拐弯处的雪坡。

MOH, M.O.H. = 1. medical officer of health 保健检查官。2. Ministry of Health (英)卫生部。

mo·hair [ˈməuhɛə; ˋmo͵hɛr] *n*. 安哥拉山羊毛;安哥拉山羊毛仿制品。

Moham. = Mohammedan.

Mo·ham·med [məuˈhæmed; moˋhæmɪd] *n*. 穆罕默德(570?—632伊斯兰教教祖)。

Mo·ham·me·dan [məuˈhæmidən; moˋhæmədən] I *a*. 穆罕默德的;伊斯兰教的。II *n*. 伊斯兰教徒,穆罕默德的信徒。-**ism** *n*.

Mo·ha·ve [məuˈhɑːvi; moˋhɑvɪ] I *n*. (*pl*. **-ves**, **-ve**) 1. 莫哈维人(居住在美国亚利桑那地区科罗拉多河两岸的印第安人)。2. 莫哈维语。II *a*. 莫哈维人的。

Mo·hawk [ˈməuhɔːk; ˋmohɔk] *n*. (纽约州中部的)印第安莫霍克族;莫霍克语;【溜冰】莫霍克步(用一冰鞋的一刀刃前进;再用另一冰鞋的另一刀刃后退)。

Mo·he·gan, Mo·hi·can [məuˈhiːgən, məuˈhiːkən; moˋhigən, moˋhikən] *n*. (原住康涅狄格州的印第安族)莫希干族[人]。

moh·ism [ˈməuˌizəm; ˋmoɪzəm] *n*. 墨翟[墨子]的学说;墨家学说。

Mo·ho [ˈməuhəu; ˋmoho] = Mohorovičić discontinuity.

Mo·hole [ˈməuˌhəul; ˋmohol] *n*.【地】超深钻。

Mo·ho·ro·vi·čić discontinuity [ˌməuhəuˈrəuvətʃitʃ; ͵mohoroˋvitʃitʃ]【地】莫霍洛维奇契不连续面,莫霍界面。

Mohs' scale [məuz; moz]【矿】莫氏硬度标。

mo·hur [ˈməuhə; ˋmohɚ] *n*. 印度旧金币名(值15 rupees)。

M.O.I. = Ministry of Information (英)新闻部。

moi [mwɑː; mwɑ] ***pro***. (F.) 我,我本人(带有幽默或自我贬低的用法)。

moi·der [ˈmɔidə; ˋmɔɪdɚ] *vt*. (英方) 1. 使混乱;迷惑,使摸不着头脑。2. 使分心,打扰。— *vi*. 1. 发呓语。2. 闲荡;瞎走。

moi·dore [ˈmɔidɔː; ˋmɔɪdor] *n*. 摩伊多(葡萄牙旧金币名)。

moi·e·ty [ˈmɔiəti; ˋmɔɪətɪ] *n*.【法】(财产等的)一半;二分之一;一部分。*only a small* ～ *of*... 仅仅一小部分。

moil [mɔil; mɔɪl] I *vi*. 劳动,辛辛苦苦做工。II *n*. 辛苦,苦工;混乱;麻烦。*toil and* ～ 辛辛苦苦做工。-**er** *n*., -**ingly** *ad*.

Moi·ra [ˈmɔirə; ˋmɔɪrə] *n*.【希神】命运。

moire [mwɑː; mwɑr] *n*. 云[波]纹绸(又叫 ～ antique)。

moi·ré [ˈmwɑːrei; mwaˋre] I *a*. 有波纹的,有云纹的;波纹的;云纹绸似的。II *n*. 1. 波纹,云纹。2. = moire.

moist [mɔist; mɔɪst] *a*. 1. 润湿的,潮湿的。2. 多雨的;【医】流出物多的;湿性的,有分泌物的。3. (眼睛)泪汪汪的;易伤感的。～ *colours* (软膏状)水彩颜料。～ *season* 雨季。～ *steam* 湿蒸气,饱和水蒸气。*be emotionally*

～容易伤感[激动]。-ly *ad*. -ness *n*.

mois·ten [ˈmɔisn; ˋmɔɪsn] *vt*., *vi*. 濡湿,弄湿;变湿。*be ～ed by rain* 被雨淋湿。～ *at the sight of* 一见…就泪眼汪汪。～ *at one's eyes* 含泪。～ ***one's clay*** [***lips***, ***throat***] 喝酒。

mois·ten·er [ˈmɔisnə; ˋmɔɪsnɚ] *n*. 湿润器。

mois·ture [ˈmɔistʃə; ˋmɔɪstʃə] *n*. 湿气,水分,潮湿;湿度;(空气中的)水蒸气;泪。～ **equivalent**【土壤】持水当量。～ **regain** 回潮。～-**free**, -**less** *a*. 没湿气[水分]的,干燥的。

mois·tur·ize [ˈmɔistʃəˌraiz; ˋmɔɪstʃəˏraɪz] *vt*. (*-ized*; *-iz·ing*) 给(皮肤、空气等)增加[提供]水分。—*vi*. 用润肤霜滋润皮肤。

Mo·ja·ve, Mo·ha·ve [məuˈhɑːviː; moˋhɑvɪ] **I** *n*. **1**. 莫哈维人。**2**. 莫哈维语。**II** *a*. 莫哈维人的。

moke [məuk; mok] *n*. 〔英俚〕驴子;笨人,傻子;〔美俚,蔑〕黑人;〔澳俚〕小马;驽马。

MOL = manned orbiting laboratory【宇】载人(绕)轨道实验室。

mol [məul; mol] *n*.【化】克分子(量) = mole[4].

mol. = molecular; molecule.

mo·la [ˈməulə; ˋmolə] *n*.【动】翻车鱼。

mo·lal [ˈməuləl; ˋmoləl] *a*.【化】**1**. (重量)克分子的。**2**. 重模的,(重量)克分子(浓度)的。～ *solution* 重模溶液。-**i·ty** [məuˈlæliti; moˋlælətɪ] *n*. 重模;(重量)克分子浓度。

mo·lar[1] [ˈməulə; ˋmolɚ] **I** *a*. 磨的,适宜于[用来]磨的;臼齿的,臼齿附近的。**II** *n*. 臼齿;〔*pl*.〕〔美俚〕牙齿。*a false* ～ 小臼齿。

mo·lar[2] [ˈməulə; ˋmolɚ] *a*.【物】质量(上)的;【化】(体积)克分子的;容模的;(体积)克分子(浓度)的。-**i·ty** [məuˈlæriti; moˋlærətɪ] *n*. 体积克分子浓度;容模。

Mo·lasse [məˈlɑːs; məˋlɑs] *n*.【地】磨砾层(相)。

mo·las·ses [məˈlæsiz; məˋlæsɪz] *n*. 〔*pl*.〕〔作单数用〕〔美〕糖浆,糖蜜。

mold [məuld; mold] = mould.

Mol·da·vi·a [mɔlˈdeivjə; mɑlˋdevɪə] *n*. 摩尔达维亚〔原苏联加盟共和国〕。-**n** **1**. *a*. 摩尔达维亚的。**2**. *n*. 摩尔达维亚人。

mold·er [ˈməuldə; ˋmoldɚ] = moulder.

mold·ing = moulding.

Mol·do·va [mɔlˈdɔvɑː; mɑlˋdɑvɑ] *n*. 摩尔多瓦〔欧洲一国家名〕。-**n** *n*., *a*.

mold·y = mouldy.

mole[1] [məul; mol] *n*. **1**.【动】鼹鼠;田鼠。**2**. 潜伏很深的间谍;在黑暗中工作的人。***as blind as a*** ～ 全盲,全瞎。～-**cast** = molehill. ～ **cricket**【虫】蝼蛄。～**hill** 鼹鼠窝,鼹鼠丘,丘垤(*make a mountain out of a* ～ *hill* 小题大做,夸大)。～ **plough** 挖沟犁,鼹鼠犁。～ **rat** 地鼠。～ **skin** 鼹鼠皮;(鼹鼠皮一样的)厚布;〔*pl*.〕鼹皮布裤。

mole[2] [məul; mol] *n*. 黑痣。

mole[3] [məul; mol] *n*. 防波堤;人工港。

mole[4] [məul; mol] *n*.【化】克分子(量),克模;衡分子。～ **fraction**【化】克分子份数。

mole[5] [məul; mol] *n*.【医】胎块。

mo·lec·u·lar [məuˈlekjulə; məˋlɛkjəlɚ] *a*. 分子的,由分子形成的,分子内[间]的。～ **attraction** 分子引力。～ **biology** 分子生物学。～ **conductivity** 克分子电导[传导]率。～ **farming** 分子养殖业〔指利用动植物研制药用化合物,亦作 ～ pharming〕。～ **film** 分子层,分子膜。～ **force**【化】分子力。～ **formula** 分子式。～ **knife**【生化】分子刀〔一种能破坏艾滋病病毒繁殖遗传指令的酶〕。～ **medicine** 分子医学。～ **rays** 分子射线。～ **sieve**【物】分子筛。～ **theory** 分子(理)论。～ **weight** 分子量。-**ly** *ad*.

mo·lec·u·lar·i·ty [məuˌlekjuˈlæriti; məˏlɛkjəˋlærətɪ] *n*. 分子状态;分子性;分子作用。

mol·e·cule [ˈmɔlikjuːl, ˈməu-; ˋmɑləˏkjul, ˋmo-] *n*.【物、化】分子;克分子;〔口〕微小颗粒。*gram* ～ 克分子。*nonpolar* ～*s* 无极(性)分子。*polar* ～*s* 有极分子。

mo·lest [məuˈlest; məˋlɛst] *vt*. 使烦恼,折磨,欺负,作弄;无故向人攀谈,恶意干涉,妨害;(对女性)动手动脚,调戏。-**er** *n*. -**ta·tion** [ˌməulesˈteiʃən; ˏmoləsˋteʃən] *n*.

mol·et [ˈmɔlit; ˋmɑlɪt] *n*. = mullet.

mo·line [məuˈlain, ˈməulin; moˋlaɪn, ˋmolaɪn] *a*. 四臂端分叉后弯的十字架的。

Moll [mɔl; mɑl] *n*. 莫尔〔女子名, Mary 的昵称〕。

moll [mɔl; mɑl] *n*. 〔俚〕妓女;〔美俚〕盗贼的姘妇,女流氓,女匪。

mol·la(h) [ˈmɔlə; ˋmɑlə] *n*. = mullah.

mol·les·cent [məˈlesnt; məˋlɛsnt] *a*. 柔软的;趋于缓和的。-**cence** *n*.

mol·li·fi·ca·tion [ˌmɔlifiˈkeiʃən; ˏmɑləfɪˋkeʃən] *n*. **1**. 平息,缓和,安慰。**2**. 使人安慰的事物;使缓和的事物。*No* ～ *of her anger appeared likely*. 她的怒气看来无法缓和。

mol·li·fi·er [ˈmɔlifaiə; ˋmɑləˋfaɪɚ] *n*. **1**. 安慰者。**2**.【医】缓和剂,镇静剂。

mol·li·fy [ˈmɔlifai; ˋmɑləˏfaɪ] *vt*. 〔罕〕使软化;缓和;减轻;使平静,平息,抚慰。

mol·lusc [ˈmɔləsk; ˋmɑləsk] *n*.【动】软体动物。

Mol·lus·ca [mɔˈlʌskə; məˋlʌskə] *n*. 〔*pl*.〕【动】软体动物(门)。

mol·lus·can [mɔˈlʌskən; məˋlʌskən] **I** *a*. 软体动物(门)的。**II** *n*. 软体动物。

mol·lus·coid [mɔˈlʌskɔid; məˋlʌskɔɪd] *n*., *a*. 软体动物(似的);拟软体动物(的)。

Mol·lus·coi·da, Mol·lus·coi·de·a [ˌmɔləsˈkɔidə, -diə; ˏmɑləsˋkɔɪdə, -dɪə] *n*. 〔*pl*.〕【动】拟软体动物类。

mol·lus·cous [mɔˈlʌskəs; məˋlʌskəs] *a*. = molluscan.

mol·lusk [ˈmɔləsk; ˋmɑləsk] *n*. = mollusc.

Moll·wei·de projection [ˈmɔːlvaidə; ˋmɔlvaɪdə]【测】摩尔魏特投影。

Mol·ly, Mol·lie [ˈmɔli; ˋmɑlɪ] *n*. 莫莉〔女子名, Mary 的昵称〕。

mol·ly [ˈmɔli; ˋmɑlɪ] *n*. 〔口〕娇嫩的男人〔男少年〕。

mol·ly·cod·dle [ˈmɔlikɔdl; ˋmɑlɪˏkɑdl] **I** *n*. 女人气的[柔弱的、没骨气的]男子;懦夫;娇生惯养的人。**II** *vt*. 溺爱,娇养。

Mo·loch [ˈməulɔk; ˋmolɑk] *n*. **1**. 莫洛克神〔古 Phoenicia 人的火神,以儿童为祭品〕;〔喻〕要求重大牺牲的可怕力量[势力]。**2**. 〔m-〕【动】(澳大利亚)四脚蛇,棘蜥。

Mo·lo·kai [ˌməuləuˈkai; ˏmoloˋkaɪ] *n*. 莫洛凯〔美国夏威夷群岛中的一岛,是麻疯病人的隔离地〕。

mo·los·sus [məˈlɔsəs; məˋlɑsəs] *n*. (诗歌中)三个长音节构成的音步。

Mo·lo·tov [ˈmɔlətɔf; ˋmɑlətɑf], **V. M.** 莫洛托夫〔1890—1986,苏联外交家和政治家〕。～ **bread basket** 〔俚〕莫洛托夫面包篮〔一种炸弹,内装许多小燃烧弹,空投后分散落下〕。～ **cocktail** 〔俚〕燃烧瓶〔一种反坦克手榴弹〕。

molt [məult; molt] *vi*., *vt*., *n*. = moult.

mol·ten [ˈməultən; ˋmoltn] **I** melt 的过去分词。**II** *a*. 熔化了的,熔融的;浇铸的。*a* ～ *image* 铸像。～ *pig* 铁水。

mol·to [ˈmɔltəu; ˋmolto] *ad*. 〔It.〕【乐】很,最。～ ***adagio*** 极慢。

Mo·luc·cas [məˈlʌkəz; məˋlʌkəz] *n*. (印尼的)摩鹿加群岛〔又叫 Spice Islands〕。

mol. wt. = molecular weight 分子量。

mo·ly[1] [ˈməuli; ˋmolɪ] *n*. **1**. (传说中有魔力的)白花黑根草。**2**.【植】黄花茖葱。

mol·y² [ˈmɔli; ˋmɑlɪ] ***n.*** 【化】钼(= molybdenum)。

mo·lyb·date [məˈlibdeit; məˋlɪbdet] ***n.*** 【化】钼酸盐。

mo·lyb·de·n·ite [mɔˈlibdinait, ˈmɔlibˈdiːnait; məˋlɪbdɪˏnaɪt, ˋmɑlɪbˋdinaɪt] ***n.*** 【矿】辉钼矿。

mo·lyb·de·num [mɔˈlibdinəm; moˋlɪbdənəm] ***n.*** 【化】钼。

mo·lyb·dic [məˈlibdik; məˋlɪbdɪk] ***a.*** 【化】钼的〔指含三价钼或六价钼的盐的〕。

mo·lyb·dous [məˈlibdəs; məˋlɪbdəs] ***a.*** 【化】二价钼的;亚钼的。

mom [mɔm; mɑm] ***n.*** 〔口〕妈妈(= mamma)。~ ***and pop store*** [***stand***] 夫妻店,家庭经营的小零售店[小摊]〔亦作 ma and pa〕。

Mom·ba·sa [mɔmˈbæsə; mɑmˋbæsə] ***n.*** **1.** 蒙巴萨岛〔肯尼亚〕。**2.** 蒙巴萨〔肯尼亚港市〕。

mome [məum; mom] ***n.*** 〔古〕笨蛋,傻瓜。

mo·ment [ˈməumənt; ˋmomənt] ***n.*** **1.** 一转眼功夫,片刻,瞬息,刹那;时刻。**2.** 时机,机会;场合;危机;当前。**3.** 重要,紧要;【哲】要素,契机。**4.**【物】矩,转矩,力矩;势头;能率;积率。**5.**【统计】动差。**6.** (历史发展的)阶段。*One* ~. = *Half a* ~. = *Wait a* ~. 等一会儿。*There is not a* ~ *to be lost*. 刻不容缓。*Go this very* ~. 现在马上去吧。*seize the* ~ 抓住机会。*matter of great* ~ 重大事件。***at a*** **~*'s notice*** 一经通知;随时;立刻,马上。***at any*** ~ 随时,无论什么时候,不知何时。***at*** **~*s*** 时时,常常。***at odd*** **~*s*** 抽暇,空闲时。***at the last critical*** ~在最后关头。***at the*** ~ 此刻[现在];(正当)那时[过去]。***at the same*** ~同时。***every*** ~时时刻刻,每一刻。***for a*** ~ 片刻,一会儿。***for*** [***at***] ***the*** ~暂时,现在。(*the man*) ***for this*** [***the***] ~能应付当前危局的(人)。***half a*** ~ 等一下,稍等片刻;马上,立刻。***in a*** ~ 立即,马上,一会儿。***in a*** ~ ***of anger*** 趁着气愤,一时气愤。***in the*** ~ ***of danger*** 一到危险关头,一有危险。~ ***of couple*** 【机】偶矩。~ ***of force*** 【物】力矩。~ ***of inertia*** 【机】惯性矩;【物】转动矩量。~ ***of stability*** 【机】安定矩。~ ***of truth*** **1.** 斗牛士击杀牛的时刻。**2.** 关键时刻〔检验人的本色,或使人面对事实的时刻〕。***of little*** ~ = ***of no*** ~不重要的,无足轻重的。***of the*** ~此刻,现在。***one*** ~ = half a ~. ***the man of the*** ~当代要人;时人。***the*** (***very***) ~〔用作连词引出时间副词子句〕一…(就) (= as soon as) (*I tell him the* ~ *he comes in*. 他一进来我就告诉他)。***to the*** (***very***) ~ 准时,不差片刻,正好。(***up***) ***on the*** ~ 一…马上就。~ **coefficient** 【机】矩系数。

mo·men·tal [məuˈmentl; moˋmɛntl̩] ***a.*** 【机】动量的;力矩的。*a* ~ *ellipse* 动量椭圆。

mo·men·ta·ri·ly [ˈməuməntərili; ˋmomənˌtɛrəlɪ] ***ad.*** 一会儿,暂时;时时刻刻;每刻。

mo·men·tar·i·ness [ˈməuməntərinis; ˋmomənˌtɛrɪnɪs] ***n.*** **1.** 顷刻,瞬息。**2.**〔现罕〕随时,经常。**3.** 随时可能发生。

mo·men·ta·ry [ˈməuməntəri; ˋmomənˌtɛrɪ] ***a.*** 瞬息间的,顷刻的,暂时的;时时刻刻的。*in* ~ *expectation* 没有一刻不盼望。

mo·ment·ly [ˈməuməntli; ˋmoməntlɪ] ***ad.*** = momentarily.

mo·men·to [məˈmentəu; məˋmɛnto] ***n.*** = memento.

mo·men·tous [məuˈmentəs; moˋmɛntəs] ***a.*** 重大的,重要的,声势浩大的(斗争)。**-ly** ***ad.*** **-ness** ***n.***

mo·men·tum [məuˈmentəm; moˋmɛntəm] ***n.*** (*pl.* ~*s*, *-ta* [-tə; -tə]) 【物】动量;【火箭】总冲量;〔口〕惰性;势头;要素,契机。*the* ~ *of attack* 进攻的锐气[劲头]。

mom·ism [ˈmɔmizəm; ˋmɑmɪzəm] ***n.*** 唯母是尊,母亲崇拜。

Momm·sen [ˈmɔmzən; ˋmɑmsn̩], **Theodor** 蒙森〔1817—1903,德国历史学家〕。

Mo·mus [ˈməuməs; ˋmoməs] ***n.*** 【希神】莫墨斯〔嘲弄之神;爱挑错儿的人〕。*a disciple* [*son*, *daughter*] *of* ~ 爱挑错儿的人;滑稽的人。

Mon [məun; mon] ***n.*** (*pl.* ~(*s*)) **1.** 孟族人〔缅甸仰光东部的一个少数民族〕。**2.** 孟族语。

mon [mɔn; mɑn] ***n.*** 〔Scot., North Eng.〕 man 的变体。

Mon. = **1.** Monday. **2.** Monastery. **3.** 〔It.〕 *Monsignor*(*e*).

mon. = **1.** monetary. **2.** monastery.

mon- *comb. f.* = mono.

Mo·na [ˈməunə; ˋmonə] ***n.*** 莫娜〔女子名〕。

mon·a·c(h)al [ˈmɔnəkəl; ˋmɑnəkl̩] ***a.*** 修道士的,僧侣的;修道生活的;修道院的。

mon·a·chism [ˈmɔnəkizəm; ˋmɑnəˌkɪzəm] ***n.*** 修道(生活);修道院制度。**-chist** ***a.***, ***n.*** 修道主义的(者)。

mon·a·chize [ˈmɔnəkaiz; ˋmɑnəˌkaɪz] ***vt.*** 使成为僧侣[修道士]。—***vi.*** 当修道士,过修道士生活。

mon·acid [mɔˈnæsid; mɑnˋæsɪd] ***a.*** 【化】一酸的。

Mon·a·co [ˈmɔnəkəu; ˋmɑnəˌko] ***n.*** **1.** 摩纳哥〔欧洲〕。**2.** 摩纳哥〔摩纳哥首都〕。

mo·nad [ˈmɔnæd; ˋmɑnæd] ***n.*** 【哲】单子,单元〔Leibnitz 哲学中的实在的、非物质的、基本单位〕;【化】一价物;一价基;【物】单轴;【生】单分体,单孢体;个体;【原】单原子元素。**-ic**, **-i·cal** ***a.***

mon·a·del·phous [ˌmɔnəˈdelfəs; ˏmɑnəˋdɛlfəs] ***a.*** 【植】单体(雄蕊)的。

mon·ad·ism, **mon·ad·ol·ogy** [ˈmɔnædizəm, ˌmɔnəˈdɔlədʒi; ˋmɑnədɪzm, ˏmɑnədˋɑlədʒɪ] ***n.*** 【哲】单子论〔德国唯心主义哲学家莱布尼兹(Leibnitz) 的学说,认为宇宙是由单子组成的〕。

mo·nad·nock [məˈnædnɔk; məˋnædnɑk] ***n.*** 【地】残丘。

mon·ak·er ***n.*** = moniker.

Mo·na Li·sa [ˈməunəˈliːsə, -zə; ˋmonə (ˋmɑnə) ˋlisə, -zə] 蒙娜·丽莎〔意大利画家达·芬奇 (*Leonardo da Vinci*) 的名肖像画名,亦称乔康达夫人 (*la Gioconda*)〕。

mo·nan·drous [mɔˈnændrəs; məˋnændrəs] ***a.*** **1.**【植】具一雄蕊的。**2.** 一夫制的。

mo·nan·dry [mɔˈnændri; məˋnændrɪ] ***n.*** 一夫制;【植】单雄蕊式。

mon·arch [ˈmɔnək; ˋmɑnɚk] ***n.*** **1.** 王,帝王,君主,元首,统治者。**2.**〔喻〕(大)王。**3.** 大花蝶。**4.**【植】单原型。*an absolute* ~专制君主。*the* ~ *of the forest* 森林之王〔树木中的橡树,动物中的狮子或老虎〕。*the* ~ *of the glen* 溪谷之王〔雄鹿〕。

mo·nar·chal [mɔˈnɑːkəl; məˋnɑrkl̩] ***a.*** 〔诗〕君主似的;帝王似的;君主政治的。**-ly** ***ad.***

mo·nar·chi·al [mɔˈnɑːkiəl; məˋnɑrkɪəl] ***a.*** = monarchal.

Mo·nar·chi·an·ism [məˈnɑːkiənizəm; məˋnɑrkɪənˌɪzəm] ***n.*** 唯一神论〔二、三世纪基督教某些教派的教义,认为三位一体的三位乃上帝的化身〕。

mo·nar·chic, **mo·nar·chi·cal** [mɔˈnɑːkik, -kikəl; məˋnɑrkɪk, -kɪkl̩] ***a.*** 君主(国)的,君主政体的,帝制的。

mon·arch·ism [ˈmɔnəkizəm; ˋmɑnɚkɪzəm] ***n.*** 君主主义;君主政治[制度]。

mon·arch·ist [ˈmɔnəkist; ˋmɑnɚkɪst] ***n.*** 君主主义者,拥护君主制度者。

mon·ar·chis·tic [ˌmɔnɑːˈkistik; ˏmɑnɑrˋkɪstɪk] ***a.*** 君主主义的,君主政治的。

mon·ar·chy [ˈmɔnəki; ˋmɑnɚkɪ] ***n.*** 君主政治,君主政体;君主国;独裁君主权,大权。*an absolute* ~君主专制制度。*a constitutional* [*limited*] ~君主立宪制度。*a despotic* ~ 专制君主政体;专制君主国。

mo·nar·da [məˈnɑːdə; məˋnɑrdə] ***n.*** 长叶薄荷 (= horsemint)。

mon·as·te·ri·al [ˌmɔnəsˈtiəriəl; ˏmɑnəˋstɪrɪəl] ***a.*** 寺院

的，修道院的。

mon·as·ter·y [ˈmɔnəstri; ˋmɑnəsˏtɛrɪ] ***n.*** 修道院，寺院，庙宇。

mo·nas·tic [məˈnæstik; məˋnæstɪk] **I** ***a.*** **1.** 修道院的；庙宇的，寺院的。**2.** 僧侣的；修道士的；修女的。**3.** 出家的；禁欲的。**II** ***n.*** 修道士；僧侣；修女；尼姑。**-ti·cal** ***a.***, **-ti·cal·ly** ***ad.***

mo·nas·ti·cism [məˈnæstisizəm; məˋnæstəˏsɪzəm] ***n.*** 寺院制度；修道生活；出家；禁欲主义。

mon·a·tom·ic [ˌmɔnəˈtɔmik; ˏmɑnəˋtɑmɪk] ***a.*** 【化】(具)单原子的；含有一个可代换原子的；一价的，独价的。

mon·au·ral [mɔnˈɔːrəl; mɑnˋɔrəl] ***a.*** **1.** 单耳(听觉)的。**2.** 单声道的。**-ly** ***ad.***

mon·ax·i·al [mɔnˈæksiəl; mɑnˈæksɪl] ***a.*** 仅有单轴的；一轴的。

mon·a·zite [ˈmɔnəˌzait; ˋmɑnəˏzaɪt] ***n.*** 【地】独居石。

Mond [mɔnd; mɑnd] ***n.*** 蒙德〔男子名〕。

mon·daine [mõuŋˈden; mʊŋˋden]〔F.〕**I** ***n.*** 社交界的时髦女人；俗气的女人。**II** ***a.*** 时髦的；俗气的。

Mon·day [ˈmʌndi, ˈmʌndei; ˋmʌndɪ, ˋmʌnde] ***n.*** 星期一，礼拜一。***a*** ～ ***morning quarterback***〔口〕放马后炮的人，事后诸葛亮。***Black*** ～〔学俚〕(放假后的)开学第一天。***blue*** ～ **1.**〔口〕烦闷的星期一〔相对于欢乐的周末而言〕；〔喻〕精神沮丧的时期。**2.** 四旬斋(Lent)前的星期一。***Mad*** ～ 忙乱的星期一〔指交易所这一天特别忙乱〕。***St.*** [***Saint***] ～ 懒懒散散、工作很少的星期一。**-ly** ***ad.***〔美〕每星期一；在任何星期一。

Mon·days [ˈmʌndiz, -deiz; ˋmʌndɪz, -dez] ***ad.*** 每星期一。

mon·day·ish [ˈmʌndiiʃ; ˋmʌndɪɪʃ] ***a.***〔口〕(由于星期日过于劳累以致)星期一不想做事的；疲倦的。

monde [mɔːnd; mɔ̃d] ***n.***〔F.〕**1.** 时髦社会；社交界上流社会(= beau ～)。**2.** 个人的生活圈子；社会。

mon·dial [ˈmɔndiəl; ˋmɑndɪəl] ***a.*** 全世界的。

mon Dieu [muŋ ˈdjəː; muŋ ˋdjɝ]〔F.〕上帝呀！哎呀！(= my God)。

mo·ne·cious [məˈniːʃəs; məˋniʃəs] ***a.*** 雌雄同株的，雌雄同体的(= monoecious)。

Mo·nel [məuˈnel; moˋnel] **metal**【冶】莫涅耳合金〔镍、铜、铁、锰的合金，有抗酸性〕。

mo·ne·tar·ism [ˈmʌnitərizəm; ˋmʌnɪtərɪzəm] ***n.***【经】货币主义〔一种主张控制货币增长率的经济学理论〕。

mo·ne·tar·ize [ˈmʌnitəraiz; ˋmʌnɪtəraɪz] ***vt.*** 使货币化。

mo·ne·tar·y [ˈmʌnitəri; ˋmʌnəˏtɛrɪ] ***a.*** 货币的；金钱的；金融的；财政(上)的。*the* ～ *system* 货币制度。*a* ～ *unit* 货币单位。***in*** ～ ***difficulties*** 财政困难。**-i·ly** ***ad.***

mon·e·tize [ˈmʌnitaiz; ˋmʌnəˏtaɪz] ***vt.*** **1.** 把…作为法定货币。**2.** 使具有货币性质。**3.** 把…铸成货币。*demonetize gold and* ～ *silver* 停止把黄金作为法定货币，而把白银作为法定货币。**-za·tion** [ˌmɔnitaiˈzeiʃən; ˏmʌnətɪˋzeʃən] ***n.***

mon·ey [ˈmʌni; ˋmʌnɪ] ***n.*** **1.** 货币；钱，金钱。**2.** 财产，财富，财力。**3.**〔主 *pl.*〕(特种)货币；通货；〔*pl.*〕〔古〕【法】金额〔常用 monies 这一特殊复数写法〕。**4.**【经】交换媒介物，货物货币。**5.** 大富翁；金融集团。**6.** (优胜)奖金。*fairy* ～ (终要变成树叶的)魔钱；拾得的钱。*paper* ～ 纸币。*ready* ～现金。*soft* ～〔美口〕纸币。*hard* ～ 硬币。*small* ～零钱。*What's the* ～? 要多少钱？价钱是多少？*Those with* ～ *should contribute* ～. 有钱出钱。*There is* ～ *in it.* 可以赚钱，有利可图。***at the*** ～ = *for the* ～. ***be in the*** ～〔俚〕有钱，富裕；(在赛狗、赛马中)得奖，赌胜，赢。***be made of*** ～ 钱多得不得了。***cheap at the*** ～ 价钱便宜。***coin*** ～〔口〕大赚其钱，暴发。***covered*** ～〔美〕国库存款。***everybody's*** [***everyman's***] ～〔口〕人人欢迎的东西 (*He's not everybody's* ～. 他不是人人都欢迎的人)。***for love or*** ～ 无论怎样都。***for*** ～ 为钱；【商】直接[现款]交易。***for my*** ～〔口〕在我看来；正合我意 (*He is the man for my* ～. 他是合我心意的人)。***for the*** ～ 照所付的代价。***get one's*** ～***'s worth*** (钱花得)合算，值得；无损失。***in the*** ～ = *be in the* ～. ***keep in*** ～ 借给钱，垫钱。***lose*** ～ 亏本 (*over*)。*make* ～ 赚钱，发财〔*cf.* ～-making〕。***make*** ～ (***out***) ***of*** 用…赚钱。～ ***crops*** 专供销售的农作物。～ ***down*** 现金，现款。～ ***for jam***〔英俚〕容易赚的钱。***M- makes the mare*** (***to***) ***go.***〔谚〕有钱能使鬼推磨；金钱万能。～ ***market*** 金融市场。～ ***of account*** 记账货币〔如美国的 mill，英国的 guinea〕。～ ***on*** [***at***] ***call*** = ***call-money*** 随时可以收回的借款。～ ***on the line***【美拳】当天卖票收入。～ ***out of hand*** = ～ down. ***M- talks.***〔美〕金钱万能。***on the*** ～〔美俚〕在最适当的时间[地点]。***out of*** ～ 拮据；吃亏 (*by*)。***out of the*** ～〔美〕赛马输掉。***raise*** ～ ***on*** 以…抵押筹措款项。***sink*** ～ 浪费金钱。***throw good*** ～ ***after bad*** 一再吃亏。～**bag** ***n.*** 钱袋，钱包；〔*pl.*〕〔口、喻〕财富，财产；〔*pl.*〕〔俚〕富翁，守财奴。～ **belt** 钱带〔里边有放钱小格子的带子〕。～ **bill** 财政法案。～ **box** 钱箱。～ **broker**, ～ **changer**, ～ **dealer** 货币兑换商。～**changing** 货币兑换(尤指外币兑换)。～**-grubber** 贪财谋利的人。～**-grubbing** 贪财谋利。～**lender** 放债的人。～**-maker** 会赚钱的人；赚钱的东西。～**making** **1.** ***a.*** 贪财谋利的，很会赚钱的；(事业等)有利的。**2.** ***n.*** 赚钱，积财。～**man** 金融专家。～ **market** 金融市场，金融界。～**matter** (金钱上的)借贷事件；〔主 *pl.*〕金钱[财政]问题。～ **order** 汇票，邮政汇票。～ **player**【美运】职业运动家。～ **position**【美运】比赛胜利者(尤指赛马的)。～ **rates** 利息。～**'s worth** 可变钱的东西；金钱上的价值。～ **spinner** (传说爬到身上就会使人走运的)财喜小蜘蛛；投机[放债]发财的人；很赚钱的东西。～(**-**)**washing** 洗钱(使非法获得的金钱取得合法地位)。～**wort**【植】铜钱状珍珠菜。

mon·eyed [ˈmʌnid; ˋmʌnɪd] ***a.*** **1.** 富有的，有钱的。**2.** 金钱(上)的。～ *interest* 金钱关系；财界，金融界；金融业者；财界人物。～ *assistance* 金钱上的援助。

mon·ey·er [ˈmʌniə; ˋmʌnɪɚ] ***n.*** 铸币人。

'mong [mʌŋ; mʌŋ] ***prep.***〔诗〕= among.

mon·ger [ˈmʌŋgə; ˋmʌŋgɚ] ***n.***〔英〕〔主要构成复合词〕…商，…贩子：fish*monger*, iron*monger*, scandal*monger*, etc.

mon·go [ˈmɔŋgəu; ˋmɑŋgo] ***n.*** (*pl.* ***-gos***) 蒙戈〔蒙古货币名，等于 1/100 图格里克〕。

Mon·gol [ˈmɔŋgɔl; ˋmɑŋgəl] ***n.***, ***a.*** 蒙古人[语]；蒙古人[语]的。

Mon·go·lia [mɔŋˈgəuliə; mɑŋˋgoljə] ***n.*** **1.** 蒙古〔亚洲〕。**2.** 内蒙古。*Inner* ～ 内蒙。*the Inner* ～ *Autonomous Region* 内蒙古自治区。

Mon·go·li·an [mɔŋˈgəuljən; mɑŋˋgolɪən] **I** ***n.*** **1.** 蒙古人[语]。**2.**【医】先天愚型病人。**II** ***a.*** **1.** 蒙古(人种)的，黄种人的。**2.**【医】(患)先天愚型病的。～ **idiocy**【医】= Mongolism. ～ **People's Republic** 蒙古人民共和国。～ **race** 黄种。

Mon·gol·ic [mɔŋˈgɔlik; mɑŋˋgɑlɪk] ***n.***, ***a.*** 蒙古人[语](的)。

Mon·gol·ism [ˈmɔŋgəlizəm; ˋmɑŋgəlɪzəm] ***n.***【医】先天性愚型〔一种先天性畸形病症，有扁平颅、斜眼、短指等症状〕。

Mon·gol·oid [ˈmɔŋgəlɔid; ˋmɑŋgəlˏɔɪd] **I** ***a.*** (像)蒙古人种的；蒙古人[族]的。**II** ***n.*** 蒙古人种，黄种人。

mon·goos(**e**) [ˈmɔŋguːs; ˋmɑŋgus] ***n.*** **1.**【动】獴哥，麝(香)猫。**2.** ～ lemur【动】獴哥狐猴(= Lemur mongoz)。

mon·grel [ˈmʌŋgrəl; ˋmʌŋgrəl] **I** ***n.*** 杂种(动植物)；(特指)杂种狗；〔蔑〕杂种，混血儿。**II** ***a.*** 杂种的，混血的。**-grel·ize** ***vt.*** 使成杂种。

M

mongst [mʌŋst; mʌŋst] ***prep.*** = amongst.
mo·ni·al [ˈməuniəl; ˋmonɪəl] ***n.*** = mullion.
Mon·i·ca [ˈmɔnikə; ˋmɑnɪkə] ***n.*** 莫妮卡〔女子名〕。
mon·ied [ˈmʌnid; ˋmʌnɪd] ***a.*** = moneyed.
mon·ies [ˈmʌnis; ˋmʌnɪz] ***n.*** 〔罕〕money 3. 的复数。
mon·i·ker, mon·i·cker [ˈmɔnikə; ˋmɑnəkɚ] ***n.*** **1.** 徒步旅行者认路的记号。**2.**〔俚〕名字;外号,绰号。
mo·nil·i·form [məuˈniliˌfɔːm; moˋnɪləˏfɔrm] ***a.*** 念珠状的;(尤指)【生】(如茎和触角的)项圈形的。
mon·ish [ˈmɔniʃ; ˋmɑnɪʃ] ***vt.*** 〔古〕**1.** 告诫;警告。**2.** 规谏。**3.** 敦促;劝告。**4.** (以警告方式)通知,提醒(= admonish)。
mon·ism [ˈmɔnizəm; ˋmɑnɪzəm] ***n.***【哲】一元论;【生】一元发生说。*idealistic* [*materialistic*] ~ 唯心[唯物]一元论。
mon·ist [ˈmɔnist; ˋmonɪst] ***n.*** 一元论者。
mon·is·tic, mon·is·ti·cal [mɔˈnistik(əl); moˋnɪstɪk(əl)] ***a.*** 一元论的。
mo·ni·tion [məuˈniʃən; moˋnɪʃən] ***n.*** **1.** 告诫,警告;(危险等的)预兆。**2.** (法院的)传票;(主教、宗教法庭的)告诫书。
mo·ni·tor [ˈmɔnitə; ˋmɑnətɚ] **I** ***n.*** **1.** 告诫物,提醒物;〔古〕忠告者;劝告[告诫、警告]者。**2.** 班[级]长,教务助理生,导生。**3.** (水利、采矿用的)水枪,喷射口。**4.**【海】浅水炮舰。**5.**【无】(对外国广播等的)监听员[器];监视器,监控器,放射能检验器;(火箭的)追踪器;【火箭】稳定装置;【影】调音员。**6.**【计】(电脑的)显示器。**7.**【动】大壁虎,巨蜥。**II** ***vi.***, ***vt.***【无】监听(外国广播);监督,监视;监控;检验,检查;调节;探索,追踪。*a pilot* ~【空】自动驾驶仪。~ **roof**, ~ **top**〔美〕(客车等的)采光屋顶,通风顶。~ **screen** 检查[选择]播送内容的电视屏。
mon·i·to·ri·al [ˌmɔniˈtɔːriəl; ˏmɑnəˋtorɪəl] ***a.*** 劝告者的;班长的;教务助理生的;使用监听器[监视器]的;劝告的,警告的。*the* ~ *system* 导生制。
mon·i·tor·ship [ˈmɔnitəˌʃip; ˋmɑnətɚˏʃɪp] ***n.*** 监听者的身份[职务];劝告者的身份[地位];警告者的身份[地位];班长的身份[职务]。
mon·i·to·ry [ˈmɔnitəri; ˋmɑnəˏtorɪ] **I** ***n.***【宗】告诫状。**II** ***a.*** 劝告的,训诫的,警告的。
mon·i·tress, mon·i·trix [ˈmɔ̃nitris, -triks; ˋmɑnətrɪs, -trɪks] ***n.*** 女的 monitor。
monk [mʌŋk; mʌŋk] ***n.*** 僧侣,修道士;【史】隐士。~**'s cloth** **1.**〔原义〕僧侣袈裟呢料。**2.**〔现义〕方平织纹的厚布〔作布帘等〕。
monk·er·y [ˈmʌŋkəri; ˋmʌŋkərɪ] ***n.*** **1.** 僧侣生涯。**2.**〔集合词〕修道士,僧侣。**3.** 修道院。
mon·key [ˈmʌŋki; ˋmʌŋkɪ] **I** ***n.*** **1.** 猴子;猿(*cf.* ape);长毛猴的毛皮。**2.** 顽童;淘气精。**3.** 打桩锤;(制造玻璃等用的)小坩埚。**4.**〔美俚〕吸毒瘾。**5.**〔英俚〕五百英镑;〔美俚〕五百美元。***have a*** ~ (***with the long tail***) ***on a house*** [***up the chimney***]〔方〕抵押房屋。***have a*** ~ ***on one's back*** **1.** 毒瘾很深。**2.** 为麻烦的问题等而苦恼。***have*** [***get***] ***one's*** ~ ***up*** = ***get a*** ~ ***on one's back***〔英俚〕生气,发脾气。~ ***money***〔美俚〕公司的临时股票;期票;外国货币。~ ***with a long tail***〔卑〕抵押。***put one's*** ~ ***up***〔英俚〕使人发怒。***suck*** [***sup***] ***the*** ~〔英俚〕插管子入酒桶里吸酒;喝酒;吸饮装在椰子壳里的酒。**II** ***vi.*** 恶戏,恶作剧,管闲事,干涉(*with*)。—***vt.*** 学样,嘲弄。~ (***about***) ***with***〔美俚〕用…逗…玩;嘲弄;瞎搞,插嘴;打搅。~ ***with a buzz saw***〔美俚〕孤注一掷,好歹干一下。~ **block**【海】附有转环的滑车。~ **bread**【植】猴面包(树、果)。~ **business**〔美俚〕狡猾的恶作剧,顽皮行为,嘲弄,胡闹,欺骗,耍花招。~ **clothes**〔美俚〕礼服,军礼服,燕尾服。~ **chocolate tree** 窄叶可可。~ **drill**〔俚〕柔软体操。~ **engine** 打桩机。~**-face** 猴子(似的)脸。~ **forecastle**【船】艏楼;前甲板。~ **flower** 沟酸浆属(*Mimulus*)植物。~ **jack** 坚硬面包果。~ **jacket** **1.** (水手穿的)紧身短上衣。**2.**〔美俚〕住院病人长睡衣。~ **meat**〔美罕俚〕罐头牛肉。~ **money**〔美俚〕公司的临时股票;期票;外国货币。~ **nut**〔英〕【植】落花生。~ **puzzle**【植】(叶尖锐,猴子也难爬上去的)智利松;智利南美杉。~***'s allowance*** 虐待。~**shines**〔美俚〕恶作剧。~ **suit**〔美俚〕制服,礼服,军装,航空装。~**swill**〔美俚〕酒。~ **wrench** 活动扳手[扳钳、扳头];引起破坏的东西(*throw a* ~ *into*〔美俚〕把活动扳手丢进机器里使不能转动,转为〕妨碍,破坏)。~**-wrench** ***vt.*** 破坏,阻挠。**-ish** ***a.*** 猴子似的;顽皮的。
Mon-Khmer [ˈməunkˈmɛə; ˋmonkˋmɛr] ***a.*** 孟—高棉语的〔澳亚语系的一个语支,包括孟语和高棉语,主要讲用区是中南半岛〕。
monk·hood [ˈmʌŋkhud; ˋmʌŋkhud] ***n.*** 修道士[僧侣]的身分[生活];〔集合词〕修道士,僧侣。
monk·ish [ˈmʌŋkiʃ; ˋmʌŋkɪʃ] ***a.*** 〔蔑〕修道士[僧侣]似的;修道院的。**-ly** ***ad.*** **-ness** ***n.***
monk's·hood [ˈmʌŋkshud; ˋmʌŋksˏhʊd] ***n.***【植】附子,舟形乌头。
mon(o)- *comb. f.* 独,单,一;【化】含一原子(*opp.* poly-; *cf.* soli-, multi-)。★ 母音前用 mon-: *mon*arch.
mono [ˈmɔnəu; ˋmɑno] ***a.*** 〔口〕单声道的(= monaural)。
mon·o·ac·id [ˌmɔnəuˈæsid; ˏmɑnoˋæsɪd] ***n.***【化】一元酸。
mon·o·a·cid·ic [ˌmɔnəuəˈsidik; ˏmɑnoəˋsɪdɪk] ***a.***【化】一(酸)价的,一元的,一酸的。
mon·o·a·tom·ic [ˌmɔnəuəˈtɔmik; ˏmɑnoəˋtɑmɪk] ***a.*** **1.**【化】单原子的;具单原子的。**2.** 包含一可交换原子[原子团]的。**3.**【生】单价的;【化】一价的,独价的。
mon·o·bas·ic [ˌmɔnəuˈbeisik; ˏmɑnəˋbesɪk] ***a.***【化】**1.** 一(碱)价的,一元的。**2.** 一代的。**-sic·i·ty** [ˌmɔnəbeiˈsisiti; ˏmɑnəbeˋsɪsətɪ] ***n.***
mon·o·car·box·yl·ic [ˈmɔnəuˌkɑːbɔkˈsilik; ˋmɑnoˏkɑrbɑkˋsɪlɪk] ***a.***【化】一元羧基的。
mon·o·car·pel·lar·y [ˌmɔnəuˈkɑːpələri; ˏmɑnəˋkɑrpəˏlɛrɪ] ***a.***【植】包含单一心皮的,具一心皮的;包含单一果片的,具一果片的。
mon·o·car·pic [ˌmɔnəuˈkɑːpik; ˏmɑnəˋkɑrpɪk] ***a.***【植】结一次果的(= monocarpous)。
mono·ceph·a·lous [ˌmɔnəuˈsefələs; ˏmɑnoˋsɛfələs] ***a.***【植】单头花序的。
Mo·noc·er·os [məˈnɔsərəs; məˋmɑsərəs] ***n.***【天】麒麟(星)座。
mon·o·cha·si·um [ˌmɔnəuˈkeiʒiəm, -ziəm; ˏmɑnoˋkeʒɪəm, -zɪəm] ***n.*** (*pl.* **-sia** [-ə; -ə])【植】单歧聚伞花序,单歧式。
mon·o·chla·myd·e·ous [ˌmɔnəukləˈmidəs; ˏmɑnokləˋmɪdɪəs] ***a.***【植】单被的,有单被花的。
mon·o·chlo·ride [ˌmɔnəuˈklɔːraid; ˏmɑnoˋklɔraɪd] ***n.***【化】一氯化物。
mon·o·chord [ˈmɔnəukɔːd; ˋmɑnəˏkɔrd] ***n.*** 一弦琴;一弦的音程测定器,和谐;一致。
mon·o·chro·mat [ˌmɔnəuˈkrəumæt; ˏmɑnəˋkromæt] ***n.***【医】全色盲者。**-ism** ***n.*** 全色盲。
mon·o·chro·mat·ic [ˌmɔnəukrəuˈmætik; ˏmɑnəkrəˋmætɪk] ***a.*** 一色的;单色光的;【物】由一波长的光形成的;【医】单色觉的,全色盲的。~ *lamp* 单色灯。
mon·o·chrome [ˈmɔnəukrəum; ˋmɑnəˏkrom] **I** ***n.*** 单色画[照片]。**II** ***a.*** 单色的,一色的。**-chrom·ist** ***n.*** 单色画家。**-chro·mic, -mi·cal** ***a.***
mon·o·cle [ˈmɔnɔkl; ˋmɑnəkl̩] ***n.*** 单片眼镜。
mon·o·cli·nal [ˈmɔnəuˈklainl; ˏmɑnəˋklaɪnəl] ***a.***【地】(地层)单斜的。
mon·o·cline [ˈmɔnəuklain; ˋmɑnəˏklaɪn] ***n.***【地】单斜褶皱[层]。
mon·o·clin·ic [ˌmɔnəuˈklinik; ˏmɑnəˋklɪnɪk] ***a.***【化】单斜(晶)的。

mon·o·cli·nous [ˌmɔnəuˈklainəs; ˏmɑnəˋklaɪnəs] *a*. 【植】雌雄(蕊)同花的。~ **flower** 雌雄同花,二性花。

mon·o·coque [ˈmɔnəukəuk; mɑnəˋkɔk] *n*. (飞机的)硬壳式结构;(汽车等的)无车架式车身。

mon·o·cot·y·le·don [ˌmɔnəuˌkɔtiˈliːdən; ˏmɑnəˏkɑtl̩ˋidn̩] *n*. 【植】单子叶植物。**-ous** *a*.

mo·noc·ra·cy [mɔˈnɔkrəsi; moˋnɑkrəsɪ] *n*. 独裁政治。

mon·o·crat [ˈmɔnəukræt; ˋmɑnəˏkræt] *n*. 独裁主义者;独裁者;〔美〕(亲英的)联邦党员。

mo·noc·u·lar [mɔˈnɔkjulə; məˋnɑkjələ] *a*. 单眼的;单眼用的 (*opp*. binocular)。*a* ~ *microscope* 单眼显微镜。

mon·o·cul·ture [ˈmɔnəukʌltʃə; ˋmɑnəˏkʌltʃɚ] *n*. 〔美〕【农】单作,单一经营,单种栽培。

mon·o·cy·cle [ˈmɔnəusaikl; ˋmɑnəˏsaɪkl̩] *n*. 独轮车。

mon·o·cy·clic [ˌmɔnəuˈsaiklik; mɑnoˋsaɪklɪk] *a*. **1.** 单环的,单周期的,单轮的。**2.** 【化】单环的,一环的。

mon·o·cyte [ˈmɔnəuˌsait; ˋmɑnoˏsaɪt] *n*. 【生】单核细胞,单核白血球。**-cyt·ic** [-ˈsitik; -ˋsɪtɪk] *a*.

mon·o·dist [ˈmɔnəudist; ˋmɑnədɪst] *n*. 单声部旋律作品的作者[歌唱者]。

mon·o·dra·ma [ˈmɔnəudrɑːmə; ˋmɑnəˏdrɑmə] *n*. 独脚戏,单人剧;单人剧剧本。

mon·o·dy [ˈmɔnədi; ˋmɑnədɪ] *n*. 【希腊剧】(悲剧的)抒情独唱;(对死者的)悼诗,挽歌;【乐】单音曲;单声部旋律的作品;无伴奏的齐唱作品。**-ic**, **-i·cal** *a*., **-i·cal·ly** *ad*.

Mo·noe·cia [məˈniːʃiə; məˋniʃɪə] *n*. 雌雄同株(植物);【动】雌雄同体。**mo·noe·cious** *a*. 雌雄同株的;雌雄同体的。

mon·o·fil·a·ment [ˌmɔnəuˈfiləmənt; ˏmɑnəˋfɪləmənt] *n*. 【纺】单丝,单纤(维)丝(= monofil)。

mon·o·fu·el [ˈmɔnəufuəl; ˋmɑnəˏfuəl] *n*. 【宇】单元燃料;单元推进剂。

mo·nog·a·mist [mɔˈnɔgəmist; məˋnɑgəmɪst] *n*. 一夫一妻主义者;主张[实行]一生一婚制者。

mo·nog·a·mous [mɔˈnɔgəməs; məˋnɑgəməs] *a*. 一夫一妻制的;一生一婚制的;【动】一雌一雄的,单配的。

mo·nog·a·my [mɔˈnɔgəmi; məˋnɑgəmɪ] *n*. 一夫一妻制;一生一婚制;单配偶,单配性。

mon·o·gen·e·sis [ˌmɔnəuˈdʒenisis; ˏmɑnəˋdʒɛnəsɪs] *n*. 【生】一元发生说;单性生殖,无性生殖。

mon·o·ge·net·ic [ˌmɔnəudʒiˈnetik; ˏmɑnədʒəˋnɛtɪk] *a*. **1.** 一元发生说的;无性生殖说的。**2.** 关于一元发生说的;关于无性生殖说的。**3.** 单殖动物的。

mon·o·gen·ic [ˌmɔnəuˈdʒenik; ˏmɑnəˋdʒɛnɪk] *a*. 【动】单基因的。**-nog·e·ny** [məˈnɔdʒini; məˋnɑdʒɪnɪ] *n*.

mo·nog·e·nism [məˈnɔdʒinizm; məˋnɑdʒənɪzəm] *n*. 人类单一起源说。

mo·nog·e·ny [mɔˈnɔdʒini; məˋnɑdʒɪnɪ] *n*. 人类一元发生说;【生】= monogenesis.

mon·o·glot [ˈmɔnəglɔt; ˋmɑnəˏglɑt] *a*., *n*. 只会说[写]一种语言的(人);只用一种语言写成的。

mon·o·gram [ˈmɔnəugræm; ˋmɑnəˏgræm] *n*. (姓名、名称等首字母组合成的)组合文字,花押字。**-ma·tic** *a*.

mon·o·graph [ˈmɔnəugrɑːf; ˋmɑnəˏgræf] *n*. 专题著作[论文],专论。**-er** *n*. 专题文章的作者。**-ic**, **-i·cal** *a*. 专题性的。**-ist** *n*. = monographer.

mo·nog·y·nous [mɔˈnɔdʒinəs; məˋnɑdʒənəs] *a*. 一夫一妻的;只有一妻的;【植】单雌蕊的;【动】单雌群的。

mo·nog·y·ny [mɔˈnɔdʒini; məˋnɑdʒənɪ] *n*. 一妻制 (*opp*. polygyny)。

mon·o·hy·drate [ˌmɔnəuˈhaidreit; ˏmɑnəˋhaɪdret] *n*. 【化】一水合物,一水化物。

mon·o·hy·dric [ˌmɔnəuˈhaidrik; ˏmɑnəˋhaɪdrɪk] *a*. **1.** 【化】一羟基的。**2.** 〔罕〕【化】一羟的,一元的(= monohydroxy)。

mon·o·hy·drox·y [ˌmɔnəuhaiˈdrɔksi; ˏmɑnəhaɪˋdrɑksɪ] *a*. 【化】一羟基的。

mon·o·i·de·ism [ˌmɔnəuˈaidiizəm; ˏmɑnəˋaɪdɪɪzəm] *n*. 【医】孤独意想。

mo·nol·a·try [mɔˈnɔletri; məˋnɑlətrɪ] *n*. 一神崇拜。

mon·o·lay·er [ˈmɔnəuˌleiə; ˋmɑnəˏleɚ] *n*. 【物】单层,单分子层。

mon·o·lin·gual [ˌmɔnəuˈliŋgwəl; ˏmɑnəˋlɪŋgwəl] **I** *a*. 用一种语言表达的,只懂一种语言的。**II** *n*. 只懂一种语言的人。

mon·o·lith [ˈmɔnəuliθ; ˋmɑnl̩ˏɪθ] *n*. 磐石,独石;独石柱[碑、像];整料。**-ic** *a*. (坚如)磐石的;铁板一块的 (*monolithic circuit* 【无】单片电路,单块电路。*monolithic unity* 坚如磐石的团结)。

mon·o·lith·ism [ˌmɔnəuˈliθizəm; ˋmɑnl̩ˏɪθɪzəm] *n*. 磐石一块,铁板一块。

mon·o·log [ˈmɔnəulɔg; ˋmɑnl̩ˏɔg] *n*. = monologue.

mono·log·ic(al) [ˌmɔnəuˈlɔdʒik(əl); ˏmɑnəˋlɑdʒɪk(əl)] *a*. **1.** 【戏】独白的。**2.** 独白式的。**3.** 滔滔不绝的。

mo·nol·o·gist [mɔˈnɔlədʒist; ˋmɑnəˏlɔdʒɪst] *n*. 独白[自言自语]的人;独演者;独自把持着说话的人。

mo·nol·o·gize [mɔˈnɔlədʒaiz; məˋnɑləˏdʒaɪz] *vi*. 【剧】独白;自言自语;独说独讲;滔滔不绝地说。

mon·o·log(ue) [ˈmɔnəlɔg; ˋmɑnl̩ˏɔg] *n*. 【剧】独白;独白场面;独脚戏剧本;(不使别人开口的)独说独讲;独白诗。

mon·o·logu·ist [ˈmɔnəlɔgist; ˋmɑnl̩ˏɔgɪst] *n*. = monologist.

mon·o·ma·ni·a [ˌmɔnəuˈmeinjə; ˏmɑnəˋmenɪə] *n*. 单狂,偏癖,偏执狂〔热中于一物或一事〕。**-ma·ni·ac** [-ˈmeiniæk; -ˋmenɪæk] *n*. 单狂者;偏执狂者。**-ma·ni·a·cal** *a*.

mon·o·mark [ˈmɔnəumɑːk; ˋmɑnəˏmɑrk] *n*. 〔英〕(用表示商品名称、地址的文字、数字作成的)注册标记[符号,代号,略名]。

mon·o·mer [ˈmɔnəmə; ˋmɑnəmɚ] *n*. 【化】单体。**-ic** [-ˈmerik; -ˋmɛrɪk] *a*.

mo·nom·er·ous [məˈnɔmərəs; məˋnɑmərəs] *a*. 【植】一基数的。

mon·o·me·tal·lic [ˌmɔnəumiˈtælik; ˏmɑnəməˋtælɪk] *a*. 【化】一金属的;【经】单本位制的。

mon·o·met·al·lism [ˌmɔnəuˈmetəlizəm; ˏmɑnəˋmɛtl̩ˏɪzəm] *n*. (货币的)单本位制 〔*cf*. bimetallism〕。

mo·no·mi·al [mɔˈnəumiəl; moˋnomɪəl] **I** *a*. 【数】一项的,单项的;【生】一个词的,单名的。**II** *n*. 【数】单项式;【生】单名。

mon·o·mo·lec·u·lar [ˌmɔnəməuˈlekjulə; ˏmɑnəməˋlɛkjəlɚ] *a*. 【物】单分子层的;【化】单(个)分子的。

mon·o·mor·phic [ˌmɔnəˈmɔːfik; ˏmɑnəˋmɔrfɪk] *a*. **1.** 单型的。**2.** 具有同型(或大体同型)结构的(= monomorphous)。

mon·o·nu·cle·o·sis [ˌmɔnəuˌnjuːkliːˈəusis, -nuː-; ˏmɑnəˏnjuklɪˋosɪs, -nu-] *n*. **1.** 传染性单核细胞增多。**2.** 单核细胞增多(= infectious mononucleosis)。

mo·noph·a·gous [məˈnɔfəgəs; məˋnɑfəgəs] *a*. 【生】单食性(的)。

mon·o·pho·bi·a [ˌmɔnəuˈfəubjə; ˏmɑnəˋfobɪə] *n*. 【医】独居恐怖,单身恐怖(症)。

mon·o·phon·ic [ˌmɔnəuˈfɔnik; ˏmɑnəˋfɑnɪk] *a*. **1.** 单音的;单音性的;单音调(乐曲)的;单音调(乐曲)性的。**2.** 单路输音的。

mo·noph·o·ny [məˈnɔfəni; məˋnɑfənɪ] *n*. **1.** 单音调乐曲。**2.** 【希腊剧】(悲剧的)抒情独唱;悼诗,挽歌;(波浪的)单调声响。**3.** 【乐】单旋律曲体;单旋律乐曲(= monody)。

mon·oph·thong [ˈmɔnəufθɔŋ; ˋmɑnəfˏθɔŋ] *n*. 单母音 〔*cf*. diphthong〕。**-al** *a*. **-ize** *vt*. (把双母音)单母音

M

化。

mon·o·phy·let·ic [ˌmɔnəufaiˈletik; ˏmɑnəfaiˋlɛtɪk] *a*. 1. 一源的,单种的。2. 由同一新型演化的。**-phy·letism** [-ˈfailitizm; -ˋfaɪlətɪzm] *n*.

mon·o·phyl·lous [ˌmɔnəuˈfiləs; ˏmɑnəˋfɪləs] *a*. 1. 【植】仅具单叶的;单叶组成的。2. 有合萼的;有合瓣的。

mono·phy·o·dont [ˌmɔnəuˈfiədɔnt; ˏmɑnəˋfaɪədɑnt] *a*. 【动】(有)不换性牙齿的,单套牙的。

Mo·noph·y·site [məˈnɔfiˌsait; məˋnɑfɪˏsaɪt] *n*. 单一性灵论者〔科普特教派的论点,论为基督的人性与神性合一〕。**-sit·ic** [-ˈsitik; -ˋsɪtɪk] *a*.

mon·o·pitch [ˈmɔnəupitʃ; ˋmɑnəˏpɪtʃ] *n*. (话声等的)单调。

mon·o·plane [ˈmɔnəuplein; ˋmɑnəˏplen] *n*. 单翼(飞)机。**-plan·ist** *n*. 单翼机飞行员。

mon·o·ple·gi·a [ˌmɔnəuˈpliːdʒiə, -ˈpliːdʒə; ˏmɑnəˋplidʒɪə, -ˋplidʒə] *n*. 【医】单瘫。**-ple·gic** [-ˈpliːdʒik, -ˈpledʒik; -ˋplidʒɪk, -ˋplɛdʒɪk] *a*.

mon·o·ploid [ˈmɔnəuˌplɔid; ˋmɑnəˏplɔɪd] *a*., *n*. 【生】单套的,单元体的;单倍体(= haploid)。~ **number** 单套数(染色体)。

mon·o·pode [ˈmɔnəuˌpəud; ˋmɑnəˏpod] **I** *a*. 仅具一足的。**II** *n*. 1. 单足生物;(尤指)(神话中的)独脚人种人。2. 【植】单轴 (= monopodium)。

mon·o·po·di·um [ˌmɔnəuˈpəudiəm; ˏmɑnəˋpodɪəm] *n*. (*pl*. **-di·a** [-ə; -ə]) 【植】单轴,单茎。**-po·dial** *a*.

mo·nop·o·lism [məˈnɔpəlizəm; məˋnɑplˌɪzəm] *n*. 垄断主义[制度]。

mo·nop·o·list [məˈnɔpəlist; məˋnɑplɪst], **mo·nop·o·liz·er** [-laizə; -laɪzɚ] *n*. 1. 独占者,垄断者;专利者。2. 〔-list〕垄断论者;专利论者。

mo·nop·o·lis·tic [məˌnɔpəˈlistik; məˏnɑpəˋlɪstɪk] *a*. 垄断[专利]的。

mo·nop·o·li·za·tion [məˌnɔpəlaiˈzeiʃən; məˏnɑplaɪˋzeʃən] *n*. 独占,垄断,包办;专利。

mo·nop·o·lize [məˈnɔpəlaiz; məˋnɑpəˏlaɪz] *vt*. 独占,垄断,包办;得到…的专利权。~ *the conversation* 独占谈话。~ *the conduct of affairs* 包办。

mo·nop·o·ly [məˈnɔpəli; məˋnɑplɪ] *n*. 1. 垄断[独占](权),专利(权)(*of*,〔美〕*on*)。2. 垄断[专利]公司;独占[专利]事业。3. 专利品。*a government* ~ 政府专利(品)。*make a* ~ *of* 独家经售;垄断。*a* ~ *capital*(*ist*) 垄断资本(家)。*the* ~ *capitalist class* 垄断资产阶级。

mon·o·pro·pel·lant [ˌmɔnəuprəˈpelənt; ˏmɑnoprəˋpɛlənt] *n*. 单元喷气燃料,单一组分的喷气机燃料。

mo·nop·so·ny [məˈnɔpsəni; məˋnɑpsənɪ] *n*. (*pl*. **-nies**) 【经】独家主顾。

mon·o·rail [ˈmɔnəureil; ˋmɑnəˏrel] *n*. 单轨;单轨铁路。

mon·o·sac·cha·ride [ˌmɔnəuˈsækəraid; ˏmɑnəˋsækəˏraɪd] *n*. 【化】单醣。

mon·o·scope [ˈmɔnəuskəup; ˋmɑnəˏskop] *n*. 【电视】单像管;存储管式示波器。

mon·o·sep·al·ous [ˌmɔnəuˈsepələs; ˏmɑnəˋsɛpələs] *a*. 【植】合萼的(= gamosepalous)。

mon·o·so·di·um glu·ta·mate [ˌmɔnəuˈsəudiəmˈgluːtəˌmeit; ˏmɑnəˋsodɪəmˋglutəˏmet] 谷胺酸钠〔俗名味精,味素〕。

mon·o·some [ˈmɔnəusəum; ˋmɑnəˏsom] *n*. 【植】单体〔指染色体〕。**-so·mic** *a*.

mon·o·sper·mous [ˌmɔnəuˈspəːməs; ˏmɑnoˋspɝməs] *a*. 【植】仅具单子的。

mon·o·sper·my [ˈmɔnəuspəːmi; ˋmɑnəˏspɝmɪ] *n*. 【动】单精受精。**-sper·mic** *a*.

mon·o·stable [ˌmɔnəuˈsteibl; mɑnəˋstebl] *n*., *a*. 单稳态(的)。~ *multivibrator* 单稳多谐振荡器。

mon·o·ste·le [ˌmɔnəuˈstiːli, ˈmɔnəustiːl; ˏmɑnəˋstilɪ, ˋmɑnəˏstil] *n*. 【植】单体中柱。**-ste·lic** *a*.

mon·o·stich [ˈmɔnəustik; ˋmɑnəˏstɪk] *n*. 1. 单行诗。2. 单行诗句。

mo·nos·ti·chous [məˈnɔstikəs; məˋnɑstəkəs] *a*. 【植】单列的。

mon·o·stome [ˈmɔnəustəum; ˋmɑnəstom] *a*. 【动】具单口的,具单吸盘的(= monostomous)。

mo·nos·tro·phe [məˈnɔstrəfi, ˈmɔnəuˌstrəuf; məˋnɑstrəfɪ, ˋmɑnəstrof] *n*. 单律诗。

mon·o·sty·lous [ˌmɔnəuˈstailəs; ˏmɑnəˋstaɪləs] *a*. 【植】仅具单花柱的。

mon·o·syl·lab·ic [ˈmɔnəusiˈlæbik; ˏmɑnəsɪˋlæbɪk] *a*. 单音节的;由单音节构成的。**-i·cal·ly** *ad*.

mon·o·syl·la·bism [ˌmɔnəuˈsiləbizəm; ˏmɑnəˋsɪləbɪzm] *n*. 单音节语使用(癖);单音节语倾向。

mon·o·syl·la·ble [ˈmɔnəuˌsiləbl; ˋmɑnəˏsɪləbl] *n*. 单音节词。*speak* [*answer*] *in* ~*s* 只冷淡的说[答] yes 或 no。

mon·o·sym·met·ric(al) [ˌmɔnəusiˈmetrik(əl); ˏmɑnəsɪˋmɛtrɪk(əl)] *a*. 1. 【化】单斜晶系的(= monoclinic)。2. 【生】两侧对称的;(生物、器官等的)从中轴可等分的(= zygomorphic)。

mon·o·the·ism [ˈmɔnəuθiːizəm; ˋmɑnəθiˏɪzəm] *n*. 一神教[论]。**-ist** *n*. 一神教信徒;一神论者。**-is·tic** *a*.

mon·o·the·is·ti·cal [ˌmɔnəuθiːˈiztikl; ˏmɑnəθiˋɪztɪkl] *a*. 信一神的,一神教的。**-ly** *ad*.

mon·o·tint [ˈmɔnəutint; ˋmɑnəˏtɪnt] *n*. = monochrome.

mon·o·tone [ˈmɔnəutəun; ˋmɑnəˏton] **I** *n*., *a*. 【语】单调音(的);(颜色、文体等的)单调(的)。**II** *vt*., *vi*. 单调地读[说、唱]。

mon·o·ton·ic [ˌmɔnəuˈtɔnik; ˏmɑnəˋtɑnɪk] *a*. 单调的。

mo·not·o·ny [məˈnɔtəni; məˋnɑtənɪ] *n*. 单音;单调;无变化,千篇一律;无聊。**-not·on·ous** [-tənəs; -ˋtnəs] *a*.

Mon·o·trem·a·ta [ˌmɔnəuˈtremətə; ˏmɑnəˋtrɛmətə] *n*. 【动】单孔目。

mon·o·treme [ˈmɔnəutriːm; ˋmɑnəˏtrim] *n*. 【动】单孔目动物〔包括鸭嘴兽和针鼹〕。**-trem·a·tous** [-ˈtremətəs, -ˈtriːmə-; ˋmɑnəˋtrɛmətəs] *a*.

mo·not·ri·chous [məˈnɔtrikəs; məˋnɑtrəkəs] *a*. 【生】单鞭毛的。

mon·o·type [ˈmɔnəutaip; ˋmɑnəˏtaɪp] *n*. 【印】1. 〔M-〕莫诺铸排机〔一种单字自动铸排机〕。2. 【生】单型;独模标本;单版画(制作法)。**-typ·ic** *a*.

mon·o·va·lent [ˌmɔnəuˈveilənt; ˏmɑnəˋvelənt] *a*. 1. 【菌】单价的。2. 【化】单价的,独价的(= univalent)。**-va·lence**, **-va·len·cy** *n*.

mon·ovu·lar [mɔˈnəuvjulə; məˋnovjəlɚ] *a*. 单卵的。~ *twins* 单卵双生。

mon·ox·id, **mon·ox·ide** [mɔˈnɔksid, mɔˈnɔksaid; məˋnɑksɪd, mɑnˋɑksaɪd] *n*. 【化】一氧化物。

Mon·roe [mənˈrəu; mənˋro] *n*. 1. 门罗〔姓氏,男子名〕。2. **James** ~ 门罗〔1758—1831,美国第五任总统〕。~ *Doctrine* 门罗主义。

Mon·roe·ism [mənˈrəuizəm; mʌnˋroɪzm] *n*. 〔美〕门罗主义。**-ist** *n*. 〔美〕门罗主义者。

Mon·ro·vi·a [mənˈrəuviə; mənˋrovɪə] *n*. 门罗维亚〔利比里亚首都〕。

Mons. = *Monsieur*.

Mon·sar·rat [ˌmɔnsəˈræt; ˏmɑnsəˋræt] *n*. 蒙萨拉特〔姓氏〕。

mon·sei·gneur, ***M-*** [ˌmɔnsenˈjəː; ˏmɑnsenˋjɝ] *n*. 〔F.〕(*pl*. ***mes·sei·gneurs***, ***M-*** [mesenˈjəːz; mesenˋjɝz]) 阁下〔对王族、大主教等的敬称〕;称为阁下的人。

mon·sieur [məˈsjəː; məˋsjɝ] *n*. 〔F.〕(*pl*. ***messieurs*** [meiˈsjəː, meˋsjə]) 先生〔和英语 Mr. 及招呼语 sir 相

M

当,略 ***M***.,***Mons***. *pl*. ***Messrs***., ***MM***.〕;绅士;〔蔑〕法国人。

Monsig. = Monseigneur; *Monsignor*.

mon·si·gnor, **Mon·si·gnor** [mɔn'siːnjə; mɑn`sinjɚ] ***n***.〔It.〕(*pl*. ***~s***, ***mon·si·gno·ri***, ***M-***) = *monseigneur*.

mon·soon [mɔn'suːn; mɑn`sun] ***n***. **1.** 季(节)风〔在印度洋和亚洲南部5—9月自西南、10—12月自东北吹的风〕。**2.** (印度的)雨季,夏季季风期。*the Indian* ~ 东亚季候风。*the dry* [*wet*] ~ 冬[夏]季季风;干[湿]季风。*a* ~ *forest* 季雨林。*the* ~ *rain* 季风雨。

mon·soon·al [mɔn'suːnl; mɑn`sunl] ***a***.【气】季风的。

mons pu·bis [ˌmɔnz'pjuːbis; ˏmɑnz`pjubɪs]〔L.〕【解】阴阜。

mon·ster ['mɔnstə; `mɑnstɚ] **I** ***n***. **1.** (想像中的)怪物〔centaur, dragon, sphinx, griffin 等〕。**2.** (尤指史前的)怪兽,巨兽〔mammoth, ichthyosaurus 等〕;畸形(生物);【医】畸胎;巨人;巨物;残忍的人,穷凶极恶的人。*a green-eyed* ~ 嫉妒。*~s of the deep* 大鱼。**II** ***a***. 巨大的。*a* ~ *ship* 巨舰。~ **man**(美式足球赛中的)自由后卫,中后卫〔无固定防区,满场跑动,拦截对方带球或接球的球员〕。~ **truck** 超巨型卡车。

mon·strance ['mɔnstrəns; `mɑnstrəns] ***n***.【天主】圣体匣。

mon·stros·i·ty [mɔns'trɔsiti; mɑn`strɑsətɪ] ***n***. 异形,畸形;怪异;怪物;异常大的东西;穷凶极恶。

mon·strous ['mɔnstrəs; `mɑnstrəs] **I** ***a***. **1.** 异形的,畸形的,巨大的。**2.** 可怕的;穷凶极恶的。**3.**〔口〕荒谬的,笑死人的。~ *crimes* 滔天罪行。**II** ***ad***.〔美口、英古〕非常,很,极。**-ly** ***ad***. **-ness** ***n***.

mon·strous·ness ['mɔnstrəsnis; `mɑnstrəsnɪs] ***n***. 异形,畸形,怪异。

mons ven·er·is [ˌmɔnz'venəris; ˏmɑnz`venərɪs] (妇女的)阴阜。

Mont. = Montana.

mon·tage [mɔn'tɑːʒ, 'mɔntidʒ; mɑn`tɑʒ, `mɑntɪdʒ] ***n***.〔F.〕**1.** 辑绘;辑绘图画。**2.**【影】剪辑画面;蒙太奇。**3.** 装配。

Mon·ta·gnard [ˌmɔntən'jɑːd; ˏmɑntən`jɑrd] ***n***. **1.** (越南中部的)山民。**2.** (美国落基山北部的)印第安部族山民。

Mon·ta·gu(e) ['mɔntəgjuː, 'mʌntəgjuː; `mɑntəˏgju, `mʌntəgju] ***n***. 蒙塔古〔姓氏,男子名〕。

Mon·tan·a [mɔn'tænə; mɑn`tænə] ***n***. 蒙大拿〔美国州名〕。

mon·tane ['mɔntein; `mɑnten] ***a***. 山多的;山区的;住在山区的。

mon·tan·ic [mɔn'tænik; mɑn`tænɪk] ***a***. ~ **acid**【化】褐煤酸;二十九(烷)酸。

mon·tan wax ['mɔntæn; `mɑntæn]【化】褐煤蜡,山蜡。

Mont Blanc [mɔŋ' blɔŋ; mɔŋ`blɑŋ]〔F.〕白朗峰〔阿尔卑斯山脉的最高峰〕。~ **ruby**【矿】红水晶(= rubasse)。

mont·bre·ti·a [mɔn'briːʃjə; mɑnt`briʃɪə] ***n***.【植】蒙布里雪氏观音兰。

mont-de-pié·té [ˌmɔ̃dəpje'te; ˏmɔ̃dəˏpje`te] ***n***.〔F.〕(*pl*. ***monts-***) 官营当铺。

mon·te ['mɔnti; `mɑnte] ***n***. (一种西班牙式)纸牌戏。*three-card* ~ (起源于墨西哥的)三张牌戏。

Mon·te, Mon·ty ['mɔnti; `mɑntɪ] ***n***. 蒙提〔男子名,Montague 的昵称〕。

Monte Carlo [ˌmɔnti'kɑːləu; ˏmɑntɪ`kɑrlo] **1.** 蒙特卡罗〔摩纳哥城市〕。**2.**【自】采用随机抽样法的。*Monte Carlo method* 蒙特卡罗法〔一种随机抽样检验法〕。

Mon·te·ne·grin [ˌmɔnti'niːgrin; ˏmɑntə`nigrɪn] **I** ***a***. 黑山(人)的,门的内哥罗(人)的。**II** ***n***. 黑山人,门的内哥罗人。

Mon·te·ne·gro [ˌmɔnti'niːgrəu; ˏmɑntə`nigro] ***n***. 黑山,门的内哥罗。

mon·te·ro [mɔn'tɛərəu; mɑn`tɛro] ***n***. (*pl*. ***-ros***) (有帽沿的)圆猎帽。

Mon·ter·rey [ˌmɔntə'rei; ˏmɑntə`re] ***n***. 蒙特雷〔墨西哥城市〕。

Mon·tes·quieu [ˌmɔntes'kjuː; ˏmɑntə`skju], **Charles** 孟德斯鸠〔1689—1755,法国政治哲学家、法学家〕。

Mon·te·vid·e·o [ˌmɔntivi'deiəu; ˏmɑntəvɪ`deo] ***n***. 蒙得维的亚〔乌拉圭首都〕。

Mont·fort ['mɔntfət; `mɑntfɚt] ***n***. 蒙特福特〔姓氏〕。

Mont·gol·fi·er [mɔnt'gɔlfiə; mɑnt`gɑlfɪɚ] ***n***. **1.** 孟高尔费〔姓氏〕。**2.** **Joseph Michel** ~ 约瑟夫、米海尔(1740—1810), **Jacques Etienne** ~ 雅克·艾甸(1745—1799)〔弟兄二人均为法国轻气球发明者〕。**3.**〔m-〕热空气气球。

Mont·gom·er·y [mənt'gʌməri; mɑnt`gʌmərɪ] ***n***. 蒙哥马利〔姓氏〕。

month [mʌnθ; mʌnθ] ***n***. (岁月的)月;一个月的时间。*a calendar* ~ 历月。*a lunar* ~ 太阴月。*a solar* ~ 太阳月。*this* ~ 本月。*last* ~ 上月(例: *He came here last* ~. 他是上月来这里的)。*the last* ~ = *the past* ~ 到今天为止的一个月(期间)(例: *I have been here the last* [*past*] ~. 我在这里已有一个月了)。*next* ~ 下一个月。*the* ~ *before last* 上上个月。*the* ~ *of July* 七月。*the* ~ *after next* 再下一个月。*for* ~ *of May* 五月份。*four times a* ~ 一月四次。***a*** ~ ***of Sundays***〔口〕很长的时间,许久(*not once in a* ~ *of Sundays* 很久很久没有…,决没有…)。***a*** ~***'s mind*** 周月(人死后一个月举行的纪念)弥撒;渴求。~ ***after*** ~ = ~ ***by*** ~ 逐月,每月,一月又一月。~ ***in***, ~ ***out*** 月月,每月。***this day*** ~ 下[上]一个月的今天。

month·ly ['mʌnθli; `mʌnθlɪ] **I** ***a***. 每月的;每月一次的;按月的。~ *pay* 月薪。*a* ~ *nurse* (照料产妇的)产褥护士。*a* ~ *rose*【植】月季花。**II** ***ad***. 每月一次,每月。**III** ***n***. 月刊;〔*pl*.〕月经。

mon·ti·cule ['mɔntikjuːl; `mɑntɪˏkjul] ***n***. 小丘,岗;火山丘;【动】小阜。

mont·mo·ril·lon·ite [ˌmɔntmə'rilənait; ˏmɑntmə`rɪləˏnaɪt] ***n***.【地】蒙脱石;蒙脱土。

Mont·re·al [ˌmɔntri'ɔːl; ˏmɑntrɪ`ɔl] ***n***. 蒙特利尔〔加拿大港市〕。**-er** 蒙特利尔市民。

Mont·ser·rat [mɔntse'ræt; ˏmɑntsə`ræt] ***n***. 蒙特塞拉特岛〔美洲〕。

mon·u·ment ['mɔnjumənt; `mɑnjəmənt] ***n***. 纪念碑,石碑;墓碑;纪念物,纪念像,纪念门,纪念馆;遗迹;遗址;遗物;不朽的功业[著作](等);标石,界石;〔古〕纪录;标记。*ancient* [*natural*] *~s* 历史[天然]纪念物[遗迹]。*the M-*〔英〕(1666年)伦敦大火纪念塔。*cultural objects and historic ~s* 文物古迹。

mon·u·men·tal [ˌmɔnju'mentl; ˏmɑnjə`mɛntl] ***a***. 纪念碑的;纪念的;巨大的,雄伟的;不朽的,不灭的;〔口〕(恶意的)非常的,极大的。*a* ~ *work* 不朽的著作[作品]。*a* ~ *inscription* 碑铭。~ *ignorance* 极端的愚蠢。**-ly** ***ad***. 用纪念碑;为纪念;〔口〕非常,极。

mon·u·men·tal·ize [ˌmɔnju'mentəlaiz; ˏmɑnjʊ`mɛntl̩ˏaɪz] ***vt***. 立碑纪念;永远传下去;树碑立传。

-mony *suf*. 表示动作、结果、状态: cere*mony*, matri*mony*, testi*mony*.

mon·zo·nite ['mɔnzənait; `mɑnzəˏnaɪt] ***n***.【地】二长岩。

moo [muː; mu] **I** ***n***. 哞〔牛叫声〕;〔美俚〕牛肉;牛。**II** ***vi***. (牛)哞哞地叫。~**-cow** ***n***.〔儿〕哞哞〔母牛〕。

M.O.O. = Money Order Office 邮汇处,邮汇部。

mooch [muːtʃ; mutʃ] ***vi***.〔俚〕鬼鬼祟祟地走(*along*);打转儿;荡来荡去,徘徊(*around*, *round*)。— ***vt***.〔美俚〕揩油;招摇撞骗,讹诈;偷偷拿走;偷取;索取。**-er** ***n***.〔美俚〕常揩油过日子的人;招摇撞骗的人;寄生虫,食客。

M

mood[1] [muːd; mud] ***n*. 1.** 〔古〕怒。**2.** (一时的)心情,情绪,心地。**3.** 〔*pl*.〕不高兴,闹脾气。**4.** 基调。*a man of ~s* 喜怒无常的人。***be in no ~ for* [*to*]** 不想…,无意…。***be in the melting ~*** 伤感得要哭,眼泪汪汪。***change one's ~*** 转换心情。***in a laughing ~*** 快快活活,高高兴兴,笑着。***in an melancholy ~*** 忧郁地,郁郁不乐地。***in a melting ~*** 心肠软化,易受感动。***in the ~ for* [*to*]** 想…,有意…。

mood[2] [muːd; mud] ***n*. 1.** 【逻、乐】论式,调式(= mode)。**2.** 【语】语气。

Mood·y [ˈmuːdi; ˋmudɪ] ***n*.** 穆迪〔姓氏〕。

mood·y [ˈmuːdi; ˋmudɪ] ***a*.** (***mood·i·er***; ***-i·est***) 动不动发脾气的,易怒的;喜怒无常的;郁郁不乐的,不高兴的。**-i·ly *ad*. -i·ness *n*.**

mool [muːl; mul] ***n*.** 〔Scot.〕**1.** 耕土,腐植土。**2.** 墓土。**3.** 墓。

moo·la(h) [ˈmuːlə; ˋmulə] ***n*.** 〔美俚〕钱。

mool·lah [ˈmuːlə; ˋmulə] ***n*.** = mullah.

mool·vie, -vee [ˈmuːlviː; ˋmulvi] ***n*.** 回[伊斯兰]教法学家;先生〔尤用于印度回[伊斯兰]教徒间〕。

moon [muːn; mun] **I *n*. 1.** 月,月球,月亮。★1. 语法上常作女性处理。2. 形容词是 lunar。**2.** 〔诗〕(一个)月,太阳月;〔诗〕月光;月状物,新月形物;(指甲的)甲弧影;卫星;(尤指)新月旗〔土耳其的国旗〕。**3.** 〔美俚〕酒,私酿的威士忌酒。**4.** 【天】月相。*a full ~* 满月。*a new ~* 新月。*a crescent ~* 蛾眉月。*a blue ~* 不可能的事物,难得遇见的事物。*There is a* [*no*] *~*. 有[没有]月亮。***bark at* (*bay*) *the ~*** (狗)咬月亮,(狂犬)吠月;瞎嚷嚷;无事自扰。***below the ~*** 月下的,尘世的。***cry for the ~*** 渴望[要求]做不到的事情[得不到的东西]。***know no more than the man in the ~*** 完全不知道。***~'s phase*** 月相,月的盈亏。***once in a blue ~*** 〔口〕极少,极难得,千载难逢。***shoot the ~*** 〔英俚〕(避债)夜逃。***the man in the ~*** 月中人〔指月面的黑斑〕;假想的人。***the old ~ in the new ~'s arms*** (因地球反光致黑暗面隐约可见的)新月,初弦月。**II *vi*.** 〔口〕懒洋洋地闲荡;出神;呆看,没精打采地东瞧西望(*about*; *around*)。— ***vt*.** 虚度时间;稀里糊涂度过(时日)(*away*)。~ **age** 月球时代(指人类登上月球的时代)。~**beam** (一线)月光。~**-blind *a*.** 夜盲的;(马的)月光盲的。~ **blindness** 【医】夜盲症;【兽医】月盲症。~**buggy** 月球车。~ **cake** (中国的)月饼。~**calf** (*pl*. ***-calves***) 怪物,畸形动物[植物];白痴。~ **car** = ~buggy. ~**craft** 月球飞船,月球航天器。~**crawler** = ~buggy. ~**-down** 〔美〕月落;月落时。~**eye** = moonblindness. ~**-eyed *a*.** = moon-blind 圆睁着双眼的。~**face** 圆脸。~**-faced *a*.** 圆脸的。~**fall** 月面降落。~**fish** 【鱼】月鲹,月鱼。~**-flight** 向月飞行。~**flower** 〔美〕月光花;〔英〕法国菊。~ **gate** (中国建筑中的)月洞门。~**head** 〔美〕笨蛋,傻瓜。~**-light 1. *n*.** 月光。**2. *a*.** 月光的;月光下的(*~light flitting* 夜逃,夜奔。*a ~light school* 〔美〕(乡村)夜校)。~**lighter** 月光团圆;〔美〕= moonshiner; 参与夜袭的人;日夜身兼两职的人。~**lighting** (月光团圆的)夜袭;月光下的活动;身兼两个职业的人。~**lit *a*.** 照着月亮的,有月亮的,月明的。~**-mad *a*.** 月狂的。~**-madness** 月狂〔因注视月亮过久发生的神经错乱〕。~**man** 登月太空人。~ **month** 太阴月。~**port** 月球火箭发射站。~**quake** 月震。~**raker** 〔英俚〕笨蛋,傻瓜;走私贩子。~**rise** 月出(时)。~**scape** 月亮的表面(景色)。~**scooper** (在月球上挖土的)宇宙车。~**scope** 卫星观察镜。~**seed family** 【植】防己科(*Menispermaceae*)蝙蝠葛属(*Menispermum*)植物。~**set** 月落(时)。~**shine 1. *n*.** 月光;荒唐的空想[计划],梦话;〔美俚〕走私酒。**2. *a*.** 月光的,月夜的;空的,无聊的。~**shiner** 〔美俚〕非法私酿[贩卖]威士忌酒的人。~**shiny *a*.** 月光照耀的,月色皎皎的;月光似的;空想的。~**ship** 月球飞船。~**shot** 向月球发射月球探测器。~**stone** 【矿】月长石。~**struck *a*.** 发狂的,神经错乱的。~**walk *n*.** 月球漫步。~**wort** 【植】**1.** 阴地蕨属(*Botrychium*)植物〔尤指月阴地蕨(*Botrychium lunarium*)〕。**2.** (= honesty)缎花属(*Lunaria*)植物〔尤指一年生缎花(*Lunaria annua*)〕。**-less *a*.** 无月光的。**-let** 小月亮;人造卫星;小卫星。

mooned [muːnd, 〔诗〕ˈmuːnid; mund, ˋmunɪd] ***a*.** 〔诗〕月亮般的;(新)月形的;有月形彩饰的。

Moo·ney [ˈmuːni; ˋmunɪ] ***n*.** 穆尼〔姓氏〕。

moon·ish [ˈmuːniʃ; ˋmunɪʃ] ***a*.** 月亮似的,三心两意的。

moon·shee [ˈmuːnʃiː; ˋmunʃi] ***n*.** 〔Hind.〕(印度籍的)语言教师;译员;秘书;雇员。

moon·y [ˈmuːni; ˋmunɪ] ***a*.** (***moon·i·er***; ***-i·est***) 月亮的;月状的;新月形的;月光下的;月光似的;恍惚的;头脑错乱的;笨的;〔美俚〕有点醉的。

moor[1] [muə; mʊr] ***n*.** 〔英〕(特指生长石南属植物的)荒野,高原沼地;〔英〕(尤指打松鸡的)猎场。~ **coal** 沼煤,泥煤。~**-cock** 公赤松鸡。~ **fowl**, ~ **game** 赤松鸡。~**hen** 母赤松鸡;鹬,水鸡。

moor[2] [muə; mʊr] **I *n*.** 停泊,抛锚;系留。**II *vt*.** (把船)系住,停住,使停泊;(把飞船)拴在系留塔上。—***vi*.** 被系住,固定;系泊,系留。

Moor [muə; mʊr] ***n*.** 摩尔人〔非洲西北部伊斯兰教民族〕。

moor·age [ˈmuəridʒ; ˋmʊrɪdʒ] ***n*.** 系泊;系泊处;系泊费。

Moore [muə; mur] ***n*.** 穆尔〔姓氏〕。

moor·ing [ˈmuəriŋ; ˋmʊrɪŋ] ***n*.** 系泊,系留;〔常 *pl*.〕系泊用具;〔*pl*.〕系泊处;〔*pl*.〕支撑物,依靠物。~ **buoy** 系泊浮筒。~ **drag** 活动锚。~ **guy** 系留索。~ **loop** 【军】沙包索圈。~ **mast**, ~ **tower** (飞船的)系留塔。~ **post** 系留柱。

moor·ish [ˈmuəriʃ; ˋmʊrɪʃ] ***a*.** 荒野的,沼地的;住在沼地的;生在沼地的。

Moor·ish [ˈmuəriʃ; ˋmʊrɪʃ] ***a*.** 摩尔人的,摩尔人式的(建筑)。~ **arch** 马蹄拱。

moor·land [ˈmuələnd; ˋmʊr,lænd] ***n*.** 〔英〕(长满石南属植物的)荒野,高沼地。

moor·stone [ˈmuəstəun; ˋmʊston] ***n*.** 松碎花岗岩。

moor·y [ˈmuəri; ˋmʊrɪ] ***a*.** 荒野(似)的;沼地的。

moose [muːs; mus] ***n*.** 〔*sing*., *pl*.〕**1.** 【动】大角麋;驼鹿。**2.** = elk. **3.** 〔M-〕= Bull Moose. ~**bird** 〔Canad.〕= Canada jay 加拿大噪鸦。~**wood** 条纹槭。

moot [muːt; mut] **I *vt*.** 讨论;提出(问题);(在假设法庭上)实习辩论。**II *n*.** 讨论;(法科学生等的)假设案件辩论会;【英史】(聚议公共问题的)讨论会。**III *a*.** 有讨论余地的,未决的。~ **court** (法学院学生实习的)模拟法庭,假设法庭。~ **hall** 【英史】集会所。

mooted [ˈmuːtid; ˋmutɪd] ***a*.** 〔美〕未决定的,有疑问的。

mop[1] [mɔp; mɑp] **I *n*.** 墩布,拖把;类似拖把的东西。*a ~ of hair* 乱蓬蓬的头发。**II *vt*.** 拿墩布拖;擦(泪、汗等)。~ ***the floor* [*the earth*] *with sb*.** 〔俚〕把(人)打得一败涂地,痛击,凌辱。~ ***up*** **1.** 擦去,揩干。**2.** 〔俚〕【军】肃清,扫荡。**3.** 〔俚〕榨取,吸取(利润等)。**4.** 打倒,痛击。**5.** 〔口〕狼吞虎咽地吃[喝]。**6.** 〔美剧〕大大成功。~**board** 【建】护壁板 = baseboard. ~**-head** 乱蓬蓬的头。~**-stick** 拖布把柄。

mop[2] [mɔp; mɑp] **I *n*.** 愁脸,搭拉脸;扭歪嘴的人。***~s and mows*** 怪相,鬼脸。**II *vi*.** 歪嘴,搭拉着脸。~ ***and mow*** 做怪相,扮鬼脸。

mop[3] [mɔp; mɑp] ***n*.** 〔英〕(秋收时的)雇工集市。

mope [məup; mop] **I *vt*., *vi*.** (使)郁郁不乐;(使)扫兴,闲荡。~ ***about*** 呆痴痴地走来走去。~ ***oneself*** 垂头丧气;烦闷。~ ***one's time away*** 闷闷不乐地度过(日子)。**II *n*.** 郁郁不乐的人,忧郁的人;〔美俚〕讨厌的人;〔*pl*.〕忧郁。***have* (*a fit of*) *the ~s*** 郁闷;闹情绪。

mo·ped [ˈməuˌped; ˋmoped] ***n*.** 摩托自行车,机动脚踏两用车。

mo·per·y [ˈməupəri; ˋmopərɪ] ***n*.** 〔美俚〕**1.** 小小的违

法行为;莫须有的罪名。**2.** 闲荡,浪费时间。

mop·ish [ˈməupiʃ; ˋmopɪʃ] ***a.*** 郁郁不乐的,忧郁的,垂头丧气的。**-ly *ad.***, **-ness *n.***

mopoke [ˈməupəuk; ˋmopok] ***n.*** **1.**【动】枭。**2.**〔澳〕笨人。

mop·pet [ˈmɔpit; ˋmɑpɪt] ***n.*** 〔儿〕(布做的)玩偶;〔口〕小孩,娃儿;巴儿狗。

mop·py [ˈmɔpi; ˋmɑpɪ] ***a.*** 拖把似的;乱蓬蓬的。

mop·ping-up [ˈmɔpiŋʌp; ˋmɑpɪŋʌp] ***a.*** 扫荡性的;扫尾的。*a* ~ *operation* 扫荡。

mop-up [ˈmɔpˌʌp; ˋmɑpˏʌp] ***n.*** 扫荡残敌,肃清残敌;扫尾工作。

mop·us [ˈməupəs; ˋmopəs] ***n.*** 〔美俚〕(现)钱。

mo·quette [məuˈket; moˋkɛt] ***n.*** 短毛绒织品〔做座垫、地毯等用〕。

mor [mɔː; mɔr] ***n.*** 粗腐植质〔森林中的浮层土壤〕。

Mor. = Morocco.

MOR = middle of the road 中间道路。

mo·ra [ˈmɔːrə; ˋmɔrə] ***n.*** (*pl.* ***-rae*** [-iː; -i], ***-ras***) **1.**【语】音节延长度。**2.**〔作诗法〕韵律节拍单位,通常用短音符(ˇ)来表示。

mo·ra [ˈmɔːrə; ˋmɔrə] ***n.*** 〔It.〕(意大利)豁拳,划拳。

mo·raine [mɔˈrein; moˋren] ***n.***【地】冰碛,冰碛层,冰川堆石。**mo·rain·ic *a.***

mor·al [ˈmɔrəl; ˋmɔrəl] **I *a.*** **1.** 道德(上)的,道义(上)的;守德行的;(特指男女关系上)品行端正的(*opp.* immoral)。**2.** 教导道德的。**3.** 精神上的(*opp.* physical, practical)。**4.** (虽未证明但)无疑的,当然的;【逻】盖然的,可能的(*opp.* demonstrative)。*a* ~ *agent* [*being*] 道德的行为者(人)。*a* ~ *victory* 精神胜利。*a* ~ *blow* 精神上的打击。~ *authority* 道义。~ *certainty* (虽不能证明但)确实可靠。~ *character* 品行。~ *courage* 信仰坚定不移的勇气,义勇。~ *culture* 德育。~ *depreciation*【机】无形损耗(*opp.* physical depreciation)。~ *education* 思想品德教育;德育。~ *faculty* [*sense*] 是非之心,良心。~ *good* 德行。~ *inexhaustibility* 百折不挠的精神。~ *law* 道德律。~ *obligations* 道义上的责任。~ *outlook* 人生观。~ *philosophy* 道德哲学,伦理学;〔古〕心理学。~ *principles* 道义。~ *rearmament* (*movement*)〔美〕重振道德运动。~ *science* 精神科学(= ~ *philosophy*)。~ *support* 精神上的支持。~ *tone* 品格。~ *virtues* 德,自然道德。**II *n.*** **1.** (寓言等的)寓意,教训;寓言剧;〔*pl.* 但通常作单数用〕修身,伦理(学);〔*pl.*〕(尤指男女间的)品行;〔罕〕= morale. **2.** 〔古〕相对者;逼肖者。*point a* ~ 用实例训导。*The boy is the very* ~ *of his father.* 这孩子活像他父亲。~ **law**【哲】道德律。~ **hazard**【保险】道德上的风险〔因被保险人的不道德或轻率而对保险公司所造成的风险〕。~ **majority**〔美〕"维护道义的大多数"〔宗教和道德观念上的一个保守群体〕。

mo·rale [mɔˈrɑːl; moˋræl] ***n.*** (军队的)士气;风纪;精神;信心,信念;道义;道德。*the* ~ *of the colony*【蜂】群势。*boost the* ~ *of* 长…的志气,给…打气。

mor·al·ism [ˈmɔrəlizəm; ˋmɑrəlɪzm] ***n.*** 道德(主义);道义;修身训言,格言。**mor·al·ist *n.*** 道德家;道学家,道德主义者;伦理学家。**mor·al·is·tic *a.*** 道学的,教训的;道德主义的。

mo·ral·i·ty [məˈræliti; moˋrælətɪ] ***n.*** **1.** 道德,道义;伦理学;〔*pl.*〕伦理;德性,德义,德行;(尤指男女间的)品行。**2.** 是非善恶;寓意,教训。**3.** (15—16 世纪的)劝善惩恶的宗教剧,寓意剧(= ~-play)。*commercial* ~ 商业道德。

mor·al·ize [ˈmɔrəlaiz; ˋmɔrəlaɪz] ***vt.*** **1.** 训导;赋与…德性,启发…的德行;德化,教化。**2.** 说道,讲道,用道德意义解释(寓言等)。— ***vi.*** 说教,讲道;给与道德上的感化。**-i·za·tion** [ˌmɔrəlaiˈzeiʃən; ˏmɔrəlɪˋzeʃən] ***n.*** **-iz·er *n.*** 说教者。

mor·al·ly [ˈmɔrəli; ˋmɔrəlɪ] ***ad.*** **1.** 道德上,从道德上看。**2.** 规规矩矩,正直地。**3.** 确实地。*be* ~ *bound to fail* 的的确确会失败。

mo·rass [məˈræs; moˋræs] ***n.*** 泥淖,沼泽;艰难,困境;堕落。~ **ore**【矿】沼铁矿。

mo·rass·y [məˈræsi; məˋræsɪ] ***a.*** 泥淖一样的。

mo·rat [ˈmɔːræt; moˋræt] ***n.*** (中世纪)桑葚调味的酒。

mor·a·to·ri·um [ˌmɔrəˈtɔːriəm; ˏmɔrəˋtorɪəm] ***n.*** (*pl.* ~*s*, ***-ri·a*** [-riə; -rɪə]) **1.**【法】延期偿付权;延缓偿付期。**2.** (行动、活动等的)暂停,暂禁。

mor·a·to·ry [ˈmɔrətəri; ˋmɔrəˏtorɪ] ***a.*** 延期偿付的。

Mo·ra·via [məˈreivjə; məˋreviə] ***n.*** 摩拉维亚〔捷克和斯洛伐克中部一地区〕。

Mo·ra·vi·an [məˈreivjən; məˋrevɪən] **I *a.*** 摩拉维亚的。**II *n.*** 摩拉维亚人;〔*pl.*〕【宗】摩拉维亚教徒,弟兄派教友。

mo·ray [ˈmɔrei, mɔːˈrei; ˋmore, moˋre] ***n.***【动】海鳝科鱼,海鳝 (moray eel)。

mor·bid [ˈmɔːbid; ˋmɔrbɪd] ***a.*** **1.** (精神上)不健全的,病态的;病态过敏性的。**2.** 关于病的;致病的;病理学的。**3.** 恶性的;可怕的;令人毛骨悚然的。~ *anatomy* 病理解剖学。*a* ~ *growth* 肿瘍。**-ly *ad.*** **-ness *n.*** (精神的)病态。

mor·bi·dez·za [ˌmɔːbiˈdetsə; ˏmɔrbɪˋdɛtsɑ] ***n.*** 〔It.〕【美术】(肤色等逼真的)柔美。

mor·bid·i·ty [mɔːˈbiditi; mɔrˋbɪdətɪ] ***n.*** **1.** 病况,病状。**2.** (一地的)发病率,致病率。

mor·bif·ic(al) [mɔːˈbifik(əl); mɔrˋbɪfɪk(əl)] ***a.*** 引起疾病的。

mor·bil·li [mɔːˈbilai; mɔrˋbɪlaɪ] ***n.*** 〔*pl.*〕【医】麻疹。

mor·ceau [mɔːˈsəu; ˏmɔrˋso] ***n.*** 〔F.〕(*pl.* ~***x*** [-z; -z]) **1.** 小片;片断。**2.** 文艺小品;【乐】作品,乐曲;小曲。

mor·da·cious [mɔːˈdeiʃəs; mɔrˋdeʃəs] ***a.*** 挖苦的,恶毒地讽刺的,尖酸刻薄的。

mor·dac·i·ty [mɔːˈdæsiti; mɔrˋdæsətɪ] ***n.*** 尖酸的讽刺,挖苦;刻薄。

mor·dan·cy [ˈmɔːdənsi; ˋmɔrdnsɪ] ***n.*** = mordacity。

mor·dant [ˈmɔːdənt; ˋmɔrdnt] **I *a.*** **1.** 讽刺的,尖酸的,尖嘴辣舌的。**2.** 媒染性的;腐蚀性的;破坏组织的。**II *n.***【染】媒染剂[料];【印】金属腐蚀剂;金箔黏着剂。**-ly *ad.***

mor·dent [ˈmɔːdənt; ˋmɔrdnt] ***n.***【乐】波音。

Mo·re [ˈmɔː; ˋmor] ***n.*** 莫尔〔姓氏〕。

Mo·ré [mɔːˈrei; moˋre] ***n.*** **1.** (苏丹中西部的)莫西人。**2.** 莫西语(= Mossi)。

more [mɔː, mɔə; mɔr, mor] **I *a.*** 〔many, much 的比较级;最高级是 most〕(*opp.* less) **1.** (数、量、程度等)更多的,较多的,更大的,更好的。**2.** 〔废〕(地位、身分等)更高的。**3.** 另外附加的,其余的,此外,还(有等)。*There was* ~ *smoke than fire.* 烟多火小。★ **1.** more 后的名词常略而不言:The ~, the merrier. 人愈多愈快活。**2.** 〔more than one + 单数名词〕M- than one person has found it so. 这样想的人不只一个。One word ~ 还有一句话。And what ~ do you want? 你还要什么(难道还不够吗)? **II *n.*** 更多的数量[程度];其余的事,附加,添加。*I hope to see* ~ *of you.* 我希望更多看到你们;我希望再看到你。*M- is meant than meets the ear.* 大有言外之意。**III *ad.*** **1.** 〔much 的比较级〕更多,更大。**2.** 〔形成二音节以上的形容词和副词的比较级〕更,格外〔例:~ *beautiful*(*ly*)〕。**3.** 再。**4.** 反而。*He was* ~ *frightened than hurt.* 他吓得厉害,伤倒不大。***a little*** ~ 再…一点。***all the*** ~ 格外,越发,更加。***and no*** ~ 不过是…罢了。(***and***) ***what is*** ~ 加之,而且。***any*** ~ 还;更;〔带否定语〕已经 (*Have you any* ~ *money?* 钱还有没有?)。~ ***and*** ~ 越来越…。~ ***brave than wise*** 有勇无谋。~ ***or less*** **1.** 有几分,有点儿(~ *or less beautiful* 颇有姿色)。**2.** 约,左右(*$100* ~ *or less* 一百元左右)。**3.** 〔在否定语后〕一点也…(*I could not*

M

afford to ride, ～ *or less*. 我根本坐不起车子)。～ **than** 多过,大过,…以上;比…更(*I went* ～ *than a mile*. 我走了一英里多路。*That is* ～ *than I can tell*. 那我就不知道了。～ *than ten years ago* 十几年前)。～ **than all** 尤其。～ **than enough** 足够;太多。～ **than ever** 越发(用功等),更多(的)。～ **... than not** (性能、状态)极其,相当,非常;(时间)往往,屡见不鲜。～ **than pleased** 十分高兴。**much** ～ 更;何况(*She knows French*, *much* ～ *English*. 她法语也懂,英语就不必说了)。**neither** ～ **nor less than** 恰,正,不多不少。**never** ～ 决不再。**no** ～ (此后)不再;死了;…也不[没有](*He is no* ～. 他死了)。**no** ～ **than** 〔than 后接名词〕只,仅仅,不过是(*no* ～ *than five* 仅五个。*no* ～ *than a puppet* 不过是个傀儡)。**no** ～ **... than** 〔than 引出子句〕和某甲一样不…,某甲不[是,能]…,某乙也不[是,能]…(*He is no* ～ *a god than we are*. 他和我们一样不是神。*He cannot speak French any* ～ *than I can*. 我不会讲法语,他也不会讲法语)。**none the** ～ = **not the** ～ 虽…仍旧[还是]…。**not any** ～ **than** = *no* ～ *than*. **not** ～ 不再…;不再有,已经没有。**not** ～ **than** 〔than 后接名词〕不超过,至多(*not* ～ *than five* 最多五个)。**not** ～ **...than** 〔than 引出从句〕不比某乙更…(*This book is not* ～ *expensive than that one*. 这本书不比那本书更贵)。**once** ～ 再一次[回]。**one** ～ 还(有)一个,再(来)一个。**or** ～ 或许更多一点,至少(*a mile or* ～ 至少一英里)。**some** ～ 再…些。**still** ～ = *much* ～: **the** ～ 越发,更。**the** ～ **and the less** 地位高的和地位低的人。**the** ～ **... because** [**as**, **that**] 因为…更。**the** ～ **... the** ～ **...** 愈…愈,越是…越是(*The* ～ *I know him*, *the* ～ *I like him*. 越是了解他,越是喜欢他)。**what is** ～ = *and what is* ～.

-more *suf*. 更…: further*more*, inner*more*. 但 ever*more*, forever*more*, never*more* 等的 *-more* 仅属加强意义。

Mo·re·a [mɔ(:)ˈriə; moˋriə] *n*. (希腊南部的)摩利亚半岛〔旧名 Peloponnesus 伯罗奔尼撒斯〕。

mo·reen [mɔːˈriːn, ˈmɔːriːn; məˋrin, ˋmɔrin] *n*. (做窗帘、帷幕等用的)云纹毛呢,云纹棉毛混纺呢。

mo·rel [mɔˈrel; məˋrel] *n*. 【植】牛肚菌;龙葵。

mo·rel·lo [məˈreləu; məˋrelo] *n*. (*pl*. ～*s*) 黑樱桃。

mo·re·o·ver [mɔːˈrəuvə; moˋrovɚ] *ad*. 况且,并且,加之,此外,又。

more·pork [ˈmɔːpɔːk; ˋmɔrpɔrk] *n*. = mopoke.

mo·res [ˈmɔːriːz; ˋmoriz] *n*. 〔L.〕〔*pl*.〕(社会)风俗,习俗,惯例;道德态度。

Mo·resque [məˈresk; məˋrɛsk] *a*. 摩尔(Moor)式装饰的。

Mor·gan[1] [ˈmɔːgən; ˋmɔrgən] *n*. (美国佛蒙特州的)摩根品种马。

Mor·gan[2] [ˈmɔːgən; ˋmɔrgən] *n*. **1**. 摩根〔姓氏,男子名〕。**2**. **Thomas Hunt** ～ 摩根〔1866—1945,美国生物学家,曾获 1933 年诺贝尔医学奖〕。

mor·ga·nat·ic [ˌmɔːgəˈnætik; ˏmɔrgəˋnætɪk] *a*. 社会身份高的男子和身份低的女子结婚的。

mor·gan·ite [ˈmɔːgəˌnait; ˋmɔrgəˏnaɪt] *a*. 【地】绝绿柱石。

mor·gen [ˈmɔːgən; ˋmɔrgən] *n*. (*pl*. ***-gen***, ***-gens***) 摩肯〔地积单位;荷兰及其属地以及南非使用,相当于二英亩。普鲁士、丹麦和挪威早先的地积单位;相当于一英亩的三分之二〕。

Mor·gen·thau [ˈmɔːgənθɔː; ˋmɔrgənˏθɔ] *n*. 摩根索〔姓氏〕。

morgue [mɔːg; mɔrg] *n*. **1**. 陈尸所,停尸室。**2**. 〔美〕(报馆等的)资料室,图画室。

morgue [mɔːg; mɔrg] *n*. 〔F.〕傲慢。～ ***anglaise*** [-ɑ̃ːŋˈgleiz; -ɑ̃ŋˋglez] 英国人特有的傲慢态度。

mor·i·bund [ˈmɔ(ː)ribʌnd; ˋmɔrəˏbʌnd] **I** *a*. 濒死的,垂死的,奄奄一息的;死气沉沉的。**II** *n*. 将死的人。**-bun·di·ty** *n*. **-ly** *ad*.

mo·ri·on[1] [ˈmɔriən; ˋmorɪˏɑn] *n*. (没有面甲的)高顶盔。

mor·ion[2] [ˈmɔriən; ˋmorɪˏɑn] *n*. 墨晶。

Mo·ris·co [məˈriskəu; məˋrɪsko] **I** *a*. Moor 式的。**II** *n*. (*pl*. ～*s*, ～*es*) 摩尔人(尤指西班牙的 Moor 人)。

Mor·i·son [ˈmɔrisn; ˋmɔrəsn] *n*. 莫里森〔姓氏〕。

Mor·ley [ˈmɔːli; ˋmɔrlɪ] *n*. 莫利〔姓氏〕。

Mor·mon [ˈmɔːmən; ˋmɔrmən] *n*. 摩门(基督复兴教)教徒;〔*pl*.〕〔美〕犹他州人的别名;一夫多妻主义者。**-ism** *n*. 摩门教。

morn [mɔːn; mɔrn] *n*. 〔诗、古〕黎明,早晨;〔Scot.〕明天。**at** ～ = in the morning. **the** ～**'s morn** 〔Scot.〕明早。

morn·ing [ˈmɔːniŋ; ˋmɔrnɪŋ] *n*. **1**. 早晨。**2**. 上午;〔废、古〕(上层社会晚餐前的)白天〔例: ～ *performance* 〔英〕(午后开演的日戏)〕。**3**. 初期,早期。**4**. 〔诗〕黎明;〔M-〕黎明的女神。*It is* ～. 天亮了。*Good* ～! 早上好! 早安! *the* ～ *of life* 青春时代。**from** ～ **till** [**to**] **night** [**evening**] 从早到晚。**in the** ～ 在早晨,在午前。**of a** ～ 往往在早上。～ **after** 〔口〕(狂饮后次日早晨的)宿醉;无节制行为的后果。～**-after pill** 后服避孕丸。～ **call** 午后的正式访问。～ **coat** 晨礼服。～ **draft** (早餐前喝的)晨酒。～ **dress 1**. 女人便服。**2**. 常礼服〔白天集会或结婚时穿的男服〕。～ **gift** (丈夫婚后第二天早晨送妻子的)晨礼。～ **glory** 【植】**1**. 牵牛花。**2**. 后劲不足者。～ **gun** 【军】晨炮,早晨升旗礼炮。～ **land** 〔诗〕东洋。～ **paper** 晨报。～ **room** (上午家属公用的)起居室〔有别于 drawing room〕。～ **sickness** 【医】孕妇晨吐。～ **star** 晓星,金星。～**tide** 〔诗〕早晨。～ **watch** 【海】早班〔自上午 4 时至 8 时〕。

Mo·ro [ˈmɔːrəu; ˋmoro] *n*., *a*. (非律宾伊斯兰教马来族之一的)摩洛族(的);摩洛语(的)。

Mo·roc·co [məˈrɔkəu; məˋrɑko] *n*. **1**. 摩洛哥〔非洲〕。**2**. 〔m-〕(*pl*. ～*s*)(摩洛哥山羊鞣制成的)摩洛哥皮。*the Levant m-* 上等摩洛哥皮。**-can** [-kən; -kən] **1**. *a*. 摩洛哥的;摩洛哥人的。**2**. *n*. 摩洛哥人。

mo·ron [ˈmɔːrɔn; ˋmɔrɑn] *n*. 白痴;〔口〕低能的人。**mo·ron·ic** [mɔːˈrɔnik; məˋrɑnɪk] *a*. 〔美〕白痴的,低能的。**mo·ron·ism**, **mo·ron·i·ty** [mɔːˈrɔniti; məˋrɑnətɪ] *n*. 白痴,低能。

Mo·ro·ni [məˈrɔni; məˋrɑnɪ] *n*. 莫罗尼〔科摩罗首都〕。

mo·rose [məˈrəus; moˋros] *a*. 愁眉苦脸的;郁闷的;不高兴的;脾气坏的;乖僻的。**-ly** *ad*. **-ness** *n*.

morph. = morphology.

morph- *comb*. *f*. = morpho-.

morph [mɔf; mɔf] **I** *n*. **1**. (动植物的)变种,变体。**2**. 【计】(电脑屏幕上的)图像变换(术)。**II** *vi*. 【计】(在电脑屏幕上)变换图像;〔口〕变来变去,变化不定。

morph·al·lax·is [ˌmɔfəˈlæksis; ˏmɔfəˋlæksɪs] *n*. (*pl*. ***-lax·es*** [-siːz; -siz]) 【动】变形再生。

mor·pheme [ˈmɔːfiːm; ˋmɔrfim] *n*. 【语】词素;语素;形素。

mor·phe·mics [mɔːˈfiːmiks; mɔrˋfimɪks] *n*. 〔*pl*.〕〔动词用单数〕词素学。

Mor·pheus [ˈmɔːfjuːs; ˋmɔrfjus] *n*. 【希神】梦神;睡神,睡梦之神。**in the arms of** ～ 在睡神怀抱中;睡着。

mor·phi·a, **mor·phine** [ˈmɔːfjə, ˈmɔːfiːn; ˋmɔrfɪə, ˋmɔrfin] *n*. 【化】吗啡。

mor·phin·ism [ˈmɔːfinizəm; ˋmɔrfɪnɪzm] *n*. 【医】吗啡中毒;吗啡瘾。

mor·phi·no·ma·ni·a [ˌmɔfinəˈmeinjə; ˏmɔrfɪnəˋmenɪə] *n*. 吗啡瘾,吗啡狂。

mor·phi·no·ma·ni·ac [ˌmɔːfinəˈmeiniæk; ˏmɔrfɪnəˋmenɪˏæk] *n*. 有吗啡瘾的人,吗啡中毒者。

mor·pho- *comb*. *f*. 表示"形状","形态": *morpho*genesis.

mor·pho·gen·e·sis [ˌmɔːfəˈdʒenisis; ˏmɔrfəˋdʒɛnəsɪs] ***n.***【动】**1.** 形态发生,形态形成。**2.** 器官发生,器官形成。**-ge·net·ic** [-dʒiˈnetik; -dʒɪˋnɛtɪk] ***a.***

mor·phol. = morphological; morphology.

mor·pho·log·ic (al) [ˌmɔːfəˈlɔdʒik(əl); ˏmɔrfəˋlɑdʒək(əl)] ***a.*** 形态学(上)的;【语】词法的,形态的。

mor·phol·o·gy [mɔːˈfɔlədʒi; mɔrˋfɑlədʒɪ] ***n.***【生、地】形态学;【语法】词法;词态学;【生】组织,形态。**-gist** ***n.*** 形态学家。

mor·pho·pho·ne·mics [ˌmɔːfəufəˈniːmiks; ˏmɔrfofəˋnimɪks] ***n.***〔动词用单数〕**1.**【语】形态音位学,词素音位学。**2.** (某语言中)词素音素变异的全类。**-pho·ne·mic** ***a.***

mor·pho·sis [mɔːˈfəusis; mɔrˋfosɪs] ***n.*** (*pl.* ***-ses*** [-siːz;-sɪz])【生】形态形成。**-phot·ic** [-ˈfɔtik; -ˋfɑtɪk] ***a.***

mor·ris [ˈmɔris; ˋmɔrɪs] ***n.*** (打扮成 Robin Hood 等传奇人物跳的)莫利斯舞。

Mor·ris [ˈmɔris; ˋmɔrɪs] ***n.*** 莫里斯〔姓氏,男子名, Maurice 的异体〕。~ **chair** 莫里斯式靠椅〔靠背斜度可自由调节〕。

Mor·ri·son [ˈmɔrisn; ˋmɔrəsn̩] ***n.*** 莫里森〔姓氏〕。~ **shelter**〔英〕屋内钢壁防空室。~ **tube** 莫利斯式枪筒。

mor·row [ˈmɔrəu; ˋmɔro] ***n.*** **1.**〔古〕早晨。**2.**〔诗〕翌日,次日,第二天。**3.** 紧接在后的时间。***on the ~ of*** 紧接着…。

Morse [mɔːs; mɔrs] **I** ***n.*** **1.** 莫尔斯〔姓氏〕。**2. Samuel Finley Breese ~** 莫尔斯〔1791—1872,美国电报机发明家〕。**3.**【电信】莫尔斯电码。**II** ***a.*** 莫尔斯电码(的)。~ **alphabet** [**code**] 莫尔斯电码。~ **instrument** 莫尔斯机。~ **receiver** 莫尔斯收报机。

morse[1] [mɔːs; mɔrs] ***n.***【动】海象。

morse[2] [mɔːs; mɔrs] ***n.*** (镶有宝石的)法衣襻扣。

mor·sel [ˈmɔːsəl; ˋmɔrsəl] ***n.*** (食物的)一口;一小片;少量;一点点;佳肴。

mort [mɔːt; mɔrt] ***n.*** **1.** 死。**2.**【猎】报告猎物已死的号角声。**3.** 三岁的鲑鱼。**4.**〔方〕许多,大量(*of*)。**5.**〔俚〕少女,女人。

mort. = mortuary.

mor·ta·del·la [ˌmɔːtəˈdelə; ˏmɔrtəˋdɛlə] ***n.*** 意大利大香肠。

mor·tal [ˈmɔːtl; ˋmɔrtl̩] **I** ***a.*** **1.** 死的;有死的,不能不死的(*opp.* immortal)。**2.** 凡人的;人的,人类的。**3.** 性命攸关的,致命的;临终的,临死的。**4.** 要堕地狱的,不能宽恕的(*opp.* venial)。**5.** 非杀不可的,不共戴天的。**6.**〔口〕冗长的,烦人的。**7.**〔口〕非常的,极大的。**8.**〔口〕〔与 all, every, no 等连用〕可能的。*Man is ~.* 人是会死的。*~ remains* 遗体,死尸。*a ~ wound* 致命伤。*a ~ disease* 绝症。*~ agony* 临死时的痛苦。*~ weapon* 凶器。*the ~ hour* 将死的时候。*a ~ combat* 你死我活的战斗;决斗。*a ~ enemy* [*foe*] 不共戴天的敌人。*two ~ hours* 长得要命的两个钟头。*~ sins* 不可饶恕的大罪。*It is of no ~ use.* 全无用处。***in a ~ funk***〔俚〕吓得要死。***in a ~ hurry***〔俚〕急急忙忙。***in ~ fear*** 极端害怕。***past all ~ aid*** 无法援救。**II** ***ad.***〔俚、方〕极,非常。**III** ***n.*** **1.** 不能不死的生物;人类;凡人。**2.**〔谑〕人。*a jolly ~* 有趣的人。**-ly** ***ad.*** 致命地;人性上;〔口〕非常,很 (*be mortally afraid* 怕得要命。*be mortally wounded* 受了致命伤)。

mor·tal·i·ty [mɔːˈtæliti; mɔrˋtælətɪ] ***n.*** 必死的命运[性质];致命性;死亡数;死亡率;大量死亡;失败数;失败率;人,人类。*the ~ from automobile accidents* 由于汽车事故造成的死亡人数。~ **table**【保险】死亡率表。

mor·tar[1] [ˈmɔːtə; ˋmɔrtɚ] **I** ***n.*** 灰泥;灰浆;胶泥;【地】碎斑结构。**II** ***vt.*** 用灰泥涂抹[接合]。

mor·tar[2] [ˈmɔːtə; ˋmɔrtɚ] **I** ***n.*** 臼,捣钵,研钵;【军】臼炮,迫击炮;【矿】(试验炸药用的)臼炮。**II** ***vt.*** 用迫击炮轰击。~-**board** 灰泥板,镘板;〔口〕学士帽;学位帽。

mort·gage [ˈmɔːgidʒ; ˋmɔrgɪdʒ] **I** ***n.***【法】抵押;抵押权;抵押契据;受押人对抵押品的权利。***on ~*** (拿房屋等)作抵押。~ **bond** 抵押债券。**II** ***vt.*** 抵押;把…许给。*~ oneself* [*one's life*] *to the revolutionary cause* 献身革命事业。

mort·ga·gee [ˌmɔːgəˈdʒiː; ˏmɔrgɪˋdʒi] ***n.***【法】接受抵押者,受押人;抵押权人。

mort·ga·ger, mort·ga·gor [ˈmɔgədʒə, ˌmɔːgəˈdʒɔː; ˋmɔrgɪdʒɚ, ˏmɔrgəˋdʒɔr] ***n.***【法】抵押人。

mor·tice [ˈmɔːtis; ˋmɔrtɪs] ***n.***, ***vt.*** = mortise.

mor·ti·cian [mɔːˈtiʃən; mɔrˋtɪʃən] ***n.***〔美〕承办丧葬的人;殡仪业者(=〔英〕undertaker)。

mor·ti·fi·ca·tion [ˌmɔːtifiˈkeiʃən; ˏmɔrtəfəˋkeʃən] ***n.*** **1.**【医】脱疽,坏疽。**2.**【宗】禁欲,节食,苦行。**3.** 耻辱,屈辱;悔恨,遗恨。**4.**〔废〕【化】中和。**5.**【植】枯斑,坏死。

mor·ti·fy [ˈmɔːtifai; ˋmɔrtəˏfaɪ] ***vt.***, ***vi.*** **1.** 抑制(情欲等)。**2.** 使悔恨,使感耻辱;伤害(感情)。**3.**【医】(使)患脱疽。**4.**【植】生枯斑,坏死。

mor·ti·fy·ing [ˈmɔːtifaiiŋ; ˋmɔrtəˏfaɪɪŋ] ***a.*** **1.** 叫人呕气的,气死人的,痛心的。**2.** 禁欲修行的。**3.** 坏疽的。

Mor·ti·mer [ˈmɔːtimə; ˋmɔrtɪmɚ] ***n.*** 莫蒂默〔男子名〕。

mor·tise [ˈmɔːtis; ˋmɔrtɪs] **I** ***n.*** **1.** 榫眼,榫孔。**2.** 固定,安定。*a ~ chisel* 榫凿。*a ~ and tenon joint* 镶榫接头。*a ~ lock* 插锁。**II** ***vt.*** 开榫眼;用榫眼接合。

mort·main [ˈmɔːtmein; ˋmɔrtmen] ***n.***【法】永久管业权〔永远不能变卖公产〕;永远保有;传统势力。

Mor·ton [ˈmɔːtn; ˋmɔrtn̩] ***n.*** 莫顿〔姓氏,男子名〕。

mor·tu·a·ry [ˈmɔːtjuəri; ˋmɔrtʃʊˏɛrɪ] **I** ***n.*** **1.** 停尸所。**2.** = morgue1. **3.**【英史】(教区牧师从已故教区居民遗产中获得的)布施。**II** ***a.*** 死亡的,纪念死的;(关于)丧葬的。*~ rites* 葬仪。*a ~ urn* 骨灰瓮。

mor·u·la [ˈmɔːrjulə, ˈmɔr-, -ulə; ˋmɔrjʊlə, ˋmɔr-, -ʊlə] ***n.*** (*pl.* ***-lae*** [-ˌliː; -ˏli])【生】桑椹胚;桑椹体。**mor·u·lar** ***a.*** **mor·u·la·tion** ***n.***

Mo·rus [ˈmɔrəs; ˋmɔrəs] ***n.***【植】桑属。

mos. = months.

mo·sa·ic [məˈzeiik; moˋze·ɪk] **I** ***n.*** **1.** 马赛克,镶嵌细工,拼花工艺;拼花图样;拼制图画;编写作品;拼制物;【建】镶嵌砖;【军】镶嵌图。**2.**【植病】花叶病。**3.**【生】嵌合体。**4.**【电视】感光镶嵌幕,嵌镶光电阴极。**II** ***a.*** 马赛克式的,镶嵌细工的;用拼花方式制成的。*~ gold* 彩色金(颜料);仿金的铜合金。*a ~ pavement* 拼花道路。*~ woolwork* 拼花绒线编织品。**III** ***vt.*** (***mo·sa·icked, mo·sa·ick·ing***) 用拼花图案装饰。

Mo·sa·ic, -i·cal [məuˈzeiik, -ikəl; moˋze·ɪk, -ɪkəl] ***a.*** 摩西 (Moses) 的。

mo·sa·i·cism [məuˈzeiːsizəm; moˋzeəsɪzəm] ***n.***【生】镶嵌性。

mo·sa·i·cist [məuˈzeiisist; moˋzeəsɪst] ***n.*** **1.** 马赛克设计者。**2.** 马赛克制作工。**3.** 马赛克销售商。

Mos·by [ˈmɔzbi; ˋmɑzbɪ] ***n.*** 莫斯比〔姓氏〕。

mos·chate [ˈmɔskeit, -kit; ˋmɑsket, -kɪt] ***a.*** 麝香味的,麝香气的。

Mos·cow [ˈmɔskəu; ˋmɑsko] ***n.*** 莫斯科〔俄罗斯首都〕。

mo·selle [məˈzel; moˋzɛl] ***n.*** (法国莫赛耳 Moselle 河流域出产的)莫赛耳白葡萄酒。

Mo·ses [ˈməuziz; ˋmozɪz] ***n.*** **1.** 摩西〔姓氏,男子名〕。**2.** (基督教《圣经》)率领希伯来人出埃及的领袖。**3.**〔喻〕领袖;立法者。**4.** 放债的犹太人。

mo·sey [ˈməuzi; ˋmozɪ] ***vi.***〔美俚〕离开,走开;闲荡,信步。*M- along!* 滚! 出去!

mo·shav [məuˈʃɑːv; moˋʃav] ***n.*** (*pl.* ***mo·sha·vim*** [ˌməuʃɑːˈviːm; ˏmoʃɑˋvim]) 私人租地集体耕作制〔以色列的一种定居方式〕。

mos·ke·neer [mɔskiˈniːə; mɑskɪˋniɚ] ***vt.***〔英俚〕(当贵东西)使当铺上当。

M

mos·ker [ˈmɔskə; ˋmɑskɚ] ***n.*** 〔英俚〕当贵东西得到便宜的人。

Mos·lem, Mus·lim [ˈmɔzlem, ˈmɔzlim; ˋmɑzləm, ˋmɑzlɪm] **I** ***n.*** (*pl.* ~*s*, ~, 〔集合词〕~)穆斯林。**II** ***a.*** 穆斯林的;伊斯兰教的。

Mos·ley [ˈmɔzli, ˈməuzli; ˋmɔzlɪ, ˋmozlɪ] ***n.*** 莫斯利〔姓氏〕。

mosque [mɔsk; mɑsk] ***n.*** 伊斯兰教寺院,清真寺。

mos·qui·to [məsˈkiːtəu; məˋskito] ***n.*** (*pl.* ~*es*, ~*s*) 蚊子;〔M-〕〔英〕蚊式轰炸机;(瑞士)蚊式地对空导〔飞〕弹;〔M-〕〔美〕New Jersey 州的别名。~ **boat** 鱼雷快艇。~ **bomb** 灭蚊弹。~**cide** 灭蚊药;灭蚊。~ **craft** 快艇。~ **curtain** [**bar, net**] 蚊帐。~ **fever** 疟疾。~ **fish** 食蚊鱼。~ **fleet** 鱼雷[轻快]艇队。~ **hawk** 蜻蜓。~ **sortie**【空】蚊式突击。

MOSS = manned orbital space station【宇】载人轨道航天站。

moss [mɔs; mɔs] **I** ***n.*** **1.**【植】苔,藓;地衣。**2.** 〔Scot.〕沼,泥淖;泥炭沼。**3.** 〔M-〕莫斯〔男子名〕。**4.** 〔美俚〕平凡的东西,守旧的人。**II** ***vt.*** 拿苔覆盖;使长满苔藓。~ **agate**【矿】藓纹玛瑙。~**back** 〔美俚〕(背上长了水草的)老乌龟;绿毛龟;〔美俚〕极端守旧的人,老顽固;〔美俚〕盲目效忠本党的政治家。~**bunker** 步鱼(= menhaden)。~ **fern**【植】水龙骨。~**-grown** ***a.*** 生了苔的;旧式的,过时的。~ **hag** 泥炭采后的废坑。~ **pink**【植】丛生福禄考。~ **rose**【植】洋蔷薇。~**trooper** (沼地)劫掠者;土匪;强盗。

Möss·bau·er effect [ˈmɔːsbauə; ˋmɔsbauɚ]【物】穆斯堡尔效应。

Mos·si [ˈmɔsiː; ˋmɔsi] ***n.*** **1.** (*pl.* ***Mos·sis***, ***Mos·si***) 莫西人〔苏丹中西部一部族名〕。**2.** 莫西语。

moss·i·ness [ˈmɔsinis; ˋmɔsɪnɪs] ***n.*** 长满藓苔。

moss·like [ˈmɔːsˌlaik; ˋmɑsˏlaɪk] ***a.*** 似苔的。

moss·y [ˈmɔsi; ˋmɔsɪ] ***a.*** (***moss·i·er***; ***-i·est***) 生了苔的;多苔的;苔状的。

most [məust; most] **I** ***a.*** 〔many, much 的最高级;比较级是 more〕(*opp.* least)。**1.** 〔常作 the ~〕(数、量、程度)最多的,最大的,最高的。**2.** 〔通例无冠词〕大概的,大多数的,大部分的。**II** ***n.*** (*pron.*) **1.** 〔常作 the ~〕。**2.** 〔通例无冠词〕最大限度;大部分;〔作复数用〕大多数人。*M- people think so.* 大多数人都这样想。~ *effective range* 最有效射程。*That is the ~ I can do.* 我能做的就仅仅这样。*M- of us know it.* 大多数人都知道。***at*** (***the***) ~ 至多,最多,充其量(不过)。***for the ~ part*** 基本上。***make the ~ of*** 充分使用;尽量使好[不好]看;极为重视;尽量称赞[贬损];把…形容尽致;尽(欢)。**III** ***ad.*** **1.** 〔much 的最高级〕最,最多。**2.** 〔主要用以形成两个音节以上的形容词、副词的最高级〕: *the ~ beautiful, cleverly.* **3.** 〔不加 the〕非常,很,极。*a ~ beautiful woman*; ~ *certainly.* **4.** 〔方、美〕差不多,几乎 = almost: ~ *any boy.* **5.** 〔尊称用语〕: *M- Noble* 〔公爵的称号〕。*the M- High* 天老爷。★形容词、副词前若有 the 则是最高级,若没有 the 则仅仅表示加重语气。~ ***and least*** (诗)全体的,统统,都,皆。***the ~ favoured nation*** (***clause***)【国际法】最惠国[条款]。

-most *suf.* 最〔用作表示位置、时间、顺序的形容词、副词、名词的词尾以形成形容词〕: end*most*, top*most*, inner*most*, ut*most*.

most·ly [ˈməustli; ˋmostlɪ] ***ad.*** 大部分,多半;通常,主要地,基本上。*They are ~ out on Sunday.* 星期天他们通常不在家。*The work is ~ done.* 工作基本上做好了。

mot [məu; mo] ***n.*** 〔F.〕(*pl.* ~*s* [-z; -z]) 警句,妙语。***bon*** ~ 良言,名言。~ ***à*** ~ [məutɑːˈməu; motɑˋmo] 逐字(对译)。~ ***d'ordre*** [ˈdɔədr; ˋdɔrdr] 命令。~ ***juste*** [ʒust; ʒust] 适当的语词。

mote[1] [məut; mot] ***n.*** 尘埃,尘屑;〔喻、古〕污点,瑕疵。~ ***and beam*** 别人的小缺点和自己的大过错。~ ***in another's eye*** 别人眼睛里的灰尘;与自己大过错相比之下别人的小缺点;不反省自己只责备别人。

mote[2] [məut; mot] ***aux. v.*** 〔古〕= may, might. *So ~ it be.* 那样也好。

mote[3] [məut; mot] ***n.*** moot 的别字。

mo·tel [məuˈtel; moˋtɛl] ***n.*** 〔美〕(专为)自驾汽车游客(开设的)旅馆〔有停车场〕(= *mo*torist's ho*tel*)。**-ing** ***n.*** "汽车旅馆式办公"〔指租赁按日收费的办公室办公〕。

mo·tet [məuˈtet; moˋtɛt] ***n.***【乐】赞美诗,圣歌;赞歌。

moth [mɔθ; mɔθ] **I** ***n.*** **1.** 蛾。**2.** 〔集合词, *sing.*, *pl.*〕蛀虫,蠹,腐蠹物。**3.** 轻快的飞机。**4.** 摧毁雷达台的导弹。~**-balls** ***n.*** 〔*pl.*〕卫生球[樟脑丸等]。~**ball fleet** 〔美俗〕预备舰队。~**-eaten** ***a.*** 虫蛀的;陈旧的。~**proof** ***a.*** 防蛀的。**II** ***vt.*** 使…防蛀。

moth·er[1] [ˈmʌðə; ˋmʌðɚ] **I** ***n.*** **1.** 母,母亲;〔常无冠词, M-〕(家人间称谓时)妈妈。**2.** 母,本源,根由。**3.** 老伯母,老大娘,老太太〔称呼年长女人时代替 Mrs. 用,如 M- Jones〕。**4.** 修女院长(= ~ superior)。**5.** 人工孵卵器。**6.** 航空母舰;航空母机;【电讯】第一模盘。**7.** 〔M-〕大猩猩(品种)苹果。*Necessity is the ~ of invention.* 需要是发明之母。*an artificial ~* 人工孵卵器〔养小鸡用〕。**II** ***a.*** 母的,母国的,本国的。*a ~ bird* 母鸟。**III** ***vt.*** **1.** 当作儿女抚养,像母亲一样照管,保育。**2.** 产,生〔通常在修辞上使用〕。**3.** 承认是(孩子)的母亲;声明自己是(小说等)的作者。**4.**【军】掩护。**every ~'s son** 〔口〕人人 = everyone, everybody. **M- Carey's chicken** [**hen**]【鸟】海燕[海雀]。~ **cell**【生】母细胞。~**-chrysanthemum** 野菊。**M- Church** 〔拟人语〕教会,所喜欢的教会;镇里最老的教会。~ **country** 本国〔对殖民地说〕,母国〔对私人说〕;父母之邦;发祥地。~ **earth** 大地;〔谑〕地,地面(*kiss the ~ earth* 跌在地上)。**M- Goose** 鹅妈妈〔**1.** 查尔斯·裴劳特(Charles Perraut)作的故事集中想像的叙述者。**2.** 1765 年前后伦敦出版的儿歌集的假想作者〕。~**hood** 母道,母亲的义务;母性;母权。**M- Hubbard** 鹅妈妈儿歌集中的女主人翁;女长大衣。~ **image** [**figure**] 心目中的母亲。~**-in-law** (*pl.* ~*s*) 婆母,岳母;〔英〕继母。~**land** 母国,祖国。**-less** ***a.*** 没有母亲的。~ **lode** 主矿脉,母脉。~**-naked** ***a.*** 像出娘胎时那样赤裸裸的。~**-of-pearl** 珍珠母,青贝,螺钿。**M- of Presidents** 〔美〕总统之乡〔指维吉尼亚州,因出过好几个总统之故〕。**M- of States** 〔美〕各州之母〔弗吉尼亚州的别名〕。~**-of-thyme**【植】欧百里香。~ **oil** (石油)原油。~ **rod** 主联杆。**M-'s Day** (美国和加拿大的)母亲节〔五月第二个星期日〕。~ **ship** 〔英〕母舰,航空母舰。~ **superior** 女修道院院长。~ **tongue** 母语,本国语,本民族语言。~ **wit** 天生的智慧;常识。~**wort**【植】益母草属。

moth·er[2] [ˈmʌðə; ˋmʌðɚ] **I** ***n.*** 醋母(= ~ of vinegar);渣滓,糟。**II** ***vt.*** 生醋母。

moth·er·ing [ˈmʌðəriŋ; ˋmʌðərɪŋ] ***n.*** 〔英〕省亲,探亲。

moth·er·li·ness [ˈmʌðəlinis; ˋmʌðɚlɪnɪs] ***n.*** 像母亲,母爱,慈母心。

moth·er·ly, moth·er·like [ˈmʌðəli, -laik; ˋmʌðɚlɪ, -laɪk] ***a.*** 母亲(似)的,母爱的,慈爱的。

moth·er·y [ˈmʌðəri; ˋmʌðərɪ] ***a.*** 醋母性的;含醋母的;像醋母的。

moth·y [ˈmɔθi; ˋmɔθɪ] ***a.*** (***moth·i·er***; ***-i·est***) 多蛾的;蛀了的,虫蛀的。

mo·tif [məuˈtiːf; moˋtif] ***n.*** 〔F.〕(艺术作品的)主题,要点,特色;动机,主旨;衣服的花边;(图案的)基本花纹;基本色彩;【物】型主。

mo·tile [ˈməutail, -til; ˋmotaɪl, -tɪl] **I** ***a.***【生】有自动力的,能动的。**II** ***n.***【心】运动型〔指人的想像力是能动的,而不仅仅是凭借视觉和听觉〕。**mo·til·i·ty** [məuˈtiliti; moˋtɪlətɪ] ***n.***【生】运动力,自动力;机动性;【化】游动(现象)。

mo·tion [ˈməuʃən; ˋmoʃən] **I** ***n.*** **1.** 运动,动,移动(*opp.*

rest)。**2.** (天体的)运行;(车、船等的)动摇;(机器的)开动,运转;【机】机械装置,机制。**3.** 动作,举动;手势;眼色;姿态;〔*pl.*〕(个人或团体的)行动,举动,活动。**4.** (议会中的)提议,动议;动机,意向;刺激;【法】申请,请求。**5.** 大便;〔*pl.*〕排泄物。**6.** 【乐】(旋律、曲调的)变移。*M-itself is a contradiction.* 运动本身就是矛盾。*All her ~s were graceful.* 她的一举一动都优美。*The ~ to adjourn was carried.* 休会的提议通过了。***in ~*** 动着,运转着,活动着。***make a ~ [~s]*** 用手势示意;提议。***~ study*** 操作研究。***of one's own ~*** 自动地,自愿地,出自本意。***on the ~ of*** 经…的动议。***put [set] in ~*** 使动,启动,发动。**II** *vi.* 打手势要求[指示](*to; towards; away*)。*~ (to) sb. to take a seat* 用手指椅子请某人坐下。— *vt.* 向某人打手势;向某人点头或摇头示意。*~ sb. away [out]* 打手势叫某人走开[出去]。~ **picture** *n.*, *a.* 电影(的),影片(的)。~ **sickness** 【医】运动病〔指晕车、晕船等〕。**-less** *n.* 不动的,静止的。

mo·tion·al [ˈməuʃənl; ˋmoʃənl̩] *a.* 运动的;由运动而生的;起动的。

mo·ti·vate [ˈməutiveit; ˋmotəvet] *vt.* 给与动机,促动,激发,诱导。**-va·tor** *n.*

mo·ti·va·tion [ˌməutiˈveiʃən; ˏmotəˋveʃən] *n.* 动机的形成;动机因素;动力。**-al** *a.* (*motivational research* 动机研究〔用于广告、销售活动〕)。

mo·tive [ˈməutiv; ˋmotɪv] **I** *a.* 引起运动的,发动的,运动的;成为(行动的)动机的。**II** *n.* **1.** 动机,动因;主旨;目的。**2.** (艺术作品的)主题;题材。***of [from] one's own ~*** 自动。**III** *vt.* **1.** = motivate. **2.** 成为(艺术作品的)主题。~ **power [force]** 动力〔电、汽力等〕;〔集合词〕机车,拖拉机。

mo·tive·less [ˈməutivlis; ˋmotɪvlɪs] *a.* 没有动机[目的、理由]的,妄动的。

mo·tiv·i·ty [məuˈtiviti; moˋtɪvətɪ] *n.* (发)动力,原动力。

Mot·ley [ˈmɔtli; ˋmɑtlɪ] *n.* 莫特利〔姓氏〕。

mot·ley [ˈmɔtli; ˋmɑtlɪ] **I** *a.* 杂色的;穿着杂色衣服的;繁杂的,混杂的;杂凑成的。**II** *n.* 杂色;(丑角穿的)杂色衣服;穿着杂色衣服的小丑。*wear (the) ~* 扮演丑角;装傻。

mot·mot [ˈmɔtmɔt; ˋmɑtmɑt] *n.* 〔动〕翠鴗〔产于美洲热带和亚热带地区〕。

mo·to·neu·ron [ˌməutəˈnjuərɔn, -nuər-; ˏmotəˋnjʊrɑn, -nʊr-] *n.* 【医】运动神经元。

mo·tor [ˈməutə; ˋmotɚ] **I** *n.* **1.** 原动者;原动力。**2.** 发动机;马达;电动机;【火箭】助推器;汽车。**3.** 【解】运动肌;运动神经。*an electric ~* 电动机。*a chemical fuel ~* 火箭发动机。**II** *a.* 使动的,发动的,原动的;【解】运动的。*~ gasoline* 动力汽油。*a ~ nerve* 运动神经。*a ~ skinner* 〔美〕汽车司机。**III** *vt.* 用汽车搬运。— *vi.* 坐汽车,开汽车。*~ a friend home* 用汽车送朋友回家。~**bicycle [bike]** 摩托(自行)车。~ **boat** 汽艇,汽船。~**boating** 乘汽艇出游;【无】汽船声〔低频寄生振荡〕。~**bus** 公共汽车。~**cab** 出租汽车。~**cade** 〔美〕汽车的长蛇阵[长列]。~**car** 汽车。~**coach** = ~bus. ~ **court** 〔美〕= motel. ~**-cross** 摩托车越野赛。~**-cycle** *n.*, *vi.* (骑)摩托车。~**cyclist** 骑摩托车的人;【军】摩托兵。~ **drawn** *a.* 汽车牵引的。~ **drive** 电机驱动系统[装置]。~**drome** 汽车试车场;汽车比赛场。~ **gen**, ~ **generator** 〔美〕电动发动机组。~ **home** 活动住宅,住房汽车。~ **hotel [inn]** (市内的)汽车酒店〔多建有停车房等〕。~ **launch** 汽艇。~**-lorry** 〔英〕运货汽车。~ **maker** 〔美〕汽车制造人[厂]。~**man** 〔美、加拿大〕(电车、电气机车的)司机;电机操作者。~ **meter** 电力测定器;汽车仪表。~**-polo** = auto-polo. ~ **pool** (军政机关)汽车集中调度场。~ **roller** 机碾。~ **scooter** 低座小摩托车。~**ship** 机船,汽船。~ **spirit** 汽油。~ **squadron** 【军】汽车队。~ **starter** (电动机)起动器。~ **torpedo boat** 鱼雷快艇。~**truck** 〔美〕运货汽车。~ **vehicle** 机动车;汽车。~**(-)voter** 汽车选民登记制〔凭驾驶执照登记注册为选民〕。~ **wag(g)on** 小卡车。**-less** *a.* 无动力的(*motorless flying* 滑翔飞行)。

mo·tor·a·ma [ˌməutəˈræmə; ˏmotəˋræmə] *n.* 新车展览。

mo·to·rial [məuˈtɔːriəl; moˋtorɪəl] *a.* 运动的,原动的;引起运动的;【解】运动神经的。

mo·tor·ist [ˈməutərist; ˋmotərɪst] *n.* 开汽车的人;乘汽车旅行的人。

mo·tor·ize [ˈməutəraiz; ˋmotəˏraɪz] *vt.* 使(车)机动化,汽车化;(废掉马车)改用汽车,摩托化;电化(铁路等)。*a ~d infantry division* 【军】摩托化步兵师。*a ~d unit* 【军】摩托化部队。

mo·to·ry [ˈməutəri; ˋmotərɪ] *a.* = motorial.

Mo·town [ˈməuˌtaun; ˋmoˏtaʊn] *a.* "汽车城"节奏的〔指一种节拍强而慢的节奏和布鲁斯舞曲;"汽车城"为美国底特律的别称〕。

Mott [mɔt; mɑt] *n.* 莫特〔姓氏〕。

motte [mɔt; mɑt] *n.* 〔美〕(大草原中的)丛林;小树林子。

mot·tle [ˈmɔtl; ˋmɑtl̩] **I** *vt.* 使成杂色,弄斑驳。**II** *n.* 斑点;斑纹;【生】斑驳病;杂色绒线[毛纱]。*~d iron* 马口铁。

mot·to [ˈmɔtəu; ˋmɑto] *n.* (*pl.* ~*es*, ~*s*) **1.** (简明的)标语;座右铭,训言,(特指刻在盾上或徽章上的)箴言。**2.** (书籍卷首或章头引用的)题词,题句;【乐】主题句。**3.** 附有题句或卦签的糖果袋。~ **kiss** 附有题句等的糖果。

mou [muː; mu] 〔单复同〕*n.* 〔Chin.〕亩 = *mu*.

mou·choir [muʃwɑːr; muʃwɑr] *n.* 〔F.〕手绢儿,手帕。

moue [muː; mu] *n.* = pout[1].

mouf·(f)lon [ˈmuːflɔn; ˋmuflɑn] *n.* 〔*sing.*, *pl.*〕摩弗伦羊〔南欧野羊〕。

mouil·lé [muːˈjei; muˋjeɪ] *a.* 【语音】颚化的。

mou·jik [ˈmuːʒik; muˋʒɪk] *n.* **1.** (俄国)农夫。**2.** 女用宽皮披肩(= muzhik)。

mou·lage [muːˈlɑːʒ; muˋlɑʒ] *n* **1.** (刑事侦察中用的)印模术,复制印痕术。**2.** 印模,印痕。

mould[1] [məuld; mold] **I** *n.* **1.** (阴)模,铸模,模型;外型;铸型;字模,字型;模制品。**2.** 形状,性格,气质;状况。**3.** 【建】(装饰)线条,花边,线脚。*a ~ of pudding* 一个布丁。***be cast in a ... ~*** 具有…的脾气,生就…的性格。***be cast in the same ~*** 性格完全相同。***of gentle ~*** 脾气温和的。**II** *vt.* **1.** 造形,翻砂,铸,放在模子里做;【建】用线条(或雕刻)装饰。**2.** 捏。**3.** 形成(性格);陶冶,训练(人格)。*~ one's own destiny* 决定自己的命运。~**(*up*)*on*** 按…的模子作。

mould[2] [məuld; mold] **I** *n.* 肥土,壤土;〔古〕土,土地。**II** *vt.* 用土覆盖。*leaf ~* 腐植质土。*a man of ~* (终要入土的)凡人,人类。*~ up (potatoes)* 拿土覆盖(马铃薯)。~**board** 犁壁;模板,型板。~**-planting** 丘植法。

mould[3] [məuld; mold] **I** *n.* 霉;霉菌,霉病。**II** *vt.*, *vi.* (使)发霉。*~ rains* 梅雨。

mould·er[1] [ˈməuldə; ˋmoldɚ] *vi.* **1.** 朽,朽坏(*away*)。**2.** 颓废,堕落;消衰,退化;吊儿郎当地度日。—*vt.* 使腐朽。

mould·er[2] [ˈməuldə; ˋmoldɚ] *n.* 模塑者,造型者;模;造型物;【印】(复制用的)电铸板。

mould·ing[1] [ˈməuldiŋ; ˋmoldɪŋ] *n.* 模塑,作模;造型;翻砂,铸造;铸造物,模塑物;〔常 *pl.*〕【建】花边,线脚,风景线。

mould·ing[2] [ˈməuldiŋ; ˋmoldɪŋ] *n.* 覆土;覆盖的土壤。

mould-loft [ˈməuldlɔft; ˋmoldlɑft] *n.* (造船厂内的)大制图室。

mould·y[1] [ˈməuldi; ˋmoldɪ] *a.* (***mould·i·er; -i·est***) 发了霉的;霉烂的;陈腐的;〔俚〕十分无聊的。

mould·y[2] [ˈməuldi; ˋmoldɪ] *n.* 〔海俚〕鱼雷,空投鱼雷。

mou·lin [ˈmuːlẽːŋ; ˏmuˋlæ̃] *n.* 〔F.〕【地】冰川锅穴。

Moul·mein [maulˈmein; mulˋmen] *n.* 毛淡棉〔缅甸港

市〕。

moult [məult; molt] I *vi*.(羽毛等)脱换,脱落。— *vt*. 使脱换(羽毛等)。II *n*. 脱换,脱落,脱皮。

Moul·ton [ˈməultən; ˋmoltən] *n*. 莫尔顿〔姓氏〕。

moul·vi [ˈmulvi; ˋmulvɪ] *n*. = moolvee, maulvi.

mound[1] [maund; maʊnd] I *n*. 堤;(尤指城堡的)护堤;土墩,土山;小山,小丘;【棒球】投球员的踏板。*the Indian* ~*s* 美洲印第安人史前时代在密西西比河东岸所筑的土墩子。*the M- City*〔美〕St. Louis 市的别名〔因土墩子很多〕。*take the* ~【棒球】作投球员。II *vt*. 筑堤;造土墩子;筑堤防御。~ **builder** *n*. 1. 筑墩者。2.〔M-Builder〕〔*pl*.〕北美五大湖地区的史前印第安人。3. 大足鹑,营冢鸟。

mound[2] [maund; maʊnd] *n*.(象征王权、王位的)宝球,宝珠;帝位的象征。

mount[1] [maunt; maʊnt] I *vt*. 1. 登,上(山、梯、王位等)。2. 骑,乘(马等)。3. 使人骑上(马),扶上(马);使做骑兵。4. 安装,装配,架(炮等);装置,装备;裱(画、地图等);镶(宝石等);封固,(把检物镜)固定在载(玻)片(slide)上,剥制(动物)。5. 准备服装、道具,上演(剧本)。6. 穿,戴。7. 测定,确定;规定。— *vi*. 1. 登,上;(血)上面孔。2. 骑马;乘(*on*)。3.(数量等)增长;增高;上升。~ *the stairs* 上楼梯。~ *a horse* 骑上马。~ *insects* 制昆虫标本。***be well*** [***poorly***] ***~ed*** 骑着好[劣]马。~ (***an offensive***) ***against*** 对…发动(攻势)。~ ***guard*** 站岗。~ ***guard over*** 守望,守卫。~ (***gems***) ***in*** 镶(宝石)在…。~ (***a gun***) ***on*** 把(大炮)安在…上。~ ***the high horse*** 趾高气扬;自大。~ ***up to*** ... (金额)增加到…。II *n*. 1. 坐骑〔马,骡;自行车等〕;〔俚〕(尤指赛马时的)骑马的机会;登,爬上;骑马。2.(衬托相片等用的)硬板纸,衬托纸,裱画纸;(家具的)边饰;(镶宝石的)宝石托;(显微镜的)载(玻)片;踏脚台;炮架,支架。3. 扇把,扇骨。4.(电子管)管脚。***get down from one's*** ~ 下马。

mount[2] [maunt; maʊnt] *n*. 1.〔书〕山,丘;〔M-〕…山,…峰〔通常略作 Mt〕。2.【手相】宫〔掌肉隆起处〕。

moun·tain [ˈmauntin; ˋmaʊntn̩] *n*. 1.(比 hill 大的)山,山岳;〔*pl*.〕山脉。2.〔the M-〕山岳党〔法国第一次革命时占据议会最高座位的左派政党〕。3. 山一样(巨大)的东西;大量。*the Rocky Mountains*〔美〕落基山脉。*rolling* ~*s* 滔天大浪。*a* ~ *of rubbish* 垃圾堆。***a*** ~ ***of*** (*difficulties*, *debts*) 山一般的(困难、债等)。***a*** ~ ***of flesh*** 大胖子。***make a*** ~ ***out of a molehill*** 小题大做。***remove*** ~***s*** 移山倒海;行奇迹,做惊人举动。***The*** ~ ***has brought forth a mouse***. = ***the*** ~ ***in labour*** 费力大收效小;雷声大雨点小。~ **artillery** 山炮;山地炮兵。~ **ash**【植】花楸,山楸属。~ **avens**【植】多瓣木,仙女木;三叶水杨梅。~ **battery** 山炮队。~ **bike** 山地自行车,山地车〔一种登山型的轻便自行车〕。~ **canary**〔美口〕小骗子。~ **cat** = cougar. ~ **chain** 山脉。~ **cloth** [**cork**, **flax**, **leather**] 石绵。~ **cranberry** = **cowberry** 牙疙瘩[越橘]。~ **crystal** 水晶。~ **deer**【动】羚羊。~ **dew** 苏格兰威士忌酒(尤指非法私造的);〔美俚〕酒,威士忌酒。~ **division** 山地作战师。~ **goat** 1.【动】石山羊。2.〔俚〕声波定位器,声纳。~ **green** 孔雀石。~ **group** 山群。~ **gun** 山炮。~**-high** *a*. 山一样高的。~ **howitzer** 山地榴弹炮。~ **laurel** 1.【植】山月桂。2. 加州桂(= California laurel)。~ **lion** = cougar. ~ **railway** 山区铁道。~ **range** 山脉。~ **rice**【植】1. 高地耐旱稻。2. 落芒草。~ **sheep**【动】野羊。~**side** 山腰;山坡。~ **sickness** 高山病,山岳病。~ **spinach** 法国菠菜。~ **spur** 山脊。**M- State** 落基山州〔美国落基山脉地区八个州之一〕。~**-stronghold** 山寨(~*-stronghold mentality* 山头主义)。~ **system** 山系。**M- (Standard) Time**(美国)山地标准时间〔落基山地区的标准时间,比格林威治时间晚七小时〕。~ **warfare** 山地战。~ **white oak** 蓝栎。~ **wine** 山地白葡萄酒(= Malaga wine)。~ **wood** 石绵,不灰木。

moun·tained [ˈmauntind; ˋmaʊntn̩d] *a*. 山一样的;多山的。

moun·tain·eer [ˌmauntiˈniə; ˌmaʊntn̩ˋɪr] I *n*. 山地人;登山家。II *vi*. 登山。**-ing** *n*. 登山(运动)。

moun·tain·ous [ˈmauntinəs; ˋmaʊntn̩əs] *a*. 山多的;山似的;巨大的。*a* ~ *country* 山国。

moun·tain·y [ˈmauntini; ˋmaʊntn̩ɪ] *a*. 1. = mountainous. 2.〔爱尔兰〕住在山地的。~ *men* 山地人。

Mount·bat·ten [mauntˈbætn; maʊntˋbætn̩] *n*. 蒙巴顿〔姓氏〕。

mount·e·bank [ˈmauntibæŋk; ˋmaʊntəˌbæŋk] *n*. 走江湖(卖假药)的人;江湖医生;江湖骗子。**-ery** 骗子行为;大话。

mount·ed [ˈmauntid; ˋmaʊntɪd] *a*. 1. 骑在马[自行车]上的。2. 装好在架子上的;贴在衬纸上的,裱上的;镶嵌的。*a* ~ *bandit* 马贼。~ *infantry* 骑马步兵。*a* ~ *point* 骑兵尖兵。~ *police* 骑警(队)。~ *units* 骑兵部队,乘车部队。*a* ~ *gun* 装好炮架的大炮。*a silver-*~ *sword* 镶银宝剑。

Mount·ie, Mount·y [ˈmaunti; ˋmaʊntɪ] *n*.〔俚〕加拿大皇家骑警。

mount·ing [ˈmauntiŋ; ˋmaʊntɪŋ] *n*.(大炮等的)架设;装置;座,架,【军】炮架;衬托纸;裱;镶嵌;装饰;攀登;登上;上马;上车;乘骑;(鸟等的)剥制;(镜检物的)装片;封固;〔*pl*.〕马具;附件,配件。*a gimbal* ~ 万向接头架。*a* ~ *block* 骑马台。

mourn [mɔːn; morn] *vi*., *vt*. 悲,悲伤,悲叹(*over*; *for*);吊,哀悼;穿丧服,戴孝。

mourn·er [ˈmɔːnə; ˋmornɚ] *n*. 1. 悲伤的人,哀伤的人,哀悼的人;守丧的人,送丧的人。2. 雇用的送丧人。3. 忏悔者。4.【拳击】眼圈被打得发黑的拳手。~***'s bench***〔美〕(教堂中供人下跪的)凳子;(教堂中的)前排座位。***the chief*** ~ 丧主;死者最近的亲属;遗嘱执行人。

mourn·ful [ˈmɔːnful; ˋmornfʊl] *a*. 悲哀似的,哀痛的;使人伤心[沮丧]的。

mourn·ing [ˈmɔːniŋ; ˋmornɪŋ] *n*. 1. 悲伤,哀悼,哀伤。2. 丧,居丧;丧服;丧章;丧帘;半旗,丧旗。*deep* ~(纯黑的)正式丧服。*half* ~(灰色的)半丧服。*a* ~ *band*(服丧所戴)黑纱。***be in*** ~ 戴着孝;〔俚〕被打得眼圈发黑;(指甲等)肮脏的,污黑的。***be out of*** ~ 服满,除服。***go into*** [***put on***, ***take to***] ~ 举哀;服丧,戴孝。***leave off*** [***go out of***] ~ 服满;除服。***nails in*** ~〔谑〕塞满污垢的指甲。***put into*** ~ 使服丧,使穿孝。~ **border**(表示哀悼的)黑边,黑框。~ **card**(服丧时用的)黑边卡片。~ **cloak**【动】蛱蝶。~**coach**(黑色的)灵柩车;出殡车。~ **dove**〔美〕(鸣声有哀感的)斑鸠。~**-paper** 黑边信纸。~**-ring**(镶有死者小像的)纪念戒指。~ **stuff** 丧服料。

MOUSE = minimum orbital unmanned satellite of the earth 不载人的最小人造地球卫星〔仪表载重五十公斤以下〕。

mouse [maus; maʊs] I *n*.(*pl*. *mice* [mais; maɪs]) 1.【动】(比 rat 小的)小鼠,耗子。2. 胆小的人。3.【计】鼠标(器),滑鼠,光标移动控制盒,〔俚〕女人;姑娘。4.〔俚〕(眼睛周围被打后留下的)青肿。5.(上下窗户用的)坠子。6.【海】缠口结。7.〔美俚〕小火箭。II *a*. 鼠灰色的。*a field* [*wood*] ~ 野鼠。*a house* ~ 家鼠。***like a drowned*** ~ 像落水鼠一样(狼狈)。~ ***and man*** 一切生物,众生(*the best-laid plans of mice and men* 最妥善的计划)。***play like a cat with a*** ~ 像猫捉耗子似地欺负[折磨]。III [mauz, maus; mauz, maus] *vi*. 1.(猫和枭)捉耗子。2. 来回窥探。3.【计】使用鼠标。— *vt*. 1. 搜捕;搜寻;探出。2.(像猫对耗子一样)欺负,虐待;扯开,撕裂;【海】用鼠装饰;(钩口)用绳子扎紧。~ **bird**【动】鼠鸟(= coly)。~ **colo(u)r** 鼠灰色。~ **deer**【动】= chevrotain. ~**-ear**【植】卷耳属;山柳菊,勿忘草。~ **hole** 耗子洞,鼠穴;狭窄的出[入]口;小房间。~ **potato**〔谑〕鼠标迷,电脑迷。~ **tail** 鼠尾巴属植物。~

trap 1. 捕鼠器;〔谑〕小屋子。2.〔美、剧〕演出技巧极坏的演员。3. 小戏院;下等夜总会。4. 防空气球网。

mous·er [ˈmauzə; ˋmauzɚ] *n*. 捕鼠动物〔猫或枭〕;来回窥探的人;〔美俚〕堕落的人;〔俚〕侦探。

mous·ey = mousy.

mous·ie [ˈmausi; ˋmausɪ] *n*. 小小耗子〔爱称〕。

mous·ing [ˈmauziŋ; ˋmauzɪŋ] *n*. 捕鼠;【海】扎钩口的绳子。

mous·que·taire [muskəˈtɛə; ˋmuskəˋtɛr] *n*.〔F.〕= musketeer.

mous·sa·ka [muːˈsɑːkə; muˋsakə] *n*. 茄片夹肉,茄合〔希腊的一道菜名:盖以白酱汁和干酪然后烤熟〕。

mousse [muːs; mus]〔F.〕I *n*. 1. 摩丝〔一种护发定型剂〕。2. 奶油冻。3.(发生海难后溢出的石油和海水形成的)胶凝物。II *vt*. 给…涂上摩丝。

mousse·line [muːsˈliːn; ˏmusˋlin] *n*.〔F.〕细棉布;木斯林玻璃〔制上等杯子用〕。

mousse·line de laine [muːsˈliːndəˈlein; musˋlindəˋlen]〔F.〕毛棉混纺薄呢。

mousse·line de soie [muːsˈliːn dəˈswɑː; musˋlindəˋswɑ]〔F.〕全丝薄纱〔用作婚礼服〕。

mous·tache [məsˈtɑːʃ, mus-; ˋmʌstæʃ, məˋs-] *n*. 1.〔常 *pl*.〕(嘴唇上面的)髭;小胡子。2.(猫等的)须。*old* ~ 老兵,富有经验的士兵。

mous·ta·chio, mus·ta·chio [məˈstɑːʃəu; məˋstɑʃo] *n*. 浓密的胡子。

Mous·te·ri·an [muːsˈtiəriən; musˋtɪrɪən] *a*.【地质】(旧石器时代)莫斯特期的。~ **culture** 莫斯特文化。

mous·y [ˈmausi; ˋmausɪ] *a*. (*mous·i·er*; *-i·est*) 耗子似的;耗子多的;鼠臭的;鼠灰色的;胆小的;缺乏活力的;(小说等)乏味的。

mouth [mauθ; mauθ] I *n*. (*pl*. ~s [mauðz; mauðz]) 1. 口,口腔,嘴。2.〔*pl*.〕口,(需要赡养的)人;(需要饲养的)动物。3. 口状物,出入口;孔,穴;枪口;河口,港口,喷火口;袋口(等);(乐器的)吹口。4. 咧嘴,怪脸,苦相;话,发言;代言人;人言,传闻,传说;〔俚〕傲慢话,厚脸。5.(啤酒等的)味儿。*Shut your* ~!〔卑〕住口! *a useless* ~ 没用的人,饭桶。*a big* ~〔美俚〕碎嘴子,说话冒失的人。*hungry* ~*s* 饥饿的人们。~ *parts*【虫】口器。***by word of*** ~ 口头通知,当面告诉,口说。***down in the*** ~ 沮丧,垂头丧气,气馁。***from hand to*** ~ 现挣现吃;仅可糊口,过一天算一天。***from*** ~ ***to*** ~ 口口相传;挨次。***give*** ~ (猎狗)吠起来。***give*** ~ ***to*** 说出,吐露。***have a foul*** ~ 嘴不干净,嘴坏。***have a good*** [***bad***, ***hard***] ~ (马)驯顺[不驯顺]。***have one's*** ~ ***made up*** (*for sth*.)〔美〕张开嘴准备吃东西;垂涎;期待,渴望得到。***in everyone's*** ~ 人人都如此说。***in*** [***with***] ***a French*** ~ 用法国腔调。***in the*** ~ ***of*** 出于…之口,据…说。***Keep your*** ~ ***shut and your ears open***.〔谚〕多听少讲。***laugh on the worng side of one's*** ~ 由得意变失意,转喜为悲。***make a*** ~ [***make*** ~***s***] ***at*** 对…咧嘴,皱眉头。***make one's*** ~ ***water*** 使垂涎,使羡慕。***open one's*** ~ 开口,开始说话。***open one's*** ~ ***too wide*** 口气过大,要求过多,要价过高。***put words into one's*** ~ 说是某人那样讲过;教某人怎样讲。***shoot off one's*** ~〔俚〕信口开河,滔滔不绝。***sound strange in one's*** ~ 某人讲就觉得奇怪。***stop sb.'s*** ~ 堵住某人的嘴;强使人停止讲话。***take the bread out of sb.'s*** ~ 夺人饭碗,夺人生计。***take the words out of sb.'s*** ~ 说出某人心里要讲的话。***with full*** [***open***] ~ 大声地。***with one*** ~〔罕〕异口同声地。

II [mauð; mauð] *vt*. 1. 说出;用演说腔调讲;附和着说;含糊地说。2. 用口衔;放进嘴里嚼;嚼;吃。3. 使(马)咬惯马嚼子。4. 用嘴接触,吻。— *vi*. 1.(特指轻蔑时的)歪嘴。2. 大声讲,叫骂;怒骂;装腔作势地讲。3.(河)注入(*in*; *into*)。~ **breeder** 非洲鲫鱼。~**feel**(对所吃食品的)口感。~**-filling** *a*.(句子)长的;夸大的。~ **friend** 口头上的朋友。~ **organ** 1. 口琴。2. = Panpipe. ~**part**【动】口器。~**-to-**~ *a*. 口对口的〔人工呼吸的一种方式〕。~**wash** 漱口水,洗口药。~**watering** *a*. 使人流馋涎的;味道好的。

-mouthed [mauðd; mauðd] *comb. f*. 有口的,嘴…的。*a foul-*~ *man* 嘴坏的人,说话刻薄的人。*a hard-*~ *horse* 不驯顺的马。

mouth·er [ˈmauðə; ˋmauðɚ] *n*. 吹牛的人,说大话的人。

mouth·ful [ˈmauθˈful; ˋmauθˏful] *n*. 满口,一口,少量(的食物);〔俚〕适当[不适当]的批评[暗示]。*You said a* ~.〔美俚〕你说得极对[真妙]。***at a*** ~ 一口。***make a*** ~ ***of*** (*sth*.) 一口吞下。

mouthing [ˈmauðiŋ; ˋmauðɪŋ] *n*. 1. 怪脸,苦相。2. 说话;夸口话。3. 使马咬马嚼子的训练。

mouth·piece [ˈmauθpiːs; ˋmauθˏpis] *n*. 1. 烟嘴口;乐器的吹口;马衔铁;口罩。2.【物】接口管;【电话】口承。3. 喉舌,发言人;代言人;〔英俚〕刑事律师,代理人。

mouth·y [ˈmauði; ˋmauðɪ] *a*. (***mouth·i·er***; ***-i·est***) 说大话的,夸口的;嘴碎的,爱说话的。**-i·ly** *ad*. **-i·ness** *n*.

mou·ton [ˈmuːtɔn; ˋmutɑn] *n*. 染色绵羊毛皮。

mou·ton·née [muːtnˈei; ˏmutəˋne] I *a*. 圆如羊背的〔指岩层〕。II *n*.【地】羊背石(= roche moutonnée)。

mov·a·bil·i·ty [ˌmuːvəˈbiliti; ˏmuvəˋbɪlətɪ] *n*. 可动,易动,可动性。

mov·a·ble [ˈmuːvəbl; ˋmuvəbl] I *a*. 可动的,可移动的;【法】动产的(*opp*. real); 变动不定的。~ *property* 动产。*a* ~ *sleeve* 活动套筒。*a* ~ *feast* 节期因年而异的节日。II *n*. 家具(*opp*. fixture);【法】〔*pl*.〕动产(*opp*. immovable)。**-ness** *n*.

mov·a·bly [ˈmuːvəbli; ˋmuvəblɪ] *ad*. 可动,易动。

move [muːv; muv] I *vt*. 1. 动,移,移动,搬动(*opp*. fix);开动;使运行;摇动。2. 感动,鼓动,激动;使感动得…;引起(人)…的兴致,打动,发动;刺激,鼓励(*to do*)。3. 提议,动议。4. 通(大便)。5. 卖,推销(货物)。— *vi*. 1. 动;生活,活动;行动;〔口〕出发。2. 摇,摇动,动摇;(机器)开动。3. 迁移,(民族)移住(*into*);(尤指)搬(家)(*in*; *into*)。4.(事件等)发展;(火车、轮船等)前进;(自然物)生长;出芽。5. 动议,提议;【象棋】走(棋子)。7. 通(大便)。8. 卖。*He* ~*d in his sleep*. 他熟睡时翻来覆去。*It's time to be moving*. 该动身了。***be*** ~***ed by*** 被…感动。***feel*** ~***d to*** 觉得想…。~ ***about*** 到处活动;动来动去;老是改变住处,老在搬家(*They* ~*d about in armed groups*. 他们组成武装小队四出活动)。~ ***aside*** 搁在旁边;除去。~ ***away*** 离开,退出。~ ***back***(使)退。~ ***for*** 动议,提议,要求。~ ***forward*** 前进。~ ***heaven and earth to*** (*do*) 想方设法,尽量努力。~ ***house*** 搬家。~***in*** 搬进。~ ***in good society*** 在上层社交中活动。~ ***in on***〔美俚〕(为了捕获而)潜近;企图从某人手中夺取对某物的控制权。~ ***off*** 离去,走掉;〔俚〕死;(货物)畅销。~ ***on***(使)继续前进,不停地向前走;〔交通警察命令〕向前! 不要站着! ~ ***one's blood*** 使人奋发。~ ***out*** 搬出,搬走;【军】开始行动。~ ***right down the car***! 往里走走! ~ ***the bowels*** 通大便。~ ***sb. to*** (*anger*; *tears*; *laughter*) 使感动得(发怒、掉泪、发笑)。~ ***to*** 搬到。~ ***up*** 提上,上升。~ ***upon*** 进逼。II *n*. 1. 动,运动,移动。2. 发展,推移。3. 搬家。4.【象棋】一着,该走的人;步骤,措施,处置,手段。***be up to every*** ~ ***on the board*** = ***be up to*** [***know***] ***a*** ~ ***or two*** = ***know every*** ~ 不落空,精明;机敏。***first*** ~ 先着,先走棋者。***get a*** ~ ***on***〔口〕赶紧,赶急;〔命令〕行动起来;快! 赶快! ***lost a*** ~ ***to*** 输了一着。***make a*** ~ 动;(准备)出发;走开;搬家;采取措施;行动;动一着(棋)。***on the*** ~ 一直在动;开始活动;(事件)正在发展。

move·a·ble [ˈmuːvəbl; ˋmuvəbl] *a*., *n*. = movable.

mov·e·list [ˈmuːvəlist; ˋmuvəlɪst] *n*. 电影小说作家。

move·ment [ˈmuːvmənt; ˋmuvmənt] *n*. 1. 运动;活动;进退,行动,动静;动摇;动作;举动;〔*pl*.〕姿势;态度。2.

M

移动,迁移。3.(市面的)活动,活跃;(行市等的)变动。4.(时代、社会等的)动向,倾向;动态;(小说、戏剧的)曲折;变化;【乐】乐章;速度;【语】节奏,韵律;(绘画、雕刻的)动势,生动效果;(诗的)韵律结构。5.【机】动程;机械装置,机构,(钟、表的)机件;(机器的)运转(状态)。6.(政治)运动。7.【军】调动,调迁;输送。8.(植物的)发芽,生长。9.通便;排泄物。*quick* ~【乐】快速调。*slow* ~【乐】徐缓调。*the temperance* ~ 禁酒运动。*The play lacks* ~. 那出戏缺乏变化。*the first* ~ *of a symphony* 交响曲第一乐章。*a dance* ~ 舞蹈的节奏。***in the*** ~ 跟着时势前进,不落伍。

mov·er [ˈmuːvə; ˋmuvɚ] ***n***. 1.(使)动的人[东西];(尤指)搬场工人[服务业];运转者;发动机,动力;主动人;鼓舞者;煽动者。2.提议人。*the first* [*prime*] ~ 主动者,发起人;发动机;动力。

mov·ie [ˈmuːvi; ˋmuvɪ] ***n***.〔常 *pl*.〕〔英俚、美口〕电影(院);影片。*go to the* ~*s* 去看电影。~ **actor** 电影男演员。~**dom** 电影界。~**goer** (常)看电影的人。~ **fan** 影迷。~ **house** 电影院。~**-land** = moviedom. ~ **maker** 电影制片者。~ **star** (电)影(明)星。~**-tone** 有声电影。

mov·ing [ˈmuːviŋ;ˋmuvɪŋ] **I** ***n***. 1. 活动,移动;煽动,感动。2.〔*pl*.〕〔口〕电影。**II** ***a***. 1. 动的;移动的。2. 使人感动的,动人的。3. 主动的,原动力的。~ **day** (房客)迁让日,(雇员)解雇日〔美国若干地方是5月1日和10月1日〕。~ *force* 动力;感染力。~ ***of the waters***〔喻〕扰嚷;兴奋;刺激;(事件发展中的)变化,阻碍。~ **picture** 影片,电影。~ **platform** 自动搬运台。~ **sidewalk** [**walk**] 自动人行道。~ **staircase** [**stairway**] 自动楼梯。~ **target**【军】活动目标。~ **vane**【空】动翼。

Mov·i·o·la, mov·ie·o·la [ˌmuːviˈəulə;ˏmuviˋolə] 一种编辑电影用(检查剪辑)的机器商标名。***n***.〔m-〕电影剪辑机。

mow[1] [məu; mo] (*-ed*; ***mown***) ***vt***. 1. 刈,割(草、麦等);收割。2. 刈倒,扫除;扫射,扫杀;扫平,摧毁 (*down*; *off*)。— ***vi***. 割,刈割。

mow[2] [məu, Am. mau; mau, mo] ***n***. 干草堆,麦秆堆;干草堆积处;谷堆。

mow[3] [mau; mau] ***n***., ***vi***. 皱眉头,(做)鬼脸〔*cf*. mop[2]〕。

M.O.W. = Ministry of Works〔英〕建筑工程部。

mow·er [ˈməuə; ˋmoɚ] ***n***. 割草人;割草机。

mow·ing [ˈməuiŋ; ˋmoɪŋ] ***n***. 1. 割草,割谷。2. 一次割下的草量。3. 饲料地。~ **machine** 割草机。

mown [məun; mon] **I** mow[1]的过去分词。**II** ***a***. 割下的。

mox·a [ˈmɔksə; ˋmɑksə] ***n***.【医】艾绒;灼烙剂;【植】艾。

mox·i·bus·tion [ˌmɔksiˈbʌstʃən;ˏmɑksɪˋbʌstʃən] ***n***. 艾灸,艾灼。*acupuncture and* ~ 针灸。

mox·ie [ˈmɔksi; ˋmɑksɪ] ***n***.〔俚〕有胆量,有气魄,坚韧不拔,刚毅。

Mo·zam·bique [ˌməuzəmˈbiːk;ˏmozəmˋbik] ***n***. 莫桑比克(旧译莫三鼻给)〔非洲〕。

Moz·ar·ab [məuˈzærəb; moˋzærəb] ***n***. 穆萨拉布〔摩尔人统治时期内被允许有抑制地奉行其宗教的西班牙基督教徒〕。**-ic** ***a***.

Mo·zart [ˈməutsɑːt; ˋmozɑrt] **Wolfgang Amadeus** 莫扎特〔1756—1791,奥地利作曲家〕。

moz·za·rel·la [ˌmɔtsəˈrelə;ˏmɑzəˋrɛlə] ***n***. 意大利干酪〔尤指用于烹饪者〕。

moz·zet·ta, mo·zet·ta [məuˈzetə; moˋzɛtə] ***n***.(天主教皇等披于法衣上的)有头巾的披肩。

moy·a [ˈmɔiə; ˋmɔɪə] ***n***.【地】火山泥(流层);泥熔岩。

moy·en ***age*** [mwaˌjɛ̃ˈnɑːʒ; mwɑˏjɛ̃ˋnɑʒ]〔F.〕中世纪。

MP, M.P. = 1. Member of Parliament〔英〕下院议员。2. military police 宪兵队; military policeman 宪兵。3. metropolitan police 首都警察队。4.〔It.〕*mezzo piano*【乐】不很轻。5. milepost 英里程标。6. motion picture 电影。7. mounted police 骑警队。8. municipal police 市警队。9. Master of Painting 绘画硕士。10. melting point 熔点,融解点。

M.Pd. = Master of Pedagogy 教育学硕士。

M.P.E. = Master of Physical Education 体育硕士。

MPEG = motion picture expert group【计】电影专家组系统。

mpg, m.p.g. = miles per gallon 英里/加仑。

M.Ph. = Master of Philosophy 哲学硕士。

mph, m.p.h. = miles per hour 英里/时。

MPO = military post office 军邮局。

MR = magneto-resistant 防磁的。

M.R. = machine rifle 自动步枪。

Mr., Mr [ˈmistə; ˋmɪstɚ] (*pl*. ***Messrs***.) …先生〔Mister 的略语,用于男子名或职衔前: *Mr. Smith*, *Mr. President*.〕。*the* ~〔美俚〕丈夫。~ ***Fix-it*** [***Fixit***]〔美俚〕办理[解决]一切的人。

MRA, M.R.A. = Moral Rearmament 道德重整运动。

MRBM = medium-range ballistic missile 中程弹道飞[导]弹。

MRCA = multi-role combat aircraft 多用途战斗机。

M.R.C.P. = Member of the Royal College of Physicians〔英〕皇家内科医师学会会员。

M.R.C.S. = Members of the Royal College of Surgeons〔英〕皇家外科医师学会会员。

MRE(s) = meals ready to eat 快餐,立即可吃的食品。

M Rep = Motor Repair 汽车修理。

mRNA = messenger RNA【生化】信使核糖核酸。

Mrs., Mrs [ˈmisiz; ˋmɪsɪz] (= Mistress) 夫人。~ **Smith** 史密斯太太。

MRV = multiple reentry vehicle【军】多弹头重返大气层运载工具。

MS = 1. manuscript. 2. Master of Science 理科硕士。3. Mississippi. 4. motor ship 内燃机船。5. mass spectrometer【物】质谱仪。

M.S. = Master of Surgery 外科硕士。

m.s., M/S = months after sight【商】见票后…月。

Ms., Ms [miz; miz] 女士(= Miss 或 Mrs.)〔用在婚姻状况不明的女子姓名前〕。

MSc, M.Sc. = Master of Science 理科硕士。

msec. = millisecond.

msg, msg. = message.

msgr, msgr. = messenger.

M.Sgt., M/Sgt., MSgt = Master Sergeant〔美〕陆军[空军、海军陆战队]军士长。

MSI = medium-scale integration【自】中规模集成电路。

m.s.l. = mean sea level 平均海平面。

MSR = missile site radar 飞[导]弹发射场雷达。

MSS = manuscripts.

MST = Mountain Standard Time 山区标准时间〔指国际时区西七区的区时〕。

Msth, Ms-Th【化】新钍(= mesothorium)。

MT = 1. mean time【天】平时〔平太阳时〕。2. metric ton 公吨。3. mechanical [motor] transport 汽车运输;【英陆军】汽车运输队。4. = MST. 5. Montana. 6. megaton.

Mt. = Mount, Mountain.

MTB = motor torpedo boat 鱼雷快艇。

M.T.C. = Mechanized Transport Corps 机械化运输兵。

MTD = mean temperature difference 平均温差。

Mtd = mounted.

mtg. = 1. meeting. 2. mortgage.

mtge. = mortgage.

mth, mth. = month.

M Tk = medium tank 中型坦克。

Mtn, mtn. = mountain.

M

Mt. Rev. = Most Reverend【宗】最尊敬的(对大主教的尊称)。
M Trk = Motor Truck.
Mts, mts. = mountains.
MTSO = mobile telephone switching office 移动电话交换站。
MTU = mobile training unit【军】巡回训练队。
MTV = music television 音乐电视。
mu [mjuː; mju] ***n.*** 希腊语的第十二字母〔M, μ〕; 百万分之一;千分之一毫米。
much [mʌtʃ; mʌtʃ] (*opp.* little) **I** ***a.*** (***more***; ***most***)〔用于修饰不可数名词〕很多的,许多的;大量的;很大程度的;(时间)长的(~ *water*, *wine*, *money*, *hope*, *courage*, *time*)。★ **1.** 主要在英国口语中,除用作肯定句主语之一或与 how, too, as, so 连用外,多用于代替 a lot of, a great quantity of, a good deal of, a great deal of 等。如: *I don't drink* ~ *wine*. 我酒喝不多〔*cf.* He drinks a great deal of wine. 他酒喝得很多〕。*Does he take* ~ *interest in it*? 他对此是否很感兴趣? **2.** 常用作反语表示 no 的意思如: M- right he has to interfere with me. 他根本没有干涉我的权力。~ ***cry and little wool*** 雷声大雨点小。**II** ***n.*** 大量,许多。*I don't see* ~ *of him*. 我不常见他。***be too*** ~ ***for one*** 〔口〕非…力所能及;干不了;受不了;搞不赢;应付不来(*He is too* ~ *for me*. 我敌他不过)。***do*** ~ ***to*** [***toward***] 对…很尽责[有利、有贡献]。***make*** ~ ***of*** 尊重,重视;充分利用;夸奖,恭维,谄媚;悉心照顾;理解。~ ***of a ...*** 了不起的(*He is not* ~ *of a scholar*. 他不是什么了不起的学者)。***M- would have more.*** 人心不足蛇吞象。***not*** ~ 〔口〕哪里的话,当然不(*Go home? Not* ~. 回家? 哪里的话)。***so*** ~ ***for ...*** 的事不必再往下说[就这样完了];…不过是这样,如果…就要吃苦头。***think*** ~ ***of*** 重视,认为了不起。***this*** ~ = ***thus*** ~ 到这里为止,这么些(是对的等)。***too*** ~ 太不像话,太过份(*That is too* ~ *of a good thing*. 那事好过了头。那个好倒好,可是受不了)。**III** ***ad.*** (***more***; ***most***) 很,非常,多;几乎,大致。*This is* ~ *better of the two*. 两个当中这个好得多。*Thank you very* ~. 多谢多谢。★修饰动词时用 very ~ 比单用 ~ 普通。***argued so*** ~ 争论够了。***as*** ~ 同样,一样,正是如此(*I think as* ~. 我也那样想)。***as*** ~ ***again as*** …的二倍。***as*** ~ (...) ***as*** 尽,尽…那样多;…跟…到同一程度(*as* ~ (*money*) *as you like* 尽你要多少。*as* ~ *as possible* 尽可能)。*as* ~ *as a single sharp rebuff* 一点点稍为尖锐的驳斥。***as*** ~ ***as to say*** 等于是说(*He gave a look as* ~ *as to say* "*Mind your own business!*" 他摆出一副好像是说"不用你管!"似的面孔)。***half as*** ~ ***again*** (***as***) (…的)一倍半。***half as*** ~ (***as***) (…的)一半。***how*** ~ 多少;什么价钱;到什么程度。***however*** ~ 不管。~ ***as ...*** 和…几乎一样;尽管,虽然。~ ***at one*** 几乎相同,几乎等价。~ ***good*** 〔主要用于否定句〕擅长,巧妙(*I am not* ~ *good at this sort of work*. 这种工作我不擅长)。~ ***less*** 何况〔否定〕(*He cannot speak French*, ~ *less Russian*. 他连法语都不会讲,俄语就更不必提了)。~ ***more*** 何况〔肯定〕。~ ***of an age*** 差不多同年纪。~ ***of a size*** 差不多大小。~ ***of a sort*** 差不多同种类的。~ ***the same*** 差不多相同。***not so*** ~ ***as*** **1.** 甚至于不[没有](*He cannot so* ~ *as write his own name*. 他甚至于自己的名字都写不来)。**2.** 与其说是…不如说是(*He is not so* ~ *a scholar as a writer*. 他与其说是学者不如说是作家)。***so*** ~ 那么多的(*I have not so* ~ *money as you think*. 我并没有你想像那么多钱)。***twice*** [***three times***] ***as*** ~ 两倍[三倍]。***without so*** ~ ***as*** 甚至于不…。
mu·cha·cha [muːˈtʃɑːtʃə; muˋtʃɑtʃə] ***n.*** (*pl.* ***-chas***) 〔Sp.〕姑娘;年青女人。**mu·cha·cho** [-tʃəu; -tʃo] ***n.*** 男孩,少年男子。
much·ly [ˈmʌtʃli; ˋmʌtʃlɪ] ***ad.*** 〔谑〕非常。
much·ness [ˈmʌtʃnis; ˋmʌtʃnɪs] ***n.*** 〔口〕很多,许多。***be much of a*** ~ 〔口〕大同小异,半斤八两。
muci- *comb. f.* 黏液。
mu·cic [ˈmjuːsik; ˋmjusɪk] ***a.*** (分泌)黏液的。~ **acid**【化】黏液酸。
mu·cid [ˈmjuːsid; ˋmjusɪd] ***a.*** 发了霉的,有霉味的。
mu·cif·er·ous [mjuːˈsifərəs; mjuˋsɪfərəs] ***a.*** 分泌黏液的,生黏液的。
mu·ci·lage [ˈmjuːsilidʒ; ˋmjuslɪdʒ] ***n.*** (植物分泌的)黏液,黏质;〔主、美〕胶水〔=〔英〕gum〕。
mu·ci·lag·i·nous [ˌmjuːsiˈlædʒinəs; ˏmjuslˋædʒənəs] ***a.*** 黏液质的,黏的;分泌黏液的。
mu·cin [ˈmjuːsin; ˋmjusɪn] ***n.***【生化】黏蛋白,黏液素。**gastric** ~胃黏液素。**-oid, -ous** ***a.***
mu·cin·o·gen [mjuːˈsinədʒən; mjuˋsɪnədʒən] ***n.***【生】黏蛋白元;黏液素原。
muck [mʌk; mʌk] **I** ***n.*** **1.** 牛马粪;粪肥;湿粪;腐植土;垃圾;污物;讨厌的东西;〔口〕肮脏,污秽;乱七八糟的状态。**2.** 拙劣[中伤]的作品;胡话;〔美俚〕钱。*a* ~ *grubber* 〔美俚〕小气鬼,吝啬鬼。***all of a*** ~ ***of sweat*** 浑身淌着臭汗。***be in*** [***all of***] ***a*** ~ 浑身是泥。***make a*** ~ ***of*** 弄脏;弄糟。***throw*** ~ ***at sb.*** 中伤某人。**II** ***vt.***, ***vi.*** **1.** 上粪,施肥;除去脏物(= *clear of* ~)。**2.** 〔口〕弄脏(*up*);〔俚〕弄糟;〔美〕用手采捞矿石。~ ***about*** 〔英〕混日子;闲荡;做笨事。~ ***up*** 〔美俚〕弄坏;搞乱;清除(污物)。~**rake** **1.** ***n.*** 粪耙;〔喻〕爱好丑闻(*the man with the* ~ 到处探听丑闻的人)。**2.** ***vi.*** 〔喻,美〕搜集并揭发名人的丑事〔尤指公务人员的贪污渎职行为〕。~**raker** 专门报导丑事的人[新闻记者]。~**-up** 〔英俚〕***n.*** 一团糟,一片混乱。~**worm** 粪蛆;守财奴;吝啬鬼;流浪儿童。
muck·a·muck[1] [ˈmʌkəmʌk; ˋmʌkəmʌk] **I** ***n.*** 〔美方〕食物。**II** ***vt.***, ***vi.*** 吃。
muck·a·muck[2] [ˈmʌkəmʌk; ˋmʌkəmʌk] ***n.*** 大人物,大亨。*a high* ~ (骄傲自大的)要人。
muck·er [ˈmʌkə; ˋmʌkɚ] ***n.*** **1.** 〔英俚〕沉重地跌落;摔倒;灾难。**2.** 〔美俚〕下流的人,无赖。**3.** 清除废矿的矿工;采矿系大学生;掘壕机,掘沟机。***come a*** ~ 〔英俚〕重重跌倒;失败,遭到不幸。***go a*** ~ 〔英俚〕滥花钱;买奢侈[高价]东西(*on*; *over*)。**-ism** ***n.*** 〔美俚〕下流行为。
muck·le [ˈmʌkl; ˋmʌkl̩] ***a.***, ***n.*** **1.** = mickle. **2.** 〔美方〕杀鱼用的棒子。
muck·luck, muc·luc [ˈmʌklʌk; ˋmʌklʌk] ***n.*** = mukluk.
muck·y [ˈmʌki; ˋmʌkɪ] ***a.*** (***muck·i·er***; ***-i·est***) 湿粪的;多腐植土的;污秽的;讨厌的;可耻的;卑劣的。
muco- *comb. f.* 黏液: *muco*protein.
mu·co·cu·ta·ne·ous [ˌmjuːkəukjuːˈteinjəs; ˏmjukokjuˋtenjəs] ***a.***【医】黏膜与皮肤的。
mu·coid [ˈmjuːkɔid; ˋmjukɔɪd] **I** ***n.*** 类黏蛋白。**II** ***a.*** 类黏蛋白的;黏液状(的)。
mu·co·pol·y·sac·cha·ride [ˌmjuːkəuˌpɔliˈsækəˌraid; ˏmjukoˏpɑlɪˋsækəraɪd] ***n.***【生化】黏多醣。
mu·co·pro·tein [ˌmjuːkəuˈprəutiːn, -ˈprəutiin; ˏmjukoˋprotin, -ˋprotɪɪn] ***n.***【生化】黏蛋白(质)。
mu·co·pu·ru·lent [ˌmjuːkəuˈpjuərjulənt; ˏmjukoˋpjurjələnt] ***a.***【医】含黏液脓的。
mu·cor [ˈmjuːkə; ˋmjukɚ] ***n.*** 毛霉(属)。
mu·co·sa [mjuːˈkəusə; mjuˋkosə] ***n.*** (*pl.* ***-sae*** [-siː; -si], ***-sas***) 黏液膜(= mucous membrane)。**-sal** ***a.***
mu·co·ser·ous [ˌmjuːkəuˈsiərəs; ˏmjukoˋsɪrəs] ***a.***【生】产生[含有]黏液乃浆液的。
mu·cos·i·ty [mjuːˈkɔsiti; mjuˋkɑsətɪ] ***n.*** 黏(性);黏液。
mu·cous [ˈmjuːkəs; ˋmjukəs] ***a.*** 黏液(似)的;黏液质的;分泌黏液的。*a* ~ *cough*【医】痰咳。*the* ~ *membrane* 黏膜。
mu·cro [ˈmjuːkrəu; ˋmjukro] ***n.*** (*pl.* ***-cro·nes*** [mjuːˈkrəuniːz; mjuˋkroniz])【植、动】短尖头;端节;锐

突。

mu·cro·nate [ˈmjuːkrənit; ˋmjukronɪt] *a*.【植、动】具短尖的；具锐突的(= mucronated)。**-na·tion** *n*.

mu·cus [ˈmjuːkəs; ˋmjukəs] *n*. (动植物的)黏液。*nasal* ~ 鼻涕。

MUD = multiuser domain【计】多用户空间。

mud [mʌd; mʌd] *n*. 泥，泥浆；泥淖；没价值的东西；污物；〔美俚〕咖啡，巧克力布丁；不清楚的电报信号；诽谤的话；恶意的攻击。*consider sb. as* ~ [*the* ~ *beneath one's feet*] 把某人当做脚下的泥，轻视某人。*His name is* ~. 他名声很坏[信用扫地]。***fling*** [***throw***] ~ ***at*** 拿泥扔…；毁谤，中伤；糟蹋，骂。***stick in the*** ~ 掉在泥坑里；墨守成规；停滞不前。~**-apron** 挡泥板。~ **bath** 泥浴。~ **cat**【动】泥鲴。~ **crack**【地】泥裂。~ **dauber**【动】泥蜂。~ **drag**, ~ **dredge** 疏浚机。~ **eel**【动】鳗螈。~**fish** 泥鱼〔泥鳅等〕。~ **flat** (退潮时露出的)泥地；泥滩。~**grass** 莎禾(属)。~**guard** (车子的)挡泥板，叶子板。~**heads** 〔*pl*.〕〔美〕Tennessee 州人的绰号。~**hen** 秧鸡科动物〔如大鹬等〕。~**hole** (道路等的)泥孔，泥坑。~ **hooks** 〔*pl*.〕〔美俚〕脚。~ **lark** 〔俚〕(退潮时)在河泥中拾破烂的人；街头流浪儿童；〔俚〕在泥道上跑得很快的马；〔英〕沼地云雀。~**-opera** 〔美俚〕马戏，野兽展览。~**-pack** 面部美容泥敷膏〔以漂土、收敛剂等制成〕。~**-puppy** 〔美〕泥狗〔美洲蝾螈〕；大鲵鱼。~**-runner** 会跑泥地的马。~ **sill** (房子的)底基，下槛；〔美南部〕出身低微的人。~ **skipper**【鱼】弹涂鱼；大弹涂鱼；飞鲨。~**slinger** 〔美俚〕毁谤者，中伤者，骂人者。~ **slinging** (政界的)诬蔑，毁谤。~ **snake**【动】蓝黑泥蛇。~**stone**【地】泥岩。~ **turtle**【动】香龟属动物。~ **volcano**【地】泥火山。~ **wort** 水芒草属。

mu·dar [məˈdɑː; məˋdɑr] *n*.【植】(缅甸、印度的)牛角瓜(树)。

mud·der [ˈmʌdə; ˋmʌdɚ] *n*. 〔美俚〕在泥地上跑得最快的马；善于在泥湿场地上比赛的运动员。

mud·di·ly [ˈmʌdili; ˋmʌdɪlɪ] *ad*. 沾满污泥地，浑身是泥，肮脏；污浊；糊涂地。

mud·di·ness [ˈmʌdinis; ˋmʌdɪnɪs] *n*. 泥污；泥泞；溷浊；(头脑的)混乱。

mud·dle [ˈmʌdl; ˋmʌdl] **I** *vt*. **1**. 〔罕〕使多淤泥；使(颜色)混浊。**2**. 使混乱，使慌张；(酒)使(脑子)糊涂。**3**. 混，混淆 (*up*; *together*)；搅拌。**4**. 弄糟。**5**. 糊里糊涂地打发；浪费 (*away*)。—*vi*. **1**. 〔古〕弄得尽是泥。**2**. 瞎搞，胡搞；胡乱对付，鬼混。**3**. (喝得)糊里糊涂。~ *a plan* 将计划弄糟。~ ***about*** 漂游浪荡；瞎搞工作。~ ***on*** [***along***] 敷衍过去，胡乱混过去，得过且过；混日子。~ ***through*** (屡次失败后)好容易达到目的。**II** *n*. 〔a ~〕混乱，杂乱；(头脑的)糊涂，昏迷。***in a*** ~ 杂乱无章，一塌糊涂；糊糊涂涂。***make a*** ~ ***of*** 弄糟。~**-headed** *a*. 昏头昏脑的；愚蠢的，笨拙的。~**-headedness** 糊涂。

mud·dler [ˈmʌdlə; ˋmʌdlɚ] *n*. **1**. 搅拌饮料的棍子。**2**. 想法[作法]糊涂的人。

mud·dy [ˈmʌdi; ˋmʌdɪ] **I** *a*. (***-di·er***; ***-di·est***) **1**. 泥多的，泥泞的；尽是泥的；脏的；泥色的。**2**. 不透明的，混浊的；模糊的(光、色、声等)。**3**. 〔罕〕不纯粹的；下流的。**4**. 混乱的；糊涂不清的，暧昧的。*a* ~ *plow* 〔美俚〕丑妇。~ *water* 〔美俚〕法国啤酒。**II** *vt*., *vi*. (使)给泥弄脏，搅混，弄浊；使头脑混乱[糊涂]。~ *a candidate's name* 损毁候选人的名声。*The first blow muddied his head*. 头一击就把他打糊涂了。~ **lark** 街头流浪汉。

mu·dir [muˈdiə; mʊˋdɪr] *n*. (埃及的)省长；(土耳其的)村长。

Muen·ster [ˈmʌnstə, ˈmun-; ˋmʌnstɚ, ˋmʊn-] *n*. 明斯特干酪〔一种半软、淡黄、味淡的干酪〕。

mu·ez·zin [mu(ː)ˈezin; mjuˋezɪn] *n*. (伊斯兰教寺院的)祷告时间报告人。

muff[1] [mʌf; mʌf] *n*. 皮手笼；手筒〔女人插手防寒用〕；【机】保温套；衬套；套筒。

muff[2] [mʌf; mʌf] **I** *n*. **1**. 笨人，笨蛋；拙劣，笨拙；【球戏】接球失误；〔美俚〕失败，错误。**2**. 〔美俚〕少女；女人。**3**. 〔美俚〕下巴胡子。**4**. 〔英〕白喉雀。***make a*** ~ ***of the business*** 把事情弄糟。***make a*** ~ ***of oneself*** 出丑，自讨人笑。**II** *vt*., *vi*. (使)失败，(使)做出笨事，弄糟；错过(机会)；【球戏】漏接(球)。

muf·fe·tee [ˌmʌfiˈtiː; ˏmʌfəˋti] *n*. 〔英〕(女人用的)绒线腕套。

muf·fin [ˈmʌfin; ˋmʌfɪn] *n*. **1**. 松饼，小松糕。**2**. (陶土制的)小盘子。**3**. 追逐年轻女人的男子。~**-bell** 〔英〕卖松饼小贩摇的铃。~**-cap** 〔英〕(慈善学校男生戴的)松饼形状的呢帽。~**-man** 〔英〕卖松饼的小贩。~**-worry** 茶话会。

muf·fin·eer [ˌmʌfiˈniə; ˏmʌfɪˋnɪr] *n*. (有盖的)松饼盘；(吃松饼时撒盐和糖用的)调味瓶子。

muf·fle[1] [ˈmʌfl; ˋmʌfl̩] **I** *vt*. **1**. 覆；裹住；用围巾围住 (*up*)。**2**. 蒙住(人的)头[眼睛](不许声张)。**3**. 捂住(铃等)断绝声音。**4**. 〔通常被动〕灭(音)，压抑，使钝。—*vi*. 〔罕〕咕哝。~ *oneself* (*up*) *well* 把自己裹得紧紧的。*a* ~*d voice* (嘴被蒙住时的)闷塞的声音。~*d curses* (嘴被蒙住时的)闷声瓮气的骂人话。**II** *n*. **1**. 拳击用手套；疯子用皮手套〔防止撕衣用〕；围巾；头巾。**2**.【机】消声罩[套]，减音器；【化】蒙焊；隔焰甑，闭(式烤)炉。~ **kiln** 隔焰窑，蒙焊窑。

muf·fle[2] [ˈmʌfl; ˋmʌfl̩] *n*. (反刍动物等的)上唇露肉部分和鼻子。

muf·fler [ˈmʌflə; ˋmʌflɚ] *n*. **1**. 围巾；头巾。**2**. (无指)厚手套；拳击用手套。**3**. 消声器，减音器。

muf·ti [ˈmʌfti; ˋmʌftɪ] *n*. 伊斯兰教法典说明官；(平时穿着制服者所穿的)便衣，便服。*in* ~ 穿着便衣。

mug[1] [mʌg; mʌg] **I** *n*. **1**. (有柄)大杯；一大杯；〔美运〕优胜杯。**2**. 〔俚、卑〕脸，嘴，皱着眉头的脸。**3**. 〔俚〕笨蛋；傻瓜；生手。**4**. 暴徒；流氓阿飞。**II** *vt*. 〔美俚〕向…装怪脸；给…拍照；对…行凶抢劫(尤指从背后袭击)。*a* ~ *of murk* 〔美俚〕一杯咖啡。*a* ~ *chaser* [*hunter*] 〔美运〕想得到优胜杯的人。*make a* ~ 皱眉头；装怪脸。~ **shot**【摄】特写镜头；面部照片；(警局存查的)嫌疑犯照片。

mug[2] [mʌg; mʌg] **I** *n*. **1**. 〔英俚〕用功的人；自充有学问的人；考试。**2**. 〔美俚〕下巴；接吻，亲嘴；(尤指警局存查的)照片。**II** *vi*. **1**. 〔英俚〕用功 (*at*)。—*vt*. 攻读(*up*)。**2**. 〔美警察俚〕拍照；亲嘴。

mugg [mʌg; mʌg] *n*. 〔美俚〕没能耐的拳击家；无赖，恶棍。

mug·gee [ˈmʌˈgiː; ˋmʌˋgi] *n*. 行凶抢劫的受害者，被行凶抢劫者。

mug·ger, **mug·gar**, **mug·ur** [ˈmʌgə; ˋmʌgɚ] *n*. **1**.【动】(印度)阔鼻鳄鱼，泽鳄。**2**. 装怪脸者。**3**. 行凶抢劫的路贼。**4**. 人像摄影家。

mug·ging [ˈmʌgiŋ; ˋmʌgɪŋ] *n*. 〔美剧〕哑剧，默剧。

mug·gins [ˈmʌginz; ˋmʌgɪnz] *n*. **1**. 蠢人，笨蛋。**2**. 一种骨牌戏；一种纸牌配套游戏。***talk*** ~***s*** 讲傻话。

mug·gy [ˈmʌgi; ˋmʌgɪ] *a*. (***-gi·er***; ***-gi·est***) 闷热的，潮湿的；〔美〕喝醉了的。**-gi·ness** *n*.

mu·ghal, **mu·ghul** [ˈmuːgəl; ˋmugəl] *n*., *a*. (= mogul)。

mug·man [ˈmʌgmən; ˋmʌgmən] *n*. 〔美俚〕照相师。

mug·wort [ˈmʌgwəːt; ˋmʌgˏwɝt] *n*.【植】艾蒿。

mug·wump [ˈmʌgwʌmp; ˋmʌgˏwʌmp] *n*. 〔美〕**1**. 〔谑〕大人物，大老板，头子。**2**. 1884 年大选时脱离共和党的人；标榜独立行动的选举人，独立分子，超然派。

Mu·ham·mad·an [muˈhæmədən; mʊˋhæmədən] *a*., *n*. = Mohammedan.

Mu·har·ram [muˈhærəm; mʊˋhærəm] *n*. = Moharram.

Muir [mjuə; mjʊr] *n*. 缪尔〔姓氏〕。

mu·jik [muːˈʒik; muˋʒɪk] *n*. = moujik.

muk·lek, **muk·luk** [ˈmʌklʌk; ˋmʌklʌk] *n*. (爱斯基摩

人穿的)海豹皮靴。

mu·lat·to [mju(:)ˈlætəu; məˋlæto] **I** *n*. (*pl*. ~*es*) 黑白混血儿;黑白混血种的后裔。**II** *a*. 黑白混血儿的;黄褐色的。

mul·berry [ˈmʌlbəri; ˋmʌl͵bɛrɪ] *n*. **1**.【植】桑,桑属;桑椹。**2**. 深紫红色。**3**. [M-]【军】(D Day 数小时内建造成的)装配式补助港[原为暗号名]。*paper* ~ 楮,构。~ **bush** (孩子们一面唱着 *Here we go round the* ~ *bush* 一面玩的)桑木林游戏。

mulch [mʌltʃ; mʌltʃ] **I** *n*.【林】林地覆盖物;护根物;地面覆盖料。**II** *vt*. 覆盖树根[地面]。~**-cover** 落叶层。

mulct [mʌlkt; mʌlkt] **I** *n*. 罚金;惩罚。**II** *vt*. 处以罚金;(用计)骗取(钱财)。~ *sb*. (*in*) *£10* 骗去某人十英镑。

mule[1] [mju:l; mjul] *n*. **1**. 骡子,马骡。**2**. 执拗的人,顽固的人。**3**.【纺】走锭精纺机。**4**. 杂种。**5**. 小型电动机车;轻便牵引机。**6**. [美俚](玉米)威士忌酒,酒。**7**. [美俚](学生用的)注解书。**8**. [美俚]走私运毒者,马仔。~ **deer**【动】大耳黑尾鹿。~**-driver** 赶骡人。~ **skinner** [美]赶骡人。

mule[2] [mju:l; mjul] *n*. 脚跟周围无帮的女(拖)鞋;无后跟的拖鞋。

mule[3] [mju:l; mjul] *n*. 冻疮。

mule[4] [mju:l; mjul] *v*., *n*. = mewl.

mu·le·ta [mu:ˈleitə, -ˈletə; muˋletɑ, -ˋletə] *n*. 斗牛士用的红布。

mu·le·teer [ˌmju:liˈtiə; ͵mjuləˋtɪr] *n*. 赶骡子的。

mul·ey, mulley [ˈmju(:)li; ˋmjulɪ] **I** *n*. 无角母牛;牝牛,乳牛。**II** *a*. 无角的;截角的。~ **saw** 直锯[锯木厂用锯的一种]。

mu·li·eb·ri·ty [ˌmju:liˈebriti; ͵mjulɪˋɛbrətɪ] *n*. 女性;女人性格,温柔;女子的身分[地位]。

mul·ish [ˈmju:liʃ; ˋmjulɪʃ] *a*. 骡子似的,执拗的,顽固的;杂种的。**-ly** *ad*. **-ness** *n*.

mull[1] [mʌl; mʌl] *n*.【纺】细软薄棉布;人造丝薄绸。

mull[2] [mʌl; mʌl] **I** *n*. [英口]失败,混乱,乱七八糟。*make a* ~ *of* 弄糟,弄坏。**II** *vt*. **1**. [英口]弄糟,弄乱,弄坏;粉碎,磨碎。**2**. [美口]仔细考虑[讨论]。— *vi*. [美口]深思熟虑(*over*)。

mull[3] [mʌl; mʌl] *vt*. [主用被动语态](加糖、香料等)烫热(酒等)。~*ed ale* 香甜的热酒。

mull[4] [mʌl; mʌl] *n*. [Scot.]鼻烟壶。

mull[5] [mʌl; mʌl] *n*. [方]母牛。

mul·lah [ˈmʌlə; ˋmʌlə] *n*. 毛拉[伊斯兰教徒间对高僧、学者的敬称];伊斯兰教的法律学家。

mull·ark·ey [mʌlˈɑ:ki; mʌlˋɑrkɪ] *n*. [美俚] **1**. 奉承,拍马屁。**2**. 不恳切的话;无聊话;胡话,梦话。

mull·ein, mul·len [ˈmʌlin; ˋmʌlɪn] *n*.【植】毛蕊花属。~ **pink**【植】毛缕。

Mul·ler [ˈmʌlə; ˋmʌlɚ] *n*. **1**. 马勒[姓氏]。**2**. **H. J.** ~ 马勒[1890—1967,美国遗传学家]。

Mül·ler [G. ˈmylə; ˋmylɚ], **P.** 穆勒[1899—1965,瑞士化学家]。

mull·er[1] [ˈmʌlə; ˋmʌlɚ] *n*. 研磨器,粉碎机;研杵;搅棒。

mull·er[2] [ˈmʌlə; ˋmʌlɚ] *n*. 烫酒的人;烫酒器。

mul·let[1] [ˈmʌlit; ˋmʌlɪt] *n*. (*pl*. ~*s*, [集合词]~)【鱼】鲻;鲱鲤科鱼。

mul·let[2] [ˈmʌlit; ˋmʌlɪt] *n*.【徽】(中有圆孔的)星形。

mul·ley [ˈmu(:)li; ˋmulɪ] *n*. = muley.

mul·li·gan [ˈmʌligən; ˋmʌlɪgən] *n*. [美俚]蔬菜烩肉。

mul·li·ga·taw·ny [ˌmʌligəˈtɔ:ni; ͵mʌlɪgəˋtɔnɪ] *n*. (印度的)咖哩肉汤(= ~ soup)。

mul·li·grubs [ˈmʌligrʌbz; ˋmʌlɪ͵grʌbz] *n*. [作单数用][口] **1**. 肚子痛。**2**. 消沉,忧郁。

mul·lion [ˈmʌliən; ˋmʌljən] *n*.【建】(窗门的)直棂,竖框。**-ed** [-d; -d] *a*. 有直棂的。

mul·lock [ˈmʌlək; ˋmʌlək] *n*. **1**. [方]废料,垃圾。**2**. [澳、方]金矿废石。**3**. 混乱的状态,一团糟。

mult-, mul·ti- [mʌlt, ˈmʌlti; mʌlt, ˋmʌltɪ] *comb. f*. 多,多倍:*multi*partite.

mul·tan·gu·lar [mʌlˈtæŋgjulə; mʌlˋtæŋgjəlɚ] *a*. 多角的。

mul·ti·ac·cess [ˌmʌltiˈækses; mʌltɪˋæksɛs] *a*.【自】同路存取的。

mul·ti·an·gu·lar [ˌmʌltiˈæŋgjulə; ͵mʌltɪˋæŋgjəlɚ] *a*. = multangular.

mul·ti-arch [ˈmʌltiˈɑ:tʃ; ˋmʌltɪˋɑrtʃ] *a*. 连拱的。*a* ~ *dam* 连拱坝。

mul·ti·bar·rel [ˌmʌltiˈbærəl; ͵mʌltɪˋbærəl] *a*. 多管(式)的。*a* ~ *rocket* 多管火箭。

mul·ti·buck·et [ˌmʌltiˈbʌkit; ͵mʌltɪˋbʌkɪt] *a*. 多斗(式)的。*a* ~ *trench digger* 多斗式挖沟机。

mul·ti·cel·lu·lar [ˌmʌltiˈseljulə; ͵mʌltɪˋsɛljəlɚ] *a*.【生】多细胞的;多室的。

mul·ti·chan·nel [ˌmʌltiˈtʃænl; mʌltɪˋtʃænl̩] *a*.【讯】多通道的,多路的,多波道的,多频道的。

mul·ti·col·o(u)red [ˌmʌltiˈkʌləd; ͵mʌltɪˋkʌlɚd] *a*. 多色的。

mul·ti·di·men·sion·al [ˌmʌltidiˈmenʃənl; ͵mʌltɪdɪˋmɛnʃənl̩] *a*. 多面的;【数】多维的。

mul·ti·dis·ci·pli·nar·y [ˌmʌltiˈdisiplinəri; ͵mʌltɪˋdɪsəplɪ͵nɛrɪ] *a*. 多种不同学科的综合训练方式的。

mul·ti·fa·ri·ous [ˈmʌltiˈfɛəriəs; ͵mʌltəˋfɛrɪəs] *a*. 形形色色的,千差万别的,五花八门的。**-ly** *ad*. **-ness** *n*.

mul·ti·fid [ˈmʌltifid; ˋmʌltəfɪd] *a*.【生】多裂的。*a* ~ *leaf*【植】多裂叶。

mul·ti·fil·a·ment [ˌmʌltiˈfiləmənt; ͵mʌltɪˋfɪləmənt], **mul·ti·fil** [ˈmʌltifil; ˋmʌltɪfɪl] *n*.【纺】复丝,多纤(维)丝。

mul·ti·flo·ra rose [ˌmʌltiˈflɔ:rə; ͵mʌltɪˋflɔrə] *n*. 蔷薇(*Rosa multiflora*)。

mul·ti·flo·rous [ˌmʌltiˈflɔ:rəs; ͵mʌltɪˋflɔrəs] *a*.【植】多花的。

mul·ti·foil [ˈmʌltifɔil; ˋmʌltɪ͵fɔɪl] *n*.【建】繁叶饰,多叶饰。

mul·ti·fold [ˈmʌltiˌfəuld; ˋmʌltə͵fold] **I** *a*. **1**. 双倍的或成几倍的。**2**. 许多的;种种的,多样的;多方面的,五花八门的(= manifold)。**II** *n*. 复写体,拷贝。

mul·ti·form [ˈmʌltifɔ:m; ˋmʌltə͵fɔrm] *a*. 多种形式的,多样的。

mul·ti·formi·ty [ˌmʌltiˈfɔ:miti; ͵mʌltɪˋfɔrmətɪ] *n*. 多形性,多样性(*opp*. uniformity)。

Mul·ti·graph [ˈmʌltigrɑ:f; ˋmʌltə͵græf] **I** *n*.【商标】轮转印刷机。**II** *vt*., *vi*. [m-]用轮转油印机印刷。

mul·ti·head·ed [ˌmʌltiˈhedid; mʌltɪˋhɛdɪd] *a*. (核武器)多弹头的。

mul·ti-in·dus·try [ˈmʌltiˈindʌstri; ˋmʌltɪˋɪndʌstrɪ] *n*. 多种经营的工业。

mul·ti·lat·er·al [ˌmʌltiˈlætərəl; ͵mʌltɪˋlætərəl] *a*. 多边的。*a* ~ *treaty* 多边条约。**-ism** *n*., **-ly** *ad*.

mul·ti·line pro·duc·tion [ˈmʌltilain prəˈdʌkʃən; ˋmʌltɪ͵laɪn prəˋdʌkʃən] (飞机的)分类生产法[一厂生产一种零件的方法]。

mul·ti·lin·e·al [ˌmʌltiˈliniəl; ͵mʌltɪˋlɪnɪəl] *a*. 多线的。

mul·ti·lin·gual [ˌmʌltiˈliŋgwəl; ͵mʌltɪˋlɪŋgwəl] **I** *a*. 多种语言[文字]的,懂多种语言[文字]的。**II** *n*. 懂多种语言[文字]的人。

mul·til·o·quent [mʌlˈtiləkwənt; mʌlˋtɪləkwənt], **mul·til·o·quous** [-kwəs; -kwəs] *a*. 多嘴的,嘴碎的,爱说话的。**-quence** *n*.

mul·ti·me·di·a [ˌmʌltiˈmi:djə; ͵mʌltɪˋmidɪə] **I** *n*. **1**.【计】多媒体。**2**. 混合舞台效果。**3**.【绘画】混合画法(= mixed media)。**II** *a*. 多媒体的,使用多种媒介[手段]的。

mul·ti·mil·lion [ˌmʌltiˈmiljən; ˏmʌltɪˋmɪljən] ***n.*** 〔常 *pl.*〕数百万。

mul·ti·mil·lion·aire [ˈmʌltiˌmiljəˈnɛə; ˏmʌltəˏmɪljənˋɛr] ***n.*** 亿万富翁,大富豪。

mul·ti-na·tion·al [ˈmʌltinæʃənl; ˋmʌltɪˏnæʃənl] ***a.*** 多民族[国家]的;多国公司的;跨国公司的。

mul·ti·no·mi·al [ˌmʌltiˈnəumiəl; ˏmʌltɪˋnomɪəl] **I** ***a.*** 【数】多项的。**II** ***n.*** 多项式。

mul·ti·nu·cle·ate [ˌmʌltiˈnjuːkliit, -eit, -ˈnuː-; ˏmʌltɪˋnjuklɪɪt, -et, -ˋnu-] ***a.*** 【生】多核的(= multinucleated, multinuclear)。

mul·ti·pack [ˌmʌltiˈpæk; ˏmʌltɪˋpæk] ***n.*** (当作一件商品出售的)多件头商品小包。

mul·tip·a·ra [mʌlˈtipərə; mʌlˋtɪpərə] ***n.*** 经产妇,再产妇,非初产妇。

mul·tip·a·rous [mʌlˈtipərəs; mʌlˋtɪpərəs] ***a.*** **1.** 一产多胎的。**2.** 经产的。**3.** 【植】多出状的。

mul·ti·par·tism [ˌmʌltiˈpɑːtizəm; ˏmʌltɪˋpɑrtɪzəm] ***n.*** 多党制。

mul·ti·par·tite [ˌmʌltiˈpɑːtait; ˏmʌltɪˋpɑrtaɪt] ***a.*** 多歧的;分为多部的;多方的,多国参加的。

mul·ti·par·ty [ˌmʌltiˈpɑːti; ˏmʌltɪˋpɑrtɪ] ***a.*** 多党的。

mul·ti·ped, mul·ti·pede [ˈmʌltiped, -piːd; ˋmʌltəˏpɛd, -pid] ***a.***, ***n.*** 多足的,多足虫[动物]。

mul·ti·phase [ˈmʌltifeiz; ˋmʌltɪˏfez] ***a.*** 多方面的;【电】多相的。

mul·ti·plane [ˈmʌltiplein; ˋmʌltəˏplen] ***a.***, ***n.*** 多翼的;多翼飞机。*a* ~ *camera* 动画摄影机。

mul·ti·ple [ˈmʌltipl; ˋmʌltəpḷ] **I** ***a.*** **1.** 多重的;复合的,复式的,多数的,多样的。**2.** 倍数的,倍。**3.** 【电】并联的;多路的,复接的。**4.** 【植】聚花的。*a man of* ~ *interests* 兴趣广博的人。**II** ***n.*** **1.** 【数】倍数。**2.** 【电】并联;多路系统。**3.** 相联成组。**4.** 成批生产的艺术品〔画、雕塑、工艺品等〕。*common* ~ 公倍数。*least common* ~ 最小公倍数。~ **antenna** 【无】复合天线。~ **bank** 【无】复接排。~**-choice** ***a.*** 多项选择的,可以从几个答案中选出正确答案的。~ **cropping** 【农】复种。~ **earth** 【无】多重接地。~ **factors** 【生】多对因子;多基因。~ **fruit** 【植】复果,繁花果。~ **modalation** 【无】复调制。~**-nozzle** ***a.*** 多喷嘴的。~**-party** ***a.*** 多党的。~ **sclerosis** 【医】多发性硬化。~ **shop** 〔英〕联号(=〔美〕chain store)。~ **star** 【天】聚星。~ **telegrams** (同时发给各方的)同文电报,通电。~ **valve** 【无】复真空管;【电】复联,并联;多路系统。~ **voting** 重复投票。

mul·ti·plet [ˈmʌltiplet; ˋmʌltɪˏplɛt] ***n.*** 【物】多重(谱)线。

mul·ti·plex [ˈmʌltipleks; ˋmʌltəplɛks] **I** ***a.*** 多部的,复合的,多样的,多重的;【电讯】多路传输的;多路复用的,【植】多褶的。**II** ***vt.***, ***vi.*** 多路传输,多路复用。**III** ***n.*** 多厅影院,多剧场影剧院。~ **telegraphy** 多路通报[电报]。~ **telephony** 多路电话。

mul·ti·pli·a·ble, mul·ti·pli·ca·ble [ˈmʌltiplaiəbl, -plikəbl; ˋmʌltəˏplaɪəbḷ, -plɪkəbḷ] ***a.*** 可增加的,可增殖的;可倍增的;可乘的。

mul·ti·pli·cand [ˌmʌltipliˈkænd; ˏmʌltəplɪˋkænd] ***n.*** 【数】被乘数。

mul·ti·pli·cate [ˈmʌltipliˌkeit; ˋmʌltəpləˏket] ***a.*** 〔现罕〕多的,多重的,多倍的。

mul·ti·pli·ca·tion [ˌmʌltipliˈkeiʃən; ˏmʌltəpləˋkeʃən] ***n.*** 增加,增殖;倍增;【数】乘法;乘法运算。~ **factor** [**constant**] 【物】放大系数;倍增常数;核燃料再生常数。~ **table** 九九表。

mul·ti·plic·a·tive [ˌmʌltiˈplikətiv; ˏmʌltəplɪˋketɪv] ***a.***, ***n.*** 趋于增加的,倍增的,增殖的;乘法的;【语法】倍数词〔double, triple 之类〕。

mul·ti·pli·ca·tor [ˈmʌltiplikeitə; ˋmʌltəplɪˏketɚ] ***n.*** 【数】乘数;【电】放大器,倍增器。

mul·ti·plic·i·ty [ˌmʌltiˈplisiti; ˏmʌltəˋplɪsətɪ] ***n.*** 多,多样,重复;多样性,重复度,多重性;复杂。*a* [*the*] ~ *of* 多重,许许多多。

mul·ti·pli·er [ˈmʌltiplaiə; ˋmʌltəˏplaɪɚ] ***n.*** **1.** 增加者,增殖者,繁殖者。**2.** 【数】乘数;【电】倍增器,扩程器,增效器,倍率器。**3.** 【经】收益增值率。

mul·ti·ply[1] [ˈmʌltiplai; ˋmʌltəˏplaɪ] ***vt.***, ***vi.*** 增殖;繁殖;(成倍)增加;【数】乘。~ *5 by 3* 以三乘五。~ **in gear** 【机】增速齿轮;增速装置(*opp.* reduction gear)。~**ing glass** 扩大镜,放大镜。

mul·ti·ply[2] [ˈmʌltipli; ˋmʌltəplɪ] ***ad.*** 复合地;多样地;多倍地;多重地;复杂地;【电】并联地,多路地。

mul·ti-ply [ˈmʌltiplai; ˋmʌltɪˏplaɪ] ***a.*** 多股的;多层的。

mul·ti·po·lar [ˌmʌltiˈpəulə; ˏmʌltəˋpolɚ] ***a.***, ***n.*** 多极的;【电】多极电磁机。

mul·ti·pole [ˈmʌltipəul; ˋmʌltɪˏpol] ***a.***, ***n.*** 【物】多极(的),复极(的)。

mul·ti·pol·y·mer [ˌmʌltiˈpɔlimə; ˏmʌltɪˋpɑlɪmɚ] ***n.*** 【化】共聚物。

mul·ti-pur·pose [ˈmʌltiˈpəːpəs; ˏmʌltɪˋpɝpəs] ***a.*** 多能的,多效应的;多用的;多方面的。

mul·ti·ra·cial [ˈmʌltiˈreiʃəl; ˋmʌltɪˋreʃəl] ***a.*** 多种族的。

mul·ti·ro·ta·tion [ˌmʌltirəuˈteiʃən; ˏmʌltɪroˋteʃən] ***n.*** 【物】变异旋光。

mul·ti·seat·er [ˈmʌltiˌsiːtə; ˋmʌltɪˏsitɚ] ***n.*** 【空】多座机。

mul·ti·shift [ˈmʌltiʃift; ˋmʌltɪˏʃɪft] ***a.*** 多班制的,轮班制的。

mul·ti·stage [ˈmʌltisteidʒ; ˋmʌltɪˏstedʒ] ***a.*** **1.** 多级(式)的。**2.** 分阶段进行的。*a* ~ *missile* 多级飞[导]弹。*a* ~ *rocket* 多级火箭。

mul·ti·state [ˈmʌltisteit; ˋmʌltɪˏstet] ***a.*** 〔美〕在许多州都有分公司的。

mul·ti·sto·r(e)y [ˈmʌltiˌstɔːri; ˋmʌltɪˏstorɪ] ***a.*** (楼)有多层的。*a* ~ *building* 多层大楼。

mul·ti·tude [ˈmʌltitjuːd; ˋmʌltɪˏtjud] ***n.*** **1.** 多,许多,大量。**2.** 大群人,群众。**3.** 【物】集;组。*as the stars in* ~ 多得像星星一样。*a* ~ *of* 许多。*the* ~ 民众,群众,大众。*Fair skin covers the* ~ *of sin.* 金玉其外,败絮其中。

mul·ti·tu·di·nism [ˌmʌltiˈtjuːdinizəm; ˏmʌltɪˋtjudnɪzəm] ***n.*** 利多主义(*opp.* individualism)。

mul·ti·tu·di·nous [ˌmʌltiˈtjuːdinəs; ˏmʌltɪˋtjudṇəs] ***a.*** 许多的;大群的,人多的;由许多部分形成的。**-ly** ***ad.*** **-ness** ***n.***

mul·ti·va·lent [ˌmʌltiˈveilənt; ˏmʌltəˋvelənt] ***a.*** 【化】多价的;多义的。**-lence** ***n.***

mul·ti·ver·si·ty [ˌmʌltiˈvəːsiti; ˏmʌltɪˋvɝsətɪ] ***n.*** (*pl.* ***-ties***) 大型综合性大学〔有很多学院,系科和附设单位〕。

mul·ti·vi·bra·tor [ˈmʌltivaiˈbreitə; ˏmʌltɪˋvaɪbretɚ] ***n.*** 【无】多谐振动器。

mul·tiv·o·cal [mʌlˈtivəkəl; mʌlˋtɪvəkḷ] **I** ***a.*** 多义的;暧昧的,含糊的;喧嚣的。**II** ***n.*** 多义语。

mul·ti·vol·tine [mʌlˈtivəltin; ˏmʌltəˋvoltin] ***a.*** 【虫】多化的。

mul·toc·u·lar [mʌlˈtɔkjulə; mʌlˋtɑkjəlɚ] ***a.*** 多眼的;(昆虫)复眼的。

mul·tum in par·vo [ˈmʌltəm in ˈpɑːvəu; ˋmʌltəm ɪn ˋpɑrvo] 〔L.〕小型而内容丰富;小中见大;大寓于小。

mul·ture [ˈmʌltʃə; ˋmʌltʃɚ] ***n.*** 给水力磨坊的报酬〔麦子或面粉的一部分〕;磨谷费。

mum[1] [mʌm; mʌm] **I** ***a.*** 无言的,沉默的,不说话的。**II** ***n.*** 〔口〕沉默。*as* ~ *as a mouse* [*an oyster*] 一点也不开口。*keep* ~ (*about it*) (严守秘密)决不开口。*Mum's the word!* 别响! 别声张! **III** ***int.*** 别说了! 别响! **IV** ***vi.*** 闭口,不讲话;演哑剧。

mum² [mʌm; mʌm] *n*. 1.〔口〕= madam. 2.〔英儿〕妈。

mum³ [mʌm; mʌm] *n*.(德国)烈性啤酒。

mum⁴ [mʌm; mʌm] *n*.〔美俚〕菊花〔chrysanthemum 的略语〕。

mum·ble [ˈmʌmbl; ˋmʌmbl̩] I *vi*., *vt*.(在嘴里)咕噜咕噜地说;闭着嘴用牙根嚼。II *n*. 咕哝,嗫嚅,含糊的话。**-bling·ly** *ad*.

mum·bler [ˈmʌmblə; ˋmʌmblɚ] *n*. 说话含糊不清的人,咕咕哝哝的人。

mum·ble·ty·peg [ˈmʌmbltiˌpeg; ˋmʌmbltɪˏpɛg] *n*. 抛刀游戏〔上抛刀子使之插入地上,(原先)输者须用牙叼出插进地里的木钉〕。

Mum·bo-Jum·bo [ˈmʌmbəuˈdʒʌmbəu; ˋmʌmboˋdʒʌmbo] *n*. 1. 摩包君婆〔西非洲黑人崇拜的守护神〕。2.〔m- j-〕迷信的崇拜物;令人畏惧的东西;迷惑人的做法;意义含糊的话;胡说八道。

mu-meson [ˈmjuːmizɔn; ˋmjuˏmɪzɑn] *n*.【原】μ 介子。

Mum·ford [ˈmʌmfəd; ˋmʌmfɚd] *n*. 芒福德〔姓氏〕。

mum·mer [ˈmʌmə; ˋmʌmɚ] *n*.(滑稽)哑剧演员;〔蔑〕戏子;爱打扮的人。

mum·mer·y [ˈmʌməri; ˋmʌmərɪ] *n*. 哑剧;假面舞;〔蔑〕虚礼;做作的表演。

mum·mied [ˈmʌmid; ˋmʌmɪd] *a*. 变成了木乃伊的。

mum·mi·fy [ˈmʌmifai; ˋmʌmɪˏfaɪ] *vt*., *vi*. 使成[变成]木乃伊;弄干保存;(使)干瘪;(使)皱缩。**-fi·ca·tion** [ˌmʌmifiˈkeiʃən; ˏmʌmɪfɪˋkeʃən] *n*. 僵化(现象)。

mum·my¹ [ˈmʌmi; ˋmʌmɪ] *n*. 1. 木乃伊;(普通)干尸;木乃伊似的人;干瘪的人。2. 木乃伊粉(刀伤药)。3.【化】(沥青中取出的)褐色颜料;普鲁士红;褐色氧化铁粉。***beat to a*** ~ 打得半死[稀烂]。~ **bag** 轻便睡袋。~ **case** 木乃伊箱。~ **cloth** 包木乃伊的麻布;〔美〕(棉[丝]毛混纺的)马米布[绉]。~ **wheat** (由木乃伊箱中所得古代麦粒繁殖成的)埃及小麦。

mum·my² [ˈmʌmi; ˋmʌmɪ] *n*.〔英、儿〕妈妈。

mump [mʌmp; mʌmp] *vi*., *vt*.〔主方〕1.(使)闹别扭;(使)郁郁不乐;装正经。2.(哭诉着)行乞,讨钱;骗。3. 咕哝。**-ish** *a*. **-er** *n*. **-ing** *a*.

mumps [mʌmps; mʌmps] *n*. 1.〔作单数用〕【医】流行性腮腺炎。2. 闹别扭;慍怒;不开心。*have the* ~ 郁郁不乐。

munch [mʌntʃ; mʌntʃ] *vt*., *vi*. 用力[大声]地咀嚼;贪馋地咀嚼。

Mun·chau·sen [mʌnˈtʃɔːzn, -ˈtʃauzn; mʌnˋtʃɔzn̩, -ˋtʃauzn̩] I *n*. 吹牛(的人)〔原为德国 Rudolph Raspe 所著冒险故事中的主人翁〕。II *a*.(故事)虚夸的。

Mün·chen [G. ˈmjuːnʃən; ˋmjunʃən] *n*. 明兴〔即 Munich 慕尼黑〕〔德国城市〕。

Mun·da [ˈmundə; ˋmʊndə] *a*.(奥亚语系)蒙达语的。

mun·dane [ˈmʌndein; ˋmʌnden] *a*. 1. 世俗的,现世的,尘世间的〔*cf*. spiritual, heavenly〕;庸俗的。2. 宇宙的。~ *affairs* 俗事。*the* ~ *era* 世界的纪元。**-ly** *ad*.

mun·dun·gus [mʌnˈdʌŋgəs; mʌnˋdʌŋgəs] *n*.〔古〕孟顿古斯烟草〔一种气味恶劣的暗黑色烟草〕。

mung·bean [ˈmɔŋˈbiːn; ˋmɑŋbin] *n*. 绿豆。

mun·go [ˈmʌŋgəu; ˋmʌŋgo] *n*.(用旧呢绒做成的)硬再生毛;短弹毛。

mun·goos(e) [mʌŋˈguːs; ˋmʌŋgus] *n*. = mongoose.

Mu·nich [ˈmjuːnik; ˋmjunɪk] *n*. 1. 慕尼黑〔德国城市〕。2. = ~ Accord. 3. 可耻的绥靖事件。~ **Accord** [**Agreement**, **Pact**] 慕尼黑协定〔1938 年英法出卖捷克而和德意签订的协定〕。

mu·nic·i·pal [mju(ː)ˈnisipəl; mjuˋnɪsəpl̩] I *a*. 1. 市的,都市的;市营的;市制的。2. 内政的〔仅用于 ~ law 国内法〕。II *n*.〔*pl*.〕地方债。*a* ~ *council* 市议会。*a* ~ *office* 市政府(办公楼)。~ *government* 市政,市政府。~ *undertakings* 市营企业。**-ism** *n*. 市自治主义。**-ist** *n*. 市自治主义者;市政当局;市政通。**-ity** [mjuːnisiˈpæliti; mjuˏnɪsəˋpælətɪ] *n*. 自治市,自治区;市政府;市政当局。

mu·nic·i·pal·ize [mju(ː)ˈnisipəlaiz; mjəˋnɪsəpl̩ˏaɪz] *vt*. 把…归市有[作市营]。**-i·za·tion** [mjuːnisipəlaiˈzeiʃən; mjuˏnɪspələˋzeʃən] *n*.

mu·nic·i·pal·ly [mju(ː)nisipəli; mjuˋnɪsəpl̩ɪ] *ad*. 市政上;市营地。*be* ~ *managed* 市营的。

mu·nif·i·cent [mju(ː)ˈnifisnt; mjuˋnɪfəsn̩t] *a*. 慷慨给予的,毫不吝啬的;宽厚的,宽大的。**-cence** *n*., **-cently** *ad*.

mu·ni·ment [ˈmjuːnimənt; ˋmjunəmənt] *n*. 1.【法】〔*pl*.〕契据,证券,文件。2. 防御[保护]手段。

mu·ni·tion [mju(ː)ˈniʃən; mjuˋnɪʃən] I *n*.〔除作定语外用复数〕军需品,军用品(尤指枪、炮、弹药);军火;(紧急时的)必需品,资金。~*s of war* 军需品。*a* ~ *plant* 军需工厂。II *vt*. 供给…军需品。**-er** *n*. 军火制造人。

mun·nion, mul·lion [ˈmʌnjən, ˈmʌljən; ˋmʌnjən, ˋmʌljən] *n*.〔古〕【建】直棂。

Mun O = Munition Officer〔美〕军械官,弹药补给主任。

Mün·ster [ˈminstə; ˋmɪnstɚ] *n*. 明斯特〔德国〕。

munt·jac, munt·jak [ˈmʌntdʒæk; ˋmʌntdʒʌk] *n*.【动】麂属(*Muntiacus*)动物。

Muntz met·al [ˈmʌnts ˈmetl; ˋmʌnts ˋmɛtl̩] *n*.(锌与铜合成的)孟次黄铜,熟铜。

mu·on [ˈmjuːɔn; ˋmjuɑn] *n*.【原】= mu-meson.

mup·pie [ˈmʌpi; ˋmʌpɪ] *n*. 玛皮士〔指城市里的中年专业技术人员〕。

mu·ral [ˈmjuərəl; ˋmjʊrəl] I *a*. 墙壁(上)的;墙壁似的,险峭的。II *n*. 墙壁;壁画;〔美〕壁饰。*a* ~ *painting* 壁画。~ **circle**【天】墙仪。~ **crown** 壁形金冠〔古罗马奖给先登上敌垒的人〕。**-ist** *n*. 壁画家;壁饰家。

Mur·cott [ˈməːkɔt; ˋmɝkɑt] *n*. 默科特柑橘〔美国柑橘培育家 *Charles Murcott*(默科特)培育的一种柑橘,果肉深黄,易剥皮,易分瓣,据认为是一杂交品种〕(= Murcot orange)。

mur·der [ˈməːdə; ˋmɝdɚ] I *n*. 1. 凶杀,杀害;屠杀;【法】谋杀;谋杀案[罪]。2. 极艰险的事。*M- will out*. 杀了人[恶事]终必败露。*The* ~ *is out*. 真相大白。~ *in the first* [*second*, *third*] *degree* 谋[故、误]杀。*judicial* ~ 合法但不公正的死刑判决。***cry blue*** ~〔俚〕大声嚷叫。***cry*** '~' 喊"杀人啦"! II *vt*. 1. 杀害;凶杀;谋杀;屠杀。2. 扼杀;糟蹋;折磨;毁坏,弄坏。~ *a song by poor singing* 拙劣的唱腔糟蹋了一首歌曲。— *vi*. 犯杀人罪。

mur·der·er [ˈməːdərə; ˋmɝdərɚ] *n*.(*fem*. ~*ess*)杀人犯,凶手。

mur·der·ous [ˈməːdərəs; ˋmɝdərəs] *a*. 杀人(用)的,行凶的;凶恶的,残忍的;厉害的,要人命的。*a* ~ *weapon* 凶器。~ *heat* 要命的炎热。

Mur·doch [ˈməːdɔk; ˋmɝdɑk] *n*. 1. 默多克〔男子名〕。2.〔苏方〕水手,海员〔苏格兰盖尔语〕。

mure [mjuə; mjʊr] *vt*. 用墙壁围绕;幽禁(*up*); = immure.

mur·ex [ˈmjuəreks; ˋmjʊreks] *n*.(*pl*. ***-rices*** [-risiːz; -rɪsiz], ***-es***)【贝】骨螺。

mu·ri·ate [ˈmjuəriit; ˋmjʊrɪˏet] *n*.〔罕〕【化】氯化物。

mu·ri·at·ic [ˌmjuəriˈætik; ˏmjʊrɪˋætɪk] *a*.【化】氯化的。~ **acid** (粗)盐酸。

mu·ri·cate [ˈmjuəriˌkeit; ˋmjʊrəket] *a*. 由于芒刺而变粗糙的(= muricated)。

mu·rid [ˈmjuərid; ˋmjʊrɪd] *n*.(*pl*. ***Mu·ri·dae*** [ˈmjuridi; ˋmjʊrɪˏdi])鼠科动物〔包括老鼠和鼷鼠〕。

Mu·ri·el [ˈmjuəriəl; ˋmjʊrɪəl] *n*. 缪丽尔〔女子名〕。

mu·rine [ˈmjuərain, -in; ˋmjʊraɪn, -ɪn] I *a*. 鼠科〔包括鼠和鼷鼠〕的。II *n*. 鼠科动物。

murk [məːk; mɝk] *n*., *a*.〔古、诗〕黑暗(的),阴暗

(的)。

murk·y [ˈməːki; ˋmɚkɪ] **a.** (***murk·i·er***; ***-i·est***) 暗,阴暗的,(雾等)浓的;阴郁的;含糊的,暧昧的。**-i·ly** ***ad.*** **-i·ness** ***n.***

Mur·mansk [muəˈmɑːnsk; mʊrˋmɑnsk] ***n.*** 莫曼斯克〔俄罗斯港市〕。

mur·mur [ˈməːmə; ˋmɚmɚ] **I** ***n.*** **1.** (浪、树叶等的)沙沙声,潺潺声,淙淙声;私语声,低语声。**2.** 咕哝,嘟哝,牢骚,怨言。**3.**【医】(不正常的)心脏杂音。**II** ***vi.*** **1.** 小声说,私语;沙沙地响。**2.** 咕哝;发牢骚,诉怨(*at*; *against*)。— ***vt.*** 低声说(秘密等)。**-er** ***n.***, **-ing·ly** ***ad.***

mur·mur·ous [ˈməːmərəs; ˋmɚmərəs] ***a.*** 小声说的;沙沙响的;低声怨语的,嘟嘟喃喃的。

mur·phy [ˈməːfi; ˋmɚfɪ] ***n.*** **1.** 〔俚〕马铃薯;〔美〕(不用时可以隐藏在墙壁里的)隐壁床,折床(= M- bed)。**2.** 〔M-〕墨菲〔姓氏〕; Murphy's Law 莫非法则(知易行难)。

mur·rain [ˈmʌrin; ˋmɝɪn] ***n.*** **1.** 炭疽热,鹅口疮,得克萨斯牛瘟(等)家畜传染病。**2.** 〔古〕瘟疫。*A* ~ *on* [*to*] *you*! = *M- take you*!〔古〕该死的! 你这遭瘟的!

Mur·ray [ˈmʌri; ˋmɝɪ] ***n.*** 默里〔姓氏〕。

murre [məː; mɝ] ***n.*** (*pl.* ~(***s***)) 海鸠(*Uria columba*)。

murre·let [ˈməːlit; ˋmɝlɪt] ***n.***【动】海雀〔主要发现于北太平洋岛屿〕。

mur·rey [ˈməːri; ˋmɝɪ] **I** ***n.*** 紫红色;桑葚色。**II** ***a.*** 紫红色的。

mur·rhine [ˈmʌrin, -rain; ˋmɝɪn, -raɪn] ***a.*** 亚宝石的,萤石的。~ **glass** 仿古罗马亚宝石器皿;精致萤石器皿。

Mur·ry [ˈmʌri; ˋmɝɪ] ***n.*** 默里〔男子名〕。

mur·ther [ˈməːðə; ˋmɝðɚ] ***n.***, ***v.*** 〔方〕= murder.

Mus. = **1.** museum. **2.** music; musical.

Mus. B., Mus. Bac. = 〔L.〕*Musicae Baccalaureus* (Bachelor of Music) 音乐学士。

Mus·ca [ˈmʌskə; ˋmʌskə] ***n.***【天】苍蝇座;【动】蝇属。

mus·ca·del [ˌmʌskəˈdel; ˏmʌskəˋdɛl] ***n.*** = muscatel.

mus·ca·dine [ˈmʌskədin; ˋmʌskədɪn] ***n.*** 麝香葡萄(酒)。

mus·ca·rine [ˈmʌskərin; ˋmʌskərin] ***n.***【化】蝇蕈碱,腐鱼毒。

Mus·cat [ˈmʌskət, ˈmʌskæt; ˋmʌskət, ˋmʌskæt] ***n.*** 马斯喀特〔阿曼首都〕。

mus·cat [ˈmʌskət, -kæt; ˋmʌskət, -kæt] ***n.*** **1.** 麝香葡萄。**2.** 麝香葡萄酒(= muscatel)。

mus·ca·tel [ˌmʌskəˈtel; ˏmʌskəˋtɛl] ***n.*** **1.** 麝香葡萄酒。**2.** 麝香葡萄(= muscat, muscadel)。

mus·cid [ˈmʌsid; ˋmʌsɪd] **I** ***a.*** 家蝇科(*Muscidae*)的〔包括家蝇〕。**II** ***n.*** 家蝇科昆虫。

mus·cle[1] [ˈmʌsl; ˋmʌsl] **I** ***n.***【解】肌(肉);体力,膂力,力气。*an involuntary* ~ 不随意肌。*a voluntary* ~ 随意肌。*a man of* ~ 大力士。***not move a*** ~ 毫不动容,神色不变。**II** ***vi.*** 〔美俚〕发挥膂力;用力挤着前进(*through*)。~ ***in*** 硬挤进;干涉,侵入;强夺。~**-bound** ***a.*** (因运动过度而)肌肉僵硬的。~ **candy** 强肌糖〔运动员服用后能增强体力的补品〕。~**-flexing** 炫耀武力。~**man** ***n.*** 〔美俚〕摔角家;体格魁梧的演员;(被雇用的)打手,保镖。~ **racket** 〔美俚〕职业摔角。~ **sense**【医】肌肉觉。**-less** ***a.*** 无肌肉的;没力气的。

mus·cle[2] [ˈmʌsl; ˋmʌsl̩] ***n.*** = mussel.

mus·col·o·gy [mʌsˈkɔlədʒi; mʌsˋkɑlədʒɪ] ***n.*** 苔藓学。

mus·co·va·do, mus·co·va·to [ˌmʌskəˈvɑːdəu, -təu; ˏmʌskəˋvedo, -to] ***n.*** 混糖。

Mus·co·vite [ˈmʌskəvait; ˋmʌskəˏvaɪt] **I** ***n.*** 〔古〕莫斯科人;俄国人。**II** ***a.*** 〔古〕莫斯科(人)的;俄国(人)的。

mus·co·vite [ˈmʌskəvait; ˋmʌskəˏvaɪt] ***n.***【矿】白云母。

Mus·co·vy [ˈmʌskəvi; ˋmʌskəvɪ] ***n.*** 〔古〕俄国。~ **duck** = muskduck.

mus·cu·lar [ˈmʌskjulə; ˋmʌskjələ] ***a.*** **1.** 肌(肉)的。**2.** 肌肉发达的,有膂力的,壮健的。*the* ~ *system* 肌肉系统。~ *motion* [*movement*] 肌肉运动。*a* ~ *strain* 肌肉过劳。~ *strength* 膂力,力气。~ **dystrophy**【医】肌肉萎缩症。~ **rheumatism**【医】肌(肉)风湿病。**-ly** ***ad.***

mus·cu·lar·i·ty [ˌmʌskjuˈlæriti; ˏmʌskjəˋlærətɪ] ***n.*** 肌肉发达,强壮;膂力。

mus·cu·la·ture [ˈmʌskjulətʃə; ˋmʌskjələtʃɚ] ***n.***【解】肌系,肌群;肌序,肌列。

Mus. D. = 〔L.〕*Musicae Doctor* (Doctor of Music) 音乐博士。

Muse [mjuːz; mjuz] ***n.*** **1.**【希神】文艺、美术、音乐等的女神;缪斯。**2.** 〔M- 或 m-〕诗思,诗才;诗,诗歌;〔m-〕〔诗〕诗人。***the*** ~***s*** 司文艺、美术等的九女神;诗神;诗歌;文艺,美文学。

muse [mjuːz; mjuz] **I** ***vi.*** **1.** 沉思,默想(*on*; *upon*)。**2.** 呆看;细心周到地说。**II** ***n.*** 〔古〕沉思,默想,冥想。*be lost in a* ~ 一味冥想。~ (*up*) *on a distant scene* 呆看远处风景。

muse·ful [ˈmjuːzfəl; ˋmjuzfəl] ***a.*** 〔古〕沉思的,默想的,冥想的。

mu·sette [mju(ː)ˈzet; mjuˋzɛt] ***n.*** **1.** 小风笛;风笛曲;风笛舞。**2.**【乐】(风琴的)簧管音栓。~ **bag** (士兵的)野战背包。

mu·se·um [mju(ː)ˈziəm; mjuˋziəm] ***n.*** 博物馆;〔美〕美术馆。~ **piece** ***n.*** 重要美术品;珍品;〔贬〕老古董〔指过时的人或物〕。

mush[1] [mʌʃ; mʌʃ] **I** ***n.*** **1.** 软块;〔美〕玉米面粥。**2.** 多愁善感;痴情;废话,胡话;〔美俚〕啰啰唆唆说情求爱。**3.** 噪声,干扰。***make a*** ~ ***of*** 〔口〕弄糟。~ ***and molasses*** 〔美〕废话,糊涂话。**II** ***vt.*** 〔方〕使成软糊状。— ***vi.*** (飞机因控制器失灵)半失速飞行;升不高。~**-mouthed** ***a.*** 〔美口〕张口结舌的,结结巴巴的。

mush[2] [mʌʃ; mʌʃ] ***n.***, ***vi.*** 〔美西北部〕坐狗拉的雪橇旅行。

mush[3] [mʌʃ; mʌʃ] ***n.*** **1.** 〔英俚〕伞;出租马车车主。**2.** 〔俚〕嘴;脸。

mush[4] [mʌʃ; mʌʃ] ***vt.*** 〔Scot.〕刻痕于。

mush·er [ˈmʌʃə; ˋmʌʃɚ] ***n.*** **1.** 赶狗拉雪橇的人。**2.** 〔英俚〕〔*pl.*〕阿拉斯加人。

mush·room [ˈmʌʃrum; ˋmʌʃrʊm] **I** ***n.*** **1.** (主指食用)蕈,蘑菇。**2.** 暴发户。**3.** 蘑菇状物;蘑菇状烟云;〔口〕(女用)蘑菇形草帽(= ~ hat);〔俚〕伞。**II** ***a.*** 蘑菇形的;雨后蘑菇似的;蘑菇一般短命的。~ *growth* 猛长。*a* ~ *millionaire* 暴发户。*a* ~ *town* 新兴城市。~ *fame* 短暂的命运。**III** ***vi.*** **1.** 迅速增长。**2.** 采集蘑菇。**3.** 子弹打扁成蘑菇形。**4.** 〔美〕(火)猛然的扩大。*go* ~*ing* 去采蘑菇。

mush·y [ˈmʌʃi; ˋmʌʃɪ] ***a.*** 柔软的;软弱的,易掉眼泪的;感伤的。**-i·ness** ***n.***

mu·sic [ˈmjuːzik; ˋmjuzɪk] ***n.*** **1.** 音乐,乐曲;乐谱。**2.** 佳调,乐音,妙音;音乐鉴赏力;(军)乐队,合唱队。**3.**【猎】狗叫声。**4.** 〔美口〕激烈的辩论,吵闹;法律制裁,惩处。*vocal* [*instrumental*] ~ 声[器]乐。*play without* ~ 不用乐谱演奏。*He has no* ~ *in himself*. 他没有音乐鉴赏力。*rough* ~ (故意使人讨厌的)吵闹,喧嚣。***face the*** ~ 临危不惧。***jerk chin*** ~ 谈话。***set*** (***a poem***) ***to*** ~ 为诗谱曲。~ **book** 乐谱。~ **box** 八音盒。~ **case** 乐谱夹子。~ **drama** 音乐戏剧〔尤指德国作曲家华格纳发展而成的具有主旋律的歌剧〕。~ **hall** 〔美〕音乐厅;〔英〕杂耍剧场。~ **paper** 五线谱纸。~ **school** 音乐学校。~ **stand** 乐谱架。~ **stool** (奏)钢琴(用)凳(子)。

mu·si·cal [ˈmjuːzikəl; ˋmjuzɪkl] **I** ***a.*** **1.** 音乐的;配乐的。**2.** 音乐似的;好听的。**3.** 爱好音乐的;精通音乐的。*a* ~ *composer* 作曲家。*a* ~ *director* 音乐指挥。*a* ~

evening 音乐晚会。*a* ～ *instrument* 乐器。*a* ～ *performance* 演奏。～ **chairs** 抢座位游戏〔游戏者在音乐伴奏下围着按人数计少一张的椅子转，音乐一停，就抢座位，每次淘汰一人并减少一张椅子〕。～ **comedy** 音乐(喜)剧。～ **drama** 音乐剧。～ **glasses** (装入不同水量形成的一组)乐杯。～ **play** 音乐剧。～ **ride** (英国近卫骑兵队)有音乐伴奏的骑马舞。～ **saw** (演奏用)钢锯。～ **soirée** 音乐晚会。**II** *n*.〔口〕**1.** (社交性的)音乐会。**2.**【影】歌舞片。**3.** 音乐(喜)剧 = ～ comedy.

mu·si·cale [ˌmjuːziˈkæl; ˏmjuzɪˋkæl] *n*.〔美〕(社交性的)音乐会，演奏会。

mu·si·cal·ly [ˈmjuːzikəli; ˋmjuzɪkəlɪ] *ad*. 音乐上，像音乐；音调佳妙，和谐。**-cal·ness** *n*.

mu·si·cas·sette [ˈmjuːzikəset; ˋmjuzɪkəsɛt] *n*. 卡式音乐录音带。

mu·si·ci·an [mju(ː)ˈziʃən; mjuˋzɪʃən] *n*. 音乐家；乐师；作曲家。**-ly** *a*. 有音乐家才能的；音乐家似的。

mu·si·col·o·gy [ˌmjuːziˈkɔlədʒi; ˏmjuzəˋkɑlədʒɪ] *n*. 音乐学，音乐研究。**-log·i·cal** *a*. **-gist** *n*.

mu·sique con·crète [mjuːziːk kəunˈkret; mjuzik konˋkrɛt] 具体音乐〔现代西欧的一个乐派作为"抽象"乐派之对，该乐派将自然声响和噪音(如乐器声、雨声等)加以改变，直接谱于磁带上〕。

mus·jid, mas·jid [ˈmʌsdʒid; ˋmʌsdʒɪd] *n*. 清真寺院，伊斯兰教寺院。

mus·ing [ˈmjuːziŋ; ˋmjuzɪŋ] *n*., *a*. 沉思(的)，冥想(的)。**-ly** *ad*.

musk [mʌsk; mʌsk] *n*. 麝香；【动】麝；【植】香沟酸浆。～ **cat** 麝香猫；〔废〕花花公子。～ **deer**【动】麝。～ **duck** (原产南美的)(澳洲)麝香鸭。～ **mallow** 麝香锦葵；黄葵。～ **melon**【植】香瓜，甜瓜。～ **ox** (北极)麝牛。～ **plant**【植】香沟酸浆。～**rat**【动】麝鼠；〔*pl*.〕〔美俚〕*Delaware* 人。～**root** 五福花(属)。～ **rose**【植】麝香蔷薇。～ **tree**, ～ **wood** 麝香树。

mus·kal·longe = muskellunge.

mus·keg [ˈmʌskeg; ˋmʌskɛg] *n*. 青苔沼泽地〔有厚层腐殖质，上面长满青苔，尤指加拿大和阿拉斯加的青苔沼泽地〕。

mus·kel·lunge [ˈmʌskiˌlʌndʒ; ˋmʌskəˏlʌndʒ] *n*. (*pl*. *-lunge*) 北美大梭鱼 (*Esox masquinongy*)〔发展于北美五大湖区和密西西比河上游，是有名的食用鱼〕(= muskie)。

mus·ket [ˈmʌskit; ˋmʌskɪt] *n*. 滑膛枪〔旧式步枪〕。～**shot** 步枪子弹；步枪射程。

mus·ke·teer [ˌmʌskiˈtiə; ˏmʌskəˋtɪr] *n*. **1.**【史】滑膛枪装备的步兵。**2.** 酒友。

mus·ke·toon [ˌmʌskiˈtuːn; ˏmʌskiˋtun] *n*.【史】短枪。

mus·ket·ry [ˈmʌskitri; ˋmʌskətrɪ] *n*. **1.**〔集合词〕滑膛枪，旧式步枪；步枪队。**2.** 步枪火力。**3.** 步枪操法〔射击法〕。

Mus·kie [ˈmʌski; ˋmʌskɪ] **Act** 美国 1970 年"防止大气污染法"的俗称。

musk·i·ness [ˈmʌskinis; ˋmʌskɪnɪs] *n*. 有麝香气。

Mus·ko·ge·an, Mus·kho·ge·an [mʌsˈkəugiən, -dʒiː; mʌsˋkogɪən, -dʒi] *a*. 摩斯科格语的〔美国东南部印第安语的一种〕。

Mus·ko·gee [mʌsˈkəugiː; mʌsˋkogi] *n*. (*pl*. *-gees*, *-gee*) **1.** 马斯科吉人。**2.** 马斯科吉语(= Creek)。

musk·y [ˈmʌski; ˋmʌskɪ] *a*. (***musk·i·er***; ***-i·est***) 麝香的，有麝香气[质]的。

Mus·lem, Mus·lim [ˈmuzlim; ˋmʌzləm] **I** *n*., **1.** 穆斯林。**2.** = Black Muslim. **II** *a*. 穆斯林的，伊斯兰教的。

mus·lin [ˈmʌzlin; ˋmʌzlɪn] *n*. **1.** 平纹细布；〔美〕棉布。**2.**〔俚〕女性，妇女。*a bit of* ～〔英口〕妇女，少女。

mus·lin delaine [ˈmʌzlin dəˈlein; ˋmʌzlɪn dəˋlen] *n*. = mousseline-de-laine.

mus·quash [ˈmʌskwɔʃ; ˋmʌskwɑʃ] *n*.【动】麝香鼠；麝鼠皮。

muss [mʌs; mʌs] **I** *vt*.〔美口〕使混乱，把…弄乱 (*up*)；弄脏，弄皱(衣服) (*up*)。**II** *n*. 混乱，杂乱；吵闹，骚乱。

mus·sel [ˈmʌsl; ˋmʌsl] *n*.【贝】蛤贝，贻贝；蚝；壳菜，淡菜。～ **plum** (深紫色的)李子。

mus·suck [ˈmʌsək; ˋmʌsək] *n*. (印度的)皮水袋。

Mus·sul·man [ˈmʌslmən; ˋmʌslmən] **I** *n*. (*pl*. ～*s*) 穆斯林。**II** *a*. 穆斯林的。

mus·sy [ˈmʌsi; ˋmʌsɪ] *a*. (***-si·er***; ***-si·est***)〔美口〕杂乱的，混乱的；吵闹的；肮脏的。

must[1] [强 mʌst, 弱 məst; mʌst, məst]〔词形无变化，三人称单数不加 s，无不定式和分词等形式，后面接不带 to 的动词不定式〕**I** *v*. *aux*. **1.** 必须，要，应当〔否定用 need not (不必)，must not (不可)〕。*I* ～ *work*. 我必须工作。*You* ～ *not do it*. 你不可以做那件事。*He* ～ *be told*. = *We* ～ *tell him*. 必须告诉他。★ 过去、未来、完成等式用 have to 的相应形式代替，如：I ～ [have to] go today (tomorrow); I had to go yesterday; I shall have to go there some day. **2.**〔必然的推断〕一定；谅必，很可能〔否定用 cannot be, could not have + p. p.〕。*He* ～ *be honest*. 他谅必是诚实的。*It cannot be true*. 那一定不可靠。*He* ～ *have arrived by this time*. 这时候他总该到了。**3.**〔主张〕一定要，坚持要。*He* ～ *always has his own way*. 他总是自行其是。**4.**〔表示不愿意发生或不耐烦〕偏要。*If you* ～, *you* ～. 你说自己一定要怎样，那也就只好怎样了。*Why* ～ *it rain on Sunday*? 偏要在星期天下雨，讨厌！*She said that she* ～ *see the manager*. 她说了她一定要见经理。**5.**〔过去的事，作为历史的现在叙述〕必须，只好。*It was too late now to retreat, he* ～ *make good his word*. 当时退缩已迟，他只好照他自己的话做了。**6.**〔过去或历史的现在〕不巧，偏偏。*Just as I was busiest, he* ～ *come bothering me*. 正在我最忙的时候，他偏要来打搅！～ ***have been*** [***done***] **1.**〔必然〕(*She* ～ *have been a beauty in her day*. 她年轻时一定是个美人。*What a sight it* ～ *have been*! 一定很好看呢！*How you* ～ *have hated me*! 你一定把我恨死了。〔间接叙述法〕*I said he* ～ *have lost his way*. 我说他一定是迷了路了)。**2.**〔～ = should 或 would surely〕(*You* ～ *have caught the train if you had hurried*. 你要是快一点就一定赶上火车了)。**3.**〔必须〕(*Applicants* ～ *have finished the middle school*. 报名者必须中学毕业)。

II [mʌst; mʌst] *n*.〔口〕必须做的事，不可不做的事；必需的东西。*This order is a* ～. 这个命令必须执行。

III *a*.〔口〕绝对需要的，不能缺少的。～ *legislation* 不可缺少的立法。*a* ～ *item* 重要项目。*a* ～ *book* 必读书。*a* ～ *subject* 必修科目。

must[2] [mʌst; mʌst] *n*. (发酵前或发酵中的)葡萄汁；新葡萄酒。

must[3] [mʌst; mʌst] **I** *n*. (象等在交配期中的)狂暴状态；交配期的象。**II** *a*. (特指象因性欲冲动而)狂暴的。

must[4] [mʌst; mʌst] *n*. **1.** 霉臭；霉。**2.** 麝香。

mus·tache [məsˈtɑːʃ; ˋmʌstæʃ] *n*. = moustache.

mus·ta·chio [məsˈtɑːʃəu; məˋstɑʃo] *n*. (*pl*. ～*s*) = mustache.

mus·tang [ˈmʌstæŋ; ˋmʌstæŋ] *n*. (美国西南平原地带的)(半)野马；〔美俚〕海员出身的海军军官；〔M-〕(美国)野马式战斗机。～ **grape** 白亮葡萄。

mus·tard [ˈmʌstəd; ˋmʌstəd] *n*.【植】芥；芥子，芥末；芥末色，深黄色；〔美俚〕热性物品；热情的人。*English* [*French*] ～ 加水[加醋]芥末。～ *and cress*〔英〕拌生菜用小芥叶。***a grain of*** ～ ***seed*** 一粒芥子；〔喻〕前途大有发展的微小事物。***cut the*** ～ (***be up to the*** ～)〔美俚〕符合要求。～ **gas** 芥子气〔一种糜烂性毒气〕。～ **greens**〔美〕芥菜叶。～ **oil** 芥子油。～ **plaster** 芥末软膏。～ **pot**, ～ **poultice** 芥末瓶。

mus·tee [mʌsˈtiː, ˈmʌstiː; mʌsˋti, ˋmʌsti] ***n*. 1.** (有八分之一黑人血统的)黑白混血儿〔白种人与有四分之一黑人血统混血儿所生的人〕(= octoroon)。**2.** 混血儿。

mus·te·line [ˈmʌstiˌlain, -lin; ˋmʌstɪˏlaɪn, -lɪn] ***a*.** 鼬鼠科 (*Mustelidae*) 的〔包括伶鼬、貂、鸡貂、水貂等〕。

mus·ter [ˈmʌstə; ˋmʌstɚ] **I *n*. 1.** (检阅点名时的)召集,集合;检阅,集合人员;群集;花名册;清单。**2.** 孔雀群。**3.**【商】样品。***pass*** [***cut the***] ~ 及格,符合要求。**II *vt*.** 调,召集(兵员),集合,集中;拼凑,振奋,鼓起(勇气等)。—***vi*.** 集合。~ ***in***〔美〕征召…入伍。~ ***out*** 使退伍。~ ***up*** 振起,鼓起。~ **book**, ~ **roll** (军队、舰队的)名册。~**-master** 检阅官。

musth [mʌst; mʌst] = must[3].

must·n't [ˈmʌsnt; ˋmʌsnt]〔口〕= must not.

must've〔口〕= must have.

must·y [ˈmʌsti; ˋmʌstɪ] ***a*.** (***-ti·er***; ***-ti·est***) 发霉的,霉臭的;陈腐的;无气力的。**-ti·ly *ad*. -ti·ness *n*.**

mut [mʌt; mʌt] ***n*.** = mutt.

mut. = mutual.

mu·ta·bil·i·ty [ˌmjuːtəˈbiliti; ˏmjutəˋbɪlətɪ] ***n*.** 可变性;易变性。~ *of human affairs* 人世沧桑。

mu·ta·ble [ˈmjuːtəbl; ˋmjutəbl̩] ***a*.** 可变的;易变的,不定的,无常的;没准性的,三心二意的。**-ness *n*. -bly *ad*.**

mu·ta·fa·cient [ˌmjuːtəˈfeiʃnt; ˏmjutəˋfeʃn̩t] ***a*.**【生】突变加强的。

mu·ta·gen [ˈmjuːtədʒən; ˋmjutədʒən] **I *n*.**【生】诱变剂[因素]。**II *a*. -gen·i·cal·ly *ad*.**

mu·ta·gen·e·sis [ˈmjutəˈdʒenisis; ˏmjutəˋdʒɛnəsɪs] ***n*.** 突变。

mu·tant [ˈmjuːtənt; ˋmjutənt] **I *a*.**【生】变异的;变异所引起的;与突变[变种]有关的,经过突变[变种]的。**II *n*.** 突变[变种]型生物;突变。

mu·tate [mjuːˈteit; ˋmjutet] ***vt*., *vi*.** (使)变异;【生】(使)突变。

mu·ta·tion [mju(ː)ˈteiʃən; mjuˋteʃən] ***n*. 1.** 变化,变异,更换;【生】突变;突变种;【语】母音变化;【乐】(提琴的)变换把位;变声;【法】让受。**2.** (人世的)浮沉,盛衰。~ **plural** 母音变化构成的复数〔men < man, geese < goose 等〕。

mu·ta·tis mu·tan·dis [mjuːˈtaːtis mjuːˈtændis; mju-ˋtetɪs mjuˋtændɪs]〔L.〕已作必要的修正。

mu·ta·tive [ˈmjuːtətiv; ˋmjutətɪv] ***a*.**【生】突变[变种]的;有突变[变种]趋势的;有突变[变种]特点的。

mutch·kin [ˈmʌtʃkn; ˋmʌtʃkn̩] ***n*.**〔Scot.〕姆尺肯〔苏格兰液衡名,稍少于一品脱〕。

mute[1] [mjuːt; mjut] **I *a*. 1.** 哑的;缄默无言的;(一时)说不出话的;(猎狗)不叫的;(金属)不响的;【法】拒绝答辩的。**2.**【语】闭止音的〔b, p, d, t, k, g 等〕;不发音的,哑音的〔如 mute 中的 e〕。*a* ~ *appeal* 无言的恳求。*stand* ~ *of malice*【法】对被控罪名拒不答辩。**II *n*. 1.** 哑子,哑吧,(尤指)又聋又哑的人;沉默的人;【法】拒绝答辩的被告人。**2.**【语】闭止音;不发音的字母。**3.** 雇用的送丧人;(没有台词讲的)无言演员。**4.**【乐】弱音器。**III *vt*.** 减弱…的声音;柔和…的色调。**-ly *ad*. -ness *n*.**

mute[2] [mjuːt; mjut] **I *vi*., *vt*.** (鸟)拉屎,排泄。**II *n*.** 鸟粪。

mu·ti·cate [ˈmjuːtiˌkeit; ˋmjutɪˏket] ***a*. 1.**【植】无芒刺的。**2.**【动】无(齿、爪等)防卫结构的(= muticious)。

mu·ti·late [ˈmjuːtileit; ˋmjutl̩ˏet] ***vt*.** 切断(手足等);使断肢;残害,毁伤,毁坏;(删去作品中的主要部分)使残缺不全。**-la·tion *n*.** (手足等的)切断;毁伤。**-til·a·tor *n*.** 切断者,毁伤者。

mu·ti·neer [ˌmjuːtiˈniə; ˏmjutn̩ˋɪr] **I *n*.** 暴动者,造反者,叛变者,反抗者;反抗长官者。**II *vi*.**〔古〕暴动;造反,叛变,反抗;反抗长官。

mu·ti·nous [ˈmjuːtinəs; ˋmjutn̩əs] ***a*.** 暴动的,叛变的,反抗的;反抗长官的,违抗命令的。**-ly *ad*.**

mu·ti·ny [ˈmjuːtini; ˋmjutn̩ɪ] **I *n*.** 暴动,造反,叛变;兵变。**II *vi*.** 暴动,造反,叛变;反抗。

mut·ism [ˈmjuːtizəm; ˋmjutɪzm̩] ***n*.**【医】哑;【心】不言症,缄默症。

mu·to·graph [ˈmjuːtəgraːf; ˋmjutəˏgræf] **I *n*.** (初期的)电影摄影机。**II *vt*.** (用电影摄影机)拍摄。

mu·to·scope [ˈmjuːtəskəup; ˋmjutəˏskop] ***n*.** (初期)电影放映机。

mutt [mʌt; mʌt] ***n*.**〔美俚〕傻子,笨蛋,无足轻重的人;杂种狗,野狗,小狗。

mut·ter [ˈmʌtə; ˋmʌtɚ] **I *n*.** 咕哝,小声低语;抱怨,怨言。**II *vt*., *vi*.** 低声说;咕哝,嘀咕,抱怨地说 (*at*; *against*);发出低沉轰隆声。~ ***and mumble*** 吞吞吐吐。~ ***away to oneself*** 喃喃自语。~ ***threats at*** 低声恐吓。~ ***to oneself*** 喃喃自语。**-er *n*. -ing·ly *ad*.**

mut·ton [ˈmʌtn; ˋmʌtn̩] ***n*.** 羊肉;〔谑〕羊;〔俚〕娼妓。***dead as*** ~ 真死,僵死。***eat*** [***take***] ***one's*** ~ ***with*** 和…共餐。***return to one's*** ~***s***〔谑〕言归正传,回到本题。~ **bird**【鸟】细嘴海燕。~ **chop** 羊排;羊肉片;〔*pl*.〕上细下圆的络腮胡子。~ **fist**〔口〕粗壮的大手;手粗大的人。~ **ham** 腊羊肉。~**head**〔口〕笨人,傻子。~ **top**〔美俚〕笨蛋。

mut·ton·y [ˈmʌtəni; ˋmʌtn̩ɪ] ***a*.** 羊肉味的;羊膻气的。

mu·tu·al [ˈmjuːtjuəl, ˈmjuːtʃuəl; ˋmjutjʊəl, ˋmjutʃʊəl] ***a*. 1.** 相互的。**2.**〔口〕共有的,共同的。~ *affection* 互爱,相爱。~ *aid* 互相援助。*a* ~ *aid team* 互助组。*a* ~ *admiration society* 一批互相吹捧的人们。*our* ~ *friend* 我们共同的朋友。*by* ~ *consent* 双方同意。~ *association* 互助会,共济会。~ *benefit and collaboration* 互惠合作。~ *preferential duties* 互惠关税。~ **capacitance**【电】互容。~ **conductance**【电】互导。~ **coupling factor** 耦合系数。~ **fund** 合股投资(公司)。~ **induction**【电】互感。~ **savings bank** 互助储蓄会。**-ly *ad*.**

mu·tu·al·ism [ˈmjuːtjuəlizəm, ˈmjuːtʃuəlizəm; ˋmjutjʊəlɪzm̩, ˋmjutʃʊəlɪzəm] ***n*.** 互助论;【生】互利共生(现象)。

mu·tu·al·ist [ˈmjuːtjuəlist; ˋmjutjʊəlɪst] ***n*. 1.** 互助论者。**2.**【生】依生生物。

mu·tu·al·i·ty [ˌmjuːtjuˈæliti, mjuːtʃuˈæliti; ˏmjutjʊ-ˋælətɪ, mjutʃʊˋælətɪ] ***n*. 1.** 相互关系,相关;(相互)依存。**2.** 同感;亲密。

mu·tu·el [ˈmjuːtjuəl, ˈmjuːtʃuwəl; ˋmjutjuəl, ˋmjutʃu-wəl] ***n*. 1.**【赛马】买中赢马者除手续费一成外分得全部赌金的方法 (= parimutuel)。**2.** 赌金计算机。

mu·tule [ˈmjuːtjuːl; ˋmjutʃul] ***n*.**【建】Doric 式檐饰。

mux [mʌks; mʌks] ***vt*.**〔美俚〕使弄糟,弄坏。

Mu·zak [ˈmjuːzæk; ˋmjuzæk] ***n*.** 音乐广播网〔通过线路向饭店、商店、工厂等用户播送录制好的背景音乐的广播系统〕。

mu·zhik, mu·zjik [ˈmuːʒik; ˋmuʒik] ***n*.** (帝俄时代的)农民。

muzz [mʌz; mʌz] ***vt*., *vi*.**〔英俚〕使(醉得)发呆;拼命用功。

muz·zle [ˈmʌzl; ˋmʌzl̩] **I *n*. 1.** (动物的)口部,口鼻;(狗、马等的)口套,口络。**2.** 枪口,炮口;喷口,喷嘴。**3.** 压制言论的事物。**II *vt*.** 上口套;封住…的嘴;使缄默;压制[箝制]…的言论;〔方〕(猪等)用嘴掘;〔方〕大口大口喝;收(帆);〔美俚〕亲嘴。*a* ~ *cover* 枪口罩。~**-loader *n*.** 前装枪[炮]。~**-loading *a*.** 前装式的,前膛的。~ **velocity** (枪弹的)初速,腔口速度。

muz·zy [ˈmʌzi; ˋmʌzɪ] ***a*.** (***-zi·er***; ***-zi·est***)〔口〕头脑混乱的;迟钝的;迷惑的;(醉得)发呆的。**-zi·ly *ad*.**

MV = **1.** market value 市面价值。**2.** mean variation 平均变化。**3.** medium voltage【电】中压。**4.** merchant vessel 商船。**5.** motor vessel 内燃机船。**6.** muzzle velocity 初速〔射炮离开口瞬间的速度〕。**7.** main verb【语

法】主要动词。

mv. = millivolt.

M.V.O. = Member of the Royal Victorian Order〔英〕维多利亚勋章获得者。

MVP = most valuable player〔美〕最高身价球员。

MW = military works 军事工程,筑垒。

M.W. = **1.** molecular weight 分子量。**2.** Most Worshipful〔英〕最尊敬的〔用于对治安法官、市参议员等的称呼〕。**3.** Most Worthy 最尊敬的。

mw. = milliwatt.

M.W.A. = Modern Woodmen of America 美国现代猎人协会。

Mx = Middlesex〔英〕米德尔塞克斯(郡)。

Mx., mx = maxwell 马克士威〔磁通量单位〕。

MX [ˈemˈeks; ˋɛmˋɛks] ***n.*** Mx (洲际)导弹(亦作 MX missile)。

my [mai, 弱 mi; maɪ, mɪ] **I** ***pro.*** **1.**〔I 的所有格〕我的。~ *and her father* 我和她俩人的父亲。~ *and her father(s)* 我的父亲和她的父亲。**2.**〔用于称呼〕~ *dear fellow* = ~ *good man* 喂,老朋友。*My Lord* [*m- l-*] [miˈlɔːd; mɪˋlɔrd] 大人,老爷〔对于贵族、主教、法官等的尊称〕。**II** ***int.***〔口〕〔表示惊奇〕***My***! = ***Oh***, ~! = ***My goodness***! 呀! 啊唷! 天哪(*My, what a mist*! 啊呀,多大的雾呀!) ***My eye***! (带有反驳或难于置信的口气)嗬! 天晓得! 去你[他]的!

my·al·gi·a [maiˈældʒiə; maɪˋældʒɪə] ***n.***【医】肌肉风湿痛,肌痛。

my·al·ism [ˈmaiəlizəm; ˋmaɪəlɪzəm] ***n.*** (西印度群岛的)巫术。

my·all [ˈmaiɔːl; ˋmaɪɔl] ***n.*** 澳大利亚洋槐。

my·as·the·ni·a [ˌmaiæsˈθiːniə; ˏmaɪəsˋθinɪə] ***n.***【医】肌无力,肌衰弱。~ **gravis**【医】重症肌无力。**-then·ic** ***a.***

myc- *comb.f.* 真菌: *myc*osis.

my·ce·li·um [maiˈsiːliəm; maɪˋsilɪəm] ***n.*** (*pl.* ***-li·a*** [-ə; -ə])【生】菌丝体。**-li·al** ***a.***

My·ce·nae·an [ˌmaisiˈniːən; ˏmaɪsɪˋniən] ***a.***【考古】(古代希腊都市)迈西尼(Mycenae)(文化)的。

my·ce·to·ma [ˌmaisiˈtəumə; ˏmaɪsəˋtomə] ***n.***【医】足分支菌病。

my·ce·to·zo·an [maiˌsiːtəˈzəuən; maɪˏsitəˋzoən] **I** ***n.***【生】黏菌性动物(= myxomycete)。**II** ***a.*** 黏菌类的(= myxomycetous)。

myco- *comb.f.* (用于子音前) = myc-.

my·co·bac·te·ri·um [ˌmaikəubækˈtiəriəm; ˏmaɪkobækˋtɪrɪəm] ***n.*** (*pl.* ***-ri·a*** [-ə; -ə])【生】分枝杆菌属。

mycol. = mycology.

my·co·log·ic, my·co·log·i·cal [ˌmaikəuˈlɔdʒik(əl); ˏmaɪkoˋlɑdʒɪk(əl)] ***a.*** 真菌学的,霉菌学的。

my·col·o·gy [maiˈkɔlədʒi; maɪˋkɑlədʒɪ] ***n.*** 真菌学,霉菌学。**-gist** ***n.***

my·co(r)·rhi·za [ˌmaikəuˈraizə; ˏmaɪkəˋraɪzə] ***n.***【微】菌根。

my·dri·a·sis [miˈdraiəsis; mɪˋdraɪəsɪs] ***n.***【医】瞳孔开大,瞳孔放大。**myd·ri·at·ic** [ˌmidriˈætik; ˏmɪdrɪˋætɪk] ***a.***, ***n.*** 瞳孔开大的(药)。

my·e·len·ceph·a·lon [ˌmaiəlenˈsefəˌlɔn; ˏmaɪəlenˋsɛfəlɑn] ***n.*** (*pl.* ***-la*** [-lə; -lə])【解】末脑,脑髓(= marrow brain)。

my·e·lin [ˈmaiəli(ː)n; ˋmaɪəlɪn] ***n.***【解】髓磷脂。**-ic** ***a.***

my·e·li·tis [ˌmaiəˈlaitis; ˏmaɪəˋlaɪtɪs] ***n.***【医】脊髓炎;骨髓炎。

my·e·lo·gen·ic [ˌmaiələuˈdʒenik; ˏmaɪələˋdʒɛnɪk] ***a.*** 生于骨髓内的;骨髓性的(= myelogenous)。

my·e·lo·gram [ˈmaiələuˈgræm; ˋmaɪəloˏgræm] ***n.*** 脊髓爱克斯线像;脊髓细胞分类计数。**-log·ra·phy** [-ˈlɔgrəfi; -ˋlɑgrəfɪ] ***n.***

my·e·loid [ˈmaiəˌlɔid; ˋmaɪəˏlɔɪd] ***a.*** **1.** 骨髓的;骨髓状的;由骨髓而来的。**2.** 脊髓的。

my·e·lo·ma [ˌmaiəuˈləumə; ˏmaɪəˋlomə] ***n.*** (*pl.* ~***s***, ***-ma·ta*** [-mətə; -mətə])【医】骨髓瘤。**-tous** [-ˈlɔmətəs, -ˈləumə-; -ˋlɑmətəs, -ˋlomə-] ***a.***

myg. = myriagram(me).

my·i·a·sis [maiˈaiəsis; ˋmaɪəsɪs] ***n.*** 蛆病。

myl [mail; maɪl] 万立升〔法国容量名〕。

My·lar [ˈmailɑː; ˋmaɪlɑr] ***n.*** 迈拉〔一种聚酯类高分子物的商品名〕。

my·lo·nite [ˈmailəuˌnait; ˋmaɪloˏnaɪt] ***n.***【地】糜棱岩。

mym [maim; maɪm] 万米〔长度单位〕。

my·na, mi·na(h) [ˈmainə; ˋmaɪnə] ***n.***【鸟】家八哥;鹩哥;秦吉了。

Myn·heer [mainˈhiə, -ˈhɛə; maɪnˋhɛr, -ˋhɛr] ***n.*** **1.**〔D.〕= Mr., Sir. **2.**〔m-〕荷兰人。

my·o·car·di·al [ˌmaiəuˈkɑːdiəl; ˏmaɪəˋkɑrdɪəl] ***a.***【解】心肌的。~ **infarction**【医】心肌梗塞。

my·o·car·di·o·graph [ˌmaiəuˈkɑːdiəˈgrɑːf, -græf; ˏmaɪoˋkɑrdɪəˏgræf, -grɑf] ***n.***【医】心肌动(描)记器。

my·o·car·di·tis [ˌmaiəukɑːˈdaitis; ˏmaɪokɑrˋdaɪtɪs] ***n.***【医】心肌炎。

my·o·car·di·um [ˌmaiəuˈkɑːdiəm; ˏmaɪəˋkɑrdɪəm] ***n.***【解】心肌(层)。**-car·di·cal** ***a.***

my·oc·lo·nus [maiˈɔklənəs; maɪˋɑklənəs] ***n.***【医】肌阵挛。**-clon·ic** [ˌmaiəˈklɔnik; ˏmaɪəˋklɑnɪk] ***a.***

my·o·e·lec·tric [ˌmaiəuiˈlektrik; ˏmaɪoɪˋlɛktrɪk] ***a.***【医】肌电位的。**-al·ly** ***ad.***

my·o·gen [ˈmaiədʒin; ˋmaɪədʒɪn] ***n.***【生化】肌浆蛋白。

my·o·gen·ic [ˌmaiəuˈdʒenik; ˏmaɪoˋdʒɛnɪk] ***a.***【解】肌原性的;肌生的。

my·o·glo·bin [ˈmaiəugləubin, ˌmaiəuˈgləubin; ˋmaɪəˏglobɪn, ˏmaɪoˋglobɪn] ***n.***【医】肌红蛋白,肌红素。

my·o·graph [ˈmaiəugrɑːf, -ˌgræf; ˋmaɪəˏgræf, -ˏgrɑf] ***n.***【医】肌动(描)记器。

my·ol·o·gy [maiˈɔlədʒi; maɪˋɑlədʒɪ] ***n.***【医】肌学。**-log·ic, -log·i·cal** ***a.***

my·o·ma [maiˈəumə; maɪˋomə] ***n.*** (*pl.* ***-mas***, ***-ma·ta*** [-mətə; -mətə])【医】肌瘤。**-tous** [-ˈɔmətəs, -ˈəumə-; -ˋɑmətəs, -ˋomə-] ***a.***

my·o·neu·ral [ˌmaiəuˈnjuərəl, -ˈnuər-; ˏmaɪəˋnjʊrəl, -ˋnʊr-] ***a.*** 有关肌神经的〔尤指有关肌纤维神经末梢的〕。

my·op·a·thy [maiˈɔpəθi; maɪˋɑpəθɪ] ***n.***【医】肌病。

my·ope [ˈmaiəup; ˋmaɪop] ***n.*** 患近视者;眼光短浅者。

my·o·pi·a [maiˈəupiə; maɪˋopɪə], **my·o·py** [ˈmaiəpi; ˋmaɪəpɪ] ***n.***【医】近视(*opp.* hypermetropia)。**-opic** [-ˈɔpik; -ˋɑpɪk] ***a.*** 近视眼的;缺乏远见的。

my·o·sin [ˈmaiəsin; ˋmaɪəsɪn] ***n.***【医】肌凝蛋白。

my·o·sis [maiˈəusis; maɪˋosɪs] ***n.***【医】瞳孔缩小,缩瞳症。

my·o·si·tis [ˌmaiəuˈsaitis; ˏmaɪoˋsaɪtɪs] ***n.***【医】肌炎。

my·o·so·tis [ˈmaiəuˈsəutis; ˏmaɪəˋsotɪs] ***n.*** 勿忘草属(*Myosotis*)植物〔包括勿忘草〕。

my·ot·ic [maiˈɔtik; maɪˋɑtɪk] ***a.***, ***n.***【医】缩瞳孔的(药)。

my·o·tome [ˈmaiəutəum; ˋmaɪəˏtom] ***n.***【解】**1.** 肌刀。**2.** 生肌节。

my·ot·o·my [maiˈɔtəmi; maɪˋɑtəmɪ] ***n.***【解】肌切开术。

my·o·to·ni·a [ˌmaiəuˈtəuniə; ˏmaɪəˋtonɪə] ***n.***【医】肌强直。**-ton·ic** [-ˈtɔnik; -ˋtɑnɪk] ***a.***

My·ra [ˈmaiərə; ˋmaɪrə] ***n.*** 迈拉〔女子名〕。

myr·i(a)- *comb.f.* 一万〔仅用于米制〕;无数。

myr·i·ad [ˈmiriəd; ˋmɪrɪəd] **I** ***n.***〔诗〕万,一万;无数,极大数量。**II** ***a.*** 无数的;众多方面的。*a* ~ *of stars* 无数的星斗。~**-minded** ***a.*** 才气纵横的,多才多艺的。

M

myr·i·a·dyne [ˈmiriədain; ˋmɪrɪəˏdaɪn] *n*.【物】万达因。

myr·i·a·gram(me) [ˈmiriəgræm; ˋmɪrɪəˏgræm] *n*. 万克(即十公斤)。

myr·i·a·li·tre, myr·i·a·liter [ˈmiriəliːtə; ˋmɪrɪəˏlitɚ] *n*. 万升。

myr·i·a·me·tre, myr·i·a·me·ter [ˈmiriəˌmiːtə; ˋmɪrɪəˏmitɚ] *n*. 万米(即十公里)。

myr·i·a·pod [ˈmiriəpɔd; ˋmɪrɪəˏpɑd] *a*., *n*. 多足(类)的;多足类动物,节足动物。

myr·i·cin [ˈmirisin; ˋmɪrəsɪn] *n*.【化】蜂酯;杨梅脂。

myr·i·o·ra·ma [ˌmiriəuˈrɑːmə; ˏmɪrɪoˋrɑmə] *n*. 万景画〔将许多小画组成的画〕;万景画会。

my·ris·tate [miˈristeit; mɪˋrɪstet] *n*.【化】十四(烷)酸盐[酯],肉豆蔻酸盐[酯]。

my·ris·tic [miˈristik; mɪˋrɪstɪk] *a*. ~ **acid** 肉豆蔻酸,十四(烷)酸。

My·ris·ti·ca [miˈristikə; mɪˋrɪstɪkə] *n*.【植】肉豆蔻属。

myr·me·co- [ˈməmikəu; ˋmɚmɪko] *comb*. *f*. 蚁。

myr·me·co·log·i·cal [ˌməːmikəuˈlɔdʒikl; ˏmɚmɪkoˋlɑdʒɪkl̩] *a*. 蚁学的。

myr·me·col·o·gy [ˌməːmiˈkɔlədʒi; ˏmɚmɪˋkɑlədʒɪ] *n*. 蚁类研究,蚁学。

myr·me·coph·a·gous [ˌməːmiˈkɔfəgəs; ˏmɚməˋkɑfəgəs] *a*. 食蚁的。

myr·mi·don [ˈməmidən; ˋmɪməˏdɑn] *n*. **1**. 盲目执行主子命令的人,顺从的部下;职业暴徒。**2**. 〔M-〕〔希神〕迈密登。*~s of the law* 〔蔑〕法律执行吏,警察(等)。

my·rob·a·lan [maiˈrɔbələn, mi-; maɪˋrɑbələn, mɪ-] *n*. **1**. 诃子(诃黎勒,藏青果)。**2**. 樱桃李(= cherry-plum)。

My·ron [ˈmaiərən; ˋmaɪrən] *n*. 迈伦〔男子名〕。

myrrh [məː; mɚ] *n*. 没药〔热带树脂,可作香料、药材〕;没药树;没药树脂。**-rhic** *a*.

myrrh·y [ˈməːri; ˋmɚrɪ] *a*. 有没药香味的。

myr·tle [ˈməːtl; ˋmɚtl̩] *n*. **1**.【植】桃金娘,番樱桃;爱神木;长春花;加州桂;铜钱状珍珠等。**2**. 〔M-〕默特尔〔女子名〕。**3**. = ~ green. *the wax* [*candleberry*] ~ 杨梅。~**-berry** 爱神木果实。~ **green** *n*. 墨绿色。

my·self [maiˈself; məˋself] *pro*. (*pl*. ***ourselves***) (我)自己;(我)亲自。**1**. 〔加重 I 的语气〕*I ~ saw it*. = *I saw it ~*. 我亲自看见的。**2**. 〔me 的反身形〕*I have hurt ~*. 我受伤了。***as for ~*** (至于)我自己,讲到我自己。***(all) by ~*** 我独自地;独力地。***I am not ~*** . 我身体不舒服;我精神不正常。***I came to ~*** . 我清醒过来了。

my·sid [ˈmaisid; ˋmaɪsɪd] *n*. 糠虾目(*Mysidacea*)动物。

My·sis [ˈmaisis; ˋmaɪsɪs] *n*. 糠虾属;〔m-〕糠虾期,幼体期。

Myst. = Mysteries.

mys·ta·gogue [ˈmistəˈgɔg; ˋmɪstəˏgɔg] *n*. 神秘教义的解释者[传播者];引人入秘教者。**-gog·ic** [-ˈgɔdʒik; -ˋgɑdʒɪk] *a*., **-go·gy** [-ˌgəudʒi; -ˏgodʒɪ] *n*.

mys·te·ri·ous [misˈtiəriəs; mɪsˋtɪrɪəs] *a*. 神秘的,不可思议的;暧昧的,可疑的;故弄玄虚的。**-ly** *ad*. **-ness** *n*.

mys·te·ri·um [misˈtiəriəm; mɪsˋtɪrɪəm] *n*.【天】神秘波源〔被认为是银河系几个区域中发出一种特别的无线电波频的羟基酸根〕。

mys·ter·y[1] [ˈmistəri; ˋmɪstrɪ] *n*. **1**. 神秘的事物,不可思议的事物。**2**. 神秘,秘密;诀窍,秘诀,秘传;玄妙,奥妙。**3**. 〔常 *pl*.〕(古代宗教中的)神秘仪式;玄义;〔*pl*.〕(基督教的)圣餐礼。**4**. 〔美口〕烤什锦。**5**. = ~ play. **6**. 疑案小说[故事,戏剧],侦探小说。*the mysteries of nature* 自然界的奥秘[奇迹]。*mysteries of a trade* 某一行业的诀窍。*mysteries of woods and rivers* 打猎和捕鱼的秘诀。***be a ~ to*** (某人)不能理解。***be wrapped in ~*** 包在秘密中。***dive into the mysteries of*** 探究…的秘密。***make a ~ of*** 把…神秘化,把…弄成秘密,卖弄玄虚。~ **play** 神秘剧〔欧洲中世纪宣传宗教的戏剧〕。~ **ship** [**boat**] 伪装猎潜舰(= Q-ship, Q-boat)。

mys·ter·y[2] [ˈmistəri; ˋmɪstərɪ] *n*. 〔英、古〕手艺,手工业;行业;行会。*the art and ~ of* …的技术和手艺〔学徒满期证书上用语〕。

mys·tic [ˈmistik; ˋmɪstɪk] **I** *a*. **1**. 神秘的,不可思议的,奥妙的;引起惊奇[畏惧]的。**2**. 秘诀的,秘法的;秘传仪式的。**3**. 神秘主义(者)的。**II** *n*. 神秘主义者。

mys·ti·cal [ˈmistikəl; ˋmɪstɪkl̩] *a*. = mystic. **-ly** *ad*. **-ness** *n*.

mys·ti·cism [ˈmistisizəm; ˋmɪstəˏsɪzəm] *n*. 神秘,玄妙;暧昧;玄想(的谬说);神秘主义;神秘教。

mys·ti·fi·ca·tion [ˌmistifiˈkeiʃən; ˏmɪstəfəˋkeʃən] *n*. 使人迷惑的事物;神秘举动[行动、现象];不可思议;迷惑;神秘化。

mys·ti·fy [ˈmistifai; ˋmɪstəˏfaɪ] *vt*. 使神秘化,蒙蔽,迷惑。***be mystified by*** 给…弄得莫名其妙。**-fing·ly** *ad*.

mys·tique [misˈtiːk; mɪsˋtik] *n*. 神秘性,神秘气氛;不可言传的性质;(技艺的)秘诀。

myth [miθ; mɪθ] **I** *n*. **1**. 神话;神怪故事。**2**. 奇人,奇事,怪物;虚构的故事;荒诞的说法。**II** *vt*. 使神化。

myth. = mythological, mythology.

myth·ic, myth·i·cal [ˈmiθik(əl); ˋmɪθɪk(əl)] *a*. 神话(式)的;神话时代的;虚构的,非现实的,想像[传说]上的。**-cal·ly** *ad*.

myth·i·cism [ˈmiθisizəm; ˋmɪθəsɪzm] *n*. 神话式的解释;神话说,神话主义。**-i·cist** *n*. 神话研究[解释]者;相信神话者。

myth·i·cize [ˈmiθisaiz; ˋmɪθəˏsaɪz] *vt*. 把…当作神话;使神话化;对…作神话解释。**-ciz·er** *n*. 编神话者;解释神化者。

mytho- *comb*. *f*. 神话。

myth·og·ra·pher [miˈθɔgrəfə, mai-; mɪˋθɑgrəfɚ, maɪ-] *n*. 神话作者。

myth·og·ra·phy [miˈθɔgrəfi; mɪˋθɑgrəfɪ] *n*. (绘画、雕刻等的)神话艺术。

mythol. = mythological; mythology.

myth·ol·og·ic, -i·cal [miθəˈlɔdʒik(əl); mɪθəˋlɑdʒɪk(l̩)] *a*. 神话(中)的;神话学(上)的;神话似的,凭空想像的,荒唐无稽的。**-i·cal·ly** *ad*.

myth·ol·o·gist [miˈθɔlədʒist; mɪˋθɑlədʒɪst] *n*. 神话学者;神话作者[编纂者]。

myth·ol·o·gize [miˈθɔlədʒaiz; mɪˋθɑləˏdʒaɪz] *vt*., *vi*. **1**. (把…)当作神话。**2**. (对…)作神话解释。**3**. 讲述(神话)。**4**. 给(神话)分类。

myth·ol·o·gy [miˈθɔlədʒi; mɪˋθɑlədʒɪ] *n*. **1**. 神话学。**2**. 〔集合词〕神话;神话集,神话志。*Greek ~* 希腊神话。

myth·o·pe·ic, myth·o·poe·ic [ˌmiθəˈpiːik; ˏmɪθəˋpiɪk] *a*. 神话时代的;创作[产生]神话的。

myth·os [ˈmaiθɔs; ˋmaɪθɑs] *n*. (*pl*. ***my·thoi*** [ˈmaiθɔːi; ˋmaɪθɔɪ]) (一个)神话;〔集合词〕神话(集);虚构的故事[事物];代表某一集体的态度、信仰等特征的类型;(文艺作品的)主题。

my·thus [ˈmaiθəs; ˋmaɪθəs] *n*. 神话 = myth.

myx(o)- *comb*. *f*. 黏液。

myx·oe·de·ma [miksiˈdiːmə; ˏmɪksɪˋdimə] *n*.【医】黏液(性)水肿。

myx·o·ma [mikˈsəumə; mɪksˋomə] *n*. (*pl*. *~s*, ***-mata*** [-mətə; mətə])【医】黏液瘤。**-tous** [-təs; -təs]) *a*.

myx·o·ma·to·sis [ˌmiksəuməˈtəusis; ˏmɪksoməˋtosɪs] *n*. **1**. 黏液瘤(菌)的存在。**2**. 多发性黏液瘤,黏液瘤病。

myx·o·my·cete [ˌmiksəumaiˈsiːt; ˏmɪksomaɪˋsit] *n*. 黏菌。

M

N

N

N, n [en; ɛn] (*pl*. ***N's***, ***n's*** [enz; ɛnz]) **1.** 英语字母表第十四字母。**2.**【印】对开〔em 字母全身的一半 = en〕。**3.** N 形物。**4.**〔n〕【数】任意数,不定数,不定量。**5.**【遗】单位(染色体)数。*an N girder* N 字桁。***to the nth*** (***power***)【数】到 n 次(幂);到极度,极端。

N 1.【罗马数字】90〔N = 90000〕。**2.**【化】= nitrogen. **3.** = North(ern)。

N., n. = **1.** name. **2.** navy. **3.** neuter. **4.** new. **5.** nominative. **6.** noon. **7.** north; northern. **8.** noun. **9.**【化】normal. **10.** National; Nationalist. **11.** Norse. **12.** November. **13.** nephew. **14.** net. **15.** note. **16.** number.

N = nuclear 核的:N-waste 核废料。

-n *suf*. = -en, -an.

'n[1]〔口〕= than.

'n[2]〔口〕= and.

NA =〔美〕National Archives 国家档案馆。

Na =【化】natrium (〔L.〕= sodium)。

N.A., NA = North America 北美洲。

NAA = National Aeronautic Association〔美〕全国航空协会。

NAACP = National Association for the Advancement of Colored People〔美〕全国有色人种协进会。

NAAFI, Naafi [ˈnæfi; ˋnæfɪ] = Navy, Army and Air Force Institutes〔英〕海陆空军小卖店经营机构。

nab [næb; næb] ***vt*.**〔口〕逮捕,拘捕;猛然抓住;抢去(东西),攫夺。

Na·bar·ro [nəˈbɑːrəu; nəˋbɑro] ***n*.** 纳巴罗〔姓氏〕。

Nab·by [ˈnæbi; ˋnæbɪ] ***n*.** Abigail 的爱称。

nabe [neib; neb] ***n*.** 本地区电影院。

na·bob, na·wab [ˈneibɔb, nəˈwɑːb; ˋnebɑb, nəˋwɑb] ***n*. 1.** 对有身分的穆斯林的尊称。**2.**【史】(印度莫卧儿帝国时代的)太守[总督]。**3.**〔古〕在印度发了大财的英国人;富翁,大财主。**4.**〔美俚〕名士。**-ism, -er·y *n*.** 财主气概[行为]。

Na·both [ˈneibɔθ; ˋnebɑθ] ***n*.** 拿伯〔《圣经》故事中的葡萄园主,国王欲占其葡萄园而把他杀死〕。**~'s vineyard** 被别人垂涎的东西。

NACA [Am.] = National Advisory Committee for Aeronautics〔美〕国家航空咨询委员会。

nac·a·rat [ˈnækəræt; ˋnækəræt] ***n*. 1.** 胭脂红,洋红。**2.** 胭脂红夏布[绉绸]。

na·celle [nəˈsel; nəˋsɛl] ***n*. 1.**【空】机舱,客舱。**2.** (轻气球的)吊篮;(飞艇的)吊舱。

nach·us, nach·as [ˈnɑːkəs; ˋnɑkəs] ***n*.**〔Heb.〕骄傲而津津乐道的事。

na·cre [ˈneikə; ˋnekɚ] ***n*. 1.** 珠母贝,珍珠母。**2.** 真珠层;真珠质。

na·cred [ˈneikəd; ˋnekɚd] ***a*.** 有珍珠层的;似珍珠(质)的。

na·cre·ous [ˈneikriəs; ˋnekrɪəs], **na·crous** [ˈneikrəs; ˋnekrəs] ***a*. 1.** 珍珠(质)的。**2.** 产生珍珠质的。**3.** 似珍珠的。

na·crite [ˈneikrait; ˋnekraɪt] ***n*.** 珍珠陶土。

N.A.D. = National Academy of Design〔美〕全国设计院。

NADGE = NATO Air Defence Ground Environment 北大西洋公约组织防空警备体系。

na·dir [ˈneidiə, -də; ˋnedɪr, -dɚ] ***n*. 1.** 天底〔天体观测者脚下正中点〕(*opp*. zenith)。**2.** 最下点,最低点。**3.** 最低温度。***at the ~ of*** 在…的最下层[低点](*His fortune was at its ~*. 他的运气坏到极点)。

nae [nei; ne]〔Scot.〕***a*., *ad*.** = no; not.

nae·vus [ˈniːvəs; ˋnivəs] ***n*.** (*pl*. ***nae·vi*** [-vai; -vaɪ])【医】痣;(一般的)斑点。*a pigmentary ~* 黑痣,黑瘤子。

NAFTA [ˈnæftə; ˋnæftə] = North American Free Trade Agreement 北美自由贸易协定。

nag[1] [næg; næg] ***n*. 1.** (骑用)小马;〔口〕(老)马;〔口〕驽马;〔美俚〕劣等赛马用马。**2.** 旧汽车。

nag[2] [næg; næg] **I *n*. 1.** 嫌言怨语;唠叨;不停的责骂。**2.**〔口〕爱唠叨的人(尤指妇女)。**II *vt*., *vi*.** (***nagged***; ***nag·ging***) **1.** 发牢骚,唠叨;责骂;老是催促;不断地找(…的)岔子。**2.** 困扰;恼人。*She nagged* (*at*) *him all day long*. 她对他终日唠叨不已。

Na·ga·sa·ki [ˌnægəˈsɑːki; ˏnægəˋsɑkɪ] ***n*.** 长崎〔日本港市〕。

nag·ger [ˈnægə; ˋnægɚ] ***n*.** 爱唠叨的人;牢骚多的女人;泼妇。

nag·ging [ˈnægiŋ; ˋnægɪŋ] **I *a*. 1.** 责天怨地的,爱唠叨的;尽找碴的。**2.** 恼人的。**II *n*.** 嫌言怨语。*~ criticism* 嫌言怨语式的批评。

nag·gish[1] [ˈnægiʃ; ˋnægɪʃ] ***a*.** 小马的;小的,劣的。

nag·gish[2] [ˈnægiʃ; ˋnægɪʃ] ***a*.** 有些爱唠叨的。

nag·gy [ˈnægi; ˋnægɪ] ***a*.** = nagging.

Na·go·ya [nɑːˈgəujɑː; nɑˋgojɑ] ***n*.** 名古屋〔日本城市〕。

na·grams [ˈneigramz; ˋnegramz] ***n*.**〔美俚〕忧郁,悲观。

nah [nɑː; nɑ] ***a*.**〔美俚〕= no.

Na·ha [ˈnɑːhɑː; ˋnɑhɑ] ***n*.** 那霸〔日本港市〕。

Na·hal [nɑːˈhɑːl; nɑˋhɑl] ***n*. 1.** 以色列的"农垦"部队。**2.** 以色列的武装"移民区"。

Na·hua [ˈnɑːwə; ˋnɑwə] ***n*.** (*pl*. ***~s***;〔集合词〕~) = Nahuatl ***a*.**

Na·huat [ˈnɑːwɑːt; ˋnɑwɑt] ***n*. 1.** (*pl*. ~(*s*)) 那瓦特族人〔墨西哥印第安人的一个部落〕。**2.** 那瓦特语。

Na·hua·tl [ˈnɑːwɑːtl; ˋnɑwɑtl] **I *n*. 1.** (*pl*. ~(*s*))〔墨西哥南部和中美洲包括阿兹特克人的印第安人〕那瓦特人。**2.** 那瓦特语。**II *a*.** 那瓦特人[语]的。

Na·hua·tlan [ˈnɑːwɑːtlən; ˋnɑwɑtlən] **I *a*.** 那瓦特语的。**II *n*.** 那瓦特语。

Na·hum [ˈneiəm; ˋneəm] ***n*.** 内厄姆〔姓氏〕。

NAI = non-accidental injury 非事故性损伤。

nai·ad [ˈnaiæd; ˋnaɪæd] ***n*.** (*pl*. ***~s***, ***nai·a·des*** [ˈnaiədiːz; ˋnaɪədiz]) **1.**【希、罗神】水精,水仙女。**2.** 女游泳者。**3.**【虫】稚虫。

naif [nɑːˈiːf; nɑˋif] ***a*.**〔F.〕= naive.

nail [neil; nel] **I *n*. 1.** 指甲,爪;喙甲。**2.** 钉。**3.** 纳尔〔旧量布尺度名,约合 5.715cm〕。***a ~ in*** [***to***] ***one's coffin*** 促人早死的事物(*drive* [*put*] *a ~ in* [*add a ~ to*] *sb.'s coffin* 促人早死,催命。*It was a final ~ in the Government's coffin*. 那是对政府的一个致命打

击)。(*as*) ***hard as ~s*** 身体强壮;冷酷无情。***be*** [***go***] ***off at he*** ~ 无法控制自己,忘形,神经失常;有点醉。***drive the*** ~ [***up***] ***to the head*** [***drive the ~ home***] 作出定论。***He must have iron ~s that*** [***who***] ***scratches a bear***. 搔熊者必具铁爪;要干危险的事,就得有充分的准备。***hit the*** (***right***) ~ ***on the head*** 说得对,中肯,一针见血,正中要害。~***s in mourning*** 有污垢的指甲。***on the*** ~〔口〕1. 立即;被捕。2. 在讨论中的(*pay on the* ~ 立即付与。*the subject on the* ~ 当前的问题)。***right as ~s*** (钉子般)直的;没错的。***to the*** [***a***] ~ 完全,彻底;极其。

II ***vt***. 1. 敲钉,钉住 (*on*; *to*)。2.〔口〕捉住,抓住;〔美俚〕逮捕;〔俚〕打。3.〔学生俚〕揭发,看穿,发觉。4. 吸引住(注意等),不放松(人家的声明等),使不能逃避。5.〔美俚〕偷。6.【棒球】使(跑垒者)被开出局。*have one's boots ~ed* (请人)在靴底上钉钉子。~ *a notice on* [*to*] *the door* 在门上钉一块告白。*be ~ed going off without leave* 被发觉擅自外出。~ ***a blow***〔美拳击〕打。~ ***a lie to the counter*** [***barn-door***] 揭发弊端,拆穿西洋镜〔从前商人把伪币钉在账柜上示众的习惯,故有此说〕。~ (*sb*.) ***down to*** (用诺言、声明等)约束某人,要求某人履行诺言 (*He was confused when we ~ed him down to his promise*. 当我们坚持要它守诺言时,他狼狈了)。~ ***it***〔美俚〕(考试)及格;成功。~ ***one's colours to the mast*** 坚持到底,极有决心;决不屈服〔原义:把舰旗钉死在桅杆上,使不能扯下来投降〕。~ ***up*** 1. 把…钉在较高处。2. 钉牢[关系](门、窗)。~**ariun** 修指甲沙龙〔修剪指甲的高级美容室〕。~**-biting** 1. 咬指甲。2. 焦虑,束手无策。~ **bomb** 钉子炸弹〔一种把钉子扎在甘油炸药棒上的土制爆炸物〕。~**brush** 指甲刷。~ **clippers** 指甲钳。~**file** 指甲锉刀。~**head** 钉头(饰)。~**-headed** ***a***. 钉头状的 (*~-headed characters* 楔形文字)。~**hole** 1. 钉眼。2. 指甲孔〔用指甲开小刀的地方〕。~**-machine** 制钉机。~**-nippers**, ~**-scissors**〔*pl*.〕指甲剪。~ **polish** 趾甲油,指甲油。~ **puller** 起钉钳。~ **set** (木工用的)钉凿。~**sick** ***a***. (板材等)因屡钉而变得不结实;钉眼渗漏的。**-less** ***a***. 无指甲的;无钉的。

nail·er [ˈneilə; ˋnelɚ] ***n***. 1. 制钉者,制钉工人。2. 敲钉人;自动敲钉机。3.〔俚〕热心(工作等)的人 (*on*; *to*);(竞赛等的)能手,好手。*a* ~ *on one's work* 热心工作的人。*a* ~ *at golf* 高尔夫球的能手。***as busy as a*** ~ 忙得很。

nail·er·y [ˈneiləri; ˋnelərɪ] ***n***. 制钉厂。

nail·ing [ˈneiliŋ; ˋnelɪŋ] **I** ***a***. 1. 敲钉用的。2.〔俚〕极好的。***a*** ~ ***stroke*** 极好的运气。**II** ***ad***.〔俚〕极好。

nain·sook [ˈneinsuk; ˋnensuk] ***n***. (印度)薄棉布;南苏克布。

Nai·ro·bi [ˌnaiəˈrəubi; naɪˋrobɪ] ***n***. 内罗毕(乃洛比)〔肯尼亚首都〕。

na·ïve, na·ive [nɑːˈiːv, naiˈiːv; nɑˋiv, naɪˋiv] ***a***. 天真的;自然的,朴素的;憨厚的。★现在以写作 naive 较普通。~ **materialism**【哲】朴素唯物论。~ **realism**【哲】朴素实在论。**-ly** ***ad***. **-ness** ***n***.

na·ïve·té, na·ïve·ty, na·ive·ty [nɑːˈiːvtei; nɑˏivˋte] ***n***. 质朴,朴素;天真;天真的行为;天真的话。

na·ked [ˈneikid; ˋnekɪd] ***a***. 1. 裸体的;露出的。2. 无,的(*of*);无叶的;【植】(种子等)裸出的;荒瘠的。3.【诗】无防备的。4. 率直的,如实的,赤裸裸的;露骨的;明白的。5. (引句等)无注释的;【法】无证据的。6.〔口〕无担保的,无保障的,风险大的。*a* ~ *dance*〔美俚〕裸体舞。~ *feet* 赤脚。*a* ~ *sword* (拔出了刀鞘的)明晃晃的刀。~ *fields* 荒地。*a* ~ *flower* 无被花。*the* ~ *eye* 肉眼。*a* ~ *heart* 赤裸裸的心。*the* ~ *truth* 明明白白的事实。*a* ~ *call* 空头股票[证券]的收兑。*a* ~ *debenture*〔英〕无担保证券。***as ~ as when one was born*** 赤条条,裸体。***stark*** ~ 赤身露体,一丝不挂。***strip*** (*sb*.) ~ 剥光。***with ~ fists*** 赤手空拳地。~ **ape** 裸猿〔出自英国人类学家 Dr. Morris 所著同名作品〕。**-ly** ***ad***. 1. 光着身子;赤裸裸地。2. 如实。

na·ked·ness [ˈneikidnis; ˋnekɪdnɪs] ***n***. 1. 裸,裸出,露出。2. 坦白;无掩饰;光秃。3.〔古、圣〕阴部(= privates)。*the* ~ *of the land* (个人、团体、国家等的)无资力[无防备]状态。

na·ked·ize [ˈneikidaiz; ˋnekɪdˏaɪz] ***vt***., ***vi***. (使)成为裸体。

na·ker [ˈneikə; ˋnekɚ] ***n***.〔古〕鼓(= kettle drum)。

NAM = National Association of Manufacturers〔美〕全国制造商协会。

Na·ma [ˈnɑːmɑː; ˋnɑmɑ] ***n***. 1. 那马部族〔西南非洲霍屯督族中的一主要部落〕。2. 霍屯督人。3. 霍屯督语。

nam·a·ble, name·a·ble [ˈneiməbl; ˋneməbl] ***a***. 1. 说得出名称的,可指名的;可命名的。2. 值得提起的;有名的。

nam·by-pam·by [ˈnæmbiˈpæmbi; ˋnæmbɪˋpæmbɪ] ***a***., ***n***. 1. 多愁善感的(人);没有决断的(人);感伤的(谈话)。2. 柔弱的(文风)浮华的(诗、文)。

name [neim; nem] **I** ***n***. 1. 名,名字,姓名;名称。2. 名声,名誉;空名,虚名;名义,名目;【逻、语法】概念的名称;名词。3. 知名之士,名士;一族,一门。4.〔*pl*.〕恶骂。*What is your* ~? 你叫什么名字? *What* ~, *please*? = *What* ~ *shall I say*? 你是怎样称呼的? *It stands in my* ~. 那是顶我的名。*a pen* ~ 笔名。*a common* ~【语法】普通名词。*an assumed* ~ 假名。*the Christian* [*first*, *given*] ~ 名字;教名,洗礼名,(对姓而言的)名。*a family* ~ 姓。*a double-barreled* ~ (以两个姓合成的)双姓。*a* ~ *ship* 同型舰中的代表舰。*an ill* ~ 臭名。*a man of* ~ 知名之士。*a man of no* ~ 无名小卒。*many great ~s* 许多名士。*a draw* ~〔美俚〕红演员。*a* ~ *scribber*〔美俚〕时评作者。***by*** ~ 1. 指名(*call by* ~ 喊名字)。2. 名叫 (*John by* ~ = *by* ~ *John* 名叫约翰)。3. 只…名字 (*know sb*. *by* ~ (没见过面)只知道某人的名字)。***by the*** ~ ***of*** 名叫…的。***call sb***. ~***s*** 骂某人。***get a*** ~ 得到名声,成名。***get*** [***win***] ***oneself a*** ~ 成名。***Give it a*** ~.〔口〕(请客时)你要什么,讲吧。***give one's*** ~ 报名。***go by*** [***under***] ***the*** ~ ***of*** 名叫…,以…的名字为人所知,以…的名义发表。***have a*** ~ ***for*** (*bravery*) = ***have the*** ~ ***of*** (*being brave*) 有(勇敢)之名。***have one's*** ~ ***up*** 有名起来;成名。***in*** ~ 名义上的,有名无实的。***in one's own*** ~ 用自己的名义,独立。***in the*** ~ ***of*** 1. 凭…的名,对…发誓 (*in the* ~ *of common honesty* 凭诚实之名(决不说谎))。2. 作…的代表,代替 (*I speak in the* ~ *of her*. 我代表她发言)。3. 为…的缘故,究竟 (*What in the* ~ *of God is it*? 这究竟是什么?)。***keep sb.'s*** ~ ***off the books*** 不让某人参加某机构。***keep one's*** ~ ***on the books*** 保留学籍,保留会籍。***leave a*** ~ ***behind*** 留名后世。***make a*** ~ ***for oneself*** 成名。***of*** ~ 有名。***of no*** ~ 无名的。***of the*** ~ ***of*** 名叫…的。***put one's*** ~ ***down for*** 写下某人认捐的款额;把某人的名字列在名单上,替某人报名(参加运动、组织等);提出某人为候选人。***send in one's*** ~ 报名申请(参加竞赛等)。***take a*** ~ ***in vain*** 滥用名字。***take sb.'s*** ~ ***off the books*** 从名册上涂去某人的名字,退学,退会。***the*** ~ ***of the game*** 事情[问题]的本质,真正重要的东西。***to one's*** ~ 属于自己的东西(*He has not a penny to his* ~. 他一个铜子儿也没有)。***to the*** ~ ***of*** 成…的名义。***under one's own*** ~ 用自己的名字(发表)。***under the*** ~ ***of*** = by the ~ of. ***without a*** ~ 1. = nameless. 2. 名字说不出来。

II ***vt***. 1. 给…命名,给…取名;喊…的名字;正确说出…的名字。2. 提名;任命;指定,说出。3.〔英〕(下院议长)指出…名字谴责。*Mr. A has been ~d for the vacancy*. A 氏被指定为继任者。*N-!* (听众要求发言人)请指出名字来!

III ***a***. 1.〔美口〕著名的。2. (作品等)据以取名的。*a*

～ *band* 著名乐队。～ **after** =〔美〕～ **for** 用(别人、别物的名字)命名。～ **the day** (女人)择定结婚日期。**not to be ～d on [in] the same day** (*with*)与…不可同日而语。～**board** 招牌;站名牌;船名牌。～**-calling** 骂人。～**check** *vt*. 提到…的名字。～**check** *vt*.〔美〕点…的名。～**child** 用某人名字命名的孩子(*his ～child* 照他的名字取名的孩子)。～ **day** 命名日;和本人同名的圣徒纪念日;〔英〕【股】结算日,交割日。～**dropper** 言谈中常以亲密、随意的口吻提到显要人物以抬高自己身价的人。～ **father** 命名父。～ **part** 【剧】和剧名同名的角色。～**-plate** 姓名牌,名称牌;(报头上的)报刊名。～**sake** 同姓名的人;(特指)沿用某人名字的人。～ **tape** 标名的布条。

name·a·ble [ˈneiməbl; ˋneməbl] *a*. = namable.

named [neimd; nemd] *a*. 被指名的,指定的。*above* ～ 上述的,上开的。

name·less [ˈneimlis; ˋnemlıs] *a*. **1.** 没有名字[名称]的;没有署名的,匿名的。**2.** 无名声的,不知名的。**3.** 难以名状的;说不出的,难以形容的。*a well-known person who shall be* ～ 暂不说明他的名字的某知名人士。*the ～ dead* 无名死者。*a ～ horror* 说不出的恐怖。**-ly** *ad*. **-ness** *n*.

name·ly [ˈneimli; ˋnemlı] *ad*. 即,就是,换句话说〔口语常说 that is to say〕。

nam·er [ˈneimə; ˋnemɚ] *n*. 命名人;指名人。

Na·mib·i·a [nəˈmiːbiə; nəˋmibıə] *n*. 纳米比亚(旧称西南非洲)(非洲)。**-i·an** *n*. 纳米比亚人。

nam·met [ˈnæmit; ˋnæmıt] *n*. = nummet.

NAMTC =〔Am.〕Naval Air Missile Test Center〔美〕海军航空飞[导]弹试验中心。

nan-, nano- *comb. f*. 表示"奈"(毫微, = 10^{-9}): *nano*second.

Na·na [ˈnɑːnɑː; ˋnɑnɑ] *n*. **1.** 巴比伦神话中的女神。**2.** 娜娜〔法国作家左拉著同名小说中的女主角,为一美貌妓女〕。

NANA = North American Newspaper Alliance 北美报业联盟。

nance, nan·cy [næns, ˈnænsi; næns, ˋnænsı] **I** *n*.〔美俚〕女子气的男子,搞同性关系的男人。**II** *a*. 女人似的,柔弱的;搞同性关系的。

Nan·cy [ˈnænsi; ˋnænsı] *n*. **1.** 南希〔女子名, Ann 的昵称〕。**2.** 南锡〔法国城市〕。

NAND [nænd; nænd] *n*. 【自】"与非"电路〔一种电子计算机逻辑电路〕。

na·nism [ˈneinizəm; ˋnenızṃ] *n*. 矮小;矮态。

nan·keen, nan·kin [næŋˈkiːn; nænˋkin] *n*. **1.** (耐穿的)本色布[原产我国南京];〔*pl*.〕本色布制裤子。**2.** 本色,淡黄色。**3.** (我国制)白底青花瓷器。

nan·no·plank·ton, na·no·plank·ton [ˌnænəuˈplæŋktən; ˏnænoˋplæŋktən] *n*. 微小浮游生物。

nan·ny [ˈnæni; ˋnænı] *n*.〔英〕(儿童的)保姆。～ **goat** 雌山羊。～ **state** 保姆国家〔指实行高福利而又对民众实行家长式控制的国家〕。

nano- *comb. f*. = nan-〔用于元音前〕表示"毫微"之意: *nano*computer【计】毫微[纳米]电子计算机。*nano*fossil【考古】(显)微[纳米]化石。*nano*tube【电子】毫微管。

nan·o·amp [ˈnænəuæmp; ˋnænoæmp] *n*. 【电】毫微[纳米]安培〔十亿分之一安培〕。

nan·o·se·cond [ˈnænəuˌsekənd; ˋnænoˏsɛkənd] *n*. 奈秒;毫微秒。

nan·o·tech·nol·o·gy [ˌneinəutekˈnɔlədʒi; ˏnenotɛkˋnɔlədʒı] *n*. 毫微[纳米]技术〔制造和测定 0.1 至 100 毫微米物件之技术〕。

na·no·watt [ˈneinəuwɔt, ˈnæ-; ˋnenoˏwɑt, ˋnæ-] *n*. 奈瓦;毫微瓦。

Nan·sen [ˈnænsn; ˋnænsṇ], **Fridtjof** 南森〔1861—1930, 挪威北极探险家、博物学家,曾获 1922 年诺贝尔和平奖〕。

Nantes [nænts, F. nɑ̃ːt; nænts, nɑ̃ːt] *n*. 南特〔法国城市〕。

Nantz [nænts; nænts] *n*.〔古〕白兰地酒。*good [right]* ～ 道地的白兰地。

Na·o·mi [ˈneiəmi; ˋneəˏmaı] *n*. 拿俄米〔女子名〕。

na·os [ˈneiɔs, ˋnɑː-; ˋneɑs, ˋnɑ-] *n*. (*pl*. **na·oi** [-ɔi; -ɔı]) **1.** 古寺院。**2.** 古寺院的内院;内殿,内堂。

nap[1] [næp; næp] **I** *n*. (尤指白天的)小睡,打盹。*take [have] a ～* 睡午觉;打一个瞌睡。**II** *vi*. (**-pp-**)〔除现在分词外罕用〕打瞌睡;疏忽。*take [catch] sb. napping* 发现人在打瞌睡;乘人不备时抓住他的疏忽[偷懒表现等]。—*vt*. 在瞌睡中度过(*away*)。

nap[2] [næp; næp] **I** *n*. (呢绒的)绒;(植物表面的)短茸毛。**II** *vt*. (**-pp-**)使起绒。

nap[3] [næp; næp] **I** *n*.〔俚〕**1.** 一种牌戏(= napoleon)。**2.** 孤注一掷。**a ～ hand** 一手可获全胜的牌;肯冒险就可获全胜的地位,机会。**go ～** 想在拿破仑牌戏中全赢 5 次;大冒险。**go ～ on** 对…孤注一掷;确信(事实等)。～ **or nothing** 成败在此一举。**II** *vt*. (**-pp-**)预测(某匹马)必赢。

na·palm [ˈneipɑːm; ˋnepɑm] **I** *n*. **1.** 凝固汽油。**2.** 凝固汽油弹。**II** *vt*. 用凝固汽油(弹)进攻,用凝固汽油燃烧。

nape [neip; nep] *n*. 颈背,后颈,项部。

na·per·y [ˈneipəri; ˋnepərı] *n*.〔Scot.〕餐巾,揩嘴布;桌布。

naph·tha [ˈnæfθə; ˋnæfθə] *n*. 【化】粗挥发油;石油脑。

naph·tha·lene, -line [ˈnæfθəliːn; ˋnæfθəˏlin], **-lin** [-lin; -lın] *n*. 【化】萘。～ **ball** 萘球,卫生丸。

naph·thene [ˈnæfθiːn; ˋnæfθin] *n*. 【化】**1.** 环烷,环烷属烃。**2.** 萘的旧名。**-then·ic** [-ˈθiːnik; -ˋθinık] *a*.

naph·thol [ˈnæfθɔl; ˋnæfθol] *n*. 【化】萘酚;含有萘环的羟基衍生物。

naph·thyl [ˈnæfθil; ˋnæfθıl] *n*. 【化】萘基,从萘衍生的一价基。

Na·pi·er [ˈneipiə; ˋnepıɚ] *n*. **1.** 纳皮尔〔姓氏〕。**2. John** ～ 纳皮尔〔1550—1617,英国数学家,对数发明者〕。**3.** 〔n-〕【物】讷〔衰耗单位〕(= neper)。

Na·pi·er·ian log·arithm [nəˈpiəriən ˈlɔgəriθəm; nəˋpırıən ˋlɔgəˏrıθəm] 【数】讷氏对数,自然对数。

na·pi·form [ˈneipifɔːm; ˋnepəˏfɔrm] *a*. 【植】芜菁状的。

nap·kin [ˈnæpkin; ˋnæpkın] *n*. (食桌上用的)餐巾,揩嘴布;〔英〕(婴儿的)尿布;〔英方〕手绢、手帕;头巾。**lay up [hide, wrap] in a ～** 藏着不用。～ **ring** (银制或骨制)揩嘴布套环。

Na·ples [ˈneiplz; ˋnepḷz] *n*. 那不勒斯〔意大利港市〕。

na·pless [ˈnæplis; ˋnæplıs] *a*. (呢绒上)没有绒毛的;磨破了的。

Na·po·le·on [nəˈpəuljən, -liən; nəˋpoljən, -lıən] *n*. 拿破仑〔全称 *Napoleon Bonaparte*, 1769—1821, 即拿破仑一世(Napoleon I), 法国皇帝。其侄,拿破仑三世(Napoleon III, 1808—1873)为 1852—1870 年在位的法国皇帝〕。

na·po·le·on [nəˈpəuljən; nəˋpoljən] *n*. **1.** 旧法国金币〔值 20 法郎〕。**2.** (每人发 5 张牌的)拿破仑牌戏〔通例叫 nap〕。**3.** (19 世纪中叶的)拿破仑式长统靴。**4.**〔美〕法国式奶油夹心千层酥。**5.** 红三叶草。**6.**〔N-〕拿破仑品种甜樱桃。

Na·po·le·on·ic [nəpəuliˈɔnik; nəˏpolıˋɑnık] *a*. 拿破仑(一世时代)的;拿破仑(一世)似的;专制的。*a ～ attitude toward one's employees* 对雇员的专横态度。～ **Code** 拿破仑法典。～ **Wars** 拿破仑一世进行的历次重大战争。**-cal·ly** *ad*.

Na·po·le·on·ism [nəˈpəuljənizəm; nəˋpoljənızəm] *n*. 拿破仑主义。

Na·po·le·on·ist [nəˈpəuljənist; nəˋpoljənıst] *n*. 拿破仑

N

主义者。

Na·po·li [It. ˈnɑːpəuli; ˋnɑpolɪ] *n*. 那波利〔即 Naples 那不勒斯,意大利港市〕。

na·poo [nɑːˈpuː; nɑˋpu] **I** *a*., *int*. **1.** 〔军俚〕完蛋了,没用了。**2.** 〔美俚〕死了〔由法语 *il n'y a plus* = there is no more 变来〕。*He's* ~. 他打死了。~ *fine* 〔美俚〕完了,去了;看不见了。**II** *vt*., *vi*. 结束,(使)完蛋;杀死。

nap·per[1] [ˈnæpə; ˋnæpɚ] *n*. 打盹的人;〔英俚〕头。

nap·per[2] [ˈnæpə; ˋnæpɚ] *n*. 拉毛工人[装置、机器]。

nap·per·kids [ˈnæpəkidz; ˋnæpɚkɪdz] *n*. 〔*pl*.〕〔美俚〕拐子。

nap·py[1] [ˈnæpi; ˋnæpɪ] *n*. 〔英口〕尿布。

nap·py[2] [ˈnæpi; ˋnæpɪ] *a*. 起毛的,起绒的;柔软的。

nap·py[3] [ˈnæpi; ˋnæpɪ] *n*. 菜盆。

nap·py[4] [ˈnæpi; ˋnæpɪ] **I** *a*. 〔Eng.〕(啤酒)起泡沫的;浓烈的。**II** *n*. 〔Eng.〕啤酒。

na·prap·a·thy [nəpˈræpəθi; nəpˋræpəθɪ] *n*. 【医】矫正疗法,推拿疗法,按摩疗法。

na·pu[1] [ˈnɑːpuː; ˋnɑpu] *n*. 【动】(爪哇、苏门答腊产之)矮麝香鹿。

na·pu[2] [nəˈpuː; nɑˋpu] *n*. 〔美俚〕= napoo.

Na·ra [ˈnɑːrə; ˋnɑrə] *n*. 奈良〔日本城市〕。

Nar·a·ka [ˈnærəkə; ˋnærəkə] *n*. 【印度神话】地狱。

narc [nɑːk; nɑrk] *n*. 〔美俚〕专捉毒品犯的便衣警察。

nar·ce·ine [ˈnɑːsiiːn; ˋnɑrsɪˏin] *n*. 【化】那碎因碱。

nar·cis·sism [nɑːˈsisizəm; nɑrˋsɪsˏɪzəm] *n*. (精神分析学中所说的)自我陶醉[崇拜];自恋。

nar·cis·sist [nɑːˈsissist; nɑrˋsɪssɪst] *n*. 自我陶醉者。**-ic** *a*.

Nar·cis·sus [nɑːˈsisəs; nɑrˋsɪsəs] *n*. **1.** (*pl*. *~es*, *-cis·si* [-ˈsisai; -ˋsɪsaɪ])【植】水仙属;[n-]水仙。**2.** 【希神】那西塞斯〔爱上自己映在水中的美丽影子以致淹死而变为水仙的美少年〕;[n-]以美貌自夸的青年。

nar·co- *comb*. *f*. 表示"麻木","失去知觉"或"(致亡)毒品"。

nar·co [ˈnɑːkəu; ˋnɑrkə] *n*. 毒品(走私)贩。

nar·co·a·nal·y·sis [ˌnɑːkəuəˈnælisis; ˏnɑrkoəˋnælɪsɪs] *n*. 精神麻醉分析。

nar·co·dol·lars [ˌnɑːkəuˈdɔləz; ˏnɑrkəˋdɑləz] *n*. 毒品美元〔通过出售毒品赚得的美元〕。

nar·co·lep·sy [ˈnɑːkəulepsi; ˋnɑrkəˏlepsɪ] *n*. 【医】嗜眠病。

nar·co·ma·ni·a [ˌnɑːkəuˈmeinjə; ˏnɑrkəˋmenɪə] *n*. 麻醉剂狂;麻醉药癖。

nar·co·sis [nɑːˈkəusis; nɑrˋkosɪs] *n*. = narcotism.

nar·co·syn·the·sis [ˌnɑːkəuˈsinθisis; ˏnɑrkoˋsɪnθɪsɪs] *n*. (精神病的)麻醉剂疗法。

nar·co·ther·a·py [ˌnɑːkəuˈθerəpi; nɑrkoˋθɛrəpɪ] *n*. 【医】麻醉疗法;睡眠疗法。

nar·cot·ic [nɑːˈkɔtik; nɑrˋkɑtɪk] **I** *a*. **1.** 麻醉(性)的;起麻痹作用的;麻醉剂的;安眠用的。**2.** 吸毒成瘾者的;护理[照料]吸毒成瘾者的。**II** *n*. **1.** 麻醉剂,麻药;安眠药;起麻痹作用的东西。**2.** 吸毒成瘾的人。

nar·co·tine [ˈnɑːkətiːn; ˋnɑrkəˏtin] *n*. 【药】鸦片宁,那可汀。

nar·co·tism [ˈnɑːkətizəm; ˋnɑrkəˏtɪzəm] *n*. 【医】麻醉(状态);麻醉作用;麻醉剂中毒,昏睡,不省人事;麻醉品嗜好。

nar·co·ti·za·tion [ˌnɑːkəutaiˈzeiʃən; ˏnɑrkətɪˋzeʃən] *n*. 麻醉。

nar·co·tize [ˈnɑːkətaiz; ˋnɑrkətaɪz] *vt*. (使)麻醉;弄弱。

nard [nɑːd; nɑrd] *n*. 【植】甘松;甘松油脂。~**grass** *n*. 亚香茅。

na·res [ˈnɛəriːz; ˋneriz] *n*. 〔*pl*.〕(*sing*. ***na·ris*** [-ris; -rɪs]) 鼻孔。

nar·g(h)i·le [ˈnɑːgili; ˋnɑrgəlɪ] *n*. (印度)水烟袋。

nark [nɑːk; nɑrk] **I** *n*. 〔英俚〕(警察的)密探;告密者(= narc)。**II** *vt*. **1.** 告…的密。**2.** 使…发怒。—*vi*. **1.** 告密。**2.** 发怒。***N- it!*** 住口! 肃静!

nark·y [ˈnɑːki; ˋnɑrkɪ] *a*. 〔俚〕易生气的。

Nar·ra·gan·sett [ˌnærəˈgænsit; ˏnærəˋgænsɪt] *n*. (旧时美国 Rhode Island 地方的)纳拉干族(人)〔北美印第安人的一支〕。

nar·rate [næˈreit; næˋret] *vt*., *vi*. 叙述,讲(故事);写[编](故事)。~ *one's adventures* 讲自己的冒险故事。
nar·rat·er *n*. 〔Am.〕= narrator 讲述者,叙述者。

nar·ra·tion [næˈreiʃən; næˋreʃən] *n*. 叙述;故事;【语】叙述法。*direct* [*indirect*] ~【语】直接[间接]叙述法。

nar·ra·tive [ˈnærətiv; ˋnærətɪv] **I** *a*. 叙述的;故事体的;善于叙述的。**II** *n*. **1.** 叙述,记事;记叙文;记叙体;叙述手法。**2.** 〔Scot.〕【法】(证件等的)事实证明部分。*a writer of great* ~ *power* 叙述手法高超的作家。~ *economy* 历史学派经济学。**-ly** *ad*. 用故事体。

nar·ra·tor [næˈreitə; næˋretɚ] (*fem*. ***-tress*** [-tris; -trɪs]) *n*. 讲述者,叙述者,讲故事者,解说员。

nar·row [ˈnærəu; ˋnæro] **I** *a*. **1.** 狭,窄,狭隘的,狭小的(*opp*. broad, wide)。**2.** 有限的,受限制的;有偏见的,气量小的,心眼儿窄的;眼光短浅的。**3.** 仅仅的,勉强的。**4.** (资力)薄弱的,贫穷的;〔英方, Scot.〕吝啬的,小气的。**5.** 精细的,严密的。**6.** 【语】窄音的。**7.** (空气)缺乏的。*have a* ~ *circle of friends* 交际不广。*in a* ~ *sense* 狭义的。~ *cloth* (52英寸以内的)窄幅布。*a* ~ *mind* 小心眼儿,小气量。*a* ~ *victory* 勉强胜利。*a* ~ *majority* 勉强的多数。*a* ~ *examination* 严格的检查。~ *circumstances* [*means*] 穷困。~ *market* 呆滞的市场。~ *vowels* 窄母音。*within* ~ *bounds* 在小范围内。***have a*** ~ ***escape*** [***shave***, ***squeak***] 九死一生。***the*** ~ ***bed*** [***cell***, ***house***] 坟墓。***the*** ~ ***way*** 正直;正义。**II** *n*. **1.** 〔常作 *pl*.〕海峡,峡谷。**2.** (场所、物品等的)狭窄部分。***the Narrows*** **1.** 达达尼尔海峡的最狭窄处。**2.** 美国纽约 Staten Islands 和 Long Islands 之间的海峡。**III** *vt*. **1.** 使狭,弄窄,收缩。**2.** 限制,缩小。~ *an argument down* 限制争论的范围。—*vi*. 变狭,变窄;【编织】收小。~**casting** **1.** 〔美〕电缆电视[有线电视]播送。**2.** 〔美〕(竞选中的)小范围拉票。~**-fisted** *a*. 吝啬的。~**-gauge(d)** *a*. 【铁路】狭轨的(*opp*. broad-gauge)。~ **minded** *a*. 气量小的,心眼儿窄的;极端保守的;思想僵化的。**-ness** *n*. 狭窄,狭小;偏狭;穷困。

nar·row·ish [ˈnærəuiʃ; ˋnæroɪʃ] *a*. 有些狭窄的。

nar·row·ly [ˈnærəuli; ˋnærolɪ] *ad*. **1.** 勉强地,好容易(才)。**2.** 严密地,仔细地。**3.** 严格地;过细地。**4.** 猛烈地。*He* ~ *escaped drowning*. 他险些儿淹死。

nar·w(h)al, nar·whale [ˈnɑːwəl; ˋnɑrhwəl] *n*. 【动】一角鲸。

nar·y [ˈnɛəri; ˋnerɪ] *a*. 〔方、美〕连…也没有。~ *a cent* 一个铜钱也没有。

NAS = National Academy of Sciences 〔美〕国家科学院。

N.A.S. = Nursing Auxiliary Service 护士辅助勤务队。

NASA = National Aeronautics and Space Administration 〔美〕国家航空和宇宙航行局。

na·sal [ˈneizəl; ˋnezl̩] **I** *a*. 鼻的;【语】鼻音的。*the* ~ *opening* 鼻孔。*the* ~ *organ* 〔谑〕鼻子。*a* ~ *discharge* 鼻涕。*a* ~ 鼻音字母。**II** *n*. **1.** 【语音】鼻音,鼻音字母[m, n, ng [ŋ]]。**2.** 【解】鼻骨。**3.** (钢盔的)护鼻。**-ly** *ad*.

na·sal·ism [ˈneizəlizəm, -zli-; ˋnezəlɪzəm, -zl̩ɪ-] *n*. 鼻音法。

na·sal·i·ty [neiˈzæliti; neˋzælətɪ] *n*. 鼻音性,鼻音。

na·sal·ize [ˈneizəlaiz; ˋnezl̩ˏaɪz] *vi*., *vt*. 发(鼻音);(使)鼻音化。**-za·tion** [ˌneizəlaiˈzeiʃən; nezəlaɪˋzeʃən] *n*.

nas·cence [ˈnæsəns; ˋnæsəns], **nas·cen·cy** [-snsi; -snsɪ] *n*. 发生,起源。

nas·cent [ˈnæsnt; ˋnæsn̩t] *a*. 发生中的,初期的;【化】初

生的,新生的。*the ~ literature and art* 萌芽状态的文艺。~ **oxygen** 原子态氧。~ **state**【化】初生态,新生态。

NASDAQ = National Association of Securities Dealers Automated Quotations (美国用计算机储存的)全国证券交易商协会自动报价表。

nase·ber·ry [ˈneizberi; ˋnezˏbɛrɪ] ***n***. (*pl*. ***-ries***) 人心果树;人心果(=sapodilla)。

Nash [næʃ; næʃ] ***n***. 纳什〔姓氏〕。

Nas·myth [ˈneizmiθ; ˋnezmɪθ] ***n***. 内史密斯〔姓氏〕。

na·so·fron·tal [neizəuˈfrʌntl; nezoˋfrʌntl̩] ***a***. 鼻额的,鼻额骨的。

na·so·phar·ynx [ˌneizəuˈfæriŋks; ˏnezoˋfærɪŋks] ***n***. 【解】鼻咽。**-pha·ryn·ge·al** [-fəˈrindʒiəl; -fəˋrɪndʒɪəl] ***a***.

Nas·sau [ˈnæsɔː; ˋnæsɔ] ***n***. 纳梭(拿骚)〔巴哈马首都〕。

nas·tic [ˈnæstik; ˋnæstɪk] ***a***. 【植】感性的。

nas·ti·ly [ˈnɑːstili; ˋnæstɪlɪ] ***ad***. 污秽,不清洁,肮脏;淫秽〔参见 nasty〕。

nas·tur·tium [nəsˈtəːʃəm; næsˋtɝʃəm] ***n***. 【植】旱金莲(花)。

nas·ty [ˈnɑːsti; ˋnæstɪ] **I** ***a***. **1**. 脏得怕人的,非常邋遢的;使人不愉快的,卑劣的,下流的;淫秽的;讨厌的。**2**. (天气)恶劣的;艰险的;痛苦的,厉害的。**3**. 难应付的;难弄的;严重的。*a ~ smell* 令人作呕的气味。~ *medicine* 难吃的药。*a ~ job* 不愉快的工作。*a ~ temper* 讨厌的脾气。*a ~ sea* 大风浪。*Don't be ~*. 不要发脾气啦。***a ~ one*** 责骂;严重的打击。***get oneself into a ~ mess*** 陷入困境。***leave a ~ taste in the mouth*** 留下讨厌的气味[印象]。(***a***) ~ ***piece of work*** 别扭行为;〔口〕下流坯;讨厌的家伙。***turn ~*** 发怒;闹别扭。**II** ***n***. **1**. 〔口〕恐怖电影,恐怖录像片。**2**. 讨厌的人[事物]。**nas·ti·ness** ***n***.

nat. = national; native; natural.

nat [næt; næt] ***n***. 〔美俚〕民族主义者。

na·tal [ˈneitl; ˋnetl̩] ***a***. 出生的,诞生的;〔诗〕故乡的。*one's ~ day* [*place*] 生日[诞生地]。

Nat·a·lie [ˈnætəli; ˋnætəlɪ] ***n***. 纳塔莉〔女子名〕。

na·tal·i·ty [neiˈtæliti; neˋtælətɪ] ***n***. 出生率,产生率。

na·tant [ˈneitənt; ˋnetn̩t] ***a***. 浮在水上的,浮游的。**-ly** ***ad***. 浮在水上。

na·ta·tion [neiˈteiʃən; neˋteʃən] ***n***. 游泳;游泳术。

Na·ta·to·res [ˌneitəˈtɔːriːz; ˏnetəˋtɔriz] ***n***. 〔*pl*.〕【动】水禽类,游禽类。

na·ta·to·ri·al [ˌneitəˈtɔːriəl; ˏnetəˋtorɪəl], **na·ta·to·ry** [-təri; -tɔrɪ] ***a***. 游泳(用)的。~ *birds* 水鸟。

na·ta·to·ri·um [ˌneitəˈtɔːriəm; ˏnetəˋtorɪəm] ***n***. (*pl*. *~s*, ***-ri·a*** [-riə; -rɪə]) 游泳池。

natch [nætʃ; nætʃ] ***ad***. 〔美俚〕自然地,当然(= naturally)。

Natch·ez [ˈnætʃiz; ˋnætʃɪz] ***n***. **1**. (*pl*. ***Natch·ez***) 纳齐兹部族人〔原是居住在美国密西西比州西南部的印第安人的一个部落,现已灭绝〕。**2**. 纳齐兹语。~ **Trace** 纳齐兹古道遗迹〔十九世纪由印第安人从美国密西西比的纳齐兹到田纳西的纳什维尔走出来的一条古道〕。

na·tes [ˈneitiːz; ˋnetiz] ***n***. 〔*pl*.〕【解】臀部。

Na·than [ˈneiθən; ˋneθən] ***n***. 内森〔姓氏,男子名〕。

Na·than·i·el [nəˈθænjəl; nəˋθænjəl] ***n***. 纳撒尼尔〔男子名〕。

nathe·less [ˈneiθlis; ˋneθlɪs], **nath·less** [ˈnæθlis; ˋnæθlɪs] **I** ***ad***. 〔古、诗〕= nevertheless. **II** ***prep***. = notwithstanding.

na·tion [ˈneiʃən; ˋneʃən] ***n***. **1**. 民族;国家;种族;〔美〕印地安人的部落(联盟)。**2**. (中世纪大学或苏格兰大学中的)学生同乡会。*the ~s* 世界各国人民。*the top industrial ~ of the world* 世界最大工业国。*the law of ~s* 国际公法。*the League of Nations* (第一次大战后成立的)国际联盟。*the United Nations* (第二次大战后成立的)联合国。*the most favoured ~ (clause)* 最惠国(条款)。***the ~s***【圣】异教徒〔指非犹太的各民族〕。~ **state** 民族国,单一民族国家。~**-wide** ***a***. 全国性的。**-hood** ***n***. 作为一个国家的地位。

na·tion·al [ˈnæʃənəl; ˋnæʃənl] **I** ***a***. **1**. 民族的;国民的;国家的;国民特有的。**2**. 国家主义的;爱国的。**3**. 国立的,国有的,国定的;全国性的。*a ~ air* [*anthem*] 国歌。*the ~ assembly* 国民代表大会。*the ~ debt* 国债。*a ~ bank* 国家银行;〔美〕(加入联邦储备银行 Federal Reserve System 有发行钞票特权的)国民银行。~ *salvation* 救国。~ *independence* 民族独立。*a ~ park* 国立公园。*a ~ enterprise* 国营企业。***go ~***〔美〕把事业扩张到全国。**II** ***n***. **1**. 国民(一分子);〔*pl*.〕(尤指侨居国外的)同国人,同胞。**2**. 〔美〕有许多支部的大学生联谊会。**3**. 〔常 *pl*.〕全国性体育比赛。***the Grand N-*** (每年三月举行的)全国性大赛马。**N- Archives** 〔美〕档案处。**N- Coal Board** 〔英〕煤炭部。**N- Convention** 〔美〕(政党为总统候选人提名而开的)全国代表大会。**N- Day** 国庆日。~ **defense** 国防。~ **domicile** 国籍。~ **economy** 国民经济。~ **emergency** 全国紧急状态,国难。~ **flag** [**ensign**] 国旗。**N- Guard** 〔美〕国民警卫队。~ **guildman** 基尔特社会主义者。~ **holiday** 国定假日;国庆日。~ **income** 国民收入。~ **independence movement** 民族独立运动。**N- Insurance** 国民保险〔英国对疾病、失业等的强制保险〕。~ **lakeshore** 〔美〕国家湖滨区〔由联邦政府划定,专供民众娱乐用〕。~ **militia** 民兵。~ **mobilization** 全国动员,总动员。~ **monument** (美国联邦政府管理的)名胜古迹〔指由美国政府保护供旅游的诸如高山、峡谷、古堡等〕。~ **park** 国家公园〔如美国的黄石公园〕。~ **policy** 国策。~ **psyche** 国民心态。~ **purse** 国富,国库。~ **revenue** 国家收入。~ **seashore** 〔美〕由联邦政府管理的海边旅行地。**N- Service** 〔英〕国民兵役。~ **socialism** 国家社会主义(即纳粹主义)。

na·tion·al·ism [ˈnæʃənəlizəm; ˋnæʃənlˏɪzəm] ***n***. 爱国心;国风,民族性,民族特征;民族主义,国家主义 (*opp*. internationalism), (尤指爱尔兰的)国家独立主义。

na·tion·al·ist [ˈnæʃənəlist; ˋnæʃənlɪst] **I** ***n***. 国家主义者;民族主义者;(爱尔兰的)民族自治论者。**II** ***a***. 国家主义的;民族主义的。*a ~ country* 民族主义国家。

na·tion·al·is·tic [ˌnæʃənəˈlistik; ˏnæʃənl̩ˋɪstɪk] ***a***. 国家主义的,民族主义的。**-ti·cal·ly** ***ad***.

na·tion·al·i·ty [ˌnæʃəˈnæliti; ˏnæʃəˋnælətɪ] ***n***. 国民性,民族性,国风;国籍,船籍;国民;国家,民族(独立)。*the minority nationalities* 各少数民族。*the question of the dual ~* 双重国籍问题。*men of all nationalities* 世界各国人民。

na·tion·a·lize [ˈnæʃənəlaiz; ˋnæʃənl̩ˏaɪz] ***vt***. **1**. 使成一国[独立国家];使国家化;使民族化。**2**. 把…收归国有[国营],使国有化。**3**. 〔罕〕使归化。**-za·tion, -r** ***n***.

na·tion·al·ly [ˈnæʃənəli; ˋnæʃənlɪ] ***ad***. 全国性地;从国民立场;举国一致;从国家立场,以国家为本位。*a ~ independent country* 民族独立国家。

na·tive [ˈneitiv; ˋnetɪv] **I** ***a***. **1**. 出生地的,本国的,本地的。**2**. 土著的,本地人的;土产的,国内的。**3**. 生来的,天赋的。**4**. 天生的,天然的;纯粹的。**5**. 天真的,纯朴的。~ *country* [*land*] 本国,祖国。~ *place* 故乡。*a ~ son* 本地人,土生土长的儿子。*a N- Son* 〔美俚〕加利福尼亚人。~ *sons of New York* 纯粹的纽约人。~ *fruit* 当地水果。*fruits ~ and foreign* 国内外的水果。~ *copper* 纯铜,自然铜。~ *rubber* 天然橡胶。***go ~*** 采取简单朴素的生活方式;作当地人,过当地生活。**II** ***n***. **1**. 土著,生在…的人 (*of*)。**2**. 〔澳〕生在澳大利亚的白种人;〔澳〕像英国种的(动植物)。**3**. 〔常贬〕土人,未开化人;当地人;当地动植物。**4**. 〔英〕(人工蚝场的)本场蚝[牡蛎]。~ **American** 土著美国人〔即印第安人〕。~**-born** ***a***. 本地[本国]生的。**-ly** ***ad***. **-ness** ***n***.

na·tiv·ism [ˈneitivizəm; ˋnetɪvɪzm̩] ***n***. **1**. 【哲】先天论,

N

天性论。2. 本土主义,排外主义。**-tiv·ist** *n*.

na·tiv·i·ty [nəˈtiviti; nəˋtɪvətɪ] *n*. 1. 出生,诞生。2. 〔N-〕耶稣诞生(图);圣诞节;圣母玛利亚诞生节。3. 【占星】算命天宫图。*cast* [*calculate*] *one's* ~ 算命。

natl. = national.

NATO [ˈneitəu; ˋneto] = North Atlantic Treaty Organization 北大西洋公约组织,北约组织。

na·tri·um [ˈneitriəm; ˋnetrɪəm] *n*. 【化】钠〔sodium 的旧名〕。

nat·ro·lite [ˈnætrəlait, ˈnei-; ˋnætrəlaɪt, ˋne-] *n*. 【地】钠沸石。

na·tron [ˈneitrən; ˋnetrɑn] *n*. 【矿】泡碱,冰碱;氧化钠;含水苏打。

nat·ter [ˈnætə; ˋnætɚ] I *vi*. 〔主英〕1. 闲谈,瞎扯。2. 发牢骚。II *n*. 谈话,交谈,闲谈。

nat·ter·jack [ˈnætədʒæk; ˋnætɚ͵dʒæk] *n*. 【动】黄条贝蟾蜍。

nat·thex [ˈnɑːθeks; ˋnɑθeks] *n*. 1. 教堂西门〔指早期基督教堂的西门,非忏悔者不许进入〕。2. 教堂前厅。

nat·ti·er [ˈnætiə; ˋnætɪɚ] *a*. natty 的比较级。~ *blue* 淡蓝色。

nat·ti·ly [ˈnætili; ˋnætɪlɪ] *ad*. 整洁,清爽。

nat·ty [ˈnæti; ˋnætɪ] *a*. (*-ti·er*; *-ti·est*) 1. (外貌、衣着)整洁的,干净的;清爽的;潇洒的。2. 灵巧的,敏捷的。**-ti·ness** *n*.

Na·tu·fi·an [nəˈtuːfiən; nəˋtuʃɪən] *a*. 西南亚中石器时代文化的。

nat·u·ral [ˈnætʃərəl; ˋnætʃərəl] I *a*. 1. 自然界的;关于自然界的。2. 天然的;未开垦的;野生的。3. 固有的,生来的,天赋的(*opp*. acquired);出乎本性的。4. 自然的,不加修饰的,不加做作的。5. 本来的;(论理上或人情上)当然的,不勉强的,常态的;普通的,平常的。6. 逼真的。7. 私生的,庶出的。8. 【乐】本位的;标明本位号的。9. 【数】自然数的;真数的。*the* ~ *day* 自然日〔由日出至日没〕。*the* ~ *forces* 自然力。~ *phenomena* 自然现象。*the* ~ *world* 自然界。*the* ~ *year* 自然年,太阳年。~ *gas* 天然气。~ *resources* 天然资源。*It is quite* ~ *that you* (*should*) *succeed* [*for you to succeed*]. 你的成功是很自然的。*Speaking comes* ~ *to him*. 他的演说流畅而自然。~ *disposition* 天性,本性。*a* ~ *gift* 天资,天禀。~ *poet* 天生的诗人。~ *vibration* 固有振动。~ *sine* 正弦真数。*one's* ~ *life* 寿命,寿限。~ *wages* 实物工资。*a* ~ *sign* 【乐】本位记号(♮)。II *n*. 1. (生来的)白痴。2. 【乐】(风琴等的)白键;本位音;本位号(♮)。3. (二十一点牌戏)一分牌就赢的两张牌。4. 〔美俚〕未曾受过训练而表演得意外出色的人,意外出色的表演;〔口〕对某方面(似乎)有天生特长的人。5. 〔美口〕可望立即成功的事物。~**-born** *a*. 天生的,生来的;本国出生的。~ **childbirth** 自然分娩法。~ **classification** 【生】自然分类。~ **frequency** 【物】固有频率。~ **guardian** 父母。~ **history** 博物学。~ **law** 自然规律;天理,自然法。~ **man** 蒙昧人。~ **number** 【数】自然数。~ **orders** (植物分类上的)目〔普通仅说作 orders〕。~ **person** 【法】自然人。~ **philosopher** 自然哲学家。~ **philosophy** 自然哲学〔旧指自然科学,尤指物理学〕。~ **right** 天赋权利,天赋人权。~ **rock** 天然沥青。~ **science** 自然科学。~ **selection** 自然淘汰,自然选择,天择。~ **system** 【植】自然分类〔根据形态的类似〕。~ **theology** 自然神学。~ **weapons** 天然武器〔爪、牙、拳等〕。~ **weight** 容积重。

nat·u·ral·ism [ˈnætʃərəlizəm; ˋnætʃərəl͵ɪzəm] *n*. 1. 自然,自然状态。2. 【哲、文艺】自然主义。3. 本能行动。

nat·u·ral·ist [ˈnætʃərəlist; ˋnætʃərəlɪst] I *n*. 1. 博物学家,(现特指)生物学家;自然主义者。2. 〔主英〕买卖玩赏动物的商人;动物标本剥制师。II *a*. = naturalistic.

nat·u·ral·is·tic [͵nætʃurəˈlistik; ͵nætʃərəlˋɪstɪk] *a*. 1. 自然的。2. 自然主义的;写实的。3. 博物学的。

nat·u·ral·i·za·tion [͵nætʃərəlaiˈzeiʃən; ͵nætʃərəlaɪˋzeʃən] *n*. 1. 顺化,归化;入国籍。2. 驯化,风土化。

nat·u·ral·ize [ˈnætʃərəlaiz; ˋnætʃərəl͵aɪz] *vt*. 1. 使归化;使入国籍;采纳(外国语言、风俗等)。2. 移养,移植(动植物)。3. 按自然规律说明,使不神秘。—*vi*. 1. 归化;土著化。2. 驯化。3. 研究博物学。*become* ~*d as a Chinese citizen* = *become* ~*d in China* 入中国籍。

nat·u·ral·ly [ˈnætʃərəli; ˋnætʃərəlɪ] *ad*. 1. 自然地。2. 生来;天然地。3. 自自然然,不做作地。4. 容易地。5. 当然,不用说。*She is* ~ *musical*. 她生来喜欢音乐。*I* ~ *accepted*. 我当然接受了。**come** ~ **to sb** (做某事)对某人很容易(*Driving comes* ~ *to him*. 他开车一点不费劲)。

nat·u·ral·ness [ˈnætʃərəlnis; ˋnætʃərəlnɪs] *n*. 1. 自然;当然;纯真。2. 【无】逼真度。

na·ture [ˈneitʃə; ˋnetʃɚ] *n*. 1. 自然(现象),大自然;自然界;自然力;〔拟人化时作 N-,作阴性用〕造化,造物主。2. 自然状态,原始状态;裸体;野生状态。3. (物体的)本质,(人、动物的)天性,本性,性格,脾性;特质,特征,性质;品种,类别;(子弹等的)大小。4. 生命力;体力,活力,精力;本能的力量,冲动;肉体的要求。5. 天理,道理。6. 自然景色,风景。7. 树脂;树液。8. 【宗】(人)尚未赎罪的状态。*all* ~ 万物。*All* ~ *looks gay*. 万物喜洋洋。*All* ~ *looks bleak*. 满目荒凉。*human* ~ 人性,人情。*the animal* ~ 兽性。*the rational* ~ 理性。*a man of good* [*ill*] ~ 脾气好[坏]的人。*N- will out*. 本性难隐。*sanguine* ~*s* (性格)快活的人,乐天派的人。*events of this* ~ 这一类事件。*Such a diet will not support* ~. 吃这种东西身体支持不住。*N- is exhausted*. 体力耗尽。**against** ~ 不自然地;奇迹地;违反自然[人性]。**by** ~ 生就,生来,本来。**by the** ~ **of things** = in the ~ of things. **call** [**necessity**] **of** ~ 自然[生理]的要求,要大小便。**contrary to** ~ = against ~. **draw from** ~ 写生。**ease** [**relieve**] ~ 解大[小]便。**freak of** ~ 造化的恶作剧〔天然的畸形〕。**in a** [**the**] **state of** ~ 在自然[野蛮]状态中,尚未开化;裸体。**in** ~ 1. 现在存在;事实上。2. 〔疑问词、否定语的加重语气〕究竟,什么地方也(没有等)(*What in* ~ *do you mean*? 你究竟是什么意思呢?)。**in the course of** ~ 依自然之势,顺乎自然。**in** [**of**] **the** ~ **of** 具有…的性质,像,类似(*His request is in the* ~ *of a command*. 他的请求简直像命令)。**in** [**by**, **from**] **the** ~ **of things** [**the case**] 在道理上,照道理说;当然,必然。**like all** ~ 〔美口〕完全。**Nature's engineering** 天工。**one of Nature's gentlemen** 地位虽低但志行高洁而有同情心的人。**one of Nature's noblemen** 〔反语〕老粗。**pay one's debt to** ~, **pay the debt of** ~ 死。**true to** ~ 逼真。~ **cure** 自然疗法。~ **deity**, ~**-god** 自然神。~ **myth** 自然神话。~ **printing** (把原物直接制成印版的)自然印刷法。~ **study** (学校)自然课。~ **worship** 自然崇拜。

-na·tured *comb.f*. "有…性质的","有…脾气的":good-*natured* 脾气好的。ill-*natured* 脾气坏的。

na·tur·ism [ˈneitʃərizəm; ˋnetʃərɪzəm] *n*. 对自然现象的崇拜;〔婉〕裸体主义。**na·tur·ist** *n*. 自然现象崇拜者;〔婉〕裸体主义者。

na·tur·o·path [ˈneitʃərəpæθ; ˋnetʃərə͵pæθ] *n*. 物理治疗家,理疗家。

na·tur·op·a·thy [͵neitʃəˈrɔpəθi; ͵netʃəˋrɑpəθɪ] *n*. 理疗,物理疗法。**-o·path·ic** [͵neitʃərəˈpæθik; ͵netʃərəˋpæθɪk] *a*.

naught [nɔːt; nɔt] *n*. 〔古〕1. 无;无价值。2. 【数】零〔作此义时通常用 nought〕。3. 〔古〕邪恶;坏人,恶人。**all for** ~ 无益,徒然。**a thing of** ~ 没价值的东西,没有用的东西。**bring to** ~ 破坏,挫败,使无效,使成泡影。**care** ~ **for** 一点不把…放在心上,丝毫不理会。**come to** ~ [**nothing**] 毫无结果,等于零;失败,枉费心机。**set at** ~ 轻视,藐视,忽视;一笔抹杀;使成泡影,完全破坏。

naught·y [ˈnɔːti; ˋnɔtɪ] *a*. (*-ti·er*; *-ti·est*) **1.** 顽皮的,淘气的,任性的,不听话的,撒野的,没规矩的。**2.** 卑劣的;猥亵的,下流的。**3.** 〔古〕邪恶的。*a* ~ *pack* 淘气鬼;坏蛋。**-ti·ly** *ad*. **-ti·ness** *n*.

nau·ma·chi·a [nɔːˈmeikiə; nɔˋmekɪə] *n*. (*pl*. ~*s*, *-chi·ae* [-ˌiː; -ˏi]) **1.** 古罗马海战演习。**2.** 古罗马海战演习场(=naumachy)。

Na·u·ru [nɑːˈuːruː; nɑˋuru] *n*. **1.** 瑙鲁(诺鲁)〔西太平洋〕。**2.** 瑙鲁〔瑙鲁首都〕。**-n** *n*. 瑙鲁人。

nau·se·a [ˈnɔːsjə; ˋnɔʒə] *n*. **1.** 恶心,作呕,晕船。**2.** 极度厌恶,引起人极度厌恶的东西。*be seized with* ~ 要吐,欲呕。

nau·se·ant [ˈnɔziːənt; ˋnɔʃɪənt] *n*. 呕吐剂。

nau·se·ate [ˈnɔːsieit; ˋnɔʒɪˏet] *vt*. **1.** 使呕吐,使恶心。**2.** 使厌恶;嫌,厌。—*vi*. **1.** 作呕。**2.** 厌恶 (*at*)。

nau·se·at·ing [ˈnɔːsieitiŋ; ˋnɔʒɪˏetɪŋ] *a*. 使人呕吐的;使人厌恶的。**-ly** *ad*.

nau·se·a·tion [ˌnɔːsiˈeiʃən; ˏnɔsɪˋeʃən] *n*. 恶心,呕。

nau·se·ous [ˈnɔːsjəs; ˋnɔʒəs] *a*. 令人作呕[恶心]的;讨厌的。**-ly** *ad*.

naut. =nautical.

nautch [nɔːtʃ; nɔtʃ] *n*. (印度专业舞女的)舞蹈(表演)。~ **girl** (印度的职业性)舞女。

nau·ti·cal [ˈnɔːtikəl; ˋnɔtɪkḷ] *a*. 海上的,航海的;船舶的;海员的,水手的。*a* ~ *almanac* 航海天文历。*a* ~ *mile* =a sea mile〔见 mile 条〕。~ *terms* 航海用语。**-ly** *ad*.

nau·ti·loid [ˈnɔːtilɔid; ˋnɔtɪlɔɪd] *n*. 鹦鹉螺目动物〔包括鹦鹉螺、船鱼、蛸船〕。

nau·ti·lus [ˈnɔːtiləs; ˋnɔtḷəs] *n*. (*pl*. ~*es*, *-li* [-lai; -laɪ]) **1.** 【动】鹦鹉螺(=pearly ~)。**2.** 【动】船鱼(=paper~); 蛸船。

nav. =**1.** naval. **2.** navigable. **3.** navigation.

Nav·a·ho, Nav·a·jo [ˈnævəhəu; ˋnævəho] *n*. (*pl*. ~*s*) **1.** (美国新墨西哥、亚利桑那、犹他等州的)印第安纳瓦霍族人;纳瓦霍语。**2.** 〔n-〕橙红色。**3.** 〔美〕超音速巡航导[飞]弹;远距离无线电领航系统。

nav·aid [ˈnæveid; ˋnæved] *n*. 助航装置[系统] (=navigational aid)。

na·val [ˈneivəl; ˋnevḷ] *a*. (有)海军的;军舰的;船的。*a* ~ *action* [*engagement*] 海战。*N- Academy* [*College*] 海军学院。*a* ~ *architect* 造船工程师。~ *architecture* 造船工程。*a* ~ *base* 海军根据地。*a* ~ *brigade* 海军陆战队。*a* ~ *cadet* 海军军官学员。*a* ~ *captain* 海军上校。*the N- Department* 〔美〕海军部。*a* ~ *engineer* (海军)轮机官。*the N- Engineering College* 海军轮机学校。~ *forces* 海军。*the N- General Board* 〔美〕海军将领会议。*the N- Intelligence Division* 〔英〕海军参谋部情报处。*a* ~ *machinis* (海军)修械师。~ *manoeuvres* 海军演习。~ *officer* 海军军官;〔美〕海关人员。*a* ~ *port* 军港。*the* ~ *powers* 海军强国。~ **stores** **1.** 海军补给品。**2.** 松脂(制品)。**-ly** *ad*.

na·val·ism [ˈneivəlizəm; ˋnevḷɪzm] *n*. 海军至上主义;海军攻势主义。**-ist** *n*. 海军至上主义者。**-istic** *a*.

nav·ar [ˈnævɑː; ˋnævɑr] *n*. 【空】指挥飞行的雷达系统。

nav·arch [ˈneivɑːk; ˋnevɑrk] *n*. 古希腊舰队指挥官。

nave[1] [neiv; nev] *n*. 【建】(教堂的)中殿,听众席;(铁路车站等建筑的)中央广场。

nave[2] [neiv; nev] *n*. (车)毂。

na·vel [ˈneivəl; ˋnevḷ] *n*. 脐;中央,中心。~ **orange** 脐橙(一端有脐状凹陷的无核橙子)。~ **string** [**cord**] 脐带。

na·vel·wort [ˈneivəlwəːt; ˋnevəlwɝt] *n*. 【植】**1.** 琉璃草属植物。**2.** 俯垂脐景天。**3.** 美洲石胡荽。

nav·i·cert [ˈnævisəːt; ˋnævɪˏsɝt] *n*. (交战国发给的)中立国船只运照,特准运照;(交战国对中立国船只的)运照制度(=~ system)。

na·vic·u·lar [nəˈvikjulə; nəˋvɪkjələ˞] **I** *a*. 船形的(尤指骨)。*the* ~ *bone* 舟骨。**II** *n*. 【解】舟骨。

navig. =**1.** navigation. **2.** navigator.

nav·i·ga·ble [ˈnævigəbl; ˋnævəgəbl] **I** *a*. **1.** (河湖等)可航行的,可通船的。**2.** (船)适于航行的,耐航行的。**3.** (气球等)可操纵航向的;适于航空的。**II** *n*. 〔罕〕飞艇。**-bil·i·ty** [ˌnævigəˈbiliti; ˏnævəgəˋbɪlətɪ] *n*. 适航性。**-bly** *ad*.

nav·i·gate [ˈnævigeit; ˋnævəˏget] *vt*. **1.** 驾驶(船舶、飞机等);导航。**2.** (人、船等)航行于;横渡。**3.** 〔美〕(稳定地)笔直走;使通过(议案等)。*She has trouble navigating the stair*. 她上下台阶(楼梯)有困难。—*vi*. 航行;航空;横穿;驾驶船舶[飞机]。*a navigating light* 航空灯。*navigating-jack* [*lieutenant*, *officer*] (海军)航海长,航海人员。

nav·i·ga·tion [ˌnæviˈgeiʃən; ˏnævəˋgeʃən] *n*. **1.** 航行;导航;领航;航海[航空]术。**2.** 〔集合词〕船。**3.** 〔古〕航路;海上交通。*aerial* ~ 空中航行。*inland* ~ 内河航行。*astro* ~ 宇宙航行;天文导航。*blind* ~ 仪表导航。*the N- Acts* 〔英〕航海条例。*There has been an increase in* ~ *through the canal*. 通过那条运河的船数增多了。~ **coal** 锅炉煤,蒸汽煤。~ **light** 飞机夜航时机身上的灯光。**-al** *a*.

nav·i·ga·tor [ˈnævigeitə; ˋnævəˏgetə˞] *n*. **1.** 航行者,航海者;(船舶、飞机的)驾驶员,领航员;海洋探险家。**2.** 航海书。**3.** 〔英罕〕=navvy. (*the*) *radar* ~ 雷达导航设备。

Nav Torp Sta =naval torpedo station 海军鱼雷艇站。

nav·vy [ˈnævi; ˋnævɪ] **I** *n*. **1.** 〔英〕(开挖运河、修筑铁路等的)工人;壮工。**2.** 掘土机;挖泥机。**3.** 〔海俚〕=navigating-officer. *a steam* ~ 蒸汽掘土机。*work like a* ~ 尽力做(讨厌的工作)。*a mere* ~*s work* (不用脑的)粗活。**II** *vi*. 做(开河、筑路的)工人。—*vt*. 掘(地)。

na·vy [ˈneivi; ˋnevɪ] *n*. **1.** 〔常 N-〕海军。**2.** 〔集合词〕海军官兵。**3.** 〔英〕海军部。**4.** 〔诗〕(商船)船队。**5.** 藏青色 =~blue. *the Royal N-* 英国海军。*the N-, Army, and Air Force(s) Institutes* 〔英〕海陆空军招待所。*the Department of the N-* = *the N- Department* 〔美〕海军部。*the secretary of the N-* 〔美〕海军部长。***bare*** ~ 〔美海军俚〕只发罐头食品的取给制度。***The N- League*** 〔英〕海军协会。~ **blue** (英国海军制服的)藏青色,深蓝色。~ **bean** 〔美〕【植】海军豆〔因美国海军中普遍食用而得名,粒小,白色,晒干〕。**N- Cross** 〔美〕海军十字勋章。~ **cut** 〔英〕切成薄片的块状板菸。**N- Day** 海军节。~ **"E" gunnery** (海军)优等射手。~ **list** 海军名簿,海军一览。~ **yard** 〔美〕海军造船厂。

naw [nɔː; nɔ] *ad*. 〔美俚〕=no.

nay [nei; ne] **I** *ad*. 〔古〕**1.** 否,不 (*opp*. yea)。**2.** 不但如是,而且〔发言时表示"好,唔,是的"等语气〕。*N-, then, I will essay it*. 好,那么我来试试看。*It is weighty*, ~, *conclusive*. 那很重要,不,有决定的作用。~ *more* 不仅…甚至…。~, ~ 〔美俚〕=no. **II** *n*. 〔古〕否,拒绝,反对;反对投票(者)。*Let your yea be yea and your* ~ *be* ~. 赞成与否请说个明白。*yea and* ~ 支支吾吾,模棱两可。*the yeas and* ~*s* 赞否(之数)。***say*** (*sb*.) ~ 跟某人说"不行";拒绝请求;禁止。***will not take*** ~ [***no***] 不许人说个"不"字,不接受否定的答案。

nay·say [ˈneisei; ˋnese] **I** *n*. 拒绝,否认。**II** *vt*. [neiˈsei; ˋneˏse] (***nay·said*** [ˈneiˈseid; ˋneˋsed]; ~·***ing***) 拒绝,否认,反对。**-er** [ˈneiseiə; ˋneˏseə˞] *n*. 反对者,否认者,拒绝者;老爱唱反调的人。

Naz·a·rene [ˌnæzəˈriːn; ˏnæzəˋrin] **I** *n*. 拿撒勒人;〔the N-〕耶稣;(犹太人及穆斯林所说的)基督教徒。**II** *a*. 拿撒勒人的。

Naz·a·reth [ˈnæzəriθ; ˋnæzərəθ] *n*. 拿撒勒〔巴勒斯坦北部古城,相传为耶稣的故乡〕。

Naz·a·rite [ˈnæzərait; ˋnæzəˏraɪt] *n*. **1.** 拿撒勒人。**2.**

N

(不剪发、不剃须、不喝酒的)古希伯来修行者。~ *hair* 长发。

naze [neiz; nez] ***n.*** 〔罕〕岬,海角。

Na·zi [ˈnɑːtsiː; ˋnɑtsi] ***n.*** (*pl.* ~*s*), ***a.*** 德国国家社会党(的),纳粹党(的),纳粹党员(的);纳粹分子(的),法西斯分子(的)。**-dom** 纳粹党的势力范围。**-fi·ca·tion** [-fiˈkeiʃən; -fɪˋkeʃən] ***n.*** 纳粹化。**-fy** [-fai;-faɪ] ***vt.*** 使纳粹化,把…置于纳粹控制或影响之下;纳粹化。**-(i)sm** ***n.*** 纳粹主义。

na·zim [ˈnɑːzim; ˋnɑzɪm] ***n.*** 纳济姆〔印度及伊斯兰教各国高级警官〕。

na·zir [ˈnɑːziə; ˋnɑzɪr] ***n.*** (印度、穆斯林国家的)法官。

N.B., NB, n. b. =**1.** 〔L.〕 *nota bene* 注意,留心(=note well)。**2.** New Brunswick 新布伦兹维克。**3.** North British 苏格兰的。

Nb =【化】niobium 铌。

NBC =National Broadcasting Company 〔美〕全国广播公司。

NbE, N by E =north by east 北偏东。

N-bomb =nuclear bomb 核弹。

N.B.R. =North British Railway 〔英〕苏格兰铁路。

NBS =National Bureau of Standards 〔美〕国家标准局。

NbW, N by W =north by west 北偏西。

N.C., NC =**1.** North Carolina 北卡罗来纳〔美国州名〕。**2.** =numerica control【自】数字控制。**3.** =network computer 网络计算机,网络电脑。

N.C., n. c.【化】=nitrocellulose 硝化纤维(火药)。

N, C.O., NCO =noncommissioned officer 军士。

N.C.U. =National Cyclists' Union 〔英〕全国自行车运动员联合会。

Nd =【化】neodymium 钕。

N.D., ND =**1.** North Dakota 北达科他〔美国州名〕。**2.** no date; not dated 无日期。

n.d. =**1.** no date; not dated 无日期。**2.** nothing doing 〔俚〕不行! 不干! 完了! **3.** no delivery 未交付,未到货;无法投递。

-nd *suf.* **1.** 〔附在动词后形成名词及形容词〕表示"(人或事物)应予…对待": rever*end*, divid*end*. **2.** 〔用于除十二外的以二结尾的顺序数词后〕表示"第二","第…二": 42*nd*(第四十二)。**3.** 用于形成名词: fie*nd*, frie*nd*.

NDAC =National Defense Advisory Committee 〔美〕国防顾问委员会。

N.Dak. =North Dakota 北达科他〔美国州名〕。

NDE =near-death experience 监死感受〔多指死而复生者所讲的感受,往往涉及见到的种种幻像〕。

Ndjamena [nˈdʒɑːmenɑː; nˋdʒɑmenɑ] ***n.*** 恩贾梅纳〔旧称 Fort-Lamy 拉密堡〕〔乍得首都〕。

N.E., NE, n. e. =**1.** northeast; northeastern. **2.** New England 新英格兰(美国东北六州之总称)。**3.** no effects 无存款。

Ne =neon【化】氖。

NEA =Northeast Airlines 〔美〕东北航空公司。

N.E.A. =National Education Association 〔美〕全国教育协会。

Ne·an·der·thal [niˈændətɑːl; nɪˋændɚ͵tɑl] ***a.***【人类】尼安得特尔人的。~ **man**【人类】尼安得特尔人。

neap [niːp; nip] **I** ***n.***, ***a.*** 小潮(的),最低潮(的)。**II** ***vi.*** (潮水)达小潮最低点。—***vt.*** (因小潮)使(船)搁浅。***be ~ed*** (船)因小潮搁浅。

Ne·a·pol·i·tan [niəˈpɔlitən;͵nɪəˋpɑlətn] **I** ***a.*** (意大利)那不勒斯(Naples)(人)的。**II** ***n.*** 那不勒斯人。~ **ice (cream)** 三色[多色]冰砖。

near [niə; nɪr] **I** ***ad.*** **1.** 近,接近,邻接(*opp.* far)。**2.** 〔口〕几乎,差不多,将近。**3.** 节省地。*He stood ~ to the door.* 他站在门附近〔在比较级和最高级之后亦常用 *to*. 如: I live ~er to the school than you. 我比你住得离学校近一些〕。*He lives very ~.* 他生活很节俭。***as ~ as*** 和…一样;在…限度内。***come ~*** 接近,赶得上,不亚于。***come*** [***go***] ***~ to ...ing*** 几乎,差点儿,差不多。***draw ~*** 接近,迫近。***far and ~*** 到处,远近。~ ***at hand*** 在手边,在近旁;即将到来。~ ***by*** 在附近。~ ***upon*** 几乎,将近(*The old man is ~ upon eighty.* 那老人将近八十了)。***not ~ so ...*** =not nearly so. ***nowhere ~*** = ***not anywhere ~*** 附近都不,远远不(*That's nowhere ~ enough.* 那是远远不够的)。

II ***prep.*** 接近,在…的近旁;快要。*sail ~ the wind* (船)抢风而驶;做危险事情。*The time draws ~ New Year.* 时节将近新年。*She came* [*went*] *~ being drowned.* 她差点儿淹死了。 *The sun is ~ setting.* 太阳快落了。*It kept him awake till ~ morning.* 这使他直到快天亮还醒着。***be ~ one's end*** 快要死,接近死期。***lie ~ one's heart*** 为某人所关怀[关切]。

III ***a.*** **1.** 近(的),接近的。**2.** 近亲的;亲密的,关系深的。**3.** 近似的,和原物难分的。**4.** (马或车的)左侧的(*opp.* off)。**5.** 近道的;直达的。**6.** 吝啬的。**7.** 〔口〕危险的。**8.** 〔美口〕仿制的,冒充的。~ *sight* 近视。*the ~ distance* (绘画等的)近景。*the ~ future* 不久的将来。*the ~(er) way* 捷径,近路。*a ~ friend* 亲密的朋友。~ *concern* (有)密切利害关系。*a ~ resemblance* 酷似。*a ~ horse* (马车)左侧的马。*a ~ guess* 相差不很多的推测。~ *silk* 〔美〕极像真丝的人造丝。*a ~ translation* 直译,接近原文的翻译。***be ~ with one's money*** 吝啬。~ ***and dear*** 极亲密的。***on a ~ day*** 日内,三五天内。

IV ***vt.***, ***vi.*** 近,接近,靠拢;迫近。~ **beer** 淡啤酒。~**by** 〔原美〕**1.** ***a.*** 附近的。**2.** ***ad.*** (靠)近〔英国分写作 ~ by〕。~ **continent** 近欧〔英国指比利时、荷兰、法国、丹麦等〕。**N- East** 近东。~ **miss**【军】**1.** 接近击中(目标)弹。**2.** 接近,但不够理想的成功。**3.** (飞机)幸免相撞。~ **point**【医】近点。~ **race** 难分上下的赛跑。~**-sighted** ***a.*** 近视的。~**-sightedness** 近视眼。~**-sonic** ***a.***【空】近音速的。~**-term** ***a.*** 近期的。~ **thing** [**escape, touch**] 九死一生,仅以身免。~ **wheel** (马车的)左轮。~ **wheeler** (四马马车的)左后马。~ **work** 精密工作〔因须接近眼睛〕。

near- *pref.* 〔Am.〕=almost: *near*-white 准白种人的; *near*-nude 差不多一丝不挂的。

Ne·arc·tic [niːˈɑːktik; nɪˋɑrktɪk] ***a.***【动、植】新北区〔包括北美洲寒带及格陵兰〕的。

near·ly [ˈniəli; ˋnɪrlɪ] ***ad.*** **1.** 近,接近;将近,大约,几乎,差不多。**2.** 好容易。**3.** 近似,密切,亲;精密。**4.** 〔罕〕细心;节俭地,吝啬地。~ *three o'clock* 将近三点钟。*She ~ fell over the cliff.* 她险些儿从崖上掉了下来。*It concerns me ~.* 这事对我有密切关系。*escape ~* 九死一生,仅以身免。***not ~*** 远不及;根本没有;相差很远(*It is not ~ so pretty as it was before.* 远不及以前漂亮。*It's not ~ enough.* 差得远。*There weren't ~ enough people to settle all that land.* 当时来这一地区移居的人根本不多)。

near·ness [ˈniənis; ˋnɪrnɪs] ***n.*** 近;接近;密切;亲近,亲密;节俭,吝啬。

neat[1] [niːt; nit] ***a.*** **1.** 干净的,整洁的;匀整的,端正的。**2.** (文字)简洁的,适当的;灵巧的,精巧的。**3.** 〔俚〕好的;美妙的。**4.** 〔英〕纯的,没搀水的;洁的。*a ~ dress* 整洁的服装。~ *weight* 净重。***as ~ as a pin*** 干干净净,非常整洁。***brandy ~*** 纯白兰地酒。***make a ~ job of it*** 做得干净利落。~ ***but not gaudy*** 〔美〕麻利的,灵巧的。~**-handed** ***a.*** 手巧的;灵活的,敏捷的。**-ly** ***ad.*** **-ness** ***n.***

neat[2] [niːt; nit] 〔古〕 ***n.*** 〔*sing.*, *pl.*〕〔集合词〕牛;牛类。~ **herd** 牧牛人。~ **house** 牛棚。~**'s foot** 牛脚〔食用〕。~**'s-foot oil** 牛脚油〔鞣革剂〕。~**'s leather** 牛皮。~**'s-tongue** 牛舌〔食用〕。

neat·en [ˈniːtn; ˋnitən] ***vt.*** 使整洁,使整齐,使干净〔常与 up 连用〕。

'neath [niːθ; niθ] ***prep.*** 〔古、诗〕= beneath.

neb [neb; nɛb] ***n.*** 〔Scot.〕(鸟的)嘴;(兽的)鼻子;(人的)口,鼻;尖端,尖头;(笔)尖。

NEB = New English Bible 新英语圣经。

Neb. = Nebraska.

neb·bish [ˈnebiʃ; ˋnɛbɪʃ] ***n.*** 〔美俚〕**1.** 无能的人;呆笨的人;胆小害臊的人。**2.** 倒霉的人,十分不幸的人。

NEbE, NE by E = northeast by east 东北偏东。

Ne·bel·trup·pe [ˈneibəltrupə; ˋnebəltrupə] ***n.*** 〔G.〕烟幕部队。

NEbN, NE by N = northeast by north 东北偏北。

Nebr. = Nebraska.

Ne·bras·ka [niˈbræskə; nəˋbræskə] ***n.*** 内布拉斯加〔美国州名〕。

Ne·bras·kan [nibˈræskæn; nəbˋræskən] ***n.*** 内布拉斯加人。

Neb·u·chad·nez·zar [ˌnebəkədˈnezə; ˏnɛbjəkədˋnɛzɚ] ***n.*** 尼布甲尼撒〔巴比仑王(605—562 B.C.),曾破坏耶路撒冷,将犹太人幽禁在巴比仑〕。

neb·u·la [ˈnebjulə; ˋnɛbjələ] ***n.*** (*pl.* ***-lae*** [-liː; -li] ~*s*) **1.**【天】星云;云状,雾影;【医】角膜翳。**2.** (小便的)溷浊;喷雾剂。*a ring* [*spiral*] ~ 环状星云。*a planetary* ~ 行星状星云。*a stellar* ~ 星云群。

neb·u·lar [ˈnebjulə; ˋnɛbjəlɚ] ***a.*** 星云(状)的。*the* ~ *theory* [*hypothesis*] 星云说〔认为太阳系是由星云状物质形成的假说〕。

neb·u·lium [niˈbjuːliəm; nəˋbjulɪəm] ***n.***【天】氙(一种假设的元素)。

neb·u·lize [ˈnebjuˌlaiz; ˋnɛbjəˏlaɪz] ***vt.*** (***-liz·ed; -liz·ing***) **1.** 使成水花,使喷水花。**2.** 喷雾;喷药水。**-zation** ***n.*** **-r** ***n.***

neb·u·los·i·ty [ˌnebjuˈlɔsiti; ˏnɛbjəˋlɑsətɪ] ***n.*** **1.** 星云状态;星云物质;星云状物。**2.** 云雾状态。**3.** 朦胧。

neb·u·lous [ˈnebjuləs; ˋnɛbjələs] ***a.*** **1.** 星云(状)的。**2.** 云雾似的。**3.** 形体不明的,朦胧的,模糊的。**-ly** ***ad.***

NEC = **1.** Nippon Electric Company 日本电气公司。**2.** National Emergency Council 〔美〕国家非常时期对策会议。

nec·es·sar·i·an [ˌnesiˈseəriən; ˏnɛsəˋsɛrɪən] **I** ***a.*** 必然论[宿命论]的。**II** ***n.*** 必然论[宿命论]者。

nec·es·sa·ri·ly [ˈnesisərili, ˌnesiˈseriəli; ˋnɛsəˏsɛrəlɪ, ˏnɛsəˋsɛrəlɪ] ***ad.*** 必定,必然;当然。*It* ~ *follows that* 必然(得出…的结论)。***not*** ~ 不一定,未必(*You don't* ~ *have to attend.* 你不一定要出席)。

nec·es·sa·ry [ˈnesisəri; ˋnɛsəˏsɛrɪ] **I** ***a.*** 必要的,不可缺的;必须的,强迫的;必然的,必定的。*a* ~ *result* 必然的结果。*a* ~ *evil* 难免的危害[坏事]。*a* ~ *house* 〔古〕厕所。***be*** ~ ***to*** [***for***] 为…所必要。***if*** ~ 如果必要的话。***It is*** ~ ***that one should*** (*do*). = ***It is*** ~ ***for one to*** (*do*). 某人必须…。**II** ***n.*** **1.** 必需品;〔the ~〕〔口〕必需的金钱[行动]。**2.** 〔美方〕厕所。*daily necessaries* 日用品。*the necessaries of life* 生活必需品。*provide* [*find*] *the* ~〔俚〕筹款。

ne·ces·si·tar·i·an [niˌsesiˈteəriən; nɪˏsɛsɪˋtɛrɪən] ***n.*** 必然论者,宿命论者。**-ism** ***n.*** 必然论,宿命论。

ne·ces·si·tate [niˈsesiteit; nəˋsɛsəˏtet] ***vt.*** **1.** 使成为必需;使需要。**2.** 强迫,迫使。*Language learning usually* ~*s conscious mimicry.* 一般地说,学习语言就要进行有意识的摹仿。*We were* ~*d to leave at once.* 我们不得不马上离开。**ne·ces·si·ta·tion** [ˌnisesiˈteiʃən; ˏnɪsɛsəˋteʃən] ***n.*** 迫使;被迫。

ne·ces·si·tous [niˈsesitəs; nəˋsɛsətəs] ***a.*** 穷;贫困的;紧迫的;必需的;不可避免的。~ *areas* 贫民区。**-ly** ***ad.***

ne·ces·si·tous·ness [niˈsesitəsnis; nəˋsɛsətəsnɪs] ***n.*** **1.** 贫困;贫乏。**2.** 必需,不可缺。**3.** 紧迫。

ne·ces·si·ty [niˈsesiti; nəˋsɛsətɪ] ***n.*** **1.** 需要,必要性。**2.** 〔常 *pl.*〕必需品。**3.** 必然(性)。**4.** 〔常 *pl.*〕贫穷;困难;危急。*physical* ~ 必然力,命运。*logical* ~ 逻辑的必然。*the doctrine of* ~ 宿命论。*N- is the mother of invention.* 需要是发明之母。***as a*** ~ 必然地。***be in dire necessities*** 穷困极了。***be under the*** ~ ***of*** (*doing*) 不得已而…;必须做某事。***bow to*** ~ 服从命运;屈服于需要。***by absolute*** ~ 万不得已。***from*** (***sheer***) ~ 因(十分)需要。***in case of*** ~ 必要时。***make a virtue of*** ~ 做非做不可的事而装成出于高尚动机。***of*** ~ 必然,必定;不得已;不可避免地(*That discussion must of* ~ *be postponed for a while.* 讨论会不得不延期举行)。~ **defence**【法】"出于无奈"辩辞〔以犯罪行为系出于无奈,否则会造成更严重后果云云所作的辩护〕。

neck[1] [nek; nɛk] **I** ***n.*** **1.** 颈,脖子;(衣)领;颈肉(尤指羊颈肉);(器物的)颈状部;【化】短管。**2.** 海峡;地峡,狭路。**3.**【建】颈弯饰。**4.**【地】岩颈。***a stiff*** ~ 固执(的人),顽固。***bend one's*** ~ 俯首听命,屈从。***break one's*** ~ 折断颈骨(致死)。***break the*** ~ ***of*** 做完(工作等的)最难部分。***fall upon sb.'s*** ~ 搂住人家的脖子(拥抱)。***escape with one's*** ~ 好容易逃脱性命。***get*** [***catch, take***] ***it in the*** ~〔俚〕大受攻击[处罚、责骂];〔美俚〕受罚,遭不幸,遭殃。***harden the*** ~ 变顽固,变刚愎。~ ***and crop*** 迅速地,急剧地;立即,马上;完全,彻底,整个地。~ ***and*** ~ (赛跑时)并驾齐驱,不分上下;〔美〕平等的。~ ***of the woods***〔美〕**1.** 森林区新村落。**2.** 近邻,附近地方,周围〔此义和树林等无关〕。~ ***oil***〔美俚〕酒。~ ***or nothing*** [***nought***] 拼命(*It is* ~ *or nothing.* 孤注一掷)。***on*** [***over***] ***the*** ~ ***of*** 紧紧跟在…的后头。***risk one's*** ~ 拼着性命。***save one's*** ~ 免受绞刑,得免一死;〔和否定连用〕无论如何不…。***speak*** [***talk***] ***through*** (***the back of***) ***one's*** ~ 说糊涂透顶的话;吹牛,说话尖锐。***tread on the*** ~ ***of*** 压服,压制,虐待。***win by a*** ~ (赛马时)以一颈之差得胜;勉强得胜。**II** ***vt.*** **1.** 割颈杀死(家禽等)。**2.** 缩小…的口径使成颈状。**3.** 〔美俚〕与…互相搂住脖子亲嘴;拥抱。—***vi.*** **1.** 〔美俚〕接吻,拥抱。**2.** 缩小。~**band** 领圈,领巾。~**beef** 牛颈肉。~**cloth** 〔古〕领饰。~ **journal**【机】轴颈。~**lace** **1.** (宝饰等做的)项圈,脖链儿。**2.** 〔俚〕绞索。**3.** 〔南非〕(处死刑用的)轮胎项圈〔套住被处死者的脖子,因其已浸透汽油,点燃后即将人烧死〕(~ *killing* 轮胎项圈火刑)。~**let** 小项圈;小皮围巾。~**-line** 领口。~**piece** **1.** 装饰性围巾(尤指皮围巾)。**2.** 颈甲〔保护脖颈的盔甲〕。~**tie** 领带;〔美俚〕绞索。~**-wear** 〔口〕颈部服饰〔如围巾,领带之类〕。

neck[2] [nek; nɛk] ***n.*** 〔英〕(地中谷物的)最后一捆。

neck·er·chief [ˈnekətʃif; ˋnɛkɚtʃɪf] ***n.*** 〔古〕围巾,围脖儿。

neck·ing [ˈnekiŋ; ˋnɛkɪŋ] ***n.*** **1.**【建】柱颈,柱颈部花边装饰。**2.** 〔美俚〕搂颈亲热。

necr(o)- *comb. f.* = corpse 死尸。

nec·ro·bi·o·sis [ˌnekrə*u* baiˈəusis; ˏnɛkrobaɪˋosɪs] ***n.***【医】渐进性(细胞)坏死。

nec·ro·gen·ic [ˌnekrə*u*ˈdʒenik; ˏnɛkrəˋdʒɛnɪk] ***a.*** 腐尸的;寄生于腐尸的;从腐尸发出的。

ne·crol·a·try [neˈkrɔlətri; nɛˋkrɑlətrɪ] ***n.*** 对死人的崇拜。

ne·crol·o·gy [neˈkrɔlədʒi; nɛˋkrɑlədʒɪ] ***n.*** 死亡表,死者名单;死亡通知;讣告。**-log·i·cal** [ˌnekrəˈlɔdʒikəl; ˏnɛkrəˋlɑdʒɪkəl] ***a.*** **-o·gist** ***n.*** 编死亡表的人;写讣告的人。

nec·ro·man·cer [ˈnekrə*u*mænsə; ˋnɛkrəˏmænsɚ] ***n.*** 巫,巫师,降神者;行妖术的人。

nec·ro·man·cy [ˈnekrə*u*mænsi; ˋnɛkrəˏmænsɪ] ***n.*** 向亡魂问卜的巫术,妖术;魔术。**-mant·ic** [-ˈmæntik; -ˋmæntɪk] ***a.***

nec·ro·pha·gi·a [ˌnekrə*u*ˈfeidʒiə; ˏnɛkrəˋfedʒɪə] ***n.*** 吃死尸肉,以腐尸为食。**ne·croph·a·gous** [neˈkrɔfəgəs; nɛˋkrɑfəgəs] ***a.***

nec·ro·pho·bi·a [ˌnekrə*u*ˈfəubiə; ˏnɛkrəˋfobɪə] ***n.*** 尸

N

体恐怖(症)。

nec·rop·o·lis [neˈkrɔpəlis; nɛˋkrɑpəlɪs] ***n*.** 大墓地(尤指古代城市或史前遗迹)。

nec·rop·sy [ˈnekrɔpsi; ˋnɛkrɑpsɪ], **nec·ros·co·py** [neˈkrɔskəpi; nɛˋkrɑskəpɪ] ***n*.** 【医】验尸;尸体剖检。

nec·ro·sis [neˈkrəusis; nɛˋkrosɪs] ***n*.** (*pl*. ***-ses*** [-siːz; -siz])【医】坏死,坏疽;骨疽;【植】枯斑,坏死。**nec·rot·ic** [neˈkrɔtik; nɛˋkrɑtɪk] ***a*.**

ne·crot·o·my [neˈkrɔtəmi; nɛˋkrɑtəmɪ] ***n*.** (*pl*. ***-mies***) **1.** 尸体解剖。**2.** 尸体切除。

nec·tar [ˈnektə; ˋnɛktɚ] ***n*.** **1.**【希神】神酒,众神饮的酒;甘美的饮料,甘露。**2.**【植】花蜜。**3.** 一种汽水。

nec·tar·e·an [nekˈtɛəriən; nɛkˋtɛrɪən], **nec·tar·e·ous** [-ˈtɛəriəs; -ˋtɛrɪəs] ***a*.** 神酒(似)的;甘美的;【植】花蜜的。

nec·tared [ˈnektəd; ˋnɛktɚd] ***a*.** 甘美的;充满神酒[甘露]的。

nec·tar·if·er·ous [ˌnektəˈriferəs; ˏnɛktəˋrɪfərəs] ***a*.**【植】分泌花蜜的。~ *glands* (植物的)蜜腺。

nec·tar·ine [ˈnektərin; ˋnɛktəˏrin] **I** ***n*.**【植】油桃。**II** ***a*.**〔古〕甘美的。

nec·ta·rous [nekˈtɛrəs; ˋnɛktərəs] ***a*.** = nektarean.

nec·ta·ry [ˈnektəri; ˋnɛktərɪ] ***n*.**【植】蜜腺;【虫】蜜管。

Ned [ned; nɛd] ***n*.** 内德〔男子名〕。

ned [ned; nɛd] ***n*.**〔美俚〕十元金币。

N. E. D., NED = New English Dictionary 牛津大词典 (= Oxford English Dictionary)。

ned·dy [ˈnedi; ˋnɛdɪ] ***n*.** **1.**〔口〕驴子,马;笨蛋,蠢货。**2.**〔N-〕〔英谑〕英国国家经济发展委员会〔源出 National Economic Development Council of Great Britain 前三字的起首字母〕。

Nedra [ˈnedrə; ˋnɛdrə] ***n*.** 内德拉〔女子名〕。

née [nei; ne] ***a*.**〔F.〕(已婚妇女的)娘家姓…。*Mrs. Smith*, ~ *Jones* 娘家姓琼斯氏的史密斯夫人。

need [niːd; nid] **I** ***n*.** **1.** 必要,需要。**2.** 缺乏,不足。**3.** 需求;需用的东西。**4.** 危急的时候,一旦有事的时候。**5.** 贫穷。*There is no* ~ *for* [*of*] *hurrying* = *There is no* ~ *to hurry*. 不用着急。*There is a great* ~ *of money*. 急需要钱。*A friend in* ~ *is a friend indeed*. 患难朋友才是真朋友。*He is in great* ~. 他穷得很。*at* (*one's*) ~ 在紧急时 (*be good at* ~ 在急需的时候有用)。***be in*** ~ ***of*** 需要。***do one's*** **~s**〔俚〕解大[小]便,解溲,撒尿。***had*** ~ (***to***) (***do***) 必须… (*I have* ~ *to go to town*. 我必须进城)。***have no*** ~ ***of*** 不需要。***If*** ~ ***be*** [***were***] 如果必要的话。***in case*** [***time***] ***of*** ~ 在紧急的时候,万一有事时。***stand in*** ~ ***of*** 需要。**II** ***vt*.** 要,需要,必须,有…的必要。*This house* ~*s repair*. 这个房子要修理了。*He* ~*s to go*. 他必须去。*Does he* ~ *to know*? 有告诉他的必要吗? —***vi*.** **1.** 生活贫困。**2.**〔古〕需要〔主要用于无人称句〕。*It* ~*s not*. 不需要。*more than* ~*s* 超过需要。*There* ~*s no apology*. 用不着辩解。*Give to those that* ~. 救济贫困者。**III** ***v. aux*.** 不得不,必须。★**1.** 在否定句或疑问句中,第三人称现在时单数也不加 s; 过去时用 had to 来代替,将来时用 will (或 shall) have to 来代替。need not (〔口〕needn't) 相当于 must 的否定形式。如: He ~ not come. 他不必来。N- she go? 她必须去吗? It ~ hardly be said that …简直用不着说。**2.** She ~ not go. 这句话,口语常说作 She doesn't ~ [have] to go. ~**-blind** ***a*.** (学校招生收费时)不考虑学生支付能力的。

need·fire [ˈniːdfaiə; ˋnidˏfaɪr] ***n*.**【条顿族神话】净火;〔Scot.〕烽火,火,狼烟,篝火。

need·ful [ˈniːdfəl; ˋnidfʊl] **I** ***a*.** **1.** 需要的,必要的,不可缺少的 (*to*; *for*)。**2.**〔古〕穷困的。**II** ***n*.** 〔the ~〕(俚)(必需的)钱,现金;必需的事物。***do the*** ~ 做该做的事。**-ly** ***ad*.** 必然地,不得已。

Need·ham [ˈniːdəm; ˋnidəm] ***n*.** 尼达姆〔姓氏〕。

need·i·ly [ˈniːdili; ˋnidɪlɪ] ***ad*.** 在贫穷中。

need·i·ness [ˈniːdinis; ˋnidɪnɪs] ***n*.** 穷困,贫穷。

nee·dle [ˈniːdl; ˋnidl] **I** ***n*.** **1.** 针,缝针;编织针。**2.** (注射、唱片等的)针;磁针,罗盘针,指针。**3.** 尖岩,尖峰;方尖碑;【化、矿】针状结晶;【植】针叶;【建】横撑木。**4.** 〔the ~〕〔英俚〕神经上的刺激;〔美俚〕麻醉毒品;注射。*a* ~*'s eye* 针鼻,针眼。*the eye of a* ~ 针眼〔指'狭缝'说〕。***get the*** ~ 急躁;恼怒。***give*** (*sb*.) ***the*** ~ 使(某人)恼怒[急躁],刺激(某人)。***have the pins and*** **~s** (脚等)发麻。***hit the*** ~ (箭)射中靶心;击中要害。***look for a*** ~ ***in a bottle*** [***bundle***] ***of hay*** 海底捞针〔徒劳无益〕。***on the*** ~ 有服用毒品瘾。***pass through the eye of a*** ~ 穿过针眼。(*as*) ***sharp as a*** ~ 非常机敏。***thread a*** ~ 穿针引线;完成一件困难的工作。**II** ***vt*., *vi*.** **1.** 拿针缝;拿针穿;【医】用针治疗。**2.** 穿过 (*through*)。**3.** (使)结晶成针状;【建】用横撑木撑住。**4.** 刺激。**5.**〔美〕加酒精(入啤酒等),加强酒性。~ **antimony** 粗锑。~**-bar** (缝纫机等的)针天心;针床;针座。~ **bath** 喷射淋浴。~ **beam**【建】簪梁。~**-beer**〔美俚〕加了酒精的啤酒。~**-book** 书形针盒。~ **case** 针盒。~**-craft** = ~ work. ~ **dam** 横栅活坝。~ **file** 什锦锉,组锉。~**fish**【鱼】颌针鱼;长喙鱼;海龙属鱼。~ **lace** 针绣花边。~ **match** 对抗心浓厚而有敌意的比赛。~**point** 针尖;针绣;针绣花边〔全称 needlepoint lace〕。~ **therapy**【医】针刺疗法。~ **time**〔主英〕(电台广播节目中编定的)播放唱片音乐的时间。~ **valve**【机】针阀。~ **woman** 针线好的妇女;做针线活的妇女;缝纫女工。~**work** 针线活,女红;刺绣,缝纫。~**-worker** ***n*.** 刺绣工;缝纫工。**-ful** ***n*.** 穿在针上的一次用线。

need·less [ˈniːdlis; ˋnidlɪs] ***a*.** 不必要的,不需要的;无用的,多余的。(*it is*) ~ *to say* [*add*]〔插入句〕不用说。**-ly** ***ad*.**

need·ments [ˈniːdmənts; ˋnidmənts] ***n*.**〔*pl*.〕〔英〕(旅行用)必需品。

need·n't [ˈniːdnt; ˋnidnt]〔口〕= need not.

needs [niːdz; nidz] ***ad*.** 必须,一定;务必〔现只与 must 连用〕。***must*** ~ **1.** 偏偏,偏要。**2.** 必须,必然,不得不 (*It must* ~ *be so*. 必然如此)。***must*** ~ ***do*** **1.** = ~ must do. **2.** 坚持说要 (*He must* ~ *come*. 他一口咬定要来)。~ ***must do*** 必须,不得不(*A man* ~ *must lie down when he sleeps*. 人睡时非躺下来不可。*N- must when the devil drives*. 魔鬼从后撵,就得向前跑;情势所迫)。

need·y [ˈniːdi; ˋnidɪ] ***a*.** (***need·i·er***; ***-i·est***) 贫穷的,贫困的。*the poor and* ~ 穷苦的人们。

ne'·er [nɛə; nɛr] ***ad*.**〔诗〕= never.

ne·'er-do-well, ne'er-do-weel [ˈnɛəduːwel, -wiːl; ˋnɛrduˏwɛl, -wil] **I** ***n*.** 没用的人,废物,饭桶。**II** ***a*.** 不中用的;无价值的。

nef [nef; nɛf] ***n*.** (食桌上搁盐、拭嘴布、匙子等用的)船形盆。

ne·far·i·ous [niˈfɛəriəs; nɪˋfɛrɪəs] ***a*.** 恶毒的;穷凶极恶的;极坏的。**-ly** ***ad*.** **-ness** ***n*.**

neg. = negative (by)。

ne·gate [niˈgeit; nɪˋget] ***vt*.** 否定,否认;取消,使无效;抹杀;使作废。

ne·ga·tion [niˈgeiʃən; nɪˋgeʃən] ***n*.** **1.** 否定,否认 (*opp*. affirmation); 拒绝,反对;反对论;消极;无,不存在。**2.**【逻】否定断定,命题的否定。~ ***of*** ~ 否定之否定。

ne·ga·tion·al [niˈgeiʃənəl; nɪˋgeʃənəl] ***a*.** **1.** 否定的;否认的;拒绝的。**2.** 对立的。**3.** 虚无的,不存在的。

ne·ga·tion·ist [niˈgeiʃənist; nɪˋgeʃənɪst] ***n*.** 否定论者。

neg·a·tive [ˈnegətiv; ˋnɛgətɪv] **I** ***a*.** **1.** 否定的,否认的;拒绝的 (*opp*. affirmative); 反对的,反面的;消极的。**2.** (*opp*. positive)【电】阴的,阴性的;负的;【数】负的;【摄】底片的;【医】阴性的。**3.**【植】(对日光或地面刺激等)有反作用的;【心理】反抗性的,不妥协的。*a* ~ *vote* 反对

票。*the* ~ *side* [*team*](讨论会的)反对方面。~ *criticism* 消极的批评。*a* ~ *plea*【法】抗辩。~ **capital** 负债。~ **charge** 阴(电)荷。~ **debt** 资本。~ **plate**【摄】底片。~ **pole**【电】负极,阴极。~ **quantity**【数】负量;〔口〕无。~ **sign**【数】负号(-)。*go* ~ 攻击[否定]对手。*on* ~ *lines* 消极地。**II** *n*. **1.** 否定词语;否定的观点;否定言论;否定回答;否定命题(等)。**2.** 消极性。**3.**【电】阴电;阴极板;【摄】底片;【数】负数,负量。*The answer is in the* ~. 回答是'不'。*Two* ~*s make an affirmative.* 两个否定等于肯定,负负得正。***answer in the*** ~ = ***return a*** ~ 回答说"不"。***decide in the*** ~ 否决。***eliminate the*** ~〔美俚〕消除自卑观念。***in the*** ~ 否定地,反对地,否认地。***prove a*** ~ 举反证。**III** *vt*. **1.** 否认;否定;驳斥;否决;拒绝;反证;反对。**2.** 使无效;抵销;使中和。~ **ad** [**commercial**]〔美〕否定性竞选宣传[广告]〔以攻击对手为主要内容〕。~ **income tax**〔美〕低收入补助。~ **interest** 倒利息〔自利息扣除的金额〕;逆利率〔存款利率减除通货膨胀率〕。~ **option**【商】消极选择权〔对自动寄来的商品具有购买或退还的权利〕。~ **proton**【物】负质子。

neg·a·tive·ly [ˈnegətivli; ˋnɛgətɪvlɪ] *ad*. 否定地;消极地。*answer* ~ 回答说不。*be* ~ *friendly* 交情(虽不好,但)还没有破裂。

neg·a·tive·ness [ˈnegətivnis; ˋnɛgətɪvnɪs], **neg·a·tiv·i·ty** [ˌnegəˈtiviti; ˏnɛgəˋtɪvətɪ] *n*. 否定[消极]性。

neg·a·tiv·ism [ˈnegətivizəm; ˋnɛgətɪvˏɪzəm] *n*. 否定论;否定态度;消极主义;怀疑主义;违拗性;【医】违拗症;抗拒症;【心】抗拒性。

neg·a·tiv·ist [ˈnegətivist; ˋnɛgətɪvɪst] *n*. 否定论者;取否定态度者;消极主义者;怀疑主义者。

neg·a·to·ry [ˈnegətɔːri; ˋnɛgəˏtorɪ] *a*. **1.** 否定的;否认的。**2.** 反面的;消极的。

neg·a·tron [ˈnegətrɔn; ˋnɛgəˏtrɑn] *n*. **1.**【物】双阳极负阻管。**2.**【物】负电子,阴电子。

neg·lect [niˈglekt; nɪˋglɛkt] **I** *vt*. 轻忽,玩忽;轻视,忽视,无视,不愿;忽略;漏做;不…(*to do*; *doing*)。**II** *n*. 疏忽;忽略;玩忽,轻忽;轻视,忽视 (*of*)。~ *of duty* 失职,玩忽职守。*Her children were in a terrible state of* ~. 她的孩子们简直没人管。*treat with* ~ 不理睬,怠慢。**-er, -or** *n*. 疏忽者,忽视者。

neg·lect·able [nigˈlektəbl; nɛgˋlɛktəbl̩] *a*. = negligible.

neg·lect·ful [nigˈlektful; nɪgˋlɛktfəl] *a*. 玩忽的,疏忽的 (*of*);不留心的,不注意的;不理睬的,不介意的,冷淡的 (*of*)。**-ly** *ad*. **-ness** *n*.

neg·li·gee, nég·li·gé [ˈnegliʒei, ˌneigliːˈʒei; ˋnɛgləˏʒe, ˏnɛglɪˋʒe] **I** *n*.〔F.〕(女人)便服,长睡衣。**II** *a*. (穿得)随便的。

neg·li·ge·able [ˈneglidʒəbl; ˋnɛglədʒəbl̩] *a*.〔罕〕= negligible.

neg·li·gence [ˈneglidʒəns; ˋnɛglədʒəns] *n*. **1.** 玩忽,疏忽;失职;【法】过失;不留心,粗心大意;不介意,冷淡。**2.** 懒散,邋遢,不整齐。**3.**【文艺】奔放不羁。*an accident out of* ~ 责任事故。*The accident was due to* ~. 事故是由于疏忽引起的。

neg·li·gent [ˈneglidʒənt; ˋnɛglədʒənt] *a*. 对…玩忽[疏忽](*of*, *in*, *about*);不留心的,粗心大意的;不检点的;随便的,懒散的。*be* ~ *of one's duty* 玩忽职守。*a writer* ~ *of punctuation* 不注意标点的作家。*be* ~ *in dress* 不讲究服饰。*One should not be* ~ *in traffic regulations*. 对交通规则不可掉以轻心。**-ly** *ad*.

neg·li·gible [ˈneglidʒəbl; ˋnɛglədʒəbl̩] *a*. 可以忽视的;无足轻重的(人);不足取的;很小的,微不足道的。*a* ~ *quantity* 可忽略的量[因素]。**-bil·i·ty** *n*. **-bly** *ad*.

ne·go·ti·a·ble [niˈgəuʃiəbl; nɪˋgoʃɪəbl̩] *a*. **1.** 可协商的,可谈的。**2.** (票据、证券等)可转让的,可流通的。**3.** (道路等)可通行的。*a* ~ *bill* 流通票据。~ *credit instruments* 流通证券。**-bil·i·ty** [niˌgəuʃiəˈbiliti; nɪˏgoʃɪəˋbɪlətɪ] *n*. 流通性,可转移性,流通能力。

ne·go·ti·ant [niˈgəuʃiənt; nɪˋgoʃɪənt] *n*. 交涉者,协商者;交易人。

ne·go·ti·ate [niˈgəuʃieit; nɪˋgoʃɪˏet] *vt*. **1.** 议定,商定,通过谈判使…。**2.** 卖[让]与;使(证券、票据等)流通,转让,兑现。**3.**〔口〕处置;处理;克服(困难等);〔口〕通过,跳通(障碍)。—*vi*. 协议,谈判,交涉 (*with*)。

ne·go·ti·a·tion [niˌgəuʃiˈeiʃən; nɪˏgoʃɪˋeʃən] *n*.〔常 *pl*.〕**1.** 协商,谈判,交涉,协定。**2.** 让与,转付,流通;交易。***be in*** ~***s with sb. over sth.*** 与某人协商某事。***break off*** ~***s*** 中断谈判。***carry on*** ~***s*** 继续交涉。***enter into*** [***upon***] ***a*** ~ ***with*** 开始和…进行谈判。

ne·go·ti·a·tor [niˈgəuʃieitə; nɪˋgoʃɪˏetɚ] *n*. (*fem*. ***-tress*** [-ʃiətris; -ʃɪətrɪs], ***-trix*** [-triks; -trɪks]) **1.** 协商者,谈判者。**2.** 让与人;交易人。

ne·go·ti·a·to·ry [niˈgəuʃiətəri; nɪˋgoʃɪəˏtorɪ] *a*. 协商的,谈判的,交涉的。

Ne·gress [ˈniːgris; ˋnigrɪs] *n*.〔贬〕女黑人。

Ne·gril·lo [niˈgriləu; nɪˋgrɪlo] *n*. (*pl*. ~*s*) (中非及南非的)矮小黑人。

Ne·grit·tic [niˈgritik; nɪˋgrɪtɪk] *a*. (像)(矮小)黑人的。

Ne·gri·to [niˈgriːtəu; nɪˋgrito] *n*. (*pl*. ~*s*, ~*es*) **1.** (分布在东南亚及大洋洲的)矮小黑人。**2.** 矮小黑人种〔包含 Negrillo〕。

ne·gri·tude [ˈnegritjuːd, ˈniːgri-; ˋnigrəˏtud, ˋnɛgrɪ-] *n*.〔亦作 N-〕对(非洲)黑人(文化)传统的自豪感。

Ne·gro [ˈniːgrəu; ˋnigro] **I** *n*. (*pl*. ~*es*) 黑人,黑种人〔目前带有贬义,一般改用 black〕。**II** *a*. **1.** 黑(种)人的;黑人住的;关于黑人的。**2.** 黑的。~ **ant**【虫】黑蚁。~ **minstrels** 黑人[化装黑人]歌舞团。

ne·gro·head [ˈniːgrəuhed; ˋnigrəˏhɛd] *n*. (压缩的)菸砖;劣等树胶。

Ne·groid [ˈniːgrɔid; ˋnigrɔɪd] **I** *a*. 黑人(似)的 (= Negroidal)。**II** *n*. 黑人。

ne·gro·land [ˈniːgrəulænd; ˋnigrəˏlænd] *n*. (非洲)黑人居住的地方。

Ne·gro·phil(e) [ˈniːgrəfail; ˋnigrəˏfaɪl] *a*., *n*. 亲[关心]黑人的(人)。**-ism** *n*. **1.** 认为黑人应有平等权利的主张。**2.** 黑人特有的发音等。

Ne·gro·phobe [ˈniːgrəfəub; ˋnigrəˏfob] *n*.〔有时作 n-〕畏惧黑人的人,强烈厌恶黑人者。**-pho·bi·a** *n*. 畏惧黑人。

ne·gus [ˈniːgəs; ˋnigəs] *n*. 尼格斯酒〔由热水、糖、柠檬、香料和酒混合成的饮料〕。

Ne·gus [ˈniːgəs; ˋnigəs] *n*. 埃塞俄比亚王的称号。

Neh·ru [ˈneiruː; ˋneru], **Jawaharlal** [dʒəˈwɑːnbərˈlɑːl; dʒəˋwɑnbɚˋlɑl] 尼赫鲁〔1889—1964,印度政治家〕。~ **coat** [**jacket**] 尼赫鲁上装〔一种窄身高领的上装〕。

neigh [nei; ne] **I** *n*. 嘶鸣声。**II** *vi*. (马)嘶。

neigh·bo(u)r [ˈneibə; ˋnebɚ] **I** *n*. **1.** 邻人,邻居;邻近的人;邻国(人)。**2.** 邻座(的人);邻接的东西。**3.** 同胞;世人。**4.** (对任何不知姓名的人的直接称呼)朋友。*a next-door* ~ 紧邻,隔壁邻居。*our* ~*s across the Channel* 海峡对面的邻人〔英国人指法国人〕。*a good* [*bad*] ~ 和邻居相处得好[不好]的人。**II** *vt*. **1.** 邻近,毗邻。**2.** 使接近,使邻近。*The building* ~*s the river*. 大楼邻近河边。—*vi*. **1.** 与…接壤,位于…附近 (*on*; *upon*)。**2.** 与…有睦邻关系 (*with*)。*The building* ~*s upon the river*. 大楼与河邻近。

neigh·bo(u)red [ˈneibəd; ˋnebɚd] *a*. 有某种邻居[环境]的。*a beautifully* ~ *city* 环境秀丽的城市。

neigh·bo(u)r·hood [ˈneibəhud; ˋnebəˏhʊd] **I** *n*. **1.** 邻近,接近;附近;周围。**2.** 四邻,街坊;街道,地区;聚居区。**3.** 近邻的人们。**4.** 邻居关系,邻人的情谊,和睦善邻[通例 good ~]。**5.**【数】邻域。*The* ~ *of the railway is a drawback*. 靠近铁路是个缺点。***in the*** ~ ***of*** **1.** 在…

的附近。**2.**〔口〕大约(*in the ~ of £100* 约一百镑)。**II *a*.**〔美〕附近的,地方的(=〔英〕local)。*a ~ newspaper* 地方报纸。~ **unit** 住宅区。~ **watch** (邻里之间的)守望相助计划〔居民有组织防止犯罪计划〕。

neigh·bo(u)r·ing [ˈneibəriŋ; ˋnebərɪŋ] ***a*.** 邻近的,附近的;邻接着的,毗邻的,接壤的。

neigh·bo(u)r·less [ˈneibəlis; ˋnebɚlɪs] ***a*.** 没邻人的;孤独的。

neigh·bo(u)r·li·ness [ˈneibəlinis; ˋnebɚlɪnɪs] ***n*.** 善邻,睦邻;和睦,亲近。

neigh·bo(u)r·ly [ˈneibəli; ˋnebɚlɪ] ***a*. 1.** 像邻人的;亲切的,和睦的,易亲近的。**2.** 住在邻近的。*live on ~ terms with* 同某人和睦相处。

Neil, Neal [niːl; nil] ***n*.** 尼尔〔男子名〕。

nei·ther [ˈnaiðə, ˈniːðə; ˋniðɚ, ˋnaɪðɚ]〔not+either〕**I *ad*. 1.**〔和 *nor* 配合使用〕两者都不…,(…不)…也不…〔动词应与最后一个名词[代名词]相一致〕。*N- he nor I know*. 他不知道,我也不知道。*N- you nor I nor anybody else has seen it*. 你我和其他任何人都没看见。**2.**〔古、方〕〔放在句尾加强前面的否定词〕也(=either)。*I don't know that ~*. 那事我也不晓得。**3.**〔用于否定条件句的结尾部分〕…也不。*If you do not go, ~ shall I*. 如果你不去,我也不去。**II *conj*.**〔古〕也不。*I know not, ~ can I guess*. 我不晓得,也猜不出来。**III *a*.** (两者)都不的,两者都不…。*N- accusation is true*. 两项责难都不对。*He took ~ side in the dispute*. 在争论中他任何一方都不参加。**IV *pro*.** 两者中无…,两者都不…。*N- of them knows*. 他们两个都不知道。~ ***flesh nor fish*** 非驴非马,不三不四。~ ***here nor there*** 无关紧要,不相干。~ ***more nor less than*** 和…完全一样;不多不少。~ ***rhyme nor reason*** 不伦不类;莫名其妙;无缘无故。

Nejd [neʒd, neid; nedʒd, ned] ***n*.** 内志〔阿拉伯中部伊斯兰教国,与 Hejaz 合并称沙特阿拉伯(沙乌地阿拉伯)(Saudi Arabia) 王国〕。

nek [nek; nɛk] ***n*.**〔南非〕山峡〔两峰间的洼处〕。

nek·ton [ˈnektən; ˋnɛktɑn] ***n*.**【动】自游生物。**-ic *a*.**

Nel·da [ˈneldə; ˋnɛldə] ***n*.** 内尔达〔女子名〕。

Nell [nel; nɛl] ***n*.** 内尔〔女子名, Helen 的爱称〕。

Nel·lie [ˈneli; ˋnɛlɪ] ***n*.** 内莉〔女子名〕。

nel·ly [ˈneli; ˋnɛlɪ] ***n*.**【鸟】大海燕。***not on your N-***〔英俚〕绝不会,不可能。

Nel·son [ˈnelsn; ˋnɛlsn] ***n*. 1.** 纳尔逊〔姓氏,男子名〕。**2. Horatio** ~ 纳尔逊〔1758—1805,英国海军大将, Trafalgar 海战的胜利者〕。

ne·lum·bo [niˈlʌmbəu; nɪˋlʌmbo] ***n*.** (*pl*. **-bos**)【植】莲属植物(=*Nelumbium*)。

ne·ma [ˈniːmə; ˋnimə] ***n*.** nematode (线虫纲动物)的缩略词。

nem·a·cide [ˈneməsaid; ˋnɛməsaɪd] ***n*.** 杀线虫剂。

nem·a·thel·minth [ˌneməˈθelminθ; ˏnɛməˋθɛlmɪnθ] ***n*.**【动】线形动物门动物。

ne·mat·ic [niˈmætik; nɪˋmætɪk] ***a*.**【物】(液晶中细长分子的位置)向列的。

nemat(o)- *comb*. *f*. 表示"线","线虫类": *nemato*logy.

nem·a·to·cyst [ˈnemətəusist; ˋnɛmətəˏsɪst] ***n*.**【动】刺丝囊(刺丝胞)。**-ic *a*.**

nem·a·to·cide [ˈnemətəusaid; ˋnɛmətəˏsaɪd] ***n*.** = nemacide.

nem·a·tode [ˈnemətəud; ˋnɛməˏtod] ***n*.** 线虫纲动物〔如钩虫、蛲虫〕。

nem·a·tol·o·gy [ˌneməˈtɔlədʒi; ˏnɛməˋtɑlədʒɪ] ***n*.** 线虫学。

Nem·bu·tal [ˈnembjutɔːl, -tæl; ˋnɛmbjəˏtɔl, -tæl] 耐波他〔pento-barbital sodium (戊巴比妥钠)的美国商标名〕。

nem. con. [ˈnem ˈkɔn; ˋnɛm ˋkɔn] =〔L.〕*nemine contradicente* [ˈniːmini: ˌkɔntrədaiˈsenti; ˋnimɪni ˏkɔntrədaɪˋsɛntɪ] 无异议地;全体一致地(=no one contradicting)。*The resolution was passed nem. con*. 决议案无异议地通过。

nem. dis(s). [ˈnem ˈdis; ˋnɛm ˋdɪs] =〔L.〕*nemine dissentiente* [ˈniːmini: diˌsentiˈenti; ˋnimɪni dɪˏsɛntɪˋɛntɪ] 无异议地;全体一致地(=no one dissenting)。

Nem·e·sis [niˈmisis; ˋnɛməsɪs] ***n*.** (*pl*. **-ses** [-siːz; -siz]) **1.**【希神】复仇[报应]女神。**2.**〔n-〕天罚;报应。**3.**〔n-〕复仇者;给以报应者。**Nem·e·sic** [niˈmesik; nɪˋmɛsɪk] ***a*.**

ne·mine con·tra·di·cen·te [ˈniːmini: kəntrədaiˈsenti:; ˋnɛməni ˏkɑntrədaɪˋsɛnti]〔L.〕= nem. con.

ne·mine dis·sen·ti·en·te [ˈniːmini:disenʃiˈenti:; ˋnɛmənidɪˏsɛnʃɪˋɛnti]〔L.〕= nem. dis(s).

ne·moph·i·la [niˈmɔfilə; nɪˋmɔfɪlə] ***n*.** 喜林草属植物〔产于美洲西部〕。

ne·ne [ˈneiˌnei; ˋneˏne] ***n*.**【动】黄颈黑雁。

N. Eng. = **1.** New England 新英格兰〔美国东北六州之总称〕。**2.** North England 北英格兰〔英国〕。

nen·u·phar [ˈnenjufɑː; ˋnɛnjʊˏfɑr] ***n*.**【植】(欧洲)白(黄)睡莲。

neo- *comb*. *f*. 表示"新","近代(的)";"复活": *neo*-impressionism.

ne·o·an·throp·ic, ne·an·throp·ic [ˌniːəuænˈθrɔpik; ˏnioænˋθrɔpɪk] ***a*.**【人类学】新人的,类新人的。

ne·o·ars·phen·a·mine [ˈni(ː)əuɑːsˈfenəmiːn; ˏnioɑrsˋfɛnəmin] ***n*.**【化】新胂凡纳明,九一四〔一种黄色粉末,可用以治疗梅毒〕。

Ne·o-Cam·bri·an [ˈni(ː)əuˈkæmbriən; ˋni(ɪ)oˋkæmbrɪən] ***a*.**【地】晚寒武纪的。

Ne·o-Cath·o·lic [ˈni(ː)əuˈkæθəlik; ˏnioˋkæθəlɪk] ***n*., *a*.** 新天主教派(的)。

Ne·o·cene [ˈni(ː)əsiːn; ˋnieˏsin] ***n*., *a*.**【地】晚第三纪(的)。

ne·o·class·ic, -si·cal [ˈni(ː)əuklæsik, -sikəl; ˋnioˋklæsɪk, -sɪkəl] ***a*.** 新古典主义的。

ne·o·clas·si·cism [ˈni(ː)əuˈklæsisizəm; ˋni(ɪ)oˋklæsɪsɪzəm] ***n*.** 新古典主义。

ne·o·co·lo·ni·al·ism [ˈni(ː)əukəˈləuniəlizəm; ˏniokəˋlonɪəˏlɪzəm] ***n*.** 新殖民主义。**-al·ist 1. *n*.** 新殖民主义者。**2. *a*.** 新殖民主义的。

ne·o·co·lo·ny [ˈni(ː)əuˈkɔləni; ˋni(ɪ)oˋkɔlənɪ] ***n*.** 新殖民地。

Ne·o-co·mi·an [ˈni(ː)əuˈkəumiən; ˋni(ɪ)oˋkomiən] ***a*.**【地】(中世代的)前绿砂期[统]的。

ne·o·con·ser·va·tive [ˌniːəukənsəvətiv; ˏniokənˋsɚvətɪv] ***n*.** 新保守主义者〔简称 neo(-)con〕。

Ne·o-Dar·win·ism [ˈni(ː)əuˈdɑːwinizəm; ˏnioˋdɑrwɪnɪzm] ***n*.** 新达尔文主义。

ne·o·dox·y [ˈni(ː)əudɔksi; ˋni(ɪ)odɑksɪ] ***n*.** 新学说,新见解。

ne·o·dym·i·um [ˌni(ː)əˈdimiəm; ˏnioˋdɪmɪəm] ***n*.**【化】钕。

Ne·o·g(a)e·a [ˌni(ː)əuˈdʒiːə; ˏni(ɪ)oˋdʒiə] ***n*.** 新热带区〔南北美热带地区〕;新界。**-n *a*.**

Ne·o·gene [ˈni(ː)əudʒiːn; ˋni(ɪ)odʒin] ***n*.**【地】晚第三纪。

ne·o·gen·e·sis [ˌni(ː)əuˈdʒenisis; nioˋdʒɛnɪsɪs] ***n*.** 新生,再生。**-ge·net·ic** [-dʒiˈnetik; -dʒɪˋnɛtɪk] ***a*.**

Neo-Geo, neo-geo [ˌniːəuˈdʒiːəu; ˏnioˋdʒio] ***n*., *a*.** (艺术上以抽象的几何线条或圆形创作的)新几何主义(的)。

Ne·o-Greek [ˈni(ː)əuˈgriːk; ˏnioˋgrik] ***a*.**【建、美】新希腊派的。

Ne·o-He·bra·ic [ˈniː(ː)əuhiˈbreiik; ˏniohɪˋbreɪk] ***n*., *a*.** 近代希伯来语(的),近代以色列语(的)。

Ne·o-Hel·len·ism [ˈniəuˈhelinizəm; ˋnioˋhɛlmɪzəm] ***n*.**

【文艺】新希腊主义。

ne·o-im·pres·sion·ism [ˈni(ː)əuimˈpreʃənizəm; ˌnio-ɪmˋpreʃənˌɪzəm] *n*. 【美】新印象主义。

Ne·o-Kant·i·an [ˈni(ː)əuˈkæntiən; ˌnioˋkæntɪən] **I** *a*. 新康德主义的。**II** *n*. 新康德主义者。

Ne·o-Kant·i·an·ism [ˈni(ː)əuˈkæntiənizəm; ˋnio-ˋkæntɪənɪzəm] *n*. 【哲】新康德主义。

Ne·o-La·marck·ism [ˈni(ː)əuləˈmaːkizəm; ˌniolə-ˋmɑrkɪzm] *n*. 【生】新拉马克学说。

Ne·o-Lat·in [ˈni(ː)əuˈlætin; ˌnioˋlætɪn] *n*. 新拉丁语(族)。

ne·o·lite [ˈni(ː)əulait; ˋni(ɪ)olaɪt] *n*. 【地】新石。

ne·o·lith [ˈni(ː)əuliθ; ˋniəˌlɪθ] *n*. (新石器时代的)新石器。

ne·o·lith·ic [ˈni(ː)əuˈliθik; ˌniəˋlɪθɪk] *a*. **1.** [N-]新石器时代的。**2.** 过时的。

ne·o·lo·gi·an [ˌni(ː)əuˈləudʒiən; ˌnioˋlodʒɪən] **I** *a*. 【宗】主张[遵守]新教义的。**II** *n*. 新教义主张者。

ne·o·log·i·cal [ˌni(ː)əuˈlɔdʒikl; ˌni(ɪ)oˋlɑdʒɪkl] *a*. 新词的,旧词新义的;新词语的使用的。**-ly** *ad*.

ne·ol·o·gism, ne·ol·o·gy [ni(ː)ˈɔlədʒizəm, -dʒi; niˋɑlə-ˌdʒɪzəm, -dʒɪ] *n*. **1.** 新词;旧词新义[新用法]。**2.** 新词[新义]的使用。**3.** 【宗】新教义的遵守[采用]。**-gist** *n*. **1.** 新词[新义]的创造者[使用者]。**2.** (= neologian)。

ne·ol·o·gis·tic, ne·ol·o·gis·ti·cal [ˌni(ː)ɔləuˈdʒistik, -tikl; ˌnioloˋdʒɪstɪk, -tɪkl] *a*. **1.** 新词的,旧词新义的。**2.** 使用新词的,使用(旧词的)新义的。

ne·ol·o·gize [ni(ː)ˈɔlədʒaiz; niˋɑləˌdʒaɪz] *vi*. 创造新词[新义];使用新词[新义];【宗】采用新说。

Ne·o-Mal·thu·si·an·ism [ˈni(ː)əumælˈθjuːzjənizəm; ˌniomælˋθjuzɪənˌɪzəm] *n*. 新马尔萨斯主义。

ne·o·mart [ˈniːəumaːt; ˋniomɑrt] *n*. 【医】新尸〔指大脑已死但其他器官仍在呼吸器等人工手段下维持活着的尸体〕。

ne·o·my·cin [ˌni(ː)əuˈmaisin; ˌniəˋmaɪsɪn] *n*. 【生化】新霉素,新链丝菌素。

ne·on [ˈniːən; ˋniɑn] *n*. **1.** 【化】氖。**2.** 氖光灯,霓虹灯。*a* ~ *lamp* 霓虹灯。*a* ~ *sign* 广告霓虹灯。

ne·o·nate [ˈniːəneit; ˋniəˌnet] *n*. 出生不满一个月的婴儿;新生婴儿。

ne·o-orth·o·dox·y [ˌni(ː)əuˈɔːθədɔksi; ˌni(ɪ)oˋɔrθə-dɑksɪ] *n*. 新正教。**ne·o-orthodox** *a*.

ne·o·phyte [ˈni(ː)əufait; ˋniəˌfaɪt] *n*. **1.** 【教会史】新入教者;【天主】新祭司。**2.** 新来者,初学者,生手;〔美〕大学一年级生。**3.** 【植】新来杂草植物;新引种植物。*The ~ must not despair of mastering the rules and procedures*. 初学的人不必在熟悉规则和程序中感到失望。

ne·o·pla·sia [ˌni(ː)əuˈpleiʒə, -ʒiə; ˌnioˋpleʒə, -ʒɪə] *n*. 【医】瘤形成。

ne·o·plasm [ˈni(ː)əuplæzəm; ˋnioplæzm] *n*. 【医】异常新生物,(尤指)赘生物,瘤。**-plas·tic** *a*. 瘤的,赘生物的;新造型主义的。

ne·o·plas·ti·cism [ˈni(ː)əuˈplæstisizəm; ˌnioˋplæstɪ-sɪzm] *n*. 【美】新造型主义。

ne·o·plas·ty [ˈni(ː)əuplæsti; ˋniəˌplæstɪ] *n*. 【外】造型术,修补术。

Ne·o-pla·to·n·ism [ˌni(ː)əuˈpleitənizəm; ˌnioˋpletn-ˌɪzəm] *n*. 新柏拉图主义。

ne·o·prene [ˈni(ː)əupriːn; ˋniəˌprin] *n*. 【化】氯丁(二烯)橡胶。

Ne·o-Re·al·ism [ˈni(ː)əuˈriəlizəm; ˌnioˋriəlˌɪzəm] *n*. **1.** 【哲】新实在论。**2.** 【文艺】新现实主义。

ne·o·sal·var·san [ˈni(ː)əuˈsælvəsæn; ˌnioˋsælvəˌsæn] *n*. 【药】九一四〔商标名,一种黄色粉末,用以治疗梅毒〕;新胂凡纳明。

Ne·o-Scho·las·ti·cism [ˈni(ː)əuskəˈlæstisizəm; ˋni(ɪ)-oskəˋlæstɪsɪzəm] *n*. 新经院哲学。

ne·ot·e·ny [ni(ː)ˈɔtini, ˈniətini; ni(ɪ)ˋɑtɪnɪ, ˋnɪətɪnɪ] *n*. 【动】幼态持续,幼期性熟。**-ten·ic** [-ˈtiːnik, -ˈtenik; -ˋtinɪk, -ˋtɛnɪk] *a*.

ne·o·ter·ic [ˌni(ː)əuˈterik; ˌnioˋtɛrɪk] **I** *a*. 现代的;崭新的;新发明的。**II** *n*. 现代人;现代作家。

ne·o-Tho·mism [ˈni(ː)əuˈtəumizm; ˋni(ɪ)oˋtomɪzm] *n*. 【哲】新托马斯主义。

ne·o·trist [ˈni(ː)əutrist; ˋni(ɪ)otrɪst] *n*. 创造新词者。

ne·o·trop·i·cal [ˈni(ː)əuˈtrɔpikəl; ˌnioˋtrɑpɪkəl] *a*. 新热带区的。

ne·o·zo·ic [ˈni(ː)əuˈzəuik; ˌniəˋzo·ɪk] *a*. 【地】新生代的。

Nep. = Neptune.

Ne·pal [niˈpɔːl; nɪˋpɔl] *n*. 尼泊尔〔亚洲〕。

Ne·pal·i [niˈpɔːli, -ˈpɔl-; nɛˋpɑlɪ, -ˋpɔl-] *n*. 尼泊尔语〔尼泊尔的印度语〕。

Nep·a(u)·lese [ˌnepɔːˈliːz; ˌnɛpəˋliz] **I** *n*. 尼泊尔人。**II** *a*. 尼泊尔(人)的。

ne·pen·the [neˈpenθi; nɪˋpɛnθɪ] *n*. 〔诗〕(古希腊传说中的)忘忧药。

ne·pen·thes [neˈpenθiːz; nɪˋpɛnθiz] *n*. **1.** 【植】猪笼草属。**2.** = nepenthe.

ne·per [ˈneipə, ˈniːpə; ˋnepɚ, ˋnipɚ] *n*. 【无】讷〔衰耗单位=8.686分贝〕。

neph·al·ism [ˈnefəlizəm; ˋnɛfəlɪzm] *n*. 完全戒酒。

neph·al·ist [ˈnefəlist; ˋnɛfəlɪst] *n*. 完全戒酒论者;〔美〕禁酒主义者。

neph·a·nal·y·sis [ˌnefəˈnælisis; ˌnɛfəˋnæləsɪs] *n*. (*pl*. *-ses* [-siːz; -siz]) 【气】云层分析;云层分析图。

neph·e·line [ˈnefəlin; ˋnɛfəlɪn], **neph·e·lite** [-lait; -laɪt] *n*. 【矿】霞石。

neph·e·lin·ite [ˈnefilinait; ˋnɛfɪlɪnaɪt] *n*. 【地】霞岩。

neph·e·lom·e·ter [ˌnefiˈlɔmitə; ˌnɛfəˋlɑmətɚ] *n*. 【化】(散射)浊度计,(散射)比浊计,混浊计。

neph·ew [ˈnevju(ː), ˈnefju(ː); ˋnɛfju, ˋnɛvju] *n*. **1.** 侄子;外甥。**2.** 〔废〕后裔(尤指孙子)。**3.** 〔婉〕(教士的)私生子。

neph·o·gram [ˈnefəgræm; ˋnɛfəgræm] *n*. 【气】云图。

ne·phol·o·gy [niˈfɔlədʒi; nɪˋfɑlədʒɪ] *n*. 【气】云学。

neph·o·scope [ˈnefəskəup; ˋnɛfəˌskop] *n*. 【气】测云器。

ne·phral·gi·a [neˈfrældʒiə; nɛˋfrældʒɪə] *n*. 【医】肾痛。

ne·phrec·to·my [neˈfrektəmi; nɪˋfrɛktəmɪ] *n*. (*pl*. *-mies*) 【医】肾切除术。

ne·phrid·i·um [neˈfridiəm; nɛˋfrɪdɪəm] *n*. (*pl*. *-phrid·i·a* [-ə; -ə]) 【解】肾,肾管。**-phrid·i·al** *a*.

neph·rite [ˈnefrait; ˋnɛfraɪt] *n*. 【矿】软玉。

ne·phrit·ic [neˈfritik; nɛˋfrɪtɪk] *a*. 肾的;肾病的,治肾病的。*the ~ stone* 肾结石。

ne·phri·tis [neˈfraitis; nɛˋfraɪtɪs] *n*. 【医】肾炎。

nephro- *comb*. *f*. 表示"肾"的意思: *nephro*tomy.

neph·ro·gen·ic [ˌnefrəuˈdʒenik; ˋnɛfrəˋdʒɛnɪk] *a*. **1.** 肾内产生的。**2.** 形成肾组织的。

neph·roid [ˈnefrɔid; ˋnɛfrɔɪd] *a*. 肾形的。

neph·ron [ˈnefrɔn; ˋnɛfrɑn] *n*. 肾元,肾单位。

ne·phro·sis [neˈfrəusis; nɪˋfrosɪs] **I** *n*. 【医】肾(变)病。**II ne·phrot·ic** [-ˈfrɔtik; -ˋfrɑtɪk] *a*.

ne·phrot·o·my [neˈfrɔtəmi; nɛˋfrɑtəmɪ] *n*. (*pl*. *-mies*) 【医】肾切开术。

ne plus ul·tra [ˈniːplʌsˈʌltrə; ˋniplʌsˋʌltrə] 〔L.〕至上,至高,无上;极致,极点,顶点。

ne·pot·ic [niˈpɔtik; nɪˋpɑtɪk] *a*. 袒护[重用]亲戚的。

nep·o·tism [ˈnepətizəm; ˋnɛpəˌtɪzəm] *n*. 袒护[重用]亲戚;任人唯亲作风;裙带关系;族阀主义。

nep·o·tist [ˈnepətist; ˋnɛpətɪst] *n*. 重用亲戚者,族阀主义者。

nep·o·tis·tic [ˌnepəˈtistik; ˌnɛpəˋtɪstɪk] *a*. 袒护亲戚的,重用亲戚的;裙带关系的。

N

Nep·tune [ˈneptjuːn; ˋnɛptjun] ***n*.** **1.**【罗神】尼普顿〔海神〕。**2.**【天】海王星。**3.** 海,海洋。**4.** (美国的)海王式巡逻机。~***'s cup*** 杯状大海绵。~***'s revel*** 赤道节。***son of*** ~ 船夫,水手。

Nep·tu·ni·an [ˈneptjuniən, -njən; nɛpˋtjunɪən, -njən] **I *a*.** **1.** 海神尼普顿的;海王星的。**2.** 〔n-〕【地】水成(论)的。**II *n*.** 〔n-〕水成论者。

nep·tun·ism [ˈneptjunizəm; ˋnɛptjunɪzəm] ***n*.**【地】岩石水成论。

nep·tun·ist [ˈneptjunist; ˋnɛptjunɪst] ***n*.**【地】岩石水成论者。

nep·tu·ni·um [nepˈtjuːniəm; nɛpˋtunɪəm] ***n*.**【化】镎〔旧译錼〕。~ **series**【化】镎系(列)。

N.E.R.A = National Emergency Relief Administration 〔美〕国家紧急救济署。

Ner·chinsk [ˈnɛətʃinsk; ˋnertʃɪnsk] ***n*.** 涅尔琴斯克〔俄罗斯城市,即尼布楚〕。

nerd [nəːd; nɝd] ***n*.** 〔美俚〕(…的)狂热爱好者,(…的)迷。*a computer* ~ 电脑迷。

Ne·re·id [ˈniəriid; ˋnɪrɪɪd] ***n*.** (*pl*. ~***s***, ~***es***) **1.**【希神】海中仙女。**2.** 〔n-〕【动】沙蚕。

ne·re·is [ˈniəriis; ˋnɪrɪɪs] ***n*.** (*pl*. ***ne·re·i·des*** [niˈriədiːz; nɪˋrɪədiz]) 沙蚕属动物。

ne·rit·ic [niˈritik; nɪˋrɪtɪk] ***a*.** 浅海的。

nerk [nəːk; nɝk] ***n*.** 〔美、加俚〕笨蛋,蠢材;令人讨厌的老古板。**-ish *a*.**

Nernst [G. nɛrnst; nɛrnst], **Walther Hermann** 内恩斯特〔1864—1941,德国物理学家、化学家,曾获 1920 年诺贝尔化学奖〕。

Ne·ro [ˈniərəu; ˋniro] ***n*.** 尼禄〔古罗马暴君,公元 37—68 年〕。

ner·o·li [ˈniərəli; ˋnɛrəlɪ] ***n*.**【化】橙花油(= ~ oil)。

Ne·ro·ni·an [niˈrəuniən; nɪˋronɪən] ***a*.** 尼禄(似)的;暴虐的;荒淫的。

ner·sy [ˈnəːzi; ˋnɝzɪ] ***a*.** 〔美俚〕声音大的,嘈杂的。

nerts, nertz [ˈnəːtz; ˋnɝtz] ***int*.** 〔美俚〕我不相信;胡说八道(= nuts)。*N- to you*! 胡说!

nerv·al [ˈnəːvəl; ˋnɝvəl] ***a*.** 神经(组织)的。

nerv·ate [ˈnəːveit; ˋnɝvet] ***a*.**【植】有叶脉的,具脉的。

ner·va·tion [ˈnəːveiʃən; nɝˋveʃən] ***n*.**【动、植】脉序。

nerve [nəːv; nɝv] **I *n*.** **1.**【解】神经。**2.** 〔诗〕筋,腱;精力,气力。**3.** 胆力,勇气;沉着,果断;大胆,胆量;〔口〕厚脸,冒昧。**4.** 〔*pl*.〕神经过敏;胆怯,忧郁。**5.** 主要部分,核心,中枢。**6.**【植】脉,叶脉;【昆虫】翅脉。**7.** 回缩性,(弹性)复原性。*a war of* ~*s* 神经战。*You have a* ~! 〔口〕无耻! *a fit of* ~*s* 神经过敏,神经病发作。*She is all* ~*s*. 她太神经过敏了。*Banks are the* ~*s of commerce*. 银行是商业的中枢。*It is trying to the* ~*s*. 精神痛苦不堪。*He does not know what* ~*s are*. 他不知道什么叫害怕;他从不紧张。***be all*** ~***s*** 神经紧张,高度不安。***brace one's*** ~ ***for an effort*** 为某项努力鼓起勇气。***get*** [***jar***] ***on one's*** ~***s*** = ***give one the*** ~***s*** 刺激神经;使人不安[心烦];惹恼人。***have a fit of*** ~***s*** 发神经病。***have iron*** ~***s*** = ***have*** ~***s of steel*** 神经坚强,有胆量。***have no*** ~***s*** (好像没神经一样)泰然自若,满不在乎。***have the*** ~***s to*** (***do***) 有…的勇气;〔口〕好意思…,厚着脸皮…。***lose one's*** ~***s*** 害怕起来;不知所措;变得慌张。***strain every*** ~ 尽心竭力。**II *vt*.** 鼓励,激励。~ ***oneself*** 鼓勇,提起精神。~ **agent** 神经毒剂。~ **air raid** (扰乱性的)神经空袭。~ **block**【医】神经传导阻滞。~**-bank** 神经库。~ **cell** 神经细胞。~ **centre,** ~ **center 1.**【解】神经中枢。**2.** 中枢,核心;要害。~ **fibre,** ~ **fiber** 神经纤维。~ **gas** (能透入皮肤、毒性剧烈的)神经错乱性毒气,神经毒气,中毒性毒气。~ **impulse** 神经冲动。~**-knot** 神经节。~ **strain** 神经过劳。~**-racking,** ~**-wracking *a*.** 使人心烦的;伤脑筋的。

-nerved [nəːvd; nɝvd] *comb. f*. 〔用以构成复合词〕**1.** 神经…的:strong*nerved*. **2.**【植】有…叶脉的;【虫】有翅脉的:five*nerved*.

nerve·less [ˈnəːvlis; ˋnɝvlɪs] ***a*.** **1.** 无力的;没生气的;(文体等)松懈的。**2.** 沉着的,镇静的。**3.**【解、动】没有神经的;【植】无叶脉的;【虫】无翅脉的。**-ly *ad*.**

ner·vine [ˈnəːviːn; ˋnɝvin] **I *a*.** **1.** 神经的。**2.** 镇定神经的。**II *n*.**【医】神经强健剂。

nerv·ous [ˈnəːvəs; ˋnɝvəs] ***a*.** **1.** 神经(方面)的,对神经起作用的。**2.** 神经过敏的,神经质的,紧张不安的,胆小的;易激动的,易怒的。**3.** 强健的,有勇气的;有力的,(文体等)简练刚劲的。*the* ~ *center* 神经中枢。~ *disorder* 神经错乱。***feel*** ~ ***about*** 以…为苦,担心…,害怕…。~ **breakdown** [**debility, depression, exhaustion, prostration**] 神经衰弱[崩溃]。~ **disease** 神经病。~ **Nellie** 〔俚〕胆小鬼;无用的人。~ **system** 神经系统。**-ly *ad*.** **1.** 神经质似地,胆怯似地。**2.** 强健地;有力地。**-ness *n*.** 神经过敏,神经质;急躁;胆小。

ner·vure [ˈnəːvjuə; ˋnɝvjur] ***n*.**【植】叶脉;【虫】翅脉。

nerv·y [ˈnəːvi; ˋnɝvɪ] ***a*.** **1.** 〔诗〕肌肉发达的,强状的。**2.** 〔美〕有勇气的,大胆的;〔俚〕冷静的;粗鲁的;脸厚的;〔俚〕刺激神经的;使人心烦的。**3.** 〔英口〕神经质的,神经紧张的;易激动的。

n.e.s., N.E.S. = not elsewhere specified 不另说明。

nes·ci·ence [ˈnesiəns, -sjəns; ˋneʃɪəns, -sɪəns] ***n*.** **1.** 无学,无知。**2.**【哲】不可知论。

nes·ci·ent [ˈnesiənt, -sjənt; ˋnɛʃənt, -sɪənt] **I *a*.** **1.** 无学的,无知的,不知的 (*of*)。**2.**【哲】不可知论的。**II *n*.** 不可知论者。

ness [nes; nɛs] ***n*.** 海岬,海角;岬(角)。

-ness *suf*. 〔附在形容词、分词、复合形容词后形成抽象名词〕表示"性质"、"状态"、"精神"、"程度":bitter*ness*, tired*ness*, up-to-date*ness*, etc.

Nes·sie [ˈnesi; ˋnɛsɪ] ***n*.** (苏格兰的)尼斯湖"怪兽"。

Nes·sus [ˈnesəs; ˋnɛsəs] ***n*.**【希神】(大力神 Hercules 用毒箭射死的)人头马腿怪物。

nest [nest; nɛst] **I *n*.** **1.** 巢;窝;窟,穴。**2.** 安息处,休息处;住处,家;避难处,隐退处。**3.** (盗贼等)的巢窟;(罪恶等的)发源地,渊薮,温床。**4.** 〔集合词〕一窝雏;(鸟、虫等的)群;(同种类物的)集合。**5.** (上下叠放着的碗、碟等的)一套 (*of*)。**6.**【地】矿巢;【建】蜂窝(混凝土缺陷)。**7.** 〔美俚〕导[飞]弹基地。*a birds* ~ 鸟巢。*a* ~ *of brigands* 一窝匪徒。*a* ~ *of tables* (大小顺次套放在一起的)一套桌子。***a mare's*** ~ 幻想的[不存在的]东西。***arouse a*** ~ ***of hornets*** 捅马蜂窝;惹麻烦;树敌招怨;犯众怒。***feather one's*** ~ 自肥;营私。***foul one's own*** ~ 说自己家里[党内]的坏话;家丑外扬。***take a*** ~ 摸巢,盗巢〔偷鸟巢里的蛋或雏〕。**II *vi*.** **1.** 筑巢;入巢,伏窝。**2.** 找鸟窝。**3.** 相互套入。**4.** 〔美俚〕蹲下来。**5.** 〔俚〕整天呆在家中足不出户。*go* ~*ing* 去找鸟窝。—***vt*.** **1.** 使入窝,使伏窝。**2.** 把(大小箱子)套起来;安顿,放置(碗碟等)。*the* ~*ed region*【数】区域套。~ **egg** 留窝蛋;〔喻〕豚子,引诱物;储备金[物]。

n'est-ce pas? [nesˈpɑː; nɛsˋpɑ] 〔F.〕不是这样的吗? 对吧?

nes·tle [ˈnesl; ˋnɛsl] ***vi*.** **1.** 〔罕〕(鸟)造窝,营巢。**2.** 舒舒服服地安顿下来;安居,安身;安卧 (*down*; *in*; *into*; *among*)。**3.** 偎依,贴靠 (*up to*; *against*)。**4.** 半隐半现地处于。*The town* ~*s among the hills*. 这个城市座落在群山之中。*The child* ~*d against* [*up to*] *his mother*. 孩子紧紧贴着妈妈。—***vt*.** **1.** 抱;使(头、脸、肩膀等)紧贴。**2.** 使安顿。~ *a baby in one's arms* 怀抱着孩子。

nest·ling [ˈnes*t*liŋ; ˋneslɪŋ] ***n*.** 刚孵出的雏,还不能离窝的雏;婴孩。

Nes·tor [ˈnestɔː, -tə; ˋnɛstɚ, -tə] ***n*.** **1.**【希神】内斯特〔特洛伊战争中希腊的贤明长老〕。**2.** 〔常作 n-〕贤明的老人;长老;耆宿 (*of*)。

Nes·to·ri·an [nesˈtɔːriən; nɛsˋtorɪən] **I** ***a*.** (五世纪君士坦丁大主教 Nestorius 创立的)聂斯托里教派的,景教的。**II** ***n*.** 景教徒。**-ism** ***n*.** 聂斯托里的宗教主张;景教。

Net [net; nɛt] ***n*.** 因特网。***supply*** ~ ***services*** 提供因特网服务。~**cast 1.** ***n*.**【计】网络播放;网络广播。**2.** ***vt*.** 网络播出。~**head** 网民,网虫,网络迷。

net[1] [net; nɛt] **I** ***n*. 1.** 网,网眼织物,(花边的)织物。**2.** 网状物,网状组织,网状系统,通信网。**3.** (乒乓、网球的)球网;落网球。**4.** 罗网,陷阱。**5.** (蜘)蛛网。*a fish* ~ 鱼网。*a mosquito-* ~ 蚊帐。*a* ~ *artist* 〔美〕网球选手。***be caught in a*** ~ 陷入罗网,上了圈套。***cast*** [***throw***] ***a*** ~ 撒网。***draw in a*** ~ 拉网。***spread one's*** ~ ***for*** (*sb*.) 给某人布置好圈套,设法叫某人上钩。***sweep everything into one's*** ~ 把可以到手的一切都攫为己有,一切尽归私囊。**II** ***vt*.** (**-*tt*-**) **1.** 用网捕,撒(网),张(网),用网覆;用网制作;用…编成网状物。**2.** 把…诱入圈套[罗网]。**3.** 〔美俚〕(努力、设法)得到(结果),捞得。**5.** 打(球)落网,触网。—***vi*.** 编网;编结网状物;〔诗〕成网状。~ *strawberries* 用网覆盖草莓。~ *a river* 在河上撒网。~ *a handsome profit* 捞到一大笔利润。*netted sunbeam* 映在水底上的网形日光。~ **ball** 少女玩的一种篮球;【乒乓球、网球】触网球。~ **surf**【计】网上冲波,网上漫游。~**-winged** ***a*.** (昆虫)有翅网脉的。~**writer** 发送电子邮件的人。

net[2] [net; nɛt] **I** ***a*.** 净的,纯的 (*opp*. gross); 无虚价的;基本的;最后的。*a* ~ *interest* 纯利,净赚。*a* ~ *loss* 纯损,净亏。*a* ~ *profit* [*gain*] 纯利润。*a* ~ *price* 实价。*at 5 dollars* ~ 实价 5 美元。~ *ton* 净吨,美吨 (2000 磅)〔英吨叫 gross ton (2240 磅)〕。~ *weight* 净重。*the* ~ *result* 最后结果。**II** ***n*.** 纯利;净值;实价;纯量,净数,净重。**III** ***vt*.** (**-*tt*-**) 得到;使得到;净得;净赚。~ *$10000 a year* 每年净赚一万元。~**-**~ ***a*., *n*.** 最后的(定论);最权威的(结论)。

neth·er [ˈneðə; ˋnɛðɚ] ***a*.** 〔古、诗〕下面的。*a* ~ *lip* 下唇。*the* ~ *millstone* 磨石的下一扇。*the* ~ *regions* 冥府,地狱,阴间;〔罕〕下界,人世间。*the* ~ *man* 〔谑〕腿。~ *garments* 〔谑〕裤子。*the N- House* 下院,众议院。***as hard as the*** ~ ***millstone*** 冷酷的;铁石心肠。~ **world** 阴间;来世;下层社会。

Neth·er·land·er [ˈneðələndə; ˋnɛðɚləndɚ] ***n*.** 荷兰人。

Neth·er·land·ish [ˈneðələndiʃ; ˋnɛðɚˏlændɪʃ] **I** ***a*.** 荷兰的;荷兰人的;荷兰语的。**II** ***n*.** 荷兰语。

Neth·er·lands [ˈneðələndz; ˋnɛðɚləndz] ***n*.** 〔*pl*.〕〔the ~〕〔*sing*., *pl*.〕荷兰〔欧洲〕(= Holland)。

neth·er·most [ˈneðəməust, -məst; ˋnɛðɚˏmost, -məst] ***a*.** 最下面的,最低的。

neth·er·ward, neth·er·wards [ˈneðəwəd, -dz; ˋnɛðɚˏwɚd, -dz] ***ad*.** 向下,向下方。

Net·i·zen [ˈnetizən; ˋnɛtɪzən] ***n*.**【计】网民〔亦作 netizen〕。

net·man [ˈnetmən; ˋnɛtmæn] ***n*.** 〔美〕网球选手。

NETR = Nuclear Engineering Test Reactor 核子工程试验反应器。

nets·man [ˈnetsmən; ˋnɛtsmən] ***n*.** 用网(捕鱼等)的人。

nett [net; nɛt] ***a*.** = net[2].

net·ted [ˈnetid; ˋnɛtɪd] ***a*.** 用网捕的,用网包的,网状的。

net·ter [ˈnetə; ˋnɛtɚ] ***n*.** 〔Am.〕= netman.

Net·tie [ˈneti; ˋnɛtɪ] ***n*.** 内蒂〔女子名,Janet 的昵称〕。

net·ting [ˈnetiŋ; ˋnɛtɪŋ] ***n*.** 网;网状(织)物;网细工;结网;撒网,网鱼;(金属)丝布。*a* ~ *needle* 结网针。*mosquito* ~ 蚊帐纱。*wire* ~ 金属网;铁纱。~ **knot** (= sheet bend) 单索花结〔绳结的一种〕。

net·tle [ˈnetl; ˋnɛtl] **I** ***n*.** 荨麻;〔喻〕使人烦恼的事,苦恼。**II** ***vt*.** 拿荨麻打,拿荨麻刺;激,惹,激怒。***grasp the*** ~ 向困难搏斗,大胆抓起棘手问题。~**-creeper** 白喉蜂雀。~**-grasper** 敢于向困难搏斗的人。~ **rash**【医】荨麻疹,风疹块。**-some** [-səm; -səm] ***a*.** 恼火的。

net·ty [ˈneti, ˋnɛtɪ] ***a*.** 网状的,网细工的。

net·work [ˈnetwəːk; ˋnɛtˏwɝk] ***n*. 1.** 网眼织物。**2.** (铁路、河道等的)网状系统,网状组织,广播网,电视网,广播[电视]联播公司。**3.**【无】网路,电路。**4.**【计】电脑网络,网。*a* ~ *of railways* 铁路网。*a* ~ *of falsehoods* 一大套谎话,谎话连篇。~ **analysis** (用数学或统计学进行的)网络分析。

net·working [ˈnetˌwəːkiŋ; ˋnɛtˏwɝkɪŋ] ***n*. 1.** 网络化。**2.**【计】电脑网络,网络系统;建网,联网。

neuk [njuːk; njuk] ***n*.** 〔Scot.〕凹角处,隐避处;角落。

neum(e) [njuːm, nuːm; njum, num] ***n*.** 中世纪教堂音乐的一种乐谱符号。**neu·mat·ic** [-ˈmætik; -ˋmætɪk] ***a*.**

neur- *comb*. *f*. 〔用于母音前〕= neuro-.

neu·ral [ˈnjuərəl; ˋnjʊrəl] ***a*.**【解】神经(系统)的;神经中枢的;【解】背的,背侧的。~ **arch**【动】髓弓。~ **canal**【解】神经沟。~ **network** [**net**]【计】模拟脑神经元网络〔一种模拟人脑神经细胞的电脑系统〕。~ **tube**【解】神经管。**-ly** ***ad*.**

neu·ral·gia [njuəˈrældʒə; njʊˋrældʒə] ***n*.**【医】神经痛。**-ral·gic** [-dʒik; -dʒɪk] ***a*.**

neu·ras·the·ni·a [ˌnjuərəsˈθiːniə, -njə; ˏnjʊrəsˋθinɪə, -njə] ***n*.**【医】神经衰弱。**-then·ic** [-ˈθenik; -ˋθɛnɪk] ***a*., *n*.** 神经衰弱的(人)。

neu·ra·tion [njuəˈreiʃən; nʊˋreʃən] ***n*.** = nervation.

neu·rec·to·my [njuəˈrektəmi; nʊˋrɛktəmɪ] ***n*.**【医】神经切除(术)。

neu·ri·lem·ma [ˌnjuəriˈlemə, nuə-; ˏnjʊrəˋlɛmə, nʊ-] ***n*.**【解】神经膜,神经鞘。

neu·rine [ˈnjuəriːn, ˈnuər-; ˋnjʊrin, ˋnʊr-] ***n*.** 神经碱。

neu·ri·tis [njuəˈraitis; njʊˋraɪtɪs] ***n*.**【医】神经炎。**-rit·ic** [-ˈritik; -ˋrɪtɪk] ***a*.**

neuro- *comb*. *f*. 〔用于辅音前〕表示"神经": *neuro*fibril.

neu·ro·act·ive [ˌnjuərəuˈæktiv; ˏnjʊrəˋæktɪv] ***a*.** 刺激神经的。

neu·ro·bi·ol·o·gy [ˌnjuərəubaiˈɔlədʒi; ˏnjʊrobaɪˋɑlədʒɪ] ***n*.** 神经生物学。

neu·ro·blast [ˈnjuərəublæst; ˋnʊrəblæst] ***n*.** 成神经细胞,神经母细胞。

neu·ro·coel, neu·ro·coele [ˈnjuərəsiːl; ˋnʊrəˏsil] ***n*.**【解】神经管腔。

neu·ro·com·pu·t·er [ˈnjuərəukəmˈpjuːtə; ˏnjʊrəkəmˋpjutəɚ] ***n*.**【计】神经(式)电脑〔模拟神经细胞和神经网络的电脑〕。

neu·ro·ep·i·the·li·um [ˌnjuərəuepiˈθiːliəm; ˏnjʊrəɛpɪˋθɪlɪəm] ***n*.**【动】神经上皮。**-the·li·al** [-liəl; -lɪəl] ***a*.**

neu·ro·fi·bril [ˌnjuərəuˈfaibril; ˏnʊrəˋfaɪbrɪl] ***n*.** 神经原纤维。**-lar·y** [-əri; -ərɪ] ***a*.**

neu·ro·gen·e·tics [ˌnjuərəudʒəˈnetiks; ˏnjʊrədʒəˋnɛtɪks] ***n*.**【医】神经遗传学。

neu·ro·gen·ic [ˌnjuərəuˈdʒenik; ˏnjʊrəˋdʒɛnɪk] ***a*. 1.** 起原于神经组织的。**2.** 神经原的,神经性的。**3.** 受神经冲动控制的。**-al·ly** ***ad*.**

neu·rog·li·a [njuˈrɔgliə, nu-; njʊˋrɑglɪə, nʊ-] ***n*.** 神经胶(质)。**-li·al** ***a*.**

neu·ro·hor·mone [njuərəuˈhɔːməun; njʊrəˋhɔmon] ***n*.**【医】神经激素。

neu·ro·hu·mo(u)r [ˌnjuərəuˈhjuːmə; ˏnjʊrəˋhjumɚ] ***n*.** 神经液。

neu·ro·lin·guis·tics [ˌnjuərəulinˈgwistiks; ˏnjʊrəlɪnˋgwɪstɪks] ***n*.**【语】神经语言学〔研究神经系统和语言之间关系的科学〕。

neu·ro·log·i·cal [ˌnjuərəuˈlɔdʒikəl; ˏnjʊrəˋlɑdʒɪkəl] ***a*.** 神经病学的。

neu·rol·o·gist [njuəˈrɔlədʒist; njʊˋrɑlədʒɪst] ***n*.** 神经病学家;神经病专科医生。

neu·rol·o·gy [njuəˈrɔlədʒi; njʊˋrɑlədʒɪ] ***n*.** 神经病学。

N

neu·ro·ma [nju'rəumə, nu-; njʊ`romə, nʊ-] *n*. (*pl*. *~s*, *-ma·ta* [-mətə;-mətə])【医】神经瘤。

neu·ro·mo·tor [ˌnjuərəu'məutə;ˏnjʊrə`motɚ] *a*. 传出神经兴奋的。

neu·ro·mus·cu·lar [ˌnjuərəu'mʌskjulə, nuər-; ˏnjʊro`mʌskjʊlɚ, nʊr-] *a*. 神经肌肉的。

neu·ron(e) ['njuərɔn; `njʊrɑn] *n*.【解】神经原,神经细胞。**neu·ron·ic** *a*.

neu·ro·path ['njuərəpæθ; `njʊrəˏpæθ] *n*.【医】神经病患者;神经质者。**-ic** *a*., *n*.

neu·rop·a·thist [njuə'rɔpəθist; njʊ`rɑpəθɪst] *n*. 神经病学家[专家、医生]。

neu·ro·pa·thol·o·gy [ˌnjuərəupə'θɔlədʒi, ˏnuər-; ˏnjʊropə`θɑlədʒɪ, ˏnʊr-] *n*. 神经病理学。**-thol·o·gist** *n*.

neu·rop·a·thy [njuə'rɔpəθi; njʊ`rɑpəθɪ] *n*. 神经(系)病。

neu·ro·phys·i·ol·o·gy [ˌnjuərəuˌfizi'ɔlədʒi; ˏnjʊroˏfɪzɪ`ɑlədʒɪ] *n*. 神经(系统)生理学。

neu·ro·psy·chi·a·try [ˌnjuərəusi'kaiətri; ˏnjʊrosɪ`kaɪətrɪ] *n*. 神经精神病学。**-at·ric** [-'ætrik;-`ætrɪk] *a*.

neu·ro-psy·chic [ˌnjuərəu'saikik; ˏnjʊrə`saɪkɪk] *a*.【医】神经与精神的。

neu·rop·ter·an [nju'rɔptərən, nuə-; njʊ`rɑptərən, nʊ-] *n*. 脉翅目昆虫〔包括蝼子,蚁狮〕。**-ter·ous** [-tərəs; -tərəs] *a*.

neu·rop·ter·ous [nju'rɔptərəs; njʊ`rɑptərəs] *a*.【虫】脉翅类的。

neu·ro·sis [njuə'rəusis; njʊ`rosɪs] *n*. (*pl*. *-ses* [-siːz; -siz])【医】神经(机能)病;精神神经病;【心】神经感动。

neu·ro·sur·ger·y [ˌnjuərəu'səːdʒəri, nuə-; ˏnjʊro`sɝdʒərɪ, nʊ-] *n*. 神经外科学。

neu·rot·ic [njuə'rɔtik; njʊ`rɑtɪk] I *a*. 神经的;神经(机能)病的;神经质的;神经过敏的。II *n*. 1. 神经病人;神经过敏者。2. 神经刺激剂。

neu·rot·o·my [nju'rɔtəmi; njʊ`rɑtəmɪ] *n*. (*pl*. *-mies*) 神经切断术;神经解剖学。

neu·ro·tox·ic [ˌnjuərəu'tɔksik, nuə-; ˏnjʊro`tɑksɪk, nʊ-] *a*. 毒害神经的。

neu·ro·tox·in [ˌnjuərəu'tɔksin, nuə-; ˏnjʊrə`tɑksɪn, nʊ-] *n*. 神经毒素。

neu·ro·trop·ic [ˌnjuərəu'trɔpik, ˌnuə-; ˏnjʊrə`trɑpɪk, ˏnʊ-] *a*. 嗜神经组织的,亲神经的,趋神经系的。

neus·ton ['njuːstɔn, 'nuː-; `njustɔn, `nu-] *n*.【动】漂浮生物。**neus·tic** *a*.

neut. = 1. neuter. 2. neutral.

neut [njuːt; njut] *n*.〔美口〕中子弹。

neu·ter ['njuːtə; `njutɚ] I *a*. 1.【语】(名词等)中性[无性]的;(动词)不及物的。2.【植、物】中性的,无性的。3.〔罕〕中立的。*the ~ gender* 中性。*a ~ noun* 中性名词。*Worker bees are ~*. 工蜂是中性蜂。*stand ~* 中立。II *n*. 1.【语】中性;中性词[名词、形容词、代名词];中性形式;不及物词。2. 无性生物[动物、植物];工蜂;去势动物。3. 中立者。~**cane**【气】中性热带气旋。

neu·tral ['njuːtrəl; `njutrəl] I *a*. 1. 中立的;中立国的。2. 不偏不倚,公平的;中庸的;中间的;不伦不类的,不明确的;不鲜艳的,暗淡的;非彩色的[指灰、黑或白色的]。3.【机】空档的;【化、电】中性的;中和的;不带电的;【植、动】无性的,无雌雄之别的。4.【语】(母音)松弛的,中性的。*a ~ state* [*zone*] 中立国[地带]。*a ~ sort of person* 无显著特征的人,平常的人。~ *equilibrium* 随遇平衡。*a ~ colour* 无彩色。*a ~ tint* 不鲜明的色彩[如灰色、青灰色]。II *n*. 1. 中立者;中立国(国民)。2.【机】(汽车等的传动装置)空档。3. 非彩色。~ **vowel**【语】中性母音[不重读的母音,如 about 中的 ə]。**-ly** *ad*.

neu·tral·ism ['njuːtrəlizəm; `njutrəlɪzm̩] *n*. 中立主义。

neu·tral·ist ['njuːtrəlist; `njutrəlɪst] *a*., *n*. 中立主义(的);中立主义者。**-ic** [-'listik; -`lɪstɪk] *a*.

neu·tral·i·ty [njuː'træliti; nju`trælətɪ] *n*. 1. 中立;中立地位;不偏不倚。2.【化】中性;中和。*armed ~* 武装中立。

neu·tral·ize ['njuːtrəlaiz; `njutrəlˏaɪz] *vt*. 1. 使中立化。2.【化、电】使中和;【物】平衡。3. 使失效,抵销;【军】压制(火力)。~ *a place* 以某地为中立地。*a ~d state* 永久中立国。**-za·tion** [ˌnjuːtrəlai'zeiʃən; ˏnjutrələ`zeʃən] *n*. 中立化,中立状态;中和;失效;平衡。**-iz·er** *n*.【化】中和剂;【电】中和器。

neu·tret·to [njuː'tretəu; nju`treto] *n*.【物】中介子。

neu·tri·no [njuː'triːnəu; nju`trino] *n*.【物】中微子。

neutro- *comb. f*. 表示"中性","中和": *neutro*sphere.

neu·tro·don ['njuːtrəudən; `njutrodən] *n*. 中和电容器。

neu·tro·dyne ['njuːtrəudain; `njutrodaɪn] I *n*.【无】中和式高频调谐放大器;衡消接收法;中和接收法。II *a*.【无】(接收机)衡消式的。*a ~ receiver* 衡消接收机。

neu·tron ['njuːtrɔn; `njutrɑn] *n*.【物】中子。~ **bomb** 中子弹。~ **number**【原子】(核内)中子数。~ **star**【天】中子星。**-ics** *n*. 中子(物理)学。

neu·tro·pe·nia [ˌnjuːtrəu'piːniə; njutro`pinɪə] *n*.【医】嗜中性白血球减少症。

neu·tro·phil, neu·tro·phile ['njuːtrəufil, -fail; `njutrəfɪl, -faɪl] I *n*.【医】嗜中性。II *a*. 嗜中性的。

neu·tro·sphere ['njuːtrəusfiə; `njutrəˏsfɪr] *n*.【天】中性圈。

Nev. = Nevada.

Ne·va ['neivə; `nevə] *n*. 内瓦〔女子名〕。

Ne·vad·a [ne'vɑːdə; nə`vædə] *n*. 内华达〔美国州名〕。**-dan** [-dən; -dən] *a*., *n*. 内华达的(人)。

né·vé ['neivei; `neve] *n*.〔F.〕(冰河上层的)碎粒冰雪,粒雪;冰原;(由碎粒冰雪形成的)万年雪。~ **line** 雪线。

nev·er ['nevə; `nɛvɚ] *ad*. 1.〔ever 的否定形式;加强否定语气;用于句首时,主谓语次序倒装〕决不,永不;从来没有,一点也不。2.〔口〕〔表示怀疑或惊异〕不会…吧;不,没有;不要。*I ~ met him before*. 从来没见过他。*He is ~ at home on Sunday*. 星期日他从不在家。*He has ~ been heard of since*. 此后再也没有听到一点儿他的消息。*N- did he break his promise*. 他从不爽约。*N- fear*! 不要怕。*N- mind*! 不必介意! 不要紧! *Better late than ~*. 晚做总比不做好。*Now or ~*. 时不可失,机不再来。*Well, I ~ ! = I ~ did!* 真想不到,真是没有见过[听说过]。*You have ~ lost the key*! 不会是丢了钥匙吧! *N- tell me*! 别跟我开玩笑啰! *He ~ so much as spoke*. 他连话都没有讲。***go to the land of ~-~*** 〔卑〕失去意识,昏过去。~ ***a*** 一个也没有。~ ***a one*** 没有一个(人)。***N- N-*** (***land*** [***country***]) 澳大利亚昆士兰州的北部,人迹稀少的地方。~ ***so***〔古〕非常;空前地;〔在条件句中〕即使。~ ***the*** 一点也不〔和比较级连用〕(*I am ~ the wiser for it*. 这样我还是一点也不懂)。~ ... ***without*** 干什么总是…(*He ~ moved a thing without replacing it exactly*. 他挪动过的东西总是要放还原地的)。~**-ending** *a*. 不断的,永不完结的,没底的。~**-failing** *a*. 不绝的,不尽的;永远不变的;永不辜负期望的。~**-get-overs** 不治之症。~**-was** *n*. (*pl*. *~-weres*)〔美俚〕从未取得成功的人。~**-waser** *n*.〔美俚〕= ~-was.

nev·er·more ['nevə'mɔː;ˏnɛvɚ`mor] *ad*. 决不再,永不再。

nev·er-nev·er ['nevə'nevə; `nɛvɚ`nɛvɚ] I *n*. 1. 边远地区,不毛之地。2. 理想的地方 (= the ~ land)。3.〔英俚〕分期付款制。II *a*. 幻想的,理想的,想入非非的。*the ~ land* 幻想中的地方。

nev·er·the·less [ˌnevəðə'les; ˏnɛvɚðə`lɛs] I *ad*. 仍然(还),不过。*I shall certainly say nothing, but it will* *come to his ears* ～. 我一定不说什么话,可是这还会传进他的耳朵里的。**II** *conj*. (尽管如此)还是,然而。*There was no news*, ～, *she went on hoping*. 尽管杳无音讯,然而她还是盼望着。

Nev·ill(e) [ˈnevil; ˋnɛvl] *n*. 内维尔〔姓氏,男子名〕。

Ne·vin [ˈnevin; ˋnɛvɪn] *n*. 内文〔姓氏,男子名〕。

Ne·vins [ˈnevinz; ˋnɛvɪnz] *n*. 内文斯〔姓氏〕。

ne·vus [ˈniːvəs; ˋnivəs] *n*. (*pl*. *ne·vi* [-vai; -vaɪ]) 痣。**ne·void** [-vɔid; -vɔɪd] *a*.

NEW = net economic welfare 〔美〕纯经济福利。

new [njuː; nju] **I** *a*. **1**. 新的,崭新的;新发现的,新发明的;新开发的。**2**. 初次(听到)的;新奇的。**3**. 新鲜的;新造的;新到的;新就任的。**4**. 改新了的,改变了的;健康恢复了的;重新开始的。**5**. 〔the ～〕〔常蔑〕现代的,新式的,摩登的。**6**. 生的,不习惯的,未熟悉的。**7**. 另加的,附加的。*a* ～ *invention* 新发明。*a* ～ *moon* 新月。*the N- Style* 新历。*the N- World* 新世界,美洲大陆。～ *milk* 新鲜牛奶。*the* ～ *rich* 暴发户。*I am* ～ *to the work*. = *The work is new to me*. 这个工作我还没有经验。*That information is* ～ *to me*. 那消息我还是初次听到。*The horse is* ～ *to harness*. 那匹马还没有养乖。***make a*** ～ ***man of*** 使…改过自新;使…恢复健康。***N-China News Agency*** 新华通讯社〔略 NCNA〕。***N-Learning*** 16 世纪文艺复兴时输入英国的希腊文艺研究。***the N- Deal*** **1**. (美国 1933 年实施的)新政。**2**. 〔口〕新的领导,新的开始,新的管理。***the*** ～ ***look*** (头发,衣服等的)新式样;〔口〕新式服装。***turn over a*** ～ ***leaf*** 革面洗心。**II** *ad*. = newly 〔主要与过去分词构成复合词〕。**III** *n*. 〔the ～〕新的东西。**New Age** *n*., *a*. 新时代(的),新潮(的)。～ **blood** 新血液〔指具有新思想又朝气蓬勃的人〕。～**-blown** *a*. (花)刚开的。～**born** *a*. 新生的,初生的,再生的,复活的。～**-build** *vt*. = rebuild. ～ **candle** 【光】烛光。～**-coined** *a*. (名词等)新造的。～ **collar** 〔美〕"新领"工人,新领阶层〔指年薪在 2–4 万美元的非白领工人〕。～**-come** *a*., *n*. 新来的(人),新到的(人)。～**-comer** 新来的人;不认识的人,陌生人。**N-Criticism** 文学新批评〔二十世纪流行的文艺分析方法,着重研究作品的语言、文学手法和结构等〕。**N- England aster** 美国紫菀(红花紫菀)〔产于北美洲东部〕。**N- England boiled dinner** 新英格兰杂烩菜〔由猪肉、腌牛肉、洋芋、洋葱、胡萝卜、白菜等烩成〕。**N- English** 新英语〔指 1750 年至今的英语〕。**N- English Bible** 圣经英国新译本〔指 1970 年出版的圣经。《新约》部分已于 1961 年出版〕。～ **fangled** *a*. 新花样的,新奇的;爱好新奇的。～**-fashioned** *a*. 新式的,新流行的。～**found** *a*. 新发现的。～**-laid** *a*. (蛋)才生的。**N- Latin** 新拉丁语〔1500 年以后的拉丁语〕。～**-made** *a*. 才做好的,重新做的。～**-married** *a*. 新婚的。～ **math** 【数】集论教学体系,基础数学集论教学法。～**-model** *vt*. 改造,改编,改组(军队、政府等)。～**-mown** *a*. 新割的。**N- Testament** (基督教《圣经》的)《新约全书》。**N- Thought** 新信念〔西方十九世纪的一种宗教信念,强调精神对健康和幸福的作用〕。～ **town** 新市镇,卫星城。**N- Wave** 新潮摇滚乐〔多为合奏合唱,歌词内容多为发泄对社会的不满〕。**-ness** *n*. 新,新奇;未熟,不惯。

New·bolt [ˈnjuːbəult; ˋnjubolt] *n*. 纽博尔特〔姓氏〕。

New·burg [ˈnjuːbəg; ˋnjubəg] *n*. 纽堡酱〔用奶油、蛋黄和酒的浓酱汁调味做的海味〕。

New Cal·e·do·ni·a [ˈnjuːˌkæliˈdəunjə; ˋnjuˏkæləˋdonjə] 新喀里多尼亚(岛)〔南太平洋〕。

New·cas·tle [ˈnjuːˌkɑːsl; ˋnjuˏkæsl] *n*. **1**. 纽卡斯尔〔澳大利亚港市〕。**2**. 纽卡斯尔〔英国港市〕。

New Delhi [njuː ˈdeli; nju ˋdɛlɪ] 新德里〔印度首都〕。

new·el [ˈnjuːəl; ˋnjuəl] *n*. **1**. 【建】(螺旋梯的)中心柱。**2**. (楼梯两端支持扶手的)望柱,起柱。

New·ell [ˈnjuːəl; ˋnjuəl] *n*. 纽厄尔〔姓氏,男子名〕。

New Eng·land [ˈnjuːˈiŋglənd; ˋnjuˋɪŋglənd] 新英格兰〔美国东北六州 *Maine*, *New Hampshire*, *Vermont*, *Massachusetts*, *Connecticut* 和 *Rhode Island* 的总称〕。

New Eng·land·er [ˈnjuːˈiŋgləndə; ˋnju ˋɪŋgləndɚ] *n*. 新英格兰人。

Newf. = Newfoundland.

New·found·land *n*. **1**. [ˌnjuːfəndˈlænd; ˏnjufəndˋlænd] 纽芬兰(岛)〔加拿大东部〕。**2**. 纽芬兰犬。

New·found·land·er [ˌnjuːˈfaundləndə; ˏnjuˋfaʊndləndɚ] *n*. 纽芬兰人。

New·fy [ˈnjuːfi; ˋnjufɪ] *n*. 〔美水手语〕纽芬兰人。

New·gate [ˈnjuːgit; ˋnjugɪt] *n*. (伦敦旧城的)新兴门监狱〔1902 年废〕。～ **frill** [**fringe**] 只留在下巴上的胡子。～ **knocker** 果菜贩从太阳穴到耳边的 6 字形毛丛。～ **saint** 死刑犯。

New Guinea [njuːˈgini; njuˋgɪnɪ] 新几内亚(岛)〔西太平洋〕。

New Hampshire [njuːˈhæmpʃiə; nju(ʊ)ˋhæmpʃɪɚ] 新罕布什尔〔美国州名〕。

New Hebrides [njuːˈhebridiːz; nju ˋhɛbrəˏdiz] 新赫布里底(群岛)〔南太平洋〕。

new·ie [ˈnjuːiː; ˋnjui] *n*. 〔美俚〕新奇的东西,新鲜东西。

new·ish [ˈnjuːiʃ; ˋnjuɪʃ] *a*. 有些新的,相当新的。

New Jersey [njuːˈdʒəːzi; nju ˋdʒɝzɪ] 新泽西〔美国州名〕。

new·ly [ˈnjuːli; ˋnjulɪ] *ad*. **1**. 〔表示时间〕新近,最近。**2**. 〔表示频率〕重新,又,再度。**3**. 〔表示方式、状态〕以新的方式。*a* ～ *wedded couple* 新婚夫妇。*a* ～ *built house* 新建住宅。*a* ～ *developed surburb* 新郊区。*a* ～ *repeated slander* 旧调重弹的诽谤。*a room* ～ *decorated* 重新装璜的房间。～ **wed** 新结婚的人。

New·man(n) [ˈnjuːmən; ˋnjumən] *n*. 纽曼〔姓氏〕。

new·mar·ket [ˈnjuːmɑːkit; ˋnjuˏmɑrkɪt] *n*. **1**. 紧身长外套。**2**. 【牌】赶新市〔一种玩法简单的纸牌戏〕。

New Mexico [njuː ˈmeksikəu; nju ˋmɛksɪko] 新墨西哥〔美国州名〕。

New Or·le·ans [njuː ˈɔːliənz; nju ˋɔrlɪənz] 新奥尔良〔美国港市〕。

news [njuːz; njuz] *n*. 〔通例作单数用〕**1**. 新闻,(新)消息;新闻报导。**2**. 新事件,奇事,奇闻。**3**. 音信。**4**. 〔N-〕〔报纸名〕…新闻报。*foreign* [*home*] ～ 国外[国内]新闻。*Is there any* ～? = *What is the* ～? 有什么新闻? *good* [*bad*] ～ 吉[凶]报。*bad* ～ 〔美俚〕账单。～ *from London* 伦敦通信。*Good* ～ *goes on crutches*. 好事不出门。*Ill* ～ *flies apace*. = *Bad* ～ *travels quickly*. 恶事传千里。*That is no* ～. 那种事并不新奇。*What you say is* ～ *to me*. 你讲的我还头一次听见。*New York N-*《纽约新闻报》。***break the*** ～ ***to*** (*sb*.) (向某人)委婉传达不幸的消息。～ **agency** 通讯社。～ **agent** 报刊经销人。～ **analyst** 新闻分析[评论]员。～ **beat** 新闻记者采访区。～**boy** 报童,送报人。～ **break** *n*. 有新闻价值的事件。～ **cameraman** 〔美〕新闻摄影记者。～**cast** 〔美〕新闻广播。～**caster** 〔美〕新闻广播员。～**casting** 〔美〕新闻广播。～ **conference** 记者招待会 (= press conference)。～ **dealer** 〔美〕= newsagent. ～**-editor** (报刊的)社会新闻编辑。～ **film** 【影】新闻片。～**-flash** 简明新闻。～**gatherer**, ～**hawk**, ～**-hound** 〔美俚〕新闻记者。～**hen** 〔美俚〕女新闻记者。～ **hole** 〔美〕新闻窗口,非广告窗口〔指报刊上仅用于刊登新闻或特写的篇幅〕。～**letter** 时事通讯;新闻信札;业务通讯。～**magazine** (电视)新闻杂志。～**maker** 〔美〕新闻人物;有新闻价值的人物[事件]。～**monger** 爱传播新闻的人;爱聊天的人。～**organ** 〔美〕报纸,新闻杂志;新闻喉舌。～ **picture** = newsfilm. ～**-print** (印报刊用的)新闻纸,白报纸。～**reel** = ～ film. ～**reeler**, ～**reelist** 新闻片摄制人。～**person** 新闻记者,新闻播音员。～**room** 〔英〕阅报室;〔美〕(报馆、广播台、电视台的)编辑部。～ **sheet** **1**. 单张报纸。**2**. = newsletter. ～**stand** 〔美〕报亭,报摊。

N

~**vendor** 报纸经销人。~**worthy** ***a***. 有新闻价值的。~-**writer** 新闻记者。-**less** ***a***. 没有新闻的。~**man** **1.** = newsboy. **2.** 新闻记者。~ **woman** 女新闻记者。

news·i·ness [ˈnjuːzinis; ˋnjuzɪnɪs] ***n***. 新闻多;饶舌。

news·paper [ˈnjuːspeipə, Am. ˈnjuːz-; ˋnjuzˏpepɚ, ˋnu-, ˋnjus-] **I** ***n***. **1.** 报,报纸。**2.** 新闻纸,白报纸。*a daily* [*weekly*] ~ 日[周]报。*a* ~ *man* 新闻记者;新闻从业员。*a* ~ *office* 报社。*the* ~ *world* 报界,新闻界。**II** ***vi***. 从事新闻工作。~-**man** 新闻记者,新闻事业经营者。~-**woman** 女新闻记者。-**dom** ***n***. 报界。

news·paper·y [ˈnjuːspeipəri; ˋnjuspepərɪ] ***a***. 报纸式的,浅薄的。

new·speak [ˈnjuːˌspiːk; ˋnjuˏspik] ***n***. (官僚政客等惯常使用的)模棱两可的官腔〔源自 G. Orwell 的一部小说〕。

news·y [ˈnjuːzi; ˋnjuzɪ] **I** ***a***. (***news·i·er***; ***-i·est***)〔口〕新闻多的,奇闻多的,爱说话的,嘴碎的。**II** ***n***.〔Am.〕= newsboy.

newt [njuːt; njut] ***n***.【动】蝾螈。

New·ton [ˈnjuːtn; ˋnjutn̩] ***n***. **1.** 牛顿〔姓氏,男子名〕。**2.** **Sir Isaac** ~ 牛顿〔1642—1727,英国科学家〕。**3.**〔n-〕【物】牛顿〔M.K.S. 制的力的单位〕;【化】牛顿〔黏度单位〕。

New·to·ni·an [njuːˈtəunjən, -niən; njuˋtonjən, -nɪən] **I** ***a***. 牛顿(学说)的。**II** ***n***. **1.** 信奉牛顿学说的人。**2.** 牛顿式望远镜。

new year [ˈnjuːˈjəː; ˋnjuˋɪr] **1.** 新年。**2.** [N- Y-] =〔美〕New Year 正月(初旬);元旦。(*I wish you*) *a happy New Year!* 恭贺新禧。*New Year's Day* 元旦。*New Year's Eve* 除夕。*New Year's gifts* 新年礼物。*New Year's greetings* [*wishes*] 新年的祝贺,贺年。

New York [ˈnjuːˈjɔːk; njuˋjɔrk] **1.** 纽约〔美国州名〕。**2.** 纽约(市)〔美国城市〕(= New York City)。

New York·er [ˈnjuːˈjɔːkə; ˋnjuˋjɔrkɚ] ***n***. 纽约市[州]人。

New Zea·land [ˌnjuːˈziːlənd; ˏnjuˋzilənd] 新西兰(纽西兰)〔大洋洲〕。

New Zea·land·er [ˌnjuːˈziːləndə; ˏnjuˋziləndɚ] ***n***. 新西兰人。

next [nekst; nɛkst] **I** ***a***. **1.** 其次的;下次的,紧接着来到的。**2.** 隔壁的。**3.**〔the ~〕任何别的。~ *Friday* = *on Friday* ~ 在下一个星期五。*Not till* ~ *time*. 下次不再吃了〔无决心戒酒或戒烟时的笑谈〕。*What is the* ~ *article?* 还要什么呢?〔商人对顾客讲的话〕。*the person* ~ (*to*) *him in rank* [*age*] 地位[年龄]次于他的人。★按现在时所说的'来年'等不用 the, 按过去时所说的'翌年'等通常都要用 the, 但在故事中或当所说语义不致发生误会时,后者也常常不用 the: ~ *week* [*month*, *year*] 来周[月、年];*the* ~ *week* [*month*, *year*] 翌周[月、年]; *the* ~ *day* [*morning*] 翌日[晨]。***as ... as the*** ~ ***fellow*** 跟任何人一样…(*I am as brave as the* ~ *fellow*. 我跟任何人一样勇敢)。***get*** ~ ***to***〔美〕知道。***in the*** ~ ***place*** 其次。~ ***best*** 其次最好的,次好的。~ ***but one*** [***two***] 第二[第三]的。~ ***door*** 邻家,在隔壁;隔壁的(*He lives* ~ *door to me*. 他住在我的隔壁。~ *door but one* 隔壁第二家)。~ ***door to*** 在…隔壁;几乎等于(*He is* ~ *door to a madman*. 他简直是一个疯子)。~ ***friend***【法】(幼儿,无法定能力者的)诉讼代理人。~ ***man*** 别人,第三者。~ ***of kin***【法】最近亲。~ ***of skin***〔美〕亲戚。~ ***to impossible*** [***nothing***, ***none***] 几乎不可能[等于没有,很少]。**II** ***n***. 下一个人[东西]。*in my* ~ (*letter*) 在我下一封信中。*To be concluded in our* ~ (*issue*). 下期续完。*He is* ~ *of kin to me*. = *He is the* ~ *of my kin*. 他是我最近的亲戚。*N-, please!* 下一位!〔促人发问或进来时用〕。**III** ***ad***. 其次,然后;下次;贴近。*When I* ~ *saw him, he was lame*. 当我第二次见他的时候,他已经跛了。*the largest city* ~ *to London* 仅次于伦敦的大都市。*He placed his chair* ~ *to me*. 他把椅子搁在我椅子的旁边。***get*** [***put***] (*sb.*) ~ ***to***〔美〕给某人知道…,把…告诉某人。***What*** ~**!** **1.** 有比这更稀奇的(事)吗!? **2.** (店员用语)还要什么? **IV** ***prep***. 在…的隔壁,贴近…,在…之次,最近于…。*He sat* ~ *me*. 他紧挨着我坐下。*I always wear flannel* ~ *my skin*. 我常穿法兰绒做贴身衣。

nex·us [ˈneksəs; ˋnɛksəs] ***n***.〔*sing.*, *pl.*〕**1.** 连系,联络;关系;连结的一系列,一组。**2.**【语】动词谓语结构;叙述关系,核心〔丹麦语言学家奥托·叶斯帕森用语〕。*the cash* ~ 现金交易关系。

Nez Per·cé [ˈnezpəˈsei, -pəːs; ˋnɛzˋpɝs] 内珀西人〔北美印第安人的部族之一〕;内珀西语。

N.F. = **1.** Newfoundland. **2.** Norman French. **3.** National Formulary〔美〕国家处方集。

n / f = no funds. 存款不足。

N.F.S. = National Fire Service〔英〕全国救火会。

N.F.U., NFU = National Farmers' Union〔英〕全国农场主联合会。

NG = **1.** National Guard〔美〕国民警卫队。**2.** no good; not good 不行。**3.** New Granada〔旧〕新格拉那达〔指原西班牙殖民地,现为委内瑞拉、哥伦比亚、巴拿马和厄瓜多尔〕。

Ng. = Norwegian.

NGO = non-govern-mental organization 非政府组织。

NGr = New Greek 新希腊语。

ngwee [ŋˈgwi; ŋˋgwɪ] ***n***. (*pl.* ***ngwee***) 昂格维〔赞比亚货币单位,等于克瓦查的 1/100〕。

N.H., NH = New Hampshire 新罕布什尔〔美国州名〕。

NHA = National Housing Agency〔美旧〕国家住房管理署。

N.Heb. = New Hebrides.

N.H.I. = National Health Insurance〔英〕国民健康保险。

N.H.K., NHK =〔Jap.〕*Nippon Hoso Kyokai* (= Japan Broadcasting Corporation) 日本广播协会。

NHP, n.h.p. = nominal horsepower 额定马力,标称马力。

N.I. = Northern Ireland 北爱尔兰。

Ni【化】= nickel 镍。

ni·a·cin [ˈnaiəsin; ˋnaɪəsn̩] ***n***.【生化】烟酸,尼克酸,抗癞皮病维生素,烟碱酸(= nicotinic acid)。

Ni·ag·a·ra [naiˈægərə; naɪˋægərə] ***n***. **1.** 尼亚加拉河〔美国与加拿大交界处的一条大河〕。**2.** 尼亚加拉瀑布(= ~ Falls);瀑布;急流;大洪水。**3.**〔n-〕滔滔不绝的谈话。***shoot*** ~ 大冒险。~ **Falls**〔美〕尼亚加拉瀑布。

ni·ai·se·rie [niˈeizəri; ˏnjɛzˋri] ***n***.〔F.〕无知,单纯,愚笨。

N.I.A.L. = National Institute of Arts and Letters〔美〕全国文学和艺术学会。

Nia·mey [ˌnjɑːˈmei; ˏnjɑˋme] ***n***. 尼亚美〔尼日尔首都〕。

nib [nib; nɪb] **I** ***n***. **1.** 钢笔尖;鹅管笔的尖端;〔古〕(鸟)嘴。**2.** (工具的)尖头,尖端。**3.**〔*pl.*〕可可豆[咖啡]的碎粒。**4.** (镰刀的)短柄。**5.**〔俚〕要人,重要人物;成功的工作。**II** ***vt***. 在…装尖头;削尖(鹅管笔);给(笔)插笔尖。

nib·ble [ˈnibl; ˋnɪbl̩] **I** ***vt***. 一点点地咬下;一点点地咬[吃];啃。—***vi***. **1.** 啃,(鱼等)一点点地咬。**2.** (对诱惑、交易等)做出有意的样子(*at*)。**3.** 吹毛求疵,找碴儿(*at*)。*tactics of nibbling away* 蚕食政策。**II** ***n***. **1.** 一点一点的咬,(鱼)试咬,(兽)(咬)一口。**2.** 咬一口的量;很少量。**3.** 不愿意似的回答。**4.**【计】(电脑)半字节(= half a byte, 亦作 nybble, 等于 4 个比特)。*glorious day for a* ~ 钓鱼的好日子。

Ni·be·lung·en·lied [ˌniːbəˈluŋənliːt; ˋnibəˏluŋənˏlit] ***n***.〔the ~〕尼伯龙根之歌〔德国民间史诗〕。

nib·lick [ˈniblik; ˋnɪblɪk] ***n***. 铁头高尔夫球棒〔现在通称为 Iron No. 9〕。

nibs [nibz; nɪbz] ***n.*** 〔美口〕自以为了不起的要人;头目。*his* ~ 那位大人[先生]。*They were careful not to offend his* ~. 他们小心翼翼,不敢冒犯这位大人。

NIC = newly-industrializing country 新工业化国家〔指近二、三十年内由农业国发展为工业化程度较高的国家〕。

ni·cad [ˈnaikæd; ˋnaɪkæd] ***n.*** 镍镉(蓄)电池〔可充电,亦作~ battery〕。

NICAM, Nicam [ˈnaikæm; ˋnaɪkæm] = near instantaneous companded audio complex 纳坎系统〔一种播放录像和高保真立体声的电视数码系统〕。~ **decorder**【计】纳坎解码器。

Nic·a·ra·gua [ˌnikəˈrægjuə; ˏnɪkəˋrɑgwə] ***n.*** 尼加拉瓜〔拉丁美洲〕。**-guan** ***a.***, ***n.*** 尼加拉瓜的(人)。

nic·co·lite [ˈnikəlait; ˋnɪkəˏlaɪt] ***n.***【矿】红砷镍矿。

Nice [niːs; nis] ***n.*** 尼斯〔法国城市〕。

nice [nais; naɪs] ***a.*** **1.** 好的,不错的,美的,漂亮的;有趣的 (*opp.* nasty); 愉快的,吸引人的;亲切的,恳切的,厚道的;有教养的;高尚的。**2.** 爱讲究,爱挑剔的,挑三拣四的。**3.** 细致的,精密的;精确的,精巧的,严格的,认真的。**4.** 敏锐的,敏感的;微妙的。**5.** 要慎重的,难决的;要手腕的。**6.**〔反语〕困难的,讨厌的。*a* ~ *dish* 好吃的菜。*a* ~ *day* 好天气。*We had a* ~ *time yesterday*. 我们昨天玩得很愉快。*He is* ~ *in his dress*. 他很讲究服装。*a* ~ *distinction* 细微的区别。*a* ~ *ear for sound* 听觉敏锐的耳朵。*a* ~ *point* 微妙之点。*a* ~ *shade of meaning* 意义的细微区别。~ *taste in art* [*literature*] 敏锐的艺术[文学]眼光。*Be* ~ *to the guests*. 对客人要周到。*That isn't* ~. 那不礼貌。*You're a* ~ *fellow, I must say*.〔反〕你真是个好家伙[讨厌的家伙]。*Here is a* ~ *mess*. 这真糟。***in a* ~ *fix*** 进退两难,非常窘困。~ **and**〔同形容词连用〕很 (~ *and cool* 很凉快。*The place is* ~ *and healthy*. 那地方很适合健康)。~ **blackberry**〔美俚〕无聊朋友,讨厌的人。~ **girl**〔美〕好女孩,有礼貌的女孩,(有时指)不活泼的女孩,一本正经的女孩。~ **going**〔美俚〕好〔表示同意〕。~**-looking** ***a.*** 漂亮的;可爱的。~ **mats**〔美剧〕日场客满。~ **money**〔美俚〕相当多的款子。**-ness** ***n.***

nice nel·ly, nice nel·lie, nice Nel·ly, nice Nel·lie [ˈnais ˈneli; ˋnaɪs ˋnɛlɪ] ***n.*** **1.** 过分拘谨的人;装得一本正经的人。**2.** 委婉语。

nice-nel·ly, nice-nel·lie, nice-Nel·ly nice-Nel·lie [ˈnaisˈneli; ˋnaɪsˋnɛlɪ] ***a.*** **1.** 过分拘谨的;装得一本正经的。**2.** 委婉语的。

nice-nel·ly·ism [ˈnaisˈneliizəm; ˋnaɪsˋnɛlɪɪzəm] ***n.*** (妇女)装得一本正经;说话委婉。

nice·ly [ˈnaisli; ˋnaɪslɪ] **I** ***ad.*** **1.** 好好地,漂亮地,精密地;机敏地;愉快地,合适地;规规矩矩地。**2.** 非常讲究地。**3.**〔口〕恰恰,恰好。*She's doing* ~.〔口〕她很好;她(身体)渐渐好了。*It suits me* ~. 那正合我意。**II** ***a.***〔口〕健康的,强健的。

Nicene [naːˈsiːn; naɪˋsin] **Council**【宗】奈斯会议〔公元325年及787年于小亚细亚都会奈斯 (Nice) 开的两次基督教会议,尤指第一次会议,会上谴责阿里安教派,并通过了基督教标准信条〕。

ni·ce·ty [ˈnaisiti; ˋnaɪsətɪ] ***n.*** **1.** 精密,正确;严密。**2.** 细微的区别,微妙之处;机敏。**3.**〔常 *pl.*〕细节。**4.**〔常 *pl.*〕雅兴,考究。*a point of extreme* ~ 极其微妙的一个论点。*the niceties of life* 生活的享受。***to a* ~** **1.** 正确地;恰恰,恰好。**2.** 精细入微地 (*judge the distance to a* ~ 判断距离很准确)。

niche [nitʃ; nɪtʃ] **I** ***n.*** **1.** 壁龛〔搁雕像、花瓶等的墙壁凹处〕;【地】雪凹。**2.** (适合个人性格、能力等的)适当地位,活动范围;【生】小生境。**3.** (市场供求情势为企业家提拱的)有利可图的缺口。***deserve a* ~ *in the temple of fame*** 可以流芳百世。***find the right* ~ *for oneself*** 适得其所;为自己谋得合适的位置[地位]。~ **analysis** 市场供求缺口之机会分析。**II** ***vt.*** **1.**〔常用被动语态〕把…放在壁龛里。**2.**〔常用被动语态或作 ~ oneself〕把自己安顿(在适当场所)。

Nich·o·las [ˈnikələs; ˋnɪkl̩əs] ***n.*** 尼古拉斯〔男子名〕。

Nichol(s) [ˈnikəl(z); ˋnɪkəl(z)] ***n.*** 尼科尔(斯)〔姓氏〕。

Nichol·son [ˈnikəlsn; ˋnɪkəlsn̩] ***n.*** 尼科尔森〔姓氏〕。

Nick [nik; nɪk] ***n.*** **1.** 尼克〔男子名, Nicholas 的昵称〕。**2.** 恶魔,魔鬼〔一般作 Old ~〕。

nick[1] [nik; nɪk] **I** ***n.*** **1.** 刻口,刻痕;缺口,微凹,裂缝,隙。**2.** 骰子掷出所要点以上的大点;〔美俚〕一对骰子的七点[十一点]。**3.**【印】(铅字边上的)沟槽。**4.**〔俚〕监狱。**5.** 恰好的时刻。***in the* ~ (*of time*)** 在恰好的时候,在紧要关头。**II** ***vt.*** **1.** 刻痕于;摘记;弄缺(刀口);切短(马尾)。**2.** 说中;恰好赶上。**3.**〔英俚〕逮捕;(掷骰子)掷出(赢点)。**4.**〔俚〕夺;偷;骗。—***vi.*** (打猎、赛跑等时)抄近路赶过 (*in*)。~ ***a hurdle***〔美运〕栏没有跳好。**(*be*) ~*ed on the whiskers***【美拳】下巴挨打。~ ***it*** 猜中,说中。~ ***in*** (打猎)抄近路追到。~ ***the time*** 恰好赶上。

nick[2] [nik; nɪk] ***n.***〔美俚〕五分镍币。

nick·el [ˈnikl; ˋnɪkl̩] **I** ***n.***【化】镍;〔美、加〕五分镍币;(一般)镍币。*a* ~ *note*〔美〕五元钞票。*a* ~ *nurser*〔美俚〕小气鬼,守财奴。***don't take any wooden* ~*s***〔美〕当心,别上当。**II** ***vt.*** (〔Eng.〕***-ll-***) 镀镍于。~**-and-dime** ***vt.***〔美口〕吝啬地对待,以节省每个铜板的方式处理(某事等)。~ **bloom** = annabergite (镍华)。~ **plate** 镀镍层。~**-plated** ***a.*** 镀镍的。~**-plating** 镀镍。~ **silver** 镍银齐〔一种镍、铜、锌的合金〕。

nick·el·if·er·ous [ˌnikəˈlifərəs; ˏnɪkəˋlɪfərəs] ***a.*** (矿石等)含镍的。

nick·el·o·de·on [ˌnikəˈləudiən; ˏnɪklˋodɪən] ***n.***〔美〕**1.** (门票一律五分的)五分戏院[电影院]。**2.** 投币式自动点唱机 (= jukebox)。

nick·el·ous [ˈnikləs; ˋnɪkəl̩əs] ***a.***【化】亚镍的,二价镍的。

nick·er [ˈnikə; ˋnɪkə] **I** ***vi.*** **1.** (马)嘶。**2.** 闷笑。**II** ***n.*** **1.** 马嘶声。**2.** 闷笑。

nick·ey [ˈniki; ˋnɪkɪ] ***n.*** 〔Am.〕= Nick.

nickle [ˈnikl; ˋnɪkl̩] ***n.*** (美国和加拿大的)五分镍币 (= nickel)。

nick·nack [ˈniknæk; ˋnɪkˏnæk] ***n.*** = knickknack.

nick·name [ˈnikneim; ˋnɪkˏnem] **I** ***n.*** **1.** 诨名,绰号。**2.** 教名 (*Christian name*) 的略称,爱称〔如称 *Elizabeth* 为 *Bess*, 称 *Robert* 为 *Bob*〕。**II** ***vt.*** **1.** 给…加诨名,给…起绰号;用诨名[爱称]称呼。**2.**〔罕〕误称。

Nic·o·bars [ˈnikəubaːz; ˋnɪkobarz] ***n.*** 〔*pl.*〕尼科巴群岛〔印度〕(= the Nicobar Islands)。

Nic·ol(l) [ˈnikəl; ˋnɪkl̩] ***n.*** 尼可耳〔姓氏〕。

Nic·ol prism [ˈnikəl prizəm; ˋnɪkəl prɪzəm]【光】尼可耳棱镜。

Ni·col·son [ˈnikəlsn; ˋnɪkəlsn̩] ***n.*** 尼科尔森〔姓氏〕。

Nic·o·si·a [ˌnikəuˈsi(ː)ə; ˏnɪkoˋsiə] ***n.*** 尼科西亚〔塞浦路斯首都〕。

ni·co·ti·a [niˈkəuʃiə; nɪˋkoʃɪə] ***n.*** **1.** = nicotine. **2.**〔诗〕烟草。

ni·co·ti·an [niˈkəuʃən; nɪˋkoʃən] **I** ***a.*** **1.** 烟草的,得自烟草的。**2.** 抽烟的。**II** ***n.***〔罕〕抽烟的人。

nic·o·tin·am·ide [ˌnikəˈtinəmaid, -ˈtiːn-; ˏnɪkəˋtɪnəˏmaɪd, -ˋtin-] ***n.***【化】烟碱醯胺,烟酰胺。

nic·o·tine [ˈnikətiːn; ˋnɪkəˏtin], **nic·o·tin** [-tin; -tɪn] ***n.***【化】烟碱,尼古丁,烟草素。

nic·o·tin·ic [ˌnikəˈtinik; ˏnɪkəˋtɪnɪk] ***a.***【化】烟碱(酸)的。~ **acid** 烟碱酸。

nic·o·tin·ism [ˈnikətiːnizəm; ˋnɪkəˏtinɪzm̩] ***n.***【医】烟碱中毒,尼古丁中毒。

nic·o·tin·ize [ˈnikətinaiz; ˋnɪkətɪnˏaɪz] ***vt.*** 使中烟碱毒。

nic·tate [ˈnikteit; ˋnɪktet], **nic·ti·tate** [ˈniktiteit; ˋnɪktɪˏtet] ***vi.*** 眨眼睛,眨巴眼儿。**-ating membrane**

N

【动】瞬膜。

nic·ta·tion [nikˈteiʃən; nɪkˋteʃən], **nic·ti·ta·tion** [ˌniktiˈteiʃən; ˏnɪktɪˋteʃən] *n*. 眨眼睛。

ni·cy [ˈnaisi; ˋnaɪsɪ] *n*. 〔儿〕糖果糕饼。

ni·da·men·tal [ˌnaidəˈmentl; ˏnaɪdəˋmɛntl̩] *a*. (软体动物)缠卵的。~ **chamber** 缠卵腔[室]。~ **gland** 缠卵腺,壳腺。

ni·date [ˈnaideit; ˋnaɪdet], *vt*. 【胚胎】(受精卵)在(子宫内)营巢,着床于(子宫)。

nid·(d)er·ing [ˈnidəriŋ; ˋnɪdərɪŋ] *a*., *n*. 〔古〕卑鄙的(人),不诚实的(人),怯懦的(人);可怜的(人)。

nid·dle-nod·dle [ˈnidlˈnɔdl; ˋnɪdl̩ˏnɑdl̩] **I** *a*. (打瞌睡时)点着头的。**II** *vi*., *vt*. (因打盹等)不断地点(头)。

nide [naid; naɪd] *n*. 雉窝(中的雏雉)。

ni·dic·o·lous [naiˈdikələs; naɪˋdɪkələs] *a*. **1**. 留在窠里的〔指鸟孵出之后一段时间仍然在窠里〕。**2**. 生活在其他禽类窠里的。

nid·i·fi·cate [ˈnidifikeit; ˋnɪdɪfɪˏket], **nid·i·fy** [-fai; -faɪ] *vi*. 作巢。**-ca·tion** [ˌnidifiˈkeiʃən; ˏnɪdɪfɪˋkeʃən] *n*.

ni·dif·u·gous [naiˈdifjugəs; naɪˋdɪfjʊgəs] *a*. (像鸡孵出后)立即离窠的。

nid-nod [ˈnidnɔd; ˋnɪdnɑd] *vi*., *vt*. (**-dd-**) (使)点着头打盹。

ni·dus [ˈnaidəs; ˋnaɪdəs] *n*. (*pl*. **-di** [-dai; -daɪ], ~**-es**) **1**. 【动】胞窝,孵卵所。**2**. 病源地,发生地,发源地。**3**. 【医】病灶。

niece [niːs; nis] *n*. **1**. 侄女;甥女。**2**. 〔婉〕教士的私生女。

ni·el·list [niˈelist; nɪˋɛlɪst] *n*. 黑金镶嵌师。

niel·lo [niˈeləu; nɪˋɛlo] *n*. (*pl*. **-li** [-liː; -lɪ], ~**es**) 黑金镶嵌术,黑金镶嵌;黑金镶嵌品。

ni·el·lo·ed [niˈeləud; nɪˋɛlod] *a*. 镶黑金的。

Nier·stein·er [ˈniəstainə; ˋnɪrstaɪnɚ] *n*. (莱茵河畔尼尔斯坦纳产的)白葡萄酒。

Nie·tzsche [ˈniːtʃə; ˋnitʃə], **Friedrich Wilhelm** 尼采〔1844—1900,德国哲学家〕。

Nie·tzsche·an [ˈniːtʃiən; ˋnitʃɪən] *a*. 尼采哲学的。

Nie·tzsche·an·ism [ˈniːtʃjənizəm; ˋnitʃjənɪzəm], **Nie·tzsche·ism** [-tʃiizəm; -tʃɪɪzəm] *n*. 尼采哲学。

nieve [niːv; niv] *n*. 〔Scot., 英方〕拳手。

niff [nif; nɪf] **I** *n*. 〔俚〕难闻的气味。**II** *vi*. 散发恶臭。

nif·fer [ˈnifə; ˋnɪfɚ] *vi*., *n*. 〔Scot.〕交换;换货;交易。

nif·tic [ˈniftik; ˋnɪftɪk] *a*. 〔美俚〕漂亮的;俏皮的。

nif·ty [ˈnifti; ˋnɪftɪ] **I** *a*. (**-ti·er**; **-ti·est**) 〔美俚〕俏皮的,漂亮的。**II** *n*. 俏皮话;漂亮东西;漂亮姑娘。*It's a* ~. 这个倒漂亮。

Ni·gel [ˈnaidʒəl; ˋnaɪdʒəl] *n*. 奈杰尔〔男子名〕。

Ni·ger [ˈnaidʒə; ˋnaɪdʒɚ] *n*. **1**. 尼日尔〔非洲〕。**2**. 〔the ~〕尼日河。**3**. 〔n-〕皂脚。~ (*seed*) *oil* 皂厂杂油。

Ni·ger-Con·go [ˈnaidʒəˈkɔŋgəu; ˋnaɪdʒəˋkɑŋgo] *n*. 尼日尔刚果语。

Ni·ger·i·a [naiˈdʒiəriə; naɪˋdʒɪrɪə] *n*. 尼日利亚(奈及利亚)〔非洲〕。**-n 1**. *n*. 尼日利亚人。**2**. *a*. 尼日利亚(人)的。

nig·gard [ˈnigəd; ˋnɪgɚd] **I** *n*. 小气鬼。**II** *a*. 〔诗〕吝啬的,小气的。**-ly** *a*., *ad*. **-li·ness** *n*.

nig·ger [ˈnigə; ˋnɪgɚ] **I** *n*. **1**. 〔口〕〔蔑〕黑人。**2**. 〔蔑〕(东印度、澳洲等处的)肤色黑的本地人。**3**. 化装黑人乐队。**4**. 〔美〕(锯木厂中的)推木机。**5**. 非洲生橡胶。**6**. 〔口〕(仪器等的)故障。**7**. (黑色)皂脚。**II** *vt*. **1**. 〔美〕耗尽(地力)。**2**. 〔英、加〕烧掉(木头)。**3**. 〔口〕受黑人影响。~ ***in the woodpile*** [***fence***] 〔美俚〕隐蔽中的事实、缺点、动机(等);秘密;令人怀疑的情况。~***s in a snowstorm*** 咖喱饭;干李子粥。***work like a*** ~ 辛苦工作。~ **driver** 〔美俚〕凶狠的矿工[伐木工]工头。~ **gin** 〔美俚〕酒。~ **head** = negro head. ~ **heaven** 〔美俚〕(戏院等的)顶层楼座。~**-lover** 同情黑人解放运动的人。~**-melodies** 黑人的歌。**-dom** 黑人身分;黑人社会。**-ish** *a*. 黑人(似)的。

nig·gle [ˈnigl; ˋnɪgl] *vi*. 〔英〕为小事花费时间[操心]。

nig·gling [ˈnigliŋ; ˋnɪglɪŋ] **I** *a*. **1**. 为小事操心的。**2**. 麻烦的。**3**. (工作等)难办的;(字等)潦草难认的。**II** *n*. 麻烦事。*petty* ~ 打小算盘。

nigh [nai; naɪ] *ad*., *a*. (~***er***; ~***est***, ***next***), *prep*., *v*. 〔古,诗、方〕= near.

night [nait; naɪt] *n*. **1**. 夜,夜间;夜晚 (*opp*. day)。**2**. 黄昏;黑夜;黑暗。**3**. 蒙昧时代;失意时代。**4**. 盲目,瞎;死。**5**. 夜晚的活动〔如晚会等〕。*last* ~ 昨晚。*the* ~ *before last* 前天的晚上。*a dirty* ~ 下雨的夜晚,暴风雨之夜。*N- falls*. 天黑了。*Good* ~! (用于晚上分别时)晚安! 再见! *He closed his eyes in endless* ~. 他的眼睛永远瞎了。*They are wrapped in the* ~ *of ignorance* [*barbarism*]. 他们完全蒙昧无知。***all*** ~ (***long***) = ***all the*** ~ ***through*** 整夜。***as black*** [***dark***] ***as*** ~ 昏黑,漆黑。***at*** [***in the***] ***dead of*** ~ 在深更半夜。***at*** ~ 在夜里,在黄昏时候;晚上〔下午六时至午夜的时间〕。***at*** ~***s*** 在夜里经常…。***by*** ~ 在夜间;趁黑夜。***far into the*** ~ 至深夜。***go forth into the*** ~ 走到黑暗处。***have*** [***pass***] ***a good*** [***bad***] ~ 睡得好[睡得不好]。***have a*** [***the***] ~ ***out*** [***off***] 在外头玩一晚上;一个晚上不上班。***in the*** ~ 在夜间。***keep*** [***last***] ***over*** ~ 保持[继续]到早上。***late at*** ~ 在深夜,在深更半夜。***make a*** ~ ***of it*** 通宵宴乐;玩到天亮。~ ***about*** 隔夜。~ ***after*** = ~ ***by*** ~ 每夜,连夜。~ ***and day*** 日夜,日夜不停地,老是。***o'*** ~***s*** (= ***of*** ~***s***, ***on*** ~***s***) 〔口、方〕= ***by*** ~, ***at*** ~ (*I cannot sleep o'* ~*s for thinking of that*. 为了担心那件事我晚上总睡不着)。***one's*** ~ ***out*** (仆人等)可以出去玩的一晚,过节的晚上,庆祝之夜。***put up for the*** ~ 投宿。***spend the*** ~ ***with*** 在…的家里过夜。***stay*** (***three***) ~***s with*** 在…家住了(三)晚上。***turn*** ~ ***into day*** 拿夜晚当白天。***under cover of*** ~ 趁夜,趁黑。~ **attire** 睡衣。~ **bell** (医院等)夜间用铃。~ **bird 1**. 夜鸟〔枭、夜鹭等〕。**2**. 夜间活动者;夜游者;夜盗。~ **blindness** 【医】夜盲症。~**-blooming** *a*. 夜间开花的。~**-boat** 夜(航客)船。~ **bomber** 【空】夜间轰炸机。~**-breeze** 晚风。~**-cap** 睡帽;〔俚〕夜酒,睡前酒;〔美〕当天最后一场比赛。~ **cart** 粪车。~ **cellar** 〔英〕低级地下酒店。~**-chair** = nightstool. ~**clothes** 〔*pl*.〕睡衣。~**club** 夜总会〔晚上喝酒跳舞的地方〕。~ **commode** = nightstool. ~ **court** 夜间法庭。~ **crawler** 〔美〕夜间爬出来的大蚯蚓。~ **crow** (枭等)夜啼鸟。~ **dog** 夜猎狗。~**-dress**, ~**-gown** 女睡衣。~ **duty** 夜勤。~**-eyed** *a*. 黑夜里能看见东西的。~**-fall** 黄昏,傍晚。~**-flower** 夜开花。~ **flying** 【空】夜间飞行。~ **game** 【棒球】夜场比赛。~ **glass** 【海】夜间用望远镜。~ **hag** 夜间飞行空中的魔女;梦魇。~**-haunted** *a*. 晚上出鬼的。~**hawk 1**. *n*. 【鸟】= nightjar; 夜间干坏事的人,夜盗;夜间工作的人;夜游的人;夜间出租马车的车夫;夜间出租汽车的司机;〔美〕= nightwrangler. **2**. *vi*. 在夜间徘徊。~ **heron** 【鸟】夜鹭。~**-jar** 【鸟】欧夜鹰。~**-key** 〔Am.〕= latchkey. ~ **landing** 【空】夜间着陆;夜间登陆。~ **latch** 夜锁〔外用钥匙、内用手开的〕。~ **letter**, ~ **lettergram** (收费低的)夜间电报,夜信电〔次日送达,略作 NLT〕。~ **life** 夜生活〔指夜间在剧场、夜总会或类似场所饮酒作乐的活动〕。~ **light** 夜明灯〔寝室或病室用〕;通夜蜡烛。~ **line** (夜间垂置水中的)夜钓绳。~ **liner** 夜间钓鱼的人。~**long** *ad*., *a*. 彻夜(的),通宵(的)。~**man** 淘粪人,净厕员;守夜人。~**-mare** [ˈnaitmεə; ˋnaɪtˏmɛr] **1**. 〔古〕睡魔。**2**. 梦魇,恶梦;可怕的事情,讨厌的人[东西];恐怖感。~**-mared** *a*. 梦魇的,做恶梦的。~**marish** [ˈnaitmεəriʃ; ˋnaɪtˏmɛrɪʃ] *a*. 恶梦[梦魇]似的。~ **owl** 【鸟】猫头鹰;夜猫子,深夜不睡的人,夜精。~ **piece** 夜景画;夜景文;夜景诗。~ **porter** (旅馆、车站等的)夜勤人员。~ **raid** 【军】夜间空袭,夜间袭击。~ **raven** 【诗】夜渡鸟〔尤指夜鹭〕。~**rid-**

er〔主美〕夜间出现的骑马歹人。～ **school** 夜校。～-**shade**【植】茄属〔有毒植物〕(*the black* ～ *shade* 龙葵。*the deadly* ～ *shade* 颠茄。*the woody* ～ *shade* 南蛇藤属)。～ **shift** 夜班(时间);〔集合词〕夜班工人。～-**shirt** (男用)睡衣。～**side** 夜面,阴面〔月球或行星背向太阳的一面〕;(事物)黑暗的一面。～-**sight** 夜间瞄准器。～ **soil** 大粪。～ **stand** 床头小桌。～ **spot**〔美口〕= nightclub. ～**stick**〔美〕夜勤警棍。～-**stool** (卧室用)便桶;尿盆。～-**stop** *vi*. (飞机)停飞过夜。～ **stop** (飞机)夜停。～ **suit** 睡衣。～ **sweat** 盗汗。～ **terror** (小孩的)夜哭。～**tide**〔诗〕夜晚;夜潮。～-**time** 夜间。～ **town** 夜市,不夜城。～**viewer** 夜间观察器,红外线观察器。～**walker** 梦游病人;夜间徘徊者;盗贼;夜间徘徊街头的妓女。～ **walking** 梦中步行,梦游病;夜间徘徊。～ **watch** 1. 守夜,值更。2. 守夜者。3. 夜班时间;〔*pl*.〕(夜晚)睡不着的时间(*in the* ～ *watches* 在那些忐忑不安的、难于入睡的夜晚)。～ **watcher** 守夜人。～ **watchman** (工厂等雇用的)守夜人。～**wear** 睡衣。～ **work** 夜间工作。～ **wrangler**〔美〕牧场的夜间看马人。

night·ie [ˈnaiti:; ˋnaɪti] *n*.〔口〕小睡衣。

Night·in·gale [ˈnaitiŋgeil; ˋnaɪtɪnˏgel] *n*. 1. 奈廷格尔(南丁格尔)〔姓氏〕。2. **Florence** ～ 南丁格尔〔1820—1910,英国女社会改良家,近代护理制度的创始人,红十字会创办人〕。

night·in·gale [ˈnaitiŋgeil; ˋnaɪtɪnˏgel] *n*. 1.【鸟】夜莺;夜间鸣叫的鸟。2. 歌喉婉转的歌手;声调好听的演说者。

night·ly [ˈnaitli; ˋnaɪtlɪ] **I** *a*. 1. 每夜的,夜夜的。2.〔诗〕夜的,夜间出来(行动、发生)的。**II** *ad*. 每夜,夜夜。～ *dews* 夜露。

nights [naits; naɪts] *ad*.〔美〕每夜;大多数夜晚。

night·y [ˈnaiti; ˋnaɪtɪ] **I** *n*.〔口〕睡衣。**II** *a*. 夜的。

night·y-night [ˈnaitiˈnait; ˋnaɪtɪˋnaɪt] *int*.〔口〕good night 的变体。

ni·gres·cence [naiˈgresəns; naɪˋgresəns] *n*. 变黑;(颜色;皮肤;眼睛等的)发黑。

ni·gres·cent [naiˈgresənt; naɪˋgresənt] *a*. 发黑的,带黑的;渐渐变黑的。

nig·ri·fy [ˈnigrifai; ˋnɪgrɪˏfaɪ] *vt*. (-*fi·ed*; -*fy·ing*) 使变黑,使成黑色。-**fi·ca·tion** [ˌnigrifiˈkeiʃən;ˏnɪgrɪfɪˋkeʃən] *n*.

nig·ri·tude [ˈnigritju:d, ˈnaig-; ˋnɪgrəˏtjud, ˋnaɪg-] *n*.〔诗〕黑;漆黑;黑色物;〔喻〕邪恶。

ni·gro·sin(e) [ˈnaigrəsi:n; ˋnaɪgrəsin] *n*.【化】尼格(洛辛)苯胺黑;粒子元。

ni·hil [ˈnaihil; ˋnaɪhɪl]〔L.〕*n*. 无,虚无,空;毫无价值的东西。～ ***ad rem*** [ædˈrem; ædˋrem] 不得要领的,牛头不对马嘴的。～ ***obstat*** [ˈɔbstæt; ˋɑbstæt] 1.【天主】无异议〔经书籍检查官审查认可的证明〕。2. 官方制裁。

ni·hil·ism [ˈnaiilizəm; ˋnaɪəlˏɪzəm] *n*. 1.【哲】虚无主义;怀疑论。2.〔N-〕(19世纪后半期俄国的)民粹主义。3. 无政府主义,恐怖手段。**ni·hil·ist** *n*., **ni·hil·is·tic** [ˌnaiiˈlistik; ˏnaɪəˋlɪstɪk] *a*.

ni·hil·i·ty [naiˈhiliti; naɪˋhɪlətɪ] *n*.〔罕〕虚无,空,无效,无力;琐事,细事。

-nik *suf*.〔对参加政治运动或支持某种思潮者表示鄙视时在该名词上冠的词尾〕…分子;…迷;以…为特征的人: film*nik*, nogood*nik*.

Ni·ke [ˈnaiki:; ˋnaɪki] *n*. 1.【希神】胜利的女神(=(罗马的)Victoria)。2. 胜利之神。3.〔美军〕奈基式地对空导〔飞〕弹。～-**Ajax** 奈基式I型地对空导〔飞〕弹。～-**Hercules** 奈基式II型地对空导〔飞〕弹。～-**Zeus** 奈基式III型地对空飞〔导〕弹。

nik·eth·a·mide [ˈnikeθəmaid, -mid; nɪˋkεθəˏmaɪd, -mɪd] *n*.【药】尼可刹米,可拉明。

Nik·kei [ˈnikei; ˋnɪke] *n*.〔Jap.〕【经】日经(平均)指数〔东京股票市场上选定的225种股票收盘价的平均指数〕。

nil [nil; nɪl] *n*. 无,零。*three goals to* ～【运】三比零。*the* ～ *method*【算术】零位法。

nil ad·mi·ra·ri [ˈnilˌædmiˈrεərai; nɪlˏædmɪˋrerɪ] [L.] 对任何事都不惊奇的态度,漫不经心,冷淡,漠视。

nil de·sp·ran·dum [ˈnilˌdespˈrændəm; nɪlˏdespəˋrændəm]〔L.〕决不绝望。

nil·gai [ˈnilgai; ˋnɪlgaɪ] *n*. = nylghau.

Nile [nail; naɪl] *n*.〔the ～〕尼罗河〔非洲〕。

Niles [nailz; naɪlz] *n*. 奈尔斯〔姓氏,男子名〕。

Nil·ky [ˈnilki; ˋnɪlkɪ] *n*. 多子女无收入之失业者〔由其复数形式 nikies (= no-income-lots of kids) 逆生而成〕。

nill [nil; nɪl] *vi*. 不愿〔只在以下句型中应用〕。*Will he*, ～ *he*, ... 不管他愿意不愿意…。*Will you*, ～ *you*, ... 不管你愿意不愿意…。—*vt*. 拒绝。

nill ni·si bo·num [ˈnilˈnaisaiˈbəunəm; ˋnɪlˋnaɪsaɪˋbonəm]〔L.〕*de mortuis nil nisi bonum* (“人死莫言过”)的缩略表示形式。

Nilo-Hamitic [ˈnailəuhæˈmitik; ˋnaɪlohæˋmɪtɪk] *a*. 尼罗哈米特语〔包括马萨伊语〕。

ni·lom·e·ter [naiˈlɔmitə; naɪˋlɑmətɚ] *n*.【工】水位计。

Ni·lo-Sa·ha·ran [ˈnailəusəˈherən; ˋnaɪlosəˋhεrən] *a*. 尼罗-撒哈拉语系的〔指包括沙里-尼罗语族的非洲语系〕。

Ni·lot·ic [naiˈlɔtik; naɪˋlɑtɪk] *a*. 尼罗河(Nile)(流域)的。

nim [nim; nɪm] *vt*., *vi*. (***nam*** [nɔm; nɑm], ***nimmed***; ***no·men*** [ˈnəumən; ˋnomən]; ***nome*** [ˈnəum; ˋnom]; ***nim·ming***)〔古〕偷,偷窃。

nim·bi [ˈnimbai; ˋnɪmbaɪ] nimbus 的复数。

nim·ble [ˈnimbl; ˋnɪmbl] *a*. (-***bler***; -***blest***) 1. 敏捷的,灵活的,灵巧的。2. 聪明的,敏锐的;机警的;敏感的。(***as***) ～ ***as a squirrel*** 身手灵活,行动敏捷。～-**fingered** *a*. 手指敏捷的,善偷窃的。～-**footed** *a*. 脚快的。～-**witted** *a*. 聪敏的,机智的。-**bly** *ad*. -**ness** *n*.

nim·bo·stra·tus [ˈnimbəuˈstreitəs, -ˈstrætəs; ˏnɪmboˋstretəs, -ˋstrætəs] *n*.【气】雨层云。

nim·bus [ˈnimbəs; ˋnɪmbəs] *n*. (*pl*. ～***es***, -***bi*** [-bai; -baɪ]) 1.【气】雨云。2. (神像头上)光轮。3. (环境或人的)光彩,气氛。4.【美术】后光。*The candidate was encompassed with a* ～ *of fame*. 候选人当时处于蜚声四起的气氛中。

nim·by, **Nim·by** [ˈnimbi; ˋnɪmbɪ] *n*. “邻闭”份子〔指反对在自己住所附近兴建大楼或有害于社区环境之其他设施(如机场、核设施等)的人,此词为 not-in-my-backyard 之缩略〕。-**ism** *n*.

ni·mi·e·ty [niˈmaiəti; nɪˋmaɪətɪ] *n*.〔罕〕过多,过剩。

nim·i·ny-pim·i·ny [ˈnimiˈpimini; ˋnɪmənɪˋpɪmənɪ] *a*. 做作的,装腔作势的;扭扭捏捏的。*A* ～ *shyness makes frankness impossible*. 装模作样不会是真正的直爽。

Nim·itz [ˈnimits; ˋnɪmɪts] *n*. 尼米兹〔姓氏〕。

Nim·rod [ˈnimrɔd; ˋnɪmrɑd] *n*. 爱打猎的人,猎迷,有名的猎人。

Ni·na [ˈni:nə; ˋninə] *n*. 尼娜〔女子名〕。

nin·com·poop [ˈninkəmpu:p; ˋnɪnkəmˏpup] *n*. 笨人;傻瓜。

nine [nain; naɪn] **I** *num*. 九,九个;第九〔用于章节页行等词之后〕。～ *tenths* 十分之九。***a*** ～ ***days' wonder*** 一时新奇,过后即忘的事物。***in the*** ～-***holes***〔美〕为难,窘困。～ ***cases*** [***times***] ***out of ten*** 十之八九,大抵。～'***s complement representation*** (十进制)反码。**II** *n*. 1. 九个一组的人或物。2. 九岁。3. 九点钟。4. 棒球队。5. 九点(的牌)。***the N-*** (***Muses***) (司文艺、美术的)缪司九女神。(***up***) ***to the*** ～***s*** 完全,完美;(衣饰)华丽。

nine·fold [ˈnainfəuld; ˋnaɪnˏfold] **I** *a*. 九倍的,九重的。**II** *ad*. 九倍,九重。

900 [nain əu əu; naɪn o o] *n*.〔美〕成人(色情)电话服务。

N

nine·pins [ˈnainpinz; ˋnaɪn͵pɪnz] ***n.*** 〔*pl.*〕〔作单数用〕九柱戏。***fall*** [***be knocked***] ***over like*** (***a lot of***) ~ 一齐倒下;东倒西歪。

nine·teen [ˈnainˈtiːn; ˋnaɪnˋtin] **I** ***num.*** (基数)十九;十九个人[物];第十九(章,页等)。**II** ***n.*** 十九岁;十九点钟。***talk*** [***go***, ***run***, ***wag***] ~ ***to the dozen*** 说个不停。

nine·teenth [ˈnainˈtiːnθ; ˋnaɪnˋtinθ] ***n.***, ***a.*** 第十九(的),十九分之一(的),(月的)十九号(的)。~ **amendment** 美国宪法赋予妇女投票权的修正案。~ **hole** 〔谑〕高尔夫球场里的酒吧间。

nine·ti·eth [ˈnaintiiθ; ˋnaɪntɪɪθ] ***num.***, ***n.*** 第九十,九十分之一。

nine·ty [ˈnainti; ˋnaɪntɪ] **I** ***num.*** 九十。**II** ***n.*** 九十岁[个]。*the nineties* 九十年代〔略作 '90s〕;九十多岁〔九十至九十九岁〕;(温度表的)九十多度〔九十至九十九度〕。~-***nine times out of a hundred*** 十有九成九,百分之九十九,几乎总是。

Nin·e·veh [ˈninivi; ˋnɪnəvə] ***n.*** 尼尼微〔古代亚述首都〕。

Nin·e·vite [ˈninivait; ˋnɪnɪvaɪt] ***n.*** 古代亚述首都尼尼微人。

nin·ja, Nin·ja [ˈnindʒə; ˋnɪndʒə] ***n.*** 〔Jap.〕"忍者"〔指受过间谍训练等的日本武士〕。**Ninja Turtle** 忍者神龟〔日本连环画中一著名英雄〕。

nin·ny [ˈnini; ˋnɪnɪ], **nin·ny·ham·mer** [ˈninihæmə; ˋnɪnɪ͵hæmɚ] ***n.*** 笨人,傻子。

ni·non [ninɔ̃; niˋnɔ̃] ***n.*** 〔F.〕尼农绸;薄绸。

Nin·ten·do [ˈnintendəu; ˋnɪntɛndo] ***n.*** 〔Jap.〕任天堂〔日本一家电脑游戏机的著名生产厂家〕。~ **Generation** 玩任天堂游戏机的一代〔指八十、九十年代的儿童〕。

ninth [nainθ; naɪnθ] **I** ***num.*** 第九(的);九分之一(的)。**II** ***n.*** (月的)第九日;【乐】第九度音程。~ *nerve* 舌咽喉神经。~ *part of a man* 〔谑〕裁缝〔从俗话 *Nine tailors make a man* 而来〕。~ **chord** 【乐】第九和弦。**-ly** ***ad.***

Ni·o·be [ˈnaiəbi; ˋnaɪəbɪ] ***n.*** **1.** 【希神】尼俄伯〔她有十四个儿子,因自夸而全被杀死,悲伤无已,后化为石头〕。**2.** 〔诗〕因丧失孩子而终身悲叹的妇女。**3.** 【植】中国百合。

ni·o·bic [naiˈəubik; naɪˋobɪk] ***a.*** 【化】铌的。

ni·o·bite [ˈnaiəbait; ˋnaɪəbaɪt] ***n.*** 【矿】铌铁矿。

ni·o·bi·um [naiˈəubiəm; naɪˋobɪəm] ***n.*** 【化】铌〔旧名 columbium〕。~ **ore** 铌矿。

ni·o·bous [naiˈəubəs; naɪˋobəs] ***a.*** 【化】亚铌的,三价铌的。

Nip [nip; nɪp] ***n.*** 〔美口〕= Niponese.

nip[1] [nip; nɪp] **I** ***vt.*** (***-pp-***) **1.** 夹,捏,掐;(马、狗等)咬。**2.** 摘取,剪断 (*off*)。**3.** 冻伤(手指等),冻死(植株);阻止,阻碍(生长等);使挫折。**4.** 〔俚〕抢去;偷;逮捕。*The crab nipped my toe.* 螃蟹夹了我的脚趾。~ ***in the bud*** 在萌芽时摘取,防患于未然;消灭于萌芽状态。—***vi.*** **1.** 夹,捏,掐,咬。**2.** (寒风等)刺骨。**3.** 〔俚〕跑,赶 (*along*; *in*; *off*; *on*)。~ ***in*** [***out***] 忽然跳进[出];插嘴 (~ *in with a smart question* 乘机提出尖锐的质问)。**II** ***n.*** **1.** 一夹,一捏,一掐,使劲的一咬;一小片。**2.** 霜害;阻碍;寒气,严寒。**3.** 讽刺,痛骂。**4.** 【海】(冰封船两边的)强压。**5.** 【地】狭缩。~ ***and tuck*** 〔美口〕竞走时不相上下。

nip[2] [nip; nɪp] **I** ***n.*** (酒等的)一口,少量。***freshen the*** ~ 〔口〕以酒解酒〔醉醒后再喝点酒〕。**II** ***vi.*** (***-pp-***) 一点儿一点儿地喝,呷。

ni·pa [ˈniːpə, ˈnai-; ˋnipə, ˋnaɪ-] ***n.*** 【植】**1.** 聂帕榈。**2.** 聂帕榈茅屋顶或聂帕果。**3.** 聂帕果汁。

nip·per [ˈnipə; ˋnɪpɚ] ***n.*** **1.** 夹[捏、掐、摘、咬]的人[东西]。**2.** (马的)前齿,(蟹等的)螯。**3.** 〔英口〕(无赖)少年;年轻的叫卖小贩;吝啬鬼,小气鬼;(行商、土工等的)帮手。**4.** 〔*pl.*〕钳子,镊子。**5.** 〔*pl.*〕〔俚〕夹鼻眼镜。**6.** 〔*pl.*〕〔俚〕手铐;脚镣。

nip·ping [ˈnipiŋ; ˋnɪpɪŋ] ***a.*** (风等)刺骨的,砭人肌肤的;讽刺的;尖刻的。

nip·ple [ˈnipl; ˋnɪpl] ***n.*** **1.** 奶头,(奶瓶的)橡皮奶头。**2.** (皮肤、山顶、金属面、玻璃面等的)乳头状突起;(枪炮的)火门;【机】喷灯喷嘴,螺纹接套。~ **shield** 乳头罩(保护疼痛的乳头)。~ **wort** 【植】稻槎菜。

Nip·po [ˈnipəu; ˋnɪpo] ***n.*** 〔美军俚〕日本人。

Nip·pon [niˈpɔn, ˈnip-; nɪˋpɑn, ˋnɪp-] ***n.*** = Japan.

Nip·pon·ese [͵nipəˈniːz; ͵nɪpənˋiz] ***n.***, ***a.*** = Japanese.

Nip·poni·an [niˈpəuniən; nɪˋponɪən] ***a.*** 日本(人)的。

nip·py [ˈnipi; ˋnɪpɪ] **I** ***a.*** (***-pi·er***; ***-pi·est***) 〔俚〕**1.** 敏捷的,伶俐的,快的。**2.** (天气等)寒冷的,刺骨的。**II** ***n.*** 〔英口〕法国里昂咖啡馆的女服务员。

nip-up [ˈnip͵ʌp; ˋnɪp͵ʌp] ***n.*** 叠肋〔杂技的一种起跳动,由仰卧一跃而起〕。

Nir·va·na [niəˈvɑːnə, nəːˈv-; nɪrˋvɑnə, nɝˋv-] ***n.*** 〔Sans.〕**1.** 【佛教】涅槃;【印度教】生命火焰的熄灭;极乐世界。**2.** 〔n-〕(自痛苦、烦恼中的)解脱。*the* ~ *Sutra* 涅槃经。

ni·sei [ˈniːˈsei; ˋniˋse] ***n.*** 〔亦作 N-〕在美国生长和受教育的第二代日本移民;双亲为日本移民的美国人。

ni·si [ˈnaisai; ˋnaɪsaɪ] **I** ***conj.*** 〔L.〕【法】要不然就,否则。**II** ***a.*** 【法】非最后的,非绝对的。***decree*** [***order***, ***rule***] ~ 在一定时日前不提出反对理由时即作确定的判决[命令、条律]。

nisi pri·us [ˈnaisaiˈpraiəs; ˋnaɪsaɪˋpraɪəs] 〔L.〕(初审)在备案法庭中由一个法官与陪审团审理的民事诉讼;〔英〕由巡回审判法官审理的民事诉讼。

Nis·sen [ˈnisən; ˋnɪsn] ***n.*** 尼森〔姓氏〕。~ **hut** 【军】(加拿大 P.N.Nissen 设计的)尼森式桶形掩体。

ni·sus [ˈnaisəs; ˋnaɪsəs] ***n.*** 〔L.〕努力,奋力,企图。

nit[1] [nit; nɪt] ***n.*** **1.** 虮,虱卵。**2.** 〔美〕没有的人,饭桶。

nit[2] [nit; nɪt] ***ad.*** 〔美俚〕= no.

nit[3] [nit; nɪt] ***n.*** 【物】尼特〔光度单位;=1 新烛光/平方米〕。

nite [nait; naɪt] ***n.*** 〔美〕= night. ~ **spot** = nitery.

ni·ter[1] [ˈnaitə; ˋnaɪtɚ] ***n.*** 〔美〕= nitre.

ni·ter[2] ***n.*** = nighter.

ni·ter·y [ˈnaitəri; ˋnaɪtərɪ] ***n.*** 〔美俚〕= night club.

ni·ton [ˈnaitɔn; ˋnaɪtɑn] ***n.*** 【化】radon (氡)的旧名。

nit-pick [ˈnitpik; ˋnɪt͵pɪk] ***vi.*** 找碴儿,挑剔。**-er** ***n.*** 爱挑剔的人。

nit-pick·ing [ˈnit͵pikiŋ; ˋnɪt͵pɪkɪŋ] ***a.***, ***n.*** 过于精细(的),挑剔(的),找碴儿(的)。

ni·trate [ˈnaitreit; ˋnaɪtret] **I** ***n.*** **1.** 【化】硝酸盐;硝酸根;硝酸酯;硝化。**2.** 硝酸盐类化肥。*ammonium* ~ 硝酸铵。*Chile* ~ 智利硝(石)。*hydrocellulose* ~ 水化纤维素硝酸酯。~ *bed* 硝石矿床。~ *nitrogen* 硝态氮。~ *of soda* 硝酸钠。~ *of silver* = *silver* ~ 硝酸银。**II** ***vt.*** 用硝酸处理,使硝化。

ni·tra·tion [naiˈtreiʃən; naɪˋtreʃən] ***n.*** 【化】硝化(作用)。*countercurrent* ~ 对流硝化。

ni·tre [ˈnaitə; ˋnaɪtɚ] ***n.*** **1.** 【化】硝石;硝酸钠(制火药用)。**2.** 智利硝石,钠硝石〔作肥料用〕。

ni·tric [ˈnaitrik; ˋnaɪtrɪk] ***a.*** 【化】氮的,含氮的;〔古〕硝石的。~ *acid* 硝酸。~ *bacteria* 硝酸细菌。~ *oxide* 氧化一氮。

ni·tride [ˈnaitraid; ˋnaɪtraɪd] ***n.*** 【化】氮化物。

ni·tri·fy [ˈnaitrifai; ˋnaɪtrə͵faɪ] ***vt.***, ***vi.*** 【化】硝化;(使)变成硝石。**-fi·er** ***n.*** 硝化(细)菌。**-ca·tion** [͵naitrifiˈkeiʃən; ͵naɪtrɪfɪˋkeʃən] ***n.*** 硝化(作用)。

ni·tril(e) [ˈnaitriːl; ˋnaɪtrəl] ***n.*** 【化】腈 (RCN)。

ni·trite [ˈnaitrait; ˋnaɪtraɪt] ***n.*** 【化】亚硝酸盐[根、酯]。

ni·tro [ˈnaitrəu; ˋnaɪtro] **I** ***a.*** 【化】含硝基的。**II** ***n.*** 硝化甘油。

nitro- *comb. f.* 表示"硝基","硝化": *nitro*acid 硝基酸。

*nitro*alkane 硝基烷。*nitro*amine 硝胺。

ni·tro·an·il·ine [ˈnaitrəuˈænilain; ˋnaɪtroˋænɪlaɪn] ***n***. 【化】硝基苯胺。

ni·tro·bac·te·ri·a [ˈnaitrəubækˈtiərə; ˋnaɪtrobækˋtɪrɪə] ***n***. 硝化细菌。

ni·tro·ben·zene [ˈnaitrəuˈbenziːn; ˏnaɪtrəˋbɛnzin] ***n***. 【化】硝基苯。

ni·tro·cel·lu·lose [ˌnaitrəuˈseljuləus; ˏnaɪtroˋseljəˏlos] ***n***. 【化】硝化纤维素,棉花火药。～ *powder* 硝化纤维素(炸药)。

ni·tro·chalk [ˌnaitrəuˈtʃɔːk; naɪtroˋtʃɔk] ***n***. 【化】钾铵硝石;白垩硝肥。

ni·tro·ex·plo·sive [ˌnaitrəuiksˈpləusiv; ˏnaɪtroɪksˋplosɪv] ***n***. 硝化火药。

ni·tro·fu·ran [ˌnaitrəuˈfjuərən, -fjuˈrɔn; ˏnaɪtroˋfjurən, -fjuˋræn] ***n***. 硝基呋喃。

ni·tro·gen [ˈnaitrədʒən; ˋnaɪtrədʒən] ***n***. 【化】氮,氮气。～ *chloride* 三氯化氮。～ *cycle* 氮循环。～ *dioxide* 二氧化一氮。～ *fixation* 固氮(作用)。～ *free extract* 无氮浸出物。～ *monoxide* 一氧化二氮,氧化亚氮。～ *mustard* 氮芥(类);含氮芥子。～ *narcosis* 氮麻醉。～ *oxide* 氧化氮。

ni·trog·e·nize [naiˈtrɔdʒənaiz, ˈnaitrədʒənaiz; ˋnaɪtrədʒənˏaɪz, naɪˋtrədʒənaɪz] ***vt***. (*-niz·ed*; *-niz·ing*) 氮化〔与氮或其化合物相化合或浸渍〕。

ni·trog·e·nous [naiˈtrɔdʒinəs; naɪˋtrɑdʒənəs] ***a***. 含氮的,氮的。～ *fertilizer* 氮肥。

ni·tro·glyc·er·in(e) [ˈnaitrəuˈglisərin; ˏnaɪtrəˋglɪsrɪn] ***n***. 【化】硝化甘油,炸油,甘油三硝酸脂。

ni·tro·hy·dro·chlo·ric acid [ˌnaitrəuˌhaidrəuˈklɔːrik; ˋnaɪtroˏhaɪdrəˋklorɪk] 王水,硝基盐酸 (= aqua regia)。

ni·trol·ic [naiˈtrɔlik; naɪˋtrɑlɪk] **acid** 【化】硝肟酸。

ni·trom·e·ter [naiˈtrɔmitə; naɪˋtrɑmətɚ] ***n***. 测氮管。

ni·tron [ˈnaitrɔn; ˋnaɪtrɔn] ***n***. 【化】硝酸灵〔制造塑胶的原料〕。

ni·tro·par·af·fin [ˌnaitrəuˈpærəfin; ˏnaɪtrəˋpærəfɪn] ***n***. 【化】硝基烷。

ni·tro·pow·der [ˈnaitrəuˈpaudə; ˋnaɪtroˋpaudɚ] ***n***. 【化】硝化火药。

ni·tros·a·mine [ˌnaitrəusəˈmiːn, -ˈæmin; ˏnaɪtrosəˋmin, -ˋæmɪn] ***n***. 【化】(某)亚硝胺。

ni·tro·so [naiˈtrəusəu; naɪˋtroso] ***a***. 【化】亚硝基的。

ni·tro·syl·sul·phu·ric, ni·tro·syl·sul·fu·ric [ˌnaitrəusilsʌlˈfjuːrik; ˏnaɪtrosɪlsʌlˋfjurɪk] ***a***. 硝酸和硫酸混合而成的。～ *acid* 【化】混酸。

ni·tro·syl [ˈnaitrəusil; naɪˋtrosəl] ***a***. 【化】亚硝醯[酰](基)的。

ni·tro·tol·u·ene [ˈnaitrəuˈtɔljuiːn; ˋnaɪtroˋtɑljʊin] ***n***. 【化】硝基甲苯〔猛烈炸药〕。

ni·trous [ˈnaitrəs; ˋnaɪtrəs] ***a***. 亚硝(酸)的;含有三价氮的。～ *acid* 【化】亚硝酸。～ *bacteria* 亚硝酸细菌。～ *oxide* 【化】一氧化二氮,笑气。

ni·tro·xyl [naiˈtrɔksil; naɪˋtrɑksɪl] ***n***. 【化】硝醯[酰](基)。

nitsky [ˈnitski; ˋnɪtski] ***ad***. 〔美俚〕= no.

nit·ty [ˈniti; ˋnɪtɪ] ***a***. (*-ti·er*; *-ti·est*) 多虱卵的,多小虫卵的。

nit·ty-grit·ty [ˈnitiˈgriti; ˋnɪtɪˋgrɪtɪ] ***n***. 〔俚〕基本事实,本质;事实。

nit·wit [ˈnitwit; ˋnɪtˏwɪt] ***n***. 〔美俚〕笨蛋,傻子。 **nit·witted** [nitˈwitid; nɪtˋwɪtɪd] ***a***.

Ni·u·e [niˈuːei; nɪˋue] **Island** ***n***. 纽埃岛(新)〔南太平洋〕。

ni·val [ˈnaivl; ˋnaɪvl] ***a***. 雪的,生于雪中的。

niv·e·ous [ˈniviəs; ˋnɪvɪəs] ***a***. 似雪的,雪白的;纯白的。

nix[1] [niks; nɪks] (*fem*. *nix·ie* [ˈniksi; ˋnɪksɪ]) ***n***. 水中精灵。**-ie** ***n***. 女水精。

nix[2] [niks; nɪks] **I** ***n***. 〔美俚〕**1**. 没有,无。**2**. 〔*pl*.〕没有邮政局的地方;无法投递的邮件,死信。**3**. 拒绝。*It must be you or* ～. 不是你才怪呢! ～ ***on*** 好了,够了(*N- on your nonsense!* 你别再胡说八道了。*N- on that tune of talk!* 再少说那样的话!)。**II** ***ad***. 不;不行,我不同意(= no)。*say* ～ *on a plan* 不同意计划。**III** ***vt***. 拒绝;禁止;否决。*The police ～ed the procession*. 警察禁止游行。

nix[3] [niks; nɪks] ***int***. 〔英学俚〕当心;(老师、班长等)来了!〔叫其他同伴当心的话〕。*keep* ～ 把风。

nix·ed [nikst; nɪkst] ***a***. 〔美俚〕被禁止的。*a* ～ *pic* 被禁映的影片。

nix·ey [ˈniksi; ˋnɪksɪ] ***ad***. 〔美俚〕= no; not at all.

Nix·on [ˈniksn; ˋnɪksn] ***n***. 尼克森〔姓氏〕。

Ni·zam [naiˈzæm; naɪˋzæm] ***n***. **1**. 尼萨〔旧时印度海得拉巴 (Hyderabad) 土邦君主的称号〕。**2**. 〔n-〕土耳其士兵。

N.J., NJ = New Jersey 新泽西〔美国州名〕。

N.L., NL = **1**. north latitude 北纬度。**2**. New Latin 新拉丁语。

n.l. = **1**. 〔L.〕 *non licet* (not permitted) 不允许。**2**. 〔L.〕 *non liquet* (not clear) 不清楚。

N. lat. = north latitude 北纬。

NLRB = National Labor Relations Board 〔美〕国家劳资关系委员会。

N.L.T. 〔美〕= night letter telegram 夜间书信电报。

NM = night message 夜间电报。

N.M., NM = **1**. New Mexico 新墨西哥〔美国州名〕。**2**. nautical mile(s) 海里。

n.m. = nuclear moment 核矩。

NMB = National Mediation Board 〔英〕全国调解局〔相当于美国的 NLRB〕。

N. Mex. = New Mexico 新墨西哥〔美国州名〕。

NMR = nuclear magnetic resonance 核磁共振。

NMU = National Maritime Union of America 〔美〕全国海员工会。

N.N.E., NNE, n.n.e. = north-northeast.

N.N.W., NNW, n.n.w. = north-northwest.

no[1] [nəu; no] **I** ***a***. **1**. 〔加在单数名词前,相当于冠词 a, an 的否定形式〕(一个也)没有。*Is there a book on the table?* 桌子上有一本书吗? — *No, there is* ～ *book there*. 没有,桌上一本书也没有。*She has* ～ *mother while he has* ～ *father*. 他没有父亲,她却没有母亲。**2**. 〔加在复数普通名词及不可数名词前〕一点儿也没有。*There are* ～ *clouds in the sky*. 天上一点儿云也没有。*She has* ～ *children*. 她一个孩子也没有。*There is* [*He has*] ～ *water* [*hope, etc*.]. 一点儿水[希望等]也没有。★No seats are left. 这类句子的强调说法是 Not a seat is left. 一个座位也没有。**3**. 〔加在不表示数量观念的普通名词、抽象名词、动名词之前〕什么也[谁也]没有。*No man is without his fault*. 谁也不会没有缺点。*No one knows*. 谁也不知道。★no one 的两个区别。如:No one can do it. 谁也不能做。No one man can do it. 无论谁,一个人是做不到的。**4**. 〔加在 be 与述语名词或其他形容词之间〕决不是…。*He is* ～ *scholar*. 他根本不是一个学者〔比较:*He is not a scholar*. 不是学者(而是…等)〕。*It is* ～ *joke*. 这决不是开玩笑。*I am* ～ *match for him*. 我决不是他的对手。*He showed* ～ *small skill*. 他显出了相当大的本事。**5**. 〔在省略句中〕不许,不可,反对,禁止。*No compromise!* 反对妥协! *No surrender!* 不要投降! *No admittance except on business*. 非公莫入。*No scribbling on the walls!* 墙上请勿涂写。*No smoking!* 请勿吸烟。*No thoroughfare*. 禁止通行。*No credit*. 不赊账。*No cards* [*flowers*]. (报丧广告)谨此报闻,恕不另讣[敬辞赠花]。**6**. 〔There is ～ +动名词〕丝毫不可能,简直没办法。*There is* ～ *denying his tale*. 他说的话是无可否认的。*There is* ～

N

saying what may happen. 简直不晓得今后情况将会怎么样。~ **bargain**〔美运〕平凡的。~ **bon**〔军俚〕不好,不行。~ **bull fighter**〔美俚〕柔弱的男子。~ **can do**〔美俚〕= I can't do it. ~ **confidence vote** 不信任投票。~ **date** (藏书签等上)无日期〔略 *n.d.*〕。~ **end of**〔口〕许多的,非常的。~ **fear**! 没有那种事! 别怕!〔拒绝请求时〕不行不行。~ **flies on**〔美俚〕活泼,有精神,机灵,聪敏 (*There are ~ flies on him*. 那家伙机灵[聪明]得很)。~ **go**〔俚〕不行,没希望,失败;〔美俚〕意见不一致 (= ~ *agreement*)。~ **got**〔美俚〕我没有。~ **great shakes**〔美俚〕普通的,平凡的,比较上不大重要的。~ **likes**〔美俚〕不欢喜;〔美剧〕收入少的;不叫座的,不成功的。~ **man's land** 没有主人的土地;【军】无人[真空]地带〔两对峙阵地间的地带〕;难于确定性质的领域。~ **two ways about it**〔美〕确实的,显著的。

II *ad*. **1.**〔用于 or 之后〕= not. *Pleasant or ~, it is true*. 无论愉快与否,事实不假。**2.**〔用于比较级之前〕一点也没有。*Things are ~ better (than before)*. 情况一点也没有(比从前)更好一些。*I can walk ~ further [longer]*. 我一点也不能再走了。~ **sooner ... than** 刚一…(就)…,才…(就)。**whether or ~ 1.** 是不是 (*Tell me whether or ~ it is true*. 请告诉我那是真是假)。**2.** 不管怎样 (*Whether or ~, I will go*. 不管怎样,我都要去)。

III *n*. (*pl*. ~(*e*)*s*) **1.** 否定,否认,拒绝。**2.**〔*pl*.〕(投)反对票(者)。*I will not take ~ (for an answer)*. 不许说不。*Two noes make a yes*. 否定的否定就是肯定。***The noes have it***. 反对票占多数。~**-account** *a*., *n*.〔美、方〕没用的(人),不足道的(人)。~**-ball** *n*., *vt*.【板球】(把…裁判为)犯规投球(应输一分)。~**-being** 不存在;非实在(的东西)。~**-brainer** 不需要费脑子的事。~**-comment** *vi*., *vt*. (对…)无可奉告〔置评〕。~**-cost** *a*.〔美俚〕免费的。~**-count** *a*.〔美方〕= no-account. ~**-frills** *a*. 仅提供最起码必需品的;无任何外加装饰的。~**-fly zone** *n*. 禁飞区。~**-go area** 禁区。~**-good** (**-er**)〔美俚〕没用的人,饭桶。~**-growth** *a*. (城市范围、人口政策等)实行无增长方针的。~**-hitter**【棒】无安打赛局。~**-knock 1.** *a*. (逮捕、搜查等)强行闯入进行的,破门而入的。**2.** *n*. 破门而入的强行搜捕。~**-load** *a*. (出售股票时)免付佣金的。~ **man 1.** = nobody. **2.**〔常作 no-man〕〔口〕不肯妥协的人,顽梗的人。~**-nonsense** *a*. 严肃的。~**-show** *n*. 预订了座位而未到的人。~**-win** *a*. **1.** 不大可能获胜的。**2.** 非竞赛性的。

no²[nəu; no] (*opp*. yes) *ad*. **1.**〔否定的回答〕不,否。*Will you come?* — No. 你来吗? ——不来。★**1.** 对否定问话给与否定回答时用。如: You haven't finished yet? — No, sir. 还没有完吗? ——还没有。**2.** 有惊奇表现。如: He even threatened to kill me. —No! —Yes, he did. 他甚至说要杀我。——不会吧! ——是真的。**2.**〔和 not 或 nor 同用,加强否定语气〕不。*A man could not lift it*, ~, *nor half a dozen*. 一个人是举不起的,不,六个人也举不起。

No【化】= nobelium 锘。

No., No, no. = number.

n.o. = natural order【生】自然分类的目(介于纲与科之间)。

No.1 [ˈnʌmbəˈwʌn; ˋnʌmbəˋwʌn] = number one. 第一;第一等,第一流;自己;自己的利益。

No·a·chi·an [nəuˈeikiən; noˋekɪən], **No·a·chic** [nəuˈeikik; noˋækɪk] *a*. 诺亚(时代)的。

No·ah¹[ˈnəuə; ˋnoə] *n*. 诺亚〔男子名〕。

No·ah²[ˈnəuə; ˋnoə] *n*.【圣】诺亚〔希伯来人的族长〕。~**'s ark** 见 *ark* 条。~**'s ark phrases**〔美〕陈辞滥调。~**'s nightcap**【植】花菱草。

no·ah·ar·cha·ic [ˌnəuəˈkeiik; ˏnoəˋkeɪk] *a*.〔美〕非常陈旧[落伍]的,〔谑〕早已过时的。

nob¹[nɔb; nɑb] **I** *n*. **1.**〔俚〕头;头上的一击。**2.** 球形门柄。**3.**【建】雕球饰。*a ~ in the fur trade* 法官。*a ~ of the first water* 第一流人物。**II** *vi*., *vt*. (**-bb-**)【拳击】打(…的)头。

nob²[nɔb; nɑb] *n*.〔俚〕富豪;贵族;上流人物。

nob·ble [ˈnɔbl; ˋnɑbl] *vt*.〔英俚〕**1.**【赛马】(为要使马不能取胜)给(马)吃毒药,使(马)成残废。**2.** (行贿)收买;诈骗;骗取(钱等)。**3.** 逮捕(犯人)。**-bler** *n*. 诈骗者;通过贿赂手段获得某方面支持的人。

nob·bler [ˈnɔblə; ˋnɑblɚ] *n*. **1.** 当头一击,击昏。**2.**〔澳俚〕一杯烈酒。

nob·but [ˈnɔbət; ˋnɑbət] *ad*.〔口〕只是,不过是。

nob·by [ˈnɔbi; ˋnɑbɪ] *a*. (**-bi·er**; **-bi·est**)〔俚〕贵族的;头面人物的;时髦的,最好的。**nob·bi·ly** *ad*.

No·bel [nəuˈbel; noˋbɛl] *n*. **1.** 诺贝尔〔姓氏〕。**2. Alfred Bernhard** [ˈɑːlfred beənɑːd; ˋalfrɛd bɛənɑrd] ~ 诺贝尔〔1833—1896,瑞典化学家,炸药创制经营者,诺贝尔奖金的创设者〕。~**-man**, ~ **Laureate** 诺贝尔奖金获得者。~ **prizes** 诺贝尔奖金。

No·bel·ist [nəuˈbelist; noˋbɛlɪst] *n*. 诺贝尔奖金获得者。

no·bel·i·um [nəuˈbeliəm; noˋbɛlɪəm] *n*.【化】锘〔102 号元素〕。

no·bil·i·a·ry [nəuˈbiliəri; nəˋbɪlɪˏɛrɪ] *a*. 贵族的。***the ~ particle*** [***prefix***] 贵族词首〔用于姓名前表示某人系贵族〕。

no·bil·i·ty [nəuˈbiliti; noˋbɪlətɪ] *n*. **1.** 高贵的身分[出身]。**2.**〔the ~〕〔集合词〕贵族(阶层);〔英〕上院议员及家族。**3.** 崇高,高贵,高尚。**4.** 庄严,雄伟。*a man of true ~* 一个真正高尚的人。

no·ble [ˈnəubl; ˋnobl] **I** *a*. (**-bler**; **-blest**) **1.** 清高的,崇高的,高尚的。**2.** 高贵的,贵族的。**3.** 宏伟的,堂皇的;华美的,壮丽的;卓越的;著名的,有名的。**4.** 贵重的 (*opp*. base)。*my ~ friend* 阁下〔演说中对贵族或有 Lord 称号的人的称呼〕。*the ~ lady* 尊夫人〔指贵族的夫人〕。*the ~ Lord* 阁下〔上院议员彼此间或对有 Lord 称号的下院议员的称呼〕。*It was planned on a ~ scale*. 计划规模宏大。*the ~ art (of self defense)* 拳击。*the ~ metals* 贵金属 **II** *n*. **1.** 贵族。**2.**【史】诺布尔金币〔英国古金币,相当于旧制 6 先令 8 便士〕;〔美工会俚〕工贼,(破坏罢工的)工头。~ **fir**【植】壮丽冷杉〔产于美国西部〕。~ **gas** 稀有气体,惰性气体。~**-minded** *a*. 心地高尚的,崇高的;气量大的,豪爽的。~**man** 贵族。~**-woman** 贵妇。**-ness** *n*. 高贵;崇高,高尚;宏大,庄严。

no·blesse [nəuˈbles; noˋblɛs] *n*.〔F.〕**1.** (法国)贵族(阶层)。**2.** 贵族身分,高贵的出身。~ ***oblige*** [əbˈliːʒ; oˋbliʒ] 位高则任重。

no·bly [ˈnəubli; ˋnoblɪ] *ad*. **1.** 崇高,高贵,出身于贵族。**2.** 华美,宏伟,壮丽。**3.** 豁达,豪爽。*a deed ~ done* 宏伟业绩。*be ~ born* 出身高贵。~*-clad attendants* 服饰豪华的侍者。*The ~ born must ~ do*. 出身高尚者行为也应高尚。

no·body [ˈnəubədi, -bɔdi; ˋnoˏbɑdɪ] **I** *pro*. 谁也不,没人;无人。*There was ~ present*. 没人出席。*Everybody's business is ~'s business*. 人人负责便是没人负责。*N- will be the wiser*. 没人会知道的。~ *else* 此外无别人。**II** *n*. (*pl*. **no·bod·ies**) 不足取的人;无名小卒;小人物 (*opp*. somebody)。*She has married a ~*. 她嫁了一个无名的人。*He is ~*. 他是一个没出息的人。

no·cake [ˈnəukeik; ˋnokek] *n*.〔美〕炒玉米粉。

no·cent [ˈnəusnt; ˋnosənt] *a*.〔废或罕〕**1.** 有害的,伤害的。**2.** 有罪的;犯罪的。

no·ci·cep·tive [ˌnəusiˈseptiv; ˏnosɪˋsɛptɪv] *a*. 疼痛的,致痛的;有疼痛反映的。

nock [nɔk; nɑk] **I** *n*. **1.** (弓的)弧口;箭的尾端[扣弦处]。**2.**【海】帆的前部上端。**II** *vt*. **1.** 给(弓)装弧口。**2.** 搭箭于(弓上)。

noct- *comb*. *f*.〔用于元音前〕= nocti-.

noc·tam·bu·lant [nɔkˈtæmbjulənt; nɑkˋtæmbjələnt] ***a.*** 梦中步行的，梦游的。**-bu·la·tion** [nɔkˌtæmbjuˈleiʃən; nɑkˏtæmbjəˋleʃən] ***n.*** 【医】梦行(症)。**-list** ***n.*** 梦行者。

noc·tam·bule [nɔkˈtæmbjuːl; nɑkˋtæmbjul] ***n.*** 梦中步行者，梦游病者。

noc·tam·bu·lism [nɔkˈtæmbjulizəm; nɑkˋtæmbjəˏlɪzəm] ***n.*** 【医】梦行。

nocti- *comb. f.* "夜"：*nocti*luca.

noc·ti·flo·rous [ˌnɔktiˈflɔːrəs; ˏnɑktɪˋflorəs] ***a.*** 夜间开花的。

noc·ti·lu·ca [ˌnɔktiˈljuːkə; ˏnɑktɪˋlukə] ***n.*** 【动】夜光虫；〔N-〕夜光虫属。

noc·ti·lu·cence [ˌnɔktiˈljuːsns; ˏnɑktəˋljusns] ***n.*** 生物(性)发光；磷花。

noc·ti·lu·cent [ˌnɔktiˈljuːsnt; ˏnɑktəˋlusənt] ***a.*** 夜间发光的。

noc·tiv·a·gant, -gous [nɔkˈtivəgənt, -gəs; nɑkˋtɪvəgənt, -gəs] ***a.*** 夜间出游的，夜间徘徊的。

nocto- *comb. f.* = nocti-.

noc·to·vi·sor [ˈnɔktəvisə; ˋnɑktəvɪsɚ] ***n.*** 红外线摄像机[望远镜]。

noc·tu·id [ˈnɔktʃuwid; ˋnɑktʃʊɪd] ***n.*** 夜蛾科昆虫〔如夜盗蛾等〕。

noc·tule [ˈnɔktjuːl; ˋnɑktʃul] ***n.*** (英国产)褐色大蝙蝠。

noc·turn [ˈnɔktəːn; ˋnɑktɝn] ***n.*** = nocturne.

noc·tur·nal [nɔkˈtəːnl; nɑkˋtɝnəl] **I *a.*** 夜的(*opp.* diurnal)；夜间(发生)的；夜出的，(花)夜开的；【乐】夜曲的。*a ~ sight* 夜景。*a ~ bird* 夜间活动的鸟。*a ~ journey* 夜间旅行。**II *n.*** 【天】夜间时刻测定器。**-ly** ***ad.*** 在夜里，每夜。

noc·turne [ˈnɔktəːn; ˋnɑktɝn] ***n.*** 夜景画；【乐】夜曲，梦幻曲；【宗】夜间礼拜；夜祷。

noc·u·ous [ˈnɔkjuəs; ˋnɑkjuəs] ***a.*** 有害的；有毒的。

nod [nɔd; nɑd] **I *vt.*** (**-dd-**) **1.** 点(头)；点头表示(同意、了解)；点头叫…过来[过去]。**2.** 使弯曲；使屈服。~ *the head* 点头。~ *assent* [*one's farewell*] 点头答应[告别]。— ***vi.*** **1.** 点头，低头；点头答应[招呼、同意、承诺、命令]。**2.** 打瞌睡；不当心弄错；(花、树等点头似地)摇摆；(房屋)倾斜。~ *to a person* 点头打招呼。(***Even***) ***Homer sometimes*** **~*s***. 〔谚〕智者千虑必有一失。~ ***to its fall*** 摇摇欲坠。~ ***and shake the spheres*** 睥睨一世。***have a nodding acquaintanceship with*** 和…只是点头之交；在…上略知一二。**II *n.*** **1.** 点头；点头礼；打瞌睡。**2.** (点头)同意。***be at*** [***dependent*** (***up***)***on***] ***sb.'s*** ~ 在某人支配下，得由某人点头而定。***Land of N-*** 睡乡；【圣】睡眠。***on the*** ~ **1.** 赊购。**2.** 未经正式手续的；有默契的，默认的。

N.O.D. = Naval Ordnance Department〔英〕海军军械司。

nod·al [ˈnəudəl; ˋnodəl] ***a.*** **1.** 节的，结的。**2.** 【物】波节的。~ **circle** 【物】波节圆。

nod·die [ˈnɔdi; ˋnɑdɪ] ***n.*** 〔美〕糊涂虫，笨货。

nod·dle[1] [ˈnɔdl; ˋnɑdl̩] ***n.*** 〔口〕头，脑袋瓜。*Dressing up doesn't fill an empty ~.* 打扮得整齐弥补不了头脑的空虚。

nod·dle[2] [ˈnɔdl; ˋnɑdl̩] ***vt.***, ***vi.*** 点(头)。

nod·dy [ˈnɔdi; ˋnɑdɪ] ***n.*** **1.** 笨人，呆子，傻瓜。**2.** 【鸟】(美国东南海岸常见的)黑燕鸥。~ **suit** 〔军俚〕防化服，防毒服。

node [nəud; nod] ***n.*** **1.** 节；结；瘤；【虫】结脉。**2.** 【植】茎节；【医】硬结肿；结，节结；【天】交点。**3.** 【数】结点，交轨点；叉点；【物】节；波节〔振动体的静止点〕；中心点。**4.** (情节的)曲折，错综复杂。*a current ~* 电流波节。

no·di [ˈnəudai; ˋnodaɪ] nodus 的复数。

nod·i·cal [ˈnəudikl; ˋnɑdɪkl] ***a.*** 【天】交点的。~ *month* 交点月。

no·dose [ˈnəudəus; ˋnodos] ***a.*** 有节的；(木材)疖疤多的。

no·dos·i·ty [nəuˈdɔsiti; nəˋdɑsətɪ] ***n.*** 节；多节；痛风结。

nod·u·lar [ˈnɔdjulə; ˋnɑdʒəlɚ], **nod·u·lat·ed** [ˈnɔdjuleitid; ˋnɑdʒəˏletɪd] ***a.*** **1.** 有节[结、瘤等]的。**2.** 【矿】结核状的；【冶】榴状的。*limestone of ~ structure* 榴状结构石灰石。~ (*graphite*) *cast iron* 【冶】球墨铸铁。

nod·u·la·tion [ˌnɔdjuˈleiʃən; ˏnɑdjəˋleʃən] ***n.*** 生节(块)；有节。

nod·ule [ˈnɔdjuːl; ˋnɑdʒul] ***n.*** 小结；小瘤；【生】小结节；【医】结核，瘤；【地】岩球，矿瘤。~ **bacteria** 根瘤(细)菌。

nod·u·lose, nod·u·lous [ˈnɔdjuləus, -ləs; ˋnɑdʒʊˏlos, -ləs] ***a.*** = nodular 1.

no·dus [ˈnəudəs; ˋnodəs] ***n.*** (*pl.* **-di** [-dai; -daɪ]) **1.** 节，结；瘤；【虫】结脉，腹隆节。**2.** 难点；(情节的)曲折，错综复杂。

No·el [ˈnouəl; ˋnoəl] ***n.*** 诺埃尔〔姓氏，男子名，女子名〕。

No·el, Now·el [nəuˈel, ˈnəuəl; noˋɛl] ***n.*** 圣诞节；〔n-〕圣诞颂歌。

no·e·sis [nəuˈiːsis; noˋisɪs] ***n.*** 【哲】纯理性的认识作用。

no·et·ic [nəuˈetik; noˋɛtɪk] **I *a.*** 【哲】智力的；纯理智的，理性的。**II *n.*** 有智力者。~***s*** 纯理性论，智能论。

nog[1] [nɔg; nɑg] **I *n.*** 木钉，木栓；木砖；【矿】木垛；垛式支架；支柱垫楔。**II *vt.*** (**-gg-**) 用木钉支柱；用木钉钉牢；在…上砌木砖。

nog[2] [nɔg; nɑg] ***n.*** 〔英方〕**1.** 一种浓烈啤酒。**2.** 〔美〕蛋酒，酒、蛋、奶等混合成的饮料(= eggnog)。

nog·gin [ˈnɔgin; ˋnɑgɪn] ***n.*** **1.** 〔古、方〕小杯；一小杯(= 1/4 pint)。**2.** 〔美方〕铅桶。**3.** 〔美俚〕头；智力，脑筋。

nog·ging [ˈnɔgiŋ; ˋnɑgɪn] ***n.*** 木架砖壁；砌在木架间的砖；壁砖。

no·how [ˈnəuhau; ˋnoˏhaʊ] **I *ad.*** 毫不，决不；无论如何不〔通常与 *can* 同用〕。*I can't do it ~.* 我决不能做。**II *a.*** 不舒服；心烦意乱。*feel ~* 感到不舒服。*look ~* 显得心烦意乱。

N.O.I.C. = Naval Officer-in-Charge 海军主管军官。

noil [nɔil; nɔɪl] ***n.*** 〔*sing.*, *pl.*〕【纺】精梳短毛；精梳落棉；针板落棉；(羊毛、丝等的)刷屑；(头发的)梳屑。

noise [ˈnɔiz; nɔɪz] **I *n.*** **1.** 声音，声响。**2.** 叫喊；嘈杂声，噪音；喧闹声；吵闹，骚动，骚扰。**3.** 〔古〕谣言，风声。**4.** 〔美〕东西〔常代替 *stuff* 用〕。*I don't like ~(s).* 我不喜欢吵闹声。~ *in the ear* 耳鸣。*Hold your ~!* 别作声！别响。***make a*** ~ 喧嚷，吵闹；扬名，轰动一时(*about*)。***make a*** ~ ***in the world*** 惹世人评论，名噪一时。***make loud*** **~*s about*** 鼓吹。***make much*** ~ ***about*** 叫嚣。***the*** [***a***] ***big*** ~〔口〕主人，东家，要人，名士；最得好评的影片[戏剧]；主要事件；耸人听闻的声明；重要歌曲节目；重磅炸弹。***The*** ~ ***goes that ....*** 〔古〕据说，据传，谣传。**II *vt.*** 哄传；谣传，传说。*It is ~d abroad that ....* 谣传…。— ***vi.*** 〔罕〕大声谈论；吵，闹。~ **limiter** 【无】杂音抑制器。~ **maker** 发出嘈杂声的人群；(狂欢时)发噪音的器物。~ **pollution** 噪音污染。~ **footprint** 噪声污染所及的地面区域。~ **proof** ***a.*** 防杂音的，隔音的。~ **suppressor** = ~ limiter.

noise·ful [ˈnɔizful; ˋnɔɪzfəl] ***a.*** 吵闹的。

noise·less [ˈnɔizlis; ˋnɔɪzlɪs] ***a.*** 没有声音的；声音很轻的；非常安静的。**-ly** ***ad.*** 静静地，轻轻地。**-ness** ***n.***

noi·sette[1] [nwɑːˈzet; nwɑˋzɛt] ***n.*** (法国)诺瓦氏(Noisette)品种蔷薇。

noi·sette[2] [nwɑːˈzet; nwɑˋzɛt] ***n.*** 〔F.〕〔常作复数用〕【烹】**1.** 小块[片]瘦肉。**2.** 在奶油中煎黄的小马铃薯片。

nois·ies [ˈnɔiziz; ˋnɔɪzɪz] ***n.*** 〔美俚〕有声电影。

nois·i·ly [ˈnɔizili; ˋnɔɪzɪlɪ] ***ad.*** 大声，吵闹地，骚然。**nois·i·ness** ***n.*** 吵闹，骚扰。

noi·some [ˈnɔisəm; ˋnɔɪsəm] ***a.*** 有害的，有毒的；有恶臭的；可厌的。**-ly** ***ad.*** **-ness** ***n.***

N

nois·y [ˈnɔizi; ˋnɔɪzɪ] ***a***. (***nois·i·er***; ***-i·est***) 1. (人、地方等)嘈杂的,喧闹的;(街道)熙熙攘攘的。2. (颜色、服装)过分鲜艳的;(文体)过分华丽[渲染]的。

No·la [ˈnəulə; ˋnolə] ***n***. 诺拉〔女子名〕。

No·lan [ˈnəulən; ˋnolən] ***n***. 诺兰〔男子名〕。

no·lens vo·lens [ˈnəulenzˈvəulenz; ˋnolɛnzˋvolɛnz] 〔L.〕无论愿意不愿意 (= willy-nilly)。

no·li me tan·ge·re [ˈnəulai miː ˈtændʒiri; ˋnolaɪ mi ˋtændʒərɪ] 〔L.〕 1. = touch-me-not【植】凤仙花属。2. 复活的耶稣和 Mary Magdalen 相会的图画。3.【医】侵蚀性溃疡;狼疮。4. 不许接触[插手](的警告)。5. 不可接触的人[物]。*a* ~ *manner* 拒绝人接近的态度。*carry a* ~ *in one's face* 摆出一副铁板面孔。

nol·le pros·e·qui [ˈnɔli ˈprɔsikwai; ˋnɑlɪˋprɑsɪˏkwaɪ] 〔L.〕【法】诉讼中止;原告[检察官]给法庭部分[全部]撤回起诉的通知。

no·lo con·ten·de·re [ˈnəuləu kənˈtendəri; ˋnolo kənˋtɛndərɪ] 〔L.〕 ***n***.【法】无罪申诉〔刑事诉讼中,被告表示不愿进行辩护,但又不承认自己有罪的申诉〕。

no·lo e·pis·co·par·i [ˈnəuləu episkəˈpεərai; ˋnolo ɪˏpɪskəˋpɛraɪ] 〔L.〕【宗】拒绝担任主教,拒任负责职位。

nol·pros [nɔlˈprɔs; ˏnɑlˋprɑs] ***vt***. 〔美〕撤回(起诉的通知),中止诉讼。

nol·pros. 〔Am.〕= *nolle prosequi*.

nom [nɔ̃; nɔ̃] ***n***. 〔F.〕名。~ ***de guerre*** [ˈnɔ̃ːm dəˈgεə; ˏnɔ̃dəˋgɛr] 假名,化名。~ ***de plume*** [-pluːm; -plum] 笔名。

nom. = 1. nomenclature. 2. nominal. 3. nominative.

no·ma [ˈnəumə; ˋnomə] ***n***.【医】水癌,走马疳,坏疽性口炎。

nom·ad [ˈnɔməd, ˈnəumæd; ˋnɑmæd, ˋnomæd] **I** ***n***. 游牧民的一员;流浪者。**II** ***a***. 游牧的;流浪的。

no·mad·ic [nəuˈmædik; noˋmædɪk] ***a***. 游牧的;流浪的。*a* ~ *way of life* 牧民生活方式。~ *children* 流浪儿童。**-al·ly** ***ad***.

nom·ad·ism [ˈnɔmədizəm, ˈnəumædizəm; ˋnɑmædˏɪzəm, ˋnomædˏɪzəm] ***n***. 游牧[流浪]生活;【生】漫游(现象)。

nom·ad·ize [ˈnɔmədaiz; ˋnomædˏaɪz] ***vi***., ***vt***. (使)过游牧生活;(使)流浪。

nom·ad·y [ˈnɔmədi; ˋnɑmədɪ] ***n***. 游牧生活(状态)。

nom·arch [ˈnɔmɑːk; ˋnɑmɑrk] ***n***. (古代埃及或现代希腊的)省[州]长。**-y** ***n***. 省[州]长管区。

nom·bles, num·bles [ˈnʌmblz; ˋnʌmblz] ***n***. 〔*pl*.〕〔古〕鹿内脏。

nom·bril [ˈnɔmbril; ˋnɑmbrɪl] ***n***.【解】脐眼。

nome [nəum; nom] ***n***. (古代埃及或现代希腊的)省[州]。

no·men [ˈnəumən; ˋnomɛn] ***n***. (*pl*. ***nom·i·na*** [ˈnɔminə; ˋnɑmənə]) 中间名字〔古罗马姓名中第一名字与第三名字(姓)之间的名字〕。

no·men·cla·tive [ˈnəumənkleitiv; ˋnomənkletɪv] ***a***. 命名的,名称的,术语的。

no·men·cla·tor [ˈnəumənkleitə; ˋnomənˏkletɚ] ***n***. 1. (科学术语等的)命名者。2. 〔古罗马〕通报来客姓名的侍从。3. 宴会中安顿座位的招待员。4. 专业辞汇集[手册]。

no·men·cla·ture [nəuˈmenklətʃə; ˋnomənˏkletʃɚ] ***n***. 1. (科学、文艺等的)(系统)命名法,记名法;命名原则;专门用语;名称,术语(集、表)。2.【军】编类名称,型别名称;〔罕〕名称;目录。*the* ~ *of music* 音乐术语。

no·mic [ˈnəumik; ˋnomɪk] ***a***. 惯用的,普通的。~ *spelling* 普通拼法。

nomin. = nominative.

nom·i·nal [ˈnɔminl; ˋnɑmənl] **I** ***a***. 1. 名字的,列名的。2. 名义上的,空有其名的;有名无实的。3. 微不足道的,轻微的。4. 名称上的;票面上的。5.【语法】名词性的。6. 按计划进行的;令人满意的。~ *capital* 名义资本。*a* ~ *par* 票面价格。*a* ~ *price* 虚价。*a* ~ *partner* 名义合伙人。~ *quotation*【商】牌价。~ *wages* 名义工资。~ *horse-power*【物】标称马力。~ *value* 票面价值。*a* ~ *list of officers* 职员名册。*a* ~ *register* 名册。**II** ***n***. 名词性的词。**-ism** ***n***.【哲】唯名论 (*opp*. realism)。**-ist** ***n***.【哲】唯名论者。**-lis·tic** ***a***.【哲】唯名论的。

nom·i·nal·ly [ˈnɔminəli; ˋnɑmənlɪ] ***ad***. 名义上,有名无实,空有其名 (*opp*. really)。*He was* ~ *the leader, but others actually wielded the power*. 名义上他是领导者,但实际上是别人掌握实权。

nom·i·nate [ˈnɔmineit; ˋnɑməˏnet] ***vt***. 1. 任命,指定;提名;推荐 (*for*)。2. 命名。3.【赛马】登记(马名)参加比赛。*He was* ~*d for President*. 他被提名为总统候选人。

nom·i·na·tion [ˌnɔmiˈneiʃən; ˏnɑməˋneʃən] ***n***. 1. 任命(权),指定(权);提名(权),推荐(权)。2.【赛马】出场马名登记。*I have a* ~ *at your service*. 我可以推荐你。*the* ~ *day* 候选人提名日。

nom·i·na·ti·val [ˌnɔminəˈtaivəl; ˏnɑmənəˋtaɪvl̩] ***a***. 主格的。

nom·i·na·tive [ˈnɔm*i*nətiv; ˋnɑmənətɪv] **I** ***a***. 1.【语法】主格的。2. [-neitiv; -netɪv] 被提名[指定]的。**II** ***n***.【语法】主格;主格语。*Is it* ~ *or elective*? 提名呢还是选举? *the* ~ *absolute*【语法】(分词的)独立主格〔如 *This being so, I did nothing*. (情况既然如此,我什么也没做)中的 this〕。

nom·i·na·tor [ˈnɔmineitə; ˋnɑməˏnetɚ] ***n***. 提名[指定、任命、推荐]者。

nom·i·nee [nɔmiˈniː; ˏnɑməˋni] ***n***. 被提名[指定、任命、推荐]者。

no·mo·graph [ˈnɔməgrɑːf; ˋnɑməˏgræf], **no·mo·gram** [ˈnɔməgræm; ˋnɑməˏgræm] ***n***. 列线图(解),(计)标图(表),诺谟图。

no·mog·ra·phy [nəuˈmɔgrəfi; noˋmɑgrəfɪ] ***n***. 1. 法律编撰术,法律编撰论。2. 图解构成术。3. 列线图解法;图算学。**-graph·ic** ***a***. **-graph·i·cal·ly** ***ad***.

no·mol·o·gy [nəuˈmɔlədʒi; noˋmɑlədʒɪ] ***n***. 1. 法理学。2. (各种科学的)理论部分,法则论。**-log·i·cal** ***a***.

nom·o·thet·ic, nom·o·thet·i·cal [ˈnɔməˈθetik, -əl; ˏnɑməˋθɛtɪk, -əl] ***a***. 1. 制定法律的。2. 以法律为根据的。3. 研究普遍性规律的科学的。

-nomy *suf*. 表示"法","学": eco*nomy*, astro*nomy*.

non [nɔn; nɑn] ***ad***. 〔L.〕非,不是 (= not)。~ ***assumpsit*** [əˈsʌm*p*sit; əˋsʌm*p*sɪt]【法】被告否认契约的答辩。~ ***compos mentis*** [ˈkɔmpəs ˈmentis; ˋkɑmpəs ˋmɛntɪs]【法】精神错乱的,发狂的。~ ***esse*** [ˈesi(ː); ˋɛsɪ] = nonexistence. ~ ***est*** (***inventus***) [ˈest (inˈventəs); ˋɛst (ɪnˋvɛntəs)] 住址不明(*He is* ~ *est*. 他地址不明)。~***-licet*** [ˈlaiset; ˋlaɪsɛt] ***a***. 〔L.〕不法的。~ ***liquet*** [ˈlaikwet; ˋlaɪkwɛt]【法】(诉讼有疑问时陪审员所作的)延期审判的评决。~ ***nobis*** [ˈnəubis; ˋnobɪs] (荣耀)不要归与我们。~ ***obstante*** [ɔbsˈtæntiː; ɑbsˋtænti] 违背法律的规定。~ ***placet*** [ˈpleiset; ˋplesɛt] 不赞成;投反对票〔教会或大学集会中的〕。~ ***plus ultra*** [plʌsˈʌltrə; plʌsˋʌltrə] 不可越境;极点,绝顶,极致 (= *ne plus ultra*)。~ ***possumus*** [ˈpɔsjuməs; ˋpɔsjuməs] 声明不可能,拒绝行动 (= we cannot)。~ ***prosequitur*** [prəuˈsekwitə; proˋsɛkwɪtɚ]【法】使未按时出席的原告败诉的缺席判决。~ ***sequitur*** [ˈsekwitə; ˋsɛkwɪtɚ] 不合理的推论,不根据前提而下的论断。~**-ism** ***n***. (戒绝一切不良嗜好的)极端禁欲主义。~**profit** 非赢利组织。

non- [ˈnɔn-; ˋnɑn] *pref*. 无,非,不〔non- 多表示简单"否定",而 in- (im-, il-, ir-), un- 等则带有积极"反对"之意: *non*human, *in*human; *non*logical, *il*logical; *non*moral, *im*moral; *non*religious, *irre*ligious〕。

Nona [ˈnəunə; ˋnonə] *n*. 诺娜〔女子名〕。
nona [ˈnəunə; ˋnonə] *n*. 【医】昏睡病。
non·a·bil·i·ty [ˈnɔnəˈbiliti; ˋnɑnəˋbɪlətɪ] *n*. 无能,没本事。
non·ab·stain·er [ˈnɔnəbˈsteinə; ˋnɑnəbˋstenɚ] *n*. 不戒酒的人;不节制的人。
non·ac·cept·ance [ˈnɔnəkˈseptəns; ˏnɑnəkˋsɛptəns] *n*. 不答应;【商】不(接受)承兑。
non·ac·cess [ˈnɔnəkˈses; ˋnɑnəkˋses] *n*. 【法】(夫妇的)不能发生性行为。
non·ac·quaint·ance [ˈnɔnəˈkweintəns; ˋnɑnəˋkwentəns] *n*. 不相识。
non·ad·mis·sion [ˈnɔnədˈmiʃən; ˋnɑnədˋmɪʃən] *n*. 拒绝入场[会,党]。
non·age [ˈnɔnidʒ, ˈnəunidʒ; ˋnɑnɪdʒ,ˋnonɪdʒ] *n*. 1. 青年时期;未成熟;早期。2. 【法】未成熟。
no·na·ge·na·r·i·an [ˌnəunədʒiˈnɛəriən; ˏnɑnədʒəˋnɛrɪən] *a*., *n*. 九十或九十多岁的(人)。
non·ag·gres·sion [ˈnɔnəˈgreʃən; ˏnɑnəˋgrɛʃən] *n*. 不侵略,不侵犯。*a* ~ *pact* 互不侵犯条约。
non·a·gon [ˈnɔnəgən; ˋnɑnəˏgɑn] *n*. 【几】九边形。
no·na·ry [ˈnəunəri; ˋnonərɪ] I *a*. 【数】九进的。II *n*. 九个一组的东西。
non·a·ligned [ˈnɔnəˈlaind; ˏnɑnəˋlaɪnd] *a*. 不结盟的。~ *nations* 不结盟国家。
non·a·lign·ment [ˈnɔnəˈlainmənt; ˏnɑnəˋlaɪnmənt] *n*. 不结盟。*the* ~ *policy* 不结盟政策。
non·an·tag·o·nis·tic [ˈnɔnænˌtægəˈnistik; ˋnɑnænˏtægəˋnɪstɪk] *a*. 非对抗性的。
non·ap·pear·ance [ˈnɔnəˈpiərəns; ˏnɑnəˋpɪrəns] *n*. (当事人或证人)不到法庭。
non·a·que·ous [ˈnɔnˈeikwiəs; ˋnɑnˋekwɪəs] *a*. 【化】非水的。
non·at·tend·ance [ˈnɔnəˈtendəns; ˏnɑnəˋtɛndəns] *n*. 不出席,不到。
non·be·ing [ˈnɔnˈbiːiŋ; ˋnɑnˋbiɪŋ] *n*. 不存在,不存在的东西(= nonexistence)。
non·bel·lig·er·en·cy [ˈnɔnbiˈlidʒərənsi; ˏnɑnbəˋlɪdʒərənsɪ] *n*. 非交战状态,非交战立场。
non·bel·lig·er·ent [ˈnɔnbiˈlidʒərənt; ˏnɑnbəˋlɪdʒərənt] I *a*. 非交战的。*the* ~ *countries* 非交战国。II *n*. 非交战国。
non-book [ˈnɔnˈbuk; ˋnɑnˋbʊk] *n*. 内容无价值的书,为满足市场需要而滥竽充数的书。
non·can·di·date [ˈnɔnˈkændideit; ˋnɑnˋkændɪdet] *n*. 沉默候选人〔尚未宣布或不愿宣布其候选人资格的人〕。
nonce [nɔns; nɑns] I *n*. 现时,目前〔本词只用于下列短语〕。*for the* ~ 目前,暂且。II *a*. 临时的,只以当时为限的。~ **word** [**noun, verb etc.**] (为某一场合或特殊需要)临时造的词[名词,动词]。
non·cha·lance [ˈnɔnʃələns; ˋnɑnʃələns] *n*. 不关心;冷淡,不激动。*with* ~ 冷淡地,漫不经心地,无动于衷地。
non·cha·lant [ˈnɔnʃələnt; ˋnɑnʃələnt] *a*. 不关心的,漫不经心的;若无其事的;不激动的,冷淡的。*assume a* ~ *air* 装作不关心的样子。**-ly** *ad*.
non·claim [nɔnˈkleim, ˋnɔnkleim; ˋnɑnˏklem, nɑnˋklem] *n*. 【法】(在规定期间内)不提出要求。
Non·Coll., non·coll [ˈnɔnkɔl; ˋnɑnkəl] *a*., *n*. 〔口〕= noncollegiate.
non·col·le·gi·ate [ˈnɔnkəˈliːdʒiit; ˋnɑnkəˋlidʒɪɪt] I *a*. 不属于学院的,(大学中)不属于任何学院的;(大学)不设学院的。II *n*. 不属于任何学院的大学生。
non·com [ˈnɔnkɔm; ˏnɑnˋkɑm] *n*. 〔口〕军士〔noncommissioned officer 的缩略〕。
non·com·ba·tant [ˈnɔnˈkɔmbətənt; nɑnˋkɑmbətənt] *n*., *a*. 非战斗人员[军医、随军牧师等](的);(战时)一般市民(的)。
non·com·bus·ti·ble [ˈnɔnkəmˈbʌstəbl; ˏnɑnkəmˋbʌstəbl̩] I *a*. 不燃的。II *n*. 不燃物。
non·com·mis·sioned [ˈnɔnˈkəmiʃənd; ˏnɑnkəˋmɪʃənd] *a*. 无委任状的,未受任命的;无军官衔的。~ *officer* 军士。
non·com·mit·tal [ˌnɔnkəˈmitəl; ˏnɑnkəˋmɪtl̩] *a*. (态度、观点等)不明朗的,不表明意见的;不承担义务的。*a* ~ *answer* 不明确的回答。*nod a vague and* ~ *assent* 模棱两可含糊其词地点头同意。
non·com·mu·ni·cant [ˈnɔnkəˈmjuːnikənt; ˏnɑnkəˋmjunɪkənt] *a*., *n*. 不受圣餐的(人);不做礼拜的(人)。
non·com·mu·nist [ˈnɔnˈkɔmjunist; ˋnɑnˋkɑmjʊnɪst] *a*. 1. 非共产主义的;非共产党员的。2. 证明不是共产党员的。
non·com·pli·ance [ˌnɔnkəmˈplaiəns; ˏnɑnkəmˋplaɪəns] *n*. 不顺从,不同意;固执。
non·com·pli·ant [ˌnɔnkəmˈplaiənt; ˏnɑnkəmˋplaɪənt] *n*. 不顺从的人,固执的人。
non compos mentis [nɔnˈkɔmpəsˈmentis; nɑnˋkɑmpəsˋmɛntɪs] 〔L.〕【法】精神失常的,精神上不适宜于处理事务的。
non·con·dens·ing [ˈnɔnkənˈdensiŋ; ˋnɑnkənˋdɛnsɪŋ] *a*. 不凝的,不能冷凝的。*a* ~ *engine* 排汽蒸汽机。
non·con·duc·ting [ˈnɔnkənˈdʌktiŋ; ˏnɑnkənˋdʌktɪŋ] *a*. 【物】不传导的;绝缘的。~ *material* 绝缘材料。
non·con·duc·tive [ˈnɔnkənˈdʌktiv; ˋnɑnkənˋdʌktɪv] *a*. 不传导的;绝缘的。
non·con·duc·tor [ˈnɔnkənˈdʌktə; ˏnɑnkənˋdʌktɚ] *n*. 【物】非导体;绝缘体。
non·con·fi·dence [ˈnɔnˈkɔnfidəns; ˋnɑnˋkɑnfədəns] *n*. 不信任。*a vote of* ~ 不信任投票。
non·con·form·ance [ˈnɔnkənˈfɔːməns; ˏnɑnkənˋfɔrməns] *n*. 不服从。~ *to the tradition of conformity* 【英史】不服从遵奉国教的传统。
non·con·form·ing [ˈnɔnkənˈfɔːmiŋ; ˋnɑnkənˋfɔrmɪŋ] *a*. 不服从国教的;非国教教徒的,新教徒的。
non·con·form·ism [ˈnɔnkənˈfɔːmizəm; ˋnɑnkənˋfɔrmɪzəm] *n*. 不遵从传统成规的作风;〔英〕不信奉国教。
non·con·form·ist [ˈnɔnkənˈfɔːmist; ˏnɑnkənˋfɔrmɪst] I *n*. 1. 〔常 N-〕〔英〕非国教徒,不信奉国教的人。2. 不符合传统规范的人。II *a*. 不信奉国教的;不墨守成规的。
non·con·form·i·ty [ˈnɔnkənˈfɔːmiti; ˏnɑnkənˋfɔrmətɪ] *n*. 1. 不墨守成规。2. 不一致,不符合。3. 【地】非整合。4. 〔常 N-〕不信奉国教;〔集合词〕新教教徒;新教教义。
non·con·sump·tive [ˈnɔnkənˈsʌmptiv; ˏnɑnkənˋsʌmptɪv] *a*. 不消耗[破坏、开发]自然资源的。
non·con·tent [ˈnɔnkənˈtent; ˋnɑnkənˏtɛnt] *n*. (英国上议院中)投反对票的活动;投反对票的议员。
non·con·ten·tious [ˈnɔnkənˈtenʃəs; ˋnɑnkənˋtɛnʃəs] *a*. 非争论性的,不大会引起争论的。
non·con·tin·u·ous [ˈnɔnkənˈtinjuəs; ˋnɑnkənˋtɪnjʊəs] *a*. 不继续的;间断的。
non·co·op·er·a·tion [ˈnɔnkəuˌɔpəˈreiʃən; ˏnɑnkoˏɑpəˋreʃən] *n*. 不合作;(印度甘地的)不合作主义。**-ist** *n*. 采取不合作态度者,不合作主义者。
non·coun·try [ˈnɔnˈkʌntri; ˋnɑnkʌntrɪ] *n*. 不存在的国家〔不被承认是国家的地理区域〕。
non·de·liv·er·y [ˈnɔndiˈlivəri; ˏnɑndɪˋlɪvərɪ] *n*. (*pl*. *-er·ies*) 无法投递;无法投递的邮件[货物];不能送达。
non·de·script [ˈnɔnˈdiskript; ˋnɑndɪˏskrɪpt] I *a*. 形容不出的;难区别的,难以归类的;不三不四的,莫明其妙的。II *n*. 不三不四的,莫名其妙的人[东西]。
non·dis·junc·tion [ˈnɔndisˈdʒʌŋkʃən; ˋnɑndɪsˋdʒʌŋkʃən] *n*. 【生】不分离,不分裂。
non·du·ra·ble [ˈnɔnˈdjuərəbl; nɑnˋdjʊrəbl̩] I *a*. 不耐用的,不耐久的。II *n*. 〔*pl*.〕不耐用物品,不耐久物品。

N

-a·bil·i·ty [nɔnˌdjuərəˈbiliti; nɑnˏdjʊrəˋbɪlətɪ] *n*.

none[1] [nʌn; nʌn] **I** ***pro*.** **1.** 〔指代人、事物或东西的一部分;可以独立使用,也可以同 of 结合;有无前行词均可,动词使用单复数形式均可〕没谁,没人;没有任何事物;没有任何一点。*There were ~ present*. 当时没人在场。*N- knows the weight of another's burden*. 彼此谁也不知道对方的难处。*There are faults from which ~ of us is (are) free*. 有些错误我们任何人都不能避免。*We should not call one a hero that is ~*. 本来不是英雄的,就不应当说成是英雄。*The children were playing, and she took care that ~ were hurt*. 孩子们正在游戏,她小心翼翼,哪一个都不叫他们受伤。*N- were left when I came*. 我来时谁都不在。*They choose ~ but the best*. 他们只选最好的。**2.** 〔同 of 结合时带有较强烈的否定意味〕…当中无论哪个都[谁都,什么都,一点也]不[没有]。*N- of us are infallible*. 我们当中无论谁都会犯错误的。*N- of them came*. 他们当中谁都没来。*N- of this money is mine*. 这笔钱没有一点是我的。*It is ~ of your business*. 这(毫)不干你的事。*N- of your impudence [cheeks]!* 不要无礼! 别厚颜无耻! *N- of this concerns me*. 这事跟我一点也没关系。*We've heard ~ of him since*. 从此以后他杳无音信。*N- of his work has been done*. 他的活儿一点也没干。*She tried on five hats, but ~ of them were attractive*. 她试戴了五顶帽子,一顶也不合适。~ **but** 只有;除…以外谁都不(*N- but fools have believed*. 除傻瓜外从来没人相信)。~ **other than** 不是别的,而是;恰恰是。**II** ***a*.** 〔古〕没有;〔= no, not any; 通常用在以元音或 h 开头的单词前〕没有。*There is ~ available*. 再无别的可弄到的东西了。*They gave me ~ other answer*. 他们对我无别的事可以奉告。*make of ~ effect* 〔古〕使无效。
III ***ad*.** 〔用于'the + 比较级'或 too, so 之前〕一点也不…,决没有。*I am ~ the better for it*. 我决未因此而好一点。*He is ~ so wise*. 他不怎样聪明。*You got home ~ too soon*. 你回来得未免太迟了。~ **the less** 虽然那样还是,仍然。

none[2] [nəun; non] *n*. nones 2 的单数。

non·ef·fec·tive [ˌnɔniˈfektiv; ˏnɑnəˋfɛktɪv] **I** *a*. **1.** 没效力的;不起作用的。**2.** 【军】无战斗力的。**II** *n*. 【军】无战斗力的兵员。

non·e·go [ˈnɔnˈegəu, -ˈi:gəu; nɑnˈigo, -ˋɛgo] *n*. 【哲】非我;客观,外界。

non·e·las·tic [ˈnɔniˈlæstik; ˋnɑnɪˈlæstɪk] *a*. 无弹性的,无伸缩性的。**-ity** [ˌnɔnilæˈtisiti; ˏnɑnɪlæˋtɪsətɪ] *n*.

non·e·lec·tive [ˈnɔniˈlektiv; ˋnɑnɪˋlɛktɪv] *a*. 不依选举(产生)的。

non·e·lec·tro·lyte [ˈnɔniˈlektrəulait; ˋnɑnɪˋlɛktrolaɪt] *n*. 【化】非电解质;不电离质。

non·e·lim·i·na·tion [ˈnɔniˌlimiˈneiʃən; ˋnɑnɪˏlɪmɪˋneʃən] *n*. 不排除,不消灭,不消除。*mutual ~* 互不并吞。

non·en·ti·ty [nɔˈnentiti; nɑnˋɛntətɪ] *n*. **1.** 不存在,非实在。**2.** 不存在的东西,非实在物,虚构;【哲】不存在的实质。**3.** 不足取[无足轻重]的人[东西]。

nones [nəunz; nonz] *n*. [*pl*.] **1.** (古罗马历)3, 5, 7, 10 月的第 7 日,其他各月的第 5 日。**2.** 【宗】9 时课〔日出后第 9 时的祈祷〕;(一日 5 次的)第 5 次(祈祷)。

non·es·sen·tial [ˈnɔniˈsenʃəl; ˏnɑnəˋsɛnʃəl] *a*., *n*. 非本质的(东西),不重要的(人)。

none·such, nonsuch [ˈnʌnsʌtʃ; ˋnʌnˏsʌtʃ] **I** *n*. **1.** 无比的事物,无以匹敌的人[东西],无双的人,典型。**2.** 〔俚〕狂妄自大的人。**3.** 【植】红色剪秋罗。**II** *a*. 〔古〕无双的,无比的。

no·net [nə*u*ˈnet; noˋnɛt] *n*. **1.** 【乐】九重奏[唱](乐曲)。**2.** 【物】九重线。

none·the·less [ˌnʌnðəˈles; ˏnʌnðəˋlɛs] *ad*. = nevertheless.

non·Eu·clid·e·an [ˈnɔnju:kˈlidiən; ˋnɑnjuˋklɪdɪən] *a*. 【数】非欧几里得的。~ *geometry* 非欧几里得几何(学)。

non·e·vent [ˈnɔniˈvent; ˋnɑnɪˏvɛnt] *n*. 大肆宣扬即将来临而并未发生的事。

non·ex·ist·ence [ˈnɔnigˈzistəns; ˏnɑnɪgˋzɪstəns] *n*. 不存在(物);非实在(物)。

non·fea·sance [ˈnɔnˈfi:zəns; nɑnˋfizṇs] *n*. 【法】不履行义务;懈怠。

non·fer·rous [ˈnɔnˈferəs; nɑnˋfɛrəs] *a*. 非铁的。~ *metals* 有色金属。

non·fic·tion [ˈnɔnˈfikʃən; nɑnˋfɪkʃən] *n*. 非小说类文学作品〔如随笔,传记等〕。

non·fi·nite [ˈnɔnˈfainait; ˋnɑnˋfaɪnaɪt] *a*. 【语法】非述语形式的,非限定的。*the ~ forms of the verb* 动词的非述语[非限定]形式〔不定式、分词和动名词〕。

non·flam·ma·ble [ˈnɔnˈflæməbl; nɑnˋflæməbḷ] *a*. 不易燃的。

non·ful·fil(l)ment [ˈnɔnfulˈfilmənt; ˏnɑnfulˋfɪlmənt] *n*. 不履行,不完成。

non·grad·ed [ˈnɔnˈgreidid; ˋnɑnˋgredɪd] *a*. **1.** 无(熟练程度)等级的。**2.** 〔美〕(教育)不分班级的。

non·he·ro [ˈnɔnhiərəu, nɔnˈhiərəu; ˋnɑnhɪro, nɑnˋhɪro] *n*. = anti-hero.

non-ho·ming [ˈnɔnˈhəumiŋ; ˋnɑnˋhomɪŋ] 【无】不归位的。

non·hu·man [ˈnɔnˈhjumən; nɑnˈhjumən] *a*. 非人类的;不属于人类的。

non·hy·gro·scop·ic [ˈnɔnˌhaigrəˈskɔpik; ˋnɑnˏhaɪgrəˋskɔpɪk] *a*. 不收湿的。

non·i·de·al [ˈnɔnaidiəl; ˏnɑnaɪˋdɪəl] *a*. 【物】非理想的。

non·i·den·ti·ty [ˈnɔnaiˈdentiti; ˋnɑnaɪˋdɛntɪtɪ] *n*. 【哲】不同一性。

no·nil·lion [nə*u*ˈniljən; noˋnɪljən] *n*. 〔英〕100 万的九次幂[乘方]〔1 后加五十四个 0 之数〕;〔美,法〕1000 的 10 次幂[乘方]〔1 后加三十个 0 之数〕。

non·in·duc·tive [ˈnɔninˈdʌktiv; ˏnɑnɪnˋdʌktɪv] *a*. 【电】无感的。*a ~ resistance* 一个无感电阻。

non·in·ter·fer·ence [ˌnɔnintəˈfiərəns; ˏnɑnɪntəˋfɪrəns] *n*. 不干涉;【电】不相互干扰。~ *in each other's internal affairs* 互不干涉内政。

non·in·ter·ven·tion [ˈnɔnintəˈvenʃən; ˏnɑnɪntəˋvɛnʃən] *n*. 不干涉(内政等);不干涉主义。**-ist** *n*.

non·i·us [ˈnɔnjəs; ˋnɑnjəs] *n*. 【机】游标,游尺。

non·join·der [ˈnɔnˈdʒɔində; nɑnˋdʒɔɪndə] *n*. 【法】(当事人的)不参预诉讼。

non·ju·ror [ˈnɔnˈdʒuə; nɑnˋdʒurə] *n*. 【英史】拒绝立誓效忠者。

non·le·gal [ˈnɔnˈli:gəl; nɑnˋligḷ] *a*. 非法律的,与法律无关的。

non·le·thal [ˈnɔnˈli:θəl; ˋnɑnˈliθəl] *a*. 不致命的,非杀伤性的。*a ~ agent* 非杀伤性化学制剂。

non·log·i·cal [ˈnɔnˈlɔdʒikəl; ˏnɑnˋlɑdʒɪkḷ] *a*. 不从逻辑得出的,不根据逻辑的。

non·lu·mi·nous [ˈnɔnˈlu:minəs; ˋnɑnˋlumɪnəs] *a*. 无光的,不发光的。

non·mem·ber [ˈnɔnˈmembə; nɑnˋmɛmbə] *n*. 非会员,非党人士。**-ship** *n*. 非会员的地位[身分]。

non·met·al [ˈnɔnˈmetl; nɑnˋmɛtḷ] *n*. 非金属。**-tal·lic** [ˈnɔnmiˈtælik; ˋnɑnmɪˋtælɪk] *a*.

non·mor·al [nɔnˈmɔrəl; nɑnˋmɔrəl] *a*. 与道德无关的。

non·ne·go·ti·a·ble [ˌnɔnniˈgəuʃjəbl; ˏnɑnnɪˋgoʃjəbḷ] *a*. 不可谈判的,无商议余地的;禁止转让的。

non·ni·trog·e·nous [ˌnɔnnaiˈtrɔdʒənəs; ˏnɑnnaɪˋtrɑdʒənəs] *a*. 不含氮的。

non·nu·cle·ar [ˈnɔnnu:kliə, nɔnˈnju:kljə; ˋnɑnnuklɪə, nɑnˋnjukljə] **I** *a*. 非核的。**II** *n*. 非核国家,只拥有常规武器的国家。~ *warfare* 常规战争。

no-no [ˈnəuˌnəu; ˋnoˏno] *n*. 〔美口〕禁忌，禁例。

non·ob·jec·tive [ˈnɔnəbˈdʒektiv; ˏnanəbˋdʒɛktɪv] *a*. 〔美〕非写实派的；不模仿自然事物的，抽象的。

non·ob·serv·ance [ˈnɔnəbˈzəːvəns; ˏnanəbˋzɝvəns] *n*. 不遵从，违反。

non obs., non obst. = *non obstante*.

non·of·fice·hold·ing [ˈnɔnˈɔfishəuldiŋ; ˋnanˋɔfɪsholdɪŋ] *a*. 没有官职的；下台的，在野的。

non·or·gas·mic [ˈnɔnɔːˈgæzik; ˋnanɔˋgæzmɪk] *a*. 【医】性欲高潮不能的。

non·par·tic·i·pat·ing [ˈnɔnpaːˈtisipeitiŋ; ˋnanparˋtɪsɪpetɪŋ] *a*. 不参加的；无分红权的。

non·pa·reil [ˈnɔnpərəl; ˏnanpəˋrɛl] **I** *a*. 无比的，无双的；无上的。**II** *n*. **1.** 无比的人[东西]。**2.** 【印】六点(*point*)活字。**3.** 粘有小白糖珠的巧克力糖；(装饰糖果、糕点等的)各色小糖珠。**4.** (用 nonpareil 命名的)一种苹果[鸟、小麦(等)]。

non·par·ti·san, non·par·ti·zan [ˈnɔnˈpaːtizən, -zæn; nanˋpartəzn, -zæn] *a*. 超党派的，不受任何党派控制的，非党人的。

non·par·ty [nɔnˈpaːti; nanˋpartɪ] *a*. 无党派的；非党的；党外的。

non·pay·ment [ˌnɔnˈpeimənt; ˏnanˋpemənt] *n*. 不支付，无支付能力。*His property was confiscated for ～ of taxes*. 他的财产因不支付税款而被没收了。

non·per·form·ance [ˌnɔnpəːˈfɔːməns; ˏnanpɚˋfɔrməns] *n*. 不履行，不实行，不完成。

non·pe·ri·od·ic [ˈnɔnˌpiəriˈɔdik; nanˏpɪrɪˋadɪk] *a*. 非周期性的。

non·plus [ˌnɔnˈplʌs; nanˋplʌs] **I** *vt*. (**-plus(s)ed; -plus(s)ing**) 使为难，使狼狈；使迷惑。**II** *n*. 狼狈，为难；迷惑；难关，窘境。***at a ～*** 进退两难，左右为难。***put* [*reduce*] *sb. to a ～*** 使某人为难，使窘困。

non·prin·ci·pled [ˈnɔnˈprinsəpld; ˋnanˋprɪnsəpl̩d] *a*. 与原则无关的，非原则的。

non·pro·duc·tive [ˈnɔnprəˈdʌktiv; ˏnanprəˋdʌktɪv] *a*. 不能生产的，无生产力的；非生产性的。

non·pro·fes·sion·al [ˈnɔnprəˈfeʃənl; ˋnanprəˋfɛʃənl̩] *a*. **1.** 无职业的；无专行的。**2.** 非科班出身的；和专门工作无关系的。**3.** 离开了职业的。*The doctor paid me a ～ visit*. 医生以普通朋友的关系来看了我。

non·pro·fit [ˈnɔnˈprɔfit; nanˋprafɪt] *a*. 非营利的。*a ～ association* 非营利团体。

non·pro·lif·er·a·tion [ˈnɔnprəˌlifəˈreiʃən; ˋnanproˏlɪfəˋreʃən] *n*. 不增生，不增殖；不扩散，防扩散(特指防核扩散)。～ **treaty** 防止核扩散条约〔略作 NPT〕。

non pros. = *non prosequitur*.

non-pros [ˌnɔnˈprɔs; ˏnanˋpras] *vt*. (**-pros·sed; -pros·sing**) 【法】对(原告)作缺席判决。

non-pro·vid·ed [ˈnɔnprəˈvaidid; ˋnanprəˋvaɪdɪd] *a*. (英国小学)不靠地方当局供给经费的。

non·rat·ed [nɔnˈreitid; nanˋretɪd] *a*. 没有等级的，没有军衔的〔尤指(美国海军)征募来的水兵〕。

non·read·er [ˈnɔnˈriːdə; ˋnanˋridɚ] *n*. 不能阅读的人；阅读能力很差的孩子。

non·rep·re·sen·ta·tion·al [ˈnɔnreprizenˈteiʃənəl; ˏnanrɛprɪzɛnˋteʃənəl] *a*. (艺术)非写实的，抽象的。**-ism** *n*. 非写实主义。

non·res·i·dent [ˈnɔnˈrezidənt; nanˋrɛzədənt] **I** *a*. 不住在工作地点的；通勤的；不寄宿的。*a ～ student* 走读生。**II** *n*. (不住在工作地点的)通勤员工；暂居的人；走读生。**-tial** [-ʃəl; -ʃəl] *a*.

non·re·sis·tance [ˈnɔnriˈzistəns; ˋnanrɪˋzɪstəns] *n*. 不抵抗(主义)；(对权力、法律等的)屈服；【电】无耗阻。

non·re·sis·tant [ˈnɔnriˈzistənt; ˏnanrɪˋzɪstənt] **I** *a*. 不抵抗(主义)的。**II** *n*. 不抵抗主义者；不主张武力抗暴者。

non·re·straint [ˈnɔnriˈstreint; ˏnanrɪˋstrent] *n*. **1.** 无约束，无拘束。**2.** (对精神病患者的)非约束性控制。

non·re·stric·tive [ˌnɔnrisˈtriktiv, ˈnɔnrisˈtriktiv; ˏnanrɪsˋtrɪktɪv, ˋnanrɪsˋtrɪktɪv] *a*. 【语法】非限制性的。

non·rig·id [nɔnˈridʒid; nanˋrɪdʒɪd] *a*. 【空】软式的；【物】非刚性的。～ *sheeting* 软质片材。～ *plastics* 非刚性塑料[塑胶]。

non·sched·uled [nɔnˈʃedʒuːld, nɔnˈskedʒuːld; nanˋʃɛdʒuld, nanˋskɛdʒuld] *a*. 未作安排的，未排定的；(客机)不定期的。*a ～ airline* 不定期航空公司。

non·sec·tar·i·an [ˈnɔnsekˈtɛəriən; ˏnansɛkˋtɛrɪən] *a*. 非宗派的；不属于任何宗教派别的。

non·sense [ˈnɔnsəns; ˋnansɛns] **I** *n*. **1.** 无意义的话，荒谬[荒唐]话，胡说；废话。**2.** 荒谬[荒唐]的念头[事情]。**3.** 胡闹。**II** *int*. 荒唐！无聊！胡扯！*None of your ～!* 别胡闹！*N-!* = *Stuff and ～!* 胡说八道！～ **book** 荒谬的书。～ **verses** [**rhymes**] 打油诗。

non·sen·si·cal [nɔnˈsensikəl; nanˋsɛnsɪkl̩] *a*. 没有意义[条理]的。

non se·qui·tur [nɔnˈsekwitə; nanˋsɛkwɪtɚ] 〔L.〕【逻】不根据前提的推理(= it does not follow)。

non·sex·ual [nɔnˈseksjuəl; nanˋsɛkʃuəl] *a*. 无性的，不论性别的。

non-sked [nɔnˈsked; nanˋskɛd] **I** *a*. 〔美口〕(客机)不定期的。**II** *n*. 〔口〕不定期客机；不定期运输机；不定期航空运输公司。*He got his training with the ～s*. 他在不定期航空公司受过训练！

non·skid [ˈnɔnskid; ˋnanˋskɪd] *a*. 防滑的，不滑的。*a ～ tread* (轮胎的)防滑轮距。

non·smok·er [ˈnɔnˈsməukə; nanˋsmokɚ] *n*. 不抽烟的人。

non·so·cial [ˈnɔnˈsəuʃəl; ˋnanˋsoʃəl] *a*. 非社交的，不爱交际的。

non·so·ci·e·ty [ˈnɔnsəuˈsaiəti; ˋnansoˋsaɪətɪ] *a*., *n*. 无工会等组织关系的(人、团体)。

non·stand·ard [ˈnɔnˈstændəd; nanˋstændɚd] *a*. 不标准的，不规范的。

non·sta·ple [ˈnɔnˈsteipl; ˋnanˋstepl̩] **I** *n*. 副产品。**II** *a*. 非主要的，副的。～ *food* [*foodstuff*] 副食品。

non·stat·ic [ˈnɔnˈstætik; ˋnanˋstætɪk] *a*. **1.** 非静止的。**2.** 【电】无静电荷的，静电荷不积聚的。**3.** 【无】不产生无线电干扰的。

non·stop [ˈnɔnˈstɔp; ˋnanˋstap] **I** *a*. 不停的，不断的；(列车、飞机等)直达的。*a ～ flight* 直达飞行。**II** *n*. 直达列车[公共汽车]。**III** *ad*. 不停地，直达地。*fly ～ from London to Paris* 由伦敦直飞巴黎。

non·stri·at·ed [ˈnɔnstraiˈeitid, nɔnˈstraieitid; ˋnanstraɪˋetɪd, nanˋstraɪetɪd] *a*. 【解】(肌肉)无横纹的。～ **muscle** (= smooth muscle) 平滑肌。

non·strik·er [ˈnɔnˈstraikə; ˋnanˋstraɪkɚ] *n*. **1.** 不参加罢工的人。**2.** 【板球】没有接着对方来球的击球员。

non·such [ˈnɔnsʌtʃ, ˈnʌnsʌtʃ; ˋnansʌtʃ, ˋnʌnˏsʌtʃ] *n*. = nonesuch.

non·suit [ˈnɔnˈsjuːt, -ˈsuːt; nanˋsjut, -ˋsut] **I** *n*. 【法】(因原告证据不足)诉讼驳回。**II** *vt*. 驳回(原告或诉案)。

non·sup·port [ˈnɔnsəˈpɔːt; ˏnansəˋport] *n*. 【法】不履行法定的抚养(或赡养)义务。

non·tox·ic [ˈnɔnˈtɔksik; nanˋtaksɪk] *a*. 无毒的。～ *plasticizer* 无毒增塑剂。

non trop·po [ˈnɔn ˈtrɔpəu; nan ˋtrɔppo] 〔It.〕【音】不太过，适度。

non-U [ˈnɔnjuː; nanˋju] *a*. 与上层阶级[上流社会]不相称[适应]的；(举止、谈吐、趣味等)非富有阶级的。

non·u·ni·form [ˈnɔnˈjuːnifɔːm; ˋnanˋjunɪfɔrm] *a*. 不一致的，不统一的；不均匀的。**-i·ty** [ˈnɔnˌjuːniˈfɔːmiti; ˋnanˏjunɪˋfɔrmətɪ] *n*.

non·un·ion [ˈnɔnˈjuːnjən; nanˋjunjən] **I** *a*. 不属于[不

N

加入]工会的;不承认工会的;不遵守工会规章的。**II** ***n.*** 【医】(骨折等)不愈合。**-ist** ***n.*** 非工会会员;非工会主义者。

non·u·ple [ˈnɔnjupl; ˋnɑnjupḷ] ***a.*** 九倍的,九重的;九个一组[一套]的。

non·u·plet [ˈnɔnjuplit; ˋnɑnjuplɪt] ***n.*** 一胎九婴。

non·use [ˈnɔnˈjuːs; ˋnɑnˋjus] ***n.*** 不使用,放弃;不形成习惯。

non·us·er [nɔnˈjuːzə; nɑnˋjuzɚ] ***n.*** **1.** 不使用。**2.**【法】弃权。**3.** 不使用者;无毒瘾者。

non·vi·a·ble [ˈnɔnˈvaiəbl; ˋnɑnˋvaɪəbḷ] ***a.*** 不能生存和成长的;不能发展和活动的。

non·vi·o·lence [ˈnɔnˈvaiələns; nɑnˋvaɪələns] ***n.*** 非暴力主义。*He is too well aware of the doubts about the efficacy of* ~. 对非暴力主义的实效的怀疑,他是深有体会和感触的。

non·vot·er [ˈnɔnˈvəutə; nɑnˋvotɚ] ***n.*** **1.** 不投票者。**2.** 无表决权的人;无投票权的人。

non·vot·ing [ˈnɔnˈvəutiŋ; ˋnɑnˋvotɪŋ] ***a.*** **1.** 不投票的,弃权的。**2.** 无投票权的,无表决权的。

non-white [ˈnɔnˈhwait; nɑnˋhwaɪt] ***n.***, ***a.*** 非白种人(的)。*the growth of* ~ *communities* 非白种人居民的增长。

non·wo·ven [ˈnɔnˈwəuvən; nɑnˋwovən] ***a.*** 非纺织的。~ *fabric* 非纺织布。

non·yl [ˈnɔnil, ˈnəu-; ˋnɑnɪl, ˋno-] ***n.*** 【化】壬(烷)基。

non·ze·ro [nɔnˈziərəu; nɑnˋzɪro] ***a.*** 非零的,非零形态的。

noo·dle[1] [ˈnuːdl; ˋnudḷ] **I** ***n.*** 笨人,傻子;〔俚〕脑袋瓜,头。**II** ***vt.*** 愚弄。**-ness** ***n.***

noo·dle[2] [ˈnuːdl; ˋnudḷ] ***n.*** 面条,鸡蛋面;粉条。

noo·dle[3] [ˈnuːdl; ˋnudḷ] ***vi.*** 〔口〕**1.** 随随便便即兴演奏乐器。**2.** 探索[钻研]某一主意;想出一个主意;思考出一个结论。**3.** (在电脑键盘上)胡乱击键。

noo·dle·head [ˈnuːdlˌhed; ˋnudḷˏhɛd] ***n.*** 笨蛋,傻瓜(= fool, simpleton, blockhead)。

nook [nuk; nʊk] **I** ***n.*** 凹角,角落;隐匿处,避难处;偏僻地方。*look in every* ~ *and corner* 到处找;查看每一个角落。**II** ***vt.*** 把…藏[放]在角落里。

noon [nuːn; nun] **I** ***n.*** **1.** 正午,中午〔此义一般不加定冠词。如:at (high) ~ 在中午〕。**2.**〔诗〕夜半,午夜。**3.** 全盛期,顶点。*a* ~ *basket* 〔美〕饭篮子(= lunch-basket)。*the* ~ *of night* 〔诗〕午夜。*the* ~ *of life* 壮年期。***as clear as*** ~ 明明白白,一清二楚。**II** ***vi.*** 〔美〕午时休息,吃午饭。~**-mark** ***n.*** 【天】(正)午标,(正)午线。

noon·day [ˈnuːndei; ˋnunˏde] **I** ***n.*** 正午,中午;全盛。**II** ***a.*** 中午的。*the* ~ *meal* 午餐。***as clear*** [***plain***] ***as*** ~ [***the sun of*** ~] 极明白;一清二楚。

noon·flow·er [ˈnuːnˌflauə; ˋnunˏflaʊɚ] ***n.*** 【植】松叶菊。

noon·ing [ˈnuːniŋ; ˋnunɪŋ] ***n.*** 〔美〕中午,正午;午餐;午休(时间)。*take one's* ~ 午休,吃午餐。

noon·tide [ˈnuːntaid; ˋnunˏtaɪd] ***n.*** **1.** 中午(= noon, noonday)。**2.**〔the ~〕最高点,全盛期。**3.**〔主持〕午夜(= midnight)。

noon·time [ˈnuːntaim; ˋnunˏtaɪm] ***n.*** **1.** 中午(= noon, noonday, noontide)。*Will he be home at* ~? 他中午在家吗?

noose [nuːs, nuːz; nus, nuz] **I** ***n.*** 套索;绞索;〔the〕绞刑;〔喻〕(夫妻等的)羁绊,束缚;圈套。*put one's neck into the* ~ 自投罗网。~*s tied round the necks of* 套在…脖子上的绞索。***The*** ~ ***is hanging.*** 〔美俚〕万事俱备。**II** ***vt.*** 用套索捕捉;处绞刑;绞死;安圈套,诱入圈套。

no·trop·ic [ˌnjuːəuˈtrɔpik; ˏnuoˋtrɔpɪk] **I** ***n.*** 【医】健脑乐。**II** ***a.*** 健脑的。

noov(e) [nuːv; nuv] ***n.***, ***a.*** 暴发户(的)〔源自法语 noveau riche〕。

N.O.P., **n.o.p.** = not otherwise provided (for) 除非另有规定。

NOP, N.O.P. = not our publication 非我社出版物。

no·pal [ˈnəupəl, ˌnəuˈpɔl; ˋnopəl, ˏnoˋpɔl] ***n.*** 胭脂仙人掌属植物(尤指胭脂仙人掌)。

no-par [ˈnəuˈpɑː; ˋnoˋpɑr] ***a.*** 无票面价值的。*a* ~ *certificate of stock* 无票面价值的公债券。

nope [nəup; nop] ***ad.*** 〔美俚〕不〔否定的答覆〕(= no[2])。

no-peck [ˈnəupek; ˋnopɛk] ***a.*** 〔美俚〕防窥视的。

nor [nɔː, 弱 no; nɔr, no] ***conj.*** (既不)…也不,(…没有)…也没有。**1.**〔和 neither 或 not 连用〕*He can neither read* ~ *write*. 他不会读也不会写。*Not a man*, ~ *a child*, *is to be seen*. 大人小孩都不见[没有]。*He can't do it*, ~ *can I*, ~ *can anybody*. 他做不来,我也做不来,任何人也做不来。**2.**〔古、诗〕〔省去 neither〕*Thou* ~ *I have made the world*. 创造这个世界的既不是你也不是我。*I cannot go*, ~ *do I want*. 我不能去,也不想去。*I have never seen her*, ~ *even heard of her*. 我从来没有看到她,也没有听说过。*He borrows not*, ~ *lends*. 他不向人借钱,也不借钱给人。*He has no mother* ~ *father*. 他没有母亲也没有父亲。**3.**〔诗〕〔nor ... nor = neither ... nor〕*N- silver* ~ *gold can buy it*. 黄金白银都买不到它。**4.**〔同主句中的否定词 not, no, never 配合,表示否定的继续,助动词与主语的排列采用倒装语序〕(不…)也不。*I said I had not seen it*, ~ *had I*. 我说我没看见那个东西,实际上我也没有看见。**5.**〔在肯定句之后,意义内容与主句一致并有所加强,也用倒装语序〕(= and ... not) 但未,但不。*The tale is long*, ~ *have I heard it out*. 故事冗长,但我也没有听到底。*I am going*, ~ *can anybody prevent it*. 我是要去的,这是任何人也阻止不了的。*They are happy*, ~ *need we worry*. 他们很幸福,我们实际上也不必担心。**6.**〔用在独立句子的句首,但与上文有衔接关系〕(因此)也不。*N- am I ashamed to confess my ignorance of what I do not know*. (因此)我是不知道的事就承认说不知道,并不害羞。**7.**〔方〕比(= than)。*Have you ever seen a nicer place* ~ *this place*? 您曾看见过比这个地方还要美好的地方吗? *I know better* ~ *you*. 我比你知道得多。

nor' [nɔː; nɔr] ***a.*** 【海】= north: ~*east*, ~*west*.

NOR [nɔː; nɔr] ***n.*** 【自】"或非"〔一种电子计算机逻辑电路〕。

Nor. = **1.** North. **2.** Norway; Norwegian. **3.** Norman.

No·ra(h) [ˈnɔːrə; ˋnɔrə] ***n.*** 诺拉〔女子名〕。

NORAD = North American Air Defense 北美空防联合司令部。

Nor·bert [ˈnɔːbət; ˋnɔrbɚt] ***n.*** 诺伯特〔男子名〕。

Nor·dic [ˈnɔːdik; ˋnɔrdɪk] **I** ***a.*** **1.** 北欧人的。**2.** (包括速度滑和飞跃动作的)北欧式滑雪赛的。**II** ***n.*** **1.** 北欧人。**2.**〔俚〕亚利安人 (Aryan)。

nor·ep·i·neph·rine [ˌnɔːrepiˈnefrin, -riːn; ˋnɔˏrɛpɪˋnɛfrɪn, -rin] ***n.*** 降肾上腺素,去甲肾上腺(激)素。

Nor·folk [ˈnɔːfək; ˋnɔrfək] ***n.*** **1.** 诺福克〔英国英格兰郡名〕。**2.** 美国东岸弗吉尼亚州一港市。~ **capon** 赤鲱。~ **dumpling** [**turkey**]〔蔑〕英国诺福克人的诨名。~ **Howard**〔英俚〕臭虫,床虱。**N- Island pine**【植】南美杉 (Araucaria excelsa)。~ **jacket** 腰部有带的男用宽上衣。

nor·i [ˈnɔːri; ˋnɔrɪ] ***n.*** 紫菜,海苔片〔一种日本海藻,包裹寿司用〕。

no·ri·a [ˈnɔːriə; ˋnɔrɪə] ***n.*** 戽水车。

nor·land [ˈnɔːlənd; ˋnɔrlənd] ***n.*** 〔英、诗〕北国,北部地方。**-er** ***n.*** 北方人。

norm [nɔːm; nɔrm] ***n.*** **1.** 规范,模范;准则;(教育)标准。**2.** (劳动)定额;【数】模方;范数。***above*** ~ 定额以上的。***below*** ~ 定额以下的。

Nor·ma [ˈnɔːmə; ˋnɔrmə] ***n*.** 诺玛〔女子名〕。

nor·mal [ˈnɔːməl; ˋnɔrml] **I *a*. 1.** 正常的,平常的,普通的;平均的。**2.** 正规的,标准的,额定的,规定的。**3.** 智力正常的,精神健全的。**4.**【化】正(链)的;中性的;规度的;当量的;【物】简正的;【几】垂直的;正交的;法线的;中性的。**5.**【生】不受感染的。**6.**【经】按成品最高成本定价的。**II *n*. 1.** 常态,正常;(人体的)正常温度;平温;平均;标准。**2.**【几】法线,垂直(线)。**3.**【物】平均量;【化】当量。***off*** ～ 离位,不正常。～ **acceleration** 法向[正交]加速度。～ **axis** 法线轴,垂直轴。～ **bud** 定芽。～ **content** [**solution**]【化】当量含量[溶液]。～ **deviate** 正态偏差。～ **distribution**【统】正态分布。～ **force** 法向力,正交力,垂直力;正常武力。～ **forest** 法正林。～ (**frequency**) **curve** (= Gaussian curve)【物】高斯曲线。～ *horse power* 正常马力。～ **infantry division** 普通步兵师。～ **line**【机】法线。～ **mode**【物】简正方式。～ **plane**【机、数】法(线)面。～ **region** 适生区。～ **school** 师范学校。～ **section**【数】正截面,正截口;【机】正断面。～ **spectrum** 匀排光谱。～ **state** (= ground state)【物】基态。～ **temperature** 标准温度,正常温度。～ **vibration** 简正振动。

nor·mal·i·ty [nɔːˈmæliti; nɔrˋmæləti], **nor·mal·cy** [-məlsi; -mlsɪ] ***n*.** 正常状态,标准;【化】当量(浓度),规度。

nor·mal·ize [ˈnɔːməlaiz; ˋnɔrml͵aɪz] ***vt*.** 使正常化,使标准化;使规格化。**-i·za·tion** [ˌnɔːməlaiˈzeiʃən; ͵nɔrmləˋzeʃən] ***n*. 1.** 正常化,标准化;【化】规定化(作用)。**2.**【冶】正火作用。

nor·mal·iz·er [ˈnɔːməlaizə; ˋnɔrml͵aɪzɚ] ***n*.** 标准化者,归一化者,规格化者。

nor·mal·ly [ˈnɔːməli; ˋnɔrməlɪ] ***ad*.** 正常情况下,通常,一般说来 (= as a rule)。

Nor·man[1] [ˈnɔːmən; ˋnɔrmən] **I *a*.** (法国西北部)诺曼底(人、民族)的。**II *n*.** 诺曼底人 (= Northman);诺曼底法兰西人;诺曼底法兰西语 (= Norman-French)。～ **English** 诺曼底英语。～ **French** 诺曼底法语。～ **Style**【建】诺曼底式〔以简朴、坚实、圆拱为特征〕。

Nor·man[2] [ˈnɔːmən; ˋnɔrmən] ***n*.** 诺曼〔男子名〕。

Nor·man·dy, Nor·man·die [ˈnɔːməndi, ˌnɔːmɑːnˈdiː; ˋnɔrməndɪ, ͵nɔrmɑ̃ˋdi] ***n*.** 诺曼底〔法国一地区〕。

Nor·man·esque [ˌnɔməˈnesk; ͵nɔrmənˋɛsk] ***a*.**【建】诺曼底式的。

Nor·man·ism [ˈnɔːmənizm; ˋnɔrmənɪzm] ***n*.** 诺曼底式(主义);对诺曼底文化的袒护。

Nor·man·ize [ˈnɔːmənaiz; ˋnɔrmən͵aɪz] ***vt*., *vi*.** (使)诺曼化。**-i·za·tion** [ˌnɔːmənaiˈzeiʃən; ͵nɔrmənɪˋzeʃən] ***n*.**

norm·a·tive [ˈnɔːmətiv; ˋnɔrmətɪv] ***a*. 1.** 标准的,规范的。**2.** 惯用法规律的。～ **grammar** 规范语法。**-ly *ad*.**

nor·mo·ten·sive [ˌnɔːməuˈtensiv; ͵nɔrmoˋtɛnsɪv] ***a*.**【医】正常血压的。

Norn [nɔːn; nɔrn] ***n*.**【北欧神】诺恩〔命运的三女神之一〕。

nor·nic·o·tine [nɔːˈnikətiːn; nɔrˋnɪkətin] ***n*.**【化】降烟碱;去甲烟碱。

Nor·ris [ˈnɔris; ˋnɔrɪs] ***n*.** 诺里斯〔姓氏,男子名〕。

Norse [nɔːs; nɔrs] **I *a*.** 斯堪的纳维亚的;挪威的,挪威人[语]的。**II *n*.** 〔the ～〕〔作复数用〕古代斯堪的纳维亚人[语];西斯堪的纳维亚人[语];北欧人[语];挪威人[语]。*N- mythology* 北欧神话。

Norse·land [ˈnɔːslənd; ˋnɔrslənd] ***n*.** 挪威的别称;北欧国家;斯堪的纳维亚。

Norse·man [ˈnɔːsmən; ˋnɔrsmən] ***n*.** 古代挪威人;古代斯堪的纳维亚人。

Norsk [nɔːsk; nɔrsk] ***a*., *n*.** = Norse.

North [nɔːθ; nɔrθ] ***n*.** 诺斯〔姓氏〕。

north [nɔːθ; nɔrθ] **I *n*. 1.** 〔通常作 the ～〕北,北方,北部。**2.** 〔N-〕英国北部;〔N-〕美国北部各州。**3.** 北半球;北极地方;〔诗〕北风;〔N-〕(大都位于北纬度地区的)经济发达国家〔集合名词,统称"北",相对于经济不发达的"南"而言,如"北南对话"即指此〕。～ *by east* [*west*] 北偏东[西]〔自正北偏东[西]11°15′〕。*in the* ～ *of* 在…的北部。*on* [*to*] *the* ～ *of* ... 在…的北面。**II *a*.** 北的,北方的,北部的;朝北的;在北方的;从北方来的,位于北方的。***be too far*** ～〔俚〕太伶俐,过于狡猾。**III *ad*.** 在北方,向北方;自北方。***due*** ～ 在正北。*lie* ～ *and south* 纵贯南北。～ *of* 在…北方。*a room facing* ～ 朝北方的房间。**N- Atlantic Treaty Organization** 北大西洋公约组织〔略作 NATO〕。**N- Britain** = Scotland〔略 *N. B.*〕。**N- Country** 英国(或英格兰的)北部;北美北部〔包括 Alaska 和加拿大的 Yukon 地区〕。**N- Island** 北岛〔新西兰两主岛之一〕。～ **land**〔诗〕北国,北方。～ **light** 从北面来的光线 (= north-light);(画室的)北窗;北极光。～ **pole** 北极。**N- Sea** 北海〔英国与西欧之间的海〕。～ **star** 北极星。

North·amp·ton·shire [nɔːˈθæmptənʃiə; nɔrθˋæmptən͵ʃɪr] ***n*.** 北安普敦郡〔英国〕。

North·ants = Northampton(shire).

north·bound [ˈnɔːθˌbaund; ˋnɔrθ͵baʊnd] ***a*.** 向北方的,北行的。

North Carolina [ˈnɔːθ ˌkærəˈlainə; ˋnɔrθ͵kærəˋlaɪnə] 北卡罗来纳〔美国州名〕。**North Car·o·lin·i·an *a*., *n*.** 北卡罗来纳州的(人)。

North·cliffe [ˈnɔːθklif; ˋnɔrθklɪf] ***n*.** 诺斯克利夫〔姓氏〕。

North Dakota [ˈnɔːθ dəˈkəutə; ˋnɔrθ dəˋkotə] 北达科他〔美国州名〕。

North Da·ko·tan [ˈnɔːθ dəˈkəutən; ˋnɔrθ dəˋkotən] ***a*., *n*.** 北达科他州的(人)。

north·east [ˈnɔːθˈiːst, ˈnɔːrˈiːst; ͵nɔrθˋist, ˋnɔrˋist] **I *n*.** 东北;东北地方;〔诗〕东北风。**II *a*.** 东北的,在东北的;自东北的。**III *ad*.** 在东北,向东北;从东北。～ *by east* [*north*] 东北偏东[北]〔自东北偏东[北]11°15′〕～**er *n*. 1.** (猛烈的)东北风。**2.** 雨帽。**-er·ly *a*., *ad*.** 向东北(的);从东北(吹来)的。**-ern *a*.** = north-easterly. **-ward 1. *ad*., *a*.** 在东北方(的),朝东北(的)。**2. *n*.** 东北地区;东北方。**-ward(s) *ad*.** 在[向]东北。**-ward·ly *ad*., *a*.** 向东北方(的);来自东北(的)。

north·er [ˈnɔːðə; ˋnɔrðɚ] ***n*.** 〔美〕(冬季吹向墨西哥湾的)寒冷的北风;南下寒潮;剧烈的北风,北来风。**-ly *ad*., *a*.** 向北(的),自北(的)。

north·ern [ˈnɔːðən; ˋnɔrðɚn] **I *a*.** (*superl*. ～*most*) 北的,北方的,住在北部的;北方特有的;〔N-〕美国北部的。**II *n*. 1.** 北方人 (= northerner)。**2.** 〔美〕北风;(自北而来的)暴风雨。*the N- States* 美国北部各州。*the* ～ *lights* 北极光。**N- Cross**【天】北十字(天鹅座)。**N- Crown**【天】北冕(星)座 (= Corona Borealis)。**N- Hemisphere** 北半球。**N- Ireland** 北爱尔兰。

north·ern·er [ˈnɔːðənə; ˋnɔrðɚnɚ] ***n*.** 北方人;〔N-〕〔美〕美国北方人。

north·ern·most [ˈnɔːðənməust; ˋnɔrðɚn͵most] ***a*.** 最北端的,极北的。

north·ing [ˈnɔːθiŋ, -ðiŋ; ˋnɔrθɪŋ, -ðɪŋ] ***n*.**【海】北进,北驶,北航;【天】(天体的)北偏,北向纬度差;北中天,北中;北赤纬。*make a very little* ～ (航行中的船)北进少许。

north·land [ˈnɔːθˈlənd; ˋnɔrθlənd] ***n*.** 〔诗〕北方,北方地方;〔N-〕(地球的)北部;〔N-〕斯堪的纳维亚半岛。

north-light [ˈnɔːθˈlait; ˋnɔrθˋlaɪt] ***n*.** 〔常 *pl*.〕北极光。

North·man [ˈnɔːθmən; ˋnɔrθmən] ***n*.** 古代斯堪的纳维亚人,北欧人;加拿大北方人;北欧海盗。

north-north·east [ˈnɔːθˌnɔːθˈiːst, ˈnɔːnɔː-; ͵nɔrθnɔrθˋist, ˋnɔrnɔr-] **I *n*.** 北东北〔正北偏东 22°30′〕。**II *ad*., *a*. 1.** 北东北(的),向北东北。**2.** 来自北东北(的),吹北东北风(的)。

N

north-north·west [ˈnɔːθˌnɔːθˈwest; ˋnɔrθˏnɔrθˋwɛst] **I** *n*. 北西北〔正北偏西 22°30′〕。**II** *ad*., *a*. **1.** 北西北(的),向北西北。**2.** 来自北西北(的),吹北西北风(的)。

north-po·lar [ˈnɔːθˈpəulə; ˏnɔrθˋpolɚ] *a*. 北极的。

North·umb = Northumberland 诺森伯兰郡〔英国〕。

North·um·bri·an [nɔːˈθʌmbriən; nɔrˋθʌmbrɪən] *a*., *n*. (英国)诺森伯兰 (Northumbria) 的(人、方言);诺森伯兰郡的(人、方言)。

north·ward [ˈnɔːθwəd; ˋnɔrθwɚd] **I** *a*. 向北的;来自北方的。**II** *ad*. 向北,向北方;来自北方。**III** *n*. 向北的方向;北方的地区。

north·ward·ly [ˈnɔːθwədli; ˋnɔrθwɚdlɪ] *ad*., *a*. 向北方(的)。

north·wards [ˈnɔːθwədz; ˋnɔrθwɚdz] *ad*. = northward (*ad*.).

north·west [ˈnɔːθˈwest, ˈnɔːˈwest; ˏnɔrθˋwest, nɔrˋwɛst] **I** *n*. 西北;西北部;西北地方;〔the N-〕美国西北部;加拿大西北部。~ *by north* 西北偏北〔西北偏北 11°15′〕。~ *by west* 西北偏西〔西北偏西 11°15′〕。**II** *a*. 西北的;向西北的;自西北的。**III** *ad*. 向西北,在西北。**N- Mounted Police** 加拿大西北部骑警队。**N- Passage** 西北航道〔从大西洋经欧亚两洲北部诸海到达太平洋的航道〕。**N- Territories** 西北地区〔加拿大北部一地区,首府为渥太华〕。**-er** 强烈的西北风。**-erly** *ad*., *a*. 向西北(的);从西北(吹来的)。**-ern** *a*. 西北的,在西北的;自西北的。**-ward** *ad*., *a*., *n*. = northwest. **-wardly** *ad*., *a*. = northwestward. **-ward(s)** *ad*. = northwest.

Nor·ton [ˈnɔːtn; ˋnɔrtn̩] *n*. 诺顿〔姓氏,男子名〕。

Norw. = **1.** Norway. **2.** Norwegian.

nor·ward(s) [ˈnɔːwəd(z); ˋnɔrwɚd(z)] *ad*., *a*., *n*. = northward(s).

Nor·way [ˈnɔːwei; ˋnɔrwe] *n*. 挪威〔欧洲〕。**N- maple** 【植】挪威槭 (*Acer platanoides*)〔美国常种此树以遮荫〕。**N- pine** (= red pine) 挪威松。**N- rat** 【动】褐家鼠 (*Rattus norvegicus*)。**N- spruce** 【植】挪威云杉 (*Picea abies*)。

Nor·we·gian [nɔːˈwiːdʒən; nɔrˋwidʒən] **I** *a*. 挪威(人、语)的。**II** *n*. 挪威人[语]。~ **elkhound** 【动】挪威猎麋犬〔挪威产中等高矮、粗短身材的猎犬,毛灰厚,尾后卷至背部〕。

nor'-west·er [ˈnɔːˈwestə; ˏnɔrˋwɛstɚ] *n*. **1.** = northwester. **2.** 一杯烧酒。**3.** 油布帽;〔美〕(水手穿的)油布外套。

Nor·wic. = Norwih.

Nos., **Nos**, **nos**, **nos.** = numbers.

nose [nəuz; noz] **I** *n*. **1.** 鼻;(动物)鼻口部;吻;嗅觉。**2.** 香气;气味 (*of*)。**3.** 管口,筒口,枪口,喷嘴;前缘,头部;船头;【空】机首;【高尔夫球】球棒头;水雷(等)头。**4.** 地角,突出部。**5.** 〔英俚〕(警察的)暗探,探员。*the bridge of the* ~ 鼻梁。*a vegetable* ~ 蒜头鼻子。*an aquiline* ~ 鹰鼻,钩鼻。***as plain as the ~ in* [*on*] *one's face*** 非常明白,一清二楚。***bite sb.'s ~ off*** 气势汹汹地回答某人。***bloody sb.'s ~*** 伤害某人自尊心,挫伤某人。***blow one's ~*** 擤鼻子。***by a ~*** 〔美〕以少许之差(输赢)。***cannot see beyond one's ~*** 鼠目寸光。***count ~s*** 数赞成人数;单依人数来决定事情。***cut* [*bite*] *off one's ~ to spite one's face*** 拿自己出气;跟自己过不去;为了跟别人呕气而伤害自己。***follow one's ~*** 笔直走;依本能行动,任性而行。***have a good ~*** 鼻子灵,嗅觉敏感。***have a ~ for news*** 善于采访新闻。***hold one's ~*** 捏鼻子。***in spite of sb.'s ~*** 不顾某人反对。***keep one's ~ clean*** 〔美〕不喝酒。***keep* [*put*, *hold*] *one's* [*sb.'s*] *~ to the grindstone*** 使自己[某人]埋头苦干。***lead sb. by the ~*** 牵着某人鼻子走。***look down one's ~ at*** 〔口〕藐视。***make a long ~ at*** (把拇指搁在鼻端,其余四指张开)对某人表示轻蔑,嘲弄某人。***make one's ~ swell*** 令人羡慕,使人忌妒。***measure ~s*** 遇见。***~ of wax*** 随人摆布的人[东西]。***not to be able to see beyond one's ~*** [*see no further than one's ~*] 眼光短浅;〔转〕鼠目寸光。***~ to ~*** 面对面。***on the ~*** 〔俚〕**1.** (赛马)跑第一。**2.** 准确,恰,正。***parson's ~*** 〔喻〕(煮熟的)鸡鸭等禽类的屁股。***pay through the ~*** 付出惊人巨款,花很多钱;付出很大代价。***poke* [*put*, *thrust*] *one's ~ into*** (*another's business*) 干涉,插手别人的事情,管闲事。***put sb.'s ~ out of joint*** 撵走某人;夺走某人的爱;破坏某人的计划;排挤某人(的职位等)。***rub sb.'s ~ in it*** 粗暴地提醒某人别忘记他所犯的错误。***snap one's ~ off*** = *bite one's ~ off*. ***speak through one's ~*** 用鼻音说话。***tell ~s*** = *count ~s*. ***turn up one's ~ at*** 瞧不起,不理会。***under one's*** (***very***) ***~*** 就在某人面前;不顾某人不高兴。***with one's ~ at the grindstone*** 费力地,辛辛苦苦做活[过日子等]。***with one's ~ in the air*** 神气活现,自高自大。

II *vt*. **1.** 闻;用鼻子品评(酒)等。**2.** 嗅出,闻出;探出,侦探出,看出 (*out*)。**3.** (船等)以头部探(路)小心前进。**4.** 用鼻子触[擦、塞入]。**5.** 〔古〕反对。**6.** 用鼻音说[唱]。~ *a job in everything* 事事都想捞一手。*The ship ~d her way through the winding channel*. 船在蜿蜒的海峡中小心驶过。—*vi*. **1.** 闻,嗅 (*at*; *about*)。**2.** 探索,打听 (*after*; *for*);干涉 (*into a matter*)。**3.** (船等)小心探索着前进。**4.** 【地】倾斜 (*in*);露出 (*out*)。**5.** 〔英〕送报告,出告。~ *ahead* 〔美运〕以少许之差领前。~ *down* [*up*] 【空】机首朝下降落[朝上上升]。~ *out* 嗅出,闻出;察觉出;〔美〕【体】以少量之差打败对方。~**-ape** 【动】长鼻猿。~**bag** 秣囊,马粮袋;〔口〕(旅行等用的)饭盒子;防毒面具。~**band** (马的)鼻羁。~**bleed** 鼻出血,衄血。~ **candy** 〔美俚〕嗅用麻醉品。~ **cone** (火箭的)头部,前锥体。~**-dive** 【空】俯冲,急降;〔喻〕(价格等的)猛跌,暴落;(事业等的)骤衰。~**-down** **1.** *a*. 【空】机首朝下的。**2.** *vi*. 把机头朝下。~ **drops** 鼻药水。~**guard** 〔美口〕鼻卫〔美式橄榄球比赛中直对对方中锋的防守中卫〕。~ **gas** 喷嚏性毒气。~ **gay** (芳香的)花束。~**-led** *a*. 任人拖着鼻子走的。~ **monkey** *n*. = noseape. ~**-to-**~ 面对面。~ **ornament** 鼻饰,鼻环。~ **paint** 〔美俚〕酒。~**-piece** 鼻羁;接(线)头;(显微镜按对物镜处的)换镜旋座[盘];(水管、风箱等的)口,嘴。~**-rag** 〔俚〕手帕。~ **ring** (牛、猪等的)鼻环,鼻圈。~**-spike** 顶针。~ **warmer** 〔俚〕短烟嘴。~**wheel** (飞机的)降落前轮。~**wing** 【解】鼻翼。**-less** *a*. **-like** *a*.

-nosed [ˈnəuzd; ˋnozd] *comb*. *f*. 〔构成复合词〕*a*. …(形)鼻子的。bottle-*nosed* 酒壶鼻子的。

nos·er [ˈnəuzə; ˋnozɚ] *n*. 〔俚〕**1.** 强逆风,顶头风。**2.** 爱管闲事的人;被雇用的密探。*a dead* ~ 猛烈的顶头风。

nose·y [ˈnəuzi; ˋnozɪ] *a*. (***nos·i·er***; ***-i·est***) = nosy.

nosh [nɔʃ; nɑʃ] **I** *vt*., *vi*. 〔俚〕吃(快餐),吃(小吃)。**II** *n*. 〔俚〕快餐,小吃。~ **up** 〔主英〕盛筵。**-er** *n*. 吃快餐[小吃]的人。

nos·i·ly [ˈnəuzili; ˋnozɪlɪ] *ad*. 好打听地;爱管闲事地。

nos·i·ness [ˈnəuzinis; ˋnozɪnɪs] *n*. 好打听;爱管闲事。

nos·ing [ˈnəuziŋ; ˋnozɪŋ] *n*. 【建】突缘饰;梯级突边;突边上的金属包覆物。

noso- *comb*. *f*. 病: *noso*graphy.

no·sog·ra·phy [nəuˈsɔgrəfi; noˋsɑgrəfɪ] *n*. 疾病记述学,病情学。

nos·o·log·ic, **nos·o·log·i·cal** [ˌnɔsəˈlɔdʒik, -əl; ˏnɑsəˋlɑdʒɪk, -əl] *a*. 疾病分类学的。**-log·i·cal·ly** *ad*.

no·sol·o·gy [nəuˈsɔlədʒi; noˋsɑlədʒɪ] *n*. 疾病分类学[表]。

nos·tal·gi·a [nɔsˈtældʒiə, -dʒjə; nɑˋstældʒɪə, -dʒjə] *n*. 怀乡病,乡愁,怀旧,留恋过去。**nos·tal·gic** [-dʒik; -dʒɪk] *a*. **nos·tal·gist** [-dʒist; -dʒɪst] *n*.

nos·toc [ˈnɔstɔk; ˋnɑstɑk] *n*. 念珠藻属植物。

nos·to·log·ic [ˌnɔstəˈlɔdʒik; ˏnɑstəˋlɑdʒɪk] *a*. 老年医学的,老年学的。

nos·tol·o·gy [nɔsˈtɔlədʒi; nasˋtalədʒɪ] *n*. 老年病学。

nos·to·ma·ni·a [ˌnɔstəˈmeiniə; ˏnastəˋmenɪə] *n*. 【心】怀乡病;留恋过去,怀旧。

Nos·tra·da·mus [ˌnɔstrəˈdeiməs; ˏnastrəˋdeməs] *n*. 1. 诺斯特拉达穆斯〔1503—1566,法国占星术士〕。2. 〔n-〕自称能卜未来吉凶的预言者。

nos·tril [ˈnɔstril; ˋnastrəl] *n*. 鼻孔;鼻孔内壁。***the breath of one's ~s*** (生命中)不可缺少的东西。***stink in sb.'s ~s*** 被某人厌恶。

nos·tril·(l)ed [ˈnɔstrild; ˋnastrɪld] *a*. 有鼻孔的。

nos·trum [ˈnɔstrəm; ˋnastrəm] *n*. 1. 注册成药;秘方。2. 骗人疗法;骗人特效药。3. 〔蔑〕(解决政治、社会问题等的)妙策;万应灵药。

nos·y [ˈnəuzi; ˋnozɪ] **I** *a*. (***nos·i·er***; ***-i·est***) 〔口〕1. 大鼻子的;好管闲事的。2. (谷草)发恶臭的;(红茶)有香味的。3. 对恶臭很敏感的。**II** *n*. 〔俚〕大鼻子〔绰号〕。***N- Parker*** 〔英俚〕爱管闲事的人。

not [nɔt, 助动词后的弱读 nt; nat] *ad*. 不。1. 〔谓语、句子的否定语〕(a)用作助动词的否定式时,常略作 n't: is*n't*, are*n't*, was*n't*, were*n't*, have*n't*, has*n't*, had*n't*, do*n't* [dəunt; dont], does*n't*, did*n't*, wo*n't* [wəunt; wont], would*n't*, sha*n't* [ʃɑːnt; ʃænt], should*n't*, ca*n't* [kɑːnt, Am. kænt; kænt, kant], may*n't*, might*n't*, must*n't* [mʌsnt; mʌsnt], ought*n't*, need*n't*, dare*n't*, used*n't* [juːsnt; jusnt]. (b) 和其他动词连用时。古语通常放在动词之后,现代语则与 do, does 连用以示否定;〔古〕*I know* ~ =〔书〕*I do* ~ [duːnɔt; dunot] *know* =〔口〕*I don't know*; 〔疑问形式〕*Is it* ~?, *Will you* ~?, *Do you* ~ (*go*)? =〔口〕*Isn't it*? *Won't you*? *Don't you* (*go*)? 2. 〔谓语以外的词、短语、从句的否定〕(a)〔在 *Litotes* (婉转反语法)及 *Periphrasis* (委婉语)中〕~ *a few* 不少。~ *a little* 不少。~ *once or* [*nor*] *twice* 不只一二次,好几次,屡次。~ *reluctant* 非常高兴;极乐意。~ *seldom* 常常。~ *without some doubt* 带着几分怀疑。(b)〔用于分词不定式之前以示否定〕*I begged him not to go out*. 我要求他不要出去。*N- knowing, I cannot say*. 我不知道,所以说不出来。3. 〔以单词用作全句的否定〕~ *any* = no, none. ~ *anybody* = nobody. ~ *anyone* = no one. ~ *anything* = nothing. ~ *anywhere* = nowhere. ~ *either* = neither. ~ *ever* = never. ~ *nearly* = by no means. *Will he come*? — *N- he* (= No, he won't)! 他会来吗? ——他不会(来)。*The French will* ~ *fight*, ~ *they*. 法国人恐怕不会打,他们不会打。4. 〔与 all, both 和 every 等连用,表示部分否定〕*N- everyone can succeed*. 不是人人都会成功的。*All is* ~ *gold that glitters*. 发亮的东西不一定都是黄金。*I don't know both*. 我并非两方面都知道〔只知道一方面〕。5. 〔否定的句子、动词、从句等的省略代用语〕*Is he ill*? — *N- at all* 他病了吗? ——一点也没病。*Right or* ~, *it is a fact*. 不管对不对,那是事实。*Is he ill*? — *I think* ~. 他是病了吗? ——我想不是病。*Will it rain tomorrow*? — *I hope* ~. 明天会下雨吗? ——希望不会。6. 〔在动词 believe, expect, fancy, fear, hope, imagine, suppose, think, trust, 副词 perhaps, probably, absolutely 等,和词组 be afraid 等后面以代表其后所否定的从句〕*I don't think it is now five o'clock yet*. 我认为现在还不到五点钟。***if*** ~ 不然的话。~ ***a*** 一个也不…(*N- a man answered*. 一个人也没有回答。~ *a breath of air* 一丝丝风也没有)。***N- at all*** 〔Eng.〕(=〔Am.〕*You are welcome*). 哪里的话,别客气。~ ***... but*** 不是…而是…(*He is* ~ *my son, but my nephew*. 他不是我的儿子,而是我的侄儿)。~ ***but that*** [***what ...***] ~〔古〕= ***but*** 然而还是,虽然,但不是不…(*I cannot do it*, ~ *but that a stronger man might*. 我不能做,但并不是说比我强的人也不能做)。~ ***dry behind the ears*** 〔美俚〕无经验的;乳臭未干的;不成熟的;未学坏的。~ ***having*** [***taking***] ***any*** 〔美俚〕无意于,不打算干(*Risk my life jaywalking*? — *No! I'm* ~ *having any*. 要我冒生命危险违章穿过马路吗? ——对不起! 我不干)。~ ***my funeral*** 〔美俚〕不关我事,不是我的责任。~ ***only ... but*** (***also***) 不仅…而且…。~ ***so*** 不是那样。~ ***so hot*** 〔美俚〕并不怎样好[聪明、漂亮、有趣、成功];普普通通。~ ***sufficient*** 〔银行退票用语〕(存数)不足〔略 N. S.〕。~ ***that ...*** 并不是((*It is*) ~ *that I dislike you*. 并非是我讨厌你。*If he said so* — ~ *that he ever did* — *he lied*. 他要是那样说——并不是说他那样说过——他便撒谎了)。~ ***that ... but that ...*** 不是(因为)…而是(因为)…。***N- that I know of***. 据我所知并不是这样。~ ***with it*** 〔美俚〕局外人。

NOTE = noe of the above 把选票上的名字全勾掉。

no·ta [ˈnəutə; ˋnotə] notum 的复数。

no·ta be·ne [ˈnəutə ˈbiːni; ˋnotəˋbinɪ] 〔L.〕〔略 N.B. 或 n. b.〕注意。

no·ta·bil·i·a [ˌnəutəˈbilie; ˏnotəˋbɪlɪə] *n*. 〔*pl*.〕值得注意的事物。

no·ta·bil·i·ty [ˌnəutəˈbiliti; ˏnotəˋbɪlətɪ] *n*. 1. 值得注意的[显著的]性质;显要人物;名人;〔罕〕值得一看的事物。2. 〔英、古〕(主妇的)当家手腕。*notabilities in political and economic circles* 政界和经济界的知名人士。

no·ta·ble [ˈnəutəbl; ˋnotəbl] **I** *a*. 1. 值得注意的,显著的;著名的,显要的;【化】可知觉的。2. 〔英常 ˈnɔtəbl; ˋnɑtəbl〕(主妇)会当家的。**II** *n*. 1. 著名人士,要人。2. 〔N-〕【法国史】法王召集参加紧急会议的知名人士。3. 〔罕〕著名事物。**-ness** *n*. **-bly** *ad*. 显著地,著名地;格外地,特别地。

no·tal·gi·a [nəuˈtældʒiə; noˋtældʒɪə] *n*. 【医】背痛。

NOT-AND gate [ˈnɔtˈænd geit; ˋnatˋænd get] *n*. 【自】"与非"门。

no·tan·dum [nəuˈtændəm; noˋtændəm] *n*. (*pl*. **~s**, ***-da*** [-də; -də]) 〔L.〕值得注意的事项或其记录;备忘录。

no·tar·i·al [nəuˈtɛəriəl; noˋtɛrɪəl] *a*. 公证人的,公证的。~ *acts* 公证手续。*a* ~ *deed* 公证证书。**-ly** *ad*. 由公证人。

no·ta·rize [ˈnəutəraiz; ˋnotəˏraɪz] *vt*. (***-riz·ed***; ***-riz·ing***) 以公证人资格证实。**-ri·za·tion** [ˌnəutəraiˈzeiʃən; ˏnotəraɪˋzeʃən] *n*.

no·ta·ry [ˈnəutəri; ˋnotərɪ] *n*. 公证人〔又称 ~ public 或 public ~〕;〔古〕书记,秘书。

no·ta·tion [nəuˈteiʃən; noˋteʃən] *n*. 1. 记号,用号,符号,标志(法),表示法。2. 【数】记数法。3. 【乐】乐谱,记谱法。4. 〔罕〕记录;注释。*broad* [*narrow*] ~【语】简略[精密]标音法。*chemical* ~ 化学符号法。*the common scale of* ~【数】十进记数法。*decimal* ~ 十进法。*binary* ~ 二进位记数法。*binary-coded decimal* ~ 用二进位编码表示的十进位计数法。**-al** *a*.

notch [nɔtʃ; natʃ] **I** *n*. 1. (V 字形的)槽口,缺口;切口;凹口;箭鞘缺口。2. 〔美〕山峡,峡谷;【地】水浪冲成的洞穴。3. (刻在棍子等上的)计数刻痕;选择器标记。4. 〔口〕等;级;〔古〕(板球等的)分数。*He is a* ~ *above the others*. 他比别人高一等。**II** *vt*. 1. 在…上开槽口[作凹口,作缺口(*into*)];作刻痕计算(比赛分数等)。2. 〔古〕(板球等)得(分)。3. 搭(箭)(*up*; *down*)。4. 砍,切;【林】劈植。~ **back** 〔美〕客货两用汽车。~**-board** 梯级搁板;【机】凹板。

notched, notchy [nɔtʃt, ˈnɔtʃi; natʃt, ˋnatʃɪ] *a*. 有凹口的;【植】粗锯齿状的;【动】尖端有缺口的;具缺刻的。

note [nəut; not] **I** *n*. 1. 备忘录,笔记,记录,略记;回想,意见。2. 注,注解,注释;按语,评论。3. 短简,便条,柬帖;(外交上的)照会,通牒;(学术上的)短文。4. (乐器的)调子,音色;样子;口气;特征。5. (人)声,(鸟)叫[鸣]声。6. 印,记号,标记,符号。7. 注意,注目。8. 暗示,提

N

示。9. 名望,显要;〔古〕污名。10. 〔常 *pl.*〕原稿,草稿。11.【乐】律音;音符,音调;(钢琴等的)键;〔诗〕调,曲调,旋律。12.【商】纸币,票据,借据。*a ~ of invitation* 请帖。*speak with a ~ of censure* 用责备的口气说。*Frankness is the chief ~ in his character*. 坦白是他性格中的主要特色。*There is the ~ of pessimism in his writings*. 他的著作带有悲观色彩。*a ~ of assurance (in his voice)* 自信的口气。*a bird's merry ~* 愉快的鸟声。*a ~ of exclamation* 惊叹符号。*a man of ~* 知名人士。*a bank-~* 银行钞票。*a ~ of hand* 期票。*£10 in ~s* 钞票十镑。***change one's ~*** 改变态度[口气]。***compare ~s*** 交换意见;对笔记。***make*** [***take***] ***~s*** [***a ~***] ***of*** 记录,记下,笔记。***make ~s of*** 作(演说等的)草稿;作标记。***sound a false ~*** = strike a false ~. ***sound a ~ of warning*** 给与警告。***sound the ~ of war*** 作主战论调。***speak from*** [***without***] ***~s*** 用[不用]草稿演说[发言]。***strike a false ~*** 做错事,说错话。***strike the right ~*** 说[做]得恰当。***take ~ of*** 注意(到),注目。***worthy of ~*** 值得注意的,显著的。**II *vt*.** 1. 笔录;记[摘]下(*down*)。2. 注目,注意(到)。3. 对…加注释;【乐】用音符记出。4. 特别提到;指明,表明。~**book** 笔记本;期票簿;笔记本式便携电脑(= ~ computer)。~**case** 〔英〕钱夹;钱包。~**head** 〔美〕印有住址的信纸;笺头。~**less *a*.** 1. 不引人注意的;不著名的。2. 音调不和谐的。~**let** 短简,短信。~**paper** 信纸;便条纸。~ **shaver** 高利贷者。~**s payable** 给债权人的期票。~**s receivable** 债务人签署的期票。

not·ed [ˈnəutid; ˋnotɪd] ***a*.** 1. 著名的,知名的(*for*)。2.【乐】附有乐谱的。**-ly *ad*.** 显著地。**-ness *n*.**

note·wor·thy [ˈnəutwəːði; ˋnot͵wɝðɪ] ***a*.** 值得注意的,显著的。*Science has recently made ~ progress especially in this field*. 特别在这一领域内,科学今天已有了显著的进步。**-thi·ly *ad*. -thi·ness *n*.**

noth·ing [ˈnʌθiŋ; ˋnʌθɪŋ] **I *n*.** 1. (什么也)没有,没有什么东西[什么事],什么东西[什么事]也不…。*N- venture, ~ have*. 不入虎穴,焉得虎子。*He is ~ of a poet*. 他一点也算不上是个诗人。*N- pleases him*. 什么都不合他的意。★修饰 nothing 的形容词放在后面。如:N- great is easy. 大事业是不容易的。2. 无,空;不存在(的东西);【数】零;无价值,无意义。*Of ~ comes ~*. 无中不能生有。*There is ~ in it*. 那是空话,毫无意义。*He has ~ in him*. 他一无可取之处。*He is five feet ~*. 他身长刚刚五英尺。3. 没价值的人[事、物],微不足道的事,琐事。*My trouble is ~ to theirs*. 我的困难比起他们来算不了什么。★作名词用时常说作 a ~, ~s. 如:He is a (mere) ~. 他完全是一个废物。the little ~s of life. 人生的琐事。whisper soft ~s 低声絮絮诉爱。4.【宗】不属任何教派的人;不信教的人;无神论者。*He is ~*. 他不属任何教派。★作此义解时仅用作表语,前面也不加冠词。

II *ad*. 毫不,决不;〔美口〕决不是。*This will help you ~*. 这对你毫无帮助。*This is ~ like as* [*so*] *good as that*. = *This is ~ near so good as that*. 这个远不及那个。*She's ~ wiser than before*. 她丝毫也不比以前聪敏。*~ daunted* 毫不畏缩。***all to ~*** 十二分,充分地。***be for ~ in*** 对…没有影响[不起作用]。***be ~ if not*** 首先;极其;是主要特征(*He is ~, if not kind*. 亲切是他主要的优点)。***be ~ to*** 对…一点关系也没有;丝毫不能和…相比(*She is ~ to me*. 我对她无所谓;我根本没有爱她)。***can make ~ of*** 不能了解,弄不懂…;看不清楚;听不清楚;对付不了,不能解决;不能利用。***come to ~*** 毫无结果,终成泡影,失败。***dance up*** (***on***) ~ 被绞死。***do ~ but*** 除了…以外什么也不干;只是…。***for ~*** 1. 徒然;白白;没有结果(*He did not go to Oxford for ~*. 他没有白进牛津大学)。2. 免费,不要钱(*I got it for ~* 免费得来)。3. 没理由地,无缘无故(*They quarrelled for ~*. 他们无端吵了一架)。***have ~ of*** 不理睬。***have ~ on sb*.** 〔美〕没有胜过某人的地方;没有关于某人的罪证,没有抓到某人的小辫子。***have ~ to do with*** 跟…毫无关系,不跟…来往。***in ~ flat*** 马上,立刻。***like ~ on earth*** 1. 了不起的,再好没有的。2. 非常奇怪的。3. 最坏的;最讨厌的。***make ~ of*** 不把…放在眼中,轻视;满不在乎;认为不在话下〔通常与 can 连用,见 can make ~ of〕。***next to ~*** 差不多没有。***no ~*** 〔用在几个否定语后〕什么都没有(*There is no bread, no butter, no cheese, no ~*. 面包也没有,奶油也没有,干酪也没有,什么都没有)。~ ***but*** = ~ ***else but*** [***than***] 只有,不过,不外,简直;〔美〕〔加强语气〕的确(*I have been working hard, ~ but*. 我拼命工作了,真的呀)。***N- doing*** 〔俚〕事情行不通,糟了! 完蛋了! 毫无办法,不行,不干〔失败或拒绝要求时说〕。~ ***flat*** 【美运】零败,吃鸭蛋。~ ***less than*** = ~ ***short of*** 完全是,不外。~ ***may come of it*** 落空。~ ***near so*** 远不及,差得远(*This building is not inferior to that one but ~ near so large*. 这建筑物并不比那一座差,只是远不及那座大)。~ ***much*** 非常少。~ ***of that kind*** 决不是那样。***N- off***! = ***N- to lose***!【海】别让船头掉向下风! ~ ***to sneeze at*** 〔美俚〕不能忽视[轻视]。~ ***to write home about*** 〔美俚〕不重要,平淡无奇。~ ***very much*** 〔口〕没有什么特别的,将就过得去;平平常常。***stop*** [***stick***] ***at ~*** 毫无顾忌;什么都做得出;不择手段。***Thank you for ~***. 〔口、讽〕不劳费心,敬谢不敏。***There is ~ for it but to*** (***do***) 除…之外别无方法。***There is ~ in it***. 1. 全是假话,不符事实;不重要,不相干,没有多少道理,没有什么意义。2. (两个竞争者之间)机会相等。***There is ~ like ...*** 什么也比不上…,没有比…更好的;远远没有,差得远。***think ~ of*** 不把…放在心里;看成平常。***to ~*** (消失得)无影无踪,(消)去。***to say ~ of ...*** 更不必说,那就根本谈不到。

noth·ing·ar·i·an [ˌnʌθiŋˈɛəriən; ͵nʌθɪŋˋɛrɪən] ***n*.** 没有信仰的人。

noth·ing·ness [ˈnʌθiŋnis; ˋnʌθɪŋnɪs] ***n*.** 1. 无,空;不存在。2. 无价值,无聊,空虚;无关紧要;琐细东西;不存在[无价值]的事物。3. 人事不省;死。

no·tice [ˈnəutis; ˋnotɪs] **I *n*.** 1. 注意;认识。2. 情报,消息;通知,预告,警告;(正式)通告;呈报。3. (辞退,解雇等的)预先通知。4. 公告,告示,布告,招贴。5. (报刊等上对戏剧,图书等的)介绍,评介,批评,短评。6. 客气;有礼的招呼。*I commend her to your ~*. 请多关照关照她。*a ~ of a call* 催缴股款通知书。*a ~ of dishonour* 退票通知书。*The new play got a favorable ~*. 那出新戏得到了好评。*He is sitting up and taking ~*. 〔口〕他忽然感到兴趣;〔谑〕他身体渐渐好了。***at a moment's ~*** 一经通知;立即,马上,随时。***at short ~*** 在短时间内,顷刻之间;(军队)得到命令后马上…,接令后立刻…。***beneath one's ~*** 被某人认为不值得注意,不值一顾。***be under ~*** 接到(解雇、辞退等的)通知。***bring to*** [***under***] ***one's ~*** 使某人注意到,使某人看见。***come into*** [***under***] ***one's ~*** 引起某人注意,给某人看见。***escape one's ~*** 逃过某人的注意,被某人疏忽;被某人看漏。***get ~*** 〔美口〕被解雇,失业。***get ~ of*** 接到…的通知。***give ~*** 通知,通告;预先通知(解雇、辞退等)(*give a week's ~* 在一星期前通知)。***give ~ of*** [***that***] 通知…。***give ~ to*** 报告。***have ~ of*** 接到…的通知。***on short ~*** 忽然;急忙。***post*** [***put up***] ***a ~*** 贴出布告(*There is a ~ posted up saying that ...* 一个布告贴了出来说…)。***public ~*** 公告,布告。***put a ~ in the papers*** 在报上登通告。***serve*** (***a***) ~ ***to*** 通知;警告。***take no ~ of*** 不注意,不理会,不管,不采取应有的措施。***take ~*** 注意;(幼儿)开始了解事物。***take ~ of sb*.** 款待某人。***Take ~ that*** (我)警告你…。***take sb.'s ~*** 接到某人通知。***till*** [***until***] ***further ~*** 在另行通知以前…。***without ~*** 不预先通知;擅自。

II *vt*. 1. 注意到,看到;留心,注意。2. 表示与(某人)认识。3. 提及,说到;(在报刊等上)介绍,评介(新书)。4. 通知…。5. 优待(儿童等);客气对待;有礼地招呼。*I didn't ~ how he was dressed*. 我没留心他穿什么衣服。*He refused to ~ me*. 他假装没看见我。*~ sb.'s services in a speech* 在报告中提到某人的功劳。*He was ~d to quit*. 他得到了离职的通知。—*vi*. 注意。*I wasn't noticing*. 我没留神。~ **board** 布告牌。**-a·ble** *a*. 引人注意的,显著的。**-a·bly** *ad*. 显著,显然。

no·ti·fi·a·ble [ˈnəutifaiəbl; ˋnotə͵faɪəbḷ] *a*. 应通知的;应具报的(传染病等)。

no·ti·fi·ca·tion [ˌnəutifiˈkeiʃən; ͵notəfəˋkeʃən] *n*. 通知,通告,布告;通告书,通知单;报告书。

no·ti·fi·er [ˈnəutifaiə; ˋnotə͵faɪɚ] *n*. 通知人,通告人。

no·ti·fy [ˈnəutifai; ˋnotə͵faɪ] *vt*. 1. (**-fied**; **-fy·ing**) 通告,宣告,布告,通知。2. 申报;报告。*I have been notified that ....* 我接到通知说…。*~ one's intention to the party concerned* 把某人意图通知有关方面。

no·tion [ˈnəuʃən; ˋnoʃən] *n*. 1. 意见,见解,想法,看法,观点;学说(= theory);打算,意图,意向,意志。2. (空泛的)理解;(空)想,奇想。3. 概念;观念。4. 〔*pl*.〕〔美〕杂货〔针线等〕;新出精巧实用小物品。5. 〔*pl*.〕英国温彻斯特(Winchester)学院特有的词汇。*Such is the common ~*. 这就是一般的见解。*I have no ~ of resigning*. 我没有辞职的意思。*I have not the haziest ~ of what he means*. 我完全不懂他究竟是什么意思。*He has a good* [*has no*] *~ of economy*. 他很懂得[完全不懂]节约(的意义)。*the first ~* 【哲】初概念。~ **counter** 〔美〕杂货柜。~ **department** 〔美〕(商店内的)杂货部。~**-store** 〔美〕杂货店。

no·tion·al [ˈnəuʃənəl; ˋnoʃənḷ] *a*. 1. 观念上的;概念上的,抽象的,纯理论的;想像中的,非现实的。2. 〔美〕空想的,幻想的;一脑门子怪念头[荒唐思想]的。3. 名义上的,象征性的。4. 【语法】表意的。**-ist** *n*. 理论家。**-ly** *ad*.

no·to·chord [ˈnəutəkɔːd; ˋnotə͵kɔrd] *n*. 1. 【动】脊索。2. 高级脊椎动物胚胎期的脊索。**-al** *a*.

No·to·gae·a [ˌnəutəˈdʒiːə; ͵notəˋdʒiə] *n*. (动物地理分区的)南界,南域〔包括新西兰、澳大利亚地区以及西南太平洋的各岛屿〕。**-an** *a*.

no·to·ri·e·ty [ˌnəutəˈraiəti; ͵notəˋraɪətɪ] *n*. 1. 有名(多指坏的方面),臭名昭著;丑名。2. 声名狼藉的人物。

no·to·ri·ous [nəuˈtɔːriəs, nə-; noˋtorɪəs, nə-] *a*. (坏的方面)有名的,臭名远扬的,臭名昭彰的,声名狼藉的。*a ~ crybaby* 有名的好哭的孩子。*a ship ~ for ill luck* 有名多灾多难的一条船。**be ~ for** 以…出名。**It is ~ that ....** …是众所周知的(事实)。**-ly** *ad*. **-ness** *n*.

no·tor·nis [nəuˈtɔːnis; noˋtɔrnɪs] *n*. 【动】南秧鸟〔新西兰的一种不能飞行的鸟〕。

no·to·un·gu·late [ˌnəutəuˈʌŋgjulit; ͵notoˋʌŋgjʊlɪt], **no·tun·gu·late** [-leit; -let] *n*. 南美有蹄类动物。

No·tre-Dame [ˌnəutrəˈdɑːm; ͵notəˋdem] *n*. 〔F.〕1. 圣母玛利亚。2. (巴黎)圣母院。

not-self [ˈnɔtself; ˋnɑtsɛlf] *n*. 【哲】非我,客观,外界(= non-ego)。

no-trump [ˈnəuˈtrʌmp; ˋnoˋtrʌmp] I *a*. 1. 无将牌的。2. 【桥牌】叫无将牌的。II *n*. 1. 叫无将牌。2. 打无将的牌。

Not·ting·ham [ˈnɔtiŋəm; ˋnɑtɪŋəm] *n*. 1. 诺丁汉〔英国城市〕。2. 诺丁汉郡〔英国郡名〕(= ~ shire)。

Notts. = Nottingham (shire).

no·tum [ˈnəutəm; ˋnotəm] *n*. (*pl*. **-ta** [-ə; -ə]) 【动】(昆虫的)背板,(动物的)背部。

not·with·stand·ing [ˌnɔtwiθˈstændiŋ, -wið-; ͵nɑtwɪθˋstændɪŋ, -wɪð-] I *prep*. 虽然,尽管…仍…。*I shall still go, ~ the rain*. 尽管下雨,我仍然要去。*this ~* 〔古〕尽管如此。II *ad*. 〔古〕虽然,尽管,还是。*There were remonstrances, but he persisted ~*. 虽遭抗议,他仍旧坚持了下去。III *conj*. 〔古〕虽然,尽管。*He went ~ (that) he was ordered not to*. 他虽被命令不许去,但他仍旧去了。

N

Nouak·chott [nuˈɑːkʃɔt; nwɑkˋʃɑt] *n*. 努瓦克肖特〔毛里塔尼亚首都〕。

nou·gat [ˈnuːgɑː; ˋnugɑ] *n*. 牛轧糖,果仁[杏仁,核桃、花生或各种干果](蛋白)糖。

nought, naught [nɔːt; nɔt] I *n*. 1. 【数】零(0)。2. 〔古、诗〕无。3. 没有价值的人[东西]。~ *decimal two* 零点二(0.2)。***bring to ~*** 使(计划等)落空。***come to ~*** 失败。***set at ~*** 蔑视,轻视;嘲笑,揶揄。II *a*. 〔古〕无价值的。III *ad*. 〔古〕毫无,决无。

Nou·mea [nuːˈmeiə; nuˋmeə] *n*. 努美阿〔新喀里多尼亚岛首都〕。

nou·me·nal·ism [ˈnjuːmənəlizm, ˈnau-; ˋnjumənəlɪzm, ˋnaʊ-] *n*. 实体主义,本体主义。**-nal·ist** *n*.

nou·me·non [ˈnauminɔn, ˈnuː-; ˋnumɪ͵nɑn, ˋnaʊ] *n*. (*pl*. **-na** [-nə; -nə]) 【哲】实体,实在,本体。**nou·menal** *a*.

noun [naun; naʊn] *n*. 1. 【语】名词。*abstract* [*material*, *common*, *proper*, *collective*, *individual*] *~s* 抽象[物质、普通、专有、集合,个体]名词。*countable* [*uncountable*] 可数[不可数]名词。*a ~ of multitude* 群体名词〔例:Are your *family* all well?〕。*a ~ of action* 动作名词〔arrival, confession〕。2. 名词代用语。3. 〔古语法〕(有屈折变化的)实词。*a ~ adjective* 形容词(= adjective)。*a ~ substantive* 名词(= noun)。

nour·ish [ˈnʌriʃ; ˋnɝɪʃ] *vt*. 1. 滋养;施肥于。2. 抚养;教养,助长。3. 怀抱(希望、怨恨)。**-er** *n*. **-ing** *a*. 滋养的,滋补的。**-ment** *n*. 食物;营养,滋养,助长,培养。

nous [naus; naʊs] *n*. 【哲】精神;理智;理性;智力;〔口〕常识。

nou·veau riche [ˈnuːvəu ˈriːʃ; ˋnuvo ˋriʃ] (*pl*. ***nouveaux riches***) 〔F.〕暴发户。

nou·veau ro·man [nuvəu rəuˈmɑːn; nuvo roˋmɑn] (*pl*. ***nou·veaux ro·mans***) 新体小说,新小说〔指 1950 年以来法国流行的反传统格式小说,以描写人物的精神状态为主〕。

nou·veau·té [nuːvəuˈtei; nuvoˋte] *n*. 〔F.〕新奇事,新事物。

nou·velle [nuːˈvel; nuˋvɛl] *n*. 〔F.〕中篇小说。

nou·velle vague [nuːˈvelˈvɑːg; nuˋvɛlˋvɑg] 〔F.〕(现代电影的)新潮(派)。

Nov. = November.

nov. = novelist.

no·va [ˈnəuvə, ˈnɔvə; ˋnovə, nɔvə] *n*. (*pl*. **~s**, **-vae** [-viː; -vi]) 【天】新星。*N- Cygni* [ˈsigniː; ˋsɪgni] 天鹅新星。

no·vac·u·lite [nəuˈvækjulait; noˋvækjʊlaɪt] *n*. 【地】均密石英岩。

No·va Sco·tia [ˈnəuvə ˈskəuʃə; ˋnovə ˋskoʃə] 新斯科舍〔加拿大省名〕。

no·va·tion [nəuˈveiʃən; noˋveʃən] *n*. 【法】(契约,义务的)更新,代替。

no·vel[1] [ˈnɔvəl; ˋnɑvḷ] *a*. 新的,新颖的;新奇的,珍奇的,异常的。*a ~ experience* 新的经验。

nov·el[2] [ˈnɔvəl; ˋnɑvəl] *n*. 1. (长篇)小说。2. 〔N-〕〔常 *pl*.〕【罗马法】新法,附律。*a love ~* 爱情小说。

nov·el·ese [ˌnɔvəˈliːz; ͵nɑvəˋliz] *n*. (低级的)小说家的陈词滥调。

nov·el·ette [ˌnɔvəˈlet; ͵nɑvḷˋɛt] *n*. 1. 中篇小说。2. 【乐】新事曲[幻想曲式的小品曲]。

nov·el·ist [ˈnɔvəlist; ˋnɑvḷɪst] *n*. 小说家。

nov·el·is·tic [ˌnɔvəˈlistik; ͵nɑvḷˋɪstɪk] *a*. 小说的。

nov·el·ize [ˈnɔvəlaiz; ˋnɑvḷ͵aɪz] *vt*. 将(剧本、事实等)编成小说;使小说化。**-i·za·tion** [ˌnɔvəlaiˈzeiʃən; ˋnɑvəlaɪˋzeʃən] *n*.

N

no·vel·la [nəuˈvelə; noˋvɛlɑ] *n*. (*pl*. ~s, -le [-le; -lɛ]) 中篇故事。
nov·el·ty [ˈnɔvəlti; ˋnɑvltɪ] *n*. 新奇,珍奇,奇异;新奇的东西[事情];【商】新颖小巧物品[玩具、服饰等]。
nov·el·wright [ˈnɔvəlrait; ˋnɑvəlraɪt] *n*. 〔蔑〕小说家。
No·vem·ber [nəuˈvembə; noˋvɛmbɚ] *n*. **1.** 十一月〔略作 Nov.〕。**2.** 通讯中用以代替字母 n 的词。
no·ve·na [nəuˈviːnə; noˋvinə] *n*. (*pl*. ~s, -nae [-niː; -ni]) 【天主】连续九天的祷告。
no·ven·ni·al [nəuˈveniəl; noˋvɛnɪəl] *a*. 每九年的。
no·ver·cal [nəuˈvəːkəl; noˋvɝkl̩] *a*. 继母(般)的。
Nov·go·rod [ˈnɔvgərɔd; ˋnɑvgərɑd] *n*. 诺夫哥罗德〔俄罗斯城市〕。
nov·ice [ˈnɔvis; ˋnɑvɪs] *n*. **1.** 初学者,新手,生手;初次出场(赛跑)的马[狗]等。**2.** 【宗】新信徒,见习修道士[修女]。
no·vi·ci·ate, no·vi·ti·ate [nəuˈviʃiit; noˋvɪʃɪɪt] *n*. **1.** 修道士[修女]的见习期;见习中的修道士[修女]。**2.** (新手的)见习(期)初学者,生手。
no·vo·bi·o·cin [ˌnəuvəˈbaiəsin; ˏnovəˋbaɪəsɪn] *n*. 【药】新生霉素。
no·vo·ca·in(e) [ˈnəuvəkein; ˋnovəˏken] *n*. 【药】奴佛卡因。
No·vo·si·birsk [ˌnəuvəsiˈbiəsk; ˏnovosəˋbɪrsk] *n*. 诺沃西比尔斯克(新西伯利亚)〔俄罗斯城市〕。
no·vus or·do se·clo·rum [ˈnəuvəs ˈɔːdəu siˈklɔːrəm; ˋnovəs ˋɔrdo sɪˋklɔrəm] 〔L.〕 = a new order of the ages.
NOW = National Organization for Women 全国妇女组织。
now [nau; naʊ] **I** *ad*. **1.** 〔现在〕(a)现在,此刻,目前。*The bell is ~ ringing*. 钟现在正在响。(b)现在(已经);按此刻情形。*It is ~ over*. 已经完了。**2.** 〔未来〕立刻,即刻,马上。*Do it ~*. 马上做吧。*I can come ~*. 我马上可以来。**3.** 〔过去〕(a)刚才,方才。★现在只用 just ~ 和〔诗〕 even ~. (b)(叙述中的)现在,那时,当时;接着,于是,然后;那时已经。*Hannibal was ~ crossing the Alps*. 汉尼拔那时正在翻越阿尔卑斯山。**4.** 〔无时间观念,表示说话者的语气,用于命令、请求、说明、警告、责骂、安慰等句中〕原来,那么;喂;嗳呀,哟。*N- what do you mean by it*? 你这究竟是什么意思呢? *N- tell me*. 那么告诉我吧。*N- Barabbas was a robber*. 却说巴拉巴斯原是个贼。*You don't mean it*, ~. 你这话不会是当真的吧。★本义的 now 多用于句首,且多用逗号。***but*** [***even***] ~ 〔古〕= just now. (***every***) ~ ***and then*** [***again***] 时常,时而,不时。***just*** ~ 方才,刚才;现在,眼下。~ ... ~ [***then***] = ... ***and again*** 时而…时而… (~ *hot*, ~ *cold* 忽热忽冷)。~ ~ = ~ ***then*** **1.** 〔口〕好啦! 行啦! 就这么样! **2.** 赶快,来吧! **3.** 喂喂,得啦〔有时是友好的抗议或是警告〕(*N-~, a little less noise, please!* 喂喂,请安静一点。*N- then, none of your nonsense*! 得啦,别说废话吧!)。***N- or never***! 机不可失,时不再来;此时不干,更待何时? ***Oh, come*** ~! 嗨,得啦! ***Really*** ~! = ***N- Really***! 嗳呀! 真的吗! 不会吧! 这倒吓了一跳! **II** *conj*. 既,既然,由于。*N- you mention it, I do remember*. 经你这样一提,我就记起来了。*N- (that) the weather is warmer, we can go outdoors*. 天气既然暖和得多,我们可以到户外去了。***Well***, ~! 〔口〕唷! 喂! 呵! 哟,好吧! **III** *n*. 〔主要用于前置词后〕此刻,目前,现在。***by*** ~ 此刻已经。***from*** ~ (***on, forward***, 等)从现在起,今后。***till*** [***up to***] ~ 迄今,到现在为止。**IV** *a*. 现在的,当今的;现任的;十分时髦的,领先于潮流的,属于新一代的。**N- account** 活期存款支票账户;能开发可转让支付命令的活期存款账户(NOW = negotiated order of withdrawal)。~**cast** 即时预报天气〔测得天气情况后即刻预报〕。**N- Generation** "新一代"人。**-ness** 现在性。
now·a·day [ˈnauədei; ˋnaʊəde] *a*. 现今的,当今的。
now·a·days [ˈnauədeiz; ˋnaʊəˏdez] **I** *ad*. 现今,现时,现在。**II** *n*. 〔古〕当今,现在。
now·a·nights [ˈnauənaitz; ˋnaʊənaɪtz] *ad*. 〔美〕在当今的夜晚。
no·way(s), no·wise [ˈnəuwei(z), ˈnəuwaiz; ˋnoˏwe(z), ˋnowaɪz] *ad*. 一点也不,决不。
Now·el, now·el [ˈnəuel; ˋnoel] *n*. 〔古〕= Noel.
no·where [ˈnəuhwεə; ˋnoˏhwεr] **I** *ad*. 什么地方都不到[没有]。*This book is ~ to be had*. 这本书什么地方都没有。*This tells us ~*. 这对我们毫无用处。**II** *n*. 无人知道的地方;没有…的地方。*He came from ~*. 他不晓得是从哪里来的。*He has ~ to go*. 他没有可去的地方。***be*** [***come in***] ~ 没有取胜的机会;〔俚〕差得远,大失败 (*His new novel is ~*. 他新写的小说是个大失败)。***can lead*** ~ 不可能有什么前途,不可能得到什么结果。***get us*** ~ (使)我们不能有所进展[不能解决问题]。~ ***near*** 离…很远,远远没有,远不及;总不如(那么好等)。
no·whith·er [ˈnəuhwiðə; ˋnoˏhwɪðɚ] *ad*. 〔古〕无论向何处都不。
no-win [ˈnəuwin; ˋnowɪn] *a*. **1.** 不大可能取胜的。**2.** 非竞赛性的,不是为输赢而进行的。
no·wise [ˈnəuwaiz; ˋnoˏwaɪz] *ad*. 〔古〕= noway.
nowt [naut; naʊt] *n*. (*pl*., *sing*. ***nowt***) 〔苏格兰〕牛,公牛。
Nox [nɔks; nɑks] *n*. 【罗神】夜之女神。
NOx [nɔks; nɑks] *n*. 氧化氮,氮的氧化物。
nox·ious [ˈnɔkʃəs; ˋnɑkʃəs] *a*. 有害的,不卫生的,有毒的;对精神上有坏影响的,使道德败坏的;引起反感的,讨厌的。*the ~ influences* 邪气,坏影响。**-ly** *ad*. **-ness** *n*.
no·yade [nwɑːˈjɑːd; nwɑˋjɑd] *n*. 溺刑,溺死刑〔如 1794 年法国南特 (Nantes) 地区把大批人淹死的处决〕。
no·yau [ˈnwaiəu, ˈnɔiəu; nwɑˋjo, ˋnɔɪo] *n*. 〔F.〕(白兰地加果仁精油制成的)白兰地果仁酒。
Noyes [nɔiz; nɔɪz] *n*. 诺伊斯〔姓氏〕。
noz·zle [ˈnɔzl; ˋnɑzl] *n*. 管嘴;喷嘴;〔俚〕鼻子。*a jet* [*propelling*] ~ 【火箭】尾喷管。
NP = **1.** no protest 【商】未拒付(票据等)。**2.** = noun phrase 名词短语。
N.P. = Notary Public 公证人。
Np = 【化】neptunium 镎。
n.p. = **1.** net personalty 纯动产。**2.** new paragraph 新段落。
NPD = Nuclear Power Demonstration Reactor 〔加拿大〕核动力示范反应堆。
NPL = National Physical Laboratory 〔英〕国家物理实验所。
n.p.or d. = no place or date 出版地点或日期不详。
n-pros 〔Am.〕= nervous prostration 神经衰弱。
n.p.t. = normal pressure and temperature 常温常压。
NPT = Nonproliferation Treaty 防止核扩散条约。
N.R. = North Riding 〔英〕约克郡北赖丁。
Nr. = near.
N.R.A. = **1.** National Rifle Association 〔英〕全国步枪射击运动会。**2.** National Recovery Administration 〔美旧〕全国(工业)复兴总署。
NRC = National Research Council 〔美〕全国科学研究委员会。**2.** National Resources Committee 〔美〕国家资源委员会。
NROTC = Naval Reserve Officers' Training Corps 〔美〕海军后备军官训练队。
NRPB = National Resources Planning Board 〔美〕全国资源计划委员会。
NRS = National Reemployment Service 〔美〕全国再就业事务局。
NRTS = National Reactor Testing Station 〔美〕国家反应

器试验站。

NS = **1.** nuclear ship 核动力船。**2.** not sufficient〔银行用语〕存款不足。

N.S.A. = National Skating Association of Great Britain 英国全国滑冰协会。

NSB = Nuclear Standards Board 核子标准委员会。

NSC = National Security Council〔美〕国家安全委员会。

NSF = National Science Foundation〔美〕国家科学基金会。

NSW = New South Wales 新南威尔士〔澳大利亚州名〕。

NT = **1.** *New Testament*（基督教《圣经》的）《新约全书》。**2.** Northern Territory 北部地区，澳北区〔澳大利亚一地区〕。

Nt【化】= niton 氡〔radon 旧称〕。

-nt *suf*.〔拉丁语系动词 + -nt→（作形容词用的）现在分词〕：domina*nt*, pleasa*nt*, prevale*nt*.

n't [nt; nt] *ad*. not 之略：could*n't*, did*n't*.

nth [enθ; ɛnθ] *a*. **1.** 第 n 号的，n 倍的；n 次的，n 阶的。**2.**〔口〕（事物发生、使用的次数、频度）最新的，最近的。**3.** 极度的，极大的。*This is the ～ time I've told you to eat slowly*. 吃饭要慢，至今我也不知告诉你多少回了。***to the ～ degree*** [***power***] **1.**【数】至 n 次。**2.** 高效能；最大限度，到极点，极度。

NTP = normal temperature and pressure 正常温度〔指摄氏 0°〕和压力〔指 760 毫米水银柱〕。

NTR = Nuclear Test Reactor 核试验反应堆。

NTSC = National Television System Committee〔美〕国家电视制式委员会。

nt.wt. = net weight 净重。

nu [njuː; nju] *n*. 希腊语的第十三字母〔N, ν；相当于英语的 n〕。

nu·ance [njuːˈɑːns, ˈnjuː-; njuˋɑns, ˋnu-] *n*.（*pl*. ～*s* [-iz; -ɪz]）（色彩、音调、意义、感情等的）细微差别，微差；细微的表情，神韵。

nu·anced [ˈnjuːɔnst, ˈnuː-, njuːˈɔnst; ˋnjuɑnst, ˋnu-, njuˋɑnst] *a*.（音调、调色、意义等）有细微差别的。

nub [nʌb; nʌb] *n*. **1.**（煤等的）小块；瘤子，疖子。**2.**〔美口〕（故事的）要点；（事、问题的）核心。*That's the ～ of it*. 要点就在这里。

Nu·ba [ˈnuːbə; ˋnubə] *n*. **1.**（*pl* ～(*s*)）努巴人〔住在苏丹中部的黑人〕。**2.** 努巴语。

nub·bin [ˈnʌbin; ˋnʌbɪn] *n*. **1.** 小块，小片。**2.**〔美〕玉蜀黍的小穗[发育不全的穗]；发育不全的东西。

nub·ble [ˈnʌbl; ˋnʌbl] *n*. 小（煤）块；瘤子，疖子。**nub·bly** *a*. 多瘤的，多疖的；块状的。

nub·by [ˈnʌbi; ˋnʌbɪ] *a*.（**-bi·er**; **-bi·est**）块状的；瘤多的；疖多的；（表面）有结子花的。*a ～ fabric* 结子花织品。**-bi·ness** *n*.

Nu·bi·a [ˈnjuːbiə; ˋnubɪə] *n*. 努比亚〔非洲东北部一地区；指苏丹北部和埃及南部的沿尼罗河地带〕。

nu·bi·a [ˈnjuːbiə; ˋnjubɪə] *n*.（女用织造的）披巾。

nu·bi·form [ˈnjuːbifɔːm; ˋnjubɪfɔrm] *a*. 云形的。

nu·bile [ˈnjuːbil, -bail; ˋnjubɪl, -baɪl] *a*.（女子）已到结婚年龄的。

nu·bil·i·ty [njuˈbiliti; njʊˋbɪlətɪ] *n*.（女子的）适婚性。

nu·bi·lous [ˈnjuːbiləs, ˈnuː-; ˋnjubɪləs] *a*. **1.** 多云的，多雾的。**2.** 不明确的，模糊的。

nu·cel·lus [njuːˈseləs, nuː-; njuˋsɛləs, nu-] *n*.（*pl*. **-cel·li** [-ai; -aɪ]）【植】珠心。**nu·cel·lar** *a*.

nu·cha [ˈnjuːkə, ˈnuː-; ˋnjutʃə, ˋnu-] *n*.（*pl*. **-chae** [-kiː; -ki]）【动】**1.** 项。**2.**（昆虫的）颈背面。**nu·chal** *a*.

nucle- *comb*. *f*. = nucleo-.

nu·cle·al [ˈnjuːkliəl; ˋnjuklɪəl] *a*. = nuclear.

nu·cle·ar [ˈnjuːkliə; ˋnjuklɪɚ] *a*. **1.** 核的，成核的；有核的。**2.**【物】原子核的；原子能的；原子弹的；核动力的。**3.**〔喻〕核心的，中心的，主要的。**4.**〔口〕愤怒的；激烈的。*The ad compaign would go ～*. 广告大战将变得异常激烈。～ **bomb** 核弹。～**-capable** *a*. 可携带核武器的。～ **club** 核俱乐部〔有核武器国家的集团〕。～ **deterrent** 核威慑力量。～ **division**【生】核分裂。～ **emulsion** 记录核轨道用的照相乳胶。～ **energy** 核能（= atomic energy）。～ **family** 核心家庭〔由父母与子女组成〕。～ **fission**【物】（原子）核分裂（作用），核裂变。～ **forces** 核力，强相互作用。～**-free zone** 无核区。～ **fuel**（促进原子核连锁反应的）核燃料。～ **fusion** 核聚变；核合成，核融合。～ **magnetic resonance** 原子核偶磁共振。～ **physics** 原子核物理学。～ **power** 核大国。～**-powered** *a*. 核动力的。～ **reactor**（原子）核反应堆。～ **sap**【生】核液（= karyolymph）。～**-tipped** *a*. 有核弹头的。～ **warhead** 核弹头。～ **winter** 核冬天〔指核战争以后全球气温会骤降〕。**-ism** 核武器主义。**-ist** *n*. 核武器主义者。

nu·cle·ase [ˈnjuːklieis; ˋnjuklɪˏes] *n*.【生化】核酸酶。

nu·cle·ate [ˈnjuːklieit; ˋnjuklɪɪt] **I** *vt*., *vi*.（使）成核。**II** [ˈnjuːkliit; ˋnjuklɪɪt] *a*. 具核的。**nu·cle·at·ed** *a*. 有核的，核形的。**nu·cle·a·tion** [ˌnjuːkliˈeiʃən; ˏnjuklɪˋeʃən] *n*.【物、化】成核（现象）；晶核过程，核子作用；集结；人工降雨作用。

nu·cle·i [ˈnjuːkliai; ˋnjuklɪˏaɪ] *n*. nucleus 的复数。

nu·cle·ic [njuːˈkliːik; njuˋkliɪk] *a*. 核的。～ *acid* 核酸。

nu·cle·in [ˈnjuːkliin; ˋnjuklɪɪn] *n*. 核素，核蛋白质。

nucleo- *comb*. *f*.〔nucleus, nuclear 以及 nucleic acid 三词有关的构词成分〕核的：*nucleo*protein.

nu·cle·o·chro·nol·o·gy [ˌnjuːkliəukrəˈnɔlədʒi; ˏnjuklɪokrəˋnɑlədʒɪ] *n*. 核子年代学〔研究化学元素由氢原子核形成之时间顺序，尤指研究恒星和行星演化时间的一门学科〕。

nu·cle·o·gen·i·sis [ˌnjuːkliəuˈdʒenisis; ˏnjuklɪoˋdʒɛnɪsɪs] *n*. 核起源。

nu·cle·o·lar [njuˈkliːələ; njuˋkliəlɚ] *a*.【生】核仁的。

nu·cle·o·lat·ed, nu·cle·o·late [njuːˈkliːəˌleitid; ˋnjuklɪəˏletɪd] *a*. 有细胞核的。

nu·cle·o·lus [njuːˈkliːələs; njuˋkliələs] *n*.（*pl*. **-li** [-lai; -laɪ]）【生】（细胞核内的）核仁。

nu·cle·o·met·er [ˌnjuːkliˈɔmitə; ˏnjuklɪˋɑmətɚ] *n*.【原】核子计。

nu·cle·on [ˈnjuːkliɔn; ˋnjuklɪɑn] *n*.【物、化】核子，单子。

nu·cle·on·ic [ˈnjuːkliˈɔnik; ˏnjuklɪˋɑnɪk] *a*. 核子的。

nu·cle·on·ics [ˌnjuːkliˈɔniks; ˏnjuklɪˋɑnɪks] *n*. 原子核物理学，核子学。

nu·cle·o·phile [ˈnjuːkliəfail; ˋnjuklɪəfaɪl] *n*. 亲核试剂。**-phil·ic** [-ˈfilik; -ˋfɪlɪk] *a*. 亲核的，亲质子的。

nu·cle·o·plasm [ˈnjuːkliəplæzm; ˋnjuklɪəˏplæzm̩] *n*.【生】核原生质。**-ic** *a*.

nu·cle·o·pro·te·in [ˌnjuːkliəuˈprəutiːn, -ˈprəutiːin; ˏnjuklɪəˋprotin, -ˋprotiɪn] *n*.【生化】核蛋白。

nu·cle·o·side [ˈnjuːkliəsaid; ˋnjuklɪəˏsaɪd] *n*.【生化】核苷。

nu·cle·o·tide [ˈnjuːkliətaid; ˋnjuklɪəˏtaɪd] *n*.【生化】核苷酸。

nu·cle·us [ˈnjuːkliəs; ˋnjuklɪəs] *n*.（*pl*. ～*es*, ***nu·cle·i*** [ˈnjuːkliai; ˋnjuklɪaɪ]）核；核心；【生】细胞核；核；【物】原子核；【化】有机化合物的原子团，环；（晶）核；【天】慧核。～ *electron* 核电子。～ *formation*（原子）（晶）核生成（作用）。

nu·clide [ˈnjuːklaid; ˋnjuklaɪd] *n*.【核】核种。**-ic** [njuːˈklaidik; njuˋklaɪdɪk] *a*.

nude [njuːd; njud] **I** *a*. **1.** 裸的，裸体的，裸出的，赤裸裸的。**2.**（房间等）没有装饰的；光秃的；（袜子等）肉色的；没有草木的；【动、植】无鳞的，无羽毛的，无叶的。**3.**【法】无效的，无偿的。*a ～ contract*【法】有条件的无效契约。*a ～ matter*【法】直率的陈述。**II** *n*.【美】裸体画[雕像]；裸体者。*the ～* 裸体（状态）。***in the ～*** 裸体的；露骨的；赤裸裸的。**III** *vt*.〔罕〕使裸。～ *it*〔美俚〕

N

脱光身体;实行裸体主义;加入裸体主义团体。**-ly** *ad*. **-ness** *n*.

nudge [nʌdʒ; nʌdʒ] *vt*., *n*. (用臂肘)轻推(促其注意);〔喻〕促…注意;接近。

nudi- [ˈnjuːdi; ˋnjudɪ] *comb*. *f*. 裸: *nudi*caul.

nu·di·branch [ˈnjuːdibræŋk; ˋnjudɪbræŋk] *n*. 裸鳃亚目动物。**-bran·chi·ate** [-ˈbræŋkiit; -ˋbræŋkɪɪt] *a*., *n*.

nu·di·caul [ˈnjuːdikɔːl; ˋnjudɪkɔl], **nu·di·cau·lous** [ˌnjudiˈkauləs; ˏnjudɪˋkaʊləs] *a*.【植】茎上无叶的,裸茎的。

nud·ie [ˈnjuːdiː; ˋnjudi] *n*.〔美俚〕廉价的黄色影片[戏剧、报刊等];卖弄色相的女演员[舞女等]。

nud·ism [ˈnjuːdizəm; ˋnjudɪzm̩] *n*. 裸体主义;裸体主义的实行。

nud·ist [ˈnjuːdist; ˋnjudɪst] *n*., *a*. 裸体主义者(的)。

nu·di·ty [ˈnjuːditi; ˋnjudɪtɪ] *n*. 裸露;裸体;〔常 *pl*.〕裸出部;【美】裸体画[像]。

nud·nik [ˈnudnik; ˋnʊdnɪk] *n*.〔美俚〕无聊的人;惹人讨厌的人。

Nu·er [ˈnuːə; ˋnuɚ] *n*. (*pl*. ***Nu·ers***, ***Nu·er***) **1**. 努尔人〔苏丹境内和埃塞俄比亚边界上的尼罗特人牧民〕。**2**. 努尔语〔属东苏丹语〕。

nuf(f), **'nuf(f)** [nʌf; nʌf] *a*., *n*., *ad*., *int*. 足够(= enough)。***nuf ced*** [sed; sɛd]〔美口〕够了! 别再说了! 说得已经够多的了! 话明白了。

nu·gae [ˈnjuːgi, -dʒi; ˋnjugɪ, -dʒɪ] *n*.〔*pl*.〕〔L.〕无聊的笑话;无聊事儿,琐事。

nu·ga·to·ry [ˈnjuːgətəri; ˋnjugəˏtorɪ] *a*. 琐碎的;没价值的,没用的;无效的;不起作用的。

nug·gar [ˈnʌgə; ˋnʌgɚ] *n*. (尼罗河上游用的)大驳船。

nug·get [ˈnʌgit; ˋnʌgɪt] *n*. **1**. (天然)块金;矿块;贵重的东西。**2**.〔美俚〕棒球。**3**.〔*pl*.〕〔美口〕金钱。*~s of wisdom* 至理名言;金言(集)。

nui·sance [ˈnjuːsns; ˋnjusns] *n*. **1**. 使人为难的行为,讨厌[有害]的东西[行为],麻烦事情。**2**. 讨厌[麻烦]的人。**3**.〔罕〕(非法)妨害,损害。*the Inspector of ~*〔英〕取缔有碍公益的巡官。*Commit no ~*. 禁止小便! *What a ~!* 真讨厌! ***indict sb. for ~*** 控告某人非法妨害。***make a ~ of oneself*** = ***make oneself a ~*** 被人讨厌;捣蛋。~ **ground**〔Can., 方〕垃圾场。~ **parameters**【统】多余参量。~ **raid** 扰乱性空袭;扰乱性袭击。~ **tax**〔美〕小额消费品税。

nuke [njuːk; njuk] **I** *n*.〔美俚〕**1**.〔*pl*.〕核武器。**2**. 核电站。**II** *vt*. 用核武器攻击;用微波炉烹调或加热(食物)。

Nu·kua·lo·fa [ˌnuːkuəˈlɔːfə; ˏnukʊəˋlɔfə] *n*. 努库阿洛法〔汤加首都〕。

N.U.J. = National Union of Journalists〔英〕全国记者协会。

null [nʌl; nʌl] **I** *a*. **1**. 无效力的,无束缚力的。**2**. 无效的,无用的,无益的;无价值的。**3**. 没特征[个性]的,没表情的。**4**.〔罕〕不存在的,没有的;零(位)的;空的。**II** *n*.【数】零,零位;空;【无】零讯号,微弱讯号。*a ~ indicator* 零示器;零位指示器。*the ~ method* 衡消法。~ ***and void***【律】无效;失效(*This check is ~ and void*. 本支票无效)。**III** *vt*. 使无效。

nul·lah [ˈnʌlə; ˋnʌlə] *n*. (印度等地的)水道;河床;干涸的河床,山峡;峡谷。

nul·li·fi·ca·tion [ˌnʌlifiˈkeiʃən; ˏnʌləfəˋkeʃən] *n*. **1**. 无效,废弃,取消,作废。**2**.【美史】州对联邦法令的拒绝执行[承认]。

nul·li·fid·i·an [ˌnʌliˈfidiən; ˏnʌləˋfɪdɪən] *n*. 无宗教信仰的人。

nul·li·fi·er [ˈnʌlifaiə; ˋnʌləˏfaɪɚ] *n*. 使…无效者,废弃者,取消者;无效论者。

nul·li·fy [ˈnʌlifai; ˋnʌləˏfaɪ] *vt*. 使无效,废弃,毁弃;取消;使无价值;抹杀。

nul·lip·a·ra [nʌˈlipərə; nəˋlɪpərə] *n*. (*pl*. *~s*, ***-lip·a·rae*** [-ˈlipəriː; -ˋlɪpəri]) 未产妇(= nulliparity)。**-lip·a·rous** [-ˈlipərəs; -ˋlɪpərə] *a*.

nul·li·pore [ˈnʌlipɔː; ˋnʌləˏpor] *n*. 红藻科植物;珊瑚藻。

nul·lity [ˈnʌliti; ˋnʌlətɪ] *n*. **1**. 无效,无效行为[证件等]。**2**. 无,全无。**3**. 无用的东西;废物〔指人或物〕。*an action of ~*【法】要求宣判契约无效的诉讼。*a ~ suit* 要求宣判结婚无效的诉讼。

nul·lo [ˈnʌləu; ˋnʌlo] *n*.【牌戏】不拿墩〔五百分牌戏中的一种叫牌法。叫这副牌的人没有对家。不拿墩,只要拿墩,就要扣掉 250 分,其他对手则每墩各加 10 分〕。

Num., **Numb.** = Numbers.

num. = numeral(s).

numb [nʌm; nʌm] **I** *a*. 麻木的,冻僵了的(*with*);没有[失去]感觉的,钝的。~ *with cold* 冻僵。*a ~ hand*〔俚〕蠢物。**II** *vt*. 使失去感觉,使麻木;使冻僵。~ **skull** = numskull. **-ly** *ad*. **-ness** *n*.

num·ber [ˈnʌmbə; ˋnʌmbɚ] **I** *n*. **1**. 数;数字;〔*pl*.〕算术。**2**. (汽车等的)号码;第…,第…卷,第…期〔通常略作 No. (复数 Nos.),用于数字之前〕。**3**. 伙伴;号子,囚犯。**4**. 数目;〔*pl*.〕大批,数量上的优势,许多,若干。**5**.【乐、韵】音律,韵律;〔*pl*.〕【乐】乐谱,调子,节奏,拍子;〔*pl*.〕【诗】诗,韵文;【语法】数。**6**.〔口〕(从多数当中挑选出来的)人,物。**7**. 一群人,一帮人。*cardinal* [*ordinal*] *~s* 基[序]数。*an even* [*odd*] *~* 偶[奇]数。*a whole* [*an integral*] *~* 整数。*the acid ~*【化】酸值。*the atomic ~* 原子序数。*a high* [*low*] *~* 大[小]数。*the science of ~s* 算术。*a telephone ~* 电话号码。*the ~ of a car* 车号。*a dead ~* 空号。*the April ~* (杂志的)四月号。*Nos. 1—5* 第一号到第五号。*No. 9* (*pill*)〔美军〕百宝丹,清导丸,通便丸。*He is not of our ~*. 他可不是我们中的一分子。*He is among the ~ of the dead*. 他也在死亡之列。*a ~ of books* 许多书。*a great* [*large*] *~ of people* 很多很多的人。*the singular* [*plural*] *~* 单[复]数。***a ~ of*** 若干;〔口〕= ***~s of*** 许多的。***back ~*** 过了期的一期报刊杂志;过时的人或事物;落后、顽固、反动的人物。***by ~*** = in ~s. ***get*** [***have***] ***sb.'s ~***〔美俚〕对某人的性格、动机等作确实的估价。***have sb.'s ~ on it***〔美俚〕注定是某人死亡的原因。***in ~*** 总共;用数字表示,在数字上。***in ~s*** (杂志等)分为数册,分数次(*The story is issued in ~s*. 那部小说是分册出版的)。***in round ~s*** 以整数[约数]表示;约莫,大概;总而言之。***lose the ~ of one's mess***〔英海军行话〕死,"报销"。***make up by ~s*** 以多为胜。~ ***one*** **1**. 头号(的),第一流(的)。**2**.〔口〕自己;自己的利益(*take care of* [*look after*] *~ one* 替自己打算)。**3**.〔口〕小便。*~s* **pool** 猜数字小赌博。***One's ~ is up***.〔俚〕某人劫数[死期]已到。***one's ~ two*** 副手,副职,接班人。***one's opposite ~*** 对等的人[物]。***out of*** [***without***] *~*(*s*) 无数的。***the ~s*** = ~s pool. ***There are ~s who ....*** …的人很多。***to the ~ of*** …多到。***win by*** (***force of***) *~s* 靠人多得胜。***without*** [***beyond***] ~ = out of ~.
II *vt*. **1**. 给…编号[记号数,加号码]。**2**. 达…之数,共计…,(人口)有…。**3**. 算入…(数)内;认为(*among*; *in*; *with*)。**4**.〔主用被动形〕已有限定,有限;〔古,雅〕数,计算。**5**. 活了…岁,足…岁。*The guests ~ 20*. 客人有二十位。*His days are ~ed*. 他(在世)的日子不多了。—*vi*. 算在…数内;计;报数。~ ***off***〔上操〕报数;〔口令〕号码! ~ **cruncher** (超大功率,能进行极复杂运算的)超级电脑。~ **dummy**〔美俚〕**1**. (旅馆)服务员。**2**. (铁路)调度员。*~ed* **account** (只认编号不认存户姓名的)银行编号账户。*~ing* **machine** 号码机,编号机。~ **plate** 号码牌。***N- Ten*** 唐宁街 10 号〔英国首相官邸,用以指英国政府〕。**-er** *n*. 编号人;计数员。

num·ber·less [ˈnʌmbəlis; ˋnʌmbɚlɪs] *a*. 1. 数不清的,无数的。2. 无号码的。

Num·bers [ˈnʌmbəz; ˋnʌmbɚz] *n*.【圣】民数记〔= *the book of* ~, 略 *Num*. 或 *Numb*.〕。

numb·fish [ˈnʌmfiʃ; ˋnʌm͵fɪʃ] *n*.【鱼】电鳗,电鳐。

num·bles [ˈnʌmblz; ˋnʌmbl̩z] *n*. 〔*pl*.〕〔古〕鹿内脏。

num·dah [ˈnʌmdɑː; ˋnʌmdɑ] *n*. 毡子鞍垫。

nu·men [ˈnjuːmən, ˈnuː-; ˋnjumən, ˋnu-] *n*. (*pl*. *-mina* [-minə; -mɪnə]) 1.【罗神】守护神。2. 引导力量[精神]。

nu·mer·a·ble [ˈnjuːmərəbl; ˋnjumərəbl̩] *a*. 可(计)数的。

nu·mer·al [ˈnjuːmərəl; ˋnjumərəl] **I** *a*. 数的;表示数的。**II** *n*. 1. 数字;【语法】数词〔*pl*.〕。2. 〔美〕(因体育运动成绩优异奖给学校中班级的)荣誉年号。*Roman* ~*s* 罗马数字。*the cardinal* [*ordinal*] ~*s* 基数[序数]词。

nu·mer·a·ry [ˈnjuːmərəri; ˋnjumə͵rɛrɪ] *a*. 数的,与数有关的。

nu·mer·ate [ˈnjuːməreit; ˋnjumə͵ret] **I** *vt*. 1. 数点;计算。2. 读(数)。**II** *a*. 识数的;有计算能力的。

nu·mer·a·ti [ˌnjuːməˈrɑːtiː; ͵njuməˋrɑrti] *n*. 〔*pl*.〕金融业内的计算天才。

nu·mer·a·tion [ˌnjuːməˈreiʃən; ͵njuməˋreʃən] *n*. 计算;读数;【数】命数法;读数法。*the* ~ *table* 数字表。

nu·mer·a·tor [ˈnjuːmereitə; ˋnjumə͵retɚ] *n*. 1.【数】(分数的)分子。2. 计算者。3. 计数器[管];示号器,回转号码机。

nu·mer·ic [njuːˈmerik; njuˋmɛrɪk] **I** *n*.【数】数,数字;分数;不可通约的比例。**II** *a*. = numerical.

nu·mer·i·cal [njuːˈmerikəl; njuˋmɛrɪkl̩] *a*. 数字的;数值的;用数字表示的。(*a*) ~ *order* 号数。*a* ~ *statement* 统计。*the* ~ *strength* 人数,兵数。~ **control**【计】(利用穿孔带对机械操作进行的)数字控制,数控。~ **keypad**【计】数字键区〔指电脑键盘右侧标示着小数点以及从 0 到 9 数字的浅色键区〕。~ **notation**【乐】数字记谱法;简谱。**-ly** *ad*. 用数字,在数字上。

nu·mer·ol·o·gy [ˌnjuːməˈrɔlədʒi, ˌnuː-; ͵njuməˋrɑlədʒɪ, nu-] *n*. 算八字术,占八卦。

nu·mer·o·scope [ˈnjuːmərəskəup; ˋnjumərəskop] *n*. 示数器;数字记录器。

nu·mer·ous [ˈnjuːmərəs; ˋnjumərəs] *a*. 1. 〔修饰单数集合名词〕由多数人形成的,人数多的。*a* ~ *army* 一支庞大的军队。*a* ~ *class* 学生人数多的一个班。2. 〔修饰复数名词〕许多的,大群的,大批的。~ *errors* 许许多多错误。3. 〔罕〕多数人们的。4. 〔古、诗〕和谐的,有节奏的。**-ly** *ad*. **-ness** *n*.

num·head [ˈnʌmhed; ˋnʌmhɛd] *n*. 〔美〕= numskull.

Nu·mid·i·a [njuːˈmidiə; njuˋmɪdɪə] *n*. 努米底亚〔北非一古国,其位置相当于现代的阿尔及利亚〕。

Nu·mid·i·an [njuːˈmidiən; njuˋmɪdɪən] **I** *a*. 努米底亚人的,努米底亚语的。**II** *n*. 1. 努米底亚人。2. 努米底亚语。~ **crane** 蓑羽鹤 (= demoiselle)。

nu·min·ous [ˈnjuːminəs; ˋnjumənəs] *a*. 1. 超自然的;神秘的;神圣的,精神上的。2. 使人深受精神影响的。

numis. = numismatics.

nu·mis·mat·ic, nu·mis·mat·i·cal [ˌnjuːmizˈmætik, -ikəl; ͵njumɪzˋmætɪk, -ɪkəl] *a*. 货币的;古钱的;金属徽章的;钱币学的。

nu·mis·mat·ics [ˌnjuːmisˈmætiks; ͵njumɪsˋmætɪks] *n*. 〔作单数用〕钱币学,古钱学;徽章学。

nu·mis·ma·tist [njuːˈmizmətist; njuˋmɪzmətɪst] *n*. 古钱学家;钱币研究家。

nu·mis·ma·tol·o·gy [njuːˌmizməˈtɔlədʒi; nju͵mɪzməˋtɑlədʒɪ] *n*. = numismatics.

num·mary [ˈnʌməri; ˋnʌmərɪ] *a*. 关于钱币的;有关货币的。

num·met [ˈnʌmit; ˋnʌmɪt] *n*. 〔英方〕午餐 (lunch)。

num·mu·lar [ˈnʌmjulə; ˋnʌmjʊlɚ] *a*. 1. 硬通货形的。2. 有关货币的 (= nummary)。

num·mu·lite [ˈnʌmjulait; ˋnʌmjʊ͵laɪt] *n*.【古生】货币化石贝。

num·mu·lit·ic [ˌnʌmjuˈlitik; ͵nʌmjʊˋlɪtɪk] *a*.【古生】货币虫的;钱币虫属的。

num·nah [ˈnʌmnɑː; ˋnʌmnɑ] *n*. = numdah.

num·skull [ˈnʌmskʌl; ˋnʌm͵skʌl] *n*. 〔口〕笨蛋;笨脑瓜。

nun [nʌn; nʌn] *n*. 1. 修女,尼姑。2.【鸟】修女(品种)家鸽;【虫】毛松虫白蛾。~*'s cloth*【纺】修女黑色薄呢。~*'s thread*【纺】细白线。~*'s veiling*【纺】修女薄纱。~ **buoy**【海】纺锤形浮标。**-hood** *n*. 修女的身分。**-like, -nish** *a*. 修女似的;温和的;贞洁的;规矩的。

Nunc Dim·it·tis [ˈnʌŋk diˈmitis; ˋnʌŋk dɪˋmɪtɪs] 〔L.〕 1.【圣】用"西面祷词" (Simeon) 开头的颂歌〔路加福音 2 章 29—32 节,俱以"安然去世"等语开头〕;辞别。2. 〔n-d-〕告别,离去;去世。*sing one's nunc dimittis* 含笑辞别〔安然去世〕。

nun·ci·a·ture [ˈnʌnʃiətʃə; ˋnʌnʃɪətʃɚ] *n*. 1. 罗马教皇使节的职位[任期]。2. 罗马教皇使团。

nun·ci·o [ˈnʌnʃiəu; ˋnʌnʃɪ͵o] *n*. (*pl*. ~*s*) 1. 罗马教皇的大使。2. 使者。

nun·cle [ˈnʌŋkl; ˋnʌŋkl̩] *n*. 〔古、方〕= uncle.

nun·cu·pate [ˈnʌŋkjupeit; ˋnʌŋkjʊ͵pet] *vt*. 口述(遗嘱、证词等)。**-pation** [ˌnʌŋkjuˈpeiʃən; ͵nʌŋkjʊˋpeʃən] *n*. 口述。**-pa·tive, -pa·to·ry** *a*.【法】口头的,口述的。

nun·na·tion, nun·a·tion [nʌˈneiʃən; nʌˋneʃən] *n*. 名词词尾上加 "n" 的变化〔如阿拉伯语的名词变化〕。

nun·ner·y [ˈnʌnəri; ˋnʌnərɪ] *n*. 女修道院;尼姑庵。

nu·per·ca·ine [ˈnjuːpəkein; ˋnjupɚken] *n*.【药】奴白卡因。

nu·phar [ˈnjuːfə; ˋnjufɚ] *n*.【植】黄睡莲。

nu·plex [ˈnjuːpleks; ˋnjuplɛks] *n*. 核动力综合企业。

nup·tial [ˈnʌpʃəl; ˋnʌpʃəl] **I** *a*. 1. 结婚的,婚姻的;婚礼的。2.【动】交配期所特有的。*a* ~ *ceremony* 婚礼。*a* ~ *flight* (蜂等)的婚飞。**II** *n*. 〔*pl*.〕婚礼。~ **plumage** (某些鸟)在交配期所长的羽毛。

N.U.R. = National Union of Railwaymen 〔英〕全国铁路工人联合会。

Nu·rem·berg, Nürn·berg [ˈnjuərəmbəːg, ˈnyrnbəːk; ˋnjuərəmbɚg, nyrnbɚk] *n*. 纽伦堡〔德国城市〕。

nurse[1] [nəːs; nɝs] **I** *n*. 1. 奶妈〔通常叫 wet ~〕;保姆〔通常叫 dry ~〕;阿妈 (= ~-maid);保育员。2. 护士,看护。3. 保护人;培养者;养成所,发祥地 (*of*)。4.【植】保护树;【虫】保护虫,保育虫;【动】世代交替的无性期的个体。***at*** ~ 交奶妈[保姆]领养中。***put out to*** ~ 托人喂养,寄养。***under a*** ~***'s charge*** 交给奶妈领着。**II** *vt*. 1. 喂奶,带养(婴儿、幼兽)。2. 看护,照料(病人)。3. 小心管理;爱惜,小心使用;养;培养;养成,助成。4. 抱(希望等)。5. 〔英〕讨好(选举区民等)爱抚;抱,搂抱。6.【撞球】将(球)凑拢。~ *a baby* 喂孩子奶。~ *a horse* (不使过劳地)爱惜用马。~ *a cat* 怀抱着猫。~ *one's knees* 抱着膝盖。*be* ~*d in luxury* 受娇养。~ *a plant* 培养植物。~ *a hatred* 怀恨。~ *the fire* 靠着火不离开。— *vi*. 看护,照料;喂奶;(小孩)吃奶。~ **balloon**【空】补助气囊。~ **cell** 营养细胞;滋卵细胞。~ **child** 养子。~ **crops** 保护作物。~ **frog**【动】产婆蛙。~**girl**, ~**maid** 照看孩子的年轻保姆。~**-keeper** 看护。~ **ship** (英国海军保护鱼雷艇,潜水艇等的)母舰。

nurse[2] [nəːs; nɝs] *n*.【动】角鲨。

nurse·ling [ˈnəːsliŋ; ˋnɝslɪŋ] *n*. 1. (特指奶妈领养的)婴儿。2. 爱儿,珍爱的东西;【植】苗木。

nurs·er [ˈnəːsə; ˋnɝsɚ] *n*. 1. 奶妈,抚养人。2. 培育者。赞助者。3. 奶瓶。

nurs·er·y [ˈnəːsəri; ˋnɝsərɪ] *n*. 1. 托儿所,育儿室。2.

N

苗床,苗圃;养鱼场;动物养殖场。3. 养成所。4.【撞球】集拢一起的球。*a day* ~ 日间托儿所。*a bush* ~ 临时苗圃。~ **garden** 苗圃。~ **governess** 兼做保姆的家庭教师,保育员。~**maid** = nursemaid. ~**-man** 园丁,花圃工、苗木培养工。~ **noodle**〔美俚〕一本正经的批评家。~ **rhyme** [**song**] 童谣,儿歌。~ **room** 育婴室。~ **school** 幼儿园。~ **tale** 童话。

nurs·ey, nurs·ie [ˈnəːsi; ˋnɝsɪ] *n.*〔儿〕阿妈。

nurs·ing [ˈnəːsiŋ; ˋnɝsɪŋ] **I** *a.* 领养(孩子)的,被领养的。**II** *n.* (职业性的)保育;护理。*the* ~ *father* [*mother*] 养父[母]。~ *profession* 护士业。*take up* ~ *as a career* 就任护士工作。~ **bottle** 奶瓶。~ **home** 私人疗养所;〔英〕小型私人医院。

nurs·ling [ˈnəːsliŋ; ˋnɝslɪŋ] *n.* = nurseling.

nur·ture [ˈnəːtʃə; ˋnɝtʃɚ] **I** *n.* **1.** 养育;培育,训练,教养。**2.** 营养物;食物。**3.** 环境因素。*nature and* ~ 本性和教养,遗传和环境。**II** *vt.* 养育,培育;教养;给…营养。**-r** *n.* 养育者;营养物。

N.U.T. = National Union of Teachers〔英〕全国教师联合会。

nut [nʌt; nʌt] **I** *n.* **1.** 坚果〔核桃、榛、栗等的果实〕坚果果仁。**2.** 难事,难题;难对付的人。**3.**【机】螺帽,螺母;【乐】弓根〔收紧弓弦的装置〕。**4.**〔美俚〕脑袋;笨蛋,傻瓜;疯子,怪人;觉得好[有趣]的东西。**5.**〔罕〕花花公子,纨袴子。**6.**〔*pl.*〕小煤块〔*cf.* nuts〕。*grass* [*ground, earth*] ~ (落)花生。**7.**【乐】(弦乐器的)琴马。**8.**【印】对开。*I have a* ~ *to crack with you*. 我有事要和你讨论。*It's the* ~*s*.〔美俚〕这倒不错。***a hard*** ~ (***to crack***) 难事,难题;难对付的人。***a tough*** ~〔俚〕有胆量的人;横蛮的家伙。***be*** (***dead***) ~***s on***〔俚〕极喜欢,极爱,是…迷,是…的能手,精通。***be*** ~***s to*** [***for***]〔俚〕是…极喜欢的东西。***do one's*** ~(***s***)〔英俚〕像疯子般行动。***don't care a*** (***rotten***) ~ 毫不在乎。***for*** ~***s***〔俚〕〔和否定语同用〕一点(不),怎么也(不)(*I can't play golf for* ~*s*. 我怎么也打不来高尔夫球)。***off one's*** ~ 神经有点不正常,有点疯狂;酩酊大醉(*go off one's* ~ 失去理智;发狂)。***on the*** ~〔美〕分文没有的。**II** *vi.* (**-tt-**) 采坚果,拾核果。*go nutting* 去拾核果。~**-burger**〔美〕碎果肉饼[排]。~**-brown** *a.* 深栗色的(尤指少女、啤酒的颜色等)。~ **butter** (坚)果仁酱〔酱油的代用品〕。~**cake**〔美〕**1.** 油煎圈饼(= doughnut)。**2.** 果仁蛋糕。~ **cracker**〔常 *pl.*〕**1.** 轧碎坚果的钳子;核桃夹子。**2.**【鸟】星鸟。**3.** (因牙齿脱落等)下巴和鼻子挤在一块的脸;瘪嘴脸(*a* ~ *cracker face*)。**4.**〔美俚〕不受欢迎的人(尤指女人)。~**gall** 五倍子,没食子。~**hatch**【鸟】䴓,五十雀。~**house**〔俚〕疯人院,精神病院。~**-meat** 坚果仁,核仁。~ **oil** 坚果油;核桃油;桐油。~**pick** *n.* **1.** 剔取坚果仁的签子。**2.**〔美俚〕精神病医生。~**s and bolts** 主要特点;基本组成部分。~ **tree** 坚果树,(尤指)榛。

nu·tant [ˈnjuːtənt; ˋnjutnt] *a.*【植】俯垂的,点垂的。

nu·tate [njuːˈteit; njuˋtet] *vi.*【植】(茎等)俯垂,下垂。

nu·ta·tion [njuːˈteiʃən; njuˋteʃən] *n.* **1.** 垂头,下垂,下俯;点头。**2.**【植】转头(运动),旋转性。**3.**【机、天】章动〔轴的微动〕。**4.**【医】点头病。~ **angle**【无】(雷达的)盘旋角。

nut·let [ˈnʌtlit; ˋnʌtlɪt] *n.* **1.** 小坚果。**2.** 樱桃核,桃核;李属核。**3.** 子房,细裂片。

nut·meg [ˈnʌtmeg; ˋnʌtmeg] *n.* **1.**【植】肉豆蔻(树)。**2.**〔美〕自负不凡的蠢货〔又叫 gilded ~〕。**3.**〔N-〕〔美〕康乃狄格(Connecticut)州的别名(= N- State)。~**apple** 肉豆蔻的果实。~ **liver**【医】豆蔻肝。~ **tree** 肉豆蔻树。

nut·meg·gers [ˈnʌtmegəz; ˋnʌtmɛgɚz] *n.*〔*pl.*〕〔美〕康涅狄格州人的别名。

nu·tra·ceu·tic·al [ˌnjuːtrəˈsjuːtikəl; ˏnutrəˋsutɪkəl] *n.* 保健食品,营养食品。

nu·tri·a [ˈnjuːtriə; ˋnjutrɪə] *n.* (南美)海狸鼠;海狸鼠毛皮。

nu·tri·ent [ˈnjuːtriənt; ˋnjutrɪənt] **I** *a.* 营养的,滋养的。**II** *n.* 营养物,营养品,养分,养料;营养剂。~ *broth* 肉汁。~ *medium* 培养基。

nu·tri·ment [ˈnjuːtrimənt; ˋnjutrəmənt] *n.* 营养物,食物。**-al** *a.* = nutrient.

nu·tri·tion [njuːˈtriʃən; njuˋtrɪʃən] *n.* **1.** 营养(作用),滋养。**2.** 营养物,食物;【农】追肥。**-al** *a.* 营养的;营养物的;食物的。**-al·ly** *ad.* 在营养上。**-ist** *n.* 营养学(专)家。

nu·tri·tious [njuːˈtriʃəs; njuˋtrɪʃəs] *a.* 有营养的,滋养的。**-ly** *ad.* **-ness** *n.*

nu·tri·tive [ˈnjuːtritiv; ˋnjutrətɪv] **I** *a.* (关于)营养的。**II** *n.* 富于营养的食物。**-ness** *n.*

nuts [nʌts; nʌts] **I** *a.*〔美俚〕笨的,蠢的,发疯的;狂热的;忙乱的。**II** *int.* 呸,不见得! 废话! 胡扯! 混蛋!〔表示讨厌、失望、拒绝、不赞成、藐视、不相信〕。***be*** (***dead***) ~ ***on, be*** ~ ***over*** [***about***] **1.** 热爱着;狂热于。**2.** 精通…的。

nut·shell [ˈnʌtʃel; ˋnʌtʃɛl] **I** *n.* **1.** 坚果的外壳。**2.** 极小的容器;窄小的房屋。**3.** 没有价值的东西,无聊的东西;小数量的东西。**4.** 最简单扼要的表现法,大要。***in a*** ~ 用一句话概括起来,极简单地,在极小范围内(*I can give it you in a* ~. 我可以用几句话加以说明)。***lie in a*** ~ 简单明了,容易理解;一言可尽,容易解决(*The whole thing lay in a* ~. 一切都非常简单明了)。**II** *a.*〔美〕简洁的,扼要的。

nut·ted [ˈnʌtid; ˋnʌtɪd] *a.* 安上螺帽的,用螺帽固定的;〔美〕没考取的。

nut·ter [ˈnʌtə; ˋnʌtɚ] *n.* 拾坚果的人;〔英俚〕古怪的人。

nut·ting [ˈnʌtiŋ; ˋnʌtɪŋ] *n.* 采拾坚果。

nut·ty [ˈnʌti; ˋnʌtɪ] *a.* **1.** 有许多坚果的,生坚果的。**2.** 有坚果味的;美味的;愉快的;内容充实的。**3.**〔俚〕古怪的;傻的;发疯的;有神经病的;可笑的;愚蠢的。**4.**〔俚〕潇洒的,漂亮的。**5.**〔俚〕狂热于…的,迷恋着…的(*on*; *upon*)。**-ti·ness** *n.*

nux [nʌks; nʌks] *n.*〔美俚〕茶。

nux vom·i·ca [ˈnʌksˈvɔmikə; ˋnʌksˋvɑmɪkə]【植】马钱子,番木鳖〔产于东印度〕;马钱子的种子。

nuz·zle [ˈnʌzl; ˋnʌzl̩] *vt.* **1.** 将鼻突入;用鼻子掘;用鼻子擦[触]。**2.** 紧挨,抱抚(示爱)。—*vi.* **1.** 用鼻子掘洞;用鼻子擦[触](*into*; *against*);用鼻子闻。**2.** 舒舒服服地蹲卧,挨紧着躺。~ ***oneself*** 使紧挨着…[舒服地]躺着。

N.W., NW, n. w. = northwest; northwestern.

NWA = Northwest Airlines〔美〕西北航空公司。

N-War = nuclear war 核战争。

NWbN, NW by N = northwest by north 西北偏北。

NWbW, NW by W = northwest by west 西北偏西。

N.W.T. = North West Territories〔加拿大〕东北地区。

n.wt. = net weight 净重。

N.Y., NY = New York 纽约〔美国州名〕;纽约(市)〔美国城市〕。

nya·la [ˈnjɑːlə; ˋnjɑlə] *n.* (*pl.* **-la**, ~**s**) 捻角羚属动物〔东非所产的一种羚〕。

nyb.ble [ˈnibl; ˋnɪbl] = nibble.

N.Y.C., NYC = New York City 纽约(市)〔美国城市〕。

nyc·ta·lo·pi·a [ˌniktəˈləupiə; ˏnɪktəˋlopɪə] *n.*【医】夜盲(症)(*opp.* hemeralopia)。**-lop·ic** *a.*

nyc·tan·thous [nikˈtænθəs; nɪkˋtænθəs] *a.* (花)夜开的。

nyc·ti·nas·ty [ˌniktiˈnæsti; ˏnɪktɪˋnæstɪ] *n.*【植】感夜性。

nyc·ti·trop·ic [ˌniktiˈtrɔpik; ˏnɪktɪˋtrɑpɪk] *a.*【植】(树叶)感夜的,夜间变更方向的。

nyc·to·pho·bi·a [ˌniktəˈfəubiə; ˏnɪktəˋfobɪə] *n.*【医】黑夜恐怖。

Nye [nai; naɪ] *n.* 奈〔姓氏〕。

nyet [njet; njɛt] ***ad***.〔Russ.〕不。～ **diplomacy** 否决外交〔指苏联常在联合国安理会运用否决权的做法〕。

nyl·ghau, nyl·ghai [ˈnilgau, -gɔː, -gai; ˋnɪlgaʊ, -gɔ, -gaɪ] ***n***.【动】印度大羚羊。

ny·lon [ˈnailən; ˋnaɪlɑn] ***n***. **1.**【纺】尼龙,耐纶。**2.**〔*pl*.〕〔口〕尼龙长袜。～ *hose* 尼龙长袜。

nymph [nimf; nɪmf] ***n***. **1.**【希神】宁芙〔半神半人的少女〕;〔诗〕美少女。**2.**【虫】若虫。**-al** ***a***. **-like** ***a***.

nym·pha [ˈnimfə; ˋnɪmfə] ***n***. (*pl*. ***-phae*** [-fiː; -fi]) **1.**【虫】若虫。**2.**〔*pl*.〕【解】小阴唇。

nym·pha·lid [ˈnimfəlid; ˋnɪmfəlɪd] **I** ***n***. 蛱蝶科动物。**II** ***a***. 蛱蝶科的。

nym·phe·an [nimˈfiːən; nɪmˋfiən], **nymph·ish** [-fiʃ; -fɪʃ] ***a***. 宁芙女神(似)的。

nymph·et [ˈnimfət, nimˈfet; ˋnɪmfət, nɪmˋfɛt] ***n***. 进入青春期的姑娘。**-ic** ***a***.

nym·pho·lep·sy [ˈnimfəlepsi; ˋnɪmfəˏlɛpsɪ] ***n***. **1.** (想得到不可得到之物的)狂乱;入迷;妄想狂;【医】情欲增盛。**2.**【医】小阴唇切除术。**-pho·lept** ***n***. 狂乱者,狂热者。**-pho·lep·tic** [ˌnimfəˈleptik; ˏnɪmfəˋlɛptɪk] ***a***. 狂乱的,热狂的;妄想的。

nym·pho·ma·ni·a [ˌnimfəˈmeiniə; ˏnɪmfəˋmenɪə] ***n***.【医】女子色狂,慕男狂,花癫,花疯。**-ni·ac** ***a***., ***n***. 慕男狂患者(的)。

nys·tag·mic [nisˈtægmik; nɪsˋtægmɪk] ***a***.【医】眼球震颤(症)的。

nys·tag·mus [nisˈtægməs; nɪsˋtægməs] ***n***.【医】眼球震颤(症)。

nys·ta·tin [ˈnistətin; ˋnɪstətɪn] ***n***.【药】制霉菌素。

NYT = *New York Times*〔美〕《纽约时报》。

Nyx [niks; nɪks] ***n***.【希神】夜之女神。

NZ = **1.** New Zealand 新西兰。**2.** New Zealand National Airways Corporation 新西兰国家航空公司。

O

O¹, o [əu; o] (*pl*. **O's, o's** [əuz; oz]) **1.** 英语字母表第十五字母。**2.** 一系列中之第十五。**3.** O 字形物;圆。**4.**【数】零。*a round O* 圆。

O² [əu; o] ***int***.〔常用大写字母〕哦! 哟! …啊! 唉! 哎呀〔表示惊讶、恐怖、赞叹、愿望等〕。*O for a rest*! 唉! 休息休息才好! *O Life*! 啊,生活! *O*! *Mr*. *John*! 唷,原来是约翰先生。***O dear*** (***me***)***!*** 哎呀! 哎唷! ***O that*** ...〔诗〕但愿…!

O., o. = **1.** old. **2.** Observer. **3.** Ocean. **4.** October. **5.** Ohio. **6.** Oregon. **7.** off. **8.** only. **9.** order. **10.** officer. **11.** *octarius*〔L.〕品脱(容量单位)。**12.** ohm【物】欧姆(电阻单位)。

o' = **1.** = of: seven o'clock 七点钟。man-o'-war 军舰。**2.**〔方〕= on: o'nights 晚上。

O' [ə, əu; ə, o] *pref*. 用于爱尔兰人姓前,表示"某人之后裔" (son of) 之意: *O'Conner*.

O- *pref*.〔用于 m 之前〕= ob-: *o*mit.

-o- *comb*. *f*.〔构成复合词〕本来只用于来自希腊语复合词,现在广泛用于科学术语(等)上;用法: **1.** 第一要素修饰第二要素: Franc*o*-British. **2.** 第一第二要素为同位: Russ*o*-Japanese war. **3.** 构成带有 *-cracy*, *-logy*, *-meter* 等希腊系词尾的衍生词 techn*o*cracy, techn*o*logy, speed*o*meter.

o/a = on account 作为部分付款。

OA = Omni-Antenna 全向天线。

o.a.d. = overall dimension 全尺寸,外廓尺寸。

oaf [əuf; of] ***n***. (*pl*. ～***s***; ***oaves*** [əuvz; ovz]) **1.**〔古〕换孩〔妖魔换置的丑小孩〕。**2.** 畸形儿;痴儿。**3.** 白痴;半傻子;呆子。

oaf·ish [ˈəufiʃ; ˋofɪʃ] ***a***. 畸形儿 (oaf)似的;痴呆的;丑陋的。

O·a·hu [əuˈɑːhuː; oˋɑhu] ***n***. 瓦胡岛〔美国夏威夷群岛中的重要岛屿〕。

Oak [əuk; ok] ***n***., ***int***., ***vt***. = O.K.

oak [əuk; ok] **I** ***n***. **1.** 栎树,橡,柽,槲;栎木,栎叶;栎树嫩叶色。**2.**〔英大学〕坚牢的(栎木)大门。**3.** 栎木家具[木器]。**4.**〔诗〕木船。**II** ***a***. 栎(木制的)。*an* ～ *table* 栎木桌子。***a heart of*** ～ 坚忍不拔的人,勇士。***Oak may fall when reeds stand the storm***.〔谚〕树大招风。***sports one's*** ～〔英学俚〕闭门谢客。***the hearts of Oak***【英海军】军舰和水兵。～ **apple**, ～ **gall** 栎五倍子。～**-leaf cluster** 橡叶簇铜质奖章〔美空军或陆军的一种奖章,银质者等于五个铜质者〕。～ **leather** 栎树皮鞣革。**O-Ridge** 橡树岭〔美国市镇,为原子能研究中心〕。～ **wilt**【植病】橡萎蔫病。

oak·en [ˈəukən; ˋokən] ***a***.〔古、诗〕栎(木制)的。

Oak·land [ˈəuklənd; ˋoklənd] ***n***. 奥克兰〔美国港市〕。

oak·let, oak·ling [ˈəuklit, -liŋ; ˋoklɪt, -lɪŋ] ***n***. 栎树苗,小栎树。

Oak·ley [ˈəukli; ˋoklɪ] ***n***.〔美俚〕= Annie ～.

oa·kum [ˈəukəm; ˋokəm] ***n***.【海】填絮,麻絮。*pick* ～ (从前让囚犯、穷人从事的)拆麻絮。

o.a.o. = off and on 断断续续。

OAO = orbiting astronomical observatory 天体观测卫星。

OAPEC = Organization of the Arab Petroleum Exporting Countries 阿拉伯石油输出国组织。

oar [ɔː, ɔə; or, ɔr] **I** ***n***. **1.** 桨;橹。**2.** 桨手,划手。**3.** 划子,船。**4.** 桨状物,桨状器官〔翼、鳍、腕等〕。*This boat pulls* [*rows*] *six* ～*s*. 这只船用六把桨划。*a pair-* [*an eight-*] ～ 双桨[八桨]船。*a good* [*bad*] ～ 好[笨]桨手。***be chained to the*** ～ 被强迫做苦工。***bend to the*** ～***s*** 用力划桨。***boat the*** ～***s*** 停划收桨。***have an*** ～ ***in every man's boat*** 任何人的事情都要插手干涉,爱管闲事。***have the labouring*** ～ 担任苦活,负担工作中最繁重或最艰苦的部分。***peak the*** ～***s*** 高举桨尾(出水中)。***pull a good*** ～ 划得一手好桨。***pull a lone*** ～ 独自干。***put*** [***thrust***] ***one's*** ～ ***in*** 干预,多管闲事。***rest*** [***lie***] ***on one's*** ～ ***s*** 搁桨停划;(暂时)歇一歇;吃老本。***ship*** [***unship***] ***an*** ～ 上[下]桨。***take*** [***pull***] ***the labouring*** ～ 担任苦活。***toss the*** ～***s*** 举桨(敬礼)。***trail the*** ～***s*** 任桨随水漂流。**II** ***vi***., ***vt***.〔诗〕划,荡(桨);像桨一样摆动(手等)。～ *one's way* 划桨前进。

oar·age [ˈɔːridʒ; ˋɔrɪdʒ] ***n***.〔诗〕划桨,划艇;划具。

oared [ɔːd; ord] ***a***. 有(…)桨的。*two-*～ 双桨的。

oar·fish [ˈɔːfiʃ; ˋɔrˋfɪʃ] ***n***. (*pl*. ～(***es***)) 皇带鱼属 (*Re-*

galecus）动物。

oar·lock [ˈɔːlɔk; ˋorˏlɑk] ***n.*** U形桨架。

oars·man [ˈɔːzmən; ˋorzmən] ***n.*** （划船比赛中的）划手；划桨能手。～**ship** ***n.*** 划船法；划船本领。

oars·wom·an [ˈɔːzwumən; ˋorzwumən] ***n.*** 女划手。

oar·y [ˈɔːri; ˋorɪ] ***a.*** 〔诗〕有桨的，桨状的。

OAS = Organization of American States 美洲国家组织。

O.A.S. = on active service 服现役。

oa·sis [əuˈeisis; oˋesɪs] ***n.*** (*pl.* ***oa·ses*** [-siːz; -siz]) **1.** （沙漠中的）绿洲；（不毛之地中的）沃洲；宜人的地方。**2.** 慰藉物。*He worked hard six days a week and looked forward to his day off as an* ～ *of rest and relaxation.* 他一星期艰苦工作六天，盼望有个假日，作为憩歇和轻松的慰藉。

oast [əust; ost] ***n.*** （烘麦芽等的）烘炉，烤房，干燥室。

oat [əut; ot] **I** ***n.*** **1.** 〔常 *pl.*〕【植】燕麦，雀麦。★ oats 是马的饲料，人吃的叫 oatmeal. **2.** 〔常作 *pl.*，用作单或复〕燕麦田；燕麦种子。**3.** 〔常作 *pl.*，用作单〕= ～-meal. **4.** 〔诗〕麦笛，牧笛；牧歌。**II** ***a.*** 燕麦做的；（燕麦）麦秆做的。***be off one's*** ～***s*** 没有胃口。***feel one's*** [***its***] ～***s*** （吃了燕麦的马）活泼地跳来跳去；〔美俚〕（人）自负，得意起来；〔美俚〕精神饱满，热情洋溢。***smell one's*** ～***s*** （马）快起来；（人）振奋起来。***sow one's wild*** ～***s*** 干年轻人的荒唐事；（年轻时）放荡；浪费青春。～**cake** 燕麦饼。～ **grass** 【植】燕麦草属植物。～**-meal** 燕麦粉；燕麦片；燕麦粥。～ **opera** = oater.

oat·en [ˈəutn; ˋotn̩] ***a.*** 〔诗〕= oat (***a.***). ～ *cakes* 燕麦饼。*an* ～ *pipe* 麦笛，牧笛。

oat·er [ˈəutə; ˋotɚ] ***n.*** 〔美俚〕西部电影[电视节目]。

Oates [əuts; ots] ***n.*** 奥茨〔姓氏〕。

oath [əuθ; oθ] ***n.*** (*pl.* ***oaths*** [əuðz; oðz]) **1.** 誓言，誓约；【法】宣誓。**2.** （咒骂、强调、发怒等时的）妄用神名，渎神的言词；诅咒；咒骂语〔God damn you! 之类〕。*an* ～ *of allegiance* 效忠宣誓。*an* ～ *of office* = *an official* ～ 就职宣誓。*a false* ～ 伪誓。***grind out an*** ～ 切齿诅咒。***make an*** ～ 立誓，宣誓。***on*** [***upon, under***] ～ = (***up***) ***on my*** ～ 发誓，必定。***put*** (***sb.***) ***on*** (***his***) ～ 使(某人)立誓。***take*** [***swear***] ***an*** ～ = make ～. ***take one's*** ～ ***that*** ... 立誓说…是千真万确的。

-oate *comb. f.* 表示有 ester（酯）存在的化合物：benz*oate*.

OAU = Organization of African Unity 非洲统一组织。

Ob [əub, ɔːb; ob, ɑb] ***n.*** （西伯利亚的）鄂毕河。***Gulf of*** ～ 鄂毕湾〔俄罗斯〕。

ob- *pref.* 表示下列诸义。**1.** 对面，颠倒（方向）：*ob*lique, *of*fer. **2.** 阻碍：*ob*stacle. **3.** 反对，抵抗：*ob*stinate, *op*pose. **4.** 抑压：*op*press. **5.** 隐蔽：*ob*fuscate, *ob*scure. ★在 m, c, f, g, p, t 前分别变为 o-, oc-, of-, og-, op-, os-.

O.B. 〔Am.〕= obie.

ob. = **1.** 〔L.〕*obiit*. **2.** 〔L.〕*obiter*. **3.** oboe.

O·ba·di·ah [ˌəubəˈdaiə; ˏobəˋdaɪə] ***n.*** **1.** 奥巴代亚〔男子名〕。**2.** 《俄巴底亚书》〔基督教《圣经》中旧约的一卷〕。

ob·bli·ga·to [ˌɔbliˈgɑːtəu; ˏɑblɪˋgɑto] **I** ***a.*** 〔It.〕【乐】（伴奏）不可缺少的，必要的〔但现在通常指可以省略的伴奏〕。**II** ***n.*** (*pl.* ～**s**, ***-ga·ti*** [-ˈgɑːtiː; -ˋgɑti]) 伴奏。

ob·bo [ˈɔbəu; ˋɔbo] ***n.*** 〔美〕观测气球。

ob·con·ic, ob·con·i·cal [ɔbˈkɔnik, -əl; ɑbˋkɑnɪk, -l̩] ***a.*** 【植】倒圆锥状的。

ob·cor·date [ɔbˈkɔːdeit; ɑbˋkɔrdet] ***a.*** 【植】（叶子）倒心形的。

obdt. = obedient.

ob·duct [ˈɔbdʌkt; ˋɑbdʌkt] ***vt.*** 【地】使（一个地块）架叠于另一地块之上，上推。

ob·du·ra·cy [ˈɔbdjurəsi, ɔbˈdjuː-; ˋɑbdjərəsɪ, ɔbˋdjʊ-] ***n.*** 顽固，执拗；冷酷。

ob·du·rate [ˈɔbdjurit; ˋɑbdjərɪt] ***a.*** 顽固的，执拗的；冷酷的。**-ly** ***ad.*** **-ness** ***n.***

O.B.E., OBE = **1.** Officer (of the Order) of the British Empire（获得帝国勋章的）英国军官。**2.** Office of Business Economics（美国商业部）商业经济管理局。

o·beah [ˈəubiə; ˋobɪə] ***n.*** （非洲、西印度群岛等地某些黑人中曾行使的）一种巫术；（作这种巫术时使用的）神物。

o·be·di·ence [əˈbiːdjəns, -diəns; əˋbidɪəns, -dɪəns] ***n.*** **1.** 服从；遵守；忠顺；〔古〕（国王等的）属下。**2.** 【天主】归依；〔集合词〕管区的信徒；（教会的）权威，管辖；管区。*filial* ～ 孝顺。*humble* ～ 恭顺。*blind* ～ 盲从。*the Roman* ～ 天主教信徒。***hold sb. in*** ～ 使某人服从。***in*** ～ ***to*** 遵从，服从。***reduce to*** ～ 使服从。

o·be·di·ent [əˈbiːdjənt, -diənt; əˋbidɪənt, -dɪənt] ***a.*** 服从的，顺从的，忠顺的，孝顺的，驯良的。***be*** ～ ***to*** 顺从，遵奉。***Your*** (***most***) ～ ***servant*** 您的恭顺的仆人；谨启（等）〔信尾用语〕。**-ly** ***ad.*** (*Yours obediently* [*Obediently yours*] = Yours ～ servant).

o·bei·sance [əuˈbeisns; oˋbesn̩s] ***n.*** 〔古〕**1.** 敬礼〔如鞠躬、屈膝礼等〕。**2.** 尊敬，服从。***do*** [***make, pay***] ～ ***to*** 向…表示敬意。***make an*** ～ ***to*** 向…致敬礼。

ob·e·lisk [ˈɔbilisk; ˋɑbl̩ˏɪst] ***n.*** **1.** （埃及的）方尖塔[碑]，方尖碑形物〔山峰、树木等〕；火山柱。**2.** 【印】剑号(†)，（古代写本中的）疑问记号〔－或÷〕。*a double* ～ 【印】双剑号(‡)。

ob·e·lize [ˈɔbilaiz; ˋɑbl̩ˏaɪz] ***vt.*** 在…上加剑号[问号]。

ob·e·lus [ˈɔbiləs; ˋɑbl̩əs] ***n.*** (*pl.* ***-li*** [-lai; ˋɑbl̩ˏaɪ]) = obelisk.

O·ber·on [ˈəubərən; ˋobəˏrɑn] ***n.*** **1.** 【中世神话】奥白龙〔Titania 的丈夫，小仙女的王〕。**2.** 【天】天王卫四(星)。**3.** 〔o-〕〔俚〕控制炸弹的雷达系统。

o·bese [əuˈbiːs; oˋbis] ***a.*** 肥胖的，肥大的。

o·bese·ness, o·be·si·ty [əuˈbiːsnis, əuˈbisiti; oˋbisnɪs, oˋbɪsətɪ] ***n.*** 肥胖，肥大；【医】肥胖症；多脂。

o·bey [əˈbei; əˋbe] ***vt.*** **1.** 服从，听(人家的)话；遵守(命令等)；照(命令)。**2.** 听由，随(理性等)行为；任(冲动等)摆布。～ *one's parents* 听父母的话。*A ship* ～*s her helm.* 船随舵行动。— ***vi.*** 服从；听话。

ob·fus·cate [ˈɔbfʌskeit; ɑbˋfʌsket] ***vt.*** **1.** 使暗淡；使模糊。**2.** 使糊涂，使迷，使困惑。**-ca·tion** [ˌɔbfʌsˈkeiʃən; ˏɑbfʌsˋkeʃən] ***n.***

ob·fus·ti·cate [əbˈfʌstikeit; ɑbˋfʌstɪket] ***vt.*** 〔美〕使困惑，使为难。

o·bi [ˈəubi; ˋobɪ] ***n.*** **1.** = obeah. **2.** （日本妇女系和服用的）宽腰带。

o·bie [ˈəubiː; ˋobi] ***n.*** 〔美口〕邮局。

ob·i·it [ˈɔbiit; ˋɑbɪɪt] ***vi.*** 〔L.〕卒，逝世〔第三人称单数过去，略为 ob.，用于死亡年月前〕。*ob. 1920* 卒于一九二〇年。

o·bit [ˈɔbit, ˈəubit; ˋobɪt, ˋɑbɪt] ***n.*** 〔古〕葬礼；〔古〕（周年）祭奠；〔美〕= obituary.

ob·i·ter [ˈɔbitə; ˋɑbɪtɚ] ***ad.*** 〔L.〕顺便，便中，附带。～ ***dictum*** (*pl.* ***ob·i·ter dic·ta***) 【法】附论（法官的附带意见）；附言，余论，附带讲的话。

o·bit·u·a·r·ist [əˈbitjuərist; əˋbɪtʃʊˏɛrɪst] ***n.*** 写死亡新闻者；死者略传的作者；讣告执笔者。

o·bit·u·a·ry [əˈbitjuəri; əˋbɪtʃʊˏɛrɪ] **I** ***a.*** 有关死亡[死者]的。*an* ～ *notice*（报上的）讣告，死亡新闻，死者略传。**II** ***n.*** 讣告；死者传略；【天主】死名簿，死者周年祭日的登记簿。

obj. = **1.** object. **2.** objection. **3.** objective.

ob·ject [ˈɔbdʒikt; ˋɑbdʒɪkt] **I** ***n.*** **1.** 物，物体，物件。**2.** 目标 (*of; for*)；目的，宗旨。**3.** 【哲】对象，客体，客观 (*opp.* subject)；【语法】宾语。**4.** 〔口〕（可笑或可怜的）人[物]。*a small* [*strange*] ～ 小[奇怪]东西。*the* ～ *of study* 研究的对象。*the direct* [*indirect*] ～ 直接[间接]受词。*What an* ～ *you have made* (*of*) *yourself!* 〔口〕你这家伙把自己搞得真不像样子！ ***attain***

[*achieve*, *gain*, *secure*] *one's* ～ 达到目的。*fail* [*succeed*] *in one's* ～ 没有达到[达到]目的。*for that* ～ 为了那个目的。*no* ～〔广告用语〕怎样都好,不成问题;没有困难(*Distance is no* ～.(待聘者)上班距离(远、近)不成问题)。*propose an* ～ *to oneself* = *set an* ～ *before one* 立志,立下目标。*with that* ～ *in view* 怀着那个目的。**II** [əb'dʒekt; əb`dʒɛkt] *vi*. **1.** 反对,抗议,表示异议(*against*, *to*)。**2.** 抱反感,不服气,有意见。— *vt*. 提出…作反对的理由(*that*)。*If you don't* ～. 假使你不反对。*I* ～.〔英下院〕我反对。*I* ～ *against him that he is a hypocrite*. 我反对他,因为他是个伪君子。～ *to* **1.** 反对(*I* ～ *to your doing that*. 我反对你做那件事)。**2.** 讨厌(*I* ～ *very much to a wet weather*. 我非常讨厌潮湿的天气)。～ **ball**【撞球】目的球。～ **glass**(显微镜等的)物镜。～ **language** 对象语言,目的语。～ **lens** = object-glass. ～ **lesson** 实物教授课;(某原理的)具体实例;可作教训的实例。～**-line** 轮廓线。～ **plate** 检镜片〔显微镜的载物玻璃片〕。～ **staff**(测量用)函尺,准尺。～ **teaching** 实物[直观]教授(法)。～ **writing** 物体文字(如结绳纪事等)。**-less** *a*. 没有目的[宗旨]的,没有物像的。

ob·jec·ti·fy [əb'dʒektifai; əb`dʒɛktə͵faɪ] *vt*. (*-fied*; *-fy·ing*) 使客观化,使具体化,体现。**-fi·ca·tion** [-'keiʃən; -`keʃən] *n*.

ob·jec·tion [əb'dʒekʃən; əb`dʒɛkʃən] *n*. **1.** 反对;异议;不承认;不情愿,嫌恶。**2.** 缺点;缺陷。**3.** 障碍,妨碍。**4.** 反对的理由。*The chief* ～ *to this book is its great length*. 这本书的主要缺点是太长。*There is no* ～ *to your leaving at once*. 你现在即刻走也不碍事。*feel an* ～ *to* (*doing*) 不愿意…。*have no* ～ *to* (*doing*) 不反对…。*make an* [*take*] ～ *to* [*against*] 对…表示异议,反对…。*open to* ～ 有可议之处,有不合理之处(*The plan is open to* ～. 该计划大有可商榷之处)。*raise an* ～ 提出抗议[异议]。

ob·jec·tion·a·ble [əb'dʒekʃənəbl; əb`dʒɛkʃənəbl̩] *a*. **1.** 引起反对的,要不得的。**2.** 令人讨厌的,令人不愉快的;有伤风化的。**-bly** *ad*.

ob·jec·tive [ɔb'dʒektiv; əb`dʒɛktɪv] **I** *a*. **1.**【哲】客观的;真实的;实在的(*opp*. subjective);外界的;如实的;无偏见的。**2.** 目的的;目标的。**3.**【语】宾格的。**4.**【医】病情除本人外也为他人感觉到的。**II** *n*. **1.** 目的,目标,任务;【军】出击目标。**2.**【语】宾格。**3.**【物】物镜。**4.** 客观事物,实在事物。*military* ～*s* 军事目标。～ **case**【语法】宾格。～ **complement**【语法】宾语补语。～ **lens** = object glass. ～ **symptom**【医】他觉症状。**-ly** *ad*. 在客观上。**-ness** *n*. 客观(性)。

ob·jec·tiv·ism [ɔb'dʒektivizəm; əb`dʒɛktɪvɪzm̩] *n*. 客观主义;客观性(*opp*. subjectivism)。

ob·jec·tiv·i·ty [͵ɔbdʒek'tiviti; ͵ɑbdʒɛk`tɪvətɪ] *n*. 客观(性);客观现实。

ob·jec·tor [əb'dʒektə; əb`dʒɛktɚ] *n*. 反对者。

ob·'jet d'art [ɔb'ʒe'dɑ; ɔb`ʒɛ`dar]〔F.〕(*pl*. ***ob'jets d'art*** [ɔb'ʒe; ob`ʒɛ]) 小美术(工艺)品;古玩。

ob·jur·gate ['ɔbdʒəːgeit; `ɑbdʒɚ͵get] *vt*. 骂,斥责,谴责。**-tion** [͵ɔbdʒəː'geiʃən; ͵ɑbdʒɚ`geʃən] *n*. **-tor** *n*. 斥责者。**-tory** *a*.

ob-gyn ['ɔbdʒin; `ɔbdʒɪn] *n*.〔口〕妇产科医师〔由 obstetrician 和 gynaecologist 二字缩合而成〕。

obl. = **1.** oblique. **2.** oblong.

ob·lan·ce·o·late [ɔb'lɑːnsiəlit, -͵leit; ɑb`lænsɪəlɪt, -͵let] *a*.【植】(叶子)倒披针形的。

ob·last ['ɔblɑːst; `ɑblæst] *n*.〔Russ.〕州,地方,区域,地区;省;外省;省会。

ob·late[1] ['ɔbleit; `ɑblet] **I** *n*. **1.** 献身教会工作的人;被父母许愿献身教会的儿童。**2.** 在修道院生活而不遵守修道士戒规的人。**3.**〔O-〕某些天主教团体的信徒。**II** *a*. 献身教会工作的。

ob·late[2] ['ɔbleit, əu'bleit; `ɑblet, ə`blet] *a*.【数】扁圆形的;扁球形的(*opp*. prolate)。**-ness** *n*.

ob·la·tion [əu'bleiʃən; ɑb`leʃən] *n*. 供奉;供献(物),祭品;圣体〔面包和葡萄酒〕供献(礼);(对教会等的)捐献。**-al**, **-la·tory** *a*.

ob·ligate ['ɔbligit; `ɑblə͵get] **I** *vt*. **1.** 使负(法律上或道义上的)义务。**2.** 强迫,强制。**3.** 使感激。**4.** 规定(某款)作还债专用。*I am* ～*d to do it*. 我有责任去做它。**II** *a*. 强制性的;有责任的;必需的;【生】专性的。～ *parasites* 专性寄生物。～ **runner** 强制性跑步者〔指为了追求健康强迫自己跑步而往往效果不佳乃至伤害自身健康的人〕。

ob·li·ga·tion [͵ɔbli'geiʃən; ͵ɑblə`geʃən] *n*. **1.** 义务;职责,责任;负担。**2.** 契约,合约;证券;债务。**3.** 恩惠,恩义。**4.** 债务,欠下的人情。*the* ～ *of tax* 纳税的义务。*be* [*lie*] *under an* ～ *to* 对…有义务;受过…的恩。*lay an* ～ *upon* 使负债务。*of* ～ 义务上的;义务性的。*meet one's* ～*s* 偿还债务。*put* [*lay*] *sb*. *under an* ～ 施恩惠给某人;使某人欠人情,使某人承担义务。*repay an* ～ 报恩。

ob·li·ga·to [͵ɔbli'gɑːtəu; ͵ɑblɪ`gɑto] *a*., *n*.〔It.〕= obbligato.

ob·lig·a·to·ry [ɔ'bligətəri; ə`blɪgə͵torɪ] *a*. **1.** 义务的;应尽的;强制性的。**2.**【生】专性的。～ *military service* 义务兵役。*an* ～ *right* 债权。*the* ～ *term* 义务年限。～ **parasitism**【生】专性寄生。**-ri·ly** *ad*.

o·blige [ə'blaidʒ; ə`blaɪdʒ] *vt*. **1.** 迫使;责成,使负债务。**2.** 施恩于,施惠于;答应…的请求;使满足(*by*, *with*);使感激;给,借(*with*)。*Your recalcitrance* ～*s firmness on me*. 你们不听话,那我就得采用果断措施。*We are much* ～*d to you for your help*. 非常感谢您对我们的帮助。*I won't* ～ *you to stay here any longer*. 你不必再待在这儿啦。*Circumstances* ～ *me to do that*. 情况使我不得不那样做。*I am sorry I cannot* ～ *you*. 很抱歉,我不能答应你的请求。*Excuse me*, *but could you* ～ *me with a match*? 对不起,请给我一根火柴好吗? *Will any gentleman* ～ *a lady*? 请哪位先生把位子让给一位女士好吗? — *vi*. 做好事,效劳。*I'll do anything within reason to* ～. 能办到的,我都愿尽力[效劳]。*be* ～*d to* **1.** 感谢((*I am*) *much* ～*d* (*to you*). 多谢多谢)。**2.** 不得已而…(*I was* ～*d to go*. 我不得不去)。～ (*one*) **by ... ing** 替人…(*Will you* ～ *me by closing the door*? 请替我关上门好吗?)。～ (*one*) **with** 给…(*O- us with your presence* [*an answer*] 务请出席[赐覆]。*Could you* ～ *me with ten dollars*? 借十块钱给我好吗?)。

ob·li·gee [͵ɔbli'dʒiː; ͵ɑblɪ`dʒi] *n*. **1.**【法】权利人,债权人,债主(*opp*. obligor)。**2.** 受惠者(*opp*. obliger)。

o·blig·ing [ə'blaidʒiŋ; ə`blaɪdʒɪŋ] *a*. 恳切的;乐于助人的;(女仆等)勤快的;〔古〕(言行等)谦和的,有礼貌的。**-ly** *ad*. **-ness** *n*.

ob·li·gor [͵ɔbli'gɔː; ͵ɑblɪ`gɔr] *n*.【法】义务人,债务人,负债人(*opp*. obligee)。

ob·lique [ə'bliːk; ə`blik] **I** *a*. **1.** 斜,倾斜的。**2.** (道德上)不正当的,邪恶的。**3.** 间接的;暗中的;不坦率的,转弯抹角的。**4.**【植】歪叶的〔两侧不对称的〕。**5.**【语法】间接(格)的。**6.**【数】非直角的;非垂直的;斜线的,斜角的,斜面的。**7.**【军】(照片)从空中倾斜摄制的。～ *dealings* 不正当交易。*the* ～ *case*【语法】间接格〔主格、呼格以外各格的总称〕。*the* ～ *narration* 间接叙述(法)。*an* ～ *plane* 斜面。*make an* ～ *reference to* 转弯抹角地说到。**II** *vi*. **1.** 倾斜,歪。**2.**【军】(成 45 度)斜进;斜行进。**III** *n*. **1.** 倾斜物。**2.**【解】斜肌(尤指腹部的肌肉)。**3.**【军】倾斜航空照片。**IV** *ad*.【军】以 45 度角。*To the right* ～, *march*!【军】向右成 45 度角,正步走! ～ **angle**【数】斜角。～ **sailing**【海】斜航。～ **wing**【航空】斜翼〔一种为减少高速飞行时风的阻力之机翼,可侧前侧后

摆动]。-ly *ad*. -ness *n*.

ob·liq·ui·ty [əˈblikwiti; ɔˋblɪkwətɪ] *n*. 1. 斜,倾斜,歪斜;倾度,倾角。2.【天】斜交。3.(说话、行为的)不明,暧昧,转弯抹角。4.(行为等的)不正,邪;精神变态。

ob·li·ter·ate [əˈblitəreit; əˋblɪtə,ret] *vt*. 1. 涂去,擦去,删去(文字等);消灭…的痕迹。2. 使消失;除去;抹杀;使淹没;使被忘却。-a·tive *a*. -a·tor *n*.

O

ob·lit·er·a·tion [ə,blitəˈreiʃən; ə,blɪtəˋreʃən] *n*. 1. 涂去,删除;清除;灭迹,消灭,淹没。2.【医】管腔闭合。

ob·liv·i·on [əˈbliviən; əˋblɪvɪən] *n*. 1. 忘却,易忘,健忘;被忘却;埋没,淹没;漠视。2. 大赦。*the Act* [*Bill*] *of O-* 大赦令。***be buried in*** ~ 全被人们忘记。***fall*** [***sink, pass***] ***into*** ~ 渐为(世人)忘却,湮没无闻。

ob·liv·i·ous [əˈbliviəs; əˋblɪvɪəs] *a*. 1. 易忘的,健忘的。2. 忘却,忘记 (*of*)。3. 不在意的,呆呆的,茫然的。4.〔诗〕使忘却的〔通过睡眠等〕。-ly *ad*. -ness *n*.

Ob·lo·mov [əbˈləuməf; əbˋloməf] *n*. 奥勃洛摩夫〔俄国作家冈察洛夫所作同名小说中的主人翁,善良而怠惰〕。-ism *n*. 沉溺于空想而一味怠惰懒散的作风。

ob·long [ˈɔblɔŋ; ˋɑblɔŋ] *n*., *a*. 长方形(的),椭圆形(的)。

ob·lo·quy [ˈɔbləkwi; ˋɑbləkwɪ] *n*. 1. 大骂,斥责。2.(由于受到强烈指责而造成的)污名,丑名,耻辱。

ob·mu·tes·cence [,ɔbmjuːˈtesns; ,ɔbmjuˋtɛsns] *n*. 死不吭声。

ob·nox·ious [əbˈnɔkʃəs; əbˋnɑkʃəs] *a*. 1. 可憎的,讨厌的。2.〔古〕易受…的。3.【法】有责任的。4. 应受谴责的。-ly *ad*. -ness *n*.

o·boe [ˈəubəu, ˈəubɔi; ˋobo, ˋobɔɪ] *n*. 1.【乐】双簧管者,欧巴。2.(风琴的)欧巴音程。

obo·ist [ˈəbəuist; ˋoboɪst] *n*. 吹双簧管者。

ob·o·lus [ˈɔbləs; ˋɑbləs] *n*. (*pl*. *-li* [-lai; -laɪ]) 〔L.〕欧布鲁斯〔古希腊价值 1/6 德拉克马的硬币;相当于 11¼ 谷(喱)的重量单位;以前欧洲通用的小硬币〕。

ob·o·vate [ɔbˈəuveit; ɑbˋovet] *a*.【植】倒卵形的〔如某些叶〕。

ob·o·void [ɔbˈəuvɔid; ɑbˋovɔɪd] *a*.【植】倒卵球形的〔指某些果〕。

O'Bri·en [əuˈbraiən; oˋbraɪən] *n*. 奥布赖恩〔姓氏〕。

obs. =1. observation. 2. observatory. 3. obsolete.

ob·scene [əbˈsiːn; əbˋsin] *a*. 1. 猥亵的,淫猥的;淫荡的。2.〔古、诗〕污秽的,丑恶的,讨厌的。~ *pictures* 淫画。*an* ~ *publication*【法】伤风败俗的刊物,淫书。*a* ~ *bird* 乌鸦。-ly *ad*.

ob·scen·i·ty [ɔbˈsiːniti; əbˋsɛnətɪ] *n*. 猥亵,诲淫;淫行,淫话。

ob·scur·ant [ɔbˈskjuərənt; əbˋskjʊrənt] I *n*. 蒙昧主义者。II *a*. 蒙昧主义的,使愚昧的。-ism *n*. 愚民政策,蒙昧主义。-ist *n*., *a*. 蒙昧主义者(的);(似)蒙昧主义的(*an obscurantist policy* 愚民政策)。

ob·scur·an·tic [,ɔbskjuˈræntik; ,ɑbskjʊˋræntɪk] *a*. 蒙昧主义的,愚民政策的。

ob·scur·a·tion [,ɔbskjuəˈreiʃən; ,ɑbskjʊˋreʃən] *n*. 1. 黑暗化,阴暗,朦胧;遮蔽;(知识等的)蒙昧化,(真理、语意的)暧昧化。2.【天】掩星,食。

ob·scure [əbˈskjuə; əbˋskjʊr] I *a*. 1. 暗(夜),黑暗的;黑夜里的;阴(天),朦胧的。2. 不清楚的,不鲜明的,不明了的,含糊的,暧昧的;难解的,晦涩的。3. 隐蔽的,偏僻的;不出名的,无名的,低微的。*an* ~ *day* 阴天。~ *yellow* 闷黄色。*an* ~ *meaning* 晦涩不明的意义。*an* ~ *retreat* 隐居处。*an* ~ *village* 穷乡僻壤。*a host of* ~ *writers* 一大群无名作家。***be of*** ~ ***origin*** [***birth***] 出身微贱。II *n*.〔诗〕阴暗,朦胧;黑夜。III *vt*. 1. 使(黑)暗。2. 遮蔽,隐藏。3. 使(发音等)暧昧[含糊、不明]。4. 使难理解;搞混。5. 掩蔽(名声等),(比较的结果,使别人)相形见绌[暗然无光]。*The sun was* ~*d by clouds*. 太阳被云遮了。~*d glass* 磨砂玻璃。—*vi*. 变模糊;隐藏起来。*This language serves to disguise and* ~. 这种话是用来文过饰非的。-ly *ad*. 暗,朦胧,暧昧;暗暗。-ness *n*. =obscurity. -r *n*.

ob·scu·ri·ty [əbˈskjuəriti; əbˋskjʊrətɪ] *n*. 1. 暗(淡);朦胧。2. 含糊,暧昧,不明;难解处,不明处,费解的话。3. 无名的人[地方];低微的人[处境]。***retire into*** ~ 隐退。***rise from*** ~ 出身微贱。***sink into*** ~ 被世人忘掉,湮没无闻。

ob·se·crate [ˈɔbsikreit; ˋɑbsɪ,kret] *vt*. (*-crat·ed*; *-crat·ing*)〔罕〕恳求,恳请,请愿。

ob·se·cra·tion [,ɔbsiˈkreiʃən; ,ɑbsɪˋkreʃən] *n*. 恳求,恳请;【宗】以 by 开始的恳求祈祷句。

ob·se·qui·al [ɔbˈsiːkwiəl; əbˋsikwɪəl] *a*. 葬[丧]礼的。

ob·se·quies [ˈɔbsikwiz; ˋɑbsɪkwɪz] *n*.〔*pl*.〕葬[丧]礼。

ob·se·qui·ous [əbˈsiːkwiəs; əbˋsikwɪəs] *a*. 谄媚的,奉承的;〔古〕顺从的;死心塌地的。*be* ~ *to the great* 巴结权贵。-ly *ad*. -ness *n*.

ob·serv·a·ble [əbˈzəːvəbl; əbˋzɝvəbl̩] I *a*. 1. 看得见的,观察得出的;常见的。2. 值得注意的,显著的。3. 可[应]庆祝的。4. 可[应]遵守的。II *n*. 1. 值得注意的东西;感觉到[看得见]的事物。2.【物】可观察量;观察算符。-bly *ad*.

ob·serv·ance [əbˈzəːvəns; əbˋzɝvəns] *n*. 1.(法律、义务、仪式等的)遵守 (*of*)。2. 仪式;(宗教)典礼;纪念,庆祝。3. 习惯,惯例。4.〔古〕恭顺。5. 教规,戒律。6.〔罕〕注意,观察。*the* ~ *of the emperor's birthday* 皇帝祝寿大典。*the* ~ *of the Sabbath* 守安息日〔宗教信徒在主日停止工作,基督教徒为星期日,犹太教徒为星期六〕。~ *of national sovereignty* 尊重国家主权。~ *of territorial integrity* 尊重领土完整。

ob·serv·ant [əbˈzəːvənt; əbˋzɝvənt] I *a*. 1. 注意,留心;盯着,看牢 (*of*)。2. 观察力敏锐的,机警的。3. 严格遵守…的 (*of*)。*an* ~ *boy* 机警的男孩子。*be* ~ *of the traffic rules* 严格遵守交通规则。*be* ~ *of one's duties* 恪尽责守。*be* ~ *to avoid danger* 注意避免危险。II *n*.〔古〕遵守者,严守者;〔O-〕【天主】(方济各会)严守教规的修道士。-ly *ad*.

ob·ser·va·tion [,ɔbzə(ː)ˈveiʃən; ,ɑbzɚˋveʃən] *n*. 1. 观察,注意;观察力;瞭望。2. 观测,实测;【海】测天;【军】观测,监视,侦察。3.(观察得的)知识,经验;〔*pl*.〕观察[观测]报告[资料]。4. 经验谈,讲话,谈话;评述,按语,短评,意见 (*on*)。5.〔口〕发言,言论。*a man of no* ~ 没有观察力的人。*an expedition of* ~ 观察队。*sampling* ~ 抽查。*service* ~ 业务检查。*a witty* [*foolish*] ~ 聪明[糊涂]话。***come*** [***fall***] ***under one's*** ~ 看见,瞧见。***keep a suspect*** [***patient***] ***under*** ~ 监视[观察]一个可疑的人[病人]。***make a few*** ~***s on*** 简单谈谈对…的几点看法。***take an*** ~【海】测天。~ **balloon**【军】观测气球。~ **car**(火车的)游览车厢。~ **check** 外部检验。~ **plane**【空】侦察机。~ **post**【军】监视哨,瞭望哨〔略为 O Pip〕。~ **station** 观察所,观察站;气象台,观象台。

ob·ser·va·tion·al [,ɔbzə(ː)ˈveiʃənəl; ,ɑbzɚˋveʃənəl] *a*. 观察[观测]的,监视的;根据观测[观察]的。-ly *ad*.

ob·serv·a·to·ry [əbˈzəːvətəri; əbˋzɝvə,torɪ] *n*. 1. 观测所,观象台,气象台,天文台。2. 观察台,瞭望台,望楼,【军】(炮台的)监视阁。

ob·serve [əbˈzəːv; əbˋzɝv] *vt*. 1. 遵守(时间,法律、习惯等);举行(仪式等);纪念,庆祝(节日、生日等)。2. 观察,观测(天体、气象等);监视(敌人行动等)。3. 通过观察认识到,注意到,看到,知道。4. 说,讲;陈述(所见);评述,评论。~ *silence* 保持沉默。~ *a rule* 遵守规则。~ *a suspected person* 监视有嫌疑的人。*Allow me to* ~ *that* .... 请允许我这样批评。*I didn't* ~ *the colors of her eyes*. 我没有注意到她眼睛的颜色。—*vi*. 1. 观察;注意。2. 陈述意见,评述,简评 (*on*; *upon*)。*I have very little to* ~ *on what has been said*. 关于刚才所听到的我没什么话好讲。*as I was going to* ~ 像我本来

想讲的。*strange to* ～ 讲起来虽奇怪。***the ～d of all observers*** 众矢之的,被大家注视的人。

ob·serv·er [əbˈzəːvə; əbˋzɝvɚ] ***n*.** **1.** 注视者;观察者;观测员;测候员。**2.** 遵守者,奉行者;(仪式等的)举行者。**3.** 观察家,评论者。**4.** 【军】观察员,观测员;机上侦察员。**5.** 监视人,见证人,目击者,旁观者;旁听者。*a plot* ～ 测绘员。*an automatic* ～【火箭】自动记录仪。

ob·serv·ing [əbˈsəːviŋ; əbˋzɝvɪŋ] ***a*.** 注意周到的;观察力敏锐的。**-ly *ad*.**

ob·sess [əbˈses; əbˋsɛs] ***vt*.** (魔鬼;妄想等)缠住,迷住;使着迷;使窘困,使烦扰[常用被动结构]。***be ～ed by*** [***with***] 被…附上[缠住,迷住心窍]。**-ive *a*.** 成见(性)的;引起成见的。

ob·ses·sion [əbˈseʃən; əbˋsɛʃən] ***n*.** 着魔;执意,积念,迷念,摆脱不了的思想[情感等]。***be under an ～ of*** 在思想[情感]上被…缠住。***suffer from an ～*** 耿耿于怀。

ob·ses·sion·al [əbˈseʃənəl; əbˋsɛʃənl̩] ***a*.** 摆脱不了的。*an ～ neurosis* 强迫观念性神经病。**-ism *n*.** (对某事物或活动的)痴迷。

ob·sid·i·an [əbˈsidiən; əbˋsɪdɪən] ***n*.** 【矿】黑曜岩。

Obsn. = observation.

ob·so·les·cent [ˌɔbsəˈlesnt; ˏɑbsəˋlɛsənt] ***a*.** (词语、习惯等)逐渐被废弃的;快要不用的;【生】废退的,萎缩的。**-les·cence *n*.** **1.** 废弃,淘汰;过时。**2.** 【生】(器官的)废退,萎缩。

ob·so·lete [ˈɔbsəliːt; ˋɑbsəˏlit] **I *a*.** **1.** 已废弃的,已不用的,已失时效的。**2.** 陈旧的,已过时的。**3.** 【生】已废退的,萎缩了的,不发育的;不明显的。*an ～ vessel* 废舰。*an ～ word* 已废的词。**II *n*.** 废词;被废弃的事物。**-ly *ad*.** **-ness *n*.**

ob·so·le·tism [ˈɔbsəliːtizəm; ˋɑbsəlitɪzm̩] ***n*.** 废弃,陈腐;废词语,废弃了的习惯[用法]。

Obsr. = observer.

ob·sta·cle [ˈɔbstəkl; ˋɑbstəkl̩] ***n*.** 障碍(物),妨害,阻碍,干扰。***an ～ to*** (*progress*) (进步)的障碍。***throw ～s in sb.'s way*** 妨害,阻碍某人。～ **course** 障碍赛跑训练场。～ **race** 障碍赛。

obstet. = **1.** obstetric(al). **2.** obstetrics.

ob·stet·ric, ob·stet·ri·cal [ɔbsˈtetrik, -kəl; əbˋstɛtrɪk, -kl̩] ***a*.** 产科(学)的,助产的。*an ～ nurse* 助产护士。

ob·ste·tri·cian [ˌɔbsteˈtriʃən; ˏɑbstɛˋtrɪʃən] ***n*.** 产科医生。

ob·stet·rics [ɔbˈstetriks; əbˋstɛtrɪks] ***n*.** 产科学,助产术。

ob·sti·na·cy [ˈɔbstinəsi; ˋɑbstənəsɪ] ***n*.** **1.** 顽固,顽强,固执,顽梗;不易克服性。**2.** [an ～] 顽固的言行 (*against*)。**3.** (病痛等)难治,难解除,难抑制。***with ～*** 顽强地,顽固地。

ob·sti·nate [ˈɔbstinit; ˋɑbstənɪt] ***a*.** 顽固的;顽强的;不易克服的;难治的。～ *resistance* 顽强的抵抗。**-ly *ad*.**

ob·sti·nate·ness [ˈɔbstinitnis; ˋɑbstənɪtnɪs] ***n*.** **1.** 固执,顽固,执拗;顽强。**2.** 抵药物性,抗治疗性。**3.** 不屈,坚持。

ob·sti·pa·tion [ˌɔbstiˈpeiʃən; ˏɑbstəˋpeʃən] ***n*.** 〔罕〕【医】便秘。

ob·strep·er·ous [əbˈstrepərəs; əbˋstrɛpərəs] ***a*.** **1.** 吵闹的,喧嚣的。**2.** 任性的,暴躁的;顽固对抗的;难驾驭的。**-ly *ad*.** **-ness *n*.**

ob·struct [əbˈstrʌkt; əbˋstrʌkt] ***vt*., *vi*.** 堵[阻]塞;遮住;妨碍;阻挠;(给…)设置障碍。～ *a passage* 堵塞通路。～ *the traffic* 阻塞交通。～ *the view* 挡住视线。～ *sb.* (*from*) *doing something* 阻挠某人做某事。**-er, -or *n*.**

ob·struc·tion [əbˈstrʌkʃən; əbˋstrʌkʃən] ***n*.** **1.** 堵塞,遮断,妨碍,阻碍,障碍;【议会】妨碍议事进程。**2.** 遮断物,障碍物。～ **guard** (火车头前的)护栏,排障器。**-ism *n*.** 故意妨碍议案通过。**-ist *n*.** 妨碍议事者。

ob·struc·tive [əbˈstrʌktiv; əbˋstrʌktɪv] **I *a*.** 引起阻塞的,妨害的,阻碍的;妨碍议事的。***be ～ to*** 成为…的障碍。**II *n*.** 妨碍物,障碍;妨碍(议事)者。**-ly *ad*.** **-ness *n*.**

ob·stru·ent [ˈɔbstruwənt; ˋɑbstruənt] **I *a*.** 〔罕〕闭塞的,阻碍的。**II *n*.** 〔罕〕【解】(体内通道的)堵塞物〔例如肾石〕。

ob·tain [əbˈtein; əbˋten] ***vt*.** 得到,获得,买到;达到(目的)。～ *a reward* 得到报酬。～ *a prize* 得奖。～ *a hearing* 得到发言机会。～ *a high price* 卖得好价钱。— ***vi*.** (习惯等)通行,流行;投合一般人心理,得到(众人)承认。*These ideas no longer* ～. 这些见解已经行不通了。*This ～s with most people*. 这是多数人公认的。**-able *a*.** 能得到的;能达到的。**-er *n*.** 获得者。**-ment *n*.** 〔古〕获得;达成。

ob·tect [ɔbˈtekt; ɑbˋtɛkt] ***a*.** 【虫】被甲的,具被的 (= obtected)。

ob·test [ɔbˈtest; ɑbˋsest] ***vt*.** 〔古〕乞,央求,恳求;请求(某人作证)。— ***vi*.** **1.** 〔罕〕抗议。**2.** 恳求。

ob·tes·ta·tion [ˌɔbtesˈteiʃən; ˏɑbtɛsˋteʃən] ***n*.** **1.** 祈求。**2.** 〔罕〕抗议。

ob·trude [əbˈtruːd; əbˋtrud] ***vt*.** **1.** 逼人接受;强行;强迫。**2.** 挤出,冲出;(乌龟)伸出(头来)。～ *one's opinions* (*up*) *on others* 把自己意见强加于人。～ *oneself* 硬管闲事,硬插手 (*upon*; *into*)。— ***vi*.** 闯入;打扰 (*upon*)。

ob·tru·sion [əbˈtruːʒən; əbˋtruʒən] ***n*.** **1.** (意见等的)强迫(别人)接受 (*on others*);强挤;强加,强求。**2.** 管闲事,多嘴;闯入;莽撞。

ob·tru·sive [əbˈtruːsiv; əbˋtrusɪv] ***a*.** **1.** 强迫人的。**2.** 爱管闲事的,爱多嘴的。**3.** 伸出的;突出的。**-ly *ad*.** **-ness *n*.**

ob·tund [əbˈtʌnd; ɑbˋtʌnd] ***vt*.** 使迟钝,使失去感觉;【医】缓和,抑制(疼痛等)。

ob·tund·ent [əbˈtʌndənt; ɑbˋtʌndənt] **I *a*.** 使感觉迟钝的;止痛的;减少疼痛的;减少刺激的。**II *n*.** 止痛药,缓和剂。

ob·tu·rate [ˈɔbtjuəreit; ˋɑbtjʊˏret] ***vt*.** 塞,闭塞;封闭,紧塞;(开炮时)密闭(炮尾)。**-ra·tion *n*.** 封闭,闭塞,紧塞。**-ra·tor *n*.** 口盖,管塞;【军】气密装置,封闭器〔炮的尾塞〕;【植】珠孔塞。

ob·tuse [əbˈtjuːs; əbˋtjus] ***a*.** **1.** 钝的,不尖的,不锐利的。【数】(角)钝的 (*opp*. acute);【植】(叶尖)钝形的,圆头的。**2.** (感觉)迟钝的,愚钝的;(印象)不鲜明的;(疼痛)不剧烈的。*an ～ angle*【数】钝角。*an ～ pain* 闷痛。*be ～ in understanding* 头脑迟钝。**-ly *ad*.**

ob·tuse·ness [əbˈtjuːsnis; ɑbˋtjusnɪs] ***n*.** **1.** 不尖,不锐利;钝。**2.** 钝角。**3.** 愚钝。**4.** 不鲜明,(疼痛)不剧烈 (= obtusity)。

ob·verse [ˈɔbvəːs; ɑbˋvɝs] **I *n*.** **1.** (货币、奖章等的)表面,正面 (*opp*. reverse);(事物两面的)较显著面;相互对应面。**2.** 【逻】换质说明法。**II *a*.** **1.** 表面的,正面的;显著面的;对应面的。**2.** 【植】(叶形)钝头形的,倒置的。*We must learn to look at problems all-sidedly, seeing the reverse as well as the ～ side of things*. 我们必须学会全面地看问题,不但要看到事物的正面,也要看到它的反面。**-ly *ad*.**

ob·ver·sion [ɔbˈvəːʃən; ɑbˋvɝʃən] ***n*.** **1.** 将表面反过来的动作。**2.** 【逻】换质法〔将 All men are mortal 改成 No men are immortal〕。

ob·vert [əbˈvəːt; əbˋvɝt] ***vt*.** **1.** 将(表面)反过来。**2.** 【逻】(用换质法)使(命题)换质。

ob·vi·ate [ˈɔbvieit, -vjeit; ˋɑbvɪˏet, -vjet] ***vt*.** 除去,排除(障碍、危险等),(事前)防止,避免。**-a·tion** [ˌɔbviˈeiʃən; ˏɑbvɪˋeʃən] ***n*.** **-a·tor *n*.**

ob·vi·o·sit·y [ˌɔbviˈɔsiti; ˏɑbvɪˋɑsətɪ] ***n*.** 不言而喻的东西。

ob·vi·ous [ˈɔbviəs, -vjəs; ˋɑbvɪəs, -vjəs] ***a*. 1.** 明显的,明白的。**2.** (感情、戏谑等)明明白白的,显而易见的;显著的。*an ~ advantage* 显著的优势。*It is ~ that you are wrong*. 显然你错了。**-ly *ad*. -ness *n*.**

ob·vo·lute [ˈɔbvəljuːt; ˋɑbvəˏlut] ***a*.**【植】跨褶的〔指叶或花瓣〕(= obvolutive)。**-lu·tion** [ˌɔbvəˈljuːʃən; ˏɑbvəˋluʃən] ***n*.**

O

O.C., OC =**1.** officer commanding 指挥官。**2.** oral contraceptive 口服避孕药。

o.c. =〔L.〕*opere citato* 见前引书 (= in the work cited)。

oc. = ocean.

o/c = outward collection 出口托收。

oc- *pref*.〔用于字母 C 前〕= ob-.

oc·a·ri·na [ˌɔkəˈriːnə; ˏɑkəˋrinə] ***n*.**【乐器】奥卡利那笛;洋埙〔陶制的蛋形笛〕。

OCAS = Organization of Central American States 中美洲国家组织。

o.c.b. = oil circuit breaker 油开关,油断路器。

Oc·cam [ˈɔkəm; ˋɑkəm] ***n*.** 奥克姆〔姓氏〕。

occas. = occasional(ly).

O'Ca·sey [əuˈkeisi; oˋkesɪ] ***n*. 1.** 奥凯西〔姓氏〕。**2. Sean ~** 希安·奥凯西〔1884—1964,爱尔兰剧作家〕。

oc·ca·sion [əˈkeiʒən; əˋkeʒən] **I *n*. 1.** (庆祝等的特殊)场合;(重大)时节,时刻。**2.** 机会;(适当的)时机〔O-〕,〔拟人语〕好机会。**3.** 原因,诱因,近因。**4.** (怒、笑等的)根据,理由,必要。**5.**〔*pl*.〕〔古〕事,事务,工作,职业。*She was the ~ of the trouble*. 她是纠纷的根源。*There is no ~ to be angry*. 没有生气的理由。*one's lawful ~s*〔古〕本职。*The national-day celebration was a great ~*. 国庆日庆祝仪式很盛大。***as ~ demands*** 遇必要时;及时。***for one's ~*** 为某人。***for the ~*** 临时。***give ~ to*** 引起,使发生。***have no ~ for*** 没有的根据。***have no ~ to*** (*do*) 没有…的理由[必要](*I had no ~ to see him*. 我没有会见他的必要)。***have ~ for*** 需要。***if the ~ arises*** [***should arise***] = ***should ~ arise*** 必要的时候。***improve the ~*** 抓紧时机,乘机说教。***in honour of the ~*** 为表示庆贺,为道贺。***on great ~s*** 在大庆[盛典]时期。***on*** [***upon***] ***~*** 有时,间或;遇必要时。***on one ~*** 曾经,有一个时候。***on several ~s*** 屡次,好几次。***on the first ~*** 一有机会。***on the ~ of*** 在…的时候,在…时。***on the present ~*** 当时。***on this ~*** 这一次。***rise to the ~*** 起来对付;善处难局。***take*** [***seize the***] ***~ to*** (*do*) 抓住…的好机会,乘机…。**II *vt*.** 惹起,引起。*His conduct ~s me great anxiety*. 他的行动使我非常担心。

oc·ca·sion·al [əˈkeiʒnəl; əˋkeʒn̩l] ***a*.** 非经常的;偶尔的;必要时的;不定期的,临时的;特殊场合的。*That sort of thing is quite ~*. 那种事是很偶然的。*an ~ writer* 应时作家。*an ~ workman* 临时雇工。**-ly *ad*.** 非经常地;偶然。**-ism *n*.**【哲】偶因论。

Oc·ci·dent [ˈɔksidənt; ˋɑksədənt] ***n*.**〔诗、古〕**1.**〔the ~〕(包括欧洲和美国在内的)西洋 (*opp*. the Orient);西方(文明)。**2.**〔the o-〕西方。

Oc·ci·den·tal [ˌɔksiˈdentl; ˏɑksəˋdɛntl̩] **I *a*. 1.** 西洋的 (*opp*. Oriental)。**2.**〔o-〕西方人[文化]的;【天】西天的。**II *n*.** 西方人;欧美人。**-ism *n*.** 西式;西方文化;西洋风味。**-ist *n*.** 西方文化研究者。**-ize *vt*.** 使西方化,欧化。**-ly *ad*.** 照西式。

oc·cip·i·tal [ɔkˈsipitl; ɑkˋsɪpətl] **I *a*.**【解】枕骨的;枕部的;【虫】后头部的。*~ bone* 枕骨。**II *n*. 1.** 枕骨。**2.** 枕部。

oc·ciput [ˈɔksipʌt; ˋɑksɪˏpʌt] ***n*.**【解】枕骨部 (*opp*. sinciput);【虫】后头。

oc·clude [ɔˈkluːd; əˋklud] ***vt*.** 使闭塞;使堵塞;封锁;遮蔽;使不发生作用;【化】吸藏,吸留;【气】使(气旋等)锢囚。—***vi*.**【医】(上齿与下齿)咬合;【气】(气旋)锢囚。*~d front*【气】锢囚锋。**oc·clu·sive *a*.**

oc·clu·sion [əˈkluːʒən, ɔ-; əˋkluʒən, ɔ-] ***n*. 1.** 闭塞。**2.**【牙】咬合;闭塞,闭合。**3.**【气】锢囚锋 (= occluded front)。**4.**【语】全闭合音。

oc·cult [ɔˈkʌlt; əˋkʌlt] **I *a*. 1.** 神秘的;玄妙的;超自然的。**2.** 秘密的;秘传的;不公开的;隐伏的;看不见的。**II *n*.**〔the ~〕秘学。*~ arts* (炼金术、占星术等的)秘术。*~ blood*【医】潜血。**III *vt*., *vi*.**【天】(使)掩(星);掩蔽;隐藏,(使)变暗。**~ing light** 连闭灯,明暗灯,隐显灯。

oc·cul·ta·tion [ˌɔkəlˈteiʃən; ˏɑkʌlˋteʃən] ***n*. 1.**【天】掩星,星蚀。**2.** 荫蔽,掩蔽,隐伏,不见;消失。

oc·cult·ism [ɔˈkəltizəm; əˋkʌltɪzm] ***n*.** 神秘学;神秘论;神秘主义。**-ist *n*.** 神秘学者;神秘主义者。

oc·cu·pan·cy [ˈɔkjupənsi; ˋɑkjəpənsɪ] ***n*. 1.** 占有;占领;占用;居住。**2.** 占有期间,居住期间。**3.**【法】据有,先占,占据;【物】占有率。*during the ~ of his post* 当他在职期间。

oc·cu·pant [ˈɔkjuːpənt; ˋɑkjəpənt] ***n*.** (土地、房屋、地位等的)占有人;居住者;【法】占据者。

oc·cu·pa·tion [ˌɔkjuˈpeiʃən; ˏɑkjəˋpeʃən] ***n*. 1.** 占有,领有;占领(状态);占据;占领军(当局);占有[占据]期间(*of*);占有权;占领地;居住。**2.** 职业;工作,事情,业务;消遣。*an ~ bridge* [*road*] 专用[占用]桥梁[道路]。*an army of ~* 占领军。*an ~ census* 职业统计调查。*domestic side-line ~s* 家庭副业。*rural subsidiary ~s* 农村副业。*men out of ~* 失业者。

oc·cu·pa·tion·al [ˌɔkjuˈpeiʃənəl; ˏɑkjəˋpeʃənl̩] ***a*. 1.** 职业的;职业引起的。**2.** 军事占领的。*an ~ disease*【医】职业病。**~ medicine** 职业病医学。**~ therapy** 工作疗法〔使患者从事一种工作(如艺术或工艺)以转移心思或矫正某种身体缺陷〕。

oc·cu·pi·er [ˈɔkjupaiə; ˋɑkjəˏpaɪɚ] ***n*.** = occupant.

oc·cu·py [ˈɔkjupai; ˋɑkjəˏpaɪ] ***vt*.** (***-pied*; *-py·ing***) **1.** 占领,占据;侵占。**2.** 住在…,使用(房间、办事处等);租用(房子等)。**3.** 占(时间、空间等);占用,占有。**4.**〔常用被动或反身结构〕使从事;使忙碌。**5.** 居(某种地位),担任(职务)。*~ a fort* 占领要塞。*~ an important position* 占重要地位。*The house is occupied*. 那房子有人住着。*Anxieties occupied his mind*. 他心里充满了焦虑。*I am occupied*. 我没有空。***be occupied*** (*in doing sth*., *with affairs*) 在做…,在忙…。***~ oneself about*** [***in*, *with***] **...** (正)从事…。**occupied fallow**【农】半休闲。

oc·cur [əˈkəː; əˋkɝ] ***vi*.** (***-rr-***) **1.** (事件等)发生。**2.** 被想到,想起。**3.** 出来,出现;存在;被发现。*An accident ~red*. 发生了一起事故。*if anything should ~* 如果发生什么事的话。*A happy idea ~red to me*. 我想起了一个好办法。*It ~red to me that ....* 我想到…。

oc·cur·rence [əˈkʌrəns; əˋkɝəns] ***n*. 1.** (事件的)发生,出现,有;【矿】存象,(矿床等的)埋藏;产地。**2.** 遭遇,事件,事故。*daily ~s* 日常发生的事。*oscillatory ~* 振荡现象。*be of frequent* [*rare*] *~* 是常[少]有的。***make allowance for unfavourable ~s*** 留有余地,以防意外。

oc·cur·rent [əˈkʌrənt; əˋkɝənt] ***a*.** 目前正在发生的;偶然发生的。

oc·cur·ring [əˈkəːriŋ; əˋkɝɪŋ] ***n*.**〔美口〕事变,事件,事故。

OCD = obsessive-compulsive disorder【医】强迫性神经官能症。

OCDM = Office of Civil and Defense Mobilization〔美〕民防国防动员署。

o·cean [ˈəuʃən; ˋoʃən] ***n*. 1.** 洋,大海;(有别于内海的)外洋。★ 英国用 sea 的地方,美国常用 ocean. 如:spend some weeks by the ocean 在海边住几个星期。**2.** (五大洋的)…洋。**3.** 一望无垠(的),茫茫(的)(*of*) 无限,无

量;〔常 *pl*.〕〔口〕极多(的),许许多多(的)(*of*)。*the Atlantic* [*Pacific*, *Indian*, *Arctic*, *Antarctic*] *O*- 大西[太平、印度、北冰、南冰]洋。★ Ocean 常可省去。如:the Atlantic [Pacific]. *a vast* ~ *of foliage* 树海。~*s of money* 大量的钱。***be tossed on an*** ~ ***of doubts*** 坠入五里雾中。***sweep back the*** ~ 做显然不可能做到的事。~**-going** *a*. 行驶外洋的,远洋的(~*-going commerce* 海外贸易)。~ **greyhound** 外洋快船(尤指定期客船)。~ **lane** [**route**]远洋航线。~ **liner** 远洋定期客轮。~ **sunfish**【动】翻车鲀(Mola mola)。~**-thermal** *a*. (利用)海洋热的。~ **tramp** 无一定航线的远洋货轮。

o·cean·ar·ium [ˌəuʃəˈnɛəriəm; ˏoʃəˋnɛrɪəm] *n*. 〔美〕大型海水水族馆。

o·ce·an·aut [ˈəuʃənɔːt; ˋoʃənɔt] *n*. 潜航员,海中作业员。

o·cean·front [ˈəuʃənfrʌnt; ˋoʃənˏfrʌnt] *n*. 海洋地带。

o·cean-gray [ˈəuʃənˈgrei; ˋoʃənˋgre] *n*., *a*. 浅灰色(的)。

O·ce·an·i·a [ˌəuʃiˈeinjə; ˏoʃɪˋænɪə] *n*. 大洋洲。

O·ce·a·ni·an [ˌəuʃiˈeiniən; ˏoʃɪˋænɪən] *a*., *n*. 大洋洲的(人)。

o·ce·an·ic [ˌəuʃiˈænik; ˏoʃɪˋænɪk] *a*. **1**. 大洋的,大海的;大洋广的,(生活)在大洋中的;大洋一样的,广阔无边的。**2**. 〔O-〕大洋洲的。

O·ce·an·i·ca [ˌəuʃiˈænikə; ˏoʃɪˋænɪkə] *n*. = Oceania.

O·ce·a·nid [əuˈsiːənid; oˋsiənɪd] *n*. (*pl*. ~*s*; *-ni·des* [ˌəusiˈænidiːz; ˏosɪˋænɪdiz]) **1**.【希神】大洋的女神。**2**. 〔o-〕海贝。

o·ce·a·nog·ra·phy [ˌəuʃiəˈnɔgrəfi; ˏoʃɪənˋɑgrəfɪ] *n*. 海洋地理学。**-graph·ic** [ˌəuʃiənə*u*ˈgræfik; ˏoʃɪənəˋgræfɪk], **-i·cal** *a*. **-nog·ra·pher** *n*. 海洋地理学家。

o·ce·an·ol·o·gy [ˌəuʃəˈnɔlədʒi; ˏoʃəˋnɑlədʒɪ] *n*. **1**. 海洋学。**2**. 海洋地理学(= oceanography.)。**-ol·o·gist** *n*. 海洋(地理)学家。

o·ce·an·aut [ˈəuʃənɔːt; ˋoʃənɔt] *n*. 潜海员,海中作业员。

oc·el·late [ˈɔsiˌleit, əuˈselit; ˋɑsəˏlet, oˋselɪt] *a*. **1**. 似脑眼的;似单眼的;似具瞳点的。**2**. 具单眼的;具瞳点的。**3**. 有斑点的。

oc·el·la·tion [ˌɔsiˈleiʃən; ˏɑsəˋleʃən] *n*. 眼状斑点。

o·cel·lus [əuˈseləs; oˋseləs] *n*. (*pl*. ***o·cel·li*** [-ai; -aɪ]) 〔L.〕**1**. (昆虫的)单眼;具瞳点。**2**. 脑眼。**3**. (孔雀尾上的)眼形花斑。

o·ce·lot [ˈəusilɔt; ˋosəˏlɑt] *n*. 豹猫〔南美、中美产〕。

och [ɔk; ʌk] *int*. 〔Ir., Scot.〕啊! 呀! 唷!

o·cher [ˈəukə; ˋokɚ] *n*. = ochre.

o·cher·ous [ˈəukərəs; ˋokərəs] = ochreous.

och·loc·ra·cy [ɔkˈlɔkrəsi; ɑkˋlɑkrəsɪ] *n*. 暴民政治,暴民的统治。**-cra·tic** [ˌɔkləˈkrætik; ˏɑkləˋkrætɪk], **-i·cal** *a*.

och·one [əˈhəun; əˋhon] *int*. 〔Scot., Ir.〕哎呀! 哎哟! 惨哉!

o·chre [ˈəukə; ˋokə] *n*. **1**.【矿】赭石〔可作颜料用〕。**2**. 赭色,黄褐色。**3**. 〔美俚〕金钱。

o·chre·ous [ˈəukriəs; ˋokrɪəs], **o·chrous** [-kərəs; -kərəs] *a*. 赭石质的;赭石色的。

o·chroid [ˈəukrɔid; ˋokrɔɪd] *a*. 似赭土的,深黄赭色的。

-ock *suf*. 小:hill*ock* 小山。

o'clock [əˈklɔk; əˋklɑk] 〔of the clock 的缩写〕…点钟。*What* ~ *is it now*? 现在几点钟? *It's just seven* (~). 刚好七点。***know what*** ~ ***it is*** 样样都晓得;熟悉情况。***like one*** ~ **1**. 非常迅速地,马上。**2**. 非常乐意地,津津有味地;很有力地;很带劲地。

O'Con·nell [ə*u*ˈkɔnl; oˋkɑnl] *n*. **1**. 奥康内尔〔姓氏〕。**2**. **Daniel** ~ 达尼尔·奥康纳尔〔1775—1847,爱尔兰民族主义运动领导者〕。

O'Con·nor [ə*u*ˈkɔnə; oˋkɑnə] *n*. **1**. 奥康纳〔姓氏〕。**2**. **Arthur** ~ 阿塞·奥康纳〔1763—1852 爱尔兰革命家〕。**3**. **Thomas Power** ~ 托马斯·波厄·奥康纳〔1848—1929 爱尔兰作家,政治家〕。

OCR = optical character recognition【计】光符号识别。

oc·re·a [ˈɔkriə, ˈəukriə; ˋɑkrɪə, ˋokrɪə] *n*. (*pl*. ***-re-ae*** [-iː; -i])【植】托叶鞘。**o·cre·ate** [-ˌeit, -it; -ˏet, -ɪt] *a*.

Oct. = October.

oct. = octave.

oct-, octa- *comb*. *f*. 八: *Octa*chord.

oc·ta·chord [ˈɔktəkɔːd; ˋɑktəˏkɔrd] *n*. 八弦琴。

oc·tad [ˈɔktæd; ˋɑktæd] *n*. 八个一组;【化】八价物;八价原素;八进制。

oc·tad·ic [ɔkˈtædik; ɑkˋtædɪk] *n*., *a*. 八个一组(的);【化】八价(的);【数】八进位(的)。

oc·ta·gon [ˈɔktəgən; ˋɑktəˏgɑn] **I** *n*.【几】八边形;八角形物;八角建筑物。**II** *a*. 八边形的。

oc·tag·o·nal [ɔkˈtægənl; ɑkˋtægənl] *a*. 八边形的。

oc·ta·he·dral [ˌɔktəˈhedrəl; ˏɑktəˋhidrəl] *a*. (有)八面的;八面体的。

oc·ta·he·drite [ˌɔktəˈhiːdrait; ˏɑktəˋhidraɪt] *n*.【地】八面石〔锐钛矿〕。

oc·ta·hed·ron [ˌɔktəˈhedrən; ˏɑktəˋhidrən] *n*. (*pl*. ~*s*, ***-he·dra*** [-drə; -drə]) 八面体。*a regular* ~ 正八面体。

oc·tal [ˈɔktl; ˋɑktl] *a*. **1**. 八的,第八的。**2**.【无】八面的,八边的;八管脚的,八进制的。

oc·tam·er·ous [ɔkˈtæmərəs; ɑkˋtæmərəs] *a*. (花的)八基数的。

oc·tam·e·ter [ɔkˈtæmitə; ɑkˋtæmɪtə] **I** *n*. 八音步诗〔由八音步组成的诗行〕。**II** *a*. 有八音步的。

oc·tan [ˈɔktən; ˋɑktn] **I** *a*. 在每第八日发生的,有一周的间隔的;隔周的。**II** *n*.【医】八日热。

oc·tane [ˈɔktein; ˋɑkten] *n*.【化】辛烷。~ **number** [**rating, value**] 辛烷值。

oc·tan·gle [ˈɔktæŋgl; ˋɑktæŋgl] *n*. 八边形;八角形(= octagon)。

oc·tan·gu·lar [ɔkˈtæŋgjulə; ɑkˋtæŋgjələ] *a*. 有八角的。

oc·ta·nol [ˈɔktənɔːl; ˋɑktənɔl] *n*.【化】辛醇。

Oc·tans [ˈɔktænz; ˋɑktænz] *n*.【天】南极(星)座。

oc·tant [ˈɔktənt; ˋɑktənt] *n*. **1**. 八分圆;八分区;卦限;八分仪;【植】八分体。**2**.【天】相对两天体成四十五度的位置。

oc·tarch·y [ˈɔktɑːki; ˋɑktɑrkɪ] *n*. (*pl*. ***-tarch·ies***) **1**. 八人执政。**2**. 八政府[王国]集团〔有时指盎格鲁-撒克逊时代英格兰的七国〕。

oc·ta·style [ˈɔktəstail; ˋɑktəˏstaɪl] *n*.【建】八柱式。

oc·ta·teuch [ˈɔktətjuːk; ˋɑktəˏtjuk] *n*. 旧约圣经的前八卷。

oc·tave [ˈɔkteiv, -tiv; ˋɑktev, -tɪv] **I** *n*. **1**.【宗】节日开始(第)八天。**2**. [ˈɔktiv; ˋɑktɪv]【乐】八音度;一音阶;高[低]八度音;低频程;【物】倍频程。**3**.【韵】十四行诗(sonnet)的起首八行;八行(体)诗。**4**. 八个一组的事物。**5**.【剑术】八种防守姿势中的第八式。**6**. 〔英〕装 $13\frac{1}{2}$ 加仑的酒桶。**II** *a*. **1**. 八个一组的;八行的。**2**.【乐】高八度音的。

Oc·ta·vi·a [ɔkˈteivjə; ɑkˋtevɪə] *n*. 奥克塔维亚〔女子名〕。

Oc·ta·vi·us [ɔkˈteivjəs; ɑkˋtevɪəs] *n*. 奥克塔维厄斯〔男子名〕。

oc·ta·vo [ɔkˈteivəu; ɑkˋtevo] *n*. (*pl*. ***-vos***) 八开,八开本〔略为 8*vo* 或 8°或 oct〕;八开纸;八开页。*a cap* ~ $4\frac{1}{2}\times7$英寸版本。*a crown* ~ $5\times7\frac{1}{2}$ 英寸版本。*an imperial* ~ $8\frac{1}{4}\times11\frac{1}{2}$ 英寸版本。*a medium* ~ $6\times9\frac{1}{2}$ 英寸版本。*a royal* ~ $6\frac{1}{2}\times10$ 英寸版本。

oc·ten·ni·al [ɔkˈtenjəl, -niəl; ɑkˋtɛnɪəl, -nɪəl] *a*. 每八

年的,八年一回的;第八年的;八年间的。

oc·tet(te) [ɔkˈtet; ɑkˋtɛt] ***n.*** 八个一组的东西;【乐】八重唱(曲);八重奏(曲);八重唱[八重奏]演出小组;【韵】十四行诗 (sonnet) 的起首八行;【物】八偶;八重线,八角(体)。

oc·til·lion [ɔkˈtiljən; ɑkˋtɪljən] ***num.*** 〔英〕百万的八次幂[乘方]〔一后加四十八个零之数〕;〔法、美〕千的九次幂[乘方]〔一后加二十七个零之数〕。

oc·tin·gen·te·na·ry [ˌɔktindʒenˈtiːneri; ˏɑktɪnˋdʒɛntɪˏnɛrɪ] ***n.*** = octocentenary.

octo- = oct-.

Oc·to·ber [ɔkˈtəubə; ɑkˋtobɚ] ***n.*** 十月。*the ~ Revolution* (苏联)十月革命(1917 年推翻克伦威尔政府中的无产阶级革命)。

Oc·to·brist [ɔkˈtəubrist; ɑkˋtobrɪst] ***n.*** 【俄史】十月党人。

oc·to·cen·te·na·ry [ˌɔktəusenˈtiːnəri; ˏɑktosɛnˋtinɛrɪ], **oc·to·cen·te·ni·al** [ˌɔktəusenˈtenjəl; ˏɑktosɛnˋtɛnjəl] ***n.*** 八百周年纪念日。

oc·to·dec·i·mo [ˈɔktəuˈdesiməu; ˏɑktoˋdɛsəˏmo] **I *n.*** (*pl.* ~*s*) 十八开,十八开本〔略 18 mo.〕。**II *a.*** 十八开的。

oc·to·ge·na·r·i·an [ˌɔktəudʒiˈnɛəriən; ˏɑktədʒəˋnɛrɪən] ***a.***, ***n.*** 八十岁的(人),八十多岁的(人)。

oc·to·nal [ˈɔktənl; ˋɑktənl̩] ***a.*** 八进位的,【韵】八音步的。

oc·to·na·r·i·an [ˌɔktəuˈnɛəriən; ˏɑktəˋnɛrɪən] ***a.***, ***n.*** 【韵】八音步的(诗句)。

oc·to·nar·y [ˈɔktənəri; ˋɑktəˏnɛrɪ] **I *a.*** 八数的,八之数组成的,八进的,用八进法的。**II *n.*** (*pl.* **-nar·ies**) **1.** 用八数所成的一组。**2.** 八行诗节;八行诗。

oc·to·pod [ˈɔktəpɔd; ˋɑktəpɑd] ***n.*** 八腕亚目 (*Octopoda*) 动物〔包括章鱼和魟鱼〕。**-an *a.***, ***n.*** **-ous *a.***

oc·to·pus [ˈɔktəpəs; ˋɑktəpəs] ***n.*** (*pl.* ~*es*, *-pi* [-pai; -paɪ]) **1.** 【动】章鱼;蛸;〔O-〕章鱼属。**2.** 周围爪牙众多的人[团体]。

oc·to·push [ˈɔktəpuʃ; ˋɑktəpuʃ] ***n.*** 水中曲棍球。

oc·to·roon [ˌɔktəuˈruːn; ˏɑktəˋrun] ***n.*** (有黑人血统八分之一的)黑白混血儿。

oc·tose [ˈɔktəus; ˋɑktos] ***n.*** 【化】辛醣。

oc·to·syl·lab·ic [ˈɔktəusiˈlæbik; ˏɑktəsɪˋlæbɪk] ***a.***, ***n.*** 八音节的(词、诗句)。

oc·to·syl·la·ble [ˈɔktəuˌsiləbl; ˋɑktəˏsɪləbl] **I *n.*** 八音节词;八音节诗句。**II *a.*** 八音节的。

oc·troi [ˈɔktrwɑː; ˋɑktrɔɪ] ***n.*** 〔F.〕(法国或印度的)入市税;入市税征收区;入市税征收所[征收员]。

O.C.T.U. = Officer Cadet Training Unit 〔英〕军官学校学员训练队。

oc·tu·ple [ˈɔktju(ː)pl; ˋɑktupl] **I *a.*** 八倍的,八重的;八部分组成的。**II *n.*** 八倍之物。**III *vt.*, *vi.*** 增加成八倍。

oc·tyl [ˈɔktəl; ˋɑktl̩] ***n.*** 【化】辛基。

oc·u·lar [ˈɔkjulə; ˋɑkjəlɚ] **I *a.*** 眼睛的,视觉上的,用眼的;眼状的。~ *demonstration* 直观演示。*an ~ witness* 目击者,见证人。**II *n.*** 目镜;〔谑〕眼睛。~**-net** 网格目镜。**-ly *ad.***

oc·u·lar·ist [ˈɔkjularist; ˋɑkjələrɪst] ***n.*** 制造假眼的人。

oc·u·list [ˈɔkjuːlist; ˋɑkjəlɪst] ***n.*** 眼科医生[专家]。

oc·u·lo·mo·tor [ˌɔkjuləuˈməutə; ˏɑkjuləˋmotɚ] **I *a.*** **1.** 眼球运动的;动眼的。**2.**【解】动眼神经的。**II *n.*** 【解】动眼神经。

O.D., **OD** = **1.** officer of the day 值日军官。**2.** overdraft, overdrawn 透支。**3.** outside diameter 外径。**4.** an overdose of drugs 过度剂量的毒品。**5.** olive drab 橄榄色。

od¹ [ɔd; ɑd] ***n.*** 假想的自然力〔德国化学家 Reichenbach 等为说明磁力、化学作用等而假定自然界存在的一种力〕。

od², 'od, Od [ɔd; ɑd] ***n.*** 〔卑〕= God. *Od's wounds!* 〔古〕他妈的! 哎呀! (= zounds)。

o·da·lisk, o·da·lisque [ˈəudəlisk; ˋodlˏɪsk] ***n.*** (伊斯兰教国家后宫里的)女奴,婢妾。

o·day [ˈəudei; ˋode] ***n.*** 〔美俚〕钱。

odd [ɔd; ɑd] **I *a.*** **1.** 奇妙的,奇特的,古怪的,可笑的。**2.** 临时的,不固定的;额外的。**3.** 余的,残余的,有零数的;带零头的,零星的。**4.** (一双、一封中的)吊单的,不全的,无配对的;零散的。**5.** 奇数的,二除不尽的;单(数)的,奇数号的。**6.** 偏僻的。*an ~ fellow* 奇人。~ *customs* 奇怪的风俗。~ *jobs* 临时工作,零活。*an ~ hand* [*man*] 临时雇工,打杂短工。*do it at ~ moments* 在有空的时间做。*sixty ~ thousand* 六万几千。*sixty thousand ~* 六万多,六万挂零。~ *money* (剩下的)零钱。*There is no contending against ~.* 寡不敌众。*an ~ glove* 单只手套。~ *numbers of a magazine* 零星本的杂志。~ *numbers* 奇数。~ *months* 大月。~ *volumes* 零本,散册。~ *moments* 余暇。***ask* [*beg*] *no ~s*** 〔美〕不要求照顾;(比赛)不要求让步。***at ~ times* [*hours*]** 在闲暇的时候,抓工夫,忙里偷闲地,用零碎的时间。***in some ~ corner*** 在某个角落里。~ ***and* [*or*] *even*** 猜单双。**II *n.*** 【高尔夫球】让转弱的对手从打球进一个洞的击球次数中减去一次击球;〔the ~〕多于对方的一次击球〔*cf.* odds〕。~**ball *a.***, ***n.*** 古怪的(人)。~**-come-short** (布的)零头;〔*pl.*〕碎屑,零碎物件。~**-come-shortly** 〔口〕不日(*one of these odd-come-shortlies* 过几天,过些时,不久)。~**-even *a.*** 〔美〕按单双日编号管理的〔如配给汽油,允许汽车上路等〕。~**job *vi.*** 干零活,打散工。~**-looking *a.*** 怪,古怪的。~ **lot** 零星货物,不成套的东西;【交易所】零星股。~ **man** (赞否各半时)额外握有表决权的一个人。~**-man-out** **1.** (三人投线)吊单者中选(法)。**2.** 和环境合不来的人。**3.** 局外人。~ **trick** 【牌戏】决胜负的最后一墩牌。**-ness *n.***

Odd-fel·low, Odd·fel·low [ˈɔdfeləu; ˋɑdˏfɛlo] ***n.*** (18 世纪英国一种近似 Free mason 的)秘密共济会的会员。

odd·ish [ˈɔdiʃ; ˋɑdɪʃ] ***a.*** 有点古怪的。

odd·i·ty [ˈɔditi; ˋɑdətɪ] ***n.*** **1.** 古怪,奇特;怪癖,怪脾气。**2.** 怪人;奇妙的东西。

odd·ly [ˈɔdli; ˋɑdlɪ] ***ad.*** **1.** 奇妙地,奇怪地。**2.** 零碎地,成奇数。**3.** 额外地,附加地。~ ***enough*** 说也奇怪。~ **even** 奇数和偶数的积。~ **odd** 奇数和奇数的积。

odd·ment [ˈɔdmənt; ˋɑdmənt] ***n.*** 零头,碎屑;〔*pl.*〕零碎物件,残余,残品;〔*pl.*〕【印】书的本文以外的部分。

odd-pin·nate [ˈɔdˈpineit; ˋɑdˋpɪnet] ***a.*** 【植】奇数羽状的〔指复叶〕。

odds [ɔdz; ɑdz] ***n.*** 〔*pl.*〕〔常用作单数〕**1.** 不平等(的东西);差额。**2.** 胜算,差异;差距,优劣之差;(优者给对方的)让步;〔美〕恩惠。**3.** 不和,相争。**4.** 希望,可能性。**5.** 赛过。**6.** 遭遇。*What's the ~?* 那有什么要紧? *The ~ are in our favour.* 我们的胜算较大。*The ~ are against you.* 形势对你不利。*It is ~ that* [〔古〕*but*]... = *The ~ are that ...* 多半,想必。*It sounds a bit over the ~.* 不会有的。*It is within the ~.* 可能有的。***ask no ~*** 〔美〕不要求照顾;(比赛中)不要求先让步。***be at ~ with*** 和…闹别扭,和…不和,和…有矛盾;处于不利的条件下(*be at ~ with fate* 遭遇不好)。***by long* [*all*] ~** 大大超过地,远远地;肯定地,无疑地。***fight against longer ~*** 以寡敌众,以弱敌强。***lay* [*give*] ~ *of* (*three*) *to* (*one*)** 以对方(一)自己(三)之比和人打赌〔赢则取三,输则赔一〕。***lay* [*give*] *the ~*** 给与有利条件,给与让步。***make no ~*** 没有不相称,平均 (*It makes* (*or is*) *no ~.* (两者)没有多大区别,怎么都好)。***make ~ even*** 除去优劣之差,拉平。~ ***and ends*** 残余,零碎物件[事情],零星杂品。***set at ~*** 使相争。***shout the ~*** 说大话。***take* [*receive*] *the ~*** (打赌时)接受有利的条件,得到让步。

odds-on [ˈɔdzˈɔn; ˋɑdzˋɑn] ***a.*** 大半有希望赢的。*an ~*

bet 大半有希望赢的打赌。*an* ～ 得人望的人。

ode [əud; od] ***n*.** 颂歌,颂诗,赋〔对意中人、物等所作的抒情诗〕;(古希腊戏剧中合唱队配合音乐舞蹈歌唱的)合唱歌。*Ode to* (*a*) *Skylark* 云雀赋。*the book of Odes* (中国的)诗经。

O·dels·thing [ˈəudelstiŋ; ˋodəlstɪŋ] ***n*.** 挪威的众议院。

O·den·se [ˈəuðənsei; ˋoðənsə] ***n*.** 奥登塞〔丹麦港市〕。

o·de·on [əuˈdiːən; oˋdiən], **o·de·um** [əuˈdiːəm; oˋdiəm] ***n*.** (*pl*. ～*s*, ***o·de·a*** [-ə; -ə]) **1.** 〔古希腊、罗马〕(有屋顶的)奏乐堂〔常被用作法庭〕。**2.** 音乐堂,戏院。

O·des·sa [əuˈdesə; oˋdɛsə] ***n*.** 敖得萨〔乌克兰港市〕。

O·dets [əuˈdets; oˋdits] ***n*.** 奥德茨〔姓氏〕。

O·dette [əuˈdet; oˋdit] ***n*.** 奥德特〔女子名, Ottilia 的爱称〕。

o·de·um [əuˈdiəm; oˋdiəm] ***n*.** (*pl*. ***o·de·a*** [əuˈdiːə; oˋdiə]) **1.** 音乐厅,剧场。**2.** (古希腊、罗马)奏乐厅,音乐堂。

od·i·c [ˈəudik; ˋodɪk] ***a*.** 颂诗的,颂歌的。

O·din [ˈəudin; ˋodɪn] ***n*.** 【北欧神话】奥丁神〔司智慧、艺术、诗词、战争的神〕。

o·di·ous [ˈəudjəs, -diəs; ˋodɪəs, -dɪəs] ***a*.** 讨厌的;可憎的;丑恶的。**-ly** ***ad*.** **-ness** ***n*.**

o·di·um [ˈəudiəm, -djəm; ˋodɪəm, -djəm] ***n*.** **1.** 憎恨,厌恶,反感;公愤;臭名;耻辱。**2.** 被憎恨的对象。*expose* (*sb*.) *to* ～ 使某人招致公愤。

o·do·graph [ˈəudəgrɑːf, -græf; ˋodəˏgræf, -græf] ***n*.** 里程表;自动记程仪,航线记录器,计步器。

o·dom·e·ter [əˈdɔmitə; oˋdɑmətɚ] ***n*.** 里程表,路程计。

od·on·tal·gi·a [ˌɔdɔnˈtældʒiə, Am. əud-; ˏodɑnˋtældʒɪə, ɔd-] ***n*.** 【医】牙痛。

-odont *suf*. 齿。

od·on·t(o)- *comb*. *f*. 牙齿。*odonto*logy.

od·on·to·blast [əˈdɔntəblæst; oˋdɑntəˏblæst] ***n*.** 【解】成牙质细胞。**-ic** ***a*.**

od·on·to·clast [əˈdɔntəklæst; oˋdɑntəklæst] ***n*.** 【解】破牙质细胞。

O·don·to·glos·sum [ɔˌdɔntəuˈglɔsəm; əˏdɑntəˋglɑsəm] ***n*.** 【植】(中南美野生的)兰属;〔o-〕兰;具有舌形唇瓣的兰花。

o·don·to·graph [əuˈdɔntəgrɑːf, -græf; oˋdɑntəˏgræf, -græf] ***n*.** **1.** 【仪】画齿规。**2.** 【医】牙面描记器。

od·on·toid [əˈdɔntɔid; əˋdɑntɔɪd] ***a*.** 齿状的,牙样的。

o·don·tol·o·gist [ˌəudɔnˈtɔlədʒist; ˏodɑnˋtɑlədʒɪst] ***n*.** 牙医师。

od·on·tol·o·gy [ˌɔdɔnˈtɔlədʒi; ˏodɑnˋtɑlədʒɪ] ***n*.** 齿科学。

o·don·to·phore [əuˈdɔntəfɔː; oˋdɑntəˏfor] ***n*.** 【解】牙嵴板。**-toph·o·ral** ***a*.**

o·dor [ˈəudə; ˋodɚ] ***n*.** 〔Am.〕= odour.

o·dor·ant [ˈəudərənt; ˋodərənt] ***n*.** 有气味的物质〔东西〕。

o·dor·if·er·ous [ˌəudəˈrifərəs; ˏodəˋrɪfərəs] ***a*.** 有香气的,香;〔口〕有气味[臭味]的。**-ly** ***ad*.**

o·dor·ous [ˈəudərəs; ˋodərəs] ***a*.** 〔诗〕= odoriferous. **-ly** ***ad*.** **-ness** ***n*.**

o·dour [ˈəudə; ˋodɚ] ***n*.** **1.** (臭或香的)气味;香,香气;臭气。**2.** 味道;迹象。**3.** 声望,名誉;名气。**4.** 香水;香料。*the* ～ *of roses* 玫瑰香。*an* ～ *of sanctity* 崇高的声誉。***be in*** [***fall into***] ***bad*** [***ill***] ～ 名誉不好[变坏]。***be in good*** ～ ***with*** 对…有威望;受…欢迎。**-less** ***a*.** 没有香气[气味]的。

ODT = Office of Defense Transportation 〔美旧〕国防运输局。

od·yl [ˈɔdil; ˋɑdɪl] ***n*.** = od[1].

O·dys·se·us [əˈdisjuːs; oˋdɪsjus] ***n*.** 【希腊】奥德修斯〔荷马史诗《奥德赛》中的主人公。曾指挥特洛伊战争,献木马计,使希腊获胜〕。

Od·ys·sey [ˈɔdisi; ˋɑdəsɪ] ***n*.** **1.** 《奥德赛》〔荷马所著史诗〕。**2.** 〔o-〕长期的漂泊[冒险旅行]。*His odyssey of passion, friendship, love, and revenge was now finished*. 他的热情、友谊、爱情和复仇的漫长历程,到此结束了。

oe- 为希腊语和拉丁语 'e-' 字母的变体,旧时在词书中写为 œ, 今多拼为 oe, 有时亦作 e, 如 *oe*cology 亦作 *e*cology.

O.E., OE = **1.** Old English 古代英语。**2.** omissions excepted 遗漏不在此限〔常印在账单上;也作 o.e.〕。

OECD = Organization for Economic Cooperation and Development 经济合作与发展组织。

oe·cist [ˈiːsist; ˋisɪst] ***n*.** (古希腊)殖民地开拓者。

oe·col·o·gy [iːˈkɔlədʒi; iˋkɑlədʒɪ] ***n*.** = ecology.

oec·u·men·i·cal [ˌiːkjuːˈmenikəl; ˏɛkjuˋmɛnɪkl] ***a*.** = ecumenical.

OED = Oxyethylene Docosanol 羟乙基二十二碳烷醇〔水温上升剂〕。

O.E.D., OED = Oxford English Dictionary 《牛津大辞典》。

oe·de·ma [iːˈdiːmə; iˋdimə] ***n*.** 【医】浮肿,水肿。

oed·i·pal [ˈiːdipəl, ˈedi-; ˋɛdəpəl, ˋidə-] ***a*.** 【心】恋母情结的。

Oe·di·pus [ˈiːdipəs, Am. ˈedipəs; ˋɛdəpəs, ˋidəpəs] ***n*.** 【希神】伊底帕斯〔底比斯王子,曾破解怪物斯芬克斯(Sphinx)的谜语,后误杀其父并娶母为妻,发觉后自刺双目,死于流浪中〕;〔喻〕解迷的人。～ **complex** 【心】恋母情结。～ **Lex** 〔英口〕伊底帕斯词典〔即电子化的《牛津英语大词典》,3 张光盘上载有 16 册该词典全部内容,系由多字综合而成〕。

O.E.E.C. = Organization for European Economic Co-operation 欧洲经济合作组织。

œil-de-bœuf [əːjədəˈbəːf; ˏɜjədəˋbɜf] ***n*.** 〔F.〕【建】圆窗。

œil·lade [əːˈjɑːd; ˏɜˋjɑd] ***n*.** 〔F.〕媚眼,秋波。

oe·nol·o·gy [iːˈnɔlədʒi; iˋnɑlədʒɪ] ***n*.** 酿酒学,酒类研究。**-log·i·cal** ***a*.** **-o·gist** ***n*.** 酒类学家。

oe·no·mel [ˈiːnəmel; ˋinəˏmɛl] ***n*.** **1.** (古希腊)蜜酒。**2.** 〔诗〕甜言蜜语,花言巧语。

o'er [əuə, ɔə; or, ɔr] ***ad*.**, ***prep*.** 〔诗〕= over.

Oer·li·kon [ˈəːlikən, -kɔn; ˋɚlɪkn, -kɑn] ***n*.** 厄利肯式自动高射炮。

oer·sted [ˈəːsted; ˋɝstɛd] ***n*.** 【电】奥斯忒〔磁场强度单位〕。～**-meter** 磁场强度计。

oe·so·ph·ag·e·al [iːˌsɔfəˈdʒi(ː)əl; ˏisəˋfædʒɪəl] ***a*.** 食道的。

oe·soph·a·gus [iːˈsɔfəgəs; iˋsɑfəgəs] ***n*.** (*pl*. ～*es*, ***-gi*** [-gai; -gaɪ]) 【解】食道。

oes·tri·ol [ˈiːstriəl; ˋɛstrɪol] ***n*.** 【生化】雌三醇 (= estriol)。

oes·tro·gen [ˈiːstrədʒən; ˋɛstrədʒən] ***n*.** 【生化】雌激素。

oes·trum [ˈiːstrəm; ˋɛstrəm], **oes·trus** [ˈiːstrəs; ˋɛstrəs] ***n*.** **1.** 机能亢进,激烈的冲动;狂热;【动】动情(期),发情(期) (*opp*. anoestrum)。**2.** 牛虻。

œuvre [ˈəːvr; ˋɝvr] ***n*.** 〔F.〕(文艺)作品。

OF = Old French 古法语。

O.F. = Odd Fellows 〔英〕一种秘密共济会的会员。

of [强 ɔv, 弱 əv, v, f; ɑv, əv] ***prep*.** **1.** 〔表示所属关系〕…的,属于…的。*the house* ～ *my elder brother* 我哥哥的家。*men* ～ *that time* 当时的人们。*the secret* ～ *success* 成功的秘密。**2.** 〔部分〕…之中的,在…中。*a friend of mine* 我的一位朋友。*one* ～ *them* 他们中间的一个。*the most dangerous* ～ *enemies* 敌人当中最危险的。*five* ～ *us* 我们当中的五个。**3.** 〔数量、程度〕…的,…数量的。*three pieces* ～ *meat* 三块肉。*a cup* ～ *tea* 一杯茶。*a ton* ～ *coal* 一吨煤。**4.** 〔材料〕…做的,用…制的。*a box* ～ *wood* 木头(制的)箱子。*a house*

O

O

～ *stone* 石头砌的房子。*made* ～ *gold* 金子做的。*make a fool* ～ *him* 拿他当傻子。*make a teacher* ～ *one's son* 把儿子训练成教师。**5.**〔表示范围、方面〕关于…,对…如何,在…方面怎样。*a story* ～ *adventures* 冒险故事。*think well* ～ *sb*. 觉得某人好。*think* ～ 想起…。*blind* ～ *one eye* 瞎一只眼。*afraid* ～ *a dog* 怕狗。*swift* ～ *foot* 脚快。*quick* ～ *eye* 眼快。*ten years* ～ *age* 年纪十岁。*inform sb*. ～ 控诉某人(什么罪)。*It is true* ～ *every case*. 在任何情况下都是真的。*What* ～ *the danger*? 危险算什么。**6.**〔同格关系〕…这个。*the city* ～ *Rome* 罗马城。*the name* ～ *James* 詹姆士这个名字。*the action* ～ *running* 跑这个动作。*the fact* ～ *my having seen him* 我见过他这个事实。*that fool* ～ *a man* 那个蠢汉。*an angel* ～ *a woman* 一个天使般的女人。*the five* ～ *us* 我们五个人。*this only son* ～ *mine* 我的这个独生子。**7.**〔距离、位置、分离、除去、摆脱〕…的,距离…。*within ten miles* ～ *London* 距伦敦十里以内。*loss* ～ *energy* 精力的消耗。*free* ～ *charge* 免费。*independent* ～ 不受…支配的。*to the north* ～ *Paris* 在巴黎的北方。*cure* [*heal*] *sb*. ～ *a disease* 医好某人的病。*steal sb*. ～ *his watch* 偷去某人的手表。**8.**〔起源、根源、原因〕…的,从,向;因…,害…。*He comes* ～ *a good stock*. 他出身好。*borrow* [*buy*, *learn*] *a thing* ～ *sb*. 向某人借[卖、学习]东西。*sick* ～ *measles* 出疹子。*die* ～ *consumption* 死于肺病。*be sick* ～ *inaction* 懒散得发腻。*be weary* ～ *life* 厌世。**9.**〔同表示性质、状态的名词搭配构成定语、表语〕…的,有…的。*a ship* ～ *800 tons* 八百吨位的船。*a girl* ～ *ten* (*years old*) 十岁的姑娘。*a matter* ～ *importance* 重要事件。*a man* ～ *ability* 有能力的人。*be* ～ *the opinion that* 认为。**10.**〔动受关系〕*the telling* ～ *lies* 说谎。*the betrayal* ～ *a secret* 泄漏秘密。*the creation* ～ *man* 创造人类。*in search* ～ *knowledge* 探求知识。*take care* ～ *one's health* 注意健康。*be glad* ～ 喜欢。**11.**〔著作或行为的主体〕*the works* ～ *Shakespeare* 莎士比亚的作品。*He is beloved* ～ *all*. 他为众人所爱戴。*It is clever* ～ *you to do so*. 你那样做真聪明。**12.**〔构成时间状语〕*He comes* ～ *an evening*. 他常在傍晚的时候来。*all* ～ *a sudden* 突然。～ *course* 当然。～ *late* 近来。～ *late years* 近年来。～ *this date*〔美〕从即日起(=〔英〕*as from this date*)。**13.**〔时间〕〔美口〕…点差几分〔=to...〕(*opp*.〔美〕after;〔英〕past)。*five minutes* ～ *four* 差五分四点。*a quarter* ～ *ten* 十点差一刻。

of- *pref*.〔用于 f 之前〕=ob-.

Ofc =**1.** office. **2.** official.

off [ɔːf, ɔf; ɔf, ɑf] **I** *ad*. **1.**〔运动〕向那边,隔开。*be* ～ 走,去,逃。*I must be* ～. 我得走了。*Where are you* ～ *to*? 你去哪里?*fly* ～ 飞去。*go* ～ 走掉〔*cf*. O- you go! 滚!〕。*run* ～ 跑掉。**2.**〔移动〕离开,脱掉(*opp*. on)。*beat* ～ 打退(敌人)。*put* ～ 延期。*ward* ～ *an attack* 挡开攻击。*come* ～ 脱落,(柄)脱掉。*get* ～ 脱(衣);下(马)。*fall* ～ (从马上)掉下来。*look* ～ 掉转视线,朝别处看。*take* ～ 脱(衣服、帽子、鞋子等)。**3.**〔断、断绝、脱落、消失〕*bite* ～ 咬下来,咬断。*clip* ～ 剪下来,剪断。*cut* ～ 割下来,切断,割掉。*cut* ～ *the gas* [*water*] 关掉煤气[自来水]。*cut* ～ *from the telephone* 挂断电话。*tear* ～ 扯下来。*The flowers were all* ～. 花全落了。*The gilt is* ～. 镀金脱落。**4.**〔静止位置、距离、时间〕隔开,隔着,在那边,有(几里)远。*a mile* ～ 有一英里路。*a little way* ～ 有一小段路。*far* ～ 远,远在。*How far* ～ *is it*? — *A great way* ～. 有多远?——很远。*only three months* ～ 只要再过三个月;只在三个月前。**5.**〔动作的完了、中止等〕…完,…光。*drink* ～ 喝完。*pay* ～ 付清。*finish* ～ 做完。*leave* ～ *work* 停止工作。*break* ～ 忽然中止,中断。*be* ～ *with* 和…断绝关系。*The game was called* ～. 比赛取消了。**6.**〔折扣〕*10 per cent* ～ *on all cash purchases* 现款购货一律九折。**7.**〔渐渐〕减少,…下来[起来]。*fall* ～ 扫兴颓丧,(利益等)减少。*cool* ～ 冷起来,(热情)低落;平静下来。*wear* ～ (精力)衰退;(衣服等)渐破。**8.**〔休息〕*I had an afternoon* ～. 我下午休息了半天。***be badly*** ～ 生活困难;贫穷;运气不佳。***be better*** ～ 处境较好,生活条件比较好,比较宽裕。***be comfortably*** ～ 收入很好,生活有保障。***be well*** ～ 生活好过,处境良好。***be worse*** ～ 情况恶化,情况更差;更加贫困。***either*** ～ ***or on*** 总之,不管怎么样。～ ***and on*** = *on and* ～ 断断续续,间歇地;偶尔;(航海)时而靠岸时而离岸地(*It rains* ～ *and on*. 雨忽下忽停)。***take oneself*** ～ 走,去,逃。

II *int*. 走开! 躲开! ***Off***! = ***Be*** ～! = ***Stand*** ～! 滚开。***Off with***〔祈使语气〕去;去掉(*Off with you*! 去你的! *Off with your cap*! 脱帽!),去! 滚!

III *a*. **1.** 远的,那一边的。*the* ～ *side of the wall* 墙那边[后面]。**2.** (特指车、马的)右侧的,右边的(*opp*. near)。*an* ～ *horse* 右边的一匹马。*the* ～ *front* [*hind*] *wheel* (马车)右边的前[后]轮。*the* ～ *side of the road* 路的右手边;【板球】打球员右前方[投球员左方]的(*opp*. on)。**3.** 离开大路的,横的;枝节的;〔仅用作表语〕掉,落。*an* ～ *road* 横街。*an* ～ *issue* 枝节问题。*the wheel is* ～ 车轮脱了。**4.** 没事的,休息的。*an* ～ *day* 休息日。*during* ～ *hours* 在闲空时。*an* ～ *season* 闲季,非生产季节。**5.** 腐坏的(鱼、肉等)。*The fish is a bit* ～. 这条鱼有点坏了。**6.**〔口〕有毛病,不对;〔美俚〕有点失常;怪的,疯的。*I was* ～ *by a week*. 我算差了一个星期。*I am feeling rather* ～ *today*. 今天总觉得不大舒服。*That old man is a bit* ～. 那个老头子有点儿怪。**7.** 偶尔,万一。*I came on the chance of finding* [*that I would find*] *you*. 我是碰巧来的。～ *flavour* 臭气,臭味。～ *gas* 废气。～ *products* 副产物。～ *side* = offside. ～ *year* (水果等的)小年;(生产的)不景气年;〔美〕非大选年。*an* ～ *year election* 中期选举。

IV *n*.【板球】(打球员的)右前方(=～ side)。

V *vt*.〔口〕通知中止(交涉、契约、计划等),中止(和人)交涉,停约、除去、杀掉。—*vi*. 走开,离开。*He* ～*ed with his coat*. 他脱去了上衣。

VI *prep*. **1.** 离开,脱离,从,由。**2.**【海】在…海面。～ *the track* 出轨。*fall* ～ *a ladder* 从梯子上掉下。～ *the stage* 离开舞台。*Keep* ～ *the grass*! 禁入草地! *be thrown* ～ *the horse* 从马上摔下来。*cut a slice* ～ *the joint* 从肉块上切一片下来。*three years* ～ *forty* 四十不足三岁。*He played* ～ *5*.〔比赛〕他让了 5 分。*5 miles* ～ *the coast of Wenchow* 在离温州海岸 5 英里的海面上。*dine* ～ *bread and butter* 吃涂有奶油的面包。～ ***one's base***〔美口〕有病的,不舒服的。～ ***one's eggs***〔美俚〕误解。～ ***one's feed***〔美俚〕无饮食。～ ***the beam***〔美俚〕不对,错误。～ ***the reel***〔美〕立即,马上。～**-book fund** 账外资金,"小金库"。～**-camera** *a*. **1.** 在电影[电视]镜头之外的。**2.** 私生活中的。～ **cast** [ˈɔːfˌkɑːst, -ˌkæst; ˋɔfˏkæst, -ˏkæst] **1.** *a*. 被抛弃的,被遗弃的;放荡的。**2.** 无用的人[物](=castoff)。～**-chance** [ˈɔːftʃɑːns; ˋɔfˏtʃæns] *n*. 不大会有的机会,万一的希望,侥幸。～**-colour** [ˈɔːfˌkʌlə; ˋɔfkʌlɚ] *a*. **1.** 不对头的。**2.** 不十分合适的;低级趣味的;有伤风化的,猥亵的。*an* ～ *joke* 下流的玩笑。～**-design** *a*. 未预计的。～**-grade** *a*. 等外,级外的,低级的。～**-duty** *a*. 下班后的,业余的。～**-gauge** *a*. 非标准的。～**-hour** *n*. **1.** 不在值勤的时间。**2.** (交通等)不拥挤的时间。～**-island** (与海岸完全脱离的)离岛。～**-key** [ˈɔːfˈkiː; ˋɔfki] *a*. **1.** 走音的,走调的。**2.** 不正常的,不适合的,不协调的。～**-limits** [ˈɔːfˈlimits; ˋɔfˈlɪmɪts] *a*. 禁止入内的〔指某种场所奉令不让某种人进入〕,不许参观的,谢绝惠顾的。～**-line** [ˈɔːfˈlain; ˋɔflaɪn] *a*. **1.**【自】离线的。**2.** 不在

铁路沿线的。~load [ˈɔːfˈləud; ˋɔflod] *vt.*, *vi*. 1. 卸货,退载;从…卸下货物。2. 发泄(忧伤、苦闷等),抒发;解除(苦闷、负担等)。3. (从枪膛中)退出子弹。4. 处理。5. 卸(货)。~mike [ˈɔːfmaik; ˋɔfmaɪk] *ad*. 在离开扩音话筒转远处;不用扩音话筒(时)。~-off-Broadway [ˈɔːfˈɔːfˈbrɔːdˌwei; ˋɔfˋɔfˋbrɔˌwe] 1. *a*. (在纽约市的小礼堂、教堂、咖啡馆等所作的)试验性、非商业性演出的;与此种演出有关的。2. *ad*. 在此种演出中;在这种方式上演的场所中。3. *n*. 此种演出。~-pollination【生】混杂授粉。~-put *vt*. 〔英俚〕使困窘,使为难。~-putting [ˈɔːfˌputiŋ; ˋɔfˌputɪŋ] *a*. 〔主英〕老是推脱的;使人懊恼的,讨厌的。~-road *a*. (车辆设计等)越野的。~take 出口;泄水处;排水渠;支管;【电】分接头。~-the-bench *a*. 法庭以外的。~-(the-)floor trader 场外交易者。~-(the-)floor trading (股票、证券等的)场外交易。~-roading 越野赛车。~-the-peg, ~-the-rack *a*. 非定做的,现成的。~-the-shelf [ˈɔːfðəˈʃəlf; ˋɔfðəˋʃɛlf] *a*. 买来就可用的〔商品,尤指军用品无需改装〕。~-the-wall *a*. 〔美俚〕异乎寻常的。~track *a*. 1. 场外进行的。2. 偏僻的。3. 铁路业务以外的。*ad*. 在场外。~-white [ˈɔːfˈwait; ˋɔfˋhwaɪt] *a*. 米色的,灰白色的,黄白色的。

off. =1. offered. 2. office; officer; official.

of·fal [ˈɔfəl; ˋɔfl] *n*. 碎屑,垃圾;食品下脚料〔碎肉等〕;内脏;下水;杂鱼,低级鱼;糠,麸(等);废料;次品。

off·beat [ˈɔːfbiːt; ˋɔfˌbit] I *a*. 次要的;不规则的;不落俗套的。II *n*.【乐】弱拍。

Of·fen·bach [ˈɔːfənbɑːk; ˋɔfənˌbɑk], **Jacques** 奥芬巴克 (1819—1880)法国歌剧作曲家。

of·fence [əˈfens; əˋfɛns] *n*. 1. 罪,罪过;【法】犯罪;违犯,违反 (*against*)。2. 无礼,侮辱;冒犯,触怒。3. 引起反感的事物。4.【军】攻击 (*opp*. defense);〔集合词〕攻击部队。5.【圣】罪源,绊脚石。*a first* ~ 初犯。*an* ~ *against decency* [*good manners*] 无礼,没规矩。*No* ~ *was meant*. 并没有触犯的意思;不是恶意讲(做)的。*O- is the best defense*. 攻击是最好的防御。***commit an*** ~ ***against*** 犯(法),违背[破坏](法律、风俗);侵犯(权利)。***give*** [***cause***] ~ ***to*** 触怒…,使…生气,得罪。***take*** ~ 见怪,生气,感到自己受委屈或侮辱。***without*** ~ 不使人见怪,不触犯人;没有生气。**-less** *a*. 不得罪人的,老实的,温和的;无力进攻的。

offend [əˈfend; əˋfɛnd] *vt*. 1. 冒犯,触犯,得罪;激怒;侮辱;伤害(…的感情)。2. 使不舒服。3. 使绊倒,使犯罪,~ *sb. unintentionally* 无意中得罪人。~ *the ear* [*eye*] 刺耳[眼],逆耳[难看]。***be*** ~***ed with*** (*sb.*) ***for*** (*his act*) [***at*** (*his words*)] (因某人的行为,言语而)发怒,生气。—*vi*. 1. 犯罪,犯过错。2. 违犯,违背(礼仪等) (*against*)。3. 引起不舒服;得罪人。~ ***against*** (*the law*) 违犯(法律)。

of·fend·er [əˈfendə; əˋfɛndɚ] *n*. 罪犯,犯人;得罪人的人,冒犯者。*a first* ~ 初犯。*a juvenile* ~ 少年犯。*an old* [*a repeated*] ~ 惯犯,累犯。~**'s tag** (由警方系在被管制者身上以随时监视其行踪的)犯罪者行踪监管电子标签。

of·fense [əˈfens; əˋfɛns] *n*. 〔Am.〕= offence.

of·fen·sive [əˈfensiv; əˋfɛnsɪv] I *a*. 1. 讨厌的,令人不快的。2. 无礼的;冒犯的;唐突的。3. 进攻(性)的,攻击的,攻势的 (*opp*. defensive)。*an* ~ *sight* [*smell*, *sound*] 令人不快的景象[气味,声音]。*an* ~ *person* 无礼的人,讨厌的人。~ *weapons* 进攻性武器。*an* ~ *defence* 进攻性的防御。*an* ~ *and defensive alliance* 攻守同盟。II *n*. 进攻,攻势。*a peace* ~ 和平攻势。*an* ~ *on a large scale* 大举进攻。***act on*** [***take***, ***assume***] ***the*** ~ 采取攻势。**-ly** *ad*.

of·fer [ˈɔfə; ˋɔfɚ] I *vt*. 1. 提供;提出;提议;伸出(手等)。2.【商】出价,开价;出售,出卖。3. 贡献,供奉。4. 企图,想要。5. 表示愿意。6. 使出现;呈现出;演出。*He* ~*ed me his seat*. 他把他的座位让给了我。~ *a few ideas* 提几点意见。~ *the house for £1000* 出售房屋要价千镑。~ *£1000 for the house* 对该屋出价千镑。~ *without engagement*【商】虚盘。~ *resistance* 进行抵抗。~ *battle to the enemy* 向敌人挑战。—*vi*. 1. 出现,呈现,自告奋勇。2. 提议;求婚。3. 献祭。4. 〔古〕企图;尝试(*at*)。***as opportunity*** ~***s*** 有机会的时候。~ ***itself*** 呈现,出现。~ ***one's hand*** 1. 伸手(给人握手)。2. 向女人求婚。~ ***up oneself*** 牺牲自己。***take the first opportunity that*** ~***s*** 一有机会就利用。II *n*. 1. 提议;提供,提出。2.【商】出价,作价;报价;发价。3. 贡献。4. 〔古〕求婚〔~ of marriage 之略〕。5. 〔古〕企图。***accept*** [***decline***] ***an*** ~ 接受[不接受]提议。***make an*** ~ (***of***) 1. 提议;提供。2. 出价。***on*** ~ 出卖。***receive an*** ~ 接受提议。**-er**, **-or** *n*.

of·fer·ing [ˈɔfəriŋ; ˋɔfərɪŋ] *n*. 1. 提议;提供。2. 贡献;供品,祭品,(给教会的)捐款。3. 礼物。4. (上市的)股票,公债;出售物。5. 课程。*a free-will* ~ 自由捐献。*a peace* ~ (要求和解[赔不是]的)友好赠品。

of·fer·to·ry [ˈɔfətəri; ˋɔfɚˌtorɪ] *n*. 1.【天主】奉献仪式;奉献歌;(英国教会收集施舍金时念的)圣语;收集施舍金。2. 献纳;捐献品;献金;捐款。

off·hand [ˈɔːfˈhænd, ˈɔf-; ˋɔfˋhænd, ˋɑf-] I *a*. 1. 临时的,即席的,无准备的;随便的。2. 唐突的,简慢的。3. 自动的,无人管理的。4. (射击)无依托立射的。*an* ~ *manner* 随随便便。~ *remarks* 随便说出的话。*act in an* ~ *way* 举止不检点。*be* ~ *with sb*. 对人简慢。II *ad*. 1. 立即;即席。2. 随便;唐突。*I can't tell* ~ *how much it will cost*. 我不能立刻告诉你它值多少钱。

off·hand·ed [ˈɔːfˈhændid, ˈɔf-; ˋɔfˋhændɪd, ˋɑf-] *a*. 〔口〕= offhand. **-ly** *ad*. **-ness** *n*.

of·fice [ˈɔfis; ˋɔfɪs] I *n*. 1. 职务,任务。2. 公职,官职;职责,任务。3. 政府机关,公署,部,司,处,局,科。4. 〔常 *pl*.〕办公室;办事处;事务处;营业处,…处;〔美〕诊室,诊所。5. 号,店,公司,〔英〕保险公司。6. 职员,全体职工。7. 〔常 *pl*.〕帮助,斡旋。8.【宗】礼拜式,仪式,祷告;祭礼;圣餐。9. 〔*pl*.〕〔口〕厨房;〔口〕厕所;〔美俚〕学生偷懒玩耍的地方;〔英空俚〕驾驶员座位。10. 〔英俚〕暗示。*the* ~ *of host* 主人的任务。*the Home O-* 〔英〕内务部。*the War O-* 〔英〕陆军部。*the Post O-* 邮政局。*the O- of Works* 工务科。*a lawyer's* ~ 律师事务所。*a box* ~ (戏院的)售票处。*a ticket* (〔英〕*booking*) ~ (车、船等的)售票处。*an inquiry* ~ 询问处。*a dentist's* ~ 〔美〕牙科诊所。*a printing* ~ 印刷所。*a fire* [*fire-insurance*] ~ 火灾保险公司。*say O-* = *say one's O-* 做祷告。***be in an*** ~ 在办事处工作。***be in*** ~ 在职;(内阁)当政,执政。***be out of*** ~ 离职;下台。***by*** [***through***] ***the good*** ~***s of*** 由…的斡旋,由…的尽力。***do sb. kind*** ~***s*** 帮某人忙。***do the*** ~ ***of*** 担任…职务。***enter upon*** ~ 就职。***fat*** ~ 肥缺。***give the*** ~ 〔俚〕暗示。***go out of*** ~ 下野,放弃政权。***hold an*** ~ = ***hold*** ~ 任职,有职,在职。***leave*** [***resign***] ~ 辞职。~ ***procedure***【计算机】管理方法。~***s of profit*** 收入好的职务,好差事。***perform the last*** ~***s*** 举行葬礼。***take*** ~ 就职,上台,掌权。***take the*** ~ 接受暗示。***the Holy O-*** (天主教的)宗教法庭。***the party in*** ~ [***out of*** ~] 执政党[在野党]。II *vt*. 〔美俚〕警告,告诉内幕。—*vi*. 〔美口〕(在办公室)办公。*Where do you* ~? 您在哪儿办公? ~**-bearer** 〔英〕官员,公务员,职员。~ **block** 办事处集中的街段。~ **boy** (办公室的)勤杂员。~ **building** [**block**] 办公大楼。~**clerk** 职员,办事员。~ **copy** 公文正本;正式抄本。~ **girl** 女职员,女办事员。~ **holder** 〔美〕官员 = office-bearer. ~ **hotelling** (租用)旅馆办公。~**-hours** 〔*pl*.〕办公时间,营业时间;〔美〕(医生的)门诊时间。~ **hunter** [**seeker**] 〔美〕谋求官职的人,猎官者。~ **procedure** (计算机的)管理方法。~ **tickler**【商】(放备忘录用的)备忘箱。~ **work** 办公室工作,事务,公

O

务。

of·fi·cer [ˈɔfisə; ˋɔfəsɚ] **I** *n*. **1**. 官员,办事员,(高级)职员。**2**.【军】军官,武官;警官;法警;【海】(商船的)船长,高级船员。**3**. 干事,理事。*a police* ~ 警官。*a public* ~ 官员。*an* ~ *of state* 〔英〕大臣。*a commanding* ~ 司令官。*a general* ~ 将级军官。*a flay* ~ (海军)将官。*a chief petty* ~【海军】〔英〕上士,〔美〕军士长。*a petty* ~ *1st* [*2nd*] *class*【海军】〔英〕中士[下士],〔美〕上士[中士]。*a military* [*naval*] ~ 陆[海]军军官。*an* ~ *of the day*【军】值日军官。*an* ~ *of the watch* 舰上值班军官。~*s and men* 官兵。*a first* ~【海】一级驾驶员,大副。~ ***of the day*** [***week***] 值日[星]官。~***'s morale*** 〔军俚〕威士忌。**II** *vt*. 〔常用被动式〕**1**. 给…配置军官[高级船员]。**2**. (做军官)指挥,统率。**3**. 管理。~ *an army* 给军队配备军官。

of·fi·cial [əˈfiʃəl; əˋfɪʃəl] **I** *a*. **1**. 职务上的,公务上的,官员的,公的;担任官[公]职的。**2**. (出自)官方的,法定的,公认的,正式的。**3**. 官气十足的;讲究形式的。**4**. 依据药典(配制)的;收入药典的。~ *duties* 公务。~ *responsibilities* 职责。*an* ~ *residence* 官邸。*an* ~ *gazette* 〔Eng.〕官方通报。*an* ~ *letter* [*note*] 公函;公文。*an* ~ *report* 公报。*an* ~ *record* 正式记录。*an* ~ *list* (*of quotation*)【商】公定行市表。~ *sanction* 批准,核准。~ *circumlocution* [*red-tape*] 官僚主义,文牍主义。*with* ~ *solemnity* 耍官腔,摆官僚架子。**II** *n*. **1**. 官员,行政人员,高级职员。**2**. 宗教法庭法官。**3**.【运】裁判。*governmental* ~*s* 政府官员。*public* ~*s* 官员。*bank* ~*s* 银行职员。~**dom** *n*. 〔集合词〕官员;官场;官派;官僚作风。**Official English** 〔美〕官方英语。~ **family** 内阁,部长们。**-ism** *n*. 官制;官派,拖拉作风等;文牍主义;官僚主义,官僚脾气。**-ize** *vt*. 使成为正式的;使经过例行手续;把…置于官方控制下。**-ly** *ad*. 以职员身分;用职权;职务上;正式。

of·fi·cial·ese [əˌfiʃəˈliːz; əˏfɪʃəˋliz] *n*. 〔美〕公文英语;官场公文体。

of·fi·ci·ant [əˈfiʃiənt; əˋfɪʃɪənt] *n*. 司仪牧师,主祭。

of·fi·ci·ar·y [əˈfiʃiəri; əˋfɪʃɪˏɛrɪ] **I** *n*. (*pl*. ***-ar·ies***) 官员团。**II** *a*. 与职务有关的,由任职而得来的。

of·fi·ci·ate [əˈfiʃieit; əˋfɪʃɪˏet] *vi*., *vt*. **1**. 执行(职务);主持(会议);做 (*as*)。**2**.【宗】(为…充当)司祭;(主持仪式)。**3**. 充当(比赛等的)裁判。~ ***as best man*** 做男傧相。~ ***as host*** 作东道主,当东。~ ***at a marriage*** 主持婚礼。

of·fi·ci·nal [ˌɔfiˈsainl, əˈfisinl; əˋfɪsɪnḷ] **I** *a*. **1**. (植物等)药用的;成药的。**2**. 依据药方的。**II** *n*. (一般)成药。

of·fi·cious [əˈfiʃəs; əˋfɪʃəs] *a*. **1**. 爱管闲事的。**2**.【外交】非官方的,非正式的 (*opp*. official)。**3**. 〔古〕亲切的,好意的;殷勤的。*an* ~ *statement* 非正式声明。**-ly** *ad*. **-ness** *n*.

off·ing [ˈɔfiŋ, ˈɔːf-; ˋɔfɪŋ, ˋɑf-] *n*. (岸上能见的远处)海上,海面,洋面;〔喻〕不远的将来。***gain*** [***keep***] ***an*** ~ 驶出海面;航行在海面上。***in the*** ~ 在海面;在附近;好像就要来似的。***take an*** ~ 驶出海面;〔口〕逃走。

off·ish [ˈɔfiʃ, ˈɔːf-; ˋɔfɪʃ, ˋɑf-] *a*. 〔口〕不亲热的,冷淡的,疏远的;刚愎的。

off-li·cence [ˈɔ(ː)fˌlaisəns; ˋɔfˏlaɪsəns] *n*. 〔英〕(不许堂饮只许外卖的)卖酒执照 (*opp*. on-license)。

off-lim·its [ˈɔ(ː)fˈlimits; ˋɔfˋlɪmɪts] *n*. 〔*pl*.〕禁止入内(地区)。

off·print [ˈɔːfprint, ˈɔf-; ˋɔfˏprɪnt, ˋɑf-] *n*., *vt*. 翻印,抽印;选刊。

off·scour·ings [ˈɔːfskauəriŋz, ˈɔf-; ˋɔfskaʊərɪŋz, ˋɑf-] *n*. 〔*pl*.〕污物;垃圾;破烂东西,废料;(人类的)渣滓。

off·set [ˈɔːfset, ˈɔf-; ɔfˋsɛt, ˋɑf-] **I** *n*. **1**. 抵销,抵销物,(优点对缺点等的)弥补,补偿 (*to*; *against*)。**2**. 分支;支脉;【植】短匐茎,侧枝。**3**.【机】偏置(管);迂回管;支管;【测】支矩;【印】胶印;背面蹭脏;【建】壁价;【地】水平断错;【船】型值;船体尺码表。**4**. 〔罕〕出发。**5**. 〔罕〕开始。**6**.【矿】纵坑道。~ *construction* 支距画图法。*an* ~ *cylinder* 偏置汽缸。*an* ~ *pipe* 偏置管,迂回管。~ *tool* 偏刀,鹅颈刀。**II** [ɔːfˈset, ɔf-; ɔfˋsɛt, ɑf-] *vt*. (***off-set***; ***-set·ting***) **1**. 抵销;(拿优点)弥补(缺点)。**2**.【印】用胶印法印刷;蹭脏(纸的)背面;【建】为…建壁阶;【机】在…作迂回管;偏置。~ *the loss* 弥补损失。~ *debits against credits* 进行借方贷方的冲账结算。—*vi*. **1**. 形成分支。**2**.【印】蹭脏背面。~ **printing** 胶印。

off·shoot [ˈɔːfʃuːt, ˈɔf-; ˋɔfˏʃut, ˋɑf-] *n*. **1**. 分枝,侧枝。**2**. 支脉;支流;横路。**3**. 衍生物 (*from*)。**4**. 旁系子孙;分支。

off·shore [ˈɔːfʃɔː, ˈɔf-; ˋɔfˋʃor, ˋɑf-] **I** *a*. (风等)(从海岸)向海面吹的;离岸的;海面上的。*an* ~ *bar* 滨外沙洲。**II** *ad*. 向海面;离岸;近海岸。~ **fund** 〔美〕海外投资。

off·side [ˈɔːfˈsaid, ˈɔf-; ˋɔfˋsaɪd, ˋɑf-] *a*. **1**. 对方界内。**2**.【足球、曲棍球等】越位(犯规) (*opp*. onside);【橄榄球】己方带球球员的前方。**3**. 〔主英〕(车马等的)右边。

off·spring [ˈɔːfspriŋ, ˈɔf-; ˋɔfˏsprɪŋ, ˋɑf-] *n*. 子女;子孙,后代;产物,结果;幼苗;(动物的)仔。

off-stage [ˈɔ(ː)fˈsteidʒ; ˋɔfˋstedʒ] *n*., *ad*., *a*. 舞台后面(的);后台(的);幕后(的)。

off·take [ˈɔfteik; ˋɔfˋtek] *n*. **1**. 排出;排出管道出口;泄水处。**2**. 支管。

off-the-re·cord [ˌɔfðəˈrekɔːd; ˏɔfðəˋrɛkəd] *a*. 不留记录的;不许发表[引用]的,非正式的。

O'Fla·her·ty [əuˈflεəti; oˋflæhəˑtɪ] *n*. 奥弗莱厄蒂〔姓氏〕。

oft [ɔːft, ɔft; ɔft, ɑft] *ad*. 〔古、诗〕经常,常常 = often. ***many a time and*** ~ 屡次,再三。~ ***repeated*** 常常重复的。~ ***told*** 常常谈起的。

of·ten [ˈɔ(ː)fn, ˈɔːftən; ˋɔfən, ˋɔftən] *ad*. 常常,往往,屡次,再三。*How* ~ *does the tram run*? 这电车多久一班? ***as*** ~ ***as*** ... 每当。***as*** ~ ***as not*** 屡次,往往。~ ***and*** ~ 屡次三番,经常。***more*** ~ ***than not*** 往往,多半,大概。★ **1**. often 一般用于动词之前, be 及助动词之后;有时也用于句末以加强语气。如: He ~ goes there. I've ~ been there. I haven't been there very ~. **2**. 方言发音中有时读作[ˈɔ(ː)ftən; ˋɔftən];在唱歌里需要唱出两个音节的地方也作[ˈɔ(ː)ftən; ˋɔftən]。

of·ten·times, oft·times [ˈɔ(ː)fəntaimz; ˋɔfənˏtaɪmz] *ad*. 〔古〕屡次,常常。

OG = **1**. Olympic Games 奥林匹克运动会,奥运会。**2**. Officer of the guard 卫兵长。

og·am [ˈɔgəm; ˋɔgəm] *n*. = ogham.

Og·den [ˈɔgdən; ˋɑgdən] *n*. **1**. 奥格登〔姓氏〕。**2**. **Charles Kay** ~ 查尔士·开伊·欧格登〔1889—1957, 英国心理学家, Basic English 的创议者〕。

og·do·ad [ˈɔgdəuˌæd; ˋɑgdoˏæd] *n*. **1**. 数目字八。**2**. 八数所成的群或组。

o·gee [ˈəudʒiː, əuˈdʒiː; ˋodʒi, oˋdʒi] *n*.【建】S形(曲)线;葱形饰;葱形拱。~ **arch** 葱形拱。~ **curve** 双弯曲线, S形曲线。

og·ham [ˈɔgəm; ˋɑgəm] **I** *n*. (古代英国及爱尔兰人的)欧甘文字;欧甘碑铭。**II** *a*. 欧甘文字的。

o·give [ˈəudʒaiv, əuˈdʒ-; ˋodʒaɪv, oˋdʒ-] *n*.【建】交错骨;尖顶穹窿;葱形饰;尖顶部;(炮弹的)蛋形部分。*false* ~【物】整流罩。**o·giv·al** *a*.

o·gle [ˈəugl; ˋogḷ] **I** *n*. 秋波,媚眼。***an*** ~ ***list*** 〔美俚〕病假表。**II** *vt*., *vi*. (对…)送秋波,(向…)施媚眼。

O·gle·thorpe [ˈəuglθɔːp; ˋogḷθɔrp] *n*. 奥格尔索普〔姓氏〕。

O gosh [əu gɔʃ; o gɑf] 〔美俚〕向左〔从法语 à gauche 变来〕。

o·gre [ˈəugə; ˋogɚ] (*fem*. ***o'gress*** [ˈəugris; ˋogrɪs]) *n*. (童话等中的)吃人魔鬼;残暴的人;丑怪的人。

o·gr(e)ish [ˈəugəriʃ; ˋogərɪʃ] *a*. 妖魔的;妖魔似的。

Og·y·gian [əuˈdʒidʒiən; oˋdʒɪdʒɪən] *a*. 史前的,太古时代的。

oh, Oh [əu; o] *int*. 哦! 啊! 呀! **1.**〔冠于人名前,起呼语作用〕*Oh Jack*! 哦! 杰克! *Oh Mary, look*! 玛丽啊,看呀! **2.**〔表示惊讶、恐惧、痛苦、快乐、悲伤等〕呀,啊。*Oh, what a surprise*! 啊,真是想不到的事! *Oh, dear*! 啊呀! *Oh, my*! 啊呀! *Oh, yes*. 啊,是的。*Oh, no*. 啊,不。★O 后常不加标点,但 Oh 后一般加逗号!

O'Hare [əuˈhɛə; oˋhɛr] *n*. 奥黑尔〔姓氏〕。

oh-dee [ˈəuˈdiː; ˋoˋdi] *vi*.〔美俚〕因为[像是]服用过量药物致死。

OHG, O.H.G. = Old High German 古代高地德语。

O·hi·o [əuˈhaiəu; oˋhaɪo] *n*. 俄亥俄〔美国州名〕。

ohm [əum; om] *n*. 欧姆〔电阻单位〕。~**-ammeter** 欧安计。~ **meter** 欧姆计[表]。**Ohm's law** 欧姆定律。

ohm·ic [ˈəumik; ˋomɪk] *a*. **1.** 欧姆的。**2.** 以欧姆计算的。**3.** 使用欧姆定律的原理装置的。

O.H.M.S. = On His (Her) Majesty's Service 为英王(女王)陛下效劳〔英国公函免付邮费的戳记〕。

o·ho [əuˈhəu; oˋho] *int*. 嗳哟! 哦嗬! 哦!〔惊喜、惊异声〕。

o·ho yes [əu jes; o jɛs] = oyes, oyez.

oi [ɔi; ɔɪ] *int*. 喂〔用于引起注意,打招呼等〕。

-oid *suf*. …状的(东西),像…的(东西),…质的:alkal*oid*, negr*oid*.

oil [ɔil; ɔɪl] **I** *n*. **1.** 油;油类;油状物〔一般是不可数名词,表示种类时则用 *pl*. 如:vegetable and animal ~s 植物油和动物油〕。**2.**〔*pl*.〕油画颜料;〔口〕油画作品。**3.**〔*pl*.〕油布;油布雨衣[衣裤]。**4.**〔美俚〕恭维话,奉承话;鬼话,油滑的话。*vegetable* [*animal, mineral*] ~ 植物[动物、矿物]油。*fixed* [*volatile*] ~ 固定[挥发]油。*crude* ~ 原油。*heavy* [*light*] ~ 重[轻]油。*machine* ~ 机器油。~ *feed* 加油。~ *feeder* 加油器。***burn*** [***consume***] ***the midnight*** ~ 用功到深夜,开夜车。***have the*** ~〔美俚〕具有讨人喜欢的态度。***paint in*** ~***s*** 画油画。***pour*** [***add, put***] ~ ***on the flame*** 火上加油;使怒气更盛;使争吵更激烈。***pour*** [***throw***] ~ ***on the*** (***troubled***) ***waters*** 劝人息怒;调停争端,平息风波。***smell of*** ~ (作品等)有煞费苦心作成的迹象。***strike*** ~ 钻探到油脉,发现油矿;〔美〕大获成功,发横财,暴富。**II** *vt*. **1.** 在…上涂油;给(机器等)上油,加油;把…浸在油中;弄滑。**2.** 使融化。**3.** 收买,行贿。—*vi*. **1.** (脂肪等)融化,熔化。**2.** (轮船等)加燃料油。***have a well-oiled tongue*** 油嘴滑舌,会说话。~ ***sb.'s hand*** [***palm***] 贿赂某人。~ ***one's tongue*** 油嘴滑舌地恭维。~ ***the wheels*** 加油在轮上;用圆滑手段[贿赂]使事情进行顺利。~ ***the whistle***〔美口〕喝一杯。~**-bearing** *a*. 产油的(~*-bearing crops* 油料作用)。~ **beetle**【动】泌油甲〔一种甲虫,受碰扰时,足肢的腺体产生一种油性分泌〕。~**berg** 漂浮在海面上的大片漏油。~**bird 1.**【动】油鸱。**2.**〔美俚〕老手;老世故。~ **box** 油箱,润滑油盒。~ **bunker** 油槽;油库;燃油舱。~**burg** (二十万吨或更大的)超级油轮。~ **burner** 燃油器;油炉;柴油舰[船];〔美俚〕耗油的旧车辆[船只];〔美俚〕常吃嚼烟的人。~ **cake** 油渣饼。~ **can** 加油器,油壶;〔美俚〕无赖;运油车。~**-carrier** 油船。~**cloth** 油布,漆布。~ **colo(u)r**〔常 *pl*.〕油画颜料;油画;油漆;油溶性染料。~ **corridor** 石油走廊〔指地下石油储量丰富之狭长地带或海上油轮航线〕。~ **crop** 油料作物。~**cup** 油杯。~ **diplomacy** (涉及石油输出国和输入国之间关系的)石油外交。~ **dorado** [dəˈrɑːdəu; dəˋrɑdo]〔美〕产油丰富的地方;油乡。~ **engine** 柴油机。~ **fever**〔美〕石油采掘热。~**field** 油田。~**-meal** 油渣粉。~ **and vinegar** 油和醋〔互不相容之物〕。~ **of joy**〔美〕酒类。~ **of vitriol** 硫酸。~ **paint** 油画颜料;油漆。~ **painting** 画油画,油画法。~**-palm** 油椰(*Elae is guineensis*)〔非洲热带地区产,其籽含椰子油〕。~**paper** 油纸。~**-plant** 油料作物。~ **press** 榨油器。~ **shale**【地】油页岩。~ **share** 石油股票。~ **sheet** 薄油层。~(-)**shock** 石油休克〔即石油能源危机〕。~**-skin 1.** 油布,防水布。**2.**〔*pl*.〕油布工装。~ **slick** (水面上的一层)浮油。~**-spring** (石)油泉[井]。~ **stick** 水面浮油。~**stone** 油磨石。~ **stove** 煤油炉。~ **tank steamer**, ~ **tanker** 油船,油轮。~**tight** *a*. 防油的,油渗不进的。~ **weapon** 石油武器〔指以停止、减少供应石油,或提高油价等手段来施加外交压力等〕。~ **well** 油井。~ **witch**〔美〕自称能发现油矿的人。**-man** 制油工;石油巨头;油商;油画颜料商。

oil·a·teer [ɔiləˈtiːə; ɔɪləˋtir] *n*.〔美〕汽车加油站的职员。

oiled [ɔild; ɔɪld] *a*. **1.** 涂了油的;油浸的;化成油状的。**2.**〔俚〕喝了酒的,有点醉的。

oil·er [ˈɔilə; ˋɔɪlɚ] *n*. **1.** 油商;涂油者,注油器,注油人,注油机;油船,油轮。**2.**〔口〕油布衣。**3.**〔口〕马屁精。**4.**〔O-〕〔美〕墨西哥人的绰号。

oil·i·ly [ˈɔilili; ˋɔɪlɪlɪ] *ad*. **1.** 油一样地;滑溜溜地。**2.** 油嘴滑舌地;会奉承地。

oil·i·ness [ˈɔilinis; ˋɔɪlɪnɪs] *n*. **1.** 油质,油气;含油,油腻。**2.** 会拍马屁;奉承。

oil·y [ˈɔili; ˋɔɪlɪ] *a*. (*oil·i·er*; *-i·est*) **1.** 油的,油质的;含油的,油多的;油腻的;油垢不堪的。**2.** 油滑的,会奉承的。

oink [ɔink; ɔɪnk] **I** *n*. 猪哼声,仿猪哼声。**II** *vi*. 学猪哼,仿效猪哼。

oint·ment [ˈɔintment; ˋɔɪntmənt] *n*. 软膏;药膏;油膏。*a fly in the* ~ 白璧之瑕;美中不足。

Oir·each·tas [ˈiərəkθəs; ˋɛrəktəs] *n*.〔Ir.〕(爱尔兰的)国家议会。

OIRT =〔F.〕*Organisation Internationale de Radiodiffusion et Télévision* 国际广播电视组织(= International Radio and Television Organization)。

O·jib·way, O·jib·wa [əuˈdʒibwei; oˋdʒɪbwe] *n*. (*pl*. ***Ojibway, Ojibwa***; ~*s*) (北美)奥吉韦印第安人。

OK, O.K. [ˈəuˈkei; ˋoˋke] **I** *a*.〔口〕好;对,不错;可以;行;阅。**II** *n*. (*pl*. ***OK's, O.K.'s***) 同意,许可,签认;阅讫,查讫(等)。*He put his OK on the shipment*. 他在装运的货物上写上"查讫"二字。**III** *vt*. (***O.K.'d***) 签上 O.K.〔表示较好等〕;(签上 O.K.)承认,同意;批准;核准。

o·ka·pi [əuˈkɑːpi; oˋkɑpɪ] *n*.【动】(似长颈鹿但颈不长的)俄卡皮鹿。

o·kay, o·keh, o·key [ˈəuˈkei; ˋoˋke] *a*., *n*., *vt*. = O.K.

oke [əuk; ok], **o·key-do·ke(y)** [ˈəukiˈdəuk(i); ˋokɪˋdok(ɪ)] *a*., *int*.〔美俚〕= O.K.

O'keef(f)e [əuˈkiːf; oˋkif] *n*. 奥基夫〔姓氏〕。

O'Kel·ly [əuˈkeli; oˋkelɪ] *n*. 奥凯利〔姓氏〕。

Ok·hotsk [əuˈkɔtsk; oˋkɑtsk], ***the sea of*** ~ 鄂霍次克海。

O·kie [ˈəuki; ˋokɪ] *n*.〔美口〕(俄克拉荷马州的)流动雇农。

O·ki·na·wa [ˌəukiˈnɑːwə; ˏokɪˋnawə] *n*. 冲绳(群岛);冲绳(岛)〔日本〕。

ok·ka [ˈɔkə; ˋɑkə] *n*. 沃克〔土耳其、约旦的一种重量单位,约等于 2¾ 磅〕。

Okla. = Oklahoma.

O·kla·ho·ma [ˌəukləˈhəumə; ˏokləˋhomə] *n*. 俄克拉荷马〔美国南部州名〕。**-n** *a*., *n*. (美国)俄克拉荷马州的(人)。~ **plum**【植】细弱李。~ **rain**〔美〕夹沙风暴。

o'kra [ˈəukrə; ˋokrə] *n*.【植】黄秋葵;秋葵纤维。

Ol. = Olympiad.

-ol *suf*.【化】(表示)醇;酚;油:naphth*ol*, phen*ol*.

O·laf [ˈəuləf, ˈɔl-; ˋoləf, ˋɑl-] *n*. 奥拉夫〔男子名〕〔Scand. 语中意为 ancestor-relics〕。

old [əuld; old] **I** ***a***. (*-er*; *-est*; 表示兄弟姊妹关系时用 ***eld·er***; ***eld·est***)。**1.** 老,上了年纪的,年老的 (*opp*. young); 衰老的,老迈的;老成的;老练的;熟练的。**2.** …岁的;…久的。**3.** 古时的,古代的 (*opp*. modern); 古老的,积年的,陈年的,多年来的,旧交的;熟悉的。**4.** (*opp*. new) 过去的,过时的;旧的;破旧的;用旧了的;旧式的,陈腐的。**5.** 〔口〕亲爱的,亲密的。**6.** 〔口〕极好的〔通常用以加强其他形容词语气〕。*grow* [*get*] ~ 老起来,上年纪。*How ~ is he?* 他多大岁数? *He is eighteen years ~.* 他十八岁。~ *in diplomacy* 擅长外交。*an ~ bachelor* 老独身汉。~ *gaolbird* 老囚犯;惯犯。*an ~ offender* 惯犯。*an ~ friend* 老朋友。*an ~ Oxonian* 牛津大学的老校友。~ *fashions* 旧式。~ *iron* 废铁。~ *jokes* 陈腐的俏皮话。~ *wine* 陈年老酒。*the ~ country* [*home*] 故乡。*the ~ thing* (老)家伙。*I had a fine ~ time*.〔口〕过得非常愉快。***an ~ head on young shoulders*** 少年老成。***any ~ thing*** 〔俚〕随便什么(东西)。***for an ~ song*** 非常便宜地。***for ~ sake's sake*** 因老交情。***in ~ time*** 在从前。***never too ~ to learn*** 活到老学到老;学无止境。***of ~ standing*** 多年的,由来已久的。***as ~ as the hill*** 很老。~ ***familiar faces*** 老相识(的人们)。***O- Lady of Threadneedle Street*** 〔英〕Bank of England 的别名。~ ***man of the sea*** 死缠着不走的人。~ ***ten in the hundred*** 高利贷。***the good ~ times*** (老人们所怀念的)过去。***the ~ gentleman = the ~ one*** 〔口〕老头儿,父亲。***the ~ year*** 去年,就要过去的一年。

II ***n***. **1.** 古时,往时。**2.** …岁的人[动物]。**3.** 〔集合词〕老年的人们;〔the ~〕古物;令人怀念的往事[风俗(等)]。*the men of ~* 古代的人们。*four-year-olds* 四岁的马。***as of ~*** 仍旧,照旧。***from of ~*** 自昔,早就。***in days of ~*** 从前,以前。***of ~*** 从前的,往时的;从前是,(老早)以前是;自古,从老早以前。~ ***and young = young and ~*** 无论老少。**O- Abe** [eib; eb]〔美〕Abraham Lincoln 的爱称。~ **age** 老年,晚年。**O- Bailey** (伦敦老贝利街的)中央刑事法院。~ **bean** [**boy, cock, chap, egg, fellow, fruit, man, thing, top**]〔俚〕(招呼)喂,老兄! 老弟! 老朋友! ~ **bird** 老手,老经验,老世故。~ **bloke** [**buffer, card, codger**]〔蔑〕不中用的老家伙,老古板,老派的人。~ **boy** 校友,老同学;(英国公学的)毕业生;〔the O- B-〕〔谑〕魔鬼。**O- Catholic** 老罗马天主教徒〔1870 年罗马天主教徒所组成的教派,不接受教皇圣明论〕。**O- Church Slavic** 古教堂斯拉夫语 (= Old Church Slavonic, Old Bulgarian)。~**-clothes-man** 旧衣商。**O- Colonials** 〔美〕Massachusetts 人的别名。~ **country** 故国〔移居外国的人对本国的称呼;特指对欧洲〕。**O- Dealer** 反对罗斯福新政的人。**O- Dirigo** [diˈriːgəu; dɪˋrigo]〔美〕Maine 州的别名。~ **doc**【军】军医长。**O- Dominion**〔美〕Virginia 州的别名。**O- Dutch** 古荷兰语。**O- English** 古代英语;【英】哥特体(铅字)。**O- English sheep-dog** 英国牧羊狗。~**fangled** ***a***. 老式的;守旧的。~**-fashioned** ***a***. 旧式的,老式的,过时的;不爱时髦的。~ **floppy**〔英空俚〕阻隔气球。~ **fogy**, ~ **fogey** 守旧者,老家伙。~**-fogyish**, ~**-fogeyish** ***a***. 老派的,守旧的。~ **folks**〔美马戏团〕猴子。**O- French** 古法语。**O- Glory** 美国国旗的俗称。~ **goat**〔美俚〕讨厌的老家伙;老色迷。~ **gold** 浅黄色。**O- Guard** 拿破仑一世的近卫队;〔美〕共和党的极端保守派;〔o- guard〕保守派,保守分子。~ **hand** 熟练工人;老手 (*at*);惯犯,老犯 (*an ~ hand at the game* 此道老手)。**O- Harry** 魔鬼。~ **hat**〔俚〕**1.** 旧式的;过时的。**2.** 老套的,陈腐的。**O- High German** 古高地德语〔标准德语〕。**o- home week 1.** 一个社区的居民邀请过去旧居民的联欢周。**2.** 旧同事[同学]的重聚联欢周。~ **horse** 咸牛肉干。**O- Icelandic** 古冰岛语。**O- Indic 1.** 古印度—雅利安语。**2.** 梵语(包括吠陀梵语)。**O- Ionic** 古爱奥尼亚语。**O- Irish** 古爱尔兰语。**O- Ironsides** 美国快速炮舰〔于 1812 年战争中服现役〕。**O- Jamica**【海】太阳。~ **Lady** 妻子;母亲;拘谨的人。~ **lag** 惯犯。**O-Latin** 古拉丁语〔指公元前 100 年以前的拉丁语〕。**O- Line**〔美〕马里兰州的别名。~**-line** ***a***. 保守的;历史性的,传统的;老资格的;老牌的。~**-liner** 守旧者,保守派的人;〔英〕〔O- L-〕保守党党员。**O- Low Franconian** 古代低地法兰克语〔莱茵河下游的法兰克人在公元 1100 年以前讲的西日耳曼语〕。**O- Low German** 古低地德语。~ **maid 1.** 老处女。**2.** 怯懦而又斤斤计较的歇斯底里性的男子。**3.**【牌】找寡妇〔一种简单的抽对子牌戏〕。~**-maidish** ***a***. 拘谨的;像老处女的。~ **man 1.** 〔an〕老头子。**2.** 〔one's〕〔口〕丈夫;父亲。**3.** 〔the〕〔口〕老板;船长;长官;【剧】老先生。**4.** 〔招呼话〕= ~ chap. **5.** 老前辈。**6.**【宗】(皈依基督教前的)旧我 (*So's your ~ man*.〔美俚〕去你的! 胡说!)。**O- Man River** "老人河"〔密西西比河的绰号〕。~ **master** 古代画家,(特指)18 世纪前的大画家(或其作品)。**O- Masters** 英国美术院冬季展览。~ **moon** 下弦月。**O- Nick** 魔鬼,恶魔,撒旦,魔王。**O- Norman French** 诺曼(第)语〔中世纪诺曼人或诺曼第人讲的法语〕。**O- Norse 1.** 古诺斯语〔14 世纪前斯堪的纳维亚人所讲的北日耳曼语〕。**2.** 古冰岛语 (= O- Icelandic)。**O- North**〔美〕北卡罗来纳州的别名。**O- North French** 古北方法语〔法国北部,尤指皮卡地和诺曼地所讲的古法语的方言〕。**O- Persian** 古波斯语。**O- Prussian** 古普鲁士语〔属波罗的语族,17 世纪时已消亡〕。~ **rose** 略带紫的[略带灰的]玫瑰色。~ **saw** 老话,民间格言。**O- Saxon** 古撒克逊语。~**-school** ***a***. 老派的,老式的。~ **school** 守旧派。**O- Scratch** 魔鬼。**O- Shake**〔美口〕莎翁,老莎士比亚 (= Shakespeare)。~ **shell**【海】水手。**O- Siwash** [ˈsaiwɔʃ; ˋsaɪwɑʃ]〔美俚〕大学。**O- Slavic** (= O- Church Slavic 古教堂斯拉夫语)。~ **sledge** (= seven-up 七点儿〔牌戏,二、三、四人玩,七点就成局〕)。~ **smoky**〔美俚〕(死刑用的)电椅。**O- Socks**〔美俚〕老兄〔爱称〕。**O- Sol**〔谑〕太阳。**O- South** 旧南方〔指美国内战以前的南方〕。**O- Spanish** 古西班牙语。~ **squaw** 冰岛 (Clangula hyemalis)。~ **stager**〔美 ~ **coon**〕经验丰富的人;识途老马,老手,过来人。~ **standers** 随舰长调动的老练水兵。~ **stuff**〔美〕陈话,听腻了的话。~ **style** ***n***. 旧式的东西;【印】旧体铅字;〔O- Style〕西洋旧历。**O- Testament** (基督教《圣经》的)《旧约全书》。~**-time** ***a***. 古时的,旧时的,老资格的。~**-timer**〔口〕老前辈;老手,老资格的人;守旧的人;上了年纪的人;〔美俚〕老朋友;可靠的朋友;可靠而有经验的人。~**tim(e)y** ***a***.〔口〕旧时的;早期的。**O- Tom** 一种杜松子酒。~ **top**〔美口〕好朋友,伙伴儿,老搭档。**O- Welsh** 古威尔斯语。~ **wife** 唠唠叨叨的老太婆。~ **wives' tale** 无稽之谈。~ **woman** 〔an〕老太婆;〔one's〕〔口〕妻,老婆;〔one's〕〔美口〕老母;〔an〕婆婆妈妈似的男人。~**-womanish** ***a***. 有老婆子性格的;适宜于老婆子的;婆婆妈妈的。~**-world** ***a***. 旧世界的,太古的;老式的;古色古香的(*~-world arrowhead* 慈姑)。**O- World** 旧世界〔欧洲、亚洲、非洲,尤专指欧洲〕;东半球。~ **year's day** 除夕。

Old·cas·tle [ˈəuldˌkɑːsl; ˋoldˏkæsl̩] ***n***. 奥尔德卡斯尔〔姓氏〕。

old·en [ˈəuldən; ˋoldn̩] **I** ***a***. 〔古〕古昔的。***in*** (***the***) ~ ***days = in ~ times*** 古昔,从前。**II** ***vt***. 〔罕〕使老,使旧。—***vi***. 变老,变陈旧。*In three months she ~ed more than she had done or 10 years before*. 她在三个月中比在以前十年还要老得快些。

old·ie, old·y [ˈəuldi; ˋoldɪ] ***n***. (*pl*. ***old·ies***)〔口〕老笑话、老话、传说、老歌子;老影子。

old·ish [ˈəuldiʃ; ˋoldɪʃ] ***a***. 有点老的,稍旧的。

Ol·do·wan [ˈɔldəwən; ˋɔldəwən] ***a***. 奥尔杜韦文化的〔奥尔杜韦是坦桑尼亚地名,于该地发掘的文物属于石器时代最早期文化产物〕。

old·ster [ˈəuldstə; ˋoldstɚ] ***n***.〔口〕上了年纪的人。

Old Test. = Old Testament.
-ole *suf*. 油。
o·lé [ɔ'lei; ɔ`le] ***int***., ***n***.〔Sp.〕好！好极了！〔看斗牛或吉普赛舞时的喝彩〕。
o·le·a ['əuliə; `olɪə] ***n***. oleum 的复数。
o·le·ag·i·nous [ˌəuli'ædʒinəs; ˏolɪ`ædʒənəs] ***a***. **1.** 含油的；油质的；油腻的；产油的；有油气的。**2.** 油嘴滑舌的，会拍马屁的。**-ness** ***n***. 含油性质。
o·le·as·ter [ˌəuli'æstə; ˏolɪ`æstɚ] ***n***.【植】胡颓子属植物。
o·le·ate ['əulieit; `olɪˏet] ***n***.【化】油酸盐；油酸脂。
o·lec·ra·non [əu'lekrənɔn, ˌəuli'kreinɔn; o`lɛkrənɑn, ˏoləkrənɑn] ***n***.【动】鹰嘴，肘突。
o·le·fin, o·le·fine ['əulifin; `oləfɪn] ***n***.【化】烯(属)烃。**-ic** ***a***.
o·le·ic [əu'liːik; o`liɪk] ***a***. 油的；油酸的。~ **acid**【化】油酸。
o·le·in ['əuliːin; `olɪɪn] ***n***.【化】油精；三油精；甘油三油酸脂。
o·len·an·der [ˌəuli'ændə; ˏolɪ`ændɚ] ***n***.【植】(欧洲)夹竹桃。
o·le·o ['əuliəu; `olɪo] ***n***.〔美〕= oleomargarine. ~ **oil**【化】油，(从动物脂肪炼成的)奶油状油。
o·le·o·graph ['əuliə*u*grɑːf; `olɪoˏgræf] ***n***. 油画式的石版画。
o·le·o·mar·ga·rin(e) ['əuliə*u*ˌmɑːdʒə'riːn; ˏolɪə`mɑrdʒərɪn] ***n***. 人造奶油，代奶油。
o·le·om·e·ter [ˌəuli'ɔmitə; ˏolɪ`ɑmətɚ] ***n***. 油比重计；量油计。
o·le·o·res·in [ˌəuliəu'rezin; ˏolɪo`rɛzn̩] ***n***.【化】含油树脂。
O·les·tra [əu'lestrə; o`lɛstrə] ***n***.〔商标〕奥利斯特拉油〔一种油脂代用品，不含胆固醇，低卡路里，供糖尿病患者等用的食物添加剂〕。
o·le·o·strut [ˌəuliə'strʌt; ˏolə`strʌt] ***n***.【空】油液空气减震器[柱]。
ol·er·i·cul·ture ['ɔleriˌkʌltʃə; `ɑlərɪˏkʌltʃɚ] ***n***. 蔬菜学。
o·le·um ['əuliəm; `olɪəm] (*pl*. ***o·le·a*** ['əuliə; `olɪə]) ***n***. **1.** 油。**2.** (*pl*. ~***s***)【化】发烟硫酸。
ol·fac·tion [ɔl'fækʃən; ɑl`fækʃən] ***n***. 嗅觉作用；嗅觉。
ol·fac·tom·e·ter [ˌɔlfæk'tɔmitə; ˏɑlfæk`tɑmɪtɚ] ***n***. 气味测量计。**-me·tric** [-'metrik; -`mɛtrɪk] ***a***. **-e·try** ***n***.
ol·fac·to·ry [ɔl'fæktəri; ɑl`fæktərɪ] **I** ***n***.〔常 *pl*.〕嗅觉，嗅觉器官，鼻。**II** ***a***. 嗅觉器官的，嗅觉的。~ **nerves** 嗅神经。~ **organ** 嗅觉器官；〔谑〕鼻子。
ol·fac·tron·ics [ˌɔlfæk'trɔniks, ˌəul-; ˏɑlfæk`trɑnɪks, ˏol-] ***n***.〔*pl*.〕〔动词用单数〕气味测定学。
Ol·ga ['ɔlgə; `ɑlgə] ***n***. 奥尔加〔女子名〕。
ol·ib·a·num [ɔ'libənəm, əu-; o`lɪbənəm, o-] ***n***. 乳香。
ol·id ['ɔlid; `ɑlɪd] ***a***. 臭的；发恶臭的。
olig(o)- *comb*. *f*. 稀，微，减，寡，少。
ol·i·garch ['ɔligɑːk; `ɑlɪˏgɑrk] ***n***. 寡头政治的执政者[支持者]。*a financial* ~ 金融寡头。**-gar·chy** [-i; -ɪ] ***n***. 寡头政治；寡头统治的国家[政权]；寡头政治集团。**-chic, -chi·cal** ***a***.
ol·i·ge·mi·a [ˌɔli'dʒiːmiə; ˏɑlɪ`dʒiˏmɪə] ***n***.【医】血量减少。
O·li·go·cene [ɔ'ligə*u*siːn; `ɑlɪgoˏsin] ***n***., ***a***.【地】渐新世(的)；渐新统(的)。
ol·i·go·chaete ['ɔligəuˌkiːt; `ɑləgoˏkit] ***n***.【动】寡毛纲(*Oligochaeta*)动物。**-chae·tous** [-ˌkiːtəs; -ˏkitəs] ***a***.
ol·i·go·clase ['ɔligəuˌkleis; `ɑlɪgoˏkles] ***n***.【地】奥长石。
ol·i·goph·a·gous [ˌɔli'gɔfəgəs; ˏɑlə`gɑfəgəs] ***a***.【动】寡食性的。
ol·i·gop·o·ly [ˌɔli'gɔpəli; ˏɑlə`gɑpəlɪ] ***n***. (*pl*. ***-lies***) 商品供应垄断〔资本主义市场少数公司或供货人搞的控制〕。**-gop·o·list** ***n***. 市场供应垄断者。**-lis·tic** [-'listik; -`lɪstɪk] ***a***.
ol·i·gop·so·ny [ˌɔliː'gɔpsəni; ˏɑlə`gɑpsənɪ] ***n***. (*pl*. ***-nies***) 商品采购垄断〔资本主义市场少数买主对市场商品采购搞的控制〕。**-so·nist** ***n***. 商品采购垄断者。**-so·nis·tic** [-'nistik; -`nɪstɪk] ***a***.
ol·i·go·sac·cha·ride [ˌɔligəu'sækəraid; ˏɑlɪgo`sækəˏraɪd] ***n***.【化】低聚醣，少醣。
ol·i·go·tro·phic [ˌɔligəu'trɔfik, -'trəufik; ˏɑləgo`trɑfɪk, -`trofɪk] ***a***. 寡营养的(指湖沼地)。**-ro·phy** [ˌɔli'gɔtrəfi; ˏɑlə`gɑtrəfɪ] ***n***.
ol·i·gu·ri·a [ˌɔli'gjuəriə; ˏɑlə`gjʊrɪə] ***n***.【医】尿少。
o·lim [əu'liːm; o`lim] ***n***.〔Heb.〕迁进以色列的犹太移民。
o·li·o ['əuliəu; `olɪˏo] ***n***. (*pl*. ~***s***)〔Sp.〕**1.**【烹】杂烩。**2.** 混杂物，杂凑，杂伴。**3.** 杂曲集；杂录。
ol·iva·ceous [ˌɔli'veiʃəs; ˏɑlɪ`veʃəs] ***a***. 橄榄的；像橄榄的(尤指颜色)；橄榄绿的。
ol·i·va·ry ['ɔlivəri; `ɑləˏvɛrɪ] ***a***.【解】橄榄形的；延髓侧突出的两橄榄个体之一的。
ol·ive ['ɔliv; `ɑlɪv] **I** ***n***. **1.**【植】齐墩果，油橄榄；橄榄树；橄榄树枝；(橄榄枝叶做的)橄榄冠 (= ~-crown)；橄榄木。**2.** 橄榄色，茶青色。**3.** 橄榄形钮扣。**4.**〔*pl*.〕【烹】小肉片菜卷。**II** ***a***. 橄榄的；橄榄色的。~ **branch** **1.** 橄榄枝〔和平[和解]的象征〕(*hold out the* [*an*] ~ *branch* 伸出橄榄枝；要求和解)。**2.**〔常 *pl*.〕〔谑〕小孩，儿童。~ **crown** (古时希腊胜利者戴的)橄榄冠。~ **drab** 草绿色；草黄色；〔美陆军〕草绿色呢制服。~ **green** 橄榄绿，茶青色。~ **oil** 橄榄油；〔美俚〕再会！〔从法语 *au revoir* 变来〕。~ **tree** 橄榄树。~ **wood** 橄榄木。
Ol·ive ['ɔliv; `ɑlɪv] ***n***. 奥莉夫〔女子名〕。
o·liv·en·ite [əu'livəˌnait, 'ɔlivə-; o`lɪvənaɪt, `ɑlɪvə-] ***n***.【矿】橄榄铜矿。
Ol·i·ver ['ɔlivə; `ɑləvɚ] ***n***. 奥利弗〔姓氏，男子名〕。~ **shield** (贴在听筒上防污染的)电话筒护纸。
ol·i·ver ['ɔlivə; `ɑləvɚ] ***n***. 脚踏铁锤。
ol·i·vet ['ɔlivet; `ɑləˏvɛt] ***n***. 人造珍珠。
ol·i·vet(te) ['ɔlivet; `ɑləˏvɛt] ***n***. 剧场用强化泛光灯。
O·liv·i·a [ɔ'liviə; o`lɪvɪə] ***n***. 奥莉维亚〔女子名〕。
ol·i·vin(e) [ˌɔli'viːn; `ɑləˏvin] ***n***.【矿】橄榄石。
ol·la ['ɔlə, Sp. 'ɔuljɑː; `ɑlə, `olja] ***n***. **1.** 土缸，土锅。**2.** 放入很多佐料做成的肉与蔬菜的炖菜。
ol·la po·dri·da ['ɔlə pɔ'driːdə; `ɑlə pə`dridə]〔Sp.〕= olio 1.
Ol·lie ['ɔli; `ɑlɪ] ***n***. 奥利〔男子名，Oliver 的昵称〕。
Ol·mec ['ɔlmek; `ɑlmɛk] **I** ***n***. (*pl*. ~(***s***)) 奥尔达克人〔墨西哥的古印第安人〕。**II** ***a***. 奥尔达克文化的〔特点是高度发展的农业，巨大的雕塑头像和雕刻玉器〕。
ol·o·gy ['ɔlədʒi; `ɑlədʒɪ] ***n***.〔常 *pl*.〕〔谑〕学问，科学；空论。
-ol·o·gy *suf*. = -logy.
O·lym·pi·a [əu'limpiə; o`lɪmpɪə] ***n***. **1.** 奥林匹亚〔希腊一地区〕。**2.** 奥林匹亚〔美国城市〕。
O·lym·pi·ad [ə*u*'limpiæd; o`lɪmpɪˏæd] ***n***.〔常用 o-〕**1.** (古希腊)四年周期〔两次奥林匹克运动会之间的四年周期。古希腊用以计算时间〕。**2.** 奥林匹克运动会。
O·lym·pi·an [ə*u*'limpiən, -pjən; o`lɪmpɪən, -pjən] **I** ***a***. **1.** 奥林匹克 (Olympus) 山的；奥林匹斯山诸神的；奥林匹斯山上似的，天上的；神仙一样的。**2.** 威仪堂堂的，气派十足的。**3.** 奥林匹克运动大会的。**II** ***n***. **1.**【希神】奥林匹斯山十二神之一。**2.** 奥林匹亚人。**3.** 奥林匹克运动会选手。
O·lym·pic [əu'limpik; o`lɪmpɪk] ***a***. 奥林匹亚的；奥林匹斯山的。***the*** ~ ***games*** **1.** (古希腊祭祀宙斯神每四年举行一次的)体育和文艺竞赛大会。**2.** 奥林匹克世界运动大会〔1896 年在雅典首次举行，以后每四年举行一次〕。

O

O·lym·pics [əu'limpiks; o`lɪmpɪks] ***n.*** 〔*pl.*〕= Olympic Games.

O·lym·pus [əu'limpəs; o`lɪmpəs] ***n.*** **1.** (希腊)奥林匹斯山。**2.**【希神】奥林匹斯山(诸神的住所)。**3.** 天。

O.M. = **1.** old measurement 旧度量制。**2.** Order of Merit〔英〕功绩勋章。

-oma *suf.* 肿,瘤:fibr*oma*.

om·a·dhaun ['ɔmədɔːn; `ɑmədɔn] ***n.*** 〔Ir.〕傻子,笨蛋。

O·ma·ha ['əuməhɑː; `omə,hɔ] ***n.*** **1.** (*pl.* ~(*s*)) 奥马哈人〔内布拉斯加东北部的印第安人〕。**2.** 奥马哈语。**3.** 奥马哈〔美国城市〕。

O·man [əu'mɑːn; o`mæn] ***n.*** 阿曼〔亚洲〕。

O·mar Khay·yám ['əumɑːkai'jɑːm; `omɑrkaɪ`ɑm] 奥马开阳〔1025? —1133,波斯诗人及天文学家〕。

o·ma·sum [əu'meisəm; o`mesəm] ***n.*** (*pl.* ***-sa*** [-sə; -sə])【解】(反刍动物的)重瓣胃。

om·ber, om·bre ['ɔmbə; `ɑmbɚ] ***n.*** **1.** 翁博牌戏〔西班牙三人玩的四十张牌的牌戏〕。**2.** 翁博牌戏的赌牌者。

om·bré ['ɔmbrei; `ɑmbre] ***a.*** (颜色)渐变的。

om·brol·o·gy [ɔm'brɔlədʒi; `ɑm`brɑlədʒɪ] ***n.*** 测雨学。

om·brom·e·ter [ɔm'brɔmitə; ɑm`brɑmətɚ] ***n.*** 雨量器。

om·buds·man ['ɔmbədzmən; ,ɑmbudz`mɑn] ***n.*** (*pl.* ***-men*** [-men; -mɛn]) 巡视官〔被委派去调查市民对官员侵犯个人权利案件的控告的政府官员〕。

Om·dur·man [,ɔmdəː'mɑːn; ,ɑmdur`mɑn] ***n.*** 恩图曼〔苏丹城市〕。

o·me·ga ['əumigə; o`megə] ***n.*** **1.** 希腊语的最后一个字母〔Ω, ω〕。**2.** (一系列中的)最后一个;终止,结局。***alpha and*** ~ 始与终,首尾,始末,全部。**Omega(-) 7, Omega Seven** 古巴在美移民中反对古巴现政府的一个恐怖主义组织。

om·e·let(te) ['ɔmlit, -let; `ɑmlɪt, -lɛt] ***n.*** 煎蛋饼,摊鸡蛋〔常对折成半月形〕。*plain* ~ 清摊鸡蛋。*savoury* [*sweet*] ~ 咸味馅[果酱馅]摊鸡蛋。***You can't make an ~ without breaking eggs.*** 不打碎鸡蛋做不出摊鸡蛋;做事不可畏首畏尾。

o·men ['əumen; `omɪn] **I** ***n.*** 前兆,预兆,兆头。*an evil* [*ill*] ~ 凶兆。*a good* ~ 吉兆。*be of good* [*bad*] ~ 兆头好[不好]。**II** ***vt.***, ***vi.*** 〔诗、修辞〕预示,预告。

o·men·tal ['əumentəl; o`mɛntl] ***a.***【解】网膜的。

o·men·tum [əu'mentəm; o`mɛntəm] ***n.*** (*pl.* ***-ta*** [-tə; -tə])【解】(肠的)网膜。

o·mer ['əumə; `omɚ] ***n.*** **1.** 欧麦〔古希伯来的干量,等于十分之一的依法〕。**2.** 〔常用 O-〕〔犹太教〕从逾越节的第二天到五旬节前一天的四十九天期间。

o·mi·cron [əu'maikrən; o`mɪkrɑn] ***n.*** 希腊字母表第十五字母〔O, o〕。

om·i·nous ['ɔminəs; `ɑmənəs] ***a.*** **1.** 预兆的,预示的(*of*)。**2.** 不吉的,不祥的,兆头坏的。*an* ~ *silence* 可怕的沉默。**-ly** ***ad.*** **-ness** ***n.***

o·mis·sible [əu'misibl, -səbl; o`mɪsəbl, -sɪbl] ***a.*** 可以省去的。

o·mis·sion [əu'miʃən; o`mɪʃən] ***n.*** **1.** 省略,删节;遗漏。**2.** 疏忽;失职。**3.**【法】不作为;懈怠;不履行法律责任(*opp.* commission)。*sins of* ~ 因未做该做的事而引起的罪责,不作为罪。

o·mis·sive [əu'misiv; o`mɪsɪv] ***a.*** **1.** 略去的,遗漏的。**2.** 忽视的,失职的,怠慢的。**-ly** ***ad.***

o·mit [əu'mit; o`mɪt] ***vt.*** (***-tt-***) **1.** (有意)省去,删去,略去。**2.** (无意中)遗漏,忽略,忘记(*to do*);怠慢,疏忽,不留神。~ *an item from a list* 自目录中略去一项。~ *to lock the door* 忘记锁门。*He ~ted making his bed.* 他忘记了铺床。**-ter** ***n.***

o·mit·tance [əu'mitəns; o`mɪtəns] ***n.*** 〔古〕遗漏。

om·ma·tid·i·um [,ɔmə'tidiəm; ,ɑmə`tɪdɪəm] ***n.*** (*pl.* ***-i·a*** [-ə; -ə])【解】小眼。**-tid·i·al** ***a.***

om·mat·o·phore [ə'mætəfɔː; ə`mætəfɔr] ***n.***【动】承眼肉茎,眼柄(= eyestalk)。

Om·mi·ad, O·may·yad [əu'maiæd; o`maɪæd] ***n.*** (*pl.* ~***s***, ***-a·des*** [-ə'diːz; -ə`diz])【阿拉伯史】倭马亚朝。

om·ni- *comb. f.* 全,总,遍:*omni*bus, *omni*potent.

om·ni·bus ['ɔmnibəs; `ɑmnə,bʌs] **I** ***n.*** **1.** 公共汽车;公共马车〔略 bus〕。**2.** (接送客人用的)旅馆汽车,旅馆马车(= hotel ~)。**3.** = ~ book. **4.** 〔口〕(旅馆等的)助理服务员。*a family* [*private*] ~ (铁路公司供应旅客的)包车[专车]。**II** ***a.*** 总括的;多项的;混合的。*an* ~ *bill* 混合议案。~ **bill** 〔美〕综合议案。~ **book** (廉价普及版本的)选集[文集]。~ **box** (戏院的)合用大包厢。~ **film** 短片集锦。~ **train** 〔美〕逢站必停的列车(= accommodation train)。

om·ni·comp·e·tent [,ɔːmni'kɔmpitənt; ,ɑmnɪ`kɑmpɪtənt] ***a.***【法】有全权的。

om·ni·di·rec·tion·al [,ɔmnidi'rekʃənl; ,ɑmnɪdɪ`rɛkʃənl] ***a.***【无】全向的,无定向的。

om·ni·far·i·ous [,ɔmni'fɛəriəs; ,ɑmnə`fɛrɪəs] ***a.*** (知识等)各种各样的,五花八门的。

om·nif·ic, om·nif·i·cent [ɔm'nifik, -fisənt; ɑm`nɪfɪk, -fɪsənt] ***a.*** 创造万物的。

om·ni·par·i·ty [,ɔmni'pæriti; ,ɑmnɪ`pærɪtɪ] ***n.*** 一切平等。

om·ni·phib·i·ous [,ɔmni'fibiəs; ,ɑmnɪ`fɪbɪəs] ***a.***【空】能在任何面上(水上、雪上、冰上、地面上)降落的。

om·nip·o·tence [ɔm'nipətəns; ɑm`nɪpətns] ***n.*** 全能,万能;无限权力;无限权威;〔O-〕(全能的)上帝。

om·nip·o·tent [ɔm'nipətənt; ɑm`nɪpətənt] **I** ***a.*** 全能的;有无限权力[威力]的;〔谑〕万能的,样样都能的;真正的,彻底的。**II** ***n.*** 万能者;〔the O-〕上帝,神。**-ly** ***ad.***

om·ni·pres·ence ['ɔmni'prezəns; ,ɑmnɪ`prɛzns] ***n.*** 无所不在,普遍。

om·ni·pres·ent ['ɔmni'prezənt; ,ɑmnɪ`prɛznt] ***a.*** 无所不在的。

om·ni·range ['ɔmni,reindʒ; `ɑmnɪ,rendʒ] ***n.***【空】全向导航台。

om·nis·ci·ence [ɔm'nisiəns; ɑm`nɪʃəns] ***n.*** **1.** 无所不知,全知。**2.** 〔O-〕【宗】无所不知者,上帝。

om·nis·ci·ent [ɔm'nisiənt; ɑm`nɪʃənt] **I** ***a.*** 无所不知的,博识的。**II** ***n.*** 〔the O-〕上帝,神。**-ly** ***ad.***

om·ni·tron ['ɔmnitrɔn; `ɑmnɪtrɑn] ***n.***【原】全能加速器。

om·ni·um ['ɔmniəm; `ɑmnɪəm] ***n.***【商】担保证券的总值;〔口〕总额;全部。~**-gatherum** [-'gæðərəm; -`gæðərəm] ***n.*** 杂凑;拼凑的一群人[一批东西]。

om·ni·vor·a [ɔm'nivərə; ɑm`nɪvərə] ***n.*** 〔*pl.*〕〔集合词〕杂食动物。

om·ni·vore ['ɔmni,vɔː; `ɑmnəvɔr] ***a.*** 杂食动物的。

om·niv·o·rous [ɔm'nivərəs; ɑm`nɪvərəs] ***a.*** **1.**【动】杂食性的〔*cf.* carnivorous, herbivorous〕。**2.** 随手采取的;滥读的。*an* ~ *reader* 无书不读的人。**-ly** ***ad.*** **-ness** ***n.***

o·mo·pha·gi·a [,əumə'feidʒiə, -'feidʒə; ,omə`fedʒɪə] ***n.*** 食生肉。**-moph·a·gist** [-'mɔfədʒist; -`mɑfədʒɪst] ***n.*** 食生肉者。**-moph·agous** [-gəs; -gəs], **-mo·phag·ic** [-'fædʒik; -`fædʒɪk] ***a.***

o·mo·plate ['əuməpleit; `omə,plet] ***n.***【解】肩胛骨。

omphalo- *comb. f.* 脐:*omphalos*.

om·pha·los ['ɔmfəlɔs; `ɑmfə,lɑs] ***n.*** **1.** 〔古希腊〕盾中央的浮凸饰;(Apollo 神殿的)半圆石祭坛。**2.** 中心点,中枢。**3.**【解】脐。

om·pha·lo·skep·sis [,ɔmfələu'skepsis; ,ɑmfəlo`skɛpsɪs] ***n.*** 意守肚脐〔东方基督教神秘主义静修教派的灵修方式〕。

on [ɔn; ɑn] **I** ***prep.*** **1.** 〔支持、接触、附属〕在…上;盖着;属于,为…的成员。~ *foot* 徒步。*go* ~ *all fours* 爬

着走。*a book to be read* ～ *a railroad train*〔美〕在火车上看的书(=〔英〕in a railway train)。～ *the table* 在桌子上。*with his hat* ～ *his head* 头上戴着帽子。*turn* ～ *a pivot* 在轴上旋转。*Have you a match* ～ *you?* 你身边有火柴吗? *The dog is* ～ *the chain*. 狗拴着链子。*He is* ～ *the committee*. 他是委员之一。*Will you be* ～ *any team?* 你想参加一个队吗? **2.**〔基础、理由、原因〕依据;靠;因…,从…得来的;(费用等)由…承担〔支付〕。*act* ～ *principle* 照原则办事。～ *one's honour* 以名誉担保。*On what ground?* 凭什么理由? *live* [*feed*] ～ 靠[吃]…生活。～ *suspicion* 因嫌疑。*borrow money* ～ *jewels* 拿宝石做抵押借钱。*a profit* ～ *sales* 销售所得的利润。*This dinner is* ～ *him*. 这顿饭由他请客。**3.**〔动作的方向、对象〕(a) 向…,朝…。*throw it* ～ *the floor* 摔在地板上。*hit him* ～ *the head* 打他的头。*make an attack* ～ *the enemy* 向敌人进攻。*steal* ～ *sb*. 偷偷逼近某人。*march* ～ *London* 向伦敦前进。*turn one's back* ～ 把背掉向…,背弃,遗弃。*lay hold* [*seize*] ～... 抓住,捉住。*leave a card* ～ *a person* 留名片给某人。*The window looks* ～ *the street*. 窗户朝街。(b)〔美〕针对…。*begin a legal fight* ～ *his opponents* 跟对方打起官司来。*confer a degree* ～ *sb*. 授予某人学位。**4.** 接近…,沿…。*the inn* ～ *the road* 路旁的旅店。*It borders* ～ *absurdity*. 那是近乎荒谬的。**5.**〔日、时〕在(某日);在(某日的晨、午、夜);和…同时,刚一…。～ *Sunday* 在星期日。～ *the morning of May 5th* 在五月五日的早晨。～ *the instant* 即刻。～ *arriving home* 一到家(就)。**6.**〔后接定冠词加某些形容词的形式表示方式、状态等〕*travel* ～ *the cheap* 花很少用费旅行。～ *the quiet* 偷偷。**7.**〔方法、状态、动作〕*hear music* ～ *the radio* 用收音机听音乐。～ *guard* [*the watch*] 看守。～ *duty* 值班。～ *sale* 出售的;上市的。*be* ～ *strike* 正在罢工。*come* ～ *horseback* 骑马来。*a house* ～ *fire* 失火的房子。*go* ～ *an errand* 办差事。*go to Tainan* ～ *business* 到台南出差。～ *the move* 动着。～ *the run* 跑着。*a bird* ～ *the wing* 飞着的鸟。～ *an official visit to a country* 对某国进行正式访问。**8.**〔联系、影响〕关于…,论述…,影响到…。*speak* ～ *finance* 讲财政问题。*take notes* ～ (= *of*) *the lectures*〔美〕听讲记笔记。*a book* ～ *grammar* 语法书。*works* ～ *philosophy* 哲学论著。*The heat told* ～ *him*. 他中了暑。*It is binding* ～ *all*. 此事人人有责。**9.**〔累加〕加。*ruin* ～ *ruin* 垮台加垮台。*loss* ～ *loss* 一再损失。*heaps* ～ *heaps* 许许多多。**10.** 冒…之险。～ *pain of death* 冒生命危险。～ ***a bender***〔美俚〕喝醉;痛饮。～ ***a bust*** [*jag*]〔美俚〕酩酊大醉。～ ***ice*** **1.** 准成功的;准赢的。**2.** 在狱中。～ ***one's high horse***〔美俚〕傲慢的,架子十足的;生气的,愤慨的;冷淡的。～ ***schedule*** 按时,准时。～ ***the air*** **1.** (正在)广播。**2.**〔美俚〕瞎谈着;哭着;闹着〔*cf*. air〕。～ ***the beach***〔美俚〕失业的〔*cf*. beach〕。～ ***the beam*** 航行正确的;运行正常的;〔美俚〕对,不错。～ ***the big green carpet***〔美俚〕(囚犯)被狱官传问。～ ***the blink***〔美俚〕**1.** 破了,坏了,有毛病,情况不好的。**2.** 喝醉的。～ ***the bones of his back*** 穷到分文没有。～ ***the book***〔美〕预定好的,预约好的。～ ***the boost***〔美俚〕冒充顾客行窃。～ ***the button***〔美俚〕**1.** 准确,确切;准时,按时。**2.** 击中下颌。～ ***the crack***〔美俚〕干强盗勾当。～ ***the cuff***〔美俚〕赊欠。～ ***the cushions***〔美俚〕生活舒服,养尊处优。～ ***the dodge***〔美〕逃过法网,逃亡。～ ***the dogs***〔军俚〕在休假。～ ***the Erie***〔美俚〕耸着耳朵;警惕着。～ ***the fence***〔美俚〕骑墙派的;迟疑不决的;守中立的。～ ***the fire***〔美〕准备[计划]中(=〔英〕～ the stocks);变更中。～ ***the floor***〔美议会〕在发言中。～ ***the fly***〔美俚〕逃亡中。～ ***the I. C.***〔美〕警惕着;当心。～ ***the in***〔美〕受欢迎,名气好。～***-the-spot meetings*** 现场会议。～ ***the wagon*** 戒酒。～ ***time***〔美〕按时,及时(*arrive at a meeting* ～ *time* 及时到会)。～ ***top of the heap*** [***world***]〔美〕大大成功;名声赫赫的;一切顺利的。

II ***ad*.** **1.**〔接触、覆盖〕上去;开(*opp*. off)。*turn* ～ *the light* [*radio, water, gas*] 开电灯[收音机、自来水、煤气]。*put* [*have*] *one's coat* ～ 穿[穿着]上衣。*On with your hat!* 把帽子戴上! **2.**〔动作的方向、时间的持续〕向前;向着;进行着,继续着。*move* ～ 继续前进。*farther* ～ 再向前。*later* ～ 后来。*It is getting* ～ *for 3 o'clock*. 快三点钟,将近三点钟。

III ***a*.**〔多用作表语〕**1.** 在进行;在发生;在活动。*The debate is* ～. 辩论正在进行。*The new play is* ～. 新戏正在上演。*The radio is* ～ (*the air*). 无线电正在广播。*He is* ～ *as Hamlet*. 他扮演哈姆雷特。*It was well* ～ *in the night*. 已经夜深了。*Breakfast is* ～ *from 8 to 10*. 早餐是 8 点到 10 点。*There's nothing* ～. 没有什么事。*What's* ～? (发生)什么事? 上演什么节目? **2.** 开着,通着,点着(*opp*. off)。*Is the water* ～ *or off?* 水开着还是关着? *Gas is* ～. 煤气开着。**3.**〔美俚〕熟悉;深知(*to*)。*I am* ～ *to your little game*. 我知道你搞的什么鬼。**4.** 有点醉意。*I am a bit* ～. 我有点醉意了。***and so*** ～ 等等。***be*** ～ ***it***〔美口〕准备就绪;决定动手。***be well*** ～ 进行得宜,进行顺利;有赌赢希望。***just*** ～ 差不多。***neither off nor*** ～ 优柔寡断的,没有决断力的;未决定的;三心两意的;没有关系的(*to*)。***off and*** ～ = ～ ***and off*** 断断续续,不规则地。～ ***and*** ～ 继续,不停地,不断地。～ ***with*** 穿上;戴上;开始;继续。

IV ***n*.**【板球】(打球人的)左边(*opp*. off)。**～-again-off-again** ***a*.** 时有时无的,断断续续的;犹豫不决的;无结论的。**on-air** ***a*.** 不通过电缆传输的,频道传输的。**～-glide** 滑移〔发音时发声器官从静止状态或一个音的发音部位滑向该音所要求的部位〕。**～-line** ***a*.**【自】在线的〔指仪器、设备直接受电子计算机的操纵〕。**～-stage** ***ad*., *a*.** 在前台(的)。**～-stream** ***ad*., *a*.** 在生产中(的)。

ON, O.N. = Old Norse 古斯堪的纳维亚语,古挪威语。

on- *comb. f*.〔与动词或动名词组成名词或形容词,重音常在第一音节〕:*on*coming, *on*fall, *on*looker.

on·a·ger[ˈɔnədʒə; ˋɑnədʒə] ***n*.** (*pl*. **～s**, **-gri** [-grai; -ˏgraɪ]) **1.**【动】(中亚细亚产)野驴。**2.** 石弩,投石器〔中世纪用〕。

o·nan·ism[ˈəunənizəm; ˋonənɪzəm] ***n*.**【医】**1.** 交媾中断。**2.** 手淫。

ONC = Ordinary National Certificate〔英国发给普通煤矿技术人员的〕国家普通合格证书。

once[wʌns; wʌns] **I** ***ad*.** **1.** 一次,一趟,一回,一遍;一倍。*I should like to see him* ～ *before I go*. 在我走以前我想看他一次。～ *a year* 每年一次。*We die but* ～. 我们不过死一次罢了。*O- bit, twice shy*. 一度被咬,再见胆小。*O- nought is nought*. 零零得零。**2.** 从前,曾经。*O- I lived in London* 我从前在伦敦住过。*I* ～ *saw him playing Hamlet*. 我曾经看过他演哈姆雷特。*a* ～ *powerful nation* 曾经强盛过的国家。**3.** 一旦…。*when* ～ *he understands* 他一旦了解时。**4.** 一次也(不),无论何时也(不)〔用于否定结构〕。*I have not seen him* ～. 我一次也没见过他。***every*** ～ ***in a while***〔美〕偶尔。***if*** ～ = ***when*** ～ 一旦…(*If we* ～ *lose sight of him, we shall never set eyes on him again*. 倘若我们一旦丢了他,就再也找不着他了)。***more than*** ～ 不只一次,好多次。***not*** ～ 一次也不…。～ ***again*** = ～ *more*. ～ ***and again***〔书〕一再,再三。～ ***and away*** = ～ *for all*. ～ (***and***) ***for all*** [***always***] 一劳永逸,限此一次;断然,爽爽快快(*I shall explain it fully* ～ *for all*. 我详细解说一次以后就不再解说了。*Tell him so* ～ *for all*. 干脆就此一次把话对他说了吧)。～ ***in a way*** [***while***] 有时,间或,偶尔。～ ***more*** 再一次,再来一次。～ ***or twice*** 一两次(*not* ～ *or twice* 一再,再

三,好几次)。~ ***over*** = ~ more. ~ ***upon a time*** 从前。

II ***conj*.** 一…(便)…,一经,一旦。*O- you begin you must continue*. 一旦开始你就不可以中断了。

III ***a*.** 从前的。*my ~ master* 我从前的主人。

IV ***n*.** 一次,一回。*O- is enough for me*. 我一次就够了。***all at ~*** 忽然,突然。***and ... at ~*** 也;同时(*interesting and instructive at ~* 既有趣又有益)。***at ~*** 立刻,马上;同时(*Come at ~*. 马上来。*at ~ interesting and instructive* 既有趣又有益)。***for that ~*** 只那一次,就是那回。***for*** (***this***) ~ 这一次(特别要),就这一回(*Do it for this ~*. 就干这一次吧)。

once-over [ˈwʌnsəuvə; ˋwʌnsovɚ] ***n*.** 〔美俚〕随随便便的看一看,草草率率的检查。*give sb. the ~* 略为看望一下某人。

onc·er [ˈwʌnsə; ˋwʌnsɚ] ***n*.** 〔英口〕(为义务关系)只做一次的人;一年只到一次的人;从一而终的女子。

on·co·gene [ˈɔnkədʒiːn; ˋɑnkədʒin] ***n*.** 致癌基因。

on·co·genesis [ɔŋkəuˈdʒenisis; ɑŋkoˋdʒenəsɪs] ***n*.** (肿)瘤形成。

on·co·ge·nic·i·ty [ˌɔŋkəudʒiˈnisəti; ˏɑŋkodʒəˋnɪsətɪ] ***n*.** 肿瘤发生性,致瘤性。

on·col·o·gy [ɔŋˈkələdʒi, ɔn-; ɑŋˋkɑlədʒɪ, ɑn-] ***n*.** 【医】肿瘤学。**-log·ic** [ˌɔŋkəˈlɔdʒik; ˏɑŋkəˋlɑdʒɪk] ***a*.** **-col·o·gist** ***n*.** 肿瘤学家。

on·com·ing [ˈɔnkʌmiŋ; ˋɑnkʌmɪŋ] ***n*.**, ***a*.** 迎面而来(的);接近(的)。*the ~ of winter* 寒冬逼临。*the ~ tide* 汹涌而来的潮水。

on-dit [ɔːnˈdiː; ɔnˋdi] ***n*.** 〔F.〕(*pl*. ~***s*** [-ˈdiː; -ˋdi]) 风闻,传说,谣传。

on·do·graph [ˈɔndəgrɑːf; ˋɑndəgræf] ***n*.** 【电】高频示波器。

on·dom·e·ter [ɔnˈdɔmitə; ɑnˋdɑmətɚ] ***n*.** 【讯】波形测量器。

one [wʌn; wʌn] **I** ***num*.** **1.** (基数)一;第一〔用于表示章节、行、页等名词之后,起前置的序数的作用〕。**2.** 一个(人),一个(事物)〔用于名词前,只起数量限定作用〕。*Once ~ is ~*. 一乘一等于一。*Line ~* 第一行。*~ half* 一半。*~ or two people* 一两个人。

II ***a*.** **1.** 独一个的,单一的。*~ hand* 一只手。*~ shot* 只出一期的杂志。*O- swallow doesn't make a summer*. 孤燕不成夏。*O- man ~ vote*. 一人一票。*No ~ man can do it*. 一个人来干,是谁也干不了的。**2.** 某(一个人)。*~ Smith* 一个叫史密斯的人。*Some ~ man must direct*. 总得有一个人指挥才行。*~ day* [*morning, afternoon, evening, night*] 有一天,改天,他日,有一个[早晨,下午,傍晚,晚上]。**3.** 一方的,一头的。*from ~ side of the room to the other* 从房间一头到另一头。**4.** 〔the ~〕唯一的。*the ~ thing needful* 唯一需要的东西。*my ~ and only hope* 我的唯一希望。**5.** 一体的,一致的;同一的;不变的。*be ~ and undivided* 是不可分的一个整体;是联合一致牢不可破的。*of ~ age* 同时代的。*I am ~* [*of ~ mind*] *with you on this*. 在这点上我和你是一致的。*It is all ~ to me*. 对我都一样[怎么都行]。*remain for ever ~* 永久不变。**6.** 〔与 one, another, the other 对比〕~ *foot in sea, and ~ on shore* 一只脚在海里,一只在岸上。*If he said ~ thing, she was sure to say another*. 他无论说什么,她总是反对。*from ~ side to the other* 从一边到另一边。***become ~*** 结合一体;成夫妇(*become ~ with the people* 和人民打成一片)。***be made ~*** 一体化;结成夫妇。***For ~ thing*** (***he drinks***). 一则(举一个例来说)(他喝酒)。***in ~ word*** 一句话,一言以蔽之,总之。***on the ~ hand*** 一方面〔常与 on the other hand 连用〕。~ ***and the same thing*** 同一个东西(一件事情)。***with*** [***in***] ~ ***voice*** 异口同声。

III ***n*.** **1.** 一岁;一点钟;一个人;独一;单位;一体。*at ~ and thirty* 三十一岁时。*at ~* (*o'clock*) 在一点钟。*by ~s* 一个一个。*~-and-twenty* (= *twenty-~*) 二十一〔同样可说 *~-and-ninety*, 但在实际上大数目是很少这样说的〕。**2.** 一击。**3.** (食物)一客。**4.** 〔口〕怪人,蠢人;胆大妄为的人。*Oh! You are a ~, telling that joke in front of the priest*. 你敢在牧师前这样开玩笑,真了不起。*You're a right ~, losing the tickets again!* 又把票丢了,真没出息。**5.** 1(号);1(的记号)。(*live*) *at No. 1 in Black Street* (住)布莱克街1号。*Your 1's* [ˈwʌnz] *are like 7's*. 你写的1总是像7。***all in ~*** 一致;一人全备(*a knife, a screwdriver, and a corkscrew all in ~* 兼备旋凿[螺丝起子]和塞拔[螺旋锥]的小刀)。***at ~*** 一致,合力,协力。***by ~s and twos*** 三三两两地。***for ~*** 至少,举个例说(*I, for ~, will not go*. 拿我来说,我就不会去)。***in ~*** 结合起来,团结一致。***in ~s*** 一个一个地。***in the year ~*** 很久很久以前。***like ~-o'clock*** 〔俚〕好得很。***make ~*** 参加,使成为一体。~ ***after another*** 一个又一个地,接连地。~ ***and all*** 每个人,谁都,全都。~ ***another*** 互相。~ ***by ~*** 一个一个,挨次。~ ***of these days*** 过几天,这几天里头;总有一天。~ ***too many*** 多余的一个;〔美口〕过量的酒。***taken ~ with another*** 总的看来。***ten to ~*** 〔多用在否定句中〕一定,必定;十之八九,多半。(***the***) ~ ***... the other*** 一个是…(另)一个是…(*O- is immoral, the other is nonmoral*. 一个是不道德,另一个是无道德)。***the ~ ... the other*** 前者是…后者是〔有时相反〕。

IV ***pro*.** 〔宾[受]格 one. 所有格 one's. 反身形 oneself〕. **1.** 人;〔古〕有人。*O- who writes is called a writer*. 写作的人就叫做作家。**2.** 〔不定代名词〕我们,任何人。*O- must observe the rules*. 我们(任何人)必须遵守规则。★这一用法的 one, 尤其是在同一句中再用时,是形式说法,一般口语常说 you: 如 One [You] can't be too careful, can ~ [〔口〕 you]? 不怕过分小心,只怕力不从心。在同一句中重说 one 时,英国正规语法仍说 one [one's, oneself], 美国习惯上则改说 he [his, him, himself] 或 she [her, herself]: 如 If ~ cuts off ~'s [〔美〕 his] nose, ~ [〔美〕 he] hurts only oneself [〔美〕 himself]. **3.** 〔装腔作势的说法〕本人,人家,我。*O- is rather busy just now*. 人家现在很忙。**4.** 〔*pl*. **ones**〕东西。*Which ~* [*~s*] *do you like? — This* [*That*] *~ will do*. 你喜欢那个?——这个[那个]好。*Give me good ~*. 给我一个好的。**5.** 〔代替前面曾说及的普通名词〕*I have lost my umbrella, I think I must buy ~*. 我丢了伞,非另买一把不可了。★这一用法的 one, 其复数为 some. one 系泛指同种物,it 则是特指同一物。*I want large ~s, not small ~s*. 我要大的,不要小的。单数的 one, 其形容词前附用冠词 a(n). 代替不可数名词时,one 可略去,仅用形容词即可。如:I like red wine better than white. 我比较喜欢红葡萄酒不喜欢白的。**6.** 〔与 another, the other 对比〕一,一个;前者。*O- succeeds where another fails*. 一个成功,一个失败。*O- is black and the other is white*. 一黑一白。*the ~ ... the other* 前者,后者。***any ~*** 无论谁。***dear*** [***little, loved***] ***~s*** 可爱的孩子们。***every ~*** 每个人,谁都。***many a ~*** 好些人。***no ~*** 没人…。***some ~*** 有人,某人。***such a ~*** 那样的人,那种人,那种家伙。***the Evil*** [***Old***] ***O-*** 魔鬼。***the Holy O-*** = ***O- above*** 上帝。**~-armed bandit** 〔俚〕吃角子老虎〔一种赌具〕。**~-base hit** 〔棒〕安全进一垒 = 〔俚〕~bagger. **~-crop system** 【农】连作制。**~-eyed** ***a*.** 独眼的;眼光狭窄的。**~fold** ***a*.** 〔罕〕= single. **~-horse** ***a*.** 单马拉的;仅有一匹马的;〔美口〕极小的;有限的;简陋的;次要的。**~-hundred-percenter** 〔美俚〕= hundred-percenter. **~-idea'd, ~-ideaed** ***a*.** 坚持一种思想的,偏狭的。**~-liner** ***n*.** 简短、机警的诙谐语。**~-man** ***a*.** 只要一个人的;只关于一个人的;个人的(*an ~-man show* 个人展览

会;独角戏)。～**-night stand** 一夜的停留演出[巡回演出,演讲者等]。～**-off** *a*. 只供使用一次的;只供一人使用的;只供在一种场合使用的。～·～ *a*. 一比一的。～**-pair** *a*.〔英〕二楼的。～**-seater** 单座的飞机[汽车]。～**-shot** *a*.〔俚〕1. 只发生一次的,只出现一次的。2. 只此一个的,不是一连串之中的。～**-sided** *a*. 单方的,一边的,只一方发达的;倾向一边的;偏于一方的;片面的,不公道的,【法】片面的,单边的 (*an ～-sided street* 一边有房子的街。*an ～-sided view* 片面的看法,偏见。*It is ～-sided to regard everything either as all positive or as all negative*. 肯定一切或者否定一切,都是片面性的)。～**-stop** *a*. 单独一处地方即可提供多种服务的。～**-stop shopping** 在一个超级市场[购物中心]一次买齐所需商品。～**-time** *a*. 过去的,一度的;只发生一次的。～**-time pad** 只使用一次的密码。～**-to-**～ *a*. 一对一的。～**-track** *a*. 1. 单轨的。2. (=one-idea'd)(*an ～-track mind* 偏狭的头脑)。～**-up 1** *a*.〔口〕胜人一筹的〔常用于短语 *be ～ on ...* 胜某人一筹〕。**2** *vt*. (**-upped, -up·ping**)〔口〕胜人一筹,优于。～**-upmanship** *n*.〔口〕胜人一筹。～**-way** *a*. 1. 单程的,单行的。～*-way street* 单行道。2. 片面的,单方面的。～**worlder** 世界大同主义者。

-one *suf*.【化】表示"酮"。

O·nei·da [əuˈnaidə; oˋnaɪdə] *n*. 1. (*pl*. ～(*s*)) 奥奈达人〔美国纽约州、威斯康辛州、安大略州的印第安人〕。2. 奥奈达语。

O'Neil(l) [əuˈniːl; oˋnil] *n*. 1. 奥尼尔〔姓氏〕。2. **Eugene Gladstone** ～ 尤·奥尼尔〔1888—1953, 美国剧作家〕。

o·nei·ric [əuˈnairik; oˋnaɪrɪk] *a*. 做梦的,与做梦有关的。

o·nei·ro·crit·ic [əuˌnairəˈkritik; oˏnaɪrəˋkrɪtɪk] *n*. 圆梦者,解梦者。**-al** *a*.

o·nei·ro·man·cy [əuˈnaiərəumænsi; oˋnaɪrəˏmænsɪ] *n*. 占梦,圆梦。

one·ness [ˈwʌnnis; ˋwʌnnɪs] *n*. 1. 独一,唯一无二,独特。2. 完整,一体;统一,一致;同一。

on·er [ˈwʌnə; ˋmʌnɚ] *n*. 1.〔俚〕无比的人[物]。2.〔俚〕猛烈的一击。3.〔英俚〕大谎。4.【板球】〔口〕一分。

on·er·ous [ˈɔnərəs; ˋɑnərəs] *a*. 繁重的,麻烦的;【法】负有法律义务的。**-ly** *ad*. **-ness** *n*.

one·self [wʌnˈself; wʌnˋsɛlf] *pro*. 1.〔反身用法〕自己,自身。*To starve ～ is suicide*. 饿自己等于自杀。2.〔加强语气〕自己,自行,亲自。*To do right ～ is the great thing*. 自己行为端正才是最重要的。***absent*** ～ 缺席。***be pleased with*** ～ 自满。***by*** ～ 独自,独力。***exert*** ～ 努力。***for*** ～ 为自己;亲自,独自 (*There are somethings one can't do for ～*. 有些事情是不能独自一人做的)。***in spite of*** ～ 不知不觉地。***of*** ～ 独自,自发地。***read*** ～ ***to sleep*** 看书看睡着了。***speak to*** ～ 自言自语。***teach*** ～ 自修。

on·fall [ˈɔnfɔːl; ˋɑnˏfɔl] *n*. 攻击,袭击。

on·flow [ˈɔnfləu; ˋɑnˏflo] *n*. 奔流,洪流。

on·go·ing [ˈɔngəuiŋ; ˋɑnˏgoɪŋ] **I** *a*. 前进的,进行的。**II** *n*. 前进,发展;〔*pl*.〕(奇怪的或不适当的)处置,行动;行为,工作,事务。

on·ion [ˈʌnjən; ˋʌnjən] **I** *n*. 1.【植】洋葱;葱头;【植】葱属。2.〔俚〕(西大西洋)百慕达 (Bermuda) 岛本地。3.〔美俚〕头,脑袋;脸;棒球。*a good ～*〔美俚〕讨人欢喜的人;不讨人嫌的朋友。*spring ～* 小葱。*Welsh ～* 大葱。**II** *vt*. 用洋葱擦(眼睛)使流泪。～ **dome**〔美〕(教堂等的)洋葱形圆顶。～**-skin** 葱皮;葱皮纸。

On·ions [ˈʌnjənz; ˋʌnjənz] *n*. 1. 阿尼恩斯〔姓氏〕。2. **Charles Talbut** ～ 阿尼恩斯〔1873—1965, 英国语言学家、词典编纂家〕。

on·ion·y [ˈʌnjəni; ˋʌnjənɪ] *a*. 洋葱似的;有洋葱气味的。

on-li·cence [ˈɔnlaisəns; ˋɑnlaɪsns] *n*. (店内可供堂饮的)酒吧营业执照 (*opp*. off-licence)。

on(-)lin·er [ˈɔnlainə; ˋɔnlaɪnə] *n*. 电脑上网者,联网者,网络用户。

on·look·er [ˈɔnlukə; ˋɑnlʊkɚ] *n*. 目击者;(袖手)旁观者;观看者。

on·look·ing [ˈɔnˌlukiŋ; ˋɑnˏlukɪŋ] *n*., *a*. 旁观(的)。

on·ly [ˈəunli; ˋonlɪ] **I** *a*. 1. 唯一的。2. 无比的,独一无二的;最适当的。*an ～ child* 独生子。*This is the ～ example* [*These are the ～ examples*] *I know*. 我知道的例子只有这一个[这些]。*one's ～ hope* 某人的唯一希望。*the ～ man present* 唯一的出席者[在场的人]。*He's the ～ man for the position*. 他是最适宜那个职位的人。

II *ad*. 1. 仅仅;只,单,才;不过。2. 结果却;不料。*I can ～ guess* [*guess ～*]. 我只能推测罢了。*O- I* [*I ～*] *can guess*. 只有我能够猜得出。*O- fancy!* 想想看罢! *He came ～ yesterday*. 他是昨天才来的。*He went to the seaside ～ to be drowned*. 他去海边游泳结果却淹死了。***if*** ～ 只要…,只要…就好了 (*If ～ he would stop talking!* 只要他不讲话就好了)。***not*** ～ ... ***but*** (***also***) 不但…而且…。～ ***by ... can ...*** 只有…才能…。～ ***just*** 好容易;刚刚才;恰好 (*I have ～ just received it*. 我才收到。*I was ～ just in time*. 我刚好赶上)。～ ***not*** 简直是;跟…差不多。～ ***too*** 极,太,非常;实在;可惜(*～ too glad* 极乐意 (*to do*)。*～ too true* 千真万确)。

III *conj*. 1. 但是,可是。2.〔与 that 同用〕除了…;要不是…。*He makes good resolutions, ～ he never keeps them*. 他决心虽好,但不能持久。*I should like to go, ～ that I am ill*. 我倒很想去,可是我有病。～ ***for*** 要是没有 (*O- for my tea, I should have had the headache*. 要是不喝茶,我又会犯头痛病了)。

O. No., O/No = order number 订单号数。

ONO, o. n. o. = or near offer〔广告用语〕或依买方接近售价的出价。

on·o·man·cy [ˈɔnəumænsi; ˋɑnomænsɪ] *n*. 依姓名算命。

on·o·mas·tic [ˌɔnəuˈmæstik; ˏɑnəˋmæstɪk] *a*. 1. 姓名的,名称的。2.【法】亲笔签名的。

on·o·mas·tics [ˌɔnəuˈmæstiks; ˏɑnəˋmæstɪks] *n*.〔作单数用〕1. 专门词汇词源学。2. 人名地名研究。

on·o·mat. = onomatopoeia.

on·o·mat·o·poe·ia [ˌɔnəumˌætəuˈpi(ː)ə; ˏɑnəˏmætəˋpiə] *n*.【语】拟声,拟声(法)构词〔cuckoo 等〕;象声词;【修】拟声法。**-poe·ic, -po·et·ic** *a*. **-po·et·i·cal·ly** *ad*.

On·on·da·ga [ˌɔnənˈdɔːgə, -ˌəun-, -ˈdɑː-; ˋɑnənˋdɔgə, -ˏon-, -ˋdɑ-] *n*. 1. (*pl*. ～(*s*)) 奥内达加族人〔北美印第安人〕,奥内达加人。2. 奥内达加语。**-gan** *a*.

ONR = Office of Naval Research〔美〕海军研究局。

on-ramp [ˈɔnræmp; ˋɑnræmp] *n*. 1. (主要公路上的)驶入坡道。2.【计】(信息高速公路的)入径。

on·rush [ˈɔnrʌʃ; ˋɑnˏrʌʃ] *n*. 突击;冲锋;(水的)奔流。

on·set [ˈɔnset; ˋɑnˏsɛt] *n*. 攻击,突击;开始,动手;【医】发作;【印】静电印刷法〔通过印版和滚筒的空隙,利用静电作用使油墨涂在纸上〕。***at the very*** ～ 刚一开始。

on·shore [ˈɔnˈʃɔː; ˋɑnˏʃor] **I** *a*. 向着海岸方面的;陆上的。**II** *ad*. 向着海岸;在陆上。

on·side [ˈɔnˈsaid; ˋɑnˋsaɪd] *a*., *ad*.【足球,曲棍球】在(不犯规的)正规位置上(的)。

on·site [ˈɔnˈsait; ˋɑnˋsaɪt] *a*. 当地的。

on·slaught [ˈɔnslɔːt; ˋɑnˏslɔt] *n*. 突击,猛袭,猛攻。

Ont. = Ontario 安大略〔加拿大省名〕。

On·tar·i·an [ɔnˈtɛəriən; ɑnˋtɛrɪən] *a*., *n*. 安大略省的(人)。

On·tar·i·o [ɔnˈtɛəriəu; ɑnˋtɛrɪˏo] *n*. 1. 安大略湖〔北美洲〕(= Lake ～)。2. 安大略〔加拿大省名〕。

O

O

on·tic [ˈɔntik; ˋɑntɪk] ***a***. 实体的。

on·to [强 ˈɔntuː, 弱(元[母]音前) -tu, (辅[子]音前) -tə; 强 ˋɑntu, 弱(元音前) -tʊ, (辅[子]音前) -tə] ***prep***. 到…上。*get* ~ *a horse* 骑到马上。★ **1.** 美国一般与前置词 into 一样,作一个词处理。英国则以分写作 on to 为普遍;美国口语中可作为 on 或 to 的代用语。如:They finally got ~ (= on) the bus. The crowd got ~ (= to) the street. **2.** 须注意勿与各有独立意义的 on 和 to 相混淆,如:They drove on to the town.

on·to·gen·e·sis [ˌɔntəuˈdʒenisis; ˏɑntəˋdʒɛnɪsɪs] ***n***. = ontogeny 1。

on·tog·e·ny [ɔnˈtɔdʒəni; ɑnˋtɑdʒənɪ] ***n***. **1.**【生】个体发生[发育]。**2.** 个体发生学,胎生学。

on·tol·o·gy [ɔnˈtɔlədʒi; ɑnˋtɑlədʒɪ] ***n***.【哲】本体论,实体论。**-log·ic, -log·i·cal** ***a***. **-o·gist** ***n***. 本体论者。

o·nus [ˈəunəs; ˋonəs] ***n***.〔L.〕义务;责任;负担;重担。~ ***probandi*** 作证的义务。

on·ward [ˈɔnwəd; ˋɑnwɚd] **I** ***a***. 前进的,向前的,向上的。**II** ***ad***. = onwards.

on·wards [ˈɔnwəːdz; ˋɑnwɚdz] ***ad***. 向前,前进;在前面。***from this day*** ~从今天起。

o·ny·mous [ˈɔniməs; ˋɑnɪməs] ***a***. 有名字的;署名的。

on·yx [ˈɔniks; ˋɑnɪks] ***n***.【矿】彩纹玛瑙,缟玛瑙;石华。~ **marble** 细纹大理石。

O/o =【商】order of.

oö- *comb. f*. 卵,蛋:*oo*cyte.

OO, O.O. = Ordnance Officer 军械军官。

O.O. [ˈdʌbl ˈəu; ˋdʌbl ˋo] (= once over)〔美〕重做,检查〔又写作 double O〕。*give the O.O.*〔美俚〕看一下;检查一下。

OOB = off-off-Broadway 纽约第三戏剧界,外外百老汇戏剧〔20 世纪与百老汇及外百老汇戏剧相对抗的纽约戏剧运动〕。

o·o·cyte [ˈəuəsait; ˋoəˏsaɪt] ***n***.【胎】卵母细胞。

OOD, O.O.D. = Officer of the Deck 舰上值班军官。

oo·dles [ˈuːdls; ˋudl̩z] ***n***.〔美口〕大量,巨额 (*of money*)。

oof [uːf; uf] ***n***.〔英俚〕金钱,财富;精力,力量。~**-bird** 财主,有钱人;财源。

oof·y [ˈuːfi; ˋufɪ] ***a***.〔英俚〕富有的,有钱的。

o·og·a·mous [əuˈɔgəməs; oˋɑgəməs] ***a***.【生】异配生殖的,异配的。**-a·my** [-mi; mɪ] ***n***.

o·o·gen·e·sis [ˌəuəˈdʒenisis; ˏoəˋdʒɛnəsɪs] ***n***.【生】卵子发生。**-ge·net·ic** [-dʒiˈnetik; -dʒɪˋnɛtɪk] ***a***.

o·o·go·ni·um [ˌəuəˈgəuniəm; ˏoəˋgonɪəm] ***n***. (*pl*. ***-ni·a*** [-niə; -nɪə], ***-ums***) **1.** 卵囊。**2.**【胎】卵原细胞。

oo-la-la [uːlaːlaː; ulɑlɑ] ***a***.〔美俚〕舒服的,舒适的;有趣的,可爱的,吸引人的。

o·o·lite [ˈəuəlait; ˋoəˏlaɪt] ***n***. **1.**【地】鲕石,鲕状岩。**2.**〔O-〕英国侏罗系的上部。

o·öl·o·gy [əuˈɔlədʒi; oˋɑlədʒɪ] ***n***. 鸟卵学;蛋学。**-gist** ***n***. 鸟卵学家。

oo·long [ˈuːlɔŋ; ˋulɑŋ] ***n***. (中国)乌龙茶。

oom [uːm; om] ***n***.〔南非〕= uncle.

oo·mi·ak [ˈuːmiæk; ˋumɪæk] ***n***. (爱斯基摩人用的)木框皮舟(= umiak)。

oom·pah, oom-pah [ˈuːmˌpaː; ˋumˏpɑ] **I** ***n***.〔拟声〕翁巴〔行进中乐队的大号所发出的低沉的节奏声〕。**II** ***a***. 作翁巴声的(= oom-pah-pah)。

oomph [uːmf; umf] **I** ***n***.〔美俚〕魅力;性感;精力。*a girl with* ~ 极迷人[性感]的女子。*The book has* ~. 这本书动人极了。**II** ***a***. 极有魅力的。*an* ~ *girl* 性感女子,极迷人的女子。

oont [uːnt; unt] ***n***.〔Hind.〕骆驼。

o·o·pho·rec·to·my [ˌəuəfəˈrektəmi; ˏoəfəˋrɛktəmɪ] ***n***. (*pl*. ***-mies***)【医】卵巢切除术。

o·o·pho·ri·tis [ˌəuəfəˈraitis; ˏoəfəˋraɪtɪs] ***n***.【医】卵巢炎。

o·o·phyte [ˈəuəˌfait; ˋoəˏfaɪt] ***n***. 有藏卵器的植物的生殖器发育期。**-phyt·ic** [-ˈfitik; -ˋfɪtɪk] ***a***.

oops [uːps, ups; ups, ʊps] ***int***. 啼!〔绊足后恢复平衡时或失言后脸色恢复自然时所发出惊叹声〕(= whoops)。

o·o·sperm [ˈəuəspəːm; ˋoəˏspɚm] ***n***.〔废〕= oöspore.

o·o·sphere [ˈəuəˌsfiə; ˋoəˏsfɪə] ***n***.【植】卵球。

o·ö·spore [ˈəuəspɔː; ˋoəˏspɔr] ***n***.【植】卵胞子;受精卵;被囊合子。

o·o·the·ca [ˌəuəˈθiːkə; oəˋθikə] ***n***. (*pl*. ***-cae*** [-siː; -si])【生】卵鞘;卵囊。**-cal** ***a***.

o·o·tid [ˈəuətid; ˋoətɪd] ***n***.【生】卵子细胞。

O.O.W.【军】= Officer of the Watch 舰上机电部门值班军官。

ooze[1] [uːz; uz] **I** ***vi***. **1.** 渗出,徐徐流出,滴出,分泌。**2.** (秘密等)泄漏 (*out*); (勇气等)渐渐消失 (*away*)。**3.** 溜走。**II** ***vt***. **1.** 渗出。**2.** 泄漏(秘密等)。~ ***out***〔美俚〕偷偷溜出。~ ***with*** (*water*) 漏(水)。**III** ***n***. **1.** 渗漏,分泌;分泌物。**2.** 鞣皮用的浸液。

ooze[2] [uːz; uz] ***n***. (海底、河底的)淤泥;沼地。

oo·zy [ˈuːzi; ˋuzɪ] ***a***. (***-zi·er***; ***-zi·est***) (有)淤泥的,渗出的;滴出的,漏出的。**ooz·i·ly** ***ad***.

OP, O.P. = observation post【军】观测所。

Op = operator.

op = out of print (书刊等)已售完;已绝版。

op. = **1.** opera. **2.** operation. **3.** opposite. **4.** opus. **5.** opposite.

op- *pref*.〔用于 p 前〕= ob-.

op, Op = op art, optical art〔口〕光效应画派〔利用几何图形等以产生各种视错觉及光效应的抽象派绘画风格〕。

OPA〔美〕= Office of Price Administration〔美旧〕物价管理局。

o·pac·i·ty [əuˈpæsiti; oˋpæsətɪ] ***n***. **1.** 不透明(体),不透明部。**2.** 意义模糊;暧昧。**3.** 愚钝。**4.**【物】不透明性[度];不反光;混浊度;暗度。**5.** 愚钝的人。

o·pah [ˈəupə; ˋopə] ***n***.【动】月鱼 (*Lampris regius*)〔产于太平洋和大西洋〕。

O·pal [ˈəupəl; ˋopl̩] ***n***. 奥珀尔〔女子名〕。

o·pal [ˈəupəl; ˋopl̩] **I** ***n***.【矿】蛋白石;(半透明的)乳色玻璃;〔*pl*.〕〔英〕轧光细棉布。**II** ***a***. 乳白的。

o·pal·esce [ˌəupəˈles; ˏopəˋlɛs] ***vi***. 发乳光。**-es·cence** ***n***. 乳光。**-es·cent, -esque** ***a***. 乳色的。

o·pa·line [ˈəupəlain; ˋoplˏaɪn] **I** ***a***. 蛋白石(似)的,发乳光的。**II** [-liːn; -lin] ***n***. 乳色玻璃;细软白布。

o·pa·lize [ˈəupəlaiz; ˋopəlaɪz] ***vt***. 使成乳色。

o·paque [əuˈpeik; oˋpek] **I** ***a***. **1.** 不透明的。**2.** (对电、热等)不传导性的。**3.** 无光泽的,(颜色)晦暗的。**4.** 含糊的;迟钝的。**II** ***n***.〔the ~〕不透明,晦暗;【建】遮檐;【摄】遮光涂料。~ **projector**【无】反射型(电视)放映机。**-ly** ***ad***. **-ness** ***n***.

op·art [ˈɔpaːt; ˋɑpart] = op.

op. cit. [ˈɔpsit; ˋɑpsɪt] = *opere citato* (〔L.〕= in the work cited) 见前引书。

OPDAR = optical detection (direction) and ranging 光学定向和测距,光雷达。

ope[1] [əup; op] ***vt***., ***vi***.〔诗〕= open.

ope[2] [əup; op] ***n***.〔美俚〕= opium.

OPEC = Organization of Petroleum Exporting Countries 石油输出国组织。

op-ed page = opposite editorial page (报纸的)社论封页版,专栏版(= Op Ed)。

o·pen [ˈəupən; ˋopən] **I** ***a***. **1.** 开着的,开放的;可进入的,可分享的 (*to*); 无盖的,敞口的;敞开的;展开的;开的;开阔的,开旷的,广漠的。**2.** 公开的,公共的,出入自由的;自由的,无限制的。**3.** 宽大的,豪爽的,豁达的;易受…的 (*to*); 议论自由的,有议论余地的;未决定的;未决算的;取舍自由的,选择自由的;【军】不设防的。**4.** 坦白的,直率的;公然的,非秘密的。**5.**(商店、展览会等)开着的;(戏院)开演着的;活动着的。**6.**【语音】开口音的;末尾为母音音节的;【乐】不用指按的,开键的;空弦的。**7.** 有空的,有空隙的;(针织品)粗疏的;【印】版面疏松的。**8.**(河等)没有冰凉的;冰雪不厉害的,(天气)温和的。**9.**〔美〕无法律限制的,公许的,(赌场)不受禁止的;不征收关税[通行税等]的,(港)自由的。**10.**【医】(大便)畅通的。*an ~ window* 开着的窗子。*an ~ boat* 无甲板的船。*an ~ car* 敞篷车。*an ~ field* 空旷的田野。*an ~ road* 畅通无阻的道路。*the ~ sea* 公海。*an ~ port* 不冻港;自由港,通商口岸。*an ~ shop*〔美〕自由雇用企业〔指可自由雇用非工会会员的工厂[商店]〕。*an ~ system* 外通系统。*an ~ winter* 无冰冻的冬天。*the ~ water in arctic regions* 北极地区的不冰封海面。*leave the matter ~* 把事情搁着暂不解决。*There are three courses ~ to us*. 我们有三条路可以走。*an ~ account* 往来账户。*an ~ season* [*time*] 渔猎解禁期。*The bowels are ~*.【医】大便畅通。***be ~ to*** **1.** 易接受(*He is ~ to advice*. 他容易接受忠告)。**2.** 易受(*The city is ~ to attack*. 该市易受攻击)。**3.** 对…开着门。***be ~ with sb. about sth.*** 关于某事对某人毫无隐瞒。***in the ~ air*** 在户外[野外]。***keep an ~ door*** [***house, table***] 欢迎来客,好客。***keep one's eyes*** [***ears***] ***~*** 留心地看着[听着];保持警惕。***~ as the day*** 光明磊落,开诚布公。***throw ~ the door to*** 送机会给…,迎接…。***with an ~ hand*** 大方,慷慨。***with ~ arms*** 张着手臂,热烈(欢迎)。***with eyes ~ = with ~ eyes*** 睁着眼睛;留神;吃惊地。***with ~ hands*** = with an ~ hand. ***with ~ mouth*** **1.** 张着口,想说。**2.** 天真地。**3.** 哑然;伸长脖子(等)。

II ***n***. 〔the ~〕空地,旷场,旷野;汪洋大海;露天,户外。***be in the ~*** 是公开的。***come*** (***out***) ***into the ~*** 公开;表明心意。***in ~*** 公然。***in the ~*** 露天,在户外。

III ***vt***. **1.** 开;打开;【医】切开,割开(腹部等);开垦,开发,开辟,启发。**2.** 公开,开放;张开(翅膀),伸开,展开;【军】疏开(队列);开始;开立;开设。**3.** 泄露;揭开;表明(*to*)。**4.** 解释,说明,论。**5.**【海】(改变船位)来到看得见…的地方。**6.**【电】断(电路)。**7.** 通(便)。*~ a door* 开门。*~ a park* 开放公园。*~ a debate* 开始辩论。*We ~ed a white pagoda to the port*.【海】左舷方面看出一座白塔来了。— ***vi***. **1.** 开;张开;裂开;(花)开;(疮等)开口;变广(大);(知识等)发达;广阔地展开;(门、窗等)通向(*to*; *into*);朝,向(*on*)。**2.** 开始(*with*);(猎狗嗅出鸟兽)吠起来;〔蔑〕(人)开口,说起话来。**3.**【海】(方向变化的结果)看得见;现出;展现。**4.** 散开;翻开;开炮。*Parliament ~s today*. 议会今天开会。*The ranks ~ed*. 队伍散开了。*O- at page 12*. 请翻开第12页。***~ fire*** (***on, at***)(向…)开炮。***~ into*** [***on, onto***] …通到,通向。***~ one's eyes*** 睁眼;吃惊;使觉悟,启发。***~ out*** 开,张开,膨胀,展开;发展,发育;展现;出现;开诚布公,倾吐衷怀;【物】加速(*~ out to each other* 互相融洽起来)。***~ the door to*** 给…大开方便之门,给…造机会。***~ up***(打)开;割开;开发(资源);揭示;展现;开辟(可能性);开始;开火;开口(说话);滔滔不绝地谈;透露。***~ upon*** 朝向,俯瞰;展望。**~-air** ***a***. 户外的,野外的,露天的;爱野外的。**~-and-shut** ***a***. 容易决定的;很简单的,很明显的(*an ~-and-shut case* 一目了然的事情)。**~-armed** ***a***. 衷心的,热诚的。**~ ballot** 无记名投票。**~ bar**(婚宴等场合)免费供应饮食的酒吧。**~ bundle** 无限维管束。**~ cast coal** 露天开采的煤。**~ chain**【化】开链。**~ champion** 公开赛的优胜者。**~ championship** 公开[锦标]赛。**~ channel** 明渠。**~ cheque** 普通支票(*opp*. crossed cheque 划线支票)。**~ circuit**【电】开路。**~-circuit** ***a***.【电】开路的(尤指公开广播的电视)。**~ city** 不设防城市。**~-collar worker** "开领"工人〔指在家办公者,尤指通过电脑远距离在家办公者,他们可敞开领口不受着装拘束,故名〕。**~ competition**【运】公开比赛。**~ country** 旷野。**~ credit** 信用贷款;信用往来。**~ cut tunnel** 露天开掘的隧道。**~-date** **1.** ***n***.(食品袋等上的)包装日期,保鲜期。**2.** ***vt***. 在(包装食品)上标明包装日期[保鲜期]。**~-dated** ***a***. 无日期限制的。**~ day**〔美〕没有应酬的日子。**~ door**【外交】门户开放。**~-eared** ***a***. 倾耳静听的。**~-end** ***a***. **1.** 开发的〔指发行不限量的随时可兑换现金的股票等〕。**2.**(借款)不受限制的。**3.** = open-ended. **~-ended** ***a***. **1.**(时间、方向、数量、数学等)没有固定限度的;广泛的,无限度的,无约束的(*an ~-ended discussion* 漫谈)。**2.** 可以变更的。**3.** 随意回答的〔选择答案的问题之对〕。**~-eyed** ***a***. 睁着眼睛的,吃惊的(*~-eyed astonishment* 大惊)。**~ face** **1.** 老老实实的面孔,和蔼的面孔。**2.**(钟表)没有盖子的一面。**~-faced** ***a***. **1.** 不掩盖的。**2.** 坦率的。**~-face pie**〔美〕无上皮馅饼。**~ fire** 明火,活火。**~ forum**(关于公众关心的问题的)公开讨论。**~-handed** ***a***. 慷慨的,豪爽的。**~ heart** 坦率的胸怀。**~-hearted** ***a***. 坦白的,直率的。**~-heart surgery** 体外循环心脏手术。**~-hearth** ***a***. **1.** 平炉的。**2.** 使用平炉的。**~ house** **1.** 家庭招待会〔宾客可随意来去〕。**2.**(学校,机关等)开放参观。**~ letter** 公开信。**~ list** 船员名册。**~ market policy**【经】市场开放政策。**~ mind** 开通的头脑;谦虚。**~-mike** ***a***. 自愿者即兴表演的。**~ marriage** "开放式"婚姻〔男女双方婚后在社交和性生活方面仍如婚前一样自由的一种约定式婚姻〕。**~-minded** ***a***. 虚心的,没有偏见的。**~-mouthed** ***a***. 张大着嘴合不拢的;呆呆的,吃惊的;吵闹的;贪馋的。**~-pit** ***a***.(矿)露天采掘的。**~-pollination** ***n***. 自然传粉〔指由风媒、虫媒等传粉〕。**~ primary** 公开预选会〔选举人不需要宣布党派关系的预选会〕。**~-punctuation**(文章的)少用标点符号。**~ question** 未决问题。**~ secret** 公开的秘密。**~ sentence**【数】开句〔包含着一个或一个以上未知量的数学方程式〕。**~ sesame** 开门咒;过关咒;〔喻〕敲门砖;护照。**~ sore**〔喻〕永远的耻辱。**~ source**【计】公开源代码。**~-space** ***a***.(家居设计)不用固定墙隔开的,使用活动墙壁或家具作分隔的。**~ stock** 可以拆散零售的成套商品〔如盘碟〕。**~ warfare**【军】野战。**~work** ***n***.(薄纱、雕刻等的)透雕细工,透孔制品[织物](*~work hose* 网眼袜)。**-ness** ***n***. 开放;公开;坦白;无私;宽大。

o·pen·a·ble [ˈəupənəbl; ˋopənəbl] ***a***. 能开的。

o·pen·er [ˈəupənə; ˋopənə] ***n***. **1.** 开的人;开始者;开具;〔美〕剥蠔刀。**2.**〔*pl*.〕〔美〕泻药。*a tin ~* 开听刀。

o·pen·ing [ˈəupniŋ; ˋopənɪŋ] **I** ***n***. **1.** 开,开放;开始,着手;开端,开头;开场,开幕。**2.** 口,孔,缝,洞;空隙;通路。**3.** 空地,空场;〔美〕林间空地。**4.**(职位的)空缺;好机会(*for*)。**5.**【象棋】开局,头几着。**6.**【律】辩护人的申办书。**7.**【商】开盘,交易开始时间。**II** ***a***. 开始的。*an ~ address* [*speech*] 开幕辞。*an ~ ceremony* 开会[开学、开幕、通车]典礼。*look out for an ~* 谋事,找就业机会。**~ stock** 期初存货。**~ sales** 开张大廉价。

o·pen·ly [ˈəupənli; ˋopənlɪ] ***ad***. 公开地;老老实实地;坦白;直率。

oper. = **1.** operation. **2.** operator.

op·er·a¹ [ˈɔpərə; ˋɑpərə] ***n***. 歌剧;〔口〕歌剧院。*a comic ~* 喜歌剧。*a grand ~* 大歌剧。*a light ~* 轻歌剧。**~ cloak** 赴剧院[夜会]穿的女大衣。**~ glass(es)** 看戏用的小望远镜。**~ hat** 歌剧帽〔可折叠的高帽〕。**~ hood** 看戏[晚会]用的女头巾。**~ house** 歌剧院。**~ window** 汽车尾座门上的小窗。

op·e·ra² [ˈɔpərə; ˋɑpərə] ***n***. 〔L.〕opus 的复数。

op·er·able [ˈɔpərəbl; ˋɑpərəbl] ***a***. **1.** 可实行的,行得通的。**2.** 可施手术的,可开刀的。**-a·bil·i·ty** [ˌɔpərəˈbiliti; ˏɑpərəˋbɪlətɪ] ***n***. **-a·bly** ***ad***.

op·er·and [ˈɔpəˌrænd; ˋɑpərˏænd] ***n***.【数】运算域。

o·pe·ra se·ri·a [ˈɔpərə ˈsiəriə, It. ˈəuperɑː ˈseriɑː; ˋɑpərə ˋsɪrɪə, It. ˋoperɑ ˋseriɑ]〔It.〕悲歌剧,正歌剧。

op·er·ate [ˈɔpəreit; ˋɑpəˏret] **I** ***vi***. **1.** 操作,工作;(机械

O

等)动作;运转。2. 起作用,生影响(*on*; *upon*);见效果;(药)见效。3.【医】动手术,开刀;用泻药。4.【军】作战,采取军事行动。5.【商】操纵市场;从事投机。**II** *vt*. 1. 开动,操纵(机器等)。2.〔美〕经营,管理。3. 完成,引起(变化等)。4. 导致,决定。5. 对…动手术,对…动刀。

op·er·at·ic [ˌɔpəˈrætik; ˏɑpəˋrætɪk] *a*. 歌剧的;歌剧式的,歌剧体的。**-i·cal·ly** *ad*.

op·er·at·ing [ˈɔpəreitiŋ; ˋɑpəretɪŋ] *a*. 1. 运行的;操作的;工作的。2. 关于业务的;营业上的;关于收支的。3 外科手术的。~ *costs* 营业费;事业费;经营成本;生产费用。~ *expenses* 业务开支;营业费。~ *funds* 流动资金。~ *personnels* 管理人员。~ **income** 营业收入。~ **lever** (大炮的)尾栓开闭杆,【机】司动杆。~ **line** 工作线,操作线。~ **room** [**table**] 手术室[台]。~ **speed** [**time**] 操作速度[时间]。~ **statement** 收支报告。~ **theatre** 手术示教室。~ **wave**【物】工作波。

op·er·a·tion [ˌɔpəˈreiʃən; ˏɑpəˋreʃən] *n*. 1. 动作,行动,活动;业务,工作;作用。2. 效果,效力;有效范围,有效期间。3【工】工序;开动,运转;操作,运用;施行,实施。4.【数】运算;【医】手术;【军】〔常 *pl*.〕军事行动,作战;〔*pl*.〕【空】地面指挥所;【商】(资金的)运用;交易;投机买卖;〔美〕经营。~ *of breathing* 呼吸作用。*regulations for technical* ~*s* 技术操作规程。*directing* ~【火箭】控制程序。*the* ~ *of a machine* 机器的运转。*a capital* ~ 大手术。*four* ~*s* (算术的)四则,加减乘除。*a base of* ~*s* 作战根据地,作战基地;策源地。*a plan of* ~*s* 作战计划。*main* ~*s* 主力战。~*s on exterior* [*interior*] *lines* 外线[内线]作战。***come*** [***go***] ***into*** ~ 开始工作,开始运转;生效。***in*** ~ 活动着;运转着;施行着。***perform an*** ~ (*on sb. for a disease*) (给某人)动(外科)手术。***put into*** ~ 实施,施行。***undergo an*** ~ 受手术。~ **sheet** (机床等的)工作说明书。~**s research**〔美〕运筹学。

op·er·a·tion·al [ˌɔpəˈreiʃənl; ˏɑpəˋreʃənl] *a*. 1. (装置,系统,工艺等)工作的,运转的。2. 可以使用的,可以工作的,可以运转的。3. 正在使用的,正在工作的,正在运转的。4. 军事行动的,准备在军事行动中使用的。~ *research* 运筹学。**-ly** *ad*.

op·er·a·tion·al·ism [ˌɔpəˈreiʃənlizm; ˏɑpəˋreʃənlɪzm] *n*.【哲】操作主义(= operationism)。亦 **op·era·tion·ism, -al·ist** *n*. 操作主义者。**-al·is·tic** *a*.

op·er·a·tion·al·ize [ˌɔpəˈreiʃənlaiz; ˏɑpəˋreʃənlaɪz] *vt*. (*-ized*; *-iz·ing*) 使工作,使运转;投入生产。**-i·za·tion** [-laiˈzeiʃən; -laɪˋzeʃən] *n*.

op·er·a·tive [ˈɔpərətiv, ˈɔpəreitiv; ˋɑpəˏretɪv, ˋɑpərətɪv] **I** *a*. 1. 工作着的,操作的,运转的。2. 起作用的;有效验的,有效力的。3.【医】手术的。4 实施的;实地的。***become*** ~ 实施,起作用(*External causes become* ~ *through internal causes*. 外因通过内因而起作用)。**II** [ˈɔpərətiv; ˋɑpərətɪv] *n*. 1. 职工,工人。2.〔美〕私人侦探。

op·er·a·tize, op·er·a·tise [ˈɔpərətaiz; ˋɑpərətaɪz] *vt*. 把…编成歌剧。

op·er·a·tor [ˈɔpəreitə; ˋɑpəˏretɚ] *n*. 1. 操作者,机务员;司机,驾驶员;【军】电话兵;【电话】接线员,话务员(= telephone ~);【电报】报务员。2. (外科)施行手术者。3. 掮客,经纪人。4.【语法】功能词。5.【数】算子,算符。6. 经营者;〔美〕工厂主,资方。7. 投机商人,骗子;精明圆滑的人。8.【剧】灯光助理员。*an* ~*'s set* 话务员的电话机。*a telegraph* ~ 电报报务员。*an unitary* ~ 公正算符。*a mine* ~ 矿山经营者,矿主。

o·per·cu·lar [əuˈpəːkjulə; oˋpɝkjulɚ] *a*. 1.【植】有盖的;有蒴盖的;有囊盖的;有孔盖的。2.【动】(鱼类)有鳃盖骨的;(软体动物)有厣的;(昆虫)有盖的。

o·per·cu·late [əuˈpəːkjulit, -leit; oˋpɝkjulɪt, -let] *a*. 有盖的;有蒴盖的;有囊盖的;有孔盖的(亦作 operculated)。

o·per·cu·lum [əuˈpəːkjuləm; oˋpɝkjuləm] *n*. (*pl*. *-la* [-lə; -lə])【植】果盖;藓盖;【动】螺的厣;(鱼的)鳃盖骨;【昆】盖。

op·e·re ci·ta·to [ˈɔpəri: saiteitəu; ˋɑpəri saɪˋteto] = op. cit.

op·er·et·ta [ˌɔpəˈretə; ˏɑpəˋrɛtə] *n*. 小歌剧,轻歌剧。

o·per·on [ˈɔpəˌrɔn; ˋɑpəˏrɑn] *n*.【生】操纵子。

op·er·ose [ˈɔpərəus; ˋɑpəˏros] *a*. 费了力气的,下了工夫的;费力的;繁忙的;勤快的;用功的。

O·phel·ia [əuˈfiːljə; oˋfiljə] *n*. 1. 奥菲丽亚〔女子名〕。2. 奥菲丽亚〔莎士比亚创作《哈姆雷特》中女主人公〕。

oph·i·cleide [ˈɔfiklaid; ˋɑfɪˏklaɪd] *n*. 类似大号的旧式铜管乐器。

o·phid·i·an [ɔˈfidiən; oˋfɪdɪən] *n*., *a*. 蛇(似的)。

ophio- *comb.f*. 表示"蛇": *ophio*logy.

oph·i·ol·a·ter [ˌɔfiˈɔlətə; ˏɑfɪˋɑlətɚ] *n*. 崇拜蛇的人。

oph·i·ol·a·try [ˌɔfiˈɔlətri; ˏɑfɪˋɑlətrɪ] *n*. 蛇崇拜。

oph·i·ol·o·gy [ˌɔfiˈɔlədʒi; ˏɑfɪˋɑlədʒɪ] *n*. 蛇类学,蛇学。

O·phir [ˈəufə; ˋofɚ] *n*.【圣】俄斐〔产金地,见旧约《列王纪》〕。

o·ph·ite [ˈɔfait; ˋɑfaɪt] *n*.【地】纤闪辉绿岩。

o·phit·ic [əuˈfitik; oˋfɪtɪk] *a*.【地】辉绿岩的。

Oph·i·u·chus [ˈɔfjuːkəs, ˈəufi-; ˋɑfɪjukəs, ˋofɪ-] *n*.【天】蛇夫(星)座。

oph·thal·mia [ɔfˈθælmiə; ɑfˋθælmɪə], **oph·thal·mi·tis** [-ˈmaitis; -ˋmaɪtɪs] *n*.【医】眼炎;结膜炎。

oph·thal·mic [ɔfˈθælmik; ɑfˋθælmɪk] **I** *a*. 眼的;眼科的;眼炎的;治眼病的。**II** *n*. 眼药。*an* ~ *hospital* 眼科医院。

oph·thal·mol·o·gist [ˌɔfθælˈmɔlədʒist; ˏɑfθælˋmɑlədʒɪst] *n*. 眼科医师。

oph·thal·mol·o·gy [ˌɔfθælˈmɔlədʒi; ˏɑfθælˋmɑlədʒɪ] *n*. 眼科学,眼科医学。**-log·i·cal** *a*.

oph·thal·mo·scope [ɔfˈθælməskəup; ɑfˋθælməˏskop] *n*.【医】眼膜曲率镜。**-scop·ic** [-ˈskɔpik; -ˋskɑpɪk] *a*. **-mos·co·py** *n*.

oph·thal·mot·o·my [ˌɔfθælˈmɔtəmi; ˏɑfθælˋmɑtəmɪ] *n*.【医】眼球切开术。

o·pi·ate [ˈəupiit; ˋopɪˏet] **I** *n*. 鸦片剂,麻醉剂。**II** *a*. 〔古〕加有鸦片的,用鸦片制的,麻醉性的,催眠性的,有镇静作用的。**III** [ˈəupieit; ˋopɪˏet] *vt*. 加鸦片麻醉;使(感觉)迟钝;使缓和。**-pi·at·ic** [-ˈætik; ˏopɪˋætɪk] *a*. 鸦片剂(一样)的。

o·pine [əuˈpain; oˋpaɪn] *vt*., *vi*.〔谑〕想,认为,以为〔常用~ that...〕;发表意见。*I* ~ *that it will rain before night*. 我想天黑以前要下雨的。

o·pin·ion [əˈpinjən; əˋpɪnjən] *n*. 1. 意见;看法;见解;〔常 *pl*.〕主张。2. 舆论(= public ~);(善恶的)判断,评价。3. (专家的)鉴定;判定。*one's political* ~*s* 政(治)见(解)。*a medical* ~ 医生的意见。*a counsel's* ~ 律师的意见。***act up to one's*** ~***s*** 遵循自己的信念而行动;照自己主张行事。***a matter of*** ~ 看法不同的问题。***be of the*** ~ ***that*** ...相信,以为,认为。***get another*** ~ 征求别人意见。***have*** [***form***] ***a bad*** [***low, mean, poor, unfavourable***] ~ ***of*** (对某人或某事)评价甚低,轻视,瞧不起。***have*** [***form***] ***a good*** [***high, favourable***] ~ ***of*** (对某人或某事)有很高的评价,重视,佩服。***have another*** ~ 请别人鉴定一下。***have no*** ~ ***of*** 不大理会,不大佩服。***have the best*** ~ 请教高明的专家。***have the courage of one's*** ~***s*** 勇敢的陈述[实行]主张。***in one's*** ~ 据某人意见。***in the*** ~ ***of*** 据…的见解。***of the same*** ~ 抱同一意见。***pass on*** ~ 下结论。***win*** (***the***) ***golden*** ~***s*** 受众人尊敬。~ **book**【商】信用调查录。~ **leader** 舆论领袖,对舆论能起导向作用的人物。~ **poll** 民意测验。

o·pin·ion·at·ed [əˈpinjəneitid; əˋpɪnjənˏetɪd] *a*. 坚持己见的,不易说服的;极自负的;教条式的。*become* ~

自以为是。

o·pin·ion·ist [əˈpinjənist; əˋpɪnjənɪst] *n*. 持有特定见解的人;持有非寻常见解[异端信仰]的人。

o·pi·oid [ˈəupiːɔid; ˋopiɔɪd] *n*.【药】类鸦片,假鸦片〔一种合成药物,药效类似吗啡〕。

O Pip, o.pip. [ˈəuˈpip; ˋoˋpɪp]〔信号用文字〕〔军口〕= observation post.

op·is·o·me·ter [ˌɔpiˈsɔmitə; ˏɑpɪˋsɑmɪtɚ] *n*. (测量地图等曲线距离用的)计图器。

op·is·thog·na·thous [ˌɔpisˈθɔgnəθəs; ˏɑpɪsˋθɑgnəθəs] *a*.【动】后口的。

o·pis·tho·graph [əˈpisθəgrɑːf; əˋpɪsθəˏgræf] *n*. 两面书写的古手稿本,(正反两面刻印有文字的)古字版。

o·pi·um [ˈəupjəm, -piəm; ˋopjəm, -pɪəm] **I** *n*. 鸦片;麻醉剂;起鸦片作用的事物;【动】寄生群落。~ **den** 鸦片窟,鸦片烟馆。~ *eating* [*smoking*] 吸鸦片。~ *habit* 鸦片烟瘾。**II** *vt*. 用鸦片处理。~**-poppy** 罂粟。**O-War** 鸦片战争。

o·pi·um·ism [ˈəupjəmizəm; ˋopɪəmɪzəm] *n*. 鸦片烟瘾,鸦片中毒。

o·pi·um·ize [ˈəupjəmaiz; ˋopjəmaɪz] *vt*. 用鸦片渗透;使麻醉。

OPL = outpost line〔美〕警戒线。

OPLR = outpost line of resistance〔美〕警戒防御线。

OPM = **1.** other people's money 别人的钱。**2.** output per man 每人产量。

Opn = operation.

op·o·del·doc [ˌɔpəuˈdeldɔk; ˏɑpoˋdɛldɑk] *n*. 肥皂樟脑涂擦剂。

o·pop·a·nax [əuˈpɔpənæks; oˋpɑpəˏnæks] *n*. 苦树脂;(用以制造香料的)卡他夫没药。

O·por·to [əuˈpɔːtuː; oˋporto] *n*. 波尔图〔葡萄牙港市〕(= Porto)。

o·pos·sum [əˈpɔsəm; əˋpɑsəm] *n*.【动】鼬〔又名负鼠〕。*play* [*act*] ~〔美俚〕装死;装蒜。~ **shrimp**【动】糠虾。

opp. = **1.** opposed. **2.** opposite.

Op·pen·heim [ˈɔpənhaim; ˋɑpənˏhaɪm] *n*. 奥本海姆〔姓氏〕。

Op·pen·hei·m·er [ˈɔpənhaimər; ˋɑpənˏhaɪmɚ] *n*. **1.** 奥本海默〔姓氏〕。**2. J.R.** ~ 奥本海默〔1904—1967,美国原子物理学家,原子弹计划主持人〕。

op·pi·dan [ˈɔpidən; ˋɑpɪdən] **I** *a*.〔罕〕城市的,城里的。**II** *n*.〔罕〕城里人,市民;(英国伊顿公学的)校外寄宿生(*opp*. colleger)。

op·pi·late [ˈɔpileit; ˋɑpɪˏlet] *vt*. 使(毛孔等)阻塞;使便秘。**-la·tion** [-ˈleiʃən; -ˋleʃən] *n*.

op·po·nen·cy [əˈpəunənsi; əˋponənsɪ] *n*. 反对,对抗。

op·po·nent [əˈpəunənt; əˋponənt] **I** *a*. 对立的,对抗的,反对的。**II** *n*. **1.** 反对者,对手,敌手。**2.**【解】对抗肌。

op·por·tune [ˈɔpətjuːn, ˌɔpəˈt-; ˏɑpɚˋtjun] *a*. 凑巧的,恰好的,时机好的;及时的,合时宜的,适切的。*at* ~ *moments* 相机。**-ly** *ad*. **-ness** *n*.

op·por·tun·ism [ˈɔpətjuːnizəm; ˏɑpɚˋtjunɪzəm] *n*. 机会主义。**-ist** *n*. 机会主义者。**-is·tic** *a*.

op·por·tu·ni·ty [ˌɔpəˈtjuːniti; ˏɑpɚˋtjunətɪ] *n*. 机会,好机会;〔罕〕凑巧,方便。*a good* [*favourable*] ~ 好机会,良机。***afford*** [***find, get, give, make, miss, seize, take***] ***an*** [***the***] ~ 给[找着,得着,给,造,失去,抓住,利用]机会(*I take every* ~ *of speaking English*. 我利用一切机会讲英语)。***at the earliest*** [***at the first, on the first***] ~ 一有机会。***equality of*** ~ 机会均等。***have an*** [***no, little***] ~ ***for doing*** [***to do***] ***sth***. 有[没有]做某事的机会。***make the most of an*** ~ 尽力利用机会。

op·pos·a·ble [əˈpəuzəbl; əˋpozəbl̩] *a*. 可反对的,可反抗的;可相对的;可使对立[面对面、头对头]的。**-bil·i·ty** [əˌpəuzəˈbiliti; əˏpozəˋbɪlətɪ] *n*.

op·pose [əˈpəuz; əˋpoz] *vt*. **1.** 反对,反抗,对抗,抗议;妨碍。**2.** 使对立,使对抗;使对照,使对比;使相对,使面对面,使头对头。~ *a scheme* 反对一个计划。*He* ~*d his arms to the blow*. 他用胳臂挡住了打击。~ *violence with violence* 用暴力对付暴力。*A swamp* ~*d the advance of the army*. 沼地阻碍了军队的前进。**-r** *n*. 反对者,反抗者,对立者。

op·posed [əˈpəuzd; əˋpozd] *a*. 反对的,敌对的,对抗的;对面的,对立的;相反的。*words* ~ *in meaning* 意义相反的词儿,反语。*Black is* ~ *to white*. 黑是白之对。~ **engine**【机】对置气缸发动机。~ **pistons**【机】对动活塞。~ **landing**【军】敌前登陆。

op·pose·less [əˈpəuzlis; əˋpozlɪs] *a*.〔诗〕反对不来的;不可抵抗的;无敌的;无可反驳的。

op·po·site [ˈɔpəzit; ˋɑpəzɪt] **I** *a*. **1.** 相对的,对面的;对立的。**2.** 背对背的,面对面的(*with*);正相反的,敌对的;不相容的(*to*; *from*)。**3.**【植】对生的;(花部)重叠的。*the tree* ~ (*to*) *the house* 房子对面的树木。~ *angles*【数】对角。*the* ~ *sex* 异性。~ *number* 职务对等的人。***in the*** ~ ***direction*** [***way***] 朝相反的方向。***on the*** ~ ***side*** 在反对方面;在敌方。**II** *n*. 相反的事物[人];反语;对立面;〔口〕对面的人。*The most extreme* ~*s have some qualities in common*. 极端相反的事物间是多少有些共性的。*I thought quite the* ~. 我想的刚刚相反。**III** *ad*. 在相反的位置,在对面。*sit* ~ *to* 坐在…的对面。*play* ~ (*to*) 作对手。**IV** *prep*. 在…的对过,在…的反对地位[场所…方向]。*sit* ~ *each other* 面对面[背对背]地坐。~ **prompter**【剧】在提词人反对方面,在演员的左首〔略 o.p.〕。

op·po·si·tion [ˌɔpəˈziʃən; ˏɑpəˋzɪʃən] *n*. **1.** 反对,敌对;对抗,抵抗;对照,对立;面对,相对;反对物;妨害。**2.** 〔the ~〕〔常 O-〕(政府的)反对党,在野党。**3.**【逻】对当;对偶。**4.**【天】冲,(月的)望。*the O-* = *His Majesty's O-*〔英〕在野党。*the O- benches*〔英〕(下院)在野党席位。***break down*** ~ 打破障碍。***in*** ~ 在野(*opp*. in office)。***in*** ~ ***to*** 反对[反抗]着。***meet with*** ~ 遇到抵抗。***offer*** ~ ***to*** 反对。**-al** *a*.

op·press [əˈpres; əˋprɛs] *vt*. **1.** 压迫;压制;虐待,欺侮。**2.** 给与沉重的感觉;使意气消沉,使气馁;使无精神。**3.** 〔古〕压倒。~ *the poor* 压迫穷人。*feel* ~*ed with the heat* 热得难受。

op·pres·sion [əˈpreʃən; əˋprɛʃən] *n*. **1.** 压迫;镇压;压制;抑制;压制物;虐待。**2.** 沉闷,忧郁;苦恼,苦闷。*relieve the* ~ *of the heart* 消除心头的沉闷。*Wherever there is* ~, *there is resistance*. 哪里有压迫,那里就有反抗。

op·pres·sive [əˈpresiv; əˋprɛsɪv] *a*. **1.** 压制的,压迫的;暴虐的。**2.** 沉重的;闷热的;忧郁的。*an* ~ *ruler* 暴虐的统治者。*The air is* ~. 空气闷热。~ *heat* 闷热。**-ly** *ad*. **-ness** *n*.

op·pres·sor [əˈpresə; əˋprɛsɚ] *n*. 压迫者,暴君。

op·pro·bri·ous [əˈprəubriəs; əˋprobrɪəs] *a*. 无礼的;鄙俗的,下流的;(话等)骂人的;该骂的;可耻的。**-ly** *ad*.

op·pro·bri·um [əˈprəubriəm; əˋprobrɪəm] *n*. **1.** 臭名,耻辱。**2.** 骂詈,责骂;轻蔑。

op·pugn [ɔˈpjuːn; əˋpjun] *vt*.〔罕〕反驳;质问;反对;抗辩;攻击;抗击。**-er** *n*. 反驳者,质问者,抗击者。

op·pug·nant [əˈpʌgnənt; əˋpʌgnənt] *a*.〔罕〕敌对的,对抗性的。**-nan·cy** *n*.

O.P.S., OPS = Office of Price Stabilization〔美旧〕物价稳定局。

op·si·math [ˈɔpsimæθ; ˋɑpsəmæθ] *n*. 年老开始学习的人。

op·sim·a·thy [ɔpˈsiməθi; ɑpˋsɪməθɪ] *n*. **1.** 晚学;接受教育晚。**2.** 年长后学得的东西。

op·sin [ˈɔpsiŋ; ˋɑpsɪŋ] *n*.【生化】视蛋白。

op·son·ic [ɔpˈsɔnik; ɑpˋsɑnɪk] *a*.【细菌】调理素的。~

action 调理(素)作用。～ *reaction* 调理素反应。

op·son·i·fy [ɔpˈsɔnifai; ɑpˋsɑnəfaɪ] ***vt***. (*-fied*; *-fying*) = opsonize. **-fi·ca·tion** ***n***.

op·so·nin [ˈɔpsənin; ˋɑpsənɪn] ***n***.【细菌】调理素;助蚀菌素。

op·so·nize [ˈɔpsənaiz; ˋɑpsənaɪz] ***vt***. (*-nized*; *-nizing*)【生化】使(细菌)易受调理素的作用。**-za·tion** ***n***.

opt. = **1.** optative. **2.** optics. **3.** optician. **4.** optional.

opt [ɔpt; ɑpt] ***vi***. 选择。～ *for* 选取;赞成。～ *out* 撤退;退出;辞职。

op·ta·tive [ˈɔptətiv; ˋɑptətɪv] **I** ***a***. 表祈愿的,希求的。*the* ～ *mood*【语法】祈愿语气。**II** ***n***.【语法】祈愿语气;表示祈愿语气的动词。**-ly** ***ad***.

op·tic [ˈɔptik; ˋɑptɪk] **I** ***a***.【解】眼的;视力的;视觉的;【物】光学(上)的。**II** ***n***. **1.** 〔谑〕眼睛。**2.** (光学仪器)镜片。**3.** 〔英〕(酒馆中罩在酒瓶上的)量酒玻璃杯。*an* ～ *angle* 视角。*the* ～ *nerve*【解】视神经。～ **axis**【理】光轴。～ **disk** 盲点。

op·ti·cal [ˈɔptikəl; ˋɑptɪkḷ] ***a***. 眼的;视觉的;视力的;帮助视力的;光学(上)的。～ *activity*【物】旋光性。*an* ～ *axis* 光轴〔线〕。*an* ～ *center* 光心。*an* ～ *square* 直角转光器。*an* ～ *illusion* 光幻视。*an* ～ *radar* 光雷达。～ **art** = op. ～ **computer** 光学电子计算机[电脑]。～ **disk**【计】光盘,光碟〔可存储视频信息,并可用激光器读出〕。～ **double** (**star**) (= double star)【天】双星。～ **fibre** 光学纤维。～ **glass** 光学玻璃。～ **isomerism** 旋光异构(现象)。～ **processor**【计】光学处理机〔一种超级电脑〕。～ **tweezer** 激光镊〔一种可用于显微操作的激光器〕。**-ly** ***ad***. 光学上,用视力。

op·ti·cian [ˈɔptiʃən; ɑpˋtɪʃən] ***n***. 光学仪器商,眼镜商。

op·ti·cist [ˈɔptisist; ˋɑptɪsɪst] ***n***. 光学家。

op·tics [ˈɔptiks; ˋɑptɪks] ***n***. 〔作单数用〕光学。

op·ti·mal [ˈɔptiməl; ˋɑptəməl] ***a***. 最适宜的;最理想的;最好的 (*opp*. pessimal)。

op·time [ˈɔptimi; ˋɑptə͵mi] ***n***. 剑桥 (Cambridge) 大学数学学位考试考中第二名或第三名的学生〔前者叫 senior ～,后者叫 junior ～〕。

op·tim·ism [ˈɔptimizəm; ˋɑptə͵mɪzəm] ***n***. 乐观主义,乐观 (*opp*. pessimism)。**-ist** ***n***.

op·ti·mis·tic, -ti·cal [͵ɔptiˈmistik, -tikəl; ͵ɑptəˋmɪstɪk, ͵ɑptəˋmɪstɪkḷ] ***a***. 乐天主义的;乐观的。**-ti·cally** ***n***.

op·ti·mi·za·tion [͵ɔptimaiˈzeiʃən; ͵ɑptəmaɪˋzeʃən] ***n***. 最佳化,最优化。

op·ti·mize [ˈɔptimaiz; ˋɑptə͵maɪz] ***vi***. 持乐观态度。～ *about the future* 对未来持乐观看法,表示乐观。—***vt***. 乐观地对待[考虑];使尽可能完善,使(劳动安排,机器运转等)发挥最大的效益;使最优化,使最佳化。

op·ti·mum [ˈɔptiməm; ˋɑptəməm] **I** ***n***. (*pl*. *～s*, *-ma* [-mə; -mə])【主、生】(成长繁殖等的)最适条件,最适度。**II** ***a***. 最适宜的。*the* ～ *temperature* 最适温度。

op·tion [ˈɔpʃən; ˋɑpʃən] ***n***. 选择,取舍,选择权,选择自由;可选择的东西;【商】(在契约有效期可附加一定贴水的)选择买卖的特权。*imprisonment without the* ～ *of a fine* 不能用罚款代替的禁锢刑。*There are three* ～*s in our college*. 我们大学里有三种选科。***at one's*** ～ 任意,随意。***have no*** ～ ***but to*** (*do*) ... 除…外别无办法,只好。***leave to one's*** ～ 随人选择。***make one's*** ～ 选择。～ **card** **1.** (商店的)专用优惠信用卡。**2.**【计】信用卡式印刷电路板。～ **market** 期货市场。

op·tion·al [ˈɔpʃnəl; ˋɑpʃənḷ] **I** ***a***. 可自由选择的;随意的,任意的;非强制的 (*opp*. compulsory)。**II** ***n***. 〔美〕选修科。*It is* ～ *with you*. 悉听尊便。**-ly** ***ad***. 随意,任意,自由。

optns. = operations.

opto- *comb*. *f*. 意为"光(电子)的"或"视觉的"。

op·to·e·lec·tron·ic [͵ɔptəuilekˈtrɔnik; ͵ɑptoɪlɛkˋtrɑnɪk] ***a***. 光电子的。**-s** ***n***. 光电子学。

op·tom·e·ter [ɔpˈtɔmitə; ɑpˋtɑmətɚ] ***n***. 视力计。

op·tom·e·trist [ɔpˈtɔmitrist; ɑpˋtɑmətrɪst] ***n***. 验光配镜师。

op·tom·e·try [ɔpˈtɔmitri; ɑpˋtɑmɪtrɪ] ***n***. **1.** 视力验定(法)。**2.** 验光配镜业,验光配镜术。**-met·ric, -met·rical** ***a***.

op·to·phone [ˈɔptəufəun; ˋɑptofon] ***n***. 听音辨光器〔可变光为音,以便盲人分辨〕。

op·to·type [ˈɔptəutaip; ˋɑptə͵taɪp] ***n***.【医】试验视力字标型。

op·tron [ˈɔptrɔn; ˋɑptrɑn] ***n***. 光导发光元件。

op·u·lence [ˈɔpjuləns; ˋɑpjələns] ***n***. 富裕;丰富,丰饶。

op·u·lent [ˈɔpjulənt; ˋɑpjələnt] ***a***. 富裕的;丰富的,丰饶的;(文章等)华丽的。*an* ～ *feast* 丰盛的酒席。～ *foliage* 茂盛的树叶。

o·pun·ti·a [əuˈpʌnʃiə, -ʃə; oˋpʌnʃɪə, -ʃə] ***n***. 仙人掌属 (*Opuntia*) 植物〔包括霸王树、仙人掌〕。

o·pus [ˈəupəs, ˈɔpəs; ˋopəs, ˋɑpəs] ***n***. (*pl*. ***o·pus·es***; ***op·e·ra*** [ˈɔpərə; ˋɑpərə]) 〔L.〕**1.** (艺术)作品。**2.** 乐曲〔按乐曲发表次序编号时用,略作 op.〕。**3.** 〔美口〕广播剧,电视剧;(一部)电影。～ *magnum* = *magnum* ～ 杰作。*Beethoven op*. 47 贝多芬作曲第 47 号。

o·pus·cule [ɔˈpʌskjuːl; ɑˋpʌskjul] ***n***. (*pl*. ～*s*) 〔F.〕小作品;小曲。

o·pus·cu·lum [ɔˈpʌskjuləm; oˋpʌskjuləm] ***n***. (*pl*. ***-la*** [-lə; -lə]) 〔L.〕= opuscule.

o·quas·sa [əuˈkwæsə; oˋkwæsə] ***n***.【动】缅因红点鲑 (*Salvelinus Oquassa*)〔产于美国缅因州西部湖里〕。

or[1] [ɔː; 弱 ə; ɔr, 弱 ɚ] ***conj***. 〔表示对前后两语词或结构的选择、区别关系〕**1.** 或,或者,还是,抑或是。*white* ～ *black* 是白呢还是黑。*white* ～ *grey* ～ *black* 白的、灰的、还是黑的。*white*, *grey*, ～ *black* 白,灰或黑。*white* ～ *black*, *red* ～ *yellow*, *blue* ～ *green* 白或黑,红或黄,蓝或绿。*Shall you be there* ～ *not*? 你是否会到那里? *any Tom*, *Dick*, ～ *Harry* 随便哪个汤姆、狄克、或哈利;不论哪个张三李四。★ (1) 有 or 联系着的几个主语全为单数时,动词用单数。如:John or Tom is wanted. (2) 主语单复不一,人称不一时,动词须与其紧接之主词相一致。如:John or I am to blame. (3) 通常不宜说 Is he or we wrong? 宜说 Is he wrong, or are we? (4) 弱音的 or [ə; ɚ], 选择意义很微弱,一般常用以表示不定意义。如:two ～ [ɔː; ɔr] three miles 两英里或三英里。*two* ～ [ə; ɚ] *three miles* 两三英里。**2.** 〔表示后一语词或结构同前面的词语有同义关系;对前面的语词作进一步阐释〕即;或者说;换句话说就是。*the culinary art* ～ *art of cookery* 烹调术即烧菜法。～ *more correctly* 说得更正确一些。～ *rather* (或者)说得更正确点。**3.** 〔在否定结构中,否定的是前后两者〕甲也不,乙也不;甲和乙都不[没有]。*He cannot read* ～ *write*. 他不会读,也不会写。*Wolves* ～ *bears are never seen in that part of the country*. 在国内的那部分地区,从来没有看到狼和熊。**4.** 〔古〕〔用于句首,起转折作用〕可是;会…吗? 再说。*Or what man of you*, *if his son asks him for a loaf*, *will give him a stone*? 你们中间,谁有儿子求饼,能给他石头吗? **5.** 〔构成让步结构〕不管…还是;…也好…也好。*Rain* ～ *shine*, *I'll go*. 不管下雨还是晴天,我一定去。**6.** 〔表示不明确的情况或约数〕左右,大概;某(地等)。*more* ～ *less* 或多或少,总有一点。*two* ～ *three pounds* 两三镑。*He's ill* ～ *something* 他大概是病了,还是怎么的。**7.** 〔在祈使语气结构后,常与 else 连用,引出相反情况〕否则,要不然。*Make haste*, *or* (*else*) *you will be too late*. 赶快,不然就太晚啦。*Do it at once*, *or else*! 不立刻动手可不行呀! ***either ... or*** 或,不是…就是 (*Can he speak either English or French*? 他能说英语或法语吗? *It must be either black or white*. 那不是黑就是白)。***or***

else 不然, 否则。 ***or ... or*** 〔诗〕= either... or, whether ... or. ***or so*** 上下, 左右, 大约; 或许 (*two miles or so* 两英里上下)。 ***or what?*** 不是吗〔多用于句末以加强语气, 相当于 isn't it?〕。 ***whether ... or*** 是…还是…, 是不是, 不管 (*I don't know whether it is true or not*. 我不知道它真不真。 *Ask him whether he will come or not*. 问他来(还是)不来)。

or² [ɔː; ɔr] ***prep.***, ***conj.*** 〔古、诗〕在…之前, 比…更早〔普通用～ ever, ～ e'er〕。

or³ [ɔː; ɔr] ***n.*** 【徽】黑金色, 黑色。

-or¹ *suf*. 表示动作、状态、性质的拉丁名词词尾(英国拼作our): favor [favour], labor [labour]. ★美国对释义为基督的 Saviour 普通仍作 -our, 对 glamour 虽也原字不变, 但也逐渐有略去 u 的倾向。

-or² *suf*. 加在拉丁语系动词(尤其是词尾 -ate 的动词)后, 造成'…人[物]', 之意的名词, 代替英语原有的 -er 或两者并用; 并用时有时 -or 比较具有专门性的意义; audit*or*, elevat*or*, tail*or*, sail*or*.

Or. = Oriental.

O.R., o.r. = owner's risk 风险所有主承担。

O·ra [ˈɔurə; ˋorə] ***n.*** 奥拉〔男子名〕。

o·ra [ˈɔːrə; ˋorə] ***n.*** 〔L.〕 os²(口, 口腔; 孔穴, 通路)的复数。

or·ach, or·ache [ˈɔːrətʃ; ˋɔrətʃ] ***n.*** 滨藜属 (*Atriplex*) 植物〔尤指法国菠菜 (*A. hortensis*)〕。

or·a·cle [ˈɔrəkl; ˋɔrəkl] ***n.*** **1.** 天启, 神谕; (古希腊的)神谕宣示所。**2.**【宗】神殿; (古犹太神神殿的)至圣所。**3.** 神使, 先知, 预言者; 大智者; 〔常谑〕圣人, 哲人。**4.** 预言; 圣言, 名言; 善断, 聪明的判断。**5.** 〔*pl.*〕基督教《圣经》。*a great* ～ *on* …方面的绝对权威。～ *bone* (*inscriptions*) 甲骨(文)。***Sir O-*** 独断的人。***work the*** ～ (贿赂僧侣而)得到自己希望的天启; (用贿赂)达到自己的目的; 用手段诱人赞助使计划实现。

o·rac·u·lar [ɔˈrækjulə; ɔˋrækjələ˞] ***a.*** **1.** 天启的, 神谕的。**2.** 天启似的, 像神谕的; 暧昧的; 谜似的。**3.** 严肃的; 明智的; 预言的; 圣言的; 装做预言者的; 宣示天启的。**-ly** ***ad.*** **-i·ty** [ɔˌrækjuˈlæriti; ɔˏrækjəˋlærətɪ] ***n.***

o·rad [ˈɔːræd; ˋɔræd] ***ad.*** 向口, 向口区。

o·ral [ˈɔːrəl; ˋɔrəl] **I** ***a.*** 口头的, 口述的; 【解】口的; 口部的; 【语】口腔发声的; 【动】口的; 前的, 前面的。～ *calisthenics* 〔美〕得意话, 用来自夸的故事。*an* ～ *examination* 口试。～ *instructions* 口授指示。*the* ～ *method* 口(头教)授法。*an* ～ *offence* 〔英国〕口臭。～ *traditions* 口碑。*an* ～ *contract* 口头合约。*the* ～ *cavity* [*opening*] 口腔。～ **administration** (药品的)口服。～ **history** 口述的历史; 口述史报道。**II** ***n.*** 〔美〕口试; 口服避孕药。**-ly** ***ad.*** 口头上。

O·ran [ɔːˈrɑːn; oˋrɑn] ***n.*** **1.** 奥兰省〔阿尔及利亚一省〕。**2.** 奥兰市〔阿尔及利亚港市〕。

o·rang [ɔːˈræŋ, ə-; oˋræŋ, ə-] ***n.*** 猩猩(= orangutan)。

Or·ange [ˈɔrindʒ; ˋɔrɪndʒ] ***a.*** 【史】奥林奇派的。**-ism** ***n.*** 奥林奇派的主张和作法。**-man** ***n.*** 奥林奇派分子〔1795年北爱尔兰的一个秘密团体的成员, 支持新教〕。

or·ange [ˈɔrindʒ; ˋɔrɪndʒ] **I** ***n.*** **1.**【植】橘香橙; 橙; 柑橙类。**2.** 橙色。**3.** 〔美俚〕棒球。*the bitter* [*sour*, *Seville*] ～ 苦橙。*the horned* ～ 佛手柑。*the king* ～ 柑。*the loose skinned* ～ 橘。*the mandarin*(*e*) [*tangerine*] ～ 中国柑橘。*the mock* ～ 山梅花。*the* ～ *pekoe* (印度、锡兰产)橙香红茶。***squeeze the*** ～ 榨干, 尽取其利, 涓滴不留。***the squeezed*** ～ 已被充分利用过的东西, 无用的糟粕; 用处不大的人物。**II** ***a.*** 橘子(一样)的; 橙色的。～ **blossom** 香橙花〔新娘子戴着表示纯洁〕。～**-colo(u)red** ***a.*** 橙色的。～ **hawkweed** (= devil's paintbrush 桔黄山柳菊)。～ **paper** 橙皮书〔英国政府一个部发布的政策性文件〕。～ **peel** 橘皮, 橙皮。～ **stick** 指甲签。～ **wood** 橙木。

or·ange·ade [ˈɔrindʒˈeid; ˋɔrɪndʒˋed] ***n.*** 橘子水; 橘子汽水。

or·ange·ry [ˈɔrindʒəri; ˋɔrɪndʒrɪ] ***n.*** 橙园; 养橙温室。

o·rang-ou·tang [əˈræŋuˈtæŋ; əˋræŋuˋtæŋ], **o·rang-u·tan** [-ˈtæn; -ˋtæn] ***n.*** 【动】猩猩。

o·rate [ɔːˈreit, ɔˈr-; oˋret, ɔˋr-] ***vi.*** 〔谑〕演说, 演讲, 用演说腔调说话。

o·ra·ti·o di·rec·ta [əˈrɑːtiəu diˈrektə; əˋrɑtɪo dɪˋrektə] 〔L.〕= direct narration.

o·ra·tion [əˈreiʃən; əˋreʃən] ***n.*** **1.** 演说, 演讲。**2.**【语】引语。***make*** [***deliver***] ***an*** ～ 演说。

or·a·ti·o ob·li·qua [əˈbliːkwə; əˋblikwə] 〔L.〕= indirect narration.

or·a·tor [ˈɔrətə; ˋɔrətə˞] (*fem.* ***-tress*** [-tris; -trɪs]) ***n.*** **1.** 演说者, 演讲者; 雄辩家, 擅长演说的人; 辩护人, 拥护者。**2.**【法】原告, 请愿人。***the Public O-*** 〔英〕(Cambridge 或 Oxford 大学的)校方发言人。

or·a·to·ri·al [ˌɔrəˈtɔːriəl; ˏɔrəˋtorɪəl] ***a.*** = oratorical.

or·a·tor·i·cal [ˌɔrəˈtɔrikəl; ˏɔrəˋtɔrɪkḷ] ***a.*** 演说(家)的; 雄辩家似的; 演说[雄辩]术的; 修辞上的。*an* ～ *contest* 演讲比赛。**-ly** ***ad.*** 演说似地; 修辞学上。

or·a·to·ri·o [ˌɔrəˈtɔːriəu; ˏɔrəˋtorɪo] ***n.*** (*pl.* ～**s**) 【乐】圣乐(歌曲); (以基督教《圣经》故事为主题的)清唱剧。

or·a·to·rize, or·a·to·rise [ˈɔrətəraiz; ˋɔrətərˏaɪz] ***vi.*** = orate.

or·a·to·ry¹ [ˈɔrətəri; ˋɔrəˏtorɪ] ***n.*** 雄辩(术), 演讲(术); 修辞; 夸张的文体。

or·a·to·ry² [ˈɔrətəri; ˋɔrətorɪ] ***n.*** **1.** 祈祷室, 小礼拜堂。**2.** 〔O-〕【宗史】奥拉托利会。

orb [ɔːb; ɔrb] **I** ***n.*** **1.** 球; 天体; 地球; 〔罕〕世界。**2.** (象征王权的)宝珠。**3.** 浑一体。**4.** 〔诗〕眼球, 眼睛; 〔罕〕圈; 环; 圆; 圆面。**5.** 轨道; (星体等的)影响范围。**II** ***vt.*** **1.** 把…作成球体, 把…弄圆。**2.** 卷, 围, 包围。

orb·ed [ɔːbd, 〔诗〕ˈɔːbid; ɔrbd, 〔诗〕ˋɔrbɪd] ***a.*** **1.** 球状的, 圆的。**2.** 有眼的。**3.** 十全的; 圆满的。**4.** 被包围着的。

or·bic·u·lar [ɔːˈbikjulə; ɔrˋbɪkjələ˞] ***a.*** 球状的, 扁圆(形)的; 浑然一体的, 完整的, 圆满的; 【植】(叶子)正圆形的。*the* ～ *bone* 【解】环骨。*the* ～ *muscle* 【解】括约肌。**-i·ty** [ɔːˌbikjuˈlæriti; ɔrˏbɪkjəˋlærətɪ] ***n.*** **-ly** ***ad.***

or·bic·u·late [ɔːˈbikjulit; ɔrˋbɪkjulɪt] ***a.*** = orbicular.

or·bit [ˈɔːbit; ˋɔrbɪt] **I** ***n.*** **1.**【天】轨道; 【解】眼窝, 眶; (鸟或昆虫的)复眼缘的颊部。**2.** (人生的)旅程, 生活过程; 势力范围。**II** ***vt.*** 使(人造卫星、宇宙飞船等)进入太空轨道运行; 环绕(天体等)作轨道运行。—***vi.*** 环行; (人造装置等)沿轨道运行, 达到轨道飞行所需的速度。～ **trajectory** 【军】轨道弹道。**-er** ***n.*** (绕)轨道飞行器。

or·bit·al [ˈɔːbitl; ˋɔrbɪtəl] ***a.*** **1.**【解】眼窝的。**2.**【天】轨道的。～ **angular momentum** 【物】轨角动量。～ **velocity** (人造卫星等)沿轨道飞行所需的速度。

orc [ɔːk; ɔrk] ***n.*** 逆戟鲸。

Or·ca·di·an [ɔːˈkeidiən, -djən; ɔrˋkedɪən, -djən] ***a.***, ***n.*** (苏格兰)奥克内群岛 (Orkney Islands) 的(人)。

or·ce·in [ˈɔːsiin; ˋɔrsɪɪn] ***n.*** 【化】苔红素, 地衣红。

orch. = orchestra.

or·chard [ˈɔːtʃəd; ˋɔrtʃə˞d] ***n.*** 果园; 果园里的全部果树; 〔美俚〕棒球场。～ **grass** 鸭茅, 鸡足草。**-ist, -man** 果树栽培家; 果园经营人。

or·ches·tic [ɔːˈkestik; ɔrˋkɛstɪk] ***a.*** 舞蹈的。

or·ches·tics [ɔːˈkestiks; ɔrˋkɛstɪks] ***n.*** 舞蹈术。

or·ches·tra [ˈɔːkistrə, -kes-; ˋɔrkɪstrə, -kɛs-] ***n.*** **1.** 管弦乐; 管弦乐队; (舞台前的)乐队席; 管弦乐队的全部乐器。**2.** 〔美〕(舞台前的)正厅前排〔又叫 ～ chairs〕; (古希腊剧场中的)合唱队席; (古代罗马剧场中舞台前面的半圆形)贵人席。～ **stalls** 〔英〕正厅前排。

or·ches·tral [ɔːˈkestrəl; ɔrˋkɛstrəl] ***a.*** 管弦乐(队)的; 供管弦乐队演奏的。～ *instruments* 管弦乐器。*an* ～ *performance* 管弦乐队的演出。**-ly** ***ad.***

or·ches·trate [ˈɔːkistreit, -kes-; ˋɔrkɪsˏtret, -kɛs-] ***vt.***, *vi*. 为(管弦乐队)谱写音乐;给…配管弦乐;使合谐地结合起来。**or·chestra·tion** [-ˈtreiʃən; -ˋtreʃən] ***n***. 为管弦乐配器;和谐的安排[组织、结合]。

or·ches·tri·na [ˌɔːkisˈtriːnə; ˏɔrkesˋtrinə], **or·ches·tri·on** [ɔːˈkestriən; ɔrˋkestriən] ***n***. (发音似的管弦乐的)桶形手摇风琴。

O

orchi-, orchido- *comb. f.* 表示"睾丸"(testicle): *orchi*tis.

or·chid [ˈɔːkid; ˋɔrkɪd] ***n***. **1.**【植】(温室栽培种)兰,兰花。**2.** 淡紫色。**3.**〔*pl*.〕〔美俚〕感谢,祝贺,恭维话,贺词。*Orchids to you for your fine performance!* 恭喜你表演得出色。

or·chi·da·ceous [ˌɔːkiˈdeiʃəs; ˏɔrkɪˋdeʃəs] ***a***. 兰(科)的;兰花般的。

or·chi·dec·to·my [ˌɔːkiˈdektəmi; ˏɔrkɪˋdɛktəmɪ] ***n***.【医】睾丸切除(术)。

or·chid·ol·o·gy [ˌɔkiˈdɔlədʒi; ˏɔrkɪˋdɑlədʒɪ] ***n***.【植】兰花栽培学。

or·chid·o·ma·ni·a [ˌɔːkidəˈmeiniə; ˏɔrkɪdəˋmenɪə] ***n***. 爱兰癖。

or·chid·o·ma·ni·ac [ˌɔːkidəˈmeiniæk; ˏɔrkɪdəˋmenɪæk] ***n***. 兰迷。

or·chid·ot·o·my [ˌɔkiˈdɔtəmi; ˏɔrkɪˋdɑtəmɪ] ***n***. (*pl*. **-mies**)【医】睾丸切开术。

or·chi·ec·to·my [ˌɔːkiˈektəmi; ˏɔrkɪˋɛktəmɪ] (*pl*. **-mies**) ***n***.【医】睾丸切除(术)。

or·chil [ˈɔːtʃil; ˋɔrtʃəl] ***n***. = archil.

Or·chis [ˈɔːkis; ˋɔrkɪs] ***n***.【植】红门兰属;〔O-〕(野生)兰;红门兰。

or·chi·tis [ɔːˈkaitis; ɔrˋkaɪtɪs] ***n***.【医】睾丸炎。

or·cin [ˈɔːsin; ˋɔrsɪn] ***n***.【化】苔黑素,苔黑酚。

or·cin·ol [ˈɔːsinəul, -nɔːl; ˋɔrsɪnol, -nɔl] ***n***. = orcin.

ord. = **1.** ordained. **2.** order. **3.** ordinance. **4.** ordinary. **5.** ordnance.

or·dain [ɔːˈdein; ɔrˋden] **I** ***vt***. **1.** (命运)注定;(法律等)规定,制定,命令。**2.** 任命(牧师、圣职)。*Nature has ~ed us mortal* [*to die*]. 自然注定我们会死。*It seemed that fate had ~ed the meeting*. 这次相会好像是命中注定的。*He ~ed that the restrictions were to be lifted*. 他下令撤销各种限制。*~ a new type of government* 制订新政府体制。*be ~ed for the priesthood* 获得牧师的职位。**II** ***vi***. 任命;命令。**-er** ***n***. **-ment** ***n***.

or·deal [ɔːˈdiːl, -ˈdiːəl; ɔrˋdil, -ˋdiəl] ***n***. (古代条顿民族间实行的)神裁法;试罪法;(人格、忍耐力等的)严峻考验;苦难的经验;折磨。*pass through a terrible ~* 渡过可怕的考验。

or·der [ˈɔːdə; ˋɔrdɚ] **I** ***n***. **1.** 次序,顺序;整齐;(社会)秩序,治安;状况,常态;健康状态;条理;会场秩序;议事程序,日程;组织,体系。**2.**〔常 *pl*.〕命令;训令;指挥,号令;【计】指令。**3.** 席次;阶级,地位;等级,品级。**4.** 牧师的地位;〔*pl*.〕牧师职。**5.** 教团,修道会;(中世纪)骑士团;结社,公会。**6.**【商】定货,定单;汇兑,汇票,汇单。**7.** 勋位,勋章。**8.** 种类;种;【生】目〔介于纲和科之间〕。**9.** 规则;规定,制度,礼法;【宗】仪式,祭礼。**10.**【建】柱式,式样;【军】整队,排队;序列,队形;【数】队,级,次,度;序模;【修】布置;调配,处理。**11.**【剧】(免费)入场券,优待券。**12.**【法】(法院等的)决议(指非最后的判决)。**13.** (转让产业的)许可证,授权证明书。*in alphabetical* [*chronological, numerical*] *~* 按 ABC [年代、号码]顺序。*the old ~* 旧制度,旧理想。*the ~ of nature* [*things*] 自然[事物]的条理。*a high ~ of culture* 高度文化。*give ~s* [*an ~*] *for sth. to be done* [*that sth. should be done*] 下命令做某事。*the military ~* 军界。*all ~s and degrees of men* 一切阶级的人们。*the higher* [*lower*] *~s* 上层[下层]阶级。*a large* [*tall, strong*] *~* 大批定货;〔俚〕艰巨的工作;不当要求。*a postal* [*money,* 〔英口〕 *postoffice*] *~* 邮汇。*the O- of the Garter* 嘉德勋位,嘉德勋章。*the standing ~s* 议事规程;【军】标准作战规定。*talents of a high ~* 优秀的才能,天才。*a battle* [*close*] *~* 战斗[密集]队形。***be on ~*** 已在订购。***by ~*** 奉命令(*by ~ of the authorities* 奉当局命令)。***call a meeting to ~*** 宣布开会。***call for ~s*** 做推销员。***call to ~*** (主席)请发言人遵守会场规则;〔美〕宣布开会。***draw*** (***up***) ***in ~*** 使排整齐。***fill an ~*** 供应订货。***get out of ~*** 损坏,发生故障。***give an ~ for*** 定(货)。***in ~ of age*** [***mexit***] 按年龄[成绩]次序。***in ~*** 整整齐齐;合规则;情况正常;健康(*The goods arrived in good ~*. 货物安全到达)。***in ~ that*** 以便,为了…起见。***in ~ to*** 为要…起见,…才能。***in short ~*** 〔美〕迅速地;在短期内;〔美〕立即,马上,毫不拖延。***keep in ~*** 整理好;保持井然有序。***keep ~*** 维持秩序。***made to ~*** 定做的。***on the ~ of*** 跟…相似的;属于…同类的。***~ of group***【数】群阶。***~ of march*** 行进序列;行军命令。***O- of Merit*** 勋章〔略 O.M.〕。***~ of the day*** (议会等的)议事日程,工作日程;日常的事,习俗,风气,惯例。***~ on ~ of*** (*sculptured figures*) 一排一排的(雕像)。***O-! O-!*** 违章!违章!〔议会等中有人违反规则时向主席提出的抗议〕;秩序!秩序!〔主席等要搅乱秩序者守秩序〕。***out of ~*** 乱,混乱,杂乱无章;不合规则;情况反常;有故障;有病,不舒服。***place an ~ with*** (*a company*) ***for*** (*sth.*) 向(某公司)定(某货)。***put*** [***set, take***] ***in ~*** 整顿,整理,修整。***rise to*** (***a point of***) ***~*** (议员)起立对议会是否遵守议事规程提出质问(通常是打断他人的发言)。***take*** (***holy***) ***~s*** 接受圣职,做牧师。***take ~s from sb.*** = ***take sb.'s ~s*** 受某人的指挥。***take ~ to*** (***do***) 采取适当手段去(做…)。***take ~ with*** 安排,处理。***take things in ~*** 依次做事。***to ~*** 定做的,照规格[计划]做的。***under the ~s of*** 在…的命令下,带着…的命令。**II** ***vt***. **1.** 命令,指令;命令去…。**2.** 购;要求供应。**3.** 整理;整顿,调整;安排,处理;建立(秩序)。**4.** (命运等)注定。**5.** 任命(某人)为牧师;授给…圣职。*~ a retreat* 下令退却。*~ a taxi to take sb. to the airport* 安排出租汽车送人到机场。*~ sth.* (*to be*) *done* [*sb. to do…, that sb.* (*should*) *do ….*] 吩咐某人做某事。★可略去过去分词前的 to be 的主要是〔美〕;that 后的假设式现在时用法为〔美〕,近来〔英〕也这样说了。*He was ~ed to Egypt*. 他被派到埃及去了。*O- arms!* 〔口令〕枪放下(立正)! *~ dinner* 叫饭,定菜。*~ one's affairs* 料理私事。*~ed alloy* 有序合金。***~ about*** [***around***] 东派西使,驱使,摆布,发号施令。***~ away*** [***back***] 命令离去[返回]。***~ from*** 向…定购(*~ some new books from England* 向英国定购几本新书)。—***vi***. **1.** 发命令,吩咐。**2.** 定货。*Please ~ for me*. 请替我点菜。~ **book** 定货簿;(英国下院的)提议通告簿;【军】命令簿。~ **cheque**【商】记名支票。~ **form** [**blank**] 定单。~ **number**【物】原子序(数)。~ **port** 商船停泊以装卸货物的港口。

or·der·li·ness [ˈɔːdəlinis; ˋɔrdɚlənɪs] ***n***. 整洁;整齐;有秩序,秩序井然;守纪律。

or·der·ly [ˈɔːdəli; ˋɔrdɚlɪ] **I** ***a***. **1.** 整洁的。**2.** 有秩序的,整齐的。**3.** 有组织的,有规则的;有纪律的;守法的;安静的。**4.**【军】有关命令的,传达的,值班的。**II** ***n***. **1.**【军】传令下士,传令兵;勤务兵;通讯员;(尤指陆军医院的)卫生员,护理员。**2.**〔英〕街道清洁工,清道夫。**III** ***ad***. 依次地,顺序地;有规则地;有条理地。~ **bin**〔英〕(路旁的)废物箱。~ **book** 命令簿。~ **man**【军】传令兵。~ **officer**【军】值班军官。~ **room** (兵营内的)文书室。

or·di·nal [ˈɔːdinl; ˋɔrdnəl] **I** ***n***. **1.** 序数(词)(*opp*. cardinal)。**2.**〔O-〕【英国国教】授任仪式书;【天主】弥撒规则书。**II** ***a***. 依次的,顺序的;【生】目(order)的。~ **number** 序数。

or·di·nance [ˈɔːdinəns; ˋɔrdṇəns] *n*. 1. 法令;训令;条令,条例。2. 布告;传统的风俗习惯。3.【宗】仪式;(尤指)圣餐式;(神或命运)注定的事。*an Imperial* ~ 〔英〕敕令。

or·di·nand [ˌɔːdiˈnænd;ˏɔrdəˋnænd] *n*.【宗】圣职候选人。

or·di·na·ri·ly [ˈɔːdnərili, ˈɔːdnrili; ˋɔrdṇɛrɪlɪ, ˋɔrdnɛrɪlɪ] *ad*. 通常,普通;大概,大抵;平凡,一般。*O- he sleeps until the last possible minute*. 他通常要尽可能睡到最后一分钟才起床。*expect sb. to be* ~ *honest* 期望某人达到一般的诚实水准。

or·di·na·ry [ˈɔːdinəri, ˈɔːdnri; ˋɔrdṇˏɛrɪ, ˋɔrdnɛrɪ] **I** *a*. 1. 普通的,平常的,正常的。2. 规定的,照常的;平凡的;拙劣的。3.〔卑〕不标致的。4.【法】直辖的。***in an*** ~ ***way*** 普通,按常例。**II** *n*. 1. 普通事,常事;常例。2.〔英〕小客店的客饭;备有客饭的小客店;便饭馆;〔美〕客店(食堂);吃客饭的人。3.【宗】礼拜仪式次序书,仪式次序;【徽】普通徽〔又叫 *honourable* ~,指 *bar, bend, chevron, cross, fess, pale* 或 *saltire*〕。4. 法官;宗教法官。5.【宗】罪犯的忏悔牧师;〔the O-〕大主教;教区主教。6.〔英〕【商】普通股。7.(前轮特大后轮特小的早期)大小轮自行车。***in*** ~ 1. 常任的,直属的(*a physician in* ~ *to the king* (国王的)侍医)。2.【海】后备的。***out of the*** ~ 不寻常的,非凡的,例外的。~ **point**【数】寻常点。~ **seaman** 新水兵,见习水兵〔略 O.S.〕。~ **signalman**〔英〕三等信号兵。~ **wave**【无】正常波。

or·di·nate [ˈɔːdiənit; ˋɔrdṇet] *n*.【几】纵标,纵坐标。

or·di·na·tion [ˌɔːdiˈneiʃən;ˏɔrdṇˋeʃən] *n*. 1. 整理;排列;分数。2. 颁布法令。3. 委任;受委任。4.【宗】圣职授任,按手礼。

or·di·nee [ˌɔːdiˈniː;ˏɔrdəˋni] *n*. 新任教会执事。

ord·nance [ˈɔːdnəns; ˋɔrdnəns] *n*.〔集合词〕1. 大炮;军械;武器。2. 军用品,军需品;〔英〕军械部门;军械署。*the Royal Army O- Corps* 英国陆军军械厂。**O- Department**〔美〕兵工署,军械处。~ **factory** (炮)兵工厂。~ **map**〔英〕陆地测量部地图。~ **officer**〔美、海军〕炮术长,军械官。~ **store** 军械库。**O- Survey**〔英〕陆地测量部。

or·do [ˈɔːdəu; ˋɔrdo] *n*. (*pl*. ~*s*, *-di·nes* [-dəniːz; -dəˏniz])【天主】弥撒祷告历〔罗马天主教对每天做弥撒和祷告做出指示的日历〕。

or·don·nance [ˈɔːdənəns; ˋɔrdənəns] *n*. 1. 配置,安排〔指绘画、建筑物等说〕。2.【法】命令,法令。

Or·do·vi·cian [ˌɔːdəˈviʃən;ˏɔrdəˋvɪʃən] **I** *n*.【地】奥陶纪;奥陶系;〔the O-〕奥陶时期;奥陶纪层。**II** *a*.【地】奥陶纪[系]的。

or·dure [ˈɔːdjuə; ˋɔrdjur] *n*. 1. 粪便;肥料;脏东西;排泄物。2. 猥亵;粗卑话;下流话。

Ore. = Oregon.

ore [ɔː, ɔə; ɔr, or] *n*. 矿;矿砂,矿石;〔诗〕金属(尤指贵金属)。***be in*** ~ 含有矿物。~ **body** 矿体。~ **carrier** 矿砂运输货船。~ **deposit** 矿床。~ **dressing** 选矿。

ö·re [ˈəurə; ˋorə] *n*. (*pl*. *öre*) 1. 欧尔〔瑞典货币单位,等于 1/100 克朗〕。2. 欧尔硬币。

ø·re [ˈəurə; ˋorə] *n*. (*pl*. *ø·re*) 1. 欧尔〔丹麦或挪威货币名,等于 1/100 克朗〕。2. 欧尔硬币。

o·re·ad, O- [ˈɔːriæd; ˋorɪæd] *n*.【希神】山精,山的女神。

o·rec·tic [ɔˈrektik; oˋrɛktɪk] *a*.【哲】欲望的,愿望的;【医】食欲的,增加胃口的。

Oreg. = Oregon.

o·reg·a·no [ɔˈregənəu, ə-; əˋrɛgəno, ə-] *n*.【植】牛至(*Origanum vulgare*)〔叶子芳香,可做调料〕。

Or·e·gon [ˈɔrigən; ˋɑrɪˏgɑn] *n*. 俄勒冈〔美国州名〕。~ **boot**〔美俚〕脚镣,附有铁球的链子。~ **fir**, ~ **pine**【植】花旗松,洋松(= Douglas fir)。**-ian** *a*. 俄勒冈州(人)的。*n*. 俄勒冈州人。

o·reide [ˈɔrid; ˋorɪaɪd] *n*. = oroide.

O·res·tes [ɔˈrestiːz; oˋrɛstiz] *n*.【希神】奥列斯特〔迈锡尼亚亚加农之子,曾杀母为父报仇〕。~ **complex**【心】弑母情结〔儿子思杀其母的欲念〕。

o·rex·is [ɔˈreksis; ɔˋrɛksɪs] *n*. 1. 欲望,愿望。2.【医】食欲(= appetite)。

orf(e) [ɔːf; ɔrf] *n*.【鱼】黑色金鱼。

org. = 1. organ. 2. organic. 3. organism. 4. organization.

or·gan [ˈɔːgən; ˋɔrgən] *n*. 1.【乐】(教堂用的)管风琴(=〔美〕pipe ~);(足踏)风琴;手摇风琴;口琴。2.(生物的)器官;人类的发音器官。3. 嗓音(尤指音量;音质说)。4. 机构;机关;机关报[杂志];喉舌;报刊。5.【机】元件,机件,工具。6.〔美军〕编制(= organization)。*a government* ~ 政府机关报。*state* ~*s* 国家机构。~*s of public security* 公安机关。*internal* ~*s* 内脏。*essential* ~*s* 花的雌雄蕊。*have a fine* [*splendid*] ~ 嗓子好。~*s of generation* [*reproduction*] 生殖器。~*s of hearing* 听觉器官。~*s of smell* 嗅觉器官。~ *of speech* 发音器官。~**-builder** 风琴制造匠人。~ **grinder** (街头的)手摇风琴师。~ **loft** 教会放置管风琴的二楼;〔美〕剧场中放置景的地方。~ **pipe** 风琴管。~ **transplant** 器官移植。

or·ga·na [ˈɔːgənə; ˋɔrgənə] *n*. organon 和 organum 的复数形式。

or·gan·die, -dy [ˈɔːgændi; ˋɔrgəndɪ] **I** *n*.【纺】蝉翼纱;玻璃纱;薄棉布。**II** *a*. 蝉翼纱[玻璃纱]制的。

or·gan·elle [ˌɔːgəˈnel;ˏɔrgəˋnɛl] *n*.【生】细胞器。

or·gan·ic [ɔːˈgænik; ɔrˋgænɪk] **I** *a*. 1.【医】器官的;器质性的;有机体的;【化】有机的(*opp*. inorganic)。2. 有组织的,有系统的;有机的;结构的;建制的;根本的;生来的,固有的。*an* ~ *disease* 器官病。~ *matter* 有机物。~ *chemistry* 有机化学。*an* ~ *whole* 有机统一体。**II** *n*. 分子有机体。~ **act** [**law**]〔美〕【法】建制法;基本法。~ **artillery**【军】建制炮兵。~**-cooled** *a*.(核反应堆)用有机化合物冷却的。~ **metal** 有机金属〔具有高导电性能的一种聚合物〕。~ **reserves**【军】后备队。~ **vegetables** (不施用农药或化肥而只使用有机肥的)天然蔬菜。**-i·cal·ly** *ad*.

or·gan·i·cism [ɔːˈgænisizm; ɔrˋgænəsɪzṃ] *n*.【生】机体说。**-cist** *n*., *a*.

or·gan·ise *v*. = organize.

or·gan·ism [ˈɔːgənizəm; ˋɔrgənɪzəm] *n*. 1. 有机体;生物(体);微生物。2. 有机组织〔社会等〕;组织;结构,构造。*the social* ~ 社会。

or·gan·ist [ˈɔːgənist; ˋɔrgənɪst] *n*. 风琴演奏者;风琴手。

or·gan·iz·a·ble [ˈɔːgənaizəbl; ˋɔrgənaɪzəbḷ] *a*. 可变为生物体的;可以组织起来的。

or·gan·i·za·tion [ˌɔːgənaiˈzeiʃən;ˏɔrgənəˋzeʃən] *n*. 1. 组织,构成;编制。2. 体制,机构;【生】生物体。3. 团体,公会,协会。4.〔美〕(政党的)委员会。*peace* [*war*] ~ 平时[战时]编制。*the* ~ *of the human body* 人体的结构。***O- of American States*** 美洲国家组织。~ **man** (组织机构内)驯服的成员;(大公司内)听话的职员。**-al** *a*.

or·gan·ize [ˈɔːgənaiz; ˋɔrgənaɪz] *vt*. 1. 组织;编组;创立,创办,发起。2.(通常用被动语态)使有器官;给与…生机,使有机化。3. 使组成工会;使加入工会。4.〔口〕使(自己思想)有条理。~ *an army* 编组军队。~ *a factory* 创办工厂。*an* ~*d body* 有机体。*the* ~*d labour*〔美〕(集合词)在编工会会员。— *vi*. 组织起来,成立组织;〔美〕参加共同事业;成立工会。*the organizing committee* 创立委员会。

or·gan·iz·er [ˈɔːgənaizə; ˋɔrgənaɪzɚ] *n*. 1. 组织者;编制者;创立人,发起人;工会组织人;【生】形成体。2.〔口〕(行政人员分档存放文件等的)公文柜;(分类记事的)备忘记事簿。3.【计】整理器。~ **bag** (行政人员使用的)

公文包。

organo- *comb.f.* 表示"器官、有机等":*organo*logy.

or·ga·no·gen·e·sis [ˌɔːgənəuˈdʒenisis; ˌɔrgənoˋdʒɛnəsɪs] *n.*【生】器官发生,器官形成。**-ge·net·ic** *a.*

or·ga·no·graph·i·cal [ˈɔːgənəuˈgræfikəl; ˋɔrgənoˋgræfɪkḷ] *a.* 器官学的;器官学有关的。

or·ga·nog·ra·phy [ˌɔːgəˈnɔgrəfi; ˌɔrgəˋnɑgrəfɪ] *n.*【生】器官学。

or·ga·no·lep·tic [ˈɔːgənəuˈleptik; ˌɔrgənoˋlɛptɪk] *a.* 1. 影响(或涉及)器官(尤指味觉、嗅觉或视觉器官)的。2. 对感官刺激敏感的。

or·ga·nol·o·gy [ˌɔːgəˈnɔlədʒi; ˌɔrgəˋnɑlədʒɪ] *n.*【医】器官学。**-log·ic, -log·i·cal** *a.* **-gist** *n.* 器官学家,器官研究者。

or·ga·no·me·tal·lic [ˌɔːgənəumiˈtælik; ˌɔrgənoməˋtælɪk] *a.*【化】有机金属的,碳金属链合的。

or·ga·non [ˈɔːgənɔn; ˋɔrgənɑn] *n.* (*pl.* **or·ga·na** [-nə; -nə], ~*s*) 1. (科学研究的)原则,研究法;方法论上的原则。2. 〔O-〕《工具论》〔希腊古代哲学家亚里士多德所著〕。

or·ga·no·sil·i·con [ˌɔːgənəuˈsilikən; ˌɔrgənoˋsɪlɪkən] *n.*【化】有机硅[矽](化合物)。

or·ga·no·sol [ɔːˈgænəsɔl; ɔrˋgænəsɑl] *n.*【化】有机溶胶。

or·ga·no·ther·a·py, or·ga·no·ther·a·peu·tics [ˌɔgənəuˈθerəpi, -ˈpjutiks; ˌɔrgənoˋθɛrəpɪ, ˌɔrgənoˌθɛrəˋpjutɪks] *n.*【医】器官疗法;内脏制剂疗法。

or·ga·no·tro·pic [ˌɔːgənəuˈtrɔpik; ˌɔrgənoˋtrɑpɪk] *a.*【医】1. 向器官的。2. 亲器官的。

or·ga·num [ˈɔːgənəm; ˋɔrgənəm] *n.* (*pl.* ~*s*, **or·ga·na** [-nə; -nə]) 1. =organon. 2.【乐】奥尔加农〔9 世纪至 13 世纪初叶的一种复调音乐〕。***Novum O-***《新工具》〔英国哲学家培根的主要著作〕。

or·gan·za [ɔːˈgænzə; ɔrˋgænzə] *n.*【纺】透明硬纱。

or·gan·zine [ˈɔːgənziːn; ˋɔrgənzin] *n.*【纺】经丝。

or·gasm [ˈɔːgæzəm; ˋɔrgæzəm] **I** *n.* 1. (感情的)极端的兴奋。2.【医】情欲亢进;【生】性交高潮。**II** *vi.* 达到性交高潮。

or·gas·ma·tron [ɔːˈgæzmətrɔn; ɔˋgæzmətrɑn] *n.* 性高潮诱导器。

or·gas·tic [ˈɔːgæstik; ˋɔrgæstɪk] *a.* 极度兴奋的;情欲亢进的。

or·geat [ˈɔːʒæt; ˋɔrʒæt] *n.* 杏仁糖浆〔作为鸡尾酒的一种配料或食品的香料,不含酒精〕;杏仁橘花香茶〔一种不含酒精的清凉甜饮料〕。

or·gi·as·ti·c [ˌɔːdʒiˈæstik; ˌɔrdʒɪˋæstɪk] *a.* 有酒神节气氛的;狂饮的;狂欢的;狂乱的。

or·gie, or·gy [ˈɔːdʒi; ˋɔrdʒɪ] *n.* 1. 〔常 *pl.*〕喧闹的宴会;纵酒宴乐。2. 〔口〕狂欢;乱舞;无节制;放荡。3. 〔*pl.*〕【古希腊,罗马】(秘密举行的)酒神节。*an ~ of bloodshed* 流血大惨剧。

org-man [ˈɔːgmən; ˋɔrgmən] *n.* 〔美口〕= organization man.

-orial *suf.* 〔构成形容词〕表示"…的","属于…的": profess*orial*, purgat*orial*.

Ori·ana [ɔriˈɑːnə; ɔrɪˋɑnə] *n.* 奥里阿娜〔女子名〕。

or·i·bi [ˈɔːribi; ˋɔrɪbɪ] *n.*【动】侏羚 (*Ourebia ourebia*) 〔产于非洲〕。

o·rie-eyed [ˈɔːriaid; ˋɔrɪaɪd] *a.* 〔美〕醉眼朦胧的。

o·riel(window) [ˈɔːriəl; ˋorɪəl] *n.*【建】凸肚窗。

o·ri·ent [ˈɔːriənt; ˋorɪənt] **I** *a.* 1. 〔诗〕东方的;东洋的。2. (太阳等)上升的;新生的。3. 光辉灿烂的;(珍珠等)光耀的。**II** *n.* 1. 〔the O-〕东方 (*opp.* occident); 亚洲;东亚、东洋;远东。2. 〔诗〕东方,东天。3. 东方产的优质珍珠;珍珠的光泽。**III** [ˈɔːrient; ˋorɪɛnt] *vt.* 1. 使(建筑物等)向东方;以东方做标准定…的位置;定…的方位;【化】使定向。2. 把(脚)向东摆,朝西摆(尸体);坐东朝西盖(教堂)。3. 摆正(地图、磁石等的)方向;〔喻〕究明(事物)的真象,正确地判断;(按照已知的事实或原则)修正;使适应(新环境)。~ *oneself* 决定自己的方针,表明态度。—*vi.* 面向东;适应形势。

o·ri·en·tal [ɔ(ː)riˈentl; ˌorɪˋɛntḷ] **I** *a.* 1. 〔O-〕东,东方的,(尤指)远东的;从东方来的,东方国家的;东方人特有的;东方式的(*opp.* occidental)。2. (珠宝等)最优质的;贵重的;有特殊光泽的;华美的。**II** *n.* 〔O-〕东亚人,东方人〔尤指中国人、日本人〕。**O- emerald** 绿玉。**O- poppy**【植】近东罂粟 (*Papaver orientale*)。**O- rug [carpet]** 东方地毯。**O- shagreen** 人造鲨鱼皮。**-ly** *ad.*

O·ri·en·tal·ism [ˌɔ(ː)riˈentəlizəm; ˌorɪˋɛntḷˌɪzəm] *n.* 1. 东方风格;东方风俗[习惯]。2. 东方知识,东方学;东方文化研究。**-ist** *n.* 1. 东方人。2. 东方通,东方学专家,东方文化研究者。

O·ri·en·tal·ize [ˌɔriˈentəlaiz; ˌorɪˋɛntḷaɪz] *vt., vi.* (使)东方化,(使)具有东方特征。

o·ri·en·tate [ˈɔːrienteit; ˋorɪɛntet] *vt.* = orient.

o·ri·en·ta·tion [ˌɔ(ː)rienˈteiʃən; ˌorɪɛnˋteʃən] *n.* 1. 向东,(礼拜时)东向;置于东端。2. (房屋等)方向;找出东方;定位,定向;取向,排列方向。3. (外交等的)方针[态度]的确定;(对周围环境等的)倾向性。4.【动】(鸽等的)回家本能;(对新环境的)适应。*a firm and correct political ~* 坚定正确的政治方向。*radio range ~* 无线电定向。

o·ri·en·teer·ing [ˌɔːrienˈtiəriŋ; ˌorɪənˋtɪrɪŋ] *n.* 越野识图比赛。

or·i·fice [ˈɔrifis; ˋɔrəfɪs] *n.* (管子等的)口,孔,锐孔,【化纤】喷丝孔。

or·i·flamme [ˈɔriflæm; ˋɔrəflæm] *n.* (古时法国的)红色王旗;(王室等的)军旗;勇气和忠诚的表征;党的标记。

orig. = 1. origin. 2. original. 3. originally.

o·ri·ga·mi [ˌɔːriˈgɑːmi; ˌɔrəˋgɑmɪ] *n.* 〔Jap.〕1. (日本传统的)折纸手工〔用纸折成花、动物等〕。2. 折纸手工品。

or·i·gan [ˈɔrigən; ˋɑrɪgən], **o·rig·a·num** [ɔˈrigənəm; ɑˋrɪgənəm] *n.*【植】牛至属植物。

or·i·gin [ˈɔridʒin; ˋɔrədʒɪn] *n.* 1. 开始,发端;根源,起源;起因,由来。2. 出身,来历;血统。3.【数】原点;起点;【解】(筋、神经的)起端。*He is a Dane by ~.* 他原籍丹麦。*He comes of Scottish ~.* 他的祖先是苏格兰人。*country of ~* 原产地。*of worker and peasant ~* 工农出身的。

o·rig·i·nal [əˈridʒənəl; əˋrɪdʒənḷ] **I** *a.* 1. 原始的,固有的,本来的;最初的,初期的。2. 原物的,原本的,原文的,原图的。3. 独创的,创造性的,别出心裁的;新颖的;崭新的,新奇的;古怪的。*an ~ bill* 原案。*an ~ edition* 原版。*one's ~ domicile* 原籍。*What does the ~ Greek say?* 希腊原文是怎么讲的? *Few plots of plays are entirely ~.* 完全独出心裁的戏剧结构很少见。**II** *n.* 1. 原物,原型,雏型,模型;原文,原作;〔罕〕起源。2. 有独创性的人。3. 怪人。***in the ~*** 用原文[原书]。~ **print** (作者自画自刻自印的)创作版画。~ **gum** 邮票背面原有的胶质。~ **house**【法】(女子的)娘家。~ **sin**【宗】原罪。

o·rig·i·nal·i·ty [ˌəridʒiˈnæliti; əˌrɪdʒəˋnælətɪ] *n.* 1. 独创性,创造力;创见;创举;独出心裁;新颖。2. 怪人;珍品。3. 原物,本物。

o·rig·i·nal·ly [əˈridʒənəli; əˋrɪdʒənḷɪ] *ad.* 1. 本来,原来;第一,最初。2. 独创地,独出心裁地。*a plant ~ African* 原产非洲的植物。*a house ~ small* 原来就小的房子。

o·rig·i·nate [əˈridʒineit; əˋrɪdʒənet] *vt.* 1. 发起;引起。2. 创办,创设;创作,创始;发明。—*vi.* 开始,发生〔起始于某事或某地多用 *from* 或 *in*; 起始于某人多用 *from* 或 *with*〕。*What ~d the Great War?* 大战的原因是什么? 大战是怎样引起的? *All genuine knowledge ~s* *in direct experience*. 一切真知都是从直接经验发源的。**-na·tion** [-ˈneiʃən; -ˋneʃən] ***n***. 开始;创作;草创;发明;起点,起因。**-na·tive** ***a***. 独创的;有创作力的;新奇的。**-na·tor** ***n***. 创作者,创设者,创办人,发起人。

Or(r)in [ˈɔrin; ˋɑrɪn] ***n***. 奥林〔姓氏,男子名〕。

o·ri·na·sal [ˌɔːriˈneizl; ˏorɪˋnezl] **I** ***a***. 【语】鼻化元〔母〕音的。**II** ***n***. 鼻化母音。

ORINS = Oak Ridge Institute of Nuclear Studies 〔美〕橡树岭原子核研究所。

o·ri·ole [ˈɔːriəul; ˋorɪˏol] ***n***. 【鸟】(欧洲)金莺;黄鹂。

O·ri·on [əˈraiən; oˋraɪən] ***n***. 【天】猎户座;【希、罗神】奥利安〔健美的猎人〕。~ *'s Belt* 猎户座的带纹三明星。~ *'s Hound* 天狼星。

or·ison [ˈɔrizən; ˋɔrɪzn̩] ***n***. 〔古、诗〕〔常 *pl*.〕祈祷。

ork [ɔːk; ɔk] ***n***. 〔美口〕= orchestra.

Or·lan·do [ɔːˈlændəu; ɔrˋlændo] ***n***. 奥兰多〔男子名 Rol(l)and 的异体〕。

orle [ɔːl; ɔl] ***n***. 【徽】盾的内边,沿着盾章的外缘。

Or·le·ans [ɔːˈliənz, ˈɔːl-; ˋɔrlɪənz, ˋɔrl-] ***n***. **1**. 奥尔良〔法国中部城市〕。**2**. (法国)奥尔良李子。**3**. 奥尔良棉毛混纺衣料。

Or·lon [ˈɔːlɔn; ˋɔrlən] **I** ***n***. 奥纶〔聚丙烯腈短纤维的商标名称〕。**II** ***n***. 〔o-〕奥纶纤维。

or·lop [ˈɔːlɔp; ˋɔrlɑp] ***n***. 最下层甲板。

Or·mazd [ˈɔːməzd; ˋɔrməzd] ***n***. 【祆教】最高的神,创世主,善灵。

or·mer [ˈɔːmə; ˋɔrmɚ] ***n***. 〔英方〕鲍鱼(= abalone)。

or·mo·lu [ˈɔːməluː; ˋɔrməˏlu] ***n***. **1**. 镀金用的金箔〔铜、锌、锡的合金〕,金色黄铜;金箔颜料。**2**. 镀金物。

Ormsby [ˈɔːmzbi; ˋɔrmzbɪ] ***n***. 奥姆斯比〔姓氏〕。

Orn = 【化】ornithin(e).

orn., **ornith.**, **ornithol.** = **1**. ornithology. **2**. ornithologic(al). **3**. ornithologist.

or·na·ment [ˈɔːnəmənt; ˋɔrnəmənt] **I** ***n***. **1**. 装饰,修饰;装饰物〔品〕。**2**. 增添光彩的人〔物、行为〕;勋章。**3**. 〔常 *pl*.〕礼拜用品。**4**. 装饰用家具。**5**. 【乐】装饰音。*a tower rich in* ~ 富于装饰的塔。*by way of* ~ 当作装饰。*personal* ~ (珠宝等)装饰品。*He was an* ~ *to his country*. 他是为国增光的人物。**II** [ˈɔːnəment; ˋɔrnəment] ***vt***. 装饰;美化。

or·na·men·tal [ˌɔːnəˈmentl; ˏɔrnəˋmɛntl̩] **I** ***a***. 装饰的;作装饰用的;增加风致〔光彩〕的。*an* ~ *plantation* 风致林。~ *writing* 装饰性的书写文字。**II** ***n***. **1**. 〔*pl*.〕装饰物。**2**. 观赏植物。**-ist** ***n***. 装饰家,设计家。**-ize** ***vt***. 装饰。**-ly** ***ad***. 装饰着,作为装饰。

or·na·men·ta·tion [ˌɔːnəmenˈteiʃən; ˏɔrnəmɛnˋteʃən] ***n***. 装饰,修饰;装饰术;〔集合词〕装饰品。

or·nate [ɔːˈneit, ˈɔːneit; ɔrˋnet, ˋɔrnet] ***a***. 装饰的,华美的;修辞上极考究的;(文体)华丽的;矫揉造作的。**-ly** ***ad***. **-ness** ***n***.

or·ner·y [ˈɔːnəri; ˋɔrnərɪ] ***a***. 〔美口〕**1**. 低劣的;卑劣的,品行坏的。**2**. 脾气坏的;爱争吵的。**3**. 平凡的;一般的。**-i·ness** ***n***.

or·nis [ˈɔːnis; ˋɔrnɪs] ***n***. 地方鸟类;地方鸟类志(= avifauna)。

ornith- 〔母音前〕, **ornitho-** *comb. f*. 表示"鸟": *ornith*oid.

or·nith·ic [ɔˈniθik; ɔrˋnɪθɪk] ***a***. 鸟的,有鸟的特征的。

or·ni·thin(e) [ˈɔːniθiːn; ˋɔrnɪˏθin] ***n***. 【生、化】鸟氨酸。

or·ni·thoid [ˈɔːniθɔid; ˋɔrnəˏθɔɪd] ***a***. 外形似鸟的,结构似鸟的。

or·ni·tho·log·ic, **or·ni·tho·log·i·cal** [ˌɔːniθəˈlɔdʒik, -kəl; ˏɔrnɪθəˋlɑdʒɪk, -kəl] ***a***. 鸟(类)学的,禽学的。

or·ni·thol·o·gist [ˌɔːniˈθɔlədʒist; ˏɔrnɪˋθɑlədʒɪst] ***n***. 鸟(类)学家,禽学家。

or·ni·thol·o·gy [ˌɔːniˈθɔlədʒi, -nai-; ˏɔrnəˋθɑlədʒɪ, -naɪ] ***n***. 鸟(类)学,禽学;鸟学论文〔著作〕。

or·ni·tho·pod [ˈɔːniθəpɔd, ɔːˈniθə-; ˋɔrnɪθəpɑd, ɔrˋnɪθə-] ***n***. 鸟脚亚目(*Ornithopoda*)动物。

or·ni·thop·ter [ˌɔːniˈθɔptə; ˏɔrnɪˋθɑptɚ] ***n***. 扑翼(飞)机(= orthopter)。

Or·ni·tho·rhyn·chus [ˌɔːniθəˈriŋkəs; ˏɔrnɪθəˋrɪŋkəs] ***n***. 【动】鸭獭属嘴兽,〔o-〕鸭嘴兽(= duckbill)。

or·ni·tho·sis [ˌɔːniˈθəusis; ˏɔrnəˋθosɪs] ***n***. 鸟传病毒病〔如鹦鹉热〕。

ORNL = Oak Ridge National Laboratory 〔美〕橡树岭国立实验室。

oro-[1] *comb. f*. 表示"山": *oro*geny.

oro-[2] *comb. f*. 表示"口": *oro*pharynx.

o·rog·e·ny [ɔːˈrɔdʒini; ɔrˋrɑdʒənɪ] ***n***. 【地】造山运动,造山作用。亦 **-gen·e·sis** [-ˈdʒenisis; -ˋdʒɛnəsɪs], **-gen·ic**, **-net·ic** ***a***.

or·o·graph·ic, **-i·cal** [ˌɔrəˈgræfik, -ikəl; ˏɔrəˋgræfɪk, -ɪkəl] ***a***. 山志的,山形的。*a* ~ *factor* 地形因素。~ **fault** 【地】山形断层。

o·rog·ra·phy [ɔˈrɔgrəfi; əˋrɑgrəfɪ] ***n***. 山志学,山岳形态学。

o·ro·ide [ˈɔːrəuid; ˋoroˏaɪd] ***n***. 铜、锡、锌等金色合金。

o·rol·o·gy [ɔˈrɔlədʒi; oˋrɑlədʒɪ] ***n***. 山理学;山岳成因学。

o·rom·e·ter [ɔˈrɔmitə; ɔˋrɑmətɚ] ***n***. 山岳气压计,山岳高度计。

o·ro·tund [ˈɔ(ː)rəutʌnd; ˋorəˏtʌnd] ***a***. (声音)朗朗的;(说话、文章等)浮夸的,做作的。

or·phan [ˈɔːfən; ˋɔrfən] **I** ***n***., ***a***. 孤儿(的),没有父母(或其中之一)的(孩子)。**II** ***vt***. 〔常用被动语态〕使成孤儿。*an* ~ *asylum* 孤儿院。*an* ~ *child* 孤儿。*children* ~*ed by the war* 战争造成的孤儿。**-age** ***n***. 孤儿院;孤儿身份〔状态〕;〔集合词〕孤儿。**-hood** ***n***. 孤儿的身份〔状态〕;(集体的)孤儿。~ **court** 〔美〕孤儿法庭。

or·phan·ize [ˈɔːfənaiz; ˋɔrfənaɪz] ***vt***. 使成孤儿。

Or·phe·an [ɔːˈfi(ː)ən; ɔrˋfiən] ***a***. 〔诗〕(希腊神话中竖琴名家)俄耳甫斯的;美好的;好听的,令人神往的,迷人的。

Or·phe·us [ˈɔːfjuːs; ˋɔrfjus] ***n***. 【希神】俄耳甫斯〔竖琴名家〕。

Or·phic [ˈɔːfik; ˋɔrfɪk] ***a***. **1**. = Orphean. **2**. 崇拜酒神的神秘教的。**3**. 〔或 o-〕神秘的。

Or·phism [ˈɔːfizm; ˋɔrfɪzəm] ***n***. 俄耳甫斯教仪〔据说是由希腊神话中的歌手俄耳甫斯创立的一种宗教和礼仪〕。

or·phrey [ˈɔːfri; ˋɔrfrɪ] ***n***. **1**. 法衣上的绣带。**2**. 精致的刺绣,精致的刺绣品。

or·pi·ment [ˈɔːpimənt; ˋɔrpɪmənt] ***n***. 【矿】雄黄,三硫化二砷。

or·pin(e) [ˈɔːpin; ˋɔrpɪn] ***n***. 【植】紫花景天。

Or·ping·ton [ˈɔːpiŋtən; ˋɔrpɪŋtən] ***n***. (英国)奥尔平顿种大鸡。

or·rer·y [ˈɔrəri; ˋɔrərɪ] ***n***. 太阳系仪。

or·ris[1] [ˈɔris; ˋɔrɪs] ***n***. 金〔银〕花边;金〔银〕刺绣。

or·ris[2] [ˈɔris; ˋɔrɪs] ***n***. 【植】**1**. 白花鸢尾,香鸢尾,菖蒲。**2**. 菖蒲根,香根鸢尾(= orrisroot)。

ort [ɔːt; ɔrt] ***n***. **1**. 〔方、古〕〔常 *pl*.〕残羹剩饭。**2**. 废品。

or·thi·con [ˈɔːθikɔn; ˋɔrθɪˏkɑn], **or·thi·con·o·scope** [ɔːθiˈkɔnɔskəup; ɔrθɪˋkɑnɑskop] ***n***. 【电视】正析(摄)像管。

orth(o)- *comb. f*. 表示"正,直;原,邻(位);正形": *ortho*chromatic; *ortho*hombic; *ortho*diazine; *ortho*paedics.

or·tho·ax·is [ˌɔːθəuˈæksis; ˏɔrθəˋæksɪs] ***n***. 【数】正轴。

or·tho·caine [ˈɔːθəukein; ˋɔrθoken] ***n***. 【药】原卡因。

or·tho·ce·phal·ic [ˌɔːθəusiˈfælik; ˏɔrθosɪˋfælɪk] ***a***. 有着高度为长度的 70.1—75% 的头颅的(= orthocephalous)。**-ceph·aly** ***n***.

or·tho·chro·ma·tic [ˌɔːθəukrəuˈmætik; ˏɔrθəkrəˋmætɪk] ***a***. 【像】正色的,现天然色的浓淡的。~ *film*

正色胶卷。

or·tho·clase [ˈɔːθəukleis; ˋɔrθəkles] ***n***. 【矿】正长石。

or·tho·di·a·zine [ˌɔːθəuˈdaiəziːn; ˏɔrθoˋdaɪəzin] ***n***. 【化】哒嗪;邻二氮苯。

or·tho·dome [ˈɔːθəudəum; ˋɔrθodom] ***n***. 【物】正轴坡面。

O

or·tho·don·tia [ˈɔːθəuˈdɔnʃiə; ˏɔrθəˋdɑnʃə] ***n***. 【医】正牙学;畸齿校整术。

or·tho·don·tics [ˌɔːθəuˈdɔntiks; ˏɔrθəˋdɑntɪks] ***n***. 〔动词用单数〕【医】正牙学(= orthodontia)。**-don·tic** ***a***. **-don·tist** ***n***. 正牙医师。

or·tho·dox [ˈɔːθədɔks; ˋɔrθəˏdɑks] ***a***. **1**. 奉正教的;正统派的;〔O-〕正教会的,希腊教会的。**2**. (尤指神学上)一般认为正当的,正统的;传统的,习俗的;习惯上的;保守的;常有的,平常的。*the O- Church* 希腊教会、东正教会。*an ~ pair of lovers* 通常的一对爱人。*~ party* 正统派。***in the ~ manner*** 正式。~ **scanning**【电】正则扫描。~ **sleep**【医】无梦睡眠。**-ly** ***ad***.

or·tho·dox·y [ˌɔːθəˈdɔksi; ˋɔrθəˏdɑksɪ] ***n***. 正教,信奉正教;正统性;正统派的观念[学说、做法等];服从一般说法。*discard the classics and rebel against ~* 离经叛道。

or·tho·e·py [ˈɔːθəuepi; ɔrˋθoɪpɪ] ***n***. 正音学;正音法;标准发音。**-ëp·ic, -i·cal** ***a***. **-ëp·ist** ***n***. 正音学者。

or·tho·gen·e·sis [ˌɔːθəuˈdʒenisis; ˏɔrθoˋdʒɛnəsɪs] ***n***. 【生】直(向)演(化);直生现象;直生论。

or·thog·na·thous [ɔːˈθɔgnəθəs; ɔrˋθɑgnəθəs] ***a***. 正颌的。**-na·thism** ***n***. 【解】正颌〔面部侧影近于垂直〕。

or·thog·o·nal [ɔːˈθɔgənl; ɔrˋθɑgənl] ***a***. **1**. 直角的,互相垂直的;正交的;直交的。**2**. (统计数字)互不相关的。*an ~ section* 正(交)剖面。

or·tho·grade [ˈɔːθəgreid; ˋɔrθəgred] ***a***. 【动】直立行走的。

or·tho·graph [ˈɔθəgrɑːf; ˋɔrθəgræf] ***n***. 正投影图;正视图。

or·thog·ra·pher, or·thog·ra·ph·ist [ɔːˈθɔgrəfə, -fist; ɔrˋθɑgrəfɚ, -fɪst] ***n***. 正字学家。

or·tho·graph·ic, -i·cal [ˌɔːθəˈgræfik, -ikəl; ˏɔrθəˋgræfɪk, -ɪkəl] ***a***. 正字法的;缀字正确的;【几】直线的,直角的;用直线投射的,用直线画的。*an ~ projection* 【几】正投影。**-i·cal·ly** ***ad***.

or·thog·ra·phy [ɔːˈθɔgrəfi; ɔrˋθɑgrəfɪ] ***n***. 正字法;缀字法;表音法;【建】面图投影;【数】正交射影。

or·tho·pae·dic, -pe·dic [ˌɔːθəuˈpiːdik; ˏɔrθəˋpidɪk] ***a***. 【医】矫形的。*an ~ hospital* [*surgeon*] 矫形医院[医师]。*~ treatment* 矫形手术。

or·tho·pae·dics [ˌɔːθəuˈpiːdiks; ˏɔrθəˋpidɪks] ***n***. 矫形学。

or·tho·pae·dy, or·tho·pe·dy [ˈɔːθəupiːdi; ˋɔrθəˏpidɪ] ***n***. 【医】矫正术,矫形术;矫形学。

or·tho·phos·phate [ˌɔːθəuˈfɔsfeit; ˏɔrθoˋfɑsfet] ***n***. 【化】正磷酸盐。

or·tho·phos·phor·ic [ˌɔːθəufɔsˈfɔːrik; ˏɔrθofɑsˋfɔrɪk] 【化】正磷酸的。*~ acid* 正磷酸。

or·tho·psy·chi·a·try [ˌɔːθəusaiˈkaiətri; ˏɔrθosaɪˋkaɪətrɪ] ***n***. 精神卫生学,行为精神病学。**-at·ric** ***a***., **-a·trist** ***n***. 精神卫生学家。

or·thop·ter [ɔːˈθɔptə; ɔrˋθɑptɚ] ***n***. 扑翼(飞)机。

Or·thop·ter·a [ɔːˈθɔptərə; ɔrˋθɑptərə] ***n***. 〔*pl*.〕【动】直翅目。

or·thop·ter·an [ɔːˈθɔptərən; ɔrˋθɑptərən] ***n***. 【动】直翅目(*Orthoptera*)动物〔包括蟋蟀、蚱蜢、蝗虫、蝉等〕。

or·thop·ter·ous [ɔːˈθɔptərəs; ɔrˋθɑptərəs] ***a***. 【动】直翅类的。

or·thop·tic [ɔːˈθɔptik; ɔrˋθɑptɪk] ***a***. 【医】矫正视轴的,矫正斜眼的〔尤指通过强化眼肌的活动〕。

or·tho·rhom·bic [ˌɔːθəuˈrɔmbik; ˏɔrθəˋrɑmbɪk] ***a***. 【物】斜方(晶)的,正交(晶)的。

or·tho·scope [ˈɔːθəuˌskəup; ˋɔrθəˏskop] ***n***. 【医】水层检眼镜。

or·tho·scop·ic [ˌɔːθəuˈskɔpik; ˏɔrθəˋskɑpɪk] ***a***. 准确显像的。

or·tho·stat·ic [ˌɔːθəuˈstætik; ˏɔrθəˋstætɪk] ***a***. 正立位置的,由正立位置引起的。*~ hypotension* 正立位血压过低。

or·thos·ti·chy [ɔːˈθɔstiki; ɔrˋθɑstɪkɪ] ***n***. (*pl*. ***-chies***) 【植】直列线。**-ti·chous** ***a***.

or·tho·tro·pic [ˌɔːθəuˈtrɔpik; ˏɔrθəˋtrɑpɪk] ***a***. **1**. 【道】支架桥面合一的〔指一种桥设计,支架结构同时也是桥面或路面〕。**2**. 【植】直生的。

or·thot·ro·pism [ɔːˈθɔtrəpizm; ɔrˋθɑtrəpɪzm̩] ***n***. 【植】直生性。

or·thot·ro·pous [ɔːˈθɔtrəpəs; ɔrˋθɑtrəpəs] ***a***. 【植】直生的〔指胚珠及其种脐、珠孔在一直线上〕。

or·to·lan [ˈɔːtələn; ˋɔrtələn] ***n***. 【鸟】蒿雀类;〔美〕食米鸟;圃鹀。

O·ru·ro [Sp. əuˈruːrəu; Sp. oˋruro] ***n***. 奥鲁罗〔玻利维亚省、省会〕。

Or·ville [ˈɔːvil; ˋɔrvɪl] ***n***. 奥维尔〔姓氏,男子名〕。

-ory[1] *suf*. 〔缀于名词、动词后构成形容词〕表示"…性质的,像…的":declamat*ory*, preparat*ory*, prefat*ory*.

-ory[2] *suf*. 表示"…所,…的地方":dormit*ory*, fact*ory*, laborat*ory*.

or·yx [ˈɔriks; ˋɔrɪks] ***n***. (*pl*. ~ *es*, 〔集合词〕~)【动】(非洲)大羚羊。

O.S., OS = **1**. old school 〔总称〕守旧派。**2**. Old Style 西洋旧历。**3**. ordinary seaman (英国海军)新水兵。**4**. Old Saxon 古撒克逊语。**5**. old series (刊物等的)旧期(号、卷)。**6**. outsize 超过普通尺寸的,特大的。**7**. out of stock 脱销。

OS = operating system 【计】操作系统。

Os 【化】osmium.

o/s = out of stock 已脱销。

os[1] [ɔs; ɑs] ***n***. 〔L.〕(*pl*. ***os·sa*** [-ə; -ə])【解、动】骨。

os[2] ***n***. 〔L.〕(*pl*. ***o·ra*** [ˈɔːrə; ˋɔrə])【解】口,口腔;孔穴;通路。

os- *pref*. 〔用于 c, t 之前〕= ob-.

O·sage [əuˈseidʒ, ˈəuseidʒ; oˋsedʒ, ˋosedʒ] ***n***. **1**. 〔*pl*.〕(***O·sag·es, O·sage***) 奥色治人〔曾一度移居米苏里州奥色治河岸,现居于俄克拉荷马州的美国印第安人〕。**2**. 奥色治语。**O- orange**【植】**1**. 桑橙树(*Maclura pomifera*)〔原生长于美国中部,常种作篱障等〕。**2**. 桑橙。

O·sa·ka [ˈɔːsəkə, əuˈsɑːkə; oˋsɑkə, oˋsɑkɑ] ***n***. 大坂〔日本港市〕。

Os·bert [ˈɔzbəːt; ˋɑzbɚt] ***n***. 奥斯伯特〔男子名〕。

Os·born(e) [ˈɔzbən; ˋɔzbɚn] ***n***. 奥斯本〔姓氏〕。

Os·can [ˈɔskən; ˋɔskən] **I** ***n***. **1**. 奥斯肯族〔古代居于意大利康帕尼亚的人〕。**2**. 奥斯肯语。**II** ***a***. 奥斯肯族的;奥斯肯语的。

Os·car[1] [ˈɔskə; ɔskɚ] ***n***. 奥斯卡〔男子名〕。

Os·car[2] [ˈɔskə; ˋɔskɚ] ***n***. **1**. 〔美〕【影】奥斯卡金像奖;〔喻〕奖(章)。**2**. 〔o-〕〔美俚〕手枪,左轮。**3**. 〔Aust.〕钱,现款。

os·cil·late [ˈɔsileit; ˋɑslˏet] **I** ***vi***. **1**. (摆似地)摆动;振动;【物】振荡。**2**. (意见等)动摇,犹豫,彷徨。**3**. 蹒跚。**4**. 【无】发杂音。**II** ***vt***. 使摆动[振动];使动摇。*an oscillating charge* [*current*] 振荡电荷[电流]。

os·cil·la·tion [ˌɔsiˈleiʃən; ˏɑsˋleʃən] ***n***. **1**. 【物】振荡,摆动,振动;振幅。**2**. 动摇,犹豫,彷徨。**3**. 蹒跚。**4**. 【无】发杂音。*the duration of ~* 振荡期间。*local ~* 本身振荡。

os·cil·la·tor [ˈɔsileitə; ˋɑslə ˏetɚ] ***n***. **1**. 摇摆者。**2**. 【电】振荡器,振动器,振动子,振动部。*a driving ~* 主

控振荡器。*a pulsed* ～ 脉冲发生器。

os·cil·la·to·ry [ˈɔsileitəri, -lətəri; ˋɑsələˏtorɪ, -lətərɪ] ***a*.** 1. 振动的,振荡的,摆动的。2. 动摇不定的。*an* ～ *circuit* 振荡电路。*an* ～ *discharge* 振荡放电。

os·cil·lo·gram [ɔˈsiləˌgræm, ə-; ˋɑsɪləˏgræm] ***n*.** 【电】示波图;波形图。

os·cil·lo·graph [ɔˈsiləgrɑːf; əˋsɪləˏgræf] ***n*.** 【电】示波器,录波器。

os·cil·lo·scope [ɔˈsiləskəup; əˋsɪləˏskop] ***n*.** 【物】示波器。**-scop·ic** [-ˈskɔpik; -ˋskɑpɪk] ***a*.**

os·cil·lo·tron [ˈɔsilətrɔn; ˋɑsɪlətrɑn] ***n*.** 电子射线(示波)管;(阴极射线)示波管。

os·cine [ˈɔsin, -ain; ˋɑsɪn, -aɪn] **I** ***a*.** 鸣禽类的〔如百灵鸟、云雀、颊白鸟〕。**II** ***n*.** 鸣禽类 (*Oscines*) 动物。

os·ci·tan·cy [ˈɔsitənsi; ˋɑsətənsɪ] ***n*.** 想睡,困倦;不活跃;冷淡,漠不关心。

Os·co-Um·bri·an [ˈɔskəuˈʌmbriən; ˋɑskoˋʌmbrɪən] ***n*.** 奥斯肯—翁布里亚语〔意大利语族的一个语支,由奥斯肯语和翁布里亚语组成〕。

os·cu·lant [ˈɔskjulənt; ˋɑskjulənt] ***a*.** 1. 〔谑〕接吻的。2. 【动】固着的;连结的;【生】中间型的。

os·cu·lar [ˈɔskjulə; ˋɑskjələ˞] ***a*.** 1. 〔谑〕嘴的;接吻的。2. 【动】孔的,吸盘的;【数】密切的。

os·cu·late [ˈɔskjuleit; ˋɑskjəˏlet] ***vi*.** 〔谑、罕〕接吻;【生】有共通性,与…接触 (*with*)。—***vt*.** 1. 【生】(通过中间物种)接触;【数】密切。2. (知识的范围等)与…有共同点。

os·cu·la·tion [ˌɔskjuˈleiʃən; ˏɑskjəˋleʃən] ***n*.** 接吻;【几】密切。

os·cu·la·to·ry[1] [ˈɔskjuleitəri, -lətəri; ˋɑskjʊləˏtorɪ, -lətərɪ] ***a*.** 〔谑〕接吻的;【几】密切的。

os·cu·la·to·ry[2] [ˈɔskjulətəri; ˋɑskjʊlətərɪ] ***n*.** = pax.

os·cu·lum [ˈɔskjuləm; ˋɑskjʊləm] ***n*.** (*pl*. **-la** [-lə; -lə]) 【动】(海绵等的)出水孔;(条虫等的)吸盘。

-ose[1] *suf*. = -ous 1. …多的:verb*ose*. 2. 爱…的:joc*ose*. 3. …性的:schist*ose*.

-ose[2] *suf*. 【化】1. 醣类名称的后缀[词尾]:cellul*ose*, fruct*ose*. 2. 蛋白质诱导体[衍生物]名称后缀[词尾]:prote*ose*.

o·sier [ˈəuʒə; ˋoʒə˞] **I** ***n*.** 【植】1. 〔英〕杞柳;柳条,柳枝。2. (美国)梾木。**II** ***a*.** 柳条的;柳条做的。～**-bed** 柳园;柳林。

os·i·fer [ˈɔsifə; ˋɑsɪfə˞] ***n*.** 〔美俚〕军官;官吏。

O·si·ris [əuˈsaiəris; oˋsaɪrɪs] ***n*.** (古埃及神话中的)地狱判官。

-osis *suf*. 表示"过程"、"状态"等意义的病名:metamorpho*sis*, neur*osis*.

-osity *suf*. 用于词尾为 -ose, -ous 的形容词后构成名词:joc*osity*, curi*osity*.

Os·lo [ˈɔzləu; ˋɑzlo] ***n*.** 奥斯陆〔挪威首都〕。

Os·man [ɔzˈmɑːn, ɔs-; ˋɑzmɑn, ɑs-] ***n*.** 1. 奥斯曼〔1259—1326,奥托曼 (Ottoman) 帝国的创建者〕。2. = Osmanli.

Os·man·li [ɔzˈmænli, ɔs-; ɑzˋmænlɪ, ɑs-] ***n*.**, ***a*.** 西支土耳其人[语](的)。

os·man·thus [ɔsˈmænθəs; ɑsˋmænθəs] ***n*.** 【植】1. 〔O-〕木犀属。2. 木犀属植物。*sweet* ～ 桂花,木犀。*orange* ～ 丹桂,金桂。

os·mic [ˈɔzmik; ˋɑzmɪk] ***a*.** 【化】锇的。

os·mics [ˈɔzmiks; ˋɑzmɪks] ***n*.** 〔用作单数〕臭味学;臭的研究。

os·mir·i·di·um [ˌɔzmiˈridiəm; ˏɑzmɪˋrɪdɪəm] ***n*.** 铱锇矿(= iridosmine)。

os·mi·um [ˈɔzmiəm, -mjəm; ˋɑzmɪəm, -mjəm] ***n*.** 【化】锇。

os·mom·e·ter [ɔzˈmɔmitə; ɑzˋmɑmɪtə˞] ***n*.** 渗透压力计。

os·mose [ˈɔzməus; ˋɑzmos] ***vt*.**, ***vi*.** (使)渗透。

os·mo·sis [ɔzˈməusis; ɑzˋmosɪs] ***n*.** 【生理】渗透(作用),渗透性。

os·mot·ic [ɔzˈmɔtic; ɑzˋmɑtɪk] ***a*.** 渗透的。～ **pressure** 渗透压(力),浓差压。**-mot·i·cal·ly** ***ad*.**

os·mous [ˈɔzməs; ˋɑzməs] ***a*.** 【化】三价锇的。

os·mund(a) [ˈɔzmənd(ə); ˋɑzmənd(ə)] ***n*.** 【植】薇。

os·na·burg [ˈɔznəbəːg; ˋɑznəˏbɝg] ***n*.** 低支纱柳条或方格棉布;粗(口)袋布。

OSO = orbiting solar observatory 太阳观测卫星。

OSP, osp = 1. 〔L.〕obiit sine prole 死时无子嗣(= he died without issue)。2. Old Spanish 古西班牙文。

os·pray, os·prey [ˈɔspri; ˋɑsprɪ] ***n*.** 1. 【鸟】鹗,鱼鹰。2. 白鹭的羽毛〔女帽业用语〕。

OSRD; O.S.R.D. = Office for Scientific Research and Development 〔美旧〕科学研究与发展局。

OSS = Office of Strategic Services 〔美〕战略情报局。

Os·sa [ˈɔsə; ˋɑsə] ***n*.** 【希神】奥萨山〔希腊东北部一山,希腊神话中巨人们妄图登天进攻天上诸神,将 Pelion 山叠于 Ossa 山之上,借以攀登 Olimpus 山〕。***heap*** [***pile***] ***Pelion upon*** ～ 难上加难,做办不到的事。

os·sa [ˈɔsə; ˋɑsə] ***n*.** **os**[1](骨)的复数。

os·se·in [ˈɔsiin; ˋɑsɪɪn] ***n*.** 【生化】骨胶原。

os·se·ous [ˈɔsiəs; ˋɑsɪəs] ***a*.** 骨的,有骨的;骨质的,骨似的。**-ly** ***ad*.**

Os·set [ˈɔset; ˋɑsɛt], **Os·sete** [ˈɔsiːt; ˋɑsit] ***n*.** 奥塞特人。

Os·set·i·a [ɔˈsetiə; ɑˋsɛtɪə] ***n*.** 奥塞特〔北高加索一地区〕。

Os·set·ic [ɔˈsetik; ɑˋsɛtɪk] **I** ***a*.** 奥塞特人的,奥塞特区的。**II** ***n*.** 奥塞特语。

Os·si·an [ˈɔsiən; ˋɑsɪən] ***n*.** 欧希安〔传说中三世纪苏格兰高地的英雄诗人〕。

Os·si·an·ic [ɔʃiˈænik; ˏɑʃɪˋænɪk] ***a*.** 欧希安 (Ossian) 式的;夸张的。

os·si·cle [ˈɔsikl; ˋɑsɪkl] ***n*.** 【解、动】小骨;小骨片。

os·si·fer [ˈɔsifə; ˋɑsəfə˞] ***n*.** = osifer.

os·sif·er·ous [ɔˈsifərəs; ɑˋsɪfərəs] ***a*.** (矿藏中)有骨的。

os·si·fi·ca·tion [ˌɔsifiˈkeiʃən; ˏɑsəfəˋkeʃən] ***n*.** 1. 【生】成骨,骨化。2. (思想等的)僵化。

os·si·frage [ˈɔsifridʒ; ˋɑsɪfrɪdʒ] ***n*.** 〔诗、古〕1. 鹗,鱼鹰。2. (南美、欧洲产)髭秃鹰。

os·sify [ˈɔsifai; ˋɑsəˏfaɪ] ***vt*.** (**-fied**; **-fy·ing**) 1. 骨化;使(像骨头一样)硬化。2. 使僵化;使无情,使冷酷;使顽固;使不进展。—***vi*.** 1. 变成骨头,骨化;硬化。2. 变成铁石心肠;变顽固,僵化。

os·so bu·co [ˈɔusəuˈbuːkəu; ˋosoˋbuko] 〔It.〕炖小牛胫〔一种意大利菜〕。

os·su·ar·i·um [ˌɔːʃuːˈɛəriəm; ˏɑʃuˋɛrɪəm] ***n*.** (*pl*. ***-ar·i·a*** [-ˈɛəriə; -ˋɛrɪə]) = ossuary.

os·su·a·ry [ˈɔsjuəri; ˋɑsjʊˏɛrɪ] ***n*.** 1. 骨瓮,骨罐。2. 藏有古代遗骨的洞穴。3. 藏骨堂。

os·te·al [ˈɔstiəl; ˋɑstɪəl] ***a*.** 骨的,骨(状)的。

os·te·i·tis [ˌɔstiːˈaitis; ˏɑstɪˋaɪtɪs] ***n*.** 【医】骨炎。

os·ten·si·ble [ɔsˈtensəbl, -sibl; ɑsˋtɛnsəbl] ***a*.** 1. 外表的,表面上的。2. 假装的;诡称的。3. 可公开的;显然的。*an* ～ *partner* 名义合伙人。*His* ～ *object was to* .... 他的表面目的是…。**-bly** ***ad*.**

os·ten·sive [ɔsˈtensiv; ɑsˋtɛnsɪv] ***a*.** 1. 用实物[动作]表示的;外表的。2. 诡称的。3. 【逻】直接证明的。*an oral-* ～ *method* 口示法,口授法。

os·ten·so·ry [ɔsˈtensəri; ɑsˋtɛnsərɪ] ***n*.** 【天主】盛圣餐面包的容器。

os·ten·ta·tion [ˌɔstenˈteiʃən; ˏɑstənˋteʃən] ***n*.** 夸示;卖弄;风头主义,讲排场,虚饰。*do sth. out of* ～ 为外表好看而做某事。

os·ten·ta·tious [ˌɔstenˈteiʃəs; ˏɑstənˋteʃəs] ***a*.** 夸示的,

O

得意扬扬地给人看的;(态度)自负的;讲排场的,虚饰的;外观美丽的,浮华的。**-ly** ***ad***.

osteo- *comb.f.* 骨:*osteo*arthritis.

os·te·o·ar·thri·tis [ˌɔstiːˌəuɑːˈθraitis; ˏɑstɪoɑrˋθraɪtɪs] ***n***.【医】骨关节炎。

os·te·o·blast [ˈɔstiəˌblæst; ˋɑstɪəblæst] ***n***.【生】成骨细胞。**-ic** ***a***.

os·te·oc·la·sis [ˌɔstiˈɔkləsis; ˏɑstɪˋɑkləsɪs] ***n***. **1.** 骨破折。**2.** 折骨术。

os·te·o·clast [ˈɔstiəklæst; ˋɑstɪəklæst] ***n***. **1.** 破骨细胞。**2.** 折骨器。

os·te·o·cran·i·um [ˌɔstiəˈkreinjəm; ˏɑstɪəˋkrenjəm]【医】骨颅。

os·te·o·gen·e·sis [ˌɔstiəˈdʒenisis; ˏɑstɪəˋdʒɛnəsɪs] ***n***.【医】骨生成,骨发生;成骨。

os·te·o·gra·phy [ˌɔstiˈɔgrəfi; ˏɑstɪˋɑgrəfɪ] ***n***. 骨论。

os·te·oid [ˈɔstiɔid; ˋɑstɪɔɪd] ***a***. 骨状的。

os·te·o·lite [ˈɔstiəlait; ˋɑstɪəlaɪt] ***n***.【矿】土磷灰石。

os·te·o·log·i·cal [ˌɔstiəˈlɔdʒikəl; ˏɑstɪəˋlɑdʒɪkl] ***a***. 骨学(上)的。

os·te·ol·o·gist [ˌɔstiˈɔlədʒist; ˏɑstɪˋɑlədʒɪst] ***n***. 骨学家。

os·te·ol·o·gy [ˌɔstiˈɔlədʒi; ˏɑstɪˋɑlədʒɪ] ***n***. 骨学。

os·te·o·ma [ˌɔstiˈəumə; ˏɑstɪˋomə] ***n***.【医】骨瘤。

os·te·o·ma·la·ci·a [ˌɔstiəumәˈleiʃə, -ʃiə; ˏɑstɪoməˋleʃə, -ʃɪə] ***n***.【医】骨软化,软骨病。

os·te·o·my·e·li·tis [ˌɔstiəuˈmaiəˈlaitis; ˏɑstɪəˏmaɪəˋlaɪtɪs] ***n***. 骨髓炎。

os·te·o·path [ˈɔstiəupæθ; ˋɑstɪəˏpæθ] ***n***. 正骨科医生,按摩医生。

os·te·op·a·thy [ˌɔstiˈɔpəθi; ˏɑstɪˋɑpəθɪ] ***n***. 疗骨术,整骨术;骨病。

os·te·o·phyte [ˈɔstiəufait; ˋɑstɪəˏfaɪt] ***n***.【医】骨赘。**-phyt·ic** [-ˈfitik; -ˋfɪtɪk] ***a***.

os·te·o·plas·tic [ˌɔstiəuˈplæstik; ˏɑstɪəˋplæstɪk] ***a***. **1.**【解】成骨的。**2.** (外科)装骨的,造骨的。**-plas·ty** ***n***.

os·te·o·po·ro·sis [ˌɔstiəupɔːˈrəusis; ˏɑstɪopəˋrosɪs] ***n***.【医】骨质疏松。

os·te·o·sis [ˌɔstiˈəusis; ˏɑstɪˋəusɪs] ***n***. 骨质生成。

os·te·o·tome [ˈɔstiəutəum; ˋɑstɪətom] ***n***.【医】骨凿。

os·te·ot·o·my [ˌɔstiˈɔtəmi; ˏɑstɪˋɑtəmɪ] ***n***. (*pl*. ***-mies***) 骨切开术,切骨术。

os·ter·moors [ˈɔstəmuːəz; ˋɑstəmuəz] ***n***.〔*pl*.〕〔美俚〕胡须。

os·ti·ak [ˈɔstiæk; ˋɑstɪæk] ***n***. =ostyak.

os·ti·ary [ˈɔstiˌeəri; ˋɑstɪˏɛrɪ] ***n***. (*pl*. ***-ar·ies***) **1.** 看门人,门房。**2.** (天主教)地位最低的神职人员。

os·ti·na·to [ˌɔstiˈnɑːtəu, It. əustiːˈnɑːtəu; ˏɑstɪˋnɑto, It. ostiˋnɑto] ***n***. (*pl*. ***-tos*** [-əuz, It. -təus; -oz, It. -tos])【乐】固定音型〔不断地重复出现的节奏型或旋律型〕。

os·ti·ole [ˈɔstiəul; ˋɑstɪol] ***n***. 小孔,孔口。**-o·lar** ***a***.

os·ti·um [ˈɔstiəm; ˋɑstɪəm] ***n***. (*pl*. ***-ti·a*** [-ə; -ə])【解】口,门,孔,心门。

ost·ler [ˈɔslə; ˋɑslɚ] ***n***. (旅馆的)马夫。

ost·mark [ɔstˈmɑːk; ˋɔstˏmark] ***n***. 前东德马克。

os·to·my [ˈɔstəmi; ˋɔstəmɪ] ***n***.【医】造口术〔如输尿管造口术等〕。

os·to·sis [ɔsˈtəusis; ɑsˋtosɪs] ***n***. 骨质生成(=osteosis)。

os·tra·cean [ɔsˈtreiʃiən; ɑsˋtreʃɪən] **I** ***a***. 牡蛎的。**II** ***n***. 牡蛎。

os·tra·cism [ˈɔstrəsizəm; ˋɑstrəˏsɪzəm] ***n***. **1.** (古希腊用投票办法将异己分子逐出国外5年或10年,并将票数记在贝壳上的)贝壳流放。**2.** 流放,放逐。**3.** 排斥。*suffer political* [*social*] ~ 被政界[社会]排斥。

os·tra·cize [ˈɔstrəsaiz; ˋɑstrəsaɪz] ***vt***. (依贝壳流放法)流放;放逐;与…绝交;排斥。

os·tra·cod [ˈɔstrəˌkɔd; ˋɑstrəˏkɑd] ***n***. 介形亚纲(*Ostracoda*)动物。

Os·tra·va [ˈɔːstrəvə; ˋɔstrəvə] ***n***. 奥斯特拉瓦〔前捷克斯洛伐克城市〕。

Os·trea [ˈɔstriə; ˋɑstrɪə] ***n***.【动】牡蛎[蚝]属。

os·trea·cul·ture [ˈɔstriəkʌltʃə; ˋɑstrɪəkʌltʃə], **os·trei·cul·ture** [ˈɔstriikʌltʃə; ˋɑstrɪɪkʌltʃɚ] ***n***. 养蚝(法)。

os·trich [ˈɔstritʃ; ˋɔstrɪtʃ] ***n***.【鸟】鸵鸟。***have the digestion of an*** ~ 食量大;胃口好。~ **belief** 掩耳盗铃的想法。~**-farm** 鸵鸟饲养场。~ **policy** 鸵鸟政策。

Os·tro·goth [ˈɔstrəˌgɔθ; ˋɑstrəˏgɑθ] ***n***. 东哥特人〔尤指公元前五世纪征服意大利的东哥特部族人〕。**-ic** [-ˈgɔθik; -ˋgɑθɪk] ***a***.

Ost·wald [ˈɔstvalt; ˋɑstvəlt] ***n***. **W.** 奥斯特瓦尔德〔1853—1932,德国物理化学家,曾获1909年诺贝尔化学奖〕。

Os·ty·ak [ˈɔstiˌæk; ˋɑstɪˏæk] ***n***. **1.** 奥斯蒂亚克人〔居于西西伯利亚的一支芬兰乌戈尔族人〕。**2.** 奥斯蒂亚克语。

Os·wald [ˈɔzwəld; ˋɑzwəld] ***n***. 奥斯瓦尔德〔男子名〕。

Os·we·go tea [ɔsˈwiːgəu; ɑsˋwigo] **1.** 大红香蜂草(*Monarda didyma*)〔产于北美〕。**2.** 大红香蜂草茶。

Oś·wie·cim [ɔːʃˈvjentsiːm; ɔʃˋvjɛntsim] ***n***. **1.** 奥斯威辛〔波兰市镇〕。**2.** 〔第二次世界大战时希特勒建立的〕奥斯威辛集中营。

O.T., OT, OT. = **1.** *Old Testament* (基督教《圣经》的)《旧约全书》。**2.** old tulerculin 旧结核菌素。

ot- *comb.f.*〔用在母音字母前〕=oto-:*ot*itis.

o·tal·gi·a [əuˈtældʒiə; oˋtældʒɪə] ***n***.【医】耳痛。

OTC **1.** =oxytetracyclin.【药】土霉素,地灵霉素。**2.** =one stop inclusive tour charter 一站全包旅行合约〔作一站旅行,一切开支全包括在内〕。

O.T.C. =Officers' Training Corps.〔英〕军官训练团。

OTE =on target [track] earnings 按工作指标[个人表现]付工资〔多用于招聘广告中〕。

OTH =over-the-horizon (雷达)超视距的,能探测地平线以外目标的。

oth·er [ˈʌðə; ˋʌðɚ] **I** ***a***. **1.** 别的,另外的,其他的;不同的(*than*; *from*);其余的;另一个的。**2.** 对方的,对面的,相反的。**3.** 其次的,第二的。**4.** 隔一个。**5.** 不久前的;以前的。*O- people think otherwise*. 别人又是另一种想法。*He has no ~ place to go to*. 他别无去处。*on the ~ side of the road* 在路对面。*the ~ thing* 相反。*the ~ way* 相反地。*the ~ day* 上回,那天,不久前的一天。*It must be one or the ~*. 二者必居其一。*the ~ night* 前几天的一个晚上。*in ~ times* 从前。**II** ***ad***. 用其他方法,另样地。*I can't do ~ than to go*. 我不去不行。***every*** ~ **1.** 每隔一(*every ~ day* 每隔一日)。**2.** 其他的…都(*every ~ boy* 其他的孩子都)。***none ~ than*** 不是别人,正是(*It was none ~ than Jones*. 不是别人正是琼斯)。***on the ~ hand*** 在另一方面,但是又。~ ***than*** **1.** 与…不同,而不是。**2.** 除了(*any ~ person than yourself* 除你以外的任何人。*I do not wish him ~ than he is*. 他就那样好了。*a world far ~ from ours* 和我们世界远不相同的世界)。~ ***things being equal*** 如果其他情形都一样。***the ~ side*** 〔美〕欧洲。***the ~ party***【法】对方。***the ~ world*** 来世。**III** ***pro***. (*pl*. ~***s***)〔*cf*. another〕**1.** 另外一个;〔*pl*.〕别的东西,别的人;其他的东西。**2.** 〔the ~(s)〕其余的一个,其他各人[各物]。*one or ~ of us* 我们当中的任何一个。*Do good to ~s*. 对他人做好事。*I must consult the ~s*. 我必须和其余的人商量。***among ~s*** 此外还有;其中也(*Smith, among ~s, was there*. 除此之外,史密斯也在那里)。***each*** ~ 互相。***know one from the*** ~ 把二者分别清楚。***of all ~s*** 所有…当中的(*on that day of all ~s* 偏偏在那天)。***one ... the*** ~ 一方面是…,另一方面是…。***one after the*** ~ 一个接一个地;(二者)相继。***some ... or*** ~ 某一…(*some man or*

~ 某一个人(非做不可等)。*Some one of us or ~ will be there*. 我们当中总会有一个人在那里的。*some time or ~* 总有一天,迟早。*Some idiots or ~ have done it*. 总是甚么傻瓜们干的那事)。***some ~s*** 另外什么人[什么东西](*Give me some ~s*. 给我另外的吧)。***the one ... the ~*** 前者是…后者是〔但有时相反〕。
IV ***ad***. 不是那样,用别的方法。*I can do no ~ than accept*. 我只好接受〔除接受外别无办法〕。*If you think ~ than logically*. 你如果不合乎逻辑地推理。~ **half** **1**. 另一部分民众(*See how ~ half lives*. 看看另一部分民众怎样生活吧!)。**2**. 配偶。

oth·er-di·rect·ed [ˈʌðədiˈrektid; ˋʌðədɪˋrɛktɪd] ***a***., ***n***. 由他人牵着鼻子走的(人),听命于他人的(人);顺从的(人),随俗的(人)。

oth·er·guess [ˈʌðəges; ˋʌðə·ˏgɛs] ***a***. 〔古、口〕别种的;不同的。

oth·er·ness [ˈʌðənis; ˋʌðənɪs] ***n***. 〔罕〕不同,相异,另一物,不同物;【哲】他,他性。

oth·er·whence [ˈʌðə*h*wens; ˋʌðə·ˏhwɛns] ***ad***. 〔古〕从别处。

oth·er·where(s) [ˈʌðə*h*weə(z); ˋʌðə·ˏhwɛr(z)] ***ad***. 〔诗〕在别处[某处];向别处[某处]。

oth·er·while(s) [ˈʌðə*h*wail(z); ˋʌðə·ˏhwaɪl(z)] ***ad***. 〔古〕在别的时候;有时候。

oth·er·wise [ˈʌðəwaiz; ˋʌðə·ˏwaɪz] **I** ***ad***. **1**. 不那样,用别的方法。**2**. 在其他方面。**3**. 在其他状态[情况]下。*I think ~*. 我是另外一种想法。*This must be done quite ~*. 这要完全改变做法才行。*be quite ~ engaged* 完全忙别的事。*He never teaches them any ~ than by example*. 他除了示范[举例]以外从来不用别的方法教他们。*I could do no ~ than laugh*. 我只好笑了。*He has a squint, but is ~ a handsome fellow*. 除斜视外,在其他各点上他是一个漂亮的人。*I know him ~ than in business*. 在生意以外我也认识他的。*Judas, ~ (called) Iscariot* 犹大,一名伊斯卡洛。
II ***conj***. 否则,不然。*Seize the chance, ~ you will regret it*. 抓住机会,否则你要后悔的。
III ***a***. **1**. 〔用作表语[述语]〕别的,另外一种的。*How can it be ~ than fatal?* 怎么能不是致命的呢? *Some are wise, some are ~*. 有聪明的,也有不聪明的。**2**. 〔用作定语[修饰语]〕在其他各方面…的;在其他不同情况下的。*his ~ equals* 在其他各方面和他不相上下的人们。***act ~ than one says*** 行不顾言;言行不一。***and ~*** 其他,等(*He helped me with advice and ~*. 他用忠告等帮助了我)。***or ~*** 或相反(*his merits or ~* (= *or demerits*)他的优点或缺点。*I am not concerned with its accuracy or ~*. 我倒不管他准确不准确)。~**-minded** ***a***. 性格两样的,兴趣[嗜好]不同的;意见不同的;与舆论相反的;思想逆潮流的。

oth·er·world·(ly) [ˈʌðəwəːld(li); ˋʌðə·ˋwɜ·ld(lɪ)] ***a***. 来世的;冥界的;修来世的;空想中的;精神上的;超俗的。

Oth·man [ɔθˈmaːn, ˈɔθmən; ɑθˋmɑn, ˋɑθmən] ***a***., ***n***. = Ottoman.

OTH radar = over-the-horizon radar 超越地平线雷达。

o·ti·at·rics [ˌəuʃiˈætriks; ˏoʃɪˋætrɪks] ***n***. 【医】耳病学。

o·tic [ˈəutik; ˋotɪk] ***a***. 【解】耳的,耳部的。~ **bit** 听窝。~ **capsule** 耳壳。~ **ganglion** 【解】耳神经节。

-otic *suf*. **1**. 患(病)的,生…的: hypn*otic*, narc*otic* 〔对应名词后缀[词尾]是 -osis〕。**2**. 似…的: Quix*otic* (< Quixote)。

o·ti·ose [ˈəuʃiəus; ˋoʃɪˏos] ***a***. **1**. 不必要的,没有用的,多余的,无效的。**2**. 〔罕〕闲着的,没事做的;懒惰的。**-ly** ***ad***. **-ness** ***n***. **o·ti·os·i·ty** [ˌəuʃiˈɔsiti; ˏoʃɪˋɑsɪtɪ] ***n***.

O·tis [ˈəutis; ˋotɪs] ***n***. 奥蒂斯〔姓氏,男子名〕。

o·ti·tis [*əu*ˈtaitis; oˋtaɪtɪs] ***n***. 【医】耳炎。~ ***externa*** [***interna***, ***media***] 外[内,中]耳炎。

o·ti·um cum dig·ni·ta·te [ˈəuʃiəm kʌmˌdigniˈteiti; ˋoʃɪəm kʌmˏdɪgnɪˋtetɪ] 〔L.〕(= leisure with dignity) 悠然自适。

OTL = output-transformerless 【无】无输出变压器的。

o·to- *comb. f*. 〔用在子音字母前〕表示"耳": *oto*logy, *oto*scope.

o·to·cyst [ˈəutəsist; ˋotəsɪst] ***n***. **1**. 【动】听泡,听囊。**2**. 【动】平衡器;(昆虫的)平衡胞。

o·to·lar·yn·gol·o·gy [ˌəutəuˌlæriŋˈgɔlədʒi; ˏotəˏlærɪŋˋgɑlədʒɪ] ***n***. 【医】耳鼻喉科。**-gist** ***n***. 耳鼻喉科医师。

o·to·lith [ˈəutəliθ; ˋotəlɪθ] ***n***. 【解】**1**. 耳石。**2**. (无脊椎动物的)听石。**-ic** ***a***.

o·tol·o·gy [*əu*ˈtɔlədʒi; oˋtɑlədʒɪ] ***n***. 耳科学。**-gist** ***n***. 耳科医生。

o·to·phone [ˈəutəfəun; ˋotəfon] ***n***. 助听器。

o·to·rhi·n·o·lar·yn·gol·o·gy [ˈ*ə*utəuˌrainəuˌlæriŋˈgɔlədʒi; ˋotoˏraɪnoˏlærɪŋˋgɑlədʒɪ] ***n***. 耳鼻喉科学。

o·to·scle·ro·sis [ˌəutə*u*skliˈrəusis; ˏotəsklɪˋrosɪs] ***n***. 【医】耳硬化。**-rot·ic** [-ˈrɔtik; -ˋrɑtɪk] ***a***.

o·to·scope [ˈəutəskəup; ˋotəˏskop] ***n***. 【医】耳镜;耳科听诊器。

O·tran·to [ɔˈtræntəu; ˋɔtrɑnto] ***n***. **Strait of** ~ (意大利与阿尔巴尼亚间的)奥特朗托海峡。

ot·ta·va [əˈtaːvə; əˋtɑvə] 〔It.〕 ***a***., ***ad***. 【音】以高[低]八度。

ot·ta·va ri·ma [ˈɔtəvəˈriːmə; əˋtɑvəˋrimə] 〔It.〕【诗】八行体(的诗)。

Ot·ta·wa [ˈɔtəwə; ˋɑtəwə] ***n***. 渥太华〔加拿大首都〕。

ot·ter [ˈɔtə; ˋɑtə·] ***n***. (*pl*. ~*s*, 〔集合词〕~) **1**. 【动】水獭;水獭皮。**2**. 一种钓具〔淡水用〕。*a common ~* 獭。*a sea ~* 海獭。~**-dog** = ~**-hound** 猎水獭用的猎狗。~**-spear** 刺水獭用的枪。

Ot·to [ˈɔtəu; ˋɑto] ***n***. 鄂图〔男子名〕。~ **cycle** 【物】四冲程循环,鄂图循环。~ **engine** 【机】四冲程发动机,鄂图发动机。

ot·to [ˈɔtəu; ˋɑto] ***n***. 玫瑰油,玫瑰精。

Ot·to·man [ˈɔtəmən; ˋɑtəmən] **I** ***a***. 旧土耳其帝国的;土耳其人的;土耳其民族的。**II** ***n***. (*pl*. ~*s*) **1**. 土耳其(族)人。**2**. 〔o-〕椅子;(无靠背的)矮脚条椅,绒垫睡椅。**3**. 楞条绸;绒脚垫;【纺】粗横棱纹织物。~ **Empire** 【史】奥斯曼帝国,鄂图曼帝国。

Ot·way [ˈɔtwei; ˋɑtwe] ***n***. **1**. 奥特韦〔姓氏〕。**2**. **Thomas ~** 托马斯·奥特韦〔1652—1685,英国剧作家〕。

O.U. = Oxford University.

oua·ba·in [waːˈbaːin; wɑˋbaɪn] ***n***. 【化】乌本(箭毒)苷。

Oua·ga·dou·gou [ˌwaːgəˈduːguː; ˏwɑgəˋdugu] ***n***. 瓦加杜古〔上沃尔特[上伏塔]首都〕。

O.U.A.M. = Order of United American Mechanics 美国机械工人联合会。

ou·bli·ette [ˌuːbliˈet; ˏublɪˋɛt] ***n***. (仅头顶有孔可以出入的)土牢,密狱。

ouch[1] [autʃ; aʊtʃ] ***n***. 〔英古〕(戒指等上的)珠座,宝石座,玉饰,金饰;扣子。

ouch[2] [autʃ; aʊtʃ] ***int***. 〔美〕哎唷! 痛呀!

ouch·y [ˈautʃi; ˋaʊtʃɪ] ***a***. 〔美俚〕神经过敏的;急躁的;脾气暴躁的。

oud [uːd; ud] ***n***. 【乐】乌得〔中东和北非弦乐器名,似琵琶〕。

ought[1] [ɔːt; ɔt] ***v. aux***. 〔oughtest 或 oughtst 是古体。现代英语用带 to 的不定式。表示过去时用完成式不定式〕应该,应当;总应该;本应,本当;早应该。*We ~ to love labour*. 我们应当爱劳动。*You ~ to know better*. 你应当更明白些。*It ~ to have been done long ago*. 这事早应该做完的。*You ~ not to do that*. 你不应当做那种事。*It ~ not to be allowed*. 那是不应该允许的。*He ~ to have arrived by this*. 他此刻应该到了。

ought[2] [ɔːt; ɔt] ***n***. 〔口〕零,全无(= nought)。
ought[3] [ɔːt; ɔt] ***n***., ***ad***. 〔古〕= aught[1].
ought·a [ˈɔːtə; ˋɔtə] 〔口〕= ought to.
oughtn't [ˈɔːtnt; ˋɔtnt] ought not 的缩合形式。
ou·gui·ya [ˈuːkwjə; ˋukwjə] ***n***. 乌吉亚〔毛利塔尼亚货币单位〕。

O

oui [wiː; wi] ***ad***. 〔F.〕是,对。
ounce[1] [auns; aʊns] ***n***. **1**. 盎司,英两,唡〔常衡 = 1/16 磅 = 28.4克;金衡 = 1/12 磅 = 31.104 克;略作 oz.〕。**2**. 液唡,流量唡(= 1/12 pint)(= fluid ～)。**3**. 少量。*an ～ of courage* 一点点勇气。*An ～ of practice is worth a pound of theory*. 一分实践当得十分理论。*That will call for every ～ of energy we have*. 这就需要我们全力以赴。
ounce[2] [auns; aʊns] ***n***. 【动】雪豹;〔诗〕山猫。
O.U.P. = Oxford University Press 〔英〕牛津大学出版社。
ouphe, ouph [auf, uːf; aʊf, uf] ***n***. 淘气的小精灵;丑妖怪;顽皮的小孩儿(= elf)。
our [ˈauə; ˋaʊr] ***pro***. 〔we 的所有格〕**1**. 我们的。**2**. 〔元首或英国教会主教用来代替 my〕我的。*～ loyal subjects* 我的忠实臣民。**3**. 〔报纸等发表意见时用〕我们的。*in ～ opinion* 我们的看法是。**4**. 正在谈的;(我们)那个。*Well, that isn't ～ business* [*affair*]. 可是,那事跟我们不相干。*～ gentleman in a black hat* (我们)那个戴黑帽子的绅士。**O- Father** 【宗】天父,上帝;主祷文。**O- Lady** 【宗】圣母玛利亚。**O- Saviour** 耶稣。
-our *suf*. = or[1].
ours [ˈauəz; ˋaʊrz] ***pro***. 〔we 的所有格代名词〕我们的(东西)。*Jones of ～* 我们的[队的或学校的]琼斯。*This orchard became ～ by purchase*. 这个果树园被我们买下了。*O- is better than yours*. 我方比你方强。★ **1**. O- is a large family. 是文语,口语说作 Our family is a large one. **2**. this our ... 是古语,现在富有感情色彩的说法是 this... of ours. 如:an old friend of ～ 我们的一个老朋友。
our·self [ˌauəˈself; ˌaʊrˋsɛlf] ***pro***. 我自己〔帝王、法官、著者等以及报刊社论中用以代替 myself〕。
our·selves [ˌauəˈselvz; ˌaʊrˋsɛlvz] ***pro***. 〔*pl*.〕**1**. 〔强势用法〕我们自己。**2**. 〔反身用语〕(把)我们自己。*We will do it ～*. 我们自己会做的。*We must not deceive ～*. 我们不可自欺。*We shall give ～ the pleasure of calling* (*on you*). 我们将高兴地去拜访(你)。*We were not ～ for sometime*. 我们有半天不能恢复常态。(***all***) ***by*** ～ 我们独自地;全靠自己地。***for*** ～ 自己,亲自(*We do everything* (*for*)～. 我们什么事都亲自做)。
-ous *suf*. **1**. 表示"多…的;…性的,有…癖的;有特质的;…似的;盛行…的":peril*ous*, rigor*ous*, graci*ous*, pomp*ous*. **2**. 【化】表示"亚…的":nitr*ous* acid 亚硝酸。
ou·sel [ˈuːzl; ˋuzl] ***n***. = ouzel.
oust [aust; aʊst] ***vt***. **1**. 逐出,撵走,驱逐(*from*; *of*)。**2**. 【法】(非法)剥夺,夺取,夺去。**3**. 代替,取代。*～ sb. from his post* 把某人撤职。*～ sb. of his inheritance* 剥夺某人的继承权。*Television has not ～ed radios*. 电视机还未能取代收音机。
oust·er [ˈaustə; ˋaʊstɚ] ***n***. **1**. 驱逐,逐出。**2**. 【法】(尤指非法的)剥夺。**3**. 驱逐[剥夺]者。
out [aut; aʊt] **I** ***ad***. **1**. 〔位置及运动的方向〕向外,向外部;在外,在外部;出去,出外,离开;离岸,向海面;(船等)开往外国。*go ～* 出去。*run ～* 跑出。*come ～* 出来。*stay ～* (在外头)不回家。*bring* [*take*] *sth. ～* 拿走东西。*leave sth. ～* 省去[遗漏](某物)。**2**. 〔同各种及物动词和不及物动词连用表示动作的极度〕完,尽;完全,彻底;到最后,显著;突出。*sell ～* 卖完。*blow ～ a candle* 吹灭蜡烛。**3**. 〔以下各解用作表语,亦可视为形容词〕出外,在外。*Her son is ～ in Canada*. 她的儿子出国在加拿大。*He is ～*. 他不在[出去了]。*anchor a mile ～* 停泊在离岸一英里处。*row ～* 划出(海面)。*be ～ at sea* 在海上航行中。**4**. 罢工;失和。*The workmen are ～*. 工人在罢工。*I am ～ with Jones*. = *Jones and I are ～*. 我跟琼斯闹翻了。**5**. 除外;离开…,被逐出,被排斥;【政】下台,下野,退位,退职;【运】退场;除去(阻碍等)。*The Tories are ～*. 托利党下台了。*The batter is ～*. 【棒球】打球员退场了。**6**. 不足,缺乏,损失。*The wine has run ～*. 酒没有了。*I am ～ fifty pounds through him*. 我为他损失了五十英镑。**7**. 消灭;熄,完,尽,到期,满期。*The fire is ～*. 火熄了。*be tired out* 筋疲力尽,累极。*before the week is ～* 在本星期内。**8**. 失常;混乱;脱出;有毛病。*The arm is ～*. 胳臂脱臼了。*My eye is a bit ～ today*. 今天眼睛有点不好。*My watch is five minutes ～*. 我的表快五分钟。*be ～ in one's calculation* 计算错误。**9**. 出世,发表;出版;出现在交际场中;现出;(花)开;(小鸡等)孵出;(秘密)暴露。*The book is ～*. 那本书出版了。*The rose is ～*. 蔷薇开了。**10**. 彻底,完全,直率,坦白;到最后,到完。*Tell him right ～*. 爽爽快快的告诉他。*hear one ～* 听完某人的话。**11**. 过时,不流行;闲着。*The frock-coats have gone ～*. 大礼服已经不流行了。*My hands are ～*. 手闲着。★美国在 help, lose, start, try, win 等动词之后,常加无意义的 out. ***be ～ at*** (***the knees***) (裤子)(膝部)破了。***be ～ for*** [***to*** (***do***)] 〔俚〕努力想得到;力图要;总想(做)…(*be ～ for a row* 准备去争吵一番。*be ～ for blood* 要打人;〔美〕期望比赛必胜,期望洗雪前耻)。***down and ～*** 落魄,败落。***have one's cry ～*** 哭个够。***have one's Sundays ～*** 星期日休息。～ ***and about*** (病后)能起床走动。～ ***and away*** 在远方,遥远;远远,大大;无比,无疑。～ ***and home*** 来回。～ ***and ～*** 毫无问题地,彻头彻尾地;彻底的,确实无疑的;绝对的,顽固不化的,坏透了的(*a scoundrel ～ and ～* 十足的无赖)。～ ***at the back*** = 〔美〕～ ***back*** 在房子后面。～ ***from under*** 〔美口〕脱离危境[困境]。～ ***here*** (老远)到这里。～ ***like a light*** 〔美俚〕喝醉。～ ***of*** 〔复合前置词〕(*opp*. in, into, within) **1**. 从…里头,从…当中,从…,出自(*come ～ of the house* 从屋子里出来。*～ of doors* 室外的,露天的;向门外,在门外。*Choose ～ of these*. 从这些当中选择罢。*one ～ of many* 许多当中的一个例子。*nine cases ～ of ten* 十有八九。*～ of Shakespeare* 出自莎士比亚)。**2**. 在…的范围外;向…达不到的地方;脱出…,变自由(*～ of date* 过时的。*～ of hearing* 在听不见的地方。*～ of sight* 看不见)。**3**. 失去…,没有(*swindled ～ of one's money* 被骗去金钱。*～ of breath* 上气不接下气。*～ of repair* 失修的。*～ of work* 失业的;失效的,不能工作的。*～ of mind* 被忘却)。**4**. 因,为了(*ask ～ of curiosity* 因好奇心而问问看)。**5**. 用…,用…做材料(*～ of one's own head* 自己想出来的。*What did you make it ～ of?* 那个你是用什么做的?)。**6**. 超出,离开(*～ of doubt* 无疑,确实。*times ～ of number* 无数次,再三再四。*born ～ of wedlock* 私生的)。**7**. 违犯,弄错(*～ of drawing* 不合画法)。～ ***of commission*** 退役的;〔美俚〕坏了的;受了伤的;有病的;没有用的;不中用的。～ ***of it*** 不加入;孤立,孤独,寂寞;窘困,不知怎样才好;脱节;弄错,搞错。～ ***of keeping*** (和周围)不调和。～ ***of line*** 不一致;不协调;不符;〔美俚〕控制不了。～ ***of the glare*** 〔美俚〕不出名,不显著。～ ***of the lot*** 【棒】惨败的;打出场外的飞球。～ ***of touch with*** 与…失去联系。～ ***there*** 向那边;远在那(边),〔口〕到战地。～ ***with*** 〔口〕拿出;说出;把…赶出去(*Out with him!* 赶他出去!)。
II ***prep***. **1**. 〔美〕通过(门、窗等)而出。*go ～ the door* 从门里出去。**2**. 〔美口〕沿着…而去。*Drive ～ High Street*. 顺着大街开去。★英国目前除雅语如诗歌尚用 from out 外,一般都用 out of. 如:From out the dungeon, came a groan. 从牢中传出呻吟的声音。

III ***n*.** **1.** 失去了地位[权势]的人;〔the ～s〕在野党。**2.** 外部,外头;外出;外观;体面。**3.**【运】守方。**4.**【印】漏排。**5.**〔美〕缺点,弱点;〔美俚〕(拳击中的)打倒;辩解,借口,离去的口实,逃脱的手段。***at the*** **～*****s*** (***with***)〔美〕跟…不和[闹翻]。***from*** **～** ***to*** **～** 从一头到另一头,全长;外径。***make a poor*** ～不成功,搞不很好。***on the*** **～*****s***〔美俚〕闹翻了脸,感情不好。***the ins and*** **～*****s*** 朝野两党;角角落落;里里外外;细节,细情,一五一十。

IV ***a*.** **1.** 外面的,外头的;外围的;远的;向外去的。**2.**〔口〕不平常的;特大的。**3.** 在野的,下台的。**4.**〔口〕过了时的。**5.**〔美俚〕时新的。**6.**〔美俚〕不省人事的,喝得烂醉的。*an* ～ *match* 外出访问比赛。*the* ～ *side*【运】守方。*an* ～ *size* (西装等)特大型。

V ***vt*.** **1.**〔口〕逐出,赶出;【拳击】打倒,击昏(= *knock* ～);【运】使退场;使出局。**2.** 把(火)弄熄[弄灭]。**3.** 揭发出(某人)为同性恋者;使(同性恋者)曝光。*Out that man!* 把那个人赶出去! *Murder will* ～. 恶事总必败露。—***vi*.** 外出;败露,破露,显露。

VI ***int*.**〔古〕表示"愤慨""谴责"等。*O- upon you!* 滚!混蛋!

out- *pref*. 加在动词、分词或动名词前表示"出","向外","在外","超过","胜过"等意,如 *out*go, *out*play.〔若为名词、形容词及分词,重音通常在 out 上,如:ˈ*out*break, ˈ*out*bound, ˈ*out*going; 若为动词,重音通常在第二音节以后,如:*out*do〕。

out·act [autˈækt; aʊtˋækt] ***vt*.** 行动上胜过。

out·age [ˈautidʒ; ˋaʊtɪdʒ] ***n*.** **1.** 出口。**2.**【商】损耗。**3.** (检修时船、机器等的)停航,停车;【电】停电。**4.** (蓄水池的)预留容量;【机】(发动机关闭后的)液体燃料剩余。

out-and-out [ˈautəndaut; ˋaʊtənaʊt] **I** ***a*.** **1.** 完全的,不折不扣的;彻底的。**2.** 公开的,明目张胆的。**II** ***ad*.** 完全;彻头彻尾。**out-and-outer** ***n*.**〔俚〕**1.** 十全十美的人;最好的样品。**2.** 极端派,过激分子。**3.** 大坏蛋;大谎。

out·ate [autˈet; aʊtˋɛt] outeat 的过去式。

out-at-el·bows [ˈautətelbəuz; ˋaʊtətɛlboz] ***a*.** 穿旧,磨破,破烂。

out·back [ˈautbæk; ˋaʊtbæk] **I** ***a*.**〔澳〕内地的。**II** ***ad*.** 向内地。**III** ***n*.** 内地。

out·bade [autˈbeid; aʊtˋbed] outbide 的过去式。

out·bal·ance [autˈbæləns; aʊtˋbæləns] ***vt*.** 在重量上胜过;优于,胜过;在效果上超过。*The bad in his character is* ～*d by the good*. 他性格中的优点胜过缺点。

out·bid [autˈbid; aʊtˋbɪd] ***vt*.** (***-bid***, ***-bade*** [-ˈbeid, -ˈbæd; -ˋbed, -ˋbæd]; ***-bid***, ***-bid·den*** [-ˈbidn; -ˋbɪdn]; ***-bid·ding***) 出价高过(别人);抢先。～ ***each other*** 互相抬高价钱。

out·board [ˈautbɔːd; ˋaʊtˏbɔrd] **I** ***a*.**【海】船外的,舷外的;(汽艇)外部装有推进机的;【空】(飞机)外侧的。**II** ***ad*.** 向船外,向舷外;(在飞机)紧靠翼尖处。*an* ～ *motor* 艇外推进机。

out·bound[1] [ˈautbaund; ˋaʊtbaʊnd] ***a*.** 开往外国[外地]的,外出的,出差的。

out·bound[2] [ˈautˈbaund; ˋaʊtˋbaʊnd] ***vt*.** 跳过。

out·bounds [ˈautbaundz; ˋaʊtbaʊndz] ***n*.**〔*pl*.〕〔废〕边境。

out·brave [autˈbreiv; aʊtˋbrev] ***vt*.** 用勇气压倒[战胜];在勇气上超过;轻视,不把…放在心上。

out·break [ˈautbreik; ˋaʊtˏbrek] **I** ***n*.** **1.** (战争、怒气等的)爆发;【虫】(虫害等)突发蔓延。**2.** 暴动,骚扰;反抗。**3.** = outcrop. **II** [autˈbreik; aʊtˋbrek] ***vi*.** (***-broke*** [-ˈbrəuk; -ˋbrok]; ***-bro·ken*** [-ˈbrəukən; -ˋbrokən]; ***-break·ing***)〔诗〕突然发生;爆发;花开。

out·breed [ˈautbriːd; ˋaʊtbrid] ***vt*.** (***-bred*** [-bred; -brɛd]; ***-breed·ing***) **1.** 使进行远系繁殖。**2.** 比…繁殖得快。

out·breed·ing [ˈautbriːdiŋ; ˋaʊtbridɪŋ] ***n*.** **1.**【动】远系繁殖。**2.**【社】族外婚。

out·build·ing [ˈautbildiŋ; ˋaʊtbɪldɪŋ] ***n*.** 外屋,副屋;〔*pl*.〕〔美〕农场办事处。

out·burst [ˈautbəːst; ˋaʊtbɝst] ***n*.** (火山、情感等的)爆发,迸发;爆炸;【化】爆燃;激增。

out·by(e) [ˈautbai; ˋaʊtbaɪ] ***ad*.**〔Scot.〕在不远的地方;在户外。

out·cast [ˈautkɑːst; ˋaʊtkæst] **I** ***a*.** 被逐出(家庭、国家)的,被排斥的;被遗弃的;无家可归的。**II** ***n*.** 被驱逐的人,被抛弃的东西;废物;无家可归的人,流浪者;流氓,无赖。

out·caste [ˈautkɑːst; ˋaʊtkæst] ***n*.** (印度)被剥夺种姓者;无种姓者;贱民。

out·class [autˈklɑːs; aʊtˋklæs] ***vt*.** 比…高一等;大大超过。*He far* ～*es the other runners in the race*. 他在比赛时远远超过其他的赛跑者。

out·clear·ing [ˈautkliəriŋ; ˋaʊtˏklɪrɪŋ] ***n*.**【商】应付票据交换额(*opp*. inclearing)。

out-college [ˈautkɔlidʒ; ˋaʊtˏkɑlɪdʒ] ***a*.**〔英〕住在大学校外的;不属于大学宿舍的。

out·come [ˈautkʌm; ˋaʊtkʌm] ***n*.** **1.** 结果;成果;后果。**2.**【理】输出口;〔喻〕出路。*The* ～ *of a war is decided by the people*. 决定战争胜败的是人民。

out·com·er [ˈautˌkʌmə; ˋaʊtˏkʌmɚ] ***n*.** 外来者,外国人,陌生人。

out·cor·ner [ˈautkɔːnə; ˋaʊtkɔrnɚ] ***n*.**【棒球】外角。

out·crop [ˈautkrɔp; ˋaʊtˏkrɑp] ***n*.**【地】(岩层等的)露头;露出地面的岩层。

out·cross [autˈkrɔs; aʊtˋkrɑs] **I** ***vt*.** 使进行异型杂交。**II** [ˈautkrɔs; ˋaʊtkrɑs] ***n*.**【生】异型杂交后代。

out·cross·ing [ˈautkrɔːsiŋ; ˋaʊtkrɔsɪŋ] ***n*.**【生】异型杂交。

out·cry [ˈautkrai; ˋaʊtˏkraɪ] ***n*.** **1.** 喊叫,喧嚷,吆喝,怒号。**2.** 叫卖;拍卖;喊价。*raise an* ～ *against* 强烈反对[抗议]。

out·curve [ˈautkəːv; ˋaʊtˏkɝv] **I** ***n*.** 外曲;外曲物;【棒球】外曲球。**II** [autˈkəːv; aʊtˋkɝv] ***vt*.**, ***vi*.** (使)外曲。

out·cut [ˈautkʌt; ˋaʊtkʌt] ***n*.** 被剪去的影片。

out·dare [autˈdɛə; aʊtˋdɛr] ***vt*.** **1.** 胆量胜过。**2.** 不怕,蔑视(= defy)。

out·date [autˈdeit; aʊtˋdet] ***vt*.** 使过时。

out·dat·ed [autˈdeitid; aʊtˋdetɪd] ***a*.** 已经不流行的;过时的;陈旧的,古风的。

out·did [autˈdid; aʊtˋdɪd] outdo 的过去式。

out·dis·tance [autˈdistəns; aʊtˋdɪstəns] ***vt*.** 把(其他赛跑者)远远抛在后头,远远超过;胜过。

out·do [autˈduː; aʊtˋdu] ***vt*.** (***-did*** [-ˈdid; -ˋdɪd]; ***-done*** [-ˈdʌn; -ˋdʌn]) 优于;凌驾,胜过;打败;制服;超越。～ ***oneself*** 得到空前成绩,打破自己以往记录;尽自己最大的努力。

out·done [autˈdʌn; aʊtˋdʌn] **1.** outdo 的过去式。**2.** ***a*.**〔美方〕激怒的,烦恼的。

out·door [ˈautdɔː; ˋaʊtˏdɔr] ***a*.** **1.** 户外的,屋外的,露天的;野外的。**2.** (医院等)院外的;〔英〕议院外的。～ *exercises* 户外运动。*an* ～ *life* 野外生活。*the* ～ *activities*〔英议院〕院外活动。

out·doors [autˈdɔːz; aʊtˋdɔrz] **I** ***ad*.** 在户外[屋外、野外];向户外[屋外、野外](*opp*. indoors)。**II** ***n*.**〔口〕户外;露天;野外;世间。

out·eat [autˈiːt; aʊtˋit] ***vt*.** (***out·ate*** [autˈet; aʊtˋɛt]; ***out·eat·en*** [autˈiːtn; aʊtˋitn]) 吃得比…多。

out·er [ˈautə; ˋaʊtɚ] (*opp*. inner) **I** ***a*.** (*superl*. ～***-most***) **1.** 外的,外部的,外面的;外侧的。**2.**【哲】客观外界的;物质的。**3.** 远离中心的。*one's* ～ *garment* 外衣。*the O- Bar*〔英〕〔集合词〕(不属于王室律师的)普通律师。*the* ～ *man*〔谑〕(人的)外貌,风度;装束。

the ~ world 外部世界,外界;世间。**II** ***n*.** 靶子环外的部分;环外命中。~ **city** 〔美〕市郊;郊区。~ **coat** 轻便大衣;外套,外衣。~ **core** (地球的)外核。~ **space** 1. 宇宙空间,外太空。2. 外层空间,星际空间。~**course** 体外性行为〔与 intercourse 相对而言〕。~ **wear** 外衣,外套[大衣、雨衣等];户外穿的服装。~ **most** ***ad*.**, ***a*.** 最外面(的),最远(的),远离中心(的),最后面(的),顶上(的);在最远处,在最后面,在顶上。

out·face [aut'feis; aʊt'fes] ***vt*.** 1. 逼视…使其将目光移开;恐吓。2. 厚着脸皮干下去,满不在乎地应付;反抗;挑(战),冒(雨)。

out·fall ['autfɔːl; 'aʊtfɔl] ***n*.** 1. 河口,流口,吐出口,落水口。2. 吵架,拌嘴,不和。3. 冲锋,突击;袭击。

out·field ['autfiːld; 'aʊt'fild] ***n*.** 1. (远离宅地的)远田,边地;(围篱以外的)外田;郊外;〔Scot.〕草地。2. 边境;未知世界。3. 〔通例 the ~〕【棒球】外场,〔集合词〕外野手(*opp*. infield)。**-er** ***n*.**【棒球】外野手。

out·fight [aut'fait; aʊt'faɪt] ***vt*.** (***out·fought*** ['aut'fɔːt; aʊt'fɔt]) 战胜,击败。

out·fight·ing ['autfaitiŋ; 'aʊtfaɪtɪŋ] ***n*.** 远距离作战。

out·fit ['autfit; 'aʊtfɪt] **I** ***n*.** 1. (旅行等的)准备;旅费;旅行用品,装置;(一定场合下穿的)全套衣装;(军事)装备;航海用具;商业用具,生财;(一般)设备,用品,工具。2. 精神准备,素养。3. 〔口〕(一般)团体;有组织的单位;旅行团;探险队;棒球队(等);采矿[筑路(等)]队;(某人手下的)全班人马;〔美军俚〕(准备出动的)部队。4. 牧场;庄园。**II** ***vt*.** (**-tt-**) 〔主用被动语态〕装备;供给;准备;配备(*with*)。

out·fit·ter ['autfitə; 'aʊt,fɪtɚ] ***n*.** 服饰用品商店;旅行用品商店;运动用品店;【船】安装机器的机工。

out·fit·ting ['autfitiŋ; 'aʊtfɪtɪŋ] ***n*.** (旅行等的)准备,装束。

out·flank [aut'flæŋk; aʊt'flæŋk] ***vt*.**【军】包抄,迂回敌侧(包围);突然胜过。*encirclement and ~ing* 包围和迂回。

out·flow ['autfləu; 'aʊtflo] ***n*.** 流出;流出物;流出口,泛滥;(语言、感情的)爆发。*stem the river's ~* 防止河水泛滥。

out·fly [aut'flai; aʊt'flaɪ] ***vt*.** (***out·flew*** [aut'fluː; aʊt'flu]; ***out·flown*** [aut'fləun; aʊt'flon]) 在飞行速度上超过。~ *the speed of sound* 超音速。

out·foot [aut'fut; aʊt'fʊt] ***vt*.** 追过,赶过;〔美〕赛船划胜。*She ~ed me in a climb up a hill*. 在一次爬山中她比我走得快。

out·fought [aut'fɔːt; aʊt'fɔt] outfight 的过去式和过去分词。

out·fox [aut'fɔks; aʊt'fɑks] ***vt*.** 瞒过,机智上胜过,比…更狡猾。

out·game [aut'geim; aʊt'gem] ***vt*.** 〔美〕比赛领先[赢]。

out·gas [,aut'gæs; aʊt'gæs] ***vt*.** (***-gassed***; ***-gas·sing***) 1. 从(行星内部向大气)放出气态物质。2. 除去…的气。

out·gen·er·al [aut'dʒenərəl; aʊt'dʒɛnərəl] ***vt*.** (〔英〕***-ll-***) 战术[谋略]胜过;使堕入术中;在领导[管理]才能上胜过。

out·giv·ing ['autgiviŋ; 'aʊt,gɪvɪŋ] **I** ***n*.** 〔美〕公开声明[发言]。**II** ***a*.** (态度)自然的,无拘无束的。

out·go [aut'gəu; aʊt'go] **I** ***vt*.** (***-went*** [-'went; -'wɛnt]; ***-gone*** [-'gɔn; -'gɑn]) 比…走得快,超过;优于,胜过。**II** ['autgəu; 'aʊtgo] ***n*.** (*pl*. ~***es***) 1. 支出,开销(*opp*. income);消耗。2. 出发,出走,退出;出口;流出。3. 结果,产品。

out·go·ing ['autgəuiŋ; 'aʊtgoɪŋ] **I** ***a*.** 1. 出发的;往外去的;退去的;即将离职的。2. 对人友好的;开朗的。*an ~ ship* 出航的船,离港船。*the ~ tide* 退去的潮水。~ *ministers* 前任部长。**II** ***n*.** 1. 〔常 *pl*. 作单数用〕支出,开支。2. 出去;外出;出发;终。3. 〔美〕声明。

out·gone [aut'gɔn; aʊt'gɑn] outgo 的过去分词。

out-group ['autgruːp; 'aʊtgrup] ***n*.** 外集团,外人集团。

out·grow [aut'grəu; aʊt'gro] ***vt*.** (***-grew*** [-'gruː; -'gru]; ***-grown*** [-'grəun; -'gron]) 1. 长得比…快[大]。2. 因年龄增加而失[脱]去,脱离…的苦痛;发展得不再需要(某事物)。*My family has outgrown our house*. 我家人口增加得房屋不够住了。*The children have outgrown their garments*. 孩子们长得衣服穿不上了。~ *a bad habit* 随着年龄增长而戒掉了一个坏习惯。~ *early friends* 长大了幼小时候的朋友也不往来了。~ *one's strength* 年龄小个子长得太大,人小个子大。—***vi*.** 生物长出。

out·growth ['autgrəuθ; 'aʊt,groθ] ***n*.** 1. 【植】枝条;瘤。2. (自然的)结果;派生物;副产物。3. (树叶等)长出,长大。*Revolution is a frequent ~ of tyranny*. 革命是暴政促成的常有结果。

out·guard ['autgɑːd; 'aʊt,gɑrd] ***n*.**【军】警戒哨。

out·guess [aut'ges; aʊt'gɛs] ***vt*.** 猜透,智胜。

out·gun [aut'gʌn; aʊt'gʌn] ***vt*.** (***-nn-***) 在武器上超过,胜过,超越。

out·haul ['authɔːl; 'aʊthɔl] ***n*.**【海】把帆扯向帆杠尾端之索。

out-her·od, out-Her·od [aut'herəd; aʊt'hɛrəd] ***vt*.** ~ *Herod* 暴虐胜过希律王;比希律王更希律王。★可同样类推说 out-Zola Zola 在某人[左拉]特征方面胜过某人[左拉]。

out·house ['authaus; 'aʊt,haʊs] ***n*.** 1. = outbuilding. 2. 〔美〕屋外厕所。

out·ing ['autiŋ; 'aʊtɪŋ] ***n*.** 外出;出游,游览,旅行;散步。~ **flannel** 软绒布。

out·island ['autailənd; 'aʊtaɪlənd] ***n*.** 群岛中的非主要岛屿。

out·jock·ey [aut'dʒɔki; aʊt'dʒɑkɪ] ***vt*.** 骗,哄人上当;用诡计胜过。

out·land ['autlænd; 'aʊt,lænd] **I** ***n*.** 1. 〔常 *pl*.〕〔废〕边远地区,偏僻地区,内地。2. 〔古〕外国。**II** ['autlənd; 'aʊt,lænd] ***a*.** 1. 遥远的,边远的,远离中心的。2. 〔古〕外国的。

out·land·er ['autlændə; 'aʊt,lændɚ] ***n*.** 外国人;外地人;外来者;陌生人;〔口〕局外人。

out·land·ish [aut'lændiʃ; aʊt'lændɪʃ] ***a*.** 外国气派的,异国风味的;奇异的;粗鲁笨拙的;〔古〕外国的;偏僻的;边远的。

out·last [aut'lɑːst; aʊt'læst] ***vt*.** 较…经久,比…持久;比…命长。

out·law ['autlɔː; 'aʊtlɔ] **I** ***n*.** 1. 丧失公权者,被剥夺法律保护的人;歹徒;惯犯;逃犯;亡命徒。2. 难驯服的动物;烈马。**II** ***vt*.** 1. 取缔;剥夺…的法律保护。2. 使失法律效力。*an ~ed debt* 〔美〕失时效的债务。

out·law·ry ['autlɔːri; 'aʊtlɔrɪ] ***n*.** 1. 法益剥夺;失时效。2. 宣布非法,非法化。3. 驱逐令,放逐。4. 逍遥法外。

out·lay ['autlei; 'aʊt,le] ***n*.** 费用,花费;支出。

out·let ['autlet, -lit; 'aʊt,lɛt, -lɪt] ***n*.** 1. 出口,出路;排水口;通风口。2. 【商】销路。3. 批发商店。4. 发泄(情感)的方法;排遣。5. 地方广播电台[电视台]。*an ~ for water* 排水孔。~ *water* 废水。*He wants an ~ for his energy*. 他需要一个发挥他的精力的去处。

out·li·er ['autlaiə; 'aʊtlaɪɚ] ***n*.** 1. 不住在工作地点的人,在工作地点外另有住宅的人。2. 离开本体的东西,分离物;【地】老围层;外露层(*opp*. inlier)。3. 门外汉;局外人。

out·line ['autlain; 'aʊt,laɪn] **I** ***n*.** 1. 外形,轮廓;轮廓线;轮廓画法,略图(画法)。2. 〔常 *pl*.〕梗概,大纲,提纲;草稿;要点;主要原则。*an ~ map* 略图。**give an ~ of** 概要说明…。**in ~** 只画轮廓(的);概略(的)(*a horse drawn in ~* 潦潦草草画成的马,马的草图)。**make an ~ of a** (*composition*) 为(作文)拟提纲。**II** ***vt*.** 1. 画轮廓;打草图,描略图。2. 概括地论述,略述。

out·live [aut'liv; aʊt`lɪv] *vt*. 1. 比…长寿,比…经久;度过…而健在。2. 老到超过…的程度;久活而失去。~ *one's contemporaries* 比同时代的人长寿。~ *one's usefulness* 衰老无用。~ *one's health* 年老多病。

out·look ['autluk; `aʊt,lʊk] I *n*. 1. 景色,风光,景致。2. 前景;展望;前途(*for*);形势。3. 见地,见解;眼界;先见;…观;观点。4. 看守,了望;看守人;了望台,望楼。*a room with an* ~ *on the sea* 望见海景的房间。*one's* ~ *on life* 某人的人生观。*the ideological* ~ 精神面貌。*the political* ~ 政治前景。**be on the** ~ (**for**) 监视着;提防着。II [aut'luk; aʊt`lʊk] *vt*. 1. 瞪着看;瞧;以目光压倒(对方)。2. 比…好看。

out·ly·ing ['autlaiiŋ; `aʊtlaɪɪŋ] *a*. 1. 在境界[围篱]外的;远离中心[主体]的,边远的。2. 无关的;题外的。

out·ma·chine [ˌautmə'ʃiːn; ˏaʊtmə`ʃin] *vt*.【军】机械化程度超过(敌人)。

out·man [ˌaut'mæn; aʊt`mæn] *vt*. (**-manned**; **-manning**) 人数胜过,在数量上超过。

out·ma·noeu·vre, 〔美〕**-neu·ver** [ˌautmə'nuːvə; ˏaʊtmə`nuvɚ] *vt*. 对…机动制胜;用谋略制胜,计谋胜过…;挫败(敌人的)阴谋。

out·march [aut'mɑːtʃ; aʊt`mɑrtʃ] *vt*. 进行得比…快[远];赶过。

out·mar·ry ['autmæri; `aʊt,mærɪ] *vt*. (**-ried**; **-rying**) (在婚姻上)高攀〔多与反身代名词连用〕。—*vi*. 与异族结婚。

out·match [aut'mætʃ; aʊt`mætʃ] *vt*. 胜过,优于,强过。*be* ~*ed in skill* 技巧方面不及别人。

out-mi·grant ['aut'maigrənt; `aʊt`maɪgrənt] I *a*. 迁徙的,迁走的,他迁的。II *n*. 迁徙者,他迁者,他迁动物。**out-mi·grate** ['aut'maigreit; `aʊt`maɪgret] *vi*. 迁徙,迁走,他迁。**-gra·tion** *n*.

out·mod·ed [aut'məudid; aʊt`modɪd] *a*. 过时的。

out·most ['autməust; `aʊt,most] *a*. = outermost.

out·ness ['autnis; `aʊtnɪs] *n*.【哲】外在性;客观存在性。

out·num·ber [aut'nʌmbə; aʊt`nʌmbɚ] *vt*. 数量上胜过,比…多。*They* ~*ed us three to one*. 他们以三与一之比在数量上超过了我们。

out-of-bounds ['autəv'baundz; `aʊtəv`baʊndz] I *adv*. 到界外。*kick a ball* ~ 把球踢到界外。II *a*. 1. 禁止入内的;不可超越的。2. 出乎意料的。3.【运】界外的。

out-of-date ['autəv'deit; `aʊtəv`det] *a*. 落后的,过时的;不适用的;不使用的,已作废的。

out-of-door(**s**) [ˌautəv'dɔːz; aʊtəv`dorz] I *a*. = outdoor. II *ad*., *n*. = outdoors.

out-of-pock·et ['autəv'pɔkit; `aʊtəv`pɑkɪt] *a*. 1. 现款支付的。2. 无钱的。3. 非预算项下开支的,预算外开支的。

out-of-the-way [autəvðə'wei; `aʊtəðə`we] *a*. 1. 边远的,偏僻的。2. 奇特的,异常的。

out-of-town·er ['autəv'taunə; `aʊtəv`taʊnɚ] *n*. 从其他城市来的参观者,他市来客。

out·pace [aut'peis; aʊt`pes] *vt*. 跑得比…快,追过;发展快过;胜过。

out·pa·tient [aut'peiʃənt; `aʊt,peʃənt] *n*. 门诊病人。

out·pen·sion·er ['autˌpenʃənə; `aʊt,pɛnʃənɚ] *n*. (救济院机关等的)院外领取年金的人。

out·per·form [autpə'fɔːm; aʊtpɚ`fɔrm] *vt*. (机器等)性能比…好。

out·place [aut'pleis; aʊt`ples] *vt*.【美】1. (在解雇某人前)先调动(该人的)职位。2. 使免职,解雇。**-ment** *n*.

out·play [aut'plei; aʊt`ple] *vt*. (在球赛中)打得比…好;(比赛中)击败,胜过。

out·point [aut'pɔint; aʊt`pɔɪnt] *vt*. (比赛)得分超过;(赛船)比…更迎风航行。

out·poll [aut'pəul; aʊt`pol] *vt*. 得到的选票超过(他人)。

out·port ['autpɔːt; `aʊt,port] *n*. 外港〔远离海滨或商业中心的海港〕;输出港。

out·post ['autpəust; `aʊtpost] *n*. 前哨;前哨基地;警戒部队。

out·pour [aut'pɔː; aʊt`por] I *vt*., *vi*. 〔诗〕(使)泻出;(使)流出。II ['autpɔː; `aʊt,por] *n*. 泻出,流出(物)。

out·pour·ing ['autpɔːriŋ; `aʊt,porɪŋ] *n*. 泻出,流出;(情感等的)流露,洋溢;迸发;〔主 *pl*.〕激动的言语。*the* ~*s of a sentimental mind* 感伤的话。

out·put ['autput; `aʊt,pʊt] *n*. 1. 产量;生产,出产,产品。2.【医】(粪便以外的)排泄物;排泄量。3.【电】发电力,输出功率;供给量。4. 输出信号。*monthly* ~ 月产量。*the* ~ *of a factory* 工厂产品。*the literary* ~ *of the year* 当年文艺作品。*a sudden* ~ *of effort* 奋发。~ **data** 输出数据。

out·rage ['autreidʒ; `aʊtredʒ] I *n*. 1. 暴举,暴行。2. 强奸,凌辱。3. 严重违法。4. 义愤,痛恨。~*s against the peasants* 鱼肉农民。*commit* ~*s* [*an* ~] *on* [*upon*] 对…[在…方面]倒行逆施;侮辱。II *vt*. 1. 伤害;虐待,迫害。2. 凌辱,强奸。3. 违反;犯(法);引起…的义愤。

out·ra·geous [aut'reidʒəs; aʊt`redʒəs] *a*. 粗暴的,残暴的;蛮横的,猖狂的,无法无天的;无耻的,令人不能容忍的;荒谬绝伦的。*commit* ~ *actions on* 对…[在…方面]倒行逆施;侮辱。**-ly** *ad*. **-ness** *n*.

out·ran [ˌaut'ræn; aʊt`ræn] outrun 的过去式。

ou·trance [uː'tɑ̃ːns; u`trɑ̃s] *n*. 〔F.〕极端,最后。*à* ~ 到底(*fight à* ~ 打到底,死战)。

out·range [aut'reindʒ; aʊt`rendʒ] *vt*. 1. 在射程上胜过,打得比…远。2. 比…看得远。

out·rank [aut'ræŋk; aʊt`ræŋk] *vt*. 〔美〕等级高于。

ou·tré ['uːtrei; u`tre] *a*. 〔F.〕逸出常轨的;失当的;过激的;奇怪的;荒诞的;夸大的。

out·reach [aut'riːtʃ; aʊt`ritʃ] I *vt*. 超出…的范围,超过;胜过;伸长。II ['autriːtʃ; `aʊtrɪtʃ] *n*. 1. 伸出;展开;达到的范围。2.〔美〕济贫工作。

out·re·lief ['autriliːf; `aʊtrɪlif] *n*. 对不住在济贫院内的贫民的施舍(=〔美〕outdoor relief)。

out·ride [aut'raid; aʊt`raɪd] *vt*. (**-rode** [-'rəud; -`rod]; **-rid·den** [-'ridn; -`rɪdn]; **-rid·ing**) 骑得比…快[好、远];骑胜;(船)冲过(风雨)。— *vi*. 在车外骑着马(跟着)。

out·rid·er ['autraidə; `aʊt,raɪdɚ] *n*. (车辆前后、左右的)骑马侍从,驾摩托车的警卫;前驱;前导。

out·rig·ger ['autrigə; `aʊtrɪgɚ] *n*.【海】(伸出船两边支桨用的)叉架;装有舷外铁架的划子[小艇];(拴绳子等用的)舷外斜木;(防止划子翻倒的)舷外浮材;【空】(支撑机翼用的)外架;承力支架,悬臂支架。

out·right ['aut'rait; `aʊt`raɪt] I *ad*. 1. 完全,彻底;公然,公开;直率地,痛快地;坦白,不客气地,露骨地。2. 即刻,马上,当场。*laugh* ~ 放声大笑。*be killed* ~ 被当场杀死。*buy* ~ 用现金购买。II ['autrait; `aʊt,raɪt] *a*. 直率的,明白的;十足的,彻底的。*give an* ~ *denial* 断然否认。*an* ~ *rogue* 彻头彻尾的恶棍。

out·ri·val [aut'raivəl; aʊt`raɪvl] *vt*. (**-ll-**) 在竞争中胜过(对手)。

out·rode [aut'rəud; aʊt`rod] outride 的过去式。

out·root [ˌaut'rut; aʊt`rʊt] *vt*. 1. 连根拔起;根绝,绝灭;赶出(住宅等)。2. 消灭;毁灭(= uproot)。

out·run [aut'rʌn; aʊt`rʌn] *vt*. (**-ran** [-'ræn; -`ræn]; **-run**; **-run·ning**) 跑胜,追过;逃走;脱离,超过;超出…界限;比…得更多选票。*let one's zeal* ~ *discretion* 过分热心实欠谨慎。*His imagination* ~*s the facts*. 他的想像脱离事实,想入非非。

out·run·ner ['autrʌnə; aʊt`rʌnɚ] *n*. 跑得更快[远、好]的人;(跟着马车跑的)侍从;辕外副马;(拉雪橇的)领头狗;先驱者。

out·rush ['autrʌʃ; `aʊt,rʌʃ] I *n*. 冲出,流出。II *vt*. 比

O

…冲得更前。

out·sail [aut'seil; aʊt`sel] *vt*. (船)航行航得比…快,追讨。

out·sat [aut'sæt; aʊt`sæt] outsit 的过去式和过去分词。

out·scrib·er [aut'skraibə; aʊt`skraɪbɚ] *n*.【无】输出记录机。

out·seg [aut'seg; aʊt`sɛg] *vt*. 〔美俚〕比…实行更激烈的种族主义。

out·sell [aut'sel; aʊt`sɛl] *vt*. (*-sold* [-'səuld; -`sold]) 卖得比…多[快、贵];比…更能推销。

out·set ['autset; `aʊtset] *n*. 开头,开端,开始。*at* [*in*] *the* ~ 在开头时。*from the* ~ 从一开始。

out·shine [aut'ʃain; aʊt`ʃaɪn] *vt*. (*-shone* [-'ʃɔn; -`ʃon]; *-shin·ing*) 比…亮,比…聪明[优秀、漂亮];胜过,优于;使相形见绌。

out·shoot [aut'ʃuːt; aʊt`ʃut] **I** *vt*. (*-shot* [-'ʃɔt; -`ʃɑt]; *-shoot·ing*) **1**. 比…更有效地射击。**2**. 射出。**II** *vi*. 突出,伸出。**III** ['autʃut; `aʊtʃʊt] *n*. **1**. 射击;突然或迅速的突出或伸出。**2**. 突出物,伸出物。**3**.【棒球】曲线球〔早期用语〕。

out·side ['aut'said; `aʊt`saɪd] (*opp*. inside) **I** *n*. **1**. 外头,外部,外面,外侧;外观;外表;外界;【电话】外线;【体】出界。**2**. 极端。**3**. 〔英〕(公共马车等的)车顶座位;车顶乘客。**4**. 〔*pl*.〕一束纸最外层上下两张。**5**. 〔美俚〕被认为跑赢机会很少的马,冷门马。*He has a rough* ~, *but a good heart*. 他外貌粗暴心地善良。*impressions from the* ~ 表面印象。*open the door from* ~ 从外头开门。*those on the* ~ 局外人;外界人士。*at the* (*very*) ~ 至多,充其量。~ *in* 里面翻到外面;彻底地。
II ['autsaid; `aʊtsaɪd] *a*. 〔仅用作表语[述语]〕**1**. 外面的,外侧的,外部的;外观上的,肤浅的;〔英〕车顶座的。**2**. 极端的,极度的;最大程度的;〔口〕最高的。**3**. 局外的,门外的,没有加入工会[协会等]的。**4**. 〔美俚〕已经出狱的。恢复了自由的。*an* ~ *broker* (交易所)场外经纪人。*an* ~ *porter* 〔英〕可以把行李送出站外的服务员。*the* ~ *edge* 用冰鞋外棱滑,极端的侮辱。*an* ~ *man* 〔美〕(替盗贼)望风的人。*an* ~ *work* (不在工作场所的)外活。*an* ~ *chance* 几乎没有希望的机会,〔美〕赛赢的机会很少。~ *help* 外来的援助,外援。~ *opinions* 外部意见;【议院】院外意见。*the* ~ *price* 最高价格。*an* ~ *wife* 情妇,外室。
III [aut'said; aʊt`saɪd] *ad*. 在外面,在外头,在外部;向户外,在户外;向海上,在海上;【体】出线,出界。*go* ~ 到户外。*Come* ~! (挑战)出来! *Outside!* (放)到外头来! *ride* ~ 〔英〕乘顶座。*get* ~ *of* 〔俚〕喝;吞;吃。~ *of a horse* 〔俚〕骑着马。
IV ['aut'said; `aʊt`saɪd] *prep*. 在[向]…的外边,…外边的;超过…的范围,在…之上,在…以上;从…;〔口〕除…外。*go* ~ *the house* 走到屋外。*go* ~ *the evidence* 牵涉到证据以外。*things* ~ *one's sphere* 本分以外的事情。*No one knows* ~ *two or three persons*. 除两三人外谁也不知道。**~-the-box** *a*. 创造性的,跳出传统格局的。

out·sid·er ['aut'saidə, aut's-; `aʊt`saɪdɚ, aʊt`s-] *n*. **1**. 外来者,外头人,局外人,没有关系的人;会外的人,党外[院外]人。**2**. 门外汉,外行;没有专门知识的人。**3**.【赛马】没有胜利希望的马[骑师]。*The* ~ *sees the best* [*most*] *of the game*. 旁观者清。

out·sight ['autsait; `aʊtsaɪt] *n*. 对外界事务的观察;观察力(*opp*. insight)。

out·sit [aut'sit; aʊt`sɪt] *vt*. (*out·sat* [-'sæt; -`sæt]; *-sit·ting*) = outstay.

out·size ['autsaiz; `aʊt,saɪz] **I** *a*. 超过标准尺寸的,特别大的(衣服鞋帽等)。**II** *n*. 特大型;特大品。**-d** *a*. (= outsize).

out·skirt ['autskəːt; `aʊtskɝt] *n*. 〔常 *pl*.〕郊外;外边。*on the* ~*s of* 在…的外边;…郊区。

out·smart [aut'smɑːt; `aʊtsmɑrt] *vt*. 〔美〕= outwit.

out·soar [aut'sɔː; aʊt`sɔr] *vt*. 飞过,飞越,翱翔于…之上。

out·sold [aut'səuld; aʊt`sold] outsell 的过去式和过去分词。

out·sole ['autsəul; `aʊt,sol] *n*. 皮鞋〔靴〕的鞋跟。

out·source [aut'sɔːs; aʊt`sɔs] *vt*., *vi*. (将…业务,工程等)外包。

out·span [aut'spæn; aʊt`spæn] **I** *vt*., *vi*. 〔南非〕(由车上)解开(牛);卸(马具)。**II** *n*. **1**. 去轭;卸马具。**2**. 牲口休息地。

out·speak [aut'spiːk; aʊt`spik] **I** *vt*. (*-spoke* [-'spəuk; -`spok]; *-spo·ken* [-'spəukən; -`spokən]) **1**. 在讲话上胜过。**2**. 大胆地说,坦率地说。**II** *vi*. 大胆、直率地说。

out·spo·ken [aut'spəukən; aʊt`spokən] *a*. 直言不讳的,坦率的;毫无保留的。~ *criticism* 坦率的批评。*an* ~ *person* 直率的人。**-ly** *ad*. **-ness** *n*.

out·spread [aut'spred; aʊt`sprɛd] **I** *vt*., *vi*. (*-spread*) (使)扩张;(使)展开;(使)伸开;传播,散布。**II** *a*. 伸开的;扩张的;展开的。

out·stand [aut'stænd; aʊt`stænd] **I** *vi*. (*-stood* [-'stud; -`stʊd]) **1**. 凸出,突出。**2**.【海】离港;向海上。**II** *vt*. **1**. 〔古〕忍耐;停留。**2**. 〔方〕抵抗,反抗;经受得起。

out·stand·ing [aut'stændiŋ; aʊt`stændɪŋ] *a*. **1**. 显著的;凸出的,杰出的。**2**. 未付的,未清的;未解决的;未完成的。**3**. (股票等)已发行和出售的。*an* ~ *fact* 显著的事实。*an* ~ *figure* 杰出人物。*an* ~ *debt* 未偿债务。~ *accounts* 未清账款。~ *check* 未兑现支票。*leave* ~ **1**. 搁着不理(*leave a good deal of work* ~ 搁着许多工作不做)。**2**. 搁置不付[不偿还]。**-ly** *ad*.

out·stare [aut'stεə; aʊt`stɛr] *vt*. **1**. 以目光镇住(对方);瞪得(某人)局促不安;瞪看着。**2**. 面对…而无惧色,挑战,对抗。

out·sta·tion ['autsteiʃən; `aʊtsteʃən] *n*. 设在边远地区的分站,边远哨所。

out·stay [aut'stei; aʊt`ste] *vt*. **1**. 比(别人)住得[逗留得]久。**2**. 久住而失去。**3**. 在持久力上超过。~ *one's welcome* 因住得[逗留]太久而讨人厌恶。

out·step [aut'step; aʊt`stɛp] *vt*. 走过;超过;逾越;过火;犯。~ *decency* 越出礼貌以外。~ *the truth* 夸大事实。

out·stretch [aut'stretʃ; aʊt`strɛtʃ] *vt*. **1**. 扩张,张开;展开。**2**. 伸展超过…。

out·stretched [aut'stretʃt; aʊt`strɛtʃt] *a*. 扩张的;伸长的。*lie* ~ *on the ground* 直挺挺躺在地上。

out·strip [aut'strip; aʊt`strɪp] *vt*. 超过;越过;追过;优于,胜过;逃脱。*overtake and* ~ 赶上并超过。

out·talk [aut'tɔːk; aʊt`tɔk] *vt*. 比…说的有力[响亮、有技巧];说败,说服。

out·think [aut'θiŋk; aʊt`θɪŋk] *vt*. (*-thought* [-'θɔːt; -`θɔt]) **1**. 思考得比…来得深入、迅速或老练。**2**. 深谋远虑地制胜…。

out·throw [aut'θrəu; aʊt`θro] **I** *vt*. (*out·threw* [aut'θruː; aʊt`θro]; *out·thrown* [aut'θrəun; aʊt`θron]) **1**. 扔出,抛出。**2**. 比…扔出得更远,更准。**II** ['autθrəu; `aʊtθrə] *n*. **1**. 扔出,迸发。**2**. 中耕翻土,翻土量。**3**. 碎料,废料。

out·thrust [aut'θrʌst; aʊt`θrʌst] **I** *vt*., *vi*. (*out·thrust* [aut'θrʌst; aʊt`θrʌst]) (使)突出,(使)冲出。**II** *a*. 突出的,冲出的。**III** ['autθrʌst; `aʊtθrʌst] *n*. 突出,冲出;突出物。

out·trade [aut'treid; aʊt`tred] *vt*. 买卖中占…的上风,占…的便宜。

out·turn ['auttəːn; `aʊt,tɝn] *n*. 产量;【林】出材率;结果。

out·val·ue [aut'væljuː; aʊt`vælju] *vt*. 比…有价值;比…更可贵。

out·vie [aut'vai; aʊt`vaɪ] *vt*. (*-vied*; *-vy·ing*) 比胜,胜

过,打败。~ *each other in study* 在学习上一个胜过一个。

out·voice [aut'vɔis; aʊt`vɔɪs] *vt*. 用大声压倒。

out·vote [aut'vəut; aʊt`vot] *vt*. 投票数胜过…,得票多于…,通过投票压倒(对方,他人)。

out·vot·er [aut'vəutə; aʊt`votɚ] *n*. 〔英〕(居住)区外(的)选举人。

out·walk [aut'wɔːk; aʊt`wɔk] *vt*. 比…走得远[快],走过;越过。

out·ward ['autwəd; `aʊtwəd] (*opp*. inward) **I** *a*. **1**. 外头的,外部的;外形的,表面的;皮毛的;明显的;可见的;公开的。**2**. 向外的,向外去的;外出的;自外得来的;外来的。**3**. 【宗】物质上的,肉体上的。*an* ~ *form* 外表,外貌。~ *reformation* 表面改革。*an* ~ *passage* [*voyage*] 出航〔*cf*. homeward〕。~ *things* 周围的事务,外界。~ *eye* 肉眼(*opp*. mind's eye)。~ ***man*** 【宗】肉体;〔谑〕衣服,丰采(等)。***to*** ~ ***seeming*** 从外表上看来。

II *n*. 〔罕〕外部;外观,外形,外表;〔*pl*.〕外在事务;周围世界。

III *ad*. = outwards. ~ ***and homeward*** 来回。~**-bound** *a*. 开往国外的,出航的(船)。**-ly** *ad*. 在外,在外面;向外面;从外面来;在物质上;外表上。**-ness** *n*. 客观存在;客观性。

out·wards ['autwədz; `aʊtwɚdz] *ad*. 在外,向外;在外部;外表上;表面上;向国外。*a ship bound* ~ 开往国外的船。

out·wash ['autwɔːʃ, -wɔʃ; `aʊt͵wɑʃ, -wəʃ] *n*. 【地】冰水沉积。

out·watch [aut'wɔtʃ; aʊt`wɑtʃ] *vt*. 看到看不见;看到最后;比…看得久。~ *the night* 通宵看守。

out·wear [aut'wεə; aʊt`wεr] *vt*. (***out·wore*** [-'wɔː; -`wɔ]; ***-worn*** [-'wɔːn; -`wɔn]) **1**. 比…经久[耐用]。**2**. 穿旧,穿破;用旧,用完,耗尽;使(人)疲倦。**3**. 耐心度过。

out·weigh [aut'wei; aʊt`we] *vt*. 比…重;比…重要;胜过,强过。*The advantages* ~ *the drawbacks*. 得多于失,优点胜过缺点。

out·went [aut'went; aʊt`wεnt] outgo 的过去式。

out·wit [aut'wit; aʊt`wɪt] *vt*. (**-tt-**) **1**. 哄骗;瞒住;给…上当;机智上胜过。**2**. 〔古〕比…更有智慧。

out·work ['autwəːk; `aʊt͵wɝk] **I** *n*. **1**. 〔常用 *pl*.〕【军】简易外围工事。**2**. 户外工作,(在单位等)外部进行的工作;外勤工作。**II** [aut'wəːk; aʊt`wɝk] *vt*. (***-worked***, ***-wrought*** [-rɔːt; -rɔt]) 在工作上胜过,比…做得快[巧]。

out·work·er ['autwəːkə; `aʊtwɝkə] *n*. 外出工作的工作人员;接工作回家做的雇员。

out·wore [aut'wɔː; aʊt`wɔr] outwear 的过去式。

out·worn [aut'wɔːn; `aʊt`worn] *a*. **1**. 〔诗〕磨坏了的,破损的。**2**. 已废的;过时的,陈腐的。**3**. 筋疲力尽的;失去忍耐的。

ou·zel, ou·sel ['uːzl; `uzl̩] *n*. 【鸟】黑鸫。*a brook* ~ 秧鸡。

ou·zo ['uːzəu; `uzo] *n*. 希腊茴香烈酒,甘露酒。

ov- *comb*. *f*. 表示"蛋,卵":*ov*al.

o·va ['əuvə; `ovə] *n*. ovum 的复数。

o·val ['əuvəl; `ovl̩] **I** *a*. 卵形的;椭圆的;【植】阔椭圆形的。**II** *n*. 卵形(物);椭圆运动场(等);【物】卵形线;【数】卵形弧,卵形线;椭圆;美式足球用球。***the O-*** 伦敦 Kennington 区的板球场。***the Oval Office*** 美国总统办公室;白宫椭圆形办公室。**-ly** *ad*. **-ness** *n*.

o·var·i·an [əu'vεəriən; o`vεrɪən] *a*. 【解】卵巢的;【植】子房的。

o·var·i·ec·to·my [əu͵vεəri'ektəmi; o͵vεrɪ`εktəmɪ] *n*. (*pl*. ***-mies***) 【医】卵巢切除术。

ovario- *comb*. *f*. 表示"卵巢":*ovario*tomy.

o·var·i·ot·o·my [əu͵vεəri'ɔtəmi; o͵vεrɪ`ɑtəmɪ] *n*. (*pl*. ***-mies***) 【医】**1**. 卵巢切除术。**2**. = ovariectomy.

o·va·ri·tis [͵əuvə'raitis; ͵ovə`raɪtɪs] *n*. 【医】卵巢炎。

o·va·ry ['əuvəri; `ovərɪ] *n*. 【植】子房;【解】卵巢。

ovate ['əuveit; `ovet] *a*. 卵圆形的(树叶);卵(体)形的。

o·va·tion [əu'veiʃən; o`veʃən] *n*. 热烈的欢迎,热烈的鼓掌,欢呼;(古罗马)小凯旋式。

ov·en ['ʌvən; `ʌvən] *n*. 灶,炉,炭窑,干燥炉;烘箱。*a coke* ~ *plant* 炼焦厂。***hot from the*** ~ 刚出炉的。***in the same*** ~ 〔俚〕处于相同的困境。~**-dry** 烘干,烤干。

ov·en·bird ['ʌvənbəːd; `ʌvən͵bɝd] *n*. 【动】灶鸟。

o·ver ['əuvə; `ovɚ], 〔诗〕**o'er** [ə, ɔə, ɔː; ɚ, or, ɔr] **I** *prep*. **1**. 越过…;越过…向外[向下];…对过的。*jump* ~ *it* 跳过它。*fall* ~ *a precipice* 从崖上掉下。*This fruit will not keep* ~ *the winter*. 这水果怕保存不到春天。*the tree* ~ *the river* 河对边的树。**2**. 在…的上面,…上的;蒙在…上,悬挂在…,支配,统治;管制;(职位)在…之上。*an umbrella* ~ *one's head* 撑在头上的伞。*She put her hands* ~ *her face*. 她用手蒙住脸。*hang* ~ ... 挂在…的上面。*have no command* ~ *oneself* 不能自制。*set him* ~ *the rest* 把他安排在其余各人之上。**3**. 全面,遍,到处。*all* ~ *the body* 浑身。*The mud splashed* ~ *the garment*. 泥溅满了衣服。*all* ~ *the world* = *all the world* ~ 世界到处〔在后一结构中,over 为副词〕。**4**. 关于,对于。*laugh* ~ *the absurdity of it* 笑它荒谬。*cry* ~ *spilt milk* 后悔无及。**5**. 一面…一面…。*talk* ~ *a cup of tea* 一面喝茶一面谈话。*go to sleep* ~ *one's work* 做着事打瞌睡。**6**. 以上。*This hat cost* ~ *£5*. 这顶帽子花了五镑多。~ ***all*** 从这头到那头;〔废〕到处,处处。~ ***and above*** 远远超过…以上;加之。~ ***my dead body*** 〔美俚〕只要我不死就不会同意。~ ***the air*** 通过无线电。~ ***the bay*** 〔美俚〕喝醉的。~ ***the hill*** 【海】在大西洋的那一边,越过水平线。~ ***the hump*** 〔美俚〕大半已完;已过难关。~ ***the top*** 过份,过度地。

II *ad*. **1**. 在上,在高处;从上向下;突出,倚靠;越过。*jump* ~ 跳过。*climb* ~ 爬过。**2**. 在那边,向那边,(越过马路、河、海等)到那边,从一处到另一处。*Take this* ~ *to the station*. 把这个拿到那边车站去。*He is* ~ *in Cuba*. 他已在古巴。*Our friends were* ~ *yesterday*. 我们的朋友们昨天来过了。*I asked him* ~. 我请过他来的。*When are you coming* ~ *to see us again*? 你什么时候再来看我们呢? **3**. 遍,多次。*brush it* ~ 刷干净。*paint it* ~ 涂遍。**4**. 倒,颠倒;翻,翻转;倒过来;〔美〕请看反面(= P.T.O.)。*fall* ~ 向前摔倒。*knock a vase* ~ 碰倒花瓶。*roll* ~ 滚动。*The milk boiled* ~. 牛奶煮得溢出来了。**5**. 太,过度,过于;而且;更,另外,剩余;…多,…余。*He is* ~ *anxious*. 他太焦急了。*I do not feel* ~ *well*. 我感到身体不太舒服。*a yard and* ~ 一码多。*give sb*. *something* ~ 另外多给某人一些东西。*I paid my bill and have several pounds* ~. 我付了账还剩了好几镑。*Five goes into seven once with two* ~. 5 除 7 得 1 剩 2。**6**. 〔用作表语[述语]〕完了,结束了;过去了;关系断绝。*The war will soon be* ~. 战争不久就要结束了。*The good old times are* ~. 好日子已经过去了。**7**. 再,重行,重复地。*Try it* ~ (*again*). 再试试看。★over 后加用 again 时主为〔英〕。*count* [*read*] ~ *again* 再数[读]。*Do that three times* ~. 把那重复做三遍。**8**. 未解决,未了结。*The matter is left* ~. 那件事还没有解决。*That can stand* ~. 那件事可以暂时搁着不管。**9**. 【板球】改变掷球方向[裁判员的命令]。(***be***) ***all*** ~ (***with***) (某人)完全完了(*It's all* ~ *with me*. 我全完啦)。~ ***again*** 再来一次,再做一遍,反复。~ ***against*** 对着,面对着,对照着。~ ***and above*** 除…以外,外加。~ ***and*** ~ 转来转去;〔主美〕反反复复,再三再四。~***-and-***~ ***addition*** 逐次加法。~ ***and*** ~ ***again*** 〔英〕三番五次,再三再四。~ ***here*** 在这边,在这里。~ ***there*** 在那边,

在那里;〔美〕在欧洲;〔大战用语〕在战地。~ ***with***〔美口〕(做)完(*get something* ~ *with* 做完某事;〔英〕*get something* ~ (*and done with*))。
III ***n*.** **1.**【板球】彼此由三柱门交互连续所投之球〔通常是6球〕;连续投球比赛。**2.** 剩余,余额。**3.**【军】远弹〔超过目标落下或爆炸的射弹〕。
IV ***a*.** **1.** 在上的,表层的人。**2.** 完了的。**3.** 剩余的。
V ***vt*.** 跳过(=leap ~),走过(=go ~)。~***-the-counter market*** 证券交易所之外的股票买卖。

over- *pref*. **1.** 太,超,过度,过度的:*over*full, *over*eat, *over*do, *over*work. **2.** 在上面(的);在外部(的),在外(的):*over*coat, *over*time, *over*all, *over*board, *over*flow. **3.** 向上,向下,到,越过,加:*over*balance, *over*haul, *over*throw, *over*whelm. **4.** 完全,全:*over*-persuade.

o·ver·a·bun·dance [ˈəuvərəˈbʌndəns; ˏovərəˋbʌndəns] ***n*.** 太多,过于丰富;多余物,奢侈品,不必要的东西。**-dant** ***a*.**

o·ver·act [ˈəuvərˈækt; ˋovəˋækt] ***vt*., *vi*.** 过度…,过分…,(把剧中角色等)演得过火。

o·ver·age[1] [ˈəuvəˈridʒ; ˋovərɪdʒ] ***n*.** (商品等)过剩;过多;超额。

o·ver·age[2] [ˈəuvəˈridʒ; ˋovəˋedʒ] ***a*.** 超龄的;旧式的,老朽的。

o·ver·all [ˈəuvərɔːl; ˋovəˏɔl] **I** ***n*.** (套头)工作服,罩衫,(妇女、小儿等的)罩衣;〔*pl*.〕〔美〕工装裤;〔*pl*.〕〔英〕【军】(军官的)紧身军裤。**II** ***a*.** 全部的,所有的,全体的,全面的,总的,综合的。*the* ~ *diameter* 全径。*the* ~ *length* 全长。*by* ~ *planning* 统筹兼顾;全面规划。~ *situation* 总的形势;全局。~ *utilization* 综合利用。**III** [ˌəuvərˈɔːl; ovəˋrɔl] ***ad*.** 全面地,总地。

o·ver·anx·i·e·ty [ˈəuvəræŋˈzaiəti; ˋovəæŋˋzaɪətɪ] ***n*.** 过虑,杞忧。

o·ver·arch [ˈəuvərˈɑːtʃ; ˏovəˋɑrtʃ] ***vt*., *vi*.** 在…上架成圆拱形。

o·ver·arm [ˈəuvərɑːm; ˋovəˏɑrm] **I** ***a*.**【棒球、板球】举手过肩的,由上朝下的;【泳】(划水时)手臂伸出水面的。**II** ***n*.**【机】横杆。

over·ate [ˈəuvəˋet; ˏovəˋet] overeat 的过去式。

o·ver·awe [ˌəuvərˈɔː; ˏovəˋɔ] ***vt*.** 使畏缩,吓住,威压。

o·ver·bal·ance [ˌəuvəˈbæləns; ˏovəˋbæləns] **I** ***vt*.** 重过;重于;价值超过;压倒;使失去平均[平衡];优于。*The gains* ~ *the losses*. 得多于失。—***vi*.** 失去平衡,歪倒下来。**II** [ˈəuvəbæləns; ˋovəbæləns] ***n*.** (重量、价值的)超额;不平衡,失均衡。*the* ~ *of exports* 出超。

o·ver·bear [ˌəuvəˈbɛə; ˏovəˋbɛr] ***vt*.** (***-bore*** [-ˈbɔː, -ˈbɔə; -boɪ, -ˋbɔr]; ***-borne*** [-ˈbɔːn; -ˋbɔn]) 压服,制服,威压;抑压;超过,压倒;压碎;【海】比他船挂更多风帆。—***vi*.** 结果实过多;繁殖过度。

o·ver·bear·ing [ˌəuvəˈbɛəriŋ; ˏovəˋbɛrɪŋ] ***a*.** 架子十足的,傲慢的,自大的;专横的;压倒的;支配的;厉害的。~ *heat* 酷热。**-ly** ***ad*.**

o·ver·bid [ˌəuvəˈbid; ˏovəˋbɪd] **I** ***vt*., *vi*.** (***-bid***; ***-bidden*** [-ˈbidən; -ˋbɪdn], ***-bid***; ***-bid·ding***) **1.**【桥牌】叫牌超过(上家)。**2.** 出价高于(别人),出价高于(物品价值)。**II** [ˈəuvəbid; ˋovəbɪd] ***n*.** 超过上家的叫牌,过高的叫牌。

o·ver·bite [ˈəuvəbait; ˋovəbaɪt] ***n*.** 覆咬合〔即上门牙和犬牙过分突出于下牙〕。

o·ver·blouse [ˈəuvəblaus; ˋovəˏblaus] ***n*.** 女式长罩衫。

o·ver·blow [ˈəuvəˈbləu; ˏovəˋblo] ***vt*.** (***-blew*** [-ˈbluː; -ˋblu]; ***-blown*** [-ˈbləun; -ˋblon]) **1.** (风等)吹散;吹落;吹过;吹起沙[雪]盖住。**2.** 吹(管乐器)过响以至基调失真。**3.** 对(转炉内)吹气时间过长。**4.** 夸张;过分渲染。—***vi*.** 狂吹;(管乐器)吹得过响。

o·ver·blown [ˈəuvəˈbləun; ˏovəˋblon] ***a*.** **1.** 被吹散[吹落]了的;被(吹起的雪)盖住了的,停了的。**2.** 被忘记的;完了的;(花)开得过盛的,已过盛期的。**3.** 夸张的;渲染过分的。**4.** 腰围过大的。

o·ver·board [ˈəuvəbɔːd; ˋovəˏbord] ***ad*.** 向船外;(自船上)到水中。***fall*** ~ 从船上掉在(水里);〔美〕从火车上掉下来。***go*** ~〔美〕过分爱好;狂热追求。***throw*** ~ 丢在船外,丢在水中;排斥,放弃。

o·ver·bold [ˈəuvəˈbəuld; ˋovəˋbold] ***a*.** 过于胆大的,鲁莽的。

o·ver·book [ˈəuvəˈbuk; ˋovəˋbʊk] ***vt*.** 预订(机票等)超出所需要的数量,超量预定。

o·ver·bore [ˌəuvəˈbɔː; ˏovəˋbɔr] overbear 的过去式。

o·ver·borne [ˌəuvəˈbɔːn; ˏovəˋborn] overbear 的过去分词。

o·ver·bought [ˈəuvəˈbɔːt; ˏovəˋbɔt] overbuy 的过去式和过去分词。

o·ver·bridge [ˈəuvəbridʒ; ˋovəbrɪdʒ] ***n*.**【建】天桥,旱桥,跨线桥。

o·ver·brim [ˈəuvəˈbrim; ˏovəˋbrɪm] ***vt*., *vi*.** (***-mm-***) (使)满出,溢出。*fill to* ~*ming* 倒的满满的,溢出了。

o·ver·build [ˈəuvəˈbild; ˋovəˋbɪld] ***vt*.** (***-built*** [-ˈbilt; -ˋbɪlt]) **1.** 建造过多。**2.** 过分讲究地建筑。**3.** 建造在…上面。**4.** 指望过度。~ ***oneself*** 屋子盖得超过自己的需要;屋子盖得多到不能卖[租]完。

o·ver·bur·den [ˌəuvəˈbəːdn; ˋovəˋbədn̩] **I** ***vt*.** 装载过多,使负担过度,使过劳;压垂。*trees* ~*ed with fruit* 果子结得过多的树。**II** [ˈəuvəbəːdn; ˋovəˏbədn] ***n*.** **1.** 过重的货物,重担,过度的负担。**2.**【地】浮盖层;覆盖层;表土。

o·ver·bus·y [ˈəuvəˈbizi; ˏovəˋbɪzɪ] ***a*.** 太忙的;过分爱管闲事的。

o·ver·buy [ˈəuvəˈbai; ˋovəˋbaɪ] ***vt*.** (***o·ver·bought*** [ˈəuvəˈbɔːt; ˋovəˋbɔt]) 买得过多[贵]。

o·ver·call [ˈəuvəˈkɔːl; ˋovəˋkɔl] **I** ***vt*.**【桥牌】叫牌叫得比…高。**II** [ˈəuvəkɔːl; ˋovəkɔl] ***n*.** 过高的叫牌。

o·ver·came [ˌəuvəˈkeim; ˏovəˋkem] overcome 的过去式。

o·ver·can·o·py [ˌəuvəˈkænəpi; ˏovəˋkænəpɪ] ***vt*.** (***-pied***; ***-py·ing***) 用帐篷遮盖。

o·ver·ca·pit·al·ize [ˈəuvəkəˈpitəlaiz, ˌəuvəˈkæpitəlaiz; ˋovəkəˋpɪtlaɪz, ˏovəˋkæpɪtəlaɪz] ***vt*.** 定[估计](资本)过大;对(事业)投资过多。

o·ver·care [ˈəuvəˈkɛə; ˋovəˋkɛr] ***n*.** 杞人忧天,过虑。

o·ver·care·ful [ˈəuvəˈkɛəful; ˋovəˋkɛrfəl] ***a*.** 太谨慎的,太小心的。

o·ver·cast [ˈəuvəkɑːst; ˋovəkæst] **I** ***vt*.** (***o·ver·cast***) **1.** 云遮掉,使阴;使暗。**2.** 包边缝拢。**3.** 过远地撒(鱼网等)。—***vi*.** 阴起来,暗起来。**II** ***a*.** 多云的,阴的;阴郁的,愁闷的。*The sky is* ~ *with black clouds*. 天空乌云密布。*a* ~ *day* 阴天。**III** ***n*.** **1.** 覆盖;阴暗的天空。**2.**【矿】风桥。**3.** (网等)过远的一撒。

o·ver·cau·tion [ˈəuvəkɔːʃən; ovəˋkɔʃən] ***n*.** 过分小心,过分谨慎。**-cau·tious** ***a*.**

o·ver·charge [ˈəuvəˈtʃɑːdʒ; ˋovətʃɑrdʒ] ***vt*., *vi*.** **1.** (向…)乱讨价;向…索费太多;滥开(账目)。**2.** 装弹(药)过多;充(电)过度;装载过多,过重。**3.** 压倒;夸张(叙述等)。~ *a lecture with facts* 讲演中事实摆得过多。

o·ver·clothes [ˈəuvəkləuz, -kləuðz; ˋovəˋkloz, -kloðz] ***n*.** *pl*. 外衣〔大衣、雨衣等〕(=outerwear)。

o·ver·cloud [ˌəuvəˈklaud; ˏovəˋklaud] ***vt*., *vi*.** **1.** (使)给云盖满;(使)变阴。**2.** (使)忧郁;(使)悲伤;使生气。**3.** 把(理解等)弄模糊。

o·ver·coat [ˈəuvəkəut; ˋovəˏkot] ***n*.** **1.** 大衣。**2.** 保护层;护膜。**3.**〔美空俚〕降落伞。**-ing** ***n*.** 大衣料子。

o·ver·col·o(u)r [ˈəuvəˈkʌlə, ˌəuvəˈkʌlə; ˋovəˋkʌlə, ˏovəˋkʌlə] ***vt*.**〔英〕给…着色过浓;润饰过度;夸张(描写等)。

o·ver·come [ˌəuvəˈkʌm; ˏovɚˋkʌm] *vt*. (*o·ver·came* [ˌəuvəˈkeim; ˏovɚˋkem]; *-come*; *-com·ing*) 1. 打败，战胜，征服；克服(困难)。2. 〔多用被动语态〕压倒，制服，…不堪(*with*; *by*)。*He was ~ by their entreaties*. 他屈从了他们的请求。*be ~ by weariness* 累倒。*be ~ with liquor* 喝醉。

o·ver·com·pen·sate [ˌəuvəˈkɔmpənseit; ˋovɚˋkɑmpənset] *vt*. 对…给予过多的补偿。—*vi*. 【心】过度补偿〔指为补偿某种生理或心理的缺陷而过分的努力〕。**-sa·tion** *n*. **-sa·tory** *a*.

o·ver·con·fi·dence [ˈəuvəˈkɔnfidəns; ˋovɚˋkɑnfədəns] *n*. 过分相信；自信过强；自负；厚脸。

o·ver·con·fi·dent [ˈəuvəˈkɔnfidənt; ˋovɚˋkɑnfədənt] *a*. 过分相信的；自信过强的；自负的；厚脸的。

o·ver-coun·ter [ˈəuvəˈkauntə; ˋovɚˋkaʊntə] *a*. (银行等)不经过交易所而卖出的(指证券等)。

o·ver·cred·u·lous [ˈəuvəˈkredjuləs; ˋovɚˋkrɛdʒʊləs] *a*. 过于轻信的。**-du·li·ty** [ˈəuvəkriˈdjuːliti; ˋovɚkrɪˋdjulətɪ] *n*. (过度的)轻信。

o·ver·crit·i·cal [ˈəuvəˈkritikəl; ˋovɚˋkrɪtəkl̩] *a*. 批评过多的，过分指摘的。

o·ver·crop [ˈəuvəˈkrɔp; ˏovɚˋkrɑp] I *vt*. (*-cropped*; *-crop·ping*) 耕种过度而弄瘦(地力)。II [ˈəuvəkrɔp; ˋovɚˋkrɑp] *n*. 耕种过度。

o·ver·crow [ˈəuvəˈkrəu; ˏovɚˋkro] *vt*. 对…自鸣得意，夸耀；压倒；胜过；打垮，打败…。

o·ver·crowd [ˌəuvəˈkraud; ˏovɚˋkraʊd] *vt*. 使(过分)拥挤，使杂沓。*an ~ed profession* 人浮于事的职业。

o·ver·crust [ˈəuvəˈkrʌst; ˏovɚˋkrʌst] *vt*. 用外皮[外壳]包[覆盖]。

o·ver·cun·ning [ˈəuvəˈkʌniŋ; ˋovɚˋkʌnɪŋ] *n*., *a*. 过分狡猾(的)。

o·ver·cu·ri·ous [ˈəuvəˈkjuəriəs; ˏovɚˋkjʊrɪəs] *a*. 过分好奇多问的。

o·ver·del·i·cate [ˈəuvəˈdelikit; ˏovɚˋdɛləkɪt] *a*. 过于微妙的，过于纤弱[细巧]的。

o·ver·de·vel·op [ˈəuvədiˈveləp; ˋovɚdɪˋvɛləp] *vt*. 1. 【摄】使显影过度。2. 使过度发展。

o·ver·do [ˌəuvəˈduː; ˋovɚˋdu] *vt*. (*-did* [-ˈdid; -ˋdɪd]; *-done* [-ˈdʌn; -ˋdʌn]) 1. 过于…，…过度；夸张。2. 〔通常用被动语态或 ~ oneself〕过度使用(体力等)，使过劳；耗尽。3. 〔通常用过去分词形式〕煮过度，烧过度。~ *exercise* 运动过度。*His politeness is overdone*. 他殷勤过度了。*The joke is overdone*. 这个玩笑开得过火了。~ *meat* 把肉煮得过老。~ ***it*** 做得过火；过劳；夸张；演得过火。~ ***oneself*** [***one's strength***] 勉强，努力过度；使尽力量。

o·ver·door [ˈəuvədɔː; ˋovɚˏdɔr] *n*. 【建】门头饰板。

o·ver·dose [ˈəuvədəus; ˋovɚˏdos] I *n*. 适量用药。II [ˈəuvəˈdəus; ˋovɚˋdos] *vt*. 使…服药过量，使…用药过量。—*vi*. 因过量服用麻醉剂而患病[死亡]。

o·ver·draft, **o·ver·draught** [ˈəuvədrɑːft; ˋovɚˏdræft] *n*. 1. 【商】透支；透支额。2. 【冶】过度通风。

o·ver·draw [ˈəuvəˈdrɔː; ˋovɚˋdrɔ] *vt*. (*o·ver·drew* [əuvəˈdruː; ovɚˋdru]; *-drawn* [-ˈdrɔːn; -ˋdrɔn]) 1. 拉(弓)过度，把…描绘过分，夸大，夸张。2. 【商】透支(存款)；过多地开(支票等)。—*vi*. 透支。

o·ver·dress [ˈəuvəˈdres; ˋovɚˋdrɛs] I *vt*. 使穿得太考究，使过度装束。II [ˈəuvədres; ˋovɚˋdrɛs] *n*. (薄)外衣。

o·ver·drink [ˈəuvəˈdriŋk; ˏovɚˋdrɪŋk] *vt*., *vi*. (*o·ver·drank* [ˈəuvəˈdræŋk; ˋovɚˋdræŋk]; *-drunk* [-ˈdrʌŋk; -ˋdrʌŋk], *-drunk·en* [-ˈdrʌŋkən; -ˋdrʌŋkn̩]) (使)喝得过度，暴饮。~ ***oneself*** 使自己喝酒过多。

o·ver·drive [ˈəuvəˈdraiv; ˋovɚˋdraɪv] I *vt*. (*o·ver·drove* [ˈəuvəˈdrəuv; ˋovɚˋdrov]; *-driven* [-ˈdrivən; -ˋdrɪvən]) 驱使过度；使负担过度；使(人)操劳过度；【无】使激励过度。II [ˈəuvədraiv; ˋovɚdraɪv] *n*. 【机】超速传动。~ *clutch* 超速离合器。

o·ver·due [ˈəuvəˈdjuː; ˋovɚˋdju] *a*. 过期(未付)的；迟到的，延误的；过度的；早就该实现的。*an ~ check* 过期支票。*The train is ~*. 火车误点了。

o·ver·dye [ˈəuvəˈdai; ˋovɚˋdaɪ] *vt*. 把…染得过久[过深]；复染。

o·ver·eat [ˈəuvərˈiːt; ˋovɚˋit] *vt*., *vi*. (*o·ver·ate* [ˈəuvəˈet; ˋovɚˋɛt]; *-eat·en* [-ˈiːtn; -ˋitn̩]) (使)吃得过多，暴食。~ ***oneself*** 吃得过多把身体吃坏。

o·ver·e·lab·o·rate [ˈəuvəriˈlæbəreit; ˏovərɪˋlæbəˏret] *vt*. 对…过分推敲；对…阐述过详。

o·ver·em·pha·size [ˈəuvəˈemfəsaiz; ˏovɚˋɛmfəsaɪz] *vt*., *vi*. (使)过分强调。

o·ver·es·ti·mate [ˈəuvərˈestimeit; ˋovɚˋɛstəˏmet] I *vt*. 估计过高；过分评价。II [ˈəuvərˈestimit; ˋovɚˋɛstəmɪt] *n*. 过高的估计；过分的评价。**-ma·tion** [-ˈmeiʃən; -ˋmeʃən] *n*. 过高的估计；过分的评价。

o·ver·ex·pose [ˈəuvəriksˈpəuz; ˋovɚɪksˋpoz] *vt*. 【摄】使过度感光；使过度受光[受辐射]。

o·ver·ex·po·sure [ˈəuvəriksˈpəuʒə; ˋovərɪkspoʒɚ] *n*. 【摄】感光过度。

o·ver·ex·tend [ˈəuvəiksˈtend; ˋovərɪksˋtɛnd] *vt*. 使伸延过长，使超过合理的限度；使承担超过能力的义务或诺言。**-ten·sion** *n*.

o·ver·fa·tigue [ˈəuvəfəˈtiːg; ˏovɚfəˋtig] I *vt*. 使疲劳过度，使筋疲力竭。II *n*. 过劳。

o·ver·feed [ˈəuvəˈfiːd; ˋovɚˋfid] *vt*., *vi*. (*o·ver·fed* [əuvəˈfed; ovɚˋfɛd]) (给)…吃得太多；给…进料过多。~ ***oneself*** 吃得过多。

o·ver·fill [ˈəuvəfil; ˋovɚfɪl] *vt*. 把…装得太满(= ~ too full)。—*vi*. 满得溢出。

o·ver·film [ˈəuvəˈfilm; ˏovɚˋfɪlm] *vt*. 把薄膜盖在…上。

o·ver·fish [ˈəuvəfiʃ; ˏovɚˋfɪʃ] *vt*. 对鱼类[鱼场]进行过分捕捞。

o·ver·flew [ˌəuvəˈfluː; ˏovɚˋflu] overfly 的过去式。

o·ver·flight [ˈəuvəflait; ˋovɚflaɪt] *n*. 飞越上空。

o·ver·flow [ˌəuvəˈfləu; ˏovɚˋflo] I *vt*. (*-flowed*, *-flown* [-ˈfluːn; -ˋflon]; *-flow·ing*) 使溢出，使泛滥，使涨满；淹没；人满得走不进(房间等)。*The river ~ed its banks*. 河水漫出堤岸。*The river ~ed several farms*. 河水淹没了几个农场。*The goods ~ed the warehouse*. 货物多得仓库堆不下了。—*vi*. 溢流，泛滥，漫出；满，充满；洋溢；(资源等)过剩。*a man ~ing with sympathy* 充满同情心的人。*a land ~ing with resources of every kind* 各种资源都很丰富的国家。~ ***with*** 充溢，充满。II [ˈauvəfləu; ˋovəflo] *n*. 1. 泛滥，溢流。2. 外溢，充溢，过多，过剩；超出额；溢出物。3. 溢洪道，排水口。*an ~ gate* 溢水口。*an ~ of population* 人口过剩。III *a*. 溢出的；充满的(= overflowing)。~ **meeting** (由于太挤而)增设的分会场。~ **weir** 越水堰，漫坝。

o·ver·flow·ing [ˌəuvəˈfləuiŋ; ˏovɚˋfloɪŋ] I *a*. 溢出的，过剩的；充满的。*a heart ~ with gratitude* 充满感激的心情。II *n*. 1. 溢出，过剩；溢出物。2. 〔常 *pl*.〕洋溢，充沛。

o·ver·fly [ˌəuvəˈflai; ˏovɚˋflaɪ] *vt*. (*-flew* [-ˈfluː; -ˋflu]; *-flown* [-ˈfluːn; -ˋflon]; *-fly·ing*) 飞行在…上空；飞越；(尤指)飞越(他国领土)作侦察；飞得比…快[远、高]。

o·ver·flight [ˈəuvəflait; ˋovɚˏflaɪt] *n*. (飞机等的)飞越上空。

o·ver·freight [ˈəuvəˈfreit; ˋovɚˋfret] I *vt*. 载货过多。II *n*. 超载；【船】超过租船合同货量的运费。

o·ver·ful·fil(l) [ˈəuvəfulˈfil; ˏovɚfulˋfɪl] *vt*. 超额生

O

产;超额完成。

o·ver·full [ˈəuvəˈful; ˋovəˋfʊl] ***a*.** 太满的,充满的;过多的;太用心…的。

o·ver·gar·ment [ˈəuvəgɑːmənt; ˋovə-ˏgɑrmənt] ***n*.** 大衣,外衣。

o·ver·gild [ˈəuvəˈgild; ˏovəˋgɪld] ***vt*.** (***-gild·ed***, ***-gilt*** [-ˈgilt; -ˋgɪlt]) 镀金在…上;〔喻〕把…染成黄金色。

o·ver·glaze [ˈəuvəgleiz; ˋovə-ˏglez] **I** ***n*.** (制陶) **1.** 第二层釉。**2.** 面釉。**II** [ˈəuvəˈgleiz; ˋovəˋglez] ***vt*.** 涂釉;涂面釉。

o·ver·gov·ern [ˌəuvəˈgʌvən; ˏovəˋgʌvən] ***vt*.** 统治;(政府等对人民)干涉过度,管制过度。

o·ver·grew [ˈəuvəˈgruː; ˋovəˋgru] overgrow 的过去式。

o·ver·ground [ˈəuvəgraund; ˋovə-ˏgraund] ***a*.** **1.** 在地面上的(*opp*. underground)。**2.** 符合现存体制下各种标准的,正统的,官方的。*an ~ route* 陆路。*be still ~* 还活着。

o·ver·grow [ˈəuvəˈgrəu; ˋovəˋgro] ***vt*.** (***-grew*** [-ˈgruː; -ˋgru]; ***-grown*** [-ˈgrəun; -ˋgron]) **1.** 〔主用被动语态〕(杂草等)在…上蔓生,丛生,长满。**2.** 〔~ oneself〕长得过度[过大、过高]。— ***vi*.** 蔓延过度;长得过大[过快]。*an ~ing city* 正在急速发展中的城市。

o·ver·grown [ˈəuvəˈgrəun; ˋovəˋgron] **1.** overgrow 的过去分词。**2.** ***a*.** (人)长得太大的,个子长得过高的;畸形发展的;(因肥大而)难看的,笨拙的;(植物)生长过度的,太繁茂的,没修剪的;(杂草等)生满的。*a garden ~ with weeds* 生满杂草的花园。

o·ver·growth [ˈəuvəgrəuθ; ˋovəgroθ] ***n*.** 繁茂,蔓延;生长过度;生长太快;【医】增生;肥大;生满某场所[建筑物上]的东西;【化】附(晶生)长。

o·ver·hand [ˈəuvəhænd; ˋovəhænd] **I** ***a*.** **1.** 从上面下手[放手]的。**2.** (打球等时)举手过肩的,向下打的;(游泳)手臂露出水面的。**3.** 【裁缝】锁缝的。*an ~ knot* 反手结〔一种绳结〕。*an ~ stroke* 两手交拍水面的游泳。**II** ***ad*.** **1.** 【球戏】举手过肩地。**2.** 【泳】拍水。**3.** 从上按住。**4.** 锁缝。**III** ***n*.** **1.** 上风,优势;胜利。**2.** 手举过肩的运动姿势。**IV** ***vt*.** 〔美〕锁缝。

o·ver·hang [ˈəuvəˈhæŋ; ˏovəˋhæŋ] **I** ***vt*.**, ***vi*.** (***-hung*** [-ˈhʌŋ; -ˋhʌŋ]) **1.** 倒悬;悬垂,吊在…上;(向…)突出[伸出]。**2.** (危险等)逼近,威胁。**3.** (用布幔等)过度装饰。*an overhung door* 吊门。*an ~ing danger* 迫近眼前的危险。**II** [ˈəuvəhæŋ; ˋovəhæŋ] ***n*.** 突出,撑出,【建】悬垂;挑出屋顶;挑出楼房;延伸量,伸出量;【空】多翼机的上翼伸出下翼的长度;(无法兑换黄金的)美元过剩额。*the ~ of a ship's stern* 船尾突出部分。

o·ver·hast·y [ˈəuvəˈheisti; ˋovəˋhestɪ] ***a*.** 过于性急的,草率的。

o·ver·haul [ˌəuvəˈhɔːl; ˏovəˋhɔl] **I** ***vt*.** **1.** 翻查;仔细检查;检修,翻修;拆修。**2.** 追上(他船);解松(船的)绳索。*be ~ed by a doctor* 受医生仔细检查。**II** [ˈəuvəhɔːl; ˋovəhɔl] ***n*.** 检查,大修。*a complete ~* 全部检查。*a general ~* 普查,大修。*a top ~* 初步检修。*undergo a thorough ~* 受彻底检查。

o·ver·head [ˈəuvəˈhed; ˋovəˋhɛd] **I** ***ad*.** **1.** 在上,在头顶上,高高地;在楼上;在空中。**2.** 从头到脚全部没入。*O- the stars were out*. 天上星星出来了。*plunge ~ into water* 扑咚地跳入水中。**II** [ˈəuvəhed; ˋovəhɛd] ***a*.** **1.** 头顶上的;架空的;架设的。**2.** 所有的,总的。**3.** 平均的。**4.** 通常开支的。*an ~ railway* 〔英〕高架铁路。*~ seam* 搭缝。*~ wires* 架空线。*~ irrigation* 人工降雨。*the ~ charges* [*expenses*] 【商】经常费,总开销。**III** [ˈəuvəhed; ˋovə-ˏhɛd] ***n*.** **1.** 企业一般管理费用。**2.** 天花板;【船】船舱的顶板。**3.** 【化】塔顶馏出物。**4.** 【体】(网球等的)扣杀。

o·ver·hear [ˌəuvəˈhiə; ˏovəˋhɪr] ***vt*.**, ***vi*.** (***-heard*** [-ˈhəːd; -ˋhɝd]) 无意中听到;偷听。**-er** ***n*.** 偷听者;无意中听到的人。

o·ver·heat [ˌəuvəˈhiːt; ˏovəˋhit] ***vt*.**, ***vi*.** 过度加热,(使)过分激动,(使)变得过热。

o·ver·hours [ˈəuvərauəz; ˋovəaurz] ***n*.** 〔*pl*.〕= overtime.

o·ver·housed [ˈəuvəˈhauzd; ˋovəˋhauzd] ***a*.** 房子太大的,住在太大的屋子里的。

o·ver·hung [ˌəuvəˈhʌŋ; ˏovəˋhʌŋ] overhang 的过去式和过去分词。

o·ver·in·dulge [ˈəuvərinˈdʌldʒ; ˋovərɪnˋdʌldʒ] ***vt*.** 过分放纵,过分姑息。**-dul·gent** [-ˈdʌldʒənt; -ˋdʌldʒənt] ***a*.** 过分放任的。**-gence** [-dʒəns; -dʒəns] ***n*.** 过度放任,放纵,姑息。

o·ver·is·sue [ˈəuvərˈisjuː; ˋovəˋɪʃu] **I** ***vt*.** 滥发(钞票、公债等)。**II** ***n*.** 滥发。

o·ver·joy [ˌəuvəˈdʒɔi; ˋovəˋdʒɔɪ] **I** ***vt*.** 〔多用被动语态〕使大喜,使狂喜。***be ~ed at*** (***with***) 听见[看见]…开心得要发狂似的。**II** [ˈəuvədʒɔi; ˋovədʒɔɪ] ***n*.** 大喜,狂喜。

o·ver·kill [ˌəuvəˈkil; ˏovəˋkɪl] **I** ***vt*.** **1.** 用过多的核力量摧毁(目标)。**2.** 重复命中。**3.** 杀尽杀绝。**II** [ˈəuvəkil; ˋovəkɪl] ***n*.** **1.** 过多的核武器摧毁力。**2.** 杀害过多。**3.** 过多;不必要的过度行动;矫枉过正。

o·ver·knee [ˈəuvəniː; ˋovə-ˏni] ***a*.** 过膝的。

o·ver·la·bo(u)r [ˈəuvəˈleibə; ˏovəˋlebə] ***vt*.** 使操劳过度,使工作过累;对…作过度用心的刻画。

o·ver·lade [ˈəuvəˈleid; ovəˋled] ***vt*.** (***-lad·ed***; ***-laden***, ***-lad·ed***; ***-lad·ing***) 使过载,使负载过重。*an overladen horse* 负载过重的马。

o·ver·la·den [əuvəˈleidn; ovəˋledn̩] ***a*.** 装货过多的;(房间)装饰[摆设]过多的。

o·ver·laid [ˌəuvəˈleid; ˏovəˋled] overlay[1]的过去式和过去分词。

o·ver·lain [ˌəuvəˈlein; ˏovəˋlen] overlie 的过去分词。

o·ver·land [ˈəuvəlænd; ˋovə-ˏlænd] **I** ***a*.** 陆上的,陆路的。*an ~ journey* 陆地旅行。*the ~ route* 陆路;〔英〕(从英国经地中海国家不绕好望角到印度的)陆上通路;〔美〕从大西洋岸横贯大陆到太平洋岸的道路。**II** [ˌəuvəˈlænd; ˋovə-ˏlænd] ***ad*.** 由陆路。

o·ver·lap [ˌəuvəˈlæp; ˏovəˋlæp] **I** ***vt*.**, ***vi*.** (***-pp-***) **1.** (与…)交搭;叠盖。**2.** (与…)部分一致[巧合],(时间等)重复,一致(*in*)。**II** [ˈəuvəlæp; ˋovəlæp] ***n*.** **1.** 重复,部分一致;交搭;重叠;复合。**2.** 覆盖物,涂盖层;【植】盖覆;【摄】重叠摄影。**3.** 【数】交叠,相交;复合。**4.** 【军】航空照片的重叠部分;【地】超复;累叠地层。

o·ver·lay[1] [ˌəuvəˈlei; ˏovəˋle] **I** ***vt*.** (***-laid*** [-ˈleid; -ˋled]) **1.** 覆,盖;铺,敷,涂;包,镀金。**2.** 盖暗,弄阴。**3.** 压制,压倒。**4.** 【印】加上衬于。**II** [ˈəuvəlei; ˋovəle] ***n*.** **1.** 【印】轮廓纸;上衬。**2.** 盖在上面的东西;被单;小台布;镀金(等)。**3.** 【军】透明图。

o·ver·lay[2] [ˌəuvəˈlei; ˏovəˋle] overlie 的过去式。

o·ver·leaf [ˈəuvəˈliːf; ˋovəˋlif] **I** ***ad*.** (纸的)反面;在次页。**II** [ˈəuvəliːf; ˋovəlif] ***n*.** 反面,次页。

o·ver·leap [ˌəuvəˈliːp; ˏovəˋlip] ***vt*.** (***-leaped*** [-ˈlept, -ˈliːpt; -ˋlɛpt, -ˋlipt], ***-leapt*** [-ˈlept; -ˋlɛpt]) **1.** 跳过,越过;[ˈəuvəˈliːp; ˋovəˋlip] 跳过头,跳出(one's mark)。**2.** 漏看,忽略,省去。*Ambition often ~s itself*. 野心常因过大而失败,抱负常因过高而不能实现。

o·ver·lie [ˌəuvəˈlai; ˏovəˋlaɪ] ***vt*.** (***-lay*** [-ˈlei; -ˋle]; ***-lain*** [-ˈlein; -ˋlen]; ***over·ly·ing*** [-ˈlaiiŋ; -ˋlaɪɪŋ]) **1.** 躺[伏]在…上面。**2.** 压在上面闷死(婴儿等)。

o·ver·live [ˈəuvəˈliv; ˏovəˋlɪv] ***vt*.** (比别人或平常寿数)活得长;比…经久。— ***vi*.** 还活着,残存。

o·ver·load [ˈəuvəˈləud; ˏovəˋlod] **I** ***vt*.** 使装载过重货物,使装载[负担]过重,超载;把(弹药等)装填过度;【电】给…过量充电。*an ~ed style* 过分夸张的文体。**II** [ˈəuvələud; ˋovəlod] ***n*.** 过重装载,过重负担;超负荷;【电】过载。

o·ver·long [ˈəuvəˈlɔŋ; ˋovɚˋlɔŋ] *a*.，*ad*. 太长,过分长(地)。

o·ver·look [ˌəuvəˈluk; ˏovɚˋlʊk] *vt*. **1**. 俯视;眺望,瞭望;(房屋等)耸出,高过…。**2**. 漏看;忽略;假装不见;宽容;放任。**3**. 监督,监视;检查;视察;照顾;检阅;读;〔罕〕随便看一遍。**4**. (蛇把蛙等)用目光震慑住,使心慌意乱。~ *a valley from a hill* 从小山上俯视山谷。~ *a fault* 宽容过失。~ … *at work* 监督…工作[劳动]。*His services have been* ~*ed for years*. 他的功绩好几年来都没有人注意到。

o·ver·lord [ˈəuvəlɔːd; ˋovɚˏlɔrd] *n*. 霸王;太上皇;大君主;封建领主[君主]。

o·ver·ly [ˈəuvəli; ˋovɚlɪ] *ad*. 〔Scot.〕过度地。

o·ver·ly·ing [ˌəuvəˈlaiiŋ; ˏovɚˋlaɪɪŋ] overlie 的现在分词。

o·ver·man [ˈəuvəmæn; ˋovɚmən] **I** *n*. **1**. 工头;(煤矿的)井内监工;头头。**2**. 调解人,公断人。**3**. 【哲】超人。**II** *vt*. 给…配备人员过多。

o·ver·man·tel [ˈəuvəmæntl; ˋovɚˏmæntl̩] *n*. 壁炉额上的饰架。

o·ver·man·y [ˈəuvəˈmeni; ˋovɚˋmɛnɪ] *a*. 过多的。

o·ver·mast·ed [ˈəuvəˈmɑːstid; ˋovɚˋmɑstɪd] *a*. 【海】桅杆太长的,桅杆过重的。

o·ver·mas·ter [ˌəuvəˈmɑːstə; ˏovɚˋmæstɚ] *vt*. 压服;克服;征服;压倒。*an* ~*ing passion* 压抑不住的强烈情感。

o·ver·match [ˌəuvəˈmætʃ; ˏovɚˋmætʃ] **I** *vt*. **1**. 优于,胜过;压倒。**2**. 和(门户等)不相称的人结婚。**II** [ˈəuvəmætʃ; ˋovɚmætʃ] *n*. **1**. 劲敌,强敌。**2**. 优劣悬殊者之间的比赛。

o·ver·mat·ter [ˈəuvəmætə; ˋovɚmætɚ] *n*. (杂志等的)存稿;多余的排版。

o·ver·meas·ure [ˌəuvəˈmeʒə; ˏovɚˋmɛʒɚ] **I** *vt*. 高估,估量过大。**II** [ˈəuvəˈmeʒə; ˋovɚˋmɛʒɚ] *n*. 过量;剩余。

o·ver·mod·est [ˈəuvəˈmɔdist; ˋovɚˋmɑdɪst] *a*. 过分谦虚的,太怕羞的。

o·ver·much [ˈəuvəˈmʌtʃ, ˈəuvəm-; ˋovɚˋmʌtʃ, ˋovɚm-] **I** *a*. 过多的。**II** *n*. 过量;剩余。**III** *ad*. 过度地;过多地。

o·ver·nice [ˈəuvəˈnais; ˋovɚˋnaɪs] *a*. 过分讲究的;吹毛求疵的;过分严格的;过于仔细[谨慎]的。

o·ver·night [ˈəuvəˈnait; ˋovɚˋnaɪt] **I** *ad*. **1**. 昨晚,昨夜一晚上。**2**. 通宵,从夜晚到天亮;一夜工夫。*stay* ~ 住一晚,过夜。**II** *a*. **1**. 昨晚的,昨夜的。**2**. 通夜的。**3**. 旅行时过夜用的。**4**. 忽然的。*an* ~ *conversation* 通夜会谈。*an* ~ *millionaire* 暴发户。**III** *n*. 〔美〕前一天的晚上。

o·ver·night·er [ˈəuvəˈnaitə; ˋovɚˋnaɪtɚ] *n*. 短途旅行用的小件行李。

o·ver·paid [ˈəuvəˈpeid; ˋovɚˋped] overpay 的过去分词。

o·ver·pass [ˌəuvəˈpɑːs; ˏovɚˋpæs] **I** *vt*. (~*ed*, *-past* [-ˈpɑːst; -ˋpæst]) **1**. 渡;过(河);通过;翻过,越过;超出(范围);违背;侵犯。**2**. 忽视;漏看。**3**. 优于,超过。*It* ~*es endurance*. 那个没法忍受得了。**II** [ˈəuvəpɑːs; ˋovɚpæs] *n*. 〔美〕【交】高架道路;立体交叉;上跨桥,天桥;上跨路。

o·ver·passed, **o·ver·past** [ˌəuvəˈpɑːst; ˏovɚˋpæst] *a*. 过去了的,结束了的。

o·ver·pay [ˌəuvəˈpei; ˋovɚˋpe] *vt*. (*-paid* [-ˈpeid; -ˋped]) 多付,多给…报酬。*The joy* ~*s the toil*. 所得的快乐超过付出的辛劳。

o·ver·peo·pled [ˈəuvəˈpiːpld; ˏovɚˋpipl̩d] *a*. 居民过多的,人口过密的。

o·ver·per·suade [ˈəuvəpəˈsweid; ˋovɚpɚˋswed] *vt*. 硬要说服(不愿听的人等)。

o·ver·pitch [ˌəuvəˈpitʃ; ˋovɚˋpɪtʃ] *vt*. **1**. 【板球】扔(球)过分接近三柱门;扔(球)过度。**2**. 夸大。

o·ver·play [ˌəuvəˈplei; ˏovɚˋple] *vt*. **1**. 把…做得过分;把…演得过火。**2**. (比赛)胜过(对方)。**3**. 【高尔夫球】打球过远。**4**. 过分依赖…的力量。

o·ver·plus [ˈəuvəplʌs; ˋovɚˏplʌs] *n*. 剩余,超出的数量;过剩;过多。

o·ver·pop·u·late [ˌəuvəˈpɔpjuˌleit; ˏovɚˋpɑpjəˏlet] *vt*. 使(某一地区)人口过剩。**-lation** [-ˈleiʃən; -ˋleʃən] *n*.

o·ver·pow·er [ˌəuvəˈpauə; ˏovɚˋpaʊɚ] *vt*. **1**. 打败,制服,压服;(精神上、肉体上)压倒。**2**. 使深深感动。**3**. 供给…过强的力量。**4**. 给…安装功率过大的发动机。*Human will can* ~ *natural forces*. 人定胜天。*The heat* ~*ed me*. 我热得受不了啦。*Your kindness* ~*s me*. 深情厚谊衷心铭感。

o·ver·pow·er·ing [ˌəuvəˈpauəriŋ; ˏovɚˋpaʊərɪŋ] *a*. 压倒(优势)的;极强大的;难抗拒的;制止不了的。*an* ~ *smell* 难闻的气味。**-ly** *ad*.

o·ver·praise [ˈəuvəˈpreiz; ovɚˋprez] **I** *vt*. 过度称赞,过奖。**II** [ˈəuvəpreiz; ˋovɚprez] *n*. 过奖;过分的称赞。

o·ver·pres·sure [ˈəuvəˈpreʃə; ˋovɚˋprɛʃɚ] *n*. **1**. 过度的重压,过度的压迫;过劳;过压,超压力。**2**. 剩余压力。

o·ver·price [ˈəuvəˈprais; ˏovɚˋpraɪs] *vt*. 对…定价过高。

o·ver·print [ˈəuvəˈprint; ˏovɚˋprɪnt] **I** *vt*. **1**. 【印】套印,添印,复印。**2**. 过量印刷;【摄】曝光过度。**3**. 在一个形像上覆印另一形像;在(邮票等)上盖印戳。**II** [ˈəuvəprint; ˋovɚˏprɪnt] *n*. **1**. 加印量。**2**. 印戳;盖过印的邮票。

o·ver·pro·duce [ˈəuvəprəˈdjuːs; ˋovɚprəˋdjus] *vt*., *vi*. (使)生产过剩。**-duc·tion** [ˈəuvəprəˈdʌkʃən; ˋovɚprəˋdʌkʃən] *n*. 生产过剩。

o·ver·proof [ˈəuvəˈpruːf; ˋovɚˋpruf] *a*. 酒精含量超过标准以上的。

o·ver·pro·tect [ˌəuvəprəˈtekt; ˏovɚprəˋtɛkt] *vt*. 过分地保护,过分地爱护(尤指对子女的溺爱)。**-ive** *a*.

o·ver·quick [ˈəuvəˈkwik; ˋovɚˋkwɪk] *a*. 过于快的。

o·ver·ran [ˌəuvəˈræn; ˏovɚˋræn] overrun 的过去式。

o·ver·rate [ˈəuvəˈreit; ˋovɚˋret] *vt*. 估计[估价]过高,高估。

o·ver·reach [ˌəuvəˈriːtʃ; ˏovɚˋritʃ] *vt*. **1**. 把(手、脚等)伸得过长;走过头,越过;赶上,追上;非分妄为致使…失败。**2**. (依靠奸诈)取胜。**3**. (马)用后脚的前端踢(前脚后跟)。*His influence* ~*ed his audience*. 他的话使听众无限感动。~ ***oneself*** 伸腰;做过火;弄巧成拙。— *vi*. **1**. (手、脚等)伸得过长;延伸过远。**2**. 过火,夸张。**3**. (马等)后蹄踢前蹄。

o·ver·re·act [ˌəuvəriˈækt; ˏovɚrɪˋækt] *vi*. 反应过度〔情绪过分强烈〕。

o·ver·read [ˈəuvəˈriːd; ˏovɚˋrid] *vt*. (*-read* [-ˈred; -ˋrɛd]) **1**. 从头读完,通读。**2**. 使读书过度而弄坏身体。

o·ver·re·fine [ˈəuvəriˈfain; ˏovɚrɪˋfaɪn] *vi*. 加工过度;区分过细。

o·ver·rent [ˈəuvəˈrent; ˏovɚˋrɛnt] *vt*. 对…地租[房租等]收得过高。

o·ver·ride [ˌəuvəˈraid; ˏovɚˋraɪd] *vt*. (*-rode* [-ˈrəud; -ˋrod]; *-rid·den* [-ˈridn; -ˋrɪdn̩]; *-rid·ing*) **1**. 蹂躏(别国等)。**2**. 蔑视,藐视(法规);制服,压倒;废弃;推翻(决议)。**3**. 奔越过;践踏过;骑着马跳过;把(马)骑累。**4**. 【外】将(断骨)重叠起来。~ *another's authority* 藐视别人职权。~ *one's commission* 滥用职权,作越权处置。

o·ver·ripe [ˈəuvəˈraip; ˋovɚˋraɪp] *a*. 过分成熟的;腐朽的,颓废的。

o·ver·rule [ˌəuvəˈruːl; ˏovɚˋrul] *vt*. **1**. 统治;压制;克服,压倒。**2**. 用权力取消(决定、方针等),废弃;推翻;驳回,批斥;否决;宣布…无效。*The claims were* ~*d*. 要求被驳回了。*Conscience may be* ~*d by passion*. 良心

O

可能为感情所支配。

o·ver·run [ˌəuvəˈrʌn; ˏovɚˋrʌn] I *vt.*, *vi.* (*-ran* [-ˈræn; -ˋræn]; *-run*; *-run·ning*) 1.(杂草等)(在…)蔓延;(害虫等)(在…)猖獗,群集(于);(使…)泛滥。2. 侵略,蚕食,蹂躏(别国等)。3. 超出,越过(范围);【机】(使)超限运转。4.〔~ oneself〕跑累;【印】因移行重排(行、栏、版面)。*be ~ with ivy* 茑萝蔓生。*be ~ with mice* 老鼠猖獗。*His speech overran the time allotted.* 他的演说超过了规定时间。~ ***the constable*** 〔口〕1. 乱花乱用;负债。2. 瞎谈不知道的事情。II [ˈəuvərʌn; ˋovɚrʌn] *n.* 1. 蔓延;猖獗,跋扈;横行为害;泛滥成灾;超越限度。2. 超出量;余额。3.【空】清除区〔机场跑道两端的备用地区〕。

o·ver·sail [ˈəuvəˈseil; ˋovɚˋsel] *vt.*, *vi.*【建】(使)连续突腰。

o·ver·saw [ˈəuvəˈsɔː; ˋovɚˋsɔ] oversee 的过去式。

o·ver·score I [ˌəuvəˈskɔː; ˏovɚˋskɔr] *vt.* 在(字、句等上或中间)划一条线。II [ˈəuvəskɔː; ˋovɚskɔ] *n.* 字、句等上或中间的线。

o·ver·sea(s) [ˈəuvəˈsiː(z); ˋovɚˋsi(z)] I *a.* 1. 来自海外的,海外的,外国的。2. 往海外的。*an ~ edition* (期刊的)海外版。*the ~ trade* 对外贸易。*an ~ broadcast program* 对(国)外(的)广播节目。*the ~ Chinese* 华侨。~ *remittance* 侨汇。II *ad.* 向海外,向国外;在海外。~ **cap**〔美军〕军便帽,船形帽。

o·ver·see [ˈəuvəˈsiː; ˏovɚˋsi] *vt.* (*-saw* [-ˈsɔː; -ˋsɔ]; *-seen* [-ˈsiːn; -ˋsin]) 1. 俯瞰;瞭望;监督,监视;检查;视察;管理;照料。2. 看漏,错过;宽恕;省略。

o·ver·se·er [ˈəuvəsi(ː)ə; ˋovɚˏsiɚ] *n.* 1. 管理员,监工,工头。2.〔英〕(做贫民救济工作的)教区低级职员。*an ~ of schools* 督学。

o·ver·sell [ˈəuvəˈsel; ˋovɚˋsɛl] *vt.* (*-sold* [-ˈsəuld; -ˋsold]) 过多地卖出(商品等);卖空(股票等);过分吹嘘。

o·ver·sen·si·tive [ˈəuvəˈsensitiv; ˋovɚˋsɛnsɪtɪv] *a.* 过分敏感[灵敏]的。

o·ver·set [ˈəuvəˈset; ˏovɚˋsɛt] I *vt.* (*-set*; *-set·ting*) 1. 翻转;推翻,颠覆。2.【印】排(版)过密。3. 镶嵌(宝石等)。II [ˈəuvəset; ˋovɚsɛt] *n.* 1. 推翻,破坏,打倒。2.〔美新闻语〕过剩稿件。

o·ver·sew [ˈəuvəsəu, ˌəuvəˈsəu; ˋovɚso, ˏovɚˋso] *vt.* (*-sewed* [-d; -d]; *-sewed*, *-sewn* [-səun; -son]) 锁(缝);管(边)。

o·ver·sexed [ˌəuvəˈsekst; ˏovɚˋsɛkst] *a.* 纵欲的,耽于色欲的。

o·ver·shad·ow [ˌəuvəˈʃædəu; ˏovɚˋʃædo] *vt.* 1. 遮阴,遮蔽;使阴。2. 使失色,夺去…的光辉,扫…的面子。3. 保护,庇护。

o·ver·shoe [ˈəuvəʃuː; ˋovɚˏʃu] *n.*〔美〕〔常 *pl.*〕套鞋。

o·ver·shoot [ˈəuvəˈʃuːt; ˏovɚˋʃut] I (*-shot* [-ˈʃɔt; -ˋʃɑt]) *vt.* 1. 把(子弹)打得过高(而未打中),打得过远;在射击上胜过;【军】弹着超越(目标);超过(界限);【空】(飞机在准备着陆时)飞过(指定地点)。2. 走过头,越过;超出(规定);逸出。3. 从高处射下。—*vi.* 1. 射击越标。2. 做得过分。~ ***oneself*** [***the mark***] 做得过分;夸张。~ ***the field*** 打猎过多致使野兽绝迹。II *n.*【自】过调量,超越度。

o·ver·shot [ˈəuvəˈʃɔt; ˏovɚˋʃɑt] overshoot 的过去式和过去分词。I *a.* 1.(水车)上射的。2. 上颌突出的。3.〔口〕喝醉的。4. 夸大的。II *n.*【纺】跳花〔一种织疵〕;浮纬花纹。

o·ver·shoul·der [ˈəuvəˈʃəuldə; ˋovɚˋʃoldə] *ad.* 回头;转过头来。

o·ver·side [ˈəuvəsaid; ˏovɚˋsaɪd] I *a.* 1. 从船边的〔指货物的装卸〕。2. 在唱片反面的。II [ˈəuvəˈsaid; ˋovɚˋsaɪd] *ad.* 从船边。***free*** ~【商】输入港船上交货价格,到港价格〔略 f. o. s.〕。

o·ver·sight [ˈəuvəsait; ˋovɚˏsaɪt] *n.* 1. 监督,监视;看管。2. 疏忽,漏失,失察,失错。***by*** (***an***) ~ 不当心,不小心;出于疏忽。***have the*** ~ ***of*** (*children*) 看管(小孩)。

o·ver·sim·pli·fy [ˈəuvəˈsimplifai; ˋovɚˋsɪmpləˏfaɪ] *vt.*, *vi.* (*-fied*; *-fy·ing*) 过分简单化〔以致歪曲、忽略了要点〕。**-pli·fi·cation** [ˌəuvəˌsimplifiˈkeiʃən; ˏovɚˏsɪmpləfəˋkeʃən] *n.*

o·ver·size [ˈəuvəˈsaiz; ˋovɚˋsaɪz] I *a.* 1. 太大的。2. 大于一般的;特别大的(= oversized)。II [ˈəuvəsaiz; ˋovɚsaɪz] *n.* 大号(物),特大号(物)。

o·ver·skirt [ˈəuvəskəːt; ˋovɚˏskɝt] *n.* 罩裙。

o·ver·slaugh [ˈəuvəslɔː; ˋovɚˏslɔ] I *n.* 1.〔英〕【军】(因另有更重要的任务而)免予执行现有任务。2.〔美〕(河川中不利于航行的)浅滩。II *vt.* 1.【军】把(某人)免除现职。2.〔美〕妨碍;阻止。3.〔美〕忽略(某人)不予任用而另用别人。

o·ver·sleep [ˈəuvəˈsliːp; ˋovɚˋslip] *vt.*, *vi.* (*-slept* [-ˈslept; -ˋslɛpt]) (使)睡过头;(使)睡得过久。

o·ver·sleeve [ˈəuvəsliːv; ˋovɚˏsliv] *n.* 袖套。

o·ver·slip [ˈəuvəˈslip; ovɚˋslɪp] *vt.* (*-pp-*) 滑过;看落,错过(机会等)。

o·ver·smoke [ˈəuvəˈsməuk; ˏovɚˋsmok] *vt.*, *vi.* (把…)弄得满是烟;(使)抽烟过度。

o·ver·sold [ˈəuvəˈsəuld; ˏovɚˋsold] oversell 的过去式和过去分词。

o·ver·soul [ˈəuvəsəul; ˋovɚˏsol] *n.*【哲】(先验论的所谓)超灵,上帝。

o·ver·speed [ˈəuvəˈspiːd; ˋovɚˋspid] I *vt.*, *vi.* (***o·ver·sped*** [ˈəuvəˈsped; ˋovɚˋspɛd]; ***o·ver·speed·ed*** [-ˈspiːdid; -ˋspidɪd]) (使)超速运行。II [ˈəuvəspiːd; ˋovɚspid] *n.* 超速。III *a.* 超速运行的。

o·ver·spend [əuvəˈspend; ˏovɚˋspɛnd] *vt.* (*-spent* [-ˈspent; -ˋspɛnt]) 用尽,耗尽;支出超过(自己的财力)。~ *one's allowance* 不量力地乱花销;入不敷出。—*vi.* 花费过多,开销太大;超支。

o·ver·spill [ˈəuvəspil; ˋovɚspɪl] *n.* 溢出物;过剩物资;过剩人口。

o·ver·spread [ˈəuvəˈspred; ˏovɚˋsprɛd] *vt.*, *vi.* (*-spread*) 铺盖;覆盖;布满;蔓延。*The sky was ~ with clouds.* 天空布满了云。*A smile ~ his face.* 他笑容满面。

o·ver·state [ˈəuvəˈsteit; ˋovɚˋstet] *vt.* 把…讲得过分;夸大,夸张。~ *one's case* 夸大自己的情况。**-ment** *n.* 言过其实;大话,夸张。

o·ver·stay [ˈəuvəˈstei; ˋovɚˋste] *vt.*, *vi.* 1.(使)逗留过久,(使)坐得过久;(使)逗留期超过签证规定期限。2.【商】勒价观望过久而坐失(良机)。~ ***one's welcome*** 逗留[坐得]过久而使人生厌。

o·ver·steer [ˈəuvəˈstiə; ˋovɚˋstɪr] *n.*(汽车)过度转向。

o·ver·step [ˈəuvəˈstep; ovɚˋstɛp] *vt.* (*-pp-*) 走过头,越过(界限),犯。~ *one's authority* 越权。

o·ver·stock [ˈəuvəˈstɔk; ˏovɚˋstɑk] I *vt.* 使存货过多;进(货)过多;(家畜)饲养过多,(鱼)放养过密。*The market is ~ed.* 市场存货过剩。II [ˈəuvəstɔk; ˋovɚˏstɑk] *n.* 进货过多;存货过剩。

o·ver·strain I [ˈəuvəˈstrein; ˏovɚˋstren] *vt.* 使伸张过度;使过度紧张;使工作过度;役使过度。~ *one's nerves* 用脑过度。—*vi.* 过度紧张,过度努力。~ *oneself* 过劳,努力过度。II [ˈəuvəstrein; ˋovɚˏstren] *n.* 过度紧张;过劳;伤力。

o·ver·strength [ˈəuvəstreŋθ; ˋovɚstrɛŋθ] I *n.* 力量过剩;人员超编。II [ˈəuvəˈstreŋθ; ˋovɚˋstrɛŋθ] *a.* 人员超编制的。

o·ver·stride [ˌəuvəˈstraid; ˏovɚˋstraɪd] I *vt.* (*-strode* [-ˈstrəud; -ˋstrod]; *-strid·den* [-ˈstridn; -ˋstrɪdn]; *-strid·ing*) 1. 跨过。2. 优于;超越;越过。3. 骑,跨;〔古〕跨过,越过(= bestride)。II *n.*【体】过大的跨步〔运

动员跨步过大会步伐不稳,速度降低〕。

o·ver·strung [ˈəuvəˈstrʌŋ; ˋovɚˋstrʌŋ] *a*. 紧张过度的,神经过敏的;(钢琴)把弦斜向交叉着装的。

o·ver·stud·y [ˌəuvəˈstʌdi; ˏovɚˋstʌdɪ] I *vt*., *vi*. (使)用功过度。II [ˈəuvəˈstʌdi; ˋovɚˋstʌdɪ] *n*. 用功过度。

o·ver·stuff [ˈəuvəˈstʌf; ˋovɚˋstʌf] *vt*. 装填…过度。*an ~ed chair* 装填得厚厚的椅子。

o·ver·sub·scribe [ˈəuvəsəbˈskraib; ˋovɚsəbˋskraɪb] *vt*. 过多定购;超额认购(公债等)。

o·ver·sup·ply [ˈəuvəsəˈplai; ˏovɚsəˋplaɪ] I *vt*. (**-plied**; **-ply·ing**) 过度供给。II [ˈəuvəsəˌplai; ˋovɚsəˏplaɪ] *n*. 供应过多。

o·vert [ˈəuvəːt, əuˈvəːt; ˋovɝt, oˋvɝt] *a*. 1. (证据等)明显的,公开的,公然的 (*opp*. covert)。2. (钱包等)开着的;(翅膀等)展开的。*an ~ act* 【法】公然的犯罪行为。*a market ~* 公开市场。

o·ver·take [ˌəuvəˈteik; ˏovɚˋtek] *vt*. (**-took** [-ˈtuk; -ˋtʊk]; **-tak·en** [-ˈteikən; -ˋtekən]; **-tak·ing**) 1. 追上;赶上;超过;赶补(欠工),赶做(限期快到的工程)。2. (暴风雨,灾难等)突然袭击。3. 打垮,压倒。*be overtaken by a storm* 遇到暴风雨袭击。*The murderer was overtaken in his crime*. 杀人犯当场被捕。*overtaking of waves* 波浪追推。***be overtaken in* [*with*] *drink*** 喝醉。***be overtaken with terror*** 被吓倒,被吓垮。

o·ver·task [ˈəuvəˈtɑːsk; ˏovɚˋtæsk] *vt*. 加重…负担,使做过重的工作;使过分辛劳。

o·ver·tax [ˈəuvəˈtæks; ˋovɚˋtæks] *vt*. 1. 对…抽税过重,过度征收。2. 使负担过重,使过度劳动,过度役使。

o·ver-the-count·er [ˈəuvəðəˈkauntə; ˋovɚðəˋkaʊntɚ] *a*. 1. 买卖双方直接交易的;(证券等)不通过交易所而直接卖给买方的。2. (药物)不需处方可出售的(= over-counter)。

o·ver·throw [ˌəuvəˈθrəu; ˏovɚˋθro] I *vt*. (**-threw** [-ˈθruː; -ˋθru]; **-thrown** [-ˈθrəun; -ˋθron]) 1. 推翻,打倒,颠覆;破坏,使瓦解;废除(制度等)。2. 【板球】投回(守门员投回之球);【棒球】过高投(球);投(球)过远。II [ˈəuvəθrəu; ˋovɚθro] *n*. 1. 倾覆;灭亡,瓦解,垮台,失败;征服。2. 【板球】暴投;【棒球】投得过高[过远]的球。***give the ~*** 推翻,灭亡。***have the ~*** 垮台,灭亡。

o·ver·throw·al [ˌəuvəˈθrəuəl; ˏovɚˋθroəl] *n*. 推翻,打倒。

o·ver·thrust [ˈəuvəθrʌst; ˋovɚθrʌst] *n*. 【地】掩冲断层,上冲断层。

o·ver·time [ˈəuvətaim; ˋovɚˏtaɪm] I *n*. 1. 超时;加班,额外工作时间;额外劳动。2. 加班费。3. 【体】(为决定胜负的)比赛延长时间。***be on ~*** 在加班。II [ˈəuvətaim; ˋovɚˏtaɪm] *ad*. 在规定(工作)时间之外。III [ˈəuvəˈtaim; ˏovɚˋtaɪm] *vt*. 使历时过久;【摄】使(曝光等)超过时间。

o·ver·tire [ˈəuvəˈtaiə; ˋovɚˋtaɪr] *vt*., *vi*. (使)过度疲劳。

o·vert·ly [ˈəuvəːtli; ˋovɝtlɪ] *ad*. 明显地;公开,公然。

o·ver·toil [ˌəuvəˈtɔil; ˏovɚˋtɔɪl] I *vt*., *vi*. = overwork *v*. II [ˈəuvətɔil; ˋovɚtɔɪl] *n*. = overwork *n*.

o·ver·tone [ˈəuvətəun; ˋovɚˏton] I *n*. 1. 【乐】陪音,泛音。2. 〔常 *pl*.〕次要的意义;联想;暗示;言外之意。3. 【无】谐波。II [ˈəuvəˈtəun; ˋovɚˋton] *vt*. 【摄】使曝光过度。

o·ver·took [ˌəuvəˈtuk; ˏovɚˋtʊk] overtake 的过去式。

o·ver·top [ˈəuvəˈtɔp; ˏovɚˋtɑp] *vt*. (**-pp-**) 高出,高耸…之上;超出,胜过。

o·ver·trade [ˈəuvəˈtreid; ˏovɚˋtred] *vi*. 过额贸易〔贸易量大于个人财力或市场需要〕。

o·ver·train [ˈəuvəˈtrein; ˏovɚˋtren] *vt*., *vi*. (使)训练过度;(使)练习时间过长。

o·ver·trick [ˈəuvəˌtrik; ˋovɚˏtrɪk] *n*. 【牌戏】比所叫的牌数多得一墩。

o·ver·trump [ˈəuvəˈtrʌmp; ˏovɚˋtrʌmp] *vt*., *vi*. 【牌戏】用较大王牌取胜。

o·ver·ture [ˈəuvətjuə; ˋovɚtʃɚ] *n*. 1. 〔常 *pl*.〕提议,建议,提案。2. 开端,序幕;【乐】序曲;前奏曲;序诗。*an ~ of marriage* 求婚。*an ~ of peace* 讲和的表示。***make ~s*** 提出建议。

o·ver·turn [ˌəuvəˈtəːn; ˏovɚˋtɝn] I *vt*., *vi*. 1. 打翻,(使)翻过来,(使)倒转。2. 颠覆;推翻;毁灭;打倒。II [ˈəuvətəːn; ˋovɚˏtɝn] *n*. 推翻;垮台,瓦解;灭亡,毁灭。*the ~ of the government* 政府的垮台。

o·ver·un·der [ˈəuvəˈʌndə; ˋovɚˋʌndɚ] I *a*. (叠筒枪)双筒上下重叠(而非并列)的。II [ˈəuvəʌndə; ˋovɚʌndɚ] *n*. 叠筒双筒枪。

o·ver·use [ˌəuvəˈjuːz; ˏovɚˋjuz] I *vt*. 把…使用过度[过久];把…用过头,滥用。II [ˈəuvəˈjuːs; ˋovɚˋjus] *n*. 过度[过久]的使用,滥用。

o·ver·val·ue [ˈəuvəˈvæljuː; ˋovɚˋvæljʊ] *vt*. 过于重视;估计过高,高估。

o·ver·view [ˈəuvəvjuː; ˋovɚˏvju] *n*. [美]概观,总的看法。

o·ver·walk [ˌəuvəˈwɔːk; ˏovɚˋwɔk] *vt*., *vi*. (使)行走过度,(使)走累。*~ oneself* 走累。

o·ver·watch [ˈəuvəˈwɔtʃ; ˋovɚˋwɑtʃ] *vt*. 1. 监视,守候。2. 〔多用被动语态〕熬夜熬累。

o·ver·wear [ˈəuvəwɛə; ˋovɚˋwɛr] *vt*. (**-wore** [-ˈwɔː; -ˋwɔ]; **-worn** [-ˈwɔːn; -ˋwɔn]; **wear·ing**) 穿破,用旧,用坏,使耗尽。

o·ver·wea·ry [ˌəuvəˈwiəri; ˋovɚˋwɪrɪ] I *a*. 过度疲劳的。II [ˈəuvəˈwiəri; ˋovɚˋwɪərɪ] *vt*. (**-ried**; **-ry·ing**) 使疲劳过度。

o·ver·ween·ing [ˈəuvəˈwiːniŋ; ˋovɚˋwinɪŋ] *a*. 自以为了不起的,自负的;傲慢的;夸大了的。**-ly** *ad*.

o·ver·weigh [ˌəuvəˈwei; ovɚˋwe] *vt*. 1. 重过;比…重要;胜过,强过。2. 给…加负担,压迫,压倒,压垮(= outweigh)。

o·ver·weight [ˈəuvəweit; ˋovɚˏwet] I *n*. 超重;偏重;优势。II [ˈəuvəˈweit; ˋovɚˋwet] *a*. 超过规定重量的,超重的。*an ~ luggage* 过重行李。III [ˈəuvəˈweit; ˋovɚˋwet] *vt*. 使…装载过重;使…负担过重;在重量上超过。

o·ver·whelm [ˌəuvəˈ*h*welm; ˏovɚˋhwɛlm] *vt*. 1. 压倒;压服;推翻;倾覆;淹没;覆盖。2. (用感情等)制服;使十分感动;使不好意思;使不知所措。*be ~ed by superior forces* 被优势兵力打垮。*be ~ed by grief* 伤心已极。*Your kindness quite ~s me*. 你的好意使我感激难言。*The boat was ~ed by the waves*. 小船给浪打翻了。

o·ver·whelm·ing [ˌəuvəˈ*h*welmiŋ; ˏovɚˋhwɛlmɪŋ] *a*. 压倒的,势不可挡的。***by an ~ majority* [*superior*]** 以压倒的多数[优势]。**-ly** *ad*.

o·ver·wind [ˈəuvəˈwaind; ˋovɚˋwaɪnd] *vt*. (**-wound** [-ˈwaund; -ˋwaʊnd]) 把(发条等)卷得太紧。

o·ver·win·ter [ˈəuvəˈwintə; ˏovɚˋwɪntɚ] I *vi*., *vt*. (使)活过冬天;(把…)保存过冬。II *a*. 整个冬季的。

o·ver·word [ˈəuvəˈwəːd; ˋovɚˏwɝd] *n*. 老重复的词句,口头禅;诗歌或乐曲的叠句,副歌。

o·ver·work [ˈəuvəˈwəːk; ˏovɚˋwɝk] I *vt*. 1. 使工作过度,使过劳;把…役使过度。2. 绣满,饰满〔只用被动语态〕。—*vi*. 工作过度,过劳。*~ a horse* 把马役使过度。*~ **oneself*** 过劳,劳累过度。II *n*. 1. [ˈəuvəˈwəːk; ˋovɚwɝk] 过度的劳动;过劳。2. [ˈəuvəwəːk; ˋovɚˏwɝk] 加班,额外工作。

o·ver·write [ˈəuvəˈrait; ˏovɚˋraɪt] *vt*. (**-wrote** [-ˈrəut; -ˋrot]; **-writ·ten** [-ˈritn; -ˋrɪtn]; **-writ·ing**) 写在…上面,写满;过度多写;用夸张、冗长的文体写…。*~ **oneself*** 因写作过多而弄坏身体[名誉等]。—*vi*. 写作过多。

o·ver·wrought [ˈəuvəˈrɔːt; ˋovɚˋrɔt] *a*. 1. 紧张过度的;兴奋过度的;神经质的。2. (作品)写作过分推敲的;不自

O

然的;装饰[刻画等]过多的;太过考究的。**3.** 过劳的。

o·ver·year·ing [ˈəuvəˈjiəiŋ; ˋovɚˋjɪrɪŋ] ***n.*** 越冬。

o·ver·zeal [ˈəuvəˈziːl; ˋovɚˋzil] ***n.*** 过度的热心。

ovi- *comb. f.* 表示"卵": *ovi*cidal.

o·vi·cid·al [ˌəuviˈsaidəl; ˏoviˋsaɪdl̩] ***a.*** 能杀卵的。

Ov·id[1] [ˈauvid; ˋɑvɪd] ***n.*** 奥维德[姓氏]。

O·vid[2] [ˈɔvid; ˋɑvɪd] ***n.*** 奥维德〔公元前48—公元17? 罗马诗人;拉丁全名为 Publius Ovidius Naso〕。

O·vid·i·an [ɔˈvidiən, -djən; oˋvɪdɪən, -djən] ***a.*** (古罗马诗人)奥维德 (Ovid) 的,奥维德风格的。

o·vi·duct [ˈəuvidʌkt; ˋovɪˏdʌkt] ***n.*** 【解】输卵管。

o·vif·er·ous [əuˈvifərəs; oˋvɪfərəs] ***a.*** 【生】有卵的,携卵的。

o·vi·form [ˈəuvifɔːm; ˋovɪˏfɔrm] ***a.*** 卵形的。

o·vig·er·ous [əuˈvidʒərəs; oˋvɪdʒərəs] ***a.*** = oviferous.

o·vine [ˈəuvain; ˋovaɪn] ***a.*** 羊(似)的;羊科的;绵羊的。

o·vip·a·rous [əuˈvipərəs; oˋvɪpərəs] ***a.*** 【动】卵生的 (*opp.* viviparous)。

o·vi·pos·it [ˌəuviˈpɔzit; ˏoviˋpɑzɪt] ***vi.*** 【昆】产卵,下子。**-sition** ***n.***

o·vi·pos·i·tor [ˌəuviˈpɔzitə; ˏoviˋpɑzɪtɚ] ***n.*** 【动】产卵器。

o·vi·sac [ˈəuvisæk; ˋovəsæk] ***n.*** **1.** 卵泡;卵囊。**2.** 受卵器(= ootheca)。

ovo- *comb. f.* 表示"卵"(= ov-): *ovo*-lactarian 只吃蛋类乳品而不食肉的素食者。

o·vo·fla·vin [ˌəuvəuˈfleivin; ˏovəˋflevɪn] ***n.*** 【化】核黄素。

o·void, o·voi·dal [ˈəuvɔid, əuˈvɔidl; ˋovɔɪd, oˋvɔɪdl̩] **I** ***a.*** 卵圆形的。**II** ***n.*** 卵形物。

o·vo·lo [ˈəuvələu; ˋovəlo] ***n.*** (*pl.* ***-li*** [-li; -ˏlɪ]) 【建】馒形饰。

O·von·ic [əuˈvɔnik; oˋvɑnɪk] **I** ***a.*** 【无】奥夫辛斯基 (Ovshinsky) 作用的,用玻璃作半导体的。**II** ***n.*** 双向开关半导体元件。**-s** ***n.*** 〔*pl.*〕〔作单数用〕交流半导体电子学。

o·vo·tes·tis [ˌəuvəuˈtestis; ˏovəˋtestɪs] ***n.*** 卵精巢。

o·vo·vi·vip·a·rous [ˌəuvəuviˈvipərəs; ˏovəvɪˋvɪpərəs] ***a.*** 卵胎生的。**-par·i·ty, -ness** ***n.*** **-ly** ***ad.***

o·vu·lar [ˈəuvjulə; ˋovjulɚ] ***a.*** 胚珠的〔指植物〕;卵子的〔指动物〕。

o·vu·late [ˈəuvjuleit; ˋovjulet] ***vi.*** 排卵。

o·vu·la·tion [ˌəuvjuˈleiʃən; ˏovjuˋleʃən] ***n.*** 排卵。**-la·to·ry** [-lətəri; -lətərɪ] ***a.***

o·vule [ˈəuvjuːl; ˋovjul] ***n.*** 【生】卵细胞;小卵;【植】胚珠。

o·vum [ˈəuvəm; ˋovəm] ***n.*** (*pl.* ***ova*** [ˈəuvə; ˋovə]) 【生】卵;卵细胞。

ow. = one way (fare).

o/w = oil in water 油水相。

ow [au; aʊ] ***int.*** 喔唷! 喔哟! 〔表示疼痛〕。

owe [əu; o] ***vt.*** **1.** 对…负有(义务、债务等),受有…的恩惠,欠。**2.** (把名誉等)归给…,归功于…,认为是靠…的力量,要感谢(某人)。*I* ~ *him $10* [*$10 to him*]. 我欠他十元。*I* ~ *you thanks.* 我得感谢你。*I* ~ *you my life.* 我受你再生之恩。*I* ~ *you an apology.* 我当向你道歉。*I* ~ *them a grudge.* 我对他们怀有怨恨。*We* ~ *to Newton the principle of graviation.* 我们全靠牛顿才知道引力的原理。*I* ~ *it to you that I am still alive.* 幸亏有你我现在才仍然活着。*She* ~*s her beauty to artificial assistance.* 她的美全靠打扮。*You* ~ *it to yourself to say it.* 这话亏你说得出口。— ***vi.*** 有支付[偿还]义务 (*for*)。*Who* ~*s for the antipasto?* 哪一位的拼盘还没有付款呢?

ow·ing [ˈəuiŋ; ˋoɪŋ] ***a.*** **1.** 该付的,未付的,欠着的。**2.** 有负于,受恩于;应归功于 (*to*)。*I paid what was* ~. 该付的都付了。*the* ~ *£10* 欠款 10 镑。~ ***to*** **1.** 由于 (*All this was* ~ *to ill health.* 这全是由于健康不好的关系所致)。★此义用 due to 较好。**2.** 〔作 *prep.* 用〕因为(*O- to the drought, crops are short.* 因为天旱收成不好)。

owl [aul; aʊl] **I** ***n.*** **1.** 【鸟】猫头鹰,鸱鸺,枭。**2.** 做夜工的人,熬夜的人;夜游子;夜生活者。**3.** 一本正经的呆子。**4.** 〔美〕深夜行驶的电车[火车等]。**5.** 〔美〕猫头鹰派〔认为核战争会因误会或估计错误而发生〕。*Don't be such a silly* ~. 别做那种傻事。***as blind*** [***stupid***] ***as an*** ~ 瞎[笨]透。***as drunk as a boiled*** ~ 〔美俚〕喝得烂醉。***bring*** [***carry, send***] ~***s to Athens*** 运枭至产枭极多的雅典;作徒劳无益的事,多此一举〔雅典盛产枭,枭为雅典守护神 Pallas 的标志〕。***fly with the*** ~***s*** 夜游。***hotter than a boiled*** ~ 〔美俚〕醉得兴奋起来的。***take*** ~ 发怒,生气。**II** ***vi.*** **1.** 〔方〕像猫头鹰般地叫[凝视]。**2.** (夜间)走私。~**-eyed** ***a.*** **1.** 黑暗中看得最清楚的。**2.** 惊讶地注视的。**3.** 〔美俚〕喝醉了的。~**-light** 微明,薄暮。~ **parrot** 鸮鹦(= kakapo)。~ **train** 〔美〕夜(行列)车。

owl·ed [auld; aʊld] ***a.*** 〔美〕喝醉了的。

owl·er [ˈaulə; ˋaʊlɚ] ***n.*** (特指夜间)走私者。

owl·et [ˈaulit; ˋaʊlɪt] ***n.*** 小猫头鹰;〔古〕猫头鹰。

owl·ish [ˈauliʃ; ˋaʊlɪʃ] ***a.*** **1.** 像猫头鹰的。**2.** 面孔严肃的;笨的(= owllike)。**-ly** ***ad.***

own[1] [əun; on] **I** ***a.*** **1.** 〔用在所有格之后以加强语气〕自己的;特有的。**2.** 珍贵的,心爱的。**3.** 〔罕〕(不与所有格连用)嫡亲的;同胞的。*He is his* ~ *man* [*master*]; *She is her* ~ *woman* [*mistress*]. 他[她]是独立自主的人[自己命运的主人]。*Every man has his* ~ *habit.* 每个人都有他特有的习惯。*The orange has a scent all its* ~. 橘子有一种独特的香味。*She is* ~ *sister to me.* 她是我的同胞姊妹。**II** ***pron.*** 〔起名词作用〕自己的东西[家属、责任、立场(等)];心爱的人。*May I not do what I will with my* ~? 我自己的东西难道不能随意处理吗? *May I have it for my* (*very*) ~? 我可以拿它当做我自己专有的东西吗? *My* ~ *did not believe it.* 连我家里的人也不相信。*And his* ~ *received him not.* 他的家属也不容他。*my* ~(我的)乖乖[爱称]。***come into one's*** ~ 取得属于自己的财产[东西];获得应有的名誉[信用等]。***do it on one's*** ~ 照自己的意思[由自己负责]做事。***get*** (***a bit of***) ***one's*** ~ ***back*** 〔口〕雪耻,报仇。***hold one's*** ~ 坚持自己立场,固守立场,不屈服(*The patient is holding his* ~. 病人还照常支持)。***love*** (***truth***) ***for its*** ~ ***sake*** 为(真理)而爱(真理)。***of one's*** ~ 自己的,自己所有的(*She had never had a room of her* ~. 她从来没有自己的住房)。***on one's*** ~ (***account***) 〔俚〕独自地;独立地;凭自己力量;主动地;自愿地。***with one's*** ~ ***eye*** 亲眼(看见)。~ **goal** **1.** 【体】踢进己方球门的球。**2.** 【喻】咎由自取的败着。

own[2] [aun; aʊn] ***vt.*** **1.** 有;拥有;持有。**2.** 承认(是…的作者、父亲、所有人,…的价值、真实等)。**3.** 顺受;服从。*a hat that nobody will* ~ 一顶无人认领的帽子。*He* ~*s that he has done wrong.* = *He* ~*s himself in the wrong.* = *He* ~*s his own fault.* 他承认他错了。*He* ~*s himself beaten.* 他认输了。— ***vi.*** 承认,自白。~ ***to*** 承认,自白(*He* ~*s to the theft.* 他承认偷东西了)。~ ***up*** 〔口〕爽爽快快承认;坦白(*You'd better* ~ *up.* 你还是爽爽快快地承认为好。~ *up to a fault* 痛痛快快地承认过失)。

own·er [ˈəunə; ˋonɚ] ***n.*** 物主,所有人;【商】货主;〔海军俚〕舰长。*a house-*~ 房主。*an* ~ *of lost property* 失主。*an* ~*-driver* 驾驶自备汽车的人。***at*** ~***'s risk*** 风险由物主负责。***the*** ~ 〔海俚〕船主。~**-occupier** ***n.*** 〔主英〕住用自己房屋的人,业主。~**ship** ***n.*** 物主身分,所有;所有权;所有制(*individual* ~*ship* 个体所有制)。

ox [ɔks; ɑks] ***n.*** (*pl.* ***ox·en*** [ˈɔksən; ˋɑksən]) 公牛,阉公牛;(一般的)牛〔不分性别的通称〕;牛属动物。★ *cf.* bull, cow, steer;〔其他的牛〕bullock, calf, heifer.

ox·ac·il·lin [ɔk'sæsilin; ɑk`sæsılın] *n*.【药】青霉素 P-12,新青霉素。

ox·a·late ['ɔksəleit; `ɑksə͵let] *n*.【化】草酸盐[酯],乙二酸盐。

ox·al·ic [ɔk'sælik; ɑks`ælık] *a*. 酢浆草的,采白浆草的。~ **acid**【化】草酸,乙二酸。

ox·a·lis ['ɔksəlis; `ɑksəlıs] *n*.【植】酢浆草。

ox·a·zine ['ɔksəziːn, -zin; `ɑksəzin, -zın] *n*.【化】恶嗪,噁畊;氧氮杂芑。

ox·blood ['ɔksblʌd; `ɑks͵blʌd] *n*. 深红色。

ox·bow ['ɔksbəu; `ɑks͵bo] *n*.〔美〕U 字形牛颈弯;(河流的)U 字形弯曲,河套(地区)。

Ox·bridge ['ɔksbridʒ; `ɑks͵brıdʒ] *n*., *a*. 牛津及剑桥大学(的)。

ox·en ['ɔksən; `ɑksən] *n*. ox 的复数。

ox·eye ['ɔksai; `ɑks͵aı] *n*. **1**. (人的)大眼睛。**2**.【植】牛眼菊;春白菊。~ **daisy**【植】春白菊,滨菊,法兰西菊。**ox-eyed** *a*. 眼睛大的。

Oxf. = Oxford.

ox·fence ['ɔksfens; `ɑksfɛns] *n*. (外围常有壕沟的坚固的)牛栏。

Ox·ford ['ɔksfəd; `ɑksfɚd] *n*. **1**. 牛津〔英国城市,牛津大学所在地〕。**2**. (英国)牛津(大学)。**3**. 〔*pl*. 通例 o-〕〔美〕= ~ shoes. **4**. 〔通例 o-〕= ~ gray. ~ **accent** 装腔作势的口音。~ **bags** [**trousers**]〔英〕宽大的裤子。~ **blue** 紫蓝色。~ **don** 牛津大学教授。~ **English** 牛津英语。~ **frame**〔英〕井字形画框。~ **gray** 深灰色。~ **man** 牛津大学受教育[出身]的人。~ **movement** 牛津运动〔在英国教会中复活天主教教义与仪式的运动,约在 1833 年发生于牛津大学,亦作 Tractarianism〕。~ **shirt** [**shirting**] 细条纹衬衫[料]。~ **shoes** (系带浅口)牛津式便鞋。

Ox·ford·shire ['ɔksfədʃiə; `ɑksfɚd͵ʃıə] *n*. 牛津郡〔英格兰中南部的一郡,首府为 Oxford〕。

ox·head ['ɔkshed; `ɑkshɛd] *n*.〔俚〕笨人,傻人。

ox·heart ['ɔkshɑːt; `ɑks͵hɑrt] *n*. 牛心樱桃〔一种心形大樱桃〕。

ox·herd ['ɔkshəːd; `ɑkshɚd] *n*. 牧牛人。

ox·hide ['ɔkshaid; `ɑks͵haıd] *n*. 牛皮。

ox·id ['ɔksid; `ɑksıd] *n*.〔罕〕= oxide.

ox·i·dant ['ɔksidənt; `ɑksədənt] *n*. 氧化剂。

ox·i·dase ['ɔksideis, -deiz; `ɑksədes, -dez] *n*. 氧化酶。**-da·sic** [-'deisik, -zik; -`desık, -zık] *a*.

ox·i·date ['ɔksideit; `ɑksə͵det] *vt*. 使氧化。

ox·i·da·tion [͵ɔksi'deiʃən; ͵ɑksə`deʃən] *n*.【化】氧化(作用),正化。~ **reduction** *n*. 氧化还原作用。

ox·ide ['ɔksaid; `ɑksaıd] *n*.【化】氧化物。*antimony* ~ 锑白,氧化锑。*deuterium* ~ 重水,氧化氘。*mercuric* ~ 氧化汞。*nitric* ~ 一氧化氮。

ox·i·dize ['ɔksidaiz; `ɑksə͵daız] *vt*.【化】**1**. 使氧化;使生锈。**2**. 使脱氧(尤指由于氧的作用)。**3**. 使增加原子价;使(原子、离子)除去电子。— *vi*. 氧化;生锈。~*d silver* 氧化银。*an oxidizing agent* 氧化剂。**-diz·a·ble** *a*. **-diz·a·tion** [͵ɔksidai'zeiʃən; ͵ɑksədaı`zeʃən] *n*.

ox·i·di·zer ['ɔksidaizə; `ɑksədaızɚ] *n*.【化】氧化剂。

ox·ime ['ɔksiːm, -sim; `ɑksim, -sım] *n*.【化】肟。

ox·im·e·ter [ɔk'simitə; ɑk`səmıtɚ] *n*.【医】血氧定量计。

ox·lip ['ɔkslip; `ɑks͵lıp] *n*.【植】高报春。

Oxon. = **1**. Oxfordshire. **2**. Oxonian.

Ox·o·ni·an [ɔk'səunjən; ɑk`sonıən] **I** *a*. 牛津(Oxford)(大学)的。**II** *n*. **1**. (英国)牛津人,牛津居民。**2**. 牛津大学的学生[毕业生]。**3**. = Oxford shoes.

ox·o·ni·um [ɔk'səunjəm; ɑk`sonıəm] *n*.【化】锌。

ox·peck·er ['ɔkspekə; `ɑkspɛkɚ] *n*. 非洲啄牛鸦。

ox·tail ['ɔksteil; `ɑks͵tel] *n*. 牛尾(尤指做牛尾汤等用的牛尾)。

ox·ter ['ɔkstə; `ɑkstɚ] *n*.〔Scot. 英方〕胳肢窝。

ox·tongue ['ɔkstʌŋ; `ɑks͵tʌŋ] *n*.〔废〕牛舌草属(*Anchusa*)植物。

oxy- *comb*. *f*. **1**. 表示"敏锐,尖锐":*oxy*cephalic. **2**. 表示"氧化":*oxy*chloride.

ox·y·a·cet·y·lene ['ɔksiə'setiliːn; ͵ɑksıə`sɛtl̩͵in] *a*.【化】氧乙炔的。~ ***blowpipe*** 氧乙炔吹管。

ox·y·ac·id [͵ɔksi'æsid; `ɑksı`æsıd] *n*.【化】含氧酸,羟基酸。

ox·y·carp·ous [͵ɔksi'kɑːpəs; ͵ɑksı`kɑrpəs] *a*.【植】尖刺果的。

ox·y·ceph·a·ly [͵ɔksi'sefəli; ͵ɑksı`sɛfəlı] *n*.【解】尖头。**-phal·ic** [-'fælik; -`fælık], **-ceph·a·lous** [-'sefələs; -`sɛfələs] *a*.

ox·y·chlo·ride [͵ɔksi'klɔːraid; ͵ɑksı`kloraıd] *n*.【化】氯氧化物。

ox·y·gen ['ɔksidʒən; `ɑksədʒən] *n*.【化】氧,氧气。~ **acid** = oxyacid 含氧酸。~ **bar** 氧吧〔一种顾客可付款吸氧以愉悦身心的日式酒吧〕。~ **helmet** (潜水、防火等用的)氧(气)帽。~ **mask** 氧(气)面罩。~ **tent** 氧气帐〔罩住病床的透明帐罩,往里输氧,以助病人呼吸〕。~ **walker** 手提式氧气箱〔供病人随身携带〕。

ox·y·gen·ate [ɔk'sidʒineit; `ɑksədʒən͵et] *vt*.【化】用氧处理,使和氧化合,充氧于。~*d water* 充氧水,过氧化氢水。**-a·tion** [ɔk͵sidʒi'neiʃən; ͵ɑksədʒən`eʃən] *n*.【化】用氧处理,氧化,充氧(作用)。

ox·y·gen·ic [͵ɔksi'dʒenik; ͵ɑksı`dʒɛnık], **oxy·gen·ous** [ɔk'sidʒənəs; ɑk`sıdʒənəs] *a*. 氧的;含氧的;似氧的;生氧的。

ox·y·gen·ize ['ɔksidʒinaiz; `ɑksədʒən͵aız] *vt*.【化】= oxygenate.

ox·y·hem·o·glo·bin [͵ɔksi'hiːmə͵gləubin; ͵ɑksı`himə͵globın] *n*.【生化】氧合血红蛋白,氧合血红素。

ox·y-house-gas ['ɔksi'haus'gæs; `ɑksı`haus`gæs] *a*. = oxy-paraffin.

ox·y·hy·dro·gen ['ɔksi'haidrədʒən; ͵ɑksı`haıdrədʒən] **I** *a*.【化】氢氧的。**II** *n*. 氢氧。~ **blowpipe** 氢氧吹管。~ **flame** 氢氧焰。

ox·y·mo·ron [͵ɔksi'mɔːrɔn; ͵ɑksı`morɑn] *n*.【修】矛盾修饰法(例:*a wise fool*, *cruel kindness*)。

ox·y·o·pi·a [͵ɔksi'əupiə; ͵ɑksı`opıə] *n*.【医】视觉敏锐。

ox·y-par·af·fin ['ɔksi'pærəfin; `ɑksı`pærəfın] *a*. (火焰)燃气与氧混合产生的。

ox·y·path·or ['ɔksipæθə; `ɑksıpæθɚ] *n*. 氧治疗器。

ox·y·phil ['ɔksifil; `ɑksıfıl] *n*. **1**. 易受酸性感染〔如嗜酸细胞,嗜酸物等〕(= acidophil)。**2**. 嗜酸(= acidophil, oxyphile)。**-ic** *a*.

ox·y·salt ['ɔksisɔːlt; `ɑksı͵sɔlt] *n*.【化】含氧盐。

ox·y·sul·fide ['ɔksi'sʌlfaid; `ɑksı`sʌlfaıd] *n*. 氧硫化物,氧代硫化物。

ox·y·tet·ra·cy·cline ['ɔksi͵tetrə'saiklin, -klain; `ɑksı͵tɛtrə`saıklın, -klaın] *n*.【药】氧四环素,土霉素。

ox·y·to·cic [͵ɔksi'təusik, -'tɔsik; ͵ɑksı`tosık, -`tɑsık] **I** *a*. 催产的〔如催产素剂〕。**II** *n*. 催产素。

ox·y·to·cin [͵ɔksi'təusin, -'tɔsin; ͵ɑksı`tosın, -`tɑsın] *n*.【生化】后叶催产素。

ox·y·tone ['ɔksitəun; `ɑksı͵ton] *a*., *n*.【希腊语法】末一音节上有重读的(词)。

oy·er ['ɔiə; ɔı] *n*.【法】(刑事案件的)听审,审判;要求听审。~ ***and terminer*** **1**. 听讼裁判庭令状〔本义为"听讼并裁判",系英国发给巡回法官等的令状中的用语〕;听讼裁判庭。**2**. 从前美国若干州的高等刑事法庭。

o·yes, o·yez [əu'jes, -z; o`ɛs, -z] *int*. 听! 静听! 肃静!〔促人注意,普通喊三次〕。

oys·ter ['ɔistə; `ɔıstɚ] *n*. **1**. 蚝,牡蛎。**2**. 鸡背肉。**3**. 〔俚〕极少开口的人。**4**. 可以从中取得个人好处的东西。***an ~ of a man*** 极少开口的人。***as close as an ~*** 嘴

紧得很,不会漏话。*as dumb as an* ~ 极少说话。*The world is sb.'s* ~. 人生最得意[最有前途]的时刻。~ **bank** [**bed, farm, field**] 牡蛎塘,养牡蛎场。~ **bar** 蚝肉菜馆。~ **bird,** ~ **catcher** 蛎鹬。~ **crab** 豆蚕科(*Pinnotheridae*)动物。~ **cracker** 牡蛎饼干〔小圆咸苏打饼干与炖牡蛎汤一起吃〕。~-**diver** 〔美俚〕洗盘子的人。~ **knife** 撬蚝刀。~**man** 〔主美〕采牡蛎人,卖牡蛎人;采牡蛎船。~ **patty** 蚝肉点心。~ **plant** 〔美〕【植】婆罗门参。~ **rake** 牡蛎耙子〔一种用于浅水中捞取牡蛎的长把弯齿耙子〕。~ **saloon** 〔美〕蚝肉菜馆。~ **shell** 1. *n*. 牡蛎壳碎粉。2. *vt*. 使(自己)关起门过日子。~ **stew** 牡蛎炖菜。~ **tongs** 采牡蛎用的挖具。~ **white** 灰乳色,牡蛎色。

oz., **oz** = ounce(s).

Oz·a·lid [ˈɔzəlid; ˋɑzəlɪd] *n*. 1. "奥萨里德"晒图机〔直接从原图或印刷品进行正面晒图的机器商标名称〕。2. 奥萨里德晒印件。

O·zark [ˈəuzɑːk; ˋozɑrk] *n*. 〔美〕密苏里 (Missouri) 州奥扎克族印第安人〔以弓术出名〕;密苏里州的别名;〔*pl*.〕密苏里州西南、阿肯色 (Arkansas) 州西北和俄克拉荷马 (Oklahoma) 州东北部的高地。

o·zo·ce·rite, o·zok·e·rite [əuˈzəukərit; oˋzokəˏraɪt] *n*. 【矿】地蜡,石蜡。

o·zone [ˈəuzəun, əuˈz-; ˋozon, oˋz-] *n*. 1. 【化】臭氧。2. 〔喻〕爽心怡神的力量;〔口〕新鲜空气。~(-)**friendly** 对大气臭氧层无危害的。~ **hole** 臭氧层空洞〔该处臭氧密度已降低到有害人类的程度〕。~ **layer** 臭氧层〔距地球表面 20—40 英里的高温层〕。~ **paper** 臭氧纸。~ **shield** 【气】臭氧层〔可防护地球上生物免遭过量紫外线辐射〕。

o·zon·ic [əuˈzɔnik; oˋzɑnɪk], **o·zo·nous** [ˈəuzəunəs; ˋozonəs] *a*. 臭氧的;似臭氧的;含臭氧的。

o·zon·ide [ˈəuzənaid; ˋozənaɪd] *n*. 【化】臭氧化物。

o·zon·ize [ˈəuzənaiz; ˋozəˏnaɪz] *vt*. 对…作臭氧处理,使含臭氧,使(氧)臭氧化。-**r** *n*. 臭氧化器。

o·zo·nom·e·ter [ˌəuzəˈnɔmitə; ˏozəˋnɑmɪtɚ] *n*. 【化】臭氧计。

o·zo·no·sphere [əuˈzəunəsfiə, -ˈzɔn-; oˋzɑnəsfɪr] *n*. 【气】臭氧层(= ozone layer)。

ozs., **ozs** = ounces.

o·zos·to·mi·a [ˌəuzɔsˈtəumiə; ˏozɑsˋtomɪə] *n*. 口臭。

Oz·zie [ˈɔziː; ˋɑzi] *n*. 〔美〕澳大利亚兵。

P

P, p [piː; pi] (*pl*. **P's, p's** [piːz; piz]) 1. 英语字母表的第十六个字母。2. P 字形(物)。3. 〔P〕【象棋】pawn 的符号。4. 〔P〕【植】亲本,【动】亲代 (parental generation) 的符号。5. 〔P〕【化】phosphorus 的符号。6. 〔P〕【物】压力,压强 (pressure) 的符号。7. 〔p〕【物】质子,氕核 (proton) 的符号。*be p and q* 上等。*mind* [*be on*] *one's P's and Q's* 谨言慎行,循规蹈矩。

P., p. = 1. pastor. 2. post. 3. power. 4. president. 5. pressure. 6. priest. 7. prince. 8. page. 9. part. 10. participle. 11. past. 12. penny. 13. per. 14. pint. 15. pole. 16. population. 17. pro. 18. 〔It.〕【乐】*piano*. 19. park. 20. progressive. 21. pipe.

PA 〔美〕= Petroleum Administration 石油管理局。

P. A. = 1. Press Association; Prosecuting Attorney 〔美〕检查官。2. particular average 【保险】单独海损。3. press agent 新闻业经理人,新闻广告员。4. power of attorney 委托书,代理权。5. Press Association, Limited 〔英〕报纸联合社。6. Purchasing Agent 采购员。

Pa = protactinium 【化】镤。

pa [pɑː; pɑ] *n*. 〔口、儿〕爸〔papa 之略〕。

Pa. = Pennsylvania.

p.a. = 1. participial adjective 【语法】分词形容词。2. 〔L.〕 *per annum* 每年。

PAA = Pan American World Airways 〔美〕泛美航空公司 (1991 年合并于 Delta 航空公司)。

pa·'an·ga [pəˈɑːŋgɑː; pəˋɑŋgɑ] *n*. 邦加〔汤加货币单位〕。

PAB, Pab 〔美〕= Petroleum Administration Board 〔美〕石油管理委员会。

PAB·A, pab·a [ˈpæbə; ˋpæbə] = para-aminobenzoic acid 对氨基苯甲酸〔解毒药〕。

pab·u·lum [ˈpæbjuləm; ˋpæbjələm] *n*. 1. 食品,养料,食粮;精神食粮。2. 柴;燃料。3. 单调乏味的文章。*mental* ~ 精神食粮〔书籍等〕。

pac [pæk; pæk] *n*. 1. 一种高统鹿皮靴;油皮鞋。2. 派克靴〔一种保温防水系带高统靴〕。

P.A.C. = Political Action Committee 〔美〕政治行动委员会。

Pac., **Pacif.** = Pacific.

pac·a [ˈpækə, ˈpɑːkə; ˋpækə] *n*. 【动】(中美,南美产)天竺鼠。

pace [peis; pes] **I** *n*. 1. 步;一步;步子;步幅〔2.5—3 英尺〕。2. 步态;步调;步速;速度;进度;【棒球】(投手的)球速。3. (文章等笔法)流畅。4. 侧对步〔马把同一边的两蹄同时并举的步法〕。5. 【建】梯台,楼梯平台。6. 〔*pl*.〕(才能等的)显示。*the geometrical* [*great*] ~ 50—60 英寸的步子。*the military* [*regulation*] ~ 【军】标准步幅,25—30 英寸的步子。*the Roman* ~ 约 58 英寸的步子。*a doubletime* ~ 跑步。*a quick* [*great*] ~ 快步。*a rattling* ~ (走得格格响的)快步。*an olderman's* ~ 大大方方的步子。*the* ~ *of the table* 【台球】球台的弹性。*at a foot's* ~ 用平常步速。*at a good* ~ 相当快地;活泼地。*at a snail's* ~ 爬行,慢吞吞地走。*do not keep* ~ *with* 跟不上;和…不相称[适应]。*go* [*hit*] *the* ~ 1. 飞快前进,急驶。2. 〔喻〕过享乐生活;挥霍。*go through one's* ~*s* 显示才能,显身手。*hold* [*keep*] ~ *with* 跟…齐步前进[并驾齐驱];向…看齐;适应。*mend one's* ~ 加快步子,赶。*off the* ~ 跑在为首者之后。*put a horse* [*sb*.] *through his* ~*s* 试马的步子;考察人的能力,使人经受考验,试验某人是否合用。*set* [*make*] *the* ~ (*for*) 1. (给…)作步调示范;定出速率;树立榜样。2. 领先,带头。3. 调整速率。*show one's* ~*s* (马)显示步法[速度];(人)显示本领。*try sb.'s* ~*s* 试某人本领。

II *vi*. 1. 慢慢地走,踱;(马)走侧对步。2. 〔美〕(比赛中)继续领先。— *vt*. 1. 踱步于。2. 步测(距离)(*off* 或 *out*)。3. 为…定步速;为…的标兵;和…并速前进。4. 使(马)练步法。~ *up and down the corridor* 在走廊里

踱来踱去。～ *it* 走,踱。～ *a room* 在室内踱步。～-**making** *n*., *a*. 定步速(的);当标兵(的)。

pa·ce [ˈpeisi; ˋpesɪ] ***prep***. 〔L.〕对不起〔陈述反对意见前的客套语〕。～ *Mr. Smith* 对不起史密斯先生(可是…)。～ *tua* [ˈtjuːei; ˋtjue] 对不起(你)[请原谅,冒昧得很](可是…)。

paced [peist; pest] *a*. **1**. …步的,步子…的〔用以构成复合词〕。**2**. 步测的。**3**. (赛马中)定了步速的。**4**. 节奏均匀的。*slow*-～ 慢步的。

pace·mak·er [ˈpeismeikə; ˋpes͵mekɚ] *n*. **1**. (赛跑等的)领跑人,带步人;定步速者,标兵;样板;引导者。**2**. 【军】整速舰;【医】电子起搏器;【解】起搏点网。

pac·er [ˈpeisə; ˋpesɚ] *n*. **1**. 慢行者;步测者;溜蹄的马。**2**. = pacemaker.

pace·set·ter [ˈpeisˌsetə; ˋpes͵sɛtɚ] *n*. = pacemaker 1.

pa·cha [ˈpɑːʃə, pəˈʃɑː; ˋpɑʃə, pəˋʃɑ] *n*. = pasha.

pa·cha·lic [ˈpɑːʃəlik; pəˋʃɑlɪk] *a*. = pashalic.

pa·chin·ko [pəˈtʃiŋkəu; pəˋtʃɪŋko] *n*. 〔Jap.〕弹球盘〔日本赌具〕。

pa·chu·co [pəˈtʃuːkəu; pəˋtʃuko] *n*. (*pl*. **-cos**) 〔Mex., Sp.〕花衣墨西哥人〔社会地位低下的墨西哥裔美国人,以好穿花衣和纹身为特殊标记〕。

pachy- *comb.f*. 表示"厚,厚度;浓厚": *pachy*derm.

pach·y·derm [ˈpækidəːm; ˋpækə͵dɝm] *n*. **1**. 厚皮动物〔象、犀、河马等〕。**2**. 〔喻〕厚脸皮的人;精神麻木的人。**-der·ma·tous** [ˌpækiˈdəːmətəs; ͵pækɪˋdɝmətəs], **-der·mous** [ˌpækiˈdəːməs; ͵pækəˋdɝməs] *a*. 皮厚的;感觉迟钝的。

pach·y·rhi·zus [ˌpækiˈraizəs; ͵pækɪˋraɪzəs] *n*. 【植】豆薯,凉薯,地瓜。

pach·y·san·dra [ˌpækiˈsændrə; ͵pækɪˋsændrə] *n*. 【植】富贵草属(*Pachysandra*)植物。

Pacif. = Pacific.

pa·cif·ic [pəˈsifik; pəˋsɪfɪk] *a*. **1**. 和平的,太平的;平时的。**2**. 爱好和平的,(性质)温和的。**3**. 〔P-〕太平洋的。*mild* ～ *breezes* 温和的微风。***the P-*** (***Ocean***) 太平洋。***the P- slope*** 〔美〕太平洋沿岸各州〔Sierra Nevada 及 Sierra Madre 以西〕。～ **blockade** 【国际法】平时封锁。**P- Rim** 太平洋地区(诸国)。**P- (Standard) Time** 太平洋标准时间〔比格林威治时间晚八小时〕。**-i·cal·ly** *ad*.

pa·cif·i·cate [pəˈsifikeit; pəˋsɪfə͵ket] *vt*. **1**. 平定;绥靖。**2**. 抚慰。

pac·i·fi·ca·tion [ˌpæsifiˈkeiʃən; ͵pæsəfəˋkeʃən] *n*. **1**. 平定;绥靖。**2**. 媾和(条约),和约。*the P- Guards* 靖卫团。

pa·cif·i·ca·tor [pəˈsifikeitə; pəˋsɪfɪ͵ketɚ] *n*. **1**. 调解人。**2**. 平定者。

pa·cif·i·ca·to·ry [pəˈsifikətəri, pəˈsifikeitəri; pəˋsɪfəkə͵torɪ, pəˋsɪfəkə͵tɔrɪ] *a*. **1**. 和解的,讲和的。**2**. 平定的。**3**. 安抚的。

pac·i·fic·ism [pəˈsifisizəm; pəˋsɪfə͵sɪzəm] *n*. = pacifism.

pac·i·fic·ist [pəˈsifisist; pəˋsɪfəsɪst] *n*. = pacifist (*n*.).

pac·i·fi·er [ˈpæsifaiə; ˋpæsə͵faɪɚ] *n*. **1**. 平定者。**2**. 使和解人。**3**. 抚慰者。**4**. (哄小孩的)橡皮奶头。

pac·i·fism [ˈpæsifizəm; ˋpæsə͵fɪzəm] *n*. **1**. 和平主义;绥靖主义。**2**. 消极态度。

pac·i·fist [ˈpæsifist; ˋpæsəfɪst] **I** *n*. **1**. 和平主义者;绥靖主义者。**2**. 持消极态度者。**II** *a*. = pacifistic.

pac·i·fis·tic [ˌpæsiˈfistik; ͵pæsəˋfɪstɪk] *a*. 和平主义的;绥靖主义的;持消极态度的。

pac·i·fy [ˈpæsifai; ˋpæsə͵faɪ] *vt*., *vi*. (**-fied**) **1**. 抚慰;使镇静。**2**. 平定,平息;绥靖;使安定。～ *a crying child* 安慰哭闹的孩子。～ *a commotion* 平定骚乱。

pack[1] [pæk; pæk] *vt*. 安插[挑选]自己人充任(委员等);拉拢,收买。～ *a committee* 纠集自己人充实委员会。～ ***cards with*** 共谋,串通。— *vi*. 共谋;串通作弊。

pack[2] [pæk; pæk] **I** *n*. **1**. 包,捆;行李;驮子。**2**. 巴克〔一包货物的标准包装量,如羊毛为 240 磅,亚麻纱为 60,000 码〕;(一季或一年中鱼、水果等的)包装量[装罐量]。**3**. 一堆;集合;大量,大堆。**4**. (纸牌等)一组,一副;(狼等的)一群,(歹人等的)一伙。**5**. 积冰,浮冰(= pack ice)。**6**. 【橄榄球】全体前锋。**7**. 【医】(水疗法的)湿布(等);(包裹疗法用的)裹布;冰袋;包扎。**8**. 【军】背包;驮包;驮载;降落伞包。**9**. 〔美〕罐头食品。**10**. 【商】包装;容器。**11**. 【电】单元;部件,组合件。**12**. 【摄】一叠装到照相机内的散页软片,软片包;一组同时曝光的彩色软片[硬片]。*a* ～ *of cigarettes* 一包[一箱]香烟。*Wolves hunt in large* ～*s*. 狼成群觅食。*It is all a* ～ *of troubles*. 尽是疙瘩事情。*a* ～ *of lies* 一片谎言。*a* ～ *of radium* 镭源。*a power* ～ 动力装置;电源组;供电部分。***spend*** [***eat***] ***the*** ～ 〔俚〕耗尽所有。

II *vt*. **1**. 包,把…打包,包装,把…包成一捆;〔美〕把…装罐头。**2**. 装填,填塞,填满(空隙)(*with*)。**3**. 压紧;集中,收集;使成一群[一组、一副]。**4**. 把…打发走;解雇(*off*)。**5**. 【医】(用裹布)包裹。**6**. 使(牲口)驮。**7**. 〔美西部〕把…(打成包)运输。**8**. 〔美〕备有;配有。**9**. 〔俚〕(拳击时)猛击(一拳)。*The car was* ～*ed with passengers*. 车里挤满了乘客。～ *clothes into a trunk* [～ *a trunk with clothes*] 把衣服装箱。～ *a donkey* 让驴子驮货。～ *a gun* 带着枪。*Meat* ～*ed in cans*. 罐头肉。— *vi*. **1**. 包装,打包。**2**. (牲口)驮货;停止活动[工作]。**3**. 变结实。**4**. 能(被)包装;做包装(运输)生意。**5**. (被解雇后)匆匆忙忙走掉(*off*, *away*)。**6**. 聚集;成群;挤。*We must* ～ *up and get ready to start*. 我们得打好行李准备动身了。*Ground* ～*s after a rain*. 雨后地面板结。～ ***a punch*** 【美棒球】有打击力。～ ***a real wallop*** = ～ ***a terrific punch*** 〔美拳〕猛打;有厉害的拳法。～ ***away*** [***off***] **1**. 辞退,解雇。**2**. 慌慌张张走掉。～***'em in*** 〔美〕(戏院)超额满座。～ ***in*** 停止。～ ***it in*** 〔俚〕**1**. 结束;承认失败。**2**. 充分利用有利条件。～ ***it up*** 〔口〕结束,停止;别讲下去了! ～ ***mustard*** 〔美俚〕砖头、灰泥等的搬运。～ (***on***) ***all sail*** 扯满全部风帆。～ ***oneself off*** (被解雇的人等)包好自己的东西匆匆走掉。～ ***up*** **1**. 把…打成包;打包。**2**. 捆好东西,收拾行李。**3**. 解雇;〔俚〕(机器)出故障;停止运转。**4**. 〔口〕收拾工具,下班。**5**. 〔俚〕死。***send*** (*sb*.) ～***ing*** 〔美俚〕解雇,辞退,撵走,叫某人立即卷铺盖。

III *a*. **1**. 搬运用的;由驮运牲畜组成的。**2**. 装满了的,填满了的。**3**. 包装用的。**4**. 〔主 Scot.〕驯良的,亲切的。*a* ～ *train* 一队驮运东西的牲口。～ **animal** 驮子,驮畜。～ **attack** (城市中顽劣青少年的)成群袭击行为〔三五成群游荡街头寻找袭击对象〕。～ **cloth** 包装布。～-**drill** 【军】驮载教练;带着全副武装往返行走〔旧军队中一种处罚〕。～-**horse** 驮马;〔喻〕做苦工的人。～**house** 仓库,堆栈;食品加工包装厂。～ **ice** 积冰;浮冰。～-**jammed** *a*. 〔美〕挤满的,客满的。～ **load** 驮载量。～**man** 小贩,负贩。～ **mule** 驼骡。～ **needle** 打包针。～**plane** 主货舱可以拆卸的飞机。～ **rape** 轮奸。～ **rat** 〔美〕**1**. 狐尾大林鼠。**2**. 旅馆的搬行李工人,侍应生。**3**. 小偷;陌生人;不可靠的人。～ **rope** 打包绳。～**sack** 旅行背包。～**saddle** 驮鞍。～**staff** 搬货工人用的支杖(*as plain as a* ～*staff* 极明显的)。～**thread** (包扎用的)粗线;双股线,缝线。～ **twine** (包扎用的)麻线。**-ed** *a*. **1**. 充满[塞满]…的〔常用以构成复合词〕。**2**. 压结实的。**3**. 挤得满满的,满座的。

pack·age [ˈpækidʒ; ˋpækɪdʒ] **I** *n*. **1**. 包装,包扎。**2**. 〔主美〕包,包裹,捆,束,组;(产品等的)(一)件,件头。**3**. 包装用物;(包装用的)管壳,外壳。**4**. (标准)部件,组件;机组;综合设备;【自】插件;【无】电晶体外壳。**5**. 包装费,打包费。**6**. 整套的广播[电视]节目。**7**. 〔俚〕(罪犯的)前科。**8**. (工会争取到的)合同上的利益〔如退休金、劳保福利等〕。*a guidance* ～【火箭】导引装置部件。
II *a*. 一揽子的。*a* ～ *deal* 一揽子交易。*a* ～ *plan* 一揽子计划。
III *vt*. **1.** 〔美〕把…打包[装箱]。**2.** 给(商品)加漂亮包装(以吸引顾客)。**3.** 给(个人、公司等)包装,为(个人、公司等)设计整体形象以达到宣传目的。～ **holiday** [**tour**] 由旅行社代办的旅行。～ **store** 瓶装酒小卖店〔所售酒仅供顾客带走外饮〕。**packaging** *n*. (效率高而美观的)包装法;打包。

pack·er [ˈpækə; ˋpækɚ] *n*. **1.** 包装者;打包工;打包商;〔主美〕罐头食品批发商,罐头食品工人。**2.** 〔美方〕赶牲口运货的人;〔澳〕驮子,驮畜。**3.** 打包机。**4.** (打牌等)作弊的人。**5.** 〔美〕(车站等处)搬行李工。**-y** *n*. 包装工厂。

pack·et [ˈpækit; ˋpækɪt] **I** *n*. **1.** 包裹;小件行李;(邮件等的)一捆;小批;袋。**2.** (定期)邮船,班轮。**3.** 〔英俚〕(打赌等中输赢的)大笔钱。**4.** 〔英俚〕倒霉的事。**5.**【计】信息包;(作为一个单位处理的)一组信息程序[数据]。*a* ～ *of letters* 一捆信。*a postal* ～ 邮包。***a surprise*** ～ 内容出人意料的小包;〔喻〕意想不到的事。***buy a*** ～ 〔英俚〕被杀。***catch*** [***cop***, ***stop***] ***a*** ～ 被子弹打死,负重伤,负伤。***get a*** ～ 受大损失。***sell sb. a*** ～ 〔俚〕向人扯谎。**II** *vt*. **1.** 把…做成包裹。**2.** 用邮船运送。～ **boat** = ～ **ship** = ～**-vessel** 邮船;班船。～ **day** 邮船开船日;邮件截止日。～**-switched** *a*. (电脑化通信系统)分组交换式的,分组接转的。

pack·ing [ˈpækiŋ; ˋpækɪŋ] *n*. **1.** 包装,打包,打行李,包扎;包装材料,包装用品;包装法。**2.** (缝隙)填料〔旧棉絮等〕。**3.** 〔美〕食品加工业;罐头业。**4.**【机】衬垫;【建】灌筑。**5.** (电视)图象压缩。**6.** 〔美〕兵士的口粮;食物。**7.**【医】包扎法;塞法。**8.** 集合。*a* ～ *mat* 草包。*the* ～ *industry* 〔美〕食品加工业;罐头工业。～ **box**, ～ **case** 货箱;【机】垫料箱。～ **charges** 打包费。～ **fraction** **1.**【化】紧束分数。**2.**【物】敛集率。～ **house** 〔美〕牲畜屠宰加工厂;食品加工厂。～ **needle** 打包针。～ **paper** 包装纸;【机】垫纸,纸垫。～ **piece** 垫片。～ **plant** = ～ house. ～ **press** 打包机,压缩机。～ **sheet** 包装布,包装纸;【医】(水疗法用的)湿布;填齿片。

pack·tong [ˈpækˈtɔŋ; ˋpækˋtɑŋ] *n*. 白铜。

Pac-Man, Pac(-)man [ˈpækmən; ˋpækmən] *n*. 〔商标〕派克曼电子游戏软件。～ **defence** [**strategy**] 派克曼防御,派克曼策略〔指面临被收购危险的公司采取反收购等以攻为守的策略〕。

pact [pækt; pækt] *n*. **1.** 合同,契约。**2.** 盟约;公约;条约。*a peace* ～ 和平条约。

pac·tion [ˈpækʃən; ˋpækʃən] *n*. 〔Scot.〕= pact.

pad¹ [pæd; pæd] **I** *n*. **1.** (防摩擦用的)衬垫,垫料,填料,缓冲物;鞍褥。**2.** 束,捆;小块。**3.** (能一张一张扯用的)便条本子[吸墨纸本等]。**4.** (动物的)肉趾;(狐、兔、狼等的)脚;〔美〕(水生植物的)大浮叶。**5.**【海】甲板垫木,(船头的)护船木。**6.** (打球时戴的)护胫[护胸等]。**7.** (钟表的)螯尖;【机】缓冲器;把手,柄;【电讯】衰减器;(火箭等的)发射台。**8.** 绣花线。**9.** 〔美俚〕床;房间;公寓。**10.** 打印台,印色盒(= stamp ～);墨滚。**11.** (简易机场的)起落地带。**12.** 〔美俚〕吸毒窝[娼妓窝等]。*a blotting* ～ 吸墨纸本。*a writing* ～ 信纸簿。*a drawing* ～ 图画纸簿。*a launch(ing)* ～【火箭】发射台。～ *money* 〔美卑〕宿费。～ *duty* 〔谑〕睡觉。***hit*** [***knock***] ***the*** ～ 〔美军俚〕上床睡觉。
II *vt*. (**-dd-**) **1.** 填,装填;填塞;在(衣内)装棉花;在(疯人室墙上)装软垫;在(鞍上)铺垫褥,衬塞;(用不必要的材料)拉长,铺张(文章),给…加补白。**2.** 黏连(纸边)(以便一张一张撕下)。**3.** 用定色机染,浸染,轧染。**4.** 浮报(名额);虚报(账目)。**5.** 减弱…的声音,使(声音)变沉闷。*a cotton-padded coat* 棉袄。～ *one's age* 虚报年龄。

pad² [pæd; pæd] **I** *n*. **1.** 〔英方〕路。**2.** 〔罕〕拦路贼,路劫盗。**3.** 慢步而行的马(= ～-nag)。**4.** (脚步等的)叭嗒叭嗒声。***a gentleman*** [***knight***, ***squire***] ***of the*** ～ 拦路强盗。**II** *vt*. (**-dd-**) 走(路)。— *vi*. 步行;轻步慢行。～ ***it*** = ～ ***the hoof*** 〔俚〕步行;跋涉;徒步走去。

pad³ [pæd; pæd] *n*. (量水果、鱼等用的)筐子,篓子。

pa·dauk [pəˈdauk; pəˋdaʊk] *n*. 紫檀木〔产于亚洲和非洲〕。

pad·ding [ˈpædiŋ; ˋpædɪŋ] *n*. **1.** 填充,填塞,装填。**2.** 填料,芯。**3.** (报纸杂志等的)补白。**4.** 定色药[法]。**5.** (文章等的)铺张。

pad·dle¹ [ˈpædl; ˋpædl̩] **I** *n*. **1.** (短而阔的)桨;桨状物;(轮船等的)蹼轮;桨板;搅棒;捣衣棒;(施杖刑的)板子;(击球用的)球板,球拍。**2.**【动】(鲸等的)鳍状肢;(蚊蛹的)尾鳍。**3.** 小闸门。**4.** 〔美口〕叭嗒叭嗒的打。**II** *vi*. **1.** 荡桨。**2.** (轮船等)用明轮行进。— *vt*. **1.** 用桨划(小船)。**2.** (用划桨的船)运送。**3.** (用桨状物)搅打;〔美口〕叭嗒叭嗒地打。～ ***one's own canoe*** 靠自己;管自己的事。～**-board** 浮板。～ **box**【船】明轮罩。～**-fish**【动】匙吻鲟;白鲟。～ **steamer** 明轮船。～**-wheel** 蹼轮;(轮船的)明轮。

pad·dle² [ˈpædl; ˋpædl̩] *vi*. **1.** 涉水,用脚玩水;用手划水。**2.** 〔古〕摆弄,抚弄(*in*; *on*; *about*)。**3.** (小孩)趔趔趄趄地走。

pad·dle foot [ˈpædl fut; ˋpædl̩ fut] (*pl*. ***pad·dle feet*** [ˈpædl fiːt; ˋpædl̩ fit]) 〔美俚〕**1.** 步兵。**2.** 空军地勤人员。

pad·dock¹ [ˈpædək; ˋpædək] **I** *n*. **1.** (练马用的)围场;(马房附近的)牧场。**2.**【矿】(井口附近的)矿石临时堆放场地。**3.** 〔澳〕围起来的土地。**II** *vt*. **1.** 把…关入围场。**2.** 临时堆集(矿石)。

pad·dock² [ˈpædək; ˋpædək] *n*. 〔古、方〕蟾蜍;蛙。

Pad·dy [ˈpædi; ˋpædɪ] *n*. **1.** Patrick〔男子名〕和 Patricia〔女子名〕的昵称;〔口〕爱尔兰人的绰号。**2.** 〔p-〕〔英口〕= paddywhack. **3.** 〔俚〕警察。～ **wag(g)on** 〔美俚〕巡逻车;囚车。～**'s hurricane** 绝对无风。～**'s land** 爱尔兰。～**'s lantern** 月亮。

pad·dy [ˈpædi; ˋpædɪ] *n*. 水稻;谷;水稻田。～**bird**【鸟】文鸟。～**field** 水稻田,水田。～**-rice** 水稻。

pad·dy·whack [ˈpædihwæk; ˋpædɪˌhwæk] *n*. 〔口〕**1.** 〔英〕大怒。**2.** 〔美〕痛打,揍;打屁股。**3.** 〔P-〕〔俚〕爱尔兰人。

Pa·di·sha(h) [ˈpædiʃɑː; ˋpɑdɪˌʃɑ] *n*. **1.** 君主,大帝〔伊朗的 Shah, 土耳其的 Sultan, (旧印度所称的)英国国王〕。**2.** 〔p-〕〔口〕有权势的人物。

pad·lock [ˈpædlɔk; ˋpædˌlɑk] **I** *n*. 挂锁,扣锁。**II** *vt*. **1.** 用挂锁锁;把…上锁。**2.** 正式关闭(公共场所等)。**-ed** *a*. 〔美〕(剧院等)奉当局命令关掉的。

pa·dre [ˈpɑːdri; ˋpɑdrɪ] *n*. 〔Sp., Pg.〕**1.** (意、西、葡和拉美等国的)神父,教士。**2.** 〔俚〕随军牧师。

pa·dro·ne [pəˈdrəuni; pɑˋdrone] *n*. (*pl*. ***-dro·ni*** [-niː; -ni], ～***s***) 〔It.〕**1.** 主人;(地中海贸易船的)船主。**2.** (*pl*. ～***s***) 〔美〕意大利搬运工人的工头;过去在美国承包意大利移民工人的包工头。**3.** 意大利旅馆老板。**4.** 意大利童丐头。

pad·u·a·soy [ˈpædjuəsɔi; ˋpædʒʊəˌsɔɪ] **I** *n*. (十八世纪流行的)棱纹花绸(衣服等)。**II** *a*. 用棱纹花绸制作的。

pae·an [ˈpiːən; ˋpiən] *n*. **1.** (古希腊)对太阳神的赞歌。**2.** 凯歌;欢乐歌,赞美歌。*a* ～ *of victory* 胜利的凯歌。

pae·deu·tics [piːˈdjuːtiks; piˋdjutɪks] *n*. 儿童教育学。

pae·di·a·tric [ˌpiːdiˈætrik; ˌpidɪˋætrɪk] *a*. 儿科学的,小儿科的。

pae·di·a·tri·ci·an [ˌpiːdiəˈtriʃən; ˌpidɪəˋtrɪʃən] *n*. 儿科医生[专家]。

pae·di·at·rics [ˌpiːdiˈætriks; ˌpidɪˋætrɪks] *n*.【医】儿科学;小儿科。

pae·di·at·rist [ˌpiːdiˈætrist; ˌpidɪˋætrɪst] *n*. = paediatrician.

pae·d(o)- *comb. f*. 表示"儿童"(= child)。

pae·do·bap·tism [ˌpiːdəuˈbæptizəm; ˏpidoˋbæptɪzm̩] *n*. 幼儿洗礼。

pae·do·bap·tist [ˌpiːdəuˈbæptist; ˏpidoˋbæptɪst] *n*. 幼儿洗礼论者。

pae·do·gen·e·sis [ˌpiːdəuˈdʒenisis; ˏpidoˋdʒɛnəsɪs] *n*. 【动】幼体生殖。**-gen·ic** [-ˈdʒenik; -ˋdʒɛnɪk], **-ge·net·ic** [-dʒiˈnetik; -dʒɪˋnɛtɪk] *a*.

pa·el·la [pɑːˈelə, Sp. pɑːˈelja; pɑˋɛlə, pɑˋɛljɑ] *n*. 肉菜饭〔一种西班牙菜饭,用大米与鸡、海味等同煮,用番红花调味〕。

pae·on [ˈpiːən; ˋpiən] *n*. 〔诗〕(由一个长[重读]音节与三个短[非重读]音节构成的)四音节的韵脚。

pae·o·ny [ˈpiəni; ˋpɪənɪ] *n*. = peony.

pae·sa·no [paiˈsɑːnəu, -ˈzɑː-; paɪˋsɑno, -ˋzɑ-] *n*. (*pl*. *-ni* [-niː; -ni], ~*s*) 同国人,同胞〔尤指意大利的同国人〕(=paesan)。

pa·gan [ˈpeigən; ˋpegən] **I** *n*. **1.** 异教徒,邪教徒;偶像信徒;非基督教徒。**2.** 没有宗教信仰的人。**II** *a*. 异教的,邪教的,异教徒的;非基督教的;无宗教信仰的。**-dom** *n*. 〔集合词〕异教徒。**-ish** *a*. 异教徒的;信奉异教的。**-ism** *n*. 异教;信奉异教,偶像崇拜。**-ize** *vt*., *vi*. (使)变成异教徒。

Page [peidʒ; pedʒ] *n*. 佩奇〔姓氏〕。

page[1] [peidʒ; pedʒ] **I** *n*. **1.** 页〔略作 p.〕;【印】一页版面;【计】网页。**2.** (报刊的)专页,专栏。**3.** 〔诗〕〔修〕〔常 *pl*.〕纪录,书,年史。**4.** (值得记的)插话;事件。*these* ~*s* 本书。*a* ~ *of history* 历史的纪录。*a fat* ~【印】空白多的版面。*a full* ~【印】没有空白的版面。*the* "*Literary Legacy*" ~《文学遗产》栏。**II** *vt*. 给…标页数,标记…的页码。— *vi*. 翻书页。**~view**【计】页视,一次网页访问。

page[2] [peidʒ; pedʒ] **I** *n*. **1.** 小听差,小侍从,侍童;〔美〕(侍候国会议员的)服务员。**2.** 王室侍从官员。**3.**【史】见习骑士。**II** *vi*. 当听差。— *vt*. **1.** 侍候,给…当听差。**2.** 〔美〕(在旅馆、俱乐部等处)侍者叫名找(人)。~**boy 1.** 做小听差的男孩。**2.** 童花头〔向下卷的齐肩女孩发型〕。~**hood**, ~**ship** 侍从[听差]的身分[地位]。

page[3] [peidʒ; pedʒ] *vt*. **1.**【无】用无线电讯号与(某人)联系。**2.** 用电子遥控器调节(电器)。**-r** *n*.【无】呼机〔一种袖珍电子装置,作通讯联系用〕。

pag·eant [ˈpædʒənt; ˋpædʒənt] *n*. **1.** 赛会,露天表演。**2.** 盛观;(穿着古装等的)壮丽的游行队伍。**3.** 虚饰;炫耀。**4.** (有山水、花鸟、人物等的)挂帐,挂布。

pag·eant·ry [ˈpædʒəntri; ˋpædʒəntrɪ] *n*. **1.** 壮观,盛观。**2.** 赛会,壮丽的游行队伍。**3.** (暂时性的)彩饰;夸耀,虚饰。

pag·i·nal, pag·i·nar·y [ˈpædʒinl, -nəri; ˋpædʒənl, -nərɪ] *a*. (每)页的,逐页对照的。*a* ~ *translation* 逐页对照的翻译。

pag·i·nate [ˈpædʒineit; ˋpædʒəˏnet] *vt*. 给…记页数,标…的页码。

pag·i·na·tion [ˌpædʒiˈneiʃən; ˏpædʒəˋneʃən] *n*. 页码标记;页数(号码)。

Pa·go Pa·go [ˈpɑːŋəu ˈpɑːŋəu; ˋpɑŋoˋpɑŋo] 帕果—帕果〔东萨摩亚首府〕。

pa·go·da [pəˈgəudə; pəˋgodə] *n*. **1.** 塔,宝塔;(卖报纸等的)宝塔式摊子。**2.** (印度从前使用的)一种金币。~**-tree 1.**【植】长成塔状的东方树木;槐;榕树(*a Japanese* ~*-tree* 槐)。**2.** (白)鸡蛋花。**3.** 〔喻〕(传说中能产金币的)摇钱树。*shake the* ~*-tree* 〔谑〕(在印度等地)发了大财。

pa·gu·rid [pəˈgjuərid, ˈpægjurid; pəˋgjʊrɪd, ˋpægjərɪd] **I** *n*. 寄生虫科(*Paguridae*)动物;寄生虫。**II** *a*. 寄生虫的(=pagurian)。

pah[1] [pɑː; pɑ] *int*. 哼!〔表示轻蔑、憎恶等〕。

pah[2] [pɑː; pɑ] *n*. (新西兰的)毛利人(Maori)村寨[村庄]。

Pah·la·vi [ˈpɑːləviː; ˋpɑləˏvi] *n*. 巴拉维语〔约在公元第三世纪至第八世纪的伊朗语〕(=Pehlevi)。

pa·ho·e·ho·e [pɑːˈhəuiˌhəui; pɑˋhoɪˏhoɪ] *n*. 〔Haw.〕绳状熔岩。

paid [peid; ped] **I** pay 的过去式及过去分词。**II** *a*. **1.** 有薪金的;受雇用的。**2.** 已付的,付清的。*all expenses* ~ 一切费用均已付清。*a* ~ *cash book* 现金支出账。***put* "~" *to*** 〔口〕结束…,了结…;付清的。

paid-in [ˈpeidin; ˋpedˏɪn] *a*. (会费等)已缴讫的。

pai·dol·o·gy [peiˈdɔlədʒi; peˋdɑlədʒɪ] *n*. 儿童学,儿童研究。

paid-up [ˈpeidʌp; ˋpedˋʌp] *a*. 已付的;付清的;(股份)已全额结清的。

pail [peil; pel] *n*. 桶,提桶;一桶的量;〔美口〕容器。*a* ~ *of milk* 一桶牛奶。*a dinner-*~〔美〕饭盒子。**-ful** *n*. 满桶,一桶之量。

pail·lasse [pælˈjæs, ˈpæljæs; pælˋjæs, ˋpæljæs] *n*. 草荐(=palliasse)。

pail·lette [pælˈjet; pælˋjɛt] *n*. (用于涂珐琅或装饰妇女服装的)闪闪发光的金属片。

pain [pein; pen] **I** *n*. **1.** 痛,疼痛;(精神上的)痛苦,忧虑,烦闷,悲痛(*opp*. pleasure)。**2.** 〔古〕罚,刑罚。**3.** 〔*pl*.〕费心,苦心;刻苦;努力;辛苦。**4.** 〔*pl*.〕产痛,阵痛。**5.** 〔美俚〕嫌恶;讨厌的人[事物]。*I have* ~*s all over*. 全身疼痛。*a* ~ *in the head* 头痛。*It gives me* ~ *to do so*. 这样做使我痛苦。*No* ~*s*, *no gains* [*profit*]. 不劳无获。~*s and penalties* 刑罚。*You may save your* ~*s*. 你不必费心。***a* ~ *in the neck*** 〔美〕讨厌或惹人生气的家伙[责任、义务]。***be an ass for one's* ~*s*** 徒劳无功。***be at the* ~*s of*** [***be at* ~*s of*** 或 ***take* ~*s***] 努力,尽力设法(*She is at* (*the*) ~*s of finding the answers*. 她在努力寻求答案)。***be in* ~** 疼痛;在苦恼中。***cause*** [***give***] (*sb*.) ~ 使痛苦。***feel no* ~ 1.** 不觉得痛。**2.**【俚】醉倒;枉费心机。***for* (*all*) *one's* ~*s*** 作为劳苦的报酬;〔反〕尽管费尽力气;费力反而(*He got little reward for his* ~*s*. 他白辛苦了。*I got a thrashing for my* ~*s*. 我费力反而挨了打)。***on*** [***upon***, ***under***] ~ ***of death*** 违则处死。***spare no* ~*s*** 全力以赴,不辞劳苦地。***take* (*much*) ~*s*** 费苦心;尽力(*He has taken* ~*s to study the problem*. 他下功夫研究那个问题)。***with great* ~*s*** 煞费苦心。
II *vt*. 使疼痛,使痛苦,使心痛。*Does your tooth* ~ *you*? 你牙痛吗? — *vi*. 〔口〕痛。*My arm is* ~*ing*. 我胳膊痛。**-ed** *a*. **1.** 疼痛的。**2.** 苦恼的,伤了感情的(*a* ~*ed expression* 痛苦的表情)。~**-killer** 〔口〕止疼药。

Pain(e) [pein; pen] *n*. 佩恩〔姓氏〕。

pain·ful [ˈpeinful; ˋpenfəl] *a*. **1.** 疼痛的,使痛苦的。**2.** 讨厌的,使人厌烦的。**3.** 费力的,(工作)困难的;〔古〕细心的,勤勉的。*the* ~ *labours of lexicographers* 编词典人的辛苦。*with* ~ *care* 煞费苦心地。**-ly** *ad*. **-ness** *n*.

pain·less [ˈpeinlis; ˋpenlɪs] *a*. 无痛的,没有痛苦的。~ *death* 没有痛苦的死;善终。**-ly** *ad*. **-ness** *n*.

pains·tak·er [ˈpeinzteikə; ˋpenzˏtekɚ] *n*. 不辞劳苦的人,苦干的人,勤勉的人。

pains·tak·ing [ˈpeinzteikiŋ; ˋpenzˏtekɪŋ] **I** *a*. **1.** (不辞)劳苦的,苦干的,辛勤的;费力的。**2.** 煞费苦心的。*be* ~ *with one's work* 苦干。**II** *n*. 苦干,刻苦,煞费苦心。**-ly** *ad*.

paint [peint; pent] **I** *n*. **1.** 颜料;涂料;油漆。**2.** 化妆品;香粉;口红;胭脂;(化装用的)油彩。**3.** 彩色;装饰,虚饰。*powder and* ~ 粉和胭脂。*a luminous* [*phosphorescent*] ~ 发光涂料。***as fresh as* ~** 精神焕发;强壮的。***as smart as* ~** 非常漂亮。***Fresh P-*** 〔美〕= ***Wet* ~** 〔英〕油漆未干! **II** *vt*. **1.** (用颜料)画;描绘;给…着色。**2.** 给…上油漆,把…涂成(某种颜色)。**3.** 涂(化妆品),搽(脂粉)。**4.** (用文字)描写,叙述(事件等);想象;

装饰。**5.**(用油漆等)涂掉;覆盖;〔喻〕粉饰。*She ~s herself thick*. 她脸上的粉搽得厚。~ *a gate green* 把门漆成绿色。~ *defects* 掩饰缺点。— ***vi*.** **1.**(用颜料等)绘画;成画题。**2.** 搽粉[胭脂],化妆。**3.**〔古〕脸红。~ *in oils* [*Indian ink*, *water colours*] 画油画[墨画、水彩画]。***as ~ed as a picture*** 搽着很厚的粉。~ ***a black*** [***rosy***] ***picture of*** 非常悲观[乐观]地叙述…。~ ***in*** 用颜色突出。~ ***it red*** 〔美俚〕把事物弄得引人注目,描写得天花乱坠。~ ***out*** (用油漆等)涂掉。~ ***sb. black*** 把某人描写成坏蛋;给某人抹黑(*He is not so black as he is ~ed*. 他并不像所说的那样坏)。~ ***the lily*** 做多余[无益]的事情,锦上添花。~ ***the town*** [***city***] ***red*** 〔俚〕(多指夜生活中的)狂欢作乐;闹酒。~**ball** 彩弹射击游戏〔一种军事游戏,双方以汽枪互射彩色染料弹丸,对方被击中后衣服上会留下彩色印渍即表示"被消灭"〕,(此种游戏中使用的)彩色弹丸。~**box** 颜料盒。~**brush** **1.** 画笔,画刷;漆刷,漆帚。**2.**【植】桔黄山柳菊;扁萼花。~ **cards** 〔美俚〕有画的扑克牌〔指 K, Q, J 等牌〕。**-less** ***a*.** 未油漆的。

paint. = painting.

paint·ed [ˈpeintid; ˋpentɪd] ***a*.** **1.** 画的;着了色的。**2.** 油漆了的。**3.** 色彩鲜明的。**4.** 搽了脂粉的。**5.** 假的,虚饰的。~ *china* 彩釉瓷器。*the P- Desert* 美国亚利桑那州的红土荒地。*a* ~ *sepulchre* 伪君子。*a* ~ *woman* 〔美〕妓女。~ **glass** 彩色玻璃。~ **lady**【动】苎胥〔蝶的一种〕;【植】红花除虫菊;波状延龄草。

paint·er[1] [ˈpeintə; ˋpentɚ] ***n*.** **1.** 画家;着色者。**2.** 油漆匠。*a lady* ~ 女画家。*a* ~*'s canvas* 画布。*a* ~ *and decorator* 油漆装饰工。*a* ~*'s brush* = paint-brush. ~**'s colic**【医】铅中毒绞痛。**-ly** ***a*.** **1.** 画家(似)的;油漆匠的。**2.** 美术的,绘画的。

paint·er[2] [ˈpeintə; ˋpentɚ] ***n*.**【海】(小船的)缆索;系船索。*a large* [*lazy*, *small*] ~ 大[小]缆索。***cut*** [***slip***] ***the*** [***one's***] ~ **1.** 解开缆索,使漂流。**2.**〔喻〕使分离;(殖民地等)和宗主国断绝关系,独立。**3.** 破诡计。

paint·er[3] [ˈpeintə; ˋpentɚ] ***n*.**【动】美洲狮(= cougar)。

paint·ing [ˈpeintiŋ; ˋpentɪŋ] ***n*.** **1.** 绘画;(一张)油画,水彩画。**2.** 画法;绘画艺术。**3.** 上色,着色;搽胭脂;涂漆。**4.** 颜料,油漆,涂料。*traditional Chinese* ~ 中国画。~**-room** 画室。

paint·ress [ˈpeintris; ˋpentrɪs] ***n*.** 女画家。

paint·y [ˈpeinti; ˋpentɪ] ***a*.** **1.**(画等)着色过度的。**2.** 被颜料[油漆]弄脏的。

pair [pɛə; pɛr] **I** ***n*.** (*pl*. ~(*s*)) **1.** 一对,一双,一套,(眼镜等的)一副;(剪子等的)一把,(裤子等的)一条。**2.** 一对男女,未婚夫妇;(动物的)偶。**3.** 系在一起的两匹马。**4.**【机】对偶,副。**5.**(成对物的)另一方。**6.**(议会)约好互相弃权的对立两派的两个议员;(比赛等中的)两人合伙关系。**7.**(纸牌等)同点子的一对。**8.**〔英方〕(楼梯等的)一段。*a* ~ *of shoes* 一双鞋。*two* ~(*s*) *of trousers* 两条裤子。*the happy* ~ 新郎新娘。*They are a pretty* ~. 他们真是好一对。*a carriage and* ~ 双马马车。*the* ~ *to this sock* 这双袜子的另一只。*a pigeon* ~ 一男一女的双胞胎;(只有)一个儿子和一个女儿。***in a*** ~ = ***in ~s*** 成双,成对。~ ***of colours***【英军】国旗和团旗。~ ***of pipes*** 〔美〕(唱歌或说话的)声音。~ ***of stairs*** [***steps***] 梯子,楼梯(*I live up two* ~ *of stairs front*. 我住在三楼前室)。~ ***royal***【牌】三张同样的牌;三颗同点的骰子。(***quite***) ***another*** [***a different***] ~ ***of shoes*** [***boots***] (完全是)另外一个问题。***take*** [***show***] ***a clean ~ of heels*** 一溜烟逃走;逃之夭夭。**II** ***vi*.** **1.** 成对,配合;交配;〔俚〕成夫妇(*with*)。**2.**(议会)相约弃权。— ***vt*.** **1.** 使成对。**2.** 使成配偶;使交配。~ ***off*** **1.** 使分成[摆成]一对一对。**2.** 两个成一组,成对而去。~ ***off with*** 〔口〕和…结婚。~ **annihilation**【物】(正负电子)对[偶]湮没。~**-horse** ***a*.** 双马的。~**-oar** ***n*.**, ***a*.** 双桨艇(的)。~**ed-associate-learning**【教】配对联想学习法〔成对地记诵单词等,通过互相联系而加强记忆〕。~ **production**【原】偶产生,对产生。

pair·ing-sea·son [ˈpɛəriŋ-ˈsiːzn; ˋpɛrɪŋ-ˋsizn̩] ***n*.** (鸟等的)交配期。

pai·sa [ˈpaisæ; ˋpaɪsæ] ***n*.** (*pl*. ***pa·ise*** [-se; -sɛ]) 派萨〔印度、巴基斯坦、卡塔尔、马斯喀特和阿曼的货币单位,等于百分之一卢比〕。

pai·sa·na [paiˈsɑːnɑː; paɪˋsɑnɑ] ***n*.** 〔Sp.〕 **1.** 女同胞。**2.**〔俚〕女伙伴。

pai·sa·no, ***pai·san*** [paiˈsɑːnəu, paiˈsɑːn; paɪˋsɑno, paɪˋsɑn] ***n*.** 〔Sp.〕 **1.** 同胞。**2.**〔俚〕同志;伙伴。**3.** 乡下人。

Pais·ley [ˈpeizli; ˋpezlɪ] ***n*.**, ***a*.**【纺】**1.**(苏格兰)佩斯利(市出产的)涡旋纹花呢(的)。**2.** 佩斯利细毛披巾[围巾](的)。~ **shawl** 佩斯利细毛围巾。

Pai·ute [ˈpaijuːt, paiˈjuːt; ˋpaɪjut, paɪˋjut] ***n*.** (*pl*. ~(*s*)) **1.** 派尤特人〔美洲的一支印地安人,居住在美国内华达、加利福尼亚东部、犹他南部和亚利桑那西北部等地〕。**2.** 派尤特语。

pa·ja·mas [pəˈdʒɑːməz; pəˋdʒæməz] ***n*.** 〔*pl*.〕宽大的睡衣裤(= pyjamas)。***the cat's*** ~ 〔美俚〕卓越的[出色的、极好的]人[事、物]。

pa·ke·ha [ˈpɑːkihə; ˋpɑkɪhə] ***n*.** (*pl*. ~(*s*))〔新西兰〕白种人。

Pa·ki·stan [ˌpɑːkisˈtɑːn; ˏpækɪˋstæn] ***n*.** 巴基斯坦〔亚洲〕。

Pa·ki·stan·i [ˌpɑːkiˈstɑːni; ˏpækəˋstænɪ] **I** ***n*.** (*pl*. ~(*s*)) 巴基斯坦人。**II** ***a*.** 巴基斯坦的。

PAL = Philippine Air Lines 菲律宾航空公司。

Pal. = Palestine.

pal [pæl; pæl] **I** ***n*.** 〔口〕伙伴,好朋友;同伙,同谋,同犯。**II** ***vi*.** (***-ll-***) 成伙伴,结成好友(*with*)。~ ***up with*** 和…结成好友;和…结伙。

pal·ace [ˈpælis; ˋpælɪs] ***n*.** **1.** 宫,宫殿。**2.**(主教)邸宅;宏伟大厦。**3.** 华丽的娱乐场所。*a* ~ *car* 〔美〕花车,豪华(火车)车厢。*a* ~ *hotel* 豪华的旅馆。*a movie* ~ 电影院。*the* (*Crystal*) *P-* 〔英口〕水晶宫。*the* ~ 宫廷显贵。~ **revolution** 宫廷政变。

pal·a·din [ˈpælədin; ˋpælədɪn] ***n*.** **1.**【法史】帕拉丁〔查理曼 (Charlemagne) 大帝部下十二武士之一〕。**2.** 干将;勇士;骑士;武士,游侠。

Pa·l(a)e·arc·tic [ˌpeiliˈɑːktik; pelɪˋɑktɪk] ***a*.** 旧北极的,古北区的〔包括欧洲、非洲、北回归线以北的阿拉伯以及喜马拉雅山脉以北的亚洲部分〕。

pa·l(a)e·eth·nol·o·gy [ˌpælieθˈnɔlədʒi; ˏpælɪɛθˋnɑlədʒɪ] ***n*.** 古[史前]人种学。

palae(o)-, **pale(o)-** 〔Gr.〕 *comb*. *f*. 表示"古,旧,原始"。

pa·lae·o·an·thro·pol·o·gy [ˈpæliəuˌænθrəˈpɔlədʒi; ˋpælɪoˏænˋθrəˈpɑlədʒɪ] ***n*.** 古人类学。**-g·i·cal** ***a*.**

pa·l(a)e·o·an·throp·ic(al) [ˌpeiliəuænˈθrɔpik(əl), ˌpæli-; ˏpelɪoænˋθrɑpɪk(l), ˏpælɪ-] ***a*.** 化石人早期形状的,与化石人早期形状有关的。

pa·l(a)e·o·bot·a·ny [ˈpæliəuˈbɔtəni; ˋpælɪoˋbɑtənɪ] ***n*.** 古植物学,化石植物学。

Pa·l(a)e·o·cene [ˈpeiliəuˌsiːn, ˈpæli-; ˋpelɪəˏsin, ˋpælɪ-] ***a*.**【地】古新的〔新生代第三纪的初期或早期的〕。*the* ~ 古新纪或该时代的岩石。

pa·l(a)e·o·crys·tic [ˌpæliəuˈkristik; ˏpælɪoˋkrɪstɪk] ***a*.** (冰、海等)长期冻结的。

pa·l(a)e·og. = palaeography.

pa·l(a)e·og·raph [ˈpæliɔgrəf; ˋpælɪˏɑgrəf] ***n*.** **1.** 古代手写本;古抄本。**2.** = paleographer.

pa·l(a)e·og·ra·pher [ˌpæliˈɔgrəfə; ˏpælɪˋɑgrəfɚ] ***n*.** 古文书学家;抄本研究者;古字体研究者。

pa·l(a)e·o·graph·ic [ˌpæliəuˈgræfik; ˏpælɪəˋgræfɪk] ***a*.** 古文(书)学的;古字体的。

pa·l(a)e·og·ra·phy [ˌpæliˈɔgrəfi; ˏpælɪˋɑgrəfɪ] ***n*.** 古

文书(学);古字体。

pa·l(a)e·o·lith [ˈpæliə*u*liθ; ˋpælɪəˏlɪθ] ***n.*** 【考古】旧石器。

pa·l(a)e·o·lith·ic [ˌpæliə*u*ˈliθik; ˏpælɪəˋlɪθɪk] ***a.*** 旧石器时代的。*the P- era* 旧石器时代。*the ~ man* 旧石器时代的人(类)。

pal(a)e·on·tol. = pal(a)eontology.

pa·l(a)e·on·tol·o·gy [ˌpælionˈtɔlədʒi; ˏpælɪɑnˋtɑlədʒɪ] ***n.*** 【地】古生物学,化石学。**-to·log·ic(al)** [ˈpæliˌɔntəˈlɔdʒik(əl); ˋpælɪˏɑntəˋlɑdʒɪk(l̩)] ***a.*** **-tol·o·gist** ***n.*** 古生物学家。

Pa·l(a)e·o·zo·ic [ˌpæliə*u*ˈzəuik; ˏpælɪəˋzoɪk] **I** ***a.*** 【地】古生代的。**II** ***n.*** 〔the ~〕古生代。

pa·l(a)e·o·zo·ol·o·gy [ˌpæliə*u*zəuˈɔlədʒi; ˏpælɪozoˋɑlədʒɪ] ***n.*** 古动物学。

pa·l(a)e·phyte [ˈpæliə*u*fait; ˋpælɪəˏfaɪt] ***n.*** 古生代植物。

pa·laes·tra, pa·les·tra [pəˈliːstrə, -ˈles-; pəˋlistrə, -lɛs-] ***n.*** (*pl.* ~*s*, ***-trae*** [-triː; -tri]) **1.** (古希腊、罗马的)角力学校。**2.** 体育场。

pa·lais de danse [pæˈlei də ˈdɑːns, F. pale də ˈdɑːŋs; pæˋle də ˋdɑns, palɛ də ˋdɑŋs] ***n.*** (特别豪华的)舞厅。

pal·an·keen, pal·an·quin [ˌpælənˈkiːn; ˏpælənˋkin] ***n.*** (东方国家旧时用人抬的)四[六]人大轿。

pal·at·a·ble [ˈpælətəbl; ˋpælətəbl̩] ***a.*** **1.** 好吃的,可口的;合口味的。**2.** 愉快的,惬意的。**-bly** ***ad.*** **-bil·i·ty** ***n.***

pal·a·tal [ˈpælətl; ˋpælətl̩] **I** ***a.*** 腭的;【语音】腭音的。**II** ***n.*** 【语音】腭音。

pal·a·tal·ize [ˈpælətəlaiz; ˋpælətl̩ˏaɪz] ***vt.*** 【语音】用腭音发(音),使腭音化。**-ization** [ˌpælətəlaiˈzeiʃən; ˏpælətəlaɪˋzeʃən] ***n.***

pal·ate [ˈpælit, -ət; ˋpælɪt, -ət] ***n.*** **1.** 【解】腭。**2.** 【植】下唇瓣。**3.** 味觉;嗜好;〔喻〕审美眼光,鉴赏力,判断。*a cleft ~* 豁嘴,缺唇。*a false ~* (实验语音学中用以调整舌腭接触部分的)人工腭。***have a delicate ~*** 爱考究,挑剔。***nice to ~*** 好吃。***suit sb.'s ~*** 合口味。***top of the ~*** 【解】悬壅垂(= uvula)。**~ bone** 【解】腭骨。

pa·la·tial [pəˈleiʃəl; pəˋleʃəl] ***a.*** 宫殿(似)的;宏伟的;壮丽的。**-ly** ***ad.***

pal·a·tine[1] [ˈpælətain; ˋpæləˏtaɪn] **I** ***a.*** **1.** 宫殿的。**2.** 宫廷官吏的;有王室特权的。**3.** 〔P-〕(享有王权的)封建领主的。**II** ***n.*** **1.** 〔P-〕古罗马的宫廷官吏;古代德国、法国的最高法官;享有王权的封建领主。**2.** 女用皮围巾[披肩]。***the P- (Hill)*** (罗马市建于其上的)帕拉坦(丘)。

pal·a·tine[2] [ˈpælətain; ˋpæləˏtaɪn] **I** ***a.*** 腭的。**II** ***n.*** 〔*pl.*〕【解】腭骨。

pal·a·to- *comb. f.* 表示"腭": *palato*-dental 前舌齿音的。

pal·a·to·gram [ˈpælətəgræm, pəˈlætəg-; ˋpælətəˏgræm, pəˋlætəg-] ***n.*** 【语音】腭位图。

pa·la·ver [pəˈlɑːvə; pəˋlævɚ] **I** ***n.*** **1.** 废话,空谈。**2.** 奉承,拍马屁;笼络;诱骗。**3.** (尤指非洲人和外来商人间的)交涉,谈判;〔俚〕事务。**II** ***vi.*** 闲谈;空谈。— ***vt.*** 哄骗;笼络。

Pa·laz·zo [pɑːˈlɑːtsəu; pɑˋlɑtso] ***n.*** (*pl.* ***-laz·zi*** [-ˈlɑːsti; -ˋlɑstɪ]) 〔It.〕豪华的宫殿,邸宅。

pale[1] [peil; pel] **I** ***a.*** **1.** 灰白的,(脸色等)苍白的。**2.** (颜色等)淡的;微暗的,(光等)弱;柔弱无力的。*a ~ moon* 朦胧的月光。*be ~ with fear* 吓得面无人色。*look ~* 脸色不好。*~ (ale)* 〔美〕淡啤酒。*~ wine* 白葡萄酒。***turn ~*** 变苍白;变淡。***as ~ as death [sheet]*** 脸色像死人一样苍白。***be ~ before [beside, by the side of]*** 在…前相形见绌;失色;变苍白;(色)变淡;变暗。**II** ***vi.*** 使变苍白,使发暗。**~eyed** ***a.*** 眼睛无神的。**~-hearted** ***a.*** 怯懦的,胆小的。**-ly** ***ad.*** **-ness** ***n.***

pale[2] [peil; pel] **I** ***n.*** **1.** 桩,(栅栏)尖板条;围篱,栅栏。**2.** 境界,范围;境内,栅内;【徽】竖贯徽章中部的线条。**3.** 〔the P-〕【史】12 世纪后并入英国的爱尔兰东部地区(= the English [Irish] Pale)。***in ~*** 纵向排列。***leap the ~*** 越界,过分。***within [out of, outside, beyond] the ~ of*** 在…的范围内[外]。**II** ***vt.*** 用桩[栅]围住,在…设围篱。

Pa·le(o)- *comb. f.* = Palae(o)-.

pa·le·a [ˈpeiliə; ˋpelɪə] ***n.*** (*pl.* ***-le·ae*** [-liiː; -lɪi]) 【植】(禾本科的)内稃;(菊科的)托苞。

pale-buck [ˈpeil-bʌk; ˋpel-bʌk] ***n.*** 【动】羚羊。

pale·face [ˈpeilfeis; ˋpelˏfes] ***n.*** 白种人〔据说是北美印第安人用语〕。

Pa·lem·bang [ˌpɑːlemˈbɑːŋ; ˏpɑlɛmˋbɑŋ] ***n.*** 巴邻旁〔印度尼西亚港市〕。

Pa·ler·mo [pəˈləːməu; pəˋlɝmo] ***n.*** 巴勒摩〔意大利港市〕。

Pal·es·tine [ˈpælistain; ˋpæləsˏtaɪn] ***n.*** **1.** 巴勒斯坦。**2.** 【圣】圣地(= Holy Land)。

Pal·es·tin·i·an [ˌpælisˈtiniən; ˏpæləsˋtɪnɪən] **I** ***a.*** 巴勒斯坦(人)的。**II** ***n.*** 巴勒斯坦人。

pa·les·tra [pəˈlestrə; pəˋlɛstrə] ***n.*** (*pl.* ~*s*, ~*e* [-triː; -tri]) = palaestra.

pal·ette [ˈpælit; ˋpælɪt] ***n.*** **1.** 调色板;(调色板上的或某画家用的)一套颜料。**2.** (中世纪铠甲的)关节板。*set the ~* 把颜料安排在调色板上。**~-knife** 调色刀。

Pa·ley [ˈpeili; ˋpelɪ] ***n.*** 佩利〔姓氏〕。

pal·frey [ˈpɔːlfri; ˋpɔlfrɪ] ***n.*** **1.** 〔古〕(普通)供乘骑的马。**2.** (供妇女骑的脚步轻快的)小马。

Pal·grave [ˈpɔːlgreiv, ˈpælgreiv; ˋpɔlgrev, ˋpælgrev] ***n.*** 帕尔格雷夫〔姓氏〕。

Pa·li [ˈpɑːli; ˋpɑlɪ] ***n.*** (印度东南部古代的)巴利语〔现已成为佛教的宗教语言〕。

pal·i·kar [ˈpælikə; ˋpælɪˏkɑr] ***n.*** (1821—1828 年独立战争时的)希腊民兵。

pal·i·mo·ny [ˈpælimәni; ˋpælimәni] ***n.*** (= pal alimony)(非婚同居者分居后法庭判决由一方付给另一方的)同居生活费。

pal·imp·sest [ˈpælimpsest; ˋpælɪmpˏsɛst] ***n.*** **1.** (可以消去旧字另写新字的)羊皮纸[石板等]。**2.** 把背面翻过来另刻的旧黄铜纪念牌。

pal·in·drome [ˈpælindrəum; ˋpælɪnˏdrom] ***n.*** **1.** 回文〔正读反读都可的语句,例如: *Madam*; *Hannah*; *Able was I ere I saw Elba* 等〕。**2.** 〔生化〕(细胞中遗传物质的)回文结构。

pal·ing [ˈpeiliŋ; ˋpelɪŋ] ***n.*** **1.** 打桩做栅栏。**2.** 〔集合词〕桩;(栅栏的)尖板条,栅,围篱;围。

pal·in·gen·e·sis [ˌpælinˈdʒenisis; ˏpælɪnˋdʒɛnəsɪs] ***n.*** **1.** 【哲】【宗】新生,再生;洗礼;轮回;历史循环论。**2.** 【生】重演(性)发生;【虫】重演(性)变态。

pal·in·ge·net·ic [ˌpælindʒiˈnetik; ˏpælɪndʒɪˋnɛtɪk] ***a.*** 【哲,宗】新生[再生]的;【生】重演性发生的;【虫】重演性变态的。**-i·cal·ly** ***ad.***

pal·i·node [ˈpælinəud; ˋpælɪˏnod] ***n.*** **1.** (否定本人旧作内容的)翻案诗。**2.** 正式打消前言。

pal·i·sade [ˌpæliˈseid; ˏpæləˋsed] **I** ***n.*** **1.** 桩,木栅,栅栏。**2.** 〔*pl.*〕(河边的)断崖。**II** ***vt.*** 用栅围绕。

pal·ish [ˈpeiliʃ; ˋpelɪʃ] ***a.*** 稍带苍白的。

pal·i·(s)san·der [ˌpæliˈsændə; ˏpæləˋsændɚ] ***n.*** (巴西)红木。

pall[1] [pɔːl; pɔl] **I** ***n.*** **1.** 棺衣;墓布;(内装尸体的)棺材;【宗】圣杯[祭台]罩布;祭服。**2.** 阴惨的东西;悲哀。**3.** 〔古〕外套,披肩。**4.** Y 字形徽章;= pallium. **5.** 遮盖物;〔喻〕幕。*a ~ of darkness* 夜幕。**II** ***vt.*** 给…盖棺衣;覆盖,包。**~bearer, ~holder, ~supporter** (丧礼中的)抬棺人;执绋人;〔美俚〕饭馆里撤盘子的人。

pall[2] [pɔːl; pɔl] ***vi.*** **1.** (酒等)走味,失味。**2.** 扫兴;丧失吸引力;令人感到腻烦;使人生厌 (*on*; *upon*)。— ***vt.*** 使

扫兴;使生厌。

Pal·la·di·an[1][pəˈleidiən; pəˋledɪən] *a*. 1.【希神】智慧女神帕拉斯 (Pallas) 的。2. 智慧的,学问的,知识的。

Pal·la·di·an[2][pəˈleidiən; pəˋledɪən] *a*. (十六世纪意大利建筑家)帕拉第奥 (A. Palladio) 的;帕拉第奥建筑形式的。

pal·lad·ic [pəˈlædik, -ˈleidik; pəˋlædɪk, -ˋledɪk] *a*.【化】钯的;四价钯的。

Pal·la·di·um [pəˈleidiəm; pəˋledɪəm] *n*. 1. 希腊智慧女神帕拉斯 (Pallas) 的神像。2. 〔p-〕(*pl*. **-dia** [-diə; -dɪə]) 守护神;保障,保护。

pal·la·dium [pəˈleidiəm; pəˋledɪəm] *n*.【化】钯。

pal·la·dous [pəˈleidəs, ˈpælədəs; pəˋledəs, ˋpælədəs] *a*.【化】亚钯的,二价钯的。

Pal·las [ˈpælæs; ˋpæləs] *n*. 1.【希神】智慧女神帕拉斯〔常作帕拉斯·雅典娜(~ Athena)〕。2.【天】小惑星。

pal·let[1][ˈpælit; ˋpælɪt] *n*. 1. 草荐;〔主美南部〕铺在地板卧铺上的小毛毡。2. 小床;地铺。

pal·let[2][ˈpælit; ˋpælɪt] *n*. 1. (陶工等用的)木抹子。2.【机】棘爪;锤垫;(电话机的)衔铁;(棘齿轮的)掣子。3.【建】制模板;【乐】(风琴等的)调节瓣。4. (画家的)调色板;(供铲车、装卸、搬运用的)货盘。

pal·let·ize [ˈpæliˌtaiz; ˋpæləˏtaɪz] *vt*. 把…放在货盘上;用货盘装运。**-i·za·tion** *n*. 货盘化。

pal·li·a [ˈpæliə; ˋpælɪə] pallium 的复数。

pal·li·al [ˈpæliəl; ˋpælɪəl] *a*.【动】(外)套膜的;【解】外皮的;大脑皮层的,大脑皮质的。

pal·liasse [pælˈjæs, ˈpæljæs; pælˋjæs, ˋpæljæs] *n*. = paillasse.

pal·li·ate [ˈpælieit; ˋpælɪˏet] *vt*. 1. (暂时)减轻(疾病等),缓和(痛苦等)。2. 掩饰(罪过等)。**-a·tion** *n*. 1. 减轻,缓和;掩饰(罪过等)。2. 起减轻[缓和]作用的东西;辩解;掩饰之词。**pal·li·a·tor** [-tə; -tɚ] *n*. 1. 减轻(疾病等)的人。2. 掩饰(罪过等)的人。

pal·li·a·tive [ˈpæliətiv; ˋpælɪˏetɪv] **I** *a*. 1. 减轻(疼痛等)的;缓和的。2. 辩解的。3.【医】姑息的;治标的。**II** *n*. 1.【医】(暂时的)减轻(剂);姑息剂;治标剂。2. 辩解;可斟酌的情况;用以作掩饰的东西。3. 姑息手段。~ **care unit**〔加〕临终者护理设备。**-ly** *ad*.

pal·lid [ˈpælid; ˋpælɪd] *a*. 1. 苍白的,没血色的。2. 病态的;无生气的。***make ... seem ~ by comparison*** 使…相形见绌。**-ly** *ad*. **-ness** *n*.

pal·li·um [ˈpæliəm; ˋpælɪəm] *n*. (*pl*. *~s*, ***pal·li·a*** [-liə; -lɪə]) 1. (古罗马哲学家等的)大披肩;(大主教的)披肩式祭服。2.【解】大脑皮层;大脑皮质;【动】外套膜;【虫】隔膜;【气】层雨云。

Pall-Mall [ˈpelˈmel, ˈpælˈmæl; ˋpɛlˋmɛl, ˋpælˋmæl] *n*. 1. 蓓尔美尔街〔伦敦一街名,街上多俱乐部〕。2. 英国陆军部〔原在蓓尔美尔街〕。

pall-mall [ˈpelˈmel, ˈpælˈmæl; ˋpɛlˋmɛl, ˋpælˋmæl] *n*. 铁圈球;铁圈球场。

pal·lor [ˈpælə; ˋpælɚ] *n*. (脸色等的)苍白,灰白。

pal·ly [ˈpæli; ˋpælɪ] *a*. 〔俚、口〕亲密的。*get ~ with sb*. 和某人要好。

palm[1][pɑːm; pɑm] **I** *n*. 1. 手掌,手心;掌尺〔以手掌的长度和宽度为尺,宽 7.6—10cm,长 18—25cm〕;(手套等的)掌部。2. 掌状物;(桨等的)扁平部;【海】掌皮,掌盘〔缝帆布时顶针用〕;锚爪。3. (赌博、变戏法时)藏牌于掌中。*sailmaker's ~* 帆工掌皮。***cross sb.'s ~*** (用钱币)在某人手心上划一个十字(把钱付给算命者);〔喻〕贿赂某人。***grease*** [***gild***, ***tickle***] ***sb.'s ~*** 向…行贿。***have an itching ~*** 〔口〕贪贿;贪财。***know sth. like the ~ of one's hand*** 对某事了如指掌。

II *vt*. 1. 用手掌抚摩;用手抚弄;〔美〕与…握手。2. (变戏法等时)把(东西)藏在手心里;哄骗,欺骗。3. (用欺骗手段)把…硬塞给[卖给]。~ ***off*** (***sth.***) ***on*** [***upon***] (***sb.***) 拿假东西硬塞[硬卖]给(人)。~ **grease** [**oil**] 〔美俚〕贿赂〔财物等〕;小费。**-ful** *n*. 一手心(的量)。

palm[2][pɑːm; pɑm] *n*. 1. 棕榈(树)。2. 棕榈枝[叶]〔胜利的标记〕;胜利。3. 优越;光荣,荣誉;奖赏;【军】荣誉勋章。*a cocoanut ~* 椰子。*a date ~* 枣椰子。***bear*** [***carry***] ***off the ~*** 得胜;获奖,博得无上的荣誉。***get the ~*** 【美体】打败竞争者。***yield*** [***give***] ***the ~ to*** 输给…一着;认输。~ **butter** 棕榈油。~ **civet** (马来群岛产)长尾麝香猫。~ **crab**【动】椰子蟹,桓蟹,尾蟹。~ **fat** 椰子油。~ **house** 温室〔栽培棕榈等用〕。~ **leaf** 棕榈叶,棕叶。~**-lily**【植】朱蕉。~ **oil** 棕榈油。~**print** 掌纹。~ **sugar** 印度赤砂糖,粗糖〔尤指椰子糖〕(= jaggery)。**P- Sunday**【宗】复活节前的星期日。~(**-**)**top** *n*, *a*. 掌上式电脑(的)。~ **wax** 棕榈蜡。

pal·ma·ceous [pælˈmeiʃəs; pælˋmeʃəs] *a*.【植】棕榈科的;棕榈状的。

Pal·ma-Chris·ti [ˈpælməˈkristi; ˋpælməˋkrɪstɪ] *n*.【植】蓖麻。

pal·mar [ˈpælmə; ˋpælmɚ] *a*. (有关)手掌的;掌中的。

pal·ma·ry [ˈpælməri; ˋpælmərɪ] *a*. 1. 最优秀的,杰出的;胜利者的。2. 最重要的,最有价值的。

pal·mate [ˈpælmit; ˋpælmet] *a*. 掌状的;【动】有蹼的。**-ly** *ad*.

pal·mat·ed [ˈpɑlmeitid; ˋpælmetɪd] *a*. = palmate.

pal·mat·i·fid [pælˈmætifid; pælˋmætəfɪd] *a*.【植】掌状半裂的。

pal·ma·tine [ˈpælmətiːn; ˋpælməˏtin] *n*.【药】巴马亭,非洲防已碱。

pal·ma·tion [pælˈmeiʃən; pælˋmeʃən] *n*. 掌状分裂;掌状部分。

Pam·e·la [ˈpæmilə; ˋpæmɪlə] *n*. 帕米拉〔女子名〕。

Palm·er [ˈpɑːmə; ˋpɑmɚ] *n*. 帕默〔姓氏,男子名〕。

palm·er[1][ˈpɑːmə; ˋpɑmɚ] *n*. 1.【宗】(旧时带着棕榈叶做的十字架从圣地回来的)朝圣者;游方僧。2. 假饵钩。3. = ~-worm. *a ~'s staff* 锡杖。~ **worm** 草毛虫,〔美〕果树毛虫。

palm·er[2][ˈpɑːmə; ˋpɑmɚ] *n*. (玩牌等时)作弊的人;变戏法的人。

Palm·er·ston [ˈpɑːməstən; ˋpɑmɚstən] *n*. 1. 帕默斯顿〔姓氏〕。2. **Henry John Temple ~** 亨利·帕默斯顿〔1784—1865,英国政治家,外交家,曾三度担任外交大臣,两度任首相〕。

pal·mette [pælˈmet; pælˋmɛt] *n*.【建】棕叶饰。

pal·met·to [pælˈmetəu; pælˋmɛto] *n*. (*pl*. *~(e)s*) 1.【植】美国矮棕榈;扇状叶的棕榈。2. 棕叶帽。**P- State** 〔美〕矮棕榈州〔南卡罗来纳州的别名〕。

pal·mi·ped, pal·mi·pede [ˈpælmiped, -piːd; ˋpælmɪˏpɛd, -pid] **I** *a*. 蹼足的。**II** *n*. 蹼足鸟,游禽类,水鸟。

palm·ist(er) [ˈpɑːmist(ə); ˋpɑmɪst(ɚ)] *n*. 看手相者。

palm·is·try [ˈpɑːmistri; ˋpɑmɪstrɪ] *n*. 1. 手相术。2. 〔谑〕(扒手等的)手指灵巧;手上功夫的变戏法。

pal·mi·tate [ˈpɑːlmiteit, pæ-; ˋpɑlməˏtet, pæ-] *n*.【化】软脂酸盐,棕榈酸盐,十六酸盐。

pal·mit·ic [pælˈmitik; pælˋmɪtɪk] *a*. 从棕榈(油)得来的。~ **acid**【化】棕榈酸,十六酸,软脂酸。

pal·mi·tin [ˈpælmitin; ˋpælmətɪn] *n*.【化】1. 棕榈精,三棕榈精,软脂。2. 甘油棕榈酸脂,甘油软脂酸酯。

palm·y [ˈpɑːmi; ˋpɑmɪ] *a*. 1. 棕榈(似)的;棕榈多的;〔诗〕棕榈荫遮的;产棕榈的。2. 兴盛的;得胜的,得意扬扬的。*one's ~ days* (已往的)得意时代,全盛时代。

pal·my·ra [pælˈmaiərə; pælˋmaɪrə] *n*.【植】扇叶树头榈 (*Borassus flabellifer*)〔生长于印度、斯里兰卡和热带非洲〕。

pal·o·mi·no [ˌpæləˈmiːnəu; ˏpæləˋmino] *n*. (*pl*. *~s*) 1. 〔美西南部〕巴洛米诺马〔脚细,毛淡黄褐色或奶油色〕。2. 淡黄褐色。

pa·loo·ka [pəˈluːkə; pəˋlukə] *n*. 1. 〔美俚〕平凡的[蹩脚的]运动员[拳师]。2. 傻子,呆子;〔蔑〕人。

pa·lo·ver·de [ˌpæləuˈvəːd; ˏpælo`vɝd] ***n.***【植】多花假紫荆（*Cercidium macrum*），兰花假紫荆（*C. torreyenum*），小叶假紫荆（*C. microphyllum*）〔产于美国西南部和墨西哥〕。

palp [pælp; pælp] ***n.*** （节足动物的）触须（= palpus）。

pal·pa·ble [ˈpælpəbl; `pælpəbl̩] ***a.*** 1. 摸得出的，可触知的；【医】可以触诊的。2. 明白的，明显的。～ *lies* 露骨的谎话。**-bly** ***ad.*** **-bil·i·ty** [-ˈbiliti; -`bɪlətɪ] ***n.***

pal·pate[1] [ˈpælpeit; `pælpet] ***vt.*** 摸认；【医】触诊。**-pation** [-ˈpeiʃən; -`peʃən] ***n.***【医】触诊，扪诊。

pal·pate[2] [ˈpælpeit; `pælpet] ***a.***【动】有触须的。

pal·pe·bral [ˈpælpibrəl; `pælpɪbrəl] ***a.*** 眼睑的；眼睑上的。

pal·pi [ˈpælpai; `pælpaɪ] ***n.*** palpus 的复数。

pal·pi·tant [ˈpælpitənt; `pælpətənt] ***a.*** 颤抖的，悸动的。

pal·pi·tate [ˈpælpiteit; `pælpəˏtet] ***vi.*** 1. （心）跳动，悸动。2. 发抖（*with*）。～ *with pleasure* 快乐得浑身颤抖。

pal·pi·ta·tion [ˌpælpiˈteiʃən; ˏpælpə`teʃən] ***n.*** 1. 颤动，跳动。2. 心跳；【医】心悸。

pal·pus [ˈpælpəs; `pælpəs] ***n.*** （*pl.* ***pal·pi*** [ˈpælpai; `pælpaɪ]）= palp.

pals·grave [ˈpælzgreiv, ˈpɔːlz-; `pɔlzˏgrev, `pɔlz-] ***n.***【德史】（在领地内享有部分王权的）独立伯爵。

pal·sied [ˈpɔːlzid; `pɔlzɪd] ***a.*** 1. 中风的，瘫痪的；麻痹的。2. 颤抖的。

pal·stave [ˈpɔːlsteiv; `pɔlˏstev] ***n.*** 青铜凿。

pal·sy [ˈpɔːlzi; `pɔlzɪ] **I** ***n.*** 1. 中风，瘫痪；麻痹。2. 颤抖，痉挛。3. 无能，无力。～ *of one side* 半身不遂。***Bell's*** ～【医】面部神经麻痹，面瘫。**II** ***vt.*** 使瘫痪；使陷入无能境地。

pal·sy-wal·sy [ˈpɔːlziˈwɔːlzi; `pɔlzɪ`wɔlzɪ] **I** ***n.*** 〔美俚〕1. 伙伴。2. 好朋友。**II** ***a.*** 非常要好的，亲密的。

pal·ter [ˈpɔːltə; `pɔltɚ] ***vi.*** 1. 骗，说模棱两可的话，搪塞过去；玩弄；敷衍了事；马马虎虎地处理。2. 讨价还价，争论不休。3. 瞎谈一通。～ *with sb.* 把某人搪塞过去。～ *with sth.* 马马虎虎地处理某事。

pal·try [ˈpɔːltri; `pɔltrɪ] ***a.*** 1. 不足取的，没有价值的；微不足道的；渺小的。2. 吝啬的；可鄙的。**-tri·ly** ***ad.*** **-tri·ness** ***n.***

pa·lu·dal, pal·u·dine [ˈpæljudl, pəˈljuːdl, ˈpæljudin, -dain; pæ`ljudl, pə`ljudl, `pæljudɪn, -daɪn] ***a.*** 1. 沼泽（多）的；沼地的；沼地上发生的。2. 疟疾的。～ *fever* 疟疾。

pal·u·dism [ˈpæludizəm; `pæljudɪzm̩] ***n.***【医】疟疾，瘴疠。

pal·y [ˈpeili; `pelɪ] ***a.*** 〔诗〕有些苍白的。

pal·y·nol·o·gy [ˌpæliˈnɔlədʒi; ˏpælə`nɑlədʒɪ] ***n.*** 孢粉学。**-no·log·i·cal** [-ˈlɔdʒikəl; -`lɑdʒɪkl̩] ***a.*** **-nol·o·gist** ***n.***

pam. = pamphlet.

pam·a·quin(e) [ˈpæməkwin; `pɑməˏkwaɪn] ***n.***【药】扑疟喹啉。

Pam·e·la [ˈpæmilə, ˈpæmələ; `pæmɪlə, `pæmələ] ***n.*** 帕梅拉〔女子名〕。

Pa·mir·i [pɑːˈmiəriː; pɑ`mɪri] ***n.*** （*pl.* ～）帕米尔高原游牧民族。

Pa·mirs [pəˈmiəz; pə`mɪrz] ***n.*** 〔the ～〕帕米尔高原。

pam·pas [ˈpæmpəz; `pæmpəz] ***n.*** 〔*pl.*〕1. 南美大草原〔南美亚马逊河以南的大草原〕。2. 〔P-〕南美大草原上的印第安居民。～[ˈpæmpəs; `pæmpəs] **grass**【植】（南美产）蒲苇。

pam·pe·an [pæmˈpiːən, ˈpæmpiən; pæm`piən, `pæmpɪən] ***a.***, ***n.*** 1. 南美大草原（的）。2. 〔P-〕南美大草原印第安人（的）。

pam·per [ˈpæmpə; `pæmpɚ] ***vt.*** 1. 纵容，娇养。2. 使满足。3. 〔古〕给…吃得过饱。～ *a child* 对孩子娇生惯养。～ *one's appetite* 拼命吃个痛快。

pam·pe·ro [pɑːmˈpɛərəu; pɑm`pero] ***n.*** （*pl.* ～***s***）滂沛罗冷风〔自安第斯山脉横扫南美大草原的强劲冷风〕。

pam·phlet [ˈpæmflit; `pæmflɪt] ***n.*** 小册子；（时事问题等的）小册子刊物。*a single-article* ～ 单行本。**-ar·y** ***a.***

pam·phlet·eer [ˌpæmfliˈtiə; ˏpæmflɪ`tɪr] **I** ***n.*** 〔常蔑〕小册子作者。**II** ***vi.*** 出版〔编写〕小册子。

pan[1] [pæn; pæn] **I** ***n.*** 1. 平底锅，盘子，盆子，蒸发皿；一满盘；一满锅；盆状器皿〔灰盆、秤盘等〕；【矿】淘盘；（火枪的）药池；铰链孔。2. 头盖。3. （表面有一层薄土的）硬质地层。4. （积水干涸后常现盐碱的）盘状凹地。5. 【海】小浮冰。6. 〔美俚〕面盘，脸。*the* ～ *of the knee* 膝盖骨。*a salt* ～ 晒盐田。***flash in the*** ～ 昙花一现。***leap*** [***fall***] ***out of the frying*** ～ ***into the fire*** 跳出锅里落进火里；才脱身小困难，又落入大灾难。***pots and*** ～***s*** 锅盘等炊事用具。***savour of the*** ～ 露出本来面目；露底。***shut one's*** ～〔俚〕闭嘴不说话；沉着，不动声色。**II** ***vt.*** (***-nn-***) 1. 用盘子淘洗（砂金）（*off*; *out*）。2. 用平底锅烧（菜）。3. 〔美俚〕得到。4. 〔美俚〕严厉批评；骂；糟蹋（名誉），向…找碴儿。— ***vi.*** 1. 淘金；产金。2. 〔口〕结果成为…（*out*）。～ *out ill* [*well*] 结果不好[好]。*How did it* ～ *out*? 〔口〕结果怎么样? ***be panned out*** 〔美俚〕力尽；破产。～ ***out*** [***off***] 选出（砂金）；〔俚〕赚钱；〔美〕结果是…。～**-fish** 煎吃的小鱼。～**-fry** ***vt.*** 用平底锅煎炸。**-ful** ***n.*** 一满锅[盘]。

pan[2] [pæn; pæn] **I** ***vt.***, ***vi.*** (***-nn-***) （电影）摇（镜头）；（使）拍摄全景。**II** ***n.*** 摇镜头；摄全景。～ ***down*** 降下〔镜头垂直下移拍摄全景〕。**III** ***a.*** 全景的。

pan[3] [pæn; pæn] ***n.*** 1. （东印度产）蒌叶〔一种胡椒〕。2. 用蒌叶制成的咀嚼物。

Pan [pæn; pæn] ***n.*** 1.【希神】潘〔牧人之神，人身、羊脚、头上有角〕。2. 自然界之精灵；基督教以前的世界。～**'s pipes** 排箫。

pan- *comb. f.* 表示"全，总，万，泛"。1. 和表示国籍，宗派等的字结合：*pan*-American. 2. 和词尾 -ism, -ish, -ic 等的衍生词结合：*pan*cosmism, *pan*-Hellenist.

Pan. = Panama.

pan·a·ce·a [ˌpænəˈsiə; ˏpænə`siə] ***n.*** 1. 万应药；秘药。2. （社会弊病等的）补救方法。**-n** ***a.***

pa·nache [pəˈnæʃ; pə`næʃ] ***n.*** 〔F.〕1. （盔等的）羽饰。2. 〔喻〕夸示，炫耀；摆架子，要派头。

pa·na·da [pəˈnɑːdə; pə`nɑdə] ***n.*** 面包粥〔以面包加糖、牛奶、调味等煮成〕；面糊〔煮汤等用〕。

Pan-Af·ri·can·ism [ˈpænˈæfrikənizəm; pæn`æfrəkənˏɪzəm] ***n.*** 泛非主义。**Pan-Af·ri·can·ist** [-nist; -nɪst] ***n.***, ***a.*** 泛非主义者（的）。

pan·age [ˈpænidʒ; `pænɪdʒ] ***n.*** = pannage.

PAN AM = Pan American World Airways 〔美〕泛美航空公司（1991 年合并于 Delta 航空公司）。

Pan·a·ma [ˌpænəˈmɑː; ˏpænə`mɑ] ***n.*** 1. （中美洲）巴拿马；巴拿马运河。2. 〔p-〕巴拿马草帽（= Panama hat）。*the* ～ *Canal* 巴拿马运河。**-ni·an** 1. ***n.*** 巴拿马人。2. ***a.*** 巴拿马（人）的。

Pan·a·ma Cit·y [ˌpænəˈmɑː ˈsiti; ˏpænə`mɑ `sɪtɪ] ***n.*** 巴拿马城〔巴拿马首都〕。

Pan-A·mer·i·can [ˈpænəˈmerikən; `pænə`mɛrəkən] ***a.*** 泛美的，全美洲（各国）的。*the* ～ *Airways* 泛美航空公司。*the* ～ *Congress* 泛美会议。*the* ～ *Day* 泛美联盟成立纪念日〔4 月 14 日〕。*the* ～ *Union* 泛美联盟〔包括二十三个美洲国家，建于 1890 年〕。**-ism** ***n.*** 泛美主义，大美洲主义。

Pan-An·gli·can [ˈpænˈæŋglikən; ˏpæn`æŋgləkən] ***a.*** 泛英国国教主义的。

pan·a·tel·(l)a [ˌpænəˈtelə; ˏpænə`tɛlə] ***n.*** 外形细长的雪茄烟。

P

pan·a·vi·sion [ˌpænəˈviʒən; ˋpænəˏvɪʒən] *n*. 宽屏幕电视;宽银幕电影。

Pa·nax [ˈpeinæks; ˋpenæks] *n*.【植】人参属。~ **ginseng** 人参。

pan·broil [ˈpænˌbrɔil; ˋpænˏbrɔɪl] *vt*. (在平锅中少放油或不放油)煎烤。

pan·cake [ˈpænkeik, ˈpæŋ-; ˋpænˏkek, ˋpæŋ-] **I** *n*. **1**. 薄煎饼,烙饼。**2**.【空】平降,平坠(着陆)。**3**. (极地洋面上的)圆形薄冰(= ~ ice)。***flat as a*** ~ 扁平的。**II** *vt*., *vi*.【空】(使)(飞机)平降。~ **coil**【电】扁平线圈。**P- Day** [**Tuesday**]〔口〕(照例要吃薄煎饼的)圣灰节〔Ash Wednesday, 四旬节的第一天〕的前一天。~ **engine** 水平对置式发动机。~ **turner** 广播电台[电视台]的唱片放送员。

P

pan·chax [ˈpænkæks; ˋpænˏkæks] *n*.【动】艳鱼。

pan·chay·at [pʌnˈtʃaiət; pʌnˋtʃaɪət] *n*. (印度)乡村行政委员会;(由大约五人组成的)乡村自治委员会。

pan·chro·mat·ic [ˌpænkrəuˈmætik; ˏpænkroˋmætɪk] *a*.【摄】全[泛]色的。~ **film** 全色胶卷[软片]。~ **plate** 全色干片。

pan·chro·ma·tise [pænˈkrəumətaiz; pænˋkroməˏtaɪz] *vt*.【摄】使成全[泛]色。

pan·cos·mism [pænˈkɔzmizəm; pænˋkɑzmɪzəm] *n*.【哲】物质[泛]宇宙论。

pan·crat·ic [pænˈkrætik; pænˋkrætɪk] *a*. **1**.【光】视界大的;(透镜)可随意调节的。**2**. (古希腊、罗马)拳击和摔跤比赛的。

pan·cra·ti·um [pænˈkreiʃiəm; pænˋkreʃɪəm] *n*. (*pl*. *-ti·a* [-ə; -ə]) (古希腊和罗马)拳击和摔跤比赛。

pan·cre·as [ˈpæŋkriəs; ˋpæŋkrɪəs] *n*.【解】胰(腺)。

pan·cre·at·ic [ˌpæŋkriˈætik; ˏpæŋkriˋætɪk] *a*. 胰(腺)的。~ **juice** [**secretion**] 胰液。

pan·cre·a·tin [ˈpæŋkriətin; ˋpæŋkrɪətɪn] *n*.【生化】胰酶(制剂)。

pan·cre·a·ti·tis [ˌpænkriəˈtaitis, ˈpæŋ-; ˏpænkrɪəˋtaɪtɪs, ˋpæŋ-] *n*.【医】胰腺炎。

pan·da [ˈpændə; ˋpændə] *n*.【动】熊猫,猫熊。*lesser* ~ 小熊猫。*giant* ~ 大熊猫。

pan·da·nus [pænˈdeinəs; pænˋdenəs] *n*.【植】露兜树属植物(= screw pine)。

Pan·de·an [pænˈdiːən; pænˋdiən] *a*. 牧神潘 (Pan) 的。*a* ~ *pipe* = Panpipe.

pan·dect [ˈpændekt; ˋpændɛkt] *n*. **1**. (某学科的)全论,全书;汇编;〔*pl*.〕法令全书。**2**.〔Pandects〕《学说汇纂》〔六世纪东罗马帝国皇帝查士丁尼 (Justinian) 下令编纂的 50 卷本罗马法学家学说摘录全书〕。

pan·dem·ic [pænˈdemik; pænˋdɛmɪk] **I** *a*. **1**. (疾病)流行全国[全世界]的;传染性的,流行性的。**2**. 一般的,普遍的。**II** *n*. (流行全国[全世界]的)传染病。

pan·de·mo·ni·um [ˌpændiˈməunjəm, -niəm; ˏpændɪˋmonjəm, -nɪəm] *n*. **1**.〔常 P-〕群魔殿,魔窟;地狱。**2**. 混乱(场所);大吵大闹,无法无天。

pan·der [ˈpændə; ˋpændɚ] **I** *n*. 拉皮条者;为妓女拉客者;妓院老板;帮人做坏事的人。**II** *vt*., *vi*. 勾引,(为…)拉皮条;怂恿,帮助(…)做(坏事);煽动;迎合 (*to*)。

pan·dit [ˈpʌndit; ˋpʌndɪt] *n*. (印度的)博学家;梵学家;〔P-〕学者〔在印度用作专称〕(= pundit)。

P. and L., P. & L., p. and l. = profit and loss account 盈亏账。

P. and O., P. & O. = Peninsular and Oriental Steam Navigation Company〔英〕半岛和东方航运公司。

Pan·do·ra [pænˈdɔːrə; pænˋdorə] *n*.【希神】潘朵拉〔主神宙斯 (Zeus) 命火神用黏土制成的地上的第一个女人〕。~**'s Box** 潘朵拉之盒〔潘朵拉下凡时宙斯神送给她的盒子,她违禁开看,使一切灾害和罪恶跑散世上,只有希望还留在里面〕;〔喻〕灾难[麻烦、祸害等]的根源。

pan·do·ra, pan·dore [pænˈdɔːrə, -ˈdɔː; pænˋdorə, -ˋdɔr] *n*. (古代)三弦琴。

pan·dow·dy [pænˈdaudi; pænˋdaʊdɪ] *n*.〔美〕(上覆酥皮的)厚苹果糕[布丁]。

pan·du·rate [ˈpændjureit, -duər-; ˋpændjəret, -dʊr-] *a*.【植】(叶子)提琴形的(= panduriform)。

pan·dy [ˈpændi; ˋpændɪ] **I** *n*., *vi*.〔Scot.〕打手心。**II** *vt*. 打…的手心。~ **bat** (打学生手心用的)藤鞭。

pane [pein; pen] **I** *n*. **1**. (一块)窗格玻璃;(棋盘等式的)长方格;长方框。**2**. (门、墙等上的)嵌板。**3**. (螺帽、钻石等的)面,边。**4**. 成为一块而互相连接的若干张邮票。**II** *vt*. **1**. 嵌玻璃于。**2**. 用染色小布片拼做(衣服)。**-d** *a*. **1**. 用布片拼做的。**2**. 嵌有…玻璃的;具有…边[面]的 (*a six-paned window* 六片玻璃的窗子)。**-less** *a*. 无窗格玻璃的。

pan·e·gyr·ic [ˌpæniˈdʒirik; ˏpænəˋdʒɪrɪk] *n*., *a*. 颂词(的),赞辞(的);称赞(的);推崇(的)。*a* ~ *on* [*upon*] *sb*. [*sth*.] 对某人[某事]的颂扬。**-i·cal** *a*. **-i·cal·ly** *ad*.

pan·e·gyr·ist [ˌpæniˈdʒirist, ˈpænidʒirist; ˏpænəˋdʒɪrɪst, ˋpænədʒɪrɪst] *n*. 颂词作者;称赞者。

pan·e·gy·rize [ˈpænidʒiraiz; ˋpænədʒəˏraɪz] *vt*., *vi*. 称赞;作(颂词);致(颂词)。

pan·el [ˈpænl; ˋpænl̩] **I** *n*. **1**. 面,板;【建】四分板,门窗材,幅板,板条;嵌板;镶板;方格;(木工)线板;【绘】(代替画布的)面板上画的画。**2**.【法】陪审员名单;全体陪审员,(合保险法规定的)地方健康保险医生名单。**3**. (广播或电视中)进行公开讨论会的小组;〔美〕(大会中的)小组委员会;一组调查对象;(对一组对象进行的)典型调查。**4**. (女衣上的)直条饰缝。**5**. 鞍褥,鞍垫;木架鞍。**6**. (一张)羊皮纸;登记簿。**7**.【摄】长方形大相片。**8**.【空】翼段,翼片。**9**.【电】配电盘,控制板;仪表盘;【军】信号布板。*a* ~ *board* 镜板。*a meter* ~ 仪表面盘。**10**.〔Scot.〕【法】刑事被告。*a power* ~ 配电盘。*a control* ~【火箭】操纵台。*a* ~*-work* 格子细工;铁工建筑;构架工程。*a* ~ *doctor* 健康保险医生。***be in the*** ~〔Scot.〕【法】在受审中。***go on the*** ~ **1**. 受健康保险医生检查。**2**. = *be in the* ~. ***on the*** ~ 登记在健康保险医生名单上的。
II *vt*. (*-l*(*l*)-) **1**. 在…上嵌板子;在(衣服等上)嵌杂色条纹,在…上置鞍垫。**2**. 选定(陪审员)。**3**.〔Scot.〕【法】对…起诉。*a* ~*ed door* 格子门。~ **discussion**〔美〕小组讨论;在(电视或广播)听众面前开的专题讨论会。~ **heating** 壁板供暖。~ **house** 设有暗门密室的妓院。~ **pin** (钉胶合板等用的)镶板钉。~ **show** 有一组名流参加的电视讨论会[游艺会等]。~ **truck** 小型运货汽车。**-ist** *n*. 专门小组成员[如评论比赛、公开讨论、参加广播(或电视)演出等的小组成员]。**-(l)ing** *n*. **1**.〔集合词〕镜板,镶木。**2**. 嵌板细工。

pan·en·the·ism [pænˈenθiːizəm; pænˋɛnθiɪzm̩] *n*. 万有在神论〔认为神包括世界而又超越世界〕。

pan·e·tel·(l)a [ˌpæniˈtelə; ˏpænəˋtɛlə] *n*. (= panatela)。

pang [pæŋ; pæŋ] **I** *n*. **1**. (肉体上的一阵)苦痛,剧痛。**2**. (精神上的一阵)极度痛苦。*the* ~*s of death* 临死的痛苦。*the* ~*s of conscience* 良心的苦责。**II** *vt*. 使剧痛;使极度痛苦,折磨。

pan·ga [ˈpɑːŋgə; ˋpɑŋgə] *n*. (非洲)带钩大切刀。

pan·gen [ˈpændʒin; ˋpændʒɪn] *n*.【生】胚芽;泛生子。

pan·gen·e·sis [pænˈdʒenisis; pænˋdʒɛnəsɪs] *n*.【生】机体再生说;泛生(子)论。

Pan-Ger·man [ˈpænˈdʒəːmən; ˏpænˋdʒɝmən] **I** *a*. 全德意志的;大德意志[日耳曼]主义的。**II** *n*. 大德国主义者。**-ism** *n*. 大德意志主义,大德意志运动。

pan·go·lin [pæŋˈgəulin; pæŋˋgolɪn] *n*.【动】鲮鲤,穿山甲。

pan·gram [ˈpæŋgræm; ˋpæŋgræm] *n*. 字母表所有的字母都出现(最好只出现一次)的句子〔一种文字游戏〕。

Pang·we [ˈpɑːŋwe; ˋpɑŋwɛ] *n*. (*pl*. ~(*s*)) (几内亚湾东海岸一带的)潘威人。

pan·han·dle[1] [ˈpænˌhændl; ˋpænˏhændl] *n*. 平底锅柄;〔原美〕突出的狭长行政区域。*the P- State* 〔美〕西维吉尼亚 (West Virginia) 州的别名。*the Gansu* ~ 甘肃走廊,河西走廊。**-rs** *n*. 〔*pl*.〕〔美〕西维吉尼亚、德克萨斯、爱达荷 (West Virginia, Texas, Idaho) 各州人的别名。

pan·han·dle[2] [ˈpænˌhændl; ˋpænˏhændl] *vt*., *vi*. 〔俚〕(在路上)(向…)讨钱。**-r** *n*. 〔俚〕乞丐,叫化子。

pan·head [ˈpænhed; ˋpænhɛd] *n*. 【机】截锥头,盘(形)头。~ **bolt** 截锥头螺栓。~ **rivet** 截锥头铆钉。**-ed** [-ˌhedid; -hɛdɪd] *a*.

Pan·hel·len·ic [ˈpænheˈliːnik; ˋpænhəˋlɛnɪk] *a*. 大希腊的,大希腊主义的。

Pan·hel·len·ism [ˈpænˈhelinizəm; pænˋhɛlɛnɪzm̩] *n*. 泛希腊主义。

pan·ic[1] [ˈpænik; ˋpænɪk] **I** *n*. **1**. 恐慌,惊慌;【商】(金融方面的)大恐慌。**2**. 〔美剧俚〕成功;热狂。**3**. 〔俚〕非常滑稽的人[事、物]。*be seized with a* ~ 恐慌起来。*get up a* ~ 起恐慌。*no* ~ 〔美剧俚〕不大高明,平凡。**II** *a*. **1**. 恐慌的,惊慌的。**2**. (恐慌心理)没来由的,无谓的;过度的。*a* ~ *price* 恐慌价格,跌落不已的价格。*a* ~ *fear* [*fright*] 无谓的恐惧。**III** *vt*. **1**. 使起恐慌。**2**. 〔美剧俚〕使狂热,使喝彩。— *vi*. 极其惊慌(*over*)。~ **button** (飞机上的)紧急按钮(*hit the* ~ *button* 在紧急情况下惊慌失措)。~**-monger** 制造恐慌的人。~**-stricken**, ~**-struck** *a*. 恐慌的,受惊恐的;狼狈的。

pan·ic[2] [ˈpænik; ˋpænɪk] *n*. 【植】稗;黍,稷,糜子(= ~ grass)。

Pan·ic [ˈpænik; ˋpænɪk] *a*. 潘神的,牧人之神的。

pan·ick·y [ˈpæniki; ˋpænɪkɪ] *a*. 〔口〕**1**. 恐慌的;吓慌了的。**2**. 易引起恐慌的。*extremely* ~ 恐慌万状。

pan·i·cle [ˈpænikl; ˋpænɪkl̩] *n*. 【植】圆锥花序;散穗花序;复总状花序。

pa·nic·u·late, pa·nic·u·lat·ed [pəˈnikjuleit, -leitid; pəˋnɪkjuˏlet, -letɪd] *a*. 具圆锥花序的。

pan·ier [ˈpæniə; ˋpænɪr] *n*. = pannier.

pan·i·fi·ca·tion [ˌpænifiˈkeiʃən; ˏpænəfɪˋkeʃən] *n*. 面包制作。

Pan·ja·bi [pənˈdʒæbi; pənˋdʒæbɪ] *n*. 旁遮普人,旁遮普语(= Punjabi)。

pan·jan·drum [pənˈdʒændrəm; pænˋdʒændrəm] *n*. 大亨,大老爷〔讥讽自命不凡者的称呼〕;摆架子的官吏,架子十足的人。

Pank·hurst [ˈpæŋkhəːst; ˋpæŋkˏhɝst] *n*. 潘克赫斯特〔姓氏〕。

pan·log·ism [ˈpænlədʒizəm; ˋpænlədʒɪzəm] *n*. 【哲】泛理论,泛逻辑主义。**pan·lo·gis·tic** [ˌpænləˈdʒistik; ˏpænləˋdʒɪstɪk] *a*.

pan·mix·i·a [pænˈmiksiə; pænˋmɪksɪə] *n*. 【生】随机交配;随机交配群体。

Pan-mun·jom [ˌpɑːnˌmunˈdʒʌm; ˏpanˏmʊnˋdʒɑm] *n*. 板门店〔朝鲜民主主义人民共和国村庄,朝鲜停战谈判会址〕。

pan·nage [ˈpænidʒ; ˋpænɪdʒ] *n*. **1**. 【英法】(林内)放猪(权);放猪费。**2**. (猪采食的)林中饲料[橡子等]。

panne [pæn; pæn] *n*. 【纺】平滑轻柔的天鹅绒,平绒。(= ~ velvet)。

pan·ni·er [ˈpæniə; ˋpænɪɚ] *n*. **1**. (挂在驮兽两旁的)驮篮;背篮。**2**. (从前用来张开女服裙部的)鲸骨框,裙撑。**3**. 野战用外科器械药品搬运篮。

pan·ni·kin [ˈpænikin; ˋpænəkɪn] *n*. **1**. 小盘子,小锅。**2**. (金属制)杯子;杯子里的东西。

pa·no·cha, pa·no·che [pəˈnəutʃə, -tʃi; pəˋnotʃə, -tʃɪ] *n*. (墨西哥)粗糖,红糖;红糖奶油核桃糖。

pan·o·ply [ˈpænəpli; ˋpænəplɪ] *n*. **1**. 全副甲胄;防护性覆盖物。**2**. 盛装,礼服。**3**. 壮丽的陈列[装饰]。**pan·o·plied** [ˈpænəplid; ˋpænəplɪd] *a*. **1**. 披戴全副甲胄的。**2**. 盛装的。

pan·op·tic [pænˈɔptik; pænˋɑptɪk] *a*. 一眼可见全貌的;一目了然的;显示全貌的。

pan·op·ti·con [pænˈɔptikɔn; pænˋɑptɪkɑn] *n*. **1**. 圆形监狱。**2**. 珍品展览室[会]。**3**. 望远显微镜。

pan·o·ra·ma [ˌpænəˈrɑːmə; ˏpænəˋræmə] *n*. **1**. (转现)全景(画);全景照片;全景装置。**2**. 概观;概论。**3**. 一连串的景象[事件]。

pan·o·ram·ic [ˌpænəˈræmik; ˏpænəˋræmɪk] *a*. 全景的,全貌的。*a* ~ *view* 全景。*a* ~ *camera* 全景照相机。*a* ~ *sight* 【军】全景瞄准镜。*a* ~ *sketch* 远景描绘图。

pan·o·ti·tis [ˈpænəˈtaitis; ˋpænəˋtaɪtɪs] *n*. 【医】全耳炎。

Pan-Pa·cif·ic [ˈpænpəˈsifik; ˋpænpəˋsɪfɪk] *a*. 泛太平洋的,全太平洋的。

Pan·pipe [ˈpænpaip; ˋpænˏpaɪp] *n*. 潘神笙;(芦杆制)排箫(= ~'s pipes)。

pan·psy·chism [pænˈsaikizəm; pænˋsaɪkɪzm̩] *n*. 【哲】泛心论,万有精神论。

Pan-Slav·ism [ˈpænˈslɑːvizəm; ˏpænˋslɑvɪzm̩] *n*. 泛斯拉夫主义。

pan·so·phism [ˈpænsəfizəm; ˋpænsəfɪzəm] *n*. 万事通。**-phist** *n*. 万事通的人。

pan·so·phy [ˈpænsəfi; ˋpænsəfɪ] *n*. **1**. 泛知,博识,万事皆知,无所不知。**2**. 〔*pl*.〕包括各种知识的体系。**3**. (自称的)万事通。**-soph·ic, -soph·i·cal** *a*.

pan·sper·mat·ism, pan·sper·my [pænˈspəːmətizəm, pænˈspəːmi; pænˋspɝmətɪzəm, pænˋspɝmɪ] *n*. 【生】胚种广布论。

Pan·sy [ˈpænzi; ˋpænzɪ] *n*. 潘西〔女子名〕。

pan·sy [ˈpænzi; ˋpænzɪ] **I** *n*. **1**. 【植】三色堇,三色紫罗兰。**2**. 〔美俚〕脂粉气的男子;搞同性恋的男子(= ~ boy)。**II** *a*. 〔美俚〕(男人)女性化的,爱打扮的,脂粉气的。**III** *vt*., *vi*. 〔美俚〕打扮 (*up*)。

pant[1] [pænt; pænt] **I** *vt*. 气喘吁吁地讲(*out*; *forth*)。— *vi*. **1**. 喘气。**2**. 心跳。**3**. 热望,渴望,想(*for*; *after*)。**4**. (机车等)喷气。**II** *n*. **1**. 气喘。**2**. 心跳。**3**. 喷气声。

pant[2] [pænt; pænt] *n*., *a*. 裤子。~ **dress** 工装裤。~ **legs** 裤管。

pant- *comb*. *f*. 〔用于元音前〕= panto-.

pan·ta- = panto-.

pan·ta·graph [ˈpæntəgrɑːf; ˋpæntəˏgræf] *n*. = pantograph.

Pan·tag·ru·el [ˌpæntəˈgru(ː)əl; ˏpæntəˋgru(ʊ)əl] *n*. 〔F.〕庞大古埃〔法国 16 世纪作家拉伯雷 (Rabelais) 所作《巨人传》中人物,粗野而喜欢嬉笑谑浪〕。**-i·an** [ˌpæntəˈgruˈeliən; ˏpæntəˋgruˋɛlɪən] *a*. 庞大古埃式的;粗野的;嬉笑谑浪的。**-ism** *n*. 粗野和嬉笑谑浪的作用。**-ist** *n*. 粗野和嬉笑谑浪的人。

pan·ta·let(te)s [ˌpæntəˈlets; ˏpæntl̩ˋɛts] *n*. **1**. (19 世纪女人的)宽松长裤。**2**. 〔美〕女裤;(骑自行车穿的)短裤。

pan·ta·loon [ˌpæntəˈluːn; ˏpæntl̩ˋun] *n*. **1**. [P-](从前意大利喜剧中戴眼镜穿窄裤的)老角;(现代哑剧中为丑角取笑对象的)傻瓜,傻老头。**2**. 〔*pl*.〕【军】(军官的)马裤;〔*pl*.〕〔美〕裤子。

pan·ta·ta [pænˈteitə; pænˋtetə] *n*. 〔俚〕要人;老板,头子。

pan·tech·ni·con [pænˈteknikən; pænˋtɛknɪkɑn] *n*. 〔英〕**1**. 家具仓库;家具陈列[出卖]所。**2**. 家具搬运车(= ~ van)。

pan·tel·e·graph [pænˈteligrɑːf; pænˋtɛləˏgræf] *n*. (早期的)有线传真电报。

pan·tel·e·gra·phy [pænˈteligrəfi; ˏpæntəˋlɛgrəfɪ] *n*. 有线传真电报(术)。

pan·the·ism [ˈpænθi(ː)izəm; ˋpænθiˏɪzəm] *n*. 【哲】泛

神论;对一切神道的崇拜,多神教;自然崇拜。**-the·ist** *n*. 泛神论者。**-the·is·tic, -is·ti·cal** [-ˈistik(əl); -ˋɪstɪk(l̩)] *a*.

pan·the·lism [ˈpænθilizəm; ˋpænθəlɪzm̩] *n*. 【哲】唯意志论,意志主义。

pan·the·on [pænˈθi(ː)ən; pænˋθɪən] *n*. 1. 【史】(古希腊、罗马供奉众神的)万神殿。2. 〔the P-〕伟人[先哲]祠。3. (一个民族信奉的)众神。4. (集团、个人、运动、党派等推崇的)英雄人物。*the British P-* 威斯敏斯特大教堂。

pan·ther [ˈpænθə; ˋpænθɚ] *n*. (*pl*. ~*s*, 〔集合词〕~) 1. 【动】豹;黑豹。2. 美洲豹(= cougar)。*a Black P-* 黑豹党人。*the Black P- Party* 黑豹党〔美国一黑人组织〕。~ **sweat** 〔美俚〕劣等酒。

pan·ther·ess [ˈpænθəris; ˋpænθərɛs] *n*. 【动】母(黑)豹。

pan·ties [ˈpæntiz; ˋpæntɪz] *n*. 〔*pl*.〕= panty.

pan·tile [ˈpæntail; ˋpæn͵taɪl] *n*. 【建】波形瓦。

pan·ti·soc·ra·cy [ˌpæntiˈsɔkrəsi; ͵pæntaɪˋsɑkrəsɪ] *n*. 理想的平等社会,大同世界。

pan·to [ˈpæntəu; ˋpænto] *n*. 〔口〕= pantomime.

pan·to- *comb*. *f*. 全部,所有,每: *panto*logy.

pan·to(f)·fle [ˈpæntəfəl; ˋpæntəfl̩] *n*. 拖鞋。

pan·to·graph [ˈpæntəgrɑːf; ˋpæntə͵grɑf] *n*. 1. 比例画图仪器,缩放仪。2. (类似缩放仪的)动臂装置。3. 【电】(电车顶上的)导电弓架。**-ic** [ˌpæntəˈgræfik; ͵pæntəˋgræfɪk] *a*.

pan·tol·o·gy [pænˈtɔlədʒi; pænˋtɑlədʒɪ] *n*. 百科全论,人类知识综合体系。

pan·to·mime [ˈpæntəmaim; ˋpæntə͵maɪm] I *n*. 1. 哑剧。2. 〔英〕(圣诞节上演的)童话剧。3. (古罗马的)哑剧演员。4. 姿势;手势;表意动作。II *vt*. 用手势传(意)。—*vi*. 演哑剧。**-to·mim·ic** [ˌpæntəˈmimik; ͵pæntəˋmɪmɪk] *a*. **-to·mim·ist** *n*. 1. 哑剧作者[演员]。2. 打手势的人。

pan·to·mor·phic [ˌpæntəˈmɔːfik; ͵pæntəˋmɔrfɪk] *a*. 变幻自若的;形态万千的。

pan·to·night [ˈpæntənait; ˋpæntə͵naɪt] *n*. 有圣诞节童话剧上演的节日[纪念日]。

pan·to·prag·mat·ic [ˌpæntəprægˈmætik; ͵pæntəprægˋmætɪk] *a*., *n*. 〔谑〕爱管闲事的(人)。

pan·to·scope [ˈpæntəskəup; ˋpæntə͵skop] *n*. 大角度照相机[凸镜]。

pan·to·scop·ic [ˌpæntəˈskɔpik; ͵pæntəˋskɑpɪk] *a*. 1. (照相机、凸镜等)大角度的。2. 眼界宽广的。*a* ~ *camera* 全景摄影机(= panoramic camera)。~ *spectacles* 全视眼镜,复眼镜。

pan·to·then·ate [ˌpæntəˈθeneit, pænˈtɔθineit; ͵pæntəˋθɛnet, pænˋtɑθɪ͵net] *n*. 【化】泛酸盐[酯]。

pan·to·then·ic [ˌpæntəˈθenik; ͵pæntəˋθɛnɪk] *a*. 【化】泛酸的。~ **acid** 【化】泛酸,本多生酸。

pan·toum [pænˈtuːm; pænˋtum] *n*. 〔Ma.〕盘头诗〔一种马来诗体〕。

pan·trop·ic(al) [pænˈtrɔpik(əl); pænˋtrɑpɪk(l̩)] *a*. 遍布于热带的。

pan·try [ˈpæntri; ˋpæntrɪ] *n*. 1. 餐具室;食品储存室;配膳室。2. 〔美俚〕胃。~**man** 饭厅管理员。

pants [pænts; pænts] *n*. 〔*pl*.〕〔pantaloons 之略〕 1. 〔美口〕裤子。2. 【英商】紧身长衬裤;(男用)短衬裤。3. 〔美〕(儿童或妇女用)紧身短衬裤。4. 【空】机轮减阻罩。*a* ~ [*landing*] *gear* 【空】裤形起落架。*wheel* ~ 机轮减阻罩。***be caught with one's*** ~ ***down*** 〔美俚〕措手不及地陷入窘况。***have ants in the*** ~ 〔美口〕烦恼,不安。***keep your*** ~ [***shirt***] ***on*** 〔美口〕沉住气,别慌;别着急;等一等。***kick in the*** ~ 受阻碍;受挫折。***wear the*** ~ (妇女)掌权当家。***with one's*** ~ ***down*** 处于尴尬境地。~**' leg** 〔美俚〕(飞机场的)风向标。~ **suit** = pantsuit.

pant·suit [ˈpæntsjuːt; ˋpænt͵sut] *n*. (上衣与裤子相配的一种)妇女旅行服。

pan·tun [pænˈtuːn; pænˋtun] *n*. 〔Ma.〕= pantoum.

pant·y [ˈpænti; ˋpæntɪ] *n*. 〔常 *pl*.〕 1. 童裤;女裤(= panties)。2. = ~ girdle. ~ **girdle** 叉式腰带。~ **hose** 女用袜裤。

pant·y·waist [ˈpæntiweist; ˋpæntɪ͵west] *n*. 1. 连衫裤童装。2. 〔美俚〕苗条柔弱的男子,女人气概的男子。

pan·zer [ˈpɑːntsə; ˋpænzɚ] I *a*. 〔G.〕装甲的,机械化的。II *n*. 装甲车,战车,坦克。*a* ~ *division* 装甲师。~ *troops* 装甲部队,机械化部队。

pap[1] [pæp; pæp] *n*. 1. 〔古、方〕奶头。2. 〔*pl*.〕奶头状双峰。

pap[2] [pæp; pæp] *n*. 1. 面包粥,奶面粥;果肉。2. 〔俚〕(官方给与的)援助,津贴;政治上的恩惠。3. 幼稚的话;纯消遣作品。*His mouth is full of* ~. 他还是个小孩子[乳臭未干]。***as easy*** [***soft***] ***as*** ~ 易如儿戏。***give*** ~ ***with a hatchet*** 1. 假装不仁慈,实际做好事。2. 假装让人尝甜头,实则给人吃苦头。

pap[3] [pæp; pæp] *n*. 〔美方〕= papa.

pap[4] [pæp; pæp] *n*. 〔口〕(跟踪名人偷拍其隐私照片出售给报刊牟利的)偷拍虫〔多为小报记者等,系 paparazzi 一词的缩略〕。

Pa·pa [pəˈpɑː; pəˋpɑ] 通讯中用以代表字母 P 的词。

pa·pa [pəˈpɑː; pəˋpɑ] *n*. 1. 〔儿〕爸爸。2. 〔美俚〕丈夫;情人。

pa·pa·ble [ˈpeipəbl; ˋpepəbl̩] *a*. 可选做教皇的。

pa·pa·cy [ˈpeipəsi; ˋpepəsɪ] *n*. 1. 罗马教皇的职位[任期、权限]。2. 〔the P-〕教皇制度[统治]。3. 教皇的继承[系谱]。

Pa·pa·go [ˌpæpəˈgəu; ͵pæpəˋgo] *n*. 1. (*pl*. ~(*s*)) 巴巴哥人〔主要居住在亚利桑那州塔克森南部的北美印第安人〕。2. 巴巴哥人的乌托阿芝特克语。

pa·pa·in [pəˈpeiin, -ˈpaiin; pəˋpeɪn, -ˋpaɪɪn] *n*. 【医】木瓜蛋白酶。

pa·pal [ˈpeipəl; ˋpepl̩] *a*. 罗马教皇的;天主教的。**P-States** 教皇辖地〔八世纪至 1870 年意大利的中部和中北部〕。**-ism** *n*. 教皇中心主义,教皇制度[统治]。**-ist** *n*., *a*. 天主教徒(的);教皇中心主义者(的)。**-ize** *vt*., *vi*. 1. (使)改信天主教;(使)变成天主教徒。2. (使)建立教皇统治。**-ly** *ad*. 由罗马教皇;按天主教方式。

Pa·pan·ic·o·la·ou [ˈpɑːpəˈniːkəlau; ˋpɑpəˋnikəlo] *n*. ~ **test** 脱落细胞巴氏染色法〔用以检查早期癌症〕。

Pa·pa·raz·zi [ˌpɑːpɑːˈrɑːtsi; ͵pɑpɑˋrɑtsɪ] 〔It.〕*n*. 〔*pl*.〕(*sing*. ***-raz·zo*** [-tsəu; -tso]) 无固定职业的摄影师。

Pa·pa·ver [pəˈpeivə; pəˋpevɚ] *n*. 罂粟属〔俗名 poppy〕。

pa·pa·ver·a·ceous [pəˈpeivəˈreiʃəs; pə͵pævəˋreʃəs] *a*. 罂粟科的。

pa·pav·er·ine [pəˈpævəˌriːn; pəˋpævə͵rin] *n*. 【化】罂粟碱。

pa·pa·ver·ous [pəˈpeivərəs; pəˋpævərəs] *a*. 罂粟(似)的;催眠的。

pa·paw [ˈpɑːpɔː; ˋpɔpɔ] *n*. 1. 【植】巴婆树;巴婆果。2. [pəˈpɔː; pəˋpɔ] = papaya.

pa·pa·ya [pəˈpaiə; pəˋpaɪə] *n*. 番木瓜(树)。

Pa·pe·e·te [ˌpɑːpiˈeitei; ͵pɑpɪˋete] *n*. 帕皮提〔法属波利尼西亚首府〕。

pa·per [ˈpeipə; ˋpepɚ] I *n*. 1. 纸;裱墙纸。2. 报纸,报。3. 收据;债券;证券;票据;汇票;钞票(= ~ money)。4. 〔*pl*.〕身份证。5. 〔*pl*.〕文件,记录;辞呈。6. 论文,论说;考题;答案。7. 〔俚〕招待券,免费入场券;〔集合词〕免费入场者。8. 〔美俚〕火车票;纸牌。9. (装有东西的)一纸包,一纸袋,一盒。10. 涂有药的纸。11. 〔俚〕一小包毒品〔尤指一小包冰毒〕。*a sheet of* ~ 一张纸。*art* ~ 铜版纸。*blotting* ~ 吸墨纸。*brown* ~ 牛皮纸。*carbon* ~ 复写纸。*craft* ~ 牛皮纸。*crape* ~ 皱纸。

glass ~ 砂纸。manifold ~ (打字、复写用)薄纸。plotting ~ 方格纸。sensitive ~ 感光纸。tracing ~ (半透明)描图纸。a daily ~ 日报。a morning [evening] ~ 早[晚]报。What do the ~s say? 报纸怎么说? good ~ 可靠的支票。state ~s 公文。value ~ 有价证券。a negotiable ~ 流通票据。collected ~s 论文集;旧信文件集。The house was largely filled with ~. 场内免费来宾拥挤不堪。a ~ of pins 一包针。**commit sth. to** ~ 把某事记录下来,写下来。**lay** ~ 使用空头支票[假钞票]。**on** ~ 纸上;统计上;理论上,名义上。**put pen to** ~ 开始写,下笔。**send in one's** ~s (特指陆海军军官)提出辞呈。**set a** ~ 出考试题目。**walking** ~s 〔美俚〕解雇通知;(朋友等的)拒绝;要人走开。**-less** *a*. (信息传播、设计、办公等)不用纸的,无纸的。

II *a*. **1.** 纸(做)的。**2.** 纸上的,假定的。*a* ~ *lantern* 灯笼。*a* ~ *war* (=~ warfare)笔战,纸上论战。*a* ~ *blockade* (只有宣言而无实力的)纸上封锁。*a* ~ *farmer* (不懂实际操作的)理论农业家。*a* ~ *army* 有名无实的军队。**III** *vt*. **1.** 用纸裱(贴),用纸覆盖,用纸包;(装钉)用纸衬里。**2.** 为…供给纸张。**3.** 用砂纸擦。**4.** 〔俚〕免费观众充塞〔剧场〕。**5.** 把…作为平装书出版。~ *a room* 用纸裱糊房间。~ *a butterfly* 把蝴蝶标本贴到纸上。—*vi*. 贴糊墙纸。~**back** 纸面本,平装本。~**backed** *a*. 纸面装的,平装的。~ **baron** (只限于一代的)挂名男爵。~**board** 卡纸板。~**bound** *a*. (书)纸面的。~ **boy** 报童,送报人。~ **bush** 【植】(=~-tree)。~ **chase** (一些人假扮兔子撒纸屑、另一些人假扮猎犬追赶的)撒纸屑追踪游戏。~ **chromatography** 【化】纸色谱法。~ **clip** 纸夹;回形针。~ **currency** 纸币。~**-cut** 剪纸。~ **cutter** 裁纸刀,切纸机。~ **file** 文件夹。~ **gold** 【经】纸黄金[即特别提款权]。~**hanger 1.** 裱糊工人,裱褙匠。**2.** 〔美俚〕使用假纸币[假支票]的人,伪造钞票的人。~**-hanging 1.** 裱糊裱墙纸;〔*pl*.〕裱糊纸。**2.** 〔美俚〕伪造支票。~ **house** 〔美俚〕有许多免费招待观众的戏剧[马戏等]。~ **knife 1.** (用象牙、木头等做的)裁纸刀。**2.** (切纸机的)切刀。~ **machine** 造纸机。~**maker** 造纸工,造纸者(~ *maker's alum* 【化】造纸明矾)。~**-making** 造纸。~ **man** 〔美俚〕不看乐谱就不会弹奏的乐师。~ **match** 纸梗火柴。~ **mill** 造纸厂。~ **money** 纸币,钞票。~ **mulberry** 【植】楮,桑科。~ **muslin** 光滑棉布。~ **nautilus** 【动】船蛸。~ **profit** (尚未实现的)纸上盈利。~ **pulp** 纸浆。~**-reed,** ~ **rush** (=papyrus)。~ **stainer** 壁纸制造人[着色人]。~**-thin** *a*. 薄如纸的;极薄弱的。~ **tiger** 纸老虎,外强中干者。~ **tree** 【植】结香。~ **twine** 纸绳。~**-weight** 压纸器,文镇,镇纸。~ **white** 多花水仙。~ **work** 文书档案工作;写作。~**worker** = ~maker.

pa·per·y [ˈpeipəri; ˋpepərɪ] *a*. 纸状的,纸质的。

pap·e·terie [ˈpæpitri:; ˋpæpɪtrɪ] *n*. 文具盒。

Pa·phi·an [ˈpeifiən; ˋpefɪən] *a*. **1.** (塞浦路斯西南部古城)帕福斯 (Paphos) (人)的。**2.** 〔p-〕性爱的;情欲的。

Pa·pia·men·to [ˌpɑ:pjɑ:ˈmentəu; ˏpɑpjɑˋmɛnto] *n*. 巴皮阿孟特语〔一种西班牙土语,其中夹杂荷兰语和葡萄牙语〕。

pap·ier collé [ˈpæpjei-kɔˈlei; paˋpje-kɔˋle] *n*. 〔F.〕拼贴画。

pap·ier-mâ·ché [ˈpæpjeiˈmɑ:ʃei; ˋpepəˋmeˋʃe] **I** *n*. 〔F.〕**1.** 【印】纸型。**2.** 制型纸〔纸浆中混入树胶等制成,具有高度韧性〕。*a* ~ *mould* 【印】纸型,纸版。**II** *a*. **1.** 制型纸做的。**2.** 人造的,假的。*a* ~ *facade* 虚饰的门面。

pa·pil·i·o·na·ceous [pəˌpiliəˈneiʃəs; pəˏpɪlɪəˋneʃəs] *a*. 【植】蝶形的,有蝶形花的。

pa·pil·la [pəˈpilə; pəˋpɪlə] *n*. (*pl*. **-lae** [-li:; -li]) 【解、植】乳头;乳头状小突起;味蕾;吐丝突;棘。

pa·pil·lar, pa·pil·la·ry, pap·il·late(d) [pəˈpilə, -ləri, pæpileit(id); pəˋpɪlɚ, -lərɪ, ˋpæpɪlˏet(ɪd)] *a*. 乳头的,乳头状突起的;乳突的。

pap·il·lo·ma [ˌpæpiˈləumə; ˏpæpəˋlomə] *n*. (*pl*. **-ma·ta** [-mətə; mətə], ~s) 【医】乳头(状)瘤。**-tous** [-təs; -təs] *a*.

pap·il·lose [ˈpæpiləus; ˋpæpəˏlos] *a*. 多乳头状小突起的;多疣的;疹状的。

pa·pism [ˈpeipizəm; ˋpepɪzm̩] *n*. 〔蔑〕教皇制度;罗马天主教。

pa·pist [ˈpeipist; ˋpepɪst] **I** *n*. 教皇至上主义者;〔蔑〕罗马天主教徒。**II** *a*. 罗马天主教(徒)的。

pa·pis·tic, pa·pis·ti·cal [pəˈpistik, -tikəl; peˋpɪstɪk, -tɪkl̩] *a*. 〔蔑〕罗马天主教的。**-ti·cal·ly** *ad*.

pa·pist·ry [ˈpeipistri; ˋpepɪstrɪ] *n*. 〔蔑〕教皇制度;罗马天主教(教义)。

pa·poose [pəˈpu:s; pæˋpus] *n*. **1.** 北美印第安人的婴儿[幼儿]。**2.** 〔美俚〕和工会会员一起工作的非会员工人。

pap·pose, pap·pous [ˈpæpəus, ˈpæpəs; ˋpæpos, ˋpæpəs] *a*. 【植】有冠毛的,冠毛的。

pap·pus [ˈpæpəs; ˋpæpəs] *n*. (*pl*. ***pap·pi*** [ˈpæpai; ˋpæpaɪ]) 【植】冠毛;柔毛。

pap·py[1] [ˈpæpi; ˋpæpɪ] *a*. 面包粥似的,半流质的;乳状的;黏糊糊的。

pap·py[2] [ˈpæpi; ˋpæpɪ] *n*. 〔美俚〕爸爸。~ **guy** 〔美俚〕(一个团体中的)长者。

pa·preg [ˈpeipreg; ˋpeprɛg] *n*. 层压纸板。

pap·ri·ka, pap·ri·ca [ˈpæprikə, pæˈpri:kə; ˋpæprɪkə, pæˋprikə] *n*. (匈牙利)红辣椒;辣椒粉。

Pap test [pæp test; pæp tɛst] *n*. 〔口〕早期子宫颈癌涂片检查(= Papanicolaou test)。

Pap·u·a [ˈpæpjuə, ˈpɑ:puɑ:; ˋpæpjʊə, ˋpɑpʊɑ] *n*. 巴布亚〔新几内亚 (New Guinea) 岛的旧名〕;巴布亚人。**Papuan** [ˈpæpjuən; ˋpæpjʊən] **1.** *n*. 巴布亚语;巴布亚人。**2.** *a*. 巴布亚(人,语)的。

Pa·pu·a New Guin·ea [ˈpæpjuə nju: ˈgini; ˋpæpjʊə nju ˋgɪnɪ] 巴布亚新几内亚[西太平洋]。**P- N- Guinean** *n*. 巴布亚新几内亚人。

pap·u·la [ˈpæpjulə; ˋpæpjʊlə] *n*. (*pl*. **-lae** [-li:; -li]) **1.** 【医】丘疹。**2.** 【动】鳃突;皮鳃;【植】小突起。

pap·ule [ˈpæpju:l; ˋpæpjul] *n*. = papula.

pap·y·ra·ceous [ˌpæpiˈreiʃəs; ˏpæpəˋreʃəs] *a*. 似纸的,薄的 (= papery)。

pa·py·ro·graph [pəˈpaiərəgrɑ:f; pəˋpaɪrəˏgræf] *n*. 复写器。

pa·py·ro·type [pəˈpaiərətaip; pəˋpaɪrəˏtaɪp] *n*. (图片等的)锌版复制。

pa·py·rus [pəˈpaiərəs; pəˋpaɪrəs] *n*. (*pl*. ***-ri*** [-rai; -raɪ]) **1.** 【植】纸莎草,大伞莎草。**2.** (古埃及人等用纸莎草造的)莎草纸。**3.** 〔*pl*.〕(莎草纸的)古写本[文稿]。

PAR = **1.** precision approach radar 【空】精确进场雷达。**2.** pulse acquisition radar 【军】脉冲搜索雷达。**3.** perimeter acquisition radar 【军】环形搜索雷达。

par[1] [pɑ:; pɑr] **I** *n*. **1.** 同等,同位,同价。**2.** (两种货币间对比的)制定等价,平价。**3.** 【商】牌价;票面金额。**4.** 定额,标准;(健康或精神的)常态;【高尔夫球】标准打数。*an issue* ~ 发行价格。*a nominal* [*face*] ~ 票面价值。~ *of exchange* (汇兑的)法定牌价;外汇平价。***above*** ~ 在票面价值以上;在标准[一般水平]以上。***at*** ~ 照票面价值,与票面价值相等。***below*** ~ **1.** 在票面价值以下;在标准[一般水平]以下。**2.** 身体不舒服。***on a*** ~ ***with*** 和…相等[同价];和…一样。***up to*** ~ 达到标准[一般水准、正常状况]。**II** *a*. **1.** 与票面价值相等的,平价的。**2.** 常态的,平均的,一般标准[水准]的。~ **value** 票面价值。

par[2] [pɑ:; pɑr] *n*. 〔口〕= paragraph (*n*.)。

par[3] [pɑ:; pɑr] *n*. = parr.

par. = **1.** paragraph. **2.** parallel. **3.** parenthesis. **4.**

parish.

par- *pref*.〔用于元[母]音前〕= para-[1].

pa·ra [ˈpɑːrɑː; ˋpɑrɑ] *n*.〔口〕= parachutist; paragraph.

Para. = Paraguay.

para-[1] *pref*. **1.** 侧,副,外,超,对,反,误: *para*llel; *para*logism. **2.**【化】对(位),聚,仲,副: *para*diazine. **3.**【医】对,副,衍: *para*typhoid.

para-[2] *pref*. 表示"保护,庇护,避难": *para*dos.

para-[3] *pref*. 表示"降落伞、伞兵": *para*operation 伞兵战。

par·a·am·i·no·sal·i·cyl·ic [ˈpærəæˌminə*u*ˌsæliˈsilik; ˋpærəəˋmɪnoˋsæləˋsɪlɪk] *a*. ~ **acid**【药】对氨基水杨酸(略作 PAS)。

par·a·bi·o·sis [ˌpærəbaiˈəusis; ˏpærəbaɪˋosɪs] *n*.【生】**1.** 异种共生。**2.** 并生。**3.** 间生态。**-bi·o·tic** [-ˈɔtik; -ˋɑtɪk] *a*.

par·a·blast [ˈpærəˌblæst; ˋpærəˏblæst] *n*.【胚】副胚层。**-ic** *a*.

par·a·ble [ˈpærəbl; ˋpærəbl̩] *n*. **1.** (道德说教性的)寓言;比喻。**2.**〔古〕格言。**3.**〔美俚〕大话。

pa·rab·o·la [pəˈræbələ; pəˋræbələ] *n*. **1.**【数】抛物线。**2.** 碗状物〔如话筒等〕。

par·a·bol·ic, -i·c(al) [ˌpærəˈbɔlik(əl); ˏpærəˋbɑlɪk(l̩)] *a*. **1.** 比喻的;寓言似的。**2.** 抛物线(状)的。

pa·rab·o·lize [pəˈræbəlaiz; pəˋræbəlaɪz] *vt*. **1.** 以寓言表示,用比喻说明。**2.** 使成抛物线。**-r** *n*.

pa·rab·o·loid [pəˈræbəlɔid; pəˋræbəˏlɔɪd] *n*.【数】抛物面;抛物体。

para·bomb [ˈpærəbɔm; ˋpærəˏbɑm] *n*. 伞投炸弹。

par·a·chor [ˈpærəkɔː; ˋpærəkɔr] *n*.【物】等张比容。

par·ach·ro·mat·ism [ˈpærəˈkrəumətizəm; ˋpærəˋkromətɪzəm] *n*.【医】色觉倒错。

par·ach·ro·nism [pəˈrækrənizəm; pærˋækrənɪzm̩] *n*. (把正确日期错误地记迟的)记迟时误(*opp*. anachronism)。

par·a·chute [ˈpærəʃuːt; ˋpærəˏʃut] **I** *n*. **1.** 降落伞;降落伞状物。**2.**【植】风散种子。**3.**【动】(蝙蝠等的)翅膜;(鳞翅目的)领片。*a heavy-duty* ~ 快速降落伞。*a free-fall* ~ 手开降落伞。*a cargo* ~ 投物伞。~ *troops* 伞兵,伞兵部队。**II** *vt*. 用降落伞投送,伞投。—*vi*. **1.** 用降落伞降落。**2.**〔美俚〕突然倾斜,突然跌下。**-r, -chut·ist** *n*. **1.**【空】跳伞者,伞兵。**2.**〔贬〕(靠各种关系被安插进某个机构的)无能冗员。**-chut·ic** [ˌpærəˈʃuːtik; pærəˋʃutɪk] *a*.

par·a·clete [ˈpærəkliːt; ˋpærəˏklit] *n*. **1.** 辩护人,调解人;安慰者。**2.**〔P-〕【宗】圣灵。

pa·rade [pəˈreid; pəˋred] **I** *n*. **1.** 游行,示威游行;(检阅时的)行进式;盛况,壮观。**2.** 陈列,展览;炫示;虚饰。**3.**【军】阅兵,检阅,阅兵式;练兵场,操场,校场。**4.**〔英〕(尤指海岸等的)散步场,运动场,广场;散步的人群。**5.**【剑】挡开;防御,守势。**6.** (城中的)院子。**7.**〔美俚〕拳赛节目。*dress* ~ 阅兵典礼。*program(me)* ~ 广播[电视]节目预告。***in front of the*** ~【美体】得冠军。***join the*** ~〔美〕学时髦。跟着大众行动。***make a*** ~ ***of*** 夸耀,炫示。***on*** ~ (演员等)全体出场。**II** *vt*. **1.** 使列队行进;在…游行。**2.** 夸耀(才能等);标榜。—*vi*. **1.** 整步行进,列队游行。**2.** 散步。**3.** 夸耀,自吹。~ *as an advocate of* 标榜为…的拥护者。~**-ground** 练兵场,校场。~ **rest** 士兵在校阅时的稍息姿势;发出稍息令。**-r** *n*. 游行者。

par·a·di·chlo·ro·ben·zene [ˌpærədaiˌklɔːrəˈbenziːn, -benˈziːn; ˏpærədaɪˏklorəˋbenzin, -benˋzin] *n*.【化】对二氯苯。

par·a·did·dle [ˈpærədidl; ˏpærəˋdɪdl] *n*.〔拟声〕咚咚哒哒声,撕边〔左右两鼓槌交替连续敲鼓声〕。

par·a·digm [ˈpærədaim, -dim; ˋpærəˏdɪm, -dɪm] *n*. **1.**【修】范例;示例。**2.**【语法】(名词、动词等的)词形变化表。

par·a·dig·mat·ic [ˈpærədigˈmætik; ˏpærədɪgˋmætɪk] *a*. 作为示范的;例证的。**-al·ly** *ad*.

par·a·di·sa·ic, par·a·di·sa·i·cal [ˌpærədiˈseik(əl); ˏpærədɪˋseɪk(l̩)] *a*. = paradisiac.

par·a·dise [ˈpærədais; ˋpærəˏdaɪs] *n*. **1.** 天堂,乐园;〔P-〕【宗】伊甸乐园(= Garden of Eden)。**2.** 地上乐园,乐土,极乐;至福。**3.** (养有鸟兽的)公园。**4.**【建】(教堂的)前院;门廊二楼;〔俚〕(戏院的)顶层座位。*a bird of* ~ 极乐鸟,风鸟。*fool's* ~ 虚幻的乐境;幻想的世界。~ **bird** 极乐鸟,风鸟。~ **fish** 极乐鱼〔一种供观赏用的热带鱼〕。**P- valley**〔美〕(美国西部的)世外桃源。

par·a·dis·e·an [ˌpærəˈdisiən, -ˈdizien; ˏpærəˋdɪsɪən, -ˋdɪzɪɛn] *a*. 天堂(似)的,乐园(似)的;极乐的。

par·a·dis·i·ac, par·a·di·si·a·cal [ˌpærəˈdisiæk, ˈpærədi ˈsaiəkəl; ˏpærəˋdɪsɪˏæk, ˏpærədɪˋsaɪəkl̩] *a*. = paradisean.

par·a·dis·i·al [ˌpærəˈdiziəl; ˏpærəˋdɪsɪəl] *a*. = paradisean.

par·a·dos [ˈpærədɔs; ˋpærəˏdɑs] *n*.【军】背墙〔在堑壕或掩体后构筑的防护土垛〕。

par·a·dox [ˈpærədɔks; ˋpærəˏdɑks] *n*. **1.** 似非而是的论点[妙语]。**2.** 反面议论,反论,悖论;疑题。**3.** 自相矛盾的话;奇谈,怪论;前后矛盾的事物。**4.**【物】佯谬。**-er, -ist** *n*. 反论家。

par·a·dox·i·cal [ˌpærəˈdɔksikəl; ˏpærəˋdɑksɪkl̩] *a*. **1.** 反论的,反面议论的。**2.** 似非而是的。**3.** 悖论的;反常的,荒谬的;自相矛盾的。**4.** 爱诡辩的。**-i·ty** [-ˈkæliti; -ˋkælətɪ] *n*. 似非而是性。**-ly** *ad*.

par·a·dox·ure [ˌpærəˈdɔksjuə; ˏpærəˋdɑksjʊr] *n*.【动】(亚洲南部产)长尾麝香猫。

par·a·dox·y [ˈpærədɔksi; ˋpærədɑksɪ] *n*. = paradoxicality.

par·a·drop [ˈpærədrɔp; ˋpærəˏdrɑp] *vt*., *n*.【空】空投,伞投。

par·aes·the·si·a [ˌpæresˈθiːʒə, -ʒiə; ˏpærəsˋθiʒə, -ʒɪə] *n*.【医】感觉异常(= paresthesia)。

par·af·fin, par·af·fine [ˈpærəfin, ˈpærəfiːn; ˋpærəfɪn, ˋpærəˏfin] **I** *n*. **1.**〔美〕(硬)石蜡。**2.**【化】链烷(属)烃。**3.**〔英〕煤油。**II** *vt*. 用石蜡涂[浸透]。~**-oil** 石蜡油;〔英〕煤油。~ **scale (wax)** 粗石蜡。

par·a·frag [ˈpærəfræg; ˋpærəfræg] *n*.【军】伞投杀伤炸弹。

par·a·gen·e·sis [ˌpærəˈdʒenisis; ˏpærəˋdʒɛnəsɪs] *n*.【地】共生,共生次序。**-net·ic** [-dʒiˈnetik; -dʒɪˋnɛtɪk] *a*.

par·a·glide [ˈpærəglaid; ˋpærəglaɪd] = parasail.

par·a·go·ge [ˌpærəˈgəudʒiː; ˏpærəˋgodʒɪ] *n*.【语音】词末附加音〔在词尾附加无意义之音: amid*st*〕。

par·a·gon [ˈpærəgən; ˋpærəˏgɑn] **I** *n*. **1.** (尽善尽美的)模范[典型]。**2.** 优秀的人[物];逸品,殊品;完人。**3.** (100克拉以上的)大钻石;特大珍珠。**4.**【印】20点铅字。*Man is the* ~ *of animals*. 人为万物之灵。*a* ~ *of beauty* 美的典型。**II** *vt*. **1.**〔诗〕比较(*with*)。**2.**〔古〕与…竞争(*with*)。**3.**〔古〕胜过,强过。

pa·rag·o·nite [pəˈrægəˌnait; pəˋrægənaɪt] *n*.【化】钠云母。**-nit·ic** [-ˈnitik; -ˋnɪtɪk] *a*.

par·a·graph [ˈpærəgrɑːf; ˋpærəˏgræf] **I** *n*. **1.** (文章的)节,段。**2.** 分段符号[¶]。**3.** (报纸的)短文,短评。*an editorial* ~ 短评。*miscellaneous* ~*s* 杂评。~ *advertisement* 新闻式广告。**II** *vt*. **1.** 把…分段。**2.** 写短文报导。—*vi*. (为报刊)写短评[杂评]。

par·a·graph·er, par·a·graph·ist [ˈpærəgrɑːfə, -fist; ˋpærəgræfɚ, -fɪst] *n*. 杂评[短评]作者。★美国多用 paragrapher.

par·a·graph·i·a [ˌpærəˈgræfiə; ˏpærəˋgræfɪə] *n*.【医】

书写倒错。

par·a·graph·ic(al) [ˌpærəˈgræfik(əl); ˏpærəˋgræfɪk(l̩)] *a*. 1. 分段的。2. 杂评的。**-cal·ly** *ad*.

Par·a·guay [ˈpærəgwai; ˋpærəˏgwe] *n*. 巴拉圭〔拉丁美洲〕。

Par·a·guay·an [ˌpærəˈgwaiən, -ˈgwei-; ˏpærəˋgweən, -ˋgwaɪ-] *n*., *a*. 巴拉圭人(的)。

par·a·he·li·ot·ro·pism [ˌpærəˌhiːliˈɔtrəpizəm; ˏpærəˏhilɪˋɑtrəpɪzəm] *n*.【植】(叶子的)偏日性。

par·a·keet [ˈpærəkiːt; ˋpærəˏkit] *n*.【鸟】长尾小鹦鹉。

par·a·kite [ˈpærəkait; ˋpærəˏkaɪt] *n*. 1. (可作降落伞用的)降落风筝。2. (观测气象等用的)无尾风筝。

par·al·de·hyde [pəˈrældihaid; pəˋrældəˏhaɪd] *n*.【化】(三)聚乙醛〔作安眠药用〕。

par·a·leip·sis, par·a·lip·sis [ˌpærəˈlaipsis, -ˈlip-; ˏpærəˋlaɪpsɪs, -ˋlɪp-] *n*. (*pl*. **-ses** [-siːz; -siz])【修】假省笔法〔省略重要部分反而起强调作用的方法〕。

par·al·lac·tic [ˌpærəˈlæktik;ˏpærəˋlæktɪk] *a*.【物、天】视差的。

par·al·lax [ˈpærəlæks; ˋpærəˏlæks] *n*.【物、天】视差。*the equatorital horizontal* ~ 赤道地平视差。

par·al·lel [ˈpærəlel; ˋpærəˏlɛl] **I** *a*. 1. 平行的;并行的(*to*; *with*);【电】并联的。2. 同一方向的,同一目的的。3. 相同的,同样的,相似的,对应的。*a* ~ *instance* [*case*] 同样的例子[情况]。*His prudence is* ~ *to his zeal*. 他固然谨慎,也同样热心。***run*** ~ ***with*** 和…平行。**II** *n*. 1. 平行线[面]。2. 相似,类似;相似物,相当的人[物]。3. 比较,对比。4. 纬度圈,纬线。5.【军】平行堑壕。6.【印】平行号〔‖〕。7.【电】并联。*the* ~ *of altitude* [*declination*, *latitude*] 平纬[赤纬,黄纬]圈。***draw a*** ~ ***between ...*** 在…之间作对比。***in*** ~ ***with*** 和…并行,和…对应。***without*** (***a***) ~ 无与匹敌的。**III** *vt*. (**-l(l)-**) 1. 使成平行;与…平行。2. 与…相匹[配得上,相应]。3. 对比,比较…(*with*)。~ **bars**【体】双杠;【机】平行杆。~ **circuit**【电】并联电路。~ **computer** 并行计算机[电脑]〔有几个处理机,能同时处理一个题目的大量运算〕。~ **feed**【电】并联馈电。~ **feeder**【电】平行馈(电)线。~ **processing**【计】并行处理。~ **resonance**【电】并联谐振。~ **ruler** 平行线规。**-ism** *n*.【计】并行计算。

par·al·le·le·p·i·ped, par·al·lel·e·pip·e·don [ˌpærəleˈlepiped, ˌpærəˌleliˈpipidən; ˏpærəˏlɛləˋpaɪpɪd, ˏpærəˏlɛlɪˋpɪpɪˏdɑn] *n*.【几】平行六面体〔常误拼作 parallelopiped, parallelopipedon〕。

par·al·lel·ism [ˌpærəˈlelizəm; ˋpærəlɛlˏɪzəm] *n*. 1. 平行。2. 相同,类似;比较;对应。3.【哲】心身平行论。4.【生、数】平行现象,平行性。5.【修】对应法,对联。

par·al·lel·o·gram [ˌpærəˈleləgræm; ˏpærəˋlɛləˏgræm] *n*.【数】平行四边形。*a period* ~ 周期格子,周期网。~ *of forces*【物】力的平行四边形。**-ic** *a*.

pa·ral·o·gism [pəˈrælədʒizəm; pəˋrælədʒɪzm̩] *n*.【逻】谬误推理,谬论;背理,反理。

pa·ral·o·gize [pəˈrælədʒaiz; pəˋræləˏdʒaɪz] *vi*. 作谬误推论。

Par·a·lym·pics [ˌpærəˈlimpiks; ˏpærəˋlɪmpɪks] *n*. 残疾人奥运会。

par·a·ly·sa·tion [ˌpærəlaiˈzeiʃən; ˏpærəlaɪˋzeʃən] *n*. 1. 麻痹,瘫痪。2. 无能为力;气馁;惊呆。

par·a·lyse, par·a·lyze [ˈpærəlaiz; ˋpærəˏlaɪz] *vt*. 1. 使麻痹,使瘫痪。2. 使无力,使无效;使气馁;使惊呆。3.【电】关闭。*be* ~*d with fear by* 被…吓瘫了,被…所吓倒。~ *one's efforts* 使努力尽成泡影。**-d** *a*. 1. 麻痹的;瘫痪的;惊呆的。2. 〔美俚〕喝得烂醉的。

pa·ral·y·sis [pəˈrælisis; pəˋræləsɪs] *n*. (*pl*. **-ses** [-siːz; -siz]) 1.【医】麻痹,瘫痪;中风。2. 无能,无气力。*infantile* ~ 小儿麻痹症。***general*** ~ 全身瘫痪。*moral* ~ 道德败坏。~ **agitans** [ˈædʒitænz; ˋædʒɪtænz]【医】震颤(性)麻痹。

par·a·lyt·ic [ˌpærəˈlitik;ˏpærəˋlɪtɪk] **I** *a*. 1. 麻痹的,患中风的。2. 无能力的。**II** *n*. 麻痹[中风]病人。

par·a·mag·net·ic [ˌpærəmægˈnetik; ˏpærəmægˋnɛtɪk] *a*.【物】顺磁(的)。~ *substance* 顺磁质。**-net·ism** [-ˈmægnitizəm; -ˋmægnɪtɪzəm] *n*.【物】顺磁性。

Par·a·mar·i·bo [ˌpærəˈmæribəu; ˏpærəˋmærəˏbo] *n*. 巴拉马利波〔苏利南首府〕。

par·a·mat·ta [ˌpærəˈmætə; ˏpærəˋmætə] *n*.【纺】棉毛呢;毛葛。

par·a·me·cin [ˌpærəˈmiːsin; ˏpærəˋmisɪn] *n*.【生化】草履(虫)素。

par·a·me·ci·um [ˌpærəˈmiːsiəm; ˏpærəˋmiʃɪəm] *n*. (*pl*. **-ci·a** [-siə, -ʃiə])【动】草履虫。

par·a·med·ic[1] [ˈpærəˌmedik; ˏpærəˋmɛdɪk] *n*. 伞兵军医;伞降医师。

par·a·med·ic[2] [ˈpærəˌmedik; ˋpærəˏmɛdɪk] *n*. 护理人员,医务辅助人员。

par·a·med·i·cal [ˌpærəˈmedikl; ˏpærəˋmɛdɪkl̩] *a*. 医务助理人员的。

par·a·ment [ˈpærəˌment; ˋpærəˏmənt] *n*. (*pl*. ~**s**, **-ta** [-tə; -tə]) (基督教的)祭衣;装饰品。

pa·ram·e·ter [pəˈræmitə; pəˋræmətɚ] *n*. 1.【数】参数,变数;参词;参项。2.【物】参量;(结晶体的)标轴。3. 〔废〕【天】通径。**-ize** *vt*. 使参数化。

par·a·met·ric [ˌpærəˈmetrik;ˏpærəˋmɛtrɪk] *a*. 参(变)数的;参量的。

par·am·e·tron [ˌpæˈræmitrɔn; pæˋræmɪtrɑn] *n*.【无】参变元件,变感元件。

par·a·mil·i·tar·y [ˌpærəˈmilitəri; ˏpærəˋmɪlɪˏtɛrɪ] **I** *a*. 1. 起军事辅助作用的;副军事性的;准军事性的。2. 半军事性秘密私人组织的。**II** *n*. 准军事部队的成员(= paramilitarist)。

par·am·ne·si·a [ˌpæræmˈniziə;ˏpæræmˋniʒə] *n*.【心】记忆错误;旧事幻现。

pa·ra·mo [ˈpærəməu; ˋpærəmo] *n*. (*pl*. ~**s**) (南美洲热带地方的,尤指安第斯山脉的)荒野高原。

par·a·morph [ˈpærəmɔːf; ˋpærəˏmɔrf] *n*.【矿】副像,同质异晶体;假晶;假形。**-ic** [ˌpærəˈmɔːfik; ˏpærəˋmɔrfɪk] *a*.

par·a·mor·phism [ˌpærəˈmɔːfizm; ˏpærəˋmɔrfɪzm̩] *n*.【矿】同质异晶现象。

par·a·mount [ˈpærəmaunt; ˋpærəˏmaʊnt] **I** *a*. 1. 最高的,至上的,首要的。2. 有最高权力的。3. 卓越的;胜过…的(*to*)。*a* ~ *chief* 帝王。***of*** ~ ***importance*** 最重要的。**II** *n*. 1. 有最高权力的人;元首;首长。2. 最高,至上,主要。*the lady* ~ 女王;射击赛女冠军。*the lord* ~ 国王。**-ly** *ad*.

par·a·mount·cy [ˈpærəmaun*t*si; ˋpærəˏmaʊntsɪ] *n*. 1. 最高权力,主权。2. 至上,最上,首要。

par·a·mour [ˈpærəmuə; ˋpærəˏmʊr] *n*. 1. 奸夫;情妇。2. 〔古、诗〕情人。

par·am·y·lum [pæˈræmiləm; pæˋræmɪləm] *n*.【生】副淀粉;裸藻淀粉。

pa·rang [pɑːˈrɑːŋ; pɑˋrɑŋ] *n*. 〔Ma.〕大而重的短刀。

par·a·noi·a, par·a·noe·a [ˌpærəˈnɔiə, ˌpærəˈniːə; ˏpærəˋnɔɪə, ˏpærəˋniə] *n*.【医】偏执狂,妄想狂。

par·a·noid [ˈpærənɔid; ˋpærənɔɪd] **I** *a*. 1. 患妄想狂的,似妄想狂的。2. 过分猜疑的;幻想狂的;被迫害妄想狂的(= paranoidal)。**II** *n*. 患妄想狂者(= paranoiac)。

par·a·nor·mal [ˌpærəˈnɔːməl; ˏpærəˋnɔrml̩] *a*. 超出科学可了解范围的,超自然的;不平常的。

par·a·nymph [ˈpærənimf; ˋpærənɪmf] *n*. 男[女]傧相。

par·a·pack [ˈpærəpæk; ˋpærəˏpæk] *n*.【军】空投包。

par·a·pet [ˈpærəpit; ˋpærəpɪt] *n*. 1. (阳台、桥等的)栏杆;女儿墙。2.【军】(构筑在堑壕和掩体前方的)胸墙,胸壁。3. 〔英方〕人行道。**-ed** [-tid; -tɪd] *a*. 筑有胸墙[栏

杆等]的。

par·aph [ˈpærəf; ˋpærəf] **I** *n*. (从前防止冒充的)花押,签名后的花押。**II** *vt*. 在…上画花押。

par·a·pha·si·a [ˌpærəˈfeiziə; ˏpærəˋfezɪə] *n*.【医】语言无序,语言错乱。

par·a·pher·na·li·a [ˌpærəfəˈneiljə, -liə; ˏpærəfəˋnelɪə, -lɪə] *n*. [*pl*.] **1**. 随身用具,行头;装饰品。**2**. 各种器具;机械附件。**3**.【法】妻子特有的动产[衣服、首饰等]。*camp* ~ 露营行装。

par·a·phrase [ˈpærəfreiz; ˋpærəˏfrez] **I** *n*. **1**. 释义;意译。**2**. [Scot.]圣经章句的诗译。**II** *vt*., *vi*. (将…)释义;意译。~ *an obscure passage* 将一段晦涩的文字加以意译。

P

par·a·phrast [ˈpærəfræst; ˋpærəfræst] *n*. 释义[意译]者。**-a·phras·tic** [ˌpærəˈfræstik; ˏpærəˋfræstɪk] *a*. 意译的;释义的。

pa·raph·y·sis [pəˈræfisis; pəˋræfəsɪs] *n*. (*pl*. **-ses** [-ˌsiːz; -ˏsiz])【植】隔丝,侧丝(菌)。

par·a·ple·gi·a [ˌpærəˈpliːdʒiə; ˏpærəˋplidʒɪə] *n*.【医】截瘫,下身麻痹。**par·a·ple·gic** [-dʒik; -dʒɪk] *a*.

par·a·prax·is [ˌpærəˈpræksis; ˏpærəˋpræksɪs] *n*. (*pl*. **-xes** [-siːz; -siz])【心】动作倒错。

par·a·prax·ia [ˌpærəˈpræksiə; ˏpærəˋpræksɪə] *n*. = parapraxis.

par·a·pro·fes·sion·al [ˌpærəprəˈfeʃənl; ˏpærəprəˋfɛʃənl] *a*., *n*. 辅助专职人员[医师]的(人)。

par·a·psy·chol·o·gy [ˈpærəsaiˈkɔlədʒi; ˏpærəsaɪˋkɑlədʒɪ] *n*.【心】灵学。

par·a·res·cue [ˈpærəˌreskjuː; ˏpærəˋrɛskju] *n*. 伞兵(对遇险者的)营救,伞投人员进行的救援。

par·a·ros·an·i·line [ˌpærərəuˈzænlin; ˏpærəroˋzænlɪn] *n*.【纺】副蔷薇苯胺,副玫瑰红。

par·a-sail, par·a·sail [ˈpærəˌseil; ˋpærəˏsel] **I** *n*. 滑翔跳伞。**II** *vi*. 作滑翔跳伞运动。

par·a·sang [ˈpærəsæŋ; ˋpærəˏsæŋ] *n*. 帕拉桑[古波斯的长度名,约合 5.5 公里或 3$\frac{1}{4}$ 英里]。

par·a·se·le·ne [ˌpærəsiˈliːni; ˏpærəsɪˋlinɪ] *n*. (*pl*. **-nae** [-niː; -ni])【气】幻月[月晕时的光轮]。

par·a·scend·ing [ˌpærəˈsendiŋ; ˏpærəˋsɛndɪŋ] *n*.【体】牵引升空跳伞[运动员佩戴已打开的降落伞由摩托车,快艇等牵引到一定高度,然后脱离牵引跳伞降落的一种体育运动]。

par·a·shah [ˈpɑːrəˌʃɑː; ˋpɑrəˏʃɑ] *n*. (*pl*. ***par·a·shoth*** [-ˌʃəut; -ˏʃot]) (犹太教堂所诵的)摩西五经中五十四段的一段(每周六安息日诵一段,一年诵完);摩西五经中的选段[专供节日诵读]。

par·a·shoot [ˈpærəʃuːt; ˋpærəˏʃut] *vi*. (***par·a·shot*** [ˈpærəʃɔt; ˋpærəˏʃɑt]) 射击敌人伞兵。**-er, par·a·shot** [ˈpærəʃɔt; ˋpærəˏʃɑt] *n*. 专打伞兵的射手。

par·a·site [ˈpærəsait; ˋpærəˏsaɪt] *n*. **1**. 寄生物;寄生虫;寄生菌;寄生植物;寄生矿物。**2**. 食客;清客,谄媚者。**3**. 反射器。~ **aeroplane** [**plane**] (飞行中由母机携带或发射的)子机。~ **drag**【空】寄生阻力。

par·a·sit·ic(al) [ˌpærəˈsitik(əl); ˏpærəˋsɪtɪk(l)] *a*. **1**. 寄生的,寄生动[植]物的;寄生体的,寄生质的;(疾病)由寄生虫引起的。**2**. 寄食的;奉承的。*a* ~ *wasp* 寄生蜂。**-cal·ly** *ad*.

par·a·sit·i·cide [ˌpærəˈsitisaid; ˏpærəˋsɪtɪˏsaɪd] **I** *a*. 杀寄生虫的。**II** *n*. 杀寄生虫药。

par·a·sit·i·cin [ˌpærəˈsitisin; ˏpærəˋsɪtəsɪn] *n*.【医】苄青霉素。

par·a·sit·ism [ˈpærəsaitizəm; ˋpærəsaɪtˏɪzəm] *n*. **1**. 寄生(现象,状态)。**2**. 阿谀,奉承。**3**.【医】寄生物传染;(寄生虫引起的)皮肤病。

par·a·sit·ize [ˈpærəsaitaiz; ˋpærəˏsaɪtaɪz] *vt*. [主用 *p*. *p*.]寄生于;侵害;为寄生虫[食客]…所烦扰。

par·a·sit·oid [ˈpærəˌsaitɔid; ˋpærəˏsaɪtɔɪd] *n*.【动】拟寄生。

par·a·si·tol·o·gy [ˌpærəsaiˈtɔlədʒi; ˏpærəsaɪˋtɑlədʒɪ] *n*. 寄生物[虫]学;寄生分子行为及心理研究。

par·a·sit·o·sis [ˌpærəsaiˈtəusis; ˏpærəsaɪˋtosɪs] *n*. (*pl*. **-ses** [-siːz; -siz]) 寄生物病,寄生虫病。

par·a·sol [ˌpærəˈsɔl, ˈpærəsɔːl; ˏpærəˋsɑl, ˋpærəˏsɔl] *n*. **1**. (女用)阳伞。**2**.【空】伞式单翼机。***the Chinese*** [***sultan's***] ~ (***trees***) 梧桐。~ **ant** 樵蚁[产于南美热带地区]。

par·a·spot·ter [ˌpærəˈspɔtə; ˏpærəˋspɑtɚ] *n*. 守望伞兵者。

par·a·sym·pa·thet·ic [ˌpærəˌsimpəˈθetik; ˏpærəˏsɪmpəˋθɛtɪk] *a*.【解、生】副交感(神经)的。

par·a·sym·pa·tho·mi·metic [ˌpærəˌsimpəˌθəumiˈmetik; ˏpærəˏsɪmpəˏθomɪˋmɛtɪk] *a*. 副交感神经性的[指药物、化学药品等而言]。

par·a·syn·ap·sis [ˌpærəsiˈnæpsis; ˏpærəsɪˋnæpsɪs] *n*.【生】(染色体的)平行联会。

par·a·syn·the·sis [ˌpærəˈsinθisis; ˏpærəˋsɪnθəsɪs] *n*.【语】双重构词[从复合词又造派生词,如 denationalize, tender-hearted 等]。**-thet·ic** [-ˈθetik; -ˋθɛtɪk] *a*.

par·a·tax·is [ˌpærəˈtæksis; ˏpærəˋtæksɪs] *n*.【语】(不用连接词的)并列结构[关系];并列排比;意合法[使几个分句不用连接词而排列起来,例如:I came, I saw, I conquered.] (*opp*. hypotaxis)。**-tac·tic** [ˌpærəˈtæktik; ˏpærəˋtæktɪk] *a*.

Par·a·tet·ran·y·chus [ˌpærətetˈrænikəs; ˏpærətɛtˋrænɪkəs] *n*.【动】(伤害橘树和胡桃树的)红蜘蛛。

pa·rath·e·sis [pəˈræθisis; pəˋræθəsɪs] *n*. (*pl*. **-ses** [-siːz; -siz]) = parenthesis.

par·a·thi·on [ˈpærəˈθaiɔn; ˏpærəˋθaɪɑn] *n*.【化】对硫磷,硝苯硫磷,拍拉息昂[用作农业杀虫剂]。

par·a·thy·roid [ˌpærəˈθairɔid; ˏpærəˋθaɪrɔɪd] **I** *a*. **1**. 甲状旁腺附近的。**2**. 甲状旁腺上或附近的四个小卵圆腺的。**II** *n*. 甲状旁腺。

par·a·troop [ˈpærətruːp; ˋpærəˏtrup] **I** *n*. [*pl*.]【军】伞兵部队。**II** *a*. 伞兵的。**-er** *n*. 伞兵。

par·a·tu·nic [ˌpærəˈtjuːnik; pærəˋtjunɪk] *n*. 伞兵上衣。

par·a·ty·phoid [ˌpærəˈtaifɔid; ˏpærəˋtaɪfɔɪd] *n*., *a*.【医】副伤寒(的)。

par·a·vane [ˈpærəvein; ˋpærəven] *n*.【军】破雷卫,防水雷器[切断锚定水雷的钢索的一种装置];防潜艇器。~ **chain** 防雷器链。~ **davits** 扫雷器吊架。

par·a·vi·on [ˌpɑːræˈvjɔ̃ːŋ; paraˋvjɔ̃] [F.]由航空邮寄[邮件标签]。

par·a·wing [ˈpærəwiŋ; ˋpærəwɪŋ] *n*. (可定点降落的)翼状降落伞。

par·bald [ˈpɑːbɔld; ˋparbɔld] *a*. 秃掉一部分的。

par·bleu [pɑːˈbləː; parˋblɜ] *int*. [F.]嗳呀! 唷!

par·boil [ˈpɑːbɔil; ˋparˏbɔɪl] *vt*. **1**. 把…煮成半熟。**2**. 使过热,晒焦(皮肤等);使热得难受。

par·buck·le [ˈpɑːbʌkl; ˋparˏbʌkl] **I** *n*. (拉上或放下大桶等用的)套拉绳。**II** *vt*. 用套拉绳拉上 (*up*);用套拉绳放下 (*down*)。

Par·cae [ˈpɑːsiː; ˋparsi] *n*. [*pl*.] (*sing*. **-ca** [-kə; -kə]) [L.]【罗神】命运三女神(= the Three Fates)。

par·cel [ˈpɑːsl; ˋparsl] **I** *n*. **1**. 包,小包,包裹。**2**.【商】(货物的)一宗。**3**.【法】(土地的)一块。**4**. [蔑](人、兽、物的)一群,一批,一组;[古]一部分。**5**. [口]赢来的[输掉的]钱。*a* ~ *of rubbish* 无聊的事。*by* ~ *post* 当包裹寄。*by* ~*s* 一点一点的。*part and* ~ (*of*) (…的)重要部分。*the* ~*s room* [美]衣帽间。**II** *vt*. ([英] **-ll-**) **1**. 分,区分;把…划成部分后分配 (*out*)。**2**. 把…作成包裹,打包,捆扎(*up*);把…拼[连]在一起。**3**.【海】用帆布条包(绳索等);用帆布条和沥青堵(缝)。~ ***out*** [***into***] 分配,分派。**III** *a*. 部分(时间)的。**IV** *ad*. [古]一部分,局部地 (= partly)。~ *blind* 半盲的。~ *drunk* 微醉

的。~ *gilt* 部分镀金的。~ **bomb** 邮包炸弹。~ **office** 包裹房。~ **paper** 包装纸。~ **post** 包裹邮件;邮包;包裹邮递。~ **post zone**〔美〕(本区内邮资相同的)包裹邮递区。

par·cel·ling〔美〕['pɑːsəliŋ; `pɑrsəlɪŋ] *n*. 1.【海】(涂了沥青油包裹绳索用的)帆布条。2. 打包。3. 划分并分配。

par·ce·na·ry ['pɑːsinəri; `pɑrsn̩,ɛrɪ] *n*.【法】共同继承。

par·ce·ner ['pɑːsinə; `pɑrsnɚ] *n*.【法】共同继承人。

parch [pɑːtʃ; pɑrtʃ] *vt*. 1. 烤;烘,使焦。2. 使干透;使极度口渴。3. 使冷干皱缩。*be ~ed with thirst* 渴得口干舌燥。—*vi*. 1. 干透;烤干;焦。2. 口渴;心烧。

parched [pɑːtʃt; pɑrtʃt] *a*. 烤干的;焦的;干透的。~ *peas* 干豌豆。~ *soil* 干透了的土地。

parch·ing ['pɑːtʃiŋ; `pɑrtʃɪŋ] *a*. 烘烤似的,燃烧般的,干燥的。~ *heat* 炎热。

parch·ment ['pɑːtʃmənt; `pɑrtʃmənt] *n*. 1. 羊皮纸;羊皮纸文件;(羊皮纸般的)上等纸。2. 羊皮纸文稿;大学毕业文凭。3. 咖啡子的皮。*vegetable* ~ (=~ paper) 假羊皮纸,硫酸纸。*virgin* ~ (用小羊皮做的)上等羊皮纸。

pard[1] [pɑːd; pɑrd] *n*.〔英古〕豹(=leopard)。

pard[2] [pɑːd; pɑrd] *n*.〔美俚〕伙伴,同伴;搭档。

par·die, par·di [pɑː'diː; pɑr`di] *ad*., *int*.〔古〕理所当然,确定不疑〔原为一种誓言〕(=pardy)。

pard·ner ['pɑːdnə; `pɑrdnɚ] *n*.〔美方〕=partner.

par·don ['pɑːdn; `pɑrdn̩] **I** *n*. 1. 原谅,饶恕,宽恕。2.【法】赦免;大赦(=general ~),特赦(=free ~)。3.【宗】赦罪;免罪符;免罪节。***a thousand ~s for*** (*doing sth*.) 千万请原谅。(***I***) ***beg your*** ~ . 请原谅,对不起〔表示:1. 道歉;2. 申述自己不同意见;3. 重音在句后时意为"对不起,请再说一遍",也可只用"Beg ~"或"Pardon",说时用升调〕。**II** *vt*. 原谅,饶恕,宽恕;【法】赦免。*P- me for interrupting* (*you*). 对不起打搅(你)了。*There is nothing to* ~. 好说好说,哪里哪里。

par·don·a·ble ['pɑːdnəbl; `pɑrdn̩əbl̩] *a*. 可以原谅的,可以饶恕的。**-bly** *ad*. **-ness** *n*.

par·don·er ['pɑːdnə; `pɑrdnɚ] *n*. 1. 宽恕者。2.【宗史】获准售卖天主教免罪符的人。

pare [pɛə; pɛr] *vt*. 1. 剥,削(果皮等);修(指甲等);削去(角、边等)(*off*; *away*)。2. (逐渐)削减,缩减,撙节(*away*, *down*)。~ *nails to the quick* 把指甲剪到肉根。~ *down expenses* 削减费用。~ *an apple* 削苹果皮。~ *a layer from a corn* 剥掉玉米的壳。

Pa·ree ['pæriː; `pæri] *n*.〔美口〕=Paris.

Pare(s) [pɛə(z); pɛr(z)] *n*. 佩尔(斯)〔姓氏〕。

par·e·gor·ic ['pærə'gɔrik; ,pærə`gɔrɪk] **I** *a*.【药】止痛的。**II** *n*.【药】止痛药;樟脑阿片酊〔小儿用止痢药〕。

paren. = parenthesis.

pa·ren·chy·ma [pə'reŋkimə; pə`rɛŋkɪmə] *n*.【解】腺细胞组织,实质,主质;【植】柔组织,薄壁组织。~ **cells** 薄壁细胞。**-l, -tous** [,pæreŋ'kimətəs; ,pærɛŋ`kɪmətəs] *a*.

parens. = parentheses.

par·ent ['pɛərənt; `pɛrənt] *n*. 1. 父亲;母亲。2.〔*pl*.〕双亲;祖先。3. (动、植物的)母体,亲本。4. 根源,本源。5. 保护者。*one's ~s* 双亲。~*-teacher association*【教】家长会。*a ~ bird* 老鸟。*a ~ company* 母公司。~ *substance* 亲体,母物。*a ~ stem* 原种。*Ignorance is the ~ of many evils*. 无知是许多罪恶的根源。**-hood** *n*. 父母的身份。**-ing** 育儿;生育;像父母对待子女般的照顾。

par·ent·age ['pɛərəntidʒ; `pɛrəntɪdʒ] *n*. 1. 亲子关系;父母身份。2. 出身;血统;家系,门第。3. 来源。***of good*** ~ 出身高贵[门第高]。***of mean*** ~ 出身微贱。

pa·ren·tal [pə'rentl; pə`rɛntl̩] *a*. 1. 亲的;父的;母的;父母(一样)的;【生】(杂种)亲本的。2. 作为来源[渊源]的。~ *love* 父母之爱。~ **home**, ~ **school** 失足儿童教养院。**-ly** *ad*. 像父母。

par·en·ter·al [pæ'rentərəl; pə`rɛntərəl] **I** *a*. 1. 非肠道的,不经肠道的。2. 不经消化道带进体内的〔如经过皮下或静脉注射〕。**II** *n*. 一种肠道外注射物。**-ly** *ad*.

pa·ren·the·sis [pə'renθisis; pə`rɛnθəsɪs] *n*. (*pl*. **-ses** [-siːz; -siz]) 1.【语法】插入成分;插入语,插句。2.〔常 *pl*.〕圆括号[( )]。3. 插曲;插剧;插话。***by way of*** ~ 附带地,顺便。***in parentheses*** 在圆括号内,附加上;附带。

pa·ren·the·size, pa·ren·the·sise [pə'renθisaiz; pə`rɛnθə,saɪz] *vt*. 1. 把…括入圆括号内,用圆括号括起。2. 在…插入插句[插话];把…作为插入语。

par·en·thet·ic, par·en·thet·i·cal [,pærən'θetik, -ikəl; ,pærən`θɛtɪk, -ɪkl̩] *a*. 1. 作为插入语[插句]的;作为附带说明(性质)的。2. 圆括号[弧形]的,弓形的;放在括号内的。3.〔喻〕插曲的,插话的。**-thet·i·cal·ly** *ad*. 作插句;插话似地。

par·er ['pɛərə; `pɛrɚ] *n*. 1. 削皮的人。2. 削皮器,削皮刀。

par·er·gon [pæ'rəːgɔn; pæ`rɝgɑn] *n*. (*pl*. **-ga** [-gə; -gə]) 1. 副业。2.【建】附属装饰;辅助装饰。3. 补遗,附录。

par·e·sis ['pærisis; pə`risɪs] *n*. (*pl*. **-ses** [-siːz; -siz])【医】1. 局部麻痹;轻瘫。2. 麻痹性痴呆(=general paresis)。

par·es·the·si·a [,pæris'θiːʒiə; ,pærəs`θiʒə] *n*.【医】感觉异常。**-thet·ic** [-'θetik; -`θɛtɪk] *a*.

pa·ret·ic [pə'retik; pə`rɛtɪk] **I** *a*.【医】1. 局部麻痹的,轻瘫的。2. 麻痹性痴呆的。**II** *n*. 局部麻痹病患者。

pa·re·u ['pɑːrei,uː; `pɑre,u] *n*.〔Tahitian〕(波利尼西亚男女穿的)彩色长裙。

par·e·ve ['pɑːrivə, -ve; `pɑrɪvə, -vɛ] *a*.【犹】素馨菜的〔无肉类或乳制品的〕。

par ex·cel·lence [,pɑːr'eksəlɑ̃ːns; pɑr`ɛksə,lɑns]〔F.〕最卓越的[地];典型的[地]。

par ex·em·ple [,pɑːr eg'zɑ̃ːmpl; pɑr ɛg`zɑ̃plə]〔F.〕例如(=for instance)。

par·fait [pɑː'fei; pɑr`fe] *n*.〔F.〕冻糕。

par·fect ['pɑːfikt; `pɑr,fɪkt] *a*.〔美俚〕=perfect.

par·fleche ['pɑːfleʃ, pɑː'fleʃ; `pɑr,flɛʃ, pɑr`flɛʃ] *n*. 1. 生皮革。2. 生皮革制品。

parge [pɑːdʒ; pɑrdʒ] *vt*. 为(密封砖、石制品的表面)涂上灰泥。**parg·ing** *n*.

par·get ['pɑːdʒit; `pɑrdʒɪt] **I** *n*.【建】1. 石膏;灰泥;粗涂灰泥;白色涂料。2. 墁饰花纹。**II** *vt*. (***par·get***(***t***)***ed***; ***par·get·***(***t***)***ing***) 在…上粗涂灰泥;涂饰。~**-work** (尤指16、17世纪的)灰泥[石膏]制品。

par·he·lic, par·he·li·a·cal [pɑː'hiːlik, ,pɑːhi'laiəkəl; pɑr`hilɪk, ,pɑrhɪ`laɪəkl̩] *a*.【气】(似)幻日的。~ **circle** [**ring**]【气】幻日环。

par·he·li·on [pɑː'hiːljən, -liən; pɑr`hilɪən, -lɪən] *n*. (*pl*. ***par·he·li·a*** [-ljə, -liə; -ljɛ, -lɪə])【气】幻日,假日〔日晕上的光轮〕。

Par·i·ah ['pæriə, 'pɑːriə; `pærɪə, `pɑrɪə] *n*. 贱民〔南部印度最下层的民众,社会地位最低〕;〔p-〕为社会所遗弃者;流浪者。

Pa·ri·an ['pɛəriən; `pɛrɪən] **I** *a*. 1. (爱琴海中盛产大理石的)帕罗斯(Paros)岛的。2.〔p-〕白色细瓷器[瓷土]的。**II** *n*. 1. 帕罗斯岛人。2.〔p-〕帕罗斯白色细瓷器[瓷土]。

pa·ri·es ['pɛəri,iːz, 'pær-; `pɛrɪ,iz, `pær-] *n*. (*pl*. **pa·ri·e·tes** [pə'raiə,tiːz; pə`raɪə,tɪz])【生】体壁。

pa·ri·e·tal [pə'raiitl; pə`raɪətl̩] **I** *a*. 1.【解】腔壁的;体壁的;颅顶部的。2.【植】周壁的,周缘的;侧膜的。3.〔美学俚〕住在校内的;大学校内的生活的。**II** *n*.【解】(颅)顶骨。

par·i-mu·tu·el ['pæri'mjuːtʃuəl; `pærɪ`mjutʃuəl] *n*.

〔F.〕**1.** 派利分成法〔赛马中扣除手续费和所得税后〕赢家分配全部赌金的方法。**2.** (按上述分享法)计算赌金的机器(= ~ machine)。

par·ing [ˈpɛəriŋ; ˋpɛrɪŋ] ***n.*** **1.** 削皮。**2.** 削下来的皮;刨花。**3.** 微少的贮蓄。*potato ~s* (削下的)洋芋皮。**~-iron** (兽医、蹄匠等用的)削蹄刀。**~-knife** 削皮刀;指甲刀。

par·i pas·su [ˈpɛəraiˈpæsjuː; ˋpɛraiˋpæsju] 〔L.〕**1.** 以同一步速[速度]。**2.** 以相同的比例。**3.** 同时。**4.** 【法】无先决权[特权],平等地。*make a ~ advance* 以同一步速前进。

P

par·i·pin·nate [ˌpæriˈpineit; ˏpærɪˋpɪnet] ***a.*** 【植】偶数羽状的〔指复叶〕。

Par·is[1] [ˈpæris; ˋpærɪs] ***n.*** **1.** 帕里斯〔姓氏〕。**2.** 【希神】帕里斯〔特洛伊王子,因诱走斯巴达王后海伦而引起特洛伊战争〕。

Par·is[2] [ˈpæris; ˋpærɪs] ***n.*** 巴黎〔法国首都〕。*~ of America* 美国的巴黎〔辛辛那提 (Cincinnati) 市的别名〕。~ **blue** 巴黎蓝。~ **Bourse** [buəs; burs]【商】巴黎证券交易所。~ **Commune**【史】巴黎公社。~ **doll** 女服裁缝用的模型人。~ **green** 巴黎绿〔颜料、杀虫药〕。~ **plaster** 塑模石膏。~ **white** 亮粉。~ **yellow** 铬黄。

par·ish [ˈpæriʃ; ˋpærɪʃ] ***n.*** **1.** 教区〔郡下的分区,每区设一教堂〕。**2.** 济贫区。**3.** 教区的全体居民;〔美〕一教会的全体信徒;〔美〕(Louisiana 州的)县。***go on the ~*** 靠教区救济。~ **child** 教区抚育的孤儿。~ **church** 〔英〕教区教堂。~ **clerk** 教区执事。~ **council** 〔英〕农村教区会。~ **lantern** 〔英方〕月亮。**~-pump** ***a.*** 教区范围的;目光偏狭的。~ **register** (教区教堂登记洗礼、命名、结婚、死亡等的)教区记事录。

pa·rish·ion·er [pəˈriʃənə; pəˋrɪʃənɚ] ***n.*** 教区居民。

Pa·ri·sian [pəˈrizjən, -ziən; pəˋrɪʒən, -zɪən] **I** ***a.*** 巴黎的,巴黎式的;巴黎人的。**II** ***n.*** 巴黎人。

Pa·ri·sienne [pərizi'en; pərɪzɪˋɛn] ***n.*** 〔F.〕巴黎女人。

par·i·syl·lab·ic, par·i·syl·lab·i·cal [ˈpærisiˈlæbik, -ikəl; ˏpærɪsɪˋlæbɪk, -ɪkl] ***a.*** (希腊语、拉丁语名词在一切词尾变化中)有同数音节的。

par·i·ty [ˈpæriti; ˋpærətɪ] ***n.*** **1.** 同等,平等。**2.** 同格,同位。**3.** 同样;类似,一致。**4.** 等量,等价。**5.** 【物】宇称(性),奇偶性。**6.** 【商】平价;价值对等。*nuclear ~* 核武器均势。*the law of ~ conservation* 【物】宇称守恒定律。*~ nonconservation* 【物】宇称不守恒。*~ of treatment* 同等待遇。***be on a ~ with*** 和…平等。***by ~ of reasoning*** 由此类推。***stand at ~*** 居于同等地位。~ **check**【自】奇偶校验。

Park [pɑːk; pɑrk] ***n.*** 帕克〔姓氏〕。

park [pɑːk; pɑrk] **I** ***n.*** **1.** 公园,…场。**2.** 囿囿;【英法】(国王特许的)猎园。**3.** 〔美〕街头广场;〔美〕运动场。**4.** 停车场;【军】(露营中放大炮、辎重等的)放置场。**5.** (放置场上所放置的)全部东西;炮兵辎重;材料厂。**6.** 养蚝所。**7.** 〔美〕(科罗拉多,怀俄明等州的)平原。**8.** 〔Scot.〕牧地,耕地。*a national ~* 国立公园。*a base-ball ~* 棒球场。*an artillery ~* 停炮场。*the P-* 〔英〕海德公园 (= Hyde P-)。

II ***vt.*** **1.** 把(某地)圈为公园[游憩场]。**2.** 把(炮车等)摆[排列]在放置场。**3.** 把(车)停在(某处);〔美俚〕把(东西)寄放在(某地),把(孩子等)交给人看管。*You may ~ your car here.* 你可以把车停在这里。*He ~ed his bag at the club.* 他把皮包摆在俱乐部里。—***vi.*** **1.** 停车;停放车辆。**2.** 〔美俚〕坐下来,安顿下来。*No ~ing here.* 此处禁止停车。***~ oneself*** 〔俚〕坐下。***~ one's frame*** 〔美俚〕休息。**~-and-ride** ***a.*** (车站附近辟出停车场)供停车和换乘公共车辆(进城上班)的。~ **home**(作为永久性住房被安置于某处的)大型活动房屋。**~ing condo**(供出租或购买的)个人泊车位。~ **land** 疏树草原。**-er** ***n.*** 停放车辆的人。

par·ka [ˈpɑːkə; ˋpɑrkə] ***n.*** 带兜帽的风雪衣,派克大衣。

Park Avenue [ˈpɑːk ˈævinjuː; ˋpɑrk ˋævɪnju] 派克大街〔美国纽约市街名,街上多大公寓,常为奢华时髦阶层的同义语〕。

Par·ker·iz·ing [ˈpɑːkəraiziŋ; ˋpɑrkəraɪzɪŋ] ***a.*** ~ **process**【冶】磷酸盐处理〔俗称磷化,钢铁防蚀法的一种〕。

Par·ker [ˈpɑːkə; ˋpɑrkɚ] ***n.*** 帕克〔姓氏,男子名〕。

par·kin [ˈpɑːkin; ˋpɑrkɪn] ***n.*** 〔英方〕麦片糖饼。

park·ing [ˈpɑːkiŋ; ˋpɑrkɪŋ] ***n.*** 〔美〕停车。~ **brake** (汽车的)手煞车。~ **light** 停车指示灯。~ **lot** 露天停车场。~ **meter** 停车计时器。~ **orbit**【宇】驻留轨道。~ **ramp** (机库前的)停机坪。~ **ticket** (违反停车规则的)罚款传票。

Par·kin·son [ˈpɑːkinsən; ˋpɑrkɪnsən] ***n.*** **~'s disease** 震颤(性)麻痹症。**~'s Law** 最大劳动量法则。

par·kin·son·ism [ˈpɑːkinsənizəm; ˋpɑrkɪnsənˏɪzm] ***n.*** **1.** 震颤(性)麻痹。**2.** 震颤(性)麻痹症 (= Parkinson's disease)。

park·ish [ˈpɑːkiʃ; ˋpɑrkɪʃ] ***a.*** 公园(似)的。

Park·man [ˈpɑːkmən; ˋpɑrkmən] ***n.*** 帕克曼〔姓氏〕。

park·way [ˈpɑːkwei; ˋpɑrkˏwe] ***n.*** 〔美〕(两旁有草地和树木的)林园式大路。

park·y [ˈpɑːki; ˋpɑrkɪ] ***a.*** 〔英俚〕寒冷的。

Parl. = Parliament; Parliamentary.

par·lance [ˈpɑːləns; ˋpɑrləns] ***n.*** **1.** 口调,腔调;(特有的)用语;说法。**2.** 〔古〕谈判;辩论。***in common ~*** 照一般的说法。***in legal ~*** 用法律上的话来说。

par·lan·do [pɑːˈlɑːndəu; parˋlando] ***n.***, ***a.*** 〔It.〕【乐】朗诵调(的)。

par·lay [ˈpɑːli, pɑːˈlei; ˋpɑrlɪ, parˋle] **I** ***vt.*** 〔美〕**1.** 把(本和利)都押作赌注。**2.** 〔口〕成功地利用;使增值。**II** ***n.*** 连本带利的赌(注)。

Par·le·men·taire [ˈpɑːləmɑ̃ːnˈtɛə; ˋpɑrləmɑ̃nˋtɛr] ***n.*** 〔F.〕军事谈判代表。

Par·ley [ˈpɑːli; ˋpɑrlɪ] ***n.*** 帕利〔姓氏〕。

par·ley [ˈpɑːli; ˋpɑrlɪ] **I** ***n.*** 会谈;(尤指与敌方的)谈判。***beat*** [***sound***] ***a ~*** (打鼓或吹号)向对方表示愿意谈判。***hold a ~ with*** (***the enemy***) 和(敌人)谈判。**II** ***vi.*** 会谈,谈判(*with*)。—***vt.*** 〔口〕讲(外国话等)。

par·ley·voo [ˌpɑːliˈvuː; ˏpɑrlɪˋvu] **I** ***n.*** (*pl.* ~*s*) 〔英谑〕**1.** 法国话。**2.** 〔P-〕法国人。**II** ***vi.*** 说法国话。

par·lez-vous [ˈpɑːleivuː; ˋparlevu] ***vi.*** 〔美俚〕讲法语〔来自法语 Parlez-vous français? 你会讲法国话吗?〕。*Can you ~?* 你会讲法语吗?

par·lia·ment [ˈpɑːləmənt; ˋpɑrləmənt] ***n.*** **1.** 议会,国会;立法机构。**2.** 〔P-〕英国[加拿大]议会;〔P-〕(1789 年法国大革命前的)最高法院。**3.** 中古世纪弗罗伦萨 (Florence) 的武人集会。**4.** 薄姜饼。*a member of P-* 〔英〕下院议员〔略作 M.P.〕。***convene*** [***summon***] ***~*** 召开议会。***dissolve P-*** 解散议会。***enter*** [***go into***] ***P-*** 成为下院议员。***open P-*** 宣布议会开会。***P- sits*** [***rises***]. 议会开会[休会]。**P- Act** 〔英〕(1911 年限制上院否决权的)议会法案。~ **cake** 薄姜饼。~ **hinge** 长羽铰链。

par·lia·men·tal [ˌpɑːləˈmentəl; ˏpɑrləˋmɛntl] ***a.*** = parliamentary.

par·lia·men·ta·ri·an [ˌpɑːləmenˈtɛəriən; ˏpɑrləmɛnˋtɛrɪən] **I** ***n.*** **1.** 议院法规专家。**2.** 议会雄辩家。**3.** 〔英〕国会议员;〔P-〕【英史】十七世纪内战时期反抗查理一世的议会党人。**II** ***a.*** 议会(派)的。

par·lia·men·ta·rism [ˌpɑːləˈmentərizəm; ˏpɑrləˋmɛntərɪzm] ***n.*** **1.** 议会主义。**2.** 议会制度。

par·lia·men·ta·ry [ˌpɑːləˈmentəri; ˏpɑrləˋmɛntərɪ] ***a.*** **1.** 议会的;国会的;议会制定的;根据议会法的。**2.** 议员的。**3.** (言语等)适合议会的;〔口〕(语气)慎重有礼的。*an old ~ hand* 精通议院法等的人。~ **agent** 〔英〕政党的法律顾问。~ **borough** 〔英〕议员选举区。~ **company**【商】公益事业公司。~ **language** (像议会里用的)慎重有礼的言语。~ **procedure** 议院法。~ **train** 〔英〕

工人减价列车，廉价列车。

par·lo(u)r [ˈpɑːlə; ˋpɑrlɚ] **I** *n*. **1.** 〔古、方〕起居室。**2.** 客厅；会客室；接待室。**3.** 〔美〕养业室；办公室；摄影室；诊室，手术室；停尸场。**4.** (旅馆等的)休息室。*a billiard* ~ 弹子房。*a dental* ~ 牙科诊室。*a beauty* ~ 美容室。*an ice-cream* ~ 冷饮店。**II** *a*. **1.** 客厅的；适于客厅使用的。**2.** 只会空谈的。~ **boarder** (出高价住在校长家里的)特别寄宿生。~ **car** 特等豪华客车车厢。~ **end** 〔美〕公事车的后部。~ **game** (猜谜答问等)室内游戏。~ **girl** = ~ maid. ~ **guest** 〔美〕受欢迎的包饭人。~ **jumping** 〔美〕盗窃。~ **maid** (负责开门、侍候餐桌的)客厅女仆。~ **match** 〔美〕(不含硫磺的)安全火柴。~ **pink** 只会空谈的温和激进派。~ [**armchair**] **socialist** 空谈的社会主义者。~ **tricks** 〔贬〕社交上的成就；为了引人注目而采取的举动。

par·lous [ˈpɑːləs; ˋpɑrləs] 〔古、谑〕**I** *a*. **1.** 危险的；靠不住的。**2.** 麻烦的；难对付的。**3.** 厉害的，精明的。**II** *ad*. 非常地，极；…得吓人。*She is* ~ *handsome*. 她潇洒极了。

par·ly [ˈpɑːli; ˋpɑrlɪ] *n*. 〔俚〕= parliamentary train.

Par·me·san [ˌpɑːmiˈzæn; ˏpɑrməˋzæn] **I** *a*. (意大利北部城市)巴马 (Parma) 的。**II** *n*. 巴马干酪 (= ~ cheese)。

Par·nas·si·an [pɑːˈnæsiən, -sjən; pɑrˋnæsɪən, -sjən] **I** *a*. **1.** (希腊)帕纳萨斯 (Parnassus) 山的。**2.** 高蹈派诗人的。*the* ~ *school* 高蹈派〔19 世纪下半叶法国诗坛的一派，鼓吹艺术至上，强调形式的谨严〕。**II** *n*. 高蹈派诗人。

Par·nas·sus [pɑːˈnæsəs; pɑrˋnæsəs] *n*. **1.** 帕纳萨斯〔希腊中部山峰名，传说为太阳神阿波罗及诗神缪斯的灵地〕。**2.** 〔总称〕文学界；诗坛，文坛。**3.** 诗，文学；诗文集。*climb* ~ 学作诗。

Par·nell [pɑːˈnel; pɑrˋnel] *n*. 帕内尔〔姓氏〕。

pa·ro·chi·al [pəˈrəukjəl, -kiəl; pəˋrokɪəl, -kjəl] *a*. **1.** 教区的。**2.** 镇村的；地方性的；狭隘的，偏狭的。*a* ~ *board* 〔Scot.〕教区(贫民救济)委员会。*a* ~ *school* 教区附属学校。

pa·ro·chi·al·ism, pa·ro·chial·i·ty [pəˈrəukjəlizm, pəˌrəukiˈæliti; pəˋrokɪəlɪzm, pəˏrokɪˋælətɪ] *n*. **1.** 教区[镇村]制度。**2.** 地方观念；眼界狭小，偏狭。

pa·ro·chi·al·ize [pəˈrəukiəlaiz; pəˋrokɪəlaɪz] *vt*. **1.** 使施行教区制。**2.** 使地方化；使眼界狭小。

par·o·dist [ˈpærədist; ˋpærədɪst] *n*. 嘲弄性模仿作品[诗文]的作者；〔贬〕不高明的模仿者。

par·o·dos [ˈpærədɔs; ˋpærədɑs] *n*. **1.** (通到乐队席的)后台过道。**2.** (古希腊戏剧中)歌唱队的上场。

par·o·dy [ˈpærədi; ˋpærədɪ] **I** *n*. **1.** (为嘲弄某作者或其诗文而改作的)滑稽性模仿诗文[作品]。**2.** 拙劣的模仿。**II** *vt*. (*-died*) **1.** 把(他人诗文)模仿成滑稽体裁。**2.** 拙劣地模仿。

pa·rol [pəˈrəul; pəˋrol] **I** *n*. 【法】口头答辩；口头言词。*prove by* ~ 口头证明。**II** *a*. 【法】口头的；没有盖章的。

pa·role [pəˈrəul; pəˋrol] **I** *n*. **1.** 誓言 (= ~ of honour)；【军】(俘虏的)释放宣誓。**2.** 【军】(卫队军官所用的)特别口令，特别暗号。**3.** 〔美〕假释许可；假释出狱；临时入境许可。**4.** 【法】= parol.
II *a*. **1.** 假释的。**2.** = parol. *break one's* ~ 违誓，企图违誓脱逃。*on* ~ **1.** (俘虏)得宣誓释放。**2.** 〔美〕暂许出狱，准许假释(出狱仍在警察管制之下)；临时入境许可。*out on* ~ 〔美俚〕(女子)离了婚的。
III *vt*. **1.** 使(俘虏)宣誓后释放。**2.** 〔美〕准许(犯人)假释出狱；许可(外国人)临时入境。**pa·rol·a·ble** *a*. 可凭宣誓释放的；可假释的。

pa·rol·ee [pəˌrəuˈliː; pəˏroˋli] *n*. 〔美〕得假释出狱的人，假释犯。

par·o·no·ma·si·a [ˌpærənəuˈmeizia; ˏpærənoˋmeʒə] *n*. **1.** 【修】(尤指同音异义的)双关语〔如 sole 和 soul〕。**2.** 文字游戏。

par·o·nym [ˈpærənim; ˋpærənɪm] *n*. **1.** 同源词〔如 wise, wisely, wisdom 等〕。**2.** (同音而拼法、语源、意义均不同的)同音形似词〔如 hair 和 hare〕。

pa·ron·y·mous [pəˈrɔniməs; pəˋrɑnəməs] *a*. (词)同词源的，同音的。

par·o·quet [ˈpærəket; ˋpærəˏkɛt] *n*. 【动】长尾小鹦鹉 (= parakeet)。

pa·rot·ic [pəˈrɔtik, -ˈrəut-; pəˋrɑtɪk] *a*. 【解】近耳的。

pa·rot·id [pəˈrɔtid; pəˋrɑtɪd] **I** *n*. **1.** 【解】腮腺，耳下腺 (= ~ gland)。**2.** (武士头盔上的)护耳。**II** *a*. 耳边的，耳下的，腮腺的。

par·o·ti·tis [ˌpærəˈtaitis; ˏpærəˋtaɪtɪs] *n*. 【医】腮腺炎。

Par·ou·si·a [ˌpɑːruːˈsiə, pəˈruːziə; pɑruˋsɪə, pəˋruzɪə] *n*. 【宗】基督再临(= second coming)。

par·ox·ysm [ˈpærəksizəm; ˋpærəksˏɪzəm] *n*. **1.** (病等的)突然发作；阵发；(感情等的)激发。**2.** (突然而来的)活动，努力。*in a* ~ *of rage* 突然发起怒来。*a* ~ *of coughing* 一阵咳嗽。

par·ox·ys·mal [ˌpærəkˈsizməl; ˏpærəkˋsɪzml̩] *a*. 发作性的；爆发性的。**-ly** *ad*.

par·ox·y·tone [pæˈrɔksitəun; pæˋrɑksəˏton] *a*., *n*. 希腊语词尾倒数第二音节有重音的(词)。

par·quet [ˈpɑːkei, ˈpɑːkit; pɑrˋke, ˋpɑrkɪt] **I** *n*. **1.** 木条镶花地板；席纹地面。**2.** 〔美〕(戏院的)前厅，正厅前排。**II** *vt*. **1.** 在…铺镶花地板。**2.** 用镶木制。~ **circle** 〔美〕(戏院的)正厅后排，后厅〔在楼厅下〕。~ **strip** 小板条。

par·quet·ry [ˈpɑːkitri; ˋpɑrkɪtrɪ] *n*. 木条镶花；镶木细工；镶花地板。

Parr [pɑː; pɑr] *n*. 帕尔〔姓氏〕。

parr [pɑː; pɑr] *n*. (*pl*. ~*s*, 〔集合词〕~)【动】幼鲑。

par·ra·keet [ˈpærəkiːt; ˋpærəˏkit] *n*. = parakeet.

par·ra·mat·ta [ˌpærəˈmætə; ˏpærəˋmætə] *n*. 毛葛；棉毛呢 (= paramatta)。

par·rel, par·ral [ˈpærəl; ˋpærəl] *n*. 【海】装于帆桁中央部两侧的索具。

par·ri·cide [ˈpærisaid; ˋpærəˏsaɪd] *n*. **1.** 杀父母(的人)；杀长上(的人)；杀主人(的人)，叛国(者)。**2.** 叛逆罪；忤逆罪。**parri·cid·al** [ˌpæriˈsaidl; ˏpærəˋsaɪdl] *a*.

Par·rish [ˈpæriʃ; ˋpærɪʃ] *n*. 帕里什〔姓氏〕。

par·rot [ˈpærət; ˋpærət] **I** *n*. **1.** 【动】鹦鹉。**2.** 学舌者，应声虫；学人行为的人。**II** *vt*. **1.** 鹦鹉学舌般复述；做…的应声虫；随声附和；机械地模仿(别人的行为)。**2.** 训练(某人)使机械地复述。~ *the textbook* 死背教科书。—*vi*. 机械地复述，死背；机械地模仿。~**-cry** 人云亦云的叫喊，学舌。~ **disease**, ~ **fever** 【医】鹦鹉病(= psittacosis)。~ **fish** 【动】隆头鱼；鹦嘴鱼。**-let** (南美)小鹦鹉。**-like** *a*. 鹦鹉般的。

par·rot·ry [ˈpærətri; ˋpærətrɪ] *n*. 学舌；机械模仿。

Par·ry [ˈpæri; ˋpærɪ] *n*. 帕里〔姓氏〕。

par·ry [ˈpæri; ˋpærɪ] **I** *vt*. (*-ried*) **1.** 挡开；避开，闪开(枪锋等)。**2.** 回避(别人的质问)。~ *a question* 避而不答，回避问题；搪塞。— *vi*. **1.** 挡开打击。**2.** 避而不答。**II** *n*. **1.** 挡开，闪避。**2.** 遁辞。

parse [pɑːz; pɑrs] *vt*. 【语】从语法上分析；解析(词句等)。

par·sec [pɑːˈsek; ˋpɑrˏsɛk] *n*. 【天】秒差距(天体距离单位，= 3.26 光年)。

Par·see [pɑːˈsiː, ˈpɑːˈsiː; pɑrˋsi, ˋpɑrˋsi] *n*. **1.** 印度祆教徒〔公元 7—8 世纪逃到印度的波斯祆教教徒的后裔〕。**2.** 祆教经典上的波斯语〔萨珊 (Sassan) 王朝时代的波斯语〕。**-ism** *n*. 印度祆教。

Par·si [ˈpɑːsiː; ˋpɑrˋsi] *n*. = Parsee.

par·si·mo·ni·ous [ˌpɑːsiˈməunjəs, -niəs; ˏpɑrsəˋmonjəs, -nɪəs] *a*. 吝啬的；过度俭省的。

par·si·mo·ny [ˈpɑːsiməni; ˋpɑrsəˏmonɪ] *n*. 吝啬，小气；过度节俭。

P

pars·ley [ˈpɑːsli; ˋparslɪ] ***n.*** 【植】欧芹,洋芫荽。

pars·nip [ˈpɑːsnip; ˋparsnəp] ***n.*** 【植】欧洲防风;欧洲防风根。

Par·son [ˈpɑːsn; ˋparsn̩] ***n.*** 帕森〔姓氏〕。

par·son [ˈpɑːsn; ˋparsn̩] ***n.*** **1.** 教区牧师。**2.**〔口〕牧师。~ *mortal*【法】终身牧师。*the ~'s nose*〔口〕(煮熟供食用的)鸡[家禽]屁股。*the ~'s week* 从本星期一到下星期六〔13天〕。~**-bird** (纽西兰的)食蜜鸟。**-age** 牧师住宅;牧师地产,牧师圣俸。**-son·ic, -son·i·cal** [-ˈsɔnik(əl); -ˋsɑnɪk(l̩)] ***a.*** (像)牧师的。

P

part [pɑːt; part] **I** ***n.*** **1.** 部分,一部分;局部(*opp.* whole)。★此义常省去不定冠词。如:a great ~ of one's money. I lost ~ of my money. **2.** (某特殊的)部分,部(*the middle ~ of the 19th century* 19世纪中期。*the upper ~ of one's face* 脸的上部);〔*pl.*〕身体的一部分(*the inner ~s* 内脏。*the ~s = the private ~s* 阴部,私处);配件,零件(*aeroplane ~s* 飞机零件。*repair ~s* 备用零件)。**3.**【数】〔前接序数词〕…分之一(*a third ~* 三分之一。*two third ~s* 三分之二。简称 *a third, two thirds*);〔前接基数词〕…分之…(*three ~s* 四分之三);〔配合比〕分(*four ~s of vinegar to one of oil* 四分醋一分油)。**4.**【数】整除部分;部分分数;部分分式。**5.**〔书籍、戏剧、诗等的〕部,篇,卷。**6.** 重要部分,要素,成分;(好、坏等的)方面。**7.**〔*pl.*〕地方,领域,附近。**8.** 关系,关心的事,任务,职责,本分;作用(*It's not my part to interfere*. 我不便干涉)。**9.** (演员的)角色;台词。**10.** (交战、争议、贸易等的)一方,…方面(*No word was spoken by either ~*. 双方都没有讲话)。**11.**〔*pl.*〕资质,才能(*a man of ~s* 有才能的人)。**12.**【乐】声部,乐曲的一部。**13.**【语】词类(*~s of speech* 词类)。**14.**〔美〕分发缝。***bear a ~ in*** 在…中有一份,参与…。***do one's ~*** 尽职责,尽自己本分。***for one's ~*** 至于某人,讲到某人,对某人来说。***for the greater ~*** 大部分,大半;在很大程度上。***for the most ~*** 在极大程度上;就绝大部分而言;多半。***have neither ~ nor lot in*** = ***have no ~ in*** 和…一点关系也没有。***in bad*** [***ill, evil***] ~ 心怀怨怒地;生气地;没有好感地。***in good ~*** 欣然;不生气地;毫无恶感地。***in ~*** 一部分地;有几成;在某种程度上,多少。***in ~s*** 分开,分次;分册;处处,到处。***in these ~s*** 在这一带,在这些地方。***on one's ~*** = ***on the ~ of sb.*** **1.** 就某人方面;就…而言,代表…。**2.** 由…表现出来的;由…所作出的(*It was a very queer conduct on the ~ of Smith*. 那是史密斯的一个怪举动。*He apologized on the ~ of his friend*. 他替他的朋友道了歉)。***on the one ~ ... on the other ~*** 一方面…,另一方面;第一点…,第二点…。~ ***and parcel*** 重要[基本]部分(*of*)。***play*** [***take, act***] ***a ~*** 扮演…角色;假装(*play the ~ of Hamlet* 扮演哈姆雷特)。***play one's ~*** 尽本分。***take a noble*** [***an active***] ~ 采取豪爽[积极]行动。***take*** (*sb.'s words*) ***in bad*** [***good***] ~ 恶[善]意解释(某人的话等)。***take ~ in*** 参加;贡献。***take ~ with, take sb.'s ~, take the ~ of sb.*** 祖护;支持。***the best ~*** 最大[最多]的部分。***the better ~*** 较大[较多]的部分;较好的办法[计策]。***the ninth ~ of a man***〔贬〕裁缝。

II ***vt.*** **1.** 分,使分开,分割;切断,断绝(关系等)。**2.**【海】斩断(缆绳、锚链等);使(缆索、锚链等)断裂。**3.** 拉开;离间。**4.** 把…分成若干份;分配。**5.** (用化学方法)分解(出)。**6.** 区别[辨别](学说、理论)。**7.**〔英方〕放弃(财产等)。~ *one's hair* 把头发分开。*A smile ~ed her lips*. 笑得她嘴唇儿绽开了。—***vi.*** **1.** 分,分开,分离;断裂;(河流等)分叉,分道。**2.** 跟…分手(*from; with*)断绝关系。**3.**【海】(缆索等)脱了。**4.** 放弃。**5.** 死。**6.**〔口〕付钱。*The clouds ~ed*. 云散开了。~ ***brass rags with***〔俚〕跟…绝交〔水手语〕。~ ***company with*** 跟…分手[绝交];跟…意见不合。~ ***friends*** 友好地分手。~ ***from*** 和…分手,〔罕〕放掉。~ ***with*** 跟…分别;解雇,辞退;卖掉(东西)。

III ***ad.*** 部分地;有几分,多少。*It is made ~ of iron and ~ of wood*. 它部分由铁部分由木而制成。

IV ***a.*** 部分的,局部的。*a part truth* 部分真理。~ **exchange** 部分交货贸易。~ **music** 合唱[合奏]乐曲。~**-off**〔加勒比英语〕隔房屏风。~ **owner**【法】(尤指船舶的)共有人。~ **singing** 重唱(法)。~ **song** 合唱歌曲〔尤指无伴奏的〕。~**-time** **1.** ***n.*** 业余时间。**2.** ***a.*** 非全日工作的,兼任的,兼职的(*opp.* full-time);定时的(*a ~-time job* 零活,非全日工作。*a ~-time high school* 定时制高等学校)。**3.** ***ad.*** 花部分时间;兼任地;兼职地。~**timer** ***n.*** 兼职者;定时制学校的学生;〔口〕零工。~**way** ***ad.*** 到某种程度;部分地。~ **work** 分册出版的作品。**-ly** ***ad.*** **1.** 部分地,不完全地。**2.** 几分,多少,在一定程度上。

part. = participle; particular.

part.adj. = participial adjective 分词形容词。

par·take [pɑːˈteik; pəˋtek] ***vi.*** (***par·took*** [-ˈtuk; -ˋtʊk]; ***par·tak·en*** [-ˈteikən; -ˋtekən]; ***-tak·ing***) **1.** 参与,参加(*of; in*)。**2.** 分享,分担;陪同(吃饭)(*of*);吃[喝]一点儿(*of*)。**3.**〔口〕吃光,喝光(*of*)。**4.** 有点…,带有某种性质[特征等](*of*)。*Will you ~ of our breakfast with us?* 和我们一道吃早饭好吗? *His manner ~s of insolence*. 他的态度有点傲慢。—***vt.*** **1.** 参加;分担;分得,分享,共享。**2.** 同吃[喝等];单独吃[喝]。~ *a meal with sb.* 同某人一道吃饭。~ *one's meal* (自己)吃饭。

par·tak·er [pɑːˈteikə; parˋtekɚ] ***n.*** 有关系的人,参与者;陪伴者;共享者;分担者(*of; in*)。

par·tan [ˈpɑːtən; ˋpartən] ***n.*** 〔Scot.〕蟹。

parted [ˈpɑːtid; ˋpartɪd] ***a.*** **1.** 分开的;分成部分的;分散的。**2.**【植】深裂的〔常用以构成复合词〕。**3.**〔古〕已死去的。

par·terre [pɑːˈtɛə; parˋtɛr] ***n.*** **1.** 花坛,花圃。**2.** (法国剧场的)正厅;(美国剧场的)池子〔在 gallery 下〕。**3.** (包括房址的)一块平地。

par·the·no·car·py [ˈpɑːθinəuˌkɑːpi; ˋparθənoˏkarpɪ] ***n.*** 【植】单性结实。**-no·car·pic** [ˌpɑːθinəuˈkɑːpik; ˏparθənoˋkarpɪk] ***a.*** **-no·car·pi·cally** ***ad.***

par·the·no·gen·e·sis [ˈpɑːθinəuˈdʒenisis; ˏparθənoˋdʒɛnəsɪs] ***n.*** 【生】单性生殖,孤雌生殖。**-no·ge·net·ic** [-dʒiˈnetik; -dʒɪˋnɛtɪk] ***a.***

par·the·nog·e·ny [ˌpɑːθiˈnɔdʒini; ˏparθəˋnadʒənɪ] ***n.*** = parthenogenesis.

par·the·no·go·nid·i·um [ˈpɑːθinəugəˈnidiəm; ˋparθɪnogəˋnɪdɪəm] ***n.*** 【生】无性生殖细胞。

Par·the·non [ˈpɑːθinən; ˋparθəˏnan] ***n.*** (希腊雅典祭祀雅典娜女神的)巴台农神殿。

Par·thi·an [ˈpɑːθiən, -θjən; ˋparθɪən, -θjən] **I** ***a.*** 【史】(伊朗北部古国)帕提亚(Parthia)人的,安息人的;〔转喻〕最后的。**II** ***n.*** 帕提亚人〔即安息人〕。~ **glance** 临死的一瞥。~ **shaft** [**arrow, shot**] 临退时发出的最后的一箭,回马箭;临走时所说的话[做的事];临退场时的台词。

par·ti [pɑːˈtiː; parˋti] ***n.*** 〔F.〕(结婚的)理想的对象,佳偶。*a good* [*an eligible*] ~ 好配偶。~ ***pris*** [ˈpriː; ˋpri] 成见,偏见。

par·tial [ˈpɑːʃəl; ˋparʃəl] ***a.*** **1.** 一部分的,局部的,不完全的。**2.** 不公平的;偏袒的。**3.** 偏爱的,特别欢喜的(*to*)。**4.**【植】后生的,再生的。~ *drought* 小旱。~ *in one's judgement* 判断不公平的。***be ~ to*** 偏爱(*He is too ~ to tobacco*. 他太欢喜抽烟了)。~ **fractions**【数】部分分数[式]。~ **pressure**【物】分压力。~ **eclipse**【天】偏蚀。~ **vacuum**【物】未尽真空。~ **tone**【音】陪音,泛音;【物】谐音。**-ly** ***ad.*** **-ness** ***n.*** = partiality.

par·ti·al·i·ty [ˌpɑːʃiˈæliti; ˏparʃɪˋælətɪ] ***n.*** **1.** 偏心,不公平。**2.** 偏爱;特殊爱好;癖好(*for, to*)。**3.** 局部性。

par·ti·ble [ˈpɑːtibl; ˋpartəbl̩] ***a.*** 可分的,可剖分的。

par·ti·ceps cri·mi·nis [ˈpɑːtiˌseps ˈkriminis; ˋpɑrtəˌseps ˋkrɪmənɪs] 〔L.〕同犯,同谋。

par·tic·i·pance, -pancy [pɑːˈtisipəns, -si; pɑrˋtɪsɪpəns, -sɪ] *n*. 参与,共享。

par·tic·i·pant [pɑːˈtisipənt; pəˋtɪsəpənt] **I** *a*. 参加的,有关系的 (*of*)。**II** *n*. 参加者,与会代表;参与国。*an active* ~ *in* 积极参加…的人。*treaty* ~*s* 条约参加国。~ **observation** (社会学家等通过参加研究对象的活动进行的)现场观察研究。

par·tic·i·pate [pɑːˈtisipeit; pəˋtɪsəˌpet] *vi*. **1.** 参与,参加,有关系;分担;共享。**2.** 有几分(…的性质等)(*of*)。~ *in a discussion* 参加讨论。—*vt*. 分享;分担。*I* ~ *your suffering and joy*. 我和你同甘共苦。**-i·pat·ing** *a*. **1.** 由多人[多方]参加的。**2.** (股票等)使持有人有权分享利益的。

par·tic·i·pa·tion [pɑːˌtisiˈpeiʃən; pɑrˌtɪsəˋpeʃən] *n*. 关系,参与,参加,加入;合作;分享。*full* ~ *in the benefit* 分享全部权益。

par·tic·i·pa·tor [pɑːˈtisipeitə; pɑrˋtɪsəˌpetə] *n*. = participant (*n*.).

par·tic·i·pa·to·ry [pɑːˈtisipətəri; pɑrˋtɪsəpəˌtorɪ] *a*. 提高参加机会的,供人分享的。~ **drama** 由观众参与演出的戏剧。~ **democracy** 分享民主制。

par·ti·cip·i·al [ˌpɑːtiˈsipiə; ˌpɑrtəˋsɪpɪəl] *a*. 【语法】分词(状)的。~ **adjective** 【语法】分词形容词。**-ly** *ad*.

par·ti·ci·ple [ˈpɑːtisipl; ˋpɑrtəsəpl] *n*. 【语法】分词。*a present* [*past*] ~ 现在[过去]分词。

par·ti·ci·pled [ˈpɑːtisipld; ˋpɑrtəsəpld] *ad*. 〔俚〕真,极,怪〔分词形咒骂语 damned 等的委婉代用语〕。*They are so* ~ *sensitive*. 他们真是太敏感了。

par·ti·cle [ˈpɑːtikl; ˋpɑrtɪkl] *n*. **1.** 颗粒,微粒;微量,极少量。**2.** 【物、数】粒子,质点。**3.** 【语法】虚词,不变词〔冠词、副词、介词、连接词、感叹词等〕;小品词〔yes, no 等〕,词缀。**4.** 〔古〕(文件中的)条,项。**5.** 【天主】一小片圣饼。*He has not a* ~ *of sense*. 他一点脑子也没有。*fundamental* [*elementary*] ~*s* 【物】基本质点,基本粒子。~ **accelerator** 【核】粒子加速器。~ **beam** 【物】粒子束(~ *beam weapons* 粒子束武器,射线武器)。~ **board** 刨花胶合板。

par·ti-col·o(u)red [ˈpɑːtikʌləd; ˋpɑrtɪˌkʌləd] *a*. **1.** 杂色的,斑驳的。**2.** 多样化的;(故事等)变化多的。

par·ti·cu·lar [pəˈtikjulə; pəˋtɪkjələ] **I** *a*. **1.** 特殊的,特别的;特有的,独特的;异常的;显著的。**2.** 特定的;个别的;各个的,各自的;独自的,个人的。**3.** 分项的,列举的。**4.** 详细的,精密的。**5.** 严格的;讲究的;苛求的;爱挑剔的。**6.** 【逻】特称的。*this* ~ *question* (特别是)这一个问题。*Why do people dislike this* ~ *tax*? 人们为什么单单讨厌这一种税呢? *my* ~ *interests* 个人利益。*Mr. P-* 〔谑〕挑三剔四的人物。*a* ~ *proposition* 【逻】特称命题。*be* ~ *about what one eats* 讲究吃喝。*be* ~ *over one's clothes* 讲究穿戴。*exact in every* ~ 正确到毫厘不差。*for no* ~ *reason* 并没有特殊理由。*from the general to the* ~ 从一般到个别。*give a full and* ~ *account* 完整而精确地说明。
II *n*. **1.** (可分类、列举的)项目;(消息等的)一条,一项,一点;某一事项。**2.** 〔*pl*.〕详细情节,细情,细目。**3.** 特色,特点;【逻】特称。*the London* ~ 伦敦的特点〔指雾〕。*give* ~*s* 详述,细讲。*go* [*enter*] *into* ~*s* 详细列出;详细叙述。*in every* ~ 在一切方面。*in* ~ 特别,尤其;一一,详细。

par·tic·u·lar·ism [pəˈtikjulərizəm; pəˋtɪkjələrɪzm] *n*. **1.** 完全忠于一党[一种制度,一种理论,一种利益]。**2.** 【宗】特殊神宠论。**3.** 允许各州[各邦]政治上独立的政策。**4.** 以单一因素阐明复杂的社会现象的倾向。

par·tic·u·lar·i·ty [pəˌtikjuˈlæriti; pəˌtɪkjəˋlærətɪ] *n*. **1.** 特别,特殊;特殊性;特性,特征;个性;癖性。**2.** 精确;细致;详细。**3.** 过分讲究;挑剔。**4.** 〔常 *pl*.〕细目;私事。

par·tic·u·lar·ize [pəˈtikjuləraiz; pəˋtɪkjələˌraɪz] *vt*., *vi*. **1.** (使)特殊化。**2.** 详述,细论;缕述。**3.** 列举,分列;特别指出;大书特书。**-lar·i·za·tion** [-ˈzeiʃən; -ˋzeʃən] *n*.

par·tic·u·lar·ly [pəˈtikjuləli; pəˋtɪkjələlɪ] *ad*. **1.** 分别,个别;特别,尤其,格外。**2.** 详细地,细致地。*I cannot go into it* ~ *now*. 我现在不能详细讲它。*a* ~ *fine day* 天气特别好。

par·tic·u·late [pəˈtikjulit, -ˌleit; pɑrˋtɪkjəlet, -ˌlet] **I** *a*. 粒子状的,微粒的,颗粒的。**II** *n*. 粒子,微粒。~ **inheritance** 【遗】单独遗传,颗粒遗传说。

part·ing [ˈpɑːtiŋ; ˋpɑrtɪŋ] **I** *a*. **1.** 临别的,临别纪念的;最后的;离去的;将要过去的;临终的,临死的。**2.** 分离的,分隔的,分开的。*a* ~ *gift* 临别纪念品。*a* ~ *reception* 欢送会。~ *words* 临别的话,临别赠言。*a* ~ *line* 分隔线。**II** *n*. **1.** 分别,离别;死亡。**2.** 分离,分裂,裂开。**3.** (道路的)岔口;(头发的)分缝;分界;分界处;分界线;分界点。**4.** 分开物,分离物;【冶】分金〔指有色金属如金银的分离〕;【机】(铸工)分离砂,分离材料。*the* ~ *of the ways* 岔口,道路分歧点;十字路口。*at the* ~ *of the ways* 处在十字路口。

par·ti·san[1], **par·ti·zan**[1] [ˌpɑːtiˈzæn; ˋpɑrtəzn] **I** *n*. **1.** 党羽,党人;同类;党派观念强的人;坚决支持者。**2.** 【军】游击队(队员)。**II** *a*. **1.** 党派性的;有偏袒的。**2.** 由一个党派组成[控制]的。**3.** 游击队的。~ **spirit** 党派性。~ **warfare** 游击战。**-ship** *n*. **1.** 党派性,对党派的效忠;党派偏见。**2.** 同类,同党。

par·ti·san[2], **par·ti·zan**[2] [ˈpɑːtizn; ˋpɑrtɪzn] *n*. 【史】(16—17 世纪)戟的一种;戟兵。

-partism *comb. f*. 表示"党派制": multi-*partism*.

par·ti·ta [pɑːˈtiːtə; pɑrˋtitə] *n*. **1.** 一种组曲〔尤指十八世纪的〕。**2.** 一种变奏曲。

par·tite [ˈpɑːtait; ˋpɑrtaɪt] *a*. **1.** 分裂的;分成若干部分的〔常组成复合词,如 bi~ 分成二分的, tri~ 分成三分的等〕。**2.** 【植】深裂的。~ **leaf** 深裂叶。

par·ti·tion [pɑːˈtiʃən; pɑrˋtɪʃən] **I** *n*. **1.** 分割;分开;被分开;区分,划分,配分。**2.** 区分线,区分物,隔开物;隔板,隔墙。**3.** 部分;隔开部分;隔开的房间。**4.** 【植】隔膜;【法】分财产;【逻】(把一个类别)分成部分。*a* ~ *line* 缝合线。*a* ~ *wall* 公墙,共有壁。**II** *vt*. **1.** 把…分成部分,分割,区分,瓜分(土地等)。**2.** (用隔板等)隔开(*off*)。~ *a house into rooms* 把房屋隔成若干房间。~ *off part of a room* 隔出房间的一部分。

par·ti·tive [ˈpɑːtitiv; ˋpɑrtətɪv] **I** *a*. **1.** 区分的;分隔的。**2.** 【语法】部分的;表示部分的。*a* ~ *adjective* 部分形容词。**II** *n*. 【语法】表示部分的词〔如: some, few, any 等〕。**-ly** *ad*.

Part·let [ˈpɑːtlit; ˋpɑrtlɪt] *n*. 〔古〕**1.** 〔拟人称语〕母鸡〔常作 Dame ~〕。**2.** 老太婆。

part·let [ˈpɑːtlit; ˋpɑrtlɪt] *n*. (16 世纪妇女穿的)打褶绣花紧身衣。

part·ner [ˈpɑːtnə; ˋpɑrtnə] **I** *n*. **1.** 合伙人;合作者,伙伴;配手,搭档 (*with*, *in*)。**2.** 配偶〔夫或妻〕。**3.** (跳舞等的)舞伴;同组伙伴。**4.** 【法】(合营事业的)合股人。**5.** 〔*pl*.〕【海】桅孔加固板,(护持)木框。*a* ~ *in crime* 共犯。*an acting* [*an active*, *a working*] ~ 担任经营业务的合股人。*a dormant* [*secret*, *sleeping*, *silent*] 隐名合伙人。~ ***for life*** 终身配偶[伴侣]。**II** *vt*. **1.** 同…合作[合伙];做…的伙伴。**2.** 使有搭档[配手]。—*vi*. 做搭档,当配手(*with*)。**-less** *a*. 无伙伴[配手]的。

part·ner·ship [ˈpɑːtnəʃip; ˋpɑrtnəˌʃɪp] *n*. **1.** 合伙[合作]关系;伙伴关系。**2.** 全体合伙[合股]人。**3.** 合伙契约。**4.** 合营公司。*a general* [*an unlimited*] ~ 普通[无限]公司。*a special* [*limited*] ~ 有限公司。***in*** ~ ***with*** 和…合伙[合作]。

par·took [pɑːˈtuk; pɑrˋtuk] partake 的过去式。

Par·tridge [ˈpɑːtridʒ; ˋpɑrtrɪdʒ] *n*. 帕特里奇〔姓氏〕。

P

par·tridge [ˈpɑːtridʒ; ˋpartrɪdʒ] ***n.*** (*pl.* ~*s*,〔集合词〕~)【动】鹧鸪;〔美〕松鸡。~ **berry**【植】蔓虎刺(果)。~**-wood** 一种红色硬木。

par·tu·ri·ent [pɑːˈtjuəriənt; parˋtjʊrɪənt] ***a.*** **1.** 产子的,生产的;临产的;多产的。**2.**〔喻〕即将形成的。*a* ~ *heifer* 临产的小母牛。

par·tu·ri·fa·cient [pɑːˌtjuəriˈfeiʃənt, -ˌtuəri-; parˏtjʊrəˋfeʃənt, -ˏturə-] **I** ***a.*** 催产的。**II** ***n.*** 催产剂。

par·tu·ri·tion [ˌpɑːtjuəˈriʃən;ˏpartjʊˋrɪʃən] ***n.*** 分娩;生产。

par·ty [ˈpɑːti; ˋpartɪ] **I** ***n.*** **1.** 党,党派;政党;结党,党派活动。**2.**【军】特遣队,分遣队,部队。**3.** (交际性质的)聚会,集会,宴会。**4.** 同行者,随行人员;同类,伙伴。**5.**【法】诉讼关系人〔原告或被告〕,当事人,一方;(证件上的)署名人;共犯者。**6.**〔俚、谑〕(一个)人。*a political* ~ 政党。*the Communist P-* 共产党。*the Socialists P-* 社会党。*the Socialist-Democratic P-* 社会民主党。*the Workers' P-* 工人党。*a reading* ~ 读书会。*a tea* ~ 茶会。*a dinner* ~ 宴会。*Dr. Johnson and his* ~ 约翰逊博士及其一行。*the parties* (*concerned*) 有关各方。*a* ~ *interested* = *an interested* ~ 关系人。*a disinterested* [*third*] ~ 非关系人,第三者。*a landing* ~ 登陆特遣队。*an old* ~〔俚〕老头儿。*the* ~ *in the white hat*〔俚〕戴着白帽子的那家伙。***be*** [***become***] ***a*** ~ ***to*** 和…发生关系,参加 (*I will never be a* ~ *to such a scheme.* 我决不参加这种计划)。***enter the*** ~ 入党。***give*** [***hold***] ***a*** ~ 举办[举行]…会;请客。***make one's*** ~ ***good*** 站稳立场;贯彻[坚持]自己主张。**II** ***vt.*** (***-tied***)〔美〕为…举行社交聚会;为…请客。*The visiting professor was cocktailed, partied and dined.* 为来访的教授举行了鸡尾酒会、晚会和晚宴。—***vi.*** 举行[参加]社交宴会。**III** ***a.*** **1.** 政党的,党派的。**2.** 社交的。**3.**【徽】分隔开的,染色的。*a* ~ *man* 党员。*a* ~ *platform* 政纲。~ *spirit* 党性。~ *standing* 党龄。~ ***per pale*** (盾徽中央)垂直分隔开的。~**-and-party** ***a.*** 当事人间的。~ **animal 1.** 热衷于社交聚会的人。**2.** 热衷于政治的人。~**-colo(u)red** ***a.*** = parti-colo(u)red. ~ **dress** 参加社交活动穿的衣服。~ **girl 1.** 社交聚会的女招待;妓女。**2.** 一心想参加社交活动的女子。~ **line 1.** (电话的)合用线;分界线;宅界。**2.**〔美〕政党路线。~ **liner** 坚持党的路线的人。~ **politics** 党派政治。~ **pooper**〔美俚〕(社交场合)令人扫兴的人。~**-spirited** ***a.*** 党性强的,有党性的,对党热心的。~ **vote**〔美〕根据本党路线所投的票。~ **wall**【法】(邻接建筑物的)界墙,通墙,公共墙。~ **whip** 在议会中督促本党党员的人。~ **wire**【讯】合用线。

par·ty·ism [ˈpɑːtiizəm; ˋpartɪɪzm̩] ***n.*** **1.** 党派性。**2.** 政党制度。*one* [*two*]*-* ~ 一[两]党制。**-ty·ist** ***n.*** 党派性强的人。

pa·rure [pəˈruə; pəˋrʊr] ***n.*** 一副首饰。

par·ve·nu [ˈpɑːvənjuː; ˋparvəˏnju] **I** ***n.*** 〔F.〕暴发户;新贵。**II** ***a.*** (像)暴发户的。

par·vis [ˈpɑːvis; ˋparvɪs] ***n.*** **1.** 教堂正门的柱廊。**2.** (建筑物,尤其是教堂前面的)天井,前庭。

par·vo·line [ˈpɑːvəliːn, -lin; ˋparvəlin, -lɪn] ***n.***【化】杷沃啉,二乙基吡啶。

pas [pɑː, F. pɑ; pɑ] ***n.*** (*pl.* ~ [pɑːz, F. pɑ; paz, F. pɑ]) 〔F.〕 **1.** 先行权;上席;优先权。**2.** 舞步;跳舞,舞。***dispute the*** ~ 争优先权。***give*** [***yield***] ***the*** ~ ***to*** 使…坐上席;让…居先;把优先权给…。~ ***de deux*** [də ˈdəː; də ˋdɝ] 〔F.〕双人舞。~ ***de trois*** [dəˈtrwɑ; dəˋtrwɑ] 三人舞。~ ***redouble*** [rəˈduːbl; rəˋdubl̩] 〔F.〕速步舞。~ ***seul*** [-səːl; -sœl] 〔F.〕单人舞。***take*** [***have***] ***the*** ~ ***of*** 坐在…的上席;比…占先;得优先权。

P.A.S., PAS, p.a.s. = para-aminosalicylic acid 对氨基水杨酸,对胺柳酸〔抗结核药〕。

Pas·cal [ˈpæskəl; ˋpæskl̩], **B.** 帕斯卡〔1623—1662,法国数学家、物理学家、哲学家〕。~**'s triangle**【数】帕斯卡三角形。

Pasch [pæsk; pæsk] ***n.***【宗】(犹太人的)逾越节〔见圣经《出埃及纪》12 章 27 节〕;逾越节用来祭神的羔羊。**2.** 复活节。

pas·chal [ˈpɑːskəl, ˈpæs-; ˋpaskl̩, ˋpæs-] **I** ***a.*** **1.** 逾越节的。**2.** 复活节 (Easter) 的。**II** ***n.*** (点复活节蜡烛用的)大烛台。~ **lamb 1.** 逾越节(宰杀吃)的小羊。**2.**〔P-Lamb〕基督;带有灵光圈的羊的图像〔象征基督〕。~ **solemnity** 复活节(前后的)周。

pas de chat [ˌpɑːdəˈʃɑː, F. pɑdəʃɑ; pɑdəˋʃɑ, pɑdəʃɑ]【芭蕾】雀跃步。

pa·se·o [pɑːˈseiəu; paˋseo] ***n.*** (*pl.* ~*s*)〔Sp.〕**1.** 散步〔尤指黄昏时散步〕;闲逛;公共大道。**2.** 斗牛士的入场式。

pash[1] [pæʃ; pɑʃ] ***n.***〔英方〕头。

pash[2] [pæʃ; pæʃ] ***vt.***〔英方〕打碎,粉碎。

pash[3] [pæʃ; pæʃ] **I** ***n.***〔美俚〕热恋〔缩略自 passion〕;(女学生的)迷恋。**II** ***vi.***〔美俚〕扮演情感激动的角色。~ **flops**〔美〕热情女郎。

pa·sha, pa·cha [ˈpɑːʃə, pəˈʃɑː; ˋpæʃə, pəˋʃɑ] ***n.***〔土耳其〕帕夏〔本义为首脑,转指伊斯兰教国家的高级官衔〕。~ ***of three tails*** [***two tails, one tail***] 最高[第二级、第三级]帕夏〔依军旗所加马尾数而言〕。**-dom** ***n.*** 帕夏的身分〔官衔〕。

pa·sha·lik, -lic [pəˈʃɑːlik; pəˋʃɑlɪk] ***n.*** 帕夏管区〔管辖权〕。

pashm [ˈpæʃəm; ˋpæʃəm] ***n.*** (西藏高原等地产的)山羊绒。

Pash·to [ˈpʌʃtəu, ˈpɑːʃ-; ˋpʌʃto, ˋpɑʃ-] ***n.*** 普什图语〔阿富汗和巴基斯坦用的印欧语系伊朗语支的语言,阿富汗的官方语言之一〕(= Pushtu, Pushto)。

pa·so do·ble [ˈpɑːsəu ˈdəubl; ˋpaso ˋdobl̩] ***n.*** (*pl.* ***paso do·bles***) **1.** 斗牛士进行曲〔斗牛士入场时或刺杀牛前的音乐〕。**2.** 斗牛士进行曲舞。

pasque·flow·er [ˈpæskflauə; ˋpæskˏflaʊɚ] ***n.***【植】白头翁;铁线海棠。

pas·quin·ade [ˌpækwiˈneid;ˏpækwɪˋned] **I** ***n.*** (贴在公共场所的)讽刺诗[文];讽刺。**II** ***vt.*** 讽刺。

pass[1] [pɑːs; pɑs] **I** ***vi.*** (~***ed*** [pɑːst; pɑst]; ~***ed***, ***past*** [pɑːst; pɑst]) **1.** 经过,通过;穿过;越过;超过;掠过;前进。**2.** (时间)流逝,推移;转化,变化 (*to*; *into*)。**3.** 及格,合格;(议案等)获得通过;被批准;得马虎过去;被宽大放过;被忽略过去。**4.** 消失,消灭;平息;停止,完;死;〔美口〕断气 (*out*)。**5.** (事件)发生,起;实行,实施。**6.** 通用,流通;以某种身分出现;被看做…,被认为是 (*for*);〔美〕(黑人后裔)自称白人。**7.**【法】做(陪审员)(*on*);宣判;下判决;讲 (*on*; *upon*)。**8.** (财产、权利等)转让(别人);(杯子等)转给(别人)。**9.** (球戏)递球,传球;练习传球;【牌】不叫牌,弃权;【剑】刺 (*on*; *upon*)。**10.**〔英〕敲丧钟。**11.**【医】(肠里的东西)排泄出来。*The days* ~*ed quickly.* 日子过得快。*I saw what was* ~*ing.* 我从头看到了尾。*It will* ~. 合格;可以。*That won't* ~. 那个不能答应。*Hot words* ~. 互相争论。*I* ~.【牌】我不要,我弃权。—***vt.*** **1.** 经过;穿过,通过;超过,横过;渡过。**2.** 使移过;使行进;过(时间);度(日)。**3.** 通;穿(针等);刺穿。**4.** (议案)通过(议会等),议决(议案等);使及格。**5.** 交,让与;传递;使传播;使通用;使流通;使用(伪币)。**6.** 宽大放过,使马虎过去;随便看一看。**7.**【法】宣告(判决);下(判断);发(誓);讲(意见、话)。**8.** 超过,胜过。**9.**〔美〕跳过;把…略过不提;忽略;省去。**10.** 不支付。**11.** 拒绝。**12.** (球戏)递(球),传(球)。**13.**【医】通(便)。*I* ~*ed my time in idleness.* 我把我的时间闲混过去了。*Please* ~ *the butter.* 请把黄油递给我。~ *a rope round a cask* 拿绳子套在桶上。*Please* ~ *your eye over this letter.* 请你看一看这封信。***bring to*** ~ 使发生,使实现;完成,实行。***come to*** ~

(事情)发生,实现。~ ***a dividend***〔美〕决定不付红利。~ ***a remark*** 开口,说话。~ ***as*** = ~ *for*。~ ***along*** 经过;再往前些。~ ***away*** 1. ***vi***. 经过;去;终止,完;废;过时;消灭;消失;死。2. ***vt***. 空费(时间等);让与(权利等)。~ ***a wet sponge over sth***. 忘记;删去。~ ***belief*** 使人不能相信。~ ***between*** (两人当中)有(磋商等)(*Nothing ~ed between us*. 我们当中没有什么事)。~ ***beyond*** 超过。~ ***by*** 1.〔by 作副词〕疏忽,忽略,不过问。2.〔by 介词〕打…旁边过去;通用(…这个名字)(*I cannot ~ by the remark in silence*. 对这句话我不能不过问)。~ ***by on the other side*** 不帮助,不同情。~ ***current*** (货币)通用;(谣言)流行。~ ***degree*** (英大学)毕业。~ ***for*** 被看做,被认为 (*He ~es for a great scholar*. 他被看做大学者)。~ ***from among us***(丢下我们)死掉。~ ***hence*** (人)死。~ ***in*** 交,付(支票等)。~ ***in one's checks***〔俚〕死。~ ***in review*** 1. 检阅,阅兵;使(军队)分列前进。2. (顺次)回想。~ ***into*** 变成 (*It has ~ed into a proverb*. 那已成了格言。~ *into disuse* 废而不用。~ *into oblivion* 淹没无闻。~ *into the shade* 名声渐渐衰落)。~ ***it***〔美〕搁着不管,不放在心上。~ ***muster*** 及格,合乎要求。~ ***off*** 1. 拿(假货)卖给 (*on sb*.)。2. 搪塞过去,敷衍过去,应付过去,混过去。3. 结束;顺利完成。4. 把…不放在心上,认为…无关紧要 (*She hated his familiarity, but ~ed it off as a joke*. 她讨厌他那种亲昵的态度,但一笑置之)。~ (*sth*. [*sb*.]) ***off as*** [***for***] 把某物[某人]冒充为。~ ***on*** [***upon***] 1. 前进,通过。2. 递,传递;传达。3. 重复。4. 欺骗,趁。5. 死,逝世。6.【剑】戳,刺。~ ***one's word*** 发誓,担保 (*to do*; *that*; *for*)。~ ***out*** 1. 出去。2.〔美俚〕(被打)昏过去;喝得烂醉;死,不复(存在);不再(出版);不能(看见,听到…)。~ ***over*** 1.〔over 作介词〕横过,经过,越过,渡过;通入;弹,拉(琴);过(日子);消磨(时光);省去。2.〔over 作副词〕交,传给,让给;忽略;免除;饶恕,放过,宽容。~ (***round***) ***the hat*** 募捐。~ ***sb***. [***sth***.] ***off as*** [***for***] ... 把某物[某人]充作…。~ ***sentence*** [***judgement***] 下判决[判断]。~ ***the baby***〔口〕推诿。~ ***the bottle*** 递酒。~ ***the buck***〔美俚〕把责任推给别人。~ ***the time of day*** (*with sb*.) 向(某人)早晚请安,同(某人)寒暄。~ ***the word*** 传达命令 (*to do*)。~ ***through*** 1. 经过,通过,穿过;经历;经验;遭受。2. 刺穿。~ ***up*** 1.〔美俚〕拒绝,绝交;放过;忽略,不理。2. 上,登。~ ***upon the merits of*** ... 评论…的是非。~ ***water*** 小便,撒尿。~***ed ball***【棒球】失误球。***try to ~ it off*** 力图搪塞(过去)。

II ***n***. 1. 免票;通行证;护照;通行[入场]许可 (*to*)。2. 及格;合格证书;(英国大学考试的)普通及格。3. 情况,形势;遭遇;危机。4. 穿过;经过;推移,变迁。5. (机器的)一次操作;(飞机、人造卫星的)一次飞过;【牌】(一次)放弃叫[补]牌;【剑】(一次)戳刺。6. 攻击,讽刺,暗讽;笑话。7. (变戏法者、催眠者的)挥手动作;欺骗;勾引手段。8. (球戏)传球动作。*No admittance without a pass*. 凭证件[票]方许入内。***come to a pretty*** [***nice***, ***fine***] ~ 陷入很困难的处境;变得很尴尬[很糟]。***make a ~ at***〔俚〕对…吊膀子;对…作勾引的表示〔尤指男对女〕;向…调情。***make ~es*** 施催眠术。***take a ~*** 接球。~ **book**〔英〕(银行)存折;顾客赊欠账簿,提货折,折子。~**-check** 门票,入场券,通行证。~ **degree** (英国大学中的)学士学位。~**-fail** 及格—不及格计分制〔不打具体分数或成绩等级,只记及格或不及格〕。~ **law** (过去南非迫害有色人种的)通行记法。~**man** (英国大学的)普通及格生。~**-word**【军】口令。

pass[2] [pɑːs; pɑs] ***n***. 1. 狭路;横路,小路;山路;关口;要隘。2. 河口,水口,渡口;涉水过渡处;(鱼箭上的)过道。***hold the ~*** 把关;维护利益;捍卫主义[事业]。***sell the ~*** 让出地位;背叛主义。**-less** ***a***. 没有路的,走不通的。

pass. 1. = passenger. 2. = passive.

pass·a·ble [ˈpɑːsəbl; ˋpæsəbl̩] ***a***. 1. 能通行的。2. 通用的;过得去的,还可以的,还好的;合格的,可用的。3. (钱币等)可流通的,真的。**-ness** ***n***.

pass·a·bly [ˈpɑːsəbli; ˋpæsəblɪ] ***ad***. 1. 可通行地。2. 还好,过得去。*a ~ good novel* 一本还算好的小说。

pass·a·ca·glia [ˌpɑːsəˈkɑːljə, ˌpæs-; ˏpɑsəˋkɑljə, ˏpæs-] ***n***. 1. 帕萨卡里亚舞〔一种慢速庄严的古代意大利舞蹈〕。2. 帕萨卡里亚舞曲。3. 以此种舞蹈为基础的曲式〔¾拍的固定复调形式〕。

pas·sade [pəˈseid; pəˋsed] ***n***.【马术】回转步。

pas·sa·do [pəˈsɑːdəu; pəˋsɑdo] ***n***. (*pl*. ~(*e*)*s*)【剑】一脚伸出在前的一刺。

pas·sage[1] [ˈpæsidʒ; ˋpæsɪdʒ] I ***n***. 1. 通行,通过;经过;转变,演变,变迁,推移;迁移,移住,(鸟的)移栖。2. 旅行;(海上、空中)航行;航行权;通行权;通行费,船费,车费。3. 通路,走廊;出入口;道路;航线,水路;行程。4. (文章等的)一节;一段;(艺术作品的)细部。5.〔美〕(议案的)通过。6.〔古〕(已发生的)事件。7. 对打;争论,讨论;〔*pl*.〕商量,密商;交流;交换。8.【医】通便。9.〔古〕逝世,死亡。10.【乐】经过句。11.【生】病原体(如病毒)的培育。*a bird of ~* 候鸟;暂时居住的人。*a ~ from that book* 那本书的一节。***a ~ at*** [***of***] ***arms*** 打架。***book*** [***engage***] ***one's ~*** 定购船票。***cut a ~*** 开路。***force a ~ through*** (*a crowd*) (在人群中)挤过去。***have a smooth*** [***rough***] ~ 航程平稳[艰险]。***have stormy ~s with*** 和…猛烈争论。***make a ~*** 1. 航海。2. (鲸鱼)移栖。***take one's ~*** 定购船票。***take ~ in*** 搭乘。***work one's ~*** 以做工抵作船费。

II ***vi***. 1. 前进;通过,穿过。2. 航海。3. 争论。~ **bird** 候鸟。~**-money** 船钱,车钱。~**way** 通路;〔美〕走廊。

pass·age[2] [ˈpæsidʒ; ˋpæsɪdʒ] I ***vt***.【马术】使(马)用斜横步前进。—***vi***. (马或骑手使马)以斜横步前进。II ***n***. 斜横步。

pas·sa·me·ter [pæˈsɑːmitə; pæˋsɑmɪtɚ] ***n***.【机】外径指示规。

pas·sant [ˈpæsənt; ˋpæsənt] ***a***.【徽】(举左前足)向右方前行之步态的。~ *gardant* [*regardant*] 用正向[左向]步态走。

pas·sa·vant [ˈpɑːsəˈvɑ̃ːŋ; ˋpɑsəˋvɑ̃ŋ] ***n***.〔F.〕通行证。

pas·sé(e) [ˈpæsei; pæˋse] ***a***.〔F.〕1. (女子等)已过盛年的;凋残的。2. 过时的,陈旧的。*a ~ belle* 老美女。

Pas·se [pæs; pæs] ***n***. 帕斯〔姓氏〕。

pas·sel [ˈpæsl; ˋpæsl̩] ***n***.〔口、方〕一批,一群〔尤指数量相当大者〕。

passe·men·terie [pasˈmɑ̃triː; pæsˋmentrɪ] ***n***.〔F.〕(衣服的)金[银]线花边;珠饰。

pas·sen·ger [ˈpæsindʒə; ˋpæsn̩dʒɚ] ***n***. 1. 乘客,(尤指)船客;旅客。2. 行人,过路人。3.〔俚〕无能船员[队员];碍手绊脚的人。***wake up the wrong ~***〔美口〕错怪了人。~ **boat** 客船。~ **car**〔指汽车〕轿车;〔指火车〕客车。~ **liner** 邮船;班船,班机。~ **list** 旅客名单。~ **liner** 班轮,邮船;班机。~ **plane**【空】客机。~**-pigeon** (能飞长距离的)北美候鸽〔已绝种〕。~ **train** (铁路)客车。

passe-partout [pɑːspɑːˈtuː, ˈpæs-; ˏpæspɚˋtu, ˋpæs-] ***n***.〔F.〕1. 无处不可通行者,通行无阻者。2. 万能钥匙。3. 嵌画片或照片的框边。4. 裱画镶框法。5. 镶画用的胶纸板。

passe·pied [pɑːsˈpjei; pɑsˋpje] ***n***.〔F.〕1. 快步舞〔法国十七世纪的一种舞蹈〕。2. 快步舞曲。

Pass·er [ˈpæsə; ˋpæsɚ] ***n***.【动】麻雀属。

pass·er [ˈpɑːsə; ˋpæsɚ] ***n***. 1. 过路人,过客;旅客;使通行(通过)的人。2. 考试及格者。3. 检验工。4.〔美俚〕使用伪币的人。

pass·er-by [ˈpɑːsəˈbai; ˋpæsɚˋbaɪ] ***n***. (*pl*. ***passers-by***) 过路人,经过者。

pas·ser·ine [ˈpæsərain; ˋpæsərɪn] I ***a***.【动】雀形目的;雀似的。II ***n***. 雀形目的鸟。

pas·si·ble [ˈpæsibl; ˋpæsəbl̩] ***a***. 易受感动的,感受力强

的〔神学用语〕。**-si·bil·i·ty** [ˌpæsiˈbiliti; ˏpæsəˋbɪlətɪ] ***n*.**

pas·sim [ˈpæsim; ˋpæsɪm] ***ad*.** 〔L.〕到处,处处,各处〔指在书中到处可见〕。*This occurs in Chaucer* ~. 这在乔叟的作品中处处可见。

pas·sim·e·ter [pæˈsimitə; pæˋsɪmɪtɚ] ***n*. 1.** 【机】内径指示规。**2.** 步测计。**3.** (车站的)自动售票器。

pass·ing [ˈpɑːsiŋ; ˋpæsɪŋ] **I *a*. 1.** 通行的,通过的;越过的;经过的;过往的;供通行的。**2.** 正在发生的;目前的,现在的。**3.** 一时的,短暂的,刹那间的。**4.** 仓促的,随便的,草率的。**5.** 偶然的,附带的。**6.** 合乎标准的;及格的。*the* ~ *time* 现在,现代。~ *events* 时事。~ *history* 现代史。*a* ~ *mark* 及格的分数。

II *n*. 1. 通过,经过。**2.** 消逝,死去。**3.** (议案的)议决;实施;(考试)及格。**4.** 遗漏,忽略。**5.** 通过的手段;穿过的地方。**6.** 摆渡,渡口。***in*** ~ 顺便(涉及),附带地(提及)。

III *ad*. 〔古〕非常,极其。~ **bell** 丧钟。~ **light** 【空】通过灯。~ **note**, ~ **tone** 【乐】经过音;补足音。~ **zone** (接力赛的)接棒区。**-ly *ad*. 1.** 暂时地。**2.** 顺便。**3.** 仓促地。**4.** 〔古〕很。

pas·sion [ˈpæʃən; ˋpæʃən] **I *n*. 1.** 激情,热情;〔the ~s〕感情〔与理智相对而言〕。**2.** 激怒,忿怒,奋激。**3.** 热恋;〔常 *pl*.〕情欲。**4.** 热心,爱好,热爱,热望(*for*)。**5.** 痛苦,悲哀。**6.** 〔the P-〕【宗】(十字架上的)耶稣的受难;〔古〕殉教。**7.** 〔废〕病痛。*Fishing is a* ~ *with him*. 他极爱钓鱼。*sexual* ~ 色情,性欲。*tender* ~ 爱情,恋爱。*one's ruling* ~ 主导感情;支配行动的动机。***be in a*** ~ 忿怒,在发脾气。***be subject to fits of*** ~ 动不动就发怒。***break*** [***burst***] ***into a*** ~ ***of*** (*tears*) 突然大(哭)起来。***fall*** [***get***] ***into a*** ~ 发怒,发脾气。***fly into a*** ~ 勃然大怒。***have a*** ~ ***for*** 对…有强烈的爱好。***up into a*** ~ = *fly into a* ~. **II *vi*.** 〔诗〕感觉[表现]热情。

pas·sion·al [ˈpæʃənəl; ˋpæʃənl] **I *a*. 1.** 热情的;感情的。**2.** 恋爱的,情欲的。**3.** 爱发脾气的,易怒的。**4.** 渴望的。**II *n*.** (基督教的)圣徒[殉教者]受难记。

pas·sion·ate [ˈpæʃənit; ˋpæʃənɪt] ***a*. 1.** 易动情的,多情的。**2.** 易怒的,急躁的。**3.** 热烈的;激昂的。**4.** 易被情欲所支配的。**-ly *ad*. -ness *n*.**

Pas·sion·ist [ˈpæʃənist; ˋpæʃənɪst] ***n*. 1.** (天主教的)受难会修道士。**2.** 〔p-〕热情的人。

pas·sion·flow·er [ˈpæʃənflauə; ˋpæʃənˏflaʊɚ] ***n*.** 【植】西番莲。

pas·sion·less [ˈpæʃənlis; ˋpæʃənlɪs] ***a*.** 没有热情的;不动情的;冷淡的;冷静的。

Pas·sion-music [ˈpæʃən-ˈmjuzik; ˋpæʃən-ˋmjuzɪk] ***n*.** 【宗】耶稣受难曲。

Pas·sion-play [ˈpæʃən-ˈplei; ˋpæʃən-ˋple] ***n*.** 【宗】耶稣受难剧。

Pas·sion Sunday [ˈpæʃən ˈsʌndi; ˋpæʃən ˋsʌndɪ] 【宗】耶稣受难日〔四旬斋 (Lent) 的第五个星期日〕。

Pas·sion·tide [ˈpæʃəntaid; ˋpæʃəntaɪd] ***n*.** 复活节前的两星期。

Pas·sion Week [ˈpæʃən ˈwiːk; ˋpæʃən ˋwik] 【宗】耶稣受难周〔复活节前的一周〕。

pas·si·vate [ˈpæsiveit; ˋpæsəvet] ***vt*.** 【冶】使钝化。**-va·tion *n*. -va·tor *n*.**

pas·sive [ˈpæsiv; ˋpæsɪv] **I *a*.** (*opp*. active) **1.** 被动的;守势的。**2.** 不抵抗的;默从的;消极的。**3.** 【语法】被动语态的;被动式的 (*opp*. active);【物、化】钝性的;钝态的;无源的;【医】虚性的;【空】不用发动机的;【法】(公债等)无利息的。*the* ~ *voice* 被动语态。~ *operations* 守势作战。~ *commerce* 【商】倚赖外国船的进出口贸易。*a* ~ *net*(*work*) 【电】无源(电)网路。*the* ~ *state* 【化】钝态。~ **congestion** 【医】虚性充血。~ **flight** 滑翔飞行。~ **bonds** 无利息公债。~ **immunity** 【医】被动免疫性。~ **resistance** 消极抵抗。~ **smoking** 被动吸烟〔指不吸烟者受吸烟者影响被动吸入烟气〕。

II *n*. 1. 〔*pl*.〕被动消极的东西;被动性。**2.** 【语法】被动语态;被动式。**-ly *ad*. -ness *n*.**

pas·siv·ism [ˈpæsivizəm; ˋpæsəˏvɪzm] ***n*. 1.** 被动的行为,被动性。**2.** 消极主义。**-ist *n*.** 消极主义者。

pas·siv·i·ty [pæˈsiviti; pæˋsɪvətɪ] ***n*. 1.** 被动;被动性;消极情绪[状态];消极怠工。**2.** 不抵抗,默从;忍受。**3.** 【物、化】钝性;钝态;无源性。**4.** 【语法】被动语态的结构。

pass·key [ˈpɑːskiː; ˋpæsˏki] ***n*.** 万能钥匙;专用钥匙;〔美〕盗贼用的钥匙;弹簧锁钥匙。*a* ~ *man* 〔美〕贼。

pas·som·e·ter [pæˈsɔmitə; pæˋsɑmɪtɚ] ***n*.** 计步器。

Pass·o·ver [ˈpɑːsəuvə; ˋpæsˏovɚ] ***n*. 1.** 【宗】(犹太人的)逾越节。**2.** 〔p-〕逾越节祭神的羔羊。**3.** 耶稣。

pass·port [ˈpɑːspɔːt; ˋpæsˏport] ***n*. 1.** 护照;通航护照;通行证;入场券[权];执照。**2.** (达到目的或获得某物的)手段,保障。***go without a*** ~ 〔美俚〕自杀。~ ***to one's favour*** 得宠[得到照顾]的手段。

pass-through [ˈpɑːsˌθruː; ˋpæsˏθru] ***n*. 1.** (厨房与食堂隔墙上的)递菜饭的小窗口。**2.** (原料成本等的)转嫁价格。

pas·sus [ˈpæsəs; ˋpæsəs] ***n*.** (*pl*. ~(*e*)*s*) 〔L.〕诗或故事的一段[一节]。

past [pɑːst; pæst] **I *a*. 1.** 过去的;完了的。**2.** 刚过去的,上(月、星期等),前(…年)。**3.** 前任的;曾任的;老练的。**4.** 【语法】过去(式)的。*the* ~ *month* 上月。*a* ~ *master* 能手,老手;(协会等的)旧会长。*the* ~ *participle* 【语法】过去分词。

II *n*. 1. 〔常 the ~〕过去,过去的事,往事。**2.** (不可告人的)过去的生活经历;可疑的经历。**3.** 【语法】过去时;(动词的)过去式。*We cannot undo the* ~. 往事不能挽回。*a man with a long* ~ 历史复杂的人。***for some time*** ~ 前些时候;最近以来。***in the*** ~ 在过去,从前。***not put it*** ~ (*sb*.) 相信(某人)可能会做(某事)。***with a*** ~ 有不可告人的经历。

III *prep*. 1. (时间)过…,(几点)多,(几岁)以上;通过,走过(某处)。**2.** (和人)错过去;(能力等的)超过。**3.** (行动等的)越过。~ *three o'clock* 三点多。*half* ~ *six* 六点半〔美语用 after〕。*an old man* ~ *seventy* 七十多岁的老人。*walk* ~ *the house* 走过那所房子。~ *endurance* 不能再忍受。~ *all belief* 简直不可思议。~ *comprehension* 费解的,无法理解的。***be*** ~ ***praying for*** (人)无可救药了。

IV *ad*. 过。*go* [*come*, *run*] ~ 打旁边走过[过来,跑过]。***be*** ~ ***due*** (火车等)误点;(支付等)误期。

pas·ta [ˈpɑːstə; ˋpɑstɑ] ***n*. 1.** (做细条实心面、通心粉、包子、饺子所用的)面团。**2.** 此种面团做的食品。

paste[1] [peist; pest] **I *n*. 1.** 糊,浆糊;面团;软糖;浓羹,酱。**2.** 糊状物;玻璃质混合物〔制人造宝石的原料〕;铅质玻璃;制陶粘土;软膏。*a bottle of* ~ 一瓶浆糊。*bean* ~ 豆(瓣)酱。*tooth* ~ 牙膏。*a man of a different* ~ 气质不同凡响的人。**II *a*.** 人造的;假的。**III *vi*. 1.** 用浆糊黏贴 (*up*; *on*; *together*);把(纸等)贴在…上。**2.** 使成面糊状。~ ***in*** 贴在(书里)。~ ***up*** 贴在…上;封上。

paste[2] [peist; pest] **I *vt*.** 〔俚〕狠狠地打;(体育比赛中)把(对方)决定性地击败。**II *n*.** (用拳头等)狠狠的一击。

paste·board [ˈpeistbɔːd; ˋpestˏbɔrd] **I *n*. 1.** 纸板;擀面板。**2.** 〔俚〕纸牌;名片。**3.** 火车票;〔美俚〕入场券,门票。~ *and rolling pin* 擀面板和擀面杖。**II *a*. 1.** 用纸板制成的。**2.** 薄弱的,不坚实的,虚有其表的;假的。*a* ~ *pearl* 人造珍珠。

pas·tel[1] [pæsˈtel, ˈpæstel; pæsˋtɛl, ˋpæstɛl] **I *n*. 1.** 彩色粉笔[蜡笔];彩色粉笔[蜡笔]画(画法);粉画(法)。**2.** 小品文,散文诗。**3.** 淡而柔和的色调。**II** [ˈpæstl; ˋpæstl] ***a*. 1.** 彩色粉笔[蜡笔]的;彩色粉笔[蜡笔]画的;粉画的。**2.** (色彩)柔和的,淡的。**3.** 虚弱的。**-list**, 〔Am.〕**-ist *n*.** 粉画家。

pas·tel[2] [pæsˈtel, ˈpæstel; pæsˋtɛl, ˋpæstɛl] ***n*. 1.** 【植】

菘蓝。2. 菘蓝染料。

past·er [ˈpeistə; ˋpestɚ] *n*. 1. 贴浆糊的人或物。2. 胶纸。

pas·tern [ˈpæstəːn; ˋpæstɚn] *n*. (马足的)骹。

paste-up [ˈpeistˌʌp; ˋpestˏʌp] *a*., *n*. 东拼西凑的文章;杂凑成的东西。

Pas·teur [pæsˈtəː; pæsˋtɝ] 巴斯德〔1822—1895, 法国化学家、细菌学家〕。~ **treatment** 【医】巴斯德狂犬病预防接种法。

pas·teur·ism [ˈpæstərizəm; ˋpæstərɪzm] *n*. 【医】巴斯德狂犬病预防接种法;巴斯德灭菌法。

pas·teur·ize [ˈpæstəraiz; ˋpæstəˏraɪz] *vt*. 【医】对…用巴斯德灭菌法消毒;给…打狂犬病预防针。**pas·teu·ri·zation** [-ˈzeiʃən; -ˋzeʃən] *n*. 巴氏灭菌法,低温灭菌。

pas·tic·cio [pæsˈtitʃəu; pɑsˋtɪtʃo] *n*. (*pl*. ~s, ***pastic·ci*** [-ˈtitʃiː; -ˋtɪtʃi]) 〔It.〕混成曲[歌];(文学、美术等的)模仿作品;东拼西凑的杂烩。

pas·tiche [pæsˈtiːʃ; pæsˋtiʃ] *n*. 〔F.〕= pasticcio.

pas·til, pas·tille [ˈpæstil, pæsˈtiːl; ˋpæstɪl, pæsˋtil] *n*. 锭剂;香锭;线香。

pas·time [ˈpɑːstaim; ˋpæsˏtaɪm] *n*. 消遣,游戏,娱乐。***by way of*** ~ = ***for a*** ~ 作消遣。

past·i·ness [ˈpeistinis; ˋpestɪnɪs] *n*. 浆糊[面团、软膏等]状态[性质]。

pas·tis [pɑːsˈtiːs; pæsˋtis] *n*. (有甘草和八角子味道的)法国无色露酒。

pas·tor [ˈpɑːstə; ˋpæstɚ] *n*. 1. (基督教的)牧师;(天主教的)大司祭;精神生活方面的指导人。2. 〔罕〕牧人,牧羊者。3. 【动】粉红椋鸟。**-ship** *n*. 牧师的职务[地位、任期]。

pas·to·ral [ˈpɑːstərəl; ˋpæstərəl] **I** *n*. 1. 牧歌,田园诗[曲、剧、画、雕刻]。2. 牧师写给教区居民的公开信〔又作 ~ letter〕。3. 田园景色。**II** *a*. 1. 牧人的。2. (土地)适于牧畜的;(诗等)描写田园生活的;牧歌似的;乡村的。3. 牧师的,主教的。~ *age* 牧畜时代。~ *area* 牧区。~ *farming* 畜牧。~ *poetry* [*poem*] 田园诗。~ *staff* 【宗】(主教的)牧杖。**-ist** *n*. 1. 田园诗[曲、剧、画等]的作者。2. 放牧者,牧畜者。3. 〔澳〕畜牧场主。**-ly** *ad*.

pas·to·ra·le [ˌpæstəˈrɑːli; ˏpæstəˋrɑlɪ] *n*. (*pl*. ~s, *-li* [-liː; -li]) 1. (欧洲旧时)描写田园生活的歌剧。2. 【乐】田园曲。

pas·to·ral·ism [ˈpɑːstərəlizəm; ˋpæstərəlɪzm] *n*. 〔诗〕 1. 田园风味。2. 牧畜主义。3. 牧歌体。

pas·tor·ate [ˈpɑːstərit; ˋpæstərɪt] *n*. 1. 牧师的职务[任期、身份]。2. 牧师团。

pas·to·ri·um [pæsˈtɔːriəm; pæsˋtorɪəm] *n*. 〔美南部〕牧师住宅。

pas·tra·mi [pəsˈtrɑːmi; pəˋstrɑmɪ] *n*. 五香熏牛(肩)肉。

pas·try [ˈpeistri; ˋpestrɪ] *n*. 1. 油酥面;油酥面皮;油酥面馅饼[点心]。2. 精制糕点。~**-cook** 糕饼师傅。

pas·tur·a·ble [ˈpɑːstʃərəbl; ˋpæstʃərəbl̩] *a*. (土地)适于作牧场的。

pas·tur·age [ˈpɑːstjuridʒ; ˋpæstʃərɪdʒ] *n*. 1. 畜牧(业)。2. 牧场;牧草。3. 〔Scot.〕放牧权。

pas·ture [ˈpɑːstʃə; ˋpæstʃɚ] **I** *n*. 1. 牧场。2. 牧草。3. 牲畜饲养,放牧。**II** *vt*. 1. 放牧;放(牛羊)吃草;(家畜)吃(牧草)。2. 把(土地)作牧场用。—*vi*. (牛羊)吃草。~**-ground,** ~**-land** 牧草。

past·y¹ [ˈpeisti; ˋpestɪ] *a*. 1. 面糊[面团]似的。2. (肌肉)松软的。3. (脸色)苍白的 (= ~-faced)。

past·y² [ˈpæsti, ˈpɑːsti; ˋpæstɪ, ˋpɑstɪ] *n*. 馅饼(尤指肉馅饼)。

PA system = public-address system 扩音装备;扩音系统,有线广播。

Pat [pæt; pæt] *n*. 1. 帕特〔男子名, Patrick 的昵称〕。2. 〔俚〕爱尔兰人。

pat¹ [pæt; pæt] **I** *n*. 1. 轻拍;轻打;抚;拍;抚摩。2. (有节奏的)轻拍声。3. (黄油等的)小块。***a*** ~ ***on the back*** 〔口〕鼓励。**II** *vt*. (*-tt-*) 1. 轻拍,轻拍…使平滑[成形]。2. 轻拍…以示抚慰[赞同等]。—*vi*. 1. 轻拍,摩,爱抚,抚 (*on*; *upon*)。2. (跑时等)发出轻拍声。~ ***oneself on the back*** (自我)满足。~ (*sb*.) ***on the back*** 拍背(表示称赞、祝贺、鼓励)。~**-ball** 1. 拍球〔类似棒球的英国球戏 (= rounders)〕。2. 拙劣无力的网球戏。~**-down search**〔美〕(用手摸被检查者衣服的)上下搜身。

pat² [pæt; pæt] **I** *a*. 1. 适当的,恰好的,合适的 (*to*)。2. 过于巧合的,人为的。3. 记得滚瓜烂熟的;准备好的。4. 〔英、方〕快活的,活泼的,神气的。5. 〔美〕可靠的;固定不变的。**II** *ad*. 1. 适当,恰好,合适;及时地。2. 立即地;流利地,顺顺溜溜地。***come*** ~ (*to*) 来得正好,正适合 (*The story came* ~ *to the occassion*. 故事恰好适合当时的场合)。***know a lesson off*** ~ 功课记得一点不差。***have*** [***know***] ~ 〔口〕1. 背熟,熟记。2. 准备好。***stand*** ~ 1. 【牌】用发到手的牌打〔不再补索新牌〕。2. 〔口〕坚持(原样)不变;固守 (*on*)。

pat. = 1. patent; patented. 2. pattern. 3. patrol.

pat·a·cake [ˈpætəkeik; ˋpætəˏkek] *n*. 1. 儿歌[童谣]的引头词。2. 手帮腔[按儿歌韵律拍手的一种游戏]。

pa·ta·gi·um [ˌpætəˈdʒaiəm, pəˈteidʒiəm; ˏpætəˋdʒaɪəm, pəˋtedʒɪəm] *n*. (*pl*. ***-gia*** [-ˈdʒiə, -ˋdʒɪə]) 【动】1. (蝙蝠类的)翅膜。2. (鳞翅目昆虫的)领片。

Pa·ta·go·ni·an [ˌpætəˈgəunjən, -niən; ˏpætəˋgonjən, -nɪən] **I** *a*. (阿根廷南部)巴塔哥尼亚(人)的。**II** *n*. 巴塔哥尼亚 (Patagonia) 的印第安人〔全世界身材最高的种族〕。

Pa·tan [ˈpɑːtən; ˋpɑtən] *n*. 帕坦〔尼泊尔城市〕。

Pat·a·vin·i·ty [ˌpætəˈviniti; ˏpætəˋvɪnətɪ] *n*. 1. 巴塔维尼亚方言的特色〔Patavium 系意大利帕多瓦 (Padua) 市的古名〕。2. 〔p-〕(一般的)方言[土话]的使用。

patch¹ [pætʃ; pætʃ] **I** *n*. 1. 补钉,补片;金属补片。2. (军服上表示所属部队的布制)臂章。3. 饰颜片,美人斑〔17、18世纪时女人贴在脸上增加美观或掩饰疤痕等的小绸片等〕;(害眼病时用的)眼罩;(伤口上的)敷裹,膏药。4. 碎片;碎屑;(文章的)一段。5. 斑点,斑纹;【医】斑。6. 小块地(上的庄稼)。7. 不中用的人,无聊的人,帮闲。8. 〔主英〕时期,季节。*a* ~ *of potatoes* 一块马铃薯地;一块地的马铃薯。***Don't put a*** ~ ***upon it***. 〔口〕别再表白啦,别掩饰啦。***make a*** ~ ***against*** 可与…相比。***not a*** ~ ***on*** 〔口〕比…差得远,远不及…。***strike a bad*** ~ 〔口〕倒霉。

II *vt*. 1. 修补,补缀;拼凑 (*up*)。2. 暂时遮掩一下 (*together*; *up*); 修理;平息(吵架等)。3. 用美人斑装饰(脸)。~ ***up*** 1. 结束,解决;制止。2. 匆忙处理。3. 拼凑。~**ing board** 【物】接线板。~ **pocket** 贴袋,明袋。~ **reef** 小而孤立的珊瑚礁。~ **test** 【医】(检验过敏症的)皮肤接触测验。~**work** 补缀品;拼凑成的东西,凑合物;编辑物。

patch² [pætʃ; pætʃ] *n*. 傻瓜。

patch·er·y [ˈpætʃəri; ˋpætʃərɪ] *n*. 补缀;补片;弥缝;拙劣的修补;拼凑物。

patch·ou·li [ˈpætʃuli(ː); ˋpætʃʊlɪ] *n*. 【植】广藿香。

patch·y [ˈpætʃi; ˋpætʃɪ] *a*. 1. 补缀(而成)的;尽是补钉的。2. 凑成的;不调合的。3. 脾气别扭的。

patd. = patented.

pate [peit; pet] *n*. 〔口〕头,脑袋;家伙,人。*a bald* ~ 秃头。*an empty* ~ 傻子。*a shallow* ~ 没头脑[浅薄]的家伙。

pâte [pɑt; pɑt] *n*. 〔F.〕浆状物〔尤指制陶瓷器的黏土〕。

pâ·té [ˈpætei, F. pate; paˋte, patɛ] *n*. 〔F.〕肉末饼。~ ***de foie gras*** [pate də fwaˈgrɑː; paˋte də fwaˋgrɑ] 肥鹅肝酱;鹅肝酱馅饼。

pa·tel·la [pəˈtelə; pəˋtɛlə] *n*. (*pl*. ~s, ***-lae*** [-liː; -li]) 1. 【解】髌,膝盖(骨);膝节;【动】杯状部;(龙虱科昆虫的)吸附节;【植】球状裸子器,小盘。2. (古代罗马的)小盘

子。

pa·tel·lar [pəˈtelə; pəˋtɛlɚ] *a*. 【解】膝盖(骨)的。~ **reflex** 【医】膝反射。

pa·tel·late [pəˈtelit; pəˋtɛlet] *a*. 膝盖状的;【植】小盘状的;【动】荷叶状的。

pa·tel·li·form [pəˈtelifɔːm; pəˋtɛlə͵fɔrm] *a*. 【植】小盘状的。

pat·en [ˈpætən; ˋpætn] *n*. 1. 【宗】圣餐盘,圣饼碟,祭碟。2. 薄的金属盘;扁盘。

pa·ten·cy [ˈpeitənsi; ˋpetnsɪ] *n*. 1. 明白,显著。2. 【医】开放(性),不闭合。3. 【语言】开音(性)。

P

pa·tent [ˈpeitənt, ˈpæt-; ˋpetnt, ˋpæt-] **I** *n*. 1. 专利(权);专利品;专利证书;专利标记;〔美〕公产让渡证。2. 独享的权利,特权。*get* [*take out*] *a* ~ *for* [*on*] (*an invention*) 得到(某项发明)的专利权[证]。
II *a*. 1. 专利的;获得专利权[证]保护的。2. 〔口〕独出心裁的,巧妙的。3. (门等)开着的;明白的,显然的;公然的;公开的。4. 开展的,扩张的;【植】张开的,伸展的。5. 〔美〕(面粉)高级的。*letters* ~ 专利证。*a* ~ *fact* 明白的事实。
III *vt*. 1. 批准给予…专利。2. 取得…的专利。~ **agent** 专利代理人。~ **ambiguity** 【法】(文件、证书的)语意暧昧不明。~ **anchor** 【海】无档锚。~ **digest** 白兰地酒。~ **flour** 上等面粉。~ **leather** 漆皮。~ **log** 【海】拖曳式计程仪。~ **medicine** (专利)成药。**P- Office** 专利局。~ **pool** 共享专利权的一组企业。~ **right** 专利权。~ **roll** 〔英〕专利特许登记簿。

pa·tent·a·ble [ˈpætəntəbl; ˋpætn̩təbl̩] *a*. 可以取得专利的,准许专利的。

pa·ten·tee [ˌpætənˈtiː, ˌpei-; ͵pætn̩ˋti, ͵pe-] *n*. 专利权获得者。

pa·tent·ly [ˈpeitəntli; ˋpetn̩tlɪ] *ad*. 显然,公然,一清二楚地。

pat·en·tor [ˈpeitəntə, ˈpæ-; ˋpætn̩tɚ, ˋpæ-] *n*. 1. 专利权的授予。2. 〔误用〕= patentee.

pa·ter [ˈpeitə; ˋpetɚ] *n*. 〔英俚〕父亲〔学童语〕。

Pa·ter [peitə; ˋpetɚ] *n*. 佩特〔姓氏〕。

pa·ter·fa·mil·i·as [ˈpeitəfəˈmiliæs; ˋpetɚfəˋmɪlɪ͵æs] *n*. (*pl*. *pa·tersfa·mil·i·as* [ˌpeitriz-; ͵petriz-]【罗马法】一家之父,男性家长〔今用作诙谐语〕。

pa·ter·nal [pəˈtəːnl; pəˋtɝnl] *a*. 1. 父亲的;像父亲的。2. 父方的;父系的;得自父亲的,世袭的。*be related on the* ~ *side* 是父方的亲戚。~ *ancestor* 〔美俚〕父亲。~ *care* 父亲(般)的关怀,父心。~ *government* 温情主义政治。*bid adieu to one's* ~ *roof* 拜别父亲独立生活。**-ly** *ad*. 父亲似的。

pa·ter·nal·ism [pəˈtəːnəlizəm; pəˋtɝnl͵ɪzm] *n*. 家长主义;(政治上的)温情主义;家长式统治;家长作风。**-nal·ist** [-ist; -ɪst] *a*., *n*. 搞家长式统治的(人)。

pa·ter·nal·is·tic [pəˌtəːnəˈlistik; pə͵tɝnlˋɪstɪk] *a*. 家长式统治的;家长作风的,家长式的。**-ti·cal·ly** *ad*.

pa·ter·ni·ty [pəˈtəːniti; pəˋtɝnətɪ] *n*. 1. 父亲的身份;父道;父性;父权;父子关系;父系。2. 〔喻〕渊源;来源;出处,作者。

pa·ter·nos·ter [ˈpætəˈnɔstə; ˋpetɚˋnɑstɚ] *n*. 1. 〔常作 Pater Noster〕【基督】主祷文,念主祷文的祷告〔尤指用拉丁文〕。2. 咒文,符咒。3. (祷告时用的)念珠。4. 念珠式钓钩〔每隔一定间隔有钩,又作 ~ line〕。*black* ~ 咒诅。*say the devil's* ~ 叽叽咕咕骂人,发牢骚。

path(ol.) = pathological; pathology.

path [pɑːθ; pæθ] *n*. (*pl*. ~*s* [pɑːðz; pæðz]) 1. (自然踏成的)路;路径;(马路边上的)人行道;(车子走不过的)小路;(竞走或自行车比赛的)跑道。2. 路线;路程;〔喻〕(人生的)道路;(思想、行为、生活的)途径,方式。3. 【天】道,带。*approach* ~ 【空】进场航线。*moon's* ~ 【天】白道。~ *of a total eclipse* 【天】全蚀带。*a* ~ *strewn with roses* 撒满玫瑰的道路,安乐的一生。*a beaten* ~ 踏出来的[走惯的]路;常规,普通方法。*break* [*blaze*] *a* (*new*) ~ 开辟一条(新)路。*cross sb.'s* ~ 碰见某人;挡住某人去路,阻碍某人。*set sb. on the right* ~ 使某人走上正路。~**-breaker** 开路人;闯将。~ **finder** 1. 探路人;开拓者;探索者。2. 导航人;导航飞机;导航雷达;【空】投照明弹的飞机。3. 〔美卑〕警察的密探。~**finding** 1. 领航;导航;寻找目标。~**way** 小路,小径。**-less** *a*. 无路的,人迹未到的。

Pa·than [pəˈtɑːn; pəˋtɑn] *n*. 帕坦人〔住在印度或印度西北边境的阿富汗族人〕。

pa·thet·ic, 〔罕〕**pa·thet·i·cal** [pəˈθetik, -kl; pəˋθɛtɪk, -kl] **I** *a*. 1. 可怜的,悲惨的,使人感动的。2. 感伤的;感情(上)的,情绪(上)的。*a* ~ *scene* (戏剧等的)悲惨场面。**II** *n*. 1. 〔the ~〕感伤性的东西。2. 〔*pl*.〕可怜的表现[动作];感伤的情绪。~ **fallacy** 感情的误置〔指对自然界现象或无生命事物的拟人化〕。**-thet·i·cal·ly** *ad*.

patho- *comb. f*. 1. 病;苦;受难。2. 热情,感情:*patho*gen, *patho*logy.

path·o·gen, **path·o·gene** [ˈpæθədʒin, ˈpæθədʒiːn; ˋpæθədʒən, ˋpæθə͵dʒin] *n*. 【生、医】病原体。

path·o·gen·e·sis [ˌpæθəˈdʒenisis; ͵pæθəˋdʒɛnəsɪs] *n*. 致病;发病。

path·o·ge·net·ic, **path·o·gen·ic** [ˌpæθədʒiˈnetik, -ˈdʒenik; ͵pæθədʒəˋnɛtɪk, -ˋdʒɛnɪk] *a*. 病原的;致病的。**-o·gen·i·cal·ly** *ad*.

path·o·ge·nic·i·ty [ˌpæθədʒiˈnisiti; ͵pæθədʒɪˋnɪsətɪ] *n*. 【医】致病力,致病原因。

pa·thog·e·nous [pəˈθɔdʒinəs; pəˋθɑdʒənəs] *a*. = pathogenetic.

pa·thog·e·ny [pəˈθɔdʒini; pəˋθɑdʒɪnɪ] *n*. 致病原因;发病。

pa·thog·no·mon·ic [pəˌθɔgnəˈmɔnik; pə͵θɑgnəˋmɑnɪk] *a*. 特殊病症的。

pa·thog·no·my [pəˈθɔgnəmi; pəˋθɑgnəmɪ] *n*. 【医、心】病征学。

pathol. = pathological; pathology.

path·o·log·ic, **path·o·log·i·cal** [ˌpæθəˈlɔdʒik, -ikəl; ͵pæθəˋlɑdʒɪk, -ɪkl̩] *a*. 病理学(上)的;病态的;由疾病引起的。~ *anatomy* 病理解剖。~ *physiology* 病理生理学。**-log·ical·ly** *ad*.

pa·thol·o·gist [pəˈθɔlədʒist; pæˋθɑlədʒɪst] *n*. 病理学家。

pa·thol·o·gy [pəˈθɔlədʒi; pəˋθɑlədʒɪ] *n*. 1. 病理学。2. 病理;病状。3. 〔喻〕反常,变态。*vegetable* ~ 植物病理学。*general* [*special*] ~ 病理总论[各论]。

pa·thom·e·ter [pəˈθɔmitə; pəˋθɑmɪtɚ] *n*. 体内电导率变化探测器。

pa·thos [ˈpeiθɔs; ˋpeθɑs] *n*. 1. (言词、作品、事件中)引起怜悯[同情]的因素;怜悯,同情,感伤力。2. 悲怆,哀婉,凄楚;【心】精神病苦。3. 偶然[暂时]因素。

path·way [ˈpɑːθwei; ˋpæθ͵we] *n*. = path.

-pathy *comb. f*. 1. 疾病。2. 疗法。3. 痛苦。4. 感情:anti*pathy*, electro*pathy*, osteo*pathy*.

Pa·tience [ˈpeiʃəns; ˋpeʃəns] *n*. 佩欣丝〔女子名〕。

pa·tience [ˈpeiʃəns; ˋpeʃəns] *n*. 1. 忍耐,容忍,忍受;忍耐力,坚韧;耐心,耐性。2. 〔主英〕多种单人牌戏之一〔又名 solitaire〕。*Have* ~! 忍耐忍耐! 再等一等! *My* ~! 〔俚〕嗳哟! 啊! *P- is a plaster for all sores*. 忍耐可以减轻一切痛苦。*be out of* [*have no*] ~ *with* 对…不能忍耐;受不了…。*lose all* (*one's*) ~ *with* 对…发脾气。*the* ~ *of Job* 极度的忍耐。*with* ~ 耐心地。

pa·tient [ˈpeiʃənt; ˋpeʃənt] **I** *a*. 1. 能忍耐的,有耐性的;容忍的。2. 勤快的,孜孜不倦的;坚韧的;受得了(饥饿、劳累等)的。3. 容许的,有…余地的。4. 被动性的。~ *of* 能忍受…的;不生气的;容许…意义的。*be* ~ *of two interpretations* 可作两种解释。**II** *n*. (接受治疗的)病人,患者;被动者;(美容院等的)顾客;〔美〕殡仪馆的尸体。in-～ 住院病人。out-～ 门诊病人。-ly ad. 忍耐地,容忍地,耐心地。

pat·i·na[1]['pætinə; ˋpætɪnə] n. (pl. ～s) 1. (青铜器上的)绿锈,古翠;【美】古色;(木器、墙壁等由年久而产生的)光泽面。2. (长久的经验[习惯]形成的)神情,外貌。

pat·i·na[2]['pætinə; ˋpætɪnə] n. (pl. -nae [-niː; -ni]) (古罗马的)盘子;(盛圣餐面包的)金属盘。

pat·i·nate ['pætineit; ˋpætəˏnet] vt., vi. 1. (使)生绿锈。2. (使)产生光泽。

pat·i·nat·ed ['pætineitid; ˋpætəˏnetɪd] a. 生了铜绿的;古色古香的。-i·na·tion [-ˈneiʃən; -ˋneʃən] n.

pat·ine ['pætn; ˋpætn̩] I n. 1. 祭碟 (= paten)。2. 古翠,绿锈 (= patina)。II [pe'tiːn; peˋtin] vt. 使生绿锈。

pat·i·nous ['pætinəs; ˋpætənəs] a. 生铜绿的;有古色的。

pa·ti·o ['pɑːtiəu; ˋpɑtɪˏo] n. (pl. ～s) 〔Sp.〕天井,院子;(连接房屋和铺有地面的)室外闲坐[就餐]处。

pa·tis·se·rie [pə'tisəri; pəˋtɪsərɪ] n. 〔F.〕= pastry.

Pat. Off. = Patent Office 〔美〕专利局。

pat·ois ['pætwɑː; ˋpætwɑ] n. (pl. *pat·ois* ['pætwɑːz; ˋpætwɑz]) 〔sing., pl.〕〔F.〕方言,土语;隐语;行话,同行语 (= jargon)。

pat·ri- comb. f. 父:patricide.

pa·tri·arch ['peitriɑːk; ˋpetrɪˏɑrk] n. 1. 家长;族长;(特指)犹太民族的祖先;(团体的)元老。2. (基督教的)早期主教〔尤指君士坦丁、亚历山大里亚、安提克、耶路撒冷等地的主教〕;【天主】罗马教皇;东正教的最高一级主教。3. (科学、学派、宗教等的)鼻祖,创始人。4. 〔pl.〕【圣】雅各 (Jacob) 的十二个儿子;亚伯拉罕 (Abraham)、以赛 (Isaac)、雅各 (Jacob) 和他们的祖先。

pa·tri·ar·chal [ˌpeitri'ɑːkəl; ˏpetrɪˋɑrkl] a. 1. 家[族]长的;(大)主教的;家长[族长、主教]管辖的;家[族]似的。2. 元老的,元老派头的;可尊敬的。*the* ～ *ideology* 宗法思想。～-**feudual** 宗法封建性的。

pa·tri·arch·ate ['peitriɑːkit; ˋpetrɪˏɑrkɪt] n. 1. 主教[家长、族长等]的职位[职务、任期、管区、住宅]。2. = patriarchy.

pa·tri·arch·ism [ˌpeitri'ɑːkizəm; ˋpetrɪˏɑrkɪzm̩] n. 家长制度;族长政治。

pa·tri·arch·y ['peitriɑːki; ˋpetrɪˏɑrkɪ] n. 1. 家长制;族长政治;族长制社会;族长管区。2. 父权制(社会)。

Pa·tri·cia [pə'triʃə; pəˋtrɪʃə] n. 帕特丽夏〔女子名,昵称为 Pat 或 Patty〕。

pa·tri·cian [pə'triʃən; pəˋtrɪʃən] I n. 1. (古罗马的)贵族 (opp. plebeian); (一般的)贵族。2. 罗马帝国的地方官;中世纪意大利的显贵。3. 有教养的人。II a. (古罗马帝国的)贵族的;(相貌等)贵族似的。

pa·tri·ci·ate [pə'triʃiit; pəˋtrɪʃɪɪt] n. 贵族阶级[地位、等级]。

pat·ri·cide ['pætrisaid; ˋpætrɪˏsaɪd] n. 杀父(行为);杀父者。-**cid·al** [ˌpætri'saidl; ˏpætrɪˋsaɪdl] a.

pat·rick ['pætrik; ˋpætrɪk] n. 1. 帕特里克〔男子名〕。2. **St.** ～ 爱尔兰的守护神。

pat·ri·co ['pætrikəu; ˋpætrɪko] n. 〔吉卜赛俚〕牧师。

pat·ri·lin·e·al [ˌpætrə'liniəl, ˌpeitrə-; ˏpætrəˋlɪnɪə, ˏpetrə-] a. 父系的。-ly ad.

pat·ri·mo·ni·al [ˌpætri'məunjəl, -niəl; ˏpætrəˋmonɪəl, -nɪəl] a. 1. 父子相传的,世袭的。2. 世袭财产的;教会生产的。～ **sea** 承袭海〔沿海国家对其自然资源可享有主权的海域,亦作～ waters〕。

pat·ri·mo·ny ['pætriməni; ˋpætrəˏmonɪ] I n. 1. 世袭财产,遗产。2. 家传;传统;继承物。3. 教堂财产[基金]。

pa·tri·ot ['peitriət, 'pæt-; ˋpetrɪət, ˋpæt-] I n. 爱国者;爱国主义者;〔P-〕〔美〕"爱国者"导弹[飞弹]〔美国的一种电脑化防空导弹,尤用于截击来袭的导弹,亦作 P-missile〕。II a. 爱国的,有爱国心的。

pa·tri·ot·eer [ˌpeitriə'tiə; ˏpætrɪəˋtɪr] n. 〔美〕(以爱国为幌子而谋私利的)"爱国"市侩。

pa·tri·ot·ic [ˌpætri'ɔtik, ˌpei-; ˏpetrɪˋɑtɪk, ˏpe-] a. 爱国的,有爱国热忱的,爱国主义的。-ti·cal·ly ad.

pa·tri·ot·ics [ˌpætri'ɔtiks; ˏpætrɪˋɑtɪks] n. 〔pl.〕1. 〔用作 sing.〕爱国的作品[演说、活动]。2. 爱国精神的表现。

pa·tri·ot·ism ['pætriətizəm, 'pei-; ˋpetrɪətɪzəm, ˋpe-] n. 爱国心,爱国主义。

pa·tris·tic, pa·trist·i·cal [pə'tristik(əl); pəˋtrɪstɪk(l)] a. 1. 早期基督教会领袖[教父]的。2. 关于早期基督教会领袖[教父]著作的,研究教父著作的。

pa·tris·tics [pə'tristiks; pəˋtrɪstɪks] n. 〔pl.〕〔用作 sing.〕早期基督教领袖[教父]著作[教义、传记]的研究;教父学。

Pa·tro·clus [pə'trɔkləs; pəˋtrɑkləs] 普特洛克勒斯〔荷马史诗《伊利亚特》中的一个英雄,特洛伊战争中为赫克托所杀〕。

pa·trol [pə'trəul; pəˋtrol] I n. 1. 巡逻,巡视,侦察。2. 巡逻兵;警察。3. 侦察队;哨舰;巡逻机队。4. 〔美〕童子军小队。5. 〔美〕囚车。**on** ～ 在巡逻,侦察中。II vt., vi. (-ll-) 巡视,巡逻,侦察;(在街上)巡游。～ *the pasture*【美棒球】守外场。～ **aviation**【空】巡逻飞行。～ **boat** 哨艇,巡逻艇。～ **car** (装有无线电话的)巡逻警车。～ **dog** 警犬。～ **leader**【军】侦察班长。～-**man** 1. 巡视者,巡逻者。2. (电线等的)保线员。3. 〔美〕外勤警察;巡警。～ **wagon** 〔美〕囚车。

pa·tron ['peitrən, 'pæ-; ˋpetrən, ˋpæ-] n. 1. 奖励者,赞助人,支持者;庇护人;恩主;【史】(艺术家等的)保护者。2. (商店的)顾客,主顾;(慈善协会等的)主席。3. 【宗】保护圣徒;守护神 (= ～ saint);(英国教会中)有授与牧师职权的人。4. 〔古罗马〕释放奴隶后的旧奴隶主;保护平民的贵族。～ **saint** 1. 保护圣徒,守护神。2. (团体等的)最初领导人;最高典范。

pat·ron·age ['pætrənidʒ; ˋpetrənɪdʒ] n. 1. 保护人[庇护人、赞助人等]的身份[影响、作用];支援,保护;赞助,奖励。2. (顾客的)光顾,惠顾。3. 以恩赐的态度施予的恩惠;沽恩,自命恩人,恩人气派。4. 圣经授与权,牧师推荐权;官职任命权。*He has a great deal of* ～ *in his hands*. 他有很大的任命权。*the P- Secretary* 〔英〕公务员铨衡长官。**take sb. under one's** ～ 使某人受自己的庇护,使某人听自己的领导。**under the** ～ **of** 在…保护下;承…栽培。

pa·tron·al [pə'trəunl, pæ't-; peˋtronl̩, pæˋt-] a. 保护的;守护神的;赞助的。

pa·tron·ess ['peitrənis, 'pæ-; ˋpetrənɪs, ˋpæ-] n. 女保护人[庇护人、赞助人等]。

pat·ron·ize ['pætrənaiz; ˋpetrənˏaɪz] vt. 1. 支援,保护,赞助。2. 光顾,惠顾。3. 对…以恩人自居;对…摆出屈尊俯就的样子。

pat·ron·iz·ing ['pætrənaiziŋ; ˋpetrənˏaɪzɪŋ] a. 恩人气派的,自命为恩人的;屈尊俯就的;神气十足的;傲慢的。-ly ad.

pat·ro·nym·ic [ˌpætrə'nimik; ˏpætrəˋnɪmɪk] I n. 1. 源于父名[祖名]的姓〔例:Johnson (= son of John), Macdonald (= son of Donald) 等〕。2. 姓。II a. 1. (前缀[词首]、后缀[词尾])表示父[祖]名的。2. (姓)源于父名[祖名]的。

pa·troon [pə'truːn; pəˋtrun] n. 1. 【美史】(荷兰统治下纽约州及新泽西州享有特权的)大庄园主。2. 〔古〕船长。

Pat's = patents.

pa·tsy ['pætsi; ˋpætsɪ] n. 〔美俚〕1. 容易受骗的人。2. 替罪羊。3. 懦夫。

pat·(t)a·mar ['pætəmɑː; ˋpætəmɑr] n. 【海】(在印度沿海从事贸易的)三角帆船。

pat·ten ['pætn; ˋpætn̩] n. 1. 木套鞋,木底靴。2. 【建】柱脚,壁脚。

pat·ter[1] ['pætə; ˋpætɚ] I vi. 1. 啪嗒啪嗒地响;(雨点)嗒

嗒地下。2. 嗒嗒地跑。—*vt*. 使发出嗒嗒声;使(水等)劈里啪啦地响。**II** *n*. (急促的)滴嗒声,滴沥声;啪嗒声,劈里啪啦声。*the ~ of little feet* 嗒嗒的小脚步声。

pat·ter[2] [ˈpætə; ˋpætɚ] **I** *n*. 1. (摊贩、魔术师等的)顺口溜,快嘴话;叽叽喳喳的谈话;饶舌。2. 行话;切口,黑话,隐语。3. (歌剧中的)滑稽顺口溜;〔美电台〕合唱后的间奏曲。4. 〔俚〕歌词;(喜剧等的)台词,说白。5. (魔术师等的)咒文〔通常作 conjuror's ~〕。**II** *vt*. 叽叽喳喳地念[讲];祷告似地说。—*vi*. 1. 喋喋不休。2. 祷告,念经。3. 念顺口溜;唱滑稽顺口溜歌曲。~ **song** (音乐喜剧中的)滑稽顺口溜歌曲。

P

pat·tern [ˈpætən; ˋpætɚn] **I** *n*. 1. 模范,榜样;典范。2. 型,模型;模式;雏型;【冶】原型。3. 花样;式样;(服装裁剪的)纸样;图案,图谱,图表;机构,结构;特性曲线;晶体点阵;(电视的)帧面图像。4. 方式;形式;格局;格调。5. (衣料等的)样品,样本,样板。6. 〔美〕一件衣料。7. (炮弹等的)散布面;靶子上的弹痕。8. (飞机的)着陆航线。*a ~ wife* 模范妻子。*a paper ~ for a dress* 女服纸样。*a machine of a new* [*an old*] ~新[旧]型机器。*a cropping* ~衣作制。***after the ~ of*** 仿…。
II *vt*. 1. 照图样做;仿造,摹制 (*after*; *upon*)。2. 给…加花样,用图案装饰。3. 〔英方〕与…相比 (*to*, *with*)。—*vi*. 形成图案。~ ***oneself after*** 模仿,学…的榜样。~ **bargaining** 工会按理想的合同方案之一同资方进行的谈判。~ **bombing**【军】定型轰炸。~**maker** 制模工;服装设计师。~ **mechanism**【纺】提花装置。~**-room**, ~**-shop** (翻砂厂等的)制模车间。**-ed** *a*. 仿造的;被组成图案的(~*ed forms*【语】仿造词)。**-ing** *n*. 图案结构,图形;(行为等的)特有型式。**-less** *a*. 无图案的。

pat·tern·ize [ˈpætənaiz; ˋpætɚnˏaɪz] *vt*. 1. 使符合型式。2. 把…构成图案。

pat·tie [ˈpæti; ˋpætɪ] *n*. = patty.

Pat·ti·son [ˈpætisn; ˋpætɪsn̩] *n*. 帕蒂森〔姓氏〕。

Pat·ty, Pat·ti, Pat·tie [ˈpæti; ˋpætɪ] *n*. 帕蒂〔女子名,Patricia 的昵称〕。

pat·ty [ˈpæti; ˋpætɪ] *n*. 1. 小馅饼 (= pâté)。2. 小片糖。~**pan** 烘馅饼锅。~ **shell** 小馅饼皮。

pat·ty-cake [ˈpætiˌkeik; ˋpætɪˏkek] *n*. 1. 儿歌[童谣]的引头词。2. 手帮腔〔按儿歌韵律拍手的一种游戏 (= patacake)〕。

pat·u·lin [ˈpætjulin; ˋpætjʊlɪn] *n*.【生化】棒曲霉素。

pat·u·lous [ˈpætjuləs; ˋpætjʊləs] *a*. 1.【植】(树枝等)平展的。2. 张开的,展开的。**-ly** *ad*. **-ness** *n*.

PAU = Pan American Union 泛美联盟。

pau·ci·ty [ˈpɔːsiti; ˋpɔsətɪ] *n*. 1. 少许,少量。2. 缺乏,贫乏。*a country marked by a ~ of resources* 一个缺乏自然资源的国家。

Paul [pɔːl; pɔl] *n*. 1. 保罗〔姓氏,男子名〕。2.【基督】使徒保罗。***rob Peter to pay*** ~ 劫甲给乙,借东还西。~ **Bunyan** [ˈbʌŋjən; ˋbʌŋjən] 1. (美国传说中的)伐木巨人。2. 〔喻〕大力士。~ **Pry** 1. 爱刨根问底的人。2. 〔英空俚〕探照灯。

Paul·a [ˈpɔːlə; ˋpɔlə] *n*. 保拉〔女子名〕。

paul·dron [ˈpɔːldrən; ˋpɔldrən] *n*. 肩甲,甲的护肩部份。

Pau·li [ˈpauli; ˋpaʊlɪ] 沃夫根·保利〔1900—1958,德国物理学家〕。~ **exclusion principle**【物】保利不相容原理。

paul·in [ˈpɔːlin; ˋpɔlɪn] *n*. 防水帆布;船舱盖布。

Paul·ine[1] [pɔːˈliːn; pɔˋlin] *n*. 保琳〔女子名〕。

Paul·ine[2] [ˈpɔːlain; ˋpɔlaɪn] **I** *a*. 1. 使徒保罗 (Paul)的。2. 保罗著作[教义]的。3. 伦敦圣保罗学校 (St. Paul's School)的。**II** *n*. 伦敦圣保罗学校的学生。

Paul·ing [ˈpɔːliŋ; ˋpɔlɪŋ] *n*. 保林〔姓氏〕。

Paul·ist [ˈpɔːlist; ˋpɔlɪst] *n*. 1.【天主】(纽约)使徒保罗传道会的神父。2. (印度)耶稣会教士。

pau·lo-post-fu·ture [ˈpɔːləupəustˈfjuːtʃə; ˋpɔləˏpostˋfjutʃɚ] *n*.【希腊语法】未来完成时;〔谑〕最近的将来。

Pau·low·ni·a [pɔːˈləuniə; pɔˋlonɪə] *n*. 1.【植】泡桐属。2. 〔p-〕泡桐树。~ **imperialis** 白桐。

paunch [pɔːntʃ; pɔntʃ] **I** *n*. 1. 肚子,腹;大肚子。2. 瘤胃〔反刍动物的第一胃〕。3. (昆虫的)囊状附器。4.【海】防摩席。***Fat ~es have lean pates***. 大腹便便,头脑空空。**II** *vt*. 把…破肚子;破腹摘出…的脏腑。

paunch·y [ˈpɔːntʃi; ˋpɔntʃɪ] *a*. 罗汉肚的,大腹便便的。

pau·per [ˈpɔːpə; ˋpɔpɚ] *n*. 1. 照救贫法得到救济的人;贫民,穷人。2.【法】(得免除诉讼费用的)贫苦起诉人;〔嘲笑语〕叫化子。~ *children* 贫穷儿童。*a ~ school* 贫民学校。**-dom, -ism** *n*. 1. 贫穷。2. 〔集合词〕穷人,贫民。

pau·per·is [ˈpɔːpəris; ˋpɔpərɪs] *n*. 〔L.〕= pauper. ***sue in forma ~***【法】作为贫民上诉。

pau·per·ize [ˈpɔːpəraiz; ˋpɔpəˏraɪz] *vt*. 把…弄穷;使成为贫民。**-i·za·tion** [ˌpɔːpəraiˈzeiʃən; ˏpɔpərəˋzeʃən] *n*. 贫困化。

Pau·ro·me·tab·a·la [ˌpɔːrəuməˈtæbələ; ˏpɔrəməˋtæbələ] *n*. 〔*pl*.〕【动】(昆虫的)渐近变态。

pau·ro·me·tab·o·lous, pau·ro·me·ta·bol·ic [ˌpɔːrəumiˈtæbələs, -ˈbɔlik; ˏpɔrəmɪˋtæbələs, -ˋbɑlɪk] *a*.【动】渐变态的。**-o·lism** *n*.

paus·al [ˈpɔːzəl; ˋpɔzəl] *a*.【语法】1. (句子结尾等时)停顿的。2. 停顿前的词形[母音形式]的。

pause [pɔːz; pɔz] **I** *n*. 1. 中止;暂停;踌躇。2. 断句;句读,段落;停读;停顿符号[句号,逗号等]。3.【乐】延长;延长号〔⌒或◡〕。***at*** [***in***] ~停止着;踌躇着。***give ~ to*** 使踌躇。***make a*** ~中止;歇一下气。**II** *vi*. 1. 停止,中止,歇气。2. 等 (*for*);踌躇。3.【乐】延长。~ ***and ponder*** 停下仔细考虑;踌躇。~ ***upon*** 在…歇一下气[停一停,想一想]。

pav [pæv; pæv] *n*. 〔口〕= pavilion.

pav·age [ˈpeividʒ; ˋpevɪdʒ] *n*. 1. 铺路,铺地。2. 铺路税。

pav·an, pav·ane [ˈpævən; ˋpævən] *n*. (16、17 世纪流行西班牙的)孔雀舞(曲)。

pave [peiv; pev] *vt*. 1. 铺(路) (*with*),作铺设…之用。2. 铺设,密布。~ ***the way for*** [***to***] 为…铺平道路;使…容易到来。

pa·vé [ˈpævei; paˋve] *n*. 〔F.〕1. 铺石路;铺筑过的地面[路面]。2. 密镶宝石。

pave·ment [ˈpeivmənt; ˋpevmənt] *n*. 1. 铺石路,〔英〕人行道 (=〔美〕sidewalk);〔美〕车道 (=〔英〕roadway)。2. 铺地,铺石;铺路材料。3.【动】铺石状构造[密生的齿列等]。*a desert* ~沙漠覆盖层。***on the*** ~无住处;被抛弃。***pound the*** ~(*s*)〔美俚〕1. 徘徊街头找工作。2. (警察)巡行街道。~ **artist** 马路画家;街头展画出售者。~**-light**【建】(地窖等的)顶窗。

pav·er [ˈpeivə; ˋpevɚ] *n*. 铺石人;铺路材料;铺路机。

pav·id [ˈpævid; ˋpævɪd] *a*. 〔罕〕害怕的,胆怯的。

pa·vil·ion [pəˈviljən; pəˋvɪljən] **I** *n*. 1. (尖顶)大帐篷;帐篷形物;穹形物。2.【建】亭子,(装饰性的)楼阁。3. (运动场内搭有帐篷的)选手席;看台;(公园等的)休息处;(医院的)隔离式病楼;(展览馆的)分馆。4. 〔古〕天盖,天空。5.【解】耳廓;外耳。6. 多角形铁石的下部(斜面)。*a water ~* 水榭。~ **hospital** 隔阻式医院。~ **roof** 四角屋顶。**II** *vt*. 给…搭帐篷(盖住);笼罩。

pav·in [ˈpævin; ˋpævɪn] *n*. 孔雀舞 (= pavane)。

pav·ing [ˈpeiviŋ; ˋpevɪŋ] *n*. 1. 铺筑过的路面[地面]。2. 铺地(工程)。3. 铺路材料。~ *in sets* [*in stone blocks*] 石块铺面。~ *with pebbles* 卵石铺面。~ **stone** 铺路石。

pav·io(u)r [ˈpeivjə; ˋpevjɚ] *n*. 1. 铺路工人。2. 铺路机。3. 铺路材料。

pav·is [ˈpævis; ˋpævɪs] *n*. (中古时期的防护全身的)大盾。

Pav·lov [ˈpɑvlɔf; ˋpævˏlɑv], **Ivan Pe·tro·vitch** 巴甫洛夫〔1849—1936,苏联生理学家〕。**-lov·i·an** [pævˈlɔviən; pævˋlovɪən] *a*. 巴甫洛夫(学说)的。

Pa·vo [ˈpeivəu; ˋpevo] *n*.【天】孔雀座(= the Peacock)。

pav·o·nine, pa·vo·ni·an [ˈpævənain, pəˈvəuniən; ˋpævəˏnaɪn, pəˋvonɪən] *a*. 孔雀(似)的;绚烂多彩的。

paw¹ [pɔː; pɔ] **I** *n*. **1.** (狗,猫等的)脚爪,爪子〔*cf*. hoof〕。**2.**〔谑〕(人的)手;〔俚〕笔迹。***a velvet*** ~ **1.** (猫的)肉爪。**2.** 笑面虎;笑里藏刀。***make somebody a cat's*** ~, ***make a cat's*** ~ ***of somebody*** 利用人做爪牙。**II** *vi*., *vt*. **1.** (用脚爪等)搔,抓,扒。**2.**〔口〕笨拙地使用;盘弄(*over*);〔美俚〕爱抚。**3.** 艰苦地行走。~ **foot** 家具的兽爪撑脚。

paw² [pɔː; pɔ] *n*.〔美口〕= papa.

PAWA = Pan American World Airways〔美〕泛美航空公司〔1991 年合并于美国 Delta 航空公司〕。

pa·waw [pəˈwɔː; pəˋwɔ] *n*., *v*. = powwow.

pawk·y [ˈpɔːki; ˋpɔkɪ] *a*. **1.**〔Scot.〕狡猾的;机警的。**2.**〔美方〕狂妄的。**-i·ly** [-li; -lɪ] *ad*. 狡猾地。**-i·ness** *n*.

pawl [pɔːl; pɔl] **I** *n*.【机】(防齿轮倒转的)爪,掣转杆;卡子;掣子;棘爪。**II** *vt*. 用卡子掣住(绞盘)。*a feeder* ~【军】拨弹钩。~ **spring** 掣动簧片。

pawn¹ [pɔːn; pɔn] *n*. (国际象棋中的)兵,卒;〔喻〕爪牙,走卒。

pawn² [pɔːn; pɔn] **I** *n*. **1.** 典,当,押。**2.** 典当物,抵押品;人质。***be at*** [***in, to***] ~ 典当着,抵押出去。***give*** [***put***] ***sth. in*** ~ 典当掉,抵押掉。**II** *vt*. **1.** 当掉,把…抵押出去。**2.**〔喻〕拿(生命、名誉等)作保证。~ ***one's word*** 许诺,答应,保证。~ ***sth. off as*** 把某物冒充为…押[拿]出去。~**broker** 当铺主,典当商。~**-broking** 典当业。~**shop** 当铺。~ **ticket** 当票;抵押凭据。

Paw·nee [pɔːˈniː; pɔˋni] *n*. (*pl*. ~(*s*)) **1.** 波尼族印第安人〔住美国普拉特 (Platte) 河沿岸一带,属喀多语族〕。**2.** (印第安人的)波尼语。

pawn·ee [pɔːˈniː; pɔˋni] *n*. 收当人;接受抵押品的人。

pawn·er, pawn·or [ˈpɔːnə; ˋpɔnɚ] *n*. 当出人,典出人。

pawn·y [ˈpɔːni; ˋpɔnɪ] *n*.〔军俚〕= water.

paw·paw [ˈpɔːpɔː; ˋpɔˏpɔ] *n*.【植】**1.** 木瓜。**2.** (美国中部和南部的)巴婆树;巴婆果(= papaw)。

PAX, P.A.X. = private automatic exchange (电话)自动小交换机。

pax [pæks; pæks] **I** *n*. **1.**【天主】(耶稣或圣母马利亚的)圣像牌;【宗】(弥撒中的)接吻礼。**2.**〔英俚〕朋友;友谊。**3.**〔P-〕【罗神】和平的女神;和平。**II** *int*.〔英学俚〕算了吧! 别吵啦,别打啦! ***be*** [***make***] ~ ***with*** 和…亲热起来。***cry*** ~ 求和。***P- America*** (第二次世界大战后的)美国强权之下的世界和平。***P- Britannica*** 英国统治下的和平。~ ***Romana***〔L.〕**1.** 罗马帝国统治下的和平。**2.** 强加于被征服民族的和平。~ ***vobis*** [ˈvəubis; ˋvobɪs], ~ ***vobiscum*** [vəuˈbiskəm; voˋbɪskəm]〔L.〕祝你们平安。

pax·wax [ˈpækswæks; ˋpæksˏwæks] *n*.〔英方〕(哺乳动物的)颈部韧带。

pay¹ [pei; pe] *vt*. (~***ed*** [peid; ped],〔罕〕***paid*** [peid; ped]) 在(船底等)上涂柏油[其他防水剂等]。

pay² [pei; pe] **I** *vt*. (***paid*** [peid; ped]) **1.** 付(款),支付;付(代价),发(薪水)。**2.** 付清,偿清,缴纳。**3.** 给…以报酬;出钱雇;酬答,报答;报偿;补偿;尽(义务等)。**4.**〔口〕报复,报(仇)。**5.** 进行(访问等),表示(敬意等),致(问候),给予(注意等)。**6.** 对…有利,合算。**7.** 有…收益;(职位等)有…报酬。**8.** (~***ed***)【海】放出(缆索等)(*away*; *out*)。~ *a doctor* 酬劳医生。~ *a visit* 访问。*The enterprise will not* ~ *you*. 这项事业怕不合算。*Submission will* ~ *you better*. 你还是服从为好(否则不利)。~ *a compliment to* 称赞,夸奖,恭维。— *vi*. **1.** 支付,偿清。**2.** 偿还,付出代价;受惩罚,得到报应(*for*)。**3.** 合算,有利,值得。~ *for the book* 付清书款。*It* ~*s to be polite*. 以礼待人不会吃亏。~ ***as you go*** **1.** 量入为出。**2.** 账单到期即付。**3.** 领到薪金即付所得税。~ ***attention to*** 关心,注意。~ ***attentions*** [***addresses***] ***to*** (***a lady***) 巴结(女人),向(女子)献殷勤。~ ***away*** **1.** 付掉。**2.**【海】放出(缆索等)。~ ***back*** 偿还;报答;向…报复(~ *sb. back in his own coin* 以其人之道还治其人之身)。~ ***by instalments*** 分期付款。~ ***court to*** 追求(女人)。~ ***down*** **1.** 即时支付。**2.** (分期付款购货时)先支付部分货款。~ ***for*** 付开销;赔偿(损失);(为某种过失)付出代价;吃亏,受到惩罚。~ ***home*** 充分报复,全力反击。~ ***in*** [***into***] 缴款;解款(入银行);捐款。~ ***in advance*** 预付。~ ***in kind*** 以实物(不拿钱)支付;〔喻〕以同物偿还,报复。~ ***off*** **1.** 偿清(债务等)。**2.** 发清(工钱);发清工钱解雇。**3.** 报复,惩罚。**4.** 使人得益,使有报偿。**5.**【海】使(船首)转向下风,(船)转向下风。**6.**【海】松出(绳索等)。~ ***it's way*** 有利可图。~ ***on delivery*** 货到付款。~ ***one's college*** 靠做工读完大学。~ ***one's way*** 作到不负债。~ ***out*** **1.** 支付,还(债)。**2.** 拿…出气,痛加责罚。**3.**【海】放松,放出(绳子)。**4.**〔美〕赚到钱。~ ***the debt of nature*** 归天,死。~ ***the fiddler***〔美〕负担费用;自作自受。~ ***the penalty*** 得报应,受罚。~ ***through the nose*** 付出过高代价。~ ***too dear for one's whistle*** 做得不偿失的事。~ ***up*** (全部或按时)付清;缴清(股款等)。***Something is to*** ~.〔美口〕情况不妙。***What is to*** ~? 出了什么事?

II *n*. **1.** 付,支付;受雇用。**2.** 薪水,工资,津贴;报酬。**3.** 偿还,报答;罚,报应。**4.** 有支付能力的人;按期付款的人。**5.** 含有富矿藏的土[岩、砂];可采矿石;产(石)油地带[层]。*full* [*half*] ~ 全[半]薪。***be good*** [***bad***] ~〔口〕(人)还债可靠[不可靠]。***hit the*** ~〔美〕掘得石油层。***in the*** ~ ***of ...*** 豢养下的,…御用下的;被…收卖。***without*** ~ 无酬的,名誉的。

III *a*. **1.** 含贵重矿物的;矿藏丰富的。**2.**〔美〕(自动)收费的,需付费的。**3.** 有关支付的。~ *ore* 富矿石。~ *rock* 含矿岩。*a* ~ *library* 收费图书馆。*a* ~ *clerk* 出纳员。~**-as-you-earn** *n*.〔英〕付工资时预扣所得税法〔略作 PAYE〕。~**-as-you-see** *a*. 付款收看选定的电视节目。~ **bill** 工资单。~ **cable** 收费有线电视。~**-check,** ~**cheque** **1.** 工资支票;薪金;工资。**2.**〔美〕播音演出的主办人。~**day** **1.** 发薪日,支付日。**2.**【商】(证券市场等的)过户结账日,交割日。~ **dirt**〔美俚〕有利可图的含金矿石[矿砂];〔喻〕有利可图的发现。~ **envelope** 工资[薪水]袋。~ **grade** (军人)薪金等级。~ **list** 薪水账。~**load** 酬载,有用负载;有效负载。~ **master** (发放薪饷的)出纳员;军需官。**P- master General**〔英〕财政部主计长;〔美〕军需部长。~**off** **1.** 发薪(日)。**2.** 结清薪水解雇。**3.**〔口〕结清,算清;了结,结束。**4.**【棒球】第 9 场。**5.**〔美俚〕分赃;报仇,报复。**6.** (事件等的)高潮。**7.** 决定性的事[因素]。**8.** 出乎意料的事情(*That was the* ~*off*. 那真是意外)。~ **office** (尤指公债利息的)偿付局。~**officer**【军】军需官。~**out** 花费,支出。~**packet** 工资袋;薪金袋。~**-per-view** 有偿点播[付费节目]服务。~ **phone** [**station**] 公用自动收费电话亭。~**roll**〔美〕**1.** 职工名册;发薪簿。**2.** 应付薪金额(*on the* ~*roll* 被雇用。*off the* ~*roll* 被解职)。**3.** (计算机的)计算报表。~**-roller**〔美〕受薪者,领津贴者〔尤指政府雇员〕。~**roll giving** 扣工资捐赠〔从税前工资中扣除的慈善捐款,可免税〕。~ **sheet** 发薪簿。~ **telephone** 自动收费公用电话。~**-TV** 收费电视。

pay·a·ble [ˈpeiəbl; ˋpeəbl̩] *a*. **1.** 可付的;(到期)应支付的。**2.** (矿山等)有利的,有开采价值的。*bills* ~ 应付票据。~ *three days after sight* 见票后三日照付。~ ***at sight*** 见票即付。~ ***on demand*** 随到随付。**-a·bly** *ad*. 可获利地。

PAYE, P.A.Y.E. = pay-as-you-earn (从薪金中扣除所得税的)所得税预扣法。

pay·ee [peiˈiː; peˋi] *n*. 收款人,受款人。

pay·er, pay·or [ˈpeiə; ˋpeɚ] *n*. 付款人。

pay·ing [ˈpeiiŋ; ˋpeɪŋ] *a*. **1.** 支付的。**2.** 有利的,有益的,

P

合算的。*a* ～ *teller* (银行)出纳员。*a* ～ *concern* 有利的事业。*a* ～ *guest* 〔英〕在私人家中付费膳宿的人。*a* ～ *in slip* 缴款通知单。

pay·ment [ˈpeimənt; ˋpemənt] ***n*. 1.** 支付;缴纳;付款额,报酬;支付物。**2.** 报偿;补偿;赔偿。**3.** 报复,报仇;惩罚。～ ***at full*** = ～ *in full*. ～ ***by instalments*** 分期摊付。～ ***in advance*** [***part***] 先付[付一部分]。～ ***in full*** 全付,付清。～ ***in kind*** 实物支付。～ ***on account*** 分期偿还。～ ***on terms*** 定期付款。***received*** ～ 货款收讫。***suspend*** ～ 无力支付,宣布破产。

Pay·ne [pein; pen] ***n*. 1.** 佩恩〔姓氏〕。**2. John Howard** ～ 约翰·H 潘恩〔1791—1852,美国演员,剧作家〕。

pay·nim [ˈpeinim; ˋpenɪm] ***n*.** 〔古、诗〕异教;异教徒〔尤指穆斯林〕;异教国。

payn·ize [ˈpeinaiz; ˋpenaɪz] ***vt*.** 给(木材)灌注药液(以提高防腐效能)。

pay·o·la [peiˈəulə; peˋolə] ***n*.** 〔美俚〕暗中给的贿赂,暗中行贿。

pay·sage [peiˈzɑːʒ, ˈpeizɑːʒ; peˋzɑʒ, ˋpezɑʒ] ***n*.** 〔F.〕 **1.** (乡间)风景。**2.** 山水画,风景画。

payt. = payment.

pa·za·za [pəˈzɑːzə; pəˋzɑzə] ***n*.** 〔美俚〕= money.

PB, P.B. = **1.** 〔L.〕 *Pharmacopoeia Britannica* 《英国药典》(= British Phamacopoeia)。**2.** Prayer Book 【宗】《祈祷书》。

Pb = plumbum 【化】铅。

p.b.i. = poor bloody infantry 〔英俚〕步兵佬。

PBX, P.B.X. = private branch exchange (电话)专用小交换机。

PC = **1.** patrol craft 巡逻舰。**2.** Post Commander 驻地司令官。

P.C., PC = **1.** police constable 〔英〕普通警员。**2.** Privy Council 〔英〕枢密院。**3.** Privy Councillor 〔英〕枢密院官员;枢密顾问官。**4.** Peace Corps 〔美〕和平队。**5.** personal computer 个人电脑。**6.** Professional Corporation 〔美〕职业公司,同行公司。

P/C, p/c = **1.** petty cash 小额现金收入(或支出);零用现金。**2.** price(s) current 市价表。

pc. = **1.** piece. **2.** price(s).

p.c. = **1.** percent. **2.** postcard; postal card.

PCB = **1.** polychlorinated biphenyls 【化】聚[多]氯联苯〔系一种极有害的污染物〕。**2.** petty cash book 【会计】零用现金簿。**3.** printed circuit board 【计】印刷电路板。

P.C.C. = **1.** Price Control Commission 〔美〕物价管理委员会。**2.** Political Consultative Council 〔中〕政治协商会议。

pcl = parcel.

PCN = personal communication net 【讯】个人通讯网络。

PCR = polymerase chain reaction 【生化】聚合酶联锁反应〔此项技术可用以复制犯罪现场发现的 DNA 小样,从而有助于破案〕。

pct. = percent.

P.D. = **1.** 〔L.〕 *per diem* 每日,按日。**2.** Police Department 警察局。**3.** Postal District 邮(政)区。**4.** potential difference (电)位差,势差。

Pd. = palladium 【化】钯。

pd. = paid 付讫。

PDA = **1.** public display of affection 当众表示感情。**2.** personal digital assistant 个人数码助手〔即电子记事簿〕。

Pd.B. = Bachelor of Pedagogy 教育学学士。

Pd D, Pd.D. = Doctor of Pedagogy 教育学博士。

P.D.I. = pilot direction indicator 飞机驾驶员航向指示器。

PDL = poverty datum line 〔英〕贫困基准线。

Pdl. = poundal 【物】磅达〔力的单位〕。

Pd.M. = Master of Pedagogy 教育学硕士。

PDP = plasma display panel 等离子体显示屏面〔一种扁平电视显示屏,其显像由集成电路片控制〕。

PDQ, pdq = pretty damn quick 〔美俚〕马上,立刻,很快。

pdr = pounder.

PDT = Pacific Daylight Time 太平洋夏季时间。

p.e. = personal estate 动产,私人财产。

pea [piː; pi] ***n*.** (*pl*. ～***s***, 〔古、英方〕～***se*** [piːz; piz]) **1.** 豌豆;豌豆类。**2.** 豌豆状物;〔美俚〕棒球。*garden* ～*s* 豌豆。*green* ～*s* 青豌豆〔做菜用〕。*split* ～*s* 去皮干豌豆〔做汤用〕。*sweet* ～ 香豌豆。*Oregon* ～ 绿豆。～ *coal* 小块煤。***as like as two*** ～***s*** 一模一样,活象。～ **bean** 豌豆。～ **coat** = ～ jacket. ～ **flour** 豌豆粉。～ **green** 青豆色,黄绿色。～ **jacket** (水手、水兵、男孩等穿的)粗呢上装。～**shooter 1.** 豆子枪,玩具枪。**2.** 〔俚〕驱逐机。～ **soup 1.** 豌豆汤。**2.** 〔美俚〕不中用的人。**3.** = ～ souper. ～**-souper** 〔英口〕(尤指伦敦的)黄色浓雾。～**-soupy *a*.** 〔英口〕(雾)黄而浓的;黄色浓雾似的。

Pea·bod·y [ˈpiːˌbɔdi; ˋpiˏbɑdɪ] ***n*.** 皮博迪〔姓氏〕。

peace [piːs; pis] ***n*. 1.** 和平;太平;平静;宁静根源;寂静。**2.** 和好,和睦;〔常 P-〕媾和,讲和;媾和条约,和约(= treaty of ～)。**3.** 〔the ～〕治安,社会秩序。**4.** 安心,安静;悠闲;沉默。*P- cannot be got by begging; it must be fought for*. 和平不能乞求,和平必须争取。*the pipe of* ～ (北美印第安人)互相传吸表示讲和的烟斗。*the piping times of* ～ 太平时代。*Do let me have a little* ～. 让我安静一下。*P-*! 安静,别吵! *P- there*! 喂! 别闹。*P- be with you*! 祝你平安! *P- to his ashes* [*memory, soul*]! 愿他安眠地下! ***at*** ～ 和平;和好,和睦;安心;安静。***be sworn of the*** ～ 被任命为治安官。***breach of the*** ～ 妨害治安。***hold*** [***keep***] ***one's*** ～ 不声不响,保持缄默。***in*** ～ 平平安安;安心(*live in* ～ 平平安安过日子)。***keep the*** (***king's*** [***queen's***]) ～ 维持治安。***leave sb. in*** ～ 不打搅某人。***let sb. go in*** ～ 放过某人,不为难某人。***make one's*** ～ ***with*** 跟…讲和[重新和好]。***make*** ～ 和好,讲和(*with*)。～ ***at any price*** 绝对和平(主义)。～ ***of conscience*** 问心无愧。～ ***with honour*** 体面[光荣]的和平。***swear the*** ～ ***against*** (*sb.*) 揭发某人图谋行凶。～ **blocade** 平时封锁。～**-breaker** 破坏和平的人;扰乱治安者。**P- Corps** 〔美〕和平队。～ **dividend** 和平红利〔指战争或军事对峙结束,削减军备开支转用于和平建设〕。～ **establishment** 【军】平时编制。～**-loving *a*.** 爱好和平的。～**maker** 调解人,和事佬;〔谑〕维持和平的工具〔手枪、军舰等〕。～**making** 调解,调停。～**monger** 〔美〕和平贩子,一味乞求和平的人。～ **offering 1.** 和平建议;和平仪式。**2.** 和解礼物。**3.** 【宗】谢恩[赎罪]供物。～ **officer** 治安官;警官。～ **pipe** = the pipe of peace. ～**time *n*., *a*.** 和平时期(的);平时(的) (*opp*. wartime)。

peace·a·ble [ˈpiːsəbl; ˋpisəbl̩] ***a*. 1.** 平和的,爱好和平的,息事宁人的,温和的,温顺的。**2.** 和平的,太平的。*in the* ～ *times* 平时。**-ness *n*. -a·bly *ad*.**

peace·ful [ˈpiːsful; ˋpisfəl] ***a*. 1.** 和平的,太平的;平时的。**2.** 宁静的,安静的。**3.** 爱好和平的,温和的。～ *coexistence* 和平共处。～ *uses of atomic energy* 原子能的和平应用。～ *penetration* 和平渗透。～ *picketing* 监视破坏罢工的纠察线。～ *times* 太平时期。**-ly *ad*. -ness *n*.**

peace·nik [ˈpiːsnik; ˋpisnɪk] ***n*.** 〔俚〕示威反战者,反战运动分子。

peach[1] [piːtʃ; pitʃ] ***vt*.** 〔俚〕告发;出卖(同伙)(*against*; *on*; *upon*)。—***vi*.** 告密。

peach[2] [piːtʃ; pitʃ] **I *n*. 1.** 桃子;桃树。**2.** 桃色,桃红色。**3.** 〔美〕桃酒。**4.** 〔俚〕受人喜欢的人[物];漂亮姑娘;好人;好东西;有功劳的人〔常用作挖苦话〕。*flat* ～ 蟠桃。*a* ～ *of a car* 一辆漂亮的车。*a* ～ *of a cook* 一位顶呱呱的厨师。**II *a*.** 桃色的。～ ***and cream*** (人)乳白色皮

肤而双颊桃红。~ **blossom** 桃花。~**blossom** 桃红色。~ **blow** 1.(中国瓷器的)紫红色釉药,桃色釉。2.紫红马铃薯。~ **brandy** 桃子酒。~**-colour(ed)** *a*. 桃色(的)。~**-tree** 桃树。

peach·er·in·o [ˌpiːtʃəˈriːnəu; ˏpitʃəˈrino] *n*. 〔美俚〕漂亮女人;了不起的人[东西]。

pea·chick [ˈpiːtʃik; ˋpiˏtʃɪk] *n*. 小孔雀。

peach·y [ˈpiːtʃi; ˋpitʃɪ] *a*. 1. 桃子(似)的;桃色的。2. 〔美俚〕漂亮的,极好的。**-i·ness** *n*.

Pea·cock [ˈpiːkɔk; ˋpikɑk] *n*. 皮科克〔姓氏〕。

pea·cock [ˈpiːkɔk; ˋpiˏkɑk] I *n*. (*pl*. ~*s*, 〔集合词〕~) 1. (雄)孔雀 (*opp*. peahen)。2. 爱虚荣的人;爱炫弄自己的人。3. 〔the P-〕【天】孔雀座 (= Pavo)。***a*** ~ ***in*** (***his***) ***pride*** 开屏孔雀;炫耀一时的人。***as proud as a*** ~ 孔雀般高傲。***play the*** ~ 炫耀自己,沾沾自喜,妄自尊大。II *vt*. 〔~ oneself〕炫耀。—*vi*. 炫耀,招摇过市,趾高气扬地走。~ **blue** 孔雀蓝(染料)。~ **ore** 黄铜矿,斑铜矿。~ **stone** 孔雀石。**-cock·y** *a*.

pea·cock·er·y [ˈpiːkɔkəri; ˋpiˏkɑkərɪ] *n*. 炫耀,招摇;虚荣,虚饰。

pea·cock·ish, pea·cock·like [ˈpiːkɔkiʃ, ˈpiːkɔklaik; ˋpiˏkɑkɪʃ, ˋpiˏkɑklaɪk] *a*. 孔雀似的;虚荣心强的;炫耀的。

pea·fowl [ˈpiːfaul; ˋpiˏfaʊl] *n*. 孔雀〔雌或雄〕。

pea·hen [ˈpiːˈhen; ˋpiˏhɛn] *n*. 雌孔雀。

peak[1] [piːk; pik] *vi*. 1. 瘦弱;消瘦,憔悴。2. 减少,缩小 (*out*)。~ ***and pine*** 消瘦;憔悴。

peak[2] [piːk; pik] I *n*. 1. 山峰,山顶;孤山。2. (胡须等的)尖儿;尖端。3. 最高点,绝顶;最大量;巅值,峰值;【物】波峰。4. (衣着等的)尖形突出部;(帽子等的)鸭舌,遮檐。5. 〔方〕岬,海角。6. 【海】斜桁尖头;船头[船尾]尖舱;锚爪。*a flood* ~ 洪峰。*the* ~ *performance* 最高生产率。*the after* ~ (船的)尾舱。~ *position* 〔美〕棒球联赛的最高名次。~ *year* 【统】最高纪录年。

II *vt*. 1. 竖起,使成峰状,使高耸。2. 使达到最高峰。3. (划船休息时)直竖(桨等);(鲸鱼)竖起(尾巴)。*She pursed her pretty lips and ~ed her eyebrows*. 她紧闭美丽的双唇,竖起眉毛。—*vi*. 1. 高耸,尖起;(桨等不划时)竖起;(鲸鱼等)翘起尾巴。2. 达到最高峰。~ **experience**【心】高峰体验,饱满体验〔极其激动的感情体验〕。~**-hour** *a*. 高峰时刻的。~**-load** 1. 【电】最大负载,高峰负荷。2. 一定时间内的最高运输[交易]量。~**-peak** 峰值中的最大值。~ **shaving** (为满足高峰时的需要)从储罐中抽出液态天然气。

peak·ed[1] [ˈpiːkid; ˋpikɪd] *a*. 1. 憔悴的,瘦削的。2. 减少的,缩小的。

peaked[2] [piːkt; pikt] *a*. 1. (帽子等)有遮檐的;有(胡须)尖的。2. 有峰的。3. 竖起的,高耸的。

peak·y[1] [ˈpiːki; ˋpikɪ] *a*. 〔俚〕消瘦了的;〔美俚〕快腐烂的。

peak·y[2] [ˈpiːki; ˋpikɪ] *a*. 有峰的,多峰的;尖的。

Peal [piːl; pil] *n*. 皮尔〔姓氏〕。

peal [piːl; pil] I *n*. 1. (雷、大炮、笑声、鼓掌声等的)响声,隆隆声。2. 钟声;钟乐;(用作乐器的)一组钟,编钟。*a* ~ *of artillery* 隆隆的炮声。*a* ~ *of thunder* 雷声隆隆。*a* ~ *of applause* [*laughter*] 一阵响亮的喝彩[哄笑]声。***ring a*** ~ 奏钟乐。II *vt*. 1. 使鸣响;大声说;夸奖;散布(谣言等)。2. 〔罕〕使耳朵变聋。—*vi*. (钟、雷等)鸣响,轰响 (*out*)。

pe·an [ˈpiːən; ˋpiən] *n*. = paean.

pea·nut [ˈpiːnʌt; ˋpiˏnʌt] I *n*. 1. 落花生;长生果;花生米。2. 〔美俚〕小人物;无聊人物;长着狮子鼻的人。3. 〔*pl*.〕(总数中的一笔)小数目;小利,小收入;小企业。II *a*. 微不足道的,渺小的。*a* ~ *politician* 〔美俚〕无聊政客,小政客。~ **butter** 花生酱。~ **gallery** 〔美俚〕(戏院的)顶层楼座〔票价最低〕。~ **oil** 花生油。

pea·pod [ˈpiːpɔd; ˋpiˏpɑd] *n*. (豌豆的)豆荚。

pear [peə; pɛr] *n*. 梨;梨树;梨形物。*balsam* ~ 苦瓜。~ **shaped** *a*. 1. 梨形的。2. (声调)圆润的,无鼻音的,清亮的。~**-tree** 梨树。

Pearl [pəːl; pɝl] *n*. 珀尔〔女子名〕。

pearl[1] [pəːl; pɝl] I *n*. 1. 珍珠;珍品;优秀典型,精华;〔*pl*.〕珍珠项链。2. 珍珠状物〔露、泪、雪白的牙齿等〕;(铁、煤等的)小片,微粒。3. 珍珠色。4. 【印】珍珠型铅字〔5 点小型活字〕;〔方〕【医】白内障,星眼。*an artificial* [*a false, an imitation*] ~ 人造珍珠,赛珍珠。*culture(d)* ~ 养殖的珍珠。*a mother of* ~ 珍珠母,珍珠贝。*the* ~ *of his country* 国家的精华[杰出人物]。***cast*** ~***s before swine*** 明珠暗投;把珍贵物送给不识货的人。

II *a*. 珍珠(制)的;珍珠似的。

III *vt*. 1. 使呈珠状,使成小圆粒,使像珍珠;把(米、麦等)制成小粒。2. 用珍珠装饰,用珍珠镶嵌。3. 使成珍珠色,使发珍珠光泽。4. 珠子似地散布于。—*vi*. 1. 采珍珠。2. 珠子般地滴下;变成珍珠形[色]。*go ~ing* 去采珍珠。~ **ash**【化】珍珠灰,粗碳酸钾。~ **barley** 大麦搓成的圆珠形小颗粒,珍珠麦。~ **button** 贝壳钮扣。~ **diver** 1. 潜水采珠人。2. 〔美俚〕洗盆子的人。~ **eye** 1. 鸟的眼睛。2. 【医】白内障。~ **fisher** 采珠人,采珠业者。~**-fishery** 采珠业;采珠场。~**-fishing** 采珠业。~ **grain** 珍珠克拉〔珍珠重量单位 = $\frac{1}{4}$ carat〕。~ **gray** 淡灰色,珍珠色。**P- Harbor** 1. 珍珠港〔美国军港〕。2. (珍珠港事件式的)偷袭。~ **oyster**【贝】珍珠贝。~**-plant**【植】紫草;麦家公。~ **powder** (化妆用)珍珠粉。~**-sago** 珠粒西米。~ **shell** 珍珠母,夜光贝,珍珠贝。~**white** 1. *a*. 珍珠般白的。2. *n*. 鱼鳞粉〔人造珍珠的原料〕;锌钡白〔一种白色颜料〕。

pearl[2] [pəːl; pɝl] *n*., *v*. = purl[2].

pearl·ed [pəːld; pɝld] *a*. 1. 〔诗〕用珍珠装饰的,镶着珍珠的。2. 变成珍珠状小粒的;珍珠似的,有珍珠色泽的。

pearl·es·cent [pəːˈlesnt; ˏpɝˋlɛsənt] *a*. 珠母般的。

pearl·ies [ˈpəːliz; ˋpɝlɪz] *n*. 〔*pl*.〕1. 大贝壳扣。2. (水果贩等穿的)钉有许多壳扣的衣服〔伦敦小贩的节日服装〕。

pearl·ite [ˈpəːlait; ˋpɝlaɪt] *n*. 1. 【冶】珠泽铁;珠光体;珠层体。2. 【地】珍珠岩。**pearl·it·ic** [pəːˈlitik; pɝˋlɪtɪk] *a*.

pearl·ized [ˈpəːlaizd; ˋpɝlaɪzd] *a*. 珠母般的。

pearl·y [ˈpəːli; ˋpɝlɪ] *a*. 1. 珍珠似的;珍珠色的。2. 产珍珠的。3. 用珍珠装饰的;珍贵的。4. 【乐】响亮的。~**-nautilus** 鹦鹉螺。

pear·main [ˈpeəmein; ˋpɛrmen] *n*. 苹果品种名。*the American Summer* ~ 祝光苹果。*the White Winter* ~ 青香蕉苹果。

Pear·son [ˈpiəsn; ˋpɪrsn] *n*. 皮尔逊〔姓氏〕。

peart [piət; pɝt] *a*. 〔美方〕愉快的,快活的;活泼的,有生气的。**-ly** *ad*.

peas·ant [ˈpezənt; ˋpɛznt] *n*. 1. 农民。★多指非英语国家的自耕农或雇农,英语国家的农民多用 farmer. 2. 庄稼人,乡下人。*a* ~ *folk* 农民。*a* ~ *farmer* 小自耕农。*landless* ~ 雇农。*a* ~ *girl* 乡下姑娘。~ **proprietor(-ship)** 自耕农(制)。

peas·ant·ry [ˈpezəntri; ˋpɛzntrɪ] *n*. 1. 〔集合词〕农民。2. 农民身分;农民特点,农村习气。

pease [piːz; piz] pea 的复数。~**-pudding** 豌豆布丁。

peas(e)·cod [ˈpiːzkɔd; ˋpizˏkɑd] *n*. 〔古〕= peapod.

peat[1] [piːt; pit] *n*. 泥炭,草炭,泥炭土。~ **bed**, ~**bog**, ~**-moor**, ~**moss** *n*. 泥炭沼。~**-reek** 泥炭烟。

peat[2] [piːt; pit] *n*. 〔古、贬〕人〔尤指女人〕。

peat·er·y [ˈpiːtəri; ˋpitərɪ] *n*. 泥炭产地;泥炭沼。

peat·y [ˈpiːti; ˋpitɪ] *a*. 1. 泥炭似的。2. 多泥炭的。

peau de soie [ˌpəu dəˈswɑː; ˏpo dəˋswɑ] 〔F.〕双面横绫缎〔法国制〕。

pea·v(e)y [ˈpiːvi; ˋpivɪ] *n*. (*pl*. ~*s*) (翻动木头用的)

钩棍,钩梃。

peb·ble [ˈpebl; ˋpɛbl] **I** *n*. **1.** 细砾,砾,卵石,石子。**2.** 水晶;水晶(做的)透镜。**3.** 粒状火药(=~-powder)。**4.** 粗鞣皮(=~d leather)。**5.** (皮革、纸张等表面仿印的)卵石花纹。***not the only ~ on the beach*** 并非独一无二的(人)。**II** *vt*. **1.** 用石子扔。**2.** 用卵石铺盖。**3.** 使纹理粗糙,使有皱纹[卵石纹]。*Scotch ~s* 玛瑙。~ **culture** 石器文化。~ **leather** 粗纹皮革。~ **powder** 粒状火药。~ **stone** 小卵石。~**-ware** 一种杂色斑纹陶器。

peb·bly [ˈpebli; ˋpɛblɪ] *a*. **1.** 卵石多的。**2.** 有卵石花纹的。

peb·rine [pebˈrin; pɛbˋrɪn] *n*. 〔F.〕蚕孢子虫病。

PEC = photo electrochemical cell【物】光电化学管。

p.e.c. = photoelectric cell 光电管,光电池。

pe·can [piˈkæn; pɪˋkɑn] *n*.【植】(美洲)薄壳山核桃(树)。

pec·ca·ble [ˈpekəbl; ˋpɛkəbl] *a*. 易犯罪的;易有过失的。**-ca·bili·ty** [ˌpekəˈbiliti; ˏpɛkəˋbɪlətɪ] *n*.

pec·ca·dil·lo [ˌpekəˈdiləu; ˏpɛkəˋdɪlo] *n*. (*pl*. ~(*e*)*s*) 轻罪;小过。

pec·can·cy [ˈpekənsi; ˋpɛkənsɪ] *n*. **1.** 有罪,犯罪;罪行。**2.** 违章,犯规。**3.**【医】病态。

pec·cant [ˈpekənt; ˋpɛkənt] *a*. **1.** 有罪的,犯罪的;邪恶的。**2.** 违章的;错误的;犯规的。**3.**【医】病态的,致病的。**-ly** *ad*.

pec·ca·ry [ˈpekəri; ˋpɛkərɪ] *n*. (*pl*. **-ries**,〔集合词〕~)【动】西貒〔美国一种野猪〕。

pec·ca·vi [peˈkɑːviː; pɪˋkevai] **I** *int*.〔L.〕我犯罪了;我忏悔。**II** *n*. (*pl*. ~*s*) 忏悔,认罪。***cry*** ~忏悔,认错。

peck[1] [pek; pɛk] *n*. **1.** 配克〔英美干量单位,等于八夸脱〕。**2.** 多量,很多。*a ~ of troubles* 很多麻烦。

peck[2] [pek; pɛk] **I** *vt*. **1.** 啄;啄起,啄穿;啄成;啄掘;啄坏。**2.** (用尖头工具)凿,琢。**3.**〔口〕匆匆忙忙地[一点一点地]吃;〔谑〕急吻一下。—*vi*. **1.** 啄;凿,琢。**2.** 一点一点地吃。**3.** 找岔子 (*at*)。**4.**〔俚〕扔(石头等) (*at*)。~ ***at*** **1.** 啄。**2.** 说…闲话,找…的岔子。~ ***out*** **1.** 啄出。**2.** 用食指按打字机的键打字〔多为美国记者的工作方式〕。**II** *n*. **1.** 啄。**2.** 啄痕;啄出的洞。**3.**〔俚〕食物;〔谑〕轻吻。**4.**〔俚〕扔石头;找岔子。**5.**〔美俚〕匆忙吃(点东西)。***off one's ~*** 失去胃口。~ ***and perch***〔俚〕吃和住。~**(ing) order**【生】禽鸟强弱次序;社会等级。

peck·er [ˈpekə; ˋpɛkɚ] *n*. **1.** 会啄的鸟;啄木鸟;啄的人。**2.** 鹤嘴锄,铁镐。**3.**〔俚〕鸟嘴,喙;穿孔器[针]。**4.**〔俚〕(人的)鼻子。**5.**〔俚〕勇气,精神。**6.**【电】替续板,簧片。***Keep your ~ up!***〔俚〕拿出精神来! 打起精神来。***put up sb.'s ~*** 气人,使人不痛快,得罪人。

peck·er·wood [ˈpekəwud; ˋpɛkɚˏwʊd] *n*. **1.** 啄木鸟(= woodpecker)。**2.**〔美南部俚〕山里人,山林居民;〔黑人用语,贬〕南方穷苦白人。

peck·ish [ˈpekiʃ; ˋpɛkɪʃ] *a*.〔口〕**1.** 饿的,肚子空的。**2.** 生气的,找岔子的。*feel* ~有点饿。

Peck·sniff [ˈpeksnif; ˋpɛkˏsnɪf] *n*. 伪君子〔英国作家狄更斯的小说 Martin Chuzzlewit 中的人物〕。

Peck·sniff·ian [pekˈsnifiən; pɛkˋsnɪfɪən] *a*. 伪善的;伪装神圣的。

peck·y [ˈpeki; ˋpɛkɪ] *a*. 有霉斑的,有蛀孔的。

Pé·cos Bíll [ˈpekəus bil; ˋpekos ˋbɪl] 配科斯·比尔〔美国西部、阿根廷传说中的放牛英雄〕。

pec·tase [ˈpekteis; ˋpɛktes] *n*.【生化】果胶酶。

pec·tate [ˈpekteit; ˋpɛktet] *n*.【化】果胶酸盐;果胶酸的盐类。

pec·ten [ˈpektən; ˋpɛktən] *n*. (*pl*. ~*s*, ***pec·ti·nes*** [-tiniːz; -tɪniz]) **1.**【动】(鸟眼的)梳膜;(昆虫的)栉。**2.**【解】耻骨。**3.**【贝】海扇,扇贝。

pec·tic [ˈpektik; ˋpɛktɪk] *a*. 果胶的,含果胶的,从果胶中得到的。~ **acid**【化】果胶酸。

pec·tin [ˈpektin; ˋpɛktɪn] *n*.【化】果胶。

pec·ti·nate, pec·ti·nated [ˈpektinit, -neitid; ˋpɛktəˏnet, -netɪd] *a*. 梳状的,齿形的。

pec·ti·na·tion [ˌpektiˈneiʃən; ˏpɛktəˋneʃən] *n*. 梳状;梳状物;梳状结构。

pec·to·ral [ˈpektərəl; ˋpɛktərəl] **I** *a*. **1.** 胸部的;戴在胸部的。**2.**【医】胸腔病的,肺病的;治肺病有效的;止咳的。**3.** 个人感情引起的;主观的。**4.** (声音)宏亮的。*a ~ remedy* 肺病药。~ *species* 止咳茶。**II** *n*. **1.** (尤指犹太祭司长的)胸饰;遮胸。**2.**【医】肺病药;止咳药。**3.**【动】胸鳍(=~ fin);胸肌。~ **cross** (教长、主教等)带在胸前的十字架。~ **fin**【鱼】胸鳍。~ **girdle** [**arch**]【动、解】肩带。~ **sandpiper**【动】纹胸滨鹬。

pec·tose [ˈpektəus; ˋpɛktos] *n*.【化】果胶糖。

pec·ul [ˈpikʌl; ˋpɪkʌl] *n*. = picul.

pec·u·late [ˈpekjuleit; ˋpɛkjəˏlet] *vi*., *vt*. 挪用,盗用,侵吞(公款等)。**-u·la·tion** *n*. **-u·la·tor** *n*. 挪用[盗用、侵吞]公款者。

pe·cul·iar [piˈkjuːljə, -liə; pɪˋkjuljɚ, -lɪə] **I** *a*. **1.** 独特的,特有的 (*to*);特别的,(兴趣等)特殊的。**2.** 特异的,罕见的,奇怪的;异常的。**3.** 个人的,(财产等)私人的。*Language is ~ to mankind*. 语言是人类所特有的。*expressions ~ to English* 英语特有的词语。~ *institution*〔美隐语〕奴隶制度。~ *motion*【天】本动。~ *people*〔总称〕**1.**【基督】上帝的特选子民〔指基督徒〕。**2.** 犹太人。**3.**〔P- People〕基督教祈祷治病派〔反对医药并相信向神祈祷即能治病〕。**II** *n*. **1.** 特有财产;特权。**2.**【宗】特殊教区。**3.**〔P-〕【基督】上帝的特选子民〔指基督徒〕;犹太人。**-ly** *ad*.

pe·cu·li·ar·i·ty [piˌkjuːliˈæriti; pɪˏkjulɪˋærətɪ] *n*. **1.** 特性,特色,特质。**2.** 癖;怪癖。**3.** 奇形怪状;特殊的东西。

pe·cu·li·um [piˈkjuːliəm; pɪˋkjulɪəm] *n*. **1.** (罗马法)给予奴隶、妻子或孩子的私产。**2.** 私产。

pe·cu·ni·a·ri·ly [piˈkjuːnjərili, -niə-; pɪˋkjunɪˏɛrɪlɪ] *ad*. 金钱上,关于金钱。

pe·cu·ni·a·ry [piˈkjuːnjəri; pɪˋkjunɪˏɛrɪ] *a*. **1.** 金钱(上)的。**2.** 应付罚金的,应罚款的。~ *aid* 资助。~ *considerations* [*reward*] 金钱报酬。~ *embarrassment* 财政困难。~ *condition* 财政,经济状况。~ *penalties* 罚金。~ *resources* 财力。***from*** [***in***] ***a ~ point of view*** 从金钱[财政]上来看。

ped *n*.〔美口〕步行者(= pedestrian)。

ped. = **1.** pedal. **2.** pedestal. **3.** pedestrian.

ped- *pref*.〔用于元[母]音前〕**1.** = pedi-. **2.** = pedo-.

-ped *suf*. 表示"足":quadru*ped*.

ped·a·gog [ˈpedəgɔg; ˋpɛdəgɑg] *n*.〔美〕= pedagogue.

ped·a·gog·ic, ped·a·gog·i·cal [ˌpedəˈgɔdʒik, -kəl; ˏpɛdəˋgɑdʒɪk, -kl] *a*. 教育学的,教授法的;教师的。~ *research group* 教研组。**-gog·i·cal·ly** *ad*.

ped·a·gog·ics [ˌpedəˈgɔdʒiks; ˏpɛdəˋgɑdʒɪks] *n*.〔*pl*.〕〔用作单〕**1.** 教育学,教授法。**2.** 教师职业。

ped·a·gogue [ˈpedəgɔg; ˋpɛdəˏgɑg] *n*. **1.** (中、小学的)老师,教员;(儿童)教育者。**2.** = pedant.

ped·a·gog(u)·ism [ˈpedəˌgɔgizəm; ˋpɛdəˏgɑgɪzəm] *n*.〔常蔑〕**1.** 儿童教授(法)。**2.** 老师派头,好为人师的教书匠习气。

ped·a·go·gy [ˈpedəgɔgi; ˋpɛdəˏgodʒɪ] *n*. **1.** 教育学,教授法。**2.** 儿童教育。**3.** 教师职业。

ped·al [ˈpedl, ˈpiːdl; ˋpɛdl, ˋpidl] **I** *a*.〔L.〕**1.** [ˈpedl; ˋpɛdl]【动】足的,脚的;踏板的。**2.** [ˈpiːdl; ˋpidl]【数】垂足(线)的。~ *brake* 脚刹车。~ *curve* [*face*] 垂足曲线[面]。**II** *n*. **1.** [ˈpedl; ˋpɛdl] (缝纫机等的)踏板;【乐】持续音。**2.** [ˈpiːdl; ˋpidl]【数】垂足线,垂足面。**III** *vt*. (***ped·al(l)ed***; ***ped·al·(l)ing***) 踏…的踏板;踩踏板转动。~ *a bicycle* 骑自行车。—*vi*. 踩踏板;骑自行车。~ *along a road* 在路上骑自行车。~ **bin**〔英〕

(用脚一踩,盖子即开的)家用小垃圾桶。~ **point**【乐】持续音(部)。~ **pusher**〔美〕**1.** 骑自行车的人,自行车比赛选手。**2.**〔~ pushers〕长及小腿的女式运动裤。

pe·dal·fer [piˈdælfə; pɪˋdælfɚ] ***n.***【地】**1.** 淋余土。**2.** 铁铝土。**-fer·ic** [ˌpedəlˈfeərik; ˏpɛdəlˋfɛrɪk] ***a.***

ped·al·o, ped·all·o [ˈpedələu; ˋpɛdəlo] ***n.*** (*pl.* **~s**) 脚踏船〔单人或双人乘坐的用脚踏板带动桨轮的小船〕(= pedal boat)。

ped·ant [ˈpedənt; ˋpɛdn̩t] ***n.*** 卖弄学问的人,书呆子,空谈家;腐儒,学究。

pe·dan·tic [piˈdæntik; pɪˋdæntɪk] ***a.*** 卖弄学问的;学究式的,迂腐的。**-ti·cism** ***n.*** 迂腐作风。

ped·an·toc·ra·cy [ˌpedənˈtɔkrəsi; ˏpɛdənˋtɑkrəsɪ] ***n.*** 腐儒政治(集团)。

ped·ant·ry [ˈpedəntri; ˋpɛdn̩trɪ] ***n.*** **1.** 卖弄学问;学究式想法。**2.** 死守陈规旧套;迂腐。

ped·ate [ˈpedit; ˋpɛdet] ***a.*** **1.**【动】具足的;具管足的。**2.** 足状的;用足的。**3.**【植】(叶子)鸟足状的。

pe·dat·i·fid [piˈdætifid, -ˈdeit-; pɪˋdætəfɪd, -ˋdet-] ***a.***【植】(叶子)鸟足状裂开的。

ped·der [ˈpedə; ˋpɛdɚ] ***n.*** 〔Scot.〕= pedlar.

ped·dle [ˈpedl; ˋpɛdl̩] ***vt.*** **1.** 贩卖,零卖,走卖,挑卖,叫卖。**2.** 传播(谣言等);兜售(理论等)。—***vi.*** **1.** 做小贩,沿街叫卖。**2.** 忙于做琐事。~ ***alibis*** [ˈælibaiz; ˋæləbaɪz]〔美俚〕托辞逃避。~ ***fish stories***〔美〕大吹自己的运动本领。***P- one's papers*** [***fish***] 不管闲事。

ped·dler [ˈpedlə; ˋpɛdlɚ] ***n.*** = pedlar.

ped·dler·y [ˈpedləri; ˋpɛdlərɪ] ***n.*** **1.** 小贩生意。**2.** 小贩的货物。

ped·dling [ˈpedliŋ; ˋpɛdl̩ɪŋ] **I** ***a.*** **1.** 商贩的,叫卖的。**2.** 琐碎的,不重要的。**3.** 小心眼儿的。~ *details* 无关宏旨的细节。**II** ***n.*** 商贩。**-ly** ***ad.***

-ped(e) *comb. f.* 表示"足": centi*pede*.

ped·er·ast [ˈpedəræst, ˈpiːdə-; ˋpɛdəræst, ˋpidə-] ***n.*** 男色者,鸡奸者。**ped·er·as·tic** ***a.*** **-as·ti·cal·ly** ***ad.***

ped·er·as·ty [ˈpedəræsti, ˈpiːdə; ˋpɛdəˏræstɪ, ˋpidə-] ***n.*** 鸡奸。

ped·es·tal [ˈpedistl; ˋpɛdɪstl̩] **I** ***n.*** **1.** 基座,底座,台,座子;架;柱脚。**2.** 根底,基础;受人尊敬的地位。**3.**【机】托轴架,支座。*the ~ of the bronze statue* 青铜塑像的底座。*a camera ~* 照像机三角架。***put*** [***set***] ***sb.*** (***up***) ***on a ~*** 非常尊敬(某人),把某人当偶像崇拜。**II** ***vt.*** (*-l(l)-*) **1.** 把…搁在架上。**2.** 给…加台脚;支持。

pe·des·tri·an [piˈdestriən; pəˋdɛstrɪən] **I** ***a.*** **1.** 徒步的,步行的。**2.** (文章等)粗俗的,枯燥的;平凡的;单调的,陈腐的。**II** ***n.*** 步行者,徒步旅行者;徒步竞走者;很能走路的人,步行主义者。~ **crossing** 人行横道。**-ism** ***n.*** **1.** 步行术,徒步旅行;徒步竞走;徒步主义。**2.** (文章的)平凡,单调。**-ize** ***vi.*** 徒步旅行,步行。

pedi-[1] *comb. f.* 表示"足": *pedi*cab.

pedi-[2] *comb. f.* 表示"儿童": *pedi*atrician.

pe·di·at·ric [ˌpiːdiˈætrik; ˏpidɪˋætrɪk] ***a.*** = paediatric.

pe·di·a·tri·cian [ˌpiːdiəˈtriʃən, pe-; ˏpidɪəˋtrɪʃən, pɛ-] ***n.*** = paediatrician.

pe·di·at·rics [ˌpiːdiˈætriks; ˏpidɪˋætrɪks] ***n.*** = paediatrics.

pe·di·at·rist [ˌpiːdiˈætrist; ˏpidɪˋætrɪst] ***n.*** = paediatrist.

ped·i·cab [ˈpedikæb; ˋpɛdɪkæb] ***n.*** (人力)三轮车。

ped·i·cel, ped·i·cle [ˈpedisəl, ˈpedikl; ˋpɛdəsl̩, ˋpɛdəkl̩] ***n.***【植】花梗;【动】肉茎,(触角的)梗节。

ped·i·cel·late, pe·dic·u·late [ˈpedisəleit, piˈdikjulit; ˋpɛdəsəlɪt, pɪˋdɪkjəlɪt] ***a.***【植】有花梗的;【动】有肉茎的,有(触角)梗节的。

pe·dic·u·lar, pe·dic·u·lous [piˈdikjulə, -ləs; pɪˋdɪkjəlɚ, -ləs] ***a.*** 满是虱子的。

pe·dic·ul·o·sis [piˌdikjuˈləusis; pɪˏdɪkjuˋlosɪs] ***n.***【医】虱病,生虱子。

ped·i·cure [ˈpedikjuə; ˋpɛdɪkˏjʊr] **I** ***n.*** **1.** 脚病治疗;足病医师,足医。**2.** 修脚。**II** ***vt.*** 修(脚),医(脚)。

ped·i·gree [ˈpedigriː; ˋpɛdəˏgri] **I** ***n.*** **1.** 血统;【生】谱系;(纯种家畜的)血统表;(家畜的)种,纯种;品种形成。**2.** 血统,家谱,家系;身家,出身,门第。**3.** (语言的)起源,词源。**4.**〔美俚〕(警察局的)犯罪档案。*a ~ seed* 原种;种子。*a ~ cattle* 纯种牛。**II** ***a.*** = pedigreed. **~-man**〔美俚〕有案可查的惯犯。

ped·i·greed [ˈpedigriːd; ˋpɛdəˏgrid] ***a.*** (家世)有来历的;(马等)血统明显的。

ped·i·ment [ˈpedimənt; ˋpɛdəmənt] ***n.*** **1.**【建】山头,人字墙;(门顶、壁炉顶等的)三角饰;【地】碛[岩]原。**-al, -ed** ***a.*** 有人字墙的,人字形的。

pe·dim·e·ter [piˈdimitə; pɪˋdɪmɪtɚ] ***n.*** = pedometer.

ped·i·palp [ˈpediˌpælp; ˋpɛdəˏpælp] ***n.***【动】须肢。

ped·lar [ˈpedlə; ˋpɛdlɚ] ***n.*** **1.** 小贩,商贩;传播(谣言等)的人。**2.**〔美俚〕(各站都停的)慢车。**pedlar's French** (盗贼等的)隐语,暗话。

ped·lar·y [ˈpedləri; ˋpɛdlərɪ] ***n.*** = peddlery.

ped·ler [ˈpedlə; ˋpɛdlɚ] ***n.*** = pedlar.

pedo- *comb. f.* = paed(o)-: *pedo*chemical 土壤化学的。

pe·do·bap·tism [ˌpiːdəuˈbæptizəm; ˏpidoˋbæptɪzm̩] ***n.*** = paedobaptism.

ped·o·cal [ˈpedəˌkæl; ˋpɛdəˏkæl] ***n.***【地】钙层土。**-cal·ic** ***a.***

pe·do·don·tics [ˌpiːdəuˈdɔntiks; ˏpidəˋdɑntɪks] ***n.*** 儿童牙科学。**-dontist** ***n.*** 儿童牙医。

ped·o·gen·e·sis [ˌpiːdəuˈdʒenisis; ˏpidoˋdʒɛnəsɪs] ***n.***【地】成土作用。**-gen·ic, -ge·net·ic** ***a.***

pe·dol·o·gy[1] [piˈdɔlədʒi; pɪˋdɑlədʒɪ] ***n.***〔美〕儿科学;小儿科。**pedo·log·ic** [ˌpiːdəuˈlɔdʒik; ˏpidəˋlɑdʒɪk], **pe·do·log·i·cal** ***a.*** **pe·do·log·i·cal·ly** ***ad.*** **pe·dolo·gist** ***n.*** 小儿科医师,儿科专家。

pe·dol·o·gy[2] [piˈdɔlədʒi; pɪˋdɑlədʒɪ] ***n.*** 土壤学。**ped·o·log·ic, ped·o·log·i·cal** ***a.*** **ped·o·log·i·cal·ly** ***ad.*** **pe·dolo·gist** ***n.*** 土壤学家。

pe·dom·e·ter [piˈdɔmitə; pɪˋdɑmətɚ] ***n.***【测】计步器,步程计。

ped·o·sphere [ˈpedəsfiə; ˋpɛdəsfɪr] ***n.*** (地球的)表土层。

ped·rail [ˈpedreil; ˋpɛdrel] ***n.*** **1.** (拖拉机等的)履带,链轨。**2.** 履带式拖拉机;履带车。

pe·dro [ˈpiːdrəu, ˈpei-; ˋpidro, ˋpe-] ***n.*** (*pl.* **~s**) 彼得牌戏〔一种纸牌戏〕。

pe·dun·cle [piˈdʌŋkl; pɪˋdʌŋkl̩] ***n.*** **1.**【植】总花梗;花梗。**2.**【解】(肿瘤或息肉的)肉茎,肉柄。**-dun·cu·lar** ***a.***

pe·dun·cu·late, pe·dun·cu·lat·ed [piˈdʌŋkjulit, -leitid; pɪˋdʌŋkjʊˏlɪt, -ˏletɪd] ***a.***【植】有(总)花梗的;【解】有肉柄的。

ped·way [ˈpedwei; ˋpɛdwe] ***n.*** (建于闹市区的)空中人行道〔多采取联接多座大楼的构建方式〕。

pee [piː; pi] **I** ***vi.***〔口〕撒尿。**II** ***n.***〔口〕尿,小便。

peek [piːk; pik] **I** ***vi.*** (从缝隙或隐蔽处)偷看,眯着眼睛看。~ *in* [*out*] *through a hole* 从小孔里向内[向外]偷看。**II** ***n.*** 偷偷的一看;一瞥。***get*** [***take***] ***a ~ at*** 偷看一下。

peek·a·boo [ˈpiːkəbuː; ˋpikəˏbu] **I** ***n.*** (逗小孩子玩的)躲猫猫(=〔美〕bo-peep)。**II** ***a.*** [ˈpiːkəˈbuː; ˋpikəˋbu] **1.** (衣服)用透明[网眼]薄织物做的。**2.** 用网眼刺绣镶边的。

peel[1] [piːl; pil] **I** ***n.*** **1.** 果皮;(蔬菜、幼苗等的)皮,嫩芽。**2.**【地】揭片。*candied ~* 蜜饯果皮。*banana ~* 香蕉皮。**II** ***vt.*** 剥(果实等的)皮,削(皮),(去)皮;剥(树皮等)(*off*)。—***vi.*** (蛇等)脱皮;(油漆、壁纸等)剥落;〔俚〕(选手)脱衣服。***keep one's eyes ~ed***〔美俚〕留神监视,睁大眼睛注视。~ ***it***〔美俚〕用足气力跑。~ ***off*** 离队,离群;【空】开始离队急降[俯冲];【海军】(护航舰)离队(攻击潜

水艇)；〔俚〕解散。～ ***off a record***〔美〕造新记录。～ ***out***〔美俚〕离开,不辞而别。***scattered and ～ed***〔古〕被劫掠。

peel[2] [piːl; pil] ***n.*** 长柄木铲〔烤面包时用的器具〕。

peel[3] [piːl; pil] ***n.***【英史】(16 世纪英格兰和苏格兰交界处的)堡寨,堡宅,堡塔。

Peel(e) [piːl; pil] ***n.*** 皮尔〔姓氏〕。

peel·er[1] [ˈpiːlə; ˋpilɚ] ***n.*** **1.** 剥皮的人,去皮机。**2.**〔美俚〕蜕皮期间的蛇(其他动物等)。**3.**〔美俚〕跳脱衣舞的演员。

peel·er[2] [ˈpiːlə; ˋpilɚ] ***n.***〔英俚〕警察;【史】爱尔兰的警官队员。

peel·ing [ˈpiːliŋ; ˋpilɪŋ] ***n.*** **1.** 剥皮,去皮;蜕皮。**2.**〔*pl.*〕(马铃薯等)剥下的皮。

peen [piːn; pin] **I** ***n.*** 锥尖,锥顶。**II** ***vt.*** 用锥尖敲打[弯、拔、打平]。

peep[1] [piːp; pip] **I** ***n.*** **1.** (小鸟、老鼠等的)唧唧声,啾啾声。**2.** (表示不满的)嘀咕。**II** ***vi.*** **1.** (小鸟等)唧唧地叫。**2.** 小声说;嘀咕。

peep[2] [piːp; pip] **I** ***n.*** **1.** 偷看;(通过小孔等)的窥视;一瞥。**2.** 窥视孔。**3.** 出现,隐约显现,露出;〔喻〕露马脚。***at the ～ of day*** 黎明时,破晓时。***have*** [***get, take***] ***a ～ at*** 偷看一下。**II** ***vi.*** **1.** (从缝隙等中)偷看,窥,窥视。**2.** (从隐蔽处)出现;(花草、太阳、月亮等)开始显出(*out*)。**3.**〔喻〕露出原形。—***vt.*** 微微探出(头等)。*Peeping Tom* (尤指下流的)偷视者;爱偷看的人,爱刨根问底的人。～**-bo** ***n.*** = peek-a-boo. ～**hole** 窥孔,透视孔;【军】瞄准孔;(坦克的)展望孔。～ **show** **1.** 西洋镜。**2.** 透过小孔看的下流表演。～**-sight** (枪炮等的)觇视孔,准门,照门。

pee·pee [ˈpiːpiː; ˋpipi] ***n.***〔儿〕小鸡。

peep·er[1] [ˈpiːpə; ˋpipɚ] ***n.*** **1.** 唧唧叫的鸟[鼠等];小鸡,小蛙。**2.** 嘀咕的人。

peep·er[2] [ˈpiːpə; ˋpipɚ] ***n.*** **1.** 偷看的人,窥视者;爱刨根问底的人;〔美俚〕私人侦探。**2.**〔*pl.*〕眼睛;〔*pl.*〕眼镜;镜子;望远镜。

pee·pul [ˈpiːpʌl; ˋpipʌl] ***n.*** (印度)菩提树 (= pipal)。

peer[1] [piə; pɪr] **I** ***n.*** **1.**〔英〕贵族〔duke, marquis, earl, viscount, baron 之一〕。**2.** 同辈,同事,伙伴;同等的人;同等地位的公民。*You will not easily find his ～s.* 他是一个无与伦比的人物。*～s of Scotland* [*Ireland*] 苏格兰[爱尔兰]贵族。*a ～ of the blood royal*〔英〕皇族上院议员。*～s of the realm* [*the United Kingdom*]〔英〕可以入上院的贵族。*the House of Peers*〔英〕贵族院,上议院。***without ～*** 无比的,无匹的。

II ***vt.*** **1.** 可与…相比,和…同等。**2.** 把…封为贵族。—***vi.*** 同等,比得上(*with*)。

peer[2] [piə; pɪr] ***vi.*** **1.** 瞪着看,凝视(*into, at*)。**2.** 朦胧出现,隐约可见;出现。*～ at the tag to read the price* 细看标签辨读出价目。*The sun ～ed through the clouds.* 太阳从云中朦胧出现了。

peer·age [ˈpiəridʒ; ˋpɪrɪdʒ] ***n.*** **1.**〔集合词〕贵族;贵族阶级。**2.** 贵族的爵位[地位、身分]。**3.** 贵族姓名录。*be raised on* [*to*] *the ～* 被封为贵族。

peer·ess [ˈpiəris; ˋpɪrɪs] ***n.*** **1.** 贵族夫人,贵族遗孀,贵妇;有爵位的妇女,命妇。**2.** 上议院议员夫人。*a ～ in her own right* (凭本身资格的)有爵妇女,女贵族。

peer·less [ˈpiəlis; ˋpɪrlɪs] ***a.*** 无比的,无双的,绝世的。**-ly** ***ad.*** **-ness** ***n.***

peet·weet [ˈpiːtˌwiːt; ˋpitˏwit] ***n.***【动】斑点矶鹬 (= spotted sandpiper)。

peeve [piːv; piv] **I** ***n.***〔美口〕**1.** 气恼,生气,怨恨。**2.** 讨厌的对象,惹人恨的东西。***have a ～ at sb.*** 生某人的气,讨厌某人。**II** ***vt.***〔口〕使恼怒,使气恼。***be ～d at sb.*** 讨厌某人,对某人生气。

peeved [piːvd; pivd] ***a.***〔美口〕恼怒的,不高兴的。**peev·ed·ly** [ˈpiːvidli; ˋpivɪdlɪ] ***ad.*** **-ness** ***n.***

pee·vish [ˈpiːviʃ; ˋpivɪʃ] ***a.*** **1.** 发怒的,恼怒的。**2.** 脾气暴躁的。**3.** 倔强的,喜欢闹别扭的。**-ly** ***ad.*** **-ness** ***n.***

pee·vit, pee·wit [ˈpiːvit, ˈpiːwit; ˋpivɪt, ˋpiwɪt] ***n.*** = pewit.

peevy [ˈpiːvi; ˋpivɪ] ***n.***【美林】(翻动木材用的)挺钩 (= peav(e)y)。

pee·wee [ˈpiːwiː; ˋpiwi] **I** ***n.*** **1.**〔美俚〕矮子;小东西。**2.** 矮小的动[植]物。**3.** = pewee. **4.**〔儿〕男女的性器官。～ **tech**〔美口〕小型电子公司。**II** ***vi.***〔儿语〕小便。

pee·wit [ˈpiːwit; ˋpiwɪt] ***n.*** = pewit.

Peg [peg; pɛg] ***n.*** 佩格〔女子名〕。

peg [peg; pɛg] **I** ***n.*** **1.** 木钉,竹钉,钉;桩,支柱;(提琴等的)弦钮,琴栓;【植】胚栓;【建】测标。**2.** 尖头物,爪;(晒衣用的)衣夹;(帽)挂。**3.** 借口,遁词,口实。**4.**〔英俚〕白兰地[威士忌]苏打水。**5.**〔*pl.*〕〔口〕腿;裤子。**6.**〔口〕木制假腿;〔美俚〕装假腿的人。**7.**〔口〕牙齿。**8.** 栓与栓的间隔;〔口〕(评选时的)等级;(物价等的)限定标准。*a hat ～* 帽挂。*a clothes ～* 晒衣夹。*a tent ～* 帐篷桩。***a ～ to hang*** (*a claim etc.*) ***on*** 提出(要求等)的借口。***a round*** [***square***] ***～ in a square*** [***round***] ***hole*** 工作安排不适当的人,不得其所的人。***be on the ～***〔口〕被拘留。***come down a ～*** 丢脸,受屈辱,降低身分。***off the ～***〔口〕(服装)现成的。***put the man on the ～***〔军俚〕把人拖到上司面前(使受处罚)。***take*** [***bring, let***] ***sb. down a ～ or two*** [***a ～ lower***] 打下某人的架子;打掉某人的傲气;杀某人的威风。

II ***vt.*** **1.** 在…上钉木钉,用木钉[短桩]钉住(*down; in; out*)。**2.** 固定,限制;限定(工资等);【股】稳住(市价);【财政】(用法令)稳住(货币价值)。**3.**〔口〕扔(石头等)。**4.** 用木桩标出(土地等)。**5.**【猎】(向狗)指示野物落下的场所。**6.**【牌戏】用竹签记(分数)。**7.**〔美俚〕暗中监视。**8.**〔口〕鉴定,识别(某人的价值)。—***vi.*** **1.** 勤快地工作 (*away*)。**2.**【牌戏】用竹签记分数。**3.** 扔石头 (*at*)。**4.** 匆忙地走。～ ***along*** [***away***] 勤快地工作,努力工作。～ ***at*** 用木桩打。～ ***down*** 用木钉把…钉在地上;用(规则等)拘束 (*to rules etc.*)。～ ***out***〔美俚〕**1.** 大失败;气力用完,完。**2.** 死,毁灭。**3.**【牌戏】赢得满分。**4.** (槌球戏中)在一盘打完时用球打中标桩。**5.** 用木桩标明(房屋、庭园等的)界线。～**board** 木栓板;构图板。～ **leg** (木制)假腿;〔口〕装假腿的人。～ **top** **1.** 陀螺。**2.**〔*pl.*〕(臀宽腿狭的)陀螺形裤子。～**-top** ***a.*** (裤子)陀螺形的。

peg·a·moid [ˈpegəmɔid; ˋpɛgəˏmɔɪd] ***n.*** 人造革;防水布。

Peg·a·sus [ˈpegəsəs; ˋpɛgəsəs] ***n.*** **1.**【希神】(诗神 Muse 的)飞马〔其足踏过之处有泉涌出,诗人饮之可获灵感〕。**2.** 诗兴,诗才。**3.** [the ～]【天】飞马座。**4.**【动】海蛾属。

Peg·gy [ˈpegi; ˋpɛgɪ] ***n.*** 佩吉〔女子名, Margaret 的昵称〕。

peg·gy [ˈpegi; ˋpɛgɪ] ***n.***〔口〕装假腿的人,独腿人。

peg·ma·tite [ˈpegmətait; ˋpɛgməˏtaɪt] ***n.***【矿】伟晶岩。

Pe·gram [ˈpiːgrəm; ˋpigrəm] ***n.*** 皮格勒姆〔姓氏〕。

peh [pei; pe] ***n.*** 希伯来语的第十七个字母。

Peh·le·vi [ˈpeilivi:; ˋpeləvi] ***n.*** 约在公元第三世纪至第八世纪的伊朗语 (= Pahlavi)。

P.E.I. = Prince Edward Island 爱德华太子岛〔加拿大〕。

peign·oir [ˈpeinwɑː; ˋpenwɑr] ***n.*** 〔F.〕(女用)宽大轻便晨衣;理发披布;浴衣。

peine [pein, F. pɛn; pen, pɛn] ***n.***〔F.〕痛苦;刑罚,处罚。***peine forte et dure*** [ˈpɛnˈfɔːt eˈdyːə; ˋpɛnˋfɔrt ɛˋdyɚ]〔F.〕(把叛国罪犯活活压死的)酷刑。

Pei·rae·us [paiˈri(ː)əs; paɪˋri(ɪ)əs] ***n.*** = Piraeus.

pe·jo·ra·tion [ˌpiːdʒəˈreiʃən; ˏpidʒəˋreʃən] ***n.*** **1.** 恶化,贬值,变劣 (*opp.* amelioration)。**2.**【语法】(加词尾或词形变化后产生的)词义转贬〔例如在 poet 一词之后加上词尾 -aster 成为 poetaster, 即作"蹩脚诗人"解〕。

pe·jo·ra·tive [ˈpiːdʒərətiv; ˋpidʒərətɪv] **I** ***a.*** 恶化的,变坏的;使带有轻蔑[贬低]意义的。*the ～ suffix-aster*

带贬意的词尾 "-aster"。**II** ***n***.【语法】轻蔑语。**-ly** ***ad***.

pek·an [ˈpekən; ˋpɛkən] ***n***.【动】(北美产)食鱼貂;食鱼貂皮。

peke [piːk; pik] ***n***. (原中国产)小狮子狗〔pekingese 的简称〕。

pe·kin [piːˈkin; ˋpikɪn] ***n***. **1**.【纺】宽条绸。**2**.〔俚〕平民,老百姓〔拿破仑一世部下士兵等的用语〕。

Pe·kin·ese [ˌpiːkiˈniːz; ˏpikɪˋniz] ***a***., ***n***. = Pekingese.

Pe·king [piːˈkiŋ, ˈpiːˈkiŋ; ˋpiˋkɪŋ, ˏpiˋkɪŋ] ***n***. 北京(市)(旧译法, = Beijing)。~ **duck** 北京鸭。~ **Man**【考古】中国猿人,北京人。

Pe·king·ese [ˌpiːkiŋˈiːz; ˏpikɪŋˋiz] **I** ***a***. 北京(人)的。**II** ***n***.〔*sing*., *pl*.〕北京人;北京话。

pe·king·ese [ˈpiːkiŋˈiːz; ˋpikɪŋˋiz] ***n***. (原中国产)小狮子狗[哈巴狗]。

pel·age [ˈpelidʒ; ˋpɛlɪdʒ] ***n***. (哺乳动物的)毛皮。

pe·la·gi·an [piˈleidʒiən; pəˋledʒɪən] **I** ***a***. 远洋的 (= pelagic)。**II** ***n***. 远洋动物,深海动物。*a* ~ *fish* 远洋鱼,深海鱼。~ *fishery* 远洋渔业。

pe·lag·ic [piˈlædʒik; pəˋlædʒɪk] ***a***. **1**. 大洋的;远洋的,深海的。**2**. 海面的;浮游的。~ *fishery* 远洋渔业。~ **larva** 海面幼虫。~ **zone** 远洋带;【动】浮游带。

pel·ar·gon·ic [ˌpelɑːˈgɔnik; ˏpɛlɑrˋgɑnɪk] ***a***. ~ **acid**【化】壬酸。

pel·ar·go·ni·um [ˌpelɑːˈgəunjəm, -niəm; ˏpɛlɑrˋgonjəm, -nɪəm] ***n***. **1**.〔P-〕【植】天竺葵属。**2**. 天竺葵属植物。

Pel·as·gi [peˈlæzdʒai; pəˋlæzdʒaɪ] ***n***.〔*pl*.〕皮拉斯基人〔曾经生活在地中海东部诸岛上的史前人〕。**-an** ***n***., ***a***. 皮拉斯基人(的)。

Pe·las·gic [peˈlæzgik, -dʒik; pɛˋlæzgɪk, -dʒɪk] ***a***. = Pelasgian (***a***.).

pe·lec·y·pod [piˈlesiˌpɔd; pɪˋlɛsɪˏpɑd] ***n***., ***a***. 瓣鳃[斧足]动物〔包括蛤、蚝等〕(的)。

pel·er·ine [ˈpeləriːn; ˏpɛləˋrin] ***n***. (女用)狭长披肩。

pelf [pelf; pɛlf] ***n***. **1**.〔蔑〕钱。**2**.〔英方〕不义之财,赃物。**3**.〔俚〕废物,破烂东西。

pel·i·can [ˈpelikən; ˋpɛlɪkən] ***n***. **1**.【鸟】鹈鹕,塘鹅。**2**. (古代炼金术士用的)鹈鹕形蒸馏器;【徽】鹈鹕印;(牙医用的)拔牙钳子。**3**.〔P-〕〔美俚〕路易斯安那 (Louisiana) 州人的别名。**4**.〔美俚〕大肚汉,贪吃的人。*a* ~ *in her piety*【徽】鹈鹕哺雏图〔啄伤胸部以血哺养其雏的鹈鹕图〕。~ **crossing**〔英〕鹈鹕式人行横道〔可由行人自己操纵红绿灯〕。~ **hook** 塘鹅钩。**P- State** 鹈鹕之州〔美国路易斯安那州的别名〕。

Pe·li·on [ˈpiːliən; ˋpilɪən] ***n***. 皮立翁山〔希腊〕。***Pile*** ~ ***upon Ossa*** 做办不到的事。

pe·lisse [peˈliːs; pəˋlis] ***n***. **1**. 轻便女大衣。**2**. (龙骑兵穿的)皮里上衣。**3**. 小孩大衣。

pel·la·gra [pəˈleigrə; pəˋlegrə] ***n***.【医】蜀黍红斑,糙皮病。**-grous** [pəˈleigrəs; pəˋlegrəs] ***a***.【医】(患)蜀黍红斑的,(患)糙皮病的。

pel·la·grin [piˈlægrin; pəˋlegrɪn] ***n***.【医】蜀黍红斑患者。

pel·let [ˈpelit; ˋpɛlɪt] **I** ***n***. **1**. (纸、面包等团成的)小球;小子弹;石弹;炮弹;小丸药;〔美俚〕(棒球用)球。**2**. (货币等的)圆浮雕。**3**.【动】肉食鸟吐出的不消化物;(啮齿动物等的)屎粒。**II** ***vt***. **1**. 用小球扔;用子弹射击。**2**. 把…弄成小球形。~ **bomb** 珠形炸弹。~ **mo(u)lding**【建】丸子饰。

pel·let·ize [ˈpeliˌtaiz; ˋpɛlətaɪz] ***vt***. 使成小球形;使成小弹丸形。**-za·tion** [-ˈzeiʃən; -ˋzeʃən] ***n***.

pel·li·cle [ˈpelikl; ˋpɛlɪkl̩] ***n***. 薄皮,表膜;(感光乳剂上的)薄膜。

pel·li·to·ry [ˈpelitəri; ˋpɛlətərɪ] ***n***.【植】(药用)墙草属植物 (*Parietaria officinalis*) (= wall pellitory)。

pell-mell [ˈpelˈmel; ˋpɛlˋmɛl] **I** ***ad***., ***a***. **1**. 乱七八糟(的),混乱(的)。**2**. 顾前不顾后(的),鲁莽(的),匆促(的)。*The enemy fled* ~ *before us*. 敌人仓皇逃窜。**II** ***n***. 纷乱,混乱,杂乱;混战。**III** ***vt***. 使混杂。—***vi***. 仓皇行走。

pel·lu·cid [pəˈljuːsid; pəˋlusɪd] ***a***. **1**. 透明的,清澄的。**2**. 明了的,明白的;易懂的;明晰的。**3**. 头脑清楚的。**-ly** ***ad***.

pel·lu·cid·i·ty [ˌpel*j*uːˈsiditi; ˏpɛluˋsɪdətɪ] ***n***. **1**. 透明度,明晰度。**2**. 易懂的程度。

Pel·man·ism [ˈpelmənizəm; ˋpɛlmənɪzəm] ***n***. **1**. 配尔曼式记忆训练法〔由配尔曼学院发明〕。**2**. 配尔曼牌戏〔一种训练记忆力的牌戏〕。**-man·ize** [ˈpelmənaiz; ˋpɛlmənaɪz] ***vt***. 用配尔曼式记忆法记忆。

pel·met [ˈpelmət; ˋpɛlmət] ***n***. (窗或门上遮帷幔挂杆的)狭长木罩[金属罩]。

Pel·o·pon·ne·sian [ˌpeləpəˈniːʃən, -ʃiən; ˏpɛləpəˋniʃən, -ʃɪən] **I** ***a***. (希腊)伯罗奔尼撒 (Peloponnesus) 半岛的。**II** ***n***. 伯罗奔尼撒人。

pe·lo·ri·a [piˈlɔːriə; pɪˋlorɪə] ***n***.【植】反常整齐花。**-ric** [piˈlɔːrik; pɪˋlɔrɪk] ***a***.

pe·lo·rus [piˈlɔːrəs; pɪˋlorəs] ***n***.【海】方位盘,哑罗经。

pe·lo·ta [piˈləutə, Sp. peˈləutɑː; pɪˋlotə, pɛˋlotə] ***n***. 回力球〔源自西班牙的一种使用柳条球拍、类似网球的球戏〕。

pelt[1] [pelt; pɛlt] **I** ***n***. **1**. (牛、羊等的)生皮,毛皮〔尤指羊皮〕。**2**. 皮衣,裘。**3**.〔谑〕(人的)皮肤。**II** ***vt***. 剥…的皮。~ **monger** 皮毛商。

pelt[2] [pelt; pɛlt] **I** ***n***. **1**. 投掷,打击。**2**. (雨、雪等的)猛降。**3**. 抨击,责问。**4**. 速度。**5**.〔英方〕大怒。***go*** (***at***) ***full*** ~ 拼命,开足马力 (*He went full* ~ *at it, and had it finished under an hour*. 他拼命地快做,不到一小时就做好了)。**II** ***vt***. **1**. (连续地)向…投击;连续打击。**2**. 投,扔。**3**. 痛加(质问、责骂等);连续抨击。—***vi***. **1**. (连续地)投,扔。**2**. (雨等)猛降。**3**.〔口〕一股劲儿向前跑,开足马力前进。

pel·tast [ˈpeltæst; ˋpɛltæst] ***n***. (古希腊)有轻盾武装的兵士。

pel·tate [ˈpelteit; ˋpɛltet] ***a***.【植】(叶)盾状的。**-ly** ***ad***.

pelt·er[1] [ˈpeltə; ˋpɛltɚ] ***n***. **1**.〔美〕皮商;剥兽皮者。**2**. (为取毛皮而饲养的)兽。

pelt·er[2] [ˈpeltə; ˋpɛltɚ] ***n***. **1**. 投掷者;投掷器;〔谑〕手枪。**2**.〔口〕(雨等的)猛下;弹雨。**3**.〔英方〕大怒。**4**.〔美〕跑得快的马。**5**. 老驽马。***in a*** ~ 大发脾气,大怒。

pelt·ing[1] [ˈpeltiŋ; ˋpɛltɪŋ] ***a***. **1**.〔英方〕盛怒的。**2**. (雨等)大下特下的。*a* ~ *rain* 倾盆大雨。

pelt·ing[2] [ˈpeltiŋ; ˋpɛltɪŋ] ***a***.〔古〕无价值的,微不足道的。

pelt·ry [ˈpeltri; ˋpɛltrɪ] ***n***. **1**. (一捆或一张)生皮,毛皮。**2**. 皮囊;皮货。**3**. 风箱。~ **monger** 毛皮商。

pel·vic [ˈpelvik; ˋpɛlvɪk] **I** ***a***.【解】骨盆的。**II** ***n***. 骨盆部。~ **fin**【鱼】腹鳍。~ **girdle**【动】腰带。

pel·vis [ˈpelvis; ˋpɛlvɪs] ***n***. (*pl*. ~**es**, **pel·ves** [ˈpelviːz; ˋpɛlviz])【解】骨盆。*the* ~ *major* = *the false* ~ 大骨盆,假骨盆。*the* ~ *minor* = *the true* ~ 小骨盆,真骨盆。

Pem·broke [ˈpembruk; ˋpɛmbrok] ***n***. **1**. 彭布罗克郡〔英国郡名〕(= ~ shire)。**2**. (一种尖耳、直腿、短尾的)威尔士小狗。**3**.〔p-〕折面桌 (= ~ table)。

pem·(m)i·can [ˈpemikən; ˋpɛmɪkən] ***n***. **1**.〔美〕干(牛)肉饼。**2**. (报告等的)摘要,提要。

pem·phi·gus [ˈpemfigəs, pemˈfai-; ˋpɛmfɪgəs, pɛmˋfaɪ-] ***n***.【医】天疱疮。

pen[1] [pen; pɛn] **I** ***n***. **1**. 笔尖;笔[笔尖和笔杆];〔古〕鹅毛(管)笔。**2**. 笔力,文体,笔法;文笔;文章。**3**. 书法家;作家。**4**.【动】雌鹄 (*opp*. cob);(乌贼的)羽状壳。**5**. 羽茎,翮。**6**.〔美俚〕伪造者 (= ~ man)。*a fountain* ~ 自来水笔。*a quill* ~ 鹅毛(管)笔。*The* ~ *catches* [*scratches*]. 这支笔刮纸。*a fluent* ~ 流畅的文体。

P

the best ～*s of the day* 当代第一流作家们。*The* ～ *is mightier than the sword*. 笔胜于刀,文比武强。～ *juice* 〔美俚〕墨水。～ *portraits* 人物描写。***draw one's*** ～ [***quill***] ***against*** 笔伐…,用笔攻击。***drive a*** ～ [***quill***] 写。***live by one's*** ～ 靠写作为生,吃笔墨饭。～ ***and ink*** 笔墨;写作。***put*** ～ ***to paper*** 拿笔写,下笔。***wield one's*** ～ 从事写作。**II** ***vt***. (***-nn-***) 写,作(文),著(书)。～**-and-ink** ***a***. **1**. 用钢笔写[画]的 (*a* ～*-and-ink drawing* [*sketch*] 钢笔画[素描])。**2**. 从事文书工作的。**3**. 〔罕〕从事文学工作的。～**-cancel** 用笔把(印花税票等)划销。～ **computer**, ～**puter**【计】笔触式电脑。～**-driver** 用笔工作的人〔抄写员;记者,作家等〕。～**-friend** 笔友。～**(-)holder** **1**. 笔杆;笔架。**2**.【体】(乒乓球运动的)直握球拍打法(亦作 penholder grip)。～**knife** 削铅笔[鹅毛笔]刀;袖珍小刀。～ **light** [**lite**] 自来水笔形手电筒。～ **name** 笔名;〔美俚〕囚犯的号码。～ **pal** = ～-friend. ～ **point** 〔美〕(钢)笔尖。～**-pusher** 〔口〕= pen-driver. ～ **rack** 笔架。～ **register**【讯】描笔式记发器〔用户电话线上的一种电子装置,可自动记录下用户电话号码、打电话日期和通话时间〕。～**top** 笔触式电脑。～ **tray** 笔盘。～**wiper** 擦笔尖布。**-ful** ***n***. (自来水笔的)一满管(墨水)。**-ner** ***n***. (文件等的)执笔人,写作人。

pen[2] [pen; pɛn] **I** ***n***. **1**. (家畜等的)围栏,槛。**2**. 一栏[一圈]家畜。**3**. 〔美口〕监狱〔penitentiary 之略〕。**4**. (西印度群岛的)开垦地,农庄,种植。**5**. 冰箱,冰房,贮藏室。**6**. 潜艇修藏坞 (= submarine ～)。**II** (***penned***, ***pent*** [pent; pɛnt]; ***-ning***) ***vt***. **1**. 把…关进栏里。**2**. 监禁 (*up*; *in*)。

pen[3] [pen; pɛn] ***n***. 雌天鹅。

P.E.N., PEN = (International Association of) Poets, Playwrights, Editors, Essayists and Novelists 国际笔会。

Pen., pen. = peninsula.

pe·nal [ˈpiːnl; ˋpinl] **I** ***a***. **1**. 刑的,刑事的;刑法上的。**2**. 受刑罚的;该受罚的,当受刑的。**3**. 作为刑罚场所的。*the* ～ *code* [*law*] 刑法。～ *servitude* 惩役;徒刑。*a* ～ *offense* 刑事罪。*a* ～ *sum* 罚款。*a* ～ *colony* [*settlement*] (流犯的)充军地。*a* ～ *farm* 劳役农场。**II** ***n***. = ～ servitude. ***do*** ～ 服徒刑。**-i·ty** [piˈnæliti; pɪˋnælətɪ] ***n***. **-ly** ***ad***. 用刑罚;刑事上。

pe·nal·ize [ˈpiːnəlaiz; ˋpinḷˏaɪz] ***vt***. **1**.【法】判…有罪;对…处以刑罚。**2**. 使处于不利地位;【体】处罚(犯规者)。**-i·zation** [-ˈzeiʃən; -ˋzeʃən] ***n***.

pen·al·ty [ˈpenlti; ˋpɛnltɪ] ***n***. **1**. 刑罚,惩罚。**2**. 罚款;违约罚金。**3**. 报应。**4**.【牌】罚点;【体】(犯规)处罚。**5**. (行为等造成的)困难、障碍、不利后果 (= handicap)。*a monetary* ～ 罚款处分。*the* ～ *area*【足球】罚球区域。*a* ～ *box*【冰球】被罚暂时下场的球员坐席。*a* ～ *kick*【足球】罚球。***on*** [***under***] ～ ***of*** 违者受…处罚。～ **clause** 〔美〕"私人冒用者必罚"〔印在政府免费邮件上的字样〕。～ **envelope** 〔美〕(其上印有"私人不得擅用,违者必罚"等字样的)免费公文信袋。～ **goal** 罚球踢中球门。～ **shoot-out**(足球)互踢点球决定胜负,点球大战。

pen·ance [ˈpenəns; ˋpɛnəns] **I** ***n***. **1**. 忏悔;悔过;(赎罪的)苦行。**2**.【天主】补赎;忏悔式。**II** ***vt***. 使苦行赎罪;处罚。

Pe·nan·ces [piˈnænsiːz; pɪˋnænsiz] ***n***. Pennsylvannia 州人的别名。

Pe·nang [piˈnæŋ; pɪˋnæŋ] ***n***. **1**. 槟榔屿〔马来西亚州名〕。**2**. 槟城〔即 George Town 乔治市〕〔马来西亚港市〕。

pe·nang [piˈnæŋ; pəˋnæŋ] ***n***. = pinang.

pen·an·nu·lar [piˈnænjulə; pɛˋnænjulɚ] ***a***. 近于环状的。

Pe·na·tes [peˈnɑːteis, peˈneitiːz; pəˋnɑtes, pəˋnetiz] ***n***. **1**.【罗神】家神。**2**. 〔p-〕家财。

Pen·can·cel [ˈpenˈkænsəl; ˋpɛnˋkænsḷ] 用笔使(印花税票等)作废。

pence [pens; pɛns] ***n***. penny 的复数。

pen·cel [ˈpensl; ˋpɛnsḷ] ***n***. 〔古〕小三角旗;小燕尾旗;狭旗。

pen·chant [ˈpɑ̃ːŋʃɑ̃ːŋ; ˋpɑ̃ŋʃɑ̃ŋ] ***n***. 〔F.〕(强烈的)倾向,嗜好,爱好 (*for*)。

pen·cil [ˈpensl; ˋpɛnsl] **I** ***n***. **1**. 铅笔;石笔;〔古〕画笔。**2**. 画风,画法。**3**.【数】束;【物】光线锥。**4**. 毛撮;铅笔形物。**5**. 〔美俚〕左轮手枪。*a hair* [*metallic*] ～ 毛[铁]笔。*Neither pen nor* ～ *can express*. 非笔墨所能形容。*a* ～ *sharpener* 削笔器。*a* ～ *pusher* 〔美俚〕书记,办事员;〔美空俚〕轰炸机领航员。*a diamond* ～ 钻石刀〔切玻璃用〕。*a beam* ～ 电子束。*a* ～ *of rays* 射线束。**II** ***vt***. (***-l***(***l***)***-***) **1**. 用铅笔写。**2**. 用画笔画。～ *the eye-brows* 画眉毛。～ **case** 铅笔盒。～ **microphone** 笔形话筒。～ **ore**【矿】笔铁矿。～ **sketch** 铅笔画;草图。～ **stone** 石笔石,滑石。～ **vase** 笔筒。～ **whipping** 〔美〕篡改证明文件。

pen·cil(l)ed [ˈpensld; ˋpɛnsḷd] ***a***. **1**. 画过细线的。**2**. 用铅笔写的;写得好看的。**3**.【物】成锥状的;【数】成束的。**4**. (禽类羽毛等)有彩色细纹的。～ *eyebrows* 用画眉笔描过的眉毛。

pen·cil·(l)er [ˈpenslə; ˋpɛnsḷɚ] ***n***. **1**. 用铅笔写[画]的人。**2**. 〔英俚〕(赛马等的)登记赌注者。

pen·cil·(l)ing [ˈpensəliŋ; ˋpɛnslɪŋ] ***n***. **1**. 铅笔[毛笔]画。**2**. 铅笔痕;细线;铅笔线花样。**3**. (墙上沿砖缝画的)白色线条。**4**. (禽羽的)彩色细纹。

pen·craft [ˈpenkrɑːft; ˋpɛnkræft] ***n***. **1**. 书法;笔迹。**2**. 措辞;文笔。**3**. 著作业。

pend [pend; pɛnd] ***vi***. 吊着;悬而未决;待决。

pend·ant [ˈpendənt; ˋpɛndənt] **I** ***n***. **1**. 下垂物,垂饰,耳环;挂表壳上系表链的环;【建】悬饰;吊灯架。**2**. 附录,附属物;(书的)姐妹篇;(成对物中的)一个;对手 (*to*)。**3**.【海】短索;旒旗;三角旗,尖旗。*a broad* ～【海】(旗舰的)小燕尾旒。**II** ***a***. = pendent (***a***.).

pend·en·cy [ˈpendənsi; ˋpɛndənsɪ] ***n***. **1**. 垂下,悬垂。**2**. 未决;未定。***during the*** ～ ***of*** 在…未定时。

pen·dent [ˈpendənt; ˋpɛndənt] **I** ***n***. = pendant. **II** ***a***. **1**. 吊着的,下垂的,悬垂的;突出的,(崖石等)悬空的。**2**. 未决的,未定的。**3**.【语法】不完全的。**4**.【植】垂头的。*a* ～ *lamp* 吊灯。*a* ～ *switch* 拉线开关。*a* ～ *rock* 悬崖。**-ly** ***ad***.

pen·den·te li·te [penˈdenti ˈlaiti; pɛnˋdɛntɪˋlaɪtɪ] 〔L.〕诉讼中。

pen·den·tive [penˈdentiv; pɛnˋdɛntɪv] ***n***.【建】穹隅。*a* ～ *dome* 三角穹圆顶。

pend·ing [ˈpendiŋ; ˋpɛndɪŋ] **I** ***a***. **1**. 悬垂的。**2**. 迫近的;紧急的。**3**. 未定的,未决的。**4**. 审理中的。～ *cases* 未决案件。*a* ～ *question* 悬案,未决问题。～ *business* 当前急务。**II** ***prep***. **1**. 当…的时候,在…中。**2**. 在…以前。～ *the negotiations* 在谈判中。～ *his return* 在他回来以前。

pen·drag·on [penˈdrægən; pɛnˋdrægən] ***n***. 王侯〔古时不列颠[威尔士]的首领〕。

pen·du·lar [ˈpendjulə; ˋpɛndʒəlɚ] ***a***. 钟摆运动的;摆动的。

pen·du·late [ˈpendjuleit; ˋpɛndʒəlet] ***vi***. 摆动;摇摆不定,犹豫。

pen·du·line [ˈpendjulin; ˋpɛndʒulɪn] **I** ***a***. **1**. (鸟巢)下垂的,吊下的。**2**. (鸟)作吊巢的。**II** ***n***. 作吊巢的鸟 (= ～ bird)。

pen·du·lous [ˈpendjuləs; ˋpɛndʒələs] ***a***. **1**. 吊着的,下垂的,悬垂的。**2**. 摇摆不定的,未决的。**-ly** ***ad***. **-ness** ***n***.

pen·du·lum [ˈpendjuləm; ˋpɛndʒələm] ***n***. **1**. (钟等的)摆。**2**. 动摇的人[物];犹豫不决的人。**3**. 吊烛架。*a simple* [*compound*] ～ 单[复]摆。*a centrifugal* ～ 离

心力调速器。*a* ～ *orbit*【物】穿核轨道。**play** ～ 处于不稳定的状态,左右摇摆。**the swing of the** ～ **1.** 摆的运动。**2.** (人心的)向背。**3.** (政党等的)一盛一衰,形势改变。

Pe·nel·o·pe [piˈneləpi, pəˈneləpi; pɪˋnɛləpɪ, pəˋnɛləpɪ] ***n*. 1.** 佩内洛普〔女子名〕。**2.**【希神】彭妮洛佩〔奥德修斯 (Odysseus) 忠实的妻子〕;贞妇。***a*** **～'*s web*** 彭妮洛佩之网;永远完不成的工作。

pe·ne·plain, pe·ne·plane [ˈpiːniplein; ˋpinə͵plen] **I** ***n*.**【地】(因地面受侵蚀而形成的)准平原。**II** ***vt*.** 使成准平原。

pe·nes [ˈpiːniːz; ˋpiniz] penis 的复数。

pen·e·tra·ble [ˈpenitrəbl; ˋpɛnətrəbl] ***a*. 1.** 可渗透的,穿得过的,能贯穿的 (*by*)。**2.** 可识破的 (*to*); 看得穿的。**-tra·bil·ity** [ˌpenitrəˈbiliti; ͵pɛnətrəˋbɪlətɪ] ***n*. 1.** 渗透性,可穿透性。**2.**【物】透明性,透明度。**3.** 可识破性。**-tra·bly** ***ad*.**

pen·e·tra·li·a [ˌpeniˈtreiliə, -ljə; ͵pɛnɪˋtrelɪə, -ljə] ***n*.** 〔*pl*.〕**1.** 内部,最深处。**2.** 内殿,内院。**3.** 秘密;私事。

pen·e·tram·e·ter [ˌpeniˈtræmitə; ͵pɛnɪˋtræmətɚ] ***n*.** = penetrometer.

pen·e·trance [ˈpenitrəns; ˋpɛnətrəns] ***n*.**【生】外显率。

pen·e·trant [ˈpenitrənt; ˋpɛnətrənt] **I** ***a*. 1.** 透入的;透彻的。**2.** 尖锐的。**II** ***n*.** 渗透剂。

pen·e·trate [ˈpenitreit; ˋpɛnə͵tret] ***vt*. 1.** 进入,渗入,突入,透过,贯穿。**2.** 渗透入;弥漫[扩散]于;(思想、感情等)深入于,打动。**3.** 看透,看穿,识破,洞察。～*d with discontent* 深为不满。～ *sb.'s meaning* 看穿某人的意思。～ *sb.'s design* 看破某人的计划。—***vi*. 1.** 穿入,刺入,渗入,透入,侵入,透过 (*into*; *through*; *to*)。**2.** 看穿,看透,识破。**3.** 渗透,弥漫,扩散。**4.** 深入人心,打动人心。

pen·e·trat·ing [ˈpenitreitiŋ; ˋpɛnə͵tretɪŋ] ***a*. 1.** 透过的,贯穿的;渗透的。**2.** (目光)锐利的;有眼光的,聪明的。**3.** (声音的)尖刺的。**4.** (伤口等)深的。*a* ～ *orbit*【物】贯穿轨道。**-ly** ***ad*.** 深入地;尖锐地。

pen·e·tra·tion [ˌpeniˈtreiʃən; ͵pɛnəˋtreʃən] ***n*. 1.** 浸透;透过;渗透力。**2.** 侵入,【军】突破;(空战中)深入敌方的飞行。**3.** 贯穿;(炮的)贯穿力;(光学机械的)透视力。**4.** 看破,洞察(力),眼光。

pen·e·tra·tive [ˈpenitreitiv; ˋpɛnə͵tretɪv] ***a*. 1.** 渗入的;贯穿的;有透入力的。**2.** (冷风等)彻骨的。**3.** (思想等)深刻的;深入人心的。**4.** 敏锐的;眼光锐利的。**-ly** ***ad*. -ness** ***n*.**

pen·e·tra·tor [ˈpenitrətə; ˋpɛnɪ͵tretɚ] ***n*. 1.** 穿入者;侵入者;渗透者。**2.**【军】侵入式飞机。

pen·e·trom·e·ter [ˌpeniˈtrɔmitə; ͵pɛnɪˋtrɑmətɚ] ***n*. 1.**【物】(测量 X 射线穿透力的)透度计。**2.**【建】贯入度仪,针入度仪。

pen·e·tron [ˈpenətrɔn; ˋpɛnɪ͵trɑn] ***n*. 1.**【物】介子〔现名 meson〕。**2.** 〔P-〕(射线)透射密度测量仪。

pen·feath·er [ˈpenfeðə; ˋpɛnfɛðɚ] ***n*.** 翮。

Peng·hu [ˈpʌŋˈhuː; ˋpʌŋˋhu] ***n*.** 澎湖〔中国台湾省〕。

pen·go [ˈpeŋgəu; ˋpɛŋgo] ***n*.** (*pl*. **-*gö*, -*gös***) 〔Hung.〕辨戈〔匈牙利从前的货币单位,1964 年为福林所代替〕。

pen·guin [ˈpeŋgwin; ˋpɛŋgwɪn] ***n*. 1.**【动】企鹅。**2.**【空】(不能飞的)滑走教练机;〔美俚〕非飞行航空人员。**3.** (第一次大战时的)英国妇女航空会会员。

pe·ni·al [ˈpiːniəl; ˋpinɪəl] ***a*.**【解】阴茎的。

pen·i·cil·late [ˌpeniˈsileit; ͵pɛnəˋsɪlet] ***a*.**【植、动】**1.** 具毛撮的,流苏状的。**2.** 有美丽花纹的。

pen·i·cil·li·a [ˌpeniˈsiliə; ͵pɛnɪˋsɪlɪə] ***n*.** penicillium 的复数。

pen·i·cil·lin [ˌpeniˈsilin, pəˈni-; ͵pɛnɪˋsɪlɪn, pəˋnɪ-] ***n*.**【药】青霉素,盘尼西林。

pen·i·cil·lin·ase [ˌpeniˈsilineis; ͵pɛnəˋsɪlənes] ***n*.**【生化】青霉素酶。

pen·i·cil·li·um [ˌpeniˈsiliəm; ͵pɛnɪˋsɪlɪəm] ***n*.** (*pl*. ～***s***, **-*li·a*** [-liə; lɪə])【微】青霉素;毛丛。

pen·in·su·la [piˈninsjulə; pəˋnɪnsələ] ***n*. 1.** 半岛。**2.** 〔the P-〕【史】(1808—1814 年西葡"半岛战争"中指)伊比利亚 (Iberia) 半岛;(第一次世界大战中指)加利波利 (Gallipoli) 半岛。

pen·in·su·lar [piˈninsjulə; pəˋnɪnsələ] **I** ***a*. 1.** 半岛(状)的。**2.** 〔P-〕伊比利亚半岛(战争)的。**II** ***n*. 1.** 半岛居民。**2.** 〔P-〕参加伊比利亚半岛战争的兵士。*the P-State* 〔美〕佛罗里达州 (Florida) 的别名。

pe·nis [ˈpiːnis; ˋpinɪs] ***n*.** (*pl*. ***pe·nes*** [ˈpiːniːz; ˋpiniz], ～***es***)【解】阴茎。

Penit. = penitentiary.

pen·i·tence [ˈpenitəns; ˋpɛnətəns] ***n*.** 后悔,忏悔,悔悟;悔罪 (*for*)。

pen·i·tent [ˈpenitənt; ˋpɛnətənt] **I** ***a*.** 后悔[悔悟、忏悟、悔罪]的。**II** ***n*. 1.** 悔过的,忏悔者。**2.**【天主】苦行会会员。**-ly** ***ad*.**

pen·i·ten·tial [ˌpeniˈtenʃəl; ͵pɛnəˋtɛnʃəl] **I** ***a*. 1.** 后悔的,忏悔的。**2.** 苦行赎罪的。**II** ***n*. 1.** = penitent. **2.**【天主】苦行赎罪规则(书)。**-ly** ***ad*.**

pen·i·ten·tia·ry [ˌpeniˈtenʃəri; ͵pɛnəˋtɛnʃərɪ] **I** ***n*. 1.**【天主】(听教徒忏悔的)听悔僧;(罗马教廷的)反省院;悔罪所。**2.** 感化院;〔美〕监狱;娼妓收容所。**II** ***a*. 1.** 悔改的。**2.** 苦行赎罪的。**3.** 〔美〕应监禁的。*the Grand P-* (罗马教廷的)反省院院长。

pen·man [ˈpenmən; ˋpɛnmən] ***n*.** (*pl*. ***penmen*** [-men; -mɛn]) **1.** 笔记者,笔者。**2.** 书法家;习字教员。**3.** 作家,文人。**4.** 〔美俚〕伪造者。**-ship** ***n*. 1.** 书法,笔法;习字;书体;笔迹;工于书法。**2.** 写作,文体。

pen·mate [ˈpenmeit; ˋpɛn͵met] ***n*.** 〔美口〕狱伴,牢友。

Penn [pen; pɛn] ***n*.** 佩恩〔姓氏〕。

Penn., Penna. = Pennsylvania.

pen·na [ˈpenə; ˋpɛnə] ***n*.** (*pl*. **-*nae*** [-iː; -i]) 羽毛;翼或鸟尾的羽翮。**-na·ceous** [peˈneiʃəs; pəˋneʃəs] ***a*.**

pen·nant [ˈpenənt; ˋpɛnənt] ***n*. 1.** 细长三角旗,小燕尾旗;【海】(勤务舰的)旒旗。**2.**【海】(从帆桁末端垂下的)短索。**3.** 〔美〕(运动比赛中三角形的)优胜锦旗;【乐】钩符 (= hook)。*a broad* ～ = a broad pendant. *a homeward-bound* ～ 归航旗。*the* ～ *chasers* 〔美〕职业棒球队。**win the** ～ 夺得锦标。

pen·nate, pen·nat·ed [ˈpeneit, ˈpeneitid; ˋpɛnet, ˋpɛnetɪd] ***a*. 1.** 有羽毛的,有翼的。**2.** 羽状的 (= pinnate)。

Pen·nell [ˈpenəl; ˋpɛnəl] ***n*.** 彭内尔〔姓氏〕。

pen·ni [ˈpeni; ˋpɛnɪ] ***n*.** (*pl*. **-*ni·a*** [-ə; -ə], ～(***s***)) 盆尼〔铜制芬兰硬币,等于 1/100 马克〕。

pen·nif·er·ous [piˈnifərəs; pɪˋnɪfərəs] ***a*.** 有羽毛的;生羽的。

pen·ni·form [ˈpenifɔm; ˋpɛnɪ͵fɔrm] ***a*.** 羽状的。

pen·ni·less [ˈpenilis; ˋpɛnɪlɪs] ***a*.** 身无分文的;穷的。

pen·nill [ˈpenil; ˋpɛnɪl] ***n*.** (*pl*. ～***ion*** [peˈniljən; pɛˋnɪljən]) (威尔士诗人会上)合竖琴调子唱的即兴诗(的一节)。

pen·non [ˈpenən; ˋpɛnən] ***n*. 1.** 细长三角旗,小燕尾旗;枪旗;〔美〕三角校旗。**2.** (一般的)旗帜。**3.** 〔诗〕(鸟类的)翼。**-ed** ***a*.** 有三角旗的。

pen·non·cel [ˈpenənsel; ˋpɛnən͵sɛl] ***n*.** 〔古〕小三角旗,小燕尾旗,狭旗 (= pencel)。

penn'orth [ˈpenəθ; ˋpɛnɚθ] ***n*.** 〔俚〕= pennyworth.

Penn·syl·va·ni·a [pensilˈveinjə, -niə; ͵pɛnslˋvenjə, -nɪə] ***n*.** 宾夕法尼亚〔美国州名〕。～ **Dutch** [**German**] 17、18 世纪时移入美国宾州的德国南部人和瑞士人;他们的子孙;他们的语言〔高地德语和英语的混合语〕;他们的民间艺术。～ **hurricane** 〔美俚〕大谎。

Penn·syl·va·ni·an [ˌpenslˈveinjən, -ˈveiniən; ͵pɛnsɪlˋvenjən, -ˋvenɪən] **I** ***a*. 1.** 宾夕法尼亚州的。**2.** 宾夕法

尼亚纪〔在密西西比纪后三叠纪前的北美古生代第六时期〕的。**II** ***n*.** **1.** 宾夕法尼亚居民。**2.**〔the ～〕宾夕法尼亚纪;宾夕法尼亚纪岩石。

Pen·ny [ˈpeni; ˋpɛnɪ] ***n*.** 彭妮〔女子名, Penelope 的昵称〕。

pen·ny [ˈpeni; ˋpɛnɪ] ***n*.** (*pl*. ***pence*** [pens; pɛns], ***pen·nies*** [ˈpeniz; ˋpɛnɪz]) **1.** 便士〔英国辅币单位,硬币 = 1/100 英镑;1971 年前旧币制 = 1/12 先令〕。★ **(a)** 表示价格的复数用 pence; 表示辅币个数的复数用 pennies. **(b)** 从 twopence 到 elevenpence 以及 twentypence 的 pence 须和前字连写,读 [-pəns; -pəns], 此外须分写成两字,读 [-ˈpens; -ˋpɛns]。**(c)** 新制在数字后时通常略作 p (如:10*p* = 10 pence); 旧制略作 d. (如: 5*d*. = fivepence)。**2.** 〔美、加拿大〕(*pl*. ***pen·nies***) = cent. **3.** 小钱;钱。**4.**【圣】一种古罗马银币〔拉丁文作 denarius, 其首字母曾作为英国旧便士的缩略号〕。～ *arcade* 〔美〕(备有娱乐机器和自动售货机的)便宜游乐场。*a* ～ *blood* 〔口〕廉价的惊险小说。*a* ～ *whistle* 便宜哨子[玩具]。*six-*～ *series* 六便士丛书。***a bad*** ～ 不受欢迎的人[物]。***a pretty*** ～ 〔口〕一大笔钱。***a*** ～ ***for your thoughts*** =〔俚〕***a*** ～ ***for 'em*** 呆呆地想什么呢。***A*** ～ ***saved is a*** ～ ***gained***. 省一文就得一文。***A*** ～ ***soul never come to twopence***. 小气鬼成不了大事。***have not a*** ～ (***to bless oneself with***) 很穷,不名一文。***In for a*** ～, ***in for a pound***. 一不做,二不休。***in*** ～ ***numbers*** 一点一点地。***not a*** ～ ***the worse*** 比以前一点不坏,一点不吃亏。～ ***number*** (一便士一本的定期出版的)侦探小说的一分册。***P- wise, pound foolish***. 小事精明,大事糊涂;贪小失大。***spend a*** ～ 〔口〕上(公共)厕所。***Take care of the pence, and the pounds will take care of themselves***. 小事留意,大事顺利。***The*** ～ ***dropped***. 目的已达到;话已听明白。***think one's*** ～ ***silver*** 〔口〕自负。***turn an honest*** ～ 挣一点正当的钱〔如干零活等〕。～**-a-line** ***a*.** 每行一便士的,稿费便宜的;(文章等)拙劣的。～**-a-liner** ***n*.** 穷文人。～**-a-lining** 〔英〕便宜稿子,无聊作品。～ **ante** 赌注小的赌博(如打扑克等);琐碎小事。～**bank** (不限最低储蓄额的)便士储蓄银行。～ **dreadful** [**blood**]〔英〕廉价惊险小说。～**-farthing** 前轮大后轮小的自行车。～ **gaff** 〔英口〕便宜小戏院[杂耍场]。～**-in-the-slot** 〔英〕一便士自动售货机。～**-pinch** ***vt*.** 〔美俚〕对…吝啬。～**-pinching** ***a*.** 〔美俚〕小气的,吝啬的。～ **post** 〔英〕一便士邮政制。～**royal**【植】薄荷属的一种植物 (～*royal mint*【植】除蚤薄荷)。～ **wedding** 〔Scot.〕贺份结婚。～**weight** 英钱〔音译"本尼威特",英国金衡, = 1.555克〕(略 dwt.) (*a* ～*weight job* 〔美俚〕偷宝石)。～**-wisdom** 省小钱。～**-wise** ***a*.** 省小钱的 (～*-wise and pound-foolish* 贪小失大)。～**wort**【植】破铜钱属植物。～**worth** [ˈpenəθ, ˈpeniwəːθ; ˋpɛnəθ, ˋpɛnɪwɝθ] ***n*.** **1.** 一便士的价值;一便士的东西,少量。**2.** 交易,买卖 (*a good* [*bad*] ～*-worth* 有利[不利]的买卖,便宜[上当]货。*get one's* ～*-worth* 对过去的牺牲得到报酬;被痛打;大受剥削。*not a* ～*worth* 一点也不…)。

pe·nol·o·gist [piːˈnɔlədʒist; piˋnɑlədʒɪst] ***n*.** **1.** 刑罚学家,罪犯教育学家。**2.** 监狱学家。

pe·nol·o·gy [piːˈnɔlədʒi; piˋnɑlədʒɪ] ***n*.** 刑罚学;监狱学。**pe·no·log·i·cal** [ˌpiːnəˈlɔdʒikəl; ˏpinəˋlɑdʒɪkl̩] ***a*.**

Pen·rose [ˈpenrəuz; ˋpɛnroz] ***n*.** 彭罗斯〔姓氏〕。

pen·sée [pɑ̃ːŋˈsei; pɑ̃ŋˋse] ***n*.** (*pl*. ～***s*** [-sei, -se]) 〔F.〕 **1.** (用文字表达出的)思想;思索,沉思,默想。**2.** 感想录;格言,箴言。

pen·sile [ˈpensail, -sil; ˋpɛnsl̩, -sɪl] ***a*.** = penduline.

pen·sion [ˈpenʃən; ˋpɛnʃən] **I** ***n*.** **1.** 退休金,恤金,养老金,生活津贴;补助费。**2.** (给学者、艺术家等的)补助金,【英国教】(缴纳教堂的)牧师酬金;临时津贴。*old-age* ～ 养老金,退休金。*retire on a* ～ 领养老金退休。**II** ***vt*.** 给…养老金[恤金、津贴等]。**III** ***a*.** 有关退休金的。～ ***off*** 发给养老金[津贴等]使退职[休]。

pen·sion [ˈpɑ̃ːŋsiɔ̃ːŋ; pɑ̃ŋˋsɪɔ̃ŋ] ***n*.** 〔F.〕 **1.** (法国、比利时等的)公寓;寄宿学校。**2.** 膳宿费。***live en*** [ɑ̃ːn; ɑ̃n] ～ 过公寓生活。

pen·sion·a·ble [ˈpenʃənəbl; ˋpɛnʃənəbl̩] ***a*.** 有领养老金[津贴等]资格[权利]的。

pen·sion·a·ry [ˈpenʃənəri; ˋpɛnʃənˏɛrɪ] **I** ***a*.** 领养老金[津贴等]的;靠养老金[津贴等]过活的;(关于)养老金[津贴等]的。**II** ***n*.** **1.** = pensioner. **2.** 被金钱收买的人;帮佣。**3.** (从前荷兰的)州长 (= Grand P-)。

pen·sio·ne [penˈsjəune; pɛnˋsjone] ***n*.** (*pl*. ***-ni*** [-ni; -nɪ]) 〔It.〕 **1.** 寄宿学校。**2.** 公寓 (= pension)。

pen·sion·er [ˈpenʃənə; ˋpɛnʃənɚ] ***n*.** **1.** 领养老金[津贴等]的人,退休的人。**2.** 随从,随员,跟班;〔罕〕雇员。**3.** 〔英〕剑桥大学的自费生。

pen·sion·less [ˈpenʃənlis; ˋpɛnʃənlɪs] ***a*.** 没有养老金[抚恤金等]的。

pen·sive [ˈpensiv; ˋpɛnsɪv] ***a*.** **1.** 沉思的。**2.** 郁郁不乐的;忧愁的,凄凉的。**-ly** ***ad*.**

pen·ste·mon [penˈstiːmən, ˈpensti-; pɛnˋstimən, ˋpɛnstɪ-] ***n*.**【植】钓钟柳属 (*Penstemon*) 植物〔草木象牙红属植物〕。

pen·ster [ˈpenstə; ˋpɛnstɚ] ***n*.** 雇佣文人。

pen·stock [ˈpenstɔk; ˋpɛnˏstɑk] ***n*.** **1.** 节制闸门,潮门,水门。**2.** 〔美〕(引水的)水渠,水槽;(水电站的)导水管。**3.** 给水栓;〔美〕救火龙头。**4.**【化】压头管线。**5.** 笔杆。

pen·sum [ˈpensəm; ˋpɛnsəm] ***n*.** 罚学生做的工作。

pent[1] [pent; pɛnt] **I** pen[2] 的过去式及过去分词。**II** ***a*.** 被幽闭的;被关闭的;郁积的。～**-up** 被抑制的,被关住的 (～*-up fury* 心中郁愤)。

pent[2] [pent; pɛnt] ***n*.** 单斜顶棚;庇檐。～ **roof** 单坡屋顶。

pent-, penta- *comb.f.* 表示"五"。

Pen·ta [ˈpentə; ˋpɛntə] ***n*.** 〔美口〕五角大厦,美国国防部。

pen·ta·chlo·ro·ni·tro·ben·zene [ˈpentəˌklɔːrəˌnaitrəuˈbenziːn; ˋpɛntəˏklɔrəˏnaɪtroˋbɛnzin] ***n*.**【化】五氯硝基苯。

pen·ta·chlo·ro·phe·nol [ˌpentəˌklɔːrəˈfiːnəul, -nɔːl; ˏpɛntəˏklɔrəˋfinol, -nɔl] ***n*.**【化】五氯苯酚。

pen·ta·chord [ˈpentəkɔːd; ˋpɛntəˏkɔrd] ***n*.** 五弦琴;五声音阶。

pen·ta·cle [ˈpentəkl; ˋpɛntəkl̩] ***n*.** = pentagram.

pen·tad [ˈpentæd; ˋpɛntæd] **I** ***n*.** **1.** 五;五个一组。**2.** 五年,五天。**3.**【化】五价元素,五价物。**II** ***a*.** 五价元素的。

pen·ta·dac·tyl, pen·ta·dac·tyl·ate [ˌpentəˈdæktil, -dækˈtilit; ˏpɛntəˋdæktɪl, -dækˋtɪlɪt] ***a*.** 有五指[五趾]的。**-dac·tyl·ism** ***n*.**

pen·ta·e·ryth·rite, pen·ta·e·ryth·ri·tol [ˌpentəiˈriθrait, -rətəul; ˏpɛntəɪˋrɪθˏraɪt, -rətol] ***n*.**【化】季戊四醇,支戊四醇。

pen·ta·gon [ˈpentəgən; ˋpɛntəˏgɑn] ***n*.** **1.** 五角形,五边形。**2.**【建】五棱堡。*a regular* ～ 正五边形。*the P-* (*Building*) 〔美〕五角大厦;美国国防部。**pen·tag·o·nal** [penˈtægənl; pɛnˋtægənl̩] ***a*.**

pen·ta·gram [ˈpentəgræm; ˋpɛntəˏgræm] ***n*.** 五角星形 (☆)。

pen·ta·graph [ˈpentəgrɑːf, -græf; ˋpɛntəgrɑf, -græf] ***n*.** 连续的五个字母 (= pantograph)。

pen·ta·grid [ˈpentəgrid; ˋpɛntəˏgrɪd] ***n*.**【无】五栅管,七极管。

Pen·tag·y·nia [ˌpentəˈdʒiniə; pɛntəˋdʒɪnɪə] ***n*.** 〔*pl*.〕【植】五雌蕊纲。

pen·tag·y·nous [penˈtædʒinəs; pɛnˋtædʒɪnəs] ***a*.**【植】(有)五雌蕊的。

pen·ta·hed·ron [ˌpentəˈhedrən; ˏpɛntəˋhidrən] ***n*.** (*pl*. ～***s***, ***-dra*** [-drə; -drə]) 【数】五面体。**-ta·he·dral**

[ˌpentəˈhedrəl; ˏpɛntəˋhidrəl] *a*.

pen·ta·hy·drate [ˌpentəˈhaidreit; ˏpɛntəˋhaɪdret] *n*. 【化】五水化物。

pen·tam·er·ous [penˈtæmərəs; pɛnˋtæmərəs] *a*. 【生】五跗节的;【植】五基数的(= 5-merous)。**-er·ism** [-rizəm; -rɪzəm] *n*.

pen·tam·e·ter [penˈtæmitə; pɛnˋtæmətɚ] I *n*. 【韵】五音步诗行。II *a*. 五音步的。

Pen·tan·dri·a [penˈtændriə; pɛnˋtændrɪə] *n*. [*pl*.] 【植】五雄蕊纲。**pen·tan·drous** [-drəs; -drəs] *a*. 五雄蕊的。

pen·tane [ˈpentein; ˋpɛnten] *n*. 【化】戊烷。

pen·tan·gle [ˈpenˌtæŋgl; ˋpɛntæŋgl] *n*. = pentagram.

pen·tan·gu·lar [penˈtæŋgjulə; pɛnˋtæŋgjʊlɚ] *a*. (有)五角的。

pen·ta·nol [ˈpentəˌnɔːl; ˋpɛntəˏnɔl] *n*. 【化】戊醇(= amyl alcohol)。

pen·ta·ploid [ˈpentəˌplɔid; ˋpɛntəˏplɔɪd] I *a*. 【生】有五倍体的。II *n*. 五倍体。**-y** *n*.

pen·ta·quine [ˈpentəkwi(ː)n, -kwin; ˋpɛntəkwin, -kwɪn] *n*. 【药】戊奎宁。

pen·tarch·y [ˈpentɑːki; ˋpɛntɑrkɪ] *n*. 1. 五头政治。2. 五国联盟。

pen·ta·stich [ˈpentəstik; ˋpɛntəˏstɪk] *n*. 五行诗,有五行一节的诗。

pen·ta·style [ˈpentəstail; ˋpɛntəstaɪl] *a*. 【建】五柱式的。

pen·ta·syl·la·ble [ˈpentəsiləbl; ˋpɛntəˏsɪləbl] *n*. 五音节。

Pen·ta·teuch [ˈpentətjuːk; ˋpɛntəˏtjuk] *n*. 【基督】《旧约全书》的首五卷。

pen·tath·lete [penˈtæθliːt; pɛnˈtæθlit] *n*. 参加五项运动的运动员。

pen·tath·lon [penˈtæθlɔn; pɛnˈtæθlən] *n*. 五项运动[田径比赛全能运动之一]。

pen·ta·tom·ic [ˌpentəˈtɔmik; ˏpɛntəˋtɑmɪk] *a*. 【化】五元的。

pen·ta·ton·ic [ˌpentəˈtɔnik; ˏpɛntəˋtɑnɪk] *a*. 【乐】五声音阶的。

pen·ta·va·lent [ˌpentəˈveilənt; ˏpɛntəˋvelənt] *a*. 1. 【化】五阶的。2. 具有五种不同的价的(= quinquevalent)。

Pen·te·cost [ˈpentikɔst; ˋpɛntɪˏkɔst] *n*. 1. (犹太人的)五旬节。2. (基督教的)圣灵降临节。**-al** [ˌpentiˈkɔstl; ˏpɛntɪˋkɑstl] *a*.

pent·house [ˈpenthaus; ˋpɛntˏhaʊs] *n*. 1. (大楼平顶上的)楼顶房间;小棚屋。2. 雨篷,遮篷;(靠墙的)单斜顶棚;庇檐;庇檐形物。*a* ~ *roof* 单坡屋顶;庇檐。*the* ~ *of the eye* 眉。***make a*** ~ ***of the eyebrows*** 皱眉头。

pen·thrit(e) [ˈpenθrait; ˋpɛnθraɪt] *n*. 【化】季戊炸药。

Pen·tium [ˈpentiəm; ˋpɛntɪəm] *n*. 【商标】奔腾[一种电脑芯片的商标名,如"奔腾 586"等]。~ *chips* 奔腾芯片。

pent·land·ite [ˈpentləndait; ˋpɛntlənˏdaɪt] *n*. 【矿】镍黄铁矿,硫镍铁矿。

pen·tode [ˈpentəud; ˋpɛntod] I *a*. 【无】五极的。II *n*. 【无】五极管。*a radio-frequency* ~ 高频五极管。*a beam* ~ 电子注管。

pen·tom·ic [penˈtɔmik; pɛnˈtɑmɪk] *a*. 【军】五群制的。

Pen·ton·ville [ˈpentənvil; ˋpɛntənvɪl] *n*. (英国伦敦的)本顿维尔(单人)监狱。

pen·to·san, pen·to·sane [ˈpentəsæn, ˈpentəsein; ˋpɛntəˏsæn, ˋpɛntəˏsen] *n*. 【化】戊聚醣,多缩戊醣。

pen·tose [ˈpentəus; ˋpɛntos] *n*. 【化】戊醣。

pen·to·thal [ˈpentəθæl; ˋpɛntəˏθæl] *n*. 【药】喷妥撒。

pent·ste·mon [pentˈstiːmən; pɛntˋstimən] *n*. 【植】锥种柳属植物;草本象牙红。

pen·tyl [ˈpentil; ˋpɛntɪl] *n*. 【化】戊(烷)基。~ **alcohol** 戊醇。

pe·nu·che, pe·nu·chi [pəˈnuːtʃi; pəˋnutʃɪ] *n*. = panocha[2].

pe·nult [piˈnʌlt; pɪˋnʌlt] *n*., *a*. 词尾倒数第二音节(的);倒数第二个(的)。

pe·nul·ti·mate [piˈnʌltimit; pɪˋnʌltəmɪt] *a*., *n*. = penult.

pe·num·bra [piˈnʌmbrə; pɪˋnʌmbrə] *n*. (*pl*. **-brae** [-briː; -bri], ~*s*) 1. 【物】半影,黑影周围的半阴影。2. (绘画中)画面浓淡相交处。3. 【天】太阳黑子周围的半暗部;(星面部的)阴影。**-bral** *a*.

pe·nu·ri·ous [piˈnjuəriəs; pəˋnʊrɪəs] *a*. 1. [古]贫穷的;贫瘠的。2. 吝啬的。**-ly** *ad*. **-ness** *n*.

pen·u·ry [ˈpenjuri, -juəri; ˋpɛnjərɪ, -jərɪ] *n*. 1. 贫穷;缺乏(*of*)。2. 吝啬。

pe·on [ˈpiːən; ˋpiən] *n*. 1. (南美的)散工,日工;(墨西哥、美国西南部)以劳力抵债的奴隶式工人。2. [ˈpjuːn, ˈpiːən; ˋpjun, ˋpiən]【印】步兵;巡警;跟班;侍役。3. (象棋)卒。

pe·on·age [ˈpiːənidʒ; ˋpiənɪdʒ] *n*. 1. 雇用日工;做日工。2. (美国东南部的)劳力偿债制。~ **labour** 偿债劳动。

pe·o·ny [ˈpiəni; ˋpiənɪ] *n*. 【植】芍药属植物。*the herbaceous* ~ 芍药。*the tree* ~ 牡丹。*blush like a* ~ 脸红。

peo·ple [ˈpiːpl; ˋpipl] I *n*. (*pl*. 1. 为 ~*s*, 其他为 ~) 1. 种族;民族。2. 人民。3. 居民;(团体、行业等中的)人们。4. [常与所有格连用](对君主而言的)臣民;教区教徒,随从;家,家属,亲属;[学]亲戚;祖先。5. [the ~]平民,老百姓。6. (一般的)人,人们;人类(*opp*. animals)。7. [作不定代名词用]人家,有的人。8. [主诗]生物。*a warlike* ~ 一个好战的民族。*the English* ~ 英国人民。*the* ~*s of Europe* 欧洲诸民族。*the* ~*'s front* 人民阵线。*the village* ~ 村民。*the* ~ *here* 这里的居民。*literary* ~ 文人们。*He has gone to his wife's* ~. 他到他丈母家去了。*My* ~ *have lived here for generations*. 我家世世代代都是住在这里。*a man of the* ~ 一个老百姓。*Few* ~ *know the truth*. 很少人知道实情。***as*** ~ ***go*** 照一般人讲。***of all*** ~ 在许多[所有]人中(偏偏…)。***P- say that*** ... 人们说,据说…。***the best*** ~ [口]上流社会人士。***the Chosen P-*** 【宗】上帝的选民[指基督徒];犹太人。
II *vt*. 1. 使人到…去住,使住满人,在…殖民。2. 把(动物)放养在(*with*)。3. [用 *p*. *p*.]住在,栖息在;布满,占据。*a thickly* [*sparsely*] ~*d country* 人口稠密[稀少]的国家。~ **journalism**(多由图片组成的)人物新闻。~ **meter** 触键式收视率统计仪[安装在电视机上,上有 8 个键,分由每个家庭成员使用,看电视时按下自己的专用键即可]。~**'s park** [美](相对于国家公园的)地区[社区]公园。~ **skills** 社交技能,待人接物的本领。~**-to-**~ *a*. 人民之间的。

pep [pep; pɛp] I *n*. [美俚]劲头,锐气,活力。*a* ~ *talk* (教练等对队员等的)精神讲话,鼓励士气的讲话。II *vt*. (**-pp-**)给…打气,刺激,鼓励(*up*)。~ **pill** [美俚]兴奋药片[尤指安非他明]。~ **rally** 鼓舞士气的集会。

P.E.P., PEP = 1. Political and Economic Planning 政治经济计划。2. personal equity plan [英]个人股本投资计划。

pep·er·i·no, pep·er·ine [ˌpepəˈriːnəu, ˈpepəriːn; ˏpɛpəˋrino, ˋpɛpərin] *n*. 【地】白榴拟灰岩。

pep·per [ˈpepə; ˋpɛpɚ] I *n*. 1. 胡椒;胡椒粉;[P-]【植】胡椒属。2. 刺激性;尖锐的批评。3. 暴躁,急性子。4. [美俚]活力,精力;劲头;勇气。*white* ~ 白胡椒。*beaten* [*ground*] ~ 胡椒粉。*the Chinese* [*Japanese*] ~ 秦椒。*the water* ~ 蓼。***take*** ~ ***in the nose*** = ***grow*** ~ 发怒,动气。II *vt*. 1. 加胡椒粉于;撒(胡椒),用胡椒调(味)。2. 乱发(质问、子弹);【美拳】接连速击。3. [罕]嘲笑;痛骂;重罚。~**-and-salt** *n*., *a*. 椒盐(的);(衣料)黑白点相间(的)。~ **box** 1. 胡椒盒[瓶]。2. 急性人。~ **caster**, ~ **castor** 胡椒瓶[盒] ~ **corn** 1. 干胡椒,胡椒

P

子。2. 无聊的东西;空有其名的地租[房租](= ~ rent);微不足道的东西。~**-grass**【植】独行菜。~ **-mill** 磨胡椒子的小罐。~**mint** 1.【植】胡椒薄荷;薄荷。2. 薄荷油。3. 薄荷糖。~**pot** 1. 胡椒瓶[盒]。2.〔俚〕急性人。3.(西印度群岛的)红辣椒炖肉;红辣椒肉菜汤。4.〔俚〕牙买加岛人。~ **spray** 辣椒喷雾剂[用于防暴等]。~ **tree**【植】木兰科植物;秘鲁乳香。~**wort**【植】胡椒草。

pep·per·y [ˈpepəri; ˋpɛpərɪ] *a*. 1. 胡椒(似)的。2.(话)辛辣的。3. 易怒的,暴躁的。

pep·py [ˈpepi; ˋpɛpɪ] *a*. 1.〔美俚〕精神饱满的;劲头十足的。2.(汽车、飞机)起动快的;高速运行性能好的。

P

-pepsia *comb. f*. 表示"消化": brady*pepsia*.

Pep·si-co·la [ˈpepsiˌkəulə; ˋpɛpsɪˏkolə] *n*.【美商标】百事可乐〔一种饮料〕。

Pep·sif·i·ca·tion [ˌpepsifiˈkeiʃən; ˏpɛpsɪfɪˋkeʃən] *n*. 使百事可乐化〔指引进名牌低档食品的美国式商业运作,饮料与快餐业尤甚〕。

pep·sin(e) [ˈpepsin; ˋpɛpsɪn] *n*.【生化】胃朊酶,胃蛋白酶。

pep·sin·ate [ˈpepsineit; ˋpɛpsɪnet] *vt*.【生化】用胃蛋白酶处理,用胃蛋白酶混合;向…注入胃蛋白酶。

pep·sin·o·gen [pepˈsinədʒən; pɛpˋsɪnədʒən] *n*.【生化】胃蛋白酶原。

pep·ster [ˈpepstə; ˋpɛpstɚ] *n*.〔美〕激起别人热情的人。

pep·tic [ˈpeptik; ˋpɛptɪk] I *a*. 1. 胃的,(帮助)消化的。2.(产生)胃(朊)酶的。3. 消化液的。II *n*. 1. 消化剂,健胃剂。2.〔*pl*.〕〔谑〕消化器官。~ *glands* 胃酶腺。

pep·ti·dase [ˈpeptideis; ˋpɛptɪˏdes] *n*.【生化】肽酶。

pep·tide, pep·tid [ˈpeptaid, -tid; ˋpɛptaɪd, -tɪd] *n*.【生化】肽;缩氨酸。

pep·ti·mist [ˈpeptimist; ˋpɛptɪmɪst] *n*.〔美〕精神饱满的人。

pep·tize [ˈpeptaiz; ˋpɛpˏtaɪz] *vt*., *vi*.【化】使胶溶。

pep·tone [ˈpeptəun; ˋpɛpton] *n*.【生化】胨,蛋白胨。

pep·to·nize [ˈpeptənaiz; ˋpɛptəˏnaɪz] *vt*. 使胨化,使蛋白胨化。**-to·ni·za·tion** [-ˈzeiʃən; -ˋzeʃən] *n*.

Pepys [piːps; pips] *n*. 佩皮斯〔姓氏〕。

Pe·quot, Pe·quod [ˈpiːkwɔt, -kwɔd; ˋpikwɑt, -kwɑd] *n*.【美史】佩科特人〔17世纪住在英格兰南部的 Algonquian 族印第安人的一支〕。

per, *per* [强 pəː, 弱 pə; 强 pɚ, 弱 pɚ] *prep*.〔L.〕1. 由,经;以,靠。2. 每,一。3. 按照,根据。*$2 ~ man* 每人两元。~ *day* [*month*, *year*] 每天[月、年]。***as ~*** = *according to*. ***as ~ usual*** 〔谑〕照常。~ ***annum*** [pəˈrænəm; pɚˋænəm] 每年。~ ***bearer*** 由来人。~ ***capita*** [ˈkæpitə; ˋkæpɪtə] 每人,按人(分配)。~ ***caput*** [ˈkæpət; kæpət] = ~ *capita*. ~ ***cent*** (***um***) [ˈsent(əm); ˋsɛnt(əm)] 每百分之(几) ~ ***contra*** [pəːˈkɔntrə; pɚˋkɑntrə] 1. 反而,相反的。2. 在另一方面;在对方。~ ***diem*** [pəːˈdaiem, -ˈdaiəm; pɚˋdaɪɛm, -ˋdaɪəm] 每日,按日。~ ***fas et nefas*** [ˈfæs et ˈneifæs; ˋfæs ɛt ˋnefæs] 无论如何。~ ***mensem*** [ˈmensem; ˋmɛnsɛm] 每月,按月。~ ***mille*** [ˈmili; ˋmɪlɪ] 每千。~ ***post*** 由邮局。~ ***procurationem*** [prɔkjuəreiʃiˈəunem; prɑkjureʃɪˋonɛm] 〔略 *p. proc.*, *p. pro.*, *p. p.*〕由…所代表;由…代理。~ ***rail*** [***steamer***] 由铁路[轮船]。~ ***saltum*** [ˈsæltəm; ˋsæltəm] 一跃。~ ***se*** [ˈsei, ˈsiː; ˋse, ˋsi] 自,自身;本来,性质上。

per. = period, person.

per- *pref*. 1. 通,总,遍: *per*fect, *per*vade. 2. 极,甚: *per*fervid. 3.【化】过,高: *per*oxide.

per·ac·id [ˈpəːˌæsid; ˋpɚˏæsɪd] *n*.【化】高酸;过酸。

per·ad·ven·ture [pərədˈventʃə; ˏpɚədˋvɛntʃɚ] I *ad*.〔古〕1. 恐怕,或者,可能。2. 偶然,万一。***if ~*** 如果…,要是…,万一…。***lest ~*** 唯恐万一,以防万一。II *n*. 1. 疑惑,疑问。2. 偶然;不确实。***beyond ~*** = ***without ~*** 无疑地,的确;必定。

per·am·bu·late [pəˈræmbjuleit; pɚˋæmbjəˏlet] *vt*. 1. 巡行,巡视;勘查。2. 走过,穿过;徘徊于。—*vi*. 闲逛,闲荡;徘徊。

per·am·bu·la·tion [pəˌræmbjuˈleiʃən; pɚˏæmbjəˋleʃən] *n*. 1. 漫步,闲荡;徘徊。2. 巡视;巡行[勘查、测量]区。3. 巡视[勘查]报告。

per·am·bu·la·tor [ˈpræmbjuleitə, pəˈræm-; pɚˋæmbjəˏletɚ] *n*. 1.〔主英〕婴儿车〔俗称 pram〕。2.【测】路程计;测程器。3. 巡视者;漫步者;徘徊者;勘查者。

per·am·bu·la·to·ry [pəˈræmbjulətəri; pɚˋæmbjələˏtorɪ] *a*. 1. 漫步的;闲荡的。2. 巡行的;巡视的,勘查的。

per an(n). = [L.] *per annum* 每年。

per·bo·rate [pəˈbɔːreit; pɚˋboret] *n*.【化】过硼酸盐。

per·bu·nan [ˈpəːb(j)unən; ˋpɚb(j)unən] *n*.【商标】别布橡胶,丁腈橡胶。

per·cale [pəˈkeil; pɚˋkel] *n*.【纺】高级密织薄纱。

per·ca·line [ˌpəːkəˈliːn, ˈpəːkəliːn; ˏpɚkəˋlin, ˋpɚkəlin] *n*.【纺】波盖勒细棉织品。

per·ceiv·a·ble [pəˈsiːvəbl; pɚˋsivəbl] *a*. 可察觉的,可看到的,可理解的,可领会的。**-a·bil·i·ty, -ness** *n*. **-a·bly** *ad*.

per·ceive [pəˈsiːv; pɚˋsiv] *vt*. 1. 察觉,发觉。2. 看见,听见。3. 领会,领悟,了解;看出,抓住(意义、真相等)。*Yes, I ~* (*what you say*). 是,不错。

per cent, per·cent [pəˈsent; pɚˋsɛnt] *n*.〔拉丁语 *per centum* 的缩略,符号为%〕1. 每百,百分之一…。2.〔*pl*.〕(…厘息)公债[投资等]。3.〔口〕百分率。7 ~ 百分之七(7%)。*get 2 ~ interest* 获二分利。*invest money in 2.5 ~s* 投资于二分五利息的公债。

per·cent·age [pəˈsentidʒ; pɚˋsɛntɪdʒ] *n*. 1.【数】百分法;百分数;百分比,百分率。2. 比例,部分。3.【商】手续费,佣金。4.〔俚〕赚头,不正当的利益;好处;用处。5.(根据统计得出的)可能性。***no ~ in*** 〔美〕没利益,没好处。~ ***of hits***【军】命中率。~ **table** 百分数表。**-wise** *ad*. 从百分比来看,在百分比上。

per·cen·tile [pəˈsentail; pɚˋsɛntaɪl] I *a*. 百分比的。II *n*. 百分位数(值);百分之一;百分比下降点。

per·cept [ˈpəːsept; ˋpɚsɛpt] *n*. 1.【哲】知觉的对象。2. 感觉;感受;印象。

per·cep·ti·ble [pəˈseptəbl; pɚˋsɛptəbl] *a*. 1. 可以感觉[感受]到的。2. 可理解的,认得出的;看得出的。3. 相当的。*quite a ~ time* 很长时间。**-ti·bil·i·ty** [pəˌseptəˈbiliti; pɚˏsɛptəˋbɪlətɪ] *n*. 感觉力,察觉力;领悟[认识]能力。

per·cep·ti·bly [pəˈseptəbli; pɚˋsɛptəblɪ] *ad*. 感觉得出地,认得出地;显然。

per·cep·tion [pəˈsepʃən; pɚˋsɛpʃən] *n*. 1.【哲】感觉(作用);感受;知觉。2. 知觉作用;感性认识;观念,概念;直觉。3. 洞察力;理解力。4.【法】(地租等的)征收;(农作物的)收获。*a man of the keenest ~* 感觉敏锐的人。*visual ~* 视觉。**-al** *a*.

per·cep·tive [pəˈseptiv; pɚˋsɛptɪv] *a*. 1. 知觉的。2. 感觉(敏锐)的;有理解力的。

per·cep·tiv·i·ty [ˌpəːsepˈtiviti; ˏpɚsɛpˋtɪvətɪ] *n*. 1. 感觉力;理解力。2. 认识能力。

per·cep·tron [pəˈseptrən; pɚˋsɛptrɑn] *n*.【无】视感控器〔类似视神经的电子仪器〕。

per·cep·tu·al [pəˈseptjuəl; pɚˋsɛptʃuəl] *a*. 知觉的,知觉力的,感性的。~ *knowledge* 感性认识(*opp*. conceptual knowledge)。*the ~ stage of cognition* 认识的感性阶段。**-ly** *ad*.

perch[1] [pəːtʃ; pɚtʃ] I *n*. 1.(鸟的)栖木;挂东西的横条。2.(尤指高处的)休息处;高位;有利地位。3.【机】(联系前后车轴的)连杆,主轴;架;驭者座;(弹药车的)车尾;

棒,竿。4. 杆〔英国长度名(=5码)〕;英国面积单位(=30¼平方码);(石头等的)体积单位(通常为16½ ft. × ½ ft. ×1ft.)。5.〔美〕虚荣心,自负;棒球场的座位。6. 皮革的鞣制,皮革破绽的弥补。7.【纺】验布架。8.【海】浮筒顶标。*come off one's* ~〔口〕失势,没落。*hop* [*drop off*, *tip over*] *the* ~〔口〕落败,死。*knock sb. off his* ~〔俚〕挫败某人;把某人毁掉。II *vi*. 1.(鸟)落,歇。2. 坐,休息(*on*; *upon*)。—*vt*. 1. 使(鸟)歇在栖木上;把(人)放置高处[危险处]〔通常用过去分词形〕。3. 验(布)。*a town ~ed on a hill* 位于山上的镇市。

perch[2] [pəːtʃ; pɝtʃ] *n*. (*pl*. ~*es*,〔集合词〕~)【鱼】河鲈。

per·chance [pə(ː)ˈtʃɑːns, -ˈtʃæns; pæˋtʃɑns, -ˋtʃæns] *ad*.〔古〕1. 偶然。2. 或许,可能。

perch·er [ˈpəːtʃə; ˋpɝtʃɚ] *n*. 1. 栖木类的鸟;在高处的人。2. 织品检查人,验布工。3.〔口〕将死的人。

Per·che·ron [ˈpɛəːʃərɔ̃ːŋ; ˋpɝtʃəran] *n*.〔F.〕(法国北部 Perche 产的)灰毛马。

per·chlo·rate [pəˈklɔːreit; pɚˋkloret] *n*.【化】过氯酸盐。~ *explosive* 过氯酸盐炸药。

per·chlo·ric [pəˈklɔːrik; pɚˋklorɪk] *a*. ~ **acid**【化】高氯酸。

per·chlo·ride [pəˈklɔːraid; pɚˋkloraɪd] *n*.【化】高氯化物。

per·cip·i·ence, per·cip·i·en·cy [pəːˈsipiəns, -ənsi; pɚˋsɪpɪəns, -ənsɪ] *n*. 1. 感觉;知觉。2. 洞察力。

per·cip·i·ent [pəːˈsipiənt; pɚˋsɪpɪənt] I *a*. 1. 感觉的,有知觉的。2. 洞察的。II *n*. 1. 感觉灵敏的人;洞察。2. 感觉者。

Per·ci·val [ˈpəːsivəl; ˋpɝsəvl̩] 珀西瓦尔〔男子名〕。

per·coid [ˈpəːkɔid; ˋpɝkɔɪd] I *a*.【鱼】鲈形类(*Percomorphi*)的〔包括鲈,翻车鲀等〕。II *n*. 鲈形类的鱼。

per·co·late [ˈpəːkəleit; ˋpɝkə͵let] I *vt*. 1. 滤,使渗滤,使渗透。2.(用渗滤壶)煮(咖啡)。3. 刺穿,穿过。—*vi*. 渗开,滤过。~ **up** 自下而上地发展经济(等)〔指发展应着重调动下层积极性,使下层人士勤奋工作,增加投资〕。II *n*. 渗出液,滤过液。

per·co·la·tion [ˌpəːkəˈleiʃən; ͵pɝkəˋleʃən] *n*. 1. 渗滤;渗透(作用);渗漏。2.【化】穿流(法)。*underground* ~ 地下渗流。

per·co·la·tor [ˈpəːkəleitə; ˋpɝkə͵letɚ] *n*. 1. 渗滤器,(尤指)咖啡渗滤壶。2. 进行渗滤的人。

per ct. =〔L.〕*per centum* 百分之…。

per cu·ri·am [pəˈkjuəriˌæm; pɚˋkjurɪəm] *a*.〔L.〕【法】法院的〔指的是整个法庭的判决意见,而不是其中某一法官的意见〕。

per·cuss [pəːˈkʌs; pɚˋkʌs] *vt*. 1. 敲,叩,击。2.【医】扣诊。

per·cus·sion [pəːˈkʌʃən; pɚˋkʌʃən] *n*. 1. 敲打,叩击;撞击;碰撞。2.(由敲打产生的)震动。3.【乐】打击;(乐队的)打击乐器组。4.【军】击发(装置)。5.【医】扣诊(法)。~ **bullet**【军】爆破炸弹。~ **cap** 雷管,发火帽。~ **fuse**【军】着发引信。~ **gun** 雷管枪。~ **instrument**【乐】打击乐器。~ **lock**【军】击发装置。~ **powder** 起爆药。~ **primer**【军】引爆药。~ **shrapnel** 着发榴霰弹。

per·cus·sion·ist [pəˈkʌʃənist; pɚˋkʌʃənɪst] *n*. 打击乐乐师。

per·cus·sive [pəːˈkʌsiv; pɚˋkʌsɪv] *a*. 1.(乐器等)敲击的。2.【医】扣诊的。3. 有强大震动力的;令人震惊的。

per·cu·ta·ne·ous [ˌpəːkju(ː)ˈteiniəs, -njəs; ͵pɝkjuˋtenɪəs, -njəs] *a*.【医】经皮的,由皮的。

per cwt. = per hundredweight 每英担。

Per·cy [ˈpəːsi; ˋpɝsɪ] *n*. 珀西〔姓氏,男子名〕。

per·die [pəˈdiː; pɚˋdi] *ad*., *int*.〔古〕必然,一定,确实〔原为一种誓言〕(=pardie)。

per·di·tion [pəːˈdiʃən; pɚˋdɪʃən] *n*. 1. 灭亡,毁灭。2.【宗】堕地狱,沉沦,永远的死;永灭;地狱。*Go to* ~! 见鬼去! 该死的!

per·du(e) [pəːˈdjuː; pɚˋdju] I *a*. 1. 看不见的;隐藏的,潜伏的,埋伏的。2.〔古〕敢死的。*lie* ~ 潜伏,埋伏。II *n*. 1. 伏兵;敢死队员。2. 很难成功的事[举动]。

per·dur·a·ble [pə(ː)ˈdjuərəbl; pɚˋdjurəbl̩] *a*. 持久的,耐久的,永久的,不朽的。**-a·bil·i·ty** *n*. **-a·bly** *ad*.

per·dure [pə(ː)ˈdjuə; pɚˋdjur] *vi*. 持久,持续。

père [pɛə; pɛr] *n*.〔F.〕1. 父。★同名父子,名后加 *père* 时为父,加 *fils* 时为子。2.〔P-〕…神父〔尊称〕。*Alexander Dumas* ~ 大仲马。

per·e·gri·nate [ˈperigrineit; ˋpɛrəgrɪ͵net] *vi*.〔古、谑〕流浪;游历,(徒步)旅行。**-gri·na·tion** [-ˈneiʃən; -ˋneʃən] *n*. 游历,(徒步)旅行;旅程;流浪。**-gri·na·tor** *n*.(徒步)旅行者;流浪者。

per·e·grin(e) [ˈperigrin; ˋpɛrəgrɪn] I *a*. 1. 外国的,外来的,舶来的;异国(风味)的。2.(鸟)移居的;(人)流浪的,漫游的。II *n*. 1.【鸟】(放鹰打猎用的)游隼(= falcon)。2. 外侨,居留外国的人;游历者。

per·emp·to·ry [pəˈrempˌtəri; pəˋrɛmptərɪ] *a*. 1. 断然的,毅然的;命令式的。2. 独断的,专横的;强制的。3.【法】绝对的,最后决定的。~ **mandamus** 强制执行命令书。**-to·ri·ly** [-ˈtɔ-; -ˋto-] *ad*. **-to·ri·ness** *n*.

per·en·nate [ˈpɛərəneit; ˋpɛrə͵net] *vi*.(植物)多年生长;持续不断地存在。**-en·na·tion** *n*.

per·en·ni·al [pəˈrenjəl; pəˋrɛnɪəl] I *a*. 1. 四季不断的,终年的;继续多年的;(青春)永驻的。2.【动】(牙齿等)不断生长的;(昆虫)活一年以上的。3.【植】多年生的。II *n*. 多年生植物。~ *river* 常流河。**-ly** *ad*. **-ni·al·i·ty** *n*.

pe·res·troi·ka [ˌperəsˈtrɔikə; ͵pɛrəsˋtrɔɪkə] *n*.〔Russ.〕(戈尔巴乔夫等推行的)"改革"。

perf. = 1. perfect. 2. perforate. 3. performer.

per·fect [ˈpəːfikt; ˋpɝfɪkt] I *a*. 1. 完全的,完美的;圆满的,理想的;纯粹的。2. 熟练的,精通的(*in*)。3. 绝对的,毋容置疑的;分毫不差的,正确的。4.〔口〕十足的;厉害的,过分的。5.【植】雌雄(蕊)同花的;具备的。6.【语法】完成的。7.【印】两面印的。8.(昆虫)性成熟的。*a* ~ *actor to play the role* 扮演这个角色的理想演员。*a* ~ *day* 一个美满快活的日子。*make a* ~ *fool of oneself* 使自己成为一个不折不扣的傻瓜。*a* ~ *tennis player* 熟练的网球家。*a* ~ *storm* 猛烈的暴风雨。**make** ~【印】两面印刷。**the** ~ **year** 犹太历。

II *n*.【语法】完成时,完成式。*the present* [*future*, *past*] ~ 现在[未来,过去]完成式。

III [pə(ː)ˈfekt, ˈpəːfikt; pɚˋfɛkt, ˋpɝfɪkt] *vt*. 1. 完成,贯彻。2. 使完全;使完美;改善,改良。3. 使熟练,使精通。~ *an invention* 完成一项声明。*be constantly ~ing one's skill* 对技术精益求精。~ **oneself in** 弄熟,精通。~ **binding**【印】无线胶黏装订。~ **gas** 理想气体。~ **press** 两面印刷轮转机。~ **square**【数】整方,完全平方。~ **stage**【生】有性阶段。~ **tense**【语法】完成时。**-or** [pə(ː)ˈfektə; pɚˋfɛktɚ] *n*.【印】两面印刷机。**-ly** *adv*. **-ness** *n*.

per·fect·i·ble [pə(ː)ˈfektəbl; pɚˋfɛktəbl̩] *a*. 1. 可以完成的。2. 可变完善的;可改善的。**-bil·i·ty** [-ˈbiliti; -ˋbɪlətɪ] *n*.

per·fec·tion [pəˈfekʃən; pɚˋfɛkʃən] *n*. 1. 完全,圆满,完备;完成;成熟;无缺;极度,极致。2. 熟习,熟练。3. 优秀人物,典型;标本。4.〔*pl*.〕才艺,美点。*Beauty is the least* ~. 美貌是优点中最微不足道的一点。***be at*** ~(果子)正熟;(菜)做得恰好。***be the*** ~ ***of*** (*folly*)(蠢)到极点,(愚蠢)之极。***come*** [***attain***] ***to*** ~ 圆熟,成熟。***to*** ~ 完全地;好极。

per·fec·tion·ism [pə(ː)ˈfekʃənizəm; pɚˋfɛkʃənɪzm] *n*. 1. 至善论,圆满论;完全论〔认为人世间可达至善境界〕。2. 过度追求尽善尽美。**-tion·ist** *n*. 1. 至善论者,圆满论者。2. 追求尽善尽美者,过分挑剔者。

per·fect·ive [pə(:)ˈfektiv; pɚˋfɛktɪv] **I** ***a*.** **1.** 使完美[圆满]的。**2.**【语法】(动词体)完成的。**II** ***n*.** 完成体(的动词)。

per·fec·to [pəˈfektəu; pɚˋfɛkto] ***n*.** 〔美〕两头尖的雪茄烟。

per·fer·vid [pəːˈfəːvid; pɚˋfɝvɪd] ***a*.** 非常热心的;热烈的;热情的。**-ly** ***ad*.** **-ness** ***n*.**

per·fid·i·ous [pəːˈfidiəs, -djəs; pɚˋfɪdɪəs, -djəs] ***a*.** 不忠实的,叛变的;背信弃义的。**-ly** ***ad*.** **-ness** ***n*.**

per·fi·dy [ˈpəːfidi; ˋpɝfədɪ] ***n*.** (*pl*. **-*dies***) **1.** 背信弃义;不忠。**2.** 叛变,出卖。

per·fo·li·ate [pə(:)ˈfəuliit; pɚˋfolɪˏet] ***a*.** **1.**【植】(叶)抱茎的,(茎)穿叶的。**2.**【动】(昆虫)具叶片的,抱茎状的。*a* ~ *leaf* 贯穿叶。**-li·a·tion** ***n*.**

Per·fo·ra·ta [ˌpəːfəˈrɑːtə; ˏpɝfəˋrɑtə] ***n*.** 〔*pl*.〕【动】有孔虫目。

per·fo·rate [ˈpəːfəreit; ˋpɝfəˏret] **I** ***vt*.** **1.** 穿孔于,凿孔于,冲孔于,穿。**2.** 在(纸)上打眼;打透(花字);打一排孔于(邮票等)。~*d paper* 穿孔纸带。*a* ~*d electrode*【电】多孔电极。~*d bricks* 多孔砖。—***vi*.** **1.** 穿孔。**2.** 穿过;贯穿;刺穿(*into*, *through*)。**II** [ˈpəːfərit; ˋpɝfərɪt] ***a*.** (邮票等)有孔的,穿孔的,有一排孔的。**-ration** [ˌpəːfəˈreiʃən; ˏpɝfəˋreʃən] ***n*.** **1.** 穿孔,贯通;打孔,打眼。**2.** 孔眼,(邮票等的)孔状接缝。

per·fo·ra·tive [ˈpəːfərətiv; ˋpɝfəˏretɪv] ***a*.** 穿孔的,穿得过的,有穿孔力的。

per·fo·ra·tor [ˈpəːfəreitə; ˋpɝfəˏretɚ] ***n*.** **1.** 穿孔器,凿孔机;剪票铗;【医】穿头器〔产科用〕。**2.** 穿孔[打眼]的人。

per·force [pəˈfɔːs; pɚˋfɔrs] **I** ***ad*.** 〔书〕必然,必要地;不可避免地。*The story is* ~ *true*. 情况属实。**II** ***n*.** 〔罕〕强制,不得已。***by*** ~ 用力,强迫。***of*** ~ 不得已。

per·form [pəˈfɔːm; pɚˋfɔrm] ***vt*.** **1.** 履行,实行,干,执行(命令、任务等);完成(事业)。**2.** 演出;表演;扮(角色);演奏。~ *one's duties* 尽责任。~ *a play* 上演一出戏。~ *a part* 演一个角色。—***vi*.** **1.** 进行,履行,实行,执行。**2.** 表演,演奏;(驯兽)玩把戏。~ *in the role of* 扮演…角色。**-form·a·ble** ***a*.** 可执行的;可完成的;可演出的。

per·form·ance [pəˈfɔːməns; pɚˋfɔrməns] ***n*.** **1.** 执行,实行,履行;完成;实现;偿还。**2.** 行为,动作,行动;工作。**3.** 性能;特性。**4.** 功绩;成绩。**5.** 演奏;弹奏;演出;(驯兽等的)表演;把戏。**6.**【物】演绩。*a* ~ *test*【机】性能试验。*high* ~ 高度准确,性能优良。*an afternoon* ~ 午后的演出,日戏。*two* ~*s a day* 一天演两场。*a fine* [*wretched*] ~ 成绩好[坏]。*put a monkey through its* ~*s* 使猴子玩种种把戏。~ *in* [*of*] *horse-manship* 马戏;马术表演。~ **index** 性能指数,演绩指数。~ **test**【心】操作测验〔用以鉴定智力的心理测验〕。

per·form·er [pəˈfɔːmə; pɚˋfɔrmɚ] ***n*.** **1.** 执行者,实行者,履行者;完成者。**2.** 演奏者,乐师;演员,歌手,卖艺人。**3.** 能手;选手。*a good promiser, but a bad* ~ 口惠而实不至的人。

per·form·ing [pəˈfɔːmiŋ; pɚˋfɔrmɪŋ] ***a*.** **1.** 实行的,完成的。**2.** 表演的;演奏的。**3.** (狗等)会玩把戏的。

per·fume [ˈpəːfjuːm; ˋpɝfjum] **I** ***n*.** **1.** 香,芳香;香味。**2.** 香水;香料。~ **dynamics** 香味动力〔使工作环境散发出宜人的芳香以激发员工的工作劲头和提高效率〕。**II** [pə(:)ˈfjuːm; pɚˋfjum] ***vt*.** 使散发香味,把…弄香;洒香水于。~ *one's hair* 给头发洒香水。***a*** ~***d talk*** 〔美讽〕坏话,骂人话。

per·fum·er [pə(:)ˈfjuːmə; pɚˋfjumɚ] ***n*.** **1.** 香料制造人;香料商。**2.** 洒香水的人[器具]。

per·fum·er·y [pə(:)ˈfjuːməri; pɚˋfjumərɪ] ***n*.** **1.** 〔集合词〕香水类,香料。**2.** 〔美〕香水。**3.** 香料制造法。**4.** 香料厂;香料商;香料店。

per·func·to·ry [pəˈfʌŋktəri; pɚˋfʌŋktərɪ] ***a*.** **1.** 敷衍塞责的,马马虎虎的。**2.** 例行公事的;不彻底的,表面的。**-to·ri·ly** ***ad*.** **-to·ri·ness** ***n*.**

per·fuse [pə(:)ˈfjuːz; pɚˋfjuz] ***vt*.** 灌,使充满;铺满,洒遍,撒满。~ *a room with radiance* 使房间光线充足。

per·fu·sion [pə(:)ˈfjuːʒən; pɚˋfjuʒən] ***n*.** **1.** 灌注,洒。**2.**【医】灌注法。

per·fu·sive [pə(:)ˈfjuːsiv; pɚˋfjusɪv] ***a*.** **1.** 洒的,洒水用的。**2.** 易散发的;能渗透的。

per·ga·me·ne·ous [ˌpəːgəˈmiːniəs; ˏpɝgəˋminɪəs] ***a*.** 羊皮纸的;羊皮纸似的;羊皮纸做的。

per·ga·ment [ˈpəːgəmənt; ˋpɝgəmənt] ***n*.** (假)羊皮纸,革纸(=~ paper)。

per·go·la [ˈpəːgələ; ˋpɝgələ] ***n*.** **1.** (用藤架等做顶的)凉亭。**2.** (藤架等底下的)小径,荫廊。**3.** 蔓棚,藤架。

perh. = perhaps.

per·haps [pəˈhæps, pəˈræps; pɚˋhæps] **I** ***ad*.** 大概,多半,大半;可能;或许,或者。*I'll come*, ~ *I won't*. 我也许来,也许不来。**II** ***n*.** 〔常 *pl*.〕偶然事件;假定,设想。*These are all* ~*es*. 这全是假定。

pe·ri [ˈpiəri; ˋpɪrɪ] ***n*.** (*pl*. ~*s*) **1.**【波斯神话】妖精,仙女。**2.** 美人。

peri- *pref*. **1.** 周围: *peri*phery. **2.** 近,迫: *peri*helion. **3.** 围绕,围入;包围: *peri*cardiac.

per·i·anth [ˈperiænθ; ˋpɛrɪˏænθ] ***n*.**【植】花被;蒴苞;总苞。

per·i·apt [ˈperiæpt; ˋpɛrɪˏæpt] ***n*.** 护符,符录。

per·i·blem [ˈperiˌblem; ˋpɛrɪˏblɛm] ***n*.**【植】皮层原。

per·i·car·di·ac, per·i·car·di·al [ˌperiˈkɑːdiæk, -diəl; ˏpɛrɪˋkɑrdɪˏæk, -dɪəl] ***a*.**【解】心包的;位于心脏周围的。

per·i·car·di·tis [ˌperikɑːˈdaitis; ˏpɛrɪkɑrˋdaɪtɪs] ***n*.**【医】心包炎。

per·i·car·di·um [ˌperiˈkɑːdjəm; ˏpɛrɪˋkɑrdɪəm] ***n*.** (*pl*. **-*dia*** [-djə; -dɪə])【解】心包;心包膜,围心膜。

per·i·carp [ˈperikɑːp; ˋpɛrɪˏkɑrp] ***n*.**【植】果皮;囊果皮。

per·i·chon·dri·um [ˌperiˈkɔndriəm; ˌpɛrɪkɑndrɪəm] ***n*.** (*pl*. **-*dri·a*** [-ə; -ə])【解】软骨膜。**-ri·al**, **-dral** ***a*.**

per·i·clase [ˈperikleis; ˋpɛrɪkles] ***n*.**【矿】方镁石。

Per·i·cle·an [ˌperiˈkliːən; ˏpɛrəˋkliən] ***a*.** **1.** (雅典政治家)培里克里斯 (Pericles) 的。**2.** 培里克里斯时代(约自公元前 495 年至 429 年)的,古雅典文化鼎盛时期的。

per·i·cli·nal [ˌperiˈklainl; ˏpɛrɪˋklaɪnl̩] ***a*.**【植】**1.** 平周的。**2.**【地】穹状的。

per·i·cline [ˈperiˌklain; ˋpɛrɪˏklaɪn] ***n*.**【矿】肖纳长石。

pe·ric·o·pe [pəˈrikəpiː; pəˋrɪkəˏpi] ***n*.** (*pl*. ~*s*, **-*pae*** [-piː; -pi]) **1.** (从书中选出的)选段,章节。**2.** (基督教)《圣经》选读。

per·i·cra·ni·um [ˌperiˈkreiniəm; ˏpɛrɪˋkrenɪəm] ***n*.** (*pl*. **-*ni·a*** [-niə; -nɪə]) **1.**【解】颅骨膜。**2.** 〔谑〕头盖骨;头颅;机智。

per·i·cy·cle [ˈperisaikl; ˋpɛrəsaɪkl̩] ***n*.**【植】中柱鞘。**-cy·clic**[-ˈsaiklik, -ˈsiklik; -ˋsaɪklɪk, -ˋsɪklɪk] ***a*.**

per·i·derm [ˈperidəːm; ˋpɛrɪdɝm] ***n*.**【植】周皮。**-al**, **-ic** ***a*.**

pe·rid·i·um [pəˈridiəm; pəˋrɪdɪəm] ***n*.** (*pl*. **-*rid·i·a*** [-ˈridiə; -ˋrɪdɪə])【植】包被。**-rid·i·al** ***a*.**

per·i·dot [ˈperidɔt; ˋpɛrɪˏdɑt] ***n*.**【矿】(浓绿色)橄榄石。

per·i·do·tite [ˌperiˈdəutait; ˏpɛrɪˋdotaɪt] ***n*.**【矿】橄榄岩。

per·i·gee [ˈperidʒiː; ˋpɛrəˏdʒi] ***n*.**【天、宇】(月球、人造卫星等运行轨道最接近地球的)近地点 (*opp*. apogee)。**-ge·al** [ˌperiˈdʒiːəl; ˏpɛrɪˋdʒiəl], **-i·ge·an** [ˌperiˈdʒiːən; ˏpɛrɪˋdʒiən] ***a*.**【天、宇】近地点的,在近地点时间的。

per·i·gla·cial [ˌperiˈgleisjəl; ˏpɛrəˋgleʃəl] ***n*.**【地】冰川周缘的。

per·i·gon [ˈperigɔn; ˋpɛrəgɑn] ***n*.**【数】周角,三百六十

度角。

per·i·gone [ˈperigəun; ˋpɛrəgon] ***n***. 【植】**1**. 花盖。**2**. = perianth. **3**. (苔藓植物的)雄器苞。

pe·rig·y·nous [pəˈridʒinəs; pəˋrɪdʒɪnəs] ***a***. 【植】子房周位的。**-y·ny** [-ni; -nɪ] ***n***.

per·i·he·li·on [ˌperiˈhiːljən, -liən; ˏpɛrɪˋhiljən, -lɪən] ***n***. (*pl*. ***-he·lia*** [-hiːliə; -hilɪə]) 【天、宇】(行星或彗星运行轨道最接近太阳的)近日点 (*opp*. aphelion); 最高点,极点。

per·il [ˈperil; ˋpɛrəl] **I** ***n***. (严重的)危险;冒险。***at one's*** ~ (若有…)咎由自取,(…,否则)自找危险 (*Resist at your* ~! 若有抵抗,咎由自取。*Keep off at your* ~! 注意站开,免遭危险。*Do it at your* ~. 要干尽管干,危险自承当)。***at the*** ~ ***of*** 冒…的危险。***in*** ~ 危急;冒着危险。***in*** ~ ***of*** 使…发生危险;有…的危险。***in the hour*** [***time***] ***of*** ~ 在危险的时刻。**II** ***vt***. (***-l***(***l***)**-**) 冒危险,拼,置…于危险中。

Pe·ril·la [pəˈrilə; pəˋrɪlə] ***n***. 【植】紫苏属。**~seed** ***n***. 紫苏籽。

per·il·ous [ˈperiləs; ˋpɛrələs] ***a***. **1**. 危险的;冒险的。**2**. 〔古〕可怕的。**-ly** ***ad***. **-ness** ***n***.

per·i·lune [ˈperiluːn; ˋpɛrəlun] ***n***. 【宇】(人造月球卫星在轨道上最接近月球的)近月点。

per·im·e·ter [pəˈrimitə; pəˋrɪmətɚ] ***n***. **1**. 【数】周,周长;周边。**2**. 周围,周界线。**3**. 【光】视野计。**4**. 【军】(军营、工事、机场等的)环形防线[防御带]。

per·i·met·ric [ˌperiˈmetrik; ˏpɛrəˋmɛtrɪk] ***a***. **1**. 周的,周长的。**2**. 视野计的,视野测定器的 (= perimetrical)。**-cal·ly** ***ad***.

pe·rim·e·try [pəˈrimitri; pəˋrɪmətrɪ] ***n***. 视野测定。

per·i·morph [ˈperiˌmɔːf; ˋpɛrəˏmɔrf] ***n***. 【矿】被壳矿物,包被矿物。

per·i·my·si·um [ˌperiˈmiʒiəm; ˏpɛrəˋmɪʒɪəm] ***n***. (*pl*. ***-si·a*** [-ə;-ə]) 【解】外肌束膜。

per·i·na·tal [ˌperiˈneitl; ˏpɛrəˋnetl̩] ***a***. 接近出生时期的,出生前后发生的。

per·i·ne·al [ˌperiˈniːəl; ˏpɛrɪˋniəl] ***a***. 【解】会阴的。

per·i·neph·ri·um [ˌperiˈnefriəm; ˏpɛrəˋnɛfrɪəm] ***n***. (*pl*. ***-ri·a*** [-riə; -rɪə]) 【解】肾包。

per·i·ne·um, per·i·nae·um [ˌperiˈniːəm; ˏpɛrəˋniəm] ***n***. (*pl*. ***-ne·a*** [-ˈniːə; -ˋniə]) 【解】会阴。**-n(a)e·al** ***a***.

per·i·neu·ri·um [ˌperiˈnjuəriəm; ˏpɛrəˋnjurɪəm] ***n***. (*pl*. ***-ri·a*** [-ə; -ə]) 【解】神经束膜。**-neu·ri·al** ***a***.

pe·ri·od [ˈpiəriəd; ˋpɪrɪəd] **I** ***n***. **1**. 时代;期;时期;期间;阶段。**2**. 〔the ~〕现代,当代。**3**. 周期;【地】纪。**4**. 终结;句号。**5**. 【语法】长复合句,圆周句;【修】掉尾句。**6**. 〔*pl*.〕美词丽句;华丽的词藻。**7**. 学时,课时,一节课;(比赛的)一节时间。**8**. 【医】过程,周期。**9**. 〔*pl*.〕月经(期)。**10**. 【数】(循环小数的)循环节。**11**. 【乐】乐段。*the transitional* ~ 过渡时期。*the warm-up* ~ 【火箭】备射阶段。*the catchwords of the* ~ 现代流行话。*a turned* ~ (字母上面的)上点。*the incubation* ~ (病的)潜伏期。*monthly* ~ 月经。***at fixed*** **~*s*** 定期。***at stated*** **~*s*** 相隔一定时期;在一定时期。***come to a*** ~ 完结。***for a*** ~ ***of time*** 一个时期,一些时候。***put a*** ~ ***to sth***. 使某事终止;取缔某事。***round a*** ~ 练句。
II ***a***. **1**. (家具、服装、建筑等)某一时代的。**2**. (小说、戏剧等)逼真地描写某一特定历史时代的。~ *furniture* 仿古家具。*a* ~ *novel* 描写特定历史时代的小说。
III ***int***. 〔口〕就这样〔强调话已经讲完了, = That's it! That's final!〕。

pe·ri·o·date [peˈraiədeit; pəˋraɪədet] ***n***. 【化】高碘酸盐。

pe·ri·od·ic[1] [ˌpiəriˈɔdik; ˏpɪrɪˋɑdɪk] ***a***. **1**. 周期的,回归的,定期的,定时的;间歇的,时时的。**2**. 某一时期的。**3**. 【修】掉尾句的,圆周句的;美词丽句的。~ **disease** 【医】周期性病。~ **function** 【数】周期函数。~ **law** 【化】周期律。~ **sentence** (主要文意最后出现的)掉尾句,圆周句〔通常指主句在最后出现的一种复合句〕。~ **structure** 循环结构。~ **system** 【化】周期系统。~ **table** 【化】元素周期表。~ **yield(s)** 隔年收获。

per·ri·od·ic[2] [ˌpəːraiˈɔdik; ˏpɪrɪˋɑdɪk] ***a***. 【化】高碘的。

pe·ri·od·i·cal [ˌpiəriˈɔdikəl; ˏpɪrɪˋɑdɪkl̩] **I** ***a***. **1**. 周期的,定期的;时常发生的,间歇的。**2**. 定期发行的,期刊的。**II** ***n***. (日报以外的)定期刊物,杂志。*a weekly* [*monthly*] ~ 周[月]刊。**-ly** ***ad***. 周期地;定期,按时。

pe·ri·o·dic·i·ty [ˌpiəriəˈdisiti; ˏpɪrɪəˋdɪsətɪ] ***n***. **1**. 定期[周期]性;间发性;周期数。**2**. 周率,频率;【电】周波;【医】定期发作;【天】定期出现;【化】周期表中的位置。

per·i·o·don·tal [ˌperiəuˈdɔntl; ˏpɛrɪəˋdɑntl̩] ***a***. 【解】**1**. 牙周的。**2**. 影响牙周齿龈、结缔组织等的。

per·i·o·don·tics [ˌperiəuˈdɔntiks; ˏpɛrɪəˋdɑntɪks] ***n***. 〔*pl*.〕〔动词用单数〕牙周病学 (= periodontia)。**-don·tic** ***a***. **-don·tist** ***n***. 牙周病学家,牙周病医师。

per·i·o·nych·i·um [ˌperiəuˈnikiəm; ˏpɛrɪoˋnɪkɪəm] ***n***. (*pl*. ***-i·a*** [-ə; -ə]) 指甲周边的表皮。

per·i·os·te·um [ˌperiˈɔstiəm; ˏpɛrɪˋɑstɪəm] ***n***. (*pl*. **~*s***, ***-tea*** [-tiə; -tɪə]) 【解】骨膜。

per·i·os·ti·tis [ˌperiɔˈstaitis; ˏpɛrɪɑsˋtaɪtɪs] ***n***. 【医】骨膜炎。

per·i·os·tra·cum [ˌperiˈɔstrəkəm; ˏpɛrɪˋɑstrəkəm] ***n***. (*pl*. ***-tra·ca*** [-kə; -kə]) 【生】壳皮层。

per·i·o·tic [ˌperiˈəutik, -ˈɔtik; ˏpɛrɪˋotɪk, -ˋɑtɪk] ***a***. 【解、动】(内)耳周围的。

per·i·pa·tet·ic [ˌperipəˈtetik; ˏpɛrəpəˋtɛtɪk] **I** ***a***. **1**. 走来走去的,徒步游历的,巡游的,逍遥的。**2**. 〔P-〕亚里士多德学派的,逍遥学派的〔由古希腊哲学家亚里士多德在学园内漫步讲学而得名〕。**II** ***n***. **1**. 徒步游历者;跑来跑去的人;〔谑〕行商,小贩。**2**. 〔P-〕逍遥学派的人。**3**. 〔*pl*.〕到处走动;游历。**-i·cal·ly** ***ad***.

Per·i·pa·tet·i·cism [ˌperipəˈtetisizəm; ˏpɛrɪpəˋtɛtɪsɪzm] ***n***. **1**. 逍遥学派[亚里士多德学派]。**2**. 〔p-〕逍遥,走动;游历习惯。

per·i·pe·tei·a, per·i·pe·ti·a [ˌperipiˈtiːə, -ˈtaiə; ˏpɛrɪpəˋtiə, -ˋtaɪə] ***n***. 剧情或命运(境遇)的巨变,突变。

pe·riph·er·al [pəˈrifərəl; pəˋrɪfərəl] ***a***. **1**. 周围的,外围的;外面的;边缘的。**2**. 【解】(神经)末梢区域的。**-ize** ***vt***. 使(某人)处于社会边缘,使成边缘人,使受社会排斥。**-ly** ***ad***.

pe·riph·er·y [pəˈrifəri; pəˋrɪfərɪ] ***n***. **1**. 周围,圆周;外面,外部,外围,边缘。**2**. 【解】(神经)末梢区域。

per·i·phrase [ˈperifreiz; ˋpɛrɪˏfrez] **I** ***vi***., ***vt***. 转弯抹角地说。**II** ***n***. = periphrasis.

pe·riph·ra·sis [pəˈrifrəsis; pəˋrɪfrəsɪs] ***n***. (*pl*. ***-ses*** [-siːz; -siz]) **1**. 【修】迂说法,转弯抹角的说法。**2**. 迂回曲折的词句。

per·i·phras·tic [ˌperiˈfræstik; ˏpɛrəˋfræstɪk] ***a***. **1**. 转弯抹角的,迂回的;冗长的,啰嗦的。**2**. 【修】迂说法的。*the* ~ *conjugation* 【语法】迂说法动词变化〔如不用 went 而用 did go〕。*the* ~ *genitive* 迂说法所有格〔如不说 Caesar's,而说 of Caesar〕。**-ti·cal·ly** ***ad***.

pe·rip·ter·al [pəˈriptərəl; pəˋrɪptərəl] ***a***. **1**. 【建】围柱式的。**2**. (飞机等运动物体的)周围气流区的。

pe·rip·ter·os [pəˈriptərɔs; pəˋrɪptərɑs] ***n***. (*pl*. ***-oi*** [-rɔi; -rɔɪ]) 【建】围柱殿,围柱式寺院[建筑物]。

pe·rip·ter·y [pəˈriptəri; pəˋrɪptərɪ] ***n***. **1**. = peripteros. **2**. (飞机等运动物体的)周围气流区。

pe·rique [piˈriːk; pəˋrik] ***n***. 上等黑色烟草〔产于美国路易斯安那州〕。

per·i·sarc [ˈperisɑːk; ˋpɛrəsɑrk] ***n***. 【动】围鞘。

per·i·scope [ˈperiskəup; ˋpɛrəˏskop] ***n***. 潜望镜〔潜水艇用〕;潜望镜镜头。

per·i·scop·ic, per·i·scop·i·cal [ˌperisˈkɔpik, -ikəl; ˏpɛrəˋskɑpɪk, -ɪkəl] ***a***. **1**. 潜望镜(用)的。**2**. (照相机

等)广角的,适于瞭望周围的;概观的。*a ～ drift angle sight* 潜望镜式偏航测角器。*a ～ lens* 大角度的镜头。*a ～ wind gauge* 潜望镜式风速计。

per·ish [ˈperiʃ; ˋperɪʃ] *vi*. 1. 灭亡;消灭,死去;暴卒。2. 枯萎;腐烂。3. 腐败,堕落。～ *in battle* 阵亡。～ *in hunger* 饿死。～ *by the sword* 〔古〕死于刀剑。—*vt*. 1. 毁坏;消灭;杀死;使死去。2. 〔常用被动式〕使非常困苦;使麻木。*We were ～ed with cold*. 我们冻得要死。*P- the thought*! 不要说啦! 得了得了! 死了心吧! 〔表示极度厌恶或反对〕。**-less** *a*. 不易死亡[消灭、枯萎、腐败]的。**-ment** *n*.

P

per·ish·a·ble [ˈperiʃəbl; ˋperɪʃəbl] I *a*. 易腐败的;不经久的;脆弱的;会枯的;会死的。II *n*. 〔*pl*.〕易腐败的东西〔尤指食物〕。**-a·bil·i·ty** [-ˈbiliti; -ˋbɪlətɪ] *n*. **-a·bly** *ad*.

per·ish·er [ˈperiʃə; ˋperɪʃɚ] *n*. 〔俚〕讨厌的家伙,混蛋。

per·ish·ing [ˈperiʃiŋ; ˋperɪʃɪŋ] I *a*. 1. 死的,灭亡的,枯死的。2. 〔俚〕(饥饿、寒冷)要命的,厉害的;悲惨的。3. 讨人厌的,要不得的。*in ～ cold* 在极度寒冷中。II *ad*. …得要命;非常,极。*It is ～ cold today*. 今天冷得要命。**-ly** *ad*.

per·i·sperm [ˈperispəːm; ˋperɪˏspɝm] *n*. 【植】外胚乳。

per·i·sphere [ˈperisfiə; ˋperɪˏsfɪr] *n*. 1. 〔美〕正圆球。2. 中心周球。3. 势力范围。

per·i·spo·me·non, per·i·spome [ˌperiˈspəuminən, ˈperispəum; ˏperɪˋspɑmɪnˏɑn, ˋperɪˏspom] I *a*. (希腊文语法中)词尾有扬抑音符的。II *n*. (*pl*. *-me·na* [-nə; -nə]) 词尾有扬抑音符的词。

perisso- *comb.f*. 表示"奇,奇数的,多余的":*perisso*dactyl(e).

pe·ris·so·dac·tyl·ate [pəˌrisəuˈdæktilit; pəˋrɪsoˋdæktḷɪt] *a*. 【动】奇蹄的。

pe·ris·so·dac·tyl(e) [pəˌrisəuˈdæktil; pəˏrɪsoˋdæktḷ] I *a*. 【动】奇蹄的。II *n*. 奇蹄类动物。**-ous** *a*.

per·i·stal·sis [ˌperiˈstælsis; ˏperəˋstælsɪs] *n*. (*pl*. *-ses* [-siːz; -siz]) 【生理】(肠壁的)蠕动。

per·i·stal·tic [ˌperiˈstæltik; ˏperəˋstæltɪk] *a*. 1. 【生理】(肠壁)蠕动的。2. 【电】在两传导体间发生的。**-ti·cal·ly** *ad*.

pe·ris·to·ma, per·i·stome [pəˈristəumə, ˈperistəum; pəˋrɪstomə, ˋperɪˏstom] *n*. 1. 【植】(藓类的)蒴齿。2. 【动】螺壳孔边;口缘,唇,口围。

pe·ris·ton [pəˈristən; pəˋrɪstən] *n*. 人造血浆。

per·i·style [ˈperistail; ˋperəˏstaɪl] *n*. 【建】周柱式;列柱廊;列柱中庭。

per·i·tec·tic [ˌperiˈtektik; ˏperɪˋtɛktɪk] *a*. 【物】包晶(体)的。

per·i·tec·toid [ˌperiˈtektɔid; ˏperɪˋtɛktɔɪd] *n*., *a*. 【物】包析(的);包析体(的)。

per·i·the·ci·um [ˌperiˈθiʃiəm; ˏperəˋθiʃɪəm] *n*. (*pl*. *-ci·a* [-ə; -ə]) 【解】子囊壳。**-ci·al** *a*.

per·i·to·ne·um, per·i·to·nae·um [ˌperitəuˈniːəm; ˏperətəˋniəm] *n*. (*pl*. *-n(a)e·a* [-ˈniːə; -ˋniə]) 【解】腹膜。**-n(a)eal** *a*.

per·i·to·ni·tis [ˌperitəˈnaitis; ˏperətəˋnaɪtɪs] *n*. 【医】腹膜炎。

pe·rit·ri·chous [pəˈritrikəs; pəˋrɪtrɪkəs] *a*. 1. 【植】周毛的〔指菌〕。2. 【动】周生鞭毛的〔指原生动物〕。**-ly** *ad*.

pe·ri·tus [pəˈriːtəs; pəˋritəs] *n*. (*pl*. *-ti* [-iː; -i]) 〔L.〕专家〔尤指作为顾问的神学家〕。

per·i·wig [ˈperiwig; ˋperəˏwɪg] *n*. 假发。

per·i·wig·ged [ˈperiwigd; ˋperəˏwɪgd] *a*. 带假发的。

per·i·win·kle[1] [ˈperiwiŋkl; ˋperəˏwɪŋkḷ] *n*. 【贝】荔枝螺,海螺,滨螺。

per·i·win·kle[2] [ˈperiwiŋkl; ˋperəˏwɪŋkḷ] *n*. 【植】长春花。

per·jure [ˈpəːdʒə; ˋpɝdʒɚ] *vt*. 1. 〔～ oneself〕使发假誓。2. 〔用被动语态〕犯伪誓[伪证]罪。*The witness ～d himself*. 证人作假证。**-d** *a*. 发假誓的,作伪证的。**-r** *n*. 发假誓的人,作伪证者。

per·ju·ry [ˈpəːdʒəri; ˋpɝdʒərɪ] *n*. 【法】伪誓,伪证(罪);大谎。**commit** ～ 犯伪证罪,发假誓。

perk[1] [pəːk; pɝk] I *vi*. 1. 抬头,昂首,伸腰,突出,翘尾巴;装腔作势(*up*);摆架子,逞能(*up*)。2. 振作;(病后)复原(*up*)。II *vt*. 1. 抬(头),伸(腰),翘(尾巴);竖(耳朵)。2. 打扮。～ *it* 傲慢,摆架子,逞能。～ **oneself up** 打扮;装腔作势;扬扬自得。III *a*. 〔罕〕= perky.

perk[2] [pəːk; pɝk] *vt*., *vi*. 〔口〕过滤,渗透〔percolate 的缩略形式〕。

perk[3] [pəːk; pɝk] *n*. 〔主英口〕津贴,赏钱〔perquisite 的缩略形式〕。

Per·kin(s) [ˈpəːkin(z); ˋpɝkɪn(z)] *n*. 帕金(斯)〔姓氏〕。

perk·y [ˈpəːki; ˋpɝkɪ] *a*. 1. 得意扬扬的。2. 装腔作势的,傲慢的,逞能的。3. 鲁莽的,莽撞的。4. 打扮得漂漂亮亮的。

per·lite [ˈpəːlait; ˋpɝlaɪt] *n*. 1. 【地】珍珠岩。2. 珠光体(= pearlite)。**per·lit·ic** [pəˈlitik; pəˋlɪtɪk] *a*.

perm [pəːm; pɝm] I *n*. 〔口〕电烫头发(= permanent wave)。*Even a ～ has its term*. 电烫的头发也有变直的时候。II *vt*. 〔口〕给…电烫头发。

per·ma·frost [ˈpəːməfrɔ(ː)st; ˋpɝməˏfrɔst] *n*. 【地】永久冻土。

per·mal·loy [ˈpəːməlɔi; ˋpɝməˏlɔɪ] *n*. 【冶】透磁合金。

per·ma·nence [ˈpəːmənəns; ˋpɝmənəns] *n*. 持久,永久;不变;永久性,耐久性。

per·ma·nen·cy [ˈpəːmənənsi; ˋpɝmənənsɪ] *n*. 1. = permanence. 2. 不变的东西;永久的地位〔终身官职等〕,终身事业。*I should not like it for a ～*. 我不打算干它一辈子。

per·ma·nent [ˈpəːmənənt; ˋpɝmənənt] I *a*. 1. 永久的,不变的,耐久的;持久的,经久的。2. 常务的,常设的(*opp*. temporary)。II *n*. 电烫发(= ～ wave)。～ **anticyclone** 【气】永久性反气旋。～ **basis** 〔美〕平时定额。～ **committee** 常务委员会。**P- Court (of International Justice)** 常设国际法庭。～ **fortification** 永久工事。～ **gas** 永久气体。～ **girl friend** 永久性女友,婚外情人,外室。～ **magnet** 永久磁铁。～ **output** 长期生产率。～ **quadrat** 定位样方。～ **rest camp** 〔美〕墓地。～ **revolution** 不断革命。～ **set** 永久定形(物);固定伸张;永久应变;最后凝结。～ **tissue** 【植】永久性组织。～ **tooth** 成人齿,恒齿。～ **wave** 电烫发。～ **way** 【铁路】轨道。**-ly** *ad*.

per·man·ga·nate [pəːˈmæŋgənit, -neit; pɚˋmæŋgənɪt, -net] *n*. 【化】高锰酸盐。～ *of potassium* 【化】高锰酸钾。

per·man·gan·ic [ˌpəːmænˈgænik; ˏpɝmænˋgænɪk] *a*. ～ **acid** 【化】高锰酸。

per·me·a·bil·i·ty [ˌpəːmiəˈbiliti; ˏpɝmɪəˋbɪlətɪ] *n*. 1. 透过性,可透性,渗透性;渗蚀度;【空】(气球气体的)透出量。2. 【物】磁导率,磁导系数(= magnetic ～)。

per·me·a·ble [ˈpəːmiəbl; ˋpɝmɪəbḷ] *a*. 能渗透[透过、穿过]的(*to*)。～ *plastics* 可透塑料。**-a·bly** *ad*. **-ness** *n*.

per·me·am·e·ter [pəːmiˈæmitə; pɝmɪˋæmətɚ] *n*. 【物】磁导计。

per·me·ance [ˈpəːmiəns; ˋpɝmɪəns] *n*. 1. 渗入,渗透,充满。2. 【物】磁导。

per·me·ant [ˈpəːmiənt; ˋpɝmɪənt] *a*. 渗入的,渗透的,充满的。

per·me·ate [ˈpəːmieit; ˋpɝmɪˏet] *vt*. 1. 渗入,透过;穿过。2. 弥漫,充满;普及。—*vi*. 渗透,渗过;普及(*in*; *through*; *among*)。**-me·a·tion** [-ˈeiʃən; -ˋeʃən] *n*.

Per·mi·an [ˈpəːmiən; ˋpɝmɪən] I *a*. 【地】二叠纪的;二叠系的。II *n*. 〔the ～〕二叠纪[系]。*the ～ period* 二

叠纪。*the* ～ *system*【地】二叠系。

per·mil·lage [pəˈmilidʒ; pɚˋmɪlɪdʒ] ***n*.** 千分率;千分比。

per·mis·si·ble [pə(ː)ˈmisəbl; pɚˋmɪsəbl] ***a*.** **1.** 可以允许[许可]的;不碍事的。**2.** 得到准许的。～ *explosives*〔美〕安全炸药。～ *load* 容许负荷。**-si·bil·i·ty** [-ˈbiliti; -ˋbɪlətɪ] ***n*.** **-si·bly** ***ad*.**

per·mis·sion [pə(ː)ˈmiʃən; pɚˋmɪʃən] ***n*.** 许,允许,答应,同意,许可,准许(*to do*)。*Ask* ～ *of your father*. 请你父亲允许吧。***ask for*** ～ 请求许可。***grant*** ～ 准许。***with*** (***your***) ～ 如果(你)允许的话。***without*** ～ 未经许可,擅自。

per·mis·sive [pə(ː)ˈmisiv; pɚˋmɪsɪv] ***a*.** **1.** 许可的,准许的;宽容的。**2.** 自由的;随意的。**3.** 纵容的。**4.**【生化】受纳的,允许复制(遗传物质等)的。*a* ～ *nod* 表示许可的点头。*a* ～ *mother* 娇惯子女的母亲。**-ly** ***ad*.**

per·mit [pə(ː)ˈmit; pɚˋmɪt] **I** ***vt*.** 许可,准许,允许,答应;默许,放任;使可能。*P- me to explain*. 请容许我解释。*No infringement will be* ～*ted*. 不许有违。～ *the escape of gases* 使得以漏气。—***vi*.** 允许,容许(*of*)。～ ***of no delay*** 不可拖延[耽搁]。～ ***of no excuse*** 不许推诿。***weather permitting*** 如果天气好的话。**II** [ˈpəːmit; ˋpɚmɪt] ***n*.** **1.** 准许证,许可证,执照。**2.** 许可,准许。

per·mit·tiv·i·ty [ˌpəːmiˈtiviti; ˏpɚməˋtɪvətɪ] ***n*.**【电】电容率,介电常数。

per·mut·a·ble [pə(ː)ˈmjuːtəbl; pɚˋmjutəbl] ***a*.** **1.** 能交换的;可置换的;可变更的。**2.**【数】可排列的。

per·mute [pə(ː)ˈmjuːt; pɚˋmjut] ***vt*.** **1.** 交换;取代,变更;置换。**2.**【数】排列。**3.** (用滤沙)软化(水)。**-ta·tion** ***n*.** **1.** 交换,互换;置换。**2.**【数】排列(*permutation and combination*【数】排列组合)。

per·mu·tite [ˈpəːmju(ː)tait; ˋpɚmjuˏtaɪt] ***n*.** 滤(水)沙,软水沙,人造沸石。

per·mu·toid [ˈpəːmju(ː)tɔid; ˋpɚmjutɔɪd] ***n*.**【化】交换体。

per·ni·cious [pəːˈniʃəs; pɚˋnɪʃəs] ***a*.** 有害的,有毒的;恶性的,致命的。*a climate* ～ *to health* 有害健康的气候。*a* ～ *scheme* 恶毒的阴谋。～ **anaemia**【医】恶性贫血。**-ly** ***ad*.** **-ness** ***n*.**

per·nick·e·ty [pəˈnikəti; pɚˋnɪkɪtɪ] ***a*.**〔口〕**1.** 爱挑剔的,吹毛求疵的。**2.** 麻烦的,难应付的;需要小心对待的。

per·noc·ta·tion [ˌpəːnɔkˈteiʃən; ˏpɚnɑkˋteʃən] ***n*.** **1.** 守夜,熬夜;彻夜不眠;整夜不归。**2.** 通宵祷告。

Per·nod [peəˈnəu; perˋno] ***n*.**〔F.〕法国绿茴香酒商标;〔p-〕法国绿茴香酒。

per·o·ne·al [ˌperəˈniəl; ˏperəˋniəl] ***a*.**【解】**1.** 腓骨的。**2.** 腓骨侧的。

Per·o·no·spo·ra·cea·e [ˌperənəuspəˈreisiˌiː; ˏpɛrənospəˋresɪˏi] ***n*.**〔*pl*.〕【植】霜霉科。

per·o·ral [pəˈɔːrəl; pəˋɔrəl] ***a*.**【医】由口的;口边的。

per·o·rate [ˈperəreit; ˋpɛrəˏret] ***vi*.** **1.** 结束演说,下结论。**2.** 作长篇演说,啰唆地讲。**-ra·tion** [-ˈreiʃən; -ˋreʃən] ***n*.** **1.** (演说等的)结论,结尾话。**2.** 夸夸其谈的演说。**-ra·tor** ***n*.** 作长篇演说的人,啰啰唆唆讲的人。

pe·ro·sis [piˈrəusis; pəˋrosɪs] ***n*.** (*pl*. ***-ses*** [-siːz; -siz]) (小鸡的)骨短粗病。**pe·rot·ic** [-ˈrɔtik; -ˋrɑtɪk] ***a*.**

per·ox·i·dase [pəˈrɔksideis, -deiz; pəˋrɑksɪdes, -dez] ***n*.**【化】过氧化酶。

per·ox·i·da·tion [pəˌrɔksiˈdeiʃən; pəˏrɑksɪˋdeʃən] ***n*.**【化】过氧化反应。

per·ox·ide [pəˈrɔksaid; pəˋrɑksaɪd] **I** ***n*.** **1.**【化】过氧化物。**2.**〔口〕过氧化氢。**II** ***vt*.**〔口〕用过氧化氢漂白(头发等)。～ *blonde*〔美俚〕漂白出一头金发的女人。～ *of hydrogen* ～ 过氧化氢[漂白、消毒剂]。

peroxy- *comb. f*. 表示"过氧":*peroxy*sulphate.

per·ox·y·sul·phate [pəˈrɔksiˈsʌlfeit; pəˋrɑksɪsʌlˏfet] ***n*.**【化】过(氧)硫酸盐。

perp [pəːp; pɚp] ***n*.**〔口〕罪犯〔perpetrator 的缩略〕。

per·pend[1] [ˈpəːpənd; ˋpɚpənd] ***n*.**【建】贯石(突出墙两面的长石);穿墙石,控石;系石。*a* ～ *wall* 单石薄墙。

per·pend[2] [pəːˈpend; pɚˋpend] ***vt*.**, ***vi*.**〔古〕细细考虑;审议。

per·pen·dic·u·lar [ˌpəːpənˈdikjulə; ˏpɚpənˋdɪkjələ] **I** ***a*.** **1.** 垂直的,直立的;【数】成直角的,正交的。**2.** 矗立的;险陡的,险峻的。**3.** [P-]【建】垂直式的。**4.**〔谑〕直站着的。*a* ～ *cliff* 绝壁。*a* ～ *line* 垂(直)线。*a* ～ *plate* 水平板。**II** ***n*.** **1.** 垂(直)线;垂直面。**2.** 垂直测器,锤规。**3.** 直立,直立姿势;廉直。**4.** [P-]【建】垂直式建筑。**5.** 绝壁。**6.**〔俚〕站着的进餐。***be out of*** (***the***) ～ 倾斜。**the** ～【数】垂直,正交。**-ly** ***ad*.** **-u·lar·i·ty** [-ˈlæriti; -ˋlærətɪ] ***n*.**

per·pe·trate [ˈpəːpitreit; ˋpɚpəˏtret] ***vt*.** **1.** 施(恶行),做(坏事);犯(过失等);犯(罪)。**2.** 胡说。～ *a pun* [*joke*]〔口〕(不考虑环境情况)瞎讲俏皮话,乱开玩笑,瞎打哈哈。**per·petra·ble** [ˈpəːpitrəbl; ˋpɚpətrəbl] ***a*.** 能做坏事(等)的。**-pe·tra·tion** [-ˈtreiʃən; -ˋtreʃən] ***n*.** 为非作歹,行凶,犯罪。**-pe·tra·tor** ***n*.** 犯人,凶手;作恶者。

per·pet·u·al [pəˈpetjuəl; pɚˋpetʃuəl] **I** ***a*.** **1.** 永久的,永恒的,无穷的;不断的,不绝的;(官职等)终身的。**2.**【园艺】四季开花的。**3.**〔口〕不停的。*a* ～ *calender* 万年历。*a* ～ *lease* 永久租地权。**II** ***n*.**【园艺】四季开花的植物;多年生草。～ **motion**【物】永恒运动。～ **rose** 四季蔷薇。**-ly** ***ad*.**

per·pet·u·ate [pə(ː)ˈpetjueit; pɚˋpetʃʊˏet] ***vt*.** 使永久存在[继续];使不朽,使不灭。

per·pet·u·a·tion, per·pet·u·ance [pəˌpetjuˈeiʃən, pəˈpetjuəns; pɚˏpetʃʊˋeʃən, pəˋpetjuəns] ***n*.** 永存;不朽,不灭。～ *of testimony*【法】证据的保存。

per·pet·u·a·tor [pəˈpetjueitə; pəˋpetʃuetɚ] ***n*.** 使永存者,使不朽的人。

per·pet·u·i·ty [ˌpəːpiˈtju(ː)iti; ˏpɚpəˋtjuətɪ] ***n*.** **1.** 永存;不灭;不朽;永恒,永远。**2.** 永存物。**3.** 终身养老金[退休金]。**4.**【法】永久所有权;(产业的)永久[长期]不得转让;永久[长期]不得转让的产业。**5.** 单利累计到等于本金的时期。*lease in* ～ 永久租地权。***in*** [***to, for***] ～ 永远,不朽。

per·plex [pəˈpleks; pɚˋplɛks] ***vt*.**〔多用被动结构〕**1.** 使窘困,使为难,使狼狈。**2.** 使纠缠,弄复杂化,使混乱,使纠缠不清。～ *an issue* 使问题复杂化。*be* ～*ed with the question* 被问题纠缠住。

per·plexed [pəˈplekst; pɚˋplɛkst] ***a*.** **1.** 为难的,困惑的,不知道怎样才好。**2.** 混乱的,纠缠不清的,疙疙瘩瘩的,复杂化的。*a* ～ *air* 为难的样子。*a* ～ *question* 错综复杂的问题。**-ly** ***ad*.** **-ness** [pəˈpleksidnis; pɚˋplɛksɪdnɪs] ***n*.**

per·plex·ing [pəˈpleksiŋ; pɚˋplɛksɪŋ] ***a*.** **1.** 使人困惑的;使人为难的。**2.** 麻烦的,复杂的。**-ly** ***ad*.**

per·plex·i·ty [pəˈpleksiti; pɚˋplɛksətɪ] ***n*.** **1.** 窘困,困惑,为难;窘态,难局。**2.** 使人困惑的事物。**3.** 纠纷,混乱。

per pro(***c***). = [L.] *per procurationem* (= by proxy) 代表,经由代理。

per·qui·site [ˈpəːkwizit; ˋpɚkwəzɪt] ***n*.** **1.** 临时津贴,临时收入;〔英〕(给仆役等的)赏钱,酒钱。**2.**【法】(庄园领主的)不定期收入;特权享有的东西。

per·qui·si·tion [ˌpəːkwiˈziʃən; ˏpɚkwəˋzɪʃən] ***n*.** (根据搜查证进行的)彻底搜查。

per·ron [ˈperən; ˋpɛrən] ***n*.**〔F.〕【建】(大建筑物门前的)露天台阶[石阶,露天梯级]。

per·ru·qui·er [peˈruːkiə; peˋrukɪr] ***n*.**〔F.〕假发师;理发师。

Per·ry [ˈperi; ˋpɛrɪ] ***n*.** 佩里〔姓氏,男子名〕。

per·ry [ˈperi; ˋpɛrɪ] ***n*.**〔英〕梨酒。

P

Pers. =**1**. Persia. **2**. Persian.

pers. =**1**. person. **2**. personal. **3**. personnel.

per·salt [ˈpəːˌsɔːlt; ˋpɝˏsɔlt] ***n***. 【化】过盐。

perse [pəːs; pɝs] ***n***., ***a***. 深灰色(的),深紫色(的)。

per·se·cute [ˈpəːsikjuːt; ˋpɝsɪˏkjut] ***vt***. **1**. (因政治、宗教上意见不同而进行)迫害,摧残。**2**. 强求,死缠着要;使为难,困扰。*Copernicus was terribly ~d for his scientific theory*. 哥白尼由于其科学理论而遭到严酷的迫害。~ *sb. with questions* 给某人出难题。

per·se·cu·tion [ˌpəːsiˈkjuːʃən; ˏpɝsɪˋkjuʃən] ***n***. **1**. 迫害;残害;【宗】迫害时期。**2**. 苛求;困扰。*be fearless in face of overt or covert ~* 在明枪暗箭的迫害面前勇敢无畏。***indulge in ~ of*** 对…大肆进行迫害。

per·se·cu·tor [ˈpəːsikjuːtə; ˋpɝsɪˏkjutɚ] ***n***. 迫害者,虐待者。

Per·se·ids [ˈpəːsiːidz; ˋpɝsiɪdz] ***n***. 〔*pl*.〕【天】英仙(座)流星群,八月流星群。

Per·seph·o·ne [pəːˈsefəni; pɚˋsɛfənɪ] ***n***. 【希神】普西芬尼〔阴间女王,冥后〕。

Per·sep·o·lis [pəːˈsepəlis; pɚˋsɛpəlɪs] ***n***. 珀塞波利斯〔波斯古都〕。

Per·seus [ˈpəːsjuːs, -sjəs; ˋpɝsjus, -sɪəs] ***n***. **1**. 【希神】柏修斯〔宙斯和达那厄 (Danae) 之子,杀死女怪美杜莎 (Medusa) 的神〕。**2**. 【天】〔the ~〕英仙座。

per·se·ver·ance [ˌpəːsiˈviərəns; ˏpɝsəˋvɪrəns] ***n***. **1**. 坚定,不屈不挠;坚持。**2**. 【宗】持续蒙受天恩。

per·se·ver·ant [ˌpəːsiˈviərənt; ˏpɝsəˋvɪrənt] ***a***. 能坚持的;愿意坚持的。

per·sev·er·ate [pə(ː)ˈsevəreit; pɚˋsɛvəret] ***vi***. 【医】患持续言语症。

per·sev·er·a·tion [pə(ː)ˌsevəˈreiʃən; pɚˏsɛvəˋreʃən] ***n***. **1**. 【医】持续言语〔指言语反复不止的病态〕。**2**. 【医】(无法停止的)专想某事。**3**. 执拗,顽梗。**-a·tive** [-reitiv; -retɪv] ***a***.

per·se·vere [ˌpəːsiˈviə; ˏpɝsəˋvɪr] ***vi***. 忍耐,熬住;百折不回,不屈不挠,坚持 (*in*; *with*)。~ *with a task* 对工作坚持不懈。~ *in one's efforts* 坚持努力。—***vt***. 支持,支撑;鼓舞。*unflagging faith that had ~d him* 曾经支撑过他的不可动摇的信念。

per·se·ver·ing [ˌpəːsiˈviəriŋ; ˏpɝsəˋvɪrɪŋ] ***a***. 坚定的,不屈不挠的,百折不回的。**-ly** ***ad***. 坚定地。

Per·shing [ˈpəːʃiŋ; ˋpɝʃɪŋ] ***n***. 珀欣〔姓氏〕。

Per·sia [ˈpəːʃə; ˋpɝʃə] ***n***. 波斯〔现称 Iran 伊朗,亚洲〕。

Per·sian [ˈpəːʃən; ˋpɝʃən] **I** ***a***. 波斯的,波斯人的,波斯语的。**II** ***n***. **1**. 波斯人;波斯语。**2**. 波斯绸。**3**. 〔*pl*.〕百叶窗(=~ blinds)。***the ~ Gulf*** 波斯湾。~ **blinds** 百叶窗。~ **carpet** [**rug**] 波斯地毯。~ **cat** 波斯猫。~ **Gulf syndrome**〔美〕海湾战争综合症〔指 1991 年对伊拉克进行波斯湾战争后,在美国士兵中出现的一种综合性健康不适症状〕。~ **lamb** 波斯羔;波斯羔皮。~ **lilac** 波斯丁香;花叶丁香。~ **powder** 杀虫粉。~ **walnut** 胡桃。~ **yellow** (**rose**) 波斯臭蔷薇。

per·si·ennes [ˌpəsiˈenz; ˏpɝzɪˋɛnz] ***n***. 〔*pl*.〕百叶窗。

per·si·flage [ˌpɛəsiˈflɑːʒ; ˋpɝsɪˋflɑʒ] ***n***. 挖苦,戏弄,嘲弄,揶揄。

per·si·fleur [ˌpɛəsiˈflə; ˏpɛrsɪˋflɝ] ***n***. 爱挖苦人的人。

per·sim·mon [pə(ː)ˈsimən; pɚˋsɪmən] ***n***. 柿子;柿树;美洲柿。***be not a huckleberry to one's ~*** 〔美〕不能和…相比。***bring down the ~*** 〔美〕得奖,拿锦旗。***rake up*** [***walk off with***] ***the ~*** 〔美〕把赢的钱带走;得奖。***That's*** (***all***) ~***s***! 〔美〕那好极了! ***The longest pole knocks the most ~s***. 〔美〕竿子最长打的柿子最多,强者常胜。

per·sist [pə(ː)ˈsist; pɚˋzɪst] ***vi***. **1**. 坚持,固执 (*in*)。**2**. 继续存在,存留。~ *in working when ill* 病中坚持工作。*He ~s in his bad habit*. 他坚决不改他的坏习惯。

per·sist·ence, per·sist·en·cy [pəˈsistəns, -si; pɚˋsɪstəns, -sɪ] ***n***. **1**. 坚持;固执;顽固。**2**. 持续性;持久;存留。**3**. 【无】持久性;(萤光屏上余辉的)保留时间。~ *of energy* 能量守恒。~ *of vision* 视觉暂留。

per·sist·ent [pəˈsistənt; pɚˋzɪstənt] ***a***. **1**. 坚持的,百折不挠的;顽固的;持久不变的。**2**. 持续性的;【植】宿存的(*opp*. deciduous);【动】持续生存的。**-ly** ***ad***.

per·snick·e·ty [pə(ː)ˈsnikiti; pɚˋsnɪkɪtɪ] ***a***. 〔口〕**1**. 过于讲究的;挑肥拣瘦的;爱小题大做的。**2**. 认真对待的,要求非常仔细处理的 (=pernickety)。

per·son [ˈpəːsn; ˋpɝsn] ***n***. **1**. 人;个人。**2**. 〔蔑〕家伙。**3**. 容貌;身体,人身;人格;本人,自身。**4**. (戏剧、小说的)人物;〔常带有修饰语〕重要人物。**5**. 【动】个体;【语法】人称;【法】自然人;法人;【神】(三位一体的)位。★表示概称的人时,女性不用 man 而用 person。*She is an attractive ~*. 她是一个吸引人的人。*a young ~* 年轻人,〔常指〕年轻女人。*He has a fine ~*. 他风度很好。*offenses against the ~* 暴行。*the natural ~*【法】自然人。*the artificial* [*legal*, *juridical*] ~【法】法人。~*s of the play* 出场人物。*chief ~s of the state* 国家的重要人物。***accept the ~ of*** 偏袒…,偏爱…。***in one's own*** [***proper***] ~ 亲自。***in ~*** **1**. 亲自。**2**. 身体上;外貌上。***in the ~ of*** **1**. 叫做…的人。**2**. 体现于…。**3**. 以…的资格;代表…。***no less a ~ than*** 身分不低于。~ ***with Aids*** 艾滋病患者〔缩写为 PWA〕。***respect of ~s*** 偏袒;区别对待;徇私。~**-hour** 工时,人时(=man-hour)。~**-to-**~ **1**. ***a***. 私人间的;(长途电话)指名受话人受话后才索费的。**2**. ***ad***. 个人间地;面对面地。

per·so·na [pəːˈsəunə; pɚˋsonə] ***n***. (*pl*. ***-nae*** [-niː; -ni]) 〔L.〕**1**. 人。**2**. (小说、戏剧中的)人物,角色。**3**. (*pl*. ~**s**)(在社交场合的)伪装外表。***dramatis ~*** 剧中人。***in propria*** [inˈprəupriə; ɪnˋproprɪə] ~ 亲自。~ (***non***) ***grata*** [ˈgreitə; ˋgretə] (不)受人欢迎的人〔指外交官而言〕。

per·son·a·ble [ˈpəːsənəbl; ˋpɝsn̩əbl̩] ***a***. 容貌漂亮的;风度好的。**-ness** ***n***.

per·son·age [ˈpəːsənidʒ; ˋpɝsnɪdʒ] ***n***. **1**. 人,个人。**2**. 名士,显贵。**3**. (历史、小说、戏剧中的)人物,角色。**4**. 〔谑〕风度。*a very singular ~* 特号怪人。*public ~s* 社会贤达。

per·son·al [ˈpəːsənl; ˋpɝsnl] **I** ***a***. **1**. 个人的,私人的;一身的,自身的。**2**. 本人的,亲自的。**3**. 身体的,容貌的。**4**. 人身的;涉及个人的;人物批评的;攻击个人的。**5**. 【语法】人称的。**6**. 【法】属于个人的,可动的 (*opp*. real)。**7**. (信件)亲启的。~ *matters* [*affairs*] 私事。(*a*) ~ *acquaintance* 个人的相识。*a ~ interview* 亲自接见。~ *appearance* 容貌,风度。~ *abuse* = *a ~ affront* [*attack*] 人身攻击。***become ~ in a dispute*** 在争论中开始攻击[批评]个人。

II ***n***. **1**. 个人,人员。**2**. 【语法】人称代名词。**3**. 〔*pl*.〕对人批评,人身攻击。**4**. 〔*pl*.〕(报刊上的)人事栏;分类人事广告版。**5**. 〔*pl*.〕【法】动产。**6**. 〔*pl*.〕【影】(演员的)初次表演。~ **action**【法】对人诉讼,要求赔偿损失的诉讼 (*opp*. real action)。~ **column** (报纸的)人事消息栏。~ **communicator** 个人通讯系统〔集手机、传真机、传呼机和笔记本式电脑于一体的小型个人通讯系统〕。~ **computer** 个人电子计算机[电脑]。~ **effects**【法】个人财产,个人所有物。~ **equation** [**error**] **1**. 【天】(观测上的)(个)人(误)差。**2**. (一般的)个人倾向,个性。~ **foul**【体】撞人犯规。~ **organizer** **1**. 多功能备忘记事簿。**2**. (配备微型电脑及相关软件的)电脑化多功能记事簿。~ **planner** 个人记事簿。~ **pronoun**【语法】人称代名词。~ **property** [**estate**]【法】动产。~ **rights** 人权。~ **service**【法】(传票等的)直接送达。~ **shopper** (商店等处)代客挑选货物的人。~ **trainer** 个人健身教练。

per·son·al·ism [ˈpəːsnəlizm; ˋpɝsnəlɪzm̩] ***n***. 个人至上论。**-al·ist** **1**. ***n***. 个人至上论者。**2**. ***a***. 个人至上论的。**-al·is·tic** ***a***.

per·son·al·i·ty [ˌpəːsəˈnæliti; ˏpɚsnˋæləti] ***n*.** **1.** 人的存在;个性,【心】性格;人格,品格,做人,为人;容貌。**2.** (有名)人物。**3.** 〔常 *pl*.〕人物批评;攻击个人(的材料)。**4.** 【地】地势,地相。**5.** 〔罕〕动产。*a man with little* ~ 个性不强的人。*a man of strong* ~ 个性强的人。*double* [*dual*] ~ 【心】双重人格。~ **cult** 个人崇拜。

per·son·al·ize [ˈpəːsnəlaiz; ˋpɚsnlˏaɪz] ***vt*.** **1.** 使个人化。**2.** 使成个人所有物。**3.** 在(物品)上标出姓名[记号]。**4.** 使人格化;【修】拟(某物)为人,使…拟人化。**-al·i·za·tion** ***n*.**

per·son·al·ly [ˈpəːsənəli; ˋpɚsnlɪ] ***ad*.** **1.** 亲自地。**2.** 作为个人,我个人,就自己而言。**3.** 作为一个人。

per·son·al·ty [ˈpəːsənəlti; ˋpɚsnˋæltɪ] ***n*.** 【法】动产 (*opp*. realty)。

per·son·ate [ˈpəːsəneit; ˋpɚsnˏet] **I** ***vt*.** **1.** 扮演,饰(剧中某角)。**2.** 假装;〔英〕冒充,冒…的名。**3.** 使(艺术品等)带有个性。**4.** 使人格化。**II** ***a*.** 【植】假面状的。

per·son·a·tion [ˌpəːsənˈeiʃən; ˏpɚsnˋeʃən] ***n*.** **1.** 扮装,假装;扮演。**2.** 假冒身分,冒名;化身。

per·son·a·tor [ˈpəːsəneitə; ˋpɚsnˏetɚ] ***n*.** **1.** 假装者;演员。**2.** 冒名者。

per·son·i·fi·ca·tion [pə(ː)ˌsɔnifiˈkeiʃən; pɚˏsɑnəfəˋkeʃən] ***n*.** **1.** 拟人,人格化;【修】拟人法。**2.** 化身,典型;活例。**3.** 体现;〔*pl*.〕表演。*the* ~ *of patriotism* 爱国典型。*an artistic* ~ *of beauty* 美在艺术(作品)上的具体表现。

per·son·i·fy [pə(ː)ˈsɔnifai; pɚˋsɑnəˏfaɪ] ***vt*.** (***-fied***) **1.** 把(某物)看做人,拟(某物)为人;赋与…以人性,使人格化。**2.** 是…的化身,象征;体现。**3.** = personate.

per·son·nel [ˌpəːsəˈnel; ˏpɚsnˋɛl] ***n*.** **1.** 全体人员,职员,班底 (*opp*. materiel)。**2.** 人事(部门)。*the* ~ *of the new cabinet* 现内阁的班底。*the bureau of* ~ 人事局。~ *department* 人事处[科]。

per·sorp·tion [pə(ː)ˈsɔpʃən; pɚˋsɔrpʃən] ***n*.** 【化】吸混(作用)。

per·spec·tive[1] [pə(ː)ˈspektiv; pɚˋspɛktɪv] **I** ***a*.** (按照)透视画法的;透视的。*a* ~ *drawing* 透视画。*a* ~ *glass* 望远镜。**II** ***n*.** **1.** 透视画法;透视画;配景,远近配置。**2.** 远景,景色,眼界。**3.** 配合,适当比例。**4.** 洞察力,眼力。**5.** 观点,看法。**6.** 希望,前途。*aerial* ~ (用色调浓淡表现的)空中透视画法。*angular* [*linear*] ~ 斜线[直线]透视画法。***in*** ~ 按照透视画法的[地];展望中的[地];正确的[地];【数】连成一行 (*see things in* ~ 正确地看待事物)。***out of*** ~ 不合透视画法;不正确地。**-ly** ***ad*.** 按照透视法;远近分明地。

per·spec·tive[2] [pə(ː)ˈspektiv; pɚˋspɛktɪv] ***n*.** 透镜,望远镜。

per·spex [ˈpəːspeks; ˋpɚspɛks] ***n*.** 塑胶玻璃,透明塑胶,【化】〔聚合的 2—甲基丙烯酸甲酯〕。

per·spi·ca·cious [ˌpəːspiˈkeiʃəs; ˏpɚspɪˋkeʃəs] ***a*.** **1.** 颖悟的;敏锐的;聪明的。**2.** 〔古〕眼光锐利的。**-ly** ***ad*.** **-ness** ***n*.**

per·spi·cac·i·ty [ˌpəːspiˈkæsiti; ˏpɚspɪˋkæsətɪ] ***n*.** 颖悟,聪明;敏锐,慧眼。

per·spi·cu·i·ty [ˌpəːspiˈkju(ː)iti; ˏpɚspɪˋkjuətɪ] ***n*.** **1.** (语言、文章等的)明晰,清楚。**2.** 〔口〕= perspicacity.

per·spic·u·ous [pə(ː)ˈspikjuəs; pɚˋspɪkjuəs] ***a*.** **1.** 明白易懂的,清楚的;说话清楚的。**2.** 〔罕〕聪明的。**-ly** ***ad*.** **-ness** ***n*.**

per·spi·ra·tion [ˌpəːspəˈreiʃən; ˏpɚspəˋreʃən] ***n*.** **1.** 出汗;发汗(作用)。**2.** 汗(水)。

per·spir·a·to·ry [pəsˈpaiərətəri; pɚˋspaɪrəˏtorɪ] ***a*.** (引起)排汗的。

per·spire [pəsˈpaiə; pɚˋspaɪr] ***vi*.**, ***vt*.** 排(汗);出(汗);发(汗)。

per·suad·a·ble [pə(ː)ˈsweidəbl; pɚˋswedəbl̩] ***a*.** 能说服的;可使相信的。**-a·bly** ***ad*.**

per·suade [pə(ː)ˈsweid; pɚˋswed] ***vt*.** 说服,劝服;使相信。~ *sb. to do* [*into doing*] 对某人作某事。~ *sb. of* [*that*] 使某人相信…。~ *oneself* 信,确信。*I am* ~*d of his innocence*. 我相信他是无罪的。—***vi*.** 被说服。*The boy* ~*s easily*. 这孩子听劝。

per·suad·er [pə(ː)ˈsweidə; pɚˋswedɚ] ***n*.** **1.** 劝说者,说服的人。**2.** 〔*pl*.〕〔俚〕踢马刺;〔美俚〕威慑物;手枪。***clap in the*** ~***s*** 用踢马刺踢马。

per·sua·si·ble [pəˈsweisibl; pɚˋswesəbl̩] ***a*.** = persuadable. **-si·bili·ty** [-ˈbiliti; -ˋbɪlətɪ] ***n*.**

per·sua·sion [pə(ː)ˈsweiʒən; pɚˋsweʒən] ***n*.** **1.** 说服,劝导。**2.** 说服力;劝说的话[论点]。**3.** 确信,信念;信仰,信条。**4.** (持某种信仰的)教派。**5.** 〔口、谑〕人种,种类;性别;阶级;〔美〕国籍。*It is my private* ~ *that he is mad*. 我个人认为他是个疯子。*a man of the Christian* ~ 基督教徒。*a man of the artist* ~ 〔谑〕艺术家。*the male* ~ 〔谑〕男性。

per·sua·sive, per·sua·so·ry [pə(ː)ˈsweisiv, -səri; pɚˋswesɪv, -sərɪ] **I** ***a*.** **1.** 有说服本领的,嘴巧的。**2.** 劝导性的;劝诱的。**II** ***n*.** 动机,诱因;劝告。**-ly** ***ad*.** **-ness** ***n*.**

per·sul·fate, per·sul·phate [pə(ː)ˈsʌlfeit; pɚˋsʌlfet] ***n*.** 【化】过(二)硫酸盐。

per·sul·fu·ric, per·sul·phu·ric [ˌpəːsʌlˈfjuərik; ˏpɚsʌlˋfjʊrɪk] ***a*.** ~ **acid** 【化】过硫酸。

PERT [pəːt; pɚt] 〔*P*(*rogram*) *E*(*valuation and*) *R*(*eview*) *T*(*echnique*)〕程序计算检查系统〔将一系列互相依赖的事情按照适当的程序安排,以便最迅速最节约地完成一个(工程)项目〕。

pert [pəːt; pɚt] ***a*.** **1.** 冒失的,没规矩的。**2.** 〔美口〕活泼的;敏捷的。**3.** (言语等)辛辣的,唐突的。**4.** (衣饰等)整齐时髦的。**-ly** ***ad*.** **-ness** ***n*.**

pert. = pertaining.

per·tain [pə(ː)ˈtein; pɚˋten] ***vi*.** **1.** 附属,属于 (*to*)。**2.** 关于,有关 (*to*)。**3.** 适合,相配 (*to*)。*It does not* ~ *to you to instruct him*. 你不适合教训他。

per·tain·ing [pə(ː)ˈteiniŋ; pɚˋtenɪŋ] **I** ***a*.** 与…有关系的,附属的…,…固有的 (*to*)。*the informations* ~*ing to the case* 有关这一事件的情报。*the infirmities* ~ *to old age* 老年常有的毛病。**II** ***n*.** 〔常 *pl*.〕附属(物)。

Perth [pəːθ; pɚθ] ***n*.** 珀斯〔澳大利亚城市〕。

per·ti·na·cious [ˌpəːtiˈneiʃəs; ˏpɚtnˋeʃəs] ***a*.** **1.** 坚持的,顽强的,不屈不挠的;孜孜不倦的。**2.** 顽固的;难消除的。**per·tinac·i·ty** [-ˈnæsiti; -ˋnæsətɪ] ***n*.** 执拗,顽固,顽强。

per·ti·nence, per·ti·nen·cy [ˈpəːtinəns, -si; ˋpɚtnəns, -sɪ] ***n*.** 恰当,适当;相关。*a speech without* ~ 文不对题的演讲。

per·ti·nent [ˈpəːtinənt; ˋpɚtnənt] **I** ***a*.** **1.** 恰当的,贴切的,中肯的。**2.** 所论的,所指的;相干的;和…有关系的,关于…的 (*to*)。~ *details* 有关的细节。~ *reply* 得当的回答。*evidences* ~ *to the case* 与案件有关的证据。**II** ***n*.** 〔常 *pl*.〕附属物;参考。**-ly** ***ad*.**

per·turb [pə(ː)ˈtəːb; pɚˋtɝb] ***vt*.** **1.** 扰乱;搅乱;使混乱[慌张];使不安。**2.** 【天】使摄动。**-a·tive** ***a*.**

per·turb·ance [pəˈtəːbəns; pɚˋtɝbəns] ***n*.** = perturbation.

per·tur·ba·tion [ˌpəːtəːˈbeiʃən; ˏpɚtɚˋbeʃən] ***n*.** **1.** 慌张,动摇;混乱。**2.** 狼狈,不安,焦虑。**3.** 引起不安[混乱]的事物;引起动摇的原因。**4.** 【天】摄动;【物】微扰。**-al** ***a*.**

per·tus·sis [pə(ː)ˈtʌsis; pɚˋtʌsɪs] ***n*.** 【医】百日咳。**-tussal** [-ˈtʌsəl; -ˋtʌsəl] ***a*.**

per·ty [ˈpəːti; ˋpɚtɪ] ***a*.** 〔美卑〕= pretty.

Pe·ru [pəˈruː, piˈruː; pəˋru, pɪˋru] ***n*.** 秘鲁〔拉丁美洲〕。

Peru., **Peruv.** = Peruvian.

pe·ruke [pəˈruːk; pəˋruk] **I** ***n*.** 长假发。**II** ***vt*.** 装(假发)。

P

pe·rus·al [pəˈruːzəl; pəˋruzl] *n*. **1.** 熟读,精读,细读。**2.**〔古〕研讨;仔细察看。*the* ～ *of a letter* 读信。

pe·ruse [pəˈruːz; pəˋruz] *vt*. **1.** 熟读,精读;细读;读。**2.**〔古〕研讨;仔细察看。**-r** *n*. 细读者;阅读者。

Pe·ru·vi·an [pəˈruːvjən; pəˋruvɪən] **I** *a*. 秘鲁(人)的;秘鲁文化的。**II** *n*. 秘鲁人。～ **bark**【植】金鸡纳(树)皮。

per·vade [pə(ː)ˈveid; pəˋved] *vt*. 扩大,蔓延,普及,弥漫,充满;渗透;发生影响;在…当中盛行。*Weariness* ～*d his whole body*. 他全身疲倦。**-va·sion** [pə(ː)ˈveiʒən; pəˋveʒən] *n*.

P

per·va·sive [pəːˈveisiv; pəˋvesɪv] *a*. 扩大的;普及的,遍布的;贯彻的,渗透的;弥漫的。**-ly** *ad*. **-ness** *n*.

per·verse [pə(ː)ˈvəːs; pəˋvɝs] **I** *a*. **1.** 乖张的,脾气别扭的;倔强的,刚愎易怒的;(东西)麻烦的。**2.** 邪恶的;不正当的,堕落的。**3.** 违背意愿的。**4.**【法】(判决等)不合法的,不当的。**II** *n*.【数、医】倒错。～ *action* 倒行逆施。～ **verdict**【法】不当判决。**-ly** *ad*. 丧心病狂地。**-ness** *n*.

per·ver·sion [pə(ː)ˈvəːʃən; pəˋvɝʒən] *n*. **1.** 曲解;误用,滥用;逆用。**2.** 恶化;败坏,堕落。**3.**【数、医】倒错,颠倒;【心】性反常行为。*sexual* ～ 性变态。

per·ver·si·ty [pə(ː)ˈvəːsiti; pəˋvɝsətɪ] *n*. **1.** 邪恶;堕落;反常。**2.** 倔强;乖僻,刚愎。

per·ver·sive [pə(ː)ˈvəːsiv; pəˋvɝsɪv] *a*. **1.** 弄颠倒的,反常的。**2.** 曲解的 (*of*)。**3.** 误人的,把人带坏的。

per·vert [pə(ː)ˈvəːt; pəˋvɝt] **I** *vt*. **1.** 使反常;颠倒。**2.** 误用,滥用;逆用;曲解;误解。**3.** 使堕落,带坏,诱惑。—*vi*. 变坏,走邪路,堕落;变成背教者 (*to*)。**II** [ˈpəːvəːt; ˋpɝvɝt] *n*. **1.** 走入邪路者,堕落者。**2.** 背教者;变质者;反常者;【心】(特指)性反常者。**-er** *n*. = pervert (*n*.).

per·vert·ed [pəˈvəːtid; pəˋvɝtɪd] *a*. **1.** 不正当的,堕落的,邪恶的。**2.** 性欲反常的。**3.** 误解的,曲解的,歪曲的。**-ly** *ad*. **-ness** *n*.

per·vert·i·ble [pəˈvəːtibl; pəˋvɝtəbl] *a*. **1.** 能曲解的,易被误解的。**2.** 能滥用的。**3.** 能被带上邪路的;易反常的。**-i·bil·i·ty** [-ˈbiliti; -ˋbɪlətɪ] *n*. **-i·bly** *ad*.

per·vi·ous [ˈpəːviəs, -vjəs; ˋpɝvɪəs, -vjəs] *a*. **1.** 能通过的;(光等)能透过的 (*to*);可渗透的。**2.** 能了解的。(对道理等)能懂的;(对影响等)能接受的;服从的 (*to*)。**3.**【动】开着的,有孔的;【植】开通的。*Glass is* ～ *to light*. 玻璃能透光。～ **bed** 透水层。**-ness** *n*. 浸透[通透]性。

pes [piːz, peis; piz, pes] *n*. (*pl*. **pe·des** [ˈpiːdiːz, ˈpediːz; ˋpidiz, ˋpɛdiz])【动】足,脚。

pe·sach [ˈpeisɑːh; ˋpesɑh] *n*. (犹太人的)逾越节 (= Passover)。

pe·sade [pəˈseid, -zɑːd; pəˋsed, -zɑd] *n*.【马术】腾空〔马前足跃起后足直立的姿势〕。

Pes·ca·do·res [ˌpeskəˈdɔːriz; ˏpɛskɑˋdɔrɪz] *n*.〔*pl*.〕"佩斯卡多尔列岛"〔某些外国人沿用的殖民主义者对我国澎湖列岛的称呼〕。

pe·se·ta [pəˈsetə; pəˋsɛtə] *n*. 比塞塔〔西班牙货币单位〕。

pes·e·wa [ˈpesiwɑː; ˋpɛsɪwɑ] *n*. (*pl*. ～(*s*)) 比塞瓦〔加纳的货币单位,等于 1/100 塞地〕。

Pe·sha·war [pəˈʃɔːə; peˋʃɑwɚ] *n*. 白沙瓦〔巴基斯坦城市〕。

pes·ky [ˈpeski; ˋpɛskɪ] *a*.〔美口〕麻烦的,讨厌的。

pe·so [ˈpeisəu; ˋpeso] *n*. (*pl*. ～*s*) 比索〔拉丁美洲一些国家和菲律宾的货币单位〕。

pes·sa·ry [ˈpesəri; ˋpɛsərɪ] *n*.【医】子宫托;子宫帽;阴道药栓。*an uterine* ～【医】子宫环。

pes·si·mal [ˈpesiməl; ˋpɛsəməl] *a*. 最坏的 (*opp*. optimal)。

pes·si·mism [ˈpesimizəm; ˋpɛsəˏmɪzəm] *n*. 悲观,悲观主义,厌世主义 (*opp*. optimism)。

pes·si·mist [ˈpesimist; ˋpɛsəmɪst] *n*. 悲观者,悲观主义者;厌世者。

pes·si·mis·tic [ˌpesiˈmistik; ˏpɛsəˋmɪstɪk] *a*. 悲观的,厌世的;悲观主义的。*take a* ～ *view of* ... 对…抱悲观见解。**-cal·ly** *ad*. 悲观地。

pes·si·mize [ˈpesimaiz; ˋpɛsəˏmaɪz] *vi*. 悲观;抱悲观主义。

pest [pest; pɛst] *n*. **1.**〔古〕疫病;鼠疫,黑死病。**2.** 有害动[植]物,害虫。**3.** 讨厌的人,害人虫。*a garden* ～ 植物寄生虫。*insect* ～*s* 害虫。*He's a regular* ～. 他是一个十足的坏蛋。***P-*** (***up***) ***on him***!〔诅咒语〕瘟死他! ～**hole** 传染病地区;瘟疫区。～**-house**【史】(尤指鼠疫病人的)隔离医院;(一般传染病人的)隔离医院,传染病医院。

Pes·ta·loz·zi [ˌpestəˈlɔtsi; ˏpɛstəˋlɑtsɪ] *n*. 海因利希·倍斯特洛齐〔1746—1827,提倡实物教学法的瑞士教育学家〕。**-zi·an** [-ən; -ən] *a*., *n*. 主张实物教授法的(人)。

pes·ter [ˈpestə; ˋpɛstɚ] *vt*. 使烦恼,使为难,折磨;纠缠。*be* ～*ed with midges* 给小蚊子烦死。

pes·ti·cide [ˈpestisaid; ˋpɛstɪsaɪd] *n*. 杀虫剂,农药。**-ti·cid·al** *a*.

pes·tif·er·ous [pesˈtifərəs; pɛsˋtɪfərəs] *a*. **1.** 传染性的;得了疫病的。**2.** 有毒的,有害的;危险的;邪恶的,危害社会的。**3.**〔美口〕讨厌的,烦死人的,纠缠不休的。**-ly** *ad*. **-ness** *n*.

pes·ti·lence [ˈpestiləns; ˋpɛstl̩əns] *n*. **1.** 鼠疫;恶疫,时疫,流行病。**2.** 祸害,洪水猛兽〔指学说等〕。**3.** 伤风败德之事。

pes·ti·lent [ˈpestilənt; ˋpɛstl̩ənt] *a*. **1.** (对社会等)有害的,破坏性的;弊病多的。**2.**〔口〕讨厌的,烦死人的。**3.** 引起传染病的;危险的,致疫的。**-ly** *ad*.

pes·ti·len·tial [ˌpestiˈlenʃəl; ˏpɛstl̩ˋɛnʃəl] *a*. **1.** 传染病(性质)的,发生[传布]瘟疫的。**2.** (对道德等)有害的,弊端多的。**3.**〔口〕讨厌的;无法无天的。**-ly** *ad*.

pes·tle [ˈpesl, ˈpestl; ˋpɛsl, ˋpɛstl̩] **I** *n*. 乳钵槌,碾槌,杵。***mortar and*** ～ 杵和臼,乳钵和乳钵槌。**II** *vt*., *vi*. (用槌)擂,(用杵)捣;研碎。

pes·tol·o·gy [pesˈtɔlədʒi; pɛsˋtɑlədʒɪ] *n*. 害虫学;鼠疫学。

pet[1] [pet; pɛt] **I** *n*. **1.** 供玩赏的动物;爱兽,爱畜。**2.** 爱物;爱子;受宠爱的人;宝贝儿。**II** *a*. **1.** 心爱的。**2.** 表示亲昵的。**3.** 得意的,拿手的。**4.**〔谑〕第一号的,特别的。*a* ～ *name* 爱称,昵称〔如称 Robert 为 Bob 或 Rob 之类〕。*my* ～ *theory* [*plan*] 我的一贯主张[得意计划]。*a* ～ *and darling work* 得意之作。***make a*** ～ ***of*** 把…当作宠儿;宠爱,爱。***one's*** ～ ***aversion*** 最讨厌的东西。**III** *vt*. (*-tt-*) 爱,宠爱,钟爱;娇养;爱抚。—*vi*.〔美俚〕拥抱,亲嘴,爱抚。

pet[2] [pet; pɛt] **I** *n*. 不高兴;烦恼;生气。***in a*** ～ 不高兴,烦恼。～ ***peeve***〔美谑〕痛处;患处;心病,弱点。***take the*** ～ 平白无故地发脾气,烦恼。**II** *vi*. (*-tt-*) 生气,不开心。

pet. = petroleum.

Pet = Peter.

PETA = portable electronic traffic analyzer 手提式电子测速器。

pet·a·byte [ˈpetəbait; ˋpɛtəbaɪt] *n*.【计】10^{15}字节。

pet·al [ˈpetl; ˋpɛtl̩] *n*.【植】花瓣。

pet·al·ine [ˈpetəlain; ˋpɛtl̩ɪn] *a*. 花瓣(状)的。

pet·al·ite [ˈpetəlait; ˋpɛtəlaɪt] *n*.【矿】透锂长石。

pet·al(l)ed [ˈpetld; ˋpɛtl̩d] *a*. 有花瓣的,…瓣的。*five-*～ (花)五瓣的。

pet·al·o·dy [ˈpetəlˌəudi; ˋpɛtəlˏodɪ] *n*.【植】花瓣状的。

pet·al·oid [ˈpetəlɔid; ˋpɛtl̩ˏɔɪd] *a*. 花瓣似的,花瓣状的;由花瓣形成的。

pet·al·ous [ˈpetələs; ˋpɛtl̩əs] *a*. 有花瓣的。

pe·tard [peˈtɑːd; pɪˋtɑrd] *n*. **1.** (古代攻城等用的)炸药包。**2.** 大花炮。***be hoist with*** [***by***] ***one's own*** ～ 害人反害己,作法自毙,搬起石头砸自己的脚。

pet·a·sos, pet·a·sus [ˈpetəsəs; ˋpɛtəsəs] ***n*. 1.** (古希腊、罗马人戴的)阔边帽。**2.**【希神】天神赫耳墨斯(Hermes)的有翼帽。

pet-cock [ˈpetˈkɔk; ˋpɛtˏkɑk] ***n*.**【机】小型旋塞;油门,汽门;手压开关;龙头。

Pete [piːt; pit] ***n*.** 皮特〔男子名 Peter 的昵称〕。

pe·te·chi·a [piˈtiːkiə; pəˋtɛkɪə] ***n*.** (*pl*. **-chi·ae** [-iː; -i])【医】瘀斑,瘀点。**-te·chi·al *a*.**

pete·man [ˈpiːtmən; ˋpitmən] ***n*.** (*pl*. **-men**)〔美俚〕强盗,撬保险箱的强盗。

Pe·ter [ˈpiːtə; ˋpitɚ] ***n*. 1.** 彼得〔男子名〕。**2.**【圣】彼得〔耶稣十二门徒之一〕;(基督教《圣经》中的)《彼得书》。***Blue* ～**【海】开船旗。～ ***Funk*** 〔美〕(拍卖者等的)囮子。～ ***Pan*** 彼得·潘〔苏格兰剧作家 Barrie 剧作中永远不会长大成人的主角〕;天真而不懂事的成年人;(儿童或妇女衣服上的)小圆领。～ ***Principle*** 攀升至无力胜任之职位的做法。～***'s fish*** 黑线鳕,海鲂。～ ***'s pence***【英史】每户每年呈交罗马教皇的税金;天主教徒自愿献给教皇的年金。***rob* ～ *to pay Paul*** 借债还债;抢甲济乙;移东补西。

pe·ter[1] [ˈpiːtə; ˋpitɚ] ***vi*.**〔口〕**1.** (水流、矿脉等)逐渐枯竭;消耗掉(*out*)。**2.** (渐渐)消失(*out*);终止。

pe·ter[2] [ˈpiːtə; ˋpitɚ] ***n*.**〔美俚〕**1.** 保险箱。**2.** 单人牢房。**3.** 麻醉品。

pe·ter·man [ˈpiːtəmən; ˋpitɚmən] ***n*. 1.** 渔夫。**2.**〔俚〕撬保险箱的强盗;窃贼;撬保险箱器具。

Pe·ters [ˈpiːtəz; ˋpetɚs] ***n*.** 彼得斯〔姓氏,男子名〕。

Pe·ters·burg [ˈpiːtəzbəːg; ˋpitɚzˏbɝg] ***n*. 1.** 彼得斯堡〔美国城市〕。**2.** 彼得堡〔俄罗斯城市〕。

pe·ter·sham [ˈpiːtəʃəm; ˋpitɚʃəm] ***n*. 1.** 靛青珠皮大衣呢;靛青珠皮呢大衣。**2.** 楞条丝带[棉带]。

pet·i·o·lar [ˈpetiələ; ˋpɛtɪəlɚ] ***a*.**【植】叶柄的;生在叶柄上的;从叶柄上伸出的。**2.**【动】(昆虫)柄的。

pet·i·o·late(d) [ˈpetiəleit(id); ˋpetɪəˏlet(ɪd)] ***a*. 1.** 有叶柄的。**2.** (昆虫)具柄的。

pet·i·ole [ˈpetiəul; ˋpɛtɪˏol] ***n*. 1.**【植】叶柄。**2.**【动】(昆虫的)柄,腹柄。

pet·i·o·lule [ˈpetiəljuːl, -əluːl; ˋpɛtɪəljul, -əlul] ***n*. 1.**【植】小叶柄。**2.** (昆虫的)小柄。

pe·tit*, pe·tit** [pəˈtiː, ˈpeti; pəˋti, ˋpɛtɪ] ***a*.**〔F.〕小的;次要的;没有价值的,琐碎的。～ ***bourgeois [ˈbuəʒwɑː; ˋburʒwɑ] 小资产阶级分子,小资产者;小资产阶级的。～ ***four*** [fɔː; fɔr] 糖霜小块蛋糕。～ ***maitre*** [ˈmeitr; ˋmetr] 花花公子,纨袴子弟。～ ***mal*** [ˈmæl; ˋmæl] 轻癫痫。～ ***point* 1.** 小花边编织法。**2.** 织景画。～ ***souper*** [ˈsuːpei; ˋsupe] 二三知己朋友的小宴。～***s soins*** [ˈswɛ̃iŋ; ˋswɛ̃ɪŋ] 小殷勤。～ ***verre*** [ˈvɛə; ˋvɛr] 小杯。

pe·tite*, pe·tite** [pəˈtiːt; pəˋtit] ***a*.**〔F.〕**1.** (女人)个子小的,娇小的。**2.** 小的,次要的。～ ***bourgeoisie [ˌbuəʒwɑˈziː; ˏbʊʒwɑˋzɪ] 小资产阶级。

pe·ti·tion [piˈtiʃən; pəˋtɪʃən] **I *n*. 1.** 请愿,请求;申请;祈求。**2.** 请愿书;诉状。*the right of* ～ 请愿权。*a* ～ *of appeal*【法】起诉状。*a* ～ *of revision*【法】上诉状。***file a* ～ *against* ...** 申请取消[停止]…。***file a* ～ *for* ...** 申请获得[实行]…。***hand in* [*send in*] *one's* ～ *to* = *lodge one's* ～ *to*** 向…申请。***present a* ～ *to*** 向…提出请愿书。***put up a* ～ *to*** (*heaven*) 向(天)祈祷。**II *vt*.** 向…请愿[祈求]。—***vi*.** 请愿,请求(*for a thing*; *to do*);祈求。

pe·ti·tion·a·ry [piˈtiʃənəri; pəˋtɪʃənɛrɪ] ***a*. 1.** 请愿的,请求的;祈求的。**2.**〔诗〕可怜的。

pe·ti·tion·er [piˈtiʃənə; pəˋtɪʃənɚ] ***n*. 1.** 请愿人,祈求人。**2.** (离婚诉讼的)原告。

pe·ti·ti·o prin·ci·pi·i [piˈtiʃiəu prinˈsipiai; pɪˋtɪʃɪo ˏprɪnˋsɪpɪˏaɪ]〔L.〕【逻】预期理由〔一种逻辑错误,以本身尚待证明的判断作为证明论题的论据〕。

pet·i·to·ry [ˈpetitəri; ˋpɛtɪtərɪ] ***a*.** 提出所有权要求的。*a* ～ *action* [*suit*] 要求所有权的诉讼。

pet·nap·ping, pet·nap·ing [ˈpetˌnæpiŋ; ˋpɛtˏnæpɪŋ] ***n*.** 偷窃猫狗〔卖供实验用〕。

Pe·tö·fi [ˈpetəfi; ˋpetəfɪ] **San·dor** 裴多菲〔1823—1849,匈牙利诗人〕。

petr- *comb*. *f*.〔用于元音前〕= petro-[1].

Pe·trar·chan [piˈtrɑːkən; pɪˋtrɑrkən] ***a*.** (十四行诗)彼特拉克文体的〔其韵脚为 abba, abba, cdc dcd 或 cde cde〕。

pet·rel [ˈpetrəl; ˋpɛtrəl] ***n*. 1.**【动】海燕〔相传这种燕子一来就有暴风雨,因此又名 storm(y) ～〕。**2.**〔喻〕一来就会发生事故的人。

pet·ri- *comb*. *f*. = petro-[1].

Pe·tri dish [ˈpiːtri ˈdiʃ; ˋpitrɪ ˋdɪʃ]【生】(陪替氏)培养皿。

Pe·trie [ˈpiːtri; ˋpitrɪ] ***n*.** 皮特里〔姓氏〕。

pet·ri·fac·tion [ˌpetriˈfækʃən; ˏpɛtrəˋfækʃən] ***n*. 1.**【地】石化(作用);化石。**2.** 发呆;茫然自失。**3.** 顽固,僵化。

pet·ri·fac·tive [ˌpetriˈfæktiv; ˏpɛtrəˋfæktɪv] ***a*.** 能使有机物石化的,有石化能力的。

pe·trif·ic [piˈtrifik; pəˋtrɪfɪk] ***a*.** = petrifactive.

pet·ri·fi·ca·tion [ˌpetrifiˈkeiʃən; ˏpɛtrəfəˋkeʃən] ***n*.** = petrifaction.

pet·ri·fy [ˈpetrifai; ˋpɛtrəˏfaɪ] ***vt*.** (**-fied**) **1.**【地】使(动植物)石化,石化(动、植物等)。**2.** 使变硬;使失去活力;使僵化;使顽固。**3.** 使迟钝;使发呆。*stand petrified* (吓得)呆呆地站着。*be petrified with terror* 吓呆。—***vi*. 1.**【地】石化;变僵硬。**2.** 吓呆。

Pe·trine [ˈpiːtrain, -rin; ˋpitraɪn, -rɪn] ***a*.** 圣彼得(Peter)的。

petro-[1] *comb*. *f*. 表示"石,岩"。

petro-[2] *comb*. *f*. 表示"石油"。

pet·ro·chem·i·cal [ˌpetrəuˈkemikl; ˏpɛtroˋkɛmək!] **I *a*.** 石油化学的;岩石化学的。**II *n*.** 石油化学产品。

pet·ro·che·mis·try [ˌpetrəuˈkemistri; ˏpɛtroˋkɛmɪstrɪ] ***n*.** 石油化学;岩石化学。

pe·tro·dol·lars [ˌpetrəuˈdɔləz; ˏpetroˋdɑlɚz] ***n*.**〔美〕石油美元〔指石油输出国积累的美元收入〕。

pe·trog·e·ny [piˈtrɔdʒini; pɪˋtrɑdʒənɪ] ***n*.**【地】岩石发生学。

pet·ro·glyph [ˈpetrəglif; ˋpɛtrəglɪf] ***n*.** 原始人石刻〔原始人刻在岩石上的物像[文字]〕。

pet·ro·graph [ˈpetrəgrɑːf; ˋpɛtrəˏgræf] ***n*.** = petroglyph.

pe·trog·ra·phy [piˈtrɔgrəfi; piˋtrɑgrəfɪ] ***n*.** 岩相学;岩类学。**pe·trog·ra·ph·i·cal** [-ˈgræfikəl; -ˋgræfɪkəl] ***a*.**

pet·rol [ˈpetrəl; ˋpɛtrəl] **I *n*. 1.**〔英〕汽油〔美国称 gasoline〕。**2.**〔废〕石油。**II *vt*.** (**-ll-**)〔英〕**1.** 给…加汽油。**2.** 用汽油消除。～**-engine** 汽油发动机。～ **station** 加油站。

pet·ro·la·tum [ˌpetrəuˈleitəm; ˏpɛtrəˋletəm] ***n*.**【化】矿脂;凡士林,石油冻。

Pet·rol·ene [ˈpetrəliːn; ˋpetrəlin] ***n*.**【化】沥青脂。

pe·tro·le·um [piˈtrəuliəm; pəˋtrolɪəm] ***n*.** 石油。*crude* [*raw*] ～ 原油,重油。～ **coal** 固体石油。～ **engine** 石油发动机。～ **ether** 石油醚。～ **jelly** 凡士林(= vaseline)。

pe·tro·le·ur [F. petrɔlœːr; petrɔˋlœr] ***n*.**〔F.〕用石油放火者。

pe·trol·ic [piˈtrɔlik; pɪˋtrɑlɪk] ***a*. 1.** 汽油的;石油的。**2.** 从石油中提炼的。**3.** 汽油发动机的。

pet·ro·lif·er·ous [ˌpetrəˈlifərəs; ˏpɛtrəˋlɪfərəs] ***a*.** 含石油的;产石油的。

pe·tro·lin(e) [ˈpetrəlin; ˋpetrəlɪn] ***n*.**【化】石油淋〔一种碳化氢〕。

pet·ro·lize [ˈpetrəlaiz; ˋpɛtrəlaɪz] ***vt*. 1.** 用石油点燃。

P

2. 用石油处理。3. 用石油覆盖(水面)。4. 用柏油铺(路)。

pe·trol·o·gy [pi'trɔlədʒi; pi`trɑlədʒɪ] *n*. 岩石学,岩理学。**pet·rolog·i·cal** [-'lɔdʒikəl; -`lɑdʒɪkəl] *a*. **pe-trol·o·gist** [-'lɔdʒist; -`lɑdʒɪst] *n*. 岩石学家。

pet·ro·nel ['petrənəl; `pɛtrənəl] *n*. (十五至十七世纪的)手枪,火枪〔一种枪筒粗的,卡宾枪似的武器〕。

pet·ro·phone ['petrəufəun; `pɛtro͵fon] *n*. 【乐】石琴。**pet·roph·onist** [-'fəunist; -`fonɪst] *n*. 石琴家。

pet·ro·pol·i·tics [petrəu'pɔlitiks; pɛtro`pɑlɪtɪks] *n*. 石油政治。

pe·tro·sal [pi'trəusəl; pɪ`trosəl] *a*. 1. 硬的,石头似的。2. 【解】位于颞骨岩部的。

pet·rous ['petrəs; `pɛtrəs] *a*. 1. 岩石(似)的,硬的。2. 【解】颞骨岩部的。

pet·ti·coat ['petikəut; `pɛtɪ͵kot] *n*. 1. 裙子;衬裙;〔*pl*.〕童装,女装。2. 〔俚〕女人,少女;〔*pl*.〕女性;〔俚〕(纸牌的)女王。3. 褶状物。*a ~ affair* 与女人有关的事件;(尤指)桃色事件。*in ~s* 1. 穿裙子的;女性的。2. 幼年时。*~ slave* 〔俚〕怕老婆的人。*under ~ government* 在妻子管辖之下。**-ed** *a*. 1. 穿着裙子的。2. 像女人的。**-ism** *n*. 老婆的管辖,女人的统治。**-less** *a*. 1. 不穿(衬)裙的。2. 不像女人的。

pet·ti·fog ['petifɔg; `pɛtɪ͵fɑg] *vi*. (**-gg-**) 1. 做讼棍,经办小件法律事务。2. 讲歪理;诡辩;挑剔。**-fog·ger** [-ə; -ə] *n*. 1. 小律师;讼棍。2. 骗子;诡辩者。**-fog·ger·y** [-gəri; -gərɪ] *n*. = pettifogging. **-fog·ging** 1. *a*. 小律师(式)的,狡诈的;卑劣的;低贱的;为小事细节而烦恼的。2. *n*. 讼棍行为[手段];狡辩;狡诈。

pet·ti·ly ['petili; `pɛtəlɪ] *ad*. 卑鄙地;偏狭地;器量小地。

pet·ti·ness ['petinis; `pɛtɪnɪs] *n*. 1. 微小,琐碎;狭小。2. 偏狭;卑劣,器量小。

pet·ting ['petiŋ; `pɛtɪŋ] *n*. 〔美俚〕拥抱,爱抚,嬉戏。~-**skirt** 〔美〕姑娘,女孩。

pet·ti·pants [petipænts; `pɛtɪpænts] *n*. 〔*pl*.〕妇女半长内裤。

pet·tish ['petiʃ; `pɛtɪʃ] *a*. 1. 不高兴的,动不动闹脾气的。2. 发脾气时说[做]的。

pet·ti·toes ['petitəuz; `pɛtɪ͵toz] *n*. 〔*pl*.〕1. (食用的)猪脚。2. 〔谑〕人的脚〔尤指小孩的脚〕。

pet·to ['pettəu; `pɛtto] *n*. (*pl*. **-ti** [-iː; -i]) 〔It.〕胸。*in ~* 在胸中,秘密。

Pet·ty ['peti; `pɛtɪ] *n*. 佩蒂〔姓氏〕。

pet·ty ['peti; `pɛtɪ] **I** *a*. 1. 小的,一点点。2. 琐碎的;渺小的;不足道的,无聊的。3. 器量小的,心眼儿小的,卑劣的。4. 小规模的;次要的;下级的。*a ~ current deposit* 零星活期存款。*a ~ dealer* 小贩。*~ expenses* 零星杂费。
II *n*. 1. 【簿记】小额。2. 〔*pl*.〕厕所。~ **bourgeois** 小资产阶级分子;小资产者;小资产阶级的。~ **bourgeoisie** 小资产阶级。~ **cash** 零用钱,零星收支。~ **jury** 小陪审团〔由十二人组成〕。~ **larceny** 【法】轻窃盗罪。~ **officer** 1. 小公务员。2. (海军的)下级官佐,军士,下士。~ **officer stoker** (海军的)锅炉下士。~ **session** 〔英〕即决法庭。

pet·u·lance, pet·u·lan·cy ['petjuləns, -si; `pɛtʃələns, -sɪ] *n*. 1. 易怒,暴躁,坏脾气;别扭,闹气;急躁言行。2. 〔古〕无礼,狂妄。

pet·u·lant ['petjulənt; `pɛtʃələnt] *a*. 1. 急躁的,易怒的,爱闹气的,脾气坏的。2. 〔古〕狂妄的;无礼的。

pe·tu·ni·a [pi'tjuːnjə, -niə; pə`tjunjə, -nɪə] *n*. 1. 【植】(南美产)矮牵牛花属植物。2. 暗紫色。

pe·tun·se [pe'tunsi; pɛ`tʊnsɛ], **pe·tun·tse, pe·tun·tze** [pe'tuntsi; pɛ`tʊntsɪ] *n*. (中国的)瓷泥〔制造瓷器用〕。

peu a peu [pəːə'pəː; pøapø; pɑɑ`pɑ; pøapø] 〔F.〕一点一点地,逐渐。

pew [pjuː; pju] **I** *n*. 1. (教堂的)条凳式座位;一家人专用包厢式座位。2. 〔*pl*.〕坐在教堂椅子上的人们;会众。3. 〔古〕(讲道者或司仪用的)讲台。4. 〔口〕椅子,座位。*Take a ~*. 请坐〔对客人讲〕。**II** *vt*. 1. 为(教堂)安座位。2. 把…围成包厢式座位。3. 使在教堂座位中就坐。~ **chair** 折叠式添座椅子。~ **opener** 教堂的领座人。~ **rent** 教堂座位费。

pew·age ['pjuːidʒ; `pjuɪdʒ] *n*. 1. 教堂条凳。2. 教堂座位费。

pe·wee ['piːwiː; `piwi] *n*. 【鸟】1. 京燕类。2. 〔美〕山鹬。

pe·wit ['piːwit; `piwɪt] *n*. 【鸟】1. = pewee. 2. 田凫。3. 红嘴鸥。

Pewks [pjuːks; pjuks] *n*. 〔美〕密苏里 (Missouri) 州人的绰号。

pew·ter ['pjuːtə; `pjutə˞] **I** *n*. 1. 【冶】白镴〔锡和铅的合金〕。2. 锡镴制器皿,白镴锅,白镴酒杯。3. 〔俚〕悬赏杯,奖金;〔美俚〕钱。**II** *a*. 白镴(制)的。~-**wort** 【植】木贼。

PF = pulse frequency 【无】脉冲频率。

pf. = 1. perfect. 2. preferred.

p.f. = 〔It.〕***più forte*** (= louder) 【乐】更大声些。

PFC, Pfc. = Private First Class 〔美〕陆军[海军陆战队]一等兵。

pfd; pfd. = preferred.

pfen·nig ['pfenig; `pfɛnɪg] *n*. (*pl*. ~*s*, ***pfen·ni·ge*** ['pfenigə; `pfɛnɪgə]) 芬尼〔德国铜币 = 1/100 mark〕。

PG = parental guidance (指电影)适合一般观众看但建议父母(对儿童观众)加以指导。

P.G. = 1. paying guest 搭伙房客。2. postgraduate (大学的)研究生。

Pg. = 1. Portugal. 2. Portuguese.

PGM = precision-guided missile 精确制导导弹[飞弹]。

Pgn., pgn = pigeon 军用鸽,通信鸽。

PH = public health 公共卫生。

P.H. = pinch-hitter (棒球赛关键时上场的)候补击球员。

Ph. = 1. phenyl 【化】苯基。2. phase.

p.h. = per hour 每小时。

pH 【化】表示氢离子浓度的倒数的对数的符号。

PHA = Public Housing Administration 〔美〕公众房产管理局。

Pha·ë·thon ['feiəθən; `feəθən] *n*. 【希神】法厄同〔太阳神赫利俄斯的儿子〕。

phae·ton ['feitn; `feətn] *n*. 1. 二马四轮轻便马车。2. 活顶游览汽车。~ **butterfly** 〔美〕火焰斑纹黑蝴蝶。

-phag, -phage *comb. f*. 表示"食,噬": bacterio*phage*.

phage [feidʒ; fedʒ] *n*. 【医】噬菌体(= bacteriophage)。

phag·e·de·na, phag·e·dae·na [͵fædʒi'diːnə; ͵fædʒə`dinə] *n*. 【医】崩蚀性溃疡。**-e·den·ic** [-'denik; -`dɛnɪk] *a*.

phago- *comb. f*. 表示"食,噬": *phago*cyte.

phag·o·cyte ['fægəsait; `fægə͵saɪt] *n*. 【生理】吞噬细胞,白血球。**-o·cyt·ic** [͵fægə'sitik; ͵fægə`sɪtɪk] *a*. **-o·cy·to·sis** [͵fægəsai'təusis; ͵fægəsaɪ`tosɪs] *n*. 噬菌(作用)。

-phagous *suf*. 表示"噬…的": creo*phagous*.

-phagy *comb. f*. 表示"常食…者": alotrio*phagy*.

phal·ange ['fæləndʒ; `fæləndʒ] *n*. 【解】指骨;趾骨 (= phalanx 4.)。

phal·an·ge·al [fə'lændʒiəl; fe`lændʒɪəl] *a*. 【解】指骨的;趾骨的。~ **joint** 【解】指[趾]关节。

pha·lan·ger [fə'lændʒə; fe`lændʒə˞] *n*. (澳大利亚的)袋貂科 (*Phalangeridae*) 动物。

pha·lan·ges [fæ'lændʒiːz; fə`lændʒiz] *n*. phalanx 的复数。

Pha·lan·gist [fə'lædʒist; fə`lædʒɪst] *n*. (黎巴嫩的)长枪党党员。

phal·an·ster·y ['fælənstəri; `fælən͵stɛrɪ] *n*. 1. 法伦斯泰尔〔法国空想社会主义者傅立叶幻想的社会主义基层组织〕。2. 法伦斯泰尔成员的公共住所。3. 类似法伦斯泰尔的组织。

phal·anx [ˈfælæŋks; ˋfelæŋks] *n*. (*pl*. ～*es*, ***pha·langes*** [fæˈlændʒiːz; fæˋlændʒiz]) **1**. (古希腊重武装步兵的)方阵。**2**. 密集队伍;集结;集团,结社。**3**. 法郎吉〔傅立叶空想社会主义的社会组织,即 phalanstery〕。**4**. (*pl*. ***pha·lan·ges***)【解】指[趾]骨;【虫】跗亚节。**5**. (*pl*. ***pha·lan·ges***)【植】雄蕊束。

phal·a·rope [ˈfælərəup; ˋfælərop] *n*.【动】瓣蹼鹬。

phal·lic, phal·li·cal [ˈfælik, -likəl; ˋfælɪk, -lɪkəl] *a*. **1**. 阴茎的。**2**. 崇拜男性生殖器的。

phal·li·cism, phal·lism [ˈfælisizəm, -lizəm; ˋfælə͵sɪzəm, -lɪzəm] *a*. 生殖器崇拜;阴茎崇拜。

phal·lus [ˈfæləs; ˋfæləs] *n*. (*pl*. ***phal·li*** [-lai; -laɪ]) **1**. (作为崇拜对象的)男性生殖器形象。**2**.【解】阴茎;阴核。

phan·er·o·gam [ˈfænərəugæm; ˋfænərə͵gæm] *n*.【植】显花植物 (*opp*. cryptogam)。

Phan·er·o·gam·i·a [ˌfænərəuˈgeimiə; ͵fænərəˋgemɪə] *n*.【植】显花植物门。

phan·er·o·gam·ic, phan·er·og·a·mous [ˌfænərəuˈgæmik, -ˈrɔgəməs; ͵fænərəˋgæmɪk, -ˋrɑgəməs] *a*. 显花的,开花的。

phan·er·o·phyte [ˈfænərəufait; ˋfænərəfaɪt] *n*.【植】高位芽植物。

phan·si·gar [ˈfænsigɑː; ˋfænsə͵gɑr] *n*. 〔Hind.〕谋财害命的暴徒 (= thug)。

phan·tasm [ˈfæntæzəm; ˋfæntæzəm] *n*. **1**. 幻像,幻影。**2**. 幽灵。**3**. 幻想,空想。**4**. 〔古〕幻觉,错觉。

phan·tas·ma [fænˈtæzmə; fænˋtæzmə] *n*. (*pl*. ～***ta*** [-tə; -tə]) = phantasm.

Phan·tas·ma·go·ri·a [ˌfæntæzməˈgɔːriə; ͵fæntæzməˋgorɪə] *n*. **1**. 幻觉效应〔尤指屏幕上形象向后缩小或骤然增大如向观众扑来的光学效应〕。**2**. 变幻不定的情景。**3**. (1802 年伦敦举行的)大幻灯会。**-ma·gor·i·al** [-ˈgɔriəl; -ˋgɔrɪəl], **-ma·gor·ic** [-ˈgɔrik; -ˋgɔrɪk] *a*. 幻影(似)的,变幻不定的。

phan·tas·mal, phan·tas·mic [fænˈtæzməl, -mik; fænˋtæzməl, -mɪk] *a*. **1**. 幻影(一样)的;幽灵(一样)的。**2**. 幻想的,空想的。**-ly** ***ad***.

phan·ta·sy [ˈfæntəsi; ˋfæntəsɪ] *n*. = fantasy.

phan·tom [ˈfæntəm; ˋfæntəm] **I** *n*. **1**. 鬼怪,妖怪;幽灵;使人害怕的东西。**2**. 错觉,妄想。**3**. 幻影,幻像;影像,印象(*of*);实际上不存在的人[物];〔美俚〕工资单上挂假名的人。**4**.【解】(人体)模型。**5**. 〔P-〕鬼怪式飞机。**II** *a*. **1**. 空的,幻想的,幻影的。**2**. 幽灵似的,鬼怪的。～ **antenna**【无】幻天线。～ **bug**【计】幻影指令〔指在特定环境下方可被激活的一种电脑程序隐蔽指令〕。～ **circuit**【电】幻像电路。～ **crystal** 先成晶体。～ **freight** 虚拟运费〔交货价格中所包括的超过了实际的运输距离的运费〕。～ **limb** (截肢后依然感到肢体存在的)幻肢(感)。～ **order** 〔美〕(武器等的)虚幻订单〔须官方批准后才有效〕。～ **tumour** (歇斯底里症患者腹部的)一时肿胀,虚瘤。～ **wire**【电】假想线路。

phar., pharm. = **1**. pharmaceutical. **2**. pharmacopoeia. **3**. pharmacy.

Phar·aoh [ˈfɛərəu; ˋfɛro] *n*. 法老〔古埃及王称号〕。～**'s chicken** [**hen**]【动】王鸡〔产于埃及等地的一种兀鹰〕。～**'s rat** [**mouse**]【动】埃及獴。～**'s serpent** 法老蛇〔一点火就呈现蛇形的化学玩具〕。**Phara·on·ic** [ˌfɛəreiˈɔnik; ͵fɛrɪˋɑnɪk] *a*.

Phar. B. = Bachelor of Pharmacy 药学士。

Phar. D. = Doctor of Pharmacy 药学博士。

Phar·i·sa·ic, Phar·i·sa·i·cal [ˌfæriˈseiik, -ikəl; ͵færəˋseɪk, -ɪkəl] *a*. **1**. 法利赛人的。**2**. 〔p-〕【圣】遵守表面教义的;拘泥(宗教)形式的;表面虔诚的,伪善的。**-i·cal·ly** ***ad***.

Phar·i·sa·ism [ˈfæriseiizəm; ˋfærəse͵ɪzəm] *n*. **1**. 法利赛人的教规[信仰,习惯];法利赛派。**2**. 〔P-〕拘泥形式;伪善。

Phar·i·see [ˈfærisiː; ˋfærə͵si] *n*. **1**. 法利赛(派)的人〔古犹太教一个派别的成员,宣称墨守传统礼仪,《圣经》中称他们为言行不一的伪善者〕。**2**. 〔p-〕(宗教上的)拘泥形式者;伪君子;伪善者。

phar·ma·ceu·ti·cal [ˌfɑːməˈsjuːtikəl; ͵fɑrməˋsjutɪkəl] **I** *a*. **1**. 制药(学)上的。**2**. 药剂师的。**3**. 应用药物的。～ *botany* 药用植物学。～ *chemistry* 制药化学,药物化学。*a* ～ *worker* 制药工人。**II** *n*. 药物。**-ly** ***ad***.

phar·ma·ceu·tics [ˌfɑːməˈsjuːtiks; ͵fɑrməˋsjutɪks] *n*. 〔*pl*.〕〔用作 *sing*.〕制药学。

phar·ma·ceu·tist, phar·ma·cist [ˌfɑːməˈsjuːtist, ˈfɑːməsist; ͵fɑrməˋsjutɪst, ˋfɑrməsɪst] *n*. 制药者,药剂师,药学家。

phar·ma·co·dy·nam·ics [fɑːməˌkəudaiˈnæmiks; ͵fɑrməkodaɪˋnæmɪks] *n*. 〔*pl*.〕〔作单数用〕药效学。**-na·mic** *a*.

phar·ma·cog·no·sy [ˌfɑːməˈkɔgnəsi; ͵fɑrməˋkɑgnəsɪ] *n*. 生药学。

phar·ma·col·o·gy [ˌfɑːməˈkɔlədʒi; ͵fɑrməˋkɑlədʒɪ] *n*. 药理学;药物学。**-col·o·gist** *n*. 药理[药物]学家。**-ma·co·log·i·cal** *a*.

phar·ma·co·poe·ia [ˌfɑːməkəˈpiːə; ͵fɑrməkəˋpiə] *n*. **1**. 处方书,药典。**2**. (一批)库存药品,(一批)备用药物。**-poe·ial** *a*.

phar·ma·cy [ˈfɑːməsi; ˋfɑrməsɪ] *n*. **1**. 配药学,药学。**2**. 制药业。**3**. 药房。**4**. (一批)备用药品。～ **jar** 药瓶。

phar·mic [ˈfɑːmik; ˋfɑrmɪk] **I** *a*. 〔美俚〕有关药物的;关于药学的。**II** *n*. **1**. 药学讲座。**2**. 药学学生。

Pharm. D. = Phar. D.

Pharm. M. = Master of Pharmacy 药学硕士。

Pharm·ing [ˈfɑːmiŋ; ˋfɑrmɪŋ] *n*. 分子药物遗传工程,基因转变技术。

Pharmt. = Pharmacist.

pha·ros [ˈfɛərɔs; ˋfɛrɑs] *n*. **1**. 〔诗〕灯塔;航线标记;标灯;望楼;炬火。**2**. 〔P-〕(从前亚历山大湾内)法罗斯(Pharos)岛上的灯塔。

pha·ryn·gal, pha·ryn·ge·al [fəˈriŋgəl, ˌfærinˈdʒiːəl; fəˋrɪŋgl, ͵færɪnˋdʒiəl] *a*.【解】咽的。～ **artery** 咽动脉。～ **tonsil** 咽扁桃体。～ **tube**【解】食管。

phar·yn·ges [fəˈrindʒiːz; fəˋrɪndʒiz] *n*. pharynx 的复数。

phar·yn·gi·tis [ˌfærinˈdʒaitis; ͵færɪnˋdʒaɪtɪs] *n*.【医】咽炎。

pharyng(o)- *comb*. *f*. 表示"咽": *pharyngo*logy.

phar·yn·gol·o·gy [ˌfæriŋˈgɔlədʒi; ͵færɪŋˋgɑlədʒɪ] *n*. 咽科学。

pha·ryn·go·scope [fəˈriŋgəskəup; fəˋrɪŋgə͵skop] *n*.【医】咽窥器,咽镜。

phar·ynx [ˈfæriŋks; ˋfærɪŋks] *n*. (*pl*. ***phar·yn·ges*** [fəˈrindʒiːz; fəˋrɪndʒiz], ～*es*)【解】咽。

phase [feiz; fez] **I** *n*. **1**. 形势,局面,状态;阶级。**2**. 方面,侧面。**3**.【天】(月等的)变相,盈亏;【物、天】相,周相,相位。**4**.【动】型,期。*a youthful* ～ 青年时期。*The problem has many* ～*s*. 这问题是多方面的。～ *distortion*【物】相畸变,周相畸变。***enter*** (***up***)***on a new*** ～ 进入一新的阶段。***from*** ～ ***to*** ～ ***during this stage*** 这一阶段中的各个时期。***in*** ～【物】相同的[地];同时协调的[地]。***out of*** ～【物】异相的[地],不同相;非同时协调的[地]。

II *vt*. **1**. 使调整相位,使定相。**2**. 使分阶段[按计划]进行。～ ***in*** 分阶段引入,逐步采用。～ ***out*** **1**. 使逐步结束;使逐步撤出;逐步淘汰;逐部停止(活动等)。**2**. (动作等的)逐步停止;逐步撤出。**3**. 逐步转入 (*into*)。～ **angle**【天】位相角。～**-contrast** *a*. 用相衬显微镜的。～ **contrast microscope**【物】相衬显微镜。～ **distortion**

(电信)相位失真。~ **indicator** 示相器。~ **meter** 相差计。~ **modulation**【无】调相,相位调制。~ **rule** 相律。~ **splitter** 分相器。~ **velocity** 相速(度)。

pha·sic [ˈfeizik; ˋfezɪk] ***a*.** **1.** 阶段的;局面的。**2.**【天,物】相(位)的。*the* ~ *development*【生】阶段发育。

phas·mid [ˈfeizmid; ˋfezmɪd] ***n*.**【动】竹节虫目(*Phasmida*)昆虫〔包括条形虫、枝状虫(*Diapheromera femorate*)〕。

phat [fæt; fæt] ***a*.**〔口〕性感的;精彩的。

phat·ic [ˈfætik; ˋfætɪk] ***a*.** (谈话)落入俗套的,无意义的,交际应酬的。**-i·cal·ly** ***ad*.**

P

Ph. B., Ph B =〔L.〕*Philosophiae Baccalaureus* 哲学学士(=Bachelor of Philosophy)。

Ph.C. =Pharmaceutical Chemist 药物化学家。

Ph.D., Ph D =〔L.〕*Philosophiae Doctor* 哲学博士(=*Doctor of Philosophy*)。

pheas·ant [ˈfeznt; ˋfɛznt] ***n*.** (*pl*. ~(*s*))【鸟】雉,野鸡。***shoot the*** ~ 加害无力自卫的人的生命[名誉];欺侮善良无辜者。~**-eyed** ***a*.** (花等)有雉羽状斑点的。~**'s-eye** ***n*.**【植】红口水仙。

pheas·ant·ry [ˈfezntri; ˋfɛzntrɪ] ***n*.** 养雉场;【建】雉舍。

Phe·be [ˈfiːbi; ˋfibɪ] ***n*.** =phoebe.

phel·lem [ˈfeləm; ˋfɛləm] ***n*.**【植】木栓。

phel·lo·derm [ˈfelədəːm; ˋfɛlədɚm] ***n*.**【植】栓内层。**-al** ***a*.**

phel·lo·gen [ˈfelədʒən; ˋfɛlədʒən] ***n*.**【植】木栓形成层(= cork cambium)。**-ge·net·ic** [-dʒiˈnetik; -dʒɪˋnɛtɪk], **-gen·ic** [-ˈdʒenik; -ˋdʒɛnɪk] ***a*.**

phen- *comb*. *f*.〔用于元音前〕=pheno-: *phen*azine.

phe·na·caine [ˈfiːnəkein, ˈfenə-; ˋfinəken, ˋfɛnə-] ***n*.**【化】芬那卡因〔即哈洛卡因,一种局部麻醉药〕。

phe·nac·e·tin(e) [fiˈnæsitin; fəˋnæsətɪn] ***n*.**【药】非那西汀,乙酰非那替汀〔一种解热镇痛药〕。

phen·a·kis·to·scope [ˌfiːnəˈkistəskəup; ˏfinəˋkɪstəˏskop] ***n*.** 诡盘〔一种玩具〕。

phen·a·kite [ˈfenəkait; ˋfɛnəkaɪt] ***n*.**【化】矽铍石(=phenacite)。

phe·nan·threne [fəˈnænθriːn; fɪˋnænθrin] ***n*.**【化】菲。

phe·nate [ˈfiːneit; ˋfinet] ***n*.**【化】(苯)酚盐,石炭酸盐。

phen·a·zine [ˈfenəˌziːn, -zin; ˋfɛnəˏzin, -zɪn] ***n*.**【化】吩嗪,(夹)二杂蒽。

phene [fiːn; fin] ***n*.**【化】=benzene.

phe·net·i·dine [fiˈnetidiːn, -din; fəˋnɛtədin, -dɪn] ***n*.**【化】氨基醚,乙氧苯胺。

phen·e·tol(e) [ˈfenitəul, -tɔl; ˋfɛnəˏtol, -tɑl] ***n*.**【化】苯乙醚,乙基苯。

Phe·ni·ci·a [fiˈniʃiə; fəˋnɪʃɪə] =Phoenicia.

phe·ni·ci·an [fiˈniʃiən, -ʃən; fəˋnɪʃɪən, -ʃən] =Phoenician.

phe·nix [ˈfiːniks; ˋfinɪks] ***n*.** =phoenix.

pheno- *comb*. *f*.〔用于辅[子]音前〕**1.**【化】苯,苯基: *pheno*barbital. **2.** 闪光,闪耀: *pheno*cryst.

phe·no·bar·bi·tal [ˌfiːnəuˈbɑːbitæl; ˏfinəˋbɑrbɪˏtæl] ***n*.**【药】苯巴比妥〔一种安眠药和镇静剂〕。

phe·no·cain [ˈfiːnəkein; ˋfinəken] ***n*.** =phenacaine.

phe·no·cop·y [ˈfiːnəˌkɔpi; ˋfinəˏkɑpɪ] ***n*.**【遗传】拟表型。

phe·no·cryst [ˈfiːnəkrist, ˈfenə-; ˋfinəkrɪst, ˋfɛnə-] ***n*.**【地】斑晶。

phe·nol [ˈfiːnɔl; ˋfinɑl] ***n*.**【化】**1.** (苯)酚,石炭酸(=carbolic acid)。**2.**〔类名词〕酚。

phe·no·lase [ˈfiːnəleis; ˋfinəles] ***n*.**【生化】酚酶。

phe·no·late [ˈfiːnəˌleit; ˋfinəlet] ***n*.**【化】(苯)酚盐,石炭酸盐(=phenate)。**-d** ***a*.** 含碳酸的。

phe·nol·ic [fiˈnɔlik; fɪˋnɑlɪk] ***n*.**【化】(苯)酚的。**-s** ***n*.** 酚醛塑料。

phe·nol·o·gy [fiˈnɔlədʒi; fɪˋnɑlədʒɪ] ***n*.** 物候学;物候现象。**phe·no·log·i·cal** [ˌfiːnəˈlɔdʒikəl; ˏfinəˋlɑdʒɪkəl] ***a*.**

phe·nol·phthal·e·in [ˌfiːnɔlˈfθæliːn; ˏfinolˋfθælin] ***n*.**【化】(苯)酚酞。

phe·nom [fiˈnɔm; fɪˋnɑm] ***n*.**〔美俚〕**1.** 好事;好东西。**2.** 杰出人材,红人〔尤指优秀运动员〕。

phe·nom·e·na [fiˈnɔminə; fəˋnɑmɪnə] ***n*.** phenomenon 的复数。

phe·nom·e·nal [fiˈnɔminl; fəˋnɑmənl] ***a*.** **1.** 现象的;可以感觉[认识]到的;来自自然现象中的;显著的。**2.** 非凡的,少有的,惊人的。~ **memory** 超人的记忆力。**-ism** ***n*.**【哲】(唯)现象论。**-ist** ***n*.** (唯)现象论者。

phe·nom·e·nal·is·tic [fiˌnɔminəˈlistik; fəˏnɑmɪnəˋlɪstɪk] ***a*.** (有关)现象论的。**-ti·cal·ly** ***ad*.**

phe·nom·e·nal·ize [fiˈnɔminəlaiz; fəˋnɑmənlˌaɪz] ***vt*.** **1.** 把…当作现象看待,把…认作现象。**2.** 用现象论解释。

phe·nom·e·nism [fiˈnɔnminizəm; fəˋnɑnmɪnɪzəm] ***n*.** =phenomenalism. **-nist·ic** ***a*.**

phe·nom·e·nol·o·gy [fiˌnɔmiˈnɔlədʒi; fəˏnɑmɪˋnɑlədʒɪ] ***n*.** 现象学。**-log·i·cal** ***a*.** **-log·i·cal·ly** ***ad*.**

phe·nom·e·non [fiˈnɔminən; fəˋnɑməˏnɑn] ***n*.** **1.** (*pl*. **-na** [-nə; -nə])【哲】现象(*opp*. noumenon);事件。**2.** (*pl*. ~*s*) 稀有现象;奇迹;珍奇;珍品;非凡的人。**3.**【医】症候。*the* ~ *of nature* 自然现象。*social* ~ 社会现象。*an infant* ~ 神童。

phe·no·thi·a·zine [ˌfiːnəuˈθaiəziːn; ˏfinoˋθaɪəzin] ***n*.**【化】吩噻嗪,夹硫氮杂蒽。

phe·no·type [ˈfiːnətaip; ˋfinəˏtaɪp] ***n*.**【生】**1.** 表现型,表型。**2.** 具有共同表型的一类有机物。

phe·nox·ide [fiˈnɔksaid; fɪˋnɑksaɪd] ***n*.**【化】(苯)酚盐,苯氧化物;石炭酸盐(=phenate)。

phe·nox·y [fiˈnɔksi; fɪˋnɑksɪ] ***a*.**【化】(含)苯氧基的。

phe·n·yl(e) [ˈfenəl, ˈfiːnəl, ˈfiːnil; ˋfɛnəl, ˋfinəl, ˋfinəl] ***n*.**【化】苯基。

phen·yl·al·a·nine [ˌfenəlˈælənin; ˏfɛnəlˋælənɪn] ***n*.**【化】苯基丙胺酸。

phen·yl·am·ine [ˌfenələˈmiːn, -ˈæmiːn; ˏfɛnələˋmin, -ˋæmin] ***n*.**【化】苯胺(=aniline)。

phen·yl·bu·ta·zone [ˌfenəlˈbjuːtəzəun; ˏfɛnəlˋbjutəzon] ***n*.**【化】苯乙丁氮酮。

phen·yl·ene [ˈfenəliːn; ˋfɛnəlin] ***n*.**【化】苯撑,次苯基。

phen·yl·ke·to·nu·ri·a [ˌfenəlˌkiːtəˈnjuəriə, ˌfiːnil-; ˏfɛnlˏkitəˋnjʊrɪə, ˏfinəl-] ***n*.**【医】苯酮尿。**-nu·ric** ***a*.**

phew [fjuː; fju, pfju] **I** ***int*.** 唷! 呸! 啐!〔表示焦躁、惊讶、嫌厌、松一口气等〕。**II** ***vt*.** 咂(舌)。

phi [fai; faɪ] ***n*.** 希腊字母表的第二十一字母〔Φ, φ 和英语 ph 相当〕;=500。***Phi Beta Kappa***〔美〕**1.** ΦBK 联谊会〔美国大学优秀生的荣誉组织〕。**2.** ΦBK 联谊会会员。***Phi Bete*** [beit; bet] = *Phi Beta Kappa*. ***Phi Bete house***〔美俚〕大学图书馆。

phi·al [ˈfaiəl; ˋfaɪəl] ***n*.** 小玻璃瓶;药瓶。

phi·bete [ˈfaibeit; ˋfaɪbet] **I** ***n*.**〔美〕Phi Beta Kappa 联谊会会员。**II** ***vi*.** 用功。

Phil [fil; fɪl] ***n*.** 菲尔〔男子名, Phil(l)ip 的昵称〕。

Phil. =**1.** Philadelphia. **2.** Philemon. **3.** Philip. **4.** Philippians 腓利比人。**5.** Philippine.

phil. =**1.** philology. **2.** philosophical. **3.** philosophy.

phil- *comb*. *f*.〔用于元[母]音前〕=philo-.

-phil(e) *suf*. **1.** 形容词后缀[词尾],表示"对…有好意"、"爱好"、"亲": Russo*phil*(*e*). **2.** 名词后缀[词尾],表示"对…有好意者"、"爱好…者": biblio*phil*(*e*).

Phila. =Philadelphia.

Phila·del·phia [ˌfiləˈdelfjə; ˏfɪləˋdɛlfjə] ***n*.** 费拉德尔菲亚〔即费城,美国宾夕法尼亚州东南部港市〕。*a* ~ ***lawyer***〔美俚〕有手腕的律师;精明的人。

phil·a·del·phus [ˌfiləˈdelfəs; ˏfɪləˋdɛlfəs] ***n*.**【植】山梅

花属植物(=mock orange)。

phi·lan·der [fiˈlændə; fəˈlændɚ] *vi*. **1**. 调戏女人,追逐女性。**2**. 玩弄(*with*)。~ *off* (男女二人)私奔。**-er** *n*. 追逐[玩弄]女性者。

phil·an·thrope [ˈfilənθrəup; ˋfɪlənθrop] *n*. 〔古〕= philanthropist.

phi·lan·throp·ic, phi·lan·throp·i·cal [ˌfilənˈθrɔpik, -ikəl; ˏfɪlənˋθrɑpɪk, -ɪkəl] *a*. **1**. 博爱的,仁爱的。**2**. 慈善的;慈善事业的。**-throp·i·cal·ly** *ad*.

phi·lan·thro·pism [fiˈlænθrəpizəm; fɪˋlænθrəpɪzm̩] *n*. 博爱主义,仁爱(= philanthropy)。**-thro·pist** *n*. 博爱主义者;慈善家。

phi·lan·thro·pize [fiˈlænθrəpaiz; fɪˋlænθrəˏpaɪz] *vt*. 使有善心;使行善。—*vi*. 行善,从事慈善事业。

phi·lan·thro·poid [fiˈlænθrəpɔid; fɪˋlænθrəpɔɪd] *n*. 〔口〕慈善基金会理事[董事]。

phi·lan·thro·py [fiˈlænθrəpi; fəˋlænθrəpɪ] *n*. **1**. 博爱(主义),慈善,善心。**2**. 〔常 *pl*.〕慈善(事业、行为、团体)。

phil·a·tel·ic, phil·a·tel·i·cal [ˌfiləˈtelik, -ikəl; ˏfɪləˋtɛlɪk, -ɪkəl] *a*. 集邮的。**-tel·i·cal·ly** *ad*.

phi·lat·e·list [fiˈlætəlist; fəˋlætl̩ɪst] *n*. 集邮者,集邮家。

phi·lat·e·ly [fiˈlætəli; fəˋlætl̩ɪ] *n*. 集邮。

-phile *suf*. = -phil.

phil·har·mon·ic [ˌfilɑːˈmɔnik, ˌfilhɑːˈm-; ˏfɪləˋmɑnɪk, ˏfɪlhɑrˋm-] **I** *a*. **1**. 欢喜音乐的。**2**. 交响乐团的,音乐团体的[多用做音乐协会、乐团等名称]。**II** *n*. **1**. 〔古〕爱音乐的人。**2**. 〔P-〕交响乐团;(交响乐团主持的)管弦乐队。**3**. (交响乐团主办的)音乐会。*the Vienna P-* 维也纳交响乐团。

phil·hel·lene, phil·hel·len·ist [ˈfilheliːn, Am. filˈhelinist; ˋfɪlhɛlin, fɪlˋhɛlənɪst] *n*. 爱希腊的人,希腊之友;(十九世纪)赞成希腊独立运动的人。

phil·hel·le·nic [ˌfilheˈliːnik; ˏfɪlhəˋlɛnɪk] *a*. 爱希腊的,亲希腊的。

phil·hel·len·ism [filˈhelinizəm; fɪlˋhɛlənɪzm̩] *n*. 爱希腊,亲希腊;希腊独立主义。

Phil. I(s). = Philippine Islands.

Phil·(l)ip [ˈfilip; ˋfɪləp] *n*. 菲利普[男子名]。***appeal from*** ~ ***drunk to*** ~ ***sober*** 请求复审[因初审在某种影响下不够郑重,故请求复审]。

Phi·lip·pi [fiˈlipai; fəˋlɪpaɪ] *n*. 腓利比[古代马其顿王菲利浦二世所建的城市,公元前 42 年安东尼、屋大维联军在此战败布鲁图等]。***meet at*** ~ 恪守危险的相会信约。***Thou shalt see me at*** ~. 等着瞧吧!〔我就要报仇雪耻了〕。

Phi·lip·pic [fiˈlipik; fəˋlɪpɪk] *n*. **1**. 〔常 *pl*.〕《斥菲利浦篇》〔古希腊德摩斯梯尼(Demosthenes)痛骂马其顿国王菲利浦二世的十二篇著名演说之一〕;《斥安东尼篇》〔古罗马西塞罗(Cicero)抨击安东尼的演说之一〕。**2**. 〔p-〕猛烈的抨击演说,痛骂,痛斥。

Phil·ip·pine [ˈfilipiːn; ˋfɪləˏpin] *n*. 菲律宾(人)的。~ **Islands** 菲律宾群岛〔亚洲〕。

Phil·ip·pine, -pin·a [ˈfilipiːn, -nə; ˋfɪləpin, -nə] *n*. **1**. 有双核的坚果〔胡桃等〕。**2**. (二人分双核果的)核果联谊游戏[习俗];玩双核果游戏的罚物〔通常多为赠品〕。

Phil·ip·pines [ˈfilipiːnz, -painz; ˋfɪləˏpinz, -paɪnz] *n*. 〔the ~〕**1**. 菲律宾群岛(= the Philippine Islands)。**2**. 菲律宾〔亚洲〕。

Phil·(l)ips [ˈfilips; ˋfɪləps] *n*. 菲利普斯〔姓氏〕。

Phil·is·tine [ˈfilistain; fəˋlɪstɪn] **I** *n*. **1**. 腓力斯人〔巴勒斯坦西南岸古国菲力斯的居民〕。**2**. 〔p-〕市侩,庸人〔指心地狭窄的实利主义者;没有教养,不懂文学、艺术的低级趣味者〕。**3**. 〔p-〕〔谑〕仇敌〔常指司法官、批评家等〕。**4**. 〔p-〕(某科知识的)门外汉;〔德国学生语〕没有进大学的人。***fall among ~s*** 大吃苦头,虎落平阳被犬欺。**II** *a*. **1**. 腓力斯人的。**2**. 〔p-〕市侩的,庸俗的;没有文化教养的;实利主义的。~ *tastes* 低级趣味。

Phil·is·tin·ism [ˈfilistinizəm, fiˈlis-; ˋfɪləstɪnɪzəm, fəˋlɪs-] *n*. **1**. 腓力斯人的风习。**2**. 〔p-〕庸人习气,市侩习性[作风];庸俗,无教养;偏狭;实利主义。*free from the slightest trace of* ~ 丝毫没有庸人习气。

Phil·lis [ˈfilis; ˋfɪlɪs] *n*. = Phyllis.

Phil·lpotts [ˈfilpɔts; ˋfɪlpɑts] *n*. 菲尔波茨〔姓氏〕。

Phil·ly [ˈfili; ˋfɪlɪ] *n*. 〔美〕费城〔Philadelphia 市的俗称〕。

philo- *comb*. *f*. 表示"爱,喜": *philo*biblic.

phil·o·bib·lic [ˌfiləˈbiblik; ˏfɪləˋbɪblɪk] *a*. **1**. 爱书的,有爱书癖的。**2**. 爱文学的。**3**. 埋头研究《圣经》的。

phil·o·den·dron [ˌfiləˈdendrən; ˏfɪləˋdɛndrən] *n*. **1**. 【植】喜林芋属(*Philodendron*)植物〔热带美洲植物〕。**2**. 任何与上述相似的植物〔广义〕。

phi·log·y·ny [fiˈlɔdʒini; fɪˋlɑdʒənɪ] *n*. 对女人的爱好,女性崇拜(*opp*. misogyny)。**-y·nous** [-nəs; -nəs] *a*. **-y·nist** *n*. 爱好[崇拜]女人的人。

philol. = philological; philology.

phi·lol·o·ger [fiˈlɔlədʒə; fɪˋlɑlədʒɚ] *n*. 语文[语言]学家。

phil·o·log·ic, phil·o·log·i·cal [ˌfiləˈlɔdʒik, -ikəl; ˏfɪləˋlɑdʒɪk, -ɪkəl] *a*. 语文[语言]学(上)的。**-i·cal·ly** *ad*.

phi·lol·o·gist [fiˈlɔlədʒist; fɪˋlɑlədʒɪst] *n*. 语文学家,语言学家。

phi·lol·o·gize [fiˈlɔlədʒaiz; fɪˋlɑləˏdʒaɪz] *vi*. 研究语文[语言]学;从语文[语言]学上论述[考察]。

phi·lol·o·gy [fiˈlɔlədʒi; fɪˋlɑlədʒɪ] *n*. **1**. 语文学;语文文献学。**2**. 语言学;历史比较语言学。**3**. 〔罕〕爱学问,爱文学。*comparative* ~ 比较语言[语文]学。

phil·o·math [ˈfiləmæθ; ˋfɪləmæθ] *n*. 爱学问〔尤指数学〕的人。

phil·o·mel [ˈfiləmel; ˋfɪləˏmɛl] *n*. 〔诗〕夜莺(= nightingale)。

Phil·o·me·la [ˌfiləuˈmiːlə; ˏfɪləˋmilə] *n*. **1**. 【希神】菲洛米拉〔雅典王 Pandion 的女儿,被神化身成夜莺〕。**2**. 〔p-〕= philomel.

phil·o·pe·na [ˌfiləˈpiːnə; ˏfɪləˋpinə] *n*. = philippine.

phil·o·pro·gen·i·tive [ˌfiləprəuˈdʒenitiv; ˏfɪlәprəˋdʒɛnətɪv] *a*. **1**. 爱子女的。**2**. 多子女的。

philos. = **1**. philosopher. **2**. philosophical. **3**. philosophy.

phi·los·o·phas·ter [fiˌlɔsəˈfæstə; fɪˏlɑsəˋfæstɚ] *n*. 假哲学家;半瓶醋哲学家。

phi·los·o·pher [fiˈlɔsəfə; fəˋlɑsəfɚ] *n*. **1**. 哲学家,哲人;贤人。**2**. 思想家,学者。**3**. 达观者,逆来顺受者。**4**. 爱卖弄大道理者。**5**. 〔古〕炼金术士。*a moral* ~ 伦理学家。*a natural* ~ 自然哲学家;物理学家。***~'s stone*** (空想中的)点金石。***take things like a*** ~ 达观世事。***You are a*** ~. 你真了不起,你真想得开。

phil·o·soph·ic, phil·o·soph·i·cal [ˌfiləˈsɔfik, -kəl; ˏfɪləˋsɑfɪk, -kəl] *a*. **1**. 哲学(家)的,哲学上的;富于哲理性的。**2**. 通哲学的;贤明的。**3**. 沉着的,冷静的;达观的,逆来顺受的。**4**. 〔古〕物理学上的。*the American Philosophical Society* 美国科学研究会。*the Philosophical Transactions* 英国皇家学会(*Royal Society*)会报。**-i·cal·ly** *ad*. **1**. 在哲学上。**2**. 贤明;镇定自若,达观。

phi·los·o·phism [fiˈlɔsəfizəm; fəˋlɑsəfɪzm̩] *n*. 伪哲学;诡辩。

phi·los·o·phist [fiˈlɔsəfist; fɪˋlɑsəfɪst] *n*. 伪哲学家;诡辩家。

phi·los·o·phize [fiˈlɔsəfaiz; fəˋlɑsəˏfaɪz] *vi*. **1**. 用哲学家的态度研究;用哲理推究,思索。**2**. 从事肤浅的说理,爱卖弄大道理。—*vt*. **1**. 使哲学化,使理论化。**2**. (用理论从哲学上)说明。

P

phi·los·o·phiz·er [fiˈlɔsəfaizə; fəˋlɑsəfaɪzɚ] *n*. **1.** 哲理家。**2.** 卖弄大道理的人。

phi·los·o·phy [fiˈlɔsəfi; fəˋlɑsəfɪ] *n*. **1.** 哲学;哲理,哲学体系。**2.** 世界观,人生观;宗旨。**3.** (某一门学科的)基本原理。**4.** 哲学家的态度,达观,泰然自若;悟道,大悟。**5.** (除医学、法律、神学外的)所有学科;〔古〕中世纪大学的高等学术。*Marxist* ~ *of dialectical materialism* 马克思主义的唯物辩证论哲学。*critical* ~ 批判哲学。*positive* ~ 实证哲学。*first* ~ (亚里士多德的)第一哲学,本体论,实体论。*mental* ~ 心理学〔现在用 psychology〕。*metaphysical* ~ 形而上学。*moral* ~ 伦理学〔现在用 ethics〕。*natural* ~ 〔古〕自然科学〔现在用 science〕,物理学〔现在用 physics〕。*the three philosophies* 物理学,伦理学,哲学。*the* ~ *of grammar* 语法原理。*use* ~ 彻悟,看破;采取哲人的态度〔指临危不惧,达观等〕。

phi·lo·tech·nic, phi·lo·tech·ni·cal [ˌfiləˈteknik, -ikəl; ˏfɪləˋtɛknɪk, -ɪkəl] *a*. 爱好工艺的。

Phil. Soc. = Philological Society.

phil·tre, phil·ter [ˈfiltə; ˋfɪltɚ] **I** *n*. **1.** 媚药,春药;有魔力的药。**2.** 诱淫巫术。**II** *vt*. **1.** 用春药迷住。**2.** 用诱淫巫术蛊惑。

phil·trum [ˈfiltrəm; ˋfɪltrəm] *n*. (*pl*. ***-tra*** [-trə; -trə]) *n*.【解】人中〔鼻唇间纵沟〕。

phi·mo·sis [faiˈməusis; faɪˋmosɪs] *n*. (*pl*. ***-ses*** [-siːz; -siz])【医】包茎。**phi·mot·ic** [-ˈmɔtik; -ˋmɑtɪk] *a*.

phiz [fiz; fɪz] *n*. 〔俚〕脸,面孔 (= physiognomy)。~ **snapper** 〔美俚〕照相师。

phle·bi·tis [fliˈbaitis; flɪˋbaɪtɪs] *n*.【医】静脉炎。

phleb·o·lite [ˈflebəlait; ˋflɛbəlaɪt] *n*.【医】静脉石。

phleb·o·lith [ˈflebəliθ; ˋflɛbəlɪθ] *n*. = phlebolite.

phle·bol·o·gy [fliˈbɔlədʒi; flɪˋbɑlədʒɪ] *n*.【医】静脉学,静脉论。

phleb·o·scle·ro·sis [ˌfləbəuskliəˈrəusis; ˏflɛbosklɪˋrosɪs] *n*.【医】静脉硬化。

phle·bot·o·mist [fliˈbɔtəmist; flɪˋbɑtəmɪst] *n*. **1.** 用静脉切开放血术治病的医师。**2.** 相信静脉切开术的人。

phle·bot·o·mize [fliˈbɔtəmaiz; flɪˋbɑtəˏmaɪz] *vt*., *vi*. (使)放血。

phle·bot·o·my [fliˈbɔtəmi; flɪˋbɑtəmɪ] *n*.【医】放血,静脉切开放血术。

phlegm [flem; flɛm] *n*. **1.** 痰。**2.** 〔古〕黏液〔古代生理学所称四种体液之一,认为此种体液型的人多迟钝〕。**3.** 冷淡;不动感情;迟钝。

phleg·mat·ic, phleg·mat·i·cal [flegˈmætik, -ikəl; flɛgˋmætɪk, -ɪkəl] *a*. **1.** (古代生理学所称)黏液质的。**2.** 迟钝的;冷淡的;不动感情的。**3.** 痰多的。*a* ~ *temperament* 迟钝的气质。**-mat·i·cal·ly** *ad*.

phleg·mon [ˈflegmən; ˋflɛgmɑn] *n*.【医】脓性蜂窝织炎。

phlegm·y [ˈflemi; ˋflɛmɪ] *a*. 痰似的;含痰的。

phlo·em [ˈfləuem; ˋfloɛm] *n*.【植】韧皮部。

phlo·gis·tic [flɔˈdʒistik; floˋdʒɪstɪk] *a*. **1.** (古代化学所说)燃素的,热素的。**2.**【医】炎的;炎症的;炎性的。

phlo·gis·ton [flɔˈdʒistən; floˋdʒɪstən] *n*. (古代化学认为可燃物中存在的)燃素,热素。

phlog·o·pite [ˈflɔgəpait; ˋflɑgəpaɪt] *n*.【化】金云母。

phlo·rhi·zin [fləˈrizin; fləˋrɪzɪn] *n*. = phlorizin.

phlo·rid·zin [fləˈrizin; fləˋrɪdzɪn] *n*. = phlorizin.

phlor·i·zin [ˈflɔːrizin, fləˈraizin; ˋflɑrɪzɪn, fləˋraɪzɪn] *n*.【化】根皮甙。

phlox [flɔks; flɑks] *n*. **1.**【植】福禄考。**2.** 〔P-〕【植】福禄考属。

phlyc·te·na [flikˈtiːnə; flɪkˋtinə] *n*. (*pl*. ***-nae*** [-niː, -ni])【医】水泡;小泡。**-nar** *a*.

phlyc·ten·ule [flikˈtenjul; flɪkˋtɛnjul] *n*.【医】小水泡。**-ten·u·lar** *a*.

Phnom Penh, Phom Penh, Pnom-Penh [ˈnɔmˈpen, pəˈnɔːmˈpen; ˋnɑmpen, pənɑmˋpɛn] 金边〔柬埔寨首都〕。

-phobe *comb. f*. 恐惧…的人,反对…的人,嫌〔厌〕恶…的人:hydro*phobe*; Germano*phobe*.

-phobia *comb. f*. = -phobe 对…的恐惧〔嫌恶〕: hydro*phobia*; Anglo*phobia*.

pho·bi·a [ˈfəubjə; ˋfobɪə] *n*. (病态的)恐惧,憎恶。

pho·bic [ˈfəubik; ˋfobɪk] *a*. **1.** (有关)病态性恐惧〔憎恶〕的。**2.** 畏缩的,怕招惹是非的。

pho·cine [ˈfəusain; ˋfosaɪn] *a*.【动】海豹的;似海豹的。

pho·co·me·li·a [ˌfəukəuˈmiːliə, -ˈmiːljə; ˏfokəˋmilɪə, -ˋmiljə] *n*.【医】短肢畸胎。**-me·lic** [-ˈmiːlik; -ˋmilɪk] *a*.

Phoe·be [ˈfiːbi; ˋfibɪ] *n*. **1.** 菲比〔女子名〕。**2.**【希神】月亮女神 (= Artemis)。**3.** 〔诗〕月亮。**4.** 〔p-〕〔美俚〕(骰子的)对五点,对梅花 (= little P-)。**5.**【天】土卫 10。

phoe·be [ˈfiːbi; ˋfibɪ] *n*.【动】(北美洲产)绯鹟。

Phoe·bus [ˈfiːbəs; ˋfibəs] *n*. **1.**【希神】太阳神 (= Apollo)。**2.** 〔诗〕太阳。**Phoe·be·an** [ˈfiːbiən; ˋfibɪən] *a*.

Phoe·ni·ci·a [fiˈniʃiə, -ʃjə; fəˋnɪʃɪə, -ʃjə] *n*. 腓尼基〔地中海东岸的古国〕。

Phoe·ni·ci·an [fiˈniʃiən; fəˋnɪʃən] **I** *a*. 腓尼基(人)的;腓尼基语的。**II** *n*. **1.** 腓尼基人。**2.** 腓尼基语。

Phoe·nix [ˈfiːniks; ˋfinɪks] *n*. 菲尼克斯〔美国 Arizona 州首府〕。

phoe·nix [ˈfiːniks; ˋfinɪks] *n*. **1.**【埃神】不死鸟,长生鸟〔相传此鸟每五百年自焚后再生〕;毁灭后会再生的事物;不死的象征。**2.** (中国古代传说中的)凤凰。**3.** 伟大天才,绝代佳人,一代尤物;完人,殊品。**4.** 〔the P-〕【天】凤凰座。**5.**【植】海枣;〔P-〕海枣属。*the Chinese* ~ 凤凰。~ **heart** 人工心脏。~ **syndrome** (公司的)起死回生〔公司破产后董事会原班人马立即组成新公司,以求摆脱原公司债务而继续经营〕。~ **tree** 梧桐。

phon [fɔn; fɑn] *n*.【物】方〔响度单位〕。

phon- *comb. f*. 〔用于元音前〕声,音:*phon*ic.

phon. = phonetics.

pho·nate [fəuˈneit, ˈfəuneit; foˋnet, ˋfonet] *vt*., *vi*. 发(音);发成(声音)。**pho·na·tion** [fəuˈneiʃən; foˋneʃən] *n*.

pho·nau·to·graph [fəuˈnɔːtəgrɑːf; fonˋɔtəˏgræf] *n*.【物】声波记振仪;声波震动记录[图表]。

phone[1] [fəun; fon] **I** *n*. 〔口〕电话;电话机〔telephone 之略〕。*hang up the* ~ 挂起电话(机)。*A* ~ *for you*. 你有一个电话。*Some one wants you on the* ~. 有人打电话给你,有人叫你接电话。*Please call him to the* ~. 请他来接电话。**II** *vt*. **1.** 〔口〕给…打电话。**2.** 打电话通知(某事)。—*vi*. 〔口〕打电话 (*to*)。~ **up** 打电话叫人。~ **book** 电话簿。~(-)**card** 电话磁卡。~ **freak** [**phreak**] (使用电子设备)偷漏电话费的人。~ **meter** 电话计数器。~ **porn**, ~ **sex** 〔口〕(需付高额费用的)色情电话热线。~ **tree** 电话树〔由一人打电话给多人的一种联络方法〕。

phone[2] [fəun; fon] *n*.【语音】单音,音素〔元音[母音]或辅音[子音]〕。*a* ~ *chart* 语音表,音素表。**pho·ne·matic** [ˌfəuni(ː)ˈmætik; ˏfonəˋmætɪk] *a*. 音素的。

-phone *comb. f*. 声音,说话: tele*phone*, micro*phone*.

pho·neme [ˈfəuniːm; ˋfonim] *n*. **1.**【语音】音素〔如 kiːp; kip (keep), kuːl; kul (cool), kɔːl; kɔl (call) 中的 k 音〕。**2.** 音,单音。

phone·me·ter [ˈfəunmiːtə; ˋfonmətɚ] *n*. (电话的)通话计数器 (= phone meter)。

pho·ne·mic [fəuˈniːmik; foˋnimɪk] *a*. **1.** 音素的;有音素特征的;以音素为根据的。**2.** 音素学的。

pho·ne·mi·cist [fəuˈniːmisist; foˋniməsɪst] *n*. 音素学家。

pho·ne·mi·cize [fəˈniːmisaiz; fəˋniməˏsaɪz] *vt*. (***-cized***; ***-ciz·ing***) 用音素符号写出[表示]。**-mi·ci·za·tion**

n. 音素化。

pho·ne·mics [fəuˈniːmiks; foˋnimɪks] *n*. 〔*pl*.〕〔用作单〕【语音】音素学。

pho·nen·do·scope [fəˈnendəuskəup; fəˋnɛndə͵skop] *n*. 扩音听诊器。

pho·net·ic [fəuˈnetik; foˋnɛtɪk] *a*. **1**. 语音(上)的;语音学的。**2**. 表示语音的;音形一致的。*international* ~ *alphabet* 国际音标。~ **notation** 标音法。~ **signs** [**symbols**] 音标,音符。~ **transcription** 标音(法)。~ **typewriter** 口授打字机,语音打字机。~ **value** 音值。

pho·net·i·cal·ly [fəˈnetikəli; fəˋnɛtɪkəlɪ] *ad*. 根据语音;在语音上;语音学上。

pho·ne·ti·cian [͵fəuniˈtiʃən; ͵fonəˋtɪʃən] *n*. 语音学家,语音学研究者。

pho·net·i·cism [fəuˈnetisizəm; fəˋnɛtəsɪzm] *n*. 音标标音法;音标拼字法[主义]。**-i·cist** *n*. 语音学家;主张按照发音拼字的人。

pho·net·i·cize [fəuˈnetisaiz; foˋnɛtɪsaɪz] *vt*. 用音标表(音),用发音符号写。

pho·net·ics [fəuˈnetiks; foˋnɛtɪks] *n*. 〔*pl*.〕〔用作单〕语音学,发音学。

pho·net·ist [ˈfəunitist; ˋfonətɪst] *n*. **1**. 语音学家,发音学家。**2**. 主张按照发音拼字的人(= phoneticist)。

phone·vi·sion [ˈfəun͵viʒən; ˋfon͵vɪʒən] *n*.【讯】电话电视〔一种收费制电视〕;(能见到对方影像的)电视电话。

pho·ney, pho·ny [ˈfəuni; ˋfonɪ] **I** *n*. 〔美俚〕**1**. 骗子;冒名顶替的人。**2**. 假货。**II** *a*. **1**. 假的,伪造的,不值钱的。**2**. 假冒的。*a* ~ *writer* 空头文学家。*a* ~ *rap* 〔美俚〕诬告。~ **man** 卖假宝石的人。**phon·i·ly** *ad*. 虚假地。**phon·i·ness** *n*. 虚假。

pho·nic [ˈfəunik, ˈfɔnik; ˋfonɪk, ˋfɑnɪk] *a*. **1**. 音的,声音的;语音的。**2**. 有声的,浊音的。*a* ~ *symbol* 音符。

pho·nics [ˈfəuniks; ˋfɑnɪks] *n*. 〔*pl*.〕〔用作单〕**1**. 声学。**2**. (以发音为重点的)基础语音教授法,发音练习。**3**. 〔罕〕= phonetics.

pho·no [ˈfəunəu; ˋfono] *n*. (*pl*. ~*s*)〔口〕= phonograph.

phono- *comb*. *f*. 〔用于辅[子]音前〕= phon-: *phono*film, *phono*gram.

pho·no·chem·is·try [ˈfəunəuˈkemistri; ͵fonoˋkɛmɪstrɪ] *n*.【化】声化学。

pho·no·deik [ˈfəunədaik; ˋfonə͵daɪk] *n*.【物】声波显示仪。

pho·no·film [ˈfəunəfilm; ˋfonə͵fɪlm] *n*. 有声电影。

pho·no·gram [ˈfəunəgræm; ˋfonə͵græm] *n*. **1**. (速记用的)表音符号;标音符号。**2**. (留声机的)唱片;【影】声带,录音片。**3**.【讯】话传电报,电话电报。

pho·no·graph [ˈfəunəgrɑːf; ˋfonə͵græf] **I** *n*. **1**. 老式留声机;机械录音机;〔美〕留声机,唱机。**2**. 〔罕〕表音字,音标字。**II** *vt*. 使灌音[录音]。~ *needle* 唱针。~ **record** 唱片。**-er** *n*. 表音速记法专家。

pho·no·graph·ic [͵fəunəˈgræfik; ͵fonəˋgræfɪk] *a*. **1**. 留声机的,唱机的。**2**. 表音的,表音速记法的。**-graph·i·cal·ly** *ad*.

pho·nog·ra·phy [fəuˈnɔgrəfi; foˋnɑgrəfɪ] *n*. **1**. 表音法。**2**. 表音速记法;速记法。

pho·no·lite [ˈfəunəlait; ˋfonə͵laɪt] *n*.【矿】响石;响岩。

pho·no·log·ic, pho·no·log·i·cal [͵fəunəˈlɔdʒik, -kəl; ͵fonəˋlɑdʒɪk, -kəl] *a*. **1**. 语音的;音位学的;音韵学的。**2**. 按照音位[音韵]学原理的。

pho·nol·o·gy [fəuˈnɔlədʒi; foˋnɑlədʒɪ] *n*. **1**. 音位学;音韵学。**2**. 语音学〔主指语音的历史研究〕。**-gist** *n*. 音位学家;音韵学家。

pho·no·ma·ni·a [͵fəunəˈmeiniə; ͵fonəˋmenɪə] *n*. 嗜杀狂;嗜害狂。

pho·nom·e·ter [fəuˈnɔmitə; foˋnɑmətɚ] *n*. 声强计,音强度计,测音计。

pho·no·mo·tor [͵fəunəˈməutə; ͵fonəˋmotɚ] *n*. (电唱机或录音机上的)电动机。

pho·non [ˈfəunɔn; ˋfonɑn] *n*.【物】声子〔晶体点阵振动能的量子〕。

pho·no·phore [ˈfəunəufɔ; ˋfonə͵for] *n*. (电)报(电)话两用机。

pho·no·phote [ˈfəunəufəut; ˋfonə͵fot] *n*. (把音波变成光波的)音波发光机。

pho·no·pore [ˈfəunəupɔː; ˋfonə͵por] *n*. = phonophore.

pho·no·re·cord [ˈfəunəu͵rekɔːd; ˋfonə͵rɛkərd] *n*. 唱片(= phonograph record)。

pho·no·scope [ˈfəunəuskəup; ˋfonə͵skop] *n*.【物】检弦器,验声器;微音器;乐音自记器。

pho·no·type [ˈfəunəutaip; ˋfonə͵taɪp] *n*. 音标铅字(体)。**-no·typ·y** [-i; -ɪ] *n*. 表音印刷法[速记法]。

pho·no·vi·sion [ˈfəunə͵viʒən; ˋfonə͵vɪʒən] *n*. = phonevision.

pho·ny [ˈfəuni; ˋfonɪ] *a*., *n*. 〔美俚〕= phoney.

phoo·ie, phoo·ey [ˈfuːi; ˋfuɪ] *int*. 〔美〕呸! 啐! 〔表示讨厌或不信〕。

-phore *comb*. *f*. 表示"带者,结者,运者": sema*phore*.

pho·re·sis [fəuˈriːsis; foˋrisɪs] *n*. 电泳现象(= cataphoresis)。

phor·mi·um [ˈfɔːmiəm; ˋfɔrmɪəm] *n*.【植】新西兰亚麻。

pho·ro·nid [fəˈrəunid; fəˋronɪd] **I** *n*. 帚虫纲(*Phoronidea*)动物。**II** *a*.【动】帚虫纲的。

pho·ro·nom·ics [͵fɔrəˈnɔmiks; ͵fɑrəˋnɑmɪks] *n*. 〔罕〕动学。

phos·gene [ˈfɔzdʒiːn; ˋfɑsdʒin] *n*.【化】光气,碳醯氯;【军】毒气(= ~gas)。~**bomb** 光气弹。

phos·gen·ite [ˈfɔzdʒinait; ˋfɑzdʒɪnaɪt] *n*.【矿】角铅矿。

phosph- *comb*. *f*. 〔用于元音前〕= phospho-: *phosph*amide.

phos·pha·mide [ˈfɔsfəmaid; ˋfɑsfəmaɪd] *n*.【化】磷醯胺。

phos·pha·tase [ˈfɔsfəteis; ˋfɑsfə͵tes] *n*.【生化】磷酸酶。

phos·pha·te [ˈfɔsfeit; ˋfɑsfet] *n*. **1**.【化】磷酸盐;磷酸酯;磷块石。**2**. (含有少量磷酸的)汽水。~ *fertilizer* 磷肥。*calcium* ~ 磷酸钙。~ *of soda* 磷酸钠。~ *rock* 磷酸盐岩。

phos·phat·ic [fɔsˈfætik; fɑsˋfætɪk] *a*.【化】(含)磷酸(盐)的。*a* ~ *deposit* 含磷沉淀物。~ *manure* 磷肥。

phos·pha·tide, phos·pha·tid [ˈfɔsfətaid, -tid; ˋfɑsfətaɪd, -tɪd] *n*.【化】磷脂。

phos·pha·tize [ˈfɔsfətaiz; ˋfɑsfə͵taɪz] *vt*. **1**. 使变成磷酸盐,用磷酸盐处理。**2**. 用磷酸处理。**-za·tion** *n*.

phos·pha·tu·ri·a [͵fɔsfəˈtjuəriə, -ˈtuər-; ͵fɑsfəˋtjʊrɪə, -ˋtʊə-] *n*.【医】磷酸盐尿。**-tu·ric** *a*.

phos·phene [ˈfɔsfiːn; ˋfɑsfin] *n*.【医】压眼闪光;光幻视。

phos·phide [ˈfɔsfaid; ˋfɑsfɪd] *n*.【化】磷化物。*hydrogen* ~ 磷化氢。

phos·phine [ˈfɔsfiːn; ˋfɑsfin] *n*.【化】**1**. 磷化氢;三氢化磷。**2**. 碱性染革黄棕。

phos·phite [ˈfɔsfait; ˋfɑsfaɪt] *n*.【化】亚磷酸盐。

phospho- *comb*. *f*. 表示"磷": *phospho*nic.

phos·pho·cre·a·tine [͵fɔsfəuˈkriətiːn, -tin; ͵fɑsfoˋkriətin, -tɪn] *n*.【化】磷(酸基)肌酸。

phos·pho·lip·id [͵fɔsfəuˈlipid; ͵fɑsfəˋlɪpɪd] *n*.【化】磷脂(= phosphatide, phospholipide)。

phos·pho·nic [fɔsˈfɔnik; fɑsˋfɑnɪk] *n*.【化】磷(酸)的。

phos·pho·ni·um [fɔsˈfəuniəm; fɑsˋfonɪəm] *n*.【化】磷(根)。

phos·pho·pro·tein [͵fɔsfəuˈprəutiːn, -tiːin; ͵fɑsfoˋprotin, -tiɪn] *n*.【化】磷朊,磷蛋白。

Phos·phor [ˈfɔsfə; ˋfɑsfɚ] *n*. 〔诗〕晓星,启明星,金星。

phos·phor [ˈfɔsfə; ˋfɑsfɚ] *n*. 黄磷;〔罕〕磷光体。~ **bronze** 磷青铜。~ **screen** 荧光屏。

P

phosphor- *comb. f.* 〔置于元[母]音前〕= phosphoro-.

phos·pho·rate [ˈfɔsfəreit;ˋfɑsfə͵ret] *vt.* 使和磷化合,给…加磷,使含磷。**-d** *a.* 含磷的。

phos·pho·resce [ˌfɔsfəˈres;͵fɑsfəˋrɛs] *vi.* 发磷光;磷似地发光;发磷火。

phos·pho·res·cence [ˌfɔsfəˈresns;͵fɑsfəˋrɛsns] *n.* **1.** 磷光(现象);磷光性;鬼火。**2.** 磷光器。

phos·pho·res·cent [ˌfɔsfɔˌresnt;͵fɑsfəˋrɛsnt] *a.* 发磷光的;磷光质的。

phos·pho·ret·ed, phos·pho·ret·ted [ˈfɔsfəretid;ˋfɑsfə͵rɛtɪd] *a.* **1.** 含(低)磷的。**2.** 与磷化合的(= phosphuret(t)ed)。

phos·phor·ic [ˈfɔsfɔrik;fɑsˋfɔrɪk] *a.* 磷的,含磷的;含有五价磷的;像磷的。~ **acid** 磷酸。

phos·pho·rism [ˈfɔsfərizəm;ˋfɑsfərɪzm̩] *n.* 慢性磷中毒。

phos·phor·ite [ˈfɔsfərait;ˋfɑsfə͵raɪt] *n.* **1.** 【化】亚磷脂肟酸。**2.** 【矿】磷灰岩,磷钙土。~ **rock** 【地】磷灰岩。

phosphoro- *comb. f.* 表示"磷,磷光,含磷的": *phosphoro*scope.

phos·phor·o·graph [ˈfɔsfərəugrɑːf, -græf;ˋfɑfərəgrɑf, -græf] *n.* 磷光画;磷光像。

phos·pho·rog·ra·phy [ˈfɔsfəˈrɔgrəfi;͵fɑsfəˋrɑgrəfɪ] *n.* 磷光画法;磷光像术。

phos·phor·ol·y·sis [ˌfɔsfəˈrɔlisis;͵fɑsfəˋrɑlɪsɪs] *n.* 【化】磷酸解(作用)。

phos·phor·o·scope [fɔsˈfɔːrəskəup, -ˈfɔr-; fɑsˋfɔrə͵skop, -ˋfɑr-] *n.* 【物】磷光镜。

phos·phor·ous [ˈfɔsfərəs;ˋfɑsfərəs] *a.* 磷的,亚磷的;含有三价磷的;含磷的。~ **acid** 亚磷酸。~**bomb** 含磷(燃烧)弹。~ **bronze** 磷青铜。~ **necrosis** 【医】磷毒性颌骨坏死。

phos·phor·us [ˈfɔsfərəs;ˋfɑsfərəs] *n.* **1.** 【化】磷。**2.** 磷光体 (= phosphor)。~ **necrosis** 【医】磷毒性颌骨坏死〔俗称 phossy jaw〕。~**pentoxide** 【化】五氧化二磷。

phos·pho·ryl·ase [ˈfɔsfəriˌleis, fɔsˈfɔːr-;ˋfɑsfərɪ͵les, fɑsˋfɔr-] *n.* 【生化】磷酸化酶。

phos·pho·ryl·ate [ˈfɔsfərileit;ˋfɑsfərə͵let] *vt.* 使磷酸化。**-ryl·ation** *n.* 磷酸化。

phos·phu·ret·(t)ed [ˈfɔsfjuretid;ˋfɑsfjə͵rɛtɪd] *a.* 【化】= phosphoret(t)ed.

phos·sy [ˈfɔsi;ˋfɑsɪ] *a.* 〔口〕磷的,磷毒性的。~ **jaw** 〔口〕磷毒性颌疽(= phosphorus necrosis)。

phot [fɔt, fəut;fɑt, fot] *n.* 【物】辐透,厘米烛光〔照明单位,=1 流明/厘米^2〕。

phot. = **1.** photograph. **2.** photographer. **3.** photographic. **4.** photography.

phot- *comb. f.* = photo.

pho·tic [ˈfəutik;ˋfotɪk] *a.* **1.** (关于)光的。**2.** (有机体)发光(性)的;靠发光(刺激)的。**3.** 透光的(尤指透日光);感光的;受光的。~ **driver** 强光防暴器〔用频频闪动的强光配合高音喇叭等驱散示威人群的一种防暴装置〕。**-s** *n.* 光学。

pho·tism [ˈfəutizəm;ˋfotɪzm̩] *n.* 【心】幻视;光幻觉;发光性。

pho·to [ˈfəutəu;ˋfoto] **I** *n.* (*pl.* ~*s*) 【口】照片 (= photograph)。~**(-)aging** 光照性皮肤老化〔长期日晒所致的皮炎〕。~**call** 〔美〕照像会议〔专为给著名人士或官员拍摄宣传照片而举行的会议〕。~**card** (印有合家欢相片和祝辞的)照片问候卡。~**finish** 〔美赛马〕(因到达终点时前后极接近,只能凭拍摄照片判断胜负的)照相终局;〔喻〕势均力敌的较量。~**Joe** 〔美空俚〕单座摄影飞机驾驶员。**II** *vt.* 〔口〕给…照相。

photo- *comb. f.* 表示"光;光电;照相(术)": *photo*chemistry, *photo*chrome, *photo*conduction.

pho·to·ac·tin·ic [ˌfəutəuækˈtinik;͵fotəækˋtɪnɪk] *a.* (发)光化射线的;能产生光化作用的。

pho·to·ac·ti·vate [ˌfəutəuˈæktiveit;͵fotəˋæktɪvet] *vt.* 【物】用光使敏化;【化】用光催化。**-ti·va·tion** *n.*

pho·to·ac·tive [ˌfəutəuˈæktiv;͵fotəˋæktɪv] *a.* 【物、化】光敏的。

pho·to·ac·tor [ˌfəutəuˈæktə;͵fotəˋæktɚ] *n.* 【无】光电变换元件。

pho·to·ad·sorp·tion [ˌfəutəuædˈsɔːpʃən;͵fotəædˋsɔrpʃən] *n.* 【物】光敏吸附。

pho·to·au·to·tro·phic [ˈfəutəuˌɔːtəˈtrɔfik;ˋfotə͵ɔtəˋtrɑfɪk] *a.* (指植物和某些微生物)光合自养的。

pho·to-beat [ˌfəutəuˈbiːt;͵fotəˋbit] *n.* 【物】光拍,光类差拍。

pho·to·bi·ot·ic [ˌfəutəubaiˈɔtik;͵fotobaɪˋɑtɪk] *a.* 【生】依光生存的。

pho·to·cat·a·list [ˌfəutəuˈkætəlist;͵fotoˋkætəlɪst] *n.* 【化】光催化剂。

pho·to·ca·tal·y·sis [ˌfəutəukəˈtælisis;͵fotokəˋtæləsɪs] *n.* 【化】光催化作用。

pho·to·cat·a·lyst [ˌfəutəuˈkætəlist;͵fotəˋkætəlɪst] *n.* 【化】光催化剂。

pho·to·cath·ode [ˌfəutəuˈkæθəud, ͵fotəˋkæθod] *n.* 【物】光阴极,光电阴极。

pho·to·cell [ˈfəutəsel;ˋfotə͵sɛl] *n.* 【物】光电管;光电池。

pho·to·ce·ram·ic [ˌfəutəusiˈræmik;͵fotəsɪˋræmɪk] *a.* 用照相图样装饰陶器的。**-s** *n.* 用照相图样装饰陶器的工艺。

pho·to·chart·ing [ˌfəutəuˈtʃɑːtiŋ;͵fotəˋtʃɑrtɪŋ] *n.* 摄影制图。

pho·to·chem·is·try [ˌfəutəuˈkemistri;͵fotəˋkɛmɪstrɪ] *n.* 光化学。**-chem·i·cal** *a.*

pho·to·chrome [ˈfəutəkrəum;ˋfotəkrom] *n.* 【摄】彩色照片。

pho·to·chro·mic [ˌfəutəuˈkrəumik;͵fotəˋkromɪk] *a.* 光致变色的,光色的。**-chro·mism** *n.* 光致变色现象。

pho·to·chro·my [ˈfəutəkrəumi;ˋfotə͵kromɪ] *n.* 【摄】彩色照相术。

pho·to·chron·o·graph [ˌfəutəuˈkrɔnəgrɑːf; ͵fotəˋkrɑnə͵græf] *n.* **1.** 活动物体照相机。**2.** 活动物体照片。**3.** 【天、物】活动物体照相计时仪。**4.** 【天】恒星中天摄影仪。**-y** [-krəˈnɔgrəfi;-krəˋnɑgrəfɪ] *n.* 活动物体照相术。

pho·to·ci·ne·sis [ˌfəutəusaiˈniːsis;͵fotəsaɪˋnisɪs] *n.* = photokinesis.

pho·to·co·ag·u·la·tion [ˌfəutəukəuˌægjuˈleiʃən;͵fotoko͵ægjəˋleʃən] *n.* 光致凝结〔利用激光等造成瘢组织,用以治疗目疾或实验〕。**-la·tor** *n.* 光致凝结器。

pho·to·com·pose [ˌfəutəukəmˈpəuz;͵fotokəmˋpoz] *vt.* 【印】照相排(版);照相排(字)。

pho·to·com·po·si·tion [ˌfəutəuˈkɔmpəˈziʃən;͵foto͵kɑmpəˋzɪʃən] *n.* 照相排版;照相排字。

pho·to·con [ˈfəutəkɔn;ˋfotəkɑn] *n.* 【无】光(电)导元件,光导器件。

pho·to·con·duc·tion [ˌfəutəukənˈdʌkʃən;͵fotokənˋdʌkʃən] *n.* 【物】光电导。

pho·to·con·duc·tive [ˌfəutəukənˈdʌktiv;͵fotokənˋdʌktɪv] *a.* 【物】光电导的。

pho·to·con·duc·tiv·i·ty [ˌfəutəukɔndʌkˈtiviti;͵foto͵kɑndʌkˋtɪvətɪ] *n.* 【物】光电导性。

pho·to·con·duc·tor [ˌfəutəukənˈdʌktə;͵fotokənˋdʌktɚ] *n.* 【物】光电导体。

pho·to·cop·i·er [ˌfəutəuˈkɔpiə;͵fotoˋkɑpɪɚ] *n.* 影印机。

pho·to·copy [ˈfəutəuˌkɔpi;ˋfotə͵kɑpɪ] **I** *n.* 影印本,照相复制本。**II** *vt.* 影印,照相复制。

pho·to·cur·rent [ˈfəutəuˌkʌrənt;ˋfoto͵kʌrənt] *n.* 【物】光电流。

pho·to·de·tec·tor [ˌfəutəudiˈtektə;͵fotodɪˋtɛktɚ] *n.*

【物】光电探测器。

pho·to·di·ode [ˌfəutəuˈdaiəud; ˏfotoˋdaɪod] *n*. 【无】光电二极管。

pho·to·dis·in·te·gra·tion [ˌfəutəudisˌintigˈreiʃən; ˏfotodɪsˏɪntəˋgreʃən] *n*. 【物】光致蜕变。

pho·to·dis·so·ci·a·tion [ˌfəutəudiˌsəusiˈeiʃən, -ʃiː-; ˏfotodɪˏsosəˋeʃən, -ʃi-] *n*. 1. 【化】光致离解。2. 【物】光致蜕变(= photodisintegration)。

pho·to·dra·ma [ˈfəutədrɑːmə; ˋfotəˏdrɑmə] *n*. 影片剧〔尤指悲剧或情节曲折紧张的故事影片〕。**pho·to·dra·mat·ic** [ˌfəutədrəˈmætik; ˏfotədrəˋmætɪk] *a*.

pho·to·dup·li·cate [ˌfəutəuˈdjuːplikeit; ˏfotoˋdjupləkɪt] I *vt*., *vi*. 照相复制。II [ˌfəutəuˈdjuːplikit; ˏfotoˋdjupləkɪt] *n*. 照相复制件。

pho·to·du·pli·ca·tion [ˌfəutəuˈdjuːpliˈkeiʃən; ˏfotoˏdjupləˋkeʃən] *n*. 照相复制术(= photocopy)。

pho·to·dy·nam·ic [fəutəudaiˈnæmik; fotodaɪˋnæmɪk] *a*. 光能作用的;光力学的。

pho·to·dy·nam·ics [ˌfəutəudaiˈnæmiks; ˏfotodaɪˋnæmɪks] *n*. 〔动词用单数〕1. (对植物的)光能作用。2. 光力学。

pho·to·e·las·tic [ˌfəutəuiˈlæstik; ˏfotoɪˋlæˋstɪk] *a*. 【物】光测弹性的。

pho·to·e·las·tic·i·ty [ˌfəutəuˌilæsˈtisiti; ˏfotoɪˏlæsˋtɪsətɪ] *n*. 光测弹性(学)。

pho·to·e·lec·tric, pho·to·e·lec·tri·cal [ˌfəutəuiˈlektrik, -trikəl; ˏfotoɪˋlɛktrɪk, -trɪkəl] *a*. 【物】光电的。~ **cell** 光电管;光电池。~ **colour analyzer** 光电析色器。~ **current** 光电流。~ **effect** 光电效应[作用]。~ **photometer** 光电光度计。

pho·to·e·lec·tric·i·ty [ˌfəutəuilekˈtrisiti; ˏfotoɪˏlɛkˋtrɪsətɪ] *n*. 【物】光电(学);光电现象。

pho·to·e·lec·tro·lu·mi·nes·cence [ˌfəutəuiˌlektrəˌljuːmiˈnesns; ˏfotoɪˏlɛktrəˏljumɪˋnɛsns] *n*. 【物】光电发光,光控场致发光。

pho·to·e·lec·tro·mo·tive [ˌfəutəuiˌlektrəˈməutiv; ˏfotoɪˏlɛktrəˋmotɪv] *a*. 【物】光电动的。~ **force** 光电动势。

pho·to·e·lec·tron [ˌfəutəuiˈlektrɔn; ˏfotoɪˋlɛktrɑn] *n*. 【物、化】光电子。

pho·to·e·lec·tron·ics [ˌfəutəuilekˈtrɔniks; ˏfotoɪlɛkˋtrɑnɪks] *n*. 〔*pl*.〕〔用作 sing.〕光电子学。

pho·to·el·e·ment [ˌfəutəuˈelimənt; ˏfotoˋɛlɪmənt] *n*. 【物】阻挡层光电池;光生伏打电池(= photovoltaic cell)。

pho·to·e·mis·sion [ˌfəutəuiˈmiʃən; ˏfotoɪˋmɪʃən] *n*. 【物】光电放射。**-to·e·mis·sive** [-ˈmisiv; -ˈmɪsɪv] *a*.

pho·to·en·grav·ing [ˌfəutəuinˈgreiviŋ; ˏfotoɪnˋgrevɪŋ] *n*. 【物】光刻;【印】照相凸版(制版术);照相感光制(凸)版。

pho·to-ex·cit·a·tion [ˌfəutəuˌeksiˈteiʃən; ˏfotəˏɛksɪˋteʃən] *n*. 【原】光致激发。

pho·to·fin·ish·ing [ˌfəutəuˈfiniʃiŋ; ˏfotoˋfɪnɪʃɪŋ] *n*. 冲洗胶卷,洗印照片。**-ish·er** *n*.

pho·to·fis·sion [ˌfəutəuˈfiʃən; ˏfotəˋfɪʃən] *n*. 【原】光致(核)分裂。

pho·to·flash [ˈfəutəuflæʃ; ˋfotəˏflæʃ] *n*. 1. (照相用)闪光灯。2. 闪光灯照片。~ **bomb** 照相闪光弹。~ **photography** 闪光(灯)摄影术。

pho·to·flood [ˈfəutəuflʌd; ˋfotəˏflʌd] *n*. 超压强烈溢光灯〔摄影用〕。

pho·to·flu·o·rog·ra·phy [ˌfəutəufluəˈrɔgrəfi; ˏfotəfluəˋrɑgrəfɪ] *n*. 【物】萤光屏图像摄影。**-flu·o·rog·raph·ic** [-ˌfluərəˈgræfik; -fluərəˋgræfɪk] *a*.

pho·to·flu·or·o·scope [ˌfəutəuˈfluːərəskəup; ˏfotəˋfluərəˏskop] *n*. 萤光屏[幕];萤光屏[幕]照相机。

pho·tog [fəˈtɔg; fəˋtɑg] *n*. 1. = photograph (*n*.). 2. = photographer. 3. = photography.

pho·to·gel·a·tin [ˌfəutəuˈdʒelətin; ˏfotəˋdʒɛlətɪn] *a*. 【印】珂罗版的。~ **process** 【印】珂罗版制版术。

pho·to·gen [ˈfəutəudʒən; ˋfotədʒən] *n*. 1. 【矿】页岩煤油。2. 【生】发光动[植]物。

pho·to·gene [ˈfəutəudʒiːn; ˋfotədʒin] *n*. 【心】后[余]像;闭眼留像(= after-image)。

pho·to·gen·ic [ˌfəutəuˈdʒenik; ˏfotəˋdʒɛnɪk] *a*. 1. 【生】发光的;发磷光的。2. 由于光而产生的;【医】(疾病)由光导致的〔如皮肤病等〕。3. 极适于拍照的,可以拍得很美的,上照的。

pho·to·ge·ol·o·gy [fəutəudʒiˈɔlədʒi; fotədʒɪˋɑlədʒɪ] *n*. 【地】摄影地质学。

pho·to·glyph [ˈfəutəglif; ˋfotəglɪf] *n*. 【印】照相雕刻版。

pho·tog·ly·phy [fəˈtɔglifi; fəˋtɑglɪfɪ] *n*. 照相雕刻术。

pho·to·gram [ˈfəutəgræm; ˋfotəgræm] *n*. 黑影照片,物影照片〔将物体放在光源和感光体之间制成〕。

pho·to·gram·me·try [ˌfəutəuˈgræmitri; ˏfotəˋgræmətrɪ] *n*. 摄影制图法;摄影测量术。**-met·ric** [-ˈmetrik; -ˋmɛtrɪk] *a*. **-gram·metri·cal·ly** *ad*. **-gram·me·trist** *n*. 摄影制图[测量]者。

pho·to·graph [ˈfəutəgrɑːf, -græf; ˋfotəˏgrɑf, -ˏgræf] I *n*. 1. 照片,相片。2. 栩栩如生的描绘,逼真的印像。*an instantaneous* ~ 瞬时快照。*have* [*get*] *one's* ~ *taken* = *sit for one's* ~ 请人拍照。*have a* ~ *taken with* 和…合影。*take a* ~ *of* 拍摄。II *vt*. 1. 为…照相,为…摄影。2. 逼真地描绘;把…深刻在印象中。—*vi*. 照相,被拍照;现在相片上。~ *badly* 照得不好;不上相。

pho·tog·ra·pher [fəˈtɔgrəfə; fəˋtɑgrəfɚ] *n*. 照相师;摄影家;摄影者。

pho·to·graph·ic, pho·to·graph·i·cal [fəutəˈgræfik, -kəl; ˏfotəˋgræfɪk, -kəl] *a*. 1. 摄影(术)的;摄影用的;照相似的。2. (描写或记述)逼真的,生动的;能详细记住所见事物的。*a* ~ *album* 照相簿。~ **camera** 照相机。~ **developer** 显像[影]剂。~ **studio** 照相馆,摄影室。**-graph·i·cal·ly** *ad*.

pho·tog·ra·phy [fəˈtɔgrəfi; fəˋtɑgrəfɪ] *n*. 摄影术;照相术。

pho·to·gra·vure [ˌfəutəgrəˈvjuə; ˏfotəgrəˋvjʊr] I *n*. 照相凹版(印刷)。II *vt*. 用照相凹版印刷。

pho·to·gun [ˈfəutəgʌn; ˋfotəˏgʌn] *n*. 光电子枪。

pho·to·he·li·o·graph [ˌfəutəuˈhiːliəugrɑːf; ˏfotəˋhilɪəˏgræf] *n*. 【天】太阳照相机。

pho·to·hole [ˈfəutəhəul; ˋfotəˏhol] *n*. 【物】光穴。

pho·to·in·duc·tion [ˌfəutəuinˈdʌkʃən; ˏfotoɪnˋdʌkʃən] *n*. 【生】光诱导。

pho·to·i·on·i·za·tion [ˌfəutəuˌaiəniˈzeiʃən; ˏfotoˏaɪənɪˋzeʃən] *n*. 光致游离(作用)。

pho·to·jour·nal·ism [ˌfəutəuˈdʒəːnəlizm; ˏfotoˋdʒɝnəlɪzm] *n*. 摄影新闻工作,摄影报导。**-jour·nal·ist** *n*. 摄影记者。

pho·to·ki·ne·sis [ˌfəutəukiˈniːsis; ˏfotokɪˋnisɪs] *n*. 【生理】趋光性。**-ki·net·ic** [-ˈnetik; -ˋnɛtɪk] *a*.

pho·to·lith [ˈfəutəliθ; ˋfotəlɪθ] I *n*. = photolithography. II *vt*. = photolithograph (*vt*.). III *a*. = photolithographic.

pho·to·lith·o·graph [ˌfəutəuˈliθəgrɑːf; ˏfotəˋlɪθəˏgræf] I *n*. 照相平版(印刷品)。II *vt*. 用照相平版印刷。**-o·graph·ic** *a*. 照相平版印刷的。**pho·to·li·thog·ra·phy** *n*. 照相平版印刷术。

pho·tol·o·gy [fəuˈtɔlədʒi; foˋtɑlədʒɪ] *n*. 光学。

pho·to·lu·mi·nes·cence [ˌfəutəuˌljuːmiˈnesns; ˏfotoˏljumɪˋnɛsns] *n*. 【电】光发光。**-mi·nes·cent** *a*.

pho·tol·y·sis [fəuˈtɔlisis; foˋtɑləsɪs] *n*. 【生】光(分)解(作用)。**pho·to·lyt·ic** [ˌfəutəˈlitik; ˏfotəˋlɪtɪk] *a*.

photom. = photometry.

pho·to·mag·net·ic [ˌfəutəumægˈnetik; ˏfotəmæg-

ˋnetɪk] *a*.【物】光磁的。

pho·to·map [ˈfəutəumæp; ˋfotə͵mæp] **I** *n*. 航空照相地图。**II** *vt*. 给(城市等)航空摄制地图。—*vi*. 航空照相制图。

pho·to·me·chan·i·cal [ˌfəutəumiˈkænikəl; ͵fotoməˋkænɪkəl] *a*. 照相制版(工艺)的。**-ly** *ad*.

pho·tom·e·ter [fəuˈtɔmitə; foˋtɑmətɚ] *n*.【物】光度计;光觉计;【摄】曝光表。

pho·to·met·ric, pho·to·met·ri·cal [ˌfəutəuˈmetrik, -rikəl;͵fotəˋmɛtrɪk, -rɪkəl] *a*. 光度计的;测量光度的;光度学的。～ *units* 测光[光度]单位。

pho·tom·e·try [fəuˈtɔmitri; foˋtɑmətrɪ] *n*. 1. 光度学。2. 光度术。

pho·to·mi·cro·graph [ˌfəutəuˈmaikrəugrɑːf; ͵fotəˋmaɪkrə͵græf] **I** *n*. 显微照相;显微照片。**II** *vt*. 为…拍摄显微照相。**-mi·crogra·phy** *n*. 显微照相术。

pho·to·mi·cro·scope [ˌfəutəuˈmaikrəuskəup; ͵fotəˋmaɪkrə͵skop] *n*. 显微照相机。

pho·to·mix·ing [ˌfəutəuˈmiksiŋ; ͵fotəˋmɪksɪŋ] *n*.【物】光混频。

pho·to·mon·tage [ˌfəutəumɔnˈtɑːʒ; ͵fotəmɑnˋtɑʒ] *n*.【摄】集成照片;集成照片制作法。

pho·to·mul·ti·pli·er [fəutəuˈmʌltiplaiə; ͵fotoˋmʌltə͵plaɪɚ] *n*.【电】光电倍增管。

pho·to·mu·ral [ˌfəutəuˈmjuərəl; ͵fotəˋmjʊrəl] *n*. (装饰用)大幅照片,壁画式照片。

pho·ton [ˈfəutɔn; ˋfotɑn] *n*. 1.【物】光子。2.【医】见光度〔网膜照明单位〕。

pho·to·neg·a·tive [ˌfəutəuˈnegətiv; ͵fotəˋnɛgətɪv] *a*.【生】负趋光性的。

pho·to·neu·tron [ˌfəutəuˈnjuːtrɔn, -ˈnuː-; ͵fotəˋnjutrɑn, -ˋnu-] *n*.【物】光(激)中子。

pho·to-off·set [ˌfəutəuˈɔːfset; ͵fotəˋɔfsɛt] *n*. 照相胶印法。

pho·to·pe·ri·od [ˌfəutəuˈpiəriəd; ͵fotəˋpɪrɪəd] *n*. 光周期。**-pe·riod·ic** [-ˌpiəriˈɔdik; -͵pɪrɪˋɑdɪk] *a*.

pho·to·pe·ri·od·ism [ˌfəutəuˈpiəriədizm; ͵fotəˋpɪrɪə͵dɪzm] *n*.【生】光周期现象 (= photoperiodicity)。

pho·to·phase [ˈfəutəfeiz; ˋfotə͵fez] *n*.【植】光照(发育阶段)。

pho·toph·i·lous [fəuˈtɔfiləs; foˋtɑfələs] *a*.【生】适光的,喜光的 (= photophilic)。**pho·to·phi·ly** *n*.

pho·to·pho·bi·a [ˌfəutəuˈfəubiə; ͵fotəˋfobɪə] *n*.【医】畏光,羞明。

pho·to·phone [ˈfəutəufəun; ˋfotə͵fon] *n*.【讯】光线电话机;光音机。

pho·to·phore [ˈfəutəufɔː; ˋfotəfɔr] *n*.【动】(发光动物的)发光器官。

pho·to·pho·re·sis [ˌfəutəufəˈriːsis; ͵fotəfəˋrisɪs] *n*.【物】光致迁动,光泳(现象)。

pho·to·pi·a [fəuˈtəupiə; foˋtopɪə] *n*.【医】光适应;眼对光调节。**-to·pic** [-ˈtəupik, -ˈtɔpik; -ˋtopɪk, -ˋtɑpɪk] *a*.

pho·to·plane [ˈfəutəuplein; ˋfotə͵plen] *n*.【空】摄影飞机。

pho·to·plas·tic [ˌfəutəuˈplæstik; ͵fotəˋplæstɪk] *a*.【物】光范性的。

pho·to·play [ˈfəutəplei; ˋfotə͵ple] *n*. 电影(剧)。

pho·to·play·er [ˈfəutəupleiə; ˋfotə͵pleɚ] *n*. 电影演员。

pho·to·play·wright [ˌfəutəuˈpleirait; ͵fotəˋpleraɪt] *n*. 电影编剧者。

pho·to·pol·y·mer·i·za·tion [ˈfəutəuˌpɔliməraiˈzeiʃən; ˋfotə͵pɑlɪməraɪˋzeʃən] *n*.【化】光致聚合(作用)。

pho·to·pos·i·tive [ˌfəutəuˈpɔzitiv; ͵fotəˋpɑzɪtɪv] *a*.【生】正趋光性的。

pho·to·print [ˈfəutəuprint; ˋfotəprɪnt] *n*. 影印;影印画。

pho·to·pro·ton [ˌfəutəuˈprəutɔn; fotəˋprotɑn] *n*.【物】光(激)质子。

pho·top·tom·e·ter [ˌfəutɔpˈtɔmitə; ͵fotɑpˋtɑmətɚ] *n*.【医】光觉计。

pho·to·ra·di·o·gram [ˌfəutəuˈreidiəugræm; ͵fotəˋredɪo͵græm] *n*. 无线电传真图片。

pho·to·re·cep·tor [ˌfəutəuriˈseptə; ͵fotorɪˋseptɚ] *n*.【生】光感受器,受光体。**-cep·tion** *n*.【生】光感受。**-cep·tive** *a*.【生】光感受的。

pho·to·re·con·nais·sance [ˌfəutəuriˈkɔnisəns; ͵fotorɪˋkɑnəsəns] *n*.【军】(空中)照相侦察。*a* ～ *satellite* 侦察卫星。

pho·to·re·cor·der [ˌfəutəuriˈkɔːdə; ͵fotorɪˋkɔrdɚ] *n*. 摄影[照相]记录器;自动记录照相机。

pho·to·re·duc·tion [ˌfəutəuriˈdʌkʃən; fotorɪˋdʌkʃən] *n*.【化】光致还原。

pho·to·re·pea·ter [ˌfəutəuriˈpiːtə; ͵fotorɪˋpitɚ] *n*. 照相复印机。

pho·to·re·sist [ˌfəutəuriˈzist; fotorɪˋzɪst] *n*.【物】光致抗蚀剂。

pho·to·sen·si·tive [ˌfəutəuˈsensitiv; ͵fotəˋsɛnsətɪv] *a*. 感光性的;光敏的。**-si·tiv·i·ty, -ness** *n*.【物】光敏性。

pho·to·sen·si·tize [ˌfəutəuˈsensiˌtaiz; ͵fotəˋsɛnsə͵taɪz] *vt*. 使具有感光性,使光敏。**-si·ti·za·tion** *n*. 光敏作用。**-r** *n*.【化】光敏剂。

pho·to·set [ˈfəutəuˌset; ˋfotə͵sɛt] *vt*. (*-set*; *-set·ting*)【印】照相排版。

pho·to·sphere [ˈfəutəusfiə; ˋfotə͵sfɪr] *n*.【天】光球;光球层。

pho·to·stat [ˈfəutəustæt; ˋfotə͵stæt] **I** *n*. 直接影印机;直接影印制品。**II** *vt*. 用直接影印机复制。

pho·to·syn·the·sis [ˌfəutəuˈsinθəsis; ͵fotəˋsɪnθəsɪs] *n*.【植】光合作用;光能合成。

pho·to·syn·the·size [ˌfəutəuˈsinθisaiz; ͵fotəˋsɪnθəsaɪz] *vt*., *vi*. (使)进行光合作用,(使)进行光能合成。

pho·to·syn·thet·ic [ˌfəutəusinˈθetik; ͵fotəsɪnˋθɛtɪk] *a*.【植】光合的。**-i·cal·ly** *ad*.

pho·to·tac·tic [ˌfəutəuˈtæktik; ͵fotəˋtæktɪk] *a*.【生】趋光性的。

pho·to·tax·is, pho·to·tax·y [ˌfəutəuˈtæksis, ˈfəutəutæksi; ͵fotəˋtæksɪs, ˋfotə͵tæksɪ] *n*.【生】趋光性。*positive* ～ 向光性。*negative* ～ 背光性。

pho·to·tel·e·gram [ˌfəutəuˈteligræm; ͵fotəˋtɛlɪgræm] *n*.【讯】传真电报。

pho·to·tel·e·graph [ˌfəutəuˈteligrɑːf; ͵fotəˋtɛlɪ͵græf] **I** *n*.【讯】传真电报(机)。**II** *vt*., *vi*. 用电报传真发送(照片)。**-ic** *a*. **-y** *n*. 电传真;光通讯。

pho·to·tel·e·phone [ˌfəutəuˈtelifəun; ͵fotəˋtɛləfon] *n*.【讯】光线电话机。

pho·to·tel·e·scope [ˌfəutəuˈteliskəup; ͵fotəˋtɛlə͵skop] *n*.【天】照相望远镜。

pho·to·ther·a·peu·tics [ˌfəutəuˌθerəˈpjuːtiks; ͵foto͵θɛrəˋpjutɪks] *n*.【医】光线疗法。

pho·to·ther·a·py [ˌfəutəuˈθerəpi; ͵fotəˋθɛrəpɪ] *n*. = phototherapeutics.

pho·to·therm·ic [ˌfəutəuˈθəːmik; ͵fotoˋθɝmɪk] *a*. 光热的;关于光和热的。

pho·to·ti·mer [ˈfəutəuˌtaimə; ˋfoto͵taɪmɚ] *n*. 1. 曝光计。2. (记录赛跑结果等的)摄影计时器。

pho·tot·o·nus [fəuˈtɔtnəs; foˋtɑtnəs] *n*.【生】光激性。**-ton·ic** [-ˈtɔnik; -ˋtɑnɪk] *a*.

pho·to·to·pog·ra·phy [ˌfəutəutəˈpɔgrəfi; ͵fototəˋpɑgrəfɪ] *n*. = photogrammetry.

pho·to·tox·is [ˌfəutəuˈtɔksis; ͵fotoˋtɑksɪs] *n*.【医】光线[波射线]损害。

pho·to·tran·sis·tor [ˌfəutəutrænˈzistə, -ˈsis-; ͵fototræn`zɪstə, -`sɪs-] *n*.【无】光电晶体管。

pho·tot·ro·pism [fəu'tɔtrəpizəm; fo`tɑtrə͵pɪzəm] *n*. 1.【植】向光性。2.【物】光色互变(现象)。

pho·tot·ropy [fəu'tɔtrəpi; fo`tɑtrəpɪ] *n*.【物】光色互变(现象)。

pho·to·tube ['fəutəutju:b; `fototjub] *n*.【无】光电管。

pho·to·type ['fəutəutaip; `fotə͵taɪp] *n*.【印】照相凸版;照相凸版制版术;照相凸版印刷品。

pho·to·type·set·ting [͵fəutəu'taip͵setiŋ; ͵fotə`taɪp͵setɪŋ] *n*. 照相排版,照相排字(= photocomposition)。**-set·ter** *n*.

pho·to·ty·pog·ra·phy [͵fəutəutai'pɔgrəfi; ͵fototaɪ`pɑgrəfɪ] *n*.【印】照相排版;照相凸版术。**-ty·po·graph·ic** *a*.

pho·to·typ·y [͵fəutəu'taipi; `fotə͵taɪpɪ] *n*.【印】照相凸版制版术。

pho·to·var·i·ster [͵fəutəu'veəristə; ͵foto`verɪstə] *n*.【物】光敏电阻。

pho·to·vi·sion [͵fəutəu'viʒən; ͵foto`vɪʒən] *n*. 电视。

pho·to·vol·ta·ic [͵fəutəuvɔl'teiik; ͵fotovɑl`teɪk] *a*.【物】光电的。

pho·to·zin·co·graph [͵fəutəu'ziŋkəgrɑ:f; ͵fotə`zɪŋkəgræf] I *n*. 照相锌版(印制品)。II *vt*. 用照相锌版印制。

pho·to·zin·cog·ra·phy [͵fəutəuziŋ'kɔgrəfi; ͵fotəzɪŋ`kɑgrəfɪ] *n*. 照相锌版术。

pho·tron·ic [fəu'trɔnik; fo`trɑnɪk] *a*.【物】(用)光电池的。

PHR = peak height ratio 峰高比。

phr. = phrase.

phras·al ['freizl; `frezl] *a*. 短语的,片语的。~ *modifier* 短语修饰语。

phrase [freiz; frez] I *n*. 1. 措辞,用语。2. 成语;名言;警句;格言,箴言。3.【语法】片语,短语,词组。4. 习惯用语。5.〔*pl*.〕空话,废话。6.【乐】短句,乐句。7.【舞】舞式。*an adjective* [*an adverb* (*ial*), *a noun*] ~ 形容词[副词、名词]片语。*a set* ~ 固定词组;成语。*an idle* ~ 空话。*We have had enough of* ~*s*. 废话已经够了。*felicity of* ~措词恰当。*speak in simple* ~用简单的话(表达)。
II *vt*. 1. 用话表示;用片语描述;把…叫做…。2.〔Scot.〕称赞,恭维;巴结。3.【乐】把…分成短句。*Thus he* ~*d it*. 他就是这样说的。~ **book** 成语集;短语集。~**-maker** 擅长创造警句者。~**-monger** 爱用陈词滥调的人,空谈主义者。~**-mongering** 空谈;讲漂亮话。

phra·se·o·gram, phra·se·o·graph ['freiziəgræm, -grɑ:f; `freziə͵græm, -͵græf] *n*. 表示片语的速记符号。

phra·se·ol·o·gist [͵freizi'ɔlədʒist; ; ͵frezɪ`ɑlədʒɪst] *n*. 喜欢咬文嚼字的人;爱用陈腐词藻的人。

phra·se·ol·o·gy [͵freizi'ɔlədʒi; ͵frezɪ`ɑlədʒɪ] *n*. 1. 用语,措词;熟语。2. 术语。3.〔集合词〕词句,表达方式。**phra·se·ol·ogist** *n*. 1. 善于措词造句的人。2. 满口陈词滥调的人。**-o·log·i·cal** [͵freiziə'lɔdʒikəl; ͵freziə`lɑdʒɪkəl] *a*. 1. 措词的,用语的,表达方式的。2. 用陈词滥调表达的。3. 喜欢用陈词滥调的。

phras·ing ['freiziŋ; `frezɪŋ] *n*. 1. 措词;表达法。2.【乐】短句的构成。

phra·try ['freitri; `fretrɪ] *n*. 1.【希腊史】(雅典的)氏族。2.【社】宗族分支〔部落中由数个奉同一图腾的氏族组成的族外通婚单位〕。

phre·at·ic [fri(:)'ætik; fri`ætɪk] *a*. 1. 井的,凿井取得的。2.【地】地下水层的。

phren., phrenol. = phrenology.

phren- *comb*. *f*. 表示"膈,心灵": *phren*algia.

phre·nal·gi·a [fri'nældʒiə; frɪ`nældʒɪə] *n*.【医】1. 精神痛苦。2. 膈痛。

phre·net·ic, phre·net·i·cal [fri'netik, -kəl; frɪ`netɪk, -kəl] *a*. 脑炎的,得脑炎的;狂乱的,发狂的;狂热的(= frenetic)。

phren·ic ['frenik; `frenɪk] *a*. 1.【解】横膈的。2.【生理】精神上的;心理的。

phre·ni·tis [fri'naitis; frɪ`naɪtɪs] *n*.【医】1. 膈炎;脑炎。2. 精神错乱,发狂;谵妄。

phreno- *comb*. *f*. = phren-.

phre·nol·o·gy [fri'nɔlədʒi; frɛ`nɑlədʒɪ] *n*. 颅相学;骨相学。**phren·o·log·ic, phren·o·log·ical** *a*. **phre·nol·o·gist** *n*. 颅[骨]相学家。

phren·sy ['frenzi; `frenzɪ] *n*., *vt*. = frenzy.

Phryg·i·an ['fridʒiən; `frɪdʒɪən] I *a*. (小亚细亚古国)弗利吉亚(Phrygia)(人)的。II *n*. 弗利吉亚人;弗利吉亚语。~ **cap** 弗利吉亚帽,垂尖圆锥帽(= cap of liberty)。

phry·nin ['frainin; `fraɪnɪn] *n*. 蟾蜍毒。

PHS, P.H.S. = 1. Public Health Service 公共保健服务。2. personal handyphone system【电信】个人手机系统。

phthal·ein(e) ['θæli:n, -iin, 'fθæl-; `θælin, -ɪɪn, `fθæl-] *n*.【化】酞。

phthal·ic ['θælik; `θælɪk] *a*. ~ **acid**【化】酞酸,苯二酸。

phthal·in ['θælin; `θælɪn] *n*.【化】酞林,酞隐(类),酚酞。

phthal·o·cy·a·nine [͵θælə'saiəni:n, 'fθæl-; ͵θælə`saɪənin, ͵fθæl-] *n*. 酞花青(染料),苯二甲蓝染料。

phthal·yl·sulph·a·thi·a·zole, phthal·yl·sulf·athi·a·zole ['θælil͵sʌlfə'θaiəzəul; `θælɪl͵sʌlfə`θaɪəzol] *n*.【药】羧苯甲酰磺胺噻唑。

phthi·o·col ['θaiəkɔl, 'fθaiə-; `θaɪəkol, `fθaɪə-] *n*.【生化】结核(菌)萘醌;结核黄素。

phthi·ri·a·sis [θi'raiəsis; θɪ`raɪəsɪs] *n*. 虱病(= pediculosis)。

phthi·sic ['θaisik, 'tizik; `θaɪsɪk, `tɪzɪk] I *n*.【医】1. 肺结核。2. 肺结核患者。II *a*. (有)肺结核的。

phthis·i·cal ['θaisikəl; `tɪzɪkl] *a*. = phthisic (*a*.).

phthis·i·o·log·y [͵θaisi'ɔlədʒi; ͵θaɪsɪ`ɔlədʒɪ] *n*.【医】痨瘵学,肺痨学。

phthi·sis ['θaisis, 'fθaisis; `θaɪsɪs, `fθaɪsɪs] *n*. (*pl*. **-ses** [-si:z; -siz])【医】肺结核;消耗性疾病。

phut(t) [fʌt; fʌt] *ad*., *n*.〔口〕啪的一声。*go* [*be gone*] ~〔俚〕1. (车胎)爆掉,泄气。2.〔喻〕失败,告吹。

phy·co·er·y·thrin [͵faikəu'eriθrin; ͵faɪkoə`rɪθrɪn] *n*.【生化】藻红朊。

phy·col·o·gy [fai'kɔlədʒi; faɪ`kɑlədʒɪ] *n*.【植】藻类学。

Phy·co·my·cete [͵faikəu'maisi:t; ͵faɪkomaɪ`sit] *n*. 藻菌纲(*Phycomycetes*)植物〔包括霜霉菌;黑霉菌〕。**-cetous** [-'si:təs; -sitəs] *a*.

phy·co·ph(a)e·in [͵faikəu'fi:in; faɪko`fiɪn] *n*.【生化】藻褐素。

phy·cox·an·thin [͵faikɔk'sænθin; ͵faɪkɑk`sænθɪn] *n*.【生化】藻黄质。

phy·la ['failə; `faɪlə] *n*. 1. phylon 的复数。2. phylum 的复数。

phy·lac·ter·y [fi'læktəri; fə`læktərɪ] *n*. 1. 护符,避邪符。2. (犹太人的)经匣。*make broad one's* ~ [*phylacteries*] 装虔诚;在人前装正经。

phy·le ['faili; `faɪlɪ] *n*. (*pl*. **-lae** [-li:; -li]) 部落,宗族〔古雅典人最大的政治划分单位〕。

phy·let·ic [fai'letik; faɪ`letɪk] *a*. 1. 部落的,种族的。2.【生】线系的,部的,门的。**phy·let·i·cal·ly** *ad*.

phyll- *comb*. *f*. 表示"叶": *phyll*ade.

-phyll *comb*. *f*. 表示"叶": sporo*phyll*.

phyl·lade ['fileid; `fɪled] *n*.【植】鳞状叶。

Phyl·lis ['filis; `fɪlɪs] *n*. 菲莉斯〔女子名〕。

phyllo- *comb*. *f*. = phyll-.

phyl·lo·ca·line [͵filə'keilin; ͵fɪlə`kelɪn] *n*.【生化】成叶素。

P

phyl·lo·clad, phy·lo·clade [ˈfiləklæd, -ˌkleid; ˋfɪləkl-æd, -ˏkled] *n*. 叶状枝(=cladophyll)。

phyl·lode [ˈfiləud; ˋfɪlod] *n*.【植】叶状(叶)柄。**phyl·lo·di·al** [-diəl; -dɪəl] *a*.

phyl·lo·er·y·thrin [ˌfiləuˈeriθrin; ˏfɪloˋɛrɪθrɪn] *n*.【生化】叶红素。

phyl·loid [ˈfilɔid; ˋfɪlɔɪd] **I** *a*.【植】叶状的。**II** *n*. 叶状枝。

phyl·lome [ˈfiləum; ˋfɪlom] *n*.【植】叶丛;初始叶;叶原体。**-lom·ic** [-ˈlɔmik, -ˈləumik; -ˋlɑmɪk, -ˋlomɪk] *a*.

phyl·loph·a·gous [fiˈlɔfəgəs; fəˋlɑfəgəs] *a*. 食叶的,以叶为生的。

phyl·lo·pod [ˈfiləpɔd; ˋfɪləˏpɑd] **I** *n*.【动】叶脚目(*Phyllopoda*)动物〔如丰年虫、兰水丰年虫(卤虾)等〕。**II** *a*. 叶脚目动物的。**phyl·lop·o·dan** [fiˈlɔpədən; fəˋlɑpədən] *n*., *a*. **phyl·lop·o·dous** [-dəs; -dəs] *a*.

phyl·lo·tax·is [ˌfiləˈtæksis; ˏfɪləˋtæksɪs] *n*.【植】叶序。

phyl·lo·tax·y [ˌfiləˈtæksi; ˋfɪləˏtæksɪ] *n*. = phyllotaxis.

-phyllous *comb*. *f*. 表示"叶…的,…叶的": mono*phyllous*.

phyl·lox·an·thin [ˌfilɔkˈsænθin; ˏfɪlɑkˋsænθɪn] *n*.【生化】叶黄素。

phyl·lox·e·ra [ˌfilɔkˈsiərə; fɪˋlɑksərə] *n*. (*pl*. **-rae** [-riː; -ri])【虫】葡蚜;〔P-〕根瘤蚜属。

phylo- *comb*. *f*. 表示"种族": *phylo*geny.

phylo·gen·e·sis, phy·log·e·ny [ˌfailəuˈdʒenisis, faiˈlɔdʒini; ˏfaɪləˋdʒɛnəsɪs, faɪˋlɑdʒənɪ] *n*. **1.**【生】系统发育(学);种族发生史;种系发生(学)(*opp*. ontogeny)。**2.** (事物的)发展史。**-gen·et·ic** [ˌfailədʒiˈnetik; ˏfaɪlədʒɪˋnɛtɪk] *a*. 系统发育的,种系发生的。

phy·lon [ˈfailɔn; ˋfaɪlɑn] *n*. (*pl*. **-la** [-lə; -lə])【生】种族。

phy·lum [ˈfailəm; ˋfaɪləm] *n*. (*pl*. **-la** [-lə; -lə]) **1.** (生物分类的)门。**2.**【语】(泛称)语系。

phys. = **1.** physical. **2.** physician. **3.** physics. **4.** physiological. **5.** physiology.

physi- *comb*. *f*. =physio-.

phys·i·at·rics [ˌfiziˈætriks; ˏfɪzɪˋætrɪks] *n*. 〔*pl*.〕〔动词用单数〕物理治疗,理疗(=physiatry)。**-at·rist** *n*. 理疗医师。

phys·ic [ˈfizik; ˋfɪzɪk] **I** *n*. **1.** 〔口〕药品,医药;(特指)泻药。**2.** 〔古〕医学;医术;医业。**3.** 〔废〕自然科学,物理学。*a dose of* ~ 一服药。**II** *vt*. **1.** 〔口〕给…吃药;给…吃泻药,使泻。**2.** 治愈。**3.** 〔俚〕虐待(敌人等);处罚。~ **nut** 麻风树。

phys·i·cal [ˈfizikəl; ˋfɪzɪkl̩] *a*. **1.** 物质的,有形的,形而下的(*opp*. psychical, spiritual, mental, moral);确凿的;外界的。**2.** 身体的,肉体的。**3.** 自然的,天然的。**4.** 依据自然规律的;自然科学的;物理学(上)的。**5.** 一味追求肉欲的。**6.** 〔废〕医药的。~ **age** 实际年龄,生理龄。~ **astronomy** 天体力学,引力天文学。~ **beauty** 肉体美。~ **chemistry** 物理化学。~ **climate** 地文气候。~ **constitution** 体格。~ **culture** [**education training**] 体育。~ **depreciation**【形】有形损耗。~ **drill** (普通)体操。~ **examination** 身体[体格]检查。~ **exercise** 体操,运动。~ **force** 力气,膂力。~ **geography** 地文学,自然地理学。~ **interpretation** 实际解说。~ **jerks** 〔俚〕= ~ drill. ~ **laws** 自然法则。~ **medicine** 物理医学。~ **pendulum**【物】变摆。~ **sciences** **1.** 物理科学。**2.** 自然科学〔指物理、化学、天文、地理〕。~ **strength** 体力。~ **therapy**【物】物理治疗法,理疗。~ **world** 外界。

phys·i·cal·ism [ˈfizikəlizm; ˋfɪzɪkəlɪzm̩] *n*.【哲】物理主义。**-cal·ist** *n*.【哲】物理主义派。

phys·i·cal·i·ty [ˌfiziˈkæliti; ˏfɪzɪˋkælɪtɪ] *n*. **1.** 肉体性。**2.** 注重肉体〔区别于精神〕。

phys·i·cal·ly [ˈfizikəli; ˋfɪzɪkəlɪ] *ad*. **1.** 按照自然规律;物理上。**2.** 物质上。**3.** 体格上,身体上。*a fine man* ~, *but a fool mentally* 一个体格好而头脑笨的人。*a* ~ *different man* 一位生理异常的男士〔实际即残疾人,一种委婉说法〕。

phy·si·cian [fiˈziʃən; fəˋzɪʃən] *n*. **1.** 医生,内科医生(*opp*. surgeon);〔美〕(一般)医师;〔口〕医学博士。**2.** 〔喻〕(精神创伤的)医治者,抚慰者。*consult a* ~ 请医生看。*one's family* ~ 家庭医师。*the* ~ *in charge* 主任医师。

phys·i·cism [ˈfizisizəm; ˋfɪzɪsɪzəm] *n*. **1.** 自然科学研究。**2.** 物理宇宙论,宇宙机械论。

phys·i·cist [ˈfizisist; ˋfɪzəsɪst] *n*. **1.** 物理学家;〔古〕自然科学家。**2.** 宇宙机械论者。

phys·i·co·chem·i·cal [ˌfizikəuˈkemikəl; ˏfɪzakoˋkɛməkl] *a*. 物理化学的。**-ly** *ad*.

phys·ics [ˈfiziks; ˋfɪzɪks] *n*. 〔通常用作单数〕**1.** 物理学。**2.** 物理过程;物理现象;物理性质;物理成分。*atomic* ~ 原子物理学。*the* ~ *of flight* 飞行的物理过程。

physio- *comb*. *f*. 表示"自然,天然;物理": *physio*gnomy, *physio*graphy, *physio*therapy.

phys·i·o·chem·i·cal [ˌfiziəˈkemikəl; ˏfɪzɪəˋkɛmɪkəl] *a*. 生理[生物]化学的。

phys·i·oc·racy [ˌfiziˈɔkrəsi; ˏfɪzɪˋɑkrəsɪ] *n*. 重农论,重农主义〔古典政治经济学的一派学说〕。

phys·i·o·crat [ˈfiziəkræt; ˋfɪzɪəˏkræt] *n*. 重农论者,重农主义者。

phys·i·og 〔美〕= physiognomy.

phys·i·og·e·ny [fiziˈɔdʒini; fɪzɪˋɔdʒɪnɪ] *n*.【生】官能发达;官能发生学。

phys·i·og·nom·ic, phys·i·og·nom·i·cal [ˌfiziəˈnɔmik, -kəl; ˏfɪzɪɑgˋnɑmɪk, -kəl] *a*. **1.** 观相术的。**2.** 相貌的。**-nom·i·cally** *ad*.

phys·i·og·no·mist [ˌfiziˈɔnəmist; ˏfɪzɪˋɑnəmɪst] *n*. 相士,相面先生。

phys·i·og·no·my [ˌfiziˈɔnəmi; ˏfɪzɪˋɑgnəmɪ] *n*. **1.** 观相术,相法。**2.** 面貌,相貌;〔卑〕面孔,脸。**3.** (土地等的)形状,外观;特色,特征。

phys·i·og·ra·phy [ˌfiziˈɔgrəfi; ˏfɪzɪˋɑgrəfɪ] *n*. 地文学,自然地理学;〔美〕地形学;自然现象志。**-ra·pher** *n*. 地文学家,地文学研究者。**phys·i·o·graph·ic, phys·i·o·graph·i·cal** *a*.

physiol. = **1.** physiological. **2.** physiologist. **3.** physiology.

phys·i·ol·a·try [ˌfiziˈɔlətri; ˏfɪzɪˋɑlətrɪ] *n*. 自然崇拜。

phys·i·o·log·ic, phys·i·o·log·i·cal [ˌfiziəˈlɔdʒik, -kəl; ˏfɪzɪəˋlɑdʒɪk, -kəl] *a*. 生理的,生理学(上)的。*a* ~ *strain*【生】生理小种。~ *saline* 生理盐水。**-log·i·cal·ly** *ad*.

phys·i·ol·o·gist [ˌfiziˈɔlədʒist; ˏfɪzɪˋɑlədʒɪst] *n*. 生理学家。

phys·i·ol·o·gy [ˌfiziˈɔlədʒi; ˏfɪzɪˋɑlədʒɪ] *n*. **1.** 生理学。**2.** 生理(机能)。

phys·i·o·ther·a·peu·tic [ˈfiziəuˌθerəˈpjuːtik; ˏfɪzɪoˏθerəˋpjutɪk] *a*. 物理疗法的,理疗的。**-tics** *n*. 物理疗法,理疗。

phys·i·o·ther·a·py [ˌfiziəuˈθerəpi; ˏfɪzɪoˋθɛrəpɪ] *n*.【医】物理疗法〔热疗、按摩等〕。

phy·sique [fiˈziːk; fɪˋzik] *n*. 〔F.〕**1.** 体格。**2.** (土地等的)地形,地势。

phy·so·stig·mine [ˌfaisəuˈstigmiːn, -min; ˏfaɪsoˋstɪgmin, -mɪn] *n*.【化】毒扁豆碱。

phy·sos·to·mous, phy·sos·to·ma·tous [faiˈsɔstəməs, ˌfaisəˈstɔmətəs; faɪˋsɑstəməs, ˏfaɪsəˋstɑmətəs] *a*.【动】通鳔的。

-phyte *comb*. *f*. 表示"植物": litho*phyte*.

Phy·tin [ˈfaitin; ˋfaɪtɪn] *n*. 植酸钙镁〔商标名〕。

phyt(o)- *comb*. *f*. 表示"植物": *phyto*chemistry.

phy·to·ben·thon [ˌfaitəuˈbenθon; ˏfaɪtoˋbɛnθɑn] ***n***. 水底植物。

phy·to·chem·is·try [ˌfaitəuˈkemistri; ˏfaɪtoˋkɛmɪstrɪ] ***n***. 植物化学。

phy·to·chrome [ˈfaitəukrəum; ˋfaɪtoˏkrom] ***n***. 植物色素〔如叶绿素〕。

phy·to·cid·al [ˌfaitəuˈsaidəl; ˏfaɪtəˋsaɪdəl] ***a***. 杀害植物的。

phy·to·cide [ˈfaitəusaid; ˋfaɪtəˏsaɪd] ***n***. 【农】除莠剂。

phy·to·coe·no·sis [ˌfaitəusiˈnəusis; ˏfaɪtosɪˋnosɪs] ***n***. (*pl*. ***-ses*** [-siːz; -siz])【植】全层群落。

phy·to·coe·no·si·um [ˌfaitəusiˈnəusiəm; ˏfaɪtosɪˋnosɪəm] ***n***. 【植】植物群落。

phy·to·com·mu·ni·ty [ˌfaitəukəˈmjuːniti; ˏfaɪtokəˋmjunɪtɪ] ***n***. = phytocoenosium.

phy·to·e·col·o·gy [ˌfaitəuiˈkɔlədʒi; ˏfaɪtoɪˋkɑlədʒɪ] ***n***. 植物生态学。

phy·to·flag·el·late [ˌfaitəuˈflædʒileit, -lit; ˏfaɪtoˋflædʒəlet, -lɪt] ***n***. 植物状鞭毛虫,匐枝状鞭毛藻。

phy·to·gen·e·sis [ˌfaitəuˈdʒenisis; ˏfaɪtoˋdʒɛnəsɪs] ***n***. 植物发生论。**-to·ge·net·ic, -to·ge·net·i·cal** ***a***.

phy·to·gen·ic [ˌfaitəuˈdʒenik; ˏfaɪtoˋdʒɛnɪk] ***a***. 植物起源的〔如泥炭、泥炭土、煤〕。

phy·tog·e·nous [faiˈtɔdʒinəs; faɪˋtɑdʒənəs] ***a***. = phytogenic.

phy·to·gen·y [faiˈtɔdʒini; faɪˋtɑdʒənɪ] ***n***. = phytogenesis.

phy·to·ge·og·ra·phy [ˌfaitəudʒiˈɔgrəfi; ˏfaɪtodʒɪˋɑgrəfɪ] ***n***. 植物地理学。

phy·tog·ra·phy [faiˈtɔgrəfi; faɪˋtɑgrəfɪ] ***n***. 叙述植物学。

phy·to·he·mag·glu·ti·nin [ˌfaitəuˌhiːməˈgluːtnin; ˏfaɪtoˏhiməˋglutnɪn] ***n***. 【医】植物血球凝集素。

phy·to·hor·mone [ˌfaitəuˈhɔːməun; ˏfaɪtəˋhɔrmon] ***n***. 植物激素(= plant hormone)。

phy·tol·o·gy [faiˈtɔlədʒi; faɪˋtɑlədʒɪ] ***n***. 植物学(= botany)。**-logic, -log·i·cal** ***a***.

phy·to·par·a·sit·ol·o·gy [ˌfaitəuˌpærəsaiˈtɔlədʒi; ˏfaɪtoˏpærəsaɪˋtɑlədʒɪ] ***n***. 植物寄生物学。

phy·to·path·o·gen(e) [ˌfaitəuˈpæθədʒin; ˏfaɪtoˋpæθədʒɪn] ***n***. 植物病菌。

phy·to·pa·thol·o·gy [ˌfaitəupæˈθɔlədʒi; ˏfaɪtopəˋθɑlədʒɪ] ***n***. 植物病理学。**-log·ic, -log·i·cal** ***a***.

phy·toph·a·gous [faiˈtɔfəgəs; faɪˋtɑfəgəs] ***a***. 【动】吃植物的,草食的。

phy·to·phar·ma·cy [ˌfaitəuˈfɑːməsi; ˏfaɪtoˋfɑrməsɪ] ***n***. 植物药剂学。

phy·to·plank·ton [ˌfaitəuˈplæŋktən; ˏfaɪtoˋplæŋktən] ***n***. 浮游植物;浮游植物(群落)。**-ic** ***a***.

phy·to·so·ci·ol·o·gy [ˌfaitəuˌsəusiˈɔlədʒi, -ʃi-; ˏfaɪtoˏsoʃɪˋɑlədʒɪ, -sɪ-] ***n***. 植物社会学。

phy·tos·ter·ol [faiˈtɔstərɔːl, -rəul; faɪˋtɑstərəl, -rol] ***n***. 植物甾醇,植物固醇。

phy·to·tax·on·o·my [ˌfaitəutækˈsɔnəmi; ˏfaɪtotækˋsɑnəmɪ] ***n***. 植物分类学。

phy·to·ther·a·py [ˌfaitəuˈθerəpi; ˏfaɪtoˋθɛrəpɪ] ***n***. 植物治疗法,本草疗法。

phy·tot·o·my [faiˈtɔtəmi; faɪˋtɑtəmɪ] ***n***. 植物解剖(学)。

phy·to·tox·e·mi·a [ˌfaitəutɔkˈsiːmiə; ˏfaɪtətɑkˋsimɪə] ***n***. 植物虫害病毒。

phy·to·tox·ic [ˌfaitəuˈtɔksik; ˏfaɪtəˋtɑksɪk] ***a***. **1.** 植物性毒素的。**2.** 对植物有毒的。**-tox·ic·i·ty** [-tɔkˈsisiti; -tɑkˋsɪsətɪ] ***n***. **1.** 植物毒性。**2.** 对植物的毒性。

phy·to·tron [ˈfaitətrɔn; ˋfaɪtətrɑn] ***n***. 人工气候室。

phy·to·zo·on [ˌfaitəuˈzəuɔn; ˏfaɪtoˋzoɑn] ***n***. 【动】植形动物,植虫。

pi[1] [pai; paɪ] ***n***. **1.** 希腊字母表的第十六字母〔Π π,和英语的 p 相当〕。**2.**【数】圆周率。

pi[2] [pai; paɪ] ***a***. 〔英学俚〕虔诚的,有道德的,宗教性的〔pious 之略〕。～**-jaw** ***n***. 〔常蔑〕说教,训话。

pi[3] [pai; paɪ] ***n***., ***vt***. 〔英〕= pie[3].

P.I. = Philippine Islands 菲律宾群岛。

PIA = Pakistan International Airlines 巴基斯坦国际航空公司。

pi·ac·u·lar [paiˈækjulə; paɪˋækjələ˞] ***a***. 赎罪的;须赎罪的;有罪的;极恶的。

pi·affe [pjæf, piˈæf; pjæf, pɪˋæf] ***vi***. (马)用慢步小跑。

pi·af·fer [ˈpjæfə, piˈæfə; ˋpjæfə˞, pɪˋæfə˞] ***n***. (马的)慢步小跑。

pi·al [ˈpaiəl; ˋpaɪəl] ***a***. 【解】软(脑脊)膜的。

pi·a ma·ter [ˈpaiəˈmeitə; ˋpaɪəˋmetə˞]〔L.〕**1.**【解】软脑(脊)膜(*opp*. dura mater 硬脑(脊)膜)。**2.** 脑,智慧。

pi·a·nette, pi·a·ni·no [piəˈnet, piəˈniːnəu; ˏpɪəˋnɛt, pɪəˋnino] ***n***. 〔方〕小型竖式钢琴。

pi·an·ism [piːˈænizm, ˈpjæn-, ˈpiːən-; piˋænɪzm, ˋpjæn-, ˋpiən-] ***n***. 弹钢琴术,钢琴技巧;钢琴演奏。**pi·an·is·tic** ***a***.

pi·a·nis·si·mo [pjæˈnisiməu, piəˈn-; pjæˋnɪsəmo, pɪəˋn-] **I** ***a***., ***ad***. 〔It.〕【乐】很轻的[地]。**II** ***n***. (*pl*. ～***s***, ***-mi*** [-miː; -mi]) 须极轻地奏出的乐句[乐段]。

pi·an·ist[ˈpiənist, ˈpjænist; ˋpɪənɪst, ˋpjænɪst] ***n***. 钢琴家;钢琴师,钢琴演奏家。

pi·a·no [piˈɑːnəu, ˈpjɑ-; pɪˋɑno, ˋpjɑ-] **I** ***a***., ***ad***. 〔It.〕【乐】轻轻的[地];微弱的[地]。**II** ***n***. 轻奏乐段。

pi·an·o [piˈɑːnəu, ˈpjænəu; pɪˋɑno, pɪˋæno] ***n***. (*pl*. ～***s***) 钢琴;〔美俚〕囚犯工作席。*a boudoir* [*cabinet*] ～ 竖钢琴。*an upright* ～ 竖钢琴。*a cottage* ～ 小竖钢琴。*a grand* ～ 大钢琴。*a piccolo* ～ 小竖钢琴。*play* [*perform*] (*on*) *the* ～ 弹钢琴。～ **accordion** 键盘式手风琴。～ **duet** 钢琴二重奏(曲)。～ **organ** 手摇式自鸣钢琴。～**phile** 钢琴爱好者。～ **player 1.** 弹钢琴的人。**2.** 钢琴自动弹奏机。～ **stool** 钢琴凳。～ **system** 分期付款购货法。～ **trio** 钢琴三重奏。

pi·an·o·for·te [piˌɑːnəuˈfɔːti, ˌpjæn-; pɪˏænoˋfɔrtɪ, ˏpɪæn-] ***n***. = piano.

pi·a·no·la[pjæˈnəulə; ˏpɪæˋnolə] ***n***. 自动钢琴。

pias. = piastre.

pi·as·(s)a·ba, pi·as·(s)a·va [ˌpiːəsɑːvə; ˏpiəˋsavə] ***n***. 纤维榈(的纤维);巴西棕(树)。

pi·as·ter, pi·as·tre [piˈæstə; pɪˋæstə˞] ***n***. **1.** 〔罕〕比塞塔〔西班牙货币〕。**2.** 皮阿斯特〔埃及、黎巴嫩、叙利亚和苏丹的货币单位〕。**3.** 〔美俚〕一元。

pi·at [ˈpaiət; ˋpaɪət] ***n***. (英国、加拿大军队中用的)一种短距离反坦克炮(= projector infantry antitank)。

pi·az·za [piˈætsə; pɪˋæzə] ***n***. (*pl*. ～***s***, 〔It.〕 ***pi·az·ze*** [ˈpjɑːtse; ˋpjɑtsɛ]) **1.** (特指意大利都市中的)广场。**2.** 〔美〕游廊,外廊(= verandah)。**3.** 〔英〕连拱廊。

pi·bal [ˈpaibəl; ˋpaɪbəl] ***n***. 【气】**1.** 测风气球(= pilot balloon)。**2.** 高空测风报告。

pi·broch [ˈpiːbrɔk; ˋpibrɑk] ***n***. (苏格兰高地人的)风笛曲。

PIC = prior informed consent 事先知悉情况下表示的同意。

pic [pik; pɪk] ***n***. (*pl*. ～***s***, ***pix*** [piks; pɪks]) 〔picture 之略〕〔美俚〕**1.** 电影。**2.** 照片。*the* ～ *mob* 电影观众。～**-parlor** ***n***. 〔美俚〕电影院。

pi·ca[1] [ˈpaikə; ˋpaɪkə] ***n***. 【印】12 点活字〔相当我国新 4 号铅字〕。

pi·ca[2] [ˈpaikə; ˋpaɪkə] ***n***. 【医】异食癖。

pic·a·dor [ˈpikədɔː; ˋpɪkəˏdɔr] (*pl*. ～***s***, ～***es*** [ˌpikəˈdɔːriːz; ˏpɪkəˋdɔriz]) ***n***. **1.** (西班牙的)骑马斗牛士。**2.** 〔喻〕老练机智的论客。

pic·a·ra [ˈpiːkɑːrɑː; ˋpikəˏrɑ] ***n***. (*pl*. ～***s***) 女流浪者。

P

pic·a·resque [ˌpikəˈresk; ˏpɪkəˋrɛsk] **I** *a*. **1.** (传奇小说)以流浪汉、歹徒等的冒险生涯做题材的。**2.** (经历等)传奇式流浪冒险的。**II** *n*. **1.** 〔常 the ～〕(16 世纪西班牙的)以歹徒、流浪汉的冒险生涯为题材的故事。**2.** 传奇式流浪冒险的事迹[人物]。*a* ～ [*picaroon*] *novel* 流浪汉小说。

pi·ca·ro [ˈpiːkɑːrəu; ˋpɪkəro] *n*. (*pl*. ～*s*) 流浪汉,亡命徒。

pic·a·roon[1] [ˌpikəˈruːn; ˏpɪkəˋrun] **I** *n*. **1.** 歹徒,强盗;窃贼。**2.** 海盗;海盗船。**II** *vi*. 做强盗;做海盗。—*vt*. 劫夺。

pic·a·roon[2] [ˌpikəˈruːn; ˏpɪkəˋrun] *n*. (加拿大樵夫用的)十字刀。

pic·a·yune [ˌpikəˈjuːn; ˏpɪkɪˋjun] **I** *n*. **1.** (原在美国路易斯安那州及南部各州流通的)西班牙小钱币;〔美〕小钱币〔尤指五分辅币〕。**2.** 〔美口〕不值钱的东西,小人物,不重要的人。**II** *a*. = picayunish.

pic·a·yun·ish [ˌpikəˈjuːniʃ; ˏpɪkɪˋjunɪʃ] *a*. 琐碎的;微不足道的;不值钱的。

Pic·ca·dil·ly [ˌpikəˈdili; ˏpɪkəˋdɪlɪ] *n*. 皮卡迪利大街〔伦敦的繁华街道〕。～ **Circus** 皮卡迪利广场〔戏院及娱乐中心〕。

pic·ca·lil·li [ˈpikəlili; ˏpɪkəˋlɪlɪ] *n*. (*pl*. ～*s*) 辣泡菜。

pic·ca·nin·ny, pick·a·nin·ny [ˈpikənini; ˋpɪkəˏnɪnɪ] **I** *n*. 黑种小孩;澳大利亚土著小孩;〔谑〕小孩。**II** *a*. 极小的。

Pic·card [ˌpiˈkɑːd; ˏpiˋkar] **A**. 皮卡德〔1884—1962, 比利时物理学家〕。

pic·co·lo [ˈpikələu; ˋpɪkəˏlo] **I** *n*. (*pl*. ～*s*) 【乐】短笛。**II** *a*. (乐器)小型的。

pice [pais; paɪs] *n*. 〔*sing*., *pl*.〕旧时印度铜币。

pic·e·ous [ˈpisiəs, ˈpaisi-; ˋpɪsɪəs, ˋpaɪsɪ-] *a*. 沥青的;似沥青的,沥青色的(尤指动物)。

pich·i·ci·a·go, pich·i·ci·e·go [ˌpitʃisiˈeigəu; ˏpɪtʃɪsɪˋego] *n*. (*pl*. ～*s*) 【动】铠鼹。

pick[1] [pik; pɪk] **I** *vt*. **1.** (用鹤嘴锄等)掘,凿,挖(洞)。**2.** (用手指)挖(鼻孔、耳朵等),挑剔(牙齿、骨头等)。**3.** 摘,掐,采,摘取(花果、棉花等);薅(草);拔(羽毛等);舐,啄;〔口〕吃。**4.** 挑选;(细心)选择(用词等)。**5.** 撬开(锁等)。**6.** 扒窃,偷,剽窃。**7.** 解,拆;扯开(麻絮等),分。**8.** 挑…的毛病,找…的碴儿,吵起(架)来,寻找(吵架的机会)(*with*)。**9.** (用指头)弹拨(弦乐器等)。～ *ground* 掘地。～ *one's teeth* 剔牙。～ *a thread off one's coat* 从衣服上摘去线头。～ *a chicken* 拔鸡毛。～ *a quarrel* (*with sb*.) 找机会(和某人)吵架。～ *fault* 挑眼,找碴儿。～ *sb.'s pocket* 扒窃。— *vi*. **1.** 凿,掘,挖,戳;啄(*at*)。**2.** 〔口〕(挑肥拣瘦地)吃。**3.** 采摘。**4.** 挑,选。**5.** 偷,窃。*Ripe grapes* ～ *easily*. 熟了的葡萄摘起来不难。～ *at the food* 吃东西挑嘴。*the* ～*ing season* 采摘季节。***have a bone to*** ～ ***with sb***., ～ ***a bone*** [美南方 ***crow***] ***with sb***. 对某人有不满之处;与某人有需要解决的争端;跟…口角[争吵]。～ ***a hole in*** = ～ *holes in*. ～ ***acquaintance with*** 偶然和人成为相识。～ ***and choose*** 挑三拣四,挑肥拣瘦。～ ***and steal*** 扒窃,偷。～ ***at*** [***on***] 〔美口〕**1.** 不断挑剔[指责,骂]某人。**2.** 拣拣吃吃。～ ***holes in*** 找…碴儿[漏洞],找…的过失,吹毛求疵。～ ***in*** **1.** (在画里)画上(阴影等)。**2.** 〔英方〕承揽,接收(要洗的衣服等)。～ ***oakum*** 拆[撕]填絮;〔喻〕做苦工。～ ***off*** **1.** 掐下,摘去,采取。**2.** 一个接一个地瞄准打中。～ ***on*** 〔美口〕**1.** 与…为难,欺负;不断责骂。**2.** 挑中,选中。～ ***oneself up*** (倒下的人)从地上爬起来;打起精神。～ ***one's steps*** 小心翼翼地走(险路)。～ ***one's way*** 拣易走处走,小心走路。～ ***one's words*** 注意措词,小心说话。～ ***out*** **1.** 挑选。**2.** 掘出,拔出,啄出。**3.** 闻出,区辨,听出;弄明白,领会,看出(文章等的意思)。**4.** 凭听来的调子弹奏(歌曲)。～ ***out with*** **1.** 装饰,使突出。**2.** (用另一种颜色)衬托(底色)。～ ***over*** 拣,分档挑选;精选。～ ***sb.'s brains*** 剽窃别人脑力劳动成果。～ ***spirit*** 提起精神。～ ***to pieces*** **1.** 拆开;扯碎。**2.** 〔喻〕刻薄批评,把…骂得一钱不值。～ ***up*** **1.** *vt*. 掘起,拾起;(车船等)在半路上搭(人);振起(精神);得到(生活费、知识等);偶然获得,四处收集,想尽办法寻求,听着;(用探照灯等)探出,找到(原来的路);听会,自然学会(言语、游戏等);(抱)起;〔口〕捉住,逮捕,(跟女人)交起朋友来,选出。**2.** *vi*. (病后)恢复健康,恢复体重,有了精神,有起色;生意好起来;(和偶然碰着的人)成为相识(*with*)(～ *up flesh* 病后长肉)。～ ***up on*** 〔美俚〕同…熟悉起来。

II *n*. **1.** 凿,掘。**2.** 选择;选择权。**3.** 〔the ～〕最好的东西,精华,精选物。**4.** 采摘的农作物。**5.** 【绘】修改。**6.** 【印】(铅字的)污点。*You can take your* ～. 你可以拣你喜欢的。***take*** [***have***, ***get***] ***the*** ～ ***of*** 任凭挑选;有…的选择权;拣,选。***the*** ～ ***of the bunch*** [***basket***] 一批中的精选品,精华。

pick[2] [pik; pɪk] *n*. **1.** 鹤嘴锄,铁镐,铁撬;用于挖掘的尖状物;〔口〕牙签。**2.** (弹弦乐器的)拨子。**3.** 撬锁工具;撬锁贼(= ～lock)。～**ax(e)** **1.** *n*. 鹤嘴锄,镐。**2.** *vt*., *vi*. (用鹤嘴锄)掘。

pick[3] [pik; pɪk] **I** *vt*. 【纺】投(梭)。**II** *n*. 纬纱;投梭。

pick·a·back [ˈpikəbæk; ˋpɪkəˏbæk] **I** *ad*. 〔口〕**1.** 在肩[背]上,背着。**2.** 在铁道平车上。*ride* ～ *on sb*. 骑在某人肩头上。**II** *a*. ～ **plane** (载于母机背上在空中飞出的)子机,寄生飞机。

pick·a·nin·ny [ˈpikənini; ˋpɪkəˏnɪnɪ] *n*. = piccaninny.

picked[1] [pikt; pɪkt] *a*. **1.** 选净的,精选的,挑选出来的,最好的。**2.** (果实等)摘下的,摘收的。**3.** (用锄、镐等)挖掘过的。～ ***to repeat*** 〔美〕有再度赛赢的希望。

picked[2] [pikt; pɪkt] *a*. 〔方〕有尖峰的;尖的。

pick·el [ˈpikəl; ˋpɪkəl] *n*. (爬山用的)冰斧。

pick·er[1] [ˈpikə; ˋpɪkɚ] *n*. **1.** 采摘者;摘棉工人,扯拔者;捡拾者,采集者;拣选者;〔美〕摘棉机。**2.** 扒手,窃贼。**3.** = pickaxe. ～***s and stealers*** 扒手和窃贼。

picker[2] [ˈpikə; ˋpɪkɚ] *n*. 【纺】清棉机;(织机)皮结。

pick·er·el [ˈpikərəl; ˋpɪkərəl] *n*. (*pl*. ～(*s*)) **1.** 【动】小狗鱼。**2.** 〔口〕= pike, pikeperch.

pick·er·el·weed [ˈpikərəlˌwiːd; ˋpɪkərəlˏwid] *n*. (北美)海寿属(拟)(*Pontederia*)植物〔尤指海寿(*P. cordata*)〕。

Pick·er·ing [ˈpikəriŋ; ˋpɪkərɪŋ] *n*. 皮克林〔姓氏〕。

pick·et [ˈpikit; ˋpɪkɪt] **I** *n*. **1.** 桩,尖桩;支柱;【电】标橛。**2.** 【军】步哨,哨兵;前哨,警戒哨[队,船,飞机];瞭望者,把风者。**3.** 〔*pl*.〕(工会罢工时的)纠察员。**4.** 【史】(罚罪犯以一足站于桩上的)站桩刑。**5.** 〔*pl*.〕〔美俚〕牙齿。*an outlying* ～ 前哨,前哨队。*a* ～ *fence* 栅栏;〔美俚〕牙齿。**II** *vt*. **1.** 用栅栏围上。**2.** 用警戒哨保卫;派…去放哨。**3.** (把马等)系在桩上。**4.** (罢工时)派纠察员监视(工厂等)。**5.** 处…以桩型。— *vi*. 放哨;担任纠察员(任务)。～**boat** 巡逻船;雷达哨艇。～ **line** **1.** 【军】哨兵线,警戒线;(罢工时的)纠察线。**2.** 拴马索。～ **pin** 拴马桩。～ **rope** 拴马索。～ **ship** 雷达警戒船。**-er** *n*. 纠察员。

Pick·et(t) [ˈpikit; ˋpɪkɪt] *n*. 皮基特〔姓氏〕。

pick·ing [ˈpikiŋ; ˋpɪkɪŋ] *n*. **1.** (用铁镐等)掘;撬开。**2.** 摘取,采集;选择,挑选。**3.** 〔*pl*.〕摘取物,采集物;挑选物;可采物;可捡物〔垃圾、废品等〕。**4.** 〔*pl*.〕摘剩的东西,落穗;剩余物。**5.** 偷窃;赃品。**6.** 〔*pl*.〕额外收入,外快。**7.** 〔*pl*.〕〔英〕(铺人行道用的)贝壳粉。**8.** 未烧透的砖。**9.** 【矿】粗选。～ ***and stealing*** 扒窃。

pick·le [ˈpikl; ˋpɪkl] **I** *n*. **1.** (腌鱼、菜等用的)盐汁,泡菜水;〔*pl*.〕酸菜、泡菜,(尤指)泡黄瓜;腌鱼。**2.** 淡酸水,酸洗液〔洗金属用〕。**3.** 〔通例带有形容词〕苦境,困境;混乱。**4.** 〔口〕顽皮孩子。**5.** 〔美俚〕烂醉。**6.** 【军】空投鱼雷。***be in a*** (***sad***, ***fine***, ***nice***) ～ 处境困难,尴尬,十分混乱。***have a rod in*** ～ ***for sb***. 蓄谋惩罚某人。***mixed*** ～***s*** **1.** 什锦酸菜。**2.** 各种不同的人[东西]的集合。**3.** 心

情非常混乱。

II *vt*. 1. 把…泡在盐水里；(用盐水等)腌制，腌渍。2. 用酸洗液洗(铸造物等)。3. 使(画)显现古色古香。4. 【海】鞭打前用盐(或醋)擦(背)。~**barrel** *n*.〔美空俚〕轰炸员练习投弹时用的目标。~ **barrel bombing**【军】极精确的轰炸。**-d** *a*. 1. 盐腌的，醋泡的。2.〔美俚〕烂醉的，酩酊大醉的。

pick·ling [ˈpikliŋ; ˋpɪklɪŋ] *n*.【化】浸酸，酸洗，浸蚀，浸洗；浸封，浸藏。*electrolytic* ~ 电渍。*a* ~ *process* 浸渍法。

pick·lock [ˈpiklɔk; ˋpɪk͵lɑk] *n*. 1. 撬锁具。2. 撬锁人，窃贼。3. 最优选手。

pick-mat·tock [ˈpikmætək; ˋpɪkmætək] *n*. (一头尖一头平的)鹤嘴锄，铁镐。

pick-me-up [ˈpikmiːʌp; ˋpɪkmi͵ʌp] *n*.〔俚〕兴奋剂；(尤指)含酒兴奋饮料。

pick-off [ˈpikɔf, ˋpɪk͵ɔf] *n*.【无】传感器，敏感元件；拣拾器；【机】自动脱模装置。

pick·pock·et [ˈpik͵pɔkit; ˋpɪk͵pɑkɪt] *n*. 扒手。*Beware of* ~*s*! 谨防扒手。

pick·purse [ˈpikpəːs; ˋpɪk͵pɝs] *n*. 1.〔罕〕扒手。2.【植】荠菜；大爪草。

pick·some [ˈpiksəm; ˋpɪksəm] *a*. 好挑剔的，爱挑三拣四的，吹毛求疵的。

pick·thank [ˈpikθæŋk; ˋpɪk͵θæŋk] *n*.〔古〕马屁精。

pick·up [ˈpikʌp; ˋpɪk͵ʌp] **I** *a*. 1.〔口〕临时拼凑成的；(菜等)凑合的。2. (球队等)挑选的。**II** *n*. 1. 拾起；掘出物。2.〔美俚〕改进，好转；复兴。3.〔美俚〕消息，情报。4.〔美俚〕刺激(品)，兴奋剂。5. (球戏)回击落地球。6. (汽车的)加速度，加快。7. 敞篷小型运货卡车。8.〔美俚〕偶然的结识，偶然结识的人；妓女。9. 临时免费搭乘他人便车的人(= hitchhiker)。10. 随便买的东西；临时准备的菜饭；遗失品。11.【无】拾波，拾音；唱头，拾波器；电视摄像(管)。12. 实况转播地点。*a live* ~ (电视)室内摄影；播送(室内)实况。*an outdoor* ~【电视】室外摄影；实况转播。~ **coil**【无】拾波线圈。

Pick·wick·i·an [pikˈwikiən, -kjən; pɪkˋwɪkɪən, -kjən] **I** *a*. 1. (英国作者狄更斯小说《匹克威克外传》中主人翁)匹克威克式善意而诙谐的。2. (学句等)别有特殊〔专门〕意义的。**II** *n*.〔the ~〕1. 匹克威克俱乐部成员。2. 爱读《匹克威克外传》的人。*in a* ~ *sense* 有隐晦〔影射，微妙，特殊，诙谐〕意义的。

pick·y [ˈpiki; ˋpɪkɪ] *a*.〔口〕过分讲究的；吹毛求疵的；爱挑剔的。

pic·nic [ˈpiknik; ˋpɪknɪk] **I** *n*. 1. 野餐，郊游；各人自带食品的宴会。2.〔俚〕愉快的时间，轻松的工作。3. (猪的)脊肉。*get up a* ~ 发起野餐[旅行]会。*go out on a* ~ 去旅行，去野餐。*It's no* ~.〔口〕这不是一件轻松事。**II** *vi*. (*pic·nicked*; *pic·nick·ing*) 去郊游，去野餐。~ **biscuit** 小而甜的饼干。

pic·nick·er [ˈpiknikə; ˋpɪknɪkɚ] *n*. 野餐者，郊游者。

pic·nick·y [ˈpikniki; ˋpɪknɪkɪ] *a*. 野餐(式)的。

pic·nom·e·ter [pikˈnɔmitə; pɪkˋnɑmətɚ] *n*. = pycnometer.

pico- *comb*. *f*. 微微，沙，毫纤〔$=10^{-12}$，略 $\mu\mu$〕: *pico*farad.

pi·co·far·ad [͵pikəˈfærəd; ˋpaɪko͵færəd] *n*.【物】微微法(拉)。

pic·o·line [ˈpikəliːn, -lin; ˋpɪkəlin, -lɪn] *n*.【化】皮考啉，甲基吡啶。

pi·cot [piːˈkəu; ˋpiko] **I** *n*. (花边、缎带等上的)饰边小环；布边图纹。**II** *vt*. 在…的边上做上小环。

pic·o·tee [͵pikəˈtiː; ͵pɪkəˋti] *n*.【英植】红边黄花[白花]；荷兰石竹。

pic·o·tite [ˈpikətait; ˋpɪkətaɪt] *n*.【矿】铬尖晶石。

pic·quet [ˈpikit; ˋpɪkɪt] **I** *n*. 1. = picket 2. 2.【军】安铁丝网的乱桩〔漩涡形铁具〕。**II** *vt*., *vi*. = picket.

pic·rate [ˈpikreit; ˋpɪkret] *n*.【化】苦(味)酸盐。

pic·ric [ˈpikrik; ˋpɪkrɪk] *a*.【化】苦(味)酸的。~ **acid**【化】苦(味)酸；2, 4, 6 三硝基酚。

pic·rite [ˈpikrait; ˋpɪkraɪt] *n*.【矿】苦橄岩。**pic·rit·ic** [-ˈritik; -ˋrɪtɪk] *a*.

pic·ro·tox·in [͵pikrəˈtɔksin; ͵pɪkroˋtɑksɪn] *n*.【化】苦毒。

PICS = platform for Internet content selection【计】因特网内容选择平台。

Pict [pikt; pɪkt] *n*. 皮克特人〔古代苏格兰东部民族〕。~ *'s houses* 地下石洞。

Pict·ish [ˈpiktiʃ; ˋpɪktɪʃ] *a*. 皮克特人的。

pic·to·graph, pic·to·gram [ˈpiktəgrɑːf, -græm; ˋpɪktə͵græf, -͵græm] *n*. 1. 象形文字，绘画文字；用象形文字所作的记录。2. 古代[史前]石壁画。3.【统】图表。

pic·to·graph·ic [͵piktəˈgræfik; ͵pɪktəˋgræfɪk] *a*. (用)象形文字的；有象形文字特征的。**-i·cal·ly** *ad*.

pic·tog·ra·phy [pikˈtɔgrəfi; pɪkˋtɑgrəfɪ] *n*. 象形文字的使用；象形文字记载法。

pic·to·ri·al [pikˈtɔːriəl; pɪkˋtorɪəl] **I** *a*. 1. 绘画的。2. 有图片的；用图片表示的。3. 图画似的，形象化的。~ *art* 绘画。*a* ~ *magazine* 画报。*a* ~ *diagram* 示意图。*a* ~ *puzzle* 画谜。**II** *n*. 画报，画刊；画页；图画邮票。**-ly** *ad*.

pic·to·ri·al·ize [pikˈtɔːriəlaiz; pɪkˋtorɪəl͵aɪz] *vt*. 用图画表示。**-ali·za·tion** [pik͵tɔːriəlaiˈzeiʃən; pɪk͵torɪəlaɪˋzeʃən] *n*.

pic·ture [ˈpiktʃə; ˋpɪktʃɚ] **I** *n*. 1. 画，图画。2. 画像；照片。3. 图画似的叙述，写照；画一般美的东西；图画似的风景，美景。4. 相似的形象；化身；体现。5. 心像；情景；局面。6. 影片；〔the ~s〕电影。7.【无】图像。*a* ~ *post-card* 美术明信片。*I had my* ~ *taken*. 我请人照了相了。*She is a* ~. 她像画一样的美丽。*He is the* ~ *of his father*. 他活像他父亲。*He is the very* ~ *of health*. 他是健康的化身(十分健康)。***be*** (***high up***) ***in the*** ~〔美俚〕出头露面；成为要人；取得成功。***come into the*** ~ 1. 出现；引起注意。2. 被牵涉到。***give a*** ~ ***of*** 把…描绘一番。***go*** ~***s***〔美〕签订演戏合同，入电影界。***go to the*** ~***s*** 看电影去。***in the*** ~ 1. 在本题之内的。2.【美体】熟练，有胜利希望。***out of the*** ~ 1. 在本题之外的，不相干的。2.〔美俚〕喝醉了的。3. 不重要的。***sit for one's*** ~ 摆好姿势让人画像[照相]。**II** *vt*. 1. 画；用图片表示。2. (形象地)描写。3. 想像。4. 把…(作为电影)拍摄。~ *to oneself* 想像。~ **book** 图画书。~ **card** 1. 花牌〔纸牌中的 K, Q, J〕。2. 美术明信片。~**drome** [~ **hall**, ~ **palace**, ~ **theatre**]〔英〕电影院。~ **element**【无】像素，像点。~ **frame** 1. 画架。2.〔美俚〕绞刑架。~ **frequency**【电视】像频，帧频。~ **gallery** 1. 绘画陈列馆；美术馆；画廊。2.〔美马戏用语〕身上刺花的人。~**-goer** 影迷。~ **hat** (女人戴的)阔边帽。~**-in-(a-)picture** 画中画〔数码式电视机屏幕上的一角能显示另一个画面，亦作 PIP〕。~ **monitor**【电视】图像监视器。~ **phone** 电视电话。~ **play** 电影剧。~ **puzzle** 画谜。~ **ratio**【电视】画面(长宽)比。~ **show** 1. 绘画展览会。2. 电影；电影院。~**some** 引人注目的；吸引人的；适宜拍照片的。~ **tube**【电视】显像管(= kinescope)。~ **window** 风景窗。~ **writing** (远古时代)用图画记载事件[通讯](的方法)；象形文字。

pic·tur·esque [͵piktʃəˈresk; ͵pɪktʃəˋrɛsk] *a*. 1. (景色等)画似的，美丽的；绚丽的；富于画趣的。2. 别致的。3. (语言)生动的，形象化的，逼真的。4. (个性)突出的，独创的。**-ly** *ad*. **-ness** *n*.

pic·tur·ize [ˈpiktʃəraiz; ˋpɪktʃə͵raɪz] *vt*. 1. 用图画表示；使绘画化。2. 使电影化；把…拍成电影。

pic·ul [ˈpikəl; ˋpɪkʌl] *n*. (*pl*. ~(*s*)) 担，百斤〔中国、泰国等重量单位〕。~**-stick** 扁担。

Pi·cus [ˈpaikəs; ˋpaɪkəs] *n*.【罗神】田园之神。

pid·dle [ˈpidl; ˋpɪdl̩] *vi*.〔英古、美〕1. 拖沓地处理[工

作]；鬼混，闲混；浪费（*away*）（精力，时间，金钱等）。**2.**〔美俚〕（学生）背错书。**3.**〔口、儿〕小便，撒尿。

pid·dling [ˈpidliŋ; ˋpɪdlɪŋ] ***a.*** 细小的，无价值的，不足道的，琐碎的。

pid·dock [ˈpidək; ˋpɪdək] ***n.*** 【动】星火蛤。

pidg·in [ˈpidʒin; ˋpɪdʒɪn] ***n.*** **1.**（不同语种的人在商业交往中形成的）混杂语言，混杂行话。**2.** 洋泾浜英语〔指旧中国上海等地使用的混杂英语〕。**3.**〔口〕事务〔business 在半殖民地时代中国的讹音字〕（= pigeon）。～ **English** 洋泾浜英语。

pi-dog [ˈpaidɔg; ˋpaɪˏdɑg] ***n.*** = pye-dog.

P

pie[1] [pai; paɪ] ***n.*** **1.** 馅饼；馅饼状物。**2.**〔美俚〕容易得到的称心东西；容易的工作。**3.**〔美俚〕不正当的得利，邪财。*a minced* ～ 肉末馅饼。***a*** ～ ***in the sky*** 乌托邦；希望中的报酬；渺茫的幸福。（***as***）***easy as*** ～〔美口〕极容易。（***as***）***nice*** [***good***] ***as*** ～ 极好。***cut a*** ～〔美〕妄加干预。***eat humble*** ～ 忍辱含垢。***have a finger in the*** ～ 干预，插手；参与其事；与某事有关系。***put one's finger into another's*** ～ 多管闲事。～ **book**〔美俚〕饭票簿。～ **card**〔美俚〕工人工会会员证。～ **chart** 馅饼形统计图〔用大小扇形表示比例〕。～ **counter**〔美俚〕（政治上的）资助[分赃]。～ **man** 卖[做]馅饼的人。～**-plant**〔方〕食用大黄〔常用做点心馅〕。～ **wagon**〔美俚〕**1.**（警察的）警备车。**2.** 流动小吃车。

pie[2] [pai; paɪ] ***n.*** **1.**【动】喜鹊。**2.** 爱说话的人。

pie[3] [pai; paɪ] **I** ***n.*** **1.**【印】杂色铅字。**2.** 混乱。**II** ***vt.*** 使混杂；弄乱（铅字、版面）。

pie[4] [pai; paɪ] ***n.*** 派〔印度的旧辅币名〕。

pie·bald [ˈpaibɔːld; ˋpaɪˏbɔld] **I** ***a.*** **1.**（马）黑白斑的，有斑纹的。**2.** 驳杂的。**II** ***n.*** **1.** 有斑纹的动物（尤指花斑马）。**2.**〔喻〕杂色。

piece [piːs; pis] ***n.*** **1.** 片；断片，碎片；一部，部分，部件。**2.**〔作量词〕一片，一幅，一匹，一块，一件，一项，一番，一段，一篇，一出，一首，一张。**3.**（艺术）作品。**4.** 炮，枪，火器。**5.** 货币，钱币；标志物；筹码。**6.**（计件工的）工作（量）；事，事项，条款。**7.**〔美俚〕点心，小吃，（饭等的）一口。**8.** 棋子。**9.** 酒杯，桶。**10.** 样品，样本；例子。**11.**〔口〕人；家伙；女人〔多带轻蔑意〕。**12.**（乐器）演奏者〔用以构成复合词〕。*a* ～ *of paper* 一张纸。*a* ～ [*two* ～*s*] *of bread* 一块[两块]面包。*a bad* ～ *of road* 一段坏路。*a fine* ～ *of painting* 一幅好画。*a night* ～ 夜景图；夜想曲。*a* ～ *of water* 一片池塘[小湖]。*an animal* [*a war*] ～ 动物[战争]画。*a field* ～ 野炮。*She is a bold* ～. 她是一个放荡的女人。*What a* ～ *of folly*! 真混蛋! *a* ～ *of impudence* 不要脸的话[举动]。*a* ～ *of work* **1.** 一件作品[产品]。**2.** 费力的工作；难事；〔口〕纷扰。***a*** ～ ***of*** ... 在某种意义[程度]上是个…，还算是一个…。***a*** ～ ***of*** (***the***) ***action***（某项活动或收益中的）一份；一杯羹。***a*** ～ ***of cake***〔口〕轻松[愉快]的事情。～ ***of eight*** 西班牙古银币。～ ***of flesh***〔口〕人，（尤指）女人。～ ***of goods***〔谑〕东西〔指女人和小孩〕。***a*** ～ ***of one's mind*** 直率的意见；指责（*give sb. a* ～ *of one's mind* 对某人坦白表示自己的意见；当面指责某人）。***all to*** ～***s*** **1.** 疲惫不堪的，虚弱已极的；神经受撼动的；惊慌而受震动的。**2.**（破得）粉碎。**3.**〔俚〕完全，充分，彻底。***by*** [***on***] ***the*** ～ 按件（计酬）。***come to*** ～***s*** 粉碎；（计划）成画饼。***cut to*** ～***s*** **1.** 切碎；使溃散。**2.** 议论某人，把（某人）批评得体无完肤。***eat a*** ～〔口〕吃零食。***fall*** [***come***, ***go***, ***tumble***] ***to*** ～***s*** 崩碎，垮碎，粉碎。***go all to*** ～***s*** 气馁沮丧。***in one*** ～ 成整块，没有接缝。***in*** ～***s*** **1.** 破碎。**2.**（意见等）分歧，不一致。***of a*** [***one***] ～（***with***）（和…）同一种类的，同型的；首尾一贯的；调和的。～ ***by*** ～ 一件一件；一点一点，逐渐。***speak one's*** ～ **1.** 朗诵。**2.**〔美口〕诉苦，提意见。**3.**〔美俚〕求婚。***take to*** ～***s*** 拆（机器），（机器）拆散。***tear*** [***break***, ***pull***, ***pick***] ***to*** [***into***] ～***s*** 把…扯[砸]得粉碎。**II** ***vt.*** **1.** 接，补；修理（*up*）。**2.** 联结，结合；拼合，拼凑（*together*）；串成（*out*）。—***vi.*** **1.**【纺】接头。**2.**〔口〕吃零食。～ ***in*** 插入，添加。～ ***on*** 接合，补足（*to*）。～ ***out*** 补足，完成。～ ***together*** 拼合，接合，综合。～ ***up*** 接合，弥缝。～**-broker** 零售商贩。～**-dyed** ***a.*** 成匹染色的。～ **goods**〔*pl.*〕【纺】匹头，布匹。～ **rate** 计件工资。～**-work** 计件工作，包工工作。～**-worker** 零工，计件工。

pi·èce-de-ré·sis·tance [ˈpjes də reiˈziːstɑ̃ːns; ˋpjɛs də ˏrezisˋtɑ̃ns] ***n.***〔F.〕**1.** 餐中主菜，主要食品。**2.** 主要事件；主要作品。

piece·meal [ˈpiːsmiːl; ˋpismil] **I** ***ad.*** 一件一件，一点一点，逐渐地（= by ～）。**II** ***a.*** **1.** 一件一件的；逐渐的。**2.** 零零碎碎的。**III** ***n.*** 断片，块。

pie·crust [ˈpaikrʌst; ˋpaɪˏkrʌst] ***n.*** **1.** 烘酥的馅饼皮。**2.** 做馅饼的糊。*Promises are, like* ～, *made to be broken.* 允诺常常是靠不住的。***as short as*** ～ 性急。

pied [paid; paɪd] ***a.*** **1.** 斑驳的，杂色的。**2.** 穿著杂色衣服的。**3.**〔美俚〕思想混乱的。

pied-à-terre [ˈpjeitɑːˈtɛə; ˏpjedaˋtɛr] ***n.***〔F.〕临时休息所；（备用的）临时寓所。

pied·mont [ˈpiːdmɔnt; ˋpidmɑnt] **I** ***a.*** 山麓的，山前地带的。*a* ～ *stream* 山脚下的溪水。**II** ***n.*** 山麓。

Pied·mont [ˈpiːdmənt; ˋpidmɑnt] ***n.*** **1.** 皮德蒙特山脉〔意大利〕。**2.** 美国皮德蒙特地区。

Pied·mon·tese [ˌpiːdmɔnˈtiːz; ˏpidmɑnˋtiz] **I** ***a.***（意大利的）皮德蒙特的；意大利人的；意大利文化的。**II** ***n.***（*pl.* ～）皮德蒙特土人；皮德蒙特居民；意大利土人；意大利居民。

pied·mont·ite [ˈpidməntait; ˋpɪdməntaɪt] ***n.***【矿】红帘石。

pied noir [pjeˈnəwɑː; pjɛdˋnwar] ***n.***（*pl.* ***pieds noirs***）〔F.〕（在阿尔及利亚的）欧洲人〔特指法国移民〕。

pie-dog [pai-dɔg; paɪ-dɑg] ***n.*** = pye-dog.

pie-eyed [ˈpaiˈaid; ˋpaɪˏaɪd] ***a.***〔美俚〕**1.** 喝醉了的。**2.** 不漂亮的。**3.**（因惊讶等）睁大了眼睛的。

Pie·gan [ˈpiːgən; ˋpigən] ***n.***（*pl.* ～(***s***)）派岗族人〔黑脚印第安人的一支〕。

pie-pow·der [ˈpaipaudə; ˋpaɪpaʊdɚ] ***n.***〔古〕行商。

pier [piə; pɪr] ***n.*** **1.** 码头；防波堤。**2.** 桥脚，墩。**3.**【建】窗间壁，户间壁，扶壁；柱，角柱。*a floating* ～ 浮码头。*a landing* ～ 码头。*an end* ～ 终端（电）杆。～ **glass** 穿衣镜；窗间镜。～ **table** 矮几〔多置于两窗间，常在窗间镜之下〕。

pier·age [ˈpiəridʒ; ˋpɪrɪdʒ] ***n.*** 码头费。

Pierce [piəs; pɪrs] ***n.*** 皮尔斯〔姓氏〕。

pierce [piəs; pɪrs] ***vt.*** **1.** 刺穿，戳穿，贯穿；刺破，穿（孔）；突入，突破。**2.** 深深打动，使感动。**3.** 看穿，看破，洞察。**4.**（出于美容目的等）在（耳、鼻等上）穿孔。*The wall is* ～*d by* [*with*] *windows.* 墙上开了窗户。～ *the enemy's line* 突破敌人阵线。*His heart was* ～*d with grief.* 他伤透了心。—***vi.*** 刺入，穿入，穿进（*into*, *through*）。～ *through the enemy's line* 突破敌人防线。

pierc·er [ˈpiəsə; ˋpɪrsɚ] ***n.*** **1.** 穿孔的人[物]；钻孔器，锥；（酒桶等的）开口器。**2.**（昆虫的）产卵管，螯针。**3.**〔俚〕锐眼。

pierc·ing [ˈpiəsiŋ; ˋpɪrsɪŋ] ***a.*** **1.** 刺穿的，贯穿的；尖锐的。**2.** 打动人心的。**3.** 观察敏锐的，洞察的，有眼光的。**4.**（评论等）尖刻的。～ *cold* 刺骨的寒冷。*a* ～ *shriek* 尖叫。*a* ～ *eye* 锐利的眼力。**-ly** ***ad.***

pier·head [ˈpiəhed; ˋpɪrˏhɛd] ***n.*** 码头外端。

Pi·er·i·an [paiˈeriən, paiˈiər-; paɪˋɪrɪən, paɪˋɪr-] ***a.***（古马其顿地名，诗神缪斯出生地）皮埃里亚的；缪斯女神的。***the*** ～ ***spring*** 缪斯女神的泉水，诗的源泉；灵感（*drink of the* ～ *spring* 诗兴大发）。

Pi·er·i·des [paiˈeridiːz; paɪˋɪrɪˏdiz] ***n.***【希神】= the Muses.

pi·er·i·dine [paiˈeridain, -din; paɪˋɛrɪdaɪn, -dɪn] ***a.***【动】粉蝶科（*Pieridae*）的〔包括白蝶〕。

Pi·erre [pi(:)ˈɛə, peə; pjɛr, pɪr] ***n.*** 皮埃尔〔男子名, Peter 的异体〕。

Pi·er·rot [ˈpiərəu; ˋpɪəro] ***n.*** (*fem.* ***pi·er·rette*** [piəˈret; pɪəˏrɛt])〔F.〕**1.** 皮耶罗〔古法国哑剧中的白衣丑角〕。**2.**〔p-〕(搽白粉、穿白衣的)丑角。

Pi·e·ta [ˌpieˈtɑ:; pjeˋtɑ] ***n.***〔It.〕圣母马利亚膝上抱着基督尸体的图画[雕刻]。

Pi·e·tism [ˈpaiətizəm; ˋpaɪətɪzəm] ***n.*** **1.** 虔信派〔17 世纪德国路德教的一个宗派〕;虔信主义。**2.**〔p-〕虔诚,虔敬。**3.** 假装虔诚。

Pi·e·tist [ˈpaiətist; ˋpaɪətɪst] ***n.*** 虔信派教徒;〔p-〕虔信的人。

Pi·e·tis·tic, Pi·e·tis·ti·cal [paiəˈtistik, -tikə; paɪəˋtɪstɪk, -tɪkəl] ***a.*** **1.** 虔信派(教徒)的。**2.**〔p-〕虔信的;假装虔诚的。

pi·e·ty [ˈpaiəti; ˋpaɪətɪ] ***n.*** **1.** 虔敬,虔诚。**2.** 孝顺,孝敬。**3.** 忠顺,恭敬;爱国。*filial* ～ 孝顺。

piezo- *comb. f.* 表示"压(力)": *piezo*crystal.

pi·e·zo·chem·is·try [paiˌi:zəuˈkemistri; paɪˏizoˋkɛmɪstrɪ] ***n.*** 压力化学,高压化学。

pi·e·zo·crys·tal [paiˌi:zəuˈkristəl; paɪˏizoˋkrɪstəl] ***n.***【物】压电晶体。**-tal·li·za·tion** ***n.***【物】加压结晶。

pi·e·zo·e·lec·tric [paiˌi:zəuiˈlektrik; paɪˏizoɪˋlɛktrɪk] ***a.***【物】压电的。～ **constant** 压电常数。～ **crystal** 压电晶体。

pi·e·zo·e·lec·tric·i·ty [paiˌi:zəuilekˈtrisiti; paɪˏizoɪlɛkˋtrɪsətɪ] ***n.***【物】压电(学);压电(现象)。

pi·e·zom·e·ter [ˌpaiəˈzɔmitə; ˏpaɪəˋzɑmətɚ] ***n.***【物】流压计,水压计,压觉计,压力计,压强计。

pi·e·zom·e·try [paiəˈzɔmitri; ˏpaɪəˋzɑmətrɪ] ***n.***【物】压力测定;流压测量(法)。

piff [pif; pɪf] ***int.*** 唏,噼〔子弹飞过声〕。

pif·fle [ˈpifl; ˋpɪfl] **I** ***vi.***〔口〕做傻事;讲废话。**II** ***n.*** 无聊事,傻事;傻话,废话,梦话。

pig [pig; pɪg] **I** ***n.*** **1.** 猪;〔美〕仔猪,猪肉;宰好的小猪,猪皮。**2.**〔口〕(猪一样)肮脏的人,嘴馋的人,贪心的人,顽固的人。**3.**〔俚〕警察;密探;荡妇。**4.** 金属块[锭];生铁,铣铁。**5.**〔美俚〕火车头;可疑的酒吧;赛马用的马(尤指劣马)。**6.** 橘子的瓤。*roast* ～ 烤小猪肉。***bring*** [***drive***] ***one's*** ～***s to a pretty*** [***a fine, the wrong***] ***market*** 卖吃亏,冒险失败;失策,失算;走错门槛,估计错误。***buy a*** ～ ***in a poke*** [***a bag***] 买下没有过目的东西,不管好坏乱买;不顾后果地承担义务,盲目负责。***go to*** ～***s and whistles*** 完蛋,失败,毁灭。***in a*** ～***'s eye*** 很少,难得;刚相反;不会的! ***in*** ～ (母猪)怀小猪的。***make a*** ～ ***of oneself*** 狼吞虎咽;大吃大喝。～ ***between sheets***〔美〕火腿夹心面包。***Pig might fly.*** 无稽之谈。～***'s eyes***〔口〕小眼睛。～***'s wash*** 泔水 (= pigwash)。～***'s whisper***〔俚〕**1.** 低声的私语。**2.** 一会儿(工夫)。***please the*** ～***s***〔谑〕如果运气好的话〔Please God 的代用语〕。***teach a*** ～ ***to play on a flute*** 教猪吹笛;做荒谬[不可能办到]的事。***when*** ～***s fly*** 永不,决不,决不可能。

II ***vt.*** (**-gg-**) (猪)下(仔)。— ***vi.*** **1.** (猪)生小猪。**2.** 猪一样聚在一块 (*together*);过猪一样的生活。～ ***it*** **1.** 猪一样聚在一块儿生活。**2.**〔美俚〕停止奔跑;放慢速度;(因胆小)退却。～ ***out***〔美俚〕吃[喝]得过多,暴饮暴食。～ **bed** **1.** 猪圈。**2.**【冶】生铁场;铸床。～**boat**〔美海俚〕潜水艇。～ **board**【体】猪身形冲浪板。～**-breeding** 养猪。～ **bucket** 喂猪桶。～ **-eyed** ***a.*** 眼睛小而凹的。～ **fight**〔美〕跳舞。～**fish**【鱼】石鲈。～ **head**〔美〕顽梗的人,顽固分子。～**-headed** ***a.*** 顽固的,梗得要命的。～**-herd** 养猪员。～**iron** **1.** 生铁。**2.**〔美俚〕私酿的劣酒。～**-jump** ***vi.*** (马)举四脚跃起。**P- Latin**〔美〕将英语词尾改成拉丁语式的说法,倒读隐语〔又作 Hog Latin〕。～**lead**【冶】铅锭。～**nut**〔英〕落花生;〔美〕光滑山核桃〔喂猪用〕。～**pen** **1.** 猪圈。**2.** 肮脏的地方。～**skin** **1.** 猪皮。**2.**〔口〕马鞍。**3.**〔美俚〕美式足球 (= football)。～ **skinner**〔美俚〕美式足球选手。～**stick** ***vi.*** (用标枪)猎野猪。～**-sticker** **1.** 猎野猪的人;猎枪。**2.**〔口〕大号小刀;〔美口〕刺刀。～**sty** **1.** 猪圈。**2.** 肮脏的住处。～ **tail**〔口〕**1.** 辫子;有辫子的人。**2.** 卷成细条的烟草。～**wash** **1.** 泔水。**2.**〔俚〕泪水。**3.**〔俚〕劣酒;坏汤;低级咖啡。～**-weed**【植】藜;苋属植物。

pi·geon[1] [ˈpidʒin; ˋpɪdʒən] **I** ***n.*** **1.** 鸽子〔包括野鸽和家鸽,诗及美国英语中多用 dove〕;鸽灰色。**2.**〔口〕易受欺骗的人,傻子,生手。**3.** (抛入空中作射击飞靶的)土圆盘,土鸽 (= clay ～)。**4.**〔美〕姑娘;年轻妇女。**5.**〔英俚〕特别关心的事。*a homing* [*carrier*] ～ 信鸽。*a stool* ～ 囮鸽;囮子;密探。～*'s blood* 深红色。～*'s milk* **1.** 鸽子用以喂小鸽的部分消化了的食物。**2.**〔谑〕愚人节那天骗人去拿的没有的东西。***fly the*** ～***s*** 送货时在路上窃取煤炭。***It's your*** ～ ***to do*** …是你的责任。***pluck a*** ～〔俚〕骗去(呆子的)钱。

II ***vt.*** **1.** 用鸽子联络[传送(信息)]。**2.**〔俚〕骗,骗取,骗(钱)。～ **breast**【医】鸡胸。～**-breasted** ***a.*** 鸡胸的。～ **carrier** **1.** 通信鸽输送兵。**2.** 鸽笼。～ **company**【军】通信鸽连。～ **express** 信鸽通信。～ **fancier** 卖[养]鸽子的人。～**gram** 鸽信。～ **hawk**【鸟】灰背隼。～**-hearted** ***a.*** 胆小的;害羞的。～**hole** **1.** ***n.*** 鸽笼的出入孔;鸽笼的区划;小房间;(写字台上的)鸽笼式文件架,分类架,分信箱。**2.** ***vt.*** 把(文件等)搁入分类架;把(文件等)整理起来保存;把…留在记忆中;搁置,搁下来不管 (*～hole the request for a new park* 把开辟新公园的请求搁置起来)。～**-livered** ***a.*** 温顺的。～**-pea** (印度的)木豆。～ **shooting** 打鸽子;飞靶射击。～**tail** ***n.***〔美〕燕尾服。～**-toed** ***a.*** 脚趾内向的。～**wing** **1.** 一种顿脚的花色舞步。**2.** 鸽翼式花色溜冰动作。

pi·geon[2] [ˈpidʒin; ˋpɪdʒɪn] ***n.*** = pidgin. ～ **English** = pidgin English.

pi·geon·ry [ˈpidʒinri; ˋpɪdʒənrɪ] ***n.*** 鸽笼,鸽舍。

pig·ger·y [ˈpigəri; ˋpɪgərɪ] ***n.*** **1.** 猪场;猪栏;肮脏地方。**2.** 猪的习性〔指肮脏、懒惰、贪吃等〕。**3.**〔总称〕猪。

pig·gie [ˈpigi; ˋpɪgɪ] ***n.***, ***a.*** = piggy.

pig·gin [ˈpigin; ˋpɪgɪn] ***n.*** **1.** 汲水桶,小水桶。**2.** 长柄杓。

pig·gish [ˈpigiʃ; ˋpɪgɪʃ] ***a.*** 猪似的,贪吃的,肮脏的;利己的;顽梗的。**-ly** ***ad.*** **-ness** ***n.***

pig·gy [ˈpigi; ˋpɪgɪ] **I** ***n.*** 小猪;〔谑〕孩子。**II** ***a.*** 猪似的;贪心的;肮脏的。～**-wig**, ～**-wiggy** ***n.***〔儿〕小猪;脏孩子。

pig·gy·back [ˈpigibæk; ˋpɪgɪˏbæk] ***ad.***, ***a.*** = pickaback.

pig·let, pig·ling [ˈpiglit, -liŋ; ˋpɪglɪt, -lɪŋ] ***n.*** 小猪(尤指猪仔)。

pig·ment [ˈpigmənt; ˋpɪgmənt] ***n.*** **1.** 颜料,色料。**2.**【生】色素。～ **granule** 色素粒。～ **rayon** 无光人造丝。

pig·men·tal, pig·men·ta·ry [pigˈmentl, ˈpigməntəri; pɪgˋmɛntl, ˋpɪgmənˏtɛrɪ] ***a.*** (含有)颜料的;色素的;分泌色素的。

pig·men·ta·tion [ˌpigmənˈteiʃən; ˏpɪgmənˋteʃən] ***n.*** **1.** 色素淀积,着色(作用)。**2.**【医】色素沉着。

pig·my [ˈpigmi; ˋpɪgmɪ] ***n.***, ***a.*** = pygmy.

pi·gno·li·a, pi·gno·li [piˈnjəuliə, -li; piˋnoljə, -lɪ] ***n.*** 可食松子。

pig·no·rate [ˈpignəreit; ˋpɪgnəret] ***vt.*** 交出[接受]…作为抵押。

pig·nus [ˈpignəs; ˋpɪgnəs] ***n.*** (*pl.* ***-no·ra*** [-nərə; -nərə])〔L.〕【法】**1.** 抵押契约,押据,当票。**2.** 典当物。

pignut [ˈpignʌt; ˋpɪgnʌt] ***n.*** 光滑山核桃;光滑山核桃树。

Pi·gou [ˈpigu; ˋpɪgu] ***n.*** 皮古〔姓氏〕。

pi·ka [ˈpaikə; ˋpaɪkə] ***n.*** 鼠兔科 (*Ochotondae*) 动物〔产于北美洲西部和亚洲高原岩石区〕。

Pike [paik; paɪk] ***n.*** 派克〔姓氏〕。

pike[1] [paik; paɪk] **I** ***n.***【史】长矛,镖枪。**II** ***vt.*** 用长矛戳

(伤、死)。*trail a* ～ 当兵,服役。

pike[2][paik; paɪk] **n.** 1. 矛头,枪尖,箭头;(走路时防滑用的)尖头杖。2. 〔英方〕(湖畔)尖峰。3. 【泳】虾式跳水。4. 〔方〕铁镐。*hit the* ～ 〔美〕出发,动身;前进。**-d a.** (有)尖的。

pike[3][paik; paɪk] **n.** 【动】梭鱼,狗鱼。

pike[4][paik; paɪk] **I n.** 1. (收通行税的)关卡;收税栅;收费门。2. 通行税。3. 税道,收税路;〔美俚〕大路。**II vi.** 〔美俚〕赶路;走,突然离开;死。

pike[5][paik; paɪk] **vi.** 〔美俚〕(跟着大赌客)小心谨慎的赌小钱。

P

pike[6][paik; paɪk] **n.** (由美国 Missiouri 州 Pike 县迁移到太平洋沿岸一带的)流浪农民。

pike·man [ˈpaikmən; ˋpaɪkmən] **n.** 1. 枪兵;使用铁镐的矿工。2. 通行税征收处的看守。

pike·perch [ˈpaikˌpəːtʃ; ˋpaɪkˏpɝtʃ] **n.** (*pl.* ～(*es*)) 鲈鲈属 (*Stizostedion*) 鱼〔如大眼鰤鲈 (*S. vitreum*)、加拿大鰤鲈 (*S. canadense.*)〕。

pik·er [ˈpaikə; ˋpaɪkɚ] **n.** 〔美俚〕1. 懦夫,临阵脱逃的人;小气鬼。2. 谨慎小心的小赌客;小投机商人。3. 流浪者。**-ish a.**

pik·er·ism [ˈpaikrizəm; ˋpaɪkrɪzəm] **n.** 〔美俚〕1. 小气,吝啬。2. 胆小。

pike·staff [ˈpaikstɑːf; ˋpaɪkˏstæf] **n.** (*pl.* **-staves** [-steivz; -stevz]) 长矛柄,枪柄;(旅行者用以防滑的)尖头杖。*as plain as a* ～ 极明白的。

pil·af(f) [piˈlɑːf; pəˋlɑf] **n.** = pilau.

pi·las·ter [piˈlæstə; pəˋlæstɚ] **n.** 【建】壁柱,半露柱。

pil·a·to·ry [piˈleitəri; pəˋletərɪ] **I n.** 生发剂。**II a.** 刺激生发的。

pi·lau, pi·law [piˈlau, piˈlɔː; pəˋlo, pɪˋlɔ] **n.** (东方的)烩肉饭〔米中加鱼或肉及调味品制成〕。

pilch [piltʃ; pɪltʃ] **n.** 尿布垫。

pil·chard, pil·cher [ˈpiltʃəd, ˈpiltʃə; ˋpɪltʃɚd; ˋpɪltʃɚ] **n.** 【动】沙脑鱼,沙丁鱼。

pile[1][pail; paɪl] **I n.** 1. 堆积,堆;火葬柴堆 (= funeral ～)。2. 大量,大批,大块;高大建筑物;〔口〕钱堆,财产。3. 【物】电堆,电池;铀堆;(连锁)反应堆。4. 【建】桩。5. 【军】叉枪。*a dry* ～ 【物】干电池,干电堆。*an uranium* ～ 铀堆。*a* ～ *of* (*books*) 一大堆(书籍)。***a*** ～ ***of bucks*** 〔美〕一盘子荞麦饼。***a*** ～ ***of dough*** 一大笔钱。***a*** ～ ***of shot*** 【数】积弹。***make a*** [***one's***] ～ 发财。**II vt.** 1. 堆 (*up*; *on*);积蓄 (*up*);堆积;层积;【军】叉(枪),架(枪)。2. 在…上堆东西。3. 【海】使(船)冲上岩礁[浅滩]。4. 【物】用反应堆处理。—**vi.** 1. 堆积;积累。2. 拥,挤;进(入) (*in*; *into*);走出 (*out*; *off*)。～ *into a car* 挤进车子里。***P- arms!*** 叉枪! 架枪! ～ ***in*** 〔美俚〕挤入(车内,屋内)。～ ***it on*** 夸张。～ ***on*** [***up***] ***the*** (*agony*) 〔口〕对(悲痛)的刻意渲染[描绘]。～ ***out*** 〔美俚〕赶紧跑掉。～ ***Pelion on Ossa*** 山上有山,困难重重〔Pelion 及 Ossa 均系希腊山名〕。～ ***up*** 1. 堆积;积聚;(汽车等)挤在一起。2. (使)(船)搁浅;(汽车、飞机等)撞毁。～**-up** 1. **n.** (数辆汽车等的)同时碰撞;(繁重任务等的)堆集。2. **vi.** (数辆汽车等)同时撞挤在一起。

pile[2][pail; paɪl] **I n.** 1. 杆木,木桩,桥桩。2. 箭头;【徽】楔形;草叶。*a* ～ *foundation* 【建】打桩屋基。*raise* [*draw*, *withdraw*] ～ 拔桩。**II vt.** 1. 打(桩);把桩打入…;用桩支撑[加固]。2. 给…装箭头。～**driver** 打桩机;打桩者。～**-dweller** 湖边桩屋居民。～**-dwelling** 湖边桩屋。

pile[3][pail; paɪl] **I n.** 1. 软毛,绒毛;毛茸。2. (布、绒的)软面。**II vt.** 使起绒。**-d a.** 有绒毛的。

pile[4][pail; paɪl] **n.** 痔疮;〔*pl.*〕痔。*blind* ～*s* 痔核。

pile[5][pail; paɪl] **n.** 〔古〕钱币的背面。***cross or*** ～ 硬币的正面或反面 (= heads or tails, 见 head 条)。

pi·le·ate, pi·le·at·ed [ˈpailiit, -tid, ; ˋpaɪlɪɪt, -tɪd] **a.** 1. 【植】有菌盖的。2. 【动】有羽冠的。

pi·le·ous [ˈpailiəs, ˈpili-; ˋpaɪlɪəs, ˋpɪlɪ-] **a.** 有毛的,多毛的,生毛的。

pi·le·um [ˈpailiəm, ˈpili-; ˋpaɪlɪəm, ˋpɪlɪ-] **n.** (*pl.* **-lea** [-ə; -ə]) 鸟头的顶部。

pi·le·us [ˈpailiəs, ˈpili-; ˋpaɪlɪəs, ˋpɪlɪ-] **n.** (*pl.* **-le·i** [-liai; -lɪaɪ]) 1. (古罗马)一种无沿帽。2. 【植】菌盖。3. 【动】(水母的)伞状盘;鸟头的顶部 (= pileum)。

pile·wort [ˈpailwəːt; ˋpaɪlwɝt] **n.** 1. 白屈菜;小白屈菜 (= celandine)。2. 白屈菜属植物。

pil·fer [ˈpilfə; ˋpɪlfɚ] **vt.**, **vi.** 偷窃,扒;小偷小摸。～**-proof a.** 防小偷的,安全的。**-er** [ˈpilfərə; ˋpɪlfərɚ] **n.** 小偷。

pil·fer·age [ˈpilfəridʒ; ˋpɪlfərɪdʒ] **n.** 1. 小偷小摸,扒窃。2. 赃品。

pil·gar·lic [pilˈgɑːlik; pɪlˋgɑrlɪk] **n.** 1. 秃头,秃顶的人。2. 被人轻视[奚落]的人,被人以虚假同情的态度对待的人。

pil·grim [ˈpilgrim; ˋpɪlgrɪm] **I n.** 1. 香客,朝圣者,参拜圣地的人。2. 游历者,旅客,流浪者。3. 最初的移民;〔美西部〕新来移民;〔P-〕1620 年移居美洲的英国清教徒。*a* ～*'s staff* 香客手杖。～(*'s*) *signs* 朝山纪念品。～*s on earth* 尘世的过客。*Pilgrim's Progress*《天路历程》〔17 世纪英国作家班扬的寓言式作品〕。*the P-* (*Fathers*) 【美史】1620 年避英国教祸而到美国创立普利茅斯 (Plymouth)殖民地的新教徒。**II vi.** 1. 朝山进香,朝圣,参拜圣地。2. 流浪。～ **shell** 海扇壳。

pil·grim·age [ˈpilgrimidʒ; ˋpɪlgrəmɪdʒ] **I n.** 1. 参拜圣地;朝圣,朝山进香。2. 人生的旅程,一生。***go on a*** ～ ***to*** 去…朝圣。***make one's*** ～ ***to*** 参拜。**II vi.** 去朝圣,去参拜圣地。

pil·grim·ize [ˈpilgrimaiz; ˋpɪlgrɪmaɪz] **vi.** 去朝圣。

pi·li [piˈliː; pɪˋli] **n.** 〔Tag.〕1. 卵橄榄。2. 卵橄榄树 (*Canarium ovatum*)。

pili- *comb. f.* 表示"毛": *pili*ferous.

pi·lif·er·ous [paiˈlifərəs; paɪˋlɪfərəs] **a.** 【生】被毛的,有毛的。

pil·i·form [ˈpilifɔːm; ˋpɪləˏfɔrm] **a.** 毛形的。

pil·ing [ˈpailiŋ; ˋpaɪlɪŋ] **n.** 1. 打桩,打桩工程。2. 桩,桩基;桩材。

Pil·i·pi·no, Fi·li·pi·no [ˌpiliˈpiːnəu; ˏpɪlɪˋpino] **n.** 他加禄语〔1962 年定为菲律宾国语〕(= Tagalog)。

pill[1][pil; pɪl] **I n.** 1. 丸,药丸;〔the ～〕(女用口服)避孕丸。2. 讨厌的东西[人];苦事。3. 〔俚〕炮弹,子弹;球;〔*pl.*〕〔英俚〕撞球战,弹子战。4. 〔美俚〕香烟;切去两端的雪茄烟;(鸦片)烟泡。5. 投票用小球。6. 【农】粒肥。7. 〔*pl.*〕〔口〕医生。***a bitter*** ～ ***to swallow*** 不能不做的苦事,不得不忍受的屈辱。***a*** ～ ***to cure an earthquake*** 软弱的措施,姑息手段,弥补政策。***gild*** [***sugar***] ***the*** ～ 加糖衣,美化讨厌的东西[人]。**II vt.** 1. 把…作成丸药;给…吃丸药。2. 〔俚〕投票反对;排斥;不录取;开除。～ **bag** 〔美俚〕医生。～ **coll** 〔美俚〕药学专科学校。～ **pad** 〔美俚〕鸦片窝,吸毒窝。～ **peddler** 〔美俚〕医生。～**roller** 〔俚〕医生,医科学生。～ **shooter** 〔美俚〕医生,药剂师。

pill[2][pil; pɪl] **vt.** 1. 〔古〕抢劫,掠夺。2. 〔方〕= peel.

pil·lage [ˈpilidʒ; ˋpɪlɪdʒ] **I n.** 抢劫,掠夺;掠夺物。**II vt.**, **vi.** 抢劫,掠夺。**-r n.** 抢劫者,掠夺者。

pil·lar [ˈpilə; ˋpɪlɚ] **I n.** 1. 柱;纪念柱;(柱)墩,柱脚;【矿】(矿井中硬炭层或岩石形成的)矿柱,煤柱。2. 柱状物〔水柱,火柱等〕。3. 〔喻〕台柱,栋梁,柱石。*a* ～ *of the state* 国家的栋梁。***be driven from*** ～ ***to post*** [***from post to*** ～] 被逼得四处奔走;到处碰壁,事事失败;被逼得走投无路。**II vt.** 1. 用柱子装饰[支持]。2. 成为…的栋梁。～**-box** 〔英〕邮筒。～**-stone** 隅石,奠基石。

pil·lar·et [ˈpilərit; ˋpɪlərɛt] **n.** 小柱。

pill·box [ˈpilbɔks; ˋpɪlˏbɑks] **n.** 1. (板纸制的)丸药盒。

2.〔英俚〕小马车,小汽车,小房屋。3.〔军俚〕独立小地堡。4.(平底无边)矮圆桶形女帽。

pil·ler [ˈpilə; ˋpɪlɚ] ***n.***〔美〕药剂师,药商。

pil·lion [ˈpiljən; ˋpɪljən] **I** ***n.*** **1.** 女用轻鞍;(骑手背后供女人乘用的)鞍褥。**2.**〔英〕(摩托车的)后座。**II** ***ad.*** 坐在后鞍上。*ride* ~ 骑后座。

pil·li·winks [ˈpiliwiŋks; ˋpɪlə,wɪŋks] ***n.*** 古代夹指刑具,拶子。

pil·lo·ry [ˈpiləri; ˋpɪlərɪ] **I** ***n.*** **1.** 颈手枷。**2.** 臭名,笑柄。***be in the*** ~ 成笑柄,遭人嘲弄。**II** ***vt.*** **1.** 把…上颈手枷示众。**2.** 使遭人嘲笑。

pil·low [ˈpiləu; ˋpɪlo] **I** ***n.*** **1.** 枕头。**2.**【机】轴枕,垫座。**3.**(棒球的)垒。**4.** 花边编织台。**5.**〔美俚〕拳击手套。***advise*** [***consult***] ***with one's*** ~ = ***take counsel of one's*** ~ 躺在床上细想一夜〔明天再说〕。**II** ***vt.*** **1.** 用…作枕头,做…的枕头;垫。**2.** 把…搁在枕上;使靠在(*on*)。— ***vi.*** 把头搁在枕头上,靠在枕上。~ **block**【机】轴台。~ **block bearing**【机】架座。~**case** 枕套。~ **fight** 打闹,小争执。~ **lace** 手编花边。~ **lava**【地】枕状熔岩。~ **pivot**【机】球面中心支枢。~ **puncher**〔美〕收拾房间的女佣人。~ **sham** 枕头饰套。~**slip** = ~case. ~ **warrior**〔俚〕枕头战士〔表面上气势汹汹实际上柔弱无能的人〕。

pil·low·y [ˈpiləui; ˋpɪləwɪ] ***a.*** 枕头似的;柔软的,一压就凹的。

pill·wort [ˈpilwəːt; ˋpɪlwɜ˞t] ***n.***【植】美洲线叶苹。

pi·lo·car·pin(e) [ˌpailəuˈkɑːpi(ː)n; ˏpaɪloˋkɑrpin] ***n.***【化】毛果(芸香)碱〔发汗、利尿剂〕。

pi·lose [ˈpailəus; ˋpaɪlos] ***a.***【动、植】软毛多的;柔毛状的。**pi·los·i·ty** [-ˈlɔsiti; -ˋlɑsətɪ] ***n.***【生】细毛被;多毛。

pi·lot [ˈpailət; ˋpaɪlət] **I** ***n.*** **1.** 领港员,舵手;【空】驾驶员,飞行员;领航员;【火箭】起动人员;指导员,领导人;〔美〕向导,带路人,带瞎丐走路的狗〔小孩〕;拳赛〔棒球俱乐部〕干事。**2.** 航线指南;罗针盘矫正器;〔美〕(机车前的)排障器。**3.**【交、建】导洞。**4.**【机、电】领示;导频;导向器;指示灯。*a chief* ~ 领港长。*an apprentice* ~ 领港见习员。*a first* [*senior*] ~ 正〔一级〕驾驶员。*a* ~ *in command*【空】机长。*a* ~*'s cockpit* 飞行员座舱。*a* ~*'s licence* 飞行员执照。*a* ~*'s log-book* 飞行员日记。*a robot* ~【空】自动驾驶仪。*a* ~ *balloon* 升力〔风向〕指示气球。***drop the*** ~ 辞退好顾问,失去良师益友。**II** ***a.*** **1.** 引导的,导向的。**2.**【机、电】辅助的,控制的。**3.**(生产等)小规模试验性质的。*a* ~ *plant*(小规模)试验厂。

III ***vt.*** **1.** 给(船只)领航〔领港〕(*on, in, over*)。**2.** 给…当向导,指导。**3.** 驾驶(飞机等)。~ **biscuit**, ~ **bread**(船中用)硬面包;硬饼干。~ **chart** 航空气象简图。~ **chute**【空】引导伞。~ **cloth**【纺】海员蓝色粗呢。~ **engine** 探路机车。~ **fish**【鱼】舟鰤。~ **flag**【海】找领港员或表示已有领港员在船上的信号旗。~**house** 操舵室,驾驶室。~ **jack** = ~ flag. ~ **jacket** 海员厚茄克。~-**officer**〔英〕空军少尉。~ **tube**【空】空速指示器。~ **whale** 巨头鲸。~ **wheel** 导轮。**-age** ***n.*** **1.** 领航,领港。**2.** 指导,向导。**3.** 领港费。**4.** 民航机驾驶术(~ *inwards* [*outwards*] 入港〔出港〕领港费)。**-ing** ***n.*** 领航,引水。**-less** ***a.*** 没有领港员〔驾驶员、舵手、领导人〕的。

Pil·sen [ˈpilzin; ˋpɪlzɪn] ***n.*** = Pizeň.

Pilt·down [ˈpiltdaun; ˋpɪltdaʊn] ***n.*** 皮尔丹〔英国地名〕。~ ***man***【人类】皮尔当人〔英国考古学家陶逊声称,他于1911年在英国 Sussex 州 Piltdown 地方发现史前人化石,称"皮尔当人",后经鉴定系伪造〕。

pil·u·lar [ˈpiljulə; ˋpɪljəlɚ] ***a.*** 药丸(状)的。

pil·ule [ˈpiljuːl; ˋpɪljul] ***n.*** 小药丸。

pil·y [ˈpaili; ˋpaɪlɪ] ***a.*** 有绒毛的;柔软的。

Pi·ma [ˈpiːmə; ˋpimə] ***n.*** (*pl.* ~(*s*)) **1.** 比马人〔北美印第安人的一个部族,居住在亚利桑那州基拉河及索尔特河流域〕。**2.** 比马人的乌托阿芝特克语。**3.**〔美〕比马棉(= ~ cotton);〔p-〕用比马棉制成的优质衣料。~ No. 1.【农】碧玛一号(小麦)。

Pi·man [ˈpiːmən; ˋpimən] **I** ***n.*** (属乌托阿芝特克语系的)比马语。**II** ***a.*** **1.** 比马语的。**2.** 比马人的。

pi·men·to [piˈmentəu; pɪˋmɛnto] ***n.*** (*pl.* ~*s*) **1.**【植】多香果(= allspice)。**2.** = pimiento.

pi·me·son [ˈpaiˈmiːzɔn; ˋpaɪmɛsən] ***n.***【原】π 介子。

pi·mien·to [piˈmjentəu; pɪˋmjɛnto] ***n.*** (*pl.* ~*s*) 甜辣椒。

pim·o·la [pimˈəulə; pɪˋmolə] ***n.*** 拌有甜辣椒的橄榄。

pimp [pimp; pɪmp] **I** ***n.*** **1.** 妓院老板,老鸨。**2.** 引人作坏事的人。**3.**〔美俚〕男妓。*a* ~ *stick*〔美俚〕香烟,烟卷儿。**II** ***vi.*** 拉皮条;为妓女拉客;帮助干坏事。

pim·per·nel [ˈpimpənel; ˋpɪmpə˞ˏnɛl] ***n.***【植】紫蘩蒌;海绿。

pimp·ing [ˈpimpiŋ; ˋpɪmpɪŋ] ***a.*** **1.** 细小的,没价值的。**2.** 小气的,卑鄙的。**3.** 病弱的。

pim·ple [ˈpimpl; ˋpɪmpl̩] ***n.***【医】丘疹,疙瘩,粉刺;小突起;脓疱。

pim·pled, pim·ply [ˈpimpld, ˈpimpli; ˋpɪmpl̩d, ˋpɪmplɪ] ***a.*** 尽是粉刺的,有疙瘩的。

pim·pon [ˈpimpɔn; ˋpɪmpɑn] ***n.***【植】苹婆〔广东凤眼果〕。

PIN = personal identification number 个人标识号〔自动提款卡等的个人密码〕。

pin [pin; pɪn] **I** ***n.*** **1.** 别针,扣针,饰针;有别针的徽章。**2.** 钉;楔;栓,销;(弦乐器上调弦的)轸子;发夹;测针;【电】插头;管脚;【海】桨架脚。**3.**〔*pl.*〕〔口〕腿。**4.**(装四加仑半的)小桶。**5.** 没价值的东西,琐碎东西。**6.** 靶心。*a safety* ~ 锁针,安全针;安全栓。*a firing* ~(枪的)撞针。*You might have heard a* ~ *fall.*(紧张得)连针掉下来也听得见(地寂静)。*There is not a* ~ *to choose between.* 没有多大差别,完全一样。***at a*** ~***'s fee*** 用极少代价。***be on one's last*** ~***s*** 快死,就要死。***be on one's*** ~***s*** 站着;健康。***be quick*** [***slow***] ***on one's*** ~***s*** 腿快〔慢〕。***in*** (***a***) ***merry*** ~ 高兴。***neat as a new*** ~ 清清爽爽的。***not care a*** ~ 一点也不在乎。***not worth a*** ~ 毫无价值。(***sit***) ***on*** ~***s*** (***and needles***) 如坐针毡〔急得要命〕。~***s and needles***(手脚的)发麻。***pull the*** ~〔美俚〕**1.** 停止工作;走开。**2.** 遗弃妻子,抛弃家属〔朋友等〕。***put*** [***keep***] ***in the*** ~〔口、俚〕**1.** 停止,作罢。**2.** 戒酒。***stick*** ~***s into*** (*sb.*) 激励某人;使(人)生气,使(人)烦恼。

II ***vt.*** **1.**(用钉等)钉住,别住,扣住(*up; together; on; to*);刺穿。**2.** 按住;按住使不能动(*against*);(用条约等)束缚住(*to*)。**3.**(用障壁等)围住,关住(*up*);〔俚〕抓住;【军】牵制。**4.** 把…归罪于(*on*)。~ ***one's faith on*** [***to***] 把信念寄托于。~ ***one's hopes on*** 把希望寄托在…上。~ (***sb.***) ***down*** (*to*) **1.** 强迫(人)承认〔履行〕条约。**2.** 用…束缚住;阻止;牵制;压住。~ ***up*** **1.** 钉住,钉起来;(用针)扣住,别住。**2.**【建】托换…的基础;加固。~ **artist**〔美俚〕堕胎手术师。~**ball** **1.** 桌上弹球戏。**2.**〔美〕球形针插。~**cushion** **1.** 针插。**2.**【无】栅形失真。~ **curl** 卷发器〔固定潮湿的发型〕。~-**curl** ***vt.*** 以卷发器卷发。~(-)**down**(通过破坏敌方地面站实现的)迫坠〔迫使敌方的导弹失控坠落〕。~ **money**(丈夫给妻女的)零用钱。~-**point** **1.** ***n.*** 针尖;极尖的顶端;极小的东西;琐事。**2.** 需准确轰炸的小目标;航空照片。**3.** ***a.*** 微小的;极准确的。**4.** ***vt., vi.*** 极精确地测定〔瞄准,轰炸〕;指出;确认。~-**prick** 针刺(的小孔);使人烦恼的小事情,刺耳的话。~-**tail**【动】针尾鸭;针尾松鸡。~-**up** **1.** ***n.*** 钉在墙上的东西;〔美俚〕被钉在墙上欣赏的女人相片。**2.** ***a.*** 可钉在墙上的;(女子)相片可钉在墙上供欣赏的,漂亮的。~-**wheel** ***n.*** **1.** 玩具风车。**2.** 彩色焰火。**3.**〔俚〕直升机。~-**work** ***n.***【纺】撚纱工艺;(针绣花边的)细小突出饰纹。

Pi·na·cea·e [paiˈneisiː; paɪˋnesɪ] ***n.*** 〔*pl.*〕【植】松科。

P

pin·a·co·the·ca [ˌpinəkəuˈθiːkə; ˏpɪnəkoˋθikə] **n.** (*pl.* ~*s*, *-cæ* [-siː; -si]) [L.] (希腊、罗马的)绘画馆。

pin·a·fore [ˈpinəfɔː, -fɔə,; ˋpɪnəfɔr, -for] **n.** (小孩、女工等的)围裙;围兜布,涎布;无袖女服。

pi·nang [piˈnæŋ; piˋnæŋ] **n.** 槟榔(树)。

pi·nas·ter [paiˈnæstə; paɪˋnæstɚ] **n.** 【植】南欧海松。

pi·ña·ta [piˈnjɑːtɑː; piˋnjɑtɑ] **n.** [Sp.] 彩饰陶罐[墨西哥人过节时将此种罐悬于天花板上,由儿童用棒击破以取得其中的玩具和糖果]。

pince-nez [ˈpɛ̃ːnsnei, ˈpæns-; ˋpɛ̃nsne, ˋpæns-] **n.** (*pl.* ***pince-nez*** [ˈpɛ̃ːnsneiz; ˋpɛ̃nsnez]) [F.] 夹鼻眼镜。

pin·cers [ˈpinsəz; ˋpɪnsɚz] **n.** *pl.* **1.** 钳子,铗子。**2.** 【动】螯;尾铗。**3.** 【军】钳形攻势[运动] (= ~(s) drive [movement])。

pin·cette [pɛ̃ːnˈset; ˏpɛ̃ˋset] **n.** (*pl.* ~**s**) [F.] (外科手术用的)小钳子;小镊子。

pinch [pintʃ; pɪntʃ] **I** ***vt.*** **1.** 捏,掐,撮,挟;(鞋子等)夹(脚);掐掉(嫩枝等);修剪 (*out, off, back*)。**2.** 折磨,使苦恼;使消瘦;使萎缩;使缩作一团。**3.** [方]削减,压缩;限制;使缺乏 (*for; in; of*)。**4.** 勒索,夺取 (*from; out of*);[俚]偷;[俚]逮捕,抓住。**5.** 【英赛马】催(马)快跑;【海】使(帆船)抢风急驶。**6.** 加入一撮(粉等)。**7.** 用杠杆撬动(重物)。*be ~ed with cold* 冷得缩手缩脚。*be ~ed with poverty* 穷困不堪。— ***vi.*** **1.** (向里)挤压,收缩 (*in*);(鞋等)紧,窄。**2.** 俭省,吝啬。**3.** (渴得、饿得,苦得)要命。**4.** 【地】(矿脉等)狭缩,变薄。~ ***and save*** 节衣缩食地攒钱。~ ***and scrape*** 东拼西凑;俭省。***be ~ed for*** (***money***) 手头拮据,缺钱等。***know*** [***feel***] ***where the shoe ~es*** 知道问题[困难]在那里。~ ***off*** 摘心,打尖;【物】箍断。~ ***out*** [***back***] 【园艺】摘心,摘除(嫩芽)。~ ***pennies*** 吝啬,节俭。

II ***n.*** **1.** 捏,掐,撮,挟【物】箍缩,收缩。**2.** 紧迫;困难,困苦;剧痛。**3.** 一撮,微量。**4.** 危机,危急。**5.** [美]矿脉的狭窄点。**6.** [俚]容易事。**7.** 撬杆。**8.** [俚]盗窃;[俚]逮捕,捕捉。*a ~ of salt* 一撮盐。*the ~ of poverty* 贫困的重压。***at*** [***in, on, upon***] ***a ~*** 在危急时。***when it comes to the ~*** 一旦危急时。***with a ~ of salt*** 有保留地,不全信地。~**bar** 撬杆。~**face** 面容消瘦的人。~**fist** 十分俭省的人;守财奴。~**-hit** ***vi.*** 【棒球】(吃紧时)代打;[喻]代表,代替。~**-hitter** 【棒球】(吃紧时出场的)代打者;(一般的)代理人,替手。~**penny** ***a.*** 吝啬的。**-ing** ***n.*** 【农】打尖,摘心。

pinch·beck [ˈpintʃbek; ˋpɪntʃbɛk] **I** ***n.*** **1.** 铜锌合金,金色黄铜。**2.** 赝品,冒牌货;廉价宝石。**II** ***a.*** **1.** 金色黄铜做的。**2.** 假的;便宜的。

pinch·ers [ˈpintʃəz; ˋpɪntʃɚz] ***n.*** [*pl.*] **1.** = pincers. **2.** [美俚]鞋子。

Pinck·ney [ˈpiŋkni; ˋpɪŋknɪ] ***n.*** 平克尼[姓氏]。

Pin·dar·ic [pinˈdærik; pɪnˋdærɪk] **I** ***a.*** **1.** (古希腊诗人)平达 (Pindar)的;平达体的。**2.** 格律谨严的。**II** ***n.*** [常 *pl.*] 平达体的诗[颂歌等]。

pin·der [ˈpində; ˋpɪndɚ] ***n.*** [美方]花生 (= peanut)。

pin·dling [ˈpindliŋ; ˋpɪndlɪŋ] ***a.*** [美方] **1.** 孱弱的,纤弱的,病弱的。**2.** 易怒的,乖张的。

pine[1] [pain; paɪn] ***n.*** 【植】**1.** 松树;松木。**2.** [口]凤梨,菠萝 (= pineapple)。*a ~ straw* [美]枯松叶。*Chinese ~* 油松。*Oregon ~* 美国松,洋松。*white ~* 枞。*a ~ tree* 松树。~ ***tree men*** [美]缅因 (Maine) 州人的绰号。***the Pine Tree State*** [美]缅因州的别名。~ **barren** [美南部]长有松林的沙地。~ **beauty** 【动】松夜蛾。~ **black** 松烟。~ **carpet** 松蛾。~ **cone** 松球,松果。~ **marten** 英国黑褐貂。~ **moth** 松毛虫。~ **needle** 松叶。~ **nut** **1.** 松果。**2.** 松子。~ **overcoat** [美俚](不值钱的)棺材。~ **resin** 松脂,松香。~ **tar** 松焦油。~ **wood** **1.** [*pl.*] 松林。**2.** 松木。

pine[2] [pain; paɪn] ***vi.*** **1.** 衰弱,憔悴,消瘦 (*out; away*)。**2.** 渴望;恋慕 (*after; for; to do*)。**3.** [古]埋怨,发牢骚。

pin·e·al [paiˈniəl, ˈpainiəl; paɪˋnɪəl, ˋpaɪnɪəl] ***a.*** **1.** 松毬状的。**2.** 【解】松果腺[体]的。*the ~ gland* [*body*] 【解】松果腺[体]。

pine·ap·ple [ˈpainæpl; ˋpaɪnæpl̩] ***n.*** **1.** 【植】菠萝,凤梨。**2.** [俚]炸弹,手榴弹。~ **cloth** 菠萝纤维布;手帕亚麻布;上浆全丝薄纱。

pi·nene [ˈpainiːn; ˋpaɪˏnin] ***n.*** 【化】蒎烯。

Pi·ner·o [piˈniərəu; pəˋnɪro] ***n.*** 皮尼罗[姓氏]。

pin·er·y [ˈpainəri; ˋpaɪnərɪ] ***n.*** 松林;菠萝温室。

pine·sap [ˈpainsæp; ˋpaɪnˏsæp] ***n.*** 水晶兰属 (*Monotropa*) 植物[包括锡杖花,鹿蹄草]。

pi·ne·tum [paiˈniːtəm; paɪˋnitəm] ***n.*** (*pl.* ***-ta*** [-tə; -tə]) **1.** 林,(收集不同种类松树的)松树栽培园。**2.** 关于松树的论文。

pine·y [ˈpaini; ˋpaɪnɪ] ***a.*** (***pin·i·er; -i·est***) = piny. *a ~ wood* [美南部]松林。

pin·feath·er [ˈpinfeðə; ˋpɪnˏfɛðɚ] ***n.*** (鸟的)幼羽,新生的羽绒毛。**-ed**, **-y** ***a.***

pin·fish [ˈpinfiʃ; ˋpɪnfɪʃ] ***n.*** (*pl.* ~(*s*)) 兔齿鲷。

pin·fold [ˈpinfəuld; ˋpɪnˏfold] **I** ***vt.*** 把…关入畜栏,监禁。**II** ***n.*** **1.** 牛栏。**2.** 禁闭室。

ping [piŋ; pɪŋ] **I** ***n.*** **1.** 砰,咻[枪弹飞过空中的声音]。**2.** 来自回声测距声纳设备的脉冲信号。**II** ***vi.*** 咻地响[飞过]。~ **jockey** 雷达兵,声纳兵。

Ping·er [ˈpiŋə; ˋpɪŋɚ] ***n.*** (研究海流的)声波发射器。

ping·er [ˈpiŋə; ˋpɪŋɚ] ***n.*** (微波炉上发出声响的)定时器;[转义]微波炉。

ping-pong [ˈpiŋpɔŋ; ˋpɪŋˏpɑŋ] ***n.*** 乒乓球。~ **effect** 乒乓效应[处理事情的踢皮球,互相推诿]。

pin·guid [ˈpiŋgwid; ˋpɪŋgwɪd] ***a.*** [谑]胖的;脂肪多的;油腻的;(土)肥沃的。

pin·head [ˈpinhed; ˋpɪnˏhɛd] ***n.*** **1.** 针头;小东西,无聊东西;傻子,笨人。**2.** [美]鸦片鬼;[美]店员;[美](铁路)扳道员。

pin·head·ed [ˈpinhedid; ˋpɪnˏhɛdɪd] ***a.*** 笨的,愚蠢的,傻的,糊涂的。**-ness** ***n.***

pin·hole [ˈpinhəul; ˋpɪnˏhol] ***n.*** 针孔,小孔,小洞。*a ~ camera* 无透镜照相机[在暗箱上开小孔,以代替透镜]。

pin·ing [ˈpainiŋ; ˋpaɪnɪŋ] ***n.*** (牛羊的)衰萎病,缺钴病;【植】憔萎病。

pin·ion[1] [ˈpinjən; ˋpɪnjən] **I** ***n.*** **1.** (鸟翼的)翼梢;翅膀;羽毛;[集合词]翮;[诗]翼。**2.** (人的)臂膀;臂绑。**II** ***vt.*** **1.** 剪断…的翮毛,捆住…的两翼。**2.** 捆住(两手);箝制,束缚。

pin·ion[2] [ˈpinjən; ˋpɪnjən] ***n.*** 【机】小齿轮。*a lazy ~* 惰轮。~ **shaft** 小齿轮轴。

pin·ite [ˈpinait, ˈpainait; ˋpɪnaɪt, ˋpaɪnaɪt] ***n.*** 【化】蒎立醇;【矿】块云母。

pi·ni·tol [ˈpainitɔːl, ˈpiniˈtəul; ˋpaɪnɪtɔl, ˋpɪnɪ-, -ˋtol] ***n.*** 【化】右旋肌醇甲醚。

pink[1] [piŋk; pɪŋk] **I** ***n.*** **1.** 【植】石竹;石竹花。**2.** 桃红色,粉红色。**3.** 化身;精华,极致。**4.** 名流;穿着入时的人。**5.** [英](猎狐用)红色上衣(料);猎狐的人。**6.** [美]私人侦探。**7.** [美俚]汽车驾驶执照;火急电报。**8.** [常 P-] [美俚]偏右的左派,左倾分子。**II** ***a.*** **1.** 粉红色的。**2.** 有点激进[左倾]的。**3.** 面红耳赤的,激怒的。**III** ***vt.***, ***vi.*** (使)变粉红色。*the Chinese ~* 石竹。*the Indian ~* 茑萝。*wear ~* 穿粉红色衣服。***in the ~*** (***of condition***) [口]极壮健;[美俚]喝醉。***the ~ of perfection*** 十全十美的东西[人]。***tickle sb. ~*** [美俚]使某人非常高兴。~**-collar** ***a.*** [美]粉红领阶层的,主要由妇女从事的职工(如护士,秘书等)的。~ **elephants** (吸毒后)幻觉。~ **English** "粉红色"英语[旁遮普语和英语的混合语]。~ **lady** 鸡尾酒[由白兰地等调制而成]。~ **slip** 解雇通知书。~ **tea** 午后茶会;社交活动。**-ly** ***ad.*** **-ness** ***n.***

pink[2][piŋk; pɪŋk] *n*. 1. 〔英〕幼小鲑鱼。2. 〔英方〕欧洲鲸鱼。
pink[3][piŋk; pɪŋk] *n*. 1. 〔废〕小孔。2. 〔罕〕刺伤;〔俚〕血。
pink[4][piŋk; pɪŋk] *vt*. 1. 刺,扎,戳(*out*)。在…穿小孔,穿饰孔。2. 在…边作饰褶〔作锯齿饰〕;〔英方〕装饰(*out*; *up*)。
pink[5][piŋk; pɪŋk] *vi*. (发动机)格登格登地响。
Pink [piŋk; pɪŋk] *n*. = Pinkerton.
pink·en [ˈpiŋkn; ˋpɪŋkn] *vi*. 成石竹色,成淡红色。
Pink·er·ton [ˈpiŋkətən; ˋpɪŋkətən] *n*. 平克顿〔姓氏〕。
pink·eye [ˈpiŋk-ai; ˋpɪŋk-aɪ] *n*. 1. (马的)流行性感冒;(人的)传染性结膜炎,眼炎,红眼。2. 澳洲阔嘴鸭。
pink·eyed [ˈpiŋkaid; ˋpɪŋkaɪd] *a*. 小眼的;(兔子等)眼发粉红色的。
Pink·er·ton [ˈpiŋkətən; ˋpɪŋkə·tən] 〔美〕平克顿私家侦探公司;便衣侦探。
Pin·kie [ˈpiŋki; ˋpɪŋkɪ] 〔美〕(平克顿私家侦探公司的)便衣侦探。
pink·ie[1][ˈpiŋki; ˋpɪŋkɪ] *n*. 〔美东部〕小(手)指。
pink·ie[2][ˈpiŋkiː; ˋpɪŋki] *n*. 尖头帆船。
pink·ish [ˈpiŋkiʃ; ˋpɪŋkɪʃ] *a*. 带粉红色的。
pink·o [ˈpiŋkəu; ˋpɪŋko] *n*. 〔美俚〕准左倾分子。
pink·root [ˈpiŋkˌruːt, -ˌrut; ˋpɪŋkˏrut, -ˏrʊt] *n*. 【植】浅赤根(*Spigelia marylandica*)〔原产美国东南部〕。
Pink·ster, Pinx·ter [ˈpiŋkstə; ˋpɪŋkstə·] *n*. 〔美〕= Whitsuntide. ~ *flower* 〔美〕粉红色杜鹃花。
pink·y [ˈpiŋki; ˋpɪŋkɪ] *a*. 粉红色的。
pin·na [ˈpinə; ˋpɪnə] *n*. (*pl*. ***pin·nœ*** [ˈpiniː, ˋpɪni]) 1. 【动】翅膀,翼,羽毛;鳍。2. 【植】羽片。3. 【解】耳廓。**pin·nal** *a*.
pin·nace [ˈpinis, -nəs; ˋpɪnɪs, -nəs] *n*. 【海】舰载艇,舢板〔常用作舰船等的供应船〕;【史】(附随大船的)二桅小船。
pin·na·cle [ˈpinəkl; ˋpɪnəkl̩] I *n*. 1. 【建】(哥德式建筑的)小尖塔;尖柱;尖端。2. 〔美〕小山;针峰。3. 极点,顶点。*a* ~ *rock* 尖岩。*the* ~ *of science* 科学尖端,尖端科学。II *vt*. 1. 使成小尖塔形。2. 把…放在高处,举起。
pin·na·cled [ˈpinəkld; ˋpɪnəkl̩d] *a*. 1. 小尖塔般耸立的;有小尖塔的。2. 在高处的。
pin·nate, pin·nat·ed [ˈpinit, -id; ˋpɪnet, -ɪd] *a*. 1. 【植】羽状的,有羽状叶的。2. 【动】有鳍的。**-ly** *ad*.
pin·nat·i·fid [piˈnætifid; pɪˋnætɪfɪd] *a*. 羽状半裂的。
pin·na·tion [ˌpinˈneiʃən; pɪˋneʃən] *n*. 【植】羽状。
pin·nat·i·sect [piˈnætisekt; pɪˋnætɪˏsɛkt] *a*. 【植】羽状全裂的。
pin·ner [ˈpinə; ˋpɪnə·] *n*. 1. 扣别针的人。2. = pinafore. 3. 【史】〔*pl*.〕(女用帽式)头巾。
pin·ni·grade [ˈpinəgreid; ˋpɪnəˏgred] I *a*. 用鳍行走的。II *n*. 用鳍〔鳍状肢〕行走的动物。
pin·ni·ped [ˈpiniped; ˋpɪnəped] I *a*. 鳍足类的。II *n*. 鳍足动物。
pin·nule [ˈpinjuːl; ˋpɪnjul] *n*. 【植】1. 小羽片。2. (棘皮动物的)羽枝。3. 【动】小鳍。**-nu·late** [-juleit; -jəlet], **-nu·lat·ed** *a*.
pin·ny [ˈpini; ˋpɪnɪ] *n*. 〔儿〕围兜,口水兜。
pi·noch·le, pi·noc·le [ˈpiːnʌkl, -ˌnɔkl; ˋpiˏnʌkl, -ˏnɑkl̩] *n*. 1. 平纳克耳牌戏〔用两副牌从9至K,并加上A牌,共48张,由二、三或四人同玩〕。2. 此种牌戏中的"Q""J"牌组〔由两张黑桃Q牌和两张方块J牌组成的一副牌〕。
pi·no·le [piˈnəulei; pɪˋnole] *n*. 〔美〕炒玉米粉。
pi·ñon [ˈpinjən, ˈpiːnjəun; ˋpɪnjən, ˋpinjon] *n*. (*pl*. ~(*e*)*s*) 〔Sp.〕(美国西部产)矮松〔子可食〕;矮松子。
pin·set·ter [ˈpinˌsetə; ˋpɪnˏsɛtə·] *n*. 1. 【滚球】球童(= pin boy)。2. 自动扶木柱器。
pin·spot·ter [ˈpinˌspɔtə; ˋpɪnˏspɑtə·] = pinsetter.
pin·ster [ˈpinstə; ˋpɪnstə·] *n*. 〔美〕玩滚球(bowling)的人。
pin·stripe [ˈpinstraip; ˋpɪnstraɪp] *n*. 1. 细条子,线条。2. 隐格布,细条子衣服。
pint [paint; paɪnt] *n*. 品脱〔液量、干量名,〔英〕= 0.57 升弱,〔美〕液量 = 0.47 升强,干量 = 0.55 升〕。
pin·ta [ˈpintə; ˋpɪntə] *n*. 【医】卡拉回线螺旋体斑病,密旋体斑病〔一种热带病,患者皮肤上发各色斑点〕。
pin·ta·do [pinˈtɑːdəu; pɪnˋtɑdo] *n*. (*pl*. ~(*e*)*s*) 橙斑马鲛(*Scomberomorus maculatus*)〔常见于佛罗里达州和古巴附近的海洋中〕。
pin·tail [ˈpinteil; ˋpɪnˏtel] *n*. 〔俚〕【鸟】尖尾凫,尖尾鸭(等)。
pin·ta·no [pinˈtɑːnəu; pɪnˋtɑno] *n*. (*pl*. ~*s*) 豆娘鱼属动物(尤指岩豆娘鱼)。
pin·tle [ˈpintl; ˋpɪntl̩] *n*. 1. 【船】舵销。2. (垂直)枢轴;(铰链、枪等的)针栓。*a* ~ *of the rudder* 舵针。
pin·to [ˈpintəu; ˋpɪnto] I *a*. 〔美〕黑白斑纹的。II *n*. (*pl*. ~(*e*)*s*) 1. 〔美西部〕黑白斑马。2. 斑豆(= ~ bean)。3. 墨西哥印第安人。
pint-size [ˈpaintˌsaiz; ˋpaɪntˏsaɪz] *a*. 小的;很小的(= pint-sized)。
pin·wale [ˈpinweil; ˋpɪnwel] *a*. (灯芯绒)细棱条的。
pin·worm [ˈpinwəːm; ˋpɪnˏwɜ·m] *n*. 【动】蛲虫。
pinx. = pinxit.
pinx·it [ˈpiŋksit; ˋpɪŋksɪt] *v*. 〔L.〕(某某)画,…笔〔画家署名用,常略作 pinx 或 pxt.〕。
pin·y [ˈpaini; ˋpaɪnɪ] *a*. (***pin·ier***; ***-i·est***) 松树(似)的;松树繁茂的。
pi·o·let [ˈpiəulei; ˋpɪole] *n*. 〔F.〕爬山用碎冰斧。
pi·on [ˈpaiɔn; ˋpaɪɑn] *n*. = pi-meson.
Pion. = Pioneer.
pi·o·neer [ˌpaiəˈniə; ˏpaɪəˋnɪr] I *n*. 1. 拓荒者,开辟者;提倡者;先锋,先驱。2. 【军】轻工兵。3. 【生】先驱生物。*a* ~ *sergeant* 工兵长。*the Youth Pioneers* 少年先锋队。II *vt*., *vi*. 开辟,开垦,开(路等);提倡,做(…的)先锋。
pi·os·i·ty [paiˈɔsiti; paɪˋɑsətɪ] *n*. 过分虔诚,假虔诚,表面虔诚。
piou·piou [pjuːˈpju; pjuˋpju] *n*. 〔F.〕〔军俚〕法国兵。
pi·ous [ˈpaiəs; ˋpaɪəs] *a*. 1. 虔诚的,信神的。2. 以宗教为口实的,以敬神为名的;伪善的。3. 〔古〕孝顺的;有善良意向的。*a* ~ *posture* 假仁假义的姿态。*a* ~ *fraud* 虔诚欺诈(为受骗者本身利益等而作的欺诈)。~**-mind** *a*. = pious. **-ly** *ad*. **-ness** *n*.
PIP 画中书〔指数码式电视机屏幕的一角能显示第二个画面,系 picture-in-(a-)picture 的缩略〕。
pip[1][pip; pɪp] *n*. 1. (苹果、梨等的)果仁,种子。2. 〔俚〕漂亮的人〔物〕。3. 〔美〕矮子。
pip[2][pip; pɪp] *n*. 1. 〔英〕(纸牌、骰子上的)点。2. 〔英俚〕(军服肩章上的)星;(簇花中的)小花;(草的)根茎;凤梨皮的一小片。3. 【讯】尖号信号,(雷达的)反射点;(荧光屏上的)脉冲。
pip[3][pip; pɪp] *n*. 1. 〔the ~〕家禽的舌病。2. 〔谑〕(人的)小毛病;〔俚〕梅毒。3. 〔俚〕烦躁;抑郁。***get*** [***give***] ***sb. the*** ~ 使发怒,使不痛快。***have the*** ~ 〔俚〕不舒服,发着脾气。
pip[4][pip; pɪp] *vt*. (*-pp-*) (小鸡)啄破(蛋壳)出来。— *vi*. 1. (小鸡)破壳而出。2. (小鸡)叽叽地叫。
pip[5][pip; pɪp] *vt*. (*-pp-*) 1. 〔俚〕反射,排斥;打败;打破(计划等),妨碍(人)。2. 射击;击死;击伤。— *vi*. 死(*out*)。
pip[6][pip; pɪp] *n*. P 字〔广播报时信号〕。~ *emma* = p.m. (午后)。
pip·age [ˈpaipidʒ; ˋpaɪpɪdʒ] *n*. 1. 用管道输送(水、瓦斯、油等)。2. 用管输送费。3. 管道,管道系统。
pi·pal [ˈpiːpəl, ˈpaipəl; ˋpipəl, ˋpaɪpəl] *n*. 菩提树(=

～-tree)。

pipe [paip; paɪp] **I** ***n*.** **1.** 管,导管,筒。**2.** 烟斗,烟袋;一袋烟。**3.** [古]笛,管乐器;【海】(水手长的)哨子(声);[*pl*.]风箱。**4.** 尖锐的声音;鸟叫声;笛声。**5.** (人体内的)血管;[口]气管,声带,喉咙;【植】茎;【矿】管状矿脉。**6.** 液量名[=105 英加仑,126 美加仑];(能装 1 pipe 的)大酒桶。**7.** [俚]容易的工作[学科]。**8.** [美俚]交谈;短信。**9.**【地】筒状火成砾岩;火山筒。*a drain* ～ 排水管。*a distributing* ～ 配水管。*light a* ～ 点一斗烟。*smoke a* ～ 吸一斗烟。***dance to sb.'s*** ～ 跟着某人亦步亦趋。***hit the*** ～ 吸毒。***put sb.'s*** ～ ***out*** 妨碍某人成功。***Put that in your*** ～ ***and smoke it***. [小声忠告后说]你仔细想想吧。***smoke the*** ～ ***of peace*** (轮流)吸和睦烟;言和。***the Queen's*** [***King's***] ～ [英]走私烟焚毁炉。

II ***vt*.** **1.** 吹(笛);(用尖锐的声音)唱,叫;【海】(吹水手长哨子)召集(*up*),吹笛子引诱。**2.** 把…装箱用管子输送。**3.** 滚边(在衣服上),镶花边(在糕饼等上)。**4.** 分株繁殖。**5.** [美俚]传递(消息等);谈论,透露;【电】(用导线或同轴电缆)传送(广播或电视节目等)。**6.** [美俚]看,瞧。～ *a song* 唱歌。～ *all hands to work* 吹哨子命令全体船员工作。— ***vi*.** **1.** 吹笛;吹口笛。**2.** 叽叽地叫,高声哭。**3.** (风)咻咻地吹。**4.**【矿】掘成圆筒形。**5.** 吸食强而纯可卡因。～ ***away***【海】吹哨子命令短艇出发。～ ***down***【海】**1.** 吹哨子停工。**2.** [美俚]停止讲话,静下来。**3.** [俚]变得较谨慎。～ ***in*** 用电讯设备传送。～ ***off*** **1.** 把某人列入黑名单。**2.** 向警察告发。～ ***one's eye***(***s***) [口]流泪,哭,号哭。～ ***up*** 开始吹;[俚]开始说[唱];装饰衣边;加快速度。～**-clay** **1.** ***n*.** (造烟管或磨皮革用的)白黏土;[喻](军队中对服装外貌等的)严格要求。**2.** ***vt*.** 用白黏土漂白。～ **cleaner** 烟斗通条。～ **course** [美俚]容易对付的课程。～**dream** [美俚]黄粱美梦,空想,幻想,痴心妄想;荒唐话[计划]。～**fest** [美]废话,闲谈。～ **fitter** 管道安装工。～**fish** 海龙。～**head** 吸毒者。～**layer** **1.** 铺管工人,自来水[煤气等]工人。**2.** [美俚]阴险的政客,阴谋家。～ **laying** ***n*.**, ***a*.** [美] = wire-pulling. ～**-light** 点烟的捻子。～ **line** **1.** ***n*.** 管路,输油管;干线,补给线。**2.** ***vt*.** 用油管输(油)(～ *line run* 油管输油量)。～ **major** 风笛乐队的主吹奏手。～ **organ** 管风琴。～ **rack** 烟斗架;【乐】(风琴的)笛管架。～**stem** **1.** 烟斗杆(管)。**2.** 形式上似烟斗杆(管)的东西。～**-stone** 北美印第安人制造烟斗用的泥质岩石。～ **wrench**【机】管板手。**-ful** ***n*.** 一袋(烟)。

pip·er [ˈpaipə; ˋpaɪpɚ] ***n*.** **1.** 吹笛人;[Scot.]风笛手。**2.**【鸟】鹨鸟;小鸡;小鸽;【鱼】魴鮄;绿鳍鱼;海胆。**3.** 气喘的马;[英]囮狗。**4.** 制[铺]管者。**5.** 滚边工;(缝纫机上的)滚边装置。***drunk as a*** ～ [口]烂醉。***pay the*** ～ 负担费用,承担后果。***pay the*** ～ ***and call the tune*** 出钱而作主,承担费用而有决定权。

piped [ˈpaipt; ˋpaɪpt] ***a*.** **1.** 有管的;管状的;用管输送的。**2.** (服装)滚边的。**3.** [美俚]烂醉的。

pi·per·a·zin(e) [piˈperəzi(ː)n; pɪˋpɛrə͵zin] ***n*.**【化】六氢吡哄,对二氮己环[痛风药]。

pi·per·ic [piˈperik; pɪˋpɛrɪk] ***a*.** 胡椒的。～ *acid*【化】胡椒酸。

pi·per·i·dine [piˈperidi(ː)n; pɪˋpɛrədin] ***n*.**【化】哌啶,氮杂环已烷,六氢吡啶。

pip·er·ine [ˈpipəri(ː)n; ˋpɪpərin] ***n*.**【化】胡椒碱[解热剂]。

pip·er·o·nal [ˈpipərənæl; ˋpɪpərə͵næl] ***n*.**【化】胡椒醛。

pi·pet, pi·pette [piˈpet; pɪˋpɛt] **I** ***n*.**【化】吸移管,吸量管,球管。**II** ***vt*.** 用吸量管吸取[移转]。*an absorption* ～ (气体)吸量管。

pip·ing [ˈpaipiŋ; ˋpaɪpɪŋ] **I** ***a*.** **1.** 吹笛的;发锐音的,高调子的;滚热沸腾的。**2.** 温和的,平静的。*the* ～ *times of peace* 太平时候。**II** ***ad*.** 滚热地。*be* ～ *hot* 滚热的;才出锅[炉、蒸笼]的。**III** ***n*.** **1.** 吹笛;管乐;笛声;尖锐声音;啭鸣;[口]哭,哭声。**2.** [集合词]管系。**3.** (糕饼的)花边;(衣服的)滚边。

pip·is·trelle, pip·is·trel [ˈpipistrel; ͵pɪpəˋstrɛl] ***n*.** 伏翼属(*Pipistrellus*)动物[北美和东半球大部分地区常见的一种蝙蝠,尤指伏翼(*P. pipistrellus*)]。

pip·it [ˈpipit; ˋpɪpɪt] ***n*.**【鸟】鹡鸰科的鸣禽,鹨。

pip·kin [ˈpipkin; ˋpɪpkɪn] ***n*.** 小瓦锅;小汲桶。

pip·pie [ˈpipi; ˋpɪpɪ] ***n*.** 因继承父母遗产而致富者[系 person inheriting parent's property 的缩略]。

pip·pin [ˈpipin; ˋpɪpɪn] ***n*.** **1.** 苹果一品种名;实生苗苹果。**2.**【植】种子。**3.** [美]美人,漂亮姑娘;令人喜爱的人[物]。*Newtown P-* 翠玉苹果。*White P-* 青龙苹果。

pip-pip [ˈpipˈpip; ˋpɪpˋpɪp] ***int*.** [英俚]再见。

pip·(p)ul [ˈpiːpəl; ˋpipəl] ***n*.** [pipal 的别字]【植】菩提树。

pip·py [ˈpipi; ˋpɪpɪ] ***a*.** (橘子等)多种子的。

pip·sis·se·wa [pipˈsisiwə; pɪpˋsɪsəwə] ***n*.** 伞形梅笠草(*Chimaphila urnbellata*)[北美的一种常绿植物]。

pip·squeak [ˈpipskwiːk; ˋpɪp͵skwik] ***n*.** [口]无足轻重的人,小人;无价值的东西,小东西。

pip·y [ˈpaipi; ˋpaɪpɪ] ***a*.** **1.** 管状的;有管的。**2.** 笛声的;发尖声的;[口]爱哭的。

pi·quan·cy [ˈpiːkənsi; ˋpikənsɪ] ***n*.** **1.** 辛辣,开胃。**2.** 泼辣;痛快;活泼。**3.** 调皮。**4.** 尖刻。

pi·quant [ˈpiːkənt; ˋpikənt] ***a*.** **1.** 辛辣的;开胃的。**2.** 泼辣的;痛快的;使人兴奋的;有趣的。**3.** 淘气的,调皮的。**4.** 讽刺的,尖刻的;惹人生气的。**-ly** ***ad*.**

pique[1] [piːk; pik] **I** ***n*.** 生气,不高兴,呕气。***in a fit of*** ～, ***out of*** ～ 赌气地;愤愤。***take a*** ～ ***against*** (*sb*.) 对…抱恶感,生某人的气。**II** ***vt*.** **1.** 使愤怒,使不高兴;损伤(自尊心),伤(感情)。**2.** 夸耀。**3.** 引起(好奇心、兴趣等)。**4.**【空】俯冲攻击。—***vi*.** 发怒,急躁。***be*** ～***d at*** 为…生气。～ ***oneself*** (***up***) ***on*** 夸,自负(～ *oneself on having a good memory* 自夸记性好)。

pique[2] [piːk; pik] ***n*.**, ***v*.**【牌】揍三十;得三十分。

pi·qué [ˈpiːkei; piˋke] ***n*.** [F.]凹凸织物,起楞布,凸纹布。～**-work** 镶花工艺。

pi·quet [piˈket; pɪˋkɛt] ***n*.** **1.** (用 7 以上 32 张牌供二人对玩的)皮克牌。**2.** [ˈpikit; ˋpɪkɪt]【军】= picket.

pi·ra·cy [ˈpaiərəsi; ˋpaɪrəsɪ] ***n*.** **1.** 海上掠夺,海盗行为。**2.** 剽窃;非法翻印;侵害版权;侵犯专利权。*literary* ～ 侵害著作权,剽窃。

Pi·rae·us, *Pei·rai·évs* [paiˈri(ː)əs, ˌpireˈefs; paɪˋriəs, ͵pireˋɛfs] ***n*.** 比雷埃夫斯[希腊港市]。

pi·rag·ua [piˈrægwə; pɪˋrɑgwə] ***n*.** **1.** 独木舟。**2.** 双桅平底船。

Pi·ran·del·lian [ˌpirənˈdeliən; ͵pɪrənˋdɛlɪən] ***a*.** 皮兰德娄的;(关于)皮兰德娄作品的;情节离奇荒诞的。

Pi·ran·del·lo [ˈpirəndeləu; pɪrənˋdɛlo], **Luigi** 皮兰德娄 [1867—1963,意大利小说家、剧作家]。

pi·ra·nha [piˈrɑːniə, -ræn-; pɪˋrɑnɪə, -ræn-] ***n*.** (南美)比拉鱼。

pi·ra·ru·cu [piˈrɑːrukuː; pɪˋrɑrʊku] ***n*.** 巨骨舌鱼[南美洲所产的一种巨鳞淡水鱼,可食用,有的可重达 500 磅,为淡水鱼中之最大者](= arapaima)。

pi·rate [ˈpaiərit; ˋpaɪrət] **I** ***n*.** **1.** 海盗;海盗船。**2.** (著作等的)剽窃者;侵害版权[专利权]者。**3.** [英]非法行走专有路线的私营公共汽车[马车]。**4.** 未经许可的广播者。*a* ～ *listener*【讯】偷听者。*a* ～ *river* 夺流河。*swear like a* ～ 破口大骂。**II** ***vt*.**, ***vi*.** **1.** 以海盗方式劫掠,掠夺。**2.** 剽窃,非法翻印。*a* ～*d edition* 翻印本,海盗版,偷印版。

pi·rat·ic, pi·rat·i·cal [paiˈrætik, -ikəl; paɪˋrætɪk, -ɪkəl] ***a*.** **1.** (像)海盗的。**2.** 剽窃的,侵害著作权的。**-i·cal·ly** ***ad*.**

pi·ric·u·lar·rin [piˈrikjuːlærin; pɪˋrɪkjulærɪn] ***n*.**【生

化】稻瘟菌素。

pirn [pəːn; pɝn] *n*. 1.【纺】纬纱管,纡子。2.〔Scot.〕(钓竿上的)线卷。*wind oneself a bonny* [*queer*] ~ 遭到困难。*wind sb. a* ~ 使人遭到困难。

pi·ro·gen [piˈrəugən; pɪˋrogən] *n*.〔*pl*.〕馅饼 (= pirogi)。

pi·ro·gi [piˈrəugi; pɪˋrogɪ] *n*.〔*pl*.〕〔Russ.〕馅饼 (= piroshki)。

pi·rogue [piˈrəug; pəˋrog] *n*. = piragua.

pir·ou·ette [ˌpiruˈet; ˏpɪruˋɛt] I *n*.【舞蹈】竖趾旋转;【马术】(马的)急转。*turn* [*perform*] *a* ~ 用脚尖旋转。II *vi*. 用脚尖旋转;表演旋转舞。

Pi·sa [ˈpiːzə; ˋpizə] *n*. 比萨〔意大利城市,城内有著名的比萨斜塔〕。**-n** *a*.

pis·all·er [ˈpiːzˈæləi; ˋpiˋzale]〔F.〕不得已而采用的手段,最后手段,应急办法。

pis·ca·ry [ˈpiskəri; ˋpɪskərɪ] *n*. 1.【法】(在他人渔区内的)捕鱼权。2. 渔场。*the common of* ~ 共渔权。

pis·ca·tol·o·gy [ˌpiskəˈtɔlədʒi; ˏpɪskəˋtɑlədʒɪ] *n*. 捕鱼学。

pis·ca·tor [pisˈkeitə; pɪsˋketɚ] *n*. 渔夫;钓鱼的人。

pis·ca·to·ri·al, pis·ca·to·ry [ˌpiskəˈtɔːriəl, ˈpiskətəri; ˏpɪskəˋtorɪəl, ˋpɪskəˏtorɪ] *a*. (爱)钓鱼的;(从事)渔业的。

Pis·ces [ˈpisiːz; ˋpɪsiz] *n*.〔*pl*.〕1.【动】鱼纲。2.〔the ~〕【天】双鱼座;双鱼宫。~ **Australis** [ɔsˈtreilis; ɑsˋtrelɪs]【天】南鱼座。

pisci- *comb. f*. 鱼。

pis·ci·cul·tur·al [ˌpisiˈkʌltʃərəl; ˏpɪsɪˋkʌltʃərəl] *a*. 养鱼(术)的。

pis·ci·cul·ture [ˈpisikʌltʃə; ˋpɪsɪkʌltʃɚ] *n*. 1. 养鱼(业);鱼类养殖。2. 养鱼术。

pis·ci·cul·tur·ist [ˌpisiˈkʌltʃərist; ˏpɪsɪˋkʌltʃərɪst] *n*. 养鱼专家。

pis·ci·na [piˈsiːnə; pɪˋsinə] *n*. (*pl*. **-nae** [-niː; -ni], ~*s*) 1. 鱼塘,养鱼池。2.〔古罗马〕浴池。3.【宗】洗礼场,洗礼盆。

pis·cine[1] [ˈpisain; ˋpɪsaɪn] *a*. 鱼的,鱼类的;似鱼的。

pis·cine[2] [ˈpisiːn; ˋpɪsaɪn] *n*. 1. = piscina. 2. 公共浴池。

pis·civ·o·rous [piˈsivərəs; pɪˋsɪvərəs] *a*. (鸟等)吃鱼的,以鱼为食的。

pis·co [ˈpiskəu; ˋpɪsko] *n*. 皮斯科酒〔秘鲁皮斯科城酿造的白兰地酒,因而得名〕。

pi·sé [ˈpiːzei; ˋpize] *n*.〔F.〕【建】砌墙黏土。

Pis·gah [ˈpizgə; ˋpɪzgə] *n*. 毗斯迦山〔基督教《圣经》传说摩西从此山眺望上帝赐给亚伯拉罕的迦南地方〕。~ ***sight*** (对得不到的东西)望洋兴叹。

pish [pʃ, piʃ; pʃ, pɪʃ] I *int*. 呸! II *n*. 呸〔轻蔑声、嫌恶声〕。[piʃ, pɪʃ] III *vt*., *vi*. (对…)嗤之以鼻,(对…)叫一声"呸"。~ ***away*** [***down***] 看不起。

pi·si·form [ˈpaisifɔːm; ˋpaɪsɪfɔrm] I *a*. 豌豆形的。II *n*.【解】豌豆骨。

pis·mire [ˈpismaiə; ˋpɪsmaɪr] *n*.【虫】蚂蚁。

pi·so·lite [ˈpaisəˌlait; ˋpaɪsəlaɪt] *n*.【矿】1. 豆石。2. 豆石沉积岩。**-lit·ic** *a*.

piss [pis; pɪs]〔卑〕I *vi*. 小便,撒尿。— *vt*. 1. 尿(血)。2. 撒尿撒脏。II *int*.〔美俚〕呸〔表示厌恶〕。***be ~ed off***〔美俚〕1. 发怒,极厌恶。2. 极疲劳。~ ***off***〔俚〕走掉;惹烦;喝醉;极端疲乏。~ ***on*** 亵渎。~ ***pins and needles***〔口〕小便极疼痛。III *n*.〔卑〕尿,小便。*a* ~ *pot* 尿壶。~ ***and vinegar*** 1. 精力,活力。2. 顽皮,淘气。**-er** *n*. 1. 小便者。2.〔美俚〕难事,苦差事。3.〔美俚〕淘气鬼〔指男孩〕。

pis·soir [piːˈswɑː; piˋswɑr] *n*.〔F.〕男小便池,男小便处〔过去巴黎街上公用的便池〕。

pis·ta·chi·o [pisˈtɑːʃiəu; pɪsˋtɑʃɪˏo] *n*. (*pl*. ~*s*) 1.【植】阿月浑子;(可作调味香料用的)阿月浑子的子 (= ~-nut)。2. 淡黄绿色。

pis·ta·reen [ˌpistəˈriːn; ˏpɪstəˋrin] I *n*. 皮斯塔林〔西班牙的古银币,通用于西班牙在美洲的属地和西印度群岛〕。II *a*.〔废〕无价值的,贱的,些小的。

piste [piːst; pist] *n*. 1. (板实的)滑雪道。2. 投木球场〔长12—15公尺,宽约4公尺的砾石场地,亦作 terrain〕。

pis·til [ˈpistil; ˋpɪstl̩] *n*.【植】雌蕊 (*opp*. stamen)。

pis·til·late [ˈpistilit; ˋpɪstl̩ɛt] *a*. 有雌蕊的;只有雌蕊的 (*opp*. staminate)。*a* ~ *flower* 雌花。

pis·tol [ˈpistl; ˋpɪstl̩] I *n*. 手枪。*a revolving* ~ 左轮(手枪)。***best the*** ~ (赛跑时)偷跑。***hotter than a*** ~〔美〕大成功。***put a*** ~ ***to sb.'s head*** 用手枪对准某人头部加以威胁。—II *vt*. (〔英〕**-ll-**) 用手枪射击[打伤]。~ **carbine** 驳壳枪。~ **grip** [**hand**] 手枪形枪把。~ **route**〔美〕用手枪打死。~**-shot** 1. 手枪射击。2. 神枪手。3. 手枪射程 (*within* [*beyond*] ~*-shot* 在手枪射程内[外])。~**-whip** *vt*. 用手枪柄打(尤指打头部)。

pis·tole [pisˈtəul; pɪsˋtol] *n*. 皮斯托尔〔西班牙古金币〕。

pis·to·leer, pis·to·lier [ˌpistəˈliə; ˏpɪstəˋlɪr] *n*. 带[用]手枪的人,手枪手。

pis·tol·graph [ˈpistlgrɑːf; ˋpɪstl̩græf] *n*. 快照(机)。

pis·ton [ˈpistən; ˋpɪstn̩] *n*. 1.【机】活塞。2.【乐】(管乐器的)直升式活塞。~**ring**【机】活塞环。~**rod**【机】活塞杆,联杆。~ **stroke** 活塞冲程。~ **valve** 活塞阀。

pit[1] [pit; pɪt] I *n*.〔美〕(桃、杏等的)核。II *vt*. (**-tt-**) 除去…的核。

pit[2] [pit; pɪt] I *n*. 1. 坑,凹地,凹处;【矿】矿井;煤坑;【植】纹孔;地下温室,窖;(染)缸。2.〔the ~〕地狱;深渊;〔方〕坟墓。3. 陷阱;〔喻〕圈套。4. (剧场的)正厅后座〔英国指正面楼厅的下面〕;正厅后座的观众。5. 斗鸡场,斗狗场(等)。6. 身体的凹窝;心窝;胳肢窝。7. 麻子。8.〔美〕(粮食交易所的)现期交易部。9. (汽车赛跑时的)加油站,车胎修理处。10.〔美〕棒球联赛的最低位。11.【军】散兵坑;靶壕;炮兵掩体。*the* ~ *of the stomach* (腹上部)心窝。*a etching* ~【冶】侵蚀陷斑。*the bottomless* ~ = *the* ~ *of darkness* = *the* ~ *of hell* 地狱。*a wheat* ~〔美交易所〕现期小麦交易部。***at the ~'s brink*** 快死。***dig a*** ~ ***for*** 设法使…落在圈套里,陷害。***shoot*** [***fly***] ***the*** ~ 1. (斗鸡等)飞出斗鸡场。2. 不付房租潜逃。II *vt*. (**-tt-**) 1.〔常用 *p.p.*〕弄凹;挖坑;打矿井;使成麻子。2. 把(蔬菜等)放在地窖里;坑陷。3. 使相斗;抵抗。*a face pitted with smallpox* 麻脸。~ *John against Paul* 使约翰反对保罗。— *vi*. 成凹;成麻子。~ **boss**〔美俚〕(矿井)工头;赌场老板。~ **bull** 铁杆斗士。~ **coal**〔英〕煤炭。~ **head**【矿】矿井口 (*the* ~ *head committee* 煤矿主和矿工共同推派代表组成的煤矿委员会。*the* ~ *head price*【商】(煤的)矿山价格)。~ **man** 矿工;矿井内机器管理员;下锯木匠;【机】〔*pl*.〕摇杆,连杆。~**mob**〔美口〕戏院的乐队。~**pan** (中美洲)独木舟。~**-prop** 矿井中用的临时木支柱。~**-saw** 双人竖拉大锯。~ **sawyer** 下面一个拉大锯的人。

pit·a·pat, pit·pat [ˈpitəˈpæt, ˈpitpæt; ˋpɪtəˏpæt, ˋpɪtˏpæt] I *ad*. 劈劈拍拍地(跑等),(心)卜卜地(跳着)。II *vi*. 劈劈拍拍地跑,(心)卜卜地跳。III *n*. 劈劈拍拍的跑声;卜卜卜的心跳声。

Pitcairn [pitˈkεən; ˋpɪtkɛrn] **Island** 皮特凯恩岛〔大洋洲〕。

pitch[1] [pitʃ; pɪtʃ] I *n*. 1. 沥青;含有沥青的物质;松脂,树脂。2. 人工合成沥青;人造树脂。*mineral* [*Jew's*] ~ 地沥青。~ *black* [*darkness*] 漆黑(的)。***Touch*** ~, ***and you will be defiled***. [***You can't touch*** ~ ***without being defiled***.] 近墨者黑。II *vt*. 用沥青涂。~ **blende** 沥青铀矿。~ **coal** 沥青煤;倾斜煤层。~**-dark** *a*. 漆黑的,黑暗的。~ **pine** (北美)油松〔采松脂的松树〕。~**stone**【地】松脂石。

pitch[2] [pitʃ; pɪtʃ] I *vt*. 1. 扔,投,抛,掷;【棒球】投球。2. 插(桩等),搭(帐篷等),扎(营),铺(路),布置(场面等),

安顿(住处)。**3.**〔常用 *p.p.*〕整顿,安排(阵容等);【乐】为…定音高[定调]。**4.**〔英〕努力推销(商品);〔口〕讲(故事)。*P- him out!* 把他赶出去! ~ *one's tent* 安顿帐篷。*a ~ed battle* 激战,互有准备的对阵战。~ ***a note*** 定音高。~ ***attack*** 攻打。~ ***(a) woo***〔美〕求爱,搂住亲嘴。~ ***it strong*** 大吹牛皮。~ ***oneself***〔口〕坐下来。~ ***sb. over the bar*** 取消某人的律师资格。— ***vi.*** **1.** 扔,投,掷;【棒球】作投球员;投球。**2.** 头朝下掉落[倒下](*on*; *into*)。**3.**【地】(地层等)向前方倾斜,倾斜。**4.** (船)前后颠簸纵摇,俯仰(*cf.* roll)。**5.** 搭帐篷,露宿;暂住;定居;布置场面。**6.** 选择,决定(*on*; *upon*);偶然碰见(*on*; *upon*)。**7.** (蜂等)歇,(马)突然跳起。**8.**【机】咬住。**9.** 吹牛,说大话。*I ~ed upon the very house that suited me.* 我找到了合适的房子。~ ***in***〔美口〕热情参加,拼命干起来。~ ***into***〔口〕猛烈攻击;大骂;开始大干特干;大吃大嚼。**II** ***n.*** **1.** 投掷;投球;投球距离。**2.** (船的)前后颠簸。**3.** 度,程度;高度;点,顶点,极点;倾斜度;倾斜,坡;【乐】音高;音高标准;【火箭】俯仰;〔喻〕态度。**4.**【机】节,齿距,节距,螺距,间距;【板球】柱的间隔;【空】螺距〔飞机螺旋桨一次旋转的前进距离〕。**5.** (路边)零售摊;摆售商品量。*the ~ of an arch* 拱高。*the axial ~* 轴节。*the ~ of a saw* 锯齿节,(锯的)齿距。*a concert* [*French*] ~【乐】高[低]音调。*a high* [*low*] ~ *sound* 高[低]音。*cry out at the utmost ~ of one's voice* 尽量地大声叫。*The voices rose to a deafening ~.* 声音大得震耳欲聋。***at concert*** ~ 处于高效能状态。***in there ~ing***〔美口〕拚命地干。***make a ~ for***〔美口〕为…说项。~ ***for the tape***〔美〕赛跑的最后冲刺。***queer the ~ for sb.*** = ***queer sb.'s*** ~〔口〕暗中破坏某人计划。***take up one's*** ~ 回到自己原位;保持一定限度。***to the highest*** [***lowest***] ~ 到最高[最低]限度。**~-and-toss** 掷钱游戏。**~-down**【火箭】俯冲。~ **farthing** 投钱戏。~ **line**【机】齿距线。~ **man**〔美〕摊贩。**~-over**【火箭】转弯。~**person** 兜揽生意者,强行推销者。~ **pipe**【乐】定调管;律管。**~-up**【火箭】上仰。~ **wheel** (和一个齿轮咬住的另一个)齿轮。

pitch·er[1] [ˈpitʃə; ˋpɪtʃɚ] ***n.*** **1.** 有柄的大水罐,柄盂。★英国多说 jug。**2.**【植】瓶状叶。*You are a little ~!* 你是个尖耳小鬼。*She has cracked her ~.* 她失身了。***Little ~s have long ears.*** 小孩子耳朵尖。***Pitchers have ears.*** 隔墙有耳〔说话要当心〕。***The ~ goes often to the well but is broken at last.*** 水壶取水,日久必破。~ **plant**【植】猪笼草,瓶子草。**-ful** (一)满水壶。

pitch·er[2] [ˈpitʃə; ˋpɪtʃɚ] ***n.*** **1.** 投掷的人;【棒球】投手。**2.** (往车上)投装(干草等)的人;〔英〕装煤人。**3.**〔英〕铺路石。**4.** 摊贩;搭帐篷卖艺的人。

pitch·fork [ˈpitʃɔːk; ˋpɪtʃˏfɔrk] **I** ***n.*** **1.** 干草叉,草耙。**2.**【乐】音叉。***rain ~s*** 下大雨。**II** ***vt.*** **1.** 用耙[叉]掻起。**2.** (突然或出其不意)推进[硬塞进,抛入](*into*)。

pitch·ing [ˈpitʃiŋ; ˋpɪtʃɪŋ] ***n.*** **1.** 铺地石,护堤石。**2.** 扔出;【棒球】投球(法)。**3.** (船的)纵摇或前后簸动;【空】俯仰。

pitch·y [ˈpitʃi; ˋpɪtʃɪ] ***a.*** (***pitch·i·er***; ***-i·est***) **1.** 沥青多的;沥青似的,黏的。**2.** 涂着沥青的。**3.** 漆黑的,黝黑的,黑褐色的。~ *wool* 原毛,含脂毛。

pit·e·ous [ˈpitiəs, -tjəs; ˋpɪtɪəs, -tjəs] ***a.*** **1.** 可怜的,凄惨的。**2.**〔古〕慈悲的。**-ly** ***ad.*** **-ness** ***n.***

pit·fall [ˈpitfɔːl; ˋpɪtˏfɔl] ***n.*** 陷坑,陷阱;诱惑;圈套;隐藏的危险;易犯的错误。

pith [piθ; pɪθ] **I** ***n.*** **1.**【植】木髓,树心;【解】髓,骨髓。**2.** 体力,力气;精力,精神;(文章的)力。**3.** 精髓,要义,要点;重要。*a man of ~* 精力饱满的人。*a matter of (great) ~ and moment* 非常重要的问题。*the ~ and marrow of an article* 文章的要点[精华]。**II** ***vt.*** **1.** 除去(茎中的)木髓。**2.** 割去脊髓弄死(牛等)。~ **cavity**【植】髓孔。

pith·e·can·thrope [ˌpiθiˈkænθrəup; ˏpɪθɪˋkænθrop] ***n.*** 【动】猿人。

pith·e·can·thro·pine [ˌpiθiˈkænθrəpain; ˏpɪθɪˋkænθrəˏpaɪn] **I** ***a.*** 猿人的(= pithecanthropoid)。**II** ***n.*** 猿人。

Pith·e·can·thro·pus [ˌpiθəkænˈθrəupəs; ˏpɪθɪkænˋθropəs] ***n.*** (*pl.* ***-pi*** [-pai; -paɪ]) 猿人属。~ ***erectus*** [iˈrektəs; ɪˋrɛktəs] 直立猿人(= Java man)。

pi·the·coid [piˈθiːkɔid; pɪˋθikɔɪd] ***a.*** **1.** (似)猿的。**2.** 狐尾猴的。

pith·less [ˈpiθlis; ˋpɪθlɪs] ***a.*** 无髓的;没气力的。

pith·y [ˈpiθi; ˋpɪθɪ] ***a.*** **1.** 有髓的,有气力的。**2.** 简洁的。**-i·ly** ***ad.*** **-i·ness** ***n.***

pit·i·a·ble [ˈpitiəbl; ˋpɪtɪəbl̩] ***a.*** **1.** 可怜的。**2.** 可怜又可笑的,卑鄙的,不足取的。**-bly** ***ad.*** **-ness** ***n.***

pit·i·er [ˈpitiə; ˋpɪtɪr] ***n.*** 怜悯者。

pit·i·ful [ˈpitif*u*l; ˋpɪtɪfəl] ***a.*** **1.** 慈悲的。**2.** 可怜的。**3.** 可怜又可笑的,卑鄙的。**-ly** ***ad.***

pit·i·less [ˈpitilis; ˋpɪtɪlɪs] ***a.*** 无情的,冷酷的。**-ly** ***ad.***

Pit·man [ˈpitmən; ˋpɪtmən] ***n.*** 皮特曼〔姓氏〕。

pi·tom·e·ter [piˈtɔmitə; pɪˋtɑmɪtɚ] ***n.*** (测量流速的)皮托压差计。

pi·ton [ˈpiːtɔn, F. piˋtɔ̃; ˋpitɑn, pɪˋtɔ̃] ***n.*** (*pl.* ***-tons*** [-tɔnz, F. -ˋtɔ̃; -tɑnz, -ˋtɔ̃]) 【登山】冰用钢锥。

Pitt [pit; pɪt] ***n.*** **1.** 皮特〔姓氏〕。**2. William** ~ 威廉·皮特〔1708—1778;1759—1806,英国政治家父子〕。

pit·tance [ˈpitəns; ˋpɪtn̩s] ***n.*** 少量食物;少量收入〔主要用于 *a mere* ~〕。

pit·ted [ˈpitid; ˋpɪtɪd] ***a.*** **1.** 有凹痕的;有麻子的。**2.**【植】具洼点的,具纹孔的。

pit·ter-pat·ter [ˈpitəpætə; ˋpɪtɚˏpætɚ] **I** ***ad.*** 拍挞拍挞地,劈劈拍拍地。**II** ***n.*** 拍挞拍挞〔连续拍击声,暴雨声〕。

pit·tite [ˈpitait; ˋpɪtaɪt] ***n.*** 【剧】正厅后座的观众。

Pitts·burgh [ˈpitsbəːg; ˋpɪtsbɚg] ***n.*** 匹兹堡〔美国城市〕。

pit·ty-pat [ˈpitipæt; ˋpɪtɪˏpæt] ***ad.*** = pitapat.

pi·tu·i·ta·ry [piˈtju(ː)itəri; pɪˋtjuəˏtɛrɪ] **I** ***a.*** **1.** (大脑)垂体的。**2.** (分泌)黏液的。**3.** (由大脑垂体所致的)异常长大的。**II** ***n.*** **1.**【解】大脑垂体。**2.**【医】大脑垂体制剂。~ **gland body** 大脑垂体。~ **membrance** 鼻黏膜。

pi·tu·i·trin [piˈtjuːitrin; pɪˋtjuətrɪn] ***n.*** 黏液腺激素。

pit·y [ˈpiti; ˋpɪtɪ] **I** ***n.*** **1.** 怜悯,同情。**2.** 可惜的事,憾事。*It is a ~* [*a thousand pities*] *that you cannot come.* 你不能来真是万分遗憾。*What a ~!* 实在可怜! 真可惜! *The ~ of it!* 可惜呀! 真遗憾! ***feel ~ for*** 可怜…。***for ~'s sake*** 请可怜可怜。***have*** [***take***] ~ (***up***) ***on*** = feel ~ for. ***in ~ of*** 因可怜…。(***the***) ***more's the*** ~ 更可惜了,更冤枉了;可惜,不幸。***out of*** ~ 出于哀怜。**II** ***vt.***, ***vi.*** (对…)觉得可怜。*He is to be pitied.* 他很值得同情。*I ~ you if you think so.* 你这样想就太可悲了〔有可耻的意思〕。

pit·y·ing·ly [ˈpitiiŋli; ˋpɪtɪɪŋlɪ] ***ad.*** 怜惜地。

pit·y·ri·a·sis [ˌpitiˈraiəsis; ˏpɪtəˋraɪəsɪs] ***n.*** 【医】糠疹,蛇皮癣。

piu [pjuː; pju] ***ad.***〔It.〕【乐】更。~ ***allegro*** [əˈleigrəu; əˋlegro] 更快。~ ***forte*** [ˈfɔːti; ˋfɔrtɪ] 更强。

piv·ot [ˈpivət; ˋpɪvət] **I** ***n.*** **1.**【机】交枢,枢轴,支轴,磨经〔磨的回转轴〕;【物】支点,支枢;扇轴儿。**2.** 枢要,中枢,中心点,要点。**3.**【军】轴兵,基准。**4.**【体】回转运动。**II** ***vt.*** **1.** 把…放在枢轴上。**2.** 使绕枢轴旋转;放在轴上;装尖轴。— ***vi.*** **1.** 依尖轴旋转;旋转。**2.** 由…而定(*on*; *upon*)。~ **axis** 摆轴。~ **bearing**【机】立式止推轴承。~ **bridge** 旋开桥;开合桥。~ **gun** 旋转炮。~ **man**【军】基准兵,轴兵。

piv·ot·al [ˈpivətl; ˋpɪvətl] ***a.*** **1.** 枢轴的。**2.** 中枢的,枢要的。*a ~ question* 中心问题。*the ~ strategy* 全局战略方针。**-ly** ***ad.***

pix [piks; pɪks] ***n.***〔*sing.*, *pl.*〕〔美俚〕(新闻)照片;影片。

pix·ie [ˈpiksi; ˋpɪksɪ] = pixy.
pix·i·lat·ed [ˈpiksileitid; ˋpɪksɪˏletɪd] *a*. 〔美、口〕有点怪的;有点神经病的。
pix·y [ˈpiksi; ˋpɪksɪ] **I** *n*. 小鬼,妖精。**II** *a*. 顽皮的。
pi·zen [ˈpaizn; ˋpaɪzn̩] *n*. 〔美俚〕威士忌酒;酒。
pizz. = pizzicato.
piz·za [ˈpiːtsə; ˋpitsə] *n*. 皮杂饼,比萨饼(一种意大利式烤馅饼)。
piz·ze·ri·a [ˌpiːtsəˈriːə; ˏpitsəˋriə] *n*. (意大利的)烤馅饼店。
piz·zi·ca·to [ˌpitsiˈkɑːtəu; ˏpɪtsɪˋkɑto] **I** *a*. 〔It.〕【乐】拨奏的。**II** *ad*. 拨奏地。**III** *n*. (*pl*. ***-ti*** [-ti(ː); -ti(ɪ)]) 拨奏曲。
piz·zle [ˈpizl; ˋpɪzl] *n*. 动物的阴茎〔过去曾做鞭子用〕。
P. J. = **1**. Police Justice 违警罪法庭法官。**2**. Presiding Judge 首席法官。**3**. Probate Judge 遗嘱检验法官。
Pj's [ˈpiːˈdʒeiz; ˋpiˋdʒez] *n*. 〔*pl*.〕〔口〕(宽大的)睡衣裤〔pyjamas 的缩略〕。
Pk = pack.
pk. = **1**. pack. **2**. park. **3**. peak. **4**. peck.
pkg. = package.
pkt. = **1**. packet. **2**. pocket.
PKU = phenylketonuria.
P. L. = **1**. Poet Laureate 〔英〕桂冠诗人。**2**. Primrose League 〔英〕樱草会。
PL = product liability 产品责任。
pl. = **1**. place. **2**. plate. **3**. plural.
plac·a·ble [ˈplækəbl; ˋplekəbl̩] *a*. 可安抚的,易劝解的,宽大的,温和的。**-bil·i·ty** [ˌplækəˈbiliti; ˏplækəˋbɪlətɪ] *n*.
plac·ard [ˈplækɑːd; ˋplækɑrd] **I** *n*. **1**. 招贴,揭示,标语,报单。**2**. 挂图,招贴画,宣传广告画。**3**. 招牌,名牌;行李牌。**II** *vt*. **1**. 在…贴招贴,在…贴公告[广告]。**2**. (用布告等)公布。**3**. 张贴,悬挂。
pla·cate [pləˈkeit; ˋpleket] *vt*. 安抚,抚慰;使和解;〔美〕得到(反对党等的)谅解。**-ca·tion** *n*.
pla·ca·to·ry [ˈpleikətəri; ˋplekəˏtorɪ] *a*. 安抚的,抚慰的。
place [pleis; ples] **I** *n*. **1**. 地方,场所,处;所在,位置;〔抽象名词〕空间 (*opp*. time)。**2**. (书中的)处所,页。**3**. 市区;市,镇,村;〔多用作专用名词〕广场,十字路口;路,街。**4**. 建筑物;住处,寓所,住宅;〔英〕乡下大宅院;〔美〕乡下小地产;本部;室,办事处。**5**. 立场,处境;地位,身分,资格;职,官职,本分;高位。**6**. 座位,席位。**7**. 【数】位,次序;【赛跑】头二三名;入选;【赛马】第二名 (*opp*. win);【足球】= place-kick. *a* ～ *of arms* 军队集合处;要塞;火药库。*a* ～ *of business* 营业处。*There is no* [*not any*] ～ *for you*. 没有你的位置,没有容纳你的余地。*Put yourself in my* ～. 请你设身处地替我想一想。*Come to my* ～ *tomorrow*. 明天请你到我家里来。*my* ～ 舍间。*at our* ～ 在我们家里。*There is always a* ～ *for you at our table*. 请你随时来吃便饭。*Calculate to 3* ～*s of decimals*. 算到小数点第三位。*The mare was beaten for a* ～ *by a short head*. 那匹母马以不到一头之差屈居第二名。***a*** ～ ***in the sun*** 有利地位;优越的立场[处境]。***a wild*** ～ ***in the road*** 〔美俚〕小城镇。***all over the*** ～ 到处。***another*** ～ 〔英〕(在下院指)上院,(在上院指)下院。***As much as my*** ～ ***is worth to do*** ... 做(那种事),我的饭碗就要打破了。***be no*** ～ ***for*** 不是…来的地方;没有…的余地(*There is no* ～ (*left*) *for doubt*. 没有怀疑的余地。*It is no* ～ *for you*. 这儿不是你来的地方)。***find*** [***lose***] ***one's*** ～ 找到[失去](书中)地方。***from*** ～ ***to*** ～ 处处。***get a*** ～【赛马】得第三名。***get*** ～***s*** 〔美俚〕到各处走动。***give*** ～ ***to*** 让位于,被…所代替。***go*** ～***s*** 〔美俚〕**1**. 出去寻乐。**2**. 表演精彩;成功,胜利。***have a soft*** ～ ***in one's heart for sb***. 对某人有爱情,对某人有好感。***in*** ～ 得其所,在适当位置;适当的。***in*** ～ ***of*** 代替。***in*** ～***s*** 多处,到处,处处。***in the first*** [***second, last***] ～ 第一[第二,最后]。***in the next*** ～ 其次,第二点。***keep people in their proper*** ～***s*** 使人安分守己。***keep sb. in his*** ～ 抑制某人;使某人安分。***know one's*** ～ 识分寸,不越分。***lose one's*** ～ 失去地位,失业。***make*** ～ 腾出地方。***make*** ～ ***for*** 给…留座位。***out of*** ～ 不得其所的;不适当的;不相称的;碍事的;失着业。***put sb. in his*** ～ 使某人不敢越轨。***take one's*** ～ 就位,就席,就座。***take*** ～ 发生;举行。***take the*** ～ ***of*** 代替某人,接替某人的位置。***the high*** ～ 祭坛;偶像。***the other*** ～ 地狱。
II *vt*. **1**. 放;安置;排列,整顿。**2**. 使就(职);任命…为(牧师)。**3**. 贷(款);投资。**4**. 发出(订单),订(货);交…出版。**5**. 把(信赖、希望等)寄托于。**6**. 定(场所[日期]);评定(等级)。**7**. 认出,想起;了解。**8**. 定(赛跑的)跑到次序〔向例到第三名为止〕;【棒球、网球】(把球)打向一定地方。**9**. 把声量、音域适当控制着说[唱]。*I will* ～ *anything at your service*. 任何东西均请随意使用。～ *one's confidence in* [*on*] *a friend* 相信朋友,信赖朋友。*I know his face, but I can't quite* ～ *him*. 我认识他的面孔,可是想不起是谁。*a very difficult person to* ～ 一个难判断其身份的人物。— ***vi***.【赛马】跑赢〔通常指头、二、三名〕。***be*** ～***d*** 【体】入选。～ ***oneself on record*** 〔美〕许下诺言,约定。～ **art** 场所艺术〔根据作品安置的环境来设计艺术作品〕。～ **brick** 半烧砖。～ **card** (宴席的)座位牌。～ **hunter** 求职者;猎官者。～ **kick** *v*.【足球】(球置地上)定位踢 (*opp*. dropkick, punt)。～ **man** 〔英〕官吏;〔蔑〕骄横的芝麻官。～ **name** 地名。**-able** *a*. 可被确定位置的。**-less** *a*. 没有固定位置的。
place aux dames [ˈplɑːs əu ˈdɑːm; ˋplɑso ˋdam] 〔F.〕妇女座;请把座位留给妇女;请让妇女先走。
pla·ce·bo [pləˈsiːbəu; pləˋsibo] *n*. **1**. 晚祷悼声[丧歌]。**2**. 安慰物,安慰剂;宽心话。
place·ment [ˈpleismənt; ˋplesmənt] *n*. **1**. 放,安置。**2**. 找职业。**3**. 定职位,安排。**4**. 【足球】定位;定位踢的球位;定位踢(= placekick)。
pla·cen·ta [pləˈsentə; pləˋsentə] *n*. (*pl*. ～***s***, ***-tae*** [-tiː; -ti]) 【解】胎盘;【植】胎座。
pla·cen·tal [pləˈsentl; pləˋsentl] **I** *a*. 【解】(有)胎盘的;【植】(有)胎座的。**II** *n*. 【动】有胎盘哺乳动物。
Plac·en·ta·li·a [ˌplæsənˈteiliə; ˏplæsənˋtelɪə] *n*. 〔*pl*.〕【动】有胎盘哺乳类,有胎盘类。
pla·cen·tate [pləˈsenteit; pləˋsentet] *a*. 【解、动】具有胎盘的;【植】具有胎座的。
plac·en·ta·tion [ˌplæsnˈteiʃən; ˏplæsənˋteʃən] *n*. **1**. 【解、动】胎盘形成。**2**. 【植】胎座式。
plac·er[1] [ˈpleisə; ˋplesɚ] *n*. **1**. 安置者,调配者。**2**. 第…名。*the sixth* ～ *in a competition* 比赛中的第六名。
plac·er[2] [ˈpleisə; ˋplesɚ] *n*. 【矿】(含金、铂等的)砂矿,砂积矿床(*opp*. lode)。～ **gold** 砂金。～ **mining** 砂矿开采。
pla·cet [ˈpleiset; ˋplesɛt] *n*. 〔L.〕赞成(票);许可,认可。*non* ～ 不赞成(票)。
plac·id [ˈplæsid; ˋplæsɪd] *a*. 平静的;宁静的;温和的。*in a* ～ *mood* 心平气和。**-ly** *ad*.
pla·cid·i·ty [plæˈsiditi; pləˋsɪdətɪ] *n*. 平静;宁静;温和。
pla·cing [ˈpleisiŋ; ˋplesɪŋ] *n*. (擅自将公司非法)出售,出盘。
plack·et [ˈplækit; ˋplækɪt] *n*. **1**. (女裙腰上的)开口〔= ～-hole〕。**2**. (女裙的)衣袋。
plac·oid [ˈplækɔid; ˋplækɔɪd] **I** *a*. 【动】板状的;有盾状鳞的。**II** *n*. 有盾鳞的鱼。
pla·fond [plaˈfɔ̃; plaˋfɔ̃] *n*. 〔F.〕**1**. 【建】天花板,顶棚。**2**. 顶棚彩画[雕刻]。
pla·gal [ˈpleigəl; ˋplegəl] *a*. 【乐】由下属和弦转成主和弦的。～ **cadence** [**close**] 变格终止。

plage [plɑːʒ; plaʒ] ***n.*** 〔F.〕海滨;海滨游乐地。

pla·gi·a·rism [ˈpleidʒiərizəm; ˋpledʒəˏrɪzəm] ***n.*** **1.** (文章、学说等的)剽窃,抄袭。**2.** 剽窃物。

pla·gi·a·rist [ˈpleidʒiərist; ˋpledʒərɪst] ***n.*** 剽窃者,抄袭者。

pla·gi·a·rize [ˈpleidʒiəraiz; ˋpledʒəˏraɪz] ***vt.***, ***vi.*** 剽窃,抄袭(别人的文章、学说等)。

pla·gi·a·ry [ˈpleidʒjəri; ˋpledʒɪˏɛrɪ] ***n.*** 〔古〕 **1.** 剽窃。**2.** 剽窃(物)。

pla·gio·clase [ˈpleidʒiəukleis; ˋpledʒɪəˏkles] ***n.*** 【矿】斜长石。

pla·gi·o·pho·tot·ro·pism [ˌpleidʒiəufəuˈtɔtrəpizəm; ˏpledʒɪofoˋtɑtrəpɪzəm] ***n.*** 【植】斜屈光性,斜向光性。

pla·gi·o·trop·ic [ˌpleidʒiəˈtrɔpik; ˏpleɑdʒɪəˋtrɑpɪk] ***a.*** 【植】斜向性的,偏途向性的〔指大多数植物的根与枝而言〕。**-trop·i·cal·ly** ***ad.***

pla·gi·ot·ro·pism [ˌpleidʒiˈɔtrəpizəm; ˏpledʒɪˋɑtrəˏpɪzəm] ***n.*** 【植】斜向性。

plague [pleig; pleg] **I** ***n.*** **1.** 时疫,瘟疫,传染病;〔the ~〕鼠疫,黑死病。**2.** 天灾,灾害,祸患;天罚。**3.** 〔口〕讨厌的人[东西],"祸虫",麻烦事情,疙瘩事。*the black* ~ 鼠疫。*the white* ~ 肺病。*the* ~ *of locusts* 蝗灾。*the* ~ *of hails* 雹灾。***be at the*** ~ 〔Scot.〕费事,费心。***P-(up) on it*** [***him***]! = ***P- take it*** [***him***]! 该死的(人)! ***What the*** [***a***] ~! 多讨厌呀! 嗳呀!
II ***vt.*** **1.** 使染瘟疫[得灾祸等]。**2.** 折磨;〔口〕麻烦,困扰。***be*** ~***d to death*** 被弄得[问题]烦死了,烦得要死。~ ***one's life out*** 拼命折磨。~ **spot** 【医】(传染性)疹子;鼠疫斑;瘟疫流行地;〔喻〕罪恶中心。~**some** ***a.*** 〔口〕麻烦的,讨厌的。

pla·gui·ly [ˈpleigili; ˋplegəlɪ] ***ad.*** 〔口〕折磨着;烦恼着;非常。*It's so* ~ *hot.* 天热得要命。

pla·guy, -guey [ˈpleigi; ˋplegɪ] **I** ***a.*** 〔口〕(***-gui·er***; ***-gui·est***) = plaguesome. **II** ***ad.*** = plaguily.

plaice [pleis; ples] ***n.*** 〔*sing.* *pl.*〕【鱼】鲽。

plaid [plæd; plæd] **I** ***n.*** (苏格兰高地人穿的)方格呢披肩;方格呢,苏格兰呢;〔罕〕格子花。**II** ***a.*** 方格花的。**-ed** ***a.*** 披着方格呢披肩的;用方格呢做的。

plain[1] [plein; plen] ***vi.*** 〔古、诗、英方〕发牢骚,诉苦;叹惜,悲伤;哀悼;悲歌,痛哭。

plain[2] [plein; plen] **I** ***a.*** **1.** 平的,平坦的。**2.** 平易的;普通的,简单的。**3.** 明白的,清楚的。**4.** 没有装饰的;平常的;朴素的;单色的,(织品)素净的;【纺】平纹的。**5.** 淡泊的,(食物等)清淡的;粗陋的。**6.** 爽直的,直率的,坦白的。**7.** 丑,难看的。**8.** 彻底的,(傻瓜)十足的。**9.** 单调的,平淡的。**10.** 【牌】(2—9 点的)普通牌的。~ *people* (没有头衔等的)普通老百姓,平民。~ *cloth* 平纹织物。~ *clothes* 便衣,便服。~ *rice* 白饭。~ *silly* 糊涂透了。***as*** ~ ***as a pikestaff*** [***the day, daylight***] 非常清楚,显而易见。***as*** ~ ***as the nose on one's face*** 清清楚楚看得见,明明白白。***in*** ~ ***English*** 用普通易懂的英语(说)。***in*** ~ ***sight*** 视界清楚,一览无遗。***in*** ~ ***terms*** [***words***] 直说,坦白说。~ ***living*** 简朴的生活。~ ***sailing*** 顺利(航行) (*cf.* plane sailing) (*It's all* ~ *sailing.* 一帆风顺,进展顺利)。~ ***speaking*** 打开天窗说亮话。~ ***words*** 〔美〕日常用语。***to be*** ~ ***with you*** 对你直说〔插入语〕。
II ***ad.*** 平;平易;明白,明了;坦白。
III ***n.*** **1.** 平地,平原,旷野。**2.** 〔英方〕(四面被建筑物包围着的)广场,小公园。**3.** 〔*pl.*〕〔美〕(落基山脉东部的)大草原。**4.** 〔诗〕战场;素织品,单色布。~ **bond** 【商】无担保债款。~ **chant** = plain-song. ~**clothes man** 便衣警察;侦探。~ **dealer** 〔罕〕率直人,爽直人,老实人。~**-dealing** ***n.***, ***a.*** 率直(的),坦白(的);光明正大(的)。~**-laid** ***a.*** (绳索)平搓的。~**-looking** ***a.*** 〔美〕= homely. ~ **song** 【宗】平歌,单旋律圣歌;定旋律。~**-spoken** ***a.*** 老实说的,直言无隐的。~ **weave** 【纺】平纹组织。~**-work** 素缝〔刺绣之对〕。**-ly** ***ad.*** **-ness** ***n.***

plains·man [ˈpleinzmən; ˋplenzmən] ***n.*** (*pl.* ***-men***) 平原居民。

plaint [pleint; plent] ***n.*** **1.** 〔诗〕悲叹,怨诉。**2.** 委屈;抗议。**3.** 【英法】控诉;诉状。**-ful** ***a.*** 哀叹的,哀诉的。

plain·tiff [ˈpleintif; ˋplentɪf] ***n.*** 【法】原告 (*opp.* defendant)。

plain·tive [ˈpleintiv; ˋplentɪv] ***a.*** 可怜的,悲哀的,忧郁的;哭诉的。*a* ~ *melody* 哀调。*a* ~ *cry* 哀鸣。**-ly** ***ad.***

plais·ter [ˈpleistə; ˋplestɚ] ***n.*** 灰泥;熟石膏;膏药(= plaster)。

plait [plæt; plet] **I** ***n.*** **1.** 褶边。**2.** 辫子;麦秆缏;辫绳。**II** ***vt.*** **1.** 在(布上)打褶。**2.** 编,(辫)。~*ed yarn* 包芯线。

plan [plæn; plæn] **I** ***n.*** **1.** 计划,设计,方案,规划;方法;进程表;时间表。**2.** 图,图面;平面图,设计图;示意图;图表;(街市)地图。**3.** 雏形,草案;轮廓,梗概。*a* ~ *of attack* [*compaign, operations*] 进攻[作战]计划。*I have a* ~ *for overcoming our difficulties.* 我有克服这些困难的方法。*The better* ~ *is to peel them after boiling.* 煮后剥皮较好。*a floor* ~ 平面图。*a raised* ~ 投影图,正面图。*a working* ~ 工作图。*a perspective* ~ 透视图。***according to*** ~ 按照计划。***form*** [***lay***] ***a*** ~ 拟计划。***in*** ~ 作为平面图。***give*** ~ ***to*** 使…发挥。
II ***vt.***, ***vi.*** **1.** 计划,设计。**2.** 制(图),绘(设计图)。**3.** 〔美〕打算 (*to*)。*planned economy* 计划经济。*planned parenthood* 计划生育。~ ***on*** 〔口〕打算,想要(~ *on going to London* 打算去伦敦)。~ ***out*** 想出,计划出。

plan- *comb. f.* 〔用于元[母]音前〕= plano-.

pla·nar [ˈpleinə; ˋplenɚ] ***a.*** **1.** 平面的;在平面上的;平的。**2.** 【数】二维的,二度的。

pla·na·tion [pleiˈneiʃən; pleˋneʃən] ***n.*** 【地】均夷作用。

planch [plɑːntʃ, plæntʃ; plɑntʃ, plæntʃ] ***n.*** 〔废、英方〕板;地板。

plan·chet [ˈplɑːntʃit; ˋplæntʃɪt] ***n.*** 造币坯。

Planck [plɑːŋk; plɑŋk], **Max Karl Ernst Ludwig** 普朗克〔1858—1947,德国物理学家〕。~ **constant** 【物】普朗克常数。

planc·ton [ˈplæŋktən; ˋplæŋktən] ***n.*** = plankton.

plane[1] [plein; plen] ***n.*** 悬铃木属树木。~ **tree** 美[法]国梧桐。

plane[2] [plein; plen] **I** ***n.*** **1.** 平面,水平面,面。**2.** (知识等的)发达程度,水平,阶段。**3.** 【空】机翼面;〔常 *pl.*〕飞机。**4.** (结晶体的)一面。**5.** 【矿】总巷道。*an inclined* ~ 斜面。*a* ~ *of polorization* 【矿】偏振(平)面,偏光面。*a* ~ *of reference* 【数】基础(平)面,对照面。*a* ~ *of symmetry* 对称面。*an elevating* ~ 【空】升降翼。*a rear* ~ 【空】尾翼,方向翼。*a robot* ~ 无人驾驶飞机。*a rotor* ~ 旋翼机。***on the same*** ~ ***as*** 和…同一水准[程度]。
II ***a.*** 平的;在平面上的,平面图的。*a* ~ *chart* 平面海图。*a* ~ *figure* 平面图。
III ***vi.*** **1.** 滑行;(比赛船等)在水面上飞一样滑跑。**2.** 〔口〕坐飞机去旅行。~ **geometry** 平面几何学。~**-milling machine** 龙门铣床。~ **polarization** 【物】平面偏振,线偏振。~ **table** 【测】平板仪,平板绘画器。

plane[3] [plein; plen] **I** ***n.*** 平刨;镘。*a jack* ~ 粗刨。**II** ***vt.***, ***vi.*** 刨平;镘平。~ **iron** 刨刀,刨铁。

plane·load [ˈpleinləud; ˋplenˏlod] ***n.*** 一飞机的人[物];飞机负载量。

plan·er [ˈpleinə; ˋplenɚ] ***n.*** **1.** 刨工。**2.** 刨床。**3.** 【印】打塞子。

plane-sailing ***n.*** [ˈpleinseiliŋ; ˋplenselɪŋ] **1.** 【海】(用平面海图的)平面航法。**2.** = plain sailing.

plan·et [ˈplænit; ˋplænɪt] ***n.*** **1.** 【天】行星 (*opp.* fixed star)。2.【占星】(左右人命运的)星相。*the major* ~*s* 大行星。*minor* ~*s* 小行星。*primary* ~*s* 一等行星。*secondar* ~*s* 卫星。*by* ~*s*〔方〕不规则;易变。~-**struck**, ~-**stricken** *a*. 1.【占星】(命运)受到行星影响的。2. 被诅咒的;带来恐慌的。

plan·e·tar·i·um [ˌplæniˈtɛəriəm; ˏplænəˋtɛrɪəm] *n*. (*pl*. ~*s*, -*ria* [-riə; -riə]) 1. 天象仪;太阳系仪。2. 天文馆。

plan·e·ta·ry [ˈplænitəri; ˋplænəˏtɛrɪ] *a*. 1.【天】行星的;由于行星作用的。2. 流浪的,不定的。3. 俗世的,现世的;地球的。4.【机】行星齿轮的。~ *days* 一星期。*a* ~ *gear* (汽车的)行星齿轮。*a* ~ *hour* 行星时。~ *motions* 行星运动。*the* ~ *system* 太阳系。

plan·e·tes·i·mal [ˌplæniˈtesiməl; ˏplænəˋtɛsəml] *n*., *a*.【天】微星(的)。~ **hypothesis** (行星形成的)微星假说。

plan·e·toid [ˈplænitɔid; ˋplænəˏtɔɪd] *n*. 小行星。-**al** [ˌplæniˈtɔidl; ˏplænɪˋtɔɪdl] *a*.

plan·e·tol·o·gy [ˈplæniˈtɔlədʒi; ˏplænɪˋtɑlədʒɪ] *n*. 行星学。

plan·form [ˈplænfɔːm; ˋplænfɔrm] *n*.【空】(飞机的)平面形状。

plan·gent [ˈplændʒənt; ˋplændʒənt] *a*. 冲到海边来的,澎湃的,哗啦哗啦响的。-**gen·cy** *n*. (尤指波浪的)澎湃声。-**ly** *ad*.

plani- *comb*. *f*. 表示"平,平面": *plani*meter.

pla·nim·e·ter [plæˈnimitə; pləˋnɪmətɚ] *n*.【数】测面仪,求积仪。

pla·nim·e·try [plæˈnimitri; pləˋnɪmətrɪ] *n*. 测面(积)学,平面几何。

plan·ish [ˈplæniʃ; ˋplænɪʃ] *vt*. 弄平;刨平,辗平,打平,锤光(金属板等);磨平;砑光(纸等)。-**ing hammer** 打平锤。

plan·i·sh·er [ˈplæniʃə; ˋplænɪʃɚ] *n*. 1. 平滑器,打平器。2. 打平者,研光者。

plan·i·sphere [ˈplænisfiə; ˋplænɪˏsfɪr] *n*. 1. 平面球体图。2.【天】步天规,星座一览图。

plank [plæŋk; plæŋk] I *n*. 1. 板,厚板〔比 board 厚,通常厚 2—6 英寸,宽 9 英寸以上〕;制板木料。2. 木板制成物。3. 支持物。4.〔美〕(政纲的)一条。5.〔美棒球俚〕= hit. ~ *bed*〔英〕(监狱等里面的)木板床。*burn the* ~*s* 长坐,久坐。*prick for a soft* ~ (海员)找最舒适的卧处。*put a* ~ *in the platform*〔美〕提作政纲之一。*step off the big* ~〔美俚〕进棺材,死亡。*walk the* ~ 1.【海】走跳板〔海盗处死俘虏的一种办法;把俘虏蒙住眼睛,然后逼使他在一个伸出舷外的跳板上前进,掉落海中〕。2. (转义)被解雇,被迫去职。
II *vt*. 1. 在…上铺板;〔口〕砰一声放下 (*down*)。2. 〔口〕立即支付(款项) (*down*; *out*)。3.〔美〕用菜板端出(烧好的鸡、鱼)。4.〔美俚〕打(球)。— *vi*. 睡光板。~ *it* 睡光板。

plank·ing [ˈplæŋkiŋ; ˋplæŋkɪŋ] *n*. 1. 铺板。2.〔集合词〕木板;地板;【船】船壳板。

plank-sheer [ˈplæŋkˌʃiə; ˋplæŋkˏʃɪr] *n*.【船】舷缘板。

plank·ter [ˈplæŋktə; ˋplæŋktɚ] *n*. 个体浮游生物。

plank·tol·ogy [plæŋkˈtɔlədʒi; plæŋkˋtɑlədʒɪ] *n*. 浮游生物学。

plank·ton [ˈplæŋktən; ˋplæŋktən] *n*.【生】浮游生物。

plan·less [ˈplænlis; ˋplænlɪs] *a*. 没有图形的;没有计划的;没有方案的。-**ly** *ad*. -**ness** *n*.

plan·ner [ˈplænə; ˋplænɚ] *n*. 计划者,订规划者,设计者。

plan·ning [ˈplæniŋ; ˋplænɪŋ] *n*. 计划,规划。*an overall* ~ 全面规划。

plano-[1] *comb*. *f*. 表示"平的,平坦的": *plano*concave.

plano-[2] *comb*. *f*. 表示"流动,游动": *plano*gamete.

plan·o·blast [ˈplænəblæst; ˋplænəˏblæst] *n*. 水螅状之水母体。

pla·no-con·cave [ˌpleinəuˈkɔnkeiv; ˏplenəˋkɑnkev] *a*. 平凹的〔一面平一面凹的〕。~ **lens** 平凹透镜。

pla·no-con·vex [-ˈkɔnveks; -ˋkɑnveks] *a*. 平凸的。~ **lens** 平凸透镜。

plan·o·gam·ete [ˈplænəgəmiːt; ˋplænəgəˏmit] *n*.【生】游动配子。

pla·nog·ra·phy [pləˈnɔgrəfi, plei-; plæˋnɑgrəfɪ, ple-] *n*. 平面印刷;平印品。-**graph·ic** *a*.

pla·nom·e·ter [pləˈnɔmitə; pləˋnɑmɪtɚ] *n*.【机】测平器,平面规。

plan·o·spore [ˈplænəspɔː; ˋplænəˏspɔr] *n*.【生】游动孢子。

plant [plɑːnt; plænt] I *n*. 1. 植物,草木 (*opp*. animal);草本;〔商用语〕树秧,苗木。2. 庄稼,作物,收获;(植物的)生育。3. 设备,装置;(工)厂,车间;(农)场;(研究所、医院、大学等的)全部设备。4. 智力工作的工具〔书籍、实验仪器等〕;方法。5.〔俚〕花招,诈欺;欺诈者。6.〔英俚〕侦探。7. (戏剧的)伏线。8.〔美俚〕假装观众的演员;(在歹徒等中布置的)内线。9. 有计划的犯罪;赃品隐藏库;歹徒巢窟;鸦片馆;(逮捕罪犯的)圈套。*a pot* ~ 盆栽植物。*flowering* ~*s* 显花植物。*ball* ~*s* 带土(秧)苗。*cabbage* ~*s* 甘蓝秧。*the humble* [*sensitive*] ~ 含羞草。*a manufacturing* ~ 制造厂。*a water* [*hydraulic*] *power* ~ 水力发电厂。*an arms* ~ 兵工厂。*a robotized* ~ 自动化工厂。*in* ~ 生长者,活着。*lose* ~ 枯死。*miss* [*fail in*] ~ 长不出;不发芽。II *vt*. 1. 栽(树、花),播(种);移植(植物);移民于(某处),殖(民)。2. 养(蚝等);放养(鱼)。3. 安,放,装,竖,插;创立,建设,设置,设立,树立;布置(内线)。4. 刺,扎,插进 (*in*; *on*);(把子弹)打进;〔俚〕给与(打击);〔拳击俚〕看准打。5. 传播,散播(新思想等),灌输 (*in*)。6.〔美俚〕埋,窝藏(赃品等);栽(赃)。7.〔俚〕把(砂金或矿砂等)放在矿里诱人来买;图谋(欺骗等)。~ *a garden* 培植庭园。~ *ideas in mind* 把思想灌输到心中。~ *one's fists in sb.'s face* 用拳头猛打某人的脸。~ *soldiers as colonists in the frontier districts* 在边境地区驻军屯垦。~ *on*〔俚〕拿假东西(卖)给人;向某人栽赃(把赃证暗藏在某人处,使他成为嫌疑犯)。~ *oneself* 占一个位置;站住;站起来。~ *out* (从盆等中)移植(到地上);隔相当的距离栽植;【造园】栽种植物遮住…。~ **cultivation** 作物栽培学。~ **culture** 作物栽培。~ **food** 植物养料;肥料。~ **hormone** 植物激素。~ **louse** 蚜虫。~-**marker** 植物名牌。~ **pathology** 植物病理学。~ **percent** 苗木成活率。~ **racket**〔美俚〕骗局。~-**school** 苗圃。~ **show**〔美〕黑人乐队的表演。-**let** 树苗,小树。

plant·a·ble [ˈplɑːntəbl; ˋplæntəbl] *a*. 1. 可以种植的,可以耕种的。2. 能建设[开辟]的;可殖民的。

Plan·tag·e·net [ˌplænˈtædʒinit; plænˋtædʒənɪt] *a*.【英史】金雀花王朝的,安茹王朝的,不兰他日奈王朝的〔指由十二世纪亨利二世即位至十五世纪理查三世死的王朝〕。

plan·tain[1] [ˈplæntin; ˋplæntɪn] *n*.【植】菜食品种香蕉,大蕉,羊角香蕉。

plan·tain[2] [ˈplæntin; ˋplæntɪn] *n*.【植】车前草。

plan·tar [ˈplæntə; ˋplæntɚ] *a*.【解】跖的,脚底的。

plan·ta·tion [plænˈteiʃən; plænˋteʃən] *n*. 1. (热带及亚热带地方的)农场,种植园,菜园,橡胶园;〔英〕造林地;栽植,造林。2.【史】移民,殖民;〔*pl*.〕殖民地。3. 创设,建设。4.〔P-〕〔美〕*Rhode Island* 的别名。*a coffee* [*rubber*, *sugar*] ~ 咖啡[橡胶,甘蔗]园。~ *fill in gaps*【林】空隙补植[自然更新]。~ **song** 北美棉花农场中黑人所唱的歌。

plant·er [ˈplɑːntə; ˋplæntɚ] *n*. 1. 种植的人;耕作的人;栽培者。2.〔美〕初期移民;(南部地方的)农场主人;种植园主;殖民者。3. (机器等的)安装人。4. 花盆。5. 种植器,播种器。6.〔美〕深深插入河底的树。

plan·ti·bod·y [ˈplɑːntibɔdi; ˋplæntɪbɑdɪ] ***n.***【生】植物抗体。

plan·ti·grade [ˈplæntigreid; ˋplæntəˏgred] **I** ***a.***【动】跖行的;跖行类的。**II** ***n.*** 跖行动物。

plant·ing [ˈplɑːntiŋ; ˋplæntɪŋ] ***n.*** **1.** 种植;造林;撒种。**2.**〔英〕【石工】奠基;【建】基础底层,基底。*ball* ~ 带土移植。~ *area* 造林面积。~ *by suckers* 分蘖造林。~ *of layers* 压条法。

plan·u·la [ˈplænjulə; ˋplænjələ] ***n.*** (*pl.* ***-u·lae*** [-liː; -li])【动】浮浪幼体。**-u·loid** [-lɔid; -lɔɪd] ***a.***

plaque [plɑːk; plæk] ***n.*** **1.** (象牙、陶瓷等制的)饰板;匾。**2.** (表示地位、名誉的)胸章;徽章。**3.**【医】斑;(噬菌体)溶菌斑;血小板。

pla·quette [plɑːˈket; plæˋket] ***n.*** 小饰板;金属印模。

plash[1] [plæʃ; plæʃ] **I** ***n.*** **1.** (水的)激溅声,哗哗声;(光的)闪动。**2.** 积水(小)坑。**3.**〔方〕倾盆大雨。**II** ***vt.***, ***vi.*** **1.** 溅泼(水)。**2.** (使)哗啦哗啦的响。

plash[2] [plæʃ; plæʃ] **I** ***vt.*** 编结(树枝)做树篱。**II** ***n.*** 编结成树篱的树枝。

plash·y [ˈplæʃi; ˋplæʃɪ] ***a.*** (***plash·i·er***; ***-i·est***) **1.** 水坑多的;尽是泥的,潮湿的。**2.** 哗啦哗啦响的。

-plasia, -plasis *comb. f.* 表示"形成,发达": hetero*plasia*.

plasm [ˈplæzm; ˋplæzəm] ***n.*** = plasma.

-plasm(a) *comb. f.* 表示"【生】生成物,产物": mela*plasm*.

plas·ma [ˈplæzmə; ˋplæzmə] ***n.*** **1.**【生理】血浆;淋巴液。**2.**【生】原生质。**3.** (做药膏用的)膏浆。**4.**【矿】半透明的绿玉髓。**5.**【物】等离子(体);等离子区。~ **panel**【计】等离子体显示屏面。**-mat·ic, -mic** ***a.***

plas·ma·gel [ˈplæzmədʒel; ˋplæzmədʒel] ***n.***【动】原生质凝胶。

plas·ma·gene [ˈplæzmədʒiːn; ˋplæzməˏdʒin] ***n.***【生】(细)胞质基因。**-genic** [-ˈdʒenik; -ˋdʒenɪk] ***a.***

plas·ma·sol [ˈplæzməsɔːl, -sɔl; ˋplæzməˏsɔl, -sɑl] ***n.***【生】**1.** 原生质溶胶。**2.** 质液。

plas·ma·tron [ˈplæzmətrɔn; ˋplæzməˏtrɑn] ***n.***【无】**1.** 等离子管;等离子流发生器。**2.** 等离子电焊机。

plas·min [ˈplæzmin; ˋplæzmɪn] ***n.***【化】胞质素,胞浆素。

plasm(o) *comb. f.* 表示"血浆,原生质": *plasmo*lysis.

plas·mo·di·um [plæzˈməudiəm; plæzˋmodɪəm] ***n.*** (*pl.* ***-dia*** [-diə; -dɪə]) **1.**【生】变形体;原质团;多核(原生)质体。**2.**【医】疟原虫。

plas·moid [ˈplæzmɔid; ˋplæzmɔɪd] ***n.***【物】等离子粒团。

plas·mol·y·sis [plæzˈmɔlisis; plæzˋmɑləsɪs] ***n.***【生】质壁分离;胞质皱缩。

plas·mo·lyze, -lyse [ˈplæzməˌlaiz; ˋplæzməˏlaɪz] ***vt.***, ***vi.***【生】(使)质壁分离;(使)胞质皱缩。

plas·mo·quine [ˈplæzməkwain; ˋplæzməˏkwaɪn] ***n.***【药】扑疟喹啉。

-plast *comb. f.* 表示"原生质;原浆": bio*plast*, proto*plast*.

plas·ter [ˈplɑːstə; ˋplæstɚ] **I** ***n.*** **1.** 胶泥,灰泥,涂墙泥。**2.** 石膏,(尤指)熟石膏〔又叫 ~ of Paris〕。**3.**【医】膏药。*adhesive* ~ 橡皮膏。*court* ~ 英国橡皮膏。*a* ~ *figure* 石膏像。~ *of Paris* 烧石膏,熟石膏。**II** ***vt.*** **1.** 涂胶泥于;(厚厚地)涂抹;用奶油[发油等]涂(*with*)。**2.** 在…上敷贴膏药。**3.**〔谑〕赔偿医药费。**4.** 加石膏除去(葡萄酒的酸味)。**5.** 黏贴;使紧贴。**6.** 安慰,抚慰。**7.** 在…上加一层掩饰。**8.**〔俚〕狠狠打击(对手等)。~ *with praise* 滥夸奖。~ **board**【建】灰胶纸拍板。~ **cast** (雕刻师的)石膏模型;【医】石膏绷带。~ **stone** (生)石膏。~ **work** 粉刷墙壁[天花板等]的工作。**-ed** ***a.*** **1.** 涂有灰泥的。**2.**〔美俚〕喝醉了的。

plas·ter·er [ˈplɑːstərə; ˋplæstərɚ] ***n.*** 泥水匠;石膏工艺品制作人。

plas·ter·ing [ˈplɑːstəriŋ; ˋplæstərɪŋ] ***n.*** **1.** 泥水工作。**2.** 石膏制品。**3.** 贴膏药。**4.** (葡萄酒的)加石膏除酸。

plas·ter·y [ˈplɑːstəri; ˋplæstərɪ] ***a.*** 胶泥[石膏]一样的。

plas·tic [ˈplæstik; ˋplæstɪk] **I** ***a.*** **1.** 造型的;塑造的;给与形态的。**2.** 可塑的,塑性的,受范的;柔软的;〔喻〕温顺的,肯听话的。**3.** 塑料[塑胶]的;塑料[塑胶]制的;合成树脂做的。**4.** 有形成力的,有创造力的。**5.**【医】整形的,成形的,修补的。**6.**【生】有适应力的;能进行新陈代谢的,构成生活组织的。~ *substances* 可塑性物质。*a* ~ *image* 塑像。*the* ~ *arts* 造型艺术;塑造术。*the* ~ *force of nature* 自然的创造力。**II** ***n.*** **1.**〔常 *pl.*〕塑料,塑胶;塑料[塑胶]制品;电木。**2.** *pl.*〔用作 *sing.* 或 *pl.*〕【医】整形外科。**3.**〔口〕(使用)信用卡。*acrylate* [*acrylic*] ~ 玻璃塑料[塑胶]。~ **bullet** 塑料子弹〔用于防暴〕。~ **clay**【地】第三期下层的中层系。~ **credit** 信用卡的使用〔以代替现金或支票〕。~ **explosive** 可塑炸药。~ **flow** 范性[塑性]流变。~ **money** 信用卡。~ **operations** 整形外科手术。~ **silverware** 塑料餐具。~ **sulphur**【化】黏性硫。~ **surgery**【医】整形外科。**-ti·cal·ly** ***ad.***

plas·ti·ca·tion [ˌplæstiˈkeiʃən; ˏplæstɪˋkeʃən] ***n.***【物】增模,增塑。

plas·ti·cine [ˈplæstisiːn; ˋplæstəˏsin] ***n.*** 塑像代用黏土。

plas·tic·i·ty [plæsˈtisiti; plæsˋtɪsətɪ] ***n.*** **1.** 黏性;可塑性;柔顺性。**2.** 适应性。**3.**【物】塑性学。

plas·ti·cize [ˈplæstisaiz; ˋplæstəˏsaɪz] ***vt.***, ***vi.*** (使)成为可塑。**-ci·za·tion** ***n.***

plas·ti·ciz·er [ˈplæstisaizə; ˋplæstəˏsaɪzɚ] ***n.*** 增塑剂,增韧剂。

plas·tid [ˈplæstid; ˋplæstɪd] ***n.***【生】**1.** 成形粒。**2.** 质体。

plas·tique [plɑːsˈtiːk; plæˋstik] ***n.***〔F.〕**1.** 塑料[塑胶]炸弹(= plastic bomb)。**2.** 造型性动作〔指舞蹈或哑剧中极其缓慢的舞姿或动作〕。

plas·ti·sol [ˈplæstisɔːl, -sɔl; ˋplæstɪsɔl, -sɑl] ***n.***【化】塑料[塑胶]溶胶。

plas·to·gene [ˈplæstədʒiːn; ˋplæstəˏdʒin] ***n.*** 质体基因。

plas·tog·raph [ˈplæstəugrɑːf; ˋplæstoˏgræf] ***n.*** 塑性变形图描记器。

plas·tom·e·ter [plæsˈtɔmitə; plæsˋtɑmətɚ] ***n.*** 塑性计。

plas·to·some [ˈplæstəsəum; ˋplæstəˏsom]【生】线粒体。

plas·tron [ˈplæstrən; ˋplæstrən] ***n.*** **1.** (女服的)胸饰,(男衬衣的)前胸衬领。**2.** (劈剑用的)护胸革;(中古的)钢制胸甲。**3.**【动】腹甲;(海胆的)盾板。

-plasty *comb. f.* 表示"形成,长成": auto*plasty*.

-plasy *comb. f.* = plasia.

plat[1] [plæt; plæt] **I** ***n.*** **1.** (作花坛等的)一块地。**2.**〔主美〕地区图,地图。**II** ***vt.***〔美〕制…的地图。

plat[2] ***n.***, ***vt.*** = plait.

plat [plɑː; plɑ] ***n.***〔F.〕(菜)一盘;菜单上的菜。

plat du jour [F. plɑdyˈʒuːr; ˏplɑdyˋʒur] ***n.*** (*pl.* ***plats du jour***)〔F.〕今日特制菜[时菜,风味菜]。

plat·an(e) [ˈplætən; ˋplætən] ***n.*** = plane tree.

plat·band [ˈplætbænd; ˋplætˏbænd] ***n.*** **1.** 花坛的花草边沿。**2.**【建】平边。

plate[1] [pleit; plet] **I** ***n.*** **1.** 厚金属板〔*cf.* sheet〕;板(片);(记有姓名等的金属)牌子,(尤指医生的)招牌,藏书牌;【印】印版;图版;另纸印插图。**2.** 金属版,电极版,铅版;金属版画。**3.** 板玻璃;【摄】底片,感光版。**4.**【史、古】锁金甲。**5.** 盘子;盆子;〔英〕金、银餐具;镀金器皿。**6.** (菜的)一盘;一顿饭菜。**7.** (做奖品用的)金杯,银杯;金银奖杯;(教会等的)捐款盘;献金,捐款。**8.** 假牙床。**9.**【建】(壁上的)横木;【棒球】投手板;本垒。**10.**【微】平皿,培养皿。**11.**【无】屏极极板,阳极。**12.** (牛的)肋肉。**13.**【动】(幼虫的)盾片;(鱼的)棱鳞。*a negative* ~ 底片;感光板。*a polarizing* ~【物】起偏振片。*a die* ~ 模板。*a die back* ~ 钢板衬片。*a door* ~ 门牌。*a family* ~ 刻有家徽、代代相传的金银餐具。*a* ~ *bat-*

tery 板极电池组。*a* ～ *of fish* 一盘鱼。*a theoretical* ～【物】理论屏。***foul a*** ～ ***with*** 和…共餐。***put up one's*** ～ 挂牌(行医)。***read one's*** ～〔美俚〕1. 做饭前祷告。2. 埋头不吭声吃饭。

II *vt*. 1. 镀;在…上覆盖金属板[装甲];给(马等)装蹄。2. 把…打成薄版;【印】给…制铅板[电版]。3.【造纸】给…上光。*copper* ～*d* 镀铜的。～ **basket**〔英〕餐具篮。～ **dinner**〔美〕全部菜都盛在一个盘子里的正餐。～ **glass**(上等)板玻璃。～ **holder**【摄】干片夹,硬片夹。～ **iron** 铁板;铁皮。～ **layer** 1. (铁路)铺路护路工。2.【印】装版工。～ **lunch**〔美〕全部菜都盛在一个盘子里的午餐。～ **mark** 1. = hallmark. 2. (印刷时因压力关系压在版画上的)铜版印。～ **matter**(通讯社发给小报馆的)电版新闻稿。～ **powder** 擦银粉。～ **printer** 铜版印刷工人。～ **printing** 铜版印刷。～ **race**〔主英〕奖杯赛马。～ **rack**〔英〕(洗后暂放的)餐具架。～**-tectonic** *a*.【地】(大地)地壳板块构造的。～ **wheel**【机】盘轮,无辐轮。**-ful** *n*. 一盘,满盘。

plat·eau [ˈplætəu, plæˈtəu; ˋplæto, plæˋto] *n*. (*pl*. *-x*, *-s* [-z; -z]) 1. 高原,台地,高地;【心】学习高原〔指学习上无进步也无退步的一段〕;〔美喻〕平稳状态[时期];停滞时期。2. 雕花托盘;饰匾;金属板;平顶女帽。3.【物】坪。

plat·ed [ˈpleitid; ˋpletɪd] *a*. 1. (铠甲等)面上装有金属片的。2. 鸳鸯布的〔指织物正反面的质料不同或颜色不同〕。3. 镀(金属)的〔尤指镀有稀有金属的〕。*silver-*～ 镀银的。

plate·let [ˈpleitlit; ˋpletlɪt] *n*. 1. 小片;小型板状物。2.【医】血小板,凝血细胞(= thrombocyte)。～ **laser** 小片状激光器〔镭射〕。

plat·(t)en [ˈplætən; ˋplætn] *n*. 1. (平压印刷机的)压印盘;(打字机的)压纸卷轴。2.【机】台板。

plat·er [ˈpleitə; ˋpletɚ] *n*. 1. 镀金匠;铁甲工。2. 光泽机。3.【赛马】劣等马。

plat·form [ˈplætfɔːm; ˋplætˏfɔrm] I *n*. 1. 台,坛;讲坛,主席台。2. 步廊;〔英〕(车站的)月台,站台;〔美〕(客车的)上下步梯;楼梯平台。3.【筑城】炮手站台;炮台座;【地】地台,台地;【油】(海洋钻井的)栈桥。4. (政党的)政纲;〔美〕(尤指选定候选人时的)政策宣言。5. 讨论会(会场);〔the ～〕演讲,演说。*a* ～ *balance* 台秤。*a launching* ～【宇】发射台。*a* ～ *ticket* 站[月]台票。*support the ministerial* ～ 支持政府党的政纲。***be at home on the*** ～ 惯于演说。

II *vt*. 1. 把…放在台上[放在高处;在…设月台]。—*vi*. 1. 起草政纲。2. 站在讲台上演说。～ **bridge**【铁路】天桥。～ **car** 平板货车,台车。～ **carriage**(搬运重物)低架台车,炮车(等)。～ **scale** [**balance**] 台秤。～ **truck** 平板大卡车。

plat·form·u·l·a [ˈplætfɔːmjulə; ˋplætfɔrmjələ] *n*. 〔谑〕演讲八股。

plat·i·na [pləˈtiːnə; ˋplætinə] *n*.【化】天然铂;铂。

plat·ing [ˈpleitiŋ; ˋpletɪŋ] *n*. 1. (电)镀,喷镀;镀金(术)。2. 镀层;外覆金属板;【船】(全部)船壳板;(兵舰等的)装甲。3.【摄】晒相。4. 悬赏赛马。～ **bath** 电镀槽。

pla·tin·ic [pləˈtinik; pləˋtɪnɪk] *a*.【化】四价铂的;铂的。～ **acid** 铂酸。～ **chloride** 氯化铂,四氯化铂。

plat·i·nif·er·ous [ˌplætiˈnifərəs; ˏplætəˋnɪfərəs] *a*. 含铂的;产铂的。

plat·i·ni·rid·i·um [ˌplætinaiˈridiəm; ˏplætɪnaɪˋrɪdɪəm] *n*.【矿】铂铱齐(铂、铱等的自然合金)。

plat·i·ni·te [ˈplætinait; ˋplætɪˏnaɪt] *n*. 代铂齐,代白金,赛白金。

plat·i·nize [ˈplætinaiz; ˋplætɪnaɪz] *vt*. 在…上镀铂;使与铂化合。～*d carbon electrode*【电】镀铂碳电极。

plat·i·no·cy·a·nide [ˌplætənəuˈsaiənaid; ˏplætənoˋsaɪəˏnaɪd] *n*.【化】氰亚铂酸盐。

plat·i·node [ˈplætinəud; ˋplætɪˏnod] *n*. 伏打电池(voltaic cell)的阴极[阴极]。

plat·i·noid [ˈplætinɔid; ˋplætɪˏnɔɪd] I *a*. 铂状的。II *n*. 1. 赛白金;合金铂。2. 铂系金属。

plat·i·no·type [ˈplætinəutaip; ˋplætɪnəˏtaɪp] *n*.【摄】铂黑印片术;铂黑照片。

plat·i·nous [ˈplætinəs; ˋplætṇəs] *a*.【化】亚铂的,二价铂的。～ *bromide* 溴化亚铂,二溴化铂。

plat·i·num [ˈplætinəm; ˋplætṇəm] *n*.【化】铂白金。～ *metals* 铂族元素。***go*** ～(唱片等)销量达百万张[上白金榜]。～ **black**(做触媒用的)铂黑,铂墨。～ **blonde**〔美〕淡金发女人;淡金黄色。～ **handshake**〔美〕付给高额退职金的解雇。～ **lamp** 白金电灯。～ **sponge** 铂棉。

plat·i·tude [ˈplætitjuːd; ˋplætəˏtjud] *n*. 1. 单调,平凡,陈腐。2. 平凡的话,滥调,俗论。*writings full of* ～*s* 满纸陈词滥调。

plat·i·tu·di·nar·i·an [ˌplætiˌtjuːdiˈnɛəriən; ˏplætəˏtjudṇˋnɛrɪən] I *a*. 平凡的,陈腐的。II *n*. 爱用陈词滥调的人。

plat·i·tu·di·nize [ˌplætiˈtjuːdinaiz; ˏplætəˋtjudɪˏnaɪz] *vi*. 讲[写]陈词滥调。

plat·i·tu·di·nous [ˌplætiˈtjuːdinəs; ˏplætəˋtjudṇəs] *a*. 平凡的;陈腐的;陈词滥调式的。～ *ponderosity*〔美〕陈腔滥调。

PLATO, Plato = programmic logic for automatic operations【计】(以电脑为基地而适应个别需要的)自动教学操作程序控制逻辑。

Pla·to [ˈpleitəu; ˋpleto] 柏拉图〔公元前 427? —347,古希腊哲学家〕。

Pla·ton·ic [pləˈtɔnik; pleˋtɑnɪk] I *a*. 1. 柏拉图(学派)的,柏拉图哲学的。2.〔常 p-〕纯精神的;纯理论的。II *n*.〔常 *pl*.〕1. = Platonist. 2. 精神恋爱故事。～ **bodies**【几】五面体。～ **love** 精神恋爱。～ **year**【天】柏拉图年〔约 26000 年的周期,经过此时期各星辰又复归原位〕。

Pla·to·nism [ˈpleitənizəm; ˋpletṇˏɪzəm] *n*. 1. 柏拉图哲学;柏拉图主义。2.〔常 p-〕精神恋爱。

Pla·to·nist [ˈpleitənist; ˋpletṇɪst] *n*. 柏拉图主义者。

Pla·to·nize [ˈpleitənaiz; ˋpletəˏnaɪz] *vi*. 信奉柏拉图哲学。— *vt*. 使信奉柏拉图哲学;根据柏拉图哲学解释。

pla·toon [pləˈtuːn; plæˋtun] *n*. 1.【军】(步兵、工兵等的)排,小队。2. (人的)一群,一组;〔美〕警察队。3.【史】排枪(队)。*a* ～ *leader* 排长。*a* ～ *sergeant*〔美军〕副排长〔级别与上士相等〕。

Platt·deutsch [ˈplɑːtdɔitʃ; ˋplɑtˏdɔɪtʃ] *n*. 德意志北部低地方言。

plat·ten [ˈplætən; ˋplætn] *n*. = platen.

plat·ter [ˈplætə; ˋplætɚ] *n*. 1.〔美、英古〕长圆形托盘,大浅盘。2.〔美俚〕(留声机)唱片;【运】铁饼;【棒球】本垒。*a* ～ *tosser*〔美〕掷铁饼选手。***on a*** ～ 1. 用盘子端上。2. 现成地;不费力地。

plat·y[1] [ˈpleiti; ˋpletɪ] *a*.【地】板状的,扁平状的。

plat·y[2] [ˈplæti; ˋplætɪ] *n*. (*pl*. ～(*s*), ***plat·ies***)(中美洲)剑尾鱼属(*Xiphophorus*)鱼。

plat·y-, plat- *comb. f*. 阔,宽,扁形,板状:*platy*cephalous 阔头的。

plat·y·hel·minth [ˌplætiˈhelminθ; ˏplætəˋhɛlmɪnθ] *n*. 扁形动物门(*Platyhelminthes*)动物〔如绦虫、肝蛭等〕。**-ic** *a*.

plat·y·po·di·a [ˌplætiˈpəudiə; ˏplætəˋpodɪə] *n*.【医】扁平足。

plat·y·pus [ˈplætipəs; ˋplætəpəs] *n*. (*pl*. *～es*, ***plat-y·pi*** [ˈplætipai; ˋplætəpaɪ])【动】鸭嘴兽。

plat·yr·rhine [ˈplætirain, -rin; ˋplætəˏraɪn, -rɪn] I *a*.【动】阔鼻类的。II *n*. 阔鼻类(*Platyrrhini*)动物。

plat·yr·rhin·i·an [ˌplætiˈriniən; ˏplætəˋrɪnɪən] *a*., *n*. 阔鼻的(人)。

plau·dit [ˈplɔːdit; ˋplɔdɪt] *n*.〔常 *pl*.〕拍手,喝彩;称赞,

赞美。

plau·si·ble [ˈplɔːzəbl; ˋplɔzəbl̩] ***a*.** **1.** (议论)好像有道理的,表面上讲得通的。**2.** 嘴巧的,会说话的。**-bil·i·ty *n*. -bly *ad*.**

plau·sive [ˈplɔːsiv; ˋplɔzɪv] ***a*.** **1.** 〔罕〕赞扬的,称誉的,称赞的。**2.** 似有理的;似诚实的,似可信的(=plausible)。

play [plei; ple] **I *vi*.** **1.** 玩,玩耍,游戏;闲逛;〔方〕罢工(*opp*. work);(动物)跳来跳去,飞来飞去,翩翩飞舞。**2.** (浪、光等)摇动,闪动,荡漾,摇晃,闪耀;(旗等)翻飞;(微笑等)浮泛(在脸上等);静静地过去(*around*; *about*)。**3.** (机器等)自由运转;(炮等)发射(*on*; *upon*);(喷泉等)喷出。**4.** 进行(比赛);适合打球;赌;打赌。**5.** 行动,举动,外置;假装;装扮;演戏,做戏,担任一个角色;(唱片、录音带等)播放;吹,奏,弹(乐器)(*on*; *upon*)。**6.** 开玩笑;嘲弄;玩弄(*with*; *on*; *upon*);发生影响。*Bees ~ about flowers*. 蜜蜂在花上飞来飞去。*a smile ~s on her lips* 她嘴唇上浮泛着微笑。*The sunlight ~s on the water*. 阳光在水上荡漾。*The imagination ~ed in our minds*. 我们浮想联翩。*The waves ~ed on the beach*. 波浪冲上了海滩。*The lawn ~s well*. 这块草地很适合打球。*The fountain ~s on Sundays*. 喷泉星期天开放。*P-!* 【球赛】比赛开始! — ***vt*.** **1.** 做(游戏),玩;打(球等);赌;和…竞争[玩耍]〔用此义既表示以球类游戏等为直接受词而在 with 后接以打玩的对方,也表示打玩的对方或单位为直接受词而在 with 或 at 后接以玩打的球类游戏等〕。**2.** 使某人上场担任某角色。**3.** 使轻快地动;使摇动,使闪动。**4.** 演(戏),饰演,扮演;弹奏,吹(乐器、曲子)。**5.** 做,行,干(鬼把戏等);举动得像…,模仿。**6.** 实行,使用;〔罕〕行使,发挥;尽(本分等)。**7.** 开玩笑;嘲弄,愚弄。**8.** 发射(炮等);放(水、烟火等);调摆(上钩的鱼);得当地操纵。**9.** 【板球】打(球);【牌戏】出(牌);【象棋】走动(棋子)。*The organist was ~ing the congregation out*. 弹风琴的弹着风琴把会众送了出去。*~ football with them*, *~ them with football* 同他们比赛足球。*Will you ~ me at chess?* 你愿意和我下棋吗? *The coach ~ed him at centre*. 教练叫他担任中锋。*~ a searchlight upon the aeroplane* 向飞机打探照灯。*~ the host* 作主人。***be ~ed out*** 〔美〕筋疲力尽,累透。***~ a double game*** 口蜜腹剑。***~ a good stick*** 会使一手好剑。***~ a lone hand*** **1.** 〔美〕独个儿工作[旅行、生活],不靠别人。**2.** 〔美运〕表演不精彩[引不起观众兴趣]。***~ advantages over sb.*** 〔美〕骗人。***~ along with*** 参与,与…合作。***~ at*** 玩,打;学…玩[取乐],比(输赢)。***~ away*** 赌掉(金钱);玩掉(时间);浪费。***~ back*** [***forward***] 【板球】把球打向后头[前头],回到三柱门方面。***~ ball*** 〔美口〕开始,着手;正正当当做,光明正大地行动。***~ both ends against the middle*** 〔美俚〕脚踏两条船;两头卖弄,从中渔利。***~ by ear*** (不会看乐谱)全靠听来的调子弹奏。***~ down*** (迎合对方的意思)放低语气(*to*);减弱;缩小某事的重要性,轻描淡写。***~ fair*** 规规矩矩比赛;光明正大的行动。***~ fast and loose*** 玩弄,反复无常。***~ for kingdom*** [***empire***] 争天下。***~ for love*** (非赌博性地)玩,打(牌等)。***~ for money*** 赌钱。***~ for time*** 争取时间。***~ foul*** [***foully, false***] 玩(打)得不规矩,作弊。***~ hard*** 行为卑鄙,不择手段。***~ high*** 大赌。***~ hookey*** 〔美〕逃学;怠工。***~ into each other's hands*** 互相渔利,互相勾结。***~ into sb.'s hands*** [***the hands of***] 故意使…占便宜;为…谋方便。***~ it*** (***low***) ***on*** (*sb*.) **=** ***~ low down on*** (*sb*.) 〔俚〕用卑劣手段骗人。***~ off*** **1.** (得分相同)进行补赛。**2.** 使某人出丑[出洋相];嘲弄某人,揭某人老底。**3.** 放射(烟火等)。**4.** 以…冒充(*as*)(*~ off a mere stone as a genuine gem upon sb*. 拿一块假宝石冒充真宝石去骗人)。**5.** 〔美〕假装有病(*The man is not ill; he is ~ing off*. 这人并不生病,他是假装的)。***~ one's hand for all it is worth*** 尽心竭力,尽全力。***~ opposite*** 扮演与主角相对的异性角色。***~ out*** 〔美〕**1.** 演完,做完。**2.** 用完,输光,使破产;使筋疲力竭。**3.** 放出,放松(绳索等)。***~ out of the cabbage*** 【美、高尔夫球】从难打的地方把球打出。***~ over one's head*** 【美运】得到预料不到的好成绩。***~ politics*** 〔美〕玩弄阴谋诡计,操纵。***~ safe*** 采取稳妥谨慎的措施。***~ the market*** 【美商】投机,买空卖空。***~*** (***the part of***) 饰演,扮演。***~ the races*** 〔美〕赌跑马。***~ up*** **1.** 〔美〕勇敢行动,大事渲染。**2.** 开始奏乐,越发使劲弹奏;(比赛等时)奋战。**3.** 〔口〕嘲弄,逗弄,耍戏,撩。***~*** (***up***) ***on*** **1.** 弹,奏,吹(笛子)。**2.** 利用(别人的恐惧心或信赖心)。***~*** (***up***)***on words*** 说俏皮话;说模棱两可的话。***~ up to*** **1.** 做…的配角,助演;帮助,支持。**2.** 〔俚〕谄媚,拍马屁。***~ with*** **1.** 以…自娱。**2.** 玩弄(火等)。

II *n*. **1.** 玩耍,游戏,娱乐;比赛。**2.** 玩笑;玩弄。**3.** 赌博;(游戏,比赛等的)方法,技巧。**4.** 失业;休业;罢工。**5.** 剧本,戏剧;话剧,戏。**6.** (投机)交易。**7.** 作用;活动范围;(才智的)运用;【机】间隙。**8.** 波动,闪动,飘动。**9.** (对工具等的)使用,运用。*a high* [*deep*] *~* 大赌。*fair ~* 公平的比赛;光明正大的行为;君子态度。*foul ~* 不规矩的比赛;卑鄙行为;小人态度。*a benefit ~* 义演。*All work and no ~ makes Jack a dull boy*. 死读书,不玩耍,孩子要变傻。*It is your ~*. 轮到你了;该你发球[走棋]了。***as good as a ~*** (戏剧似的)有趣。***at ~*** 在玩,正在游戏。***be in full ~*** 正在起劲,正在开足马力转动。***bring*** [***call***] ***into*** (***full***) ***~*** (充分)利用,使(充分)发挥作用,使(尽量)活动。***come into ~*** 开始活动,开始起作用。***give*** (***full***) ***~ to*** (*one's speciality*) 发挥[发扬](其所长)。***give sb. a ~*** 〔美〕努力想得到某人的信任。***go to the ~*** 去看戏。***hold*** [***keep***] ***sb. in ~*** 使人工作下去;牵制(敌人等)。***in ~*** **1.** 开玩笑。**2.** 【球赛】在比赛中;在工作;(牌)尚未打出。***make a ~ for*** 〔美口〕想方设法引诱。***make good ~*** 精神勃勃地[顺利地]进行[行动]。***make ~*** **1.** 【赛马】调摆追者。**2.** 加紧工作;起作用,发生效果。**3.** (拳击赛中)猛击对手。**4.** 领先。***out of ~*** 失业;【球赛】死球〔暂停比赛〕。***~ of colours*** 闪色,幻色,变彩,光彩幻现。***~ of words*** 诡辩;玩弄词藻。***~ on*** [***upon***] ***words*** 说双关语,说俏皮话。**~act *vi*.** **1.** 演戏。**2.** 假装;装扮。**3.** 装腔作势。**~ actor** 〔蔑〕演员。**~back** (录音等的)播放,放音。**~bill** 海报;剧场节目单。**~ book** 剧本。**~ boy** **1.** 〔美口〕花花公子,荡子,玩耍哥儿。**2.** 〔英方〕小丑;滑头。**~-by-~ *a*.** (比赛时)现场报道[评述]的;详细叙述的。**~clothes** 平常穿的衣服。**~ club** 高尔夫球棒。**~-date**(由家长安排的儿童们的)游戏约会。**~ day** 休息日;〔英〕(煤矿工人等的)假日。**~fellow** 玩耍朋友,游伴。**~game** 儿戏;〔喻〕幼稚的东西。**~girl** 爱交际游乐的女子。**~goer** 爱看戏的人,常看戏的人。**~going** 看戏。**~ground** (学校的)运动场;游乐地;(儿童)游戏场;公园(*the ~ground of Europe* 欧洲游乐场〔瑞士的别名〕)。**~house** 戏院,剧场;儿童游戏馆。**~land** (=~ground)。**~let** 短剧,独幕剧。**~list *vt*.** 将(唱片)排进播放节目表。**~mate**= playfellow. **~-off** 【运】最后决赛。**~pen** 婴儿圈栏〔供幼儿在内爬着玩的轻便圈栏〕。**~-right** 上演权。**~ room** 〔美〕(儿童的)游戏室。**~-some *a*.** 爱开玩笑的。**~suit** (妇女、儿童)运动衫,运动裤。**~ therapy** 【心】演剧疗法;游戏疗法。**~thing** 玩具;〔喻〕被玩弄的人[东西],玩物。**~ time** 游戏时间,娱乐时间。**~-white** 〔南非〕冒充白人的混血儿。**~-wright**, **~writer** 剧作家,编剧家。**~write *vi*.** 〔美〕写剧本。**~writing** 剧本创作。**-dom** 〔美〕戏剧界。**-ful *a*.** 爱游戏的,爱开玩笑的;滑稽的;开玩笑的。

pla·ya [ˈplɑːjə; ˋplɑjə] ***n*.** 【地】干盐湖。

play·a·ble [ˈpleiəbl; ˋpleəbl̩] ***a*.** 可演奏的;适宜于竞技表演的。

play·er [ˈpleiə; ˋpleɚ] ***n*.** **1.** 游戏的人;选手;〔英〕【板球】〔P-〕职业选手(*opp*. Gentleman)。**2.** 演员;演奏人。

3. 唱机。4. 为了消遣而干…的人;赌徒;懒人。*a seeded* ～ 种子选手。*Players versus Gentlemen*〔英〕职业选手对业余选手。*a record* ～ 电唱机。～ **piano** 自动(演奏的)钢琴。**-dom** *n*.〔美〕演员界,剧界。

play·ing-card [ˈpleiiŋkɑːd; ˋpleɪŋkɑrd] *n*. (一张)纸牌。

play·ing-field [ˈpleiiŋfiːld; ˋpleɪŋfild] *n*. (野外)运动场。

pla·za [ˈplɑːzə; ˋplæzə] *n*.〔Sp.〕(西班牙都市中的)广场;集市场所。

plbg. = plumbing.

-ple *suf*. 表示"重,倍":tri*ple*.

plea [pliː; pli] *n*. 1. 恳求,请求,请愿;祷告。2. 辩解;托词,口实。3.【法】抗辩,答辩。***cop a*** ～ 避重就轻地主动认罪。***make a*** ～ ***for*** 主张;请求。***on*** [***under***] ***the*** ～ ***of*** [***that***] 借口…。***The Court of Common Pleas*** 1. (英国的)高等民事法庭。2. (美国某些州的)中级民事[刑事]法庭。

pleach [pliːtʃ; plitʃ] *vt*. 编结(树枝);编。

plead [pliːd; plid] (～*ed*,〔美口〕***pled*** [pled; plɛd]) *vt*. 1. 辩护;辩论;答辩;抗辩。2. 主张;解释。— *vi*. 1. 辩护;辩论;抗辩,解释。2. 恳求,求情。～ ***ignorance*** 以不知道情况为借口。～ [***not***] ***guilty*** [不]服罪。～ ***poor mouth***〔美〕(有人催款[捐款]时)装穷。～ ***against*** 反驳;劝人不要…。～ ***for*** 恳求(～ *for sb.'s favour* 替某人说情)。～ ***with*** 向…恳求,说情(*for*)。

plead·a·ble [ˈpliːdəbl; ˋplidəbəl] *a*. 可辩护的,可作为抗辩的理由的。

plead·er [ˈpliːdə; ˋplidɚ] *n*. 1.【法】辩护人,律师。2. 代为求情者。

plead·ing [ˈpliːdiŋ; ˋplidɪŋ] I *n*. 1. 辩论,辩护。2. 诉讼程序。3.〔*pl*.〕【法】诉状。4. 调停,说项。II *a*. 恳求的,请求的。**-ly** *ad*.

pleas·ance [ˈplezəns; ˋplɛzṇs] *n*. 1. (特指邸宅内的)大庭园。2.〔古〕= pleasure.

pleas·ant [ˈpleznt; ˋplɛznt] *a*. (～*er*; ～*est*) 1. 愉快的,快乐的,舒适的,快活的。2. 活泼的,可爱的。3.〔古〕滑稽的,有趣的。～ *spoken*〔美〕说的有趣,说起来有趣。～ *to the eye* [*taste*] 好看[吃]。***have*** [***spend***] ***a*** ～ ***time*** 愉快地度过。***make oneself*** ～ 处世灵活,八面玲珑。**-ly** *ad*. **-ness** *n*.

pleas·an·try [ˈplezntri; ˋplɛzntrɪ] *n*. 玩笑;幽默,诙谐。

please [pliːz; pliz] *vt*. 1. 使高兴,使欢喜,使快乐,使满足;中…的意。2.〔祈使语气〕请。*One can't* ～ *everybody*. 一个人不可能使人人满意。*Come in*, ～. 请进来。*P- take a seat*. 请坐。— *vi*. 1. 欢喜,中意;觉得好。2. 讨好;讨人喜欢,有趣。*He is anxious to* ～. 他一心想讨好。*I shall do exactly as I* ～. 我将完全按照我自己的意思去做。*The play* ～*s*. 这戏有趣。***as you*** ～ 随你的意思,随你喜欢。***be easily*** ～***d*** 容易说话。***be*** ～***d in*** 欢喜,爱…。***be*** ～***d to*** (*do*) 乐意;〔敬语〕承蒙;肯(*He was* ～*d not to believe me*.〔带挖苦的敬语〕他不肯相信我的话)。***be*** ～***d with*** 喜欢。***if you*** ～ 1. 请劳驾;对不起(*I will wash my hands, if you* ～. 对不起,我要方便一下)。2. 你看多奇怪,竟…(*Now, if you* ～, *he expects me to pay for it*. 你看多奇怪,他还打算我来掏腰包哩)。～ ***God*** 如果运气好的话。～ ***oneself*** 满意,高兴;随意去做(*P- yourself*. 请便)。***to*** ～ ***me*** 看在我面上。

pleased [pliːzd; plizd] *a*. 对…高兴,对…满意(*with*)。*I'm quite* ～ *with your success*. 我为你的成功十分高兴。***be as*** ～ ***as Punch*** 非常高兴。

pleas·ing [ˈpliːziŋ; ˋplizɪŋ] *a*. 舒适的,愉快的;满意的;惹人喜欢的,可爱的。**-ly** *ad*.

pleas·ur·a·ble [ˈpleʒərəbl; ˋplɛʒrəbḷ] *a*. 令人快乐的,愉快的,舒适的。**-ness** *n*.

pleas·ur·a·b·ly [ˈpleʒərəbli; ˋplɛʒərəblɪ] *ad*. 快乐地,愉快地。

pleas·ure [ˈpleʒə; ˋplɛʒɚ] I *n*. 1. 愉快,快乐,满意;愉快的事情。2. 娱乐;(尤指)肉体上的快乐,享受,欢乐。3. 意志,欲求,希望。4. 恩惠,厚道。*a man of* ～ 逍遥快活的人。*a life given up to* ～ 纵情享受的生活。*It is our* ～ *to submit the balance-sheet*. 现呈上资产负债表。*Is it your* ～ *to go at once?* 你愿意立刻去吗? ***ask sb.'s*** ～ 问人来意。***at one's*** ～; ***at*** ～ 随意,随时(*You may go or stay at* ～. 去留都听你的便)。***consult sb.'s*** ～ 询问[顾到]某人的意愿。***do sb. the*** ～ (***of***) 讨好某人,使高兴,赏光(*Will you do me the* ～ *of coming to dinner with me?* 请赏光同我一起去吃饭好吗?)。***during one's*** ～ 在高兴的时候。***for*** ～ 为取乐,为消遣。***give*** ～ ***to*** 使…高兴。***have the*** ～ ***of*** (*doing*)〔敬语〕幸得…,乞(*May we have the* ～ *of your company?* 敬请出席)。***take*** (***a***) ～ ***in*** 高兴地;以…为乐;欣然(*I take* ～ *in sending you a copy*. 兹送上副本一份)。***with*** ～ 高兴(*I read of your success with* ～. 看到你成功的消息非常高兴)。II *vt*. (使)高兴;(使)欢喜;(使)满意。— *vi*. 1. 高兴,喜欢。2. 游荡,沉溺于享乐;〔口〕游览。～ **boat** 游船。～**-dome** 富丽堂皇的大厦[旅馆等]。～ **garden**, ～ **ground** 游乐场;公园。～ **principle**【心】(精神分析中的)快乐原则。～ **seeker** *n*. 追求享乐的人。～ **seeking** *n*. *a*. 玩乐(的);寻欢作乐(的)。～ **trip** 游览。

pleat [pliːt; plit] I *n*. (衣服上的)褶。***put sb. in*** ～***s***〔英俚〕使(某人)大为恼火。II *vt*. 1. 使打褶。2. 把…编成辫。

pleat·er [ˈpliːtə; ˋplitɚ] *n*. 打褶人;褶裥机〔尤指缝纫机上打褶用的机件〕。

pleb [pleb; plɛb] *n*.〔俚〕1. 老百姓,平民。2.〔美〕军官学校[海军学校]的一年级生;大学一年级生。

plebe [pliːb; plib] *n*.〔美俚〕= pleb 2.

ple·be·ian [pliˈbiːən; plɪˋbiən] I *n*.【古罗马史】庶民,平民(*opp*. patrician)。II *a*. 平民的;下等的,下贱的,鄙俗的。*a* ～*'s bank* 平民银行。**-ism** *n*. 平民身份[气习]。**-ize** *vt*. 使平民化。

pleb·i·scite [ˈplebisit, -sait; ˋplɛbɪsɪt, -saɪt] *n*. 公民投票;【古罗马史】全民表决。**-sci·tar·y** *a*.

plebs [plebz; plɛbz] *n*. (*pl*. ***plebes*** [ˈpliːbiz; ˋplibɪz])〔L.〕1. 古罗马的下层阶级。2. 平民,庶民;百姓。

plec·tog·nath [ˈplektɔgnæθ; ˋplɛktɑgnæθ] I *n*.【动】愈颌类(固颌类)(*Plectognathi*)鱼。II *a*.【动】愈颌类的。

plec·trum [ˈplektrəm; ˋplɛktrəm] *n*. (*pl*. ～*s*, ***-tra*** [-trə; -trə]) 1. (弦乐器的)拨子。2.【动】距。

pled [pled; plɛd]〔口、方〕plead 的过去式及过去分词。

pledge [pledʒ; plɛdʒ] I *n*. 1. 公约;誓约;〔the ～〕戒酒的誓约;(政党领袖等的)诺言;〔美口〕宣誓入会者。2.【法】抵押权,抵押,典当;抵押品。3. (表示友谊的)干杯。4. 保证;(好意或友情的)表示。*the P- to the Flag*〔美〕对国旗宣誓。*a* ～ *of affection* [*love*] 爱情的象征;子女。***be*** [***lie***] ***in*** ～ 在抵押中。***be under*** ～ 发了誓。***give*** [***lay, put***] (*sth*.) ***to*** [***in***] ～ 抵押,典当。***in*** ～ ***of good faith*** 当作好意[信义]的表示。***redeem one's*** ～ 履行信约。***take a*** ～ 发誓。***take out of*** ～ 赎回。***take*** [***sign***] ***the*** ～ 发誓戒酒。***under*** ～ (*of secrecy*) 发誓(守秘密)。II *vt*. 1. 使发誓,保证。2. 典当,抵押。3. 为…干杯。4.〔美口〕使入会(作后补会员)。～ *oneself to secrecy* 发誓守秘密。～ *one's word* [*honour*] 发誓;保证。～ *the honourable guest* 为贵宾干杯。***be*** [***stand***] ～***d to*** 对…保证。**-r** *n*.

pledg·ee [pledʒˈiː; plɛdʒˋi] *n*. 接受抵押的人。

pledg·er, pledg·or [ˈpledʒə; ˋplɛdʒɚ] *n*. 1. 抵押者;典当人。2. (戒酒等的)发誓人。3. 举酒干杯的人。

pledg·et [ˈpledʒit; ˋplɛdʒɪt] *n*. (包扎伤口用)小拭子。

-plegia, -plegy *comb. f*. 表示"瘫,麻痹":hemi*plegia*, para*plegia*.

Plé·iade [pleˈjad; plɛˋjad] *n*.〔F.〕1. 七星社〔十六世纪

法国七位喜欢运用古典格式的诗人所组成〕。**2.** 七名人(= pleiad)。

Plei·a·des, Plei·ads [ˈplaiədiːz, ˈplaiədz; ˋplaɪəˏdiz, ˋplaɪədz] *n*. 〔*pl*.〕 **1.** 【希神】阿特拉斯 (Atlas) 的七个女儿,后化为天上七星。**2.** 【天】昴(宿)星团;〔喻〕七区头;七颗明星。

plein-air [ˌpleinˈɛə;ˏplenˋɛr] *a*. (绘画、绘画法)直接利用外光描绘的,外光主义的,外光派的〔法国十九世纪的一种印象画派〕。**-ism** *n*. **-ist** *n*.

Plei·o·cene [ˈplaiəsiːn; ˋplaɪəˏsin] *a*., *n*. 【地】上新世(的)。

plei·o·tax·y [ˈplaiətæksi; ˋplaɪəˏtæksɪ] *n*. 【植】花轮增多。

plei·ot·ro·py [plaiˈɔtrəpi; plaɪˋɑtrəpɪ] *n*. 【遗】(基因)多效性(= pleiotropism)。**-ic** [ˈplaiəˈtrɔpik; ˋplaɪəˋtrɑpɪk] *a*. **-trop·i·cal·ly** *ad*.

Pleis·to·cene [ˈplaistəusiːn; ˋplaɪstəˏsin] *n*., *a*. 【地】更新世(的)。

Plen. = Plenipotentiary.

ple·na·ry [ˈpliːnəri; ˋplinərɪ] *a*. **1.** 十足的,完全的;无条件的,绝对的。**2.** 全体出席的;有全权的;【法】正式的(*opp*. summary)。~ *indulgence* 【天主】大赦。~ *power* [*authority*] 全权。*a* ~ *meeting* [*session*] 全体会议,大会。**-ri·ly** *ad*.

ple·ni·lune [ˈpliːnəluːn; ˋplinəlun] *n*. 〔诗〕满月,望月;满月之时。

ple·nip·o·tence [pləˈnipətəns; pləˋnɪpətəns] *n*. 全权;全部主权。**-o·tent** *a*.

plen·i·po·ten·tia·ry [ˌplenipəˈtenʃəri; ˏplɛnəpəˋtɛnʃərɪ] **I** *n*. 全权大使,全权委员。**II** *a*. 有全权的;(权力等)绝对的。*an ambassador extraordinary and* ~ 特命全权大使。*a minister* ~ 全权公使。

plen·ish [ˈpleniʃ; ˋplɛnɪʃ] *vt*. 〔Scot.〕 **1.** 充,充满,充填。**2.** 给(房屋)安置设备。**3.** 养家畜于(农场)。

plen·i·ti·tude [ˈplenititjuːd; ˋplɛnɪtətjud] *n*. = plenitude.

plen·i·tude [ˈplenitjuːd; ˋplɛnəˏtjud] *n*. **1.** 充分,完全。**2.** 充实,充满;丰富,多;(权力等的)绝顶;【医】(胃等的)胀满。*the moon in her* ~ 【徽】满月。*in the* ~ *of his power* 当他权力的最高峰时。

plen·i·tu·di·nous [ˌpleniˈtjuːdinəs, -ˈtuːd-; ˏplɛnɪˋtjudɪnəs, -ˋtud-] *a*. **1.** 丰满的,充足的。**2.** 肥壮的,结实的。

plen·te·ous [ˈplentjəs, -tiəs; ˋplɛntjəs, -tɪəs] *a*. 〔诗〕= plentiful. ~ *crops* 丰收。*a* ~ *year* 丰年。

plen·ti·ful [ˈplentiful; ˋplɛntɪfəl] *a*. 丰富的。*a* ~ *harvest* 丰收。**-ly** *ad*. **-ness** *n*.

plen·ty [ˈplenti; ˋplɛntɪ] **I** *n*. 多,丰富;充分。*a year of* ~ 丰年。*There is* ~ *of time*. 时间很充裕。**in** ~ 多,丰富;充分(*live in peace and* ~ 过太平富裕的日子。*We are in* ~ *of time*. 我们有充分时间)。~ **of** 很多的(*There is* ~ *of food*. 食物很充足)。**II** *a*. 〔口、方〕〔通常用作表语[主词补语]〕充裕的,足够的;很多的。*This is* ~. 这就很多了。~ [***plentiful***] ***as blackberries*** 很多很多的,多得不得了。**III** *ad*. 〔口〕十分,充分。*The house is* ~ *large enough*. 那房子足够大了。

ple·num [ˈpliːnəm; ˋplinəm] **I** *n*. (*pl*. ~**s**, **-na** [-nə; -nə]) **1.** 充满物质的空间 (*opp*. vacuum);充实,充满。**2.** 【物】高压间。**3.** 全体会议。**II** *a*. 增压的。~ *method* (*of ventilation*) 压力通风法。~ **gauge** 通风计。~ **system** 压力通风系统。

ple·och·ro·ism [pliˈɔkrəuizəm; plɪˋɑkroɪzəm] *n*. 【理】多向色性。**-chroic** [-ˈkrəuik; -ˋkroɪk] *a*.

ple·och·ro·ma·tism [ˌpli(ː)əˈkrəumətizəm; ˏpliəˋkromətɪzəm] *n*. 【物】多向色性。

ple·o·mor·phism [ˌpli(ː)əˈmɔːfizəm; ˏpliəˋmɔrfɪzəm] *n*. **1.** 【植】多型(现象)。**2.** 【动】多态性;多态现象(= poly morphism)。**-mor·phic**, **-mor·phous** *a*.

ple·o·nasm [ˈpli(ː)ənæzəm; ˋpliəˏnæzəm] *n*. 【修】冗词,冗句,冗言〔如 a false lie〕。**-nas·tic** *a*. 烦冗的;重复的,赘语的。

ple·o·pha·gous [pli(ː)ˈɔfəgəs; pli(ɪ)ˋɑfəgəs] *a*. **1.** 吃多种食物的。**2.** (寄生虫)寄生于多种动[植]物的。

ple·o·pod [ˈpliːəpɔd; ˋpliəˏpɑd] *n*. 【动】(甲壳类幼虫的)腹足;(成虫的)后足。

ple·rome [ˈpliərəum; ˋplɪrom], **ple·rom** [ˈplirəm; ˋplɪrəm] *n*. 【植】中柱原。

ple·si·o·saur, ple·si·o·sau·rus [ˈpliːsiəsɔː, -ˈsɔːrəs; ˋplisɪəˏsɔr, -ˋsɔrəs] *n*. (*pl*. **-ri** [-rai; -raɪ]) 【古生】蛇颈龙。

ples·sor [ˈplesə; ˋplɛsɚ] *n*. 叩诊锤(= plexor)。

pleth·o·ra [ˈpleθərə; ˋplɛθərə] *n*. **1.** 过多,过剩。**2.** 【医】多血,多血症,多血质。**-thor·ic** *a*.

ple·thys·mo·graph [pliˈθizməgrɑːf, -græf; plɪˋθɪzməˏgrɑf, -græf] *n*. 【医】体积描记器。**-ic** *a*. **-y** *n*.

pleu·ra [ˈpluərə; ˋplʊrə] *n*. (*pl*. **-rae** [-riː; -ri]) **1.** 【解】胸膜,肋膜;【动】肋部。**2.** (昆虫的)侧板。**pleu·ral** *a*.

pleu·ri·sy [ˈpluərisi; ˋplʊrəsɪ] *n*. 【医】肋膜炎,胸膜炎。*dry* [*moist*] ~ 干性[湿性]肋膜炎。**-rit·ic** [-ˈritik; -ˋrɪtɪk] *a*.

pleu·ro·dont [ˈpluːrədɔnt; ˋplʊrəˏdɑnt] **I** *a*. 偏齿的〔如某些蜥蜴〕。**II** *n*. 偏齿动物。

pleu·ro·dyn·i·a [ˌpluərəuˈdiniə; ˏplʊrəˋdɪnɪə] *n*. 【医】胸膜痛,肋肌痛。

pleu·ron [ˈpluərɔn; ˋplʊrɑn] *n*. (*pl*. ***pleu·ra*** [-rə; -rə]) 【动】(甲壳类的)横突起;(昆虫的)侧板。

pleu·ro·pneu·mo·ni·a [ˌpluərəunju(ː)ˈməunjə; ˏplʊrənjəˋmonɪə] *n*. 【医】胸膜肺炎。

pleu·rot·o·my [pluˈrɔtəmi; plʊˋrɑtəmɪ] *n*. (*pl*. **-mies**) 胸膜切开术。

pleus·ton [ˈpluːstɔn; ˋplustɑn] *n*. 水漂生物。**-ic** [-ˈtɔnik; -ˋtɑnɪk] *a*.

plew [pluː; plu] *n*. 海狸皮。

-plex *comb*. *f*. 表示"含…个厅[楼层]"之意。

plex·i·form [ˈpleksifɔːm; ˋplɛksəˏfɔrm] *a*. 网状的,丛状的;复杂的。

plex·i·glass [ˈpleksiglɑːs; ˋplɛksɪˏglæs] *n*. 有机玻璃〔源自商标名〕。

plex·im·e·ter [plekˈsimitə; plɛksˋɪmətɚ] *n*. 【医】叩诊板。

plex·or [ˈpleksə; ˋplɛksɚ] *n*. 【医】叩诊锤。

plex·us [ˈpleksəs; ˋplɛksəs] *n*. (*pl*. ~(*es*)) **1.** 【解】(神经、淋巴管或血管的)丛。**2.** 纠纷。*the solar* ~ 太阳神经丛。*the spinal* ~ 脊柱静脉丛。

plf., **plff.** = plaintiff.

pli·a·ble [ˈplaiəbl; ˋplaɪəbl] *a*. **1.** 柔韧的,易弯的,柔软的。**2.** 柔顺的;圆通的。**-bil·i·ty** [ˌplaiəˈbiliti; ˏplaɪəˋbɪlətɪ] *n*. 柔韧(性),柔顺(性)。**-ab·ly** *ad*.

pli·ant [ˈplaiənt; ˋplaɪənt] *a*. = pliable. **-an·cy**, **-ness** *n*. **-ly** *ad*.

pli·ca [ˈplaikə; ˋplaɪkə] *n*. (*pl*. ***pli·cae*** [ˈplaisiː; ˋplaɪsi]) **1.** 【解】褶,(皱)襞。**2.** 【医】纠发病。

pli·cate, pli·cat·ed [ˈplaikit, ˈplaikeitid; ˋplaɪket, ˋplaɪketɪd] *a*. 【植、动】有皱襞的,有褶的;折扇状的。

pli·ca·tion [plaiˈkeiʃən; plaɪˋkeʃən] *n*. **1.** 褶,摺叠。**2.** 【植】折扇式。**3.** 【地】皱纹,细褶皱。

pli·ca·ture [ˈplikətʃə; ˋplɪkətʃɚ] *n*. 摺,摺叠;皱摺(= plication)。

pli·é [pliːˈei; plɪˋe] *n*. 【芭蕾】蹬。

pli·er [ˈplaiə; ˋplaɪɚ] *n*. **1.** 努力工作的人,勤奋的人。**2.** 定期来回盘运的车[船]。**3.** 【诗】驾驶者;【海】逆风换抢的帆船。

pli·ers [ˈplaiəz; ˋplaɪɚz] *n*.〔用作 *sing*., *pl*.〕钳子,老虎钳,手钳。(*a*) *cutting* ~ 钢丝钳。*a pair of* ~ 一把钳子。*a round-rose* ~ 圆头钳。

plight[1] [plait; plaɪt] **I** *n*. 保证;誓约;婚约。**II** *vt*. **1.** 保证;发誓。**2.**〔~ oneself〕定婚。*She ~ed herself to him*. 她和他订婚了。*~ed lovers* 山盟海誓的一对情人。~ *one's faith* [*promise*, *troth*, *word*, *honour*] 牢牢约定,说定,山盟海誓。

plight[2] [plait; plaɪt] *n*. (困难)处境,状况,状态;苦境,悲惨命运。*What a* ~ *to be in*! 真不得了啦! *in a sorry* ~ 在狼狈不堪的处境中。

plim [plim; plɪm] *vt*., *vi*. (*plimmed*; *plim·ming*)〔英方〕**1.** (使)膨胀 (*out*)。**2.** (使)丰满。

plim·soll [ˈplimsəl; ˋplɪmsəl] *n*.〔*pl*.〕〔澳〕橡皮底帆布鞋。

Plim·soll [ˈplimsəl; ˋplɪmsl] *n*. **1.** 普利姆索尔〔姓氏〕。**2. Samuel** ~ 萨·普利姆索尔〔1824—1898,英国船运改革者,世称 the Sailor's Friend〕。

Plim·soll mark [ˈplimsəlˈmɑːk; ˋplɪmsəlˋmark] *n*.【海】(商船上显著标明的)载重线标志〔亦作 ~ line〕。

pling [pliŋ; plɪŋ] *vi*.〔美〕做叫化子。— *vt*. 乞讨。

plink [pliŋk; plɪŋk] **I** *n*.〔拟声〕轻而尖的玎玲声。**II** *vt*., *vi*. **1.** (使钢琴、班卓琴等)发出玎玲声。**2.** (向铁盒或类似目标)射击;乱射。**-er** *n*.

plink-ponk [ˈpliŋk-pɔŋk; ˋplɪŋk-paŋk] *n*.〔谑〕白葡萄酒。

plinth [plinθ; plɪnθ] *n*. **1.**【建】柱基,柱脚;壁脚板。**2.** 像座,底座。

Plin·y [ˈplini; ˋplɪnɪ] *n*. 普林尼〔人名〕。~ **"the Elder", Gaius Plinius Secundus** 老普林尼〔23—79,古罗马政治家,百科辞典编集者〕。~ **"the Younger", Gaius Plinius Caecilius Secundus**〔小普林尼 62(?)—113 著作家,政治家,雄辩家〕。

Pli·o·cene [ˈplaiəsiːn; ˋplaɪəˏsin] *n*., *a*. = pleiocene.

pli·o·film [ˈplaiəfilm; ˋplaɪəˏfɪlm] *n*. (制雨衣等用的)氢氯化橡胶膜〔源自商标名〕。

pli·o·tron [ˈplaiətrɔn; ˋplaɪəˏtrɑn] *n*.【无】功率电子管〔原商标名〕。

plis·sé, *plis·se* [pliˈsei; plɪˋse] *n*. **1.** 褶裥,打褶〔使棉布、尼龙等起皱的最后一道工序〕。**2.** (起皱的)纤维织品。

P.L.M. = Paris-Lyons-Mediterranéan Railway. (法国)巴黎—里昂—地中海铁路。

PLO = Palestine Liberation Organization 巴勒斯坦解放组织。

plod [plɔd; plɑd] **I** *vi*. (*plod·ded*; *plod·ding*) **1.** 沉重地走 (*on*; *along*)。**2.** 努力从事;勤苦工作[用功] (*at*)。~ *through the desert* 在沙漠里跋涉。~ *at one's books* 勤苦读书。*He's plodding away day and night*. 他一天到晚在勤苦工作。~ *through a task* 苦干到底。*a ~ding genius* 勤学苦练的人才。— *vt*. 沉重地走(路)。~ *one's weary way* 拖着疲劳的脚步走。**II** *n*. **1.** 沉重的脚步[脚步声]。**2.** 勤苦工作,辛苦,劳苦。

plod·der [ˈplɔdə; ˋplɑdɚ] *n*. **1.** 沉重地走的人;勤苦工作的人。**2.**【化】蜗压机。

Plo·esti [plɔːˈjeʃt; plɔˋjɛʃt] *n*. 普洛耶什特〔罗马尼亚城市〕。

-ploid *suf*. 表示"【生】…倍(染色)体":poly*ploid* 多倍体。

ploms [plɔmz; plɑmz] *n*.〔口〕自怜;自卑心理〔*p*oor *l*ittle *o*ld *m*e *s*yndrome 的缩略〕。

plonk[1] [plɔŋk, plʌŋk; plɑŋk, plʌŋk] = plunk.

plonk[2] [plɔŋk; plɑŋk] *n*.〔澳俚〕廉价的劣等酒。

plop [plɔp; plɑp] **I** *vt*., *vi*. (*plopped*; *plop·ping*) (使)噗通一声掉落,(使)砰一声爆开[弹出];(使)噗噗地沉下去。**II** *n*. 噗通声;砰的一声。**III** *ad*. 噗通一声,噗噗地,砰的一声。*fall* ~ *into the water* 噗通一声掉落水中。*The cork came out* ~! 塞子砰的一声拔出了。~ **art** 随便放置艺术〔不考虑作品放置环境是否相宜的艺术设计〕。

plo·sion [ˈpləuʒən; ˋploʒən] *n*.【语音】破裂(发音)。**plo·sive** *n*., *a*. 破裂音(的),爆发音(的)。

plot[1] [plɔt; plɑt] **I** *n*. **1.** 阴谋(事件),策划。**2.** (小说、戏剧等的)情节。**3.**【炮兵】测算表。*hatch a* ~ 策划阴谋。*be privy to a* ~ 参与阴谋。*The* ~ *thickens*. 情节复杂起来了。**II** *vt*. (*-tt-*) **1.** 密谋,图谋;策划。**2.** 绘(图);画(设计图)。**3.** 把…记入(海图)。**4.** 拟定(剧本等的)情节。— *vi*. 图谋,策划 (*for*; *against*)。

plot[2] [plɔt; plɑt] **I** *n*. **1.** 小块地,一块地;一块地上的作物。**2.**〔美〕地基;基址图;【军】标绘(图)。*an experimental* ~ 试验田。*reserved private ~s* 自留地。*a garden* ~ 园地。*a* ~ *of barley* 一块大麦地。*a radar* ~ 雷达测绘板;雷达情报站。**II** *vt*. (*-tt-*) 区划(土地);划分。~ *out one's time* 分配自己的时间。

plot·tage [ˈplɔtidʒ; ˋplɑtɪdʒ] *n*. 一块地皮的面积。

plot·ter [ˈplɔtə; ˋplɑtɚ] *n*. **1.** 策划者;阴谋者。**2.** 绘迹器。**3.** 标图员;制图者。*a curve* ~ 曲线描绘器。

plot·ting [ˈplɔtiŋ; ˋplɑtɪŋ] *n*. **1.** 测绘;标图。**2.** 标航路。~ **paper** 方格绘图纸。~ **scale** 绘图比例尺。

plough, 〔美〕**plow** [plau; plaʊ] **I** *n*. **1.** 犁;犁形器具;排雪机;【矿】煤犁,刨煤机;【建】路犁;(木工用的)沟刨;【印】手动式切书机。**2.** 耕作,农业;耕地。**3.**〔the P-〕【天】北斗七星。**4.**〔英俚〕(主考人评定)不及格。*a two-wheeled double-share* ~ 双轮双铧犁。*a cable-towed* ~ 绳索牵引犁。***be at the*** ~ 在种田。***beat*** [***follow***, ***hold***] ***the*** ~ 种田。***go to one's*** ~ 作自己的事。***look back from the*** ~ 中止,停止。***put*** [***lay***, ***set***] ***one's hand to the*** ~ 开始工作。***take a*** ~〔英口〕不及格。***under the*** ~ 在耕作下。**II** *vt*. **1.** 犁,耕;开(沟),作(畦);【木工】挖沟(槽)。**2.** 使(额头)起皱。**3.** 开(路);破(浪)前进。**4.**〔英口〕使不及格。**5.** 投(资)。*a face ~-ed with wrinkles* 起皱的脸。— *vi*. **1.** 犁;耕;(土地)适于耕种。**2.** 开路;分开积雪等前进 (*through*);钻研。**3.** 刻苦前进 (*through*)。**4.**〔英口〕考试不及格。*The land ~s hard after the drought*. 旱后田难犁。***be ~ed*** 考不及格。~ ***a*** [***one's***] ***lonely furrow*** = ~ ***one's furrow alone*** (脱离组织)单独行动;过孤独生活,离群索居。~ ***around***〔美口〕试探,打探。~ ***back*** 把(草等)犁入土中;把(利润)再投资。~ ***down*** 犁倒。~ ***into*** 奋力投入(工作)。~ ***in*** [***into***] ***the land*** 犁进去。~ ***one's way*** 奋力前进。~ ***the sand***(***s***) [***air***] 白费气力。~ ***the waves*** 破浪前进。~ ***under*** 使消失;埋葬掉。~ ***up*** 犁翻,掘翻。~ ***with sb.'s heifer*** [***ox***] **1.** 利用别人的牛给自己耕地。**2.** 利用他人资财。~**back**〔主美〕利润再投资;利润再投资额。~**boy** 耕地时牵牛的孩子;农家子;庄稼汉。~ **head** = ploughshare. ~**land**〔英〕**1.** (可)耕地。**2.** = hide[3]. ~**man** (*pl*. ~**men**) *n*. 耕地人,庄稼汉。~**share** 犁头;犁铧。~**staff** 小铲。~**tail** 犁柄;农活,耕作(*at the ~tail* 在种田)。~ **wright** 制犁[修犁]人。

Plough-Mon·day [ˈplauˈmʌndi; ˋplaʊˋmʌndɪ]【英史】主显节 (Epiphany)〔1 月 6 日〕后的星期一〔过去英国某些地方在这一日开始耕作〕。

Plov·div [ˈplɔːvdif; ˋplɔvdɪf] *n*. 普罗夫迪夫〔保加利亚城市〕。

plov·er [ˈplʌvə; ˋplʌvɚ] *n*.【鸟】鸻科鸟;鸻。

plow [plau; plaʊ] *n*., *vt*., *vi*.〔美〕= plough.

ploy [plɔi; plɔɪ] *n*. **1.** (为了得到利益而使用的)花招;(挫敌的)策略,手法。**2.** (社交性的)玩乐。

PLU = people like us〔美〕像我们这类人。

plu. = plural.

pluck [plʌk; plʌk] **I** *vt*. **1.** 拨,扯(羽毛等);采,摘,掐(花、果实)。**2.** 拉,拖,拉下,拖开。**3.** 鼓起(勇气等) (*up*)。**4.**〔口〕抢,夺 (*away*; *off*),诈取,讹诈。**5.**

【地】(冰川)冲走(岩石),拔蚀。6. 拨响(琴弦)。7.〔英大学俚〕使不及格。~ *sb. by the sleeve* 拉…的袖子。— *vi.* 猛拉(*at*);想抓住,捉(*at*)。*A drowning man ~s at a straw.* 溺水的人连稻草也要抓。**get ~ed** 考不及格,落第。~ **a pigeon** 骗取愚人金钱。~ **asunder** 扯开。~ **away**[**off**] 扯去,撕去。~ **down** 拆毁(建筑物),(把某人)拖下来。~ **out** 拔出;揭露。~ **up** 1. 连根拔去,根绝。2. 提高,鼓起(勇气)。**II** *n.* 1. 拔;扯。2.(牛等的)内脏。3.〔口〕胆子,勇气。4.〔俚〕不及格。5.【摄】鲜明。*a hard ~ed man* 冷酷无情的人。*a good-~ed man* 有勇气的人。

P

pluck·less [ˈplʌklis; ˋplʌklɪs] *a.* 没勇气的。

pluck·y [ˈplʌki; ˋplʌkɪ] *a.* (*-i·er; -i·est*) 1. 有勇气的,有胆量的。2.【摄】清晰的,鲜明的。**-i·ly** *ad.* **-i·ness** *n.*

plug [plʌg; plʌg] *n.* 1. 塞子;(龋齿等的)填塞物。2. 救火龙头,消防栓;(内燃机的)火花塞;【军】火门闩;枪口盖;【海】锚链孔塞子,疏水塞子。3.【电】插塞,插头;针形接点;抽水马桶的抽水装置。4. 板烟。5.【地】岩颈。6.〔美俚〕废马,老马;废物;〔美口〕陈货。7.〔美俚〕用功学生。8.〔美俚〕高礼帽。9.〔美俚〕(插在广播或电视节目里的)讨厌的广告。10.〔美俚〕一拳。*chewin' ~* 橡皮糖。**pull the ~** 中断,停止,取消。**II** *vt.* (**-gg-**) 1. 塞,填塞,堵(*up*)。2.〔俚〕开枪打死[打伤];〔俚〕用拳头打,殴打。3.〔美俚〕反反复复硬叫人听[看];利用无线电做广告。— *vi.* 1.〔俚〕勤苦工作;用功。2. 开枪射击。3.【电】插上插头。~ **along**〔美俚〕勤苦工作下去。~ (**away**) **at sth.** 拼命地干着(某项工作)。~**-and-play** *n.*, *a.*【计】即插即用(的)。~**-in** 1. *n.*【无】插座;【计】插件。2. *vt.* 接通电源。~ **bush**【无】插头衬套。~ **cock** 旋塞。~ **cord**【电】1. 插头(软)线。2. 塞绳。~**-ended trunk**【无】插头收端中继线。~ **fuse**【电】插塞式熔丝,插入式保险丝。~ **hat**〔美俚〕高礼帽。~ **rod** 塞杆。~**-ugly**〔美俚〕(城里的)流氓,恶棍,暴徒。~**-up line** (电话的)障碍试验线。

plug·ger [ˈplʌgə; ˋplʌgɚ] *n.* 1.【医】(牙科医生用)填充器;填塞物。2.【矿】凿岩机。3.〔美俚〕用功学生;勤苦工作的人。4. 捧场者;(电台的)商业广告播音员;宣传员。

plum [plʌm; plʌm] **I** *n.* 1.【植】李子;李树;梅。2. 酒馅巧克力。3.(制糕饼用的)葡萄干。4. 糖果。5. 酱紫色。6. 最好的东西,最好的地方,精华。7.〔英俚〕十万镑,大财产;(不小的)额外利益,奖品。8.〔美〕重要职位。**II** *ad.*〔美〕充分,完全(= plumb)。~ *ripe* 熟透。~ **cake** 葡萄干糕饼。~ **locoed**〔美〕思想癫狂的,非常入迷的。~ **pudding**[**duff**] 葡萄干布丁。~ **tree** 李树;〔美〕利益的来源〔如政治恩惠和职位〕。

plum·age [ˈpluːmidʒ; ˋplumɪdʒ] *n.* 1.【动】〔集合词〕羽毛。2. 漂亮衣服。*full-~d* 羽毛长齐的。

plu·mas·sier [pluːˈmæsiə, -siei; pluˋmæsɪr, -sɪe] *n.* 〔F.〕〔罕〕羽毛制品商,羽毛商人。

plumb [plʌm; plʌm] **I** *n.* 铅锤,测锤,线砣;垂直。**off ~ = out of ~** 不垂直,歪斜。**II** *a.* 1. 垂直的;公正的。2.〔口〕彻底的,完全的,绝对的。~ *nonsense* 荒唐透顶之事,毫无意义之事。~ *nuts*〔美〕完全神经病的人;低能到极点的人。**III** *ad.* 1. 垂直地。2. 恰恰,正。3.〔美口〕完全。*fall ~ down* 垂直落下。~ *southwards* 正南,向正南。~ *in the face of* 正对着。**IV** *vt.* 1. 用铅锤检查(是否垂直);使垂直(*up*)。2. 用测铅测(水深),测量。3. 查明;看穿,看出。4. 给…装铅,灌铅以增加…的重量。5. 给…铺自来水管[煤气管]。6. 焊。*No eye can ~ those depths.* 谁也看不到那样的深度。— *vi.* 1. 垂直悬挂。2. 作(铅)管工。~ **bob** 铅锤,线锤。~ **line** 铅锤线;标准。~**-line** *vt.* 1. 用铅锤线测量(…的垂直度)。2. 探测,检查。~ **rule**【建】垂规。**-less** *a.*〔诗〕深不可测的,无底的(大洋等)。

plum·bag·i·nous [plʌmˈbædʒinəs; plʌmˋbædʒɪnəs] *a.* (像)石墨的,含石墨的。

plum·ba·go [plʌmˈbeigəu; plʌmˋbego] *n.* (*pl.* ~*s*) 1. 石墨。2.【植】琉璃茉莉属的植物。

plum·bate [ˈplʌmbeit; ˋplʌmbet] *n.*【化】铅酸盐。

plum·be·ous [ˈplʌmbiəs; ˋplʌmbɪəs] *a.* 铅的;似铅的;含铅的;铅色的。*a ~ crucible* 石墨坩埚。

plumb·er [ˈplʌmə; ˋplʌmɚ] *n.* 1. 管子工,铅工;铅管(铺设)工人。2.〔美〕(调查政府人员泄密情况的)堵防泄密人员。~**-block**【机】轴台。

plumb·er·y [ˈplʌməri; ˋplʌmərɪ] *n.* 1. 制铅工业;铅器(工艺)。2. 铅管工;铅(管)厂。

plum·bic [ˈplʌmbik; ˋplʌmbɪk] *a.* 1.【化】铅的,含铅的;【化】四价铅的,高铅的。2.【医】由于铅毒的。~ **acid** 高铅酸,四氢氧化铅。~ **oxide** 氧化铅。

plum·bif·er·ous [plʌmˈbifərəs; plʌmˋbɪfərəs] *a.* 产铅的;含铅的。

plumb·ing [ˈplʌmiŋ; ˋplʌmɪŋ] *n.* 1. 制铅工业;铅管制造。2. 铅管铺设,铅管工程;自来水工程。3. 管件,铅管类。4. 铅锤测量。5. 波导设备,波导管。6.〔the ~〕抽水马桶。

plum·bism [ˈplʌmbizəm; ˋplʌmbɪzm̩] *n.*【医】慢性铅中毒。

plum·bite [ˈplʌmbait; ˋplʌmbaɪt] *n.*【化】亚铅酸盐。

plum·bous [ˈplʌmbəs; ˋplʌmbəs] *a.* 铅的;二价铅的。

plum·bum [ˈplʌmbəm; ˋplʌmbəm] *n.*【化】铅〔略 Pb〕。

plume [pluːm; plum] **I** *n.* 1.(长而美的)羽毛;羽衣。2. 羽毛饰;荣誉的表征。3.【虫】羽状毛;【植】羽状部,羽状圆锥花,冠毛。4.【空】卷流。**borrowed ~s** 借来的衣服,空名(*adorn oneself with borrowed ~s* 穿借来的衣服,虚装门面)。**II** *vt.* 1.(鸟)整理(羽毛);用羽毛装饰。2.〔~ oneself〕借衣服装饰;自夸(*upon*)。3. 使形成羽毛状。

plume·let [ˈpluːmlit; ˋplumlɪt] *n.* 小羽毛,幼毛;【植】= plumule.

plum·met [ˈplʌmit; ˋplʌmɪt] **I** *n.* 测锤(钓丝的)坠子;线锤;铅锤线;锤规;重压物。**II** *vi.* 笔直掉下;骤然跌落。~**-level** 锤准器。

plum·my [ˈplʌmi; ˋplʌmɪ] *a.* 1. 李子多的;李子似的;加葡萄干的。2.〔英口〕有利的;极好的,高级的。3.(声音)圆润的。

plu·mose, plu·mous [ˈpluːməus, ˈpluːməs; ˋplumos, ˋpluməs] *a.* 羽毛状的;有羽毛的。

plump[1] [plʌmp; plʌmp] **I** *a.* 肥胖的,(女人等)丰满的;(钱包等)鼓起的。**II** *vt.*, *vi.* (使)肥胖,(使)膨胀,使(水果等)长饱满(*out; up*)。**-ly** *ad.* **-ness** *n.*

plump[2] [plʌmp; plʌmp] **I** *vi.* 1. 噗通地掉落(*down; into; upon*)。2. 突然跳进。3.(把自己全部选票)投选一人;绝对赞成(*for*)。— *vt.* 1. 噗通地放落。2. 唐突地说出(*out*)。3. 为…说好话。**II** *n.* 沉重的坠落;〔Scot.〕阵雨。**III** *a.* 直率的,莽撞的;唐突的(话等);完全的(假话等)。*a ~ refusal* 断然拒绝。*a ~ lie* (明目张胆的)大谎话。~ *and plain* 露骨的。**IV** *ad.* 1. 噗通地,沉重地。2. 突然,蓦地。3. 直接了当地,坦白地。*sit down ~* 噗通一声坐下。*come ~ upon the enemy* 突然袭击敌人。*Say it out ~!* 老老实实讲出来吧! **-ly** *ad.* **-ness** *n.*

plump[3] [plʌmp; plʌmp] *n.*〔古〕群,队,众。

plump·er[1] [ˈplʌmpə; ˋplʌmpɚ] *n.* 1. 使肥胖[膨胀]的东西;(瘪嘴人含用的)鼓腮物。2.(鞣皮用的)除酸剂;除酸工人。

plump·er[2] [ˈplʌmpə; ˋplʌmpɚ] *n.* 1. 急剧重落;猛跌。2. 把全数选票投选一候选人(的人)。3.〔俚〕大谎;特大东西。

plump·y [ˈplʌmpi; ˋplʌmpɪ] *a.* (*-i·er; -i·est*) 丰满的,肥胖的。

plu·mule [ˈpluːmjuːl; ˋplumjul] *n.* 1.【植】胚芽。2.【动】(鸟的)绒毛;(鳞翅目昆虫的)香羽鳞。

plum·y [ˈpluːmi; ˋplumɪ] *a.* (*-i·er; -i·est*) 1. 有羽毛

的;似羽毛的;用羽毛装饰的。2. 绒毛(状)的。

plun·der [ˈplʌndə; ˋplʌndɚ] **I** *vt.*, *vi.* 掠夺,抢劫;偷,私吞。**II** *n.* 1. 抢劫,掠夺。2. 掠夺物,赃品;〔口〕赚头,利益。3. 〔美〕家具,行李。～**-bund** 〔美口〕剥削公众利益的集团。**-able** *a.*

plun·der·age [ˈplʌndəridʒ; ˋplʌndərɪdʒ] *n.* 【法】抢劫,掠夺,(尤指)盗用船货;劫掠品。

plun·der·er [ˈplʌndərə; ˋplʌndərɚ] *n.* 抢劫者,掠夺者;盗窃者。

plunge [plʌndʒ; plʌndʒ] **I** *vt.* 1. 使投入;插进,扔进;浸入(*into*)。2. 使陷入;使遭受;使埋头…,使投身(*in*; *into*)。3. 【园艺】将(花盆)埋入地中。～ *a room into darkness* 突然使屋子一团漆黑。— *vi.* 1. 跳进,掉进,钻进(*into*);冲(*into*; *down*; *up*);不顾前后地干起来(*into*)。2. 下降,急降。3. (马)猛烈前冲;跃起后蹄倒竖起来;(船)前后颠簸。4. 〔俚〕盲目投资;滥赌;借债(～*into*)。～ *into the river* 跳入河中。～ *into war* 投入战斗。*plunging deeper and deeper* 愈陷愈深。**II** *n.* 1. 跳进,插进。2. 猛冲,蛮干;冒险,断然手段。3. 〔俚〕投机,赌博。4. 〔古〕为难,困难。5. 〔罕〕大雨。6. (船的)前后颠簸;马跃起后蹄倒竖。*at a* ～ 进退两难。*take the* ～ 冒险尝试;蛮干;毅然从事。～ **bath** 大浴池;全身浴。

plung·er [ˈplʌndʒə; ˋplʌndʒɚ] *n.* 1. 跳进水中的人;潜水人;突入者。2. 【枪炮】(后膛枪的)撞针杆;【机】柱塞,活塞;插棒式铁心;(波导管)短路器。3. 〔俚〕骑兵。4. 〔俚〕滥赌的人;盲目的投机家;鲁莽的人。～ **pump** 柱塞泵。

plung·ing [ˈplʌndʒiŋ; ˋplʌndʒɪŋ] *a.* 跳进的;向前猛冲的;俯射的。～ **fire** (火炮等的)俯射,瞰射。

plunk [plʌŋk; plʌŋk] **I** *vt.* 1. 〔口〕砰的投掷;使砰地坠落;砰砰地弹(弦等)。2. 〔美〕猛打,猛推,猛戳。— *vi.* 1. 砰砰地响。2. 砰地坠落。3. 支持(*for*)。～ *down* 1. 猛地放下;突然落下。2. 砰地坐下。3. 付款。**II** *n.* 砰的声音;啪的打声[打击];〔美俚〕美元一元。**III** *ad.* 砰地,噗通地。

plup. = pluperfect.

plu·per·fect [ˈpluːˈpəːfikt; pluˋpɝfɪkt] *n.*, *a.* 【语法】过去完成式(的)。

plur. = plural.

plu·ral [ˈpluərəl; ˋplurəl] **I** *a.* 复数的(*opp.* singular);二以上的。**II** *n.* 【语法】复数(形);复数词。～ **livings** 【宗】兼俸。～ **marriage** 一夫多妻,一妻多夫。～ **vote** 双重投票,复投票。**-ly** *ad.*

plu·ral·ism [ˈpluərəlizəm; ˋplurəlɪzm] *n.* 1. 复数,多种。2. 【宗】(在数个教堂)兼职。3. 双重投票。4. 【哲】多元论。**-ral·ist** *n.* 〔英〕兼职者;双重投票(权)者;多妻主义者;【哲】多元论者。**-ral·is·tic** *a.*

plu·ral·i·ty [pluəˈræliti; pluˋrælətɪ] *n.* 1. 复数;多数;大多数;过半数;〔美〕(当选人对次多票者的)超过票数。2. 〔英〕兼管数教堂;兼职。3. 一夫多妻。

plu·ral·ize [ˈpluərəlaiz; ˋplurəlˏaɪz] *vt.* 使成复数(形);以复数形表示。— *vi.* 1. 成为复数。2. 〔英〕兼管数教堂;兼数职。

plu·ral·ly [ˈpluərəli; ˋplurəlɪ] *ad.* 以复数形式。

plu·ri·ax·i·al [ˌpluəriˈæksiəl; ˏplurəˋæksɪəl] *a.* 【植】多轴的。

plus [plʌs; plʌs] (*opp.* minus) **I** *prep.* 加,加上。*Four* ～ *one equals five* [4+1=5]。四加一等于五。**II** *a.* 1. 【数】加的,正;【电】阳;【植】(菌丝体)阳性的,雄性的;【商】贷方的。2. 〔口〕(同等物中)略大[高]的;标准以上的。3. 〔口〕有增益的。4. 【高尔夫球】让分的,先加分的。*the* ～ *sign* 加号,正号。*a* ～ *quantity* 正数,正量。*on the* ～ *side of the account* 【商】在账户的贷方。*I found myself* ～ *nearly* £100. 我多得了将近百镑。*B* ～ B^+的成绩。**III** *n.* 1. 【数】加号;正数;正量;正型。2. 附加物,多余;剩余;利益。3. 【高尔夫球】优者的让步。～**-fours** 〔*pl.*〕〔俚〕〔英〕(打高尔夫球穿的)灯笼裤。

plush [plʌʃ; plʌʃ] **I** *n.* 长毛绒;〔*pl.*〕长毛绒裤。*on the* ～ 舒服,舒舒服服的。**II** *a.* 1. 长毛绒(做)的。2. 〔俚〕豪华的;漂亮的;舒服的。**-ly** *ad.* **-y** *a.*

Plu·tarch [ˈpluːtɑːk; ˋplutɑrk] *n.* 蒲鲁塔克[46—120,希腊历史学家,传记作家,以其作品《名人传》著名]。

plu·tar·chy [ˈpluːtɑːki; ˋplutɑrkɪ] *n.* 1. 富豪统治,财阀统治。2. 财阀;财政寡头。

plute [pluːt; plut] *n.* 〔美口〕富豪,财阀,有钱人;〔*pl.*〕富豪阶级。

plu·te·us [ˈpluːtiəs; ˋplutɪəs] *n.* (*pl.* **-te·i** [-ai; -aɪ]) 【动】长腕幼虫[海胆类]。

Plu·to [ˈpluːtəu; ˋpluto] *n.* 1. 【罗神】冥王;阴间之神。2. 〔the ～〕【天】冥王星。

plu·to [ˈpluːtəu; ˋpluto] *n.* 1. 放射性检查计。2. 【军】海上搜索与救援飞机。

PLUTO = pipeline under the ocean (二次大战时英法两国间的)海底输油管。

plu·toc·ra·cy [pluːˈtɔkrəsi; pluˋtɑkrəsɪ] = plutarchy.

plu·to·crat [ˈpluːtəkræt; ˋplutəˏkræt] *n.* 财阀,富豪政治家。**-ic** *a.* 富豪统治的;财政寡头的,财阀(般)的。

plu·to·graph·y [pluːˈtɔgrəfi; pluˋtɑgrəfɪ] *n.* (专门描写富人生活的)富豪作品。

Plu·to·ni·an [pluːˈtəunjən; pluˋtonɪən] *a.* 1. 阴间的,地府的。2. 〔罕〕【地】火成的。3. 冥王星的。

Plu·ton·ic [pluːˈtɔnik; pluˋtɑnɪk] *a.* 1. 【罗神】冥王的;冥府的,阴间的。2. 冥王星的。3. 〔常 p-〕【地】深成的,深发的;深成岩体的;火成的。～ **earthquake** 深源地震。～ **rocks** 深成岩。～ **theory** 地壳火成论。

plu·to·nism [ˈpluːtəunizm; ˋplutənɪzm] *n.* 1. 【地】火成论。2. 钚射线伤害。

plu·to·ni·um [pluːˈtəuniəm; pluˋtonɪəm] *n.* 【化】钚。～ **bomb** 钚弹[使用钚元素的原子弹]。

Plu·tus [ˈpluːtəs; ˋplutəs] *n.* 【希神】财神。

plu·vi·al [ˈpluːviəl; ˋpluvɪəl] *a.* 1. 雨的,多雨的。2. 【地】洪水的,雨成的。～ **age** 洪积世。

plu·vi·an [ˈpluːviən; ˋpluvɪən] *a.* 多雨的;下雨的。

plu·vi·om·e·ter [ˌpluːviˈɔmitə; ˏpluvɪˋɑmətɚ] *n.* 雨量计。

plu·vi·o·met·ric, plu·vi·o·met·ri·cal [ˌpluːviəˈmetrik, -rikəl; ˏpluvɪəˋmɛtrɪk, -rɪkl] *a.* 雨量计的;测定雨量的。

plu·vi·ose [ˈpluːviːəus; ˋpluvɪos] *a.* 雨的,多雨的(= pluvious)。**-os·i·ty** [-ˈɔsiti; -ˋɑsətɪ] *n.* 雨量多。

ply[1] [plai; plaɪ] *vt.* (**plied**) 1. 勤苦经营,努力从事;勤用(器具、武器等)。2. 拼命给…加(煤、柴等);硬逼人(吃菜等);死劝,硬要(*with*);(提出质问等)攻击;缠扰。3. (船等)来回于,往返于。～ *an oar* 使劲划。～ *one's books* 用功读书。～ *a man with liquor* 硬劝人喝酒。— *vi.* 1. (船、马车等)来往,来回兜揽(*between*; *from*; *to*);(搬运员、船夫等)接客,等客(*at*)。2. 勤苦工作,出力;兜卖(*in*)。3. 赶,向前冲;【海】逆风换抢;〔主诗〕(船)前进。*a* ～*ing taxi* 野鸡汽车。～ *between* (车船等)来回于…之间,走…线。

ply[2] [plai; plaɪ] *n.* 1. 襞;股,绹,厚,层。2. 倾向,性癖,癖。*three* ～ *thread* 三股(头的)线。*take a* ～ 有倾向,有习癖。

Ply·mouth [ˈpliməθ; ˋplɪməθ] *n.* 1. 普利茅斯[英国港市]。2. 普利茅斯[蒙特塞拉特岛(英)首府]。～ **Brethren** 【宗】普里木斯教友会[1830年前后形成于英国普利茅斯的基督教的一派]。～ **Rock** 1. 传说中美国第一批移民至美洲登陆处。2. 普利茅斯品种鸡。

ply·wood [ˈplaiwud; ˋplaɪˏwud] *n.* 胶合板;层板。*exterior* ～ 耐火胶合板。

Plzen [ˈpʌlzenjə; ˋpʌlzɛnjə] *n.* 皮耳森[捷克城市]。

PM, P.M. = 1. paymaster (发放薪饷的)出纳员;军需官。2. permanent magnet 永久磁铁。3. police magistrate

违警罪法庭推事。**4.** postmaster 邮政局长;驿站站长。**5.** postmortem. **6.** prime minister 总理;首相。**7.** provost marshal 宪兵司令。**8.**〔L.〕*post meridiem* 下午,午后(=afternoon)。**9.** Pacific Mail〔英〕太平洋邮船公司。**10.** Past Master (行会、俱乐部等的)前任主持人。**11.** photomultiplier 光电倍增管。

Pm =【化】promethium.

pm. = premium.

p.m. = **1.**〔L.〕*post meridiem* 下午,午后(=afternoon)。**2.** postmortem. **3.** per minute 每分钟。**4.**〔L.〕*pro memoria* 为了纪念,以作纪念。**5.** purpose made 特制的,特殊用途的。

P

P.M.G. = **1.** Pall-Mall Gazette〔英〕《蓓尔美尔街官报》。**2.** Paymaster General 军需部长。**3.** Postmaster General 邮政总长。**4.** Provost Marshal General〔美〕宪兵(总)司令。

pmh = per man-hour 每人每小时。

p.m.h. = production per man-hour 每人每小时的产量。

pmk = postmark 邮戳。

PMLA = Publications of the Modern Language Association of America《美国现代语言学协会会刊》(期刊名称)。

P.M.O. = Principal Medical Officer〔英〕主治军医。

P.M.R.A.F.N.S. = Princess Mary's Royal Air Force Nursing Service〔英〕皇家空军玛丽公主护士队。

PN, p.n. = **1.** promissory note【商】本票,期票。**2.** please note 请注意。

PNA = pentose nucleic acid【生化】戊糖核酸。

pneum. = pneumatic; pneumatic(s).

pneum- = pneumo-.

pneu·ma [ˈnjuːmə; ˋnumə] *n.* **1.** 呼吸。**2.** 精神,灵魂。**3.**〔P-〕【神】圣灵。

pneu·mat·ic [njuːˈmætik; njuˋmætɪk] **I** *a.* **1.** 空气的;似空气的,气体的;空气学(上)的。**2.**【机】压缩空气推动的;汽动的;风动的。**3.** 装满空气的。**4.** 有气胎的;【动】有气腔的。**5.**〔罕〕【神】灵的。**II** *n.* 气胎;〔口〕有气胎的自行车;(风琴的)管。～ **brake** 气闸;风闸。～ **cushion** 气枕,气垫。～ **dispatch** (信件、电报等的)气(力输)送。～ **drill** 风钻。～ **hammer** 气(压)锤。～ **jack** 气力起重机,气压千斤顶。～ **perforator** 气压钻孔机。～ **tire** 气胎。**-i·cal·ly** *ad.*

pneu·mat·ic·i·ty [ˌnjuːməˈtisiti; ˏnjuməˋtɪsətɪ] *n.*【生】有气腔。

pneu·mat·ics [njuːˈmætiks; njuˋmætɪks] *n.*【物】气体力学。

pneumato- *comb. f.* 表示"空气;气体;呼吸;精神;圣灵":*pneumato*logy.

pneu·ma·to·gen·i·c [ˌnjuːmətəuˈdʒenik; ˏnjumətoˋdʒɛnɪk] *a.* 气成的。～ *minerals* 气成矿物。

pneu·ma·tol·o·gy [ˌnjuːməˈtɔlədʒi; ˏnuməˋtɑlədʒɪ] *n.* **1.**【医】气体(治疗)学。**2.**【物】气体力学。**3.**【宗】灵物学;圣灵论;〔古〕心理学。

pneu·ma·tol·y·sis [ˌnjuːməˈtɔlisis, ˌnuː-; ˏnjuməˋtɑləsɪs,ˏnu-] *n.*【地】气化(作用)。**-to·lyt·ic** [-təˈlitik; -təˋlɪtɪk] *a.*

pneu·ma·tom·e·ter [ˌnjuːməˈtɔmitə; ˏnuməˋtɑmətɚ] *n.*【医】呼吸量测定器。

pneu·ma·to·phore [njuˈmætəufɔː; njuˋmætofɔr] *n.* **1.**【植】出水通气根。**2.**【动】气囊;浮囊。**3.**【医】救生氧气袋。

pneu·ma·to·ther·a·py [ˌnjuːmətəuˈθerəpi; ˏnumətoˋθɛrəpɪ] *n.*【医】气体疗法。

pneu·mec·to·my [njuːˈmektəmi; nuˋmɛktəmɪ] *n.*【医】肺部分切除术。

pneumo- *comb. f.* 表示"肺":*pneumo*coccus.

pneu·mo·ba·cil·lus [ˌnjuːməubəˈsiləs; ˏnumobəˋsɪləs] *n.* (*pl.* **-li** [-lai; -laɪ]) 肺炎杆菌。

pneu·mo·coc·cus [ˌnjuːməˈkɔkəs; ˏnjuməˋkɑkəs] *n.* (*pl.* **-cocci** [-ˈkɔksai; -ˋkɑksaɪ]) 肺炎双球菌。**-coccal** [ˈ-kɔkl; -ˋkɑkl], **-coc·cic** [-ˈkɔksik; -ˋkɑksɪk] *a.*

pneu·mo·co·ni·o·sis [ˈnjuːməˌkəuniˈəusis, ˏnjuməˏkoniˋosɪs, ˋnu-] *n.*【医】肺尘埃沉着病,肺尘病。

pneu·mo·en·ceph·a·lo·gram [ˌnjuːməenˈsefələuˈgræm; ˏnjumoɛnˋsɛfəloˋgræm] *n.*【医】脑蛛网膜下腔充气。

pneu·mo·gas·tric [ˌnjuːməˈgæstrik; ˏnjuməˋgæstrɪk] **I** *a.*【解】**1.** (关于)肺和胃的。**2.** 迷走神经的。*a* ～ *ganglion* 气胃神经节。～ *nerves* 迷走神经。**II** *n.* 迷走神经。

pneu·mo·graph [ˈnjuːməgrɑːf; ˋnjuməgræf] *n.*【医】呼吸描记器。

pneu·mo·nec·to·my [ˌnjuːməˈnektəmi; ˏnjuməˋnɛktəmɪ] *n.* (*pl.* **-mies**) 肺切除术。

pneu·mo·ni·a [nju(ː)ˈməunjə; njuˋmonjə] *n.*【医】肺炎;急性肺炎(=acute ～)。*double* ～ 双肺炎。*single* ～ 单肺炎。

pneu·mon·ic [nju(ː)ˈmɔnik; njuˋmɑnɪk] *a.* 肺的;【医】(患)肺炎的。

pneu·mo·ni·tis [ˌnjuːməuˈnaitis; ˏnjuməˋnaɪtɪs] *n.* 肺炎;局部急性肺炎。

pneu·mo·no·ul·tra·mi·cro·scop·ic·sil·i·co·vol·ca·no·co·ni·o·sis [ˈnjuːmənəuˌʌltrəˌmaikrəsˈkɔpikˈsilikəvɔlˈkeinəuˌkəuniˈəusis; ˋnjumənoˏʌltrəˏmaɪkrəsˋkɑpɪkˋsɪlɪkəvɑlˋkenoˏkoniˋosɪs] *n.*【医】矽酸盐沉着病,肺尘病。

pneu·mor·rha·gia [ˌnjuːməuˈrɑːdʒiə; ˏnjumoˋrædʒɪə] *n.*【医】肺出血。

pneu·mo·tho·rax [ˌnjuːməuˈθɔːræks; ˏnjuməˋθoræks] *n.*【医】气胸。*artificial* ～ 人工气胸。

pneu·mo·tro·pism [nju(ː)ˈmɔtrəpizəm; njuˋmɑtrəpɪzm] *n.*【医】亲肺,肺向性。**-trop·ic** [-ˈtrɔpik; -ˋtrɑpɪk] *a.*

p-n junction [ˈpiːˈenˈdʒʌŋkʃən; ˋpiˋenˋdʒʌŋkʃən]【物】p-n结。

Pnom Penh [nɔmˈpen; ˈnɔːmˈpen; ˋnɑmˋpɛn, ˋnɔmˋpɛn] 金边(=Phnom Penh)。

pnxt. = pinxit (=painted it).

PO, p.o. = **1.** petty officer 海军军士。**2.** postal order〔英〕邮政汇票。**3.** post office 邮局。**4.** Pilot Officer〔英〕空军少尉。**5.** power output 功率输出。**6.** Province of Ontario〔加拿大〕安大略省。**7.** Public Office (国家机关或社会团体的)办公处。

Po = polonium【化】钋。

po [pəu; po] *n.*〔儿语〕便盆 = chamber-pot.

poach[1] [pəutʃ; potʃ] *vt.* **1.**〔英〕偷猎,偷偷捕(鱼);(为偷猎而)侵入。**2.**【赛跑】用不正当手段取得(有利的起步);【网球】抢打(该由 partner 打的球)。**3.** 把(土地)践踏成泥浆。**4.**【制纸】加水调匀浓度。**5.**【化】漂洗。**6.** 把(棒,手指等)戳入 (*into*)。— *vi.* **1.** 偷猎,偷偷捕鱼;〔美口〕物色高级人才。**2.** 走路陷入泥中。**3.**【网球】抢打。～ *in other people's business* 侵犯别人权限。～ *for fresh ideas* 抄袭(别人著作中的)新观点。

poach[2] [pəutʃ; potʃ] *vt.* 水煮(荷包蛋)。～*ed eggs* 水煮荷包蛋。

poach·er[1] [ˈpəutʃə; ˋpotʃɚ] *n.* **1.**〔英〕偷猎者。**2.** 侵犯他人权限的人。

poach·er[2] [ˈpəutʃə; ˋpotʃɚ] *n.* 浅碟煮荷包蛋器。

poach·y [ˈpəutʃi; ˋpotʃɪ] *a.* (*poach·i·er*; *poach·i·est*) 潮湿的,(泥土)湿而软的。

POB, P.O.B. = post-office box 邮政信箱。

POC = port of all (沿途)停靠港。

poc·co·sin [pəˈkəusin; pəˋkosn] *n.* (美国东南部的)沼泽地。

po·chard [ˈpəutʃəd; ˋpotʃɚd] *n.*【鸟】潜鸭;红头潜鸭。

pock [pɔk; pɑk] **I** ***n***.【医】痘疱,痘疮;痘凹。**II** ***vt***. 使留有痘痕,使有麻点。

pock·et [ˈpɔkit; ˋpɑkɪt] **I** ***n***. **1.** 衣袋;钱袋;(袋鼠等的)袋;小袋;【军】袋形阵地(中的部队)。**2.** 金钱,财富,资力;零用钱。**3.**【撞球】球囊;(羊毛等的)一袋〔约 168—224 磅〕;【采】矿穴,窝矿,矿袋;矿石块;【机】套。**4.** 凹处,穴;〔美〕峡谷。**5.**【空】(大气中的)气阱(= air-~)。**6.** 小航室;煤库。**7.**【赛马、赛跑】被其他马[人]挤轧的不利地位。*a deep* ~ 充足的财力。*an empty* ~ 两手空空;穷光蛋。*a high* ~*s* 〔美俚〕高个子,长人。***be in*** ~ 手头有钱;赚钱;剩下钱(*I am 5s. in* ~. = *I am in* ~ *by 5s*. 我手头有 5 先令)。***be out of*** ~ 手头没有钱;赔钱。***have sb. in one's*** ~ 可以左右某人。***keep one's hands in one's*** ~ 不做事,偷懒。***line one's*** ~***s*** 赚大钱,肥私囊。***out-of-*** ~ ***expenses*** 用现金付出的费用;实际支出。***pay out of one's own*** ~ 自己掏腰包支付。***pick a*** ~ 扒窃。(***be prepared to***) ***put one's hand in one's*** ~ (准备)用钱,出钱。***put one's pride in one's*** ~ 忍辱,抑制自尊心。***suffer in one's*** ~ 赔钱,亏损。**II** ***a***. **1.** 袖珍的,小型的。**2.** 金钱上的。**3.** 秘密的。*a* ~ *battleship* 袖珍战列舰。*a* ~ *edition* (图书的)袖珍版;小型的东西。*a* ~ *pistol* 小手枪;〔俚〕小酒瓶。**III** ***vt***. **1.** 把…装在衣袋内;包藏。**2.** 盗用,侵吞。**3.** 忍受(侮辱等)。**4.**〔美〕阻挠,搁置(议案等)。**5.** 抑制,藏住(感情等)。**6.** 任意摆布,操纵。**7.**【撞球】把球打进(球囊)。**8.**【赛跑】自前后妨碍(跑的人),四面挤轧。~**-book 1.** 皮夹子;〔美、喻〕钱包;金钱。**2.**〔英〕笔记簿;袖珍本。~ **borough** (英国旧时)由个人[家族]操纵的选区。~ **edition 1.** 袖珍本[版]。**2.** 小东西。~**-handkerchief 1.** (衣袋中的)手帕。**2.** 小型物。~**-hunter**〔美〕骗子。~ **knife** 小刀。~ **money** 零用钱。~ **office** 小型便携式办公设备〔包括手机、手提式电脑等〕。~ **phone** 袋装电话。~ **piece** (搁在衣袋里的)吉利钱〔多半是古钱〕。~**-size(d)** ***a***. 尺寸相当小的〔尤指适应于放在口袋中的尺寸〕。~**veto** ***vt***.〔美〕(总统)搁置议案,拒绝签署。**-ful** ***n***. (*pl*. ~***fuls***) 一袋〔指量〕。

pock·e·ta·ble [ˈpɔkitəbl; ˋpɑkɪtəbl̩] ***a***. 衣袋里装得下的;可供私用的;能隐藏起来的。

pock·et·y [ˈpɔkiti; ˋpɑkətɪ] ***a***. **1.** 有凹入处的;囊形的,有囊状特征的。**2.**【矿】袋状分布的。

pock·mark [ˈpɔkmɑːk; ˋpɑkˏmɑrk] **I** ***n***. 痘痕,麻点。**II** ***vt***. **1.** 使布满痘痕。**2.** 使密密麻麻地布满。

pock·marked, pock·pitted, pock·y [ˈpɔːkmɑːkt, -pitid, -pɔki; ˋpɑkˏmɑrkt, -pɪtɪd, -pɑkɪ] ***a***. 有麻窝的。

po·co [ˈpəukəu; ˋpoko] ***a***. (使用语言)无性别歧视的〔politically correct 的缩略〕。

po·co [ˈpəukəu, ˈpɔːkəu; ˋpoko, ˋpɔko] ***ad***.〔It.〕【乐】稍,少许,略。~ ***largo*** [***presto***] 略慢[快]。~ ***a*** ~ 渐渐,慢慢。

po·co·cu·ran·te [ˌpəukəukjuəˈrænti; ˏpokoˋkurænti] **I** ***a***.〔It.〕无动于衷的;满不在乎的;漠不关心的。**II** ***n***. 满不在乎的人;漠不关心的人。

po·co·cu·ran·tism [ˌpəukəukjuəˈræntizəm; ˏpokokuˋræntɪzm] ***n***. 满不在乎,不关心,不热心。

pod[1] [pɔd; pɑd] **I** ***n***. **1.**【植】荚,荚果。**2.** 蚕茧;蝗虫的卵囊。**3.** (捕鳗鱼的)袋网。**4.**【空】容器;塔门吊舱;(发动机)吊舱;(翼梢等上的)发射架;(宇宙船的)可分离的舱。**5.**【矿】近圆柱形矿体,扁豆形矿体;透镜形矿体。**6.**〔口〕肚子(= belly)。~ *bearing plant* = ~*ded plant* 豆科植物。**II** ***vt***. (**-dd-**) 剥(荚)。—***vi***. 成荚,结荚;生蒴(*up*)。~**mall** 小商场,小型购物中心。~ **pepper**【植】朝天椒。

pod[2] [pɔd; pɑd] **I** ***n***. (海豹、鲸等的)小群。**II** ***vt***. 把(海豹等)赶到一块。

pod[3] [pɔd; pɑd] ***n***.【机】**1.** (某些钻头及螺旋钻的)纵槽;有纵槽的螺旋钻。**2.** 手摇钻的钻头承窝。

POD, P. O. D. = **1.** pay on delivery【商】货到付款。**2.** post office department 邮政部门。**3.** port of debarkation 下船港口,卸载港口。**4.** *Pocket Oxford Dictionary*《袖珍牛津辞典》。

pod(o)- *comb. f*. 表示"足":*podo*theca.

-pod(e) *suf*. 表示"有足的"。

po·dag·ra [ˈpɔdəgrə, pəˈdægrə; ˋpɑdəgrə, poˋdægrə] ***n***.【医】足痛风。**-dag·ral, -dag·ric** ***a***.

pod·ded [ˈpɔdid; ˋpɑdɪd] ***a***. **1.** 有荚的;结荚的;生于荚中的。**2.**〔喻〕富裕的,生活宽裕的,小康的,安乐的,舒适的。

po·des·ta [pəuˈdestə, It. ˌpəudeˈstɑː; poˋdɛstə, ˏpodɛˋstɑ] ***n***. **1.**【史】中世纪意大利的城镇长官。**2.** 意大利城市小官员。**3.** 法西斯时代意大利的市长。

podge [pɔdʒ; pɑdʒ] ***n***. 矮胖的人。

podg·y [ˈpɔdʒi; ˋpɑdʒɪ] ***a***. (***podg·i·er***; ***-i·est***)〔英〕矮胖的。

po·di·a·trist [pəuˈdaiətrist; poˋdaɪətrɪst] ***n***. 足病医生。

podi·a·try [pəuˈdaiətri; poˋdaɪətrɪ] ***n***.【医】足病学;足医术。

po·dite [ˈpɔdait; ˋpɑdaɪt] ***n***.【动】肢节。**po·dit·ic** [pɔˈditik; pɑˋdɪtɪk] ***a***.

po·di·um [ˈpəudiəm; ˋpodɪəm] ***n***. (*pl*. ***-dia*** [-diə; -dɪə]) **1.**【建】墩座墙。**2.** 角斗场和前座间的矮墙。**3.**〔美〕乐队指挥台。**4.** 屋内墙边的一圈长椅。**5.**【动】足,(乌贼的)管足;【植】叶柄。

-podium *comb. f*. 表示"足;足状部分":pseudo*podium*.

pod·o·car·pus [ˌpɔdəˈkɑːpəs; ˏpɑdəˋkɑrpəs] ***n***.【植】罗汉松属 (*Podocarpus*) 植物。

pod·o·phyl·lin [ˌpɔdəˈfilin; ˏpɑdəˋfɪlɪn] ***n***.【药】鬼臼树脂〔可作泻药〕。

pod·o·phyl·lum [ˌpɔdəˈfiləm; ˏpɑdəˋfɪləm] ***n***. **1.** 鬼臼属植物。**2.** 鬼臼根〔可作泻剂〕。

pod·o·the·ca [ˈpɔdəθiːkə; ˋpɑdəθikə] ***n***. (*pl*. ***-cae*** [-siː; -si])【鸟】脚鞘。

Po·dunk [ˈpəudʌŋk; ˋpodʌŋk] ***n***.〔美谑〕小镇。

pod·zol [ˈpɔdzɔːl, -zɔl; ˋpɑdzɔl, -zɑl] ***n***.〔地〕灰壤,灰化土(= podsol)。**-ic** ***a***.

pod·zol·i·za·tion, pad·sol·i·za·tion [ˌpɔdzɔːlaiˈzeiʃən; ˏpɑdzolaɪˋzeʃən] ***n***. 灰壤化作用。**pod·zol·ize** [ˈpɔdəzəlaiz; ˋpɑdəzəlaɪz] ***vt***. 使灰壤化。

Poe [pəu; po] ***n***. **1.** 波〔姓氏〕。**2. Edgar Allan** ~ 爱伦·坡〔1809—1849,美国诗人,短篇小说家,批评家〕。

po·em [ˈpəuim, ˈpəuem; ˋpoɪm, ˋpoəm] ***n***. 诗,韵文(*opp*. prose); 诗一样的作品;富有诗意的东西。*a prose* ~ 散文诗。*compose a* ~ 作诗。*Their lives are a* ~. 他们的生活就是一首诗。

po·e·sy [ˈpəuizi, ˈpəuezi; ˋpoɪsɪ, ˋpoəzɪ] ***n***. **1.**〔古、诗〕作诗(法);诗歌,韵文。**2.** 诗才。

po·et [ˈpəuit, ˈpəuet; ˋpoɪt, ˋpoət] ***n***. 诗人;诗人一样的人,空想家。*a minor* ~ 小诗人。~ **laureate**〔英〕桂冠诗人。**Poets Corner 1.** 诗人区〔伦敦 Westminster Abbey 的南隅,有英国大诗人坟墓和纪念碑〕。**2.**〔p-corner〕〔美谑〕厕所。**3.**〔谑〕(报纸上的)诗歌栏。~**'s narcissus**【植】口红水仙。

poet. = **1.** poetical. **2.** poetry.

po·et·as·ter [pəuiˈtæstə, pəue-; poɪˋtæstɚ, poə-] ***n***. 蹩脚诗人;自封的诗人。

po·et·ess [pəuˈitis; poˋɪtɪs] ***n***. 女诗人。

po·et·ic, -i·cal [pəuˈetik(əl); poˋɛtɪkl] **I** ***a***. 诗的,韵文的;有诗意的;诗人(一样)的。★ poetic 主指内容、本质方面;poetical 主指形式方面。*poetical works* 诗集。*poetic genius* [*faculty*] 诗才。*a poetical person* 有诗人风度的人。*poetic justice* 劝善惩恶;理想的赏罚。*poetic license* 诗的破格。**II** ***n***. = poetics. **-i·cal·ly** ***ad***.

po·et·i·cize [pəuˈetisaiz; poˋɛtəˏsaɪz] ***v***. = poetize.

po·et·ics [pəu'etiks; po`ɛtɪks] ***n***. **1**. 诗法,诗学,诗论。**2**.〔the P-〕亚里士多德 (Aristotle) 写的《诗论》。

po·et·ize ['pəuitaiz, 'pəuet-; `po·ɪt,aɪz, `poət-] ***vi***. **1**. 作诗。**2**. 用诗赞美。— ***vt***. 使成诗;使诗化;有诗意地说。

po·et·ry ['pəuitri, 'pəuetri; `po·ɪtrɪ, `poətrɪ] ***n***. **1**. 诗,诗歌,韵文;诗集。**2**. 作诗(法)。**3**.〔P-〕诗神,缪斯神 (= the Muse)。**4**. 诗意,诗情;有诗意的事物。*satiric* ~ 讽刺诗。*epic* ~ 叙事诗。*historical* ~ 史诗。*lyric* ~ 抒情诗。*prose* ~ 散文诗。

POGO = polar orbiting geophysical observatory 极轨道地球物理观测卫星。

P

po·go ['pəugəu; `pogo] ***n***. (*pl*. ~*s*) **1**. 弹簧单高跷〔一种运动用具,又叫 ~-stick〕;弹簧单高跷游戏。**2**. (音乐伴奏下的)原地跳跃舞蹈。

po·go·ni·a [pə'gəuniə, -'gəunjə; pə`gonɪə, -`gonjə] ***n***. **1**. (美洲的)红朱兰 (*Pogonia ophioglossides*)。**2**. 红朱兰花。

pog·o·nip ['pɔgənip; `pɑgənɪp] ***n***.【气】冻雾。

pog·rom ['pɔgrəm; `pogrəm] **I** ***n***.〔Russ.〕(有组织的)大屠杀;集体迫害〔尤指帝俄时代对犹太人的大屠杀〕。**II** ***vt***. 大屠杀;集体迫害。**-ist** ***n***. 大屠杀的组织者[参加者]。

po·gy ['pəugi; `pogɪ] ***n***. (*pl*. **-gies**)【动】步鱼;玫瑰海鲫。

po·i ['pəui; pɔɪ] ***n***. (*pl*. ~*es*) (夏威夷的)芋粉酱。

poign·an·cy ['pɔinjənsi, 'pɔinən-; `pɔɪnjənsɪ, `pɔɪnən-] ***n***. **1**. 辛辣;尖锐,刻薄。**2**. 强烈;深刻。

poign·ant ['pɔinənt; `pɔɪnənt] ***a***. **1**. 尖锐的,强烈的;辛辣的;尖酸刻薄的;痛快的。**2**. 生动的,(记忆)活鲜鲜的。*a* ~ *question* 苛刻的质问。~ *regret* 深沉的懊悔。~ *remarks* 尖锐的批评。~ *sarcasm* 尖酸刻薄的讽刺。~ *tears* 忍不住的眼泪。**-ly** ***ad***.

poi·kil·it·ic [,pɔiki'litik; ,pɔɪkɪ`lətɪk] ***a***.【地】嵌晶结构的,嵌晶状的。

poi·kil·o·ther·mal [pɔi,kiləu'θə:ml, ,pɔkələu-; ,pɔɪkəlo`θɝməl, ,pɑkəlo-] ***a***.【动】冷血的 (= poikilothermic)。**-ther·mism** ***n***. 冷血。

poi·lu ['pwɑ:lu:; `pwɑlu] ***n***.〔F.〕〔俚〕(法国)兵。

Poin·ca·re [pwɛ̃ŋkɑ:'rei, F. pwɛkare; pwæka`re, pwɛ̃kare] **1**. 普安卡雷(姓氏)。**2**. **J.H.** ~ 普安卡雷〔1854—1912,法国数学家〕。**3**. **Raymond** ~ 朋加莱〔1860—1934,法国政治家,曾代总统〕。

poin·ci·a·na [,pɔinsi'ænə; ,pɔɪnsɪ`ænə] ***n***. **1**. 黄蝴蝶属 (*Poinciana*) 植物。**2**. 凤凰木 (= royal poinciana)〔一种热带树〕。

poin·set·ti·a [pɔin'setiə, -'setə; pɔɪn`sɛtɪə, -`sɛtə] ***n***.【植】一品红 (*Euphorbia pulcherrima*);猩猩木;大戟属植物。

point [pɔint; pɔɪnt] **I** ***n***. **1**. 尖头,尖端;尖头器具;〔美〕笔尖;接种针,雕刻针,编织针;小岬,小地角;【拳击】下巴。**2**.【几】点;【数】小数点;切点;【语】标点;句号;【乐】点符;(寒暑表等的)度;程度。**3**.【赛马】标点;分数。**4**. 时刻,霎那。**5**. 地点;位置;目标,目的。**6**. 条款,细目;特点,特征;要点,旨趣;〔美〕要领;论点;(故事、笑话等的)高潮,妙处。**7**.〔*pl*.〕【铁路】轨闸,转轨器,道岔扳子;〔英〕〔*pl*.〕路轨总点;〔美〕站;【海】方位;罗经点;两罗经点间的差度〔1 point = 11$\frac{1}{4}$〔度〕〕;【狩】(猎狗)指示猎获物的姿势。**8**【印】点〔活字大小的单位,约一英寸的七十二分之一〕;【商】点,磅音〔物价、股票价格涨落的单位〕。**9**.【军】尖兵;【机】岔尖;【板球】三柱门右方前面的防守人。**10**.〔美〕(大学)学分。**11**.【语音】= diacritical mark. **12**.【乐】短促曲调;军号短调讯号;(弦乐器)弓的顶端,弓尖。*the weakest* [*best*, *strongest*] ~ 最大缺[优]点。*a* ~ *of contact*【机】接触点;【数】切点。*the eye* ~ 出射点。*a full* ~ 句号。*At this* ~ *he got up*. 这时[说到这里]他从床上跳了起来。*There is no* ~ *in doing that*. 那没有做的必要。*What is the* ~ *of getting angry?* 发脾气有什么用处呢? *Cotton has gone down several* ~*s*. 棉花跌了好几档了。*a buck of ten* ~*s* 有十叉角的鹿。***a*** ~ ***of honour*** 体面攸关的事。***at all*** ~***s*** 充分,完全,彻底;在各方面 (*be beaten at all* ~*s* 彻底被打垮)。***at swords'*** ~***s*** 敌对状态;剑拔弩张。***at*** [***on***] ***the*** ~ ***of*** 将近[就要]…的时候;接近,靠近(*at the* ~ *of death* 濒死时候。*on the* ~ *of starting* 正要出发的时候)。***at the*** ~ ***of the sword*** 用武力;在武力威胁之下。***away from the*** ~ = *off the* ~. ***be*** (***up***) ***on the*** ~ ***of*** (***... ing***) 正要…的时候,正打算。***beat on*** ~***s***【拳击】靠得分打胜。***beside the*** ~ = *off the* ~. ***carry*** [***gain***] ***one's*** ~ 达到目的;说服别人。***catch the*** ~ ***of*** 了解[抓住]…的要点。***come to a*** ~ **1**. (猎狗)停住向猎物所在方向示意。**2**. 变尖。***come to the*** ~ 到紧要关头,说到要点。***cut to a*** ~ 弄尖,削尖。***from*** ~ ***to*** ~ 从一个点到另一个点;〔罕〕逐项;详细。***get one's*** ~ 抓住某人话中要点。***give*** ~ ***to*** 按上一个尖;削尖;增强,强调。***give*** ~***s to sb***. = ***give sb***. ~***s*** **1**. 让…占优势,让分给对方;〔口〕强过某人。**2**. 给与有益的劝告。***give the*** ~【剑】戳进。***grow to a*** ~ 顶端逐渐尖下去。***in*** ~ 适当的;中肯的;当前的,待解决的 (*a case in* ~ 恰当的例子)。***in*** ~ ***of*** 说到,关于;就…而言;…上 (*in* ~ *of fact* 事实上)。***keep to the*** ~ 扣住要点;(祈使)别绕圈子,别离题。***knotty*** ~ 难点,困难的地方。***lack*** ~ 抓不住要点。***make a*** ~ **1**. (比赛)得一分。**2**. 立论;证明论点。**3**. 照预想一样使受到感动。**4**. (猎狗)作看见猎获物的姿势。***make a*** ~ ***of*** = ***make a*** ~ ***that...*** = ***make it a*** ~ 主张,强调;重视;决心,必定。***make one's*** ~ 达到目的;【猎】对直跑。***make the*** ~ ***that*** …大意好像是说。***miss the*** ~ 抓不着要点;不得要领。***not to put too fine a*** ~ ***on it*** 坦白地说,直截了当地说。***off the*** ~ 离开本题,不切要领。~ ***by*** ~ 逐一,一点一点地,详细。~ ***for*** ~ 一一,细细,正确地。~ ***of order***【议会】议事规程问题。~ ***of view*** 观点,见地,见解。***rise to a*** ~ ***of order***〔会议用语〕(议员)起立提出程序问题。***score a*** ~ 得一分;获得利益[有利地位]。***see one's*** ~ = ***get one's*** ~. ***see the*** ~ 懂得…的要点。***stand*** (***up***) ***on*** ~〔罕〕过分刻板[拘泥]。***strain*** [***stretch***] ***a*** ~ 超出范围;破例;通融,作重大让步;牵强附会。***the*** ~ ***run to*** [***sailed from***]【海】目的[出发]地。***to the*** ~ 露骨;中肯,扼要 (*brief and to the* ~ 简明扼要)。***to the*** ~ ***of***... 达到…的程度。(***a joke***) ***without any*** ~ (笑话)平平无奇的。**II** ***vt***. **1**. 削尖(铅笔等);弄尖;给…装上尖头;使尖锐;强调,使增加力量。**2**. 指向;使对准;把…对准;注意;指点(路);(猎狗)站住以头指向(猎获物所在处);指出。**3**. 圈点;给…加句点;给…加元[母]音符号;给…打小数点。**4**. (泥水工)用泥灰涂抹,嵌填(接缝)。— ***vi***. **1**. 用手指人。**2**. 暗示,指示,表明,显示 (*at*; *to*)。**3**. 瞄准;对着;面向。**4**. 有…的倾向 (*toward*)。**5**. (猎狗)站住瞻望猎获物所在处。**6**.【海】张帆抢风开行。**7**. (疮等)起脓头。*It is rude to* ~. 用手指人是不礼貌的。~ ***in*** 用锄掏(粪)。~ ***off*** 打标点分开。~ ***out*** 指示,指出,提醒。~ ***over*** 用锄播(土)。~ ***up***〔美〕强调出…;使显眼。~**-and-click** **1**. ***n***.【计】(鼠标的)点击。**2**. ***vi***., ***vt***.【计】点击(鼠标)。~**-and-shoot** 傻瓜相机。~ **constable**〔英〕交通警察。~ **count**【桥牌】数点子。~ **duty** (警察)值勤;站岗。~ **guard** (篮球场上)负责组织进攻的后卫。~ **lace** 针绣花边。~**-of-sale** ***a***. (商店中)出售处的〔缩写为 POS〕。~ **rationing** 计点配给制。

point-blank ['pɔintblæŋk; `pɔɪnt`blæŋk] **I** ***a***. **1**. (枪)近距离平射的,直射的;水平瞄准的。**2**. 直截了当的,干脆的。*a* ~ *refusal* 直截了当的拒绝。**II** ***ad***. **1**. 平射,直射。**2**. 直截了当地;立即。*fire* ~ 平射。*refuse* ~ 断然拒绝。**III** ***n***. 直射(点)。

point d'ap·pui ['pwɛ̃:ndæ'pwi:; ,pwæda`pwi] ***n***.〔F.〕支点;【军】据点;战线据点;集合点;策源地;〔喻〕论据。

point-de·vice, point-de·vise [ˈpɔint dəvais; ˋpɔɪntdɪvaɪs] *a.*, *ad.* 〔古〕极正确的[地];非常精致的[地]。

pointe [pwænt; pwɛ̃nt] *n.* (*pl.* ***pointes*** [pwænt; pwænt]) *n.* 〔F.〕【芭蕾】足尖站立的姿式。

point·ed [ˈpɔintid; ˋpɔɪntɪd] *a.* **1.** 尖的,尖角的;尖锐的。**2.** 严厉的;直截了当的。**3.** 显然的。**4.** 中肯的。**5.** 突出的。~ *architecture* 尖拱式建筑(法)。**-ly** *ad.*

Pointe-Noire [pwæntˈnwɑː; pwæntˋnwɑr] *n.* 黑角〔刚果港市〕。

Point·er [ˈpɔintə; ˋpɔɪntɚ] *n.* 〔美〕西点 (West Point) 军官学校学员。

point·er [ˈpɔintə; ˋpɔɪntɚ] *n.* **1.** 指示者;指示物;(钟、表的)指针;教鞭;〔口〕线索;暗示;点子。**2.** 能站住用鼻尖指示猎获物所在处的猎狗。**3.** 〔*pl.*〕(the P-)【天】(大熊星座中的)两颗指极星。**4.** 【军】(大炮)瞄准手;(捕鲸船桅头的)鲸位指示器。**5.** 〔口〕广告索引(=~ad)。**6.** 【铁路】闸柄。~ **fire** 【军】直接瞄准射击。

poin·til·lism [ˈpwæntilizəm; ˋpwæntəlɪzm̩] *n.* 【美】(法国印象派)点画法。**-til·list** *n.* 点画家。

point·ing [ˈpɔintiŋ; ˋpɔɪntɪŋ] *n.* **1.** 弄尖。**2.** 指示;瞄准。**3.** 标点法;标点。**4.** (砖缝的)嵌填,勾缝。**5.** 【医】脓头,穿头。

point·less [ˈpɔintlis; ˋpɔɪntlɪs] *a.* **1.** 〔古〕无尖头的,钝的。**2.** 不对劲儿的;无力的。**3.** 不得要领的;空洞的;无意义的。**4.** (比赛)没有得分的。**5.** 【植】无芒的。*a* ~ *sword* 〔古〕钝剑。*a* ~ *joke* 索然无味的笑话。**-ly** *ad.* **-ness** *n.*

points·man [ˈpɔintsmən; ˋpɔɪntsmən] *n.* (*pl.* ***-men***) 〔英〕**1.** 【铁路】扳道岔人,扳闸员。**2.** (交通岗上的)交通警察。

point-to-point [ˈpɔinttəˈpɔint; ˋpɔɪnttəˋpɔɪnt] *a.* **1.** (赛马等)越过原野的。**2.** 逐点的。**3.** 【无】定向传送的。*a* ~ *race* 越野赛跑。

point·y [ˈpɔinti; ˋpɔɪntɪ] *a.* (***-i·er***; ***-i·est***) **1.** 非常尖的。**2.** 多尖的,全是带尖的。~ **head** 〔美口,贬〕尖脑袋〔指知识分子〕。

poise [pɔiz; pɔɪz] **I** *vt.* **1.** 使重量相等,使平衡。**2.** 作(投标枪一样的)姿势,使(头等)保持一定姿势[位置]。**3.** 〔罕〕仔细考虑。**4.** 使悬而不决,踌躇。**5.** 使悬着不动。~ ***oneself on*** 在…上面保持身体的重心以免倒下。— *vi.* 保持平衡;悬着。**II** *n.* **1.** 平衡。**2.** 歪头姿势。**3.** 安定,平静;沉着;自信。**4.** 犹豫不决,踌躇;虚悬。**5.** 法码,秤锤。**6.** 【化】泊〔黏度单位〕。

poised [pɔizd; pɔɪzd] *a.* **1.** 沉着的,有威严的,有自信心的。**2.** 保持平衡的,平稳的。**3.** 悬空的,盘旋的。*be* ~ *on the brink of disaster* 处变不惊。

poi·son [ˈpɔizn; ˋpɔɪzn] **I** *n.* **1.** 毒;毒药。**2.** 毒害;弊病;有害的主义[学说、风气(等)]。**3.** 〔俚〕劣酒。**4.** 抑制剂。*slow* [*cumulative*] ~ 慢性毒药。*aerial* ~ 瘴气。*What's your* ~? 〔俚〕你喝什么(酒)? *hate like* ~ 〔口〕痛恨;极端厌恶。**II** *vt.* **1.** 放毒于;涂毒于;毒害;毒杀;使中毒。**2.** 玷污,伤害,败坏(计划、名誉等)。**3.** 阻碍;抑制。**4.** 弄坏(机器等)。~ ***one's mind*** 对…发生恶感,毒害某人的思想;使沾染上坏习气。— *vi.* 放毒,投毒。~ **fang** (蛇等的)毒牙。~ **gas** 【军】毒气。~ **gland** 毒腺。~ **hemlock** 【植】毒参;芹叶钩吻。~ **ivy** = ~**-oak** 栎叶毒漆树。~**-pen** *a.* 〔俚〕恶意中伤的;匿名写的。~ **sumac** 【植】美国毒漆。

poi·son·er [ˈpɔiznə; ˋpɔɪzn̩ɚ] *n.* 毒害者,毒杀者;放毒者。

poi·son·ing [ˈpɔizniŋ; ˋpɔɪznɪŋ] *n.* 中毒;毒害;布毒;…毒。*mercury-* ~ 水银毒。*lead-* ~ 铅中毒。

poi·son·ous [ˈpɔiznəs; ˋpɔɪznəs] *a.* **1.** 有毒的,有害的。**2.** 有恶意的;恶毒的。**3.** 恶臭的。**4.** 〔口〕不愉快的,讨厌的。*a* ~ *dose* 中毒量。*a* ~ *gas bomb* 毒气弹。*a* ~ *smell* 臭味。*an absolutely* ~ *horse* 一匹极凶猛的马。**-ly** *ad.*

poi·trine [pwɑˈtrin; pwɑˋtrɪn] *n.* 〔F.〕胸部,胸膛〔尤指妇女丰满的乳房〕。

pok·a·ble [ˈpəukəbl; ˋpokəbl̩] *a.* **1.** 可以戳的。**2.** 能激励的。

poke[1] [pəuk; pok] **I** *vt.* **1.** (用手指、棍子等)戳、刺(*in*; *up*; *down*),戳进。**2.** 伸出(头、指等);把…指向[推向]。**3.** 拨,添(火等)。**4.** 激励(马等)。**5.** 〔美俚〕打,殴。— *vi.* **1.** 戳,刺(*at*)。**2.** (头等)伸出;好事,多嘴;探听;打听。**3.** 摸索着走;闲逛。**4.** 【板球】小心慢打。~ (*up*) *the dying fire* 拨燃快熄的火。~ ***about*** **1.** 〔美〕(在书中等)找查。**2.** 闲荡。**3.** 多查多问。~ ***and pry*** 管闲事,探查消息。~ ***fun at*** 〔口〕开…的玩笑,嘲弄。~ ***into*** 干涉;刺探;挑剔。~ ***one's head*** 向前伸头;向前弯腰。~ ***one's nose into*** 干涉,管…的闲事,插手。**II** *n.* **1.** 戳,刺;〔美俚〕一拳,一击。**2.** 〔美〕(牛等的)颈轭。**3.** 〔美俚〕懒人;讨厌的家伙。**4.** (救世军女军官等的)帽子的撑边;有撑边的女帽〔又叫 ~-bonnet〕。~ **nose** 〔美〕爱啰啰嗦嗦打听人家事情的人。

poke[2] [pəuk; pok] *n.* **1.** 〔古〕= pocket. **2.** 〔主方〕小袋;钱袋;钱包;钱〔尤指个人所有的全部钱钞〕。**3.** (鱼的)鳔。***buy a pig in a*** ~ 瞎买东西,隔山买牛。

poke[3] [pəuk; pok] *n.* = pokeweed.

poke·ber·ry [ˈpəukˌberi; ˋpokˏbɛrɪ] *n.* (*pl.* ***-ries***) 【植】美国商陆 (= pokeweed)。

pok·er[1] [ˈpəukə; ˋpokɚ] **I** *n.* **1.** 戳火的人;火钳,拨火棍。**2.** 烙划用具。**3.** 〔英俚〕(牛津、剑桥大学的)副校长的权标,(队前)持权标的人。***as stiff as a*** ~ (态度)呆板。***by the holy*** ~ 〔谑〕立誓,一定。**II** *vt.* 用烙画做(图案)。~ **drawing** 烙画术。~ **picture,** ~ **work** 烙画。

pok·er[2] [ˈpəukə; ˋpokɚ] *n.* 〔罕、美俚〕妖怪。

pok·er[3] [ˈpəukə; ˋpokɚ] *n.* 【纸牌】扑克。~ **face** 一本正经的面容;面无表情的人。~**-faced** *a.* 扑克面孔的,脸上没有表情的。~ **pan** 〔美〕能毫无表情地表演戏剧的演员。

poke·root [ˈpəukˌruːt, -ˌrut; ˋpokˏrut, -ˏrʊt] *n.* = pokeweed.

poke·weed [ˈpəukˌwiːd; ˋpokˏwid] *n.* 【植】美国商陆 (*Phytolacca americana*)〔产于北美,其根和果有毒〕。

pok·ey [ˈpəuki; ˋpokɪ] *n.* (*pl.* ~, ***pok·ies***) 〔美俚〕监狱。

pok·(e)y [ˈpəuki; ˋpokɪ] *a.* (***pok·i·er***; ***-i·est***) **1.** 没有神气的;迟钝的;【生】生长缓慢的。**2.** (房间、场所等)闷人的,窄小的,肮脏的。**3.** (工作、职业等)微贱的,无聊的。**4.** 无趣味的。

pol [pɔl; pɑl] *n.* **1.** 老资格的政客,党派政治老手。**2.** = politician.

Pol. = Poland; Polish.

pol. = political; politician; politics.

po·lac·ca, pola·cre [pəuˈlækə, -ˈlɑːkə; poˋlækə, -ˋlɑkə] *n.* (地中海的)三桅商船。

Po·lack [ˈpəulæk; ˋpolæk] **I** *n.* **1.** 〔蔑〕波兰血统的人。**2.** 〔古〕波兰人。**II** *a.* 〔口〕= Polish.

Po·land [ˈpəulənd; ˋpolənd] *n.* 波兰〔欧洲〕。

po·lar [ˈpəulə; ˋpolɚ] **I** *a.* **1.** (南、北)极的,地极的;近地极的。**2.** 【物、化】(有)极的;磁极的;有磁性的。**3.** 【几】极线的。**4.** 【化】极化的,离子化的;(多)极性的。**5.** 中轴一样的;中心的;(像北极星那样)有指向意义的。**6.** (性格)正相反的。**II** *n.* 【几】极线;极面。~ **circles** 极圈。~ **bear** 北极熊,白熊。~ **beaver** 〔俚〕白髯人。~ **body** 【解】极体。~ **cap** 【天】极冠。~ **curve** 【数】配曲线。~ **distance** 【天】极距。~ **front** 【气】极锋。

polari- *comb. f.* 表示"极": *polari*scope.

po·lar·im·e·ter [ˌpəuləˈrimitə; ˏpoləˋrɪmətɚ] *n.* 【物】偏振计,旋光计,极化计。

po·lar·i·me·tric [pəuˌlæriˈmetrik; poˏlærɪˋmɛtrɪk] *a.* 【物】测定偏振[旋光、极化]的。

P

po·lar·i·me·try [ˌpəulə'rimitri; ˏpolə'rɪmɪtrɪ] *n*.【物】偏振测定法;旋光测定法;极化测定术。

Po·la·ris [pəu'lɛəris; po'lɛrɪs] *n*.【天】北极星。

po·lar·i·scope [pəu'læriskəup; po'lærəˏskop] *n*. 偏振光镜,旋光计。

po·lar·i·scop·y [pəu'læriskəupi; po'lærɪskopɪ] *n*. = polarimetry.

po·lar·i·ty [pəu'læriti; po'lærətɪ] *n*. **1.**【物】(分)极性,磁性引力;(光的)偏极;极体;【数】配极(变换);【生】(茎与根的)反向性,极性。**2.** (性格的)正反对。**3.** (思想、感情等的)归向,倾向。*a ~ inverting amplifier* 倒像放大器。~ **therapy**【医】体能极性疗法〔通过节食、运动和心理治疗以缓解机能障碍症的非传统疗法〕。

po·lar·i·za·tion [ˌpəulərai'zeiʃən; ˏpolərə'zeʃən] *n*. **1.** 两极分化。**2.**【物、天】极化;极化强度。**3.**【物】偏振(化)。*a ~ cell* 极化电池。*atomic ~* 原子极化强度。*orientation ~* 定向极化。*a ~ microscope* 偏振显微镜。

po·lar·ize, po·lar·ise ['pəuləraiz; 'poləˏraɪz] *vt*. **1.** 给与…极性,使归极。**2.** 使(光)偏振。**3.** 使(语言等)有特殊意义[用途]。**4.** 使两极分化。*a ~d bell* 极化电铃。*~d light* 偏振。*a polarizing circuit* — *vi*. (物质)偏振;【电】(金属等)极化;两极分化;赋极电路。**-iz·abil·i·ty** [ˌpəuləˌraizə'biliti; ˏpoləˏraɪzə'bɪlɪtɪ] *n*. **-iz·able** *a*.

po·lar·iz·er ['pəuləraizə; 'poləˏraɪzɚ] *n*.【物】起偏(振)镜,起偏光镜。

po·lar·o·gram [pəu'lærəgræm; po'lærəgræm] *n*. 极谱。

po·lar·o·graph [pəu'lærəgrɑːf; po'lærəgræf] *n*.【物】极谱记录器,极谱仪旋光计。

po·lar·og·ra·phy [ˌpəulə'rɔgrəfi; ˏpolə'rɑgrəfɪ] *n*.【化】极谱法,极谱学。**-graph·ic** *a*. **-graph·i·cal·ly** *ad*.

po·lar·oid ['pəulərɔid; 'poləˏrɔɪd] *n*.【物】(人造)偏振片〔防止闪光用〕。

po·lar·on ['pəulərɔn; 'poləˏrɑn] *n*.【物】极化子。

pol·der ['pəuldə; 'poldɚ] *n*. 堤围泽地,垸,圩圩。

pole[1] [pəul; pol] **I** *n*. **1.** 棒,杆,竿〔通常为十英尺以上圆杆〕。**2.** 旗竿;钓竿;【运】(撑竿跳的)竿;桅杆;电线杆;(车的)辕杆;理发师的招牌杆。**3.** 杆〔长度名,等于五码半〕。*a tent ~* 帐篷的中心支柱。*a punt ~* (撑船的)篙子。***climb up the greasy ~*** 处理困难工作。***under* [*with*] (*bare*) *~s***【海】不张帆。***up the ~***〔俚〕**1.** 微狂的。**2.** 进退两难。**II** *vt*. **1.** 用棒支持;用棒推;用篙撑;架(豆蔓等)。**2.** 用(竹)杆挑。— *vi*. 用篙撑船。~ **jumping** [**vault**] 撑竿跳。

pole[2] [pəul; pol] *n*. **1.**【天、地】极;极地;北极星;【物】极点,顶点。**2.**【电】电极;磁极。**3.** 两极端〔指性格、学说等〕。**4.** 天空。*the North* [*South*] *~* 北[南]极。*the positive* [*negative*] *~* 阳[阴]极。***be ~s asunder*** 截然相反,南辕北辙。(*Our opinions and theirs are ~s asunder*. 我们双方的意见截然相反)。***from ~ to ~*** 全世界(*English is spoken from ~ to ~*. 英语在世界各国都通用)。~ **piece** 极靴,磁极片。~ **star**【天】北极星;指导人;指导原理;有吸引力的中心;目标。~**ward(s)** *ad*. 向极。

Pole [pəul; pol] *n*. 波兰人。

pole·ax(e) ['pəulæks; 'polˏæks] **I** *n*.【史】战斧;钺;【海】短把斧;杀牛斧。**II** *vt*. 拿斧砍倒。

po·leis ['pəulais; 'polaɪs] polis 的复数。

pole·cat ['pəulkæt; 'polˏkæt] *n*. (*pl*. ~(**s**)) **1.**【动】鸡貂;臭猫〔鼬类〕。**2.**〔古〕妓女。

pol. [**polit.**] **econ.** = political economy.

po·lem·ic [pɔ'lemik; po'lɛmɪk] **I** *n*. **1.** 攻击,驳斥;〔*pl*.〕争论,论战,辩论(术);〔*pl*.〕(神学上的)论证法。**2.** 争论者,论客。~***s on paper*** 打笔墨官司。**II** *a*. 论战的,辩论的;喜欢争论的。*a ~ writer* 爱论战的作者。**-i·cal** *a*. **-ly** *ad*.

po·lem·i·cist [pə'lemisist; pə'lɛmɪsɪst] *n*. 争论者,争辩者,善辩论者(= polemist)。

po·lem·i·cize [pəu'lemisaiz; po'lɛmɪsaɪz] *vi*. = polemize.

pol·e·mist ['pɔləmist; 'pɑləmɪst] *n*. 争论者,善辩论者。

pol·e·mize ['pɔlimaiz; 'pɑləˏmaɪz] *vi*. 争论,辩驳,笔战。

po·len·ta [pəu'lentə; po'lɛntə] *n*.〔It.〕大麦粥;粟粉粥;玉米粥。

pol·er ['pəulə; 'polɚ] *n*. **1.** 辕马(= pole horse)。**2.** 以竿撑船的人。

po·lice [pə'liːs; pə'lis] **I** *n*. **1.** 警察;〔集合词〕警务人员。**2.** 治安,公安。**3.**【火箭】校正,修正。**4.**【美军】(兵营内的)打扫,整顿;内务值勤;内务值勤人员。*ten ~* = ten policemen 十名警察。*campus ~* 校园警卫。*the harbour* [*marine*] *~* 水上警察。*the metropolitan ~ department* 市公安厅,市警处。*the ~ office*〔英〕警察局。*a ~ officer* 警官。*the military ~*〔美〕宪兵队。*mounted ~* 骑警队。*a ~ agent* (法国等的)警察。*the ~ station* 警察(分)局。*a ~ box* [*stand*] (警察)岗亭。*a ~ inspector* 巡官。*The ~ are on his track*. 警察正在搜捕他。**II** *vt*. **1.** 在…实施警察制度;在…设置警察;维持…的秩序。**2.** 统治,管辖。**3.**【火箭】校正,修正。**4.**【美军】打扫,整顿。~ **constable**〔英〕普通警员。~ **court** 违警罪法庭。~ **dog** 警犬。~ **force**〔集合词〕警察(力量)。~ **justice**, ~ **magistrate** 违警罪法庭法官。~**man** **1.** 警察;【矿山】看守矿井的人。**2.**【化】淀帚。~ **offence** 违警罪。~ **post** 派出所。~ **state** 警察国家。~ **trap** (管制车速的)岗哨。**-woman** 女警察。

pol·i·clin·ic [ˌpɔli'klinik; ˏpɑlɪ'klɪnɪk] *n*. (医院的)门诊部;(有教授作顾问的)学生私人诊所。

pol·i·cy[1] ['pɔlisi; 'pɑləsɪ] *n*. **1.** 政策,政纲;方针,方向;方法。**2.** 策略;权谋;智慧;精明的行为。**3.**【军】政治,行政。**4.**〔Scot.〕〔常 *pl*.〕别墅的附属庭园。*a domestic ~* 国内政策,内政方针。*a foreign ~* 对外[外交]政策。*non-alignment ~* 不结盟政策。*policies of war and aggression* 侵略政策和战争政策。*a cold war ~* 冷战政策。*a ~ of strength* 实力政策。*the Party's general and specific ~* 党的方针政策。*Honesty is the best ~*. 正直是最明智的。***for reasons of ~*** 出于策略上的原因。~ **maker** 制定政策的人。

pol·i·cy[2] ['pɔlisi; 'pɑləsɪ] *n*. **1.** 保险单。**2.**〔美〕(由抽签决定的)彩票。*a life* [*fire*] *~* 人寿[火灾]保险单。*a floating ~* 总保(险)单。*a valued ~* 确定保险单。*an open ~* 预定保险单。***play ~***〔美〕打彩,抽彩。***take out a ~ on one's life*** 加入人寿保险。~ **racket**〔美〕彩票(= numbers pool)。~ **shop**〔美〕抽彩的商店[场所]。~ **holder** 保险客户。

pol·ing ['pəuliŋ; 'polɪŋ] *n*. **1.**【冶】还原,吹气。**2.**【电】立杆,架线路。

po·li·o ['pəuliəu; 'polɪo] *n*. 脊髓灰质炎 = poliomyelitis.

pol·i·o·my·e·li·tis [ˌpɔliəumaii'laitis; ˏpɑlɪoˏmaɪəˏlaɪtɪs] *n*. 脊髓灰质炎,小儿麻痹症。*acute anterior ~* 小儿麻痹。

po·lis ['pəulis, 'pɔlis; 'polɪs, 'pɑlɪs] *n*. (*pl*. ***po·leis*** [-leis, -eis; -laɪs, -aɪs]) (古希腊的)城邦。

-polis *suf*. 表示"都市": metro*polis*.

Po·lish ['pəuliʃ; 'polɪʃ] *a*., *n*. 波兰(人)的;波兰语(的)。

pol·ish ['pɔliʃ; 'pɑlɪʃ] **I** *vt*. **1.** 磨光,擦亮,抛光。**2.** 使简练,使醇化,使优美;推敲;润饰(文章等)(*up*)。~ *one's boots* (*up*) 擦亮皮鞋。*a ~ing mill* 碾米厂。— *vi*. **1.** 发亮。**2.** 变优美。***be ~ed***〔美俚〕喝醉。~ ***away*** [***off***, ***out***] 擦去。~ ***off*** 很快做好(吃完等);〔口〕很快杀掉。

~ *the mug* 〔美俚〕洗脸。~ **up** 完成;〔口〕改善,改进。**II** *n*. **1.** 磨擦;光泽。**2.** 擦亮粉,上光剂,亮油,亮漆。**3.** 优美;修养;推敲。*give it a* ~ 把它擦一擦。*Many of his poems lack* ~. 他的诗作有许多是不够精练的。*shoe* [*boot*] ~ 鞋油。

pol·ished [ˈpɔliʃt; ˋpɑlɪʃt] *a*. **1.** 擦亮的,光亮的,磨光的。**2.** 优美的;精练的。~ *rice* 白米。

pol·ish·er [ˈpɔliʃə; ˋpɑlɪʃɚ] *n*. 磨光工人;磨光器。

polit. = political; politics.

po·lite [pəˈlait; pəˋlaɪt] *a*. (*-lit·er*; *-est*) **1.** 有礼貌的;殷勤的,恳切的;斯文的;文雅的;有教养的。**2.** (文章等)推敲过的,精练的,优美的。~ *society* 讲究礼貌的场合[交际场所];上流社会。*the* ~ *thing* 规矩礼貌。~ *letters* [*literature*] 纯文学。**do the** ~ 〔口〕硬装文雅,竭力做出彬彬有礼的样子。**say sth. ~ about** 恭维。**-ly** *ad*. **-ness** *n*.

pol·i·tesse [ˌpɔliˈtes, F. pɔliˈtɛs; ˏpɑlɪˋtɛs] *n*. 〔F.〕文雅,斯文;彬彬有礼。

pol·i·tic [ˈpɔlitik; ˋpɑləˏtɪk] *a*. **1.** 精明的;机敏的,狡猾的;有手腕的。**2.** (话等)巧妙的,适当的。**3.** 〔古〕政治上的,国家的。*a* ~ *move* 适当的处置。*a body* ~ 〔罕〕国家。**-ly** *ad*.

po·lit·i·cal [pəˈlitikəl; pəˋlɪtɪkḷ] *a*. **1.** 政治(上)的;政策(上)的;政治学(上)的。**2.** 行政上的;政党的,有政治组织的。*a* ~ *writer* 政论作家;政治记者。*a* ~ *view* 政治见解。*a* ~ *offense* [*prisoner*] 政治犯[犯人]。~ *rights* 政权。*a* ~ *party* 政党。*a* ~ *meeting* 政治集会。**~ly correct** 〔美〕政治上正确的〔指语言使用上极力避免使用性别或种族歧视的词语,例如用 chairperson 来代替 chairman 等,有时会因过分而显得可笑〕。~ **economy** 政治经济学。~ **expedients** 权谋。~ **posturing** 政治作秀,(为赢得选票等而就热点问题)作政治表态。~ **pluralism** 政治多元化。~ **science** 政治学。**-ly** *ad*. **1.** 政治上;政策上。**2.** 精明,巧妙。

po·lit·i·cal·ize [pəˈlitiklaiz; pəˋlɪtɪkḷˏaɪz] *vt*. 使政治化,使具有政治性,使带政治色彩。**-za·tion** *n*.

pol·i·ti·cian [ˌpɔliˈtiʃən; ˏpɑləˋtɪʃən] *n*. **1.** 政治家。**2.** 〔蔑〕政客;〔美〕政治贩。*crafty* ~*s* 阴谋家。

po·lit·i·cize [pəˈlitisaiz; pəˋlɪtəˏsaɪz] *vi*. 从事政治活动;谈论政治。— *vt*. 使政治化;从政治上处理。

pol·i·tick [ˈpɔlitik; ˋpɑlətɪk] *vi*. 进行政治活动,谈论政治。**-er** *n*. 进行政治活动的人。

pol·i·tick·ing [ˈpɔlitikiŋ; ˋpɑlətɪkɪŋ] *n*. 政治活动〔尤指竞选和拉选票的活动〕。

po·lit·i·co [pəˈlitikəu; pəˋlɪtɪˏko] *n*. (*pl*. ~(*e*)*s*) 政客;专搞党派政治的人。

po·lit·i·co- *comb*. *f*. 表示"政治…上的": *politico*geographical 政治地理上的。

pol·i·tics [ˈpɔlitiks; ˋpɑləˏtɪks] *n*. **1.** 〔作单数用〕政治学;政治。**2.** 〔作复数用〕政界;行政工作;政治运动;战略,政策;政见;政治关系;政治斗争;利害,动机,目的。**3.** 〔作单数用〕经营,管理。**4.** 〔作复数用〕政纲,政见。*lunar* ~ 不切实际的问题。*power* ~ 强权政治。*engaged in* ~ 从事政治活动。*It is not practical* ~. 这没有再谈论的价值。*play* ~ 要阴谋诡计,为自己打算。*with* [*put*] ~ *in command* 政治领先。

Po·l(l)itt [ˈpɔlit; ˋpɑlɪt] *n*. 波利特〔姓氏〕。

pol·i·ty [ˈpɔliti; ˋpɑlətɪ] *n*. **1.** 政体,国体。**2.** 国家,政府;行政;制度。*civil* ~ 国家行政机构[组织]。

Polk [pəuk; pok] *n*. 波克〔姓氏〕。

polk [pɔlk; polk] *vi*. 〔口〕跳波尔卡舞。

pol·ka [ˈpɔlkə; ˋpolkə] **I** *n*. **1.** (波希米亚的)波尔卡舞(曲)。**2.** 女人紧身短上衣。**II** *vi*. 跳波尔卡舞。~ **dot** (衣料上的)圆点花纹。

poll[1] [pəul; pol] **I** *n*. **1.** 〔古;谑〕脑袋;人,人数。**2.** 纳税人[选举人]名册。**3.** 投票,投票数;〔*pl*.〕〔美〕投票处。**4.** 人头税。**5.** [P-]〔美〕民意测验所。**6.** (锤等的)宽平端。*a gray* [*snow-white*] ~ 白头。*a heavy* [*light*, *poor*] ~ 高[低]得票率。*How stands the* ~? 投票情形怎样? **at the head of the** ~ 得票最多。**go to the** ~ 到投票处去投票。~ **of** ~**s** 民意测验的比较。**take a** ~ 投票表决。**II** *vt*. **1.** 把(选民)登记入名册。**2.** (候选人)得(票);查(票);投(票)。**3.** 作…的民意调查。**4.** 剪短(头发);锯下(家畜的角);〔古〕剪(毛,枝,草等)。— *vi*. 投票。~*ing place* [*booth*] 投票所。~ **book** 选举人名册。~ **tax** 人头税。

poll[2] [pɔl; pɑl] *n*. 〔俚〕剑桥 (*Cambridge*) 大学普通毕业生〔又作 ~*man*〕。*go out in the P-* 拿到普通学位。*a* ~ *degree* 普通学位。

poll[3] [pəul; pol] *a*. 【法】当事人一方作成的。*a deed* ~ 单独盖章证书。

Poll [pɔl; pɑl] *n*. **1.** 〔称呼名〕鹦鹉。**2.** 〔口〕= Mary. **3.** 〔p-〕〔口〕妓女。~ **parrot** 鹦鹉;瞎说白扯的人。

poll·a·ble [ˈpəuləbl; ˋpoləbḷ] *a*. 可以修剪的,可以剪去头[角]的;可以投票的。

pol·lack [ˈpɔlək; ˋpɑlək] *n*. 【鱼】绿鳕。

pol·lard [ˈpɔləd; ˋpɑlɚd] **I** *n*. **1.** 截去了梢的树;脱角鹿[牛],无角兽。**2.** 糠,含有少许面粉的糠。**II** *vt*. 剪去…的树梢。

polled [pəuld; pold] *a*. 剪去了树梢的;剪了毛[发]的;秃头的;锯了角的;(牛等)无角(品种)的。*the P- Angus* = Aberdeen Angus.

poll·ee [pəuˈliː; polˋi] *n*. 〔美〕受民意测验的人。

pol·len [ˈpɔlin; ˋpɑlən] **I** *n*. **1.** 【植】花粉。**2.** 【虫】粉面。**II** *vt*. 授粉给;传粉给;用花粉掩盖。

pol·len·o·sis, pol·li·no·sis [ˌpɔliˈnəusis; ˏpɑləˋnosɪs] *n*. 枯草热 (= hay fever)。

pol·lex [ˈpɔliks; ˋpɑlɛks] *n*. (*pl*. ***pol·li·ces*** [-əˈsiːz; -əˋsiz]) 【解】拇指。**pol·li·cal** [-ikl; -ɪkl] *a*.

pol·li·nate [ˈpɔlineit; ˋpɑləˏnet] *vt*. 【植】给…授粉;传花粉给。

pol·li·na·tion [ˌpɔliˈneiʃən; ˏpɑləˋneʃən] *n*. 【植】传粉,授粉(作用)。*artificial* ~ 人工授粉。

pol·li·nif·er·ous [ˌpɔliˈnifərəs; ˏpɑləˋnɪfərəs] *a*. 【植】**1.** 有花粉的,生花粉的。**2.** 适于传粉的。

pol·lin·i·um [pəˈliniəm; pəˋlɪnɪəm] *n*. (*pl*. *-i·a* [-ə; -ə]) 【植】花粉块。

pol·li·nize [ˈpɔlinaiz; ˋpɑləˏnaɪz] *vt*. (*-niz·ed*; *-niz·ing*) = pollinate. **-r** *n*.

pol·li·no·sis [ˌpɔliˈnəusis; ˏpɑləˋnosɪs] *n*. 【医】花粉病,枯草热。

pol·li·wig, pol·li·wog [ˈpɔliwig, -wəg; ˋpɑlɪwɪg, -wɑg] *n*. 〔口〕= tadpole.

Pol·lock [ˈpɔlək; ˋpɑlək] *n*. 波洛克〔姓氏〕。

pol·lock [ˈpɔlək; ˋpɑlək] *n*. = pollack.

pol·loi [ˈpɔlɔi; pəˋlɔɪ] *n*. 〔*pl*.〕〔Gr.〕人民,民众。***Hoi*** ~ = *the* ~ 一般民众,群众。

poll·ster [ˈpəulstə; ˋpolstɚ] *n*. 〔美〕民意测验所;民意测验录编者;选举预测人。

pol·lu·tant [pəˈluːtənt; pəˋlutnt] *n*. 污染物〔尤指放入水中和空气中的有害的化学物质〕。

pol·lute [pəˈluːt, -ˈljuːt; pəˋlut] *vt*. **1.** 弄脏,污染;玷污,亵渎。**2.** 败坏(品性),使堕落。

pol·lu·tion [pəˈluːʃən, -ˈljuː-; pəˋluʃən] *n*. **1.** 污染(作用)。**2.** 腐败,堕落。*nocturnal* ~ 【医】梦遗(精)。~ **disease** 污染病。

Pol·lux [ˈpɔləks; ˋpɑləks] *n*. 【天】北河三(双子座 β 星)。

Pol·ly[1] [ˈpɔli; ˋpɑlɪ] *n*. = poll parrot.

Pol·ly[2] [ˈpɔli; ˋpɑlɪ] *n*. 波莉〔女子名, Mary 的昵称〕。

Pol·ly·an·na [ˌpɔliˈænə; ˏpɑlɪˋænə] *n*. 〔有时也作 p-〕遇事过分乐观的人〔源出美国作家 Eleanor Porter 所作小说〕。

pol·ly·wog [ˈpɔliwɔg; ˋpɑlɪˏwɑg] *n*. = polliwog.

po·lo [ˈpəuləu; ˋpolo] *n*. **1.** 马球。**2.** 水球 (= water

P

~)。~ **shirt** (开领短袖式)马球衬衫。~ **stick** 马球棍。**-ist** *n*. 马球[水球]运动员。

Po·lo [ˈpəuləu; ˋpolo], **Marco** 马可波罗〔1254—1324, 意大利旅行家〕。

pol·o·naise [ˌpɔləˈneiz; ˏpoləˋnez] *n*. 1. 波罗奈兹〔波兰慢步舞(曲)〕。2. 波兰连衫裙;四股装饰花线。

po·lo·ni·um [pəˈləuniəm; pəˋlonɪəm] *n*.【化】钋。

po·lo·ny [pəˈləuni; pəˋlonɪ] *n*. 半熟干香肠。

pol·sci. = political science.

pol·ter·geist [ˈpɔltəgaist; ˋpoltəˏgaɪst] *n*. [G.] (*pl*. ~*er* [-ə; -ə]) (迷信者认为造成各种噪音的)吵闹鬼。

P

polt·foot [ˈpəultfut; ˋpoltfʊt] *n*., *a*. 弯脚(的)。

pol·troon [pɔlˈtruːn; pɑlˋtrun] I *n*. 胆小鬼。II *a*. 胆子小的。

pol·troon·er·y [pɔlˈtruːnəri; pɑlˋtrunərɪ] *n*. 怯懦。

poly- *comb. f*. 表示"多,复;聚": *poly*gamy; *poly*genesis.

pol·y [ˈpɔli; ˋpɑlɪ] *n*. 〔口〕1. 工艺学校(= polytechnical school)。2. 聚酯纤维(= polyester fibre)。

pol·y·a·del·phous [ˌpɔliəˈdelfəs; ˏpɑlɪəˋdɛlfəs] *a*.【植】多体雄蕊的。

pol·y·am·ide [ˌpɔliˈæmaid; ˏpɑlɪˋæmaɪd] *n*.【化】聚醯胺。

pol·y·an·drous [ˌpɔliˈændrəs; ˏpɑlɪˋændrəs] *a*. 1. 一妻多夫的。2.【植】具多种雄蕊的;【动】一雌多雄的。

pol·y·an·dry [ˈpɔliændri, pɔliˈæn-; ˋpɑlɪˏændrɪ, -ˏpɑlɪˋæn-] *n*. 1. 一妻多夫制。2.【动】多雄,一雌多雄(配合);【植】多雄蕊。**-drist** *n*. 多夫女人。**-drous** *a*.

pol·y·an·thus [ˌpɔliˈænθəs; ˏpɑlɪˋænθəs] *n*.【植】1. 西樱草。2. 多花水仙。

pol·y·ar·ch·y [ˈpɔliɑːki; ˋpɑlɪˏɑrkɪ] *n*. 多头政治(*opp*. oligarchy)。

pol·y·a·tom·ic [ˌpɔliəˈtɔmik; ˏpɑlɪəˋtɑmɪk] *a*.【化】多原子的,多元的,多碱的,多酸的。

pol·y·au·tog·ra·phy [ˌpɔliɔːˈtɔgrəfi; ˏpɑlɪɔˋtɑgrəfɪ] *n*. 〔古〕石印术。

pol·y·bas·ic [ˌpɔliˈbeisik; ˏpɑlɪˋbesɪk] *a*.【化】多碱(价)的;多元的;多代的。

pol·y·bas·ite [ˌpɔliˈbeisait; pəˋlɪbəˏsaɪt] *n*. 硫锑铜银矿。

pol·y·car·bon·ate resin [ˌpɔliˈkɑːbənit; ˏpɑlɪˋkɑrbənɪt] 聚碳酸脂。

pol·y·car·pel·lar·y [ˌpɔliˈkɑːpiˌleəri; ˏpɑlɪˋkɑrpəˏlɛrɪ] *a*.【植】多心皮的。

pol·y·car·pic [ˌpɔliˈkɑːpik; ˏpɑlɪˋkɑrpɪk] *a*.【植】1. 结多次果的。2. 多心皮的(= polycarpous)。**-car·py** [-pi; -pɪ] *n*.

pol·y·cen·trism [ˌpɔliˈsentrizm; ˏpɑlɪˋsɛntrɪzəm] *n*. 多中心主义。**-cen·tric** *a*. **-cen·trist** *a*., *n*. 主张多中心主义的(人)。

pol·y·chaete [ˈpɔlikiːt; ˋpɑlɪkit] *n*.【动】多毛纲(*Polychaeta*)动物。**-chae·tous** *a*.

pol·y·chlo·ro·prene [ˌpɔliˈklɔ(ː)rəpriːn; ˏpɑlɪˋklɔrəprin] *n*.【化】聚氯丁烯;氯丁橡胶。

pol·y·chres·tic [ˌpɔliˈkrestik; ˏpɑlɪˋkrɛstɪk] *a*. (药品等)有多种用途的;多能的;(话)有多种意义的。

pol·y·chro·mate [ˌpɔliˈkrəumit; ˏpɑlɪˋkromɪt] *n*.【化】多色物质。

pol·y·chro·mat·ic [ˌpɔlikrəuˈmætik; ˏpɑlɪkroˋmætɪk] *a*. 多色的;【矿】变色的。

pol·y·chrome [ˈpɔlikrəum; ˋpɑlɪˏkrom] I *a*. 多色的;彩饰的;彩印的,多色印刷的。II *n*. 1. 彩色画;彩像;多色,色彩配合。2.【药】七叶灵。

pol·y·chro·my [ˈpɔlikrəumi; ˋpɑlɪˏkromɪ] *n*. (雕刻、建筑等的)彩饰;彩画法。

pol·y·clin·ic [ˌpɔliˈklinik; ˏpɑlɪˋklɪnɪk] *n*. 综合医院。

pol·y·cot·y·le·don [ˌpɔliˌkɔtəˈliːdən; ˏpɑlɪˏkɑtəˋlidən] *n*.【植】多子叶植物。**-don·ous** *a*.

pol·y·cy·clic [ˌpɔliˈsaiklik, -ˈsiklik; ˏpɑlɪˋsaɪklɪk, -ˋsɪklɪk] *a*. 1.【生】多轮的。2.【化】多环的。

pol·y·cy·the·mi·a [ˌpɔlisaiˈθiːmiə; ˏpɑlɪsaɪˋθimɪə] *n*.【医】红血球增多(症)。

pol·y·dac·tyl [ˌpɔliˈdæktl; ˏpɑlɪˋdæktəl] I *a*. 多指[趾]的[畸形的]。II *n*. 多指的人;多趾动物。**-tyl·ism**, **-ty·ly** *n*. **-tyl·ous** *a*.

pol·y·dip·si·a [ˌpɔliˈdipsiə; ˏpɑlɪˋdɪpsɪə]【医】烦渴。

pol·y·dy·mite [pəˈlidimait; pəˋlɪdɪmaɪt] *n*.【矿】辉镍矿。

pol·y·em·bry·o·ny [ˌpɔliˈembriəni; ˏpɑlɪˋɛmbrɪənɪ] *n*.【医】多胚,一卵多胎。

pol·y·ene [ˈpɔliiːn; ˋpɑlɪin] *n*.【化】聚烯,多烯[烃]。**-e·nic** [-ˈiːnik; -ˋinɪk] *a*.

pol·y·es·ter [ˌpɔliˈestə; ˏpɑlɪˋɛstə] *n*. 聚酯。~ *fibres* 聚酯纤维。

pol·y·es·ter·i·fi·ca·tion [ˈpɔliesˌterifiˈkeiʃən; ˋpɑlɪɛsˏtɛrɪfɪˋkeʃən] *n*.【化】聚酯;聚酯化(作用)。

po·ly·eth·y·lene [ˌpɔliˈeθiliːn; ˏpɑlɪˋɛθɪlin] *n*.【化】聚乙烯。

pol·y·foam [ˈpɔlifəum; ˋpɑlɪfom] *n*. 泡沫塑料。

pol·y·flu·or·tetra·eth·y·lene [ˈpɔlifluəˌtetrəˈeθiliːn; ˋpɑlɪfluəˏtɛtrəˋɛθɪlin] *n*.【化】聚四氟乙烯。

po·lyg·a·la [pəˈligələ; pəˋlɪgələ] *n*. 远志属植物(= milkwort)。

po·lyg·a·mist [pəˈligəmist; pəˋlɪgəmɪst] *n*. 多配偶论者〔尤指一夫多妻主义者〕;多配偶的人。

po·lyg·amize [pəˈligəmaiz; pəˋlɪgəmaɪz] *vi*. 实行多配偶制。

po·lyg·a·mous [pəˈligəməs; pəˋlɪgəməs] *a*. 1. 多配偶的;一夫多妻的;一妻多夫的。2.【动】分配性的,一雄多雌的。3.【植】雌雄同株的;杂性的。

po·lyg·a·my [pəˈligəmi; pəˋlɪgəmɪ] *n*. 1. 多婚(制);多配偶;一夫多妻;一妻多夫。2.【植】雌雄同株;杂性式。3.【动】多配性,一雄多雌。

pol·y·gene [ˈpɔlidʒiːn; ˋpɑlɪdʒin] *n*.【生】多基因。**-gen·ic** [-ˈdʒenik; -ˋdʒɛnɪk] *a*.

pol·y·genes [ˌpɔlidʒiːnz; ˋpɑlɪdʒinz] *n*. *pl*.【遗】多对因子,多基因(= multiple factors)。**-gen·ic** [-ˈdʒenik; -ˋdʒɛnɪk] *a*.

pol·y·gen·e·sis [ˌpɔliˈdʒenisis; ˏpɑlɪˋdʒɛnəsɪs] *n*. 1.【生】多元发生说。2. 有性生殖。

pol·y·gen·y [pəˈlidʒini; pəˋlɪdʒənɪ] *n*. (人种起源的)多源发生。**-gen·ist** *n*. 多元发生说者。

pol·y·glot [ˈpɔliglɔt; ˋpɑlɪˏglɑt] I *a*. 1. 数国语言的;用数国语言写的;多种语言混合组成的。2. 讲[懂]数国语言的。II *n*. 1. 用数国语言写的书;〔特指〕数国语言对译的圣经。2. 会讲数国语言的人。

pol·y·glot·tal, **pol·y·glot·tic**, **pol·y·glot·tous** [ˌpɔliˈglɔtl, -tik, -təs; ˏpɑlɪˋglɑtl, -tɪk, -təs] *a*. 1. 用数国语言写的。2. 会讲好几国话的。

pol·y·glot·tism [ˌpɔliˈglɔtizəm; ˋpɑlɪˋglɑtɪzəm] *n*. 数种文字的使用;通晓数种语言。

pol·y·gon [ˈpɔligən; ˋpɑlɪˏgɑn] *n*.【几】多边形,多角形。*a regular* ~ 正多边形。**-lyg·o·nal** [ˈpəligənl; ˋpɑlɪgənl] *a*. 多边多角形的(地面龟裂)。

po·lyg·o·num [pəˈligənəm; pəˋlɪgənəm] *n*.【植】蓼属(*Polygonum*)植物;蓼。

pol·y·graph [ˈpɔligrɑːf; ˋpɑlɪˏgræf] I *n*. 1. 复写器。2. 多种波动描记器;测谎器。3. 多产作家;论集,著作集。II *vt*. 用测谎器测试(嫌犯等)。**-ic**, **-i·cal** *a*.

po·lyg·y·nous [pəˈlidʒinəs; pəˋlɪdʒənəs] *a*. 1. 多雌的,一夫多妻的。2.【植】多雄蕊(植物)的;多花柱的。

po·lyg·y·ny [pəˈlidʒini; pəˋlɪdʒənɪ] *n*. 一夫多妻;【植】杂性式;【动】多雌,一雄多雌。

pol·y·hed·ron [ˌpɔliˈhedrən; ˏpɑlɪˋhidrən] *n*. (*pl*.

-dra [-drə; -drə], ～*s*)【几】多面体;【拓】可剖分空间。**-hed·ral** *a*.

pol·y·his·tor [ˌpɔli'histə; ˏpɑlɪˋhɪstɚ] *n*. 博学者,博识者,硕学。

pol·y·hy·dric [ˌpɔli'haidrik; ˏpɑlɪˋhaɪdrɪk] *a*.【化】多羟(基)的。

pol·y·hy·drox·y [ˌpɔli'haidrɔksi; ˏpɑlɪˋhaɪdrɑksɪ] *n*.【化】多羟(基)。

pol·y·i·so·prene [ˌpɔli'aisəuˌpriːn; ˏpɑlɪˋaɪsoˏprin] *n*.【化】聚异戊二烯。

pol·y·math ['pɔlimæθ; ˋpɑlɪˏmæθ] *n*. 学识渊博的人。**-ic** *a*.

pol·y·mer ['pɔlimə; ˋpɑlɪmɚ] *n*.【化】聚合体,聚合物,多聚物。*high molecular* ～*s* 高聚物,高分子聚合物。**-ic** *a*.

pol·y·mer·ase ['pɔlimәreis; ˋpɑlɪmәres] *n*.【生化】聚合酶。

pol·y·me·ride [pə'limәraid; pəˋlɪmәraɪd] *n*. = polymer.

pol·ym·er·ism [pə'limərizəm; pəˋlɪmərɪzṃ] *n*.【化】聚合(性),聚合(现象)。

pol·y·mer·ize ['pɔliməraiz; ˋpɑlɪmәˏraɪz] *vt*., *vi*.【化】(使)聚合,(使)成同式异量。**-za·tion** *n*. 聚合(作用),聚合度。

po·lym·er·ous [pə'limərəs; pəˋlɪmərəs] *a*.【植】多基数的。

pol·y·me·thy·lene [ˌpɔli'meθiliːn; ˏpɑlɪˋmeθɪlin]【化】聚甲撑,多亚甲基。

pol·y·morph ['pɔlimɔːf; ˋpɑlɪˏmɔrf] *n*. 多形体;多晶型物。

pol·y·mor·phic [ˌpɔli'mɔːfik; ˏpɑlɪˋmɔrfɪk] *a*. = polymorphous.

pol·y·mor·phism [ˌpɔli'mɔːfizəm; ˏpɑlɪˋmɔrfɪzṃ] *n*. 1. 多形性(现象)。2.【化】(同质)多晶型(现象);【生】多态性(现象)。

pol·y·mor·pho·nu·cle·ar [ˌpɔliˌmɔːfə'nuːkliə; ˏpɑlɪˏmɔrfəˋnuklɪr] *a*. 多形核的。

pol·y·mor·phous [ˌpɔli'mɔːfəs; ˏpɑlɪˋmɔrfəs] *a*. 1. 多形的。2.【化】多晶型的。

pol·y·myx·in [ˌpɔli'miksin; ˏpɑlɪˋmɪksɪn] *n*.【药】多黏菌素。

Pol·y·ne·sia [ˌpɔli'niːzjə; ˏpɑləˋniʒə] *n*. 波利尼西亚〔中太平洋的岛群〕。

Pol·y·ne·si·an [ˌpɔli'niːziən, -zjən; ˏpɑləˋniʒən, -ʃən] I *a*. 1. 波利尼西亚(人)的。2. [p-]多岛的。II *n*. 波利尼西亚人。

po·lyn·i·a [pə'liniə; pəˋlɪnɪə] *n*. (北冰洋)冰原中的水圈。

pol·y·no·mi·al [ˌpɔli'nəumiəl, -mjəl; ˏpɑlɪˋnomɪəl] I *a*. 1.【动、植】多词学名的。2.【数】多项式的。II *n*. 1.【动、植】多词学名。2.【数】多项式。*a* ～ *expression* 多项式。

pol·y·nu·cle·ar [ˌpɔli'njuːkliə, -'nuː-; ˏpɑlɪˋnjuklɪɚ, -ˋnu-] *a*. 多核的 (= polynucleate)。

po·lyn·ya [pə'linjə, 'pɔlinjɑː; ˋpɑlɪnɪə, ˋpɑlɪnjɑr] *n*.【地】冰前沼;冰隙,冰穴〔海水面未结冰处〕。

pol·yp ['pɔlip; ˋpɑlɪp] *n*. 1. (水螅型)珊瑚虫;水生小动物。2.【医】鼻息肉;(子宫)蒂肉。

pol·y·par·y [ˌpɔli'pɛəri; ˋpɑlɪˏpɛrɪ] *n*. (*pl*. **-par·ies**) (水螅型)珊瑚虫(群栖而成的)岩 (= polyparium)。

pol·y·pep·tide [ˌpɔli'peptaid; ˏpɑlɪˋpɛpˏtaɪd] *n*.【化】多肽缩多氨酸。

pol·y·pet·al·ous [ˌpɔli'petələs; ˏpɑlɪˋpɛtḷəs] *a*.【植】离瓣的。

pol·y·pha·gi·a [ˌpɔli'feidʒiə; ˏpɑlɪˋfedʒɪə] *n*. 1.【医】多食症;贪食。2.【动】杂食性。**-lyph·a·gous** *a*.

pol·y·phase ['pɔlifeiz; ˋpɑlɪˏfez] *a*.【电】多相的。*a* ～ *dynamo* [*motor*] 多相发电[电动]机。

Pol·y·phe·mus [ˌpɔli'fiːməs; ˏpɑlɪˋfiməs] *n*.【希神】波吕斐摩斯〔独眼巨人〕。

pol·y·phone ['pɔlifəun; ˋpɑlɪˏfon] *n*. 1. 多音字母[符号]〔如 lead 中的 ea 既读 [iː]又读[e]〕。2.【乐】百音盒。

pol·y·phon·ic, po·lyph·o·nous [ˌpɔli'fɔnik, pə'lifənəs; ˏpɑlɪˋfɑnɪk, pəˋlɪfənəs] *a*. 1. 多音的;(标音字)可以发多种音的。2.【乐】复音的;复调的;对位(法)的。

po·lyph·o·ny [pə'lifəni; pəˋlɪfənɪ] *n*. 1. 多音【语】(一个字母[符号]的)多种发音。2.【乐】复调音乐;对位法。**-pho·nist** ['pɔlifəunist; ˋpɑlɪfonɪst] *n*.【乐】复调乐曲作曲者;口技演员。

pol·y·phy·let·ic [ˌpɔlifai'letik; ˏpɑlɪfaɪˋlɛtɪk] *a*.【生】多源的。**-i·cal·ly** *ad*.

pol·yp·ide, pol·yp·ite ['pɔlipaid, -pait; ˋpɑlɪpaɪd, -paɪt] *n*. 1.【动】个虫。2.【动】水螅型珊瑚虫;息肉 (= polyp)。

pol·y·ploid ['pɔliplɔid; ˋpɑlɪˏplɔɪd] I *n*.【生】多倍体。II *a*. 多倍体的。

pol·y·pod ['pɔlipɔd; ˋpɑlɪpɑd] I *a*.【动】多足(类)的。II *n*. 多足类动物。

Pol·y·po·di·um [ˌpɔli'pəudiəm, -djəm; ˏpɑlɪˋpodɪəm, -djəm] *n*.【植】水龙骨属。

pol·y·po·dy ['pɔlipəudi; ˋpɑlɪˏpodɪ] *n*.【植】水龙骨。

pol·y·poid, pol·yp·oi·dal ['pɔlipɔid, ˌpɔli'pɔidəl; ˋpɑlɪpˏɔɪd, ˏpɑlɪˋpɔɪdəl] *a*.【动】螅形的;【医】息肉[蒂肉]样的。

pol·y·pous ['pɔlipəs; ˋpɑlɪpəs] *a*. = polypoid.

pol·y·pro·pyl·ene [ˌpɔli'prəupiliːn; ˏpɑlɪˋpropɪlin] *n*.【化】聚丙二醇酯,聚丙烯。

pol·yp·tych ['pɔliptik; ˋpɑlɪptɪk] *n*. 四联画[雕刻]屏;多联画[雕刻]屏。

pol·y·pus ['pɔlipəs; ˋpɑləpəs] *n*. (*pl*. **-pi** [-pai; -paɪ]) 1.【动】水螅体。2.【医】(鼻子、子宫等的)息肉,蒂肉。

pol·y·rhythm ['pɔliˌriðm; ˋpɑləˏrɪðəm] *n*.【乐】复合节奏。**-ic** *a*.

pol·y·sac·cha·ride, pol·y·sac·cha·rose [ˌpɔli'sækəraid, -əs; ˏpɑlɪˋsækəˏraɪd, -əs] *n*.【化】多糖(类)。

pol·y·sa·pro·bic [ˌpɔlisə'prəubik; ˏpɑlɪsəˋprobɪk] *a*.【生】多腐生活的〔指原生动物〕。

pol·y·se·my [ˌpɔli'siːmi; ˋpɑlɪˏsimɪ] *n*. 一词多义;有多种解释。**-se·mous** ['pɔlisiməs; ˋpɑlɪsɪməs] *a*.

pol·y·some ['pɔlisəum; ˋpɑlɪsom] *n*.【生】多体〔指染色体〕。

pol·y·so·mic [ˌpɔli'səumik; ˏpɑlɪˋsomɪk] *a*.【遗】多体生物的。

pol·y·stome [ˌpɔlistəum; ˋpɑlɪstom] I *a*.【动】多口的;多口类的。II *n*. 多口类动物。

pol·y·style ['pɔlistail; ˋpɑlɪˏstaɪl] I *a*.【建】多柱式的。II *n*. 多柱式;多柱式建筑物。

pol·y·sty·rene [ˌpɔli'staiəriːn; ˏpɑlɪˋstaɪrin] *n*.【化】聚苯乙烯。

pol·y·sul·phide, pol·y·sul·fide [ˌpɔli'sʌlfaid; ˏpɑlɪˋsʌlfaɪd] *n*. 多硫化物。

pol·y·syl·lab·ic, pol·y·syl·lab·i·cal [ˌpɔlisi'læbik, -ikəl; ˏpɑləsɪˋlæbɪk, -ɪkəl] *a*. 多音节的;多音节词的。

pol·y·syl·la·ble ['pɔliˌsiləbl; ˋpɑləˏsɪləbḷ] *n*. 多音节词。

pol·y·syn·de·ton [ˌpɔli'sinditən; ˏpɑlɪˋsɪndətɑn] *n*.【修】连词叠用。

pol·y·syn·the·sis, -y·syn·thet·ism [ˌpɔli'sinθisis, -sin'θetizəm; ˏpɑlɪˋsɪnθəsɪs, -sɪnˋθɛtɪzəm] *n*. 多数综合,高级综合;【语】多式综合词。

pol·y·syn·thet·ic [ˌpɔlisin'θetik; ˏpɑlɪsɪnˋθɛtɪk] *a*.【语】多式综合的。

pol·y·tech·nic [ˌpɔli'teknik; ˏpɑləˋtɛknɪk] I *a*. 多种工艺的;多种科技的。*a* ～ *exhibition* 工艺品展览会。*a*

P

～ *school* 科技[工艺]学校。II *n*. 综合性工艺学校[大学]。

pol·y·the·ism [ˈpɔliθiːizəm; ˋpɑləθiˏɪzəm] *n*. 多神教;多神论,多神主义 (*opp*. monotheism)。**-the·ist** *n*. 多神论者;多神教徒。**-the·is·tic** *a*.

pol·y·thene [ˈpɔliθiːn; ˋpɑlɪθin] *n*. 聚乙烯 (= polyethylene)。

pol·y·to·nal·i·ty [ˌpɔlitəuˈnæliti; ˏpɑlɪtoˋnælətɪ] *n*.【乐】多调性;多音色。

pol·y·troph·ic [ˌpɔliˈtrɔfik; ˏpɑlɪˋtrɑfɪk] *a*. 多型发酵的;多滋的;(细菌等)广食性的。

pol·y·tropic [ˌpɔliˈtrɔpik; ˏpɑlɪˋtrɑpɪk] *a*.【动】多花采蜜的。

pol·y·trop·y [ˈpɔlitrɔpi; ˋpɑlɪtrɑpɪ] *n*.【化】多变性。

pol·y·typ·ic [ˌpɔliˈtipik; ˏpɑlɪˋtɪpɪk] *a*. 1.【生】多型的。2. 多分支的。

pol·y·un·sat·u·rat·ed [ˌpɔliʌnˈsætjureitid; ˏpɑlɪʌnˋsætjʊretɪd] *a*.【化】多不饱和的〔指有一个以上的双键或三键有机化合物的;还能溶解更多溶质的〕。

pol·y·u·re·thane [ˌpɔliˈjuəriθein; ˏpɑlɪˋjuərɪθen] *n*.【化】聚氨基甲酸脂;聚氨酯(类)。

pol·y·u·ri·a [ˌpɔliˈjuəriə; ˏpɑlɪˋjʊrɪə] *n*.【医】多尿症。**-u·ric** *a*.

pol·y·va·lent [ˌpɔliˈveilənt; ˏpɑlɪˋvelənt] I *a*.【化、生】多价的。II *n*.【生】多价(染色)体。**-lence** *n*.

pol·y·vi·nyl [ˌpɔliˈvainil; ˏpɑlɪˋvaɪnɪl] *n*., *a*. 聚乙烯化合物[基](的)。～ *alcohol* 聚乙烯醇。～ *chloride* 聚氯乙烯。～ *resin* 聚乙烯(基类)树脂。

pol·y·vi·nyl·i·dene [ˌpɔlivaiˈniliˌdiːn; ˏpɑlɪvaɪˋnɪləˏdin] *a*.【化】聚乙烯叉的。

pol·y·wa·ter [ˌpɔliˈwɔːtə; ˏpɑlɪˋwɔtɚ] *n*. 聚合水〔如水溶胶、污染水〕。

pol·y·zo·a [ˌpɔliˈzəuə; ˏpɑlɪˋzoə] *n*.【动】群栖虫,苔藓虫。

pol·y·zo·an [ˌpɔliˈzəuən; ˏpɑlɪˋzoən] *n*. 外肛亚纲动物 (= ectoproct)。

pol·y·zo·ar·i·um [ˌpɔlizəuˈeəriən; ˏpɑlɪzoˋɛrɪəm] *n*. (*pl*. **-i·a** [-ə; -ə])【动】1. 苔藓虫的群体。2. 苔藓虫群体的骨骼。

pom[1] [pɔm; pɑm] *n*. = Pomeranian dog.

pom[2] [pɔm; pɑm] I *n*. 砰的一声。II *vi*. 发砰砰声。

pom·ace [ˈpʌmis; ˋpʌmɪs] *n*. (榨汁后剩下的)苹果渣;鱼渣;蓖麻油渣。

po·ma·ceous [pəuˈmeiʃəs; poˋmeʃəs] *a*. 苹果的,梨果的;似苹果的,似梨果的。

po·made [pəˈmaːd, pəuˈm-; poˋmed, poˋm-] I *n*. 润发香脂[香油]。II *vt*. 用润发香脂[香油]搽。

po·man·der [pəuˈmændə; ˋpomændɚ] *n*. 香丸;香盒,香袋。

Po·mard [pəˈmaː; pɑˋmar] *n*. = Pommard.

po·ma·tum [pəˈmeitəm; poˋmetəm] *n*., *vt*. = pomade.

pom·be [ˈpɔmbi; ˋpɑmbɪ] *n*. 〔Swahili〕(非洲)小米啤酒。

pome [pəum; pom] *n*. 梨果〔如苹果、李、榅桲〕。

pome·gran·ate [ˈpɔmgrænit; ˋpʌmˏgrænɪt] *n*.【植】石榴(树)。

pom·e·lo [ˈpɔmiləu; ˋpɑməˋlo] *n*.【植】柚、栾,文旦;(*pl*. ～*s*) 葡萄柚。

Pom·er·a·ni·an [ˌpɔməˈreinjən; ˏpɑməˋrenɪən] I *a*. 旧德国波米兰尼亚 (Pomerania) 州的。II *n*. 1. 波米兰尼亚人。2. (尖嘴,竖耳,有光滑长毛的)波米兰尼亚小狗 (= ～ dog)。

pom·er·on [ˈpɔməˌrɔn; ˋpɑməˏrɔn] *n*.【物】玻密子。

pom·fret [ˈpɔmfrit; ˋpɑmfrɪt] *n*.【鱼】黑脊鲳鱼,银鲳;乌鲂。

po·mi·cul·ture [ˈpəumikʌltʃə; ˋpomɪˏkʌltʃɚ] *n*. 果树栽培。

po·mif·er·ous [pəuˈmifərəs; poˋmɪfərəs] *a*. 生长梨果的。

Pom·mard [pɔˈmaː; pɑˋmar] *n*. 〔F.〕(法国)波马红葡萄酒。

pom·mel [ˈpʌml; ˋpʌml] I *n*. 1. (刀把)头。2. 鞍头,马鞍前桥。3. 球,球形装饰。II *vt*. (*-ll-*) (用刀把头等)打;用拳头连打。～ *to a jelly* 痛打。

pom·my, pom·mei [ˈpɔmi; ˋpɑmɪ] I *n*. 〔澳、新西兰俚〕〔贬〕英国人〔尤指新来的英国移民〕。II *a*. 英国的。

Po-Mo, po-mo [ˈpəuməu; ˋpomo] *n*. 后现代主义 (= post-modernism)。

po·mol·o·gy [pəuˈmɔlədʒi; poˋmɑlədʒɪ] *n*. 果树学;果树栽培法。

Po·mo·na [pəˈməunə; pəˋmonə] *n*.【罗神】果树女神。～ **green** 嫩绿色。

pomp [pɔmp; pɑmp] *n*. 1. 华丽,壮观;盛大的仪式,华丽的行列。2. 〔*pl*.〕虚荣;浮华;虚饰;浮夸。*do anything with* ～ 体面漂亮地做。

pom·pa·dour [ˈpɔmpəduə; ˋpɑmpəˏdor] *n*. 1. 一种往上梳拢的头发样式。2. 低领圆角女背心。3. 鸭蛋青色。4.【纺】小花卉纹。

pom·pa·no [ˈpɔmpənəu; ˋpɑmpəˏno] *n*.【鱼】(北美)卵鲹。

Pom·pe·i·an [pɔmˈpiːən; pɑmˋpeən] I *a*. (古意大利)庞培城 (Pompeii)的;〔美〕庞培(壁画)式的。II *n*. 庞培人。

Pom·peii [pɔmˈpei; pɑmˋpe·i] *n*. 庞培〔被维苏威火山灰埋掉的意大利古都〕。

Pom·pey [ˈpɔmpi; ˋpɑmpɪ] 庞培 (Gnaeus Pompeius Magnus) ～ **the Great** 庞培〔106—48B.C.,罗马将军,第一次三头政治的首领之一〕。

pom·pi·er [ˈpɔmpjə; ˋpɑmpɪr] I *n*. 救火梯。II *a*. 救火员用的。

pom·pom [ˈpɔmpɔm; ˋpɑmˏpɑm] *n*. 〔俚〕高射机关炮;排发炮。

pom·pon [ˈpɔ̃ːmpɔːŋ; ˋpɑmpɑn] *n*. 〔F.〕1. (军帽的)毛球;绒球,丝球〔妇女、儿童鞋帽上装饰〕。2.【植】绒球菊花;(生圆形小花的)大丽花。

pom·pos·i·ty [pɔmˈpɔsiti; pɑmˋpɑsətɪ] *n*. 1. 豪华,华丽。2. 自大;夸大;傲慢;自负;摆架子。

pom·po·so [pɔmˈpəusəu; pɑmˋposo] *a*., *ad*. 〔It.〕【乐】庄重的[地]。

pom·pous [ˈpɔmpəs; ˋpɑmpəs] *a*. 1. 豪华的,盛大的,壮丽的。2. 浮华的;夸大的;自负的;傲慢的。～ *prolixity* 喜用长字的习惯;冗长的言词。**-ly** *ad*. **-ness** *n*.

pon. = pontoon.

'pon [pɔn; pɑn] ***prep***. = upon.

Pon·ca [ˈpɔŋkə; ˋpɑŋkə] I *n*. 1. (*pl*. ～(*s*)) 1. 彭加人〔在内布拉斯加州和俄克拉荷马州保留地的美洲印第安人部落〕。2. 彭加语。II *a*. 彭加人的。

ponce [pɔns; pɑns] *n*. 〔俚〕= pimp.

pon·ceau [ˈpɔnsəu; pɑnˋso] *n*. 1.【植】丽春花。2. 深红,朱红。3. 酸性朱,丽春红〔染料商品名〕。

pon·cho [ˈpɔntʃəu; ˋpɑntʃo] *n*. (*pl*. ～*s*) 1. (南美人穿的)穗饰披巾。2. (橡胶)雨衣。～ **cloth** (宿营用)防雨厚毛毯;军用防雨披风。

pond [pɔnd; pɑnd] I *n*. 池塘;鱼塘。*the big* [*herring*] ～ 〔谑〕北大西洋。II *vt*. 把…挖成池塘;堵(溪流)水成池 (*back*; *up*)。—*vi*. (水)蓄积成池。～ **fish** 塘鱼。～ **life** 池中小动物〔尤指无脊椎动物〕。～ **lily** 睡莲。～ **snail**【贝】生殖于池中的螺〔尤指膀胱螺属〕。～ **weed**【植】眼子菜;角果藻。

pond·age [ˈpɔndidʒ; ˋpɑndɪdʒ] *n*. (池塘或水库的)蓄水量。

pon·der [ˈpɔndə; ˋpɑndɚ] *vi*. 仔细考虑;沉思,默想 (*on*; *over*; *upon*)。*With the great seriousness he*

~ed upon the problem. 他极其严肃地仔细考虑问题。— *vt*. 衡量,估量。*He ~ed his words thoroughly*. 他说每一句话都要仔细掂量。**-a·tion** [-reiʃən; -reʃən] *n*.

pon·der·a·bil·i·ty [ˌpɔndərəˈbiliti; ˏpandərəˋbɪlətɪ] *n*. 可称性;可衡量性;可估量性;可估计性。

pon·der·a·ble [ˈpɔndərəbl; ˋpandərəbl̩] **I** *a*. **1**. 可称的,有重量的;可衡量的。**2**. 可估量的;可估计的。**3**. 值得一称的;值得一想的。*a ~ body* 有质体。**II** *n*.〔the ~s〕**1**. 有考虑价值的事件,预先考虑过的事件。**2**. 有重量的东西。

pon·der·ance, ***pon·der·ancy*** [ˈpɔndərəns, -si; ˋpandərəns, -sɪ] *n*. **1**. 重量;重要。**2**. 严重。

pon·der·o·sa (pine) [ˌpɔndəˈrəusə; ˏpandəˋrosə] **1**. 美国黄松(*Pinus ponderosa*)。**2**. 美国黄松木。

pon·der·os·i·ty [ˌpɔndəˈrɔsiti; ˏpandəˋrasətɪ] *n*. 重,沉重;冗长,呆板。

pon·der·ous [ˈpɔndərəs; ˋpandərəs] *a*. **1**. 极重的;沉重的;笨重的。**2**. (谈话、文章等)冗长的,沉闷的(*opp*. light, gay)。**-os·i·ty** *n*. 沉重;冗长,沉闷。**-ly** *ad*. **-ness** *n*.

po·ne[1] [ˈpəuniː; ˋponi] *n*.【牌戏】**1**. (双人牌戏中)发牌者的对手。**2**. (桥牌戏等玩法中的)庄家右边签牌的人。

pone[2] [pəun; pon] *n*.〔美南部〕**1**. (椭圆形)玉米饼(= corn ~)。**2**. 玉米面甜糕。

pong [pɔŋ; paŋ] *vi*., *n*.〔英俚〕发恶臭;名誉臭,坏透,讨厌透(= stink)。

pon·gee [pənˈdʒiː; panˋdʒi] *n*. **1**. 类茧绸的织物。**2**. 茧绸,柞丝绸。**3**. 府绸。~ **silk** 绢。

pon·gid [ˈpɔndʒid; ˋpandʒɪd] *n*. 类人猿科动物。

pon·go [ˈpɔŋgəu; ˋpaŋgo] *n*. (非洲)类人猿;〔俚〕黑猩猩。

pon·iard [ˈpɔnjəd; ˋpanjɚd] **I** *n*.〔古〕短剑,匕首。**II** *vi*., *vt*. 用短剑戳。

Pons [pɔnz; panz] *n*. 庞斯〔姓氏〕。

pons [pɔnz; panz] (*pl*. ***pontes*** [-tiːz;-tiz]) *n*.〔L.〕桥;【解】脑桥。~ ***asinorum*** [-ˌæsiˈnɔːrəm; -æsˋnorem] = asses' bridge〔见 ass 条〕。~ ***Varollii*** [-vəˈrəuliai; -vəˋrolɪaɪ]【解】脑桥。

Pon·tic [ˈpɔntik; ˋpantɪk] *a*. **1**. 庞塔斯(*Pontus*)的〔庞塔斯原为小亚细亚的国家,位于黑海之南〕。**2**. 黑海的。

pon·ti·fex [ˈpɔntiˌfeks; ˋpantəˏfɛks] *n*. (*pl*. ***pon·tifi·ces*** [pɔnˈtifisiːz; panˋtɪfəˏsiz])(古罗马的)最高祭司团成员;教长;大祭司。

pon·tiff [ˈpɔntif; ˋpantɪf] *n*. **1**.【天主】教皇;主教;(古代犹太)大祭司;(古代罗马)高僧团长。**2**. (某一问题的)权威,泰斗;自以为是权威的人。*the Supreme [Sovereign] P-* 罗马教皇。

pon·tif·i·cal [pɔnˈtifikəl; panˋtɪfɪkl̩] **I** *a*. **1**. 教皇[大祭司、主教等]的。**2**. 傲慢武断的。**II** *n*. **1**.〔*pl*.〕主教仪典书。**2**.〔*pl*.〕(天主教的)祭服;(主教的)徽章。*in full ~s* 穿着(教皇)礼服。

pon·tif·i·ca·li·a [pɔnˌtifiˈkeiliə; panˏtɪfɪˋkelɪə] *n*.〔*pl*.〕主教的祭服。

pon·tif·i·cate [pɔnˈtifikit; panˋtɪfɪkɪt] **I** *n*. 教皇[主教、高僧]的职位[任期]。**II** [-keit; -ket] *vi*. **1**. 以主教身份执行(仪式)。**2**. 装作绝对正确的样子;发表武断的意见。

pon·ti·fy [ˈpɔntifai; ˋpantəfaɪ] *vi*. 担任教皇;发挥威权(= pontificate)。

pon·til [ˈpɔntil; ˋpantɪl] *n*. (取熔融玻璃用的)铁杆(= punty)。

Pon·tius Pi·late [ˈpɔntʃəs ˈpailət; ˋpantʃəs ˋpaɪlət] *n*. **1**. 彼拉多〔钉死耶稣的古代罗马的犹太总督〕。**2**.〔美俚〕法官;典当商。

pont·lev·is [pɔntˈlevis, pɔ̃ːlvi; pantˋlɛvɪs, pɔ̃lvɪ]〔F.〕吊桥。

pon·ton [ˈpɔntən; ˋpantn̩] *n*.〔美军〕= pontoon.

pon·to·neer, **pon·to·nier** [ˌpɔntəˈniə; ˏpantəˋnɪr] *n*.【军】架桥兵;浮桥架设人。

pon·toon[1] [pɔnˈtuːn; panˋtun] **I** *n*. **1**.【军】平底船,浮舟〔架浮桥用〕;趸船;浮桥(= ~bridge);浮筒;起重机船;驳船。**2**. (水中工程用)潜水钟[箱];沉箱。**II** *vt*., *vi*. (在…上)架浮桥;用浮桥渡(河)。

pon·toon[2] [pɔnˈtuːn; panˋtun] *n*.〔英〕【牌戏】二十一点。

po·ny [ˈpəuni; ˋponɪ] **I** *n*. **1**. 矮小的马,矮种马;〔口〕矮马。**2**.〔美大学俚〕(特指拉丁文、希腊文的)注释本;考试作弊用的夹带;自学参考书〔*cf*.〔英〕crib〕。**3**.〔英俚〕二十五镑〔主赌博用语〕。**4**. 小杯子,一小杯;小个子女人;小火车头;小型汽车。**5**.〔美〕少量酒。**II** *a*. 小(型)的。***play the ponies***〔美俚〕赌赛马。~ **chorus**〔美〕少女合唱队。~ **engine** 小火车头。~ **express** (美国西部的)用小马快递的邮政制度;〔美〕拉丁文讲座。~ **tail** 少女或妇女的马尾发型。**III** *vt*., *vi*. (**-nied**)〔美俚〕**1**. 用注解书学习。**2**. 支付,清偿(*up*)。

POO, **P.O.O.** = post-office order〔英〕邮政汇票。

pooch [puːtʃ; putʃ] *n*.〔美俚〕狗,(特指)杂种狗。

pood, **poud** [puːd; pud] *n*. 普特〔前苏联衡量单位 = 16.38 公斤〕。

poo·dle [ˈpuːdl; ˋpudl] **I** *n*. (身上毛修剪成球饰状的)长卷毛狗。**II** *vt*. 修剪狗毛使成球饰状。

poof [puf; puːf] *int*. **1**. 喔哟〔表示突然消失或出现的感叹词〕。**2**. 呸! 啐!〔表示焦急、讥笑或轻蔑的感叹词〕(= pooh)。

pooh [puː; pu] *int*. 呸! 啐!〔表示焦急、讥笑、或轻蔑之意〕。

Pooh-Bah [ˈpuːˈbaː; ˏpuˋba] *n*. 公私兼职极多的人〔Gibert 所编歌剧 *The Mikado* 中的人物〕。

poohed [puːd; pud] *a*.〔美俚〕筋疲力尽的,累透的。

pooh-pooh [puːˈpuː, ˈpuˈpuː; puˋpu, ˋpuˋpu] **I** *vt*. 轻视,藐视,瞧不起。*He ~ed the idea*. 他藐视那个意见。**II** *int*. 呸呸! 啐啐! ~ *theory*〔语〕(语言起源的)感叹词说,语言感情反应说。

poo·ja [ˈpuːdʒə; ˋpudʒə] *n*. = puja.

poo·ka, **phoo·ka** [ˈpuːkə, ˈfuːkə; ˋpukə, ˋfukə] *n*.〔爱〕马形妖怪。

poo·koo, **pu·ku** [ˈpuːkuː; ˋpuku] *n*. (中非南部产)红羚羊。

pool[1] [puːl; pul] **I** *n*. **1**. (天然)水坑,水塘;水池子,沉淀池;游泳池;龙潭。**2**.〔美〕油田地带;石油层;瓦斯层;煤坑。**3**.【医】淤血。***the P- (of London)*** 泰晤士河伦敦桥正下面的水域。**II** *vt*. **1**. 在…中形成塘[池];使(血)郁积。**2**. (凿石时)开(楔眼)。**3**. 采(煤等);将(煤)从下面挖掘出来。

pool[2] [puːl; pul] **I** *n*. **1**.〔英〕赌博性质的撞球。**2**. 赌注;放赌注处。**3**. 拼份子赌博;合伙生产[经营、投资](者);合伙人所出的份子。**4**.【剑术】各场接力联战。**5**. 集中备用物资。**6**.〔美俚〕停车场。**II** *vt*. **1**. 合伙经营,合办;以(资金等)入股;集中(智慧等)。**2**. 共享。~ *together our efforts* 协力。—*vi*. 合伙经营。~ **room** **1**. 台球房。**2**. (对在远处举行的赛马、拳击等下注的)公开赌场。~ **table** 撞球桌。

poon, **poon-wood** [puːn, ˈpuːnwud; pun, ˋpunwud] *n*.【植】胡桐〔造船用〕。

poop[1] [puːp; pup] **I** *n*.【海】船尾;船尾楼;船尾楼甲板。**II** *vt*. (浪)冲打(船)尾;使船尾受(浪)冲打。

poop[2] [puːp; pup] *n*., *vt*. = pope[2].

poop[3] [puːp; pup] *n*.〔俚〕蠢货,傻子(= nincompoop)。

poop[4] [puːp; pup] **I** *vi*.〔俚〕放屁;【军俚】开炮(*off*)。**II** *n*.〔俚〕汽车喇叭声;放屁声;炮声。

poop[5] [puːp; pup] *vt*.〔口〕〔常用 *p. p.*〕使筋疲力尽;使喘不过气来。

poop[6] [puːp; pup] *n*.〔俚〕(官方或非官方的)情报,消息。~ *sheet* 专题材料简编。

poop·er [ˈpuːpə; ˋpupɚ] *n*. 翻过船尾的大浪。**~-scoop-**

er〔美〕粪杓。

poor [puə; pʊr] ***a*.** **1.** 穷,贫穷的 (*opp*. rich, wealthy)。**2.** (收获)少,差,不够。**3.** (衣裳)破旧的,不体面的;卑劣的,(酒等)粗劣的;(演说者等)拙劣的。**4.** 萎靡的;不健康的;不愉快的;〔口〕瘦;(身体)弱;(精神)差;(土地)贫瘠的。**5.** 不幸的 (*opp*. fortunate); 不利的 (*opp*. favourable); 已故的,亡…。**6.** 胆小的;可怜的;卑贱的,不足道的,无聊的。*the* ~ 穷苦人;贫民阶级。*urban* ~ 城市贫民。*a* ~ *crop of apples* 苹果歉收。*a* ~ *three days' holiday* 仅仅三天假。*a* ~ *£1 a week* 一星期仅一镑。*a* ~ *ore* 贫矿,~ *soil* 瘠地。*in my* ~ *opinion* 愚见以为。照我的肤浅看法。~ *in spirit* 懦弱的;卑怯的。*a* ~ *conductor* 不良(电)导体。~ *digestion* 消化不良。~ *health* 身体虚弱。~ *pens* 劣笔。*a* ~ *speech* 拙劣的演说。~ *So-and-so* 已故某某。*the* ~ *man's side* (*of the river*)〔口〕(伦敦泰晤士河)南岸。*a* ~ *crumb* [*potato*]〔美〕没趣的人。*My* ~ *old mother used to say* ... 先母常常说…。~ *fellow* [*thing*]! 可怜虫。~ *house* 贫民院,养育院。***as*** ~ ***as a church mouse*** = ***as*** ~ ***as Job's turkey*** 穷到极点;一贫如洗。***have a*** ~ ***chance for*** 做[得]某事[物]的机会不大。***have a*** ~ ***memory*** 记意力不好。~ **box** (教堂的)济贫捐款箱。~ **law** 贫民救助法,济贫法。~ **pay**〔美〕经济上信用不佳的人。~ **rate** 救贫税。~**-spirited** ***a*.** 胆小的,懦弱的。~ **white** (**trash**) (美国南部各州)穷苦的白种人。

poor·ly **I** ***pred*., *a*.** 〔口〕身体不舒服。*He is* (*looking*) *very* ~. 他身体好像很不好。**II** ***ad*.** 下贱;没有大成就;贫穷;不体面;不够;贫弱;拙劣。~ ***off*** 日子不好过。***think*** ~ ***of*** 不佩服,不认为好。

poor·mouth [puəˈmauθ; purˋmauθ] ***vi*.** 〔口〕哭穷。—***vt*.** 把…说得一钱不值。

poor·ness [ˈpuənis; ˋpurnɪs] ***n*.** 贫穷;缺乏;拙劣;不够;粗劣,卑劣;不毛,硗瘠。~ *of supply* 供给差。~ *of character* 人格卑劣。

POP = printing-out paper【摄】(利用光照直接显影的)印相纸。

pop[1] [pɔp; pɑp] **I** ***vi*.** (*-pp-*) **1.** 砰砰地响;劈劈拍拍地响;砰的一声打出去 (*at*); 爆裂。**2.** 突然进去[出去],突然动起来 (*in*; *out*; *up*)。**3.** (眼珠)突出。~ *into one's mind* 忽然想起来。—***vt*.** **1.** 使砰砰的响;开枪打,砰的一声打。**2.**〔美〕(将玉米等)炒爆。**3.** 突然伸出[推动、放下] (*in*, *out*; *down*)。**4.**〔英俚〕典当,抵押。~ *a question* 突然提出质问。~ *corn* 炒玉米。~ ***in*** 突然进去,突然访问。~ ***off*** 突然出去;忽然不见;突然死掉 (~ *off the hooks*〔口〕死掉)。~ ***out*** (火,把火)突然灭掉;突然伸出;〔俚〕(突然)死掉。~ ***the question***〔口〕(乘机向女方)要求结婚;求婚。**II** ***n*.** **1.** 砰,劈劈拍拍(声);枪声;开枪;〔口〕手枪。**2.**〔口〕汽水,香槟酒(等)。**3.** 斑点〔羊等的记号〕。**4.**〔英俚〕典当。**5.**〔美俚〕爸爸;〔口〕大爷,老爹。~ ***quiz***〔美〕突然而来的考试。***in*** ~ (东西)在当铺里。**III** ***ad*.** 砰地(一声);突然,出其不意地。*go* ~ 砰地一声响;死掉;破掉。~ **corn** 玉米花;炒用玉米。~**-eyed** ***a*.** 〔美〕突眼的,眼球突出的;(吓得)睁大了眼睛的。~ **fly**【棒球】内野飞球。~ **gun** 纸枪,木塞枪,汽枪;【蔑】没有用[打不出]的枪。~**-off** 大声讲话的人;乱说乱讲的人。~ **over** (加奶油馅的)薄空心松饼。~**-rock** 流行摇摆舞音乐。~ **shop**〔俚〕当铺。~ **test**〔美俚〕突然袭击式的测验。~**-up**【棒球】内野飞球 (= pop fly)。~ **valve**【机】突开阀。~ **wine**〔美〕(苏打)汽酒。

pop[2] [pɔp; pɑp] **I** ***a*.** 〔口〕流行的;普及的;大众的;演唱流行歌曲的。**II** ***n*.** 流行音乐〔popular music 之略〕。*a* ~ *concert*〔美〕大众音乐会〔主要演奏半古典派音乐或古典派轻音乐〕。~ **culture** 大众文化。~ **dao** [**trio**]〔美〕流行性的双重唱双人戏[三重唱、三人戏]。~ **warbler**【美】流行歌星。

pop. = population; popular(ly)。

Pope [pəup; pop] ***n*.** **1.** 波普〔姓氏〕。**2.** **Alexander** ~ 蒲伯〔1688—1744,英国诗人〕。

pope[1] [pəup; pop] ***n*.** **1.** 〔有时作 P-〕罗马教皇。**2.** 教皇一样的人〔自认为或被认为一贯正确的人〕。**3.** (希腊正教的)教区牧师。**-dom** **1.** 罗马教皇的职权[管区、领地、在职的时期等]。**2.** 教皇政治。**3.**〔蔑〕= popery.

pope[2] [puːp; pup] **I** ***n*.** (一打就极痛或发麻的)腿的要害处。*take sb.'s* ~ 打某人腿上要害处。**II** ***vt*.** 〔常用 *p.p.*〕打(某人)腿上要害处。

pop·er·y [ˈpəupəri; ˋpopərɪ] ***n*.** 〔蔑〕罗马天主教教义;天主教教皇制度。

pope's-eye [ˈpəups-ai; ˋpops-aɪ] ***n*.** (牛、羊等的)腿部淋巴腺。

pope's-head [ˈpəupshed; ˋpopshɛd] ***n*.** 长柄笤帚。

pope's-nose [ˈpəupsnəuz; ˋpopsˏnoz] ***n*.** 【烹】(煮熟的)鸡[鸭、家禽的]屁股。

pop·in·jay [ˈpɔpindʒei; ˋpɑpɪnˏdʒe] ***n*.** **1.** 爱漂亮的人;花花公子;自负的人。**2.**〔英方〕绿毛啄木鸟;〔古〕鹦鹉;杆上的鸟形靶子。

pop·ish [ˈpəupiʃ; ˋpopɪʃ] ***a*.** 〔蔑〕罗马天主教教义的;教皇制度的。

pop·lar [ˈpɔplə; ˋpɑplɚ] ***n*.** 【植】杨属植物;白杨;杨木。*the white* [*silver*] ~ 银白杨。*the Chinese white* ~ 毛白杨。*the Lombardy* ~ 钻天杨,毛杨。*the trembling* ~ = aspen.

Pop·lar·ism [ˈpɔplərizəm; ˋpɑplərˏɪzəm] ***n*.** 救济过多的济贫政策。

pop·lin [ˈpɔplin; ˋpɑplɪn] ***n*.** 府绸;毛葛。~ *broché* 织花府绸;织花毛葛。*cotton* ~ 棉府绸。

pop·lit·e·al, pop·lit·ic [pɔpˈlitiəl, pɔpˈlitik; pɑpˋlɪtɪəl, pɑpˋlɪtɪk] ***a*.** 【解】腿弯部的,腘窝部的。

pop·pa [ˈpɔpə; ˋpɑpə] ***n*.** 〔美俚〕爸爸。

pop·per [ˈpɔpə; ˋpɑpɚ] ***n*.** **1.** 〔美〕爆玉米的锅。**2.** 爆破者。**3.** 爆竹,枪。**4.** 炮手,射手。

pop·pet [ˈpɔpit; ˋpɑpɪt] ***n*.** **1.** 〔方〕玩偶;〔英方〕宝宝〔对小孩的爱称〕。**2.**【机】(车圆的)托架;提升阀;【海】(船竣工入水时的)垫架,支架;船弦桨架垫片。~**head**【机】随转尾座。

pop·pied [ˈpɔpid; ˋpɑpɪd] ***a*.** **1.** 罂粟多的;用罂粟装饰的。**2.** 起麻醉作用的。**3.** 被麻醉了的;昏昏睡的。

pop·ping [ˈpɔpiŋ; ˋpɑpɪŋ] **I** ***n*.** **1.** 爆音。**2.**【板球】打球员线 (= ~ crease)。**II** ***a*.** **1.** (眼睛)鼓出的。**2.** 间歇的。**3.** 活跃的。

pop·ple [ˈpɔpl; ˋpɑpl] **I** ***vi*.** (海水等)起泡沫;波动;忽沉忽浮;荡漾着微波流动。**II** ***n*.** 波动,涟漪。

pop·py[1] [ˈpɔpi; ˋpɑpɪ] ***n*.** 【植】罂粟属植物;鸦片;芙蓉红。*the field* [*red*] ~ 虞美人。*the garden* ~ 观赏罂粟。*the opium* ~ 可制鸦片的罂粟。*the Californian* ~ 金英花。~ **cock**〔美俚〕胡话,废话 (*the* ~ *cock season*【棒球】春天练球季)。~ **head** 罂粟的头;【建】罂粟状装饰;顶花饰〔特指教堂座位上的〕。

pop·py[2] [ˈpɔpi; ˋpɑpɪ] ***n*.** 〔美俚〕爸爸 (= popea)。

pop·si·cle [ˈpɔpsikl; ˋpɑpsəkḷ] ***n*.** 〔美俚〕**1.** 冰棍,棒冰。**2.** = motorcycle.

pop·sy(-wop·sy) [ˈpɔpsi(wɔpsi); ˋpɑpsɪ(wɑpsɪ)] ***n*.** 〔称呼〕好宝宝〔尤指女孩〕。

pop·u·lace [ˈpɔpjuləs; ˋpɑpjəlɪs] ***n*.** 人民,老百姓;大众;〔蔑〕下层民众,群氓。

pop·u·lar [ˈpɔpjulə; ˋpɑpjəlɚ] **I** ***a*.** **1.** 人民的,民众的,大众的,民间的。**2.** 通俗的,普通的,平易的。**3.** 有人望的,得人心的,有名气的;受欢迎的;流行的;大众化的;(民间)流传的;便宜的,低廉的。**4.**〔美俚〕自以为了不得的,骄傲的。*the* ~ *voice* 群众呼声。*the* ~ *front* [*P-Front*] 人民阵线。*a* ~ *edition* 普及版,廉价版。~ *election* 普选。*a* ~ *hero* 众望所归的英雄。~ *lectures* 通俗讲话。~ *prices* 廉价。~ *science* 通俗科学。*a* ~

song 流行歌曲。*a* ～ *writer* 受人欢迎的作家。*He is* ～ *in society*. 他在社会上是有名望的。*be* ～ *with* 受…欢迎,在…间名声好。*in* ～ *language* 用普通话;用通俗语言。**II** *n*. 大众音乐会 (= ～ concert)。**-ly** *ad*. 一般地,普通地;通俗地;通过民众地。

pop·u·lar·es [ˌpɔpjuˈlɛəriːz; ˏpɑpjəˋlɛriz] *n*. 〔L.〕〔*pl*.〕(古罗马的)民众。

pop·u·lar·i·ty [ˌpɔpjuˈlæriti; ˏpɑpjəˋlærətɪ] *n*. 名气,名望;通俗性;大众性;流行;普及。*enjoy general* ～ 享盛名,受欢迎,得众望。

pop·u·lar·i·za·tion [ˌpɔpjuləraiˈzeiʃən; ˏpɑpjələraɪˋzeʃən] *n*. 通俗化,简单化;普及,推广。

pop·u·lar·ize [ˈpɔpjuləraiz; ˋpɑpjələˏraɪz] *vt*. 使通俗化;使大众化;推广,使普及;使流行,使受欢迎。**-er** 1. 普及者,推广者。2. 普及读物。

pop·u·late [ˈpɔpjuleit; ˋpɑpjəˏlet] *vt*. 使人口聚居在…中;移民于;殖民于;居住于…中。*densely* [*sparsely*] ～*d* 人口稠密[稀少]的。— *vi*. (人口)繁殖,增加。

pop·u·la·tion [ˌpɔpjuˈleiʃən; ˏpɑpjəˋleʃən] *n*. 1. 人口;人口总数;全体居民;人口的聚居。2. 物的全体[总数];【生】虫口;种群(量);群体;族,组,个数;【统】对象总体,全域。3. 【物】布居;密度。4. 〔罕〕殖民。*varietal* ～*s* 品种群体。～ **dynamics** 群体动态。～ **biology** 群体生物学〔研究动植物群体的分布情况等〕。～ **explosion** 人口爆炸,人口骤增。

pop·u·lous [ˈpɔpjuləs; ˋpɑpjələs] *a*. 人口稠密的,人口多的;挤满的。**-ly** *ad*. 人口稠密地。**-ness** *n*. 人口稠密。

p.o.r. = pay on return【商】返回后付款。

por·bea·gle [ˈpɔːˌbiːgl; ˋpɔrˏbigḷ] *n*. 【鱼】青鲛,鼠鲨。

porce·lain [ˈpɔːsəlin, -lein; ˋporslɪn, -len] **I** *n*. 瓷(料);〔总称〕瓷器。**II** *a*. 1. 瓷(器)的。2. 精美的。3. 脆的;易碎的。*electrical* ～ 绝缘瓷。*a* ～ *shell*【动】宝贝属贝类;玛瑙贝。*a* ～ *insulator*【电】陶瓷绝缘子。～ **clay** 瓷土,高岭土。～ **enamel** 搪瓷。～ **glaze** 瓷釉。

porce·lain·ize [ˈpɔːsəlinaiz; ˋporslɪnˏaɪz] *vt*. 1. 把…做成瓷器。2. 涂瓷于(金属器皿)。

porce·lain·ous, por·cel·la·ne·ous, por·cel·lan·ic, por·cel·la·nous [ˈpɔːsəlinəs, ˌpɔːsəˈleiniəs, -səˈlænik, pɔːˈselənəs; ˋporsəlɪnəs, ˏporsəˋlenɪəs, -səˋlænɪk, porˋselənəs] *a*. 瓷器(似)的,瓷质的。

porch [pɔːtʃ; portʃ] *n*. 1. (有顶棚的)门廊,大门内停车处,门口。2. 〔美〕走廊,游廊。3. 【无】(脉冲)边沿。4. 〔the P-〕公元前4世纪斯多噶派哲学家芝诺 (Zeno)对弟子讲学的柱廊;斯多噶学派,斯多噶哲学。～ **climber** 〔美〕小偷。**-ed** *a*. 有门廊的。

por·cine [ˈpɔːsain; ˋporsaɪn] *a*. 猪的;像猪的;肮脏的。

por·cu·pine [ˈpɔːkjupain; ˋporkjəˏpaɪn] *n*. 1. 【动】豪猪,箭猪。2. 【纺】梳麻机。～ **anteater**【动】食蚁蝟,针鼹。～ **fish**【动】鱼虎,针鲀。～ **grass**【植】大蓟。

pore[1] [pɔː, pɔə; por, por] *vi*. 1. 注视,细看。2. 用心阅读;细心研究 (*on*; *over*)。3. 沉思,默想。— *vt*. 因凝视过度而使(眼睛)疲劳。～ *one's eyes out* 因读书过度以致眼睛疲劳。

pore[2] [pɔː; por] *n*. 毛孔;气孔,细孔。**at every** ～ 全身,浑身。**sweat from every** ～ 1. 极热。2. (因害怕、兴奋等)冒汗,受惊,兴奋。

por·gy [ˈpɔːdʒi; ˋporgɪ] *n*. (*pl*. ～, **por·gies**)【动】大西洋鲷;钉头鱼;尖口鲷。

po·rif·er·an [pɔːˈrifərən, pə-; poˋrɪfərən, pə-] **I** *n*. 海绵动物门[多孔动物门] (*Porifera*) 动物。**II** *a*. 海绵动物门的,多孔动物门的。

po·rif·er·ous [pɔːˈrifərəs; poˋrɪfərəs] *a*. 1. 有孔的。2. 【动】多孔动物的,海绵动物的。

po·rism [ˈpɔːrizəm; ˋporɪzṃ] *n*. 【数】不定命题定理;(希腊几何学的)系,系论。

pork [pɔːk; pork] *n*. 1. 猪肉〔尤指未腌过的〕。2. 〔古〕猪(= hog, swine)。3. 〔美俚〕支持政党上台所分到的好处,政治分肥。*mess* ～ 上好猪肉。***P- chops hang high***. 〔美〕萧条的冬季又来了。～ **barrel**〔美俚〕(议员为讨好支持者而私给的)政治分肥〔如促使政府拨款用于地方的水利、公共建筑等福利事项〕。～ **butcher** (杀猪的)屠户。～ **chop** 猪排。～ **chopper**〔美俚〕被会员认为是只图私利的工会领导人。～ **pie** 1. 猪肉馅饼。2. 卷边低平顶毡帽(= porkpie hat)。

pork·er [ˈpɔːkə; ˋporkɚ] *n*. 食用猪;肥小猪。

pork·et [ˈpɔːkit; ˋporkɪt] *n*. 乳猪,小猪。

pork·ling [ˈpɔːkliŋ; ˋporklɪŋ] *n*. 小猪,乳猪。

pork·y [ˈpɔːki; ˋporkɪ] *a*. 猪肉(一样)的;〔口〕肥的。

porn, por·no [pɔːn, ˈpɔːnəu; porn, ˋporno] *n*. = pornography.

por·nog·ra·phy [pɔːˈnɔgrəfi; porˋnɑgrəfɪ] *n*. 春宫,春画;色情文学[电影];娼妓风俗志。**por·no·graph·ic** [ˌpɔːnəˈgræfik; ˏpornəˋgræfɪk] *a*.

por·o·mer·ic [ˌpɔːrəˈmerik; ˏporəˋmɛrɪk] *n*. 一种人造革〔常用作鞋、行李箱、腰带等的面子〕。

po·ro·plas·tic [ˌpɔrəuˈplæstik; ˏpɑroˋplæstɪk] *a*. 多孔而可塑的。

po·ros·i·ty [pɔːˈrɔsiti; poˋrɑsətɪ] *n*. 1. 多孔性。2. 【物】孔积率;孔度,隙度。3. 多孔部分;多孔结构;多孔的东西。

po·rot·ic [pəˈrɔtik; pəˋrɑtɪk] **I** *a*. 【医】多孔性的;(骨质)疏松的。**II** *n*. 治骨折药,促生骨痂药。

por·ous [ˈpɔːrəs; ˋporəs] *a*. 1. 多孔的;有气孔的;〔喻〕漏洞多的。2. 能渗透的。3. 素烧(瓷)的。**-ly** *ad*. **-ness** *n*.

por·phyr·a·tin [pɔːˈfiərətin; porˋfɪrətɪn] *n*. 【化】卟啉的金属络合物。

por·phyr·i·a [pɔːˈfiəriə; porˋfɪrɪə] *n*. 【医】卟啉病。

por·phy·rin [ˈpɔːfərin; ˋporfərɪn] *n*. 【生化】卟啉(类)。

por·phy·rit·ic [ˌpɔːfiˈritik; ˏporfɪˋrɪtɪk] *a*. 【地】斑岩的,斑状的。

por·phy·roid [ˈpɔːfirɔid; ˋporfəˏrɔɪd] *n*. 【矿】残斑岩。

por·phy·rop·sin [ˌpɔːfiˈrɔpsin; ˏporfɪˋrɑpsɪn] *n*. 【生化】视紫质。

por·phy·ry [ˈpɔːfiri; ˋporfərɪ] *n*. 【地】斑岩。

por·poise [ˈpɔːpəs; ˋporpəs] **I** *n*. 1. 【动】海豚。2. 前后振动;波动。*a school of* ～*s* 一群海豚。**II** *vi*. 1. (船)在水面急行。2. (鱼雷)在水面急驶。

por·rect [pəˈrekt; pəˋrɛkt] **I** *a*. (平)伸出的;延伸的。**II** *vt*. 1. 伸出。2. 〔教会法用语〕提出(文书等)。

por·ridge [ˈpɔridʒ; ˋpɔrɪdʒ] *n*. 〔英〕1. 粥,稀饭,麦片粥。2. (肉菜加大麦等煮的)汤。***do one's*** ～〔英俚〕服刑期。***keep*** [***save***] ***one's breath to cool one's*** ～ 省点力气少开口,少说话〔说也无用〕。

por·ri·go [pəˈraigəu; pəˋraɪgo] *n*. 【医】头疮,发癣。

por·rin·ger [ˈpɔrindʒə; ˋpɔrɪndʒɚ] *n*. 粥碗,汤钵;(供儿童用的)单柄金属浅杯[浅碗]。

port[1] [pɔːt; port] *n*. 1. 港;港口;〔喻〕避难港;避难所,休息处。2. (特指有海关的)港市;输入港;通商口岸。3. 机场,航空站。*a close* ～〔英〕河港。*a free* ～ 自由港。*a naval* ～ 军港。*an open* ～ 1. 对外贸易港。2. 不冻港。*a warmwater* [*an ice-free*, *a non-freezing*] ～ 不冻港。*clear a* ～ 出港。*enter* ～ 入港。*in* ～ 在港,停泊中的。*leave* (*a*) ～ = clear a ～. *make* [*reach*] (*a*) ～ 入港。*P- Arthur* 旧时外国人对我国旅顺港的称呼。～ *of arrival* 到达港。～ *of call* (沿途)停靠港。～ *of coaling* 装煤港。～ *of delivery* 卸货港,交货港。～ *of departure* 出发港。～ *of destination* 到达港,目的港。～ *of discharge* [*unloading*] 卸货港。～ *of distress* 避难港。～ *of embarkation* 启航港。～ *of entry* 进口港。～ *office* 港务局。～ *of registry* 船籍港。～ *of sailing* 启航港。～ *of shipment* 装货港。*touch* (*at*) *a* ～ 靠港。**any** ～ **in a storm** 遇难时任何港口都是好的;〔喻〕穷途之策。～ **admiral**〔英〕军港司令。～ **bar** 河[港]口的洲;港口防材;装货口门闩。～ **charges**

P

〔*pl.*〕入港税。～ **town** 港市。

port[2]〔pɔːt; port〕*n*. 1.（从前军舰上的）炮门；【海】（商船的）上货口，舱门；（船边的）舷窗。2.〔Scot.〕门，入口；城门。3.（工事等的）射击孔；炮眼；枪眼；展望口。4.【机】汽门，汽口；水门。5.【徽】门印。*an exhaust* ～【机】排气口。*a stream* ～【机】汽门。～**hole** 1. 射击孔；炮眼。2. 舷窗；舱口。

port[3]〔pɔːt; port〕I *n*. 1. 态度；举止，样子，风采。2. 含意；意义。3.【军】持枪姿势〔枪筒向上，自左肩至右胯斜持枪〕。II *vt*. 1. 持（枪）。2.〔古〕搬运。***P- arms!***〔口令〕持枪。

port[4]〔pɔːt; port〕I *n*.（船、飞机的）左舷（*opp*. starboard）。*the* ～ *watch* 床位在左舷的船员的值班。*a* ～ *engine* 左侧发动机。*a* ～ *plane*〔*wing*〕左翼。***on the*** ～ ***bow*** 在左舷船首。***on the*** ～ ***quarter*** 在左舷船尾。***put the helm to*** ～ 转左舷。II *vt*.〔主要作命令语〕转（舵）向左〔使船头右转〕。—*vi*. 转舵向左。***P- the helm!***〔命令〕左舵！～**side** *a*. 左边的；左派的；〔美俚〕惯用左手的。～**sider**〔美俚〕左撇子；【垒球】左手投手。

port[5]〔pɔːt; port〕*n*.（葡萄牙）（红）葡萄酒〔有时也作褐色或白色酒（＝～ wine）〕。

port[6]〔pɔːt; port〕*vt*.【计】移植〔无需修改即将软件等原样转移至另一系统〕。

Port. = Portugal; Portuguese.

port. = portable.

porta-, porto- *pref*. 表示"便携式的，轻便的，手提式的"之意。

por·ta·bil·i·ty〔ˌpɔːtəˈbiliti; ˏportəˋbɪlətɪ〕*n*. 可携带性，轻便。

port·a·ble〔ˈpɔːtəbl; ˋportəbl̩〕I *a*. 可搬运的；便于携带的；手提式的，轻便的。*a* ～ *barometer* 轻便晴雨表。*a* ～ *railway* 轻便铁路。II *n*. 1. 手提式打字机〔收音机、电视机〕。2. 便携式电脑。3. 活动房屋。**-a·bly** *ad*.

port·age〔ˈpɔːtidʒ; ˋportɪdʒ〕I *n*. 1. 搬运；运输。2. 搬运物，货物。3. 水陆联运，联运路线。4.〔古〕运费。*the mariner's* ～（船上准许水手存放所带私货的）物品寄存处〔旧时常以此种方式代替付水手工资〕。II *vt*., *vi*. 在连水陆路间搬运（船、货物）。

Por·tal〔ˈpɔːtəl; ˋportl̩〕*n*. 波特尔〔姓氏〕。

por·tal〔ˈpɔːtəl; ˋportl̩〕I *n*. 1.（大建筑物的）入口；正门；桥门；隧道门。2.〔诗〕门，入门。3.【解】门静脉。4.【计】网络出入口，门户站点〔指万维网上提供查寻服务的网站〕。II *a*.【解】门的；肝门的；门静脉的，关于门脉的。～ *vein* 门脉，门静脉。～**-to-**～ 按照从进厂矿到出厂矿的全部时间计算的。～**-to-**～ **pay** 进出厂统含的计时工资。

por·ta·men·to〔ˌpɔːtəˈmentəu; ˏportəˋmɛnto〕*n*.（*pl*. ***-ti***〔-ti; tɪ〕）〔It.〕【乐】滑音，延音。

port·ance〔ˈpɔːtns; ˋportns〕*n*.〔古〕人的行为，举止或品格。

por·ta·tive〔ˈpɔːtətiv; ˋportətɪv〕*a*. 1. 可携带的；可搬运的。2. 有力搬动的；用作支撑的。3.〔古〕携带用的。

Port-au-Prince〔ˌpɔːtəuˈprins; ˏportoˋprɪns〕*n*. 太子港〔海地首都〕。

port·cul·lis〔pɔːtˈkʌlis; portˋkʌlɪs〕I *n*.（城堡的）吊闸，吊门。II *vt*. 1. 在…上装吊门。2. 用吊门关闭。

Port-de-France〔pɔːtdəˈfrɑːns; portdəˋfrɑns〕*n*. 法兰西堡〔尼提尼克岛首府〕。

Porte〔pɔːt; port〕*n*.（帝制时代的）土耳其政府（＝the Sublime ～ 或 the Ottoman ～）。

porte-co·chère〔ˈpɔːtkəuˈʃεə; ˋportkəˋʃɛr〕*n*.〔F.〕车辆出入门道；门内停车处。

port(e)·cray·on〔pɔːtˈkreiən; portˋkreən〕*n*.〔F.〕粉笔或蜡笔的（金属）笔夹。

por·temon·naie〔ˈpɔːtˌmʌni; ˏportˏmɔˋnɛ〕*n*.〔F.〕皮夹子；小钱包。

por·tend〔pɔːˈtend; porˋtɛnd〕*vt*. 成为…的前兆，预示，预兆；给…以警告。*Black clouds* ～ *a storm*. 乌云为暴风雨的前兆。

Por·te·ño〔pɔːˈteinjəu; porˋtenjo〕*n*. 布宜诺斯艾利斯〔阿根廷首都〕人。

por·tent〔ˈpɔːtent; ˋportɛnt〕*n*. 1. 预兆，凶兆；不祥之兆。2. 怪事，怪物；奇迹。

por·ten·tous〔pɔːˈtentəs; porˋtɛntəs〕*a*. 1. 预兆的；不吉的。2. 可惊的，怪异的；奇特的；可怕的。3.〔谑〕（沉默等）严肃的。4.〔蔑〕自命不凡的；妄自尊大的。**-ly** *ad*.

Por·ter〔ˈpɔːtə; ˋportɚ〕*n*. 波特〔姓氏，男子名〕。

por·ter[1]〔ˈpɔːtə; ˋportɚ〕*n*. 看门人，门房。

por·ter[2]〔ˈpɔːtə; ˋportɚ〕*n*. 1. 搬运工人；〔车站〕行李搬运员；（大饭店等中的）服务员；〔美〕卧车〔餐车〕服务员。2.（银行、商店中的）杂务工，清洁工。*a* ～*'s knot* 搬运工肩垫。～**house**〔美〕1.（从前的）小酒馆；饭馆。2. 上等牛排（＝～house steak）。

por·ter[3]〔ˈpɔːtə; ˋportɚ〕*n*.〔英〕黑啤酒（＝～'s beer）。

por·ter·age〔ˈpɔːtəridʒ; ˋportərɪdʒ〕*n*. 1. 搬运（行李）；搬运业。2. 搬运费。

port·fire〔ˈpɔːtfaiə; ˋportˏfaɪr〕*n*.（烟火、烽火、矿山用炸药等的）点火装置，导火筒，引火具。

port·fo·li·o〔pɔːtˈfəuljəu, -liəu; portˋfolɪo, -lɪo〕*n*.（*pl*. ～*s*）1. 纸夹；文件夹；公事包。2. 部长〔大臣〕的职位。3.〔美〕有价证券一览表〔明细表〕；（保险）业务量〔业务责任〕。4.（艺术家等的）代表作选辑。*a minister without* ～ 不管部部长〔大臣〕。***hold the*** ～ 担任部会政务委员。～ **insurance**【经】有价证券保险〔指在股票落价时即将股票期货售出的策略〕。

Port Harcourt〔pɔːt ˈhɑːkət; portˋhɑrkət〕哈科特港〔尼日利亚港市〕。

Por·tia〔ˈpɔːʃjə; ˋporʃɪə〕*n*. 1. 波西娅〔女子名〕。2. 莎士比亚剧《威尼斯商人》中的女主人翁；〔喻〕女律师。

por·t·i·co〔ˈpɔːtikəu; ˋportɪˏko〕*n*.（*pl*. ～(*e*)*s*）【建】（有圆柱的）门廊。

por·tière〔pɔːˈtjεə; ˏportɪˋɛr〕*n*.〔F.〕门帘，门帷。

por·tion〔ˈpɔːʃən; ˋporʃən〕I *n*. 1. 一部分。2. 一份，一般；（饭菜）一客。3.【法】分得的财产。4. 嫁妆，妆奁。5.〔仅用单数〕命运。*one* ～ *of roast beef* 烤牛肉一客。*a* ～ *of*（*land*）一部分地，若干（土地）。II *vt*. 1. 把…分成份额；分配（*out*）。2. 给…嫁妆。3. 命运注定。**-less** *a*. 得不到分配物的〔尤指遗产〕的；没有嫁资的。

Port·land〔ˈpɔːtlənd; ˋportlənd〕*n*. 1. 波特兰〔姓氏〕。2. 波特兰〔美国港市〕。3. 波特兰监狱〔英国 *Dorsetshire* 的监狱〕（＝～ prison）。～ **cement** 水泥。～ **stone**（英国波特兰岛产的）建筑用石灰石，波特兰石。

port·li·ness〔ˈpɔːtlinis; ˋportlɪnɪs〕*n*. 肥胖；魁伟。

Port Louis〔ˈpɔːt ˈluː(ː)i(s); ˋport ˋlu(ʊ)ɪ(s)〕路易港〔毛里求斯首都〕。

port·ly〔ˈpɔːtli; ˋportlɪ〕*a*. 1. 肥胖的；粗壮的；魁梧的。2.〔方〕仪表堂堂的。*a* ～ *belly* 罗汉肚，大肚子。*a lady of* ～ *presence* 身量肥胖的女人。

port·man·teau〔pɔːtˈmæntəu; portˋmænto〕I *n*.（*pl*. ～***s***，～***x***〔-z; -z〕）1.（两开绞合）旅行皮包〔皮箱〕。2.〔喻〕（两词音义合并的）混成词〔＝～ word; 如 Oxbridge 由 Oxford 和 Cambridge 二字组成〕。II *a*. 多用途的；多性质的。

Port Mores·by〔pɔːt ˈmɔːzbi; portˋmorzbɪ〕莫尔斯比港〔巴布亚新几内亚首府〕。

Por·to〔ˈpɔːtu; ˋportʊ〕*n*. 波尔图〔葡萄牙港市〕。

Port-of-Spain〔ˈpɔːtəvˈspein; ˋportəvˋspen〕*n*. 西班牙港〔特立尼达和多巴哥首都〕。

Porto-Novo〔ˈpɔːtəuˈnəuvəu; ˋportoˋnovo〕*n*. 波多诺伏〔贝宁首都〕。

Por·to Ri·can〔ˌpɔːtəuˈriːkən; ˋportəˋrikən〕*a*., *n*. 波多黎各岛的（人）。

Por·to Ri·co〔ˌpɔːtəu ˈriːkəu; ˏportəˋriko〕*n*. 波多黎各岛〔在西印度群岛〕。

por·trait [ˈpɔːtrit; ˋportret] ***n*.** **1.** 肖像,肖像画;相片。**2.** 雕像;半身像。**3.** 人物描写;生动的描绘。**4.** 类型,模型,标本。~ **painter** 肖像画家。

por·trait·ist [ˈpɔːtritist; ˋportretɪst] ***n*.** 肖像画家,肖像制作者;摄影者。

por·trai·ture [ˈpɔːtritʃə; ˋportrɪtʃɚ] ***n*.** **1.** 肖像画法。**2.** 肖像画;照相;肖像画集。**3.** 生动的描绘;(人物)描写(法)。*in* ~ 所描写的。

por·tray [pɔːˈtrei; porˋtre] ***vt*.** **1.** 画(人物、风景),画(肖像)。**2.** 描绘;描写;描述。**3.** 【剧】扮演,饰演。

por·tray·al [pɔːˈtreiəl; porˋtreəl] ***n*.** **1.** 画;描写,叙述。**2.** 画像;肖像。

port·reeve [ˈpɔːtriːv; ˋportˏriv] ***n*.** **1.** 【英史】市长;(现在英国某些市镇的)副市长;执行官;副镇长。**2.** 港市的长官。

por·tress [ˈpɔːtris; ˋportrɛs] ***n*.** **1.** 女看门人,女门房。**2.** 女杂务工;女帮工。

Port Sa·id [ˈpɔːt ˈsaid; portˋsed] 塞得港〔埃及港市〕。

Port-Sa·lut [ˈpɔːsæˈluː, F. pɔːrsaˈly; ˋporsæˋlu, porsaˋly] ***n*.** 一种半硬全脂黄乳酪(=port du salut)。

Ports·mouth [ˈpɔːtsməθ; ˋportsməθ] ***n*.** 朴次茅斯〔英国、美国港市〕。

Port Sudan [ˈpɔːt su(ː)ˈdɑːn; ˋport su(ʊ)ˋdɑn] 苏丹港〔苏丹港市〕。

Port Swettenham [ˈpɔːt ˈswetnəm; ˋportˋswetnəm] 巴生港〔即瑞天咸港,马来西亚港市〕。

Por·tu·gal [ˈpɔːtjugəl; ˋportʃəgl̩] ***n*.** 葡萄牙〔欧洲〕。

Por·tu·guese [ˌpɔːtjuˈgiːz; ˋportʃəˏgiz] **I** ***a*.** 葡萄牙的;葡萄牙人的;葡萄牙语的。**II** ***n*.** 葡萄牙人[语]。~ **man-of-war** 【动】僧帽水母。

por·tu·lac·a [ˌpɔːtjuˈlɑːkə, -ˈlækə; ˏportjəˋlɑkə, -ˋlækə] ***n*.** 【植】半支莲(*Portulaca grandiflora*)。

Port Vila [pɔːt ˈviːlə; portˋvilə] ***n*.** 维拉港〔新赫布里底群岛首府〕。

POS = point of service 保健服务点。

pos. = positive; possessive.

po·sa·da [pɔːˈsɑːðɑː; poˋsɑdə] ***n*.** (*pl*. ~*s* [-ðɑːs; -ðɑs]) (Sp.) 小旅馆,客栈。

P.O.S.B. = Post-Office Savings Bank 邮政局储蓄银行。

pose[1] [pəuz; poz] **I** ***n*.** **1.** (画像、表演、拍照时的)姿态,姿势。**2.** 心理状态,精神状态。**3.** 矫揉造作;装腔作势;伪装。**4.** (玩骨牌戏时)打的第一张牌。*His diligence is a mere* ~. 他的勤奋不过是装样子罢了。***a dramatic*** [*stage*] ~【剧】亮相。***strike*** [***put on***] ***a*** ~ 装腔作势。**II** ***vi*.** **1.** 采取某种态度[姿态]。**2.** 做作,装腔作势;极力装作…,冒充(*as*)。**3.** (玩骨牌戏时)打第一张牌。—***vt*.** **1.** (艺术家)使(模特儿等)作某种姿势;使…摆好姿势;把…摆正位置。**2.** 拿出(要求等);提出(问题)。~ **... against ...** 把…同…对立起来。~ ***for a photograph with*** 摆好姿势同…合影。

pose[2] [pəuz; poz] ***vt*.** 盘问;(提出难题)难住(人)。

Po·sei·don [pɔˈsaidən; poˋsaɪdn̩] ***n*.** 【希神】**1.** 波塞顿〔海神〕。**2.** 海神式导弹(=~ missile)。

Po·sen [ˈpəuzən; ˋpozən] ***n*.** =Poznan.

pos·er[1] [ˈpəuzə; ˋpozɚ] ***n*.** 装腔作势的人;伪装者。

pos·er[2] [ˈpəuzə; ˋpozɚ] ***n*.** **1.** 提出难题的人;考试员。**2.** 难题;怪题。

po·seur [pəuˈzəː; poˋzɝ] ***n*.** 〔F.〕=poser[1].

po·sey [ˈpəuzi; ˋpozɪ] **I** ***n*.** =posy. **II** ***a*.** 装门面的,矫饰的。

posh [pɔʃ; pɑʃ] **I** ***a*.** 〔英俚〕**1.** 亮晶晶的;漂亮的,优雅的;时髦的;最好的;第一流的。**2.** 豪华的;奢侈的。**II** ***vt*.** 把…打扮起来(*up*)。**III** ***int*.** 呸〔表示蔑视〕。~**-looking** ***a*.** 漂亮的。**-ism** ***n*.** 奢侈主义。**-ly** ***ad*.** **-ness** ***n*.**

pos·it [ˈpɔzit; ˋpɑzɪt] **I** ***vt*.** **1.** 〔主用被动语态〕安置,布置;安排。**2.** 【逻】断定;论断;假定。**II** ***n*.** **1.** 安置。**2.** 论断。

posit. = position; positive.

po·si·tion [pəˈziʃən; pəˋzɪʃən] **I** ***n*.** **1.** 位置;方位;地点。**2.** 处境,情况;状态,形势,局面。**3.** 姿态,姿势。**4.** 地位,身份;职位;职务。**5.** 态度,观点,立场;见解;论点,主张;命题。**6.** (音节中的)元音位置。**7.** 【军】发射阵地;阵地;战略要点。**8.** 【乐】(左手在提琴指板上的)把位。*the neutral* ~【汽车】空挡。*people of* ~ 有身份的人们。*What is the* ~ *of the affairs?* 形势怎么样? *a directory* ~ (电话)查号台。*The* ~ *was stormed*. 阵地遭受猛袭。~ *warfare* 阵地战。***a ready*** ~【军】射击准备姿势。***be in a*** ~ ***to*** 在可以…的地位;能够…。***be in*** ~ 在应有位置,在适当地位,无障碍;照规定姿势。***be out of*** ~ 不在应有位置,有障碍;未照规定姿势。***get*** [***go***] ***into*** ~【军】进入阵地。***in my*** ~ 在我的立场;(对于)像我这样立场的(人)。***jockey for*** ~ **1.** (赛马时)挤其他骑师以占有利位置。**2.** 〔喻〕以(欺诈)手段图谋私利。***maneuver for*** ~ 调动军队争取有利地位。***put sb. in a false*** ~ 使(某人)处于违反原则行事[被误解]的地位。***presume on one's*** ~ 倚仗地位。***take up the*** ~ ***that ...*** 主张…。**II** ***vt*.** **1.** 把…放在适当位置;规定…的位置,给…定位。**2.** 【军】屯(兵),驻扎(部队)。~ **buoy** 雾标,指示浮标。~ **light** (飞机的)指示灯;锚位灯。~ **paper** 表明对问题所持见解的论文。

po·si·tion·al [pəˈziʃənəl; pəˋzɪʃənl] ***a*.** **1.** 位置(上)的;地位的。**2.** 【军】阵地的。~ *warfare* [*fighting*]【军】阵地战。~ **error** (钟表等的)位置误差。

pos·i·tive [ˈpɔzətiv, -zi-; ˋpɑzətɪv, -zɪ-] **I** ***a*.** **1.** 确实的,明确的;确定的;无条件的(*opp*. qualified, implied, inferential);绝对的,无疑问的,断然的。**2.** 有自信的;过分自信的,独断的。**3.** 积极的;建设性的;肯定的(*opp*. negative)。**4.** 〔口〕十足的,纯粹的。**5.** 现实的,实在的,实际的(*opp*. speculative, theoretical)。**6.** 【物、数】正的;【物】阳性的;【化】盐基性的。**7.** 【摄】正片的。**8.** 【哲】实证的。**9.** 【语法】原级的。**10.** 【生】(刺激源)向性的,趋性的。**11.** 〔用作表语[主词补语]〕一定,确信(*to do*; *that*)。~ *proof* [*evidence*] 确实的证据。*a* ~ *fact* 无可怀疑的事实。~ *orders* 绝对命令,强制的命令。*a* ~ *sort of person* 刚愎自用的人。*a* ~ *mind* 实事求是的人。*Are you sure? Yes, I'm* ~. 真的吗?当然了。*She is* ~ *to come tomorrow*. 她明天一定来。*I am* ~ *that he is right*. 我确信他说的对。***in a*** ~ ***way*** 从正面,由积极方面。***be*** ~ ***about*** [***of***] 确信,确知(~ *of the approach of a violent revolutionary storm* 确信一场猛烈的革命风暴的来临)。**II** ***n*.** **1.** 实在;确实;明确性;绝对性;积极性;正面。**2.** 【语法】原级。**3.** (电池的)阳极;【摄】正片。**4.** 【数】正量。~ **adjective** [**adverb**] 原级形容词[副词]。~ **charge** 【物】阳电荷。~ **check** 【经】积极限制。~ **column** 【电】阳辉区,阳极区。~ **degree** 【语法】原级。~ **electricity** 阳电,正电。~ **law** 【法】成文法。~ **number** 【数】正数。~ **organ** **1.** (管风琴的)伴唱键盘。**2.** 座式管风琴。~ **philosophy** 实证哲学,实证论。~ **pole** 正极,阳极。~ **pressure** 【机】正压力。~ **rays** 【理】阳射线,正电射线。~ **reaction** 阳性反应;正反应;正反力。~ **sign** 【数】正号〔即 +〕。**-ly** ***ad*.** 确实,必定;断然;绝对,积极。**-ness** ***n*.** = positivity.

pos·i·tiv·ism [ˈpɔzitivizəm; ˋpɑzətɪvˏɪzəm] ***n*.** **1.** 【哲】〔通例 P-〕实证哲学;实证论;实证主义。**2.** 明确性,确实性;积极性。

pos·i·tiv·ist [ˈpɔzitivist; ˋpɑzətɪvɪst] ***n*.** 实证论者;实证主义者。

pos·i·tiv·i·ty [ˌpɔziˈtiviti; ˏpɑzəˋtɪvətɪ] ***n*.** **1.** 确实;确信;积极性。**2.** 【物】正性。

pos·i·tron [ˈpɔzitrɔn; ˋpɑzɪˏtrɑn] ***n*.** 【物】正子,阳电子,正电子。

pos·i·tro·ni·um [ˌpɔziˈtrəuniəm; ˏpɑzɪˋtronɪəm] ***n*.**

【电】电子偶素,阳[正]电子素。

po·sol·o·gy [pəuˈsɔlədʒi; pəˋsɑlədʒɪ] *n*.【医】配药学,剂量学。**pos·o·log·ic** [ˌpɔsəˈlɔdʒik; ˏpɑsəˋlɑdʒɪk] *a*. **po·sol·o·gist** [-ˈsɔlədʒist; -ˋsɑlədʒɪst] *n*. 配药学家。

poss. = 1. possession. 2. possessive. 3. possible. 4. possibly.

pos·se [ˈpɔsi; ˋpɑsɪ] *n*. 1. 武装队;(警察等的)一队;【法】民兵,民团 (= ~ comitatus)。2.〔口〕乌合之众,暴徒。3. 可能性;潜在力。*in* ~ 可能地。~ **comitatus** [ˌkɔmiˈtɑːtəs; ˏkɑmɪˋtɑtəs] (州长、郡长等可随时召集的)地方民团。

pos·sess [pəˈzes; pəˋzɛs] *vt*. 1. 具有(能力、性质等),掌握(知识等);据有,占有,拥有(财产、房屋等);使占有,使拥有 (*of*, *with*)。2. (鬼等)缠,附;(情欲等)迷住。3. (在身心方面)克制,抑制;保持(镇定等);维持(平衡等)。4. 使沾染 (*with*); 使被任意摆布,支配(人)。*What ~es you to do such a thing*? 你怎么干出那样的事情来了? ~ *one's mind in peace* 使人心胸保持宁静。***be ~ed*** 被(鬼等)缠上,迷住。***be exclusively ~ed by*** 在…把持下。***be ~ed by*** [***with***] 被(鬼怪、思想等)缠住,迷住。***be ~ed of*** 拥有,据有。***like all ~ed*** 〔美〕疯狂地,猛烈地,拚命地,热烈地。***like one ~ed*** 像着了魔的人一样。~ ***oneself*** 自制,镇静。~ ***oneself of*** 获得;据有,把…占为己有。~ ***one's soul in patience*** 硬是耐着性子等待。~ ***sb***. ***of sth***. 使某人占有[拥有]某物。

pos·ses·sion [pəˈzeʃən; pəˋzɛʃən] *n*. 1. 有,所有,拥有;【法】占有。2.〔*pl*.〕占有物,所有物;〔*pl*.〕财产;所有权。3.〔常 *pl*.〕领地,属地,殖民地。4. 着迷,着魔。5. (足球等比赛中某一队员的)暂时控制住球。6.〔罕〕自制,泰然自若。*a man of great ~s* 大财主。*personal ~s* 个人财物。*The keys are in his* ~. 钥匙他拿着。*He is in full* ~ *of his senses*. 他显得极泰然自若。***come into sb.'s*** ~ , ***come into the*** ~ ***of sb***. 被某人占有,落入某人手中。***come into*** ~ ***of sth***. 获得[占有]某物。***get*** ~ ***of*** 拿到,占有,占领。***in*** ~ (物)被据有;(人)据有。***in*** ~ ***of sth***. 占有某物。***in the*** ~ ***of sb***. 为某人所有。***P- is nine points of the law***. 现实占有,败一胜九〔指在诉讼中占有者总占上风〕。***rejoice in the*** ~ ***of*** 幸而有…。***take*** ~ ***of*** 占领,占有 (*He took* ~ *of his new house*. 他已住进他的新房子了)。***the man in*** ~ 占有者,封查执行官。~**-minded** *a*. 贪心的,想把一切据为己有的。

pos·ses·sive [pəˈzesiv; pəˋzɛsɪv] **I** *a*. 1. 所有的,占有的,占有欲的;表示所有的。2.【语法】(词、词组、形态变化等)所属关系的,所有格的。**II** *n*.【语法】〔the ~〕所有格;所有格的词,物主代词,(表示)所属关系的词(或词组等)。*the* ~ *case*【语法】所有格,属格。~ **adjective**【语法】所有格形容词。~ **pronoun**【语法】物主代词。**-ly** *ad*. **-ness** *n*.

pos·ses·sor [pəˈzesə; pəˋzɛsɚ] *n*. 持有人,占有人,所有人。

pos·ses·so·ry [pəˈzesəri; pəˋzɛsərɪ] *a*. 占有的;所有(者)的;所有性的。*a* ~ ***action*** 确认所有权的诉讼。*a* ~ ***title to land*** 土地占有权。

pos·set [ˈpɔsit; ˋpɑsɪt] *n*. 牛奶甜酒〔热牛奶加酒等,旧时常用以治感冒等〕。

pos·si·bil·i·ty [ˌpɔsəˈbiliti; ˏpɑsəˋbɪlətɪ] *n*. 1. 可能,可能性。2.〔常 *pl*.〕可能(发生)的事情;〔*pl*.〕希望。***a bare*** ~ 万一的事情。***be within*** [***out of***] ***the bounds*** [***range***] ***of*** ~ …是可能[不可能]的。***by any*** ~ 1. 万一,也许〔带条件词〕。2. 决不会〔带否定词〕。***by some*** ~ 或许,也许。***There is no*** ~ ***of***... 没有…的希望[可能]。

pos·si·ble [ˈpɔsəbl; ˋpɑsəbl] **I** *a*. 1. 可能有的,也许会有[发生]的;潜在的。2. 可能实行的,做得到的,想得到的。3. 合理的,可以允许的。4.〔口〕相当的,不坏的;可以接受的;还算过得去的。*all the assistance* ~ 一切可能支援。*the highest* ~ *speed* 最大速度。*It is* ~ *that he knows*. 他也许知道。***a*** ~ ***person*** 能胜任(做某事)的人。***as ... as*** ~ 尽量…,尽可能…。***if*** ~ 可能的话。~ ***of*** 可能…的。***with the least delay*** ~ 尽快。**II** *n*. 1. 〔the ~〕可能性,潜在性。2.〔常 *pl*.〕可能的人[物],可能有的事。3. (射击等中)最高分。4.〔*pl*.〕〔俚〕必需物品;金钱。5. 候补人,预备队员,生力军。6. 全力。*~s to probables* 预备队员对候补队员。***do one's*** ~ 尽全力。***score a*** ~ (射击等中)得最高分。

pos·si·bly [ˈpɔsəbli; ˋpɑsəblɪ] *ad*. 1. 可能地;合理地。2. 或者,也许。3. 无论如何,万万,不管怎样〔用于否定句和疑问句〕。*He may* ~ *recover*. 他也许会好。*I cannot* ~ *do it*. 那件事我无论如何也不能做。

pos·sum [ˈpɔsəm; ˋpɑsəm] **I** *n*.〔美口〕鼩,负鼠 (= opossum)。***come*** ~ ***over sb***.〔口〕欺骗某人,瞒哄某人。***play*** [***act***] ~ 装死;装病;装傻;假装不知。**II** *vi*.〔美口〕= play ~. ~ **belly**〔美俚〕火车车箱底下的贮藏室;车辆底部的藏物处。

pos·sy [ˈpɔsi; ˋpɑsɪ] *n*.〔军俚〕阵地〔position 的缩略语〕。

Post [pəust; post] *n*. 波斯特〔姓氏〕。

post[1] [pəust; post] **I** *n*. 1. 柱,桩,杆;标竿。2. (赛马等)起跑标,终点标;【矿】矿柱;煤柱;厚砂岩层;厚石灰岩层。3. (剑桥大学的)不及格榜。4. (枪的)准星。5.【计】黏贴的文字,贴子。*a lamp* ~ 路灯杆。*a sign* ~ 标竿。***be in the wrong*** [***right***] ***side of the*** ~ 干得不对[对]。***beat sb. at the*** ~【赛跑】最后一刻胜过某人。***between you and me and the*** ~ 你知我知,切勿外泄。***deaf as a*** ~ 全聋。***kiss the*** ~ 深夜回来被关在门外。~ ***and railing*** 木栅。**II** *vt*. 1. 把(布告等)贴在(柱子等)上 (*up*); 贴出(布告等);【计】(在网上)黏贴(文章等),把…贴上公告板,公布。2. 公布(某船迟到、行踪不明等)。3. (出布告)公开揭发[谴责]。4. 把…登入榜;(剑桥大学)贴出(不及格榜)。5.〔美〕公告(地内)禁猎;(出布告等)禁止进入(某地)。***P- no bills***. (此处)禁止招贴。~ ***one's land***〔美〕贴告示地内禁猎。~**-mill** 风车。

post[2] [pəust; post] **I** *n*. 1.〔主英〕邮政;邮寄;(一批)邮件 (*cf*.〔美〕mail); 邮件的一次发送[收进]。2. 邮政法,邮政制度。3.〔英〕邮政局;邮筒;信箱。4.〔方〕邮递员;快件递送员;邮车;驿站,驿馆;〔古〕驿马。5.〔英〕(20×16 英寸的)信笺尺寸。6. …邮报[作报名]。*I had a heavy* ~ *yesterday*. 我昨天收到很多邮件。*Take the letter to the* ~. 请把这封信投到邮筒里。*the Washington P-* 华盛顿邮报。~ ***and telecommunication*** 邮电。***by*** ~ 由邮寄 (*send by* ~ 邮寄)。***by return of*** ~【史】回信请交来人带回;(现指)由下一班回程邮递带回。***catch*** [***miss***] ***the*** ~ 赶上[没有赶上]发信时间。**II** *vt*. 1.〔主英〕邮寄,投邮。2. 用驿马送,急送。3. 誊(账),过(账);登入(总账)。4.〔通例用被动语态〕使熟悉;使了解,使懂得(新知识等)。— *vi*. 1.〔古〕骑驿马旅行。2. 赶紧走,飞快走过。3.【马术】跟着马动。***be well ~ed up*** [~ ***oneself up***] ***in*** 通晓,熟悉。~ ***off*** [***over***] 赶紧出发。~ ***up sales*** 把销售金额登入总账。**III** *ad*. 用急件[驿马];赶紧地,火速的。*ride* ~ 骑驿马赶路;催马快跑。~ **bag**〔英〕邮袋。~ **boat**〔英〕邮船;客船。~ **box**〔英〕信箱;邮筒。~**boy** 1. 邮递员。2. = postilion. ~ **card**〔英〕(不需贴邮票的邮局发行)官制明信片 (=〔美〕postal card); (非邮局发行的)商制明信片〔附有图画,需贴邮票〕。~ **chaise**〔古〕驿马车。~**code** 1. *n*. 邮政编码。2. *vt*. 为(某一邮区)提供邮政编码。~**-free** *a*. 免邮费的;邮费付讫的。~**haste** *n*., *ad*. 赶紧,火速,火急。~**-horn** (18、19 世纪)驿车上用的喇叭。~**-horse** 驿马。~ **house** 驿馆。~**man** 邮递员,邮差。~**-mark** 1. *n*. 邮戳。2. *vt*. (将邮票)盖销。~**master** 邮政局长。~**mistress** 女邮政局长。~ **office** 邮政局 (*a* ~ *office box* 邮政信箱〔略 P.O.B.〕。*a* ~ *office order* 邮政汇票〔略 P.O.O.〕。*a* ~ *office savings bank* 邮政储金局。

a ~ *office stamp* 邮政日戳)。~**-paid** ***a***. 邮费付讫的。~**rider** 1.(过去)骑马投送邮件的人,驿使。2. 邮政。~ **road** 驿路。~ **time** 邮件递送[到达、截止]时间;邮件收发时间。~ **town** 有邮局的市镇;(备有驿马的)驿站。

post[3][pəust; post] **I** ***n***. 1.(被指定的)地位,岗位;职位,职守。2.【军】哨所,站;哨兵警戒区;〔转义〕哨兵,卫兵。3. 基地,驻(屯)地;兵营;营区。4.【美军】守备队;复员军人分会。5.(特种股票)交易所。6.【英军】(睡眠)熄灯号。7. 商埠;贸易站;租界。*a radar* ~ 雷达哨。*the* ~ *of duty* 工作岗位,职守。*a vigorous, militant command* ~ 朝气蓬勃的战斗指挥部。*the first* ~ 头遍熄灯号〔九点半〕。*the last* ~ 末次熄灯号〔十点〕。***at one's*** ~ 在任所;在岗位上。***fill*** (***up***) ***a*** ~ 就任。***hold a*** ~ ***at*** 在…任职。***keep the*** ~ 守住岗位。***resign*** [***remain at***] ***one's*** ~ 退[留]职。***proceed to one's*** ~ 赴任。***take*** ~ 各就各位。***stick to one's post*** 坚守岗位。**II** ***vt***. 1. 配置(哨兵等)。2.【英史】任命(20 门炮以上舰船的舰长等)。3.(隆重地)把(国旗)带往指定地。4. 把…作赌注。~ **captain**【英史】小军舰的舰长。~ **exchange**〔美军〕营地服务商店〔略作 PX〕。

post [pəust; post] ***ad***.〔L.〕在后。~ ***bellum*** [ˈbeləm; ˋbɛləm] 战后。~ ***factum*** [ˈfæktəm; ˋfæktəm] 事后。~ ***meridiem*** [məˈridiəm; məˋrɪdɪəm] 午后〔略作 P.M., p.m., PM〕。~ ***mortem*** [ˈmɔːtem; ˋmɔrtɛm] 死后;事后。~ ***obitum*** [ˈɔbitəm; ˋɑbɪtəm] 死后。

post. = postal.

post- *pref*. 表示"后,次": *post*axial, *post*war.

post·age [ˈpəustidʒ; ˋpostɪdʒ] ***n***. 邮费。~ *due* 欠(邮)资。~ *free* 邮寄免费。~ *paid* 邮费付讫。*inland* ~ 国内邮资。~ **stamp** 邮票。~ **meter**(加盖"邮资已付"的)自动邮资盖印机。

post·al [ˈpəustəl; ˋpostl̩] **I** ***a***. 邮政的;邮政局的。*The International* [*Universal*] *P- Union* 万国邮政联盟。**II** ***n***.〔美口〕明信片。~ **card**〔美〕(邮局制的)明信片〔上面印有邮票〕。~ **clerk**〔美〕邮局运员。~ **course** 函授课程。~ **insurance** 简易保险。~ **matters** 邮件。~ **order**〔英〕邮政汇票。~ **package** 小包邮件。~ **savings** 邮政储金。

post·al·i·za·tion [ˌpəustəlaiˈzeiʃən; ˏpostəlaɪˋzeʃən] ***n***.(像邮费那样)远近运费均一化。

post·a·tom·ic [ˈpəustəˈtɔmik; ˏpostəˋtɑmɪk] ***a***. 第一颗原子弹爆炸之后的;原子能发现以后的。

post·ax·i·al [pəustˈæksiəl; postˋæksɪəl] ***a***.【解,动】轴后的。

post-bel·lum [pəustˈbeləm; postˋbɛləm] ***a***. 战后的;美国南北战争以后的。

post·ca·va [ˌpəustˈkeivə, -kɑː-; ˏpostˋkevə, -kɑ-] ***n***. (*pl*. **-vae** [-viː; -vi])【解】后腔静脉。**-l** ***a***.

post-clas·si·cal [ˈpəustˈklæsikəl; ˋpostˋklæsɪkl̩] ***a***.(希腊、罗马文学艺术的)古典时代后的。

post·date [ˈpəustˈdeit; ˏpostˋdet] **I** ***vt***. 1. 把日期填迟(若干天);在…上填事后日期,填迟…的日期。2. 在…之后到来,接在…的后面。**II** [ˈpəustdeit; ˋpostdet] ***n***.(证券等的)事后日期,比实际填迟的日期(*opp*. predate)。

post·di·lu·vi·an [ˌpəustdaiˈluːviən; ˏpostdɪˋljuvɪən] ***a***., ***n***.(基督教《圣经》中所说)世界大洪水(Deluge)之后的(人)。

post·doc·tor·al [ˌpəustˈdɔktərəl; ˏpostˋdɑktərəl] ***a***. 博士后的(取得博士学位后从事更高深研究的);从事比博士级工作更高深的研究工作的。

post·en·try [ˈpəustˌentri; ˋpostˏɛntrɪ] ***n***. 1.(赛马)后补手续书。2.【簿】补记账目。

post·er[1] [ˈpəustə; ˋpostɚ] **I** ***n***. 1.(贴在墙壁等上的)广告(画);海报,标语,招贴。2. 贴标语[广告、传单等]的人。**II** ***vt***. 贴[传单、广告等];用招贴宣传。~ **child** [**boy, girl**]代表(人物),典型(人物)〔指海报等上的人物形象〕。

post·er[2] [ˈpəustə; ˋpostɚ] ***n***. 1. 驿马。2.〔古〕急件递送员;匆匆忙忙的旅客。

poste res·tante [ˈpəustˈrestɑ̃ːnt; ˏpostrɛsˋtɑnt]〔F.〕1.(信封上附注的)留局待领邮件。2.〔主英〕(邮局的)待领邮件科;待领邮件业务。

pos·te·ri·or [pɔsˈtiəriə; pɑsˋtɪrɪɚ] **I** ***a***.(地位上)后面的(*opp*. anterior);(时间上)在后的,(次序上)其次的(*to*)(*opp*. prior);【动】尾部的;【解】背部的;【植】接近茎轴处的。~ *to the year 1972* 一九七二年以后的。*various events that happened* ~ *to the end of the war* 战后继之发生的种种事件。**II** ***n***. 1. 后部。2.〔*sing*.,〔古〕*pl*.〕臀部,屁股。**-ly** ***ad***. 在后部,在背后。

pos·te·ri·or·i·ty [pɔsˌtiəriˈɔriti; pɑsˏtɪrɪˋɑrətɪ] ***n***.(时间、位置、次序上的)在后。

pos·ter·i·ty [pɔsˈteriti; pɑsˋtɛrətɪ] ***n***.〔集合词〕1. 后裔,子孙。2. 后世,后代。*write for* ~ 为后代写作。

pos·tern [ˈpəustəːn; ˋpostɚn] ***n***. 1.(城、教堂等的)后门,边门;便门。2. 边道;(城堡的)地下暗道;逃路。

post·face [ˈpəusfis; ˋposfɪs] ***n***.(刊物等的)编后记。

post·fix [ˈpəustfiks; ˋpostfɪks] **I** ***n***. 1. 后加物。2.【语法】后缀词尾。**II** [pəustˈfiks; postˋfɪks] ***vt***. 把…加在后面;加后缀于;加词尾于。

post·form [pəustˈfɔːm; postˋfɔrm] ***vt***. 把(加工后的薄板材)再制成一定形状。

post·gan·gli·on·ic [ˌpəustˌgæŋgliˈɔnik; ˏpostˏgæŋglɪˋɑnɪk] ***a***.【解】后神经节的。

post·gla·cial [ˈpəustˈgleisjəl; postˋgleʃəl] ***a***. 冰期后的。

post·grad·u·ate [ˈpəustˈgrædjuit, Am. ˈpəu*st*ˈgrædʒuit; ˋpostˋgrædjuɪt, postˋgrædʒuɪt] **I** ***a***. 大学毕业后的;大学研究院的。*the* ~ *course* 研究学科。*the* ~ *research institute* 研究院。*a* ~ *student* 研究生。**II** ***n***. 研究生。

post hoc, er·go prop·ter hoc [ˈpəusthɔkˈəːgəuˈprɔptəhɔk; ˋposthɑkˋɚgoˋprɑptəhɑk]〔L.〕在此之后,因此。

post·hu·mous [ˈpɔstjuməs; ˋpɑstʃuməs] ***a***. 1. 父死后生的,遗腹的。2. 著作者死后出版的。3. 身后的,死后的。*a* ~ *child* 遗腹子。*one's* ~ *name* 讳,谥号。~ *works* 遗著。***confer*** ~ ***honours on*** 追赠,谥封,追认…为。**-ly** ***ad***. 死后,身后。

post·hyp·not·ic [ˌpəusthipˈnɔtik; ˏposthɪpˋnɑtɪk] ***a***. 催眠后的,进入昏睡状态后的时期的。~ **suggestion**【医】催眠后暗示。

pos·tiche [pɔsˈtiːʃ; pɔsˋtiʃ] **I** ***a***.〔F.〕1. 伪造的,假冒的,人为的,人造的。2. 过分装饰的。**II** ***n***. 1. 代替物;伪造物。2. 虚假;矫饰。3. 假发。4.(建筑物等上的)多余的添加物,画蛇添足似的东西。

pos·ti·cous [pɔsˈtaikəs; pɑsˋtaɪkəs] ***a***.【植】在后的;外附的。

pos·til [ˈpɔstil; ˋpɑstɪl] ***n***.(基督教《圣经》的)旁注;注解。

pos·til·(l)i·on [pəsˈtiljən; poˋstɪljən] ***n***.(四马以上马车的)前排左马骑手,左马驭者。

post·im·pres·sion·ism [ˈpəustimˈpreʃənizəm; ˏpostɪmˋprɛʃənɪzm] ***n***.【美】后期印象派。**-sion·ist** 1. ***n***.【美】后期印象派画家。2. ***a***. 后期印象派的。

post·li·min·i·um, post·lim·i·ny [ˌpəustliˈminiəm, -ˈlimini; ˏpostlɪˋmɪnɪəm, -ˋlɪmɪnɪ] ***n***.【国际法】战后财产恢复权;【罗马法】(俘虏等回国后的)公民资格恢复权。

Post-it, Post-It [ˈpəu*st*it; ˋpo*st*ɪt] ***n***.〔商标〕玻斯提〔一种边沿涂有不干胶的便条纸,可随贴随撕下〕。

post·lude [ˈpəustljuːd; ˋpostˏlud] ***n***. 1.【乐】(*opp*. prelude)后奏曲;尾曲;(乐曲的)结尾部。2. 教堂做礼拜后的风琴独奏。

Post·mas·ter-Gen·er·al [ˈpəu*st* mɑːstəˈdʒenərəl; ˋpo*st* mɑstɚˋdʒɛnərəl] ***n***.〔英〕邮政大臣;〔美〕邮政部长。

post·me·rid·i·an [ˈpəustməˈridiən; ˏpostməˋrɪdɪən] ***a***.

午后的,午后发生的(*opp*. antemeridian)。

post·mil·len·ni·al [ˌpəustmiˈleniəl; ˌpostməˋlɛnɪəl] ***a***. 【宗】一千至福年(millennium)后的。

post·mil·len·ni·al·ism [ˌpəustmiˈleniəlizəm; ˌpostməˋlɛnɪəlˌɪzəm] ***n***. 【宗】一千至福年后基督再临说。

post-mor·tem [ˈpəustˈmɔːtəm; ˌpostˋmɔrtəm] **I** ***a***. **1**. 死后的。**2**. 事后的。*a* ~ *table* 验尸台。**II** ***n***. **1**. 尸体解剖,验尸。**2**. 事后的调查分析(= ~ examination)。

post·na·tal [ˈpəustˈneitl; postˋnetḷ] ***a***. 出生后的;初生婴儿的。

post·na·tus [ˈpəustˈneitəs; ˋpostˋnetəs] ***n***. (*pl*. ***-nati*** [-ˈneitai; -ˋnetaɪ]) **1**. 某大事件后出生的人;发表《独立宣言》(1776年)后出生的美国人。**2**. 〔废〕〔*sing*.〕次子。

post·nup·tial [ˈpəustˈnʌpʃəl; postˋnʌpʃəl] ***a***. 结婚后的。**-ly** ***ad***. 婚后。

post-o·bit [ˈpəustˈɔbit, Am. pəustˈəubit; postˋobɪt, ˋpostˋɑbɪt] **I** ***a***. 死后生效的。**II** ***n***. 死后偿还借据〔以应得遗产做抵押的借据〕(= ~ bond)。

post·or·bit·al [ˌpəustˈɔːbitl; ˌpostˋɔrbɪtḷ] **I** ***a***. 【解,动】眶后的。**II** ***n***. 眶后骨。

post·op·er·a·tive [ˈpəustˈɔpərətiv, -ˈɔprə-, -əreitiv; postˋɑpərətɪv, -ˋɑprə-, -əretɪv] ***a***. 手术后的。**-ly** ***ad***.

post·par·tum [ˌpəustˈpɑːtəm; ˌpostˋpartəm] ***a***. 产后的。

post·pone [pəustˈpəun; postˋpon] ***vt***. **1**. 使延期,延缓;搁置(*until*, *till*, *to*, *for*)。**2**. 把…视为次要,把…放在次要地位(*to*)。**3**. 【语法】把(某种词等)放在后面[句尾]。— ***vi***. 【医】(疟疾等)延迟发作[复发]。*postponing of military service* 缓役。**post·pon·a·ble** ***a***. 可延缓的。**-r** ***n***. 延迟者,使延缓者。**-ment** ***n***. 延期,延迟;搁置。

post·po·si·tion [ˈpəustpəˈziʃən; ˌpostpəˋzɪʃən] ***n***. **1**. 【语法】后置词。**2**. 后置。**-al** ***a***.

post·pos·i·tive [ˈpəustˈpɔzitiv; postˋpɑzətɪv] **I** ***a***. 【语法】置于词后的,附加于另一词的;与前词接合的;词尾的。**II** ***n***. 【语法】后置词。**-ly** ***ad***.

post·pran·di·al [ˈpəustˈprændiəl; postˋprændɪəl] ***a***. 〔谑〕饭后的。

post·sce·ni·um [ˈpəustˈsiːniəm; ˋpostˋsinɪəm] ***n***. (戏院的)后台。

post·script [ˈpəusskript, ˈpəuskript; ˋpos·skrɪpt; ˋposkrɪpt] ***n***. **1**. (信的)再者,又及;附言〔略作 P.S., PS., PS 或 p.s.〕。**2**. (书等的)补遗,附录;跋。**3**. 英国广播协会(B.B.C.)新闻报告的结束语。

post-synch [ˈpəustsiŋk; ˋpostsɪŋk] ***vt***., ***vi***. (为电影)后期录音[配音]。

pos·tu·lant [ˈpɔstjulənt; ˋpɑstʃələnt] ***n***. **1**. 【宗】圣职[牧师职]申请人。**2**. 〔罕〕申请者。

pos·tu·late [ˈpɔstjuleit; ˋpɑstʃəˌlet] **I** ***vt***. **1**. (认为当然而)主张,(认为自明之理而)假定;(作为先决条件而)要求。**2**. 【宗】要求上级任命[指定]。**3**. 根据上级批准而任命[指定]。**4**. 【数】公设,假设。*the claims* ~*d* 要求事项。— ***vi***. 假定;要求(*for*)。**II** [ˈpɔstjulit; ˋpɑstʃəlɪt] ***n***. **1**. 假定。**2**. 基本要求;先决[必要]条件。**3**. 【数】公设,假设;(作图的)公准。**4**. 基本原理。

pos·tu·la·tion [ˌpɔstjuˈleiʃən; ˌpɑstʃəˋleʃən] ***n***. **1**. 假定。**2**. 要求。**3**. 【宗】须经上级批准的任命[指定]。**-al** ***a***.

pos·tu·la·tor [ˈpɔstjuˌleitə; ˋpɑstʃəˌletɚ] ***n***. **1**. 假定者。**2**. 要求者。**3**. (要求批准圣职的)申请人。

pos·ture [ˈpɔstʃə, -tjuə; ˋpɑstʃɚ, -tjʊr] **I** ***n***. **1**. 姿势,姿态;态度。**2**. 精神准备;心情,心境。**3**. 形势,情形(*of*)。*a* ~ *of defense* 守势。*the present* ~ *of affairs* 目前形势,时局。**II** ***vt***. 使作出某种姿态[态度]。— ***vi***. 取某种姿势[态度];故作姿态。~**-maker** 杂技演员。~**-master** 柔软体操教师。**pos·tur·al** ***a***.

pos·tur·er [ˈpɔstʃərə; ˋpɑstʃərɚ] ***n***. **1**. 作出某种姿态的人;装腔作势者。**2**. 杂技演员。

pos·tur·ize, pos·tur·ise [ˈpɔstʃəraiz; ˋpɑstʃərˌaɪz] ***vi***. 取某种姿势,装作…的样子(*as*)。

post·vac·cin·al [ˌpəustˈvæksinəl; ˌpostˋvæksɪnəl] ***a***. 【医】种牛痘后的,接种后的。

post·war [ˈpəustˈwɔː; ˋpostˋwɔr] ***a***. 战后的(*opp*. prewar)。~ *problems* 战后问题。

po·sy [ˈpəuzi; ˋpozɪ] ***n***. **1**. 花束。**2**. 〔古〕(刻在戒指里圈上的)诗句,题铭。

pot [pɔt; pɑt] **I** ***n***. **1**. 壶,瓶,罐;钵,(深)锅。**2**. 【冶】坩埚。**3**. 一壶[钵、瓶、罐、锅]之量。**4**. 壶中物;酒;饮酒;酗酒。**5**. 花盆;尿壶;罐状物;烟囱罩;捕鱼篓,捕虾笼;〔美俚〕高顶帽子。**6**. 〔俚〕(赌钱时的)巨款;赌注总额;(一个团体的)基金总额;纸牌戏的一局。**7**. 〔俚〕大人物;大肚子。**8**. 【运】银杯,银盾,奖品。**9**. $15\frac{1}{2}\times12\frac{1}{2}$英寸大小的纸张。**10**. 【地质】壶穴,水穴。**11**. 〔美俚〕电位计。**12**. 〔俚〕(地狱的)深渊。**13**. 〔俚〕近距离射击,随手射击(= ~-shot)。**14**. 〔美俚〕大麻叶。*a big* ~ 要人,名人。*brazen and earthen* ~*s* 阔老和穷人;名人和无名小卒。*A little* ~ *is soon hot*. 壶小易热;量小易怒;人小火气大。*A watched* ~ *never boils*. 心急水不沸。***betray the*** ~ ***to the roses*** 露出马脚,泄露秘密。***boil the*** ~ 挣钱糊口,谋生。***call each other*** ~ ***and kettle*** 互相谩骂。***crush a*** ~ 设宴。***go into the melting*** ~ 经受锻炼。***go to*** ~ 〔俚〕没落,(营养等)衰弱;被毁坏;垮掉;破产;毁灭。***If you touch*** ~, ***you must touch penny***. 一律不赊。***in one's*** ~, ***in the*** ~ 喝醉。***make a*** ~ ***of money*** 发大财。***make one's*** ~***s and pans of one's property*** 败尽财产去讨饭。***make the*** ~ ***boil***, ***keep the*** ~ ***boiling*** **1**. 谋生,维持生活,挣钱糊口。**2**. 保持热度,继续猛干;兴致勃勃(玩下去)。~***s and pans*** 炊事用具,瓶瓶罐罐。***put a quart into a pint*** ~ 白费劲,做不可能的事。***put the*** ~ ***in*** 在…中发大财。***put the*** ~ ***on*** 在…上赌巨款。***The*** ~ ***calls the kettle black***. 乌鸦骂猪黑,只知责怪别人而不知自己有同样的缺点或过失。***take a*** ~ ***at*** (***a bird***) 用枪乱打(鸟)。

II ***vt***. (***-tt-***) **1**. (用锅等)煮,炖。**2**. 把…装入壶内[罐内](保存)。**3**. 把…栽在花盆里。**4**. 删节;摘录。**5**. (为取得食物)而向(动物)射击;乱射;猎获;〔口〕得到。**6**. 【台球】把(球)打入袋内。~ *an heiress* 〔俚〕得到一个嗣女。~ *a rabbit* 打兔子。— ***vi***. **1**. 射击;乱射(*at*)。**2**. 〔古〕喝酒。~ **ale** 酒糟。~ **barley** 去壳大麦。~**bellied** ***a***. 罗汉肚的;大肚皮的。~**belly** 罗汉肚;大腹便便的人。~**boil** ***vi***. 〔俚〕(为混饭吃而)粗制滥造文艺作品。~**-boiler** 〔俚〕(文学艺术上的)骗钱作品,为混饭吃而写作的作品[作者]。~**-bound** ***a***. (植物)根系长满一花盆的;没有发展余地的。~ **boy** 〔英〕(尤指啤酒馆的)服务员。~**companion** 酒友。~ **experiment** 盆栽试验。~**-gang** 〔美〕聚在一处吃饭的一群无业游民。~**-garden** 菜地。~**-hanger**= pothook. ~ **hat** 高帽,(硬顶)礼帽。~**head** 〔俚〕麻醉品吸者,吸毒者。~ **herb** 野菜;家种蔬菜;调味香草。~**holder** (保暖用的)布壶套。~**hole** **1**. 【地】锅穴,壶穴,地壶〔河床岩石上的壶形洞〕。**2**. 路面的凹窝,车印。~**hole politician** 注重干实事的政治家〔如注重修桥补路而不事浮夸〕。~**hook** **1**. 锅钩〔挂锅用〕。**2**. 潦草难看的字(~ *hooks and hangers* 初学写字时写成的字;潦草难看的字)。~ **house** **1**. ***n***. 啤酒店;小酒馆。**2**. ***a***. 小酒馆的,下等的(*the manners of a* ~*house* 作风粗野。*a* ~ *house politician* 小政客)。~**hunter** **1**. 随手乱打的猎人。**2**. 〔口〕以获得奖品为目的的运动员。~ **lead** (涂赛船底用的)石墨。~**-lids** 〔*pl*.〕〔美俚〕铙钹(= cymbals)。~**luck** 便饭,现成饭菜;〔美俚〕客人带来的菜(*take* ~*luck with friends* 同朋友吃便饭)。~**man** = ~boy. ~ **metal** **1**. 铸铁,锅铁;铜铅合金。**2**. (熔解时着色的)有色玻璃。~**pie** 锅贴,烤馅饼;加团子的烩肉菜汤。~ **plant** 盆栽植物。~ **roast** 〔美〕炖肉,焖肉。~**-roast** ***vt***. 炖。~**sherd** (考古学上有价值的)陶器碎片。~**-shot** **1**. ***n***. (为取得食物而进行

的)打猎;近距离狙击;乱射,乱打(*take a ~-shot at a rabbit*〔喻〕好歹试试看);肆意[突然]的抨击。**2.** *vt.*, *vi.* (向…)乱射;肆意抨击。~**-spinning** (化纤的)离心式纺丝。~**-still 1.** (没有汽套的)罐式蒸馏器。**2.** 非法酒坊。~**stone**【矿】粗皂石;块滑石〔史前人用以做器皿〕。~**-valiant** *a.* 酒后胆壮的。~**-valour** 酒后之勇。~**waller**【英史】(1832年以前)自己成家而具有选举权的人。~**walloper 1.** = potwaller. **2.**〔美俚〕厨师;洗锅工。**3.**【海】厨师下手;〔英俚〕笨手笨脚的人。**-ful** *n.* 一壶,一锅,一钵,一罐。

pot. = potential.

po·ta·ble [ˈpəutəbl; ˋpotəbḷ] **I** *a.*〔谑〕可以喝的,适合饮用的。~ *water* 饮用水。**II** *n.*〔*pl.*〕饮料,酒。**-bil·i·ty** [-ˈbiliti; -ˋbɪlətɪ], **-ness** *n.*

po·tage [pɔˈtɑːʒ; pɔˋtɑʒ] *n.*〔F.〕浓汤,肉汁。

potam(o)- *comb. f.* 表示"河": *potamo*logy.

po·tam·ic [pəuˈtæmik; pəˋtæmɪk] *a.* 河流的,江河的。

pot·a·mol·o·gy [ˌpɔtəˈmɔlədʒi; ˏpɑtəˋmɑlədʒɪ] *n.* 河流学,河川学。

pot·a·mom·e·ter [ˌpɔtəˈmɔmitə; ˏpɑtəˋmɑmɪtɚ] *n.*【电】水力计。

pot·ash, po·tass [ˈpɔtæʃ, pɔˈtæs; ˋpɑtˏæʃ, poˋtæs] *n.* **1.**【化】钾碱,碳酸钾,氢氧化钾。**2.** = potassium. *caustic* ~ 苛性钾碱〔氢氧化钾的俗称〕。*muriate of* ~ 氯化钾。~ **fertilizer** 钾肥。~ **soap** 钾皂。

po·tas·si·um [pəˈtæsjəm; pəˋtæsɪəm] *n.*【化】钾。~ **carbonate** 碳酸钾。~ **chlorate** 氯酸钾。~ **chloride** 氯化钾。~ **nitrate** 硝酸钾。~ **oxide** 氧化钾。~ **permanganate** 高锰酸钾,灰锰氧。

po·ta·tion [pəuˈteiʃən; poˋteʃən] *n.* **1.** 一饮;一杯;畅饮。**2.**〔常 *pl.*〕喝酒;酒宴;(酒类)饮料。

po·ta·to [pəˈteitəu; pəˋteto] *n.* (*pl.* ~*es*) **1.**【植】马铃薯,土豆。**2.**〔美〕甘薯。**3.**〔俚〕(趾头戳破的)袜子洞。**4.**〔美俚〕一元钱。**5.**〔美俚〕头;难看的脸。**6.**〔美俚〕(垒)球。*sweet* [*Spanish*] ~ 甘薯,白薯,山芋。*white* [*Irish*] ~〔美〕马铃薯。*Canada* ~ 菊芋。*a* ~ *digger* 马铃薯收获机。***a hot*** ~ 棘手的问题。~***es and point*** (肉少得可怜的)一锅马铃薯炖肉。***quite the*** ~, ***the clean*** ~〔俚〕恰好的,正合适的事物。***small*** ~***es*** [***a small*** ~]〔美俚〕微不足道的人[东西]。~ **blight** 马铃薯早疫[晚疫]病。~ **box**〔俚〕嘴。~ **chip** 炸马铃薯薄片。~**-head**〔美俚〕笨蛋。~ **masher 1.** 熟马铃薯捣烂器。**2.** 木柄手榴弹。**3.**〔美俚〕鼓槌;煮熟的鸡[鸭]腿。**4.**〔俚〕干扰雷达的天线。~ **plug** 斜面马铃薯培养基。~ **ring**〔爱〕垫碗、钵的银圈。~ **trap** = ~ box.

po·ta·tory [ˈpəutətəri; ˋpotəˏtorɪ] *a.* 饮酒的;有酒癖的。

pot-au-feu [pɔtəuˈfə; pɑtoˋfə] *n.*〔F.〕肉菜汤〔汤中肉菜另盘上桌〕。

pot·e·ca·ry [ˈpɔtəkəri; ˋpɑtəkərɪ] *n.*〔主英方〕药剂师,药房(= apothecary)。

po·teen [pəuˈtiːn; poˋtin] *n.*〔Ir.〕私造威士忌酒。

po·tence, po·ten·cy [ˈpəutəns, -tənsi; ˋpotns, -tnsɪ] *n.* **1.** 潜能,潜力,能力。**2.** 势;力量;权力,权威,权势。**3.** (药品等的)效力,效验。**4.** 有权势的人;神力。**5.** 生殖力,性能力。

po·tent [ˈpəutənt; ˋpotnt] *a.* **1.**【诗、修饰】有力的,强有力的;有势力的。**2.** (药等)有效力的;烈性的;(议论等)使人心服的。**3.** (茶等)浓的。**4.** (男性)有生殖力的。**-ly** *ad.*

po·ten·tate [ˈpəutənteit; ˋpotnˏtet] *n.* **1.** 有权势的人;富权者。**2.** 统治者;君主。**3.** 强盛的国家。

po·ten·tial [pəˈtenʃəl; pəˋtenʃəl] **I** *a.* **1.** 可能的;【语法】可能语气的。**2.** 潜在的;有潜势的;【物】位的,势的。**3.**〔罕〕有力的。*The seed is the* ~ *flower and fruit.* 种子是潜在的花和果实。**II** *n.* **1.** 可能(性);【语法】可能语气。**2.** 潜在力;潜势;【物】位,势;电势,电位。*partial* ~ 化学势。~ **difference**【物】位差,势差;电位差。~ **energy**【物】位能,势能。~ **genius** 有天才素质的人。~ **hill**【数】位垒,势垒。~ **infinity**【数】潜无穷。~ **mood**【语法】可能语气。~ **share**【商】权利股。~ **transformer** (测量用)变压器。**-ly** *ad.* 潜在地,有潜在可能性地。

po·ten·ti·al·i·ty [pəˌtenʃiˈæliti; pəˏtenʃɪˋælətɪ] *n.* 可能性,潜在的可能;潜能,潜势;〔*pl.*〕潜力。*tap potentialities* 挖掘潜力。*bring all potentialities into full play* 充分发挥一切潜力。

po·ten·tial·ize [pəˈtenʃəlaiz; pəˋtenʃəlˏaɪz] *vt.* **1.** 使具有潜在的可能性;使成为潜在的。**2.**【物】使成为势能[位能]。**-i·za·tion** [-ˌtenʃəlaiˈzeiʃən; -ˏtenʃəlaɪˋzeʃən] *n.*

po·ten·ti·ate [pəˈtenʃieit; pəˋtenʃɪˏet] *vt.* 赋与…以力量;使加强;使(药物等)更有效力。— *vi.* 有加强[提高效力]的作用。

po·ten·til·la [ˌpəutənˈtilə; ˏpotənˋtɪlə] *n.*【植】委陵莱属植物(= cinquefoil)。

po·ten·ti·om·e·ter [pəˌtenʃiˈɔmitə; pəˏtenʃɪˋɑmətɚ] *n.*【电】电位计,电势计;【讯】分压器。*a balance* ~【火箭】随从[伺服]系统电位计。

po·ten·ti·o·stat [pəˈtenʃiəstæt; pəˋtenʃɪəˏstæt] *n.*【物】恒(电)势器。

poth·e·car·y [ˈpɔθiˌkeri; ˋpɑθəˏkerɪ] *n.*〔英方、古〕药剂师,药铺。

po·theen [pɔˈθiːn; poˋθin] *n.* = poteen.

poth·er [ˈpɔðə; ˋpɑðɚ] **I** *n.*〔书〕**1.** 喧扰,骚动;忙乱。**2.** 弥漫的尘土;蒙蒙烟雾;云烟。**3.** 烦恼。***be in a*** ~ 心神不宁。***make*** [***raise***] ***a*** ~ 引起骚动。**II** *vt.* 使烦恼;使心神不安。— *vi.* 喧扰;忙乱。

po·tiche [pəuˈtiːʃ; poˋtiʃ] *n.* (*pl.* ***po·tiches*** [pəuˈtiːʃ; poˋtiʃ])〔F.〕瓷(花)瓶;(有盖瓶式)瓷缸。

po·ti·cho·ma·ni·a [ˌpɔtiʃəˈmeiniə; ˏpɑtɪʃəˋmenɪə] *n.* **1.** 热衷于花瓶的仿造。**2.** 日本陶器仿造(法)。

po·tion [ˈpəuʃən; ˋpoʃən] *n.* **1.** (药的)一服,一剂。**2.** 一服麻醉药[毒药]。*a sleeping* ~ 一服安眠药。

pot·latch [ˈpɔtˌlætʃ, -ˌlæʃ; ˋpɑtˏlætʃ, -ˏlæʃ] *n.* **1.**〔常用 P-〕冬季赠礼节〔美洲印第安人冬季的第一个节日〕;在该节日里分配或交换的礼物。**2.**〔美口〕庆宴,宴会。

Po·to·mac [pəˈtəumək; pəˋtomək] *n.* 波托马克河〔美国、流经华盛顿〕。

po·tom·e·ter [pəˈtɔmetə; pəˋtɑmətɚ] *n.*【气】蒸腾计。

pot·pour·ri [pəuˈpuri(:), F. pɔːpuriː; poˋpuri(ɪ), pɔpʊri] *n.*〔F.〕**1.** 百花香〔干燥的花瓣加香料,用于熏房间〕。**2.** 混杂物;肉菜杂烩。**3.**【乐】集成曲,杂曲;(文学作品等的)杂集,杂录。

Pots·dam [ˈpɔtsdæm, Ger. ˈpɔːtsdɑːm; ˋpɑtsdæm, ˋpɔtsdɑm] *n.* 波茨坦〔德国一城市,柏林市西南旧离宫所在地〕。~ ***Declaration*** (1945年7月盟国敦促日本无条件投降的)波茨坦宣言。

pot·sy [ˈpɔtsi; ˋpɑtsɪ] *n.*〔美方〕小孩(独脚)跳踢石子的游戏,"跳房子"游戏,"踢房子"游戏,"跳方"游戏(= hopscotch)。

pot·tage [ˈpɔtidʒ; ˋpɑtɪdʒ] *n.*〔古〕(蔬菜或菜肉)浓汤(= potage)。***a mess of*** ~ 见 mess 条。

pot·ted [ˈpɔtid; ˋpɑtɪd] *a.* **1.** 盆栽的。**2.** 瓶装的;装成罐头的。**3.**〔美俚〕喝醉的;因吸食大麻毒剂而醉倒的。*a* ~ *plant* 盆栽植物。~ *jam* 瓶装果酱。~ *meat* 加味罐头碎肉。*a* ~ *play* 短剧。

pot·teen [pɔˈtiːn; pɑˋtin] *n.* = poteen.

pot·ter[1] [ˈpɔtə; ˋpɑtɚ] *n.* **1.** 陶工;〔英方〕陶器小贩。**2.** 罐头制造人。~**'s asthma** [**bronchitis**]【医】陶工喘症[支气管炎]。~**'s clay** 陶土。~**'s field** 义冢地,公共墓地。~**'s lathe** 陶器旋床。~**'s wheel** 陶工旋盘。~**'s work** [**ware**] 陶器。

pot·ter[2] [ˈpɔtə; ˋpɑtɚ] *vi.* **1.** 稀里糊涂地混日子,吊儿郎当地[磨磨蹭蹭地]做事(*at*; *in*)。**2.** 慢条斯理地走;闲逛;闲荡(*about*)。~ *over a task* 磨洋工。~ *about the*

P

house all day 在屋子里整天磨蹭。—vt. 混(日子),浪费(时间)(away)。~ away one's time 混日子,磨时间。

pot·ter·y [ˈpɔtəri; ˋpɑtəɪ] n. 1.〔集合词〕陶器类。2. 陶器厂[作坊]。3. 陶器制造(法)。a ~ casting 陶器铸坯。the Potteries 陶器区〔英国斯塔福德郡(Staffordshire)北部陶器出产地〕。

pot·ting [ˈpɔtiŋ; ˋpɑtɪŋ] n. 1. 陶器制造。2. 装壶,装瓶。3. 盆栽。

pot·tle [ˈpɔtl; ˋpɑtl] n. 1.〔古〕罐〔液量名(=2 quarts)〕。2.(相当于一个容量的)一壶(葡萄酒)。3.(装草莓等的)小果篮。

P

pot·to [ˈpɔtəu; ˋpɑto] n. (pl. ~s)【动】(中非的)树熊猴(Perodicticus potto)。

POTS = plain old telephone service【电信】老式普通电话服务。

pot·ty[1] [ˈpɔti; ˋpɑtɪ] a.〔英俚〕1. 零零碎碎的,琐碎的;微不足道的。2.(试题)容易的。3. 傻的,发疯似的;拚命[疯狂]追求的;着迷的(about)。4. 傲慢的;势利的。a ~ set of questions 一组容易回答的问题。be ~ about 迷恋。~ little 一点点,琐碎的。

pot·ty[2] [ˈpɔti; ˋpɑtɪ] n. (小孩用的)便罐;尿壶。~-chair (小孩用的)大便坐椅。

pouch [pautʃ; paʊtʃ] I n. 1.(随身携带的)小袋,囊;烟草袋;〔Scot.〕衣袋;〔古〕钱包。2. [pautʃ, puːtʃ; paʊtʃ, putʃ]【军】皮制弹药盒。3. 邮袋。4.【医】水疱。5.【动】(有袋类的)育儿袋,肚囊;(某些猴子的)颊袋;囊状部;【虫】翅陷;【解】陷凹;憩室;【植】短角。6.〔口〕酒钱,小账。II vt. 1. 把…装入袋中,把…占为己有。2. 把…做成袋状;使鼓起。3.(鱼、鸟)吞进。4.〔俚〕赏酒钱给…,付小账给…。5. 缩拢(袋口等)。~ the mouth 噘着嘴。— vi. 1.(衣服的一部)成袋状;膨胀。2.(鸟等)吞食。3. 用邮袋递送。

pouched [pautʃt; paʊtʃt] a. 有袋的;袋形的;悬垂如袋的。~ animals 有袋类动物。

pouch·y [ˈpautʃi; ˋpaʊtʃɪ] a. 袋状的,囊状的,似囊的。**pouch·i·ness** n.

pou·drette [puːˈdret; puˋdrɛt] n. (由粪肥、木炭、石膏混合成的)杂肥。

pouf, pouff, pouffe [puːf; puf] n. 1.(十八世纪流行的)有高发髻的妇女精巧发饰。2. 衣服上四周有褶皱中间隆起的部分。3. 有厚褥的(睡)椅;厚实的大坐垫,蒲团。

pou·lard(e) [puːˈlɑːd; puˋlɑrd] n. 割去卵巢催肥的母鸡,肉鸡;肥育母鸡。~ wheat 圆锥小麦〔美国的一种饲料〕。

poule [puːl; pul] n. [F.]〔俚〕妓女(=prostitute)。

poulp(e) [puːlp; pulp] n. [F.]【动】章鱼。

poult [pəult; polt] n. (鸡、火鸡等的)雏,幼禽。

poult-de-soie [ˈpuːdəˈswɑː; ˏpudəˋswɑ] n. [F.]波纹绸,绉绸。

poul·ter·er [ˈpəultərə; ˋpoltərə] n.〔英〕鸡贩;家禽贩,野禽贩。

poul·tice [ˈpəultis; ˋpoltɪs] I n.【医】泥罨[泥敷]剂。II vt.【医】敷泥罨[敷]剂于。

poul·try [ˈpəultri; ˋpoltrɪ] n.〔集合词〕家禽〔鸡、火鸡、鹅、鸭等〕(opp. game);鸡类。~ farm 家禽饲养场;鸡场。~-man (以营利为目的的)饲养家禽的人;家禽商。

pounce[1] [pauns; paʊns] I vt. 扑过去抓住。—vi. 1. 猛扑;飞扑(upon);猛抓(at)。2.(对人的过错等)急忙抓住,攻击(on; upon)。II n. 1.(猛禽等的)猛扑,抓。2.(猛禽等的)利爪。make a ~ (up)on 猛扑向。on the ~ 正要扑过去。

pounce[2] [pauns; paʊns] I n. 1.(从前用来防止墨水洇开的)吸墨粉。2.(绣工撒在镂花模板上以印出图案花样的)印花粉。II vt. 1. 在(纸)上撒吸墨粉。2. 用印花粉印出(底样);(在金属板、布等上)打成浮凸花样;在(布等上)打孔;在…上作孔饰。3. 用擦粉把(纸面、帽子面等)打光。

Pound [paund; paʊnd] n. 庞德〔姓氏〕。

pound[1] [paund; paʊnd] I n. 1. 磅〔英国重量名,称一般用品的叫"常衡磅"(avoirdupois ~)=16 盎司或 453.6 克,略作 lb. 或 lb. av.;称金银或药品的叫"金衡磅"(troy ~)=12 盎司或 37.32 克,略作 lb. t.;称药品的叫"药衡磅"(apothecaries' ~,与金衡磅等重,略作 lb. ap.)〕。2. 英镑〔英国货币单位,又名 ~ sterling, =20 旧先令,1971 年取消先令后=100 便士,略作 £ 或 L〕。3. 镑〔某些国家的货币单位〕。five ~s [~] 五英镑〔可写作 £5〕。a five-~ note 一张五英镑钞票。a ~ note 一张一英镑钞票。a ~ of flesh 合法但不合情理的要求;要求偿还一磅肉〔源出莎士比亚戏剧《威尼斯商人》〕。by the ~ 按每磅(计价)。claim one's ~ of flesh 逼人还债。in for a penny, in for a ~ 一不做,二不休。in the ~【商】每磅(贴水多少)。Mischief comes by ~s and goes away by ounces. 祸害易来难去。penny wise and ~ foolish 小事聪明,大事糊涂,小处精明,大处马虎。pay twenty shillings in the ~ 全数付清。~ for [and] ~ 均等地。II vt. 验称(货币等的)重量。~ cake (用面粉、白糖、奶油等主要用料各 1 磅或等量做成的)蛋糕。~ foolish a. 大数目上马虎的;省小失大的。~ Scots【史】1 先令 8 便士。~s, shillings, and pence 金钱〔略 L.s.d. 或 £. s. d.〕。~ sterling 英镑。

pound[2] [paund; paʊnd] I n. 1.(收留迷失犬、牛等待领的)官设兽栏。2.(关禁无执照等的家畜的)牲畜栏;(放置充公物品等的)待赎所;〔喻〕监牢,拘留所。3. 养鱼塘,养龙虾池;鲜活龙虾出售处。4.〔方〕积水。5.【猎】危险地位。II vt. 1.〔古〕把(走失的牲畜等)关进兽栏(up);〔喻〕监禁,拘留(up)。2.〔古〕筑坝拦(水)。~ the field 设栅栏使牲畜跳不过去。

pound[3] [paund; paʊnd] I vt. 1. 捣碎,舂烂,把…捣成粉。2.(连续)猛击;乱敲;砰砰砰地乱弹(钢琴等),乱奏(曲子)。3.(不断重复地)灌输(into)。4.(沉重地)沿着…行走;持续地沿着…移动。—vi. 1. 连续不断地打,乱打;打破;接连不断地开炮(at; on; away);(心)砰砰地跳。2. 步子沉重地走(along);发轰隆声地航行[飞行]。3.(持续地)苦干。~ away at 1. 乱打;接连不断地炮击;批评,抨击。2. 拚命地干(工作)。~ home (to) 把(道理等)反复灌输给…。~ one's ear〔美俚〕睡觉。~ out 连续猛打出(字),猛弹出(曲子等)。~ the side walk [pavement]〔美俚〕1. 徘徊街头找职业,找工作做。2.(警察)巡行街道。II n. 连续打击;砰砰的打击(声)。

pound·age[1] [ˈpaundidʒ; ˋpaʊndɪdʒ] n. 1. 每英镑应纳的手续费或佣金。2. 按磅计算的重量[收费数]。3.(企业总收益中的)工资比额。

pound·age[2] [ˈpaundidʒ; ˋpaʊndɪdʒ] n. 1.(领回走失牲畜时付的)官设兽栏收容费。2.(收容走失牲畜的)官设兽栏。3. 拘留,监禁。

pound·al [ˈpaundl; paʊndəl] n.【物】磅达〔力的单位〕。

pound·er[1] [ˈpaundə; ˋpaʊndə] n. 1.〔用作复合词〕…磅重的东西[人];发射…磅重炮弹的炮。2. 付…英镑的人;有…英镑财产[收入]的人;…英镑的东西。a 200-~ 体重 200 磅的人;有 200 英镑收入的人。a ring which is a 2,000 ~ 价值 2000 英镑的戒指。

pound·er[2] [ˈpaundə; ˋpaʊndə] n. 1. 连续猛打的人;捣[舂]的人;捣[舂]的工具,杵。2.【无】鞭状天线。a stone ~ 石碓。

Pou·part [ˈpəupɑːt; ˋpopɑrt] n. 波帕特〔姓氏〕。

pour [pɔː, pɔə; pɔr, pɔr] I vt. 1. 注,倒,灌,泻,喷散(液体、粉粒、光线等);流(血等);倾注;源源不断地输送。2. 使冒着(枪林弹雨等);大施(恩惠等)。3. 尽情唱(歌);尽情说,任意说,发泄,倾吐。4.(用话)安抚;使(锐气、意气等)沮丧。5. 浪费。P- yourself another cup of tea. 请再倒杯茶喝。~ out the tea 倒茶。The river ~s itself *into the sea*. 这条河流入大海。— *vi*. **1**. 流出,注出;倾泻(*forth*; *out*; *down*);(雨等)倾盆而下。**2**. 扩大,传开;蜂拥而来;源源而来(*in*)。**3**. 在茶桌上当主妇〔西方习俗,招待客人时多由家庭主妇斟茶〕。***It never rains but it ~s***.(雨)不下就不下,一下就下大;祸不单行。***in the ~ing rain*** 在倾盆大雨之下。~ ***cold water on*** 泼冷水,使(人)沮丧,使(人)扫兴。~ ***forth abuses on sb***. 把某人骂得狗血喷头,大骂某人。~***ing rain*** 倾盆大雨。~ ***it on***〔美俚〕**1**. 大肆吹捧。**2**. 加油干。**3**. 飞快前进。~ ***oil on the fire***[***flames***] 火上加油。~ ***oil upon troubled waters*** 平息风波,排解纠纷,调停。~ ***on the coal***〔美俚〕(飞机等)急飞,急驶。~ ***oneself out*** 倾诉自己的想法[感情等],倾诉衷曲。~ ***out grievances*** 诉苦。**II** ***n***. **1**. 注出,流出;大雨。**2**.【铸】浇注,灌铸;(已熔金属的)一次浇注量。~ **point** (润滑油等的)流动点〔保持流动状态的最低温度〕。

pour·boire [ˈpuəbwɑː; ˋpʊr͵bwɑr] ***n***.〔F.〕酒钱,小账。

pour·er [ˈpɔːrə; ˋpɔrɚ] ***n***. **1**. 倒(茶等)的人。**2**. 浇铸工。

pour·par·ler [puəˈpɑːlei; pʊrˋparlɪ] ***n***.〔F.〕〔常 *pl*.〕(外交上的)预备性谈判,非正式会谈。

pour·point [ˈpuəpɔint; ˋpʊr͵pɔɪnt] ***n***. (14 世纪男子穿的)紧身棉马甲。

pousse-ca·fé [ˌpuːskæˈfei, F. puskɑfe; ͵puskɑ ˋfe, pʊskɑˋfɛ] ***n***.〔F.〕(*pl*. ~***s*** [-ˈfeiz, F. puskɑfe; -ˋfez, pʊskɑfɛ]) **1**. 在餐后咖啡之后喝的(甜)酒。**2**.〔美〕(同一杯里注入比重不同的酒形成的)五色酒。

pous·sette [puːˈset; puˋset] **I** ***vi***. (互相拉着手)跳环舞。**II** ***n***. 拉手环舞〔一种乡村舞蹈〕。

pou sto [ˈpau ˈstəu; ˋpuˋsto]〔Gr.〕***n***. **1**. 立足地,立足点。**2**. 根据地,基础〔来自阿基米德 (Archimedes) 所说他如有一块立足地即可推动地球一语〕。

pout[1] [paut; paʊt] **I** ***n***. **1**. 噘嘴。**2**.〔常 *pl*.〕生气,不高兴。***be in the ~s*** = ***have the ~s*** 噘着嘴,绷着脸,赌着气。**II** ***vt***. **1**. 噘(嘴);张开(羽毛等)。**2**. 噘着嘴说。— ***vi***. **1**. 噘嘴,绷脸;发脾气。**2**. 凸起;鼓起;膨胀;胸膛凸出。**-y** ***a***. 生气的。

pout[2] [paut; paʊt] ***n***.【动】大头鱼类〔如鳕、棉鳚、鲶等〕。

pout·er [ˈpautə; ˋpaʊtɚ] ***n***. **1**. 撅嘴的人,绷脸的人;发脾气的人。**2**.【动】凸胸鸽。

pov·er·ty [ˈpɔvəti; ˋpɑvɚtɪ] ***n***. **1**. 贫穷。**2**. 缺乏,缺少,贫乏,不足(*of*, *in*);(土地的)贫瘠,不毛。**2**. 虚弱;低劣。*come to* ~ 变穷。~ *of blood*【医】贫血。~ *in vitamins* 维生素不足。***live in genteel*** ~ 家贫而要面子摆阔。~ **level**【经】贫困水平线〔在此水平以下者为贫困〕。~**-striken** ***a***. 为穷所苦恼的,贫困的;贫穷的;贫乏的;(计谋等)极空泛的。

POW, P.O.W. = prisoner of war 战俘。

pow[1] [pəu, pau; po, paʊ] ***n***.〔主 Scot.〕脑袋。

pow[2] [pau; paʊ] ***int***. 砰〔表示射击、爆炸声等的拟声词〕。

pow·der [ˈpaudə; ˋpaʊdɚ] **I** ***n***. **1**. 粉,粉末。**2**. (搽脸的)香粉;牙粉;发粉。**3**. (一服)药粉;粉剂;散。**4**. 尘土,泥屑;雪糁。**5**. 炸药,火药;〔喻〕推动力;打击力;(打击对方所需的)力量。**6**.〔美俚〕一杯酒。**7**.〔*pl*.〕〔美俚〕逃跑;溜掉。**8**.〔美俚〕老板的命令。***burn*** ~〔美俚〕射击,开枪。***food for*** ~ 炮灰。***foolish*** ~〔美俚〕海洛英。***grind***[***reduce***] ***to*** ~ 磨碎;粉碎。***keep one's*** ~ ***dry*** 准备,万一,做好准备。***take a*** ~〔美俚〕逃掉;离开。***Put more*** ~ ***into it***! 加油! 加一把劲! ***put on*** ~ 搽粉。***smell of*** ~ 闻过火药味,有实战经验。***smell*** ~ 吸收实战经验。***wear*** ~ 撒发粉。

II ***vt***. **1**. 把…作成粉,使成粉末,磨碎。**2**. 撒粉于;搽粉于;用粉状物覆盖(*with*)。**3**. 用圆点图案装饰。— ***vi***. **1**. 变成粉末。**2**. 搽香粉[发粉]。**3**.〔美俚〕逃走。~ ***up***〔美俚〕喝。~ **and shot 1**. 弹药,军需品。**2**. 费用,劳力(*not worth* ~ *and shot* 得不偿失,不值得费力。*waste* ~ *and shot* 白费力气)。~ **blue** 氧化钴〔一种深蓝色颜料〕;(洗衣用的)粉末大青[花绀蓝];深蓝色。~ **box** 化妆盒;粉盒。~**-cart** 弹药车。~ **chamber** (炮弹里的)药室。~ **diagram** 粉末照相,粉末图。~ **down** (昆虫的)粉冉羽。~ **factory**[**mill**] 火药(制造)厂。~ **flask** 火药瓶,火药筒〔打猎用〕。~ **horn** 牛角制火药筒。~ **keg** (金属制)小型火药箱;易爆炸物。~ **magazine** 火药库。~ **metallurgy**【冶】粉末冶金术。~ **monkey** (从前军舰中)搬火药的少年;〔美谑〕装炸药的人,使用炸药的人。~ **photography** 粉末照相术。~ **puff 1**. 粉扑〔搽粉用〕;〔转义〕花花公子;〔美俚〕傻姑娘,浅薄无聊的女子;女性化的男子。**2**. 机灵的拳手;轻敲,轻打。~ **rocket** 固体燃料火箭。~ **room 1**.〔婉〕妇女盥洗室;女厕所。**2**. (军舰的)火药室。~ **snow** 雪糁。~ **waggon**〔美〕把枪身切短的猎枪。

pow·dered [ˈpaudəd; ˋpaʊdɚd] ***a***. **1**. 弄成粉的。**2**. 涂了白粉的;有小白斑的。**3**.〔美俚〕喝醉了的。~ **coal** 粉煤,煤末。~ **milk** 奶粉。~ **sugar** (作清凉饮料用的)粉末砂糖。

pow·der·y [ˈpaudəri; ˋpaʊdərɪ] ***a***. **1**. 粉的,粉状的。**2**. 满是粉的;布满尘埃的。**3**. 容易变成粉的。~ *mildew* 白粉菌,白粉病。**pow·der·i·ness** ***n***.

Powel(l) [ˈpəuəl; ˋpoəl] ***n***. 鲍威尔〔姓氏〕。

pow·er [ˈpauə; ˋpaʊɚ] **I** ***n***. **1**. 力,力量;能力;体力,精力;(生理)机能;〔常 *pl*.〕才能。**2**. 势力,权力,权限;威力;政权;权能。**3**. 有力人物,有势力者;有影响的机构。**4**. 兵力;军事力量;大国,强国。**5**.【数】幂,乘方。**6**. (透镜的)放大力。**7**.【法】委任权,委任状。**8**.【机】动力,机力;简单的机械;电力;电(能)源;功率;率;能量;生产率。**9**.〔口、方〕许多,大量。**10**.〔*pl*.〕神,恶魔。*the* ~ *of vision* 视力。~ *of muscle* 力气。*a man of varied ~s* 多才多艺的人。*the air* ~ 空军兵力。*The third* ~ *of 2 is 8*. 2 的三次方是 8。*treaty ~s* 缔约国。*the Great* (*World*) *Powers* (世界)列强。*super ~s* 超级大国。*the party in* ~ 当权政党,执政党。*a* ~ *of attorney* 委任状。*a full* ~ 全权证书。*a* ~ *of representation*【法】代理权。*dispersive* ~【光】色散率。*mechanical* ~ 机械力。*labour* ~ 劳动力。*motive* ~ 原动力,动力。~ *fuel* 动力燃料。*He did a* ~ *of work*.〔口〕他做了许多的事情。*I saw a* ~ *of people*.〔口〕我看见许多人。*It has done me a* ~ *of good*. 这给我很大的帮助。~*s of darkness* 魔鬼。***a*** ~ ***of*** 许多的。***be in one's*** ~ 在…的权力范围之内。***beyond one's ~s*** 力量达不到;不能胜任。***come into*** ~ 掌权,上台。***do all in one's*** ~ 尽力做。***fall into the*** ~ ***of*** 落在…手中。***have*** (*sb*.) ***in one's*** ~ 控制住某人,可随意支配[摆布](某人)。***have***[***hold***] ~ ***over*** 支配,领导。***in*** ~ 执政的,在朝的,当权的。***More*** ~ ***to your elbow***[***to you***]. 加油干,好好干。***out of one's*** ~ 力所不及。***out of*** ~ 在野(的)。***tax sb.'s ~s to the utmost*** 需要某人尽力。***the*** ~ ***of the keys***【基督教】司钥权,教皇享有的最高教权。***the ~s that be***〔谑〕当局。**II** ***vt***.〔美〕给…装发动机,赋与…以动力;用动力发动。~**boat** 机动艇;摩托艇(= motorboat)。~ **brake** 动力刹车。~ **dive**【空】全力俯冲。~ **dressing** 女强人式着装〔指妇女在着装上力求端庄、严肃以显示其职业身份、地位、权势等〕。~ **game** 权术。~ **gas** 动力气体。~ **grids** 电力输送网。~ **hitter 1**.【棒球】力量型击球手。**2**.〔喻〕强人,铁腕人物(*a female* ~ *hitter* 女强人)。~ **house** 发电厂;〔美〕强有力者。~ **lathe** 动力车床。~ **loom** 机动织机。~**-off**【火箭】(发动机)停车。~ **plant**[**station**] 发电厂;发动机,动力装置。~ **politics** 强权政治。~ **series**【数】幂级数。~ **shovel** 挖土机;机铲。~ **structure** 权力结构。~ **take-off** 动力输出装置。~ **tower** 发电塔〔即太阳能发电站配置的镶镜高塔〕。~ **transmission** 输电。~(-) **walk 1**. ***n***. 快步走锻炼。**2**. ***vi***. 作快步走锻炼。

pow·ered [ˈpauəd; ˋpaʊɚd] ***a***. **1**.〔构成复合词〕以…为动力的;有…马力的。**2**. 装有发动机的;用动力推动的。*a high-~ engine* 高马力发动机。

P

P

pow·er·ful [ˈpauəful; ˋpauəfəl] **I** *a*. **1**. 有力的,强大的。2. (药等)有效力的;作用大的。**3**. 有权力的,有势力的;有权威的,有影响的,(演讲等)动人的。**4**. 〔口、方〕很多的,相当的;(头痛等)厉害的。**II** *ad*. 〔美〕非常,很。*a ~ lot of* 〔口〕许许多多。**-ly** *ad*.

pow·er·less [ˈpauəlis; ˋpauəlɪs] *a*. **1**. 无力的,无能的(*to do*)。**2**. 无依靠的;虚弱的;无效力的;无权力的。**3**. 无资源的。**4**. 无活动能力的,麻痹的。**-ly** *ad*. **-ness** *n*.

Pow·nall [ˈpaunl; ˋpaunl̩] *n*. 波纳尔〔姓氏〕。

pow·wow [ˈpauˌwau; ˋpauˏwau] **I** *n*. **1**. (北美印第安人的)祭司,巫师。**2**. (北美印第安人的)祛病祈祷;预祝典礼〔出发打猎、打仗前的跳舞、狂欢〕。**3**. 〔美俚〕(政治等方面的)会谈,讨论;社交集会;〔英俚〕(作战时的)军官会议。**II** *vi*. **1**. (北美印第安人)做祛病祈祷;举行预祝狂欢。**2**. 〔美俚〕开会;商量(*about*)。— *vt*. (北美印第安人)用巫术治(病)。

Pow·ys [ˈpəuis; ˋpoɪs] *n*. 波伊斯〔姓氏〕。

pox [pɔks; pɑks] *n*. (*pl*. ~(*es*)) **1**. 【医】痘;(皮)疹;脓疱;〔古〕天花。**2**. 〔俚〕〔the ~〕梅毒。**3**. 瘟疫。**4**. 【植】疮痂病。*chicken ~* 水痘。***A ~ on*** [***of***] ***you*** [***him***]! 遭瘟的! 该死的! ***What a ~***! 嗳呀! ~ **marks** 痘瘢,麻瘢。

Poz·nan, **Poz·nań** [ˈpəuznæn, Pol. ˈpoznɑn; ˋpozˏnɑnjə] *n*. 波兹南〔波兰城市〕。

poz·z(u)o·la·na [ˌpɔtsəˈlɑːnə, It. ˌpɔttzɔːˈlɑːnə; ˏpɑtsəˋlɑnɑ, pɔttzɔˋlɑnə] *n*. 〔It.〕 **1**. 【地】白榴火山灰〔作胶泥用〕。**2**. (与火山灰混合制成的)一种胶合水泥。

poz·zo·la·nic [ˌpɔtsəˈlɑːnik; ˏpɑtsəˋlɑnɪk] *a*. 【化】凝硬性的;火山灰的。~ *action* (水泥的)凝硬作用。

poz·zy [ˈpɔzi; ˋpɑzɪ] *n*. 〔军俚〕果酱。

PP = **1**. parcel post 包裹邮递;包裹邮务处;〔总称〕邮包,包裹邮件。**2**. past participle 过去分词。**3**. postpaid 邮费付讫的。**4**. prepaid 已预付。**5**. personal property 【律】动产。**6**. power plant 发电站[厂];动力设备。

P.P. = parish priest 教区牧师。

pp = **1**. pages. **2**. 〔L.〕 *per procurationem* 由…所代表。**3**. 〔It.〕 *pianissimo*.

ppb, **p.p.b.** = parts per billion 十亿分之一。

PPC, **ppc** = **1**. 〔F.〕 *pour prendre congé* 离开;告别(= to take leave)。**2**. picture postcard 美术明信片。

ppd = **1**. postpaid 邮费付讫的。**2**. prepaid 已预付。

pph = pamphlet.

PPI = plan position indicator 平面位置雷达指示器。

p.p.i. = **1**. parcel post insured 挂号邮政包裹。**2**. picks per inch 【纺】纬/英寸。

P.P.M. = picks per minute 【纺】纬/分。

ppm, **p.p.m.** = parts per million 百万分率。

ppr., **p.pr.** = present participle 现在分词。

P.P.S. = **1**. Parliamentary Private Secretary 〔英〕政务次官。**2**. 〔L.〕 Post postscrip 再附言。

PPs, **pps** = pulses per second 脉冲/秒。

ppt = precipitate 沉淀;沉淀物。

PP-WP = Planned Parenthood-World Population 计划生育-世界人口组织。

P.Q. = **1**. Province of Quebec 〔加拿大〕魁北克省。**2**. personality quotient 【心】人格商(数)。

PR = public relations (通过宣传手段建立的)与公众的联系,对外联络;公关;公关人士。

P.R. = **1**. payroll 工资发放名册。**2**. Parliamentary Reports 〔英〕议会议事录。**3**. prize ring 拳击场;拳击(练习)。**4**. proportional representation (选举的)比例代表制。

Pr = praseodymium 【化】镨。

Pr. = **1**. Prince. **2**. preferred stock 〔美〕优先股。**3**. 〔F.〕 *Provençal*.

pr. = **1**. pair. **2**. power. **3**. preferred. **4**. present. **5**. pronoun. **6**. price. **7**. printed. **8**. priest. **9**. primary. **10**. printer.

PRA = Public Roads Administration 〔美旧〕公路管理局。

P.R.A. = President of the Royal Academy 英国皇家艺术学会会长。

praam [prɑːm; prɑm] *n*. = pram².

prac·tic [ˈpræktik; ˋpræktɪk] *a*. = practical.

prac·ti·ca·bil·i·ty [ˌpræktikəˈbiliti; ˏpræktɪkəˋbɪlətɪ] *n*. **1**. 实行的可能性,实用性,可行性。**2**. 实用物。

prac·ti·ca·ble [ˈpræktikəbl; ˋpræktɪkəbl̩] *a*. **1**. 切实可行的,行得通的;实际的;实用的。**2**. (桥等)可以通行的;适用的;【剧】(窗、门等舞台布景)实际能用的。**-ness** *n*. **-bly** *ad*.

prac·ti·cal [ˈpræktikəl; ˋpræktɪkl̩] *a*. **1**. 实地的,事实上的,实际上的(*opp*. theoretical)。**2**. 实践的,实地经验过的,练习过的,经验丰富的,老练的。**3**. 实用的,应用的;注重实用的;〔贬〕只讲实用的。**4**. (人等)有用的,会做事的,能干的。**5**. 有实效的;可行的。**6**. 实事求是的,注重实行的。~ *considerations* 需要切实考虑的事情,实际问题。~ *duty* 实际工作。*the ~ rulers* 事实上的统治者。*a ~ joker* 耍弄别人的人。~ *experience* 实际经验。~ *politics* 实际政治,行得通的政治。~ *minds* 讲求实际的头脑;注重实际的人。***be not ~*** 不实际,不能落实。***for*** (***all***) ***~ purposes*** 实际上。~ **joke** 恶作剧,戏弄人的鬼把戏。~ **nurse** 从实际工作中锻炼出来的护士〔未曾正式登记的〕。~ **piece** 〔美剧〕像实物一样的布景。~ **shooting** 实弹模拟射击运动。~ **unit** 【物】实用单位。~ **wisdom** 常识。**-ness** *n*.

prac·ti·cal·ism [ˈpræktikəlizəm; ˋpræktɪkəlɪzm̩] *n*. 求实主义;实用主义。

prac·ti·cal·i·ty [ˌpræktiˈkæliti; ˏpræktɪˋkælətɪ] *n*. **1**. 实际;实用;实用性;实践性。**2**. 实物;实例。

prac·ti·cal·ly [ˈpræktikəli; ˋpræktɪkl̩ɪ] *ad*. **1**. 实际上;实用上;事实上,实际上。**2**. 从实际出发;通过实践。**3**. [ˈpræktikli; ˋpræktɪklɪ] 〔口〕差不多;几乎;简直。*P- speaking, there is no more to be done*. 实际地讲,没有别的办法可行了。*It's summer ~*. 这天气简直像夏天了。

prac·tice¹ [ˈpræktis; ˋpræktɪs] *n*. **1**. 实行,实践,实施;实际;实用;做法,技术。**2**. 习惯,惯例,常规。**3**. 练习,演习,实习,实验;老练,熟练。**4**. (医生、律师等的)业务,开业;生意,主顾。**5**. 【数】实算。**6**. 〔常 *pl*.〕〔古〕策略,诡计,欺诈。**7**. 【法】诉讼手续。**8**. 【宗】仪式。*A plausible idea, but will it work in ~?* 主意倒好,然而能实行吗? *a common ~* 风气;常例。*bureaucratic ~s* 官僚主义作风。*the old ~s* 过去的一套,老一套。*social ~* 社会实践。*a blank* [*firing*] *~* 空弹[实弹]演习。*sharp ~* 狡诈[不正当]的手段。*The doctor has a large ~*. 这个医生病人很多。***a matter of common*** [***daily***] ***~*** 寻常的事。(***do***) ***~*** (*in music* [*at the nets*]) 练习(音乐[网球])。***in ~*** **1**. 实际上,事实上;在实践中。**2**. 在不断练习中;练习充足;熟练。**3**. 在开业中。***in ~ if not in profession*** 虽不明讲但实际如此。***It was the ~***. 这就是当时的习惯。***make a ~ of*** 老是;经常进行…;以…为惯用手段。***out of ~*** 久不练习,荒疏。***P- makes perfect***. 熟能生巧。***put*** [***bring***] ***in*** [***into***] ***~*** 实行。***reduce to ~*** 实施。~ **teacher** (本人是学生的)实习教师。~ **teaching** (师范学院学生等的)教学实习。

prac·tice² [ˈpræktis; ˋpræktɪs] *vt*., *vi*. 〔美〕= practise.

prac·ticed [ˈpræktist; ˋpræktɪst] *a*. 〔美〕= practised.

prac·ti·cian [prækˈtiʃən; prækˋtɪʃən] *n*. **1**. 实行者,开业者,经营事业者。**2**. 有实际经验的人,熟手。

prac·ti·cum [ˈpræktikəm; ˋpræktəkəm] *n*. 实习课,实践课。

prac·tise [ˈpræktis; ˋpræktɪs] *vt*. **1**. 搞;实行;实践;实施;常做;惯常进行。**2**. 练习,实习;训练,使练习。**3**. 开业从事。~ *law* [*medicine*] 开业当律师[医生]。~

pupils in singing 教学生唱歌。~ *economy* 节约。— ***vi*.** **1.** 实践;实行。**2.** 练习;实习(*on*; *at*; *with*)。**3.** 开业,挂牌行医[当律师等]。**4.** 〔古〕策划阴谋。~ *as a barrister* = ~ *at the bar* 挂牌做律师。~ *at* [*on*] *the piano* 练钢琴。~ *with the rifle* 练习打步枪。~ ***on*** [***upon***] 利用(别人弱点);欺骗(某人)。

prac·tised [ˈpræktist; ˋpræktɪst] ***a*.** **1.** 经验丰富的。**2.** 精通的,熟练的;老练的。*a* ~ *hand* 熟手,老手。*the* ~ *in trade* 善于经商的人们。

prac·tis·ing [ˈpræktisiŋ; ˋpræktɪsɪŋ] ***a*.** 正在从事某种职业[活动]的,开业的。*a* ~ *physician* [*lawyer*] 开业医师[律师]。

prac·ti·tion·er [prækˈtiʃənə; prækˋtɪʃənɚ] ***n*.** **1.** 开业者〔尤指医生、律师等〕;老手。**2.** 从事者,实践者;实习者,练习者。**3.** 〔古〕策士,策划阴谋者。*a private* ~ 开业医生。*a general* ~ 普通医生。

prae- *pref*. 〔多用于拉丁语及与古代罗马事物有关的词前〕〔L.〕= pre-.

prae·co·cial, 〔Am.〕 **pre·co·cial** [priˈkəuʃəl; prɪˋkoʃəl] ***a*.** 【动】孤生的〔新孵出来的小鸟即长了羽毛并能自己找食的〕。

prae·dial [priːˈdiəl; ˋpridɪəl] ***a*.** = predial.

prae·fect [ˈpriːfekt; ˋprifɛkt] ***n*.** = prefect.

prae·mu·ni·re [ˌpriːmjuˈnaiəri; ˏprimjəˋnaɪrɪ] ***n*.** **1.** (英国古代法律中的)擅自行使教皇司法权罪,蔑视王权罪。**2.** 命令行政司法官传犯蔑视王权罪者的令状。

prae·no·men [priːˈnəumen; priˋnomen] ***n*.** (*pl*. **~*s***, ***prae·nom·i·na*** [priːˈnəuminə; priˋnomɪnə]) 【古罗马】本名,第一个名字〔相当于后来的教名(Christian name),如 Caius Julius Caesar 的 Caius〕。

prae·pos·tor, **pre·pos·ter** [priːˈpɔstə; priˋpɑstɚ] ***n*.** 〔英〕(某些公学(public school)的)班长,级长。

prae·sid·i·um [priˈsidiəm; prɪˋsɪdɪəm] ***n*.** = presidium.

prae·tor, 〔Am.〕 **pre·ter** [ˈpriːtə; ˋpritɚ] ***n*.** 【罗马史】执政官;(仅次于执政官的)地方长官。

prae·to·ri·an, 〔Am.〕 **pre·to·ri·an** [priːˈtɔːriən; prɪˋtorɪən] ***n*.**, ***a*.** **1.** (古罗马)执政官(的);地方长官(的)。**2.** 〔常作 P-〕(古罗马皇帝的)禁卫军(的)。

prag·mat·ic [prægˈmætik; prægˋmætɪk] **I** ***a*.** **1.** 好管闲事的,爱多事的。**2.** 刚愎自用的,独断的;自负的。**3.** 【哲】实用主义的。**4.** 重实效的;实际的。**5.** 国务的,国事的;团体事务的。**6.** 研究史迹的相互关系的。~ *lines of thought* 实用主义的想法。*the* ~ *sanction* 构成基本法的诏书,国事诏书。**II** ***n*.** **1.** 爱管闲事的人。**2.** 专断的人。**3.** 国事诏书。**4.** 〔废〕实务家,实际家。**pragmat·i·cal** ***a*.** **prag·mat·i·cal·ly** ***ad*.**

prag·mat·i·cism [prægˈmætisizəm; prægˋmætɪsɪzəm] ***n*.** 【哲】实用主义。**-mat·i·cist** ***n*.** 实用主义者。

prag·mat·ics [prægˈmætiks; prægˋmætɪks] ***n*.** 语用学,(语言)实用学〔研究语言符号和其使用者关系的一种理论,符号学的一个部分〕。

prag·ma·tism [ˈprægmətizəm; ˋprægməˏtɪzəm] ***n*.** **1.** 【哲】实用主义。**2.** 实用的观点和方法。**3.** 好管闲事;独断(性);自负。

prag·ma·tist [ˈprægmətist; ˋprægmətɪst] ***n*.** **1.** 【哲】实用主义者,实用主义哲学的信奉者。**2.** 请求实际的人。**3.** 爱管闲事的人。

prag·ma·tis·tic [ˌprægməˈtistik; ˏprægməˋtɪstɪk] ***a*.** 实用主义的。

prag·ma·tize [ˈprægmətaiz; ˋprægməˏtaɪz] ***vt*.** 把(空想的事物)实际化,使现实化;合理地解释(神话等)。

Prague, **Pra·ha** [prɑːg, ˈprɑːhɑː; preg, ˋprɑha] ***n*.** 布拉格〔捷克首都〕。~ **Spring** 布拉格之春〔指 1968 年捷共的自由化改革政策导致苏联 1969 年出兵的事件〕。

Praia [ˈprai·ɑː; ˋpraɪ·ɑ] ***n*.** 普拉亚〔佛得角首都〕。

prai·rie [ˈpreəri; ˋprɛrɪ] ***n*.** **1.** (特指美国中西部的)大草原。**2.** 牧场,草原地带。**3.** 〔美方〕林中空地。*the call of the* ~ 大草原的诱惑。~ *fire* 燎原大火,野火。~ *oyster* [*cocktail*] 加调料生吃的蛋。~ **chicken** [**hen**] 北美松鸡。~ **dog** [**marmot**] 【动】(北美产)草原土拨鼠,草原犬鼠。**P- Provinces** 草原诸省〔加拿大的 Manitoba, Saskatchewan, Alberta 诸省的别名〕 ~ **schooner** 【美史】(早期在草原地带用的)篷盖大马车。~ **squirrel** = ~ dog. ~ **value** (不含劳动、资本等的)自然地价。**P-State** 〔美〕草原之乡〔美国伊利诺斯州的别名〕。~ **wag(g)on** = ~ schooner. ~ **wolf** 【动】草原狼。

prais·a·ble [ˈpreizəbl; ˋprezəbl] ***a*.** 可称赞的;值得赞扬的,可嘉许的。**-ness** ***n*.** **prais·a·bly** ***ad*.**

praise [preiz; prez] **I** ***n*.** **1.** 称赞;赞扬,表扬;〔*pl*.〕赞词,赞美的话。**2.** 【宗】(对上帝的)崇拜,赞美,尊崇。**3.** 〔古〕值得称赞的人[物];〔古〕可称赞的地方[理由]。***a service of*** ~ 【宗】赞美礼拜。***be above*** [***beyond all***] ~ 赞美不尽的。***be loud*** [***warm***] ***in sb.'s*** **~(*s*)** 热烈颂扬某人。***bestow*** [***give***] ~ 称赞(*on*; *upon*)。***chant*** [***sing***] ***the*** **~*s of sb*.** 颂扬[歌颂]某人。***P- be to God***! 感谢上帝! ***in*** ~ ***of*** 称赞[赞美,歌颂]…。***more*** ~ ***than pudding*** 恭维多而实惠少。***pudding rather than*** ~ 宁要实惠,不要恭维。***say in sb.'s*** ~ 称赞某人说。***sing one's own*** **~*s*** 自吹自擂。***win high*** ~ 受到高度赞扬。**II** ***vt*.** **1.** 称赞,赞扬,表扬,歌颂;吹捧。**2.** 【宗】赞美(上帝)。***God be*** **~*d***! 谢天谢地。~ ***sb. to the skies*** 把某人捧上天。**-er** ***n*.** 赞美者,赞扬者;吹捧者。**-less** ***a*.** 没有赞扬的。

praise·ful [ˈpreizful; ˋprezful] ***a*.** **1.** 满是称赞话的;赞不绝口的;赞扬的;歌颂的。**2.** 有称赞价值的。**-ness** ***n*.**

praise·wor·thy [ˈpreizˌwəːði; ˋprezˏwɝðɪ] ***a*.** 值得赞扬的,值得钦佩的,可嘉许的。**-thi·ly** ***ad*.** **-thi·ness** ***n*.**

Pra·krit [ˈprɑːkrit, ˈpræ-; ˋprɑkrɪt, ˋpræ-] ***n*.** 帕拉克里语〔印度中部及北部的方言,古时与梵文并存或起源于梵文〕。

pra·line [ˈprɑːliːn; ˋprɑlin] ***n*.** 果仁糖;胡桃糖,杏仁糖。

prall·tril·er [ˈprɑːltrilə; ˋprɑltrɪlɚ] ***n*.** 【乐】回波音(= inverted mordent)。

pram[1] [præm; præm] ***n*.** **1.** 〔英口〕婴儿车,童车〔perambulator 的缩称〕。**2.** 〔俚〕(送牛奶的)手推车。

pram[2], **praam** [prɑːm; prɑm] ***n*.** **1.** (波罗的海沿岸一带的)平底货船;平底炮艇。**2.** (斯堪的纳维亚一带的)大船上附带的小艇。

prance [prɑːns; præns] **I** ***vi*.** **1.** (马)腾跃。**2.** (人)傲然跃马前行。**3.** 高视阔步,神气十足地走[骑马];欢跃;快活地走[骑马](*about*)。**II** ***vt*.** 使(马)腾跃。**III** ***n*.** **1.** (马的)腾跃。**2.** 昂首阔步;神气十足的态度。**3.** 欢跃;欢跃的舞蹈动作。

pranc·er [ˈprɑːnsə; ˋprɑnsɚ] ***n*.** **1.** 腾跃前进的人[马]。**2.** 烈性[慓悍]的马;骑烈马者;〔俚〕骑马士官;马贼。**3.** 欢快的舞蹈者,欢跃者。

pran·di·al [ˈprændiəl, -djəl; ˋprændɪəl, -djəl] ***a*.** 〔谑〕膳食的,正餐的。

prang [præŋ; præŋ] 〔英空俚〕 **I** ***vt*.** **1.** 使(飞机、车辆等)砰地撞坏[坠毁];投弹命中(目标);轰炸。**2.** 撞,击。— ***vi*.** (飞机)坠毁。**II** ***n*.** 〔俚〕 **1.** (飞机的)猝然坠地,坠毁。**2.** 命中目标的轰炸,炸中。**3.** 大功。

prank[1] [præŋk; præŋk] ***n*.** **1.** 开玩笑;恶作剧,鬼把戏。**2.** 不正常的动作;(机器等)不规则的转动。*They are up to their old* **~*s*.** 他们又在玩鬼把戏了。***play*** **~*s on*** 向…开玩笑,戏弄,对…玩鬼把戏。

prank[2] [præŋk; præŋk] ***vt*.** **1.** 把…打扮漂亮,盛装(*up*)。**2.** 装饰。~ *oneself up* [*out*] *with the best clothes* 穿着最漂亮的衣服。*meadows* **~*ed*** *with flowers* 花朵盛开的牧场。— ***vi*.** 打扮得漂漂亮亮。

prank·ish [ˈpræŋkiʃ; ˋpræŋkɪʃ] ***a*.** 爱开玩笑的;顽皮的;恶作剧的。

prank·ster [ˈpræŋkstə; ˋpræŋkstɚ] ***n*.** 开玩笑的人,恶

P

作剧的人。

prase [preiz; prez] *n*. 【矿】葱绿玉髓;绿石英。

pra·se·o·dym·i·um [ˌpreiziəuˈdimiəm; ˏpreziəˋdɪmɪəm] *n*. 【化】镨。

prate [preit; pret] I *vi*., *vt*. 唠唠叨叨地讲;瞎说,瞎胡诌;空谈;(把无聊事情)大谈特谈。*merely* ~ *about it* 只是空谈[胡扯]一阵。II *n*. 唠叨,多嘴;无聊话。**prating** *a*. **prat·ing·ly** *ad*.

prat·er [ˈpreitə; ˋpretɚ] *n*. 多嘴的人;唠唠叨叨的人;空谈者。

pra·tie [ˈpreiti; ˋpretɪ] *n*. 〔Ir.〕〔常 *pl*.〕马铃薯(= potato)。

P

pra·tique [ˈprætiːk; præˋtik] *n*. 〔F.〕(检疫后发给的)无疫入港许可证。

prat(t) [præt; præt] *n*. 〔美俚〕屁股。~ **kick** 〔美俚〕屁股上的裤袋。

prat(t)·fall [ˈprætˌfɔːl; ˋprætˏfɔl] *n*. 〔美俚〕1. 屁股着地的跌跤。2. 倒霉;丢脸;可耻的失败。

prat·in·cole [ˈprætiŋkəul, ˈprætn-; ˋprætɪŋkol, ˋprætn̩-] *n*. 【动】燕鸻。

Pratt [præt; præt] *n*. 普拉特[姓氏]。

prat·tle [ˈprætl; ˋprætl] I *vi*. 1. 像小孩般颠三倒四地说话;发出连续而无意义的声音。2. 空谈,瞎聊,唠叨。—*vt*. 天真地说;轻率地说。II *n*. 1. 孩子般颠三倒四的话;连续而无意义的声音。2. 空谈,废话,无聊话。

prat·tler [ˈprætlə; ˋprætlɚ] *n*. 1. 喁喁学语的小孩;小孩般幼稚地讲话的人。2. 空谈者,瞎聊的人。

prau [prau, ˈprɑːuː; praʊ, ˋprɑʊ] *n*. 马来人的一种快帆船(= proa)。

Prav·da [ˈprɑːvdə; ˋprɑvdə] *n*. 〔俄〕《真理报》。

prav·i·ty [ˈpræviti; ˋprævətɪ] *n*. 〔古〕1. (食物的)腐烂。2. 腐败;堕落;邪恶。

prawn [prɔːn; prɔn] I *n*. 【动】明虾,对虾;斑节虾。II *vi*. 捉对虾。

prax·e·ol·o·gy [ˌpræksiˈɔlədʒi; ˏpræksɪˋɑlədʒɪ] *n*. 人类行为学。

prax·is [ˈpræksis; ˋpræksɪs] *n*. (*pl*. ***prax·es*** [-siːz; -siz]) 1. 习惯,惯例,常规。2. 练习,实习;实践;应用。3. (语法等的)例题集,练习问题集。

pray [prei; pre] *vi*. 1. 请求,恳求(*for*)。2. 祷告,祈祷(*to*)。~ *for pardon* 请求原谅。*He is past* ~*ing for*. 他是不可救药了。— *vt*. 1. 请求;恳求;祈求,祈祷。2. 请[I ~ you 之略]。*What is the use of that*, ~? 请问那有什么用处呢? *Tell me the reason*, ~. 请把理由告诉我吧。***P- come with me***. 请跟我来。***P- consider that ...*** 请想想看。~ ***down*** [***out***] 祈祷求神降伏(某人)。~ ***for rain*** 求雨。~ ***for sb***. 为某人祈祷。~ ***in aid of*** 〔古,雅〕求…帮助。~***ing insect*** 螳螂。

pray·er[1] [ˈpreiə; prer] *n*. 恳求者;祷告者。

pray·er[2] [prɛə; prer] *n*. 1. 祈祷,祈求;恳求。2. 〔常 *pl*.〕祈祷式;祈祷文,祈祷语句。3. 所祈祷[恳求]的事物。4. 〔*pl*.〕祝福。5. 〔口〕极渺茫的成功希望。***be at one's*** ~***s*** 正在祈祷。***evening*** ~ 晚祷。***morning*** ~ 晨祷。***say one's*** ~***s*** = ***give*** ~***s*** 祈祷,祷告。***the house of*** ~ 教堂。***the Lord's P-*** 【宗】主祷文。***the unspoken*** ~ 默祷,心中的愿望。***wrestle in*** ~ 热忱祈祷。~ **bones** 〔美俚〕膝盖。~ **book** 祈祷书。~ **breakfast** 早餐祷告会。~**-machine** [~**-mill**] = ~-wheel. ~ **meeting** 祷告会。~ **rug** [**mat**] (穆斯林祈祷时用的)跪毯。~**-wheel** 【佛教】地藏车,祈祷轮。**-less** *a*. 不祷告的,不虔诚的。

prayer·ful [ˈprɛəfʊl; ˋprerfəl] *a*. 常常祷告的,虔诚的。**-ly** *ad*. **-ness** *n*.

pre- *pref*. 表示"前,先,预先": *pre*history, *pre*pay, *pre*school, *pre*vent.

preach [priːtʃ; pritʃ] I *vi*. 1. 布讲,讲道,布道,传道。2. 宣扬,宣传,鼓吹。3. 谆谆劝诫,唠叨地劝说。— *vt*. 1. 讲(道);说(教);讲(学)。2. 教,劝告,规戒。3. 提倡,鼓吹,宣传。4. 由于说教而(讲得口干舌燥等)。*Practise what you* ~. 躬行己言,身体力行,以身作则。~ ***a funeral*** 〔口〕致悼辞。~ ***a sermon*** 讲道;〔喻〕劝诫,说教。~ ***against*** 对…作反宣传。~ ***at*** [***to***] ***sb***. 对某人谆谆告诫。~ **down** 贬损;当众谴责,当众折服[否决掉],驳倒。~ ***the Gospel*** 布讲福音。~ ***to deaf ears*** 对聋子讲道;对牛弹琴。~ ***up*** 称赞,赞扬;推崇;吹捧。II *n*. 〔口〕讲道,说教;训诫。

preach·er [ˈpriːtʃə; ˋpritʃɚ] *n*. 1. 讲道者;说教者;传教师。2. 训诫者,警告者。3. 宣传者;鼓吹者。4. 〔the P-〕【圣】《传道书》;《传道书》作者。

preach·i·fy [ˈpriːtʃifai; ˋpritʃəˏfaɪ] *vi*. (***-fied***) 〔口〕(令人生厌地)训诫;说教。

preach·ing [ˈpriːtʃiŋ; ˋpritʃɪŋ] I *n*. 1. 讲道;说教;训诫。2. 布道术,讲道法。3. 有人布道的礼拜。II *a*. 布道的,说教的;训诫的。~ **shop** 〔美俚〕教堂。

preach·ment [ˈpriːtʃmənt; ˋpritʃmənt] *n*. 〔口〕(冗长的)讲道,说教。

preach·y [ˈpriːtʃi; ˋpritʃɪ] *a*. 〔口〕爱讲道的;喜欢说教的;说教性的;讲道似的。**-i·ly** *ad*. **-i·ness** *n*.

pre·ac·quaint [ˈpriːəˈkweint; ˋpriəˋkwent] *vt*. 预先通知,预告。**pre·ac·quaint·ance** *n*.

pre·act [ˈpriːˈækt; ˋpriˋækt] *vt*. 提前,超前(行动);预作用。

pre·a·dam·ic [ˈpriːəˈdæmik; ˏpriəˋdæmɪk] *a*. = preadamite (*a*.).

pre·ad·am·ite [ˈpriːˈædəmait; priˋædəmˏaɪt] I *a*. 1. (基督教《圣经》所云人类始祖)亚当以前的。2. 亚当以前的人的。II *n*. 1. 亚当以前的人。2. 相信亚当以前已有人存在者。

pre·ad·o·les·cence [ˈpriːˌædəuˈlesns; ˏpriædəˋlɛsns] *n*. 青春期以前的时期[约 9—12 岁]。

pre·ad·o·les·cent [ˈpriːˌædəuˈlesnt; ˏpriædəˋlɛsnt] I *a*. 青春期以前一段时期的。II *n*. 处于青春期以前一段时期的少年。

pre·am·ble [priːˈæmbl; ˋpriæmbl] I *n*. 1. 序,绪言;(条约等的)前言。2. 预兆性事件;开端,端倪。II *vi*. 作序言[绪论]。***without*** ~ 开门见山地,直截了当地。

pre·am·bu·late [priːˈæmbjuleit; priˋæmbjəlet] = preamble (*vi*.).

pre·am·pli·fi·er [ˈpriːˈæmplifaiə; priˋæmpləˏfaɪɚ] *n*. 【电】前置放大器。

pre·an·nounce [ˌpriːəˈnauns; ˏpriəˋnaʊns] *vt*. 预告,事先宣告。

pre·ar·range [ˈpriːəˈreindʒ; ˏpriəˋrendʒ] *vt*. 预先安排;预先协商;预定。**-ment** *n*.

pre·as·signed [ˈpriːəˈsaind; ˋpriəˋsaɪnd] *a*. 预先指定的;预先分配[分派]的。

pre·a·tom·ic [ˈpriːəˈtɔmik; ˏpriəˋtɑmɪk] *a*. 原子弹和原子能使用前的,核时代以前的。

pre·au·di·ence [ˈpriːˈɔːdjəns; priˋɔdɪəns] *n*. (英国法律中一方律师在法庭上的)优先发言权。

pre·ax·i·al [ˈpriːˈæksiəl; ˏpriˋæksɪəl] *a*. 【解】轴前的。

pre-bat·tle [ˈpriːˈbætl; ˋpriˋbætl] *a*. 战斗前的,交战前的。~ **formation** 接敌队形。~ **intelligence** 战前侦察。

pre·book [ˈpriːbuk; ˋpribuk] *vt*. 预订;预约。

preb·end [ˈprebənd; ˋprɛbənd] *n*. 1. 牧师会会员的俸禄;供给牧师会会员俸禄的教会财产[土地、什一税、捐献等]。2. 受俸牧师;名誉受俸牧师。**-al** *a*.

preb·en·da·ry [ˈprebəndəri; ˋprɛbəndˏɛrɪ] *n*. 〔英〕受俸牧师;名誉受俸牧师。

prec. = preceded; preceding.

Pre·cam·bri·an [priːˈkæmbriən; priˋkæmbrɪən] I *a*. 【地】前寒武纪的。II *n*. 〔the ~〕前寒武纪。

pre·can·cel [priːˈkænsəl; priˋkænsl] I *vt*. (~(***l***)***ed***, ~(***l***)***ing***) 在使用前盖销(邮票)。II *n*. 在使用前盖销的

邮票。**-cel·la·tion** [-ˈleiʃən; -ˋleʃən] *n.*

pre·can·cer·ous [priːˈkænsərəs; priˋkænsərəs] *a.* 可能致癌的;癌症前期的。*a ~ mole* 可能致癌的痣。

pre·car·i·ous [priˈkɛəriəs; priˋkɛrɪəs] *a.* **1.** 不确定的,靠不住的;危险的,(生活等)不安定的。**2.** (推测等)可疑的;前提有问题的,根据不充足的。**3.** 〔古〕由他人摆布的。*a ~ living* 愁吃少穿[朝不保夕]的生活。*a ~ life* 不安定的生活。*the ~ life of a fisherman* 极危险的渔民生活。*~ privileges* 随时均有被取消可能的特权。*a ~ foothold* 不稳定的立足点。*a ~ assumption* [*assertion*] 靠不住的假定[论断]。**-ly** *ad.* **-ness** *n.*

pre·cast [ˈpriːˈkɑːst; priˋkæst] *vt.*, *a.* 【建】预制(的);预浇铸(的)。*~ reinforced concrete beams* 预制钢筋混凝土梁。

prec·a·tive, prec·a·to·ry [ˈprekətiv, -təri; ˋprɛkətɪv, -ˏtorɪ] *a.* 恳求的;【语法】祈求的。*~ words* (遗嘱中的)拜托话,恳求话。**precatory trust** 【法】(有约束力的)遗托。

pre·cau·tion [priˈkɔːʃən; priˋkɔʃən] **I** *n.* **1.** 小心,警惕,谨防,预防。**2.** 预防措施。***by way of ~*** 为小心起见,为了预防。***take ~s against*** 谨防,小心;对…采取预防措施。**II** *vt.* 使提防;预先警告。

pre·cau·tion·al, pre·cau·tion·a·ry [priˈkɔːʃənəl, -ʃənəri; priˋkɔʃənl, -ʃənərɪ] *a.* 预有戒备的,预防的。*~ measures* 预防措施。

pre·ca·va [ˌpriːˈkeivə, -kɑː-; ˏpriˋkevə, -kɑ-] *n.* (*pl.* **-vae** [-viː; -vi]) 【解】前腔静脉。**-val** *a.*

pre·cede [pri(ː)ˈsiːd; priˋsid] *vt.* **1.** 领先于,居先于,在…之先。**2.** 在…之上;优于;比…重要。**3.** 在…前加上;为…加上引言(*by*, *with*)。*We were ~d by our guide.* 我们跟着向导走。*Economy ~s every other problem.* 经济问题优先于所有其他问题。—*vi.* 在前面,领先,居先。*the words that ~* 上述的话。**pre·ced·a·ble** *a.*

pre·ced·ence, 〔罕〕 **pre·ced·en·cy** [pri(ː)ˈsiːdəns, -si; priˋsidns, -sɪ] *n.* **1.** 领先,先行,先在;在前。**2.** 上位,上座,上席。**3.** 优先,优越;优先权。**4.** (按地位的)先后次序。*Economic problems must take ~ of other questions.* 经济问题应作首要问题处理。*the order of ~* 席次,位次。*quarrel about ~* 席次之争。***give ~ to*** 把主席让给…,承认…的优越。***take*** [***have the***] ***~ of*** [***over***] 在…之上,优于。

prec·e·dent[1] [ˈpresidənt; ˋprɛsədənt] *n.* **1.** 先例,前例;惯例。**2.** 【法】判例。*There is no ~ for it.* 那是没有前例的。*without ~* 无前例的,空前的。***have no ~ to go by*** 无先例可循。***set*** [***create***] ***a ~ for*** 为…开先例。**-less** *a.* 没有前例的。

pre·ce·dent[2] [priˈsiːdənt; priˋsidənt] *a.* 在前的,在先的;优先的。***a condition ~*** (财产转让,合同生效等之前的)先决条件。

prec·e·dent·ed [ˈpresidəntid; presəˏdɛntɪd] *a.* 有先例(可援)的(*opp.* unprecedented)。

prec·e·den·tial [ˌpresiˈdenʃəl; ˏprɛsəˋdɛnʃəl] *a.* **1.** 先例的,作为先例的。**2.** 有先例的;预先的。

pre·ced·ing [pri(ː)ˈsiːdiŋ; priˋsidɪŋ] *a.* **1.** 在前的,在先的(*opp.* following)。**2.** 上述的。*~ crops* (轮作中的)前作(物)。*the ~ years* 前几年。*in the ~ chapter* 在前章。

pre·cen·sor [ˈpriːˈsensə; ˋpriˋsɛnsɚ] *vt.* (书籍出版、影片放映或新闻发布前)预先审查。

pre·cen·tor [pri(ː)ˈsentə; priˋsɛntɚ] *n.* (教堂歌咏班的)指挥人;领唱人。

pre·cept [ˈpriːsept; ˋprisɛpt] *n.* **1.** 训导,告诫;格言,箴言;戒律。**2.** (技术上的)格式;规程;方案。**3.** 【法】命令书,令状。***Practice*** [***Example***] ***is better than ~.*** 实例优于口训;以身作则胜于口头训导。

pre·cep·tive [priˈseptiv; priˋsɛptɪv] *a.* **1.** 教训的;告诫的。**2.** 【法】令状的。

pre·cep·tor [priˈseptə; priˋsɛptɚ] *n.* **1.** 训导者,导师。**2.** 教师,(美某些大学的)导师;校长;(带实习生的)辅导医生。**3.** 【史】圣殿骑士团 (Knights Templars) 的教堂长。**-to·ri·al** [-ˈtɔriəl; -ˋtorɪəl] *a.* (*a preceptorial system* 导师制)。

pre·cep·to·ry [priˈseptəri; priˋsɛptərɪ] *n.* 【史】圣殿骑士团的教堂;圣殿骑士团地方分团[管辖区];圣殿骑士团地方分团的产业。

pre·cep·tress [priˈseptris; priˋsɛptrɪs] *n.* 女导师;女教师;女校长。

pre·cess [priˈses; priˋsɛs] *vi.* 向前运动;【天】(按岁差)向前运行;【机】旋进。

pre·ces·sion [priˈseʃən; priˋsɛʃən] *n.* **1.** 前行,先行。**2.** 前进运动,进动;【天】岁差。*~ of the equinoxes* 【天】(分点)岁差。**-al** *a.* 岁差的;进动的。

pre·choose [priːˈtʃuːz; priˋtʃuz] *vt.* (***pre·chose*** [priːˈtʃəuz; priˋtʃoz], ***pre·cho·sen*** [priːˈtʃəuzən; priˋtʃozən]) 预先选定,预先选择。

pre-Chris·tian [ˈpriːˈkristjən, ˈpriːˈkrisʃən; ˋpriˋkrɪstʃən, ˋpriˋkrɪsʃən] *a.* 基督(教)以前的。

pré·cieuse [preˈsjuːz; preˋsjœz] **I** *n.* 〔F.〕(17世纪沙龙中的)女学者;社交界附庸风雅和卖弄学问的妇女。**II** *a.* (妇女)附庸风雅的,过分文雅的,装模作样的。

pré·cieux [preˈsjuː; preˋsjœ] *a.* 〔F.〕= precieuse (*a.*).

pre·cinct [ˈpriːsiŋkt; ˋprisɪŋkt] *n.* **1.** (建筑物等的)围地,附近范围;〔英〕(教会的)会内,(寺院的)院内;境域内;〔*pl.*〕境界。**2.** 〔美〕(县以下的)管区;〔美〕(选举)区,分界,分区。**3.** 〔*pl.*〕(城镇的)周围,附近,郊区。*city ~s* 市区。*an election ~* 选区。*a police ~* 警察管区。*a shopping ~* 商业区。

pre·ci·os·i·ty [ˌpreʃiˈɔsiti; ˏprɛʃɪˋɑsətɪ] *n.* (措词用句的)过分雕琢,过分讲究;矫揉造作。

pre·cious [ˈpreʃəs; ˋprɛʃəs] **I** *a.* **1.** 高价的,昂贵的;贵重的;宝贵的,珍贵的。**2.** 可爱的,宝贝的。**3.** 非常,极;大大的,十足的,彻底的。**4.** 〔反语〕好的,没价值的。**5.** (工艺等)过分精雕细琢的;(文章等)过分讲究的,咬文嚼字的。*the ~ metals* 贵金属。*~ stones* 宝石。*~ memories* 珍贵的纪念品。*My ~ darling!* 我的心肝宝贝! *A ~ friend you have been.* 〔讽刺话〕你真是个宝贝朋友。*a ~ fool* 大傻瓜。***a ~ deal*** 〔口〕非常,极。***make a ~ mess of sth.*** 把某事弄成一团糟。**II** *n.* 〔称呼用语〕可爱的人。***My ~!*** 我的亲爱的! **III** *ad.* 〔口〕非常,极。*It is ~ cold.* 冷极了。*There is ~ little of it.* 只有一点点,极少极少。**-ly** *ad.* **-ness** *n.*

prec·i·pice [ˈpresipis; ˋprɛsəpɪs] *n.* **1.** 悬崖,绝壁;断崖边。**2.** 危地,危急处境,危机。***be*** [***stand***] ***on the brink of a ~*** 处于灾难的边缘。

pre·cip·i·ta·ble [priˈsipitəbl; priˋsɪpətəbl] *a.* 【化】沉淀性的,能使沉淀的。**pre·cip·i·ta·bil·i·ty** [priˌsipitəˈbiliti; priˏsɪpɪtəˋbɪlətɪ] *n.* 【化】沉淀性,沉淀度。

pre·cip·i·tance, pre·cip·i·tan·cy [priˈsipitəns, -si; priˋsɪpətəns, -sɪ] *n.* 急躁;慌张;仓卒;〔*pl.*〕轻率行为。

pre·cip·i·tant [priˈsipitənt; priˋsɪpətənt] **I** *a.* **1.** 很快落下的;陡斜地落下的;倒落的。**2.** 急躁的;(病)急,(行动)突然的;(举动)轻率的。**II** *n.* 【化】沉淀剂,沉淀试药。**-ly** *ad.*

pre·cip·i·tate [priˈsipiteit; priˋsɪpəˏtet] **I** *vt.* **1.** 把…倒摔下去,把…猛然扔下。**2.** 使(人)突然陷入(某种状态)(*into*);使突然发生。**3.** 拼命催促,促成,促使(危机等)早现。**4.** 【化】使沉淀;【物】使(水蒸气)凝结。*~ sb. into misery* 使某人一下子陷入苦海。*~ a disaster* 闯下一个大祸。*~ a war* 发动[挑起]战争。*~ **oneself into*** (*danger*) 使自己一下子陷入(危险)。*~ **oneself upon*** [***against***] 猛袭,突击(敌人)。**II** [priˈsipitit; priˋsɪpɪtɪt] *a.* **1.** 猛然落下的,倒栽下的;陡斜地落下的;猛冲的;(水

流)湍急的。2. 慌张的,急躁的,轻率的。III [pri'sipitit; prɪ`sɪpɪtɪt] n.【化】沉淀物;【物】凝结的水蒸气〔指雨、雪、露等〕;降水。-ly [pri'sipititli; prɪ`sɪpɪtɪtlɪ] ad. **pre·cip·i·tat·ing** a. 1. 急落的;猛冲的。2.【化】起沉淀作用的,导致沉淀的。

pre·cip·i·ta·tion [priˌsipi'teiʃən; prɪˏsɪpə`teʃən] n. 1. 猛然摔下,落下。2. 猛冲;急躁,轻率,鲁莽。3.【化】沉淀(作用);降雨(量);(雨、雪等的)降落。~ **hardening**【冶】沉淀硬化,弥散硬化。

pre·cip·i·ta·tor [pri'sipiteitə; prɪ`sɪpɪtetə] n. 1. 催促的人[物];促进者。2.【化】沉淀器;沉淀剂;除尘器;电滤器;滤尘器。3. 沉淀器操作者。

P

pre·cip·i·tin [pri'sipitin; prɪ`sɪpətɪn] n.【生化】沉淀素。

pre·cip·i·tin·o·gen [priˌsipi'tinədʒən; prɪˏsɪpɪ`tɪnədʒən] n.【生化】沉淀素原。**-gen·ic** [-'dʒenik; -`dʒɛnɪk] a.

pre·cip·i·tous [pri'sipitəs; prɪ`sɪpətəs] a. 1. 险峻的,绝壁的;陡峭的;急转直下的,突然而来的。2. 急躁的,鲁莽的,轻率的;仓卒的。**-ly** ad.

pré·cis ['preisiː; pre`si] I n. (pl. ***pré·cis*** ['preisiːz; `presiz]) 〔F.〕(文章或讲话的)摘要,提要;大意,梗概。II vt. 作…的摘要,摘取…的大意。

pre·cise [pri'sais; prɪ`saɪs] a. 1. 准确的,精确的。2. 清楚的,(言语等)清晰的;(区分等)明确的。3. (数量上)恰好的,丝毫不差的。4. 〔加强语气〕恰好的,正是的。5. 合规则的,正式的,正规的;没错的。6. 古板的;拘泥的,严格的。***at the ~ moment*** 恰恰在那个时刻。***to be ~*** 〔用作插入语〕确切地讲。**-ly** ad. 1. 正好,恰恰,恰 (*~ly because* 正因为)。2. 精确地;明白地;严格地。3. 刻板地,拘泥(陈规)地,呆板地。4. 〔表示同意时用〕的确那样,一点不错 (*Precisely so*. 正是这样)。**-ness** n. 1. 精确,准确,确切。2. 呆板,拘泥。

pre·ci·sian [pri'siʒən; prɪ`sɪʒən] n. (尤指宗教方面)严格遵守规则的人;清教徒。

pre·ci·sion [pri'siʒən; prɪ`sɪʒən] I n. 精密,精确性;严格;精密度;【修】精确。*arms of ~* 装有瞄准仪的枪炮。II a. 精确的,精密的。*~ apparatus* 精密仪器。*a ~ balance* 精密天平。*a ~ fire* 准确射击。

pre·ci·sion·ist [pri'siʒənist; prɪ`sɪʒənɪst] n. 拘泥于道德的人;讲究语言精确的人。

pre·clas·si·cal ['priː'klæsikəl; pri`klæsɪkḷ] a. (特指希腊、罗马文学的)古典时期以前的。

pre·clin·i·cal ['priː'klinikəl; pri`klɪnɪkḷ] a.【医】临诊前期的,临床前的。

pre·clude [pri'kluːd; prɪ`klud] vt. 1. 排除,预防,消灭,杜绝。2. 阻断(路等),阻止;使不可能,妨碍。*A prior engagement will ~ them from coming*. 他们因为有约在先,不能来了。*so as to ~ all doubts* 为了消除疑点。**-clu·sion** [pri'kluːʒən; prɪ`kluʒən] n. **-clu·sive** [-'kluːsiv; -`klusɪv] a.

pre·co·cious [pri'kəuʃəs; prɪ`koʃəs] a. 1. (人)早熟的,早慧的;发育过早的。2. (植物等)早成的,(花)早开的。**-ly** ad. **-ness** n.

pre·coc·i·ty [pri'kɔsiti; prɪ`kɑsətɪ] n. (人的)早熟,过早发育;(植物的)早成。

pre·cog·ni·tion ['priːkɔg'niʃən; ˏprikɑg`nɪʃən] n. 1. 预知,预见。2. 〔Scot.〕【法】(对证人或证据的)预先审查。

pre-Co·lum·bi·an ['priːkə'lʌmbiən; ˏprikə`lʌmbɪən] a. 哥伦布以前的〔指哥伦布发现美洲以前的西半球的任何时期〕。

pre·com·pose ['priːkəm'pəuz; ˏprikəm`poz] vt. 预作(诗歌等)。

pre·com·pres·sion ['priːkəm'preʃən; `prikəm`prɛʃən] n. 预先压缩,预压力。

pre·con·ceive ['priːkən'siːv; ˏprikən`siv] vt. 预见;事先打好(主意等)。*~d prejudices* 先入之见,偏见。

pre·con·cep·tion ['priːkən'sepʃən; ˏprikən`sɛpʃən] n. 1. 预想,预见。2. 先入之见,偏见。**-al** a.

pre·con·cert ['priːkən'səːt; ˏprikən`sɝt] vt. 预定;预先商定;预先同意。*a ~ed plan* 预定的计划。**-ed** [-tid; -tɪd] a. 预先商定的。

pre·con·demn ['priːkən'dem; ˏprikən`dɛm] vt. (不调查证据)先预定…有罪。

pre·con·di·tion ['priːkən'diʃən; ˏprikən`dɪʃən] I n. 前提,先决条件。II vt. 1. 把…预先安排[准备]好。2. 预先处理。3. 使…先作好思想准备。**-ing** n. 预处理。

pre·co·nize ['priːkənaiz; `prikəˏnaɪz] vt. 1. 宣告,声明;公布。2. 指名召唤。3. (教皇)正式公布批准任命(新任主教)。**pre·co·ni·za·tion** ['priːkənai'zeiʃən; `prikənaɪ`zeʃən] n.

pre·con·quest ['priː'kɔŋkwest; pri`kɑnkwɛst] a.【英史】诺曼 (Norman) 人征服英国(1066年)前的。

pre·con·scious ['priː'kɔnʃəs; `pri`kɑnʃəs] n., a.【心】前意识(的)。

pre·con·sid·er·a·tion ['priːkənˌsidə'reiʃən; ˏprikənˏsɪdə`reʃən] n. 预先考察,事先考虑。

pre·con·tract ['priː'kɔntrækt; pri`kɑntrækt] I n. 预约,先约;〔古〕(具有法律效力的)订婚,婚约。II ['priːkən'trækt; `prikən`trækt] vi. 预约,〔古〕订婚(约)。— vt. 预先规定;〔古〕同…预订婚约。

pre·cook [priː'kuk; pri`kʊk] vt. 预先烹调,预煮,预烧。

pre·cool ['priː'kuːl; pri`kul] vt. 预先冷冻〔货物打包或装船前进行冷冻〕。

pre·cor·di·al ['priː'kɔːdjəl; `pri`kɔrdɪəl] a.【解】心前区的。

pre·cor·di·um [priː'kɔːdjəm; pri`kɔrdɪəm] n. (pl. ***-dia*** [-djə; -djə])【解】心前区。

pre·cos·tal ['priː'kɔstəl; ˏpri`kɑstəl] a.【解】在肋骨前的。

pre·cur·sive [pri(ː)'kəːsiv; prɪ`kɝsɪv] a. = precursory.

pre·cur·sor [pri(ː)'kəːsə; prɪ`kɝsɚ] n. 1. 前辈,前驱,先锋;前任。2. 预兆;先兆。3. 预报器。4.【原】前驱波;初级粒子。

pre·cur·sory [pri(ː)'kəːsəri; prɪ`kɝsərɪ] a. 1. 前驱的,先锋的,前辈的,前任的。2. 预兆的,预报的。3. 开端的,作预备的;初步的。

pred. = predicate; predicative(ly).

pre·da·cious, pre·da·ceous [pri'deiʃəs; prɪ`deʃəs] a. = predatory.

pre·dac·i·ty [pri'dæsiti; prɪ`dæsətɪ] n.【动】捕食性,食肉性。

pre·date ['priː'deit; pri`det] vt. 1. 倒填…的日期,填早于…的日期。2. 在日期上早于[先于] (*opp*. postdate)。*~ the check by three days* 把支票的日期填早三天。

pre·da·tion [pri'deiʃən; prɪ`deʃən] n. 1. 掠夺的行为。2. 捕食其他动物的生存方法。

pred·a·tor ['predətə; `prɛdətɚ] n. 以掠夺为生的人;捕食其他动物的动物,食肉动物。

pred·a·to·ry ['predətəri; `prɛdəˏtorɪ] a. 1. (战争等)以掠夺为目的的,掠夺(性)的;掠夺成性的。2.【动】捕食其他动物的,食肉的。*a ~ war* 掠夺性战争。*a ~ ruffian* 强盗。*~ birds* 食肉禽。**-to·ri·ly** ['predə'tɔrili; `prɛdə`tɑrɪlɪ] ad. **-to·ri·ness** n.

pre·dawn ['priː'dɔːn; pri`dɔn] a. 黎明前的。

pre·de·cease ['priːdi'siːs; ˏpridɪ`sis] I vt. (比某人)先死;死在(某事件)之前。*~ one's father* 比父亲先死。— vi. 先死。II n. 先死,早死。

pre·de·ces·sor ['priːdisesə; ˏprɛdɪ`sɛsɚ] n. 1. 前任;前辈;〔古〕祖先。2.【农】前作;【数】前趋。3. (被取代的)原先的东西。*It will share the fate of its ~*. 它将遭受与前者同样的命运,它将重蹈覆辙。

pre·de·fine ['priːdi'fain; `pridɪ`faɪn] vt. 预先规定[确定]。

pre·del·la [priˈdelə; prɪˋdɛlə] *n*. (*pl*. **-le** [-li; -lɪ]) 祭坛台座[台阶];祭坛台座垂直面上的绘画[雕刻]。

pre·de·pres·sion [ˈpriːdiˈpreʃən; ˋpridɪˋprɛʃən] **I** *a*. 经济萧条期以前的。**II** *n*. 萧条期以前的时期。

pre·des·ig·nate [ˈpriːˈdezigneit; priˋdɛzɪgˏnet] *vt*. 预先指示。**pre·des·ig·na·tion** [-ˈneiʃən; -ˋneʃən] *n*.

pre·des·ti·nar·i·an [pri(ː)ˌdestiˈnɛəriən; prɪˏdɛstəˋnɛrɪən] **I** *n*. 宿命论者,命定论者。**II** *a*. 宿命论(者)的;宿命的。**-ism** *n*. 宿命论,命定论。

pre·des·ti·nate I [pri(ː)ˈdestineit; prɪˋdɛstəˏnet] *vt*. **1**. 预先注定,命中注定。**2**. 〔古〕预先确定。**II** [pri(ː)ˈdestinit; pri(ɪ)ˋdɛstnɪt] *a*. **1**. 被预先注定的;被命运注定的,宿命的。**2**. 〔古〕预定的。

pre·des·ti·na·tion [pri(ː)ˌdestiˈneiʃən; prɪˏdɛstəˋneʃən] *n*. 前定,预定;命运,前世因缘;【宗】命定论,宿命论。

pre·des·tine [pri(ː)ˈdestin; prɪˋdɛstɪn] *vt*. 预先指定,预先决定;命中注定。

pre·de·ter·mi·nate [priːdiˈtəːminit; pridɪˋtɝmənɪt] *a*. 预定的,先定的。*the* ～ *will of* …的预定意志。

pre·de·ter·mine [ˈpriːdiˈtəːmin; ˏpridɪˋtɝmɪn] *vt*. **1**. 预定,先定,注定。**2**. 预先决定…的方向;使先存偏见。**-nation** [-ˈneiʃən; -ˋneʃən] *n*.

pre·di·al [ˈpriːdiəl; ˋpridɪəl] **I** *a*. **1**. 土地的;与土地有关的;固定资产的,与固定资产有关的;有土地的。**2**. 与耕种有联系的;乡村的。**3**. 佃户的;隶属于土地的。～ *serfs* 农奴。**II** *n*. 农奴。

pred·i·ca·bil·i·ty [ˌpredikəˈbiliti; ˏprɛdɪkəˋbɪlətɪ] *n*. 可断定性;可断定为…的属性。

pred·i·ca·ble [ˈpredikəbl; ˋprɛdɪkəbl̩] **I** *a*. 可断定性;可断定为…的属性的 (*of*)。*Length is* ～ *of a line*. 长度是线的属性。**II** *n*. **1**. 可被作为属性而断定的东西;同类对象的共同属性。**2**. 〔*pl*.〕【逻】宾词;〔the ～〕(特指亚里士多德逻辑学中的)五种宾词(“类”、“种”、“特异性”、“固有性”、“偶然性”)。

pre·dic·a·ment [priˈdikəmənt; prɪˋdɪkəmənt] *n*. **1**. 境遇,状况;穷境,苦境;危境。**2**. 【逻】(可)被论断的事物,种类;〔*pl*.〕(亚里士多德逻辑学中的)十大范畴。*be in an awkward* ～ 处困境中。

pred·i·cant [ˈpredikənt; ˋprɛdɪkənt] **I** *a*. 讲道的,说教的。**II** *n*. (天主教多明我会的)说教神父。

pred·i·cate [ˈpredikit; ˋprɛdɪkɪt] **I** *n*. **1**. 【语法】谓语,述语。**2**. 【逻】谓项,述项,述词,宾词。**3**. 本质;属性。**II** *a*. 谓语的,述语的;谓项的,述项的。**III** [ˈpredikeit; ˋprɛdɪket] *vt*. **1**. 论断,断言;断定…为某物的属性;断定某物有…的属性 (*about*; *of*)。**2**. 〔美〕使(声明、行动等)依据于 (*on*; *upon*),使基于。**3**. 宣言,宣布,声明。**4**. 意味着,具有…的含义。**5**. 【语法】表述。—*vi*. 断言 (*of*)。*Can anything be* ～*d about a non-existent thing*? 能够表述不存在的东西吗? (*We*) ～ *of the motive that it is good*. (我们)断言这个动机是好的。

pred·i·ca·tion [ˌprediˈkeiʃən; ˏprɛdɪˋkeʃən] *n*. **1**. 断定;判断。**2**. 【语法】谓语,述语;述语的表述,述谓。

pred·i·ca·tive [priˈdikətiv; ˋprɛdɪˏketɪv] **I** *a*. **1**. (在某一事物的属性方面)起论断作用的;论断性的。**2**. 【语法】谓语的,表语的,用作谓语[表语]的。*a* ～ *adjective* [表语]形容词。**II** *n*. 【语法】表语;表语性。**-ca·tiv·i·ty** [priˌdikəˈtiviti; prɪˏdɪkəˋtɪvətɪ] *n*. 表语性。**-ly** *ad*.

pred·i·ca·to·ry [ˈpredikətəri; ˋprɛdəkəˏtorɪ] *a*. **1**. 说教的,说教性的。**2**. 断定的,论断性的。**3**. 宣言的。

pre·dict [priˈdikt; prɪˋdɪkt] *vt*., *vi*. 预言,预告,预报,预示。～ *rain for tomorrow* 预告明天有雨。～ *a good harvest* 预告丰年。

pre·dict·a·ble [priˈdiktəbl; prɪˋdɪktəbl̩] *a*. 可预言的;可预报的。**pre·dict·a·bil·i·ty** [priˌdiktəˈbiliti; prɪˏdɪktəˋbɪlətɪ] *n*. **-a·bly** *ad*.

pre·dic·tion [priˈdikʃən; prɪˋdɪkʃən] *n*. **1**. 预言,预告。**2**. 被预言的事物。**3**. 【气】预测,预报。*weather* ～ 天气预报。

pre·dic·tive [priˈdiktiv; prɪˋdɪktɪv] *a*. 预言性的;(成为)前兆的。

pre·dic·tor [priˈdiktə; prɪˋdɪktɚ] *n*. **1**. 预言者;预报者。**2**. 【军】活动目标预测器;水雷发射预测器。**3**. 【气】预报因子。

pre·di·gest [ˈpriːdiˈdʒest, priːdaiˈdʒest; ˏpridəˋdʒɛst, pridaɪˋdʒɛst] *vt*. **1**. 把(食物)弄得容易消化;预先消化。**2**. 使简化易懂。**pre·di·ges·tion** [ˈpriːdiˈdʒestʃən, -dai-; ˋpridɪˋdʒɛstʃən, -daɪ-] *n*.

pre·di·lec·tion [ˌpriːdiˈlekʃən; ˏpridl̩ˋɛkʃən] *n*. 嗜好,偏好;偏爱 (*for*)。*have a* ～ *for* (*opera*) 特别爱好(歌剧)。

pre·dis·pose [ˈpriːdisˈpəuz; ˏpridɪsˋpoz] *vt*. **1**. 预先处理[处置,安排]。**2**. 是…造成…的基础[原因],使先倾向于;使先爱好,使先适应。**3**. 使容易感染;使易接受(病)。*A cold* ～*s one to other diseases*. 伤风容易使人患别的病。*be* ～*d to* 本来爱好…,有…的倾向;易患…病。**-d** *a*. **1**. 先倾向于…的。**2**. 事先安排好的。

pre·dis·po·si·tion [priːˌdispəˈziʃən; ˏpridɪspəˋzɪʃən] *n*. **1**. 倾向,天性,素质;癖性,资质 (*to*)。**2**. 【医】诱因 (*to*)。

pred·nis·o·lone [predˈnisələun; prɛdˋnɪsəlon] *n*. 【药】氢化泼尼松,去氢氢化可的松,强的松龙,Δ[1]-去氢皮质醇。

pred·ni·sone [ˈprednisəun; ˋprɛdnɪson] *n*. 【药】泼尼松,Δ[1]-皮质酮。～ **acetate** 【药】醋酸泼尼松,去氢可的松,强的松,乙酸 Δ[1]-皮质酮。

pre·dom·i·nance [priˈdɔminəns; prɪˋdɑmənəns] *n*. **1**. 优越,优势。**2**. 卓越,出众;显著,突出。

pre·dom·i·nant [priˈdɔminənt; prɪˋdɑmənənt] **I** *a*. **1**. 主要的;突出的;最显著的。**2**. 掌握主权的;有力的,有效的。**3**. 占优势的,支配其他的 (*over*),卓越的。**4**. 流行的。*a* ～ *idea* 主导思想。*a* ～ *colour* 主色。**II** *n*. 【生】特优生物,特优种。**-ly** *ad*.

pre·dom·i·nate I [priˈdɔmineit; prɪˋdɑməˏnet] *vi*. 统治;居支配地位,(数量上)占优势 (*over*)。*a mixed feeling in which jealousy* ～*s* 嫉妒占优势的复杂感情。*a garden in which dahlias* ～ 大丽花最多的花园。—*vt*. 支配,统治。**II** [priˈdɔminit; prɪˋdɔmɪnɪt] *a*. = predominant. **pre·dom·i·nat·ing·ly** *ad*.

pre·dom·i·na·tion [priˌdɔmiˈneiʃən; prɪˏdɑməˋneʃən] *n*. = predominance.

pre·doom [ˈpriːˈduːm; ˋpriˋdum] *vt*. 〔古〕命中注定,预先判处。

pre-e·lect [ˈpriːiˈlekt; ˏpriɪˋlɛkt] *vt*. 预选。

pre-e·lec·tion [ˈpriːiˈlekʃən; ˏpriɪˋlɛkʃən] **I** *n*. **1**. 〔古〕预选;优先的选择。**2**. 预定。**II** *a*. 选举前的。～ *promises* 选举前的许诺。

preem [priːm; prim] *n*. 〔美俚〕(电影、戏剧、电视节目等的)初次上演,首轮放映。

pree·mie [ˈpriːmiː; ˋprimɪ] *n*. 〔口〕早产儿〔尤指体重未超过 $5\frac{1}{2}$ 磅者而言〕。

pre-em·i·nence [pri(ː)ˈeminəns; prɪˋɛmənəns] *n*. 杰出,卓越。

pre-em·i·nent [pri(ː)ˈeminənt; prɪˋɛmənənt] *a*. 优秀的,杰出的,卓越的,显著的。**-ly** *ad*.

pre·em·pha·sis [ˈpriːˈemfəsis; priˋɛmfəsɪs] *n*. 【无】预加重,预修正,(频应)预矫。

pre-empt [pri(ː)ˈempt; prɪˋɛmpt] *vt*. **1**. 以先买权取得。**2**. 〔美〕为取得先买权预先占据(公地)。**3**. 〔喻〕先占,先取。— *vi*. (桥牌中)先发制人地叫牌〔故意叫得很高使对方为难〕。

pre-emp·tion [pri(ː)ˈempʃən; prɪˋɛmpʃən] *n*. **1**. 先买;(个人购买公地的)先买权。**2**. 先取;先占。

pre-emp·tive [pri(ː)ˈemptiv; prɪˋɛmptɪv] *a*. **1**. 先买的,有先买权的。**2**. (桥牌中叫牌、战争等)先发制人的。

P

a ~ *bid*【桥牌】先发制人的叫牌〔故意叫高以阻止对方叫牌〕。*a* ~ *war* 先发制人的战争。

preen [priːn; prin] *vt*. **1.** (鸟)用嘴理(毛)。**2.** 〔~ oneself〕(人)打扮(自己)。**3.** 〔~ oneself〕(人)夸耀(自己)。— *vi*. **1.** 把自己打扮得漂漂亮亮。**2.** 自满,自负,自我夸耀。

pre·en·gage [ˈpriːinˈgeidʒ; ˌpriɪnˋgedʒ] *vt*. **1.** 先订,预约;(以先订的婚约)约束。**2.** 先得,先占。**3.** 使先入为主,使偏向。**-ment** *n*.

pre·es·tab·lish [ˈpriːisˈtæbliʃ; ˌpriəsˋtæblɪʃ] *vt*. 预先设立[制定],预定,先定。

P

pre-es·ti·mate [pri(ː)ˈestimeit; pri(ɪ)ˋɛstɪmet] **I** *vt*. 预测,预估,预算。**II** [pri(ː)ˈestimit; pri(ɪ)ˋɛstɪmɪt] *n*. 预测,预估,预算。

pre-ex·am·ine [pri(ː)igˈzæmin; pri(ɪ)ɪgˋzæmɪn] *vt*. 预试,预考;预先检查。**pre-ex·am·i·na·tion** [pri(ː)igˌzæmiˈneiʃən; pri(ɪ)ɪgˌzæmiˋneʃən] *n*.

pre-ex·ist [ˈpriːigˈzist; ˌpriɪgˋzɪst] *vi*. 先(存)在。— *vt*. 先于…而存在。

pre-ex·ist·ence [ˈpriːigˈzistəns; ˌpriɪgˋzɪstəns] *n*. **1.** 先在,先存〔尤指所谓灵魂与肉体结合前的存在〕。**2.** 前世。**pre-ex·ist·ent, pre-ex·ist·ing** *a*.

pref. = **1.** preface; prefaced. **2.** preference; preferred. **3.** preffix.

pre·fab [ˈpriːˈfæb; ˋpriˋfæb] **I** *n*. 〔口〕预制房屋;活动房屋(=prefabricated house)。**II** *a*. 预制的,预构的(= prefabricated)。

pre·fab·ri·cate [ˈpriːˈfæbrikeit; priˋfæbrəˌket] *vt*. **1.** 预制。**2.** 〔美〕用预制构件建筑[制造]。**3.** 预先构思。*~d parts* 预制构件。*~d structures* 预制结构。*a ~d house* (构件均预先制成,到施工现场装配即建成的)预制房屋,活动房屋。**pre·fab·ri·ca·tion** [priːˌfæbriˈkeiʃən; priˌfæbrɪˋkeʃən] *n*.

pref·ace [ˈprefis; ˋprɛfɪs] **I** *n*. **1.** 序,绪言;前言;引语;开端。**2.** 〔P-〕【宗】(弥撒的)序诵,序祷。**II** *vt*. **1.** 给…作序。**2.** 开始,导致;作为…的开端。—*vi*. 作序,写序文。~ *one's remarks by a cough* 先咳嗽一下然后开始讲话。

pre·fade [priˈfeid; priˋfed] *vt*. 【纺】使(新的纺织品或衣服)预退色〔显出已经退色的模样,如牛仔服多用此法处理〕。

pref·a·to·ri·al, pref·a·to·ry [ˌprefəˈtɔːriəl, ˈprefətəri; ˌprɛfəˋtorɪəl, ˋprɛfəˌtorɪ] *a*. **1.** 序言的;引言性的。**2.** 位于前面的。*prefatory remarks in a speech* 演说的开场白。

prefd. = preferred stock 〔美〕优先股。

pre·fect [ˈpriːfekt; ˋprifɛkt] *n*. **1.** (古罗马的)行政长官;(陆、海军)司令官;总督。**2.** (现代法国的)省长;(日本的)县知事。**3.** (英国某些公立学校、美国某些私立学校负责维持秩序的)班长。~ *of police* 巴黎警察总监。**pre·fec·tor·al** [priˈfektərəl; priˋfɛktərəl], **pre·fec·tori·al** [ˌpriːfekˈtɔːriəl; prifɛkˋtorɪəl] *a*.

pre·fec·tur·al [ˈpriːfektjurəl; priˋfɛktʃərəl] *a*. **1.** 专区的;(日本的)县的;(法国的)省的。**2.** (日本的)县知事的;(法国的)省的。

pre·fec·ture [ˈpriːfektjuə, -tʃuə; ˋprifɛktʃə] *n*. **1.** 古罗马高级文武长官[法国省长、日本县知事]的职位[任期、管区、官邸]。**2.** 级长的职位[任期]。**3.** 专区;县;府;(法国的)省。

pre·fer [priˈfəː; priˋfɝ] *vt*. (**-rr-**) **1.** (比较起来)喜欢…(而不喜欢…);宁可…(而不…);比起…来还是…好;宁愿选择;更喜欢(*to, above, before*)。**2.** 提起,提出(声明、请求、控诉等)。**3.** 提升,提拔;任命;录用;推荐,介绍。**4.** 【法】给与(某债权人等)优先获得偿付权。**5.** 建议;申请。*I ~ water to wine*. 我喜欢水不喜欢酒。~ *working to sitting idle* 喜欢干活而不喜欢闲呆着。~ *the country to the town* 比起城市来还是乡下好。~ *a claim to property* 提出一项财产要求。~ *charge against sb*. 控告某人。*a ~red share* [*stock*]【商】优先股。★ **1.** prefer 后接 rather than 的习惯用法: *He ~red to do this rather than that*. 他说宁愿做这个,不愿做那个。**2.** 比较部分常有省略: ~ *to wait* (*rather than go at once*) (与其马上就走)还是等一等的好。~ *to leave it alone* = ~ *that it should be left alone* 还是听其自然的好。~ **sb. for** 提升某人为…。

pref·er·a·ble [ˈprefərəbl; ˋprɛfrəbl̩] *a*. 更可取的;更好的(*to*);略胜一筹的。*Poverty is ~ to ill-health*. 贫穷比不健康好一点。

pref·er·a·bly [ˈprefərəbli; ˋprɛfərəblɪ] *ad*. 宁可,宁愿;最好;更可取地。*I might travel by York or ~ by Preston*. 我想旅途中经过约克,但最好是经过普雷斯顿。

pref·er·ence [ˈprefərəns; ˋprɛfərəns] *n*. **1.** 优先选择;偏爱。**2.** 优先选择物,偏爱物。**3.** 【法】优先权;特惠〔特指关税〕;(债权人)受优先偿还的权利;选择机会。**4.** 一种牌戏。*This is my ~*. 我喜欢这个。**by** [**for**] ~ 喜欢,选择。**have a ~ for** [**to**] 喜欢…,认为…更好。**in ~ to ...** 比…先,比起…来宁愿。~ **of sth. to** [**over**] **another** 宁要某物而不要另一物。~ **bond** [**share, stock**] 〔英〕优先公债[股]。

pref·er·en·tial [ˌprefəˈrenʃəl; ˌprɛfəˋrɛnʃəl] **I** *a*. **1.** 优先的;优待的;优先选择的;差别制的。**2.** (国际贸易等方面)特惠的。**II** *n*. **1.** 优先权。**2.** 特惠税率。~ **pairing** 【生】偏向配对。~ **right** 优先权。~ **shop** 〔美〕优先(雇工会会员的)工厂。~ **species** 【生】适宜种。~ **stock** 优先股。~ **system** = ~ voting. ~ **tariff** [**duties**] 特惠关税。~ **voting** 选择选票制〔选择者可在选票中注明对被选举人的优先选择次序〕。**-ism** *n*. 关税特惠主义。**-ist** *n*. 关税特惠主义者。

pre·fer·ment [priˈfəːmənt; priˋfɝmənt] *n*. **1.** 升级,提升。**2.** 〔古〕(购置财产等的)优先权。**3.** (神父等的)高位;肥缺。**4.** (控告等的)提出。

pre·fig·u·ra·tion [ˌpriːfigjuˈreiʃən; ˌprifɪgjəˋreʃən] *n*. **1.** 预示,预兆。**2.** 预想。**3.** 原型。**pre·fig·u·ra·tive** [ˈpriːˈfigjurətiv; ˋpriˋfɪgjurətɪv] *a*.

pre·fig·ure [ˈpriːˈfigə; priˋfɪgjɚ] *vt*. **1.** (通过形象)预示,预兆。**2.** 预想;预见;预言。**pre·fig·u·ra·tive** *a*.

pre·fix I [ˈpriːfiks; ˋpriˌfɪks] **I** *n*. **1.** 【语法】前缀,词首;前加成分〔如 prefix 的 pre-〕。**2.** 人名前用的尊称〔Mr., Dr., Sir. 等〕。**3.** 【数】首标。**II** [priːˈfiks; priˋfɪks] *vt*. **1.** 把…放在前头;作…的前缀;给…附加标题。**2.** 〔古〕预先指定,预先任命。*Quotations are ~ed to the chapters*. 各章前头附有引文。**-al** *a*. **pre·fix·al·ly** *ad*.

pre·flight [ˈpriːˈflait; ˋpriˋflaɪt] *a*. 【空】在起飞之前的。~ *instructions* 起飞前的指示。

pre·form [ˈpriːˈfɔːm; priˋfɔrm] **I** *vt*. **1.** 预先形成[决定]。**2.** 把…初步加工,对(宝石等)粗加工。**II** [ˈpriːfɔːm; ˋprifɔrm] *n*. 初步加工的成品;压片;雏形,塑坯预塑;(录音用)盘料;经过粗琢的宝石。

pre·form·a·tion [ˈpriːfɔːˈmeiʃən; ˌprifɔrˋmeʃən] *n*. **1.** 预先形成。**2.** 【生】胚中预存说,预成说(*opp*. epigenesis)。

pre·for·ma·tive [ˈpriːˈfɔːmətiv; priˋfɔrmətɪv] **I** *a*. **1.** 使预先形成的。**2.** 【语法】以前缀[词首]为特征的;前缀[词首]的。**II** *n*. 【语法】前缀,词首。

pre·fron·tal [ˈpriːˈfrʌntl; priˋfrʌntl] **I** *a*. 【解】前额的,额叶前部的;前额骨的。**II** *n*. 前额骨。

pre·gan·gli·on·ic [priˌgæŋgliˈɔnik; prɪˌgæŋglɪˋɑnɪk] *a*. 【动】前神经节的。

pre·gla·cial [ˈpriːgleisjəl; priˋgleʃəl] *a*. 【地】冰河期前的。

preg·na·ble [ˈpregnəbl; ˋprɛgnəbl̩] *a*. 可攻克的,易占领的;易受攻击的,有弱点的。*a ~ fortress* 易攻破的堡垒。*a ~ idea* 有毛病的主意。*the only ~ point* 唯一

的弱点。**preg·na·bil·i·ty** [ˌpregnəˈbiliti; ˏpregnəˋbɪlətɪ] ***n.***

preg·nan·cy [ˈpregnənsi; ˋpregnənsɪ] ***n.*** **1.** 怀孕,妊娠;怀孕期;(事件等的)蕴酿。**2.**〔喻〕丰富,丰满;含蓄,(内容)充实,富有意义。~ **cell** 孕细胞。

preg·nant [ˈpregnənt; ˋpregnənt] ***a.*** **1.** 怀着孕的,有孕的,怀胎的。**2.** 意义深长的,(话等)有含蓄的。**3.** 包藏着[孕育着](重大结果)的;充满…的 (*with*)。**4.** 富于想像的,富于发明才能的,聪明的,有创造力的。**5.** 富于成果的。**6.**〔古;诗〕多产的,丰饶的。*a ~ construction*【修】简洁体〔如将 *Let him go out*. 说成 *Let him out*.〕。*the ~ year* 丰年。**-ly** ***ad.***

preg·phone [ˈpregfəun; ˋpregfon] ***n.*** 孕妇传话器〔类似扩音器,孕妇可通过该装置对胎儿说话进行胎教〕。

pre·heat [ˈpriːˈhiːt; priˋhit] ***vt.*** 预热(炉、灶等)。**-er** ***n.*** 预热器。

pre·hen·sile [priˈhensail; prɪˋhɛnsl] ***a.*** **1.**【动】(足、尾等)适于抓拿的,适于缠卷的,(有)捕握(力)的。**2.** 善于领悟的,有洞察力的。*a ~ arm* (头足类的)捉脚。*the ~ tail of a monkey* 猿猴的卷尾。~ *poets* 有特殊洞察力的诗人们。

pre·hen·sion [priˈhenʃən; prɪˋhɛnʃən] ***n.*** **1.**【动】抓住,捕捉,把握。**2.**【心】理解,领悟。

pre·his·tor·ic, pre·his·tor·i·cal [ˈpriː*h*isˈtɔrik, -ikəl; ˏpriɪsˋtɔrɪk, -ɪkəl] ***a.*** **1.** 史前的,(有记载的)历史以前的。**2.**〔口〕陈旧不堪的;旧式的;陈腐的。**-i·cal·ly** ***ad.***

pre·his·to·ry [ˈpriːˈhistəri; priˋhɪstərɪ] ***n.*** **1.** (历史记载以前的)史前史。**2.** (导致事件、危机等的)背景。**3.** 史前学;史前考古学。

pre·hu·man [ˈpriːˈhjuːmən; priˋhjumən] ***a.*** 人类以前的。

pre·ig·ni·tion [ˈpriːigˈniʃən; ˏpriɪgˋnɪʃən] ***n.***【机】(内燃机内的)提前点火,预燃(作用);过早点火。

pre·judge [ˈpriːˈdʒʌdʒ; priˋdʒʌdʒ] ***vt.*** 预先判断,过早判断;【法】不审而判。**-judg(e)·ment** ***n.***

pre·ju·di·ca·tion [ˈpriːˌdʒuːdiˈkeiʃən; ˋpriˏdʒudɪˋkeʃən] ***n.*** **1.** 预先判断;预先判决;草率的判断。**2.**【法】判例。

prej·u·dice [ˈpredʒudis; ˋprɛdʒədɪs] **I** ***n.*** **1.** 偏见,成见;歧视。**2.**【法】损害,伤害;不利。*Divest you of your ~.* 扫除你的偏见。***be swayed by*** ~ 为偏见所左右。***have a ~ against*** (*sb.*) 对(某人)有偏见。***have a ~ in favour of*** ... 祖护,偏爱。***in*** [***to the***] ***~ of*** 有损于,不利于。***without*** ~ **1.** 无偏见。**2.**【法】不违背;不使(合法权利等)受损害。**II** ***vt.*** **1.** 使抱偏见,使怀成见。**2.** 侵害,伤害,损害。*His manner ~d his audience against* [*in favour of*] *him.* 他的态度使听众对他发生了反感[好感]。*You ~d your chances of success.* 你糟蹋了你的前途。

prej·u·diced [ˈpredʒudist; ˋprɛdʒədɪst] ***a.*** 抱有偏见的,有成见的,有偏心的。*a ~ opinion* 偏见。*the least ~ in sizing up situations* 最能不抱偏见地估计形势。*be ~ against* [*in favour of*] 对…抱反感[好感]。

prej·u·di·cial [ˌpredʒuˈdiʃəl; ˏprɛdʒəˋdɪʃəl] ***a.*** **1.** 引起偏见的,有成见的。**2.** 有损害的,不利的。*a course of action ~ to sb.'s interest* 不利于某人的诉讼。**-ly** ***ad.***

prel·a·cy [ˈpreləsi; ˋprɛləsɪ] ***n.*** **1.** [the ~]〔集合词〕主教(团);高级教士(团) (= prelates)。**2.** 主教[高级教士]的地位[职务、管辖区]。**3.**〔贬〕主教统治,主教监管制。

prel·ate [ˈprelit; ˋprɛlɪt] ***n.*** **1.** 高级教士[教长,主教]。**2.**〔美〕教士,牧师。**3.**【史】修道院长。**pre·lat·ic, pre·lat·ical** [priˈlætik(əl); prɪˋlætɪk(əl)] ***a.***

prel·at·ess [ˈprelitis; ˋprɛlɪtɪs] ***n.*** **1.** 女修道院长。**2.**〔谑〕主教太太。

pre·law [ˈpriːˈlɔː; priˋlɔ] ***a.***〔美〕法科预科的;修习法科预科的。*a ~ student* 法科预科学生。

pre·lect [priˈlekt; prɪˋlɛkt] ***vi.*** (特指大学讲师)讲演,讲述,讲课。**-lec·tion** [-ˈlekʃən; -ˋlɛkʃən] ***n.***

pre·lec·tor [priˈlektə; prɪˋlɛktɚ] ***n.***〔主英〕(大学)讲师。

pre·li·ba·tion [ˈpriːlaiˈbeiʃən; ˏprilaɪˋbeʃən] ***n.*** 试尝,预尝〔通常作比喻用〕。

pre·lim [priˈlim; prɪˋlɪm] ***n.***, ***a.***〔俚〕大学考试(的),初试(的)〔preliminary 的缩略形式〕。

pre·lim·i·na·ry [priˈlim*i*nəri; prɪˋlɪməˏnɛrɪ] **I** ***a.*** **1.** 预备的;初步的,初级的。**2.** 序言性的,绪言的。*a ~ examination* 初试,预考〔学生普通说作 prelim〕。~ *expenses* 开办费。~ *hearing*【法】预审。~ *remarks* 前言;开场白。**II** ***n.*** **1.**〔常 *pl.*〕初步,开端;预备行为[步骤、措施],准备。**2.**〔*sing.*〕入学初考,预考。**3.**【体】预赛;淘汰赛;(主赛前的)次要比赛〔如拳击〕。**4.**〔常 *pl.*〕正文前的书页[内容]。***without preliminaries*** 直截了当地,单刀直入地。**III** ***ad.*** 预先 (= preliminarily)。**pre·lim·i·na·ri·ly** [priˈlim*i*nərili, Am. priˌlimiˈnerili; prɪˋlɪmɪnərɪlɪ, Am. prɪˏlɪmɪˋnɛrɪlɪ] ***ad.***

pre·lit·er·ate [priˈlitərit; prɪˋlɪtərɪt] ***a.*** 没有文字的社会的,有文字社会前的。

pre·load·ed [priˈləudid; prɪˋlodɪd] ***a.***【计】(电脑中的处理程序等)事先安装的。

prel·ude [ˈpreljuːd; ˋprɛljud] **I** ***n.*** **1.**【乐】序曲,前奏曲。**2.** 开场戏;序幕;序言。**3.** 前兆,预兆。**II** ***vt.*** **1.** 成为…的序曲[序幕];奏(序曲)。**2.** 为…作序;开头;成为…的前兆。— ***vi.*** 奏序曲;唱开场戏;成为序幕;成为前兆 (*to*)。*He ~d with some banal remarks.* 他讲了一些老套话作为开场白。

pre·lu·di·al [priˈl*j*uːdiəl; prɪˋl*j*udɪəl] ***a.*** **1.** 序言(式)的;序幕(式)的;序曲(式)的。**2.** 先导的;前兆的,预兆的。

pre·lu·sion [priˈluːʒən; prɪˋluʒən] ***n.*** 序言 (= prelude ***n.***)。

pre·lu·sive [priˈl*j*uːsiv; prɪˋljusɪv] ***a.*** **1.** 前奏曲的;序幕的;序言的 (*to*)。**2.** 先导的;成为先驱的;成为前兆的。**-ly** ***ad.***

pre·lu·so·ry [priˈl*j*uːsəri; prɪˋlusərɪ] ***a.*** = prelusive.

prem. = premium.

pre·man [ˈpriːmæn; ˋpriˏmæn] ***n.*** (*pl.* ***pre·men*** [ˈpriːˈmen; ˋpriˋmɛn]) (假定为人类直系祖先的)一种古灵长类动物。

pre·mar·i·tal [ˈpriːməˈraitəl, priːˈmæritəl; priməˋraɪtəl, prɪˋmærətl] ***a.*** (结)婚前的。

pre·ma·ture [ˌpreməˈtjuə, ˌpriːməˈtjuə; ˏpriməˋtjur, ˏpriməˋtʃur] **I** ***a.*** **1.** 早熟的;不成熟的。**2.** 过早的,不到期的;时机未成熟的。*a ~ birth* 早产。*a ~ death* 夭亡。*a ~ decision* 过早的决定。**II** ***n.*** **1.** 早产的婴儿。**2.** 过早爆发的炮弹。**3.** 过早发生的事物。

pre·ma·tu·ri·ty [ˌpreməˈtjuəriti, ˌpriːməˈtjuəriti; ˏprɛməˋtjurətɪ, ˏpriməˋtjurətɪ] ***n.*** **1.** 早熟(性);不成熟。**2.** 不到期;过早,时机未成熟;(花的)早开。

pre·max·il·la [ˌpriːmækˈsilə; ˏprimækˋsɪlə] ***n.*** (*pl.* ***-lae*** [-iː; -i])【解】切牙骨。**-il·lar·y** [-ˈmæksiləri; -ˋmæksəlɛrɪ] ***a.***

pre·med [ˈpriːmed; ˋprimɛd] **I** ***a.***〔美〕医科大学预科的〔premedical 的缩略形式〕。**II** ***n.*** 医科大学预科(学生)。

pre·med·i·cal [ˈpriːˈmedikəl; priˋmɛdɪkl] ***a.***〔美〕医科大学预科的。

pre·med·i·tate [pri(ː)ˈmediteit; prɪˋmɛdəˏtet] ***vt.***, ***vi.*** 预先思考,预谋,预先策划。

pre·med·i·tat·ed [pri(ː)ˌmediˈteitid; prɪˋmɛdəˏtetɪd] ***a.*** 预先想过的,预先策划的,有预谋的。*a ~ murder* 谋杀。**-ly** ***ad.***

pre·med·i·ta·tion [pri(ː)ˌmediˈteiʃən; ˏprimɛdəˋteʃən] ***n.*** 预想,预谋;预先策划。

prem·i·er [ˈpremjə, -miə; ˋprimɪɚ, -mjɚ] **I** ***n.*** 总理,首

相。**II** ***a*.** **1.** 第一的,首位的,首要的。**2.** 最先的,最早的。*take the* ～ *place* 占第一位,占首席。*the* ～ *minister* 〔古〕首相。**-ship** ***n*.** 首相[总理]的职务[任期]。

pre·mière [ˈpremieə; priˋmɪr] **I** ***n*.** 〔F.〕**1.** 首次演出;(演出的)第一天,开场日;初次的展出。**2.** (舞蹈、戏剧等的)女主角。***give*** ～ ***of*** 首次演出。**II** ***vi*.** 初次演出;(名演员等)首次登台。**III** ***a*.** 首要的,第一的。

pre·mil·len·ni·al [ˈpriːmiˈleniəl; ˋprimɪˋlɛnɪəl] ***a*.** 【宗】千年至福期前的;基督再临以前的;现世的。**-ism** ***n*.** 千年至福期前基督再临论。

prem·ise I [ˈpremis; ˋprɛmɪs] ***n*.** **1.** 【逻】前提〔常作 premiss〕。**2.** 〔*pl*.〕【法】(理由等的)前提,根据,缘起部分;〔*pl*.〕【法】控诉事实;前述事件,让渡物件;证件前款〔如当事人姓名、让渡物件、让渡理由等〕。**3.** 〔*pl*.〕房屋(及其附属基地、建筑等);院内,屋内。*the major* [*minor*] ～【逻】大[小]前提。*business* ～*s* 事务所,办公室。*the back* [*front*] ～ 后[前]院。***on*** [***in***] ***the*** ～***s*** 只供店内喝〔指酒等〕。***live on the*** ～***s*** 住在楼内。**II** [priˈmaiz; prɪˋmaɪz] ***vt*.** **1.** 预述(条件等);引导(论述等)。**2.** 提出…作为前提[条件]。**3.** 假定。～ *one's argument with a bit of history* 引证一点历史作为立论的前提。— ***vi*.** 作出前提。

prem·iss [ˈpremis; ˋprɛmɪs] ***n*.** 【逻】前提 (= premise ***n*.** **1.**)。

pre·mi·um [ˈpriːmjəm, -miəm; ˋprimɪəm] ***n*.** **1.** 超票面价格,溢价;加价;贴水,升水。**2.** 奖赏,奖励;奖金;奖状,奖品;【桥牌】奖分。**3.** 保险费。**4.** 佣金;(利息;工资等以外的)酬金。**5.** 额外费用。**6.** 学费;习艺费。*a* ～ *for* 为…而发的奖金。***at a*** ～ (股票)以超过票面以上的价格;〔喻〕非常需要,极受重视 (*opp*. at a discount) (*It sells at a* ～ *of 20 percent*. 这是加二卖出的)。***pay a*** ～ ***for*** 付…佣金。***put*** [***set***, ***place***] ***a*** ～ ***on*** 诱发;助长,促进;鼓励;奖励。～ **bond** 溢价债券。**P- Bonds** 〔英〕政府有奖债券〔但无利息〕。～ **note** 保险费付款期票。～ **system** 职工奖金制度。～ **tariff** 保险率表。

pre·mo·lar [ˈpriːməulə; priˋmolɚ] ***n*.**, ***a*.** 【解】前磨牙(的),前臼齿(的)。

pre·mon·ish [ˈpriːmɔniʃ; priˋmɑnɪʃ] ***vt*.**, ***vi*.** 〔罕〕预先警告;预先劝告。

pre·mo·ni·tion [ˌpriːməˈniʃən; ˏpriməˋnɪʃən] ***n*.** **1.** 预先的警告[告诫],预诫。**2.** 预感;前兆,征兆。

pre·mon·i·tor [priˈmɔnitə; prɪˋmɑnɪtɚ] ***n*.** **1.** 预先警告[告诫]者。**2.** 预兆,征兆。

pre·mon·i·to·ry [priˈmɔnitəri; prɪˋmɑnəˏtorɪ] ***a*.** **1.** 预先警告[告诫]的。**2.** 前兆的。**3.** 【医】前驱的,先兆的,先期的。

pre·morse [pri(ː)ˈmɔːs; pri(ɪ)ˋmɔrs] ***a*.** 【植】(叶、根等)啮蚀状的。

pre·mune [pri(ː)ˈmjuːn; pri(ɪ)ˋmjun] ***a*.** **1.** 显示抗病(力)的。**2.** 【医】预免疫的。

pre·mu·ni·tion [ˌpriːmjuːˈniʃən; ˏprimjuˋnɪʃən] ***n*.** **1.** 〔古〕预防;抗病(力)。**2.** 【医】预免疫。

pre·na·tal [ˈpriːˈneitl; priˋnetl̩] ***a*.** 出生前的,胎儿期的。

pre·nom·i·nate I [pri(ː)ˈnɔmineit; pri(ɪ)ˋnɑmɪˏnet] ***vt*.** 〔废〕预先命名,预先提到。**II** [pri(ː)ˈnɔminit; pri(ɪ)ˋnɑmɪnɪt] ***a*.** 〔废〕预先提到的,预先命名的。

pre·no·tion [pri(ː)ˈnəuʃən; priˋnoʃən] ***n*.** 〔罕〕先见之明,预知,预想。

pren·tice [ˈprentis; ˋprɛntɪs] **I** ***n*.** 〔古〕〔口〕定期学徒〔apprentice 之略〕。～ ***hand*** 生手 (*try one's* ～ *hand at* 做做试一试看)。**II** ***a*.** 〔古〕〔口〕学徒的。**III** ***vt*.** 〔古〕〔口〕使做学徒。

pre·nup [priːˈnʌp; priˋnʌp] ***n*.** 〔口〕婚前协议〔结婚前男女双方就财产、婚后权利和义务等签订的协议〕。

pre·nup·tial [pri(ː)ˈnʌpʃəl; pri(ɪ)ˋnʌpʃəl] ***a*.** **1.** 结婚前的,婚礼前的。**2.** 【动】交配前的。

pre·oc·cu·pan·cy [pri(ː)ˈɔkjupənsi; priˋɑkjəpənsɪ] ***n*.** **1.** 先占据,先取;先占权。**2.** 专心致志,全神贯注;(事情)极繁忙。

pre·oc·cu·pa·tion [pri(ː)ˌɔkjuˈpeiʃən; priˏɑkjəˋpeʃən] ***n*.** **1.** 先占据,先取。**2.** 偏见,成见。**3.** 专心,全神贯注;出神。**4.** 使人全神贯注的事;首先要做的事,急务。***take one's*** ～ ***with*** 全神贯注于,专心致志于。

pre·oc·cu·pied [pri(ː)ˈɔkjupaid; priˋɑkjəˏpaɪd] ***a*.** **1.** 专心一意的,全神贯注的;(为某事)出神的;心思重重的。**2.** 被先占的。**3.** 【生】(种和属的名称)不能再以新义使用的。

pre·oc·cu·py [pri(ː)ˈɔkjupai; priˋɑkjəˏpaɪ] ***vt*.** (***-pied***) **1.** 先占领,先取。**2.** 〔常用被动语态〕吸引住,迷住;使出神;使全神贯注;使专心于;使抱偏见。*His mind is preoccupied with private cares*. 他一脑袋全是私心。

pre·op·er·a·tive [ˈpriːˈɔpərətiv; ˋpriˋɑpərətɪv] ***a*.** (外科)手术前的。**-ly** ***ad*.**

pre·or·dain [ˈpriːɔːˈdein; ˏpriɔrˋden] ***vt*.** **1.** 预先注定,命该,命中注定。**2.** 预先规定。

prep [prep; prɛp] **I** ***n*.** **1.** 〔学俚〕预备功课;家庭作业〔*preparation* 之略〕。**2.** 〔美〕预备学校,预科 (= ～ *school*);预科学生 (= ～ *student*)。**II** ***a*.** 〔美口〕预备的,准备的(= preparatory)。*a* ～ *school* 预备学校。**III** ***vi*.** (***-pp-***) 〔口〕进预备学校;进行预备学习[训练];自修。— ***vt*.** 预备,准备,为(病人)做(手)术前(的)准备。

prep. = **1.** preposition. **2.** preparation. **3.** preparatory.

pre·pack [ˈpriːˈpæk; priˋpæk] ***n*.**, ***vt*.** = prepackage.

pre·pack·age [pri(ː)ˈpækidʒ; priˋpækɪdʒ] **I** ***vt*.** (出售前)将(食品或其他商品)按标准重量或单位包装。**II** ***n*.** (食品等出售前用透明纸等)预先作好的包装。

pre·paid [ˈpriːˈpeid; priˋped] ***a*.** (运费、邮资等)先付的,付讫的。*a telegram with reply* ～ 覆电费先付的电报。

prep·a·ra·tion [ˌprepəˈreiʃən; ˏprɛpəˋreʃən] ***n*.** **1.** 准备,预备;〔常 *pl*.〕准备工作[措施];预修,预习 (*for*);预习时间;(对…的)准备。**2.** (药、菜等的)配制,备办;制剂,配制品;配制好的食物。**3.** 【乐】准备调(音)。**4.** (进行解剖、病理等实验的)标本。**5.** 节日的前夜。*The* ～*s are complete*. 准备妥当了。～ *of gunpowder* 火药的配制。～ *of soil* 整地。***be in*** ～ 在准备中;在编辑中 (*The dictionary is in* ～. 这部字典在编辑中)。***in*** ～ ***for*** 作为…的准备。***make*** ～***s against*** 为对付…作准备。***make*** ～***s for*** 为…作准备。～**-room** 〔美〕(殡仪馆的)尸体防腐室。

pre·par·a·tive [priˈpærətiv; prɪˋpærətɪv] **I** ***a*.** 准备的,预备的;筹备的 (*to*)。**II** ***n*.** **1.** 预备,准备;筹备。**2.** 【军、海】(用鼓、号角等发出的)准备信号,预备号。**-ly** ***ad*.**

pre·par·a·to·ry [priˈpærətəri; prɪˈpærətərɪ] **I** ***a*.** 准备的,预备的;筹备的。*a* ～ *committee for a congress* 大会的筹备委员会。*a* ～ *course* 预科。～ *formation* 【军】准备姿势。**II** ***n*.** 〔英〕(为升入高级中学作准备的)私立预科学校;〔美〕大学预科。*a* ～ *school* 〔英〕补习学校;〔美〕大学预科。～ ***to*** 作为…的准备,在…之前。**III** ***ad*.** 在先前;作为准备 (*to*)。**pre·par·a·to·ri·ly** [priˈpæritərili, Am. priˌpærəˈtɔːrili; prɪˋpærɪtərɪlɪ, prɪˏpærəˋtɔrɪlɪ] ***ad*.**

pre·pare [priˈpɛə; prɪˋpɛr] ***vt*.** **1.** 准备,预备;筹备;布置;备办;温习(功课)。**2.** 锻炼(身体等);训练。**3.** 编写;配备,装备(旅行团、军队等)。**4.** 配制,制造(药等),调制。**5.** 使有准备,使作准备。**6.** 作出,制订。**7.** 【乐】调(音)。～ *lessons* 准备功课。～ *a boy for an examination* 叫孩子准备考试。～ *a prescription* 配药。～ *a meal* 做饭。～ *oneself for bad news* 对坏消息作好思想准备。— ***vi*.** **1.** 预备,作好准备(*for*)。**2.** (心中)有思想(*for*)。～ *for the worst* 以防万一。***be*** ～***d for*** [***to*** (*do*)] 准备着。(*I am* ～*d for anything*. 我已作好应急准备。*My son is preparing for the army*. 我的儿子

正准备参军)。~ *the table* 布置餐桌,准备开饭。

pre·pared [priˈpɛəd; prɪˋpɛrd] *a*. 1. 有准备的,准备好的。2. 精制的,特别处理过的。~ *position*【军】既设阵地。**-ly** [priˈpɛədli, Am. priˈpɛəridli; prɪˋpɛrdlɪ, prɪˋpɛrɪdlɪ] *ad*.

pre·pared·ness [priˈpɛədnis, Am. priˈpɛəridnis; prɪˋpɛrɪdnɪs, -ˋpɛrdnɪs] *n*. 1. 有准备,作好准备。2. 〔美〕扩军,备战。*a* ~ *campaign* 扩军运动。*a* ~ *parade* 扩军运动游行。*strengthen* ~ *against war* 加强战备。*P- averts peril*. 有备无患。

pre·par·ing [priˈpɛəriŋ; prɪˋpɛrɪŋ] *a*. 预备的,准备的;制备的。~**-room** *n*. =〔美〕preparation-room.

pre·pay [ˈpriːˈpei; priˋpe] *vt*. (***pre·paid*** [ˈpriːˈpeid; ˋpriˋped]) 预付,先付(运费、利息、邮资等)。~ *a reply to a telegram* 预付电报覆电费。~**-set** 投币自动售物装置。**-pay·a·ble** *a*. 可预付的。**-ment** *n*.

pre·pense [priˈpens; prɪˋpɛns] *a*. 预先考虑过的;故意的〔用在名词后〕。***of malice*** ~【法】蓄意伤害[中伤];预谋(*to kill a man of malice* ~ 预谋杀人)。**-ly** *ad*. 有计划地,故意。

pre·plan [ˈpriːˈplæn; priˋplæn] *vt*., *vi*. 预先计划[打算,规划]。

pre·pon·der·ance, pre·pon·der·an·cy [priˈpɔndərəns, -si; prɪˋpɑndrəns, -sɪ] *n*. (数量、重量、力量、影响、重要性上的)优势;优越。~ *of force at the crucial point*【军】集中优势兵力于要害目标。***have the ~ over*** 比…占优势。

pre·pon·der·ant [priˈpɔndərənt; prɪˋpɑndərənt] *a*. (数量、重量、力量、影响、重要性上)占优势的;压倒的(*over*)。**-ly** *ad*.

pre·pon·der·ate [priˈpɔndəreit; prɪˋpɑndəˏret] *vi*. 1. 数量上超过;重量超过;(天平)倒向一方。2. (智力、权力等)超过,压倒(*over*)。— *vt*. 〔古〕重过;压倒。

prep·o·si·tion [ˌprepəˈziʃən; ˏprɛpəˋzɪʃən] *n*.【语法】介词,前置词。

prep·o·si·tion·al [ˌprepəˈziʃənəl; ˏprɛpəˋzɪʃənl] *a*.【语法】前置词的,介词的。*a* ~ *phrase* 前置词短语。**-ly** *ad*.

pre·pos·i·tive [priˈpɔzitiv; prɪˋpɑzətɪv] I *a*.【语法】前置的;前缀[词首]的。II *n*.【语法】前置词语;前缀[词首]词语。

pre·pos·i·tor [priˈpɔzitə; prɪˋpɑzətɚ] *n*. = praepostor.

pre·pos·sess [ˌpriːpəˈzes; ˏpripəˋzɛs] *vt*. 1. 使预先具有,使充满(某种感情,思想等)。2. 〔常用被动语态〕(人、态度等)使先有好感;使偏爱。3. 使某人对某事先有反感[偏见](*against*)。*He is ~ed with a queer idea*. 他有一种奇怪的偏见。*She* [*Her manners*] *~ed me in her favour*. 她[她的态度]给我留下了好印象。*I was quite ~ed by his appearance*. 他的仪表使我十分喜欢。

pre·pos·ess·ing [ˌpriːpəˈzesiŋ; ˏpripəˋzɛsɪŋ] *a*. 使人喜欢的,可爱的;有吸引力的;给人好感的。**-ly** *ad*.

pre·pos·ses·sion [ˌpriːpəˈzeʃən; ˏpripəˋzɛʃən] *n*. 1. 预先形成的印象[信念];偏爱,袒护;偏见。2. 全神贯注;着迷。3. 〔古〕先占,先领。

pre·pos·ter·ous [priˈpɔstərəs; prɪˋpɑstərəs] *a*. 1. 是非颠倒的,反常的,乖戾的;十分荒谬的,不合理的,可笑的;愚蠢的。2. 〔古〕次序颠倒的。*It is* ~! 岂有此理! **-ly** *ad*.

pre·pos·tor [priːˈpɔstə; priˋpɑstɚ] *n*. = praepostor.

pre·po·tence, pre·po·ten·cy [priˈpəutəns, -si; prɪˋpotns, -sɪ] *n*. 1. 优越的力量[权势];优势。2.【生】优先遗传(力)。

pre·po·tent [priˈpəutənt; prɪˋpotnt] *a*. 1. 力量极优越的;优势的。2.【生】有优先遗传力的。

prep·pie [ˈprepi; ˋprɛpɪ] I *a*. 〔美〕1. 未熟的。2. 傻,笨。II *n*. (大学)预科生。

prep·ping [ˈprepiŋ; ˋprɛpɪŋ] *n*. 〔美口〕运动前的练习。

prep·py [ˈprepi; ˋprɛpɪ] = preppie.

pre·pran·di·al [ˈpriːˈprændiəl; priˋprændɪəl] *a*. 饭前的。

pre·pref·er·ence [ˈpriːˈprefərəns; priˋprɛfərəns] *a*. (证券等)最优先的。~ *shares* [*stocks*] 最优先股。

pre·prim·er [ˈpriːˈprimə; ˋpriˋprɪmɚ] *n*. 1. 学前儿童识字书。2. 基础入门之书;初学者所用的书。

pre·pro·ces·sor [priːˈprəusesə; priˋprosesɚ] *n*.【计】预处理程序。

prep·ster [ˈprepstə; ˋprɛpstɚ] *n*. 中学校[大学预科]的运动选手。

pre·puce [ˈpriːpjuːs; ˋpripjus] *n*. 1.【解】(阴茎的)包皮。2.【虫】阴(茎)端膜。**pre·pu·tial** [priˈpjuːʃəl; prɪˋpjuʃəl] *a*.

Pre-Raph·a·el [ˈpriːˈræfiəl; ˋpriˋræfɪəl] *a*.【美】1. (十九世纪英国)拉斐尔前派的。2. 拉斐尔之前时期的。*the* ~ *Brotherhood* (英国19世纪的)拉斐尔前派社。

Pre-Raph·a·el·ite [ˈpriːˈræfəlait; priˋræfəˏlaɪt] *a*., *n*. 前拉斐尔时期(画派)的(画家)。

Pre-Raph·a·el·it·ism [ˈpriːˈræfəlaitizəm; ˋpriˋræfəlaɪtɪzəm] *n*.【美】拉斐尔前派的艺术主张[思潮]。

pre·re·cord [ˈpriːriˈkɔːd; ˏpriːrɪˋkɔrd] *vt*. (无线电与电视)预先录制(广告、节目等)。

pre·re·lease [ˈpriːriˈliːs; ˏpriːrɪˋlis] *n*. 1. (电影的)预映。2. (蒸汽机的)提前排汽。

pre·req·ui·site [ˈpriːˈrekwizit; priˋrɛkwəzɪt] I *a*. 必须先具备的,必要的;先决条件的(*to*)。*a* ~ *fund of knowledge* 必须先具有的知识储备。II *n*. 必要条件;前提;先决条件(*for*)。

pre·rog·a·tive [priˈrɔgətiv; prɪˋrɑgətɪv] I *n*. 1. 特权;特典;君权,帝王的大权[又作 royal ~];天赋的特权[能力等]。2.【史】优先投票权。3. 特性,特点;显著的优点。*the* ~ *of mercy* 赦免权。***within one's ~ to do*** 是某人的特权[自由](*It is within his* ~ *to leave* 离席是他的自由)。II *a*. 1. (有)特权的;依照特权享有的。2.【罗马史】有优先投票权的。*a* ~ *right* 特权。~ **court** 1.【英史】(审查遗嘱等的)大主教法庭。2.【美史】(英国殖民统治时期)总督委任组成的法庭。

Pres. = President.

pres. = 1. present. 2. presidency; president. 3. presumptive.

pres·age [ˈpresidʒ; ˋprɛsɪdʒ] I *n*. 1. 预示;前兆。2. 预知,先见(之明);预感。3. 〔古〕预言。***of evil*** ~ 不吉利的。II [ˈpresidʒ, priˈseidʒ; ˋprɛsɪdʒ, prɪˋsedʒ] *vt*. 1. 成为…的前兆,预示;预先警告;预言。2. 预知,预感。*The lowering clouds* ~ *a storm*. 暗云低沉是暴风雨的前兆。— *vi*. 预言;〔古〕有预感。

pres·age·a·ble [priˈseidʒəbl; prɪˋsedʒəbl] *a*. 能预言的,可预知的。

Presb. = Presbyter(ian).

presby- *comb*. *f*. 1. 老,老者: *presby*opia. 2. 长老: *Presby*terian.

pres·by·cu·sis, pres·by·cou·sis [ˌprezbiˈkjuːsis, ˌpres-; ˏprɛzbəˋkjusɪs, prɛs-] *n*.【医】老年性耳聋。

pres·by·ope [ˈprezbiəup; ˋprɛzbɪˏop] *n*.【医】老花(眼)者;远视者。

pres·by·o·pi·a [ˌprezbiˈəupiə, -pjə; ˏprɛzbɪˋopɪə, -pjə] *n*.【医】远视(眼),老花(眼)。

pres·by·op·ic [ˌprezbiˈɔpik; ˏprɛzbɪˋɑpɪk] *a*. 远视眼的,老花眼的。

pres·by·ter [ˈprezbitə; ˋprɛzbɪtɚ] *n*.【宗】1. (早期基督教的)地方教会监察者。2. (基督教长老会的)长老。3. (英国圣公会的)牧师,司祭。

pres·byt·er·ate [prezˈbitəreit; prɛzˋbɪtəˏret] *n*.【宗】1. 长老的职位,长老的职权。2. 长老会。

pres·by·te·ri·al [ˌprezbiˈtiəriəl; ˏprɛzbəˋtɪrɪəl] *a*.【宗】

全体长老的;长老制的。

Pres·by·te·ri·an [ˌprezbiˈtiəriən; ˏprɛzbəˋtɪrɪən] **I** ***a.*** 【宗】**1.** 〔p-〕长老制的。**2.** 长老会的。*the ~ Church* 基督教的长老会。**II** ***n.*** **1.** 长老会教友。**2.** 〔p-〕长老制主义者。**-ism** ***n.*** 长老制,长老派的信仰[主张]。

pres·by·ter·y [ˈprezbitəri; ˋprɛzbəˏtɛrɪ] ***n.*** 【宗】**1.** 长老会;长老会教务评议会[管辖区]。**2.** (大教堂的)司祭席;祭坛。**3.** (天主教神父)住宅。

pre·school [ˈpriːˈskuːl; ˋpriˋskul] **I** 〔美〕***a.*** (小)学前的,学龄前的。**II** ***n.*** 幼儿园,保育园。**-er** ***n.*** 学龄前儿童。

pres·ci·ence [ˈpresiəns; ˋprɛʃɪəns] ***n.*** 预知,先见。

pres·ci·ent [ˈpresiənt; ˋprɛʃɪənt] ***a.*** 预知的,有先见之明的;有见识的 (*of*)。**-ly** ***ad.***

pre·sci·en·tif·ic [ˈpriːˌsaiənˈtifik; ˏprisaɪənˋtɪfɪk] ***a.*** 近代科学出现前的;科学方法应用前的。

pre·scind [priˈsind; prɪˋsɪnd] ***vt.*** **1.** (过早或突然地从整体中)割去;使某甲同某乙分开 (*from*)。**2.** 【哲】孤立地观察[考虑];抽象地思索。**3.** 〔古〕使中断[断绝]。*happiness ~ed from pleasure and self-indulgence* 超脱开享乐与自我放纵的幸福。— ***vi.*** 离开,脱离;不加考虑 (*from*)。

Pre·scott [ˈpreskət; ˋprɛskət] ***n.*** 普雷斯科特〔姓氏〕。

pre·scribe [prisˈkraib; prɪˋskraɪb] ***vt.*** **1.** 命令,指示,指挥;规定。**2.** 处(方),开(药);劝行(某种疗法等);嘱咐,建议。**3.** 【法】使(过限期而)失效[不合法]。*penalties ~d by law* 法律规定的刑罚。*~ the treatment* 建议采取该种治疗。— ***vi.*** **1.** 命令,指挥,指令;规定。**2.** 开药,处方 (*for*)。**3.** 【法】(通过长期占有等而)要求(权利等) (*for, to*);(因过期限而)失效[不合法]。*~ for a patient in a fever* 给热病患者开药方。**-er** ***n.*** 处方者,开药者;建议者。

pre·script [ˈpriːskript; ˋpriˋskrɪpt] **I** ***n.*** 命令,训令;规定;法令。**II** [priˈskript, ˈpriːskript; prɪˋskrɪpt, ˋpriskrɪpt] ***a.*** 指示的,命令的;规定的。

pre·scrip·ti·ble [priˈskriptəbl; prɪˋskrɪptəbl] ***a.*** **1.** 可以治疗的,有疗效的。**2.** (根据传统或长期使用等而)要求权利的,(根据长期使用等而)获得权利的。*a ~ illness* 可治疗的疾病。

pre·scrip·tion [priˈskripʃən; prɪˋskrɪpʃən] ***n.*** **1.** 命令,训令,指示;规定;法规;(应守的)旧习惯。**2.** 【医】药方,处方;处方的药。**3.** 【法】(依据传统或长期使用等而)要求权利;(由于长期使用等而)获得权利。*a medical ~* 药方。***make a ~*** 开药方。***make up the ~*** 抓药,配方。***the negative ~*** 【法】可提出诉讼[要求]的法定期限。***the positive ~*** 【法】(在法定期限内等的)长期使用,长期占有;(由于长期使用等而获得的)权利。***write out a ~ for*** 为…开药方。

pre·scrip·tive [priˈskriptiv; prɪˋskrɪptɪv] ***a.*** **1.** 规定的;指示的,命令的。**2.** 【法】依照时效的,因时效而得的;由于长期使用而获得的。**3.** 惯例的;约定俗成的。*a ~ right* 【法】(由于长期使用而获得的)时效权利。*~ grammar* 规范性语法 (*opp.* descriptive grammar)。**-ly** ***ad.***

pre·se·lec·tive [ˈpriːsiˈlektiv; ˋprisɪˋlɛktɪv] ***a.*** (汽车齿轮)预选式的。

pres·ence [ˈprezns; ˋprɛzns] ***n.*** **1.** 在,存在,实在;存在的人[物]。**2.** 出席,列席,到场;参加;会同 (*opp.* absence)。**3.** (人)面前,眼前;〔the ~〕御前,驾前;接近。**4.** 见面,谒见;〔古〕接见室(= ~-chamber)。**5.** 鬼,妖怪,精灵。**6.** 相貌,姿容;态度,风采,风度。*all foreign military ~* 一切外国的军事存在。*Your ~ is requested.* 请你出席,敬请光临。*a man of (a) noble ~* 有威仪的人。*a man of no ~* 其貌不扬的人。***be admitted to sb.'s ~*** 被允许谒见[会见]某人。***be banished from sb.'s ~*** 被斥退。***in the ~ of*** 在…之前,在…面前;面临着…。***~ of mind*** 镇静,沉着。***saving your ~*** (在你面前)说句冒昧的话,恕我冒昧。***with (great) ~ of mind*** 泰然,毅然,镇定自若地。~**-chamber** [**room**] (君主、显要人物的)接见厅;客厅,会客室。

pres·ent[1] [ˈprezənt; prɪˋzɛnt] **I** ***a.*** **1.** 在座的,出席的,在场的,到(场)的;现存的,存在的 (*opp.* absent)。**2.** 现在的,今天的,当前的,目前的 (*opp.* past, future)。**3.** 当面的,该,本,此;意念中的,正在考虑中的。**4.** 〔古〕立刻有用的,应急的,即刻的。*P-!* (点名时回答)到! *P-, Sir [Ma'am].* 来了〔主人、顾客招唤时的回答〕! *All ~ assented.* 出席者一致赞成。*those here ~* 在座各位。*the ~ tense* 【语法】现在时(态)。*the ~ Cabinet* 现(任)内阁。*the ~ volume* 本书。*the ~ writer* 本作者,笔者。*a ~ wit* 机智,急智。***at the ~ time [day]*** = ***in the ~ day*** 在现在,在今天。***be ~ to the mind*** 放在心里,不忘记。***in the ~ case*** 在这件事中;在这种情况下。***~ company excepted*** 在座各人除外。***the ~ worth of*** (*£100 in 12 years*) (十二年后会变成一百镑的)现在的金额。**II** ***n.*** **1.** 现在,目前 (*opp.* past, future)。**2.** 【语法】现在式。**3.** 〔*pl.*〕【法】本文,本证件。***at ~*** 目前,现在。***by these ~s*** 【法】〔谑〕根据本文件 (*Know all men by these ~s that, ...* (等等)特给此(文件)为证)。***for the ~*** 眼前;暂且。***until the ~, up to the ~*** 至今,到现在为止。~ **company** 出席者。~**-day** ***a.*** 现代的,当代的。~ **participle** 【语法】现在分词。~ **perfect** 【语法】现在完成式(的);现在完成式的动词。~ **tense** 【语法】现在时(态)。

pres·ent[2] [ˈpreznt; ˋprɛznt] ***n.*** 赠品,礼物;赠送。*a birthday ~* 寿礼,生日礼物。*a New Year's ~* 年礼。***make a ~ of sth. to sb.*** 把某物赠送某人 (*Will you make me a ~ of your photograph?* 你可以送我一张照片吗?)。***make [give] a ~ to sb.*** 给某人送礼。

pre·sent[3] [priˈzent; prɪˋzɛnt] **I** ***vt.*** **1.** 呈献;赠送,给予。**2.** 交出,提出;出示;呈递;交给(收据等);兑(支票等)。**3.** 显示;呈现出;陈述;描述。**4.** 提供(机会等);引起(困难等)。**5.** 引见,介绍;披露,宣布。**6.** 上演(戏剧);使扮演。**7.** (拿武器)对准;瞄准 (*at*);举枪(敬礼)。**8.** 【法】控告;控诉。**9.** 【宗】举荐(牧师任圣职)。*~ an album to sb.* = *~ sb. with an album* 送某人一本照相簿。*~ an appearance of* 给人以…的印象。*P- my compliments to (him).* 请替我问候(他)。*Allow me to ~ Mr. X to you.* 让我给你介绍 X 先生。***~ a cheque [bill]*** (为领款)交出支票[票据]。***P- arms!*** 【军】举枪。***~ itself*** 出现;呈现;(主意等)浮现脑中。***~ oneself*** 出席(会议等),参加(考试等);出现(在听众面前等);到场。— ***vi.*** **1.** (举枪)瞄准;举枪致敬。**2.** 【宗】行使牧师推荐权。**3.** 【医】(分娩时婴儿)露出,先露。***Present!*** 【军】瞄准。**II** ***n.*** **1.** 拿枪对准,瞄准;瞄准时枪的位置;举枪的姿势。**2.** 举枪致敬。

pre·sent·a·bil·i·ty [priˌzentəˈbiliti; prɪˏzɛntəˋbɪlətɪ] ***n.*** 漂亮,中看,拿得出;适于赠送。

pre·sent·a·ble [priˈzentəbl; prɪˋzɛntəbl] ***a.*** **1.** 拿得出去的,像样的;漂亮的;见得了人的,中看的;有规矩的,有礼貌的。**2.** 适于赠送的。**3.** 可介绍的,可推荐的。

pres·en·ta·tion [ˌprezenˈteiʃən; ˏprɛznˋteʃən] ***n.*** **1.** 赠送,献礼;授予;授予仪式;〔罕〕赠品,礼物。**2.** 提出;呈递。**3.** 介绍,引见,谒见;〔英〕(特指入宫)晋谒。**4.** (牧师的)举荐,举荐牧师权。**5.** 表现;外观,外貌,仪表;【无】图像;显示,扫瞄。**6.** 【哲】【心】表象,直觉,观念。**7.** 发表;表示;展示;陈述,描述。**8.** 【剧】演出,上演。**9.** 【医】先露,产式,胎位。**10.** 【商】(支票等的)提出,交兑 (= presentment)。***give a ~ of*** 对…作陈述。***payable on ~*** (支票等)交银行即可兑现。~ ***of colours [medals]*** 授军旗[勋章]仪式。***the ~ of credentials*** 呈递国书。~ **copy** 赠本,献本。~ **day** (大学)学位授予日。

pres·en·ta·tion·al [ˌprezənˈteiʃənəl; ˏprɛznˋteʃənəl] ***a.*** **1.** 直觉的;表象(论)的;观念的。**2.** 上演的,演出的。**3.** (词、语等)描述性的。

pres·en·ta·tion·ism [ˌprezənˈteiʃənizəm; ˏprɛznˋteʃənɪzm̩]【心、哲】表象论,表象主义。

pres·en·ta·tion·ist [ˌprezənˈteiʃənist; ˌprɛzənˋteʃənɪst] *n*. 表象论者,表象主义者。

pre·sent·a·tive [priˈzentətiv; prɪˋzɛntətɪv] *a*. 1. 起呈现作用的。2.【宗】有举荐牧师权的。3.【哲】直觉的;表象的;(美术等)抽象的。

pres·ent-day [ˈprezəntˈdei; ˋprɛzntˋde] *a*. 当代的;现在的,当前的。~ *English* 当代英语。

pres·en·tee [ˌprezənˈtiː; ˌprɛzənˋti] *n*. 1. 受赠者。2. 被推荐者;【宗】被举荐为牧师的人。3. (入宫等)晋谒者。

pre·sent·er [priˈzentə; prɪˋzɛntə] *n*. 1. 赠送者,呈献者。2. 提出者;具呈人。3. 推荐者。4.〔英〕(电台或电视台的)节目主持人〔美国英语为 anchor〕。

pre·sen·ti·ent [priˈsenʃiənt, -ʃənt; prɪˋsɛnʃɪənt, -ʃənt] *a*. 预觉的,预感的(*of*)。

pre·sen·ti·ment [priˈzentimənt; prɪˋzɛntəmənt] *n*. (不祥的)预感,预觉。*a* ~ *of danger* 对危险的预感。

pre·sen·tive [priˈzentiv; prɪˋzɛntɪv] *a*.【语法】(文字)直接表达概念的,直(接表)示的(*opp*. symbolic)。

pres·ent·ly [ˈprezəntli; ˋprɛzntlɪ] *ad*. 1. 不久,一会儿。2.〔方〕〔美〕现在,目前,时下。3.〔古〕马上,立刻;作为直接结果,必然地。*They will be here* ~. 他们马上就到这里。*You will know all about it* ~. 你不久就会了解事情的底细。*He is* ~ *out of the country*. 他现在出国了。

pre·sent·ment [priˈzentmənt; prɪˋzɛntmənt] *n*. 1. 陈述,叙述;呈示;【心】表象。2. (戏剧的)上演,演出;呈现;展示(物);描写;画,肖像。3.【商】(支票、汇票等的)提出,交兑;出示。4.〔罕〕赠送(物)。5.【法】陪审官的报告;【宗】(主教来视察时教区委员的)陈诉。

pre·ser·va·ble [priˈzəːvəbl; prɪˋzɝvəbl̩] *a*. 可保存[保管、保护]的;可储藏的。

pres·er·va·tion [ˌprezə(ː)ˈveiʃən; ˌprɛzəˋveʃən] *n*. 1. 保存;保管;储藏;保护,防腐。2. 保持;维护。*the* ~ *of one's health* 保持健康。*the* ~ *of peace* 维护和平。~ *from decay* 防腐。**be in fair** [**poor**] ~ 保存得好[不好]。

pre·serv·a·tive [priˈzəːvətiv; prɪˋzɝvətɪv] I *a*. (能)保存的;储藏的;防腐的 (*from*; *against*)。II *n*. 1. 预防法;预防药;防腐剂。2. 起维护作用的因素[原则等],防…物。*Salt is a* ~ *for meat*. 盐是肉类的防腐剂。

pre·serv·a·tize [priˈzəːvətaiz; prɪˋzɝvətaɪz] *vt*. 给(食品等)施行防腐,给…加防腐剂。

pre·serve [priˈzəːv; prɪˋzɝv] I *vt*. 1. 保存,保藏,防腐;保管(贵重品等);保留。2. 保持,维持;保护,维护。3. 腌(肉等);渍(果物);把…做成罐头;储藏。4. 把…放在心里,不忘记,使(名声、作品等)流传。5. 禁猎;把…圈为禁猎地。~ *health* 保持健康。*She is well-preserved*. 她保养得好[显得很年轻]。~ *order* 维持秩序。~ *fruit* 把水果做成果酱。~ *fruit in sugar* 把水果做成蜜饯。~ *fish in* [*with*] *salt* 用盐腌鱼。*These woods are* ~*d*. 此处林场禁止打猎。— *vi*. 1. 做蜜饯;做果酱;制罐头。2. 禁猎;圈禁地。II *n*. 1.〔常 *pl*.〕保藏物;糖脯,蜜饯,果酱;罐头。2.〔常 *pl*.〕禁猎地;(私有的)猎物,鱼塘。3. 独占的活动范围[领域]。4. 防护物;〔*pl*.〕护目镜;遮光眼镜,防尘眼镜。*poach on another's* ~*s* 侵犯别人的活动[利益等]范围[领域]。**-d** *a*. 1. 腌制的,制成蜜饯[果酱、罐头]的。2. 得到保存的;受维护的。3. 禁猎的。4.〔美俚〕喝醉的。

pre·serv·er [priˈzəːvə; prɪˋzɝvə] *n*. 1. 保存者;保持者;保护者。2. 防腐物;防护物。3. 罐头制造人;蜜饯制造人。4.〔英〕禁猎地主管人;鸟兽保护者。

pre·set [ˈpriːˈset; priˋsɛt] *vt*. (*pre·set*; *-set·ting*) 预先装置;预调,调整。

pre-shrunk [ˈpriːˈʃrʌŋk; priˋʃrʌŋk] *a*.【纺】(布料等)已预缩的,下水后不会再缩的。

pre·side [priˈzaid; prɪˋzaɪd] *vi*. 1. 作会议主席;作议长,作会长(*at*; *over*)。2. 统辖;指挥;负责;主持 (*at*, *over*)。3. 主奏 (*at*)。~ *over a meeting* 主持会议。~ *at a public dinner* 主持宴会〔充当宴会的主人〕。— *vt*. 管理。~ *naval affairs* 主管海军事务。**-r** *n*. 主席,会议主持者。

pres·i·den·cy [ˈprezidənsi; ˋprɛzədənsɪ] *n*. 1. 总统[主席、议长等]的职位[任期]。2. 统辖;主宰,支配。3.〔P-〕〔美〕总统直辖的政府机构。4.【史】管辖区〔旧英属印度的马德拉斯等三大管区之一〕。5. (摩门教的)三人评议会。

pres·i·dent [ˈprezidənt; ˋprɛzədənt] *n*. 1. 总统。2. 总裁;长官;主席;议长;【法】院长;庭长。3. 会长;校长;〔英〕大学院长;〔美〕大学校长。4.〔美〕(银行等的)行长;董事长;总经理,社长。5.【史】州长,知事;(殖民地)总督。*the Lord P- of the Board of Trade*〔英〕商务大臣。*the Lord P- of the Council*〔英〕枢密大臣。*the P- of the U. N. General Assembly* 联合国大会主席。

pres·i·dent-e·lect [ˈprezidəntiˈlekt; ˋprɛzɪdəntɪˋlɛkt] *n*. 即将就任的总统,新当选(尚未就职)的总统,当选总统。

pres·i·dent·ess [ˈprezidəntis; ˋprɛzɪdəntəs] *n*. 1. 女总统[总裁、议长、董事长、校长等]。2. 总统[总裁、议长、董事长、校长等]的夫人。

pres·i·den·tial [ˌpreziˈdenʃəl; ˌprɛzəˋdɛnʃəl] *a*. 1. 总统[总裁、议长、董事长、校长等](职务)的。2. 统辖的,支配的,监督的,指挥的。3. 有总统气派的。*the* ~ *chair* 总统[总裁、议长、校长、董事长等]的职位[地位]。*a* ~ *election* 总统选举。~ *electors* 总统选举人。*a* ~ *postmaster*〔美〕总统任命的邮政局长。*the* ~ *term* 总统[议长、董事长、校长等]的任期。*a* ~ *timber*〔美〕有做总统资格的人。*the* ~ *year*〔口〕(总统)大选年。~ **government** 总统制政体。**-ly** *ad*. 以总统[议长、校长等]的资格;有总统气派地。

pres·i·dent·ship [ˈprezidəntˌʃip; ˋprɛzədəntˌʃɪp] *n*.〔英〕总统[议长、会长、社长、总经理、总裁、校长等]的职位[任期]。

pre·sid·ing [priˈzaidiŋ; prɪˋzaɪdɪŋ] *a*. 主席的,主持会议的,首席的。~ **judge** 审判长,首席法官。~ **officer** (选举投票所的)监选员。

pre·sid·i·o [priˈsidiəu; prɪˋsɪdɪˌo] *n*. (*pl*. ~*s*)〔Sp.〕1. 要塞,卫戍区。2. 流放地,充军地。

pre·sid·i·um [priˈsidiəm; prɪˋsɪdɪəm] *n*. (*pl*. ***pre·sid·i·a*** [priˈsidiə; prɪˋsɪdɪə]) 主席团;常务委员会。

pre·sig·ni·fy [ˈpriːˈsignifai; priˋsɪgnəˌfaɪ] *vt*. 预示,预告。

pre·soak [ˈpriːˈsəuk; ˋpriˋsok] I *vt*. 事先浸泡;【农】预浸。II *n*.【农】预浸剂。**-ing**【农】浸种。

press[1] [pres; prɛs] I *vt*. 1. 压,按,揿,扳;推动;(用熨斗)熨平;贴(邮票等)。2. 绞榨,压榨;榨取,挤(葡萄汁等);压碎。3. 使贴紧;压紧;紧抱,紧握。4. 坚持;坚决进行;贯彻,严厉执行(法律等)。5. 敦促;谆谆劝说,逼人接受(意见等);把…强加于人。6. 强迫;勒索,强募,强要。7. 催逼;压迫,进逼(敌人等);使苦恼;使窘迫;虐待,折磨,逼,困。8. 聚集;拥挤。9. 强调,加重(语气等)。10. 压倒;抑制(感情等)。11.〔古〕使深为感动。12. 印刷;用模子压制。~ *the trousers* 烫裤子。*Wine is* ~*ed from the grapes*. 葡萄酒是榨葡萄汁制成的。~ *a child to one's breast* 把孩子紧紧抱在怀里。~ *the argument* 坚持这个论点。~ *home an argument* 反复说明论点使对方接受。~ *sb. into confession* 逼人招供。~ *sb. for money* 向某人勒索钱财。*be hard* ~*ed* 被逼紧,被紧攻,陷困境。— *vi*. 1. 压,重压(*on*; *against*)。2. 奋勇前进,突进,赶上前 (*on*; *forward*)。3. 催迫,勒索,强要;迫切要求 (*for*)。4. (事情)紧急;(时间)紧迫。5. 密集,拥挤 (*up*; *round*)。6. 侵入,蚕食。7. 使感觉,给与印象,影响。8. 承压,受压。*The shoe is* ~*ing on my*

P

toe. 我的鞋子挤脚。*I must ~ for an answer*. 请速赐覆。*The matter ~es*. 事情紧急。*Time is ~ing*. 时间紧迫。*Have you any business that ~es*? 你有什么要紧事没有? *The argument ~ed upon the judgement*. 那场争论影响到了判决。***be ~ed for*** 穷于,困于,缺少,缺乏(*be ~ed for funds* 缺少资金。*be ~ed for time* 时间紧迫)。~ ***an attack*** 强袭。~ ***about*** [***around***] ***sb***. 拥挤[密集]在某人周围。~ ***back*** 推回去,击退。~ ***for*** 催促,催逼,催索;(时间)迫促;(资金)短少〔多用被动式 *be ~ed for*〕。~ ***forward*** [***ahead***] 突进,推进;奋力前进;向前挤。~ ***hard upon*** 进逼,压迫,穷追。~ ***home*** 极力主张。~ ***on*** [***upon***] **1**. 向前挤,赶紧向前走。**2**. 坚决推进。~ ***on*** [***forward***] ***with*** 加紧,决心继续(~ *on with one's work* 加紧干)。~ ***one's way*** 奋力前进,坚持前进,向前挤。~ ***sail*** 扯满所有风帆。~ ***the button*** 按电铃;动手干。~ ***the matter to a division*** 坚持要把事情弄个明白。~ ***the words*** 坚持字面意义。~ ***sb***. ***to death*** 把某人折磨致死。

II ***n***. **1**. 压;按;揿;挤;紧握;熨。**2**. 绞榨,压榨;冲床,压床,压力机,压榨机;吐丝器。**3**. 印刷机;印刷术;印刷厂;印刷(业),出版。**4**. 〔the ~〕〔集合词〕(包括报刊、广播、电视、通讯社等的)新闻报导[评论];报纸;定期刊物,杂志;出版物;出版社;通讯社;新闻界;出版界;〔集合词〕期刊编者,报馆记者;言论出版。**5**. 急迫;紧急;繁忙。**6**. 拥挤,杂沓;人丛,群众;白刃战,混战。**7**. 柜,衣橱;书橱。**8**. 【机】夹具;(网球拍等的)夹子。**9**. 【举重】推举。*a hydraulic ~* 水压机。*a drill* [*punching*] ~ 钻[冲]床,*the ~ of work* 繁忙的工作。*a rotary ~* 滚筒印刷机。*the local ~* 地方报刊。***a ~ of*** 密集的,拥挤的(*a ~ of people* 拥挤的人群)。***at ~ time*** 在发稿时,到发稿时为止。***at*** (***the***) ~, ***in ~***, ***come to the ~*** 已付印;印刷中。***correct the ~*** 改正校样;校对。***freedom*** [***liberty***] ***of the ~*** 言论出版的自由。***give to the ~*** 在报上发表。***go to*** (***the***) ~ 付印。***have a good ~*** 在报上得到好评。***in*** (***the***) ~ 在印刷中。***make one's way through the ~*** 挤过人丛。***off the ~*** 已印好;已发行。***out of ~*** 绝版,卖光。~ ***of sail*** 【海】吃满风的帆。***send to*** (***the*** ~) 付印。***stop the ~*** 用重要消息代替已排好的次要消息。***write for the ~*** 给报纸写文章。~ **agent** (剧团等的)新闻广告员;宣传员。~ **board** 皮纸板;压板。~ **boys** 〔美〕体育记者。~**-button** 电钮,按纽。~ **box** 新闻记者席。~ **clipping** [**cutting**] (一份)剪报。~ **communique** 新闻公报。~ **campaign** [**stunt**] (为竞选等而进行的)报纸宣传。~ **conference** 记者招待会。~ **gallery** (特指英国下院的)记者席。~ **kit** 新闻包〔记者招待会上散发的新闻材料包〕。~ **law** 新闻条例;〔常 *pl*.〕出版法。~**man** **1**. 印刷工人,印刷厂经营者。**2**. 烫衣人;熨衣工。**3**. 榨葡萄[油]的人。**4**. 〔英〕新闻记者。~ **mark** **1**. ***n***. (图书馆书目上的)书架号码。**2**. ***vt***. 在(书上)加号码,给(书)编号。~ **photographer** 摄影记者。~ **proof** 清样;机样。~ **reader** 清样校对(员)。~ **release** **1**. (通讯社发布的)通讯稿。**2**. (向记者发布的)新闻稿。~ **representative** 〔美〕新闻发布组长。~ **revise** 末校。~**room** **1**. 印刷室。**2**. (政府机构中的)记者室。~ **telegram** 新闻电报。~ **time** (新闻等的)截止时间。~**work** **1**. 印刷(工作);印刷业务。**2**. 〔集合词〕印刷物,印刷品。**-er** ***a***. 压具,压者(尤指熨衣工)。

press[2] [pres; prɛs] **I** ***n***. 【史】强迫征募,抓壮丁。**II** ***vt***. 【史】**1**. 强迫…服兵役[劳役]。**2**. 征用。~ (*things*) *into the service of* 强制征用(实物)。~ **gang** 抓兵队。~**-gang** ***vt***. 强征…入伍[服劳役]。~ **money** 【史】新兵入伍安家费。

press·ing [ˈpresiŋ; ˋprɛsɪŋ] **I** ***a***. **1**. (工作、要求等)急迫的,紧急的,迫切的。**2**. (邀请等)恳切的。*a ~ business* 急事。*a ~ danger* 紧迫的危机,燃眉之急。**II** ***n***. **1**. 压;按。**2**. 压榨;催逼。**3**. 冲压;冲压件;模压制品。**4**. 唱片;同一批压制的唱片。*He required no ~*. 他不需要催迫。**-ly** ***ad***. **-ness** ***n***.

pres·sor [ˈpresə; ˋprɛsɚ] **I** ***a***. 【医】加压的,增高血压的。**II** ***n***. 增压物质。

pres·sure [ˈpreʃə; ˋprɛʃɚ] **I** ***n***. **1**. 压;按;挤;榨。**2**. 【物】压力,压强;大气压力;电压。**3**. 精神压力,政治[经济、舆论等]压力。**4**. 压迫,强制。**5**. 紧急,急迫;繁重,繁忙。**6**. 艰难,为难,困苦。*atmospheric ~* (大)气压(力)。*downward* [*upward*] ~ 向下[向上]压力。*high blood ~* 高血压。~ *for money* 金融紧迫;缺钱。*financial ~* 财政困难。*the ~ of the crowd* 人群的拥挤。*the ~ of affairs* 事务繁忙。***at high*** [***low***] ~ 紧张[松懈,疲塌]。***bring ~ to bear upon***, ***exert ~ upon*** 对…施加压力。***put ~ on*** [***upon***] ... 对…施加压力,压迫…。***the ~ of the times*** 不景气,时势的艰难。***under the ~ of*** 在…的压力下;逼不得已。***work at high ~*** 紧张地工作;使劲干。**II** ***vt***. **1**. 对…施加压力;迫使。**2**. 使(机舱等)增压;密封。~ **cabin** 【空】增压舱,气密座舱。~**-cook** ***vt***., ***vi***. 用高压锅[压力锅]烹调。~ **cooker** 高压锅,加压蒸(汽速)煮器。~ **ga(u)ge** 气压计,压强计;(火炮药室内的)膛压表。~ **group** 压力集团〔对立法者和公众施加压力以影响立法和政策的集团〕。~ **point** 【医】压迫止血点。~**suit** 增压(衣)服〔高空飞行用〕。~ **vessel** 压力容器〔锅炉等〕。

pres·sur·ize [ˈpreʃəraiz; ˋprɛʃəˏraɪz] ***vt***. **1**. 对…加压力;使压入(油井等)。**2**. 使(机舱)增压;密封;使(飞机中)保持接近于正常气压。

pres·sur·i·za·tion [ˌpreʃəraiˈzeiʃən; ˏprɛʃəraɪˋzeʃən] ***n***. **1**. 压力输送,挤压。**2**. 气密,密封。**3**. 增压;加压。

prest [prest; prɛst] **I** ***n***. 〔废〕应募金〔= prest money, 尤指发给应募服役英国陆、海军新兵的一笔钱〕。**II** ***a***. 〔废〕准备好的。

pre·ster·num [priˈstəːnəm; prɪˋstɝnəm] ***n***. 【动】(昆虫的)前腹片;前胸骨;前腹板(= manubrium)。

pres·ti·dig·i·ta·tion [ˈprestiˌdidʒiˋteiʃən; ˏprɛstɪˏdɪdʒɪˋteʃən] ***n***. 变戏法,魔术。

pres·ti·dig·i·ta·tor [ˌprestiˈdidʒiteitə; ˏprɛstɪˋdɪdʒɪˏtetɚ] ***n***. 变戏法的人,魔术师。

Pres·tige [ˈprestidʒ; ˋprɛstɪdʒ] ***n***. 普雷斯蒂奇〔姓氏〕。

pres·tige [presˈtiːʒ, -ˈtiːdʒ; ˋprɛstidʒ, -tidʒ] ***n***. 威信,威望,声望;声誉;(财势的)显赫。*the political ~ and influence* 政治声势。*national* [*military*] ~ 国家[军事]声誉。

pres·tig·ious [ˌpresˈtiːdʒəs, -ˈtidʒjəs; ˏprɛsˋtɪdʒɪəs, -tɪdʒjəs] ***a***. **1**. 〔古〕魔术的,欺骗的。**2**. 有威信的,有声誉的。

pres·tis·si·mo [presˈtisiməu; prɛsˋtɪsəˏmo] **I** ***ad***., ***a***. 〔It.〕【乐】最快,极快,更急速。**II** ***n***. 最快速度。

pres·to [ˈprestəu; ˋprɛsto] **I** ***ad***. 赶快,快,立刻,转眼之间〔变戏法时用语〕。***Hey ~***, ***pass***! 快,变了! 说变就变! ***P-***! ***chango*** [ˈtʃeindʒəu; ˋtʃendʒo]! 快! 快! 变! 〔魔术师用语〕;剧变,迅速的变化。**II** ***a***. 快,迅速的,变戏法似的。

pres·to [ˈprestəu; ˋprɛsto] **I** ***a***., ***ad***. 〔It.〕【乐】快,急速。**II** ***n***. (*pl*. ~*s*) 急板。

Pres·ton [ˈprestən; ˋprɛstən] ***n***. **1**. 普雷斯顿〔男子名〕。**2**. 普雷斯顿〔英国港市〕。

pre·stress [ˈpriːˈstres; priˋstrɛs] **I** ***n***. 预应力。**II** ***vt***. 对…预加应力。~*ed concrete* 预应力混凝土。~ **unit** 预应力构件。

pre·sum·a·ble [priˈzjuːməbl; prɪˋzuməbl] ***a***. 可推测的,可假定的;像有的,像是的;可能的。

pre·sum·a·bly [priˈzjuːməbli; prɪˋzuməblɪ] ***ad***. 推测起来;假定;大概,大抵,可能。*He knows, ~, what is best for him*. 他总该知道怎样对他最有利吧。

pre·sume [priˈzjuːm; prɪˋzum] ***vt***. **1**. 假定,假设;推测;认为,以为;想像,猜想。**2**. 敢于,胆敢,擅敢〔用于第一人称时多半为客套话〕。**3**. 足以推定,意味着。*I ~ he* *isn't coming*. 我想他不会来了。*You had better* ～ *no such thing*. 你最好不要这样想当然。*May I* ～ *to ask ...?* 请问…。—*vi*. 1. 设想,推测,相信。2. 擅自行动,放肆〔用于第一人称时多为客套话〕。3. 不正当地利用;倚靠,恃(*on*, *upon*)。～ *upon sb.'s good nature* 利用某人性情好。～ *upon a short acquaintance* 凭着一面之交就和人亲热起来。*Mr. Johnson, I* ～? 您就是约翰逊先生吧? ***You*** ～. 你这人真不客气[冒昧、脸厚]。

pre·sumed [priˈzjuːmd; prɪˋzjumd] ***a***. 假定的;推测的。

pre·sum·ed·ly [priˈzjuːmidli; prɪˋzjumɪdlɪ] ***ad***. 据推测,大概。

pre·sum·er [priˈzjuːmə; prɪˋzjumɚ] ***n***. 1. 假定者,推测者。2. 冒昧的人。

pre·sum·ing [priˈzjuːmiŋ; prɪˋzjumɪŋ] ***a***. 1. 自以为是的,专横的。2. 不客气的;冒昧的;放肆的;傲慢的。**-ly *ad*.**

pre·sump·tion [priˈzʌmpʃən; prɪˋzʌmpʃən] ***n***. 1. 推测,猜测,臆断,假定;设想,想像。2. 专横,自以为是;不客气,跋扈,冒昧,放肆,无礼;傲慢,自大。3.【法】事实的推断〔根据已知事实作出的推断〕(= ～ of fact)。*The* ～ *is that he will refuse*. 看起来他会拒绝的。*I have never heard of such* ～. 从来没有听说过如此无礼的事。～ ***of fact***【法】事实的推断。～ ***of law***【法】1. 法律上的假定。2. (在一定情况下普遍适用的)法定推论。

pre·sump·tive [priˈzʌmptiv; prɪˋzʌmptɪv] ***a***. 1. 推测的,假定的。2. 可据以推定的。***an heir*** ～ 假定继承人〔如有血统更近的继承人出生时,即失去继承权〕。～ **evidence**【法】推定证据。**-ly *ad*.** 据推测。

pre·sump·tu·ous [priˈzʌmptjuəs; prɪˋzʌmptʃʊəs] ***a***. 1. 放肆的,不客气的,跋扈的,冒昧的。2. 自以为是的,专横的,傲慢的。*It is too* ～ *of you to say so*. 你这样说话太放肆了。**-ly *ad*.**

pre·sup·pose [ˌpriːsəˈpəuz; ˏprisəˋpoz] ***vt***. 1. 预先假定;预料,预想;推测;猜想。2. 以…为前提;含有。***Effects*** ～ ***causes***. 有结果必有原因。***Success*** ～***s diligence***. 勤勉为成功的先决条件。

pre·sup·po·si·tion [ˌpriːsʌpəˈziʃən; ˏprisʌpəˋzɪʃən] ***n***. 1. 预想(的事),猜测(的事)。2. 预先假定(的事)。3. 前提;先决条件。

pret. = preterit(e).

pret [pret; prɛt] ***a***. (服装)现成的,非订做的。

pre·teen [ˈpriːˈtiːn; ˋpriˋtin] ***a***., ***n***. 未满十三岁的(孩子),青春期以前的(孩子)。

pre·tence [priˈtens; prɪˋtɛns] ***n***. 1. 借口,口实,托辞,假托。2. 假装,假做作,虚伪。3. 虚饰,虚装门面。4. (无理的)要求,虚假的理由(*to*)。5. 自命,自称;自吹。6. 〔罕〕目的,企图。*He wished to be relieved of his post on the* ～ *of ill health*. 他想托病辞职。*There are no* ～*s about him*. 他一点不虚伪。***devoid of all*** ～ 毫不虚伪[不做作]地。***false*** ～***s***【法】欺诈(手段)。***make a*** ～ ***of*** .... 假装,装做…。***on the*** ～ ***of*** = ***under*** (***the***) ～ ***of*** 托辞,借口,拿…做口实。***on the slightest*** ～ 借着一点点口实。

pre·tend [priˈtend; prɪˋtɛnd] ***vt***. 1. 假托,借口;假装,装做;(戏剧等中)装扮。2. 诈,骗…说(*that*);自命,自称;要求,妄想。*We must not* ～ *to know when we do not know*. 不要强不知为知。～ *ignorance* 假装不知道,装聋作哑。— ***vi***. 1. 以…自居;自封,自称;要求,妄想,觊觎(*to*);求婚(*to*)。2. 假装,装作。～ *to beauty* [*learning*] 自以为是美人[学者]。*It's no use* ～*ing*. 装假是没用的。～ *to the throne* 觊觎王位。～ ***to a woman*** [***her hand***] 〔古〕企图和(身分高的)女人结婚。

pre·tend·ed [priˈtendid; prɪˋtɛndɪd] ***a***. 1. 虚假的,虚伪的。2. 假装的;假冒的;号称为…的,所谓的。3. 传说的,听说的。～ *sickness* 假病。*a* ～ *friend* 虚伪的朋友。**-ly *ad*.**

pre·tend·er [priˈtendə; prɪˋtɛndɚ] ***n***. 1. 假装者;冒充者;冒牌学者;骗子。2. 妄求者,妄想者,觊觎者;觊觎王位者。*He is a* ～ *to philosophy*. 他是一个冒牌哲学家。***the Old P-***【英史】老僭君〔指 1715 年觊觎英国王位的詹姆士·爱德华·斯图亚特 (James Edward Stuart),詹姆士二世的儿子〕。***the Young P-***【英史】小僭君〔指 1745 年觊觎英国王位的查理·爱德华 (Charles Edward),詹姆士二世之孙,"老僭君"之子〕。

pre·tense [priˈtens; prɪˋtɛns] ***n***. 〔美〕= pretence.

pre·ten·sion[1] [priˈtenʃən; prɪˋtɛnʃən] ***n***. 1. 抱负,意图;自负;自夸的长处;自命,自称。2. 虚饰,假装,做作;虚荣。3. (有根据的)要求;主张;资格;权利。4. 借口,托词;口实。***have no*** ～***s to*** 无权主张[要求],不能称为,说不上是。***make no*** ～***s to*** 不摆…的架子;不自诩…。***of the most humble*** ～***s*** (人)极朴实的。***without*** ～ (人)朴实的;不自负的。

pre·ten·sion[2] [priˈtenʃən; prɪˋtɛnʃən] ***vt***.【建】预张,预拉,给…加预应力。～*ed concrete* 预应力混凝土。

pre·ten·tious [priˈtenʃəs; prɪˋtɛnʃəs] ***a***. 1. 自负的,狂妄的,自命不凡的;自夸的。2. 虚伪的,矫饰的,做作的。*a* ～ *manner* 妄自尊大,盛气凌人。～ *literary style* 矫揉造作的文体。**-ly *ad*. -ness *n*.**

preter- *pref*. 表示"过,超": *preter*natural, *preter*sensual.

pre·ter·hu·man [ˌpriːtə(ː)ˈhjuːmən; ˏpritɚˋhjumən] ***a***. 超人的;异乎常人的。

pret·er·ist [ˈpretərist; ˋprɛtərɪst] ***a***., ***n***. 1.【基督教】认为《启示录》的预言已经实现的(人)。2. 发思古之幽情的(人)。

pret·er·it(e) [ˈpretərit; ˋprɛtərɪt] **I *n***.【语法】过去〔略作 pret.〕;过去时(态);过去式的动词。**II *a***. 1.【语法】过去的。2. 〔古、谑〕过去的,已往的。*the* ～*-present tense*【语法】过去形现在式〔如 can, may, must, shall 等本属过去形,今则用为现在式〕。*the* ～ *tense*【语法】过去时(态)。

pre·ter·i·tion [ˌpriːtəˈriʃən; ˏprɛtəˋrɪʃən] ***n***. 1. 遗漏,疏漏;忽略;省略,不提(*of*)。2.【宗】上帝对不宠爱者的忽视。3.【修】暗示忽略法〔例如说 I will not mention his rudeness. 等〕。4.【法】遗嘱中不提某些有继承权者。

pre·ter·mis·sion [ˌpriːtə(ː)ˈmiʃən; ˏpritɚˋmɪʃən] ***n***. 置之不问;疏忽;遗漏;省略。

pre·ter·mit [ˌpriːtə(ː)ˈmit; ˏpritɚˋmɪt] ***vt***. (**-tt-**) 1. 对…置之不问;把…忽略过去;遗漏,略去。2. 中断,中止。

pre·ter·nat·u·ral [ˌpriːtə(ː)ˈnætʃərəl; ˏpritɚˋnætʃərəl] ***a***. 超自然的;异常的,奇异的,不可思议的。**-ly *ad*.**

pre·ter·sen·su·al [ˌpriːtə(ː)ˈsensjuəl; ˏpritɚˋsɛnʃʊəl] ***a***. 感觉不到的;超感觉的。

pre·test [ˈpriːtest; ˋpriˏtɛst] **I *n***. (产品等的)预先试验;(对学生等的)预先测验。**II *vt*., *vi***. [priˈtest; prɪˋtɛst] 预先试验[测验]。

pre·text [ˈpriːtekst; ˋpritɛkst] **I *n***. 1. 借口,口实,托词。2. 假象,掩饰(*for*)。***find a*** ～ ***for*** 为…找口实。***make a*** ～ ***of*** 以…作口实。***on some*** ～ ***or other*** 用某种借口。***on*** [***under***, ***upon***] ***the*** ～ ***of*** 以…为借口,托词。**II *vt***. [priˈtekst; prɪˋtɛkst] 借口,假托。

pre·tone [ˈpriːtəun; ˋpriton] ***n***.【语音】重读音节前的音节[母音]。

pre·tor [ˈpriːtə; ˋpritɚ] ***n***. = praetor.

Pre·to·ri·a [priˈtɔːriə; prɪˋtorɪə] ***n***. 比勒陀利亚〔南非(阿扎尼亚)首府〕。

pre·to·ri·an [priːˈtɔːriən; prɪˋtorɪən] ***n***., ***a***. = praetorian.

pre·treat [ˈpriːˈtriːt; ˋpriˋtrit] ***vt***. 预先处理。**-ment *n*.** 预处理。

pre·tri·al [ˈpriːˈtraiəl; ˋpriˋtraɪəl] **I *a***.【法】审判前的。*a* ～ *motion* 审判前的申请[动议]。**II *n***. 〔美〕审判前的预备会议。

pret·ti·fy [ˈpritifai; ˋprɪtɪˏfaɪ] ***vt***. (***-fied***) 1. 〔蔑〕过分

P

修饰;过分润饰,雕琢(文章等)。2.〔蔑〕美化。

pret·ti·ly [ˈpritili; ˋprɪtɪlɪ] *ad*. 1. 漂亮地,可爱地。2. 有礼貌地,潇洒地,文雅地。3. 优美地;愉快地。4. 好地,妙地。5. 机灵地。6. 贴切地。7. 相当多地。*be ~ dressed* 穿得漂亮,穿得花哨。*ask ~* 恭恭敬敬地问。

pret·ti·ness [ˈpritinis; ˋprɪtɪnɪs] *n*. 1. 漂亮,可爱;漂亮的东西。2.(文章、风度等的)优美,潇洒。3. 好,妙。4. 机灵。5. 贴切。

pret·ty [ˈpriti; ˋprɪtɪ] I *a*. 1. 漂亮的,俊俏的,(女子)标致的;(男子)清秀的,潇洒的;(场所、物件等)整洁的,精致的;(花园、山谷等)可爱的;秀丽的,美丽的。2. 优柔的,(男性)女人气的。3. 优美的;悦耳的;有趣的;(游戏等)愉快的。4. 好的,妙的;〔反语〕好〔表示糟糕的,拙劣的〕。5. 机灵的;巧妙的;狡猾的;贴切的,恰当的。6.〔俚、方〕相当的,好多的。7.〔古〕(军人等)魁伟的,英勇的。*a ~ fellow* 优柔的[女人气的]家伙。*a ~ child* 可爱的孩子。*a ~ story* 有趣的故事。*a ~ boy*〔美俚〕(马戏团的)保镖;漂亮男子,女性化的男子。*~ ways* 讨人喜欢的态度。*a ~ sum of money* 相当多的钱。*A ~ mess you have made!* 你弄得真糟!*a ~* ***how d'you do*** 麻烦事;〔反语〕好事。*a ~* ***kettle of fish*** 乱七八糟。*a ~* ***penny*** 一大笔钱。***Here is a ~ go!*** 这事真糟!***Here is a ~ mess*** [***business, muddle***]! 这成个什么样子! II *ad*. 相当,颇;还;〔反〕非常。*I am ~ well*. 我很好。*I am ~ sick of it*. 这个叫我厌烦极了。~ ***much*** 1.〔口〕几乎,全部。2. 非常。~ ***much the same thing*** 差不多一样。~ ***soft***〔美俚〕容易的,便当的;合算的。~ ***soon*** 很快。***sit ~*** 处于极有利地位;〔美俚〕成功;过舒服日子。III *n*. 1. 心肝,宝贝〔对子女、妻子的称呼,说作 *my ~! my pretties!*〕。2.〔*pl*.〕〔美〕漂亮东西,衣饰。3.【高尔夫球】球的正规通路。4.(玻璃杯的)凹条花纹。*She has put on all her pretties*. 她打扮得花枝招展。*fill up to the ~* 把酒斟到齐杯子的凹条花纹处(倒满约三分之一杯)。~**-pretty** 1. *a*. 装饰过分的,漂亮得俗气的;只想漂亮的;娇柔造作的。2. *n*.〔*pl*.〕小装饰品,中看不中用的便宜货。**-ish** *a*. 有些漂亮的,有点可爱的;好像不错的。**-ism** *n*.(文体、态度等的)娇柔造作,过分讲究修饰。

pre·tu·ber·cu·lous [ˌpriːtju(ː)ˈbəːkjuləs; ˏpritjuˋbɝkjələs] *a*.【医】结核发生前的。

pre·typ·i·fy [priːˈtipifai; priˋtɪpəˏfaɪ] *vt*. (**-fied**) 预示,预告,预表。

pret·zel [ˈpretsəl; ˋprɛtsl̩] *n*. 1. 椒盐卷饼;纽结形盐饼干。2.〔美俚〕(乐器)法国号。*a ~ bender*〔美俚〕吹法国号的人〔原意为卷盐卷饼的人〕。

prev. = previous(ly).

pre·vail [priˈveil; prɪˋvel] *vi*. 1. 胜,压倒,占优势;占上风,胜过(*over*; *against*);成功,奏效。2. 普遍;传开,盛行,流行,普及。3. 说服,劝说(*on*; *upon*; *with*)。*This custom does not ~ now*. 这种风俗现在已经不流行了。*Can't I ~ upon you to have another helping of pie*? 你再吃一块馅饼好吗? *I cannot ~ upon him*. 我说服不了他。*~ over* [*against*] *the enemy* 战胜敌人。

pre·vail·ing [priˈveiliŋ; prɪˋvelɪŋ] *a*. 1. 盛行的,流行的;当时的,目前的;一般的,普通的。2. 占优势的,主要的,有效的,显著的,有势力的,有力的。*the ~ fashions* 流行的式样。*a ~ opinion* 普遍的意见。~ **wind**【气】盛行风。**-ly** *ad*. **-ness** *n*.

prev·a·lence [ˈprevələns; ˋprɛvələns] *n*. 1. 流行,盛行,普遍。2.〔罕〕优势,卓越。

prev·a·lent [ˈprevələnt; ˋprɛvələnt] *a*. 1. 流行的,盛行的;一般的,普通的;广布的,蔓延的。2.〔罕〕优势的。*Whooping cough is very ~ just now*. 百日咳正在广泛流行。**-ly** *ad*.

pre·var·i·cate [priˈværikeit; prɪˋværəˏket] *vi*. 支吾,搪塞,推诿,撒赖。**-ca·tion** *n*. **-ca·tor** *n*. 支吾者,搪塞者,推诿者。

pre·ven·ient [priˈviːnjənt; prɪˋvinjənt] *a*. 1. 前,先,以前的;领先的。2. 预期的(*of*)。3. 预防的(*of*)(= preventive)。

pre·vent [priˈvent; prɪˋvɛnt] *vt*. 1. 阻止,阻挡;制止;妨碍(*from*)。2. [priːˈvent; priˋvɛnt] 预防;〔古〕先做,预先,迎合(愿望),预先应付(问题);【宗】引领。*Rain ~ed the game*. 下雨妨碍了比赛。*~ him from going* = *~ his* [*him*] *going* 阻止他走。*~ sb. from injuring himself* 预防某人弄伤自己。— *vi*. 妨碍;阻止。*if nothing ~s* 如果没有什么妨碍的话。

pre·vent·a·ble [priˈventəbl; prɪˋvɛntəbl̩] *a*. 可阻止的;可预防的。**-bil·i·ty** *n*. 预防可能性。

pre·vent·a·tive [priˈventətiv; prɪˋvɛntətɪv] *a*., *n*. = preventive.

pre·vent·er [priˈventə; prɪˋvɛntɚ] *n*. 1. 防止者;预防者;防护设备,预防物,预防法,预防药。2. 阻止者;妨碍物。3.【海】辅助索,保险索。

pre·ven·tion [priˈvenʃən; prɪˋvɛnʃən] *n*. 1. 阻止,制止;妨碍,阻碍;妨碍物。2. 预防;预防法;*P- is better than cure*.【谚】医病不如防病。***by way of ~*** 作为预防;为预防起见。

pre·ven·tive [priˈventiv; prɪˋvɛntɪv] I *a*. 预防的(*of*);防止的;防护的。II *n*. 1. 防护物;预防法;预防措施;预防剂。2.〔古〕沿岸缉私员。*~ medicine*【医】预防医学;预防药。*a ~ war*【军】先发制人的战争。*~ maintenance*【机】定期维修。***the P- Service***〔英〕沿岸海关缉私队。

pre·view [ˈpriːvjuː; ˋpriˏvju] I *n*. 1. 预观;预映,试映;预演,试演;(展览会的)预展;预习。2.(电影)预告片。II *vt*. 预观;预映,试映;预演;预展;预习。

pre·vi·ous [ˈpriːvjəs, -viəs; ˋprivɪəs] I *a*. 1. 先,前;以前的(*opp*. following)。2.〔口〕过早的,过急的。*on the ~ night* 在前一晚。*You have been a little too ~*. 你稍微急了一点。***P- Examination***(剑桥大学的)文学士学位初考。~ ***question***(议会中的)先决问题[动议]。II *ad*. 在前,在先,在…以前(*to*)。*He died ~ to my arrival*. 他在我到达以前就故去了。**-ly** *ad*. 在前,在以前;预先(*previously designated* 预先指定的)。**-ness** *n*.

pre·vise [priˈvaiz; prɪˋvaɪz] *vt*. 1. 预先警告,预告。2. 预知,预先看到。

pre·vi·sion [pri(ː)ˈviʒən; prɪˋvɪʒən] *n*., *vt*. 预见,预知。**-al** *a*. 有先见之明的,预先就知道的。

pre·vo·cal·ic [ˌpriːvəuˈkælik; ˏprivoˋkælɪk] *a*. 元[母]音前的。

pre·vo·ca·tion·al [ˌpriːvəuˈkeiʃənl; ˏprivoˋkeʃənl] *a*. 为入职业学校作准备的。*~ course* 为进入职业学校作准备的课程。

Pre·vost [preiˈvəu, ˈprevəust; preˋvo, ˋprɛvost] *n*. 普雷沃(斯特)〔姓氏〕。

pre·vue [ˈpriːvjuː; ˋpriˏvju] *n*., *vt*. = preview.

pre·war [ˈpriːˈwɔː; priˋwɔr] I *a*. 战前的(*opp*. postwar)。II *ad*. 在战前。

prex(y) [ˈpreks(i); ˋprɛks(ɪ)] *n*.〔美俚〕(大学)校长,(学院)院长,(橄榄球俱乐部的)会长。

prey [prei; pre] I *n*. 1. 被捕食的动物。2. 牺牲者,牺牲品。3. 捕获;捕食;〔古〕战利品,掠夺品,赃物。*a ~ to circumstances* 境遇的牺牲品。*a beast* [*bird*] *of ~* 肉食兽[鸟],猛兽[禽]。***become the ~ of*** = ***fall a ~ to*** 被…捕食;成了…的牺牲品;被…所俘;被…折磨(*He fell a ~ to melancholy*. 他为忧郁所折磨)。***make a ~ of*** 把…当做食物,把…当做捕获物。***seek after one's ~*** 打食,寻找捕获物;寻求战利品。II *vi*. 1.(猛兽、猛禽等)攫食,捕食(*on*, *upon*)。2. 劫掠,掠夺,诈取(*on*, *upon*)。3.(疾病等)使人慢慢衰弱,消耗,折磨;使苦恼,损害(*on*, *upon*)。*Foxes ~ on rabbits*. 狐狸捕食兔

子。~ *upon the defenseless villages* 抢掠无防备的村庄。*Care ~ed (up) on her health*. 忧虑损害了她的健康。

prez [prez; prɛz] ***n***. 〔美俚〕**1**. = president. **2**. …大王〔对特别精于自己行业者的称呼〕。

pri. = **1**. private. **2**. primary. **3**. prison.

Pri·am [ˈpraiəm; ˋpraɪəm] ***n***. 普利安〔荷马史诗《伊利亚特》中被联军围攻的特洛伊国王〕。

pri·ap·ic [praiˈæpik; praɪˋæpɪk] ***a***. **1**. 〔有时作 P-〕阴茎的,崇拜男性生殖器的 (= phallic)。**2**. 非常雄劲的,很有丈夫气的,很有男性气的。

pri·a·pism [ˈpraiəpizəm; ˋpraɪəpɪzm] ***n***. 【医】**1**. 胀阳症。**2**. 好色。

Pri·a·pus [praiˈeipəs; praɪˋepəs] ***n***. **1**. 【希、罗神】男性生殖神〔酒神和爱神之子〕。**2**. 〔p-〕男性生殖器;(鱼的)交换器。

Price [prais; praɪs] ***n***. 普赖斯〔姓氏〕。

price [prais; praɪs] **I** ***n***. **1**. 价格,价钱;市价;代价;费用。**2**. 报酬;悬赏;交换物;〔美俚〕钱;(为取得某物而付出的)牺牲。**3**. 赌金比率,赌注与赢款的差额。**4**. 〔古〕价值,贵重。~*s (of commodities)* 商品价格,物价。*a cash* ~ 现金价格。*a cost* ~ 成本价格,原价。*a market* ~ 市价。*a famine* ~ 缺货时的市价。*a fixed [set, settled]* ~ 定价。*a net* ~ 实价。*the* ~ *asked* 开价,喊价。*a reduced [bargain]* ~ 廉价;有折扣的价格。*the selling* ~ 售价。*the trade* ~ 同行价格。*the wholesale [retail]* ~ 批发[零售]价格。*a stable* ~ 价格稳定。*the* ~ *of money* 贷款利率;延期日息。*a unit* ~ 单价。***at a*** ~ 付很大代价。***at any*** ~ 不惜任何代价。***at a fair*** ~ 售价公平。***at the*** ~ ***of*** 拼着…;以…的代价。***beyond [above, without]*** ~ 无价的,极贵重的。***fetch a high*** ~ 可以卖得高价。***get a good*** ~ ***for*** 好价卖出。***give a long*** ~ ***for*** 高价买。***make a*** ~ 讨价,开价;定价。***pay a heavy*** ~ 付高价。***raise [reduce] a*** ~ 涨[减]价。***set [put] a*** ~ ***on sb.'s head [life]*** 悬赏缉拿某人[悬赏要某人的命]。***set a*** ~ ***(up) on sth***. 给某物批上价格。***set high [little, no]*** ~ ***on*** 重视[不重视]。***What*** ~ ***...?*** 〔英俚〕**1**. (赛马时走红的马)跑赢的希望怎样?〔喻〕你以为怎么样?有可能…吗?(*What* ~ *fine weather tomorrow?* 〔口〕明天天气会好吗)。**2**. …算什么东西?…有什么用处[价值]呢?〔嘲笑会被吹捧而遭到失败的某事物〕。

II ***vt***. 〔口〕**1**. 给…定价。**2**. 问…的价。**3**. 给…估价。**4**. 由于要价过高而使…。~ ***one's goods [oneself] out of market*** 由于要价过高而失掉销路。~ **control** 价格管制,物价控制。~ **current** (股票或物品的)行市表。~-**cutter** (为挫败竞争者等的)削价者。~ **cutting** 减价,削价。~ **index** 物价指数。~ **level** 物价水平。~ **list** 定价表。~-**proof** ***a***. 价格保证公道的。~ **tag**, ~ **ticket** 价格标签。~ **support** 〔美〕**1**. 价格维持〔通常由政府采取措施对预定的价格标准的维持〕。**2**. 价格补助金〔为维持一定价格而发放的贷金〕。~ **war** 价格战〔一再削价的商品竞争〕。~ **work** 按件计值的工作。

priced [praist; praɪst] ***a***. 有定价的;定价的。*a* ~ *catalogue* 有定价的目录。*high-*~ 高价的。*low-*~ 廉价的。

price·less [ˈpraislis; ˋpraɪslɪs] ***a***. **1**. 无价的,千金难买的,极贵重的。**2**. 〔英口〕非常有趣的;极荒谬的,不成话的。*a perfectly* ~ *evening* 一个十分难得的[极愉快的]夜晚。*It's perfectly* ~ *to hear them abuse each other*. 听他们相骂实在是有趣。*She is* ~, *isn't it?* 她有些不像话,是吗?

price·y [ˈpraisi; ˋpraɪsɪ] ***a***. 〔英口〕昂贵的,高价的。

prick [prik; prɪk] **I** ***vt***. **1**. 扎,刺,戳穿。**2**. 刺伤;扎痛,刺痛;刺激;使痛心,使(良心等)受责备。**3**. (马、狗等)侧(耳),竖(耳)。**4**. 〔古〕用踢马刺踢(马),驱策。**5**. 在…上穿小孔;在…上穿孔作标记;(在名单等上做小记号)挑选出;选择;选任。**6**. 插(苗) (*out*; *in*)。**7**. 【海】缝合(帆、篷);(在海图上)测量(距离)。**8**. 追踪(兔等)。*The pin ~ed her finger*. 针刺破了她的手指。*My duty ~s me on*. 责任感激励着我。— ***vi***. **1**. 扎,刺,被刺;(感到)刺痛。**2**. 〔古〕策马前进 (*on*; *forward*)。**3**. (葡萄酒等)变酸。**4**. (耳朵)耸立,竖立;朝上。*My conscience ~s*. 我受良心责备。~ ***a bubble*** 戳破肥皂泡;揭穿真相。~ ***down*** 选择。~ ***for a soft plank*** 【海】在船上找寻舒适的卧处。~ ***near*** 跟…匹敌,与…并驾齐驱。~ ***off [out]*** **1**. (在航海地图上)记上船的位置、进路。**2**. 挑选出。**3**. 移植(幼苗)。~ ***sb. for*** 遴选[选任]某人为。~ ***up*** **1**. (用灰泥等)粗涂,打底子。**2**. 【海】(风)厉害起来。~ ***up oneself*** 打扮自己;炫耀自己。~ ***up the [one's] ears*** (狗)竖耳,(人)侧着耳朵听。**II** ***n***. **1**. 扎,刺;扎痛,刺痛;刺伤;(良心的)责备,悔恨。**2**. 刺痕;刺点,刺孔;(箭靶的)靶心;【乐】符点;野兔的足迹。**3**. (植物的)刺;(动物)突出的器官。**4**. 尖形器具[武器];〔古〕锥,刺;踢马刺;(赶牲口用的)刺棍。***kick against the ~s*** 螳臂挡车,以卵击石;作无益的抵抗。***the ~s of conscience*** 良心的责备,内心的悔恨。~-**eared** ***a***. (狗)竖耳的;(人)耳朵显露的(尤指英国十七世纪不戴假发的圆颅党成员)。~ **song** 〔古〕(16、17 世纪英国的)乐谱。~-**up** ***a***. 漂亮的。

prick·er [ˈprikə; ˋprɪkɚ] ***n***. **1**. 刺[扎、戳]的人。**2**. 供刺[扎、穿孔]用的工具;锥子;通针;【电】触针。**3**. 〔古〕轻骑兵。

prick·et [ˈprikit; ˋprɪkɪt] ***n***. **1**. (双角笔直未生叉的)二岁雄鹿。**2**. 烛台,蜡烛扦。

prick·ing [ˈprikiŋ; ˋprɪkɪŋ] ***n***. 刺;刺痕;刺痛感。

prick·le[1] [ˈprikl; ˋprɪkl̩] **I** ***n***. **1**. (动植物皮上的)刺,棘。**2**. 刺痛;刺戳。**II** ***vt***., ***vi***. (使)感到刺痛。*He ~d all over*. 他浑身刺痛。

prick·le[2] [ˈprikl; ˋprɪkl̩] ***n***. 柳条篮子。

prick·ly [ˈprikli; ˋprɪklɪ] ***a***. **1**. 多刺的;针刺般痛的。**2**. 易动怒的;敏感的。**3**. 刺手的,难办的。~-**ash** 花椒。~ **heat** 痱子。~ **pear** 【植】霸王树;仙人球[霸王树的梨状果实]。

Pride [praid; praɪd] ***n***. 普赖德〔姓氏〕。

pride [praid; praɪd] **I** ***n***. **1**. 自大,骄傲,傲慢。**2**. 自尊(心);自豪;得意,自满。**3**. 足以夸耀的东西,引以自豪的人[东西]。**4**. 最优秀部分;精华〔指一部分人等〕。**5**. 全盛(期);顶点;〔诗〕豪华,美观;装饰。**6**. (马等的)精力,血气。**7**. (禽兽的)群。**8**. 〔古〕(牝兽的)交尾期。**9**. (孔雀的)开屏;【徽】孔雀开屏。*a proper* ~ 自尊心;自豪感。*a false* ~ 妄自尊大,狂妄。*P- goes before a fall*. = *P- will have a fall*. 骄者必败。*a mother's* ~ 母亲的得意孩子。*in the* ~ *of one's years [life]* 在全盛时期,正年富力强。*a* ~ *of peacocks* 一群孔雀。***a peacock in his*** ~ 正在开屏的孔雀。***be puffed up with*** ~ 妄自尊大。***give [yield]*** ~ ***of place to*** 使…占第一位,把第一位让给…。***hold*** ~ ***of place*** 占第一位。***in*** ~ ***of grease*** (猎物)正肥,正适宜于狩猎。~ ***of China*** 檀香。~ ***of the desert*** 骆驼。~ ***of one's youth*** 青春。~ ***of place*** 傲慢;高位;(尤指鹰的)飞翔。~ ***of the morning*** 早晨的雾或阵雨〔天晴的预兆〕。~ ***of the world*** 〔古〕虚荣。***put one's*** ~ ***in one's pocket*** 压抑住自尊心,忍辱。***take (a)*** ~ ***in*** 以…自豪;对…感到满意。**II** ***vt***. 〔~ oneself〕使得意。~ ***oneself on [upon]*** 以…自豪,自夸…(*She ~s herself on her cooking*. 她自夸会做菜)。-**ful** ***a***. 骄傲的;得意的,自傲的。

prie-dieu [ˈpriːdjəː; ˋpridjɚ] ***n***. (*pl*. **prie-dieux** [ˈpriːdjəː(z); ˋpridjɚ(z)]) 〔F.〕**1**. 祷告台。**2**. 祷告椅(= ~ chair)。

pri·er [ˈpraiə; ˋpraɪɚ] ***n***. 刺探[打听]者;窥探者。

priest [priːst; prist] **I** ***n***. **1**. 祭司;教士;神父,牧师;僧人;术士。**2**. (学术领域等的)大师,宗师。**3**. 〔主 Ir.〕(用来打死已上钩的鱼的)打鱼槌。*a* ~ *of art* 艺术宗师。***a*** ~ ***of Bacchus*** 酒鬼。***the ~'s Crown*** 〔英方〕蒲公英。

P

II *vt*. 使成为教士,使做僧人;任命…为祭司[神父]。～**-craft** 教士[僧侣]的权术[谋略]。～**-ridden** *a*. 受教士支配[压制]的。**-hood** *n*. 1. 教士[祭司等的]职位[身分]。2. 〔集合词〕全体教士。**-like** *a*. 像教士的;适于教士的。

priest·ess ['pri:stis; `pristɪs] *n*. (基督教以外的)尼姑;女祭司;女术士。

Priest·ley ['pri:stli; `pristlɪ] *n*. 普里斯特利〔姓氏〕。

priest·ling ['pri:stliŋ; `pristlɪŋ] *n*. 小教士;小僧;小祭司。

priest·ly ['pri:stli; `pristlɪ] *a*. 教士的;像教士的;适于教士的。**-li·ness** *n*.

prig[1] [prig; prɪg] *n*. 1. (讲话、态度等)一本正经的人;爱充学者[教育家]的人。2. 讨厌的人。

prig[2] [prig; prɪg] I *n*. 〔俚〕小偷,扒手。II *vt*. (*-gg-*) 〔俚〕偷。— *vi*. 〔Scot.〕争论;讨价还价。

prig·ger·y ['prigəri; `prɪgərɪ] *n*. 1. 自负,自命不凡,沾沾自喜。2. 一本正经,古板。

prig·gish ['prigiʃ; `prɪgɪʃ] *a*. 1. 骄傲的,自命不凡的,自负的。2. 一本正经的,死板的。**-ly** *ad*.

prig·gism ['prigizəm; `prɪgɪzm̩] *n*. 1. 自负。2. 一本正经;死板。

prill [pril; prɪl] I *n*. 金属小球,金属颗粒。II *vt*. 1. 使(固体物)变成小珠状[小颗粒]。2. 使(粒状或晶体状材料)变为流体。

prim [prim; prɪm] I *a*. 1. 整洁的。2. 一本正经的;丝毫不苟的;古板的。II *vt*. (*-mm-*) 1. 使(面孔)摆出一本正经的样子。2. 整洁地打扮,装饰。— *vi*. 装出一本正经的模样。**-ly** *ad*. **-ness** *n*.

prim. =1. primary. 2. primate. 3. primitive.

pri·ma ['pri:mə; `primə] *a*. 〔It.〕第一的,主要的。～ ***ballerina*** [ˌbæləˈri:nə; ˏbæləˋrinə] 芭蕾舞的主要女演员。～ ***buffa*** ['bufə; `bufə] (歌舞喜剧的)主要女歌星。～ ***donna*** ['dɔnə; `dɑnə] (*pl*. ～ ***donnas***, ***prime donne*** ['pri:meiˈdɔnei; `primeˋdɑne]) 1. (歌剧的)首席女演员,音乐会的主要女歌手。2. 〔美俚〕爱虚荣的人,傲慢的人,神经质的人(尤指女人)。

pri·macy ['praiməsi; `praɪməsɪ] *n*. 1. 第一位,首位;卓越。2. (英国教会)大主教的职务[地位];(罗马天主教)教皇的最高权力。

pri·mae·val [praiˈmi:vəl; praiˋmivl] = primeval.

pri·ma fa·ci·e ['praiməˈfeiʃii(:); `praɪmə `feʃɪˏi] 〔L.〕1. 初看时,一见之下,乍看起来;据初次印象。2. 自明的。3.【法】足以构成案件[事实等]的。***prima facie case***【法】表面上证据确凿的案件。***prima facie evidence***【法】表面上确凿的证据,初步证据。

pri·mage[1] ['praimidʒ; `praɪmɪdʒ] *n*. 1. 运费贴补〔运费以外的费用〕。2.【海】货主送给船长的酬金。

pri·mage[2] ['praimidʒ; `praɪmɪdʒ] *n*. 水分诱出量〔汽锅中随蒸气排出的水量〕。

pri·mal ['praiməl; `praɪml] *a*. 1. 第一的,最初的,原始的。2. 首位的,主要的;根本的。**-ly** *ad*.

pri·ma·quine ['praiməˈkwi:n; `praɪməˋkwin] *n*.【化】首喹。

pri·ma·ri·ly ['praimərili, Am. praiˈmerili; `praɪmərɪlɪ, `praɪˏmerəlɪ] *ad*. 1. 首先,最初;原来。2. 主要地;根本上。

pri·ma·ry ['praiməri; `praɪˏmerɪ] I *a*. 1. 第一的,最初的,初级的;初等的;基本的;基层的。2. 主要的,为首的,第一位的。3. 原始的,根本的;原著的,第一手的;(颜色)原色的。4. 初步的 (*opp*. secondary); 预备的。5.【医】初期的,第一期的。6.【电】一次的;原的;第一级的。7.【生】初生的;【地】原生的,原成的,结晶岩的,最下层的。8.【化】伯的;连上一个碳原子的;(无机盐)一代的。9.【语法】语根的;一级语结的。*a matter of* ～ *importance* 头等重要的事情。～ *meaning of a word* 一个词的原义。II *n*. 〔常 *pl*.〕1. 居首位的事物,主要事物。2. 〔美〕候选人选拔会;初选。3. 原色;原色感。4. (油漆等的)底子。5.【天】主星;(有卫星的)行星。6.【电】原线圈;初级线圈。7.【动】〔*pl*.〕鸟翼末节上的羽毛,初级飞羽;(昆虫的)前翅。8.【语法】一级语结〔叶斯帕森用语,指句中可用作主语、宾语的成分,包括名词、代词、分句以及不定式结构等〕。～ **accent**【语音】第一重音。～ **accumulation**【经】原始积累。～ **algebra** 准质[准素]代数。～ **battery** [**cell**] 一次电池,原电池。～ **care** 初级保健〔指对疾病或健康状况的初步诊断和治疗〕。～ **coil** 初级线圈,原线圈。～ **colours** 原色。～ **cost** 成本。～ **cuticula** 外表皮。～ **education** 初等教育,小学教育。～ **election** 〔美〕预选(会)。～ **grades** 小学低年级。～ **group**【地】古生界。～ **laws** 〔美〕预选会规则。～ **meeting** [**assembly**] 〔美〕预选会。～ **minerals** 原生矿物,未氧化的矿物。～ **oil**【化】初级油,原油。～ **pest** 主要害虫。～ **products** 农产物,原料品。～ **road** (公路中的)干线。～ **salt**【化】一代盐。～ **school** 小学校。～ **shock**【医】原发休克。～ **star**【天】主星。～ **tenses**【语法】主要时态〔指拉丁文和希腊文语法中的现在、将来、完成和将来完成时[式]〕。

pri·mate[1] ['praimit; `praɪmɪt] I *n*. 1. (英国教会的)大主教,首席主教,监督长。2. 〔古〕首领。*P- of England* 约克大主教。*P- of all England* 坎特伯雷大主教。

pri·mate[2] ['praimeit; `praɪmet] *n*. 灵长目动物。

Pri·ma·tes [praiˈmeiti:z; praiˋmetiz] *n*. 〔*pl*.〕【动】灵长目〔包括人、猿等〕。

prime[1] [praim; praɪm] I *a*. 1. 最初的;第一的,首位的;首要的,主要的;原始的;基本的;原有的。2. 最好的,第一流的,头等的;〔英俚〕漂亮的。3. 血气旺盛的,青春的。4.【数】质数的,素数的。*the* ～ *agent* 主因。***feel*** ～ 很神气。***of*** ～ ***importance*** 最重要的。II *ad*. 好极,妙极。III *n*. 1. 初期,最初。2. 春;青春,壮年;盛时,全盛期。3. 精华,最好部分 (*of*); 上等。4. 〔古〕黎明。5. 上撇号,符号〔′〕,(记时的)分号〔例:6′5″=6 分 5 秒〕;英尺号〔3′5″=3 英尺 5 英寸〕;重音符号。6.【数】质数,素数。7. (击剑中八个防御姿势中的)第一姿势〔刺〕。8.【天主教】(午前六时的)晨祷。9.【乐】同度。***in*** ～ ***of grease*** = in pride of grease 〔见 pride 条〕. ***in the*** ～ ***of life*** [***manhood***] 在壮年,年富力强。***the*** ～ ***of the moon*** 新月。***the*** ～ ***of the year*** 春天。***the*** ～ ***of youth*** 青春的全盛期〔12 岁到 28 岁〕。～ **cost** 原价,主要成本;进货价格。～ **meridian** 本初子午线。～ **minister** 总理,首相。～ **ministry** 总理[首相]的职权[地位]。～ **mover** 1. 原动力;主导力。2. 倡议者。3.【电】原动机;〔美军俚〕强力牵引车;【哲】第一动因。～ **number**【数】质数,素数。～ **number theorem**【数】素数定理。～(-)**plus** *a*.【经】最优惠贷款利率再附加一定百分比的。～ **pump**【机】起动汽油泵。～ **rate** 最优惠(贷款)利率。～ **time** 〔美〕(电视等观众最多的)黄金时刻。～ **vertical**【天】卯酉圈。**-ly** *ad*. 〔口〕很好,极好。**-ness** *n*.

prime[2] [praim; praɪm] *vt*. 1. (旧时)为…装雷管,为…装火药;装填,灌注。2. 事先为…提供消息[情报];事先给…指示。3. 〔口〕使尽量吃,使尽量喝(酒等) (*with*)。4. 在…上涂底子,在…上涂头道油漆。5. 〔英方〕修剪(树枝);采摘(烟叶)。6. 使准备好。7. (注入水或油等)使起动,使汽水混合。*fully* ～*d with the latest news* 掌握了最新的消息。～ *the pump* 起动油泵;〔美,喻〕采取措施促使事物发展(尤指以政府资金促使就业人数的增加和经济的发展)。— *vi*. 1. (旧时)装火药(准备开枪);装雷管(准备开炮)。2. (水随蒸汽)进入汽缸,汽水共腾。3. 事先提供消息。4. 涂底子,涂头道漆。5. 修剪树枝,采摘烟叶。

prim·er[1] ['praimə; `praɪmɚ] *n*. 1. 初级读本,初学书;初阶,入门(书);(尤指宗教改革前的)小祷告书。2. ['primə; `prɪmɚ]【印刷】10 点或 18 点活字的旧称。*great* ～ 18 点铅字。*long* ～ 10 点铅字。

prim·er[2] ['praimə; `praɪmɚ] *n*. 1. 装填火药者;装雷管

者；起动油泵者。2.【机】初给器；发火极；发火药；导火线；爆管，雷管；火帽；底火。3. 底漆，首涂油。4.【生化】引体。

pri·me·ro [priˈmeərəu; priˋmɛro] *n*. 普利麦罗纸牌戏〔十六与十七世纪流行的一种纸牌戏〕。

pri·meur [priːˈməː; priˋmɝ] *n*.〔F.〕〔常 *pl*.〕(果类的)初熟；初上市(的水果、蔬菜)；早来的消息。

pri·me·val [praiˈmiːvəl; praiˋmivl] *a*. 早期的，原始(时代)的，太古的。*a* ~ *forest* 原始森林。**-ly** *ad*.

prim·ing [ˈpraimiŋ; ˋpraɪmɪŋ] *n*. 1. 装雷管，装火药；点火药，起爆药。2. 涂底漆，底子，底漆。3. (汽机的)蒸贱，飞沫；汽水开发；(汽缸、唧筒等的)引动水；起动注油。4. 引动，起爆，发火，点火。5. (知识的)速成灌输。6. (事先)提供消息[情报]。7. (加在啤酒中的)一种浓糖溶液。~ **can** 注油器。~ **carburetor** 起爆汽化器。~ **powder** 起爆药。

pri·mip·a·ra [praiˈmipərə; praiˋmɪpərə] *n*. (*pl*. ~*s*, ***-rae***[-riː; -ri])【医】初产妇；只生过一个孩子的妇女。**pri·mi·par·i·ty** [ˌpraimiˈpæriti; ˏpraɪməˋpærətɪ] *n*. 初产。**pri·mip·ar·ous** [praiˈmipərəs; praiˋmɪpərəs] *a*. 初产的。

prim·i·tive [ˈprimitiv; ˋprɪmətɪv] I *a*. 1. 原始的，上古的；早期的。2. 古风的，老式的；粗糙的，简单的；幼稚的，未开化的，不发达的。3. 纯朴的，自然的。4. 原来的，基本的，非派生的 (*opp*. derivative)；最初的，第一位的 (*opp*. secondary)。5.【生】初生的；【地】初期的。6. 自学出来的；由自学的艺术家创作的。~ *men* 原始人。*the* ~ *mode of life* 原始生活方式。*a* ~ *mode of dressing* 朴素的服装。~ *colours* 原色。*the* ~ *chord*【乐】基础和音。~ *rocks* 原成岩。~ *soil* 生荒地。II *n*. 1. 原(始)人；原始事物。2.【语法】原词，根词；【数】本原，原始。3. 早期艺术家(作品)；模仿早期风格的艺术家；原始派艺术家。4.〔P-〕文艺复兴期前的画家(作品)；自学而成的艺术家(作品)；风格质朴的艺术家。5.〔P-〕〔英〕原始卫理公会派教徒 (= P- Methodist)。**-ly** *ad*. **-ness** *n*.

prim·i·tiv·ism [ˈprimitivizəm; ˋprɪmətɪvˏɪzəm] *n*. 1. (生活方式上的)原始主义。2. (艺术或艺术家的)原始风格；尚古主义。**-tiv·ist** *n*., *a*.

pri·mo[1] [ˈpriːməu, It. ˈpriːmɔː; ˋprimo] *n*. (*pl*. ~*s*, It. **-mi**[-mi; -mɪ])〔It.〕【乐】(重奏或重唱的)第一部，主要部。

pri·mo[2] [ˈpraiməu; ˋpraɪmo] *ad*., *a*.〔L.〕第一(的)，首先(的)。

primo- *comb*. *f*. 表示"始，原始，主部，第一"：*primo*genitor, *primo*geniture, *primo*dium.

pri·mo·gen·i·tor [ˌpraiməuˈdʒenitə; ˏpraɪməˋdʒɛnətɚ] *n*. 始祖；祖先。

pri·mo·gen·i·ture [ˌpraiməuˈdʒenitʃə; ˏpraɪməˋdʒɛnətʃɚ] *n*. 长子身分；【法】长子继承权[继承法]。

pri·mor·di·al [praiˈmɔːdjəl; praiˋmɔrdɪəl] *a*. 原始的，初生的，初发的，最初的；(从)原始时代存在的；基本的。~ *customs* 原始时代的风俗。~ (*germ*) *cell*【植】原生殖细胞。**-ly** *ad*.

pri·mor·di·um [praiˈmɔːdiəm; praiˋmɔrdɪəm] *n*. (*pl*. ***-di·a*** [-ə; -ə])【胚】原基。

primp [primp; prɪmp] *vt*., *vi*.〔美〕(过分讲究地)打扮，装饰。

prim·rose [ˈprimrəuz; ˋprɪmˏroz] I *n*. 1.【植】报春花属植物；樱草；樱草花。2. 樱草色，淡黄色。II *a*. 1. 樱草的。2. 樱草色的，淡黄色的。3. 樱草多的。4. 华美的；欢乐的。***the*** ~ ***path*** [***way***] 1. 享乐之路；追求安逸享受的堕落生活；放荡生活。2. 看来容易和恰当却容易出错的行动步骤。**P- Dame** 樱草会的女会员。**P- Day** 樱草节〔英国保守党政治家迪斯累利 (Disraeli) 的忌辰〕。**P- League**【英史】樱草会〔为纪念保守党政治家迪斯累利而成立的一个组织〕。~ **yellow** 樱草色。

prim·u·la [ˈprimjulə; ˋprɪmjulə] *n*.【植】报春花属植物。

pri·mum mob·i·le [ˈpraimʌm ˈmɔbiliː; ˋpraɪməm ˋmɑbəˏli] *n*.〔L.〕1. 原动天，第十层天〔古希腊天文学家托勒密的天动说中的最外层天体，带动所有天体转动〕。2.〔喻〕原动力；行动[运动]的主因。

pri·mus[1] [ˈpraiməs; ˋpraɪməs] I *n*.〔P-〕苏格兰主教派教会的主教。II *a*. 第一的，首位的；(英国男子学校同姓学生中)最年长的，资格最老的。*Jones* ~ 最年长的琼斯。~ ***inter pares*** [ˈintə ˈpeəriːz; ˋɪntɚ ˋpɛriz] 同事中资格最老的，同辈中居首位的。

pri·mus[2] [ˈpraiməs; ˋpraɪməs] *n*. 普利姆斯汽化炉〔一种燃烧汽化油的轻便炉子，商标名〕。

prin. = 1. principal; principally. 2. principle.

prince [prins; prɪns] *n*. 1. 王子；王孙；皇族；亲王。2. (英国以外的)公爵，侯爵，伯爵；…公；…侯。3. (封建时代的)诸侯；(作为小附属国统治者的)公。4.〔诗〕帝王，君主。5. 宗匠，大家，名家；大王，巨头。6.〔口〕好人。*P- Bismarck* 俾斯麦公爵。*a* ~ *of the blood* (*royal*) 皇族。*the P- Imperial* 皇太子。*the Crown P-* 皇太子，王储。*the* ~ *of poets* 诗坛名家。*the* ~ *of bankers* 银行大王。*a merchant* ~ 富商，豪商。***as happy as a*** ~ 极幸福的。***live like a*** ~ 生活(像王侯似地)豪华。***manners of a*** ~ 高贵的态度。~ ***among men*** 正人君子。***P- of Denmark*** 丹麦王子〔指莎士比亚笔下的 Hamlet〕(*Hamlet without the P- of Denmark* 没有 *Hamlet* 的 *Hamlet* 剧，失去了本质[存在意义]的东西)。***P- of Peace*** 耶稣。~ ***of the air*** [***the world***, ***darkness***, ***evil***] 魔王。***P- of the*** (***Holy Roman***) ***Church***【天主教】红衣主教的称号。***P- of Wales*** 威尔斯亲王〔英国皇太子的称号〕。**P- Albert** (**coat**)〔美口〕大礼服。~ **bishop** 兼任主教的公[侯]国君主。~ **charming** 女子理想中的求婚者；对女子献假殷勤的男子。~ **consort** 女王的丈夫，伴君。**P- Regent** 摄政王。~ **royal** 太子〔王或女王的长子〕。**-dom** 王子[诸侯等]的地位[权力，领土]。**-kin**, **-let** 幼君；小公子。**-like** *a*. 像王侯的，像王子的；高雅的，有威严的。**-ling** = -let. **-ship** 王子[诸侯等的]身份[职位]。

prince·ly [ˈprinsli; ˋprɪnslɪ] *a*. 1. 像王侯的，像贵公子的；高贵的；有威仪的。2. 堂皇的；壮丽的；豪华的；奢侈的。3. 王侯的，王子的。**-li·ness** *n*.

prin·ceps [ˈprinseps; ˋprɪnsɛps] *a*.〔L.〕1. 第一的，最初的。2.【解】主要的。*editio* ~ 初版。

prin·ce's-feath·er [ˈprinsizfeðə; ˋprɪnsɪzˋfɛðɚ] *n*.【植】硬穗苋；荭草。

prin·ce's-met·al [ˈprinsizmetl; ˋprɪnsɪzmɛtl] *n*. 黄铜，一种铜锌合金。

prin·cess[1] [prinˈses; ˋprɪnsɪs] *n*. 1. 公主；王妃；王族女性成员；亲王夫人。2. (英国以外的)公爵[侯爵]夫人。3. 英国国王[女王]的孙女。4. 女巨头；女名家。5.〔古〕女王。★ princess 作修饰语用时读作 [ˈprinses; ˋprɪnsɛs]。*a* ~ *of seamstresses* 著名女缝衣师。***a Crown P-*** 皇太子妃。***a*** ~ ***of the blood*** 女王族。***P- of Wales*** 英国太子之妃。***P- regent*** 女摄政王。~ **royal** 大公主。**-ship** 公主[王妃等]的身份[地位]。

prin·cess[2], **prin·cesse** [prinˈses, ˈprinses; prɪnˋsɛs, ˋprɪnsɛs] *n*., *a*. 紧身连衣裙(的)。~ **dress** [**petticoat**, **slip**] 紧身连衣裙。

prin·ci·pal [ˈprinsəpəl, -sip-; ˋprɪnsəpəl; -sɪp-] I *a*. 1. 主要的，首要的，最重要的；第一的。2. 领头的；负责人的，首长的。3. 资本的，本金的，作为本钱的。*the* ~ *actor* 主要演员，主角。*the* ~ *boy* [*girl*] (哑剧中)扮演男[女]主角的女演员。*the* ~ *offender*【法】主犯。*the* ~ *sum* 资本，本金，本钱。~ *operations* 主力战。~ *clause*【语法】(复合句中的)主句。~ *order*【化】主序模。~ *parts*【语法】(动词的)主要变化形式〔现在、过去式及过去分词〕。~ *sentence*【语法】主句 (= ~ clause)。~ *tone*【乐】主音。II *n*. 1. 长；长官；首长；负责人；校

P

长;社长;会长。**2.** 主动者;决斗的本人 (*opp*. second); 主要演员,主角;【法】主犯;本人;(经纪人、代理人、受委托人所代表的)委托人 (*opp*. agent, surety)。**3.**【商】资本,本金 (*opp*. interest, dividend); 基本财产 (*opp*. income)。**4.**【建】(主要)屋架;主构,主材。**5.**【乐】主音栓;(音乐会的)主奏者,独奏者,独唱者,主演者。**6.** (艺术作品的)主题;特征。*a lady* ~ 女校长。*I must consult my* ~. 我必须同委托人商量。~ **and interest** 本利。**a ~ in the first** [**second**] **degree** 主[从]犯。

prin·ci·pal·i·ty [ˌprinsiˈpæliti; ˏprɪnsəˋpælətɪ] ***n*.** **1.** 公国,侯国;封邑。**2.** 公国君主的职位[统治权、领地]。**3.** 〔*pl*.〕【宗】九级天使中的一级。***the P-*** 英国威尔斯(Wales)的俗名。

prin·ci·pal·ly [ˈprinsəpəli, -sip-; ˋprɪnsəpl̩ɪ, -sɪp-] ***ad*.** 主要,大抵。

prin·ci·pate [ˈprinsipit; ˋprɪnsɪˏpet] ***n*.** **1.** 最高权力。**2.** 古罗马早期帝政[略带共和政治色彩]。**3.** (古罗马帝国)执政者的权力[任期];公国君主的统治权。**4.** 公国;封邑,领地。

prin·cip·i·um [prinˈsipiəm; prɪnˋsɪpɪəm] ***n*.** (*pl*. ***-cip·i·a*** [-piə; -pɪə]) 原理,原则;〔*pl*.〕基本原理[原则];初步;基础。

prin·ci·ple [ˈprinsəpl, -sipl; ˋprɪnsəpl, -sɪpl] ***n*.** **1.** 原理,原则。**2.** 主义;政策;〔常 *pl*.〕道义;节操。**3.** 本质,本体,根源;本原,源泉。**4.** 本性,本能;天然的性能;天赋的才能;动因,素因。**5.**【化】素,要素;精。*the* ~ *of dividing to move and uniting to fight* 【军】分进合击原则。*the* ~*s of political economy* 政治经济学原理。*the first* ~ 第一原理,本体。*the first* ~ *of all things* 万物的本原。*a man of* ~ 有原则的人,正派人。*good* [*right, moral*] ~*s* 道义。*a vital* ~ 精力。*guiding* ~*s* 方针。*the bitter* ~【化】苦味素。*the* ~ *of causality* 因果律。*the* ~ *of contradiction*【逻】矛盾律。***against one's*** ~ 违反自己的原则。***as a matter of*** ~ 作为原则的问题。***by*** ~ 按照原则,原则上。***in*** ~ 原则上,大体上。***of*** ~ 有原则的。***on*** ~ 按照原则,根据原则 (*I refuse on* ~ 我拒绝是按原则办事[并无恶意])。***on the*** ~ ***of*** 根据…的原则。***stick to one's*** ~*s* 坚持原则。

prin·ci·pled [ˈprinsəpld; ˋprɪnsəpl̩d] ***a*.** 原则的,原则性的,有原则的;有节操的。*high-* ~ 有高度道德原则的,原则性强的。*loose-* ~ 原则性差的,无主见的,意志薄弱的。

prin·cox [ˈprinkɔks; ˋprɪnkɑks] ***n*.** 〔古〕纨袴子,花花公子。

prink [priŋk; prɪŋk] ***vt*.** **1.** 给…梳妆打扮,把…打扮漂亮,把…装饰漂亮 (*up*)。**2.** (鸟)用嘴理(毛)。— ***vi*.** **1.** 化妆,打扮得漂亮 (*up*)。**2.** 〔英方〕卖俏,装腔作势;扭扭捏捏地走。

print [print; prɪnt] **I *vt*.** **1.** 印;刻;盖上(印等)。**2.** 印刷(书、画等);把…付印;出版,刊行,发行(书籍等)。**3.** 印染,在(布等上)印花样;印(花)。**4.** 把…写成印刷字体。**5.** 把…铭记在心。**6.**【摄】印,晒印(相片);复制(电影拷贝等) (*out; off*)。~ *a kiss on her cheek* 在她脸上亲一亲。~ *a book* 出版一本书。~ *a newspaper* 发行一种报纸。~*ed matter* 印刷品。*a* ~*ed circuit* 印刷电路。~*ed goods* 印花布。*P- your name in block capitals*. 请用印刷体大写字母写姓名。~ (*sth*.) *on one's memory* 把(某事)铭记在心。— ***vi*.** **1.** 印刷;出版;以印刷为业。**2.** (相片等)晒出;现出;晒相;复制。**3.** 用印刷体写字。*This paper* ~*s badly*. 这种纸很难印底片。~ ***out*** (印刷机)不断地印出。**II *n*.** **1.** 印刷;印刷术;印刷业。**2.** 图片;晒图;版画。**3.** 〔主美〕出版物,报纸;印出的字体,印刷字体。**4.** 痕迹,印象;〔*pl*.〕〔美俚〕指纹;【地】印痕。**5.**【摄】(从底片晒出的)相片;照片;正片。**6.** 印花布;印花布服装;(用模型制出的)压制品。**7.** 印章;打印器;印模;【冶】铸模;型心座。**8.** 版本;印次。*a clear* ~ 清晰的印刷字体。*daily* ~*s* 日报。*weekly* ~*s* 周刊(杂志)。*write the address in* ~ 用印刷体写住址。*a finger* ~ 指印,指纹。*a foot* ~ 脚印,足迹。*cotton* ~ 印花布。*India* ~ 印度花纹印花布。*a* ~ *of butter* (模压成的)一块黄油。*a blue* ~ 蓝相片;蓝图。***appear*** [***come out***] ***in*** ~ 印成,印出来。***in*** ~ 已出版的;(书等)在出售中的;(书等)尚有供应的 (*Is the book in* ~? 这本书还买得到吗?)。***in cold*** ~ 已用活字印成(白纸黑字);〔喻〕不能再更动,没有变更的余地。***in large*** [***small***] ~ 用大号[小号]活字印刷的。***lie like*** ~ 撒大谎。***out of*** ~ (书等)已脱销;已绝版。***put into*** ~ 付印,出版。~ **effect** (录音)复制效应,转印效应。~ **hand** 用印刷体写的字。~ **journalism** 〔美〕报刊新闻工作〔有别于电视、广播新闻工作〕。~**-out**【自】印出(指以打印方式表示的计算机计算结果)。~**-seller** 版画[图片]商。~ **shop** 版画[图片]店;印刷所。~**works** (棉布等的)印染厂,印花布厂。

print·a·ble [ˈprintəbl; ˋprɪntəbl̩] ***a*.** **1.** 可印刷的,印得出来的;可翻印的。**2.** 适宜于出版的。**-bil·i·ty** [ˌprintəˈbiliti; ˏprɪntəˋbɪlɪtɪ] ***n*.**

print·er [ˈprintə; ˋprɪntɚ] ***n*.** **1.** 印刷(业)者;印刷商;印刷工人,排字工人。**2.** 印染者,印花工。**3.** 印刷机;【摄】晒片机,印像机;【讯】印字机。~*'s devil* 印刷厂学徒工。~*'s dozen* 十三。~*'s error* 排错〔略作 P.E., p.e.〕。~*'s ink* 油墨。~*'s mark* (版权页等上)出版商的商标。~*'s pie* 活字的乱堆;〔喻〕混乱 (*make* ~*'s pie of* 搞乱…)。***the public*** ~ 〔美〕印刷局局长。~ **gram** 印字电报。

print·er·y [ˈprintəri; ˋprɪntərɪ] ***n*.** **1.** 印染厂。**2.** 印刷所,印刷厂。

print·ing [ˈprintiŋ; ˋprɪntɪŋ] ***n*.** **1.** 印刷;版;印刷术;印刷业;印刷品;〔*pl*.〕供印刷用的纸。**2.** 〔美〕印刷次数,版次;(书等的一次)印数。**3.** 〔美〕印刷体一样的字。**4.**【纺】印花,印染。**5.**【摄】晒片;(电影拷贝等的)复制。*colour* ~ 彩印。*phosphor* ~ 荧光屏涂磷。*smoke* ~ 静电印刷。*three-coloured* ~ 三色版印刷(术)。~ **ink** 油墨。~ **house** 印刷厂。~ **machine** 印刷机。~ **office** 印刷所。~ **paper** 印刷用纸,道林纸;相片纸。~ **press** (电动)印刷机;印刷厂。

print·less [ˈprintlis; ˋprɪntlɪs] ***a*.** 无印迹的,不留印痕的。

print·mak·er [ˈprintˌmeikə; ˋprɪntˏmekɚ] ***n*.** 制版工人;(尤指)版画制作者。**-mak·ing *n*.** 制版;版画制作。

pri·on [ˈpriːɔn; ˋpriɑn] ***n*.**【生化】朊病毒,感染性蛋白质。

Pri·or [ˈpraiə; ˋpraɪɚ] ***n*.** 普赖尔〔姓氏〕。

pri·or[1] [ˈpraiə; ˋpraɪɚ] **I *a*.** **1.** 〔用作前置定[修饰]语〕在前的;优先的。**2.** 〔与 to 连用〕在…之前 (*opp*. posterior); 比…优先[重要]。~ *engagement* 预先的约会。~ *claims* 优先要求权。*This duty is* ~ *to all others*. 这个职务比其他一切职务都重要。**II *ad*.** 居先,在前 (*to*)。*I called on her* ~ *to my departure*. 我动身前去看过她。**-ly *ad*.**

pri·or[2] [ˈpraiə; ˋpraɪɚ] ***n*.** **1.** 小修道院院长,大修道院的副院长。**2.**【史】(十三世纪意大利诸共和国的)行政长官。**-ship *n*.** 小修道院院长[共和国行政长官]的职务[地位、任期]。

pri·or·ate [ˈpraiərit; ˋpraɪərɪt] ***n*.** **1.** = priorship. **2.** = priory.

pri·or·ess [ˈpraiəris; ˋpraɪərɪs] ***n*.** 小修女院院长;大修女院的副院长。

pri·or·i·ty [praiˈɔriti; praɪˋɔrətɪ] ***n*.** **1.** (时间、顺序上的)先,前。**2.** 较重要;上席;上位;重点,优先(权);先取权。**3.** 优先配给;优先考虑的事。*establish an order of* ~ 确定讨论项目的次序。*give* ~ *to* 把优先权让给…。~ *of one's claim to another's* 某人的要求比另一人的更重要。***according to*** ~ 依照次序,依次。***take*** ~ ***of*** 比…居先;得…的优先权。~ **construction** 近期[首期]建筑。

pri·o·ry [ˈpraiəri; ˋpraɪərɪ] ***n*.** 小修道院;小的女修道

院。*a* ～ *alien* 从属于外国大修道院的小修道院(=an alien ～)。

Pris·ci·an [ˈpriʃiən; ˋprɪʃɪən] *n*. 普里兴〔六世纪活跃于君士坦丁堡的拉丁语语法学家,被奉为语法学鼻祖〕。***break*** [***knock***] ～***'s head*** 违反语法规则,犯语法错误。***Shade of*** ～! 气死普里兴!〔闹语法笑话时的感叹语〕。

Pris·cil·la [priˈsilə; prɪˋsɪlə] *n*. 普丽西拉〔女子名〕。

prise [praiz; praɪz] *vt*., *n*. =prize.

pri·sere [ˈpraisiə; ˋpraɪsɪə] *n*.【植】正常演替系列。

prism [ˈprizəm; ˋprɪzəm] *n*. **1**.【数】棱柱(体),角柱(体);【物】(结晶)柱。**2**. 棱镜;棱晶。**3**.【物】分光光谱;〔*pl*.〕光谱的七色;折光物体。*an oblique* [*a regular*, *a right*, *a triangular*] ～ 斜[正、直、三角]棱柱。*cross* ～*s* 正角棱镜。～ *glasses* 棱镜双目望远镜。*a reversing* ～ 反像棱镜。*a* ～ *of first* [*second*] *order*【物】(结晶)第一[第二]柱。

pris·mat·ic, pris·mat·i·cal [prizˈmætik, -kəl; prɪzˋmætɪk, -kəl] *a*. **1**. 棱柱(形)的。**2**. 用棱镜分析的,分光的。**3**. 虹色的;射出七色光彩的;灿烂的。**4**.【物】斜方晶系的。～ *colours* 光谱的七色。～ *powder* 棱形火药。**-i·cal·ly** *ad*.

pris·moid [ˈprizmɔid; ˋprɪzmɔɪd] *n*. 平截头棱锥体。**-moi·dal** *a*.

prism·y [ˈprizəmi; ˋprɪzmɪ] *a*. **1**. 棱柱(似)的,棱镜的。**2**. 棱镜七色的,虹色的;五光十色的,灿烂的。

pris·on [ˈprizn; ˋprɪzn] **I** *n*. **1**. 监狱;拘留所,羁押室,禁闭室。**2**. 监禁,禁闭。***break*** (***out of***) ～ 越狱。***cast*** [***put***] ***sb***. ***into*** ～ 把某人下狱,把某人关进牢里。***escape from*** ～ 越狱逃跑。(***lie***) ***in*** ～ 在狱中。***send*** [***take***] ***sb***. ***to*** ～ =cast sb. into ～. **II** *vt*.〔诗〕〔方〕**1**. 监禁;关押。**2**. 紧紧抱住。～ **bird**〔口〕囚犯;惯犯,积犯。～ **breaker** 越狱者。～ **breaking** [**breach**] 越狱。～ **camp** 战俘集中营;苦役拘禁地。～ **editor** (报上负法律责任的)署名编辑。～ **fever**【医】斑疹伤寒。～ **house**〔主喻〕监狱,牢房。～ **van** 囚车。

pris·on·er [ˈpriznə; ˋprɪznə] *n*. **1**. 囚犯;刑事被告;拘留犯,羁押犯;俘虏。**2**. 被夺去自由的人[动物]。*a state* [*political*] ～ = *a* ～ *of state* 政治犯。*He made her hand a* ～. 他握住她的手不放。*a* ～ *to one's room* [*chair*] 病人[困在椅子上的残废者]。*My work kept me a* ～ *all summer*. 整个夏天,我的工作忙得不可开交。～ ***at large*** 在无法逃走处(如船上、营房等)许与相当自由的囚犯;(只准在船上或营房内自由走动的)受约束处分的军人。～ ***at the bar*** 刑事被告。***give oneself up a*** ～ 投降;自首;自投罗网。***make sb***. ～ 俘虏某人。～ ***of war*** 战俘。***take*** (*sb*.) ～ 俘虏(某人)。***yield oneself*** ～ 投降。～**s'**〔美 ～**'s**〕**bars** [**base**] 抢阵地[捉俘虏]游戏。

priss [pris; prɪs] *vi*.〔美口〕**1**. 做事严肃谨慎。**2**. 穿得讲究整洁。

pris·sy [ˈprisi; ˋprɪsɪ]〔美口〕*a*. **1**. 严肃谨慎的;刻板的。**2**. 服装讲究整洁的。**3**. 纤柔的;娇气的;缺乏男子气的。

pris·tine [ˈpristain; ˋprɪstin] *a*. **1**. 原始时代的,原始的;太古的;早期的。**2**. 原来的;纯朴的;未受腐蚀的。～ *innocence* 天真无邪。**-ly** *ad*.

prith·ee [ˈpriði(:); ˋprɪðɪ] *int*.〔古、口〕请,求求你〔pray thee 的别字〕。

Pritt [prit; prɪt] *n*. 普里特〔姓氏〕。

prit·tle-prat·tle [ˈpritl ˈprætl; ˋprɪtl ˋprætl] **I** *n*. **1**. 空谈,废话。**2**. 碎嘴子,饶舌者。**II** *vi*. 空谈;饶舌。

priv. =private(ly); privative.

pri·va·cy [ˈpraivəsi; ˋpraɪvəsɪ] *n*. **1**. 隐退,隐避,隐居。**2**.〔古〕隐居处,隐退处。**3**. 秘密,私下。*He must have disturbed your* ～. 他一定打搅你的幽静生活了〔真对不起〕。***in the*** ～ ***of one's thoughts*** 在内心深处。***in*** ～ 隐避地;秘密地。***in strict*** ～ 完全私下的[地]。***live in*** ～ 过隐居生活。

pri·vat·do·cent, pri·vat·do·zent [priˈvɑːtdəuˈtsent; prɪˋvɑtdoˋtsent] *n*. (*pl*. **-en** [-ən; -ən]) (在德国等的大学中)无薪俸的讲师〔不支薪俸,仅以学生的学费为报酬者〕。

pri·vate [ˈpraivit; ˋpraɪvɪt] **I** *a*. **1**. 私的,私人的,个人的,私用的,专用的。**2**. 秘密的;保密的;非公开的;(信件等)亲启的。**3**. (财产等)私有的;私营的;民间的;(学校等)私立的。**4**. 平民的;无官职的;士兵的。**5**. (地方等)隐蔽的,幽僻的。**6**. 不宜公开谈论[显露]的。**7**.〔古〕隐遁的。～ *life* 私生活。～ *coach* [*teacher*, *tutor*] 家庭教师;私人教师。～ *property* 私有财产。～ *ownership* 私有制。*a* ～ *secretary* 私人秘书。*a* ～ *car* 自备汽车。～ *business* 个人的事,私事。～ *affairs* = ～ *concerns* 私事,隐秘的事。*a* ～ *door* 便门。～ *clothes* 便服。～ *information* 非正式消息。*Keep the news* ～. 这个消息请守秘密。*We are quite* ～ *here*. 这里就不怕被人看见了。*a* ～ *citizen* 平民。*a* ～ *soldier* 士兵,列兵。***a*** ～ ***member*** (***of Parliament***) 非内阁阁员的普通议员。***as a*** ～ ***person*** 以个人身分。***for*** ～ ***reasons*** 仅仅私下地,不能给外人知道。***for sb***.***'s*** ～ ***ear*** 秘密地(*This is for your* ～ *ear*. 这是私下只跟你一个人讲的)。***in one's*** ～ ***capacity*** 以个人身分。**II** *n*. **1**. 列兵;〔美陆军、海军陆战队〕二等兵;士兵,〔英陆军〕二等兵。**2**.〔古〕私人,个人。**3**.〔*pl*.〕阴部,生殖器。*a basic* ～〔美陆军〕三等兵。*a* ～ *first class*〔美陆军、海军陆战队〕一等兵。***in*** ～ 秘密地(*criticism in* ～ 背后批评)。～ **bill** [**act**]【议会】有关个人利害的议案〔英国也指阁员以外的议员所提的议案〕。～ **detective**〔美〕人事调查所员,私人侦探。～ **detective agency**〔美〕私人侦探所,人事调查所。～ **eye**〔美俚〕= ～ detective. ～ **parts** 阴部,私处。～ **practice** 私人开业。～ **school** 私立学校。～ **secretary** 私人秘书。～ **soldier** 列兵,士兵。～ **theatricals** 业余戏剧演出。～ **view** (绘画等的)预展。～ **treaty** (买卖双方直接议定条件的)财产出让契约。**-ly** *ad*. 私下,秘密,一个人。

pri·va·teer [ˌpraivəˈtiə; ˌpraɪvəˋtɪr] **I** *n*. **1**. 私掠船〔战时特准掠捕敌方商船的武装民船〕。**2**. 私掠船船长;〔*pl*.〕私掠船船员。**II** *vi*. 私掠巡航。～**sman**〔美〕私掠船船长,私掠船船员。**-ing** *n*. 私掠巡航,掠捕敌方商船。

pri·va·tion [praiˈveiʃən; praɪˋveʃən] *n*. **1**. 缺乏;(生活必需品的)匮乏;穷困;困难,艰难。**2**. 剥夺,褫夺;没收;丧失。**3**.【逻】(积极性的)缺性。*suffer many* ～*s* 吃尽苦头,备尝艰辛。*die of* ～ 穷死。*Cold is the* ～ *of heat*. 冷就是缺热性。

pri·va·tism [ˈpraivitizəm; ˋpraɪvətɪzm] *n*. 利己主义〔只关心与自己直接利益有关的事情〕。**-va·tist, -tis·tic** *a*. **-ti·za·tion** *n*. **-va·tize** [-taiz; -taɪz] *vt*. 使利己主义化,使只顾自己。

priv·a·tive [ˈprivətiv; ˋprɪvətɪv] **I** *a*. **1**. 剥夺的,褫夺的。**2**. 缺乏某种性质的。**3**.【语法】表示缺性的;否定的,反义的。**II** *n*. **1**.【语法】缺性语〔voiceless, dumb 等〕;否定的前缀[后缀]〔un-, -less 等〕。**2**.【逻】缺性概念〔blindness, dumbness 等〕。

priv·et [ˈprivit; ˋprɪvɪt] *n*.【植】水蜡树,女贞。

priv·i·lege [ˈprivilidʒ; ˋprɪvlɪdʒ] **I** *n*. **1**. 特权,优惠,特别照顾,特别待遇;特殊荣幸。**2**. 特别处理;特许,特免。**3**. (对公司股票的)优惠增购权。*the* ～ *of Parliament*〔英〕议会[议员]的特权。*a breach of* ～ 对(国会议员等)特权的侵犯。*water* ～ 用水权。*the* ～ *of citizenship* 公民权。*exclusive* ～ 专有特权。***a bill of*** ～ 贵族要求贵族阶级审判的申请书。***a writ of*** ～ (因民事诉讼被扣押的人的)特赦状。～ ***of sb***.***'s friendship*** 和…交际的光荣。***the*** ～ ***of clergy***【史】**1**. 教士的特权〔犯罪时可不受普通法院审判〕。**2**. 知识阶级的特权〔初次犯罪时可免予判刑〕。**II** *vt*. 给…以特权;特许;特免(*from*)。～ *sb*. *from arrest* 特免某人不受逮捕。～ **cab** 特许在车站接客的马车。**-r** *n*. 享受特权者。

priv·i·leged [ˈprivilidʒd; ˋprɪvlɪdʒd] *a*. **1**. 特权的;有特权的;特殊待遇的。**2**. 特许的;专用的。**3**. 特免的;(由于特殊情况)不受一般法规制约的。**4**. 【天主教】(祭坛等)庆祝大赦的弥撒中特设的。*the* ~ *few* 少数享受特权者。*a* ~ *communication* 法律上无论何时皆可拒绝公开的(医生与病人、律师与委托人间等的)通信。

priv·i·ly [ˈprivili; ˋprɪvəlɪ] *ad*. 暗中;私下,秘密地。

priv·i·ty [ˈpriviti; ˋprɪvətɪ] *n*. **1**. 暗中参与;私下知悉;默契 (*to*); 秘密,私事。**2**. 【法】(对同一权利)有合法利益的人之间的相互关系;(对合同等因与当事人的一方有关系而产生的)非当事人的利益。~ *to the plot* 暗中参与阴谋。*with his* ~ *and consent* 得到他的同意。***with the*** ~ ***of*** 通知,告诉。***without the*** ~ ***of***... 不通知,不告诉。

priv·y [ˈprivi; ˋprɪvɪ] **I** *a*. **1**. (物、地方等)秘密的;隐蔽的;(行为)暗中参与的,和…有勾结的 (*to*)。**2**. 个人的;私人的。*I was made* ~ *to it*. 我心里明白那件事。**II** *n*. **1**. 【法】有利害关系的人。**2**. 〔古〕厕所。***be*** ~ ***to*** (*a plot*) 参与(阴谋)。**P- Council** 枢密院。**P- Councellor** [**Councillor**] 枢密顾问官。~ **parts** 阴部。~ **purse 1**. 〔英〕(王室的)私财;内库。**2**. 〔P- Purse〕英国皇室司库〔全称是 *Keeper of the P- Purse*〕。~ **seal** 〔英〕御玺〔加 the〕。**P- Seal** = Lord P- Seal 掌玺大臣。

prix [priː; pri] *n*. 〔*sing*., *pl*.〕〔F.〕**1**. 奖金;奖品。**2**. 价格。~ ***fixe*** [fiːks; fiks] (一客)份饭;份饭价格。**P- Goncourt** 龚古尔奖金〔法国的文艺奖金〕。

prize[1] [praiz; praɪz] **I** *n*. **1**. 奖赏;奖品;赠品;奖金。**2**. 争夺物;值得竞争的目标;〔口〕极好的东西。*the Nobel P-* 诺贝尔奖。*Good health is an inestimable* ~. 健康是无价之宝。**II** *a*. **1**. 悬赏的;作为奖品的;得奖的。**2**. 〔口〕非常的;了不起的。*a* ~ *cup* 奖杯。*a* ~ *idiot* 可以得奖的大傻瓜,头号傻瓜。*a* ~ *poem* 得奖诗。***carry off*** [***gain***, ***take***, ***win***] ***a*** ~ 得奖。***draw a*** ~ ***in the lottery*** 摸彩。***gain the*** ~***s of a profession*** 得到优薪高位。***pick up a*** ~ ***at a sale*** 大减价时买到极好东西。***play one's*** ~ 谋私利。***run*** [***play***] ~***s*** (为得奖赏)参加赛跑(比赛)。~ **essay** 得奖论文。~ **fellow** 得到奖学金的学生。~ **fellowship** 成绩优异奖学金。~ **fight**(**ing**) 职业拳击。~ **fighter** 职业拳击家。~**man** 得奖人。~ **ring** 拳击场;职业拳击赛。~ **scholarship** = ~ fellowship. ~**winner** 获奖人。**-less** *a*. 未获奖的;成绩平庸的。

prize[2] [praiz; praɪz] *vt*. **1**. 珍视,宝贵;珍藏。**2**. 〔古〕评价;估价。~ *security above all else* 安全第一。

prize[3] [praiz; praɪz] **I** *n*. **1**. 捕获(尤指战时在海上捕获敌方的船、货等)。**2**. 捕获品,战利品;(战时在海上)捕获的敌船[货物等]。**3**. 意外的收获,横财。***become*** (***the***) ~ ***of*** [***to***] 为…所捕获。***make*** (***a***) ~ ***of*** (战时)缉捕(船货等)。**II** *vt*. 捕拿,缉捕;捕获。~**-court** 处理战时海上捕获物的海军军事法庭。~ **crew** 战时海上押送捕获船的船员。~ **master** 捕获船押送官。~**-money** (战时海上捕获敌方船货者应得的)捕获赏金。

prize[4] [praiz; praɪz] **I** *vt*. 〔英方〕用杠杆推动;撬开 (*open*; *out*; *up*; *off*)。**II** *n*. 〔英方〕杠杆,撬棍;杠杆作用。

priz·er [ˈpraizə; ˋpraɪzɚ] *n*. 〔古〕(比赛中)争夺奖品的人。

pro[1] [prəu; pro] *n*. (*pl*. ~s) 〔口〕内行,专家;〔美〕职业选手。*a golf* ~ 高尔夫球的职业选手。

pro[2] [prəu; pro] **I** *n*. (*pl*. ~s) 投票赞成者;赞成方面的意见[理由];赞成的(投)票。***the*** ~***s and cons*** 赞成论与反对论;赞成与反对的理由;赞成者与反对者。**II** *ad*. 站在赞成方面;正面地 (*opp*. con)。~ ***and con*** 赞成与反对。~**-and-con** *vt*., *vi*. 辩论。

pro [prəu; pro] *prep*. 〔L.〕**1**. 为…的。**2**. 按…;随…,视…。~ ***bono publico*** [ˈbəunəu ˈpʌblikəu; ˋbono ˋpʌblɪˏko] 为了公益。~ ***forma*** [ˈfɔːmə; ˋfɔrmə] 形式上;【商】估计的,假定的(~ *forma account sales* 估计卖出计算书。~ *forma invoice* 估价单)。~ ***hac vice*** [hækˈvaisi(ː); hækˋvaɪsi(ɪ)] 只此一回,只为这个场合。~ ***memoria*** [miˈmɔːriə; mɪˋmɔrɪə] 提醒。~ ***patria*** [ˈpeitriə; ˋpetrɪə] 为祖国。~ ***rata*** [ˈreitə; ˋretə] 按比例的;成比例地。~ ***renata*** [riːˈneitə; riˋnetə] 【法】临时地[的] (*a meeting held* ~ *renata* 临时举行的会议)。~ ***tanto*** [ˈtæntəu; ˋtænto] 至此,到这个程度[范围]。~ ***tem***. = ~ ***tempore*** [ˈtemperi; ˋtɛmpəˏrɪ] 当时(的);暂时(的);临时(的) (*the* ~ *tem*. *secretary* 临时秘书)。

pro. = **1**. probation. **2**. probationer. **3**. prohibitionist. **4**. prostitute.

PRO = public relations officer 〔美军〕对外联络官。

pro-[1] *pref*. **1**. 代,副:*pro*noun, *pro*consul. **2**. 亲,赞成,偏袒: *pro*-American. **3**. 出,向前,在前:*pro*duce, *pro*pel, *pro*fane. **4**. 按,照:*pro*portion. **5**. 公开: *pro*claim.

pro-[2] *pref*. 表示"〔位置、时间〕前,先": *pro*gnathous, *pro*logue.

pro·a [ˈprəuə; ˋproə] *n*. (马来群岛的)快速帆船。

prob. = probable; probably; problem.

prob·a·bi·lism [ˈprɔbəbilizəm; ˋprɑbəbəlɪzm] *n*. **1**. 【哲】盖然论;或然说。**2**. 【宗】盖然说〔一种天主教教义,认为在神学权威有分歧时,可遵从任何一位神学大师的阐释〕。

prob·a·bi·lis·tic [ˌprɔbəbiˈlistik; ˏprɑbəbɪˋlɪstɪk] *a*. **1**. (天主教教义)盖然论的,或然说的。**2**. 概率的,几率的。

prob·a·bil·i·ty [ˌprɔbəˈbiliti; ˏprɑbəˋbɪlətɪ] *n*. **1**. 或有;或然性。**2**. 【哲】盖然性〔在 certainly 和 doubt 或 posibility 之间〕。**3**. 【数】几率,概率,或然率。**4**. 或有的事;可能的结果。**5**. 〔*pl*.〕〔美俚〕天气预测。*What are the probabilities*? 有几分把握? *The probabilities are against us* [*in our favour*]. 趋势对我们好像不利[有利]。*hit* ~ 命中率。***in all*** ~ 很可能,大概,多半,十之八九。~ ***of*** (*missile survival*) (飞弹不被击落的)概率。***The*** ~ ***is that***... 大概是…,很可能是…。***There is every*** ~ ***of*** [***that***]... 多半有,多半会。***There is no*** ~ ***of*** [***that***]... 很难有,很难会。

prob·a·ble [ˈprɔbəbl; ˋprɑbəbl] **I** *a*. 像有的,像确实的;很可能的,或然的,大概的;有希望的。★ probable 所指的可能性比 possible 或 likely 所指的要大一些。*Successs is possible but hardly* ~. 成功是可能的,但不一定。**II** *n*. 很可能被选中[获胜]的人;很可能的事[情况]。***It is*** ~ ***that***... 也许是,恐怕是 (*It is* ~ *that he forgot*. 他也许是忘记了)。~ **candidate** 大有希望的候选人。~ **cost** 大约的费用。~ **error** 概差,或然误差;【数】机差;【物】可几[可能]误差;【天】或然差。~ **evidence** 大概确实的证据。~ **zone** 【军】预期命中地带。

prob·a·bly [ˈprɔbəbli; ˋprɑbəblɪ] *ad*. 大概,或许,很可能。

proband [ˈprəubænd; ˋprobænd] *n*. 家谱中发支始祖 (= propositus)。

pro·bang [ˈprəubæŋ; ˋprobæŋ] *n*. 【外】除鲠器,食管探子。

pro·bate [ˈprəubit; ˋprobɪt] **I** *n*. 【法】**1**. 遗嘱检验。**2**. 验讫的遗嘱。*the* ~ *court* 遗嘱检验法庭。**II** [ˈprəubeit; ˋprobet] *vt*. 〔美〕**1**. 检验(遗嘱)。**2**. 对(犯人)予以缓刑。~ **duty** 立遗嘱人死后的动产税。

pro·ba·tion [prəˈbeiʃən; proˋbeʃən] *n*. **1**. 检定,检验,验证,查验。**2**. 考验(期),见习(期);试用(期);预备期;〔美〕(处罚学生的)试读期。**3**. 察看(以观后效)。**4**. 【法】缓刑。***on*** ~ **1**. (作为)试用,作为见习。**2**. 察看;【法】缓刑。***place*** (*an offender*) ***on*** [***under***] ~ 对(犯人)缓刑。~ **officer** 缓刑犯的监视官。~ **system** 缓刑制。

pro·ba·tion·al, pro·ba·tion·a·ry [prəˈbeiʃənəl, -ʃənəri; proˋbeʃənḷ, -ʃənərɪ] *a*. **1**. 试用的;见习的;

(会员等)非正式的;(党员)预备期的。2.【法】缓刑(中)的。3.察看(以观后效的)。*a probationary officer* = probation officer. *a* ~ *member* 非正式会员。

pro·ba·tion·er [prəˈbeiʃənə; proˋbeʃənɚ] *n*. 1. 试用人员,见习生,练习生;试读生;候补牧师;候补会员[党员、社员等]。2. 缓刑中的罪犯。

pro·ba·tive [ˈprəubətiv; ˋprobətɪv] *a*. 1. 检验的,鉴定的;试验中的。2. 证明的;作证据用的。*a* ~ *letter* 证明信。

pro·ba·to·ry [ˈprəubətəri; ˋprobəˏtorɪ] *a*. = probative.

probe [prəub; prob] I *n*. 1.【医】探针;探示器;取样器;【物】试探电极。2.【医】(对伤处等的)针探,探查;刺探;探索;试探;查究 (*into*);〔美〕调查;试样。3.【空】(飞机)空中加油管。4.【宇】探测器;探测飞船。*a lunar* ~ 月球探测器。II *vt*. 1. 用探针[探测器]探查。2. 刺探;调查,探查,查究。~ *a matter to the bottom* 彻底调查一件事。— *vi*. (用探针)探查;探索;查究,深查 (*into*)。~ *deeply into* 深入调查。

prob·er [ˈprəubə; ˋprobɚ] *n*. 探测器;探示器。

prob·it [ˈprɔbit; ˋprɑbɪt] *n*.【统计】正规偏差值〔一种计算平均数的偏差的统计单位〕。

pro·bi·ty [ˈprəubiti; ˋprobətɪ] *n*. 正直,诚实。

prob·lem [ˈprɔbləm; ˋprɑbləm] I *n*. 1. 问题,课题;疑难问题;令人困惑的情况。2.【数、物】习题;作图题。3. (象棋的)布局问题。*the* ~ *of unemployment* 失业问题。*His whole conduct is a* ~ *to me*. 他的一切行为我都不理解。II *a*. 1. 成问题的;难处理的。2. 关于社会问题的。*a* ~ *child*【心】问题儿童;难管教的孩子。*a* ~ *novel* [*play*] (反映社会问题等的)问题小说[戏剧]。**sleep on** [**upon, over**] **a** ~ 把问题留到第二天解决。

prob·lem·at·ic, prob·lem·at·i·cal [ˌprɔbliˈmætik, -ikəl; ˏprɑbləˋmætɪk, -tɪkl] *a*. 1. 有问题的;可疑的;疑难的;未定的,未可预断的。2.【逻】盖然性的,或然性的。**-i·cal·ly** *ad*. **-s** *n*. 〔*pl*.〕复杂而问题很多的种种事情。

pro·bos·cid·e·an, pro·bos·cid·i·an [ˌprəubəˈsidiən; ˏprobəˋsɪdɪən] I *n*. 长鼻目 (*Proboscidea*) 动物〔如象、(第三纪产的)乳齿象〕。II *a*. 长鼻目的。

pro·bos·cis [prəuˈbɔsis; proˋbɑsɪs] *n*. (*pl*. **-cides** [-sidiːz; -sɪdiz]) 1. (象等的)鼻子。2. (昆虫的)喙,吻。3.〔谑〕(人的)大鼻子。~ **monkey** 天狗猴。

proc. = 1. proceedings. 2. process. 3. proctor.

pro·caine [ˈprəukein, prəuˈkein; ˋproken, proˋken] *n*.【药】普鲁卡因。

pro·cam·bi·um [prəuˈkæmbiəm; proˋkæmbɪəm] *n*.【植】原形成层。**-bi·al** [-biəl; -bɪəl] *a*.

pro·carp [ˈprəukɑːp; ˋprokɑrp] *n*.【植】果胞系。

pro·ca·the·dral [ˌprəukəˈθiːdrəl; ˏprokəˋθidrəl] *n*.【宗】作为主教礼拜堂的教区教堂,主教教堂。

pro·ce·dur·al [prəˈsiːdʒərəl; proˋsidʒərəl] *a*. (法律)程序上的,程序性的。~ *details* 程序上的细节。*reject on* ~ **grounds** 根据程序上的理由予以拒绝。**-ist** 拘泥于程序者,刻板的程序主义者。

pro·ce·dure [prəˈsiːdʒə; prəˋsidʒɚ] *n*. 1. 工序,过程,步骤。2. 程序,手续;方法;诉讼程序;(议会的)议事程序。3. 行为,行动,传统的做法;(外交、军队等的)礼仪,礼节。4.〔罕〕进行。*the code of civil* [*criminal*] ~ 民事[刑事]诉讼法。*legal* ~ 法律诉讼程序。*radio* ~ 无线电通讯工作规则。*setup* ~【自】准备程序。

pro·ceed [prəˈsiːd; prəˋsid] I *vi*. 1. 前进;进行;出发,赴。2. 动手,开始,着手。3. 继续进行;继续做下去;继续讲下去。4. 发出,发生,出自 (*from*)。5. 办理手续,处置;进行诉讼程序,起诉。6.〔英大学〕升学位,取(硕士以上)学位 (*to*)。~ *to London* 去伦敦。~ *to the next business* 着手另一工作。*Please* ~ *with your story*. 请讲下去。*diseases that* ~ *from dirt* 因为不清洁引起的疾病。~ **against** 控诉(某人)。~ **on** [**upon**] 照…进行。~ **to do sth**. 开始做某事。~ **to the degree** 得硕士学位。~ **with one's work** 继续干下去〔尤指停顿一段时间后〕。II [ˈprəusiːd; ˋprosid] *n*. 〔*pl*.〕(从事某种活动或变卖财物等的)收入;货款收入,卖得金额;收益。*gross* ~*s* 营业总收入。*He sold his house and lives on the* ~*s*. 他卖了房子靠房款收入过日子。

pro·ceed·ing [prəˈsiːdiŋ; prəˋsidɪŋ] *n*. 1. 进行;进程;程序。2. 行为,行动;活动;做法,手段;处理。3. 〔*pl*.〕诉讼程序。4. 〔*pl*.〕事项,项目。5. 〔*pl*.〕记录,会议录,会报,会刊,学报;(科学文献)汇编。*a high-handed* ~ 高压手段。*suspicious* ~*s* 鬼鬼祟祟的行径。*the* ~*s of a club* 俱乐部年报。**dispossess** ~**s** 〔美口〕(房屋等的)腾让诉讼。**institute** [**take**] **legal** ~**s against** 对…提起诉讼,控告。**oral** ~**s** 口头辩论。

P

pro·ce·phal·ic [ˌprəusiˈfælik; ˏprosəˋfælɪk] *a*.【动】头前部的,与头前部有关的。

pro·cer·coid [prəuˈsəːkɔid; proˋsɝkɔɪd] *n*.【动】原尾幼虫。

pro·cess[1] [ˈprəuses, Am. ˈprɔses; ˋprosɛs, ˋprɑsɛs] ★后接 of 时,读作 [ˈprəusis; ˋprosɪs] I *n*. 1. 进行,经过;过程,历程;作用。2. 处置,方法,步骤;加工处理,工艺程序,工序;制作法。3.【摄】照相制版法;照相版图片;三原色印刷。4.【法】诉讼程序;法律手续;被告传票,传票。5.【解】(动植物机体的)突起,隆起,突。*the* ~ *of growth* 生长过程。*a mental* [*psychological*] ~ 心理作用。*labour-consuming* ~ 重体力劳动。*film* ~ 影片加工。*offset* ~ 胶印法。*legal* ~ 法律手续。*vermiform* ~【解】阑尾,蚓突。**in** ~ 进行着 (*changes in* ~ 正在发生的变化)。**in** ~ **of time** 随着时间的推移;逐渐地。**in** (**the**) ~ **of** 在…的过程中 (*in* ~ *of construction* 正在建筑中)。**serve a** ~ **on** 对…发出传票。II *a*. 1. 经过特殊加工的;(用化学方法等)处理过的。2. 照相制版的;三色版的。3. (电影镜头等)有幻觉效应的。III [ˈprəuses; ˋprosɛs] *vt*. 1. 加工;处理,办理;初步分类;储藏(腌肉等);(用化学方法)处置(废物等)。2. 用照相版影印。3. 对…提起诉讼;用传票传审。*a* ~*ing tax* 〔美〕(农产品)加工税。*a* ~*ing plant* 炼油厂,石油加工厂。~ **engraving**【印】三色版。~ **ink** 三色版油墨。~ **plate**【印】套色版。~ **printing** 彩色套印。~ **server** 递送传票的司法人员。~ **shot**【摄】伪装镜头〔如地震等的特技镜头〕。~**ing unit**【计算机】运算器。

pro·cess[2] [prəˈses; prəˋsɛs] *vi*. 〔口〕排队走,列队行进〔procession 之略〕。

pro·ces·sion [prəˈseʃən, prəu-; prəˋsɛʃən, pro-] I *n*. 1. (人、车、船等的)行列,队伍。2. (队列的)行进;游行,进行,前进,先行;发出;【宗】圣灵的发出。3. (运动中)轻易取胜;不认真对付而速败的行为。*a funeral* ~ 送葬队伍。*form a* ~ 排成行列。*go in* ~ 排成队去。*parading* ~ 游行队伍。II *vi*. 排队前进。— *vt*. 沿着(街道)列队行进。**-ary** *a*. **-ist** *n*.

pro·ces·sion·al [prəˈseʃənəl; prəˋsɛʃənl] I *a*. 队伍的,列队行进的。II *n*.【宗】列队行进时唱的圣歌,行列仪式书。

pro·ces·sor [ˈprəusesə; ˋprɑsɛsɚ] *n*. 1. 〔美〕农产品加工者;进行初步分类的人。2. (数据等的)分理者;【自】信息处理机。

pro·cès-ver·bal [ˈprɔseveəˈbɑl; prəˋsɛverˋbɑl] *n*. (*pl*. **-verbaux** [vɛəˈbo; verˋbo]) 〔F.〕 1. 官方报告书。2.【法】检察官的调查报告书。3. (会议)记录,议事录。

pro·chro·nism [ˈprəukrənizəm; ˋprokrənɪzm] *n*. (所记日期比事件实际发生日期早的)记时早的错误。

pro·claim [prəˈkleim; proˋklem] *vt*. 1. 宣布,公布,宣告,通告,公告。2. 声明;表示,显示。3. 赞扬,歌颂。4. 宣布禁止(集会等);通告隔离[隔断](某一地区)。~ *him a traitor* 宣布他为叛徒。~ *war* 宣战。~ *a victory* 宣告胜利。~ *one's opinions* 发表意见。*His man-*

ners ～ *him a scholar*. 从他的举止可以看出他是一个学者。～ *a meeting* 宣布集会为违法,禁止集会。～ *a district* 宣布对(某一地区)加以法律管制。**-er** *n*.

proc·la·ma·tion [ˌprɔkləˈmeiʃən; ˏprɑkləˋmeʃən] *n*. 1. 宣布,公布。2. 声明;宣言,布告,公告;宣言书,声明书。3. 〔古〕自白。*issue* [*make*] *a* ～ 发表公告[声明]。～ *of neutrality* 宣布中立。～ *of martial law* 宣布戒严。～ *of war* 宣战。

pro·clam·a·to·ry [prəˈklæmətəri; proˋklæməˏtorɪ] *a*. 宣言的,布告的,公告的。

pro·cli·max [prəuˈklaimæks; proˋklaɪmæks] *n*. 【生】原顶极群落。

pro·clit·ic [prəuˈklitik; proˋklɪtɪk] **I** *a*. 连接发音的〔即一个字与其后面的重读字组成一个语音单位而发音的,如 *once and for all* 中的 *for*〕。**II** *n*. 连接读音词。

pro·cliv·i·ty [prəˈkliviti; proˋklɪvətɪ] *n*. 1. 倾向,性癖,脾气 (*to*; *towards*; *for*; *to do*)。2. 〔古〕敏捷。*a* ～ *to vice* 作恶的倾向。*warlike proclivities* 好战癖。

pro·con·sul [prəuˈkɔnsəl; proˋkɑnsḷ] *n*. 〔古罗马〕地方总督;〔主英〕(殖民地的)总督。

pro·con·sul [prəuˈkɔnsəl; proˋkɑnsəl] *n*. 代理领事。

pro·con·su·lar [prəuˈkɔnsjulə; proˋkɑnsḷɚ] *a*. 总督的,总督管辖下的。

pro·con·su·late, pro·con·sul·ship [prəuˈkɔnsjulit, -səlʃip; proˋkɑnslɪt, -slʃɪp] *n*. 总督的职位[任期]。

pro·cras·ti·nate [prəuˈkræstineit; proˋkræstəˏnet] *vi*., *vt*. 耽搁,拖延,迁延,因循。

pro·cras·ti·na·tion [prəuˌkræstiˈneiʃən; proˏkræstəˋneʃən] *n*. 耽搁,拖延,因循。*P- is the thief of time*. 拖延就是浪费时间。

pro·cras·ti·na·tor [prəuˈkræstineitə; proˋkræstənetɚ] *n*. 拖延者。

pro·cre·ant [ˈprəukriənt; ˋprokrɪənt] *a*. 生殖的;产生的;多产的。

pro·cre·ate [ˈprəukrieit; ˋprokrɪˏet] *vt*. 1. 生(儿女),生殖,生育。2. 产生(新种等);制造(谣言等)。— *vi*. 生殖。

pro·cre·a·tion [ˌprəukriˈeiʃən; ˏprokrɪˋeʃən] *n*. 生产,生育,生殖。

pro·cre·a·tive [ˈprəukrieitiv; ˋprokrɪˏetɪv] *a*. 生殖的,有生殖力的;产生的;多产的。

pro·cre·a·tor [ˈprəukrieitə; ˋprokrɪˏetɚ] *n*. 生育者;生殖者。

Pro·crus·te·an [prəuˈkrʌstiən; proˋkrʌstɪən] *a*. 1. 【希神】普罗克拉斯提斯的。2. 〔喻〕用暴力使人就范的;强求一致的。～ *treatment* 粗暴对待。**the** ～ **bed** 强求一致的制度[政策]。

Pro·crus·tes [prəuˈkrʌstiːz; proˋkrʌstiz] 【希神】普罗克拉斯提斯〔传说中的强盗,常使被劫者卧铁床上,比床长者斩去过长部分,比床短者,强行与床拉齐〕。

pro·cryp·tic [prəuˈkriptik; proˋkrɪptɪk] *a*. 【动】有原隐色的,有保护色的。～ **colour** 原隐色。～ **beetle** 有保护色的甲虫。

procs. = proceedings.

proc·to·dae·um, proc·to·de·um [ˌprɔktəˈdiəm; ˏprɑktəˋdɪəm] *n*. (*pl*. **-dae·a** [-ə; -ə], **-dae·ums**) 【动】肛道。**-dae·al** *a*.

proc·tol·o·gy [prɔkˈtɔlədʒi; prɑkˋtɑlədʒɪ] *n*. 【医】直肠病学。**-to·log·ic** [-təˈlɔdʒik; -təˋlɑdʒɪk], **-to·log·i·cal** *a*. **-to·lo·gist** *n*.

proc·tor [ˈprɔktə; ˋprɑktɚ] *n*. 1. 代理人;【法】代诉人;(宗教、海事、离婚、遗嘱等的)王室的讼监。2. 〔英〕(大学的)学监;监考人。**King's** [**Queen's**] **P-** 王室的讼监〔英国对王室有权监察离婚、遗嘱等案件的官员〕。

proc·to·ri·al [prɔkˈtɔːriəl; prɑkˋtorɪəl] *a*. 1. 讼监的;代理人的;代诉的。2. 学监的。

proc·tor·ize [ˈprɔktəraiz; ˋprɑktəˏraɪz] *vt*. (学监)处罚(学生)。— *vi*. 执行学监任务。

proc·to·scope [ˈprɔktəskəup; ˋprɑktəˏskop] *n*. 直肠镜,肛门镜。**-scop·ic** [-ˈskɔpik; -ˋskɑpɪk] *a*. **-tos·copy** [-ˈtɔskəpi; -ˋtɑskəpɪ] *n*. 直肠镜观察术。

pro·cum·bent [prəuˈkʌmbənt; proˋkʌmbənt] *a*. 1. 平伏的。2. 【植】爬地的,匍匐的;俯卧的。

pro·cur·a·ble [prəˈkjuərəbl, prɔˈk-; proˋkjurəbḷ, prɑˋk-] *a*. 可以得到的。

proc·u·ra·cy [ˈprɔkjurəsi; ˋprɑkjərəsɪ] *n*. (*pl*. **-cies**) 1. 代理(权)。2. 代理人职位[任务]。

pro·cur·al [prəˈkjuərəl; prəˋkjurəl] *n*. 获得,取得。

pro·cur·ance [prəˈkjuərəns; prəˋkjurəns] *n*. 1. 获得,取得;获得[实现]的手段。2. 代理。

proc·u·ra·tion [ˌprɔkjuəˈreiʃən; ˏprɑkjəˋreʃən] *n*. 1. 获得,取得。2. 【法】代理(权);(对代诉人的)委任;〔罕〕委任状;(寺院等献给巡临主教的)巡视费。3. (借款的)介绍费,佣金。4. 娼妓介绍业。

proc·u·ra·tor [ˈprɔkjuəreitə; ˋprɑkjəˏretɚ] *n*. 1. 【法】代理人;代诉人。2. 〔古罗马〕地方财政官。*a chief* ～ 检察长。**-ship** *n*. 检察官的职位。**-to·ri·al** [-ˈtɔriəl; -ˋtɑrɪəl] *a*. **-to·ry** *a*.

pro·cure [prəˈkjuə; proˋkjur] *vt*. 1. (努力)取得,获得;实现,达成。2. 〔古,诗〕招致,引起。3. 介绍(娼妓)。— *vi*. 介绍娼妓,拉皮条。*His pride* ～*d his downfall*. 骄傲使他身败名裂。**-ment** *n*. 1. 取得,获得;达成,成就;获;娼妓介绍。2. 〔美〕(政府的)征购,采购。

pro·cur·er [prəˈkjuərə; proˋkjurɚ] *n*. (*fem*. **-cur·ess** [-ˈkjuəris; -ˋkjurɪs]) 1. 取得者,获得者。2. 娼妓介绍人,拉皮条者。

Pro·cy·on [ˈprəusiɔn; ˋprosɪɑn] *n*. 【天】南河三(小犬座 α)。

prod[1] [prɔd; prɑd] **I** *n*. 1. 刺针;锥;竹签;刺棒。2. 刺,戳。3. 刺激(物);促使;推动。*give sb. a sharp* ～ *on the shoulder* 在某人的肩膀上猛戳一下。*under the* ～ *of conscience* 在道德心的促使下。**on the** ～ 〔美俚〕大发脾气。**II** *vt*. (**-dd-**) 1. 刺戳。2. 刺激起,惹起,促使,激励,使苦恼。～ *a lazy boy into quick action* 催促一个懒男孩动作快一点。*This thought* ～*ded me out of bed*. 一想起这一点就促使我从被窝爬了起来。— *vi*. 刺,戳 (*at*, *into*)。*She* ～*ded into her memory at his suggestion*. 他一提醒,她就想起来了。

prod[2] [prɔd; prɑd] *n*. 神童,异人,天才 (= prodigy)。

prod. = produce(d); product.

pro·de·li·sion [ˌprəudiˈliʒən; ˏprodɪˋlɪʒən] *n*. 首元[母]音的省略〔如 I am 省作 I'm 等〕。

prod·i·gal [ˈprɔdigəl; ˋprɑdɪgḷ] **I** *a*. 1. 非常浪费的,挥霍的,奢侈的。2. 丰富的;大量的;富于 (*of*, *with*)。3. 不吝惜的;十分慷慨的。～ *expenses* 冗费。*the* ～ *son* 浪子。*be* ～ *of smiles* 笑声不绝。*May is* ～ *with flowers*. 五月里百花盛开。**II** *n*. 1. 浪费者;浪子。2. 【动】军曹鱼。*play the* ～ 挥霍;逛荡。**-ly** *ad*.

prod·i·gal·i·ty [ˌprɔdiˈgæliti; ˏprɑdɪˋgælətɪ] *n*. 1. 浪费,挥霍;奢侈。2. 慷慨;豪爽。3. 丰富,大量。*a man of wonderful* ～ *of ability* 多才多艺的人。

prod·i·gal·ize [ˈprɔdigəlaiz; ˋprɑdɪgəlaɪz] *vt*. 浪费,挥霍。

pro·di·gious [prəˈdidʒəs; prəˋdɪdʒəs] *a*. 1. 巨大的,庞大的。2. 可惊的,奇妙的;非常的,异常的。*a* ～ *opportunity* 绝好的机会。**-ly** *ad*.

prod·i·gy [ˈprɔdidʒi; ˋprɑdədʒɪ] **I** *n*. 1. 奇事,奇迹,怪事;奇物,怪物;奇观,壮观。2. 非凡的人,奇才,天才;神童,天才儿童;绝代美人。3. 〔古〕预兆。**II** *a*. 天才的,非凡的。*an infant* [*child*] ～ 神童。*a* ～ *violinist* 天才提琴家。*a* ～ *of learning* 非凡的学者。*a* ～ *of energy* 精力异常充沛的人。

prod·ro·mal, pro·drom·ic [ˈprɔdrəməl, prəˈdrɔmik;

ˋprɑdrəməl, prəˋdrɑmɪk] *a*. 前驱病状的。

pro·drome [ˈprəudrəum; ˋprodrom] *n*. 1.【医】前驱症状。2. 序论;序卷 (*to*)。

pro·duce [prəˈdjuːs; prəˋdjus] **I** *vt*. 1. 生,产生;生产;结(果实)。2. 制造;制(图);创作;作(诗);出版(书)。3. 产生,引起。4. 拿出,提出(证据等);展现;出示。5. 演出,上演(戏剧等);(电影)制片;放映;【数】连结,延长(线),扩展(面)。*The soil ~s grain*. 这块地出产粮食。*a producing lot* 〔美俚〕电影制片厂。~ *one's railroad ticket* 拿出[出示]火车票。~ *a play* 公演戏剧。~ *a war* 引起战争。— *vi*. 生产;创作。*With all his scholarship, he seems unable to ~*. 他学识渊博,但好像没有创作力。**II** [ˈprɔdjuːs; ˋprɑdjus] *n*. 1. 生产,出产;产额,产量。2. 物产;产品,农产品;制品,作品。3. 成果,结果。*the agricultural ~* 农产品。*the ~ of the fields* 农作物。

pro·duced [prəˈdjuːst; prəˋdjust] *a*. 引长的,畸形伸长的。

pro·duc·er [prəˈdjuːsə; prəˋdjusɚ] *n*. 1. 生产者;制造者 (*opp*. consumer)。2.【英影】制片人;〔美〕(为演出出资的)演出者;舞台监督;(广播等节目的)安排人;〔美〕戏院老板。3. 发生器;煤气发生炉。4.【讯】振荡器。5. (油)生产井。

pro·duc·i·ble [prəˈdjuːsəbl; prəˋdjusəbl̩] *a*. 1. 可生产[制造]的。2. 可上演的。3. 可提出的。4. 可延长的。**pro·duc·i·bil·i·ty** [prəˌdjuːsəˈbiliti; prəˏdjusəˋbɪlətɪ] *n*.

prod·uct [ˈprɔdəkt; ˋprɑdəkt] *n*. 1. 产物,产品;制品;产量;出产。2. 结果,成果。3. 创作,作品。4.【化】生成物;【数】积,乘积。*natural ~s* 天然产物。*agricultural ~s* 农产品。*residual ~* 副产物。*40 is the ~ of 5 and 8*. 40 是 5 和 8 的积。~ **liability** (制造商应该负的)产品责任。

pro·duc·tion [prəˈdʌkʃən; prəˋdʌkʃən] *n*. 1. 生产,产生;【物】(粒子的)生成;制造;(电影的)摄制;(戏剧的)演出;著作。2. 产品,制品;作品;总产量;成果。3. 提出,提供,拿出。4.【数】延长(线)。5. 大事张罗,小题大做。6. 电影制片。*a means of ~* 生产资料。*full ~* 成批生产。*pre-~* 试生产。*line ~* 流水作业法,连续作业法。*standard ~* 标准产额。*go* [*be put*] *into ~* 开始生产。***make a ~ of*** [***out of***] 对…小题大做。~ **cost** 生产成本;制片费用。~ **line** 流水作业线。~ **quota** 生产指标。

pro·duc·tique [prəˈdʌktik; prəˋdʌktɪk] *n*. (将机器人和电脑等应用于制造业的)生产现代化。

pro·duc·tive [prəˈdʌktiv; prəˋdʌktɪv] *a*. 1. 生产的,生产性的;有生产力的;多产的。2. 产生[出产]…的 (*of*)。~ *labour* 生产劳动。~ *forces* 生产力。*an age ~ of great men* 伟人辈出的时代。~ *of great annoyance* 会产生巨大麻烦的。~ *soil* 沃土,肥地。*a ~ writer* 多产作家。**-ly** *ad*. **-ness** *n*.

pro·duc·tiv·i·ty [ˌprɔdʌkˈtiviti; ˏprodʌkˋtɪvətɪ] *n*. 1. 多产,丰饶。2. 生产率;生产能力。*labour ~* 劳动生产率。*raise ~* 提高生产率。

pro·em [ˈprəuem; ˋproɛm] *n*. 开场白;序言;开端。

pro·en·zyme [prəuˈenzaim; proˋɛnzaɪm] *n*. 酶原 (= zymogen)。

prof [prɔf; prɑf] *n*. 〔美俚〕= professor.

Prof. = Professor.

pro·fa·na·tion [ˌprɔfəˈneiʃən; ˏprɑfəˋneʃən] *n*. 1. 亵渎神圣;玷污;滥用,误用;使用亵渎的言语。2. [*pl*.] 亵渎的言语。

pro·fane [prəˈfein; prəˋfen] **I** *a*. 1. 亵渎神圣的,不敬的;好咒骂的。2. (与宗教无关或鄙视宗教)世俗的;粗俗的;污秽的。3. 异教的,邪教的。4. 未受秘传的;外行的。~ *language* 亵渎的言语。*the ~ (crowd)* 俗众。~ *persons* 俗人。**II** *vt*. 亵渎,玷污(神圣)滥用,误用。**-ly** *ad*.

pro·fan·i·ty [prəˈfæniti; prəˋfænətɪ] *n*. = profanation.

pro·fer·ment [prəuˈfəːmənt; proˋfɝmənt] *n*.【化】前酵素,生酶素。

pro·fess [prəˈfes; prəˋfɛs] *vt*. 1. 表示,明言,声言,宣布;承认;〔~ oneself〕自称。2. 假装,佯装。3. 表明信仰。4. 以…为业;〔英〕教授(化学等)。~ *oneself to be a poet* 自称是诗人。~ *ignorance* 假装[自称]不知道。~ *language* 教授语文。~ *medicine* 行医。— *vi*. 声言,宣言;表明信仰;承认;〔英口〕(在大学)教书。

pro·fessed [prəˈfest; prəˋfɛst] *a*. 1. (无神论者)公然表示自己观点的;公开声称的。2. 专业的,专门的。3. 假装的,表面上的,自称的。4. 已立誓信教的。**-ly** *ad*.

pro·fes·sion [prəˈfeʃən; prəˋfɛʃən] *n*. 1. 职业,(特指)知识性专门职业 (*opp*. trade, business)。2. 声明,宣言,(信仰等的)自白,表白;入教宣誓;自认,自称。3. 〔the ~〕同业,同行;〔俚〕戏剧界同人。4. 信仰表白,立誓信教。*medical ~* 医疗职业。*He is a doctor by ~*. 他的职业是医生。*Spare me these ~s*. 请别逼我讲这件事吧。***by ~*** 职业是。***in practice if not in ~*** 虽不明讲而实际如此。***the (learned) ~s = the three ~s*** 神学、医学及法学三种职业。***the oldest ~*** 〔谑〕卖淫。**-less** *a*. 没有职业的。

pro·fes·sion·al [prəˈfeʃənəl; prəˋfɛʃənl̩] **I** *a*. 1. 职业的,专业的,专职的 (*opp*. amateurish); 本职的,专门的。2. 从事(需要知识修养的)专门职业的;业务上的;同行中的。*a ~ politician* 职业政治家。*a ~ singer* 职业歌唱家。~ *education* 职业教育。~ *skill* 专业技术。*a ~ man* 专家。**II** *n*. (有知识修养的)专门职业者;职业画家[演员等],职业选手〔简称 pro〕;内行,专家 (*opp*. amateur)。~ **carer** (专门给人照顾家中老弱病残者的)专职护理。~ **competence** 专长,专业知识;专才。~ **etiquette** 同行间遵守的规矩。~ **jealousy** 同行间的妒忌。**-ly** *ad*.

pro·fes·sion·al·ism [prəˈfeʃənəlizəm; prəˋfɛʃənl̩ɪzm] *n*. 内行派头,专家气派;职业特性;职业选手气派[身分、特性];职业化。

pro·fes·sion·al·ize [prəˈfeʃənəlaiz; prəˋfɛʃənl̩ˏaɪz] *vt*. (使)职业化,(使)专业化;专门处理;用职业选手参加(比赛)。

pro·fes·sor [prəˈfesə; prəˋfɛsɚ] *n*. 1. (大学)教授〔略 Prof.〕;〔美口〕(男性)先生,老师。2. 〔俚、谑〕(魔术、拳击、跳舞等的)专家。3. 声明者;自称者;表白信仰者。4. 〔美俚〕(在酒吧间等处)下等场所弹奏钢琴者。*a ~ emeritus* (退职或退休后的)名誉教授。*a ~ extraordinary* 临时教授。*an assistant ~* 助理教授。*an associate ~* 副教授。*a ~'s chair* 讲座;教授的职位。*He is a professor of history at my university*. 他是我们大学的历史教授。

pro·fes·sor·ate [prəˈfesərit; prəˋfɛsərɪt] *n*. 1. 教授的职务[任期]。2. (大学的)全体教授;教授会;教师会 (= professoriate [prɔfiˈsɔːriit; profɪˋsorɪɪt])。

pro·fes·so·ri·al [ˌprɔfeˈsɔːriəl; ˏprofɛˋsorɪəl] *a*. 教授的;教授似的;学者气的,教条式的。*a ~ lecturer* 教授级讲师。**-ly** *ad*.

pro·fes·so·ri·ate [ˌprɔfeˈsɔːriit; ˏprofɛˋsorɪɪt] *n*. = professorate.

pro·fes·sor·ship [prəˈfesəʃip; prəˋfɛsɚˏʃɪp] *n*. 教授的职务[地位]。

prof·fer [ˈprɔfə; ˋprɑfɚ] **I** *vt*. 1. 提供,贡献;提出。2. 赠送,奉送。3. 表示愿意,自告奋勇(做某事)。~ *a gift* 献礼物,送礼。*I ~ to help him*. 我愿意帮助他。**II** *n*. 建议,提议;贡献;提供物。

pro·fi·cien·cy [prəˈfiʃənsi; prəˋfɪʃənsɪ] *n*. 精通,熟练 (*in*)。~ *in music* 擅长音乐。*attain ~ in English* 精通英语。

pro·fi·cient [prəˈfiʃənt; prəˋfɪʃənt] **I** *a*. 熟练的,精通…

的(*at*; *in*)。*be* ~ *at English* 精通英语。**II** ***n***. 熟练者,能手,老手,专家(*in*)。**-ly** ***ad***.

pro·file [ˈprəufail, -fiːl; ˋprofaɪl, -fil] **I** ***n***. **1**. 剖面,半面,(雕像等的)侧面;侧面像。**2**. 外形,轮廓;外观,形象;型;【空】翼型,翼(剖)面。**3**. (人物)素描;人物简介;传略;简介,简况。**4**. 纵断面图,侧面图;【地】断面;(人)形象。*She has a fine* ~. = *She is fine in* ~. 她侧面看很美。*low* ~低姿态(形象)。*draw in* ~ 画侧面[轮廓]。*soil* ~ 土壤剖面图。**II** ***vt***. **1**. 画…的轮廓。**2**. 作…的纵断面图,…的侧面图。**3**.【机】铣出…的轮廓。**4**. 为(某人)写传略。

P

pro·fil·ist [ˈprəufailist, -fiːl-; ˋprofaɪlɪst, -fil-] ***n***. 侧面图绘制者;侧面像画家。

pro·fil·o·me·ter [ˌprəufiˈlɔmitə; ˏprofəˋlamɪtɚ] ***n***.【机】轮廓曲线仪;表面光度仪;纵断面测绘器(= profilograph)。

prof·it [ˈprɔfit; ˋprɑfɪt] **I** ***n***. **1**. 〔常 *pl*.〕赢余,利润,赚头(*opp*. loss); 利润率。**2**. 〔常 *pl*.〕红利。**3**. 得益,益处。*gross* ~(*s*) 总利润,毛利。*clear* [*net*] ~ 纯利润,净利。***at a*** ~ 获利,赚钱。***in*** ~〔英方,澳〕(乳牛)在产乳期。***make a*** ~ ***on*** 在…上头赚钱。***make one's*** ~ ***of*** 利用,使对自己有利。***reap*** **~*s at the expense of others*** 损人利己。***small*** **~*s and quick returns*** 薄利多销。***to one's*** ~ = ***with*** ~ 有益。**II** ***vt***. 有利于,有益于。*What will it* ~ *me*? 对我有什么好处呢? — ***vi***. 得益;获利,赚钱;利用(*by*; *from*; *of*); 有用。*You may* ~ *by the experience of others*. 你可以吸取别人的经验教训。*I* ~*ed by his confusion to make my escape*. 我趁他忙乱的时候逃走了。~ **and loss**【统】损益。~ **and loss account** 损益账。~**-and-loss** ***a***. 损益的(~-and-loss statement 损益计算书)。~ **center** 能创造利润的部门。~**-hungry** ***a***. 贪求利润的。~ **margin** 利润率。~ **sharing** 分红制。~ **taking** (股票买空卖空)获利了结;(有利可图即将股票脱手的)抛售。

prof·i·ta·ble [ˈprɔfitəbl; ˋprɑfɪtəbl] ***a***. **1**. 有益的;有用的。**2**. 有利可图的,可赚钱的,合算的。**-it·a·bil·ty** [ˌprɔfitəˈbiliti; ˌprɑfətəˋbɪlətɪ] ***n***. **-ness** ***n***. **-bly** ***ad***.

prof·i·teer [ˌprɔfiˈtiə; ˏprɑfəˋtɪr] **I** ***n***. (尤指战时的)奸商,发横财的人,暴发户;(生活必需品的)投机商人。**II** ***vi***. 取得不正当的利益,牟取暴利。~*ing merchants* 奸商。**-ing** ***n***. 不当利得,投机活动。

prof·it·less [ˈprɔfitlis; ˋprɑfɪtlɪs] ***a***. **1**. 无利的;无利可图的。**2**. 无益的,无用的。**-ness** ***n***. **-ly** ***ad***.

prof·li·ga·cy [ˈprɔfligəsi; ˋprɑfləgəsɪ] ***n***. **1**. 放荡;堕落;荒淫。**2**. 极度的浪费;恣意的挥霍。

prof·li·gate [ˈprɔfligit; ˋprɑfləgɪt] **I** ***a***. **1**. 放荡的;堕落的;荒淫的。**2**. 极度浪费的。**II** ***n***. **1**. 放荡的人,浪子。**2**. 恣意挥霍的人。

prof·lu·ent [ˈprɔfluənt; ˋprɑfluənt] ***a***. 辞藻丰富文体流畅的;流利的,流畅的。

pro for·ma [prəuˈfɔːmə; proˋfɔrmə] 〔L.〕形式上。

pro·found [prəˈfaund; prəˋfaʊnd] **I** ***a***. **1**. (渊等)深。**2**. (哲理、诗等)深奥的;(意义等)深远的,意味深长的。**3**. 学识渊博的,造诣深的;深谋远虑的。**4**. (兴趣等)深厚的;深刻的;深切的;深深的;极度的,(注意等)充分的;来自心底的。**5**. 谦恭的,谦卑的。*a* ~ *sleep* 熟睡。*a* ~ *scholar* 渊博的学者。*a* ~ *statesman* 深谋远虑的政治家。~ *sympathy* 深厚的同情。*a* ~ *bow* 深深一躬。***make a*** ~ ***curtesy*** [***reverence***] 恭恭敬敬地行礼。***take a*** ~ ***interest*** 感到很大的兴趣;十分关切。**II** ***n***. 〔诗〕〔the ~〕深海,大洋;深渊;(灵魂)深处。**-ly** ***ad***. 深深地;深奥地;恳切地;郑重地(*a* ~*ly scientific attitude* 高度科学的态度)。

Prof. Reg. = Regius Professor.

pro·fun·di·ty [prəˈfʌnditi; prəˋfʌndətɪ] ***n***. **1**. 深,深度;深处;〔诗〕深渊。**2**. 深奥;深刻;深厚。**3**. 〔常 *pl*.〕深奥的事物;深刻的思想;意义深刻的话。

pro·fuse [prəˈfjuːs; prəˋfjus] ***a***. (*-fus·er*; *-fus·est*) **1**. 大方的,豪爽的,十分慷慨的。**2**. 奢侈的,挥霍的,浪费的(*in*; *of*)。**3**. 很多的;充沛的;过多的;极其丰富的。*He was* ~ *in thanks*. 他谢了又谢。~ *hospitality* 丰盛的款待。**-ly** ***ad***. **-ness** ***n***.

pro·fu·sion [prəˈfjuːʒən; prəˋfjuʒən] ***n***. **1**. 大量,充沛,丰富。**2**. 豪爽,慷慨,大方。**3**. 浪费,挥霍,奢侈。***a*** ~ ***of*** 很多的,大量的。***in*** ~ 丰富地,大量地。

prog[1] [prɔg; prɑg] **I** ***n***. 〔俚〕搜寻、偷窃或乞讨来的食物。**II** ***vi***. (**-gg-**) **1**. 搜寻、偷窃或乞讨食物。**2**. 伺机偷窃。

prog[2] [prɔg; prɑg] **I** ***n***. 〔英〕(大学的)学监。**II** ***vi***. (**-gg-**) 行使学监的职权,处罚(学生)。

prog[3] [prɔg; prɑg] ***n***. 〔英口〕节目(= program)。

pro·gen·i·tive [prəuˈdʒenitiv; proˋdʒɛnətɪv] ***a***. 繁殖的;有生殖力的。

pro·gen·i·tor [prəˈdʒenitə; proˋdʒɛnətɚ] ***n***. **1**. (人及动植物的)祖先;先驱;前辈。**2**. (抄本的)原书;【物】原(始)粒子。

pro·gen·i·tress [prəuˈdʒenitris; proˋdʒɛnɪtrɪs], **pro·gen·i·trix** [prəuˈdʒenitriks; proˋdʒɛnɪtrɪks] ***n***. (动植物的)雌性祖先;(人的)女性始祖[先驱,先辈]。

prog·e·ny [ˈprɔdʒini; ˋprɑdʒənɪ] ***n***. **1**. 子孙,后代。**2**. 成果,结果。**3**.【物】次级粒子。

pro·ges·ta·tion·al [ˌprəudʒesˈteiʃənl; ˏprodʒɛsˋteʃənl̩] ***a***.【化】孕酮的,孕激素的。

pro·ges·ter·one [prəuˈdʒestərəun; proˋdʒɛstəˏron] ***n***.【化】孕(甾)酮,孕激素;黄体酮[激素]。

pro·ges·tin [prəuˈdʒestin; proˋdʒɛstɪn] ***n***. 孕激素;黄体制剂;孕(甾)酮。

pro·ges·to·gen [prəuˈdʒestədʒən; proˋdʒɛstədʒən] ***n***.【生化】孕激素类。

prog·gins [ˈprɔginz; ˋprɑgɪnz] ***n***. 〔俚〕= prog[2].

pro·glot·tid [prəuˈglɔtid; proˋglɑtɪd] ***n***.【动】节片。

pro·glot·tis [prəuˈglɔtis; proˋglɑtɪs] ***n***. (*pl*. ***-tides*** [-tidiːz; -tɪdiz]) (绦虫的)节片。

prog·nath·ic, prog·na·thous [prɔgˈnæθik, prɔgˈneiθəs; prɑgˋnæθɪk, prɑgˋnəθəs] ***a***. **1**. 突颚的,下巴突出的。**2**.【动】(昆虫)前口式的。**-thism** ***n***.【解】突颚。

prog·no·sis [prɔgˈnəusis; prɑgˋnosɪs] ***n***. (*pl*. ***-ses*** [-siːz, -siz]) **1**. 预测。**2**.【医】预后,判病结局(*opp*. diagnosis)。

prog·nos·tic [prɔgˈnɔstik; prɑgˋnɑstɪk] **I** ***a***. **1**. 预兆的,预示…的(*of*)。**2**.【医】预后的,(症状)预示后果的。*be* ~ *of failure* 预示失败。**II** ***n***. **1**. 征兆,前兆。**2**. 预测,预知。**3**.【医】预后症状。

prog·nos·ti·cate [prɔgˈnɔstikeit; prɑgˋnɑstɪˏket] ***vt***., ***vi***. **1**. 由前兆[症状]预知,预言,预测。**2**. 预示;预兆,有…的兆头。**-ca·tion** ***n***. **1**. 预言,预测。**2**. 前兆;症状。**-ca·tor** ***n***. 预言者,预测者。

prog·nos·ti·ca·tive [ˌprɔgˈnɔstikeitiv; prɑgˋnɑstəˏketɪv] ***a***. 预知的;能预知…的(*of*)。~ *of a dream* 预知未来的梦。*The solar eclipse was thought* ~ *of the fall of the country*. 日蚀过去被认为是国家灭亡的预兆。

pro·gram·mat·ic [ˌprəugrəˈmætik; ˏprogrəˋmætɪk] ***a***. **1**. 有纲领的,纲领性的。**2**. 标题音乐的。**3**. 计划性的。

pro·gramme, 〔美〕**pro·gram** [ˈprəugræm; ˋprogræm] **I** ***n***. **1**. 程序表;节目单,说明书;(演出)节目;要目,大纲。**2**. 〔英〕(政党的)纲领,方案。**3**. 规划,计划,打算。**4**. 工作进度表,课程表;〔美〕时间表。**5**.【自】程序〔用 program〕。**6**. 序,绪言。**7**. 〔古〕公告,布告。*a theatre* [*broadcasting*, *television*] ~ 演出[广播,电视]节目。*a live* ~【电视】实况广播[电视],室内广播节目。*an outdoor* ~ 室外广播节目。*a common* ~ 共同纲领。*What is the* ~ *for today*? 今天有些什么活动? *a television* [*broadcasting*] ~ 电视[广播]节目。*What's on the* ~? 有些什么节目? ***a full*** ~ 忙得团团转的工作

[约会(等)]。**draw up a** ~ **of work** 拟定课程表[工作进度表]。**put in the** ~ 排入节目里。**II** *vt*.〔罕〕制定(进度表),排(节目);拟(计划);【自】为…编制程序,使按程序工作。*linear programming* 线性规划。*program(m)ed instruction* 循序渐进的教学(法)。*program(m)ed learning* 利用有习题解答的教科书进行的自学;(按书本规定或计算机安排)循序渐进的自学。~ **girl** 卖戏剧节目单的女子。~ **music** 标题音乐。~ **picture**【影】加映副片;普通作品。~ **trading**〔美〕程控交易〔以电脑程序监控股票和期货交易〕。

pro·gram·mer [ˈprəugræmə; ˋprogræmɚ] *n*.〔美〕**1.** 节目编排者;订计划者。**2.**【自】程序设计员;程序设计器。

pro·gress [ˈprəugres; ˋprɑgrɛs] **I** *n*. **1.** 前进,进行。**2.** 上进,进步;进度;进展,增长,发展;经过;【生】发育,进化。**3.**〔古〕(特指王侯的)视察,巡行,游历。*the* ~ *of mankind* 人类的进步。~ *in* [*of*] *knowledge* 知识的进步。*the* ~ *of events* 事件的经过。**in** ~ 进行中,还没有完的。**make** ~ **1.** 进行,前进。**2.** 进步,进展(*make no* ~ *in one's studies* 研究没有进展)。**II** [prəˈgres; prəˋgrɛs] *vi*. 前进,进行;进步;发达(*in*)。~ *in one's health* 健康在好转。*We are* ~*ing fairly with the work*. 我们正在顺利地进行着工作。

pro·gres·sion [prəˈgreʃən; prəˋgrɛʃən] *n*. **1.** 前进,进行。**2.**〔罕〕进步,改进,发展;进展状态。**3.**【数】级数;【乐】(乐音或和弦的)相继进行;(各声部的)和谐进行。*arithmetical* ~【数】等差级数,算术级数。*geometrical* ~【数】等比级数,几何级数。*in geometrical* ~ 按几何级数,加速度地。**in** ~ 连续,相继。**mode of** ~ 步法,游法。**-al** *a*.

pro·gres·sion·ist, pro·gress·ist [prəˈgreʃənist, -ˋgresist; prəˋgrɛʃənɪst, -ˋgrɛsɪst] *n*. 提倡进步者;进化论者;进步党派成员;革新主义者;改良主义者。

pro·gres·sive [prəˈgresiv; prəˋgrɛsɪv] **I** *a*. **1.** 前进的;渐进的,发展的;递增的,累进的。**2.** 进步的,上进的,进取的,改进的;进步主义的,进步党的。**3.**【医】进行性的。**4.**【语法】进行(时)的。~ *elements* 进步人士。~ *methods* 新方法。**II** *n*. **1** 进步分子,进步人士,进步论者;革新主义者;改良主义者;[P-]进步党党员。~ **assimilation**【语音】顺行同化。~ **form** (时态之)进行式。~**jazz** 渐进式爵士乐〔流行于本世纪五十年代〕。~ **lens** 渐变透镜〔双焦点或多焦点,可通过焦点渐变在各个距离上清晰成像〕。~ **rate** 累进税率。~ **taxation** 累进税制。~ **wave**【无】行波。**-ly** *ad*. **-ness** *n*.

pro·gres·siv·ism [prəˈgresivizəm; prəˋgrɛsɪvɪzm] *n*. **1.** 进步人士的政见。**2.** 顺序渐进的教育理论。**3.**〔P-〕进步党的主义。

pro·hi [ˈprəui; ˋproɪ] =〔美〕prohibition.

pro·hib·it [prəˈhibit; proˋhɪbɪt] *vt*. 不准许,禁止;阻止,防止。~*ed articles* [*goods*] 违禁品。~*ed degrees* (因同血缘而禁止通婚的)禁婚亲等。*It was* ~*ed on pain of death*. 违者处死。*P- him from coming* [*his coming*]. 别让他来。*Smoking strictly* ~*ed*. 严禁吸烟。**-er,**〔美〕**-or** *n*. 禁止者;阻止者。

pro·hi·bi·tion [ˌprəuiˈbiʃən, ˌprəuhi-; ˏproəˋbɪʃən, ˏprohɪ-] *n*. **1.** 禁止;禁令。**2.**【法】(上级法院禁止下级法院对无权审理的案件起诉的)诉讼中止令。**3.**〔美〕禁酒;[P-]【美史】禁酒时期。~ **law**〔美〕禁酒法。**P- Party**〔美〕禁酒党。~ **state**〔美〕禁酒州。**-ism** *n*. 禁酒主义;〔美〕保护贸易主义。**-ist** *n*. 禁酒主义者;[P-]〔美〕禁酒党党员;保护贸易论者。

pro·hib·i·tive [prəˈhibitiv, prəu-; prəˋhɪbɪtɪv, pro-] *a*. **1.** 禁止的;禁止性的;抑制性的。**2.** (价格)非常高的。*a* ~ *tax* 寓禁税。~ *inhibition* 超限抑制。*a* ~ *price* 高得使人不敢买的价格。

pro·hib·i·to·ry [prəˈhibitəri, prəu-; prəˋhɪbəˏtorɪ, pro-] *a*. =prohibitive.

pro·ject [prəˈdʒekt; ˋprɑdʒɛkt] **I** *vt*. **1.** 投掷,抛出;发射(炮弹等);喷射。**2.** 使突出,使凸出。**3.** 设计,规划,计划,打算,筹划。**4.** 投影;于…上映。**5.**【数】作…的投影图;把…画成投影状。**6.** 表明…的特点;生动地表演。**7.**【心】使(思想、感情)形象化[具体化]。**8.**【化】投入(*into*; *on*)。~ *motion pictures on the screen* 放电影。~ *the rebuilding of a street* 计划改造街道。~ *oneself* 突出自己;使自己显得像…(*as*);没想自己处于(*into*)。*a* ~*ed route* 预定路线。*a* ~*ed area* 投射面积。— *vi*. 突出,伸出。*The upper storey* ~*s over the street*. 二楼伸出街上。**II** [ˈprɔdʒekt; ˋprɑdʒɛkt] *n*. **1.** 规划,方案,计划,设计。**2.** 科研[建设]项目;课外自修项目。**3.** 工程;事业,企业。*irrigation* ~*s* 灌溉工程。*build irrigation* ~*s* 兴修水利工程。*water conservancy* ~*s* 水利工程。*abovenorm construction* ~*s* 限额以上的建设项目。*the* ~ *method* (要求学生独立思考的)构想教授法。*a* ~ *engineer* 设计工程师。*a harebrained* ~ 轻率的想法。

pro·jec·tile [ˈprɔdʒektail, prəˈdʒek-; prəˋdʒɛktl̩, prəˋdʒɛk-] **I** *n*. **1.** 抛射体。**2.** 射弹。**3.** 导弹,飞弹,火箭。*an atomic* ~ 原子炮弹;轰击原子粒子。*a nuclear* ~ 核弹头飞弹。*a cosmic* ~ 宇宙射线粒子。*a rocket* ~ 喷气火箭;火箭弹。**II** [prəˈdʒektail; prəˋdʒɛktaɪl] *a*. **1.** 抛射的,发射的;射弹的。**2.** 可抛射的;推进的。**3.**【动】(触角等)能伸出的。~ *force* 推进力。

pro·ject·ing [prəˈdʒektiŋ; prəˋdʒɛktɪŋ] *a*. 突出的,凸出的。*a* ~ *eye* 凸眼。*a* ~ *tooth* 暴牙。

pro·jec·tion [prəˈdʒekʃən; prəˋdʒɛkʃən] *n*. **1.** 射出,投掷,发射,喷射。**2.** 投射;投影,投影法;(地图)投影图制法;【影】放映。**3.** 凸出;凸出部;凸出物。**4.** 设计,规划,计划。**5.** (根据已知资料或观察所作的)预测,推测,估计。**6.**【心】投射;(思想等的)形象化,具体化。**7.**【心】想像。**8.**【冶】金属的嬗变。*central* [*perspective*] ~ 透视投影。*orthogonal* [*oblique*] ~ 正[斜]投影。*a* ~ *booth* [*room*]〔美〕放映室。*a* ~ *machine* 放映机。*a* ~ *lantern* 幻灯,映画器。*the* ~ *of the lower lip* 下唇凸出。**-ist** *n*. **1.** 制投影图的人;地图绘制者。**2.** 电影[幻灯]放映员;电视播放员。

pro·jec·tive [prəˈdʒektiv; prəˋdʒɛktɪv] *a*. **1.** 投影的,射影的。**2.** 凸出的,突出的。**3.**【心】投射的。*the* ~ *power of the mind* 想像力。~ **geometry** 投影几何。

pro·jec·tor [prəˈdʒektə; prəˋdʒɛktɚ] *n*. **1.** 设计者,规划人,计划者。**2.** 投机公司的发起人,骗子。**3.** 投射器,发射装置。**4.** 探照灯;幻灯;放映机。**5.** 放映技师。**6.** (制图)投射线。*a flame* ~【军】喷火器。*a microfilm* ~ 缩微胶片放大器。*a supersound* ~ 大功率扬声器。

pro·jet [proˈʒei; proˋʒɛ] *n*.〔F.〕**1.** 设计,计划。**2.** (条约或法律的)草案。

prol. = prologue.

pro·lac·tin [prəuˈlæktin; prəˋlæktɪn] *n*.【生化】催乳激素。

pro·la·mine [prəuˈlæmin, ˈprəuləmiːn, -min; proˋlæmɪn, ˋproləmɪn, -mɪn] *n*.【化】醇溶朊。**-la·min** [-min; -mɪn].

pro·lan [ˈprəulæn; ˋprolæn] *n*.【药】绒膜促性腺激素。

pro·lapse [ˈprəulæps; prəˋlæps] **I** *n*.【医】=prolapsus. **II** *vi*.【医】脱出,脱垂。

pro·lap·sus [prəuˈlæpsəs; prəˋlæpsəs] *n*.〔L.〕【医】脱肛,(子宫的)脱出,脱垂,下垂。

pro·late [ˈprəuleit; ˋprolet] *a*. **1.**【数】扁长的;延长的;长球形的(*opp*. oblate)。**2.** 扩大的,扩展的。**3.**【语法】=prolative.

pro·la·tive [prəuˈleitiv; proˋletɪv] *a*.【语法】补足谓[述]语的,表述性的。*the* ~ *infinitive* 表述性不定式〔如 He must go, willing to go 的 go, to go〕。

prole [prəul; prol] *a*., *n*.〔主英口〕无产阶级的,无产阶级(=proletarian)。

pro·leg [ˈprəuleg; ˋproˏlɛg] ***n.***【动】腹足;原足。

pro·le·gom·e·non [ˌprəuləˈgɔminən; ˏproliˈgamɪnən] ***n.*** (*pl.* ***-na*** [-nə; -nə])〔常 *pl.*〕序,序言,绪论 (*to*)。**-gom·e·nous** ***a.*** 序的,绪言的;有长序的,绪言冗长的。

pro·lep·sis [prəuˈlepsis, -ˈliːp-; prəˋlɛpsɪs, ˋlip-] ***n.*** (*pl.* ***-lep·ses*** [-ˈlepsiːz, ˋlɛpsiz]) **1.**【修】预辩法。**2.**【语法】预期的叙述;预期描写法。**3.**【哲】感觉概念。**4.** 预期;早记日期。

pro·lep·tic [prəuˈleptik, -ˈliːp-; prəˋlɛptɪk, ˋlip-] ***a.*** **1.** 预想的。**2.** 预辩的,预驳的。**3.**【语法】预期叙述法的;(形容词)预期描写法的。**4.**【医】提早发作的;早发的。

pro·les [ˈprəuliːz; ˋproliz] ***n.***〔集合词〕〔*pl.*〕〔L.〕子孙,后代。

pro·le·taire [ˌprəuleˈtɛə; ˏproleˋtɛr] ***n.*** = proletarian.

pro·le·tar·i·an [ˌprəuleˈtɛəriən; ˏproləˋtɛrɪən] ***n.***, ***a.*** 无产阶级(的) (*opp.* bourgeoisie); 无产者(的)。～ *dictatorship* 无产阶级专政。**-ism** ***n.*** 无产阶级性;无产者的地位。

pro·le·tar·i·an·ize [ˌprəuliˈtɛəriənaiz; ˏproləˋtɛrɪənˏaɪz] ***vt.*** (***-iz·ed***; ***-iz·ing***) 使无产阶级化;作为无产阶级对待。**-za·tion** [-ˈzeiʃən, ˋzeʃən] ***n.*** 无产阶级化。

pro·le·tar·i·at(e) [ˌprəuleˈtɛəriət; ˏproləˏtɛrɪət] ***n.*** 无产阶级(*opp.* bourgeoisie);【罗马史】最下层社会。*the dictatorship of the* ～ 无产阶级专政。*the black-coated* ～ 劳动知识分子。

pro·le·ta·ry [ˈprəulitəri; ˋproləˏtɛrɪ] ***n.***, ***a.***〔罕〕【史】(古罗马)最下层阶级的公民(的)。

pro·li·cide [ˈprəulisaid; ˋproləˏsaɪd] ***n.*** 杀害胎儿[婴儿]。**-cid·al** [-ˈsaidl; ˋsaɪdl] ***a.***

pro·lif·er·ate [prəuˈlifəreit; proˋlɪfəˏret] ***vi.*** **1.**【生】分芽繁殖,细胞分裂繁殖;增殖;增生;多育。**2.** 激增;扩散。— ***vt.*** 使激增;使扩散。～ *nuclear weapons* 扩散核武器。**-a·tion** [prəuˌlifəˈreiʃən; proˏlɪfəˋreʃən] ***n.*** **-a·tive** ***a.***

pro·lif·er·ous [prəuˈlifərəs; proˋlɪfərəs] ***a.***【植】分芽繁殖的;【动】(珊瑚等的)分枝繁殖的;【医】增生性的;扩散性的,增生的,多育的。

pro·lif·ic [prəˈlifik; prəˋlɪfɪk] ***a.*** **1.** 多育的,结果实的;有生产力的;富于创造力的;多产…的 (*of*)。**2.** 肥沃的;丰富的;富于…的 (*in*)。*a family* ～ *of children* 多子女的家庭。*a* ～ *writer* 多产作家。*an age* ～ *in great poets* 大诗人辈出的时代。**-i·cal·ly** ***ad.*** **-ness** ***n.***

pro·lin(e) [ˈprəuliːn; ˋprolɪn] ***n.***【化】脯氨酸,氮戊氨酸。

pro·lix [ˈprəuliks, prəuˈliks; ˋprolɪks, proˋlɪks] ***a.*** 冗长的,啰唆的。**-lix·i·ty** ***n.*** 冗长,啰唆。

pro·loc·u·tor [prəuˈlɔkjutə; proˋlakjətɚ] ***n.*** **1.** 代言人,发言人。**2.** (尤指宗教会议的)议长,主席。

pro·log [ˈprəulɔg; ˋprolɔg] ***n.***, ***v.*** = prologue.

pro·log·ize [ˈprəuləgaiz; ˋprolɔgˏaɪz] = prologuize.

pro·logue [ˈprəulɔg; ˋprolɔg] **I** ***n.*** **1.** 序,序诗;(戏剧的)开场白;序幕 (*opp.* epilogue)。**2.** 序幕性事件 (*to*)。**II** ***vt.*** **1.** 作…的序;为…加上序诗;作(戏剧等的)开场白。**2.** 成了…的开端。

pro·logu·ize [ˈprəuləgaiz; ˋprolɔgˏaɪz] ***vi.*** 作序;作序诗;作开场白。

pro·long [prəˈlɔŋ; prəˋlɔŋ] ***vt.*** **1.** 延长;拉长,拖长;引伸。**2.** 将(元[母]音等)拉长发音。**3.** 拖延,延期。～ *one's life* 延长寿命。

pro·lon·gate [prəuˈlɔŋgeit; prəˋlɔŋget] ***vt.*** 延长;拉长;拖延 (= prolong)。

pro·lon·ga·tion [ˌprəulɔŋˈgeiʃən; ˏprolɔŋˋgeʃən] ***n.*** **1.** 延长;延期。**2.** (发音的)拉长,拖长。**3.** 延长部分。

pro·longe [prəuˈlɔndʒ; proˋlandʒ] ***n.***【军】(拉炮用带钩的)缆绳。

pro·lu·sion [prəuˈljuːʒən; proˋluʒən] ***n.*** **1.** 序幕,序乐;绪论,绪言。**2.** 预演;预习;试讲。**-lu·so·ry** [-ˈluːsəri; -ˋlusərɪ] ***a.***

prom [prɔm; pram] ***n.*** **1.**〔英口〕= promenade concert. **2.**〔美〕(大学的)跳舞会。*a* ～ *trotter*〔美〕经常参加舞会的学生。

prom. = promenade; promontory.

prom·e·nade [ˌprɔmiˈnɑːd; ˏpraməˋned] **I** ***n.*** **1.** 散步,(骑马)闲逛,(开车)兜风。**2.** (特指骑马或乘车的)队伍。**3.** 散步场所;散步甲板。**4.**〔美〕(大学的)跳舞会〔略 prom〕。**5.** (正式舞会开始前全体参加者的)列队绕场(礼)。**II** ***vi.*** **1.** 散步;运动。**2.** (骑马,开车)兜风。**3.** (舞会中)列队(绕场)行进。～ *about* 炫耀地游逛。— ***vt.*** **1.** 在…散步。**2.** 炫耀地带领着人散步[兜风]。～ *the street* 逛街,逛马路。～ **concert** (部分听众可一面散步一面听的)逍遥音乐会。～ **deck** 散步甲板。**-r** ***n.***

Pro·me·the·an [prəˈmiːθiən; prəˋmiθɪən] ***a.*** **1.** (像)普罗米修斯 (Prometheus) 的。**2.** 赋与生命的;有创造力的;勇于创新的。

Pro·me·theus [prəˈmiːθjuːs; prəˋmiθjəs] ***n.***【希神】普罗米修斯〔因盗取天火给世人而被宙斯神锁在山崖上,每日遭神鹰啄食肝脏,夜间伤口愈合,天明神鹰复来。但他始终坚毅不屈〕。

pro·me·thi·um [prəˈmiːθiəm; prəˋmiθɪəm] ***n.***【化】钷〔略 Pm;旧名 illinium 钷〕。

prom·i·nence, -cy [ˈprɔminəns, -si; ˋpramənəns, -sɪ] ***n.*** **1.** 突起;凸出。**2.** 凸出物;突出的部分[地方]。**3.** 显著,杰出,卓越;著名。**4.**【天】日珥。*give* ～ *to* 重视,突出。

prom·i·nent [ˈprɔminənt; ˋpramənənt] ***a.*** **1.** 突起的;(眼、牙等)凸出的。**2.** 突出的;显著的;杰出的;卓越的;显眼的。**3.** 重要的,著名的。～ *eyes* 凸眼。～ *teeth* 暴牙,虎牙。*a* ～ *paunch* 罗汉肚。*a* ～ *figure* 知名人士。*a* ～ *politician* 杰出的政治家。**-ly** ***ad.***

prom·is·cu·i·ty [ˌprɔmisˈkjuːiti; ˏpramɪsˋkjuətɪ] ***n.*** **1.** 混杂(性),混乱,混淆。**2.** (男女)乱交。

pro·mis·cu·ous [prəˈmiskjuəs; prəˋmɪskjuəs] ***a.*** **1.** 杂乱的,混杂的。**2.** 不加区别的;不分男女的;男女乱交的。**3.**〔口谑〕偶然的,没有目的的。～ *bathing* 男女混浴。～ *sexual relations* 乱交。～ *hospitality* 不加区别的款待。***at a*** ～ ***manner*** 胡乱,不分青红皂白地。***take a*** ～ ***stroll*** 漫步,没有目的地散步。**～-like** ***ad.***〔谑〕偶然。**-ly** ***ad.*** (*I dropped in* ～*ly.* 我是随便来串门子的)。

prom·ise [ˈprɔmis; ˋpramɪs] **I** ***n.*** **1.** 允许,诺言;约束,字据;约定事项;允诺的东西。**2.** (前途有)希望;(有)指望。*an express* ～ 订明的契约。*an implied* ～ 默契。*I claim your* ～. 请把允诺的东西给我吧。*writers of* ～ 有前途[希望]的作家 (*cf.* sterile)。*There is every* ～ *of success.* 大有成功的希望。***the Land of P-***【圣】上帝许给亚伯拉罕的地方〔即迦南〕;福地;想望之乡。***the P-*** 上帝给亚伯拉罕的允诺。***afford*** ～ ***of*** (使)有…的希望。***break a*** (***one's***) ～ 不守诺言;违约。***give*** [***show***] ～ ***of*** 有…的希望,使抱有…的希望。***keep a*** [***one's***] ～ 遵守诺言,践约。***make a*** ～ 约定;许诺。***put*** (*sb.*) ***off with fair*** ～ 哄开,骗人走开。**II** ***vt.*** **1.** 约,约定,订约;约好给,许给;允诺,答应。**2.** 有…的希望;给人以…的指望。**3.**〔只用于第一人称〕断定,保证。**4.**〔～ oneself〕指望;指望获得;确信会有。～ *sb. sth.* 许给某人某物。*I* ～ *you, it will not be so easy.* 包你不会那么容易。*These discussions* ～ *future storm.* 这些争论有引起未来风波的危险。— ***vi.*** **1.** 允诺;作出保证;**2.** 有希望,有指望,有前途。*It is one thing to* ～ *and another to perform.* 约是约做是做。～ *well* 前途有希望;(庄稼)有丰收希望。***be*** ～***d to*** 许配给,给…做未婚妻。***the Promised Land*** = *the Land of* ～.

prom·is·ee [ˌprɔmiˈsiː; ˏpramɪˋsi] ***n.***【法】受约人。

prom·is·er [ˈprɔmisə; ˋpramɪsɚ] ***n.*** 作出诺言的人。

prom·is·ing [ˈprɔmisiŋ; ˋpramɪsɪŋ] ***a.*** 有出息的;有前

途的;有希望的;有指望的。*a* ～ *youth* 有希望的青年。*a* ～ *future* 远大的前途。*a* ～ *sky* 十拿九稳的晴天。*They are intelligent and* ～. 他们聪明有为。**in a** ～ **state** [**way**] **1.** 有希望的。**2.** (病人)在开始复原中。**3.** 〔口〕有孕,有喜。

prom·i·sor [ˈprɔmisə, ˌprɔmiˈsɔː; ˋprɑmɪsˏɔr, ˏprɑmɪsˋɔr] *n.* 【法】立约人,订约者。

prom·is·so·ry [ˈprɔmisəri; ˋprɑməˏsorɪ] *a.* 表示允诺的;约定的;【商】约定支付的。～ **note**【商】期票;本票。

pro·mo [ˈprəuməu; ˋpromo] *n.* (*pl.* ～*s*) 〔美口〕宣传,推广;促销(= promotion)。

prom·on·to·ried [ˈprɔməntərid; ˋprɑməntərɪd] *a.* 形成海角的;有海角的,有岬的。

prom·on·to·ry [ˈprɔməntəri; ˋprɑmənˏtorɪ] *n.* **1.** 海角,岬。**2.**【解】隆突,荐骨岬。

pro·mor·phol·o·gy [ˌprəumɔːˈfɔlədʒi; ˏpromɔrˋfɑlədʒɪ] *n.* 【生】原形学。

pro·mote [prəˈməut; prəˋmot] *vt.* **1.** 增进;提倡,发扬,助长,促进;振兴,奖励;引起。**2.** 提升,使升级,使晋级,提拔。**3.** 发起,创立(企业等);〔美〕筹划(不正当事业)。**4.** 努力使(议案)通过。**5.** 宣传,推广(商品等)。**6.** 〔美俚〕(用不正当手段)获得。**7.** (象棋)使升格〔如小卒变为女王〕。～ *digestion* 促进消化。～ *sb. captain* 提升某人作上尉。*be* ～*ed to the next grade* 升到下年级。*Milk* ～*s health*. 牛奶有助于健康。

pro·mot·er [prəˈməutə; prəˋmotɚ] *n.* **1.** 增进者,助长者;振兴者,奖励者;后援人;(通常指恶意的)煽动者。**2.** (企业等)发起人;推销者。**3.**【化】促进剂,助催化剂。**4.** (宗教裁判的)起诉人。～*s of progress* 促进派。*a company*～ 投机性公司发起人。

pro·mo·tion [prəˈməuʃən; prəˋmoʃn] *n.* **1.** 增进,促进;助长;发扬;振兴,奖励。**2.** 提升;升级。**3.** (企业等的)发起;举办。**4.** (商品等的)宣传,推广。**5.** (推销中的)产品。～ *of disorder* 引起混乱。～ *expenses*【商】开办费。～ *shares* 发起人股份。*a* ～ *worker* 推销员。*This electric toothbrush is our latest promotion*. 这种电牙刷是敝公司的最新产品。**be on one's** ～ 有缺即可提升的;为了提升而表现自己。**get** [**obtain**] ～ 升级。

pro·mo·tive [prəˈməutiv; prəˋmotɪv] *a.* **1.** 促进性的;增进的,助长的,奖励的。**2.** 提升的。**3.** 发起的;创立的。**4.** 宣传的,推广的。

prompt [prɔmpt; prɑmpt] **I** *a.* **1.** 敏捷的,迅速的;即刻的,(回答等)及时的。**2.**【商】即期付款的。(*come to*) *a* ～ *decision* (作出)迅速的决定。*be* ～ *to obey* [*carry out an order*] 即刻服从[执行]命令。～ *cash payment*【商】即期付现。**II** *n.* 刺激物;(给演员的)提示,提词;【商】(期货的)付款日期,交割日期。**III** *vt.* **1.** 刺激,鼓励,怂恿,煽动,唆使,挑拨。**2.** 激起,唤起(思想感情等)。**3.** 提醒,指点,给(演员)提词。～*ed by instinct* [*necessity*] 为本能[需要]所驱使。**IV** *ad.* 准时地,正好。*at seven o'clock* ～ 在七时正。～ **book**【剧】提词用的剧本。～ **box**【剧】提词人藏身处。～ **day**【商】交割日。～ **delivery**【商】即交,即送。～ **note**【商】期货金额及交割日期通知单。～ **sale**【商】期货交易。～ **side** 提白员所在的方面;〔英〕舞台上演员的左方;〔美〕演员的右方。**-ly** *ad.* **-ness** *n.*

prompt·er [ˈprɔmptə; ˋprɑmptɚ] *n.* **1.** 激励者,鼓舞者;唤起者。**2.**【剧】(台词的)提白员,提词员。

prompt·ing [ˈprɔmptiŋ; ˋprɑmptɪŋ] *n.* **1.** 刺激,鼓励;煽动;唤起;驱使。**2.** 暗示,提示,提词。*the* ～*s of conscience* 良心的驱使。*under the* ～*s of sb.* [*sth.*] 在某人[某事]的激励下。

prompt·i·tude [ˈprɔmptitjuːd; ˏprɑmptəˏtjud] *n.* 敏捷,迅速,机敏;果断。*with great* ～ 极其敏捷地。*Their own* ～ *in retreating at the critical moment saved them*. 他们自己在危急的时刻迅速退却,这才得以避免被歼灭。

prom·ul·gate [ˈprɔməlgeit; prəˋmʌlget] *vt.* **1.** 颁布,公布(法令等)。**2.** 传播;宣传;发表。**-ga·tion** [ˌprɔməlˈgeiʃən; ˏpromʌlˋgeʃən] *n.* **-gator** *n.*

pro·mulge [prəuˈmʌldʒ; prəˋmʌldʒ] *vt.* 〔古〕= promulgate.

pro·my·ce·li·um [ˌprəumaiˈsiːliəm; ˏpromaɪˋsilɪəm] *n.* (*pl.* **-li·a** [-ə; -ə])【植】先菌丝。

pron. = pronominal; pronoun; pronounced; pronunciation.

pro·na·tal·ist [prəuˈneitəlist; proˋnetəlɪst] *a.* 鼓励提高人口出生率的;鼓励生育的。

pro·nate [ˈprəuneit; ˋpronet] *vt.* (*-nat·ed*; *-nat·ing*) **1.** 使(手、前肢)翻转向下,旋前;内转。**2.** 使俯,使伏。— *vi.* 俯,伏。

pro·na·tion [prəuˈneiʃən; proˋneʃən] *n.* 【生理】(手的)旋前(作用),内转(作用)(*opp.* supination)。

pro·na·tor [prəˈneitə; prəˋnetɚ] *n.* 【解】旋前肌。

prone [prəun; pron] *a.* **1.** 俯伏的;平伏的 (*opp.* erect, supine);向前弯曲的。**2.** 有…癖的,易…的,有…倾向的;易害…的 (*to*)。**3.** 倾斜的,坡陡的。*lie* ～ 平伏。*fall* ～ 向前跌倒。*a* ～ *surface* 下面。*be* ～ *to anger* 动辄发怒。*be* ～ *to think that* 总认为。**be less** ～ **to** 不致老是…。**be** ～ **to err** 易犯过失。～ **bombing** 俯冲轰炸。～ **position**【军】卧倒姿势。～ **pressure method** 俯伏人工呼吸法。**-ly** *ad.*

prone·ness [ˈprəunnis; ˋpronnɪs] *n.* **1.** 俯伏;屈,前屈,下屈。**2.** 倾向,脾性,嗜好。

pro·neph·ros [ˈprəuˈnefrɔs; proˋnefrɑs] *n.*【动】前肾。**-neph·ric** *a.*

prong [prɔŋ; prɔŋ] **I** *n.* **1.** 尖头;尖头物;叉(齿),股。**2.** 干草叉;(麋鹿的)角。**3.**【物】射线(径迹);(真空管的)插脚。**II** *vt.* **1.** 刺,掘翻(泥土等);用耙耙。**2.** 给…装上尖头[叉齿等]。

pronged [prɔŋd; prɔŋd] *a.* 有尖的,有叉的。

prong·horn [ˈprɔŋhɔːn; ˋprɔŋˏhɔrn] *n.* (*pl.* ～(*s*))【动】(美国产)叉角羚。

pro·no·grade [ˈprəunəgreid; ˋpronəˏgred] *a.* 爬行的,匍行的。

pronom. = pronominal.

pro·nom·i·nal [prəˈnɔminl, prəu-; prəˋnɑmənl̩, pro-] *a.* 【语法】代(名)词的;代(名)词性的。～ **adjective** 代名形容词〔指一个由代名词变成的形容词,如 my, her 等,或指有时用作代词有时用作形容词者,如 each, this 等〕。**-ly** *ad.*

pro·non·ce [prəunɔnˈsei; pronɑnˋse] *a.* 〔F.〕显著的;显眼的;夸张的。

pro·noun [ˈprəunaun; ˋpronaʊn] *n.* 【语法】代(名)词。*a personal* ～ 人称代词。*a reflexive* ～ 反身代词〔myself 等〕。

pro·nounce [prəˈnauns; prəˋnaʊns] *vt.* **1.** 发…的音。**2.** 宣判,宣告(刑罚、赦免等);演讲,讲述。**3.** 断言,断定(*on*; *upon*)。*The patient was* ～*d out of danger*. 病人已告脱险。～ **a curse** (**up**) **on** 诅咒。～ ***sentence of death*** (**up**) **on** ... 宣判…死刑。— *vi.* **1.** 发音。**2.** 代表意见;作出判断;表态 (*on*)。*a word difficult to* ～ 发音难的词。～ *against* 对…表明反对意见。～ *for* = ～ *in favour of* 表明赞成意见。

pro·nounce·a·ble [prəˈnaunsəbəl; prəˋnaʊnsəbl̩] *a.* 可发音的;读得出的。

pro·nounced [prəˈnaunst; prəˋnaʊnst] *a.* 决然的,断然的,强硬的;明白的,显著的。～ *opinions* 强硬的意见。*a* ～ *improvement* 显著改进。**-ly** *ad.*

pro·nounce·ment [prəˈnaunsmənt; prəˋnaʊnsmənt] *n.* **1.** 宣告;表示。**2.** 声明,公告;决定,判决。～*s on the matter* 对有关问题的表态意见。

pro·nounc·ing [prəˈnaunsiŋ; prəˋnaʊnsɪŋ] *a.* 发音的;表示发音的。*a* ～ *dictionary* 发音词典,正音词典。

pron·to ['prɔntəu; ˋprɑnto] ***ad.*** 〔美俚〕立刻,马上;很快地。*They told him to get out of there and ~.* 他们通知他离开那里而且要马上离开。*I thought that you'd be along pretty ~.* 我原来以为你会很快就来的。

pro·nu·cle·us [prəu'nju:kliəs, -'nu:-; proˋnjuklɪəs, -ˋnu-] ***n.*** (*pl.* ***-cle·i*** [-ai; -aɪ])【动】原核。**-cle·ar** ***a.***

pro·nun·ci·a·m(i)en·to [prəˌnʌnsiə'mentəu; prəˏnʌnsɪəˋmento] ***n.*** (*pl.* *~(e)s*) 宣言(尤指西班牙语国家起义者的宣言);檄文;声明;公告。

pro·nun·ci·a·tion [prəˌnʌnsi'eiʃən; prəˏnʌnsɪˋeʃən] ***n.*** 发音(法)。*The tongue is one of the organs for ~.* 舌是发音器官之一。*He has a good ~.* 他的发音很好。*An introduction to the ~ of American English.* 美国英语发音法入门。

proof [pru:f; pruf] **I** ***n.*** **1.** 证明;证据;【法】证件;【法】(口头或书面)证词,证言。**2.** 检验,考验;验算;检定的品质[强度等]。**3.** 试管。**4.**【印】校样,印样。**5.** (酒精的)标准强度。**6.** (甲胄等的)耐力,坚牢强度,不贯穿性。**7.**【摄】样片;样张。**8.** [Scot.] 审问。**9.**【数】证,证明,证法。*The ~ of the pudding is in the eating.* 布丁好坏一吃即知;空谈不如实验。*Here is ~ positive.* 有确实证据。*a foul ~* 错字很多的校样。*a foundry ~* (压型前的)清样。*an artist's* [*engraver's*] *~* 版面印样。*stand a severe ~* 经受严格的考验。*afford ~ of* 提供证据。*armour of ~* 戳不通的坚牢的铠甲。***below ~*** 不合格。***bring* [*put*] *to the ~*** 试,试验。***have ~ of shot*** 能防弹,能避弹。***in ~ of*** 作…的证据。***~ positive of his intention*** 他的企图的确证。***read the ~*** 校对。**II** ***a.*** **1.** 试验过的,有保证的;(酒)合标准的,规定的。**2.** 校样的。**3.** (子弹等)不入的,耐…的,防…的。*a ~ coin* 标准货币,制钱。*a ~ sample* 样品。*~ against the severest weather* 经得起任何酷烈天气的。*~ against the pricks of all temptations* 不为任何诱惑所动的。**III** ***vt.*** 使经得住,使(布等)耐久[不漏水(等)]。*~ed cloth* 防水布。~ **mark** (枪等的)验讫记号。~ **plane** 验电板。~**read** ***vt.***, ***vi.*** 〔美〕校对。~**reader** 校对员。~**-reading** 校对。~ **sheet** 校样。~ **spirit** 含标准酒精的酒〔英国的标准含酒精成分为 57.1%,美国为 50%〕。~**-test** ***vt.*** 试验,检验〔武器等〕。**-less** ***a.*** 无证据的。

-proof *suf.* 表示"耐,防(等)":*acid-~* 耐酸的。*air-~* 密封的。*dust-~* 防尘的。*fire-~* 防火的。*radar-~* 反雷达的。*slander-~* 听了坏话不会生气的。*sound-~* 隔音的。*water-~* 防水的。

Prop. = propeller.

prop. = properly; property; proposition.

prop[1] [prɔp; prɑp] **I** ***n.*** **1.** 支柱。**2.** 支持者,拥护者,后援者,后盾,靠山。**3.** 晾衣绳支柱 (= clothes-~)。**4.** 〔美俚〕腿。*pit ~s*【矿】坑木。*He is the only ~ of mine.* 他是我的唯一的靠山[支柱]。*the main ~ of a state* 国家的栋梁。**II** ***vt.*** (**-pp-**) 支持;把…靠着。*He ~ped his cane against the wall.* 他把自己的手杖靠墙立着。*~ up* (把…)撑住;给…撑腰。— ***vi.*** (马等)前腿突然挺直地停住。

prop[2] [prɔp; prɑp] ***n.***【剧】道具(= property)。

prop[3] [prɔp; prɑp] ***n.*** 〔英盗贼俚语〕钻石别针。

prop[4] [prɔp; prɑp] ***n.*** 〔口〕【空】螺旋桨 (= propeller)。~**-fan**【航】螺旋桨式风机〔由喷气发动机推动,有多个叶片〕。

pro·pae·deu·tic, -ti·cal [ˌprəupi'dju:tik, -tikəl; ˏpropɪˋdjutɪk, -tɪkl] **I** ***a.*** 初步的,预备的,预料的。**II** ***n.*** 预备学科[项目],预料。

pro·pae·deu·tics [ˌprəupi:'dju:tiks; ˏpropɪˋdjutɪks] ***n.*** 〔*pl.*〕预备知识,基础知识。

prop·a·ga·ble ['prɔpəgəbl; ˋprɑpəgəbl] ***a.*** **1.** 可传播的;可宣传的。**2.** 可以繁殖的。*be ~ by seed* 种子繁殖的。**-bil·i·ty** [ˌprɔpəgə'biliti; ˏprɑpəgəˋbɪlətɪ] ***n.*** **-ness** ***n.***

prop·a·gand [ˌprɔpə'gænd; ˏprɑpəˋgænd] ***vt.*** 〔美〕宣传。

prop·a·gan·da [ˌprɔpə'gændə; ˏprɑpəˋgændə] **I** ***n.*** **1.** 〔口〕宣传;宣传计划;宣传方法;传播。**2.** 宣传部,宣传机关。**3.** 〔the P-〕【天主】布教总会[学校]。***make ~ for*** 为…宣传。***set up a ~ for*** 设立…的宣传机关。**II** ***vt.***, ***vi.*** = propagandize.

prop·a·gan·dism [ˌprɔpə'gændizəm; ˏprɑpəˋgændɪzəm] ***n.*** 宣传;宣传事业;宣传(法)。

prop·a·gan·dist [ˌprɔpə'gændist; ˏprɑpəˋgændɪst] **I** ***n.*** 宣传者;宣传人员。**II** ***a.*** 宣传的。**-ic** ***a.***

prop·a·gan·dize [ˌprɔpə'gændaiz; ˏprɑpəˋgændaɪz] ***vt.***, ***vi.*** 宣传;传播;(对…)进行宣传。

prop·a·gate ['prɔpəgeit; ˋprɑpəˏget] ***vt.*** **1.** 增殖,繁殖。**2.** 普及,传播;宣传。**3.** 使(光、音、地震等)波及,传达。**4.** 传染,使蔓延;遗传(特征等)。**5.**【物】传播。*The weeds ~ themselves rapidly.* 杂草繁殖极快。*~ disease* 传染疾病。— ***vi.*** 增殖,繁殖;普及,传播,蔓延。**-ga·tion** ***n.***

prop·a·ga·tor ['prɔpəgeitə; ˋprɑpəˏgetɚ] ***n.*** 增殖者;传播者;宣传者。

pro·pane ['prəupein; ˋpropen] ***n.***【化】丙烷。

pro·pa·none ['prəupənəun; ˋpropənon] ***n.***【化】丙酮 (= acetone)。

pro·par·ox·y·tone [ˌprəupæ:'rɔksitəun; ˏpropæˋrɑksɪˏton] **I** ***a.*** (词)从词尾倒数第三音节上有重音的。**II** ***n.*** 从词尾倒数第三音节上有重音的词。

pro pa·tri·a [prəu'peitriə; proˋpetrɪə] 〔L.〕为了祖国。

pro·pel [prə'pel; prəˋpel] ***vt.*** (**-ll-**) 推,推进,驱使。*~ling power* 推进力。*be ~led by steam* 由蒸气推进。

pro·pel·lant [prə'pelənt; prəˋpelənt] ***n.*** 推进物,推进剂;(枪炮的)发射火药;喷气燃料。*high-energy ~* 高能燃料。*work horse ~*【火箭】通用燃料。

pro·pel·lent [prə'pelənt; prəˋpelənt] **I** ***a.*** 推进的。**II** ***n.*** = propellant.

pro·pel·ler, pro·pel·lor [prə'pelə; prəˋpelɚ] ***n.*** **1.** 推进者。**2.** (汽船、飞机的)螺旋桨,推进器;暗轮汽船。

pro·pend [prəu'pend; proˋpend] ***vi.*** 〔废〕倾向于,有意于 (*to*; *toward*)。

pro·pene ['prəupi:n; ˋpropin] ***n.***【化】丙烯 (= propylene)。

pro·pen·si·ty [prə'pensiti; prəˋpensətɪ] ***n.*** 倾向,嗜好,脾性,癖 (*to*; *for*)。*a ~ to extravagance* [*for gambling*] 奢华[赌博]的癖好。

prop·er ['prɔpə; ˋprɑpɚ] **I** ***a.*** **1.** 适当的,相当的;正当的,应该的;正式的,正常的。**2.** 有礼貌的;规矩的。**3.** 固有的,特有的,独特的 (*to*)。**4.** 本来的,真正的;严格意义上的〔用于名词后面〕。**5.**【语法】专有的;〔古〕自己的;【天】自身的。**6.**【纹】本色的。**7.** 〔英口〕纯粹的,完全的。**8.** 〔古〕漂亮的,优美的。**9.**【宗】仅限节日应用的。*I dislike ~ children.* 我不喜欢一本正经的孩子。*The book hardly belongs to literature ~.* 这本书不好说是纯文学书。*the dictionary ~* 辞典正文。*temperature ~ to August* 八月特有的气温。*Ferosity is ~ to tigers.* 凶猛是老虎的天性。*a peacock ~*【纹】天然色彩的孔雀(纹章)。*architecture ~* (不包含雕刻、管道等加工工程的)主体纯粹建筑。*There will be a ~ row about it.* 这个事情要引起一场大乱子来的。*a ~ man* 〔古〕漂亮的男子。*quite a ~ book* 一本极好的书。***as you think ~*** 你认为怎么合适就…。***at a ~ time*** 在适当的时候。***in the ~ sense of the word*** 按照这个词的本来意义。***in the ~ way*** 用适当方法。***paint sb. in sb.'s ~ colours*** 老老实实批评某人。~ ***for the occasion*** 合时宜。**II** ***ad.*** 〔方〕适当地,好好地;非常,很;完完全全地;彻底地。**III** ***n.*** 〔常 *pl.*〕【宗】特定礼拜仪式,特祷;特

赞。~ **circle**【数】真圆,常态圆。~ **function**【数】特征函数,常义函数。~ **mass**【物】静质量。~ **motion**【天】自行。~ **names**【语】专有名称。~ **noun**【语法】专有名词。

pro·per·i·spo·me·non [ˈprəuˌperiˈspəuminən; ˏproperɪˈspɑmɪˏnɑn] *a.*, *n.* (*pl.* **-na** [-nə; -nə])【希腊语法】词尾倒数第二音节上有变长音符的(词)。

pro·per·din [ˈprəupədin; ˋpropədɪn] *n.* (血液中)一种能消灭细菌和病毒的血清。

prop·er·ly [ˈprɔpəli; ˋprɑpəlɪ] *ad.* **1.** 适当,相当;当然,正正当当;整整齐齐。**2.** 完全,非常。*He very ~ refused.* 他正正当当地拒绝了。*I thrashed him ~.* 我狠狠打了他一顿。~ ***speaking*** = ***to speak*** ~ 严格地说来,本来。

prop·er·tied [ˈprɔpətid; ˋprɑpətɪd] *a.* **1.** 有财产的。**2.**【剧】使用道具的。

prop·er·ty [ˈprɔpəti; ˋprɑpətɪ] *n.* **1.** 财产;资产;所有物;所有地,地产;所有,所有权。**2.** 性质,特征,属性,特性;【逻】非本质特性。**3.**〔*pl.*〕【剧】道具;〔英〕服装。*a man of ~* 有产业者。*real ~* 不动产。*movable* [*personal*] *~* 动产。*Is this your ~?* 这是你的东西吗? *The secret is common ~.* 那个秘密人人知道。*literary ~* 著作权,版权。*the properties of soda* 碳酸钠[苏打]的特性。~ ***in copyright*** 版权所有。~ **animal**〔美〕【剧、影】惯于演出的动物。~ **man** [**master**]【剧】小道具管理员。~ **owner** 地主,业主。~ **tax** 财产税。

pro·phase [ˈprəufeiz; ˋproˏfez] *n.*【动】(有丝分裂)前期。

proph·e·cy [ˈprɔfisi; ˋprɑfəsɪ] *n.* 预言;预言能力;【宗】预言书。

proph·e·sy [ˈprɔfisai; ˋprɑfəˏsaɪ] *vt.*, *vi.* (**-sied**) 预言,预示。

proph·et [ˈprɔfit; ˋprɑfɪt] *n.* **1.** 预言者;〔诗〕先知;预言者。**2.** (主义等的)提倡者,主张者。**3.**〔俚〕(赛马输赢的)预测者。*a weather ~* 天气预报员。***the P-*** **1.** (伊斯兰教祖)穆罕默德。**2.** 约瑟·史密斯 (Joseph Smith)〔1805—1844,美国摩门教的开山鼻祖〕。***the Prophets*** 《旧约》中的各预言书或其作者。

proph·et·ess [ˈprɔfitis; ˋprɑfɪtɪs] *n.* 女预言者。

pro·phet·ic, pro·phet·i·cal [prəˈfetik, -ikəl; prəˋfɛtɪk, -ɪkəl] *a.* 预言(者)的。**-i·cal·ly** *ad.*

proph·y·lac·tic [ˌprɔfiˈlæktik; ˏprofəˋlæktɪk] **I** *a.*【医】预防(性)的。**II** *n.* **1.**【医】预防药;预防法。**2.** 避孕用品[药物]。

proph·y·lax·is [ˌprɔfiˈlæksis; ˏprofəˋlæksɪs] *n.*【医】预防(法)。

pro·pine [prəˈpiːn, prəu-; prəˋpin, pro-] **I** *vt.*〔Scot.〕〔古〕赠送(礼品)。**II** *n.*〔Scot.〕〔古〕礼品。

pro·pin·qui·ty [prəˈpiŋkwiti; proˋpɪnkwətɪ] *n.* **1.** (地点的)相近,邻近。**2.** (时间的)接近;迫切。**3.** (血统上的)近亲。**4.** (性质、性情等的)近似,类似。

pro·pi·o·nate [ˈprəupiəneit; ˋpropɪəˏnet] *n.* 丙酸盐,丙酸酯。

pro·pi·ti·ate [prəˈpiʃieit; prəˋpɪʃɪˏet] *vt.* **1.** 劝解;抚慰;调和,调解。**2.** 向…讨好,邀宠于;【宗】向(上帝)赎罪。**-ation** *n.* **1.** 劝解,抚慰。**2.** 邀宠;【宗】赎罪。

pro·pi·ti·a·tor [prəˈpiʃieitə; prəˋpɪʃɪˏetə] *n.* **1.** 劝解的人,调解人。**2.** 邀宠者;【宗】赎罪者。

pro·pi·ti·a·to·ry [prəˈpiʃiətəri; prəˋpɪʃɪəˏtorɪ] **I** *a.* **1.** 劝解的,调解的。**2.** 邀宠的;【宗】赎罪的。**II** *n.* = mercy-seat. **-to·ri·ly** *ad.*

pro·pi·tious [prəˈpiʃəs; prəˋpɪʃəs] *a.* **1.** 顺利的,幸运的;有利于…的;适合的 (*for*; *to*; *towards*);吉利的。**2.** 慈祥的,慈悲的。*a ~ sign* [*omen*] 吉兆。*~ to the undertaking* 有利于任务[事业]的成功。*~ weather for journey* 适合旅行的好天气。*~ wind* 顺风。**-ly** *ad.* **-ness** *n.*

prop·jet [ˈprɔpdʒet; ˋprɑpˏdʒɛt] *n.* 涡轮螺桨发动机,涡轮螺桨飞机 (= turboprop)。

prop·man [ˈprɔpmæn; ˋprɑpmæn] *n.* (*pl.* **-men**) 道具管理员 (= property man)。

prop·o·lis [ˈprɔpəlis; ˋprɑpəlɪs] *n.* 蜂胶。

pro·pone [prəˈpəun; prəˋpon] *vt.*〔Scot.〕提议;陈述。

pro·po·nent [prəˈpəunənt; prəˋponənt] **I** *n.* **1.** 提议者;主张者。**2.** 支持者;辩护者。**3.**【法】遗嘱检验申请人。**II** *a.* 建议的;支持的;辩护的。

pro·por·tion [prəˈpɔːʃən; prəˋporʃən] **I** *n.* **1.** 比,比率;【数】比例。**2.** 相称,平衡,调和,配合。**3.** 份;部分。**4.**〔*pl.*〕大小,面积,容积。*the ~ of births to the population* 出生率。*direct* [*inverse*] *~* 正[反]比例。*a large ~ of the earth's surface* 地球表面的大部分。*due* [*proper*] *~* 调和,相称。***do a sum in*** [***by***] ~ 按比例计算。***in admirable*** ~ 非常均衡。***in*** ~ ***to*** [***as***] 与…成比例;与…相称;按…的比例(越…越…)。***of fine ~s*** (高楼等)堂皇的。***of gigantic ~s*** 巨大的。***out of*** (***all***) ~ ***to*** 和…不相称[不成比例]。***sense of*** ~ 能作出公允判断的能力;辨别轻重缓急的能力。**II** *vt.* **1.** 使相称,使均衡。**2.** 摊派,分配。~ *the expenses to the receipts* 量入为出。

pro·por·tion·a·ble [prəˈpɔːʃənəbl; prəˋporʃənəbl] *a.* 可配合的,相称的,相当的,成比例的 (*to*)。**-bly** *ad.*

pro·por·tion·al [prəˈpɔːʃənl; prəˋporʃənl] **I** *a.* (成)比例的;相称的,平衡的,调和的 (*to*)。*a ~ number* 比例数。*a ~ error* 相对(比例)误差(率)。**II** *n.*【数】比例项,比例量。***be directly*** [***inversely***, ***reciprocally***] ~ ***to*** 与…成正[反]比例。~ **representation** (选举上的)比例代表制。~ **sampling** 比例抽样。**-ist** *n.* **1.** 主张实行比例代表制者。**2.** (人力、物力等的)分派比例的安排者。**-ly** *ad.* 按比例地,相应地,相配合地;比较地。

pro·por·tion·al·i·ty [prəˌpɔːʃəˈnæliti; prəˏporʃənˋælətɪ] *n.* 比例(性);均衡(性);相称。

pro·por·tion·ate [prəˈpɔːʃənit; prəˋporʃənɪt] **I** *a.* 相称的,成比例的,相当的。**II** *vt.* 使相称,使成比例,使相当;使适应 (*to*)。~ *punishment to crimes* 按罪量刑。**-ly** *ad.*

pro·por·tioned [prəˈpɔːʃənd; prəˋporʃənd] **I** *a.* 相称的,配合得…的;成比例的。*an evenly ~ share* 公平的分配。*well-~* 相称的,很匀称的。*ill-~* 不相称的,不成比例的。

pro·por·tion·ment [prəˈpɔːʃənmənt; prəˋporʃənmənt] *n.* 比例,相称,调和,匀整。

pro·pos·al [prəˈpəuzəl; prəˋpozl] *n.* **1.** 申请;提议,建议;提案。**2.** 求婚。**3.**〔美〕投标。*a counter ~* 对案,反提案。*sealed ~s* (密封)投标。***agree to a*** ~ 同意某项建议(提案)。***make a*** ~ (***of marriage***) 求婚。***make*** [***offer***] ~***s of*** [***for***] (***peace***) 求(和)。

pro·pose [prəˈpəuz; prəˋpoz] *vt.* **1.** 申请;提议,建议,提出。**2.** 推荐,提名。**3.** 计划,打算。**4.** 求(婚)。*~ a motion* 提出一项动议。*I wish to ~ a toast to our friendship.* 我建议为我们的友谊干杯。*We ~d him for* [*as*] *candidate.* 我们推荐他为候选人。*~ a riddle* 出谜。*I do not ~ to stay long at Shanghai.* 我不打算在上海久住。*~ marriage to a girl* 向一个姑娘求婚。— *vi.* **1.** 打算,作出计划。**2.** 求婚 (*to*)。*Man ~s, God disposes.*〔谚〕谋事在人,成事在天。

pro·pos·er [prəˈpəuzə; prəˋpozə] *n.* 申请者,提议者,建议者,提案国。

prop·o·si·tion [ˌprɔpəˈziʃən; ˏprɑpəˋzɪʃən] **I** *n.* **1.** 提议,建议;主张。**2.**【逻】命题;【修】主题;【数】定理。**3.**〔口〕企业,事业。**4.**〔口〕商品。**5.**〔口〕事情,工作;家伙。*an absolute* [*a predicative*, *a categorical*] *~*【逻】定言命题,直言判断。*a major* [*minor*] *~*【逻】大[小]前题。*a paying ~* 赚钱生意。*a queer ~* 怪事。*He is a tough ~.* 他是一个难对付的家伙。**II** *vi.*〔美俚〕提议,

P

建议。**-al** ***a*****. -al·ly** ***ad*****.**

pro·pos·i·tus [prəˈpɔzitəs; proˋpɑzətəs] ***n*****.** (*pl*. ***-ti*** [-tai; -taɪ]) 族谱中发支的始祖。

pro·pound [prəˈpaund; prəˋpaʊnd] ***vt*****. 1.** 提议,建议。**2.**【法】(为求确定合法性向有关方面)提出(遗嘱)。**-er** ***n*****.**

propr. = proprietary; proprietor.

pro·prae·tor, pro·pre·tor [prəuˈpriːtə; proˋpritɚ] ***n*****.** 省长〔作过罗马(军事)执政官后被派任为省的行政官〕。

pro·pri·e·ta·ry [prəˈpraiətəri; prəˋpraɪə͵tɛrɪ] **I** ***a*****. 1.** 所有(人)的。**2.** 有财产的。**3.** 专有的,独占的,专利的。**II** ***n*****.** 〔古〕**1.** 所有人,所有团体。**2.** 所有权;所有物。**3.** 专卖药品。**4.**【美史】(独立前英王特许独占某块殖民地的)领主。～ **articles** 专利品。～ **class** 资产阶级;(尤指)地主阶级。～ **company 1.** (亦略作 **Pty**)(占有其他公司全部或大部分的)控股公司,持股公司。**2.** 土地兴业公司。～ **medicine** 特许专卖药品。～ **rights** 所有权。

pro·pri·e·tor [prəˈpraiətə; prəˋpraɪətɚ] ***n*****. 1.** 所有人;业主。**2.** 地主;【美史】(独立前,英王特许独占某块殖民地的)领主。*landed* ～ 地主。*a lord* ～ 大地主。*a peasant* ～ 自耕农。**-ship** ***n*****.** 所有权。

pro·pri·e·to·ri·al [prəˌpraiəˈtɔːriəl; prə͵praɪəˋtorɪəl] ***a*****.** 所有(权)的。**-ly** ***ad*****.**

pro·pri·e·tress [prəˈpraiətris; prəˋpraɪətrɪs] ***n*****.** 女所有人〔业主,地主等〕。

pro·pri·e·ty [prəˈpraiəti; prəˋpraɪətɪ] ***n*****. 1.** 妥当,适宜,适当;正当,恰当。**2.** 礼节;〔the proprieties〕礼仪,规矩。*I doubt the* ～ *of the term*. 我怀疑这个术语是否适当。*a breach of* ～ 失礼行为。*observe the proprieties* 遵守礼节;依照社交惯例。***with*** ～ 按照礼节,正当,适当。

pro·pri·o·cep·tive [ˌprəupriəˈseptiv; ͵proprɪəˋsɛptɪv] ***a*****.**【动】固有感受的,本体感受的。

pro·pri·o·cep·tor [ˌprəupriəˈseptə; ͵proprɪəˋsɛptɚ] ***n*****.**【动】本体感受器。

pro·pri·o mo·tu [ˈprəupriəu ˈməutju; ˋproprɪ͵o ˋmotu]〔L.〕自愿。

pro·proc·tor [prəuˈprɔktə; proˋprɑktɚ] ***n*****.** 〔英大学〕副学监。

props [prɔps; prɑps] ***n*****.** 〔*pl*.〕〔英俚〕【剧】小道具。

prop·to·sis [prɔpˈtəusis; prɑpˋtosɪs] ***n*****.** (*pl*. ***-ses*** [-siːz; -siz])【医】突出,脱出,前垂,凸出(尤指眼球凸出)。

pro·pul·sion [prəˈpʌlʃən; prəˋpʌlʃən] ***n*****.** 推进(力)。*a* ～ *engineer* 动力装置工程师。*jet* ～ 喷气推进。

pro·pul·sive [prəˈpʌlsiv; prəˋpʌlsɪv] ***a*****.** 推进的,促进的,有推进力的。

pro·pul·sor [prəˈpʌlsə; prəˋpʌlsɚ] ***n*****. 1.** 喷气式发动机,推进器。**2.** 推进物;火箭的推进燃料。

pro·pyl [ˈprəupil; ˋpropəl] ***n*****.**【化】丙基。**-ic** ***a*****.**

pro·pylae·um [ˌprɔpiˈliːəm; ͵prɑpəˋliəm] ***n*****.** (*pl*. ***-laea*** [-ˈliːə; -ˋliə])(常用 *pl*.)(神殿等的)入口。*the Propylaea* 希腊雅典卫城 (Acropolis) 的入口。

pro·pyl·ene [ˈprəupiliːn; ˋpropəlin] ***n*****.**【化】丙烯。

prop·y·lite [ˈprɔpilait; ˋprɑpəlaɪt] ***n*****.**【地】青磐岩。

pro·pyne [ˈprəupain; ˋpropaɪn] ***n*****.**【化】丙炔。

pro ra·ta [prəuˈrɑːtə, -ˈreitə; proˋrɑtə, -ˋretə] ***a*****., *ad*****.** 按比例的[地]。

pro·rate [prəuˈreit; proˋret] ***vt*****.** 〔美〕按比例分配;摊派。

pro·ro·ga·tion [ˌprəurəˈgeiʃən; ͵prorəˋgeʃən] ***n*****.** (议会的)闭会;休会。

pro·rogue [prəˈrəug; proˋrog] ***vt*****., *vi*****.** (尤指英国议会)(使)休会;(使)闭会。*Parliament stands* ～*d*. 议会在休会中。

pros. = prosody.

pros- *pref*. **1.** 前,向(…方面);加之。**2.** (靠)近。

pro·sage [ˈprəusidʒ; ˋprosɪdʒ] ***n*****.** 无肉香肠;素肠。

pro·sa·ic [prəuˈzeiik; proˋzeɪk] ***a*****. 1.** 散文的,散文体的(*opp*. poetic);没有诗意的。**2.** 单调的,平凡的;使人厌倦的,无聊的。**3.** 如实的。*a* ～ *life* 枯燥无味的生活。**-i·cal·ly** ***ad*****.**

pro·sa·i·cism, pro·sa·ism [ˈprəuzeiisizəm, ˈprəuzeiizəm; ˋprozeɪsɪəm, ˋprozeɪzm] ***n*****. 1.** 散文体。**2.** 平凡,枯燥。

pro·sa·ist [ˈprəuzeiist; ˋprozeɪst] ***n*****. 1.** 散文家。**2.** 平凡的人,没有诗意的人。

Pros. Atty. = prosecuting attorney.

pro·sce·ni·um [prəuˈziːniəm; proˋsinɪəm] ***n*****.** (*pl*. ***-nia*** [-niə; -nɪə]) **1.** (舞台的)幕前部分。**2.** 〔古〕(希腊、罗马剧场的)舞台。**3.** 〔泛指〕前部;显著地位。～ **box** 舞台前部的包厢。

pro·sciut·to [prəˈʃuːtəu, It. prəuˈʃuːttəu; proˈʃuto, It. proˋʃutto] ***n*****.** (意大利的一种熏过的、切得很薄的)五香火腿。

pro·scribe [prəuˈskraib; proˋskraɪb] ***vt*****. 1.** 使丧失公权,使失去法律保护。**2.** 放逐。**3.** 禁止;排斥。**4.** 〔古〕公布(被处罚者的)姓名;宣布…(公民)为国家的敌人并取消对他的法律保护。

pro·scrip·tion [prəuˈskripʃən; proˋskrɪpʃən] ***n*****. 1.** 公权剥夺。**2.** 放逐。**3.** 禁止;排斥。**4.** 〔古罗马〕宣布…为公敌的公告。**-tive** ***a*****.**

prose [prəuz; proz] **I** ***n*****. 1.** 散文 (*opp*. verse)。**2.** 平凡,单调,普通。**3.** 枯燥无味的话,无聊的议论。**4.**【天主】续唱。**5.** 〔英〕(学生的)译成外语的练习。*a* ～*-poem* 散文诗。*the* ～ *of life* 平凡的人生。*I've got 2 French* ～*s to do before tomorrow morning*. 明天上午以前我还要做两道译成法语的练习题。**II** ***vt*****., *vi*****.** 用散文写;(将诗)译成散文;平淡无趣地写;啰啰唆唆地讲。

pro·sect [prəuˈsekt; proˋsɛkt] ***vt*****.**【医】解剖(尸体)作示范教学。

pro·sec·tor [prəuˈsektə; proˋsɛktɚ] ***n*****.** (为准备实物示教的)尸体解剖者。

pros·ecute [ˈprɔsikjuːt; ˋprɑsɪ͵kjut] ***vt*****. 1.** 彻底进行(调查、研究学问等),推行,执行,从事;经营,做(买卖等)。**2.** 控告,对…提起公诉;依照法律手续要求执行(权利)。～ *the war against* 对…作战。— ***vi*****. 1.** 起诉,告发。**2.** 作检察官。*Trespassers will be* ～*d*. 〔告示〕违者法办。**prosecuting attorney** 〔美〕检察官。

pros·e·cu·tion [ˌprɔsiˈkjuːʃən; ͵prɑsɪˋkjuʃən] ***n*****. 1.** 实行,执行,贯彻;营业。**2.** 控告,起诉,检举。**3.** 〔the ～〕原告及其律师的总称 (*opp*. defense)。*the* ～ *of a trade* 从事一门行业。*a criminal* ～ 刑事诉讼。*a malicious* ～ 诬告。*start a* ～ *against sb*. 检举某人。***the Director of Public P-s*** 〔英〕检察官。

pros·e·cu·tor [ˈprɔsikjuːtə; ˋprɑsɪ͵kjutɚ] ***n*****.** (*fem*. ***-trix*** [-triks; -trɪks]) (*pl*. ***-tri·ces*** [-trisiːz; -trɪsiz]) **1.** 实行者。**2.**【法】起诉人,告发人,检举人。*a public* ～ 检察官。

pros·e·lyte [ˈprɔsilait; ˋprɑsl͵aɪt] **I** ***n*****. 1.** 新入教者;(意见、思想、政党等的)改宗者。**2.** 〔古〕从邪教皈依犹太教者。**II** ***vt*****., *vi*****. 1.** (使)改变(意见、思想等)。**2.** 〔美〕劝诱(运动员);搜罗(人员)。

pros·e·ly·tism [ˈprɔsilitizəm; ˋprɑslaɪt͵ɪzəm] ***n*****.** 改宗;(政治信仰等的)改变。

pros·e·ly·tize [ˈprɔsilitaiz; ˋprɑsəlaɪt͵aɪz] ***vt*****.** 使改宗[转向、变节]。

pro·sem·i·nar [prəuˈseminɑː; proˋsɛmɪnar] ***n*****.** (为未毕业的高材生开设的)研究班。

pros·en·ceph·a·lon [ˌprɔsenˈsefəlɔn, -lən; ͵prɑsɛnˋsɛfəlɑn, -lən] ***n*****.** (*pl*. ***-la*** [-lə; -lə]) 前脑;壮年人发达的脑部〔包括间脑和大脑半球〕(= forebrain)。**-phal·ic** ***a*****.**

pros·en·chy·ma [prɔsˈeŋkimə; prɑsˋɛŋkɪmə] ***n*****.**【植】长轴组织;锐端细胞组织。**-chym·a·tous** [-ˈkimətəs;

-ˋkɪmətəs] *a*.

pros·er [ˈprəuzə; ˋprozɚ] *n*. 1. 散文家;写平凡事物的人。2. 唠唠叨叨的人。

Pro·ser·pi·na, Pros·er·pine [prəˈsəːpinə, ˈprɔsəpain; proˋsɝpɪnə, ˋprɑsɚˏpaɪn] *n*. 【罗神】= Perse phone.

pros·et·ry [ˈprəuzitri; ˋprozɪtrɪ] *n*. 〔美〕散文诗。

pros·i·fy [ˈprəuzifai; ˋprozɪˏfaɪ] *vt*. 1. 把…改成散文;使散文化。2. 使平庸化。— *vi*. 1. 写散文。2. 变得平庸无奇。

pros·i·ly [ˈprəuzili; ˋprozɪlɪ] *ad*. 散文般地;平淡无味地,啰啰唆唆地。

pros·i·ness [ˈprəuzinis; ˋprozɪnɪs] *n*. 1. 散文体。2. 平凡,单调。

pro·sit [ˈprəusit, ˈprəuzit; ˋprosɪt, ˋprozɪt] *int*. 为…健康干杯! 祝你健康! 〔尤指德国人祝酒时的用语〕。

pro·slav·er·y [prəuˈsleivəri; proˋslevrɪ] *a*. 赞成奴隶制度的。

pro·so [ˈprəusəu; ˋproso] *n*. 〔Russ.〕黍,稷 (= millet)。

pro·so·di·al, pro·sod·ic, pro·sod·i·cal [prəˈsəudiəl, -ˈsɔdik, -ikəl; prəˋsodɪəl, -ˋsɑdɪk, -ɪkəl] *a*. 诗体学的;韵律学的;作诗法的。**-i·cal·ly** *ad*.

pros·o·dist [ˈprɔsədist; ˋprɑsədɪst] *n*. 韵律学者;诗体学者。

pros·o·dy [ˈprɔsədi; ˋprɑsədɪ] *n*. 韵律学;作诗法;诗体学。

pros·o·po·p(o)e·ia [prɔˌsəupəˈpiːə; proˏsopəˋpiə] *n*. 【修】拟人法;(使虚幻人物)具体化。

pros·pect I [ˈprɔspekt; ˋprɑspɛkt] *n*. 1. 眼界,风景,景色;展望;(房屋的)方向。2. 希望,前途;远见;预料。3. 形势;情景,景色。4. 〔美〕可能成为顾客[应征者]的人。5. 探矿有希望的地区。6. 矿石样品。7. 试掘;【地】勘探。*command a fine* ~ 景致好。*a house with a southern* ~ 朝南的房子。*a youth with bright* [*rosy*] ~*s* 前途远大的青年。*The job offers good* ~*s*. 这工作很有前途。*Industrial modernization opens up broad* ~*s for youth*. 工业的现代化为青年开辟广阔的前程。*Things offer a gloomy* ~. 形势不佳。*strike a good* ~ 挖到旺矿。***in*** ~ 可以预料到,有希望 (*We have a pleasant time in* ~. 我们前途乐观)。***in*** [***within***] ~ (***of***) 可期待,在望,有希望。**II** [prəusˈpekt; prɑsˋpɛkt] *vt*. 勘探(矿藏),找(金矿等)。—*vi*. 1. 试掘 (*for*)。2. (矿产量)有希望。~ *a mine* 勘探矿藏。~ *for oil* 勘探石油矿。*a mine* ~*ing ill* [*well*] 一个没有[有]开采前途的矿山。

pro·spec·tive [prəˈspektiv; prəˋspɛktɪv] *a*. 1. 将来的,未来的 (*opp*. retrospective)。2. 有希望的;预期的。*my* ~ *son-in-law* 我将来的女婿。**-ly** *ad*.

pro·spec·tor [ˈprɔsˈpektə; ˋprɑspɛktɚ] *n*. 探矿者;(指望将来的)投机家。

pro·spec·tus [prəsˈpektəs; prəˋspɛktəs] *n*. 1. (创办学校、公司等的)计划书,意见书,发起书。2. (讲义等的)大纲,(计划书等的)样本。3. (即将出版的书等的)内容介绍,简介。

pros·per [ˈprɔspə; ˋprɑspɚ] *vi*., *vt*. (使)兴隆,(使)繁荣;(使)成功。*conditions* ~*ing the business* 使生意兴隆的条件。~ *in business* 生意兴隆。*Everything he does* ~*s with him*. 他做事样样顺当。*a* ~*ing breeze* 顺风。

pros·per·i·ty [prɔsˈperiti; prɑsˋpɛrətɪ] *n*. 兴隆,繁荣,旺盛;〔*pl*.〕顺遂,幸福 (*opp*. adversity)。*national* ~ 国家的兴旺。*I wish you all* ~. 祝你诸事顺遂。

pros·per·ous [ˈprɔspərəs; ˋprɑspərəs] *a*. 兴隆的,繁荣的,昌隆的;幸福的,运气好的;顺遂的,良好的。~ *weather* 绝好天气。*in a* ~ *hour* 恰好,刚好。*bring a plan to a* ~ *issue* 使计划顺利成功。**-ly** *ad*.

prost [prəust; prost] *int*. 为…健康干杯! 祝你健康! 〔尤指德国人祝酒时的用语〕(= prosit)。

pros·ta·glan·din [ˌprɔstəˈglændin; ˏprɑstəˋglændɪn] *n*. 【化】前列腺素。

pros·tate [ˈprɔsteit; ˋprɑstet] *n*., *a*. 【解】前列腺(的)。

pros·ta·tec·to·my [ˌprɔstəˈtektəmi; ˏprɑstəˋtɛktəmɪ] *n*. (*pl*. **-mies**) 【医】前列腺切除术。

pros·ta·tism [ˈprɔstətizəm; ˋprɑstətɪzəm] *n*. 前列腺慢性病(尤指前列腺肿大引起对排尿的阻塞)。

pros·ta·ti·tis [ˌprɔstəˈtaitis; ˏprɑstəˋtaɪtɪs] *n*. 【医】前列腺炎。

pros·the·sis [ˈprɔsθisis; ˋprɑsθɪsɪs] *n*. (*pl*. ***pro·theses*** [-siːz; -siz]) 1. 【语法】词首增添字母[音节]〔如 belove 中的 b〕。2. 【医】修复术,弥补术;假体。3. 【化】取代,置换。*dental* ~ 假牙。

pros·thet·ic [prɔsˈθetik; prɑsˋθɛtɪk] *a*. 1. 【语法】词首增添字母[音节]的。2. 【医】修复术的。3. 【化】非朊基的。

pros·thet·ics [prɔsˈθetiks; prɑsˋθɛtɪks] *n*. 〔动词用单数〕(假肢、假眼、假牙)装补学,修复学。**pros·the·tist** [ˈprɔsθiːtist; ˋprɑsθətɪst] *n*. (假牙等的)装补专家。

pros·tho·don·tics [ˌprɔsθəˈdɔntiks; ˏprɑsθəˋdɑntɪks] *n*. 〔动词用单数〕牙修复术 (= prosthodontia)。**-don·tic** *a*. **-don·tist** *n*. 镶牙专家。

pros·ti·tute [ˈprɔstitjuːt; ˋprɑstəˏtjut] **I** *n*. 妓女;卖身投靠的人,出卖贞操的人。**II** *a*. 卖淫的;堕落的。**III** *vt*. 使卖淫,卖(身);出卖(名誉等);滥用(能力等)。~ *oneself* 沦为娼妓。— *vi*. 卖淫,卖身。

pros·ti·tu·tion [ˌprɔstiˈtjuːʃən; ˏprɑstəˋtjuʃən] *n*. 卖淫;出卖灵魂;滥用。*illicit* ~ 私娼。*licensed* [*public*] ~ 公娼(制度)。

pro·sto·mi·um [prəuˈstəumiəm; proˋstomɪəm] *n*. (*pl*. ***-mi·a*** [-ə; -ə]) 【动】口前叶。

pros·trate [ˈprɔstreit; ˋprɑstret] **I** *a*. 1. (为表示屈服)拜倒在地下的。2. 打败了的,屈服的,降伏的。3. 沮丧的;筋疲力尽的。4. 【植】匍匐性的,爬地的,平卧的。*They laid the Republicans* ~. 他们使共和党人屈服了。*be* ~ *with fatigue* 筋疲力竭。**II** [prɔsˈtreit; prɑsˋtret] *vt*. 1. 使倒伏,使平卧;弄倒,(风)吹倒,吹翻。2. 〔~ oneself〕拜倒,平伏。3. 使屈服,推翻。4. 使衰弱,使筋疲力尽,使累透。~ *oneself before sb*. 拜倒人前,对…五体投地。*be* ~*d by the heat* 热得昏倒。

pros·tra·tion [prɔsˈtreiʃən; prɑˋstreʃən] *n*. 1. 拜倒;平伏。2. 疲劳;【医】虚脱,衰弱。*general* [*nervous*] ~ 全身[神经]衰弱。

pro·style [ˈprəustail; ˋprostaɪl] **I** *a*. 【建】柱廊式的。**II** *n*. 柱廊;柱廊式建筑。

pros·y [ˈprəuzi; ˋprozɪ] *a*. (***-i·er***; ***-i·est***) 散文(体)的,枯燥无味的,啰唆的。

Prot. = Protectorate; Protestant.

prot- *comb. f*. = proto.

pro·tac·tin·i·um [ˌprəutækˈtiniəm; ˏprotækˋtɪnɪəm] *n*. 【化】镤。

pro·tag·o·nist [prəuˈtægənist; proˋtægənɪst] *n*. 1. (戏剧的)主角;(小说的)主人翁。2. 领导者,首唱者,首创者。

Pro·tag·o·ras [prəuˈtægəræs; proˋtægərəs] *n*. 普罗塔哥拉〔481—411? B.C.,古希腊智者派哲学家〕。

pro·ta·mine, pro·ta·min [ˈprəutəmiːn, -min; ˋprotəmin, -mɪn] *n*. 【化】鱼精朊,鱼精蛋白;鱼卵胺。

pro·tan·o·pi·a [ˌprəutəˈnəupiə; ˏprotəˋnopɪə] *n*. 红色盲。**-tan·op·ic** [-ˈɔpik; -ˋɑpɪk] *a*.

prot·a·sis [ˈprɔtəsis; ˋprɑtəsɪs] *n*. (*pl*. ***-a·ses*** [-əsiːz; -əsiz]) 【语法】条件从[子]句 (*opp*. apodosis)。**protat·ic** [prəˈtætik; prəˋtætɪk] *a*.

prote- *comb. f*. = proteo-.

Pro·te·an [prəuˈtiːən; ˋprotɪən] *a*. 1. 【希神】普罗秋斯 (Proteus) 神(似)的。2. 〔p-〕千变万化的;变化不定的;(演员)能演好几种角色的;【动】变形虫的。*a* ~ *per-*

former 多面手演员。

pro·te·ase [ˈprəutieis; ˋprotɪes] *n*. 【化】蛋白酶。

pro·tect [prəˈtekt; prəˋtɛkt] *vt*. 1. 保护,包庇,守护;警戒;防止(危险、损害等)。2. 【机】装保险器(在枪等上)。3. 【经】(对外货征收重税)保护(国内产业)。4. 【商】准备支付(汇票)。*a ~ed state* 保护国。*~ed trade* 保护贸易。*~ sb. from* [*against*] *danger* 保护某人免遭危险。— *vi*. 有保护作用。

pro·tec·tion [prəˈtekʃən; prəˋtɛkʃən] *n*. 1. 保护,保卫,防御,掩护,包庇,照顾 (*from*; *against*)。2. 保护者,防护物 (*against*);〔美俚〕(歹徒向人索取的)保护费。3. 护照,通行证;〔美〕(国籍)护照;通行证。3. 【经】保护贸易制,保护政策。*~ against cold* 防寒用具。*~ against moths* [*lightning*] 除虫,避(雷)。*~ at halts* 驻军警戒。*~* **on move** 行军警戒。**under the** *~* **of** 在…保护下,受…保护,托…照顾。

pro·tec·tion·ism [prəˈtekʃənizəm; prəˋtɛkʃənɪzm] I *n*. 【经】保护贸易主义,保护主义,保护政策。**-ist** *n*. 赞成保护贸易主义者。II *a*. 保护贸易主义的。

pro·tec·tive [prəˈtektiv; prəˋtɛktɪv] *a*. 1. 保护的,防护的。2. 保护贸易的。~ **clothing** 防毒服。~ **colouring** 【动】保护色。~ **mimicry** [**resemblance**] 【动】保护性拟态。~ **potential** 自卫能。~ **reflex** 防卫反射。~ **system** 保护关税制。~ **tariff** 保护(性)关税。~ **trade** 保护贸易。**-ly** *ad*. **-ness** *n*.

pro·tec·tor [prəˈtektə; prəˋtɛktɚ] *n*. 1. 保护人,拥护者。2. 防护器,保护装置;【棒球】胸甲。3. 【英史】摄政;〔the P-〕护国公。*a point ~* 铅笔套。*Lord P-* 护国公〔英国十七世纪摄政者克伦威尔父子 Oliver Cromwell 和 Richard Cromwell 的称号〕。

pro·tec·tor·al [prəˈtektərəl; prəˋtɛktərəl] *a*. 保护者的;保护国的;摄政的。

pro·tec·tor·ate [prəˈtektərit; prəˋtɛktərɪt] *n*. 1. 摄政的职位,摄政期间;〔the P-〕护国公执政时期。2. 保护领地,保护国;(强国对弱小国家的)保护制度。

pro·tec·to·ry [prəˈtektəri; prəˋtɛktərɪ] *n*. 【天主】贫儿收容所,少年感化院。

pro·tec·tress [prəˈtektris; prəˋtɛktrɪs] *n*. 女保护者。

pro·té·gé [ˈprəuteʒei, ˈprɔ-; ˋproteʒe, ˋprɑ-] *n*. (*fem*. *-gée* [-ʒei; -ʒe]) 被保护人;手下;门徒。

pro·teid [ˈprəutiːd; ˋprotiɪd] *n*. 【化】= protein.

pro·tein [ˈprotiːn; ˋprotiɪn] *n*. 【化】朊,蛋白(质)。~ **engineering** 【生化】蛋白质工程〔通过基因拼接等手段制造新药或改良农产品等〕。

pro·tein·aceous, -tein·ic, -tei·nous [ˌprəutiˈneiʃəs, -ˈtinik, ˈprəutinəs; ˏprotɪəˋneʃəs, -ˋtɪnɪk, ˋprotɪnəs] *a*. 朊的,蛋白质的。

pro·tein·ase [ˈprəutineis, ˈprəutiːi-; ˋprotɪnes, ˋprotiɪ-] *n*. 蛋白酶。

pro·tein·ate [ˈprəutineit; ˋprotɪnet] *n*. 蛋白化合物。

pro·tein·oid [ˈprəutinɔid; ˋprotɪnɔɪd] *n*. 【化】类蛋白(质)。

pro·tein·u·ri·a [ˌprəutiːnˈjuəriə, ˌprəutiin-; ˏprotinˋjuərɪə, ˏprotɪɪn-] *n*. 蛋白尿(症)。

proteo- *comb. f*. 表示"朊,蛋白质": *proteo*lysis.

pro·te·o·clas·tic [ˌprəutiəuˈklɑstik; ˏprotɪoˋklɑstɪk] *a*. (分)解蛋白的。

pro·te·ol·y·sis [ˌprəutiˈɔlisis; ˏprotɪˋɑləsɪs] *n*. 【生化】蛋白水解作用。**-lyt·ic** [-ˈlitik; -ˋlɪtɪk] *a*.

pro·te·ose [ˈprəutiəus; ˋprotɪos] *n*. 【化】朊间质,䏲。

Prot·er·o·zo·ic [ˌprɔtərəˈzəuik; ˏprɑtərəˋzoɪk] *n*., *a*. 【地】元古代[元古界](的)。

pro·test [prəˈtest; prəˋtest] I *vi*. 1. 声明,断言,坚决主张。2. 抗议,声明反对,提出异议。3. 〔古〕说,讲。— *vt*. 1. 坚决主张,坚决声明,坚持 (*that*);证明说,发誓说。2. 【商】拒付(票据)。3. 〔美〕向…提出抗议。*~ friendship* 发誓说友情不变。*~ one's innocence* [*that one is innocent*] 坚决声明无罪。II [ˈprəutest; ˋprotest] *n*. 1. 声明,断言。2. 抗议(书),不服;(期票等的)拒付说明。*a ~ for non-acceptance* [*nonpayment*] 拒收[拒付]说明。**enter** [**lodge**, **make**] **a** *~* **against** 向…提出抗议。**under** ~ 不情愿地,抗议着,在异议下。

Prot·es·tant [ˈprɔtistənt; ˋprɑtɪstənt] I *a*. 1. 新教徒的。2. 〔p-〕提出抗议的,表示不服的。II *n*. 1. 新教徒。2. 〔p-〕抗议者。

Prot·es·tant·ism [ˈprɔtistəntizəm; ˋprɑtɪstəntˏɪzm] *n*. 1. 新教;耶稣教。2. 〔集合词〕新教徒。3. 新教徒的制度[教义]。

Prot·es·tant·ize [ˈprɔtistəntaiz; ˋprɑtəstənˏtaɪz] *vt*., *vi*. (使)改信新教,(使)新教化;(使)成新教徒。

pro·tes·ta·tion [ˌprəutesˈteiʃən; ˏprɑtəsˋteʃən] *n*. 1. 声明,断言,主张 (*of*; *that*)。2. 抗议,异议(的提出);拒绝 (*against*)。

pro·test·er [prəˈtestə; prəˋtestɚ] *n*. 1. 声明者。2. 抗议者,提出异议者;拒付(期票等)者。

pro·test·ing·ly [prəˈtestiŋli; prəˋtestɪŋlɪ] *ad*. 抗议地,不服地。

Pro·teus [ˈprəutjuːs; ˋprotjus] *n*. 1. 【希神】普罗秋斯,变幻无定的海神。2. 〔p-〕容易变的东西;三心二意的〔反复无常的〕人;【动】变形虫〔阿米巴的旧名〕。3. 【动】盲螈属。~ **syndrome** 【医】普罗秋斯综合症〔包括骨隆突、骨生长增速不均、脚上皮肤皱纹过多等症状〕。

pro·tha·la·mi·on, pro·tha·la·mi·um [ˌprəuθəˈleimiən, -miəm; ˏproθəˋlemɪˏɑn, -mɪəm] *n*. (*pl*. *-mi·a* [-ə; -ə]) 祝婚歌,洞房赞。

pro·thal·li·um [prəˈθæliəm; prəˋθælɪəm] (*pl*. ***pro·thal·li·a*** [prɔˈθæliə; prɑˋθælɪə]) *n*. 【植】原叶体。

proth·e·sis [ˈprɔθisis; ˋprɑθəsɪs] *n*. 1. 【语法】词首增添字母[音节] (= prosthesis)。2. 【东正教】圣餐桌;圣餐的准备;圣餐的施舍。

pro·thon·o·tar·y [prəuˈθɔnətəri, ˌprəuθəˈnəutəri; proˋθɑnətərɪ, ˏproθəˋnotərɪ] *n*. (*pl*. *-tar·ies*) 1. 法院的首席书记。2. 【天主】罗马教皇的书记教士。

pro·tho·rax [prəuˈθɔːræks; proˋθɔræks] *n*. (*pl*. *-rax·es*, *-ra·ces* [-əˌsiːz; -əˏsiz]) 【动】前胸;前胸节。**-rac·ic** [-ˈræsik; -ˋræsɪk] *a*.

pro·throm·bin [prəuˈθrɔmbin; prəˋθrɑmbɪn] *n*. 【生化】凝血酶原。

pro·tist [ˈprəutist; ˋprotɪst] *n*. 【生】原生生物。**-tis·tan** *a*., *n*.

pro·ti·um [ˈprəutiəm; ˋprotɪəm] *n*. 【化】氕。

pro·to- *comb. f*. 表示"第一,主要,原始,最初": *proto*-Arabic 原始阿拉伯人的。

pro·to·ac·tin·i·um [ˌprəutəuækˈtiniəm; ˏprotəækˋtɪnɪəm] *n*. 【化】镤〔protactinium 的旧名〕。

pro·to·col [ˈprəutəkɔl; ˋprotəˏkɑl] I *n*. 1. 议定书;调查书,始末记。2. (条约等的)草案,草约;(罗马教皇诏书等的)首尾程式。3. 〔the P-〕法国外交部的礼宾司。II *vt*., *vi*. 1. (把…)记入议定书。2. 打(草稿),拟(草案)。

pro·to·his·to·ry [ˌprəutəuˈhistəri; ˏprotoˋhɪstərɪ] *n*. 1. 史前时期。2. 史前人类学。

pro·to·hu·man [ˌprəutəuˈhjuːmən; ˏprotoˋhjumən] *a*. 古时类人猿的,早期原始人的。

pro·to·lith·ic [ˌprəutəuˈliθik; ˏprotəˋlɪθɪk] *a*. 原始石器时代的。

pro·to·mar·tyr [ˌprəutəuˈmɑːtə; ˏprotoˋmɑrtɚ] *n*. 第一个殉道者[殉教者]。

pro·ton [ˈprəutɔn; ˋprotɑn] *n*. 【物】(正)质子;氕核,氢核始基;精朊胨。*~ decay* 质子衰变。*~-force* 质子间力。*~-scattering* 质子互致散射。

pro·to·na·tion [ˌprəutəˈneiʃən; ˏprotəˋneʃən] *n*. 质子注入。

pro·to·ne·ma [ˌprəutəuˈniːmə; ˏprotəˋnimə] *n*. (*pl*.

-*ma·ta* [-mətə; -mətə])【植】原丝体。-**l** *a*.

pro·to·ne·phrid·i·um [ˌprəutəuniˈfridiəm; ˏprotoniˋfrɪdɪəm] *n*.【动】原肾;原肾管。

pro·ton·o·tar·y, pro·thon·o·tar·y [prəuˈtɔnətəri; proˋtɑnətərɪ] *n*. (*pl*. -*tar·ies*) = prothonotary.

pro·to·nymph [ˈprəutəuˌnimf; ˋprotoˏnɪmf] *n*.【动】第一若虫。-**al** *a*.

pro·to·path·ic [ˌprəutəuˈpæθik; ˏprotoˋpæθɪk] *a*.【生理】(皮肤的)初感的;原始的,初期的。

pro·to·phyte [ˈprəutəfait; ˋprotəfaɪt] *n*.【植】原生植物,单细胞植物。

pro·to·plasm [ˈprəutəplæzəm; ˋprotəˏplæzəm] *n*.【生】原生质;原浆;细胞质。-**plas·mat·ic, -ic** *a*.

pro·to·plast [ˈprəutəplæst; ˋprotəˏplæst] *n*. 原人;原物;原生动物;【生】原生质体。

pro·to·ste·le [ˈprəutəstiːl, -stiːli; ˋprotəstil, -stilɪ] *n*.【生】原生中柱。-**ste·lic** *a*.

pro·to·troph·ic [ˌprəutəuˈtrɔfik; ˏprotəˋtrɑfɪk] *a*.【生】原始营养的,原养型的(固氮细菌),不需有机营养的。

pro·to·type [ˈprəutətaip; ˋprotəˏtaɪp] *n*. **1**. 原型;典型;样板;模范,标准。**2**. 试制型式;样机;样品;【物】原器。-**typ·al, -typ·ic, -i·cal** *a*.

prot·ox·ide [prəuˈtɔksaid; proˋtɑksaɪd] *n*. 初氧化物,低(价)氧化物。

pro·to·xy·lem [ˈprəutəzailəm, -lem; ˋprotəzaɪləm, -lɛm] *n*.【植】原生木质部。

Pro·to·zo·a [ˌprəutəuˈzəuə; ˏprotəˋzoə] *n*. [*pl*.]【动】原生动物门。

pro·to·zo·an, pro·to·zo·ic [ˌprəutəuˈzəuən, -ˈzəuik; ˏprotəˋzoən, -ˋzoɪk] **I** *n*. 原生动物 (= protozoon)。**II** *a*. 原生动物的。

pro·to·zo·ol·o·gy [ˌprəutəuzəuˈɔlədʒi; ˏprotəzoˋɑlədʒɪ] *n*. 原生动物学。

pro·to·zo·on [ˌprəutəuˈzəuən; ˏprotəˋzoɑn] *n*. (*pl*. *pro·to·zo·a* [-ə; -ə]) 原生动物。-**al** *a*.

pro·tract [prəˈtrækt; proˋtrækt] *vt*. **1**. 拖长,延长。**2**. (用比例尺半圆规)画(线),画(角),制(图)。**3**.【解】伸出,突出 (*opp*. retract)。~ *one's stay for some weeks* 多逗留几个星期。~*ed disease* 拖得很久的病。*a* ~*ed test* 疲劳试验。*a* ~*ed warfare* 持久战。

pro·tract·ile [prəˈtræktail; proˋtræktɪl] *a*. (动物器官等)可伸长的。

pro·trac·tion [prəˈtrækʃən; proˋtrækʃən] *n*. **1**. 拖延;伸长,延长。**2**. 制图。

pro·trac·tor [prəˈtræktə; proˋtræktɚ] *n*. **1**. 半圆规,分度规,量角器。**2**.【解】牵引肌。**3**.【外】异物取除器;钳取器。**4**. 使延长的人。*a bevel*(*ed*) ~ 角度尺,斜角规,活动量角器。

pro·trude [prəˈtruːd; proˋtrud] *vt*., *vi*. (推)出;(使)突出;(使)伸出 (*beyond*)。~ *one's tongue* 伸出舌头。*protruding eyes* 凸眼。

pro·trud·ent [prəˈtruːdənt; proˋtrudənt] *a*. 突出的,伸出的。

pro·tru·sile [prəˈtruːsail; proˋtrusɪl] *a*. 可突出的,可伸出的。

pro·tru·sion [prəˈtruːʒən; proˋtruʒən] *n*. **1**. 突出,伸出;突起;隆起。**2**. 突起部,隆起物。

pro·tru·sive [prəˈtruːsiv; proˋtrusɪv] *a*. 突出的,伸出的;突兀的;触目的。

pro·tu·ber·ance [prəˈtjuːbərəns; proˋtjubərəns] *n*. 突起;突出部;瘤,节疤,疙瘩。*a solar* ~【天】日珥。*a* ~ *on a tree* 树节疤。*a cancerous* ~ 癌肿。

pro·tu·ber·ant [prəˈtjuːbərənt; proˋtjubərənt] *a*. 凸出的,突起的,隆起的;显著的。

pro·tu·ber·ate [prəuˈtjuːbəreit, -ˌtuː-; proˋtjubəˏret, -ˏtu-] *vi*. (-*at·ed*; -*at·ing*) 凸出,隆起,突起。

pro·tyle, pro·tyl [ˈprəutail; ˋprotaɪl] *n*.【化】(不可分)原质[想像中认为构成原素的物质]。*the* ~ *theory* (物质)单元(学)说。

proud [praud; praʊd] **I** *a*. **1**. 傲慢的,骄傲的。**2**. 有自尊心的,自重的;有见识的。**3**. 自豪的,得意的,高兴的,引以为荣的 (*of*)。**4**. 光荣的,漂亮的,高尚的,堂皇的。**5**. 溢出的;涨水的;凸现出来的。**6**. [古]勇敢的;[诗](马等)活蹦乱跳的。*a* ~ *man* 傲慢的人。*He is too* ~ *to ask questions*. 他太骄傲,总不问人。*a* ~ *father* (因有好儿子而)得意的父亲。*a* ~ *sight* 壮丽景色。*a* ~ *achievement* 辉煌的成就。*a* ~ *occasion* 隆重的场合。*a* ~ *tailor* [方]金翅雀。**as** ~ **as Punch** [*a peacock*] 扬扬得意。**be** ~ **of** 以…自豪,对…感觉得意[光荣] (*I am* ~ *of his acquaintance*. 我因认识他而觉得自豪)。~ **flesh** (伤口长好后凸出的)疤;【医】浮肉。**too** ~ **to fight** 战争有违自尊心,不屑战争。**II** *ad*. [口] = proudly. **do one** ~ [口]给面子,使欢喜 (*You do me* ~. (你这样说)令我感到荣幸。*It will do me* ~. 这将使我很满意)。**do oneself** ~ 干得漂亮,有面子;得意;养尊处优。~-**hearted** *a*. 骄傲的,傲慢的。-**ly** *ad*.

Prou·dhon [pruːˈdɔŋ, F. pruˈdɔ̃; pruˋdɑŋ, ˏpruˋdɔ̃], **P**. **J**. 蒲鲁东[1809—1865,法国经济学家和社会学家]。

Prou·dhon·ism [pruːˈdɔŋizəm; pruˋdɔŋɪzəm] *n*. 蒲鲁东主义。-**ist** *n*. 蒲鲁东主义者。

Proust [pruːst; prust] *n*. 普鲁斯特[姓氏]。

Prov. = **1**. Proverbs. **2**. Province. **3**. Provençal. **4**. Provence.

prov. = **1**. provincial. **2**. provisional. **3**. provost.

prov·a·ble [ˈpruːvəbl; ˋpruvəbl] *a*. 可证明的;可证实的。-**bly** *ad*. -**ness** *n*.

prove [pruːv; pruv] *vt*. (-**d**; -**d**, [古、美] ***prov·en*** [ˈpruːvən; ˋpruvən]) **1**. 证明,证实;【法】验证,检定。**2**. 试验;检验(武器的效力)。**3**. 勘察,探明。**4**.【数】证,证明,验算,检算。**5**.【印】打(校样)。**6**. [古]体验。~ *oneself worthy of confidence* 证明有信用;不负信赖。~ *a gun* 试炮。*the proving ground*【军】试炮场,打靶场。~*d reserves* (石油、天然气等的)已探明储量。*I* ~*d the extreme depths of poverty*. 我体验过极贫苦的生活。— *vi*. 结果是…,成为…;试验。*He* ~*d* (*to be*) *a swindler*. 他原来是个骗子。~ **up** (*on a claim*) 具备(提出某某要求的)条件。~ **up to the hilt** 充分证明。

prov·en [ˈpruːvən; ˋpruvən] **I** [古、美] prove 的过去分词。**II** *a*. 被证明了的。**not** ~ [Scot.]【法】证据不足。

prov·e·nance [ˈprɔvinəns; ˋprɑvənəns] *n*. 起源,出处;原产地。*of doubtful* ~ 出处可疑的。

Prov·en·çal [ˌprɔvɑ̃ːnˈsɑːl; ˏprovənˋsɑl] **I** *a*. (法国)普罗旺斯州 (Provence) (人)的。**II** *n*. 普罗旺斯人[语]。

Pro·vence [prɔˈvɑ̃ːns; ˋprɑvɛns] *n*. 普罗旺斯[法国东南一地区,中世纪时以诗歌与武侠著称]。

prov·en·der [ˈprɔvində; ˋprɑvəndɚ] *n*. 饲料,粮草,秣;[谑](人的)食物。

pro·ve·ni·ence [prəuˈviːniəns, -ˈviːnjəns; proˋvinɪəns, -ˋvinjəns] *n*. [美] = provenance.

pro·ven·tric·u·lus [ˌprəuvinˈtrikjuləs; ˏprovɪnˋtrɪkjuləs] *n*. (*pl*. -**li** [-ˌlai; -ˏlaɪ])【动】**1**. 鸟的前胃。**2**. 蚯蚓和龙虾的前胃。

prov·er [ˈpruːvə; ˋpruvɚ] *n*. **1**. 试验装置。**2**.【印】打校样的工人。**3**. [古]证明者。

prov·erb [ˈprɔvəb, -əːb; ˋprɑvɝb, -ɝb] *n*. **1**. 谚语,古语;俗话;箴言。**2**. 话柄,笑柄。**3**. 人人知道的事情;有名的事情。**4**. 俚谚剧。**5**. [*pl*.] 俚谚游戏。*His punctuality is a* ~. = *He is a* ~ *for punctuality*. 他严守时间是有名的。*The* (*Book of*) *P-s* (基督教《旧约全书》)《箴言》。**as the** ~ **goes** [**runs**] 俗话说。**pass into a** ~ **1**. 成为谚语。**2**. 成话柄。**to a** ~ 弄到出名 (*He is punctual to a* ~. 他严守时间是人所共知的)。

P

pro-verb [ˈprəuvəːb; ˋprovɚb] *n*.【语法】代动词。
pro·ver·bi·al [prəˈvəːbiəl; prəˋvɝbɪəl] *a*. 1. 谚语(式)的。2. 已成话柄的。3. 出名的,天下闻名的。*the* ~ *London fog* 有名的伦敦雾。
pro·ver·bi·al·ist [prəˈvəːbjəlist; prəˋvɝbɪəlɪst] *n*. 善用谚语的人;谚语作者;集谚者。
pro·ver·bi·al·ly [prəˈvəːbjəli; prəˋvɝbɪəlɪ] *ad*. 1. 如谚语所说。2. 广泛地,一般(所知道)地。*Why, medicine is* ~ *nasty*. 药当然难吃啰。
pro·vide [prəˈvaid; prəˋvaɪd] *vt*. 1. (为某人)提供,供应某物(*for sb*.);(以某物)供给某人,(以某物)装备另一物(*with*)。2. (条约,法律等)规定(*that*)。3.【宗史】任命,指定…做候补牧师(*to*)。4.【法】考虑,酌量(*for*)。5.〔古〕准备,预备。~ *food and clothes for one's family* 为家里人供应衣食。~ *one's family with food and clothes* 以衣食供应家里人。~ *children with a good education* 为儿童提供良好的教育条件。~ *a car with radio* 给汽车装上无线电设备。*Sheep* ~ *us with wool*. 羊供给我们羊毛。*She was* ~*d for, at any rate*. 她总算有了一个着落。— *vi*. 1. 作准备(*for*);预防(*against*)。2. 赡养;提供生计(*for*)。3. 规定(*for*);禁止(*against*)。~ *for old age* 防老。~ *against accident* 以防万一。~ *for one's children* 抚养子女。*The constitution* ~*s for an elected two-chamber legislature*. 宪法规定设置经选举产生的两院制立法机构。~ ***oneself*** 自备,自办。
pro·vid·ed [prəːˈvaidid; prəˋvaɪdɪd] **I** *conj*. 倘若…,只要,在…条件下。*I will come* ~ (*that*) *I am well enough*. 我身体好一定来。**II** *a*. 预备好的;由…供给的。~ **school**〔英〕(靠地方税维持的)公立小学校。
Prov·i·dence [ˈprɔvidəns; ˋprɑvədəns] *n*. 普罗维登斯〔美、加城市〕。
prov·i·dence [ˈprɔvidəns; ˋprɑvədəns] *n*. 1.〔常 P-〕神意,天道,天命;〔P-〕神,上帝。2.〔罕〕精明,深谋远虑;节约。3.【古】准备。*a visitation of P-* 天灾。***a special*** ~ 1. 天助,天佑。2. 自然力,命运。
prov·i·dent [ˈprɔvidənt; ˋprɑvədənt] *a*. 1. 有先见之明。2. 精明的,节俭的。*He is* ~ *of his money*. 他用钱很节省。**-ly** *ad*.
prov·i·den·tial [ˌprɔviˈdenʃəl; ˏprɑvəˋdɛnʃəl] *a*. 神意的;天佑的,幸运的。**-ly** *ad*. 照天意,靠天佑。
pro·vid·er [prəˈvaidə; prəˋvaɪdɚ] *n*. 1. 供给者,准备者。2. 需供养家庭的人。*a lion's* ~【动】豺狼(= jackal);为虎作伥的人;被人利用的人,爪牙。*a universal* ~ 杂货商。*a good* ~ 能使家属丰衣美食的人。
pro·vid·ing [prəˈvaidiŋ; prəˋvaɪdɪŋ] *conj*. = provided.
provinc. = provincial.
prov·ince [ˈprɔvins; ˋprɑvɪns] *n*. 1. 省,州;〔*pl*.〕地区,地方;〔the ~s〕乡下。2. 本分;职责;(学问等的)范围。3.【宗】大教区;【罗马史】(国外)行省;(旧时)英国在北美的殖民地。*one's native* ~ 故乡。*London and the* ~*s*〔英〕中央和(全国各)地方。***be within one's*** ~ 在某人职权内,是某人的本分。***in the*** ~***s*** 在地方上,在乡下。
pro·vin·cial [prəˈvinʃəl; prəˋvɪnʃəl] **I** *a*. 1. 地方的,乡下的。2. 省的,州的;领地的。3. 乡下气的;鄙俗的,粗野的;地方性的,褊狭的。4.〔英〕大教区的。*a* ~ *accent* 土腔。*a* ~ *paper* 地方报。**II** *n*. 地方居民,乡下人;【英宗】(管辖教区的)大主教。**-ly** *ad*.
pro·vin·cial·ism [prəˈvinʃəlizəm; prəˋvɪnʃəlˏɪzəm] *n*. 1. 乡下气,粗野。2. 土腔,方言。3. 地区性,褊狭;地方感情,乡土观念。4. 地方主义。
pro·vin·cial·ist [prəˈvinʃəlist; prəˋvɪnʃəlɪst] *n*. 1. 地方居民,外省人;乡下人。2. 地方主义者。
pro·vin·ci·al·i·ty [prəˌvinʃiˈæliti; prəˏvɪnʃɪˋælətɪ] *n*. 1. 地方风尚。2. 乡下气,土气;粗野。
pro·vin·cial·ize [prəˈvinʃəlaiz; prəˋvɪnʃəlˏaɪz] *vt*., *vi*. (使)地方化,(使)带乡下气;(使)乡土化人;用方言[土腔]讲。
pro·vi·sion [prəˈviʒən; prəˋvɪʒən] **I** *n*. 1. 预备,准备,设备(*for*; *against*);供应,(一批)供应品;生活物质;储备物资。2.〔*pl*.〕食品,粮食。3.【法】规定,条项,条款。*an express* ~【法】明文(规定)。*the* ~*s of lease* 租借条款。***according to the*** ~***s of the Act*** 据该法令各条(所说)。***make ample*** ~ ***for*** 充裕地供养。***make*** ~ 预备,准备(*against*)。***run out of*** ~***s*** = ***short of*** ~***s*** 粮食缺乏。**II** *vt*. 向…供应粮食[必需品]。~ **merchant** 食品商人。**-er** *n*. 粮食筹办员。**-ment** *n*. 粮食供应。
pro·vi·sion·al [prəˈviʒənl; prəˋvɪʒənl̩] *a*. 假定的,暂时的,临时的。*a* ~ *consent* 假答应。~ *charter* 临时执照〔证书〕。*a* ~ *government* 临时政府。~ *headquarters* 行营。*the P- 37th Division* 暂编第 37 师。*a* ~ *order* 紧急命令。*a* ~ *treaty* 临时条约。**-ly** *ad*.
pro·vi·sion·al·i·ty [prəˌviʒəˈnæliti; prəˏvɪʒənˋælətɪ] *n*. 临时性,暂时性。
pro·vi·sion·a·ry [prəˈviʒənəri; prəˋvɪʒənˏɛrɪ] *a*.〔罕〕= provisional.
pro·vi·so [prəˈvaizəu; prəˋvaɪzo] *n*. (*pl*. *-sos*, *-soes*) 附带条款,附文;条件,但书,限制性条款。*I make it a* ~ *that*... 以…为附带条件。*with the* [*a*] ~ *that*... 以…为条件。
pro·vi·sor [prəˈvaizə; prəˋvaɪzɚ] *n*. 1. 伙食采办者。2.【宗】(尤其指未出缺的)圣职的被委任者。3.【天主】副主教,代理主教。
pro·vi·so·ry [prəˈvaizəri; prəˋvaɪzərɪ] *a*. 1. 有附文的;有附带条件的。2. 临时的,暂定的。*a* ~ *clause* 附文;附带条款;限制性条款,保留条款。
pro·vi·ta·min [prəuˈvaitəmin; proˋvaɪtəmɪn] *n*.【生化】维生素原,原维生素。
pro·vo [ˈprəuvəu; ˋprovo] *n*. (*pl*. *-vos*) 青年无政府主义者〔在一些欧洲国家内自由地组织起来的无政府主义运动的青年〕。
pro·voc·a·ble, pro·vok·a·ble [prəˈvəukəbl; prəˋvokəbl̩] *a*. 易受刺激[煽动、挑拨]的。
pro·vo·ca·teur [prɔvɔkatœːr; prɔvɔkatœːr] *n*. [F.] (*fem*. *-trice* [-tris; -trɪs]) 坐探,奸细,内奸(= *agent* ~);(故意煽动肇事的)破坏分子,煽动者。
prov·o·ca·tion [ˌprɔvəˈkeiʃən; ˏprɑvəˋkeʃən] *n*. 1. 触怒;挑拨,挑衅;刺激,煽动;诱发。2. 惹人恼火的事;刺激的原因。3. 愤怒,发怒,发脾气。~ *and estrangement* 挑拨离间。***at the slightest*** ~ = on the slightest ~. ***give*** ~ 激怒,使发怒。***make*** ~ ***against*** 挑衅。***on the slightest*** ~ 动不动就…,并不因为什么了不起的事就…。***under*** ~ 在愤怒下。***without*** ~ 无缘无故。~ **method** 诱发试验法。
pro·voc·a·tive [prəˈvɔkətiv; prəˋvɑkətɪv] **I** *a*. 1. 气(人)的,使人生气的,寻衅的,挑衅的;挑拨性的,刺激性的,(言语、态度等)煽动性的。2. 使引起…的(*of*);引起争论[议论、兴趣等]的。~ *behaviour* 惹人恼火的行为。*be* ~ *of mirth* 引人发笑。**II** *n*. 刺激物;兴奋剂。**-ly** *ad*.
pro·voke [prəˈvəuk; prəˋvok] *vt*. 1. 触怒,使愤怒,激怒。2. 成为…的原因,引起。3. 驱使,逼使;激发,煽动某人做某事(*to sth*., *to do sth*.)。*Don't allow yourself to be* ~*d*. 你不要激动;你别发火。~ *riot* 引起骚乱。~ *indignation* 激起义愤。*This is thought-provoking*. 这是耐人寻味的[颇有启发性的]。~ *sb*. *to anger* 惹怒某人。*Oppression* ~*d the people to rebellion*. 压迫逼得老百姓们起来造反了。**-r** *n*.
pro·vok·ing [prəˈvəukiŋ; prəˋvokɪŋ] *a*. 气人的,叫人冒火的,难熬的,叫人焦躁的。**-ly** *ad*.
pro·vo·lo·ne [ˌprəuvəˈləuni, ˌprɔvə-; ˏprovəˋlonɪ, ˏprɑvə-] *n*. [It.] 意大利熏干酪〔一种硬的浅色干酪,梨形,通常用烟熏制成〕。
prov·ost [ˈprɔvəst; ˋprɑvəst] *n*. 1.〔英〕(牛津剑桥等大

学某些学院的)院长;〔美〕教务长。2.【史】大教堂主监;修道院长;宗教团体首领。3.〔Scot.〕市长。4.(德国城市新教教会的)牧师。5.[prəˈvəu; prəˋvəu]【军】宪兵 ~ **court** 宪兵法庭。~ **marshal** 宪兵司令。**P- Marshal Department** 宪兵司令部。~ **sergeant** 宪兵军士。

prow[1][prau; praʊ] *n*. 船首,舳;飞机头部;〔诗〕船。

prow[2][prau; praʊ] *a*.〔古〕英勇的,威风凛凛的。

prow·ess [ˈprauis; ˋpraʊɪs] *n*. 英勇;威力;本事。*show one's* ~ 显威风;显本事。

prowl [praul; praʊl] **I** *vi*. 1.(小偷等)鬼鬼祟祟地踱来踱去;(觅食的野兽)悄悄地荡来荡去。2.徘徊(*about*)。— *vt*. 1.在…鬼鬼祟祟地荡来荡去。2.在…徘徊。**II** *n*. 1.(野兽)到处觅食;(小偷)四处探头探脑。2.徘徊;潜行。*be* [*go*] *on the* ~(尤指小偷伺机)踱来踱去。*take a* ~ 荡来荡去。~ *car*〔美〕警备车。

prowl·er [ˈpraulə; ˋpraʊlɚ] *n*. 荡来荡去的人,徘徊者;秘密警察;小偷(等)。

prox. =〔L.〕*proximo*.

prox·i·mal [ˈprɔksiməl; ˋprɑksəml̩] *a*. 1.【解】近身体中心的;近基的;近轴的 (*opp*. distal)。2.最接近的,近似的。**-ly** *ad*.

prox·i·mate [ˈprɔksimit; ˋprɑksəˏmet] *a*. 1.最接近的,近似的。2.即将到来[发生]的。*the* ~ *cause* 近因,直接原因。~ *principles* 近似成分。*the* ~ *grade* 次一级。**-ly** *ad*.

prox·i·me ac·ces·sit [ˈprɔksimi ækˈsesit; ˋprɑksɪmɪ ækˋsesɪt] (*pl*. ***accesserunt*** [-ˈsiərənt; ˋsɪərənt]) 〔L.〕(赛跑等的)第二名;第二。*I was* [*I got a*] *proxime accessit*. 我得了第二。

prox·im·e·ter [prɔkˈsimitə; prɑkˋsɪmɪtɚ] *n*.【空】着陆高度计。

prox·im·i·ty [prɔkˈsimiti; prɑkˋsɪmətɪ] *n*. 接近,邻近;临近;接近度,距离;亲近 (*to*)。~ *of blood* 近亲。***in close*** ~ (***to***) 与…极接近,紧靠。***in the*** ~ ***of*** 在…附近。~ **effect** 邻近效应。~**-fused**【火箭】备有近爆引信的,装有近发[无线电]引信的。~ **talks** 毗邻会谈〔谈判双方各自占用相邻近而被分隔开的场所,由调停人来往传话进行的外交会谈〕。

prox·i·mo [ˈprɔksiməu; ˋprɑksɪmo] *ad*.〔L.〕下月〔略 *prox*.〕。*on the 10th prox*. 下月十日。★现在多用 next month.

prox·y [ˈprɔksi; ˋprɑksɪ] *n*. 1.代理(权);代表(权);代理投票。2.代理人,代表人;代用品。3.(对代理人的)委托书。***by*** ~ 用代理人,由代表。***stand*** [***be***] ~ ***for*** 做…的代理人,代表…。

prs. = 1. pairs. 2. printers.

PRT = personal rapid transit 个人高速公共交通系统〔一种自动化小客车,乘客可随时按电钮停车下车〕。

prtd. = printed.

prtg. = printing.

prude [pruːd; prud] *n*. 过分拘谨的人,显得[装作]正经的人〔尤指女人〕。

Pru·dence [ˈpruːdəns; ˋprudns] *n*. 普鲁登丝〔女子名〕。

pru·dence [ˈpruːdəns; ˋprudns] *n*. 1.小心,谨慎。2.精明。3.节俭。***in common*** ~ 应有的小心。***use*** ~ 采取慎重态度。

pru·dent [ˈpruːdənt; ˋprudnt] *a*. 1.小心的,慎重的,顾虑周到的,稳健的。2.世故的,精明的。3.节俭的,会打算的。*be modest and* ~ 谦虚谨慎。**-ly** *ad*.

pru·den·tial [pru(ː)ˈdenʃəl; pruˋdɛnʃəl] **I** *a*. 1.谨慎的;考虑周到的。2.备咨询的。*a* ~ *committee*〔美〕(学校、教会等的)咨询委员会。**II** *n*.〔*pl*.〕必须慎重的事;慎重的考虑。**-ism** *n*. 谨慎第一。**-ist** *n*. 谨慎小心的人。**-ly** *ad*.

pru·d·er·y [ˈpruːdəri; ˋprudərɪ] *n*. 过分拘谨;装正经,假正经。

prud'homme [pruːˈdɔm; pruˋdɑm] *n*.〔F.〕1.【法】劳资纠纷调解委员。2.行家,里手。

prud·ish [ˈpruːdiʃ; ˋprudɪʃ] *a*. 1.过分拘谨的。2.一本正经的,假正经的。**-ly** *ad*.

pru·i·nose [ˈpruːinəus; ˋpruənos] *a*.【植】具白粉的,具果霜的。

prune[1] [pruːn; prun] *vt*. 1.修剪(树枝),剪除,伐除 (*down*);砍去 (*away*; *off*)。2.省去(费用等);删掉,除去(多余部分)。~ *a writing of superfluous words* 删去文章中的冗语。

prune[2] [pruːn; prun] *n*. 1.洋李脯,梅干。2.深紫红色的。3.〔美〕没趣的人,讨厌的人;蠢货。***full of*** ~***s***〔美俚〕傲慢的;完全错误的,胡诌的。~ **peddler**〔美〕食品商,食品店员。~ **picker**〔美〕果园工人。~**s and prisms** 装腔作势;矫揉造作的(人或言语)。

prune[3] [pruːn; prun] *vt*.〔罕〕= preen.

pru·nel·la[1] [pru(ː)ˈnelə; pruˋnɛlə] *n*. 英国普鲁涅拉斜纹薄呢。

pru·nel·la[2] [pru(ː)ˈnelə; pruˋnɛlə] *n*. 1.【医】鹅口疮,霉菌性口炎。2.〔P-〕【植】夏枯草属。

prun·ing [ˈpruːniŋ; ˋprunɪŋ] *n*. 1.(树等的)修剪。2.【电】切断分路。~ **hook** 修枝钩镰。~ **shears** 剪枝剪。

pru·ri·ence, pru·ri·en·cy [ˈpruəriəns, -si; ˋprʊrɪəns, -sɪ] *n*. 1.好色。2.渴望,热望。

pru·ri·ent [ˈpruəriənt; ˋprʊrɪənt] *a*. 1.好色的。2.〔罕〕渴想的。3.(枝、芽等)伸得过长的。**-ly** *ad*.

pru·ri·go [pruəˈraigəu; prʊˋraɪgo] *n*.【医】痒疹。

pru·ri·tus [pruəˈraitəs; prʊˋraɪtəs] *n*. 瘙痒。**pru·rit·ic** [-ˈritik; -ˋrɪtɪk] *a*.

Prus(s). = Prussia(n).

Prus·sia [ˈprʌʃə; ˋprʌʃə] *n*.【史】普鲁士。

Prus·sian [ˈprʌʃən; ˋprʌʃən] **I** *a*. 普鲁士(人)的;普鲁士式的〔指训练严酷的、军国主义的和妄自尊大的〕。**II** *n*. 1.普鲁士人。2.(古)普鲁士语。~ **blue**【化】普鲁士蓝;绀青色。

Prus·sian·ism [ˈprʌʃənizəm; ˋprʌʃənɪzm] *n*. 大普鲁士主义〔特指普鲁士统治阶级的专横、黩武主义和严酷纪律性〕。

Prus·sian·ize [ˈprʌʃənaiz; ˋprʌʃənˏaɪz] *vt*. 使普鲁士化〔尤指严格的纪律和服从权威方面〕。**-i·za·tion** *n*.

prus·si·ate [ˈprʌʃiit; ˋprʌʃɪɪt] *n*.【化】氰化物;亚铁氰化物;铁氰化物;氢氰酸盐。

prus·sic [ˈprʌsik; ˋprʌsɪk] *a*.【化】(从)氰化物(得来)的。~ **acid**【化】氢氰酸,氰化氢。

pru·ta [ˈpruːtɑ, pruːˈtɑː; ˋprutɑ, pruˋtɑ] *n*. (*pl*. ***prutot*** [-ˈtəut; -tot]) 普鲁达〔以色列的辅币单位,相等于 1/1000以色列镑〕。

pry[1] [prai; praɪ] **I** *vi*. (***pried***) 眼睛盯着看,盯;窥探;刺探,打听 (*into*)。**II** *n*. 1.窥视;窥探。2.爱刺探的人。~ ***about*** 到处窥探。~ ***into other people's affairs*** 打听别人的事情。~ ***out*** 探出(别人秘密等)。

pry[2] [prai; praɪ]〔美、英方〕**I** *n*. 撬具;杆子,杠杆。**II** *vt*. (用杠杆等)撬,撬起,撬动;(用尽方法)使脱离。

pry·er [ˈpraiə; ˋpraɪɚ] *n*. 窥探者,打听(别人事情)者 (= prier)。

pry·ing [ˈpraiiŋ; ˋpraɪɪŋ] *a*. 窥视的;窥探的;爱刺探的。

Prynne [prin; prɪn] *n*. 普林〔姓氏〕。

pryth·ee [ˈpriðiː; ˋprɪðɪ] *int*.〔古语、口〕请,求求你 (= prithee)。

PS., p.s. = postscript.

P.S., PS = 1. passenger steamer 客轮。2. permanent secretary 常任书记。3. privy seal〔英〕御玺;Privy Seal = Lord Privy Seal〔英〕掌玺大臣。4. public school (英国的)公学;(美国的)公立中学[小学]。5. police sergeant 警官,巡官。6. prompt side〔英〕舞台上演员的左方;〔美〕舞台上演员的右方。7. postscript. 8. per second 每秒。

Ps. = Psalms.

ps. = 1. pieces. 2. pseudonym.

p/s; p/s. = periods per second 周/秒。

PSI = personized system of instruction【教】个人化教学系统。

psalm [sɑːm; sɑm] **I** *n*. 1.【宗】赞美诗,圣诗,圣歌。2. 〔P-〕〔*pl*.〕【圣】《诗篇》。**II** *vt*. 用赞美诗祝贺。~ **book** = Psalter. **-ist** *n*. 赞美诗[诗篇]作者;〔the Psalmist〕《诗篇》作者,大卫 (David) 王。

psal·mo·dy [ˈsælmədi, ˈsɑːmə-; ˋsɑmədɪ, ˋsɑmə-] *n*. 【宗】唱赞美诗;赞美诗集。**-ic, -i·cal** *a*. **-dist** *n*. 唱赞美诗的人;赞美诗作者。

P

Psal·ter [ˈsɔːltə; ˋsɔltɚ] *n*. 1.【圣】《诗篇》。2. 〔p-〕(祷告用的)分印诗篇。

psal·te·ri·um [sɔlˈtiəriəm; sɔlˋtɪrɪəm] *n*. (*pl*. **-ri·a** [-ə; -ə]) 重瓣胃 (= omasum)。

psal·ter·y [ˈsɔːltəri; ˋsɔltrɪ] *n*. 1. (14—15 世纪的)八弦琴。2. 〔P-〕 = Psalter.

psam·mite [ˈsæmait; ˋsæmaɪt] *n*. 〔罕〕【地】砂屑岩 (= sandstone)。**-mit·ic** [-ˈmitik; -ˋmɪtɪk] *a*.

psam·mon [ˈsæmɔn; ˋsæmɑn] *n*. 【生态】适砂[喜砂]生物。

psam·mo·phile [ˈsæməfail; ˋsæməfaɪl] *n*. 喜砂性生物[有机体],适砂植物。

psam·mo·phyte [ˈsæməfait; ˋsæməfaɪt] *n*. 砂生植物。

pse·phite [ˈsiːfait; ˋsifaɪt] *n*. 砾质岩。**-phit·ic** [-ˈfitik; -ˋfɪtɪk] *a*.

pse·phol·ogy [siːˈfɔlədʒi; siˋfɑlədʒɪ] *n*. 选举学[对选举结果的统计估价]。**-log·i·cal** [-ˈlɔdʒikl; -ˋlɑdʒɪkl̩] *a*. **-gist** *n*.

pse·pho·man·cy [ˈsiːfəmænsi; ˋsifəmænsɪ] *n*. 石(子)(占)卜。

pseud. = pseudonym.

pseu·de·pig·ra·pha [ˌsjuːdiˈpigrəfə, ˏsuː-; ˏsjudəˋpɪgrəfə, ˏsu-] *n*. 〔*pl*.〕〔亦作 P-〕圣经的模拟作品,圣经的伪仿作品〔所写的虽是经中的人物但不是圣典的正经〕。**-phous** [-fəs; -fəs] *a*.

pseud(o)- *comb. f*. 表示"伪,拟,假,赝": *pseudo*archaic; *pseudo*classical; *pseudo*-martyr; *pseudo*- plastic.

pseu·do [ˈ*p*sjuːdəu; ˋsjudo] *a*. 〔口〕假,伪,冒充的。

pseu·do·al·um [*p*sjuːdəuˈæləm, ˌsuː-; sjudoˋæləm, ˏsu-] *n*. 假矾。

pseu·do·ar·cha·ic [*p*sjuːdəuɑːˈkɑːik; ˏsudoɑrˋkeɪk] *a*. 拟古的。

pseu·do·carp [ˈ*p*sjuːdəukɑːp, ˈsuː-; ˋsjudəkɑrp, ˋsu-] *n*. 假果 (= false fruit)。**-ous** *a*.

pseu·do·clas·sic [*p*sjuːdəuˈklæsik, ˌsuː-; ˏsjudəˋklæsɪk, ˏsu-] **I** *a*. 拟古典的,伪古典的。**II** *n*. 拟古典的东西。

pseu·do·clas·si·cism [ˈ*p*sjuːdəuˈklæsisizəm; ˏsjudəˋklæsəsɪzm] *n*. 拟古体;拟古典主义;伪古典主义。

pseu·do-dem·o·crat·ic [ˈpsjuːdəuˌdeməˈkrætik; ˋsjudoˏdɛməˋkrætɪk] *a*. 假民主的。

pseu·do·graph [ˈ*p*sjuːdəugrɑːf; ˋsjudoˏgræf] *n*. 伪书,冒名著作。

pseu·do·her·maph·ro·dite [*p*sjuːdəuhəˈmæfrədait, ˌsuː-; ˏsjudohɚˋmæfrədaɪt, ˏsu-] *n*. 【医】假两性畸形。**-dit·ic** [-ˈditik; -ˋdɪtɪk] *a*. **-dit·ism, -rod·ism** *n*.

Pseu·do·la·rix [*p*sjudəuˈlæriks; sjudoˋlærɪks] *n*. 【植】金钱松属。

pseu·dol·o·gy [*p*sjuːˈdɔlədʒi; sjuˋdɑlədʒɪ] *n*. 谎话;说谎。

pseu·do-mar·tyr [*p*sjuːdəuˈmɑːtə; sjudoˋmɑrtɚ] *n*. 伪殉教者。

pseu·do·morph [ˈ*p*sjuːdəmɔːf; ˋsjudəmɔrf] *n*. 1.【矿】假晶,假同晶,赝形体。2. 假象,伪形。**-ic, -ous** *a*.

pseu·do·nym [ˈ*p*sjuːdənim; ˋsjudn̩ˏɪm] *n*. 假名;(特指作者的)笔名。

pseu·do·nym·i·ty [ˌpsjuːdəuˈnimiti; ˏsjudəˋnɪmətɪ] *n*. 使用假名[笔名];签有假名[笔名]。

pseu·don·y·mous [*p*sjuːˈdɔniməs; sjuˋdɑnəməs] *a*. 用假名[笔名]写的;签有假名[笔名]的;用假名[笔名]的。

pseu·do·plas·tic [ˌ*p*sjuːdəuˈplæstik; ˏsjudoˋplæstɪk] *n*. 类塑料,代塑料,假塑性体。

pseu·do·po·di·um [*p*sjuːdəuˈpəudiəm; ˏsjudəˋpodɪəm] *n*. (*pl*. **-di·a** [-ə; -ə]) 【动】假足,伪足 (= pseudopod)。**-dop·o·dal** [-ˈdɔpədəl; -ˋdɑpədəl] *a*.

pseu·do·preg·nan·cy [ˌ*p*sjuːdəuˈpregnənsi; ˏsjudoˋpregnənsɪ] *n*. (*pl*. **-cies**)【医】假孕。**-preg·nant** *a*.

pseu·do·salt [*p*sjuːdəuˈsɔːlt, suː-; sjudoˋsɔlt, su-] *n*. 假盐[不能电离的盐]。

pseu·do·sci·ence [*p*sjuːdəuˈsaiəns; ˏsjudoˋsaɪəns] *n*. 假科学,伪科学。**-sci·en·tif·ic** *a*.

pseu·do·scope [ˈ*p*sjuːdəskəup; ˋsjudəˏskop] *n*. 【物】幻视镜 (*opp*. stereoscope)。

p.s.f., psf = pounds per square foot 每平方英尺上的磅数,磅/英尺²。

pshaw [pʃɔː; ʃɔ] **I** *int*. 啐! 哼! 〔表示轻蔑、讨厌、急躁〕。**II** *n*. 啐[哼]的声音。**III** *vi*., *vt*. 啐一声 (*at*);用鼻子哼的一声应付。

PSI = pollution standard index【环保】污染标准指数〔0–50 表示空气质量尚可,100 以上则对人健康有害,200 以上则为严重危害健康〕。

psi [*p*sai; saɪ] *n*. 希腊语的第二十三字母〔Ψ、ψ,相当于英语的 ps〕。

p.s.i., psi = pounds per square inch 每平方英寸上的磅数,磅/英寸²。

psia = 1. pounds per square inch absolute 绝对压强〔磅/英寸²〕。2. pounds per square inch of area 磅/平方英寸面积。

psi·lan·thro·py, psi·lan·thro·pism [*p*saiˈlænθrəpi, -pizəm; saɪˋlænθrəpɪ, -pɪzəm] *n*. 耶稣凡夫论。

psi·lo·cin [ˈ*p*sailəsin; ˋsaɪləsɪn] *n*. 【生化】裸头草辛,二甲-4-羟色胺。

psi·lo·cy·bin [ˌ*p*sailəˈsaibin; ˏsaɪləˋsaɪbɪn] *n*. 【生化】裸头草碱,二甲-4-羟色胺磷酸。

psi·lom·e·lane [*p*saiˈlɔmilein; saɪˋlɑməlen] *n*. 硬锰矿。

psi·lo·sis [*p*saiˈləusis; saɪˋlosɪs] *n*. 【医】脱发症,秃头病;口炎性腹泻。

psit·ta·cine [ˈ*p*sitəsain, -sin; ˋsɪtəsɪn, -sɪn] *a*. 鹦鹉的,似鹦鹉的。**-ly** *ad*.

psit·ta·co·sis [*p*sitəˈkəusis; ˏsɪtəˋkosɪs] *n*. 【医】鹦鹉病,鹦鹉热。

P.S.N.C. = Pacific Steam Navigation Company〔英〕太平洋轮船海运公司。

pso·as [ˈ*p*səuəs; ˋsoəs] *n*. (*pl*. **pso·ai**, **pso·ae** [ˈsəuai, -iː; ˋsoaɪ, -i]) 【解】腰肌。

pso·cid [ˈ*p*səusid; ˋsosɪd] *n*. 啮虫科 (*Psocidae*) 昆虫。

pso·phom·e·ter [*p*səuˈfɔmitə; soˋfɑmɪtɚ] *n*. 【物】噪音计;测听器。

pso·ra·le·a [*p*sɔ(ː)ˈreiliə; sɔ(ə)ˋrelɪə] *n*. 【植】食用补骨脂 (*Psoralea esculenta*)。

pso·ri·a·sis [*p*sɔ(ː)ˈraiəsis; səˋraɪəsɪs] *n*. 银屑病,牛皮癣。**pso·ri·at·ic** [ˌ*p*sɔ(ː)riˈætik; ˏsɔ(ə)rɪˋætɪk] *a*.

PSS, P.SS. = postscripts.

psst [ps; ps] *int*. 喂! 〔引起别人注意的感叹词〕。

PST, P.S.T. = Pacific Standard Time 太平洋标准时间〔美国太平洋沿岸等地采用的西八区时间〕。

psyc [saik; saɪk] *n*. 〔美口〕= psychology.

psych [saik; saɪk] *vt*. (**~ed**; **~ing**)〔俚〕1. 使精神纷乱[失调];使感情激动〔常与 *up* 连用〕。2. 用精神分析法治疗 (= psycho-analyse)。3. 用直觉或按照心理学的方法分析…的动机或行动以便智胜(对手)。4. 〔~ oneself〕使作好精神准备。~ *a table-tennis opponent*

以心理分析的方法智胜乒乓球对手。～ ***out***〔美俚〕**1.** 吓坏了,吓糊涂了。**2.** 装精神失常进行逃避。

psych. = psychological; psychology.

psy·chas·the·ni·a [ˌsaikæsˈθiːniə; ˏsaɪkæsˋθinɪə] ***n.*** 精神衰弱症。**-then·ic** [-ˈθenik; -ˋθɛnɪk] ***a.***

psy·che [ˈpsaiki(ː); ˋsaɪkɪ] ***n.*** **1.**〔P-〕【希神】爱神 Eros 所爱的美女〔灵魂的化身〕。**2.** 灵魂,精神。**3.**【虫】(属蓑蛾科的)一种蛾。

psy·che·de·li·a [ˌsaikiˈdiːliə; ˏsaɪkɪˋdilɪə] ***n.*** **1.** 幻觉剂〔服用后可使人兴奋的一种麻醉剂〕。**2.** 服用幻觉剂的人。

psy·che·del·ic [ˌsaikiˈdelik; ˏsaɪkɪˋdɛlɪk] **I** ***a.*** **1.** 引起幻觉的,幻觉的。**2.** 幻觉剂的。**II** ***n.*** 幻觉剂。**-cal·ly** ***ad.***

psy·chi·at·ric, psy·chi·at·ri·cal [ˌsaikiˈætrik(əl); ˏsaɪkɪˋætrɪk(əl)] ***a.*** 精神病学的;医精神病的。

psy·chi·a·trist [saiˈkaiətrist; saɪˋkaɪətrɪst] ***n.*** 精神病医生;精神病学者。

psy·chi·a·try [saiˈkaiətri; saɪˋkaɪətrɪ] ***n.*** 精神病学;精神病治疗法。

psy·chic, psy·chi·cal [ˈsaikik(əl); ˋsaɪkɪk(l̩)] **I** ***a.*** **1.** 精神的,灵魂的;心理的 (*opp.* physical);【心】心理(现象)的。**2.** 对超自然力量敏感的;通灵的。～ *phenomena* 心灵现象。**II** ***n.*** **1.** 灵媒;巫师,巫婆;对超自然力量敏感的人;通灵的人。**2.** 精神上的现象;超自然的现象。

psy·chics [ˈsaikiks; ˋsaɪkɪks] ***n.***〔口〕心理学;心灵研究。

psy·cho [ˈsaikəu; ˋsaɪko] (*pl.* ***-chos***) ***n.*** **1.** 精神分析(学)。**2.** 精神(性)神经病患者。**3.** 精神变态者。～**biography** 精神分析传记〔从精神分析角度写下的个人生活故事〕。～**prison** (关押犯罪性精神错乱者的)精神病院。～**geriatrics** 老年精神病学。

psy·cho(-) *comb. f.* 表示"灵魂,精神,心理": *psycho*analysis, *psycho*biology.

psy·cho·a·cous·tics [ˌsaikəuəˈkuːstiks; ˏsaɪkoəˋkustɪks] ***n.***〔动词用单数〕心理声学。**-cous·tic, -cous·ti·cal** ***a.***

psy·cho·ac·tive [ˌsaikəuˈæktiv; ˏsaɪkoˋæktɪv] ***a.*** (药剂)对神经起显著[特殊]作用的。

psy·cho·a·nal·y·sis [ˌsaikəuəˈnæləsis; ˏsaɪkoəˋnæləsɪs] ***n.*** 精神分析(学)。**-an·alyst** ***n.*** 精神分析学家。**-an·a·lyt·ic(al)** [-əˈlitik(əl); -əˋlɪtɪk(əl)] ***a.*** 精神分析的。

psy·cho·bi·ol·o·gy [ˌsaikəubaiˈɔlədʒi; ˏsaɪkobaɪˋɑlədʒɪ] ***n.*** **1.** 心理生物学。**2.** 生物心理学。**-log·i·cal** [-ˈlɔdʒikl; -ˋlɑdʒɪkl̩] ***a.***

psy·cho·chem·i·cal [ˌsaikəuˈkemikl; saɪkoˋkɛmɪkl̩] **I** ***n.*** 精神病的治疗药物。**II** ***a.*** 精神病治疗药物的。

psy·cho·del·ic [ˌsaikəuˈdelik; ˏsaɪkoˋdɛlɪk] **I** ***a.*** 引起幻觉的,幻觉的;幻觉剂的。**II** ***n.*** 幻觉剂 (= psychedelic)。

psy·cho·dra·ma [ˌsaikəuˈdrɑːmə; ˏsaɪkəˋdrɑmə] ***n.*** 心理剧〔一种可使患者的感情得以发泄从而达到治疗效果的戏剧〕。

psy·cho·dy·nam·ic [ˌsaikəudaiˈnæmik; ˏsaɪkodaɪˋnæmɪk] ***a.*** 心理动力的。**-nam·ics** ***n.*** 心理动力学。

psy·cho·gen·e·sis [ˌsaikəuˈdʒenisis; ˏsaɪkoˋdʒɛnəsɪs] ***n.*** 心理发生。

psy·cho·gen·ic [ˌsaikəuˈdʒenik; ˏsaɪkoˋdʒɛnɪk] ***a.*** 心理发生的,心理(起源)的;由心理冲突引起的。**-al·ly** ***ad.***

psy·cho·graph [ˈsaikəgrɑːf; ˋsaɪkəˏgræf] ***n.***【心】心理图案。

psy·cho·ki·ne·sis [ˌsaikəukiˈniːsis; ˏsaɪkokɪˋnisɪs] ***n.***【心】(灵学研究的)由于思想作用而影响客观事物的能力。**-net·ic** [-ˈnetik; -ˋnɛtɪk] ***a.***

psychol. = psychological; psychologist; psychology.

psy·cho·lin·guis·tics [ˌsaikəuliŋˈgwistiks; ˏsaɪkolɪŋˋgwɪstɪks] ***n.*** 心理语言学。

psy·cho·log·i·cal [ˌsaikəˈlɔdʒikəl; ˏsaɪkəˋlɑdʒɪkl̩] ***a.*** 心理学(上)的;精神(现象)的。～ *warfare* 心理战。*the* ～ *moment*【心】心理上的适当瞬间;〔口〕最适当的时机;紧要关头。**-ly** ***ad.***

psy·chol·o·gism [saiˈkɔlədʒizəm; saɪˋkɑlədʒɪzm] ***n.*** **1.** 心理说,对心理因素的注重。**2.** 心理学专门用语。

psy·chol·o·gist [saiˈkɔlədʒist; saɪˋkɑlədʒɪst] ***n.*** 心理学者;心理学家。

psy·chol·o·gize [saiˈkɔlədʒaiz; saɪˋkɑləˏdʒaɪz] ***vi.*** 研究心理学。— ***vt.*** 从心理学的角度来解释;用心理学分析。

psy·chol·ogy [saiˈkɔlədʒi; saɪˋkɑlədʒɪ] ***n.*** **1.** 心理学。**2.** 心理。**3.** 心理学论著;心理学体系。*child* ～ 儿童心理学。*comparative* [*criminal, experimental*] ～ 比较[犯罪,实验]心理学。

psy·chom·e·ter [saiˈkɔmitə; saɪˋkɑmɪtɚ] ***n.*** 用脑时间测定计;智力测验器。

psy·cho·met·rics [ˌsaikəˈmetriks; ˏsaɪkoˋmɛtrɪks] ***n.***〔动词用单数〕心理测验学 (= psychometry)。**-tri·cian** ***n.***

psy·chom·e·try [saiˈkɔmitri; saɪˋkɑmətrɪ] ***n.*** **1.** 心理测验(学);用脑时间测定法;智力测验。**2.** 触物卜卦;心灵占卜术。

psy·cho·mi·met·ic [ˌsaikəumiˈmetik; ˏsaɪkomɪˋmɛtɪk] ***a.***【心】拟精神病的。

psy·cho·mo·tor [ˌsaikəuˈməutə; ˏsaɪkoˋmotɚ] ***a.*** **1.** 痉挛的〔精神作用对运动神经(肌)产生影响的〕。**2.** 癫痫病状的〔发作特点是病人出现复杂的行为〕。

psy·cho·neu·ro·sis [ˌsaikəunjuəˈrəusis; ˏsaɪkonjʊˋrosɪs] ***n.*** (*pl.* ***-ses*** [-siːz; -siz])【医】精神(性)神经病。

psy·cho·path [ˈsaikəupæθ; ˋsaɪkəˏpæθ] ***n.*** 精神变态者,心理病者。

psy·cho·path·ic [ˌsaikəuˈpæθik; ˏsaɪkəˋpæθɪk] **I** ***a.*** 精神病态的,心理变态的。**II** ***n.*** 精神变态者,心理病者。～ **hospital** 精神病院。

psy·cho·pa·thol·o·gy [ˌsaikəupəˈθɔlədʒi; ˏsaɪkopəˋθɑlədʒɪ] ***n.*** 精神病理学,心理病理学。

psy·chop·a·thy [saiˈkɔpəθi; saɪˋkɑpəθɪ] ***n.*** 精神变态,心理变态。

psy·cho·phar·ma·col·o·gy [ˌsaikəuˌfɑːməˈkɔlədʒi; ˏsaɪkoˏfɑrməˋkɑlədʒɪ] ***n.*** 精神药理学。**-log·ic, -log·i·cal** ***a.***

psy·cho·phys·ics [ˈsaikəuˈfiziks; ˏsaɪkoˋfɪzɪks] ***n.*** 心理物理学,心物学。

psy·cho·phys·i·ol·o·gy [ˈsaikəuˌfiziˈɔlədʒi; ˏsaɪkoˏfɪzɪˋɑlədʒɪ] ***n.*** 心理[精神]生理学。

psy·cho·sex·u·al [ˌsaikəuˈsekʃuəl; ˏsaɪkəˋsɛkʃʊəl] ***a.*** (精神上)有性的特性的〔与肉体上相对而言〕。**-sex·u·al·i·ty** [-ˈæliti; -ˋælətɪ] ***n.***

psy·cho·sis [saiˈkəusis; saɪˋkosɪs] ***n.*** (*pl.* ***-ses*** [-siːz; -siz]) **1.** 精神病,精神错乱,精神变态。**2.** (由于环境、情况等而引起的)精神上极度的紧张、不安。

psy·cho·so·cial [ˌsaikəuˈsəuʃəl; ˏsaɪkoˋsoʃəl] ***a.*** 社会心理的〔指社会环境影响下的个人心理变化〕。

psy·cho·sur·ger·y [ˌsaikəuˈsəːdʒəri; ˏsaɪkoˋsɝdʒərɪ] ***n.*** 精神(病)外科学。

psy·cho·tech·nol·o·gy [ˈsaikəutekˈnɔlədʒi; ˋsaɪkotɛkˋnɑlədʒɪ] ***n.*** 心理技术学。

psy·cho·ther·a·peu·tics [ˌsaikəuˌθerəˈpjuːtiks; ˏsaɪkoˏθɛrəˋpjutɪks] ***n.*** [*pl.*]〔动词用单数〕心理疗法,精神疗法 (= psychotherapy)。**-peu·tic** ***a.***

psy·cho·ther·a·py [ˈsaikəuˈθerəpi; ˏsaɪkoˋθɛrəpɪ] ***n.***【医】精神疗法,心理疗法,(尤指)催眠疗法。

psy·chot·ic [saiˈkɔtik; saɪˋkɑtɪk] **I** ***a.*** 精神病的,有精神病的。**II** ***n.*** 精神病患者。

psy·cho·tox·ic [ˌsaikəuˈtɔksik; ˏsaɪkoˋtɑksɪk] ***a.***【药】精神麻醉品的〔如能损伤大脑的酒精等〕。

psy·cho·trop·ic [ˌsaikəuˈtrɔpik; ˏsaɪkoˋtrɑpɪk] **I** ***a.***

(药物)治疗精神病的。**II** *n*. 治精神病的药。

psy·chrom·e·ter [sai'krɔmitə; saɪ`krɑmətə·] *n*. (干湿球)湿度计。

psy·chro·phil·ic [ˌsaikrəu'filik; ˏsaɪkrə`fɪlɪk] *a*.【生】嗜冷性的。**-phile** [-fail; -faɪl] *n*.

psy·co·graph ['saikəugrɑːf, -ˏgræf; `saɪkogræf, -ˏgræf] *n*.【心】**1.** 性格特点描记图。**2.** 精神作用记录。

psyl·la ['silə; `sɪlə] *n*. 叶虱科(*Psyllidae*)昆虫。

psy·war ['saiwɔː; `saɪwɔr] *n*. 心理战(= psychological warfare)。

P.T. = **1.** Physical Training 体育锻炼。**2.** post town 设有邮局的市镇。**3.** Pupil Teacher (小学)见习教师。

Pt = platinum【化】铂。

pt. = **1.** part. **2.** payment. **3.** pint. **4.** point. **5.** port.

p.t. = potential transformer 变压器,电压互感器。

PTA, P.T.A. = Parent-Teacher Association〔美〕学生家长和教师联谊会。

ptar·mi·gan ['tɑːmigən; `tɑrməgən] (*pl*. **-gan(s)**) *n*.【鸟】雷鸟(松鸡类)。

ptbl. = portable.

P T boat ['piː 'tiː bəut; `pi `ti bot] = patrol torpedo boat〔美〕鱼雷快艇;〔喻〕(篮球比赛中)矮小灵活的后卫。

Pte. = Private 列兵;〔英〕陆军二等兵;〔美〕陆军[海军陆战队]二等兵。

pter·i·dol·o·gy [ˌ*p*teri'dɔlədʒi; ˏtɛrə`dɑlədʒɪ] *n*. 蕨类植物学。**-log·ical** [-'lɔdʒikl; -`lɑdʒɪkl̩] *a*. **-gist** *n*.

pter·i·do·phyte ['*p*teridəuˌfait, tə'ridə-; `tɛrədoˏfaɪt, tə`rɪdə-] *n*. 蕨类植物(*Pteridophyta*)。**-phyt·ic** [-'fitik; -`fɪtɪk], **-doph·y·tous** [-'dɔfitəs; -`dɑfɪtəs] *a*.

pter·id·o·sperm ['*p*teridəuspəːm; `tɛrɪdospɝm] *n*. 种子蕨(= seed fern)。

ptero- *comb. f*. 表示"翼": *ptero*dactyl.

pter·o·dac·tyl [ˌ*p*terəu'dæktil; ˏtɛrə`dæktɪl] *n*.【古生】飞龙目动物;翼手龙;无尾飞龙。

pter·o·pod ['*p*terəpɔd; `tɛrəˏpɑd] **I** *a*. 翼足目的。**II** *n*. 翼足目(*Pteropoda*)动物。**-an** *a*., *n*.

pter·o·saur ['*p*terəsɔː; `tɛrəsɔr] *n*. 飞龙目动物(= pterodactyl)。

pte·ryg·i·um [*p*tə'ridʒiəm; tə`rɪdʒɪəm] *n*. (*pl*. **-i·ums, -i·a** [-ə; -ə])【医】翼状胬肉。**-ryg·i·al** *a*.

pter·y·goid ['*p*terigɔid; `tɛrəˏgɔɪd] **I** *a*. **1.** 翅形的。**2.** 翼突的。**II** *n*. 翼骨或翼突。

pter·y·la ['*p*terilə; `tɛrələ] *n*. (*pl*. **-lae** [-ˌliː; -ˏli])【动】羽区。

Ptg, Ptg. = Portugal; Portuguese.

ptg, ptg. = printing.

ptis·an ['tizən, ti'zæn; `tɪzən, tɪ`zæn] *n*. **1.** 大麦(与其他配料同煮的)汤,大麦茶。**2.** 煎汤〔如草药汤药等〕。

PTO, P.T.O., p.t.o. = please turn over 见反面,见下页。

Ptol·e·ma·ic [ˌtɔli'meiik; ˏtɑlə`meɪk] *a*. **1.** (古埃及)托勒密(Ptolemy)王朝的。**2.** (公元前二世纪古希腊天文学家)托勒密(Ptolemy)体系的;天动说的。*the* ~ *system* 托勒密体系,天动说。

Ptol·e·ma·ist [ˌtɔli'meiist; ˏtɑlə`meɪst] *n*. 托勒密体系[天动说]信奉者。

pto·ma·in(e) ['təumein; `tomen] *n*.【化】尸碱;尸毒。**P- Domain**〔美军俚〕食堂。~ **poisoning** 食物中毒。**P-Tillie** [**Tommy**]〔美俚〕小酒馆的老板。

pto·sis ['*p*təusis; `tosɪs] *n*.【医】上睑下垂。

pts, pts. = **1.** parts. **2.** payments. **3.** pints. **4.** points. **5.** ports.

PTSD = post-traumatic stress disorder【医】创伤后精神压力症。

PTV = public television (非商业性的)公营电视。

pty·a·lin ['taiəlin; `taɪəlɪn] *n*. 唾液淀粉酶。

pty·a·lism ['taiəlizəm; `taɪəlɪzm̩] *n*. 唾液分泌过多,多涎。

Pu = plutonium【化】钚。

pub [pʌb; pʌb] *n*.〔英〕= public house;〔美〕= publisher. ~**-crawl** *vt*., *vi*.〔英俚〕(在…)喝通关,从一家喝到一家地逛酒店。

pub. = **1.** public. **2.** publication; published; publisher; publishing.

pu·ber·ty ['pjuːbə(ː)ti; `pjubətɪ] *n*. **1.** 发身;发情期,青春期;青春,妙龄。**2.**【植】开花期。*the age of* ~ 发情期〔英法律男14岁,女12岁〕。*arrive at* ~ 到青春期。

pu·ber·u·lent [pju'berulənt; pjʊ`bɛrjʊlənt] *a*.【动】柔毛覆盖的。

pu·bes ['pjuːbiːz; `pjubiz] *n*.〔*sing*., *pl*. 同〕**1.** 阴毛;阴阜。**2.**【动,植】柔毛。

pu·bes·cence [pju(ː)'besns; pju`bɛsn̩s] *n*. **1.** 发情期。**2.**【植,动】短柔毛;柔毛。

pu·bes·cent [pju(ː)'besnt; pju`bɛsnt] **I** *a*. **1.** 青春的,妙龄的,发情期的,发身期的。**2.**【植、动】有柔毛的。**II** *n*. 发情期的人。

pu·bic ['pjuːbik; `pjubɪk] *a*. 阴毛的;阴阜的。*the* ~ *bone* 耻骨。【动】*the* ~ *region* 阴部。

pu·bis ['pjuːbis; `pjubɪs] *n*. (*pl*. **-bes** [-biːz; -biz]) **1.**【解】耻骨。**2.**【动】(昆虫)前胸侧部。

publ. = publication; published; publisher; publishing.

pub·lic ['pʌblik; `pʌblɪk] **I** *a*. (*opp*. private) **1.** 公共的,公众的,公用的;人民的,社会的,国家的;政府的,公营的,公立的。**2.** (会等)公开的,当众的;人人知道的,知名的,突出的。**3.**〔罕〕国际上的。**4.**〔英〕大学的;(有别于各分科学院时说的)全校的。~ *good* [*benefit*, *interests*] 公益。~ *life* 社会生活,公共生活。*at the* ~ *expense* 用公费。*in the* ~ *eye* 公然。*make a* ~ *protest* 提公开抗议。*make* ~ 发表,公布。**II** *n*. **1.**〔the ~〕人民,国民,公众,社会。**2.** (某一方面的)大众,群众;…界,…帮,…社会;(文学家等的)爱读者,爱好者。**3.**〔英口〕酒吧,客栈。*The* ~ *is the best judge*. 公众是最好的判断者。*the British* ~ 英国社会,一般英国人。*the musical* [*sporting*] ~ 音乐[运动]界。***give to the*** ~ 出版,印行(书等)。***in*** ~ 公然,当众。***the general*** ~ = ***the*** ~ ***at large*** 公众。~ **act** 公法。~ **address system** 扩音装置,有线广播系统。~ **affairs** 公众事务。~ **assistance institution**〔英〕贫民收容所。~ **auction** 拍卖。~ **bath** 公共浴室,澡堂。~ **bidding**〔美〕投标。~ **bill** 公共关系法案。~ **body** 公共团体。~ **bond** 公债券。~ **comfort station**〔美〕公厕。~ **debt** [**bond**] 公债。~ **defender** 公设辩护人[指律师]。~ **domain**〔美〕官产,公地;公有财产;不受版权[专利权]限制的状态。~ **education** 学校教育;〔英〕公学教育。~ **enemy** 公敌;社会公敌。~ **enemy number one**〔美〕第一号罪犯;万分可恶的人。~ **examination**〔英〕大学考试。~ **funds**〔英〕公债。~ **health** 公共卫生。~ **holiday** 公定假日。~ **house**〔英〕客栈;〔英〕酒吧。~ **latrine** 公厕。~ **international law** 国际公法。~ **law** 公法。~ **lecture** 公开演讲。~ **library** 公立[公共]图书馆。~ **loan** 公债。~**-minded**[**-spirited**] 热心公益的。~ **morality** 风纪。~ **nuisance**【法】公妨犯;社会的害物。~ **offence** 政治犯。~ **officer** 公务员。~ **opinion** 舆论;民意。~ **opinion poll** 民意测验。~ **orator**〔英〕(大学的)代表人,秘书长。~ **park** 公园。~ **pay telephone** 公用电话。~ **peace** 公安。~ **prosecutor**〔英〕检察官。~ **relations** (工厂、公司等的)(与)公众(的)关系[联系]。~ **right** 公权。~ **sale** 拍卖。~ **scandal** 众所周知的丑事。~ **school**〔美〕公立学校;〔英〕公学,私立(寄宿制大学预备)学校。~ **servant** 公仆,公务员;从事公用事业的个人[团体]。~**-service corporation**〔美〕公用事业公司。~ **speaking** 演说(术)。~ **spirit** 热心公益的精神。~

street 公路,大路。~ **utility** 公用事业。~ **way** 公路。~ **welfare** 公安,治安,公共福利。~ **woman** 妓女。~ **works** 〔美〕公共[市政]工程;公共建筑。**-ly** *ad*. 公然,公开,当众;由公众;由政府(出资、持有等)。

pub·li·can [ˈpʌblikən; ˋpʌblɪkən] *n*. 1. (古罗马的)收税官。2. 〔英〕客栈[酒馆]老板。

pub·li·ca·tion [ˌpʌbliˈkeiʃən; ˏpʌblɪˋkeʃən] *n*. 1. 公布,颁布,发布,发表。2. 发行,出版。3. 发行物,出版物,刊物。*the list of new ~s* 新书[新刊]目录。*a monthly* [*weekly*] ~ 月[周]刊。

pub·li·cist [ˈpʌblisist; ˋpʌblɪsɪst] *n*. 1. 国际法专家[研究者]。2. 政论家,政论学家;政治记者;新闻发布官员。

pub·lic·i·ty [pʌbˈlisiti; pʌbˋlɪsətɪ] *n*. 1. 公开(性);传开,出名。2. 宣传;宣扬。3. (向新闻界散发的)宣传材料;广告。*the ~ department* 宣传部。***avoid*** [***shun***] ~ 避免惹人注意,不想出名。***court*** [***seek***] ~ 自我宣传,求名,沽名钓誉。***give ~ to*** 公开,宣传,宣扬。~ **agent** [**man**] 广告员;(演员等的)宣传员。~ **hound** 〔美〕爱在报上露名的人。

pub·li·cize [ˈpʌblisaiz; ˋpʌblɪˏsaɪz] *vt*. 〔美〕发表,公布;宣传,为…做广告。

pub·li·phone [ˈpʌblifəun; ˋpʌblɪfon] *n*. 〔口〕公用电话。

pub·lish [ˈpʌbliʃ; ˋpʌblɪʃ] *vt*. 1. 公开,发表;宣布(结婚等)。2. 公布,颁布。3. 发行;出版;刊印。4. 出版…的著作。5. 〔美〕使用(伪钞等)。— *vi*. 1. 出版;发行。2. (著作人)发表著作。~ ***or perish*** 不出版(作品)就会灭亡〔指作家如长期不发表作品就会被人忘却〕。**-a·ble** *a*. 可发表的;适于出版的。

pub·lish·er [ˈpʌbliʃə; ˋpʌblɪʃɚ] *n*. 1. 出版者,发行人,出版社。2. 公布者,发表者;〔美〕办报者。

pub·lish·ing [ˈpʌbliʃiŋ; ˋpʌblɪʃɪŋ] *a*., *n*. 出版(业)(的)。*a ~ house* 出版社。

pub·lish·ment [ˈpʌbliʃment; ˋpʌblɪʃmənt] *n*. 〔罕〕= publication.

puc·coon [pəˈkuːn; pəˋkun] *n*. 1. 紫草(= gromwell)。2. 〔古〕美洲血根草(= bloodroot)。3. 〔古〕紫草染料。

puce [pjuːs; pjus] *a*., *n*. 深褐色(的)。

puck[1] [pʌk; pʌk] *n*. 1. [P-] (莎士比亚戏剧《仲夏夜之梦》中的)喜欢恶作剧的小妖精。2. 淘气的小孩,顽童。

puck[2] [pʌk; pʌk] *n*. (冰上运动用的)冰球[硬橡皮圆盘]。

puck[3] [pʌk; pʌk] *n*. 1. 〔英〕脾脱疽〔相传由蚊母鸟引起的家畜病〕。2. 蚊母鸟。

puck·a [ˈpʌkə; ˋpʌkə] *a*. 〔印度〕1. 分量足的。2. 纯良的;真正的,可靠的。3. 上等的,第一流的。4. 坚牢的,(房屋等)永久性的。*a ~ general* 终生陆军上将。

puck·er [ˈpʌkə; ˋpʌkɚ] I *vt*. 折叠,使起皱纹;撅(嘴等),皱(眉头)(*up*)。— *vi*. 1. 成褶子,皱起来;缩拢(*up*)。2. 〔口〕烦闷,为难。~ ***up one's brows*** 皱起眉头来。~ ***up the mouth*** 撅起嘴来。II *n*. 1. 褶子,皺,皱纹。2. 〔口〕狼狈;惶惑。***in a*** ~ 慌慌张张。***in ~s*** 起皱,有褶缝。

puck·er·stop·ple [ˈpʌkəˈstɔpl; ˋpʌkɚˋstɑpl̩] *vt*. 〔美〕使着慌,使为难。

puck·er·y [ˈpʌkəri; ˋpʌkərɪ] *a*. 皱起的,易皱褶的。

puck·ish [ˈpʌkiʃ; ˋpʌkɪʃ] *a*. 顽皮的,恶作剧的。**-ly** *ad*. **-ness** *n*.

pud [pʌd; pʌd] *n*. 〔儿语〕手手;(小孩的)手;(猫、狗等的)前脚。

pud·ding [ˈpudiŋ; ˋpʊdɪŋ] *n*. 1. 布丁〔西餐中一种甜点心〕;〔喻〕物质的报酬。2. 香肠。3. 【海】(由帆布等制成的护船用的)船尾碰垫。4. (窃贼给狗吃的)毒肝(等)。5. 〔美卑〕侥幸。*The proof of the ~ is in the eating*. 布丁好坏,一尝便知〔谚语〕。*Indian* ~ 玉米布丁。***more praise than*** ~ 恭维多而实惠少,假恭维。~ ***rather than praise*** 恭维不如实惠。***~s and pies*** 眼睛。~ **cloth** (蒸布丁用的)布丁布。~ **face** 扁圆呆板的脸。~**-faced** *a*. 面孔扁圆呆板的。~ **head** 笨人,蠢货。~**-headed** *a*. 愚笨的,蠢的。~ **heart** 懦夫,精神萎靡的人。~ **house** 〔俚〕胃,肚子。~ **pie** 肉布丁。~ **stone** 【矿】圆砾岩。**-y** [ˈpudiŋi; ˋpʊdɪŋɪ] *a*. 布丁一样的;沉闷的;迟钝的;愚笨的。

pud·dle [ˈpʌdl; ˋpʌdl̩] I *n*. 1. (路上的)水坑。2. (黏土和沙捣成的)胶土。3. 〔俚〕混乱。4. 〔美口〕商品分类目录〔相对于总目录 pool 而言〕。II *vt*. 1. 弄脏,把…弄得泥糊糊。2. 把…做成胶土;用胶土涂塞。3. 搅拌(熔铁),搅炼。4. 【农】湿土培育(稻秧等)。— *vi*. 1. 搅泥浆;在泥水中泼溅[打滚](*about*; *in*)。2. 撒尿。~ **furnace** 搅炼炉,炼铁炉。~ **jumper** 〔美俚〕小型(公共)汽车;小火车;小汽艇;〔美军俚〕吉普车(= jeep);小型低空侦察机。~**-poet** 打油诗人。

pud·dler [ˈpʌdlə; ˋpʌdlɚ] *n*. 搅炼者;搅炼棒;搅炼炉。

pud·dling [ˈpʌdliŋ; ˋpʌdlɪŋ] *n*. 1. 涂胶;捣成泥浆;和泥。2. 【冶】(铣铁)精炼(法),搅炼炼铁(法);搅炼(作用)。

pud·dly [ˈpʌdli; ˋpʌdlɪ] *a*. 1. (路等)水坑多的。2. 〔罕,方〕尽是泥的,溷浊的;脏的。

pu·den·cy [ˈpjuːdənsi; ˋpjudn̩sɪ] *n*. 羞怯,害羞;拘谨。

pu·den·dum [pjuːˈdendəm; pjuˋdendəm] *n*. (*pl*. ***-denda*** [-də; -də]) 1. 女性外生殖器;阴部。2. 〔*pl*.〕外生殖器。**pu·den·dal** [-dl; -dl̩] *a*.

pudge [pʌdʒ; pʌdʒ] *n*. 〔口〕矮胖子;矮胖的动物;短而粗的东西。

pudg·y [ˈpʌdʒi; ˋpʌdʒɪ] *a*. (*-i·er*; *-i·est*) 〔口〕圆胖的;矮胖的。**-i·ly** *ad*. **-i·ness** *n*.

pu·dic·i·ty [pjuːˈdisiti; pjuˋdɪsətɪ] *n*. 羞怯,害羞;贞洁,淑贞。

puds·y [ˈpʌdzi; pʌdzɪ] *a*. = pudgy.

pu·eb·lo [puˈebləu, ˈpwebləu; puˋɛblo, ˋpweblo] *n*. 〔Sp.〕(*pl*. ~*s*) 1. (美国西南部或墨西哥等)印第安人的村庄〔集体住所、城镇〕。2. 〔P-〕住集体住所的印第安人。3. (操西班牙语的美洲国家中的)村庄[城镇]。

pu·er·ile [ˈpjuərail; ˋpjuəˏrɪl] *a*. 孩子气的;幼稚的;不成熟的;傻的。**-ly** *ad*.

pu·er·il·ism [ˈpjuːərilizəm; ˋpjuərəˏlɪzm̩] *n*. 孩子气,幼稚〔尤指成年人〕。

pu·er·il·i·ty [ˌpjuəˈriliti; ˏpjuəˋrɪlətɪ] *n*. 1. 幼稚;孩子气;愚蠢。2. 〔*pl*.〕幼稚的言行。3. 【法】幼年〔7—14岁〕。

pu·er·per·al [pju(ː)ˈəːpərəl; pjuˋɝpərəl] *a*. 【医】生产的,分娩的。~ *fever* 【医】产褥热。

pu·er·pe·ri·um [ˌpju(ː)əˈpiəriəm; ˏpjuɚˋpɪrɪəm] *n*. 产后期,产褥期。

Puer·to Ri·co [ˈpwəːtəuˈriːkəu; ˏpwɛrtəˋriko] 波多黎各(岛)〔拉丁美洲〕。

puff [pʌf; pʌf] I *n*. 1. 一吹[喷];噗的一吹[喷];一阵,一股(气味、烟雾等);吹[喷]的声音;(烟等)一喷的分量。2. 噗的一声膨胀起来;膨胀起来的东西[部份]。3. 被子;鸭绒被。4. 夸奖,吹嘘,自我宣传。5. 粉扑〔又叫 powder-~〕。6. (奶油)松饼。7. 〔美俚〕广告。8. 〔美俚〕向女性献殷勤的人。*a ~ of the wind* 一阵风。*get a good ~ of one's book* 著作大受称赞。*newspaper ~s* 报纸上的浮夸性广告,吹捧性短文[书评等]。II *vi*. 1. 噗噗地喷气,噗噗地喷烟(*out*; *up*);噗噗地喷着气开动;喘气;喘着气走。2. 膨胀,噗地膨起(*up*; *out*)。3. 〔古〕哼的一声用鼻音应酬(*at*);(拍卖时)把价钱哄抬上去。~ *and blow* [*pant*] 喘气。~ *away at one's cigar* 一口口猛喷着雪茄烟。~ *out* 喘着气说;(烟)噗噗噗地喷。*The engine ~ed out of the station*. 火车头噗噗地喷着气驶出车站。— *vt*. 1. 喷(烟等),噗噗地吹去(灰尘等)。2. 〔口〕使喘气。3. 使噗的一下膨起;使自满,使得意(*up*);乱夸,瞎吹;(拍卖时)把(价钱)哄抬上去。~ *out a candle* 吹熄蜡烛。*I was frightfully ~ed by the run*. 我跑得气都喘不过来了。*be ~ed out* [*up*] *with self-importance* 自以为了不起而摆架子。~**adder**

P

(南非)膨身蛇〔怒时身体膨大的大毒蛇〕。~ **ball**【植】马勃(菌);马勃菌状短裙,汽球状裙子。~ **box** 粉(扑)盒子。~**-puff** 噗噗〔烟等喷出声〕;〔儿语〕火车头。**-ing** **1.** ***n***. 噗噗吹;夸奖;【拍卖】虚价。**2.** ***a***. 乱夸奖的。

puff·er [ˈpʌfə; ˋpʌfɚ] ***n***. **1.** 吹气的人[物]。**2.** 瞎吹乱夸的人。**3.** 拍卖行的囮子,抬价人。**4.**【鱼】河豚。**5.**〔儿〕火车噗噗,火车头。**6.**【矿】小绞车;小绞车工。

puff·er·y [ˈpʌfəri; ˋpʌfərɪ] ***n***. 夸大的称赞,吹嘘,夸奖;吹捧的广告。

puf·fin [ˈpʌfin; ˋpʌfɪn] ***n***. **1.**【鸟】善知鸟;海鹦。**2.**【植】马勃(菌)。

puff·i·ness [ˈpʌfinis; ˋpʌfɪnɪs] ***n***. **1.** 膨胀。**2.** 自夸,自满;夸张。

puff·y [ˈpʌfi; ˋpʌfɪ] ***a***. (***-i·er***; ***-i·est***) **1.** 膨起的,肿胀的;肥胖的。**2.**〔罕〕骄傲的,夸大的。**3.** 喘气的;容易气急的。**4.** 噗一声吹的;一阵的。**-i·ly** ***ad***.

pug[1] [pʌg; pʌg] **I** ***n***. **1.** 巴儿狗;狮子鼻。**2.**〔爱称〕狐,兔子,猴子(等)。**3.**〔英〕小火车头。**4.**〔英〕高级仆役,管家。**II** ***a***.〔美〕**1.** 舒服的,贴身的。**2.** 往上翘的。

pug[2] [pʌg; pʌg] **I** ***n***. **1.** (制砖瓦等用的)泥料;隔音土。**2.** 捏土机,捣泥机。**II** ***vt***. (***-gg-***) **1.** (制砖瓦)捣[捏](黏土);涂塞泥料。**2.**【建】涂(灰泥)阻止传音。~ **mill** 捣泥机,搅拌机。

pug[3] [pʌg; pʌg] **I** ***n***.〔印度用英语〕(野兽的)足迹。**II** ***vt***. (***-gg-***) 寻找(野兽的)足迹。

pug[4] [pʌg; pʌg] ***n***.〔俚〕(职业)拳击家,拳师。

pugg·a·ree, pugg·ree, pug·gry [ˈpʌgəri, -gri; ˋpʌgərɪ, -grɪ] ***n***.〔印度〕= pugree.

pug·ging [ˈpʌgiŋ; ˋpʌgɪŋ] ***n***. **1.** 捏合;捣制窑泥。**2.**【建】隔音层;隔音材料,阻声灰泥。

pugh [pjuː; pju] ***int***. 呸!〔表轻蔑、憎恶等〕。

pu·gil·ism [ˈpjuːdʒilizəm; ˋpjudʒəˏlɪzəm] ***n***. (空手打的)拳击。

pu·gil·ist [ˈpjuːdʒilist; ˋpjudʒəlɪst] ***n***. **1.** 拳击家,拳师。**2.** (争论中的)劲敌,厉害的对手。**-ic** ***a***.

pug·na·cious [pʌgˈneiʃəs; pʌgˋneʃəs] ***a***. 爱吵架的,好斗的。**-naci·ty** ***n***. 好斗性。

pug·ree [ˈpʌgriː; ˋpʌgri] ***n***.〔印度用英语〕轻头巾;帽沿遮阳布。

puis·ne [ˈpjuːni; ˋpjunɪ]〔主英〕**I** ***a***. 晚辈的;年小的;下位的;【法】后的,其次的 (*to*)。**II** ***n***. 陪席法官;晚辈。*a ~ judge* 陪席法官。

pu·is·sance [ˈpju(ː)isns; ˋpjuɪsns] ***n***.〔诗,古〕力,权力,威力,势力,精神。

pu·is·sant [ˈpju(ː)isnt; ˋpjuɪsnt] ***a***.〔诗,古〕有力的,有势力的,有权力的,强大的。

pu·ja, poo·ja [ˈpuːdʒɑː; ˋpudʒɑ] ***n***. **1.** (印度教的)偶像礼拜,宗教仪式。**2.**〔印度用英语〕〔常 *pl*.〕祈祷文。

puke [pjuːk; pjuk] **I** ***n***. **1.** 呕吐;呕出物;催吐剂。**2.** 绰号。**3.** 可唾弃的人;令人作呕的人[事物、情形]。**II** ***vi***. 吐,呕;呕出 (*up*)。*mewling and puking* 哽咽,抽抽噎噎地哭。

puk·ka(h) [ˈpʌkə; ˋpʌkə] ***a***. = pucka. ~ **gen**〔军俚〕可靠的情报 (*opp*. duff gen)。

pul [puːl; pʊl] ***n***. (*pl*. ~(***s***)) 普尔〔阿富汗的货币单位,相当于 1/100 的阿富汗尼〕。

Pu·la [ˈpuːlɑː; ˋpulɑ] ***n***. 普拉〔南斯拉夫港市〕。

Pu·las·ki [puˈlæski; pʊˋlæskɪ] ***n***.〔美〕(消防员、伐木工人等用的)斧镐〔源出美国林场主 Edward ~〕。

pul·chri·tude [ˈpʌlkritjuːd; ˋpʌlkrɪˏtjud] ***n***.〔罕〕体态美,美丽,漂亮(指人)。**-tu·di·nous** ***a***.

pule [pjuːl; pjul] ***vi***. (小鸡等)叽叽地叫;(婴儿等伤心地)抽噎地哭泣。

pu·li [ˈpuːli; ˋpulɪ] ***n***. (*pl*. ***pu·lik*** [-liːk; -lik], ***pu-lis***) [Hung.] 匈牙利粗毛狗〔用来看守农物〕。

Pul·it·zer [ˈpulitsə; ˋpjulɪtsɚ] ***n***. 普利策〔姓氏〕。~ **Prize** 普利策奖金〔美国的一种在文学、艺术和新闻界内颁发的奖金〕。

pull [pul; pʊl] **I** ***vt***. **1.** 拉,拖,牵,曳 (*opp*. push);勒(马)。**2.** 拽住;扽;扯破,扯开。**3.** 拔去(鸡等的)毛;拔(牙齿、瓶塞等) (*up*);摘,采(苹果等);搬走,移开。**4.** 摇(橹),荡(桨);摆渡(旅客);(船)有…桨。**5.** 吸引,招徕(顾客);获得(援助等)。**6.**〔俚〕捉拿(罪犯);(警察)突袭(赌窟等)。**7.** 抽出(刀子)。**8.** 完成(计划等)。**9.** 玩(手段等);干…(勾当)。**10.**【印】用手印刷,打(校样)。**11.**【赛马】勒马减速而故意跑输;【板球】从三柱门的 *off* 方面把(球)打到 *on* 方面;【高尔夫】把(球)打向左面;【拳击】猛击不中;【运】扭伤(脚筋等);拉伤(肌肉)。**12.** 呈现(面容)。**13.**〔口〕取消;撤回;撤销。~ *a fowl* [*hide*] 拔鸟毛[皮上的毛]。~ *sb. by his ear* 扯某人的耳朵。~ *a cart* 拉车。~ *a tooth* 拔牙。*The boat ~s four oars*. 这条船有四把桨。~ *tricks* 耍欺诈手段。*a game ~ing a large crowd* 一场吸引了许多人的比赛。~ *a ligament in one's leg* 扭伤一条腿。*She ~ed the letter to pieces*. 她把信扯成碎片。~ *a knife* 拔刀。— ***vi***. **1.** 拉,拖;被拔;被拉。**2.** 能被拉[拖、拔];(被拖着)动;行驶;(船)被划;划船 (*away*; *for*; *out*)。**3.** 一口喝下去 (*at*);抽烟 (*at*)。**4.** 马咬嚼子不听话。**5.** 吃力地前进。**6.** 得到后援。**7.** 吸引住顾客;(就职等时)提携提携。**8.** (赛跑时)超过对方。*The fish ~s on the line*. 鱼拉钓丝。~ *up the hill* 吃力地爬山。~ *at a pipe* 抽烟。*The drawer won't ~ out*. 抽屉拉不开。*a train ~ing out of the station* 一列开出车站的火车。~ ***a boner***〔美俚〕失错;弄错,闹大笑话,出丑。~ ***a fast one*** (***on sb***.)〔美〕对…行骗,诈取。~ ***a line***〔美俚〕话多起来,嘴碎起来。~ ***a*** (***long***) ***face*** 板起面孔,拉下面孔。~ ***a poor mouth***〔美俚〕装穷拒绝付款[捐款]。~ ***a shut-eye***〔美俚〕喝醉。~ ***about*** = ~ ***and haul*** 乱拖;拖来拖去。~ ***apart*** [***asunder***] 扯断(索子等);劝开(吵闹)。~ ***at a rope*** 套住绳子拉。~ ***back*** 拉回来,退;节省,收缩;改变主意,不守诺言。~ ***caps*** [***wigs***] 打架。***P- devil***, ~ ***baker***! [***P- dog***, ~ ***cat***!]〔拔河赛〕(鼓励双方)大家加油! ~ ***down*** **1.** 挣钱,赚。**2.** 压低,贬低。**3.** 拆坏(房子等);(疾病使人)衰弱;推翻,打倒(政府等) (~ *down one's house about one's ears* 自取灭亡)。***P-down your jacket*** ! 镇定。~ ***foot***〔俚〕逃走。~ ***for***〔美口〕帮助;声援。~ ***in*** **1.** 使后退,缩(头等)。**2.** 节省(费用)。**3.** (火车等)到站;船靠近(海岸)。**4.** 逃走,离开。***P- in your ears*** [***barber pole***, ***horns***, ***neck***]!〔美俚〕不要你管闲事! 住嘴! ~ ***it*** = ~ foot. ~ ***off*** **1.** 忙着脱(衣服、鞋等)。**2.** (竞争)得胜,得(奖)。**3.** 做好,完成;协定。**4.**〔美〕干,实行。**5.** 开(船);(船)离开 (*from* shore)。**6.** 走开,逃走;释放 (~ *off one's hat to* 脱帽招呼)。~ ***on*** 穿上(衣服),戴(手套),穿(袜子)。~ ***oneself together*** 定定心,恢复精神,重新振作。~ ***oneself up*** 自制;急忙止住。~ ***one's freight***〔美俚〕急速出发;离开。~ ***one's leg***〔美俚〕**1.** 逗,惹,嘲弄。**2.** 诳骗。~ ***sb.'s nose*** = ~ ***sb***. ***by the nose*** 牵人鼻子[侮辱的动作]。~ ***sb.'s sleeve*** = ~ ***sb***. ***by the sleeve*** 拉某人袖子使注意。~ ***one's weight*** 尽自己的力量做。~ ***out*** **1.** 拔(牙等)。**2.** 拖长(谈话等)。**3.** 把船划出;(车、船等)开出;(人)出发。**4.**〔美〕离(职)。**5.**【空】(飞机的)改出动作(由俯冲姿势变成水平姿势)。**6.** (抽屉等)脱出。~ ***out of the fire*** 使转败为胜。~ ***over*** **1.** (把衣裳)从头上套下来穿。**2.** 推翻(桌子等)。**3.**〔口〕把(车)靠拢路边。~ ***round*** (使)恢复健康,医好…的病。~ ***sth***. ***on sb***. 在…方面欺骗某人。~ ***the chestnuts out of the fire*** 火中取栗,为他人作牺牲品。~ ***the iron-man stunt***【美运】在同一运动会中参加好几个比赛项目。~ ***the strings*** [***wires***] 在幕后拉线,在幕后操纵。~ ***through*** **1.** ***vt***. 使克服困难,使渡过难关 (*Good nursing ~ed him through*. 看护周到使他脱离险境)。**2.** ***vi***. 渡过难关,克服困难,脱离险境;(竞争时)赶过,追过。~ ***to*** [***in***] ***pieces*** **1.** 扯碎。**2.** 批评得一文不值,谩骂。~ ***to-***

gether 1. 通力合作,同心协力去做。2. 拼凑。~ **up** 1. *vt*. 拔出(树、桩等);根绝,勒住(马),拉住(马车等);吃力地攀登;〔口〕制止,责骂,责备 (*He was ~ed up for his error*. 他因过失受到了责骂)。2. *vi*. (马、人力车、马车等等)停止,刹住。~ **up lame** 〔美〕(赛马的马)跑得慢。~ **up to** [**with**] …追上,赶上。

II *n*. 1. 拉,拖,牵引。2.【骨牌】抓牌;扣(枪的)板机。3. 拉力,牵引力,(月等的)引力;〔美〕(对人的)吸引力,魅力。4. 〔口〕一划,划游。5. 〔口〕(酒的)一杯,〔英〕(烟的)一口;〔英〕(酒馆中给顾客)额外添加的酒。6. 把柄,把手,(枪的)拉绳;(啤酒水压机的)挺棍 (= beer-~), 啤酒泵。7.【赛马】(故意要输而)勒住马,放慢。8.【印】手印样,校样。9.【高尔夫球】左弯球。10. 〔俚〕利益,好处;照顾;门路,关系。*A good education gives a man a great ~*. 良好的教育能给人很大好处。*have a ~ with the police* [*on the governor*] 跟警察[州长]有关系。*It's along ~ to the top of the building*. 爬上楼顶很吃力。*a ~ at a cigar* 吸一口雪茄。*a wooden ~ for a drawer* 抽屉的木把手。**give a ~ at** 拉(拖)…。**have** [**take**] **a ~ at the bottle** [**a pipe**] 〔口〕喝一杯[吸一口]。**have the ~ of** [**over**] 胜过,强于。**the long ~** (酒等的)添送。~**-back** 1. 〔口〕障碍,不利,弱点。2. 反动家伙。3. 撤回。~**-date**(包装食品袋上标明的)保鲜期。~**-over** (无领无扣的)套衫,绒线套衫。~ **tag** (开罐等用的)拉片。~**-through** 1. (一头拴有布的)枪筒清扫绳。2.【军口】瘦长汉子。~**-up** 1. (马车的)停车处,休息处;停止,休息。2.【空】(飞机的)拉起动作,急升动作(特指从平飞位置转入急升的动作);【体】(单杠)引体向上。

pulled [puld; puld] *a*. 1. 扯下来的,摘下来的。2. 拔去了毛的。3. 健康衰退了的,没有精神的。~ *bread* 面包渣儿。~ *figs* 用手指拉成扁而圆的无花果果干。

pull·er [ˈpulə; ˋpulɚ] *n*. 1. 拉的人;摘的人,拔的人。2. 拔具,拉出器。3. 划手。4. 难勒制的马。5. 〔美〕私酒运入人。~**-in** 〔美俚〕顾客招揽员,拉生意的人。

pul·let [ˈpulit; ˋpulɪt] *n*. 1. (孵出后不到一年的)小母鸡。2. 〔英〕(食用)毛蛤。3. 〔美俚〕小姑娘。

pul·ley [ˈpuli; ˋpulɪ] I *n*.【机】滑车,滑轮,皮带轮。*a compound ~* 复滑车。*a differential ~* 差动滑车。*a driven ~* 从动滑车。*a driving ~* 主动滑车。*a fast* [*fixed*] *~* 固定滑车。*an idle* [*a loose*] *~* 游滑车。*a movable ~* 动滑车。II *vt*. 1. 用滑车举起;用滑车推动。2. 给…装滑车。

Pull·man[1] [ˈpulmən; ˋpulmən] *n*. 普尔曼[姓氏]。

Pull·man[2], **pull·man** [ˈpulmən; ˋpulmən] *n*. (*pl*. ~*s*)【铁道】(G. M. Pullman 设计的设备特别舒适的)普尔门式火车卧车〔又叫 ~ car〕。*a side door ~* 〔美〕有盖货车。

pul·lu·late [ˈpʌljuleit; ˋpʌljəlet] *vi*. 1. 萌芽,发芽;成长。2. 繁殖;发生;发达。**-la·tion** *n*.

pul·ly-haul [ˈpulihɔːl; ˋpulɪhɔl] *vt*., *vi*. 〔英口〕(竭力)拖,拉。**-y** *n*., *a*. 〔英口〕拖(的),拉(的)。

pul·mom·e·ter [pulˈmɔmitə; pʌlˋmɑmətɚ] *n*. 肺(容)量计。

pul·mo·na·ry [ˈpʌlmənəri; ˋpʌlmənɛrɪ] *a*. 1. 肺的。2. 有肺的。3. 肺状的,像肺的。4. 对肺有影响的。*the ~ artery* [*veins*] 肺动[静]脉。~ *complaints* [*diseases*] 肺病。~ *tuberculosis* 肺结核。

pul·mo·nate [ˈpʌlmənit; ˋpʌlməˌnet] I *a*. 有肺的;【动】有肺类的。II *n*. 有肺类的(动物)。

pul·mon·ic [pʌlˈmɔnik; pʌlˋmɑnɪk] I *a*. 1. 肺的。2. 肺病的,肺炎的。II *n*. 1. 肺病药。2. 肺病病人。

pul·motor [ˈpʌlməutə; ˋpʌlˌmotɚ] *n*. 人工呼吸器。

pulp [pʌlp; pʌlp] I *n*. 1. 果肉;(植物的)髓。2. 牙髓。3. 纸浆;浆状物;【冶】矿浆。4. 〔美俚〕〔常 *pl*.〕庸俗杂志。*a ~ cavity* 牙髓腔。*a ~ saver* 纸浆回收机。*a ~ mill* 纸浆厂。~ *wood* 制(纸)浆木材。II *a*. 〔美俚〕(杂志)低级趣味的。**beat one to a ~** 打瘫某人,狠揍某人。**be reduced to ~** 1. 成纸浆,成软块。2. 累得瘫软。III *vt*. 1. 把…捣成浆状;把…制成纸浆。2. 取出(咖啡豆的)果肉。— *vi*. 成浆状。

pulped [pʌlpt; pʌlpt] *a*. 〔美俚〕被打得要死的。

pulp·er [ˈpʌlpə; ˋpʌlpɚ] *n*. 1 (咖啡豆的)果肉采集器。2. 搅碎[碎浆]机。

pulp·i·fy [ˈpʌlpifai; ˋpʌlpəˌfaɪ] *vt*. 1. 使成纸浆。2. 使软烂,使柔软。

pulp·i·ness [ˈpʌlpinis; ˋpʌlpɪnɪs] *n*. 1. 浆状;果肉状。2. 稀烂;柔软性。

pul·pit [ˈpulpit; ˋpulpɪt] *n*. 1. 讲道坛;〔the ~〕〔集合词〕教士,牧师;传教。2. (捕鲸船的)标枪舌。3. 〔英空俚〕飞机驾驶员座位。4. (机器)操纵台。*a ~ banger* [*smiter, thumper*] 〔美俚〕牧师。

pul·pit·eer [ˌpulpiˈtiə; ˌpulpɪtˋɪr] I *n*. 〔蔑〕讲道的,说教者。II *vi*. 说教,讲道。

pul·pit·er [ˈpulpitə; ˋpulpɪtɚ] *n*. 讲道者,牧师。

pulp·less [ˈpʌlplis; ˋpʌlplɪs] *a*. 无浆的;干燥的。

pulp·ous, pulp·y [ˈpʌlpəs, ˈpʌlpi; ˋpʌlpəs, ˋpʌlpɪ] *a*. 果肉(状)的,肉多的,浆状的,浆多的;柔软的。

pul·que [ˈpu(ː)lki:, Sp. ˈpuːlkei; ˋpulki, ˋpulke] *n*. (墨西哥人所饮的)龙舌兰酒。

pul·sant [ˈpʌlsnt; ˋpʌlsənt] *a*. 1. (心脏)跳动的,(脉)搏动的,有节奏地震动(或鼓动)的。2. 发抖的,颤动的。

pul·sar [ˈpʌlsɑː; ˋpʌlsɑr] *n*.【天】脉冲星。

pul·sate [pʌlˈseit, ˈpʌlseit; pʌlˋset, ˋpʌlset] *vi*. 1. (脉等)搏动,(心脏)跳动,悸动,有规律地拍击;【电】脉动,脉冲,波动。2. 震动。— *vt*. 筛选(钻石)。*a pulsating* [*pulsatory*] *current*【电】脉冲电流。

pul·sa·tile [ˈpʌlsətail; ˋpʌlsətl] I *a*. 1. 脉动的,搏动的,跳动的。2. (乐器)敲打的。II *n*.【乐】敲打乐器〔鼓等〕。

pul·sa·tion [pʌlˈseiʃən; pʌlˋseʃən] *n*. 1. 脉搏,悸动;跳动,颤动;【电】脉动。2.【罗马法】(不痛程度的)殴打。

pul·sa·tive, pul·sa·to·ry [ˈpʌlsətiv, -təri; ˋpʌlsətɪv, -tərɪ] *a*. = pulsatile.

pul·sa·tor [ˈpʌlseitə, pʌlˈseitə; ˋpʌlsetɚ, pʌlˋsetɚ] *n*. 〔L.〕脉动器。

pul·sa·to·ry [ˈpʌlsətəri; ˋpʌlsəˌtorɪ] *a*. 能跳动的;有跳动特征的;跳动的。

pulse[1] [pʌls; pʌls] I *n*. 1. 脉搏;有节奏的跳动;【动】脉冲(波);脉动。2. 意向;倾向。3.【乐】拍子,律动。*His ~ was at a hundred*. 他的脉搏(每分钟)一百次。*a galloping ~* 急脉。*a high ~* 强脉。*a long* [*slow*] *~* 缓脉。*a weak ~* 弱脉。*an action ~* (火箭)触发脉冲。*a carry ~* 进位脉冲。*a driving ~* 起动脉冲。**feel sb.'s ~ = have one's fingers on the ~ of sb**. 按某人的脉;探某人的意向。**stir sb.'s ~s** 鼓动某人的情绪;使人兴奋。**with quickened ~s** 心跳得更快地。II *vi*. 脉跳动;震动;脉动。— *vt*. 使发生脉冲;用脉冲输送(血等)(*in*; *out*)。~ **code**【无】脉冲(编)码。~ **frequency**【无】脉冲频率。~**-jet** 脉动式空气喷气发动机。~**-on** *n*. 启动。~ **radar** 脉冲雷达。~ **ripple** [**ringing**]【物】脉动。

pulse[2] [pʌls; pʌls] *n*. 〔*sing*., *pl*.〕豆类;豆。

pulse·less [ˈpʌlslis; ˋpʌlslɪs] *a*. 1. 没有脉搏的。2. 没有生气的;不活动的。

pul·sim·e·ter [pʌlˈsimitə; pʌlˋsɪmɪtɚ] *n*. 1.【医】验脉器,脉搏计。2.【物】脉冲计。

pul·som·e·ter [pʌlˈsɔmitə; pʌlˋsɑmətɚ] *n*. 1. 蒸汽吸水机;气压唧筒。2.【动】脉震计,脉冲计。3.【医】验脉器,脉搏计。

pul·ver·iz·a·ble [ˈpʌlvəraizəbl; ˋpʌlvəˌraɪzəbl] *a*. 可以粉碎的。

pul·ver·i·za·tion [ˌpʌlvəraiˈzeiʃən; ˌpʌlvəraɪˋzeʃən] *n*. 研末(作用),粉碎(作用)。

pul·ver·i·za·tor [ˈpʌlvəraizeitə; ˋpʌlvəraɪzetɚ] *n*. 粉

碎器。

pul·ver·ize [ˈpʌlvəraiz; ˋpʌlvəˏraɪz] *vt*. 1. 把…磨成粉状,弄碎。2. 把(水等)喷成雾。3. 粉碎(议论等)。~*d soap stone* 滑石粉。— *vi*. 成粉,碎。

pul·ver·iz·er [ˈpʌlvəraizə; ˋpʌlvəˏraɪzɚ] *n*. 1. 粉碎机,研磨机。2. 喷雾器。3. 粉碎者。

pul·ver·ous [ˈpʌlvərəs; ˋpʌlvərəs] *a*. 粉的;粉状的;满是粉末的。

pul·ver·u·lent [pʌlˈverjulənt; pʌlˋverjələnt] *a*. 1. 粉的,灰尘的,满是粉末[灰尘]的。2. (岩石等)脆的。3. 【植】如被尘的。

P

pul·vil·lus [pʌlˈviləs; pʌlˋvɪləs] *n*. (*pl*. *-li* [-ai; -aɪ]) 【动】1. 垫。2. (昆虫的)毛垫。**pul·vil·lar** *a*.

pul·vi·nate [ˈpʌlvineit, -nit; ˋpʌlvənet, -nɪt] *a*. 1. 垫子形的。2. 【植】具叶枕的。**-ly** *ad*.

pul·vi·nus [pʌlˈvainəs; pʌlˋvaɪnəs] *n*. (*pl*. *-ni* [-nai; -naɪ]) 【植】叶座;叶枕。

pu·ma [ˈpjuːmə; ˋpjumə] *n*. 【动】美洲狮(皮)。

pum·e·lo [ˈpʌmiləu; ˋpʌməlo] *n*. 柚,文旦(=pomelo)。

pum·ice [ˈpʌmis; ˋpʌmɪs] I *n*. 轻石,浮石;浮岩;泡沫岩〔亦作 ~ stone, 多用于去污和磨光〕。II *vt*. 用浮石磨,用轻石擦(=pumicate, pumicestone)。

pu·mi·ceous [pjuːˈmiʃəs; pjuˋmɪʃəs] *a*. 浮石的,像轻石的;轻石质的。

pum·mel [ˈpʌml; ˋpʌml] *vt*. =pommel.

pum·me·lo [ˈpʌmiləu; ˋpʌməlo] *n*. =pomelo.

PUMP =politically upwardly mobile personality 政治新星,政治上有望晋升人士。

pump[1] [pʌmp; pʌmp] *n*. (浅口无带的)轻舞鞋。

pump[2] [pʌmp; pʌmp] I *n*. 1. 泵,抽(水)机,唧筒;抽机作用,抽动;抽运;泵声。2. 〔口〕盘问,用话套话;盘问者,善于探听消息的人。3. 〔卑、俚〕反应迟钝的人,呆子。4. 〔美俚〕心。5. 〔喻〕(昆虫的)吸盘。*a bicycle* ~ 打气筒。*a breast* ~ 吸奶器。*a feed* ~ 给水泵。*a force* [*pressure*] ~ 压力泵,压水泵。*a fore* ~ 预抽真空泵。*fetch a* ~ 用水灌满抽机排去空气然后抽水。*For all my* ~*s, he did not tell the truth; he is truly a* ~. 盘来问去,总不实说;他实在是个牛皮筋。II *vt*. 1. 用泵抽(水等);抽干(井等);绞(脑筋)。2. 〔俚〕把(秘密等)盘问出来,诱问出来。3. 用打气筒(给车胎)打气(*up*);把(子弹)打进。4. 把(功课等)塞进(脑中),注入。5. 〔口〕使疲倦,使喘气。~ *a ship* 抽出船底的水。*a* ~*ed tree* 腐心木。— *vi*. 1. 用泵(抽水),用泵增压,抽动。2. 被盘问出来。3. (像泵柄一样)上下运动;(寒暑表水银柱)猛升猛降。4. 喷出。5. 〔口〕卖力气。***be*** ~***ed out*** 累得喘不过气来。***prime the*** ~ 1. (政府)以增大开支刺激经济复苏。2. 对(企业等)的经营管理予以支援。~ ***abuses upon sb***. 破口骂人。~ ***away at*** 努力干。~ ***out*** 抽空。~ **brake** 泵柄;液压制动器。~ **handle** *n*. 1. 泵柄。2. 〔俚〕手,手杆,胳臂。3. 〔俚〕使劲的握手。~**-handle** *vt*. 〔口〕使劲握手。~ **priming** 经济刺激开支。~ **room** 1. (温泉等处的)矿泉水饮用处。2. (供水处等的)水泵房。**-age** *n*. 泵的抽水量。**-ship** *vi*., *n*. 〔海俚、卑〕小便,撒尿。

pumped [pʌmpt; pʌmpt] *a*. 1. 〔俚〕喘得上气不接下气的。2. 〔俚〕兴奋的,紧张的。

pump·er [ˈpʌmpə; ˋpʌmpɚ] *n*. 1. 用泵人;司泵员。2. 〔美〕用泵抽的油井。

pum·per·nick·el [ˈpumpənikl; ˋpʌmpɚˏnɪkl] *n*. 裸麦粗面包。

pump·kin [ˈpʌmpkin; ˋpʌmpkɪn] *n*. 1. 【植】南瓜;南瓜藤。2. 〔口〕夜郎自大的蠢货;〔美俚〕〔some ~s〕重要人物,大亨;重要的东西。3. 〔美俚〕脑袋瓜。*a* ~ *center* 〔美〕幻想中的典型孤村。~ ***and squash*** 南瓜。~**-ash** 【植】绒毛白蜡树。~ **head** 〔美〕笨蛋,傻瓜。~**-seed** 1. 南瓜子;西葫芦子。2. 太阳鱼〔产于北美〕。~ **time** 由兴旺突然转向衰落的时刻〔源自童话《灰姑娘》中大马车到午夜时刻又变回来成为南瓜〕。

pun[1] [pʌn; pʌn] I *n*. 双关俏皮话,双关语。II *vi*. (-*nn*-) 用双关语(*on*, *upon*)。~ *on a word* 一语双关。— *vt*. 以双关语劝说。

pun[2] [pʌn; pʌn] *vt*. (-*nn*-) 〔英方〕把(土,碎石等)捣结实[夯实](*up*)。

pu·na [ˈpuːnɑː, Sp. ˈpuna; ˋpunɑ, ˋpʊna] *n*. 1. 山间高原,尤指南美贫瘠干冷高原。2. 〔*pl*.〕普那草原,南美安第斯山西部草原。

Pun·a·kha [ˈpunəkə; ˋpunəkə] *n*. 普那卡〔不丹县名〕。

Punch [pʌntʃ; pʌntʃ] *n*. 1. 潘趣〔英国木偶戏 Punch and Judy 中的主角,背驼,鼻长而钩, Judy 是他的妻子,时常和他吵架〕。2. (英国 1841 年创刊的)《笨拙画报》。***as pleased*** [***proud***] ***as*** ~ 扬扬得意[神气十足]。

punch[1] [pʌntʃ; pʌntʃ] I *n*. 1. 冲压机,冲床,冲孔(机),穿孔(机)。2. 打印器;剪票铗;大钢针。3. (冲或打出的)孔[切口]。*a* ~ *press* 冲床,冲孔机。*a calculating* ~ 穿孔计算机。*a conductor's* ~ 剪票铗。***put more*** ~ ***into*** 加强。II *vt*. (用压穿器)穿孔,冲孔;(用打印器)打印;(用票铗)剪票。*have one's ticket* ~*ed* 剪了票。~ ***in*** (***out***) 用记时钟在考勤卡上打印上(下)班时间。~**(ed) card** [**tape**] 【统计】(统计机上用的)穿孔卡片。

punch[2] [pʌntʃ; pʌntʃ] I *vt*. 1. 用拳头打,殴打;(用肘)推;(用棒)捅。2. 〔美西部〕赶(家畜)。— *vi*. 用拳猛击;用力击;用力按。II *n*. 1. 拳打,殴打。2. 〔俚〕(语言、小说等的)力量;效果;精力;魄力。*There was not much* ~ *in his remarks*. 他的话没啥力量。***get a*** ~ ***on the head*** 头上挨一拳。***pull the*** ~***es*** 〔美俚〕故意不用力打,故意让对手打胜。~ **line** (击中要害的)警句,妙语。

punch[3] [pʌntʃ; pʌntʃ] *n*. 1. 〔英〕(英国 Suffolk 地方产的)矮小肥胖的驮马(=Suffolk punch)。2. 〔英方〕矮胖子;粗而短的东西。

punch[4] [pʌntʃ; pʌntʃ] *n*. 1. (果汁、香料、奶、茶、酒等搀和的)香甜混合饮料;多味果汁饮料。2. 饮香甜混合饮料的聚会。3. =~ bowl. 4. (东印度的)五人会议。~ **bowl** 1. 混合香甜饮料的大酒钵。2. (山间)圆形凹地。3. 〔美俚〕拳击场。~ **ladle** 舀香甜混合饮料用的长柄勺。

punch·board [ˈpʌntʃˌbɔːd; ˋpʌntʃbɔrd] *n*. 抽彩盘。

punch-up [ˈpʌntʃʌp; ˋpʌntʃʌp] *n*. 〔主英俚〕1. 一场吵闹的殴斗;吵闹;怒骂。2. 打群架;吵闹声;隆隆声。

punch·drunk [ˈpʌntʃdrʌŋk; ˋpʌntʃˏdrʌŋk] *a*. 1. 〔美俚〕(拳赛中)被打得头昏眼花的;惶惑的。2. 夜郎自大的,过于自信的。3. 自私的。

pun·cheon[1] [ˈpʌntʃən; ˋpʌntʃən] *n*. 1. 短柱;(煤矿坑内的)架柱,支柱。2. 〔美〕(圆木料对剖成的)半圆木料。3. 打印器;打孔器。4. 石凿,凿子。

pun·cheon[2] [ˈpʌntʃən; ˋpʌntʃən] *n*. (72—120 加仑的)大桶,一大桶的分量。

punch·er [ˈpʌntʃə; ˋpʌntʃɚ] *n*. 1. 穿孔的人。2. 穿孔机;打印器。3. 〔俚〕服务员。4. 〔美〕=cowboy.

Pun·chinel·lo [ˌpʌntʃiˈneləu; ˏpʌntʃəˋnɛlo] *n*. (*pl*. ~(*s*)) 1. (意大利木偶喜剧的)丑角。2. =Punch. 3. 〔p-〕滑稽人;矮胖子;怪模怪样的男子[东西]。

punch·ing-bag, punch·ing·ball [ˈpʌntʃiŋbæg, -bɔːl; ˋpʌntʃɪŋbæg, -bɔl] *n*. (练习拳击用的)吊索,吊球。

punch·y [ˈpʌntʃi; ˋpʌntʃɪ] *a*. (***punch·i·er***; ***punch·i·est***) 〔美口〕1. 有力的;精力旺盛的,生气勃勃的。2. (拳击中)被打得晕头转向的,摇摇晃晃的,惶惑的(=punchdrunk)。

punct. =punctuation.

punc·tate, punc·tat·ed [ˈpʌŋkteit, -teitɪd; ˋpʌŋktet, -tɪd] *a*. 【动、植】有斑点的,有细孔的,具刻点的,具点的;细孔状。

punc·til·io [pʌŋkˈtiliəu; pʌŋkˋtɪlɪˏo] *n*. (*pl*. ~*s*) 1. (仪式等的)细节。2. 死板,拘板,拘泥形式。

punc·til·i·ous [pʌŋ*k*ˈtiliəs; pʌŋkˋtɪlɪəs] *a*. 礼仪烦琐的;死板的,拘泥形式的。**-ly** *ad*.

punc·tu·al [ˈpʌŋ*k*tjuəl; ˋpʌŋktʃuəl] *a*. 1. 严守时刻的,不误期限的,准时的,如期的;准确的。2. = punctilious. 3.【几】点的。*as* ~ *as the clock* 时间准确(的)。~ *to the minute* 一分不差。*a* ~ *light source* 点光源。**-ly** *ad*. 1. 按时,如期。2. 郑重其事地;〔古〕死板地。

punc·tual·i·ty [ˌpʌŋ*k*tjuˈæliti; ˏpʌŋktʃuˋælətɪ] *n*. 严守时间;敏捷,守信用。

punc·tu·ate [ˈpʌŋ*k*tjueit; ˋpʌŋktʃuˏet] *vt*. 1. 加标点于,标点(文章)。2. 加重(语气等);强调。3. 间断;不时打断(演说等)。~ *one's talk with sobs* 边哭边讲,抽抽噎噎地讲。*Each word was* ~*d by a blow*. 字字拍桌,慷慨激昂。— *vi*. 点标点。**-a·tor** *n*. 点标点者。

punc·tu·a·tion [ˌpʌŋ*k*tʃuˈeiʃən; ˏpʌŋktʃuˋeʃən] *n*. 1. 标点;标点法;全部标点符号。2. 〔Semitic 语〕元[母]音点法。3.【动】斑点。*close* [*open*] ~ 精细[简略]标点法。~ **marks** [**points**] 标点符号。

punc·tu·late [ˈpʌŋ*k*tjuleit, -lit; ˋpʌŋktʃələt, -lɪt] *a*.【生】具小点的;有细小孔的。**-la·tion** *n*.

punc·tum [ˈpʌŋ*k*təm; ˋpʌŋktəm] *n*. (*pl*. **-ta** [-tə; -tə])【解,植】细穿孔,点,斑点,刻点。

punc·ture [ˈpʌŋktʃə; ˋpʌŋktʃɚ] I *n*. 1. 刺,扎,戳。2. 穿孔,刺痕,刺伤;扎伤。3.【动】刻点;细孔,小点。4. (车胎等的)刺孔。II *vt*. 1. 用针等刺,戳通,穿孔,击穿,打穿。2. 揭穿。— *vi*. (车胎等)刺破,穿孔。

pun·dit [ˈpʌndit; ˋpʌndɪt] *n*. 1. (印度的)学者,梵学者。2. 〔谑〕博学的人;空谈家。

pung [pʌŋ; pʌŋ] *n*. 〔美方〕方箱形雪车。

pun·gent [ˈpʌndʒənt; ˋpʌndʒənt] *a*. 1. 辣的,刺鼻的,(味等)刺激性的。2. 尖酸刻薄的,泼辣的。3.【生】尖形的;尖锐的。~ *sarcasm* 尖酸刻薄的讽刺。**pun·gen·cy** [-i; -ɪ] *n*.

Pu·nic [ˈpjuːnik; ˋpjunɪk] I *a*. 1. 古迦太基 (Carthage) (人)的。2. 没有信义的,反复无常的。II *n*. 古迦太基语。~ **apple** 石榴。~ **faith** 反叛,背信弃义。(*the*) ~ **Wars** 罗马和迦太基间的三次布匿战役。

pu·ni·ness [ˈpjuːninis; ˋpjunɪnɪs] *n*. 1. 短小;弱小。2. 次要,不足道。

pun·ish [ˈpʌniʃ; ˋpʌnɪʃ] *vt*. 1. 罚,处罚;惩罚;〔口〕严厉对付,严厉批评。2. (比赛)使大败,痛击(对手);〔~ oneself〕吃大亏,吃苦头。3. 〔口〕【赛马】乱糟踏(马)。4. 〔口〕大吃大喝,大量消耗。~ *sb. for his crime* 处罚某人。~ *sb. with* [*by*] *death* 处某人死刑。~ *an opponent* 严厉抨击[对付]反对者。*The enemy was severely* ~*ed*. 敌人被打得惨败。~ *one's food* 大吃。~ *the bottle* 喝干(一瓶酒等)。— *vi*. 处罚,惩罚。

pun·ish·a·ble [ˈpʌniʃəbl; ˋpʌnɪʃəbl̩] *a*. 该罚的;可受惩罚的。**-bly** *ad*.

pun·ish·er [ˈpʌniʃə; ˋpʌnɪʃɚ] *n*. 处罚者,惩罚者。

pun·ish·ing [ˈpʌniʃiŋ; ˋpʌnɪʃɪŋ] *a*. 1. 处罚的,惩罚的。2. 猛打的。3. 辛苦的。*a* ~ *assault* 猛攻。*a* ~ *blow* 狠狠的一击。

pun·ish·ment [ˈpʌniʃmənt; ˋpʌnɪʃmənt] *n*. 1. 罚,刑罚(*for*; *on*);惩罚。2. 〔口〕给吃苦头。3.【拳击】痛击;【运】使疲劳。*capital* ~ 死刑。*corporal* ~ 体刑。*disciplinary* ~ 惩戒。*inflict* [*impose*] *a* ~ *upon a criminal* 处罚犯人。

pu·ni·tion [pjuːˈniʃən; pjuˋnɪʃən] *n*. = punishment.

pu·ni·tive, pu·ni·to·ry [ˈpjuːnitiv, -təri; ˋpjunətɪv, -ˏtorɪ] *a*. 刑罚的,惩罚的。*a* ~ *expedition* 征伐,讨伐。~ *actions against* 讨伐…的战争。*a* ~ *force* 讨伐军。~ *justice* 因果报应。**-ness** *n*. 惩办主义。

Pun·ja·bi [pʌnˈdʒɑːbi; pʌnˋdʒæbɪ] *n*. 1. 旁遮普人。2. 旁遮普语。

punk[1] [pʌŋk; pʌŋk] *n*. 〔古〕妓女,娼妇。

punk[2] [pʌŋk; pʌŋk] I *n*. 〔美俚〕1. (引火用的)朽木。2. 无聊话,无聊人物,无聊东西。3. 鬅克[庞克]族〔七十年代兴起的思想和服饰都很怪异的青年〕;年轻无知的人;小伙子。4. 不中用的拳师;面包。II *a*. 〔美俚〕没价值的,低劣的;不适当的。*a* ~ *pusher* 〔美〕乡村工人的工头。~ **rock** 鬅克[庞克]摇滚乐。**-er** *n*. 鬅克摇滚乐迷。

pun·ka(h) [ˈpʌnkə; ˋpʌŋkə] *n*. 〔Hind.〕1. (棕榈叶做的)扇子。2. (吊在天花板上的)布风扇。~**-wallah** 拉布风扇的人。

pun·kie [ˈpʌŋki; ˋpʌŋkɪ] *n*. 〔美〕虻的一种。

pun·kin [ˈpʌŋkin; ˋpʌŋkɪn] *n*. 〔美〕= pumpkin. ~**head** = pumpkin-head.

pun·ner [ˈpʌnə; ˋpʌnɚ] *n*. (夯地用的)硪,夯。

pun·net [ˈpʌnit; ˋpʌnɪt] *n*. (阔而浅的)扁篮。

pun·ning·ly [ˈpʌniŋli; ˋpʌnɪŋlɪ] *ad*. 一语双关地。

pun·ny [ˈpʌni; ˋpʌnɪ] *a*. 〔美〕一语双关的。

pun·ster [ˈpʌnstə; ˋpʌnstɚ] *n*. 善于说双关话的人。

punt[1] [pʌnt; pʌnt] 〔英〕I *n*. 方头平底船。II *vt*. 1. 用篙撑(方头平底船等)。2. 用平底船装运。— *vi*. 1. 坐方头平底船走。2. 撑方头平底船。

punt[2] [pʌnt; pʌnt] I *vt*., *vi*.【足球】踢(从手上放下的未落地的球)。II *n*. 踢悬空球。~**-about** 足球练习(用球)。

punt[3] [pʌnt; pʌnt] I *vi*. (纸牌等)向庄家下赌注;【赛马】赌。II *n*. = punter.

pun·ter, punt·ist [ˈpʌntə, -ist; ˋpʌntɚ, -ɪst] *n*. 下赌注的人。

pun·to [ˈpʌntəu; ˋpʌnto] *n*. 1. 点 (= point)。2.【剑术】一刺;【裁缝】一针。

pun·ty [ˈpʌnti; ˋpʌntɪ] *n*. (制玻璃时取熔融玻璃用的)铁杆。

pu·ny [ˈpjuːni; ˋpjunɪ] *a*. (**-ni·er**; **-ni·est**) 1. 短小的;弱小的,微弱的。2. 不足道的,次要的。

pup[1] [pʌp; pʌp] I *n*. 1. 小狗,小海豹,小狐狸(等)。2. 〔俚〕(狂妄自大的)小伙子。*a conceited* [*an uppish*] ~ 狂妄自大的小伙子。*be in* ~ (母狗)怀胎。*sell sb. a* ~ 骗某人;卖骗人东西给人。II *vi*., *vt*. (**-pp-**) (母狗)生(小狗),下(仔)。~ **tent** 〔美〕楔形帆布小帐篷。

pup[2] [pʌp; pʌp] *n*. 〔俚〕低功率干扰发射机。

pup[3] [pʌp; pʌp] *n*. 〔俚〕学生 (= pupil)。

pu·pa [ˈpjuːpə; ˋpjupə] *n*. (*pl*. ~*s*, **pu·pae** [-piː; -pi]) 蛹。

pu·pal [ˈpjuːpəl; ˋpjupl̩] *a*. 蛹的。

pu·pate [ˈpjuːpeit; ˋpjupet] *vi*.【动】化蛹。**-pa·tion** *n*.

pu·pil[1] [ˈpjuːpl, ˈpjuːpil; ˋpjupl̩, ˋpjupɪl] *n*. 1. 学生〔指中、小学生,大学生叫 student〕。2.【罗马法】(不满 25 岁的)被监护人;【苏格兰法】幼年人〔不满 14 岁(男)或 12 岁(女)的被监护人〕。~ **load** 一名教师负责的学生总数。~ **teacher** (小学校的)实习老师,小先生。**-(l)a·ry** *a*.

pu·pil[2] [ˈpjuːpl, ˈpjuːpil; ˋpjupl̩, ˋpjupɪl] *n*.【解】瞳孔;【物】光瞳。**-ar**, **-(l)ary** *a*.

pu·pil·(l)age [ˈpjuːpilidʒ; ˋpjupl̩ɪdʒ] *n*. 1. 学生身分;幼年人身分。2. 幼年时代,半开化状态。

pu·pil·lar·i·ty, pu·pi·lar·i·ty [ˌpjuːpiˈlæriti; ˏpjupəˋlærətɪ] *n*.【苏格兰法】少年期。

pu·pip·a·rous [pjuˈpipərəs; pjuˋpɪpərəs] *a*. 蛹生的。

pup·pet [ˈpʌpit; ˋpʌpɪt] *n*. 1. 木偶。2. 傀儡;(行动、思想等)受别人操纵的人。*a glove* [*hand*] ~ (套在手上表演的)布袋木偶。*a* ~ *government* 傀儡政府。~ **play**, ~ **show** 木偶戏。~ **valve** [**clack**]【机】提升阀、随转阀。

pup·pet·eer [ˌpʌpiˈtiːə; ˏpʌpɪˋtɪr] *n*. 操纵傀儡的人。

pup·pet·oon [ˈpʌpituːn; ˋpʌpɪtun] *n*. (电影的)木偶片。

pup·pe·try [ˈpʌpitri; ˋpʌpɪtrɪ] *n*. 1. 〔总称〕木偶,傀儡。2. 木偶戏;假面宗教戏。3. (小说中的)假想人物。4. 虚假,假装。

Pup·pis [ˈpʌpis; ˋpʌpɪs] *n*. 〔the ~〕【天】船尾(星)座。

pup·py [ˈpʌpi; ˋpʌpɪ] *n*. **1.** 〔儿语〕小狗〔又叫 ~-dog〕;幼小的动物。**2.** 狂妄自大的小伙子;呆笨的花花公子。**3.** 〔*pl*.〕〔美俚〕脚。~**dom**, ~**hood** 小狗的状态(或时代);逞能的时代。~ **love** = calflove. **-ish** *a*. 小狗似的;爱俏的,爱打扮的;逞能的。**-ism** *n*. 小狗一般的行为;傲慢,逞能;浮华。

pur- *pref*. = pro-.

pur. = **1.** purchaser; purchasing. **2.** pursuit.

pu·ra·na [puˈrɑːnə; puˋrænə] *n*. 〔常用 P-〕印度史诗〔指印度关于创世、神、万物进化等十八篇史诗中任何一篇〕。

Pur·beck [ˈpəːbek; ˋpɝbɛk] *n*. **1.** (英国 Dorset 郡的)珀贝克半岛。**2.** 珀贝克石(= ~ stone [marble])。~ **marble** 珀贝克大理石〔一级珀贝克石〕。~ **stone** 珀贝克硬石灰石〔像大理石,建筑用〕。

pur·blind [ˈpəːblaind; ˋpɝˏblaɪnd] **I** *a*. **1.** 半瞎的,近视眼的。**2.** (脑筋)迟钝的。**3.** 〔古〕全盲的。**II** *vt*. **1.** 使成半瞎。**2.** 使愚钝。**-ness** *n*.

Pur·cell [ˈpəːsl; ˋpɝsl̩] *n*. 珀塞尔〔姓氏〕。

Pur·chas [ˈpəːtʃəs; ˋpɝtʃəs] *n*. 珀切斯〔姓氏〕。

pur·chas·a·ble [ˈpəːtʃəsəbl; ˋpɝtʃəsəbl̩] *a*. **1.** 可买的;买得起的,能买到的。**2.** 可以收买的。

pur·chase [ˈpəːtʃəs; ˋpɝtʃəs] **I** *vt*. **1.** 买,购买。**2.** 努力取得,(付出代价)赢得。**3.** 【法】(用继承以外的方法合法地)购置,取得。**4.** 【海】用滑车(等)举起。*a purchasing agent* 〔美〕办庄,代购人,采购主任。*a purchasing guild* [*association*] 购买合作社。*purchasing power* 购买力。~ *freedom with blood* 以血的代价赢得自由。**II** *n*. **1.** 买进,购买;购得物,买进物。**2.** (靠自己努力、流血等)挣得的[争取到的]东西;【法】(非继承性的房屋、地产的)购买,获得,取得;获得物。**3.** (以全年收益做单位计算的)价格;(土地等的)每年收益。**4.** 【美史】政府收买[出售]的地区。**5.** 买卖,交易;【史】买卖军职的作法。**6.** 【机】起重装置,扩力装置;复滑车,杠杆;(杠杆等的)支点;〔喻〕人情,门路。**7.** 【海】绳索;绞辘;滑轮。**8.** 紧握,紧抓。~ *and sale* 买卖。*make a* ~ 买件东西。*It is a recent* ~ *of mine*. 那是我前几天买来的。*I cannot get any* ~ *on it*. 我找不到什么门路。*The estate was sold at ten year's* ~. 田庄以相当于十年间土地收入的价钱售出。***not worth an hour's*** ~ (人)性命危在旦夕(*His life is not worth an hour's* ~. 他命在垂危)。~ **tax** 〔英〕消费品零售税。

pur·chas·er [ˈpəːtʃəsə; ˋpɝtʃəsɚ] *n*. 买主,购买人。

pur·dah [ˈpəːdɑː; ˋpɝdə] *n*. 〔印度〕**1.** (印度等地女人闺房用的)帷幔。**2.** 〔the ~〕妇女隔幔的深闺习惯[制度]。**3.** (做帷幔用的)蓝白条花布。

pure [pjuə; pjʊr] *a*. **1.** 纯的,纯粹的;清一色的(*opp*. mixed);单一的,同质的;道地的;【生】纯血统的,纯种的。**2.** 纯理论的;抽象的(*opp*. applied)。**3.** 清洁的,无垢的;清白的,清廉的,贞淑的;洗练的,文雅的。**4.** 十足的,完全的。**5.** 【乐】音调纯正的;【语音】单元音的;【希腊语法】(语根)以元音收尾的,(元音)连接其他元音的,(辅音)不连接其他辅音的。~ *gold* 纯金。~ *descent* 纯血统。~ *of* [*from*] *taint* 没有污点的。~ *white* 纯白。*the* ~ *in* [*of*] *heart* 心地纯洁的人们。*a* ~ *Englishman* 道地的英国人。~ *English* 纯正英语。~ *science* 理论科学,纯(粹)科学。~ *mathematics* 理论数学。~ *nonsense* 十足的废话。*a* ~ *accident* 纯属意外的事件。*out of* ~ *necessity* 仅仅是由于需要。~ ***and simple*** 单纯的;纯粹的,十足的。~ **bred** *a*., *n*. 纯种的(动物、家畜、植物)。~ **line** 【生】纯系。**-ness** *n*. 纯粹;纯度;清白。

pu·rée [ˈpjuərei; pjʊˋre] **I** *n*. 〔F.〕**1.** 菜泥;果泥;肉泥;酱。**2.** (把菜、肉等煮烂捣碎滤过的)纯汁浓汤。**II** *vt*. 把…做成浓汤[酱等]。

pure·ly [ˈpjuəli; ˋpjʊrlɪ] *ad*. **1.** 清洁地;纯洁地。**2.** 贞淑地。**3.** 完全,全然,单。

pur·fle [ˈpəːfl; ˋpɝfl̩] **I** *n*. (衣服的)镶边,花边;【建】边缘饰。**II** *vt*. **1.** 〔古〕给…装饰边。**2.** 在…边上刺绣。**3.** 美化。**4.** 【徽】用毛皮给…镶边[作里子]。

pur·fling [ˈpəːfliŋ; ˋpɝflɪŋ] *n*. (特指弦乐器的)镶边。

pur·ga·tion [pəːˈgeiʃən; pɝˋgeʃən] *n*. **1.** 洗清,净化。**2.** 涤罪,洗罪。**3.** (吃泻药)通便。**4.** 〔古〕(自行发誓或依审判法)雪冤,证明无罪。

pur·ga·tive [ˈpəːgətiv; ˋpɝgətɪv] **I** *a*. **1.** 洗清的,净化的。**2.** 便通的。**3.** 〔古〕证明无罪的。*a* ~ *medicine* 泻药。**II** *n*. 泻药。

pur·ga·to·ri·al [ˌpəːgəˈtɔːriəl; ˏpɝgəˋtorɪəl] *a*. 炼狱的;(在炼狱中)涤罪的。

pur·ga·to·ry [ˈpəːgətəri; ˋpɝgəˏtorɪ] **I** *a*. **1.** 洗清的;净化的。**2.** 涤罪的。**II** *n*. **1.** 【天主】死后涤罪处,炼狱。**2.** 临时惩罚所[涤罪所];暂时的苦难。

purge [pəːdʒ; pɝdʒ] **I** *vt*. **1.** 使(身、心)清净(*of*; *from*);清洗,清(党),整(党),肃清,扫除(*away*; *off*)。**2.** (用药)泻,使(人)通便。**3.** 【法】证明…无罪,雪(冤);服满(刑期)。**4.** 〔古〕赎(罪)。— *vi*. **1.** 变清净。**2.** 证明无罪。**3.** 泻下。~ *a party of undesirable members* [~ *undesirable members from a party*] 清除党内不合格分子。~ *one of suspicion* 把某人的嫌疑洗脱干净。~ *oneself of a charge* 辩明,剖白。**II** *n*. **1.** 清洗,净化。**2.** 【政】肃整。**3.** 药泻。*the party* ~ 清党[整党]运动。

purg·er [ˈpəːdʒə; ˋpɝdʒɚ] *n*. **1.** 清洗者。**2.** 泻药。**pur·gee** [pəːˈdʒiː; pɝˋdʒi] *n*. 被清洗者。

pur·i·fi·ca·tion [ˌpjuərifiˈkeiʃən; ˏpjʊrəfəˋkeʃən] *n*. **1.** 清洗,洗净;净化(作用)。**2.** 提纯,精制。**3.** 【宗】涤罪;洁身;斋戒;洁礼,祓;【天主】洁杯式。*the P- of the Virgin Mary* = Candlemas.

pu·ri·fi·ca·tor [ˈpjuərifikeitə; ˋpjʊrəfɪˏketɚ] *n*. 【宗】圣器揩布,圣器帕。

pu·ri·fi·ca·to·ry, pu·ri·fi·ca·tive [ˈpjuərifikeitəri, -tiv; pjəˋrɪfɪkəˏtorɪ, -tɪv] *a*. **1.** 使洁净的;净化的。**2.** 洁身的,涤罪的。**3.** 精炼的,精制的。

pu·ri·fi·er [ˈpjuərifaiə; ˋpjʊrəˏfaɪɚ] *n*. **1.** 使洁净的人[物];精炼者。**2.** 精炼用品;清洗装置;净化器;提纯器。

pu·ri·fy [ˈpjuərifai; ˋpjʊrəˏfaɪ] *vt*. (**-fied**) **1.** 使纯净,使洁净,净化;清除(*from*; *of*)。**2.** 使清洁身心;涤(罪)。**3.** 使(语言)纯正。**4.** 精炼,提纯,精制。— *vi*. 纯净;洁净。

pu·rin(e) [ˈpjuəri(ː)n; ˋpjʊrin] *n*. 【化】嘌呤,尿(杂)环;四氮杂茚。~ **nucleotide** 嘌呤核苷酸。

pur·ism [ˈpjuərizəm; ˋpjʊrɪzəm] *n*. 语言纯正;语言纯正癖者所使用的词语。**pur·ist** *n*. 语言纯正癖者。**pur·is·tic** *a*.

Pu·ri·tan [ˈpjuəritən; ˋpjʊrətn̩] **I** *n*. **1.** 【宗史】清教徒。**2.** 〔p-〕清教徒似的人;道德上极端拘谨的人。**II** *a*. 清教徒(似)的,极端拘谨的。~ *simplicity* 清教徒式的简朴。***the*** ~ ***city*** 〔美〕Boston 市的别名。

pu·ri·tan·ic, pu·ri·tan·i·cal [ˌpjuəriˈtænik, -ikəl; ˏpjʊrəˋtænɪk, -kl̩] *a*. **1.** 〔P-〕清教徒的;清教主义的。**2.** 〔p-〕宗教[道德]上极端拘谨的。**-i·cal·ly** *ad*.

Pu·ri·tan·ism [ˈpjuəritənizəm; ˋpjʊrətn̩ˏɪzəm] **I** *n*. **1.** 清教,清教徒气质的习俗和教义;清教主义。**2.** 〔p-〕(宗教、道德上)极端的拘谨。

pu·ri·tan·ize [ˈpjuəritənaiz; ˋpjʊrətn̩ˏaɪz] *vi*., *vt*. (使)变成清教徒。

pu·ri·ty [ˈpjuəriti; ˋpjʊrətɪ] *n*. **1.** 纯净,纯洁,纯粹,清洁;清白,清廉;贞洁。**2.** (语言等的)纯正。**3.** 【化】纯度。

purk [pəːk; pɝk] *vt*., *vi*. 〔美俚〕渗滤(= percolate)。

purl[1] [pəːl; pɝl] **I** *n*. **1.** (溪水等的)潺潺声。**2.** 涡纹。**II** *vi*. (溪水等)潺潺地流;潺潺地响。

purl[2] [pəːl; pɝl] **I** *n*. **1.** (绣边等所用)金银丝。**2.** 绣边;金[银]绣边;流苏。**3.** (编织物的)反编,倒编。**II** *vt*. **1.** 用金银丝绣。**2.** 用绣边[流苏]装饰;镶以金[银]绣边。

3. 反编。

purl[3][pəːl; pɚl] *n*. 【史】苦艾啤酒;搀有杜松子酒的热啤酒。

purl[4][pəːl; pɚl] *vt*., *n*. 〔口、方〕(马等)使(人)翻倒[颠倒]。

purl·er [ˈpəːlə; ˋpɚlɚ] *n*. 〔口〕倒落。*come* [*take*] *a* ~ 头朝地落下,倒栽葱跌下。

pur·lieu [ˈpəːljuː; ˋpɚlu] *n*. 1. 〔英史〕森林边缘地〔归原主所有〕。2. 常出入的场所。3. 〔*pl*.〕范围;界限。4. 郊外,近郊。5. 贫民窟。~ *men* 〔古〕御猎场内的土地所有人。***the dusty ~s of the law*** 律师常出入的场所;法律事务。

pur·lin(e) [ˈpəːlin; ˋpɚlɪn] *n*. 【建】檩(条);桁条。

pur·loin [pəːˈlɔin; pɚˋlɔɪn] *vt*., *vi*. 偷窃。

pu·ro·my·cin [ˌpjurəuˈmaisn; ˏpjuroˋmaɪsn̩] *n*. 【生化】嘌呤霉素。

purp [pəːp; pɚp] *n*. 〔美俚〕小狗,狗。

pur·ple [ˈpəːpl; ˋpɚpl̩] I *a*. 1. 紫色的;紫红色的;〔古〕深红色的。2. 〔诗〕鲜红的,血腥的。3. 帝王的。4. 词藻华美的。*turn ~ with rage* 气得脸色发紫。~ *wine* 红葡萄酒。*a ~ patch* [*passage*] 浮词丽句。II *n*. 1. 紫色;〔古〕紫红色 (= Tyrian [royal]~)。2. 紫衣;紫袍;〔the ~〕帝位,王权,高位;红衣主教的职位。3. 【动】紫螺。4. 皇族,贵族。5. 〔*pl*.〕【医】紫斑。***be born in the ~*** 生在帝王[王侯贵族]家。***be raised to the ~*** 升为红衣主教。***marry into the ~*** 嫁到显贵人家。III *vt*. 使成紫色。— *vi*. 变紫。**P- Heart** 〔美〕(给受伤兵士的)紫心勋章。~ **passion** 〔美俚〕暗中被爱着的人。

pur·plish, pur·ply [ˈpəːpliʃ, -pli; ˋpɚplɪʃ, -plɪ] *a*. 带紫的。

pur·port [ˈpəːpət, -pɔːt; ˋpɚport] I *n*. 1. (文件、演说等的)意义;要旨,大意,要领。2. 〔罕〕目的。II *vt*. 1. 意味着,有…的意义,大意是…。2. 声称。3. 〔罕〕意欲,意图。*The letter ~s that* ...信上写着…。*a document ~ing to be official* 据称是官方发布的文件。

pur·pose [ˈpəːpəs; ˋpɚpəs] I *n*. 1. 目的,宗旨,意向。2. 决意,意志,决心。3. 用途,效果;意义。4. (讨论中的)论题。*an all-~s army* 〔美〕全能军。*honesty of ~* 认真。*He is wanting in ~*. 他意志薄弱。***answer the*** [***one's***] ~ 适合目的,管用。***be at cross ~s*** 彼此不合;观点分歧。***be firm*** [***infirm***, ***weak***] ***of*** ~ 意志坚强[薄弱],有[无]决断力。***bring about*** [***attain***, ***accomplish***, ***carry***] ***one's*** ~ 达到目的。***for the ~ of*** 为…。***from the*** ~ 〔古〕不得要领,不中肯。***miss one's*** ~ 达不到目的。***of set*** ~ 有计划地,故意。***on*** ~ 故意;意欲,为要。***serve the*** [***one's***] ~ = answer the [one's] ~. ***speak from the*** ~ 说得不中肯。***to no*** [***little***] ~ 全无[很少]效果,完全[几乎]白费,徒,空 (*I laboured to no ~*. 我白干了)。***to some*** [***good***] ~ 相当[很]成功。***to the*** ~ 剀切地,得要领地 (*speak to the ~* 讲得剀切,说得中肯)。***to this*** ~ 在这一意义上。II *vt*. 想,企图,打算(做);决心(做)。*I ~ coming* [*to come*] *next week*. 我想下星期来。**be ~d** 〔古〕想…,打算…,决心。~**-made** *a*. 特制的,定做的。

pur·pose·ful [ˈpəːpəsful; ˋpɚpəsfʊl] *a*. 1. 有目的的;故意的。2. 意志坚强的;果断的。3. 有意义的,意味深长的。4. 重大的。*a ~ character* 果断的性格。**-ly** *ad*. 有目的地,自觉地。**-ness** *n*. 自觉性。

pur·pose·less [ˈpəːpəslis; ˋpɚpəslɪs] *a*. 1. 无目的的;无对象的。2. 无决心的。3. 无意义的;无益的。**-ly** *ad*.

pur·pose·ly [ˈpəːpəsli; ˋpɚpəslɪ] *ad*. 故意,特意。

pur·pos·ive [ˈpəːpəsiv; ˋpɚpəsɪv] *a*. = purposeful.

pur·pu·ra [ˈpəːpjurə; ˋpɚpjʊrə] *n*. 1. 【医】紫癜(病)。2. 〔P-〕【动】荔枝螺属。

pur·pure [ˈpəːpjuə; ˋpɚpjʊr] *n*. 【纹】紫色〔以左方上部至右方下部的对角线表之〕。

pur·pu·ric [pəːˈpjuərik; pɚˋpjʊrɪk] *a*. 1. 【医】紫癜(性)的。2. 【化】红紫(酸)的。3. 紫(色)的。~ **acid** 【化】红紫酸。

pur·pu·rin [ˈpəːpjurin; ˋpɚpjʊrɪn] *n*. 【化】红紫素。

purr [pəː; pɚ] I *vi*. (猫)得意似地咕噜咕噜叫;(人)高兴得喉咙咕噜咕噜响;(器物)咕噜咕噜响。— *vt*. 咕噜咕噜地叫[说、弄响]。II *n*. 咕噜咕噜的响声。

pur sang [ˈpjuəˈsɑ̃ːŋ; pyrˋsɑ̃] 〔F.〕纯种的;纯粹的;真正的,道地的。*The artist pur sang is a rarity*. 真正的艺术家很少。

purse [pəːs; pɚs] I *n*. 1. 钱包,钱袋。2. 金钱;资财,资力;国库;悬赏金,奖金;〔美俚〕拳师的收入。3. 钱袋一样的东西;(女用)手提包。4. 【解】囊,囊状部。*a cold* [*a lean*, *a light*, *an ill-lined*] ~ 空虚的钱包;贫穷。*a heavy* [*long*, *well-filled*, *well-lined*] ~ 充实的钱包;富裕。*sword and ~* 武力和财力。*the public ~* 国库。*~s under the eyes* (老年人眼睛下面的)眼垂,眼泡皮。*give a ~* 赠奖,捐款。***have a common ~*** 有公共基金。***make*** (***up***) ***a*** ~ 募捐。***One cannot make a silver ~ out of a sow's ear***. 巧妇难为无米之炊。***open one's*** ~ 解囊,出钱。***put up a*** ~ 赠奖,捐款。II *vt*. 1. 使缩拢,抽紧。2. 〔古〕把…放进钱袋。~ (*up*) *one's lips* [*mouth*] 撅嘴。— *vi*. 缩拢,皱起。~**-bearer** 1. 保管银钱的人;出纳员。2. 〔英〕在大法官前捧持国玺的人。3. 有袋类动物。~**-crab** (以椰子为食的)椰子蟹。~ **net** 袋网。~ **pride** 自负有钱。~**-proud** *a*. 夸耀富有的。~ **seine** (用两条船拖的)大型袋网。~ **strings** 〔*pl*.〕钱袋的扣绳;钱财 (*hold the ~ strings* 掌管银钱出入。*loosen the ~ strings* 乱花钱,浪费。*tighten the ~ strings* 扎紧钱袋,节省)。**-ful** *n*. 一钱袋。

purs·er [ˈpəːsə; ˋpɚsɚ] *n*. (轮船、班机等的)事务长;〔古〕(军舰的)军需官;出纳员。

pur·si·ness [ˈpəːsinis; ˋpɚsɪnɪs] *n*. 1. (因肥胖而引起的)气急;肥胖。2. (因富有而引起的)傲慢。

purs·lane [ˈpəːslin; ˋpɚslɪn] *n*. 【植】马齿苋。

pur·su·a·ble [pəˈsjuːəbl; pɚˋsjuəbl̩] *a*. 1. 可追求的,可追赶的。2. 可实行的,可从事的,可继续进行的。

pur·su·ance [pəˈsjuːəns; pɚˋsuəns] *n*. 1. 追,追踪,尾追;追求。2. 奉行,推行;实行,履行;贯彻。*the ~ of truth* 追求真理。*consistent ~ of* 坚定不移的奉行。***in ~ of*** 依…,按…;履行,推行。

pur·su·ant [pəˈsjuːənt; pɚˋsuənt] I *a*. 1. 追赶的。2. 依据的,按照的 (*to*)。3. 随后的。~ *to the rules* 按照规则。II *ad*. 依、按照 (*to*)。**-ly** *ad*. 从而,因此。

pur·sue [pəˈsjuː; pɚˋsu] *vt*. 1. 追,追赶,追踪;紧跟着,纠缠;【军】追击。2. 求,追求。3. 继续,奉行,推行,实行,从事;经营;贯彻;采取(方针等)。4. 走(路等)。~ *the enemy* 追赶敌人。*Detraction ~s the great*. 人大招物议,树大惹风吹。~ *knowledge* 求知。~ *knowledge under difficulties* 苦学。~ *a calling* 从事一种职业。~ *a subject* 继续讨论。~ *a plan* 贯彻计划。~ *the proper legal law* 采取法律上的正当手段。— *vi*. 1. 追,追随 (*after*)。2. 继续(说)。3. 〔Scot.〕起诉 (*for*)。

pur·su·er [pəˈsjuːə; pɚˋsuɚ] *n*. 1. 追赶者;追求者。2. 实行者;研究者。3. 〔英〕【法】原告。

pur·suit [pəˈsjuːt; pɚˋsut] *n*. 1. 追赶,追踪;驱逐;追击;追求。2. 实行;经营。3. 事务;职业,工作;研究。4. 〔美〕【军】歼击机,驱逐机 (= ~ plane)。~ *troops* 追击部队。*daily ~s* 日常事务。*mercantile* [*commercial*] *~s* 商业。*literary ~s* 文学工作[研究]。***in hot*** ~ 穷追。***in ~ of*** 寻求,追求 (*in ~ of health* 为了健康)。

pur·sui·vant [ˈpəːsivənt; ˋpɚswɪvənt] *n*. 1. 纹章院属官;〔废〕王使,国使。2. 〔诗〕从者,随员。

pur·sy[1] [ˈpəːsi; ˋpɚsɪ] *a*. (*-si·er*; *-si·est*) (因肥胖而)气急的;肥胖的。

pur·sy[2] [ˈpəːsi; ˋpɚsɪ] *a*. 1. 缩拢的;有皱褶的。2. 有钱的,夸耀富有的。

pur·te·nance [ˈpəːtinəns; ˋpɝtɪnəns] *n*. 〔古〕(屠宰后的家畜的)内脏。

pu·ru·lence, -cy [ˈpjuəruləns, -si; ˋpjʊrələns, -sɪ] *n*. 1. 化脓,脓性。2. 脓,浓液。

pu·ru·lent [ˈpjuərulənt; ˋpjʊrələnt] *a*. 化脓的;脓性的。

pur·vey [pəːˈvei; pɚˋve]〔英〕*vt*. 供给,供应,备办(伙食)。— *vi*. (为…)办伙食 (*for*)。

pur·vey·ance [pəˈveiəns; pəˋveəns] *n*. 1. 承办[供应]伙食。2. 伙食,食物。3.【英史】王室食物征发权。

pur·vey·or [pəˈveiə; pɚˋveɚ] *n*. 〔英〕(军队、王室等的)粮食筹办员;伙食办理员;【史】食物征发官。

P

pur·view [ˈpəːvjuː; ˋpɝvju] *n*. 1. (法令等的)范围,界限;应用范围,权限。2. 视界,眼界。3.【法】要项,条项 (*opp*. preamble)。*fall within the* ~ *of Art*. (*1*) 该按第(一)条办理。*within* [*outside*] *the* ~ *of* 在…的范围内[外]。

pus [pʌs; pʌs] *n*. 脓,脓液。

Pu·san [ˈpuːˈsɑːn; ˋpusɑn] *n*. 釜山〔南韩港市〕。

Pu·sey [ˈpjuːzi; ˋpjuzɪ] *n*. 普西〔姓氏〕。

Pu·sey·ism [ˈpjuːziizəm; ˋpjuzɪˏɪzəm] *n*. 〔贬〕(E. B. Pusey 等发起的)牛津运动 (Tractarianism)。**-ite** *n*. 参加牛津运动的人。

push [puʃ; pʊʃ] **I** *vt*. 1. 推(门等) (*opp*. pull; draw); 推动(车子等);刺出(剑、手杖等)。2. 大力推进,进行。3. 使延伸,使伸出;发(芽),生(根) (*out*; *forth*)。4. 强求,赖着要;追求(目的等)。5. 驱使,逼迫,催促(某事达到…程度,某人做某事)〔后接介词 to, 或 into doing, to do〕。6. 拼命挣(家当),扩充(营养);〔俗〕增加 (*up*)。7. 使引人注意;推荐(人);推销(货);〔俚〕贩卖(毒品)。8.【撞球】推撞。9. 使(某人)在金钱等方面受窘,对难题感到困惑〔常用被动结构〕。~ *a car* 推车。*trees* ~*ing their roots into the ground* 深深扎根于土中的树。*They draw some people in*, ~ *others out*. 他们拉拢一些人,排挤一些人。~ *one's claims* 竭力要求。~ *it* 〔口〕死乞白赖地要求。~ *a person* 推荐人。~ *one's business* 努力做生意;扩展事业。~ *one's wares* 强卖商品。*He* ~*ed me to pay*. 他逼我付款。— *vi*. 1. 推;挤。2. 推行。3. 伸展,扩展;增加。4. 竭力争取 (*for*)。5. 〔古〕用角触。*The door* ~*es easily*. 这门一推就开。~ *past* 挤了过去。*dock* ~*ing far out into the sea* 远远伸入海中的码头。~ *for higher wages* 争取提高工资。***be*** ~***ed around*** 被摆布;被支使;被欺负。***be*** ~***ed for*** (*money*) 困于(金钱);拮据。~ ***away*** 推开。~ ***back*** 推回,捅回。~ ***in*** 1. 推进;推进去。2. (小艇)靠近岸。~ ***off*** 1. 用浆推岸把船撑开。2. 〔口〕离去,回去 (*It is time for us to* ~ *off now*. 现在是我们回去的时候了)。~ ***on*** 1. 费力地前进。2. 赶快完成任务等 (*with*)。~ ***one's way*** 排开路前进(~ *one's way in the world* 奋斗成名)。~ ***open*** 推开。~ ***out*** 1. *vt*. 推出,发出(芽等),伸展(根等)。2. *vi*. (岬向海中)突出。~ ***over*** 推倒。~ ***round the ale*** 传递啤酒。~ ***the mark skyward*** 〔美俚〕创新记录。~ ***through*** 1. 完成(事务)。2. 冲过,穿过。3. (树叶等)长出。~ ***up the daisies*** 〔美俚〕被埋葬。~ ***up to*** 逼近。

II *n*. 1. 推,(用剑、棒等)刺,戳;推进。2. 突进,冲进;猛攻,打击。3. 推力;〔口〕精力,毅力;〔口〕努力,苦干,奋发。4. 迫切,紧急,危机,紧急关头。5. 后援,推荐。6. 〔俚〕人群;伙伴;有力集团。7. 〔英俚〕贼党,流氓集团。8.【台球】推球;【棒球】触击。9.【计】(能使网页创造者将内容传送给订户的)推送技术。*I gave him a good* ~. 我使劲给他一击。*a bell* ~ 电铃按钮。*P- generally succeeds in business*. 在事业中埋头苦干多半成功。***at a*** ~ 临危;急迫时。***at one*** ~ 一推,一下子。***at the first*** ~ 第一;在开始攻击时。***be in the*** ~ 是集团中一份子;熟悉情况。***bring to the*** ~ 使陷绝境。***come to the*** ~ 临到紧急关头;陷入绝境。***get the*** ~ 〔俚〕被解雇。***give a*** ~ 给推一把;给予打击。***give the*** ~ 〔俚〕解雇。***make a*** ~ 奋发,加油。~ ***and go*** 〔口〕精力饱满的,肯做肯干的 (*a man of* ~ *and go*)。***put to the*** ~ 使陷绝境;使受到严重考验。~**ball**【运】推球〔球重 48 磅以上〕。~**-bicycle** [〔俚〕**-bike**]〔英〕自行车,脚踏车 (*opp*. motorbike)。~ **button**〔美〕电钮,按钮;开关。~**-button** *a*. 按钮的;按动电钮操纵的。~ **car**〔美〕(铁路上的)四轮手推车。~**-cart** (商贩的)手推车;坐椅式手推车。~ **cycle** = ~ bicycle. ~**-down** 1.【空】推下。2.【自】后进先出存储器,叠式存储器。~**-halfpenny** [ˈheipəni; ˋhepənɪ] 一种在长桌上推移钱币等物的游戏。~**-in crime**〔美〕推人入室的暴力抢劫。~**mobile**〔美〕手推车。~ **money**〔美〕推销佣金。~**over** 1. 〔美俚〕极简单的工作[问题];闲差事。2. 容易说服的人,容易打倒的拳击对手,弱敌。3. 年轻荡妇。4. (导弹、火箭)沿弹道水平方向的位移。~**-pin**〔美〕圆钉;(小孩玩的)弹图钉游戏。~**-pull** *a*.【电子】推挽式的。~**-up** *n*.【体】俯卧撑。

push·a·ble [ˈpuʃəbl; ˋpʊʃəbl̩] *a*. 可以推的。

push·er [ˈpuʃə; ˋpʊʃɚ] *n*. 1. 推者;挤者。2. 推杆;后推火车头。3.【空】(螺旋桨在后的)推进式飞机。

push·ful [ˈpuʃful; ˋpʊʃfʊl] *a*. 〔口〕精力充沛的,富有进取精神的;肯做肯干的。

push·i·ness [ˈpuʃinis; ˋpʊʃɪnɪs] *n*. 〔美〕精神,精力;毅力,冲力。

push·ing [ˈpuʃiŋ; ˋpʊʃɪŋ] *a*. 推的,推进的;奋进的;活跃的,有干劲的。**-ly** *ad*.

Push·kin [ˈpuːʃkin; ˋpʊʃkɪn], **Alexander Sergeevich** [ˌɑːlekˈsɑːndə seəˈgejəvitʃ; ˏɑlɛkˋsɑndɚ sɛrˋgɛjəvɪtʃ] 普希金(或译普式庚)〔1799—1837,俄国诗人、散文家、剧作家〕。

Push·tu [ˈpʌʃtuː; ˋpʌʃtu] *n*. 普什图语 (= Pashto)〔阿富汗和巴基斯坦用的印欧语系伊朗语支的语言,阿富汗的官方语言之一〕。

push·y [ˈpuʃi; ˋpʊʃɪ] *a*. 〔美〕前进的,有进取精神的,有干劲的。

pu·sil·la·nim·i·ty [ˌpjuːsiləˈnimiti; ˏpjusl̩əˋnɪmətɪ] *n*. 怯懦;胆小;无气力。**-lan·i·mous** [-ˈlæniməs; -ˋlænəməs] *a*.

puss [pus; pʊs] *n*. 1. 小猫咪〔爱称,呼唤用语〕。2. 〔口〕少女,小姑娘。3. 〔英〕兔子;老虎。4. 〔美俚〕脸,嘴。*a sly* ~ (要提防的)狡猾女郎;〔美〕姑娘气的青年。***the*** ~(**-**)***in***(**-**)***the***(**-**)***corner*** 〔美〕抢壁角游戏。~ **moth** 天社蛾的一种。

puss·ley, puss·ly [ˈpʌsli; ˋpʌslɪ] *n*.【植】马齿苋 (= purslane)。

pus·sy[1] [ˈpʌsi; ˋpʊsɪ] *a*. 脓多的;脓一样的 (= pursy)。

puss·y[2] [ˈpusi; ˋpʌsɪ] *n*. 1. 〔儿〕猫咪 (= puss)。2. (褪色柳等的)葇荑花序。3. 抢壁角游戏。***play*** ~ 飞机躲在云里。~ ***gut*** 〔美〕肥胖的大汉子;笨汉。~ ***wants a corner*** 抢壁角游戏。~**cat** 猫咪。~ **willow**【植】褪色柳。

Puss·y·foot [ˈpusifut; ˋpʊsɪˏfʊt] **I** *vi*. 〔美俚〕偷偷地走,轻轻地走;抱骑墙态度。**II** *a*. 〔美俚〕骑墙的;主张绝对禁酒的。**III** *n*. 〔美俚〕1. 抱骑墙态度的政治家。2. 禁酒主义者。3. 潜行者。

pus·tu·lant [ˈpʌstjulənt; ˋpʌstʃələnt] **I** *a*. 致脓疱形成的。**II** *n*. 起脓疱剂。

pus·tu·lar [ˈpʌstjulə; ˋpʌstʃəlɚ] *a*.【医】小脓疱的;有小粒点的,满布小粒点的。

pus·tu·late [ˈpʌstjuleit; ˋpʌstʃəˏlet] **I** *vt*., *vi*. (使)生小脓疱。**II** *a*. 满布小粒点的。

pus·tule [ˈpʌstjuːl; ˋpʌstʃʊl] *n*. 1.【医】小脓疱。2.【动、植】色点;小疱。

pus·tu·lous [ˈpʌstʃuləs; ˋpʌstʃʊləs] *a*. = pustular.

put[1] [put; pʊt] (*put*; *put·ting*) **I** *vt*. 1. 搁,放,安,摆;放进,加入,搀进 (*to*; *in*)。~ *milk to* [*in*] *tea* 加牛奶在茶里。~ *a saddle on a horse* 把鞍子放在马上。~ *a man in gaol* 把人关进牢里。2. 使贴近,使接近,使靠近。~ *a glass to one's lips* 把杯子贴在嘴唇上。~ *a* *cow to a bull* 使母牛跟公牛交尾。**3.** 装,安。～ *a handle to a knife* 把刀把安装在刀上。**4.** 套(马拉车),拴(马)。～ *a horse to a cart* 把马套上车。**5.** 做成,整理成,使成(某种状态)。～ *a room in order* 收拾房间。～ *to sleep* 使入睡。～ *to flight* 打退,击溃。～ *a man into a rage* 使人发怒。～ *to death* 处死。～ *names in alphabetical order* 依字母次序排列名字。**6.** 使转向特定方向。～ *a horse to a fence* 使马跳过围栅。～ *one's mind to* [*on*] *a problem* 集中心思考虑问题。～ *the rudder to port* 搬外舵(把舵转向左舷)。**7.** 使从事。～ *a boy out in service* 把孩子送去做帮工。**8.** 应用,运用。*put one's skill to good use* 善于运用技术。**9.** 委托,交给,托付。～ *a child into his hands* 把孩子托付给他。**10.** 写上,写下来;记录,记入,登记;盖(印),签(名)。～ *something on paper* 写到纸上,留下记录。**11.** 叙述,表明;说明,陈述;翻译。*The case was* ～ *cleverly*. 事情陈述得很巧妙。*I don't know how to* ～ *it*. 我不晓得怎样表述才好。*How shall I* ～ *it?* 我怎样说才好呢? ～ *one's ideas into words* 把思想用言语表现出来。～ *it into Chinese* 把它翻译成汉语。**12.** 提出(问题),加以(质问);建议,提议。～ *a question to sb.* 向某人提个问题。～ *a thing before sb.* 向某人建议,向某人说一件事。～ *it to sb.* 问某人,征求某人意见,要某人承认。**13.** 估计;算定;认为。～ *one's income at £3,000 a year* 估计某人收入为一年三千镑。**14.** 使负(责任、罪等);使蒙受(耻辱等);加以(责难等)。*put sb. to trial* [*shame*] 使某人受考验[蒙耻]。*put sb. in the wrong* 归咎于某人。**15.** 使受到(制止等)。～ *a stop* [*an end, a period*] *to* 停止,制止。**16.** 抽(税);下(赌注)。～ *a tax on gasoline* 征收汽油税。～ *three dollars on the favourite horse* 在热门马上下三元赌注。**17.** 掷,投,丢;抛;捅出(武器),刺,戳;〔古〕推,推进。～ *the shot* 【运】推铅球。～ *a knife into it* 把小刀戳进去。**18.** 为…配(曲等)。～ *that famous poem to music* 为那首名诗配曲。**19.** 使渡过(河等)。～ *a boat across a river* 使船渡河。**20.** 使(家畜)吃,限(人)吃 (*to; on; upon*)。— *vi*. **1.** (船等)前进,驶向 (*to; for*);(河水等)流入;流出。**2.** (植物)发芽。**3.** 出发;匆忙离开;〔美口〕逃走 (*for; out*)。**be** ～ **to it** 〔口〕左右为难,进退两难。～ **about 1.** *vt*. 使转变方向;公布,宣布,散布;〔Scot. 口〕使苦恼,使心烦,使窘,使混乱 (= ～ out)。**2.** *vi*. (掉头)折回;【海】掉转航路(方向,船头) (～ *oneself about* 为难)。～ **a bug** [**flea**] **in one's ear** 〔美俚〕通过告知秘密来唆使[煽动];使担忧。～ **a crimp in** 〔美俚〕破坏计划,妨害,捣蛋。～ **across 1.** 美满完成,弄成功;堂堂开张。**2.** 〔美俚〕使人接受,使承认;欺骗人,使人上当。～ **a half-Nelson on** 〔美〕把对方带到不利的地位。～ **a large number of runs together** = ～ **two and two together** 推断。～ **aside** 挪开,撇开,避开;扔弃;排除 (～ *aside one's difficulties* 排除困难)。～ **asunder** 分开,拆散。～ **at** 估量作。～ (*sb.*) **at his ease** 使宽心[放心,安心]。～ **away 1.** *vt*. (a) 拿开,收掉,贮存,留下来(以后用)。(b) 排斥;扔掉,忘记;进(医院、监狱等)。(c) 抛弃,放弃。(d) 〔俚〕吃光,喝光 (～ *away a gallon of beer* 喝光1加仑啤酒);(船)开行。(e) 〔俚〕当,押;葬;反叛;告密。**2.** *vi*. (船)开行 (～ *away for Shanghai* 开往上海)。～ **back 1.** *vt*. 放在原来地方,送回;使退回,拨慢,拨回(钟、表的)针;使退步,妨碍,阻碍;延迟;羁押(犯人)。**2.** *vi*. 回去,折回;〔喻〕变年轻。～ **by 1.** 避开(人、质问等);搁在一边,推脱,置之不理。**2.** 积蓄,储存。～ **down 1.** 放下。**2.** 镇压;制止,使沉默。**3.** 削减,减,节省;降级,剥夺职权。**4.** 记下;登记(作申请人) (*Put me down for £5*. 请记下我认5镑)。**5.** 以为,认为 (*as; for*)。**6.** 归,担,推给 (*to*) (*He* ～ *the mistake down to me*. 他把错误推给我)。**7.** 〔口〕大喝。**8.** (飞机)着陆。～ **down the drain** 〔口〕浪费。～ **down in black and white** 白纸黑字写下。～ **for** 以…为目标前进。～ **forth 1.** *vt*. 突出,长出,伸出;放(光);表现,发挥,拿出(力量等);陈列;出版,发行;建议。**2.** *vi*. 发芽;〔诗〕出发。～ **forward 1.** 建议,提倡;促进,振兴;推举(候补人等)。**2.** 使突出,使显眼。～ **heads together** 讨论,商量。～ **... home 1.** 戳进;撵走。**2.** 坚持[贯彻]到底。～ **in 1.** *vt*. 插(嘴);替人说(话),吹嘘吹嘘 (～ *in a word for a friend* 替朋友辩护);提出(要求、文件等);加以(打击等);使就任,任命,请(家庭教师等)花费(时间)。**2.** *vi*. (船)入港,靠码头;进来,访问 (～ *in at a port* 入港)。～(*sb.*) **in** [**into**] **a junk** 吓(某人)。～ (*sb.*) **in a fix** [**hole**] 使某人陷入绝境。～ **in for** 申请,做候补人。～ **in force** 实施。～ **in hand** 着手,动作。～ **in mind of** 提醒,使想起。～ **in motion** 开动。～ **in one's two cents' worth** 〔美俚〕发表自己的意见,参加谈话[讨论]。～ **into 1.** 插入;注入。**2.** (船)入港,开进。～ **into shape** 使体现。～ **it across** (**him**) 严厉批评[责备]。～ **it aptly** 说得好。～ **it in another way** 用另一方式说,换句话说。～ **it on** 〔口〕讨高价;乱吹牛;假装。～ **it on ice** 〔美俚〕忘记。～ **it over** 〔美俚〕成功,考试及格。**not to** ～ **it past** (*sb.*) 〔美口〕**1.** 认为某人能做某事。**2.** 认为那是某人的本分。～ **it** (**to sb.**) **that** (向某人)建议。～ **it to** (*sb.*) 征求(某人)意见。～ **it where the flies won't get it** 〔美俚〕喝(酒)。～ **off 1.** *vt*. 拿走,拿开;脱(衣帽等);避开,推辞,推脱(人、要求);搁置;使等;拖,延期 (*till; until; to*);拿(假货等)骗人,使人上当 (*on; upon*);排斥,黜免,驱逐,丢弃;谏止 (*from*);妨碍,反叛,出卖;使为难;使没有精神去…,使厌恶 (*be* ～ *off one's meals* 不想吃饭)。**2.** *vi*. (船…船员等)离岸,出发,动身。～ **on 1.** 穿上(衣服),戴上(眼镜)。**2.** 增加(体重、速度等) (～ *on flesh* 长肉。～ *on the pace* 赶紧走。～ *on weight* 增加体重);(比赛等中)得(分) (*to*)。**3.** 装,假装 (*His modesty is all* ～ *on*. 他的谦虚全是假的)。**4.** 赌 (～ *£5 on a horse* 赌某马5镑)。**5.** 使走快,拨快 (～ *the clock on* 把钟拨快)。**6.** 任命。**7.** 使工作;煽动,教唆,撺掇。**8.** 上演(剧本)。**9.** 把(罪)推给。**10.** 推荐,介绍 (*to*)。～ **on an act** 〔美俚〕假装。～ **on airs** 摆架子。～ **on lugs** 〔美俚〕装腔作势,摆架子。～ **on steam 1.** 使劲,加油。**2.** 开动,投入生产。～ (*sb.*) **on to** 〔口〕向某人点明…。～ **on the dog** [**ritz**] 〔美〕摆架子,逞威。～ (*sb.*) **on the pan** 〔美俚〕骂,责备。～ **one's back up 1.** (美橄榄球)抵抗,顶住。**2.** 激怒。～ **oneself out of the way** 自找麻烦。～ **oneself outside of** 〔美俚〕吃,喝。～ **oneself over** (*an audience*) 使(听众)理解[接受、欢迎]。～ **out 1.** *vt*. 拿出,长出,发出(芽等);迁移,移植(树苗);转让,交出;逐出,赶出,撵走,解雇;伸出(手);熄(火),灭火;表现,表示,发挥;交给(人);出产;完成;作出;发行,出版;使出场(比赛);弄脱(关节),使脱臼;贷出(款子),投资,花费,存款;触怒,惹,使窘,使为难;【棒球】使打出界外,使出局。**2.** *vi*. 开船;〔美〕出发,发芽;突然跑掉。～ **out of action** 歼灭,消灭。～ **out of service** 关,停止。～ (*sb.*) **out of the way** 除掉(某人);把(某人)关进牢监。～ **over 1.** (船)渡过去。**2.** 延期。**3.** (使戏剧、政策等)成功[得到好评]。**4.** 〔美俚〕顺利完成。～ **paid to** 〔口〕认为…已了结[解决]了,毁掉了…。～ **right** 订正;医治(病人)。～ **the acid on** 〔美俚〕试。～ **the bee on** 〔美俚〕**1.** 骗去…的钱,找借口赖债。**2.** 把…打昏过去。～ **the crimp in** 〔美俚〕**1.** 领头,打败。**2.** 自由驱使。～ **the cross on** 〔美俚〕决定杀死。～ **the finger on** 〔美俚〕向警察局出卖[告密]。～ **the game on ice** 〔美运〕保持胜利。～ **the heat on** 〔美俚〕**1.** 使成不愉快的注意对象,使窘,使为难,盘问,折磨。**2.** = ～ the finger on. ～ **the muffler on** 〔美俚〕使住嘴,使沉默。～ **through 1.** 完成,做好(工作等)。**2.** 戳穿。**3.** 使(议案等)通过。**4.** 使受(考验等)。**5.** 接通(电话) (*Put me through to X*. 请接X先生)。～ **together 1.** 编辑;拼拢。**2.** 比较考虑,合计。**3.** 使结婚。～ **to it** 折磨,使为难,使烦恼;强制 (*be* ～ *to it* 非常困

P

苦)。~ ***to rights*** 〔美〕整理,整顿。~ (*sb.*) ***to the door*** 辞退,解雇(某人)。~ ***up*** **1.** ***vt.*** (a) 挂,升(帆、旗等);贴(广告等);打(伞);吊(蚊帐);撑开(帐篷);盖,造(房子)。(b) 作(祷告),提出(请求)。(c) 收拾;收藏,插入刀鞘 (~ *up the sword* 收刀;停止战争);掩藏;(将汽车等)开进车房。(d) 包捆,打包。(e) 涨(价)。(f) 上演(剧本)。(g) 交去拍卖;拿去卖。(h) 提名候选人,推荐。(i) 留宿;得到食宿。(j) 梳(头)。(k) 配,配制(药等)。(l)【赛马】雇用…做骑师。(m) 鼓动,唆使;(打猎时)赶出野兽。(n) 通知,暗示 (*to*);〔俚〕计划,密谋。(o) 公布(结婚的预告)。**2.** ***vi.*** 投宿(~ *up at an inn* 住旅馆);提名竞选;〔美俚〕付钱;下赌注。~ ***up the shutters*** 停业。~ ***upon*** 欺骗;压迫。***P- up or shut up!*** 〔美〕拿出确实证据否则免开尊口! ~ (*sb.*) ***up to*** 唆使(某人)…,煽动(某人)…,告诉,教。~ ***up with*** 忍住,熬住,隐忍迁就。~ (*sb.*) ***wise*** 〔美俚〕使(某人)想某事,点醒,点悟。**II** ***n.*** **1.** 推;刺,戳;投,掷,扔。**2.** 一扔的距离。**3.**【交易所】使按限价卖出 (*opp.* call)。~ *and call* 限价买卖,强买,强卖。~**-down** **1.** 平定。**2.** 贬低(的话)。**3.** (飞机的)降落。~**-off** **1.** 辩解,遁辞,推诿。**2.** 延期,拖延。~**-on** 〔美俚〕哄骗,假话。~**-up** ***a.*** 〔美俚〕预谋的,预先商定的 (*a* ~ *job* 阴谋,奸计)。~**-upon** ***a.*** **1.** 受虐待的。**2.** 被愚弄的。

put[2] [put; put] ***a.*** 〔美口〕固定的,不动的。

put[3] [put; put] ***v.***, ***n.*** = putt.

pu·ta·men [pjuːˈteimən; pjəˋtemən] ***n.*** (*pl.* ***-mi·na*** [-minə; -mɪnə]) 【植】(核果的)内果皮,核;【动】(卵壳内的)硬膜;壳。

pu·ta·tive [ˈpjuːtətiv; ˋpjutətɪv] ***a.*** 推断的;假定的。*the ~ author of a book* (真实作者难考的)一本书的假定作者。**-ly** ***ad.***

pute [pjuːt; pjut] ***a.*** 〔古〕单纯的。

pu·te·al [ˈpjuːtiəl; ˋpjutɪəl] ***n.*** (古罗马的)井栏。

put·log, put·lock [ˈputlɔg, -lɔk; ˋput͵lɔg, -lɑk] ***n.*** 【建】脚手架跳板(短)横木;支踏脚板的横木,踏脚桁。

put-on [ˈputɔn; ˋput͵ɔn] **I** ***a.*** 假装的,伪装的。*a ~ smile* 假笑。**II** ***n.*** 〔俚〕**1.** (利用别人的轻信)欺骗或愚弄人的行为。**2.** (对读者或观众进行戏弄的)滑稽剧,滑稽小说;模仿剧,模仿小说。

put-put, putt-putt [ˈpʌtˈpʌt; ˋpʌtˋpʌt] **I** ***vi.*** (***put-putted***; ***put-put·ting***) (汽艇、摩托车等)发出噗噗声。**II** ***n.*** **1.** 〔口〕(车辆、发动机等发出的)噗噗声。**2.** 移动东西或操作时可能发出的声音。

pu·tre·fa·cient [ˌpjuːtriˈfeiʃənt; ͵pjutrəˋfeʃənt] **I** ***a.*** 容易腐败的。**II** ***n.*** 【医】腐败剂,化脓剂。

pu·tre·fac·tion [ˌpjuːtriˈfækʃən; ͵pjutrəˋfækʃən] ***n.*** **1.** 腐败,腐化(作用)。**2.** 腐败物。

pu·tre·fac·tive [ˌpjuːtriˈfæktiv; ͵pjutrəˋfæktɪv] ***a.*** **1.** 容易腐败的。**2.** 使腐臭的,致腐的。

pu·tre·fy [ˈpjuːtrifai; ˋpjutrə͵faɪ] ***vt.*** (***-fied***) 使化脓;〔罕〕使腐烂,使腐败。— ***vi.*** 化脓;腐烂,腐败,发霉;堕落。

pu·tres·cence [pjuːˈtresns; pjuˋtresns] ***n.*** **1.** 腐败,腐化,堕落。**2.** 正在腐烂的东西。

pu·tres·cent [pjuːˈtresnt; pjuˋtresnt] ***a.*** **1.** 将腐烂的,开始腐烂的。**2.** 关于腐烂的。

pu·tres·ci·ble [pjuːˈtresibl; pjuˋtresəbl] ***a.*** 会腐臭的,容易腐败的。

pu·tres·cine [pjuːˈtresiːn, -in; pjuˋtresin, -ɪn] ***n.*** 【化】腐胺。

pu·trid [ˈpjuːtrid; ˋpjutrɪd] ***a.*** **1.** 已腐烂的;恶臭的,肮脏的;堕落的。**2.** 〔口〕(行为、态度等)讨人嫌的,使人不愉快的。*a perfectly ~ book* 极枯燥的书。*turn ~* 烂掉。~ **fever** 斑疹伤寒。~ **sore throat** 白喉;坏疽性咽炎。**-ly** ***ad.***

pu·trid·i·ty [pjuːˈtriditi; pjuˋtrɪdətɪ] ***n.*** **1.** 霉烂,腐败(物)。**2.** 堕落。

putsch [putʃ; pʊtʃ] ***n.*** 〔G.〕仓促起义[暴动],民变,暴动。

putsch·ism [ˈputʃizəm; ˋputʃɪzəm] ***n.*** 盲动主义。

putsch·ist [ˈputʃist; ˋputʃɪst] ***n.*** 仓促起义的人,盲动主义者。

putt [pʌt; pʌt] **I** ***vt.***, ***vi.*** 【高尔夫球】把(球)轻轻打进洞里。**II** ***n.*** 【高尔夫球】轻打。

put·tee [ˈpʌti; ˋpʌtɪ] ***n.*** (布或皮的)绑腿。

put·ter[1] [ˈpʌtə; ˋpʌtɚ] ***n.*** 【高尔夫球】轻击棒;轻打者。

put·ter[2] [ˈputə; ˋputɚ] ***n.*** **1.** 置放者。**2.** 【采】搬运工,推车工。

put·ter[3] [ˈputə; ˋputɚ] ***vi.***, ***n.*** 〔美口〕磨蹭,拖拉,偷懒;瞎忙。**-er** ***n.*** 拖拉者,偷懒者;瞎忙者。

put·tie [ˈpʌti; ˋpʌtɪ] ***n.*** = puttee.

put·ti·er [ˈpʌtiə; ˋpʌtɪɚ] ***n.*** 用油灰(装窗玻璃)的人。

put·ting[1] [ˈputiŋ; ˋpʌtɪŋ] ***n.*** 投掷。

put·ting[2] [ˈpʌtiŋ; ˋpʌtɪŋ] ***n.*** 【高尔夫球】打球入洞。~ **green** [**ground**] 离球洞三十码以内的地区。~ **hole** 球洞。

put·to [ˈpuː(t)təu; ˋputo] ***n.*** (*pl.* ***put·ti*** [-ti; tɪ]) 〔It.〕(巴罗克 *baroque* 新奇艺术风格中的)肥胖的年轻男天使或神童之形象;爱神裸体像(尤指有翅者)。

put·too [ˈpʌtuː; ˋpʌtu] ***n.*** 〔印度〕普妥粗羊绒呢。

put·ty [ˈpʌti; ˋpʌtɪ] **I** ***n.*** **1.** 油灰[装窗玻璃等用]。**2.** (擦玻璃或金属用的)去污粉;宝石磨粉〔又叫 jewellers' ~〕。*glazier's ~* 镶玻璃窗的油灰。*plasterers' ~* 涂底油灰。**II** ***vt.*** (***-tied***) 用油灰涂固[结合、涂平]。~**-blower** 〔美俚〕(小孩用铁管做的)铁炮。~ **face** 〔美俚〕呆脸;呆子,白痴。~**-head** 〔美口〕蠢货。~**-looking** ***a.*** 带灰色的。~ **medal** 油灰(做的)奖章,微功奖。~ **powder** (擦玻璃或金属用的)去污粉。

puy [pwiː; pwi] ***n.*** 〔F.〕【地】死火山锥。

puz·zle [ˈpʌzl; ˋpʌzl] **I** ***vt.*** 使为难,使迷惑;使伤脑筋;使混乱。*I am ~d what to do.* 我不知怎样办才好。~ ***one's brains*** [***oneself***] ***about*** [***over***] ***sth.*** 为…大伤脑筋,拼命想…。— ***vi.*** 为难 (*about*; *over*);伤脑筋 (*over*)。~ ***out*** 解决(难题等)。~ ***through*** 摸索着通过。**II** ***n.*** 难题,迷惑;(字谜、书谜等的)谜。***in a ~*** (*about sth.*) (为某件事情)为难。~ **headed** ***a.*** 昏头昏脑的;思想混乱的。~ **ring** 益智环[如九连环等]。**-dom** ***n.*** 为难;苦境。**-ment** ***n.*** **1.** 为难,迷惑。**2.** 难题;谜。

puz·zler [ˈpʌzlə; ˋpʌzlɚ] ***n.*** **1.** 使人为难的人[物]。**2.** 难题。

puz·zling [ˈpʌzliŋ; ˋpʌzlɪŋ] ***a.*** 使为难的;费解的;莫名其妙的。**-ly** ***ad.***

PVA =【化】**1.** polyvinyl acetate 聚醋酸乙烯酯。**2.** polyvinyl alcohol 聚乙烯醇。

PVC = polyvinyl chloride【化】聚氯乙烯。

PVS = persistent vegetative state【医】(无法恢复的)植物人状态。

Pvt. = Private 列兵;〔英〕陆军二等兵;〔美〕陆军[海军陆战队]二等兵。

PW = prisoner(s) of war 战俘。

PWA, P.W.A. = **1.** Public Works Administration 〔美〕公共工程署。**2.** a person with aids 艾滋病患者。

P.W.D. = **1.** Psychological Warfare Division 〔美〕心理作战部。**2.** Public Works Department 〔美〕公共工程处。

Pwr; pwr = power.

pwt. = pennyweight.

PX = **1.** please exchange 请交换。**2.** post exchange 〔美〕陆军消费合作社。

pxt; pxt. = 〔L.〕*pinxit* …画,…作[画家署名用语]。

pya [pjɑː; pjɑ] ***n.*** (*pl.* ***pyas***) 缅分[等于 1/100 缅元 (Burmeskyat)]。

py·ae·mi·a [paiˈiːmiə, -mjə; paɪˋimɪə] ***n.*** 【医】脓毒性,脓血症。**py·ae·mic** ***a.***

pyc·nid·i·um [pikˈnidiəm; pɪkˋnɪdɪəm] *n*. (*pl*. **-i·a** [-ə; -ə]) 分生孢子器。**-nid·i·al** *a*.

pyc·no·gon·id [ˌpiknəˈgonid; ˏpɪknəˋgɑnɪd] *n*. 海蜘蛛类 (*Pycnogonida*) 动物。

pyc·nom·e·ter [pikˈnɔmitə; pɪkˋnɑmətɚ] *n*. 【物】比重瓶;比重管;比重计。

Pye [pai; paɪ] *n*. 派伊〔姓氏〕。

pye-dog, pi(e)-dog [ˈpaidɔg; ˋpaɪˏdɔg] *n*. (东南亚)野狗。

pye-eyed [ˈpaiaid; ˋpaɪaɪd] *a*. 〔美俚〕醉醺醺的。

py·e·li·tis [ˌpaiəˈlaitis; ˏpaɪəˋlaɪtɪs] *n*. 【医】肾盂炎。

py·e·lo·gram [ˈpaiələgræm; ˋpaɪələgræm] *n*. 肾盂 X 线照片。

py·e·log·ra·phy [ˌpaiəˈlɔgrəfi; ˏpaɪəˋlɑgrəfɪ] *n*. 肾盂照相术。

py·e·lo·ne·phri·tis [ˌpaiəˌləuniˈfraitis; ˏpaɪəlonəˋfraɪtɪs] *n*. 肾盂肾炎。

py·e·mi·a [paiˈiːmiə; paɪˋimɪə] *n*. = pyaemia.

py·gid·i·um [paiˈdʒidiəm; paɪˋdʒɪdɪəm] *n*. (*pl*. **-i·a** [-ə; -ə]) 【动】尾节,尾板;(介壳虫)臀板。

pyg·mae·an, pyg·me·an [pigˈmiən; pɪgˋmɪən] *a*. **1**. (在古代历史和传说中所说的,居住在非洲、亚洲的一种身体矮小的民族)俾格米人的。**2**. 现代非洲、亚洲的身体矮小的黑人的。**3**. (人、动物、植物等身体或枝干)小得奇特的,侏儒的。**4**. 微不足道的,无足轻重的人[物]的 (= pygmy)。

Pyg·ma·li·on [pigˈmeiljən; pɪgˋmelɪən] *n*. 【希神】皮格梅隆〔塞浦路斯国王;热恋自己雕的少女像〕。

pyg·moid [ˈpigmɔid; ˋpɪgmɔɪd] *a*. 似俾格米人的〔尤指身体矮小的〕。

pyg·my [ˈpigmi; ˋpɪgmɪ] **I** *n*. **1**. 矮人;矮小动物;智力低劣的人。**2**. 〔P-〕矮小黑人,俾格米人 (= pagm(a)ean)。**II** *a*. **1**. 矮小的。**2**. 不足道的;小规模的。**3**. 〔P-〕俾格米人的,矮小黑人的。*our* ~ *effort* 我们的微小努力。

pyg·my·ism [ˈpigmiizəm; ˋpɪgmɪɪzm̩] *n*. 矮小,矮小的状态。

py·ja·mas [pəˈdʒɑːməz, pi-; pəˋdʒæməz; pɪ-] *n*. 〔*pl*.〕〔英〕(宽大的)睡衣裤;(印度人等的)宽松裤。

pyk·nic [ˈpiknik; ˋpɪknɪk] *a*. 肩宽矮胖体型的。

Pyle [pail; paɪl] *n*. 派尔〔姓氏〕。

py·lon [ˈpailən; ˋpaɪlɑn] *n*. **1**. (古埃及的)塔门。**2**. 【电】(高压线的)桥塔;【空】(飞机场的)标塔;标杆,路标灯;硬式飞艇的螺桨架;悬臂,支架。*a slab* ~【火箭】流线型发射架。

py·lo·rec·to·my [ˌpailəˈrektəmi; ˏpaɪləˋrɛktəmɪ] *n*. (*pl*. **-mies**) 幽门切除术。

py·lo·rus [paiˈlɔːrəs; pəˋlorəs] *n*. (*pl*. **-ri** [-rai; -raɪ]) 【解】幽门。**py·lor·ic** *a*.

Pym [pim; pɪm] *n*. 皮姆〔姓氏〕。

pymt; **pymt**. = payment.

pyo- *comb*. *f*. 表示"脓": *pye*mia.

py·od [ˈpaiəd; ˋpaɪəd] *n*. 热电偶,温差电偶。

py·o·der·ma [ˌpaiəˈdəːmə; ˏpaɪoˋdɝmə] *n*. 脓皮病。**-der·mic** *a*.

py·o·gen·e·sis [ˌpaiəˈdʒenisis; ˏpaɪəˋdʒɛnəsɪs] *n*. 【医】酿脓,生脓。**-gen·ic** *a*.

py·oid [ˈpaiɔid; ˋpaɪɔɪd] *a*. 脓的,脓状的。

py·o·ne·phri·tis [ˌpaiə*u*niˈfraitis; ˏpaɪonɪˋfraɪtɪs] *n*. 【医】化脓性肾炎。

Pyong·yang [ˈpjɔŋˈjæŋ; ˋpjʌŋˋjɑŋ] *n*. 平壤〔朝鲜民主主义人民共和国首都〕。

py·or·rhoe·a [ˌpaiəˈriə; ˏpaɪəˋrɪə] *n*. 【医】脓溢[漏],(尤指)齿槽脓溢[漏]。

pyorrhoea al·vi·o·la·ris [ˌpaiəˈriə ælˌviːəˈlɛəris; ˏpaɪəˋrɪə ælˏvɪəˋlɛrɪs] 【医】牙槽脓溢。

py·o·sis [paiˈəusis; paɪˋosɪs] *n*. 【医】化脓,脓溃。

pyr- = pyro-.

pyr·a·can·tha [ˌpiərəˈkænθə, ˌpairə-; ˏpɪərəˋkænθə, ˏpaɪrə-] *n*. 【植】火棘属植物;欧洲火棘 (firethorn)。

py·ral·i·did [paiˈrælidid, pə-; paɪˋrælədɪd, pə-] **I** *a*. 【动】螟蛾科的。**II** *n*. 螟蛾科蛾 (= pyralid)。

pyr·a·mid [ˈpirəmid; ˋpɪrəmɪd] **I** *n*. **1**. 金字塔。**2**. 【数】角锥,棱锥;【结晶】锥;【解、动】角锥形器官;【园艺】剪成角锥形的果树。**3**. 【运】叠罗汉。**4**. 〔*pl*.〕〔英〕开盘时使球摆成金字塔形的撞球。*a regular* [*right*] ~ 正[直]角锥。*a truncated* ~ 斜截头角锥。**II** *vi*. **1**. 成金字塔形状。**2**. 【交易所】用累进式手法扩大交易;步步升级。— *vt*. **1**. 使成金字塔形状。**2**. (按累进方式)抬高价格,用累进方式经营。**3**. 使步步升级。**-ist, -al·ist** *n*. **1**. 埃及金字塔研究者。**2**. 对埃及金字塔持神秘观点者。

py·ram·i·dal [piˈræmidl; pɪˋræmədl̩] **I** *a*. 金字塔状的;角锥的;锥体的。**II** *n*. 【解】楔骨。**-ly** *ad*.

pyr·a·mid·ic, pyr·a·mid·i·cal *a*. = pyramidal.

py·ran [ˈpairæn; ˋpaɪræn] *n*. 【化】吡喃,氧(杂)芑。

py·rar·gy·rite [paiˈrɑːdʒirait; paɪˋredʒəraɪt] *n*. 硫锑银矿,深红银矿。

pyre [paiə; paɪr] *n*. 火葬柴堆;火葬燃料。

py·rene[1] [ˈpairiːn; ˋpaɪrin] *n*. **1**. 小坚果。**2**. 分核。

py·rene[2] [ˈpairiːn; ˋpaɪrin] *n*. 【化】芘;嵌二萘。

Pyr·e·nees [ˌpirəˈniːz; ˋpɪrəˏniz] *n*. 比利牛斯山脉〔法国、西班牙交界处山脉名〕。**Pyr·e·ne·an** [ˌpirəˈniːən; ˏpɪrəˋnɪən] *a*., *n*. 比利牛斯山的(居民)。

py·re·noid [paiˈriːnɔid; paɪˋrinɔɪd] *n*. 【植】淀粉核。

py·re·thrin [paiˈriːθrin; paɪˋriθrən] *n*. 【化】除虫菊酯。

py·re·thrum [paiˈriːθrəm; paɪˋriθrəm] *n*. **1**. 【植】红花除虫菊 (*Chrysanthemum coccineum*)。**2**. 除虫菊粉。

py·ret·ic [paiˈretik; paɪˋrɛtɪk] **I** *a*. 【医】(害)热病的;治疗热病的。**II** *n*. 解热剂,退热药。

pyr·e·tol·o·gy [ˌpaiərəˈtɔlədʒi; ˏpɪrəˋtɑlədʒɪ] *n*. 热病学。

py·rex [ˈpaiəreks; ˋpaɪrɛks] *n*. 派热克斯玻璃,硼硅酸玻璃〔原是一种耐热玻璃的商标名〕。

py·rex·i·a [paiəˈreksiə; paɪˋrɛksɪə] *n*. 【医】热;发热;热病。

py·rex·ic [paiəˈreksik; paɪˋrɛksɪk] *a*. 热病的。

pyr·he·li·om·e·ter [ˌpaiəhiːliˈɔmitə; ˏpaɪrhɪlɪˋɑmətɚ] *n*. 【气】(直接)日射强度计;日照计,太阳热量计。

pyr·i·din(e) [ˈpiridiːn; ˋpɪrɪˏdin] *n*. 【化】吡啶,氮(杂)苯〔治喘病用〕。

pyr·i·dox·al [ˌpiəriˈdɔksəl; ˏpɪrɪˋdɑksəl] *n*. 吡哆醛,维生素 B_6醛。

pyr·i·dox·a·mine [ˌpiəriˈdɔksəmi(ː)n; ˏpɪrɪˋdɑksəmɪn] *n*. 吡哆胺,维生素 B_6胺。

pyr·i·dox·in(e) [ˌpiəriˈdɔksin, -si(ː)n; ˏpɪrɪˋdɑksɪn, -sin] *n*. 【化】吡哆醇,吡哆素;【药】维生素 B_6,抗皮炎素。

pyr·i·form [ˈpiərifɔːm; ˋpɪrəˏfɔrm] *a*. 梨状的。

py·rim·i·dine [paiˈrimidiːn; paɪˋrɪmɪdin] *n*. 【化】嘧啶,间二氮(杂)苯。

py·rite [ˈpairait; ˋpaɪraɪt] *n*. (*pl*. **py·ri·tes** [paiˈraitiːz; paɪˋraɪtiz]) 黄铁矿,天然的二硫化铁。

py·ri·tes [paiˈraitiːz; pəˋraɪtiz] *n*. 〔*sing*., *pl*.〕【矿】硫化矿类;黄铁矿 (= iron ~); 白铁矿 (= white iron ~); 黄铜矿 (= copper ~); 黄锡矿 (= tin ~)。**py·rit·ic, py·ri·tous** *a*.

py·ri·to·he·dron [piˌraitəˈhiːdrən; pɪˏraɪtəˋhidrən] *n*. 【矿】五角十二面体。

py·ro [ˈpaiərəu; ˋpaɪro] *n*. 【化】焦棓酚,五倍子酚;连苯三酚(= pyrogallol)。

pyro- *comb*. *f*. 表示"火,热,高温,焦": *pyro*chemistry.

py·ro·cat·e·chol [ˌpaiərə*u*ˈkætikɔːl; ˏpaɪrəˋkætəkol] *n*. 邻苯二酚 (= pyrocatechin)。

py·ro·cer·am [ˌpaiərə*u*səˈræm; ˏpaɪrosəˋræm] *n*. 派洛塞拉姆钢化玻璃〔一种抗高温的防碎玻璃,用作炊具、火箭锥形头等,原商标名〕。

P

py·ro·chem·i·cal [ˌpaiərəuˈkemikl; ˏpaɪroˋkɛməkl] *a*. 高温化学的。**-ly** *ad*.

py·ro·chem·is·try [ˌpaiərəuˈkemistri; ˏpaɪroˋkɛmɪstrɪ] *n*. 高温化学。

py·ro·clast·ic [ˌpaiərəuˈklæstik; ˏpaɪroˋklæstɪk] *n*., *a*.【地】火成碎屑物(的)。

py·ro·con·den·sa·tion [ˌpaiərəuˌkɔndənˈseiʃən; ˏpaɪroˏkɑndənˋseʃən] *n*. 热缩(作用)。

py·ro·con·duc·tiv·i·ty [ˌpaiərəuˌkɔndʌkˈtiviti; ˏpaɪroˏkɑndʌkˋtɪvətɪ] *n*. 高温导电性。

py·ro·crys·tal·line [ˌpaiərəuˈkristəlin; ˏpaɪroˋkrɪstəlɪn] *a*.【地】火成晶质。

pyr·o·dy·nam·ics [ˌpaiərəudaiˈnæmiks; ˏpaɪrodaɪˋnæmɪks] *n*. 爆发力学,爆发动力学。

py·ro·e·lec·tric [ˌpaiərəuiˈlektrik; ˏpaɪroɪˋlɛktrɪk] **I** *a*. 热电(学)的。**II** *n*. 热电物质。**-i·ty** [-ˈtrisiti; -ˋtrɪsətɪ] *n*. 热电(现象);热电学。

py·ro·gal·late [ˌpaiərəuˈgæleit; ˏpaɪroˋgælet] *n*.【化】焦棓酸盐,焦五倍子酸盐。

py·ro·gal·lic [ˌpaiərəuˈgælik; ˏpaɪrəˋgælɪk] *a*. 焦棓性的,焦五倍子性的。~ *acid*【化】焦棓酸,焦五倍子酸;焦棓酚,焦五倍子酚。

py·ro·gal·lol [paiərəuˈgæləul, -gəˈlɔul; ˏpaɪrəˋgælol, -gəˋlol] *n*.【化】焦棓酸,焦五倍子酸,焦棓酚,焦五倍子酚。**py·ro·gen** [ˈpaiərədʒin; ˋpaɪrədʒən] *n*. **1**.【医】热原,致热质。**2**.【化】焦精〔一种染料〕;热精。

py·ro·gen·ic, py·rog·e·nous [ˌpaiərəuˈdʒenik, paiəˈrɔdʒinəs; ˏpaɪrəˋdʒɛnɪk, paɪˋrɑdʒɪnəs] *a*. **1**. 高热的,高温反应的。**2**.【地】火成的(= igneous)。

py·rog·nos·tics [ˌpaiərɔgˈnɔstiks; ˏpaɪrɑgˋnɑstɪks] *n*. 〔*pl*.〕(用吹管测定的)矿物特性〔如可熔性、焰色等〕。

py·ro·graph [ˈpaiərəugrɑːf; ˋpaɪrəˏgræf] *n*. 烙画;烫画;裂解色谱;热谱。

py·ro·graphy [ˌpaiəˈrɔgrəfi; paɪˋrɑgrəfɪ] *n*. 烙画(法);烫画(法);裂解色谱法;热谱法。

py·rol·a·try [ˌpaiəˈrɔlətri; paɪˋrɑlətrɪ] *n*. 对火(神)的崇拜;拜火教。

py·ro·lig·ne·ous [ˌpaiərəuˈligniəs; ˏpaɪrəˋlɪgnɪəs] *a*. 焦木的;干馏木材而得的。

pyr·ol·o·gy [paiəˈrɔlədʒi; paɪˋrɑlədʒɪ] *n*. 热工学。

py·ro·lu·site [ˌpaiərəuˈluːsait; ˏpaɪrəˋlusaɪt] *n*. 软锰矿。

py·rol·y·sis [paiˈrɔlisis; paɪˋrɑləsɪs] *n*. 热解(作用)高温分解。**-lyt·ic** [-ˈlitik; -ˋlɪtɪk] *a*. **-lyt·i·cal·ly** *ad*.

py·ro·mag·net·ic [ˌpairəumægˈnetik; ˏpaɪromægˋnɛtɪk] *a*.【物】热磁的(= thermomagnetic)。

py·ro·man·cy [ˈpaiərəumænsi; ˋpaɪrəˏmænsɪ] *n*. 火占术,火卜。

pyr·o·ma·ni·a [ˌpaiərəuˈmeiniə; ˏpaɪrəˋmenɪə] *n*. 放火狂。**-ni·ac** *a*., *n*. 放火狂的;放火狂(者)。

py·ro·met·al·lur·gy [ˌpairəumeˈtælədʒi; ˏpaɪroˋmɛtəˏlɝdʒɪ] *n*. 热冶学;热冶术,火法冶金学。

py·ro·met·a·mor·phism [ˌpaiərəuˌmetəˈmɔːfizəm; ˏpaɪroˏmɛtəˋmɔrfɪzm] *n*.【地】高热变质。

py·rom·e·ter [ˌpaiəˈrɔmitə; paɪˋrɑmɪtɚ] *n*.【物】高温计。**-rom·e·try** [-ˈrɔmitri; -ˋrɑmətrɪ] *n*. 高温测定(法),测高温术。

py·ro·mor·phite [ˌpairəuˈmɔːfait; ˏpaɪrəˋmɔrfaɪt] *n*. **1**.【矿】磷氯铅矿。**2**.【地】火成结晶。

py·rone [ˈpairəun; ˋpaɪron] *n*.【化】哌喃。

py·ro·nine [ˈpairəuniːn, -nin; ˋpaɪronin, -nɪn] *n*.【化】焦宁;二苯氧(杂)芑胺[染料]。

py·rope [ˈpairəup; ˋpaɪrop] *n*. 镁铝榴石(红榴石)。

py·ro·pho·bi·a [ˌpaiərəuˈfəubiə; ˏpaɪrəˋfobɪə] *n*.【医】畏火症。

py·ro·phor·ic [ˌpaiərəuˈfɔːrik; ˏpaɪrəˋfɔrɪk] *a*. 引火的;生火花的。

py·ro·phos·phate [ˌpairəuˈfɔsfeit; ˏpaɪroˋfɑsfet] *n*. 焦磷酸盐(或脂)。

py·ro·pho·tom·e·ter [ˌpairəufəuˈtɔmitə; ˏpaɪrofoˋtɑmɪtɚ] *n*. 高热光度计。

py·ro·phyl·lite [ˌpairəuˈfilait; ˏpaɪrəˋfɪlaɪt] *n*.【矿】叶蜡石。

py·ro·sis [paiˈrəusis; paɪˋrosɪs] *n*.【医】胃灼热。

py·ro·stat [ˈpairəustæt; ˋpaɪrəstæt] *n*. 高温(保持)器。

py·ro·sul·phate, py·ro·sul·fate [ˌpairəuˈsʌlfit; ˏpaɪrəˋsʌlfet] *n*. 焦硫酸盐。

pyrotech. = pyrotechnics.

py·ro·tech·nic, py·ro·tech·ni·cal [ˌpaiərəuˈteknik, -nikəl; ˏpaɪrəˋtɛknɪk, -nɪkəl] *a*. **1**. 烟火制造术的。**2**. 烟火(一般)的;(才智等)辉煌灿烂的,天花乱坠的。~ **sponge** 发火絮。

py·ro·tech·nics [ˌpaiərəuˈtekniks; ˏpaɪrəˋtɛknɪks] *n*. 烟火制造技术;火花;(聪明、才智、口才等的)辉煌灿烂,天花乱坠;善辩的口才。

py·ro·tech·nist [ˌpaiərəuˈteknist; ˏpaɪrəˋtɛknɪst] *n*. 烟火制造人。

py·ro·tech·ny [ˈpaiərəutekni; ˋpaɪrəˏtɛknɪ] *n*. **1**. 烟火制造术。**2**. 焰火的施放。

py·ro·tox·in [ˌpaiərəuˈtɔksin; ˏpaɪrəˋtɑksɪn] *n*. 热毒素。

py·rox·ene [paiˈrɔksiːn; ˋpaɪrɑkˏsin] *n*.【矿】辉石。

py·rox·e·nite [paiˈrɔksinait; paɪˋrɑksənaɪt] *n*.【矿】辉岩。

py·rox·y·lin(e) [paiˈrɔksilin; paɪˋrɑksəlɪn] *n*.【化】焦木素,火棉,低氮硝化纤维素。

Pyr·rhic [ˈpirik; ˋpɪrɪk] *a*. (古希腊伊皮鲁斯 (Epirus) 国王)比鲁斯 (Pyrrhus) 王的。~ **victory** 付出极大牺牲而得到的胜利〔Pyrrhus 在 280—279 B.C. 打败了罗马军队,但牺牲极大〕。

pyr·rhic [ˈpirik; ˋpɪrɪk] *n*., *a*. **1**. (古希腊的)战舞(的)。**2**.【韵】二短音步(的);抑抑格(的)。

Pyr·rho·nism [ˈpirənizəm; ˋpɪrənɪzm] *n*. (希腊哲学家)庇罗 (Pyrrho) 的怀疑说;极端怀疑主义。**-nist** *n*. 极端怀疑主义者。

pyr·rho·tite [ˈpiərəutait; ˋpɪrətaɪt] *n*. 磁黄铁矿。

pyr·rhu·lox·i·a [ˌpiərəuˈlɔksiə; ˏpɪroˋlɑksɪə] *n*.【动】凤头红蜡嘴雀 (*Pyrrhuloxia sinuata*)〔产于美国西南部和墨西哥北部〕。

pyr·role [ˈpiərəul; ˋpɪrol] *n*.【化】吡咯。

py·ru·vate [paiˈruːveit; paɪˋruvet] *n*. 丙酮酸盐[酯]。

Py·thag·o·ras [paiˈθægərəs; pɪˋθægərəs] 毕达哥拉斯〔580? —? 500 B.C., 希腊哲学家、数学家〕。

Py·thag·o·re·an [paiˌθægəˈriːən; pɪˏθægəˋriən] *a*., *n*. 毕达哥拉斯的(信徒)(的);毕达哥拉斯哲学的。~ **bean** 莲子。~ **proposition** [**theorem**]【数】毕达哥拉斯定理,勾股定理。~ **table** (乘法)九九表。

Py·thag·o·re·an·ism [piˌθægəˈriːənizəm; pɪˋθægəˏriənɪzm] *n*. 毕达哥拉斯哲学。

Pyth·i·an [ˈpiθiən, -θjən; ˋpɪθɪən, -θjən] **I** *a*. **1**. (古希腊)达尔菲 (Delphi) 地方的。**2**. (达尔菲地区)阿波罗 (Apollo) 神殿的。**3**. 祀奉阿波罗神的女巫的。**4**. 阿波罗神附身的。**5**. 被阿波罗所杀的巨蟒的。~ **games** 在达尔菲每四年举行一次的古代希腊四大运动会之一。~ **oracle** 阿波罗神附身所作的宣示。**II** *n*. 〔the P-〕**1**. 达尔菲的居民。**2**. 阿波罗神。**3**. 祀奉阿波罗神的女巫。

Py·thon [ˈpaiθən; ˋpaɪθɑn] *n*. **1**.【动】蚺蛇属,蟒蛇属。**2**.【希神】(被 Apollo 神杀掉的)巨蟒。**3**. 〔p-〕巫;预言者。

py·tho·ness [ˈpaiθənəs; ˋpaɪθənɪs] *n*. **1**. 女巫。**2**. 希腊达尔菲地方祀奉阿波罗神的女巫。

py·thon·ic [paiˈθɔnik; paɪˋθɑnɪk] *a*. **1**. 神托的,预言的。**2**. 蚺蛇的,蟒蛇的。

py·u·ri·a [paiˈjuəriə; paɪˋjurɪə] *n*.【医】脓尿。

pyx [piks; pɪks] **I** *n*. **1.** 【天主】圣体容器,圣饼盒。**2.** (英国造币局的)货币样品箱,货币检查箱。**II** *vt*. **1.** 将(货币样品)收入货币检查箱。**2.** 检查(铸造的货币)。*the trial of the* ~ 货币样品的检查。

pyx·id·i·um [pikˈsidiəm; pɪksˋɪdɪəm] *n*. (*pl*. *-id·i·a* [-iə; -ɪə]) **1.** 【植】盖果。**2.** 【天】= Pyxis.

pyx·ie [ˈpiksiː; ˋpɪksi] *n*. 【植】沙盖花(*Pyxidanthera barbulata*)〔原产于美国大西洋沿岸平原〕。

pyx·is [ˈpiksis; ˋpɪksɪs] *n*. (*pl*. *pyx·ides* [ˈpiksidiːz; ˋpɪksɪdiz]) **1.** 小箱;化妆盒,宝石盒。**2.** 【植】盖果;【解】杯状窝,髀凹。

Pyx·is [ˈpiksis; ˋpɪksɪs] *n*. 〔the ~〕【天】罗盘(星)座。

Q

Q, q [kjuː; kju] (*pl*. *Q's*, *q's* [kjuːz; kjuz]) **1.** 英语字母表第十七字母。**2.** 〔Q〕Q 字形。**3.** 〔Q〕(滑冰动作中的)Q字形旋转。**4.** 【剧】提示(= cue)。**5.** 品质因数,Q值,佳度。**6.** 〔Q〕= queen〔在国际象棋和纸牌中〕。*in a merry Q* 快快活活地。*mind one's P's and Q's* 谨言慎行。**Q-boat, Q-ship** 【军】伪装猎潜舰。**Q-correction** 【天】Q 补偿角,北极星高度补偿角。**Q department** 军需部。**Q fever** 【医】Q 热,昆士兰热。**Q-meter** 【无】Q 表,品质因素表。

Q. = Quebec.

Q., q. = **1.** queen. **2.** question. **3.** quart; quarter; quarterly; quarto. **4.** quasi. **5.** query. **6.** quintal. **7.** quire. **8.** quotient.

Q. and A. = questions and answers 问与答。

Qa·tar [ˈkɑːtər; ˋkɑtɑr] *n*. 卡塔尔〔亚洲〕。

Q.B., QB = Queen's Bench 英国高等法院。

QC, Q.C. = Queen's Counsel 〔英〕(女王的)王室法律顾问。

Q(-)clearance (接触核武器机密资料的)绝密级许可证。

q.d. = **1.** 〔L.〕*quasi dicat* 好像应该说(= as if one should say)。**2.** 〔L.〕*quasi dictum* 好像说过了(= as if said)。

Q.E. = 〔L.〕*quod est* 这就是(= which is)。

QEA = Qantas [ˈkwɔntæs; ˋkwɑntæs] Empire Airways 〔澳〕康达斯帝国航空公司。

Q.E.D., QED = 〔L.〕*quod erat demonstrandum* 【数】这就是所要证明的(= which was to be demonstrated),证完,证讫。

Q.E.F., QEF = 〔L.〕*quod erat faciendum* 【数】这就是所要做的(= which was to be done),作毕,作讫。

Q.E.I., QEI = 〔L.〕*quod erat inveniendum* 【数】这就是所要寻求的(= which was to be found out),求毕,求讫。

QF, QF. = **1.** quick-firing 【军】急射的,速射的。**2.** quick-firer 速射枪[炮]。

qi [tʃiː; tʃi] *n*. 〔Chin.〕气。

Qi·gong [tʃiːˈkəuŋ; tʃiˋkoŋ] *n*. 〔Chin.〕(中国的)气功。

qing·hao·su [ˌtʃiŋhauˈsuː; ˏtʃɪŋhaʊˋsu] *n*. 〔Chin.〕青蒿素〔一种抗疟疾的中药〕。

qin·tar [kinˈtɑː; kɪnˋtɑr] *n*. 昆塔〔阿尔巴尼亚货币名,等于1/100 列克〕。

ql. = quintal.

q.l. = 〔L.〕*quantum libet* 〔药剂处方用语〕随意量(= as much as is desired)。

QM, Q.M. = quartermaster **1.** 【军】军需军官,军需主任。**2.** 【海】(兼管信号等的)舵手,航信士官。

QMC, Q.M.C. = Quartermaster Corps 〔美〕(陆军)军需兵。

QMG, Q.M.G. = Quartermaster General 陆军军需兵司令兼军需局局长。

QMS, Q.M.S. = quartermaster sergeant 军需军士。

qoph [kəuf; kof] *n*. = koph 〔希伯来语第十九个字母〕。

Qo·ran [kəuˈrɑːn, -ˈræn, kɔː-; koˋrɑn, -ˋræn, kɔ-] *n*. 可兰经(= Koran)。

q.p., q.pl. = 〔L.〕*quantum placet* 〔药剂处方用语〕随意量(= as much as is desired)。

qr. = **1.** quarter. **2.** quire.

q.s. = **1.** 〔L.〕*quantum sufficit* 〔药剂处方用语〕适量,足量(= a sufficient quantity)。**2.** quarter section 约四分之一平方英里的土地〔= 160 英亩〕。

QT, Q.T., q.t. = 〔俚〕quiet. *on the* ~ 秘密地,私下地。

qt. = **1.** quantity. **2.** quart.

qto. = quarto.

qts. = quarts.

qu. = **1.** quasi. **2.** quart. **3.** quarter; quarterly. **4.** queen. **5.** query; question.

qua [kwei; kwe] *conj*. 〔L.〕以…的资格[身份];作为。*He did it not* ~ *father, but* ~ *judge*. 他不是用父亲身份而是用法官身份处理此事的。

quack[1] [kwæk; kwæk] **I** *n*. **1.** 嘎嘎〔鸭叫声〕。**2.** 大声闲谈;嘈杂声,吵闹声。**II** *vi*. **1.** (鸭)嘎嘎地叫。**2.** 大声闲谈,聊天。

quack[2] [kwæk; kwæk] **I** *n*. **1.** 庸医,江湖医生。**2.** 骗子;大言不惭的人;假充内行的人。*a* ~ *doctor* 庸医。~ *medicines* [*remedies*] 骗钱药[疗法]。*a* ~ *politician* 空头政客,骗人的政客。**II** *vt*. **1.** 卖(假药)。**2.** (用广告等)大肆吹嘘。—*vi*. **1.** 用行医方式骗钱。**2.** 用广告骗人;大言不惭,吹牛。

quack·er·y [ˈkwækəri; ˋkwækərɪ] *n*. **1.** 江湖医生的治疗,庸医的医术。**2.** 自我吹嘘,大话;骗子行为。

quack·ish [ˈkwækiʃ; ˋkwækɪʃ] *a*. **1.** (像)庸医的;江湖医生(一样)的;一知半解的。**2.** 大言不惭的,胡吹的;骗人的。

quack-quack [ˈkwækˈkwæk; ˋkwækˋkwæk] *n*. **1.** 嘎嘎(鸭叫声)。**2.** 〔儿〕鸭子。

quack·sal·ver [ˈkwækˌsælvə; ˋkwækˏsælvɚ] *n*. 〔古〕庸医;骗子(= quack[2] *n*.)。

quad [kwɔd; kwɑd] **I** *n*. **1.** 四方院子;〔俚〕监狱。**2.** = 【印】quadrat. **3.** = quadruple. **4.** = quadrant. **5.** 【电讯】四心线组。**II** *vi*., *vt*. (*-dd-*) 【印】用空铅填满(字行)。~ **bike** 四轮摩托车〔供娱乐或运动用〕。

quadr- *comb*. *f*. = *quadri-*.

quad·rable [ˈkwɔdrəbl; ˋkwɑdrəbḷ] *a*. 【数】可用有限代数项表示的;可用等价平方表示的。

quad·ra·ge·nar·i·an [ˌkwɔdrədʒiˈnɛəriən; ˏkwɑdrədʒɪˋnɛrɪən] *a.*, *n.* 四十(多)岁的(人);四十至四十九岁的(人)。

Quad·ra·ges·i·ma [ˌkwɔdrəˈdʒesimə; ˏkwɑdrəˋdʒɛsəmə] *n.*【宗】1. 四旬斋的第一个礼拜天〔普通叫 ~ Sunday〕。2.〔废〕四旬斋。**-l** *a.*

quad·ran·gle [kwɔˈdræŋgl; ˋkwɑdræŋgḷ] *n.* 1. 四角形,四边形(特指正方形及矩形)。2.(大学等的)四方院子;围着四方院子的建筑物。3.(美国国家陆地测量局颁布的)标准地形图上的一方格〔通常为南北 27 公里,东西 18—24 公里〕。

quad·ran·gu·lar [kwɔdˈræŋgjulə; kwɑdˋræŋgjulɚ] *a.* 四角形的;四边形的。**-ly** *ad.* 成四边形。

quad·rant [ˈkwɔdrənt; ˋkwɑdrənt] *n.* 1.【数】象限;圆周的四分之一,九十度弧;四分之一圆。2.【天,海】象限仪。3.【生】四分体。4. 长度单位(= 10,000 kilometres)。5. 扇形体;【机】扇形齿轮。~ **elevation**【军】(炮的)仰角;水平射角。**quad·ran·tal** [kwɔˈdræntl; kwɑˋdræntḷ] *a.*

quad·ra·pho·nic [ˌkwɔdrəˈfəunik; ˏkwɑdrəˋfonɪk] *a.*(唱片、录音带等)四声道录音放音的。

quad·rat [ˈkwɔdræt; ˋkwɑdrət] *n.* 1.【印】(用以填空的无字面)空铅,衬铅,嵌块〔略 quad〕。2.【农】样方〔用来进行生态调查的一块长方形地〕。*an em* [*m*] ~ 全身空铅[阔铅块]。~ *an en* [*n*] ~ 对开空铅[狭铅块]。*a census* ~ 普查样方。

quad·rate [ˈkwɔdrit; ˋkwɑdrɪt] I *a.* 1.【动、解】方骨的。2. 正方形的,方形的。~ *algebra* 方代数。*a* ~ *lobe* (脑髓的)方叶。II *n.* 1. 正方形;方形。2.【解】方骨,方肌。III [kwɔˈdreit; kwɑˋdret] *vt.*, *vi.* 1.(使)适合;(使)一致(*with*; *to*)。2.【数】将(圆)作成等积正方形;(使)成正方形(*with*)。

quad·rat·ic [kwəˈdrætik; kwɑdˋrætɪk] I *a.* 1.【数】二次的。2. 方形的。II *n.* 1.【数】二次方程式;二次项。2.〔*pl.* 作单数用〕【数】二次方程式论。~ **equation** 二次方程式。~ **sieve**【数】二次节法〔一种简化数学难题的方法〕。

quad·ra·ture [ˈkwɔdrətʃə; ˋkwɑdrətʃɚ] *n.* 1.【数】求积分,求面积。2.【天】矩;(月的)上[下]弦;方照。3.【物】正交;转象差;九十度相位差。*the* ~ (*of the circle*) 圆积法[作与圆等积的正方形]。*phase* ~【物】转象相差,九十度相位差。

quad·ren·nial [kwɔˈdrenjəl; kwɑdˋrɛnɪəl] I *a.* 继续四年的;每四年一次的。II *n.* 1. 每四年一次的事件。2. 连续四年的时间。3. 第四周年;四周年纪念。**-ly** *ad.*

quad·ren·ni·um [kwɑːˈdreniəm; kwɑdˋrɛnɪəm] *n.* (*pl.* ~*s*, *-nia* [-niə; -nɪə]) 四年为一期的时间。

quadri- *comb. f.* 1. 四,第四: *quadri*lateral. 2.【数】平方,二次: *quadri*c.

quad·ric [ˈkwɔdrik; ˋkwɑdrɪk] I *a.*【数】二次的;二次曲面的。II *n.*【数】二次;二次曲面。

quad·ri·cen·ten·ni·al [ˌkwɔdrisenˈteniəl; ˏkwɑdrɪsɛnˋtɛnɪəl] I *a.*(第)四百周年的。II *n.* 四百周年纪念(日、节)。

quad·ri·ceps [ˈkwɑːdriseps; ˋkwɑdrəsɛps] *n.*【解】四头肌。**quadri·cip·i·tal** [ˌkwɑːdriˈsipitl; ˏkwɑdrəˋsɪpətḷ] *a.*

quad·ri·fid [ˈkwɔdrifid; ˋkwɑdrɪfɪd] *a.*【动、植】四分裂的;分成四部份的。~ *petal*【植】四分裂花瓣。

quad·riga [kwəˈdriːgə; kwɑdˋraɪgə] *n.* (*pl.* *-gae* [-dʒiː; -dʒi])〔古罗马〕四马双轮战车。

quad·ri·lat·er·al [ˌkwɔdriˈlætərəl; ˏkwɑdrəˋlætərəl] I *a.* 1. 四边(形)的。2. 四方面的。II *n.* 1.【数】四边形。2. 方形物,方形地;【军】(四边有四座堡垒防御的)方形要塞[地区]。

quad·ri·lin·gual [ˈkwɔdriˈliŋgwəl; ˏkwɑdrɪˋlɪŋgwəl] *a.* 用四种语言(说或写)的;由四种语言形成的。

qua·drille [kwəˈdril, kə-; kwəˋdrɪl, kə-] I *n.* 1. 四对舞,方舞;四对舞曲。2. "打四十张"〔18 世纪流行的由四人玩四十张牌的一种牌戏〕。II *a.*(图案等)形成许多大小相等的方格的,方眼的。

quad·ril·lion [kwɔˈdriljən; kwɑdˋrɪljən] *num.*〔英、德〕百万的四次幂[乘方]之数〔1 后有 24 个 0 之数〕;〔美、法〕千的五次幂[乘方]之数〔1 后有 15 个 0 之数〕。

quad·ri·no·mial [ˌkwɔdriˈnəumiəl; ˏkwɑdrɪˋnomɪəl] I *a.*【数】四项的。II *n.* 四项式。

quad·ri·par·tite [ˌkwɔdriˈpɑːtait; ˏkwɑdrɪˋpɑrtaɪt] *a.* 1. 分成四部份的;由四部份[四人]形成的。2. 由四方参加的;四方面的。*a* ~ *treaty* 四国条约。

quad·ri·ple·gi·a [ˌkwɑːdriˈpliːdʒiə; ˏkwɑdrəˋplidʒɪə] *n.*【医】四肢麻痹。**quad·ri·ple·gic** [-ˈpliːdʒik, -ˈpledʒik; -ˋplidʒɪk, -ˋplɛdʒɪk] *n.* 四肢麻痹症患者。

quad·ri·sect [ˈkwɑːdrisekt; ˋkwɑdrəˏsɛkt] *vt.* 把…四等分。

quad·ri·syl·lable [ˈkwɔdriˌsiləbl; ˋkwɑdrəˏsɪləbḷ] *n.*【语音】四音节词。**quad·ri·syl·lab·ic** [-siˈlæbik; -sɪˋlæbɪk] *a.* 四音节的。

quad·riv·a·lence, quad·riv·a·len·cy [ˌkwɔdriˈveiləns, -lənsi; ˏkwɑdrɪˋvɛləns, -lənsɪ] *n.*【化】四价。

quad·ri·va·lent [ˌkwɔdriˈveilənt; ˏkwɑdrəˋvɛlənt] *a.*【化】四价的。

quad·riv·i·al [kwɔˈdriviəl; kwɑdˋrɪvɪəl] *a.* 1. 四路交叉的。2.(中世纪大学之)四高级学科的〔算术、几何、天文、音乐〕。

quad·riv·ium [kwɔˈdriviəm; kwɑdˋrɪvɪəm] *n.*【史】(中世纪大学的)四高级学科[算术、几何、天文、音乐]。

quad·rode [ˈkwɔdrəud; ˋkwɑdrod] *n.*【无】四级管。

quad·roon [kwɔˈdruːn; kwɑdˋrun] *n.* 1. 黑人[异种],(血统占四分之一的)混血儿〔尤指黑白混血儿〕。2.(动、植物)前一代杂交的杂种。

quadru- *comb. f.* = quadri-: *quadru*mana.

quad·ru·ma·na, quad·ru·mane [kwɔˈdruːmənə, kwɔˈdrumein; kwɑˋdrumənə, ˋkwɑdrumen] *n.*(人类之外的)灵长类动物,四足具有手的功能的动物〔如猿、猴等〕。**-nous** [-nəs; -nəs] *a.*

quad·rum·vir [kwɔˈdrʌmvə; kwɑdˋrʌmvɚ] *n.* 四人团体[小组]的成员之一。

quad·rum·vi·rate [kwɔˈdrʌmvərit; kwɑdˋrʌmvərɪt] *n.* 四人团体[小组]。

quad·ru·ped [ˈkwɔdruped; ˋkwɑdrəˏpɛd] I *n.*【动】四足动物(尤指哺乳动物)。II *a.* 有四足的;四足动物的。

quad·ru·pe·dal [kwɔˈdruːpidəl; kwɑdˋrupɪdḷ] *a.*【动】有四足的;四足动物的。

quad·ru·plane [ˈkwɔdruplein; ˋkwɑdrʊˏplen] *n.* 四翼飞机。

quad·rup·le [ˈkwɔdrupl; ˋkwɑdrupḷ] I *a.* 1. 四倍的。2. 四重的;由四部份组成的。3.【乐】四节拍的。*a size* ~ *to* [*of*] *that of the earth* 地球四倍大的大小。II *n.* 四倍,四倍量。III *vt.*, *vi.*(使)成四倍;以四乘。~ **time** [**rhythm, measure**]【乐】四拍子。**-ness** *n.*

quad·ru·plet [ˈkwɔdruplit; ˋkwɑdrʊˏplɪt] *n.* 1. 四件一套。2.〔*pl.*〕四胞胎,四生子。3. 四胞胎中的一个孩子。4. 四人同乘的自行车。

quad·ru·plex [ˈkwɔdrupleks; ˋkwɑdrʊˏplɛks] I *a.* 1. 四倍的,四重的。2.【电】四心电缆的;(同一线路中)四重信号的;【生】四式的。II *n.* 四工电讯机;【生】四式,四显性组合。

quad·ru·pli·cate [kwɔˈdruːplikit; kwɑdˋruplɪkɪt] I *a.* 1. 四倍的,四重的;反复四次的。2.(文件等)一式四份的;第四(份)的。3.【数】四次方的。II *n.* 1. 一式四份中的一份。2.〔*pl.*〕一式四份的文件。*in* ~ 一式四份地。III [kwɔˈdruːplikeit; kwɑdˋruplɪˏket] *vt.* 使成四倍,使成四重;使成一式四份。**quadru·pli·ca·tion** [kɔˌdruːpliˈkeiʃən; kɑˏdruplɪˋkeʃən] *n.*

quad·ru·ply [ˈkwɔdrupli; ˋkwɑdrʊplɪ] *ad.* 四重地,四

倍地。

quae·re [ˈkwiəri; ˋkwɪrɪ] **I** ***vt.*** 〔L.〕〔用于祈使句〕问，调查；查询；敢问，请问。*Quaere more about it.* 再仔细查查。*But ～, is it true?* 不过请问这是真的吗？**II** ***n.*** 〔古〕疑问，询问，问题〔略 qu.〕。

quaes·tio vex·a·ta [ˈkwestʃiəu vekˈsɑːtə; ˋkwestʃɪo vɛkˋsɑtə] 〔L.〕难题；争执中的问题。

quaes·tor [ˈkwiːstə; ˋkwɛstɚ] ***n.*** **1.** (古罗马的)检察官。**2.** 财务官。**-to·ri·al** [-ˈtɔːriəl; -ˋtorɪəl] ***a.***

quaff [kwɑːf, kwɔf; kwæf, kwɑf] **I** ***vt., vi.*** 〔诗〕一口喝干(酒等)，咕咚咕咚地喝。～ ***off*** [***out, up***] 喝干；大口大口喝。**II** ***n.*** 一饮而尽，痛饮；一饮而尽的酒。**-able** ***a.*** 可畅饮的；可饮用的。

quag [kwæg; kwæg] ***n.*** **1.** 泥沼，沼地。**2.** 困境。

quag·ga [ˈkwægə; ˋkwægə] ***n.*** 【动】南非斑驴〔现已绝种〕。

quag·gy [ˈkwægi; ˋkwægɪ] ***a.*** **1.** 沼泽地的；泥泞的。**2.** 软的；松弛的。

quag·mire [ˈkwægmaiə; ˋkwæg͵maɪr] ***n.*** = quag.

qua·haug, qua·hog [ˈkwɔːhɔg; ˋkwɔhɔg] ***n.*** (美国大西洋沿岸所产的)一种圆蛤，帘蛤。

quai [ke; kɛ] ***n.*** 〔F.〕= quay.

Quai d'Orsay [ˌkei dɔːˈsei; ͵ke dɔrˋse] **1.** 巴黎塞纳河边一码头。**2.** 〔the ～〕法国外交部〔因法国外交部在上述码头对面而得名〕；法国外交(政策)。

quaich, quaigh [kweik; kwek] ***n.*** 〔Scot.〕双耳小浅酒杯。

quail[1] [kweil; kwel] ***n.*** (*pl.* ～(***s***)) **1.** 【动】鹌鹑。**2.** 〔美俚〕女大学生；漂亮姑娘。*a bevy of ～s* 一群鹌鹑[姑娘]。*a ～ pipe* (引诱鹌鹑的)鹑笛。*a ～ call* 鹑笛声。～**-roost** 〔美俚〕(大学)女生宿舍。

quail[2] [kweil; kwel] ***vi.*** 沮丧；畏缩 (*at; before; to*)。— ***vt.*** 〔古〕使沮丧；使畏缩。

Quain [kwein; kwen] ***n.*** 奎恩〔姓氏〕。

quaint [kweint; kwent] ***a.*** **1.** 离奇有趣的，古雅的；优雅的；奇妙的。**2.** (工艺制作等)灵巧的。*a ～ old house* 一座古雅的老房子。**-ly** ***ad.*** **-ness** ***n.***

quake [kweik; kwek] **I** ***vi.*** **1.** 摇动，震动。**2.** 打战，抖，发抖 (*with, from, for*)。～ *with fear* 吓得发抖。～ *with cold* 冷得打战。*The earth suddenly began to ～.* 大地突然摇晃。**II** ***n.*** **1.** 摇动，震动；〔口〕地震。**2.** 战栗。**quaking ash** 【植】白杨。**quaking aspen** 【植】颤杨。**quaking concrete** 塑性混凝土。**quak·ing·ly** ***ad.***

Quak·er [ˈkweikə; ˋkwekɚ] ***n.*** (*fem.* **-ess** [-ris; -rɪs]) **1.** (基督教的一个教派)贵格会教徒，教友会教徒，公谊会 (the Society of Friends) 教徒；像教友派教徒的人。**2.** 〔q-〕发抖的人。**3.** 〔美〕费拉德尔菲亚人。～ *City* 〔美〕费拉德尔菲亚 (Philadelphia) 市的别名。～ *gun* 木制假枪。～ *oats* 燕麦片，老人牌麦片。～*s'* [～] *meeting* **1.** 教友派教徒的祈祷会。**2.** 沉默会；倾向沉默的集会。～**-bird** 【动】纯黑信天翁。～**-moth** ***n.*** 英国夜蛾。

Quak·er·ish [ˈkweikriʃ; ˋkwekərɪʃ] ***a.*** **1.** 像教友派教徒一样的。**2.** 朴实的；严谨的；艰苦的。

Quak·er·ism [ˈkweikrizəm; ˋkwekər͵ɪzəm] ***n.*** 教友派；教友派教义。

Quak·er·ly [ˈkweikəli; ˋkwekɚlɪ] **I** ***a.*** = Quakerish. **II** ***ad.*** 像教友派教徒一样地。

quak·y [ˈkweiki; ˋkwekɪ] ***a.*** **1.** 易震动的。**2.** 战栗的。

qual. = qualitative.

qual·i·fi·ca·tion [ˌkwɔlifiˈkeiʃən; ͵kwɑləfəˋkeʃən] ***n.*** **1.** 授权，批准；资格，职权 (*for*)。**2.** 条件，限制，限定；保留，斟酌。**3.** 身分证明书，执照，工作证。**4.** 形容，评定；称呼，称作，认作。*Nothing but has ～ of some kind.* 无任何性状[限定条件]的东西[事物]是不存在的。*The statement requires ～.* 这项声明须加斟酌。*medical ～s* 医生执照。***without*** ～ 无限制地，无条件地，无保留地。～ **shares** 【商】资格股。

qual·i·fi·ca·to·ry [ˈkwɔlifikətəri; ˋkwɑləfɪ͵ketərɪ] ***a.*** **1.** 赋与资格的；资格上的。**2.** 带有条件的；有限制的。

qual·i·fied [ˈkwɔlifaid; ˋkwɑlə͵faɪd] ***a.*** **1.** 有资格的，胜任的，适当的；经过检定的，得到许可的。**2.** 有限制的，有条件的。**3.** 〔俚〕十足的，无比的。*a ～ fool* 大傻瓜。***be ～ for*** 有…的资格；适于担任…。***in a ～ sense*** 在一定意义上；有点，有些。～ **acceptance** 【商】(票据的)条件承兑。**-ly** ***ad.*** **-ness** ***n.***

qual·i·fi·er [ˈkwɔlifaiə; ˋkwɑlə͵faɪɚ] ***n.*** **1.** 合格的人[物]。**2.** 限定者。**3.** 预选赛，资格赛。**4.** 【语法】修饰词〔如形容词、副词等〕。

qual·i·fy [ˈkwɔlifai; ˋkwɑlə͵faɪ] ***vt.*** (**-fied; -fy·ing**) **1.** 使具有资格；授法权予，准予；使适宜，证明…合格。**2.** 限制，斟酌，缓和；(把酒等)搀淡。**3.** 把…当做，把…叫做。**4.** 【语法】限定[形容，修饰]。～ *one's anger* 息怒。～ *spirits with water* 用水搀淡酒。～ *sb. as scoundrel* 把…叫做坏蛋。— ***vi.*** **1.** (通过考试、宣誓等)取得资格，具备合格条件。**2.** 〔美〕宣誓就职；宣誓。～ ***as*** **1.** 取得…的资格。**2.** 宣誓作…。～ ***oneself for*** 取得…的资格，准备好…的条件。～**ing examination** (资格)检定考试。

qual·i·ta·tive [ˈkwɔlitətiv; ˋkwɑlə͵tetɪv] ***a.*** **1.** 质的，质量上的。**2.** 性质上的。**3.** 【化】定性的，定质的 (*opp.* quantitative)。～ **analysis** 定性分析。～ **relation** 种别关系。～ **sound changes** 【语音】音质变化。**-ly** ***ad.*** **1.** 性质上；质量上。**2.** 用定性方法。

qual·i·ty [ˈkwɔliti; ˋkwɑlətɪ] **I** ***n.*** **1.** 质，质量；性质，特质；品质，品位。**2.** 优质，美质，优点。**3.** 才能，能力，技能，素养。**4.** 品种。**5.** 身份，地位；〔古、俚〕高位，名门；〔the ～〕〔古〕身分高贵的人们 (*opp.* the common people)。**6.** 【物】音值，音色；(色泽的)鲜明(性)。**7.** 【逻】(命题的肯定或否定)性质。*the ～ of inspiring confidence* 受人信任的品质。*This is the best ～ of cigars.* 这是最好的雪茄。***give a taste of one's*** ～ 显本领。***have many good qualities*** 有许多长处。***have*** ～ 优秀。***of good*** [***poor***] ～ 优质[劣质]的。**II** ***a.*** **1.** 优质的，高级的。**2.** 上流社会的。～ **circle** 质量攻关小组[研讨会]。～ **control** 质量控制，质量管理。～ **of stand** 【林】林位。～ **of steam** 【物】蒸汽干度。～ *products* 高质量产品。～ **time** 〔美口〕宝贵时光(指父母亲排除工作干扰和外界杂务，专心致志地与孩子们亲热欢聚的时间)；不受干扰地与他人欢聚的一段时间。

qualm [kwɑːm, kwɔːm; kwam, kwɔm] ***n.*** **1.** 一阵眩晕，眼花；恶心。**2.** 不安，疑惧；(良心的)责备。～*s of seasickness* 晕船。*He has no ～s about lying.* 他撒谎毫不内疚。

qualm·ish [ˈkwɑːmiʃ, kwɔː-; ˋkwamɪʃ, kwɔ-] ***a.*** **1.** 有点发晕的，有点恶心的。**2.** 有点不安的；有点受良心责备的。

quan·da·ry [ˈkwɔndəri; ˋkwɑndrɪ] ***n.*** 窘，困惑，左右为难；窘境，狼狈的处境。*I was put in a great* [*in rather a*] ～. 我简直为难死了。

quand même [kɑ̃ˈmɛm; kɑ̃ˋmɛm] 〔F.〕即使，纵令，还是，无论如何。

quang·o·cra·cy [kwæŋˈgɔkrəsi; kwæŋˋgɑkrəsɪ] ***n.*** 〔英〕半官方机构统治。

quant[1] [kwɑːnt, kwænt; kwɑnt, kwænt] **I** ***n.*** (英国平底船用的)平顶篙〔顶端有平顶防止其陷入泥中的篙〕。**II** ***vt., vi.*** 用平顶篙撑(船)。

quant[2] [kwɑːnt, kwænt; kwɑnt, kwænt] ***n.*** 〔口〕股市分析员 (= ～ jock)。

quant. = quantitative.

quan·ta [ˈkwɔntə; ˋkwɑntə] ***n.*** quantum 的复数。

quan·tic [ˈkwɔntik; ˋkwɑntɪk] ***n.*** 【数】齐次多项式。

quan·ti·fi·ca·tion [ˌkwɔntifiˈkeiʃən; ͵kwɑntəfɪˋkeʃən] ***n.*** 定量；【逻】附量，量化。

quan·ti·fi·er [ˈkwɔntifaiə; ˋkwɑntə͵faɪɚ] ***n.*** 【逻】限

量词〔用 all, some 等语词以及前缀[词首]、符号等表示〕。

quan·ti·fy [ˈkwɔntifai; ˋkwɑntə͵faɪ] *vt*. (*-fied*; *-fying*) 1. 确定…的数量, 表示…的数量; 用数量表示 (*opp*. qualify)。2.【逻】用量词限定(全称、特称等的命题)。

quan·tile [ˈkwɔntail, -til; ˋkwɑntaɪl, -tɪl] *n*.【统】分位数。

quan·ti·tate [ˈkwɔntiteit; ˋkwɑntətet] *vt*. 测定[估计]…的数量; 用数量表示。**-ta·tion** *n*.

quan·ti·ta·tive [ˈkwɔntitətiv; ˋkwɑntə͵tetɪv] *a*.【数】量的; 定量的。*the* ～ *limits that determine the qualities of things* 决定事物质量的数量界限。～ **analysis** 定量分析。～ **genetics** 数量遗传学〔亦称 population genetics, 即群体遗传学〕。～ **inheritance**【生】数量遗传。～ **sound changes**【语音】音量变化。**-ly** *ad*.

Q

quan·ti·ty [ˈkwɔntiti; ˋkwɑntətɪ] *n*. 1. 量 (*opp*. quality); 分量, 数量; 额;【物】值, 参量。2. 〔*pl*.〕大量, 大宗, 大批, 许多。3. 定量, 定额。4.【数】量; 表示量的数字[符号];【逻】(名词、特别是命题主语的)量。5.【韵】音节的长短; 表示音节长短的符号;【语音】(元[母]、音节等的)音量。6.【法】期限。*a known* ～ 已知数。*an unknown* ～ 未知数;〔喻〕难预测的人[物]。*a negligible* ～ 可忽略的量;〔喻〕无足轻重的人〔物〕; 可忽略的因素。*a* ～ *of* 一些。*in quantities* 大量。*in* ～ 很多。～ **goods**【经】数量财。～ **mark**【语音】(标于元[母]音上的)音量号。～ **surveyor**【建】估算师, 估料师。

quan·tiv·a·lence [ˌkwɔntiˈveiləns; ͵kwɑntɪˋveləns] *n*.【化】化合价。

quan·tize [ˈkwɔntaiz; ˋkwɑntaɪz] *vt*. 1.【数】用基本数的倍数表示。2.【物】使量子化, 用量子论的术语表示。**～d bubble**【物】量子化磁泡。**-za·tion** [ˌkwɔntaiˈzeiʃən; ͵kwɑntaɪˋzeʃən] *n*. 量子化。

quan·tiz·er [ˈkwɔntaizə; ˋkwɑntaɪzɚ] *n*.【自】数字转换器, 编码器; 量子化(变化)器。*a binary* ～【自】二进位数字转变器。

quan·tom·e·ter [kwɔnˈtɔmitə; kwɑnˋtɑmɪtɚ] *n*.【自】冲击电流计; 电量计; 辐射强度测量计; 光子计数器, 光量计; 剂量计。

quan·tum [ˈkwɔntəm; ˋkwɑntəm] *n*. (*pl*. *-ta* [-tə; -tə]) 1. 量, 额; 定量, 定额; 份; 总量。2.【物】量子。*have one's* ～ *of* 充分尝到…, 充分得到…。～ *libet* [ˈlibet; ˋlɪbɛt] 随意量[略 quant. lib. 或 q.l., 药方用语]; 随意。～ *meruit* [ˈmeruit; ˋmɛruɪt] 按照劳力价值。～ *placet* [ˈpleiset; ˋplesɛt] = ～ *libet* 〔略 q. p.〕。～ *sufficit* [ˈsʌfisit; ˋsʌfɪsɪt] 足量〔略 quant. suff. 或 q.s., 药方用语〕; 充足的份量, 尽量。～ **chemistry** 量子化学。～ **chromodynamics** 量子色动力学。～ **electronics** 量子电子学。～ **equivalence**【物】量子当量。～ **mechanics** 量子力学。～ **physics** 量子物理学。～ **theory**【物】量子论。～ **tunnel(l)ing**【物】量子隧道贯穿〔指电子穿透势垒的现象〕。～ **yield**【物】量子产量。

qua·qua·ver·sal [ˌkweikwəˈvəːsəl; ͵kwekwəˋvɝsl̩] *a*.【地】(地层从中心)向四方倾斜的。**-ly** *ad*.

quar·an·tine [ˈkwɔrəntiːn; ˋkwɔrən͵tin] I *n*. 1. (对港口船舶的)停船检疫, 留验; (防传染病而对人、畜等的)隔离, 封锁。2. 停船期间, 检疫期间。3. 检疫停船港; 检疫所[局]; 隔离医院。4. 四十日间。5. (英国旧时法律规定的)寡妇居留期间〔丈夫死后得留住夫家四十天的期限〕。*a* ～ *flag* 检疫旗〔黄色, 单旗表示无疫病, 双旗表示有疫病〕。II *vt*. 1. 对…进行检疫。2. 封锁, 隔离; 使孤立。3. 命令停船留验。～ *aggressor nations* 孤立侵略国。～ **measures** 植物检疫工作。

quar·en·den, quar·en·der [ˈkwɔrəndən, -də; ˋkwɑrəndən, -dɚ] *n*. (英国 Devonshire 及 Somersetshire 等地产的)红苹果。

quark [ˈkwɑːk; ˋkwɑrk] *n*. 夸克〔假设的带电核粒子, 为已知的粒子如质子及中子等的基本构成部分〕。

Quar·les [kwɔːlz; kwɔrlz] *n*. 夸尔斯〔姓氏〕。

quar·rel[1] [ˈkwɔrəl; ˋkwɔrəl] I *n*. 1. 争吵, 口角, 吵闹, 不和, 不睦; 反目。2. 吵闹的原因[理由]; 怨言。*espouse sb.'s* ～ = *fight one's* ～*s for sb*. 帮着某人吵闹。*find* ～ *in a straw* 吹毛求疵, 找碴儿, 鸡蛋里找骨头, 寻事生非。*fix* [*fasten*] *a* ～ *on* 向某人进行寻衅, 向人找碴儿吵闹。*have a* ～ *with* 和…争吵。*have no* ～ *against* [*with*] 对…无怨言, 对某人无所责难。*in a good* ～ 在理由正大的争论下 (*I will do anything in a good* ～. 只要有理我甚么都干)。*make up a* ～ 和解, 言归于好。*pick* [*seek*] *a* ～ *with* 向…找碴儿吵闹。*pick* ～*s* 闹意气。*take up another's* ～ 助长别人争吵。II *vi*. (英-*l*(*l*)-) 1. 争吵, 争论 (*with*; *about*; *for*); 不和。2. 责备, 埋怨 (*with*)。～ *with* 和(人)吵, 和…争论, 埋怨 (*A bad workman* ～*s with his tools*. 工人无能, 埋怨工具。*Do not* ～ *with Providence*. 不要怨天)。～ *with one's bread and butter* 自暴自弃, 厌弃自己的职业。**-er** *n*.

quar·rel[2] [ˈkwɔrəl; ˋkwɔrəl] *n*. 1.【史】方镞箭, 角镞箭。2. 小块方形[菱形]玻璃。3. (石工的)凿子; 方头物。

quar·rel·(l)er [ˈkwɔrələ; ˋkwɔrəlɚ] *n*. 争吵者, 好争吵的人。

quar·rel·some [ˈkwɔrəlsəm; ˋkwɔrəlsəm] *a*. 好争吵的, 好争论的。**-ly** *ad*. **-ness** *n*.

quar·ren·den [ˈkwɔrəndən; ˋkwɑrəndən] *n*. = quarenden.

quar·ri·er [ˈkwɔriə; ˋkwɑrɪɚ] *n*. = quarryman.

quar·ry[1] [ˈkwɔri; ˋkwɑrɪ] I *n*. 1. 采石场, 石坑, 石矿。2. 知识的泉源; 消息[资料、引文等]的出处。～ *stone* 石块, 乱石。II *vt*., *vi*. (*-ried*; *-ry·ing*) 1. 采(石), 挖掘。2. (从)(书等中)苦心找出(证据等); 苦心寻找(记录等)。**quar·ri·er** *n*. 采石工人。

quar·ry[2] [ˈkwɔri; ˋkwɑrɪ] *n*. 1. 猎获物。2. 〔喻〕追求物; 复仇的对象, 寻找中的仇人。

quar·ry[3] [ˈkwɔri; ˋkwɑrɪ] *n*. 1. 菱形[方形]玻璃[石、瓦等]。2. 机制花砖。

quar·ry·man [ˈkwɔrimən; ˋkwɑrɪmən] (*pl*. *quar·ry·men* [-men; -mɛn]) *n*. 采石工人。

quart[1] [kwɔːt; kwɔrt] *n*. 1. 夸脱〔液量单位, = 1/4 gallon, 约 1.14 升; 干量单位, = 1/8 peck〕。2. 一夸脱的容器; 一夸脱的啤酒。*He still takes his* ～. 他现在还是照常喝大满杯的啤酒。*try to put a* ～ *into a pint pot* 想把一夸脱倒入一品脱的瓶子; 想做不可能做的事情。

quart[2] [kɑːt; kɑrt] *n*. 1. (剑术中的)右胸开脱〔八种防御姿势中的第四种架式。手掌向上, 剑尖指向对手右胸〕。2.【牌】四张同花顺。*a* ～ *major* 最大的四张同花顺〔ace, king, queen, knave〕。～ **and tierce** 剑术研究。

quart. = quarterly.

quart- *comb*. *f*. 表示"四": *quart*er.

quar·tan [ˈkwɔːtən; ˋkwɔrtn] I *a*. (疟疾)每逢第四天发生的, 每隔三天发一次的。II *n*.【医】三日疟。

quar·ta·tion [kwɔːˈteiʃən; kwɔrˋteʃən] *n*.【化】(硝酸)析银法。

quarte [kɑːt; kɑrt] I *n*. 〔F.〕【剑术】= quart. II *vi*., *vt*.【剑术】(采用手掌向上、剑尖指向对手右胸的姿式时)将(头部等)仰向后。

quar·ter [ˈkwɔːtə; ˋkwɔrtɚ] I *n*. 1. 四分之一。★3/4 通常不说 three-fourths 而说 three ～s. 2. 一刻钟, 十五分钟; 一季〔四季结账期之一〕; 每三个月的付款;〔主 Scot.〕一学期〔一年分四学期〕;【天】弦〔月球公转期的四分之一〕;【乐】四分音符。3. 〔英〕夸特〔谷量单位, 约 2.909 公石; 衡量单位, 1/24 英担〕。4. 〔美、加拿大〕二角五分(= 1/4 dollar); 二角五分银币; 1/4 英里; 1/4 码; 1/4 呎; 1/4 磅; 1/4 平方英里的土地 (= ～-section)。5.【运】1/4 英里的赛跑; (橄榄球赛的) 1/4 场 (= ～-back)。6. 罗盘针四方位基点之一〔东、西、南、北〕, 方位, 方角; (机器零件的)相互垂直。**7**. 方向,方面;地域,地方;区,市区,街。**8**. (供给、救助、消息的)来源,出处。**9**. 〔*pl*.〕寓所,住处;〔*pl*.〕【军】营房,驻地,营盘,宿舍;〔*pl*.〕岗位。**10**.鸟兽四分后的一肢;〔*pl*.〕受刑者被四分肢解后的一肢;〔*pl*.〕(人、马等的)腰,臀部。**11**.【海】船侧后半部〔正横与船尾的中间部分〕,船尾部。**12**.【建】间柱〔柱与柱间的小柱〕;【纹】盾形的四分之一。**13**. 英国海峡殖民地征收财产税、所得税的标准单位〔25 镑〕。**14**. (特指对投降者的)饶命,免死,慈悲;宽大,宽恕,减轻。*cut an apple in ~s* 把苹果切成四分。*a ~ to* [*past*] *nine* 九点差[过]一刻。*the four ~s of the globe* 全世界。*the first* [*last*] ~ 上[下]弦。*What ~ is the wind in*? 风是从哪一方面吹来的? 形势如何? *Lies the wind in that ~*? 形势是这样的吗? *I had the news from a good ~*. 这个消息是从可靠方面听来的。*There is no help to be looked for in that ~*. 从那方面得不到什么援助。*workers' living ~s* 工人宿舍。*industrial ~s* 工业区。*residential ~s* 住宅区。*licensed* [*gay*] *~s* (低级下流娱乐场所汇聚的)风化区。***a bad ~ of an hour*** 不愉快的一刻。***a ~ and five*** $5\frac{1}{4}$ 吋。***a ~ less five*** $4\frac{3}{4}$ 吋。***a ~ right*** [***left***]【军】靠右[左]1/4 直角。***ask for*** [***cry***] ***~s*** 请求饶命。***at close ~s*** **1**. 迫近,逼近,接近;在仔细观察之下。**2**.【军】短兵相接,白刃战。***beat to ~s***【海】使各就岗位。***beat up the ~s of*** 突然访问。***call to ~s***【军】使各就各位。***from every ~*** [***all ~s***] 从四面八方。***give ~*** 不杀,饶命。***Give no ~***! 格杀勿论! ***in all ~s*** [***every ~***] 到处,处处。***not a ~*** 完全不是(*not a ~ so* [*as*] *good as* 远不及)。***on the ~***【海】在船尾方面。***strike the ~s*** (钟)敲一刻钟。***take up one's ~s*** **1**. 投宿,住宿 (*in*, *with*)。**2**. (水兵)进入岗位。**II** ***vt***. **1**. 把…四分,把…四等分。**2**. 使住宿;使(军队)扎营;使筹办食宿。**3**.【海】使各就岗位。**4**. 四裂肢体(动物、罪犯)。**5**. 将(别家纹章)加在自己盾牌的一角上,将(盾)用纵横线加以四分。**6**. (猎狗为搜寻猎获物)纵横奔跑于(某地区)。**7**. 使(机器零件)相互垂直。— ***vi***. **1**. 驻扎,扎营 (*at*, *with*)。**2**. 变更位置;各就岗位。**3**. (猎狗)搜找猎物。**4**.【海】(风从斜后方)吹来。**5**. (机器零件)相互垂直。~ ***oneself on*** [***with***] 投宿在…[和…同住]。~**back** ***n***.【橄榄球】四分卫〔在 forwards 和 half-backs 之间〕;进攻时指挥本队的选手。~ **bell** 每十五分钟一响的铃。~ **bill**【海】战斗部署表。~ **binding** (书的)皮脊[布脊]装订。~ **blood** ***n***., ***a***. 四分之一杂种(血统的)。~ **boards** 〔*pl*.〕舰尾的防波板。~**-bound** ***a***. 皮脊[布脊]装订的。~**-bred** ***a***. (牛、马等)四分之一纯血统的。~**-butt**【台球】短小的球棒。~ **day** 四季结账日〔英格兰与爱尔兰是 Lady Day (3 月 25 日), Midsummer Day (6 月 24 日), Michaelmas (9 月 29 日), Christmas (12 月 25 日),苏格兰是 Candlemas (2 月 2 日), Whitsunday (5 月 15 日), Lammas (8 月 1 日), Mastinmas (11 月 11 日);美国是 1、4、7、10 月的 1 日〕。~**-deck** **1**.【海】后甲板。**2**. 〔the ~-deck〕高级船员们,军官们。~ **horse** 1/4 英里赛跑马。~**-hour** **1**. 一刻钟的期间。**2**. (某时的)15 分钟前[后]。~**-jack** = quartermaster. ~ **light** (车辆的)边窗。~ **line**【海】军舰的雁行式阵形。~**master** **1**.【海】舵手。**2**.【军】军需(官)〔略 Q.M.〕(*~master corps* 辎重兵,辎重队。*~-master service* 后方勤务)。~**master-general** 兵站总监〔略 Q.M.G.〕(*Quarter-master-general to the Forces* 〔英〕军需署署长)。~**-master-sergeant** 辎重军士〔略 Q.M.S.〕。~ **mile** 1/4 英里〔尤指赛跑的距离〕。~**-miler** 1/4 英里赛跑选手。~ **note**【乐】四分音符。~**-phase** ***a***.【电】二相的。~ **plate**【摄】照相干片〔$3\frac{1}{4}\times 4\frac{1}{4}$ 英寸〕;同尺寸的照片。~ **saw** ***vt***. 把(木头)打直锯成四块。~ **section** **1**. 〔美、加拿大〕【测量】约 1/4 平方英里的土地(=160 英亩)。**2**. 四分之一。~ **sessions** 〔*pl*.〕一年开四次的州法庭。~**staff** 铁头木棒〔古时英国农民两头包铁的武器〕。~ **tone**【乐】四分音〔semitone 之半〕。~ **wind**【海】从斜后方吹来的风,船尾风。**-age** ***n***. **1**. 按季收付的款项;季度工资[税、津贴]。**2**. 供给军队的住处。**3**. 供宿。**4**. 住宿费。**-ing** [ˈkwɔːtəriŋ; ˋkwɔrtərɪŋ] **1**. ***n***. 四等分;(罪犯的)四裂肢解;【军】扎营的分派;【纹】联姻纹章(的配合);【建】间柱;【机】成直角;【天】月球向上弦、满月、下弦的移变。**2**. ***a***.【海】(风)从斜后方吹来的;【机】成直角的。**-ly** **1**. ***a***. 按季的,一年四次的,每季的;【海】(风)向船尾吹的;【纹】(盾面)分为四部份的。**2**. ***ad***. 一年四次,一季一次,按季;【纹】(盾面)纵横四分地。**3**. ***n***. 季刊,按季出版物。

quar·tered [ˈkwɔːtəd; ˋkwɔrtəd] ***a***. **1**. 四分的,四等分的。**2**. 提供住处的。**3**. (把木头)纵向锯成四片再锯成木板的。

quar·ter·fi·nal [ˌkwɔːtəˈfainl; ˏkwɔrtəˋfaɪnl] **I** ***a***.【运】复赛的。**II** ***n***. 复赛,四分之一决赛。**-ist** ***n***. 参加四分之一决赛的选手[队]。

quar·tern [ˈkwɔːtən; ˋkwɔrtən] ***n***. **1**. 夸脱仑〔液量单位 (=1/4 pint, gill);谷量单位 (=1/4 peck, stone)〕。**2**. 四等分,四分之一。**3**. (用 1 quartern 面粉做成、重 4 磅的)大面包,四磅面包〔又作 quartern-loaf〕。

quar·tet, quar·tette [kwɔːˈtet; kwɔrˋtɛt] ***n***. **1**.【乐】四重奏,四重唱;四部合奏[唱]曲;四部合奏[唱]者。**2**. 四件一组,四个一副[一套]。**3**.【生】四集体;四分孢子;【物】四重线。

quar·tic [ˈkwɔːtik; ˋkwɔrtɪk] **I** ***a***.【数】四次的。**II** ***n***. 四次齐式;四次(乘)幂。

quar·tile [ˈkwɔːtail, -tl; ˋkwɔrtaɪl, -tl] ***n***., ***a***. **1**.【统】四分位数(的);四分位数一组(的)。**2**.【天】方照(的);弦(的);二天体直径差 90 度(的)。

quar·to [ˈkwɔːtəu; ˋkwɔrto] **I** ***n***. (*pl*. **~s**) (纸等的)四开〔$7\times 8\frac{1}{2}$ 至 10×13 英寸,略作 4 to 或 4°〕;四开书本。**II** ***a***. 四开(本)的。*a ~ edition* 四开本版。*a ~ paper* 四开的纸。

quartz [kwɔːts; kwɔrts] ***n***.【矿】石英,水晶。*milky ~* 乳石英。*smoky ~* 烟水晶。*violet ~* 紫石英。*water ~* 泡水晶。~**(-halogen) lamp** 石英(卤素)灯。~ **clock** 石英晶体钟。

quartz·if·er·ous [kwɔːˈtsifərəs; kwɔrtˋsɪfərəs] ***a***.【矿】石英质的,含石英的。

quartz·ite [ˈkwɔːtsait; ˋkwɔrtsaɪt] ***n***.【矿】石英岩。

qua·sar [ˈkweisɑː; ˋkwesɑr] ***n***.【天】类星体;类星射电源。

quash[1] [kwɔʃ; kwɑʃ] ***vt***.【法】取消,废除,使无效。

quash[2] [kwɔʃ; kwɑʃ] ***vt***. **1**. 捣碎,压碎。**2**. 压制,镇压;平息。

quash·ee, quash·ie [ˈkwɔʃi; ˋkwɑʃɪ] ***n***. (特指西非)黑人。

qua·si [ˈkwɑːzi(ː), ˈkweisai; ˋkwezɪ, ˋkwesaɪ] **I** ***ad***. **1**. 在某一意义上,有点,几乎。**2**. 恰如,宛如,就像是。**3**. 就是说,即〔略作 q. 或 qu.,尤用以作语源上的说明〕。*He was ~ a prisoner*. 他就像一个犯人。*Earls of Wilbraham, ~ wild boar ham* 威尔白莱罕(即"野猪大腿肉")伯爵家。**II** ***a***. 好像是的;似乎是的,类似的。*He was a ~ artist*. 他有点儿像画家。*a ~ governmental agency* 类似政府机关的一个机构。

quasi- *pref*. 表示"类似,准,拟": *quasi*judicial. ★汉译可较灵活。如 *~-cholera* 拟似霍乱。*~-contract* 准契约。*~-war* 准战争。*~-conductor* 半导体。*~-sovereign state* 半独立国。

qua·si·at·om [ˌkweisaiˈætəm; ˏkwesaɪˋætəm] ***n***.【物】准原子〔一种类似原子而存在时间极短暂的核粒子〕。

qua·si·chol·er·a [ˌkwɑːzi(ː)ˈkɔlərə; ˏkwɑzɪ(i)ˋkɑlərə] ***n***.【医】拟似霍乱。

qua·si-his·tor·i·cal [ˌkwɑːzi(ː)hisˈtɔrikəl; ˏkwɑzɪ(i)-hɪsˋtɑrɪkəl] ***a***. 带有历史性质的。

qua·si-ju·di·cial [ˌkwɑːzi(ː)dʒuːˈdiʃəl; ˏkwesaɪdʒu-ˋdɪʃəl] ***a***. 准司法性的,具有部份立法权的。

qua·si-leg·is·la·tive [ˌkwɑːzi(ː)ˈledʒislətiv; ˏkwesaɪ-

ˋlɛdʒɪsletɪv] *a*. 准立法性的,具有部份立法权的。

Qua·si·mo·do [ˌkwɑːzi(ː)ˈməudəu; ˏkwɑzɪ(i)ˋmodo] *n*.【基督教】复活节后的第一个星期日。

qua·si-of·fi·cial [ˈkwɑːzi(ː)əˈfiʃəl; ˋkwɑzɪ(i)əˋfɪʃəl] *a*. 半官方的。

qua·si-op·ti·cal [ˈkwɑːzi(ː)ˈɔptikəl; ˋkwɑzɪ(i)ˋɔptɪkəl] *a*. 准光(学)的。～ **wave**【物】准光波。

qua·si-pub·lic [ˈkwɑːzi(ː)ˈpʌblik; ˏkwesaɪˋpʌblɪk] *a*. (公司、企业等)私营公用事业的。

qua·si-shawl [ˈkwɑːziʃɔːl; ˋkwɑzɪʃol] *n*. 类似围巾的东西。

qua·si-sov·er·eign [ˌkwɑːziˈsɔvrin; ˏkwɑzɪˋsɑvrɪn] *a*. 半独立的,半主权的。

quas·qui·cen·ten·ni·al [ˌkwɔskwisenˈteniəl; ˏkwɑskwɪsɛnˋtɛnɪəl] *n*. 第一百二十五周年纪念日。

quass [kvɑːs, kwɑːs; kvɑs, kwɑs] *n*. 克瓦斯(= kvass)〔一种用面包或水果发酵制成的俄式清凉饮料〕。

quas·sia [ˈkwɔʃə; ˋkwɑʃɪə] *n*. 1.【植】苦树;〔Q-〕苦木属。2. 苦树木料[树皮、根];由苦树采取的苦味液。3. 啤酒苦味剂。～**-wood** *n*. 苦木。

qua·ter·cen·te·na·ry [ˌkwætəsenˈtiːnəri; ˏkwetɚˋsɛntɚˏnɛrɪ] *n*. 四百周年(纪念)。

qua·ter·na·ry [kwəˈtəːnəri; kwəˋtɝnərɪ] I *a*. 1. 四个一组的;由四部份组成的;第四的。2.【化】四元的;四价的;季的;【数】四进制的。3.〔Q-〕【地】第四纪〔系〕的。II *n*. 1. 四;四个一组的东西;第四组组成部分。2.〔Q-〕【地】第四纪。3.【数】四进制。*the Pythagorean* ～ 毕达哥拉斯四元数〔即 1+2+3+4,结果恰巧是 10〕。

qua·ter·ni·on [kwəˈtəːnjən, -niən; kwəˋtɝnjən, -nɪən] *n*. 1. 四,四个一组;四组物;四人一组。2. 四张对折的一沓纸;对折两次的一张纸。3.【数】四元数;〔*pl*.〕四元法。

qua·ter·ni·ty [kwəˈtəːniti; kwəˋtɝnətɪ] *n*. 1. 四,四个一组;四人一组。2.【宗】四位一体。

quat·rain [ˈkwɔtrein; ˋkwɑtren] *n*.【韵】四行诗,四行一节的诗。

qua·tre [ˈkɑːtə; ˋkɑtɚ] *n*. (纸牌、骨牌、骰子的)四点。

quat·re·foil [ˈkætrəfɔil; ˋkætɚˏfɔɪl] *n*. 1. (苜蓿等)四叶片的叶子;四瓣的花朵。2.【建】四叶式;【纹】四叶形。～ **crossing** (道路的)四叶式交叉。

quat·tro·cen·tist [ˌkwætrəuˈtʃentist; ˏkwætroˋtʃɛntɪst] *n*. 十五世纪的意大利艺术家[作家]。

quat·tro·cen·to [ˌkwætrəuˈtʃentəu; ˏkwɑttroˋtʃɛnto] *n*.〔常 Q-〕十五世纪(风格)〔词义是 1400 年代,即欧洲文艺复兴的初期〕。

qua·ver [ˈkweivə; ˋkwevɚ] I *vi*. 1. 震动,颤动。2. (特指声音)颤抖。— *vt*. 颤抖着说[唱],用颤音演奏(*out*)。II *n*. 1. 颤音;颤声。2.【乐】八分音符。

qua·ver·ing, qua·ver·ous [ˈkweivəriŋ, -rəs; ˋkwevərɪŋ, -rəs] *a*. 颤抖的;颤声的。

qua·ver·ing·ly [ˈkweivəriŋli; ˋkwevərɪŋlɪ] *ad*. 颤抖着声音,用颤声。

qua·ver·y [ˈkweivəri; ˋkwevərɪ] *a*. 颤音多的,颤声的。

Quay [kwei; kwe] *n*. 奎伊〔姓氏〕。

quay [kiː; ki] *n*. 码头,埠头。～**side** *n*. 码头区〔常作修饰语,如 ～*side building* 等〕。

quay·age [ˈkiːidʒ; ˋkiɪdʒ] *n*. 1. 码头使用税[费]。2. 码头空位;码头用地,码头面积。3.〔总称〕一组码头。

Que. = Quebec.

quean [kwiːn; kwin] *n*. 1.〔Scot.〕(未婚)妇女;少女。2. 厚脸女人,轻佻妇女(尤指妓女)。

quea·sy, quea·zy [ˈkwiːzi; ˋkwizɪ] *a*. 1. (食物等)使人作呕的,(船等)使人眩晕欲吐的。2. (人)易呕吐的,要呕的,易反胃的。3. 心软的;顾虑重重的;(良心等)易不安的。**quea·si·ly** *ad*. **quea·si·ness** *n*.

Quebec [kwiˈbek; kwɪˋbɛk] *n*. 1. 魁北克〔加拿大省名〕。2. 魁北克〔加拿大港市〕。

que·bra·cho [keiˈbrɑːtʃəu; keˋbrɑtʃo] *n*. (*pl*. ～*s*)【植】1. 破斧树(*Schinopsis lorentzii*)〔产于美洲热带地区〕。2. 白坚木(*Aspidosperma quebracho-blanco*)〔产于南美洲〕。3. 破斧树材[树皮];白坚木材[树皮]。

Quech·ua [ˈketʃwɑː, -wə; ˋkɛtʃwɑ, -wə] *n*. (*pl*. ～(*s*)) 1. 凯楚阿人〔南美安第斯高原各国的印第安人〕。2. 凯楚阿语。**Quech·uan** *n*., *a*. 凯楚阿人[语](的)。

Quech·u·ma·ran [ˈketʃuməraːn; ˋkɛtʃumərɑn] *n*. 凯楚阿马兰语系。

Queen [kwiːn; kwin] *n*. 奎恩〔姓氏〕。

queen [kwiːn; kwin] I *n*. 1. 皇后,王后。2. 女王,女皇,女帝;女酋长;女首脑。★在位君主是女王时,成语中的 King 可改用 Queen. 如 King's Bench [Counsel 等]可说作 Queen's Bench [Counsel 等]。3. (因权力、地位、相貌等而被尊崇的)出众的妇女;(神话等中的)女神;圣母玛利亚;爱人,情人;心爱的女子〔指妻、女等〕。4. (社交界等的)…皇后,名媛;"美女比赛"第一名,尤物;〔喻〕精华,上品;胜地。5. (纸牌或象棋中的)后;(蚂蚁、蜜蜂等的)女王;雌猫(等)。6.〔美俚〕乱搞同性恋爱的男子,女性化的男人。7.〔空军俚〕操纵无人驾驶飞机(drone)的指挥机。*Q- Anne Style* (18 世纪初期建筑,家具等的)安女王式。*Q- Anne is dead*. 老早听腻了;(消息等)早知道了。*Q- of Grace*【基督教】圣母玛利亚。～ *of hearts* 1.【牌戏】心牌女王。2. 美人。～ *of heaven* 天后〔希腊神话中主神宙斯之妻朱诺(Juno)的别称〕。～ *of love* 爱神〔希腊神话中维纳斯(Venus)的别称〕。～ *of night* 1. 夜神,月神〔希腊神话中司狩猎女神、月神狄安娜(Diana)的别称〕。2. 月。～ *of the Adriatic* 亚德里亚海之后〔意大利城市威尼斯(Venice)的别称〕。～ *of (the) May* 五月女王〔指五月一日花魁日游戏中被选中为女王的女子, = May-queen〕。～ *of the meadows* 草原女王〔即【植】绣线菊 = meadow-sweet〕。*Q- of the seas* 海上之王〔指旧时英帝国〕。*Q- of the West* 西部之王〔美国辛辛那提(Cincinnati)市的别名〕。～*-right colony*【蜂】有王群。*Queen's Bench* 英国高等法院。*Queen's Club* 英国肯辛顿(Kensington)的运动场。*Queen's colour* 英军的团旗。*Queen's Counsel* 英国王室法律顾问。*Queen's omnibus*〔俚〕巡警车,囚车(= Black Maria)。～*'s ware* 英国产的奶油色陶器。～*'s weather* 晴天。*to the* ～*'s taste* 尽善尽美地,完美地,使人无可挑剔地。II *vt*. 1. 立…为女王[王后],使即女王位。2. 以女王的身份统治。3.【象棋】使(卒子)达底线后变为王后。— *vi*. 1. 成为女王;作为女王而统治。2.【象棋】卒子达底线后变为王后。～ *it* 做女王统治,像女王一般地动作(～ *it over [among] girls* 在女孩中称王)。～ **ant** 蚁王,雌蚁。**Q- Bee [Duck]** 无线电操纵的靶机[靶舰]。～ **bee** 蜂王;〔喻〕社交界女王。～**cake** 夹有葡萄干的心形小软饼。～ **consort** 皇后,王妃。～ **dowager** (皇)太后〔已故君主之妻〕。～ **mother** 1. (皇)太后〔在位君主之母〕。2. (生有太子或公主的)现任女王。～ **post**【建】双柱架。～ **regent** 1. 摄政王后。2.〔罕〕女皇。～**regnant** (执政的)女皇,女帝,女王。～**-size** 大号的,仅次于特大号的。～ **wasp** 雌蜂,蜂王。**-dom** 1. 女王统治的王国。2.〔罕〕女王[王后]的身份[地位]。**-hood [-ship]** 女王[王后]的地位[身份,统治期间]。**-less** *a*. 无女王[王后]的。**-like** *a*. = queenly *a*.

queen·ing [ˈkwiːniŋ; ˋkwinɪŋ] *n*. 1. 立为女王[王后]。2.〔英〕王后苹果〔苹果的一个品种〕。

queen·li·ness [ˈkwiːnlinis; ˋkwinlɪnɪs] *n*. 女王般的威严,女王般的作风。

queen·ly [ˈkwiːnli; ˋkwinlɪ] I *a*. (像)女王的,俨然女王的,有威严的。II *ad*. 女王[王后]般地。

Queens·ber·ry [ˈkwiːnzbəri; ˋkwinzbərɪ] *n*. 昆斯伯里〔姓氏〕。～ **rules** 标准拳击规则(= Marquis ～ of rules)。

Queensland [ˈkwiːnzlənd; ˋkwinzˏlænd] *n*. 昆士兰〔澳大利亚州名〕。

queer [kwiə; kwɪr] I *a*. 1. 奇妙的,奇怪的。2.〔口〕可

疑的,费解的。**3.** 眩晕的,眼花的,(身体)觉得不舒服的;有点神经失常的;〔英俚〕喝醉了的。**4.**〔美俚〕假的,伪造的;无价值的。**5.**〔美俚〕搞同性恋爱的;(男子)女性化的。**6.** 对…着了迷的(*for*, *on*, *about*)。*That's* ~! 那倒奇怪! *a* ~ *character* 可疑的人物。*a* ~ *transaction* 不正当的交易。***a* ~ *fish* [*card*]** 怪人,疯子。***be* ~ *in the head*** 头脑失常。***feel* ~** 觉得不舒服。***in Q-Street*** 〔俚〕背着债;(财政)陷入绝境;名誉不好。**II** ***n*.** **1.**〔美俚〕〔the ~〕假钞票,伪钞,伪币。**2.**〔美俚〕搞同性恋爱的男子。***pass the* ~** 使用伪币。***on the* ~** 犯伪钞制造罪。**III** ***vt*.** **1.**〔俚〕糟蹋,弄糟,破坏。**2.** 使觉得不舒服;使陷入窘境;使处于危险地位。*Bad food ~ed the party*. 饭菜不好使宴会大为减色。~ ***sb.'s pitch*** = ~ ***the pitch for sb*.** 〔英口〕暗中破坏某人计划。**-ish** ***a*.** 有点古怪[可疑、不舒服]的。**-ly** ***ad*.** **-ness** ***n*.**

quell [kwel; kwɛl] **I** ***vt*.** 〔书〕**1.** 镇压(叛乱等),压制;平息。**2.** 镇定,消除,减轻(激动、恐惧等)。**II** ***n*.** 〔古〕屠杀。**quell·able** ***a*.** 可平定的;可消除的。**-er** ***n*.** 镇压者,平息者。

quel·que chose [kelkəˈʃəuz; kɛlkəˋʃoz]〔F.〕小事,琐事。

Que·moy [ˈkweiˈmɔi; kweˋmɔɪ] ***n*.** 金门(岛)〔中国福建省岛屿〕。

quench [kwentʃ; kwɛntʃ] ***vt*.** **1.** (主持)熄灭(火、光);扑灭。**2.** 压制,遏制,抑制;解(渴)。**3.**【机】把…淬火,使骤冷;使淬硬;淬炼;【物】淬熄。**4.**〔俚〕迫使(反对者)沉默,使无话可说。~ *one's thirst* 解渴。~ *a fire* 弄灭火。~ *eyesight* 减弱视力。~ *an uprising* 镇压起义。~ ***smoking flax*** 弄熄冒着烟的火,中止充满着希望的计划。

quench·a·ble [ˈkwentʃəbl; ˋkwɛntʃəbl̩] ***a*.** **1.** 可熄灭的,可冷却的。**2.** 镇压得了的;抑制得住的。**-ness** ***n*.**

quench·er [ˈkwentʃə; ˋkwɛntʃɚ] ***n*.** **1.** 熄灭者,扑灭者。**2.** 灭火器;猝灭器;骤冷器;猝火剂。**3.** 抑制者;压制者[物]。**4.**〔口〕解渴物,饮料。

quench·ing [ˈkwen*t*ʃiŋ; ˋkwɛntʃɪŋ] ***n*.**【机】淬火;【物】淬熄。~ **effect** 淬炼效应。~ **machine** 淬火机。~ **medium** 淬火剂;骤冷剂。~ **oil** 淬火油。

quench·less [ˈkwentʃlis; ˋkwɛntʃlɪs] ***a*.** **1.** 难弄熄的;不(可)冷却的。**2.** 难镇压的;难抑制的。

que·nelle [keˈnel; kəˋnɛl] ***n*.** 肉丸子;鱼圆子。

Quen·tin [ˈkwentin; ˋkwɛntɪn] ***n*.** 昆廷〔男子名〕。

quer·ce·tin [ˈkwəːsitin; ˋkwɝsətɪn] ***n*.**【化】栎精;栎皮黄素。**quercet·ic** [kwəˈsetik, -ˈsiːt-; kwəˋsɛtɪk, -ˋsit] ***a*.**

quer·cine [ˈkwəːsin, -sain; ˋkwɝsɪn, -saɪn] ***a*.** 栎树的;橡树的;槲树的。

quer·cit·ron [ˈkwəːsitrən, kwəˈsitrən; ˋkwɝsɪtrən, kwɝˋsɪtrən] ***n*.** **1.** 美洲黑栎的内层皮。**2.** 栎皮粉。

quer·i·mo·ni·ous [ˌkweriˈməuniəs; ˏkwɪrɪˋmonɪəs] ***a*.** = querulous.

que·rist [ˈkwiərist; ˋkwɪrɪst] ***n*.** 讯问者,质问者。

quern [kwəːn; kwɝn] ***n*.** 手(推的)磨。~**stone** 磨石(= millstone)。

quer·u·lous [ˈkweruləs; ˋkwɛrələs] ***a*.** 爱抱怨的;爱发牢骚的;易发脾气的。**-ly** ***ad*.**

que·ry [ˈkwiəri; ˋkwɪrɪ] **I** ***n*.** **1.** 质问;询问;疑问,怀疑。**2.** 敢问,请问〔在疑问句前单独使用〕。**3.**【印】(打在原稿或校样上的)疑问号〔?〕〔亦可写作 query, 通常略作 qu. 或 qy.〕。*Q-, was the money ever paid?* 请问这钱付过了没有? **II** ***vt*.** (***-ried***; ***-ry·ing***) **1.** 问,询问(*whether*; *if*);质问。**2.** 把…作为问题提出,对…表示怀疑。— ***vi*.** 质问,询问;表示怀疑,在(校样等上)加疑问符号。

ques. = question.

quest [kwest; kwɛst] **I** ***n*.** **1.** 找,寻找,搜索,追求,探求。**2.** (特指中世纪骑士的)追求物。**3.**〔英方〕审问;〔古〕验尸;验尸陪审团。***in* ~ *of*** 为求…,为寻求…(*He has come in* ~ *of employment*. 他来找工作)。**II** ***vi*.** **1.** (狗等)跟踪搜寻,四处找(*about*)。**2.** 追求,探索。— ***vt*.** 〔诗〕寻求,探索(*out*)。

ques·tion [ˈkwestʃən; ˋkwɛstʃən] **I** ***n*.** **1.** 问,询问,发问;质问。**2.**【语法】疑问句。**3.** 疑问;疑义,疑窦。**4.** 问题;议题;争论点;悬案;(法庭等上的)争端。**5.** (把问题)付表决;付表决的问题。**6.** 审问;〔古〕拷问。*a direct* ~ 直接疑问句。*an indirect* [*oblique*] ~ 间接疑问句。*a rhetorical* ~ 反诘句。*a* ~ *of time* 时间问题。*leading* ~【法】诱供,诱导询问。*the Eastern* ~ 东方问题。*The* ~ *is* ...题是…。***an open* ~** 未解决的问题,容许讨论的问题。***a* ~ *at* [*in*] *issue*** 悬案,争持的问题。***a* ~ *of* ~*s*** 首要问题。***a previous* ~** (议会中的)先决问题[动议]。***a sixty-four dollar* ~** 最重要的问题。***begging* (*of*) *the* ~** 用未经证明的假定来辩论。***beside the* ~** 在本题之外,离题。***beyond* (*all*) ~** 毫无疑问;一定,当然。***call in* ~** 怀疑,表示异议,表示不服;要求…的证据。***come into* ~** 成为问题,成为有实际重要性。***foreign to the* ~** = beside the ~. ***in* ~** **1.** 议论中的,该…,本…。**2.** 可怀疑,被争论,成为问题的。***make no* ~ *of*** = ***make no* ~ *but that* ...** 对…不加怀疑。***out of* ~** = beyond ~. ***out of the* ~** 不在考虑之列,谈不上;根本不可能。***past* ~** = beyond ~. ***pop the* ~**〔俚〕求婚。***put a* ~ *to*** 向…质问,质问…。***put the* ~** 提付表决;要求表决。***put to the* ~**〔古〕加以拷问。***Question***! 〔公开集会等中的叫声〕**1.** 请注意正题,离题了!〔促发言人言归本题〕。**2.** 有疑问! 有异议!〔表示疑问或不赞成〕。~***s and commands*** 问答游戏。***starred* ~** 要求口头答复的质问〔因英国国会中要求口头答复时附加星印〕。***That is not the* ~.** 那是另外一个问题,那是另外一回事,那是题外话,那和我们的讨论无关。***There is no* ~ (*but*) *that* ...**那的确是…的;…是没有怀疑余地的。***There is no* ~ *of* ...** **1.** …是毫无疑问的。**2.** …是不可能的。***to the* ~** 针对论题;对题,切题。***without* ~** 毫无疑问。**II** ***vt*.** **1.** 询问;讯问;审问。**2.** 怀疑,对…表示疑问,对…提出疑问。**3.** 争论。**4.** 分析;探究,研究(事实)。~ *sb.'s honesty* 怀疑某人是否诚实。— ***vi*.** 询问;探问;探究。***It cannot be* ~*ed but that*...** …无怀疑的余地;…是确实的。~ **mark** = ~ **stop** 疑问号〔?〕。~-**master** (广播或电视等中)答问节目的主持人。~ **time** (英国议会中议员对大臣提问题的)质询时间。**-er** ***n*.** 询问者;讯问者;审问者。**-less** ***a*.** **1.** 无疑的。**2.** 无异议的。**-lessly** ***ad*.** 无疑地,的确。

ques·tion·a·ble [ˈkwestʃənəbl; ˋkwɛstʃənəbl̩] ***a*.** 可疑的;(人)靠不住的,(品德等)有问题的。**-a·bly** ***ad*.**

ques·tion·a·ry [ˈkwestʃənəri; ˋkwɛstʃənˏɛrɪ] **I** ***a*.** 询问的,探问的,疑问的。**II** ***n*.** 〔美〕= question(n)aire.

ques·tion·ing·ly [ˈkwestʃəniŋli; ˋkwɛstʃənɪŋlɪ] ***ad*.** 质问的,像讯问似地,疑惑地,诧异地。

ques·tion·(n)aire [ˌkwestiəˈnɛə, -tʃə-; ˏkwɛstɪənˋɛr, -tʃə-] ***n*.** 〔F.〕**1.** (调查情况用的)一组问题;问题单。**2.** 调查表,征求意见表。**3.** 用调查表进行的调查。

ques·tor [ˈkwestə, ˈkwiːs-; ˋkwɛstɚ, ˋkwis-] ***n*.** = quaestor.

Quetta [ˈkwetə; ˋkwɛtə] ***n*.** 奎达〔巴基斯坦城市〕。

quet·zal [ketˈsɑːl, ˈketsəl; kɛtˋsɑl, ˋkɛtsəl] (*pl*. ~(*e*)*s* [ketˈsɑːleis; kɛtˋsɑles]) ***n*.**【动】克沙尔鸟〔中美产,尾特长,羽美,为危地马拉的国鸟〕。

Quet·zal·co·a·tl [ketˌsɑːlkəuˈɑːtl; kɛtˏsɑlkoˋɑtl̩] ***n*.** (墨西哥印第安人)阿兹台克人信奉的主神。

queue [kjuː; kju] **I** ***n*.** **1.** 发辫,辫子。**2.**〔英〕(顺序等车、购物的)行列,长队;车队。***form a* ~** 排队。***in a* ~** 排成一行。***jump the* ~** 不按次序排队;企图获得优惠待遇。**II** ***vt*.** 把(头发)梳成辫子。— ***vi*.** 〔英〕排(成)队,排队等候(*on*; *up*)。~ *up at a bus stop* 在公共汽车站排队。

que·zal [keˈsɑːl; kɛˋsɑl] ***n*.** = quetzal.

Quezon City [ˈkeizɔn ˈsiti; ˋkesɔn ˋsɪtɪ] 奎松城〔菲律宾城市〕。

quib·ble [ˈkwibl; ˋkwɪbl] **I** *n*. **1**. 遁词,狡辩;支吾,模棱两可的说法。**2**. 吹毛求疵的意见。**3**. 〔古〕双关话。**II** *vi*. **1**. 推托,推诿,讲模棱两可的话;狡辩。**2**. 讲双关话。 **quib·bler** *n*. **1**. 推诿[狡辩]的人。**2**. 讲双关语的人。 **quib·bling·ly** *ad*.

quiche Lor·raine [kiːʃ ləuˈren; kiʃ loˋrɛn] (*pl*. ***quiches*** [kiːʃ; kiʃ] ***Lorraine***)〔F.〕洛林糕〔用干酪,腌肉等做成的奶蛋糕〕。

Quick [kwik; kwɪk] *n*. 奎克〔姓氏〕。

quick [kwik; kwɪk] **I** *a*. **1**. 快,迅速的,急速的 (*opp*. slow); 短时间的。**2**. 敏捷的;机敏的,聪明的,伶俐的;(眼睛等)敏锐的。**3**. 生动的,活泼的。**4**. 性急的,易怒的,易发脾气的。**5**. 〔古、方〕活着的;(水等)流动的;有孕的(尤指胎动期)。**6**. 含矿石的;(资本等)生利的;〔美〕(商品等)可立即转换成现金的。**7**. 〔古〕(火烧得)旺盛的,(火焰)熊熊的。**8**. (路)弯的,(坡)陡的。*He did a ~ mile*. 他用快步走了一英里。*a ~ march*【军】齐步行进。*Q- at meal*, *~ at work*. 吃得快,做得快。*Be ~!* 赶快! *a ~ child* 伶俐的孩子。*a ~ eye* 慧眼。*a ~ temper* 急性子。*~ wits* 急智,机智。*a ~ hedge* 活篱,树篱。*~ water*〔罕〕流水。***in ~ succession*** 紧接着。***be ~ at figures*** 算得快。***be ~ on the draw*** **1**. 动辄就拿出武器。**2**. 〔美俚〕脑子快。***~ and dirty*** 粗制滥造的,质量很差的。***~ of hearing*** [***sight***] 耳朵[眼睛]尖的。***~ of temper*** = ***~ to take offence*** 易怒的。***~ with child***〔原作 ***with ~ child***〕感到胎动。**II** *ad*. 快速。***as ~ as thought*** [***lightning***] 一眨眼工夫,霎时间,风驰电掣般。**III** *n*. **1**. (有感觉的)活肉,(特指指甲下的)肉根,指甲肉;伤口的嫩皮;感情的中枢,感觉最敏锐的地方;痛处。**2**. 要害,本质;核心。**3**. 〔古〕生物,活物。**4**. 彻头彻尾。**5**. 〔英〕插条 (= quickset)。***the ~ and the dead*** 生者与死者。***to the ~*** **1**. 触到活肉 (*cut the fingernail to the ~* 剪指甲剪着了肉)。**2**. 彻骨,入骨,痛切地。**3**. 真正,彻头彻尾;道地 (*He is a cockney to the ~*. 他是道地的伦敦人。*He is a Tory to the ~*. 他是一个彻头彻尾的保守党。*Your coolness cuts me to the ~*. 你的冷淡真使我伤心)。**~-change** *a*. 善变的〔指演员能在同一戏中扮演几种不同的角色〕。**~-eared** *a*. 耳朵尖[敏锐]的。**~-eyed** *a*. 眼睛尖的。**~-fence** 树篱。**~ fire**【军】速射。**~-firer** 速射枪[炮]。**~-firing**, **~-fire** *a*. 速射的。**~-freeze** *vt*. 使(生鲜食品)速冻。**~ grass** (长得极快的)鹅观草。**~lime** 生石灰。**~print** 速印〔指信纸、信封、目录等小型商业用品的快速印刷〕。**~sand** 流沙;〔喻〕复杂危险的情况。**~-scented** *a*. 嗅觉敏锐的。**~set**〔英〕**1**. *a*. 树篱的。**2**. *n*. (主指山楂的)树篱;〔集合词〕做树篱用的树,山楂树。**~-sighted** *a*. 眼睛尖,眼快的。**~-silver** **1**. *n*. 水银,汞;〔喻〕快活的性格,易变的脾气;三心两意的人。**2**. *vt*. 涂水银(在玻璃上做镜子)。**3**. *a*. 水银似的,易变的。**Q- Snap**〔商标〕快拍相机〔由日本富士公司推出的一种预先装好胶卷的简易相机,拍完后连同相机一道送去冲洗〕。**~ step** **1**.【军】齐步。**2**. 快速进行曲;轻快舞步。**3**. 〔美俚〕拉痢。**~-tempered** *a*. 性急的,急性子的。**~ time** 快步〔英国陆军一分钟 128 步;美国陆军一分钟 120 步〕; **~-witted** *a*. 富于机智的,机敏的;敏捷的。**-ly** *ad*. **-ness** *n*.

quick·en [ˈkwikən; ˋkwɪkən] *vt*. **1**. 加快,加速。**2**. 使变活,使复活,使有生命,使苏醒。**3**. 使活跃,使有生气,鼓舞,刺激。**4**. 使(曲线)更弯;使(斜坡)更陡。*~ one's appetite* 开胃,刺激食欲。— *vi*. **1**. 变快,快速。**2**. 变活,苏醒。**3**. 变活泼,变生动。**4**. 感觉胎动;(孕妇)进入胎动期。*The pulse ~s*. 脉搏快起来了;〔喻〕兴奋起来了。

quick·en·ing [ˈkwikəniŋ; ˋkwɪkənɪŋ] **I** *a*. 加快的,使活的,使苏醒的;使活泼的,使振作的。**II** *n*. 胎动初期〔受孕后第十八周左右〕。

quick·ie [ˈkwiki; ˋkwɪkɪ]〔美俚〕**I** *n*. **1**. 匆匆做成的事。**2**. 粗制滥造的影片[文艺作品]。**3**. 短促的接吻。**4**. 匆忙的旅行。**5**. (酒的)一饮而干。**6**. 未经工会同意的罢工 (= ~ strike)。**II** *a*. 快的,迅速的;简短的。*a ~ training course* 速成训练班。

quid[1] [kwid; kwɪd] *n*. 〔*sing*., *pl*.〕〔英俚〕一镑金币,金镑;一镑。*half a ~* 半镑。

quid[2] [kwid; kwɪd] *n*. (咀嚼用的)一块烟草块;咀嚼物。

quid·dity [ˈkwiditi; ˋkwɪdətɪ] *n*. **1**. (人、事物的)本质;实质。**2**. 遁辞,诡辩,狡辩。**3**. 莫名其妙的言行,怪癖;怪想法。

quid·nunc [ˈkwidnʌŋk; ˋkwɪdˏnʌŋk] *n*. **1**. 爱搬弄是非的人;爱闲扯的人。**2**. 爱问长问短的人,爱打听[传播]新闻的人。

quid pro quo [ˈkwid prəu ˈkwəu; ˋkwɪd pro ˋkwo]〔L.〕**1**. 补偿物;交换物;赔偿;报酬;报复。**2**. 代替物;相等物。**3**. 〔罕〕弄错。

quién sa·be [kiːn ˈsæbi; kjɛn ˋsɑbɛ]〔美〕打在牛身上的秘密烙印〔原意有"有谁会知道呢?"〕。

qui·es·cence, **qui·es·cen·cy** [kwaiˈesns, -ˈesnsi; kwaɪˋɛsns, -ˋɛsnsɪ] *n*. **1**. 不动,静止。**2**. (蚕等的)休眠,静止期。**3**. 寂静,沉默。**4**. (疾病的)被遏制状态。*the ~ period* 休眠期。

qui·es·cent [kwaiˈesnt; kwaɪˋɛsnt] *a*. **1**. 不动的,静止的。**2**. (蚕等)静止期的,休眠的。**3**. 寂静的,沉默的。**4**. (疾病等)被遏制的,无症状的。*a ~ point*【物】静点。**-ly** *ad*.

qui·et [ˈkwaiət; ˋkwaɪət] **I** *a*. **1**. 静的,恬静的,平静的。**2**. (生物)不动的,安静的。**3**. 肃静的,寂静的。**4**. (市面)萧条的;(比赛等)松懈的。**5**. (态度、举止等)镇静的,沉着的;温和的。**6**. (社会)太平的,安定的,平稳无事的;(环境、生活方式等)单调的,无变化的;闲适的,从容的。**7**. 不显眼的,朴素的,素静的 (*opp*. loud)。**8**. 秘密的,私下的,暗地里的;转弯抹角的;藏在心里的。**9**. (街道等)僻静的。**10**. 非正式的。*a ~ sea* 平静的海。*Be ~!* = *Keep ~!* 请安静! 肃静! *a ~ cup of tea* 安闲享用的一杯茶。*nice ~ people* 稳重的人们。*~ resentment* 闷在肚子里的火气,闷气。*~ colours* 素静的颜色。***have a ~ dig at*** (*sb*.) 暗中讽刺某人一下。***keep*** (*sth*.) ***~*** (对某事)保守秘密。**II** *n*. **1**. 寂静,肃静。**2**. 稳静;沉静,沉着。**3**. 沉默。**4**. 安静,休养,静养。**5**. 和平,平稳,安定,太平。*rest and ~* 休息。***at ~*** 平稳地,平静地。***in ~*** 安静地,和平的。***on the ~*** 私下,暗地里,秘密〔美俚略作 on the q. t.〕。**III** *vt*. **1**. 使静,使宁静。**2**. 抚慰,安慰。**3**. 使缓和,平息,使镇定。— *vi*. 平静,变静,变稳 (*down*)。**~ conscience** 自问无愧的良心。**~ irony** 转弯抹角的讽刺。**~ room** 禁闭式病房〔精神病院中安置狂暴患者的类似于禁闭室的病房〕。**-ize** *vt*. 给…隔音;使隔音。**-ly** *ad*. **-ness** *n*.

qui·et·en [ˈkwaiətn; ˋkwaɪətn̩] *vt*., *vi*. 〔俚〕= quiet *vt*., *vi*.

qui·et·er [ˈkwaiətə; ˋkwaɪətɚ] *n*.【机】防音装置。

qui·et·ism [ˈkwaiətizəm; ˋkwaɪətɪzm] *n*.【宗】**1**. 寂静教〔17 世纪一种基督教的神秘主义教派〕。**2**. 无为主义,清静无为。**-ist** *n*. **1**. 寂静教徒。**2**. 安于清静的人,主张清静无为者。**quiet·is·tic** *a*.

qui·e·tude [ˈkwaiətjuːd; ˋkwaɪəˏtjud] *n*. 寂静;平静;宁静;沉着。

qui·e·tus [kwaiˈiːtəs; kwaɪˋitəs] *n*. **1**. 死,灭亡;寂灭;死的解脱。**2**. (债务,义务等的)偿清,解除,理清;〔古〕清欠收据。**3**. 平息;制止。**4**. 静止状态;休眠。*give a ~ to a rumour* 杜绝谣言。*get one's ~* 死。*give sb. his ~* 杀死。

quiff[1] [kwif; kwɪf] *n*. 〔英俚〕(搽油梳在额前的)一绺卷发。

quiff[2] [kwif; kwɪf] *n*. 〔方、美〕一阵风;一口烟〔whiff 的

别字〕。

quiff[3] [kwif; kwɪf] ***n*.** 〔美俚〕姑娘,女人;轻佻的女子;下等娼妓。

Qui·h(a)i [ˈkwaiˈhi; ˋkwaɪˋhaɪ] ***n*.** 〔印度〕久住印度的英国人。

quill [kwil; kwɪl] **I** ***n*.** **1.** 翮,羽毛管,羽茎;(翼或尾部的)翮羽。**2.** 翮笔,鹅毛笔;翮制弦拨,(钓鱼的)浮漂,羽毛制的牙签。**3.**〔常 *pl*.〕(猬或豪猪的)刺。**4.** (芦茎等做的)芦笛。**5.**【纺】线轴;纡管;纬管;【机】套筒轴。**6.** (桂皮或金鸡纳皮等的)一小卷。**7.** (炸药的)导火线。***drive the*** ~ 挥毫,写字。**II** ***vt*.** **1.** 在(布)上做管状褶。**2.** 把(线)卷在线轴上。**3.** (用羽毛管等)刺穿;拔掉…的羽毛管。**4.**〔俚〕拍…的马屁。~ **covert** 翮〔鸟翮根部细毛〕。~ **driver**〔谑〕吃笔墨饭的;(特指)录事,抄写员。~**wort** ***n*.**【植】水韭。

quil·lai·a, quil·laj·a, quil·lai [kiˈlaiə, -ˈlai; kɪˋlaɪə, -ˋlaɪ] ***n*.** 皂树;皂树皮 (=soapbark)。

quill·back [ˈkwilbæk; ˋkwɪlbæk] ***n*.**【动】(*pl*. ~(*s*)) 鲤型亚口鱼属 (*Carpiodes*)。

Quil·ler [ˈkwilə; ˋkwɪlɚ] ***n*.** 奎勒〔姓氏〕。

Quil·ler-Couch [ˈkwiləˈkuːtʃ; ˋkwɪlɚˋkutʃ] ***n*.** 奎勒—库奇〔姓氏〕。

quil·let [ˈkwilit; ˋkwɪlɪt] ***n*.** 〔古〕遁辞;细微差别。

quill·ing [ˈkwiliŋ; ˋkwɪlɪŋ] ***n*.** **1.** 网眼纱褶裥边[边饰]。**2.**【纺】卷纬(工艺)。

quilt [kwilt; kwɪlt] **I** ***n*.** 被子,毛被,驼绒被,鸭绒被;被状物。**II** ***vt*.** **1.** 缝(被),绗(被);绗缝(衣服)。**2.** 用垫料填塞后缝拢;将(钞票等)缝进衣服里。**3.** 在(多层布等)上缝出花样。**4.** 用摘抄等方法编辑;东拼西凑地做。**5.**〔方〕殴打。— ***vi*.** 制被;缝被。**-er** ***n*.** **1.** 缝被子的人。**2.** (缝纫机上的)绗缝附件。

Quilt·er [ˈkwiltə; ˋkwɪltɚ] ***n*.** 奎尔特〔姓氏〕。

quilt·ing [ˈkwiltiŋ; ˋkwɪltɪŋ] ***n*.** **1.** 被子绗缝。**2.** 被子料。**3.** (衣服上的)管状褶裥。**4.**〔方〕殴打。**5.**〔美〕= ~ bee. ~ **bee** [**party**]〔美〕(妇女聚在一起缝被子的)大家缝聚会。~ **cotton** 棉胎用棉。

quin [kwin; kwɪn] ***n*.** =quintuplet.

qui·na [ˈkwainə; ˋkwaɪnə] ***n*.** 金鸡纳(皮)。

qui·na·ry [ˈkwainəri; ˋkwaɪnərɪ] **I** ***a*.** 五的;五个的;五个一组的;第五位的。**II** ***n*.** 五个一套[一组]。

qui·nate[1] [ˈkwaineit; ˋkwaɪnet] ***a*.**【植】(复叶)由五枚小叶片组成的。

qui·nate[2] [ˈkwaineit; ˋkwaɪnet] ***n*.**【化】奎尼酸。

Qui·nault [ˈkwinəlt; ˋkwɪnəlt] ***n*.** 奎纳尔特〔姓氏〕。

quince [kwins; kwɪns] ***n*.**【植】榅桲,榅梨,榅桲树。

quin·cen·te·na·ry, quin·gen·te·na·ry [ˌkwinsenˈtiːnəri, -dʒenˈtiːnəri; kwɪnˋsɛntɪˏnerɪ, -dʒɛnˋtinərɪ] ***n*.**, ***a*.** 第五百周年(的);五百周年纪念(的)。

quin·cun·cial [kwinˈkʌnʃəl; kwɪnˋkʌnʃəl] ***a*.** **1.** (骰子、纸牌的)五点形的,梅花形的。**2.**【植】五叶[五瓣]叠覆排列的〔二在外,二在内,一个半在外半在内〕。**-ly** ***ad*.** 成梅花形;叠覆排列地。

quin·cunx [ˈkwinkʌŋks; ˋkwɪnkʌŋks] ***n*.** **1.** (五点排列成的)梅花形。**2.**【植】(果树、灌木的)梅花形栽法。**3.**【植】五叶[瓣]的叠覆排列。

quin·cunx·ci·al [kwinˈkʌŋksiəl; kwɪnˋkʌŋksɪəl] ***n*.** =quincuncial.

Quin·c(e)y [ˈkwinsi; ˋkwɪnsɪ] ***n*.** 昆西〔姓氏〕。

Quin(n) [kwin; kwɪn] ***n*.** 奎恩〔姓氏〕。

quin·dec·a·gon [kwinˈdekəgən; kwɪnˋdɛkəgɑn] ***n*.**【数】十五角形,十五边形。

quin·de·cen·ni·al [ˌkwindiˈseniəl; ˏkwɪndɪˋsɛnɪəl] **I** ***a*.** **1.** 每十五年发生一次的。**2.** 持续十五年的。**II** ***n*.** **1.** 十五年期间;十五周年。**2.** 十五周年纪念活动。

quin·i·a [ˈkwiniə; ˋkwɪnɪə] ***n*.**【医】=quinine.

quin·ic [ˈkwinik; ˋkwɪnɪk] ***a*.** ~ **acid**【药】金鸡纳酸;【化】奎尼酸。

quin·i·dine [ˈkwinidiːn, -din; ˋkwɪnədin, -dɪn] ***n*.**【化】奎尼定。

qui·nine, quin·in [kwiˈniːn, ˈkwiniːn, Am. ˈkwainain; kwɪˋnin, ˋkwɪnin, ˋkwaɪnaɪn] ***n*.**【药】奎宁;【化】金鸡纳碱。*a Q- Jimmy*〔美俚〕林场医生。

qui·nin·ism, qui·nism [kwiˈniːnizəm, ˈkwainizəm; kwɪˋninɪzəm, ˋkwaɪnɪzm] ***n*.** 金鸡纳[奎宁]中毒。

quin·na·tsal·mon [ˈkwinætˈsæmən; ˋkwɪnætˋsæmən] ***n*.**〔美〕【鱼】大鳞大麻哈鱼〔太平洋沿岸产〕。

qui·no·a [kiˈnəuə; kɪˋnoə] ***n*.**【植】昆诺阿藜 (*Chenopodium quinoa*)〔产于安第斯山脉地区,印第安人种之以食其粟〕。

quin·oid [ˈkwinɔid; ˋkwɪnɔɪd] ***n*.**【化】醌式,醌型。

qui·noi·dine [kwiˈnɔidiːn, -din; kwɪˋnɔɪdin, -dɪn] ***n*.**【化】奎诺酊。

quin·o·line [ˈkwinəliːn, -in; ˋkwɪnəlin, -ɪn] ***n*.**【化】**1.** 喹啉,氮(杂)萘。**2.** 喹啉衍生物。**quin·o·lin·ic** ***a*.**

qui·none [kwiˈnəun, ˈkwinəun; kwɪˋnon, ˋkwɪnon] ***n*.**【化】**1.** 醌,苯醌。**2.** 醌类。

qui·non·i·mine [kwiˈnɔnimiːn, -min; kwɪˋnɔnɪmin, -mɪn] ***n*.**【化】醌亚胺。

quin·o·noid [ˈkwinənɔid, kwiˈnəunɔid; ˋkwɪnənɔɪd, kwɪˋnonɔɪd] ***a*.**【化】醌型结构状的。

quinqua- *comb*. *f*. 表示"五" (=quinque-)。

quin·qua·ge·nar·i·an [ˌkwiŋkwədʒiˈnɛəriən; ˏkwɪnkwədʒɪˋnɛrɪən] ***a*.**, ***n*.** 五十至五十九岁的(人)。

quin·qua·ge·nar·y [ˌkwinkwəˈdʒinəri; kwɪnˋkwædʒɪˏnerɪ] **I** ***a*.** 五十岁的。**II** ***n*.** 五十岁的人;五十周年纪念。

Quin·qua·ges·i·ma [ˌkwinkwəˈdʒesimə; ˏkwɪnkwəˋdʒɛsəmə] ***n*.**【基督教】四旬斋前的星期日,复活节前的第五十日 (=~ Sunday)。

quin·quan·gu·lar [kwiŋˈkwæŋgjulə; kwɪnˋkwæŋgjulɚ] ***a*.**〔古〕有五角的,五角形的。

quinque- *comb*. *f*. 表示"五": *quinque*nnial.

quin·que·fo·li·o·late [ˌkwiŋkwəˈfəuliəlit, -leit; ˏkwɪnkwəˋfolɪəlɪt, -let] ***a*.**【植】有五小叶的。

quin·quen·ni·ad [kwiŋˈkweniæd; kwɪnˋkwɛnɪˏæd] ***n*.** =quinquennium.

quin·quen·ni·al [kwiŋˈkweniəl, -njəl; kwɪnˋkwɛnɪəl, -njəl] **I** ***a*.** **1.** 每五年(一次)的。**2.** 持续五年的。**II** ***n*.** **1.** 五周年纪念;每五年一次的事。**2.** 持续五年的在职期间。~ **valuation** (决定财产税征收额的)五年一次的估价。

quin·quen·ni·um [kwiŋˈkweniəm; kwɪnˋkwɛnɪəm] (*pl*. ~**s**, ***-nia*** [-niə, -nɪə]) ***n*.** 五年,五年的时间。

quin·que·par·tite [ˌkwinkwiˈpɑːtait; ˏkwɪnkwɪˋpɑrtaɪt] ***a*.** 分为五部份的;由五部份组成的。

quin·que·reme [ˈkwiŋkwəriːm; ˋkwɪnkwɪˏrim] ***n*.** (古罗马的)五层橹船。

quin·que·va·lence, quin·que·va·len·cy [ˌkwiŋkwiˈveiləns, -ˈveilənsi; ˏkwɪnkwəˋveləns, -ˋvelənsɪ] ***n*.**【化】五价。

quin·que·va·lent, quin·qui·va·lent [ˌkwiŋkwiˈveilənt; ˏkwɪnkwɪˋvelənt] ***a*.**【化】五价(原子)的。

quin·qui·na [kwiŋˈkwainə; kwɪnˋkwaɪnə] ***n*.** =quina.

quins [kwinz; kwɪnz] ***n*.** 〔口〕=quintuplets.

quin·sied [ˈkwinzid; ˋkwɪnzɪd] ***a*.**【医】感染扁桃体周脓肿的。

quin·sy [ˈkwinzi; ˋkwɪnzɪ] ***n*.**【医】扁桃体周脓肿。

quint[1] [kint; kwɪnt] ***n*.** **1.**【纸牌】同花顺。**2.** [kwint; kwɪnt]【乐】五度;五度音;(提琴的) E 弦[第一弦]。***a*** ~ ***major*** 同花大顺〔A, K, Q, J, 10〕。***a*** ~ ***minor*** 同花小顺〔J, 10, 9, 8, 7〕。

quint[2] [kwint; kwɪnt] ***n*.** 〔美口〕=quintuplet.

quint[3] [kwint; kwɪnt] ***n*.** 〔美俚〕男子篮球队。

quin·tain [ˈkwintin; ˋkwɪntɪn] ***n.*** **1.**【史】(中世纪的)刺矛靶。**2.** 骑马用刺矛靶练刺。

quin·tal [ˈkwintəl; ˋkwɪntl] ***n.*** **1.** 公担(=100 公斤)。**2.** 英担〔英国为 112 磅,美国为 100 磅〕。

quin·tan [ˈkwintən; ˋkwɪntən] **I** ***n.***【医】五日热。**II** ***a.*** 每五天的,每逢第五天发生一次的。

Quin·tard [ˈkwintɑːd; ˋkwɪntɑrd] ***n.*** 昆塔德〔姓氏〕。

quinte [kɛ̃nt; kɛ̃nt] ***n.*** 〔F.〕【剑】(击剑八种姿势中的)第五种防守架式。

quin·tes·sence [kwinˈtesns; kwɪnˋtɛsns] ***n.*** **1.** (古代哲学所说的空气,水,火,土以外的)第五原质。**2.** 精华;精髓;典型,典范。**3.** (物质的)本体,实体,本质,实质,原质。*the ~ of beauty* 美的典型。

quin·tes·sen·tial [ˌkwintiˈsenʃəl; ˏkwɪntɪˋsɛnʃəl] ***a.*** **1.** 精华的,精髓的。**2.** 典型的,典范的,最完美的。

quin·tette, quin·tet [kwinˈtet; kwɪnˋtɛt] ***n.*** **1.**【乐】五部曲;五部合奏,五重奏;五部合唱;五部合奏队;五部合唱队。**2.** 五人一组;五件一套。**3.**【物】五重线。**4.** 〔美俚〕男子篮球队。

quin·tile [ˈkwintil, -tail; ˋkwɪntɪl, -taɪl] **I** ***a.***【天】(两天体的)五分之一对座的(相隔 72 度)。**II** ***n.***【天】五分之一对座。

quin·til·lion [kwinˈtiljən; kwɪnˋtɪljən] ***num.*** 〔英、德〕百万的五次幂[乘方]〔1 后有 30 个 0 的数〕;〔美、法〕千的六次幂〔乘方〕〔1 后有 18 个 0 的数〕。

quints [kwints; kwɪnts] ***n.*** 〔美〕= quintuplets.

quin·tuple [ˈkwintju(ː)pl; ˋkwɪntjupl] **I** ***a.*** **1.** 五的;五倍的;五重的;由五个部份组成的。**2.**【乐】五拍子的。**II** ***n.*** **1.** 五倍量。**2.** 〔罕〕五个一套。**III** ***vt.*** 使成五倍,以五乘之。— ***vi.*** 成为五倍。

quin·tuplet [ˈkwintjuplit; ˋkwɪntəplɪt] ***n.*** **1.** 五人一组,五件一套。**2.** 〔*pl.*〕五胞胎;五人自行车。

quin·tu·pli·cate [kwinˈtjuːplikit; kwɪnˋtjuplɪkɪt] **I** ***a.*** **1.** 五倍的,五重的。**2.** 一式五份的;第五(份)的。**II** ***n.*** **1.** 五倍的数[量]。**2.** 一式的五份;一式五份中的一份;第五份。**III** [kwinˈtjuːplikeit; kwɪnˋtjuplɪket] ***vt.*** **1.** 把…作成一式五份。**2.** 使成五倍。

quip [kwip; kwɪp] **I** ***n.*** **1.** 讥讽,挖苦话。**2.** 妙语;好笑的话。**3.** 奇行;怪物,好笑的东西。**4.** 遁辞(=quibble)。**II** ***vt.*** (***-pp-***) 讥讽,嘲弄。— ***vi.*** **1.** 讥讽。**2.** 讲妙语[双关语等]。

qui·pu [ˈkwiːpu; ˋkipu] ***n.*** (古秘鲁的)结绳语〔以颜色和形状各不相同的绳结记事、记数等〕。

quire[1] [kwaiə; kwaɪr] ***n.*** (纸的)一刀〔24 张;略 qr.〕;(装订时)对折的一叠纸;(中世纪抄本等的)四张对折的纸。***in ~s*** **1.** 书页折好尚未装订的。**2.** 按(纸张)的刀数。

quire[2] [kwaiə; kwaɪə] ***n.***, ***vi.***, ***vt.*** 〔古〕= choir.

Qui·rey [ˈkwaiəri, ˈkwiəri; ˋkwaɪərɪ, ˋkwɪərɪ] ***n.*** 奎厄里〔姓氏〕。

Quir·i·nal [ˈkwirinəl; ˋkwɪrənl] ***n.*** 罗马七丘之一;(建在该丘上的)意大利皇宫,〔转义〕意大利政府〔宫廷〕〔相对于梵帝冈教廷而言〕。

Qui·ri·tes [kwiˈraitiːz; kwɪˋraɪtiz] ***n.*** 〔*pl.*〕古罗马平民。

quirk [kwəːk; kwɝk] **I** ***n.*** **1.** 双关话;遁辞,口实;讥讽话。**2.** 不定心,奇想;奇癖。**3.** (书写等的)花体。**4.** 三角形物;菱形窗玻璃。**5.** 突然的弯曲[扭曲]。**6.**【建】(鸟喙饰的)深槽。**7.**【乐】急转。**8.** 〔美俚〕见习空军飞行员。*a ~ moulding*【建】鸟喙饰。**II** ***vt.*** **1.** 嘲讽。**2.** 使弯曲。**3.** 挥鞭急打。**4.**【建】在(装饰线条等)上作成深槽。— ***vi.*** **1.** 弯曲,扭曲。**2.** 古怪地说话[行动]。**-y** ***a.*** **1.** 诡诈的。**2.** 突兀的;离奇的,古怪的。

quirt [kwəːt; kwɝt] **I** ***n.*** 〔美〕(附有长条皮瓣的)短柄马鞭。**II** ***vt.*** 用马鞭鞭打[驱赶]。

quis·le [ˈkwizl; ˋkwɪzl] ***vi.*** 卖国,做卖国贼;当傀儡政府头子。

quis·ling, quis·ler [ˈkwizliŋ, -lə; ˋkwɪzlɪŋ, -lɚ] ***n.*** 卖国贼,叛国分子,傀儡政府头子〔源于挪威法西斯党魁吉斯林 (Vidkun Quisling),他在第二次世界大战时卖国通敌,任纳粹侵占挪威后的傀儡政府头子〕。

quis·ling·ism [ˈkwizliŋizəm; ˋkwɪzlɪŋzəm] ***n.*** 卖国,叛国,通敌。

quis·lin·gite [ˈkwizliŋgait; ˋkwɪzlɪŋgaɪt] **I** ***n.*** 卖国贼,叛国分子。**II** ***a.*** 卖国的,叛国的。

quit [kwit; kwɪt] **I** (***quit·ted*** [ˈkwitid; ˋkwɪtɪd], ***quit***) ***vt.*** **1.** 放弃(信仰、行动、工作等);〔美〕停止。**2.** 退出(屋外),离开(本国、军队等);告别(亲友等)。**3.** 偿清,还清,偿还(借款等);尽(义务等);〔诗〕报答,酬答。**4.** 解除,免除。**5.** 〔~ oneself〕〔古〕使行动,表现。*~ office* 辞职。*Q- your nonsense!* 不要胡说! *Death ~s all scores.* 一死百了。*~ love with hate* 以恨报爱。*Q- you like men.* 〔古〕举动须如大丈夫。— ***vi.*** **1.** (租借人、房客等)迁出租借地,搬出,迁走。**2.** 停止,作罢;认输。**3.** 〔口〕辞职。*give notice to ~* 通知迁出[离职]。*have notice to ~* 接到迁出通知书。*~* ***hold of*** 放开,放掉,搁开。*~* ***oneself*** 表现得…。*~* ***oneself of*** (*fear*) 消除(恐惧)。*~* ***score with*** 和…了结债务,结清账目;向…报复。*~* ***the scores*** 报仇雪恨。**II** ***a.*** 〔仅用作表[述]语〕**1.** 被释放,被宣告无罪。**2.** 自由的;摆脱了…的。**3.** 被免除了…的,了清债务的;尽了义务的。***be ~ for*** 只因…就逃脱[得免](*He was ~ for a ducking.* 他因钻入水中而逃脱)。***be*** [***get***] *~* ***of ...*** 免除…,摆脱…,了清…(*get ~ of one's debts* 了清债务)。*~* ***of*** (*thirty*) (年龄)(三十)开外。**III** ***n.*** **1.** 离开,退出。**2.** 退职,辞职。

qui tam [ˈkwai ˈtæm; ˋkwaɪ ˋtæm] 〔L.〕【法】要求取得罚金的起诉〔此项罚金由起诉人与官方均分〕。

quitch [kwitʃ; kwɪtʃ] ***n.***【植】匍匐根草(= couch-grass)。

quit·claim [ˈkwitkleim; ˋkwɪtˏklem] **I** ***n.*** **1.** 放弃权利[要求]。**2.** (产权等的)转让契约。**II** ***vt.*** (通过转让契约)放弃[转让]对…的合法权利。

quite [kwait; kwaɪt] ***ad.*** **1.** 完全,十分,彻底,真正,的确。**2.** 事实上;差不多;可以说(是…),简直和…一样。**3.** 颇,相当,有点儿,或多或少。**4.** 〔口〕很,极。*~ the opposite* 正相反。*Q- right.* 好,行,完全对。*Oh, ~.* = *Q- so!* 对啦! 是啊! 不错! 正是这样! *I was ~ by myself* [*~ alone*]. 只有我一个人。*He is ~ a man.* 他真是个男子汉。*You are getting ~ a big boy now.* 你已经不小了。*It's ~ too delightful.* 真是太叫人高兴了。*He* [*She*] *isn't ~.* 〔英口〕= *He* [*She*] *isn't ~ a gentleman* [*lady*]. 他[她]不像是一个绅士[贵妇人];他[她]不像是一个正人君子[正派女人]。***not ~*** 有点不…(*not ~ proper* 有点不妥)。***not ~ the thing to do*** 不太合适,有点不好(但是没有办法)。***not ~ well*** 还有点不好。*~* ***a few*** 〔美〕相当[多]的,很不少。*~* ***other*** [***another***] 完全不同的。*~* ***some*** 〔美〕非常多。*~* ***the thing*** 时髦,时新。

Quit·man [ˈkwitmən; ˋkwɪtmən] ***n.*** 奎特曼〔姓氏〕。

Quito [ˈkiːtəu; ˋkito] ***n.*** 基多〔厄瓜多尔首都〕。

quit·rent [ˈkwitrent; ˋkwɪtˏrɛnt] ***n.*** (封建时代的)免役税。

quits [kwits; kwɪts] ***a.*** 〔仅用作表语〕(因报复或偿清而)两相抵消了的;恢复原状的;成平局的,不分胜负的;对等的,旗鼓相当的。***be ~ with*** 向…报复[报仇],和…弄成平局,不分胜负。***call it ~*** = ***cry ~*** 互无胜负;(打架等时)同意罢休;停做某事声言作罢。***double or ~*** (连赌两次时的)加倍(输赢),(输赢)相消。***We are ~ now.*** 现在咱俩清账了;现在谁也没有对不起谁的地方了。

quit·tance [ˈkwitəns; ˋkwɪtns] ***n.*** **1.** (债务,义务等的)免除,解除,宽免。**2.** 免除债务[义务]的证书,收据。**3.** 报酬;赔偿;报答;报复。***Omittance is no ~.*** 不催账并不就是销账。

quit·ter [ˈkwitə; ˋkwɪtɚ] ***n.*** 〔美口〕轻易中止[放弃](竞争、计划、义务等)的人;半途而废的人;懒人;意志薄弱的人,懦夫。

quit·ting-time [ˈkwitiŋtaim; ˋkwɪtɪŋtaɪm] ***n.*** 〔美〕下班时间。

quit·tor [ˈkwitə; ˋkwɪtɚ] ***n.*** 马踢疡,马蹄疽。

quiv·er[1] [ˈkwivə; ˋkwɪvɚ] **I** ***vi.*** (人、叶、声、光等)轻微地颤抖,震颤,抖动,颤动。— ***vt.*** 使震颤;使颤动;(云雀等)抖动(翅膀)。**II** ***n.*** **1.** 抖动,颤动;颤音。**2.** 一闪。

quiv·er[2] [ˈkwivə; ˋkwɪvɚ] ***n.*** **1.** 箭袋,箭筒。**2.** 箭筒中的箭。**3.** (能装一套东西的)容器。**4.** 大群;大队。*a ～ full of children* 子女多的大家庭。***have an arrow*** [***a shaft***] ***left in one's*** ～ 还有本钱,还有办法可想。***have one's*** ～ ***full*** 本钱充足。

quiv·er[3] [ˈkwivə; ˋkwɪvɚ] ***a.*** 〔古〕迅速的,敏捷的;活泼的。

quiv·er·ful [ˈkwivəf*u*l; ˋkwɪvɚfʊl] ***n.*** **1.** 满箭筒的箭。**2.** 大量,许多。**3.** 〔谑〕大家庭。

quiv·er·ing [ˈkwivəriŋ; ˋkwɪvərɪŋ] ***a.*** 颤抖的。**-ly** ***ad.***

qui vive [kiːˈviːv; kiˋviv] 〔F.〕〔哨兵的查问口令〕你是什么人? 你是哪一边的? ***on the qui vive*** 警戒着。

Quix·ote [ˈkwiksət, -səut, Sp. kiˈhɔːte; ˋkwɪksət, -sot, kɪˋhote] ***n.*** **1.** (堂)吉诃德〔西班牙作家塞万提斯(Cervantes)所作小说《堂吉诃德》(Don Quixote)中的主人公〕。**2.** 狂热的空想家;愚侠;时代落伍者。

quix·ot·ic, quix·ot·i·cal [kwikˈsɔtik, -kəl; kwɪksˋɑtɪk, -kl] **I** ***a.*** **1.** 〔q- 或 Q-〕(堂)吉诃德式的。**2.** 骑士气派的,愚侠的;空想的。**II** ***n.*** 〔*pl.*〕= quixotism. **quix·ot·ical·ly** ***ad.***

quix·ot·ism, quix·ot·ry [ˈkwiksətizəm, -tri; ˋkwɪksətɪzm, -trɪ] ***n.*** (堂)吉诃德式的行为[思想、性格];愚蠢的侠义行为,愚妄。

quiz [kwiz; kwɪz] **I** ***n.*** (*pl.* ***quiz·zes*** [-iz; -ɪz]) **1.** 〔英〕开玩笑,恶作剧;挖苦,嘲笑。**2.** 〔英〕爱开玩笑的人,淘气鬼;挖苦者,嘲弄者。**3.** 〔美〕(教师的)考问,提问;小型考试;测验;(广播节目中的)问答比赛;猜谜;难题。**4.** 〔罕〕怪人,相貌怪的人;举止奇特的人。***a drop*** [***shotgun***] ～〔美〕突击测验。**II** ***vt.*** (**-zz-**) **1.** 对…开玩笑,挖苦,嘲弄。**2.** 冷笑着或无礼地盯着…看,好奇地看,张望。**3.** 〔美〕考问,考试,对(学生)进行测验;给…出难题。**4.** 盘问。～ **bee** [**game**] 〔美〕(广播、电视节目中的)问答比赛。～ **kid** 〔美〕参加电台问答比赛节目的孩子,聪明孩子;神童。～ **master** (问答比赛节目的)主持人,提问者。～ **program(me)** 问答比赛节目。～**zing glass** 带柄单眼镜。

quiz·zable [ˈkwizəbl; ˋkwɪzəbl̩] ***a.*** 可挖苦的,可嘲笑的。

quiz·(z)ee [kwiˈziː; kwɪˋzi] ***n.*** 参加问答比赛的人,被测验者。

quiz·zer [ˈkwizə; ˋkwɪzɚ] ***n.*** **1.** 嘲笑者,挖苦者,戏弄者。**2.** 〔美〕主持测验者,提问者。**3.** (广播、电视中的)问答比赛节目。

quiz·zi·cal [ˈkwizikəl; ˋkwɪzɪkl] ***a.*** **1.** 专爱挖苦人的。**2.** 问询的,困惑的。**3.** 古怪的,滑稽的。**-ly** ***ad.***

quo·ad hoc [ˈkwəuæd ˈhɔk; ˋkwoæd ˋhɑk] 〔L.〕 **1.** 关于这一点,在这一点上。**2.** 到此为止,到这个程度[范围]。

quod [kwɔd; kwɑd] **I** ***n.*** 监牢,监狱。*in* [*out of*] ～ 入[出]狱。**II** ***vt.*** 把…关进牢里。

quod [kwɔd; kwɑd] ***pro.*** 〔L.〕= which. ～ ***erat demonstrandum*** [ˈeræt ˌdemənˈstrændəm; ˋɛræt ˏdɛmənˋstrændəm] 【数】这就是所要证明的,证完,证讫〔略作 Q. E. D.〕。～ ***erat faciendum*** [ˌfeiʃiˈendəm; ˏfeʃɪˋendəm] 【数】这就是所要做的,作毕,作讫〔略作 Q. E. F.〕。～ ***erat inveniendum*** [inˌveniˈendəm; ɪnˏvɛnɪˋendəm] 〔略作 Q. E. I.〕【数】这就是所要寻求的,求毕,求讫。～ ***est*** [est; ɛst] 这就是,即。～ ***vide*** [ˈvidei; ˋvaɪdɪ] 见…,参看…〔书籍等中的参照用语,略作 q. v., = which see〕。

quod·li·bet [ˈkwɔdlibet; ˋkwɑdlɪbɛt] ***n.*** **1.** 【乐】幻想曲;各种旋律的随意混合。**2.** (神学、经院哲学等中的)微妙的争论点;关于微妙问题的辩论。

quoif [kɔif; kɔɪf] ***n.*** = coif.

quoin [kɔin; kɔɪn] **I** ***n.*** 【建】**1.** (房屋的)突角,外角;(墙壁接合处的)隅石;(拱门等的)楔形石;楔形支持物。**2.** (夹紧版面或防止圆桶滚动等的)楔子。**II** ***vt.*** **1.** 用隅石砌牢;给…装嵌隅石。**2.** 用楔形物支持;打楔子夹紧[固定]。**-ing** ***n.*** (接合墙壁等平面的)外角构件。

quoit [kɔit; kwɔɪt] **I** ***n.*** **1.** 铁环,绳圈。**2.** 〔*pl.*〕〔作单数用〕掷(铁)环[绳圈]游戏。*deck ～s* (甲板上玩的)掷绳圈。**II** ***vt.*** 掷(铁环等),抛(绳圈等)。

quo ju·re [kwəuˈjuəri; kwoˋjʊərɪ] 〔L.〕以什么权利?

quo mo·do [kwəuˈməudəu; ˋkwomədo] 〔L.〕 **1.** 以何种方式? **2.** 用…这样一种形式。

quon·dam [ˈkwɔndæm; ˋkwɑndəm] ***a.*** 曾经是(演员、朋友等)的;以前的,过去的。～ *lovers* 过去的恋人,旧情人。*a ～ singer* 过去的歌唱家。

Quon·set [ˈkwɔnsit; ˋkwɑnsɪt] 〔美〕(用瓦楞铁预制件构成的)半圆拱形活动房屋〔商标名〕(= ～ hut)。

quor. = quorum.

quo·rate [ˈkwɔrit; ˋkwɑrɪt] ***n.*** 〔英〕(开庭、开会等)达到法定人数的。

quo·rum [ˈkwɔːrəm; ˋkworəm] ***n.*** **1.** (英国旧时法庭开庭时必须达到的)法定治安法官人数;〔总称〕治安法官。**2.** (会议等的)法定人数。**3.** 选出的一群人;特选队员。***form*** [***lack***] ***a*** ～ 形成[不足]法定人数。

quot. = quotation, quoted.

quo·ta [ˈkwəutə; ˋkwotə] ***n.*** **1.** 份,担任部份,分得部份。**2.** 定额,比额;(入口货等的)限额,控制额。***hiring ～s*** 〔美〕雇员分配额〔指政府为企业单位等规定的雇员中各人种的比额〕。～ ***quickie*** 〔英〕(按照影片限额法摄制的)额定影片,廉价影片。***the*** ～ ***system*** 定额分配制。

quot·a·ble [ˈkwəutəbl; ˋkwotəbl̩] ***a.*** 可引用的,有引证价值的。**-a·bil·i·ty** [ˌkwəutəˈbiliti; ˏkwotəˋbɪlɪtɪ] ***n.*** **-ness** ***n.***

quo·ta·tion [kwəuˈteiʃən; kwoˋteʃən] ***n.*** **1.** 引用,引证;引用语,语录 (*from*)。**2.** 【商】行市,行情,时价;行市表;估价单。**3.** 【印】(填空白的)空铅,嵌块。**4.** = ～ mark. ～ **mark(s)** 〔*pl.*〕引用号,引号〔即“”或‘’〕。

quo·ta·tive [ˈkwəutətiv; ˋkwotətɪv] ***a.*** **1.** 引用的,引证的。**2.** 喜欢引用的。

quote [kwəut; kwot] **I** ***vt.*** **1.** 引用(他人文章);引证,引述,举(例)。**2.** 把…放入引号,用引号把…括起来。**3.** 【商】喊(价),报(价),开(价);给…估价为。*It is ～ed at £5.* 这在市面上开价 5 镑。— ***vi.*** **1.** 引用 (*from*)。**2.** 喊价,报价,开价;估价。**II** ***n.*** 〔口〕**1.** 引用句,引文。**2.** 引号。**3.** 报价,估价表。***pipe a*** ～ 杜撰引文,编造引文。～ **mark** = quotation mark.

quot·er [ˈkwəutə; ˋkwotɚ] ***n.*** **1.** 引用者,引证者。**2.** 估价者,报价者,开价者。**3.** 保险单红利计算员。

quote·wor·thy [ˈkwəutˌwəːði; ˋkwotˏwɝðɪ] ***a.*** 有引用价值的,值得引证的。

quoth [kwəuθ; kwoθ] ***vt.*** 〔古、谑〕说 (= said)〔第一人称和第三人称的直说法过去式,用如 ～ I [he, she] 我[他,她]说。偶然也用如 ～ we [they] 我们[他们]说。常置于主语前,插在引用语句的前后或当中〕。*Q- the raven, "Nevermore".* 老鸦说:“决不!”

quoth·a [ˈkwəuθə; ˋkwoθə] ***int.*** 〔古〕〔带有轻蔑、卑视、讥笑、惊讶等意义〕真的! 的确!

quo·tid·ian [kwəuˈtidiən, ˌkwɔ-; kwoˋtɪdɪən, ˏkwɑ-] **I** ***a.*** **1.** 每日的,每天发生的。**2.** 司空见惯的,平凡的。**II** ***n.*** **1.** 司空见惯的事,天天发生的事。**2.** 【医】日发疟 (= ～ fever)。

quo·tient [ˈkwəuʃənt; ˋkwoʃənt] ***n.*** **1.** 【数】商。**2.** 份

额,应分得的部分。*intelligence* ~ 智商。~ **group**【数】商群。

quo·ti·e·ty [kwəu'taiiti; kwo`taɪətɪ] ***n*.** 率,系数。

Quo Va·dis [kwəu 'vɑːdis; `kwo `vedɪs] ***n*.** 〔L.〕《君往何处》〔描写罗马暴君尼禄时代的历史小说,1859 年波兰作家显克维支 (Henryk Sienkiewicz) 所作〕。

quo wor·ran·to ['kwəu wɔ'ræntəu; `kwo wɔ`rænto] 〔L.〕【法】**1.** (旧时英国法庭所发)责问某人根据什么行使职权[享受特权]的令状。**2.** (旧时)收回被僭用的职位[特权]的诉讼。**3.** 为收回被僭占的职位[特权]而提起的公诉。

Quran, Qur'an [ku'rɑːn; kʊ`rɑn] ***n*.** = Koran.

q.v.[1] = 〔L.〕 *quod vide* 参看,另见,见。

q.v.[2]〔医疗处方〕多少随便 (= as much as you wish)。

qy. = query.

R

R, r [ɑː; ɑr] (*pl*. ***R's***, ***r's*** [ɑːz; ɑrz]) **1.** 英语字母表第十八字母。**2.** 〔R〕R 字形(之物)。**3.** 〔R〕中世纪罗马数字的 80。**4.** 〔R〕〔美〕(电影)需成年人带领入场〔17 岁以下青少年不能单独观看〕,R 级 (= restricted)。$\bar{R}$ = 80 000。*the 'r'* [*R*] *months* 九月到四月〔牡蛎当令的季节,月名都含有 r 字〕。***the three R's*** (作为初等教育基础的)读写算 〔*r*eading, w*r*iting, a*r*ithmetic〕。

R = **1.** 〔L.〕 recipe【医】处方。**2.** radical. **3.** Reaumur. **4.** 〔L.〕 *Rex*, *Regina*. **5.** radius. **6.** ratio. **7.** resistance. **8.** retree. **9.** roentgen. **10.** range. **11.** registered. **12.** rifle. **13.** regulating.

R. = **1.** Royal. **2.** Republic; Republican. **3.** range. **4.** radio. **5.** ratio. **6.** resistance. **7.** rabbi. **8.** retarder. **9.** 〔L.〕 *Rex*, *Regina*.

r = **1.** refrigerator. **2.** rod.

r. = **1.** railway, railroad. **2.** right. **3.** river. **4.** road. **5.** r(o)uble. **6.** rupee. **7.** rare. **8.** residence. **9.** retired. **10.** rubber. **11.** rabbi. **12.** rood. **13.** runs.

R.A., **RA** = **1.** rear admiral 海军少将。**2.** Regular Army〔美〕正规陆军。**3.** regular army 常备军,正规军。**4.** Royal Academician〔英〕皇家艺术院会员。**5.** Royal Academy〔英〕皇家院。**6.** Royal Artillery〔英〕皇家陆军炮兵。**7.** right ascension【天】赤经。

R/A = refer to acceptor【商】询问承兑人。

Ra[1] [rɑː; rɑ] ***n*.**【埃神】太阳神。

Ra[2] = radium【化】镭。

r.a. = radioactive 放射性的。

Ra A = radium A【化】镭 A〔即 Po^{218}〕。

R.A.A.F., **RAAF** = Royal Australian Air Force (皇家)澳大利亚空军。

Ra-B = radium-B【化】镭 B.

Ra·bat [rə'bɑːt; rə`bɑt] ***n*.** 拉巴特〔摩洛哥首都〕。

ra·bat [rə'bæt; rɑ`bɑ, rə`bæt] ***n*.** (某些牧师服用的,长及前胸,内衬牧师白领的)黑色短披肩。

ra·ba·to [rə'beitəu, -'bɑː-; rə`beto, -`bɑ-] ***n*.** (*pl*. ***-tos***) 披肩领子,(细麻布或花边织物)大衬领〔翻下遮住前胸及肩背,流行于十六、十七世纪〕。

rab·bet ['ræbit; `ræbɪt] **I** ***n*.** (木板的)凸凹,槽口;半边槽;半槽[企口]接合[使榫舌与槽口密接]。**II** ***vt*.** 在…挖槽口;嵌接。—***vi*.** 半槽接合 (*on*, *over*)。~ **joint** 半槽[企口]接合。

rab·bi ['ræbai; `ræbaɪ], **rab·bin** ['ræbin; `ræbɪn] ***n*.** **1.** 犹太法学博士。**2.** 先生,老师〔犹太人尊称用语〕。**3.** 犹太教教士。*the rabbins* 2—13 世纪的犹太法学家们。

rab·bin·ate ['ræbinit; `ræbɪnɪt] ***n*.** 犹太法学博士[犹太教教士]的身分[职位];〔集合词〕犹太法学博士们;犹太教教士们。

rab·bin·ic(al) ['ræbinik(əl); ræ`bɪnɪkl] ***a*.** 犹太法学博士[犹太教教士]的,犹太法学博士式的;犹太法学博士的语风的。*rabbinical literature* 犹太教法典 (Talmud) 之后的希伯来文学。

rab·bin·ism ['ræbinizəm; `ræbɪn,ɪzəm] ***n*.** 犹太法学博士的学说;犹太法学博士的语风;死钻牛角尖的学风。

rab·bin·ist, **rab·bin·ite** ['ræbinist, -ait; `ræbɪnɪst, -aɪt] ***n*.** 信奉犹太法学博士学说者;犹太教旧教徒。

rab·bit[1] ['ræbit; `ræbɪt] **I** ***n*.** **1.** 兔,家兔;野兔;兔皮。**2.** 胆小的人,懦夫。**3.** 〔英口〕笨拙的球员。**4.**【军】由工厂中偷出来的东西。***breed like ~s*** 像兔子一样多生孩子。**dead** ~ 没价值的东西。***like ~s in a warren*** (居民)稠密,拥挤不堪。***run like a ~*** 一溜烟地跑掉。**II** ***vt*.** **1.** 打兔子,猎兔。— ***vi*.** 兔子似地聚拢 (*together*)。*go ~ing* 去打兔子。~ **burrow** 野兔穴。~ **ears** **1.**【电视】兔耳形[室内 V 形]天线。**2.** 〔美〕(运动员)对场外观众嘲讽的敏感。~ **fever**【医】兔热病。~ **fish** 银鲛。~ **food**〔美俚〕生菜;凉拌菜。~ **heart**〔美〕懦夫。~ **hutch** 兔棚。~ **punch**【美拳击】向颈背猛打的一拳。~('s) **foot**〔美〕(迷信者认为有护符作用,会带来好运的)兔子后足。~ **twister**〔美〕乡下佬。~ **warren** 养兔场。**-er** ***n*.** 捕兔者。

rab·bit[2] ['ræbit; `ræbɪt] ***vt*.** 〔卑〕〔常用命令语气〕咒骂,诅咒。*Odd ~ it*! = *'Od ~ 'em*! 讨厌! 讨厌的家伙!

rab·bit·ry ['ræbitri; `ræbɪtrɪ] ***n*.** 兔群,养兔业。

rab·bit·y ['ræbiti; `ræbɪtɪ] ***a*.** 像兔子一般的;多兔子的。

rab·ble[1] ['ræbl; `ræbl] **I** ***n*.** **1.** 临时聚集起来的人,乌合之众,暴民。**2.** [the ~]〔蔑〕低级阶层,贱民。**3.** (动物等的)一群;(东西)混乱的一堆。*a ~ of books* 一堆乱书。**II** ***vt*.** 聚众袭击[暴动]。

rab·ble[2] ['ræbl; `ræbl] **I** ***n*.**【冶】(制铁用)搅拌棒;【矿】(长柄)耙。**II** ***vt*.** (用拨火棒)搅拌。

rab·ble[3] ['ræbl; `ræbl]〔英方〕***vt*.**, ***vi*.** 急促地说[读];絮絮地说 (*forth*; *off*; *out*; *over*)。

rab·ble·ment ['ræblmənt; `ræblmənt] ***n*.** 一群临时聚集成的人群;喧扰,暴动。

rab·ble-rous·er ['ræbl,rauzə; `ræbl,rauzə] ***n*.** (暴乱、暴动等的)煽动者,蛊惑民心的政客。**-rous·ing** ***a*.**, ***n*.**

Rab·e·lais ['ræbəlei; ,ræbl`e], **François** 拉伯雷〔1490—1533,法国讽刺作家〕。

Rab·e·lai·si·an, **Rab·e·lae·si·an** [,ræbə'leiziən; ,ræbl`ezɪən] **I** ***a*.** (法国讽刺滑稽作家)拉伯雷式的;粗野的。**II** ***n*.** 拉伯雷崇拜者[模仿者、研究者]。

rab·id ['ræbid; `ræbɪd] ***a*.** **1.** 狂怒的,狂暴的,疯狂的;过激的,激烈的,狂热的。**2.** 恐水病的,患狂犬病的。~ *hate* 愤恨。*a ~ dog* 疯狗。**-ly** ***ad*.**

ra·bid·i·ty, rab·id·ness [rəˈbiditi, ˈræbidnis; ræˋbɪdətɪ, ˋræbɪdnɪs] ***n*.** 1. 猛烈;蛮横,不讲理,顽固。2. 患狂犬病;疯狂。

ra·bi·es [ˈreibiːz, ˈræ-; ˋrebiz, ˋræ-] ***n*.**【医】狂犬病。

Ra. C = radium C【化】镭 C。

R.A.C., RAC = 1. Royal Armoured Corps〔英〕皇家装甲兵。2. Royal Automobile Club〔英〕皇家汽车俱乐部。

rac·coon [rəˈkuːn; ræˋkun] ***n*.** = racoon.

race[1] [reis; res] **I *n*.** 1. 竞赛;赛跑;赛艇;赛马;〔*pl*.〕赛马会,跑马会;竞赛;疾走。2. 路程,行程;经历,人生路程,一辈子,(日、月的)运行;时间的经过。3. 急流,急潮,小海峡。4. (水车等的)沟,水道;(织机的)梭道,走梭板;【机】轴承套,夹圈,座圈;【空】螺桨滑流,激流。*a rat* ~ 激烈的竞争。*go to the* ~*s* 看赛马去。*an armament* ~ 扩军竞赛。*consolation* ~【体】安慰赛。*His* ~ *is nearly run*. 他的一生快完了。**open** ~ 自由参加的赛跑。***play the*** ~***s***〔美〕赌赛马。***ride a*** ~ 举行赛马,出场赛马。***row a*** ~ 划船比赛。***run a*** ~ 赛跑。***sail a*** ~ 帆船竞赛。***selling*** ~ 拍卖胜利马的赛马。***with a strong*** ~ 凶猛地,猛烈地。**II *vi*.** 1. 赛跑,竞走;竞赛(*with*);疾走;以赛马为业。2. (螺旋桨、马达等)空转。—***vt*.** 1. 使拼命跑;使赛跑。2. 努力想跑过…,和…赛跑。3. 为赛马输光(财产)(*away*);使(马达等)空转。~ *the bill through the House* 使议案匆匆[迅速]通过。~ ***against*** 和…赛跑,和…竞赛。~**about** (比赛用的)快艇,跑车。~ **ball** 赛马会附带举行的跳舞会。~ **card** 赛马次序表。~**course** 1. 〔英〕跑马场,赛马场;赛船水道。2. (水车的)沟。~ **cup** 奖杯,优胜杯。~ **glass** (看赛马用的)小型望远镜。~ **ground** 赛马场,赛跑场。~ **horse** 赛马的马;【鸟】河鸭;【虫】螳螂(*a* ~ *horse bill*〔美〕开给来兑款支票的支票)。~ **meeting** 赛马会;赛跑会。~ **rotation**【机】空转。~ **track**【体育】跑道。~ **walking** 竞走,步行比赛。~**-way** (矿山等的)导水路,(水车的)水道;电线保护管。

race[2] [reis; res] **I *n*.** 1. 人种;种族,民族。2. 氏族,家族,家系,系统;门第。3. 种类,…们,阶层;〔诗〕子孙,后裔。4. (生物的)类;人类;【动、植】属,种类。5. 人种的特性;(文体等的)特征;(酒的)特殊风味。*the Jewish* ~ 犹太人种。*the white* ~ 白(色人)种。*the* ~ *of poets* 诗人们。*the feathered* [*finny*] ~ 鸟[鱼]类。*The wine has a certain* ~. 这个酒有一种特殊风味。**II *a*.** 人种的,种族的。*a* ~ *prejudice* 种族偏见。*the* ~ *problem* 人种[种族]问题[美国尤指黑人的问题]。*a* ~ *riot* 因种族歧视引起的暴动。~ **suicide** 种族自杀〔把出生率控制过低而引起某一种族的逐渐消亡〕。

race[3] [reis; res] ***n*.** (生姜等的)根。

ra·ce·mate [reiˈsiːmeit, rə-; reˋsimet, rə-] ***n*.**【化】外消旋盐,外消旋酒石酸盐。

ra·ceme [rəˈsiːm; reˋsim] ***n*.**【植】总状花序;【化】外消旋体[物]。

ra·ce·mic [rəˈsiːmik; rəˋsimɪk] ***a*.**【化】外消旋的,消旋的;得自葡萄的。~ **acid**【化】外消旋酸;外消旋酒石酸。~ **compound**【化】外消旋化合物。

rac·e·mism [ˈræsimizəm, reiˈsiːmizəm; ˋræsəmɪzəm, reˋsimɪzəm] ***n*.** 1.【化】(外)消旋性。2. = racemization.

rac·e·mi·za·tion [ˌræsimiˈzeiʃən; ˏræsəmɪˋzeʃən] ***n*.**【化】(外)消旋(作用);【考古】(化石标本的)消旋作用年代测定法。

rac·e·mose, rac·e·mous [ˈræsiməus, -məs; ˋræsəˏmos, -məs] ***a*.**【植】总状的;【解】葡萄状的。

rac·er [ˈreisə; ˋresɚ] ***n*.** 1. 赛跑者;疾走者;赛马者,比赛用快艇,比赛用自行车(等)。2.【动】(美洲)黑蛇。3.【军】火炮转台。

race·run·ner [ˈreisrʌnə; ˋresˏrʌnɚ] ***n*.**【动】鞭尾蜥(*Cnemidophorus sexlineatus*)〔主要发现于南美洲和北美洲〕。

Ra·chel [ˈreitʃəl; ˋretʃəl] ***n*.** 1. 雷切尔〔女子名〕。2.【圣】拉结〔雅各(Jacob)的妻子〕。3. 〔美〕(女)犹太人。

ra·chet = ratchet.

ra·chil·la [rəˈkilə; rəˋkɪlə] ***n*.** (*pl*. **-lae** [-iː; -i])【植】小穗轴;小花轴。

ra·chis [ˈreikis; ˋrekɪs] ***n*.** (*pl*. ~**es** [ˈreikisiz; ˋrekɪsɪz], ***ra·chi·des*** [ˈreikidiːz; ˋrekɪdiz])【解】脊椎,脊柱;【植】花序轴,叶轴;【动】羽轴;分脊。

ra·chi·tis [ræˈkaitis; rəˋkaɪtɪs] ***n*.**【医】佝偻病,脊柱炎;【植】萎缩病。

ra·cial [ˈreiʃəl; ˋreʃəl] ***a*.** 人种(上)的,种族的;种族间的。~ *antipathies* [*characteristics, prejudice*] 种族反感[特质,偏见]。**-ly *ad*.**

rac·i·ly [ˈreisili; ˋresəlɪ] ***ad*.** 1. 保持原味地。2. 活泼地。3. 爽脆,干脆,痛快,尖锐泼辣地。4. 〔美〕近乎淫猥地。

Racine [rɑːˈsiːn; rɑˋsin], **Jean Baptiste** 莱辛〔1639—1699,法国剧作家〕。

rac·i·ness [ˈreisinis; ˋresɪnɪs] ***n*.** 1. 保持原味。2. 活泼,有趣。3. 爽气,痛快,尖锐泼辣。4. 挑逗性。

rac·ing [ˈreisiŋ; ˋresɪŋ] ***n*.** 竞赛;赛跑;赛马;赛艇;【机】空转。*a* ~ *man* 赛马狂。*the* ~ *world* 赛马界。*a* ~ *boat* 竞赛用艇。*a* ~ *cup* 奖杯。~ **colours** (赛马)骑师(衣服)的颜色。~ **form**〔美俚〕赛马消息。~ **track**【体】滑冰比赛场。

ra·cism [ˈreisizəm; ˋresɪzəm] ***n*.** 1. 种族主义。2. 种族歧视[隔离、迫害]。

ra·cist [ˈreisist; ˋresɪst] **I *n*.** 种族主义者。**II *a*.** 种族主义的;种族歧视[隔离、迫害]的。

rack[1] [ræk; ræk] **I *n*.** 1. (火车等的)行李(网)架;各种搁架[枪架、帽架、笔架等],工具架;【海】结绳架;【军】(飞机的)炸弹架;【海】餐具架;防止转动架;【机】齿条,齿轨;饲草架,马槽。2. (从前拉脱犯人四肢关节的)拉肢拷问台,拉肢刑架;拷问;(精神上或肉体上的)巨大痛苦。*a clothes* ~ 衣架。*a torpedo net* ~ 鱼雷防御网架。*a launching* ~【火箭】发射导轨。*an underwing* ~【火箭】翼下发射导轨。***by*** ~ ***of eye*** 依据目测估量,照估计。***come*** [***stand up***] ***to the*** [***one's***] ~ 听天由命。***in a high*** ~ 在高位。***live at*** ~ ***and manger*** 过豪华[富裕]生活。***off the*** ~ (衣服)做好了的,现成的。***on the*** ~ 正在受拷问;忧虑,害怕(*My ingenuity is on the* ~ *to find a good excuse*. 我正在绞尽脑汁找借口)。***put sth. on the*** ~ 使极度紧张;使受到严格考验。***put sb. to*** [***on***] ***the*** ~ 对…加以拷问。**II *vt*.** 1. 对(犯人)拉肢拷问;扭伤。2. 使过分紧张,使苦痛,折磨。3. 剥削,榨取(佃户);使(地力)变瘦。4. 把…做成架子。5. 把…搁在架子[台子]上;把(马)拴在马槽上。*a cough that* ~*s one's whole body* 仿佛要扯碎全身的激烈的咳嗽。*a* ~*ing headache* 要爆炸似的头痛。***be*** ~***ed with pain*** 苦痛不堪。~ ***one's brains*** 绞尽脑汁,费尽心机。~ ***rent from sb*.** 勒索过高地租剥削某人。~ ***up*** 1. 获得(胜利);得(比分)(~ *up 20 points in the first half* 前半场得 20 分。~ *up a victory* 获得胜利)。2. 彻底击败。3. 把马拴[系]起来喂草料。~ **car**【铁路】多层平板车皮〔运输汽车用〕。~ **rail** 齿。~ **railway**,〔美〕~ **railroad** 齿轨铁路。~**-rent** 1. ***vt*.** 收取(盘剥性地租[租金])。2. ***n*.** 盘剥性地租,额外地租。~**-renter** 收取[支付]高额租金的人。~ **wheel** 大齿轮。

rack[2] [ræk; ræk] ***n*.** 〔古〕破坏,荒废。***go to*** ~ ***and ruin*** [***manger***] 走向毁灭[荒废](= wrack)。

rack[3] [ræk; ræk] **I *n*.** 行云团;〔废〕行雾。**II *vi*.** (云)随风飘动。

rack[4] [ræk; ræk] **I *n*.** (马的)轻跑,小步跑。**II *vi*.** (马)轻跑。

rack[5] [ræk; ræk] ***vt*.** 把(酒槽中的酒)榨出(*off*);将(酒)装瓶。

R

rack[6] [ræk; ræk] *n*. = arrack.

rack·a·bones [ˈrækəbəunz; ˋrækəˏbonz] *n*. 〔用作单数〕〔美〕骨瘦如柴的人[动物]。

rack·et[1], **rac·quet** [ˈrækit; ˋrækɪt] **I** *n*. **1**. (网球等的)球拍。**2**. 〔*pl*.〕〔作单数用〕(四周有围墙的)拍打回力网球,硬壁回力球。**3**. 球拍形雪球;(走泥地时用的)马穿的木鞋。*a* ~ *swinger* 〔美〕回力网球选手。**II** *vt*. 用球拍打。

rack·et[2] [ˈrækit; ˋrækɪt] **I** *n*. **1**. 喧骚,吵闹,嚷闹;扰嚷;喧骚嘈杂的集会;狂欢。**2**. 考验,困难的立场[经验];辛酸经历。**3**. 〔俚〕行业,职业,工作;事情。**4**. 〔美俚〕勒索金钱,讹诈,敲诈,骗局。*the publishing* ~ 出版业。*What's his* ~? 他做什么工作? *What's your* ~? 请问贵干? *What's the* ~? 什么事? 怎么啦? *It isn't my* ~. 这不关我事。***give away the*** ~ 没提防把秘密泄漏出去。***go on a*** ~ 纵情欢闹。***kick up a*** ~ = ***make a*** ~ 惹乱子,大吵大闹。***stand the*** ~ ***of*** 经受得住考验,负责;偿付[承担]费用。**II** *vi*. 嚷闹,吵闹,纵情欢闹。

rack·et·eer [ˌrækiˈtiə; ˏrækɪtˋɪr] **I** *n*. 〔美俚〕讹诈钱财的歹徒。**II** *vi*. 勒索金钱,恐吓,讹诈。

rack·et·y [ˈrækiti; ˋrækɪtɪ] *a*. **1**. 喧闹的;放荡的;寻欢作乐的。**2**. 摇晃的;不可靠的。

R

rack·ing [ˈrækiŋ; ˋrækɪŋ] *a*. 拷问的;折磨人的,难忍受的。*a* ~ *pain* 难以忍受的痛苦。

rack·le [ˈrækl; ˋrækl] *a*. 〔Scot.〕**1**. 不受管束的,刚愎的;任性的,鲁莽的;激烈的。**2**. 精力旺盛的,强健的。

ra·con [ˈreikən; ˋrekɑn] *n*.【无】雷达信标 (= radar beacon)。

rac·on·teur [rækənˈtəː; ˏrækɑnˋtɝ] *n*. 〔F.〕善于讲轶事[故事]的人;爱说话的人,健谈家;说书的。

ra·coon [rəˈkuːn; ræˋkun] *n*.【动】浣熊;浣熊毛皮。~ **dog**【动】貉。

rac·quet [ˈrækit; ˋrækɪt] *n*. = racket[1]. ~ **ball** (硬壁回力球戏所用的)回力球。

rac·quet·eer [ˌrækiˈtiːə; rækɪˋtiɚ] *n*. 〔美俚〕网球选手。

rac·y [ˈreisi; ˋresɪ] *a*. **1**. 保持原味的,有风味的,芳醇的,芬芳的;新鲜的;道地的。**2**. 爽气的,痛快的;泼辣的。**3**. 〔美〕猥亵的。~ *of the soil* 有道地风味的;干脆的,直截了当的;生动活泼的;刺激的。**-i·ly** *ad*. **-i·ness** *n*.

Ra-D = radium-D【化】镭 D。

Rad., **rad.** = radical; radio.

rad. = 〔L.〕*radix*【植】根。

rad [ræd; ræd] *n*.【物】拉德〔吸收辐射剂量单位〕。

ra·da·me·ter [ˈreidɑːmiːtə; ˋredɑmitɚ] *n*. 防撞雷达设备[装置]。

ra·dar [ˈreidə; ˋredɑr] *n*. 〔美〕【无】〔radio detecting and ranging 之略〕雷达,无线电探测器 (=〔英〕radiolocator)。*air search* ~ 防空[空中搜索]雷达。*air surface vessel* ~ 飞机用水面舰船搜索雷达。*beam-transmitter* ~ 定向瞄准雷达。*missile* ~ 弹载雷达;跟踪导[飞]弹的雷达。*long-range* ~ 远程雷达。~ *control* 雷达控制。~ *installation* 雷达装置。*laser* ~ 激光[雷射]雷达。*a* ~ *set* 雷达装置。***below*** [***beneath***] ***the*** ~ 不引人注意,在视线之外。★ radar 是不可数名词。~ **beacon** 雷达信标。~ **fence** 雷达警戒网。~**-homer** 自动瞄准[导航]雷达弹头;自动瞄准雷达。~**man** 雷达员。~ **picket** 装有雷达设备的警戒船或飞机。~**scope** 雷达显示[示波]器。~ **screen** 雷达荧光屏[幕];〔喻〕备受公众注意的地方。~**-tracking** *a*. 雷达追踪的。~ **trap** (受到交通警严密监视的)雷达监控路段。

Rad·cliffe [ˈrædklif; ˋrædklɪf] *n*. 拉德克利夫〔姓氏〕。

RADCM = radar countermeasures 反雷达措施。

rad·dle[1] [ˈrædl; ˋrædl] **I** *n*.【矿】代赭石。**II** *vt*. 用赭石,胭脂等涂 (= ruddle)。

rad·dle[2] [ˈrædl; ˋrædl] *vt*. 编织;交织。

ra·di·ac [ˈreidiæk; ˋredɪæk] *n*. 辐射计。~ **meter** 辐射剂量计。

ra·dial [ˈreidjəl; ˋredɪəl] **I** *a*. **1**. 光线的;光线状的。**2**. 放射的,辐射(状)的。**3**. 镭的。**4**.【数】半径的;【物】径向的;【解】桡骨的;【植】射出花的,射出状的。**II** *n*. **1**. 放射部。**2**. 桡骨神经[动脉]。**3**. 子午线轮胎。~ **arrangement**【植】间隔排列。~ **axle** 转向轴。~ **drill** 旋臂钻床。~ **engine** 星形发动机。~ **flux**【物】辐射通量。~ **heating** 辐射能热。~ **motion** 径向运动。~ (**ply**) **tire** 放射状轮胎。~ **velocity** 径向速度;【天】视向速度。**-ly** *ad*.

ra·di·al·ized [ˈreidiəlaizd; ˋredɪəlaɪzd] *a*. 放射(状)的。

ra·di·an [ˈreidjən; ˋredɪən] *n*.【数】弧度。

ra·di·ance, **ra·di·an·cy** [ˈreidjəns, -si; ˋredɪəns, -sɪ] *n*. 发光,光辉;(眼睛或脸色的)光彩;辐射;照射(作用)。

ra·diant [ˈreidjənt; ˋredɪənt] **I** *a*. **1**. 发光的,放热的。**2**. 放射的,辐射的;【动、植】辐射形的。**3**. 照耀的,辉煌的,灿烂的;满面春风的,容光焕发的;极漂亮的。**II** *n*. 光源,光点;光体;【天】(流星的)辐射点。~ *energy* [*heat*] 辐射能[热]。~ *ray* 辐射线。*the* ~ *sun* 耀眼的太阳。*a* ~ *smile* 满脸微笑。~ ***with joy*** 喜形于色。**-ly** *ad*.

ra·di·ate [ˈreidieit; ˋredɪˏet] **I** *vi*. **1**. 发光;辐射;射出,发散;放射热。**2**. 向周围扩展。—*vt*. **1**. 辐状射出,辐射,放射,发散。**2**. 使向周围扩展。**II** [ˈreidiit; ˋredɪɪt] *a*. 射出的,辐射状的;【动、植】辐射形的。

ra·di·a·tion [ˌreidiˈeiʃən; ˏredɪˋeʃən] *n*. **1**. 发光,射光,放热,放射,发射。**2**.【物】辐射;放射物;辐射线[热、能];照射(作用)。**3**.【动、植】辐射形;【测】射出测量法;【医】射线疗法。*direct* [*indirect*] ~ 直接[间接]放热。*electromagnetic* ~ 电磁辐射。*solar* [*terrestrial*] ~ 太阳[地球]放射热。~ **field**【物】辐射场。~**-meter** 伦琴计,X 射线计。~**-proof** *a*. 防辐射的。~**-sickness** 辐射病,射线中毒。~**-sterilized** *a*. 辐射消毒的。~**-thermometer** 辐射计。

ra·di·a·tive [ˈreidieitiv; ˋredɪˏetɪv] *a*. **1**. 发光的,放热的;放射的,发射的。**2**.【物】辐射性的。

ra·di·a·tor [ˈreidieitə; ˋredɪˏetɚ] *n*. **1**. 辐射体,辐射器,放热物。**2**. 散热器,暖气管;(汽车引擎的)水箱,冷却器;【电】辐射暖房装置;【无】发射天线。*an electric* ~ 电热器。*a full* ~ 黑体,全辐射体。*a spherical* ~ 全向辐射器。*an active* [*reactive*] ~ 有源[无源]辐射器。

rad·i·cal [ˈrædikəl; ˋrædɪkl] **I** *a*. **1**. 基本的,根本的;固有的,本来的;重要的,主要的;最初的;彻底的。**2**. 〔常 R-〕激进的,急进的,过激的,极端的。**3**.【植】根生的;【化】基的,原子团的;【语】根词的;语根的;【数】根的;【乐】根音的。**II** *n*. **1**. 激进分子,激进主义者;〔R-〕激进党派成员。**2**.【语】词根;词干,(中国字的)偏旁,部首;【化】根,基,原子团;【数】根数;根号;【乐】根音。*a* ~ *principle* 基本原理。~ *defects* 生来的缺点。*a* ~ *treatment* 彻底疗法,根治法。~ *measures* 激烈手段。*a R- party* 激进派。~ *growths* [*hairs*, *leaves*] 根生物[根生毛,根生叶]。~ **centre**【数】等幂心,根轴心。~ **chic** 〔美俚〕(时髦人物)与激进派交往的风尚。~ **sign**【数】根号。~ **word**【语】根词。**-ism** 激进主义。**-i·za·tion** [ˌrædikəlaiˈzeiʃən; ˏrædɪkəlaɪˋzeʃən] *n*. 激进。**-ize** *vt*., *vi*. 使激进,变激进,相信激进主义,成为激进主义者。**-ly** *ad*.

rad·i·cand [ˈrædikænd; ˋrædəˏkænd] *n*.【数】被开方数。

rad·i·cle [ˈrædikl; ˋrædɪkl] *n*.【古生】胚根;【化】基;根。

ra·dii [ˈreidiai; ˋredɪˏaɪ] *n*. **1**. radius 的复数。**2**. 辐管;辐部。

ra·dio [ˈreidiəu; ˋredɪˏo] **I** *n*. **1**. 无线电讯[电报,电话];无线电,射电。**2**. 无线电广播;无线电(广播)台。**3**. 收音机。*listen* (*in*) *to the* ~ 听无线电。~ *message* 无线电通讯。**II** *vt*., *vi*. 用无线电传送[广播];(向…)作无线电广播[传送];用 X 射线拍照;用镭医治。~ **actor** 广播剧演员。~**amplifier** 无线电高频放大器。~ **apparatus** 无线电报[电话]机。~ **astronomy**【天】射电天文学。~

autocontrol 无线电自控。~**autogram** *n*. 无线电传真。~ **beacon** 无线电航空信标。~ **beam** 无线电射束。~-**bearing** 无线电定向[方位]。~ **broadcast** *vi*., *vt*.【无】(对…)作广播。~-**broadcaster** 无线电广播员;无线电广播机。~**broadcasting** 无线电广播(~*broadcasting station* 广播电台)。~**cast** *vt*. = radiobroadcast. ~ **channel** 无线电频道[波道],射电波道。**R- City**〔美〕纽约市洛克菲勒中心娱乐地区。~ **communication** 无线电(通)讯,射电通讯。~ **compass** 无线电罗盘。~ **compass station** 无线电方位信标站。~-**controlled** *a*. 无线电控制[操纵]的。~-**detector**【无】无线电探测器,雷达。~ **direction finder** 无线电探向器。~ **echo sounding** 无线电回波测深。~**electronics** 无线电电子学。~ **facsimile** 无线电传真。~**fication** 无线电化。~ **field**【无】射电场,无线电场。~ **frequency**【无】射(电)频(率)。~ **goniometer** 无线电测向计,无线电罗盘,无线电方位计。~ **goniometric station** 无线电测向所。~**gram** 无线电报;射线照片;〔口〕= radio-gramophone;〔英〕= X-ray。~ **gramophone** 收音、电唱两用机。~ **intercepts** 无线电情报侦译术。~ **interference** 无线电干扰。~**ite**〔美〕无线电广播员。~ **knife**【医】高频手术刀。~**location** 无线电定位(法)。~**locator**〔英〕= radar. ~**man** 无线电员[兵]。~ **merits** 无线电话的质量。~ **metal** 无线电高导磁性合金。~ **meteorograph** 无线电气象自记器。~-**meteorography** 无线电气象自记法。~**moppet**〔美〕电台儿童演员。~**news** 广播新闻。~ **operator** 无线电报员。~**page** *vt*.〔美〕用无线电找(人)。~ **parts** 无线电零件。~**phone** 无线电话(机)。~ **phonograph** 收音电唱两用机。~**photo**, ~**photograph** 无线电传真照片。~**photography** 无线电传真(术)。~ **play** 广播剧。~ **press** 广播报。~ **pulsar**【天】射电脑卫星。~**quiet** *a*. 不产生无线电干扰的。~ **range** 无线电轨[信标],射电轨;无线电航向信标,等信号区无线电信标;无线电测得距离。~ **range beacon** 航线无线电指标。~ **receiver** = ~-**receiving set** 无线电接收机。~ **service code** 无线电电码。~ **set** 无线电接收[发报]机。~ **sonde** = radiometeorograph. ~ **spectrum**【无】射频频谱。~-**stat** 中放晶体滤波式超外差接收机。~ **station** 无线电台,广播电台。~ **studio** 无线电播音室。~**telegram** 无线电报。~ **telegraph** 1. *n*. 无线电报(机)。2. *v*. 向…发无线电报。~**telegraphic** *a*. 无线电报(术)的,用在无线电报上的。~**telegraphy** 无线电报(术)。~ **telemetric** *a*. 无线电遥测的。~ **telemetry** 无线电遥测学。~**telephone** *n*., *vt*., *vi*. 无线电话(机);打无线电话。~**telephony** 无线电话(术)。~ **telescope**【天】射电望远镜。~**teletype(writer)** 无线电电传打字电报机[设备]。~**television** 无线电电视。~-**transparent** *a*. 在 X 光照射中不显影的,容许射线通过的。~ **tube** 无线电真空管。

ra·di·o- [ˈreidiəu; ˋredɪo] *comb*. *f*. 1. 放射;辐射。2. 光线。3. 半径。4. 桡骨。5. 镭。6. 无线电。

ra·di·o·ac·tin·i·um [ˈreidiəuækˈtiniəm; ˏredɪoækˋtɪnɪəm] *n*.【化】射锕〔略 Rd Ac; 即钍^{227}〕。

ra·di·o·ac·ti·vate [ˈreidiəuˈæktiveit; ˏredɪoˋæktəvet] *vt*. 使带放射性。

ra·di·o·ac·tive [ˈreidiəuˈæktiv; ˏredɪoˋæktɪv] *a*.【物】放射性(引起)的。~ **dating**【地】放射衰变年代鉴定。~ **decay** 放射衰变。~ **dust** 放射性尘埃。~ **fallout** 放射性微粒回降。~ **isotope** 放射性同位素。~ **series** 放射系列。-**ac·tiv·i·ty** *n*. [-ækˈtiviti; -ækˋtɪvətɪ] 放射性;放射(现象)。

ra·di·o·as·say [ˈreidiəuəˈsei; ˋredɪoəˋse] *n*. 放射性测量。

ra·di·o·au·to·gram [ˈreidiəuˈɔːtəgræm; ˋredɪoˋɔtəˏgræm] *n*. = radioautograph.

ra·di·o·au·to·graph [reidiəuˈɔːtəˌgrɑːf, -græf; redɪoˋɔtəˏgrɑf, -græf] *n*.【原】放射自显照相[相片],自动射线照相,射线显迹图(= autoradiograph)。-**ic** *a*. -**y** [-ɔːˈtɔgrəfi; -ɔˋtɑgrəfɪ] *n*. 放射自显照相术,自动射线照相术。

ra·di·o·bi·ol·o·gy [ˈreidiəubaiˈɔlədʒi; ˏredɪobaɪˋɑlədʒɪ] *n*. 放射生物学。

ra·di·o·car·bon [ˈreidiəuˈkɑːbən; ˏredɪoˋkɑrbən] *n*.【化】放射性碳。

ra·di·o·car·di·o·gram [ˈreidiəuˈkɑːdiəgræm; ˏredɪoˋkɑrdɪəˏgræm] *n*.【医】放射能心电图。

ra·di·o·car·di·og·ra·phy [ˈreidiəuˌkɑːdiˈɔgrəfi; ˏredɪoˏkɑrdɪˋɑgrəfɪ] *n*.【医】放射能心电图测定。

ra·di·o·ce·ram·ic [ˈreidiəusiˈræmik; ˏredɪosɪˋræmɪk] *n*. 高频瓷。

ra·di·o·chem·is·try [ˈreidiəuˈkemistri; ˏredɪoˋkɛmɪstrɪ] *n*.【化】放射化学。

ra·di·o·el·e·ment [ˈreidiəuˈelimənt; ˏredɪoˋɛləmənt] *n*.【化】放射性元素。

ra·di·o·ge·net·ics [ˈreidiəudʒiˈnetiks; ˏredɪodʒɪˋnɛtɪks] *n*. 放射遗传学。

ra·di·o·gen·ic [ˈreidiəuˈdʒenik; ˏredɪoˋdʒɛnɪk] *a*. 1.【原】放射[辐射]产生的。2. 适合于广播的。

ra·di·o·gram [ˌreidiəuˈgræm; ˋredɪəˏgræm] *n*. 1. 无线电报。2.【物】射线照片。3.〔口〕收音电唱两用机。

ra·di·o·graph [ˈreidiəugrɑːf; ˋredɪəˏgræf] I *n*. 射线照片,X 光照片。II *vt*. 给…拍摄射线照片。-**ic** [-ˈgræfik; -ˋgræfɪk] *a*. -**y** *n*. 射线[X 光]照相术。

ra·di·o·heat·ing [ˈreidiəuˈhiːtiŋ; ˋredɪoˋhitɪŋ] *n*. 射频加热。

ra·di·o·i·so·tope [ˈreidiəuˈaisətəup; ˏredɪoˋaɪsətop] *n*.【原】放射性同位素。-**i·so·top·ic** [ˌreidiəuˌaisəˈtɔpik; ˏredɪoˏaɪsəˋtɑpɪk] *a*.

ra·di·o-la·bel [ˈreidiəuˈleibl; ˋredɪoˋlebl] I *vt*. 对…作放射性同位素示踪。II *n*. 示踪放射性同位素。

ra·di·o-la·bel(l)ed [ˈreidiəuˈleibld; ˋredɪoˋlebḷd] *a*.【原】放射性同位素示踪[标记]的。

ra·di·o·lar·i·an [ˌreidiəuˈleəriən; ˏredɪoˋlɛrɪən] *n*.【动】放射虫〔一种放射虫目(*Radiolaria*)深海单细胞动物〕。

ra·di·o·lo·ca·tion [ˈreidiəuləuˈkeiʃən; ˏredɪoloˋkeʃən] *n*. 1. 无线电定位。2. = radar.

ra·di·ol·o·gy [ˌreidiˈɔlədʒi; ˏredɪˋɑlədʒɪ] *n*.【物】放射学,辐射学;X 线学;【医】放射科,X 线科。-**o·gist** *n*. 放射线学家;【医】放射科医师。

ra·di·o·lu·cent [ˈreidiəuˈluːsnt; ˏredɪoˋlusənt] *a*. 射线可透射的。-**cenc·y** *n*.

ra·di·o·lu·mi·nes·cence [ˈreidiəuˌljuːmiˈnes ns; ˏredɪoˏljumɪˋnɛsns] *n*. 射线[辐射]发光(现象)。

ra·di·ol·y·sis [ˌreidiˈɔlisis; ˏredɪˋɑlɪsɪs] *n*.【化】辐射分解,放射性分解,射解作用。-**o·lyt·ic** [-əˈlitik; -əˋlɪtɪk] *a*.

ra·di·om·e·ter [ˌreidiˈɔmitə; ˏredɪˋɑmətɚ] *n*.【物】辐射计;放射量测定器;射线检查器。

ra·di·o·mi·crom·e·ter [ˈreidiəumaiˈkrɔmitə; ˏredɪomaɪˋkrɑmɪtɚ] *n*. 辐射微热计。

ra·di·o·mi·met·ic [ˌreidiəumiˈmetik; ˏredɪomɪˋmɛtɪk] *a*. 模拟辐射的〔引起与辐照相同作用的〕。

ra·di·on [ˈreidiɔn; ˋredɪɑn] *n*.【物】(放)射(微)粒。

ra·di·on·ics [ˌreidiˈɔniks; ˏredɪˋɑnɪks] *n*. 射电电子学;电子管学。

ra·di·o·nu·clide [ˌreidiəuˈnjuːklaid, -ˈnuː-; ˏredɪoˋnjuklaɪd, -ˋnu-] *n*.【化】放射性核素。

ra·di·o·nym [ˈreidiəunim; ˋredɪonɪm] *n*.〔美〕无线电民用波段者的绰号。

ra·di·o·paque [ˌreidiəuˈpeik; ˏredɪoˋpek] *a*. (X 线、γ 线等)射线[辐射]透不过的(= radio-opaque)。-**pac·i·ty** [-ˈpæsiti; -ˋpæsɪtɪ] *n*.

ra·di·o·phare [ˈreidiəufɛə; ˋredɪoˏfɛr] *n*. 1. 与船舶通信的无线电台。2. 无线电信标。3. 雷达探照灯。

R

ra·di·o·phar·ma·ceu·ti·cal [ˌreidiəuˌfɑːməˈsjuːtikl, -ˈsuːt-; ˏredɪoˏfɑrməˋsjutɪkl̩, -ˋsut-] *n*.【医】放射性药品,放射性药剂。

ra·di·o·scope [ˈreidiəuskəup; ˋredɪoˏskop] *n*. 放射镜;剂量测定验电器。

ra·di·os·copy [reidiˈɔskəpi; ˏredɪˋɑskəpɪ] *n*. 放射性试验[检查];X光线透视检查法。

ra·di·o·sen·si·tive [ˌreidiəuˈsensitiv; ˏredɪoˋsɛnsɪtɪv] *a*.【医】对辐射敏感的;可被射线杀死[摧毁]的。**-tiv·i·ty** *n*.

ra·di·o·stron·ti·um [ˌreidiəuˈstrɔnʃiəm, -tiəm; ˏredɪoˋstrɑnʃɪəm, -tɪəm] *n*.【化】放射性锶。

ra·di·o·tel·e·type, ra·di·o·tel·e·type·writ·er [ˌreidiəuˈtelitaip, -raitə; ˏredɪoˋtɛlɪtaɪp, -raɪtɚ] *n*. 无线电电传打字电报机;无线电电传打字电报设备。

ra·di·o·tel·lu·ri·um [ˈreidiəuteˈljuəriəm; ˏredɪotɛˋljʊrɪəm] *n*.【化】射碲。

ra·di·o·thal·li·um [ˈreidiəuˈθæliəm; ˏredɪoˋθælɪəm] *n*.【化】射铊。

ra·di·o·ther·a·peu·tics [ˈreidiəuˌθerəˈpiuːtiks; ˋredɪoˏθɛrəˋpjutɪks] *n*.【医】放射疗法[治疗];镭锭[X线]治疗(科)。

R

ra·di·o·ther·a·py [ˈreidiəuˈθerəpi; ˋredɪoˋθɛrəpɪ] *n*. = radiotherapeutics. **-a·pist** *n*. 放射科医师。

ra·di·o·ther·my [ˈreidiəuˈθəːmi; ˋredɪoˏθɝmɪ] *n*.【医】热放射疗法。

ra·di·o·tho·ri·um [ˈreidiəuˈθɔːriəm; ˏredɪoˋθɔrɪəm] *n*.【化】(放)射(性)钍。

ra·di·o·vi·sion [ˈreidiəuviʒən; ˋredɪoˏvɪʒən] *n*.〔废〕电视 (= television)。

rad·ish [ˈrædiʃ; ˋrædɪʃ] *n*.【植】小红萝卜。*horse* ~ 辣根。*pickled* ~ 盐渍萝卜,萝卜泡菜。

ra·dium [ˈreidjəm; ˋredɪəm] *n*.【化】镭。~ **emanation** 镭(放)射气,氡(= radon)。

ra·di·um·ther·a·py [ˈreidjəmˈθerəpi; ˋredɪəmˋθɛrəpɪ] *n*.【医】镭疗法;放射疗法。

ra·di·us [ˈreidjəs; ˋredɪəs] *n*. (*pl*. **ra·di·i** [-ai; -aɪ]) 1. 半径;半径范围。2.【解】桡骨。3. (车轮的)辐;【物】辐射线;【无】径向射线;辐射物;(六分仪等的)针;【纺】杼。4.【植】射出花。*within a ~ of three miles* 在周围三英里以内。*the flying* ~ 飞行半径;(加一次油的)飞行距离。*a ~ of action*【军】行动[活动]半径[所及范围];航程;续航距离;续航力。~ *of convergence*【数】收敛半径。~ *of curvature*【数】曲率半径。~ **vector**【数、物】矢径,辐;位置矢量。

ra·dix [ˈreidiks; ˋredɪks] *n*. (*pl*. **-es** *or* **rad·i·ces** [-disiːz; -dɪsiz]) 1. 根本。2.【数】基数;根值;记数根;【植】根;【语】词根。

ra·dome [ˈreidəum; ˋredom] *n*.【无】雷达天线罩。

ra·don [ˈreidɔn; ˋredɑn] *n*.【化】氡〔由镭裂变后生成的放射性元素,旧名 radium emanation〕。~ **daughters** 氡放射性衰变产物〔香烟烟尘中的一种放射性微粒,对被动吸烟者的健康有害〕。

rad·u·la [ˈrædʒulə; ˋrædʒulə] *n*. (*pl*. **-lae** [-liː; -li]) 【动】齿舌。**-lar** *a*.

ra·dux [ˈreidʌks; ˋredʌks] *n*. 1.【数】计数制的基数。2.【空】远距双曲线低频导航系统。

RAE; R.A.E. = Royal Aircraft Establishment〔英〕皇家航空研究所。

Rae [rei; re] *n*. 雷〔姓氏,女子名,Rachel 的昵称〕。

Ra-F = radium-F【化】镭 F。

R.A.F., RAF = Royal Air Force〔英〕皇家空军。

Ra·fael, Raph·a·el [ˈræfeiəl; ˋræfeəl] *n*. 拉斐尔〔男子名〕。

ra·fale [ræˈfɑːl; rɑˋfɑl] *n*.〔F.〕【军】(排炮的)迅猛射击。

raff [ræf; ræf] *n*. 1. 社会底层的人(们)。2.〔方〕大量,大批,许多。3. 垃圾,废料。

raf·fi·a [ˈræfiə; ˋræfɪə] *n*. 1.【植】(马达加斯加)酒椰树 (*Raphia ruffia*)。2. 酒椰叶的纤维;酒椰纤维帽。~ **palm** = raffia.

raf·fi·nate [ˈræfineit; ˋræfəˏnet] *n*. (石油)(提炼过程中的)残油液。

raf·fi·nose [ˈræfinəus; ˋræfənos] *n*. (由甜菜根,棉子等提炼的)棉子糖。

raff·ish [ˈræfiʃ; ˋræfɪʃ] *a*. 1. 放荡的,颓废的;声名狼藉的。2. 粗俗的;艳丽而俗气的。

raf·fle[1] [ˈræfl; ˋræfl] **I** *n*. (义卖)抽彩出售。**II** *vi*. 加入抽彩。~ *for an auto* 抽彩买汽车。— *vt*. 用抽彩办法出售(商品等) (*off*)。~ *off a piece of furniture* 以抽彩法出售一件家具。

raf·fle[2] [ˈræfl; ˋræfl] *n*. 1. 废物;杂物;碎屑。2. (船上的)绳索什具。3.〔美俚〕业余窃贼。

raf·fle·si·a [ræˈfliːʒiə, -ʒə, -ziə; ræˋfliʒɪə, -ʒə, -zɪə] *n*.【植】大花草属 (*Rafflesia*) 植物〔产于马来西亚〕。

raft[1] [rɑːft; ræft] **I** *n*. 1. 筏,桴,槎,木排。2.【军】(登陆用的)浮桥。3.〔美〕(妨碍航行的)流木,浮冰,水鸟群(等)。4.【动】(昆虫的)卵筏。*on a* ~〔美俚〕以烤面包垫底 (*Adam and Eve on a* ~ 烤面包垫底炒蛋)。**II** *vt*. 1. 把(木料等)编成筏子。2. 筏运(木材等);用筏子航行。— *vi*. 乘筏子去;使用筏子。

raft[2] [rɑːft; ræft] *n*.〔美口〕大量。*a ~ of trouble* 很多麻烦。

raft·er[1] [ˈrɑːftə; ˋræftɚ] **I** *n*.【建】椽。*an angle* ~ 角椽。***from cellar to*** ~ 遍屋子,屋里到处。**II** *vt*. 1. 给…装椽子。2. 把(木材)作成椽子。3.〔英〕犁(地)使草泥等顺着一边堆成畦。

raft·er[2] [ˈrɑːftə; ˋræftɚ] *n*. 筏夫,撑木排的人。

rafts·man [ˈrɑːftsmən; ˋræftsmən] *n*. (*pl*. **-men** [-men; -mɛn]) = rafter[2].

rag[1] [ræg; ræg] *n*. 1. 破布,烂布,碎布;破碎帆布;擦布,抹布。2.〔蔑、谑〕(破旧的)手帕,旗子,帐篷,小块风帆;报纸,钞票,衣服(等);〔*pl*.〕破烂的衣裳,〔美俚〕衣服。3. 少量。4.〔美俚〕卑劣的人。5.〔口〕= ragtime. 6. (橘子的)橘络。7.〔the R-〕〔英俚〕陆军[海军]俱乐部。*a ~ of cloud* 一片残云。*There is not a ~ of evidence*. 毫无证据。*He has not a ~ to his back*. 他衣不蔽体。~ *currency* [*money*] 纸币。***chew the*** ~〔美俚〕嚼舌头;发牢骚。**(*be*) *cooked to ~s*** 煮得稀烂。***glad ~s***〔口〕(个人所有的)最好的一套衣服。***in ~s*** 成碎片;穿着破衣服 (*go in ~s* 服装破烂,穿着破烂衣服)。***It was like a ~ to a bull***. 像拿红布给牛看一样(越发使它发火)。***part brass ~s with sb***.〔俚〕不再同某人保持亲密关系,同某人疏远了。***spread every ~ of sail*** 挂起所有的风帆。***take the ~ off***〔美〕强过,超过。***torn to ~s*** 被撕碎。***without a*** ~ 分文没有。~**-and-boneman** 收买破烂东西的。~ **baby** 碎片做成玩具娃娃。~ **bag** 放破布的袋,破烂(东西)。~ **cutting** (烟叶的)切丝。~ **doll** = ~ baby. ~ **fair** 旧货市场,旧衣市场。~**man** 收买破布废纸的人;拾破布废纸的人;〔废〕恶魔。~**-rolling** 布滚油漆法〔用布上漆以达到特定表面效果的一种室内装饰艺术〕。~ **paper** (破布制的)优质纸。~ **picker** 拾破布废纸的人。~**rug** 碎呢(拼成的)地毯。~**s-rock**〔美口〕拉格摇摆舞乐。~**tag (and bobtail)**〔俚〕〔集合词〕衣服褴褛的人们;下层社会;乌合之众。~**-time** 1.【美乐】(1890~1915 年间流行的)切分乐曲〔大量采用黑人音乐,旋律采用切分法 (syncopation) 作成,以节奏迅速,拍子清楚为特色,可称为最早的爵士音乐〕;爵士音乐[舞蹈]。2. *a*. 可笑的,滑稽的;无忧无虑的。~ **top**〔美俚〕敞篷汽车。~ **trade**〔美俚〕制衣工业。~**-waggon**〔蔑〕帆船。~**weed**【植】豚草属植物。~ **wheel** 抛光布轮。~**wort**【植】千里光属植物。

rag[2] [ræg; ræg] **I** *vt*. (**-gg-**)〔英俚〕1. 糟蹋,欺负;骂。2. 愚弄,逗,撩,惹;开玩笑。— *vi*. 1. 吵闹,扰嚷。2. 指

责,欺负人。3. 瞎开玩笑。II *n*. 〔俚〕(大学生等的)顽皮,开玩笑,恶作剧;嚷闹。*I only said it for a* ～. 我不过是说笑罢了。

rag³ [ræg; ræg] *n*. 石板瓦;〔英〕(可作成石板瓦的)石炭页岩。

ra·ga [ˈrɑːgə; ˋrægə] *n*. 拉迦〔印度的一些传统曲调,具备特有的音程、韵律和装饰音等,常用以作即席演奏[唱]〕。

rag·a·bash [ˈrægəbæʃ; ˋrægə͵bæʃ] *n*. 不中用的人,废物;乌合之众。

rag·a·muf·fin [ˈrægəˌmʌfin; ˋrægə͵mʌfɪn] *n*. 1. 衣服褴褛的人;流浪儿童。2. 【鸟】山雀。

rag·a-zine [͵rægˈziːn;͵rægˋzin] *n*. 小报。

rag·bolt [ˈrægbəult; ˋræg͵bolt] *n*. 【机】棘螺栓。

rage [reidʒ; redʒ] I *n*. 1. 愤激,愤怒。2. 激烈,猛烈;(风等的)狂暴。3. 热望,渴望;热心,热狂,疯狂;〔口〕战争狂。4. 〔古〕(诗人、预言者等的)灵感,热情;(音乐的)兴奋。5. (战时精神的)昂扬,热烈。6. 〔口〕狂欢作乐(的聚会)。7. (行动的)白热化。8. 〔口〕时兴东西。*the* ～ *of the wind* 风的狂暴。*the* ～ *of hunger* 非常饿。**be (all) the** ～ 大流行,风靡一时 (*Table tennis became all the* ～ *from then*. 从那时以来乒乓球就流行起来)。***burst into a*** ～ ***of tears*** [***grief***] 嚎啕大哭。***fly into a*** ～ 勃然大怒。***have a*** ～ ***for*** 对…具有狂热爱好。***in a*** ～ 一怒之下。II *vi*. 1. 发怒 (*at*; *upon*; *against*)。2. 发狂;(发狂)大嚷大叫。3. 〔Scot.〕大骂。4. 放肆,尽情做;狂欢作乐;(风)狂吹,(浪)汹涌;(疫病等)猖獗,(战争)猛烈进行;大流行,风行。— *vt*. 使怒;使狂暴。～ *oneself* 狂暴起来。～ *itself out* (暴风雨等)平息下来。

rag·ged [ˈrægid; ˋrægɪd] *a*. 1. (衣衫等)破烂的,褴褛的;穷相毕露的。2. 外形参差不齐的,凹凸不平的;(毛、发)乱蓬蓬的;粗糙的。3. 不调和的;刺耳的。4. 不完善的,有缺点的。*a* ～ *sheep* 乱羊毛。*a* ～ *hip* (瘦马的)骨架突露的臀部。～ *sounds* 刺耳的声音。***on the*** ～ ***edge*** 〔美〕在危险状态中,在穷困[失败]的边缘。～ **robin** 【植】布谷鸟剪秋罗。～ **school** 〔英古〕贫民学校。～ **time** (赛艇划法或训练中的)不齐整。**-ly** *ad*. **-ness** *n*.

rag·ged·y [ˈrægidi; ˋrægədɪ] *a*. 有点破烂的,不大完整的,褴褛样的。

rag·ger [ˈrægə; ˋrægɚ] *n*. 1. 〔英口〕恶作剧者;胡闹者。2. 〔美俚〕新闻记者。

rag·gie [ˈrægiː; ˋrægi] *n*. 〔水手俚〕非常友好[亲密]的朋友。

rag·ging [ˈrægiŋ; ˋrægɪŋ] *n*. 〔口〕欺负;开玩笑,恶作剧,(学生的)胡闹。

rag·gle-tag·gle [ˈræglˈtægl; ˋrægl͵tægl] *a*. 1. (衣衫等)破烂的。2. (节目等)七拼八凑的;混杂的。

rag·gy [ˈrægi; ˋrægɪ] *a*. 〔美俚〕不公平的,不正当的。

rag·i, rag·gee, rag·gy [ˈrægiː; ˋrægi] *n*. 【植】龙爪稷(穇子,鸭脚粟) (*Eleusine coracana*) 〔产于非洲和印度,其粟可食〕。

rag·ing [ˈreidʒiŋ; ˋredʒɪŋ] *a*. 发怒的,愤怒的;狂暴的;猛烈的,猖獗的。**-ly** *ad*.

Rag·lan [ˈræglən; ˋræglən] *n*. 拉格伦〔姓氏〕。

rag·lan [ˈræglən; ˋræglən] *n*. (袖缝直达领部的)拉格伦式[套袖]大衣。

ra·gout [ˈræguː; ræˋgu] I *n*. 【烹】浓味蔬菜炖肉。II *vt*. (***-gout·ed*** [-ˈguːd; -ˋgud]; ***-gout·ing*** [-guːiŋ; -guɪŋ]) 把…做成浓味蔬菜炖肉。

rah [rɑː; rɑ] *int*. = hurrah.

ra·hat la·koum [ˈrɑːhæt ləˈkuːm; ˋrɑhæt læˋkum] *n*. 土耳其甜糕饼。

rah-rah [ˈrɑːˈrɑː; ˋrɑˋrɑ] I *a*. 〔美口〕1. (在大学足球赛中)热烈喝彩的,啦啦队的。2. 大学(生)的。II *n*. 〔美俚〕传统的大学生精神。～ **skirts** 〔美〕啦啦队超短裙〔一种荷叶边超短裙,女啦啦队员的流行服装〕。

raid [reid; red] I *n*. 1. (骑兵队等的)急袭,袭击;突击;(军舰等的)游击;(盗贼、狐等的)侵入。2. (警察的)抄查,围捕。*an air* ～ 空袭。*a* ～ *on a bank* 抢劫银行。*make a* ～ *into* 侵入,袭击。*make a* ～ *on* [*upon*] 抄查,围捕。II *vt*., *vi*. 攻入,袭击 (*into*);(警察)抄查,围捕 (*on*; *upon*)。～ ***the market*** (散布谣言等)搅乱市面以便卖出股票等。**~ing party** 【军】挺进队,突击队。

Raids = recently acquired income deficiency syndrom 〔谑〕近期获得收入缺损综合症〔指近期个人收入锐减,仿 aids 艾滋病一词创造出的幽默用语〕。

raid·er [ˈreidə; ˋredɚ] *n*. 袭击者;侵入者;抄查员;(市场的)扰乱者。

rail¹ [reil; rel] I *n*. 1. (围栏等的)横木,横档;(钉帽架等用的)横条,栏杆,扶手;〔*pl*.〕围栏。2. 轨道;钢轨;铁路;〔*pl*.〕铁路股票。*a towel* ～ (钉在墙上的)挂毛巾的横木。*a* ～ *advice* (铁路)到货通知单。*zero-length* ～ 【火箭】超短型导轨。**by** ～ 乘火车,用火车。***get*** [***go***] ***off the*** **~s** 出轨;越轨。***off the*** **~s** 出轨;扰乱秩序;〔喻〕发狂;越轨 (*He is a very reliable person*; *he has never gone off the* **~s**. 他这人十分可靠,从来不越轨逾矩)。***ride*** (***sb***.) ***on a*** ～ 〔美〕(把人)捆在横杆上抬着赶走〔一种私刑〕。***run off the*** **~s** 出轨,脱轨。II *vt*. 1. 用围栏围 (*in*; *off*),用栏杆围住,装栏杆于。2. 在…铺铁轨;用铁路运输。— *vi*. 坐火车旅行。～ **car** 单节机动有轨车。～ **chair** (铁路的)轨座。～ **fence** 栅栏,篱墙。～ **man** 铁路员工,(装卸货时打信号的)码头工人。～-**motor** 1. *n*. 【铁路】摩托交通车,摩托客车。2. *a*. 铁路公路联运的。

rail² [reil; rel] *n*. 【动】秧鸡。

rail³ [reil; rel] *vi*. 咒骂,责备;抱怨 (*against*; *at*)。

rail·age [ˈreilidʒ; ˋrelɪdʒ] *n*. 铁路运费;铁路运输。

rail·head [ˈreilhed; ˋrel͵hɛd] *n*. 【铁路】轨道终点;【军】军需品的铁路运输终点[兵站基点]。

rail·ing¹ [ˈreiliŋ; ˋrelɪŋ] *n*. 栏杆;围栏,栅栏;扶手;做栏杆用的木料。

rail·ing² [ˈreiliŋ; ˋrelɪŋ] *n*., *a*. 咒骂(的);责备(的);抱怨(的)。

rail·ler·y [ˈreiləri; ˋrelərɪ] *n*. 挖苦,讥笑。

rail·road [ˈreilrəud; ˋrel͵rod] I *n*. 〔美〕1. 铁路。★英国说 railway; 市内轻轨铁路美国也说 railway。2. 【火箭】轨道设备,滑轨装置。3. (包含车辆、房产、建筑物等说的)铁路设施;铁路公司;〔集合词〕铁路员工。*a* ～ *bridge* 铁路桥梁。*a* ～ *car* 铁路车辆。*a* ～ *carriage* (铁路)客车车厢。*a* ～ *train* 火车列车。*a* ～ *fare* 火车费。*a* ～ *tariff* 火车运费。*a* ～ *stock* 〔美〕铁路股票。*a* ～ *tie* (铁路)枕木。～ *trousers* 〔美军俚〕有金线条的裤子。II *vt*. 1. 在…铺设铁路;用铁路运输。2. 〔美口〕急急忙忙送去;使(议案等)草草通过。3. 捏造罪证拘禁。— *vi*. 1. 在铁路上服务。2. 坐火车旅行。～ **flat** (没有各间分别进出的走廊的)一间接一间的套房,列车式套房。～ **spike** 铁路道钉。～ **worm** 苹果蝇蛆(一种果实害虫)的俗名。**-er** 〔美〕铁路职工;铁路铺设技术员;坐火车旅行的人。**-ing** 1. 铁路建设事业[工程]。2. 铁路经营管理。3. 〔美俚〕仓猝完成。

rail-split·ter [ˈreilˌsplitə; ˋrel͵splɪtɚ] *n*. 将木头截成横木的人。***The Rail-Splitter*** 林肯的绰号。

rail·way [ˈreilwei; ˋrel͵we] I *n*. 1. 〔英〕铁路;铁路系统,铁道部门。2. 〔美〕(市内)轻轨(铁路)。*an aerial* ～ 高架铁道。*a broad-gauge* [*narrow-gauge*] ～ 阔轨[狭轨]铁路。*a high level* [*a surface*, *an underground*, *a submarine*] ～ 高架[地上,地下,海底]铁路。*a* ～ *accident* 铁路事故。*a* ～ *engine* 机车,火车头。*a* ～ *man* 铁路员工。*a* ～ *novel* (坐火车旅行时看的)轻松小说。*a* ～ *porter* (车站上的)搬运工;〔美〕卧车服务员。*a* ～ *rug* 火车旅行用绒毯。*a* ～ *station* 火车站。*a* ～ *suboffice* 铁路分局〔略 R.S.O.〕。II *vi*.

R

〔英〕坐火车旅行。— *vt*. 在…铺设铁路。~ **letter**〔英〕由铁道部门运送的信件。~ **market**〔英〕铁道股票交易。~ **sleeper** [**tie**]（铁路）枕木。

rai·ment [ˈreimənt; ˋremənt] ***n***.〔诗〕衣服。

rain[1] [rein; ren] **I** ***n***. **1**. 雨，下雨；〔*pl*.〕阵雨。**2**. 雨天；〔the ~s〕(热带地方的)雨季；〔the ~s〕大西洋北纬 4—10 度的多雨地带。**3**.（雨一样的）降落物。**4**.〔俚〕电子流。*a drizzling* ~ 细雨。*fine* ~ 毛毛雨。*a heavy* [*light*] ~ 大[小]雨。*It looks like* ~. 像要下雨。***a* ~ *of*** (*ashes*, *tears*, *blows*, *kisses*)（下雨一样的）一阵(灰，眼泪，打击，吻)。***in the*** ~ 在雨中，冒着雨。~ ***or shine*** 无论晴雨，风雨无阻；必然地；确定不疑地。**II** ***vi***. 下雨〔通例用 it 为主语〕；雨一般地落下。*It* ~*s in*.（房屋）漏雨；雨飘进来。*It has* ~*ed over*. 雨停了。*It never* ~*s but it pours*. 不下则已，一下倾盆；〔喻〕祸不单行；发生大灾祸。— ***vt***. 使像雨一样地落下；厚施(恩惠等)。*It* ~*s blood*. 血流如注。*Her eyes* ~*ed tears*. 她泪下如雨。~ *benefits upon sb*. 给(某人)很大恩惠。~ ***off***〔英〕= ~ *out*. ~ **out** 因下雨阻碍，因下雨而取消(*The meeting was* ~*ed out*. 大会因雨停开)。~**band** 雨带〔太阳光谱中黄色部份的黑带〕。~**bow 1**. 虹。**2**.〔美俚〕美妙的梦想。**3**. 五彩药片[药丸]〔一种巴比妥类安眠药〕(= ~bow pill)（*all the colours of the* ~*bow* 种种颜色。*a primary* ~*bow* 虹。*a secondary* ~*bow* 霓。*a* ~*bow trout* 虹鳟鱼)。~**bow coalition** 彩虹联盟〔少数派结成的联盟〕。~ **box**【剧】雨声装置，雨声箱。~ **cap** 雨帽。~ **cape** 雨披。~ **check**〔美〕(比赛因雨停止时的)留待下次补看比赛的票根；〔美俚〕延期举行；顺延；死刑的改为无期徒刑（*Since you can't join us for dinner*, *we'll give you a* ~ *check*. 既然您不能和我们一起参加宴会，我们就延期举行了)。~ **cloud** 雨云。~**cloth** 防雨布。~**coat** 雨衣。~ **doctor** 祈雨法师。~**drop** 雨滴。~**fall** 下雨，雨量。~ **forest**（热带多雨地区茂密的)雨林。~ **gauge** 雨量计。~ **glass** 晴雨表。~**maker 1**. = **rain doctor**〔美空俚〕气象学家。**2**.〔美俚〕"呼风唤雨者"〔指有特殊背景、能招揽到大生意的经理等〕。~**-making** 人工降雨。~ **out**（比赛、表演因雨）中断；暂停；(对大气尘埃的)冲洗，消除。~**proof 1**. ***a***. 防雨的，不透雨的。**2**. ***n***.〔英〕雨衣。**3**. ***vt***. 使能防雨。~ **room**〔俚〕淋浴室。~ **shadow**（山坡背面降雨极少的)雨影区。~ **sprout 1**. 水落管，排水口。**2**. 海龙卷，龙卷风卷起的水柱。~**-storm** 暴风雨。~**tight** ***a***. = rainproof. ~ **wash** 雨水的冲刷；被雨水冲走的东西。~**water** 雨水。~**wear** 防雨布。~**worm 1**. 蚯蚓。**2**.【医】耙行疹。**-less** ***a***.

rain·i·ness [ˈreininis; ˋrenɪnɪs] ***n***. 多雨。

rain·y [ˈreini; ˋrenɪ] ***a***. (*rain·i·er*; *-i·est*) 下雨的，常下雨的，多雨的，含雨的；像要下雨的。*a* ~ *day* 雨天；萧条[遭难，穷困]的时候；万一的时候（*save* [*lay up*] *against a* ~ *day* 以备万一，未雨绸缪)。*a* ~ *season* 雨季。*a* ~ *district* 多雨地区。*a* ~ *street* 雨天的湿淋淋街道。

raise [reiz; rez] **I** ***vt***. **1**. 抬起，举起(重物等)；升(旗等)；使起立，竖起(柱子等)；捞起，打捞(沉船)。**2**. 建造，建立(纪念碑等)，造起(房子)；使(雕刻物上的形象等)浮起，凸起。**3**. 踢起，扬起(灰尘等)，溅起(泥)，喷起(烟)；(用酵母等)使膨起；【纺】把(布)拉绒，使起绒。**4**. 抬高(价钱、租金)；增高(温度)；提高(声音)；叫起。**5**. 提升，加薪；使事业成功；使上进；(一朝有事时)使(市民、国民等)奋起。**6**. 引起，掀起(动乱、悲剧等)；惹起，使发(笑等)；提起，提出(问题、异议等)。**7**. 征收(捐税等)，征(兵)，招集；筹(款等)。**8**. 栽培，种植，出产(谷类等)；饲养(家畜等)；养育，教育(子女)。**9**.【军】解除(包围或封锁)。**10**.【海】(指船只航近而)使(陆地等)渐渐出现。**11**.【数】使自乘。**12**. 使复活，叫醒，提醒；使出现。**13**.〔美〕任命。**14**.〔美〕增加(赌注)。*Not a voice was* ~*d in opposition*. 一声反对都没有。~ *the white flag* 举[升]起白旗投降。~ *one's eyes* 抬眼观看，仰视。~ *a private from the ranks* 把一个列兵提升为下士。~ *one's spirits* 打起精神。~ *a smile* [*blush*] 使微笑[脸红]。~ *money* 筹款。~ *cloth* 把布起绒毛。*A deliverer was* ~*d up*. 救星(突然)出现。*Where was he* ~*d*? 他是在哪儿长大的？*stock raising* 家畜饲养。*late raising* 抑制栽培。— ***vi***. **1**. 起身，立起。**2**. 升高。**3**.〔口〕咳出痰。**4**. 提高赌注[叫价]。***be* ~*d in the barn*** 缺乏教养，粗野无礼。~ ***a check***〔美〕涂改支票[增加金额]。~ ***a dust*** 扬起灰尘；引起骚动；瞒人眼目。~ ***Cain*** [***hell***, ***the devil***, ***the mischief***]〔俚〕引起风波，闹出问题。~ ***colour*** 改染。~ ***oneself*** 长高；发迹，露头角。~ ***one's glass to*** 为(某人)举杯祝酒。~ ***one's hat*** 举帽行礼。~ ***one's head*** 抬一抬头(表示在座)。~ ***one's voice* 1**. 在人群中发言（*No one* ~*d his voice*. 一个不响)。**2**. 提高嗓子说；(愤怒着)提高声音。~ ***one's voice against*** 向…抗议。~ ***sand***〔美〕起风潮，惹出事情。~ ***the ante*** [ˈænti; ˋæntɪ]〔美〕提价。~ ***the city against*** [***upon***] 发动市民抵抗。~ ***the colours***〔美〕走漏计划。~ ***the lid***〔美俚〕熟视无睹，放松禁令。~ ***the roof***〔美俚〕引起风波；大声叫喊，吵闹。~ ***the wind*** 起风波；〔喻〕筹款。~ ***to a*** [***third***] ***power*** 使自乘[自乘到三次幂]。**II** ***n***.〔美〕**1**. 升起，抬起；登高。**2**.（道路等的)高起处，隆起处；【矿】天井。**3**. 增加；加价；加薪，加赌注。**4**.〔俚〕(钱等的)筹措；筹募。*make a* ~ 筹办；筹款，凑钱。

raised [reizd; rezd] ***a***. **1**. 加高了的；凸起的，浮雕的；发过酵的，鼓起的，高起的。**2**.〔美〕受过教育的。*a* ~ *bottom*（升、斗等的)垫高了的底。~ *tissue* 起毛布。*a* ~ *beach*（因冲积而)上升的海滩。*a book in* ~ *type* 凸字书，点字书。~ *work* 浮雕工艺。*a* ~ *cheque* 涂改过的(金额增大了的)支票。~ *pastry* 发面点心。*a* ~ *pie* 发面饼。

rais·er [ˈreizə; ˋrezɚ] ***n***. **1**. 举起者，提出者，提高者(等)。**2**.（资金等的)筹集者。**3**. 饲养者，栽培者。**4**.（面包厂等的)发酵工人；酵母。

rai·sin [ˈreizn; ˋrezn] ***n***. **1**.〔常 *pl*.〕(无核)葡萄干。**2**. 闪光紫蓝色。~ **tree**【植】枳椇。

rai·son d'é·tat [rezɔŋ deˈtɑ; rɛzɑŋ dɛˋtɑ]〔F.〕外交理由，政治理由。

rai·son d'être [F. ˈreiz ɔːn ˈdeitr; ˋrezɔn ˋdɛt]〔F.〕存在的理由。

rai·son·né [F. rɛzɔnei; ˏrɛˏzɔˋne] ***a***.〔F.〕合理[有组织地]排列的，分门别类的。*a catalogue* ~ 分类目录。

raj [rɑːdʒ; rɑdʒ] ***n***.〔印〕主权，支配，统治。

Ra·jab [rəˈdʒæb; rəˋdʒæb] ***n***.（伊斯兰教历)七月。

ra·ja(h) [ˈrɑːdʒə; ˋrɑdʒə] ***n***.〔Hind.〕(印度等的)邦主，王公；(马来亚的)酋长。

Ra·ja·stha·ni [ˌrɑːdʒəsˈtɑːni; ˏrɑdʒəsˋtɑnɪ] ***n***.〔Hind.〕拉贾斯坦语。

Raj·put, **Raj·poot** [ˈrɑːdʒput; ˋrɑdʒput] ***n***. 拉其普特人〔自称是刹帝利（Kshatriya）后裔的印度北部一民族〕。

rake[1] [reik; rek] **I** ***n***. **1**. 耙子；耙地机。**2**. 火钩，火拨。**3**.【林】流材挡栅。*a horse* ~ 马拉耙。**II** ***vt***. **1**. 用耙子耙拢，用耙子耙；耙除，扫除（*off*）；耙到一块（*up*; *together*）；〔废〕在(种子等上)盖上土；〔方〕用土压(火)。**2**. 遍搜，到处找；探讨。**3**. 掠过，擦过。**4**. 看透；俯瞰，眺望。**5**.【军】扫射，纵射。— ***vi***. **1**. 用耙子工作。**2**. 搜求，到处找（*in*; *into*; *among*）；拼命收集。***as lean*** [***thin***] ***as a*** ~ 瘦得只有皮包骨头。~ ***among*** [***in***, ***into***] ***old records*** 翻查古老记录[文献等]。~ ***and scrape*** 拼命攒钱[搜刮]。~ ***down***〔美〕申斥。~ ***in the dough***〔美〕发财。~ ***out* 1**. 搜集(情报)。**2**.（把火)耙出；扫除。~ ***over the coals***〔美俚〕责骂。~ ***up* 1**. 搜集；搜出，挑剔出来。**2**. 压灭(火)。

rake[2] [reik; rek] **I** ***n***. **1**.【海】船首[船尾]的突出部分；船尾柱；舵前部的倾斜；(桅、烟囱等)向船尾方向的倾斜

(度)。2.【矿】罅隙;倾侧;斜脉,【空】倾度。II *vi*.(桅杆、烟囱等)倾斜。— *vt*. 使(桅杆等)向后倾斜。

rake[3] [reik; rek] I *n*. 荡子,浪子。II *vi*. 放荡,游荡。III *a*. 放荡的,淫乱的,无赖的。~ **hell**〔古〕荡子,游荡儿,浪子;无赖。~**-off**〔美俚〕(通常指不合法的)利益;油水;佣金,手续费,回扣(等)。

rak·er [ˈreikə; ˋrekɚ] *n*. 1. 用耙子耙的人;耙地机。2. 清道夫;【军】纵射炮。3.〔美俚〕大胆的人。

ra·ki, ra·kee [rɑːˈki, ˈræki; rəˋkɪ, ˋrækɪ] *n*. (用葡萄汁制成的)拉基烧酒。

rak·ish[1] [ˈreikiʃ; ˋrekɪʃ] *a*. 1.【海】(像海盗船一样)轻快的。2. 时髦的,漂亮的。**-ly** *ad*.

rak·ish[2] [ˈreikiʃ; ˋrekɪʃ] *a*. 放荡的,游荡的。**-ly** *ad*.

râle, rale [rɑːl; rɑl] *n*.〔F.〕【医】(肺的)水泡音;罗音;(临死时的)喉鸣。

Ra·le(i)gh[1] [ˈrɔːli; ˋrɔlɪ] *n*. 1. 罗利〔姓氏,男子名〕。2. **Sir Walter** ~ 罗利爵士〔1552? —1618,英国政治家,历史家〕。

Ra·le(i)gh[2] [ˈrɔːli; ˋrɔlɪ] *n*. 罗利〔美国北卡罗来纳州首府〕。

rall. = rallentando [rælenˈtændəu; ˏrælənˋtændo] *a*., *ad*.〔It.〕【乐】渐慢。

ral·li·car(t) [ˈrælikɑː, -kɑːt; ˋrælɪˏkɑr, -kɑr(t)] *n*.〔英〕(四人坐)二轮小马车。

Rall's Janet [ˈrɔːlz ˈdʒænit; ˋrɔlz ˋdʒænɪt]〔美〕一种晚熟耐藏的苹果。

ral·ly[1] [ˈræli; ˋrælɪ] I *vt*. (*-lied, -ly·ing*) 1. 召集,纠合,团结。2. 重整(队伍);挽回(颓势)。2. 振奋(精神);集中(力量);恢复(元气);激励。~ *world opinion against nuclear weapons* 重新调动世界舆论反对核武器。~ *one's followers to action* 纠合追随者行动起来。*They rallied their energies for the counter-attack*. 他们奋起反攻。— *vi*. 1. 重行集合;挽回颓势,重整旗鼓;恢复气力。2.【网球】(将球)打回去。~ *from an illness* 病愈恢复。~ *in price* 物价回升。~ *round* 聚集在…的周围,团结在…的周围。II *n*. 1. 重新集合;挽回颓势,重新振作;恢复气力。2.〔美口〕群众大会[集会];示威行动。3.【网球】连续打回。4. 汽车竞赛。~ **cross**(环绕短跑道进行的)汽车赛场比赛。~ **master** 汽车竞赛的组织者[指挥者]。~**ing cry** 战斗口号,呐喊。~**ing point** 振作点,恢复点。**-ist** 参加汽车竞赛者。

ral·ly[2] [ˈræli; ˋrælɪ] *n*., *vt*., *vi*. (*-lied*; *-ly·ing*) 嘲笑,挖苦。

Ralph [reif, rælf; ref, rælf] *n*. 拉尔夫〔男子名〕。

R.A.M. = Royal Academy of Music〔英〕皇家音乐学院。

RAM = random-access memory【计】随机存取存储器〔数据存取可随意选择的电脑存储器〕。

ram [ræm; ræm] I *n*. 1. (没有阉过的)公羊;〔R-〕【天】白羊宫。2. (从前攻城用的)撞墙车;撞角〔装在军舰舰首的铁嘴〕;有撞角的军舰;【建】(打桩用的)撞槌;夯槌。3.【机】作动筒;(压力机的)压头,速度头;压力扬吸机;活塞。*a* ~ *cat*〔英方〕公猫。*a* ~ *compartment*【海】舰首隔室。*a* ~ *engine* 打桩机。~ *jet* 冲压喷气(发动机)。***milk the*** ~ 做徒劳无益的事。II *vt*. (*-mm-*) 1. 用撞墙车撞;用撞角撞;撞 (*against*; *at*; *on*; *into*)。2. 撞入;打入 (*down*; *in*; *into*);撞倒;把(地)夯固;(用通条)把(火药)填进(枪炮)(*with*);坚持推行;迫使别人接受,灌输。~ *one's head against a wall* 把头撞在墙壁上。~ ***the argument home*** 反复说明论旨使充分了解。~ ***up***【火箭】向上运送,用起重机吊起。~**-raid** 1. *n*. 飞车闯入(商店等)的抢劫。2. *vt*.(飞车)闯入…并进行抢劫。

Ram·a·dan [ˌræməˈdɑːn; ˏræməˋdɑn] *n*. = ramazan.

Ra·man [ˈrɑːmən; ˋrɑmən] *n*. 拉曼〔姓氏〕。

ra·mark [ˈreimɑːk; ˋremɑrk] *n*.【无】雷达指点标〔连续发射脉冲,为 radar marker 的缩合词〕。

Ra·ma·ya·na [rɑˈmaiənɑ, rɑˈmɑːjənə; rɑˋmaɪənɑ, rɑˋmɑjənə] *n*.《罗摩衍那》〔印度古代梵语叙事诗〕。

Ram·a·zan [ræməˈzɑːn; ræməˋzɑn] *n*.【伊斯兰教】莱麦丹月,斋月〔伊斯兰教教历太阴年第九月莱麦丹月禁食戒斋〕。

ram·ble [ˈræmbl; ˋræmbl̩] I *n*. 1. 漫步;散步;徘徊。2.〔罕〕漫谈,闲谈。***on*** [***upon***] ***the*** ~ 在散步。II *vi*. 1. 漫步,散步 (*about*, *over*);徘徊。2. 闲聊天,漫谈;写随笔。3. (草木等)蔓延。~ ***on*** 长谈。— *vt*. 在…上漫步。*He spent the morning rambling woodland paths*. 他一上午在林间小径漫步。

ram·bler [ˈræmblə; ˋræmblɚ] *n*. 1. 漫步者。2. 漫谈者。3.【植】蔓生植物;攀缘蔷薇;〔the R-〕(十八世纪 Dr. Samual Johnson 主办的)《漫步者》(双周刊)。

ram·bling [ˈræmbliŋ; ˋræmblɪŋ] *a*. 1. 漫步的。2. (谈话)不着边际的,漫无限制的;(思想等)散漫的;(生活等)放浪的。3. (房屋、街市等)不规则的,不整齐的。4.【植】攀缘的。

Ram·bo [ˈræmbəu; ˋræmbo] *n*. 兰博;兰博式的英雄人物〔美国作家 David Morrell 所著小说《第一滴血》(First Blood)中的主人公,孔武有力的孤胆英雄〕。*a* ~ *killer* 兰博式杀手。**-ism** *n*. 兰博主义〔指凭借个人本领以暴力达到目的的做法〕。

Ram·bouil·let [ˈræmbəˌlei, F. rɑ̃buiˈjɛ; ˋræmbəˏle, rɑ̃bʊɪˋjɛ] *n*.【动】(法国)兰勃羊。

ram·bunc·tious [ræmˈbʌŋkʃəs; ræmˋbʌŋkʃəs] *a*.〔美俚〕粗暴的,蛮横的,无法无天的。

ram·bu·tan [ræmˈbuːtn; ræmˋbutn̩] *n*.【植】红毛丹树 (*Nephelium lappaceum*)〔产于马来亚〕;红毛丹果。

R.A.M.C., RAMC = Royal Army Medical Corps〔英〕皇家陆军军医队。

ram·e·kin, ram·e·quin [ˈræmkin; ˋræməkɪn] *n*. 1. 干酪蛋糕〔以乳酪面包屑,鸡蛋等烘烤而成的食品〕。2. 烘烤干酪蛋糕用的烤盘。

ra·men·tum [rəˈmentəm; rəˋmɛntəm] *n*. (*pl*. *-ta* [-tə; -tə])【植】小鳞片。

ra·mi [ˈreimai; ˋremaɪ] *n*. ramus 的复数。

ram·ie, ram·ee [ˈræmi; ˋræmɪ] *n*.【植】苎麻。

ram·i·fi·ca·tion [ˌræmifiˈkeiʃən; ˏræməfəˋkeʃən] *n*. 1. 分枝,分叉;分歧;分裂;分枝状;分枝式;分枝法。2. 支流,支派;分派;区分,门类。3. 衍生物;结果,后果。

ram·i·form [ˈræmiˌfɔːm; ˋræməˏfɔrm] *a*. 枝形的,枝状的。

ram·i·fy [ˈræmifai; ˋræməˏfaɪ] *vt*. (*-fied*; *-fy·ing*)〔常用被动结构〕使分枝,使分叉;分派;使交错。*Railways are ramified over the country*. 铁路线分布全国。— *vi*. 生枝,分叉;被分派,分歧;交错。~ *into a labyrinth* 分枝成迷宫状。

ram-jet en·gine [ˈræmdʒetˈendʒin; ˋræmdʒɛtˋɛndʒɪn]【空】冲压式喷气发动机。

ram·mer [ˈræmə; ˋræmɚ] *n*. 1. 使用夯槌等的人。2. 撞槌;夯槌;(枪炮)通条,装填器。3.〔美俚〕臂膊。

ram·mish [ˈræmiʃ; ˋræmɪʃ] *a*. 1. 公羊一般的。2. 臭气强烈的,膻臊的;气味浓烈的。3. 好色的。

Ra·mon [rəˈməun, ˈreimən; rəˋmon, ˋremən] *n*. 雷蒙〔男子名,Raymond 的异体〕。

Ra·mo·na [rəˈməunə; rəˋmonə] *n*. 雷蒙娜〔女子名〕。

ra·mose [rəˈməus; rəˋmos], **ra·mous** [ˈreiməs; ˋreməs] *a*. 生了枝的,多枝的;枝状的。

ramp[1] [ræmp; ræmp] I *vt*. 1.【纹】(狮子等)用后脚直立;作恫吓姿势;猛扑;暴跳,乱冲。2.【植】(植物)繁茂。II *n*. (纹章上狮子等的)猛扑姿势;〔口〕愤怒。

ramp[2] [ræmp; ræmp] I *vt*.【建】在…设斜面[斜路、坡];把…弄弯曲(使适于倾斜)。— *vi*. 减少,降低。II *n*. 1. (连结高低互异的两条十字路的)坡道,斜路;(筑城)斜坡。2. 倾斜装置,斜轨;【建】楼梯扶手的弯斜部分。3.【讯】接线夹,接线端钮。4.【空】(客机的)舷梯。

ramp[3][ræmp; ræmp]〔英俚〕**I** *vt*. 向(…)索取高价,诈骗,诈取。**II** *n*. 诈骗,索高价。

ramp[4][ræmp; ræmp] *n*.【植】北美野韭 (*Allium tricoccum*)。

ramp·act·or [ˈræmpæktə; ˋræmpæktɚ] *n*. 跳击夯。

ramp·age [ræmˈpeidʒ; ˋræmpedʒ] **I** *n*. (因发怒等)暴跳;狂暴行为。*be* [*go*] *on the* ~ 暴跳如雷,狂怒,处于极端愤激状态。**II** *vi*. 暴跳,暴怒。

ram·pa·geous [ræmˈpeidʒəs; ræmˋpedʒəs] *a*. 暴跳的,暴怒的,狂暴的。

ram·pan·cy [ˈræmpənsi; ˋræmpənsɪ] *n*. (疾病等的)蔓延;猖獗;繁茂;(狮子等用后脚的)跳起,直立。

ram·pant [ˈræmpənt; ˋræmpənt] *a*. **1**. (兽类)跳起的;直立的;【纹】(狮子)跳起用后脚直立着的。**2**. 蔓延的;猖狂的,猖獗一时的;激烈的;暴怒的;(植物)繁茂的。*a lion* ~【纹】跃立狮形。~ *gardant*【纹】朝正面用后脚站立着的。~ *regardant*【纹】用后脚站立着头往后面看的。**-ly** *ad*.

ram·part [ˈræmpɑːt; ˋræmpɑrt] **I** *n*. 堡垒,壁垒,城墙,防御物。**II** *vt*. 用堡垒[城墙]围绕,筑城围住;防御,保护。

ram·pike [ˈræmpaik; ˋræmˌpaɪk] *n*.〔加拿大〕高大的死树(尤指被火烧黑了的无枝的树)。

ram·pi·on [ˈræmpjən; ˋræmpɪən] *n*.【植】匍匐风铃草。

ramps [ræmps; ræmps] *n*. = ramp[3].

ram·rod [ˈræmrɔd; ˋræmˌrɑd] *n*. **1**. (火药枪的)通条,推弹杆;洗杆。**2**.〔俚〕瘦长的人。

Ram·say [ˈræmzi; ˋræmzɪ] *n*. **1**. 拉姆齐〔姓氏〕。**2**. **Sir William** ~ 拉姆齐〔1852～1916,英国化学家,氦的发现者〕。

Rams·den [ˈræmzdən; ˋræmzdən] *n*. 拉姆斯登〔姓氏〕。

ram·shack·le [ˈræmˌʃækl; ˋræmʃækl̩] *a*. **1**. 要倒似的,要塌似的;(马车、房子等)摇摇晃晃的。**2**. 无定见的,没主意的;朝三暮四的;放荡的,任性的。

ram·son [ˈræmzən; ˋræmzn̩] *n*.【植】熊葱,阔叶葱;〔*pl*.〕熊葱头。

ram·u·lose [ˈræmjuˌləus; ˋræmjʊlos] *a*. 多小枝的。

ra·mus [ˈreiməs; ˋreməs] *n*. (*pl*. **-mi** [-mai; -maɪ])【生】支,分支。

ran [ræn; ræn] run 的过去式。

R.A.N., **RAN** = Royal Australian Navy (皇家)澳大利亚海军。

Rance [rɑːns; ræns] *n*. 兰斯〔姓氏〕。

ranch(e) [ræntʃ, rɑːntʃ; ræntʃ] **I** *n*.〔美〕大牧场,大农场;〔集合词〕牧场工作人员。**II** *vi*.〔美〕经营牧场;在牧场工作。— *vt*. **1**. 在…经营牧场。**2**. 在牧场饲养。~ **house** (农场主,牧场主的)场内住房;(附有车库的)平房建筑。~**man** = rancher.

ranch·er [ˈræntʃə; ˋræntʃɚ] *n*.〔美〕牧场主;牧场工人。

ran·che·ria [ˌræntʃəˈriːə; ˏræntʃəriə] *n*.〔美〕**1**. (墨西哥的)牧场主[工人]的住房。**2**. 牧人小村。**3**. 印第安人村落。

ran·che·ro [rænˈtʃɛərəu; rænˋtʃero] *n*. (*pl*. **-ros**) **1**.〔美〕= rancher. **2**. 小农场主。

ranch·ette [ˌrænˈtʃet; ˏrænˋtʃɛt] *n*. 小农场,小牧场。

ran·cho [ˈræntʃəu; ˋræntʃo] *n*.〔美〕**1**. 棚屋,简陋的小房子;小村庄,(尤指旅客的)投宿地。**2**. (美西南部)牧场。

ran·cid [ˈrænsid; ˋrænsɪd] *a*. **1**. (指油脂变质后的特有怪味)哈喇的;腐臭的,酸腐的。**2**. 不愉快的,讨厌的。**-ly** *ad*.

ran·cid·i·ty [rænˈsiditi; rænˋsɪdətɪ] *n*. 哈喇;腐臭;酸败(度)。

ran·cor·ous [ˈræŋkərəs; ˋræŋkərəs] *a*. 充满[表示]仇恨的,憎恨的;有遗恨的。**-ly** *ad*.

ran·cour [ˈræŋkə; ˋræŋkɚ] *n*. 深仇,怨恨,憎恨。

rand [rænd; rænd] *n*. **1**. (垫在皮鞋后跟上的)斜面衬皮,衬底。**2**. 石桥。**3**.〔英方〕田边,地头。**4**. 兰特〔南非,博茨瓦纳等国的货币单位〕。**the R-** (南非)河边高地〔尤指德兰士瓦 (Transvaal) 的约翰内斯堡 (Johannesburg) 市附近的产金丘陵〕。

Ran·dal(l) [ˈrændl; ˋrændl̩] *n*. 兰德尔 (= Randolph)。

ran·dan[1] [rænˈdæn; rænˋdæn] *n*. (居中一人双桨,头尾二人单桨的)三人小艇(划法)。

ran·dan[2] [rænˈdæn; rænˋdæn] *n*.〔俚〕乱闹,傻闹,纵情嬉闹;〔罕〕爱乱闹的人,好纵情嬉闹的人。*go on the* ~ 嬉戏喧闹,狂饮,纵酒作乐。

R and B = rhythm and blues 拍子清楚,节奏简单的布鲁斯乐曲。

R & C = receiving and classification 接收与分类。

R and D, **R & D** = research and development 研究与发展。

Ran·dolph [ˈrændɔlf; ˋrændɑlf] *n*. 伦道夫〔姓氏,男子名〕。

ran·dom [ˈrændəm; ˋrændəm] **I** *n*.〔罕〕胡乱行为,偶然的[随便的]行动[过程]。**II** *a*. **1**. 任意的,胡乱的,随便的;(话等)信口乱说的;(人等)偶然碰到的。**2**. 随机的;【物】无规则的;(石工)(大小)不齐的。*a* ~ *guess* 瞎猜。*a* ~ *shot* 乱射(的子弹);流弹。**at** ~ 碰运气地;无目标地,漫无目的地。~ **access**【计】随机存取。~ **masonry** (随石头不同大小堆砌的)堆砌泥瓦工。~ **mating** 随机交配。~ **sampling** 随机取样。~ **variable**【数、统】随机变数。~ **walk**【数】随机游动。**-i·ci·ty** *n*. 随机性,无规性。

ran·dom·ize [ˈrændəmaiz; ˋrændəmˌaɪz] *vt*. (**-iz·ed**; **-iz·ing**) **1**. 使形成不规则分布;完全打乱。**2**.【数、统】使随机化;使不规则化;随机选择。**-i·za·tion** [ˌrændəmaiˈzeiʃən; ˏrændəmaɪˋzeʃən] *n*.

R. & P. Sec. = Radio and Panel Section【军】无线电及信号布板通信组。

R and R, **R & R** **1**. = rest and recuperation (leave)【美军】(正常例假以外的)休整假期。**2**. rock'n'roll 摇滚舞(曲)。

Ran·dy [ˈrændi; ˋrændɪ] *n*. 兰迪〔男子名,Randolph 的昵称〕。

ran·dy [ˈrændi; ˋrændɪ] **I** *a*. **1** [Scot.] 粗暴的,吵闹的,(女人)说话大声的。**2**.〔方〕(牛等)横暴的。**3**.〔方〕淫乱的。**II** *n*.〔Scot.〕**1**. 强横的乞丐;吵闹的女人,暴躁的女人。**2**.〔方〕大吵大闹。

ra·nee [rɑːˈniː; ˋrɑnɪ] *n*.〔Hind.〕女邦主,王后,王妃,邦主妃 (= rani)。

rang [ræŋ; ræŋ] ring 的过去式。

range [reindʒ; rendʒ] **I** *vt*. **1**. 排列;整理(头发等)。**2**. 使归类[班、行、队];把…分类。**3**.〔用被动形或反身形〕加入,站住…的一边 (*with*; *against*)。**4**.〔古、诗〕在…徘徊,在…走来走去,到处寻找;【海】巡逻(沿岸等)。**5**. (用枪、望远镜等)对准(目标);瞄准;(炮术)试(炮),试(射程)。~ *books on a shelf* 把书排列在书架上。~ *the forest for game* 在森林中跑来跑去猎取猎物。***be ~d according to size*** 按大小顺序排列。***be ~d against*** [***among***] 站在…的反对方向[…的一伙内]。~ ***oneself*** **1**. (放荡后因结婚而)改过自新。**2**. 得到固定职业。~ ***oneself on the side of*** 做…的伙伴。~ ***oneself with*** 做…的伙伴,与…做伙伴。— *vi*. **1**. 开列,进行;成直线 (*with*);(山脉等)相连,连绵;(动植物等)分布,蔓延,散布 (*from*... *to*);(子弹)能打到,达到。**2**. 加入,站在…的一边 (*with*; *against*);与…为伍 (*with*)。**3**. 徘徊,走来走去,跋涉 (*in*; *over*; *through*);【海】巡航。**4**. (思想、研究等)到达,涉及。**5**.【军】测距,试射测距;射程为。**6**. (在某范围内)变动,升降 (*between*; *from*... *to* ...)。~ *north and south* 绵亘南北。*The gun* ~*s 3 miles*. 这炮能打三英里远。*The thermometer* ~*s from 45° to 50°*. 温度表的升降幅度是从 45 度到 50 度。***ranging fancy*** 动摇的爱情,水性杨花。**II** *n*. **1**.

(山脉、房屋等的)排列;连续;绵亘。**2.** (同种物的)一批,一套,一堆。**3.** 方向;范围,区域;(动植物的)分布[繁殖]区域;生存期间;放牧区域,牧场;知识范围;音域;幅度,差度;限度,极限;【数】变程,量程;值域;全距。**4.** 作用[有效]半径,距离;射程;靶子场,射击场。**5.** 等级,类别,种类,部类。**6.** 徜徉,徘徊。**7.** (能同时利用余热烧水、烤面包的)多用铁灶;火格子;梯级。**8.** 〔美〕公地测量中相距六英里的两子午线间的一排市镇。*a ~ of buildings* 一排房子。*the ~ of politics* 政界。*a high* [*lower*] *~* 大[小]比例,大[小]刻度。*the ~ of a thermometer* 温度表的(升降)幅度。*the ~ of one's voice* 音域;声音所能达到的范围。*the effective ~* 有效射程。*foul the ~ finding* (放烟幕)扰乱测距工作。*a projectile* [*proving, rocket*] *~* 炮兵[军用、火箭]靶场。*a ~ boss* 〔美〕(在某一地段内)看守放牧牲畜的人。*a ~ rider* 〔美〕牧童;山村看守人。*~ cattle* 放牧的牲畜。*a ~ forecast* 【商】(棉花的)收成估计。*a ~ of the cable* 抛锚时所必需的一定长度的锚链。*an electronic ~* 电子炉。***a low ~ of prices*** 低档价钱。***at long*** [***short***] ***~*** 在远距离[近距离]。***go over the ~*** 〔美〕死。***in ~ with*** 和…开排着;和…同一方向。***in the ~ of*** 在…范围内。***out of one's ~*** 能力达不到的;在知识以外的,不能办到的。***out of*** [***within***] ***~*** 在射程外[内]。***within the ~ of*** 在…的射程内,…能力达得到的,…所能的。~ **ability** (火箭的)射程。~ **coal** 块煤。~ **finder** 测远仪,测距器;【军】(测定由枪炮至目标间距离的)光学测距仪。~ **hammer**【林】打号槌。~**land** 牧场,放牧地。~ **oil** 厨房用燃料器。~ **radar** 雷达测距计。~ **party**【军】监靶官。~ **pole** 测量标杆。~**-setting**【军】射程表尺数。~ **table**【军】射程表;可凑成大桌子的许多小桌子之一。~ **taker**【军】测距员。

rang·er [ˈreindʒə; ˋrendʒɚ] ***n*.** **1.** 荡来荡去的人,徘徊者。**2.** 〔英〕御林看守人;〔美〕护林员。**3.** 【美军】突击队员;(防守广大地域的)游击兵,游骑兵;〔*pl*.〕游骑队。**4.** 〔英〕老资格的女童子军。~ **district**【林】护林区。**-ing** 试射;定向;测距。

rang·(e)y [ˈreindʒi; ˋrendʒɪ] ***a*.** **1.** 〔美〕(动物)走来走去的。**2.** 个子细长的,长脚的。**3.** 广阔的。**4.** 〔澳〕山脉连绵的,多山的。

Ran·goon [ræŋˈguːn; ræŋˋgun] ***n*.** 仰光〔缅甸首都〕。

ra·ni [ˈrɑːni; ˋrɑnɪ] ***n*.** (印度的)王妃;邦主妃;女王;女邦主;公主。

ran·id [ˈrænid; ˋrænɪd] ***n*.**【动】蛙科 (*Ranidae*) 动物。

rank[1] [ræŋk; ræŋk] **I** ***n*.** **1.** 列,排;【军】行列;〔*pl*.〕阵线,队伍,军队;〔*pl*.〕士兵,列兵。**2.** 阶层,等级,地位;身份;高级;显贵。**3.** 次序,顺序;【统】秩;(棋盘的)横格。**4.**【语】语结级位〔叶斯帕森语,按语、词和结构在句中所起作用而分为三级,即一级语结 (primary)、二级语结 (secondary) 和三级语结 (tertiary)〕。*the front* [*rear*] *~* 前[后]排。*people of all ~s* 各阶层的人们。*a man of high* [*no*] *~* 地位高[低]的人。*~s and ratings* 官兵。*within the ~s of the people* 在人民内部。***be in the first ~*** 是第一流的。***break ~s*** 落伍;走出队伍,出列;溃散。***close the ~s*** **1.** 使队伍靠拢。**2.** 〔喻〕紧密团结。***fall into ~*** 排队,列队。***give first ~ to*** 把…放在第一位。***keep ~*** 维持秩序。***other ~s*** 普通士兵们。***~ and fashion*** 上流社会。***~ and file*** 队伍,行伍,士兵(群众);民众,老百姓,普通人。***rise from the ~s*** 由士兵升为军官;行伍出身;布衣起家。***serve in the ~s*** 服兵役。***take ~ of*** 在…之上。***take ~ with*** 和…并列,和…并肩。**II** ***vt*.** **1.** 排列,使成横排。**2.** 把…分类,分等级,使归类。**3.** 〔美〕强过,胜过,先于,在…之上。*~ one's ability very high* 把某人能力评得很高。— ***vi*.** **1.** 并列;位于 (*among*; *with*);排列;排队前进 (*off*; *past*)。**2.** 〔美〕占第一位。**3.** 〔英〕(对破产者财产)有要求权。*~ among the Great Powers* 跻身于世界强国之林。

rank[2] [ræŋk; ræŋk] ***a*.** **1.** 繁茂的,蔓延的;过于肥沃的。**2.** 臭极的,恶臭的。**3.** 〔贬意〕极端(恶劣,下流等)的;真正的,十足的,很厉害的,讨厌的。**4.** 卑鄙的;猥亵的。**5.** 〔口〕难制御的,倔强的。**6.**【法】〔古〕过重的,过份的。*a garden ~ with weeds* 杂草滋生的院子。*The land is too ~ to grow corn.* 土地过肥不宜种谷类〔徒长枝叶,结实稀少〕。*tall ~ grass* 长得很高的草。*~ fraud* 大骗局。*~ nonsense* 荒唐到极点的事情〔胡说〕。*~ pedantry* 好像样样都懂的臭样子。*~ poison* 剧毒。*a ~ traitor* 大叛徒,巨奸。**-ly** ***ad*.** **-ness** ***n*.**

rank·er [ˈræŋkə; ˋræŋkɚ] ***n*.** 〔英〕兵;(特指)出身行伍的军官。

Ran·kine [ˈræŋkin; ˋræŋkɪn] ***a*.** 兰(金)氏温标的〔用华氏度数表示的绝对温标〕。~ **cycle**【物】兰金循环。~**'s formula**【物】兰金公式。

rank·ing [ˈræŋkiŋ; ˋræŋkɪŋ] **I** ***n*.** 顺序;【统】秩评定。**II** ***a*.** 第一流的;首席的;高级的;干部的。*a ~ officer* 高级军官。*a ~ player* 一级选手。

ran·kle [ˈræŋkl; ˋræŋkl] ***vi*.** **1.** 〔古、诗〕痛。**2.** 红肿。**3.** (怨恨,失望等)使心痛,压在胸口[心头]。— ***vt*.** 激怒;使怨恨。

RANN = Research Applied to National Needs 〔美〕国民需求应用研究〔英国的一项全国性科研项目〕。

ran·sack [ˈrænsæk; ˋrænsæk] ***vt*.** **1.** 细搜,遍处搜索,翻来复去地找。**2.** 洗劫,掠夺,劫掠。**3.** 仔细思索。

Ran·som [ˈrænsəm; ˋrænsəm] ***n*.** 兰瑟姆〔姓氏〕。

ran·som [ˈrænsəm; ˋrænsəm] **I** ***n*.** **1.** 赎,赎取,赎身。**2.** 赎金;罚款。**3.** 讹诈,威胁。**4.** 〔古〕赎罪。***a king's ~*** 巨款。***hold sb. to*** [***for***] ***~*** 绑票,勒取赎金。**II** ***vt*.** **1.** 赎,赎回,赎出,赎(身)。**2.** 赎(罪)。**3.** 向…勒索赎金;绑(某人的)票进行勒索。**4.** 〔现罕〕得赎金后释放(某人)。~ **bill**, ~ **bond**【国际法】(被捕获船舶的)赎回证书〔有此证书的船只此后即通行无阻,可不再受同一国家其他船只的侵袭〕。

rant [rænt; rænt] **I** ***n*.** 大话,夸口话;叫喊,叫声;怒吼;〔Scot.〕欢嚷吵闹。**II** ***vi*.** 说粗暴话,大声叫喊;咆哮,怒吼;做戏似地说;说大话;大声讲道[祈祷];怒骂。*~ and rave* 大声叫嚷。— ***vt*.** 夸口说,大声说。*~ out one's denunciation* 激昂地指责。

ran·tan [ˈræntæn; ˋrænˏtæn] ***n*.** 〔俚〕敲打声;〔美〕喝酒吵闹。

ran·tan·ker·ous [rænˈtæŋkərəs; rænˋtæŋkərəs] ***a*.** 〔美〕倔强的,乖僻的。

rant·er [ˈræntə; ˋræntɚ] ***n*.** **1.** 大言壮语的人;粗声大气(喧闹)的人。**2.**【宗、史】(英国共和制时代狂热地排斥一切教会,牧师,宗教仪式的)喧骚派教徒;(早期美以美教派大声祈祷或说教的)狂热派教徒[牧师]。**3.** 〔Scot.〕喧嚷的艺人[歌手]。

ran·u·la [ˈrænjulə; ˋrænjʊlə] ***n*.** 舌下囊肿。

ra·nun·cu·lus [rəˈnʌŋkjuləs; rəˋnʌŋkjʊləs] ***n*.** (*pl*. *~es*, **-li** [-lai; -laɪ])【植】毛茛属植物 (= buttercup)。

ranz-des-vaches [ˌrɑ̃ndeiˈvɑːʃ; ˏrɑ̃(s)deˋvɑʃ] ***n*.** 〔F.〕(阿尔卑斯山区牧人用角笛吹奏召集牛羊的)召牛调。

raob [ˈreiəb; ˋreəb] ***n*.** 无线电探空仪观测。

R.A.O.C., **RAOC** = Royal Army Ordnance Corps 〔英〕皇家陆军军械兵。

rap[1] [ræp; ræp] **I** ***n*.** **1.** 重敲,拍;敲(门)声,拍(桌)声(等)。**2.** 〔美俚〕监禁,处罚,责骂。***beat the ~*** 〔美俚〕逃过刑事责任。***get a ~ on*** [***over***] ***the knuckles*** 受谴责,受申斥,受责骂。***give sb. a ~ on*** [***over***] ***the knuckles*** 申斥,责骂。***take the ~*** 挨骂。**II** ***vt*.** (***-pp-***) **1.** 用力敲,嘭嘭地敲[拍]。**2.** 突然讲出,出其不意地说,严厉地说。**3.** 〔美〕斥责,苛评。~ ***out*** 严厉地说,突然说出;把(意思等)用敲击声表现出来;敲奏(钢琴);击倒。— ***vi*.** **1.** 敲(门) (*at*, *on*)。**2.** 发急促尖锐声。**3.** 说粗野话。

rap[2] [ræp; ræp] ***n*.** **1.** (从前爱尔兰通用的)半便士私铸货币。**2.** 〔口〕一文(也不),一点儿(也不)。*do not care a*

R

~ 一点也不在意。

rap[3][ræp; ræp] *vt*. (*rapped*, *rapt* [ræpt]; *rap·ping*) 1. 使心荡神移,使神往,迷住〔多用被动结构〕。2.〔古〕抢去,夺去。~ *and rend* [*ren*, *run*, *ring*, *wring*] (想方设法地)获得;强夺。

rap[4][ræp; ræp] **I** *vi*. (*-pp-*)〔美俚〕自由而坦率地谈论;交谈(*to*);理解。**II** *n*. 交谈;谈论。~ **parlour** 交谈处,洽谈处;〔美俚〕(妓女的)卖淫处。~ **session** (非正式的)小组讨论会[座谈会]。~ **sheet**〔美俚〕警方档案。

R.A.P. = Regimental Aid Post〔英〕团救护所。

ra·pa·cious [rəˈpeiʃəs; rəˋpeʃəs] *a*. 1. 强夺的,掠夺的,剥削性的;贪婪的。2.【动】(猛禽等)捕食动物的。**-ly** *ad*.

ra·pac·i·ty [rəˈpæsiti; rəˋpæsətɪ] *n*. 强夺,掠夺(性);贪婪。

R.A.P.C., **RAPC** = Royal Army Pay Corps〔英〕皇家陆军财务队。

rape[1][reip; rep] *n*. (榨汁后制醋用的)葡萄渣;制醋用的滤器。~ *wine* 渣汁葡萄酒,二汁葡萄酒。

rape[2][reip; rep] **I** *n*. 1.〔古、诗〕强夺,抢夺,掠夺。2.【法】强奸。**II** *vt*., *vi*. 1. 抢,强夺,掠夺。2. 强奸。~ *and rend* = *rap and rend*.

rape[3][reip; rep] *n*.【植】芸薹,油菜。~ **cake** 菜子饼。~ **oil** 菜油。~ **seed** 菜子。

Raph·a·el [ˈreifl, ˈræfeil; ˋræfɪəl] *n*. 1. 拉斐尔〔姓氏〕。2. **Santi** [**Sanzio**] ~ 拉斐尔〔1483～1520,意大利画家〕。

Raph·a·el·esque [ˌræfeiəˈlesk; ˌræfɪəlˋɛsk] *a*. 意大利画家、建筑家拉斐尔 (Raphael) 风格的。

ra·phe [ˈreifi:; ˋrefi] *n*. 1.【解】缝际。2.【植】脊;种脊,珠脊。

ra·phi·a [ˈreifiə, ˈræfiə; ˋrefɪə, ˋræfɪə] *n*. = raffia.

ra·phide [ˈreifid, ˈræfid; ˋrefɪd, ˋræfɪd] *n*. (*pl*. *raph·i·des* [ˈræfidi:z, ˈreifidz; ˋræfɪdiz, ˋrefɪdz])【植】针晶体。

rap·id [ˈræpid; ˋræpɪd] **I** *a*. 1. 快。2. 敏捷的,麻俐的,快手快脚的(工人等)。3. 峻险的(坡等)。4.【摄】感光快的。*a* ~ *stream* 急流。*a* ~ *thinker* 颖慧的思想家。*a* ~ *journey* 匆促的旅行。*a* ~ *decline* 急性肺痨。**II** *n*.〔常 *pl*.〕急流;滩,碛;湍流。~**-fire**, ~**-firing** *a*. 速射(用)的。~**-firer** 速射炮[枪]。~ **reaction force** 快速反应部队。~ **transit**〔美〕高速交通系统。~ **water**〔美〕水流加速液〔消防抽水设备中的一种无毒聚合物悬浮体,混于水中能减少摩擦力,从而加速水的流动〕。**-ly** *ad*. 快,迅速,敏捷,立刻。**-ness** *n*.〔罕〕= rapidity.

ra·pid·i·ty [rəˈpiditi; rəˋpɪdətɪ] *n*. 迅速,急速,敏捷;速度。

ra·pi·er [ˈreipiə; ˋrepɪɚ] *n*. (旧时决斗用的)轻巧细长的剑。*a* ~ *thrust* 用剑戳;妙语,妙论。*a* ~ *glance* 目光锐利的一瞅。

rap·ine [ˈræpain; ˋræpɪn] *n*. 劫掠,掠夺;【林】滥伐。

rap·ist [ˈreipist; ˋrepɪst] *n*. 强奸犯。

rap·pa·ree [ˌræpəˈri:; ˌræpəˋri] *n*. 1.【史】十七世纪爱尔兰革命时的民兵〔非正规军〕。2. 强盗,海盗,流寇,散兵;游民。

rap·pee [ræˈpi:; ræˋpi] *n*. 粗鼻烟。

rap·pel [ræˈpel, rə-; ræˋpɛl] **I** *n*. 坐式下降法〔指登山者用双绳一端系于山上,一端系在自己身上。从悬岩陡壁滑下〕。**II** *vi*. (*-pelled*; *-pel·ling*) 用绳绕双腿下降。

rap·pen [ˈrɑ:pən; ˋrɑpən] *n*. (*pl*. *-pen*) 分〔瑞士货币单位"分"的德语名称〕。

rap·per [ˈræpə; ˋræpɚ] *n*. 叩击者[物],(尤指)敲门者;敲门锤。

rap·port [ræˈpɔ:t; ræˋport] *n*.〔F.〕1. 关系;友好关系;和好,和睦,亲善。2. 降神术中的与神鬼灵魂交往。*be on* [*in*] ~ *with* 跟…和好(一致)。

rap·por·teur [ˌræpɔ:ˈtuə, F. rapɔrˈtœ:r; ˌræporˋto, rɑporˋtœr] *n*. 指定为委员会(或大会)起草报告等的人。

rap·proche·ment [ræˈprɔʃmɑ̃:ŋ; rɑprɔ̃ʃˋmɑ̃] *n*.〔F.〕和解,和睦;(恢复或建立)友好关系;恢复国交。

rap·scal·lion [ræpˈskæljən; ræpˋskæljən] *n*. 恶棍,无赖,流氓。

rapt [ræpt; ræpt] **I** rap[3]的过去式及过去分词。**II** *a*. 1. 被夺去的(*away*; *up*)。2. 销魂的,着迷的;热心的,全神贯注的;发狂似的,狂喜的。*be* ~ *in wonder* 惊异得目瞪口呆。*listen with* ~ *attention* 入迷地听。~ *to the seventh heaven* 欢天喜地。

rap·to·rial [ræpˈtɔ:riəl; ræpˋtorɪəl] **I** *a*.【动】捕食动物的(鸟兽等);食肉的;猛禽类的。**II** *n*. 猛禽。*a* ~ *bird* [*beast*] 猛禽[兽]。

rap·ture [ˈræptʃə; ˋræptʃɚ] *n*. 狂喜;〔常 *pl*.〕欢天喜地。*recall childhood's* ~*s of delight* 回忆幼时快乐。*be in* [*go into*] ~*s over* [*about*] 狂喜,欢天喜地。*fall* [*go*] *into* ~*s over* 对…发起迷来。~ *of the deep* 1. 深海晕眩。2.【医】氮麻醉(法)(= nitrogen narcosis)。

rap·tured [ˈræptʃəd; ˋræptʃɚd] *a*. 欢天喜地的;高兴得不得了的。

rap·turous [ˈræptʃərəs; ˋræptʃərəs] *a*. 狂喜的,欢天喜地的,兴高采烈的,热烈的。(*a shout of*) ~ *applause* 热烈的鼓掌(喝彩)。**-ly** *ad*.

ra·ra a·vis [rɛərəˈævis; ˋrɛrəˋevɪs] (*pl*. ***ra·rae·ves*** [ˈrɛəˈri:ˈeivi:z; ˋrɛriˋeviz])〔L.〕少见的鸟;稀有事物[人物];怪人;神童;珍品。

rare[1][rɛə; rɛr] **I** *a*. 1. 稀少的;(空气等)稀薄的;(群岛、星等)稀疏的。2. 稀有的,珍奇的;极好的,珍贵的。3.〔口〕非常有趣的。*It is no* ~ *thing*. 那不算什么稀奇。*a* ~ *book* 珍本。~ *earths*【化】稀土族。~ *metals* 稀有金属。*You are a* ~ *one*. 你是一个难得的[了不起的]人。*I had* ~ *fun with him*. = *We had a* ~ *time of it, he and I*. 我和他过得极快乐。(**kind**) *in a* ~ *degree* 极(亲切的)。*in* ~ *cases* = *on* ~ *occasions* 难得;偶尔。~ *and*〔口〕非常(*I was* ~ *and hungry*. 我非常饿)。**II** *ad*.〔口、诗〕非常,很,极。*a* ~ *fine view* 极好的风景。

rare[2][rɛə; rɛr] *a*.〔美〕(肉)烹调得嫩的,半熟的。

rare·bit [ˈrɛəbit; ˋrɛrˏbɪt] *n*. = Welsh rabbit.

rar·ee show [ˈrɛəri: ʃəu; ˋrɛri ʃo] *n*. 1. 西洋镜。2. 杂耍;街头表演。

rar·e·fac·tion [ˌrɛəriˈfækʃən; ˏrɛrəˋfækʃən] *n*. 稀少,稀薄;纯净;【化】稀疏(作用)。**-tive** *a*.

rar·e·fy [ˈrɛərifai; ˋrɛrəˏfaɪ] *vt*. (*-fied*; *-fy·ing*) 把(气体)弄稀薄;使(人格、精神等)纯洁;使(思想等)精细。~ *one's earthly desires* 涤除尘俗的欲念。— *vi*. 变稀薄;变纯洁。

rare·ly [ˈrɛəli; ˋrɛrlɪ] *ad*. 极,极少有地,极精彩地;难得,很少(*opp*. often)。*I* ~ *meet him*. 我难得遇到他。

rare·ness [ˈrɛənis; ˋrɛrnɪs] *n*. 稀奇;稀薄;珍奇,珍贵。

rare·ripe [ˈrɛəraip; ˋrɛrˏraɪp] **I** *a*. 早熟的。**II** *n*. 早熟;早熟的水果[蔬菜]。

rar·i·ty [ˈrɛəriti; ˋrɛrətɪ] *n*. 奇事,珍品,奇物;稀薄,稀少。

Raro·tonga [ˌrɑ:rəuˈtɔŋgə; ˏræroˋtɑŋgə] *n*. 拉罗通加〔库克群岛首都〕。

ras·bo·ra [ræzˈbɔ:rə; ræzˋborə] *n*.【动】波鱼。

R.A.S.C., **RASC** = Royal Army Service Corps〔英〕皇家陆军补给与运输勤务队。

ras·cal [ˈrɑ:skəl; ˋræskl] **I** *n*. 1. 恶棍,坏蛋,流氓。2.〔谑〕家伙。**II** *a*. 无赖的,无耻的;〔罕〕卑鄙的。*the* ~ *rout*〔古〕平民。*You lucky* ~. 你这幸运的家伙。

ras·cal·dom [ˈrɑ:skəldəm; ˋræskldəm] *n*. 流氓[歹徒]集团;流氓行为;卑鄙龌龊的事。

ras·cal·ism [ˈrɑ:skəlizəm; ˋræsklɪzəm] *n*.〔罕〕= rascality.

ras·cal·i·ty [rɑːsˈkæliti; ræsˋkælətɪ] ***n***. 罪恶勾当;无赖行为;流氓行为[习气]。

ras·cal·lion [rɑːsˈkæljən; ræsˋkæljən] ***n***. 恶棍,流氓,歹徒。

ras·cal·ly [ˈrɑːskəli; ˋræsklɪ] **I** ***a***. 恶棍的,流氓的,歹徒的;无赖的;卑鄙的,无耻的。**II** ***ad***. 无赖地;卑鄙地。

rase [reiz; rez] ***vt***. 〔罕〕= raze.

rash[1] [ræʃ; ræʃ] ***a***. 轻率的,鲁莽的;性急的;过早的,未成熟的。*be* ~ *enough* 胆敢;贸然。~ *advance* 冒进。**-ly** ***ad***. **-ness** ***n***.

rash[2] [ræʃ; ræʃ] ***n***. 【医】**1**. (皮)疹。**2**. 同时大量出现的事件。*a heat* ~ 热疹。*a nettle* ~ 荨麻疹。*the* ~ *of student disturbances* 连续发生的学生闹事事件。

rash·er [ˈræʃə; ˋræʃɚ] ***n***. 煎咸肉[火腿]片。

ra·so·ri·al [rəˈsɔːriəl; rəˋsorɪəl] ***a***. 【动】搔拨类的〔如鸡〕;鹑鸡类的。

rasp [rɑːsp; ræsp] **I** ***n***. **1**. 粗锉,木锉;【机】锉机;锉磨而发出的刺耳声音。**2**. (心里的)焦急,烦躁。**II** ***vt***. **1**. 用粗锉锉(*off*; *away*);粗锉,粗刮,粗擦;把…弄得刺耳地响。**2**. 伤(人感情),使焦急,使急躁;用急躁刺耳的声音说(*out*)。— ***vi***. 锉,磨擦;嘎嚓嘎嚓地响。**-er** [-ə; -ɚ] ***n***. **1**. 木锉;锉刀;(甜菜根的)磨碎器。**2**. 【猎】(难于飞越的)高墙,障碍。**3**. 〔俚〕令人讨厌的人[东西]。

rasp·ber·ry [ˈrɑːzbəri; ˋræzˏbɛrɪ] **I** ***n***. **1**. 【植】悬钩子;木莓,山莓。**2**. 红光暗紫色。**3**. 〔美俚〕咂舌头嘲笑的声音,讥笑;谴责。***get the*** ~ 被(咂舌头)嘲笑。***hand*** [***give***] ***sb***. ***the*** ~ (咂舌头)嘲笑某人。**II** ***a***. 紫红色的。~**-canes** (次年结果的)悬钩子的新枝。~ **vinegar** 树莓醋。

rasp·ing [ˈrɑːspiŋ; ˋræspɪŋ] ***a***. 锉的;嘎嘎响的;使人烦躁的。*a* ~ *voice* 刺耳的语声。

rasp·y [ˈrɑːspi, ˈræs-; ˋræspɪ] ***a***. (***rasp·i·er***; ***rasp·i·est***) **1**. 发刺耳声的;使人烦躁的。**2**. 易怒的。**-i·ness** ***n***.

ras·sle [ˈræsl; ˋræsl̩] ***n***., ***vi***., ***vt***. (***-sled***; ***-sling***) 〔方,口〕摔跤 (= wrestle)。

rass·ling [ˈræsliŋ; ˋræslɪŋ] ***n***. 〔口,方〕= wrestling.

ras·ter [ˈræstə; ˋræstɚ] ***n***. 【电视】光栅,(无图像的横线)屏面;【摄】網板。~ **display** 【自】光栅显像〔电子计算机输出的一种图形显像〕。

ra·sure [ˈreiʒə; ˋreʒɚ] ***n***. 削除,抹掉,作过删除的痕迹 (= erasure)。*There are many* ~*s in the manuscript*. 原稿中有许多删除的痕迹。

RAT = rocket-launched antisubmarine torpedo 火箭发射式反潜鱼雷。

rat[1] [ræt; ræt] **I** ***n***. **1**. 【动】鼠〔比 mouse 要大〕。**2**. 〔俚〕(患难时的)脱党者,退会者,变节者,叛徒,卑劣的人;〔俚〕接受低于工会规定工资的工人,不参加罢工的工人,工贼;〔美俚〕特务。**3**. 〔美口〕(衬在头发下的)假发卷。**4**. 〔*pl*.〕〔美俚〕发酒疯。**5**. 〔美俚〕街头青少年流氓;下流女人。***as drunk*** [***poor***, ***weak***] ***as a*** ~ 喝得酩酊大醉[穷得身无分文,弱得气力毫无]。***die like a*** ~ 被毒死。***have a*** ~ ***in the garret*** [***attic***] 〔口〕头脑不正常,有点精神病。***like a drowned*** ~ 像落汤鸡,浑身湿透。***like a*** ~ ***in a hole*** 像瓮中之鳖。***smell a*** ~ 觉得可疑,发觉,看出苗头。**II** ***vi***. (***-tt-***) **1**. (特指用狗)捕鼠。**2**. 变节,脱党;〔俚〕接受低于工会规定的工资工作,不参加罢工,接替罢工工人的位置,破坏罢工;〔美俚〕叛变,告密,做特务。~ ***on*** 出卖。~ ***out*** 〔俚〕背信弃义地撤回(支持等)。~ **bite fever** 【医】鼠咬热。~ **cheese** (工厂制造的)硬奶酪。~ **face** 〔美〕奸险人物。~ **fink** 可鄙的人 (= fink)。~ **firm** 雇用破坏罢工工人的工厂。~ **guard** 【海】(船索上的)防鼠装置。~ **pack** 街头青少年流氓团伙。~ **poison** 杀鼠药。~ **race** 〔美俚〕费神的日常工作。~ **run** (汽车的)绕小路走。~ **trap** **1**. 捕鼠夹。**2**. 〔英空俚〕气球防空网。**3**. (自行车)有齿脚蹬。**4**. 陷入绝境。**5**. 〔口〕肮脏破烂的房屋。

rat[2] [ræt; ræt] ***vt***. (***-tt-***) 〔俚〕诅咒,责骂。***R- me if I'll do it***. 绝对[砍了我的头也]不干。

rat·a·ble [ˈreitəbl; ˋretəbl] ***a***. **1**. 可估价的,可评价的。**2**. 〔英〕应征税的。**3**. 按比例(计算)的。*the* ~ *value* 征税额。**-bili·ty** [ˌreitəˈbiliti; ˏretəˋbɪlətɪ] ***n***. 〔英〕纳税义务;估价。**-bly** ***ad***.

rat·a·fia, rat·a·fee [ˌrætəˈfiə, -fiː; ˏrætəˋfɪə, -ˋfi] ***n***. 果酒〔用樱桃仁等调味的甜酒〕;果酒味饼干。

rat·al [ˈreitl; ˋretl̩] 〔英〕**I** ***n***. 征税价格,纳税额。**II** ***a***. 征税价格的,纳税的。

RATAN = radar and television aid to navigation 用于导航的雷达和电视设备。

ra·tan [ræˈtæn; ræˋtæn] ***n***. = rattan.

rat·a·plan [ˌrætəˈplæn; ˏrætəˋplæn] **I** ***n***. 咚咚〔鼓声〕。**II** ***vt***. (***-nn-***) 敲(鼓),用鼓敲奏。— ***vi***. (鼓)咚咚地响。

rat-a-tat [ˈrætəˈtæt; ˋrætəˋtæt] ***n***. 砰砰〔敲门声等〕。

ratch·et, ratch [ˈrætʃit, rætʃ; ˋrætʃɪt, rætʃ] **I** ***n***. **1**. 【机】棘齿;棘爪;(尤指钟表、机器的)棘轮,制轮,棘轮机构。**2**. 〔喻〕为使收入增长不可逆转所采取的强制手段。**II** ***vt***. 把…造成棘齿形,于…作棘齿,在…上刻锯齿。~ **brace** 扳钻。~ **effect** 断断续续的进展[增长等]。~ **wheel** 棘轮,制轮,闸轮。

rate[1] [reit; ret] **I** ***n***. **1**. 比率,率;速度,进度;程度;(钟的快慢)差率。**2**. 价格;行市,行情;估价,评价;费,费用,运费。**3**. (船或船员的)等级。**4**. 〔常 *pl*.〕捐税;〔英〕地方税。**5**. 程度,方式,情况,样子。*the birth* [*death*] ~ 出生[死亡]率。*the seed* ~ 播种率。*the fuel* ~ 燃料消耗率。~ *cutting* 减低运费[保险费]。*the* ~ *of interest* 利率。*the rotation* ~ 转速。~*s of exchange* = *exchange* ~*s* 外汇率,汇价,汇兑行情。*postal* ~*s* 邮费。*railroad* ~*s* 铁路运费。~ *of profit* 利润率。~ *of surplus value* 剩余价值率。*the first* ~ 头等的,上等的。*Things are going first-*~. 事情进行顺畅。~*s and taxes* 地方税和国税。*the poor* ~ 〔英〕贫民救济税。***at a good*** [***terrible***] ~ 以相当[惊人]的速度。***at a great*** ~ 以高速度,飞快地;大大地,非常地。***at a high*** [***low***] ~ 以高[低]价 (*live at a high* ~ 生活豪华)。***at all*** ~***s*** 无论如何,一定要。***at an easy*** ~ 非常容易地,毫不费力地。***at any*** ~ 总而言之,无论如何。***at that*** [***this***] ~ 〔口〕那[这]种样子,照那[这]种情形 (*If you go on at that* ~, *you will injure your health*. 你如果照这样子继续下去,你会损害健康的)。***at the*** ~ ***of*** 按…的比例;以…的速度。***be*** (***come***) ***on the*** ~***s*** (贫民)受救济。***by no*** ~ 决没有…。***give special*** ~***s*** 各(特惠)折扣。~ ***of climb*** 【空】上升速度。**II** ***vt***. **1**. 估价,评价〔常用被动语态〕。**2**. 看做,认为。**3**. 征(地方)税;定(船、船员的)等级;测定(钟表等的)快慢;〔美〕给…批分数;〔美〕按一定运费运输。**4**. 〔美俚〕有…的价值[资格],值得。~*d age* 【保险】标准年龄。~*d current* 额定电流。~*d horse-power* 额定马力。~ ***up*** (按危险情况)提高保险费。— ***vi***. **1**. 被估价,被评价。**2**. 有(某种)价值。**3**. 列于(某一)等级,列入。*The ship* ~*s as a ship of the line*. 该舰船列入战列舰级。~ ***with sb***. 得某人好评。~**-cap** ***vi***. 〔英〕限定税额。~ **card** (列举收费标准的)广告费卡。~**-meter** 速率计;(辐射)强度计。~ **payer** 〔英〕纳(地方)税人。~**-war** 减价竞争。

rate[2] [reit; ret] ***vt***., ***vi***. 申斥,斥责,骂。

rate[3] [reit; ret] ***vt***., ***vi***. 〔方〕= ret.

rate·a·ble [ˈreitəbl; ˋretəbl̩] ***a***. = ratable.

ra·tel [ˈreitel; ˋretəl] ***n***. 【动】(南非)蜜獾。

rat·er[1] [ˈreitə; ˋretɚ] ***n***. **1**. 某一等级的人[物];…吨的比赛艇。**2**. 定等级者;估价者,评价者。*a 10-*~ 十吨快艇。*a first-*~ 一流人物;头等货。

rat·er[2] [ˈreitə; ˋretɚ] ***n***. 责骂者,抱怨者。

rat·fish [ˈrætˌfiʃ; ˋrætˏfɪʃ] ***n***. (*pl*. ***-fish***, ***-fish·es***) 【动】银鲛属 (Chimaera) 的鱼。

rath[1] [rɑːθ; rɑθ] ***n***. 【考古】(爱尔兰古代族长住所的)围墙,山寨围垣。

R

rath², **rathe** [reið; reð] ***a*.** 〔诗、古〕快的,敏捷的;比普通时刻早的;早开的,早生的,早熟的。

Rat·haus [ˈrɑːthaus; ˋrætha us] ***n*.** 〔G.〕市[镇]议会厅。

rath·er I [ˈrɑːðə; ˋræðɚ] ***ad*.** **1.** 〔与动词连用〕宁愿,宁可,毋宁。**2.** 稍微,有点;相当,颇;比较地说。★在形容词+名词的结构中带有不定冠词时,rather 通常可位于不定冠词之前,也可位于其后。**3.** 〔与 or 连用〕说得更恰当点,更确切地说。**4.** 相反地,反而,倒不如说…更好[更合理]。**5.** 〔与连词 than 配合〕(与其…)不如(好)。**6.** 〔用作表[述]语〕更应当,更应该,当然。*I would* ~ *not go*. 我宁可不去。*Which would you* ~ *have, tea or coffee*? 你喜欢喝茶,还是喝咖啡呢? *I'd* ~ *he was married to somebody else*. 我宁愿他同别的人结婚。*He's done* ~ *well*. 他做得相当好。*This one is* ~ *too large*. 这个稍微大一些。*That is* ~ *an unusual question*. (= *a* ~ *unusual question*) 这是一个相当异常的问题。*He got home late last night, or* ~ *early this morning*. 他昨天半夜里,更确切地说,今天一清早才回到家。*He was no better, but* ~ *grew worse*. 他的病情未见好转,反而更恶化了。*It's not generosity,* ~ *self-interest*. 这不是慷慨,相反,这是自私。*He is honest* ~ *than clever*. 与其说他聪明,不如说他老实。*It is* ~ *cold than not* [*otherwise*]. (不管怎么说)天就是很冷。*I had* ~ *go than stay to be insulted*. 我宁可去,也不愿留着受辱。*He insisted on staying* ~ *than go*. 他坚持要留下来,而不愿意去。*It is* ~ *for us to be here dedicated to the great task remaining before us*. 我们更应当在这里献身于摆在我们面前的伟大事业。**II** [ˈrɑːˈðə; ˋrɑˋðɚ] ***int*.** 怎么不,当然。*Have you been here before*? — *R*-! 你以前到这儿来过吗?——当然来过。***had*** [***would***] ~ ... ***than*** (与其…)不如。~ ***than*** 而不。~ ***too*** ...稍微…一点 (*This one is* ~ *too large*. 这个稍微大一点)。***the*** ~ ***that*** [***because***] 尤其因为…(就更加)。

rat·hole [ˈræthəul; ˋræt͵hol] ***n*.** **1.** 被老鼠咬成的洞。**2.** 鼠穴。**3.** 狭小龌龊的地方。(***go***) ***down the*** ~ 白白浪费。

raths·kel·ler [ˈrɑːtskelə; ˋrɑts͵kɛlɚ] ***n*.** 〔G.〕**1.** 〔R-〕市议会厅的地下室餐厅[啤酒厅]。**2.** 〔美〕德国式地下室餐馆[咖啡馆、酒吧]。

rat·i·cide [ˈrætisaid; ˋrætɪ͵saɪd] ***n*.** 杀鼠药。

rat·i·fi·ca·tion [ˌrætifiˈkeiʃən; ͵rætəfəˋkeʃən] ***n*.** 批准,认可;追认。

rat·i·fi·er [ˈrætifaiə; ˋrætə͵faɪɚ] ***n*.** 批准者,认可者;追认者。

rat·i·fy [ˈrætifai; ˋrætə͵faɪ] ***vt*.** (***-fied***; ***-fy·ing***) 批准,认可(代理商等);追认。~ *an amendment to a constitution* 批准宪法修正案。

ra·ti·né [ˌrætˈnei; ͵rætˋne], **ra·tine** [ræˈtiːn; ræˋtin] ***n*.** 【纺】平纹结子花呢,珠皮大衣呢。

rat·ing¹ [ˈreitiŋ; ˋretɪŋ] ***n*.** **1.** 分等级;定等级;估价;估计;分摊,分配;【电】测定,计算;〔美〕(考试的)批分数。**2.** 额定值,定额;参量;工作能力;(商店的)信用程度;〔英〕地方税征收额。**3.** 【海】(船舰或海员的)等级;(汽车等的)规格;〔*pl*.〕〔英〕刚入伍的船员。**4.** (电台、电视台经调查确定的)节目受欢迎的程度。*a nominal* ~ 标准规格。*a power* ~ 额定功率。

rat·ing² [ˈreitiŋ; ˋretɪŋ] ***n*.** 叱责,斥责。*give a sound* ~ 严厉申斥一顿。

ra·ti·o [ˈreiʃiəu; ˋreʃɪo] **I** ***n*.** (*pl*. ~***s***) **1.** 比,比率,比值;比例;系数。**2.** 【经】复本位制中金银的法定比价。*the* ~ 3:2 (读作 *the* ~ *of three to two*) 3 对 2 之比。*arithmetical* ~ 公差,算术比。*direct* ~ 正比。*inverse* [*reciprocal*] ~ 反比。*current* ~ 电流比,电流变换系数。*nutritive* ~ 营养率。**II** ***vt*.** **1.** 用比例方式表达;求出…的比值;使…成比例。**2.** 将(相片)按比例放大或缩小。

ra·ti·oc·i·nate [ˌrætiˈɔsineit; ͵ræʃɪˋɑsn͵et] ***vi*.** 推理,推论;推断;用三段论法推论。

ra·ti·oc·i·na·tion [ˌrætiˌɔsiˈneiʃən; ͵ræʃɪ͵ɑsnˋeʃən] ***n*.** 推理,推论。

ra·ti·oc·i·na·tive [ˌrætiˈɔsineitiv; ͵ræʃɪˋɑsɪ͵netɪv] ***a*.** 推理的,推论的;爱推论的,好议论的。

ra·tion [ˈræʃən; ˋræʃən] **I** ***n*.** **1.** (供应物等的)限额,定额,定量;饲料配(给)量。**2.** 〔常 *pl*.〕(一般人或动物尤指兵员的)每日口粮;食物;军粮,军肉;粮食。*the iron* [*emergency*] ~ 【军】紧急用的浓缩食物;随身干粮。***be put on*** ~***s*** 实行配给供应制;计口授粮。***on short*** ~***s*** 处于配给量不足的限制下。**II** ***vt*.** (按额定分量)配给;给与…一天口粮;供给(兵士)伙食;限定(粮食等)。*The army is well* ~*ed*. 部队给养很好。~ **book** 配给供应本。~**-bread** 配给面包,军用面包。~ **export** 限额输出。~ **system** 配给制,供给制。

ra·tion·al [ˈræʃənl; ˋræʃənl̩] **I** ***a*.** **1.** 理性的。**2.** 推理的;有理性的;懂道理的,讲道理的;合理的,合道理的;纯理论的。**3.** 【数】有理的。*the stage of* ~ *knowledge* 理性认识阶段 〔*cf*. perceptual〕。*Man is a* ~ *being*. 人是理性动物。*the* ~ *faculty* 推理力。*a* ~ *man* 有理性的[言行合理的]人。~ *conduct* 合理的行为。*a* ~ *explanation* 合乎情理的解释。**II** ***n*.** **1.** 【数】有理数。**2.** 合理的事物;理性。**3.** 懂道理的人,人类。**4.** 〔*pl*.〕〔英〕合理的服装 (= ~ dress)。~ **expression** 【数】有理式。~ **analysis** 【化】示构分析。**-ly** ***ad*.**

ra·ti·on·a·le [ˌræʃiəˈnɑːli; ͵ræfəˋnæl] ***n*.** 理论的说明;基本原理;理论基础 (*of*)。

ra·tio·nal·ism [ˈræʃənəlizəm; ˋræʃənl̩͵ɪzəm] ***n*.** 【哲】理性主义,唯理论 (*opp*. empiricism)。

ra·tion·al·ist [ˈræʃənlist; ˋræʃənl̩ɪst] **I** ***n*.** 理性主义者,唯理论者。**II** ***a*.** = rationalistic.

ra·tion·al·is·tic [ˌræʃənəˈlistik; ͵ræʃənl̩ˋɪstɪk] ***a*.** 理性主义(者)的;唯理论(者)的。

ra·tion·al·i·ty [ˌræʃəˈnæliti; ͵ræʃəˋnælətɪ] ***n*.** 合理性;推理力;理由;〔*pl*.〕合理的意见[行动]。

ra·tion·al·i·za·tion [ˌræʃənəlaiˈzeiʃən; ͵ræʃənəlɪˋzeʃən] ***n*.** **1.** (尤指事业等的)合理化,合理状态。**2.** 理论解释。**3.** 【数】有理化;【心】文饰(作用)。~ *proposals* 合理化建议。

ra·tion·alize [ˈræʃənəlaiz; ˋræʃənl̩͵aɪz] ***vt*.** **1.** 使合理,合理化。**2.** 据理[在理论上]解释。**3.** 【数】使成为有理数,使消根。**4.** 【心】文饰。*a* ~*d unit* 【物】核理单位。— ***vi*.** **1.** 据理说明[行动]。**2.** 实行合理化。**3.** 文过饰非。

ra·tion·ing [ˈræʃəniŋ; ˋræʃənɪŋ] ***n*.** 定量配给。

rat·ite [ˈrætait; ˋrætaɪt] **I** ***a*.** 【动】平胸类 (*Ratitae*) 的,无龙骨的。**II** ***n*.** 平胸类鸟〔如食火鸡;鸵鸟等〕。

rat·lin(e)s, **rat·lings** [ˈrætlinz, -liŋz; ˋrætlɪnz, -lɪŋz] ***n*.** 〔*pl*.〕【海】绳梯横索。

rato, **RATO** [ˈreitəu; ˋreto] ***n*.** 火箭辅助起飞;起飞补助火箭 〔rocket-assisted take-off 的首字母缩略词〕。~ **unit** 火箭辅助起飞装置。

ra·toon [ræˈtuːn; ræˋtun] **I** ***n*.** 【植】截根苗。**II** ***vi*.** 发[长出]截根苗。

rats [ræts; ræts] ***int*.** 〔俚〕瞎扯。*Oh,* ~! 胡说。

rats·bane [ˈrætsbein; ˋræts͵ben] ***n*.** 杀鼠药〔特指亚砷酸〕;某些有毒植物的通称。

RATT = radioteletype.

rat·tail [ˈrætteil; ˋræt͵tel] **I** ***a*.** 鼠尾状的,细长的,一端逐渐变细的 (= rattailed)。**II** ***n*.** 【动】长尾鳕。

rat·tan [rəˈtæn; ræˋtæn] ***n*.** 藤,藤条;藤杖。

rat-tat, **rat-tat-tat**, **rat-tat·too** [ˈrætˈtæt, -tət-ˈtæt, -təˈtuː; ͵rætˋtæt, -tətˋtæt, -təˋtu] ***n*.** = rat-a-tat.

rat·teen [ræˈtiːn; ræˋtin] ***n*.** 【纹】平纹结子花呢;珠皮大衣呢〔流行于十八世纪英国〕。

R

rat·ten [ˈrætn; ˋrætn] *vt*. (工人在劳资争议时)用瘫痪工厂的战术迫使(资方)同意劳方要求,用隐藏或破坏机件的战术迫使(雇主)同意工会的要求。

rat·ter [ˈrætə; ˋrætɚ] *n*. 1. 捕鼠者;捕鼠猫[狗];捕鼠机。2. 〔俚〕叛变者,告密者,变节者,叛徒,工贼(等)。

rat·tish [ˈrætiʃ; ˋrætɪʃ] *a*. 鼠的,似鼠的,具有老鼠特性的。

rat·tle [ˈrætl; ˋrætl̩] **I** *vi*. 1. (硬物相碰或敲打时)格格地响。2. 卡嗒卡嗒地赶马车。3. (人或车)飞跑,疾走(*along*; *by*; *in*; *out*; *over*; *down*)。4. (临死的人)喉咙呼噜呼噜地响。5. 喋喋不休地讲(*on*; *away*; *along*; *about*)。*He ~d at the door*. 他把门推得格格地响。— *vt*. 1. 使格格地响。2. 急促地讲[吟诵](话、诗等)(*away*; *off*; *out*; *over*; *through*)。3. 匆匆忙忙做好,赶着完成(工作等)。4. 使(人)振作(*up*)。5. 〔口〕使狼狈[慌张];使烦恼。6. 打草赶出猎物。7. 破口烂骂。~ *a bill through the House* 使议案匆匆通过。*Nothing ~d him*. 什么事都惊动不了他。~ *foxes* 打草赶出狐狸。**II** *n*. 1. 卡嗒卡嗒声;格格声。2. (喉咙的)呼噜声;〔the ~s〕【医】哮吼〔一种喉炎,= croup〕。3. 喋喋不休(的话);喋喋不休的人。4. 格格地响的东西;响荚植物,响环,嘎吱嘎吱响的玩具;(响尾蛇的)音响器官。5. 高声吵闹。6. 响(亮程)度。~ **-box** 1. 响盒[玩具]。2. 【植】金链花猪屎豆。3. 〔美〕喋喋不休的人。~ **brain** = ~ **head** = ~ **pate** 糊涂虫。~**-snake** 〔美〕【动】响尾蛇(~ *snake and polecat* 〔美〕时常吵闹的两个人)。~ **stone** 铃石。~ **trap** 1. (格格响的)破马车;破汽车。2. 〔*pl*.〕破烂东西。3. 〔俚〕嘴;多嘴的人。

rat·tled [ˈrætld; ˋrætl̩d] *a*. 〔美俚〕兴奋的,狼狈的,慌张的。

rat·tler [ˈrætlə; ˋrætl̩ɚ] *n*. 1. 格格响的东西。2. 饶舌者。3. 〔美〕响尾蛇。4. 〔口〕极好的东西。5. 倾盆大雨。6. 〔美〕货运列车。7. 〔美俚〕有轨电车。8. 磨砖机。

rat·tling [ˈrætliŋ; ˋrætl̩ɪŋ] **I** *a*. 1. 格格地[卡嗒卡嗒]响的。2. 〔口〕活泼的,快活的;迅速的。3. 〔口〕巨大的,非常好的。4. 【商】原有响声〔对有松动声的包装的声明〕。~ *fun* 喧嚷;喝酒的嚷闹。*a ~ wind* (吹得窗子)卡嗒卡嗒响的风。*a ~ pile of money* 一大堆钱。**II** *ad*. 〔口〕极,很,非常。~ *big distance off* 极远极远。*I had a ~ good dinner*. 吃了一顿极好的饭。**at a ~ pace** 用很快速度。

rat·tly [ˈrætli; ˋrætlɪ] *a*. 作格格响的,吵闹的。

rat·ton [ˈrætən; ˋrætn̩] *n*. 〔Scot.〕老鼠〔尤指褐家鼠;黑家鼠〕。

rat·toon [ræˈtuːn; ræˋtun] *n*., *vi*. = ratoon.

rat·ty [ˈræti; ˋrætɪ] *a*. 1. 老鼠似的,老鼠特有的。2. 老鼠多的。3. 〔俚〕破烂的,可怜的,悲惨的;可卑的;〔英俚〕爱发脾气的。*a ~ smell* 老鼠臭味。*a ~ house* 闹耗子的房屋。

rau·cous [ˈrɔːkəs; ˋrɔkəs] *a*. 沙声的;粗声的;吵闹的。**-ly** *ad*. **-ness** *n*.

raugh·ty [ˈrɔːti; ˋrɔtɪ] *a*. 〔英口〕= rorty.

raunch [rɔntʃ; rɑntʃ] *n*. 粗野;粗俗。

raun·chy [ˈrɔːntʃi, ˈrɔn-; ˋrɔntʃɪ, ˋrɑn-] *a*. 〔美俚〕1. 质量不好的,邋遢的,便宜的,草率的。2. 赤裸裸地描写两性关系的,猥亵的;有伤风化的;粗野的;粗俗的。**-i·ness** *n*.

rau·wol·fi·a [rɔːˈwulfiə, rau-; rɔˋwulfɪə, raʊ-] *n*. 【植】1. 萝芙木属(*Rauwolfia*)印度萝芙木〔热带有毒植物〕。2. 【药】蛇根木(*Rauwolfia serpentina*)根部粉剂[浸剂]〔可提取萝芙木碱等〕。

rav·age [ˈrævidʒ; ˋrævɪdʒ] **I** *n*. 1. 破坏,荒废。2. 暴力。3. 〔常 *pl*.〕破坏的残迹,灾害,损害。*the ~s of time* 年久荒废。**II** *vt*., *vi*. 1. 摧残,蹂躏,破坏,使荒废。2. 劫掠。*a countenance ~d by time* 年老衰颓的面容。

R.A.V.C., **RAVC** = Royal Army Veterinary Corps 〔英〕皇家陆军兽医队。

rave[1] [reiv; rev] **I** *vi*. 1. (狂人一般)说胡话,说梦话,叫喊,叫嚣,嚷(*about*; *against*; *at*; *of*; *for*)。2. (海、风等)狂暴,咆哮;发狂似地讲;激赏,狂喜(*about*; *of*)。3. 大跳锐舞。~ *about* [*of*] *one's misfortunes* 叹惜自己倒霉。~ *against one's fate* 抱怨自己的命运。~ ***with fury*** 大发脾气,激怒。— *vt*. 〔多用反身代词〕(风)使自己咆哮得…,(人)使自己讲得[闹得]…。~ *itself out* (暴风等)咆哮后停息。~ *oneself hoarse* 叫嚷得嗓子都哑了。~ *oneself to sleep* 闹得疲倦地睡着了。**II** *n*. 1. (人、风、浪的)狂闹;怒吼;狂闹声。2. 〔俚〕狂热,入迷。3. 锐舞;锐舞舞会〔青少年马拉松式的疯狂舞会〕。***no ~*** 〔美剧〕不大成功(指戏剧)。***a ~ review*** 〔美〕捧场的评论。~**-up** 疯狂的晚会。

rave[2] [reiv; rev] *n*. 〔常 *pl*.〕(马车、卡车上为便于多装货物而设置的)围子,围栏,围板。

rav·el [ˈrævəl; ˋrævl̩] (〔英〕**-ll-**) **I** *vt*. 1. 解开,拆开(缠绕着的东西);理清,弄明白(错综复杂的事件)(*out*)。2. 使纠缠,使纷乱。— *vi*. 1. (编织物等)散开,脱开;(纠纷、混乱)解决;(困难)解除(*out*)。2. 纠结,缠绕,纷乱。*a hem to prevent its ~ling out* 防止散开的边。*the ~led skein of life* 错综复杂的人生。**II** *n*. 纠结,缠绕;(绳、织物等)散开的一端;错杂,混乱。

rave·lin [ˈrævlin; ˋrævlɪn] *n*. 【筑城】半月堡。

ra·vel·ling [ˈrævəliŋ; ˋrævl̩ɪŋ] *n*. 解,拆;解开;散开的线。

rav·el·ment [ˈrævlment; ˋrævl̩mənt] *n*. 缠结,纠缠,混乱。

ra·ven[1] [ˈreivən; ˋrevən] **I** *n*. 1. 【动】渡鸦,大乌鸦。2. 〔R-〕【天】乌鸦座。**II** *a*. 黑而亮的,乌亮的,(头发等)乌黑的。~ *locks* [*hair*] 黑发。

ra·ven[2] [ˈrævən; ˋrævən] **I** *n*. 1. 强夺,劫掠,抢劫。2. 强夺物,赃。**II** *vi*. 1. 掠夺,到处抢劫(*about*)。2. 往来捕食(*for*; *after*)。— *vt*. 狼吞虎咽地吃。

rav·en·ing [ˈrævniŋ; ˋrævənɪŋ] **I** *a*. 贪婪地捕食的,掠食的。**II** *n*. = ravin.

rav·en·ous [ˈrævinəs; ˋrævənəs] *a*. 1. 贪食的,贪婪的。2. 饿极了的;渴望的。**-ly** *ad*. **-ness** *n*.

rav·in(e) [ˈrævin; ˋrævɪn] *n*. 1. 〔诗〕劫掠。2. 掠夺物,赃物。3. 大嚼。*a beast* [*bird*] *of ~* 猛兽[禽]。

ra·vine [rəˈviːn; rəˋvin] *n*. 沟壑,深谷,峡谷,山涧。

rav·ing [ˈreiviŋ; ˋrevɪŋ] **I** *a*. 1. 说胡话的。2. 疯狂的,怒吼的,狂暴的。3. 令人醉心[痴心]的;〔美口〕非常的,(美人)绝代的。*a ~ lunatic* 胡说胡讲的疯子。*a ~ storm* 凶猛的暴风雨。*a ~ beauty* 绝代佳人。**II** *ad*. 胡说乱讲地;疯狂地。*be ~ mad* 胡说乱讲地发疯。**III** *n*. 〔常 *pl*.〕胡话。

ra·vi·o·li [ˌræviˈəuli; ˏrɑvɪˋolɪ] *n*. 〔*pl*.〕〔It.〕【烹】煮合子〔像中国的饺子,但为圆形或方形,煮熟后浇上番茄沙司吃〕。

rav·ish [ˈræviʃ; ˋrævɪʃ] *vt*. 1. 强夺;抢去,攫去;〔诗〕(死神)把(人)从人世夺去。2. 使心荡神移;使出神;使销魂,使狂喜。3. 强奸。**-ing** *a*. 引人入胜的;令人狂喜的,销魂的。**-ing·ly** *ad*. **-ment** *n*.

raw [rɔː; rɔ] **I** *a*. 1. (肉等)生的;未煮过的;未加工的,粗的;不搀水的,(酒精等)纯净的。2. 未开化的;未熟的,生硬的,无经验的;未经训练的,不完备的。3. (伤处等)皮肤绽开的,露出了肉的。4. 露骨的;〔口〕猥亵的。5. 〔俚〕苛刻的,不当的;刺痛的,针刺似的。6. 阴冷的,湿冷的,冷冰冰的。~ *brick* (未烧的)砖坯。~ *fish* 生鱼。*a ~ cocoon* 鲜茧。~ *silk* 生丝。~ *coal* 原煤。~ *cotton* 原棉,籽棉。~ *cloth* (未漂白的)原色布。~ *sugar* 粗糖。~ *spirits* 纯酒。~ *judgement* 不成熟的判断。*a ~ recruit* 生手,新手;新兵。*a ~ hand* 新手;莽撞的小伙子。*a nose ~ from rubbing* 擦破了皮的鼻子。*a ~ weather* 阴冷的天气。***be ~ to one's work*** 对工作还不熟练。***pull a ~ one*** 〔美俚〕讲下流的话;讲逗趣的故事。**II** *n*. 1. 擦破了皮的地方,皮开肉绽的地方,痛处。

2. 生的食物;纯酒;〔pl.〕粗糖;生牡蛎。**touch sb. on the ~** 触到某人痛处,触犯,大伤感情。**III vt.**〔罕〕(特指将马背的皮)擦破,使皮开肉绽。~ **boned a.** 瘦削的,骨瘦如柴的。~ **crop tillage system** 中耕农作制。~ **data** 原始数据。~ **deal**〔美〕不公平的待遇;凶狠的处置。~ **head** (哄孩子说的)妖怪 (*~ head and bloody bones* 骷髅头和下面交叉的大腿骨〔死的象征〕)。~ **hide** 1. *n.* 生皮;生皮鞭,皮条;皮索。2. *a.* 生皮(制)的。3. *vt.*〔美〕用皮条抽打,欺负。~ **material** 原料。~ **milk** 未经杀菌的牛奶。~ **ship**【海】新服役舰只。~ **umber** 生赭土。~ **silk** 生丝。**-ness** *n.*

Ra·wal·pin·di [ˌrɑːvəlˈpindiː; ˏrɑvəlˋpɪndi] *n.* 拉瓦尔品第〔巴基斯坦城市〕。

ra·win [ˈreiwin; ˋrewɪn] *n.* 1. 无线电测风;无线电测风仪。2. 测到的风向风速。~ **sonde** 无线电探空测风仪。

raw·ish [ˈrɔːiʃ; ˋrɔɪʃ] *a.* 有些生的,煮得不很熟的。

Raw·lin·son [ˈrɔːlinsn; ˋrɔlɪnsn] *n.* 罗林森〔姓氏〕。

Ray [rei; re] *n.* 雷〔姓氏,男子名, Raymond 的昵称〕。

ray[1] [rei; re] **I** *n.* 1. 光线,射线,热线;〔诗〕光辉,闪烁,曙光,一线光明。2. 辐射状物;辐助;【植】星状毛分枝,伞形花序枝;【动】鳍刺;魟;【几】半直线。*actinic ~s* 光化射线。*anode* [*cathode*] *~s* 阳极〔阴极〕线。*Becquerel ~s* 柏克勒尔射线〔法人 Becquerel 发现的镭等的放射线,有 α rays, β rays, γ rays〕。*cosmic ~s* 宇宙线。*electric ~s* 电子束;电磁波。*H ~s* 氢离子束。*infra-red ~s* 红外线。*ultra-violet ~s* 紫外线。*Roentgen ~s* = *X ~s* *X* 光线。*a star with six ~s* 六角星。*a ~ of hope* 一线希望。*a ~ of truth* 一丝真理。**II** *vt.* 1. 放射,照射,投射。2.〔俚〕给…照 X 光像片。— *vi.* 放射光线;(思想、希望等)闪现。**-less** *a.*

ray[2] [rei; re] *n.*【动】(短鼻)鹞鱼〔*cf.* skate[2]〕。*a whip ~* 魟。

ray·a(h) [ˈrɑːjə; ˋrɑjə] *n.* 非穆斯林的土耳其人〔尤指土耳其的基督教徒〕。

rayl [reil; rel] *n.*【物】雷(耳)〔1 牛顿/米^2 声压能产生 1 米/秒质点速度的声阻抗率(值)〕。

Ray·leigh [ˈreili; ˋrelɪ] *n.* 雷利〔姓氏〕。

Ray·mond [ˈreimənd; ˋremənd] *n.* 雷蒙德〔姓氏,男子名〕。

ray·on [ˈreiɔn; ˋreɑn] *n.* 嫘萦,人造丝;人造纤维;人造纤物。

rayon·nant [ˈreiənənt; ˋreənənt] *a.* 1. 射出光线的。2.【建】(窗格等)辐射式的。

raze [reiz; rez] *vt.* 1. 消除,磨灭(记忆等);毁坏,毁灭,夷平(城市房屋等)。2.〔罕〕微伤,擦伤。

ra·zee [reiˈziː; reˋzi] *vt.*, *n.*【史】拆除上面一层〔几层〕甲板使船身减低(的船)。

ra·zon [ˈreizɔn; ˋrezɑn] *n.*〔俚〕导弹,飞弹。

ra·zor [ˈreizə; ˋrezɚ] *n.* 剃刀。*a safety ~* 安全剃刀。***as sharp as a ~*** 厉害的,机警的。***skin a ~*** 做不可能做的事。~ **back** 尖突的背脊;尖峰耸立的山脉;剃刀鲸;〔美〕半野猪。~ **bill**【鸟】尖嘴海鸦。~ **edge** 1. (剃刀的)刀口;锐锋;尖锐的山背。2. 危机,危急时候〔情况〕(*on a ~ edge* [*~'s edge*] 在危险关头)。~ **fish**【动】隆头鱼科的一种鱼。~ **grinder** 剃刀磨石。~ **shape**〔美〕准备好了的。~ **shell**【动】竹蛏。~ **strop** 磨刀皮带,荡刀皮。**~-thin** *a.* 极薄的、其薄如纸的。

razz [ræz; ræz] *n.*, *vt.*〔美俚〕嘲笑;讥笑;逗惹;责备。*give sb. the ~* 嘲笑,奚落。*get the ~* 被嘲笑,被奚落。

raz·zia [ˈræziə; ˋræzɪə] *n.* 1. 侵略,袭击,劫掠。2. 掳掠奴隶的远征。

raz·zle-daz·zle [ˈræzldæzl; ˋræzl ˏdæzl] **I** *vt.*〔英俚〕1. 使混乱。2. 使酩酊大醉。3. 欺骗。**II** *n.*〔俚〕1. 烂醉。2. 混乱,慌张失措;嬉戏胡闹,喝酒嚷闹。3. 波动式旋转木马。*go on the ~* 狂饮,纵酒作乐。

razz·ma·tazz [ˈræzmətæz; ˋræzməˏtæz] *n.*〔俚〕1. 愉快的精神;精力,活力;兴奋。2. 令人眼花缭乱的动作(或场面),卖弄。

R.B. = Rifle Brigade〔英〕步枪旅;步兵旅。

Rb = rubidium【化】铷。

R.B.A. = Royal Society of British Artists 英国皇家艺术家协会。

RBC = red blood cell【解】红血球,红(血)细胞。

RBE = relative biological effectiveness 相对生物效应。

R-boat [ˈɑːbəut; ˋɑrbot] *n.* (德国的)快速扫雷艇。

RBT = random breath test (对开车人进行的)任意呼吸测试(以测出是否饮酒)。

RC = resistance capacitance (电)阻(电)容。

R.C., RC = 1. Red Cross 红十字(会)。2. research centre 研究中心。3. right centre (舞台)中央偏右方。4. Roman Catholic 罗马天主教的;罗马天主教徒。5. reinforced concrete【建】钢筋混凝土。6. Reserve Corps〔美〕后备军。

r.c. = remote control 遥控。

RCA = Radio Corperation of America 美国无线电公司。

R.C.A.F., RCAF = Royal Canadian Air Force (皇家)加拿大空军。

R.C.C. = Radio Chemical Centre〔英〕放射化学中心。

R.C.Ch., RCC, RCCH = Roman Catholic Church 罗马天主教会。

RCD = residual current device【电】剩余电流装置。

rcd = received.

RCM = 1. radar countermeasures 反雷达措施。2. radio countermeasures 无线电干扰措施。

R.C.M. = Royal College of Music〔英〕皇家音乐专科学校。

R.C.M.P., RCMP = Royal Canadian Mounted Police (皇家)加拿大骑警队。

R.C.N., RCN = Royal Canadian Navy (皇家)加拿大海军。

R.C.O. = Royal College of Organists〔英〕皇家管风琴学院。

r-col·o(u)red [ˈɑːkʌləd; ˋɑrˏkʌlɚd] *a.*【语音】带 r 音色彩的〔如 further 中的 u 和 e〕。

R.C.P. = Royal College of Physicians〔英〕皇家内科医师学会。

rcpt. = receipt.

R.C.S. = 1. Royal College of Surgeons〔英〕皇家外科医师学会。2. Royal Corps of Signals〔英〕皇家通信兵(部队)。

Rct = Recruit.

R.C.V.S. = Royal College of Veterinary Surgeons〔英〕皇家兽医学会。

R.D. = 1. Royal Dragoons〔英〕皇家龙骑兵团。2. rural delivery〔美〕乡村免费邮递。

R/D, R.D. = refer to drawer【商】请询问出票人,请与出票人接洽。

Rd., rd. = 1. road. 2. rod. 3. round. 4.【物】rutherford. 5. reduce. 6. rendered.

RDA = recommended dietary allowance 推荐饮食量。

RdAc =【化】radioactinium 射锕。

RDB = Research and Development Board〔美〕研究发展局。

R.D.C. = Royal Defence Corps〔英〕皇家保卫团。

R.D.C.A. = Rural District Councils' Association〔英〕乡村区议会联合会。

RDF = 1. radio direction finder 无线电测向器,无线电定向仪。2. radio direction finding 无线电探向,无线电测向。

RDP = ration distribution point〔美〕给养分配站。

RDS = radio data system【无】无线电数据系统〔甚高频信号广播用的编码信息系统〕。

Rd Th = radiothorium【化】射钍,放射性钍。

RE, R.E. = 1. real estate 不动产,房地产。2. Royal Engineers〔英〕皇家陆军工兵。**3.** Royal Exchange 伦敦交易所。**4.** rare earths 稀土元素。**5.** Reformed Episcopal (基督教)新主教派的。

Re = rhenium【化】铼。

re. = **1.** (with) reference (to). **2.** rupee.

re[1] [riː, rei; re, ri] ***n.***【乐】全音阶的长音阶第二音〔相当于音名 D〕。

re[2] [riː; ri] ***prep.*** 关于〔原法律和商业用语,现在用作口语〕。~ *your esteemed favour of 6th inst.*〔商、口〕关于本月六日专函〔旧式信函用语〕。*I want to speak to you* ~ *your behaviour.*〔口〕关于你的行为,我想跟你谈一谈。***in*** ~ 关于(*in* ~ *Bardell vs. Pickwick* 关于巴德尔对皮威克的诉讼)。~ (*Brown*) 关于(布劳恩案)。

re[3] [riː; ri]〔拉〕事物〔拉丁语 res 的夺格〕。~ ***infecta*** 事情未成。~ ***integra*** (事物等)完整如初。

re- *pref.* [ri, re, riː; rɪ, rɛ, ri] **1.** 相互,报复: *re*act, *re*venge. **2.** 反对: *re*sist, *re*volt. **3.** 后,在后: *re*lie, *re*main. **4.** 隐退,秘密: *re*cluse, *re*ticent. **5.** 离,去,下: *re*miss, *re*side, *re*tail. **6.** 反复,加强语气: *re*double, *re*search, *re*solve. **7.** 否定: *re*sign, *re*veal. **8.** 又,再,从新,重行: *re*adjust, *re*issue, *re*capture, *re*-entrance. ★〔发音〕**1.** 表示"再""又"等意义,且其后音节开头字母系母音或 *h* 时读 [riː; ri] (*re*hearse [riˈhəːs; rɪˋhɝs] 例外)。**2.** 表示其他意义,且重音在其后一音节时读 [ri; rɪ]: *re*turn [riˈtəːn; rɪˋtɝn]. **3.** 其后为辅[子]音开头的弱音节时读 [re; rɛ]: *re*collect [ˌrekəˈlekt; ˏrɛkəˋlɛkt]. ★加 hyphen 的用法: **1.** 欲与原来已有的词有所区别: *re*-pair〔*cf.* repair〕, *re*-cover〔*cf.* recover〕. **2.** 加强"反复""再"的意义: make and *re*-make, search and *re*-search. **3.** 常在元[母]音前,尤其在元[母]音 e 前: *re*-enter, *re*-assure〔常作 *re*assure〕。

're [ɑ, ə; ɑ, ɚ] = are〔如 *we're*; *you're*; *they're*〕.

REA =〔美〕Rural Electrification Administration〔美〕农村电气化管理局。

reach [riːtʃ; ritʃ] **I** ***vt.*** **1.** 到,抵,到达(特定地点,目的地等),(长度等)达到…;(子弹等)打中;扩展到…,延及…,(作为结果或结论而)达到…;〔美俚〕和…通讯,和…得到联络。**2.** 伸(手等) (*out*; *to*; *toward*); 伸手拿;伸手送达,交给,递给;给予。**3.** 取得,打动,感动(人心等);〔美俚〕行贿而收买到。*Your letter* ~*ed me yesterday.* 你的信昨日到达。*The rule does not* ~ *the case.* 这条规则不适用于那种情况。*R- me that book.* 请把那本书递给我。*Would you* ~ *me the salt, please?* 请把盐递给我好吗? *He is liable to be* ~*ed by flattery.* 他容易被谄媚奉承所打动。***as far as the eye can*** ~ 就眼力所能及,极目,满目。~ ***bottom*** 到底;查明,打听出来。~ ***down one's hat*** 伸手脱帽。~ ***land*** (渡洋而来的船等)好容易到达陆地;找到稳固的立脚点。~ ***sb.'s conscience*** 打动某人的良心。~ ***sb.'s ears*** 落入某人耳里,给某人听到。— ***vi.*** **1.** 伸手抓(东西);(企图拿到某物等而)伸展身体;(手脚)向前伸出;(草木向某方向)伸长,蔓延。**2.** 竭力想得到,竭力想达到(目的等)。**3.** (在时间、空间或程度范围上)扩展,达到 (*to*; *into*)。**4.**〔古〕抵达,到达。**5.**【航】横风行驶。~ ***after*** [***at***, ***for***] 竭力想达到,竭力想得到[拿到]。~ ***out*** **1.** 伸(手);伸手(拿…) (*for*)。**2.** (手)伸向前;(草木向…)生长。**II** ***n.*** **1.** 伸手(抓东西),伸展身体;手脚所能伸的限度;宽窄,广袤;到达,到达距离;(枪、炮弹等的)射程,所能及的限度,极度。**2.** 理解力,智力;力量。**3.** 区域,领域,范围,有效范围,势力范围;(河流二湾曲间眼所能及的)直线流域,(运河二闸门间的)河段,河流流程;〔美〕岬。**4.** 一次努力;【海】横风行驶;一气儿进行的航程。*a* ~ *of grassland* 一大片草原。*He has a wonderful* ~ *of imagination.* 他具有很丰富的想像力。*the upper* [*lower*] ~*es of a river* 河的上[下]游。***beyond*** [***above***] ***one's*** ~ 达不到,够不着;力量不及。***have a wide*** ~ 范围宽广。***make a*** ~ ***for*** (*sb.*, *sth.*) 向…伸出手去;企图抓住。***out of one's*** ~ = *beyond one's* ~. ***out of*** ~ ***of danger*** 脱离危险。***within easy*** ~ ***of*** 在容易达到…的地方,在…的附近 (*My house is within easy* ~ *of the station.* 我家离车站很近[在车站附近])。***within one's*** ~ 在够得着的地方;力量能做到的;能得到的。

reach-me-down [ˈriːtʃmidaun; ˋritʃmɪˏdaʊn] **I** ***a.***〔口〕现成的;穿旧了的,别人用过的。**II** ***n.*** **1.**〔常 *pl.*〕现成衣服;旧衣服。**2.**〔*pl.*〕〔美〕裤子。

re·act[1], **re-act** [ri(ː)ˈækt; rɪˋækt] ***vt.*** 再做,重做;再演,重演。

re·act[2] [riˈækt; rɪˋækt] ***vi.*** **1.** 反应;发生反作用 (*to*)。**2.**【化】反应 (*on*, *upon*);【物】反拨 (*against*; *upon*)。**3.** 反抗;【军】反攻。**4.** 反动,倒退,复古。~ ***against*** 反抗。~ ***upon*** 对…起反应,作用于… (*Tyranny* ~*s upon the tyrant.* 对于暴虐者反应也是暴虐行动)。

re·act·ance [ri(ː)ˈæktəns; rɪˋæktəns] ***n.*** 反作用力;【电】电抗;电抗器。

re·act·ant [riːˈæktənt; rɪˋæktənt] ***n.***【化】反应物。

re·ac·tion [ri(ː)ˈækʃən; rɪˋækʃən] ***n.*** **1.** 反作用,反应;反冲;反动力。**2.**【政】反动,倒退;复古(运动)。**3.**【化】反应,【物】反应力,反作用力;【无】反馈,回授;反向辐射;【医】反应;副作用,后效应;(紧张兴奋后的)无气力,虚脱。**4.**【商】猛跌。**5.**【军】反击。*action and* ~ 作用与反作用。*the* ~ *of mental on material things* 精神对于物质的反应。*chain* ~ 连锁反应。*nuclear* ~ (原子)核反应。*rocket* ~ 火箭推力[后坐力]。*a* ~ *type wavemeter*【无】吸收式波长计。

re·ac·tion·ar·y [ri(ː)ˈækʃənəri; rɪˋækʃənˏɛrɪ] **I** ***a.*** **1.** 反动的,倒退的;保守的。**2.**【化】反应的。~ *elements* 反动分子。**II** ***n.*** 反动分子;保守分子。

re·ac·tion·ism [ri(ː)ˈækʃənizəm; rɪˋækʃənɪzm̩] ***n.*** 反动思想;极端保守主义;复古主义。

re·ac·tion·ist [ri(ː)ˈækʃənist; rɪˋækʃənɪst] **I** ***n.*** 反动分子,复古主义者,保守主义者。**II** ***a.*** 反动的。

re·ac·ti·vate [ri(ː)ˈæktiveit; riˋæktɪˏvet] ***vt.*** (***-vat·ed***, ***-vat·ing***) **1.** 使恢复活动,使复活。**2.**【海】使复航。— ***vi.*** 重新活跃起来,重新活动起来。**re·ac·ti·va·tion** [ri(ː)ˌæktiˈveiʃən; rɪˏæktɪˋveʃən] ***n.***

re·ac·tive [ri(ː)ˈæktiv; rɪˋæktɪv] ***a.*** **1.** 反动的,倒退的,复古的。**2.** 反应的;反作用的;反冲的;【电】电抗的;【化】反应性的,活性的。*a* ~ *current* 无效电流。~ *power* 无功电力。**re·ac·tiv·i·ty** [ˌri(ː)ækˈtiviti; ˏrɪækˋtɪvətɪ] ***n.*** **-ly** ***ad.*** **-ness** ***n.***

re·ac·tor [ri(ː)ˈæktə; rɪˋæktɚ] ***n.*** **1.** 反应者,被试验者;【医】有(阳性)反应的人[动物]。**2.**【电】碍圈,扼流圈;电抗器;【化】反应器;【物】反应堆。*a fast* ~ 快中子反应堆。

read[1] [riːd; rid] (***read*** [red; rɛd]) **I** ***vt.*** **1.** 阅读,朗读,诵读;【议会】宣读(议案);照谱唱[奏] (*aloud*; *out*; *off*)。**2.** 辨读,辨认(暗号等);解答(谜等);(用计算机等)读出(信息的意义;密码等);(看脸色等)察觉,了解。**3.** 显示[钟点,度数等]。**4.** 能读,看得懂(拉丁语等);阅悉,读知(某事)。**5.** 读给人听;读着使…。**6.** 把(一段文字)解释为;把(文献中某一字句)读作,写作,印作。**7.**〔主为牛津大学学生语〕学,研究 (*up*)。*R- me* (*off*) *the list.* 请把名单给我念一遍。~ *a bill for the first time* 一读议案。*For* "*paper*" ~ "*proper.*" paper 应(读)作 proper. ~ *a book for sb.* 为某人代读一本书。~ *the child to sleep* 读书引孩子睡觉。~ *his silence as consent* 把他的沉默认为是同意。~ ***a dream*** 解释一个梦。~ ***men's hearts*** 了解[考察]人们的心理。~ ***off*** 读(出);数。~ ***one's shirt***〔美俚〕找衬衫缝中的虱子。~ ***oneself hoarse*** 读哑嗓子。~ ***oneself in*** 当众朗读誓约等后而就任。~ ***out*** 大声读;【自】读出〔指把计算机存储器中的资料取出等〕。~ ***out of a book*** = ~ *from a* book. ~ **sb. a lesson** [**lecture**] 训斥某人。~ **sb.'s face** 观察某人的脸色(而猜测他的内心)。~ **sb.'s hand** 看某人手相。~ **sth. else into sth.** = ~ **into sth. sth. else** 用别种观点[说法]解释某种观点[说法];把某种观点理解为别种观点〔多指曲解〕(*You are ~ing more than was intended into what he said*. 你歪曲了他讲话的真实意图)。~ **the future** 预言未来。~ **the Scriptures to sb.** 〔美俚〕对某人下命令;断言;发誓;责斥,命令。~ **the signs of the times** 观察时势。~ **to** 读书给…听(*Children like to be ~ to*. 小孩子喜欢人读书给他们听)。~ **up** 专攻(某科目);重点读一科目。~ **up on some subject** 系统地研究某一科目。— **vi.** **1.** 阅读,读书;学习,勤学,用功;朗读,诵读,宣读;讲读。**2.** 可读,值得读;使(读者或听者)感动。**3.** (某一文句)具有某种意义,可作某种解释。**4.** (某一文句)具有某种形式,由某些词组成。*The thermometer ~s 90°*. 寒暑表的示度是90度。~ *law* 研究法律。*The ticket ~s to Beijing via Shanghai*. 车票上写明经上海到北京。*The play ~s better than it acts*. 这出戏阅读比上演有趣。*He who runs may ~*. 跑着的人都能辨读;简明易懂。**be ~ out of** 被宣告开除。~ **about** = ~ *of*. ~ **back** 【军】重复,复述。~ **between the lines** 体会出字里行间之意;看出言外之意。~ **for degree** [**honours**] 为得学位[成为优等生]而用功。~ **from a book** 选书中一段朗读。~ **in a book** 读一本书读得入迷。~ **like** 可读作…,读了可认为…,可解释作。~ **of** 读知,阅悉(某事)。~ **through** (从头到尾)读完。~ **to oneself** 默读。~ **with sb.** 有老师陪着温习功课;(做家庭教师)陪某人读书。**II n.** 读书;(一次的)读书时间。**have a good** [**quiet, long, short**] ~ 舒畅地[安静地,长时间,短时间]读书。**take a quick** [**short**] ~ **at a book** 匆匆忙忙读一本书,读一会儿书。~**-in n.** **1.** 【自】写入。**2.** 宣读活动〔如议员在国会宣读某种文件以表示反对某议案等〕。~**-mostly memory** 【计】主读储存器。~**-only memory** 【计】(固定[永久性])只读储存器〔其数据不能被程序指令所改变〕。~**-out** **1.** 【机】(仪表等的)测量结果输出值,示值读数;【自】读出。**2.** (宇宙飞船等的)发回资料。**3.** 宣告开除。

read[2] [red; rɛd] **I** read 的过去式及过去分词。**II a.** **1.** 被朗读的。**2.** 读知的。**3.** 博识的;博览的;造诣深的。*a well-~ man* 博学者。(**deeply, well**) ~ **in** 精通(某一学科)。**little** [**slightly**] ~ **in** 略通。

Read(e) [riːd; rid] **n.** 里德〔姓氏〕。

read·a·ble [ˈriːdəbl; ˈridəbl̩] **a.** **1.** 易读的。**2.** 值得一读的。*a ~ book* 值得一读[读起来有趣]的书。~ *handwriting* 易读的[易看懂的]笔迹。**-bil·i·ty** [ˌriːdəˈbiliti; ˌridəˋbɪlətɪ] **n.** **1.** (书等)易读;值得读。**2.** (字迹等的)清晰,清楚。**3.** 【军】清晰程度。**-bly ad.**

re·ad·dress [ˈriːəˈdres; ˌriəˋdrɛs] **vt.** **1.** 重写(姓名、地址,更改姓名、地址等)。**2.** 再讲,再致(辞)。**3.** 〔~ oneself〕重新致力于,重新着手 (*in*)。

read·er [ˈriːdə; ˋridɚ] **n.** **1.** 读者,朗读者。**2.** 讲读者;(英国大学及法学协会的)讲师;〔美〕(大学教授的)助教;读经师〔通常称 lay-~〕。**3.** 读出器,读数镜,读数装置,指数仪表。**4.** 出版社的出版物审稿人〔通常叫 *publisher's ~*〕;阅览者,评阅者;校对人。**5.** 好学者。**6.** (谜的)解答人。**7.** (学校用的)读本;文选。*a great ~* 很爱读书的人;读很多书的人。*gentle ~s* 各位读者〔著者对读者的称呼〕。*a French ~* 法语读本。~**'s marks** 校对符号。~**ship** 读者的身份;〔美〕(杂志、报纸的)读者人数 (*cf*. circulation)。

read·i·ly [ˈredili; ˋrɛdlɪ] **ad.** 容易地;欣然,爽爽快快地,毫不勉强地,毫不犹豫地。*He would ~ die for his motherland*. 他为祖国死也甘心。

read·i·ness [ˈredinis; ˋrɛdɪnɪs] **n.** 容易;迅速;敏捷;欣然应允,愿意;准备,有预备。~ *to assume responsibility* 负责精神。**get** (**up**) **everything in ~ for** 为…准备齐全。**hold in ~** 经常有准备。**in ~** (**for**) … 准备妥当。~ **of wit** 机敏。**with ~** 欣然;爽快地;迅速地。

Read·ing [ˈrediŋ; ˋrɛdɪŋ] **n.** 雷丁〔姓氏〕。

read·ing [ˈriːdiŋ; ˋridɪŋ] **I n.** **1.** 阅读;读书;讲读;朗读,讲读会,读书会;(议会议案的)宣读。**2.** 读物。**3.** 学识;(尤指)书本知识。**4.** (谜、气候等的)判断,解释;(诗文词句等的)理解含义。**5.** (晴雨表等的)读数,示数,示度。**6.** (考证异本等时所见的)异文;(某节某处的)读法;(剧本人物的)演出法;(音乐的)演奏法。*a penny ~* (从前乡下举办的、门票极低的)朗诵会,歌唱会。~*s from Dickens* 狄更斯作品朗读会[选读]。~*s in politics* 政治读本。*a good* [*dull*] ~ 优良的[无聊的]读物。*the first ~* 初读会〔决定议案可否审议〕。*the second ~* 二读会〔决定议案采纳与否〕。*the third ~* 三读会〔决定所修正议案的成立与否〕。*What is your ~ of the fact?* 你对于这件事情的看法怎样? *a man of vast ~* 博学的人。**II a.** 读书的,爱书的,用功的。*a ~ man* 〔英〕爱读书的人。~ *matter* (报章、杂志的)读物,记事。*the ~ public* 读书界。~ **book** 读本。~ **desk** 书桌;阅览桌。~ **glass** (看小字用的)放大镜。~ **lamp** 台灯。~ **notice** (排在报纸第一页底部的)小广告。~ **room** (图书馆等的)阅览室;(印刷厂的)校对室。~ **wand** 电子读码棒〔可读出和记录零售商品标签产上的电子编码信息〕。

re·ad·just [ˈriːəˈdʒʌst; ˌriəˋdʒʌst] **vt.** 重做,再整理,(再)调整。**-ment n.**

read·y [ˈredi; ˋrɛdɪ] **I a.** (**read·i·er**; **-i·est**) **1.** 〔用作表语[主词补语]准备[预备]…的,下了决心…的,随时可以…的,即将…,动辄…的,已作好准备[预备]的;心中准备好的,打定了主意的。**2.** 现成的,现有的;迅速的,当面的,(答复等)即时的;敏捷的;巧于…的 (*at*);容易的,轻便的,简便的,立刻可用的;容易得到的。**3.** 【军】摆好放枪姿势的。*clothes ~ for wearing* 准备好待穿的服装。~ *for sea* 已作好航行准备的。*R-? Go!* (赛跑口令)预备!跑! *R-, present, fire!* (射击口令)预备!瞄准!放! *I am ~ to risk my life*. 我随时可以拼掉这条命。*You are ~ to speak ill of men*. 你动不动就讲人家坏话。*The boat is ~ to sink*. 这条船就要沉了。*a ~ pen* [*writer*] 倚马文章[快笔]。~ *wit* (应对如流,随机应变的)机智。~ *money* 现金。**be not ~ to** 来不及。**too ~ to promise** 轻易许诺。**find ~ acceptance** 被欣然接受,得到爽快的允诺;马上被相信。**get... ~** = *make... ~*. **give a ~ consent** 马上答应。**hold oneself ~ to** 正准备要…。**make ~** **1.** 作好准备。**2.** 整装 (*for*)。~ **about!** 【海】掉头准备。~ **all!** 【军】各就各位! ~ **at excuses** 随时都能找到借口;善于辩解的。~ **at** [**to**] **hand** 在手边。~ **for** 预备好。**the readiest way to do it** 做这事的最简便的方法[捷径]。**too ~ to suspect** 疑心太重。**II n.** 〔the ~〕**1.** 【军】射击准备。**2.** 〔俚〕现金(= ~ money)。**come to the ~** 托枪。**hold the rifle at the ~** 预备开枪。**plank down the ~** 〔俚〕付现款。**III ad.** **1.** 〔多与过去分词连用或用连字符连结,如 ~*-made*, ~*-built* 等〕预先,准备好。**2.** 〔多用比较级或最高级〕迅速,欣然,爽快。*be ~ packed = be packed ~* 预先包扎好。*the child that answers readiest* 回答最快的孩子。**IV vt.** 使预备[准备]好。~ **up** 〔俚〕即付现款。~**-faded a.** (牛仔服等)做成已褪色样子的,预褪色的。~**-for-service** 〔美〕= ~**-made** **1. a.** (服装等)现成的;预先准备好的,(意见等)听来的。**2. n.** 现成艺术品〔艺术家在实在生活中选出的实物,并不作任何加工〕。~**-mix a.** 预先拌好的。~ **room** (航空母舰上飞行员出发前的)接受命令室。~**-to-wear a.** 〔美〕马上就可用的,现成的。~**-wash** 〔俚〕强效可卡因。~**-witted a.** 机敏的,有机智的,能随机应变的。

re·af·firm [ˈriːəˈfəːm; ˌriəˋfɝm] **vt.** 重申,再断言,再肯定。

Rea·gan [ˈreigən; ˋregən], **Ronald** (**Wilson**) 里根,罗纳德(·威尔逊)(1911—),美国第40任总统(1981—1989)。~ **Doctrine** 里根主义〔指里根宣示的遏制苏联的外交政

策]。

re·a·gent [ri(:)ˈeidʒənt; rɪˋedʒənt] *n*. 1.【化】试药,试剂;反应物。2. 被试验者。*a ~ bottle* 试药瓶。

re·ag·gre·gate [riˈægrigeit; rɪˋægrɪˏget] I *vt*. 使重新聚集(为一个整体,一个分子等)。II *n*. 重新聚集体[分子]。**-ga·tion** [riˈægriˈgeiʃən; rɪˏægrɪˋgeʃən] *n*.

re·a·gin [riˈeidʒin; rɪˋedʒɪn] *n*.【医】反应素。

re·al[1] [riəl, ˈriːəl; ˋriəl, rɪl] I *a*. 1. 真实的,真正的(*opp*. sham);实际的,现实的(*opp*. ideal);事实上的,实质上的(*opp*. nominal);【哲】实在的。2. 真诚的。3.【法】不动产的,关于物的。4.【数】= ~-valued. *a ~ man* 真诚的人;真正的人。*effect a ~ cure* 根治。***the ~ thing* [*stuff*]** 道地货,原装货,上等货。II *n*. 〔the ~〕实在;现实;实物;实情;【数】实数。III *ad*. 〔美口〕真,真正,实在。*I am ~ pleased to meet you*. 遇见了你真高兴。~ **action** 物权讼诉。~ **capital** 实际资本。~ **credit** 实际信用。~ **estate** 不动产,房地产(*a ~ estate agent* [*broker*] 房地产经纪人)。~ **green** 〔美俚〕大量的钱,大笔款项。~ **image**【物】实像。~ **life** 现实生活。~**life** *a*. 实际的,真实的;非想像的。~ **money** 实价货币;现金。~ **number**【数】实数。~ **property** = ~ estate. ~ **right** 物权。~ **school** 实业学校。~ **tennis** 室内网球。~ **time** (真)实时(间),实际时间。~-**time** *a*. 实时的;快速的。~-**valued**【数】实数的。~ **wages** 实质工资〔根据购买力来衡量的工资〕。

re·al[2] [ˈriːəl; ˋriəl] *n*. 1. (*pl*. ~s [-z; -z];〔Sp.〕*-es* [ˈreɑːles; ˋreɑlɛs]) 从前西班牙及其领地所通用的小钱币(=1/8 peso)。2. (*pl*. *reis* [reis; rez]) 从前葡萄牙、巴西的货币单位。

re·al·gar [riˈælgə; rɪˋælgɚ] *n*. 1.【矿】雄黄,鸡冠石。2.【化】二硫化二砷。

re·a·lign [ˌriəˈlain; ˏrɪəˋlaɪn] *vt*., *vi*. (使)重新排列,(使)重新组合。

re·al·ism [ˈriəlizəm, ˈriːəl-; ˋrɪəlˏɪzəm, ˋriəl-] *n*. 1.【文艺】现实主义;写实主义;【哲】实在论,唯实论;【教】实学主义;【法】实体主义。2. 现实性。

re·al·ist [ˈriəlist; ˋrɪəlɪst] I *n*.【文艺】现实主义者[作家];【哲】实在论者,唯实论者;【教、数】实学主义者。II *a*. = realistic.

re·al·is·tic [riəˈlistik; ˏrɪəˋlɪstɪk] *a*. 1.【哲】实在论(者)的;【文艺】现实主义的。2. 逼真的;栩栩如生的。*a ~ novel* 现实主义的小说。**-ti·cal·ly** *ad*.

re·al·ity [ri(:)ˈæliti; rɪˋælətɪ] *n*. 1.【哲】现实,实在,实体,本体。2. 真实;事实;现实性。3. 逼真。*the objective ~* 客观现实[物质世界]。*the subjective ~* 主观的实在[精神世界]。*reproduced with startling ~* 仿造得和原物分辨不出的。***become a ~*** 实现;成为现实。***in ~*** 事实上,实际上;实在,真正。***make sth. a ~*** 实现某事,落实。~ **TV** 社会写实电视节目。

re·al·iz·a·ble [ˈriəlaizəbl; ˋrɪəlˏaɪzəbl] *a*. 1. 可实现的,可实行的;可确实感觉到的。2. 可变为不动产的;可换成现钱的。

re·al·i·za·tion [ˌriəlaiˈzeiʃən; ˏrɪələˋzeʃən] *n*. 1. (理想等的)实现,现实化,实在化;成就;亲身体会,真正认识。2. 赚头,实得。3. 把钱换成不动产;把财产[商品]换成钱,变卖。***have a full* [*a true*] *~ of*** 充分认识到某事,真正了解到某事。

re·al·ize [ˈriəlaiz; ˋrɪəˏlaɪz] *vt*. 1. 实现,实行(希望、计划等)。2. 实认,实感,领悟,了解,体会。3. 使显得逼真;如实表现,写实。4. 赚到,实得(若干钱);变卖。5.【经】实现〔把商品卖出,收回货币〕。*He could not ~ his own danger*. 他认识不到他自己的危险。— *vi*. 变卖;变现。*The sale of his picture ~d £20000*. 他的画卖了两万镑。

re·al·ly [ˈriəli; ˋrɪəlɪ] *ad*. 真,真正,实在,果真。*R-?* 真的吗? 哦? 果真吗? *R-!* 实在的! 真的! *~ and truly* 果真,的的确确,千真万确。*Not ~!* 不会吧! *Well ~!* 哎呀,真是这样[真想不到]! *If that is ~ the case*. 假如真是如此。*Tell me what you ~ think*. 把你的真心话告诉我吧。

realm [relm; rɛlm] *n*. 1. 王国,国土。2. 领域,区域,范围。3. (学术的)部门,界;(动植物分布的)圈,带。*~ of necessity* 必然王国。*the Defense of the R- Act* 英国国防令。*the laws of the ~* 国法。*the coin of the ~* 国币。*persons who are out of the ~* 在国外的人们。*the ~ of poetry* 诗的领域。*ideological ~* 思想领域。*the ~ of sleep* 梦的世界。

Re·al·po·li·tik [reiˈɑːlˌpəuliˈtiːk; reˋɑlˏpolɪˋtik] *n*. 〔G.〕现实政策;实力政策。**-er** 现实政治家。

Re·al·schu·le [reiˈɑːlˌʃuːle; reˋɑlˏʃulɛ] *n*. 〔G.〕(德国的)实科中学〔与着重古典语教育相对,着重理工,现代语〕。

re·al·tor [ˈriːəltə; ˋriəltɚ] *n*. 〔美〕房地产经纪人〔尤指全国房地产同业公会会员〕。

re·al·ty [ˈriəlti, ˈriːəl-; ˋrɪəltɪ, ˋriəl-] *n*. 不动产,房地产。

ream[1] [riːm; rim] *n*. 1. (纸的)令。★20 刀为一令,计 480 张,称 short ~;白报纸加损耗为 500 张,称 long ~;印刷用纸再加印刷损耗为 516 张,称 printer's [perfect] ~。2. 〔*pl*.〕〔口〕大量的纸[著述]。*He wrote ~s (and ~s) of verse*. 他写了很多很多的诗。

ream[2] [riːm; rim] *vt*. 1. (用绞刀)绞大(枪的口径等)。2. 折进(子弹壳等的)边。3. 挖除(不良部份)。4. 榨取(果汁)。

ream[3] [riːm; rim] *n*. 〔英方〕生奶油。

ream·er [ˈriːmə; ˋrimɚ] *n*. 1.【机】扩孔锥,绞刀,绞床;整孔钻。2. 果汁压榨器。

re·an·i·mate [ˈriːˈænimeit; riˋænəˏmet] *vt*. 使苏生,使复活;鼓舞,激励。**-ma·tion** [-ˈmeiʃən; -meʃən] *n*.

reap [riːp; rip] *vt*., *vi*. 1. 刈取,收割,采收。2. 得到,获得(努力的结果)。3. 遭到(报应);得到(报偿)。*~ grain* [*fruit*] 收割粮食[采收水果]。***~ as* [*what*] *one sows* [*has sown*]** 自食其果;种瓜得瓜种豆得豆,善因善果,恶因恶果。***~ experience*** 取得经验。***~ the fruits of one's actions*** 自作自受。***~ where one has not sown*** 不劳而获,侵占别人的劳动成果。***sow the wind and ~ the whirl wind*** 恶有恶报;干坏事必将受到严厉的报应。~-**ing hook** (收割用)镰刀。~**ing machine** 收割机。**-er** *n*. 收割者;收获者;收割机。

re·ap·pear [ˈriːəˈpiə; ˏriəˋpɪr] *vi*. 再现,再出,再发生。**-ance** *n*.

re·ap·point [ˈriːəˈpɔint; ˏriəˋpɔɪnt] *vt*. 1. 再任命,使复职。2. 重新约定;重新指定。**-ment** *n*.

re·ap·por·tion [ˈriːəˈpɔːʃən; ˏriəˋporʃən] *vt*. 重新分派,重新分配。**-ment** *n*.

re·ap·praise [ˈriːəˈpreiz; ˏriəˋprez] *vt*. (*-praised*, *-prais·ing*) 重新评价,重新估价,重新鉴定,重新考虑。**re·prais·al** *n*.

rear[1] [riə; rɪr] I *n*. 1. 后,后部,背面,背后(*opp*. front);(舰队或军队的)后方;后尾;殿后部队,后卫。2. 〔英口〕厕所[男子专用语]。3. 〔口〕屁股。***at the ~ of*** = ***in* (*the*) *~ of*** 在…之后,在…的后方,在…的背后。***bring* [*close*] *up the ~*** 殿后;走在后头。***follow in the ~*** 跟在后头。***front and ~*** 前前后后。***go to the ~*** 绕到后面。***hang on the ~ of*** 紧紧尾随(敌人)背后(伺机袭击)。***see* (*sth*.) *far in the ~*** 看见(某物)远远在后头。***send sb. to the ~*** 把某人送到后方。***take* (*the enemy*) *in* (*the*) *~*** 袭击(敌人)后方,从背后袭击敌人。II *a*. 后(方)的,背面的,背后的,殿后的。*the ~ gate* 后门。*a ~ rank*【军】后列。*~ service*【军】后方勤务。III *vi*. 〔英口〕上厕所去。~ **admiral** 海军少将。~-**end** *vi*. (汽车)追尾,撞入(前车后部)。~ **guard**【军】后卫。~ **vassal** 陪臣。~ **most** *a*. 最后的。

rear[2] [riə; rɪr] *vt*. 1. 举起,竖起,树立(旗竿等);建设,建

立(纪念碑等)。2. 饲养(家畜等);抚养,教养(孩子);栽培(作物)。3.〔古〕提高声音(叫喊、歌唱等)。~ *the* [*its, his*] *head* 抬头;(人)显露头角;(恶意等)显露出来。*The mountains ~ed their crests into the clouds.* 山顶高耸入云。~ *pigs* 养猪。— *vi*. 1. (马等)用后脚站起。2.〔方〕现出,出现。

rear·er [ˈriərə; ˋrɪrɚ] *n*. 1. 养育员,饲养员。2. 喜欢用后脚直立起来的马。

re·arm [ˈriːˈɑːm; ˋriˋɑrm] *vt*., *vi*. (使)重新武装,(使)重整军备;(使)配备新式武器。**re·ar·ma·ment** *n*.

rear·mouse [ˈriəˌmaus; ˋrɪrˏmaʊs] *n*. (*pl*. *-mice*) = reremouse.

re·ar·range [ˈriːəˈreindʒ; ˏriəˋrendʒ] *vt*. 重新整顿,重新布置,重新排列。— *vi*.【化】(分子)重排。**-ment** *n*.

re·ar·rest [ˈriːəˈrest; ˋrirˋrɛst] *vt*., *n*. 重新逮捕[拘留]。

rear·ward [ˈriəwəd; ˋrɪrwɚd] **I** *ad*. 在后方,向后方。**II** *n*. 后方,后部,背后;后卫。*in* [*at*] *the* ~ 在后卫;在后部[背后]。*in* [*on*] *the* ~ *of* 在…的后方,在…的后卫。**III** *a*. 向后方的;在末尾的。

rear·wards [ˈriəwədz; ˋrɪrwɚdz] *ad*. = rearward.

rea·son [ˈriːzn; ˋrizn] **I** *n*. 1. 理由,原因,缘故,动机。2. 理性,理智;智慧;合理(的行为)。3. 正常的思想,健全的思想,健全的议论[判断],常识,正常的事物。4. 道理,条理;理论,辩论,推论。5.【逻】论据,论点;前提,小前提。6. 理解力,判断力,理性直觉力。7. 实际的事情,可实行的事情。*bereft of* ~ 失去理智,疯狂;失掉知觉。*It is neither rhyme nor* ~. 莫名其妙。*It is without rhyme or* ~. 毫无道理,无缘无故。***as*** ~ ***was*** 根据情理。***be restored to*** ~ 恢复理智。***bring to*** ~ 使明白道理,使服从道理。***by*** ~ ***of*** 凭…的理由,因为。***by*** ~ (***that***) 因为,由于。***come to*** ~ 清醒过来。***for a*** ~ ***of state*** 以国家的利益为理由〔指执政者的借口〕。***for no other*** ~ ***than that*** [***but this***] 单单因为(这一理由)。***for*** ~***s of*** 因为。***give*** ~***s for*** 说明…的理由。***have*** ~ ***for*** [***to do***] 有必须的理由,有理由去(做),…(做)是对的,…(做)是当然的。***hear*** ~ = *listen to* ~. ***in*** (***all***) ~ 合理;正当 (*It is not in* ~ *to expect me to do so.* 要我做这样的事是没有道理的。*I will do anything in* ~. 只要是有道理的事我都答应去做)。***listen to*** ~ 服从道理,听从。***lose one's*** ~ 失去理性,发狂。***out of all*** ~ 不合理,不对头;不可理喻的。***stand to*** ~ 得当,合道理。***There is*** ~ ***in*** .... (某事)有道理 (*There is* ~ *in what you say.* 你讲得有道理)。***with or without*** ~ 无论有理与否。***with*** ~ 有道理;合乎情理。**II** *vt*. 1. 论证;推论,论断,推究。2. 说服 (*down*; *out of*; *into*); 向…解释。~ ***oneself into perplexity*** 不能自圆其说。~ ***out a conclusion*** 推论出一个结论。~ ***sb. down*** 说服某人。~ ***sb. into compliance*** 劝某人顺从,说服某人。~ ***sb. out of his fears*** 劝人不要怕。— *vi*. 1. 论究,推理,推论,推究 (*about*; *of*; *from*; *upon*)。2. 劝说 (*with*)。~ *with sb. for* [*against*] *sth.* 因赞成[反对]某点同某人讲道理。

rea·son·a·ble [ˈriːznəbl; ˋriznəbl] *a*. 1. 合理的;明白道理的,懂道理的;有理性的。2. (要求等)适当的;(价钱等)不高的;适度的。*a* ~ *man* 明白道理的人。*a* ~ *creature* [*being*] 有理智的动物[人]。*You must be* ~. 你别胡说八道,你该讲讲道理。**-bly** *ad*. **-ness** *n*.

rea·son·ing [ˈriːzəniŋ; ˋriznɪŋ] **I** *n*. 推论,推理;论究,论断;理论,论证;论法。**II** *a*. 能推理的;有关推理的。*the* ~ *power* 推理力。*a* ~ *creature* 理性动物,人类。

rea·son·less [ˈriːznlis; ˋriznlɪs] *a*. 不明道理的;不合理的,没有理性的。

re·as·sem·ble [ˈriːəˈsembl; ˏriəˋsɛmbl] *vt*. 重新召集;重新装配;调整。— *vi*. 重新集合。

re·as·sert [ˈriːəˈsəːt; ˏriəˋsɝt] *vt*. 再断言,再主张,再申明。~ ***oneself*** 重申自己的主张。**-tion** *n*.

re·as·sess [ˈriːəˈses; ˏriəˋsɛs] *vt*. 1. 对…再估价,再估定,再评价。2. 再征税。**-ment** *n*.

re·as·sign [ˈriːəˈsain; ˏriəˋsaɪn] *vt*. 再指定;再分配;再让与;交还。**-ment** *n*.

re·as·sume [ˈriəˈsjuːm; ˏrɪəˋsjum] *vt*. 1. 再取,取回。2. 再担任,重就,再接受。3. 再设想,再假定。— *vi*. (中断后)再开始说。**re·as·sump·tion** [ˈriːəˈsʌmpʃən; ˏriəˋsʌmpʃən] *n*.

re·as·sur·ance [ˈriːəˈʃuərəns; ˏriəˋʃʊrəns] *n*. 1. 再保证,自信,安心。2.〔英〕再保险。

re·as·sure [ˌriːəˈʃuə; ˏriəˋʃʊr] *vt*. 1. 再向…保证;使安心。2.〔英〕再对…进行保险。*People are ~d.* 人心安定了。

re·a·ta [ri(ː)ˈɑːtə; rɪˋɑtə] *n*. = riata.

Re·au·mur [ˈreiəmjuə; ˋreəˏmjʊr] **I** *n*. 1. 列欧穆〔法国姓氏,特指 René Antoine Ferchault de ~ 法国物理学家,生物学家,1683—1757〕。2. 列氏温度计〔以零度为冰点,80 度为沸点〕。*a temperature of more than 55°* ~ [*55° R.*] 列氏 55 度以上的温度。**II** *a*. 列氏(温度计)的〔略 R.〕。

reave, reive [riːv; riv] (~*d*, *reft* [reft; rɛft]) *vt*., *vi*.〔古、诗〕掠夺,劫掠〔多用 reive〕;抢劫 (*away*; *from*; *of*)。*parents* (*who were*) *reft of their children* 被夺去了[死去了]孩子的父母。~ *the neighbours of their cattle* 夺取邻人的牲畜。

Reb [reb; rɛb] *n*. 犹太人的尊称〔相当于"先生",与姓名连用〕。

reb [reb; rɛb] *n*.〔美口〕(美国南北战争中的)南军士兵 (= rebel)。

Re·ba [ˈriːbə; ˋribə] *n*. 丽巴〔女子名, Rebecca 的昵称〕。

re·bap·tism [riːˈbæptizəm; riˋbæptɪzm̩] *n*. 再洗礼;重新命名。

re·bap·tize [ˈriːˈbæptaiz; ˏribæpˋtaɪz] *vt*. 1. 给…再施洗礼。2. 给…重新取名。

re·bar·ba·rize [ˈriːˈbɑːbəraiz; ˋriˋbɑrbərˏaɪz] *vt*. 使重新变野蛮,使回到野蛮时代。

re·bar·ba·tive [riˈbɑːbətiv; rɪˋbɑrbətɪv] *a*. 令人讨厌的;容貌可怕的,狰狞的。

re·bate[1] [ˈriːbeit, riˈbeit; ˋribet, rɪˋbet] **I** *n*. 1. 折扣,回扣。2.〔英古〕减少。*the* ~ *system* 运费回扣制。**II** [riˈbeit; rɪˋbet] *vt*. 1. 给…回扣,打…的折扣。2.〔英古〕减少;削弱。3.〔美古〕使钝(刀刃)。

re·bate[2] [riˈbeit, ˈræbit; rɪˋbet, ˋræbɪt] *n*., *vt*. = rabbet.

re·ba·to [rəˈbɑːtəu; rəˋbɑto] *n*. = rabato.

re·ba·tron [ˈrebətrɔn; ˋrɛbətrɑn] *n*.【无】大功率电子聚束(加速)器。

re·bec, re·beck [ˈriːbek; ˋribɛk] *n*.【乐】雷别克〔中世纪的一种弓拉的梨形三弦乐器,由此演变而成小提琴〕。

Re·bec·ca[1] [riˈbekə; rɪˋbɛkə] *n*. 丽贝卡〔女子名〕。

Re·bec·ca[2] [riˈbekɑ; rɪˋbɛkɑ] *n*.【无】雷别卡〔一种飞机询问应答器〕。

reb·el [ˈrebəl; ˋrɛbl̩] **I** *n*. 造反者,反叛者;起义者,反抗者;〔美〕(内战时期的)南方人。**II** *a*. 造反的,反叛的。*the* ~ *army* 叛军。**III** [riˈbel; rɪˋbɛl] *vi*. 造反,反叛;反抗,不服从;厌恶 (*against*; *at*)。*The stomach ~s against too much food.* 胃不能接受过多的食物。

reb·el·dom [ˈrebldəm; ˋrɛbl̩dəm] *n*. 1. 发难地〔反叛者控制或据守的区域;尤指美国南北战争中的南方各州〕。2.〔集合词〕叛乱者,起义者。3. 叛乱(行为)。

re·bel·lion [riˈbeljən; rɪˋbɛljən] *n*. 造反,叛乱,起义;反抗。***rise in*** ~ 造起反来,起义。***rise in*** ~ ***against*** 起来造…的反。***the R-*** 1.【英史】= the Great R- 大叛乱 (1642—1660)。2.【美史】= the Civil War 南北战争。

re·bel·lious [riˈbeljəs; rɪˋbɛljəs] *a*. 1. 造反的;反抗的。2. 有叛变倾向的;企图叛变的。3. (事物)难控制的,难驾驭的;(病)难治的,顽固的。**-ly** *ad*. **-ness** *n*.

re·bel·low [ˈriːˈbeləu; riˋbɛlo] ***vi.***, ***vt.*** 〔诗〕(风等)(使)发回响;(使)回声轰鸣。

re·bind [ˈriːˈbaind; riˋbaɪnd] ***vt.*** (***re·bound*** [ˈriːˈbaund; ˋriˋbaʊnd]) 1. 重捆,重绑。2. 重新装订。

re·birth [ˈriːˈbəːθ; riˋbɝθ] ***n.*** 再生,复生,复活;【宗】轮回,转生。

re·boot [riˈbut; rɪˋbʊt] ***vt.*** 【计】重新启动。

reb·o·ant [ˈrebəuənt; ˋrɛboənt] ***a.*** 【诗】大声反响的,回音轰响的。

re·born [ˈriːˈbɔːn; riˋbɔrn] ***a.*** 再生的,复活的;更新的,复兴的。

re·bound[1] [ˈriːˈbaund; riˋbaʊnd] rebind 的过去式和过去分词。

re·bound[2] [riˈbaund; rɪˋbaʊnd] **I** ***vi.*** 1. (球等)弹回,回跳;【篮球】擦板入篮。2. 回响;复兴,重新振作;回到原地。3. (在蹦床上)作蹦跳运动。*Our evil example will ~ upon ourselves*. 我们的坏榜样会回到我们自己头上的〔意为结果自己受害〕。**II** ***n.*** 1. 弹回,跳回。2. 反应。3. 重新振作。*take a ball on the ~* 抓住反跳回来的球。***take sb. at* [*on*] *the ~*** 利用某人有某种反应等机会影响某人(*His courageous words took his depressed supporters on the ~*. 他趁机用豪言壮语鼓舞了那些沮丧消沉的支持者)。**-er** ***n.*** 蹦跳床〔蹦跳运动用的小型蹦床〕。

re·bo·zo [riˈbəuzəu, Sp. reˈbouθəu; rɪˋboso, rɛˋboθo] ***n.*** (*pl.* ***-zos*** [-zəuz, Sp. -θəus; -zoz, -θos]) 长披巾〔西班牙和美洲说西班牙语妇女包头和肩〕。

re·branch [ˈriːˈbrɑːntʃ; riˋbræntʃ] ***vi.*** 形成次级分支。

re·broad·cast [ˈriːˈbrɔːdkɑːst; riˋbrɔdˏkæst] ***vi.***, ***vt.***, (~(***ed***)) ***n.*** 【无】再播送,重播;转播。

re·buff [riˈbʌf; rɪˋbʌf] ***vt.***, ***n.*** 1. 拒绝,驳斥。2. 击退。3. (对希望、计划等的)阻碍,挫折。

re·build [ˈriːˈbild; riˋbɪld] ***vt.*** (***-built*** [-ˈbilt; -ˋbɪlt]) 再建,重建;使复原;改建;改造;改变。— ***vi.*** 重建。

re·buke [riˈbjuːk; rɪˋbjuk] ***vt.***, ***n.*** 指责,非难,谴责,惩戒。*give* [*administer*] *a ~* 谴责。*without ~* 无可非难,无可指责(地)。

re·bus [ˈriːbəs; ˋribəs] ***n.*** 谜;画谜,字谜。

re·but [riˈbʌt; rɪˋbʌt] ***vt.*** 1. 【法】反驳,驳回;揭露,戳穿。2. 〔罕〕击退,逐回,阻止(攻击等)。— ***vi.*** 举反证。**~ing evidence** 【法】反证。

re·but·tal [riˈbʌtl; rɪˋbʌtəl], **re·but·ment** [riˈbʌtmənt; rɪˋbʌtmənt] ***n.*** 【法】反驳;反证。

re·but·ter [riˈbʌtə; rɪˋbʌtɚ] ***n.*** 1. 反驳者。2. 【法】(被告的)第三答辩;反证。

rec. = 1. receipt. 2. received. 3. recipe. 4. record; recorded; recorder; recording. 5. reclamation.

re·cal·ci·trance [riˈkælsitrəns; rɪˋkælsɪtrəns] ***n.*** 固执;顽强,顽抗;难驾御,不听话。

re·cal·ci·trant [riˈkælsitrənt; rɪˋkælsɪtrənt] ***a.***, ***n.*** 倔强的(人),顽抗的(人),不顺从的(人)。

re·cal·ci·trate [riˈkælsitreit; rɪˋkælsɪˏtret] ***vi.*** 反抗,顽抗;不顺从;〔罕〕踢回。**-tra·tion** [riˌkælsiˈtreiʃən; rɪˏkælsɪˋtreʃən] ***n.***

re·cal·cu·late [riˈkælkjuleit; rɪˋkælkjəˏlet] ***vt.*** (***-lat·ed***, ***-lat·ing***) 重新计算,再核算。**-la·tion** [riˌkælkjuˈleiʃən; rɪˏkælkjəˋleʃən] ***n.***

re·ca·les·cence [ˌrikəˈlesns; ˏrɪkəˋlɛsns] ***n.*** 【冶】再辉,复辉。**re·ca·les·cent** ***a.***

re·call [riˈkɔːl; rɪˋkɔl] **I** ***vt.*** 1. 叫回,召回,召还。2. 取消,撤销,撤回。3. 使复活,恢复,挽回,拿回。4. (使)想起;(使)回忆。5. 〔美〕(依据一般投票)罢免(官吏)。*~ an ambassador* 召回大使。*~ a decree* 撤销法令。*~ sb. to a sense of his duties* 唤起某人责任心。*~ what was said* 想起说过的事情。***~ to life*** 使复活。***~ to one's mind*** 回忆,想起。**II** ***n.*** [riˈkɔːl; ˋriˏkɔl, rɪˋkɔl] 1. 叫回;(大使等的)召回,召还。2. 取消,撤回,撤销。3. 恢复。4. 回忆,回想。5. 【军】归队信号;收操号;集合号(号声)。6. (音乐会等中的)再演,再来一次。7. 【电讯】二次呼叫。8. 招艇旗;招艇信号。9. 〔美〕罢免(权)。10. (制造商因产品有问题等)公开收回出厂产品,返修请求。11. 【计】信息检索(能力)。*beyond* [*past*] *~* 收不回的,挽回不了的。

re·cant [riˈkænt; rɪˋkænt] ***vt.*** 改变,取消,撤回(主张等)。— ***vi.*** 取消主张;收回前言;撤回声明;公开认错。

re·can·ta·tion [ˌriːkænˈteiʃən; ˏrikænˋteʃən] ***n.*** 撤消,取消;改变信仰,改变主张,收回前言[意见]。*to exact ~s from prisoners of war* 要战俘认罪。*make a public ~* 公开认错;(登报)自首。

re·cap[1] [ˈriːkæp, riːˈkæp; ˋriˏkæp] **I** ***vt.*** 翻新,翻造(轮胎)。**II** ***n.*** 再生轮胎。

re·cap[2] [ˈriˌkæp; rɪˋkæp] **I** ***n.*** = recapitulation. **II** ***vt.***, ***vi.*** (***-capped***, ***-cap·ping***) = recapitulate.

re·cap·i·tal·ize [ˈriːkəˈpitəlaiz; riˋkæpɪtlˏaɪz] ***vt.*** (***-iz·ed***, ***-iz·ing***) 再投资;改变[调整]资本结构。

re·cap·i·tal·i·za·tion [ˈriːkəˌpitəlaiˈzeiʃən; riˏkæpɪtlɪˋzeʃən] ***n.*** 【经】资本额的调整。

re·ca·pit·u·late [ˌriːkəˈpitjuleit; ˏrikəˋpɪtʃəˏlet] ***vt.***, ***vi.*** 扼要重述,概括。

re·ca·pi·tu·la·tion [ˈriːkəˌpitjuˈleiʃən; ˏrikəˏpɪtʃəˋleʃən] ***n.*** 1. 扼要的重述。2. 【乐】再现部。**~ theory** 【生】重演说,反复说。

re·ca·pit·u·la·tive, re·ca·pit·u·la·to·ry [ˌriːkəˈpitjuleitiv, ˌriːkəˈpitjuleitəri; ˏrikəˋpɪtʃəˏletɪv, ˏrikəˋpɪtjuləˏtorɪ] ***a.*** 摘要的,扼要重述的。

re·cap·ture [ˈriːˈkæptʃə; riˋkæptʃɚ] **I** ***n.*** 1. 重新获得;恢复,夺还;收回物,夺回物。2. 征收。**II** ***vt.*** 1. 重新获得;收复,夺还。2. 征收。3. 想起;再经历;再体验。

re·cast [ˈriːˈkɑːst; riˋkæst] **I** ***vt.*** 1. 改铸,再铸;改作,改造。2. 再计算。3. 重新分派(角色)。**II** ***n.*** 1. 改铸;重做,改做。2. 再计算。3. 重新分配角色。

rec·ce [ˈreki; ˋrɛkɪ], **rec·co** [ˈrekəu; ˋrɛko], **rec·cy** [ˈreki; ˋrɛkɪ], **re·con** [ˈriːkɔn; ˋrikɑn] ***n.*** 〔军俚〕搜索,侦察〔reconnaissance 的缩略〕。

recd., **rec'd.** = received.

re·cede[1] [ri(ː)ˈsiːd; rɪˋsid] ***vi.*** 1. 后退,退却(*opp.* proceed)。2. 退缩;缩小,减退。3. 收回意见;退出(某种活动)(from)。4. (价值、品质等)跌落,低落;变坏。*the receding tide* 退潮。*a receding forehead* 脱发渐多的前额。***~ from one's position*** 退职。***~ in importance*** 重要性减小。***~ into the background*** 退居不重要地位;(问题)失去重要性。

re·cede[2] [ˈriːˈsiːd; ˏriˋsid] ***vt.*** 归还(领土等)。

re·ceipt [riˈsiːt; rɪˋsit] **I** ***n.*** 1. 接受,接收;收条,收据;〔常 *pl.*〕收入,收益,进款。2. 〔旧〕配方,制法。3. 〔古〕收税所。*I beg to acknowledge ~ of your letter*. 接奉尊函〔商业信件等用语〕。*a shipping ~* 送货收条。*the gross ~s* 总收入。***be in ~ of*** 【商】已收到…。***on* (*the*) *~ of*** 一俟收到。***upon* (*the*) *~ of*** = *on* (*the*) *~ of*. **II** ***vt.***, ***vi.*** (给…)出收据;(给…)开收条;签收。

re·ceipt·or [riˈsiːtə; rɪˋsitɚ] ***n.*** 领收者,领受的人;〔尤指〕【法】受委托而领收有关财产的人。

re·ceiv·a·ble [riˈsiːvəbl; rɪˋsivəbl] **I** ***a.*** 应收的,该接收的,该接受的;可信的。*bills ~* 应收票据(*opp.* bills payable)。**II** ***n.*** 〔*pl.*〕应收款项[票据]。**-a·bil·i·ty** [riˌsiːvəˈbiliti; rɪˏsivəˋbɪlətɪ], **-ble·ness** ***n.***

re·ceive [riˈsiːv; rɪˋsiv] ***vt.*** 1. 领受,接到,收到,得到(信、命令、请帖等);接受(欢迎,招待,请愿,建议,惩罚,损伤等)。2. 承受;顶住,支住(敌人、重量等)。3. 容纳,收容。4. 听从(警告等),领悟;承认,信任(报告等)。5. 迎接,接见(人);欢迎,招待,款待。6. 收买(赃物)。7. 【网球】接(球);打回。*~ letters* [*orders*] *from sb.* 接到某人的信[命令等]。*~ the enemy's cavalry* 迎击敌人骑兵。*~ sb. into the Trade Union* 接受某人为工会

R

会员。*a hole large enough to ~ three men* 足够容纳三人的一个大洞。~ *sb. in audience* 赐见,召见。*He ~d the contents of Jack's pistol.* 他被杰克用手枪打死了。*It deserves more attention than it ~s.* 世人应该更加注意这件事才好。**be ~d into sb.'s favour** 得到某人的宠爱。— **vi.** 1. 领受,接收。2. 接见,接待。3.【通讯】接收,收听,收看电视。4.【网球】接球,打回去。5.【宗】受圣餐。*He ~s on Sunday.* 他在礼拜天接见客人。~ **with open arms** 热烈欢迎。

re·ceived [riˈsiːvd; rɪˋsivd] **a.** 被容纳的,被接收的,被公认的;标准的。*R- Standard English* 标准英语。*the ~ text (of a book)* (某书的)标准版本。

re·ceiv·er [riˈsiːvə; rɪˋsivə] **n.** 1. 接受者。2. 收税人,收税官。3. 招待人。4. 窝家,收买赃赃的人。5. 应战者。6.【法】破产案产业管理人,(争执财产等的)委托管理人。7.【化】接收器,容器;【机】蓄汽室,收汽室;接受器;接收机,收报机,收音机,收话机,听筒;电视机,(电视)接收机。*a dual range ~* 长短波收音机。*The ~ is as bad as the thief.* 窝家跟贼一样坏。

re·ceiv·ing [riˈsiːviŋ; rɪˋsivɪŋ] I **n.** 1. 接收。2. 收买贼赃。II **a.** 接受的;收报的。~ **aerial** [**antenna**]【无】接收天线。~ **blanket**〔美〕洗澡后包婴儿的浴巾。~ **line** 正式场合列队欢迎客人的主人或主宾。~ **office**〔英〕邮件收寄处。~ **set**【无】收音机;电视接收机。~ **order**【法】法院委派破产者产业管理人的委任书。~ **ship**【海军】新兵练习舰。~ **station** 收报电台。~ **teller** (银行的)收款员。

re·cen·cy [ˈriːsnsi; ˋrisnsɪ] **n.** 新近。

re·cen·sion [riˈsenʃən; rɪˋsɛnʃən] **n.** 修订;校订本;修订版。

re·cent [ˈriːsnt; ˋrisnt] **a.** 1. 新近的;近来的。2. 近代的。3.〔R-〕【地】全新世的。**-ly ad.**

re·cep·ta·cle [riˈseptəkl; rɪˋsɛptəkl] **n.** 1. 容器。2. 贮藏所,仓库。3.【植】花托;囊托;(分泌液的)贮器。4.【电】插座,插孔。*a collection ~* 收钱箱。*a lamp ~*【无】管座。

re·cep·tion [riˈsepʃən; rɪˋsɛpʃən] **n.** 1. 接收;收容。2. 接见,招待(会),欢迎;欢迎会。3. 入会,入会许可。4. 所受待遇。5. 承认,公认。6. 领悟,感受。7.【无】接收(力)。*a warm ~* 热烈的接待;猛烈的抵抗。*a ~ area* 空袭避难人收容区,躲警报的地区。*a favourable ~* 好评。**give a ~ to** 招待,欢迎。**have a great faculty of ~** 领会力很强。**hold a ~** 举行欢迎会。~ **centre** (新兵等的)报到站。~ **chamber** = ~ room. ~ **clerk**〔美〕(旅馆等的)接待员。~ **desk** (旅馆的)接待处。~ **committee** 接待委员会。~ **day** 接见日,会客日。~ **order** (麻疯医院的)病人入院命令。~ **room** 客厅,会客室,接待室。**-ist n.**〔美〕(照相馆、牙科医院等的)接待员。

re·cep·tive [riˈseptiv; rɪˋsɛptɪv] **a.** 1. 接受的,接纳的,容纳的。2. 有接受力的,有容纳力的,善于接受的,敏悟的。3. 感受的;感官的。**-ly ad.** **-ness n.**

re·cep·tiv·i·ty [risepˈtiviti; rɪ,sɛpˋtɪvətɪ] **n.** 感受性;理解力。

re·cep·tor [riˈseptə; rɪˋsɛptə] **n.**【生】感受器;受体;【化】接受器;受纳体;【电】感受器;接收器。~ **site**【生】受体位点〔药物等的作用在细胞中见效的部位〕。

re·cess [riˈses; rɪˋsɛs] I **n.** 1. 休息,歇息;(议会的)休会(期间);〔美〕(大学等的)短暂的休假。2. 隐居处;〔*pl.*〕幽深处,深底。3.(山脉、海岸等的)凹进处,山限,水限;壁龛;壁凹;【解】(器官的)凹处,隐窝。4.【史】条约,条令。*the noon ~* 午休。**at ~** 在休息时间。**go into ~** 休会。**in the inmost ~es of** 在…的最深处。**in the secret ~es of one's heart** 在内心深处。II **vt.** 使凹进;把…搁在深处,隐藏。— **vi.**〔美〕(暂时)休会,休课,休庭。

re·ces·sion[1] [riˈseʃən; rɪˋsɛʃən] **n.** 1. 撤退,后退;退出,退离。2. 凹处。3.(工商业的)衰退;(价格的)暴跌。4.(墙壁等的)凹处。5.【基督教】(做完礼拜后牧师和唱诗班)退场时的行列。

re·ces·sion[2] [riːˈseʃən; ,riˋsɛʃən] **n.** (占领地等的)交还。

re·ces·sion·al [riˈseʃənl; rɪˋsɛʃənəl] I **a.** 1. 后退的;撤退的。2.(赞美歌等)在礼拜结束后退场时唱的。3. 休会[休课,休庭]的。II **n.** (礼拜结束后退场时唱的)赞美歌(= ~ hymn);(礼拜结束时奏的)退场音乐(= ~ music)。

re·ces·sive [riˈsesiv; rɪˋsɛsɪv] I **a.** 后退的,倒退的;逆行的;【生理】衰退的;【生】隐性的:*a ~ character*【生】隐性性状。II **n.**【生】隐性性状。~ **accent** 逆行重音〔重音由词尾向前移的历史音变〕。

Rech·a·bite [ˈrekəbait; ˋrɛkə,baɪt] **n.**【圣经】1. 利甲族 (Rechab) 的后裔〔见旧约《耶利米书》;相传该族人民不喝酒〕。2.〔转义〕禁酒者。

re·charge [ˈriːˈtʃɑːdʒ; riˋtʃɑrdʒ] I **vt.** 1.【电】给…再充电;再装填(弹药等);再装载。2. 再袭击。3. 重行告发;再控告。II **n.** 再袭击;再装火药。

ré·chauf·fé [riˈʃəufei, F. reʃofe; ,rɪʃoˋfe, reʃofɛ] **n.** (*pl.* ~*s* [-fe; -fɛ])〔F.〕1. 回锅菜。2.(文章、小说等的)改头换面工作。

re·cher·ché [rəˈʃeəʃei; rəˋʃɛrʃe] **a.**〔F.〕1. 考究的,煞费苦心的;精选的,上好的,优秀的;珍贵的,罕有的,难得的。2.(文字等)推敲过的;雕琢的;太讲究的;娇揉造作的。

re·cid·i·vism [riˈsidivizəm; rɪˋsɪdə,vɪzəm] **n.**【法】累犯,惯犯〔指所犯罪行〕。

re·cid·i·vist [riˈsidivist; rɪˋsɪdəvɪst] **n.**【法】累犯,惯犯〔指犯罪的人〕。

rec·i·pe [ˈresipi; ˋrɛsəpɪ] **n.** 1.【医】处方;照处方配成的药。2. 食谱;配方,制法;秘诀,秘法。*a ~ for living long* 长寿秘诀。

re·cip·i·ence [riˈsipiəns; rɪˋsɪpɪəns], **re·cip·i·en·cy** [riˈsipiənsi; rɪˋsɪpɪənsɪ] **n.** 接受,领受,容纳。

re·cip·i·ent [riˈsipiənt; rɪˋsɪpənt] I **a.** 容纳的,接受的;感受性强的。II **n.** 接受者;感受者;容纳者;容器。

re·cip·ro·cal [riˈsiprəkəl; rɪˋsɪprəkl] I **a.** 1. 相互的,交互的;可易的,互易的;酬答的。2.【数】倒数的,反商的。~ *help* 互助。*on ~ terms* 互惠地,按互惠条件。II **n.** 1. 互相关联的事物。2.【数】倒数,反商;乘法逆元素。~ **action** 交互作用。~ **cone**【数】配极锥面。~ **cross**【生】正反交,反交。~ **expression**【数】倒数式。~ **levelling** 对向水准测量。~ **love** 相爱。~ **pronoun**【语法】相互代词。~ **proportion** [**ratio**] 反比(例)。~ **symbiosis**【生】互惠共生。~ **treaty** 互惠条约。**-ly ad.**

re·cip·ro·cate [riˈsiprəkeit; rɪˋsɪprə,ket] **vt., vi.** 1. 互换,交换;酬答,报答 (*with*)。2.【机】往复,来回。~ *favours* 互相照应。*a reciprocating engine*【机】往复式发动机。*reciprocating motion* 往复运动。

re·cip·ro·ca·tion [ri,siprəˈkeiʃən; rɪ,sɪprəˋkeʃən] **n.** 1. 交互作用;交换;报答。2. 来回,往复运动。

re·cip·ro·ca·tor [riˈsiprəkeitə; rɪˋsɪprə,ketə] **n.** 1. 报答者。2. 往复机件。

rec·i·proc·i·ty [,resiˈprɔsiti; ,rɛsəˋprɑsətɪ] **n.** 相互关系;交互作用;互换;互惠主义;相互的利益[义务、权利];【哲】相关性,相互性;【化】倒易,可逆性;【数】互反性,互易性。*a ~ treaty* 互惠条约。

re·ci·sion [riˈsiʒən; rɪˋsɪʒən] **n.** 废除,取消,撤回。

re·cit·al [riˈsaitl; rɪˋsaɪtl] **n.** 1. 朗诵,吟诵。2. 叙述;详述,细说;叙事,故事。3.【法】(契约等中)陈述[证明]事实的部份。4.【乐】独奏[独唱](会)。

rec·i·ta·tion [,resiˈteiʃən; ,rɛsəˋteʃən] **n.** 1. 详述,叙述。2. 朗诵;朗诵诗文;背诵的诗[文章]。3.〔美〕背诵;口头答问。*a ~ room*〔美〕教室,课堂。

rec·i·ta·tive[1] [ˈresiteitiːv; ,rɛsətəˋtiv] **a.** 1. 朗诵的,吟诵的。2. 叙述的,讲述的。

rec·i·ta·tive[2] [,resitəˈtiv; ˋrɛsə,tetɪv] I **a.**【乐】宣叙调

的。**II** ***n***.【乐】宣叙调;(歌剧等中的)宣叙部。

re·cite [ri'sait; rɪ`saɪt] ***vt***., ***vi***. **1**.(在听众前)吟诵,朗诵(诗文等)。**2**. 讲,陈述,细说;列举。**3**.【法】在借据(等)上复述(事实)。**4**.〔美〕背诵(功课)。

re·cit·er [ri'saitə; rɪ`saɪtə] ***n***. 背诵者,朗诵者;朗诵集。

re·cit·ing-note [ri'saitiŋnəut; rɪ`saɪtɪŋnot] ***n***.【乐】朗吟符,朗吟调。

re·civ·i·lize ['riː'sivilaiz; `ri`sɪvɪl,aɪz] ***vt***. 使恢复文明。

reck [rek; rɛk] ***vi***., ***vt***.〔古〕〔仅否定句或疑问句用〕**1**. 注意,留心。**2**.(与…)发生关系,相干。*He ~s not of danger*. 他不注意危险。*What ~s it*? (= *It ~s not*.) 这有什么关系呢? ***What ~s he*** [***What ~s it***, ***him***] ***if***...? 即使…和他又有什么相干? (*What ~s he if the sky should fall*? 天垮下来他也不在乎)。

reck·less ['reklis; `rɛklɪs] ***a***. 不注意的;满不在乎的;鲁莽的,轻率的,不顾一切的。***be ~ of*** 不注意(*be ~ of the consequences* 毫不顾及后果)。**-ly** ***ad***. **-ness** ***n***.

reck·on ['rekən; `rɛkən] ***vt***. **1**. 计算;总计(*up*); 合计达…;算入,列入,加入(*among*; *in*; *with*)。**2**. 评定(*up*); 断定(*that*); 把…看做,认为(*as*; *for*; *to be*)。**3**.〔古〕(把某事)归咎于(某人),把…推到(某人身上)(*to*)。**4**.〔主美〕想;料想。*He is not ~ed among the leaders*. 他不算领导成员。*I ~ 53 of them*. 我算起来一共是五十三。*R- from 5 to 100*. 由五数到一百。*be ~ed as prosperous* 被认为兴隆繁荣。*~ sb. wise* 认为某人聪明。— ***vi***. **1**. 计算;支付,结算(*with*, *for*); 正确评定。**2**. 依靠,指望(*on*; *upon*)。**3**.〔主美〕想,料想,想像〔主作插句用〕。*He will come soon*, *I ~*. 我想他会来的。~ ***with*** **1**. 和…算账,和…结算。**2**. 将…加以考虑,重视。~ ***without one's host*** **1**. 不是当着店主人的面结账;〔喻〕不考虑重要因素而作出决定。**2**. 打如意算盘,不顾困难。

reck·on·er ['rekənə; `rɛkənə] ***n***. 计算者;计算便览(= ready ~)。

re·ck·on·ing ['rekəniŋ; `rɛkənɪŋ] ***n***. **1**. 计算,算账,结算;估计;(酒馆等的)账单。**2**. 报应,惩罚。**3**.【海】(由天文观测的)船位推算。*Even ~ makes lasting* [*long*] *friends*. 彼此无账友情久长。***a dead ~*** 仅凭测程器和罗盘进行的船位推算。***A Dutch ~*** 单方面有利的结账;〔喻〕一厢情愿的事。***be out in*** [***of***] ***one's ~*** 计算错误;估计错误。***pay the ~*** 付账。***the day of ~*** **1**. 结账日。**2**. 报应到来的日子;最后审判日。

re·clad ['riː'klæd; `ri`klæd] reclothe 的过去式和过去分词。

re·claim [ri'kleim; rɪ`klem] **I** ***vt***. **1**. 要求归还…,收回。**2**. 把(鹰)养乖,叫回。**3**. 矫正,改正,使悔改;教化,感化。**4**. 开垦,填筑。**5**. 利用;翻造,再生,回收(废物)。*~ land from the sea* 填海拓地。*a ~ed ground* 填筑地。*~ed* (*India-*) *rubber* 再生(橡)胶。— ***vi***. **1**.〔古〕抗辩。**2**. 悔改,改邪归正。**II** ***n***. **1**. 矫正;改造;悔改,改邪归正;教化。**2**. 开垦。**3**. 再生[回收]利用。**4**.〔罕〕收回,取回。***past*** [***beyond***] ~ 不可救药,无法改造。

re-claim ['riː'kleim; ri`klem] ***vt***. 要求收回,要求恢复;试图取回。

re·claim·a·ble [ri'kleiməbl; rɪ`kleməbl] ***a***. **1**. 可收回[取回]的。**2**. 可养乖的;可矫正的;能悔改的。**3**. 可开垦的,可填筑的。**4**. 可利用[回收]的。

rec·la·ma·tion [ˌreklə'meiʃən; ˏrɛklə`meʃən] ***n***. **1**. 收回的请求;收复,取回;矫正;驯服;教化。**2**. 开垦,填筑。**3**.(废物的)翻造,再生;回收;土壤改良。*~ of waste land* 开垦荒地。*~ of desert* 治理沙漠。

ré·clame ['reiklɑːm; ˏre`klɑm] ***n***. [F.] 自我宣传,沽名钓誉;虚名。

rec·li·nate ['reklineit; `rɛklənet] ***a***.【植】(叶片)下垂的,(枝条)拱垂的。

re·cline [ri'klain; rɪ`klaɪn] ***vt***.(将头、身体等)靠(在某物上)。*I lay ~d upon the grass*. 我躺在草地上。— ***vi***. **1**. 靠,躺(*upon*)。**2**.〔罕〕倚靠,信赖(*upon*)。*Being tired out*, *he ~d on the couch*. 他疲倦极了,横躺在沙发椅上。

re·clin·er [ri'klainə; rɪ`klaɪnə] ***n***. **1**. 倚靠者,斜倚者,横卧者。**2**. 活动躺椅(= reclining chair)。

re·clo·ser [riː'kləuzə; ri`klozə] ***n***.【电】自动开关,自动接入继电器;反复充电设备。

re·clothe ['riː'kləuð; ri`kloð] (***-d***, ***-clad*** [-klæd; -klæd]) ***vt***. **1**. 使再穿;使重新穿。**2**. 使换衣。

re·cluse [ri'kluːs; `rɛklus] **I** ***a***. 隐居的,遁世的;孤寂的,(生活等)寂寞的。**II** ***n***. 隐居者,隐士,遁世者。**-clusive** ***a***.

re·clu·sion [ri'kluːʒən; rɪ`kluʒən] ***n***. **1**. 幽居,隐退。**2**. 单独监禁。

re·coal ['riː'kəul; `ri`kol] ***vt***., ***vi***.(给…)再供给煤,(给…)重新添煤,(给…)再装煤。

re·coat ['riː'kəut; `ri`kot] ***vt***.(用油漆等)重新涂(一层)。

rec·og·ni·tion [ˌrekəg'niʃən; ˏrɛkəg`nɪʃən] ***n***. **1**. 认识;识出;识别;面熟,认得;招呼。**2**. 承认,认可。**3**. 褒奖,表扬;感谢,酬劳。*My ~ of him was immediate*. 我一见就认得是他。***beyond*** [***out of***] ~ (…得)使人认不出,(…得)完全改了模样,面目全非。***escape*** ~ 使人认不出。***give a passing*** ~ 打一个过路招呼。***in ~ of*** 承认…而,为酬答…而,按照(功劳等)… (*He is rewarded in ~ of his services*. 他因功受奖)。***receive*** [***meet with***] ***much*** ~ 大受赏识,大受注意。***win ~ from*** 赢得(某人的)赏识,博得(某人的)好评。~ **signal**【军】识别讯号。

rec·og·niz·a·ble ['rekəgnaizəbl; `rɛkəgˏnaɪzəbl] ***a***. **1**. 可认识[识别]的。**2**. 面熟的,好像认得的。**3**. 可承认[公认]的。**-bil·i·ty** [ˌrekəgˌnaizə'biliti; ˏrɛkəgˏnaɪzə`bɪlətɪ] ***n***. **-bly** ***ad***.

re·cog·ni·zance [ri'kɔgnizəns; rɪ`kɑgnɪzəns] ***n***. **1**. 承认。**2**.【法】保证书,具结;保释金。*enter into ~s* 具结,保证。

re·cog·ni·zant [ri'kɔgnizənt; rɪ`kɑgnɪzənt] ***a***. 认识到的;表示赏识的;表示承认…的(*of*)。

rec·og·nize ['rekəgnaiz; `rɛkəgˏnaɪz] ***vt***. **1**. 认识;认别;认出,看出;招呼。**2**. 承认;赏识;表扬;感谢,酬劳。**3**.〔美〕认可…发言。**4**. 认清;确认;自己承认。**5**. 公认。*~ the independence of a new state* 承认一个新国家。*He ~d that he was beaten*. 他认输了。*He was so much changed that I hardly ~d him*. 他变得我几乎认不出了。*I refuse to ~ him any longer*. 我以后不再睬他了。~ *services* 记功。— ***vi***.〔美〕【法】具结,提交保证书。

re·cog·ni·zee [riˌkɔgni'ziː; rɪˏkɑgnə`zi] ***n***.【法】接受具结书的人。

rec·og·niz·er ['rekəgˌnaizə; `rɛkəgˏnaɪzə] ***n***. 承认者。

re·cog·ni·zor [rikɔgni'zɔː; rɪˏkɑgnə`zɔr] ***n***.【法】写具结书的人。

re·coil [ri'kɔil; rɪ`kɔɪl] **I** ***n***. **1**. 反跳,跳回,倒退;(枪的)反撞,反冲,后座;反冲力,后座力。**2**. 退缩,畏缩,退却(*from*)。**3**. 报应。**II** ***vi***. **1**. 反跳,跳回,倒退,后坐。**2**. 撤退,退却,畏缩(*from*; *before*; *at*)。~ (*up*) *on oneself* (害人)反害己,自食其果。*The advancing troops ~ed before the counter-attack*. 前进部队遭遇反攻而退却。

re·coil·less [ri'kɔillis; rɪ`kɔɪllɪs] ***a***.【军】无后坐力的。

re·coin ['riː'kɔin; ri`kɔɪn] ***vt***. 重铸(硬币)。**~age** ***n***. 重铸;重铸的硬币。

re·col·lect [ˌrekə'lekt; ˏrɛkə`lɛkt] ***vt***. 想起;回想,追忆;想到;〔~ oneself〕使(自己)想起一时忘掉的事。— ***vi***. 回忆,记忆。

re-col·lect ['riːkə'lekt; ˏrikə`lɛkt] ***vt***. **1**. 再集合。**2**. 使镇定;鼓(劲),振作(勇气)。***be ~ed*** 沉着。~ ***oneself*** (使自己)镇定下来。— ***vi***. 重新集合。

R

re·col·lec·tion [ˌrekəˈlekʃən; ˏrɛkəˋlɛkʃən] ***n*.** **1.** 回忆,回想;记性,记忆力;〔常 *pl*.〕回想起来的事物。**2.** 心境平静。**3.**【宗】冥想。***beyond*** [***past***] ~ 想不出,记不得。***in one's*** ~ 记得。***have no*** ~ ***of*** 无…的记忆,忘记了。

re·col·our, re·col·or [ˈriːˈkʌlə; ˋriˋkʌlɚ] ***vt*.** 给…重新着色。

re·com·bi·nant [riˈkɔmbinənt; rɪˋkɑmbɪnənt] ***n*.**【遗】重组器官,复合器官。~ **DNA**【生化】重组脱氧核糖核酸。

re·com·bine [ˈriːkəmˈbain; ˏrikəmˋbaɪn] ***vt*.** 重新结合[化合];重组。**re·com·bi·na·tion** [ˈriːˌkɔmbiˈneiʃən; ˋriˏkɑmbəˋneʃən] ***n*.**

re·com·mence [ˈriːkəˈmens; ˏrikəˋmɛns] ***vt*., *vi*.** (使)重新开始;从头再做。**-ment** ***n*.**

rec·om·mend [ˈrekəˈmend; ˏrɛkəˋmɛnd] ***vt*.** **1.** 推荐,推举,介绍。**2.** (行为、性质)使人欢喜;使受欢迎。**3.** 劝,劝告,忠告(人)(*to do*; *that*)〔现多用 commend〕。**4.** 托,委托。*Can you* ~ *me a good cook*? 你可以介绍我一个好厨师吗? ~ *sb*. *as a servant* [*for a post*] 推荐某人做仆人[就任某职]。*Her manners* ~ *her to high and low alike*. 她的态度使上上下下的人都喜欢她。*Your plan has very little to* ~ *it*. 你的计划几乎毫无可取的地方。*I* ~ *you to take a holiday*. 我劝你休假吧。*the* ~*ed variety* 优良品种。~ ***one's own person*** 自荐。**-able** ***a*.** 可以推荐的;该赞许的,明智的。

rec·om·men·da·tion [ˌrekəmenˈdeiʃən; ˏrɛkəmɛnˋdeʃən] ***n*.** **1.** 推荐,介绍;介绍信。**2.** 特长;可取之处。**3.** 劝告。*speak in* ~ *of sb*. [*sth*.] 口头推荐某人[某物]。*sb*.*'s personal* ~*s* 某人的特长。*long-playing* ~*s* 受推荐的一些密纹唱片。*follow sb*.*'s* ~*s* 听从某人的劝告。

rec·om·mend·a·to·ry [ˌrekəˈmendətəri; ˏrɛkəˋmɛndəˏtorɪ] ***a*.** **1.** 推荐的。**2.** 特长的。**3.** 劝告的。*a* ~ *letter* 介绍信。

re·com·mis·sion [ˈriːkəˈmiʃən; ˏrikəˋmɪʃən] ***vt*.** 使(已退伍的人员、军舰等)再服役。

re·com·mit [ˈriːkəˈmit; ˏrikəˋmɪt] ***vt*.** **1.** 再干,再犯(罪);把…再关进监狱。**2.** 再委托,再委任。**3.** 重新提出(议案等)。**-ment, -tal** ***n*.**

rec·om·pense [ˈrekəmpəns; ˋrɛkəmˏpɛns] **I** ***n*.** 报应;报酬;回报;回礼;偿还;赔偿。**II** ***vt*.** 酬答,回报;偿还,赔偿。~ *him for his services* = ~ *his services* 酬答他的勤劳。~ (*him for*) *his loss* 赔偿他的损失。

re·com·pose [ˈriːkəmˈpəuz; ˏrikəmˋpoz] ***vt*.** **1.** 改组(内阁等);改写(诗文等)。**2.** 使安静,使镇定。**3.**【印】改排,重排。~ *a quarrel* 把争吵平息下来。

re·con [ˈriːkɔn; riˋkɑn] ***n*.** = recco; reconnaissance.

rec·on·cil·a·ble [ˈrekənsailəbl; ˋrɛkənˏsaɪləbl] ***a*.** 有和解[调停]希望的;可顺从的;可调和的,可使一致的。

rec·on·cile [ˈrekənsail; ˋrɛkənˏsaɪl] ***vt*.** **1.** 使和解,使和好(*to*; *with*);调停,排解(争端等)。**2.** 使顺从,使满足,使安心。**3.** 使一致,使调和 (*to*; *with*)。**4.**【宗】使(场所等)洁净。**5.**【造船】使(木板)接缝平滑。~ *persons to each other* = ~ *sb*. *to* [*with*] *another man* 使(某人与另一人)和解。*How can you* ~ *it to your conscience*? 你这样做,问心无愧吗? ~ *one's statement with one's conduct* 使言行一致。***be*** ~***d*** 言归于好,和解。***be*** ~***d to*** = ~ ***oneself to*** 甘心…,服从,顺从(*one's fate*)。

rec·on·cile·ment [ˈrekənsailmənt; ˋrɛkənˏsaɪlmənt], **re·con·cil·i·ation** [-siliˈeiʃən; -ˏsɪlɪˋeʃən] ***n*.** 调停;和解,调和,一致;服从,顺从。

rec·on·cil·er [ˈrekənsailə; ˋrɛkənsaɪlɚ] ***n*.** 调解人。

rec·on·cil·ia·tor·y [ˌrekənˈsiliətəri; ˏrɛkənˋsɪlɪəˏtorɪ] ***a*.** 调解的;和解的;调和的;顺从的。

rec·on·dite [riˈkɔndait, ˈrekən-; rɪˋkɑnˏdaɪt, ˋrɛkən-] ***a*.** **1.** 奥妙[深奥]的;(作品等)难解的。**2.** 看不出来的,隐藏着的。

re·con·di·tion [ˈriːkənˈdiʃən; ˏrikənˋdɪʃən] ***vt*.** **1.** 修理,检修;修改;改革。**2.** 重建,恢复;(重行)调整。

re·con·firm [ˈriːkənˈfəːm; ˏrikənˋfɝm] ***vt*.** 再证实;再确认。

re·con·nais·sance [riˈkɔnisəns; rɪˋkɑnəsəns] ***n*.** **1.** 侦察,搜索。**2.** 踏勘;勘察,探查;【植】概测。**3.** 侦察队;侦察车。*high* ~ 高空侦察。~ *in force* 强行侦察。*a* ~ *machine* [*airplane*] 侦察(飞)机。

rec·on·noi·ter, 〔美〕**-tre** [ˌrekəˈnɔitə; ˏrikəˋnɔɪtɚ] ***vt*., *vi*.** **1.**【军】侦察;搜索。**2.** 踏勘(土地)。

re·con·quer [ˈriːˈkɔŋkə; riˋkɔŋkɚ] ***vt*.** 再征服;夺回,克复。

re·con·sid·er [ˈriːkənˈsidə; ˏrikənˋsɪdɚ] ***vt*., *vi*.** 重新考虑。**-a·tion** [ˈriːkənˌsidəˈreiʃən; ˏrikənˏsɪdəˋreʃən] ***n*.**

re·con·sign·ment [ˌriːkənˈsainmənt; ˏrikənˋsaɪnmənt] ***n*.** **1.** 再交付,再委托;再寄售,再托卖。**2.** (在运输中对原提单上的路线、目的地、收货人等的)改变委托事项。

re·con·sti·tute [ˈriːˈkɔnstitjuːt; riˋkɑnstəˏtjut] ***vt*.** **1.** 重新构成[组成、编制、制定]。**2.** 重新编成。**3.** 恢复(脱水食物的)水分。

re·con·struct [ˈriːkənˈstrʌkt; ˏrikənˋstrʌkt] ***vt*.** **1.** 重建,再建;改造;复兴。**2.** 使在想像中重现;推想;设想。~ *a crime* (经过调查及推理等)设想犯罪情况。**re·con·struc·tion** ***n*.** **1.** 重建;改造;复兴。**2.** 〔美〕南北战争后南部各州的重建。

Re·con·struc·tion·ism [ˌrikɔnˈstrʌkʃənizəm; ˏrɪkɑnˋstrʌkʃənˏɪzəm] ***n*.** **1.** (美国南北战争后)提倡重建的运动。**2.**【宗】(犹太教)重建运动〔发生于 20 世纪,目的在于使犹太教传统与时代相适应〕。

re·con·vene [ˈriːkənˈviːn; ˏrikənˋvin] ***vt*., *vi*.** 再召集。

re·con·vert [ˈriːkənˈvəːt; ˏrikənˋvɝt] ***vt*.** **1.** 使重新皈依;使恢复党籍,使重新入党。**2.** 使恢复原状。**re·con·ver·sion** ***n*.**

re·con·vey [ˌriːkənˈvei; ˏrikənˋve] ***vt*.** 取回,送还,归还。**-ance** ***n*.**

re·cord[1] [ˈrekɔːd; ˋrɛkɚd] **I** ***n*.** **1.** 记录;记载。**2.**【法】案卷;档案;证据,证明;诉状;公判录。**3.** 履历,经历,阅历。**4.** 成绩;(运动比赛的)最高记录。**5.** (留声机的)唱片;录了音的磁带。*a matter of* ~ 有案可查的事件。*His* ~ *is against him*. 他的履历不好(对他不利)。*school* ~*s* 学业成绩。***a*** ~ ***run*** 打破记录的赛跑。***bear*** ~ ***to*** 给…作证,保证。***beat*** [***break, cut***] ***the*** ~ 打破前例,打破记录。***call to*** ~ = *take to* ~. ***go on*** ~ **1.** 被记录下来。**2.** 公开表明见解。***have a good*** ~ 履历好;信誉[名声]好。***hold the world's*** ~ 保持世界记录。***in*** ~ 有记录在案,记录上被登记(*the greatest earthquake in* [*on*] ~ 有记录以来最大的地震,空前的大地震。*It is in* ~ *that* ....…是有先例的)。***keep to the*** ~ **1.** 依据判例判决。**2.** 不扯到题外。***leave on*** ~ 留在记录上。***off the*** ~ 〔美〕不得发表的;不可以公开的;非正式的(*This is off the* ~. 这是非正式的谈话〔政治家用语〕)。***put*** [***place***] ***on*** ~ = *leave on* ~. ***put*** [***place***] ***oneself on*** ~ **1.** 取得卓著的成绩,出类拔萃。**2.** 表示意见,指出。***set*** (***up***) ***a new*** ~ 创新记录。***take to*** ~ 使…作证人,求…证明。***the greatest ... on*** ~ 有史以来最大的,前所未闻的。***travel out of the*** ~ **1.** 不依据判例判决。**2.** 扯到题外。**II** [riˈkɔːd; rɪˋkɔrd] ***vt*.** **1.** 记录,记载;登记,挂号;叙述,报告;给…录音;印记;永久留下。**2.** (寒暑表等)表示(度数)。**3.** (鸟)低声唱(歌)。*a* ~*ed statement* 正式声明。— ***vi*.** **1.** 记录;登记。**2.** 进行录音;被录音。~ **breaker** 打破记录的人,创新记录者。~ **breaking** ***a*.** 打破记录(的),空前的。~ **changer** 自动换片装置。~ **holder** (最高)记录保持人。~ **library** 收藏唱片的全部。~ **player** 电唱机。**-a·ble** ***a*.** 可记录的,值得记录的(*a* ~*able CD* 一张可录式光碟)。

re·cord·er [riˈkɔːdə; rɪˋkɔrdɚ] ***n*.** **1.** 记录者,记录员;市

法院法官。**2.** 自动记录器;(电报的)收报机;录音机;录音技师。**3.**〔常 *pl.*〕舌簧八孔直笛。*a wire* ~ 钢丝录音器。*a tape* ~ 磁带录音机。

re·cord·ing [riˈkɔːdiŋ; rɪˋkɔrdɪŋ] **I** *a.* (从事)记录的;自记的。*a* ~ *secretary* 记录员。*a* ~ *altimeter*【空】自记高度计。*a* ~ *mechanism* 自记装置。**II** *n.* (自动)记录,录音;唱片;录了音的磁带;录音的节目。*sound* ~ 录音。*disc* [*film*] ~ 唱片[胶片]录音。*wire* [*tape*] ~ 钢丝[磁带]录音。***play back the*** ~ 放录音。

re·cord·ist [riˈkɔːdist; rɪˋkɔrdɪst] *n.* 录音员。

re·count¹ [riˈkaunt; rɪˋkaʊnt] *vt.* **1.** 详细讲,细述。**2.** 列举。

re·count² [ˈriːˈkaunt; ˏriˋkaʊnt] **I** *vt.* 重新点数,再数。**II** *n.* (投票等的)重数,重计。

re·count·al [riˈkauntl; rɪˋkaʊntl̩] *n.* 再数,重数;叙述。

re·coup [riˈkuːp; rɪˋkup] *vt.* **1.** 扣除。**2.** 收回,使赔还;补偿,赔偿。**3.** 重获。~ *sb.* (*for*) *his loss* = ~ *sb.'s loss* 赔偿某人损失。~ *oneself* 收回用费[损失]。— *vi.* 补偿损失。

re·coup·ment [riˈkuːpmənt; rɪˋkupmənt] *n.* **1.** 扣除。**2.** 赔偿。

re·course [riˈkɔːs; rɪˋkɔrs] *n.* **1.** 依赖,依靠,利[使]用,求助(*to*)。**2.**【法】追索权;偿还要求。**3.**〔罕〕所依靠的物[人]。***have*** ~ ***to*** ...求助于…,依靠…,用…。***without*** ~【法、商】无追索权的;(汇票等)背书人[签证人]不负追索之责。

re·cov·er [riˈkʌvə; rɪˋkʌvɚ] **I** *vt.* **1.** 克复,恢复。**2.** 收回,取回,挽回(失去或被夺去之物);回收(废料);重新获得[找到](失传的技术等);找到,搜出(失踪的尸体等)。**3.** 使痊愈,使复原;使清醒,使复活。**4.** 赔偿(损失等);取得(损害赔偿等)。**5.** 使和解,安抚,怀柔。**6.** 使悔改。**7.** 填海造(地),围垦。~ *one's feet* [*legs*] (跌倒后又)站起来。~*ed acid* 回收酸。~*ed wool* 再生毛。~ *one's losses* 弥补[挽回]损失。~ *land from the sea* 填海拓地。*R- arms*!【军】还原(由瞄准转为预备放的口令)! ~*ed area* 收复区。~ *oneself* 清醒过来;心定下来;手脚恢复自由;重行站稳。~ *the meaning of* 发现…的意义。~ *the wind of* 重新追寻到(猎物的)臭迹。— *vi.* **1.** 恢复;痊愈 (*from*; *of*); 苏生,清醒。**2.**【击剑】恢复开始时姿势。**3.**【法】胜诉。**II** *n.*【击剑等】恢复开始时姿势。*at the* ~ 恢复开始姿势。

re-cov·er [ˈriːˈkʌvə; ˏriˋkʌvɚ] *vt.* 重新盖;改装(伞等的)面子,改装[更换]封面。

re·cov·er·a·ble [riˈkʌvərəbl; rɪˋkʌvərəbl̩] *a.* 可取回的;可恢复的;可回收的,可医好的。~ **reserve**【矿】可采储量。

re·cov·er·y [riˈkʌvəri; rɪˋkʌvərɪ] *n.* **1.** 重获;复得;恢复,收回,回收。**2.** 还原,复原;痊愈;苏生;矫正。**3.** 回缩。**4.** 填地。**5.**【法】胜诉。~ **room** (观察开过刀的病人或分娩后的孕妇的)恢复室。~ **plant** (废料)回收设备,再生工厂。

rec·re·ance [ˈrekriəns; ˋrɛkrɪəns] *n.* 求饶;怯懦;背叛变节。

rec·re·ant [ˈrekriənt; ˋrɛkrɪənt] **I** *a.* 求饶的;怯懦的;不忠的;变节的。**II** *n.* 胆小鬼,懦夫;背叛者,变节者。

re-create [ˈriːkriˈeit; ˋrikrɪˏet] *vt.* 再创造,再创作;改造,重做。

rec·re·ate [ˈrekrieit; ˏrɛkrɪˋet] *vt.* 使恢复精神;使得到休养;使得到消遣。~ ***oneself with*** 以…消遣(~ *oneself with baseball* 打棒球消遣)。— *vi.* 静养,休养;消遣。

re-cre·a·tion [ˈriːkriˈeiʃən; ˏrɛkrɪˋeʃən] *n.* 再创造,再创作;重新创造;再创造的事物。

rec·rea·tion [ˌrekriˈeiʃən; ˏrɛkrɪˋeʃən] *n.* 休养;娱乐,消遣。*a* ~ *ground* 休养地;娱乐场。*a* ~ *room* 娱乐室。**-al** *a.* *recreational vehicles* 娱乐车辆。

rec·re·a·tive [ˈrekrieitiv; ˋrɛkrɪˏetɪv] *a.* 适合休养的;消遣的,娱乐的。

rec·re·ment [ˈrekrimənt; ˋrɛkrɪmənt] *n.* 〔现罕〕渣滓,废物。**-al** *a.*

re·crim·inate [riˈkrimineit; rɪˋkrɪməˏnet] *vt.*, *vi.* 反责;反(控)诉。**re·crim·i·na·tion** [riˌkrimiˈneiʃən; rɪˏkrɪməˋneʃən] *n.*

re·crim·i·na·tive, -to·ry [riˈkrimineitiv, -təri; rɪˋkrɪməˏnetɪv, -ˏtorɪ] *a.* 反责的;反控诉的。

rec room [ˈrekrum; ˋrɛkrum] 〔口〕= recreation room.

re·cross [ˈriːˈkrɔ(ː)s; riˋkrɔs] *vt.* 再横过,再越过,再渡;横越[横渡]回来。

re·cru·desce [ˌriːkruːˈdes; ˏrikruˋdɛs] *vi.* (病、痛等)复发;(内乱等)再发作。

re·cru·des·cence [ˌriːkruːˈdesns; ˏrikruˋdɛsns] *n.* 再痛;(病等的)复发。

re·cru·des·cent [ˌriːkruːˈdesnt; ˏrikruˋdɛsn̩t] *a.* 又痛起来的(伤等);复发的(病等),更加重了的。

re·cruit [riˈkruːt; rɪˋkrut] **I** *vt.* **1.** 添补,补充(兵员);招募(新兵),征求(新成员),征收,吸收(党员)。**2.** 补养,保养(身体),恢复体力。**3.** 把食品装入(船内)。~ ***oneself*** 休养,静养。— *vi.* **1.** 招募新兵[人员],征求新成员。**2.** 补充,恢复健康;保养。**3.** 装入食品。*a* ~*ing sergeant* 征兵军士。~*ing ground* 征兵地区。***go to the country to*** ~ 到乡下去休养,易地疗养。**II** *n.* 新兵,新成员,新加入者,新学生。*a raw* ~ 初学者,新手,生手。**-ment** *n.*

Rec. Sec., rec. sec. = recording secretary 记录秘书。

rect. = **1.** receipt. **2.** rectangle; rectangular. **3.** rectified. **4.** rector; rectory.

rect- *comb. f.* = recti-.

rec·ta [ˈrektə; ˋrɛktə] rectum 的复数。

rec·tal [ˈrektəl; ˋrɛktl̩] *a.*【解】直肠的;近直肠的。

rec·tan·gle [ˈrektæŋgl; ˋrɛktæŋgl̩] *n.*【数】矩形,长方形。

rec·tan·gu·lar [rekˈtæŋgjulə; rɛkˋtæŋgjəlɚ] *a.* 矩形的,长方形的;成直角的。~ **distribution**【统】均匀分布。

recti- *comb. f.* 直,正;【电】整流。

rec·ti·fi·a·ble [ˈrektifaiəbl; ˋrɛktəˏfaɪəbl̩] *a.* **1.** 可矫正[改正,校正]的;可整顿的。**2.**【电】可整流的;【化】可精馏的。**3.**【几】(曲线)可求长的。

rec·ti·fi·ca·tion [ˌrektifiˈkeiʃən; ˏrɛktəfəˋkeʃən] *n.* **1.** 改正,校正,订正;矫正,纠正,整顿。**2.**【电】整流;矫频;【化】精馏,提纯。**3.**【数】求长法。~ **campaign** [**movement**] 整风运动。

rec·ti·fi·er [ˈrektifaiə; ˋrɛktəˏfaɪɚ] *n.* **1.** 改正者,校正者,订正者,更正者;矫正者,纠正者,整顿者。**2.**【电】整流器;检波器;检波管;纠[校]正仪;【化】精馏器。*a ignition* ~【机】点火管。*a plate* ~【无】屏极检波器;屏压整流器。

rec·ti·fy [ˈrektifai; ˋrɛktəˏfaɪ] *vt.* **1.** 改正,校正,订正,更正;矫正,纠正;整顿。**2.**【化】精馏,提纯;【电】整流,检波。**3.**【数】求(曲线的)长。**4.**【机】调整,拨准(表等)。*rectified alcohol* [*spirits*] 纯酒精。*a* ~*ing detector*【无】整流检波器。*a* ~*ing plane*【数】从切[平]面。*a* ~*ing surface*【数】伸长曲面。

rec·ti·lin·e·al, -e·ar [ˌrektiˈliniəl, -iə; ˏrɛktəˋlɪnɪəl, -ɪr] *a.* 直线的;沿直线的;形成直线的。

rec·ti·tis [rekˈtaitis; rɛkˋtaɪtɪs] *n.*【医】直肠炎。

rec·ti·tude [ˈrektitjuːd; ˋrɛktəˏtjud] *n.* **1.** 正直,公正。**2.** 正确。**3.**〔罕〕直。

rec·to [ˈrektəu; ˋrɛkto] *n.* (*pl.* ~*s*) 书籍的右页〔单数页〕;纸张的正面(*opp.* verso)。

rec·to·cele [ˈrektəsiːl; ˋrɛktəˏsil] *n.*【医】直肠(向阴道)突出。

rec·tor [ˈrektə; ˋrɛktɚ] *n.* **1.** (美国国教中掌管财产及税收的)教区长;〔美〕(新教主教派的)教区牧师;【天主】

R

教区长;修道院院长。2. 校长〔尤指德国大学的校长,英格兰限指牛津大学 Exeter and Lincoln Colleges 的院长,苏格兰指中学校长〕。*Lord R-* 〔Scot.〕(每三年选举一次的)大学名誉校长〔相当于英格兰的 Chancellor〕。~**-ship** = rectorate.

rec·tor·ate [ˈrektərit; ˋrɛktərɪt] *n*. 教区长(等)的职位[任期]。

rec·to·ri·al [rekˈtɔːriəl; rɛkˋtorɪəl] *a*. 教区长(等)的。

rec·to·ry [ˈrektəri; ˋrɛktərɪ] *n*. 教区长(等)的住宅[职位、辖区、俸禄]。

rec·trix [ˈrektriks; ˋrɛktrɪks] *n*. (*pl*. ***rec·tri·ces*** [ˈrektrisiːz, rekˈtraisiːz; ˋrɛktrɪsiz, rɛkˋtraɪsiz])【动】尾羽,舵羽。

rec·tum [ˈrektəm; ˋrɛktəm] *n*. (*pl*. ***rec·ta*** [ˈrektə; ˋrɛktə])【解】直肠。

rec·tus [ˈrektəs; ˋrɛktəs] *n*. (*pl*. ***-ti*** [-tai; -taɪ])【解】(眼、颈、大腿等部的)直肌。

re·cum·ben·cy [riˈkʌmbənsi; rɪˋkʌmbənsɪ] *n*. 1. 靠着,斜倚;躺着;休息。2. 依靠;依赖。

re·cum·bent [riˈkʌmbənt; rɪˋkʌmbənt] I *a*. 1. 靠着的;横卧的。2. 不活动的,懒惰的。II *n*. 〔口〕座位斜靠式自行车。**-ly** *ad*.

re·cu·per·a·bil·i·ty [riˌkjuːpərəˈbiliti; rɪˏkjupərəˋbɪlətɪ] *n*. 1. 恢复力,复原力。2.【化】可回收性。

re·cu·per·ate [riˈkjuːpəreit; rɪˋkjupəˏret] *vt*. 1. 恢复(健康、元气);使复原。2.【化】同流换热;回收。— *vi*. 1. (健康)复原。2. 弥补损失。

re·cu·per·a·tion [riˌkjuːpəˈreiʃən; rɪˏkjupəˋreʃən] *n*. 1. 恢复,复原。2. 弥补,挽回。3.【化】同流换热(法),同流节热,继续收热(法)。

re·cu·per·a·tive [riˈkjuːpəreitiv; rɪˋkjupəˏretɪv] *a*. 1. 恢复的;复原的;有复原力的。2. (火炉等)有保热装置的;同流换热的,复热的。

re·cur [riˈkəː; rɪˋkɝ] *vi*. (**-rr-**) 1. (问题、困难等)再发生;(疾病等)复发;来来去去,翻来覆去。2. 回想;回头讲(*to*);(思想等)重新浮现在心上(*to*)。3.【数】递归,循环。4.〔罕〕倚赖,求助,借助。~ *in* [*on*, *to*] *the mind* [*memory*] 又浮现在心上,想起。~**ring decimals** 循环小数。

re·cur·rence [riˈkʌrəns; rɪˋkɝəns] *n*. 1. 复回,重现,再发;来去,反复,隐现。2.【数】递归,循环;回想。3.〔罕〕倚赖。*a* ~ *formula* 递推[递演]公式,循环公式。*have* ~ *to arms* 用武力解决。

re·cur·rent [riˈkʌrənt; rɪˋkɝənt] I *a*. 1. 复回的,复现的,再发的。2. 时常来的,周期性发作的;循环的;时时想起的;【解、植】逆向的;回归的。II *n*.【解】回归动脉,回归神经,(尤指)上下喉头神经。~ **fever**【医】回归热。~ **nerves** 回归神经。~ **parent** 回交亲本。**-ly** *ad*.

re·cur·sion [riːˈkəːʃən; rɪˋkɝʒən] *n*.【数】递归(式);递推,循环。**-sive** *a*. **-sive·ly** *ad*. **-sive·ness** *n*.

re·cur·vate [riˈkəːvit; rɪˋkɝvet] *a*.【植】反曲的,反弯的。

re·curve [riːˈkəːv; riˋkɝv] *vt*. 使反曲,使反弯,使向后弯曲。— *vi*. 反弯;(风、水流等)折回。

rec·u·sancy [ˈrekjuzənsi; ˋrɛkjʊznsɪ] *n*. 抗拒;不服从;不服权威;【英史】不遵奉国教。

rec·u·sant [ˈrekjuzənt; ˋrɛkjʊznt] I *a*. 1. 不服从的,抗拒的。2.【英史】不遵奉国教的。II *n*. 1. 抗拒者,不顺从舆论[一般习惯]的人。2.【英史】不遵奉国教者。

re·cuse [riˈkjuːz; rɪˋkjuz] *vt*. (**-cused**, **-cus·ing**)〔罕〕宣布反对(审判员、陪审员或法庭),(提出某种理由)要求撤换(审判员等)。

rec vee [ˈrekviː; ˋrɛkvi]〔口〕= a recreational vehicle 游玩车辆,家庭旅行汽车。

re·cy·cle [riːˈsaikl; riˋsaɪkl] *vt*., *n*. 1. (使)再循环。2. (使废物回收后)反复利用。3. 整修,改建。

red[1] [red; rɛd] I *a*. (***red·der***; ***red·dest***) 1. 红色的,赤色的。2. 赤热的,(面孔)因…而胀红的(*with*)。3. 血腥的,血淋淋的(*with*);(战争等)残酷的。4.〔常 R-〕红的,革命的;共产主义的。5.【磁石】(指)北极的。6.〔英〕英国的〔由于地图上常把英国领土染成红色〕。~ *meat* 红肉,牛羊肉〔*cf*. white meat〕。~ *wine* 红葡萄酒。*a* ~ *battle* 血战。*The Chinese R- Army* 中国的红军。***as*** ~ ***as blood*** [***scarlet***, ***a turky-cock***] 胀红了脸。***become*** ~ = *turn* ~. ***paint the town*** ~ 痛饮;胡闹。~ *with* (*anger*) (气得)满脸通红。***turn*** ~ 变红,红了脸。II *n*. 1. 红,赤色;红色绘画颜料。2. 红布,红衣;〔美〕印第安人;〔R-〕〔美〕红头发的人;(台球的)红球。3. 共产党(员);共产主义者;左派。4.〔*pl*.〕月经。5.〔美〕一分(钱)。6.〔the ~〕〔美〕赤字,亏空,负债〔*cf*. the black〕。7.〔R-〕【英史】红舰队〔从前英国红、白、蓝三舰队之一〕。***be in*** (***the***) ~〔美〕亏蚀。***come out of the*** ~〔美〕开始赚钱,获利。***go into*** (***the***) ~〔美〕出现赤字,发生亏蚀。***see*** ~〔口〕激怒,生气。~**-bag** *a*. 内装传染性医院垃圾的,"红袋"垃圾的。~**-bait** *vt*.〔政俚〕给(人)扣红帽子,加以迫害[攻击]。~**-baiter**〔政俚〕给(人)扣红帽子的人。~**-baiting** *n*., *a*.〔政俚〕给人扣红帽子(的)。~**-ball**〔美〕特快车。~**-blind** *a*. 红盲的。~ **-blooded** *a*.〔美〕健壮的;精神好的;有勇气的;(小说等)情节紧张的。**R- Book** (红皮)社会名人录。~ **box**〔英〕大臣用红色文件匣。~ **breast**【鸟】欧鸲,知更鸟。~**brick**, ~**-brick** 1. *a*. (别于牛津和剑桥的)新大学的,新学院的;〔尤指〕地方设立的新大学的。2. *n*. 新大学,新学院。~**bud**【植】紫荆。~**bug**【动】红恙螨;红蝽。~**cap** 1.〔美〕(火车站、飞机场上戴红帽子的)搬运员。2.〔英口〕宪兵。3.〔Scot.〕妖怪,魔鬼。4.〔英〕金翅雀。~ **card**【足球】红牌(警告)。~**-card** *vt*.【足球】对…亮红牌(警告)。~ **cent**〔美口〕铜币(*I don't care a* ~ *cent*. 我毫不在乎)。~ **chip** (香港的)红筹股。~**coat**〔口〕【英史】英国兵,红衣兵。**R- Corners**〔前苏联〕红角,文化室。**R- Crescent**〔土耳其〕红新月会〔相当于红十字会〕。~ **cross** 圣乔治 (St. George) 十字架〔英国国徽〕;〔R- C-〕十字军徽章,十字军;〔R- C-〕红十字,红十字会;〔美俚〕吗啡。**R- Cross Society** 红十字会。~ **devil**〔美俚〕【药】速可眠〔丙烯戊巴比妥钠〕红色药丸。~**-dog** *vt*. 1. = Blitz. 2. (在金罗美牌戏中)使(对手)得零分。3.【足球】从边线带(球)插入球门区。~ **ear**【动】红耳太阳鱼〔产于美国中部和东南部〕。~ **eye** 1. 红眼鱼。2.〔美俚〕蕃茄汁;酒;下等浓威士忌酒。~**-eye** *n*.〔美口〕(熬)夜班;(熬)飞机夜航航班。~ **fescue**【植】紫羊茅。~ **fig**【植】红榕。~ **fish**【动】鲑鱼;海鲋。~ **flag** 红旗〔革命旗;危险信号旗;开战旗〕;激人发怒的东西。~ **gold**〔古、诗〕纯金;货币,现金。**R- Guard**〔苏联〕赤卫军。~ **hands** 血腥的[杀人的]手。~**-handed** *a*. 血手淋淋的,残忍的;现行犯的(*be caught* [*taken*] ~*-handed* 当场被捕)。~ **hat** 红帽,红衣主教。~**head** 红头发的人;【动】(美国产)红头啄木鸟(= redheaded woodpecker)。~ **headed** *a*. 头发红的;〔美俚〕大怒的。~ **legs** 拳参。~**-letter** *a*. 红字的;(日历上)用红字表示的(纪念日,节日等)。~**-light** 红灯;危险信号;【空】红色航空灯。~**-light district**〔美俚〕红灯区,风化区。~**-line** *vt*.〔美〕(以拒绝贷款、抵押、保险等)歧视,将…列入不受优待的范围。(**the**) **R- Sea** 红海。~ **herring** 1. 熏青鱼。2. 无关紧要的题外的话(*draw a* ~ *herring across the track* 提出无关系的问题使人的注意离开本题)。~**-hot** 1. *a*. 炽热的,灼热的;热烈的;非常激动的。2. *a*. 最新的。3. *n*. 红肠面包。~**-hot miracle**〔美〕意料之外的结果〔如赛跑得胜的马等〕。**R- Indian** [**man**] (红)印第安人。~ **ink** 红墨水;〔俚〕赤字;损失;〔俚〕廉价红葡萄酒。**R- International** 第三国际〔1919—1944〕。~ **knees**【植】蓼。~ **lamp** 红灯〔医师或药房夜间的门灯;(马路等的)停止通行信号,危险信号〕。~ **lane**〔儿语〕〔俚〕咽喉。~ **lattice**〔古〕红格子〔有执照的酒馆的标识〕;〔转义〕酒馆。~ **lead**【矿】铅丹,红丹,四

氧化三铅;〔美俚〕番茄酱。~ **neck**〔美俚〕乡下佬;(美国)南部农民。~ **noise**〔美俚〕番茄汤。~ **out**【空】红视〔飞行员因急剧推捍头部充血而视觉变红〕。~ **paint**〔美俚〕番茄酱。~ **pepper** 辣椒。~ **phosphorus**【化】赤磷,红磷。~**-pole**, ~**poll** 1.【动】金翅雀。2.〔*pl*.〕无角赤牛。~ **precipitate**【化】红色沉淀物;红色氧化汞。~ **prussiate**【化】赤血盐,铁氰化物。~ **rag** 1. 使人发怒的东西〔源自斗牛士手拿的那逗牛发怒的红披肩〕。2. 破红旗〔反对派诅咒"~ flag"的话〕。3.(小麦的)锈病。~ **ribbon Bath** 勋章;(法国)荣誉团勋章;勋章的红绶;佩带红绶勋章者。~ **root**【植】西风古;美洲茶。~ **ruin** 战祸。~ **sanders** [**saunders**, **sandalwood**]【植】紫檀。~ **shank**【鸟】赤足鹬(*run like a* ~ *shank* 飞一样地跑)。~ **shift**【天】红移,红向移动。~ **shirt**【意史】红衫党人〔十九世纪意大利加里波的之信徒〕。~**-shirt** 1. *vt*.〔美俚〕取消(球员)比赛资格〔一年后可再恢复其资格〕。2. *n*. 大学选手〔通常指延期毕业以进行训练的大学生体育尖子〕;被取消比赛资格的球员。~**-short** *a*.【冶】(铁)因热而脆的,热脆性的。~ **skin**〔贬〕(北美)印第安人。~ **snow** 红雪〔北极和阿尔卑斯山上被红藻染红的雪〕。~ **soldier** 穿红衣的兵;(皮肤变红的)猪霍乱;患猪霍乱的猪。~ **spider** 红蜘蛛〔棉花害虫〕。~ **spruce**【植】云杉。(**the**) **R- Square** 红场。~ **start**【鸟】红尾鸲。~ **tab**〔俚〕英国参谋军官。~ **tag** 特价,大减价。~ **tape** *n*., *a*.(扎文件的)红带(的);官僚作风(的),文牍主义(的)。~**-tapery**, ~**-typism** *n*. 官样文章,官僚作风,文牍主义。~**-tapist** *n*. 不离俗套的人,官僚[文牍]主义者。~ **tiger** 美洲虎。~ **top**【植】小糠草,红顶草。~**-top** *a*.(报纸栏目等)套红的。~ **triangle** 红三角〔Y. M. C. A. 的标识〕= Y. M. C. A. ~ **turkey**〔美俚〕刚煎好的法兰克福香肠。~ **ware**【植】掌状昆布〔可食用〕。~ **water** 1.(海湖中因红色微生物造成的)赤潮。2.【兽医】(牛的)血尿病(= texas fever)。~**-wing**【动】红翼歌鸫。~**wood**【植】1.〔美〕红杉。2. 红树,红木〔作染料用〕。**-ness** *n*. 红,红色。

red[2] [red; rɛd] *n*. 镇静剂。

re·dact [riˈdækt; rɪˋdækt] *vt*. 编辑,编纂(原稿等);编写;拟订(公告、通告等)。~ *a proclamation* 草拟宣言。**-tor** *n*. 编辑者;校订者。

re·dac·tion [riˈdækʃən; rɪˋdækʃən] *n*. 1. 编辑;编写;校订,改订。2. 改订本。

re·dan [riˈdæn; rɪˋdæn] *n*.【筑城】凸角堡。

redd[1] [red; rɛd] *vt*., *vi*. (*redd* 或 *red·ded*, *red·ding*)〔口或方〕整理,弄整洁〔常与 *up* 连用〕。

redd[2] [red; rɛd] *n*. 鳟鱼或鲑的产卵区。

redd[3] [red; rɛd] *vt*. 整顿,收拾。

red·den [ˈredn; ˋrɛdn̩] *vt*. 使红;使脸红。— *vi*. 变红;脸红。

red·dish [ˈrediʃ; ˋrɛdɪʃ], **red·dy** [ˈredi; ˋrɛdɪ] *a*. 带红色的,淡红的,微红的。

red·dle [ˈredl; ˋrɛdl̩] *n*., *vt*. (*-dled*, *-dling*) = raddle, ruddle.

rede [riːd; rid] I *vt*.〔古、方〕1. 忠告,劝告。2. 打算,企图。3. 解释,说明(谜、梦等)。4. 讲述。II *n*. 1. 忠告。2. 企图。3. 解释,说明。4. 故事。

re·deem [riˈdiːm; rɪˋdim] *vt*. 1. 买回(已卖之物等),赎回(典质物等),赎出(身体);挽回,恢复(名誉、权利、地位等)。2. 偿还,还清(债务等),收回(纸币等)。3 赎(罪);补救,弥补(缺点、过失等);【宗】(上帝)使免罪;拯救,救出(*from*; *out*; *of*);超度(众生)。4. 履行(契约),尽(义务)。~ *land from the sea* 填海拓地。*a* ~*ing point* [*feature*] 足以弥补缺点的特色,可取的地方,长处。~ *oneself* 用钱赎回人身。~ ***sth***. ***from*** 补救…的(缺点)。

re·deem·a·ble [riˈdiːməbl; rɪˋdiməbl] *a*. 可赎回[买回]的;可救的;可偿还的;可赎的,可补救的。*a* ~ *paper money* 可兑现的纸币。

re·deem·er [riˈdiːmə; rɪˋdimə] *n*. 1. 买回者,赎当者,赎身者;赎罪者。2.〔the R-〕【宗】救世主〔指耶稣基督〕。

re·de·mand [ˌridiˈmɑːnd, -ˈmænd; ˌridɪˋmɑnd, -ˋmænd] *vt*. 1. 再要求,再请求,再询问。2. 要回,要求交还。

re·demp·tion [riˈdempʃən; rɪˋdɛmpʃən] *n*. 1. 赎回,赎买;赎身。2. 履行,实践;偿还,(票据的)兑现。3. 赎罪;【宗】救济,超度。4. 补救;补偿之物;可取的地方,长处。5.〔英〕(地位、资格的)出钱购买。*a policy of* ~ 赎买政策。*That blow was* [*proved*] *his* ~. 他受了那个打击就改过自新了。***beyond*** [***past***, ***without***] ~ 无恢复希望的,不可救药的;难超度的。***by*** ~ 出钱(获得资格等)。***in the year of our*** ~ ...耶稣纪元…年,公元…年。~ **fund** 偿债基金。

re·demp·tion·er [riˈdempʃənə; rɪˋdɛmpʃənə] *n*.〔美〕(殖民地时代)出卖劳力抵作赴美船资的人。

re·demp·tive [riˈdemptiv; rɪˋdɛmptɪv], **-to·ry** [-təri; -tərɪ] *a*. 1. 赎回的,买回的,赎买的,赎身的。2. 偿还的。3. 救世的,拯救的;赎罪的。

Re·demp·tor·ist [riˈdemptərist; rɪˋdɛmptərɪst] *n*.(罗马天主教)传道会会员。

re·de·ploy [ˌriːdiˈplɔi; ˌridɪˋplɔɪ] *vt*., *vi*. 转移(军队、劳动力等);(使)重新布置。**-ment** *n*. 转移;(为加强生产力所采取的)调整措施。

re·de·scribe [ridiˈskraib; ˌrɪdɪˋskraɪb] *n*. 重新描述,完全重作描述〔尤指对生物学中的分类法〕。**-scrip·tion** *n*.

re·de·vel·op [ridiˈveləp; ˌrɪdɪˋvɛləp] *vt*. 1. 再发展。2. 重点恢复(破败的地区);恢复(一个地区的)经济发展。促进(一个地区的)经济发展。3.【摄】再[重新]显影。— *vi*. 再[重新]发展。**-ment** *n*.

re·di·a [ˈriːdiə; ˋridɪə] *n*. (*pl*. *re·di·ae* [-diːi; -dɪi])【动】雷蚴,雷迪幼虫。

re·dif [reiˈdiːf; reˋdif] *n*.(土耳其的)预备兵。

re·dif·fu·sion [ˈriːdiˈfjuːʒən; ˋridɪˋfjuʒən] *n*.【无】(电视节目等接收后的)播放,转播。~ **station**(有线)广播台,广播站。

red·in·gote [ˈrediŋgəut; ˋrɛdɪŋˌgot] *n*. 1. 大礼服,长大衣。2. 女式骑装外衣。

red·in·te·grate [reˈdintigreit; rɪˋdɪntəˌgret] *vi*., *vt*.(使)复原,(使)复旧,(使)更新。**-gra·tion** [reˌdintiˈgreiʃən; rɪˌdɪntəˋgreʃən] *n*. 恢复原状,复原,复旧,更新;【心】重整作用。

re·di·rect [ˈriːdiˈrekt; ˌridəˋrɛkt] *vt*. 1. 使改寄,更改(信件等)姓名地址。2. 再查问(证人等)。3. 使再回到,使折回;使改方向;使改道。

re·di·rec·tion [ˈriːdiˈrekʃən; ˌridəˋrɛkʃən] *n*. 1. 改寄,更改姓名地址;新姓名地址。2. 折回;归还。

re·dis·count [riːˈdiskaunt; riˋdɪskaunt] I *vt*. 再打折扣,再贴现。II *n*. 1. 再打折扣,再贴现。2. 再打折扣(商业)票据,再贴现票据。**-able** *a*. 可再打折扣[贴现]的。

re·dis·cov·er [ˈriːdisˈkʌvə; ˌridɪˋskʌvə] *vt*. 再发现;重新发现。

re·dis·trib·ute [ˈriːdisˈtribju(ː)t; ˌridɪˋstrɪbjʊt] *vt*. 重新分配,再分配;重新划分。

re·dis·trict [riːˈdistrikt; riˋdɪstrɪkt] *vt*. 重新划分(区域)(尤指重划选区)。

re·div·ide [ˈriːdiˈvaid; ˌridɪˋvaɪd] *vt*., *vi*. 重新[再]分配[划分]。

red·i·vi·vus [ˌrediˈvaivəs; ˌrɛdəˋvaɪvəs] *a*. 复活的,复生的,再兴的,再生的。*a Napoleon* ~ 拿破仑的再世。

Red·mond [ˈredmənd; ˋrɛdmənd] *n*. 雷德蒙〔姓氏〕。

re·do [ˈriːduː; riˋdu] *vt*. (*re·did* [ˈriːˈdid; riˋdɪd]; *re·done* [ˈriːˈdʌn; riˋdʌn]) 1. 再做,重做。2. 重新布置[装饰]。

red·o·lence [ˈredəuləns; ˋrɛdl̩əns] *n*. 1. 芬芳,芳香。2. 怀旧,怀念已往。

red·o·lent [ˈredəulənt; ˋrɛdl̩ənt] *a*. 1. 芬芳的,芳香

的;有…香味[气味]的 (*of*)。2. 令人想起[回忆、联想到]…的。~ *of the past* 令人想起往事的。

re·dou·ble [ri(:)ˈdʌbl; riˋdʌbl] *vt*. 1. 使加倍;加强。2. 再折叠。3. 使发反响。4. 重复,再说。~ *one's efforts* 加倍努力。— *vi*. 1. 激增,加强。2. 反响。3. 重折,重选。4.【桥牌】再加倍。

re·doubt [riˈdaut; rɪˋdaʊt] *n*.【军】多面堡,棱堡;(有护墙等的)防守阵地。

re·doubt·a·ble [riˈdautəbl; rɪˋdaʊtəbl]〔古〕**re·doubt·ed** [-id; -ɪd] *a*. (敌手等)可畏的,可怕的;不容轻视的;令人敬畏的。

re·dound [riˈdaund; rɪˋdaʊnd] *vi*. 1. 抬高,增加(信用、利益等)。2. (利益等)归于…,及于… (*to*);回到…,返还… (*upon*)。3. 发生,起来。*The sins of the fathers do not ~ to the children*. 父罪不及子。*His praises ~ upon himself*. 他称赞人,人也称赞他。

red·ox [ˈredɔks; ˋrɛdɑks] *n*.【化】氧还反应,氧化还原反应(=oxidation-reduction)。

re·draft [ˈriːdrɑːft; riˋdræft] *n*. 1.【商】(代替退票另加手续费的)新汇票。2. 新草案,新稿。

re·dress [riːˈdres; riˋdrɛs] I *n*. 1. 救济。2. 调整;调正,纠正,矫正。3. 赔偿。II *vt*. 1. 救济(受损害等的人)。2. 调整;调正,修整;革除(错误,弊病等);弥补,补救。3. 赔偿(损害、损失等);医治(疾病等)。~ *the balance* 恢复平衡;矫正不平衡状态。

re-dress [riːˈdres; riˋdrɛs] *vt*. 1. 再给…穿上。2. 重新包扎(伤处)。

re·duce [riˈdjuːs; rɪˋdjus] *vt*. 1. 减少,减轻,节减;缩短,缩小;降低,贬低;使没落,使落魄。2. 使降服,征服,克服;攻陷(城市等)。3. 使衰弱,使退化。4. 使变为,使成为,迫使,使不得不。5. 把…归类[分类,整理]。6.【数】简化,约简;化为;缩减;折合。7.【化】还原;【冶】提炼,精炼;从(原油)中蒸去轻质油。8.【医】使(脱臼等)复位,使复原。9. 使适合,使适应,使一致。10.【火箭】整理(测量结果等);译解(代号等)。11.【生】使(细胞)减数分裂。12.【摄】把(底片等)减薄,减低强度。13.【语音】把(重读音)变为非重读音。~ *production* 减少生产。*a map on ~d scale* 按比例缩小了的地图。~ *wine to two-thirds by boiling* 将葡萄酒煮沸浓缩成三分之二。~ *the temperature* 降低温度。~ *prices* 减低价格。*be ~d to a shadow* 消瘦得像一个影子似的。*be in a very ~d state* 非常衰弱。*be ~d to nothing* [*to a skeleton*] 瘦成骨架子。*a ~d family* 破落户。~ *sb. to terror* [*tears*] 使…恐怖[流泪]。~ *to reason* 使明理。~ *the animals to classes* 把动物分类。~ *one's discourse into* [*to*] *writing* 把谈话写成文章。~ *a house to ashes* 使房屋化为灰烬。~ *a compound to its components* 将化合物分解成各成分。***at a ~d price*** 廉价。***have the dislocation*** (***shoulder***) ***~d*** 请人将脱臼(肩骨)复位。***in ~d circumstances*** 没落。***on a ~d scale*** 小规模地。~ ***a fraction***【数】约分。~ ***an equation***【数】解方程式。~ ***a rule to practice*** 使条文变成实践。~ ***oneself into*** 陷入…的地步。~ ***the establishment*** (公司,机关等)裁员。~ ***to an absurdity*** 使变成荒谬。~ ***to assert*** [***asserting***] ***an absurdity*** 使陷于不得不讲荒唐话的地步;使窘迫得语无伦次。~ ***to discipline*** 恢复秩序,平定,使归顺。~ ***to order*** [***chaos***] 使秩序井然[乱七八糟]。~ ***to powder*** 把…弄成碎粉。~ ***to subjection*** 征服。~ ***to the ranks*** 把…降为兵。— *vi*. 体重减轻;【生】减数分裂。**reducing agent** 还原剂。**reducing division**【生】减数分裂。

re·duc·er [riːˈdjuːsə; riˋdjusɚ] *n*. 1. 缩小物。2. 渐缩管;减压阀;退黏剂;【化】还原器,还原剂;【摄】减薄剂。

re·duc·i·ble [riˈdjuːsəbl; rɪˋdjusəbl] *a*. 1. 可减少的,可缩减的;可贬低的;可降低的。2.【数】可简化的,可约的。3.【化】可还原的。4.【医】(脱臼等)可复位的。

re·duc·ing [riˈdjuːsiŋ; rɪˋdjusɪŋ] *n*. 1. 减肥法。2.【化】还原,减低。3.【数】折合;化简。~ **agent** 还原剂。

re·duc·tase [riˈdʌkteis, -teiz; rɪˋdʌktes, -tez] *n*.【化】还原酶。

re·duc·ti·o ad ab·sur·dum [riˈdʌkʃiəu ædəbˈsəːdəm; rɪˋdʌkʃɪo͵æd æbˋsɝdəm] [L.] = reduction to absurdity【逻】归谬(证)法,间接证明法。

re·duc·tion [riˈdʌkʃən; rɪˋdʌkʃən] *n*. 1. 缩小,减少;降级,降位;(刑罚等的)轻减;减速;减价,折扣。2. (城市、国家等的)陷落,投降,被征服、变成 (*to*; *into*)。3. 破落,没落;【物】衰减。4. 类别;碎矿;提炼。5.【数】简化,约简,缩减;化归。6. (测量结果的)整理,(代号等的)译解;【无】订正。7.【化】还原法,改格法;【摄】减薄。*a 10% ~* 九折。*great ~s in prices* 大减价。*the ~ of armaments* 裁(减)军(备)。*ascending* [*descending*] ~ 由小[大]单位改成大[小]单位的换算法。~ *to absurdity* = *reductio ad absurdum*. ~ **division**【生】减数分裂(=meiosis)。~ **potential**【化】还原单位,还原电势。

re·duc·tion·ism [riˈdʌkʃənizm; rɪˋdʌkʃənɪzm] *n*. 1. 简化法;简化论。2. 归纳主义〔以演绎无生命物质的理化用词来解释一切生物过程的作法〕。**-ist** *n*., *a*. 1. 简化论者(的)。2. 归纳主义者(的)。**-tion·is·tic** *a*.

re·duc·tive [riˈdʌktiv; rɪˋdʌktɪv] I *a*. 1. 缩减的;还原的;简化(成)的。2. 还原艺术的,抽象艺术的。II *n*.【化】还原剂,脱氧剂。

re·duc·tor [riˈdʌktə; rɪˋdʌktɚ] *n*.【化】还原器;还原剂;【无】减速器;减压器。

re·dun·dance, -dan·cy [riˈdʌndəns, -si; rɪˋdʌndəns, -sɪ] *n*. 1. 过多,冗余,过剩(物),累赘。2. 冗语。3.【自】多余度,冗余度;冗余位;【无】冗余码;多余信息。4.【宇航】(在某一配件失灵时能提供备用件的)后备能力。

re·dun·dant [riˈdʌndənt; rɪˋdʌndənt] *a*. 1. 过多的,冗余的,冗长的(文章等);累赘的;丰富的(食物等);过剩的。2. 后备的〔指特别多配备的配件,以防整个机件中这一配件发生故障〕。~ *words* 冗词,赘语。*a ~ population* 过剩人口。~ **verb** (时态有一种以上拼法的)一态多型动词〔如 light,其过去式可写作 lit 或 lighted〕。**-ly** *ad*.

re·du·pli·cate [riˈdjuːplikeit; rɪˋdjupləˏket] I *vt*. 1. 使加倍;重复。2.【语法】使重复(音节);重叠音节形成(派生词)。— *vi*. 重复。II *a*. 重复的;加倍的;重叠的;【植】外向镊合状的。

re·du·pli·ca·tion [riˌdjuːpliˈkeiʃən; rɪˏdjupləˋkeʃən] *n*. 加倍;重复;【语法】重叠。**-tive** *a*.

re·du·vi·id [riˈdjuːviːid, -duː-; rɪˋdjuvɪɪd, -du-] *n*.【动】食虫椿象科 (*Reduviidae*) 昆虫。

re·dye [ˈriːdai; riˋdaɪ] *vt*. 重染,再染。

ree·bok [ˈriːbɔk; ˋribɑk] *n*.【动】(南非)短角羚羊。

re-ech·o [ri(:)ˈekəu; riˋɛko] I *vt*., *vi*. 1. (使)再发回声,(使)回声传回,反响。2. 响遍,轰传,哄动。II *n*. (*pl*. ~*es*) 回声的反响,再回声。

reech·y [ˈriːtʃi; ˋritʃɪ] *a*.〔古、方〕烟熏的,煤烟熏黑的,污秽的,败坏的,恶臭的。

Reed [riːd; rid] *n*. 1. 里德〔姓氏,男子名〕。2. **Walter** ~ 里德〔1851—1902,美国军医,黄热病原发现者〕。

reed [riːd; rid] I *n*. 1.【植】芦苇,芦秆,苇丛;〔主英〕盖屋顶用的麦秸。2. 芦笛,牧笛。3. 牧歌。4.〔诗〕矢,箭。5.〔常 *pl*.〕【乐】簧片;簧[管]乐器。6.【纺】杼,筘,钢筘;【建】芦饰;小凸嵌线;【矿山】引火管。*the ~s* 乐队中的簧乐器。***a broken*** [***bruised***] ~ 折断的芦苇杆;〔喻〕不可靠的人[物]。***lean on a*** ~ 倚赖不可靠的人[物]。II *vt*. 1. 用茅草[麦秸、芦苇]盖(屋顶);用芦苇装饰。2. 把簧装(在乐器上)。~ **mace**〔英〕【植】香蒲。~ **organ**【乐】簧风琴。~ **pipe** 牧笛;舌管,簧管。~ **relay**【无】笛簧继电器〔电子电话交换系统中用作开关部件〕。~ **stop**【乐】簧管音栓。

reed·ed [ˈriːdid; ˋridɪd] *a*. 1. 芦苇覆盖的;芦苇丛生的。

2. 有沟的,有凹槽的。

reed·ing [ˈriːdiŋ; ˋridɪŋ] *n*. 【建】小凸嵌线,芦饰,小凸嵌线装饰〔如圆柱上的装饰〕。

re·ed·u·cate, re-ed·u·cate [riːˈedʒju(ː)keit; riˋɛdʒəˏket] *vt*. (*-cat·ed*; *-cat·ing*) 再教育。**-ca·tion** [riˌedʒju(ː)ˈkeiʃən; rɪˏɛdʒəˋkeʃən] *n*. **-ca·tive** *a*.

reed·y [ˈriːdi; ˋridɪ] *a*. (*-i·er*; *-i·est*) 1. 多芦苇的,芦苇丛生的;芦苇做的;芦苇状的。2. 细长的。3. 像芦笛声音的。

reef[1] [riːf; rif] *n*. 1. 【地】暗礁,礁脉;沙洲。2. 【矿】矿脉;含金石英脉。

reef[2] [riːf; rif] I *n*. 【海】(便于减少受风面积的)缩帆部,榫帆部。*let* [*skake*, *take*] *out the* ~*s* 放开帆篷。*take in a* ~ 收缩帆篷;〔喻〕缩减(用费等);慎重行事。II *vt*. 收缩(帆篷)。~ **knot** 【海】缩帆结,平结,方结。~**-point** 【海】缩帆索。

reef·er [ˈriːfə; ˋrifɚ] *n*. 1. 缩帆者。2. 〔英俚〕海军候补士官生;〔美俚〕海军学校学员。3. 平结,方结,缩帆结(= reef-knot)。4. (水手穿的)对襟双排钮短上衣(= ~ jacket)。5. 〔美俚〕大麻卷烟(= marijuana cigarette)。6. 〔美俚〕冰箱,冷藏汽车;冷藏车箱;冷藏船。

reek [riːk; rik] I *n*. 1. 〔主 Scot.〕烟。2. 热气,水蒸气。3. 恶臭;腐臭的空气。4. 雾。*the* ~ *of tobacco* 烟臭味。*amid* ~ *and squalor* 在恶臭和污秽之中。II *vi*. 冒烟;冒水蒸汽,冒热气;冒血腥气;放恶臭,冲鼻子 (*of*; *with*)。~ *of garlic* 发出大蒜的臭气。~ *with gore* 染满淤血。~ ***of affectation*** 摆臭架子。~ ***of blood*** 冒血腥气。~ ***of murder*** 杀气腾腾。— *vt*. 用烟熏;散发(烟、水汽等);发出…的气息。*Her manner* ~*s prosperity*. 她的风度显出有钱的样子。

reek·ing [ˈriːkiŋ; ˋrikɪŋ] *a*. 冒烟的,烟雾腾腾的,热气腾腾的;发臭的;冒血腥气的;新鲜的(血等)。

reek·y [ˈriːki; ˋrikɪ] *a*. 冒烟的,烟雾沉沉的,烟熏熏的;熏黑的;冒蒸汽的;发臭的。

reel[1] [riːl; ril] I *n*. 1. 【纺】卷线车,纺车;绕线筒。2. 〔英〕(钓丝的)卷轴,线框;(线、铁丝、胶片、纸、铅管等的)一卷;【机】线轴;电缆盘,影片盘,磁带盘;(影片的)一盘,卷〔1000—2000 英尺〕。3. 刈割机上的夹杆器。*a picture in six* ~*s* 六盘长的影片。*two* ~*s of motion picture films* 两盘电影片。~ *boss* 〔美〕影片公司的经理。***off the*** ~ (线等)陆续放长;滔滔不绝地,继续不断地(*tell a story off the* ~ 滔滔不绝地讲故事)。II 1. *vt*. 【纺】卷(线),纺(线),缫(丝)(*off*)。2. 收卷轴拉近(鱼、测程线等) (*in*; *up*)。— *vi*. (蟋蟀等)唧唧地叫。~ ***in*** [***up***] (将上钩的鱼、测程线等)收卷轴拉近[拉起]。~ ***off*** 从纺车上把线拉出;(用茧)缫(丝);滔滔不绝地讲。~***ing frame and comber*** 【纺】梳麻机。

reel[2] [riːl; ril] I *n*. 摇摆,蹒跚;眩晕。***the*** ~ ***of vice and folly around us*** 在我们周围乱动的邪恶和愚蠢。***without a*** ~ ***or a stagger*** 脚步稳定地。II *vi*. 摇摆,摇摇摆摆地走 (*about*; *along*); 眼花,眩晕;摇动,动摇。*My brain* ~*s*. 我的头晕。*The drunkard* ~*ed down the street*. 那醉汉在街上摇摇欲倒地走。— *vt*. 1. 使眩晕。2. 在…上蹒跚而行。

reel[3] [riːl; ril] I *n*. (苏格兰高地人的)双人对舞(曲);〔美〕弗吉尼亚舞〔一种乡村舞蹈, Virginia Reel 的简称〕。II *vi*. 跳双人对舞。

re-elect [ˈriːiˈlekt; ˏriəˋlɛkt] *vt*. 重选,改选。

re-elec·tion [ˈriːiˈlekʃən; ˏriəˋlɛkʃən] *n*. 重选,改选。

reel·er [ˈriːlə; ˋrilɚ] *n*. 1. 【纺】摇纱工;缫丝工;【纺】摇纱机;缫丝机。2. 〔英俚〕警察。3. …卷的影片。*a three-reeler* 一部三卷胶片组成的影片。

re-el·i·gi·ble [ˈriːˈelidʒəbl; riˋɛlədʒəbl̩] *a*. 可以重选的;可改选的;可再任命的。

reel·ing·ly [ˈriːliŋli; ˋrilɪŋlɪ] *ad*. 摇摇摆摆地,蹒跚地;头晕眼花地;动摇不定地。

re-en·able [ˈriːiˈneibl; ˋriɪˋnebl̩] *vt*. 使再能…;重新授权给。

re-en·act [ˈriːiˈnækt; ˏriɪnˋækt] *vt*. 1. 再制定,再用法律规定。2. 再扮演。**-ment** *n*.

re-en·force [riːinˈfɔːs; ˏriɪnˋfors] *vt*. = reinforce.

re-en·gine [ˈriːˈendʒin; ˋriˋɛndʒɪn] *vt*. 更换(船只等的)发动机。

re-en·ter [ˈriːˈentə; riˋɛntɚ] *vt*. 1. 再进入;再加入;再登记。2. 【雕刻】加深(不清楚的线条等);加印印刷品的颜色。3. 【法】收回(贷出物)。4. (角等)凹入。*The spacecraft* ~*ed the atmosphere*. 宇宙飞船[太空船]重返大气层。— *vi*. 1. 再入,又进去。2. 收回所有权;重新占有。

re-en·trant [riːˈentrənt; riˋɛntrənt] *a*., *n*. 1. 再进去(的)。2. 【筑城】凹角(的)。~ **angle** 凹角。~ **foam** 〔口〕可摺叠泡沫塑料〔其纤维可任意扭曲而不断裂〕。

re-en·try [riːˈentri; riˋɛntrɪ] *n*. 1. 再进入。2. 【法】所有权的收回。3. 【宇】重返大气层。4. 【牌戏】可以重占优势的大牌(= ~ card)。

Reese [riːs; ris] *n*. 里斯〔姓氏〕。

re-estab·lish [ˈriːisˈtæbliʃ; ˏriəˋstæblɪʃ] *vt*. 重建;使复元;使复职,使复原。**-ment** *n*.

reeve[1] [riːv; riv] (~*d* 或 ***rove*** [rouv; rov]) *vt*. 1. 【海】穿(绳入孔等) (*through*); 穿(绳)入孔结牢 (*in*; *on*; *round*; *to*)。2. 把(棍子等)插进(洞内)。3. (船)穿过(浮水、浅滩等)。

reeve[2] [riːv; riv] *n*. 1. 〔英史〕地方官,镇长,区长;〔加拿大〕(村会的)主席。2. 【采】矿工领班。

reeve[3] [riːv; riv] *n*. 【动】雌流苏鹬〔*cf*. ruff〕。

re-ex·am·ine [ˈriːigˈzæmin; ˏriɪgˋzæmɪn] *vt*. 再考试,重考,复试;复查,再调查,再检查,再审查;再审。**-i·na·tion** *n*.

re-ex·change [ˈriːiksˈtʃeindʒ; ˏriɛksˋtʃendʒ] I *n*. 1. 再交换,再交易。2. 【商】退汇(要求);要求退汇的金额。II *vt*. 再交换;掉换;换回。

re-ex·port [ˈriːeksˈpɔːt; ˏriɪksˋport] I *vt*. (将进口货)再输出,再出口。II [riːˈekspɔːt; riˋɛksˏport] *n*. 再输出,再出口;再出口的货物;〔*pl*.〕再出口额。**-a·tion** *n*.

ref. = 1. referee. 2. reference; referred. 3. reformation; reformed; reformer. 4. refining. 5. refunding. 6. refrigeration; refrigerator. 7. refrain.

re·face [ˈriːˈfeis; riˋfes] *vt*. 1. 重修(房屋等的)门面。2. 换(衣服的)面子。

re·fash·ion [ˈriːˈfæʃən; riˋfæʃən] *vt*. 再作,重作,改制,改做;改变(形式等);给…以新形式。**-ment** *n*.

re·fect [riˈfekt; rɪˋfɛkt] *vt*. 〔废〕(通过饮食)使精力恢复,使精神振作。

re·fec·tion [riˈfekʃən; rɪˋfɛkʃən] *n*. 消遣,休养;(吃饮食)恢复精神,提神;小吃;茶点。

re·fec·to·ry [riˈfektəri; rɪˋfɛktərɪ] *n*. (神学院、修道院等的)饭厅,食堂。*a* ~ *table* 长条餐桌。

re·fer [riːˈfəː; rɪˋfɝ] *vt*. (*-rr-*) 1. 把…提交,交付,委托,付托(事件、问题等)(*to*)。2. 叫…去打听,叫某人参看,叫某人查询,叫某人注意 (*to*); 叫…到某处或某人处 (*to*), 查询某事 (*for*); 让…过目,使…参看;使…注意(事实等) (*to*)。3. 把某人叫做 (*as*), 将…归因于…,认为,是起因于[由于]…,将…归入,认为,属于(某物、某类、某地、某人、某时代等) (*to*)。~ *oneself to* 依赖,求助于。*The dispute was* ~*red to the United Nations*. 这项争论已提交联合国。~ *a bill to a committee* 把议案提交委员会。*For further particulars I* ~ *you to my secretary*. 详细情况请问我的秘书。*She often* ~*s questions to me*. 她常拿问题来问我。~ *sb. to the dictionary* 叫某人去查字典。*All these are* ~*red to as animals*. 这些都叫做动物。*Zoologists* ~ *barnacles to Crustancea*. 动物学家把螺蛳归入甲壳类。— *vi*. 1. 借助,参考,参看,引证,引用;翻阅,查看(账簿等) (*to*)。2. 有关系,涉及 (*to*); 说到,提到;打听,查询〔特别是品行、

能力等〕(*to*)。**3.** 使注意,指点,指示。*The asterisk* ～*s to a footnote*. 星号表示参看附注。*all the documents* ～*ring to this matter* 有关这一事件的一切文件。～ *to a dictionary* 查阅字典。*The figure* ～*s to chapters* [*pages*]. 数字表示章数[页码]。～ *to drawer* 【商】请与出票人接洽〔略 R.D., R/D〕。

re·fer·a·ble [riˈfəːrəbl; ˋrɛfərəbl] ***a.*** 可交付的;可归因于…的;可归入…的,可借助的,可依赖的;可参考的;可说及的,与…有关的(*to*)。*This disease is* ～ *to microbes*. 这个病是由细菌引起的。

ref·er·ee [ˌrefəˈriː; ˏrɛfəˋri] **I *n.*** 公断人,仲裁人;【法】(受法庭委托的)审查人,鉴定人;(足球等的)裁判员。**II *vt.*, *vi.*** (为…)担任仲裁;(为…)担任裁判。

ref·er·ence [ˈrefərəns; ˋrɛfərəns] **I *n.*** **1.** (对委员、审查人等的)委托;委托项目[范围]。**2.** 说到,论到,提到。**3.** 参考;参考书;附注,引证;基准,依据;关系。**4.** (关于人品、能力等的)查询,咨询,询商;可供查问的人;证明人,介绍人;(身份、能力等的)证明书,介绍书,服务经历,鉴定书。**5.** 参看符号〔如 asterisk*, obelisk †, section §, parallel ‖, paragraph π 等〕(= ～ marks)。*the commission's terms of* ～ 委员会的职权。*R- was made to me*. 提到了我;所指的是我。*You make no* ～ *to your plan in your letter*. 你信里没有提到你的计划。*a book of* ～ = *a* ～ *book* 参考书。*Who are your* ～*s*? 你的证明人都是谁? ***bear*** ～ ***to*** = *have* ～ *to*. ***give a*** ～ ***to*** 提到,介绍。***have*** ～ ***to*** 和…有关系。***in*** ～ ***to*** 关于。***load one's pages with*** ～***s*** (在著作中)引用大量参考资料[文献]。***make*** ～ ***to*** 说到,涉及,提到;参考;查问;介绍。***with*** ～ ***to*** 关于。***without*** ～ ***to*** 不管,不论(*without* ～ *to age or sex* 无论男女老少)。**II *vt.*** 加注,附加注脚;给(书等)列出参考书目[注明资料来源]。～ **Bible** 附有参读章节注释的圣经。～ **buoy** 基准浮标。～ **frame** 参考系;坐标系统;(电子计算机的)计算系统。～ **gauge** 校对量规。～ **library** (不外借图书的)参考书阅览室。～ **mark** 参照符号;【建】参考标记。～ **point** 控制点;衡量的标准。～ **pressure** 参考压力。～ **room** 图书参考室。

ref·er·en·dary [ˌrefəˈrendəri; ˏrɛfəˋrɛndərɪ] **I *n.*** 【英史】(宫廷、教廷中负有审查或顾问职责的)审查官,咨询官;【罕】公断人。**II *a.*** 公民投票的。

ref·er·en·dum [ˌrefəˈrendəm; ˏrɛfəˋrɛndəm] ***n.*** (*pl.* ～*s*, *-da* [-də; -də]) **1.** (决定政策可否等的)公民表决;投票(权);公民所投的票。**2.** (大使对本国政府的)请示书。

ref·er·ent [ˈrefrənt; ˋrɛfrənt] ***n.*** **1.** 被谈到的事物、概念等。**2.** 【语】语词所指的对象。

ref·er·en·tial [ˌrefəˈrenʃəl; ˏrɛfəˋrɛnʃəl] ***a.*** 参考(用)的,有参考文献的,有附注[傍注]的;咨询的;有关的。

re·fer·ra·ble, -ri·ble [riˈfəːrəbl; rɪˋfɝəbl] ***a.*** = referable.

ref·er·ral [riˈfəːrəl; rɪˋfɝəl] ***n.*** **1.** 介绍,指引,指点,指示;职业介绍,工作[职务]指派。**2.** 受指点[指示]者,被介绍[指派]者。**3.** (对病人、病症等的)转诊[转科]介绍。

re·fill [ˈriːˈfil; riˋfɪl] ***vt.*, *vi.*** 再装满;再灌满;再填;再补充。

re·fi·nance [ˈrifiˈnæns, riˈfainæns; ˏrɪfɪˋnæns, rɪˋfaɪnæns] ***vt.*** (*-nanc·ed*, *-nanc·ing*) 对…再供给资金。

re·fine [riˈfain; rɪˋfaɪn] ***vt.*** **1.** 精炼,精制,提炼;纯化,提纯。**2.** 使高尚,使优美,使精致,使优雅;琢磨(文章等),推敲。**3.** 除去缺点,改善,美化。— ***vi.*** **1.** 变纯粹,澄清;(言语、举动等)变高尚;变优雅。**2.** 改善、弄得更好,精益求精(*on*, *upon*)。**3.** 应用精密的语言[思想];细加区别;详细讲(*on*, *upon*)。

re·fined [riˈfaind; rɪˋfaɪnd] ***a.*** 精炼的,精制的;高尚的,优雅的,洗炼的;极微妙的,精密的,正确的。～ *salt* 精盐。～ *sugar* 精制糖。～ *distinctions* 微妙的区别。～ *cruelty* 阴险刻毒的残忍。**-ly *ad.***

re·fine·ment [riˈfainmənt; rɪˋfaɪnmənt] ***n.*** **1.** 精炼,提炼,提纯,纯化,精制;净化;纯净,精美。**2.** 高尚,优雅;改善。**3.** (思想、推理、议论等的)精密,微妙;细微的区别;极致。*a person of* ～ 高尚的人。*a* ～ *of cruelty* 阴险刻毒之极的残忍。

re·fin·er [riˈfainə; rɪˋfaɪnɚ] ***n.*** **1.** 精炼者,精制者,提炼者。**2.** 精炼机,精制机,精研机;(纤维的)匀浆机。**3.** 过于精细的人,精密地推论的人。

re·fin·er·y [riˈfainəri; rɪˋfaɪnərɪ] ***n.*** 精炼厂;炼糖厂;精炼设备。*a sugar* ～ 制糖厂。

re·fin·ish [ˈriːˈfiniʃ; riˋfɪnɪʃ] ***vt.*** 再修整,再修光,再抛光,修整(木、金属物的)表面。**-er *n.***

re·fit [ˈriːˈfit; riˋfɪt] **I *vt.*** 整修(船等);重新装修,改装。— ***vi.*** (船等)进行整修,进行改装。**II *n.*** (特指船的)整修;改装。**-ment *n.***

refl. = **1.** reflection; reflective(ly). **2.** reflex; reflexive.

re·flate [riˈfleit; rɪˋflet] ***vt.*, *vi.*** (使)通货再膨胀。**re-fla·tion *n.***

re·flect [riˈflekt; rɪˋflɛkt] ***vt.*** **1.** 【物,计】反射(光、热、声音等)。**2.** (镜子等)映现(影像等);反响,反照;〔喻〕反映;表现。**3.** 招致,带来,博得(信用等);使蒙受(羞辱等)(*on*, *upon*)。**4.** 转移(视线等);折转(纸角等);(球等)弹回。**5.** 反省,深思熟虑,仔细想。*The sidewalks* ～ *heat on a hot day*. 在热天,人行道反射热气。*Her actions* ～ *her thought*. 她的行为反映她的思想。*clouds* ～*ed in the water* 映在水里的云影。*His conduct* ～*ed great credit* (*up*) *on him*. 他的行为给他带来了很大荣誉。～ *the eyes from* 把眼睛避开。～ *how to get out of a difficulty* 盘算怎样渡过难关。— ***vi.*** **1.** 【物,计】反射。**2.** 反映;反响。**3.** 反省,熟虑,沉思,仔细想,回顾(*on*, *upon*)。**4.** 反应;非难,谴责,中伤,诽谤;(行为等)发生坏影响,丢脸(*on*, *upon*)。*His conduct* ～*s on his parents*. 他的行为使他父母丢脸。**-ing·ly *ad.***

re·flec·tance [riˈflektəns; rɪˋflɛktəns] ***n.*** 【物】反射比;反射能力[系数]。

re·flec·tion [riˈflekʃən; rɪˋflɛkʃən] ***n.*** **1.** 【物,计】反射;反射波[光,热,音,色]。**2.** 反映;反影,映像,(映在水等中的)影像;〔喻〕学人样的人,极像…的人,逼肖的形象[言语、动作、思想]。**3.** 反省,熟虑,沉思,回顾;〔*pl.*〕感想,意见;【心】(神经等的)反射作用。**4.** 非难,谴责;丢脸,耻辱(*on*, *upon*)。**5.** 折转;弹回;【解】翻转(处),折转(处)。*theory of* ～ 反映论。*an angle of* ～ 反射角。*He is simply a* ～ *of his father*. 他完全是他父亲的复本。*I have a few* ～*s to offer on what you have said*. 我对你的发言提供几点意见。***be lost in*** ～ 沉思。***cast a*** ～ ***on*** 谴责…,成为…的耻辱。***on*** [***upon***] ～ 仔细想,反省;对…不利,使…名誉受影响,使…蒙受耻辱;中伤,影射(*On* ～, *I doubt whether I was right*. 细细想起来我倒怀疑我讲的是否正确了)。***without*** (***due***) ～ 不经思考,轻率。**-al *a.***

re·flec·tive [riˈflektiv; rɪˋflɛktɪv] ***a.*** **1.** 反射的,反照的,反映的,反光的。**2.** 能反省的;反省性的,熟虑的。**3.** 反射性的,相互的。**4.** 〔罕〕【语法】= reflexive. ～ **power** 反射率[力]。**-ly *ad.***

re·flec·tor [riˈflektə; rɪˋflɛktɚ] ***n.*** **1.** 反射物,反射器;反光镜;【原】反射层;【天】反射望远镜。**2.** (习惯、感情等的)反映(者)。**3.** 〔罕〕反省者,回想者,沉思者。*a* ～ *lamp* 反光灯。*The newspaper is a true* ～ *of public opinion*. 报纸是舆论的真实反映(者)。

re·flec·tor·ize [riˈflektəˌraiz; rɪˋflɛktərˏaɪz] ***vt.*** (*-iz·ed*, *-iz·ing*) **1.** 使能反射光线。**2.** 装反射器(或反射镜)。

re·flect·os·cope [riˈflekˈtəskəup; rɪˋflɛkˋtəskop] ***n.*** 超声探伤仪;反射测试仪。

re·flet [rəˈfle; rəˋflɛ] ***n.*** (陶瓷器物表面的)光泽,光彩。

re·flex [ˈriːfleks; ˋriflɛks] **I *a.*** **1.** 反射的,反射性的,有反应的,有反射作用的。**2.** 反作用的(效果、音响等)。**3.**

R

反省的;回想的。4.(叶、茎等)折转的,反曲的。5.【无】来复式的。6.【数】优角的。II *n*. 1.(光、热的)反射,(本质等的)反映,显现;反射光;(镜子等反映的)影像,映像。2.【生理,心】反射作用。3.【无】来复;来复式收音机[接收机];来复式增幅装置。~ *action* 反射作用,反射运动。~ *angle* 优角。~ *arc*【生】反射弧。~ *camera* 反光镜照相机。~ *condenser* 回流冷凝器。~ *receiver* 来复式收音机。III [riˈfleks; rɪˋflɛks] *vt*. 把…折转[折回];【无】给…加来复式增幅装置。

re·flex·i·ble [riˈfleksəbl; rɪˋflɛksɪbl] *a*. 可反射的;可折射性的。

re·flex·ion [riˈflekʃən; rɪˋflɛkʃən] *n*. = reflection.

re·flex·ive [riˈfleksiv; rɪˋflɛksɪv] I *a*. 1. = reflex. 2. = reflective. 3.【语法】反身的。II *n*.【语法】反身动词[代词]。~ ***law*** 自反律。**-ly** ***ad***.

re·float [ˈriːˈfləut; riˋflot] *vt*. 使(沉没或搁浅的船)再浮起来;打捞。— *vi*. 再浮起。*~ing operations* 打捞工程。

re·float·a·tion [ˈriːfləuˈteiʃən; ˌrifloˋteʃən] *n*. (沉船、搁浅的船)打捞;离礁。

ref·lu·ence [ˈrefluəns; ˋrɛfluəns] *n*. 倒流,逆流;退潮。

ref·lu·ent [ˈrefluənt; ˋrɛfluənt] *a*. (潮水、血液等)逆流的,倒流的,回流的;退潮的。

re·flux [ˈriːflʌks; ˋriˌflʌks] *n*. 1. 回流,反流,倒流,逆流;退潮。2.【化】回流加热。*the flux and ~ of the tides* [*fortune*] 潮水的涨落;〔喻〕(人、事物的)荣枯盛衰。

re·focil·late [riːˈfɔːsileit; riˋfɔsəlet] *vt*. 使振作精神,使复苏。

re·foot [ˈriːˈfut; riˋfʊt] *vt*. 换(袜子等的)底子。

re·for·est [ˈriːˈfɔrist; riˋfɔrɪst] *vt*., *vi*. 重新造林。

re·form [riˈfɔːm; rɪˋfɔrm] I *vt*. 1. 改革,改良,革新(制度、事业等)。2. 矫正(品性等),使悔改;改造;改正(错误等)。3.救济,救治,铲除(弊害、紊乱等)。4.【化】重整〔指将石油等裂化〕。~ ***oneself*** 改过自新,自我改造。— ***vi***. 改过自新,改邪归正;改善,面目一新。~ ***school*** 〔美〕少年感化院。II *n*. 1. (社会、政治等的)改革,改良,改进,改造,革新。2.(误谬的)改正;(品行等的)感化,矫正,悔改。*agrarian* (*land*) ~ 土地改革。*democratic ~s* 民主改革。**R- Bill** [**Act**] (1832年英国的)选举法修正法案[条令]。**R- Church** (基督教)新教。**-ism** *n*. 改良主义。**-ist** *n*., *a*. 改良主义者[的]。

re-form [ˈriːˈfɔːm; ˌriˋfɔrm] *vt*., *vi*. 再作,重作;改编(军队等);(飞机在攻击后)重新编队。

re·form·a·ble [riˈfɔːməbl; rɪˋfɔməbl] *a*. 可改革的;可改正的;可革除的;可矫正的,可感化的。

ref·or·ma·tion [ˌrefəˈmeiʃən; ˌrɛfəˋmeʃən] *n*. 1. 改造;改革,改良,改善,革新;矫正。2.〔the R-〕(欧洲16—18世纪)宗教改革(运动),基督教改革(运动)。

re-for·ma·tion [ˈriːfɔːˈmeiʃən; ˌrifəˋmeʃən] *n*. 再构成;重新组成;重作,再作,再造。

re·form·a·tive [riˈfɔːmətiv; rɪˋfɔrmətɪv] *a*. 1. 改革的,改良的;改造的。2. = reformatory.

re·form·a·to·ry [riˈfɔːmətəri; rɪˋfɔrməˌtorɪ] I *a*. 起改革[革新]作用的;起改良作用的。II *n*. 教养院;〔英〕妓女改造所。

re·formed [riˈfɔːmd; rɪˋfɔrmd] *a*. 改正了的,改造了的;〔R-〕【宗】改革派的。

re·form·er [riˈfɔːmə; rɪˋfɔrmə] *n*. 改革者,革新者;〔R-〕宗教改革者;选举法修正论者。

re·fract [riˈfrækt; rɪˋfrækt] *vt*.【物】(水、玻璃等)折射(光线等);【化】分析(硝石);测定…的折射度。*a ~ing angle* 折射棱角。*~ing power* 折射率[力]。*a ~ing telescope* 折射望远镜。

re·fract·a·ble [riˈfræktəbl; rɪˋfræktəbl] *a*. 可折射的,折射性的。

re·frac·tion [riˈfrækʃən; rɪˋfrækʃən] *n*. (光、音波等的)屈折,折射;折射作用;折射度;【天】蒙气差,折光差;【化】硝石杂物含有率(测定)。*astronomical* ~ 空中屈折。*terrestrial* ~ 地上屈折。*index of* ~ 折射率,屈折率。**-al** ***a***.

re·frac·tive [riˈfræktiv; rɪˋfræktɪv] *a*. 折射(光线等)的,有屈折[折射]力的。~ *index* 折射率,屈折率;折光指数。

re·frac·tom·e·ter [ˌriːfrækˈtɔmitə; ˌrifrækˋtɑmətə] *n*.【物】折射计;屈光计。

re·frac·tor [riˈfræktə; rɪˋfræktə] *n*. 折射器;折射望远镜;折射透镜。

re·frac·to·ri·ly [riˈfræktərili; rɪˋfræktərəlɪ] ***ad***. 倔强地,顽强地,执拗地;顽固地;难熔化地。

re·frac·to·ry [riˈfræktəri; rɪˋfræktərɪ] I *a*. 1. 不听话的,难驾驭的,倔强的,执拗的。2. 加工困难的;难处理的;【医】难医的,难治疗的(病、伤等);无刺激反应的(神经);不感受病毒的,能抵抗(疾病等)的。3.耐熔的,耐火的(矿、金属等)。II *n*. 1. 倔强的人。2. 耐火矿石[金属];耐熔质。~ *matter* 耐火材料。*a ~ brick* 火砖。

re·frain[1] [riˈfrein; rɪˋfren] *vi*. 1. 抑制,自制,忍住。2. 戒除(烟、酒等)。3. 避免;避开。~ *from* (*smoking*) 戒(烟)。*I cannot ~ from laughing*. 我忍不住好笑。~ *from unprincipled argument* 不作无原则的争论。— *vt*. 抑制。~ *oneself* 抑制自己,忍住。

re·frain[2] [riˈfrein; rɪˋfren] *n*. (诗歌、乐曲每节收尾的)叠句,反复句,叠句的乐曲;口头禅。***take up the ~ of*** 为…帮腔。

re·frame [ˈriːˈfreim; ˌriˋfrem] *vt*. 1. 再构造;重新制订。2. 给某物装上新框架。

re·fran·gi·ble [riˈfrændʒibl; rɪˋfrændʒəbl] *a*. 屈折(性)的,可折射的。**-bil·i·ty**, **-ness** ***n***.

re·fresh [riˈfreʃ; rɪˋfrɛʃ] *vt*. 1. (磨光表面等)使变新,使焕然一新;翻新。2. (雨、微风等)使清新;使爽快,使清。3.(娱乐、饮食、休息等)使(人)心神爽快,使神清气爽,使精神振作,使精神恢复。4.恢复(记忆),使重新明了,使(火等)再旺盛;给(电池)充电;给(船)被充给养。~ *oneself with a cup of tea* 喝一杯茶提神。~ *a storage battery* 给蓄电池充电。— ***vi***. 1. (因饮食、休养等)恢复精神,觉得神清气爽,觉得爽快。2.〔口〕吃东西,喝一杯(酒);(船等)补装粮食[饮用水](等)。

re·fresh·er [ˈriˈfreʃə; rɪˋfrɛʃə] I *n*. 1. 使心神清爽的东西[人];饮料,食物;〔口〕冷饮料;酒;使恢复记忆的东西。2.〔英〕(诉讼长期不决时的)律师额外酬劳。3.〔美〕(温习性的)补习科(= ~ course)。4.最新科技资料。II *a*. 〔美〕温习的,进修的;(科技资料)最新的。

re·fresh·ing [riˈfreʃiŋ; rɪˋfrɛʃɪŋ] *a*. 使人身心爽快的,使人精神振作的;使人耳目一新的。*a ~ breeze* 使人凉爽的微风,清风。*a ~ drink* 清凉饮料。~ *innocence* 可爱的天真。**-ly** ***ad***.

re·fresh·ment [riˈfreʃmənt; rɪˋfrɛʃmənt] *n*. 1. 提神;精神恢复,身心爽快,心旷神怡。2.〔常 *pl*.〕提神物;饮食,点心。*take some ~s* 吃点东西。*R-s provided*. 备有茶点。~ **car** (火车的)餐车。~ **room** (车站、火车中的)餐室。**R- Sunday** 四旬斋(*Lent*)中的第四个礼拜天。

re·frig·er·ant [riˈfridʒərənt; rɪˋfrɪdʒərənt] I *a*. 解热的,使清凉的;冷却的。II *n*. 清凉剂,凉药;清凉饮料;冷却剂,冷冻剂,致冷剂。

re·frig·er·ate [riˈfridʒəreit; rɪˋfrɪdʒəˌret] *vt*. 1. 解热,消热,使冷,使清凉。2. 冷藏,冷冻,冰镇(鱼、肉等)。*a refrigerating machine* 冷冻机,冷冻装置。*a ~d van* 冷藏车。

re·frig·e·ra·tion [riˌfridʒəˈreiʃən; rɪˌfrɪdʒəˋreʃən] *n*. 消热,清凉;冷却(法);冷藏(法),冰冻,致冷;致冷学。

re·frig·er·a·tive [riˈfridʒəreitiv; rɪˋfrɪdʒəˌretɪv] *a*. 消热的,清凉的;致冷的,冷却的。

re·frig·er·a·tor [riˈfridʒəreitə; rɪˋfrɪdʒəretə] *n*. (电)冰箱;致冷器,冷藏库;制冰机;冷冻机。~ *car*【铁道】冷

藏车(厢)。

re·frig·er·a·to·ry [riˈfridʒərətəri; rɪˋfrɪdʒərə͵torɪ] **I** ***a*.** 致冷的;消热的;冷却的。**II** ***n*.** 冷却器,(电)冰箱;冷藏室;制冰机;冰冻机。

re·frin·gent [riˈfrindʒənt; rɪˋfrɪndʒənt] ***a*.** 【物】折射的。**-gen·cy, -gence** ***n*.**

reft [reft; rɛft] **I** *reave* 的过去式及过去分词。**II** ***a*.** 〔诗〕被夺去的,被掠夺的;失去了的。

re·fu·el [riːˈfjuəl; riˋfjuəl] ***vt*., *vi*.** (给…)加油[燃料]。~ *station* 加油站。

ref·uge [ˈrefjuːdʒ; ˋrɛfjudʒ] **I** ***n*.** **1.** 避难;庇护,保护;庇护者;避难所,隐匿处,藏身处;〔英〕(马路中的)完全岛。**2.** 可倚靠的人[物];慰藉物。**3.** 口实,借口。**4.** 权宜之计,应急办法;【医】救急(疗)法。*a harbour of* ~ 避风港。*a house of* ~ 难民收容所。*He is the* ~ *of the distressed*. 他是不幸者的朋友。***the last*** ~ 最后的托词。***find a*** ~ 找到避难所[躲避处]。***give*** ~ ***to*** 隐匿,包庇,庇护。***seek*** ~ ***in flight*** 逃难。***seek*** ~ ***with sb*.** 求某人庇护,逃难到某人处。***take*** ~ ***in*** 避难到;求助于…,求安慰于…,用…支吾过去。**II** ***vt*.** 〔古〕庇护。— ***vi*.** 躲避,避难。

ref·u·gee [͵refju(ː)ˈdʒiː; ͵rɛfjuˋdʒi] **I** ***n*.** (特指逃避战祸或政治、宗教迫害的)难民,避难者,亡命者;逃亡者。**II** ***a*.** 避难的,逃难的。**III** ***vi*.** 避难,逃难。

re·ful·gence [riˈfʌldʒəns; rɪˋfʌldʒəns] ***n*.** 辉煌,灿烂。

re·ful·gent [riˈfʌldʒənt; rɪˋfʌldʒənt] ***a*.** 辉煌的,灿烂的。**-ly** ***ad*.**

re·fund [riːˈfʌnd; riˋfʌnd] **I** ***vt*., *vi*.** 退还,偿还。**II** [ˈriːfʌnd; ˋrifʌnd] ***n*.** 退还,偿还;退款。**-ment** ***n*.**

re·fur·bish [riːˈfəːbiʃ; riˋfɝbɪʃ] ***vt*.** **1.** 重新擦亮。**2.** 再刷新;整修;翻新。

re·fur·nish [ˈriːˈfəːniʃ; riˋfɝnɪʃ] ***vt*.** **1.** 再供给;供给新装备。**2.** 【植】剪顶枝嫁接(果树等)。

re·fus·a·ble [riːˈfjuːzəbl; rɪˋfjuzəbl̩] ***a*.** 可拒绝的。

re·fus·al [riˈfjuːzəl; rɪˋfjuzl̩] ***n*.** **1.** 拒绝,谢绝,固辞,不允,不承认。**2.** 优先取舍[选择]权;优先购买权。*a* ~ *to obey orders* 违抗命令。*the* ~ *of an invitation* 谢绝邀请。***ask for the*** ~ ***of*** 要求优先权。***buy the*** ~ ***of*** 付定钱,买得优先权。***give sb. a flat*** ~ 断然拒绝。***give the*** ~ ***of*** 给与优先[选择]权(*I will give you the* ~ *of my offer till the end of the month*. 对我提议[要价]是否采纳[同意]请于本月底以前决定)。***have the*** ~ ***of*** 获得先买权;获得取舍权。***take no*** ~ 不许说不,逼人答应。

re·fuse[1] [riˈfjuːz; rɪˋfjuz] ***vt*.** **1.** 拒绝,谢绝,固辞,辞退,推辞,不受。**2.** 不肯(承认、服从等);拒婚〔主指女子拒绝男子〕。**3.** (马)不肯跳过(沟、篱等)而突然停住;(机件等)发生故障失效。**4.** 【牌戏】因无同花的牌而出别的牌。**5.** 【军】(交战前)撤回(翼军),撤出(不重要的阵地)。**6.** 否认,放弃。~ *sb. satisfaction* 拒不赔偿;拒绝某人的要求。~ *sb. money* 拒绝借钱给某人。~ *a suitor* 拒绝求婚者。~ *a gift* 拒受礼物。~ *one's consent* 不同意,不答应。~ *to burn* (柴等)烧不着。~ *to shut* (门等)关不上。— ***vi*.** **1.** 拒绝。**2.** (马)不肯跃过。**3.** (纸牌)打不出同花牌。**~nik** ***n*.** **1.** 未获准移民国外的(前苏联)居民。**2.** 拒绝与当局合作的人,持不同政见者。

ref·use[2] [ˈrefjuːs; ˋrɛfjus] **I** ***n*.** 废料,糟粕,渣滓,垃圾;废物。**II** ***a*.** 无用的,无价值的,垃圾的,废料的。*kitchen* ~ 厨房垃圾。~ *oil* 废油。*a* ~ *consumer* [*destructor*] 垃圾焚毁炉。**~-up** 垃圾堆。

re·fus·er [riˈfjuːzə; rɪˋfjuzɚ] ***n*.** 拒绝者,推辞者;不信奉国教者;不肯跳过沟渠[篱笆等]的马。

ref·ut·a·ble [ˈrefjutəbl, riˈfjuːt-; ˋrɛfjutəbl̩, rɪˋfjut-] ***a*.** 可驳倒的;有错误的。**-bly** ***ad*.**

ref·u·tal [riˈfjuːtəl; rɪˋfjutl̩] ***n*.** 驳斥,反驳。

ref·u·ta·tion [͵refjuːˈteiʃən; ͵rɛfjuˋteʃən] ***n*.** 驳斥,驳倒。

re·fute [riˈfjuːt; rɪˋfjut] ***vt*.** 驳斥,驳倒(某论点,对方)。*His doctrine was* ~*d down to the last point*. 他的学说被驳得体无完肤。

Reg. = **1.** Regina. **2.** Regiment.

reg. = **1.** Regent. **2.** regiment. **3.** region. **4.** register; registered; registrar; registry. **5.** regular; regulation; regulator.

re·gain [riˈgein; rɪˋgen] **I** ***vt*.** **1.** 取回,夺回,收复,恢复(失物、失地、健康等);回收。**2.** 再到,回到(某地、某种状态)。~ *consciousness* 清醒过来;恢复知觉。~ *one's feet* [*footing*, *legs*] (跌倒的人)重新站起来。**II** ***n*.** **1.** 收回;复得;夺回,收复;恢复。**2.** (纤维的)回潮(率)。

re·gal[1] [ˈriːgəl; ˋrigl̩] ***a*.** **1.** 王的;帝王(般)的。**2.** 庄严的,堂皇的,凛然的。*the* ~ *office* 王位。*live in* ~ *splendour* 生活得像帝王一样奢华。**-ly** ***ad*.**

re·gal[2] [ˈriːgəl; ˋrigl̩] ***n*.** (16世纪可携带搬动的)小风琴。

re·gale [riˈgeil; rɪˋgel] **I** ***vt*.** 盛宴招待,款待;使欢悦,使快乐;使心满意足(*with*)。~ *oneself with drink* [*a cigar*] (高兴地)喝酒,抽[雪茄]。— ***vi*.** 享受好滋味;吃喝,享用(*on*);大大欢喜。**II** ***n*.** 〔古〕盛宴;山珍海味,佳肴。**-ment** ***n*.**

re·ga·li·a[1] [riˈgeiliə; rɪˋgelɪə] (*sing*. **re·gale** [riˈgeiliː; rɪˋgeli]) ***n*.** 〔*pl*.〕 **1.** 王室徽章;王位的标记〔王冠、王节、宝剑等〕;(等级、协会等的)标记,纹章,勋章。**2.** 〔史、古〕王室特权,王权。**3.** 华丽的服装。***in full*** ~ 威风凛凛。

re·ga·li·a[2] [riˈgeiljə; rɪˋgelɪə] ***n*.** (古巴产的)优质大雪茄烟。

re·gal·ism [ˈriːgəlizəm; ˋrigəlɪzm̩] ***n*.** 王权至上论〔尤指宗教事务方面〕。

re·gal·i·ty [riːˈgæliti; riˋgælətɪ] ***n*.** 王位;国王的地位[身份];〔*pl*.〕王权;王国。

re·gard [riˈgɑːd; rɪˋgɑrd] **I** ***n*.** **1.** 注重,注意,留意;考虑,关心(*to*);注目,注视,凝视;牵挂,惦念(*for*)。**2.** 尊重,尊敬;敬意,好意,厚意,好感;名誉,声名。**3.** 事项,关系。**4.** 〔*pl*.〕致意,问候,请安。*Give my* (*best*) ~*s to*.... 请代问候…。*With kindest* ~*s to you all*. 向各位问候。***have a*** ~ ***for*** 尊敬;考虑到,顾到;重视。***have*** ~ ***to*** 顾到,注意(*R- must be had to his wishes*. 须照顾到他的愿望)。***hold sb. in high*** [***low***] ~ 尊敬[藐视]某人。***in sb.'s*** ~ 关于某人,对于某人。***in*** ~ ***of*** [***to***] 关于,对于;为了答复…;关于,在…方面;取决于…的,…对…的影响。***in this*** [***that***] ~ 在这[那]一点上,关于这[那]件事。***pay*** (***no***) ~ ***to*** (不)考虑;(未)顾到;(不)尊敬;(不)注意。***turn one's*** ~ ***on sb*.** 把目光[注意力]转向某人。***with*** ~ ***to*** [***of***] = *in* ~ *to*. ***with*** ~ ***to*** 关于;对于;为了答复。***without*** ~ ***to*** [***for***] 不顾…,与…无关,不遵守。

II ***vt*.** **1.** 看,瞧,注视,凝视,注意;关心。**2.** 考察,考虑;顾虑;(用爱情、憎恨等)对待,看待。**3.** 〔主要用于否定句〕重视,尊重;尊敬,敬重。**4.** 把…看做,把…视为,把…认为(*as*...)。**5.** 和…有关系。*Many passed, but none* ~*ed her*. 许多人走过去了,没有一人注意她。~ *a matter from every point of view* 从各方面去考察一个问题。~ *a situation with anxiety* 担忧局势。*He does not* ~ *my advice*. 他不重视我的劝告。~ *him as a friend* 把他看做朋友。*The matter does not* ~ *you at all*. 这事和你毫无关系。***as*** ~***s*** 关于,至于。— ***vi*.** 〔罕〕注意,留意。

re·gard·ant [riˈgɑːdənt; rɪˋgɑrdənt] ***a*.** **1.** 【纹】回头向后看的(动物的姿态)〔*cf*. gardant〕。**2.** 〔古、诗〕注视的,留心的,谨慎的。*keep a* ~ *eye upon* 对…仔细观察。

re·gard·ful [riˈgɑːdful; rɪˋgɑrdfʊl] ***a*.** **1.** 对…留心,注意周到,谨慎(*of*)。**2.** 表示敬意的,恭敬的(*for*)。*be* ~ *of one's promises* 守约。

re·gard·ing [riˈgɑːdiŋ; rɪˋgɑrdɪŋ] ***prep*.** 关于。~ *the* *future of reform* 关于改革的前途。

re·gard·less [riˈgɑːdlis; rɪˋgɑrdlɪs] **I** ***a*.** **1.** 不重视的,不尊敬的;不注意的,不留心的,不顾虑的,不关心的。**2.** 不受注意的;毫无价值的。～ ***of*** 不管,不顾,不拘,不注意(*I shall go* ～ *of the weather*. 无论天气好坏我都要去)。**II** ***ad*.** 〔口〕〔用于省略句中〕不顾一切地;无论如何;不惜费用地。***be got up*** [***be dressed***] ～不惜花费地打扮。**-ly** ***ad*.**

re·gat·ta [riˈgætə; rɪˋgætə] ***n*.** **1.** (威尼斯大运河上举行的)狭长平底船的比赛。**2.** 赛艇会。

re·ge·late [ˈriːdʒileit, ˌriːdʒiˈleit; ˋridʒəˏlet, ridʒəˋlet] ***vi*.** 【物】(已溶解的碎冰)再凝冻,重新冻结,覆冰。**-lation** ***n*.** 【物】覆冰(现象)。

re·gen·cy [ˈriːdʒənsi; ˋridʒənsɪ] ***n*.** **1.** 摄政;摄政期间;摄政管辖区;摄政权;摄政团。**2.** 〔古〕政权,统治。**3.** 〔美〕(州立大学)评议员的职位。*the R-* 【史】英国(1811—1820年的或法国1715—1723年的)摄政时期。

re·gen·er·a·cy [riˈdʒenərəsi; rɪˋdʒenərəsɪ] ***n*.** **1.** 再生,新生,更生,复生。**2.** 刷新,革新。**3.** 悔悟,洗心。

re·gen·er·ate [riˈdʒenəreit; rɪˋdʒɛnəˏret] **I** ***a*.** **1.** 再生的,新生的。**2.** 革新的。**3.** 改造了的,回心转意的。**II** [-nəreit; -nəret] ***vt*.** **1.** 使再生,使复生,使新生。**2.** 使悔悟。**3.** 改造,革新(社会、国家等)。**4.** 回收(废热、废料等);【无】使回授,使反馈。～*d rubber* 再生橡胶。— ***vi*.** **1.** 再生。**2.** 悔悟。*Nails are constantly regenerating*. 指甲不断地新生。

re·gen·er·a·tion [riˌdʒenəˈreiʃən; rɪˏdʒɛnəˋreʃən] ***n*.** **1.** 再生,新生。**2.** 悔悟。**3.** 改造,革新。**4.** 回收。**5.** 【化】交流换热(法);【物】正回授[反馈]放大。～ ***through one's own efforts*** 自力更生。

re·gen·er·a·tive [riˈdʒenərətiv; rɪˋdʒɛnəˏretɪv] ***a*.** **1.** 再生的;使更生的。**2.** 使悔悟的。**3.** 更新的。**4.** 【机】回热式的;【电】回授的,反馈的;【化】交流换热(的)。*a* ～ *furnace* 回热炉;交流换热炉。

re·gen·er·a·tor [riˈdʒenəreitə; rɪˋdʒɛnəˏretɚ] ***n*.** **1.** (使)新生的人[物]。**2.** 更新者;改革者。**3.** 【机】交流换热器,蓄热器;回热器;【电】再生器;再发器。

re·gen·e·sis [riːˈdʒenisis; riˋdʒɛnəsɪs] ***n*.** 再生,新生;更新。

re·gent [ˈriːdʒənt; ˋridʒənt] **I** ***a*.** **1.** 摄政的〔通常用于名词后〕。**2.** 〔美〕担任(大学)评议员职位的。**3.** 〔罕〕统治的。**II** ***n*.** **1.** 摄政者。**2.** 〔罕〕统治者,支配者。**3.** 〔美〕(州立大学的)评议员,(Harvard大学的)学监;〔英史〕(牛津、剑桥大学)辅导讨论的文学士。*the Prince R-* 摄政王。*the Queen R-* 摄政女王。～**ship** 摄政王的地位[任期]。

re·ger·mi·nate [ˈriːˈdʒəːmineit; riˋdʒɝməˏnet] ***vi*.** 再发芽;重新生长。**re·ger·mi·na·tion** ***n*.**

re·ges [ˈriːdʒiːz; ˋridʒiz] ***n*.** rex 的复数。

reg·gae [ˈreˌgei; ˋreˏge] ***n*.** 【乐】一种源出西印度群岛,带有勃鲁斯音乐成分的,节拍强烈的通俗音乐。

reg·i·cid·al [ˌredʒiˈsaidl; ˏrɛdʒəˋsaɪdl̩] ***a*.** 弑君的。

reg·i·cide [ˈredʒisaid; ˋrɛdʒəˏsaɪd] ***n*.** 弑君(行为);弑君者。*the R-s* **1.** 处死英王查里一世(Charles I)的国会议员团。**2.** 处死法王路易十四(Louis XIV)的革命党员。

ré·gie [reiˈʒiː; ˏreˋʒi] ***n*.** 〔F.〕(烟、盐等的)专卖局;(公共事业的)官营,官办。～**book** (记有舞台导演说明的)导演须知。

re·gime, ré·gime [reiˈʒiːm; rɪˋʒim] ***n*.** **1.** 制度,社会组织;政权,政体;统治(时期)。**2.** 管理;方法;状态。**3.** 【医】养生法;(病人等的)生活规则。*the Parliamentary* ～ 议会制度。*establish a new* ～ 建立新秩序。***during the ...*** ～ 在…统治时代。***under the*** ～ ***of*** 在…的制度下。

reg·i·men [ˈredʒimen; ˋrɛdʒəˏmɛn] ***n*.** **1.** 【医】摄生,食物疗法,养生法;(给病人等特定的)生活规则。**2.** 支配,统治;政体,政权,社会制度。**3.** 管理办法;事物的所处状况。**4.** 【语法】支配。*the water* ～ 水分状况。

reg·i·ment [ˈredʒimənt; ˋrɛdʒəmənt] **I** ***n*.** **1.** 【军】团。**2.** 〔常 *pl*.〕大群,大量。**3.** 〔罕〕统治,支配。**II** ***vt*.** **1.** 把…编成团。**2.** 使(职工、劳动者等)受组织训练,组织起来;组织化,系统化;把…编成组;编入(团、团体)。*an education that* ～*s children* 使儿童受到组织训练的教育。

reg·i·men·tal [ˌredʒiˈmentl; ˏrɛdʒəˋmɛntl̩] **I** ***a*.** 【军】团的。**II** ***n*.** 〔*pl*.〕军服;特种团队的军服和徽章。*a* ～ *colour* 团旗,军旗。*a* ～ *district* 团管区。～ *headquarters* 团本部。

reg·i·men·ta·tion [ˌredʒimenˈteiʃən; ˏrɛdʒəmɛnˋteʃən] ***n*.** **1.** 【军】团的编制。**2.** 编制,类别;组织化,规格化;组织训练。

Re·gi·na[1] [riˈdʒainə; rɪˋdʒaɪnə] ***n*.** 〔L.〕女王〔略 R.,或 Reg.〕。★用于布告等的署名或在王室对臣民的诉讼案件中用作女王称号〔*cf*. Rex〕。

Re·gi·na[2] [riˈdʒainə; rɪˋdʒaɪnə] ***n*.** 丽贾纳〔女子名〕。

re·gi·nal [riˈdʒaiəl; rɪˋdʒaɪnl̩] ***a*.** 〔L.〕女王(一样)的;拥护女王的。

Reg·i·nald [ˈredʒinəld; ˋrɛdʒɪnəld] ***n*.** 雷金纳德〔男子名〕。

re·gion [ˈriːdʒən; ˋridʒən] ***n*.** **1.** 地方,地域,地带;地区;行政区,管辖区,区;左近,邻近;(大气、海水等的)层,界,境。**2.** 【解、动】(身体的)局部,部位。**3.** (学问等的)范围,领域。**4.** 〔罕〕天空。*a fertile* ～ 肥沃地带。*a desert* ～ 沙漠地带。*forest* ～*s* 森林地带。*the lower* [*infernal, nether*] ～*s* 地狱。*the middle* [*lower, upper*] ～ *of the air* 大气的中[下、上]层。*the operating* ～ 工作范围。***in the*** ～ ***of*** 在…附近,在…的左右(*in the* ～ *of 45 dollars* 四十五美元左右)。

re·gion·al [ˈriːdʒənəl; ˋridʒnəl] ***a*.** 地方(性)的;地方主义的;区域(性)的;局部的。**-ism** ***n*.** 地方习惯,地方制度;地方主义。**-ly** ***ad*.**

ré·gis·seur [ˌreiʒiˈsəː; reʒɪˋsœr] ***n*.** 〔F.〕导演;舞台监督。

reg·is·ter [ˈredʒistə; ˋrɛdʒɪstɚ] **I** ***n*.** **1.** 记录,注册,登记,挂号。**2.** (人口动态,户籍等的)登记簿,注册簿;【商】船籍登记簿;海关证明书。**3.** 自动记录器;【自】寄存器;自动记录的数。**4.** 〔美〕记录员,登记员,注册员。**5.** (暖房的)通风装置;调温装置。**6.** 【印】所印纸张两面行;线等位置的相符;彩色版各种颜色的准确套合;【摄】感光板[软片]与焦点玻璃片间的位置的相符。**7.** 【乐】(人声与乐器的)声域,音区;音栓;声域的一部分;(风琴的)整调器,音栓。**8.** 【语言】语域,使用域;专用语言,特殊场合使用语言。*a hotel* ～ 住客登记簿。*a* ～ *of members* 股东登记名簿。*a line* ～ (电话)用户计次器。*a cash* ～ 现金出纳机。*a program* ～ (计算机的)程序寄存器。*in close* ～【电视】精确配准。***be on the*** ～〔美〕有嫌疑,被怀疑;受到注意。**II** ***vt*.** **1.** 记录,登记,注册;(信件等)挂号。**2.** 牢记心上。**3.** (寒暑表等)示度,指示;(机器等)自动记录;【印、电视】对准,套准,配准。**4.** 〔美〕(电影演员等)做(喜、怒等的)表情。～ *a letter* 把信交付挂号寄发。～ *oneself* (在选举人名册等上)登记自己姓名。～ *luggage on a railway* 〔英〕把行李交铁路托运。～ *a vow* 立誓。～ ***a bull's eye*** 打中(靶子的)黑圈。— ***vi*.** **1.** 〔美〕登记姓名。**2.** 【印、电视】对准,套准,配准。**3.** (电影演员)做表情。**4.** 〔口〕留下印象;受到注意。～ ***at a hotel*** 〔美〕住旅馆时登记。～ ***at the congress*** 向大会报到。～ **office** = registry 3.

reg·is·tered [ˈredʒistəd; ˋrɛdʒɪstɚd] ***a*.** 登记过的,注过册的;记名的;挂号的。*a* ～ *design* [*trade-mark*] 注册图案[商标]。*a* ～ *letter* 挂号信。～ *post* [〔美〕*mail*] 挂号邮件。*a* ～ *reader* 预约读者,订阅者。*a* ～ *nurse* 〔美〕领有执照的护士。～ *horses* [*cattle, dogs*] (其血统业经登记认可的)立案马[牛、狗]。～

ballots 记名投票。*a* ～ *bond* 记名债券[证券]。*a* ～ *certificate of shares* 记名股票。

reg·is·tra·ble [ˈredʒistrəbl; ˋrɛdʒɪstrəbl] *a*. **1**. 可注册的;(邮件)可挂号的。**2**. (感情)可表达的。**3**. (印刷品)可对齐的,可套准的。

reg·is·trant [ˈredʒistrənt; ˋrɛdʒɪstrənt] *n*. (商标,专利权等的)登记者;注册人;挂号人;被登记者;被注册者。

reg·is·trar [ˌredʒisˈtrɑː; ˋrɛdʒɪˏstrɑr] *n*. 记录员,登记员,注册员,户籍员;(专管学生学籍、成绩等的)注册干事;负责登记股票转让的信托公司。*the Registrar-General* 〔英〕(伦敦)户籍处[注册处]处长。

reg·is·tra·tion [ˌredʒisˈtreiʃən; ˏrɛdʒɪˋstreʃən] *n*. **1**. 记录,登记,注册;〔美〕签到,报到;(信件等的)挂号;记名;(寒暑表等的)示度,读数。**2**. 【乐】音栓配合法。**3**.【印、电视】(正反面版面的)对准,(彩色的)套准,(图像的)配准。*a* ～ *fee* 挂号费;登记费。

reg·is·try [ˈredʒistri; ˋrɛdʒɪstrɪ] *n*. **1**. 记录,登记,注册;(船舶登记证上的)国籍。**2**. 记录簿,登记簿。**3**. 记录处,登记处,注册处;〔英〕户籍处。**4**. 佣工介绍所〔又叫 *servants'* ～ (*office*)〕。*a* ～ *fee* 〔美〕= a registration fee. *be married at a* ～ (不举行仪式)登记结婚。

re·gi·us [ˈriːdʒiəs; ˋridʒɪəs] *a*. 〔L.〕王的;钦定的。*a R-professor* (牛津、剑桥)钦定讲座教授。

reg·nal [ˈregnl; ˋrɛgnəl] *a*. (某王)在位时的,统治时期的,朝代的;王国的;王的。*the* ～ *day* 即位纪念日。*the third* ～ *year* 即位第三年。

reg·nant [ˈregnənt; ˋrɛgnənt] *a*. **1**. 〔通例用于名词后〕(帝王等)在位的,统治的,支配的。**2**. 优势的,有力的;流行的;广泛的。*the Queen R-* 执政[当朝]女王。

reg·o·lith [ˈregəliθ; ˋrɛgəlɪθ] *n*. 【地】风化层,土被,表皮土(= mantlerock)。

re·gorge [riˈgɔːdʒ; rɪˋgɔrdʒ] *vt*. **1**. 吐出。**2**. 〔罕〕吞回。**3**. 使倒流。— *vi*. 倒流,涌回。

reg·o·sol [ˈregəˌsɔːl, -sɔl; ˋrɛgəˏsɔl, -sɑl] *n*. 【地】表面土,浮土。

re·grant [riˈgrænt; rɪˋgrænt] **I** *vt*. 重新许可,再答应,再承认;再次授与。**II** *n*. 再答应,重新承认;再次的补助金。

re·grate [riˈgreit; rɪˋgret] *vt*. 囤积;售出(商品等)。**-tor** *n*. 囤积居奇者。

re·gress [ˈriːgres; ˋrigrɛs] **I** *n*. **1**. 回归,退回。**2**. 【法】复归(权)。**3**. 退化,退步。**4**. 回顾。**5**. 【天】= regression. **II** [riˈgres; rɪˋgrɛs] *vi*. **1**. 后退,倒退;退回;【天】退行。**2**. 复归,回归。

re·gres·sion [riˈgreʃən; rɪˋgrɛʃən] *n*. **1**. 复归,回归。**2**. 退步,退化。**3**.【天】退行。**-sive** *a*. **-sive·ly** *ad*.

re·gret [riˈgret; rɪˋgrɛt] **I** *n*. **1**. 遗憾,抱歉;后悔,悔恨;痛惜,惋惜,哀悼 (*at*; *for*; *over*; *of*)。**2**. 〔常 *pl*.〕〔美〕(对于邀请等的)婉言辞谢〔回帖〕。***express*** ～ ***at*** 惋惜…,表示…可惜。***express*** ～ ***for*** 对[为]…表示抱歉,为…道歉。***have no*** ～***s*** 没有遗憾,没有后悔。***hear with*** ～ ***of*** [***that***] 听到觉得后悔[惋惜、失望]。(***much***) ***to my*** ～ 非常抱歉。***refuse with many*** ～***s*** [***much*** ～] 非常抱歉地谢绝。***send*** ～***s*** [***a*** ～] (尤指对请帖)发出辞谢信。**II** *vt*. **1**. 怀念,想念(快乐的童年、故乡等);悼念,哀悼(死去的亲友等)。**2**. 悔恨,后悔,懊悔(过错、失去的机会等);以(不能…)为憾,抱歉,抱憾。*I* ～ *that I did not take your advice*. 我懊悔没有听你的劝告。***I*** ～ ***(to say) that....*** 我很遗憾…,很抱歉… (*I* ～ *to say that I am unable to help you*. 我很抱歉不能帮助你)。***It is to be regretted that....*** 使人遗憾的是…;真可惜…;真可怜…。

re·gret·ful [riˈgretful; rɪˋgrɛtfl] *a*. **1**. 悔恨的,后悔的,惋惜的,有遗憾的,抱歉的。**2**. 怀念的;依依不舍的,依恋的。*a* ～ *apology* 道歉。**-ly** *ad*.

re·gret·a·ble, re·gret·ta·ble [riˈgretəbl; rɪˋgrɛtəbl] *a*. 使人后悔的,可惜的,可悲的,可叹息的,令人抱歉的,令人遗憾的,令人过意不去的。**-bly** *ad*.

re·group [ˈriːˈgruːp; riˋgrup] *vt*. **1**. 重新聚合;重行编组。**2**. 【军】变更(军队)的部署。—*vi*. **1**. 重行组合。**2**. 【军】变更部署。

regs 〔美〕= regulations 海军学校规则。

Regt. = **1**. Regent. **2**. Regiment.

reg·u·la·ble [ˈregjuləbl; ˋrɛgjələbl] *a*. 可调整的,可调节的;可控制的。

reg·u·lar [ˈregjulə; ˋrɛgjələ] **I** *a*. **1**. 有规则的,有规律的;有秩序的,井井有条的,整齐的;正规的,正式的。**2**. 端正的,匀称的,调和的,和谐的;首尾一贯的,一律的。**3**. 不变的,一定的;常例的,平常的;习惯的,非偶然的;定期的,定时的。**4**.【军】常备的,正规的。**5**. 合格的,得到营业执照的,挂牌的(医师等),公认的。**6**.【语法】按规则变化的。**7**.【数】等边等角的;【结晶】等轴的;〔立体〕各面大小形状相等的;【植】整齐的(花)。**8**.【宗】受教规束缚的;属于教团的。**9**. 〔口〕十足的,真正的,名符其实的;彻底的。**10**. 〔美口〕诚实的,可靠的。～ *procedure* 正规手续。*a* ～ *member* 正式会员。～ *people* 生活有规律的人〔尤指大便、月经有定时的〕。*a* ～ *pulse* 规则脉。～ *features* 端正的面貌。*a* ～ *customer* 老主顾。～ *holidays* 正式假日。～ *service* 定期航行,定期开车(等)。*the* ～ *army* 正规军,常备军。*a* ～ *verb* 规则动词。*a* ～ *hero* 真正的英雄。*a* ～ *rascal* 十足的恶棍。*a* ～ *fellow* [*guy*] 〔美口〕受大家欢迎的人;(用钱)手松的人;有趣的家伙。***keep*** ～ ***hours*** 过有规律的生活。

II *ad*. **1**. 有规则地,定期地,经常地。**2**. 完全,非常。*He comes* ～. 他经常来。*It happens* ～. 这经常发生。*He is* ～ *angry*. 〔卑〕那家伙生气极了。

III *n*. **1**. 〔常 *pl*.〕正规兵,常备兵;(球队的)正式队员。**2**. 〔口〕长期雇工;固定职工;老主顾,常客。**3**.【宗】修道士。**4**. 〔美〕(某党派的)忠诚支持者。**5**. 〔俚〕〔*pl*.〕赃物的份儿。～ **bedtime** 规定[通常]的睡眠时间。～ **coast** 平直岸。～ **contributor** 定期[经常]撰稿人。～ **course** (学校的)本科。～ **curve**【数】正弧。～ **five**【篮球】主力队员。～ **forest**【林】同龄林。～ **marriage** (按仪式举行的)正规[合法]结婚。～ **planting**【农】方形种植。～ **practitioner** 合格的开业医生[律师]。～ **publications** 定期刊物。～ **stock**【交易所】现货。～ **reflection**【物】单向反射。～ **subscriber** (期刊)长期订户。～ **way** (交易所的)普通交易。**-ly** *ad*.

reg·u·lar·i·ty [ˌregjuˈlæriti; ˏrɛgjəˋlærətɪ] *n*. 有规则;整齐(度);调和;一定不变;正规;(合乎)规格;规律性;经常,定期。

reg·u·lar·i·za·tion [ˌregjuləraiˈzeiʃən; ˏrɛgjələraɪˋzeʃən] *n*. 正规化,秩序化,组织化;整理,调整;合法化。

reg·u·lar·ize [ˈregjuləraiz; ˋrɛgjələˏraɪz] *vt*. **1**. 使有规律;使规则化,使有秩序,使有组织。**2**. 整理,调整。**3**. 使合法。

reg·u·late [ˈregjuleit; ˋrɛgjəˏlet] *vt*. **1**. 规定,管制,控制。**2**. 整顿;使有条理,使整齐。**3**. 调节(温度、速度等);调准,校准,对准(机器、钟表等);【化】调节。

reg·u·la·tion [ˌregjuˈleiʃən; ˏrɛgjəˋleʃən] **I** *n*. **1**. 规则,规程,规章,条例。**2**. 控制,管理,限制,(情欲等的)节制。**3**. 调整,调节,整顿。**4**. 校准;稳定;【电】变动率;【火箭】导向;【生】调整〔指胚胎发育物质的重新分配〕;(维持早期胚胎正常发育的)调节机制。**II** *a*. **1**. 正规的,规定的,正式的。**2**. 正常的,普通的。*In many cases* ～*s alone will not work*. 单靠行政命令,在许多情况下就行不通。*detailed* ～*s* 详细规定[章程],细则。*laws and* ～*s* 法令。*draft* ～*s* 条例草案。*staff* ～*s* 人事条例。*a* ～ *cap* [*uniform*] 制帽[制服]。*a* ～ *game* 正式比赛。～ *speed* 规定速率。*the* ～ *mourning* 正式悼念仪式。*of the* ～ *size* 普通大小[尺寸]的。

reg·u·la·tive [ˈregjuleitiv; ˋrɛgjəˏletɪv] *a*. **1**. 管理的;管制的,规定的。**2**. 调整的;调节的;整理的。**-ly** *ad*.

reg·u·la·tor [ˈregjuleitə; ˋrɛgjə͵letɚ] ***n.*** 1. 管理者。2. 调整者;整理者。3. 校准者;【机】调整器,校准器,调节器;【无】稳定器;【化】调节剂;【代】调节基因;(钟表的)整时器;标准钟。4. 原则,标准。5. 【英史】选举调查[监视]委员。

Reg·u·lus [ˈregjuləs; ˋrɛgjʊləs] ***n.*** 雷古拉斯〔Marcas Atilius ~, 罗马大将〕。

reg·u·lus [ˈregjuləs; ˋrɛgjʊləs] ***n.*** 1. 〔R-〕【天】(狮子座 a)轩辕十四。2. (*pl.* ***-lus·es***, ***-li*** [-lai; -laɪ])【化、冶】锑块;金属渣;熔块。

re·gur·gi·tate [ri(ː)ˈgəːdʒiteit; rɪˋgɝdʒə͵tet] ***vt.***, ***vi.*** 1. (使)掷还,(使)丢回;(使)喷回;(使)回流。2. (婴儿)吐(奶);(使)反胃;(使)反哺;(使)反刍。**-ta·tion** ***n.*** 回流,回涌;【动】反刍,反胃,回吐;【医】心脏瓣口(血液)反流。

re·gust·ed [riˈgʌstid; rɪˋgʌstɪd] ***a.*** 〔美俚〕= disgusted.

re·ha·bil·i·tant [͵riːhəˈbilitent; ͵rihəˋbɪlətənt] ***n.*** 在康复中的病残者。

re·ha·bil·i·tate [͵riːhəˈbiliteit; ͵rihəˋbɪlə͵tet] ***vt.*** 1. 使复原;使复权[复职、复位]。2. 使恢复。3. 改善,复兴,修理。~ *oneself* 恢复名誉,昭雪。

re·ha·bil·i·ta·tion [ˈriːhəˈbiliˈteiʃən; ͵rihə͵bɪləˋteʃən] ***n.*** 1. 复权,复职,复位。2. 善后;平反,恢复名誉,昭雪。3. 恢复,复兴,改善。

re·han·dle [ˈriːˈhændl; riˋhændl̩] ***vt.*** 1. 再处理。2. 改造;改铸。3. 重新整顿。

re·hash [ˈriːˈhæʃ; riˋhæʃ] **I** ***vt.*** 1. 重新剁碎(肉等)。2. (特指利用旧文学材料)改作,重作,重讲。**II** ***n.*** (旧东西的)改作;用旧材料改编的作品。~ *of platitude* 滥调翻新。

re·hear [ˈriːˈhiə; riˋhɪr] (***-heard*** [-ˈhəːd; -ˋhɝd]) ***vt.*** 1. 再听。2. 【法】复审,再审。

re·hears·al [riˈhəːsəl; rɪˋhɝsl] ***n.*** 1. 背诵。2. (经验等的)详述,复述。3. (音乐演出等的)练习;排练;排演。*a ~ of one's experiences* 介绍经验。*a (full) dress ~* 【剧】彩排。*a full ~* 【剧】全体排演。*a public ~* 【剧】公开预演。

re·hearse [riˈhəːs; rɪˋhɝs] ***vt.*** 1. 背诵;反复讲,再三讲;讲述,详述;学嘴,照样讲(别人讲的话)。2. 练习,排练;排演,预演。3. 列举;总计。— ***vi.*** 1. 朗诵,背诵。2. 练习,预演;排演。

re·heat [ˈriːˈhiːt; riˋhit] ***vt.*** 再热,对…重新加热。

re·house [ˈriːˈhauz; riˋhaʊz] ***vt.*** 给…提供新房子,给…安排新房子。

re·hu·man·ize [ˈriːˈhjuːmənaiz; riˋhjumə͵naɪz] ***vt.*** 使改邪归正,使成正经人。

re·hy·drate [riːˈhai͵dreit; riˋhaɪdret] ***vt.*** (***-drat·ed***, ***-drat·ing***)【化】再水合,再水化。**-dra·tion** ***n.***

Reich [raik; raɪk] ***n.*** 〔G.〕帝国,国;德国,(德意志)帝国。*the First R-* 第一(神圣罗马)帝国〔962—1806〕。*the Second R-* (德国 Bismarck 当权时代的)第二帝国〔1871—1919〕。*the Third R-* (纳粹统治下的)第三帝国〔1933—1945〕。

Reichs·mark [ˈraiksmaːk; ˋraɪks͵mark] ***n.*** (*pl.* ***~s***, ***~***) 〔G.〕德国旧马克。

Reichstag [ˈraikstaːg; ˋraɪks͵tag] ***n.*** 〔G.〕(旧德意志帝国)国会;(旧德意志共和国)国民议会。

Reichsweshr [ˈraiksvεə; ˋraɪks͵vεr] ***n.*** 〔G.〕(1919 年组成的德国)国防军;德国军队。

Reid [riːd; rid] ***n.*** 里德〔姓氏,男子名〕。

re·i·fy [ˈriːifai; ˋriə͵faɪ] ***vt.*** (***-fi·ed***, ***-fy·ing***)【哲】使(抽象的概念)具体化。**-ca·tion** ***n.***

reign [rein; ren] **I** ***n.*** 1. (帝王等的)统治,支配;朝代,在位时代;统治权,支配权。2. 势力,权势。3. 领域,范围。*during five successive ~s* 一连五个统治者统治时代中。*His ~ was a gentle one.* 他在位时期很太平。*Night resumes her ~.* 黑夜重临。*the ~ of law in nature* 自然规律的支配。***the R- of Terror*** 【法史】恐怖时期〔1793—1794〕。***under*** [***in***] ***the ~ of*** …在位时期。**II** ***vi.*** 1. 掌握权力,统治,君临,支配 (*over*)。2. 称霸,有巨大势力。3. 盛行,大大流行,通行。*the ~ing beauty* 绝代佳人,当代第一美女。*~ing sovereign* 在位君主。

re·im·burse [͵riːimˈbəːs; ͵riɪmˋbɝs] ***vt.*** 偿还,付还,赔还,赔偿,补偿。**-ment** ***n.***

re·im·port [ˈriːimˈpɔːt; ͵riɪmˋport] **I** ***vt.*** 再输入(输出品等),再进口。**II** [ˈriːˈimpɔːt; riˋɪmport] ***n.*** 再输入,再进口;〔常 *pl.*〕再进口货。**-ta·tion** [͵riːimpɔːˈteiʃən; ͵riɪmporˋteʃən] ***n.*** 再进口货。

re·im·pose [ˈriːimˈpəuz; ͵riɪmˋpoz] ***vt.*** 再征收(停征的税等)。**re·im·po·si·tion** ***n.***

re·im·pres·sion [͵riimˈpreʃən; ͵riɪmˋprɛʃən] ***n.*** 【印】再版,重版。

rein [rein; ren] **I** ***n.*** 1. (皮)缰,缰绳。2. 〔常 *pl.*〕驾驭(法);统治(手段);拘束物;控制(权),箝制,牵制。***assume*** [***drop***] ***the ~s of government*** 执掌[放弃]政权。***draw ~ = draw in the reins*** 收紧缰绳(勒住马);放弃努力;节省费用。***drive*** [***ride***] ***with a loose ~*** 放松缰绳;放任,纵容。***gather up one's ~s*** 勒紧缰绳。***give ~*** [***the ~s***] ***to*** 让马自由走;使…自由发挥;给…自由,放任,纵容(*He gave ~ to his fancy.* 他一味空想)。***hold a ~ on*** (*one's appetites*) 抑制(食欲)。***hold*** [***keep***] ***a tight ~ over*** [***on***] 紧紧地控制,对…严加约束。***hold the ~s*** 掌握(政权等)。***take the ~s*** 掌权,支配,有决定权,作领导人。***throw*** (***up***) ***the ~s to*** = *give ~ to*. **II** ***vt.*** 1. 给(马)套上缰绳;用缰绳勒住。2. 控制,支配,约束;箝制;抑制(情欲等)。~ ***back*** 勒(马)后退。~ ***in*** [***up***] 勒住(马);控制,约束,抑制。*Rein your tongue.* 住嘴! —***vi.*** 1. (马)顺从缰绳。2. 勒缰绳使马止步[慢行] (*in*, *up*); 止住;放慢 (*in*, *up*)。*a horse that ~s well* 易于驾驭的马。

re·in·car·nate [riːˈinkaːneit; ͵riɪnˋkarnet] **I** ***vt.*** 1. 再赋与新的肉体。2. 使化身,使转生。**II** [-ˈkaːnit; -ˋkarnɪt] ***a.*** 再具肉身的;化身的,转生的。

re·in·car·na·tion [ˈriːinkaːˈneiʃən; ˋri͵ɪnkarˋneʃən] ***n.*** 再具肉体;化身,再生;再投胎;再体现。

rein·deer [ˈreindiə; ˋrendɪr] ***n.*** (*pl.* ~, ***~s***)【动】驯鹿。

reinf. = reinforced.

re·in·fect [ˈriːinˈfekt; ͵riɪnˋfɛkt] ***vt.*** 使再感染。**-fection** ***n.***

re·in·force [͵riːinˈfɔːs; ͵riɪnˋfors] **I** ***vt.*** 1. 增兵,增援。2. 增强,加固,补强;补充,增加;添加,补足。~ *a fortress* 增援要塞。~ *a party* 加强党的力量[组织]。*~d concrete* 钢筋混凝土。*reinforcing bar(s)* [*iron*] 钢筋。~ *one's health* 增进健康。~ *provisions* 补充粮食。—***vi.*** 求援;得到援助。**II** ***n.*** 加固物。

re·in·force·ment [͵riːinˈfɔːsmənt; ͵riɪnˋforsmənt] ***n.*** 1. 增强,加固;补强物,强化物;补给品。2. 增援,支援;〔*pl.*〕增援部队,援军;救援舰。*a stub ~* 【电】撑杆;帮桩,接腿。*a concrete ~ worker* 钢筋工人。

re·ink [ˈriːˈiŋk; ͵riˋɪŋk] ***vt.*** 重新加墨水[油墨]于。

rein·less [ˈreinlis; ˋrenlɪs] ***a.*** 无缰的;不受勒制的,无拘束的,放纵的,自由的。

reins [reinz; renz] ***n.*** 〔*pl.*〕〔古〕1. 肾脏;腰部。2. 感情,爱情,激情。

re·in·state [ˈriːinˈsteit; ͵riɪnˋstet] ***vt.*** 1. 使复原;使恢复;使复任,使复位,使复职。2. 使恢复健康。3. 修补,修理。*be ~d in an office* [*to lost privileges*] 复职[恢复特权]。**-ment** ***n.***

re·in·sur·ance [ˈriːinˈʃuərəns; ͵riɪnˋʃʊrəns] ***n.*** 再保险,转保险;分保;再保险金额。

re·in·sure [ˈriːinˈʃuə; ͵riɪnˋʃʊr] ***vt.*** 再保险;再承受保险;分保。*the ~d* 再保险者。

re·in·te·grate [ˈriːˈintigreit; riˋɪntɪˏgret] *vt*. 使重新完整,恢复;重建,复兴;再统一,再团结。**-gra·tion** [ˈriːˌintiˈgreiʃən; ˋriˏɪntɪˋgreʃən] *n*.

re·in·ter [ˈriːinˈtəː; ˏriɪnˋtɝ] *vt*. 重埋,改葬。

re·in·ter·pret [ˌriːinˈtəːprit; ˏriɪnˋtɝprɪt] *vt*. 再解释〔尤指给…以不同的解释〕。**-ation** *n*.

re·in·tro·duce [ˈriːˌintrəˈdjuːs; ˏriɪntrəˋdjus] *vt*. 再介绍;再提出;再引入。

re·in·vent [ˈriːinˈvent; ˋriɪnˋvɛnt] *vt*. 重新改变(自己的兴趣、人生观等)。~ ***oneself*** 重塑自我。~ **the wheel** 从事不必要的重复劳动。

re·in·vest [ˈriːinˈvest; ˏriɪnˋvɛst] *vt*. **1**. 再投资于;重新投资于。**2**. 再授与;再委任 (*with*); 归还。**3**. 再围攻。**-ment** *n*.

re·in·vig·or·ate [ˈriːinˈvigəreit; ˏriɪnˋvɪgəˏret] *vt*. 使恢复生气,使再活跃,使恢复精神[体力],使重新振作。**-or·a·tion** [-reiʃən; -reʃən] *n*.

reis [reis; res] *n*. 〔*pl*.〕real 2.的复数。

re·is·sue [ˈriːˈisjuː, ˈriˈiʃjuː; riˋɪʃjɚ, riˋɪʃɚ] **I** *vt*., *vi*. 再发出(证券、汇票等),再发行(书籍等);重行发布。**II** *n*. 重新发行;改版。

re·it·er·ate [riːˈitəreit; riˋɪtəˏret] *vt*. 反复,反复讲;反复做;重申;重作。

re·it·er·a·tion [riːˌitəˈreiʃən; riˏɪtəˋreʃən] *n*. 反复;重复;重申;〔主英〕【印】反面印刷。

re·it·er·a·tive [riːˈitərətiv; riˋɪtəˏretɪv] **I** *a*. 反复的。**II** *n*. 【语法】反复动作词〔如从 prate 变成的 prattle 等〕;重叠语〔如 dillydally, pell-mell 等〕。

reive [riːv; riv] *v*. = reave.

reiv·er [ˈriːvə; ˋrivɚ] *n*. 抢夺者,掠夺者。

re·ject I [riˈdʒekt; rɪˋdʒɛkt] *vt*. (*opp*. accept) **1**. 拒绝,抵制;不受理,不接受;驳回,否决,否认。**2**. 退掉;丢弃,除去,滤去。**3**. (胃)吐出,呕出(食物)。**4**.【物】拒斥。*His view has been ~ed*. 他的意见已被否决了。*Sorting-machine ~s all defective specimens*. 精选机挑除一切有瑕疵的制品。~ *a literary contribution* 退稿。~ *a vote* 否决所投之票〔视为无效〕。**II** [ˈriːdʒekt; ˋridʒɛkt] *n*. 废品,下脚料;不合格者;被剔除者。*reduction in the number of ~s and seconds* 废品次品率降低。

re·jec·ta·men·ta [riˌdʒektəˈmentə; rɪˏdʒɛktəˋmɛntə] *n*. 〔L.〕〔*pl*.〕**1**. 垃圾,废物。**2**. (被冲到岸上的)海草,漂浮物。**3**. 排泄物。

re·ject·er [ˈriˈdʒektə; rɪˋdʒɛktɚ] *n*. 丢弃者;排除者;拒绝者;否决者;呕吐者。

re·jec·tion [riˈdʒekʃən; rɪˋdʒɛkʃən] *n*. **1**. 抛弃,排除,退回;废弃。**2**. 抵制;拒斥;拒绝;排泄物,呕出物。**3**.【统】否定;否决;【法】驳回;【电讯】阻碍。~ *and waste* 返工和浪费。**-ist** *n*. 拒绝派〔反对以色列进行任何谈判的阿拉伯人〕。

re·jec·tor [riˈdʒektə; rɪˋdʒɛktɚ] *n*. **1**. = rejecter. **2**.【无】带阻滤波器;抑制器。

re·jig·ger [ˈriːˈdʒigə; riˋdʒɪgɚ] *vt*. 〔英口〕重新安排;更新装备(工厂等)。

re·joice [riˈdʒɔis; rɪˋdʒɔɪs] *vi*. **1**. 欢喜,高兴;快乐,欢乐 (*at*; *in*; *to do*; *over*)。**2**. 欢呼,宴乐;庆祝,欢庆。~ ***in*** 〔谑〕拥有,享有(~ *in health* 身体健康。~ *in the name of* 名叫…。~ *in one's youth* 年轻)。— *vt*. 使欢喜,使高兴,使快乐。***be ~d to hear*** [***at hearing***] 听到而欢喜[高兴](*I am ~d to hear of your success*. 听到你的成功我很高兴)。

re·joic·ing [riˈdʒɔisiŋ; rɪˋdʒɔɪsɪŋ] *n*. **1**. 喜悦,欢喜,高兴。**2**. 〔*pl*.〕欢呼,欢声;庆祝;欢庆;宴乐。**-ly** *ad*.

re·join[1] [ˈriːˈdʒɔin; ˏriˋdʒɔɪn] *vt*. **1**. 使再接合,使再聚合 (*to*, *with*)。**2**. 再参加,再加入,重返(队伍等);重逢。~ *one's colours* 重归队伍。~ *one's regiment* [*ship*] 归队。— *vi*. 照原样接合;再结合,重逢,复聚,重聚。

re·join[2] [riˈdʒɔin; rɪˋdʒɔɪn] *vt*. (再)回答说,答应,答复。— *vi*. **1**. 回答,答辩。**2**.【法】(被告)再次答辩,抗辩。

re·join·der [riˈdʒɔində; rɪˋdʒɔɪndɚ] *n*. **1**. 回答,答辩;回嘴。**2**. (被告的)第二答辩。

re·ju·ve·nate [riˈdʒuːvineit; rɪˋdʒuvəˏnet] *vi*., *vt*. **1**. (使)回复青春;(使)恢复精神,(使)复壮;(使)年轻化;(使)翻身。**2**.【化】(使)(黏胶)嫩化;【地】(使)回春;(使)再生。**-na·tion** *n*. 恢复过程;复壮作用[现象];嫩化。

re·ju·ve·na·tor [riˈdʒuːvineitə; rɪˋdʒuvəˏnetɚ] *n*. **1**. 回复青春的人。**2**. 复活器;复壮剂;【化】嫩化剂。

re·ju·ve·nesce [ˌriːdʒuːviˈnes; rɪˏdʒuvəˋnɛs] *vi*., *vt*. (使)回复青春;【生】(使)复壮。

re·ju·ve·nes·cence [ˌriːdʒuːviˈnesns; rɪˏdʒuvəˋnɛsns] *n*. 回复青春,回春,更新;【生】复壮(现象)。

re·ju·ve·nes·cent [ˌriːdʒuːviˈnesnt; rɪˏdʒuvəˋnɛsnt] *a*. (使)回复青春的;(使)恢复活力的;(使)复壮的。

re·ju·ve·nize [riˈdʒuːvinaiz; rɪˋdʒuvəˏnaɪz] *v*. = rejuvenate.

re·kin·dle [ˈriːˈkindl; riˋkɪndl̩] *vt*., *vi*. **1**. 再点火;重新燃起;重新燃烧。**2**. 〔喻〕使再振作精神;使重新激起[引起]。

REL = rate of energy loss 能量损耗率。

-rel, -erel *suf*. 表示"小","少","轻":cocker*el*.

rel. = **1**. relative; relatively. **2**. religion; religious.

re·lapse [riˈlæps; rɪˋlæps] **I** *n*. **1**. 复旧,故态复萌;退步;堕落;累犯。**2**.【医】再发,旧病复发。**II** *vi*. **1**. 回复(原来坏习惯等),故态复萌;(重新)堕落,退步;恶化;沉陷。**2**. (病)再发,复发 (*into*)。*relapsing fever* 【医】回归热。

re·late [riˈleit; rɪˋlet] *vt*. **1**. 讲,叙述(故事等)。**2**. 把…与…关联起来;显示…与…的关系;使联系 (*to*, *with*)。**3**. 〔通例用被动语态〕使结成亲戚。*Curious to ~, the giraffe has no voice*. 说来奇怪,长颈鹿不会出声。***be ~d to*** 和…有(亲戚)关系。— *vi*. **1**. 关联,有关系 (*to*)。**2**. 符合 (*with*)。**3**. 与…相适应;与…友好相处。*These remarks ~ to the industrial modernization*. 这些话涉及工业的现代化。*unable to ~ to one's environment* 不能适应环境。~ *well to people* 人缘好。

re·lat·ed [riˈleitid; rɪˋletɪd] *a*. **1**. 所叙述的,所说的。**2**. 相关的,有关系的〔尤指有亲戚关系的〕。**3**.【乐】和声的。**-ness** *n*.

re·la·tion [riˈleiʃən; rɪˋleʃən] *n*. **1**. 说话,叙述,报告;故事。**2**. 关系,联系;〔*pl*.〕(利害)关系,交情;〔*pl*.〕国际关系。**3**. 亲戚关系;亲戚。**4**.【法】告发;追溯效力。**5**. 比率,比数。**6**. 〔*pl*.〕男女关系;性关系。*diplomatic ~* 外交关系。*the ~s of production* 生产关系。*social ~s* 社会关系。*the ~ between cause and effect* 因果关系。*the ~ of father and son* 父子关系。*Is he any ~ to you?* 他是你的亲戚吗? ***bear no ~ to*** = ***be out of all ~ to*** 和…无关,和…完全不称。*The outlay seems to bear no ~ to the object aimed at*. 这费用似乎和预期目的完全不相称。***have ~s with*** 和…有(某种)关系。***have ~ to*** 有关;和…有关系(*The report has ~ to a state of things now past*. 这个报告是关于现在已经过去的事件的)。***in*** [***with***] ***~ to*** 关于…,就…而论。***make ~ to*** 提及…,读到…。~ ***by marriage*** 姻亲,裙带关系。

re·la·tion·al [riˈleiʃənəl; rɪˋleʃənl̩] *a*. 有关系的;亲戚的;(特指语法上)表示关系的。**-ly** *ad*.

re·la·tion·ship [riˈleiʃənʃip; rɪˋleʃənˏʃɪp] *n*. **1**. 亲戚,亲戚关系。**2**. 关系,联系。**3**. 〔婉〕男女关系〔指男女之间的暧昧关系〕。

rel·a·tive [ˈrelətiv; ˋrɛlətɪv] **I** *a*. **1**. 关于…的,与…有关系[联系]的。**2**. 相对的;相关的;以(他物)为准的,相应的,成比例的 (*to*); 相比较的。**3**. 附条件的。**4**. 切合本问题的(例证)。**5**.【乐】关系的〔指有相同调号的〕;【语法】表示关系的。II *n*. 1. 亲戚，亲属。2. 关系物；有关事项。3. 相对物。4.【语法】关系词。*What are the ~ merits of the two?* 两者相较的优劣如何？ ~ *velocity* 相对速度。*to assign tasks according to their ~ importance and urgency* 按轻重缓急安排工作。*a different yet ~ reason* 虽不同但有连带关系的理由。*without some more ~ proof* 倘无更恰当的证据。**be ~ to** 和…相应，和…成比例，和…有关系，随…而转移（*Value is ~ to demand*. 价值随需要而转移）。~ **adjective** [**adverb, pronoun**] 关系形容词[副词，代名词]。~ **terms** 相对词语〔例：strong, weak〕。

rel·a·tive·ly [ˈrelətivli; ˋrelətɪvlɪ] *ad*. 1. 关系上；相对；相互。2. 比较上；按…比例说，比较…地。*an engine ~ powerful to its weight* 就重量而论马力较大的发动机。

rel·a·tiv·ism [ˈrelətivizəm; ˋrelətɪvɪzm̩] *n*. 相对性；相对主义，相对论。

rel·a·tiv·ist [ˈrelətivist; ˋrelətɪvɪst] *n*. 相对论者。

rel·a·tiv·is·tic [ˌreləti'vistik; ˏrelətəˋvɪstɪk] *a*. 相对论(性质)的。

rel·a·tiv·i·ty [ˌreləˈtiviti; ˏreləˋtɪvətɪ] *n*. 相关(性)；互相依存；相对性；相对论。*the general* [*restricted, special*] *theory of ~* 广义[狭义]相对论。

rel·a·tiv·ize [ˈrelətiˌvaiz; ˋrelətəˏvaɪz] *vt*. (*-iz·ed*; *-iz·ing*) 把…相对起来考虑，把…作为相对物描述，把…作为相对物处理。**-i·za·tion** *n*.

re·la·tor [riˈleitə; rɪˋletɚ] *n*. 〔L.〕 1. 叙述者，讲说者。2.【法】原告，告发人。

re·lax [riˈlæks; rɪˋlæks] *vt*. 1. 松弛(肌肉等)，放松(紧握的手等)；使软弱无力。2. 缓和，放宽，减轻(刑罚等)。3. 使松懈，减少(注意、努力等)。4. 使休息；使(心里)轻松，使舒畅，宽(心)。— *vi*. 1. 松弛；放松。2. 缓和，放宽。3. 变得不拘束；变得从容。4. 休养；休息；娱乐。5. 通便。*thinking that ~es the will to fight* 松懈战斗意志的思想。*a ~ed throat* 咽喉炎。*a ~ing climate* 使人懒洋洋的气候。*You must not ~ in your efforts*. 你不能松懈；你要继续努力。~ *one's attention* 疏忽，懈怠。~ *one's pace* 放慢步伐。~ *the bowels* 通便。

re·lax·ant [riˈlæksənt; rɪˋlæksənt] I *a*. 放松的，弛缓的〔尤指减轻肌肉的紧张程度〕。II *n*.【医】弛缓剂。

re·lax·a·tion [ˌriːlækˈseiʃən; ˏrilæksˋeʃən] *n*. 1. (精神等的)松弛；放松；【物】张弛；弛豫。2. (刑罚等的)减轻，放宽。3. 休养，休息，解闷，娱乐。4. 松懈；宽舒；缓和。5. 衰弱，精力减退。

re·lax·ed [riˈlæksid; rɪˋlæksɪd] *a*. 1. 松懈的，不严格的。2. 放松的，得到安宁的。3. 随意的，自在的，不拘束的。

re·lax·ed·ly [riˈlæksidli; rɪˋlæksɪdlɪ] *ad*. 松弛的。

re·lax·in [riˈlæksin; rɪˋlæksɪn] *n*.【医】松弛激素。

re·lay I [riˈlei; rɪˋle] *n*. 1. 接替的马；驿马；接替的狗；(备有接替马匹的)旅馆。2. 接替；接替人员；补给供应。3. 分程递送；传达；转运；【军】递骑；【体】接力赛跑。4. [ˈriːlei; ˋrile]【电】替续器；【机】继动器；【无】转播的无线电节目。*work in* [*by*] *~s* 轮班工作。*a fresh ~ of workers* 刚接班的一批工人。*a key ~* 键控继电器。*a radar ~* 雷达中继站。II [ˈriːlei; riˋle] *vt*. 1. 用驿马递送；分程递送；使接替。2. 供给接替马匹；供给新材料。3. [riːˈlei; riˋle] 传达；【无】转播。— *vi*. 1. 得到接替[补充]。2. 传达；转播。*a ~ing station*【无】转播电台。~ **broadcast**【无】转播。~ **race** 接力赛跑。~ **station**【电信】中继站[局]。

re-lay [ˈriːˈlei; ˏriˋle] *vt*. (*-laid*, *-lay·ing*) 1. 再放，重放；重铺。2. 再征收(税等)。3. 再给穿上，使重穿，重涂。

re·lease [riˈliːs; rɪˋlis] I *vt*. 1. 放(箭等)，投(炸弹)；解放，释放(囚犯、俘虏等)；使免除；救出；解除(痛苦、债务等)(*from*)。2.【法】放弃；让与(权利、财产等)。3.【机】吐出，放出；【农】推广。4.【物，电】释放；断开；断路器。5. 发表(消息)；发行(新影片、书刊等)。*He is ~d at five o'clock*. 他五点钟就下班了。II *n*. 1. (炸弹等的)投掷，投下。2. 释放；解脱；解除，免除。3. 救出，救济；安慰。4.【法】弃权，让渡(证书)。5.【机】放气装置；放气时间；吐出，放出。6. 发表；发售(物)；(影片的)发行上映。7. 发布的消息；发行的书[刊物、影片等]。*a news ~* 新闻稿。*a happy ~* 幸福的解脱〔尤指久病后的死〕。*This medicine will give you ~ from pain*. 这药吃后会减轻你的疼痛。

re-lease [riːˈliːs; riˋlis] *vt*. 重订契约出租；再出租。

re·leas·ee [riˌliːˈsiː; rɪˏlisˋi] *n*.【法】(权利或财产的)受让人；被免除债务者。

re·lea·sor [riˈliːsə; rɪˋlisɚ] *n*.【法】放弃权利者；(权利或财产的)让与人。

rel·e·gate [ˈreligeit; ˋreləˏget] *vt*. 1. 命令撤离，驱逐(出境)；〔古〕充军；降职，贬黜；丢弃，束之高阁。2. 使归属(某类、某级)。3. 委托，移交(事件)；指示(某人向某人打听)。

rel·e·ga·tion [ˌreliˈgeiʃən; ˏreləˋgeʃən] *n*. 充军；降职，贬黜；归属；(事件的)移交，委托；指示问讯处。

re·lent [riˈlent; rɪˋlent] *vi*. 变温和，变宽厚；心平气和；发慈悲心，动怜悯心(*towards*)；减弱，缓和。**-ing·ly** *ad*. 温和地；心平气和地；怀着怜悯心；宽厚地，随和地。

re·lent·less [riˈlentlis; rɪˋlentlɪs] *a*. 1. 狠心的，冷酷的，残忍的，酷虐的，毫不留情的。2. 坚韧的，不屈不挠的；不懈的。**-ly** *ad*.

re·let [riːˈlet; riˋlet] I *vt*. (*-let*; *-let·ting*) 再出租；续租；转租。II *n*.〔英〕转租的房屋。

rel·e·vance, -van·cy [ˈrelivəns, -si; ˋreləvəns, -sɪ] *n*. 1. 有关系；适当，适切。2. 实质性；现实意义；实质作用。*His answer bore little ~*. 他的回答无关痛痒。**have ~ to** 和…有关。

rel·e·vant [ˈrelivənt; ˋreləvənt] *a*. 1. 有关的；适当的，贴切的，中肯的(*to*)。2. 成比例的；相应的。3. 有重大意义[作用]的，实质性的。**not ~ to the present question** 和目前的问题无关的。**-ly** *ad*.

re·le·vé [rələˈvei; rələˋve] *n*.〔F.〕(正餐上用的)开胃菜。

re·li·a·bil·i·ty [riˌlaiəˈbiliti; rɪˏlaɪəˋbɪlətɪ] *n*. 可靠性，安全性，确实(性)。~ **trials** (汽车等的)耐用[可靠]试验。

re·li·a·ble [riˈlaiəbl; rɪˋlaɪəbl̩] *a*. 可靠的，确实的。*It is reported on ~ authority that* .... 据可靠方面消息…。**-bly** *ad*.

re·li·ance [riˈlaiəns; rɪˋlaɪəns] *n*. 信赖，信任；信心；依靠(*in*; *on*, *upon*)；所信赖的人[物]；寄托。*No ~ is to be placed on his word*. 他的话靠不住。**have** [**place**] **~ upon** 信赖…。**in ~ on** 信赖…而(*I waited in ~ on your promise*. 我相信你答应过的话而等待着)。

re·li·ant [riˈlaiənt; rɪˋlaɪənt] *a*. 信赖的，信任的，依靠的(*on*; *upon*)；信赖自己的；依靠自己的；自力更生的。

rel·ic [ˈrelik; ˋrelɪk] *n*. 1.〔常 *pl*.〕遗物；遗迹；遗风。2. (殉教者的)圣骨，圣物，遗宝。3. 纪念物，遗念；〔*pl*.〕〔古、诗〕遗骨，遗骸；尸体。4.【古生】残遗体；残遗种〔如水杉〕；【地】残余。*unearthed ~s* 出土文物。~ *species*【生】孑遗种。~ *fauna* 残遗动物群。

rel·ict [ˈrelikt; ˋrelɪkt] *n*. 1.〔古〕寡妇。2.【古生】残遗体；残遗种；【地】残余。

re·lief[1] [riˈliːf; rɪˋlif] *n*. 1. (难民、贫民等的)救助，救济，救护；救济品。2. (痛苦、忧虑等的)解除，减轻；【化】减压。3. 慰藉，安慰，安心；解闷，消遣。4. 调班，换班，替换；替换者，接班者，接班兵；救援，解围；救兵，援兵；【军】换防；接防部队。5.【电】卸载；释放；【机】放泄；离隙。6.〔婉〕性满足。*a ~ fund* 救济(基)金。*This medicine will give you ~*. 这药会使你舒服的。*A comic scene follows by way of ~*. 接着来一个喜剧场面以资调剂。**feel a sense of ~** 放下心，如释重负。**find ~ from** 从…中摆脱出来。**for the ~ of** 为了救济…。**give a**

R

sigh of ～ 宽慰地舒一口气。***to my great*** ～ 使我大为欣喜[放心]的是。～ **valve** 保险阀,安全阀。～ **works** 失业救助工程〔如修筑道路等〕。

re·lief[2] [riˈliːf; rɪˋlif] ***n*.** **1.**【雕刻】凸起;浮起,浮雕;浮雕品;【绘画】人物凸现,轮廓鲜明。**2.** 鲜明,生动,显著,卓越。**3.** 地形,地势,起伏;【筑城】壁高;【摄】调剂画面。*high* [*grand*] ～ 高[深]浮雕。*low* ～ 低[浅]浮雕。*His deeds stand out in* ～. 他功绩显赫。*micro-*～ 小区地形,小区起伏。***blank wall without*** ～ (无门无窗的)平墙。***bring*** [***throw***] ***into*** ～ 使突出,使鲜明,使显著。***bring out the fact in full*** ～ 把事实十分鲜明地摆出来。***in*** ～ 浮雕一般;鲜明地,显著地。***stand out in bold*** [***strong***] ～ 鲜明地突现出来。*The snowy Alps stand out in bold* ～ *against the blue sky*. 白雪皑皑的阿尔卑斯山在蓝色天空的衬托下鲜明地耸立着。～ **map** 模型地图;地形[势]图。～ **printing** 凸版印刷。～ **telescope**【军】体视望远镜。～ **television** 立体电视。

re·li·er [riˈlaiə; rɪˋlaɪɚ] ***n*.** 信赖者;依靠者。

re·liev·a·ble [riˈliːvəbl; rɪˋlivəbl] ***a*.** **1.** 可减轻的;可解除的,可安慰的。**2.** 可援救的。**3.** 可刻成浮雕的。

re·lieve [riˈliːv; rɪˋliv] ***vt*.** **1.** (从危险、痛苦等中)救出,使脱离,解脱。**2.** 救济,救助(难民等);供应食品[物资]给。**3.** 援救(被围城市等)。**4.** 使安心,使放心,安慰。**5.** 减少,减轻,缓和,除去(忧虑、恐惧等)。**6.** 使调班[换班],使(哨兵、卫兵等)交班休息;免除(职务),免职(*from*; *of*)。**7.** 使变化多趣,使能消愁解闷。**8.** 使浮现,使突出;使显目,衬托,使互相对照。*I am* [*feel*] *much* ～*d to hear it*. 我听了感到十分宽慰。～ *sb. from pain* 解除某人的痛苦。*You shall be* ～*d at 10:30*. 你十点半钟下班。*a black bodice* ～*d with white lace* 用白花边作衬托的黑胸衣。***be*** ～***d of*** 被解除…,消失(*He was* ～*d of his post* [*of his post at his own request*]. 他撤职[辞职]了)。*Let me* ～ *you of your bag*. 让我替你拿这个提包。～ ***guard*** 换岗。～ ***nature*** [***the bowels***, ***oneself***] 解手,大便,小便。～ ***sb. of his purse***〔谑〕扒去某人钱包。— ***vi*.** **1.** 救济。**2.** 接班,接防。**3.** 突出。**4.** 解除。

re·liev·er [riˈliːvə; rɪˋlivɚ] ***n*.** 解除苦痛的人;救助者,救济者;救济物;慰藉物;缓和装置;接替者。

re·lie·vo [riˈliːvəu; rɪˋlivo] ***n*.** (*pl*. ～*s*)【雕刻】浮雕;浮雕品。*in* ～ = in relief.

re·li·gion [riˈlidʒən; rɪˋlɪdʒən] ***n*.** **1.** 宗教;宗派。**2.** 信仰。**3.** 宗教[修道]生活。**4.** 心爱的事物;一心追求的目标。**5.** 有关良心的事;(自己感到)应做的事。**6.**〔罕〕宗派仪式;〔罕〕教团,僧团。*liberty of* ～ 宗教自由。*the established* ～〔英〕国教。*the Mohammedan* ～ 伊斯兰教。***enter into*** ～ 加入教团,做修士;做教士;出家。***experience*** [***get***] ～〔美俗、谑〕皈依宗教。***lead the life of*** ～ 过修士生活。***make a*** ～ ***of*** (*doing*) = ***make it*** ～ ***to*** (*do*) 自己认为必须做…。

re·li·gion·ism [riˈlidʒənizəm; rɪˋlɪdʒənɪzəm] ***n*.** **1.** 笃信宗教;狂热信仰。**2.** 伪装的虔信宗教(模样)。

re·li·gion·ist [riˈlidʒənist; rɪˋlɪdʒənɪst] ***n*.** **1.** 宗教家;热心宗教的人,宗教狂;笃信宗教的人。**2.** 假信徒。

re·li·gi·os·i·ty [riˌlidʒiˈɔsiti; rɪˏlɪdʒɪˋɑsətɪ] **I** ***n*.** **1.** 信仰宗教的特性〔尤指笃信宗教,宗教狂〕。**2.** 虚伪的虔信态度。**II re·li·giose** [-ˌəus; -ˏos] ***a*.**

re·li·gious [riˈlidʒəs; rɪˋlɪdʒəs] **I** ***a*.** **1.** 宗教(上)的。**2.** 笃信的,虔诚的。**3.** 修道(院)的;(属于)教团的。**4.** 严正的,认真的;凭良心的。**5.**【诗】神圣的。**II** ***n*.** 修士,修女,出家人。*a* ～ *house* 修道院。*a* ～ *question* 宗教问题。*the* ～ 笃信宗教的人;修士,修女。***with*** ～ ***care*** [***exactitude***] 非常细心[严谨]地。**-ly** ***ad*.** **-ness** ***n*.**

re·line [ˈriːˈlain; riˋlaɪn] ***vt*.** **1.** 换(衣服的)里子,换衬里。**2.** 重新划线。**3.**【军】换(炮的)内筒。

re·lin·quish [riˈliŋkwiʃ; rɪˋlɪŋkwɪʃ] ***vt*.** **1.** 作罢,废除,撤回;放松(计划、政策、信仰、希望等)。**2.** 放开,放松(所握之物)。**3.** 让出(权利、财产等)。～ *bad habits* 戒除不良习惯。**-ment** ***n*.**

rel·i·quary [ˈrelikwəri; ˋrɛləˏkwɛrɪ] ***n*.** 圣骨盒,遗骨盒;圣物盒;遗物盒。

rel·ique [ˈrelik; ˋrɛlɪk] ***n*.**〔美、古〕= relic.

re·liq·uiae [riˈlikwiiː; rɪˋlɪkwɪˏi] ***n*.**〔L.〕〔*pl*.〕**1.** 遗骨,遗物;遗著。**2.**【地】化石;【植】(经久不落的)枯叶,残花。

rel·ish [ˈreliʃ; ˋrɛlɪʃ] **I** ***n*.** **1.** 味,味道,滋味,风味,美味。**2.** 嗜好,兴趣 (*for*);食欲,胃口;玩味,赏玩。**3.** 调味品,佐料;引起兴趣的东西。**4.** (…的)气味 (*of*);少量。**5.** 意味,寓意,含意。*Hunger gives* ～ *to any food*. 肚子饿了什么都好吃。*give* ～ *to* 添加滋味;增加兴趣。*Food has no* ～ [*loses its* ～] *when one is ill*. 病中什么都不好吃。***have no*** ～ ***for*** 不喜欢,对…不感兴趣。***with*** ～ 津津有味地,有趣地。**II** ***vt*.** **1.** 津津有味地吃,品味,领略;喜欢,爱好,享受。**2.** 加味,调味。*Hunger will* ～ *the plainest fare*. 肚饿糠好吃,饥不择食。*He does not* ～ *my advice*. 他不喜欢听我的劝告。— ***vi*.** 有(…的)味道,有…的风味 (*of*);有(…的)气味 (*of*)。

re·live [ˈriːˈliv; riˋlɪv] ***vi*.** 再生,苏醒,复活。— ***vt*.** (尤指凭想像)使再现,重新生活,重新体验。～ *one's life* 重新生活。

re·load [ˈriːˈləud; riˋlod] ***vt*.**, ***vi*.** 再装货;再装填;再装弹。

re·lo·cate [riːˈləukeit; riˋloket] ***vt*.** **1.** 重新安置[配置],改放。**2.**【军】调动。**3.**〔美〕强制疏散。**re·lo·ca·tion** ***n*.**

Rel. Pron.; **rel. pron.** = relative pronoun 关系代词。

re·lu·cent [riˈljuːsənt; rɪˋlusənt] ***a*.** **1.** 返照的,反射的。**2.** 光辉的,明亮的。

re·luct [riˈlʌkt; rɪˋlʌkt] ***vi*.**〔罕〕**1.** 作斗争 (*against*);反抗、反对 (*at*)。**2.** 不愿意,勉强。

re·luc·tance, **-tan·cy** [riˈlʌktəns, -si; rɪˋlʌktəns, -sɪ] ***n*.** **1.** 厌恶,嫌厌。**2.** 不情愿,勉强。**3.**〔罕〕抵抗,反抗 (*to*; *at*)。**4.**【电】磁阻。***with*** ～ 不情愿地,勉强地。***without*** ～ 欣然,甘愿。

re·luc·tant [riˈlʌktənt; rɪˋlʌktənt] ***a*.** **1.** 厌恶的,嫌厌的,不高兴的;不情愿的,勉强的(同意、答复等)。**2.** 难处理的;难加工的;难得到的。**3.**〔罕〕反抗的,抵抗的。*be* ～ *to discard* 舍不得丢弃。*give sb*. ～ *assistance* 勉勉强强帮人的忙。～ *followers* 胁从分子。*The soil is hard and* ～ *to the plough*. 地硬难耕。**-ly** ***ad*.**

rel·uc·tiv·i·ty [ˌreləkˈtiviti; ˏrɛləkˋtɪvətɪ] ***n*.**【物】磁阻率。

re·lume, **re·lu·mine** [riːˈljuːm, riˈluːmin; riˋlum, rɪˋlumən] ***vt*.**〔古、诗〕再点燃;使重新照亮;使重新明亮。

re·ly [riˈlai; rɪˋlaɪ] ***vi*.** **1.** 倚赖,依靠,仗恃。**2.** 信任,信赖 (*on*, *upon*)。～ *on one's own efforts* 依靠自己努力。～ *on food and water to live* 依靠食物跟水维生。～ ***upon a broken reed*** 依赖不可靠的东西。～ ***upon it*** 放心吧(*You may* ～ *upon it that he will be here*. 请相信他一定会来的)。

REM [rem; rɛm] (= rapid eye movement) ***n*.** (*pl*. ***REMS***)【心】眼的迅速跳动〔指人做梦时眼的跳动〕。

rem. = remittance.

rem [rem; rɛm] (= roentgen equivalent, man) ***n*.** (*pl*. ***rem***)【物】雷姆,仑目,人体伦琴当量。

re·mail·er [ˈriːˈmeilə; ˋriˋmelɚ] ***n*.**【计】回邮器。

re·main [riˈmein; rɪˋmen] **I** ***vi*.** **1.** 剩余,剩下;遗留,留下;活着(未死)。**2.** 逗留(在某处)(*in*; *at*; *with*)。**3.** 搁着不动,搁置;尚待…;留待…;依然,仍然…;继续存在,现存。**4.** 终属,归于 (*with*)。*This* ～*ed over from yesterday's dinner*. 这是昨天晚饭吃剩的。*I* ～*ed three weeks in Paris*. 我在巴黎逗留了三个星期。*She* ～*s unmarried*. 她仍然没有结婚。*Much* [*Little*] *now* ~*s to be done*. 还有许多事[没有什么事]待做。***I*** ~ ***yours truly*** [***sincerely***, ***etc***.] 你永远忠实的, 谨上〔信尾客套话〕。***It*** ~***s to be proved that....*** (…) 尚待证明。***Nothing*** ~***s but to....*** 只要…就行了(*Nothing* ~*s but to draw the moral*. 只要引出其中的教训就行了)。~ ***abroad*** 滞留在国外。~ ***at home*** 留在家里, 留在国内。~ ***at one's post*** 留在岗位上。~ ***faithful*** 保持忠诚。~ ***with*** 在…的权限内, 在…的手里, 属于, 归于, 终属。**II** ***n***.〔常 *pl*.〕**1**. 剩余物; 遗物, 遗迹; 余额。**2**. 残余人物; 遗嘱。**3**. 遗体, 遗骨。**4**. 遗稿。**5**. 遗风。**6**.【古生】化石。*the* ~*s* [*a* ~] *of a temple* 一座寺庙的遗迹。*the* ~*s of an army* 残兵败将; 残部。

re·main·der [riˈmeində; rɪˋmendɚ] **I** ***n***. **1**. 剩余物, 残余, 剩余; 剩下的人, 残留者, 其余的人。**2**.【数】余部, 余项; 余数。**3**.【法】残留权。**4**.(爵位等的)继承权。**5**. 卖剩的书籍、商品存货; 处理品。**6**.〔*pl*.〕遗址, 遗迹, 废墟; 遗风, 遗痕。*the* ~ *of one's life* 余生, 晚年。**II** ***a***. 剩余的; 留存下的。*the* ~ *biscuit* 吃剩的饼干。*If you divide 10 by 3, the* ~ *is 1*. 用三除十, 余数是一。**III** ***vt***.〔美〕将…作处理品廉价出售。**-ship** ***n***.【法】残留权, 继承权。

re·make [ˈriːˈmeik; riˋmek] **I** ***vt***. 再作, 再制; 重造, 改造, 改作, 修改, 翻新。**II** ***n***. 重制; 翻新; 改造, 修改; 重制物; 重新摄制的影片。

re·man [ˈriːˈmæn; riˋmæn] ***vt***. **1**. (给船只、军舰、炮台等)重新配备人员。**2**. 使重新像男子汉; 使重新有勇气。

re·mand [riˈmɑːnd; rɪˋmænd] **I** ***n***. **1**. 召回; 送回。**2**.【法】还押(命令); 被还押者; 案件的发回。**II** ***vt***. **1**. 送回, 送还; 叫回, 召回, 命令归回。**2**.【法】还押(被告、嫌疑犯); 押候; 发回(案件)至下级法院。~ **home**〔英〕青少年拘留所。

rem·a·nence [ˈremənəns; ˋrɛmənəns] ***n***.【电】剩余磁感应, 剩磁, 顽磁。

rem·a·nent [ˈremənənt; ˋrɛmənənt] ***a***. 残余的, 剩余的。

re·mark [riˈmɑːk; rɪˋmɑrk] **I** ***n***. **1**. 注意, 观察。**2**. 话, 言语; 评论, 意见。*worthy of* ~ 值得注意。*the* ~*s column* 备注栏。*a theme of general* ~ 议论纷纷的事情。*Did you make a* ~? 你有没有说过什么话[发表意见]? ***make a*** ~ ***on*** 就…说一说[表示一点意见]。***make no*** ~ 什么也不说。***make*** ~***s*** 说东道西; 评论; 演说。***pass a*** ~ 表示一点意见, 略陈所见。***pass without*** ~ 置之不理, 置若罔闻, 默认。**II** ***vt***. **1**. 注意到, 看见, 觉得, 发觉。**2**. 说, 讲; 陈述(注意到的事情等)。*I* ~*ed the heat as soon as I entered the room*. 一进房间就觉得热。*as* ~*ed above* 如上所述; 前面已说过。— ***vi***. **1**. 留意。**2**. 评论, 谈论, 议论(*on*, *upon*)。

re·mark·a·ble [riˈmɑːkəbl; rɪˋmɑrkəbl] ***a***. 值得注意的, 惊人的; 显著的; 非凡的, 非常(好)的, 异常的, 出众的, 奇异的。*He is* ~ *for precocity*. 他早熟得惊人。*She makes herself too* ~. 她这人锋芒毕露。*a* ~ *work* 极出色的工作[作品]。**-bly** ***ad***.

Re·marque [rəˈmɑːk; rəˋmɑrk] ***n***. **1**. 雷马克〔姓氏〕。**2**. **Erich Maria** ~ 雷马克〔1898—1970, 美国小说家, 原籍德国, 《西线无战事》的作者〕。

re·marque [riˈmɑːk; rəˋmɑrk] ***n***.〔F.〕【印】**1**. (注在印版边上的)轮廓略图[记号]。**2**. 带有轮廓略图的印版或校样。

re·mar·riage [ˈriːˈmæridʒ; riˋmærɪdʒ] ***n***. 再娶; 再嫁; 再婚。

re·mar·ry [ˈriːˈmæri; riˋmærɪ] ***vt***., ***vi***. (使男或女)再结婚; 再娶; 再嫁。

re·mast [ˈriːˈmɑːst; riˋmæst] ***vt***. 换船桅。

re·match [ˈriːˈmætʃ; riˋmætʃ] ***n***. (体育运动项目的)复赛; 重赛。

rem·blai [rɑ̃ːmˈblei; rɑ̃mˋble] ***n***.〔F.〕填筑(铁道路基的)土方。

Rem·brandt [ˈrembrænt; ˋrɛmbrænt], **van Rijn** [**Ryn**] 伦布兰〔1609—1669, 荷兰画家〕。

R.E.M.E., **Reme** [ˈriːmi; ˋrimɪ] = Royal Electrical and Mechanical Engineers〔英口〕皇家电气和机械工程师部队。

re·me·di·a·ble [riˈmiːdiəbl; rɪˋmidɪəbl] ***a***. 可医治的; 可挽回的, 可补救的; 可纠正的; 可修补的。**-bly** ***ad***.

re·me·di·al [riˈmiːdjəl; rɪˋmidɪəl] ***a***. **1**. 医治(用)的, 治疗上的。**2**. 挽回的, 补救的; 纠正(用)的; 修补(用)的; 补习的。**-ly** ***ad***.

re·me·di·a·tion [riˌmidiˈeiʃən; rɪˏmidɪˋeʃən] ***n***.【教】补习, 辅导。**-al** ***a***.

rem·e·di·less [ˈremidilis; ˋrɛmɪdɪlɪs] ***a***. 治不好的; 不能挽回的; 无法纠正的; 无法修补的。

rem·e·dy [ˈremidi; ˋrɛmədɪ] **I** ***n***. **1**. 医药; 药品; 医疗, 疗法。**2**. 补救(法), 纠正(法)(*for*)。**3**.【法】(损失的)赔偿; 补偿。**4**.(硬币的)公差。***be past*** [***beyond***] ~ 无可救药的, 医不好的。***There is no*** ~ ***but....*** 除…外别无办法。**II** ***vt***. **1**. 医治, 疗治。**2**. 补救, 纠正, 改善, 减轻, 克服, 消除(弊病等)。**3**. 修补, 修理; 赔偿。

re·mem·ber [riˈmembə; rɪˋmɛmbɚ] ***vt***. **1**. 记起, 想起, 回忆起(*opp*. forget); 记着, 记得; 记着去…; 谙记。**2**. 牢记, 记住, 铭记; 铭感, 感谢; 酬劳, 赏赐, 送礼。**3**. 致意, 问候。*I can't* ~ *your name*. 我想不起你的名字了。*I* ~ *seeing him once*. = *I* ~ *that I saw him once*. 我记得见过他一次。*Please* ~ *to call me at six*. 请别忘记六点钟叫我。~ *a child on its birthday* 给孩子生日送礼。~ ***sb***. ***in one's will*** 在遗嘱中把一部分财产赠给某人。***R- me to....*** 请向…致意。~ ***oneself*** 醒悟, 反省, 检查自己过失; 想起; 记起。— ***vi***. 记起, 想起, 追想, 回忆; 记着, 记得; 有记忆力。***if I*** ~ ***right***(***ly***) 我没记错的话; 我记得的确是那样的。~ ***of***〔美〕记得…, 想起。

re·mem·brance [riˈmembrəns; rɪˋmɛmbrəns] ***n***. **1**. 记忆; 回忆, 回想; 记忆力。**2**. 纪念, 追忆; 纪念品; 纪念碑; 备忘录。**3**.〔*pl*.〕致意, 问候。***bear*** [***keep***] ***in*** ~ 记在心里, 记着。***bring to*** ~ 使记起[想起]。***call to*** ~ 想起。***come to*** ~ 回忆起, 想起。***escape one's*** ~ 记不起了; 忘记。***give my*** ~***s to*** 请代问候…。***have in*** ~ 记得。***have no*** ~ ***of*** 一点也记不得…。***in*** ~ ***of*** 为纪念…; 回忆…。***pass from sb.'s*** ~ 忘记。***put in*** ~ 使想起。**R- Day**〔英〕休战纪念日。

re·mem·branc·er [riˈmembrənsə; rɪˋmɛmbrənsɚ] ***n***. **1**. 使想起的人[物], 提醒者; 纪念品; 备忘录。**2**. 记录官。*the City R-*〔英〕伦敦市议会代表。*the King's* [*Queen's*] *R-*〔英〕皇室债款的征收官〔旧时英国的高等法院官吏〕。

re·mex [ˈriːmeks; ˋrimɛks] ***n***. (*pl*. ***rem·i·ges*** [ˈremidʒiːz; ˋrɛmədʒiz]) (鸟的)飞羽。

rem·i·ges [ˈremiˌdʒiːz; ˋrɛmədʒiz] ***n***.〔*pl*.〕(*sing*. ***remex*** [ˈriːmeks; ˋrimɛks])【动】飞羽。**-gial** [riˈmidʒiəl; rɪˋmɪdʒɪəl] ***a***.

re·mil·i·ta·rize [ˈriːˈmilitəraiz; riˋmɪlətəˏraɪz] ***vt***. 使重新武装, 再武装。**-za·tion** ***n***.

re·mind [riˈmaind; rɪˋmaɪnd] ***vt***. 使想起, 使记起, 提醒(*of*; *that*; *how*)。*You* ~ *me of your father*. 你使我想起你的父亲。*Please* ~ *me to call her up before ten*. 请提醒我在十点以前给她打电话。

re·mind·er [riˈmaində; rɪˋmaɪndɚ] ***n***. **1**. 使人回想起某人[事]的东西; 提醒者, 提醒物。**2**. 提示, 信号, 通知。**3**.【商】催询单。*a* ~ *slip* 催询单。*a* ~ *tray* 意见箱。*a gentle* ~ 暗示。

re·mind·ful [riˈmaindfʊl; rɪˋmaɪndfʊl] ***a***. 留意的, 注意的; 使想起的, 提醒注意…的(*of*)。

Rem·ing·ton [ˈremiŋtən; ˋrɛmɪŋtən] ***n***. 雷明顿〔姓氏〕。

rem·i·nisce [ˌremiˈnis; ˏrɛməˋnɪs] ***vi***. 追忆[缅怀]往事(*of*)。— ***vt***. 追忆[怀旧]地说[写](往事)。

rem·i·nis·cence [ˌremiˈnisns; ˏrɛməˋnɪsns] ***n*.** **1.** 回想,追忆,回忆;怀念,记忆力,回想力;怀念的事物;一星半点的回忆线索,暗示者;潜在意识。**2.**〔*pl*.〕回忆往事的谈话;经验谈;回忆录。**3.**引起联想的相似物。*The scene awakens ~s of my youth*. 这景象唤起我年轻时的往事。~ *of the war* 大战回忆录。

rem·i·nis·cent, rem·i·nis·cent·i·al [ˌremiˈnisnt, -snʃəl; ˏrɛməˋnɪsnt, -snʃəl] **I *a*.** **1.** 怀旧的,回忆的。**2.** 喜谈往事的。**3.**暗示…的,提醒的;使人联想…的(*of*)。*The old man was* ~. 那老年人爱谈往事。*His writings were* ~ *of ancient classical writers*. 他的作品很像古代的古典作家。**II *n*.** 回忆者,回忆录作者;追记前事者。**-ly *ad*.**

re·mint [ˈriːˈmint; riˋmɪnt] ***vt*.** 改铸;重铸(货币)。

re·mise[1] [rəˈmiːz; riˋmiz] **I *n*.** **1.**【击剑】再刺,重刺。**2.**(高级)出租马车;马车房。**II *vi*.**【击剑】再刺,重刺。

re·mise[2] [riˈmaiz; riˋmaɪz] ***vt*.** (*-mised*; *-mising*)【法】让渡,让与(权利、财产等),立契出让。

re·miss [riˈmis; riˋmɪs] ***a*.** **1.** 怠慢的,疏忽的,不留心的。**2.** 慢吞吞的,迟缓的,倦怠的。*be* ~ *in one's duties* 玩忽职守。**-ness *n*.**

re·mis·si·ble [riˈmisibl; riˋmɪsəbl̩] ***a*.** **1.** 可宽恕的,可饶恕的;可赦免的。**-bil·i·ty *n*.**

re·mis·sion [riˈmiʃən; riˋmɪʃən] ***n*.** **1.** 宽恕,饶恕,(负债、捐税等的)免除;免罪,赦免。**2.** (怒气、紧张等的)缓和,松弛;减退,(病痛等的)减轻,平息。**3.**〔罕〕寄钱,汇款;(事件的)交付;延期。**R- Thursday**【宗】洗足星期四。**-sive *a*.**

re·mit [riˈmit; rɪˋmɪt] ***vt*.** (*-mit·ted* [-ˈmitid; -ˋmɪtɪd]; *-mit·ting* [-ˈmitiŋ; -ˋmɪtɪŋ]) **1.** 汇寄,付(款);送交(行李等);开发(支票)。**2.**【法】(将案件)发回下级法院;(把事件)转移(某方面取决)(*to*);指示(某人)去问(某人)[参考(某书)]。**3.**使复原,恢复原状。**4.**饶恕,赦免,免除,减轻(罚金、捐税等)。**5.** 缓和,减退,停止(苦痛、注意、努力等)。**6.** 展期,延期(以便重新调查)。**7.**〔古〕再拘押。**8.**〔古〕释放(犯人)。**9.**〔古〕放弃。~ *one's anger* 息怒。~ *the siege* 解围。*I* ~ *money to my family every month*. 我每月给家里汇款。~ *one's efforts* 轻松,不费劲。— ***vi*.** **1.** 汇款,寄款,付款。**2.** (病痛等)减退,和缓,减轻。*kindly* ~【商】祈即付款。*Her pain began to* ~. 她的疼痛开始缓和了。

re·mit·tal [riˈmitl; riˋmɪtl] ***n*.** **1.** 赦免;免除。**2.** 减轻。**3.**【法】(案件的)发回,移转。

re·mit·tance [riˈmitəns; riˋmɪtns] ***n*.** **1.** 汇款;汇款额;支付(金额)。**2.**【法】(案件的)发回,移转。*make* ~ 汇款,开发(支票等)。*a* ~ *man* 〔英〕侨居外国靠本国汇款生活的人[游手好闲不务正业的懒人]。

re·mit·tee [riˌmiˈtiː; rɪmɪˋti] ***n*.** 汇款领取人。

re·mit·tent [riˈmitənt; riˋmɪtnt] **I *a*.** 弛张的;忽轻忽重的(病等)。**II *n*.**【医】弛张热(=~ fever)。

re·mit·ter [riˈmitə; riˋmɪtɚ] ***n*.** **1.** 汇款人,出票人。**2.**【法】(诉讼案件的)移转。**3.**〔罕〕复权,复位,复旧。

rem·nant [ˈremnənt; ˋrɛmnənt] **I *n*.** **1.** 剩余,残余,余物,残屑;剩货;零头;碎布;〔常 *pl*.〕残存者,幸存者。**2.** 余烬;遗迹,遗风。*the* ~*s of a feast* 筵席的残汤剩菜。*a* ~ *of the feudal times* 封建时代的遗留物,封建残余。**II *a*.** 剩余的,残余的,残留的。

re·mod·el [ˈriːˈmɔdl; riˋmɑdl] (〔英〕*-ll-*) ***vt*.** 重新塑造;重作,改造;改作(剧本);改编(军队);改变(行为等)。~ *a barn into a house* 把谷仓改成住宅。*a* ~*led army* 经过改编的军队。

re·mo·lade [ˌreiməˈlɑːd; ˏreməˋlɑd] ***n*.** = rémoulade.

re·mold [ˈriːˈməuld; riˋmold] ***vt*.** 〔美〕= remould.

re·mon·e·tize [ˈriːˈmʌnitaiz; riˋmɑnɪˏtaɪz] ***vt*.** 把(某种金属)重新作货币通用。

re·mon·strance [riˈmɔnstrəns; riˋmɑnstrəns] ***n*.** 抗议;抗辩,规谏,规劝,诤谏,忠告,劝告;【史】谏书。*the Grand R-*【英史】(1641 年的)大抗议书。***make*** ~ ***with sb*. *against*** [***on***] ***his*** ... 对某人…的抗议[劝告]。***say in*** ~ ***that*** 抗议说…。

re·mon·strant [riˈmɔnstrənt; rɪˋmɑnstrənt] **I *a*.** 抗议的;诤谏的,忠告的。**II *n*.** 抗议者;诤谏者,忠告者。

re·mon·strate [riˈmɔnstreit; rɪˋmɑnstret] ***vi*.** 表示异议,抗议;抗辩(*against*);忠告,规劝,诤谏,苦谏(*with*; *on*; *upon*)。— ***vt*.** 抗议[抗辩]地说。**-stration** [ˌrimɔnsˈtreiʃən; ˏrɛmɑnˋstreʃən] ***n*.** **-stra·tive** [-strətiv; -strətɪv] ***a*.** **-tor *n*.**

rem·on·toir, rem·on·toire [ˌremənˈtwɑː; ˏrɛmənˋtwɑr] ***n*.** (钟表的)摆锤均衡键。

rem·o·ra [ˈremərə; ˋrɛmərə] ***n*.** **1.**【动】鲫鱼。**2.** 阻碍,障碍物。

re·morse [riˈmɔːs; rɪˋmɔrs] ***n*.** **1.** (对罪恶的)后悔,悔恨,良心的责备,自责。**2.**〔古〕慈悲,怜悯;同情心。***without*** ~ **1.** 毫不后悔地,毫无遗憾地。**2.** 无情地;不宽恕地。

re·morse·ful [riˈmɔːsful; rɪˋmɔrsfəl] ***a*.** **1.** 后悔的,悔恨的,深受良心责备的。**2.**〔古〕慈悲的;怜悯的。**-ly *ad*.**

re·morse·less [riˈmɔːslis; rɪˋmɔrslɪs] ***a*.** **1.** 无情的;无慈悲心的;冷酷的;残忍的。**2.** 不懊悔的,不悔恨的。**-ly *ad*.**

re·mote [riˈməut; rɪˋmot] ***a*.** (*-mot·er*; *-est*) **1.** 遥远的,远距离的;偏僻的,边远的(*from*)。**2.** 很久以前[以后]的。**3.**疏远的;远缘的,(血缘)关系淡薄的(亲戚等),远房的;间接的。**4.** 大不相同的,悬殊的,别种的(*from*)。**5.** 细微的,稀少的,漠然的,模糊的(观念等);看上去决不会发生的,可能性极少的。**6.** 稀毛的。**7.** 遥控的。*a village* ~ *from a city* 离城市远的一个乡村。*the* ~ *regions of the earth* 天涯地角。*a* ~ *ancestor* 远祖。*a* ~ *kinsman* 远亲。*a* ~ *cause* 远因。*a* ~ *effect* 间接影响。*be* ~ *and cold in one's manner* 态度冷淡。*a* ~ *resemblance* 微似。~ *sensing* 遥感。***have only a very*** ~ [***have not the*** ~***st***] ***conception*** [***idea***] ***of what he means*** 对他的意思只有一点点了解[全无了解]。***live*** ~ 住在偏僻的乡下。~ **ages** 古代。~ **control**【无】遥控。~ **damages**【法】间接损害。~ **possibility** 极少的可能性。~ **sensor** 太空遥感器〔指人造卫星、航天飞机等所装备的各种遥测仪器〕。**-ly *ad*.** **-ness *n*.**

re·mo·tion [riˈməuʃən; rɪˋmoʃən] ***n*.** **1.** 移动。**2.**〔废〕分离,离开。

ré·mou·lade [ˌreiməˈlɑːd; ˏreməˋlɑd] ***n*.** 加料的蛋黄酱〔用作凉菜或色拉的调味品〕。

re·mould [riːˈməuld; riˋmold] ***vt*.** 改型,重造,改造,改铸,改塑。*to* ~ *our world outlook* 改造我们的世界观。*ideological* ~*ing* 思想改造。

re·mount [riːˈmaunt; riˋmaʊnt] **I *n*.** 新马,接替的马;新补充的马群,新马的补充。**II *vi*., *vt*.** **1.** 再骑(马)。**2.** 再登上(山、梯等)。**3.**重新供给马;重新安置(炮);重镶(宝石等);重新裱装(照片等)。**4.** 回溯,回到(某时代、地点等)。

re·mov·a·ble [riˈmuːvəbl; rɪˋmuvəbl] **I *a*.** **1.** 可移动的;可拆装的。**2.** 可去除的;可撤职的。**II *n*.**〔英〕(爱尔兰的)非终身治安法官(=~ magistrate)。**-bil·i·ty *n*.**

re·mov·al [riːˈmuːvəl; rɪˋmuvl] ***n*.** **1.** 移动,迁移;撤退;折卸。**2.** 排除;除去;切除;杀害;【林】皆伐,终伐。**3.** 撤职;调职。~ **sod right** 林地刈草权。~ **van** 搬运卡车〔特别是供搬家用〕。

re·move [riˈmuːv; rɪˋmuv] **I *vt*.** **1.** 移动,迁移。**2.** 拿走,撤去,收拾(碗碟等);脱掉(衣服等),拿下(眼镜等);扫除,消除,除去,洗清(疑虑、污点等);〔委婉话〕除掉,杀掉,暗杀。**3.**使退出,使离开(某处);免职,撤职。**4.**【法】移交(案件)。**5.** 窃取,偷。*There was soup and fish*,

~*d by boiled chicken and bacon*. 接在汤和鱼之后,换上来的是煮鸡和咸肉。*This will* ~ *the last doubts*. 这会将最后的疑虑一扫而光。~ *sb. from office* 免去某人职务。**be ~d from school** 被勒令退学,被开除。~ **a name from a list** 把姓名从名单中勾消,开除。~ **furniture** 替人搬家(为业)。~ **oneself** 走开,离开。~ **one's hat** 脱帽〔打招呼,表示敬意〕。— **vi. 1.** 移动;搬家,迁居 (*from ... to*)。**2.**〔诗〕跑开,离去,消失。*Truth has ~d from the earth*. 真理荡然无存。**II n. 1.** 移动;〔英〕迁移,搬家〔美国通常说 move〕。**2.** 距离,路程,间隔;阶段,等级;亲戚等次。**3.**〔英〕(学校的)升级;(charterhouse 学校等的)中间学级,中班。**4.**〔英〕下一道菜;收去的杯盘;收碗[盘]。*action but one* ~ *from crime* 差一点就犯罪的行为。*He is but one* ~ [*few* ~*s*] *from me*. 他和我隔着一代[两三代]。*Three* ~*s are as bad as a fire*. 搬家三次等于失火一次。

re·moved [riˈmuːvd; rɪˋmuvd] **a. 1.** (亲族关系)隔了…代的。**2.** 远离的;远隔的;无关的(与 *from* 连用)。*They are not many degrees* ~ *from the brute*. 他们跟禽兽相差不远。*a first cousin once* ~ 嫡堂[嫡表]兄弟[姐妹]的子女。*a first cousin twice* ~ 嫡堂[嫡表]兄弟[姐妹]的孙子女。*a cousin forty times* ~ 很远的本家[亲戚]。

re·mov·er [riˈmuːvə; rɪˋmuvɚ] **n. 1.** 搬运工;搬家公司。**2.** 脱离器;【化】脱膜剂;去…剂。**3.**【法】(案件的)移送。**4.**〔罕〕迁居者,调差者。

Rem·sen [ˈremsn; ˋrɛmsn] **n.** 雷姆森〔姓氏〕。

re·mu·da [riˈmuːdə; rɪˋmudə] **n.** (大牧场里供牧人每日外出乘骑的)加鞍备用马群。

re·mu·ner·ate [riˈmjuːnəreit; rɪˋmjunəˏret] **vt.** 报酬,酬劳;给…赔偿[补偿]。*His trouble is sufficiently ~d*. 他的辛苦得到十分优厚的报酬。

re·mu·ner·a·tion [riˌmjuːnəˈreiʃən; rɪˏmjunəˋreʃən] **n.** 报酬,酬劳;赔偿,补偿。

re·mu·ner·a·tive [riˈmjuːnərətiv; rɪˋmjunəˏretɪv] **a.** 有报酬的,有利的,合算的。~ *work* 有报酬的工作。

Re·na [ˈriːnə; ˋrinə] **n.** 丽娜〔女子名〕。

re·nais·sance [rəˈneisəns, F. rənsɑ̃ːs, 〔美〕reneˈsɑ̃ːns; ˏrɛnəˋzɑns, F. rənsɑ̃s, 〔美〕rɪˋnesns] **I n. 1.** 复兴;新生;复活。**2.**〔the R-〕(14—16 世纪欧洲的)文艺复兴(期);文艺复兴期(的美术、建筑)式样。**II a.**〔R-〕文艺复兴(时代)的,文艺复兴式的。*R- architecture* 文艺复兴时期[风格]的建筑。

re·nal [ˈriːnl; ˋrinl̩] **a.** 肾脏(部)的。~ *calculus*【医】肾结石。~ *capsule* 肾上腺。~ *colic* 肾绞痛。~ *corpulse* 肾小体,肾球。

re·name [ˈriːˈneim; riˋnem] **vt.** 给…重新命名;给…改名。

Ren·ard [ˈrenəd; ˋrɛnɚd] **n.** = Reynard.

re·nas·cence [riˈnæsns; rɪˋnæsns] **n. 1.** 更生,再生;复活,复兴。**2.**〔R-〕= Renaissance.

re·nas·cent [riˈnæsnt; rɪˋnæsn̩t] **a.** 新生的,再生的;复兴的,复活的;四季青春的。

ren·con·tre [renˈkɔntə; rɛnˋkɑntɚ] **n. 1.** 偶遇,邂逅。**2.** 决斗,冲突;遭遇战;论战,论争。

ren·coun·ter [renˈkauntə; rɛnˋkauntɚ] **I n.** = rencontre. **II vt., vi. 1.** 偶然碰见,邂逅。**2.** (与…)交战,(与…)冲突。

rend [rend; rɛnd] (**rent** [rent; rɛnt]) **vt. 1.** 割裂,劈开,使分裂,使分离。**2.**〔古〕(因愤怒)扯破,撕碎(头发、衣服等)。**3.** (悲伤等)撕裂,扯乱(心肠等);伤…的感情。**4.** 剥(树皮)。**5.** 抢去,强夺 (*off, away, from, out of, up*)。**6.** (声音)刺破,响彻。*The party was rent in two*. 这个政党分裂成两派。*Her heart was rent by conflicting emotions*. 她的心被矛盾的感情搅乱。*Infants were rent from their mother's arms*. 婴儿从母亲手里被抢走。**be rent in two** 分成两份。~ **apart** [**asunder**] = ~ **in** [**to**] **pieces**〔古、诗〕扯碎。~ **one's garments** [**hair**] 扯破衣服[扯乱头发]。— **vi.** 裂开,劈开,寸断,分裂。~ **the air** (喊声等)震天。

ren·der [ˈrendə; ˋrɛndɚ] **I vt. 1.** 报答,报复;归还,付还;交付,交纳。**2.** 提出,开出,拿出(账单、理由等)。**3.** 给与(帮忙等);表示(敬意等)。**4.** 让与,让出,放弃;移交,托付。**5.** 致使。**6.** 表现,描写(个性等),演出,演奏(音乐等);翻译 (*into*)。**7.** 反映,反响,反应。**8.** 提取(脂肪),炼(油)。**9.** 放出,放松(滑车上的索子)。**10.**【建】给…初涂[打底];粉刷;给…抹灰。~ *good for evil* 以德报怨。*You have ~ed great service*. 你们作了很大的贡献[帮了很大的忙]。~ *a bill* 开出账单。~ *judgement* 宣判。~ *sb. famous* 使某人出名。*My efforts were ~ed futile*. 我的努力全落空了。*Poetry can never be adequately ~ed in another language*. 诗从来不能贴贴切切翻译成另一种语言。**an account ~ed**【商】开出而未付账单。~ **a fortress** = ~ *up a fortress*. ~ **an account of** 讲述…,说明…。~ (*sb.*) **a service** 帮(某人)忙。~ **good for evil** 以德报怨。~ **him service** = ~ **service to sb.** 为某人效劳[服务]。~ **oneself up to** 投降。~ **thanks to** 感谢,报答。~ **up** 放弃,让出。~ **up a fortress** 放弃要塞。**II n. 1.**〔罕〕(地租、房租等的)缴纳。**2.**【建】(墙壁的)初涂,打底;粉刷;抹灰。**3.** 精制油。

ren·der·ing [ˈrendəriŋ; ˋrɛndərɪŋ] **n. 1.** 翻译,译文;表现,描绘;演出,演奏。**2.** 提炼,炼油,熬油。**3.** (墙壁的)初涂,打底;粉刷;抹灰。**4.** (滑车上绳索的)放出。

ren·dez·vous [ˈrɔndivuː; ˋrɑndəˏvu] **I n.**〔*sing.*, *pl.*〕**1.**【军】指定集合地;集合基地;集合,结集。**2.** 约会,聚会,约会地点[时间];幽会处。**3.** 太空船的会合(点)。**II vi.** (尤指在约定地点)会合,会见,集合,聚会。

ren·di·tion [renˈdiʃən; rɛnˋdɪʃən] **n. 1.**〔美〕翻译,重显,再现,复制;演出,演奏。**2.** 施行;给予。**3.**〔罕〕(犯人的)引渡;(城市等的)放弃。

ren·dzi·na [renˈdʒiːnə; rɛnˋdʒinə] **n.** 黑色石灰土。

Re·ne [ˈrenei; ˋrɛne] **n.** 雷内〔男子名〕。

ren·e·gade [ˈrenigeid; ˋrɛnɪˏged] **I n.** 叛教者,改信伊斯兰教的基督教徒;变节者,叛徒,脱党者。**II a.** 叛教的,变节的。**III vi.** 背叛,变节;脱党;背教。

ren·e·ga·do [ˌreniˈgeidəu, -ˈgɑː-; ˏrɛnəˋgedo, -ˋgɑ-] **n.** (*pl.* **-does**)〔古语〕= renegade.

re·ne·go·ti·ate [ˌriniˈgəuʃiːˌeit; ˏrɪniˋgoʃiˏet] **vi., vt.** (**-at·ed**, **-ating**) 重新商议,重新谈判〔尤指对契约的复审,以免订约一方获得超额利润〕。**-a·ble a. -a·tion n.**

re·neg(u)e [riˈniːg; rɪˋnig] **I vt.** 否认;放弃 (*one's country*);拒绝。— **vi. 1.**【牌戏】有某种花色的牌可跟而(故意或无意)违反规则出另一花色的牌。**2.**〔喻〕食言,背信,违约。**II n.**【牌戏】有某种花色的牌可跟而违反规则不跟。

re·new [riˈnjuː; rɪˋnju] **vt. 1.** 翻新(旧物),更新。**2.** 使(精神)一新;使复活,使苏生;恢复(青春等);再兴,重建。**3.** 重新想起;重新开始,再开始(攻击等);重做;反复。**4.** 重订,更改(契约等);换取(新的东西),更换;再补给,补充。*a coat ~ed in places* 东缝西补的上衣。~ *correspondence* [*efforts*, *game*] 再开始通讯[努力、游戏]。~ *the garrison* 增援守军。*A snake ~s its skin*. 蛇蜕皮。~ *one's health* 恢复健康。~ *one's old friendship with* 和…重温旧情。~ *one's youth* 回复青春。— **vi.** 恢复原状;重新开始;继续;展期。

re·new·a·ble [riˈnju(ː)əbl; rɪˋnjuəbl̩] **a. 1.** 可翻新的。**2.** 可恢复[复活]的,可再生的。**3.** (契约等)可延期[更新]的。**4.** 可重新开始的。*a* ~ *natural resource* 可再生的自然资源。

re·new·al [riˈnju(ː)əl; rɪˋnjuəl] **n. 1.** 更新。**2.** 复活,恢复,复新。**3.** 再开始。**4.** 重做;(票据等的)更换;(契约等的)重订,延期。~ **of term of office** 连任。

ren·i·form [ˈreniˌfɔːm, ˈriːni-; ˋrɛnəˏfɔrm, ˋrinə-] **a.**

R

肾形的。

re·nig [ri'nig; rɪ`nɪg] *v.*, *n.* 〔美俚〕= reneg(u)e.

re·nin ['riːnin; `rinɪn] *n.* 【生化】肾素;高血压蛋白原酶。

re·ni·tent [ri'naitnt, 'renitənt; rɪ`naɪtənt, `rɛnətənt] *a.* **1.** 抵抗压力的。**2.** 顽抗的。**re·ni·ten·cy** *n.*

ren·min·bi ['ren'min'biː; `rɛn`mɪn`bi] *n.* 〔Chin.〕(中国的)人民币。

ren·net[1] ['renit; `rɛnɪt] *n.* **1.** (晒干的)小牛皱胃的内膜〔制干酪用〕;(小牛皱胃中的)凝乳。**2.** 【化】= rennin.

ren·net[2] ['renit; `rɛnɪt] *n.* 〔英〕(原产法国的)王后苹果。

ren·nin ['renin; `rɛnɪn] *n.* 【生化】粗制凝乳酶。

Re·no ['riːnəu; `rino] 离诺〔美国有名的"离婚城市",在内华达州西部,凡欲离婚者,只须在该市住满三个月,即可离婚〕。***go to*** ~ 离婚。

re·no·gram ['riːnəgræm; `rinə͵græm] *n.* 【医】肾爱克斯线(造影)照片。

re·nog·ra·phy [riː'nɔgrəfi; ri`nɑgrəfɪ] *n.* 【医】肾爱克斯线照相术,肾造影照片。**-no·graph·ic** *a.*

re·nounce [ri'nauns; rɪ`naʊns] *vt.* **1.** 抛弃,放弃,背弃。**2.** 不承认,否认;与(儿子等)断绝关系。~ *the world* 退隐。~ *one's peerage* 放弃贵族地位。— *vi.* **1.** 【法】放弃权利[财产、地位等]。**2.** 【牌戏】(因打不出应跟的花色而)垫牌。**3.** 正式投降。

re·no·vas·cu·lar [ˌrinə'væskjulə; ͵rɪnə`væskjələ˞] *a.* 【医】肾血管的。~ *hypertension* 肾血管高血压。

ren·o·vate ['renəuveit; `rɛnə͵vet] **I** *vt.* **1.** 弄新,刷新,革新;翻新;重做,改做,再制。**2.** 修理,修补;改善。**3.** 恢复;使精神一新。**4.** 弄干净,使清洁。*a ~d tyre* 再生轮胎。**II** *a.* 恢复的,革新的,翻新的。

ren·o·va·tion [ˌrenəu'veiʃən; ͵rɛnə`veʃən] *n.* **1.** 革新;更新,复壮。**2.** 修理,修补。**3.** 清扫。**-va·tor** *n.* 革新者;修理者(等)。

re·nown [ri'naun; rɪ`naʊn] *n.* **1.** 声誉,名望,声望。**2.** 〔古〕传说,传闻。*a man of* ~ 知名之士,名人。*have great* ~ *for* 因…出名。*of great* [*high*] ~ 有名。

re·nowned [ri'naund; rɪ`naʊnd] *a.* 有名的,著名的,有声望的。

rens·se·laer·ite ['rensiləˌrait, ˌrensi'liəˌrait; `rɛnsɪlə͵raɪt, ͵rɛnsɪ`lɪə͵raɪt] *n.* 【化】假晶滑石。

rent[1] [rent; rɛnt] **I** *n.* 地租;房租;〔美〕(一般的)租借;租金,租费;〔口、美〕出租地;出租房屋。***for*** ~ 〔美〕出租的。**For R-** 招租〔广告用语〕。**II** *vt.* 付地租[房租等];租用,把…租给某人 (*to*);向…租入 (*from*),向某人收租。~ *one's tenants low* 向租户收低价租金。— *vi.* 出租。*This apartment ~s cheaply.* 这套公寓房间租价便宜。~**(-)a(-)crowd**[**mob**] (出于闹事等目的)花钱雇来的人群[暴徒]。~ **charge** 【法】地租。~**-free** *a.*, *ad.* 不收租金的[地],不付租金。~ **roll** 租册;租金总额。~ **service** 【史】地租服役;代替租金的劳役。~ **strike** (租户因房租过高,房屋失修等)拒付房租。

rent[2] [rent; rɛnt] *n.* **1.** (衣服等的)裂缝,破缝,绽线处;(云等的)裂隙;谷,峡谷;【地】断口。**2.** (意见等的)分裂,分歧;(关系等的)破裂。

rent[3] [rent; rɛnt] **I** *v.* rend 的过去式及过去分词。**II** *a.* 撕裂的;分裂的。

rent·a·ble ['rentəbl; `rɛntəbl] *a.* 可出租的,可租借的。

rent·al ['rentl; `rɛntl] *n.* 地租总额;租金总额,租费,收入;〔罕〕租折,租册。~ **condominium** 供租赁的公寓套间。~ **library** **1.** 〔美〕收取租借费的图书馆。**2.** (商店附设的)租书处。

rente [F. rɑ̃ːt; rɑ̃t] *n.* 〔F.〕年金,每年的收入;定期收入;〔*pl.*〕长期公债;公债年利。

-rent·ed ['rentid; `rɛntɪd] *a.* *suf.* 租金…的: *high-* [*low-*] ~ 租金高[低]的。

rent·er ['rentə; `rɛntə˞] *n.* 承租人,租户,佃户,房客;〔美〕(一般)出租人;租借人;【影】影片经租商。

ren·tier ['rɔntiei; ͵rɑ̃`tje] *n.* 〔F.〕领年金的人;靠债券[地租、房租]利息生活的人。

re·num·ber ['riː'nʌmbə; ri`nʌmbə˞] *vt.* 重编…的号码,给…重标号码。

re·nun·ci·a·tion [riˌnʌnsi'eiʃən; rɪ͵nʌnsɪ`eʃən] *n.* **1.** 放弃;抛弃,废弃;弃权;否认状;【法】(对权利等的)放弃声明书。**2.** 不承认,拒绝,否认。**3.** 断念;自制;出家。**-tive** *a.*

ren·voi [ren'vɔi; rɛn`vɔɪ] *n.* (政府对外国人,特别是外交官)驱逐出境。

re·oc·cu·py ['riː'ɔkjupai; ri`ɑkjə͵paɪ] *vt.* (**-pied**) **1.** 再占领,收复;再占用;再住。**2.** 再从事。*the reoccupied area* 收复区。**-pa·tion** *n.*

re·om·e·ter [ri'ɔmitə; rɪ`ɑmɪtə˞] *n.* = rheometer.

re·o·pen ['riː'əupən; ri`opən] *vt.* **1.** 再开,重开。**2.** 再开始;重新进行(辩论、讨论、考虑等)。*The matter is settled and cannot be ~ed.* 这件事已经作了决定,不能再予讨论。— *vi.* 再开,重开。*School ~s on Monday.* 星期一开学。

re·or·der [ri'ɔːdə; ri`ɔrdə˞] **I** *n.* 再定货。**II** *vt.* **1.** 再订购,再定货。**2.** 重新整理;重新整顿,重新安排。— *vi.* 再订购同类货品。

re·or·gan·ize ['riː'ɔːgənaiz; ri`ɔrgə͵naɪz] *vt.*, *vi.* 改组,改编,整编;改造,改革;整理。**-za·tion** *n.*

reo·vi·rus [ˌriːəu'vaiərəs; ͵rio`vaɪrəs] *n.* 【医】呼吸道肠道病毒。

rep[1] [rep; rɛp] *n.* 【纺】棱纹平布。

rep[2] [rep; rɛp] *n.* **1.** 〔俚〕浪子;堕落者。**2.** 〔美俚〕代表。**3.** 〔美俚〕名誉;名声,名气。

rep[3] [rep; rɛp] *n.* 〔学俚〕默唱,背诵的诗句(等)〔repetition 之略〕。

rep[4] [rep; rɛp] *n.* 【原】物体伦琴当量〔电离辐射剂量〕。

rep[5] [rep;rɛp] *n.* 一次重复动作〔源自 repetition〕。

Rep. = **1.** Representative. **2.** Republic; Republican.

rep. = **1.** repeat. **2.** report; reported; reporter. **3.** repair. **4.** representative. **5.** reprint.

re·pack·age [ri'pækidʒ; ri`pækədʒ] *vt.* (**-aged**; **-aging**) 重新打包,重新包装。

repaid [riː'peid, ri-; ri`ped, rɪ-] repay 的过去式及过去分词。

re·paint I [riː'peint; ri`pent] *vt.* **1.** 重新涂(油漆)。**2.** 重画。**II** ['riːpeint; `ripent] *n.* (画面)重新着色的部分;重新漆过的高尔夫球。

re·pair[1] [ri'pɛə; rɪ`pɛr] **I** *n.* **1.** (房屋、衣服等的)修理,修补;〔*pl.*〕修理工作。**2.** (健康等的)恢复;(错误等的)改正,订正,矫正;(伤害等的)赔偿,补偿。*The shop is closed during ~s.* 本店进行装修,暂停营业。*Repairs done while you wait.* 修理来件,立等可取。*big* [*capital*, *heavy*] ~ 大修。*operating* ~ 日常维护检修。*permanent* ~ 大[治本、永久]修理。***beyond*** ~ 无法修理(的)。***in bad*** ~ 维修不善,失修。***in good*** ~ 维修良好,修理认真,完好可用。***in*** ~ 维修良好(*Keep roads in* ~ 保持道路的维修良好)。***out of*** ~ 长年缺乏维修,失修。***past*** ~ = *beyond* ~. ***under*** ***~s*** 在修理中(的)。**II** *vt.* **1.** 修理,修补。**2.** 赔偿,补偿。**3.** 使恢复;改正,订正,矫正;治疗。*a ~ing lease* 租户自负修理责任的租约。~ *a mistake* 改正错误。~ *a wound* 治伤。~**man** 修理工。~ **planting** 补植。~ **ship** 修理船。

re·pair[2] [ri'pɛə; rɪ`pɛr] **I** *n.* **1.** 常去之处,人来人往的地方,热闹场所。**2.** 依赖,依靠。***have*** ~ ***to*** 依靠,依赖。***a place of great*** [***little***] ~ 游人杂沓[稀少]的地方,热闹[僻静]场所。**II** *vi.* **1.** 去,往,赴,时常去 (*to*);大伙儿去,群集,聚拢。**2.** 依靠,依赖 (*to*; *for*)。

re·pair·a·ble [ri'pɛərəbl; `rɛpərəbl] *a.* 可修理的;可赔偿[补偿]的;可挽回[恢复]的。

re·pair·er [ri'pɛərə; rɪ`pɛrə˞] *n.* 修理工人,修补者。

re·pand [ri'pænd; rɪ`pænd] *a.* 【植】残波状的〔指叶缘〕。

re·pa·per [ˈriːˈpeipə; ˋriˋpepɚ] *vt*. 1. 重新用纸裱糊(墙壁等)。2. 用纸重新包;重新供给纸张。

rep·a·ra·ble [ˈrepərəbl; ˋrɛpərəbl] *a*. 可修补的;可赔偿的;应由(某人)修理[赔偿]的。**-bly** *ad*.

rep·a·ra·tion [ˌrepəˈreiʃən; ˏrɛpəˋreʃən] *n*. 赔偿(款项);修理〔现在多用 repair〕;〔*pl*.〕修理工作,维修工程〔现在多用 repairs〕。***demand ~ for*** 要求赔偿。***make ~ for*** 对…作出赔偿。***~s in kind*** 货物赔偿。

rep·a·ra·tive, re·par·a·to·ry [ˈrepərətiv, riˈpærətəri; rɪˋpærətɪv, rɪˋpærəˏtorɪ] *a*. 修理的;赔偿的;恢复的;弥补的。

rep·ar·tee [ˌrepɑːˈtiː; ˏrɛpɚˋti] *n*. 敏捷的回答,巧妙的回答;应对敏捷(的才能)。

re·par·ti·tion [ˈriːpɑːˈtiʃən; ˏriparˋtɪʃən] I *n*. 1. 分配,区分,摊分。2. 再分配,再区分,再分割,再瓜分。II *vt*. (再)分配,(再)区分,(再)分割。

re·pass [ˈriːˈpɑːs; riˋpæs] *vt*., *vi*. 再通过[经过],再渡过(河、海等);在回程中又通过[渡过];再通过(议案等)。*pass and ~* 往返。**-age** *n*.

re·past [riˈpɑːst; rɪˋpæst] I *n*. 膳食,饭餐;饮食;就餐时间。*a dainty* [*rich*] *~* 盛餐,筵席。*a light* [*slight*] *~*便餐。II *vi*. 就餐;设宴。

re·pat·ri·ate [riːˈpætrieit; riˋpetrɪˏet] I *vt*. 遣送回国,送回本国。— *vi*. 回国。II *n*. 被送回本国的人。

re·pat·ri·ation [ˈriːˌpætriˈeiʃən; ˋriˏpætrɪˋeʃən] *n*. 遣送回国,遣返。

re·pay [ri(ː)ˈpei; rɪˋpe] *vt*., *vi*. (**-*paid*** [-ˈpeid; -ˋped]) 1. 付还,偿还。2. 报答,回敬;报复。~ *a visit* 回访。~ *a salutation* 答礼。**-ment** *n*. 1. 偿还。2. 报答;报复,复仇。3. 赔款。

re·pay·a·ble [ri(ː)ˈpeiəbl, ri-; rɪˋpeəbḷ] *a*. 可付还的;可报答的;应报复的。

re·peal [riˈpiːl; rɪˋpil] I *n*. (法令等的)废除,作废,取消,撤销;撤回;【英史】撤销合并运动;〔美〕废除禁酒法。II *vt*. 废除,作废,取消,撤销,撤回(法律、判决、决议等);召回。

re·peal·er [riˈpiːlə; rɪˋpilɚ] *n*. 废除[撤销]者,撤销论者;【英史】合并撤销论者。

re·peat [riˈpiːt; rɪˋpit] I *n*. 1. 再说,再做,重演;(尤指应听众要求的)再演;重播。2.【乐】复奏[复唱]部分;反复符号。3.【商】(同样货物的)再供给;再定货。4. 拷贝,复制。5. (花纸等的)重复的花样。II *vt*. 1. 反复,重说,再三讲;重做。2. 照样传达(别人的话),照样讲;复述,背诵,复诵。~ *an error* 一错再错。*History ~s itself*. 历史反复重演。*Please don't ~ this to anybody*. 请不要对别人再提此事。~ ***oneself*** 反复做[讲]同样事情。— *vi*. 1. 重复说[做]。2. (枪)连打。3. (小数等)循环。4. 〔美〕在同一选举中投几次票〔违法行为〕。

re·peat·ed [riˈpiːtid; rɪˋpitɪd] *a*. 反复的,再三的。**-ly** *ad*.

re·peat·er [riˈpiːtə; rɪˋpitɚ] *n*. 1. 重复某一行动者;重复发生的事物。2. 背诵者;复述者。3. 连珠枪;连发枪。4.【数】循环小数。5. 〔美〕在同一选举中投几次票者。6. 〔美〕重考者;重修(某课程)者;留班生。7. (每小时或每15分钟报时一次的)自鸣钟。8.【电】重发器,转发器,(替续)增音机,中继器;复示器。9. 累犯,惯犯。*a reverse ~*【机】反围盘。

re·peat·ing [riˈpiːtiŋ; rɪˋpitɪŋ] *a*. 反复的;循环的;连发的。*a ~ instrument* 复测仪。*a ~ rifle* 连发枪。*a ~ watch* 打簧表。*a ~ ship* 信号船。

re·pel [riˈpel; rɪˋpɛl] *vt*. (**-*pelled*** [-ˈpeld; -ˋpɛld]; **-*pelling*** [-ˈpeliŋ; -ˋpɛlɪŋ]) 1. 逐退,击退(敌军等)。2. 反驳;抵抗(诱惑等);抵制;拒绝,推却(请求、建议等)。3.【物】反拨,排斥,弹回。4. 使厌恶,使不快;使反感。*Water ~s oil*. 水排斥油。*A study which ~s you is invaluable*. 使你望而生畏的研究倒是大有用处的。— *vi*. 1. 被排斥,被击退。2. 引起反感。*Evil odors invariably ~*. 臭味总是使人不愉快。

re·pel·lent [riˈpelənt; rɪˋpɛlənt] I *a*. 1. 排斥的;防水的;【化】防止的;相斥的。2. 拒人于千里之外的(表情等);令人厌恶的。II *n*. 1. 反拨力,排拒力。2. 防水布。3.【医】消肿药;驱虫剂。*moth ~* 防蛀剂。**-lency, -lence** *n*. **-ly** *ad*.

re·pent[1] [riˈpent; rɪˋpɛnt] *vt*. (对某事或行为感到)悔恨,后悔,〔古〕使后悔〔多用于无人称句,有时用反身代词〕。~ *one's injustice to another* 对于对某人的不公正的态度感到悔恨。~ *an imprudent act* 后悔行为粗暴。~ *having said slanderous and false things about sb*. 后悔对某人说了些污蔑不实之词。*He repenteth him of the evil*. 他对罪恶感到后悔。*It ~s me that I did it*. 我很后悔做了这事。*R- what's past; avoid what is to come*. 痛悔过去,慎防将来。— *vi*. 后悔;【宗】忏悔(*of*);悔悟;悔改。~ *of having missed a good opportunity to learn* 后悔失去一个学习的好机会。*too late to ~* 后悔已晚。*I have nothing to ~ of*. 我没有什么好后悔的。*a man who ~s of his thoughtlessness* 一个对自己的粗心大意有所悔悟的人。

re·pent[2] [ˈriːpənt; ˋripənt] *a*.【植】匍匐生根的;【动】爬行的。

re·pent·ant [riˈpentənt; rɪˋpɛntənt] *a*. 对…感到懊悔[忏悔](*of*)。*be ~ of sth*. 对…表示后悔。**-tance** *n*.

re·peo·ple [ˈriːˈpiːpl; riˋpipl] *vt*. 使人重新居住,使新居民居住于;给…重新提供家畜。

re·per·cus·sion [ˌriːpə(ː)ˈkʌʃən; ˏripɚˋkʌʃən] *n*. 1. 反击,击退。2. 弹回;返回;(事件、声音的)反响,影响。3. 散肿法;消疹法;浮动诊(胎)法。4.【乐】(赋格曲中间插段后的)主题的再现,答句,(音调或和弦的)重复。

rep·er·toire [ˈrepətwɑː; ˋrɛpɚˏtwar] *n*. 1. (排好待演的)常备剧目,演奏节目;保留节目。2. 全部技能;所有组成部分。*instruction ~*【计算机】指令系统。~ **company** 拥有大量常备剧目的剧团。

rep·er·to·ry [ˈrepətəri; ˋrɛpɚˏtorɪ] *n*. 1. = repertoire. 2. 仓库,贮藏所,宝库;(尤指知识等的)贮藏,搜集;贮藏物。

re·pe·ruse [ˈriːpəˈruːz; ˏripəˋruz] *vt*. 重读,再读,重新细读,重新审读。**-ru·sal** *n*.

rep·e·tend [ˈrepiˌtend, ˌrepiˈtend; ˋrɛpəˏtɛnd, ˏrɛpəˋtɛnd] *n*. 1. 重复的声音[词、短语];(诗与乐曲的)叠句,副歌。2.【数】小数的循环节。

rep·e·ti·tion [ˌrepiˈtiʃən; ˏrɛpɪˋtɪʃən] *n*. 1. 反复,重复;重说,再讲;背诵;背诵文[诗];再现,再演。2.【乐】复唱,复奏,重奏。3. 副本,拷贝;模仿物。**-al, -ar·y** *a*. 反复的。

rep·e·ti·tious [ˌrepiˈtiʃəs; ˏrɛpɪˋtɪʃəs] *a*. 反复的,重复的;啰嗦的。**-ness** *n*.

re·pet·i·tive [riˈpetitiv; rɪˋpɛtɪtɪv] *a*. 反复的,重复的,重说的;复唱的,复奏的。**-ly** *ad*.

re·phrase [riˈfreiz; rɪˋfrez] *vt*. (**-*phras·ed***; **-*phrasing***) 改变说法;重新措词。

re·pine [riˈpain; rɪˋpaɪn] *vt*. 发牢骚,诉苦(*at*; *against*);渴望改变困难处境等而想望,向往(*for*)。

repl. = replacement 补充。

re·place [ri(ː)ˈpleis; rɪˋples] *vt*. 1. 放回原处[原位]。2. 还,送还,赔偿(钱、书等)。3. 使复职[复位]。4. 代替,接任,取代。5. 调换,替换;给与替手[代用品]。6.【化】置换。*a thing hard to ~* 难替换之物。**-able** *a*. 可放回原处的;可替换的,可代替的。**-ment** 复位,归还;【军】补充;替换,替代;代换;替换物;代替物;代替者;补充人员[兵员];【化】移位;置换;取代;【地】交代(作用)(*replacement level* 更替基准线〔为维持一定数量的人口所需要的出生率〕)。

re·plant [ˈriːˈplɑːnt; riˋplænt] *vt*. 1. 改种;移植,补种,补播。2. 使复位。3.【医】再植(断肢等)。**-ta·tion** *n*.

re·play I [ˈriːˈplei; riˋple] *vt*. 重新举行(比赛);重演;再

播放。II [ˈriːplei; ˋriple] *n*. 重赛;重演;(录音、电影等的)重放。

re·plead·er [riˈpliːdə; riˋplidɚ] *n*.【法】1. 第二次申诉。2. 再诉权。3. 法院要求诉讼双方进行第二次申诉的令状。

re·plen·ish [riˈpleniʃ; rɪˋplɛnɪʃ] *vt*. 1. 再斟满,再装满(*with*)。2. 装足,装满,补充(钱袋等);加强。3.〔古〕使牲口[人和动物]众多。~ *the fire* 添燃料,加火。~ *the earth* 使土地上充满生物。**-er** *n*. 补充者;【电】补电器;【摄】显像剂,显影剂。**-ment** *n*. 再斟满,再装满,新补给;充满,充实,补充,供给。

re·plete [riˈpliːt; rɪˋplit] *a*. 1. 充分供应的,饱满的;吃饱了的;塞满的(*with*)。2.〔罕〕充分的,完全的。~ *state of soil* 土壤充水状态。

re·ple·tion [riˈpliːʃən; rɪˋpliʃən] *n*. 1. 充满,充实,吃饱;满足。2.【医】多血。*to* ~ 饱,满满,充分。

re·plev·in [riˈplevin; rɪˋplɛvɪn] I *n*.【法】没收物[扣押物]的发还[收回];收回(不该没收的)物件的诉讼;发还物件的命令。II *vt*. = replevy.

re·plev·y [riˈplevi; rɪˋplɛvɪ] I *vt*. 1.【法】经诉讼收回(被没收的物件等)。2. 凭令状取回(被扣押物品)。3.〔罕〕保释;准许保释。— *vi*. 凭令状取回被扣押物。II *n*. 发还扣押物的命令。

R

rep·li·ca [ˈreplikə, riˈpliːkə; ˋrɛplɪkə, rɪˋplikə] *n*. 1. 复制品〔特指由原作者自己照前一作品作成的〕;摹本,拷贝。2. 逼真的东西,一模一样的东西。3.【乐】(主题的)反复;(乐谱中的)重复句。*a* ~ *of his father* 跟父亲长得一模一样的子女。**-ble** *a*. 可重复[重演]的,可反复再现的。

rep·li·cate [ˈreplikit; ˋrɛplɪkɪt] I *a*.【植】折转的。II *n*.【统】重复实验中的一次。III [-ˈkeit; -ˋket] *vt*. 1.【植】折转。2. 重复,反复,复制。3.〔罕〕回答。

rep·li·ca·tion [ˌrepliˈkeiʃən; ˏrɛplɪˋkeʃən] *n*. 1. (尤指对答辩的)回答;【法】(原告对被告抗辩的)答辩。2. (绘画等的)复制,摹写;拷贝,复制品。3.【统】重复(实验)。3.【植】折转;折缝。4. 反响。**-ca·tive** *a*.

re·pli·er [riˈplaiə; rɪˋplaɪɚ] *n*. 回答者,答复者。

re·ply [riˈplai; rɪˋplaɪ] I *n*. 答复,回答;(用行动等)应战;反响;【法】(原告对被告抗辩的)答辩。*in* ~ (*to*) 为答复…;作为…的答复。*make* ~ 回答。~ *paid* 附回信邮费;(拍电人已将)回电费付讫。II *vi*. 答复,回答(*to*);【法】(原告)答辩;应付;应战;反响。~ *to the enemy's fire* 对敌人炮火加以回击。~ *for* 代表…答辩[回答,答谢祝酒]。— *vt*. 回答。*He replied that he would not do that*. 他回答说他不愿做那件事。

ré·pon·dez s'il vous plait [reipɔ̃ːˈdeisiːl vuːˈple; repɔ̃ˋdesilvuˋplɛ]〔F.〕乞赐复〔请帖用语,通常略作 R.S.V.P.〕。

re·port [riˈpɔːt; rɪˋport] I *vt*. 1. 告知,报告,汇报;报导(新闻、调查结果等);发表,公布,发表公报。2. 传达(人的话);转述;传说,传闻;品评。3. 记录(讲演等以备发表)。4. (向当局)报到(等);揭发,告发(某人不法行为等)。*It is ~ed that ....* 据说…,据传…。*He was ~ed killed*. 据说他已阵亡[被杀]。*~ed speech*【语法】间接引语。*be badly* (*well*) *~ed of* 名气坏[好]。*move to ~ progress* (以防碍议事为目的而)提议中止讨论。~ *oneself* 报到,到差;出席。~ *progress* 报告经过。— *vi*. 1. 报告,呈报,回报(*on*);作报告,打报告,就…提出报告(*on*; *upon*)。2. (新闻记者)采访,访问,通讯,报导。3. 报到,到差。~ *for duty* [*work*] 报到,上班,上工。~ *for the Times* 担任泰晤士报的通讯记者,给泰晤士报写通讯。~ *to at* 到…报到;到校,上学。~ *to the police* 向警察报告。II *n*. 1. (调查、研究后的)报告(书)(*on*);(政府机关等的)公报;(学校的)成绩报告单;(报纸等的)通讯,报导。2.【议会】记录;速记;【法】〔*pl*.〕审判记录;意见书;(给上级法院的)申请书,案件[判例]汇编。3. 传说,传闻,社会上的评论,名气,名声。4. 响声,爆炸声,枪炮声。*idle ~s* 无根据的传说。*a matter of common* ~ 大家都知道的传闻。*The rifle went off with a loud* ~. 枪砰的一声打了出去。*a* ~ *on* 关于…的报告。*as* ~ *has it* [*goes*] 据说。*have a good* [*bad*] ~ (学生)成绩好[不好]。*make* ~ 报告(调查结果等)。*of good* ~ 名声好的,评价好的。*The* ~ *goes* [*runs, has it*] *that ....* 据说,据传。*through good and evil* ~ 不顾毁誉褒贬;不管名声好坏。~ **card** (学生)成绩报告单。~ **stage** (英国议会)委员会的报告会;第三读会。

re·port·age [ˌrepɔːˈtaːdʒ; rɪˋportɪdʒ] *n*. 1. 新闻采访,新闻报导。2. 报告文学,报导文体。

re·port·ed·ly [riˈpɔːtidli; rɪˋportɪdlɪ] *ad*. 据报导,据传说。

re·port·er [riˈpɔːtə; rɪˋportɚ] *n*. 报告者;呈报者;采访记者,新闻通讯员;审判[议事]记录员;指示器。**-tori·al** [ˌrepəˈtɔːriəl; ˏrɛpɚˋtorɪəl] *a*.

re·pos·al [riˈpəuzəl; rɪˋpozəl] *n*. (信用等的)托付,信托。

re·pose[1] [riˈpəuz; rɪˋpoz] *vt*. 把(希望等)寄托在…;〔罕〕委托。~ *trust* [*confidence*] *in* [*on*] *sb*. [*sth*.] 信任某人[某情况]。

re·pose[2] [riˈpəuz; rɪˋpoz] I *vi*. 1. 休息,安歇;睡,安睡;〔喻〕永眠,长逝。2. 躺着,横卧;蕴藏;处于。3. 建立于,基于(*on*; *upon*)。4. 倚靠,信赖(*on*; *in*)。*The statue ~s on a pedestal*. 雕像安在台座上。*The scheme ~s on a revival of trade*. 这个计划以活跃贸易为基础。~ *in sleep* [*death*] 睡着[永眠]。~ *on a bed of down* [*roses*] 过奢侈生活。~ *on the past* 留恋过去;缅怀往昔。— *vt*. 使休息,使安睡(*on*; *in*)。~ *one's head on the pillow* 将头靠枕休息。~ *oneself* 休息,歇息,睡觉。~ *oneself on a bed* 躺在床上。II *n*. 1. 休息,睡眠;静止;平静,安静;休养,静养;永眠,长逝。2. (色彩等的)恬静;(态度的)镇静,悠闲,泰然自若。3. 信用,信赖。*make* [*seek, take*] ~ 休息。*a volcano in* ~ 休止的火山。

re·pose·ful [riˈpəuzful; rɪˋpozfl̩] *a*. 平静的,安静的;泰然自若的。**-ly** *ad*.

re·pos·it [riˈpɔzit; rɪˋpɑzɪt] *vt*. 1. 保存,贮藏。2.〔罕〕使复位,放回原位;归还;取代;改变…的位置。

re·po·si·tion[1] [ˌriːpəˈziʃən; ˏripəˋzɪʃən] *n*. 1. 安置,保存,保藏。2.【医】复位术。

re·po·si·tion[2] [ˌriːpəˈziʃən; ˏripəˋzɪʃən] *vt*. 换位;改变位置[主张、态度、立场等]。

re·pos·i·to·ry [riˈpɔzitəri; rɪˋpɑzəˏtorɪ] *n*. 1.〔英〕仓库,贮藏所;〔罕〕(美术品等的)陈列所[室],博物馆;店铺;墓室;贮物器;(知识等的)宝库;学识见闻广博的人。2. 受人信托的人,心腹,亲信。*He was a* ~ *of all her secrets*. 她的一切秘密她都肯告诉他;他是她完全信赖的人。*The book* [*man*] *is a* ~ *of curious information*. 这书里有[这人晓得]许多奇事。

re·pos·sess [ˈriːpəˈzes; ˏripəˋzɛs] *vt*. 再占有,取回,复得(被夺之物);使恢复。~ *oneself of* 使自己重新占有…;取回,恢复。

re·post [riːˈpəust; rɪˋpost] *n*., *v*. = riposte.

re·pot [ˈriːˈpɔt; riˋpɑt] *vt*. 移植到别的花盆里,换盆。

re·pous·sé [ripuːˈse; rəpuˋse]〔F.〕I *a*. 1. (金属细工所锤成或冲压出)凸纹形的。2. 凸纹饰的。II *n*. 1. 凸纹(面)。2. 凸纹制作(术)。

repp [rep; rɛp] *n*. = rep[1].

repr. = representing; reprinted; reproduction.

rep·re·hend [repriˈhend; ˏrɛprɪˋhɛnd] *vt*. 责难,指摘,谴责;申斥。

rep·re·hen·si·ble [ˌrepriˈhensəbl; ˏrɛprɪˋhɛnsəbl̩] *a*. 应受谴责的。**-bly** *ad*.

rep·re·hen·sion [ˌrepriˈhenʃən; ˏrɛprɪˋhɛnʃən] *n*. 谴责;指摘;申斥。

rep·re·sent [ˌrepriˈzent; ˏrɛprɪˋzɛnt] **vt.** **1.** (用文章等)描述;(用绘画等)表现,描写,描画;象征;意指,表示,意味。**2.** 把…讲述为(*as*);声称自己是(*oneself as*; *to be*);认为…是(*as*)。**3.** 相当于,比拟。**4.** 上演(戏等);扮演(某角色)。**5.** 代表,代理;被选为议员。~ *ideas by words* 用言语表达思想。*I am not what you ~ me to be.* 我并不是像你所说的那种人。*They ~ed him as the chief conspirator.* 他们说他是主谋者。*He ~ed himself as a philosopher.* 他声称自己是哲学家。*We ~ed this plan easy, but it was not.* 我们原以为这计划很容易,但实际并非如此。*Camels are ~ed in the New World by llamas.* 在美洲相当于骆驼的是美洲驼。*members ~ing urban constituencies* 市选议员。**~ sth. to oneself** 想像出某事物。**~ oneself as** [**to be**] 声称自己是…。— **vi.** 提出异议。

re-pre·sent [ˈriːpriˈzent; ˏripriˋzɛnt] **vt.** 再赠送;再提出;再上演(戏剧等)。

rep·re·sen·ta·tion [ˌreprizenˈteiʃən; ˏrɛprɪzɛnˋteʃən] **n.** **1.** 表示,表现,描画,描写;画像,肖像;雕像,想像,想像力;【心】表象。**2.** 上演,演出;扮演。**3.** 〔常 *pl.*〕说明,陈述;主张,断定;建议,提议;抗议。**4.** 代理,代表;选举区民代表;〔集合词〕代表人。**5.** 【物】图像;显像;描绘;扫描。**6.** 【法】(权利、债务的)继承;(促使另一方订契约的)陈述。*a symbolic ~* 象征性的图象,象征物。*a coded ~* 代码。**make a ~ against** 向…抗议。**make a ~ to** 向…说明。**make ~ to** 向…交涉。

rep·re·sen·ta·tion·al [ˌreprizenˈteiʃənl; ˏrɛprɪzɛnˋteʃənl] **a.** **1.** 表现的,再现的,表象的。**2.** 扮演的,反映客观现实的艺术的。**-ly ad.**

rep·re·sen·ta·tion·al·ism [ˌreprizenˈteiʃənlizm; ˏrɛprɪzɛnˋteʃənlˏɪzəm] **n.** **1.** 表现论。**2.** 【哲】再现说〔头脑只有通过概念或思想才能理解客观事物的理论〕。**-tion·al·ist n.**, **a.**

rep·re·sent·a·tive [ˌrepriˈzentətiv; ˏrɛprɪˋzɛntətɪv] **I a.** **1.** 表示的;表现的,描写的;象征的。**2.** 能代表…的;可作…的典型[模范]的(*of*)。**3.** 代理的,代表的,代议制的。**4.** 相当[类似](另一种属)的。~ *art* 描绘自然或生活的艺术。*a ~ body* 代表团。*a ~ chamber* [*house*] 代议院。**in a ~ capacity** 以代表资格。**II n.** **1.** 代表,代理(人);继任者,继承人;议员;〔美〕众议员;驻外代表[大使,公使,领事]。**2.** 类似物;样本,标本;典型。*a legal* [*personal*] ~ 遗嘱执行人,法定代理人。*a real* [*natural*] ~ 承继人。*the House of Representatives* 〔美〕众议院。**-ly ad.**

re·press [riˈpres; rɪˋprɛs] **vt.** **1.** 镇压(叛乱等)。**2.** 抑制,压抑(欲望等);忍住,熬住,止住(笑、眼泪等);【心】把(冲动等)压入(潜意识)。**-er, -or n.** **-i·ble a.**

re-press [riːˈpres; ˋriˋprɛs] **vt.** 再压。

re·pressed [riˈprest; riˋprɛst] **a.** **1.** 被抑制的,受约束的。**2.** 被镇压的。~ **memory** 【心】被(压)抑(的)记忆。

re·pres·sion [riˈpreʃən; rɪˋprɛʃən] **n.** **1.** 镇压;制止。**2.** 抑制。*the ~ of a cough* 制止咳嗽。*R- made him behave worse.* 受抑制使他表现得更糟。

re·prieve [riˈpriːv; rɪˋpriv] **I n.** 【法】缓刑;死刑缓刑期[命令];〔喻〕(死、痛苦等的)暂免,暂止,暂减,暂缓。**II vt.** 【法】缓期执行(死刑),暂缓处刑;暂免,暂缓,暂止。

rep·ri·mand **I** [ˈreprimɑːnd; ˋrɛprəˏmænd] n. (特指当权者进行的)严责,谴责,惩戒;申斥。**II** [ˈre-, repriˈmɑːnd; ˋrɛ-, rɛprəˋmænd] **vt.** 申斥,谴责,惩戒。

re·print **I** [ˈriːˈprint; riˋprɪnt] **n.** **1.** 再版;重印;翻版。**2.** (刊物中论文的)单行本,抽印材料。**3.** 已不通用的邮票的重印版。**II** [ˈriːprint, -ˈprint; ˋriprɪnt, -ˋprɪnt] **vt.** **1.** 再版;重印;翻印。**2.** (刊物中论文的)单独抽印。**3.** 转载。

re·pris·al [riˈpraizəl; rɪˋpraɪzl] **n.** **1.** (特指国家间的)暴力性报复,报复行为;【史】(对敌国人民、财产的)报复性劫掠。**2.** 〔罕〕〔主 *pl.*〕赔偿,赔款。*letters* [*a commission*] *of ~* 报复性拘捕证。*make ~(s)* 进行报复。

re·prise [riˈpraiz; rɪˋpraɪz] **I n.** **1.** 【法】〔常 *pl.*〕从贵族所有地每年收入中扣除的费用〔租费、恩俸等〕。**2.** 【乐】反复(句)〔尤指奏鸣曲乐章的主题〕。*beyond* [*above, besides*] *~s* 付完租费(等)后剩下的。**II vt.** **1.** 重演,重奏,重复,重映。**2.** 〔古〕夺回。**3.** 〔古〕赔偿。

re·pro [ˈriːprəu; ˋripro] **n.** (*pl.* **-pros**) reproduction proof 的缩略词(= repro proof)。

re·proach [riˈprəutʃ; rɪˋprotʃ] **I n.** **1.** 责备,责骂,谴责;耻辱,污辱(*to*)。**2.** 〔*pl.*〕【宗】应答圣歌。*a term of ~* 侮蔑话;责难的话。*the mute ~ in his eyes* 他眼睛里现出的无言谴责。*The state of the roads is a ~ to civilization.* 道路的这种状态是文明的耻辱。**beyond ~** 无可非议地,漂亮地,出色地。**bring down ~ upon** 玷污,毁损。**bring** [**draw**] **~** (**up**) **on** 使成为…的耻辱。**heap ~es on** 痛骂,痛责。**II vt.** 责备,责骂,谴责;使丢脸;损伤…的体面。*His eyes ~ me.* 他用眼睛责备我。**-a·ble a.** 应受责备的;可责备的。**-less a.**

re·proach·ful [riˈprəutʃful; rɪˋprotʃfl] **a.** 谴责的;责备的;应受斥责的;〔古〕可耻的。**-ly ad.** **-ness n.**

rep·ro·bate [ˈreprəubeit; ˋrɛprəˏbet] **I vt.** **1.** 拒绝,排斥。**2.** 谴责。**3.** 【宗】(上帝)摒弃;(天)罚。**II a.** 为上帝摒弃的;邪恶的,堕落的。**III n.** 为上帝摒弃的人;堕落的人;恶棍。

rep·ro·ba·tion [ˌreprəuˈbeiʃən; ˏrɛprəˋbeʃən] **n.** **1.** 拒绝,排斥。**2.** 反对,异议;斥责。**3.** 【宗】摈弃。

re·pro·cess [ˈriːˈprəuses; riˋprɑsɛs] **vt.** 重新处理;再加工;使再生;回收(废料)。

re·pro·duce [ˌriːprəˈdjuːs; ˏriprəˋdjus] **vt.** **1.** 再生产;再现。**2.** 复制,复写;仿造。**3.** 再演;再版;转载;翻印。**4.** 生殖,繁殖。~ *oneself* 生殖,繁殖。— **vi.** **1.** 繁殖,生殖。**2.** 进行再生产;复制。

re·pro·duce·a·ble, re·pro·duc·i·ble [ˌriːprəˈdjuːsəbl, -ibl; ˏriprəˋdjusəbl, -ɪbl] **a.** 能再生产的;能复制的;能繁殖的。

re·pro·duc·er [ˌriːprəˈdjuːsə; ˏriprəˋdjusɚ] **n.** **1.** 再现设备。**2.** 扬声器。

re·pro·duc·tion [ˌriːprəˈdʌkʃən; ˏriprəˋdʌkʃən] **n.** **1.** 再生产,再现;【心】再生作用。**2.** 复制(品),复写,仿造;转载;翻印。**3.** 生殖,繁殖。~ *by division* [*ramification, gemmae*] 分裂[分枝、芽胞]生殖。~ *by tending treatments* 【林】抚育更新。~ **proof** 【印】照相制版用样张。

re·pro·duc·tive [ˈriːprəˈdʌktiv; ˏriprəˋdʌktɪv] **a.** **1.** 生殖的。**2.** 再生产的,再现的。**3.** 多产的。~ *organs* 生殖器官。**-ly ad.**

re·pro·gram [ˈriːˈprəugræm; ˋriˋproˏgræm] **vt.** 改编[重编](程序),程序重调。

re·prog·ra·phy [riːˈprɔgræfi; riˋprɑgræfɪ] **n.** 复印,翻印。**-pher n.** **-graph·ic a.**

re·proof¹ [riˈpruːf; rɪˋpruf] **n.** 责备,谴责。**in ~ of** 对…加以责备。

re·proof² [riˈpruːf; rɪˋpruf] **vt.** **1.** 重新上防水胶。**2.** 【印】重新打样。

re·prov·al [riˈpruːvəl; rɪˋpruvl] **n.** = reproof¹.

re·prove [riˈpruːv; rɪˋpruv] **vt.** 责骂,谴责,训斥(*for*)。~ *sb. to his face* 当面责备某人。

re-prove [riːˈpruːv; riˋpruv] **vt.**, **vi.** 再证明。

re·prov·ing·ly [riˈpruːviŋli; rɪˋpruvɪŋlɪ] **ad.** 谴责地。

re·pro·vi·sion [ˈriːprəˈviʒən; ˋriprəˋvɪʒən] **vt.** 再给…食品,补充粮食给…。

reps [reps; rɛps] **n.** = rep¹.

rep·tant [ˈreptənt; ˋrɛptənt] **a.** 【植】匍匐的;【动】爬行的。

rep·tile [ˈreptail; ˋrɛptl] **I a.** **1.** 匍匐的,爬行的;爬虫类的。**2.** 卑劣的。**II n.** **1.** 爬虫,爬行动物。**2.** 卑劣的人。

Rep·til·ia [repˈtiliə; rɛpˋtɪlɪə] **n.** 〔*pl.*〕【动】爬虫纲。

R

rep·til·i·an [rep'tiliən; rɛp'tɪlɪən] **I** ***a*.** **1.** (像)爬行动物的;(像)爬虫类的。**2.** 卑劣的。**II** ***n*.** 爬行动物;爬虫。

Repub. = Republic; Republican.

re·pub·lic [ri'pʌblik; rɪ'pʌblɪk] ***n*.** **1.** 共和国;共和政体。**2.** …圈,…界,…坛。**3.**〔古〕国家。*the ~ of letters* 文学界,文坛。

re·pub·li·can [ri'pʌblikən; rɪ'pʌblɪkən] **I** ***a*.** **1.** 共和政体的,共和国的;共和主义的;〔R-〕〔美〕共和党的。**2.**【动】群栖的(鸟等)。**II** ***n*.** 共和主义者;拥护共和政体者;〔R-〕〔美〕共和党员。*the R- Party*〔美〕共和党。**-ism** ***n*.** 共和政体;共和主义;(美国)共和党的政策。**-ize** ***vt*.** 使成共和政体,使成共和国。

re·pub·li·ca·tion ['ri:ˌpʌbli'keiʃən; ˌripʌblɪ'keʃən] ***n*.** 再版(的书);再发表,再发行。

re·pub·lish ['ri:'pʌbliʃ; ri'pʌblɪʃ] ***vt*.** **1.** 再出版;再发表;再发行。**2.**【法】重新订立(遗嘱)。

re·pu·di·ate [ri'pju:dieit; rɪ'pjudɪˌet] ***vt*.** **1.** (古代)休(妻),与(妻)离婚,遗弃(妻子);逐(子),断绝(父子)关系。**2.** 不承认,不接受,否定,批判,推翻(建议);驳斥,驳倒;拒绝(要求等)。**3.** (尤指政府等)拒付(公债等);赖(债)。

re·pu·di·a·tion [riˌpju:di'eiʃən; rɪˌpjudɪ'eʃən] ***n*.** **1.** 休妻;逐子。**2.** 拒绝;(国家、政府的)赖债,拒付公债。**3.** 推翻,批判,驳斥。

re·pu·di·a·tor [ri'pju:dieitə; rɪ'pjudɪˌetɚ] ***n*.** 抛弃者;否认者;拒绝支付者,赖债者。

re·pugn [ri'pju:n; rɪ'pjun] ***vt*., *vi*.** 〔罕〕(使)厌恶;反对(*against*)。

re·pug·nance, -nan·cy [ri'pʌgnəns, -si; rɪ'pʌgnəns, -sɪ] ***n*.** 厌恶,反感(*to*, *against*; *towards*);反对;矛盾,冲突(*of*; *between*; *to*; *with*)。

re·pug·nant [ri'pʌgnənt; rɪ'pʌgnənt] ***a*.** **1.** 令人厌恶的,令人讨厌的(*to*),不得人心的。**2.** 冲突的(*to*);与…不一致的,不调和的(*with*)。**3.** 反抗的;抱反感的。

re·pulse [ri'pʌls; rɪ'pʌls] **I** ***vt*.** **1.** 反击[打退](敌人等);推开;驳倒;挫败(对方)。**2.** 排斥;拒绝,谢绝。**II** ***n*.** 反击;打退;击退;拒绝;【物】拒斥。*meet with* [*suffer*] (*a*) ~ 被拒绝[击退]。

re·pul·sion [ri'pʌlʃən; rɪ'pʌlʃən] ***n*.** **1.** 反击,反驳。**2.** 排斥,拒绝。**3.** 嫌恶,嫌忌。**4.**【物】反斥,推斥;斥力。**5.**【医】(疮肿等的)消散;分离倾向,分散性。*feel ~ for sb*. 觉得某人讨厌。

re·pul·sive [ri'pʌlsiv; rɪ'pʌlsɪv] ***a*.** **1.** (令人)厌恶的,讨厌的(*to*)。**2.** 情绪上有抵触的;排斥的;【物】推斥的,斥力的。*a ~ smell* 讨厌的气味。*~ forces* 斥力。**-ly** ***ad*.**

rep·u·ta·ble ['repjutəbl; 'rɛpjətəbl̩] ***a*.** 名气好的,有名声的;可尊敬的,高尚的;规范的。*a man of ~ character* 人格高尚的人。**-bly** ***ad*.**

rep·u·ta·tion [ˌrepju(:)'teiʃən; ˌrɛpjə'teʃən] ***n*.** 名气,名声,名誉;名望,信誉,声望。*a man of ~* 有名望的人。*a man of no ~* 默默无闻的人;没有声望的人。*build up a ~* 博得名声。*enjoy a high ~ as a man of science* 享有盛名的科学家。***have a good*** [***poor***] ~ 名誉好[坏]。***have a ~ for = have the ~ of*** 因…而著名,以…闻名,有…的名气。***live up to one's ~*** 不负盛名;行为与名声相符。***lose*** [***ruin***] ***one's ~*** 名誉扫地。

re·pute [ri'pju:t; rɪ'pjut] **I** ***n*.** 名誉,名声,名望,信用。*know sb. by ~* 由传闻中知道某人。*authors of ~* 有名的作家们。***of good*** [***bad***] ~ 名誉好[坏]的,有[无]信用的。***through good and evil ~*** 不管毁誉褒贬,不管人家怎样讲,不管舆论如何。**II** ***vt*.** **1.** 〔古、诗〕以为,认为。**2.** 看做;称为;评价。*He is ~d* (*as*, *to be*) *honest*. 一般都认为他老实。*He is ill* [*well*] *~d of*. 他名誉不好[好]。

re·put·ed [ri'pju:tid; rɪ'pjutɪd] ***a*.** **1.** 名誉好的,有名气的。**2.** 号称…的,被称为…的,据说是…的。*~ gin* 驰名的杜松子酒。*sb.'s ~ father* 据说是某人的父亲〔真假不明〕。*a ~ pint* 号称一品脱装的(酒等)。**-ly** ***ad*.** 据一般批评,据说。

re·quest [ri'kwest; rɪ'kwɛst] **I** ***n*.** **1.** 请求,恳求,恳请;要求,需要。**2.** 要求物,需要品,请求之事;请求文,请愿书。*I have a ~ to make of you*. 我有事求你。*You shall have your ~*. 你要的东西会给你的,会答应你的请求的。***at sb.'s ~*** 应某人请求。***be in*** (***great***) ~ (非常)需要。***by ~*** 照需要;依照请求;应邀,如嘱(*She will sing by ~*. 她将应邀歌唱)。***come into ~*** 出现需要,受人需要。***make*** (***a***) ***~ for*** 请求,恳请。***on ~*** 承索(即寄等)。**II** ***vt*.** (郑重或正式)请求,要求,恳求,恳请(*sth*.; *sb. to do*; *that* ...)。*~ a loan from the bank* 请求银行借款。*Your presence is immediately ~ed*. 即请光临[驾临,出席]。*May I ~ your attention?* 请您注意! *Gentlemen are ~ed not to smoke*. 先生们请勿吸烟。*I ~ them to stop making such a noise*. 我请求他们别这样吵闹。*I ~* (*of him*) *that he* (*should*) *leave*. 我恳请他离开。*We ~ that no flowers be sent*. 敬辞花圈〔讣文中用语〕。***as ~ed*** 依照请求。

re·quick·en ['ri:'kwikən; 'ri'kwɪkən] ***vt*., *vi*.** (使)苏醒;(使)重新振作。

req·ui·em ['rekwiem; 'rikwɪəm] ***n*.** **1.** 〔R-〕【宗】安魂弥撒(曲)。**2.** 安魂曲,挽歌。**3.** 安息,平安,平静。

re·qui·es·cat in pace [ˌrekwi'eskæt in 'peisi; ˌrɛkwɪ'ɛskæt ɪn 'pesɪ] 〔L.〕愿灵安眠〔基督教徒墓碑用语,略R.I.P.〕。

re·quire [ri'kwaiə; rɪ'kwaɪr] ***vt*.** **1.** 需要。**2.** 要求;请求,命令。*Will you ~ breakfast earlier than usual?* 〔英〕你需要比平常早一点开早饭吗? *They ~ me to come*. 他们要我来。*He ~s medical care*. 他需要治疗。*The emergency ~s that it should be done*. 事情紧急,非这样做不可。*All passengers are ~d to show their tickets*. 所有乘客都必须出示车票。***It ~s that*** .... 有…的必要。— ***vi*.** 需要;请求,要求。***if circumstances ~*** 遇必要时。

re·quired [ri'kwaiəd; rɪ'kwaɪrd] ***a*.** 〔美〕必修的(大学课程)。

re·quire·ment [ri'kwaiəmənt; rɪ'kwaɪrmənt] ***n*.** **1.** 要求,需要。**2.** 要求物,必需品;需要量;必要条件,资格(*for*)。*the detailed ~s* 详细规格。*meet the ~s of the times* 适应当时需要。*the first ~* 第一要件。

req·ui·site ['rekwizit; 'rɛkwəzɪt] **I** ***a*.** 必要的,必需的,需要的(*to*; *for*)。**II** ***n*.** 必需品;要素,要件(*for*; *of*)。*a quality ~ to a scientist* 科学家必不可少的品质。*the number of votes ~ for him to be elected* 他当选的不可少的票数。

req·ui·si·tion [ˌrekwi'ziʃən; ˌrɛkwə'zɪʃən] **I** ***n*.** **1.** 要求,请求,命令,必要条件;【国际法】引渡犯人的要求。**2.** 需要;【军】征购,征用,征发。**3.** 通知书;调拨单;申请书,请求书;召唤书。***be in*** [***under***] ~ 另有需要,现在无空。***bring*** [***call***, ***place***] ***into ~ = put in ~ = lay under ~*** 征收,征发,征用。***~ of land*** 征用土地。**II** ***vt*.** 要求,强制使用;【军】征发;命令征发;召集。

re·quit·al [ri'kwaitl; rɪ'kwaɪtl̩] ***n*.** 报答;报复,复仇;罚;报答的行动;酬谢之物;〔罕〕赔偿,补偿。***in ~ of*** [***for***] 作为…的报酬,为酬谢…,为报复…。

re·quite [ri'kwait; rɪ'kwaɪt] ***vt*.** 报答,酬谢,报酬;报复(*for*; *with*);补偿。***~ like for like*** 用同样手段报答,以恩报恩,以怨报怨;以牙还牙。

re·ra·di·a·tion [ˌri:reidi:'eiʃən; ˌrɪredɪ'eʃən] ***n*.** 【物】再辐射。

re·read ['ri:'ri:d; ri'rid] (***-read*** [-'red; -'rɛd]) ***vt*.** 重新读,再读。

rere-arch [ˈriəˈɑːtʃ; ˌrɪrˋartʃ] *n*. 【建】背拱,内拱(= rear arch)。

re·re·cord [ˈriːriˈkɔːd; ˌririˋkɔrd] *vt*. (录音)再录,重录。

re·re·cord·ing [ˈriːriˈkɔːdiŋ; ˌririˋkɔrdɪŋ] *n*. 再录音。

rere·dos [ˈriədɔs; ˋrɪrdɑs] *n*. 〔英〕祭坛背后的装饰品(= altar-piece)。

re-re·fine [ˈriːrəˈfain; ˌrirəˋfaɪn] *vt*. 再精炼。~*d oil* 再生润滑油。

re·re·lease [ˈriːriˈliːs; ˋrirɪˌlis] *n*. 【影】= reissue.

rere·mouse [ˈriəˌmaus; ˋrɪrˌmaʊs] *n*. (*pl*. **-mice** [-ˌmais; -ˌmaɪs]) 〔古语〕蝙蝠(= bat)。

re·route [riˈruːt, -ˈraut; riˋrut, -ˋraʊt] *vt*. (**-rout·ed**; **-rout·ing**) 按新路线发送,改道发送。

re·run I [ˈriːˈrʌn; riˋrʌn] *vt*. (**-ran**, **-run·ning**) 重新开动,重新进行〔尤指首轮放映后的影片或电视片的再度上映〕。II [ˈriːˌrʌn; ˋriˌrʌn] *n*. 1. 再开动,再进行。2. 再度上映的影片或电视片。

res [riːz; riz] *n*. 〔*sing*., *pl*.〕〔L.〕物,实体,物件;事,事件;财产。~ ***angusta domi*** [æŋˈgʌstə dəuˈmai; æŋˋgʌstə doˋmaɪ] 家境贫困。~ ***judicata*** [dʒuːdiˈkeitə; dʒudɪˋketə] 已决事件。

res. = 1. reserve. 2. residence. 3. resort. 4. resolution.

re·sad·dle [ˈriːˈsædl; riˋsædl] *vt*. 给…再装鞍子。

re·sail [ˈriːˈseil; riˋsel] *vt*. 再航行。— *vi*. 开回;再航行。

re·sal·a·ble [riˈseiləbl; riˋseləbl̩] *a*. 可再卖的,可转卖的。

re·sale [ˈriːseil; riˋsel] *n*. 再卖;转卖。

re·scind [riˈsind; rɪˋsɪnd] *vt*. 1. 废除,作废,取消,撤销,解除。2. 〔古、主喻〕扫除,删除。

re·scis·sion [riˈsiʒən; rɪˋsɪʒən] *n*. 1. 取消,撤销,解除,废除。2. 【法】解约。**-scis·so·ry** [-ˈsisəri; -ˋsɪsərɪ] *a*.

re·script [ˈriːskript; ˋriskrɪpt] *n*. 1. (罗马皇帝或教皇的)书面答复;诏书,政令布告。2. 再写,重写;重写的东西;〔美〕【法】副本。

res·cue [ˈreskjuː; ˋrɛskju] I *vt*. 1. 救,援救,营救,救出(俘虏等)。2. 【法】劫出(囚犯),夺回(没收物)。3. 维护。*He ~d the child from drowning*. 他救起了一个溺水的孩子。II *n*. 1. 援救,营救,救济。2. 【法】(囚犯的)劫出,(没收物的)非法夺回。*a ~ party* 援救队。*a ~ home* 娼妓救济所,济良所。~ *work* (对妇女、儿童的)救济事业。***go*** (***come***) ***to the*** ~ 进行援救,营救。

res·cu·er [ˈreskju(ː)ə; ˋrɛskjuɚ] *n*. 救助者,援救者;救星。

re-search [riːˈsəːtʃ; ˋriˋsɝtʃ] *vt*., *vi*. 再调查,再搜索(*sth*., *into sth*.)。

re·search [riˈsəːtʃ; ˋrisɝtʃ] I *n*. 1. 仔细搜索(*for*, *after*)。2. 〔常 *pl*.〕研究,调查,探测;追究。*literary* [*scientific*] *~es* 文学[科学]研究。*basic* ~ 理论研究。*a scholar of great* ~ 非常有研究的学者。*be engaged in* ~ 从事研究。*scholastic* ~ 繁琐的追究。II *vt*., *vi*. 追究;调查,研究(*sth*., *into sth*.)。

re·seat [ˈriːˈsiːt; riˋsit] *vt*. 1. 使再坐下;使复职。2. 增设座位;换装座面。~ *oneself* (站起来后)又坐下来。*The boy's trousers want ~ing*. 这个孩子的裤子后座部得修换了。

re·seau, ré·seau [reiˈzəu; reˋzo] *n*. (*pl*. **-seaux** [-ˈzəuz, -zəu; -ˋzoz, -zo]) 1. 网状物;【天】网格;【气】世界气象网。2. (花边织物的)网眼地纹组织。3. 【摄】滤(光)屏。

re·sect [ri(ː)ˈsekt; rɪˋsɛkt] *vt*. 【医】切除。**-tion** *n*. 切除(术)。

re·se·da [ˈresidə; rɪˋsɪdə] *n*. 1. 【植】木樨草。2. 灰绿色。

re·seg·re·ga·tion [ˈriːˌsegriˈgeiʃən; ˌrisɛgrɪˋgeʃən] *n*. 恢复种族隔离。

re·sell [ˈriːˈsel; riˋsɛl] (**re·sold** [ˈriːˈsəuld; riˋsold]) *vt*. 再出售;转卖。

re·sem·blance [riˈzembləns; rɪˋzɛmbləns] *n*. 相似(*to*; *between*; *of*);相似性;相似点;相似程度;外表,外观,外形,样子;肖像,像。*He has a strong ~ to his father*. 他极像他父亲。*He was of fine ~*. 他外表很好。

re·sem·ble [riˈzembl; rɪˋzɛmbl̩] *vt*. 1. 像,类似,相似。2. 〔古〕比拟,譬喻(*to*)。3. 〔罕〕使像(某人,物)。4. 〔古〕仿造,摹写,画肖像。*They ~ each other in shape*. 他们形态相像。

re·send [riˈsend; riˋsɛnd] *vt*. (**-sent**, **-send·ing**) 再送,再寄;重派;再发;退还,送还。

re·sent [riˈzent; rɪˋzɛnt] *vt*. 憎恨,愤恨。

re·sent·ful [riˈzentful; rɪˋzɛntfl] *a*. 愤怒的,愤慨的;易发脾气的,易怒的;显然不满的。**-ly** *ad*. **-ness** *n*.

re·sent·ment [riˈzentmənt; rɪˋzɛntmənt] *n*. 愤怒,愤慨;怨恨,憎恨。*harbor* [*cherish*] ~ (*against*) 对…怀恨。

re·ser·pine [riˈsəːpin, -piːn, ˈresəˌpiːn; rɪˋsɝˌpɪn, -pin, ˋrɛsəpɪn] *n*. 【药】利血平。**re·ser·pi·nized** *a*. 用利血平治疗[处理]过的,被投给过利血平的。

res·er·va·tion [ˌrezə(ː)ˈveiʃən; ˌrɛzɚˋveʃən] *n*. 1. (权利等的)保留;保留下来的权利;条件,限制,除外条件,但书。2. 〔常 *pl*.〕(房间、座位等的)包定,租定,预定,预约。3. 〔古〕隐讳。4. 保留地;专用地;禁猎地;〔美、加拿大〕(给印第安人指定的)居留地。5. 【宗】留给(病人等的)一部分圣餐。6. (教皇对)圣职任命权的保留;(高级圣职者对)特殊罪恶赦免权的保留。7. 【法】(让与或贷借财产时的)特殊权益保留权;保留权益。***make ~s*** 定座,定房间(等);附保留条件;声名。***without*** ~ 直率地,坦白地;无条件地。***with ~s*** 有保留地(*I agree with you, but with some ~s*. 我同意你,不过有几点要保留[除外])。***write for ~s*** 写信去预定座位(等)。

R

re·serve [riˈzəːv; rɪˋzɝv] I *vt*. 1. 保留;留下(以备后用、享受等)。2. 预定,预约,租定,包,定(座位、房间等)。3. 贮藏,储备。4. 把…除外,附加但书,限制。5. 改期(宣判等)。6. 订约保留(某种权益)。7. 〔罕〕让活着;救命。8. 【宗】留出(部分圣餐);保留(特赦权)。9. 注定。*All rights ~d*. 所有权利全部保留;版权所有,不许翻印。*This discovery was ~d for Columbus*. 一直等到哥伦布才来完成这一发现。*A great future is ~d for you*. 远大的前程等着你。*All seats ~d*. 所有座位必须预定。~ ***oneself for*** 养精蓄锐以待。II *n*. 1. 贮藏,保存;保留;储备,预备。2. 备用人力[资源];贮藏物。3. 保留地;预备林;猎区。4. 【军】〔常 *pl*.〕后备兵;后援部队;后援舰队;预备舰队;【运】预备队员,候补选手;(博览会等的)预备奖品。5. 【商】准备金,公积金。6. 自制,虚心,谨慎;斟酌,限制,条件,例外。7. 缄默;隐讳,隔阂,冷淡,不坦白。8. 【染】防染物;(电镀用的)防镀剂。9. 【采】埋藏量,(石油)贮量。10. 限价,最低价格。11. 【生化】(溶液,血液等的酸或碱的)储量。*He has a great ~ of energy*. 他绰有余力;他精力充裕。*the first* ~ 预备役[军]。*the second* ~ 后备役[军]。*the gold* ~ (发钞银行的)黄金储备。*proved* ~ 【采】探明贮量。~ *cell* 补充细胞。***be placed on the*** ~ (军舰)被编入后备舰队。***break down all*** ~ (无保留地)消除一切隔阂。***call up the ~s*** 召集预备役。***in*** ~ 留下的,预备的,备用的。***have*** [***keep***] ***in*** ~ 留作预备。***place a ~ upon a house*** 给房子标上拍卖的最低价格。***place to*** ~ 留作备用款[公积]。***with all*** ~ [***all proper ~s***] 有保留地(*We publish this with all ~*. 本处公布此事确否待证)。***throw off*** ~ 消除隔阂。***with*** ~ 有保留地;有条件地;有限制地。***without*** ~ 不客气地,坦白地,直言不讳地;无限制地,无保留地(*sale without ~* 不限价拍卖)。III *a*. 后备的,准备的,多余的。*one's ~ strength* 潜力。*a ~ bank* 〔美〕准备银行,储备银行。*a ~ city* 〔美〕(市内国立银行保有一定黄金储备的)准备市。*a ~ fund* 储备金,公积金。*a ~ tank* 【机】后备油箱。*a ~ tooth* 永久齿。*a ~ price* 最低拍卖限价。~ *speed* 〔美军俚〕最大速度。～ **clause** 保留条款〔职业运动员与某一团体签立的合同中,该团体保有自动延长合同期限,以及解约前该运动员一切活动全部受约束的条款〕。～ **officer** 预备军官。

re·served [riˈzəːvd; rɪˋzɝvd] ***a*** . **1.** 保留的,留作专用的;包定的,预定的,预约的。**2.** 有隔阂的,有保留的;缄默的;有节制的,谨慎的;冷淡的。**3.** 储藏着的,保存着的。*a ～ seat* 预定的座位。*a ～ car* 包定的汽车。*a ～ army* 后备军 (*opp*. active army)。a ～ *price* 最低拍卖价格。**-ly** ***ad*** .

re·serv·ist [riˈzəːvist; rɪˋzɝvɪst] ***n*** . 后备役军人。

res·er·voir [ˈrezəvwɑː; ˋrɛzə-ˏvɔr] **I** ***n*** . **1.** 贮藏所;贮气筒;贮水池,水库;贮水槽,水槽;贮存器;贮油器,油筒,油箱;贮墨管;【解】贮液囊。**2.** (知识、精力等的)贮藏,蓄积。*an air ～* 气槽。*a depositing* [*settling*] *～* 澄清池。*a distributing ～* 配水池。*a receiving ～* 集水池。*a storing ～* 贮水池。*a seminal ～*【解】贮精囊。*the Ming Tomb R-* 十三陵水库。*a ～-pen* 自来水笔。**II** ***vt*** . 贮藏;在…设贮藏所[贮水槽]。

re·set [ˈriːˈset; ˋriˏsɛt] ***vt*** . , ***n*** . 重新安放,重新安装;重排(铅字);重镶,重嵌(宝石);重磨(刀具等);【电讯】重调,重安设;【物】(使)复位,转接;零位设置;【医】重接(断骨),接骨;【园艺】移栽(植物)。*a ～ button* 重复起动按钮。

re·set·tle [ˈriːˈsetl; riˋsɛtl̩] ***vt*** . 使重新安居;使在新地方定居;使再殖民。～ *oneself* 再坐下来 (*in*; *on*);使(纠纷等)恢复安定,再度澄清。— ***vi*** . 再坐下,再就席。**-ment** ***n*** .

resh [reiʃ; reʃ] ***n*** . 希伯来语第二十个字母。

re·shape [ˈriːˈʃeip; riˋʃep] ***vt*** . 给…以新形态[新方针];改造。— ***vi*** . 采取新形式;打开新局面。*Affairs are gradually reshaping themselves*. 事情在慢慢地转变着。

re·ship [ˈriːˈʃip; riˋʃɪp] ***vt*** . 把…再装上船;重新装船;把…改装别船。～ *oneself* 再上船,换搭另一船。— ***vi*** . 再上船;(船员)签订另一次航行合同。

re·ship·ment [ˈriːˈʃipmənt; riˋʃɪpmənt] ***n*** . (货物的)重装,转载,换船;重装货物;重装量。

re·shuf·fle [ˈriːˈʃʌfl; riˋʃʌfl̩] **I** ***vt*** . **1.** 重新洗(牌)。**2.** 〔喻〕改组(政府等),重新安排[布置](事件)。**II** ***n*** . **1.** (牌的)重洗。**2.** 〔喻〕(政府等的)改组;重新配置,(事件的)重新安排。

re·sid [riˈzid; rɪˋzɪd] ***n*** . 【石油】残油,渣油。

re·side [riˈzaid; rɪˋzaɪd] ***vi*** . **1.** 住,居住 (*in*; *at*);(官吏)留驻,驻在。**2.** (性质)存在,具备 (*in*);(权力、权利等)属于,归于 (*in*)。*The real power ～s in the people*. 真正的权力属于人民;真正的力量在于人民。

res·i·dence [ˈrezidəns; ˋrɛzədəns] ***n*** . **1.** 居住,居留;驻在;居住期间;宅邸,公馆;(权利等的)所在。**2.** (污染物质等在介质中的)留存,滞留。*R- is required*. 须居住在任所。*an official ～* 官邸。*Desirable family ～ for sale*. 优良住宅出售〔广告文〕。***have*** [***keep***] ***one's*** ～ 住,居住。***in*** ～ (官吏)驻在(任地);住在官邸;(大学教职人员)寄宿(校内)。***take up one's*** ～ (***in***) 住入…,住进…。

res·i·dent [ˈrezidənt; ˋrɛzədənt] **I** ***a*** . **1.** 居住的 (*at*; *in*; *abroad*)。**2.** 驻节的。**3.**【动】不迁徙的(鸟兽等)(*opp*. migratory)。**4.** 固有的;内在的。**5.**【计】常驻的,常存于内存中的。*the ～ population* 居民,现住人口。～ *aliens* 外侨。*the ～ physician of a hospital* 住院医生。*a ～ minister* = *a minister ～* 驻节公使〔地位仅次于全权公使〕。*a ～ tutor* 住家家庭教师。***be*** ～ ***at*** [***in***] 住在…。***whether*** ～ ***at home or abroad*** 无论住在国内国外。**II** ***n*** . 住户,居民,侨民;驻扎官;驻节公使;【动】留鸟。*foreign ～s* 外侨。*summer ～s* 避暑客。

res·i·den·tial [ˌreziˈdenʃəl; ˏrɛzəˋdɛnʃəl] ***a*** . 住宅的;适宜作住宅的;关于居住的。*a ～ district* [*quarter*, *section*] 住宅区。**-ly** ***ad*** .

res·i·den·tia·ry [ˌreziˈdenʃəri; ˏrɛzəˋdɛnʃɪˏɛrɪ] **I** ***a*** . 居住的(人民等);应留在任地的,驻在的。**II** ***n*** . 居住者;【宗】住守教堂的牧师〔又名 canon ～〕;住院僧。

re·sid·u·al [riˈzidjuəl; rɪˋzɪdʒuəl] **I** ***a*** . 残余的,剩下的;残留的;残渣的;未加说明的;【数】残数的,留数的。**II** ***n*** . **1.** 残余;【数】残数,留数;余差;渣滓;【地】残丘;【心】记忆痕迹,【医】后遗症。**2.** 上演税〔商业电影等每次重新上演付给作家及演员等的酬金〕。～ **current device**【电】剩余电流装置〔一种极灵敏的可切断电流的断路器,缩写为 RCD〕。～ **error**【数】残差。～ **oil**【石油】残油。～ **products** 副产物。～ **property**【法】剩余财产,余产。

re·sid·u·a·ry [riˈzidjuəri; rɪˋzɪdʒuˏɛrɪ] ***a*** . 残余的,剩余的;残渣的;【法】接受[处理]剩余财产的,余产的。～ *odds and ends* 剩下的零碎东西,零头。*a ～ estate*【法】余产。*a ～ legatee* 余产承受人。

res·i·due [ˈrezidjuː; ˋrɛzəˏdju] ***n*** . 残余,残渣,余款;【林】废材,木屑;【法】剩余遗产,余产;【化】残基;滤渣;余渣,残余物;【数】残数,留数,余数。***for the*** ～ 至于其余;说到其他。

re·sid·u·um [riˈzidjuəm; rɪˋzɪdʒuəm] ***n*** . (*pl*. ***re·sid·u·a*** [riˈzidjuə; rɪˋzɪdjuə]) **1.** 残余,剩余物;【化】残渣,残留物;残留产物;残(渣)油副产品;【数】剩余;残差。**2.**【法】余产。**3.** 社会底。**4.** 社会渣滓。

re·sign [riˈzain; ˏriˋsaɪn] ***vt*** . **1.** 辞去(职务)。**2.** 放弃,抛弃(权利等);让出(工作等)。**3.** 〔用反身代词或用被动语态〕委身给,听从,服从。**4.** 委托,把…交托给 (*to*)。*He ～ed his seat to a lady*. 他给一位女士让座。*be ～ed to one's fate* 听天由命了。～ ***one's child to sb.'s care*** 委托某人照顾自己的孩子。***be ～ed to a state of lagging behind*** 甘居下游,自甘落后。***not*** ～ ***oneself to*** 不甘心。～ ***oneself to*** 听任;只好(做某事) (*to sth*., *to do*) (～ *oneself to waiting* [*to wait*] *till next morning* 只好等到明天再说。～ *oneself to extinction* 束手待毙。～ *oneself to another's guidance* 听任别人指导。*We must ～ ourselves to doing without a domestic help*. 我们只好不用仆人)。— ***vi*** . **1.** 辞职,退职,退出 (*from*)。**2.** 服从。～ (*from*) *one's office* 〔美〕辞职。～ *to one's fate* 听天由命。

re-sign [riːˈsain; riˋzaɪn] ***vt*** . 重新签署。

res·ig·na·tion [ˌrezigˈneiʃən; ˏrɛzɪgˋneʃən] ***n*** . **1.** 辞职,退职,让位;辞呈。**2.** 抛弃,断念。**3.** (对于命运等的)听从,服从,听任。***accept sb.'s*** ～ 准予辞职。***give in*** [***hand in***] ***one's*** ～ = *send in one's* ～. ***meet one's fate with*** ～ 听天由命。～ ***under instruction*** 着令免职。***send in*** [***tender***] ***one's*** ～ 提出辞呈。

re·signed [riˈzaind; rɪˋzaɪnd] ***a*** . **1.** 〔被动用法〕已辞职的,已告退的;已放弃的。**2.** 〔反身被动用法〕听从…的(摆布);(断了某念头而)决心[只好]做某事的〔后接介词 to, 美国口语中可接不定式〕。*be ～ to die* 决心一死。**-ly** ***ad*** .

re·sile [riˈzail; rɪˋzaɪl] ***vi*** . **1.** 跳回,弹回;有弹力,能恢复原状;很快就恢复(精神),恢复愉快情绪。**2.** 折回,回来。**3.** (契约等)被撤回,取消 (*from*);畏缩,躲避;怕 (*from*)。

re·sil·i·ence, -en·cy [riˈziliəns, -si; rɪˋzɪlɪəns, -sɪ] ***n*** . 跳回,弹回;弹性;恢复工;精神恢复(力)。

re·sil·i·ent [riˈziliənt; rɪˋzɪlɪənt] ***a*** . **1.** 跳回的,弹回的;有弹性的。**2.** 能立刻恢复精神的;心情开朗的。～ *steel* 弹性钢。

res·in [ˈrezin; ˋrɛzn] **I** ***n*** . 树脂;松脂;树脂状沉淀物。～ *opal*【矿】脂光蛋白石。*acrylate* [*acrylic*] ～ 玻璃状可塑物。**II** ***vt*** . 涂树脂;用树脂处理。～ *tapping* 采收树脂。

res·in·ate [ˈreziˌneit; ˋrɛzɪˏnet] ***vt*** . (***-at·ed***; ***-at·ing***) 用树脂浸透[处理]。

res·in·if·er·ous [ˌreziˈnifərəs; ˏrɛznˋɪfərəs] *a*.【化】含有树脂的,含脂的。

res·in·oid [ˈreznˌɔid; ˋrɛzɪˏnɔɪd] **I** *a*.【化】似树脂的。**II** *n*. 1. 树脂型物。2. 树胶脂(= gum resin)。

res·in·ous [ˈrezinəs; ˋrɛznəs] *a*. 1. 树脂质的;含树脂的;用树脂做的。2.〔罕〕【电】阴电性的,负电性的。~ *electricity* 阴电。

res·i·pis·cence [ˌresiˈpisəns; ˏrɛsəˋpɪsəns] *n*. 认错;悔过自新。

re·sist [riˈzist; rɪˋzɪst] **I** *vt*. 1. 抵抗,反抗,抗拒,敌对,抵御,阻止,击退(敌人、侵略等);妨碍,阻碍。2. 忍耐(艰苦等);抵制(疾病等);〔主与否定语连用〕忍住(笑等)。3. 反对,不赞成(提案等);蔑视,违背(法律等)。*~ing force* 抵抗力。~ *heat* 耐热。*a cement that will ~ damp* 抗[耐]湿水泥。~ *law* 违抗法律。*I cannot ~ a joke*. 我听了一个笑话总忍不住要笑出来;我想起一个笑话总忍不住要说出来。*I can never ~ strawberries and cream*. 我一看见奶油草莓就非吃不可。— *vi*. 抵抗;反对;抵制。**II** *n*. 防染剂,(印染花布用的)排色物;防蚀用涂料;防腐剂。

re·sist·ance [reˈzistəns; rɪˋzɪstəns] *n*. 1. 抵抗,反抗,抗拒,抵御;敌对,抵抗力,反抗力,阻力,【生】抗病性。2.【电】电阻;阻抗;电阻器。*electric ~* 电阻。*abrasive ~* 耐磨力[度]。*dead ~* 吸收[消耗,镇流]电阻。*passive ~* 无源电阻;消极抵抗。***a piece of ~*** 主要品,压轴,出类拔萃的东西;主菜,压桌菜(= pièce de résistance)。***make some* [*no*] *~*** 进行[不]抵抗。***offer* [*put up*] *~ to* [*against*]** 抵抗。~ ***welding*** 电阻焊接,电焊。***take the line of least ~*** 采取阻力最小的路线;采取最省力的方法。~**-box** 电阻箱[器]。

re·sist·ant [riˈzistənt; rɪˋzɪstənt] **I** *a*. 抵抗的;耐久的,稳定的。**II** *n*. 抵抗者;有抵抗力的东西;防染剂,防腐剂。

re·sist·i·ble [riˈzistəbl; rɪˋzɪstəbl̩] *a*. 可抵抗的,可反抗的,可反对的;抵抗得住的。

re·sis·tive [riˈzistiv; rɪˋzɪstɪv] *a*. = resistant.

re·sis·tiv·i·ty [ˌri:zisˈtiviti; ˏrizɪsˋtɪvətɪ] *n*. 抵抗力;抵抗(性);【电】电阻率;电阻系数,比阻。

re·sist·less [riˈzistlis; rɪˋzɪstlɪs] *a*. 1. 不可抗的;不可避免的。2. 不抵抗的;无抵抗力的。**-ly** *ad*.

re·sist·o·jet [riˈzistəˌdʒet; rɪˋzɪstəˏdʒɛt] *n*. 电阻加热电离式发动机。

re·sis·tor [riˈzistə; rɪˋzɪstɚ] *n*.【电】电阻(器)。

re·sole [ˈri:ˈsəul; riˋsol] *vt*. 给(鞋)换底[换前掌]。

re·sol·u·ble [riˈzɔljubl; rɪˋzɑljəbl̩] *a*. 1. 可分解的,可溶解的(*into*)。2. 可解决的。

res·o·lute [ˈrezəlju:t; ˋrɛzəˏlut] **I** *a*. 坚决的,毅然的;坚定的。**II** *n*. 坚定的人,果敢的人。**-ly** *ad*.

res·o·lu·tion [ˌrezəˈlju:ʃən; ˏrɛzəˋljuʃən] *n*. 1. 决心,果断;坚定,刚毅。2. (议会等的)决定,决议(案);【法】〔罕〕判决;(疑问等的)解决,解答。3. 分解,溶解;解析,离析;变形,变化,转化。4.【医】(疮肿等的)消散;〔罕〕松弛。5.【乐】由不谐和音转变为谐和音;【诗】用二短音节代替一长音节。6.【机】分解力;【自】分辨(力)。*a man of no ~ of character* 意志不坚定的人。*visual ~* 目力分辨率。*come to a ~ = from* [*make, take*] *a ~* 决心。*make good ~s* 下定改好的决心。*pass a ~ in favour of* [*against*] 通过赞同[反对]…的决议。

res·o·lu·tive [ˈrezəlju:tiv; ˋrɛzəˏljutɪv] **I** *a*. 使溶解的,使分解的;【医】消散的;【法】解除的。**II** *n*. 消散药。*a ~ clause* [*condition*]【法】解除条款[条件]。

re·solv·a·bil·i·ty [riˌzɔlvəˈbiliti; rɪˏzɑlvəˋbɪlətɪ] *n*. 1. 分解[溶解]的可能;可分析性;可溶解性。2. 可解决性。

re·solv·a·ble [riˈzɔlvəbl; rɪˋzɑlvəbl̩] *a*. 1. 可解析的;可溶解的。2. 可解决的。

re·solve [riˈzɔlv; rɪˋzɑlv] **I** *vt*. 1. (使)下决心,决议。2. 决定;决议。3. 使分解,使解体;解析,溶解(化合物)。4. 使消释;解释(疑惑等),解决(问题等);分辨。5. 变成,转化为。6. 消退(炎症等)。7.【乐】使不谐和音转变为谐和音。*This discovery ~d us to go*. 是这一发现使我们决心去的。*I ~d to give up smoking*. = *I ~d that I would give up smoking*. 我决心戒烟了。*It was ~d that* ....(会议)议决…。~ *doubts* 使疑惑冰释。*be ~d to* (*do*) ...决心(做…)。~ *itself into* 分解成,还原;终归成为(*The House ~d itself into a committee*. 整个议会已改变成委员会了)。*resolving power*【物】分辨本领;分辨率。— *vi*. 1. 决心,决定(*on, upon*)。2. 分解,解体;溶解;解析;分辨;还原。3. 归结于,变成,成为(*into*)。4. (疮肿)消散。5.【乐】变成谐和音。6.【法】失效,消失。*She ~d on making an early start*. 她决定早早出发。**II** *n*. 决心,坚定,不屈不挠,刚毅;〔美〕(议会等的)议决。*a man of ~* 刚毅的人。*deeds of high ~* 果敢的行为。***keep one's ~*** 坚持。***make a ~*** 下决心。

re·solved [riˈzɔlvd; rɪˋzɑlvd] *a*. 坚决的,断然的;决心的。**-ly** *ad*.

re·solv·ent [riˈzɔlvənt; rɪˋzɑlvənt] **I** *a*.【医、化】使分解的;有溶解力的;消散性的。**II** *n*. 1. 分解物;溶剂;消散药;【数】预解(式)。2. (事件等的)解决办法。

re·solv·er [riˈzɔlvə; rɪˋzɑlvɚ] *n*. 1. 下决心者。2. 解决者;解答者。3. 分解器;【化】溶剂,溶媒。

res·o·nance [ˈrezənəns; ˋrɛznəns] *n*. 1. 回声,反响;【物】共鸣,共振;【无】(波长的)调谐。2.【化】中介(现象)。3.【医】叩响。4.【天】(同一天体的两种运动间或两个天体运动间的)同步。*atomic ~* 原子共振。*fission ~* 裂变反应共振。~ **box**, ~ **chamber**【物】共振箱。~ **level**【物】共振级。

res·o·nant [ˈrezənənt; ˋrɛznənt] *a*. 共振的;能共鸣的;反响的,有回声的。**-ly** *ad*.

res·o·nate [ˈrezəˌneit; ˋrɛzəˏnet] *vi*. (*-nat·ed*; *-nat·ing*) 1. 回响,共鸣,反响。2. 产生共鸣,产生反响;产生共振。3.【天】同步运动。— *vt*. 使共鸣,使反响,使共振。

re·sona·tor [ˈrezəneitə; ˋrɛzəˏnetɚ] *n*. 谐振器,共鸣器。

re·sorb [riˈsɔ:b; rɪˋsɔrb] *vt*. 1. 再吸收,再吸入,重新吸收,再吞。2. 消溶。**-sorp·tion** [-ˈsɔ:pʃən; -ˋsɔrpʃən] *n*. **-sorp·tive** *a*.

res·or·cin·ol [riˈzɔ:siˌnəul, -nɔ:l; rɛzˋɔrsɪˏnol, -nɔl] *n*.【化】间苯二酚,雷琐辛(= resorcin)。

re·sort [riˈzɔ:t; rɪˋzɔrt] **I** *n*. 1. 热闹场所,娱乐场;常去[人多]的地方,胜地。2. 常去;人多;人群。3. 倚靠,凭藉;手段。*a place of great ~* 人们常去的热闹地方。*a place of public ~* 娱乐场所。*a fashionable ~* 高级游乐地。*a holiday ~* 假日游乐地。*a health ~* 疗养地。*a pleasure ~* 游乐胜地。*a ~ of thieves* 贼窝。*a summer* [*winter*] *~* 避暑[避寒]地。*A carriage was the only ~*. 乘马车是唯一的办法。*He encouraged the ~ of scholars*. 他鼓励学者常去访问。***have ~ to*** (*force*) 用(武力),动(武)。***in the last ~*** 作为最后的一着[手段],终于。***without ~*** 无计可施。**II** *vi*. 1. 去,常去,群往,会集(*to*)。2. 倚靠,凭藉,采用(某种手段)。*the inn to which he was known to ~* 他常去的客栈。~ ***to*** (***armed force***) 使用(武力),诉诸(武力)。***without ~ing to*** (***force***) 不使用(武力)。

re-sort [ˈri:ˈsɔ:t; ˏriˋzɔrt] *vt*. 把…再分类,再分级。

re·sound [riˈzaund; rɪˋzaund] *vi*. 回响;反响(*with*);(名声等)轰传,传遍(*through*)。*Radios ~ from every house*. 家家户户传出收音机的广播声。— *vt*. 1. 反响;使回响。2. 高声响;使(某地)充满声响。3. 赞扬;传播。

re·sound·ing [riˈzaundiŋ; rɪˋzaundɪŋ] *a*. 1. 反响的,共鸣的;响亮的,宏亮的。2. 彻底的,完全的。3. 夸张的,虚夸的。*a ~ victory* 彻底的胜利,完全的胜利。**-ly** *ad*.

re·source [riˈsɔ:s; rɪˋsors] *n*. 1. 〔*pl*.〕资源;物力,财力。2. 方法,手段;机智,智谋,才略。3. 消遣,娱乐。*natu-*

R

ral ~*s* 自然资源。*hidden* ~*s* 地下资源。*Flight was his only* ~. 他只有逃走一法。*Reading is a great* ~ *in illness*. 读书是病中极好消遣。*He is lost without* ~. 他彻底完蛋[失败]了。***a man of no*** ~***s*** 无资力的人;毫无办法的人;闲极无聊的人。***at the end of one's*** ~***s*** 山穷水尽;无计可施。***be full of*** ~***(s)*** 富有机智。*be thrown on one's own* ~*s* 除独自努力外别无他法。**-ful** ***a***. **-ful·ly** ***ad***.

re·spect [ris'pekt; rɪ`spɛkt] **I** ***n***. **1.** 尊敬,尊重;〔*pl*.〕敬意,问候,请安。**2.** 注意,关心。**3.** 关系;着眼点,方面;细目。**4.**〔古〕偏袒;事由,动机,目的。***give one's*** ~***s to*** 向…致候。***have*** ~ ***for*** 尊敬;尊重,重视。***have*** ~ ***to*** 关心;筹划;与…有关系。***hold in*** ~ 尊敬。***in all*** ~***s*** = ***in every*** ~ 无论从哪方面[哪一点]来看;在各方面。***in no*** ~ 无论在哪方面[哪一点]都不是…;完全不是…。***in*** ~ ***that*** 因为…;如果考虑到…。***in*** ~ ***to*** [***of***] 关于,就…来说,对…有影响的。***in that*** [***this***] ~ 在那一[这一]方面。***no*** ~ ***of persons with*** 对…无所偏袒。***pay one's*** ~***s to*** 向…请安,向…致敬〔常作反语用〕,拜望,拜访。***pay*** ~ ***to*** 斟酌,考虑,关心。***send one's*** ~***s to*** 向…问候。***win the*** ~ ***of all*** 处处受人尊敬。***with all*** ~ ***for your opinion*** 你的意见很好;可是…。***with*** ~ ***to*** = *in* ~ *to*. ***without*** ~ ***to*** [***of***] 不考虑…,不管…。**II** ***vt***. **1.** 尊敬;尊重;不侵犯,不妨害。**2.** 注意,重视,关心。**3.** 关于。~ *sb.'s silence* 尊重别人的沉默;不随便跟人谈话。~ *privileges* [*property, neutral territory*] 尊重[或不侵犯]特权[所有权、中立地带]。***as*** ~***s*** 关于,说到。~ ***oneself*** 自重。

re·spect·a·bil·ity [ris,pektə'biliti; rɪ,spɛktə`bɪlətɪ] ***n***. **1.** 可尊敬,人格高尚,品行端正;威望;尊严,体面。**2.** 可尊重的事物;可尊敬的人;有身分[名望]的人;〔谑〕一本正经的人。**3.**〔*pl*.〕礼仪,习俗。

re·spect·a·ble [ris'pektəbl; rɪ`spɛktəbḷ] ***a***. **1.** 可尊敬的,可尊重的,人格高尚的,品行端正的;有身分的,有相当地位的,有名望的。**2.** 相当大的,可观的,不少的(数量等)。**3.** 不难看的,体面的,大方的,相当好的。**4.** (举止、态度等)过分高雅的,一本正经的,装腔作势的。*the* ~ 有身分的人们。*a* ~ *income* 相当大的[不少的]收入。~ *clothes* 体面的[相当好的]衣服。*a* ~ *hill* 相当大的小山。*a* ~ *painter* 相当有名的画家。*a* ~ *minority* 不小的少数。*He is too* ~ *for my taste*. 那个人太高雅了,我不喜欢。**-bly** ***ad***.

re·spect·ant [ris'pektənt; rɪ`spɛktənt] ***a***.【徽】(动物)面对面的;向后看的。

re·spect·er [ris'pektə; rɪ`spɛktɚ] ***n***. 尊重者;势利的人。***be no*** ~ ***of persons*** 对任何人一律看待(*The law is no* ~ *of persons*. 法律面前人人平等)。~ ***of persons*** 势利鬼,趋炎附势的人。

re·spect·ful [ris'pektful; rɪ`spɛktfəl] ***a***. **1.** 尊重人的,表示敬意的;谦恭的,有礼貌的,殷勤的。**2.**〔古〕可尊敬的。***be*** ~ ***of tradition*** 尊重传统。***be*** ~ ***to age*** 尊敬老人。***keep*** [***stand***] ***at a*** ~ ***distance*** 有礼貌地离着一点;〔喻〕保持一定距离;敬而远之。

re·spect·ful·ly [ris'pektfuli; rɪ`spɛktfulɪ] ***ad***. 恭敬地,殷勤地。*Yours* (*very*) ~ = *R- yours* 谨上,敬礼〔信末用语〕。

re·spect·ing [ris'pektiŋ; rɪ`spɛktɪŋ] ***prep***. 关于…;由于,鉴于。*I am at a loss* ~ *his whereabouts*. 关于他的下落,我一无所知。

re·spec·tive [ris'pektiv; rɪ`spɛktɪv] ***a***. 各自的,各个的,各有分别的。*A and B contributed the* ~ *sums of 4d. and 3d*. A 和 B 的捐款分别是四便士和三便士。*All men have their* ~ *duties*. 各人有各人的职责。

re·spec·tive·ly [ris'pektivli; rɪ`spɛktɪvlɪ] ***ad***. 各自,各别,分别。*The first and second prizes went to Mary and George* ~. 头奖归玛丽所得,二奖归乔治所得。

re·spell ['riː'spel; ri`spɛl] ***vt***. 再拼(单词);以别种形式(尤指按语音系统)另拼(单词)。

re·spir·a·ble ['respiərəbl, ris'paiərəbl; `rɛspɪrəbḷ, rɪ`spaɪrəbḷ] ***a***. **1.** 可呼吸的,适于呼吸的。**2.** 能呼吸的。**-bil·i·ty** ***n***.

res·pi·ra·tion [respi'reiʃən; ,rɛspə`reʃən] ***n***. 呼吸;【生理】呼吸作用。*artificial* ~ 人工呼吸。

res·pi·ra·tor ['respəreitə; `rɛspə,retɚ] ***n***. **1.** 口罩;【军】防尘口罩;防毒面具;【化】滤毒罐。**2.**〔美〕人工呼吸装置。*a canister* ~ 防毒面具。

re·spir·a·to·ry [ris'paiərətəri; rɪ`spaɪrə,torɪ] ***a***. 呼吸(作用)的。~ *organs* 呼吸器官。

re·spire [ris'paiə; rɪ`spaɪr] ***vi***. **1.** 呼吸。**2.** 休息;透一口气。**3.**〔罕〕生存,生活。— ***vt***. **1.** 呼吸。**2.**〔罕〕散发(香气等),表现(情绪等);悄悄透露(爱情等)。

res·pi·rom·e·ter [,respi'rɔmitə; ,rɛspə`rɑmətɚ] ***n***.【医】呼吸(运动)计。**-try** ***n***.【医】呼吸(运动)计量(法)。**-tric** ***a***.

res·pite ['respait, Am. 'respit; `rɛspaɪt, `rɛspɪt] **I** ***n***. **1.** 延期;【法】缓刑。**2.** 暂停;休息,休养;休息期间。*grand a* ~ *to a condemned man* 对判刑的人宣布缓刑。***put in*** ~ 延期,暂缓。***toil without*** ~ 不断地工作。**II** ***vt***. **1.** 延期,缓期执行(死刑)。**2.** 使休息,使(苦痛等)暂时停止,使缓和一下。**3.**【军】停付(军人)薪饷;停付(薪金)。

re·splend·ence, -en·cy [ris'plendəns, -si; rɪ`splɛndəns, -sɪ] ***n***. 辉煌,光辉,光彩。

re·splend·ent [ris'plendənt; rɪ`splɛndənt] ***a***. 辉煌的,灿烂的。~ *with jewels* 带着耀眼的宝石。~ *achievements* 辉煌的成就。~ *in full uniform* 穿着耀眼的全副军装。

re·spond [ris'pɔnd; rɪ`spɑnd] **I** ***vi***. **1.** 答,回答;响应(*to*)。**2.**【宗】(会众对牧师)唱和[例行应答]。**3.** 答应(要求等),应付(敌人等),(对刺激等)感应,反应。**4.**【法】承担责任;〔美〕负责,赔偿。**5.**〔罕〕符合(希望等)。~ *by a nod* 点头答应。~ *for the masses* 代表群众致谢辞。~ *to the cheers of the crowd* 向欢呼的群众挥手致意。~ *with a left hander*【拳击】用左手回击。~ *in damages* 赔偿损失。~ *to the controls* (飞机)好驾驶,对操纵反应灵敏。~ *unsoundly to* 对…不起劲。— ***vt***. 回答,响应;〔美〕应负…的责任,履行;〔古〕一致,符合。~ *the judgement of the court* 履行法院判决。*His great deeds* ~*ed his great speeches*. 他的巨大事业体现[符合]了他的豪言壮语。**II** ***n***.【宗】应唱圣歌;【建】(柱、拱基等的)对称;壁联。

re·spond·ence, -en·cy [ris'pɔndəns, -si; rɪ`spɑndəns, -sɪ] ***n***. **1.** 相应,适合,符合。**2.** 作答;回答;反应;响应。

re·spond·ent [ris'pɔndənt; rɪ`spɑndənt] **I** ***a***. **1.** 回答的;有反应的,响应的,感应的。**2.**【法】被告的。**3.**〔古〕符合的。**II** ***n***. **1.** 回答者;答辩者;提案辩护者。**2.**【法】(特指离婚诉讼的)被告。**3.**【生理】(对外来刺激的)反应,反射。*The knee jerk is a typical* ~. 膝反射是一种典型反射。

res·pon·den·tia [,respɔn'denʃiə; ,rispɑn`dɛnʃɪə] ***n***. 船货抵押借款;冒险借款。

re·spond·er [ri'spɔndə; rɪ`spɑndɚ] ***n***. **1.** 响应者,回答者。**2.**【电】应答机。

re·sponse [ri'spɔns; rɪ`spɑns] ***n***. **1.** 回答,答复。**2.**【宗】应唱圣歌。**3.** (因刺激等引起的)感应,反应,反响;应验;【物】响应;【无】灵敏度,感扰性;特性曲线。*His oratorical efforts evoked no* ~ *in his audience*. 他的雄辩在听众中不起反响。***call forth no*** ~ ***in sb.'s breast*** 在某人心中不起反应。***in*** ~ ***to*** 应…而,答…而。***make no*** ~ 不回答。

re·spon·si·bil·i·ty [ri,spɔnsə'biliti; rɪ,spɑnsə`bɪlətɪ] ***n***. **1.** 责任;责任心;职责,义务 (*of*; *for*);负担。**2.**〔美〕义务履行能力,偿付能力。**3.**【无】响应性[度]。*the person with overall* ~ *in the locality* 一个地区的总负

责人。*be relieved of one's* ～[*responsibilities*](被)解除责任。*decline all* ～ *for* 声明对…不负任何责任。*lack of* ～ 无人负责现象。*on one's own* ～ 自作主张地。*take* [*assume*] *the* ～ *of* [*for*] 负起…的责任。*take the* ～ *upon oneself* 自己承担起责任来。

re·spon·si·ble [riˈspɔnsəbl; rɪˋspɑnsəbl̩] *a*. **1**. 有责任的,应负责任的(*to* sb.; *for a* thing)。**2**. 能负责的,可靠的;懂道理的,明白是非的。**3**. 责任重的(地位等)。*have a* ～ *position* 担任要职。～ *government* 责任政府制。*I am not* ～ *to you for my actions*. 我的行为我没有向你说明的义务。*a* ～ *face* 一本正经的面孔。**hold sb**. ～ **for** 使某人负担…的责任。**make oneself** ～ **for** 负起…的责任。～ **for** 为…负责;是造成…的原因。**-bly** *ad*.

re·spon·sion [risˈpɔnʃən; rɪˋspɑnʃən] *n*. **1**. 〔*pl*.〕〔英〕(牛津大学)B.A. 学位初试〔俗称 smalls〕。**2**. 大学的公开讨论会。**3**. 〔罕〕回答。

re·spon·sive [risˈpɔnsiv; rɪˋspɑnsɪv] *a*. 回答的;表示回答的;反应迅速的,易反应的,共鸣的,敏感的;唱应答歌的。*a* ～ *glance* 带有回答意义的一瞥。**-ly** *ad*. **-ness** *n*.

re·spon·so·ry [risˈpɔnsəri; rɪˋspɑnsərɪ] *n*. 【宗】应答歌。

res·pu·bli·ca [resˈpʌblikə, -ˈpu:bli:-; rizˋpʌblɪkə, -ˋpubli-] [L.] *n*. 国家,联邦,共和国。

res·sen·ti·ment [rəˌsɑ:nti:ˈmɑn; rəsɑntiˋmɑn] *n*. 〔F.〕【社】(阶级、阶层或集团间的)仇恨,憎恶。

rest[1] [rest; rɛst] **I** *n*. **1**. 休息,休养,【军】稍息。**2**. 停止,静止;安静,安稳;安心。**3**. 睡眠;长眠;死。**4**. 休息处,安歇处,住处;床。**5**. 台,架,托,支柱;(枪炮的)瞄准台。**6**. 停顿;【乐】休止;休止符。*the day of* ～ 休息日;假日;星期日;【宗】安息日。*a good night's* ～ 一夜的充分休息;一晚好睡。*a tripod* ～ 三脚架。*an eighth* ～ 八分休止符。**at** ～ 静止的,安宁的,心情安定的;长眠,死;解决了的,不必再谈的(*a volcano at* ～ 静止的火山)。*bring a machine to* ～ 停止机器。*go to one's* ～ 永眠,死。*go to* ～ 去睡;去休息。*lay to* ～ 安葬;完全消除;完全解决。*put at* ～ 使安心;使休息;予以解决。*retire to* ～ 去睡;去休息。*set at* ～ = *put at* ～. *set sb.'s mind at* ～ 安定人心,使安心。*set up one's* ～ 居住,定居。*take a* ～ 休息一下。*take* (*one's*) ～ 休息,睡觉,就寝。**II** *vi*. **1**. 休息,歇息;静止,停止;〔美〕【法】停止举证。**2**. 躺,靠(*on*; *upon*; *against*)。**3**. 搁在,安置在(台上等);根据,以…为基础(*on*; *upon*)。**4**. 睡,长眠,死。**5**. 信赖;安心,满足(于某事)(*on*; *upon*)。**6**. (成功、决定)系于,在于,在…的权限内(*with*)。**7**. 归于。*I* ～*ed well*. 我睡得好。*I am* ～*ed and refreshed*. 我精神恢复了。*I cannot* ～ *under an imputation*. 我不能甘受诬陷。*Science* ～*s on phenomena*. 科学以现象为根据。*The matter cannot* ～ *here*. 这个事情不能就此搁置不管。～ *in oneself* 依靠[信赖]自己。～ *in peace* 安静永眠。～ *in pieces* 〔美〕炸死。～ *on* [*upon*] 被支持在…上,搁在…上,以…为基础,依靠,信任;(目光等)停留在…上,落在…上。～ *on one's arms* 枕戈待旦,警惕着。～ *on one's oars* (停划)靠着桨暂时休息;喘一口气,休息一下。～ *on* [*in*] *sb.'s promise* 相信[指望]某人的诺言。～ *with* 取决于,属于…的权限(*The decision* ～*s with you*. = *It* ～*s with you to decide*. 决定在你。*The honours* ～*ed with him*. 荣誉归他)。— *vt*. **1**. 使休息,使歇息,(使)休养;使轻松,使恢复精神;使平静;【军】使稍息。**2**. 安放,搁置;把…靠在(*on*; *against*)。**3**. 〔美〕【法】对…停止举证。～ *the ladder against the wall* 把梯子靠在墙上。～ *oneself* 休养。～ *the* [*sb.'s*] *case* 〔美〕对某人某案停止举证。～ **cure** 【医】(特指精神病的)卧床疗养法。～ **day** 休息日;假日;〔罕〕星期日;【宗】安息日。～ **energy** 【物】静能。～ **house** 客栈;休养所;〔美俚〕监狱。～ **mass** 【物】静质量。～ **period** 【生】休眠期。～ **room** (车站、戏院的)休息室;〔美〕厕所。**-ful** *a*. 平静的,安静的,悠闲的。

rest[2] [rest; rɛst] **I** *n*. **1**. 〔the ～〕其余,其他,残余部分。**2**. 〔the ～〕〔作复数处理〕残留的人;其余的人[物]。**3**. 〔英〕【银行】〔the ～〕公积金,准备金。**4**. 【网球】连续回击(时间)。*You know the* ～. = *The* ～ *needs no telling*. 其余不必再说。**among the** ～ 其中,尤其(*myself among the* ～ 我也是其中之一)。**and** (**all**) **the** ～ (**of it**) 其他一切,等等。**as to the** ～ 至于其余各点[其他方面]。**for the** ～ 其后,至于其余(*for the* ～ *of one's life* 就其余生。*for the* ～ *of the day* 在这天的其余时间)。**II** *vi*. 〔与表语[主词补语]连用〕依然是,仍旧是;保持;〔古〕留下。*The mistakes* ～ *uncorrected*. 错误仍旧没有更正。～ **assured** 请放心(*R-* [*You may* ～] *assured that I will do my best*. 请放心,我一定尽力)。～ **satisfied** [**content**] 满意[心满意足]。

re·stamp [ri:ˈstæmp; riˋstæmp] *vt*. 另[重新]盖印;另贴邮票。

re·start [ri:ˈstɑ:t; riˋstɑrt] *vt*., *vi*. 重新开始。

re·state [ˈri:ˈsteit; riˋstet] *vt*. 重申;再声明;重新陈述。**-ment** *n*.

res·tau·rant [ˈrestərɔ̃:ŋ, -rɔnt; ˋrɛstərənt, -ˏrɑnt] *n*. 餐馆;(大旅馆等的)餐厅。*a* ～ *car* 餐车。

res·tau·ra·teur [ˈrestɔ(:)rəˈtə:; ˏrɛstərəˋtɚ] *n*. 〔F.〕餐馆老板。

rest·har·row [ˈresthærəu; ˋrɛstˏhæro] *n*. 【植】芒柄花(属)。

res·ti·form [ˈrestiˌfɔ:m; ˋrɛstəˏfɔrm] *a*. 【解】索状的。

rest·ing [ˈrestiŋ; ˋrɛstɪŋ] *a*. **1**. 不动的,静止的;沉默的。**2**. 【植】休眠的,静止的。**3**. 【生理】静止的,不积极分裂的。～ **place** [ˈrestiŋpleis; ˋrɛstɪŋples] *n*. **1**. 休息所[室]。**2**. 坟墓。**3**. 【建】= landing. *the last* ～ *place* 坟墓。

res·ti·tute [ˈrestitju:t; ˋrɛstəˏtjut] *vt*., *vi*. **1**. 赔偿(损失等);归还(夺去物等)。**2**. 〔罕〕恢复,复旧。

res·ti·tu·tion [ˌrestiˈtju:ʃən; ˏrɛstəˋtjuʃən] *n*. **1**. 赔偿;归还;复职。**2**. 恢复;【物】(因弹性体的)复原;【化】复原取代(作用)。**3**. 【法】要求恢复原状的诉讼。*make* ～ 赔偿损失,归还。～ **nucleus** 再组核。～ **of conjugal rights** 【法】夫妇同居权的恢复。～ **suit** 【法】恢复夫妇同居权的诉讼。

res·tive [ˈrestiv; ˋrɛstɪv] *a*. 烈性的(马);难驾驭的;不听话的。*a* ～ *person* 倔强的人。**-ly** *ad*. **-ness** *n*.

rest·less [ˈrestlis; ˋrɛstlɪs] *a*. 不安定的,坐卧不宁的;动作不停的;得不到休息的,不休息的;不睡的。*a* ～ *heart* 烦乱不宁的心。*a* ～ *child* 不肯安静的孩子。*a man of* ～ *energy* 精力充沛[不停活动]的人。～ *waves* 动荡不停的波浪。～ **cavy** (拉丁美洲)野狼鼠。～ **leg syndrome** 【医】静坐不适症。**-ly** *ad*.

re·stock [ˈri:ˈstɔk; riˋstɑk] *vt*. 使重新进货;再储存。

re·stor·a·ble [risˈtɔ:rəbl; rɪˋstorəbl̩] *a*. 可恢复原状的;可恢复的;可再兴的;可归还的。

res·to·ra·tion [ˌrestəˈreiʃən; ˏrɛstəˋreʃən] *n*. **1**. (领土等的)恢复,光复;复位,复职;复旧,复古;复兴;归还。**2**. 【建】修复,照原样修复的建筑物;(受损美术品等的)修复,修补;(古动物的)再造,复原。**3**. 复辟;〔the R-〕(英国1660年查理二世的;法国大革命后布尔蓬王朝的)复辟;(日本的)明治维新。*the* ～ *of peace* [*health*] 和平[健康]的恢复。*the* ～ *of a picture* 画的修复。

re·stor·a·tive [risˈtɔ:rətiv; rɪˋstorətɪv] **I** *a*. 复原的;复兴的;恢复健康[元气]的;滋补的。**II** *n*. 恢复剂,补药;补品。**-ly** *ad*. **-ness** *n*.

re·store [risˈtɔ:; rɪˋstor] *vt*. **1**. 拿回原处,恢复原状;复旧;恢复;复活,复兴,再兴(制度、习惯等),使复位,使复职,使复辟。**2**. 归还。**3**. 修理,修补,重建,修复;再造,复原(古生物),补正,校补(书籍中的缺失文字等)。**4**. 使恢复健康[元气],使恢复意识。～ *order* 恢复秩序。～ *to its owner* (把拾物等)归还原主。～ *sb*. *to life* 使人苏

R

醒过来。*be ~d out of all recognition* 修复得一点也认不出。

re·stor·er [ris'tɔːrə; rɪ`storə] *n*. 复原者;修补者;修建者;【无】恢复设备;复位器。*a hair* ~ 生发药。*tired nature's sweet* ~ 睡眠。

re·strain [ris'trein; rɪ`stren] *vt*. **1**. 压抑,抑制。**2**. 制止,防止,禁止。**3**. 拘束,束缚;羁押,监禁。**4**. 限定,限制。*She ~ed tears with difficulty*. 她好容易才忍住了眼泪。*~ sb. from interference* 制止某人干涉。*~ sb. of his liberty* 剥夺某人自由,束缚某人自由。*~ oneself* 自制;克己,忍耐。**-er** *n*. 抑制者;【化】抑制剂。

re·strain·a·ble [ris'trenəbl; rɪs`trɛnəbl̩] *a*. 可抑制的,可遏制的,可制止的。

re·strain·ed [ris'treind; rɪ`strend] *a*. 受限制的;受约束的;克制的,谨严的;忍耐的,拘束的。**-ly** [-li; -lɪ] *ad*.

re·straint [ri'streint; rɪ`strent] *n*. **1**. (活动等的)克制,抑制,制止;禁止。**2**. 拘束,束缚,桎梏;拘束力,牵制力;羁押,监禁。**3**. 自制;拘泥;(表现、记述的)严谨。**4**. 限制。***be beyond*** ~ 不能抑制。***be held in*** ~ 受监禁。***be under*** ~ (尤指精神病人)被拘禁中。***free from*** ~ 无束缚的,自由的。***in*** ~ ***of*** 以便制止。***keep under*** ~ 抑制,束缚。***place under*** ~ 监禁。***put under*** ~ 拘禁,送进疯人院。~ ***of princes*** 【海上保险】出港[入港]的禁止。***with*** ~ 用克制态度。***without*** ~ 无拘束地,自由地;放纵地,肆无忌惮地。

re·strict [ris'trikt; rɪ`strɪkt] *vt*. 限制,限定(*to*; *within*; *in*);制止,禁止。*I am ~ed by time*. 我受时间限制。*I am ~ed to advising*. 我只限于劝导。**-ed** *a*. 有限制的,范围狭窄的;〔美军〕一般保密的(*It has a very ~ed application*. 它的应用范围很窄。*a ~ed area* 禁止通行地区;【美军】闲人止步(地区)。*~ed materials* (内部)参考资料)。**-ed·ly** *ad*.

re·stric·tion [ris'trikʃən; rɪ`strɪkʃən] *n*. **1**. 限制,限定。**2**. 拘束,束缚;自制。**3**. 【逻】限定。*impose* [*lay down*, *place*, *put*] *~s on* 对…加以限制。*remove* [*withdraw*] *~s* 取消限制。*without ~s* 无限制地。

re·stric·tion·ism [ri'strikʃənizm; rɪ`strɪkʃən͵ɪzm] *n*. 限制主义〔如限制贸易的政策,限制移民的政策等〕。**-ist** *n*., *a*.

re·stric·tive [ris'triktiv; rɪ`strɪktɪv] **I** *a*. 限制的;限定的,特定的。**II** *n*. 【语法】限制性词语。**-ly** *ad*. **-ness** *n*.

re·struc·ture [ri'strʌktʃə; rɪ`strʌktʃə] *vt*. (***-tured***; ***-tur·ing***) 重新组织,调整,改组。**re·struc·tur·ing** *n*. 改革〔尤指前苏联戈尔巴乔夫时期实行的改革,与 perestroika 同义〕。

re·stud·y ['riːstʌdi; `ristʌdɪ] *vt*., *n*. 再学习;重新学习;重新估计;重新研究。

re·stuff ['riː'stʌf; ri`stʌf] *vt*. 再充填,重新填塞。

re·sult [ri'zʌlt; rɪ`zʌlt] **I** *n*. **1**. 结果,效果,效验,成效;成绩;〔*pl*.〕【体】比分。**2**. 【数】计算的结果,答案。**3**. 〔美〕(立法机构等的)决议,决定。*to lead to good ~s* 引出好的结果。*The ~ was that* .... 结果是…。***as a*** ~ ***of*** (作)为…的结果。***bring about*** [***yield***] ***good ~s*** 得到好结果[好成绩]。***give out the ~s*** 发表成绩。***in the*** ~ 结果。***meet with good ~s*** 取得好结果。***without*** ~ 无效地,毫无结果地。**II** *vi*. **1**. 结果为(*in*),由…而造成[产生](*from*)。**2**. 归结为,导致(*in*)。*Love ~s in marriage*. 恋爱终归于结婚。*Nothing has ~ed from my efforts*. 我的努力毫无结果。*~ in* (*failure*) 终于(失败)。

re·sult·ant [ri'zʌltənt; rɪ`zʌltənt] **I** *a*. **1**. 〔尤指由若干相反力量所造成〕作为最后结果的;作为后果而产生的。**2**. 【物】组合的,合成的。**II** *n*. **1**. 结果;后果。**2**. 合力,合成力;合成[运动];【物】合量;组合;【化】生成物,(反应)产物;【数】结式;消元式。

re·sult·ful [ri'zʌltful; rɪ`zʌltfl̩] *a*. 有结果的,有效果[效验]的,有效的。

re·sult·less [ri'zʌltlis; rɪ`zʌltlɪs] *a*. 无结果的,无效果[效验]的,无益的。

re·sum·a·ble [ri'zjuːməbl; rɪ`zjuməbl̩] *a*. 能恢复的,能取回的;能再开始的。

re·sume [ri'zjuːm; rɪ`zum] *vt*. **1**. 拿回,取回,收回(给人的东西等);恢复(自由等);重占(场所等);再穿用(衣服等);再开始用(烟管等)。**2**. 重新开始(已停的事),继续(中断的谈话等)。**3**. 扼要说,摘要叙述。**4**. 重新获得工作(work),复职(office),收复失地(lost territory)。*~ a pipe* (把烟斗再点着)又抽起烟斗来了。*The House ~d work*. 议会(休会后)又开会了。~ ***one's seat*** 回位,回到原位,归席。~ ***one's spirits*** 恢复精神。~ ***the thread of one's discourse*** 言归正传,回到谈话的本题。— *vi*. 重新开始;再讲,继续讲;扼要讲。*Let us ~ where we left off*. 让我们回头来再接下去讲。*Well, to ~*. 好,接下去讲。

ré·su·mé ['rezju(ː)mei; ͵rɛzu`me] *n*. 〔F.〕摘要,梗概;(求职时等所写的)个人简历。

re·sum·mon ['riː'sʌmən; ri`sʌmən] *vt*. 再[重新]召集;【法】再传唤。**-s** *n*. 再召集;【法】再传唤。

re·sump·tion [ri'zʌmpʃən; rɪ`zʌmpʃən] *n*. **1**. 取回,收回;再占领。**2**. 再开始,继续;再使用。**3**. 〔罕〕摘要,概要。

re·sump·tive [ri'zʌmptiv; rɪ`zʌmptɪv] **I** *a*. **1**. 恢复的,取回的,收回的;恢复精神的。**2**. 再开始的。**3**. 摘要的。**II** *n*. 〔古〕补药。**-ly** *ad*.

re·su·pi·nate [ri'sjuːpineit; rɪ`supə͵net] *a*. 【植】(叶等)翻转的,颠倒的;仰卧的;【古生】双曲形。**-na·tion** *n*.

re·su·pine [͵risuː'pain; ͵risu`paɪn] *a*. 仰卧的。

re·sur·face [ri'səːfis; ri`sɝfɪs] *vt*. (***-faced***; ***-fac·ing***) 重换新面,铺新路面。— *vi*. 重新露面,(潜艇)重新露出水面。

re·surge [ri'səːdʒ; rɪ`sɝdʒ] *vi*. 再起;复活,苏醒。

re·sur·gent [ri'səːdʒənt; rɪ`sɝdʒənt] *a*., *n*. 复活的[者];复兴(的)。**-gence** *n*. 复活。

res·ur·rect [re͵zə'rekt; ͵rɛzə`rɛkt] *vt*. 使复活;复兴;〔口〕掘墓偷(尸),偷挖(尸体)。— *vi*. 复活。

res·ur·rec·tion [͵rezə'rekʃən; ͵rɛzə`rɛkʃən] *n*. **1**. 〔the R-〕【宗】耶稣的复活;(最后审判日的)人类的复活〔又叫 general ~〕。**2**. 复活;复兴,再起,恢复,再用,再流行。**3**. 〔口〕掘墓偷尸,发掘尸体。~ *man* (掘墓)盗尸者。~ *pie* 〔英俚〕用剩菜做的馅饼。**-al** *a*. 复活的;耶稣复活的;复活节的。**-ism** *n*. (为解剖而)掘墓盗尸。**-ist** 偷尸人。

re·sur·vey **I** ['riːsə(ː)'vei; ͵risə`ve] *vt*. 再[重新]测量,再勘查;复查;再看一遍。**II** ['riː'səːvei; ri`sɝve] *n*. 再测量;再勘查;复查。

re·sus·ci·tate [ri'sʌsiteit; rɪ`sʌsə͵tet] *vi*., *vt*. (使)复活;(使)复兴;(使)恢复精力。

re·sus·ci·ta·tion [ri͵sʌsi'teiʃən; rɪ͵sʌsə`teʃən] *n*. 复活,回生;复兴,再兴。**-ta·tive** *a*.

re·sus·ci·ta·tor [ri'sʌsi͵teitə; rɪ`sʌsə͵tetə] *n*. 使苏醒(或复活)的人[物];〔尤指〕【医】复苏器。

ret [ret; rɛt] *vt*., *vi*. (***ret·ted*** ['retid; `rɛtɪd], ***ret·ting*** ['retiŋ; `rɛtɪŋ]) 沤(麻、肥料等);受潮湿腐烂。*flax ~ting* 亚麻浸洗[脱胶]。

ret. = **1**. retired. **2**. returned.

re·ta·ble [ri'teibl; rɪ`tebl̩] *n*. 祭坛后部的高架〔供放十字架、灯、装饰品等〕。

re·tail ['riːteil, riː'teil; `ritel, ri`tel] **I** *n*., *a*. 零售(的)。*a ~ dealer* 零售商人。*a ~ shop* 零售店。*~ trade* 零售业。*the ~ sales department* 零售营业部。***at*** [***by***] ~ 零卖。**II** *ad*. 零卖。*He buys wholesale and sells ~*. 他整买零卖。**III** [riː'teil; ri`tel] *vi*. 零售,零卖。— *vt*. **1**. 零售,零卖。**2**. 传播,转述,到处宣扬(丑事、新闻等)。~ **park** 商店林立的绿化区,园林化

购物中心。～ **politics**“零售式”竞选活动〔指竞选者四处活动,开会、讲演和接触选民等〕。

re·tail·er [riːˈteilə; rɪˋtelɚ] ***n.*** **1.** 零售店,零售商。**2.** 到处散布闲话的人。

re·tain [riˈtein; rɪˋten] ***vt.*** **1.** 保留;保持;保有;维持。**2.** 留住;挡住。**3.** 记住。**4.** 雇用,聘用(律师等)。～ *an appearance of youth* 保有年轻的外貌。～ *one's presence of mind* 镇定自若。*~ed object*【语法】保留宾语〔如:He was given a book 中的 book, 和 A book was given him 中的 him〕。*~ing fee* 预诉辩护费。*~ing force*【军】牵制队。*~ing wall* (防止沙土崩溃的)护堤壁,撑壁。*~ing works* 拦水工程;蓄水工程。**-able** ***a.*** 能保持[保有,留住]。

re·tain·er [riˈteinə; rɪˋtenɚ] ***n.*** **1.**【史】(诸侯等的)家臣,侍从,随从;门客。**2.** 随军商人(等)。**3.** 保持者;保留者。**4.** 保留物;保留权;预约辩护费;律师的预聘。**5.**【机】承盘;导圈,护圈;挡板;(滚动轴承的)保持架。***become ~ of*** 投靠。

re·take [ˈriːˈteik; riˋtek] **I** ***vt.*** (***-took***; ***-taken***) 再取,重新拿起;夺回,抢回,克服;【摄】再摄影,改拍,重拍,补摄。**II** ***n.***【摄】改拍,重拍;补摄;重拍的场面。

re·tal·i·ate [riˈtælieit; rɪˋtælɪˏet] ***vi.*** (向某人)报复(*upon*, *against*);为某事进行反击,倒算(*for*)。— ***vt.*** 征收报复关税。

re·tal·i·a·tion [riˌtæliˈeiʃən; rɪˏtælɪˋeʃən] ***n.*** 报复,反击,倒算。

re·tal·i·a·tive, re·tal·i·a·to·ry [riˈtæliətiv, -lieitəri; rɪˋtælɪətɪv, -lɪətərɪ] ***a.*** 报复(性)的。

re·tard [riˈtɑːd; rɪˋtɑrd] **I** ***vt.*** 弄慢,延缓,延迟,使停滞,推迟;使耽误,妨碍,阻止;【物、工】减速。*Lack of science and education ~s social progress.* 缺乏科学和教育会妨碍社会进步。— ***vi.*** (潮水涨退等)迟延;耽误;迟到。**II** ***n.*** 迟延,迟滞,耽误;妨碍,阻止。***in ~*** 迟延,耽搁,阻碍。***keep at ~*** 使迟延,耽误,阻碍,妨碍发达[进步]。

re·tard·ant [riˈtɑːdənt; rɪˋtɑrdənt] **I** ***n.*** 阻止物,迟延物〔指化学上的抑止剂〕。**II** ***a.*** (使)延迟的。

re·tar·date [riˈtɑːdeit; rɪˋtɑrdet] ***n.*** 智力发展迟于正常的人[儿童],智力迟钝者。

re·tar·da·tion [ˌriːtɑːˈdeiʃən; ˏritɑrˋdeʃən] ***n.*** 迟延,推迟,迟滞;阻碍;迟延程度,妨碍量;【物】减速度,妨碍物;【心】发育迟缓;迟钝。

re·tard·a·tive, re·tard·a·to·ry [riˈtɑːdətiv, -təri; rɪˋtɑrdətɪv, -tərɪ] ***a.*** 减速的,使迟延的,阻碍的。

re·tard·ed [riˈtɑːdid; rɪˋtɑrdɪd] ***a.*** 发展迟缓的〔尤指智力迟钝的〕。

re·tard·er [riˈtɑːdə; rɪˋtɑrdɚ] ***n.*** 延迟者[器];【化】延迟剂,阻滞剂。

retch [riːtʃ, retʃ; retʃ] **I** ***vi.*** 作呕,发恶心,干呕。— ***vt.*** 呕吐。**II** ***n.*** 恶心,要呕时的声音。

retd; retd. = **1.** retained. **2.** returned.

re·te [ˈriːtiː; ˋriti] ***n.*** (*pl.* ***-ti·a*** [-iə; -ɪə])【解】网,膜层。

re·tell [ˈriːˈtel; riˋtel] ***vt.*** (***-told*** [-ˈtəuld; -ˋtold]) 再讲,重讲,重述;重数;(用不同方式)复述。

re·tene [ˈriːtiːn, ˈretiːn; ˋritin, ˋretin] ***n.***【化】惹烯,1—甲—7—异丙基菲。

re·ten·tion [riˈtenʃən; rɪˋtenʃən] ***n.*** **1.** 保留,保持,(意见等的)保留。**2.** 保持力,记忆力;保留物。**3.**〔古〕拘押,监禁;扣留。**4.**【医】分泌闭止,停滞;闭尿;固位。**5.**【保险】保有额。～ *of snow* 积雪。*the seizure and ~ of power* 权力[政权]的夺取和保持。

re·ten·tive [riˈtentiv; rɪˋtentɪv] ***a.*** **1.** 保持(热等)的,(对…)有保持力的(*of*);保持湿气的,易潮湿的。**2.** 记性好的,记忆力强的。**3.**【医】固位的。*a ~ faculty* 记忆力。*a ~ memory* 好记性。

re·ten·tiv·i·ty [ˌriːtenˈtiviti; ˏritenˋtɪvətɪ] ***n.*** **1.** 保持力。**2.**【物】顽磁性。

re·ten·ue [rətəˋnuː, F. retny; rətəˋnu, retny] ***n.***【法】克制,节制;谨慎。

re·think [riˈθiŋk; riˋθɪŋk] ***vt.*** (***-thought*** [-ˈθɔːt; -ˋθɔt]; ***think·ing*** [-ˈθiŋkiŋ; -ˋθɪŋkɪŋ]) 再思考,重新考虑。

re·ti·a [ˈriːʃiə; ˋrɪʃɪə] ***n.*** rete 的复数。

re·ti·a·ri·us [riʃiˈeəriəs; ˏrɪʃɪˋerɪəs] ***n.*** (*pl.* ***-ri·i*** [-ˌai; -ˏaɪ]) (古罗马持三叉戟和网的)角斗士。

re·ti·a·ry [ˈriːʃiəri; ˋrɪʃɪˏerɪ] **I** ***n.*** **1.** 结网蜘蛛。**2.** (古罗马)持三叉戟带网角斗士。**II** ***a.*** 网(状)的;结网的;以网为武器的;巧于纠缠的。

ret·i·cence, ret·i·cency [ˈretisəns, -si; ˋretəsn̩s, -sɪ] ***n.*** 沉默,缄默;寡言;含蓄;保留。

ret·i·cent [ˈretisənt; ˋretəsn̩t] ***a.*** 沉默的;爱缄默的;有保留的,含蓄的(*of*, *about*, *on*)。*be ~ about* [*on*] *the matter* 对该问题保持沉默。*be ~ of one's opinion* 有保留意见。**-ly** ***ad.***

ret·i·cle [ˈretikl; ˋretəkl] ***n.***【光】(光学仪器上的)分划板,标线片;标线,十字线。

ret·i·cul- *comb. f.* 表示"网,小网": *reticul*ar.

re·tic·u·la [riˈtikjuələ; rɪˋtɪkjələ] ***n.*** reticulum 的复数。

re·tic·u·lar [riˈtikjulə; rɪˋtɪkjəlɚ] ***a.*** **1.** 网状的。**2.**【生】网状结缔[组织]。**3.** 复杂的,错综的,交错的。**-ly** ***ad.***

re·tic·u·late [riˈtikjulit; rɪˋtɪkjəlɪt] **I** ***a.*** 网状的。**II** [-leit; -let] ***vt.***, ***vi.*** (使)成网状。

re·tic·u·la·tion [riˌtikjuˈleiʃən; rɪˏtɪkjəˋleʃən] ***n.*** 网状,格子状;网状物,网状组织;(绘画等的)方眼复写法。

ret·i·cule [ˈretikjuːl; ˋretɪˏkjul] ***n.*** **1.** (女用)网状手提包。**2.**【光】(光学仪器上的)十字线,标线片(= reticle)。

re·tic·u·lo·cyte [riˈtikjuləuˌsait; rɪˋtɪkjələˏsaɪt] ***n.***【解】网织红血球,网状细胞。**-cy·tic** [-ˈsitik; -ˋsɪtɪk] ***a.***

re·tic·u·lo·en·do·the·li·al [ritikjuləuˌendəuˈθiːliəl; rɪˏtɪkjəloˏendoˋθilɪəl] ***a.***【解】网状内皮组织的。

re·tic·u·lose [riˈtikjuləus; rɪˋtɪkjəlos] ***a.*** = reticulate (***a.***)

re·tic·u·lum [riˈtikjuləm; rɪˋtɪkjələm] ***n.*** (*pl.* ***re·tic·u·la*** [-lə; -lə]) **1.** 网状物,网状构造[组织]。**2.** (反刍动物的)蜂巢胃。**3.**〔R-〕【天】网罟座。

re·ti·form [ˈriːtifɔːm; ˋritɪˏfɔrm] ***a.*** 网状的;有交叉线的。

ret·i·na [ˈretinə; ˋretn̩ə] ***n.*** (*pl.* ***~s***, ***-nae*** [-niː; -ni])【解】视网膜。～ **identification** 视网膜鉴定〔通过视网膜鉴定人的身份的方法〕。**-l** ***a.***

ret·i·nac·u·lum [ˌretiˈnækjuləm; ˏretəˋnækjələm] ***n.*** (*pl.* ***-u·la*** [-lə; -lə])【生】支持带。**-u·lar** [-lə; -lɚ] ***a.***

ret·ine [ˈretiːn; ˋretin] ***n.***【生化】抑制碱〔抑制体内细胞生长的物质〕。

ret·in·ene [ˈretiniːn; ˋretɪˏnin] ***n.***【生化】视黄素,视黄醛。

ret·i·ni·tis [ˌretiˈnaitis; ˏretəˋnaɪtɪs] ***n.***【医】视网膜炎。

ret·i·nos·co·py [ˌretiˈnɔskəpi; ˏretəˋnɑskəpɪ] ***n.*** 爱克斯线透视检查法;视网膜镜检法(= skiascopy)。**-scop·ic** [-ˈskɔːpik; -ˋskɑpɪk] ***a.***

ret·i·nue [ˈretinjuː; ˋretn̩ˏju] ***n.***〔集合词〕随员,扈从。

ret·i·nu·la [riˈtinjulə; rɪˋtɪnjulə] ***n.*** (*pl.* ***ret·i·nul·ae*** [-liː; -li]) (昆虫复眼的)小网膜。

re·tire [riˈtaiə; rɪˋtaɪr] **I** ***vi.*** **1.** 后退,退却;(部队等主动)撤退;退去,离开。**2.** 退隐,退休,退职,退役,告退。**3.** 就寝,去睡觉。**4.** (浪等)向后退,(海岸等)缩进。*He ~d from office in disgrace.* 他受处分撤职。～ ***for the night*** 上床去睡,就寝。～ ***from the service*** 辞职;退役。～ ***from the world*** 退隐;出家,做和尚。～ ***in disorder*** 溃退。～ ***in good order*** 秩序良好地退却。～ ***into oneself*** 不和人交际,退隐;沉默。～ ***on a pension*** 领

退休金退休。~ **to bed** [**to rest**] 去就寝。~ **under the age clause** 因年老退休。—**vt**. **1**.【军】(令)撤退。**2**. 收回(纸币等)。**3**. 使退职,使告退。**II n**. 退隐;〔罕〕退隐所;【军】退兵信号。*sound the* [*a*] ~ 吹退兵号。

re·tired [ri'taiəd; rɪ`taɪrd] **a**. **1**. 告退的,退职的,退休的,退役的;歇了业的。**2**. 退隐的;与世隔绝的。**3**. 秘密的;僻远的;幽静的。*a* ~ *general* 退职将军。*the* ~ *list* 退伍军官[退职人员]名册。~ *pay* = *a* ~ *allowance* 退休金,退职金。*a* ~ *life* 退隐生活。*a* ~ *valley* 幽谷。**go on the** ~ **list** 退休,退职,退役。**place** [**put**] **on the** ~ **list** 使退职,使退役。**-ness n**.

re·tir·ee [riˌtaiə'riː; rɪ`taɪri] **n**. 退休者,退职者(= retirant)。

re·tire·ment [ri'taiəmənt; rɪ`taɪrmənt] **n**. **1**. 退休,退职,退役。**2**. 退却(*from*)。**3**. 退休[隐]处;幽静地方,偏僻地方。**4**. (通货等的)收回。*live in* ~ 过退休生活。~ **community** (主要供老年人居住的)退休社区。~ **pay** 退休金,退役补贴。

re·tir·ing [ri'taiəriŋ; rɪ`taɪrɪŋ] **a**. 退休的,退职的;不爱交际的,谦让的,退却的。~ *pension* 退休金;养老金。*a* ~ *room* 休息室;〔尤指〕厕所。~ *board*【军】退役调查委员会。**-ly ad**.

R

re·told [riː'təuld; ri`told] retell 的过去式及过去分词。

re·took ['riː'tuk; ri`tʊk] retake 的过去式。

re·tool ['riː'tuːl; ri`tul] **vt**., **vi**. **1**. 改进[更换较好的]工具,在机器上作改进〔以适应新产品的生产〕。**2**. (为适应新形势)重新组织。

re·tor·sion [ri'tɔːʃən; rɪ`tɔrʃən] **n**.【国际法】报复,反斥,回报〔尤指国际法中受害国对侵害国的报复〕。

re·tort[1] [ri'tɔːt; rɪ`tɔrt] **I vt**. **1**. 回嘴,反责。**2**. 反驳;照样报复。*He ~ed the invectives* [*sarcasm*] *on her*. 他用恶言还击她。~ *blow for blow* 以牙还牙。—**vi**. 反击,回嘴,反驳(*on*, *upon*, *against*)。*She ~ed upon him*, *saying he was to blame*. 她反驳他,说他不好。**II n**. 回嘴,反责;(议论的)反攻,反驳;报复。*quick at* ~ 善于回嘴的。

re·tort[2] [ri'tɔːt; rɪ`tɔrt] **n**.【化】干馏釜,甑,杀菌釜。~ **pouch** 闭口密封袋〔可将食物密封,使其在非低温情况下仍能长期保存〕。

re·tor·tion [ri'tɔːʃən; rɪ`tɔrʃən] **n**. **1**. 扭转,拧转。**2**.【国际法】= retorsion.

re·touch ['riː'tʌtʃ; ri`tʌtʃ] **vt**., **n**. **1**. 再碰[接]触。**2**. 润色,修饰,修改(文章,绘画等)。**3**.【摄、印】修描(底片,照片,照相版等)。

re·trace [ri'treis; rɪ`tres] **vt**. **1**. 折回,折返,退回。**2**. 探源,调查追溯。**3**. 回想,回忆;回顾,回头看,重看。**4**. 重新再描摹。~ *one's steps* 折回;重做。~ *a book* 再从头阅读,再回到前面某处重新阅读。~ *one's steps* [*ways*] 顺原路返回。

re·tract[1] [ri'trækt; rɪ`trækt] **vt**. 缩进。*A cat ~s its claws*. 猫缩进它的爪子。~ *one's tongue* 缩进舌头。

re·tract[2] [ri'trækt; rɪ`trækt] **vt**. 取消;撤消,撤回,收回(命令、前言等)。—**vi**. 取消前言,食言,撤回。~ *from an engagement* 取消约会。

re·tract·a·ble [ri'træktəbl; rɪ`træktəbl] **a**. **1**. 能缩进的;伸缩自如的。**2**. 可取消的,可撤回的。*a* ~ *landing wheel* [*gear*]【空】伸缩起落轮[架]。

re·trac·ta·tion [ˌriːtræk'teiʃən; ˏritræk`teʃən] **n**. **1**. (意见等的)取消,撤回。**2**. 缩进;缩回。**3**.【拓】保核收缩。

re·trac·tile [ri'træktail; rɪ`træktl] **a**. (爪等的)伸缩自如的;能缩进的。

re·trac·til·i·ty [ˌriːtræk'tiliti; ˏritræk`tɪlətɪ] **n**. 伸缩性;可缩进性。

re·trac·tion [ri'trækʃən; rɪ`trækʃən] **n**. **1**. (爪等的)缩进(*opp*. protrusion)。**2**. 缩回;取消,撤回。

re·trac·tive [ri'træktiv; rɪ`træktɪv] **a**. (能)缩进的。

re·trac·tor [ri'træktə; rɪ`træktə] **n**. **1**. 取消前言者,食言者。**2**.【解】牵缩肌;【外】牵开器,牵开绷带。**3**. (枪炮的)抽筒器,抽(弹)壳。

re·tread ['riː'tred; ri`trɛd] **I vt**.【汽车】翻新修补,热补(轮胎)。**II n**. **1**. 热补过的轮胎。**2**.〔美俚〕再服兵役者。*a ~ing plant* 轮胎修补厂。

re-tread ['riːtred; ri`trɛd] (**re-trod** ['riː'trɔd; `ri`trɑd]; **re-trod·den** ['riː'trɔdn; `ri`trɑdn], **re-trod**) **vt**. 再踏上;重走,再走上(路途),走回头路。

re·treat [ri'triːt; rɪ`trit] **I n**. **1**. 退却;退兵;退却信号,(日没时的)回营号[鼓]。**2**. 隐退;隐退处,躲藏处,避难处;(兽、盗贼等的)潜伏处,巢窟。**3**. (醉汉,疯子等的)收容所。**4**.【宗】静修;默想。**5**.【空】(翼等的)向后倾斜。*He lives in a quiet* ~. 他住在一个幽静的地方。*a mountain* ~ 山庄。*a summer* ~ 避暑地。**beat a** ~ 发出收兵的信号;撤退,退却,放弃不干,打退堂鼓。**be in full** ~ 总退却,全线溃败。**be beyond** ~ 没有后退的可能。**blow** [**sound**] **the** [**a**] ~ 吹退却号,下令退却。**cover the** ~ 掩护退却。**cut off the** ~ 截断退路。**go into** ~ 到修道院里静修(一个时期)。**make a** ~ 撤退。**make good one's** ~ 安全撤退;顺利地脱身。**II vi**. **1**. 后退,退却,撤退。**2**. 隐退。**3**. 退缩;(眼睛等)凹进。**4**. 撤回,撤销,作罢,放弃。**5**.【空】向后倾斜。~ *before the enemy* 被迫撤退。—**vt**. 使退回,缩回(象棋的棋子等)。

re·treat·ism [ri'triːtizəm; rɪ`tritɪzəm] **n**. 退却主义,逃跑主义。

re·tree [ri'triː; rɪ`tri] **n**. 次品纸张〔在包装外面英国标有 XX,美国标有 R 记号〕。

re·trench [ri'trentʃ; rɪ`trɛntʃ] **vt**. **1**. 节省,减省,削减,缩减,减少(经费等);删除,省略(字句等);截去,割去,修剪。**2**.【筑城】设内郭,筑内墙。—**vi**. 俭约,节省。**-ment n**. **1**. 节约,缩减,紧缩;删除,省略。**2**.【筑城】内郭,内墙;内线防御工事。

re·tri·al ['riː'traiəl; ri`traɪəl] **n**. **1**.【法】再审;复审。**2**. 再实验;再试验;重新实验[试验]。

re·tri·bu·tion [ˌretri'bjuːʃən; ˏrɛtrə`bjuʃən] **n**. 报复,惩罚;报应;果报;报酬,报答。*the day of* ~ 最后的审判日;报应到来的时候。

re·trib·u·tive, **re·trib·u·to·ry** [ri'tribjutiv, -təri; rɪ`trɪbjətɪv, -ˏtorɪ] **a**. 报应的;报复的;惩罚的。**-tive·ly ad**.

re·triev·al [ri'triːvəl; rɪ`trivl] **n**. (可)取回,(可)恢复,(可)挽回;(可)修补,(可)修正,(可)更正;(可)弥补,(可)补偿。*beyond* ~ 不能补救的,不能挽回的。

re·trieve [ri'triːv; rɪ`triv] **I vt**. **1**. 取回,恢复,挽回(失物、名誉等)。**2**. 补偿,弥补(损失等);更正(错误等)。**3**. (从灾难中等)救出,拯救(*from*)。**4**. 想起(忘记的事情)。**5**. (猎狗将猎获物)找回;拉回(钩鱼线)。~ *freedom* 恢复自由。~ *one's character* 恢复名誉。~ *an error* 更正错误。—**vi**. (猎狗)找回猎获物;拉回钩鱼线,恢复;精神恢复。**II n**. 恢复,挽回。*beyond* [*past*] ~ 无可挽回地,无法补救地。**-ment n**. = retrieval. **-vable a**.

re·triev·er [ri'triːvə; rɪ`trivə] **n**. 恢复者;重新得到者;衔回猎物的犬。

retro- *pref*. 表示"向后,倒退,追溯": *retro*gress, *retro*rocket.

ret·ro ['retrəu; `rɛtro] **n**. (老式服装、音乐等的)重新流行,复旧,怀旧。

ret·ro·act [ˌretrəu'ækt; ˏrɛtro`ækt] **vi**. **1**. 逆动,反作用。**2**.【法】追溯(既往);有追溯效力。

ret·ro·ac·tion [ˌretrəu'ækʃən; ˏrɛtro`ækʃən] **n**. **1**. 逆动;反作用。**2**.【法】追溯效力。**3**.【化】逆反应。

ret·ro·ac·tive [ˌretrəu'æktiv; ˏrɛtro`æktɪv] **a**. **1**. 逆动的;反作用的。**2**.【法】追溯既往的,有追溯力的。**3**. 补发增加工资的。*a* ~ *law* 有追溯力的法律。**-tiv·i·ty**

[-ˈtiviti; -ˋtɪvətɪ] *n*. **-ly** *ad*.

ret·ro·cede[1] [ˌretrəuˈsiːd; ˏrɛtroˋsid] *vt*. 交还,退还。

ret·ro·cede[2] [ˌretrəuˈsiːd; ˏrɛtroˋsid] *vi*. 1. 后退,退却。2.【医】(疾病)内攻;(器官)内移。

ret·ro·ces·sion [ˌretrəuˈseʃən; ˏrɛtrəˋsɛʃən] *n*. 1. 交还;后退。2.【医】(疾病)内攻;(器官等)内移。3.【保险】再再保险,三重保险。

ret·ro·choir [ˈretrəuˌkwaiə; ˋritroˏkwaɪr] *n*. (大教堂的)祭坛后面的地方;圣歌队席位的后面。

ret·ro·cog·ni·tion [ˈretrəuˈkɔgniʃən; ˏrɛtrəkɑgˋnɪʃən] *n*. (超过常态感知能力的)异常回溯性知觉。

re-trod [ˈriˈtrɔd; riˋtrɑd] retread 的过去式和过去分词。

re-trod·den [ˈriːˈtrɔdn; rɪˋtrɑdn̩] re-tread 的过去分词。

ret·ro·fire [ˈretrəˌfaiə; ˋrɛtroˏfaɪr] *vt*., *vi*., *n*. (**-fired**; **-fir·ing**) (制动火箭的)点火发动。

ret·ro·fit [ˈretrəˌfit; ˋrɛtrəˏfɪt] I *n*. (飞机等的)式样翻新。II *vt*., *vi*. (**-fit·ted**; **-fit·ting**) (对…)作翻新改造。

ret·ro·flex [ˈretrəufleks; ˋrɛtrəˏflɛks] I *a*. 反曲的,翻转的;【语音】卷舌的。II *n*.【语音】卷舌音。

ret·ro·flex·ion, -flec·tion [ˌretrəuˈflekʃən; ˏrɛtrəˋflɛkʃən] *n*. 1. 翻转,反曲。2.【医】子宫后屈。3.【语音】卷舌(音)。

ret·ro·gra·da·tion [ˌretrəugrəˈdeiʃən; ˏretrəgreˋdeʃən] *n*. 后退,倒退;逆行;退步,退化;退减(作用)。

ret·ro·grade [ˈretrəugreid; ˋrɛtrəˏgred] I *a*. 后退的,倒退的;反的,倒转的;逆行的;退步的,退化的。II *vi*. 后退,倒退;逆行;退步,退化;堕落。~ *metamorphosis* [*development*]【生】退化。~ *motion*【天】逆行。*in a* ~ *order* 以相反次序,颠倒地。III *ad*. 后退地;向后地;颠倒地。*flow* ~ 倒流。

ret·ro·gress [ˈretrəugres, ˌretrəuˈgres; ˋrɛtrəˏgrɛs, ˏretrəˋgrɛs] *vi*. (*opp*. progress) 1. 倒退,退步,衰退。2.【生】退化。

ret·ro·gres·sion [ˌretrəuˈgreʃən; ˏrɛtrəˋgrɛʃən] *n*. 后退,倒退,退步,消退,堕落,衰微;【生】退化;【天】逆行(运动);【化】逆反应。*Persist in progress and oppose* ~! 坚持进步,反对倒退! **-sive** *a*.

ret·ro·len·tal [ˌretrəuˈlentl; ˏrɛtrəˋlɛntl̩] *a*.【解】眼晶状体后面的。

ret·ro·pack [ˈretrəupæk; ˋrɛtroˏpæk] *n*. 制动[减速]发动机;(由火箭组成的)制动[减速]装置。

ret·ro-rock·et [ˈretrəurɔkit; ˋretroˏrɑkɪt] *n*. 制动火箭,减速火箭。

re·trorse [riˈtrɔːs; rɪˋtrɔrs] *a*.【生】下向的,倒向的。**-ly** *ad*.

ret·ro·spect [ˈretrəuspekt; ˋrɛtrəˏspɛkt] I *n*. 1. 回顾(*opp*. prospect)。2. 怀旧,追忆。3. 追溯力。4. 对证,参照。*It is pleasant in* (*the*) ~. 回想起来令人愉快。*The* ~ *was depressing*. 回想起来令人沮丧。II *vi*., *vt*. 〔罕〕回顾;回想,追忆。III *a*. = retrospective.

ret·ro·spec·tion [ˌretrəuˈspekʃən; ˏrɛtrəˋspɛkʃən] *n*. 回顾,回想;(过去事实等的)对证。

ret·ro·spec·tive [ˌretrəuˈspektiv; ˏrɛtrəˋspɛktɪv] *a*. 1. 回顾的,怀旧的;爱追溯既往的。2.【法】有追溯力的。*a* ~ *law*【法】追溯法。**-ly** *ad*.

re·trous·sé [rəˈtruːsei; ˏrɛtruˋse] *a*. 〔F.〕(鼻子)朝上翘的;尖端向上弯的。

ret·ro·ver·sion [ˌretrəuˈvəːʃən; ˏrɛtrəˋvɝʃən] *n*. 1. 回顾;向后转,倒退。2. (器官的)翻转,后倾[特指子宫的后倾]。

ret·ro·vert [ˌretrəuˈvəːt; ˏrɛtrəˋvɝt] *vt*. 使翻转;使后倾。**-ed** *a*. (子宫等)后倾的。

re·try [ˈriːˈtrai; riˋtraɪ] *vt*. 1. (重新)再试。2.【法】再审,重审。

ret·si·na [ˈretsinə; ˋrɛtsɪnə] *n*. (带松脂香味)希腊红(白)葡萄酒。

ret·ter·y [ˈretəri; ˋrɛtərɪ] *n*. 沤麻场。

ret·ting [ˈretiŋ; ˋrɛtɪŋ] *n*. (亚麻)浸渍(法),沤麻。

re·turn [riˈtəːn; rɪˋtɝn] I *vi*. 1. 回转,回来,回去,返回,折回 (*to*)。2. 再来,又来;复发,回复,恢复。3. 回头说正经话,回到本题,言归正传。4. 送还,归还(原主)。5. 回答,回嘴,回骂。*He has gone never to* ~. 他一去不回。*The property* ~*ed to the original owner*. 财产已归还原主。~ *to duty* 回到岗位。~ ***from a digression*** 把说开去的话拉回来,言归正传。~ ***home*** 回家;回乡;回国。~ ***to dust*** 死。~ ***to one's muttons*** 回到本题,言归正传。~ ***to oneself*** 苏醒;醒悟。— *vt*. 1. 归还,送还,送[放]回(原处),(光、声等)反射,反响。2. 报复;回礼,报答,酬答。3. 回答说;反驳道;答辩;回骂。4. 汇报,报告,呈报。5. 选举(为议员等)。6.【牌戏】(响应搭档者)跟出(同花色的牌);【网球】将(球)打回。7.【法】(陪审员)答复。8.【建】(使墙壁、嵌线等)向侧面转延。~ *one's income at $200* 申报收入额是两佰元。~ *a soldier as killed* 呈报某兵士已阵亡。*a* ~*ing officer* 〔英〕负责选举的官员。~ *a compliment* 回礼,还礼;报复。~ ***sb. to Parliament*** 选举某人为议员。~ ***a profit*** 产生收益[利润]。~ ***a visit*** 回拜。~ ***good for evil*** 以德报怨。~ ***kindness with ingratitude*** 恩将仇报。~ ***like for like*** 以牙回牙,以眼还眼,一报还一报。~ ***swords*** 纳剑入鞘。~ ***thanks*** (对宴会,祝酒等)答谢。***To*** ~ 〔用作插入语〕闲语休讲,言归正传。

II *n*. 1. 归来,回去;回家,还乡,归国;复归,回归;再发,复发;来回,回程;【电】回路。2. 退还,归还,付还,送还。3. 还报,报复;还礼,报答;回答,答复;回骂,反唇相讥。4. 报告(书),汇报,申报;〔主 *pl*.〕统计表;【物】输出量。5. (议员的)选出,当选。6. 〔常 *pl*.〕赢利,利润,赚头;报酬。7.【法】送回。8.【建】(嵌线等的)转延,侧面。9. 〔*pl*.〕〔英〕(用废料制成的)再生板烟。10. 〔口〕= ~ ticket 来回票。(*I wish you*) *Many happy* ~*s* (*of the day*)! (敬祝)多福多寿。*election* ~*s* 选举结果,选举报告书。*official* ~*s* 公报。*Small profits and quick* ~*s*. 薄利多销〔商店广告用语〕。*a third-class* ~ (*ticket*) (*to*) *London* (到)伦敦(的)三等来回(票)一张。***at*** (***the***) ~ ***of the year*** 过了年就。***bring*** [***yield***] ***a prompt*** [***quick***] ~ 利润回来得快。***by*** ~ (***of post***) 请即回示。***in*** ~ 作报复[报酬,回答,报答];作替换。***in*** ~ ***for*** 作…的报酬[回礼]。***make a*** ~ 作报告[汇报]。***make*** ~ ***for*** 报答…。***secure a*** ~ 当选(为议员)。***without*** ~ 无赚头,无利润。***write in*** ~ 写回信。~ **circuit**【电】回路。~ **game** [**match**] (同样两个球队的)再赛。~ **of health** [**an illness**] 恢复健康;(旧病)复发。~ **passenger** [**voyage, cargo**] 回程的乘客[行程,货载]。~ **postcard** 来回明信片。~ **ticket** 〔主英〕来回票。~ **visit** 回访,答拜,回拜。

re·turn·a·ble [riˈtəːnəbl; rɪˋtɝnəbl̩] *a*. 1. 可返回的。2. 可回答的;应返还的。3. 应报告的。4. 可多次利用的;可回收的。5.【法】应送回[答辩]的。

re·turned [riˈtəːnd; rɪˋtɝnd] *a*. 被送回的;已归来的;已回国的。~ *empties* 退回的空箱[空桶(等)];〔英谑〕归国牧师。*a* ~ *overseas Chinese* 归国华侨。

re·turn·ee [ritəːˈniː; rɪˏtɝˋni] *n*. 1. (服刑后)释放回来的人。2. (从国外服役后)回国军人。3. 从国外回来的人。4. 回校复学的学生。

re·turn·less [riˈtəːnlis; rɪˋtɝnlɪs] *a*. 1. 回不来的。2. 没有报酬的,赚不到钱的。3. 没有报告的;没有回答的。

re·tuse [riˈtjuːs; rɪˋtjus] *a*.【植】(叶)微凹形的;凹端的。

ret·zi·na [ˈretsinə; ˋrɛtsɪnə] *n*. = retsina.

Reu·ben [ˈruːbin; ˋrubɪn] *n*. 鲁本[男子名]。

re·une [riːˈjuːn; rɪˋjun] *vi*. 〔美俚〕重新聚会。

re·u·ni·fy [ˈriːˈjuːnifai; rɪˋjunəˏfaɪ] *vt*., *vi*. (**-fi·ed**; **-fy·ing**) (使)重新统一,(使)重新团结。**-fi·ca·tion** [ˌriːjuːnifiˈkeiʃən; ˏrijunɪfɪˋkeʃən] *n*.

Ré·un·ion [riːˈjuːnjən; rɪˋjunjən] *n*. 留尼汪(岛)〔非洲〕。

R

re·un·ion [ˈriːˈjuːnjən; riˋjunjən] ***n*.** **1.** 复合,再结合,再合并,再统一;和解。**2.** 重聚,(亲友等的)聚会,恳亲会。*a family* ~ 亲属的团聚。*a college* ~ (大学)校友联欢会。**-ist *n*.**

re·u·nite [ˈriːjuːˈnait; ˏrijuˋnaɪt] ***vt*., *vi*.** (使)再联合;(使)重聚;(使)再结合。

re-up [ˈriːˈʌp; riˋʌp] ***vt*., *vi*.** (***-upped***; ***-up·ping***)〔美俚〕再服兵役,再入伍。

re·used [ˈriːˈjuːzd; riˋjuzd] ***a*.** 再生的。~ *wool* 【纺】旧呢片再生毛。

Reu·ters [ˈrɔitəz; ˋrɔɪtɚz] ***n*.** (英国)路透(通讯)社。

rev [rev; rɛv] **I *n*.** 〔口〕(发动机的)旋转。**II *vi*., *vt*.** (使)变速。~ ***down*** [***up***] 使(马达)转得慢点[快点]。

Rev. =**1.** Revelation. **2.** Reverend.

rev, rev. =**1.** revenue. **2.** reverse(d). **3.** review(ed). **4.** revised; revision. **5.** revolution.

re·va·lo·ri·za·tion [ˈriːˌvæləraiˈzeiʃən; ˏrivælərɪˋzeʃən] ***n*.** 【经】(通货膨胀后对资产或通货的)重行估价。

re·val·u·ate [ˈriːˈvæljueit; riˋvæljuˏet] ***vt*.** (***-at·ed***; ***-at·ing***) 再估价,重新评价[估价]。**-a·tion *n*.**

re·val·ue [ˈriːˈvæljuː; riˋvælju] ***vt*.** 对(货币等)再估价;对…重新估价[评价]。

re·vamp [ˈriːˈvæmp; riˋvæmp] ***vt*.** 补钉,补缀;修理,修补;〔美口〕改制;翻新;改装(书等);给(鞋等)换新面。

re·vanche [rəˈvɑ̃ːnʃ, F. rəvɑ̃ːʃ; rəˋvɑ̃nʃ, rəˋvɑ̃ʃ] ***n*.** 〔F.〕报复;复仇战。

re·vanch·ism [riˈvɑːnʃizəm, -ˈvɑːntʃ-; rɪˋvænʃɪzəm, -væntʃ-] ***n*.** (促使战败国企图收复失地的)复仇主义。**-ist *a*., *n*.**

re·veal [riˈviːl; rɪˋvil] **I *vt*.** **1.** 显露,揭露,揭发,剖明;告诉,透露,泄露(秘密等),给,看。**2.** (神)默示,启示。~ *a secret* 泄露秘密。*~ed religion* 【宗】天启宗教〔指信仰有一个有意志的神的任何宗教,如犹太教,基督教等〕。*A man's work ~s him*. 由作家的作品可看出作家其人。*It was soon ~ed to him how much he needed her cooperation*. 他很快就明白他是多么需要同她合作。~ ***itself*** 出现。~ ***oneself*** 讲出姓名,表明身分。~ ***one's identity*** 揭示身分。**II *n*.** **1.** 显露,启示。**2.** 【建】窗侧壁【外抱】;门侧。**3.** (汽车的)窗框。**-a·ble *a*. -ment *n*.**

re·veal·er [riˈviːlə; rɪˋvilɚ] ***n*.** 显示者;揭露者;【宗】启示者。

re·veil·le [riˈvæli; ˋrɛvˏli] ***n*.** 【军】起床号,起床鼓;(一天的第一次)列队、集合。

rev·el [ˈrevl; ˋrɛvḷ] **I *vi*.** (〔英〕***-ll-***) **1.** 欢宴,纵酒狂欢,闹饮。**2.** 狂喜,得意扬扬;极爱,沉迷(艺术等)(*in*)。— ***vt*.** 宴饮作乐浪费掉(钱、时间)。~ *in luxury* [*mischief*, *vice*] 爱奢华[捣蛋、干坏事]。~ *away the time* 狂欢作乐虚度光阴。~ *it* 纵酒狂欢;欢宴。**II *n*.** 〔常 *pl*.〕宴会;狂欢,欢乐。*the Master of the Revels* (王室、法学院等的)宴会主持人。~ *rout* 〔古〕参加宴会的人们。

rev·e·la·tion [ˌreviˈleiʃən; ˏrɛvḷˋeʃən] ***n*.** **1.** 揭发,暴露;泄露;显示;被揭露出来的事物;意外的发现[新事,新经验]。**2.** 【宗】天启,启示,默示;圣经;〔the Revelations〕(基督教《圣经》中的)《启示录》。*It was a ~ to me*. 这真是一件料想不到的事情。*What a ~!* 这真是一个意外! **-al *a*.** **1.** 暴露的;显示的。**2.** 意外发现的。**3.** 天启的,启示的。**-ist *n*.** 启示论者;启示录作者。

rev·e·la·tor [ˈrevileitə; ˋrɛvəˏletɚ] ***n*.** 〔美〕= revealer.

rev·e·la·to·ry [ˈrevilətəri, riˈvelətəri; ˋrɛvələˏtorɪ] ***a*.** **1.** 揭露的。**2.** 能启示…的 (*of*)。*a ~ account of their home life* 对他们家庭生活的揭露性的叙述。*a poem ~ of his deep, personal sorrow* 能表明他的深沉的个人悲痛的一首诗。

rev·el·(l)er [ˈrevlə; ˋrɛvəlɚ] ***n*.** 参加欢宴的人,纵酒狂欢的人,大喝大闹的人;荡子。

rev·el·ry [ˈrevlri; ˋrɛvəlrɪ] ***n*.** 纵酒狂欢,宴饮作乐;欢宴。

rev·e·nant [ˈrevənənt; ˋrɛvənənt] ***n*.** 〔F.〕**1.** 幽灵。**2.** 久别归来的人。

re·venge [riˈvendʒ; rɪˋvɛndʒ] **I *n*.** 报仇,雪恨;仇恨;报仇[报复]的机会;【运】雪耻赛(的机会)。*counter-attack in ~* 反攻倒算。*give sb. his ~* 给输方一个雪耻赛的机会。***get*** ~ 报仇。***have*** [***take***] ***one's*** ~ 复仇,报仇。***in*** ~ ***of*** [***for***] 为报复…而。***meditate*** ~ 企图报仇。***seek one's*** ~ (***up***) ***on*** 找机会向…报仇。***threaten*** ~ 声言要报仇,以报仇威胁。**II *vt*.** 〔~ oneself 或用被动语态〕报复,报仇;替…报仇。***be ~d*** (***up***)***on sb*.** = ~ ***oneself*** (***up***)***on sb*.** 对…进行报复[报仇]。~ ***a wrong*** 申冤雪恨。~ ***wrong with wrong*** 以牙还牙,报仇。— ***vi*.** 报仇 (*upon*, *on*)。

re·venge·ful [riˈvendʒful; rɪˋvɛndʒfḷ] ***a*.** 仇恨深的,不共戴天的,一心要报仇的;报仇的,报复的。**-ly *ad*.**

rev·e·nue [ˈrevinjuː; ˋrɛvəˏnju] ***n*.** **1.** (国家的)岁入;税收;(土地、财产等的)收入,收益,所得;(个人的)固定收入;〔*pl*.〕总收入;收入项目;财源。**2.** 税务署;〔美俚〕税务官。*the Public R-* 国库岁入。*defraud the ~* 漏税,逃税。~**cutter** (海关的)缉私船。~ **duty** = ~ tax. ~ **officer** 税务员。~ **stamp** 印花税票。~ **tax** 税收。

re·verb [riˈvəːb; rɪˋvɝb] ***n*.** = reverberation 3.

re·ver·ber·ant [riˈvəːbərənt; rɪˋvɝbərənt] ***a*.** 反响的;回荡的;【物】交混回响的;反射的。

re·ver·ber·ate [riˈvəːbəreit; rɪˋvɝbəˏret] ***vi*.** **1.** 反响,混响;反射;(球等)弹回。**2.** (反射炉)返焰。**3.** 〔罕〕抱反感。— ***vt*.** **1.** 使反响;使回荡;使反射。**2.** 使返焰;用返焰[反射]炉处理。*a reverberating peal of thunder* 雷的隆隆声。**-a·tive *a*.**

re·ver·ber·a·tion [riˌvəːbəˈreiʃən; rɪˏvɝbəˋreʃən] ***n*.** **1.** 反响,回荡;余韵;反射;反射热,反射光。**2.** (反射炉的)返焰;返焰炉处理法。**3.** 【物】交混回响,混响,余响。

re·ver·ber·a·tor [riˈvəːbəreitə; rɪˋvɝbəˏretɚ] ***n*.** 反射炉,返焰炉;反射器,反射灯,反射镜。

re·ver·ber·a·to·ry [riˈvəːbərətəri; rɪˋvɝbərəˏtorɪ] **I *a*.** **1.** 回响的。**2.** 反射的。**3.** 返焰(炉)的,发射炉的。**II *n*.** 反射炉,返焰炉。

re·vere[1] [riˈviə; rɪˋvɪr] ***vt*.** 尊敬,崇敬。

re·vere[2] [riˈviə; rɪˋvɪr] ***n*.** = revers.

Re·vere [riˈviə; rɪˋvɪr] ***n*.** 里维尔〔姓氏〕。

rev·er·ence [ˈrevərəns; ˋrɛvərəns] **I *n*.** **1.** 尊敬,崇敬。**2.** 威望,〔古〕敬礼;鞠躬。**3.** 〔your R-; his R-〕〔古、谑〕大师;尊敬的…阁下。*at the ~ of* 对…尊敬地。***bow in humble*** ~ 必恭必敬地鞠躬。***do*** [***make***] ***to*** 〔废〕= *pay ~ to*. ***feel*** ~ ***for*** 觉得…可敬。***hold ... in*** [***regard ... with***] ~ 敬畏某人,尊敬某人。***make a profound*** ~ 恭恭敬敬行礼,深深鞠躬。***pay*** ~ ***to*** 尊敬,向…致敬。***saving your*** ~ 〔古〕恕我冒昧(地讲);请原谅。**II *vt*.** 尊敬,崇敬;敬畏。

rev·er·end [ˈrevərənd; ˋrɛvərənd] **I *a*.** **1.** 应受尊敬的,可尊敬的,可敬畏的。**2.** 大师,法师〔对僧侣、牧师的尊称、略作 Rev. 或 the Rev.;对教长用 the Very R-,对主教 (bishop) 用 Right R-,对大主教 (archbishop) 用 Most R-〕。**3.** 教士的,圣职的。**4.** 〔古〕恭敬的,表示敬畏的。*the ~ gentleman* 那个牧师。**II *n*.** 〔常 *pl*.〕教士,牧师。*the ~s and right ~s* 牧师和主教们。

rev·er·ent [ˈrevərənt; ˋrɛvərənt] ***a*.** **1.** 尊敬的,虔诚的,谦恭的。**2.** 〔美俚〕(威士忌酒)烈性的。**-ly *ad*.**

rev·er·en·tial [ˌrevəˈrenʃəl; ˏrɛvəˋrɛnʃəl] ***a*.** 表示尊敬的,出于虔诚的。**-ly *ad*.**

rev·er·ie [ˈrevəri; ˋrɛvərɪ] ***n*.** **1.** 冥想,沉思;空想,幻想,白日梦;梦想,妄想,奇想。**2.** 【乐】幻想曲。***be lost in*** (***a***) ~ 想得出神,正在做白日梦。***fall into*** (***a***) ~ = ***indulge in*** ~ 沉溺于不实际的空想中。

re·vers [riˈviə, riˈvɛə, 〔*pl*.〕riˈviəz, riˈvɛəz; rɪˋvɪr, rɪˋvɛr, 〔*pl*.〕rɪˋvɪrz, rɪˋvɛrz] ***n***. 〔*sing*., *pl*.〕〔F.〕翻领,翻边,翻袖(等)。

re·ver·sal [riˈvəːsəl; rɪˋvɝsəl] ***n***. **1**. 颠倒,倒转,反转,逆转,反向;反复。**2**.【法】撤消。**3**.【摄】正负片之间的转换。*That would be a* ~ *of the order of host and guest*. 这就主客颠倒了。*a* ~ *of wind* 风向突然逆转。*a thrust* ~【火箭】推力反向装置。

re·verse [riˈvəːs; rɪˋvɝs] **I** ***vt***. **1**. 使颠倒,使倒转,使反转;使翻转;翻(案)。**2**. 掉换,交换。**3**. 使成正相反的东西,完全改变。**4**.【机】使倒退,使绕行,使倒开。**5**.【法】撤消,推翻。~ *an engine* 倒车。~ *a motion* [*policy*] 使运动倒转[完全改变政策]。~ *an order* 颠倒次序。~ *positions* 掉换位置。*R- arms*! 倒枪!〔行葬礼时使枪口向地的命令〕。*a* ~*d line*【物】自蚀(光线)谱。~ *the verdict* 翻案。~ *the charge* 让接电话的人付电话费。~ ***oneself*** 完全改变自己主张,使逆转。— ***vi***. 颠倒,倒转,反转,倒退;逆转;反向;【机】回动;(跳舞时)向左转。**II** ***a***. **1**. 反对的,相反的,倒转的,颠倒的;翻转的,反面的,背后的;朝后的;反卷的;反向的,倒开的,回动的,逆流的。**2**.【生】倒卷的,左卷的。***in the* ~ *direction*** 朝着相反的方向。***in* ~ *order*** 次序颠倒地。**III** ***n***. **1**. 反对,相反。**2**. (硬币等的)反面,背面(*opp*. obverse)。**3**. 倒转,颠倒;反向;【机】回动;回动装置[齿轮]。**4**. (枪等的)托尾。**5**. 逆境,倒霉,不幸,挫折,失败。**6**.【剑术】倒击,倒刺。**7**.【跳舞】左转。*the very* ~ 正相反。*the* ~*s of fortune* 运气不佳;灾难,不幸。*With others the* ~ (*of this*) *happens*. 其他各人遭遇完全相反。***in*** ~ 相反;【军】在阵后,在[从]背面。***meet with*** ~***s*** 遭受挫折;倒霉;失败;吃败仗。***on the*** ~ (汽车)倒开着。***quite the*** ~ 正相反。***suffer*** [***sustain***, ***have***] ***a*** ~ 遭受失败;被打败,吃败仗。***take in*** ~ 从背面攻击。**-d** ***a***. 颠倒的;撤销了的。**IV** ***ad***. = reversely 颠倒地,翻转地,反对地,(和这)相反地,在另一方面。~ **commuting** 逆向乘车上下班〔指从城里去郊区上班〕。~ **fire** 背面火力[炮击]。~ **import** 逆向进口〔指进口由本国设在国外的子公司生产或加工的产品〕。~ **turn**【空】(方向的)急转。

re·vers·i·bil·i·ty [riˌvəːsəˈbiliti; rɪˏvɝsəˋbɪlətɪ] ***n***. 可逆(性);正反[表里]两用,(命令、判决等)可撤销性。

re·vers·i·ble [riˈvəːsəbl; rɪˋvɝsəbḷ] **I** ***a***. **1**. 可转换[掉换]的;可翻转的,正反[表里]两用的;可逆的。**2**. 可取消的,可废弃的。**II** ***n***. (正反一样的)双面织物;晴雨两用大衣;正反两用式上衣。*a* ~ *carpet* 双面地毯。*a* ~ *raincoat* 两面用雨衣。

re·vers·ing [riˈvəːsiŋ; rɪˋvɝsɪŋ] ***a***. 回动的,倒进的。*a* ~ *key*【电】换向电钥。*a* ~ *lever*【机】回动杆。

re·ver·sion [riˈvəːʃən; rɪˋvɝʒən] ***n***. **1**. 回复;复原;逆演;颠倒,反转。**2**.【生】回复变异;返祖(现象);返祖遗传,隔世遗传。**3**.【橡胶】(硫化)还原。**4**. 未来[复归]享有权;继承权;(约满后财产还给原主的)复归,财产复归。**5**. (可在一定期间后或死后得到的)复归储金[退休金、恤金、人寿保险金等]。**6**.〔古〕剩余。***in*** ~ 以让与人死亡[约定期间届满]为条件(的);将来应归某人所有的;将来应实现的。~ ***to type*** 隔世遗传,间歇遗传,返祖性。**-al** [-ʃənl; -ʃənl], **-ary** [-ʃnəri; -ʃnərɪ] ***a***. **1**. 回复的,复原的,复归的。**2**. 隔世遗传的,返祖遗传的。**3**. 将来应享有的,应继承的;归属原主的。**-er** ***n***. 有将来享有权的人,继承权人。

re·vert [riˈvəːt; rɪˋvɝt] **I** ***vi***. **1**. 恢复原状;回复(旧习惯等);复辟,复归(原主等)(*to*)。**2**. 回到原来话题(*to*)。**3**. 回想(*to*)。**4**.【生】回复变异;返祖遗传,隔世遗传(*to*)。**5**. 归属,继承。— ***vt***. 使颠倒,使绕行,使(眼睛等)转向后。**II** ***n***. **1**. 恢复原来信仰的人。**2**. 归属,继承。**-ant** ***n***.【生】回复突变体〔通过突变回复到早先类型的有机体〕。

re·vert·i·ble [riˈvəːtəbl; rɪˋvɝtəbḷ] ***a***. 可回复的;(财产等)应归还的,可归复的;可逆的;可回溯的。**-i·bil·i·ty** ***n***.

rev·er·y [ˈrevəri; ˋrɛvərɪ] ***n***. = reverie.

re·vest [riˈvest; rɪˋvɛst] ***vt***. **1**. 使重新具有(财产、权力、职位);再授予(给予)(财产、权力、职位等)。**2**. 重新投资。— ***vi***. 重新拥有,重归原主〔指财产、权力等〕。

re·vet [riˈvet; rɪˋvɛt] ***vt***. (用砖石等)遮护,铺盖(堤防等)。~ *a trench* 用砂包、鹿砦等巩固壕沟。**-ment** ***n***.【筑城】被覆;拥壁;护岸。

re·view [riˈvjuː; rɪˋvju] **I** ***vt***. **1**. 再看,再阅,复阅;重行检查,再验查;检查;审查,观察。**2**. 检阅(军队)。**3**. 评论(新书等)。**4**. 温习,复习(功课等)。**5**.【法】复审,再审。**6**. 回顾;回忆;写回忆录。**7**.〔古〕校改,校订,修订,改订。— ***vi***. 评论,写评论;做评论员。**II** ***n***. **1**. (再)检查;检阅;观察,校阅。**2**. 复习,温习;习题。**3**. 评论;书评;评论杂志。**4**. 阅兵;阅兵式,阅舰式。**5**.【法】复审。**6**. 回顾,回忆;反省。**7**. = revue. *the Board of R-* (影片等的)审查局。*a court of* ~ 复审法庭。***give a general*** ~ ***of*** 概括地谈谈。***hold a military*** ~ 举行阅兵式。***in*** ~ 检查中。***pass*** [***march***] ***in*** ~ **1**. (队伍行进)受检阅。**2**. (被)检查;(被)回顾(*pass events in* ~ 对事件一一检查)。***the years under*** ~ 回顾中那些年代。**-a·ble** ***a***. 应检查的,可评论的。

re·view·al [riˈvjuːəl; rɪˋvjuəl] ***n***. 复查;校阅;评论;复习。

re·view·er [riˈvjuːə; rɪˋvjuɚ] ***n***. **1**. 评论家,评论员,评论作者。**2**. 校阅者。**3**. 检阅者;阅兵者。

re·vile [riˈvail; rɪˋvaɪl] ***vt***., ***vi***. 辱骂,漫骂;诽谤。**-r** ***n***. 谩骂者。

re·vis·al [riˈvaizəl; rɪˋvaɪzḷ] ***n***. 修订,校订;修订本;【印】校对。

re·vise [riˈvaiz; rɪˋvaɪz] **I** ***vt***. **1**. 修订,校订;校阅。**2**. 再检查;修正,改变(意见等)。**3**.【生】对…重新分类。~*d and enlarged* 修订增补的。*a* ~*d edition* 修订版。*the Revised Version* (基督教)《圣经》钦定英译本的修订本〔1881—1885 年出版,略 R. V. 或 Rev. Ver.〕。*the Revised Standard Version* (基督教)《圣经》修订版标准英译本〔1952 年出版于美国〕。**II** ***n***. **1**. 校订,订正。**2**.【印】再校样。

re·vis·er, re·vis·or [riˈvaizə; rɪˋvaɪzɚ] ***n***. **1**. 校订者,修订者;修正者;检查员。**2**.【印】校对员。

re·vi·sion [riˈviʒən; rɪˋvɪʒən] ***n***. **1**. 校订,订正,修订;修改,修正。**2**.【印】校对;再校。**3**. 校订本;修订本。**4**. 复审,上诉。**5**.〔R-〕= (the) Revised Version. **-al**, **-ary** ***a***. **1**. 校订的,校正的,修订的;修改的,修正的。**2**. 校对的。**-ism** ***n***. 修正主义。**-ist** **1**. ***n***. 修正主义者。**2**. ***a***. 修正主义的。

re·vis·it [ˈriːˈvizit; riˋvɪzɪt] ***vt***., ***n***. 再访问;再参观;重临,重游,回到。

re·vi·so·ry [riˈvaizəri; rɪˋvaɪzərɪ] ***a***. **1**. 校订的;修订的,修改的,修正的。**2**. 校对的。

re·vi·tal·ize [ˈriːˈvaitəlaiz; riˋvaɪtḷˏaɪz] ***vt***. 使恢复元气;使有新的活力;使新生;复兴。

re·viv·a·ble [riˈvaivəbl; rɪˋvaɪvəbḷ] ***a***. 能苏醒的,能复生的;可复兴的;可恢复的。

re·viv·al [riˈvaivəl; rɪˋvaɪvḷ] ***n***. **1**. 苏醒;更生,再生,复活;复兴;再流行。**2**.【宗】信仰复兴;〔R-〕文艺复兴;【剧】(旧戏等的)重新上演。**3**.【法】(契约等的)再生效。*the* ~ *of learning* [*letters*, *literature*] 文艺复兴。**-ism** ***n***. **1**.【宗】信仰复兴运动。**2**. 复兴精神。**-ist** ***n***. **1**.【宗】信仰复兴运动者。**2**. 复兴者。

re·vive [riˈvaiv; rɪˋvaɪv] ***vi***. **1**. 苏醒,更生,再生,复活。**2**. 恢复,更新;恢复精神,振奋。**3**. 复兴,再兴;再流行;再生效。**4**.【化】再生,复原;(金属)还原。— ***vt***. **1**. 使苏醒,使复活。**2**. 使恢复;使(重新)振作精神,使重新活跃。**3**. 使复兴,使再兴;使再流行;使再生效。**4**. 回想起;重新上演(旧戏等)。**5**.【化】使再生,复原,还原。~ *an*

R

old play 重演旧戏(使再受人欢迎)。

re·viv·er [riˈvaivə; rɪˋvaɪvɚ] ***n***. 使复活[复兴]者;〔俚〕刺激性饮料,兴奋剂;酒;生色剂。

re·viv·i·fi·ca·tion [ri(:)ˌvivifiˈkeiʃən; rɪˏvɪvəfəˋkeʃən] ***n***. **1.** 苏醒,复活。**2.**【化】复原(作用),再生(作用)。

re·viv·i·fy [ri(:)ˈvivifai; rɪˋvɪvəˏfaɪ] ***vt***. **1.** 使苏醒,使复活;使恢复精神,使振作,使有生气。**2.**【化】使复原,使再生。— ***vi***. = revive.

rev·i·vis·cence [ˌreviˈvisns; ˏrɛvɪˋvɪsns] ***n***. 苏醒,复活;再生;精神[活力]的恢复。

re·vi·vis·cent [ˌreviˈvaisənt; ˏrɛvɪˋvɪsnt] ***a***. 苏醒的,复活的;恢复精力的。

re·vi·vor [riˈvaivə; rɪˋvaɪvɚ] ***n***.【法】恢复诉讼。

rev·o·ca·ble [ˈrevəkəbl; ˋrɛvəkəbl] ***a***. 可废除[撤销,解除]的。**-bly** ***ad***.

rev·o·ca·tion [ˌrevəˈkeiʃən; ˏrɛvəˋkeʃən] ***n***. 废除,取消,解除;(对契约、建议等)撤销;〔古〕召还,唤回。

rev·o·ca·to·ry [ˈrevəkətəri; ˋrɛvəkəˏtorɪ] ***a***. 废除的,撤销的,解除的。*a* ~ *action*【法】解除契约诉讼。

re·voice [riˈvɔis; riˋvɔɪs] ***vt***. (***-voiced***; ***-voic·ing***) **1.** (用语言)重新表达,应答;把(声音)反射回来。**2.** 调校(风琴管等)。

R

re·vok·a·ble [riˈvəukəbl; rɪˋvokəbl] ***a***. = revocable.

re·voke [riˈvəuk; rɪˋvok] **I** ***vt***. **1.** 取消,撤销,收回,作废,废除,解除(命令、权利、诺言等)。**2.**〔古〕唤回,召还。~ *verbal evidence* 翻供。— ***vi***.【牌戏】(不跟出同样花色的牌而)犯规另出他牌。**II** ***n***. **1.**【牌戏】(不跟出同样花色的牌)犯规另出他牌。**2.**〔罕〕取消,废弃。***beyond*** ~ 不能取消的。***make a*** ~【牌戏】犯规另出他牌。

re·volt [riˈvəult; rɪˋvolt] **I** ***n***. **1.** 反叛,造反;起义。**2.** 反抗,反对。**3.** 反感,对抗情绪,厌恶。***in*** ~ 反抗着。***raise a righteous*** ~ 起义。***rise in*** ~ 起来反抗,起义。**II** ***vi***. **1.** 反抗;反叛;起义;造反。**2.** 恶心,感觉不快,反感,嫌恶 (*at*; *against*; *from*)。~ *against the authority* 反抗当局。~ *from one's allegiance* 反叛,对…不再忠诚。~ *to the enemy* 投敌。*Common sense* ~*s against* [*at*, *from*] *such measures*. 这种处置违反常情。*The stomach* ~*s at such food*. 这种食物使人恶心。—***vt***. 使恶心;使嫌恶;使反感。

re·volt·ed [riˈvəultid; rɪˋvoltɪd] ***a***. 反叛的;造反的;起义的,起来反抗的。

re·volt·ing [riˈvəultiŋ; rɪˋvoltɪŋ] ***pred***., ***a***. **1.** 反叛的;造反的;叛乱的;反抗的;起义的。**2.** 使人厌恶的,令人恶心的。*It is* ~ *to* .... 那是违反…的。*This is* ~ *to me*. 这使我讨厌死了。

rev·o·lute[1] [ˈrevəljuːt; ˋrɛvəˏljut] ***a***.【植】外卷的;【动】后旋的。

rev·o·lute[2] [ˈrevəljuːt; ˋrɛvəˏljut] ***vi***.〔俚〕干革命。

rev·o·lu·tion [ˌrevəˈluːʃən; ˏrɛvəˋluʃən] ***n***. **1.** 革命;剧烈的变革。**2.** 回转,绕转,旋转;转数;周期;一转;【天】运行,周转,公转。*the industrial* ~ 产业革命,工业革命。*palace* ~ 宫廷政变。*violent* ~ 暴力革命。*the R-* = the English [French] ~ 英国[法国]革命。*technical* ~ 技术革命。*the* ~ *of the seasons* 季节的循环。*the* ~ *of the moon around the earth* 月球绕着地球的公转。*The earth completes one* ~ *each day*. 地球每天完成一次自转。~***s per minute*** 〔略 r. p. m.〕【物】每分钟转数。**-ism** ***n***. 革命主义[学说、原理]。**-ist** ***n***., ***a***. 革命者(的),革命家(的),革命论者(的)。

rev·o·lu·tion·a·ry [ˌrevəˈljuːʃənəri; ˏrɛvəˋluʃənˏɛrɪ] **I** ***a***. **1.** 革命的,大变革的,革命性的。**2.** 旋转的。*the R-War* 〔美〕独立战争。~ *sweep* 革命气概。**II** ***n***. 革命家[者]。

rev·o·lu·tion·ize [ˌrevəˈljuːʃənaiz; ˏrɛvəˋluʃənˏaɪz] ***vt***. 使革命化;引起革命;鼓吹革命思想;革新;彻底改革。**-i·za·tion** [-ˈzeiʃən; -ˋzeʃən] ***n***. **-d** ***a***. 革命化的;被彻底改革的。

re·volve [riˈvɔlv; rɪˋvɑlv] ***vi***. 旋转,绕转;运行,周转;【天】公转,循环。*The earth* ~*s both round* [*about*] *the sun and on its own axis*. 地球又公转又自转。*Seasons* ~. 时令循环周而复始。*a mechanism for revolving the turntable* 回转桌的回转装置。— ***vt***. **1.** 使旋转;使周转。**2.** 细想,转念头,盘算。~ *a problem* (*in one's mind*) 反复思考问题。

re·volv·er [riˈvɔlvə; rɪˋvɑlvɚ] ***n***. **1.** 旋转者;旋转式装置。**2.**【冶】转炉。**3.** 转[左]轮手枪。*a six-chambered* ~ 六响左轮。*the policy of the big* ~ (用报复关税等)威吓政策。

re·volv·ing [riˈvɔlviŋ; rɪˋvɑlvɪŋ] **I** ***a***. 回转的;周转性的;旋转(式)的,轮转式的;循环的。**II** ***n***.【游泳】滚泳。*a* ~ *bookstand* 旋转书架。*a* ~ *door* 旋转门。~ ***fund*** (贷借经常保持平衡的)周转基金。

Rev. stat. = revised statutes 经过修订的(新)章程(法规)。

re·vue [riˈvjuː; rɪˋvju] ***n***. 〔F.〕 **1.** 时事讽刺剧,活报剧。**2.** 轻歌舞剧。

re·vul·sion [riˈvʌlʃən; rɪˋvʌlʃən] ***n***. **1.** (感情等的)激变,急变;突发变乱。**2.**〔罕〕(资本等的)突然收回;突然的分离。**3.** 嫌恶,反感。**4.**【医】(尤指用相反刺激剂的)诱导(法)。

re·vul·sive [riˈvʌlsiv; rɪˋvʌlsɪv] **I** ***a***.【医】诱导的。**II** ***n***.【医】诱导药[剂];诱导器具。

Rev. Ver. = Revised Version 〔见 revise 条〕。

re·ward [riˈwɔːd; rɪˋwɔrd] **I** ***n***. **1.** 报酬,酬劳,奖赏,酬金 (*for*)。**2.** 报答;报应;惩罚。*offer* [*give*] ~ *to sb*. *for sth*. 为某事给某人以报酬。*in* ~ *for* 为酬答…,作为…的奖赏。**II** ***vt***. **1.** 酬劳,奖赏 (*for*; *with*)。**2.** 报答;惩罚。***be*** ~***ed by success*** 获得了成功。~ ***sb***. ***for sth***. 为某事报答某人。~ ***according to sb.'s deserts*** 论功行赏;给予应得的赏罚。— ***vi***. **1.** 报答。**2.** 报复。**-ing** ***a***. 有价值的,有益的。**-less** ***a***. 无报酬的,白费气力的,徒劳的。

re·wind [riˈwaind; rɪˋwaɪnd] **I** ***vt***. (***-wound***; ***-winding***) 重新卷绕〔尤指倒卷影片等〕。**II** ***n***. **1.** 重卷物。**2.** 重卷。

re·wire [riˈwaiə; riˋwaɪr] ***vt***., ***vi***. (***-wired***; ***-wir·ing***) **1.** 再接电线,接新电线〔尤指给房子、马达等装新线〕。**2.** 再发报,重新发报。

re·word [ˈriːˈwəːd; riˋwɝd] ***vt***. 重说;改说;改变…的措词。

re·work [riˈwəːk; riˋwɝk] ***vt***. 再作;重做;重写;再工作;再加工。

re·write I [ˈriːˈrait; riˋraɪt] vt. (***-wrote*** [ˈriːˈrəut; rɪˋrot], ***-writ·ten*** [ˈriːˈritn; riˋrɪtn]) 书面答复;重写;再写;改写,修改。**II** [ˈriːrait; ˋriraɪt] ***n***. 改写[重写]的文稿。

re·writ·able ***a***.【计】(电脑存储器尤指光盘)可重写的,存储内容可洗去或修改的。**-man** ***n***. (报馆等的)改写加工编辑。

Rex [reks; rɛks] ***n***. 雷克斯〔男子名〕。

Rex [reks; rɛks] ***n***. 〔L.〕 **1.**〔英〕王,君主〔略 R., 常用于诉讼案件中,如: George R. = King George Rex V. Jones 国王对琼斯,即对琼斯提出公诉的刑事案件〕。**2.**〔俚〕控制导弹的脉冲系统。**3.** (比利时的法西斯党)国王党,列克斯党。

rex [reks; rɛks] ***n***.【古生】霸王龙〔恐龙的一种〕。

rex·ine [ˈreksiːn; ˋrɛksin] ***n***. 人造封面布;人造革沙发套。

Rey·kja·vik [ˈreikjəviːk; ˋrekjəˏvik] ***n***. 雷克雅未克〔冰岛首都〕。

Rey·nard [ˈrenəd; ˋrenɚd] ***n***. (民间故事中的)列那狐;〔r-〕狐狸。~ *the Fox* (中世纪流行的)《列那狐故事》。

Reyn·old [ˈrenəld; ˋrɛnəld] ***n***. 雷诺〔男子名, Reginald 的异体〕。

Reyn·olds [ˈrenəldz; ˋrɛnl̩dz] ***n*.** 雷诺兹〔姓氏〕。

RF = **1**. radio frequency 射频，无线电频率。**2**. range finder【摄，军】(测定目标距离的)测距计，光学测距仪。**3**. rapid-fire (枪等)速射的。**4**. 〔F.〕*République Française* 法兰西共和国。

R.F. = **1**. right field【棒球】右外场，右外野。**2**. right fielder【棒球】右场手，右外野手。

R.F.A. = Royal Field Artillery 〔英〕皇家野战炮兵。

RFC = Reconstruction Finance Corporation 〔美旧〕复兴金融公司。

R. F. C. = Royal Flying Corps 〔英旧〕皇家陆军航空队。

R. F. D. = Rural Free Delivery 〔美〕乡村免费邮递。

RG = registered (bonds).

R. G. A. = Royal Garrison Artillery 〔英〕皇家要塞炮兵。

R. G. S. = Royal Geographical Society 〔英〕皇家地理学会。

R. H. = **1**. relative humidity 相对湿度。**2**. right-handed 右手的，右方的。

R. H. = **1**. Royal Highlanders 〔英〕皇家苏格兰高地团。**2**. Royal Highness 〔英〕殿下。

Rh = Rhodium【化】铑。

R. H. A. = Royal Horse Artillery 〔英〕皇家骑炮兵。

rhab·do·coele [ˈræbdəˌsiːl; ˋræbdəˏsil] ***n*.**【动】单肠类(*Rhabdocoela*)动物。

rhab·do·man·cy [ˈræbdəmænsi; ˋræbdəˏmænsɪ] ***n*.** 棍卜〔用探矿杖占测矿物的迷信活动〕。

rhab·do·my·o·ma [ˈræbdəumaiˈəumə; ˏræbdomaɪˋomə] ***n*.** (*pl*. ***-ma·ta*** [-mətə; -mətə])【医】横纹肌瘤。

rha·chis [ˈreikis; ˋrekɪs] ***n*.** = rachis.

Rhad·a·man·thine [ˌrædəˈmænθain; ˏrædəˋmænθɪn] ***a*.** **1**. 像冥府判官似的。**2**. 铁面无私的。

Rhad·a·man·thus [ˌrædəˈmænθəs; ˏrædəˋmænθəs] ***n*.**【希神】拉达曼斯〔宙斯(Zeus)神与欧罗巴(Europa)之子，阴间的判官；铁面无私的法官〕。

Rhae·to-Ro·man·ic [ˌriːtəurəuˈmænik; ˏritoroˋmænɪk] **I** ***n*.** (瑞士东南部和意大利北部所讲)拉蒂亚罗曼斯方言。**II** ***a*.** 拉蒂亚罗曼斯方言的。

rham·nose [ˈræmnəus; ˋræmnos] ***n*.**【化】鼠李糖。

rhap·so·dic, rhap·sod·i·cal [ræpˈsɔdik(əl); ræpˋsɑdɪk(l)] ***a*.** **1**. 狂文的；狂诗的。**2**. 热狂的；狂喜的；夸张的。**3**. 狂乱的，混乱的。**-cal·ly** ***ad*.**

rhap·so·dist [ˈræpsədist; ˋræpsədɪst] ***n*.** **1**. 〔古希腊〕吟诵史诗者，吟游诗人。**2**. 狂热的写作者[说话者]；狂诗[狂想曲]作者。

rhap·so·dize [ˈræpsədaiz; ˋræpsəˏdaɪz] ***vi*.** 用狂诗[狂文]描写；吟诵狂诗；作狂文[狂诗]；作狂想曲；狂热地讲(*about*; *on*; *over*)。— ***vt*.** 狂热地吟诵；狂热地说。

rhap·s·o·dy [ˈræpsədi; ˋræpsədɪ] ***n*.** **1**. 〔古希腊〕适于一次吟诵的史诗[叙事诗]的一节〔尤指荷马史诗 Odyssey 或 Iliad 中的〕。**2**. 狂文，狂诗；狂话；【乐】狂想曲。**3**. 狂喜。***go into rhapsodies*** 狂热地说[写]；夸张地说。

rhat·a·ny [ˈrætni; ˋrætənɪ] ***n*.** (*pl*. ***-nies***)【植】拉檀根〔南美一种豆科植物的根，含丹宁酸，可用于鞣革〕。

rhd. = railhead 铁路终点。

rhe [ri; rɪ] ***n*.**【物】流值〔流度绝对单位，动力黏单位厘泊的倒数，有时亦指厘沲的倒数〕。

Rhe·a [ˈriə, ˈriːə; ˋrɪə, ˋriə] ***n*.** **1**. 丽亚〔女子名〕。**2**.【希神】宙斯的母亲。**3**. 〔r-〕【动】(南美产)三趾鸵鸟。

Rhe·in [ˈrain; ˋriɪn] ***n*.** 〔G.〕= Rhine.

Rhein·gold [ˈrainˌgəuld, G. ˈrainˌgɔːlt; ˋraɪnˏgold, ˋraɪnˏgɔlt] (北欧神话)莱茵金〔秘藏的黄金，原由莱茵仙女守护，后为尼柏龙矮人和西格夫里特所得〕。

Rhe·n·ish [ˈriːniʃ, ˈren-; ˋrinɪʃ, ˋrɛn-] **I** ***a*.** 莱茵(Rhine)河的。**II** ***n*.** 莱茵白葡萄酒(= Rhine wine)。

rhe·ni·um [ˈriːniəm; ˋrinɪəm] ***n*.**【化】铼〔Re〕。

rheo- *comb*. *f*. 表示"流"：*rheo*logy.

rhe·o·base [ˈriəˌbeis; ˋrɪəˏbes] ***n*.**【生理】基强度。**-basic** ***a*.**

rhe·ol·o·gy [riˈɔlədʒi; rɪˋɑlədʒɪ] ***n*.**【物、化】(研究物质流动、变形、弹性、黏性、可塑性的)流变学；液流学。

rhe·om·e·ter [riːˈɔmitə; rɪˋɑmətɚ] ***n*.**【电】电流计；【医】血流速度计；【物】流变仪。

rhe·o·phile [ˈriəˌfail; ˋrɪəˏfaɪl] ***n*.**【生】急流生物〔生活在流水中的动物或植物〕。**-oph·i·ly** [-ˈɔfili; -ˋɑfɪlɪ] ***n*.**

rhe·o·scope [ˈriːəskəup; ˋriəˏskop] ***n*.**【电】验电器。

rhe·o·stat [ˈriːəstæt; ˋriəˏstæt] ***n*.**【电】变阻器；电阻箱。

rhe·o·tax·is [ˌriəˈtæksis; ˏrɪəˋtæksɪs] ***n*.**【动】趋流性。**-tac·tic** ***a*.**

rhe·o·tome [ˈriːətəum; ˋriəˏtom] ***n*.**【电】周期断流器。

rhe·o·tron [ˈriːətrɔn; ˋriəˏtrɑn] ***n*.**【物】= betatron.

rhe·o·trope [ˈriːətrəup; ˋriəˏtrop] ***n*.**【电】电流转换开关。

rhe·ot·ro·pism [riˈɔtrəpizm; rɪˋɑtrəˏpɪzm̩] ***n*.**【生】向流性。**-trop·ic** [-əˈtrɔpik; -əˋtrɑpɪk] ***a*.**

rhe·sus [ˈriːsəs; ˋrisəs] ***n*.**【动】(印度)恒河猴，罗猴(= ~ monkey)。**R- factor**【医】(在人和罗猴红血球中发现的)凝血素，Rh 因子(= Rh factor)。

rhet. = rhetoric(al)。

rhe·tor [ˈriːtə; ˋritɚ] ***n*.** 〔古希腊〕修辞学教师[大师]；雄辩家，演说家。

rhet·o·ric [ˈretərik; ˋrɛtərɪk] ***n*.** 修辞学；辩论法；雄辩术；华丽的文词；花言巧语；辩才；修辞学书。

rhe·tor·i·cal [riˈtɔrikəl; rɪˋtɔrɪkl] ***a*.** (符合)修辞学的，修辞上的；华丽的，夸张的(文风)。*a ~ question* 修辞性疑问(句)，(不期望得到回答的)反问，反诘〔例如：Who cares? (= Nobody cares)〕。**-ly** ***ad*.**

rhet·o·ri·cian [ˌretəˈriʃən; ˏrɛtəˋrɪʃən] ***n*.** **1**. 修辞学者；雄辩家。**2**. 说话浮夸的人；词藻华丽浮夸的作家。

Rhe·um [ˈriːʌm; ˋriʌm] ***n*.**【植】大黄属。

rheum, rheu·ma [ruːm, ˈruːmə; rum, ˋrumə] ***n*.**【医】**1**. 稀黏液，黏膜分泌物〔鼻涕、泪等〕。**2**. (鼻黏膜)感冒。**3**. 〔*pl*.〕风湿痛。~ **epidemic** 流行性感冒。**-y** ***a*.**

rheu·mat·ic [ru(ː)ˈmætik; ruˋmætɪk] **I** ***a*.**【医】(害)风湿病的。**II** ***n*.** **1**. 风湿病人。**2**. 〔*pl*.〕〔口〕风湿痛。~ *fever* [*gout*] 急性关节风湿病。*a ~ paper* 风湿膏药。~ *walk* 风湿病人的步态。**-i·cal·ly** ***ad*.**

rheu·ma·tism [ˈruːmətizəm; ˋruməˏtɪzəm] ***n*.**【医】风湿病。*acute* [*chronic*] ~ 急性[慢性]关节风湿病。*articular* [*muscular*] ~ 关节[肌肉]风湿病。

rheu·ma·tiz [ˈruːmətiz; ˋrumətɪz] ***n*.** 〔口〕= rheumatism.

rheu·ma·toid [ˈruːmətɔid; ˋruməˏtɔɪd] ***a*.** 风湿性的；害风湿病的；患风湿性关节炎的；类风湿病的。~ **arthritis** 类风湿性关节炎。

rheu·ma·tol·o·gy [ˌruːməˈtɔlədʒi; ˏruməˋtɑlədʒɪ] ***n*.**【医】风湿病学。**-tol·o·gist** ***n*.**

rheum·y [ˈruːmi; ˋrumɪ] ***a*.** **1**. 分泌黏液的；黏膜分泌液的；黏液过多的。**2**. 鼻黏膜感冒〔鼻炎、鼻伤风〕的。**3**. 潮湿的；多湿气的(空气)；阴冷的。

R. H. G. = Royal Horse Guards 〔英〕皇家近卫骑兵团。

rhig·o·lene [ˈrigəliːn; ˋrɪgəˏlin] ***n*.**【药】列可冷〔局部麻醉药〕。

rhi·nal [ˈrainl; ˋraɪnl̩] ***a*.**【解】鼻(腔)的。~ *cavities* 鼻腔。

Rhine [rain; raɪn] ***n*.** 莱茵河。~ *wine* (莱茵)白葡萄酒。~**-stone** 莱茵水晶石；假金钢钻。

rhi·nen·ceph·a·lon [ˌrainenˈsefəlɔn; ˏraɪnɛnˋsɛfəlɑn] ***n*.** (*pl*. ***-la*** [-lə; -lə])【解】嗅脑。**-phal·ic** [-ˈfælik; -ˋfælɪk] ***a*.**

rhi·ni·tis [raiˈnaitis; raɪˋnaɪtɪs] ***n*.**【医】鼻(黏膜)炎。

rhi·no[1] [ˈrainəu; ˋraɪno] ***n*.** 〔英俚〕钱。*ready* ~ 现钱。

rhi·no[2] [ˈrainəu; ˋraɪno] ***n*.** (*pl*. ***~s***) **1**. 〔口〕=

R

rhinoceros. **2.** 〔美海军口〕(可作登陆浮桥用的)自动箱船。
rhino- *comb. f.* 表示"鼻,鼻腔":*rhino*laryngology.
rhi·noc·e·ros [rai'nɔsərəs; raɪ'nɑsərəs] (*pl.* ~*es*, ~) *n.* 【动】犀牛。
rhi·no·lar·yn·gol·o·gy [ˌrainəuˌlærin'gɔlədʒi; ˌraɪno-ˌlærɪn'gɑlədʒɪ] *n.* 鼻喉科学。**-o·gist** *n.*
rhi·nol·o·gy [rai'nɔlədʒi; raɪ'nɑlədʒɪ] *n.* 【医】鼻科学。
rhi·no·phar·yn·gi·tis [ˌrainəuˌfærin'dʒaitis; ˌraɪno-ˌfærɪn'dʒaɪtɪs] *n.* 【医】鼻咽炎。
rhi·no·plas·ty ['rainəˌplæsti; 'raɪnəˌplæstɪ] *n.* 【医】鼻成形术。**-plastic** *a.*
rhi·nor·rhe·a [ˌrainə'riːə; ˌraɪno'rɪə] *n.* 【医】鼻液溢。
rhi·no·scope ['rainəskəup; 'raɪnəˌskop] *n.* 【医】鼻(窥)镜。
rhi·nos·co·py [rai'nɔskəpi; raɪ'nɑskəpɪ] *n.* 【医】鼻镜检查法;鼻腔检查。
rhi·no·vi·rus ['rainəu'vairəs; 'raɪno'vaɪrəs] *n.* 【医】鼻病毒。
rhi·zo·bi·um [rai'zəubiəm; raɪ'zobɪəm] *n.* (*pl.* **-bi·a** [-ə; -ə]) 【生】根瘤菌〔如豆和车轴草根部所生〕。
rhi·zo·cal·ine [ˌraizəu'keiliːn; ˌraɪzə'kelin] *n.* 【植】成根素。
rhi·zo·car·pous [ˌraizə'kɑːpəs; ˌraɪzə'kɑrpəs] *a.* 【植】根部多年生而茎叶每年生的〔指多年生草本植物而言〕。
rhi·zo·ceph·a·lan [ˌraizə'sefələn; ˌraɪzə'sɛfələn] *n.* 【动】根头目(*Rhizocephala*)。**-ceph·a·lous** *a.*
rhi·zoc·to·ni·a [ˌraizɔk'təuniə; ˌraɪzɑk'tonɪə] *n.* 【生】丝核菌。
rhi·zo·gen·ic [ˌraizə'dʒenik; ˌraɪzə'dʒɛnɪk] *a.* 【植】生根的(= rhizogenous, rhizogenetic)。
rhi·zoid ['raizɔid; 'raɪzɔɪd] **I** *a.* 【植】似根的。**II** *n.* 假根。**-al** *a.*
rhi·zo·ma, rhi·zo·me [rai'zəumə; raɪ'zomə] *n.* (*pl.* **-ta** [-tə; -tə]) 【植】根茎,地下茎。
rhi·zo·mor·phous [ˌraizə'mɔːfəs; ˌraɪzə'mɔrfəs] *a.* 【植】似根的,根形的。
rhi·zo·pod ['raizəˌpɔd; 'raɪzəˌpɑd] *n.* 【动】肉足(虫)纲(*Sarcodina*)动物。**-al, -ous** *a.*
rhi·zo·pus ['raizəpəs; 'raɪzəpəs] *n.* 【生】根霉属(*Rhizopus*)菌;根霉。
rhi·zo·sphere ['raizəˌsfiə; 'raɪzəˌsfɪr] *n.* 【生态】根围。
rhi·zot·o·my [rai'zɔtəmi; raɪ'zɑtəmɪ] *n.* (*pl.* **-mies**) 【医】脊神经根切断术。
rho [rəu; ro] *n.* **1.** 希腊语第十七个字母〔ρ 相当于英语的 r〕。**2.** 【原】ρ 介子(= rho meson)。
rhod- *comb. f.* 表示"玫瑰,红"。
Rho·da ['rəudə; 'rodə] *n.* 罗达〔女子名〕。
rho·da·mine ['rəudəmiːn, -min; 'rodəmin, -mɪn] *n.* 【染】若丹明,玫瑰精,盐基桃红,呖呒。
Rhode Island ['rəud'ailənd; rod'aɪlənd] *n.* 罗德岛州〔美国州名〕。**Rhode Island Red** 〔美〕红毛罗德鸡〔卵肉兼用品种〕。**Rhode Island White** 〔美〕白毛罗德鸡〔与红毛罗德鸡近似,但为白羽〕。
Rhodes [rəudz; rodz] *n.* 罗兹〔姓氏〕。
Rho·de·sia [rəu'diːzjə; ro'diʒɪə] *n.* 罗得西亚〔津巴布韦的旧称〕。
Rho·di·an ['rəudiən, -djən; 'rodɪən, -djən] **I** *a.* (地中海的)罗得岛的;罗得骑士的。**II** *n.* 罗得岛人;罗得骑士。*the* ~ *law* 罗得海商法〔世界最古的海上法〕。
rho·dic ['rəudik; 'rodɪk] *a.* 【化】铑的〔尤指四价的〕。
rho·di·um ['rəudiəm, -djəm; 'rodɪəm, -djəm] *n.* 【化】铑。
rhodo- *comb. f.* = rhod-.
rho·do·chro·site [ˌrəudə'krəusait; ˌrodo'krosaɪt] *n.* 【矿】菱锰矿。
Rho·do·den·dron [ˌrəudə'dendrən; ˌrodə'dɛndrən] *n.* 【植】杜鹃花属,〔r-〕杜鹃花。
rho·do·lite ['rəudəˌlait; 'rodəˌlaɪt] *n.* 【矿】红榴石〔柘榴石(*garnet*)的变种,常用作宝石〕。
rho·do·my·cin [rəudə'maisin; rodə'maɪsɪn] *n.* 〔L.〕【化】玫红霉素。
rho·do·nite ['rəudənˌait; 'rodəˌnaɪt] *n.* 【矿】蔷薇辉石〔有时用作装饰品〕。
rho·do·plast ['rəudəˌplæst; 'rodəˌplæst] *n.* 【生】藻红体。
rho·dop·sin [rəu'dɔpsin; ro'dɑpsɪn] *n.* 【生理】(眼球视网膜上的)视玫红质,视紫红质。
rho·dous ['rəudəs; 'rodəs] *a.* 铑的;含铑的。
rhomb [rɔm; rɑm] *n.* 【数】菱形,斜方形;【结晶】斜方六面体。
rhom·ben·ceph·a·lon [ˌrɔmben'sefəˌlən; ˌrɑmbɛn'sɛfəlɑn] *n.* 【解】后脑(= hindbrain)。
rhom·bi ['rɔmbai; 'rɑmbaɪ] *n.* rhombus 的复数。
rhom·bic, rhom·bic·al ['rɔmbik(əl); 'rɑmbɪk(l̩)] *a.* 菱形的;斜方形的,正交(晶)的。
rhom·b(o)- *comb. f.* 表示"菱形":*rhomb*hedron.
rhom·bo·hed·ral [ˌrɔmbə'hedrəl; ˌrɑmbə'hɛdrəl] *a.* 斜方六面体的;【化】棱形的;三角晶的。
rhom·bo·hed·ron [ˌrɔmbə'hedrən; ˌrɑmbə'hidrən] *n.* (*pl.* **-dra** [-drə; -drə]) 【结晶】斜方六面体,菱面体。
rhom·boid ['rɔmbɔid; 'rɑmbɔɪd] *n.*, *a.* 【数】偏菱形(的);长斜方形(的)。
rhom·boi·dal ['rɔmbɔidl; rɑm'bɔɪdəl] *a.* 【数】偏菱形的,长斜方形的。
rhom·boi·de·us [rɔm'bɔidiəs; rɑm'bɔɪdɪəs] *n.* (*pl.* **-de·i** [-ˌai; -ˌaɪ]) 【解】脊胛肌。
rhom·bus ['rɔmbəs; 'rɑmbəs] *n.* (*pl.* **-bi** [-bai; -baɪ], ~*es*) 【数】菱形,斜方形;菱面体。
rhon·chus ['rɔŋkəs; 'rɑŋkəs] *n.* (*pl.* **-chi** [-kai; -kaɪ]) 【医】干啰音;鼻音;(临死时的)喉鸣(= râle)。**-chal, -chi·al** *a.*
Rhon·dda ['rɔndə; 'rɑndə] *n.* 朗达〔姓氏〕。
rho·ta·cism ['rəutəsizm; 'rotəsɪzm̩] *n.* 以 r 取代其他音或变他音为 r。
R. Hq = Regimental Headquarter 【军】团部。
R. H. S. = **1.** Royal Historical Society 〔英〕皇家历史学会。**2.** Royal Horticultural Society 〔英〕皇家园艺学会。**3.** Royal Humane Society 〔英〕皇家人文科学学会。
rhu·barb ['ruːbɑːb; 'rubɑrb] *n.* **1.** 【植】大黄;食用大黄;大黄根〔药用〕。**2.** 〔美俚〕争吵;激烈的争论;(比赛中的)抱怨。~**ing 1.** *a.* 〔英〕(舞台后部演员)造成人声嘈杂效果的。**2.** *n.* 嘈杂的人声。
rhumb [rʌm; rʌm] *n.* 【海】罗盘方位;罗盘方位二点间的角距;罗盘方位线;恒角线(= ~ line)。
rhum·ba ['rʌmbə; 'rʌmbə] *n.* = rumba.
rhyme [raim; raɪm] **I** *n.* **1.** 韵,脚韵。**2.** 同韵语。**3.** 〔常 *pl.*〕韵文,诗。*single* [*male*, *masculine*] ~ 单韵,阳性韵〔如 disdain, complain, 仅末音节押韵〕。*double* [*female*, *feminine*] ~ 二重韵,阴性韵〔如 motion 和 notion, 前后两个音节都押韵〕。*imperfect* ~ 不完全韵〔*love*, *move*; *phase*, *race* 等〕。*a nursery* ~ 摇篮曲。*a* ~ *slinger* 〔美〕诗人。***neither* ~ *nor reason***, ***without* ~ *or reason*** 杂乱无章;莫名其妙;无缘无故。**II** *vi.* 作诗,作韵文;押韵;(和某字)叠韵,同属一韵(*to*; *with*);(诗、音乐)和谐。— *vt.* 用韵文[诗]写;写(诗、韵文);把(故事、感想等)作成诗;写(押韵诗);使押韵;用…作韵脚;使合韵。~*d verse* 押韵诗(*opp.* blank verse 无韵诗)。*a rhyming dictionary* 诗韵辞典,韵府。
rhyme·less ['raimlis; 'raɪmlɪs] *a.* 无韵的;不押韵的。
rhym·er, rhym·ist, rhyme·ster ['raimə, -ist, -stə; 'raɪmɚ, -ɪst, -stɚ] *n.* 作诗的人;打油诗人。
rhyn·cho·ce·pha·li·an [ˌriŋkəusi'feiliən; ˌrɪŋkosɪ'felɪən] **I** *a.* 【动】喙头目(*Rhynchocephalia*)的。**II** *n.*

【动】喙头目。

rhy·o·lite [ˈraiəˌlait; ˋraɪə͵laɪt] *n*.【地】流纹岩。

Rhys [riːs; ris] *n*. 里斯〔姓氏〕。

rhythm [ˈriðəm, ˈriθəm; ˋrɪðəm, ˋrɪθəm] *n*.【诗】抑扬,节奏;韵律;【乐】节拍;节奏的格调;律动;【美】(色彩变化、浓淡配置等的)调和,匀称,和谐、有节奏的变化,有规律的循环运动;【医】节律;周期性。*the* ~ *of a sentence* 文句的抑扬顿挫。***play*** [***sing***] ***in quick*** ~ 用快调奏乐[歌唱]。

rhyth·mic, rhyth·mi·cal [ˈriðmik(əl); ˋrɪðmɪk(əl)] *a*. 有抑扬顿挫[节奏、韵律]的;韵律[节奏、配合]匀整和谐的,格调优美的;周期性的,间歇的,有规则地循环的。~ **gymnastics**【体】韵律操〔指用缎带、环、短棒等器具表演的有节奏的体操〕。**-cal·ly** *ad*. 有节奏地;按照拍子。

rhyth·mic·i·ty [riðˈmisiti; rɪðˋmɪsətɪ] *n*. 速度均匀,韵律,节奏性。

rhyth·mics [ˈriðmiks; ˋrɪðmɪks] *n*. 〔动词用单数〕韵律学。

rhyth·mist [ˈriðmist; ˋrɪðmɪst] *n*. 通韵律的人,作韵文的人;富有韵律的诗人[作曲家];有节奏感的人。

rhythm·less [ˈriðəmlis; ˋrɪðəmlɪs] *a*. 无韵律[节奏]的;不合拍子的。

rhy·ti·dec·to·my [ˌritəˈdektəmiː; ͵rɪtəˋdɛktəmi] *n*. 整容手术〔如除去脂肪沉淀物、拉紧皮肤等以达到整容目的〕。

rhy·ton [ˈraitɔn; ˋraɪtɑn] *n*. (一种古希腊的)角状杯。

R. I., RI = **1.** Rhode Island 罗德岛〔美国州名〕。**2.** Rotary International "扶轮国际"。**3.**〔L.〕*Rex et Imperator* (= King & Emperor)国王和皇帝。**4.**〔L.〕*Regina et Imperatrix* (= Queen & Empress) 女王和女皇。**5.** Royal Institution〔英〕皇家学会。

R. I. A. = Royal Irish Academy 爱尔兰皇家研究院。

ri·a [ˈriə; ˋriɑ] *n*.【地】溺河。

ri·al [ˈraiəl; rɪˋɔl] *n*. 里亚尔〔伊朗货币单位〕。

rial·to [riˈæltəu; rɪˋælto] *n*. (*pl*. ~*s*) **1.** 交易所;市场。**2.** (威尼斯的)里亚尔托岛〔商业中心区〕;(威尼斯大运河上通里亚尔托岛的)大石桥。**3.**〔R-〕纽约百老汇戏院区。*What news on the R-?* 有什么新闻没有?

ri·ant [ˈraiənt; ˋraɪənt] *a*. (主要指风貌、风景等)含笑的,喜气洋溢的,欢乐的;悦目的。

ri·a·ta [riˈɑːtə; rɪˋɑtə] *n*.〔美〕(牧童用的)套索。

rib[1] [rib; rɪb] **I** *n*. **1.**【解】肋骨;【烹】排骨。**2.** (船等的)肋材;(叶)主脉;叶肋。**3.** (昆虫的)翅脉;(鸟的)羽翮。**4.**【空】(翼)肋;【建】(圆拱的)弯梁,肋拱;(桥的)横梁;伞骨,扇骨;【采】矿壁;【机】力骨;变梁;【装订】书背凸带。**5.**〔谑〕心上人,妻子;〔美俚〕姑娘,少女。**6.** (布上的)棱线,棱纹,凸条,罗纹,山嘴;(在沙滩上的)浪痕,铁。*false* [*floating*] ~【解】假肋,游肋,浮肋。*true* [*sternal*] ~【解】真肋。*cooling* ~*s* 散热片。~*s of beef* 大块牛排。*Poke sb. in the* ~*s* (用肘)碰触某人肋骨一下使注意。***smite under the fifth*** ~ 戳进心脏,戳死。**II** *vt*. **1.** 装肋于;给…装肋材;用肋骨[肋材]包围。**2.** 起棱;【农】作垄。~ **flange** 肋凸缘。**~let** 凸肋〔固定于船侧以减少浪潮阻力〕。

rib[2] [rib; rɪb] **I** *vt*.〔俚〕开…的玩笑,戏弄。**II** *n*.〔俚〕开玩笑,戏弄;讽刺[滑稽]诗文。*tickle the* ~*s* 使人大笑。

rib- *comb. f*. 表示"有关核糖的"。

rib·ald [ˈribəld; ˋrɪbḷd] **I** *n*. 讲下流猥亵话的人;开下流玩笑的人。**II** *a*. 下流的,猥亵的,嘴脏的,不敬的;开下流玩笑的。

rib·ald·ry [ˈribəldri; ˋrɪbḷdrɪ] *n*. 下流;下流话,猥亵话;下流的笑话。

rib·and [ˈribənd; ˋrɪbənd] *n*.〔古、英〕= ribbon.

rib·band [ˈribbænd; ˋrɪb͵bænd] *n*.【船】带板;木桁。

rib·bed [ribd; rɪbd] *a*. 呈肋骨形的;用肋状物支撑的;起棱的;有罗纹的。

rib·bing [ˈribiŋ; ˋrɪbɪŋ] *n*. **1.**〔集合词〕叶肋,肋材,翅脉,垄。**2.** 肋材的装配[排列];(建筑等)肋材构架;作垄。**3.**〔美俚〕开玩笑,挖苦。

rib·ble-rab·ble [ˈribəlˌræbl; ˋrɪbḷ͵ræbḷ] *n*. **1.** 瞎嚷,胡言乱语。**2.** 暴民。

rib·bon [ˈribən; ˋrɪbən] **I** *n*. **1.** 缎带,丝带;带。**2.** (勋章的)饰带,绶带;【军】勋表〔佩于军服左上袋上方代表所得勋章的彩色条带〕;帽带。**3.** 带状物;(打字机的)墨带;(钟表的)发条;钢条卷尺;带状切片;【木工】条板;碎片;【船】= ribband. **4.**〔*pl*.〕〔口〕缰绳。*the blue* ~ (英国 *Garter* 勋章的)蓝绶带;最高荣誉的标记;禁酒会会员的徽章。*the red* ~ (*Bath* 勋章的)红绶带。*a* ~ *of road* 一条道路。***be torn to*** ~***s*** 撕成碎片。***handle*** [***take***] ***the*** ~***s*** 牵马,赶马车。***hang in*** ~***s*** 裂成碎片吊着。~ ***brake***【机】带状制动器。~ **building** [**development**] (从都市通到郊外干道两旁的)带状建筑。~ **fish**【动】带鱼。~ **speaker** 带式扬声器〔一种高保真扬声器〕。**II** *vt*. **1.** 装上丝带,用丝带装饰;加上带状条纹。**2.** 把…撕成长带,撕碎。— *vi*. 形成带状。

ri·bes [ˈraibiːz; ˋraɪbiz] *n*.【植】醋栗。

rib·grass [ˈribˌgrɑːs, -græs; ˋrɪb͵grɑs, -græs] *n*.【植】长叶车前草 (*Plantago lanceolata*)。

ri·bi·tol [ˈraibitɔl; ˋraɪbɪtɑl] *n*.【化】核糖醇。

ri·bo·fla·vin [raibəuˈfleivin; ͵raɪbəˋflevɪn] *n*.【化】核黄素,维生素 B_2,维生素 G。

ri·bo·nu·cle·ase [ˌraibəuˈnjuːkliˌeis, -ˈnuː-; ͵raɪboˋnjuklɪ͵es, -ˋnu-] *n*.【生化】核糖核酸酶。

ri·bo·nu·cle·ic acid [raibəunjuˈkliːik ˈæsid; raɪbonjəˋkliɪk ˋæsɪd] *n*.【生化】核糖核酸(略 RNA)。

ri·bose [ˈraibəus; ˋraɪbos] *n*.【化】核糖。

ri·bo·side [ˈraibəsaid; ˋraɪbə͵saɪd] *n*.【化】核糖甙[苷]。

ri·bo·some [ˈraibəˌsəum; ˋraɪbə͵som] *n*.【生化】核糖体。**-so·mal** *a*.

ri·bo·tide [ˈraibətaid; ˋraɪbə͵taɪd] *n*.【化】核糖酸。

ri·bo·zyme [ˈraibəzaim; ˋraɪbəzaɪm] *n*.【生化】核酶,酶性核糖核酸。

rib·wort [ˈribˌwəːt; ˋrɪb͵wɝt] *n*.【植】长叶车前草 (*Plantago lanceolata*)。

R.I.C. = Royal Irish Constabulary 爱尔兰皇家警察。

Ri·car·do [riˈkɑːdəu; rɪˋkɑrdo] *n*. **1.** 里卡多〔姓氏〕。**2.** David ~ 大卫·李嘉图〔1772—1823,英国经济学家〕。**-dian** *a*. 李嘉图学说[学派]的。

Rice [rais, riːs; raɪs, ris] *n*. 赖斯〔姓氏〕。

rice [rais; raɪs] **I** *n*. 稻,水稻;米;米饭。*a* ~ *seeding bed* 秧田。*broken* ~ 碎米。*cargo* ~ 糙米。*cleaned* ~ 白米。*polished* ~〔英〕= *faced* ~〔美〕上白米。*glutinous* ~ 糯米。~ *bran* 米糠。~ *in the husk* 谷子,稻子。*early* [*middle-season, late*] ~ 早[中、晚]稻。~ *sprouts* 稻秧。*paddy* ~ 水稻。*upland* ~ 陆稻,旱稻。~ *blast* 稻瘟病。*Canada* [*India, wild*] ~ 菰。*false* ~ 鞘糠草。**II** *vt*. 用压粒器把(熟马铃薯等)压成碎粒。~**bird**【动】(美国产)禾花雀;芙蓉鸟;爪哇麻雀。~ **flour** 米粉。~ **milk** 米粉牛奶。~ **paper** 卷烟纸;通草纸;宣纸。~ **pudding** 米饭布丁。~**stem** 稻杆 (*a* ~*-stem borer* 水稻螟虫)。~ **transplanter** 水稻插秧机。~ **water** (供病员喝的)稀粥,米汤。

ric·er [ˈraisə; ˋraɪsɚ] *n*. (把熟马铃薯压成碎粒的)压粒器。

rich [ritʃ; rɪtʃ] *a*. **1.** 富有的,富裕的,有钱的。**2.** 富于…的 (*in*); 丰富的,大量的 (*in*; *with*)。**3.** 肥沃的,丰饶的;出产丰富的(土地等)。**4.** 华美的,奢侈的,高价的,昂贵的。**5.** 富有某种美好之处的 (*with*)。**6.** 富有滋味的;意味深长的。**7.** 芳醇的,芳烈的(酒等);浓厚的,油腻的。**8.** 浓艳的,鲜艳的(颜色)。**9.** 洪亮的,圆润的(声音等);强烈的(香等)。**10.**〔口〕好笑的,有趣的;荒唐的。**11.**〔和过去分词连用〕= richly. *the* ~ 富人;有钱人。~ *and poor* 不论贫富。*a* ~ *ore* 富矿,好矿。*a* ~ *mine* 贮量丰富的矿山。*a* ~ *harvest* [*crop*] 丰收。~ *soil*

沃土,肥壤。~ *dresses* 华美的衣服。~ *dishes* 丰富的菜肴。~ *milk* 浓厚的牛奶。~ *allusions* 意味深长的典故〔喻指〕。*be* ~-*clad* 穿得漂亮华贵。*a* ~-*bound book* 装订豪华的书。*That's* ~!〔口〕真有意思! 真可笑! 真荒唐! ***as* ~ *as a Jew* [*as Croesus*]** 非常有钱的。***be* ~ *in* ...** 富于…。**-ness** ***n.***

Rich·ard [ˈritʃəd; ˋrɪtʃɚd] ***n.*** 理查德〔姓氏,男子名〕。~ ***Roe***【法】诉讼中不知姓名的当事人〔参见 John Doe〕。~***'s himself again.*** 又是好好的理查德了〔指从疾病、失望、恐怖中恢复正常〕。

Rich·ards [ˈritʃədz; ˋrɪtʃɚdz] ***n.*** 理查兹〔姓氏〕。

Rich·ard·son [ˈritʃədsn; ˋrɪtʃɚdsn] ***n.*** 理查森〔姓氏〕。

rich·en [ˈritʃn; ˋrɪtʃən] ***vt.*** 使富有;使浓;使(混合燃料)可燃成分更高。

rich·es [ˈritʃiz; ˋrɪtʃɪz] ***n.*** 〔*sing.*, *pl.*〕〔常 *pl.*〕财富,财宝;丰富。*the* ~ *of knowledge* 知识的宝库。

rich·ly [ˈritʃli; ˋrɪtʃlɪ] ***ad.*** 富裕地;丰饶地;浓厚地;浓郁地;华美地;〔主要和 deserve 连用〕充分地;完全地;彻底地。*He* ~ *deserved a thrashing.* 他挨揍活该。

Richter scale [ˈritʃə skeil; ˋrɪtʃɚ skel]【地】里氏地震强度表〔强度分级〕。

ri·cin [ˈraisin, ˈris-; ˋraɪsɪn] ***n.***【生化】蓖麻蛋白;蓖麻子白蛋白〔会凝集红血球〕。

ric·in·o·le·ic [ˌrisinəˈliːik; ˏrɪsənəˋliɪk] ***a.***【化】蓖麻油酸。

ric·in·o·le·in [ˌraisinˈəuliːin; ˏraɪsɪnˋolɪɪn] ***n.***【生化】甘油三蓖麻醇酸酯。

rick[1] [rik; rɪk] ***n.***, ***vt.*** 〔英〕禾堆,干草堆;堆成草堆。~ ***barton*** 〔英〕干草堆积场。

rick[2] [rik; rɪk] ***v.***, ***n.*** 〔英〕= wrick.

rick·ets [ˈrikits; ˋrɪkɪts] ***n.*** 〔*sing.*, *pl.*〕【医】软骨病,佝偻病。

rick·ett·si·a [riˈketsiə; rɪˋkɛtsɪə] ***n.*** (*pl.* ***-si·ae*** [-iː; -i], ***-si·as***)【微】立克次氏体。**-l *a.***

rick·et·y [ˈrikiti; ˋrɪkətɪ] ***a.*** (***-et·i·er***; ***-i·est***) **1.** 佝偻病[软骨病]的;患佝偻病的;似佝偻病的。**2.** 蹒跚的,东倒西歪的,摇晃的;虚弱的。

rick·ey [ˈriki; ˋrɪkɪ] ***n.*** 〔美〕利克酒;利克水〔酸橙汁、糖、酒、汽水的混合饮料〕。

rick·rack, ric·rac [ˈrikræk; ˋrɪkˏræk] ***n.*** 波状[曲折]花边。

rick·sha, rick·shaw [ˈrikʃə, -ʃɔː; ˋrɪkʃɔ, -ʃɔ] ***n.*** 人力车,黄包车。*a* ~ *man* 人力车夫。

rick·y-tick [ˈrikiˈtik; ˋrɪkɪˋtɪk] ***a.*** 〔俚〕**1.**【乐】单调而快速的〔如二十世纪二十年代的一种民间音乐〕。**2.** 老式的,过时的 (= ricky-ticky)。

ric·o·chet [ˈrikəʃet, -ʃei; ˏrɪkəˋʃɛt, -ʃe] **I *n.*** (石片、枪弹等接触地面、水面后的)跳飞;漂;跳飞的石片;【军】跳弹。~ *fire* [*firing*] 跳弹射击,跳射。*a* ~ *shot* 跑弹。**II *vi.*** (〔英〕***-tt-***)跳飞;漂掠。— ***vt.*** 使跳飞,用跳弹射击。

ri·cot·ta [riˈkɔtə, It. riːˈkəutɑː; rɪˋkɔtə, riˋkotɑ] ***n.*** (意大利制)乳清干酪。

ric·tus [ˈriktəs; ˋrɪktəs] ***n.*** **1.**【动】嘴裂,(鸟或动物)张嘴时的阔度。**2.** (此种)裂口。**3.** 露齿裂嘴,龇牙咧嘴。**-tal *a.***

rid[1] [rid; rɪd] (***rid*** [rid; rɪd]; ***rid·ded*** [ˈridid; ˋrɪdɪd]; ***rid·ding***) ***vt.*** **1.** 使脱除,使摆脱 (*of*; *from*)。**2.** 〔方〕除去,扫除;收拾干净(房间、饭桌) (*up*);打发掉(工作等) (*off*, *away*)。**3.** 〔古〕救,救出。*The world is well* ~ *of him.* 那个家伙死得好。*He is* ~ *of fever.* 他的烧退了。***get* [*be*] ~ *of*** 摆脱;除去,驱除,拔除(眼中钉) (*I can't get* ~ *of this cold.* 伤风总是不好)。

rid[2] [rid; rɪd] 〔古〕ride 的过去式和过去分词。

rid·a·ble [ˈraidəbl; ˋraɪdəbl] ***a.*** 可以骑的(马);可以骑马过去的(路、河等)。

rid·dance [ˈridəns; ˋrɪdṇs] ***n.*** 摆脱;除去,驱除。*a good* ~ 拔除得好;可喜的摆脱。*He is a good* ~. 他这家伙不在的好。*make clean* ~ *of* 把…扫除干净[一扫而光]。

rid·den [ˈridn; ˋrɪdn] **I** ride 的过去分词。**II *a.*** 受…支配的,受…虐待的,受…折磨的,…横行的。*a country* ~ *by soldiers* 军人跋扈的国家。

ri·dent [ˈraidnt; ˋraɪdnt] ***a.*** 〔罕〕笑的。

rid·dle[1] [ˈridl; ˋrɪdl] **I *n.*** 谜;谜语,哑谜;莫名其妙的事情,闷葫芦;莫名其妙的人。*propound* [*propose*, *ask*] *a* ~ 出谜。*solve* [*find out*, *guess*] *a* ~ 解谜,猜谜。*speak in* ~*s* 令人摸不着头脑地说。**II *vt.*** 解(谜),猜。*Riddle me a* [*my*] ~, *what is this?* = *Riddle me*, ~ *me what it is.* 给你猜一个谜,你猜这是什么谜? — ***vi.*** 出谜;令人摸不着头脑地说。

rid·dle[2] [ˈridl; ˋrɪdl] **I *n.*** 粗筛。**II *vt.*** 用筛分选(卵石等),筛分。**2.** (子弹等把船等)打得枪眼像筛子一样。**3.** 精查,细查(证据、真伪);连连质问(使人为难),(列举事实)问倒(人)。*The door was* ~*d with shot.* 门被子弹打得尽是窟窿。

rid·dling [ˈridliŋ; ˋrɪdlɪŋ] ***a.*** 谜似的,费解的,莫名其妙的,令人摸不着头脑的。

ride [raid; raɪd] (***rode*** [rəud; rod]; ***ridden*** [ˈridn; ˋrɪdn]) **I *vi.*** **1.** 骑(马)去,坐(车)去;骑,乘,坐;骑马;骑自行车去(旅行)。**2.** 当骑兵,在骑兵队服务。**3.** (骑师赛马前穿着骑装)在马上有若干重量。**4.** (马乖乖地)给骑(等),骑(乘,坐)着(舒服、不舒服等)。**5.** 背,背去,(车等)载,载去。**6.** 浮,漂,像浮(在空中、水上),(船)停泊;(月、太阳)上升,挂;被支持着动;【导弹】乘波。**7.** (折断的骨头等)叠上;【彩印】套上。**8.** 〔美俚〕(事情)进展顺利。~ *in* [*on*] *a carriage* [*train*, *ship*] 坐车[火车,船]。~ *on a bicycle* 骑着自行车走。*He* ~*s in Life Guards.* 他在近卫骑兵队服务。~ *12 stone* (指赛马骑师)穿着骑装有 12 英担重。~ *well* [*hard*] (道路等)好[不好]骑行,(车)好[不好]乘坐。*Let it* ~. 〔美俚〕听其自然。— ***vt.*** **1.** 骑,乘,坐,跨;驾驭(马等);破(浪)前进(等)。**2.** 乘马[车等]经过(某处)。**3.** 支配,控制。**4.** 压迫;使痛苦,折磨〔通常用过去分词,*cf.* ridden〕。**5.** 〔美〕给坐着去,载去,载运。**6.** 系(船),使停泊。~ *a bicycle* 骑自行车。*Spectacles* ~ *his nose* 眼镜架在鼻子上。*I was ridden by a nightmare.* 我被梦魇压住了。~ ***a gravy train*** 〔美〕多取,多拿。~ ***a man down like the maintack*** 使人过分疲劳。~ ***a method* [*jest*] *to death*** 把一种方法用得过多以致失却效用,(笑话)讲得过分反而乏味。~ ***a race*** 赛马,赛车。~ ***and tie*** 两人轮流骑一匹马〔一人骑至某处即拴马留给另一人,自己徒步前进〕。~ ***at*** 骑马驶向。~ ***at single anchor*** 抛单锚停船。~ ***at the ring*** 跑马(用枪)挑(取高悬的)圈[环]。~ ***away*** = ~ off. ~ ***bareback*** 骑没鞍子的马。~ ***behind*** 骑在背后。~ ***bodkin*** 乘在两人当中。~ ***double*** 两人骑一匹马[一辆自行车]。~ ***down*** 骑马穷追[赶上];骑马踏坏[撞倒];克服;打败;把马骑死;过度驱使。~ ***for a fall*** 蛮干,自讨苦吃,自取灭亡。~ ***herd*** 〔美西部〕(牧童)骑马看管牧群;(一般)看管,保护。~ ***off*** 岔开去。~ ***off on* (*side issues*)** 岔到枝节问题上去;回避要点。~ **(*sb.*) *on a rail*** 令人骑在木棍上被扛着游街〔作为惩罚〕。~ ***sb. off***【马球】驱马插入球和对手中间阻止对手打球。~ ***one's horse at a fence*** 策马向篱笆跑去〔准备跳过去〕。~ ***one's horse to the enemy*** 骑马向敌人冲锋。~ ***one's horse to death*** 把马骑死;把自己的得意话讲得过分而惹人讨厌。~ ***on the wind* [*waves*]** (船)迎风[破浪]前进。~ ***out*** **1.** (船等)安然冲过风暴。**2.** 平安渡过困难。~ ***over*** 蹂躏;威吓,压倒;跳(越)过;(赛马)从容胜过;骑马而来。~ ***roughshod over*** 大摆架子,趾高气扬;蹂躏,欺凌,为所欲为,横行霸道。~ ***rusty*** 变顽固,倔强地反抗。~ ***sth. to death*** (把某事物)使用过分,反而得不到效果。~ ***the beam*** 沿着波束所示航线飞行。~ ***the bumpers* [*buffers*]** 〔美俚〕(站在货车与货车连接

处)偷乘火车。~ *the deck* 〔美俚〕(扒在客车顶上)偷乘火车。~ *the fence* 骑马巡视牧场周围并检修篱笆。~ *the goat* 〔口〕加入秘密团体。~ *the line* 〔美俚〕(在无篱笆的牧场与牧场间)做看守。~ *the rods* [*tickets*]〔美俚〕(钻在棚车里面)偷乘火车。~ *the shoe leather express* 〔美俚〕走路去。~ *the whirlwind* (天使)御旋风;叱咤风云;趁革命机会。~ *to hog* [*pig*] 猎野猪。~ *to hounds* (猎狐时)骑马紧跟着猎狗追赶;猎狐。~ *up* (身上的衣服等)向上拱,缩上去;(衣领)露出(衣外);(领带)松开;走样。~ *up to* 骑马[坐车]赶到…跟前。

II *n*. 1. 骑乘,乘坐;骑马旅行;乘车[船等]旅行;搭乘时间。2. (森林等中的)马道;跑马场。3.【军】补充骑兵队。4.〔美俚〕汽车;轻松自由的节奏。*give sb. a* ~ 让(人)骑马[乘车]。*go for a* ~ 去骑一骑,乘车转一圈。*have* [*take*] *a long* ~ 骑马[乘车]走很远一段路。*take for a* ~ 〔美俚〕用汽车诱出杀害;欺骗。

rid·er [ˈraidə; ˋraɪdɚ] I *n*. 1. 骑马的人;善于骑马的人;骑师;〔古〕跑生意的,行商。2.〔古〕骑士,武士;驯马师;马贼。3. 附款;附笔;(特指议会三读会的)追加条款。4. (精密天平上的)游(动砝)码。5. 制导器;【数】系;〔口〕乘波导[飞]弹;【几】应用习题;(机械装置的)上部;夹层;【海】(加固船体的)盖顶木料[钢板];【园艺】接穗;【建】(支墙)斜撑。*by way of* ~ 作为…的追加,作为附款。**-ship** 全体乘客;乘客数。**-less** *a*. 没人骑的;没主人的(马);无附款的,无追加条款的。

ridge [ridʒ; rɪdʒ] I *n*. 1.【动】脊;脊背。2. 山脊;岭,岗;分水岭,山脉。3. 屋脊;(犁沟与犁沟间的)犁垄;田塍;鼻梁;隆起线;【筑城】斜堤脊;【铸造】沟,注沟;(气象图上)狭长的高压带(脊)。II *vt*. 装屋脊;作垄,培土;使(面上)起皱纹;种在垄上。—*vi*. 成垄;起皱纹。~ **beam**, ~-**piece**, ~**pole** 栋梁,栋木。~ **roof** = gable roof. ~ **tile** 脊瓦。~ **tree**【建】栋木。~ **way** 山顶上的路,山脊路;田塍路。

Ridge [ridʒ; rɪdʒ] *n*. 里奇〔姓氏〕。

ridg·y [ˈridʒi; ˋrɪdʒɪ] *a*. (-*er*; -*i·est*) 有脊的;成垄的;隆起的。

rid·i·cule [ˈridikjuːl; ˋrɪdɪkjul] I *n*. 嘲笑,愚弄,揶揄;〔古〕笑柄。*bring into* ~ = *cast* [*pour*] ~ *upon* = *cover with* ~ = *hold up to* ~ = *turn into* [*to*] ~ 嘲笑,讽刺,挖苦(*He was held up to* ~. 他被人嘲弄。*He turns everything into* ~. 他把一切都当作笑话看待。*pour* ~ *on sb*. 嘲笑某人)。II *vt*. 嘲笑,奚落;愚弄;讥刺,挖苦。

ri·dic·u·lous [riˈdikjuləs; rɪˋdɪkjələs] *a*. 可笑的,滑稽的;该嘲笑的;荒谬的。~ *in dress* [*shape*] 衣服[形状]好笑的。*the* ~ 可笑的事物。**-ly** *ad*. **-ness** *n*.

rid·ing[1] [ˈraidiŋ; ˋraɪdɪŋ] *n*. 区〔英国约克郡的行政区,有东西北三区〕。*the Three Ridings* (英国)约克郡。

rid·ing[2] [ˈraidiŋ; ˋraɪdɪŋ] *n*. 骑马;乘车;马道,跑马场。*take a* ~ 骑马,乘车。~ *hawse full*【海】船在停泊中前后簸动致海水由锚链孔打入。*radar beam* ~ 波束导航。~ **bitts**【海】系缆柱。~-**habit** 女骑装。~ **lamp**, ~ **light**【海】锚位灯,停泊灯。~ **master** 马术教练[教官]。~ **school** 马术学校。~ **suit** 骑装。

Rid·ley [ˈridli; ˋrɪdlɪ] *n*. 里德利〔姓氏〕。

ri·dot·to [riˈdɔtəu; rɪˋdɑto] *n*. (*pl*. -*tos*) 舞蹈会,歌舞会〔十八世纪英国流行的社交聚会,常为一种化装舞会〕。

Rid·path [ˈridpɑːθ; ˋrɪdpæθ] *n*. 里德帕斯〔姓氏〕。

Ri·el [riˈel, riːl; rɪˋɛl, rɪl] *n*. 瑞尔〔柬埔寨货币单位〕。

Ries·ling [ˈriːzliŋ; ˋrɪzlɪŋ] *n*. 一种浓烈的莱茵白葡萄酒。

ri·fa·ci·men·to [riˌfɑtʃiˈmentəu; riˌfɑtʃiˋmɛnto] *n*. 〔It.〕(*pl*. ***ri·faci·men·ti*** [-ˈmentiː; -mɛnti]) 改编,改写。

rif·am·pi·cin [ˌrifæmˈpaisən; ˏrɪfæmˋpaɪsən] *n*.【药】利福平(= rifampin)。

rif·a·my·cin [ˌrifəˈmaisən; ˏrɪfɑˋmaɪsən] *n*.【药】利福霉素。

rife [raif; raɪf] *a*.〔用作 *Pred*.〕流行的,盛行的;普遍的;大量的,丰富的。*be* [*grow*, *wax*] ~ *with* (*idioms*) 富于,充满(习语等)。*used to be* ~ 过去很盛行。

Riff [rif; rɪf] *n*. 1. = Rif, Er. 2. (北非的)里弗族。**-i·an** *n*., *a*. 里弗人(的)。

riff [rif; rɪf] *n*. (爵士音乐的)即与反复片段。—*vi*. 反复演奏即兴段。

rif·fle [ˈrifl; ˋrɪfl] I *n*. 1.【采】(沙金采集槽的)捕沙沟。2.〔美〕(河中)急流;波纹。*make the* ~ 成功地渡过河流或急滩;成功地战胜困难;成功,胜利。II *vt*., *vi*. 1. 流过(浅滩);使起涟漪。2. (用拇指)翻(书页等)。3. 快速洗(纸牌)。

riff·raff [ˈrifræf; ˋrɪfˏræf] *n*. 地痞,流氓;(人类的)渣滓;废物,碎屑。

ri·fle[1] [ˈraifl; ˋraɪfḷ] I *n*. 步枪;来福枪,膛线枪〔和滑膛枪区别〕;来福线,膛线;〔*pl*.〕步枪队。II *vt*. 在(枪膛)内制来福线;用步枪[来福枪]射击。~**bird** (叫声像枪声一样的)噬鸣飞鸟。~ **corps** 志愿步枪队。~-**green** *n*., *a*. 暗绿色(的)。~ **ground** 步枪射击[打靶]场。~**man** 1. 步兵;步枪射手。2. = ~ bird. ~-**pit**【军】散兵壕。~ **range** 步枪射击[打靶]场;步枪射程。~ **scope** 步枪上的望远瞄准器。~**shot** 步枪子弹;步枪射手;步枪射程。

ri·fle[2] [ˈraifl; ˋraɪfḷ] *vt*. 搜劫;抢劫一空;偷去;(顺手)带走。~ *the drawers and show cases* 翻箱倒柜,抢劫一空。~ *a person of his belongings* 搜劫某人的行李。—*vi*. 搜劫;抢劫;掠夺。

ri·fle·ry [ˈraifləri; ˋraɪflrɪ] *n*. 步枪打靶(练习)。

ri·fling [ˈraifliŋ; ˋraɪflɪŋ] *n*. 1. (在枪膛里)制来福线。2. 来福线,膛线。

rift [rift; rɪft] I *n*. 1. 裂口,罅隙,空隙,裂缝。2.【地】断裂;断层线;长狭谷;河流浅石滩。3. 分裂,不和。*a little* ~ *within the lute* 嫌隙;最初的分歧;发狂的预兆〔神志开始不清〕。II *vt*., *vi*. 破开,裂开,劈开。~ **valley**【地】地堑;裂谷。

rig[1] [rig; rɪg] I *n*. 1.【海】索具,装具,装备;舣装;帆缆的配备;帆装,帆具,索具;帆式。2.〔口〕服装。3.〔美〕设备,装配,配备;配好了马的马车;准备好的马车。4. 钻探设备[平台];凿井机器;【矿】钻塔,钻车。5.〔口〕钓鱼用具[设备]。*a working* ~ 工作服。*a* ~ *of the day* 时装。*a test* ~【空】试验台。II *vt*. 1.【海】装上索具(帆桩,帆桁等);配备,装备;【空】装机身[机翼]。2.〔口〕穿(美服)(*out*; *up*)。3. 临时赶造,草草做成(*up*)。—*vi*. (船)装上索具(*out*; *up*)。~ **out** 装饰,打扮。~ *up a tent* 赶忙撑起一个帐篷。~ *up a military force* 调兵遣将。

rig[2] [rig; rɪg]〔口〕I *n*. 1. 捣蛋,恶作剧;嘲弄,戏弄;欺骗。2. 阴谋,诡计。3.【商】垄断,囤积。*run a* [*the*] ~, *run one's* ~*s* 恶作剧,捣蛋(*upon*)。II *vt*. 用不正当手段操纵,控制;(为欺骗目的而)事先决定[安排];〔口〕欺骗。~ *the market* 操纵市价,垄断(证券等)市价。~ *an election* 操纵选举。

rig[3] [rig; rɪg] *n*. 发育不全[部分阉割]的动物。

Ri·ga [ˈriːgə; ˋrigə] *n*. 里加〔拉脱维亚港市〕。

rig·a·ma·role [ˈrigəməˌrəul; ˋrɪgəməˏrol] *n*. 冗长的废话,无聊的啰唆话,没条理的文章,烦琐的仪式程序(= rigmarole)。

ri·ga·to·ni [ˌrigəˈtəuni, It. ˌriːgɑːˈtəuniː; ˏrɪgəˋtonɪ, ˏrɪgɑˋtonɪ] *n*. 小肉龙〔一种条状肉馅的面食〕。

Ri·gel [ˈraidʒl; ˋraɪdʒḷ] *n*.【天】参宿七。

rig·ger [ˈrigə; ˋrɪgɚ] *n*. 1. 装配工人;【海】索具装配人;【空】机身装配员。2.【机】束带滑车;【建】脚手架安全装置。3. 骗子;垄断市价[操纵物价]的人。

rig·ging [ˈrigiŋ; ˋrɪgɪŋ] *n*. 1.【海】索具;装置,设备;【空】机身装配;(舞台用)索具;传动用装置。2.〔口〕衣服,服装。*a* ~ *band*【空】装配带,座带。*a* ~ *shop*【空】装配

厂。*climb the* ～〔美俚〕发脾气;发怒。

right [rait; raɪt] **I** *a*. **1.** 右,右方的,右侧的,右派的(*opp*. left)。**2.** 正当的,当然的(*opp*. wrong)。**3.** 不错的;正确的;真的;真正的;(布的)正面的。**4.** 笔直的,直角的(*opp*. olique)。**5.** 恰好的,合适的,适当的,得当的,妥当的,顺当的,顺利的;秩序井然的,井井有条的。**6.** 健康的,健全的;精神正常的。**7.**〔罕〕(人、性格)正直的;公正的;〔美〕同情的;有好意的。**8.**〔古〕合法的。～ *and left* 左右的,两方的。*the R- Wing(s)* 右派,保守派。*That's* ～. 好;〔口〕就是那样。*R-*!〔口〕= *R- you are*. 说得对;〔回答命令、提议〕是,知道了,对。*R- oh*! = righto. *the* ～ *side of cloth* 布的正面。～ *arm* 得力助手。*Mr*. [*Miss*] *R-*〔口〕很相配的丈夫[妻子]。～ *amount* 需要量,适量。*a* ～ *angle* 直角。*a* ～ *line* 直线。*I am not quite* ～. 我身体不大舒服。*He is not* ～ *in his head*. 他神志不正常。***a fault on the*** ～ ***side*** 可以原谅的过失,小缺点。***act a*** ～ ***part*** 采取正当行动。***all*** ～ 好;圆满;确实。***All's*** ～. 万事顺利,一切都好。***as*** ～ ***as a trivet*** [***as rain***] 非常健康;〔美〕好极了。***at*** [***on, to***] ***one's*** ～ ***hand*** 在右方。***at*** ～ ***angles with*** 和…成直角。***do the*** ～ ***thing*** 做正确的事情,做得对。***get it*** ～ (使)真正[正确]理解,(使)了解清楚。***get on the*** ～ ***side of*** 得到…的喜爱[宠爱]。***get*** [***make***] ～ 改正,弄正,弄好。***give the*** ～ ***hand of fellowship*** 接纳为友;同意入伙。***in one's*** ～ ***mind*** [***senses***] 精神正常。***on the*** ～ ***side of*** (***fifty***) (50岁)以下,(50岁)不到。***put oneself*** ～ 说明自己的正确立场[真正用意](*I put myself* ～ *with him*. 我向他说明他对我的误解)。***put one's*** ～ ***hand to the work*** 认真[尽力]做事。***put*** ～ 改正,恢复健康[秩序],弄好;修理;矫正,订正。***put the*** (～) ***saddle on the*** ～ ***horse*** 责备应该责备的人。～ ***D.A.***〔美俚〕老实公正的地方检察官〔D. A. = district attorney〕。～ ***forward*** = ～*in*. ～ ***guy***〔美俚〕忠实可靠的人。～ ***halfback***【足球】右前卫。～ ***in***【足球】右内锋。～ ***or wrong*** 无论对与不对,无论怎样,一定。～ ***side out*** 正面向外。～ ***side up*** 正面朝上。***set oneself*** ～ = *put oneself* ～. ***set*** ～ = *put* ～. ***the*** ～ ***man in the*** ～ ***place*** 人地两宜;人得其位,位得其人。***the*** ～ ***way*** 正路(*to*);最正当[适当、有效]的方式[做法];真相;〔用作状语〕正当地,适当地。

II *ad*. **1.** 一直,笔直;一直,始终。**2.** 正当地,公正地;正确地,准确地;无误地;真实地,真正地。**3.** 适当地,得当地;正好地,恰好地;当然地;顺当地,顺利地;完全,全然;恰好,正好。**4.** 立刻,马上。**5.** 向右,向右侧。**6.**〔古、俗〕非常,很。**7.**〔尊称〕*the R- Honourable*, 见 honourable 条。*It sank* ～ *to the bottom* 直沉到底。*I guessed* ～. 我猜中了。*It serves you* ～. 真是活该,真是报应。～ *well* 非常好。***be rotten*** ～ ***through*** 完全腐烂。***come*** ～ 改正,变好;实现。***do a thing*** ～ 好好干,认真做。***go*** ～ 进行得顺利。***go*** ～ ***home*** 直接回家。***go*** ～ ***on*** 一直前进,向前突进。***if I remember*** ～ 如果我没有记错的话。***look neither*** ～ ***nor left*** 目不斜视。***Right about***!〔口令〕向后转! ～ ***along***〔美〕不停地,不断地。～ ***and left*** 向左又向右;向四面八方,从四面八方;(拳击等的)乱打。～ ***away***〔美〕立刻,马上。～ ***down*** 一直朝下;明明白白地,不隐瞒地;很,十分;无风。***Right dress***!〔口令〕向右看齐! ～ ***here***〔美〕现在就在这里;即刻。～ ***in the middle of one's work*** 正在工作中。～ ***in the wind's eye*** 迎风。～ ***now***〔美〕现在,目前;方才,刚刚。～ ***off***〔美〕即刻;全然。～ ***off the bat***〔美俚〕立刻。～ ***off the reel***〔美俚〕立刻;慌忙;新鲜的。～ ***on***〔美俚〕**1.** 对啊! **2.** 老于世故。～ ***on time*** 准时。～ ***opposite*** 正对面,正相反。～ ***out of the feed box***〔美俚〕最新情报〔尤指关于赛马的〕。～ ***over*** (***the way***) 在(道路的)正对过。～ ***smart*** (***of***)〔美〕大量的,很多的。～ ***straight***〔美〕即刻。～ ***there*** 就在那里。***Right turn***!〔口令〕向右转! ～ ***up and down***【海】风平浪静;直率认真地。***send sb. to the*** ～ ***about*** 一口谢绝,拒绝(某人)。***turn out*** ～ 顺利起来;碰巧。***turn*** ～ 转往右面。***turn*** ～ ***round*** 转一个圈。

III *n*. **1.** 右,右面,右边,右侧;【军】右翼;右边的东西;〔美〕【海军】右舷。**2.** 〔R-〕【政】(从主席台上看去)右座议员[党员];右翼[右派](分子);保守派,保守分子。**3.** 正,正当;正义,公理,公道;公正;正当行为;正确,准确,无误;〔*pl*.〕正当状态[秩序];〔*pl*.〕事情的真相。**4.** 权利;〔常 *pl*.〕(董事对新股的)优惠权。**5.** 正面。～(*s*) *and wrong*(*s*) 是非曲直。*the* ～*s of a matter* [*the case*] 事情的真相。*absolute* ～*s* 绝对权。*civil* ～*s* 公民权。*the* ～ *of flights beyond*【空】以远权。*the* ～ *of visit* (*and search*)【法】(交战国在公海上的)搜查权。***be in*** ～ ***with*** = *get in* ～ *with*. ***the Bill of Rights***【英史】**1.**《权利法案》〔1689年公布的英国君主立宪制的根本法文件〕。**2.**《人权法案》〔1789年美国通过的美国宪法的第一次修正案〕。***bring to*** ～*s* 使复原状,改正;规劝。***by*** (***good***) ～ 正当地,当然。***by*** ～ ***of ...*** 依…,以…的权限[理由]。***by*** ～*s* 根据正当权利。***claim a*** ～ ***to*** 要求…的权利。***confuse*** ～ ***with wrong*** 混淆是非。***do*** (*sb*.) ～ 公平对待(某人),正当批评(某人)。***get in*** ～ ***with***〔美〕得到…的喜爱。***go to the*** ～ ***about*** 向后转;扭转[转变]局面[主义、政策等]。***have a*** [***the***] ～ ***to do*** [***of doing***] 有权做…;应该做…。***have a*** [***no***] ～ ***to*** (***sth.***) 有[没有]要求(某事物)的权利。***have a*** [***no***] ～ ***to do*** [***of doing***] 有[没有]做…的资格[权利],应该[不应该]做…。***have*** ～〔罕〕正当,有理。***in one's*** (***own***) ～ 依据自己的权利;依据自己生来应有的权利。***in*** ～ ***of*** = *by* ～ *of*. ***in the*** ～ 有理,正当。***keep to the*** ～ 靠右边走;走正路。***of*** ～ = *by* ～. ***put to*** ～*s* = *set to* ～*s*. ～ ***of way*** 通行权;(车、船)先行权;(消防车等的)优先通行权;〔美〕铁路[公路、电路]用地。***set to*** ～*s* 整理,整顿,改正;纠正。***sit on the R-*** 是右座[右方,右翼,右派,保守党]议员。***stand on*** [***upon***] ***one's*** ～*s* 坚持自己权利。***to the*** ～ 向右面。***turn to the*** ～ 向右拐(弯)。***turn to the*** ～ ***about*** = *go to the* ～ *about*.

IV *vt*. **1.** 弄直,扶直,竖立,扶起,扶正。**2.** 改正,修正,纠正,改善;整理。**3.**〔美〕把(舵)转向右舷。**4.** 使复权,使恢复名誉;报复;救济,拯救(被压迫者等)。～ ***itself*** 恢复常态,(重新)站平,摆平。～ ***oneself*** 辩明,表白,伸雪。—*vi*. (歪斜的船等)复原,恢复正常;站平,摆平。～**-about 1.** *n*. 反相的方向;向后转;(态度;主义;政策等的)转变,改变。**2.** *a*., *ad*. 向后转的[地]。**3.** *vi*., *vt*. (使)向后转(*Right-about face* [*turn*]!【军】〔口令〕向后转! *send to the* ～*-about* 拒绝;使溃退;驱逐;立刻解聘[免职])。～**-angled** *a*. 直角的。～**-down** *a*., *ad*. 彻底的[地];真正的[地](*a* ～*-down scoundrel* 十足的恶棍。*I was* ～*-down sorry*. 十分抱歉)。～**-hand** *n*. **1.** 亲信;得力的助手。**2.**〔古〕有实权的地位;荣誉地位。～**-hand** *a*. 右手的;右边的;用右手的;非常得力的,心腹的,倚为股肱的(*a* ～*-hand man* 自己右边的同排的人;心腹,左右手,得力的助手;〔美〕没趣味的主人)。～**-handed 1.** *a*. 惯用右手的;用右手的;向右旋转的,右旋性的;〔罕〕可原谅的(～*-handed screw* 右旋螺钉。～*-handed fault* 可原谅的过失[缺点])。**2.** *ad*. 用右手。～**-hander** 惯用右手的人;向右旋转的东西;〔口〕用右手的一击。～ **heart**【生】右心房。～**-hearted** *a*. 正直的,诚实的。～**-minded** *a*. 有正义感的;公正的。～**-mindedness** 正直,正义感,诚实的。～ **sailing**【海】(直向)基点方位航行法。～**-to-lifers** 反对堕胎者。～**-to-work** *a*. (法律等)禁止强行要求工人加入工会的;禁止工会垄断雇用工人的。～**ward** *ad*., *a*. 向右,向右边;向右的,右的。～**wards** *ad*. 向右。～ **whale**【动】露脊鲸。～**-wing** *a*. 右翼的。～**-winger** 右翼分子。

right·en [ˈraitn; ˋraɪtn] *vt*. 使恢复正常,整顿。*lack the agility to* ～ *oneself at once* 缺乏立刻恢复正常的敏捷性。

right·eous [ˈraitʃəs; ˋraɪtʃəs] ***a*** . 1. 正直的,公正的,正义的。2. 正当的,当然的。*the* ~ 好人,正人君子。~ *indignation* 义愤。**-ly** ***ad*** . **-ness** ***n*** .

right·ful [ˈraitful; ˋraɪtfəl] ***a*** . 1. 正直的,正义的。2. 正当的,当然的;合法的;正统的。3. 恰当的,合适的。*a* ~ *cause* 正义。*one's* ~ *position* 当然的地位。**-ly** ***ad*** . **-ness** ***n*** .

right·ism [ˈraitizəm; ˋraɪtɪzm] ***n*** . 1. 〔常 R-〕右派纲领[言论、观点]。2. 对右派观点的赞同;右派思潮。

right·ist [ˈraitist; ˋraɪtɪst] ***n*** ., ***a*** . 右派分子(的),右倾分子(的),保守分子(的)。~ ***ideas*** 右倾[派]思想。

right·ly [ˈraitli; ˋraɪtlɪ] ***ad*** . 正义地,正直地,正当地;正确地;恰当地;当然。

right·ness [ˈraitnis; ˋraɪtnɪs] ***n*** . 正直,诚实;正义,公正;正确(性);恰当。

right·o [ˈraitəu, raiˈtəu; ˋraɪto, raɪˋto] ***int*** . 〔主英口〕是! 对! 好!

rig·id [ˈridʒid; ˋrɪdʒɪd] ***a*** . 1. 坚硬的,强直的,硬性的,僵硬的 (*opp*. flexible, elastic)。2. 坚定的,固定不动的。3. 严格的,严正的,严肃的,严厉的;严密的(实验等)。4. 刚直的;顽固的;不屈的。5. 【物】刚性的;【空】硬式的(飞船)。~ *in one's views* 意志坚定。~ *discipline* 严格的训练。~ *adherence to rules* 严守规则。*a* ~ *body* 【物】刚体。**-ly** ***ad*** . **-ness** ***n*** .

ri·gid·i·fy [riˈdʒidiˌfai; rəˋdʒɪdəˏfaɪ] ***vt*** ., ***vi*** . (***-fied***; ***-fy·ing***) 使[变]坚硬,使[变]顽固,(使)僵化,使[变]坚固。**-fi·ca·tion** [ˌridʒidifiˈkeiʃən; ˏrɪdʒɪdɪfəˋkeʃən] ***n*** .

ri·gid·i·ty [riˈdʒiditi; rɪˋdʒɪdətɪ] ***n*** . 1. 坚硬,强直;僵硬;【物】刚性,刚度。2. 刚直;顽固,强硬。3. 严格,严厉,严峻,严肃;严密,精密。

rig·ma·role [ˈrigmərəul; ˋrɪgməˏrol] **I** ***n*** . 鬼话,冗长的废话,无聊的啰唆话;冗长的文章。**II** ***a*** . 乱七八糟的,条理不清的;无聊的。

rig·or [ˈrigə; ˋrɪgɚ] ***n*** . 〔美〕= rigour.

rig·or [ˈraigɔː; ˋraɪgɔr] ***n*** . 〔L.〕【医】寒战,发冷,冷颤;强直,僵硬。~ ***mortis*** 【医】尸僵[死后僵硬]。

rig·or·ism [ˈrigərizm; ˋrɪgərɪzəm] ***n*** . 过分严厉,严肃主义,严格主义。**-ist** ***n*** .

rig·or·ous [ˈrigərəs; ˋrɪgərəs] ***a*** . 1. 严格的,严肃的;严厉的。2. 严峻的,严酷的,苛刻的;凛烈的。3. 严密的,精确的。

rig·our [ˈrigə; ˋrɪgɚ] ***n*** . 1. 严格,严肃;严厉,严酷,苛刻;苛刻行为;横暴行为。2. (法律等的)严格执行;严密,精密。3. 艰苦,困苦;〔常 *pl*.〕(气候等的)严酷,凛烈。*execute a law with* ~ 严厉执法。*with the utmost* ~ *of the law* 最严格地依法(办理等)。*the* ~ *of winter* [*punishment*] 冬天的严寒[处罚的严厉]。**-ism** ***n*** .

rig-out [ˈrigˈaut; ˋrɪgˋaʊt] ***n*** . 〔英俚〕一套服装。

Rigs·dag [ˈrigzdɑːg; ˋrɪgzˏdɑg] ***n*** . (丹麦的)国会。

Rig-ve·da [rigˈveidə; rɪgˋvedə] ***n*** . 〔Sans.〕梨俱吠陀〔印度最古经典四吠陀之一〕;赞颂。

R.I.I.A. = Royal Institute of International Affairs 〔英〕皇家国际问题研究所。

rijst·ta·fel, rijs·ta·fel [ˈraisˌtɑːfəl; ˋraɪsˏtɑfəl] ***n*** . 〔D.〕【烹】印尼式饭菜〔以米饭为主食,配有各种菜肴和各种调味酱汁的吃法〕。

Riks·dag [ˈriksdɑːg; ˋrɪksˏdɑg] ***n*** . (瑞典或芬兰的)国会。

rile [rail; raɪl] ***vt*** . 1. 〔美〕搅浑,搅浊。2. 〔口〕惹怒,激怒,使急躁。

Ri·ley [ˈraili; ˋraɪlɪ] ***n*** . 赖利〔姓氏,男子名〕。

ri·li·e·vo [riliˈeivəu; rɪˋljɛvo] ***n*** . 〔It.〕浮雕,凸雕。

rill[1] [ril; rɪl] **I** ***n*** . 〔诗〕小河,小溪,细流。**II** ***vi*** . 像小河一般流。

rille, rill[2] [ril; rɪl] ***n*** . 【天】(月面)谷,沟纹。

rill·et [ˈrilit; ˋrɪlɪt] ***n*** . 小溪,细流。

rim [rim; rɪm] **I** ***n*** . 1. (圆形器皿的)边,缘;轮圈,辋圈,轮辋,轮缘;眼镜框,帽边(等)。2. 【海】水面,海面。*the golden* ~ 王冠。*the sea's* ~ 水平线。**II** ***vt*** . 装边(缘),装轮圈;〔美俚〕欺骗,诳骗。~**-brake** 轮圈煞车。~ **land** 【地理】(中心地区的)边缘地带。

rimble-ramble [ˈrimblræmbl; ˋrɪmbl̩ræmbl̩] ***n*** ., ***vi*** . 〔美〕(说)没意思的话,(说)傻话。

rime[1] [raim; raɪm] **I** ***n*** . 1. 〔诗〕白霜,雾凇。2. 结晶,凝结的外壳。**II** ***vt*** . 使盖上霜。

rime[2] [raim; raɪm] ***n*** ., ***vi*** ., ***vt*** . = rhyme.

rime riche [riːmˈriːʃ; rimˋriʃ] (*pl*. ***rimes riches*** [riːmˈriːʃ; rimˋriʃ]) 【诗】(完)全韵 (= perfect rhyme)。

rim·fire [ˈrimˌfaiə; ˋrɪmˏfaɪr] ***a*** . 弹药筒的,子弹筒的〔指底火装在底部边上的弹药筒〕。

rim·i·fon [ˈrimifən; ˋrɪmɪfən] ***n*** . 【药】雷米封,异烟肼〔肺结核特效药〕。

rim·less [ˈrimlis; ˋrɪmlɪs] ***a*** . 无边(缘)的;(眼镜)无框的。

ri·mose, ri·mous [ˈraiməus, -məs; ˋraɪmos, -məs] ***a*** . 【植】有裂缝的,多罅裂的。

rim·ple [ˈrimpl; ˋrɪmpl̩] ***n*** ., ***vt*** ., ***vi*** . (***-pled***; ***-pling***) 〔罕〕皱纹;皱起;生皱;弄皱。

rim·y [ˈraimi; ˋraɪmɪ] ***a*** . 下了霜的,白霜[雾凇]盖满了的。

rind [raind; raɪnd] **I** ***n*** . 1. 外皮,果皮,菜皮;树皮;皮壳;熏肉皮;干酪皮;鲸皮。2. 外观,外表。**II** ***vt*** . 剥…皮;削…皮。~ **gall** 树皮上的伤痕。

rin·der·pest [ˈrindəpest; ˋrɪndɚˏpɛst] ***n*** . 【兽医】牛瘟,牛疫。

Rine·hart [ˈrainhɑːt; ˋraɪnhɑrt] ***n*** . 赖恩哈特〔姓氏〕。

ring[1] [riŋ; rɪŋ] **I** ***n*** . 1. 圈,环,轮;戒指,指环,耳环,鼻圈,镯子(等);【运】吊环。2. 轮状物;【植】年轮;(羊齿类的)环带。3. 赛马场,竞技场,运动场;(赛马的)赌客席;马戏场;(动物展览会的)陈列场;〔the ~〕拳击场,拳师帮伙。3. 〔主美〕(政治、商业上的)党派,圈子,帮,集团。4. 【化、数】环,圈。*a betrothal* ~ 订婚戒指。*a heavy* ~ 承力环。*a* ~ *counter* 环形计数器。*an annual* ~ 【植】年轮。*an inner* ~ 骨干分子小圈子。***be in the*** ~ ***for*** 参加…的竞选。***close the*** ~ ***around*** 【军】缩紧包围。***hold*** [***keep***] ***the*** ~ 保持中立,保持不干涉态度。***in a*** ~ 成圆地,团团地。***lead the*** ~ 领头,发起。***make a*** ~ 围成圈;结成小集团操纵市场。***make*** [***run***] ~***s round sb***. 〔俚〕抢在某人之前;容易地击败某人,大大地胜过。***meet in the*** ~ 比赛拳击[摔跤]。***puff out*** ~***s of smoke*** 喷烟成圈圈,吐烟圈。***ride*** [***run***] ***at the*** ~ 跑马挑圈。~***s in water*** 一圈一圈的水纹。***sit in a*** ~ 坐成一圈。***toss one's hat in the*** ~ 参加竞选。**II** ***vt*** . 1. 给套上环;给戴上戒指,给穿上鼻圈。2. 围住,包围 (*in*; *round*; *about*)。3. 【园艺】环剥(树皮);把(洋葱)切成圈。4. 使马兜着圈子跑。5. (投环游戏)套住。~ ***a quoit*** (投环游戏)投环。~ (***up***) ***cattle*** 骑马把牛围赶在一块儿。—***vi*** . 成环状;(鹰等)盘旋飞翔;(狐、兔等)兜圈子奔跑。~ **armour** 连环甲,锁子甲。~ **bolt** 【机】环端螺栓。~**-dove** 【动】斑尾林鸽。~**-fence** 1. ***n*** . 围墙,围栅;束缚,限制。2. ***vt*** . 保证(资金等)的安全,保护(基金等)。~**-finger** 无名指〔尤指左手的,结婚戒指通常戴在这里〕。~ **hunt** 烧火围猎。~ **leader** (尤指暴动、违法行为等的)领头人,首领。~ **like** ***a*** . 似环的,环状的。~**-lock** 密码锁;暗码锁。~**-man** 〔英〕(赛马的)马票掮客。~**-master** 马戏团领班。~ **neck** 颈上有环纹的鸟、蛇等。~**-necked** ***a*** . 【动】颈上有环纹的。~ **net** (捕鱼用)围网。~ **road** 环形道路;环城公路。~ **side** (马戏场等的)场缘前座;可以近望的地点。~**-streaked** ***a*** . (身上)有环纹的。~**-tailed** ***a*** . 尾上有环纹的。~**toss** 投环游戏,套圈游戏。~**worm** 【医】轮癣,金钱癣。

ring[2] [riŋ; rɪŋ] **I** ***vt*** . (***rang*** [ræŋ; ræŋ]; ***rung*** [rʌŋ; rʌŋ]) 1. 鸣,敲(钟),摇[按](铃);敲钟[摇铃]报知,敲钟[按铃]叫(人);给…打电话。2. 使响遍;大声讲,唠唠叨

叨讲;说来说去。~ *an alarm* 敲警钟。~ ***down***【剧】鸣铃闭幕;使[宣布]结束;使[宣布]告终。~ ***in*** [***out***] 打铃上班[下班];(鸣钟)迎进(新年)[送出(旧岁)];以不正当手段引入。~ ***a bell*** 引起反应[共鸣]。~ ***one's own bell*** 自夸自赞。~ ***sb.'s praises*** 大声夸赞某人。~ ***the bell***〔口〕成功;得…赞许(*with*)。~ (***the***) ***changes*** 变花样形式收到同样效果;用正常的程序作出不同花样形式;把同一事情翻来覆去地说(*He likes to ~ the changes on his old story*. 他喜欢翻来覆去地说他的老一套)。~ ***the glim***〔美俚〕开灯。~ ***the knell*** 敲丧钟;宣告废除[没落](*of*)。~ ***up***〔英〕打电话给某人(*sb*.);【剧】鸣铃开幕(*the curtain*)。~ ***up a win***〔美〕记录胜利;得胜。—***vi***. **1**. (钟、铃等)鸣,响;敲钟,摇铃,敲钟[摇铃]叫人(*for*)。**2**. 反响,鸣响,响遍;名气大。~ *at the door* 按门铃。~ *for the nurse* 按铃叫护士。*The woods rang with their shouts*. 树林里响遍了他们的叫声。*A shot rang out*. 传来一声枪响。*ears* ~ 耳朵叫,耳鸣。~ ***again*** 轰响,反响。~ ***false*** [***true***] 似乎是假的[真的];可以断定是假货[真货]。~ ***in one's ears***(语声等)还留在耳朵里,声犹在耳。~ ***in one's heart*** [***fancy***] 铭记在心;留在记忆里。~ ***off*** 挂断电话;〔美〕停止说话;静默。~ ***to*** [***for***] ***dinner*** 摇吃饭铃。~ ***with one's fame*** 名声传遍。**II** ***n***. **1**. (钟,铃等的)鸣,响,鸣声,响声;(性质、真伪等的)声音;(文章、言语等的)韵调,格调,腔调,口气。**2**. (教堂的)一套钟,钟声。*There is a ~ at the door*. 有人按门铃。*Give me a ~ this afternoon*. 今天下午给我一个电话。*His words have the ~ of truth*. 他的话听来像是真的。***answer sb.'s*** ~ 接某人打来的电话。***give the bell a*** ~ 按一按铃。***have a ~ of*** 有…的声音,有…的风韵[意味],有…的腔调,是…的口气。***have a false*** ~ 声音不对,是假钱,是假货,品质低劣。***have the true*** [***right***] ~ 声音好[对],是真币,是真品,有实力,有真正价值。

ring-a-ding [ˈriŋəˌdiŋ; ˋrɪŋəˏdɪŋ] **I** ***a***. 〔拟声〕〔俚〕疯狂刺激的,振奋的。**II** ***n***. 〔俚〕**1**. 疯狂的刺激性,狂饮。**2**. 具有疯狂刺激性的人[物]。

ringed [riŋd; rɪŋd] ***a***. **1**. (镶)有环[轮、圈]的;轮状的;用环[圈]装饰的。**2**. 被包围的。**3**. 戴着戒指的。**4**. 正式结[订]了婚的。

rin·gent [ˈrindʒənt; ˋrɪndʒənt] ***a***.【植、动】开口(状)的。

ring·er [ˈriŋə; ˋrɪŋɚ] ***n***. **1**. 敲钟[摇铃]的人;鸣钟[铃]装置;电铃。**2**. 〔口〕成功(者)。**3**. 〔美俚〕冒名(用捏造的记录)出场比赛的人[动物];〔喻〕极相像的人;骗子。*That man is a ~ for so-and-so*. 那个人很像某人。

ring·hals [ˈriŋhæls; ˋrɪŋhæls] ***n***. (*pl*. ***-hals***, ***-halses***)【动】唾蛇(*Haemachates haemachatus*)〔产于南非〕。

ring·let [ˈriŋlit; ˋrɪŋlɪt] ***n***. **1**. 小环;小圈。**2**. (长)鬈发。

ring·let·ed [ˈriŋlitid; ˋrɪŋlɪtɪd] ***a***. 有(长)鬈发的;成(长)鬈发状的。

ring·ster [ˈriŋstə; ˋrɪŋstɚ] ***n***. 〔美口〕同党(的人);(政治等)集团的成员。

rink [riŋk; rɪŋk] **I** ***n***. (室内)溜冰场;(冰上)溜石游戏场;(草地)木球场。*a skating* ~ 溜冰场。**II** ***vi***. (在溜冰场中)溜冰〔尤指穿四轮溜冰鞋溜冰〕。**-er** ***n***.

rink·y-dink [ˈriŋkiˈdiŋk; ˋrɪŋkɪˋdɪŋk] ***a***., ***n***. 〔俚〕劣等的(东西),便宜的(东西),破旧的(东西),陈腐的(东西)(= rinkytink)。

rinse [rins; rɪns] **I** ***n***. 漱洗;漂洗,漂清。**II** ***vt***. 漱(口);(用清水)刷;涮掉,冲洗掉(*out*; *away*);用开水冲服(*down*)。—***vi***. 漂净。~ *out one's mouth with water* 用水漱口。~ (*the soap*) *out of washed clothes* 把洗过的衣服(中的肥皂水)漂去。*give sth. a* ~ 漂清[冲洗]某物。

rins·ing [ˈrinsiŋ; ˋrɪnsɪŋ] ***n***. 〔常用复数〕**1**. (冲洗,漂清用的)清水、漂洗池;漂洗过东西的水。**2**. 残渣,渣滓,剩余物(= dregs)。**3**. 冲洗,漂清。

RINT [rint; rɪnt] = radio intelligence【军】无线电侦察。

Rio de Ja·nei·ro [ˈri(:)əu də dʒəˈniərəu; ˋriodə dʒəˋnɪro] ***n***. 里约热内卢〔巴西港市,州名〕。

Ri·o Gran·de [ˈri:əuˈgrændi; ˏriəˋgrænd] ***n***. (美国和墨西哥之间的)格兰得河。

ri·ot [ˈraiət; ˋraɪət] **I** ***n***. **1**. 骚乱;暴动;暴乱,骚动;混乱。**2**. 放荡;闹饮,嘈闹的宴会,喝酒狂闹。**3**. (植物、疫病等的)蔓延。**4**. 五色缤纷;喧嚣嘈杂。**5**. 〔美口〕非常成功的戏剧。**6**. (想像、感情等的)奔放。**7**. (猎狗)闻错猎物臭迹乱追。*The garden was a ~ of colour*. 园花竞艳,五色缤纷。*a ~ of sound* 声音嘈杂。*a ~ of emotion* 感情的奔放。*race* ~ 〔美〕种族骚动。***get up a*** ~ = ***raise*** [***start***] ***a*** ~ 闹乱子,挑起暴动。***read the R-Act*** 下令解散;〔口〕严重警告[告诫]。***run*** ~ 猎狗认错猎物臭味乱跑,〔转义〕追来追去;越出常轨,放肆,横行无忌;放纵自己的想像;猖獗;(花)盛开(*His tongue runs* ~. 他胡言乱语,讲话放肆)。**II** ***vi***. **1**. 骚乱,暴动。**2**. 闹饮;喝酒喧闹;放荡(*in*)。—***vt***. 花天酒地混(日子);挥霍;因放荡花光(*out*; *away*)。**R- Act**【英史】骚乱取缔令。~ **call**(警察因发生骚乱的)紧急召集。~ **gun**(驱散骚乱人群用的)连发短枪,防暴枪。~ **police** 防暴警察。~ **shield** 防暴盾牌。

ri·ot·er [ˈraiətə; ˋraɪətɚ] ***n***. **1**. 闹乱子的人,骚乱者,暴徒。**2**. 闹饮者,喝酒狂闹的人;放荡的人。

ri·ot·ous [ˈraiətəs; ˋraɪətəs] ***a***. 扰乱性的;暴动的;闹饮的,喝酒狂闹的;放荡的;吵闹的;奔放不羁的;五色缤纷的;(植物等)茂盛的。~ *fancy* 胡思乱想;想入非非。

rip[1] [rip; rɪp] **I** ***vt***. (***ripped***; ***rip·ping***) **1**. 扯裂,割裂(*up*);剥去,拆去,割掉,扯掉(*off*; *away*; *out*);划破;撕开,割开(*open*)。**2**. 劈开,直锯,解(木材);凿开(洞穴等)。**3**. 使绽线。**4**. 暴露;穷究,寻根究底。—***vi***. **1**. 裂开,破开;绽开。**2**. 〔口〕突进,横撞直闯;任意行动。**3**. 〔口〕乱说乱讲,乱骂。~ (*the seams of*) *a garment* 拆衣裳。~ *open a bag* 拆开袋子。*let things* ~ 搁置不管,任其自然;开足马力。*Let her* [*it*] ~. 别管它,让它去。~ ***and tear*** 狂怒;胡闹。~ ***into*** 攻击,批评。~ ***off*** 扯掉;〔口〕偷窃;骗取。~ ***out*** (*an oath*)〔口〕狠狠发出咒骂语。~ ***out*** [***off***] ***the lining*** 扯去里子。~ ***up the back***〔口〕背后中伤。**II** ***n***. **1**. 扯裂;绽线;破裂;裂口,裂缝。**2**. = ripsaw. ~ **cord**【空】开伞索;(气球放气的)拉索。~**-off**〔口〕偷窃;骗取。~ **panel**【空】(气球的)裂瓣;【机】裂幅。~**-roaring** [**-roarious**] ***a***. 〔美俚〕非常热闹的;喧闹的。~ **saw** 粗齿锯。~ **snorter**〔俚〕喧闹狂暴的人[事物];突出的人[物]。

rip[2] [rip; rɪp] ***n***. 劣马,废马;废物;〔口〕浪子,荡子。

rip[3] [rip; rɪp] ***n***. 巨澜。~ **current**, ~**-tide** 岸边巨澜的回流,激流。

rip[4] [rip; rɪp] ***n***. 清管器;刮板,刮刀。

R.I.P. = 〔L.〕*Requiescat* [*Requiescant*] *in pace* (= *May he / she* [*they*] *rest in peace*). 愿灵安眠〔墓碑用语〕。

ri·par·i·an [raiˈpɛəriən; rɪˋpɛrɪən] **I** ***a***. 河岸[河边]的;【动】岸栖的。**II** ***n***. 河岸土地所有人。

ripe [raip; raɪp] **I** ***a***. **1**. 成熟的。**2**. 成人的;圆熟的,老练的。**3**. 时机成熟的,已准备妥当的。**4**. 红润丰满的(嘴唇等)。**5**. 已养肥(可宰食)的(动物);醇美可口的(酒);熟透的。**6**. 【医】(疖等)已化脓的;(白内障等)可开刀的。**7**. 〔俚〕喝得烂醉的。*Soon ~, soon rotten*. 熟得早,烂得快;〔喻〕早慧早衰。*a person of ~ years* 成年人,大人。***at the ~ age of*** 以…的高龄。***be ~ for*** …的时机成熟;渴想…。***die at a ~ age*** 享高年而死。***an opportunity ~ to be seized*** 时机成熟,可乘的好机会。~ **beauty** 妙龄。~ **wine** 醇酒。**II** ***vt***., ***vi***. 〔主诗〕= ripen. **-ly** ***ad***. **-ness** ***n***.

rip·en [ˈraipən; ˋraɪpən] ***vi***. 成熟;长成(*into*)。—***vt***. 使成熟;催熟;【医】使(疖等)化脓〔适于开刀〕。**-er** ***n***.【化】催熟剂。

Ri·pley [ˈripli; ˋrɪplɪ] ***n.*** 里普利〔姓氏〕。

Rip·man [ˈripmən; ˋrɪpmən] ***n.*** 里普曼〔姓氏〕。

ri·post(e) [riˈpəust; rɪˋpost] **I *n.*** **1.**【剑术】敏捷的回刺。**2.** 机敏迅速的回答[应对]。**II *vt.*, *vi.*** **1.** 敏捷回刺。**2.** 机敏迅速的应对[回答]。

rip·per [ˈripə; ˋrɪpɚ] ***n.*** **1.** 扯裂者;拆缝线用具;拆屋顶用具;粗齿锯。**2.**〔英俚〕非常好的人[物]。

rip·ping [ˈripiŋ; ˋrɪpɪŋ] **I *a.*** **1.** 扯裂的。**2.**〔英俚〕非常好的,绝妙的。*a ~ pace* 极快的速度。*We had a ~ good time.* 我们过了一段快活极了的时光。**II *ad.***〔英俚〕极好地,绝妙地。

rip·ple[1] [ˈripl; ˋrɪpl̩] **I *n.*** **1.** 涟漪,皱波,涟波;涟波声,潺潺声;细小急流;(头发等的)波浪形,鬈曲;(沙上的)波痕(= ~ mark);【动】脉动,波动。**2.**〔美俚〕钱。~ *cloth* 波纹细呢,绒毛织物。*a ~ of laughter* 一阵(嘻嘻哈哈的)笑声。*a ~ of conversation* 咕咕哝哝的谈话声。*make the ~*〔美〕发财。**II *vt.*** 使起涟漪[波纹];卷(头发),(把头发)弄成波浪形,使作潺潺声。—***vi.*** 起涟漪[波纹];作潺潺声。***rippling through***【物】行波传送。~ **effect** 涟漪效应〔指一点一点地逐步扩大影响〕。~ **mark** (砂岩等上的)波痕;【植】波状纹。

rip·ple[2] [ˈripl; ˋrɪpl̩] ***n.*, *vt.*** 麻梳;用麻梳梳(去麻子)。

rip·plet [ˈriplit; ˋrɪplɪt] ***n.*** 小涟漪,小波纹。

rip·ply [ˈripli; ˋrɪplɪ] ***a.*** 起涟漪的,有波纹的;潺潺响的。

rip·rap [ˈripˌræp; ˋrɪpˏræp] **I *n.*** **1.** (防冲)乱石筑成的地基或堤坝。**2.** (防冲)乱石。**II *vt.*** (***-rapped; -rapping***) **1.** 在…上堆(防冲)乱石。**2.** 用(防冲)乱石加固。

Rip·u·ar·i·an [ˌripjuˈwɛəriən; ˏrɪpjəˋwɛrɪən] ***n.*, *a.*** (四世纪初叶移居于)莱茵河畔的法兰克族人(的)。

Rip Van Winkle [ˈripvænˈwiŋkl; ˏrɪpvænˋwɪŋkl] 里普·万·温克尔〔美国作家欧文(W. Irving)作 *Sketch Book* 中一篇故事题名及其主人翁;时代落伍的人〕。

RISC, Risc, risc [risk; rɪsk] = reduced instruction set computer [computing]【计】简化指令系统计算机[精简指令集运算]。

rise [raiz; raɪz] **I *vi.*** (***rose*** [rəuz; roz]; ***risen*** [ˈrizn; ˋrɪzn̩]) (*opp.* fall, sink) **1.** 上升,升起;(日、帆等)现出,出来;(地势)向上斜,隆起。**2.** 起身〔口语说 get up〕;起立,立起〔口语说 stand up〕,耸起;直立;浮起。**3.** (声音等)提高,变高;(面包等)膨胀,发起来;(物价等)高涨,腾贵;增大;涨水,涨潮,起浪。**4.** 反抗;义愤;恶心。**5.** 兴起;起源,发端;发生。**6.** (植物)出芽,生长。**7.** 成功,发迹,出头,高升,升进;上进。**8.** 苏醒,复活。**9.** 撤离,退出,撤退;散会。*Morning* [*Dawn*] *~s.* 天亮了。*The tide ~s.* 潮水上涨。*The tower ~s 80 feet.* 塔高 80 英尺。*The house rose at the actors.* 全场起立对演员鼓掌喝彩。*The wind rose rapidly.* 风突然吹了起来。*His anger rose at that remark.* 听见那话他就生气了。*My gorge* [*stomach*] *~s at it.* 我一看见这东西就恶心。*I can't ~ to it.* 没有干那个的气力[情绪]。*My heart ~s.* 我的情绪好起来了。*They rose from a siege.* 他们停止(对某地的)围困而撤走。~ ***above*** 凌驾…之上;超越…;摆脱。~ ***again*** (***from the dead***) 死而复生。~ ***and fall*** 盛衰,兴亡。~ ***before*** [***in***] ***the mind*** (想像等)在头脑里浮现,在心里发生。~ ***from the ranks*** (军官)出身行伍;布衣起家。~ ***from the table*** 吃好了饭离开饭桌。~ ***in sb.'s opinion*** [***estimation***] 受某人器重;在某人心目中信用[声誉]增加。~ ***in arms*** [***rebellion***] 武装起义[反抗,暴动]。~ ***in the world*** 出头,发迹。~ (***1,000 feet***) ***out of the sea*** 海拔(1000 英尺)。~ ***to a fence*** 马纵身跃起准备过篱笆。~ ***to fame*** 出名。~ ***to greatness*** 成为伟大人物。~ ***to one's eyes*** 哭肿眼睛。~ ***to one's feet*** 站起来。~ ***to the bait*** [***fly***] (鱼)上钩;(人)被诱惑,上当。~ ***to the occasion*** [***emergency***] 随机应变;起而应付紧急事件。~ ***to the requirement*** 符合要求,胜任。~ ***with the larks*** 早起,黎明即起。—***vt.*** **1.** 举高,提高,抬高,擢升;〔美〕登(山)。**2.** (将鱼)诱出水面;使(鸟)飞起;使(兽)跳起;【海】驶近(另一船)使慢慢在地平线上出现。**3.**〔俗〕养育,饲养。**4.**〔罕〕使苏醒,使复活。**II *n.*** **1.** 上升;(日、月、星的)出来;(鱼吞饵时的)浮出;【猎】鸟出窝。**2.** 斜坡;隆起(地)。**3.** 涨价,腾贵;增加(量);涨水;升级;加薪。**4.** 苏醒,复活。**5.** 发迹,出头;上进,进步。**6.** 起源,发源;兴起,发生。**7.**【建】倾斜高,梯高,矢高。*a ~ of land* 高地。*He asks for a ~.* 他要求加薪。***at ~ of sun*** [***day***] 日出时候。***buy for the ~*** 看涨而买进。***get a ~ from***〔美俚〕惹怒人。***get*** [***have, take***] ***a ~ out of sb.*** 激怒某人;挖苦某人;把某人当笑柄。***give ~ to*** 使发生,引起,惹起。***have a ~ in life = make a ~*** 发迹,出头。***on the ~*** 在涨;在增加;好转。~ ***and fall*** 盛衰;兴亡;高低,抑扬。***take its one's ~ in*** [***among, from***] 始于,发端于。

ris·en [ˈrizn; ˋrɪzn̩] **I** rise 的过去分词。**II *a.*** 升起的;复活的。*the ~ sun* 升起的太阳。

ris·er [ˈraizə; ˋraɪzɚ] ***n.*** 起来的人;反抗者,起义者;【空】起飞装置;【机】(铸件)冒口;上升装置;【建】(梯级的)起步板,登板。*an early* [*a late*] ~ 起得早[晚]的人。

ris·i·ble [ˈrizibl; ˋrɪzəbl̩] ***a.*** **1.** 能笑的;善笑的;爱笑的。**2.** 可笑的。*a ~ animal* 会笑的动物。

ris·i·bil·i·ty [ˌriziˈbiliti; ˏrɪzəˋbɪlətɪ] ***n.*** **1.** 可笑性。**2.** 笑癖。**3.**〔美〕〔*pl.*〕对可笑事物的敏感性。

ris·ing [ˈraiziŋ; ˋraɪzɪŋ] **I *a.*** **1.** 上升的;渐渐上升的(坡等)。**2.** 上涨的;腾贵的;增大的,增加的;涨水的。**3.** 升进的;新进的,前途有望的(作家等);如日之升的,勃兴的,正在发展中的。*the ~ sun* 朝日。*a ~ ground* 台地。*a ~ market* 上涨的行情。*a ~ novelist* 新进小说作家。*the ~ generation* 年轻的一代。**II *prep.*** (年龄)将近…的;〔美口〕(数量)不下…的;…以上的,超过…的。*He is ~ ten.* 他快十岁了。*R- (of) a thousand men were killed.* 一千以上的人被杀害了。**III *n.*** **1.** 上升;起床;起立;出现;苏醒,复活。**2.** 坡,坡地;高地。**3.** 起义,反抗。**4.**〔方〕瘤,疮肿,疙瘩。**5.** 闭会,散会。*the ~ of the sun* 日出。*the ~ of the mother* 子宫病;歇斯底里。

risk [risk; rɪsk] **I *n.*** **1.** 风险,危险;冒险。**2.**【保险】(损失的)风险(率);保险金额;被保险人,被保险物。***at all ~s = at any*** [***whatever***] ~ 无论冒什么危险,一定,无论如何。***at one's own ~*** 对可能发生的后果自己负责,自担风险。***at owner's*** [***buyer's***] ~ 由所有人[购买者]负责。***at the ~ of*** 冒着…的危险。***run ~s*** [***a ~***] 冒险;***run*** [***take***] ***the ~ of*** 冒…的危险。***take a ~*** [***~s***] 冒险;【保险】承保…的险。***take no ~s*** 慎重行事。**II *vt.*** 冒…的危险;拼着,赌着(性命);好歹试试看,冒险去干。~ *a battle* 冒险一战。~ *one's fortune* [*life*] 拼着财产[性命]。~ *the jump* 大着胆子跳跳看。~ *sb.'s anger* 冒着某人可能会生气的风险;抱着受某人责备的决心试试看。~ *it* 豁出去。~**-benefit ration** 利弊比,风险—收益比。~ **capital** 冒风险投资的资本(= venture capital)。

risk·ful [ˈriskfəl; ˋrɪskfʊl] ***a.*** 危险(多)的。

risk·i·ly [ˈriskili; ˋrɪskɪlɪ] ***ad.*** **1.** 冒险地。**2.** 近乎淫猥地。

risk-mo·ney [ˈriskmʌni; ˋrɪskmʌnɪ] ***n.*** (由于出纳工作中难免少收多付等差错,银行等给出纳员的)差错补贴。

risk·y [ˈriski; ˋrɪskɪ] ***a.*** (***-i·er; -i·est***) **1.** 危险的;冒险的,孤注一掷的。**2.**〔口〕近乎猥亵的(作品等;=〔F.〕***risqué***)。

Ri·sor·gi·men·to [riˌsɔːdʒiˈmentəu; rɪˏsɔrdʒɪˋmɛnto] ***n.***〔It.〕(十九世纪为解放和统一意大利的)复兴运动,复兴时代。

ri·sot·to [riˈsɔtəu; rɪˋsɔto] ***n.***〔It.〕洋葱、鸡肉等煨饭。

ris·qué [riˈskei; rɪsˋke] ***a.***〔F.〕近乎淫猥的;有伤风化的。

ris·sole [ˈrisəul; ˋrɪsol] ***n.***〔F.〕炸肉卷,炸丸子;油炸包子。

R

Ri·ta [ˈriːtə; ˋritə] *n*. 丽塔〔女子名, Margaret 的昵称〕。

ri·tar·dan·do [ˌriːtɑːˈdændəu; ˏritɑrˋdændo] *a*., *ad*.〔It.〕【乐】渐缓〔略 rit., ritard.〕。

Rit·chie [ˈritʃi; ˋrɪtʃɪ] *n*. 里奇〔姓氏〕。

rite [rait; raɪt] *n*. 仪式,典礼,礼仪;习惯,惯例;〔R-〕【宗】礼拜式。*the burial* [*funeral*] *~s* 丧礼。*the conjugal* [*marriage*, *nuptial*] *~s* 婚礼。*the ~s of hospitality* 招待客人的礼节。*the ~ of passage* (某些民族习俗中的)进年庆祝仪式〔如成年典礼之类〕;一生中值得庆祝的大事 (=〔F.〕le rite de passage)。

ri·tor·nel·lo [ˌritəˈneləu, It. ˌriːtɔːˈneləu; ˏrɪtəˋnɛlo, ˏrɪtɔrˋnɛlo] *n*. (*pl*. **-los**; It. ***-li*** [-li; -lɪ])【乐】**1**.间奏。**2**. 副歌。

rit·u·al [ˈritjuəl; ˋrɪtʃuəl] **I** *a*. 仪式的,礼仪的;典礼的;宗教仪式的。~ *murder* 杀人祭神〔以人为牺牲〕。**II** *n*. 仪式;典礼。**-ism** *n*. 教会仪式,礼拜式;仪式主义;仪式学,仪式研究。**-ist** *n*. 精通仪式的人;墨守教会仪式者;仪式主义者。

rit·u·al·is·tic [ˌritjuəˈlistik; ˏrɪtʃuəlˋɪstɪk] *a*. 仪式的;仪式主义的。**-ti·cal·ly** *ad*.

rit·u·al·ize [ˈritʃjuəˌlaiz; ˋrɪtʃuəlˏaɪz] *vi*. (***-ized***; ***-izing***) 参加仪式,参加典礼。—*vt*. **1**. 使进行仪式,使奉行仪式。**2**. 使仪式化。**-za·tion** *n*.

Ritz [rits; rɪts] *n*. **1**. 里兹大饭店〔以豪华著称的瑞士大旅馆〕。**2**.〔r-〕〔美俚〕豪华,摆场,炫耀。***put on ritz*** 摆阔气,讲豪华。

ritz·y [ˈritsi; ˋrɪtsɪ] *a*. (***-i·er***; ***-i·est***)〔美俚〕时新的,时髦的,最新式的,漂亮的,高级的;骄傲的。**rit·zi·ly** *ad*.

Riv. = river.

riv·age [ˈrividʒ; ˋrɪvɪdʒ] *n*.〔古〕河岸,海滨。

ri·val [ˈraivəl; ˋraɪvḷ] **I** *n*. 竞争者,对手,敌手;匹敌者,对等的人[物]。*a ~ in love* 情敌。*without a ~* 无与匹敌,无敌。**II** *a*. 竞争的,对抗的。~ *suitors* 情敌;相竞争的求婚者。**III** *vt*., *vi*. (〔英〕***-ll-***) 竞争,对抗;匹敌。

ri·val·ry, **ri·val·ship** [ˈraivəlri, -ʃip; ˋraɪvḷrɪ, -ʃɪp] *n*. 竞争,对抗。*friendly ~* 友谊竞赛。***contend in ~*** 互相倾轧[争胜]。***enter into ~ with*** 和…开始竞争。

rive [raiv; raɪv] **I** *vt*. (~***d***; ***riv·en***, ~***d***) **1**. 扯裂,撕开,劈开。**2**. 扭去,拧去 (*from*; *away*; *off*)。**3**. 使苦恼,使烦恼。—*vi*. 裂开,分裂。**II** *n*.〔英方〕裂缝,裂罅;〔废〕裂片,碎片。

riv·el [ˈrivəl; ˋrɪvḷ] *vt*., *vi*. (〔英〕***-ll-***)〔古〕弄皱;皱起来,皱缩;干瘪。

riv·en [ˈrivən; ˋrɪvən] rive 的过去分词。

riv·er[1] [ˈrivə; ˋrɪvɚ] *n*. **1**. 河,江。*R- Thames* 或 *the R- Thames* 泰晤士河; *the Hudson R-*〔美〕哈得孙河。*the R- of Jordan* 约旦河。*the Yangtze R-* 长江,扬子江。**2**. 巨流;〔*pl*.〕大量。**3**.〔the ~〕生与死的界河,阴阳河。***a ~ rat***〔美俚〕住在河边低地的人。***a ~ novel*** = roman-fleuve. ***He at last crossed the ~***. 他终于死了。~***s of blood*** 血流成河,大量的血[杀伤]。***over the ~***〔美俚〕再会〔由法语 *au revoir* 变来〕。***row sb. up Salt River***〔美政俚〕使失败;使落选。***sell down the ~***〔美〕陷害,欺骗。***send up the ~***〔美俚〕开进监狱。~**basin** (江河的)流域。~ **bed** 河床。~ **boat** 江轮;内河船只。~**god** 河神。~**head** 河源。~**horse**【动】河马。~ **sand** 河沙。~**side** 河边,河畔。~ **wall** 河堤。~**word(s)** *a*., *ad*. 向河的[地]。

riv·er[2] [ˈraivə; ˋraɪvɚ] *n*. 劈木工人。

riv·er·ain [ˈrivərein; ˋrɪvɚˏren] **I** *a*. 河的,河边的;住在河边的。**II** *n*. 住在河边的人。

riv·er·ine [ˈraivərain, -in; ˋrɪvɚˏraɪn, -ɪn] *a*. **1**. 河岸上的,水滨的,靠近河边的。**2**. 河流的,河状的。

riv·et [ˈrivit; ˋrɪvɪt] **I** *n*. 铆钉。**II** *vt*. **1**. (用铆钉)铆,铆接 (*down*; *in*; *on*; *together*); 敲打(螺栓)使成铆钉头。**2**. 固结,加深(爱情、友谊等)。**3**. 集中(目光、注意力)(*on*; *upon*);吸住人心,使心醉。~ *one's attention* [*eyes*] *upon* 集中注意…。~ **gun** (自动)铆钉枪。**-ed** *a*. 用铆钉钉牢的;〔美俚〕结了婚的 (*a ~ed error* 根深蒂固的错误。*~ed hatred* 深恨)。**-er** *n*. 铆工(工人);铆钉枪。

Riv·i·er·a [ˌriviˈɛərə; ˏrɪvɪˋɛrə] *n*. 〔the ~〕**1**. 里维埃拉〔法国东南部和意大利西北部沿地中海的假日游憩胜地〕。**2**. (气候温和的)沿海游憩胜地。

riv·i·ère [riviˈɛə; riˋvjɛr] *n*.〔F.〕宝石项链。

riv·u·let [ˈrivjulit; ˋrɪvjəlɪt] *n*. 小河,溪流。

Ri·yadh [riːˈjɑːd; rɪˋjɑd] *n*. 利雅得〔沙特[沙乌地]阿拉伯首都〕。

ri·yal [riˈjɑːl, -ˈjɔːl; rɪˋjɑl, -ˋjɔl] *n*. (*pl*. ***-yals***) 里亚尔〔沙特[沙乌地]阿拉伯、卡塔尔、也门货币单位〕。

R.M., **RM** = **1**. Royal Marines〔英〕皇家海军陆战队。**2**. resident magistrate〔爱〕受薪治安推事。

rm. = **1**. ream. **2**. room.

R.M.A., **RMA** = **1**. Royal Military Academy〔英〕皇家陆军军官学校。**2**. Rubber Manufacturers' Association〔美〕橡胶制造业协会。

RMB = Renminbi (中国的)人民币。

R.M.C., **RMC** = Royal Military College〔英〕皇家陆军学院。

R.M.L.I. = Royal Marine Light Infantry〔英〕皇家海军陆战队轻步兵。

RMS = root-mean-square【数】均方根(值)。

R.M.S., **RMS** = **1**. Royal Mail Steamer 英国邮船。**2**. Royal Mail Service 英国邮政。**3**. Railway Mail Service 铁道邮政。

rms. = rooms.

Rmt = remount 新补充的马匹。

R.N., **RN** = **1**. registered nurse 注册护士。**2**. Royal Navy〔英〕皇家海军。

Rn = radon【化】氡。

RNA = ribonucleic acid【生化】核糖核酸。

R.N.C. = Royal Naval College〔英〕皇家海军学院。

R.N.D. = Royal Naval Division〔英〕皇家海军局。

R.N.R. = Royal Naval Reserve〔英〕皇家海军后备队。

R.N.S.S. = Royal Naval Scientific Service〔英〕皇家海军科学研究部。

R.N.V.R. = Royal Naval Volunteer Reserve〔英〕皇家海军志愿后备队。

R.N.Z.A.F., **RNZAF** = Royal New Zealand Air Force (皇家)新[纽]西兰空军。

R.N.Z.N., **RNZN** = Royal New Zealand Navy (皇家)新[纽]西兰海军。

ROA = record of achievements 学习成绩记录。

roach[1] [rəutʃ; rotʃ] *n*.【鱼】斜齿鳊,(欧洲)石斑鱼。***sound as a ~*** 非常健壮。

roach[2] [rəutʃ; rotʃ] *n*. **1**. 蟑螂 (= cockroach)。**2**.〔美俚〕大麻制成的烟卷烟蒂。~ *clip* 大麻烟卷夹子。

roach[3] [rəutʃ; rotʃ] **I** *vt*. **1**. 梳(发)使成拱状。**2**. 切短(马鬃等)使竖立。**II** *n*.【海】横帆下缘的弧形切口。~ **back** 弓形背〔尤指马背〕。

road [rəud; rod] **I** *n*. **1**. 路,道路;街〔略 Rd.〕;公路;行车道;路程,行程。**2**.〔美〕铁路。**3**. 方法,手段,办法;(走向成功、失败等的)道路,途径。**4**.【海】〔常 *pl*.〕(开放)锚地,海中停泊处。**5**.〔the ~〕〔美剧俚〕纽约以外的任何地方〔巡回剧团经常旅行的路线和演出的城镇〕;〔美推销员俚〕旅行路程。*a main ~* 大街,干道。*beaten ~* 走惯了的路;〔喻〕惯例,常规办法。*royal ~* 捷径。*by ~* 经由公路(而非铁路,空路)。*the rule of the ~* 交通规则。*a gentleman* [*knight*] *of the ~*〔谑〕拦路强盗。*All ~s lead to Rome*. 条条道路通罗马。***break a ~*** 开路前进;排除困难前进。***for the ~*** 为了送行,祝一路平安。***get out of the*** [***sb.'s***] ***~*** 不妨碍;让开道路给…走过。***get sth. out of sb.'s*** [***the***] ***~*** 扫清,消除,赶走。

give (*sb*.) *the* ～ 让路;给通过;辞退某人。*go on the* ～ = *take the* ～. *go over the* ～〔美俚〕被判徒刑。*hit the* ～〔美俚〕上路;离去。*in sb.'s* ～ 拦着…的路;〔口〕阻碍着。*on the* ～ 在旅行中;〔美〕(剧团等)在巡回演出中。*out of the common* ～ *of* 离开…常规,逸出…的常轨。～ *agent* 〔美〕拦路强盗;小贩。*take the* ～ 出发,启程,动身;流浪;〔古〕做强盗;(剧团)去巡回演出。*take the* ～ *of sb*. 居某人之上。*take to the* ～ 出发旅行;〔英古〕做拦路强盗。

II *vt*. (狗)闻着臭迹追。～**bed** 〔美〕1. (铁路)路基,路床。2. 铺路材料[碎石,沙子]。3. 供车辆行驶的路面部分;行车道。～**block**【军】路障。～**book** 路程[旅行]指南。～ **discipline**【军】行车纪律。～ **hog** *vi*., *n*. 乱开汽车(的人);妨碍其他车辆行驶(的司机);〔美〕流浪人。～**house** 〔美〕小旅馆,客栈。～ **kill** 1. 路上被轧死的动物。2. 〔喻〕穷途末路者。～ **lamp** 路灯。～ **louse**, 〔*pl*.〕～ **lice** 〔美俚〕微型汽车。～ **map** 街道地图,路线图,行车地图。～**mender** = ～ man. ～ **metal** 铺路碎石。～ **rage** 马路怒火〔行车时某一开车者对另一开车者不满而产生的愤怒〕。～ **roller** 压路机。～ **runner**【动】槲鸡。～ **scraper** 平路机。～ **sense** 安全行车本领。～**show** 巡回演出;〔美俚〕【影】(票价较高的)特别献映。～**side** *n*., *a*. 路旁(的),路边(的)(树木等)。～ **sister** 〔美〕流浪女人。～ **sprinkler** 洒水车。～**stead**【海】(开敞)锚地。～**ster** 1. 早期无后座的敞篷汽车;跑车。2. 可以走长途的车马[自行车]。3. 停泊在海中的船。4. 走惯某条路的人;徒步旅行者;流浪者;马车夫;拦路强盗。～**test** 1. *vt*. 对(车辆)进行路上试车;实骑试验(自行车等),实作试验(才能等)。2. *n*. (对车辆的)实地路检;(对人的能力的)实作检验。～**train** (运货)汽车队。～**way** 道路;车行道;【林】运材路;铁路。～**work**【运】越野长跑训练。～**-worthy** *a*. 适于走长途的(马、车等);(人)能旅行的。**-er** *n*. 1. 修路工人;清道夫。2. = ～ster. **-man** *n*. 修路工人。

road·a·bil·i·ty [ˌrəudəˈbiliti; ˏrodəˋbɪlətɪ] *n*. (车辆的)行车稳定性;行车舒适性;(行车时的)操纵灵便性。

Road Town [ˈrəud taun; ˋrodˏtaʊn] *n*. 罗得城〔英属维尔京群岛首府〕。

roam [rəum; rom] *n*., *vi*., *vt*. 漫游,游历,游荡,漫步,闲逛。～**-a-phone** 便携式电话机,漫游式电话机。**-ing** *n*.【电讯】漫游。

roan[1] [rəun; ron] *a*., *n*. 灰斑[白斑]栗色皮毛的(马);花毛的(马或其他动物)。

roan[2] [rəun; ron] *n*. (装订书籍用的)柔软羊皮。

roar [rɔː, rɔə; rɔr, ror] **I** *vi*. 1. (猛兽尤指狮子)吼,咆哮;(海、风等)呼啸,怒号;(人)喊叫,呼号,吆喝;〔美〕诉苦。2. 狂笑,哄笑,大笑。3. 轰鸣,反响。4. (马)喘鸣。～ *with laughter* 哄堂大笑。*You need not* ～. 你不必那么大声嚷嚷。—*vt*. 1. 大声讲[唱]。2. 大声喊叫而造成某情况。3. 使轰鸣。～ *out an order* 大声发出命令。～ *down* 哄下;大声压倒某人讲话声。～ *oneself hoarse* 喊哑嗓子。*The driver pressed on the accelerator, savagely* ～*ing the engine*. 司机踩下油门踏板,引擎轰鸣。**II** *n*. 吼(声),咆哮;怒号;叫唤,呼叫;喧哗,鼓噪,大笑声;轰鸣。*a* ～ *of anger* 怒骂声。*in a* ～ 大声鼓噪着。*set the table in a* ～ 引起全桌(的人)哄堂大笑。

roar·er [ˈrɔːrə; ˋrorɚ] *n*. 1. 吼者,咆哮者;怒号者。2.【兽医】患喘鸣症的马。3. 〔美俚〕极好的人物[东西];暴风雨;吵闹多言的人;鲁莽[好动武]的人;强壮的人;低劣的运动员[拳击家];喷油井。

roar·ing [ˈrɔːriŋ; ˋrorɪŋ] **I** *n*. 咆哮,怒号,喧噪;【兽医】(马的)喘鸣症。**II** *a*. 1. 吼叫的,咆哮的,怒号的,轰鸣的;暴风雨的(夜等)。2. 喧哗的,鼓噪的,吵闹的。3. 〔口〕兴旺的,(生意)兴隆的。～ *applause* 雷鸣一般的鼓掌喝彩。*a* ～ *night* 暴风雨之夜,纵酒狂闹之夜。***drive a*** ～ ***trade*** 生意兴隆。***in*** ～ ***health*** 非常健康,精神饱满。～ **blade** 〔古〕荡子,浪子。～ **forties** (北纬40°左右的)大西洋暴风雨带。～ **game** (苏格兰人玩的)冰上滚石戏。

roast [rəust; rost] **I** *vt*. 1. (在火上)烤,炙,烧(肉);烘;(用文火)焙;(用热沙)炒。2.【冶】锻烧,焙烧。3. 〔俚〕讥刺,挖苦;〔美〕责备。～ *oneself* 挨着火烤身子。～ *one's hands* 烘手。—*vi*. 烤;炙;烘;炒;烤好;变热;烤得发烫。**II** *a*. 烤的,烘的,炒的。～ *beef* 烤牛肉。～ *ducks* 烤鸭。**III** *n*. 1. 烤肉;烧肉;烤食聚餐会;烤,烘,炒。2. 〔俚〕挖苦,愚弄;逗乐。3.【冶】锻烧,焙烧。*a cold* ～ 〔古〕没价值的东西。***rule the*** ～ 当家;做主人;执牛耳,指挥。

roast·er [ˈrəustə; ˋrostɚ] *n*. 烤[烘、炒]的人[用器];锻烧炉,焙烧炉;烤用的食物[鸡、小猪等]。

roast·ing [ˈrəustiŋ; ˋrostɪŋ] *a*. 1. 适于烤食的;烤肉用的。2. 天气酷热的。～ *jack* 旋转烤肉叉。*a* ～ *July* 炎热的七月。～**-spit** 〔俚〕刺刀。

Rob [rɔb; rɑb] *n*. 罗布〔男子名,Robert 的昵称〕。

Rob. = Robert.

rob [rɔb; rɑb] *vt*. (**-bb-**) 强夺,掠夺;盗劫;抢夺,夺取,剥夺,使丧失 (*of*);【矿】滥掘。～ ***sb. of*** 使…丧失,剥夺…的… (～ *sb. of his money* 抢人钱财。*The shock* ～*bed him of speech*. 他震惊得说不出话来)。～ *a safe* 盗劫金库[保险柜]。～ ***Peter to pay Paul*** 抢了东家给西家;东挪西借;借钱还债。—*vi*. 抢劫,劫掠;掠夺。

rob·a·lo [ˈrɔbəˌləu, ˈrəubə-; ˋrɑbəlo, ˋrobə-] *n*. (*pl*. **-los**, **-lo**)【动】锯盖鱼科鱼〔尤指锯盖鱼〕。

rob·and [ˈrɔbənd; ˋrɑbənd] *n*.【海】系帆绳索。

rob·ber [ˈrɔbə; ˋrɑbɚ] *n*. 盗贼,强盗。～ **baron** 1. (封建时代)对路过自己领地的旅客进行抢劫的封建主。2.【美史】十九世纪末靠残酷剥削致富的美国资本家。～ **fly**【动】食虫虻,盗蝇。

rob·ber·y [ˈrɔbəri; ˋrɑbərɪ] *n*. 抢夺,劫夺;【法】强盗[盗劫]罪。*daylight* ～ 白昼抢劫,光天化日之下的抢劫;明目张胆的掠夺,剥削。*To ask such prices is sheer* ～. 要这样的价钱简直是明火执仗的抢劫。

Rob·bins [ˈrɔbinz; ˋrɑbɪnz] *n*. 罗宾斯〔姓氏〕。

robe [rəub; rob] **I** *n*. 1. 长袍,罩袍;晨衣,浴衣;〔商店用语〕长连衣裙。2. 〔*pl*.〕衣服。3. 〔常 *pl*.〕礼服,法衣,官服,制服。4. 〔诗〕被盖。5. 〔美〕(毛皮)短围裙。*the long* ～ (法官、牧师的)长袍。*the short* ～ 〔废〕军服。～*s of office* = *official* ～*s* 制服。*gentlemen of the long* ～ 律师们,法官们。*the* ～ *of night* 夜幕。*both* ～*s* 长袍阶级和兵士,文人和武人。*either* ～ 文人或武人。***follow the*** ～ 充任律师。**II** *vt*., *vi*. (给…)穿上;装扮;穿法衣。

robe-de-cham·bre [rɔbdəˈʃɑːmbr; ˏrɔbdəˋʃɑ̃brə] 〔F.〕 *n*. (*pl*. ***robes-de-cham·bres*** [-br; -br]) 晨衣,化妆时穿的长衣。

Rob·ert [ˈrɔbət; ˋrɑbɚt] *n*. 1. 罗伯特〔男子名,昵称为 Bert, Bertie, Bobby, Dob, Dobbin, Rob, Robin〕。2. 〔英口〕警察。

Ro·ber·ta [rəuˈbəːtə; roˋbɚtə] *n*. 罗伯塔〔女子名〕。

Ro·berts [ˈrɔbəts; ˋrɑbɚts] *n*. 罗伯茨〔姓氏〕。

Ro·bert·son [ˈrɔbətsn; ˋrɑbɚtsn] *n*. 罗伯逊〔姓氏〕。

Robe·son [ˈrəubsn; ˋrobsn] *n*. 1. 罗伯逊〔姓氏〕。2. **Paul** ～ 罗伯逊〔1898—1976 美国黑人歌唱家〕。

Rob·in [ˈrɔbin; ˋrɑbɪn] *n*. 罗宾〔男子名,女子名, Robert 和 Roberta 的昵称〕。

rob·in [ˈrɔbin; ˋrɑbɪn] *n*.【动】鸲鸟,知更鸟〔又叫 ～ redbreast〕;〔美〕鸫。～*s egg blue* 〔美〕绿蓝色。～ **snow** 〔美〕春天的小雪。

Rob·in Good·fel·low [ˈrɔbin ˈgudfeləu; ˋrɑbɪn ˋgudˏfɛlo] (英国民间传说中专门跟人捣蛋的)小妖怪,小精灵。

Rob·in Hood [ˈrɔbinˈhud; ˋrɑbɪnˋhud] 罗宾汉〔英国中古传说中的侠盗〕。***sell Robin Hood's pennyworth*** 像义贼一般廉价卖东西给人。

R

Rob·ins [ˈrəubinz, ˈrɔbinz; ˋrobɪnz, ˋrɑbɪnz] ***n***. 罗宾斯〔姓氏〕。

Rob·in·son [ˈrɔbinsn; ˋrɑbɪnsn] ***n***. 鲁宾逊〔姓氏〕。

Rob·inson Cru·soe [ˈrɔbinsn ˈkruːsəu; ˋrɑbɪnsn ˋkruso] 鲁宾逊〔英国小说家 Daniel Defoe 所著《鲁宾逊漂流记》一书中主人公〕。*Robinson Crusoe and Friday*〔美〕教堂[剧场]过道中两旁的两个座位。

ro·ble [ˈrəublei; ˋroble] ***n***. 【植】(美国西南部的)栎树〔尤指加州白栎(*Quercus lobata*)〕。

ro·blitz [ˈrəublits; ˋroblɪts] ***n***. 无人飞机闪击轰炸。

ro·bomb [ˈrəubɔm; ˋro͵bɑm] ***n***. = robot bomb.

rob·o·rant [ˈrɔbərənt; ˋrɑbərənt] **I** ***a***. 起强壮作用的。**II** ***n***. 【医】强壮剂。

ro·bot [ˈrəubɔt, ˈrɔbət; ˋrobət, ˋrɑbət] ***n***. **1**. 机器人。**2**. 自动机,自动仪器,自动控制导[飞]弹,遥控设备。*an electronic* ～ 电子自动装置。*a* ～ *airplane* 无线电操纵飞机,无人飞机。*a* ～ *bomb* 自动操纵的飞弹。*a* ～ *bomber* 遥控轰炸机,无人驾驶轰炸机。

ro·bot·is·tic [ˌrəubəˈtistik; ͵robəˋtɪstɪk] ***a***. 机器人似的;自动化的。

ro·bot·ize [ˈrəubətaiz; ˋrobət͵aɪz] ***vt***. **1**. 使自动化。**2**. 使像机器人一样地行事。

R

ro·bur·ite [ˈrəubəˌrait; ˋrobəraɪt] ***n***. 【化】罗必赖特〔一种炸药〕。

ro·bust [rəˈbʌst; roˋbʌst] ***a***. **1**. 强壮的,强健的,雄壮的,粗壮的。**2**. (运动等)费力的。**3**. 坚定的;健全的。**-ly** ***ad***. **-ness** ***n***.

ro·bus·tious [rəuˈbʌstʃəs; roˋbʌstʃəs] ***a***. **1**. 强壮的。**2**. 粗野的;刚愎自用的。**3**. 〔美〕猛烈的。

roc [rɔk; rɑk] ***n***. **1**. (阿拉伯、波斯传说中的)大怪鸟。**2**. 〔R-〕〔俚〕(海军用)无线电制导的电视瞄准导[飞]弹,"大鹏"式制导炸弹。*a* ～*'s egg* 乌有之物。

R.O.C. = Royal Observer Corps〔英〕皇家对空观察队〔民防组织〕。

Ro·ca [ˈrəukɑ; ˋrokə] ***n***. 罗卡角〔在葡萄牙西部,欧洲大陆的最西端〕。

roc·am·bole [ˈrɔkəmˌbəul; ˋrɑkəm͵bol] ***n***. 【植】胡蒜(*Allium scorodoprasum*)〔欧洲的一种圆葱〕。

Ro·chelle [rəuˈʃel; roˋʃɛl] ***n***. 罗谢尔〔姓氏,女子名〕。～ **salt** 罗谢尔盐,四水(合)酒石酸钾钠。

roche mou·ton·née [rɔʃ mutɔne; rɑʃ mutɑnɛ] 【地】羊背石。

roch·et [ˈrɔtʃit; ˋrɑtʃɪt] ***n***. 【宗】紧身法衣。

rock[1] [rɔk; rɑk] ***n***. **1**. 岩,岩石,磐石,岩壁;卵石;〔常 *pl*.〕〔美口〕石子儿;暗礁,岩礁。**2**. 〔the R-〕直布罗陀(Gibraltar)的别名。**3**. 〔喻〕靠山,护符。**4**. 〔喻〕隐藏的危险[困难],祸根。**5**. = ～ cake, ～ candy. **6**. 〔英〕硬糖果;硬干酪。**7**. 〔美〕用来投掷的石头;〔美俚〕金刚钻,宝石(等);〔美俚〕一块钱;〔*pl*.〕钱。**8**. 〔俚〕礴〔一种结晶状可卡因〕。*a needle of* ～ 巉岩。*a sunken* ～ 暗礁。*Rocks ahead*! 前面有暗礁! 危险! *an almond* ～ 杏仁味硬糖。***as firm as a*** ～ = ***like a*** ～ 安如磐石,坚定不移,屹然不动。***built*** [***founded***] ***on*** ～ 建立在岩石上的;基础坚固的。***driven on the*** ～ 触礁。***on the*** ～***s*** 触礁;搁浅;手头拮据;进退两难;〔美俚〕分文没有的,破了产的。***run*** [***strike***] ***upon the*** ～***s*** = ***thrown on the*** ～ 触礁。***see*** ～***s ahead*** 看到前途的暗礁,看到前途的危险。***split on a*** ～ 在暗礁上撞得粉碎;完全破灭[失败]。***the Rock of Ages*** 【宗】永久的磐石〔原为基督教会一首赞美诗的题目,现指耶稣和基督教〕。～ **and rye** 加有冰糖和水果片装瓶的裸麦威士忌酒。～ **away** 四轮轻便马车。～ **bass** 【动】岩阳鱼,岩鲈。～ **bottom** ***n***., ***a***. 岩底(的);最底下(的);底细,底蕴,真相(～*-bottom prices*〔俚〕最低价钱)。～**-bound** ***a***. 岩包围着的,岩多的。～ **brake** 【植】珠蕨。～ **cake** 糖衣脆皮小饼。～ **candy** 〔美〕冰糖(=〔英〕sugar candy)。～**-climbing** 【爬山】爬岩(术)。～ **cod** 【动】岩鳕;鲉。～ **cork** 软木状石绵。～**-crusher** 碎石机;【牌戏】一手实力强大的好牌。～ **crystal** 【矿】石英,水晶。～ **dove**, ～**-pi·geon** 【动】野鸽。～ **drill** 凿岩机;开石钻。**R- English** 直布罗陀英语。**R- fever** 【医】马尔他热病。～ **fish** 【鱼】生活在海底岩石间的鱼类之一〔石鲔;鲉;石斑鱼等〕。～ **floor** 【地】岩原。～ **garden** (种植岩生植物的)岩石[假山]庭园。～ **goat** 野山羊。～**-hewn** ***a***. 岩石凿成的。～ **hind** 【动】岩石斑鱼。～**-hound** 〔美口〕奇石采集者。～ **jock** (高难度)攀岩运动爱好者。～ **leather** 一种石绵。～ **maple** 【植】糖槭树。～ **oil** 石油。～ **rabbit** **1**. = hyrax. **2**. = pika. ～**-ribbed** ***a***. 有岩层的;多岩脊的;岩石突露的;顽强的;坚定不移的;僵硬的。～ **rose** 【植】**1**. ***n***. 岩蔷薇。**2**. ***a***. 半日花科的。～ **salmon** 【动】角鲨。～ **salt** 岩盐。**R- scorpion** 磐石蝎〔直布罗陀人的绰号,有贬意〕。～ **slide** 【地】岩滑,塌方。～ **snake** 锦蛇。～ **squirrel** 【动】岩黄鼠;巨松鼠。～ **tar** 原油。～ **tripe** 【植】石耳属植物。～ **wool** 石绵,石绒。～ **work** 粗面石工;岩壁;爬岩术;石块砌筑;堆石工艺;假山。

rock[2] [rɔk; rɑk] **I** ***vt***. **1**. 摇,摇动,使振动。**2**. 【采】摇选。**3**. 摇引…入睡;抚慰。**4**. 使感动,打动;使震动,使震惊。*He* ～*ed back and forth in his chair*. 他坐在椅子上前前后后地摇。～ *the baby to sleep* 摇婴儿入睡。*a* ～*ing gait* 摇摇摆摆的步态。—***vi***. **1**. 摇动,动摇;振动;摇摆;蹒跚。**2**. 感动;震动。**II** ***n***. **1**. 摇;动摇。**2**. 摇摆,摇摆舞曲。～ **and roll** 摇摆舞(曲)。～**-fest** 摇摆舞音乐节。～ **opera** 摇摆舞音乐剧。～**shaft** 摇臂轴。**-ism** ***n***. 摇滚乐。

rock[3] [rɔk; rɑk] ***n***. 〔古〕(手纺用)卷线杆。**R- day** 开纺日〔Twelfth day 的翌日〕。

Rock·e·fel·ler [ˈrɔkifelə; ˋrɑkɪ͵fɛlɚ] ***n***. 洛克菲勒〔姓氏〕。

rock·er [ˈrɔkə; ˋrɑkɚ] ***n***. **1**. 摇的人;摇摇篮的人。**2**. 摇杆,摇轴;〔美〕摇椅;摇木马;【动】摇移器;【化】振荡器;【采】摇选台。**3**. 【溜冰】弯底冰鞋;【航】龙骨弯曲的船。**4**. 〔俚〕头,脑袋。**5**. 摇摆舞音乐歌曲[歌手、歌迷]。**6**. = rocking-turn. ***off one's*** ～ 〔俚〕发疯。

rock·er·y [ˈrɔkəri; ˋrɑkərɪ] ***n***. 假山;有假山的园林。

rock·et[1] [ˈrɔkit; ˋrɑkɪt] **I** ***n***. 火箭;火箭弹,火箭发动机;火箭式投射器;〔英俚〕斥责。*a carrier* [*freight*] ～ 载运火箭。*an antitank* ～ 反坦克火箭。*a moon* ～ 月球火箭。*an outer-space* ～ 外层空间宇宙[外太空]火箭。*a photon* ～ 光子火箭。*a sounding* ～ 探测火箭。*a* ～ *signal* 火箭信号。**II** ***vt***. 用火箭运载;用火箭轰击。—***vi***. (鸟等)直升飞起;(马或骑手)向前猛冲,(物价)猛涨。～ **base** 火箭(发射或试验)基地。～ **bomb** 火箭(推动的)炸弹。～ **jet** 火箭喷管;火箭喷气流。～ **launcher** [**gun**] 火箭发射装置[发射筒]。～ **motor** 火箭发动机。～ **plane** 火箭(发射)飞机。～**-propelled** 火箭推进的。～ **propulsion** 火箭推进。～ **range** 火箭靶场;火箭试验区。～ **science** 火箭科学;〔喻〕艰深的学问;〔喻〕复杂伤神的工作。～ **scientist** **1**. 火箭专家。**2**. (能承担高难度工作的)能人,高人。～ **ship** 火箭宇宙飞船[太空船]。～ **sonde** 【气】火箭探空仪。～ **target** 火箭靶机。

rock·et[2] [ˈrɔkit; ˋrɑkɪt] ***n***. 【植】芝麻菜;紫花南芥。

rock·et·eer [ˌrɔkiˈtiə; ͵rɑkəˋtɪr] ***n***. 〔美〕火箭专家;火箭制造人。

rock·et·er [ˈrɔkitə; ˋrɑkətɚ] ***n***. **1**. 惊起向上直飞的猎鸟。**2**. = rocketeer.

rock·et·ry [ˈrɔkitri; ˋrɑkətrɪ] ***n***. **1**. 火箭学;火箭技术;火箭研究。**2**. 火箭〔总称〕。

rock·i·ly [ˈrɔkili; ˋrɑkəlɪ] ***ad***. 岩石一般;多岩。

rock·i·ness [ˈrɔkinis; ˋrɑkɪnɪs] ***n***. **1**. 坚如岩石,坚硬性。**2**. 冷酷无情。**3**. 摇晃性。

rock·ing [ˈrɔkiŋ; ˋrɑkɪŋ] ***a***. 摇动的,来回摇摆的。～ **chair** 摇椅。～ **horse** 摇木马。～ **turn** 【溜冰】摇转〔从弧线外侧扭转身体用同侧冰鞋刃滑回来〕。

Rock·ing·ham [ˈrɔkiŋəm; ˋrɑkɪŋəm] ***n***. 罗金厄姆〔姓

氏〕。

rock'n'roll [ˈrɔknˈrəul; ˋrɑkənˋrol] ***n.*** 摇滚舞(曲)(= rock and roll)。

rock·oon [rɔˈkuːn, ˈrɔkuːn; rɑˋkun, ˋrɑkun] ***n.*** **1.** (由气球带到空中发射的)气球火箭。**2.** 火箭(探空)气球。

rock·y[1] [ˈrɔki; ˋrɑkɪ] ***a.*** (***-i·er***; ***-i·est***) **1.** 岩石的;岩石重叠的,岩石多的。**2.** 磐石一般的;泰然不动的;冷酷的,无情的,铁石心肠的。**3.** 障碍重重的;困难的。the *R- Mountains* =〔口〕*the Rockies*〔美〕落基山脉。~ **desert** 沙漠,戈壁。

rock·y[2] [ˈrɔki; ˋrɑkɪ] ***a.*** **1.** 摇摆的;不稳的;不安定的。**2.**〔俚〕头晕目眩的;(因虚弱、酒醉,被猛击等)站不稳的。**-i·ly** ***ad.*** **-i·ness** ***n.***

ro·co·co [rəˈkəukəu; rəˋkoko] **I** ***n.*** 【美】(法国18世纪以浮华纤巧为特色的)罗可可式;罗可可式建筑;浮华纤巧俗气的装饰。**II** ***a.*** 罗可可式的;俗不可耐的;浮华纤巧的。

ROD = rewritable optical disc【计】可重写光盘〔其内存信息可由激光读出并加以编辑的光盘〕。

rod [rɔd; rɑd] ***n.*** **1.** 枝,一节树枝。**2.** 棍棒;杆;竿;钓竿。**3.** 杖,魔杖;鞭,体罚。**4.** 职标,权标;笏;权力,威力。**5.**【机】杆,拉杆,推杆,连杆;测量杆,照尺;避雷针。**6.**〔主、美〕杆〔=5½码=5.0292公尺〕;平方杆〔=30¼平方码〕;【解】(网膜内的)杆状体;【生】杆状菌,杆状染色体。**7.**〔美俚〕(左轮)手枪。**8.**【圣】种族;家系;血统;子孙。**9.**〔美俚〕旧汽车改装成的跑车〔= hot rod〕。*a calculating* ~ 计算尺。***give the*** ~ 鞭打。***have a*** ~ ***in pickle for sb.*** 伺机惩罚(某人)。***kiss the*** ~ 俯首受罚,甘心受刑。***make a*** ~ ***for one's own back*** [***for oneself***] 自找麻烦,自找苦吃,自作孽。***ride*** [***take***] ***the*** ~***s*** (躲在货车车厢下的棒轴上)偷乘火车。~ **cell**【生】杆细胞。~ **license**〔加拿大〕鲑鱼税。~**man** (用钓竿)钓鱼者;【测】标杆员,立尺员;〔美俚〕执枪强盗。

rode [rəud; rod] ride 的过去式。

ro·dent [ˈrəudənt; ˋrodnt] **I** ***a.*** **1.** 咬的,嚼的;【动】啮齿目的。**2.**【医】侵蚀性的(溃疡等)。**II** ***n.*** 【动】啮齿动物。

ro·den·tial [rəuˈdenʃəl; roˋdɛnʃəl] ***a.*** **1.**【动】啮齿目的。**2.**【医】侵蚀性的。

ro·dent·i·cide [rəuˈdentiˌsaid; roˋdɛntəˏsaɪd] ***n.*** 杀鼠剂,杀啮齿类剂。

ro·de·o [rəuˈdeiəu; ˋrodiˏo]〔美〕***n.*** **1.** (集中牛马的)圈地;(为打烙印的)驱集牛马。**2.** 牧人马术表演;摩托车花式表演。

Rod·er·ic(k) [ˈrɔdərik; ˋrɑdərɪk] ***n.*** 罗德里克〔男子名〕。

Rod·ger [ˈrɔdʒə, ˈrəudʒə; ˋrɑdʒɚ, ˋrodʒɚ] ***n.*** 罗杰〔男子名〕。

Rod·gers [ˈrɔdʒəz; ˋrɑdʒɚz] ***n.*** 罗杰斯〔姓氏〕。

Rod·ney [ˈrɔdni; ˋrɑdnɪ] ***n.*** 罗德尼〔姓氏;男子名〕。

rod·o·mon·tade [rɔdəmɔnˈteid; ˏrɑdəmɑnˋted] **I** ***n.*** 大话。**II** ***vi.*** 吹牛,说大话。**III** ***a.*** 说大话的,吹牛的。

roe[1] [rəu; ro] ***n.*** (*pl.* ~***s***,〔集合词〕~)【动】牝麅鹿,狍(= ~ deer)。~**buck** 雄狍。

roe[2] [rəu; ro] ***n.*** (鱼类、甲壳类、两栖类的)卵,卵块。*hard* ~ 卵。*soft* ~ (雄)鱼精。

Roent·gen [ˈrentgən; ˋrɛntgən], **Wilhelm Conrad** 伦琴〔1845—1923,德国物理学家,伦琴射线的发现者〕。

roent·gen [ˈrentgən, ˈrɔntjən, ˈrʌntdʒən; ˋrɛntgən, ˋrɑntjən, ˋrʌntdʒən] **I** ***n.*** 伦琴射线,爱克斯[X]射线。**II** ***a.*** 伦琴(射线)的,X射线的。*a* ~ *photogram* [*photograph*] X[爱克斯]射线照片。~ *rays* 爱克斯[X]射线。

roent·gen·ize [ˈrentgənaiz; ˋrɛntgənˏaɪz] ***vt.*** 爱克斯线照射。

roentgeno- *comb. f.* 表示"伦琴射线的": *roentgenogram*.

roent·gen·o·gram, roent·gen·o·graph [ˈrentgənəgræm, ˈrɔntˈgenəgrɑːf; ˋrɛntgənəˏgræm, ˋrɛntgənəˏgræf] ***n.*** 伦琴射线照片。

roent·gen·og·ra·phy [ˌrentgeˈnɔgrəfi; ˏrɛntgənˋɑgrəfɪ] ***n.*** 爱克斯射线[伦琴射线]拍摄技术。

roent·gen·ol·o·gy [ˌrɔntgeˈnɔlədʒi; ˏrɛntgənˋɑlədʒɪ] ***n.*** 爱克斯射线学。

roent·gen·o·sco·py [ˌrɔntgənˈɔskəupi; ˏrɛntgəˋnɑskəpɪ] ***n.*** 爱克斯射线透视术;萤光屏检查。

roent·gen·o·ther·a·py [ˌrɔntgənəˈθerəpi; ˏrɛntgənəˋθɛrəpɪ] ***n.*** 爱克斯射线疗法。

roe·stone [ˈrəustəun; ˋroston] ***n.*** 【矿】鲕状岩;鱼卵石(= oolite)。

ROFL = roll on the floor laughing【计】笑得在地板上打滚〔网民们彼此在网上聊天时常用的缩略语之一,此类网上缩略语如今已流行多种〕。

Rog. = Roger.

ro·ga·tion [rəuˈgeiʃən; roˋgeʃən] ***n.*** **1.**〔古罗马〕法案的提出;法律草案。**2.**〔*pl.*〕【宗】连祷,祈求。~ **flower**【植】= milkwort.

Rog·er [ˈrɔdʒə; ˋrɑdʒɚ] ***n.*** 罗杰〔男子名〕。*Jolly* ~ (黑底白骷髅的)海盗旗。

rog·er [ˈrɔdʒə; ˋrɑdʒɚ] ***int.*** 知道了! 收到了!〔无线电话通讯用语〕;〔俚〕好! 对! 行!

Rog·ers [ˈrɔdʒəz, ˈrəudʒəz; ˋrɑdʒɚz] ***n.*** 罗杰斯〔姓氏,男子名〕。

Ro·get [ˈrɔʒei; roˋʒe] ***n.*** 罗热〔姓氏〕。

rogue [rəug; rog] **I** ***n.*** **1.** 歹徒,恶棍;流氓,无赖;乞丐;骗子。**2.** 爱捉弄人者;淘气孩子,小淘气。**3.** 家伙〔爱称〕。**4.** 离群的象,离群的野兽;(赛马或行猎时的)腿懒的马。**5.**【生】变劣;【园艺】变劣了的实生苗;劣种。*a* ~ *and vagabond* 身体健壮的乞丐。*a* ~*s' gallery* (警察局里的)前科犯相片陈列室。~*'s yarn*〔英海军〕标识(用)绳股。***play the*** ~ 行恶作剧,淘气。**II** ***vt.*** **1.** 骗,欺诈。**2.**【农】间苗;【育种】去劣;去杂,淘汰。—***vi.*** **1.** 流浪,游荡;行骗。**2.**【农】淘汰劣种[杂种]。~ **program**【计】"痞子"程序,捣乱程序〔指含有病毒的程序,多为电脑黑客所编〕。

ro·guer·y [ˈrəugəri; ˋrogərɪ] ***n.*** **1.** 流氓[无赖]行为,坏行为;欺骗。**2.** 淘气,捣鬼。

ro·guish [ˈrəugiʃ; ˋrogɪʃ] ***a.*** **1.** 流氓的,无赖的。**2.** 淘气的,捣鬼的,恶作剧的。**-ly** ***ad.*** **-ness** ***n.***

roi [rwɑ; rwɑ] ***n.*** (*pl.* ~***s*** [rwɑ; rwɑ]) (F.) 王。***le*** ~ ***le veut*** [ləˈrwɑːləˈvə; ləˋrwɑləˋvə] 照准 (= the king wills it)。***le*** ~***s' avisera*** [ləˈrwɑːsɑːlˈviːzərɑː; ləˋrwɑsɑˋvizərɑ] 缓议〔= the king will consider〕。~ ***fai·ne·ant*** [-ˈfeineiɑ̃ːŋ; -ˋfeneɑ̃ŋ] (*pl.* ***rois fai·ne·ants*** [-fenex; -fɛnɛs]) 徒拥虚名的国王[议长],傀儡(首领)。

roil [rɔil; rɔɪl] ***vt.***〔美〕**1.** 搅浑;搅乱。**2.** 惹怒,使生气。—***vi.*** 动荡。

roil·y [ˈrɔili; ˋrɔɪlɪ] ***a.*** **1.** 浑浊的。**2.** 生气的,易怒的。**3.** 动荡的。

roi·nek [ˈrɔinek; ˋrɔɪnɛk] ***n.***〔南非〕新来移民;〔南非、蔑〕英国兵。

roist·er [ˈrɔistə; ˋrɔɪstɚ] ***vi.*** **1.** 摆架子,欺侮人。**2.** 嚷闹;闹饮。**-er** ***n.*** 喧闹者;闹饮者。

Ro·land [ˈrəulənd; ˋrolənd] ***n.*** **1.** 罗兰〔男子名〕。**2.** 勇士罗兰〔与奥利佛 (Oliver) 各为查理大帝手下十二勇士之一〕;〔喻〕勇将。***a*** ~ ***for an Oliver*** 旗鼓相当;势均力敌。

role, rôle [rəul; rol] ***n.*** **1.** (演员扮演的)角色。**2.** 任务;作用。*the leading* ~ 主角。***fill the*** ~ ***of*** 担负…的任务。***play an important*** ~ ***in*** 在…中起重要作用。~ **model** (克尽职守的)工作模范。~**-playing game**【计】角色扮演游戏〔在电子游戏中扮演不同角色〕。

Rolf(e) [rɔlf, rəuf; rɑlf, rof] ***n.*** 罗尔夫〔男子名,Rudolph 的异体〕。

roll [rəul; rol] **I** *vt*. **1.** 滚,转,推滚(桶、车轮等),使(烟、尘土)滚滚上升,滚滚推进(浪、水等);滚动,溜转(眼睛)。**2.** 卷,卷成圆形,弄圆;包卷,卷拢,卷捆,卷起(*in*; *into*; *up*)。**3.** 滚压(草地);辗,轧,辗平,辗薄;用面棍辗薄[擀薄]。**4.** 擂(鼓);用卷舌发(r 音)。**5.** 使左右摇摆。**6.** (在心里)盘算,翻来覆去细想。**7.** 〔美俚〕趁人睡着[喝醉]时偷窃。*The chimney* ~*s up smoke*. 烟囱滚滚冒烟。*She* ~*ed the string into a ball*. 她把线卷成一团。*The boy* ~*ed himself up in a blanket*. 这孩子拿毯子把身体裹了起来。*He* ~*ed himself from side to side*. 他左右摇晃。—*vi*. **1.** 滚转,旋转,滚去,滚动前进;坐车去。**2.** 彷徨,流浪。**3.** 波动,起伏,弯转;(岁月)周而复始,移变。**4.** 横摇,摆动,左右颠簸(*opp*. pitch);(船)左右摇摆着航行,(人)踉踉跄跄地走。**5.** 卷起;变圆;卷拢(*up*; *together*);展延。**6.** (雷)隆隆地响;(言语)滔滔不绝;(鸟)啭。**7.** (动物)打滚;(眼睛)转动。**8.** (烟)滚滚上升;(雾)消散。*The carriage* ~*ed along*. 马车隆隆走过。*Bills* ~ *up*. 账单堆积。*Years* ~ *on* [*by*]. 岁月流逝。~ ***around*** 〔美口〕(时光)流逝;周而复始;按时到临。***be*** ~***ing in luxury*** [***money***] 十分奢华[有钱]。~ ***sb. over*** 把某人打翻[撞倒]在地。~ ***and pitch*** (船)左右前后摇摆。~ ***back*** 使退却,击退;压平(物价)。~ ***down*** 滚下来,流下来。~***ed gold*** (辗压成的)金箔。~***ed steel*** 轧过的薄钢板。~ ***in*** **1.** (预约者、捐款等)滚滚而来;(浪)滚滚打来;大量进来。**2.** 〔俚〕飘然到来;到达。**3.** 〔美〕睡;退下。~ ***into*** 卷成(一团);交混成(一体)。~ ***one's own*** 〔美俚〕卷自己的香烟;自行生活。~ ***oneself up*** 卷成一团。~ ***out*** **1.** 滚出;动身,离开。**2.** 伸出,展开。**3.** 〔美〕起床。**4.** 不及格被开除。**5.** 朗诵;声音宏亮地唱。~ ***over*** 使滚;滚;〔美棒球〕得分。~ ***the bones*** 闲谈;吹牛。~ ***up*** **1.** 卷起(袖子);包卷。**2.** 积贮,攒(钱)。**3.** 缩成圆球,团拢。**4.** (烟等)袅袅上升。**5.** (车)前进;到达;〔澳〕蜂拥而来;〔口〕(人)出现(某处),登场;来到约定地点。**6.** 〔美〕起床(*A carriage* ~*ed up to the inn*. 一辆马车驶至旅店前停下)。~ ***your hoop*** 〔美〕当心自己的事。

II *n*. **1.** 滚,滚动,旋转;波动,起伏;摇摆,蹒跚。**2.** (雷等的)轰鸣,隆隆声,(鼓的)疾擂,连敲;(诗、散文等的)朗朗可诵的格调。**3.** 卷物,卷轴;纸;卷;一卷。**4.** (学校、军队等的)点名簿;名单,细目单;公文,案卷;记录;目录。**5.** 卷制品,面包卷,肉卷,烟卷(等)。**6.** 滚筒机、辗压机、压路机,卷扬辘轳;【装订】压型机。**7.** 【建】(柱头的)漩涡饰。**8.** 【空】横[侧]滚。**9.** 〔美俚〕一卷钞票,钱。**10.** 【乐】(和弦)琶音。*the* ~ *of thunder* 雷鸣。*a toilet* ~ 一卷手纸。*a* ~ *of printing-paper* 一卷印刷用纸。*a* ~ *of cloth* 一卷呢绒,成卷的一匹布。*a* ~ *of bread* (早点用的)面包卷儿。*He has* ~*s of fat on him*. 他浑身胖得圆滚滚的。(*vote*) ***by*** ~ ***call*** 唱名(表决)。***call the*** ~ 点名。***in the*** ~ ***of*** 载于…名单[目录]中,跻身…之列。***on the*** ~***s*** 在名单中。***on the*** ~***s of fame*** 在名人录里,在名人之列。***the*** ~ ***of honour*** 阵亡将士名簿[单]。***strike off the*** ~***s*** 消去(律师)名册中名字;开除。~ **angle** 倾斜角。~**away** *a*. 附有轮子并可折叠推动搬移的(*a* ~*away bed* 有轮子、可搬移的床)。~**back** 压平物价;击退。~ **bar** 【机】辗棍,辗杆。~**booster** 【火箭】绕纵轴助推器[加速器]。~**cage** 翻车防护罩〔车内保护开车人用的金属丝网〕。~**call** 点名;【军】点名号。~ **cumulus** 层积云。~ **film** 摄影胶卷。~**-mop** 腌鲱鱼。~**-out** (新飞机)初次出厂[展出]。~ **past** (军事检阅中)重武器行进。~**-top desk** 拉盖书桌。~**way** 滚木坡;(在河岸上)一堆待运圆木。

Rol·land [rɔːˈlæŋ; rɔˋlɑ̃], **Romain** 罗曼·罗兰〔1866—1944,法国小说家,音乐评论家,剧作家〕。

roll·a·way [ˈrəuləˌwei; ˋroləˏwe] *a*. 可折叠滚动的。*a* ~ *bed* 带轱辘的折叠床。

roll·er [ˈrəulə; ˋrolɚ] *n*. **1.** 使滚转的人;滚转物;滚筒;【印】墨辊,印色辊;(地图等的)轴,卷轴;辊子,转子,滚轴,滚子,辊;轧滚;镇压器,压路机;〔方〕擀面棍;布卷,绷带卷。**2.** (暴风雨后打来的)大浪。**3.** 【动】啭舌金丝雀;鹳鸽。**4.** 〔美〕警察。~ **bandage** 绷带卷。~ **bearing** 【机】滚柱轴承。~ **lap** 【纺】皮辊花。~**-skate** 四轮滑行鞋,溜冰鞋。~ **ski** 四轮滑雪板。~ **towel** (套在横木架或滚筒上供擦手用的)环状毛巾。

roll·ey [ˈrɔli; ˋrɑlɪ] *n*. = rulley.

rol·lick [ˈrɔlik; ˋrɑlɪk] **I** *vi*. 嘻嘻哈哈地闹着玩,欢闹。**II** *n*. 嬉戏;说笑;欢闹;高兴。**-ing, -some** *a*.

Rol·lin [ˈrɔlin; ˋrɑlɪn] *n*. 罗林〔男子名,Rol(l)and 的异体〕。

roll·ing [ˈrəuliŋ; ˋrolɪŋ] **I** *a*. **1.** 旋转的;滚动的;波动的,起伏的;滔滔地流的;隆隆响的。**2.** 卷起的。**3.** 左右摇摆的。**4.** 〔美〕起伏不平的(土地等)。**5.** 〔美俚〕有钱的,钱多的。*the* ~ *smoke* 滚滚浓烟。*the* ~ *sea* 波涛滚滚的大海。*a* ~ *collar* 翻领。*the* ~ *seasons* 周而复始的季节。**II** *n*. **1.** 滚动;旋转;横摇。**2.** 辗压,轧。**3.** 轰鸣,隆隆声;啭鸣声。~ **barrage** 【军】徐进弹、幕射击。~ **bridge** 滚轮活动桥。~ **hitch** 【海】轮结〔一种绳结〕。~ **hospital** 【军】随军医院。~ **kitchen** (设置在卡车上的)流动厨房〔俗叫 soup-kitchen〕。~ **mill** 轧钢厂;轧钢机。~ **pin** 擀面棍。~ **press** 滚筒印刷机;轧光机;(橡胶)压延机。~ **stock** (铁路或汽车运输机构的)全部车辆。~ **stone** 无定居的人;见异思迁的人。~ **strike** 持续罢工。

Rol·lo [ˈrɔləu; ˋrɑlo] *n*. 罗洛〔男子名〕(L. = Rolf)。

ro·ly-po·ly [ˈrəuliˈpəuli; ˋrolɪˏpolɪ] **I** *n*. **1.** 〔英〕果酱布丁卷。**2.** 滚圆肥胖的人[动物]。**3.** 滚球。**II** *a*. 胖得圆滚滚的(孩子等)。

Rom [rɔm; rɑm] *n*. (*pl*. ***Ro·ma*** [ˈrɔmə; ˋromə]) = gypsy.

Rom. = **1.** Roman. **2.** Romance. **3.** Romanic. **4.** *Romans* (基督教《圣经》,《新约》中的)《罗马人书》(= *Epistle to the Romans*)。

rom. = 【印】roman.

ROM = read-only memory 【计】只读存储器。

Ro·ma·ic [rəuˈmeiik; roˋme·ɪk] *n*., *a*. 现代希腊语(的);有关现代希腊的。

ro·maine [rəuˈmein; roˋmen] *n*. 【植】长叶莴苣。

Ro·man [ˈrəumən; ˋromən] **I** *a*. **1.** (古)罗马的;(古)罗马人的;(古代)罗马人气概[风度]。**2.** (罗马)天主教的。**3.** 〔r-〕罗马字的,罗马体铅字的;正体字的;罗马数字的。~ *arch* 半圆拱。~ *architecture* 罗马式建筑。~ *balance* [*beam*, *steelyard*] (普通的)天平。~ *candle* 手持燃放的焰火筒。~ *Catholic* 罗马天主教的;天主教徒。~ *Catholicism* 天主教。~ *cement* 天然水泥。~ *Curia* 罗马教廷。~ *holiday* 以看别人受苦为乐的娱乐。~ *Law* 罗马法。~ *letter* [*type*] 罗马字体,正体(铅)字。~ *mosaic* 镶嵌玻璃。~ *nose* 鼻梁高的鼻子。~ *numerals* 罗马数字〔I=1, V=5, X=10, L=50, C=100, D=500, M=1000, 从大到小顺列者为各数相加之和: MDCLXVI=1666, 大小倒列者为二数相减之差: XC=90, MCM=1900〕。~ *order* 【建】罗马柱型,混成柱型。~ *pitch* 25°的屋顶斜面。~ *school* 拉斐尔(Raphael)画派。~ *vitriol* 罗马矾〔即硫酸铜〕。**II** *n*. **1.** (古)罗马人。**2.** 天主教徒。**3.** 拉丁语。**4.** 〔r-〕【印】罗马字,罗马体铅字,正体铅字〔略 rom.〕。*an Emperor of the* ~*s* 神圣罗马帝国皇帝。

ro·man [roˈmɑ̃; ˏroˋmɑ̃] *n*. 〔F.〕(中世纪在法国发展起来的)韵文小说;传奇小说。~ ***à clef*** [nɑˈklei; nɑˋkle] 影射小说。~***-fleuve*** [fləːv; fləv] 家世小说(=〔英〕saga novel)。

ro·mance [rəuˈmæns, ro-; rəˋmæns, ro-] **I** *n*. **1.** 中世纪骑士故事;冒险故事,传奇,虚构小说。**2.** 小说般的事迹;浪漫史,风流事迹,恋爱故事。**3.** 传奇式的生活[世界、情调等];空想癖;杜撰,虚构。**4.** 【乐】浪漫曲。**5.** 〔R-〕= *R- language* 罗曼(斯)语,拉丁系语言〔包括意大利语、葡萄牙语、罗马尼亚语、法兰西语、西班牙语等〕。

R

the ~s about King Arthur 亚瑟王故事。*travel in search of ~* 寻找奇遇的旅行。**II** ***a***. 〔R-〕拉丁系语言的。**III** ***vi***. **1.** 讲[写]虚构故事。**2.** 吹牛;空想,妄想。**3.** 〔口〕谈情说爱;追求异性。—***vt***. 〔口〕和…恋爱;追求(异性)。

ro·manc·er [rəˈmænsə; rəˋmænsɚ] ***n***. **1.** = romancist. **2.** 爱空想的人;爱瞎吹的人。

ro·manc·ist [rəuˈmænsist; rəˋmænsɪst] ***n***. 虚构故事作者,传奇小说作家。

Rom·an·es [ˈrɔmənez; ˋrɑmənɛz] ***n***. 【语言】(吉普赛的)罗马乃斯语,吉普赛语。

Ro·man·esque [ˌrəuməˈnesk; ˏroməˋnɛsk] **I** ***n***. **1.** 【建】罗马式建筑;罗马式绘画[雕刻]。**2.** 〔罕〕拉丁系语言。**II** ***a***. **1.** 【建】罗马式的;罗马风格的。**2.** 拉丁语系的。**3.** 〔r-〕传奇小说的;空想的。

Ro·ma·nia [rəuˈmeinjə; roˋmenjə] ***n***. 罗马尼亚〔欧洲〕。

Ro·ma·nian [ˈrəuˈmeinjən, rəuˈmeiniən; roˋmenɪən, roˋmenjən] **I** ***a***. 罗马尼亚的。**II** ***n***. **1.** 罗马尼亚人。**2.** 罗马尼亚语。

Ro·man·ic [rəuˈmænik; roˋmænɪk] **I** ***a***. **1.** (古代)罗马(人)的。**2.** 拉丁语系的。**II** ***n***. 拉丁系语言。

Ro·man·ish [ˈrəumaniʃ; ˋromanɪʃ] ***a***. 〔蔑〕罗马天主教(徒)的。

Ro·man·ism [ˈrəumənizəm; ˋromənˏɪzəm] ***n***. **1.** 〔常蔑〕天主教。**2.** (罗马天主教)教义[教规]。**3.** 古罗马气质[制度]。**4.** 【建】罗马式。

Ro·man·ist [ˈrəumənist; ˋromənɪst] ***n***. **1.** 天主教徒。**2.** 古罗马掌故学家。**3.** 罗马法学者[专家]。**4.** 拉丁系语言学者。

Ro·man·ize [ˈrəumənaiz; ˋromənˏaɪz] ***vt***. **1.** 使罗马化;使拉丁化。**2.** 使天主教化。**3.** 〔r-〕用罗马字写,用罗马体[正体]铅字印刷。—***vi***. **1.** (古)罗马化;拉丁化。**2.** 成为天主教徒。**3.** 使用拉丁字母。**-i·za·tion** [-ˈzeiʃən; -ˋzeʃən] ***n***.

Ro·ma·no- [rəuˈmeinəu; roˋmɑno] *pref*. 表示"罗马的"。

Ro·mansh, R(o)u·mansh [rəuˈmænʃ, ruːˈmænʃ; roˋmænʃ, ruˋmænʃ] ***n***., ***a***. 瑞士东部所用拉丁语系方言(的)。

ro·man·tic [rəˈmæntik; roˋmæntɪk] **I** ***a***. **1.** 【文艺史】〔常 R-〕浪漫主义的(*opp*. Classical, Realistic 等)。**2.** 传奇(式)的;小说般的;情节离奇的。**3.** 空想的,虚构的;怪诞的,想入非非的;不实际的,难实行的(计划等)。**4.** 谈情说爱的,多情的,风流的,香艳的。**II** ***n***. **1.** 浪漫主义者,浪漫派诗人[艺术家]。**2.** 〔*pl*.〕浪漫思想[行为]。*the R- school* 【文艺】浪漫(主义)派。**-ti·cal·ly** ***ad***.

ro·man·ti·cism [rəˈmæntisizəm; roˋmæntəˏsɪzəm] ***n***. **1.** 传奇小说体裁;虚构,空想;传奇性;浪漫精神[倾向]。**2.** 浪漫主义(*opp*. classicism 等)。**-cist** ***n***. 浪漫主义者[作家,艺术家]。

ro·man·ti·cize [rəˈmæntisaiz; roˋmæntəˏsaɪz] ***vt***., ***vi***. (使)浪漫化;(使)幻想化。

Rom·a·ny [ˈrɔməni; ˋrɑmənɪ] ***n***., ***a***. 吉普赛(Gipsy)(的);吉普赛语(的)。*deep ~* 纯粹的吉普赛语。*~ rye* 与吉普赛人结伙,能说吉普赛话的非吉普赛人。

ro·maunt [rəuˈmɔnt, -ˈmɔːnt; roˋmɑnt, -ˋmɔnt] ***n***. 〔古〕传奇诗或故事;骑士故事。

Rom. Cath. = Roman Catholic.

Rome [rəum; rom] ***n***. **1.** 罗马〔意大利首都〕。**2.** 古罗马城;罗马城邦;古罗马(帝国)。*All roads lead to ~.* 条条大道通罗马;殊途同归。*When in ~, do as the Romans do.* 入国问禁,入境从俗。*fiddle while ~ is burning* 罗马大火漠不关心。*~ was not built in a day.* 罗马不是一天建成的;伟业非一日之功。

Ro·me·o [ˈrəumiəu; ˋromɪˏo] ***n***. 罗密欧〔莎士比亚戏剧《罗密欧与朱丽叶》中的男主人翁〕。

Rome·ward [ˈrəumwəd; ˋromwɚd] ***a***., ***ad***. 向天主教(的);向罗马。

Rome·wards [ˈrəumwədz; ˋromwɚdz] ***ad***. = Romeward.

Rom·ish [ˈrəumiʃ; ˋromɪʃ] ***a***. = Romanish.

Rom·ney [ˈrɔmni; ˋrɑmnɪ] ***n***. 罗姆尼〔姓氏〕。

romp [rɔmp; rɑmp] **I** ***n***. **1.** 乱蹦乱闹;顽皮嬉闹,顽皮嬉闹的孩子〔尤指女孩〕;顽童。**2.** 【赛马】轻快的飞跑;轻易的胜利。**II** ***vi***. **1.** 顽皮嬉闹;〔美学生语〕跳舞。**2.** 轻易地取胜;【赛马】轻快地飞跑(*along*; *past*)。*~* ***away with it*** 〔美剧〕获得大成功。*~* ***home*** = *~* ***in*** 〔俚〕(赛马时)轻松愉快地得胜。

romp·er [ˈrɔmpə; ˋrɑmpɚ] ***n***. **1.** 嬉戏的人,顽皮不羁的女孩。**2.** 〔*pl*.〕(小孩穿的一种宽松)连裤外衣。

romp·ish, romp·y [ˈrɔmpiʃ; ˋrɑmpɪʃ] ***a***. 顽皮嬉闹的,乱蹦乱闹的。

Rom·u·lus [ˈrɔmjuləs; ˋrɑmjələs] ***n***. 【古罗马传说】古罗马的建国者〔Mars 的儿子,古罗马人的守护神〕。

Ro·na, Rho·na [ˈrəunə; ˋronə] ***n***. 罗娜〔女子名〕。

Ron·ald [ˈrɔnəld; ˋrɑnəld] ***n***. 罗纳德〔男子名, Reginald 的异体〕。

Ron·da [ˈrɔndə; ˋrɑndə] ***n***. 朗达〔女子名〕。

ron·deau [ˈrɔndəu; ˋrɑndo] ***n***. **1.** 【诗】二韵叠句短诗〔主体由 13 行或 10 行构成,其最初二行在中间及末尾构成重复出现的叠句,基本形式为"a a b b a, a a b 叠句, a a b b a 叠句"〕。**2.** 【乐】回旋曲(= rondo)。

ron·del [ˈrɔndl; ˋrɑndl] ***n***. 【诗】由 14 行构成的二韵叠句短诗〔最初二行与第 6, 7 行及第 13, 14 行相同〕。

ron·de·let [ˈrɔndeˌlet; ˋrɑndɛˏlɛt] ***n***. 【诗】五行或七行短叠句诗。

ron·do [ˈrɔndəu; ˋrɑndo] ***n***. (*pl*. *~s*) 〔It.〕【乐】回旋曲。

ron·dure [ˈrɔndʒə; ˋrɑndʒɚ] ***n***. 〔罕,诗〕圆形,圆形物,弧线。

Ro·ne·o [ˈrəuniəu; ˋronɪo] ***n***., ***vt***. (用)复写机(复写)〔商标名〕。

Ron·nie [ˈrɔni; ˋrɑnɪ] ***n***. **1.** 罗尼〔男子名, Ronald 的昵称〕。**2.** 罗妮〔女子名, Veronica 的昵称〕。

Rönt·gen ***n***. = Roentgen.

rood [ruːd; rud] ***n***. **1.** 【宗】十字架上的基督像;〔the ~〕〔古〕(处死耶稣的)十字架。**2.** 长度单位〔= 5½—8 码〕;地积单位(= ¼英亩)。*Not a ~ remained to him.* 没有寸土留给他。***by the*** (***holy***) *~* 的确,一定。*~* **arch** (教堂里)十字梁隔屏正中的圆拱。*~* **loft** (教堂里的)十字架神龛。*~* **screen** (教堂里设置在圣坛与会堂之间,以示分隔的)十字梁隔屏。

roof [ruːf; ruf] **I** ***n***. **1.** 屋顶,房屋;家屋。**2.** (放行李的)车顶;笠形罩。**3.** 上颌。**4.** 最高部,顶部;【矿】顶板。**5.** 【空】(飞机)机身上的包皮;担任空中掩护的飞机;〔口〕(飞机的)绝对上升限度。*the ~ of heaven* 天空。*the ~ of the world* 世界的屋脊。***full to the*** *~* 塞满一屋。***hit the*** *~* [***ceiling***] 勃然大怒[狂怒]。***left*** [***be***] ***without a*** *~* 无家可归。***raise the*** *~* 〔俚〕喧闹;闹翻了天;大声诉苦[发怨言]。***under sb.'s*** *~* 寄住某人家里。***under a*** *~* ***of foliage*** 在树荫下。***under the*** *~* ***of*** 住在…的家里,寄…的篱下,在…的照应下。**II** ***vt***. 给…盖屋顶;像屋顶一样盖着;放入屋里;保护,庇护。*~* **garden** 屋顶花园。*~* **spotter** (对敌机的)屋顶瞭望员。*~* **tax** 人头税,人丁税。*~* **top** 屋顶。*~* **tree** 栋梁;屋脊梁。**-less** ***a***. 无屋顶的;无家的,无住处的。

roof·age [ˈruːfidʒ; ˋrufɪdʒ] ***n***. 屋顶用材[用料]。

roofed [ruːft; ruft] ***a***. 有屋顶的;…屋顶的。*a ~ wagon* 有盖货车。*a thatch-~ house* 茅草顶房。*a flat-~ house* 平顶房。

roof·er [ˈruːfə; ˋrufɚ] ***n***. **1.** 〔口〕盖屋顶的人;盖屋顶的厚板。**2.** 〔英、口〕客人给主人道谢的信。

roof·ing [ˈruːfiŋ; ˋrufɪŋ] ***n***. **1.** 屋顶;盖屋顶;屋顶用材

料。2. 覆盖;保护。~ *felt* 【建】油毛毡。

rook[1] [ruk; rʊk] **I** *n*. 1. 【鸟】白嘴鸦;〔北英〕乌鸦。2. 赌棍;骗子。**II** *vt*. (用赌博)骗(钱);诈骗;敲竹杠。*They ~ed me £10 for my berth*. 他们敲了我十英镑的卧铺费。

rook[2] [ruk; rʊk] *n*. 【国际象棋】军,堡垒。

rook·er·y [ˈrukəri; ˋrukərɪ] *n*. 〔英〕1. 白嘴鸦[海豹、企鹅等]群(的栖居处)。2. 公寓;贫民窟。3. 同类人[物]的集中处。

rook·ie, rook·y[1] [ˈruki; ˋrʊkɪ] *n*. 〔军俚〕新兵;新手,新队员,新来者。*a ~ cop* 〔美俚〕新来的警察。

rook·y[2] [ˈruki; ˋrʊkɪ] *a*. 有白嘴鸦的;白嘴鸦多的。

room [rum, ruːm; rʊm, rum] **I** *n*. 1. 室,房间。2. 场所,席位,位置,地位,空间。3. 余地,余裕;机会。4. 〔*pl*.〕一套房间;寄宿舍;出租的房间。5. 屋子里的人们;一屋子[满座](的人们)。*an upper ~* 顶楼房间。*a single* [*double*] *~* 单人[双人]房间。*a strong ~* 保险库。*There is ~ for one more*. 还可以容纳一个人。*I would rather have his ~ than his company*. 他不在反而好。~ *for doubt* 怀疑的余地。*set the ~ in a roar* 使一屋子的人哄然大笑。*give ~* 腾地方(位置),让开,移开,挪开一点。***in sb.'s ~ = in the ~ of sb***. 处于某人的地位,代替某人,代…而。***leave ~ for evasion*** 留下推诿余地。***make ~ for*** 让地位[位置]给…。***no ~ to turn in = no ~ to swing a cat*** 地方狭窄;无转身余地。~ ***of reconciliation*** (天主教会的)忏悔室〔忏悔者和神甫可在室内面对面相见,亦可隔着屏风交谈〕。***parcels ~*** 衣帽[物件]寄存处。~ ***to rent*** 〔美俚〕傻瓜。***take ~s at*** 在…租房间。***take up too much ~*** 占用地位过多。**II** *vi*. 〔美〕占有[租有]房间,在房间里;投宿,住宿,寓居,同住 (*at*; *with*; *together*)。**II** *vt*. 留…住宿,留住(客人)。~(*ing*) *house* 〔美〕公寓;供寄宿的房屋。~ ***and board*** (供)膳宿,吃住 (*He receives wages plus ~ and board*. 他除工资外还享受膳宿待遇)。~ **clerk** (旅馆里的)预定、登记房间的职员。~ **mate** 〔美〕同房间的人。~**-to-room** *a*. 室对室的 (*~-to-~ telephone* 各室互通电话)。~ **service** 送酒菜等到房间的旅馆的服务(部)。

roomed [ru(ː)md; rumd] *a*. 有…间房间的。

room·er [ˈruːmə; ˋrumɚ] *n*. 〔美〕(旅馆、公寓里的)寄宿者,房客。

room·ette [ru(ː)ˈmet; rumˋɛt] *n*. 〔美〕(铁路卧车的)单人小室。

room·ful [ˈru(ː)mfəl; ˋrum͵fʊl] *n*. 满房间;一屋子的人;满场的人,满座。

room·ie [ˈruːmi; ˋrumɪ] *n*. 住在同一房间里的人。

room·y [ˈruːmi; ˋrumɪ] *a*. (*-i·er*; *-i·est*) 宽敞的,广阔的;有很多空间的。**-i·ly** *ad*. **-i·ness** *n*.

roor·back, roor·bach [ˈruəbæk; ˋrʊrbæk] *n*. 〔美〕(对选举中的政敌或可能出任本人所想获得的职位的人的)诽谤性谣言。

roose [ruːz, Scot. röz; ruz, röz] *n*., *vt*., *vi*. 〔英方〕称赞,赞美。

Roo·se·velt [ˈrəuzəvelt, ˈruːsvelt; ˋrozə͵vɛlt, ˋrusvɛlt] *n*. 1. 罗斯福〔姓氏〕。2. **Franklin Delano ~** 佛兰克林·迪拉诺·罗斯福〔1882—1945, 1933—1945 任美国第三十二任总统〕。3. **Theodore ~** 赛奥多尔·罗斯福〔1858—1917, 美国第二十六任总统〕。

roost [ruːst; rust] **I** *n*. 1. 栖架;鸡埘,鸡棚,鸡舍;同栖的一群家禽。2. 栖息处;卧室;床;〔口〕旅舍。***at ~*** 歇着;睡着。***come home to ~*** 还归原主;得到恶报 (*Curses come home to ~*. 害人反害己)。***go to ~*** 去歇;去睡。***rule the ~*** 当家,作主;跋扈,称雄,居首。**II** *vi*. 栖息;进窝;〔美〕歇着;睡着;投宿;过夜;〔口〕就座,坐下。—*vt*. 为…设置栖息处,把…送去栖息。

roost·er [ˈruːstə; ˋrustɚ] *n*. 1. 〔美、方〕雄鸡。2. 狂妄自负的人。3. 飞机问答机。

Root [ruːt; rut] *n*. 鲁特〔姓氏〕。

root[1] [ruːt; rut] **I** *n*. 1. (草木、毛发等的)根;根菜,食用菜根;根茎,地下茎;块根;有根植物,草木,草;〔*pl*.〕根菜类;(山)麓。2. 根本,根源,原因;本质;基础,根柢;【语】词根;根词;【数】根数,根。3. 祖先;【圣】子孙。4. 【乐】和弦基音。*the ~ of a tooth* 牙根。*the ~ of all evil* 祸根。***the ~ of a gem*** 玉根〔毛玉的非玉部分〕。*a cubic* [*second, square*] *~* 立方[平方]根。***at*** (***the***) ~ 根本上。***be at the ~ of*** 是…的根本[基础]。***by the ~***(***s***) 连根,从根部,从根源 (*pull up by the ~s* 连根拔除,根除)。***get at*** [***go to***] ***the ~ of*** 追究…的根底,追查…的真相。***lay the axe to the ~ of*** 根本改革;治本。~ ***and branch*** 完全,都;彻底地,急进地。***strike at the ~ of*** 打击…的根部,彻底摧毁。***strike*** [***take***] ~ 生根;扎根;固定,固着。***to the ~***(***s***) 充分地;竭力地;彻底地。**II** *vi*., *vt*. (使)生根;(使)固定;(使)固着;〔喻〕深深种下,使根深蒂固。*Terror ~ed him to the spot*. 吓得他呆立不动。~ ***up*** [***out***] 连根拔除(杂草等);肃清(反叛等)。**III** *a*. 根的;根本的。*a ~ idea* 根本思想。~ **borer** 钻根害虫。~ **cellar** 块根储藏窖。~ **climber** 根部攀缘植物。~ **crop** 块根作物〔马铃薯、萝卜等〕。~ **infinitive** 【语法】动词的无 "to" 不定式。~ **let** 幼根,细根,根枝。~ **nodule** (**bacteria**) 根瘤(菌)。~ **rot** 根腐病。~ **stock** 1. 【植】根茎;砧木。2. 根源,起源。~ **tubercle** 根瘤。

root[2] [ruːt; rut] *vt*., *vi*. (猪等)用鼻子掘(地);搜寻 (*for*)。*R-, hog, or die*. 〔美〕拼命干啊,不然就得饿死。

root[3] [ruːt; rut] *vi*. 〔美俚〕应援,声援;支持,赞助;欢呼,喝彩。

root·age [ˈruːtidʒ; ˋrutɪdʒ] *n*. 生根;固定;根源。

root·ed [ˈruːtid; ˋrutɪd] *a*. 生了根的;有根的;根深蒂固的;固定的。**-ly** *ad*.

root·er [ˈruːtə; ˋrutɚ] *n*. 〔美俚〕(比赛时的)声援者,啦啦队;拔根者,拔根器。

root·le [ˈruːtl; ˋrutḷ] *vt*. (猪)用嘴拱土。—*vi*. 翻,寻找。

root·less [ˈruːtlis, ˈrut-; ˋrutlɪs] *a*. 无根的。**-ly** *ad*. **-ness** *n*.

root·y[1] [ˈruːti; ˋrutɪ] *a*. 1. 根多的。2. 根状的。

root·y[2] [ˈruːti; ˋrutɪ] *n*. 〔英军俚〕面包。

ROP = 1. 〔常作 rop〕run-of-paper (由编辑)随意决定登载位置的。2. record of production 生产记录。

rope [rəup; rop] **I** *n*. 1. (通常指 1—10 英寸以上粗细的)索子,麻索 (*cf*. cable; cord)。2. 绳〔长度名 = 20 英尺〕。3. 套索;测量索;绞首索;〔the ~〕绞刑;缢死。4. 一串;(啤酒等液体中的)丝状黏质,菌丝束。5. 干扰雷达用的长反射器。6. 〔*pl*.〕(拳击的)围栏索。7. 〔*pl*. the ~s〕秘诀,内幕。8. 〔美俚〕劣质雪茄烟;项圈。~ *of sand* 靠不住的东西。***be at*** [***come to***] ***the end of one's ~*** 山穷水尽,日暮途穷;智穷力竭;一精二光。***be outside the ~s*** 〔俚〕不懂秘诀[内情];是门外汉。***dance on the ~s*** 〔俚〕被绞死。***get on to the ~s*** 熟识适当手续。***give sb. a ~'s end*** 鞭打某人。***give*** (***sb.***) (***plenty of***) ~ 放任。***give*** (***sb.***) ~ ***enough*** (***to hang himself***) 放任(某人)使他自取灭亡。***give the calf more ~*** 〔美〕给予较多的自由,听其自便,别管。***know the ~s*** 熟悉内幕,懂得秘诀。***learn the ~s*** 摸到窍门[线索],弄清内幕。***name not a ~ in his house that hanged himself*** 在有人吊死的人家莫说绳子;要避免提及别人的忌讳[隐痛]。***on the high ~s*** 得意扬扬;精神饱满;骄傲。***on the ~*** (登山者)互相用绳子联系着。***on the ~s*** 被击倒在(拳击场的)围栏索上;〔俚〕使窘困[毫无办法];即将完蛋。***put*** (***sb.***) (***up***) ***to the ~s*** 把窍门[线索]指点给(某人)。***show sb. the ~s*** 指点某人窍门[线索]。

II *vt*. 1. 用绳绑[捆、缚]。2. (爬山者等)用绳系住(身体)。3. 拉绳分隔,用索子围住 (*in*; *off*)。4. 用绳拉;拉运;〔美俚〕引诱。5. 勒着马慢跑。6. 〔美西部〕用套索

R

捕捉(牛马等)。—*vi*. 1. 拧成绳。2. 生黏丝。3.〔英〕故意让对方赛赢。~ **in**〔美俚〕引诱,诱惑,诱入圈套。**~-a-dope** (拳击比赛中抓住机会靠在围栏上的)短暂休息(以伺机反攻);〔喻〕以逸待劳。~**dancer** 走钢索的演员。~**dancing** 走钢索。~ **end** (打人的)鞭子。~ **ferry**【军】绳渡。~ **ladder** 绳梯。~**line** *n*. 1.(警察等在某些场合拉起的)安全警卫线;隔离线。2.〔美俚〕(竞选者、要人等与安全线外人群致意的)隔线亲民。~**manship** 走索技术;爬绳技术。~ **quoit** (投环戏用的)(麻索)环。~**'s-end** (笞刑用的)鞭子。~ **skipping** 跳绳。~**walk** = ropery. ~**walker** 走钢索的演员。~ **walking** 走钢索。~**way** 架空索道。~ **yard** = ropery. ~ **yarn** 旧绳子解开的绳线;无足轻重的小事物(*Rope-Yarn Sunday*【军】星期五下午的衣物缝补假,一星期内不工作的一个下午)。

rop·ery [ˈrəupəri; ˋropəri] *n*. 绳厂,制索厂。

rop·i·ness [ˈrəupinis; ˋropɪnɪs] *n*. 可拉成丝;黏性。

rop·y [ˈrəupi; ˋropɪ] *a*. (*-i·er*; *-i·est*) 1. 像绳子的;可做绳子的;能拉长的。2. 胶黏的,黏韧的。3. 坚牢的,粗壮结实的。

Roque·fort [ˈrɔkfɔːt; ˋrokfɚt] *n*. (洛克福)羊乳干酪。

ro·que·laure [ˈrɔkəlɔː, F. rɔkˈlɔr; ˋrɑkəˏlɔr, rɑkˋlor] *n*. 一种十八世纪男式齐膝外套。

ro·quet [ˈrəuki, -kei; ˋrokɪ, -ke] *n*., *v*.【槌球】(使)自己的球碰到(别人的球)。

ror·qual [ˈrɔːkwəl; ˋrɔrkwəl] *n*.【动】鳁鲸(= finback)。

ror·ty [ˈrɔːti; ˋrɔrtɪ] *a*.〔英俚〕愉快的,快乐的,有趣的;喜爱娱乐的。*have a ~ time* 过得愉快。

Ro·sa [ˈrəuzə; ˋrozə] *n*. 罗莎〔女子名〕。

ro·sace [ˈrəuzeis; ˋrozes] *n*. 蔷薇花[圆花]图样;【建】圆花窗;圆浮雕;圆花饰。

ro·sa·ceous [rəuˈzeiʃəs; roˋzeʃəs] *a*.【植】蔷薇科的;蔷薇花形的;玫瑰色的,玫瑰香的。

Ros·a·lie [ˈrɔzəli; ˋrɑzəlɪ] *n*. 罗莎莉〔女子名〕。

Ros·a·lind [ˈrɔzəlind; ˋrɑzlɪnd] *n*. 罗莎琳德〔女子名〕。

Ros·a·line [ˈrɔzəlin; ˋrɑzəlɪn] *n*. = Rosalind.

ros·an·i·line [rəuˈzænilin, -ˌiːn, -ˌain; roˋzænəˏlin, -ˏɪn, -ˏaɪn] *n*.【化】品红碱,玫苯胺。

ro·sar·i·an [rəuˈzeəriən; rəˋzɛrɪən] *n*. 1. 蔷薇[玫瑰]栽培者。2.〔R-〕【天主】念珠祈祷会会员。

Ro·sa·rio [rəuˈsɑːrjəu; rɔˋsɑrjo] *n*. 罗萨里奥〔阿根廷港市〕。

ro·sar·i·um [rəuˈzeəriəm; roˋzɛrɪəm] *n*. (*pl*. *ro-sar·i·a* [-iə; -ɪə]) (L.) 蔷薇[玫瑰]园,蔷薇花坛。

ro·sa·ry [ˈrəuzəri; ˋrozərɪ] *n*. 1.【天主】念珠;念珠祈祷。2. 蔷薇冠。3. 玫瑰园;蔷薇花坛。4. 佳句集。

Ros·coe [ˈrɔskəu; ˋrɑsko] *n*. 1. 罗斯科〔姓氏,男子名〕。2.〔r-〕〔美俚〕手枪。

ros·coe·lite [ˈrɔskəulait; ˋrɑskolaɪt] *n*.【矿】钒云母。

Rose [rəuz; roz] *n*. 罗斯〔姓氏,女子名〕。

rose[1] [rəuz; roz] **I** *n*. 1.【植】蔷薇,玫瑰;蔷薇科植物;蔷薇[玫瑰]花。2. 蔷薇[玫瑰]色,淡红色;〔*pl*.〕玫瑰色的脸色;玫瑰香,玫瑰香料。3.〔喻〕舒服,安乐,愉快。4.【纹】(象征英国的)五瓣蔷薇花样;(装饰等)蔷薇花样;玫瑰结。5.【建】圆花饰,车轮窗,圆花窗。6. 玫瑰形钻石;(喷壶的)莲蓬头,喷嘴。7.【医】〔the ~〕丹毒。8.【海】(罗盘等的)刻度盘;罗经卡。9.【机】停座器;【电】灯线盒。*Every ~ has its thorn*. = *No ~ without a thorn*. 没有无刺的玫瑰,没有十全十美的幸福。*the Alpine ~*【植】石南。*the Chinese ~ = the ~ of China*【植】月季花。*the ~ of May*【植】白水仙。*a blue ~* 蓝玫瑰,虚有之物,办不到的事。*She has quite lost her ~s*. 她脸上的玫瑰色完全消失了。*It is not all ~s*. = *It is no bed of ~s*. 并非一切都轻松愉快[十全十美];未必完全安逸。*a wind ~*【空】风图。***a* [*the*] *bed of ~s*** 称心如意的境遇;安乐窝。***as welcome as the ~ in May*** 像五月的玫瑰那样可爱[受欢迎]。***gather* (*life's*) *~s*** 追求欢乐。***the Golden ~***【宗】金玫瑰〔教皇于四旬斋中对某国元首或城市特别颁赠,象征祝福的赠物〕。***path strewn with ~s*** 欢乐的一生,一帆风顺的遭遇。***the ~ of* (*the party*)** (一群人中)最漂亮的美人。***the white ~ of innocence* [*virginity*]** 白玫瑰似的纯洁。***under the ~*** 秘密地;暗中地;私下地。***the Wars of the Roses***【英史】蔷薇战争。**II** *vt*. 1.(运动等把脸色等)弄红,使成为玫瑰色〔通常用被动语态〕;把(羊毛等)染成玫瑰色。2. 使有玫瑰香味。**~-acacia**【植】毛洋槐。~ **aphid**【动】蔷薇长管蚜。~ **apple**【植】蒲桃。~ **bay**【植】夹竹桃;石南。~**bed** 玫瑰花坛[圃]。~ **beetle**【动】吉丁虫。~ **bit**【机】梅花钻。**~-breasted grosbeak**【动】红斑胸腊嘴雀。~ **bud** 玫瑰的骨朵;〔美俗〕初次出入社交场所的少女。~**bush** 蔷薇[玫瑰]丛。~ **campion**【植】毛剪秋罗(= mullein pink)。~ **chafer** [**bug**]【动】蔷薇鳃[玫瑰]金龟子。**~-colo(u)red** *a*. 玫瑰色的;乐观的。**~-diamond** 二十四面钻石。~ **drop** 酒糟鼻。~ **engine** 车制曲线花样的车床附件。~ **fever** [**cold**]【医】枯草热。**~-fish** 许多红色食用鱼的通称〔如鲈鲉,拟石首鱼,无鳔鲉等〕。~ **geranium**【植】头状天竺葵。~ **leaf** 玫瑰花瓣(*a crumpled ~ leaf* 幸福中的小折磨)。~ **mallow**【植】木槿属。~**mary**【植】迷迭香(属)。~ **moss**【植】半支莲(= portulaca)。~ **of Jericho**【植】含生草。~ **of Sharon**【植】木槿;〔主英〕大萼金丝桃。~ **oil** 玫瑰油,玫瑰香水。~**ola**【医】蔷薇[玫瑰]疹。~ **pink** 1. *n*. 玫瑰色,玫瑰色颜料。2. *a*. = ~coloured. **~-pipe** 滤吸管。**~-rash**【医】= ~ ola. ~ **quartz**【矿】蔷薇石英。~**red** *a*. 玫瑰红的。~ **scale**【动】蔷薇白边蚧。~ **slug**【动】蔷薇黏叶蜂。~ **water** 玫瑰香水;奉承话;温和的处置,优柔的办法[手段]。~**water** *a*. 像玫瑰香水的;温和的,感伤的;优雅的,优美的。~ **window**【建】车轮窗,圆花窗。~ **wood**【植】黄檀(属);花梨树;黄檀[花梨]木;青龙木。

rose[2] [rəuz; roz] rise 的过去式。

rosé [rəuˈzei; roˋze] *n*. 玫瑰葡萄酒。

ro·se·ate [ˈrəuziit; ˋrozɪɪt] *a*. = rose-coloured.

Rose·bery [ˈrəuzbəri; ˋrozbərɪ] *n*. 罗斯伯里〔姓氏〕。

Rose·mar·y [ˈrəuzməri; ˋrozˏmɛrɪ] *n*. 罗斯玛丽〔女子名〕。

rose·mar·y [ˈrəuzməri; ˋrozˏmɛrɪ] *n*. (*pl*. *-mar·ies*) 1.【植】迷迭香。2. 艾菊(= costmary)。

ro·se·o·la [rəuˈziːələ; roˋziələ] *n*.【医】蔷薇疹;玫瑰疹。

ro·ser·y [ˈrəuzəri; ˋrozərɪ] *n*. 蔷薇园,玫瑰园;玫瑰花坛[花圃]。

Ro·setta [rəuˈzetə; roˋzɛtə] *n*. 罗塞塔〔女子名〕。

Rosetta stone [rəuˈzetəstəun; roˋzɛtəston] 罗塞塔石〔1799 年在埃及 Rosetta 地方发现的碑石。用象形文字、古埃及俗语和希腊语三种文字写成,由此得到解释古埃及象形文字的初步依据〕。

ro·sette [rəuˈzet; roˋzɛt] *n*. 1. 玫瑰花结,蔷薇花缨缝;蔷薇花饰。2.【建】圆花饰;圆花窗;【电】插座,(天花板)接线盒。3.【植】莲座(叶)丛(= rose-diamond)。*peanut ~* 花生丛簇病。

Rosh Ha·sha·na [ˌrɔʃhəˈʃɑːnə; ˏrɑʃhəˋʃɔnə] *n*. 犹太新年。

Ro·si·cru·cian [ˌrəuzikruˈʃən, ˌrɔzi-; ˏrozəˋkruʃən, ˏrɑzɪ-] **I** *n*. 1. 炼金[占星]术士〔十七、十八世纪一些自称属于会玄术的秘密会社的人〕。2. 其他类似会社的成员。**II** *a*. 玄术[炼金术、占星术等]的。**-ism** *n*.

ros·in [ˈrɔzin; ˋrɑzn] **I** *n*. 松脂,松香;树脂。**II** *vt*. 用松脂擦(提琴弓弦);用松脂封。~ **oil**【化】树脂油,松香油。~**weed**【植】松香草(*Silphium laciniatum*);松脂植物的泛称。

ros·i·nan·te, ro·zi·nan·te [ˌrɔziˈnænti; ˏrɑzɪˋnæntɪ] *n*. 老弱瘦马,不中用的马。

Ross [rɔs; rɔs] *n*. 罗斯〔姓氏,男子名〕。

Ross. = 〔Scot.〕Ross and Cromarty 罗斯克罗马太郡〔苏格兰北部一个郡〕。

ross [rɔs; rɑs] ***n.*** (树皮上)粗糙带鳞状的表面。

Ros·set·ti [rɔˈseti; roˋsɛtɪ] ***n.*** 罗塞蒂〔姓氏〕。

ros·tel·late [ˈrɔstlˌeit, -it; ˋrɑstlˏet, -ɪt] ***a.*** **1.**【植】有蕊喙的;有小喙的。**2.**【动】有顶突的;有小喙的(虱)。

ros·tel·lum [rɔsˈteləm; rɑsˋtɛləm] ***n.*** (*pl.* ***-tel·la*** [-ə; -ə]) **1.**【植】蕊喙;小喙。**2.**【动】顶突;小喙(虱)。**-tel·lar** [-ə; -ə] ***a.***

ros·ter [ˈrəustə; ˋrɑstɚ] ***n.***【军】花名册;勤务簿;名册;登记簿。

Ros·tock [ˈrɔstɔk; ˋrɑstɑk] ***n.*** 罗斯托克〔德国港市〕。

Ros·tov [ˈrɔstɔv; ˋrɑstɑv] ***n.*** 罗斯托夫〔俄罗斯港市〕(= ~-on-Don 顿河畔罗斯托夫)。

ros·tra [ˈrɔstrə; ˋrɑstrə] ***n.*** rostrum 的复数。

ros·tral [ˈrɔstrəl; ˋrɑstrəl] ***a.*** **1.**【动】喙的,嘴的;有嘴的。**2.**【建】(圆柱等)附有喙形船首装饰的。*a ~ column* (雕有敌舰艇首花样的)海战纪念柱。*a ~ crown*【古罗马】(赠给海战中第一个跃登敌艇的将士的)海战功勋冠。

ros·trate, ros·trat·ed [ˈrɔstreit, -tid; ˋrɑstret, -tɪd] ***a.*** **1.**【动】有喙的,有嘴状突起的。**2.**【建】有嘴状装饰的,有喙形船首装饰的。

ros·tri·form [ˈrɔstrifɔːm; ˋrɑstrɪˏfɔrm] ***a.*** 喙形,嘴状。

ros·trum [ˈrɔstrəm; ˋrɑstrəm] ***n.*** (*pl.* ***-tra***, ***~s***) **1.** (古罗马装在舰首用以撞击敌艇的)喙形舰首。**2.**〔*pl.*〕(有敌舰舰首装饰的)舰首讲坛;讲坛;主席台;检阅台。**3.**【动】喙,嘴;嘴状突起。**4.**【医】镊子,钳子。*take the ~* 登坛。

ros·y [ˈrəuzi; ˋrozɪ] ***a.*** (***-i·er***; ***-i·est***) **1.** 蔷薇[玫瑰]色的;粉红色的;玫瑰一样香的;用蔷薇装饰的。**2.** 光明的,有希望的;会幸福的;情况好的,乐观的;〔美〕滥醉的。*a ~ blush (face)* 玫瑰红的(脸)。*~ about the gills* (酒后等)脸色红润。*~ cheeks* 红润的脸颊。*~ finch*【动】粉红岭雀。*the ~ future* 光明的将来。*~ views* 乐观的想法。**-i·ly** ***ad.*** **-i·ness** ***n.***

rot [rɔt; rɑt] **I** ***vi.*** (***-tt-***) **1.** 腐烂;朽坏;枯萎;(尤指囚犯)虚弱,消瘦;(羊)生肝蛭病;腐败,堕落。**2.**〔英俚〕说胡话,说讽刺话,说挖苦话。***be only ~ting*** 一味胡说;只不过是开玩笑。*~* ***off*** [***away***] (树枝等)枯死,凋落。—***vt.*** **1.** 使腐朽[烂];使枯萎;沤制(亚麻等)。**2.** 糟蹋,弄糟;完全破坏(计划等)。**3.**〔英俚〕讽刺,挖苦,取笑。*~ it* [*um*, *'em*] 糟了! 胡说! 见鬼! *R- it! I forgot to bring my book with me.* 糟了! 忘记带书来了。*Rot the luck!* 弄糟了。**II** ***n.*** **1.** 腐朽,腐烂;腐败,堕落。**2.**【植】腐烂病;【兽医】〔the ~〕羊肝蛭病,羊瘟;【医】消耗性疾病。**3.**〔英俚〕胡话,无聊(愚蠢、糊涂、荒唐)的事情。**4.** (板球赛等的)料不到的失败。**5.** 令人沮丧的事;失败。*the black ~ on sweet potato*【农】甘薯黑斑病。*Don't talk ~!* 别胡说! *It is perfect ~ to trust him.* 相信他简直是荒唐。*Rot!*〔俚〕胡说,废话;蠢话,蠢事(= tommyrot)。*What ~ that it is not open on Sundays!* 星期天老不开演[开门]真是荒唐! *A ~ set in.* 士气不振而成败局。

ro·ta [ˈrəutə; ˋrotə] ***n.*** **1.**〔主英〕花名册,勤务簿。**2.**〔英〕值班,轮班。**3.** 轮唱。**4.**〔R-〕【天主】最高法庭。

ro·ta- *comb. f.* 表示"旋转","转动","轮转"。

ro·ta·me·ter [ˈrəutəˌmiːtə; roˋtæmətɚ] ***n.*** 转子流量计,转子流速计。

Ro·tar·i·an [rəuˈtɛəriən; roˋtɛrɪən] ***a.***, ***n.*** 扶轮社(Rotary Club)的(社员);扶轮社社员(的);"扶轮国际"的(成员)。

ro·ta·ry [ˈrəutəri; ˋrotərɪ] **I** ***a.*** 旋转的,轮转的。*a ~ press* [*machine*] 轮转印刷机。*a ~ fan* 扇[吹]风机。*the R- Club* 扶轮社["扶轮国际"(R- International)的旧称;现指"扶轮国际"的各地分社]。*~ Cultivator*【农】旋(转中)耕机。**II** ***n.*** **1.** 轮转(印刷)机。**2.** 环行交叉路。**3.**〔the R-〕"扶轮国际"。**~-wing aircraft**【空】旋翼飞机。

ro·ta·scope [ˈrəutəskəup; ˋrotəskop] ***n.*** (高速)转动机械观察仪。

ro·tat·a·ble [ˈrəuteitəbl; ˋrotetəbl] ***a.*** 可旋转[转动,轮转]的。

ro·tate [rəuˈteit; ˋrotet] ***vi.*** **1.** 旋转;轮转;循环。**2.**【天】自转。**3.** 轮流,交替,轮换。—***vt.*** **1.** 使旋转[轮转];使循环。**2.** 使轮流,使轮换;使交替。**3.**【农】轮作。

ro·ta·tion [rəuˈteiʃən; roˋteʃən] ***n.*** **1.** 旋转;轮转;循环。**2.**【天】自转。**3.**【物】旋度。**4.** 轮流,轮换;交替。**5.**【农】轮作;【林】轮伐(期)。***by*** [***in***] *~* 轮换,轮流。

ro·ta·tion·al [rəuˈteiʃənəl; roˋteʃənl] ***a.*** **1.** 旋转的;轮流的,循环的。**2.**【农】轮作的。*~* **inertia**【物】转动惯量。*~* **grazing**【农】循环[轮换]放牧。

ro·ta·tive [ˈrəutətiv; ˋrotətɪv] ***a.*** 旋转的,转动的;循环的,轮流的。

ro·ta·tor [rəuˈteitə; ˋrotetɚ] ***n.*** **1.** 旋转器,旋转部。**2.**【冶】旋转反射炉。**3.**【物,电】转子。**4.** (*pl.* ***~es***)【解】rotatory (轴)转肌。

ro·ta·to·ry [ˈrəutətəri; ˋrotəˏtorɪ] ***a.*** **1.** (使)转旋的,(使)循环的。**2.** 使轮流的。**3.**【物】旋光的。*~* **dispersion**【物】旋光色散。*~* **power** 旋光力,旋光本领。

ROTC = Reserve Officers' Training Corps〔美〕后备军官训练队。

rotch(e) [rɔtʃ; rɑtʃ] ***n.***【动】扁脚海雀(*Plantus alle*)〔产于北极和北大西洋沿岸〕。

rote[1] [rəut; rot] ***n.*** **1.** 死记,死背。**2.** 机械方法;刻板办法;固定程序。***by*** *~* 死记;机械地(*do by ~* 呆板地做。*have* [*get*, *learn*] *by ~* 死记)。

rote[2] [rəut; rot] ***n.***【乐】= rotte.

ro·te·none [ˈrəutnˌəun; ˋrotənon] ***n.***【化】鱼藤酮。

rot·gut [ˈrɔtgʌt; ˋrɑtˏgʌt] **I** ***n.***〔美俚〕劣酒;下等威士忌酒。**II** ***a.*** 劣质的。

Roth·en·stein [ˈrəuθənstain; ˋroθənˏstaɪn] ***n.*** 罗森斯坦〔姓氏〕。

rô·ti [ˈrɔti; ˏroˋtɪ] ***n.***〔F.〕烤肉。

ro·ti·fer [ˈrəutifə; ˋrotɪfɚ] ***n.***【动】轮虫纲。**-al**, **-ous** ***a.*** **-an** ***a.***, ***n.***

ro·ti·form [ˈrəutiˌfɔːm; ˋrotəˏfɔrm] ***a.*** 轮形的,轮状的。

ro·tis·ser·ie [rəuˈtisəri; roˋtɪsərɪ] ***n.*** **1.** 熟肉店,烤肉店。**2.** 电转烤肉架。

rot·l [ˈrɔtl; ˋrɑtl] ***n.*** (*pl.* ***ar·tal*** [ˈɑːtɑːl; ˋɑrtɑl], ***rotls***) 罗特尔〔穆斯林国家重量单位,标准因地而异,差别约在一磅到五磅之间〕。

ro·to [ˈrəutəu; ˋroto] ***n.*** (*pl.* ***-tos***)〔美〕= rotogravure.

ro·to·chute [ˈrəutəʃuːt; ˋrotəˏʃut] ***n.***【空】(减速)螺旋桨降落伞。

ro·to·graph [ˈrəutəgrɑːf; ˋrotəˏgræf] ***n.***【摄】**1.** 轮转印片机;旋印照片。**2.** (将正本转为反像而直接拍摄的)翻拍照片。

ro·to·gra·vure [ˌrəutəgrəˈvjuə; ˏrotəgrəˋvjʊr] ***n.***〔美〕**1.** 轮转凹板印刷术[品]。**2.** (报纸的)凹版图画副刊。

ro·tor [ˈrəutə; ˋrotɚ] ***n.*** **1.**【电机】转子 (*cf.* stator);动片,转片。**2.**【空】水平旋翼。**3.**【物】旋度。**4.** (风筒船的)风筒,旋转圆筒。**5.**【气】滚轴气团〔水平方向上绕轴旋转的湍流气团〕。**~craft**【空】旋翼飞机(= rotary-wing aircraft, ~ plane)。**~turner**【航空】旋翼调节器〔可调节直升机旋翼轴周围的重力分布以排除机身的振动〕。

ro·to·till [ˈrəutətil; ˋrotətɪl] ***vt.*** 使用旋耕机碎土。

Ro·to·till·er [ˈrəutəˌtilə; ˋrotəˏtɪlɚ] ***n.*** 旋耕机商标名,旋转碎土器商标名,〔r-〕旋耕机,旋转碎土器。

rot·te [ˈrɔtə; ˋrɑtə] ***n.*** 洛特琴〔中世纪的一种拨乐器〕。

rot·ten [ˈrɔtn; ˋrɑtn] ***a.*** **1.** 腐败的,腐朽的;腐烂的;不干净的,邋遢的;臭的。**2.** 腐朽的,堕落的。**3.** 破烂的;不坚固的,不牢的,脆的,易碎的;虚弱的,不健全的。**4.**〔俚〕劣等的,无用的,不可靠的;坏的,不愉快的。**5.** (羊)患肝蛭病的;害了羊瘟的。**6.**〔古、方〕潮湿的,下雨的。*a ~ municipal government* 腐败的市政府。*a ~ show*

〔美〕蹩脚的演出。*a* ～ *deal*〔美〕不公平的待遇。～ *to the core* 腐败透顶。～ *weather* 恶劣的天气。***Something is*** ～ ***in the state of Denmark***. 这里有点古怪[不对头]的事情。～ **borough**【英史】(有权选民太少的)有名无实的选举区。**R- Row** (伦敦 *Hyde Park* 中的)练马林荫路〔常简称 the Row〕。～ **stone** 磨石。**-ly** ***ad***. **-ness** ***n***.

rot·ter [ˈrɔtə; ˋrɑtɚ] ***n***. **1**.〔英俚〕没用的人,废物;无赖,下流坯。**2**. 自动瞄准干扰发射机。

Rot·ter·dam [ˈrɔtədæm; ˋrɑtɚˏdæm] ***n***. 鹿特丹〔荷兰港市〕。

ro·tund [rəuˈtʌnd; roˋtʌnd] ***a***. (***-er***; ***-est***) **1**. 近圆形的。**2**. 胖得圆滚滚的,胀得圆圆的;(嘴等)张得圆圆的。**3**. (声音)洪亮的,圆润的。**4**. 铺张的,(文体等)华丽的。**-ly** ***ad***.

ro·tun·da [rəuˈtʌndə; roˋtʌndə] ***n***. (有圆顶的)圆形建筑物;圆形大厅。

ro·tun·di·ty [rəuˈtʌnditi; roˋtʌndətɪ] ***n***. **1**. 球状,圆形;圆物。**2**. 肥胖。**3**. (声音的)洪亮。**4**. (言语的)圆熟。**5**. (文体等的)铺张,华丽。

ro·tu·rier [F. ˌrotyˈrjei; ˏrɔˏtyˋrje] ***n***.〔F.〕平民。

r(o)u·ble [ˈruːbl; ˋrubl̩] ***n***. 卢布〔俄罗斯等国货币单位〕。

rou·é [ruːˈei; ruˋe] ***n***.〔F.〕荡子,浪子。

Rou·en [ˈruːɑ̃ːŋ; ruˋɑn] ***n***. 鲁昂〔法国城市〕。

rouge[1] [ruːʒ; ruʒ] **I** ***n***. **1**. 胭脂,唇膏,口红。**2**. 粉红,过氧化铁粉,铁丹。**II** ***vt***. ***vi***. (在…上)搽胭脂,搽口红;弄红;变红。**III** ***a***.〔罕〕红的〔只用于: ***R- Croix*** [krwɑː; krwɑ]〔英〕纹章局四属官之一,其纹章为圣乔治红十字〕。***R- Dragon***〔英〕纹章局四属官之一,其纹章为亨利七世赤龙。

rouge[2] [ruːdʒ; rudʒ] ***n***.【橄榄球】〔Eton 校语〕**1**. 扭夺(= scrummage)。**2**. 一分〔带球越过球门界线三次〕。

rouge-et-noir [ˈruːʒeˈnwɑːr; ˋruʒeˋnwɑr] ***n***.〔F.〕(用纸牌玩的)猜红黑。

rough [rʌf; rʌf] **I** ***a***. **1**. 粗糙的(*opp*. smooth);凹凸的,崎岖不平的(*opp*. level)。**2**. 粗毛的,多毛的,蓬乱的(头发)。**3**. 狂暴的(风雨等);汹涌的(海水等);激烈的。**4**. 粗鲁的,粗暴的,无礼的。**5**. 粗陋的,粗杂的。**6**. 未完成的,未加工的,未琢磨的;粗制的。**7**. 草率的,粗枝大叶的,大体的。**8**. 刺耳的,难听的(声音);刺眼的;难看的。**9**. 涩的,难吃的。**10**.〔口〕辛苦的,难受的,难忍的(*on*)。**11**.【希腊语法】带"h"音的,送气的。*a* ～ *skin* 粗糙的皮肤。*a* ～ *road* 崎岖不平的道路。*a* ～ *weather* 狂风暴雨的天气。～ *manners* 粗暴的态度。～ *work* 粗暴的举动;粗活。～ *word* 粗话。～ *accommodation* 粗陋的设备。*the* ～*er sex* 男性。*a* ～ *circle* 不精确的圆。*a* ～ *estimate* 粗略的估计。*a* ～ *guess* 瞎猜。～ *music* (捣蛋的)大声喧闹。*a* ～ *landscape* 荒芜[极难看]的景色。～ *claret* 味涩的红葡萄酒。～ *coal* 粗煤,原煤。～ *materials* 原料。～ *rice* 糙米。～ *coating* 粗抹的底子;灰泥粗糙的表面。*a* ～ *leaf*【植】(在子叶之后生出的)真叶,糙叶。～ *makeshifts* 勉强临时对付办法。*a* ～ *life* 艰苦的生活。*a* ～ *but hearty welcome* 虽然不周到但是诚心诚意的欢迎。***be*** ～ ***on sb***. 对某人粗暴苛刻;欺侮某人;使某人倒霉。***call sb***. ～ ***names round*** 乱七八糟的,庞杂的。～ ***and tough*** 强壮的,结实的。～ ***going***〔美,运动〕苦战。***give sb. a lick with the*** ～ ***side of one's tongue*** 严厉责备,申斥。***have a*** ～ ***time*** (***of it***) 吃苦头,受苦受难,备尝辛酸。

II ***ad***.〔口〕粗,粗糙地;粗暴地;粗话谩骂某人;用坏话骂某人。***play*** ～ (比赛中)动作粗暴。***treat sb***. ～ 对人态度粗暴。***cut up*** ～ 狂暴起来,闹起来,暴跳起来。***live*** ～ 艰苦地生活。

III ***n***. **1**. 粗糙的东西,崎岖不平的地面;(马蹄上的)防滑钉;〔the ～〕【高尔夫球】障碍区域。**2**. 未加工[粗加工]状态。**3**.〔英〕粗暴的人。**4**. 虐待;艰难困苦。**5**. 粗矿,废矿。**6**. 草图;要略。***in the*** ～ 未加工(的),未完成(的);杂乱的[地];无准备的[地];大体上;处于日常状态;〔美高尔夫球〕处于障碍地区。***over*** ～ ***and smooth*** 不管甘苦难易;无论高低起伏;到处。***take the*** ～ ***with the smooth*** 是好是歹,一起承受。***the*** ～(***s***) ***and the smooth***(***s***) 人世的苦乐;幸与不幸。

IV ***vt***. **1**. 弄粗,弄粗糙;弄成崎岖不平;使(羽、毛等)倒竖(*up*);弄成乱七八糟,搅乱。**2**. 粗制,草草作成,使略具雏形(*out*)。**3**. (铁蹄上)装防滑钉;粗暴地对待,虐待;讲粗鲁话,粗暴地说;惹怒;使发脾气。**4**. 写概略(*in*);拟定大体的计划(*out*)。**5**. 驯(马);使(动物)受饥寒。～ ***sb***. ***up the wrong way*** 惹怒某人。～ ***it*** 胡闹;含辛茹苦,忍受辛苦。—***vi***. 变粗糙;粗鲁行事。～**-and-ready** ***a***. 只管快不管好的;潦草塞责的(*the* ～*-and-ready rule* 只管快不管好的作法[主张])。～**-and-tumble** **1**. ***a***. 乱七八糟的,混乱的,杂乱的;莽撞的。**2**. ***n***. 混战;战斗,漫无计划的生活。～ **bluegrass**【植】粗茎莓系草。～**cast** ***vt***., ***n***.【建】粗作,粗制;粗涂,打底子;打底用灰泥;(拟定)大体方案。～ **cut** 粗切的菸叶。～**-cut** 乱切的;粗切的。～ **diamond**〔喻〕外表粗鲁的人。～**-dry** ***vt***. 晒干(衣服)不烫。～ **fish** 非食用鱼,无经济价值的鱼。～**-footed** ***a***. 脚上有羽毛的(鸟)。～**-hearted** ***a***. 无同情心的,硬心肠的。～**-hew** (～**-hewed**; ～**-hewn**, ～**-hewed**) ***vt***. 粗切,粗削;粗制。～**-hewn** ***a***. 粗制的;粗糙的;粗鲁的。～ **house** **1**. ***n***.〔原美俚〕(学生的)乱闹。**2**. ***vt***., ***vi***. 吵闹,叫嚣;虐待。～**-legged** ***a***. 脚上有毛的(马、鸟等)。～ **luck** 恶运,倒霉。～ **neck**〔美俚〕粗暴的人,蛮横的人。～ **quarter** (**of the town**) 城市的贫民区。～ **rice** 稻谷。～ **rider** ***n***. 驯马人;劣马骑手;非正规的骑兵;〔R-R-〕【美史】美西战争时的义勇骑兵。～ **scuff**〔美俚〕粗暴的人,暴徒。～**shod** ***a***. 穿钉靴的;钉着防滑铁蹄的(马);残酷无情的(*ride* ～*shod over* 对…大摆架子;骑在…脖子上作威作福,对…恣意妄为,对…横行霸道)。～**spoken** ***a***. 说话粗鲁的。～ **stuff**〔美俚〕暴力行为;下流行为;色情文字。～**-up**〔俚〕动武;打架。～ **wrought** ***a***. 潦草作成的,粗制的。

rough·age [ˈrʌfidʒ; ˋrʌfɪdʒ] ***n***. **1**. 素材,(粗)原料。**2**. 粗糙食物中的纤维质,富含纤维质的粗食,食用糠;(美国西部)粗草料。

rough·en [ˈrʌfən; ˋrʌfən] ***vt***. 弄粗糙,使崎岖不平。—***vi***. 变粗糙,变得崎岖不平。

rough·ish [ˈrʌfiʃ; ˋrʌfɪʃ] ***a***. **1**. 有点粗糙的。**2**. 有点粗暴的;有点不好听的。

rough·ly [ˈrʌfli; ˋrʌflɪ] ***ad***. 粗糙地;粗暴地;粗俗地;粗略地。～ *estimated* 粗略地估计起来。～ *speaking* 粗略地说来。

rough·ness [ˈrʌfnis; ˋrʌfnɪs] ***n***. **1**. 粗糙;凹凸不平,崎岖;蓬乱。**2**. 粗暴;狂风暴雨。**3**. 未加工。**4**. 难听,刺耳;味涩;不调和。**5**. 概略。**6**.【工】粗糙程度。

rou·lade [ruːˈlɑːd; ruˋlɑd] ***n***. **1**.【乐】华彩经过句。**2**. (牛肉片馅的)肉卷。

rou·leau [ruːˈləu; ruˋlo] ***n***. (*pl*. ～**s**, ～**x** [-z; -z]) **1**. 一卷东西;(用纸卷包着的)一卷硬币;〔*pl*.〕一卷丝带。**2**.【军】柴捆。**3**.【医】缗线状红血球簇。

rou·lette [ru(ː)ˈlet; ruˋlɛt] ***n***. **1**. 轮盘赌;(轮盘赌用的)转轮。**2**. (雕刻家的)点线压制轮;粗网纹压制轮;(邮票)骑缝虚线压制轮。**3**.【数】一般旋轮线。**4**. 转轮式卷发器。

roum [ruːm; rum] ***n***. room 的一种旧拼写法。

Roum. = Roumania(n) = Rumania(n).

Rou·mansh [ru(ː)ˈmænʃ; ruˋmænʃ] ***n***. = Romansh.

roun·ce·val, **roun·ci·val** [ˈraunsivəl; ˋraʊnsɪvəl] ***n***.【植】大豌豆。

round[1] [raund; raʊnd] **I** ***a***. **1**. 圆形的;球形的;圆筒形的;弧形的,半圆(形)的。**2**. 兜圈子的,一周的;来回的。**3**. 完全的;十足的;完整的,无零头的。**4**. 数目不小的,巨额的。**5**. 流畅的,嘹亮的。**6**. 轻快的,迅速的;活泼的。

R

7. 率直的,坦白的;不客气的,严厉的;断然的,毅然的。8.【语音】圆唇音的,撮口音的。*a* ~ *face* 圆脸。*a* ~ *dance* 圆舞。*a* ~ *arch*【建】半圆拱。*a* ~ *lie* 十足的谎话。*a* ~ *dozen* 恰好[整整]一打。*a* ~ *number* 整数〔10,100,1000 等〕。*a good* ~ *whipping* 一顿狠打。~ *dealing* 光明正大的做法。*a* ~ *unvarnished tale* 坦白话,真情实话。~ *hand* 圆体楷书〔*cf*. running hand〕;楷书书法。***at a* ~ *pace*** 轻快矫健的步子。***be* ~ *with*** 对…露骨地讲,老老实实跟…讲。***bring up with a* ~ *turn***【海】套住索子使(船)停止;使突然停止,突然阻止。***have a* ~ *scolding*** 被大骂一顿。***in good* ~ *terms*** 直率地(说)。***in* ~ *numbers*** 大概算起来,大略。

II ***n*.** 1. 圆形物,球;环。2. (散步、喝酒等的)一圈,一巡,一转;(人的)一团,一伙。3. 巡视,巡逻,巡视路线;巡逻区域;【军】巡逻队。4. 环行路,圆路。5. 周围,范围。6. 周转;循环。7. 牛腿肉。8. (梯子、椅子脚等的)横档。9.【建】圆形嵌线;【雕】〔the ~〕立体雕刻(*opp*. relief)。10. (工作的)一件;(比赛的)一次,一回(合),一场,一局,(谈判等的)一轮,(欢呼的)一阵,(弹药的)一发,一颗;(枪炮等的)(一次)齐发;排射;(事情、行动等的)一连串,一系列。11.【乐】轮唱;圆舞(曲)。*this earthly* ~ (这个)地球。*The news goes the* ~. 消息传遍。*the* ~ *of knowledge* 知识的范围。*the daily* ~ (*of life*) 日常生活[工作、事务]。*three* ~*s of cheers* 三次欢呼。*a live* ~ 实弹。*a training* ~ 教学[试验]用导[飞]弹。***draw from the* ~** 照着立体模型描绘。***go for a good* ~** 兜一个大圈子。***go* [*make*] *one's* ~*s*** 1. 兜圈子,巡回;走遍。2. (医生)巡视病房;(邮递员)按户投送。***go* [*pace, walk*] *the* ~(*s*)** 巡回,走遍;传遍。***make the* ~ *of*** 巡视。***in all the* ~ *of Nature*** 在自然界的整个范围内,在世界各处。***in the* ~** 雕刻成立体(的),栩栩如生的,表现无余的。***play a* ~** 赛一次。***~ after ~ of cheers*** 一阵一阵欢呼。***serve out a* ~ *of brandy to all hands*** 拿白兰地酒给大家都斟上。***take a* ~** 走一转,兜个圈子;散步。

III ***ad*.** 1. 旋转,回转,团团转,循环往复,周而复始;兜着圈子。2. (在)周围,在附近;到处;在四方。3. 走整整一圈;从头至尾;传遍;挨次。4. 朝反方向;转过来。5. 绕弯儿地,绕道,迂回。6. 到某(指定)地点。*turn* ~ 旋转,团团转。*three inches* ~ 周围三英寸。*all the neighbours for a mile* ~ 周围一英里以内的人们。*Glasses* (*went*) ~. 每人都给了一杯酒。*spread destruction* ~ 向四面八方进行破坏。*all the country* ~ 全国。***all* ~** 周围,到处;四面八方。***all the year* ~** 一年到头。***ask sb*. ~** 邀人来家。***bring* ~** 1. 使苏醒过来。2. 说服过来。3. 拿到…去(*to*)。***come* ~** (从某处)转来,兜回来;恢复(神志);复元;到来;来到(*Easter soon comes* ~ *again*. 复活节很快又要来了)。***come* ~ *to sb.'s view*** 同意某人意见。***cut round* [*around*]** 〔俚〕故意卖弄[显示]。***go a long way* ~** 绕远路走,兜着圈子去。***go* ~** 绕着走;迂回着走;运行;(食物等)人人分到(*enough food to go* ~ 食品充足人人有份)。***hand* ~** 传递给每一个人。***look* ~** 往周围一看;回头看。***order a carriage* ~** 叫马车过来。***right* ~** 周围,到处;四面八方。***~ about*** 成圆圈,在周围,在四面八方;绕着,迂回着;向相反方向;大约。***~ and* ~** = (加强语气的) *round*. ***show one* ~** 带人到处游览。***sleep the clock* ~** 连续睡一整天。***turn* (*short*) ~** (忽然)转过身来。***win* (*sb*.) ~** 把某人拉到[争取到]自己方面。

IV ***prep*.** 在…的周围;在…的四面八方;在…各处;向…四周;围(绕)着…;绕过;在…的附近;(在时间方面)横贯过。*a tour* ~ *the world* 环球旅行。~ *the corner* 在拐弯的地方。*the country* ~ *Beijing* 北京近郊。***argue* ~ *and* ~ *a subject*** 只在问题表面兜圈子〔不深入问题核心〕。***get* [*come*] ~ *sb*.** 智胜某人;诱骗人。***go* ~ *the papers*** 报上普遍登载。***~ the clock* = *the clock* ~** 整天整夜;昼夜不停地。

V ***vt*.** 1. 弄圆,弄成圆形;使胀得圆圆的。2. 完成,使圆满。3. 环绕;(船)绕过(某处),迂回(某处);拐(弯);包围,围住;〔罕〕使旋转。4. 骑马赶拢(畜群)(*up*)。5.【语音】发圆唇音。6. 使成整数;【数】把…四舍五入。***~ in***【海】(把索缆)拉上来。***~ off*** 弄圆;完成,使成熟;使完美;使圆满;愉快地度过。***~ on sb*.** 骂某人,说某人坏话,攻击某人;告某人的密,出卖某人。***~ on one's heels*** 用脚后跟支住而转身,转过身来。***~ out*** 1. 〔美〕= *round off*. 2. 使胖得圆滚滚的。***~ to*** 1.【海】使船掉头迎风停下。2. 恢复健康[体力]。***~ up*** 弄成圆球;使数目恰好;使成一个整数;赶拢,赶在一块儿;兜捕;逮捕。—***vi*.** 1. 变圆;弯曲。2. 成熟,长饱满。3. 巡视,巡逻;绕转,拐弯,回过头来。~ **about** 1. ***a*.** 绕大圈子的,迂回的(路等);转弯抹角的,委婉的;包围着的,广泛包含的;长胖了的。2. ***n*.** 迂回曲折的路,远路;转弯抹角的说法,婉转的说法;周游,圆形物,圆场,圆形阵营;团团围住的树篱;圆背靠椅;〔英〕旋转木马;〔英〕环状交叉路;〔美〕(男用)短上衣(*lose on the swings what you make on the* ~-*about* 转木马得来打秋千失去;一手得来,一手失去;结果落空)。~ **angle**【数】(360 度)周角。~**-arm** ***a*., *ad*.** 手臂齐肩的[地]。~ **clam**【动】(北美)蛤蜊(= quahog)。**Roundhead**【英史】圆头党人〔1642—1652 英国内战时反对贵族的清教徒议会党人〕。~ **heel(s)** 〔俚〕性行为随便的女人。~ **house** 1.【海】后甲板舱室。2. 〔美〕(中央有调车转台的)圆形机车库。3.【史】拘留所。4. 〔美俚〕把胳臂弯成弧形打出去的一拳;〔美棒球俚〕大弯球。~ **let** 小圆圈。~**-off** 舍去零数。~ **robin** 1. (看不出签名人先后的)环形签名请愿[抗议]书。2.【运】循环赛。~ **shot** (旧时的)圆球形炮弹。~**-shouldered** ***a*.** 弯腰曲背的。~ **steak** 一刀[一块]牛腿肉。~ **table** 圆桌会议;协商会议,出席圆桌会议的人们。~**-the-clock** ***a*., *ad*.** 昼夜不停的(地);连续二十四小时的(地)。~ **top** 桅楼。~ **trip** 〔英〕周游;〔美〕来回(的旅程)。~**-trip** ***a*.** 〔美〕来回的。~**up** 1. 〔美、澳〕畜群驱集;赶拢一块的牲畜,赶拢家畜的人;兜捕,围捕,逮捕(犯人)。2. 综述;摘要。~ **worm** 蛔虫。

round[2] [raund; raʊnd] ***vi*., *vt*.** 〔古〕低声讲,悄悄地说。~ *sb*. *in the ear* 对着某人耳朵悄悄地讲。

round·ed [ˈraundid; ˋraʊndɪd] ***a*.** 1. 圆的;丰满的,匀称的。2. (兴趣)多样的;(能力)强的,多面的。3.【语音】圆唇的。4.【数】四舍五入的。*a well* ~ *person* 有多方面兴趣[能力]的人。**-ness** ***n*.**

roun·del [ˈraundl; ˋraʊndl] ***n*.** 1. 圆形物;环;小圆盘;圆楯;圆形纹章;【建】小圆窗,串珠花边;【筑城】圆形棱堡。2.【诗】= rondeau. 3. 圆舞。

roun·de·lay [ˈraundilei; ˋraʊndəˏle] ***n*.** 1. 鸟的啼啭声。2.【乐】反复重唱的民歌,回旋曲。3. 圆舞。

round·er [ˈraundə; ˋraʊndɚ] ***n*.** 1. 〔口〕绕行者,巡行者。2. 〔美俚〕累犯;无业游民;酒鬼;〔美〕乱花钱的人。3. 加工成圆形的人[工具]。4. 〔英〕〔*pl*.〕〔作单数用〕软球棒球。5. 〔英〕〔R-〕卫理公会牧师。

round·ish [ˈraundiʃ; ˋraʊndɪʃ] ***a*.** 稍圆的,圆圆的。

round·ly [ˈraundli; ˋraʊndlɪ] ***ad*.** 1. 圆圆地,滚圆地。2. 充分,完全,全面地。3. 坦白地,率直地,露骨地;严厉地;毫不容情地;断然。4. 迅速地;大略。*go* ~ *to work* 热心工作。*scold* ~ 严厉谴责。*He* ~ *asserted that it is true*. 他(完全)断言这是真的。

round·ness [ˈraundnis; ˋraʊndnɪs] ***n*.** 1. 圆,圆形,球形,圆筒状。2. 完满,圆满;完整;丰富。3. 率直,坦率;严厉。

rounds·man [ˈraundzmən; ˋraʊndzmən] ***n*.** (*pl*. **-men**) 〔英〕推销员,跑街;〔美〕巡官;守夜人。

roup[1] [ruːp; rup] ***n*., *vt*.** 〔Scot.〕拍卖。

roup[2] [ruːp; rup] ***n*.**【兽医】1. (家禽的)感冒;鸡瘟[疫]。2. (家禽的)哑声病;哑声。**-y** ***a*.**

rouse[1] [rauz; raʊz] **I** ***vt*.** 1. 叫(人)起来;使跳起来,赶出(猎物)。2. 叫醒;使觉醒;惊醒;鼓励,鼓舞,激励,振起。

3. 激发(感情);惹怒,使发脾气。4. 搅动〔液体使发酵,如在啤酒制造中〕。5.【海】用力拉 (*up*)。—*vi*. 1. 醒来;跳起来,飞起来;【军】起床。2. 奋起;活动起来。~ ***and bitt*** [***shine***]!【军】起床。~ ***oneself*** 振作精神,奋起。~ ***to action*** 使奋起。***want rousing*** 需要刺激,懒惰。II *n*. 1. 觉醒;奋起。2.〔英〕【军】起床号。~**-about** = roustabout 2.

rouse[2] [rauz; raʊz]〔英古〕*n*. 满杯;干杯;闹饮。***give a*** ~ 举杯祝酒。***take one's*** ~ 狂饮乱闹。

rous·er [ˈrauzə; ˋraʊzɚ] *n*. 1. 唤起者;使觉醒者;使惊醒的东西。2.〔俚〕惊人的话[行为];大谎。

rous·ing [ˈrauziŋ; ˋraʊzɪŋ] *a*. 1. (使)觉醒的;鼓励的,使兴奋的。2. 烧起的(火);活泼的,兴旺的(贸易等)。3.〔口〕惊人的,异常的。*a* ~ *lie* 弥天大谎。~ *cheers* 热烈的欢呼。

Rous·seau [ˈruːsəu; ruˋso], **Jean Jacques** 卢梭〔1712—1778,法国哲学家,启蒙思想家〕。**-ism** *n*. 卢梭的学说[社会契约说]。

roust [raust; raʊst] *vt*. 1. 撵出,赶出,驱逐 (*out*)。2. 唤醒;激动,鼓舞 (*up*)。—*vi*. 1. 勤快地工作。2.〔俚〕扒窃。

roust·a·bout [ˈraustəbaut; ˋraʊstə͵baʊt] *n*. 1.〔美〕码头工人;(矿山、牧场等的)杂工;(炼油厂的)非[半]熟练工人;〔美〕马戏团场地工。2.〔澳〕干零碎杂活的人〔尤指牧羊场的打杂工 = rouseabout〕。

rout[1] [raut; raʊt] I *n*. 1. 混乱的群众[集会];【法】非法集会。2.〔英〕盛大的晚会。3.〔古〕团队。4. 溃败,溃散。*put to* ~ 打垮,击溃。II *vt*. 1. 打垮,击破,击溃;使溃退。2. 逐出,赶出。

rout[2] [raut; raʊt] *vt*., *vi*. 1. = root. 2. (从床上)唤起,拉出。3. 挖掘出;刳刨。**-er** *n*. 刳刨者;刳刨工具。

route [ruːt; rut] I *n*. 1. 路;路线,路程;航线。2.【军】[raut; raʊt]出发令,开拔令。***en*** ~〔F.〕= *on* ~. ***give the*** ~ 下令出发。***on*** ~ 在途中。***on the*** ~ 在途中。***take one's*** ~ 向…行进。II *vt*. 1. 给…规定路线[次序,程序]。2. 由某一路线发送。~ **formation**【军】行军队形。~**man** 专在某一条路线上营业的推销员。~ **march**【军】便步行军。~**-proving flight**【空】新航线试飞。

rou·ter[1] [ˈrautə; ˋraʊtɚ] *n*. 刳刨者,刳刨工具〔尤指(a)刳空刨 (= router plane)。(b) 一种刳刨机〕。

rout·er[2] [ˈrautə; ˋraʊtɚ] *n*.【计】路由(选择)器〔相当于网上交通警的一种布线程序〕。

rou·tine [ruːˈtiːn; ruˋtin] I *n*. 例行公事,日常工作;常规;惯例;程序。*the day's* ~ = *daily* ~ 日常工作。*He can only follow the old* ~. 他只会照常规办事。*a test* ~ 检验程序。*the input* ~【计】输入程序。~**-car** 定期汽车。~**-time** 授课时间。II *a*. 日常的,常规的,一定不变的。

rou·tin·eer [ˌruːtiniə; ͵rutiˋnɪr] *n*. 1. 墨守成规者;事务主义者。2.【无】定期测试装置。

rou·tin·ism [ruːˈtiːnizm; ruˋtinɪzm] *n*. 墨守成规,事务主义。**-ist** *n*.

rou·tin·ize [ruːˈtiːnaiz; ruˋtinaɪz] *vt*. (*-ized*, *-iz·ing*) 使程序化,常规化,习惯化。**-za·tion** [-ˈzeiʃən; -ˋzeʃən] *n*.

roux [ruː; ru] *n*. 油脂(尤指黄油)面粉糊〔用于加浓羹汤等〕。

ROV = remotely operated vehicle 遥控操作的小型潜艇〔用于海洋探索〕。

rove[1] [rəuv; rov] *vi*. 1. 盘桓,徘徊,流浪,漂泊。2. (眼睛)转来转去。3. (爱情、权利等)不断地变动。4.【弓术】随走随选目标射箭;用活饵钓(鱼)。—*vt*., *n*. 徘徊(于),流浪(于)。***on the*** ~ 徘徊着,流浪着。~ ***the woods*** 漫游森林。*His eyes* ~*d round the room*. 他的眼睛环视着房间的每个角落。

rove[2] [rəuv; rov] I *vt*. 穿过孔拉;梳;纺(成粗纱)。II *n*. 粗纱;【船】(敲弯钉头用的)垫圈。

rove[3] [rəuv; rov] reeve 的过去式及过去分词。

rov·en [ˈrəuvn; ˋrovn] reeve (1. 穿(绳索)。2. 穿(绳)入孔系牢)的过去分词的异体。

rove-o·ver [ˈrəuvˌəuvə; ˋrov͵ovɚ] I *a*.【韵】转接韵的〔前一行末尾的超韵律音节与第二行的第一音节组成一个音步,形成不间断的韵〕。II *n*. 转接韵诗。

rov·er [ˈrəuvə; ˋrovɚ] *n*. 1. 徘徊者,漫游者,漂泊者,流浪者。2. 海盗;海盗船。3.【弓术】远处的临时目标。4.〔英〕(音乐会等的)站位。5. (橄榄球的)外场守场员。6. (17 岁以上的)童子军。*shoot at* ~*s* 乱射;射远处的临时目标。

rov·ing[1] [ˈrəuviŋ; ˋrovɪŋ] *n*. 1. 粗纱。2. 粗纺。

rov·ing[2] [ˈrəuviŋ; ˋrovɪŋ] *a*. 流浪的;流动的;无定所的,不固定的。*a* ~ *ambassador* 巡回大使。*a* ~ *correspondent* 流动通讯员。*a* ~ *mission* 巡回特派团。*a* ~ *patrol* 游动哨。~*-rebel ideology* 流寇主义。

row[1] [rəu; ro] I *n*. 1. (一)排,(一)行;一排(座位);行列,横列。2. (两旁或一旁有房屋的)路,街〔英国常用作某种行业占用的街道、地区〕。3.【无】天线阵。4.〔the R-〕〔英〕= Rotten R- 伦敦海德公园中的骑马道。***It doesn't amount to a*** ~ ***of beans***.〔美、俚〕这实在不算什么。***at the end of one's*** ~〔美〕沦落不堪;万不得已。***have a hard*** [***long***] ~ ***to hoe***〔美〕有麻烦事,有巨大任务。***hoe one's own*** ~〔美〕做自己的事情,自扫门前雪。***in a*** ~ 成一排;连续,一连串。***in*** ~***s*** 排列着。***in the front*** ~ 在头排;〔美〕胜人一等的,优秀的。II *vt*. 使成行,使成排 (*up*)。~ **house** 联立[成排]房屋的一幢。

row[2] [rəu; ro] I *vt*. 1. 划(船),用…划,划运;摆渡。2. 划船去参加(竞渡等);赛划。*Shall I* ~ *you to the shore*? 要我来把你划运到岸边吗? *The boat* ~*s six oars*. 小艇用六把桨划。***look one way and*** ~ ***another***〔俚〕看东划西,声东击西。~ ***a fast stroke*** 拼命划。~ ***a race*** 竞渡,赛艇。~ ***bow*** [***stroke***, ***five***] (*in the boat*) 担任(小艇)前桨手[整调手,五号划手]。~ ***down*** 划着赶上。~ ***dry*** 不溅水地划;空划。~ ***in the eight*** 作八人小艇选手出场。~ ***in the Oxford boat*** 作牛津大学选手去赛艇。~ ***in the same boat*** 同划小船;同干一工作,有同一处境,抱同样见解;风雨同舟。~ ***out*** 使划累。~ ***over*** 划赢。~ ***30 to the minute*** 一分钟划三十次。~ ***up Salt River***〔美〕使反对党失败。~ ***wet*** 水花四溅地划。—*vi*. 1. 划船,荡桨,摇橹。2. 参加竞渡[赛艇];赛划。II *n*. 划,一划,划船,划船旅行;划程。

row[3] [rau; raʊ] I *n*.〔口〕吵嚷,吵架,争吵;谴责;打架;*What is the* ~? 吵嚷些什么? 怎么啦? *We've had awful* ~*s now and then*. 我们常常争吵的很厉害。***get into a*** ~ 挨骂,被斥责。***have a*** ~ ***with*** 和…争吵。***Hold your*** ~!〔口〕住口! 别吵! ***kick up a*** ~ = ***make a*** ~ 起哄,吵闹;抗议。***make a*** ~ ***about*** 因…谴责。***pick a*** ~ ***with*** 和…争吵。II *vt*.〔口〕责骂,申斥,责备。~ *sb*. *up*〔美〕责备某人。—*vi*.〔口〕争吵,吵闹。

row·an, **row·an·ber·ry** [ˈrəuən, ˈrau-, -beri; ˋroən, ˋraʊ-, -bɛrɪ] *n*.【植】1. 欧洲花楸 (*Sorbus aucuparia*)。2. 美洲花楸。3. 花楸果。

row·an·tree [ˈrəuəntriː, ˈrauən-; ˋroəntri, ˋraʊən-] *n*. 1. (欧洲)山楸。2. (美洲)花楸。

row·boat [ˈrəubəut; ˋro͵bot] *n*. 用桨划的船;划艇,划子。

row-de-dow, **row·dy·dow** [ˈraudiˈdau; ˋraʊdɪˋdaʊ] *n*.〔口〕吵闹,喧嚷。

row·dy [ˈraudi; ˋraʊdɪ] I *n*. 凶暴的人;无赖;〔美俚〕钱。*a young* ~ 阿飞。II *a*. (*-di·er*; *-di·est*) 凶暴的,粗暴的;吵闹的。**-ism** *n*. 吵闹[粗暴]的行为;流氓作风。**-di·ly** *ad*. **-di·ness** *n*., **-ish** *a*. 有点吵闹的;有点粗暴的。

row·dy-dow·dy [ˈraudiˈdaudi; ˋraʊdɪˋdaʊdɪ] *a*. 喧哗的,吵闹的。

Rowe [rəu; ro] *n*. 罗〔姓氏〕。

R

row·el [ˈrauəl; ˋrauəl] **I** ***n***. (踢马刺上的)齿轮,距轮;【兽医】插环打脓。**II** ***vt***. (〔英〕***-ll-***) 用距轮刺;插入插环打脓器。

row·en [ˈrəuən; ˋrauən] ***n***. **1.** 留茬(放牧)田。**2.** 上茬作物;再生草。

Ro·we·na [rəuˈiːnə; roˋinə] ***n***. 罗伊娜〔女子名〕。

row·er [ˈrəuə; ˋroɚ] ***n***. 划船的人,划手。

row·ing [ˈrəuiŋ; ˋroɪŋ] ***n***. 划船。*a* ~ *boat* 划艇。*a* ~ *club* 划船俱乐部。~**-machine** 练划台。

Row·land [ˈrəulənd; ˋrolənd] ***n***. 罗兰〔男子名〕。

Row·ley [ˈrəuli; ˋrolɪ] ***n***. 罗利〔姓氏〕。

row·lock [ˈrʌlək; ˋroˏlɑk] ***n***. 桨架,桨叉。

Rox·burgh(e) [ˈrɔksbərə; ˋrɑksˏbɚə] ***n***. 【印】罗克斯布拉装订式〔熨金皮书脊,布或纸封面,外切口与底切口为毛边的书籍装订〕。

rox·y [ˈrɔksi; ˋrɑksɪ] ***n***. 〔美学生语〕地质学教授。

Roy [rɔi; rɔɪ] ***n***. 罗伊〔男子名〕。

roy·al [ˈrɔiəl; ˋrɔɪəl] **I** ***a***. **1.** 王的,女王的,王室的。〔R-〕(英国)皇家的。**2.** 受王保护的,敕立的,敕许的,敕定的。**3.** 像王的;高贵的,庄严的;大模大样的。**4.** 极好的,极佳的,无上的,高级的,盛大的(宴会、欢迎等)。**5.** 大型的,非常大的;非常重要的,地位非常高的。**6.** 浓艳的(颜色等)。*His* [*Her*] *R- Highness* 殿下〔间接提到时用〕。*the Princess R-* 大公主。*a* ~ *princess* 公主。*the* ~ *family* [*household*] 王室,皇家,皇族。*the* ~ *blood* 王族。*a* ~ *feast* 盛宴。*a battle* ~ 大规模的战争;大混战。***have a*** ~ ***time*** 非常愉快。***in*** ~ ***spirits*** 精神很好。***live in*** ~ ***state*** [***splendor***] 生活豪华。**R- Academician** (英国)皇家艺术院院士。**R- Academy** (英国)皇家艺术院〔略 R.A.〕。**R- Air Force** (英国)皇家空军〔略 R. A. F.〕。**R- Anthem** 英国国歌。~ **arch** 共济会 (Freemasonry) 中的一种级别。**R-Army** (英国)皇家陆军。**R- Army Medical Corps** (英国)皇家陆军医疗队〔略 R.A.M.C.〕。**R- Army Ordnance Corps** (英国)皇家陆军军械队〔略 R.A.O.C.〕。**R- Army Pay Corps** (英国)皇家陆军财务队〔略 R.A.P.C.〕。**R- Army Service Corps** (英国)皇家陆军补给与运输勤务队〔略 R.A.S.C.〕。**R- Army Veterinary Corps** (英国)皇家陆军兽医队〔略 R.A.V.C.〕。**R- Artillery** (英国)皇家陆军炮兵〔略 R.A.〕。~ **blue** 品蓝,红光蓝。**R- Botanic Gardens** (伦敦)皇家植物园。~ **burgh** 〔Scot.〕敕许自治邑。**R- Canadian Mounted Police** 加拿大骑警。~ **cell** (白蚁巢中的)王房。**R- Corps of Signals** (英国)皇家通讯兵〔略 R.C.S.〕。**R- Courts of Justice** (伦敦)高等法院。~ **duke** 王室公爵〔指有公爵爵位的王子〕。**R- Engineers** (英国)皇家陆军工兵〔略 R.E.〕。~ **evil** 瘰疬。**R- Exchange** 伦敦交易所〔略 R.E.〕。~**-fern** 【植】王紫萁。**R- Field Artillery** (英国)皇家陆军野战炮兵〔略 R.F.A.〕。~ **flush** 【牌戏】最大的五张同花顺。**R- Flying Corps** (英国)皇家飞行队〔略 R.F.C.〕。**R- Humane Society** 英国溺水者营救会〔略 R.H.S.〕。**R- Institution** 英国科学知识普及会〔略 R.I.〕。**R- Irish Constabulary** 爱尔兰皇家警察队〔略 R.I.C.〕。~ **jelly** (蜜蜂的)王浆。**R- Marines** (英国)皇家海军陆战队〔略 R.M.〕。**R- Marine Artillery** (英国)皇家海军陆战炮兵〔略 R.M.A.〕。**R- Martyr** 【英史】查理 (Charles) 一世。~ **mast** 【船】最上桅。**R- Military College** (英国)皇家陆军军官学校〔略 R.M.C.〕。**R- Naval Air Service** (英国)皇家海军航空队〔略 R.N.A.S.〕。**R- Naval Reserve** (英国)皇家海军后备队〔略 R.N.R.〕。**R- Navy** (英国)皇家海军〔略 R.N.〕。~ **octavo** 八开纸〔$6\frac{1}{2}\times10$ 英寸〕。~ **palm** (古巴)王棕。~ **paper** 24×19 英寸的纸;25×20 英寸的印刷纸。~ **purple** 深紫色。~ **road** 捷径 (*There is no* ~ *road to knowledge*. 学问上没有平坦的大道[捷径])。~ **sail** 【船】最上桅帆。**R- Society** (英国)皇家学会。~ **stag** 有十二以上角叉的鹿。~ **standard** 〔英〕王旗。**II** ***n***. **1.** 〔口〕王族,皇族。**2.** = ~ paper. **3.** 【海】= ~ mast; = ~ sail. **4.** = ~ stag. **5.** 〔*pl*.〕〔the Royals〕(英国)皇家步兵第一团 (= the R- Scots); (英国)皇家海军陆战队 (= the R- Marines)。

roy·al·ism [ˈrɔiəlizəm; ˋrɔɪəlɪzəm] ***n***. 尊王主义,保王主义;保皇,忠君。

roy·al·ist [ˈrɔiəlist; ˋrɔɪəlɪst] **I** ***n***. 保皇党员;【英史】保王党,查理一世党;【美史】(独立战争时的)英国军队,英国方面的人;〔R-〕〔美〕死而后已的人。*an economic* ~ 保守的实业家。**II** ***a***. = **roy·al·is·tic** 尊王主义的,保皇党员的。

Roy·al(l) [ˈrɔiəl; ˋrɔɪəl] ***n***. 罗亚尔〔姓氏,男子名〕。

roy·al·ly [ˈrɔiəli; ˋrɔɪəlɪ] ***ad***. 作为王,像王;庄严地,高贵地;挥金如土地。

roy·al·ty [ˈrɔiəlti; ˋrɔɪəltɪ] ***n***. **1.** 为王;王位;王德,王威;王道,王者;〔集合词〕皇族,王族;〔常 *pl*.〕王的特权,王权;王国;王的领土。**2.** 版税;上演税;铸币税;矿区使用费;特许权使用费。**3.** 堂皇,庄严,高贵。

Royce [rɔis; rɔɪs] ***n***. 罗伊斯〔姓氏,男子名〕。

roys·ter [ˈrɔistə; ˋrɔɪstɚ] ***vi***. = roister.

roz·zer [ˈrɔzə; ˋrɑzɚ] ***n***. 〔英俚〕警察。

RP = **1.** radiophotography 无线电传真术。**2.** rocket projectile 火箭弹。**3.** refilling point 补给所。

R.P. = **1.** reply paid 回电费付讫。**2.** regius Professor 〔英〕(英国大学中担任希腊文等)钦定讲座教授。

r.p. = relative poisoning 相对中毒。

RPF = 〔F.〕*Rassemblement du Peuple Français* (= *Reunion of French People*) 法兰西人民联盟。

RPI = retail price index 【商】零售物价指数。

r.p.m., rpm = revolutions per minute 每分钟转数。

R.P.O. = Railway Post Office 铁路邮局。

RPS = revolutions per second 转/秒。

rpt = report.

RPV = remotely piloted vehicle 遥控飞行器。

R.Q. = respiratory quotient 【医】呼吸商。

R.R. = **1.** railroad. **2.** Right Reverend 可尊敬的…〔对主教的尊称〕。**3.** rural road 乡村道路。

Rr = rear.

R.R.C. = **1.** Royal Red Cross 英国红十字会。**2.** Rubber Reserve Commission 〔美〕橡胶储备委员会。

RR Ly·rae var·i·a·bles [ˌɑːˌɑː ˈlairiː ˈvɛəriəblz; ˏɑrˏɑr ˋlaɪri ˋvɛrɪəbl̩z] 【天】天琴 RR 型(变)星。

RRS = Radiation Research Society 〔美〕辐射研究学会。

RS = Revised Statutes 〔加拿大〕《修整法案》〔指 1867 年加拿大由英殖民地变为自治领的法案〕。

R.S., RS = **1.** Royal Society 〔英〕皇家学会。**2.** Recording Secretary 秘书记录员。**3.** Royal Scots (Regiment) 〔英〕皇家苏格兰团,皇家步兵第一团。

Rs = **1.** rupees. **2.** rivers.

r.s. = reed space 【纺】筘幅。

RSC = Reactor Safeguards Committee 反应堆安全技术委员会。

R.S.F.S.R. = Russian Soviet Federated Socialist Republic (前苏联的)俄罗斯苏维埃联邦社会主义共和国。

R.S.M. = **1.** Regimental Sergeant Major 〔英〕团部军士长。**2.** Royal Society of Medicine 〔英〕皇家医学会。

R.S.O. = Railway Sub-Office 铁路分局。

R.S.S. = 〔L.〕*Regiae Societatis Socius* 〔英〕皇家学会会员。

RSVP, r.s.v.p. = 〔F.〕*répondez s'il vous plaît* (请帖等用语)请答复 (= please reply)。

RT, R.T., R/T = **1.** radiotelegraphy 无线电报术。**2.** radiotelephony 无线电话术。

rt. = right.

R.T.C. = Royal Tanks Corps 〔英〕皇家坦克兵。

Rt. Hon. = Right Honourable 〔英〕可尊敬的〔对有爵位者的尊称〕。

RTOL = reduced take-off and landing【航】短距离起落〔指在不到标准跑道 1/2 长的条件下的起落〕。

R.T.R. = Royal Tank Regiment〔英〕皇家坦克团。

Rt. Rev. = Right Reverend 尊敬的〔对主教的尊称〕。

RTT = radioteletype.

R.U. = Rugby Union〔英〕橄榄球联合会。

Ru = ruthenium【化】钌。

Ru·an·da [ruˈwɑndə; ruˋɑndə] ***n*.** **1.** (*pl*. ***-das***, ***-da***) 卢旺[安]达人〔住在卢旺[安]达和刚果的班图人〕。**2.** 卢旺[安]达人用的班图语。

ruat·cae·lum [ˈruːætˈsiːləm; ˋruætˋsiləm]〔L.〕即使天塌下来也罢。

rub[1] [rʌb; rʌb] **I** ***vt*.** **1.** 擦,摩擦;使相擦;抚摩;揩拭;把…摩擦得(干净、光亮等)。**2.** 用…擦;擦上,涂上 (*on*, *over*)。**3.** 触痛,惹怒(某人)。**4.** 擦掉,擦去 (*out*, *off*)。**5.** 拓印,摹拓(碑石等)。**6.**〔美俚〕杀害。~ ***away*** 擦掉,揩掉;消除。~ ***down*** **1.** 用力擦遍(全身),擦干净;按摩。**2.** 彻底梳刷(马毛)。**3.**〔口〕(警察等对人)全身搜查。~ ***in*** 把…用力擦进去;〔俚〕反反复复说。~ ***it in***〔美俚〕反反复复提别人的不愉快的事情;(故意)触人痛处。~ ***noses*** 用鼻互擦〔某些民族寒暄方式〕。~ ***off*** 擦掉,擦去。~ ***one's hands*** 搓手〔满足等的表情〕。~ ***out*** **1.** 擦掉,磨去 (~ *out the pencil marks from the picture* 擦掉插图上的铅笔印)。**2.**〔美俚〕杀死。~ ***shoulders*** 肩肩相擦,接触;交际 (*with*)。~ (*sb*.) ***the right way*** 迎合(某人),使…高兴[满意]。~ (*sb*., *the hairs*, *the fur*) ***the wrong way*** 惹怒(某人),使焦急。~ ***up*** 擦,磨擦;温习;拌和,调(颜料等);想起。—***vi*.** **1.** 摩擦,擦到 (*on*, *against*)。**2.** 被擦掉 (*off*, *out*)。**3.** (皮肤等)擦痛,擦破;(衣服等)磨损。**4.** 引得恼火[烦恼]。~ ***against one's grain*** 使人生气[烦恼]。~ ***along*** **1.** (两人或两人以上)平安相处。**2.** (一个人)过得去。

II ***n*.** **1.** 擦,磨擦。**2.** 障碍,阻碍,困难。**3.**【滚木球戏】(场所的)不平坦,崎岖;球碰到障碍物滚歪。**4.** 伤害感情的东西;暗讽,讥刺,挖苦。**5.**〔方〕磨(刀)石。*There's the* ~. 问题难就难在这里。*a* ~ *of* [*on*] *the green* 球碰到障碍物滚歪。***give a thing a*** ~ ***with*** 用…擦,用…磨。~***s and worries of life*** 人世的辛酸。~***down*** **1.** 擦全身。**2.** 按摩 (*have a* ~ *down with a wet towel* 用湿毛巾擦全身)。~ **rail** (汽车等防止擦坏的)摩擦横档。~ **stone** 磨石,磨刀石。

rub[2] ***n*.** 〔the ~〕= rubber[2].

rub. = ruble.

rub·a·dub [ˈrʌbədʌb; ˋrʌbəˏdʌb] **I** ***n*.** 咚咚(鼓声)。**II** ***vi*.** (鼓)咚咚地响。

Ru·bai·yat [ˈruːbiˌjɑːt, -bai-;ˏrubiˋjɑt, -baɪ-] ***n*.**《鲁拜集》〔古波斯诗人莪默·伽亚谟所作的每节四行的长诗〕。~ **stanza** 抑扬格五音步的四行诗节〔韵律为 a a b a〕。

ru·basse [ruːˈbɑːs, -ˈbæs; ruˋbɑs, -ˋbæs] ***n*.**【矿】红水晶。

ru·ba·to [ruːˈbɑːtəu; ruˋbato] **I** ***a*.**, ***ad*.**【乐】表演者随意改变音符的;节奏自由的。**II** ***n*.** (*pl*. ***-tos***) **1.** 表演者随意改变音符的时值。**2.** 节奏自由的演奏风格。

rub·ba·boo, **rub·a·boo** [ˈrʌbəˌbuː; ˋrʌbəˏbu] ***n*.** 烩干肉饼,烩牛肉干〔有时加面粉使汤更加浓稠〕。

rub·ber[1] [ˈrʌbə; ˋrʌbɚ] **I** ***n*.** **1.** 摩擦者;磨者;摩擦物,磨光器;按摩师;(土耳其浴室的)擦背人;(洗澡用)毛巾。**2.** 擦具;粗锉;磨石,砥石,磨砂。**3.** 橡胶;橡胶状物;橡皮;橡皮擦子;黑板擦;〔英〕抹布,掘布。**4.**〔*pl*.〕橡皮鞋;〔美〕橡皮套鞋;【棒球】〔俚〕本垒。**5.** 挖苦,讥讽;阻碍,困难;不幸,倒霉。**6.**〔美俚〕职业刺客,凶手。~ *cement* 树胶胶水。*reclaimed* ~ 再生橡胶。*a* ~ *check* [*cheque*]〔美俚〕空头支票。~ *cloth* 橡皮布。~ *drink*〔美〕酒醉呕吐前的最后一口[一杯]酒。~ *heel*〔美俚〕侦探。~ *insertion sheets* 夹布橡皮。~ *insulated copper wire* 皮(电)线。~ *joint*〔美俚〕低级下流的舞厅。~ *plant* 橡胶植物。~ *sole* 橡胶(鞋)底。~ *solution* 橡胶胶水。**II** ***vt*.** 涂橡胶于…。—***vi*.**〔美俚〕= rubberneck. ~ **bullet** (防暴用的)橡皮子弹。~**stamp** ***n*.** **1.** 橡皮图章;〔喻〕瞎盖图章(的人)。**2.** 机器一样传达命令的人。**3.** 陈腔滥调。

rub·ber[2] ***n*.**【纸牌】(三盘或其他成单的盘数构成的)一局;〔the ~〕三盘两胜,三盘分输赢。*have a* ~ *of bridge* 打三盘[一局]桥牌。

rub·ber·ize [ˈrʌbəraiz; ˋrʌbəˏraɪz] ***vt*.** 给…涂上橡胶,用橡胶处理。

rub·ber·neck [ˈrʌbənek; ˋrʌbɚˏnɛk] **I** ***n*.**〔美俚〕**1.** 橡皮套管。**2.** 伸长脖子看的人,好围观的人;游览者。*Two cars smashed together and a cluster of* ~*s gathered around*. 两辆汽车相撞,一群好奇的人围拢起来观看。**II** ***a*.**〔美俚〕供游览用的。*a* ~ *bus* 游览汽车。**III** ***vi*.** 好奇观览,伸长脖子看;游览,观光。*She* ~*ed through Shanghai last month*. 她上月游览了上海。**-er** ***n*.**

rub·ber-stamp [ˌrʌbəˈstæmp; ˏrʌbɚˋstæmp] **I** ***vt*.** **1.** 在…上盖橡皮图章。**2.**〔口〕不加思考就赞同[批准](计划、建议、文件等)。*They expect the board to* ~ *their findings*. 他们期望理事会能不加思考就赞同他们的调查结论。**II** ***a*.** **1.** 盖橡皮图章的。**2.**〔口〕不加思索而批准的;经例行公事式地批准的。

rub·ber·y [ˈrʌbri; ˋrʌbərɪ] ***a*.** (形态、性质等)似橡胶的。**-i·ness** ***n*.**

rub·bing [ˈrʌbiŋ; ˋrʌbɪŋ] ***n*.** 摩擦、研磨、按摩、摹拓(片)。~ *from a tablet* 碑板等的拓本。

rub·bish [ˈrʌbiʃ; ˋrʌbɪʃ] **I** ***n*.** 碎屑,垃圾,废物;拙劣的作品,无聊的想法,荒唐的事情。*a good riddance of bad* ~ 眼中钉[讨厌的人]离开好。*He is talking* ~. 他在说废话。*This book is* ~. 这本书不行。*Oh*, ~! 〔蔑〕真无聊! 废话! **II** ***vt*.** **1.** 轻视;蔑视。**2.** 消灭;销毁。

rub·bish·ing, **rub·bish·y** [ˈrʌbiʃiŋ, -ʃi; ˋrʌbɪʃɪŋ, -ʃɪ] ***a*.** 碎屑的,垃圾的,废物的;无聊的,没价值的。

rub·ble [ˈrʌbl; ˋrʌbl] ***n*.**【建】毛石,块石;碎石,卵石,粗石;碎砖,瓦砾。~ **work**【建】毛石工(程);乱石工(程)。**-bly** ***a*.** 由毛石砌成的;碎石状的,碎石多的。

rube [ruːb; rub] ***n*.**〔美俚〕乡下佬,土包子。

ru·be·fa·cient [ruːbiˈfeiʃənt; ˏrubəˋfeʃənt] ***a*.**, ***n*.**【医】(使皮肤)发红的;发红药〔外用〕。

ru·be·fac·tion [rubiˈfækʃən; ˏrubəˋfækʃən] ***n*.** (用引赤药后)皮肤的发红。

ru·be·fy [ˈruːbifai; ˋrubəˏfaɪ] ***vt*.** 使红;使(皮肤)发红。

Rube Gold·berg [ˈruːb ˈgəuldbəːg; ˋrub ˋgoldbɝg] **1.** 鲁宾〔Reuben L. Goldberg (1883—1970)美国漫画家〕。**2.**〔美〕杀鸡用牛刀的,小题大做的〔喻用繁琐办法做简单的事〕。

ru·bel·la [ruːˈbelə; ruˋbɛlə] ***n*.**【医】风疹,流行性蔷薇疹。

ru·bel·lite [ruːˈbelait; ruˋbɛlaɪt] ***n*.**【矿】红电气石,红碧玺〔用作宝石〕。

Ru·ben [ˈruːbin; ˋrubɪn] ***n*.** 鲁宾〔男子名〕。

Ru·bens [ˈruːbəz; ˋrubɪnz], **Peter Paul** 鲁本斯〔1577—1640,荷兰画家〕。

ru·be·o·la [ruːˈbiːələ, ˌruːbiˈəulə; rəˋbiələ, ˏrubɪˋolə] ***n*.**【医】麻疹。

ru·bes·cent [ruːˈbesnt; ruˋbɛsn̩t] ***a*.** 变红的,发红的。**-cence** ***n*.**

Ru·bi·con [ˈruːbikən; ˋrubɪˏkɑn] ***n*.** (原为意大利一河名)〔r-〕【皮克牌】比对手早得百分。***cross*** [***pass***] ***the*** ~ 采取断然手段[行动];下重大决心;破釜沉舟。

ru·bi·cund [ˈruːbikənd; ˋrubəˏkʌnd] ***a*.** (脸色等)红润的。

ru·bi·cun·di·ty [ˌruːbiˈkʌnditi; ˏrubəˋkʌndətɪ] ***n*.** 发红,红。

ru·bid·i·um [ru(ː)ˈbidiəm; ruˋbɪdɪəm] ***n*.**【化】铷〔Rb〕。~**-strontium dating**【地】铷锶年代测定法〔通过测定标本中铷放射衰变为锶的时间以确定地质标本的年

龄〕。

ru·bied [ˈruːbid; ˋrubɪd] ***a***. 红玉色的,深红的。

ru·big·i·nous, ru·big·i·nose [ruːˈbidʒinəs, -nəus; ruˋbɪdʒənəs, -nos] ***a***. 锈色的,赤褐色的,棕红色的。

Ru·bik [ˈruːbik; ˋrubɪk] ***n***. 鲁比克〔匈牙利一教师名〕。~**'s Clock** 鲁比克钟,魔钟〔一种智力玩具,难度超过魔方〕。~**'s Cube** 魔方。

ru·ble [ˈruːbl; ˋrubl̩] ***n***. = rouble.

ru·bric [ˈruːbrik; ˋrubrɪk] **I** ***n***. **1**. 红字,红色印刷;红字标题。**2**. 礼拜规程;规程,例式。**II** ***a***. **1**. 用红字写[刻]的。**2**. 印红字的。*a* ~ *day* 节日。**-i·ty** [ruːbˈrisiti; rubˋrɪsətɪ] ***n***. **1**. 变红。**2**. 礼教。

ru·bri·cal [ˈruːbrikəl; ˋrubrɪkl̩] ***a***. 礼拜规程的;用红色印刷[标明]的;朱红的。

ru·bri·cate [ˈruːbrikeit; ˋrubrɪˏket] ***vt***. 用红字写,用红色印刷,加红字标题;制定礼拜规程。**-ca·tor** ***n***. 加红字标题的人。

ru·bri·ca·tion [ˌruːbriˈkeiʃən; ˏrubrɪˋkeʃən] ***n***. 红色印刷;红字标题;用红字写的东西。

ru·bri·cian [ruːˈbriʃən; ruˋbrɪʃən] ***n***. 墨守教仪者。

Ru·by [ˈruːbi; ˋrubɪ] ***n***. 鲁比〔女子名〕。

ru·by [ˈruːbi; ˋrubɪ] **I** ***n***. **1**. 【矿】红宝石,红玉;(钟表里的)宝石(轴承)。**2**. 红宝石色,鲜红色。**3**. 〔英〕细铅字〔相当于美国的 agate, 中国的七号铅字〕。**4**. 红葡萄酒;(脸上的)红酒刺;【拳击】血;〔*pl*.〕嘴。***above rubies*** 极贵重的。**II** ***vt***. 把…弄红;把…涂染成红色。**III** ***a***. 红宝石(色)的,鲜红色的。~ **copper** 赤铜矿。~ **glass** 红玻璃。~ **laser** 红宝石光激光[镭射]器。~ **wedding** 红宝石婚〔结婚后第 40 年〕。

ruche [ruːʃ; ruʃ] ***n***. 〔F.〕(花边、纱等的)褶带,褶边,褶饰。**ruch·ing** ***n***. 褶裥饰边(料)。

ruck[1], **ruck·le** [rʌk, ˈrʌkl; rʌk, ˋrʌkl̩] **I** ***vt***. 弄皱。—***vi***. 变皱,起皱。**II** ***n***. 皱,褶。

ruck[2] [rʌk; rʌk] **I** ***n***. **1**. 多数,多量;群;散乱的人群。**2**. 【赛马】落伍马群。**3**. 〔美俚〕碎屑,废物。**4**. 〔the ~〕群众;一般的人,普通人;一般事物。**II** ***vt***. 把…堆起来。

ruck·le [ˈrʌkl; ˋrʌkl] **I** ***n***. (尤指人将死时的)喉鸣,喘鸣。**II** ***vi***. 发喉鸣声。

ruck·sack [ˈruksæk; ˋrʌkˏsæk] ***n***. 帆布背包。

ruck·us [ˈrʌkəs; ˋrʌkəs] ***n***. 〔美口〕吵闹,吵嚷;乱动,骚动。*raise a* ~ 引起一场争吵。

ruc·tion [ˈrʌkʃən; ˋrʌkʃən] ***n***. 〔常 *pl*.〕〔口〕吵闹,骚动。

Rud·beck·i·a [rʌdˈbekiə; rʌdˋbɛkɪə] ***n***. 【植】金光菊属。

rudd [rʌd; rʌd] ***n***. 【鱼】赤睛鱼。

rud·der [ˈrʌdə; ˋrʌdɚ] ***n***. (船等的)舵;【空】方向舵;指针;领导人,指导者;麦芽浆搅拌棒;【动】尾羽。*an internal* ~ 【火箭】燃气舵。~**fish** 追船鱼。~**post** [ˈrʌdəˌpəust; ˋrʌdɚˏpost] ***n***. 【船】**1**. 舵柱。**2**. 上舵杆,舵头。~**stock** [ˈrʌdəˌstɔk; ˋrʌdɚˏstɑk] ***n***. 【船】上舵杆,舵头。**-less** ***a***. 无舵的,无领导者的。

rud·de·va·tor [ˈrʌdəveitə; ˋrʌdəˏvetɚ] ***n***. 【空】方向升降舵。

rud·di·ness [ˈrʌdinis; ˋrʌdɪnɪs] ***n***. 红色,红。

rud·dle [ˈrʌdl; ˋrʌdl̩] **I** ***n***. 【矿】代赭石,红土;赭色。**II** ***vt***. 用红土在(羊身上)作记号;涂红土于。

rud·dle·man [ˈrʌdlmən; ˋrʌdl̩mən] ***n***. (*pl*. ***-men*** [-men; -mɛn]) 卖代赭石(赤铁矿)的人。

rud·dock [ˈrʌdək; ˋrʌdək] ***n***. 【鸟】知更鸟,鸥鸲。

rud·dy [ˈrʌdi; ˋrʌdɪ] **I** ***a***. (***-di·er***; ***-di·est***) **1**. 红的;微红的;红润的;血色好的。**2**. 〔俚〕讨厌的,可恶的。**II** ***ad***. 非常,很。~ *health* 强壮,健康。*a* ~ *youth* 容光焕发的少年。**III** ***vt***., ***vi***. (使)变红。~ **duck** (北美)红鸭。~ **squirrel** 红松鼠。

rude [ruːd; rud] ***a***. **1**. 粗陋的,粗笨的;未加工的。**2**. 原始的,蒙昧的;野蛮的。**3**. 粗暴的,粗鲁的;无礼的。**4**. 残暴的,猛烈的;厉害的;突然的。**5**. 芜杂的;荒凉的;大略的,不正确的;不成样子的,难看的;不熟的,拙劣的;未完成的,粗制的。**6**. 强壮的,健壮的(*opp*. delicate)。*a* ~ *beginning* 草率的开始。~ *cotton* 原棉。*a* ~ *drawing* 草图。*a* ~ *plenty* 粗糙物品一大堆。~ *produce* 天然产物。~ *petroleum* 原油。~ *fare* 粗陋的食物。~ *savages* 未开化的野蛮人。~ *simplicity* 质朴。*a* ~ *man* 粗人。~ *classification* 大致的分类。*a* ~ *blast* 一阵狂风。~ *scenery* 荒野景色。~ *times* 原始时代。~ *health* 健壮。~ *version* 粗略的译文。*a* ~ *writer* 拙劣的作家。***be*** ~ ***to*** 对…粗暴无礼。***say*** ~ ***things*** 说无礼话。**-ly** ***ad***. **-ness** ***n***.

ru·der·al [ˈruːdərəl; ˋrudərəl] **I** ***n***. 宅旁杂草,道旁杂草。**II** ***a***. 杂草似的。

rudes·by [ˈruːdzbi; ˋrudzbɪ] ***n***. (*pl*. ***-bies***) 〔古语〕鲁莽汉,粗鲁的人。

ru·di·ment [ˈruːdimənt; ˋrudəmənt] ***n***. **1**. 基本,基本原理[知识];〔*pl*.〕初步,入门。**2**. 【生】(器官的)原基;退化[痕迹]器官。*the* ~*s of grammar* 语法入门。*the* ~*s of civilization* 文明的萌芽。

ru·di·men·tal, -ta·ry [ˌruːdiˈmentl, -təri; ˏrudəˋmɛntl̩, -tərɪ] ***a***. 根本的;基本的;初步的,开端的;原状的,发育不全的;残留的。*a rudimentary knowledge* 初步知识,起码的知识。*a rudimentary organ* 退化器官,痕迹器官。**-ta·ri·ly** [-ˈtærili; -ˋtærəlɪ] ***ad***.

Ru·dolph, Ru·dolf [ˈruːdɔlf; ˋrudɑlf] ***n***. 鲁道夫〔男子名〕。

Ru·dy [ˈruːdi; ˋrudɪ] ***n***. 鲁迪〔男子名, Rudolph 的昵称〕。

rue[1] [ruː; ru] **I** ***n***. 〔古〕悲叹;悔恨;后悔。**II** ***vt***., ***vi***. 悲叹;后悔,懊悔,悔恨。*You shall* ~ *it*. 你要后悔的。~ *the loss of opportunities* 后悔失掉机会。

rue[2] [ruː; ru] ***n***. 【植】芸香。

rue·ful [ˈruːfəl; ˋrufʊl] ***a***. 悲伤的;可怜的;悔恨的;沮丧的。*the knight of the R- Countenance* 愁容骑士〔指唐·吉诃德(*Don Quixote*)〕。**-ly** ***ad***. **-ness** ***n***.

ru·fes·cent [ruːˈfesnt; ruˋfɛsənt] ***a***. 带红色的,带有红色的。**ru·fes·cence** ***n***.

ruff[1] [rʌf; rʌf] ***n***. **1**. (伊利莎白 (Elizabeth) 时代流行的)皱领;皱领状物。**2**. 鸟兽的颈毛。**3**. 【鸟】有皱领状颈毛家鸽;流苏鹬。

ruff[2] [rʌf; rʌf] ***n***. 【鱼】鲈鲉。

ruff[3] [rʌf; rʌf] **I** ***n***. 勒弗牌戏〔一种早期的纸牌戏〕。**II** ***vt***. 用王牌胜过。—***vi***. 出王牌。

ruf·fi·an [ˈrʌfjən, -fiən; ˋrʌfjən, -fɪən] **I** ***n***. 暴徒,恶棍,流氓;〔俚〕无线电盲目投弹系统。**II** ***a***. 凶恶的,残暴的。**-ism** ***n***. 流氓习气;暴徒行为。**-ly** ***a***. 流氓般的,歹徒似的;凶恶的,残忍的,凶暴的。

ruf·fle[1] [ˈrʌfl; ˋrʌfl̩] **I** ***vt***. **1**. (将布、纸等)弄皱;兴波作浪;(鸟发怒等时)颤动身体竖起羽毛;搅乱,扰乱,弄乱(头发);洗(牌)。**2**. 使着急,使发躁,使发脾气,惹怒。**3**. 做褶纹;加褶边。~ *up the feathers* [*plumage*] 颤动身体竖起羽毛;惹怒,使生气;发怒,生气。—***vi***. **1**. 起皱,变皱;生浪,起浪;(旗等)飘动。**2**. 生气,发脾气,着急,发躁。**3**. 自大,摆架子。**II** ***n***. **1**. 褶边;褶边状物;皱纹;(鸟的)颈毛;(兽的)头毛。**2**. 兴波作浪,微波,波纹。**3**. 动摇,混乱;急躁;〔罕〕吵闹,骚动。***put in a*** ~ 使躁急不安;激怒。***without*** ~ ***or excitement*** 不吵不闹。

ruf·fle[2] [ˈrʌfl; ˋrʌfl̩] **I** ***n***. 【军】(鼓的)轻擂声。**II** ***vt***. 轻擂,轻击(铜鼓)。

ruf·fler [ˈrʌflə; ˋrʌflɚ] ***n***. 起皱机;(缝纫机上的)打裥装置;〔俚〕骄傲自大的人。

ru·fous [ˈruːfəs; ˋrufəs] ***a***. 赤褐色的。

Ru·fus [ˈruːfəs; ˋrufəs] ***n***. 鲁弗斯〔男子名〕。

rug [rʌg; rʌg] **I** ***n***. **1**. (整块皮制成的)皮毡;小地毯;〔尤指 hearth-~〕;〔英〕(围盖膝的)围毯,车毯。**2**. 地毯式草皮。**3**. 〔美俚〕男子假发。**4**. 〔俚〕反雷达干扰发射机。***cut a*** ~ 〔美俚〕跳摇滚舞。***pull the*** ~ ***from under*** 破

R

坏…的计划。II *vt*. 用厚毯包。～ **joint**〔美俚〕高级豪华的夜总会。

ru·ga [ˈruːgə; ˋrugə] *n*. (*pl*. **-gae** [-dʒiː; -dʒi])【生, 解】皱, 皱襞。

ru·gate [ˈruːgeit; ˋruget] *a*. 皱的, 有折痕的。

Rug·bei·an [rʌgˈbi(ː)ən; rʌgˋbiən] *n*. (英国)拉格比市市立学校的学生[毕业生]。

Rug·by [ˈrʌgbi; ˋrʌgbɪ] *n*. **1.** 拉格比市〔英格兰中部城市〕。**2.** 橄榄球; 橄榄球戏〔*cf*. socker = ～ football〕。

rug·ged [ˈrʌgid; ˋrʌgɪd] *a*. (*superl*. **~est**) **1.** 毛蓬松的; 凹凸不平的, 高低不平的, 崎岖的; 嵯峨的。**2.** 有皱纹的, 皱眉蹙额的(脸等)。**3.** 粗鲁的, 粗暴的。**4.** 粗眉大鼻的, 丑陋的; 刺耳的, 难听的; 严厉的, 严格的(教师等)。**5.** 辛苦的, 艰难的(生活等);〔罕〕狂风暴雨的, 恶劣的(气候)。**6.**〔美口〕强壮的, 结实的。*a* ～ *beard* 蓬松的胡子。*a* ～ *life* 艰难的生活。～ *manners* 粗鲁而朴质的态度。*a* ～ *road* 崎岖不平的路。～ *honesty* 率直, 坦白。～ *kindness* 粗鲁而朴实的好意。**-ly** *ad*. **-ness** *n*.

rug·ge·dize [ˈrʌgidaiz; ˋrʌgɪˏdaɪz] *vt*. 使(机器等)坚固; 使耐用。**-di·za·tion** [ˌrʌgidaiˈzeiʃən; ˏrʌgɪdaɪˋzeʃən] *n*.

rug·ger [ˈrʌgə; ˋrʌgɚ] *n*. 〔英俚〕rugby (football) (橄榄球; 橄榄球戏)的变体。

ru·gose, ru·gous [ˈruːgəus, -gəs; ˋrugos, -gəs] *a*.【生】有皱纹的, 多皱的, 皱层的。

ru·gos·i·ty [ruːˈgɔsiti; ruˋgɑsətɪ] *n*. 皱纹, 皱纹多(状态)。

Ruhr [ruə; rʊr] *n*. **1.** 鲁尔〔德国一地区〕。**2.**〔the ～〕鲁尔河〔莱茵河支流〕。

ru·in [ˈruin, ˈruːin; ˋruɪn] I *n*. **1.** 毁灭, 灭亡; 瓦解, 崩溃; 没落, 破产, 败落; (女人的)堕落; 没落者, 破产者; 毁坏, 破坏。**2.**〔*pl*.〕废墟, 遗迹, 旧址; 毁灭[灭亡]的原因, 祸根。**3.**〔*pl*.〕损失。**4.**〔卑〕劣等杜松子酒〔通常叫 blue ～〕。*the crash of* ～ 可怕的倒塌声。*He is but the* ～ *of what he was*. 他现在(穷困潦倒)不像当年那样容光焕发了。**be the ～ of** 成为…毁灭的原因。**bring to ～** 使失败, 使没落。**come [fall, go] to ～** 毁灭, 灭亡; 崩溃; 破坏掉。**lay in ～** 使荒废, 弄成废墟。**lie in ～s** 成为废墟。**go to rack and ～** 陷于毁灭。II *vt*. **1.** 使破产; 诱奸。**2.** 破坏, 毁灭。**3.** 使没落, 使堕落。～ **oneself** 毁掉自己。～ **one's prospects** 断送某人前程。—*vi*. 破产; 堕落; 变成废墟;〔古、诗〕倒栽葱落下来。

ru·in·ate [ˈruːəˌneit; ˋruɪˏnet] I *vt*., *vi*. (**-at·ed, -at·ing**)〔古语〕使破产, 灭亡, 毁坏, 瓦解, 崩溃; 堕落。II *a*.〔古〕破坏了的, 毁坏了的, 破产的, 没落的, 堕落的。

ru·in·a·tion [ru(ː)iˈneiʃən; ˏruɪnˋeʃən] *n*. 毁灭, 灭亡; 没落, 破产; 毁坏; 毁灭的原因, 祸根。*The olive is spoken of as the* ～ *of martini*. 有人认为橄榄会使马丁尼酒走味。

ru·ined [ˈru(ː)ind; ˋruɪnd] *a*. 破坏了的, 毁坏了的, 灭亡了的; 破产的, 没落的; 堕落的。*a* ～ *city* 一座破坏了的城市。～ *hopes* 破灭了的希望。

ru·in·ous [ˈruinəs, ˈruːinəs; ˋruɪnəs] *a*. 破坏性的, 招致毁灭的; 没落的; 破坏的; 已成废墟的。*a* ～ *heap* 倾圮的一堆, 废墟。**-ly** *ad*.

rul·a·ble [ˈruːləbl; ˋruləbḷ] *a*. 可统治的;〔美〕规章上允许的。

rule [ruːl; rul] I *n*. **1.** 规则, 规定; 法则, 定律; 章程, 规章; 标准; (教会等的)教规, 条例, 教条; 常例, 惯例。**2.** 统治, 支配;【法】命令; (对某一案的)裁决, 裁定。**3.** 尺, 画线板;【印】线, 线条。**4.**【数】解法。**5.**〔the ～s〕【英史】(允许囚犯交付保证金后迁往居住的)狱旁特区。*the* ～(*s*) *of the road* 交通规则。*a hard and fast* ～ 严厉的规则; 精密的标准。*Exception proves the* ～. 有例外就证明有规则。*a carpenter's* ～ (木工)折尺。*a dotted* [*wave*] ～【印】点线; [波]线。*the golden* ～ 金科玉律。*make it a* ～ *to* (*rise early*) 惯于(早起); 照例(起得早)。*R- Britannia* 英国的爱国国歌。～ *of force* 武力政治。～ *of three* 比例的运算法则。～ *of thumb* 手工业方式; 靠经验估计。～ *test* (石油产品的)简单评价法。~*s of decorum* 礼法。**as a ～** 通常, 照例。**break ~s** 破例, 犯规。**by ～** 按规则。**by ～ and line** 准确地, 精密地。**work to ～** (故意)死扣规章而降低生产。II *vt*. 统治, 控制, 支配; 管理; 规定; 判定; (用尺)画线。*the* ~*d class* 被统治阶级。～ *paper with lines* 在纸上画线。~*d paper* 划线纸。～ *the roast* [*roost*] 当领袖。**be ~d by** 听从…的忠告[指导]。～ **against** 不许; 否决。～ **off** 划线隔开, 不准参加比赛。～ **out 1.** (用直线)划去。**2.** 排除在外; 拒绝考虑; 使…不可能。*Bad weather* ~*d the picnic out for that day*. 天气不好使那天的野餐告吹了。—*vi*. 控制, 统治, 支配 (*over*); 裁决, 决定;【商】(价格)稳定, 经常。*prices* ~*d high* 行市一直高。*Crops* ～ *good*. 庄稼情况一般都不错。～ **over** 治理…; 统治…。~**-driller** 教法呆板的教员。～ **joint** 肘垫; (曲尺等只能朝单一方向弯折的)活动接头。～ **monger** 拘泥规则的人。~**-of-three** *a*. 按比例计算的。**-less** *a*. 无规则的, 无约束的。

rul·er [ˈruːlə; ˋrulɚ] *n*. **1.** 统治者, 支配者。**2.** 尺, 画线板。～ **ship** *n*. 统治者的地位[职权]。

rul·ing [ˈruːliŋ; ˋrulɪŋ] I *a*. 统治的, 支配的, 管辖的; 主要的, 主导的, 优势的, 有力的; 普遍的, 流行的, 一般的, 平均的(价格等); 划线用的。II *n*. 统治, 管辖;【法】判决; (用尺的)划线[量度]; 划出的线。*a* ～ *passion* 占统治地位的感情, 主要动机。*the* ～ *class* 统治阶级。*the* ～ *spirit* 主动者, 首脑。*the* ～ *price* 市价, 时价。*accept the* ～ 服从判决。*give a final* ～ 作出最后决定。~**pen** 直线笔, 鸭嘴笔。

rul·ley [ˈrʌli; ˋrʌlɪ] *n*.〔英〕四轮卡车。

rum[1] [rʌm; rʌm] *n*. 朗姆酒, 甘蔗酒;〔美俚〕酒。*a* ～ *hound*〔美俚〕酒鬼, 醉鬼。～ **row**〔美口〕酒类走私船。~**runner**〔美口〕酒类走私贩; 酒类走私船。~**-running**〔美口〕酒类走私。

rum[2] [rʌm; rʌm] *a*. (**-mer**; **-mest**)〔英俚〕奇怪的; 难对付的, 危险的; 蹩脚的。*feel* ～ 觉得不妙; 觉得害怕, 觉得奇怪。*a* ～ *go* 可疑的情况。*a* ～ *start* 惊人事件。*a* ～ *customer* 危险的家伙; 奇怪的家伙。**-ly** *ad*.

Rum. = Rumania.

Ru·ma·ni·a(n) [ruːˈmeiniə(n); ruˋmenɪən] *n*., *a*. 罗马尼亚(人)(的), 罗马尼亚语(的)。

rum·ba [ˈruːmbə; ˋrʌmbə] I *n*. **1.** (古巴的)伦巴舞〔交际舞的一种〕。**2.** 伦巴舞曲。II *vi*. 跳伦巴舞。

rum·ble[1] [ˈrʌmbl; ˋrʌmbḷ] I *n*. (闷雷、电车、肚子等的)隆隆声, 辘辘声; 噪声; 吵闹声, 喧哗声; (随员坐的)马车后座; (汽车在篷后的)活动座位〔又叫 ～ seat〕。II *vt*., *vi*. (使)隆隆[辘辘]地响; (使)车子轱辘轱辘地跑 (*along*; *by*); 闹, 为患。*My guts* ～. 〔俚〕我的肚子咕噜咕噜地响。**-bling** *n*. & *a*.〔俚〕打闹; 隆隆声(的), 辘辘声(的)。～ **strip** 起皱狭长路段〔可使汽车行驶时发出隆隆声并猛烈颤动, 以使开车人集中注意力警惕前方车辆〕。~**-tumble** *n*. 咯噔咯噔动动摇摇的车; 咯噔咯噔的摇动, 厉害的摇动。

rum·ble[2] [ˈrʌmbl; ˋrʌmbḷ] *vt*.〔英俚〕看穿, 看破。

rum·bus·tious [rəmˈbʌstʃəs; rʌmˋbʌstʃəs] *a*.〔英口〕吵闹的, 喧嚣的。

ru·men [ˈruːmen; ˋrumɪn] *n*. (*pl*. **ru·mi·na** [-minə; -mɪnə])【动】(反刍动物的)瘤胃。

ru·mi·nant [ˈruːminənt; ˋrumənənt] I *a*. 反刍的, 反刍动物的; 沉思默想的, 左思右想的。II *n*. 反刍动物。

ru·mi·nate [ˈruːmineit; ˋruməˏnet] *vi*., *vt*. 反刍; 深思, 沉思, 左思右想 (*about*; *of*; *on*; *upon*; *over*)。**-na·tor** *n*. 沉思默想的人, 好思考的人。

ru·mi·na·tion [ˌruːmiˈneiʃən; ˏruməˋneʃən] *n*. 反刍; 思索; 沉思, 默想。

ru·mi·na·tive [ˈruminətiv; ˋruməˏnetɪv] *a*. 沉思默想

R

的,左思右想的。**-ly** ***ad***.

rum·mage [ˈrʌmidʒ; ˋrʌmɪdʒ] **I** ***vt***., ***vi***. 翻查,抄查,搜查;搜出,抄出(*out*; *up*);(为搜查)乱翻,翻箱倒柜;(海关人员)检查(船内)。**II** ***n***.(尤指海关人员的)翻查,搜查,搜遍(船内),查遍,抄遍,杂物,七零八碎的东西。~ **sale** 捐赠物品拍卖;处理品廉价出售。

rum·mag·er [ˈrʌmidʒə; ˋrʌmɪdʒɚ] ***n***. 翻查人,搜查人;检查人。

rum·mer [ˈrʌmə; ˋrʌmɚ] ***n***. 大杯酒。

rum·my[1] [ˈrʌmi; ˋrʌmɪ] ***a***. (***-mi·er***; ***-mi·est***)〔英俚〕= rum[2].

rum·my[2] [ˈrʌmi; ˋrʌmɪ] ***n***. **1**. 兰米牌戏。**2**.〔俚〕怪人。

rum·my[3] [ˈrʌmi; ˋrʌmɪ] **I** ***n***.〔美俚〕酒徒,无赖。**II** ***a***. 兰姆酒(一样)的。

ru·mour, 〔美〕**ru·mor** [ˈruːmə; ˋrumɚ] **I** ***n***. 谣言,传闻,流言。*R- has it that* [*says that*].... 据谣传…。*the author of the* ~ 造谣者。*The* ~ *ran that* .... 谣传…。*start a* ~ 造谣。*spike a* ~ 辟谣。**II** ***vt***.〔常用被动语态〕谣传。*It is* ~*ed that* .... 谣传…,听说…。

ru·mour·mon·ger [ˈruːməˈmʌŋɡə, -ˌmɔŋ-; ˋrumɚˏmʌŋɡɚ, -ˏmɑŋ-] ***n***. 传布谣言者,造谣者,谣言贩子。**-ing** ***n***. 造谣。

rump [rʌmp; rʌmp] ***n***.(鸟兽的)臀部,尾部;〔谑〕(人的)臀部;〔英〕(牛的)大腿肉;残余物,渣滓;〔the R-〕= R-Parliament【英史】残余议会。~ **steak**〔英〕牛腿扒。

rum·ple [ˈrʌmpl; ˋrʌmpl̩] **I** ***vt***.(把织物、纸等)弄皱;(把头发等)弄乱。—***vi***. 变皱,起皱。**II** ***n***.〔罕〕皱纹,褶子。**-ply** ***a***. 弄皱的,弄乱的。

rum·pus [ˈrʌmpəs; ˋrʌmpəs] ***n***. **1**.〔口〕喧嚷;吵闹。**2**.〔英俚〕比赛。*raise a* ~ 引起骚乱。~ ***room***(地下)晚会室,游戏室,娱乐室。

run[1] [rʌn; rʌn] **I** ***vi***. (*ran* [ræn; ræn]; *run*) **1**. 跑,奔,奔驰;【空】滑行。**2**. 赶,赶去。**3**. 逃,逃走,逃亡。**4**. 参加赛跑;当候选人,参加竞选。**5**.(时间)经过,过去。**6**.(事等)进行;运转,运行;(火车、船等)走,开行,行驶;(路)通到(某地)。**7**. 来回跑,往来。**8**.(植物)爬,蔓延;(鱼群)洄游,溯流而上(产卵);(孩子等)长大,生长,发达。**9**.(河、血、鼻涕等)流;(墨水等)渗开;(金属、蜡烛等)熔化,熔解。**10**. 变(冷、热、干、胖等);陷入(危险、负债等),染上(邪恶等)。**11**. 很快地蔓延,扩大;传闻,传布,(谈话等)涉及,谈到(某题目);略一过目,匆匆浏览。**12**.(机器等)转动,开动;滑走,滑动;(旅馆等)营业。**13**. 倾向,偏向。**14**. 有效力;通用,适用;(戏等)连演;继续。**15**. 写着,说明。**16**.【乐】急奏。**17**.(诗句、口才等)流畅,流利。**18**. 平均是,大体是。*He who* ~*s may read* (*it*). 跑着都读得出,明显易懂。*The train* ~*s daily*. 火车每天开行。*The river* ~*s clear* [*thick*]. 这条河流清澈[混浊]。*Shelves ran round the walls*. 架子靠墙四面摆满。*The child's nose* ~*s*. 这孩子流鼻涕。*A thought ran through my mind*. 我脑子里闪过一个念头。*His eyes ran down the page*. 他看了看这一页。*His letter* ~*s as follows*. 他的信这样写着。*So the story runs*. 据说(事情)就是这样的。*The play will* ~ (*for*) *thirty nights*. 这戏将连演一个月。*How your tongue* ~*s!* 瞧,你讲个没完。—***vt***. **1**. 使跑;跑去。**2**.(使)逃走,想逃开。**3**. 催赶;追,追赶,追猎。**4**. 使(船)来回行驶,(用车、船)运输;开(会、车等);经营,办,管理(旅馆、学校等);指挥。**5**. 把(绳子等)穿过,通过(某物);刺;戳,撞;碰;突破(封锁线);顺利通过(岗哨等)。**6**. 流(血、泪等);倒,注(水、铅等入桶,模型等);铸(子弹等);熔化(金属等)。**7**. 举…做候选人;举出(候选人);和…赛跑,使(马)参加赛跑。**8**. 使处(于)(*into*);冒(危险等)(risks, the risk of);使陷入(困难、负债等)。**9**. 划,划定(界线等);砌(隔墙),装(隔板)。**10**. 急急忙忙地缝。**11**. 想下去,思索。**12**. 走私,秘密输入[出]。**13**.〔口〕欺负,挖苦。**14**.〔口〕生(热)。**15**.〔美〕登(广告);(比赛)连续得分。*We will* ~ *you for $ 50 a side*. 我们各赌50元来赛跑吧。*The fever must* ~ *its course*. 这种热病要经过一定过程才会好。~ *a race* 赛跑。~ *errands*(为别人)跑腿,跑差使。~ *cattle* 把家畜赶到牧场。~ *a scent* 追赶猎物。~ *a hare to earth* [*ground*] 把兔子追到洞里。~ *a hotel* 经营旅馆。~ *a cord through* 穿绳子。~ *a cart into a wall* 把车撞到墙上。~ *sb. into trouble* 使某人为难。~ *a blockade* 冲破封锁。~ *the rapids* 过急滩。***cut and*** ~〔口〕奔逃。***have*** ~ ***one's course*** 了结一生。***let things*** ~ ***their course*** 听其自然。~ ***a simile too far*** 把一个明喻用得太牵强。~ ***across*** 遇到,碰见。~ ***after*** 碰上,撞上;偶然遇见,碰见;终于对…不利。~ ***aground***〔船〕搁浅。~ ***ahead of*** 赶过,超过。~ ***at*** 向…扑过去,攻击…。~ ***at the nose*** [***mouth***] 流鼻涕[口水]。~ ***away*** 逃,逃走,逃脱;私奔;(事情)进行不顺利,弄不好,失去控制。~ ***away from*** 学生从(学校)逃出,逃学;水兵从(船里)逃出;放弃(主义等);远远超过(其他竞争者)。~ ***away with*** 拐走,偷去;带着…逃跑,和…私奔;贸然接受(别人意见等);消耗(金钱时间等)(*Don't let your feelings* ~ *away with you*. 你不要被感情驱使[不要感情用事])。~ ***away with it***〔美〕好好儿地做成功,顺利办妥。~ ***back*** 跑回来;(家谱等)上溯到(*to*)。~ ***back over the past*** 想起过去,回顾过去。~ ***before*** 被(敌人)追着逃走;好过,胜过;预料,预想(~ *before one's horse to market* 市场未到先想赚钱)。~ ***before the wind***【海】顺风行驶。~ ***behind*** 跑在…的后头,落后(~ *behind one's expenses* 钱不够用,入不敷出)。~ ***by the name of*** 通用…这个名字,以…这个名字见知于世。~ ***close*** 赶上,追上,紧逼;是…的劲敌,不在…之下。~ ***down*** **1**. 跑下来,下乡;(钟表等)停止;衰弱(*I am* [*feel*] *much* ~ *down*. 累极了)。**2**. 追上,赶上(人、猎物);找出,搜出;讲坏话,诽谤;撞倒;【海】撞沉;压倒;威压;【化】馏出。~ ***dry*** 干;(奶、水等)不出;在干燥的情况下操作;干涸。~ ***false***(猎狗不跟着臭迹跑而)直朝着猎物奔去。~ (*money*) ***fine*** 尽量省钱。~ ***for*** 去叫(…);参加…的竞选,做…的候选人。~ ***for an office*** 做候补人;钻营作官,运动作官,〔美〕参加竞选。~ ***for it*** 逃出,逃脱(危险)。~ ***for one's life*** 拼命逃跑;好容易逃脱。~ ***foul of*** 与…撞上;与…冲突。~ ***full***【海】一帆风顺地行驶。~ ***hard*** = ~ *close*. ~ ***high***(市价等)上涨;(海浪等)汹涌;激昂。~ ***idle***(机器)空转,白转。~ ***in*** **1**. 跑进;(火车)进站;流入;注入;〔口〕(到某处)顺便访问一下(*to*);互相扭住;一致,同意(*with*)。**2**. 赶进;捉进牢里;〔口〕(使)某人当选;【印】(不分段的)接排,连排;【机】试车;试转。~ ***into*** **1**. 跑进,陷入,冲进;(河)注入(海);撞上;到达;和…合并;倾向(~ *into a lot of money* 要花费很多钱。*the readers* ~ *into millions* 读者人数多到以百万计。~ *into five editions* 出到第五版)。**2**. 戳进,插进(~ *something into the ground* 把某物插入地里)。**3**. 使陷入(~ *sb. into* 使人陷入…)。~ ***its course*** 跑到,跑完;(病)痊愈。~ ***low*** 消耗尽;缺乏。~ ***neck and neck*** 并肩跑。~ ***off*** **1**. 逃走;流出,溢出;(火车等)出轨;(话等)离题,越轨。**2**. 放出;使流出;流利地念[写,叙述];举行(赛跑的)决赛;【印】印刷;(用机器)制造。~ ***off at the mouth***〔美俚〕喋喋不休,说个不完。~ ***off with*** = ~ *away with*. ~ ***on*** **1**.〔*on* 副词〕继续,继续作用[有效];说个不停;【印】印完;(排印材料)不另行,接排;连排。**2**.〔*on* 前置词〕(话等)牵涉到(某问题);搁(浅),触(礁);(到银行去)挤兑。~ ***sb. off his legs*** 使某人疲于奔命。~ ***out*** **1**. 跑出;跑累;突出;流出;冲出;(钟等)停止,终止,尽,满期;花光,用光;(稿子付排结果)超出预定篇幅;【海】(绳子)散开;扩张。**2**.【棒球】使跑垒者出场;决定…的胜负。**3**.【机】溢流;偏转。**4**.【空】放下(起落架襟翼)。**5**.【印】把(一段的第一行)排成向左伸出。**6**.【印】用空铅[点线]填入。~ ***out of*** 用光…,缺乏。~ ***out the clock***(足、篮球赛中)为保持领先地位而拖时间;〔喻〕奉行安全而呆板的策略。~ ***over*** **1**. 溢出;泛出;(人)走近(*to*)。**2**. 略一过目,匆匆忙忙看一遍;想

想看;概括地讲;匆匆排练,急奏(乐谱)。3.(车辆等)辗过(人)。~ *ragged*〔美俚〕工作过度,筋疲力尽,累透。~ *short* 用完;缺乏。~ *small* 大概都小,生得小。~ *the streets* 逛马路;流浪街头。~ *the show*〔口〕总管[主管]某事;称霸,逞威,发挥权势,新奇玩意儿大展览。~ *through* 1. 扎穿,刺穿,戳穿,穿过。2. 匆匆忙忙看一遍。3. 不间断地排练,略一过目。4. 花光,浪费(财产等);(将文字等)划线涂掉。5. 普及到,遍达;(铁路)贯通,贯串。~ *time fine* 尽量省时间。~ *to* (数量等)达…;陷于(毁灭、衰亡等);〔口〕(人)有(购买、支付等的)资力,(钱)足够(应付事业、费用等)。~ *to arms* 急忙拿起武器。~ *to extremes* 走极端。~ *to fat* 发胖。~ *to leaves* 生叶子,变成叶子。~ *to meet one's troubles* 杞忧,自苦。~ *to seed* (菜)开了花不能吃;要结子了;〔转为〕盛时已过。~ *together* 混合。~ *up* 1. 跑上去;赶快;迅速长大;(价格)上涨,腾贵;(债款等)增加;(数目)达到…;(弄湿的布等)缩短;末赛跑输。2. 抬高(市价等);升(旗等);盖,造,急造(房屋等);增加(费用、债款等)。~ *up against* 撞上,碰上。~ *up to* 跑到;匆匆忙忙去;(数目)达到。~ *upon* 偶然碰到,意外地碰见;(思想等)时时刻刻集中(在某问题上)。~ *wide* (鱼)成群游回近海。~ *wild* 蔓延;狂暴起来;放肆起来,撒起野来;放荡。~ *with the hare and hunt with the hound(s)* 一面跟着兔子跑一面帮着猎狗咬,两边讨好,骑墙。

II *n*. 1. 跑,奔跑;逃亡,逃走;跑拢;赛跑;打猎;航行;(短期)旅行;跑速;跑的气力;【空】滑行;滑行距离。2. 进行;行程;航程,船舶一昼夜的航程;【空】(投弹前的)直线飞行;【铁路】区间。3. 延续,继续,蝉联;联结;(戏的)连演;【美】(杂志的)连载,发表。4. 流出,淌;流量;【美】小河,水路;水管。5.(银行的)挤兑(*on*);订购踊跃,畅销;流行。6.(山脉、水流等的)方向,趋向,(矿脉的)走向,方位;(市场的)趋势;(事件的)经过;(工厂的)作业,工作,工作时间,产额。7.(普通的)人,物,事件;种类,类型,品质。8.(动物的)通路;(牛、羊的)圈;放牧场。9.(产卵期的鱼的)迁徙,洄游,奔上水;迁徙中的鱼群[鸟群、兽群]。10. 使用的自由,出入的自由。11.【球戏】得分,一分;【棒球】场分,得分。12.【乐】急奏;律动;〔美〕(袜子的)梯形抽丝[绽线]。13.〔美〕【纺】纶(1 盘司长 100 码为 1 纶)。14.【船】船尾尖部。*The train makes a ~ of 100 miles in 2 hours*. 火车两小时跑 100 英里。*a ~ on the Continent* 到欧洲大陆去的短期旅行。*a ~ of a mile* 一英里路程。*a ~ of wet weather* 阴雨连绵。*a ~ of luck* 一连串的好运气。*There was a great ~ to see the new comer*. 许多人跑拢来看新来的人。*a great ~ on the new novel* 新出版小说的畅销。*the ~ of events* 事态的趋势;形势。*the heat ~*【电】发热试验。*the common ~ of mankind* 普通人,常人。*It's all in the day's ~*. 应看作正常[普通]的事。*the ordinary [common] ~* 普通人,普通物品[事件]。*the ~ of the mine* 粗煤。*a poultry ~* 养鸡场。***at a ~*** 跑着。***a bill at the long ~*** 长期支票。***by the ~ = with a ~*** 突然,忽然。***get the ~ upon***〔美〕奚落,挖苦。***give a good ~*** 使尽量跑。***have a good [great] ~*** 大受欢迎,非常流行,盛行。***have a long [short] ~*** 影片放映时间长[短]。***have a ~ for one's money*** 不白费力;不白花钱。***have the ~ of one's teeth***(多半作为劳动报酬)可免费吃饭。***in the long ~*** 最后,结果,归根到底。***keep the ~ of***〔美〕和…并肩而行[并驾齐驱],不落…之后。***let sb. have his ~*** 给某人自由,听任某人自由去做。***level ~*** 水平飞行。***no ~ left*** 气力用完了(*no more ~ left in him* 他再也跑不动了)。***put sb. to the ~*** 使…逃走。***Sunday ~***〔美俚〕1. 长距离。2.(流动售货员的)星期日的旅行。

run[2] [rʌn; rʌn] run 的过去分词。

run[3] [rʌn; rʌn] *a*. 刚出海的,刚捉上来的(鱼),榨取的(蜜等);熔化的,液化的;铸的;〔俚〕走私的。~ *goods* 私货。

run·a·bout [ˈrʌnəbaut; ˋrʌnə͵baut] **I** *n*. 1. 流浪者,游民。2.〔美〕无盖小马车;轻快小汽车;小汽艇;小型飞机;幼童。*trial ~*【机】试车。**II** *a*. 徘徊的,流浪的,跑来跑去的。~ ***on sentence*** 1.(该用连接词)错用逗号的句子。2. 乱加从句的冗长句子。***on the ~*** 在逃走中;在跑着时。***take a ~ to the city*** 到城里去一趟。~ ***of gold*** 富金脉。

run·a·gate [ˈrʌnəgeit; ˋrʌnə͵get] *n*.〔罕〕游民,瘪三;逃亡者,亡命者;变节者,叛徒。

run·a·round [ˈrʌnəraund; ˋrʌnə͵raʊnd] *n*. 1.〔俚〕借口。2. 躲闪,回避,逃避。3. 藐视,冷待。

run·a·way [ˈrʌnəwei; ˋrʌnə͵we] **I** *n*. 逃走者,逃亡者;阻不住的奔马,逃马;逃走,逃亡,私奔。**II** *a*. 逃走的,逃亡的,私奔的;容易跑赢的(马);节节上涨的(物价)。*a ~ chin* 凹下巴。*a ~ ring* 按铃逃〔按了铃就逃,和人家开玩笑〕。*a ~ star*【天】速逃星〔双星之一爆炸为超新星时,以直线方向高速飞离原处〕。

run·back [ˈrʌnˌbæk; ˋrʌn͵bæk] *n*.【足球】断球后带球回跑。

run·ci·ble [ˈrʌnsəbl; ˋrʌnsəbl̩] *a*. 有利刃的。

run·ci·nate [ˈrʌnsinit; ˋrʌnsɪnɪt, -͵net] *a*.【植】下向锯齿形的;倒向羽裂的。

Run·di [ˈruːndi; ˋrʌndɪ] *n*. 1.(*pl*. **-dis**, **-di**) 布隆迪人〔住在布隆迪的班图人〕。2. 布隆迪人用的班图语〔布隆迪和卢安达所用的两种商业语言之一〕。

run·dle [ˈrʌndl; ˋrʌndl̩] *n*. 1. 梯级。2. 灯笼齿轮的齿。3. 绞盘头。

rund·let [ˈrʌndlit; ˋrʌndlɪt] *n*.〔古语〕1. 小桶。2. 隆勒〔液体容量单位,相当于 18 美国加仑〕。

run-down [ˈrʌnˈdaun; ˋrʌnˋdaʊn] **I** *a*.〔美〕伤身体的,累人的;荒废的;(钟等)停了的。**II** *n*. 削减人员,裁员。

Rund·rei·se [ˈruntraizə; ˋruntraɪzə] *n*.〔G.〕环游。*a ~ ticket* 环游车票。

rune [ruːn; run] *n*.〔常 *pl*.〕北欧古字;北欧古诗;芬兰古诗;神秘;神秘的符号。

rung[1] [rʌŋ; rʌŋ] ring[2] 的过去分词。

rung[2] *n*. 1. 梯级,梯子(等)的横档;车辐;〔罕〕(船的)地板料。2.(地位等的上升)一级。*the lowest [topmost] ~ of Fortune's ladder* 倒霉[幸运]之至。

ru·nic [ˈruːnik; ˋrunɪk] **I** *a*. 1. 北欧古字的;古北欧人的;古北欧风的。2.(符号等)有神秘性[魔术性]的。**II** *n*. 北欧古字碑文。

run-in[1] [ˈrʌnin; ˋrʌn͵ɪn] *n*. 插入物;(印件上的)插补段落,(主要词目下的)附加词目;【军】(发动机)试车;【军】飞机向目标(或指定地点)的飞行。

run-in[2] [ˈrʌnin; ˋrʌn͵ɪn] *n*.〔美〕争论,口角;第二道门;【橄榄球】抢球冲进对方球门界线拿球触地。

run·let[1] [ˈrʌnlit; ˋrʌnlɪt] *n*. = rundlet.

run·let[2], **run·nel** [ˈrʌnlit, ˈrʌnl; ˋrʌnlɪt, ˋrʌnl̩] *n*. 小河,水沟。

run·ner [ˈrʌnə; ˋrʌnɚ] *n*. 1. 跑的人;赛跑者;交通员;通讯员,情报员;使者;(银行等的)收款员;善跑的马;乘用马;赛跑马。2. 逃走的人;破坏封锁的船;走私者,买卖私货的人。3.(火车等的)司机。4.〔美〕接客员;兜揽员,推销员,跑街。5.(习车、溜冰鞋等的)滑走部;【机】转子,滚子;【冶】流道。6.【英史】警察,巡捕;【植】纤匐枝,蔓;蔓生草本植物;【鸟】走禽类鸟;秧鸡;鲹属的鱼;黑蛇。7.(铺走廊的)长条地毡,(铺在条桌中部的)长条桌布;(袜子的)梯形绽线。8.【海】游动绞辘。~ **bean**〔英〕红花菜豆。

run·ner-up [ˈrʌnərˈʌp; ˋrʌnɚˋʌp] *n*.【运】亚军,第二名;决赛失败者;(在竞选等中)占第二位的人;(拍卖时)喊高货价的人;【高尔夫球】末赛输者。

run·ning [ˈrʌniŋ; ˋrʌnɪŋ] **I** *a*. 1. 跑的,边跑边走的;流动的,流体的;【机】操作中的;现在的,现行的;【植】纤匐的,攀缘的。2. 继续的,连接的。3. 草草的,仓促而草率的;出脓的(伤等)。*a ~ fight* (海上的)追击战。*four days ~* 接连四天。*the ~ month* 本月。***at the ~***

pace 用跑步。II *n*. 1. 奔跑;赛跑;跑力;【棒球】跑垒。2. 流出;出脓。3. 开动,运转;经营,管理。4.【植】匍匐,长纤匐枝。5.〔口〕短期旅行。*idle* ~【机】空转。***in the*** ~ 参加赛跑;有胜的希望。***make the*** ~ 使(熟练马)带领着(生马)跑;向导。***out of the*** ~ 不参加赛跑;没有胜的希望。***take up the*** ~ (马)从半路起尽力跑;率先领导。~ **account** 流水账。~ **board**〔美〕(汽车两旁的)踏(脚)板。~ **commentary** [**comments**] (散见书中的)评注,注解;(电台的)时事评述。~ **cost** 运转费用[成本];营业费用。~ **fire** 连续跑火。~ **frequency** 转速。~ **gear**【机】驱动装置;【海】驱动船具。~ **hand** 草书。~ **head** [**line, title**] 栏外标题,书楣标题。~ **knot** [**noose**] 一扯就紧的活结[套绳]。~ **mate** (熟马带着跑的)练跑马;〔美〕副职候选人;〔口〕(某人的)密友。~ **meter** 延米,纵长米。~ **plate**【机】踏板。~ **repair** 小修小配。~ **shed**〔英〕圆形机车车库。~ **test** 试探性试验,行车试验。~ **time** 操作时间。~ **water** 流水;自来水。

run·ny [ˈrʌni; ˋrʌnɪ] *a*. (**-ni·er, -ni·est**) 1. 液状的。2. 流黏液的。*a* ~ ***nose*** 流鼻涕的鼻子。**-ni·ness** *n*.

run-off [rʌnˈɔːf; ˋrʌn,ɔf] *n*. (同分者之间的)决赛;〔美〕(地表)径流,径流量。

run-of-paper [ˈrʌnəvpeipə; ˋrʌnəvˋpepə] *a*. (由报纸编辑)随意决定刊载位置的。

run-of-the-mill [ˈrʌnəv ðəˈmil; ˋrʌnəvˋmɪl] *a*. 普通的,一般性的,不突出的,不出色的。

run-of-the-mine, run-of-mine [ˈrʌnəv (ðə) ˈmain; ˋrʌnəvˋmaɪn] *a*. 1. (煤)不按规格、质量分等级的。2. 普通的,不出色的。

run·on [ˈrʌnɔn; ˋrʌn,ɑn] *n*., *a*. 追加(的),连续接排(的)。~ *entries* 接排词目。

run-o·ver [ˈrʌnəuvə; ˋrʌnˋovɚ] *a*. 超篇幅而需转页的。

run·o·ver [ˈrʌnəuvə; ˋrʌn,ovɚ] *n*. 超篇幅的排印材料;(报刊等文章的)转页部分。

runt [rʌnt; rʌnt] *n*. 1. 小牛;矮小的家畜。2. 矮人;〔蔑〕矮子。3. 特大品种家鸽。4.〔苏格兰、英方〕植物的硬茎,腐朽的根;老牛,干瘪老太婆。

run·way [ˈrʌnwei; ˋrʌn,we] *n*. 1.〔主美〕跑道;飞机跑道。2. 河床;(滑运木材等用的)滑路;(窗框等的)滑沟。3.〔美〕动物来往的路;【剧】演员由观众席间上场的通道。4. (在T形台上作的)时装表演。

Run·yon [ˈrʌnjən; ˋrʌnjən] *n*. 拉尼恩〔姓氏〕。

ru·pee [ruːˈpiː; ruˋpi] *n*. (印度等国的货币单位)卢比;卢比银币。

Ru·pert [ˈruːpət; ˋrupət] *n*. 鲁珀特〔姓氏,男子名〕。

ru·pes·trine, ru·pic·o·lous, ru·pic·o·line [ruːˈpestrin, -ˈpikələs, -ˈlain; ruˋpɛstrɪn, -ˋpɪkələs, -ˋlaɪn] *a*.【生】生长或居住在岩石丛中的。

ru·pi·ah [ruːˈpiːə; ruˋpiə] *n*. 卢比,盾〔印尼货币单位〕。

rup·ture [ˈrʌptʃə; ˋrʌptʃɚ] I *n*. 裂断,破裂;决裂,断绝,闹翻;【医】脱肠,疝。***come to a*** ~ (交涉)破裂,决裂;闹翻脸。***have a*** ~ 有疝气。II *vt*. 弄破,使破裂;断绝(关系等);使不和,闹翻;【医】使患脱肠症。~***d duck***〔美俚〕二次大战从军纪念章。—*vi*. 裂开,破裂;断绝。

ru·ral [ˈruərəl; ˋrurəl] *a*. 乡下的,农村(风味)的 (*opp*. urban);地方的;农业的。~ *life* 农村生活。*a* ~ *district*〔英〕地方自治区。~ *economy* 农业经济。~ **dean**〔英〕(主管若干教区的)乡村牧师。~ **free delivery**〔美〕农村地区免费邮递。~ **route** (乡村免费邮递区的)邮道。**-ly** *ad*.

ru·ral·ist [ˈruərəlist; ˋrurəlɪst] *n*. 过田园生活的人,提倡田园生活的人。

ru·ral·ism, ru·ral·i·ty [ˈruərəlizm, ruəˈræliti; ruˋrælətɪ] *n*. 1. 田舍风味,乡村风味。2. 田园生活。3. 农村习语,乡村特色。

ru·ral·ize [ˈruərəlaiz; ˋrurəl,aɪz] *vt*., *vi*. 弄[变]成乡村风味;(使)田园化;过田园生活。

Rus. = Russia; Russian.

ruse [ruːz; ruz] *n*. 策术,谋略,阴谋诡计。

ru·sé [ˈruːzei; ˋruze] *a*. 〔F.〕玩弄策术的,狡猾的。

Rush [rʌʃ; rʌʃ] *n*. 拉什〔姓氏〕。

rush[1] [rʌʃ; rʌʃ] I *vi*. 1. 向前猛进,冲,突进;突击,冲击,袭击 (*on*; *upon*)。2. 匆匆忙忙地走[通过、旅行]。3. 迫不及待地要,冒冒失失地做;突然出现[发生]。—*vt*. 1. 使向前冲,使猛进;突破,冲破;赶,驱;催促;赶紧做[执行、进行];赶紧送,急送。2. 冲锋夺取,袭击;冲破;【足球】带球冲到球门;〔美俚〕热烈地追求;拚命巴结;〔美学生语〕款待(新会员)。*He ~es into things*. 他做事冒失。*R- this order please*. 请赶快办理订货单。~ ***a bill through*** 使议案匆匆通过。~ ***at*** 向…冲过去。~ ***headlong*** 冒进。~ ***harvest*** 抢收。~ ***plant*** 抢种。~ ***in*** 冲进,跑进,跳进,踏进。~ ***into extremes*** 走极端。~ ***in upon one's mind*** 忽然浮现在心里。~ ***out*** 赶制出来。~ ***out of the room*** 冲出屋子。~ ***to a conclusion*** 轻率下结论。~ ***to arms*** 急取武器。II *n*. 1. 突进,猛进;突击,突破。2. 蜂拥而至;激增,猛长;繁忙。3. 抢购,抢订。4.【足球】带球冲破敌阵冲到球门(的人)。5.〔美〕(大学各年级学生间抢夺旗子等的)揪扭,乱斗;〔美学生语〕上好成绩,几乎得一百分。6.【影】试映影片。7.〔美俚〕热烈的追求,殷勤,体贴。8.〔俚〕(服用毒品后立即产生的)瞬间强烈快感。*a* ~ *of water* 奔流。*a* ~ *of wind* 一阵急风。*a* ~ *of blood to the head* 脑溢血。*a great* ~ *of work* 工作繁忙。*a* ~ *of buds* 芽猛长。***be in a*** ~ 大忙特忙。***with a*** ~ 哄地一下子,猛地 (*They came in with a* ~. 他们一哄而入)。III *a*.〔主美〕猛冲的,蜂拥而来的;赶紧完成[执行]的(命令等)。~ **hours** (上班、下班时)交通拥挤的时刻;(公共车辆)高峰时间。~ **job** 急件。~ **order** 加急订单。

rush[2] [rʌʃ; rʌʃ] I *n*.【植】灯心草,蔺;没价值的东西。***not care a*** ~ 满不在乎。***not worth a*** ~ 毫无价值。II *vt*. 铺灯心草于;用灯心草做。~ **bearing**〔英〕献堂纪念节。~**candle** 灯心草蜡烛。~**light** 灯心草蜡烛;黯淡的亮光;微光;微弱的知识;微不足道的人。

rush·ee [rʌˈʃiː; rʌʃˋi] *n*. (大学生联谊会的)拉进对象。

rush·y [ˈrʌʃi; ˋrʌʃɪ] *a*. (**-i·er; -i·est**) 灯心草多的;灯心草做的;铺满灯心草的。

rusk [rʌsk; rʌsk] *n*. 1. 干面包片,脆饼干。2.〔R-〕腊斯克〔姓氏〕。

Rus·kin [ˈrʌskin; ˋrʌskɪn] *n*. 1. 拉斯金〔姓氏〕。2. **John** ~ 约翰·拉斯金〔1819—1900,美国作家,美术评论家,社会改革家〕。

Russ [rʌs; rʌs] *a*., *n*.〔古〕= Russia(n).

Russ. = Russia(n).

Rus·sell [ˈrʌsl; ˋrʌsl] *n*. 1. 拉塞尔〔姓氏〕。2. **Bertrand** ~ 贝特兰·罗素〔1872—1970,英国数学家、哲学家〕。

rus·set [ˈrʌsit; ˋrʌsɪt] I *a*. 枯叶色的,黄褐色的,赤褐色的;手织的;〔古〕乡下式的,简陋的。II *n*. 枯叶色,黄褐色,赤褐色;赤褐色手织土布(衣服);赤褐色冬苹果。

rus·set·y [ˈrʌsiti; ˋrʌsɪtɪ] *a*. 枯叶色的,赤褐色的。

Rus·sia [ˈrʌʃə; ˋrʌʃə] *n*. 1. = the Russian Empire. 2. = 前苏联。3. = (现今的)俄罗斯联邦。4. 〔r-〕= ~ leather (做书皮用的)俄国皮。

Rus·sian [ˈrʌʃən; ˋrʌʃən] *a*., *n*. 俄国的;俄国人(的),俄语(的)。~ **boots** 长统靴。~ **dandelion** 橡胶草。~ **Federation** 俄罗斯联邦〔简称俄罗斯〕。~ **olive**【植】沙枣。~ **Revolution** 俄国革命〔指俄国1905年的二月革命,亦指俄国1917年的十月革命〕。~ **Socialist Federated Soviet Republic** (原)俄罗斯苏维埃联邦社会主义共和国〔略 R.S.F.S.R.〕。

Rus·sian·ize [ˈrʌʃənaiz; ˋrʌʃən,aɪz] *vt*. 使俄罗斯化。

Rus·sify [ˈrʌsifai; ˋrʌsə,faɪ] *vt*. = Russianize.

Rus·so- *comb. f*. 表示"俄国": *the ~-Japanese War* 日俄战争。

rust [rʌst; rʌst] I *n*. 1. 锈;锈色。2. 铁锈;【植】锈菌,锈病。3. 荒废,停滞,无活动。*a life of* ~ 疲塌懒散的生

活。the ~ of idleness 懒癖;惰性。talents left to ~ 白有才能,怀才不遇。**be in** ~ 生着锈。**gather** ~ 生锈。**get [rub] the ~ off** 把锈擦掉。**keep from** ~ 使不生锈。**II** *vi*. 生锈;【植】害锈病;(不用的结果)变钝,变荒废,变呆;变成锈色。*Better wear out than ~ out*. 与其锈坏不如用坏,与其闲死不如忙死。—*vt*. 使生锈,使腐蚀;使钝,使弱。**Rust Belt**〔英口〕"铁锈"地带〔指工业衰退的地带〕。**~-coloured** *a*. 铁锈色的,赤褐色的。**~proof** *a*. 抗锈的,防锈的,不锈的。**-a·ble** *a*. 会生锈的。**-less** *a*. 无锈的,不锈的。

rus·tic [ˈrʌstik; ˋrʌstɪk] **I** *a*. **1**. 乡村的,乡下的。**2**. 质朴的,朴素的。**3**. 粗鲁的,没礼貌的。**4**. (石工等)粗面的;圆木造的;(古代拉丁字体)粗俗体的。~ *simplicity* 纯朴。*a ~ bridge* 独木桥。~ *tobacco* 黄花烟。*a ~ seat* 粗木椅。~ *work* (用天燃树根树枝等建造成的)圆木结构;【石工】粗面石堆砌。**II** *n*. 乡下人,农夫;粗汉。

rus·ti·cal [ˈrʌstikəl; ˋrʌstɪkəl] *a*. 〔古〕乡村的,土气的,粗俗的;做工粗糙的〔rustic 的变体〕。

rus·ti·cal·ly [rʌsˈtikəli; ˋrʌstɪklɪ] *ad*. 照乡下式样;质朴地,不加修饰地;粗鲁地。

rus·ti·cate [ˈrʌstikeit; ˋrʌstɪˏket] *vi*. 到乡下去,下乡;在乡下住。—*vt*. **1**. 使在乡下住,把…送到乡下去。**2**. 〔英大学〕勒令…停学。**3**. 使成粗面石堆砌。

rus·ti·ca·tion [ˌrʌstiˈkeiʃən; ˏrʌstɪˋkeʃən] *n*. 下乡;乡村生活。

rus·tic·i·ty [rʌsˈtisiti; rʌsˋtɪsətɪ] *n*. **1**. 乡下式,乡村风味;乡村生活;质朴,朴素。**2**. 粗鲁,撒野,礼貌。*He was ashamed of his own ~ in that distinguished company*. 在那伙人当中他因自己粗俗而惭愧。

rust·ily [ˈrʌstili; ˋrʌstɪlɪ] *ad*. 生着锈;用哑声。

rust·i·ness [ˈrʌstinis; ˋrʌstɪnɪs] *n*. 生锈。

rus·tle [ˈrʌsl; ˋrʌsl̩] **I** *vi*. **1**. (树叶、纸等)沙沙地[飒飒地]响;绸衣沙沙沙地摩擦着走 (*along*)。**2**. 〔美俚〕快快干,勤奋工作;〔原美西部〕偷牲畜。—*vt*. **1**. 使作沙沙[飒飒]声,沙沙地抖动[抖落]。**2**. 〔美俚〕快干,迅速取到;〔原美西部〕偷(牛马等)。~ **in silks** 穿着绸衫。**II** *n*. 沙沙声,飒飒声。

rus·tler [ˈrʌslə; ˋrʌslɚ] *n*. 〔美俚〕活动分子,活跃分子;偷牲畜的贼。

rus·tling [ˈrʌsliŋ; ˋrʌsl̩ɪŋ] *n*. 沙沙[飒飒]的声音;〔美〕偷牲畜。**-ly** *ad*.

rust·y[1] [ˈrʌsti; ˋrʌstɪ] *a*. **1**. 生了锈的,上锈的;腐蚀了的。**2**. 由锈而成的,因锈而生的;【植】患锈病的。**3**. 锈色的;褪了色的;陈旧的。**4**. (因不使用)变得不能用的,变荒疏的,变拙劣了的,变钝了的。*His Greek is a little ~*. 他的希腊语生疏了。*He is getting ~*. 他渐渐落伍了。**-i·ly** *ad*. **-i·ness** *n*.

rust·y[2] [ˈrʌsti; ˋrʌstɪ] *a*. 〔方〕发脾气的,恼怒的。*He turned ~*. 他发火了。**cut up** ~ 发脾气的。

rust·y[3] [ˈrʌsti; ˋrʌstɪ] *a*. 有腐烂臭味的,开始腐烂的。

rut[1] [rʌt; rʌt] **I** *n*. **1**. 车辙,车印。**2**. 定例,常例,常轨,惯例,老规矩。**get into a** ~ 陷入一定格式。**go on in the same old** ~ 老是干同一样事情。**move in a** ~ 照惯例行动,干老工作。**II** *vt*. 在…上留下车印;在…挖沟。

rut[2] [rʌt; rʌt] **I** *n*. (雄鹿、雄羊等的)发淫,发疯,起兴;发淫期,发淫期的鸣声。**at [in] the** ~ 在发淫。**go to (the)** ~ 发淫。**II** *vi*. 发淫,起兴,动情。

ru·ta·ba·ga [ruːtəˈbeigə; ˏrutəˋbegə] *n*. 【植】大头菜。

ruth [ruːθ; ruθ] *n*. 〔古〕同情,怜悯;悔恨。**-ful** *a*. 充满同情的,悲哀的。

Ruth [ruːθ; ruθ] *n*. **1**. 露丝〔女子名〕。**2**. 【圣】大卫的女祖先。**3**. 【圣】《路得记》〔旧约全书的一篇〕。

ru·the·ni·um [ruːˈθiːniəm; ruˋθinɪəm] *n*. 【化】钌。

Ruth·er·ford [ˈrʌðəfəd; ˋrʌðɚfɚd] *n*. **1**. 卢瑟福〔姓氏〕。**2**. 〔r-〕卢〔放射性强度单位,略作 rd.〕。

ruth·less [ˈruːθlis; ˋruθlɪs] *a*. 无情的,残忍的。**-ly** *ad*. **-ness** *n*.

ru·ti·lant [ˈruːtilənt; ˋrutələnt] *a*. 发红色火光的。

ru·tile [ˈruːtiːl; ˋrutil] *n*. 【矿】金红石。

ru·tin [ˈruːtin; ˋrutɪn] *n*. 【药】芸香苷;卢丁。

Rut·land [ˈrʌtlənd; ˋrʌtlənd] *n*. 拉特兰市〔美国佛蒙特州西部一城市〕。

Rut·ledge [ˈrʌtlidʒ; ˋrʌtlɪdʒ] *n*. 拉特利奇〔姓氏〕。

rut·tish [ˈrʌtiʃ; ˋrʌtɪʃ] *a*. 发淫的;好色的。

rut·ty [ˈrʌti; ˋrʌtɪ] *a*. 车印多的。

R.V. = Revised Version (of the Bible).

R-value R 值〔绝缘材料阻挡热流的阻力计算单位〕。

R.V.O. = Royal Victorian Order.

R.W. = Right Worshipful; Right Worthy.

Rwan·da [ruˈɑːndə; ruˋɑndə] *n*. 卢旺达,卢安达〔非洲〕。

R.W.S. = Royal Society of Painters in water-colours.

Rx [ˈɑːreks; ˋɑrˋeks] *n*. **1**. 处方。**2**. 〔喻〕解决方案。

Ry. = Railway(s).

-ry, -ery *suf*. 构成名词: **1**. 表示"性质、行为"。例: pedant*ry*, brave*ry*. **2**. 表示"境遇,身分"。例: slave*ry*. **3**. 表示"货物的种类"。例:perfume*ry*. **4**. 表示"制造所、饲养所"。例:bake*ry*.

Ry·der [ˈraidə; ˋraɪdɚ] *n*. 赖德〔姓氏〕。

rye [rai; raɪ] *n*. 【植】**1**. 裸麦〔面包原料、牲畜饲料〕;〔美俗〕裸麦威士忌酒。**2**. 绅士,〔特指〕吉卜赛绅士,和吉卜赛人要好的人。~ **bread** 黑面包。~ **grass** *n*. 【植】毒麦〔做粮草用〕。

ryke [raik; raɪk] *vi*. 〔Scot.〕到,达。

Ry·land [ˈrailənd; ˋraɪlənd] *n*. 赖兰〔姓氏,男子名〕。

ry·ot [ˈraiət; ˋraɪət] *n*. 〔英印〕农夫。

R.Y.S. = Royal Yacht Squadron.

Ryu·kyu [ˈrjuːˈkjuː; ˋrjuˋkju] *n*. 琉球(群岛)〔日本〕。**-an** *n*. 琉球民族;琉球人。

ryve [raiv; raɪv] *vi*. 戳通。

S

S

S, s [es; ɛs] (*pl*. *S's*, *s's*, *Ss*, *ss* [ˈesiz; ˋɛsɪz]) **1**. 英语字母表第十九字母。**2**. S 字形, S 形物。**3**. 〔S〕【化】元素硫的符号 (= sulphur)。**4**. 〔S〕〔美〕(学业成绩的)良好等级 (= satisfactory)。**5**. 〔S〕中世纪罗马数字中的 7 或 70。**6**. 〔S〕有色情内容(sex)影片[电视片]的符号。*the collar of S* [*SS*, *Ss*, *esses*], S 字状连锁颈章〔最早为英国兰加斯特王族,以后为伦敦市长等权贵所佩用〕。*an S-hook* S 形钩子。*an S curve* S 形曲线。

S., s. = **1**. saint. **2**. school. **3**. society. **4**. Sabbath. **5**. Saturday. **6**. Saxon. **7**. Senate. **8**. September. **9**.

〔It.〕*Signor*. **10.** Socialist. **11.** south; southern. **12.** Submarine. **13.** Sunday. **14.** second(s). **15.** section. **16.** see. **17.** series. **18.** shilling(s). **19.** sign. **20.** singular. **21.** son. **22.** steamer. **23.** substantive.

's [(浊辅音后) z,(清辅音后) s]〔口〕= is, has, does, us: *He's a boy. He's done it. What's he say about it? Let's go.*

-'s [(浊辅[子]音后) z,(清辅[子]音后) s,(咝音后) iz;z, s,ɪz] **1.**〔古〕= God's: *'sblood* (= God's blood)! 真的! 哼! **2.** 字母、数字等略语的复数:*3's*, *M.P.'s*. **3.** 作名词所有格:*cat's*, *Tom's*. **4.** 加于数字、字母、缩写词之后构成复数:*Ph. D.'s* [*Ph. D.s*] 哲学博士们。*1980's* [1980s] 二十世纪八十年代。

-s [(浊辅[子]音后) z,(清辅[子]音后) s;z,s] *suf.* **1.** 名词复数在词末加 -s: *cats*, *dogs*. **2.** 行为动词第三人称单数现在一般时在词末加 -s: *He jumps. It rains.* **3.** 副词词尾:*always*, *indoors*, *needs*, *forwards*.

S.A. = **1.** Salvation Army【宗】救世军。**2.** sex appeal 性感。**3.** small-arms 轻武器。**4.** South Africa 南非。**5.** South America 南美洲。**6.** South Australia 南澳大利亚。**7.**〔G.〕*Sturmabteilung* (= storm detachment)〔旧〕(希特勒纳粹党的)冲锋队。

Sa =【化】元素钐的符号 (= Samarium)。

Sa. = Saturday.

s.a. = **1.** (〔L.〕*secundum artem* = according to art, in accordance with the rules of the art) 依常规。**2.** (〔L.〕*sine anno* = without year or date) 无年代,无日期。**3.** small-arms 轻武器。**4.** subject to approval 有待批准。

S

SAA, S.A.A. = small arms ammunition 轻兵器弹药,轻武器弹药。

SAAM = small arms ammunition 轻兵器弹药,轻武器弹药。

Saar [sɑː; sɑr] *n.* **1.** [the ~] 萨尔河〔西欧〕。**2.** 萨尔〔德国州名〕(= ~land)。

Saar·brück·en [ˈsɑːbrukən; ˌzɑrˋbrʊkən] *n.* 萨尔布鲁根〔德国城市〕。

SAB = Science Advisory Board〔美〕科学咨询委员会,科学顾问委员会。

Sab. = Sabbath.

sab [sæb; sæb]〔英口〕**I** *n.* 反对杀戮动物者〔尤指反对猎狐运动的人〕;动物保获运动的参加者。**II** *vi.* 参加(阻止猎狐等的)动物保护运动〔系 sabotear 的缩略〕。

Sa·ba [ˈseibə; ˋsebə] *n.*【史】塞巴〔阿拉伯南部一古国,今也门〕。

Sa·ba·e·an [səˈbi(ː)ən; səˋbiən] *a.*, *n.* **1.** 塞巴地方的(人)。**2.**〔误用〕= Sabian.

sab·a·dil·la [ˈsæbəˌdilə; ˋsæbəˌdɪlə] *n.* **1.**【植】沙巴藜芦〔*Schoenocaulon officinale* 墨西哥和中美产有毒百合科植物〕。**2.** 沙巴达子〔沙巴藜芦的干熟种子,用以杀灭害虫〕。

Sa·bah [ˈsɑːbɑː; ˋsɑbɑ] *n.* 沙巴〔马来西亚州名〕。

Sa·ba·han [səˈbɑːhən; səˋbɑhən] **I** *n.* 沙巴人。**II** *a.* 沙巴的。

Sa·ba·ism [ˈseibiizəm; ˋsebɪɪzm] *n.* 拜星;星辰崇拜。

Sab·a·oth [sæˈbeiɔθ, ˈsæbeiɔθ; ˋsæbɪˌɑθ] *n.*〔*pl.*〕【圣】万军;万民。*the Lord of* ~【圣】上帝。

sab·bat [ˈsæbət; ˋsæbət] *n.*〔常作 S-〕= Sabbath 4.

Sab·ba·tar·i·an [ˌsæbəˈtɛəriən; ˌsæbəˋtɛrɪən] **I** *a.* (严守)安息日的。**II** *n.* **1.** 严守安息日的犹太人。**2.** 严守星期日为安息日的基督教徒。**3.** 认定星期六为安息日的基督教徒。**-ism** *n.* 严守安息日习惯。

Sab·bath [ˈsæbəθ; ˋsæbəθ] *n.* **1.** 安息日〔犹太人及少数基督教徒是星期六,一般基督教徒是星期日〕。**2.**〔s-〕休息;静寂。**3.** 安息年;休息时。**4.** (传说中每年一次在夜半举行的)魔女的聚会;恶魔的聚会 (= Witches' Sabbath)。*the great* [*holy*] ~ 复活节前一日。*a s- of sound* 静寂。*keep* [*break*] *the* ~ 守[不守]安息日的。*~-day's journey* 安息日行程〔约三分之二英里〕;〔喻〕轻便旅行。~**-breaker** 不守安息日的人。~ **day** 安息日。~ **School** 星期日[安息日]学校,主日学校,星期日教授宗教课程的学校。

Sab·bat·ic [səˈbætik; səˋbætɪk] *a.*, *n.* = sabbatical.

Sab·bat·ical [səˈbætikəl; səˋbætɪkl] **I** *a.* **1.** 安息日(般)的。**2.**〔s-〕安息的,休息的。*s- leave*〔美〕(大学教授每七年享受一年的)休假。~ *year* (古代犹太人每七年休耕一年的)安息年;〔美〕(大学教授的)休假年。**II** *n.* **1.** (古犹太人的)安息年;(大学教授的)休假年;休假。**2.**〔*pl.*〕星期天穿的衣服,节日服装。**-ly** *ad.*

Sa·be·an [səˈbi(ː)ən; səˋbiən] *a.*, *n.* = Sabaean.

Sa·bel·li·an [səˈbeliən; səˋbɛlɪən] *n.* **1.** 塞贝里人〔包括塞宾人和萨摩奈人在内的古意大利一个部族集团中的成员〕。**2.** 塞贝里语。

sa·ber [ˈseibə; ˋsebɚ] *n.*, *vt.*〔美〕= sabre.

Sa·bi·an [ˈseibiən; ˋsebɪən] *n.*, *a.* **1.** 萨比教徒(的)〔在古兰经中,与伊斯兰教徒、犹太教徒和基督教徒并列,信仰真主〕。**2.**〔误用〕拜星教徒(的)。**-ism** *n.* **1.** 萨比教。**2.** = Sabaism〔误用〕。

Sa·bin [ˈsæbin, ˈseibin; ˋsæbɪn, ˋsebɪn] *n.* 萨宝〔姓氏〕。

sa·bin [ˈseibin; ˋsebɪn] *n.*【声】沙平,赛宝〔声吸收单位〕。

Sa·bine [ˈsæbain; ˋsebaɪn] *n.*, *a.* **1.** 萨拜恩〔姓氏〕。**2.**〔古代意大利住在亚平宁 (Apennines) 山区的〕赛宝人(的)。**3.** 塞宝语(的)。

sa·ble [ˈseibl; ˋsebl] **I** *n.* **1.**【动】黑貂;黑[紫]貂皮;(黑)貂(尾)毛画笔;〔常 *pl.*〕黑貂皮大衣。**2.**【徽】〔诗〕黑色;〔*pl.*〕〔诗〕丧服。**II** *a.* **1.** 黑貂皮(制)的。**2.**〔诗〕黑的;阴暗的;阴森可怕的。*His S- Majesty* [*Excellency*]〔谑〕魔王。~ **antelope** *n.*【动】貂羚。~**fish** *n.*【动】裸盖鱼。

sa·bled [ˈseibld; ˋsebl̩d] *a.* **1.** 穿着丧服的。**2.** 黑色的。

SABMIS = seaborne anti-ballistic missile intercept system 舰载反弹道导[飞]弹截击系统。

sab·ot [ˈsæbəu; ˋsæbo] *n.* **1.** (法、比等国农民穿的)木鞋,木屐;木底鞋。**2.**【军】炮弹软壳;【机】镗杆,衬套;【建】桩靴。**-ed** *a.* 穿木鞋的〔指农民〕。

sab·o·tage [ˈsæbətɑːʒ, -ˈtidʒ; ˋsæbəˌtɑʒ, -tɪdʒ] **I** *n.* 怠工;(劳资纠纷、战争中的)胡乱破坏。*engage in* ~ 从事破坏。**II** *vt.*, *vi.* (对…)怠工 (*on*);破坏,阻挠。~ *peace* 破坏和平。

sab·o·teur [ˌsæbəˈtəː; ˌsæbəˋtɝ] *n.*〔F.〕怠工者,破坏者。

sa·bra [ˈsɑːbrə; ˋsɑbrə] *n.* 在以色列出生的人。

sa·bre,〔美〕**sa·ber** [ˈseibə; ˋsebɚ] **I** *n.* **1.** (骑兵的)军刀,马刀。**2.** 骑兵;〔*pl.*〕骑兵队。**3.**〔the ~〕武力;军法;黩武政治。*have 3000 ~s* 有三千骑兵。*by the* ~ 用武力。**II** *vt.* **1.** 用军刀斩[砍、杀]。**2.** 把…用骑兵武装起来。~ *one's way* (用军刀)杀开一条路。~**-cut** 用军刀斩;军刀伤口[疤]。~ **jet** 佩刀式喷气战斗机〔F-86 型战斗机〕。~**-rattler** 鲁莽的黩武主义者,张牙舞爪的人。~**-rattling** *a.* 耀武扬威的,张牙舞爪的。~ **saw** 轻便[手提]电锯。~**-toothed** *a.* 有军刀式上犬齿的。~**-toothed tiger**【古生】剑齿虎。

sab·re·tache [ˈsæbətæʃ; ˋsebɚˌtæʃ] *n.*【军】(挂在骑兵军官佩刀带左方的)佩囊。

sab·u·lite [ˈsæbjulait; ˋsæbjʊˌlaɪt] *n.* 一种烈性炸药〔爆炸力约为普通炸药的三倍〕。

sab·u·lous [ˈsæbjuləs; ˋsæbjʊləs] *a.* **1.** 多沙的;含沙的;沙质的;沙状的。**2.**【医】(尿)沉淀多的,有粒状物的。

SAC = Strategic Air Command〔美〕战略空军司令部。

sac [sæk; sæk] *n.* **1.**【生】囊,液囊。**2.** 上衣 (= sack)。~ **fungus** 子囊菌。

sac·a·ton [ˌsækəˈtəun; ˌsækəˋton] *n.*〔美〕【植】赖特氏鼠尾粟 (*Sporobolus wrightii*)〔一种粗草,美国西南部和墨西哥作饲料用〕。

sac·cade [sæ'kɑːd; sæˋkɑd] ***n*.** **1.** (阅读等时眼睛的)飞快跳阅,扫视,眼急动,眼跳跃。**2.** 急速勒马。

sac·cadic [sæ'kɑːdik; sæˋkɑdɪk] ***a*.** 跳阅的,扫视的。

sac·cate ['sækeit; ˋsæket] ***a*.**【生】囊状的,有囊的。

sac·char- *comb. f.* 表示"糖的,糖精的":*sacchar*ase.

sac·cha·rase ['sækəreis; ˋsækəres] ***n*.**【生化】蔗糖酶(=invertase)。

sac·cha·rate ['sækəreit; ˋsækəˏret] ***n*.** **1.**【化】糖质酸盐。**2.** 糖合物,糖与金属氧化物的化合物。

sac·char·ic [sæ'kærik; səˋkærɪk] ***a*.**【化】**1.** 糖合物的。**2.** 从糖合物取得的。**3.** 糖质的。~ **acid**【化】糖质酸;糖二酸。

sac·cha·ride ['sækəraid; ˋsækəˏraɪd] ***n*.**【化】糖化物;糖类。

sac·cha·rif·er·ous [ˌsækə'rifərəs; ˏsækəˋrɪfərəs] ***a*.**【化】含糖的;产糖的。

sac·char·i·fy ['sækərifai; səˋkærəˏfaɪ] ***vt*.** (***-fied***)【化】把…制成糖;使糖化。

sac·cha·rim·e·ter [ˌsækə'rimitə; ˏsækəˋrɪmətɚ] ***n*.**【化】(旋光)检糖计。

sac·cha·rin ['sækərin; ˋsækərɪn] ***n*.** 糖精。**-ize** ***vt*.** 加糖精于;用糖精使…变甜。

sac·cha·rine ['sækərain, -riːn; ˋsækəˏraɪn, -ˏrɪn] **I** ***a*.** **1.** 糖(质)的。**2.** 太甜的。**3.** (十分)甜蜜的。**4.** 巴结的,逢迎的,讨好的,奉承的。**II** ['sækərin; ˋsækərɪn] ***n*.** 糖精(=saccharin)。~ **diabetes** 糖尿病。~ **sorghum** 甜高粱。

sac·cha·rize ['sækəraiz; ˋsækəˏraɪz] ***vt*.** 糖化;使发酵。

sac·cha·ro- *comb. f.* =sacchar-.〔用于子音前〕。

sac·cha·roid ['sækərɔid; ˋsækəˏrɔɪd] **I** ***a*.**【地】结构纹理像砂糖状的。**II** ***n*.** 粒状物;砂糖状物。

sac·cha·roi·dal [ˈsækərɔidl; ˋsækəˏrɔɪdḷ] ***a*.** =saccharoid ***a*.**

sac·cha·rom·e·ter [ˌsækə'rɔmitə; ˏsækəˋrɑmətɚ] ***n*.**【化】(旋光)检糖计。

sac·cha·ro·my·cete [ˌsækərəu'maisiːt; ˏsækərəˋmaɪsit] ***n*.**【植】酵母菌。

sac·cha·rose ['sækərəus; ˋsækəˏros] ***n*.**【化】蔗糖。

sac·cu·lar ['sækjulə; ˋsækjʊlɚ] ***a*.**【生】囊状的。

sac·cu·late(d) ['sækjuleit(id); ˋsækjəˏletɪd] ***a*.** 成囊的;袋状的;分成囊状的。**-la·tion** [ˌsækju'leiʃən; ˏsækjəˋleʃən] ***n*.**

sac·cule ['sækjuːl; ˋsækjul] ***n*.**【生】小囊,〔尤指〕耳迷路的球囊。

sac·cu·lus ['sækjuləs; ˋsækjuləs] ***n*.** (*pl*. ***-li*** [-lai; -laɪ])〔L.〕=saccule.

sac·er·do·tal [ˌsæsə'dəutl; ˏsæsɚˋdotl] ***a*.** **1.** 僧侣的;祭司的;祭司制的。**2.** 主张僧侣掌握大权的。**-do·cy** [-dəusi; -ˏdosɪ] ***n*.**〔罕〕(= sacerdotalism). **-ism** ***n*.** 祭司制度,僧侣政治。**-ly** ***ad*.**

sa·chem ['seitʃəm; ˋsetʃəm] ***n*.** **1.** (某些北美印第安人的)酋长。**2.**〔谑〕大老板,首领,巨头。**3.**〔美〕(纽约市民主党组织)坦慕尼协会 (Tammany Society) 的干事。

sa·chet ['sæʃei; sæˋʃe] ***n*.** **1.** 香囊;香袋。**2.** 香粉。

sack[1] [sæk; sæk] **I** ***n*.** **1.** (通常指亚麻或大麻等制的)袋,包;麻袋;硬纸袋。**2.** (旧时妇女穿的)宽身长袍;宽短外衣。**3.**〔美俚〕床,卧铺铺位。**4.**【棒球】垒。**5.** 撒克〔重量单位,=101.6 公斤〕。**6.**〔the ~〕〔英俚〕解雇,革职。*Nothing comes out of the ~ but what was in it*. 袋子里有什么才能倒出什么;无中不能生有。***a sad*** ~〔美俚〕**1.** 好心办错事的兵[人]。**2.** 难处的人,讨人厌的女孩。***buy a cat in the*** ~ 买封在口袋里的猫;不看清货物瞎买。***get*** [***have***] ***the*** ~〔俚〕被解雇;被拒绝。***give*** (*sb*.) ***the*** ~〔英俚〕解雇(某人);抛弃(情人等)。***hit the*** ~〔美俚〕就寝,睡觉。***hold the*** ~ **1.** 被留下来独担罪责。**2.** 只分得最差的一份,两手空空,上当受骗。**II** ***vt*.** **1.** 把…装进袋里;装袋运输。**2.**〔口〕解雇;把…驱逐出校,开除;抛弃(情人等)。**3.**〔口〕侵吞。**4.**〔口〕〔竞赛〕打败;胜过。**5.** (美式橄榄球中在前锋线后)抱摔(对方的四分卫等球员)。~ ***in*** [***out***]〔美俚〕上床睡觉,睡个痛快。~**but** 中世纪低音喇叭。~**cloth** **1.** (粗)麻布,麻袋布。**2.** 丧服(~*-cloth and ashes* 悲哀,深深懊悔)。~**coat**〔美〕男式便装短上衣。~**-race**【运】袋囊赛跑〔腿上套着袋子的跳跃式竞走〕。~ **suit**〔美〕= ~ coat. ~**time**〔美俚〕睡眠时间。**-er** ***n*.** **1.** 制(或装)袋工人。**2.**【棒球】守垒员。**-ful** ***n*.** **1.** 满袋,一袋。**2.** 一大堆。**-ing** ***n*.** **1.** 袋布,粗麻布。**2.**〔美俚〕守垒。

sack[2] [sæk; sæk] **I** ***vt*.** 抢劫;掠夺。**II** ***n*.** 掠夺(物)。*put to the* ~ 掠夺。**-er** ***n*.** 掠夺者。

sack[3] [sæk; sæk] ***n*.** (从前西班牙输出的)干白葡萄酒。***one half-pennyworth of bread to an intolerable deal of*** ~ 吃的面包太少,喝的汤汤水水太多;无关紧要的东西太多。

sack·less ['sæklis; ˋsæklɪs] ***a*.** **1.**〔古〕无罪的。**2.**〔Scot.〕垂头丧气的,软弱的;头脑愚钝的。

Sack·ville ['sækvil; ˋsækvɪl] ***n*.** 萨克维尔〔姓氏〕。

sack·y ['sæki; ˋsækɪ] ***a*.** (衣服)宽大的,像布袋似的。

sacque [sæk; sæk] ***n*.** **1.** (妇女穿的)宽短外衣。**2.**〔古〕(妇女穿的)宽长服。**3.** (婴儿的)短上衣〔通常系在脖子上〕(=sack[1])。

sa·cral ['seikrəl; ˋsekrəl] ***a*.**【解】骶骨[荐骨]的。*the* ~ *vertebrae* 荐椎。

sa·cral·ize ['sækrəlaiz, 'seikrəlaiz; ˋsækrəlˏaɪz] ***vt*.** 使神圣化;使神圣。**-za·tion** [-'zeʃən; -ˋzeʃən] ***n*.**

sac·ra·ment ['sækrəmənt; ˋsækrəmənt] **I** ***n*.** **1.** 圣礼。**2.** 神圣的东西;神秘;神圣的宣誓;(古罗马军队的)入队宣誓。**3.**〔the S-〕圣餐(礼);圣体;圣餐面包〔英国国教、罗马天主教通常把这叫做 the Blessed [Holy] S-〕。*the* ~ *of the altar* 圣餐面包;圣物。***administer the*** ~ 行圣餐礼。***go to*** ~ 参加圣餐礼。***take the*** ~***s*** 发誓,宣誓。**II** ***vt*.**〔主用被动语态〕使发誓,使宣誓。

sac·ra·men·tal [ˌsækrə'mentl; ˏsækrəˋmɛntl] **I** ***a*.** **1.** 神圣的。**2.** 圣礼的;圣餐礼的;重视圣礼的;重视圣餐礼的。**3.** 发过誓的。**4.** 象征性的。**II** ***n*.** **1.** 类似圣礼的仪式(如用圣水等)。**2.**〔*pl*.〕圣餐礼用具(如十字架等)。~ **elements** 圣餐礼的面包和葡萄酒。~ **rites** 圣餐礼。~ **wafers** 圣饼,圣餐面包。**-ism** ***n*.** 重视圣礼(的信仰、教义)。**-ist** ***n*.** 重视圣礼者。

sac·ra·men·tar·i·an [ˌsækəmen'tɛəriən; ˏsækrəmenˋtɛrɪən] **I** ***a*.** **1.** 重视圣礼的;圣餐的。**2.** 圣餐形式论者的。**II** ***n*.** 重视圣礼者;圣餐形式论者。

sac·ra·men·ta·ry [ˌsækrə'mentəri; ˏsækrəˋmɛntərɪ] **I** ***n*.** **1.** =sacramentarian (***n*.**). **2.**〔*pl*.〕圣礼书。**II** ***a*.** =sacramentarian (***a*.**).

Sac·ra·men·to [ˌsækrə'mentəu; ˏsækrəˋmɛnto] ***n*.** 萨克拉门托〔美国城市〕。

sa·crar·i·um [sə'krɛəriəm; səˋkrɛrɪəm] ***n*.** (*pl*. ***-ri·a*** [-riə; -rɪə]) **1.** (古罗马)神龛。**2.**【宗】圣堂。**3.**【天主】(带有排水设备用以处理洗礼圣水用的)水盆。

sa·cré ['sækrei; sækre] ***vi*.**〔F.〕(***-d***; ***-ing***)〔法国人〕骂一声该死的[傻瓜(等)];骂人,咒人。

sa·cred ['seikrid; ˋsekrɪd] ***a*.** **1.** 神圣的 (*opp*. profane);宗教的 (*opp*. secular);上帝的,神的。**2.** (动物、植物等)被崇为神物的;不可侵犯的。**3.** 献给…的;供献给…的。*a* ~ *disease* 疯癫。*a* ~ *number* (宗教上)神秘的数字〔特指 7〕。*a* ~ *place*【法】坟墓。*the* ~ *cat* (古埃及的)神猫。*the* ~ *beetle* = scarab. *a monument* ~ *to the memory of sb*. (某人的)纪念碑。***be*** ~ ***from*** 免除,不受。***hold*** ~ 尊重,保护。~ **baboon**【动】阿拉伯狒狒;阿比西尼亚猩猩 (=hamadryad)。~ **book** [**writing**] 圣曲,宗教经典〔包括一个宗教的律法,如可兰经、圣经〕。~ **college** (罗马教廷)枢密院。~ **cow** **1.** (印度的)神牛。**2.**〔喻〕不可批评[冒犯]的人或物。~ **mushroom** 祭神蕈〔美洲几种可以引起幻觉的蕈类之一,常被用于印

S

第安人的祭神仪式中〕。~ **music**［**poetry**］圣乐［诗］。**-ly** *ad*.

sac·ri·fice［ˈsækrifais; ˋsækrəˏfaɪs］**I** *n*. 1. 牺牲,供品,祭品。2. 供奉,献祭;〔喻〕损失。3. 供作牺牲,牺牲行为,献身,舍身。4.【宗】基督的献身〔指耶稣之钉死在十字架上〕;圣餐。5.【商】大贱卖。6.【棒球】(为了他人进垒而特意轻击的)牺牲打(=~bunt, ~ hit)。***at the*** ~ ***of*** 以…为牺牲,牺牲…而。***fall a*** ~ ***to*** 成为…的牺牲品。***fear no*** ~ 不怕牺牲,付出…的代价。***make all*** ~***s*** 不惜一切牺牲。***make*** ~***s***［***a*** ~］***to*** 为…牺牲。***make the*** ~ ***of*** 以…为牺牲。***sell at a*** ~ 亏本出售。***the great***［***last***］~ 阵亡,战死,为国捐躯。**II** *vt*. 1. 牺牲;把…奉献给…(*for*; *to*)。2. 廉价卖出。— *vi*. 1. 牺牲,献祭。2.【棒球】作牺牲打。~ **fly**【棒球】(为了使跑垒的人得分而打出的)牺牲飞球。

sac·ri·fi·cial［ˌsækriˈfiʃəl; ˏsækrəˋfɪʃəl］*a*. 1. (供作)牺牲的,供奉的,献祭的。2.〔罕〕献身的,舍身的。3.〔俚〕亏本卖的。**-ly** *ad*.

sac·ri·lege［ˈsækrilidʒ; ˋsækrəlɪdʒ］*n*. 1. 亵渎(神物);窃取圣物。2.【法】渎圣罪。

sac·ri·le·gious［ˌsækriˈlidʒəs; ˏsækrɪˋlɪdʒəs］*a*. 亵渎(神物)的;窃取圣物的;有罪孽的。**-ly** *ad*.

sa·cring［ˈseikriŋ; ˋsekrɪŋ］*n*.【宗、古】圣餐礼。~ **bell** 圣餐铃。

sac·rist［ˈseikrist; ˋsekrɪst］*n*.【宗】圣器保管人。

sac·ris·tan［ˈsækristən; ˋsækrɪstən］*n*. 1. = sacrist. 2.〔古〕教堂司事(= sexton)。

S

sac·ris·ty［ˈsækristi; ˋsækrɪstɪ］*n*. (教堂的)圣器(保藏)室。

sac·ro·il·i·ac［ˌseikrəuˈiliæk; ˏsækroˋɪlɪæk］**I** *a*.【解】骶骼的;骶骨与骼骨之间的关节的。**II** *n*. 骶骨与骼骨之间的关节(或软骨)。

sac·ro·sanct［ˈsækrəusæŋkt; ˋsækroˏsæŋkt］*a*. 神圣不可侵犯的。

sac·ro·sanc·ti·ty［ˌsækrəuˈsæŋktiti; ˏsækrəˋsæŋktətɪ］*n*. 神圣不可侵犯。

sa·cro·sci·at·ic［ˌseikəusaiˈætik; ˏsekəsaɪˋætɪk］*a*.【解】骶骨和坐骨的。

sa·crum［ˈseikrəm; ˋsekrəm］*n*. (*pl*. ~*s*, ***sa·cra***［-krə; -krə］)【解】骶骨,荐骨。

sad［sæd; sæd］*a*. 1. 悲哀的,悲伤的;凄惨的,可悲的,可怜的。2.〔俚、谑〕糟透了的,不可救药的。3.〔古〕认真的。4. 黯淡的,(颜色等)阴郁的。5.〔罕、方〕(面包、饼等)发得不好的;黏糊糊的。6.〔美俚〕二流的,次等的。*feel* ~ 悲伤。*a* ~*der and a wiser man* 吃过苦学了乖的人;饱经忧患的人。***in*** ~ ***earnest***〔古〕认真地。***It is*** ~ ***that…*** 遗憾的是…。***make*** ~ ***work of it*** 大失败,弄得糟透。~ **dog**〔蔑、谑〕不可救药的家伙,糟透了的家伙,无赖,流氓。~ **to say** 可悲的是。~**-coloured** *a*. 黯淡的,阴郁的。~ **sack**〔美口〕冒失鬼。**-ly** *ad*.

SADARM, Sadarm［ˌsædˈɑːm; ˏsædˋɑm］= sense and destroy armor【军】辨向穿甲炮弹〔装有雷达辨向器,用于摧毁敌方坦克〕。

sad·den［ˈsædn; ˋsædn］*vt*. 使悲哀,使悲伤,使阴郁,使黯淡。— *vi*. 悲伤(起来);阴郁(起来);黯淡起来。*Do not* ~ *your friends and gladden your enemies*. 勿使亲者痛仇者快。

sad·dle［ˈsædl; ˋsædl］**I** *n*. 1. 马鞍;(脚踏车(自行车)等的)鞍。2. (羊等的)带肋［脊］骨的肉。3. 鞍形架,鞍状物。4.【地】鞍部;马鞍形山;鞍状构造。5.【物】谐振曲线的凹谷。6.【船】圆枕木;【机】凹座,轴鞍,鞍座板;滑动座架;滑板;锅炉座。7.【电】电线杆的托架;【建】浮桥的托梁;(门口的)踏板。*an axle* ~【机】轴鞍。*a cylinder* ~ 鞍形汽缸座。*the Gr. S-*(长江口外的)马鞍山群岛。***be at home in the*** ~ 善于骑马。***be cast out of the*** ~ 免职。***for the*** ~(马)骑用的。***get into the*** ~ 骑上马;就职。***in the*** ~ 骑着马;在职;统辖着,控制着,掌着权。***lost the*** ~ 从马上摔下来。***put the*** ~ ***on the right***［***wrong***］***horse*** 1. 责备应该［不该］责备的人。2. 夸奖应该［不该］夸奖的人。**II** *vt*. 1. 加鞍,上鞍。2. 给背上,使负担(责任等)。~ *sb. with a task* 使某人担负某一任务。~**back** 1. 鞍状峰。2.【建】鞍形屋顶。3.【动】鞍背动物;黑背鸥;北海豹。~**-backed** *a*. 1. 鞍状的;(动物等)背部呈鞍形的。2. (鸟、鱼)背部有鞍状花纹的。3.【地】有鞍部的。~**-bag** 鞍囊,马褡裢。~ **block** (**anesthesia**)【医】鞍基麻醉〔产妇分娩时的腰脊麻醉,有久乘鞍马的麻木感觉〕。~**-bow** 鞍的前穹;鞍的后穹。~**-cloth** 鞍垫［褥］。~ **function**【数】鞍式函数。~**-horse** 骑用马。~ **roof**【建】鞍形屋顶。~ **shoe**〔美〕鞍背鞋〔深色鞋背和白色鞋带的皮鞋〕。~ **soap** 皮革皂。~ **sore** 鞍疮。~**-tree** 1. 鞍框。2.【植】(北美)鞍叶桉(树);美国鹅掌楸。**-less** *a*.

sad·dler［ˈsædlə; ˋsædlɚ］*n*. 1. 鞍工,马具师;马具制造［贩卖］人。2.【军】(骑兵团的)鞍工兵。3.〔美俚〕骑用马。

sad·dler·y［ˈsædləri; ˋsædlərɪ］*n*. 1.〔总称〕鞍具;马具。2. (放)马具室。3. 马具店;马具业。

Sad·du·cee［ˈsædjusiː; ˋsædʒəˏsi］*n*. 撒都该人〔基督时代犹太教中以僧侣、贵族为主的派别中的人,只承认摩西五书之成文法而不承认传说律法及复活、来世等教义〕。**-an** *a*. 撒都该人的。**-ism** *n*.

sa·dhe［ˈsɑːdiː, ˈtsɑː-; ˋsɑdi, ˋtsɑ-］*n*.〔Heb.〕希伯来语字母表的第十八个字母(= tsadi)。

sa·dhu［ˈsɑːduː; ˋsɑdu］*n*. (印度的)圣人,哲人;苦行高僧,苦行者,禁欲主义者。

Sa·die［ˈseidi; ˋsedɪ］*n*. 塞迪〔女子名,Sara(h) 的昵称〕。

sad·i·ron［ˈsædˌaiən; ˋsædˏaɪɚn］*n*. (实心)熨斗,烙铁。

sa·dism［ˈsɑːdizm; ˋsædɪzəm］*n*. 1.【心】(对异性的)残暴色情狂,施虐淫(*opp*. masochism)。2.〔美〕残忍癖。**sa·dist** *n*., *a*. 残暴色情狂者(的);施虐淫者(的);〔美〕有残忍癖者(的)。**sa·dis·tic**［-ˈdistik; -ˋdɪstɪk］*a*.

sad·ness［ˈsædnis; ˋsædnɪs］*n*. 1. 悲哀,悲伤,忧愁,忧伤。2. 愁眉苦脸,心境恶劣,心情恶劣。3. 认真。***in sober***［***good***］~ 认真地。

sad·o·mas·o·chism［ˌseidəuˈmæsəkizəm, ˌsædəuˈmæzə-; ˏsædoˋmæsəkɪzm］*n*.【心,医】施虐—受虐狂〔口语中亦作 sado-maso〕。**-chist** *n*. **-chis·tic** *a*.

sae［sei; se］*ad*.〔Scot.〕= so.

SAEF = stock exchange automatic execution facility (伦敦交易所中用以处理小指令的)证券交易所自动报行系统。

SAF = Strategic Air Force〔美〕战略空军。

sa·fa·ri［səˈfɑːri; səˋfɑrɪ］*n*. 1. (徒步)旅行(队),(科学考察,游猎)远征(队)(特指在非洲东部)。2. (服装的)非洲旅行装式样。~ **park**〔英〕= animal park.

safe［seif; sef］**I** *a*. 1. 安全的,安稳的;无危险的。2. 确实的,一定的。3. 安全,平安〔作 *arrive*, *come* 等的表语用〕。4. 谨慎的,稳健的,可靠的;小心翼翼的。5.【棒球】不会死的,安全的〔安抵某垒的〕(*opp*. out)。6.【自】稳定的。*I saw him* ~ *home*. 我送他平安到家。*It is* ~ *to get warmer as the day goes on*. 天气确实一天比一天暖和了。*He is* ~ *to get in*. 他肯定会当选。*get a person* ~ 抓牢某人。*a* ~［*good*］*catch*【棒球】灵巧的接球员。*a* ~ *first* 稳拿第一的人。*S- bind*, ~ *find*. 藏得牢,找得着。***be*** ~ ***from***(*attack*; *infection*)没有受到(攻击、传染)的危险。***It is*** ~ ***to say that ....*** 不妨说,说…准不会错。***on the*** ~ ***side*** 谨慎［安全,可靠］地(*It's best to err on the* ~ *side*. 即使错,最好也错在谨慎上面)。***play*** ~ 采取四平八稳的办法。~ ***and sound*** 平安无恙,安全。**II** *n*. 1. 保险箱,安全容器,纱厨,纱罩;〔美俚〕冰箱。2. 马鞍防擦皮。~ **area**［**haven**］(为动乱地区平民设置的禁止战争活动的)安全区。~**-blowing** 爆破保险箱进行盗窃。~**-conduct**. 1. *n*. (特指战时的)通行证,(军用)护照;安全证〔免受逮捕或

伤害)。2. *vt*. 发护照给;护送,保卫。~ **cracking** 撬盗保险箱。~ **deposit** 保险仓库,信托仓库。**~-deposit** *a*. 安全保管的(*a ~-deposit company* 信托公司。*a ~-deposit box* [*vault*] 银行地下室中备人租用的保险箱)。**~guard** 1. 保护,赶卫,守护。2. 防护设施,装置;安全保护物,防护物(*against*)。3. 卫兵;警卫船。4. 通行证;(军用)护照,安全证〔免受逮捕或伤害〕(=~-conduct)。5.【机】护轮轨条;排障器。6. 保护措施,保证条款。7. (美反弹道导[飞]弹系统的)卫兵式导[飞]弹(*~guarding duties* 〔英〕保护关税。*~guard against* 防止)。**~keeping** 保护,保管(*be in ~keeping with sb*. 在某人处保管着)。~ **keep** *vt*. 妥善保管[保存,保护]。~ **light**【摄】(暗房用)安全灯。~ **load**【工】安全载荷。~ **one**= ~'**un**【赛马】包跑第一的马,稳赢的马。~ **operation** 安全操作。~ **room** 安全室〔指情报人员、秘密警察等使用的不会受到监视的房屋〕。~ **seat** (候选人准能被选出的)可靠的选举区。~ **winner** 稳赢的人[马]。**-ly** *ad*.

safe·ty [ˈseifti; ˋseftɪ] *n*. 1. 安全;平安,稳安,保险。2. (枪等的)保险器,安全瓣;〔口〕低座脚踏车[自行车](=~-bicycle)。3. 安全设备,保险装置。4.【棒球】安全打。*public ~* 公安。~ *explosive* 安全炸药。*a gun at ~* 上了保险的枪。*a ~ device* [*apparatus*] 保险装置。*There is ~ in numbers*. 人多较安全;大家一致行动起来成功的希望较大。*coefficient* [*factor*] *of ~* 安全系数。***flee for ~*** 避难。***in ~*** 平安地。***play for ~*** 稳扎稳打,谨慎行事。***S- first!*** 安全第一! ***Seek ~ in flight*** 避难。***with ~*** 安全地,平安地。~ **action** 保安措施。**~-arresting** 安全制动。~ **belt** 安全带;【海】救生带。~ **bicycle** (低座的)安全自行车。~ **check** 安全检查。~ **computing**【计】(可防止病毒侵入的)电脑的安全管理操作法。~ **curtain** (戏院的)消防幕。~ **cut-off** 安全开关。~ **cut out** 保安断路器。~ **film** (电影等用)不燃性[安全]胶片。~ **fuse**【电】安全熔断器,保险丝;保险信管,安全导火线。~ **glass** 不碎玻璃(= triplex glass)。~ **island** [**zone**] (马路中间的)安全岛[地带]。~ **lamp** (矿山用)安全灯。**~-light**【摄】(暗室用)安全灯。~ **match** 安全火柴。~ **net** 安全网;(防止经济损失等的)安全保证,保险。~ **pin** 保险销,安全销,别针。~ **razor** 保险剃刀。~ **relay** 保安继电器,闭锁继电器。~ **sex** (事先采取预防措施以避免感染性病的)安全性交。~ **valve** 保险阀;〔喻〕缓和紧张状态的手段(*sit on the ~ valve* 按住保险阀;压住性子;采取高压性的权宜措施)。~ **switch** 紧急开关,保险开关。~ **zone** = ~ **island**.

saf·fi·an [ˈseifiən; ˋsæfɪən] *n*. 一种着色的特制山羊革,摩洛哥革(=~ leather)。

saf·flow·er [ˈsæflauə; ˋsæˏflaʊɚ] *n*. 1.【植】红花。2. 红花染料。~ **oil** 红花油。

saf·fron [ˈsæfrən; ˋsæfrən] *n*., *a*. 1.【植】藏红花(色的),番红花(色的)。2. 深黄(色的),橘黄(色的)。~ **oil** 藏红花油。**~-tritonia**【植】观音兰。**-y** *a*.

saf·ing [ˈseifiŋ; ˋsefɪŋ] *a*.【宇航】〔发生动力故障等机件失灵情况下〕能自动恢复安全状态的,保障安全的。

S.Afr. = South Africa(n).

saf·ra·nin(e) [ˈsæfrənin; ˋsæfrənɪn] *n*.【化】(碱性)藏[桃]红(染料)。

saf·role [ˈseifrəul; ˋsæfrol] *n*.【化】黄樟脑,黄樟素。

sag [sæg; sæg] **I** *vi*. (*-gg-*) 1. (桥、梁等)陷下,压弯;(门)成一边高一边低状;(蜡烛等)弯曲;(绳、天花板等)松弛,下垂;(裙子下摆等)松垂,弛垂;(土地等)下陷,陷没。2. (物价等)下跌。3. 〔喻〕萎顿;消衰;(情绪)低落;疲沓,松懈。4.【海】漂流(特指船向下风流去)。— *vt*. 使下陷,压弯;使下垂[下落],【海】使漂流。**II** *n*. 1. 弯下,下垂;下沉,下陷。2. 垂度。3. (物价的)下跌。4.【海】随风漂流。

sa·ga [ˈsɑːgə; ˋsɑgə] *n*. 1. (中世纪冰岛或挪威的)散文体叙事[故事];北欧英雄传说。2. 〔口〕长篇故事,冒险故事;英雄故事。3. 〔多卷本〕家世小说〔=~ novel〕。

sa·ga·cious [səˈgeiʃəs; səˋgeʃəs] *a*. 1. 聪明的,明智的,敏锐的;精明的。2. (动物等)灵敏的,〔特指〕嗅觉敏锐的。**-ly** *ad*. **-ness** *n*.

sa·gac·i·ty [səˈgæsiti; səˋgæsətɪ] *n*. 聪明,明智;敏锐,精明。

sag·a·more [ˈsægəmɔː; ˋsægəˏmor] *n*. 北美印第安部落的酋长〔次于酋长的二头目〕。

SAGE = semiautomatic ground environment 半自动地面防空警备体系。

Sage [seidʒ; sedʒ] *n*. 塞奇〔姓氏〕。

sage[1] [seidʒ; sedʒ] **I** *a*. 1. 聪明的,明智的,贤明的;精明的。2. 〔谑〕像煞聪明的;道貌岸然的。**II** *n*. 〔常谑〕圣人,贤人,哲人。*the ~ of the village* 〔谑〕三家村学究。*the seven ~s* 希腊七贤〔通常指 *Solon*, *Thales*, *Pittacus*, *Bias*, *Chilo*, *Periander* 及 *Cleobulus* 〕。**-ly** *ad*. **-ness** *n*.

sage[2] [seidʒ; sedʒ] *n*.【植】1. 鼠尾草;鼠尾草[洋苏]叶〔药用、食用〕。2. 一串红〔又称 scarlet ~〕。3. = sagebrush. ~ **cock**【动】雄性艾草鸡。~ **green** 灰绿色。~ **grouse**【动】(北美西部荒漠地带的)艾草鸡。~ **hen**【动】母艾草鸡;〔S- H-〕〔美俚〕Nevada 州人的诨名。~ **oil** 洋苏叶油。~ **rat** 原鼠;〔美俚〕艾原居民。~ **tea**【药】鼠尾草煎汁〔用作健胃剂〕。

sage·brush [ˈseidʒbrʌʃ; ˋsedʒˏbrʌʃ] *n*. 1. 蒿子。2.【植】山艾〔美国西南荒漠地带所产的一种灰绿色灌木〕。**S-state** 艾草州〔美国 Nevada 州的别名〕。

sag·ger, sag·gar [ˈsægə; ˋsægɚ] **I** *n*. 1. (陶瓷工业用的)烧箱,烧盆。2. (制造烧箱的)黏土。**II** *vt*. 用烧箱[盆]烘。

sag·gy [ˈsægi; ˋsægɪ] *a*. (*-gi·er*, *-gi·est*) 倾斜的;松弛的;下垂的。

Sagh·a·lien [ˌsægəˈliːn; ˋsɑgɑˋljɛn] *n*. 库页岛(= Sakhalin)。

Sa·git·ta [səˈdʒitə; səˋdʒɪtə] *n*. 1.【天】天箭(星)座。2. 〔s-〕【数】矢。3. 〔s-〕【动】箭虫。

sag·it·tal [ˈsædʒitl; ˋsædʒɪtl] *a*. 1. 箭的,矢状的。2.【解】(颅顶骨)矢状缝合的;纵分的;矢形面的,纵分面的。**-ly** *ad*.

Sag·it·tar·i·us [ˌsædʒiˈtɛəriəs; ˏsædʒɪˋtɛrɪəs] *n*.【天】人马(星)座。

sag·it·tar·y [ˈsædʒitəri; ˋsædʒəˏtɛrɪ] *n*. (*pl*. *-taries*) 1. 弓箭手。2.【希神】半人半马的怪物。3. 〔S-〕【天】半人马(星座)(= centaur)。

sag·it·tate [ˈsædʒiteit; ˋsædʒɪˏtet] *a*.【植】镞形的,箭头形的。

sa·go [ˈseigəu; ˋsego] *n*. (*pl*. *~s*) 1. 西[壳,谷]米〔用西米椰子茎髓做成的淀粉质食品〕。2.【植】西[壳,谷]米椰子(=~ palm)。

Sa·hap·tin [sɑːˈhæptin; sɑˋhæptɪn] *n*. 1. (*pl*. *~(s)*) 萨哈泼丁人〔北美印第安一个部族集团的成员〕。2. 萨哈泼丁语。3. 由萨哈泼丁语和内珀西(*Nez Percé*) 语组成的语族。亦作 **Sa·hap·tian** [-tiən; -tɪən].

Sa·ha·ra [səˈhɑːrə; səˋhɛrə] *n*. 1. (非洲)撒哈拉大沙漠。2. 〔s-〕沙漠,荒野。**Saha·ran, Saha·rian, Saharic** *a*.

Sa·hib [ˈsɑːhib; ˋsɑ·ɪb] *n*. 1. 大人,老爷〔旧时印度人对欧洲人的尊称〕;〔S-〕先生(= Mr., Sir, 用于职称或人名后): *colonel S-* 上校先生; *Jones S-* 琼斯先生。2. 〔口〕绅士; *a pucka* [*pukka*] ~ 〔常谑〕真正的欧洲人; *Jone S-* 道地的绅士。

said [sed; sɛd] **I** say 的过去式及过去分词。**II** *a*. 上述的。*the ~ witness* 该证人。

Sa·i·da [ˈsɑːidɑː; ˋsɑɪdɑ] *n*. 赛伊达〔即 Sidon 西顿,黎巴嫩港市〕。

sai·ga [ˈsaigə; saɪˋgɑn] *n*.【动】高鼻羚羊[赛加羚羊] (*Saiga tatarica*) 〔产于俄罗斯东南部和西伯利亚西南

部草原〕。

Sai·gon [saiˈgɔn; saɪˋgɑn] ***n***. 西贡〔越南港市,胡志明市的旧称〕。

sail [seil; sel] **I** ***n***. **1.** 帆,〔集合词〕(船上)全部风帆,全帆(= sails)。**2.** 帆船;〔集合名词〕船只(= ships);【空】滑翔机。**3.** 〔*pl*.〕缝帆员;〔英海军俚〕帆具官。**4.** 扬帆行驶,航行。**5.** 航行距离,航程;航行力。**6.** 帆形物;(风车等的)翼板;〔诗〕(鸟的)翼;(鹦鹉螺的)触手。*a set* ~ 已张开的风帆。*a riding* ~ 停泊用小帆。*a* ~ *taken aback* (逆风吹翻过来的)反帆,逆帆。*a* ~ *well taut* 绷紧了的帆。*a shoulder-of-mutton* [*leg-of-mutton*] ~ 三角帆。*S- ho*! 看,有帆! *a fleet of twenty* ~ 二十条船的一个船队[舰队]。*ten days'* ~ *from*... 离…有十天航程。***at full*** ~(***s***) 张起所有的帆;开足马力。***back*** [***brace aback***] ***the*** ~***s*** 使成反帆[逆帆]。***be under*** ~ 在航行中。***bend the*** ~ 将(帆)绑在桁上[支索上]。***brail*** [***clue***] ***up a*** ~ 卷帆。***bring a*** ~ ***to*** 将帆绑在桁上。***carry a press of*** ~ 张满风帆。***carry a*** ~ 张着风帆。***carry*** ~ ***well*** 张满风帆。***crowd*** [***clap on***] (***all***) ~(***s***) 扯起异常多(所有)的风帆。***douse*** ~ = strike ~. ***fill the*** ~***s*** 使帆吃满风,(风)满帆。***furl a*** ~ 叠帆,收卷风帆。***get in a*** ~ 收下一张帆。***get under*** ~ 开船。***go for a*** ~ 乘船游览。***haul down a*** ~ 落帆,下帆。***haul in one's*** ~***s*** 退出比赛,回避。***hoist a*** ~ 张起一张帆。***hoist*** ~ 扯起所有风帆;〔喻〕逃跑。***in full*** ~ 张满帆的。***in*** ~ 扬着帆;乘帆船;在帆船上。***keep full*** ~***s*** 张着所有的风帆。***lower a*** ~ 落下一张帆。***lower one's*** ~ (下帆)投降;认输,甘拜下风。***make*** ~ 急加帆;扬帆,出航,开船;〔口〕逃跑。***more*** ~ ***than ballast*** 华而不实。***put on*** [***pack*** (***on***)] ***all*** ~ 扯起所有的帆;竭尽全力。***set*** ~ ***for*** 开船,驶往…,乘船往…。***shorten*** ~ 减(少风)帆;抑制(欲望、野心等),放慢速度。***solar*** ~ 太阳反射器〔在星际飞行中利用太阳能的一种设备〕。***spread the*** ~***s*** 张帆。***strike*** ~ 〔为行敬礼或因急风〕急下帆;屈服,投降;认输;减少排场。***take in*** ~ = shorten ~. ***take the wind out of one's*** ~***s*** [***the*** ~***s of***] 抢(他船)上风;〔喻〕先发制人。***trim the*** [***one's***] ~***s*** 调整风帆;随机应变地处置,机动处理。***under*** ~ 扬帆而驶;航行中。***with all*** ~***s set*** = ***with every*** ~ ***set out*** 张起全部风帆。

II ***vi***. **1.** 扬帆行驶,航行;开船;坐船旅行。**2.** (水禽)游泳;(鸟、云等)轻快地飞,浮游。**3.** (尤指妇女)步态优美地走。— ***vt***. **1.** 扬帆行驶,航行。**2.** 驾驶(船);漂浮(玩具船)。**3.** (鸟等)飞行(空中)。~ ***a race*** 进行帆船比赛。~ ***against the wind*** 逆风驶船;处逆境;违抗潮流。~ ***away*** **1.** 〔美〕慌忙启程。**2.** 逸散,挥发。~ ***before the wind*** 顺风行驶;一帆风顺;走运,处顺境。~ ***close to*** [***near***] ***the wind*** **1.** 切风[几乎逆风]行驶。**2.** 俭约地处事,简朴地生活。**3.** 冒昧地行动;几乎犯法[违背道德准则]。~ ***in*** **1.** 驶入港口;〔口〕毅然出面(~ *in and settle the dispute* 毅然出面排解纠纷)。**2.** 开始行动;攻击,责叱。~ ***in company*** = ~ under convoy. ~ ***in the same boat*** 同舟共济;干同一工作;有同一处境,抱同样见解。~ ***into*** **1.** 大摇大摆地[庄严地]走进,突然闯入。**2.** 〔俚〕攻击,辱骂,殴打。**3.** 精力充沛,效率高地投入(某项工作)。~ ***large*** 满帆行驶。~ ***on one's bottom*** 自主地航行;〔喻〕独立自主。~ ***one's own boat*** 独立自主地行动;走自己的路。~ ***out*** 开船。~ ***over*** 跳过;【建】突出。~ ***right before the wind*** 顺风行驶;一帆风顺。~ ***round*** 返航。~ ***under convoy*** 在护送下结队航行。~ ***under false colours*** (海盗等)挂着冒牌旗子航行。~ ***under the Chinese flag*** 搭乘中国船。~ **arm** 风车翼板。~ **axle** 转动风车翼板的轴。~**board** 小型风帆船,风帆滑水板。~**-boat** 〔美〕帆船(=〔英〕~ing boat)。~**cloth** 帆布;篷布;苫布。~**-fish** 【动】东方旗鱼〔背鳍如帆〕。~**-flying** 【空】滑翔飞行。~**-maker** 缝帆员;〔英海军〕缝帆兵;〔美海军〕掌帆长。~ **needle** 缝帆用的针。~**-plane** **1.** ***n***. 滑翔机。**2.** ***vi***. 滑翔飞行。

sail·er [ˈseilə; ˋselə] ***n***. 帆船。*a good* [*fast*] ~ 速度快的船。*a heavy* [*bad, poor, slow*] ~ 速度慢的船。

sail·ing [ˈseiliŋ; ˋselɪŋ] ***n***. **1.** 扬帆行驶,航行;开船。**2.** 航行方法,航海术;滑翔。*fixed* ~*s* 定期航行。*Hours of* ~ *will be announced daily*. 开船时刻每日公布。*aerial* ~ 航空术,飞行。*current* ~ 潮流航法。*great-circle* ~ 大圈航法。*Mercator's* ~ 马氏航法,渐长纬度航法。*middle-latitude* ~ 中分纬度航法。*parallel* ~ 等距航法。*plane* ~ 平面航法。***plain*** [***smooth***] ~ 一帆风顺,轻而易举。~**-boat** 〔美〕帆船。~ **flight** 【空】滑翔飞行。~**-master** 〔英〕(游艇的)、〔美〕(军舰的)领航员。~**off** 帆船比赛。~ **orders** 〔*pl*.〕(船长的)开船命令。~ **ship**, ~ **vessel** 帆船。

sail·or [ˈseilə; ˋselɚ] ***n***. **1.** 海员,航海者;水手,水兵。**2.** 〔美〕老兄。**3.** 〔口〕= ~ hat. *a leading* ~ 〔英〕一等水兵。*an able* [*full*] ~ 〔英〕二等水兵。*an ordinary* ~ 新水兵。*a bad* [*good*] ~ 晕船[不晕船]的人。*What kind of* (*a*) ~ *are you*? 你晕船不晕船? ~ **boy** 小水手;见习水手。~ **collar** 水手领〔领口背部宽而方〕。~ **hat** 水手帽;宽檐草帽〔妇女或儿童用〕。~**'s book** 航海指南。~**'s choice** 〔美〕黑棘鬣鱼;海摩伦鱼。~**s' home** 海员旅舍〔收费低廉〕。~**'s knot** 水手结,水手领结。~ **suit** 男童的水手装。

sail·or·ing [ˈseiləriŋ; ˋselərɪŋ] ***n***. 海员生活;航海(生涯);水手工作。

sail·or·ly [ˈseiləli; ˋselɚlɪ] ***a***. 像水手的。

sail·or·man [ˈseiləmæn; ˋselɚ͵mæn] ***n***. 〔谑〕= sailor.

sain [sein; sen] ***vt***. 〔古、方〕划十字于…之上以祈福避灾。

sain·foin [ˈseinfɔin; ˋsenfɔɪn] ***n***. 【植】红豆草,驴喜豆。

Sains·bury [ˈseinzbəri; ˋsenzbərɪ] ***n***. 塞恩斯伯里〔姓氏〕。

saint [seint, 弱 sənt; sent] **I** ***n***. **1.** 神圣的人;圣者;(教会正式尊崇的)圣徒。**2.** 道德崇高的人;圣人;圣者[徒]似的人。**3.** (被认为已进入天堂的)死者。**4.** 上帝的选民,基督教教徒。**5.** 〔S-〕[seint, sənt; sent]〔用于人名,地名前,单数略作 St., S. 复数略作 SS 或 Sts.〕圣…。*I am no* ~. 我不是圣人。*He is a* ~ *of a man*. 他是一个圣人。***All Saints' Day*** 万圣节〔11月1日〕。***It would provoke*** [***try the patience of***] ***a*** ~ 这话[事、行为等]连圣徒听了都会生气〔葬礼用语〕。***keep St. Monday*** 〔英〕星期天喝醉星期一请假。***play the*** ~ 假装信徒。***St. Agnes's Eve*** 圣女埃格尼斯节前夜〔一月二十日之夜,传说少女在这天夜晚行某种仪式就可以看到未来丈夫的模样〕。***St. Andrew's cross*** X 形十字架(形)。***St. Anthony's cross*** T 形十字架(形)。***St. Anthony's fire*** 皮肤病,皮炎;丹毒,麦角中毒。***St. Bernard*** 圣比纳品种救护犬。***St. George's cross*** 白底红色希腊教会十字架(形)。***St. James's*** (伦敦)圣詹姆士宫;圣詹姆士宫附近的高级住宅区;英国宫廷。***St. John's-bread*** 【植】角豆荚(= carob)。***St. John's-wort*** 【植】小连翘。***St. Lubbock's Day*** 〔英〕(St. Lubbock 法案中所规定的)公假日。***St. Luke's summer*** = ***St. Martin's summer*** 晚秋(十月二十八日前后)风和日暖的天气。***St. Michael*** (大西洋东部 *Azores* 群岛的)子少皮薄的橘子。***St. Peter's chair*** 教皇的职位。***St. Vitus's dance*** 【医】舞蹈病〔主要指小孩的抽搐〕。***the departed*** ~ 蒙上帝召唤弃我而去的故人(指死者)。**II** ***vt***. 〔通例用被动语态〕(教会正式宣布)列[尊]…为圣徒,把…视为圣徒[圣者]。

Saint-Denis [seint ˈdenis; sent ˋdɛnɪs] 圣但尼〔留尼汪岛(法)首府〕。

saint·dom [ˈseintdəm; ˋsentdəm] ***n***. **1.** 圣徒身份[地位]。**2.** 〔集合词〕圣徒。**3.** 圣洁。

saint·ed [ˈseintid; ˋsentɪd] ***a***. **1.** 列为圣徒的,成为神圣的。**2.** 神圣的。**3.** 升了天的〔称呼死者的委婉说法〕。*my* ~ *mother* 先母。

saint·ess [ˈseintis; ˋsentɪs] *n*. 女圣徒,圣女。
saint·hood [ˈseinthud; ˋsent͵hʊd] *n*. = saintdom.
saint·ly [ˈseintli; ˋsentlɪ] *a*. 像圣徒的;道德高尚的;神圣的;圣洁的。
Saints·bury [ˈseintsbəri; ˋsentsbərɪ] *n*. 森茨伯里〔姓氏〕。
saint's-day [ˈseintsdei; ˋsentsde] *n*. 纪念某一圣徒的日子〔节假日〕。
saint·ship [ˈseintʃip; ˋsent·ʃɪp] *n*. 圣徒的地位[品格]。
Saint-Si·mon [sæŋsiˈmɔŋ, F. sɛ̃siˈmɔ̃; sɛ̃siˋmɔ̃], **C. H.** 圣西门〔1760—1825,法国空想社会主义者〕。
Saint-Si·mon·ian [səntsiˈməuniən;͵sɛ̃saɪˋmonɪən] *n*., *a*. 圣西门主义者(的);空想社会主义者(的)。**Saint-Si·mon·ism** *n*. 圣西门主义,空想社会主义。
Saint-Si·mon·ist *n*. = Saint-Simonian (*n*.)。
Sai·pan [saiˈpɑːn; saɪˋpɑn] *n*. **1.** 塞班岛〔西太平洋〕。**2.** 塞班〔马里亚纳群岛、加罗林群岛、马绍尔群岛(美托管)首府〕。
saith [seθ; sɛθ] says 的古体。
sake [seik; sek] *n*. 缘故,理由,目的,关系。★现常在 for the ~ of …, for …'s ~ 中应用;修饰 sake 的名词的尾音是[s]时,常省去所有格的 s: *for goodness' ~. for the ~ of health* 为了健康。***art for art's*** ~ 为艺术而艺术。***for all*** [***both***] ***our*** ~***s*** 为了大家[你我双方]。***for any*** ~ 无论如何,好歹。***for appearance'*** ~ = ***for the*** ~ ***of appearance*** 为了面子,面子上。***for form's*** ~ 形式上。***for God's*** [***Christ's***, ***goodness'***, ***heaven's***, ***mercy's***] ~ 千万,务请。***for old*** ~***'s*** ~ 为了老交情,看从前交情的面上。***for pete's*** ~〔俚〕= for God's ~. ***for the*** ~ ***of*** [***for one's*** ~] 为…起见,为了…。***Sakes*** (***alive***)!〔方,美俚〕天呀! 吓我一跳! ***without*** ~ 无缘无故,毫无理由地。
sa·ke, ***sa·ké***, ***sa·ki*** [ˈsɑːki; ˋsɑkɪ] *n*.〔Jap.〕日本清酒。
sa·ker [ˈseikə; ˋsekɚ] *n*.【动】猎隼〔用于放鹰行猎〕。
Sa·kha·lin [͵sækəˈliːn, -ˈlin; ͵sækəˋlin, -lɪn] *n*. 萨哈林岛〔即库页岛〕。
sa·ki [ˈsɑːki; ˋsɑkɪ] *n*.【动】(南美)粗尾猿。
sa·ki·a [ˈsækiə; ˋsækɪə] *n*.〔Arab.〕水车〔用于农田灌溉〕。
Sal [sɑːl; sɑl] *n*.【植】〔印度〕娑罗双树,柳安(亦作 Saltree)。
sal[1] [sæl; sæl] *n*. **1.**【化、药】盐。**2.**【地】矽铝带,矽铝质。~ **ammoniac** 氯化铵,硇砂。~ **soda** 苏打,十水(合)碳酸钠。
sal[2] [sæl; sæl] *n*.〔俚〕= salary.
Sa·la [ˈsɑːˈlɑː; ˋsɑlə] *n*. 撒拉族,撒拉族人。
sa·laam [səˈlɑːm; səˋlɑm] **I** *n*. 额手礼〔伊斯兰教用右手摩额鞠躬的礼〕;敬礼,敬意。**II** *vt*., *vi*.(向…)行额手礼。
sal·a·bil·i·ty [͵seiləˈbiliti; ͵seləˋbɪlətɪ] *n*. 畅销;销路。
sal·a·ble [ˈseiləbl; ˋseləbl̩] *a*. 有销路的;畅销的。
sa·la·cious [səˈleiʃəs; səˋleʃəs] *a*. **1.**(人)好色的,淫荡的。**2.**(书、画、写作、言谈)诲淫的。**-ly** *ad*. **-ness** *n*. **sa·lac·i·ty** *n*.
sal·ad [ˈsæləd; ˋsæləd] *n*. **1.** 色[沙]拉〔凉拌生菜〕;色[沙]拉用蔬菜。**2.**〔美、方〕(特指)莴苣,生菜。~ **days** 没有经验的少年时代,少不更事的时期。~ **dressing** 色[沙]拉用调料〔植物油、醋、香料等的混合〕。~ **oil** 色[沙]拉油〔多用净纯橄榄油〕。
Sa·lade [səˈlɑːd; səˋlɑd] *n*. = sallet.
sal·a·man·der [ˈsæləmændə; ˋsælə͵mændɚ] *n*. **1.**(传说中的)火蛇;火怪,火精。**2.**〔俗〕能耐高热的人[物],不怕炮火的军人;吞火的魔术师。**3.**【动】蝾螈。**4.** 拨火棒。**5.**〔美俚〕耐火保险箱〔又称 ~ safe〕。**6.**【徽】火兽。**7.**〔口〕(烤肉或烘糕饼等用的)烤盘。**8.**【冶】(高炉)炉底铁块。
sal·a·man·drine, **-dri·an** [͵sæləˈmændrin, -driən; ͵sæləˋmændrɪn, -drɪən] **I** *a*. **1.** 像火蛇[蝾螈等]一样的。**2.** 耐火的,耐热的。**II** *n*. **1.** 耐火物,耐热的人。**2.** 蝾螈类。
sa·la·mi [səˈlɑːmi(ː); səˋlɑmɪ] *n*.(意大利式的)萨拉米香肠〔一种蒜味咸腊肠〕。~ **technique** "萨拉米香肠"式贪污术〔财务人员在电脑上通过四舍五入法将存款金额化为整数以侵吞其余额。源出从多根香肠上各截下一小片的鼠窃狗偷手段〕。
sal·an·gane [ˈsæləngæn; ˋsælən͵gæn] *n*.【鸟】(筑可食用"燕窝"的)金丝燕。
sa·lar·i·at(e) [səˈlɛəriæt; səˋlɛrɪ͵æt] *n*. 薪水阶级,薪水阶层。
sal·a·ried [ˈsælərid; ˋsælərɪd] *a*. **1.** 拿薪金的。**2.** 有薪金的。*a ~ man* 靠薪水生活者。*a ~ office* 有薪金的职位。
sal·a·ry [ˈsæləri; ˋsælərɪ] **I** *n*. 薪水,薪金,薪俸。★ salary 指公职人员、职员等拿按年、按月计算的"年薪"或"月薪"。工人等拿的"工资"叫做 wages 一般按日、按时或按件计算。*a ~ man* 领薪族(= *a salaried man*)。***draw one's*** ~ 领薪水。**II** *vt*. (***-ried***)〔常用被动语态〕发…薪水,付…薪水。
sale [seil; sel] **I** *n*. **1.** 卖,出卖,出售。**2.** 拍卖;贱卖(尤指季末存货的大减价)。**3.** 销路。**4.** 销数,销售额。**5.**【法】买卖契约。*a ~ for* [*on*] *cash* = *a cash ~* 现金出售。*a ~ on credit* [*account*] 赊销。*a public* [*an open*] ~ 拍卖。*forced ~* 强制拍卖。*a trade ~* 同行拍卖。*the season of ~s* 出清存货的季节。*a grand* [*bargain*] ~ 大廉价。***at*** ~(书店同行间)照定价七折。***dispose of*** (***sth***.) ***by*** ~ 卖掉(某物)。***dull of*** ~ 滞销,销路不好。***easy of*** ~ 畅销,销路好。***find no*** ~ 无销路。***have*** [***meet with***, ***command***] ***a ready*** [***good***] ~ 畅销。***for*** ~ 出售(的)。***no*** ~〔美俚〕不;我不赞成,我不来。***not for*** ~ 非卖品;不出售的。***offer for*** ~ 供应销售。***on*** ~ **1.** 出售(的),待售(的)。**2.** 廉价出售(的),拍卖(的)。***put up for*** ~ 拿出拍卖。~ ***by area***【林】场地上立木全部出卖。~ ***by bulk*** 估堆卖,成批出售。~ ***of work***(教友等举行慈善性质的)义卖。~ ***or*** [***and***] ***return*** 剩货保退〔指批发给零售商的货物〕。~ **price** 廉价。~**-ring** 聚集在拍卖人周围的人。~**-room** = ~**sroom.** ~**s departments** 营业部。~**s resistance**〔美俚〕无销路,无订购户,滞销,(公众的)不愿购买。~**s talk** **1.** 兜售的话。**2.**〔喻〕游说。~**s tax** 营业税。~ **yard** 买卖家畜的围场。
sale·a·ble [ˈseiləbl; ˋseləbl̩] *a*. = salable.
sal·ep [ˈsælep; ˋsælɛp] *n*. 色列普淀粉〔从兰科植物球根提制,可供药用及食用〕。
sal·e·ra·tus [͵sæliˈreitəs; ͵sæləˋretəs] *n*.〔美〕(烹调用)小苏打,发酵粉。
sales·clerk [ˈseilzklɑːk; ˋselz͵klɝk] *n*.〔美〕= salesperson.
sales·girl [ˈseilzgəːl; ˋselz͵gɝl] *n*.〔美〕女售货员,女店员。
sales·la·dy [ˈseilzleidi; ˋselz͵ledɪ] *n*.〔美〕= saleswoman.
sales·man [ˈseilzmən; ˋselzmən] *n*. (*pl*. ***-men***) **1.** 售货员,店员。**2.**〔美〕推销员,跑街。*a dead ~*〔英〕肉店,屠户。*an insurance ~*〔美〕保险公司的跑街。**-ship** *n*. 售货术;推销术。
sales·per·son [ˈseilspəːsn; ˋselz͵pɝsn] *n*. (*pl*. ***-people***)〔美〕**1.** 店员,营业员,售货员。**2.** 推销员。
sales·room [ˈseilzrum; ˋselz͵rum] *n*.〔美〕**1.** 货品陈设室;售货处。**2.** 拍卖处。
sales·woman [ˈseilzwumən; ˋselz͵wʊmən] *n*. (*pl*. ***-wom·en***) **1.** 女店员。**2.**〔美〕女推销员,女跑街。
sali- *comb. f*. 表示"盐": *sali*ferous.
Sa·li·an [ˈseiliən; ˋselɪən] **I** *a*. **1.**【古罗马】战神祭司的。

2.（四世纪时居于 Ijssel 河沿岸、作为法兰克人一支的）撒利族的。*a* ～ *hymn* 战神赞歌。**II** ***n*.** 撒利族。

Sal·ic [ˈsælik; ˋsælɪk] ***a*.** 1. 撒利族的。2. 撒利族法典的。～ **law**【法】撒利族法典〔尤指其中禁止妇女继承土地的规定〕；撒利法〔法国和西班牙禁止女性继承王位的法律〕。

sal·i·cin [ˈsælisin; ˋsæləsɪn] ***n*.**【化】水杨甙；柳醇。

sal·i·cyl [ˈsælisil; ˋsæləsɪl] ***n*.**【化】水杨基，邻羟苄基。

sa·lic·y·late [sæˈlisileit; ˋsælə͵sɪlet] **I** ***n*.**【化】水杨酸盐[脂]。**II** ***vt*.** 加水杨酸。

sal·i·cyl·ic [ˌsæliˈsilik; ͵sæləˋsɪlɪk] ***a*.**【化】水杨酸的。～ **acid** 酸。～ **aldehyde** 水杨醛。～ **amide** 水杨醯胺。

sa·li·ence, -cy [ˈseiljəns, -si; ˋselɪəns, -sɪ] ***n*.** 1. 凸出，突起。2. 跃起，跳跃。3. 喷出，射出，发出。4.【军】突出部，突角。5.〔喻〕特征，特点，特色，卓越，显著。

sa·li·ent [ˈseiljənt; ˋselɪənt] **I** ***a*.** 1. 显著的，卓越的，惹人注目的。2. 凸出的，突起的。3. 跃起的，跳跃的。4.（泉水等）喷出的，涌出的。5.【徽】前脚腾空作跳跃状的。**II** ***n*.** 凸角；【筑城】突出部。*a* ～ *feature*（海岸线、脸形的）突出部分。～ *features* [*points*, *characteristics*] 特色，特征，特点。**-ly** ***ad*.**

sa·li·en·ti·an [ˌseiliˈenʃiən; ͵selɪˋɛnʃɪən] **I** ***n*.**【动】无尾目动物〔包括蛙、蟾等〕。**II** ***a*.** 无尾目的。

sa·lif·er·ous [səˈlifərəs; səˋlɪfərəs] ***a*.**（地层）含[产]盐的。

sal·i·fi·a·ble [ˈsælifaiəbl; ˋsæləfaɪəbḷ] ***a*.**【化】能变成盐的。

sal·i·fi·ca·tion [ˌsælifiˈkeiʃən; ͵sæləfaɪˋkeʃən] ***n*.**【化】成盐作用。

sal·i·fy [ˈsælifai; ˋsælə͵faɪ] ***vt*.** 1. 使变咸，使含有盐分；【化】盐化。2. 使成盐；使与盐化合。

Sa·li·i [sæliai; sælɪaɪ] ***n*.** *pl*. 撒利族法兰克人。

sa·lim·e·ter [sæˈlimitə; səˋlɪmətɚ] ***n*.**【化】盐(液比)重计。

sa·li·na [səˈlainə; səˋlaɪnə] ***n*.**【地】盐沼，盐地，盐湖，盐碱滩。

sa·line [ˈseilain, səˈlain; ˋselaɪn] **I** ***a*.** 1. 盐的；含盐的；盐性的，咸的。2. 盐渍的；【医】盐水注射人工流产法。**II** [səˈlaɪn; səˋlaɪn] ***n*.** 1. 盐沼，咸湖，盐泉；盐皮；盐碱滩；盐田，盐地，制盐所，盐场。2.【医】盐水；含盐泻药。～ *matter* 盐分。～ *taste* 咸味。3.【医】盐水注射人工流产法。*normal* ～ 生理盐水。

sa·lin·i·ty [səˈliniti; səˋlɪnətɪ] ***n*.** 盐分；盐浓度，咸度；含盐量。

sal·i·nom·e·ter [ˌsæliˈnɔmitə; ͵sælɪˋnɑmətɚ] ***n*.** 1.【化】盐(液比)重计，盐液密度(比重)计。2.【电】(电导)调浓器。

Sa·lique [səˈliːk; ˋsælɪk] ***a*.** = Salic.

Salis·bur·y [ˈsɔːlzbəri; ˋsɔlz͵bɛrɪ] ***n*.** 1. 索尔兹伯里〔津巴布韦(原罗德西亚)首都〕，索尔兹伯里〔英国城市〕。2.（英格兰 Wiltshire 郡的）索尔兹伯里平原〔又称 ～ Plain〕。***as plain as*** ～ 明明白白地。～ **steak** 汉堡牛排，牛肉饼（= Hamburger）。

Sa·lish [ˈseiliʃ; ˋselɪʃ] ***n*.** 1. 撒利希语族〔北美印第安语，包括十五个语支〕。2. 讲此语族语言的人。3. "平头"印第安人（= flathead）。4. 撒利希语。亦作 **Sa·lish·an** [-ən; -ən].

sa·li·va [səˈlaivə; səˋlaɪvə] ***n*.** 涎，唾液。*eject* ～ 吐唾沫。

sal·i·var·y [ˈsælivəri; ˋsæləverɪ] ***a*.**（分泌）唾液的。*a* ～ *gland*【解】涎腺，唾(液)腺。

sal·i·vate [ˈsæliveit; ˋsælə͵vet] ***vt*.**, ***vi*.**（使）分泌（过多）唾液，（使）流口水。**-va·tion** [ˌsæliˈveiʃən; ͵sæləˋveʃən] ***n*.**【医】流涎，多涎(症)。

salle [sɑːl, sæl; sal, sæl] ***n*.**〔F.〕大厅。～ ***à manger*** [ˈsæləˈmɑ̃ːnʒei; ͵salaˋmɑ̃ʒe] 餐厅；茶室，咖啡室。～ ***d'attente*** [ˈsældæˈtɑ̃ːnt; ͵saldaˋtɑ̃t]（车站的）候车室。

sal·len·ders [ˈsæləndəz; ˋsæləndɚz] ***n*.** *pl*. 马跗关节的干性皮疹。

sal·let [ˈsælit; ˋsælɪt] ***n*.**（15 世纪带护颈的）轻盔。

sal·low[1] [ˈsæləu; ˋsælo] **I** ***a*.**（肤色）灰黄的。**II** ***n*.** 灰黄色，土色。**III** ***vt*.**, ***vi*.**（使）成[变成]灰黄色。**-ish** ***a*.** 略带灰黄色的。**-ness** ***n*.**

sal·low[2] [ˈsæləu; ˋsælo] ***n*.** 1.【植】阔叶柳，黄华柳，山毛柳。2. 柳枝，柳条。

sal·ly [ˈsæli; ˋsælɪ] **I** ***n*.** 1.（被围军队的）突围，出击。2. 远足；外出；旅行。3.（感情等的）迸发，突发。4.（脱口而出的）俏皮话，警句。5. 戏谑，开玩笑，恶作剧。6.【建】凸出部；钝角。*make a* ～ *into* 到…去逛。*a* ～ *wit* 脱口而出的俏皮话[警句]。**II** ***vi*.** 1. 突围，冲出，出击（*out*）。2. 动身，出发（*forth*, *off*, *out*）。～ **port**【筑城】暗门，（碉堡等的）出击口；（备失事用的）太平门。

Sal·ly [ˈsæli; ˋsælɪ] ***n*.** 萨莉〔女子名，Sarah 的昵称〕。～ **Lunn, s- lunn** 萨莉·伦恩饼〔一种趁热抹上黄油食用的茶点，源于 1797 年英国巴思（Bath）一位名叫萨莉·伦恩的女子沿街出卖的甜饼〕。

sal·ma·gun·di [ˌsælməˈgʌndi; ͵sælməˋgʌndɪ] ***n*.** 1. 酸辣鱼肉杂烩〔意大利菜肴〕。2.〔喻〕杂凑，大杂烩。

sal·mi [ˈsælmi; ˋsælmɪ] ***n*.** 五香野味〔烧天鹨、鹌等，加大量调味烧烤后并以葡萄酒蒸煮〕。

salm·on [ˈsæmən; ˋsæmən] **I** ***n*.**（*pl*. ～，〔罕〕～*s*）1. 鲑，大麻哈鱼。2. 鲑肉色，橙红色，淡红色。*chum* [*dog*] ～ 大麻哈鱼。**II** ***a*.** 鲑肉色的，橙[淡]红色的。～ **colo(u)r** 鲑肉色，橙[淡]红色。～ **trout**【鱼】1.（一种似鲑的）鳟（= brown trout）。2. 硬头鳟（= steel head）。

sal·mo·nel·la [ˌsælməˈnelə; ͵sælməˋnɛlə] ***n*.**（*pl*. ***-nellae*** [-iː; -i]，***-nella***，***-nel·las***）【生】沙门氏菌属细菌。

sal·mo·nel·lo·sis [ˌsælməˈneləusis; ͵sælmənəˋlosɪs] ***n*.**【医】沙门氏菌病〔沙门氏菌属引起的传染病〕。

sal·mo·noid [ˈsælmənɔid; ˋsæmənɔɪd] **I** ***a*.**【动】1. 似鲑的。2. 鲑鱼属的，鲑亚目的〔包括鲑鱼、白鲑等〕。**II** ***n*.** 鲑科鱼；（尤指）鲑鱼。

sal·ol [ˈsæləul; ˋsælol] ***n*.**【化】萨罗，水杨酸苯酯〔用作保护皮肤的药剂〕。

Sa·lo·me [səˈləumi; səˋlomɪ] ***n*.** 1. 萨洛米〔女子名〕。2.【圣】莎乐美〔希律王（Herod）之女，以其舞使希律王着迷，允其所请将施洗者约翰斩首并将首级赐给她，见马太福音〕。3.《莎乐美》〔王尔德（Oscar Wilde）根据圣经故事用法文写的剧本〕。

Sa·lo·mon·ic, Sa·lo·moni·an [ˌsæləˈmɔnik, -ˈməunjən; ͵sæləˋmɑnɪk, -monjən] ***a*.** 所罗门（Solomon）王的，所罗门王似的。

sal·on [ˈsæl ɔ̃ːŋ; saˋlɔ̃] ***n*.**〔F.〕1. 沙龙，客厅。2.（尤指巴黎上流社会妇女客厅中举行的）招待会。3. 名流集会。4. 美术展览会。〔the S-〕（每年举行一次在世美术家作品的）巴黎美术展览会。5.（营业性的）厅，院。*a beauty* ～ 美容院。*literary* ～*s* 文艺沙龙。～ **music** 一种室内轻音乐。

Sa·lo·ni·ka, Sa·lo·ni·ca [səˈlɔnikə; ͵sæləˋnikə] ***n*.** 萨罗尼加，萨洛尼卡〔希腊港市〕。

sa·loon [səˈluːn; səˋlun] ***n*.** 1.（旅馆、轮船等的）大厅，客厅。2.（旅客机的）客室；〔英〕（火车的）客厅式豪华车厢〔又叫 ～ car，～ carriage〕。3. 大轿车〔又叫 ～ car =〔美〕*sedan*〕。4.〔英〕高级酒店（= ～-bar）；〔美〕酒吧（=〔英〕public house）。5.〔英〕（公众出入的）…厅，…店，…场(等)。*a dining* ～〔英〕餐车；〔美〕（轮船的）餐厅。*a* ～ *cabin* 头等船。*a family* ～ 专用客车。*a refreshment* ～ 饮食店。*a hair-dressing* ～ = *a hair dresser's* ～ 理发店[馆]。*a shooting-* ～ 靶子厅。～ **deck** 头等船客专用甲板。～**keeper**〔美〕酒吧老板，酒店主人。～ **pistol** [**rifle**] 打靶枪。

sa·loon·ist [səˈluːnist; səˋlunɪst] ***n*.** 1.〔美〕= saloon-keeper. 2. 酒吧的老主顾，酒店的常客。

sa·loop [səˈluːp; səˋlup] ***n*.** 1. 色列普茶〔用 salep 或 sassafras 做的热饮料〕。2. = salep.

Sal·op [ˈsæləp; ˋsæləp] ***n.*** 【动】英国萨洛普郡 (Shropshire) 绵羊。

Sa·lo·pi·an [səˈləupiən, -pjən; səˋlopɪən] **I** ***a.*** **1.** 萨洛普郡 (Shropshire) 的。**2.** 萨洛普郡人的。**3.** Shrewsbury 公学的。**II** ***n.*** **1.** 萨洛普郡居民。**2.** Shrewsbury 公学的学生。

sal·pa [ˈsælpə; ˋsælpə] ***n.*** (*pl.* *~s*, *-pae* [-piː;-pi]) 【动】萨尔帕属的被囊动物,萨尔帕。亦作 **salp.**

sal·pi·glos·sis [ˌsælpiˈglɔsis; ˏsælpɪˋglɑsɪs] ***n.*** 【植】喇叭舌草〔一种茄科观赏植物,原产南美智利等地〕。

sal·pin·gec·to·my [ˌsælpinˈdʒektəmi; ˏsælpɪnˋdʒɛktəmɪ] ***n.*** (*pl.* ***-mies***) 【医】输卵管切除术。

salping- *comb. f.* 【医】输卵管的,耳咽管的:*salping*itis.

sal·pin·gi·tis [ˌsælpinˈdʒaitis; ˏsælpɪnˋdʒaɪtɪs] ***n.*** 【医】输卵管炎;耳咽管炎。

salpingo- *comb. f.* = salping.

sal·pin·gos·to·my [ˌsælpinˈgɔstəmi; ˏsælpɪŋˋgɑstəmɪ] 【医】输卵管造口术。

sal·pinx [ˈsælpiŋks; ˋsælpɪŋks] ***n.*** (*pl.* ***sal·pin·ges*** [-pindʒiːz;-pɪndʒiz]) **1.** 【解】输卵管 (= Fallopian tube)。**2.** 咽鼓管,欧氏管 (= Eustachian tube)。**sal·pin·gi·an** [-ˈpindʒiən; -ˋpɪndʒɪən] ***a.***

sal·si·fy [ˈsælsifi; ˋsælsəfɪ] ***n.*** 【植】婆罗门参〔其根可食,有牡蛎的味道〕。

SALT [sɔːlt; sɔlt] = Strategic Arms Limitation Talks 限制战略武器会谈。

salt [sɔːlt; sɔlt] **I** ***n.*** **1.** 盐,食盐。**2.** 【化】盐;酸类和盐基化合物。**3.** 〔*pl.*〕盐剂,药用盐,〔特指〕泻盐 (= Epsom ~s)。**4.** 俏皮话,讽刺;机智。**5.** 要素,精华。**6.** 趣味,滋味,风味,刺激(品)。**7.** (老练的[富有经验的])水手〔通例叫 old ~〕。**8.** 〔俚〕(餐桌上的)小盐缸,盐瓶 (= ~-cellar)。**9.** 现实[慎重、有保留]的态度。**10.** 盐沼;盐碱滩 (= ~ marsh)。*common* [*culinary*, *table*] ~ 食盐。*white* ~ 精盐。*a dose of* ~ 一付泻药。*smelling ~s* (提神的)嗅盐,碳酸铵。***above*** [***below***, ***beneath***, ***under***] ***the*** ~ 坐上席[下席]〔从前长餐桌中间摆盐缸,上面一半算是上席〕;受[不受]尊敬。***be faithful*** [***true***] ***to one's*** ~ 忠于自己的雇主。***cast*** [***lay***, ***put***, ***throw***, ***drop a pinch of***] ~ ***on the tail of*** 诱捕;巧妙地捕捉。***earn one's*** ~ 自立,自食其力。***eat sb.'s*** ~ = ***eat*** ~ ***with sb.*** 做某人的(食)客;吃某人的饭;依赖某人。***in*** ~ 撒了盐的;盐腌的。***not made of*** ~ 不是盐做的,遇水不溶的。***spill*** ~ 把盐撒落在餐桌上〔被认为是恶兆〕。***the*** ~ ***of the earth*** 社会中坚〔源出《圣经》〕。***with a grain of*** ~ 有保留地,须打折扣的,须视为是夸大的 (*His statement must be taken with a grain of* ~. 他的话要打一个折扣听取[不能全信])。***worth one's*** ~ 称职,胜任,不是吃白饭的。**II** ***a.*** **1.** 盐的,含盐份的。**2.** 咸的,有咸味的。**3.** 盐腌的,盐渍的。**4.** (土地等)灌进海水的;生长于咸水中的。**5.** (眼泪等)饱含痛苦的。**6.** (俏皮话等)犀利的,痛快的,辛辣的,尖刻的。**7.** (话等)猥亵的,下流的。**8.** 〔俚〕(账款等)浮报的,以少报多的。*The dish is too* ~. 这盘菜太咸。*a* ~ *pasture* 海水淹过的牧场。***as*** ~ ***as fire*** 极咸。***rather too*** ~ 〔俚〕太贪暴利。

III ***vt.*** **1.** 给…加盐,给…调味。**2.** 撒盐(使路上的雪溶化)。**3.** 〔口〕(以盐)腌;保存。**4.** 储蓄。**5.** 使(话等)有风趣[力量]。**6.** 〔用被动语态〕使(马或人)服水土。**7.** 以盐喂…给(羊等)盐吃。**8.** 【化】用盐类处理。**9.** 〔俚〕给(劣矿)移入别处良矿石作伪装;〔商俚〕(用伪品)冒充,(用劣货)骗卖。**10.** 虚报,浮报(价钱),浮记(账款)。~ *a mine* 移入别处良矿伪装矿山〔使人误以富矿购买〕。~ *an account* 〔商俚〕浮报账款。~ *books* 浮记盈余。~ *prices* 讨虚价,开虚价。~ ***away*** [***down***] **1.** 腌制。**2.** 积蓄,储蓄。**3.** 〔美〕投资。**4.** 〔美俚〕大骂一顿。~ ***in*** 盐(助)溶。~ ***out*** 【化】盐析;加盐分离。**~-and-pepper** **1.** ***n.*** (黑白点相间的)椒盐色(织物),芝麻呢。**2.** ***a.*** 椒盐色的;〔美口〕由黑人和白人混合组成的。~ **box** 斜盖盐箱;(17—19 世纪初美国新英格兰地区的一种)盐箱形楼房。~**bush** 【植】滨藜属 (*Atriplex*) 植物〔生于盐碱地或沙漠〕。~ **cake** 盐饼,芒硝,粗制硫酸钠。**~-cat** 盐块(喂鸽子的)含盐饲料。~ **cellar** (餐桌上的)盐瓶,小盐缸;〔俚〕脖子基部两边的窝,脖根窝。~ **dome** 【地】盐穹,盐丘。~ **glaze** 【化】盐釉。~ **grass** 【植】盐草属 (*Distichlis*) 植物〔尤指拉美海滨盐草 (*Distichlis spicata*)〕。~ **horse** [**junk**] 【海】腌牛肉。~ **lake** 咸水湖。**S- Lake City** 〔美〕盐湖城。~ **lick** 动物爱舐食的含盐地。~ **marsh** 盐泽,盐沼。~ **mine** 岩盐产地,岩盐坑。~**-pan** **1.** 盐锅。**2.** 盐田。**3.** 〔*pl.*〕= ~ **works.** ~**-peter**, **~petre** 【化】硝石,芒[火]硝,钾硝,硝酸钾 (*Chile ~peter* 智利硝,硝酸钠。*~peter rot* 湿墙上生的白斑)。~ **pit** 盐田。~ **rheum** 〔美〕湿疹。**S- River** (美国 Arizona 中部的)咸河;〔美喻〕政治上失败,政治生命结束 (*row sb. up S- River* 结束某人的政治生命)。~ **spoon** 盐匙。~ **temperature** 【冶】盐浴温度。~ **water** ***n.*** **1.** 咸水,海水。**2.** 〔谑〕泪。**~-water** ***a.*** **1.** 咸水的。**2.**(鱼等)咸水产的。~ **well** 盐井。**~works** 〔*sing. pl.*〕盐场。~ **wort** 【植】(生于海边或盐沼)藜科植物,尤指猪毛菜和海莲子。**-less** **1.** 无盐的,无咸味的。**2.** 无味道的。**-ness** ***n.***

SALT = Strategic Arms Limitation Talks 限制战略核武器会谈。

sal·tant [ˈsæltənt; ˋsæltənt] **I** ***a.*** **1.** 跳跃的,舞蹈的。**2.** 【徽】(兽)跳跃状的。**II** ***n.*** 【生】突变形,菌落突变形。

sal·ta·rel·lo [ˌsætəˈreləu; ˏsæltəˋrɛlo] ***n.*** **1.** 萨尔塔列洛舞〔意大利的一种轻快的舞蹈名〕。**2.** 萨尔塔列洛舞曲。

sal·ta·tion [sælˈteiʃən; sælˋteʃən] ***n.*** **1.** 跳,跳跃。**2.** 舞蹈。**3.** 脉动。**4.** 【生】突变;菌落局变;不连续变异。**5.** 【地】河底滚沙。

sal·ta·to·ri·al [ˌsæltəˈtɔːriəl; ˏsæltəˋtorɪəl] ***a.*** **1.** 跳跃的;舞蹈的。**2.** (动物)适于跳跃的。~ *exercises* 跳跃活动。~ *legs* 善跳的腿。

sal·ta·to·ry [ˈsæltətəri; ˋsæltəˏtorɪ] ***a.*** **1.** 跳跃的。**2.** 舞蹈的。**3.** 跃进的。*the* ~ *art* 舞蹈(艺)术。*her* ~ *talent* 她的舞蹈才能。

salt·ed [ˈsɔːltid; ˋsɔltɪd] ***a.*** **1.** 腌的;加了盐的,有咸味的。**2.** 〔俚〕(马等)得过瘟病而有免疫性的。**3.** 有经验的,熟练的。**4.** 〔俚〕(矿山等)伪装过的。**5.** 〔俚〕冒销的,骗卖的。

salt·er [ˈsɔːltə; ˋsɔltɚ] ***n.*** **1.** 制盐者。**2.** 卖盐者,盐商。**3.** 盐田[盐井]职工。**4.** 腌制者。**5.** 干货商。

salt·ern [ˈsɔːltən; ˋsɔltɚn] ***n.*** 盐田;盐场。

salt·er·y [ˈsɔːltəri; ˋsɔltərɪ] ***n.*** **1.** 盐场。**2.** 腌鱼场。

sal·tier [ˈsæltiə; ˋsæltɪr] ***n.*** = saltire.

sal·ti·grade [ˈsæltigreid; ˋsæltəˏgred] ***a.*** **1.** 有适应于跳跃的腿的。**2.** 借跳跃移动的。

salt·ine [sɔːlˈtiːn; sɔlˋtin] ***n.*** (盐精)梳打饼干。

sal·tire [ˈsæltaiə; ˋsæltɪr] **I** ***n.*** 【徽】X 形十字;圣安得列 (St. Andrew) 十字。**II** ***a.*** 成 X 形的。

salt·ish [ˈsɔːltiʃ; ˋsɔltɪʃ] ***a.*** 带有咸味的,略带咸味的。

sal·tus [ˈsæltəs; ˋsæltəs] ***n.*** **1.** 急变;急转,中断。**2.** 【逻】跳越(推论步骤而作)判断,速断,逻辑的飞跃。

salt·y [ˈsɔːlti; ˋsɔltɪ] ***a.*** (***-i·er***; ***-i·est***) **1.** 有盐味的;有海洋味的。**2.** 富有(航海)经验的。**3.** 刺激的,辛辣的,有趣的,富于机智的。**4.** (马等)难驾驭的。**-i·ness** ***n.*** 咸性。

sa·lu·bri·ous [səˈljuːbriəs; səˋlubrɪəs] ***a.*** (气候等)有益健康的。**-ly** ***ad.*** **-ness** ***n.***

sa·lu·bri·ty [səˈljuːbriti; səˋlubrətɪ] ***n.*** 有益健康。

sa·lud [sɑːˈluːd; sɑˋlud] ***int.*** 〔Sp.〕祝你健康,干杯。

sa·lu·ki [səˈluːki; səˋlukɪ] ***n.*** (猎羚羊用的)萨路基猎狗〔亦作 Saluki. 产于波斯和阿拉伯等地〕。

Sa·lus·bury [ˈsɔːlzbəri; ˋsɔlzbərɪ] ***n.*** 索尔兹伯里〔姓氏〕(= Salisbury)。

S

sal·u·ta·ry [ˈsæljutəri; ˋsæljəˏtɛrɪ] ***a*.** **1.** 有益健康的。**2.** 有益的。

sal·u·ta·tion [ˌsælju(:)ˈteiʃən; ˏsæljəˋteʃən] ***n*.** **1.** 问候,致意,祝贺,道别,招呼〔现多用 greeting, welcome〕。**2.** (书信开始的)称呼,敬称。**3.**〔罕〕敬礼〔现用 salute〕。*a word of* ~ 欢迎辞(等)。*the Angelic S-* = the Ave Maria. **-al** ***a*.**

sa·lu·ta·to·ri·an [səˌluːtəˈtɔːriən; səˏlutəˋtorɪən] ***n*.** 〔美〕行毕业礼时代表致辞的(第二名)毕业生〔*cf*. *valedictorian*〕。

sa·lu·ta·to·ry [səˈluːtətəri; səˋlutəˏtorɪ] **I** ***a*.** 行礼的,致意的,致敬的,祝贺的。**II** ***n*.** 〔美〕(通常由第二名毕业生作的)毕业致辞;欢迎辞;祝辞。

sa·lute [səˈluːt; səˋlut] **I** ***vt*.** **1.** 向…敬礼,向…(放礼炮)致敬,向…致意。**2.** 欢迎,祝贺。**3.**〔古〕对(来人)吻手,吻脸〔表示敬意〕。**4.** (景象,声音等)迎着…而来,呈现在…的面前。~ *a flag* 向国旗致敬。*The lark* ~*s the dawn*. 云雀(以歌声)迎接天明。~ *sb*. *with cheers* 欢呼迎接某人。~ *the enemy with a volley* 用排炮[密集火力]迎接敌人。— ***vi*.** **1.** 行礼,点头,招呼,致敬。**2.** 祝贺。**3.** 放礼炮。*Salute!* 〔信未用语〕敬礼! **II** ***n*.** **1.** 行礼,招呼,敬礼。**2.** 礼炮,举枪,举刀(礼)。**3.** 喝彩;〔古〕表示致敬的吻手或吻脸〔又称 chaste ~〕。*a* ~ *of 21 guns* 二十一响的礼炮。***acknowledge a*** ~ 答礼。***at the*** ~ 以敬礼姿势。***come to the*** ~【军】行敬礼。***exchange*** ~***s*** 互致敬礼,互鸣礼炮。***fire a*** ~ 鸣礼炮。***national*** ~ **1.** 为国旗[国家元首]鸣放的 21 响礼炮。**2.**〔美〕〔独立纪念日鸣放相当于所有州数的〕国庆礼炮(= ~ to the Union)。***stand at*** (***the***) ~ (比赛前的)立正敬礼,立正致敬。***take the*** ~ (元首、将军等高级官员)接受敬礼,还礼,行答礼。

salv. = salvage.

Salv. = Salvador.

sal·va·ble [ˈsælvəbl; ˋsælvəbḷ] ***a*.** **1.** 可挽救的,可抢救的。**2.** (船、货等)可打捞的。

Sal·va·dor [ˈsælvədɔː; ˋsælvəˏdɔr] ***n*.** 萨尔瓦多[拉丁美洲]。

Sal·va·do·ran [ˌsælvəˈdɔːrən; ˏsælvəˋdɔrən], **-do·ri·an** [-ˈdɔːriən; -ˋdɔrɪən] ***a*.**, ***n*.** 萨尔瓦多的[人]。

sal·vage [ˈsælvidʒ; ˋsælvɪdʒ] **I** ***n*.** **1.** (海上遇险的)海员海难救助,船舶救助,货物救助。**2.**【商】海难救助酬金,救货费,救难费。**3.** 被救船舶,(海难的)被救财货。**4.**【保险】(可抵补一部分损失额的)残余财货。**5.** 沉船打捞工作,救难工作。**6.** (从火灾或其他灾难中抢救出来的)被救货物,被救财产。**7.** 救济;救助;救难。**8.** 废物利用。**9.**〔美俚〕偷。*a* ~ *boat* 海难救助船。*a* ~ *company* 海难救援公司。~ *corps* (保险公司的)救火队。~ *money* [*charges*] 援救费。**II** ***vt*.** **1.** (从海难、火灾等中)救出。**2.** 打捞(沉船)。**3.** 抢救(财产)。**4.** 把…(从危难中)解救出来;解决…的困难。**5.**【医】救,治。**6.**〔美、俚〕把…据为己有;偷。~ **archaeology** 古物抢救工程。

sal·var·san, S- [ˈsælvəsən; ˋsælvəˏsæn] ***n*.** 【医】"六〇六",洒尔佛散〔= arsphenamine, 治梅毒的特效药,最先由 Paul Ehrlich (1854—1915)加以运用〕。

sal·va·tion [sælˈveiʃən; sælˋveʃən] ***n*.** **1.** 救助,拯救,救济。**2.** 救济者;救济品;救助的工具。**3.** 解救办法,救济措施。**4.**【宗】得救,超度。**5.** 救星,救世主。**6.** 救出来的东西,劫余之物。***be the*** ~ ***of*** 是…的劫余之物。***find*** ~ **1.** 信教,皈依;改宗。**2.**〔谑〕找到改变态度的借口。***S- Army*** (1865 年创建的基督教)救世军。***work out one's own*** ~ 独立自救,自寻出路。**-ism** ***n*.** 救世主义[救世军的教义]。**-ist** **1.** ***n*.** 救世军传道师。**2.** ***a*.** 救世军(式)的。

salve[1] [sɑːv; sæv] **I** ***n*.** **1.** 药膏;软膏。**2.** 缓和物,安慰物〔同 for 连用〕。**3.** 安慰。**4.**〔俚〕奉承。**II** ***vt*.** **1.**〔古〕用药膏医治,给…敷药膏。**2.** 缓和(恶劣感情等);减轻(痛苦);安慰(良心等)。**3.**〔古〕掩饰,遮掩(缺点等)。**4.** 解除(困难等);消除(疑惑、矛盾等)。**5.**〔美俚〕奉承。~ *a sore* 减轻痛苦。

salve[2] [sælv; sælv] ***vt*.** 营救(难船),抢救(火灾中物资);救助,救护。

sal·ve [ˈsælvi; ˋsælvɪ] 〔L.〕 ***int*.** 万岁! 好! 有福了!〔原意为"你好!"欢呼祝贺或祝人安好的呼声或用语〕。

sal·ver [ˈsælvə; ˋsælvə˞] ***n*.** (金、银、铜制的或电镀的,端食品或放置信件,名片等的)托盘,盘子。**~form, ~-shaped** ***a*.**【植】高脚托盘状的,(花冠)管状的〔上端边缘扁平展开〕。

sal·vi·a [ˈsælviə; ˋsælvɪə] ***n*.**【植】鼠尾草。

sal·vif·ic [sælˈvifik; sælˋvɪfɪk] ***a*.** 救人的,救世的,救苦救难的。**-al·ly** ***ad*.**

sal·vo[1] [ˈsælvəu; ˋsælvo] ***n*.** (*pl*. ~***s***) **1.**〔英〕保留;保留条款。**2.** 口实,遁词,托词。**3.** (名誉等的)保全手段,(感情等的)缓和方法。

sal·vo[2] [ˈsælvəu; ˋsælvo] ***n*.** (*pl*. ~***s***, ~***es***) **1.** (礼炮或射击的)齐发,齐鸣,齐射,(炸弹、伞兵等的)齐投,连续投。**2.** 一阵(热烈鼓掌);齐声欢呼,同声喝彩。**3.** 突然爆发。**4.**【军】(炮兵的)翼次射。*The performance won a* ~ *of applause*. 演出博得一阵喝彩。~ **bombing** 齐投轰炸。~ **fire** 集中射击。**~-switch** ***n*.** 齐投开关。

sal vo·la·ti·le [sæl vəuˈlætili; ˋsæl voˋlætḷˏi]【化】碳酸铵(水),挥发盐〔一种提神药,主要成分是碳酸铵〕。

sal·vor [ˈsælvə; ˋsælvə˞] ***n*.** **1.** 救难者,救助人员,打捞人员。**2.** 救援船,打捞船。

Sam [sæm; sæm] ***n*.** 萨姆〔男子名,Samuel 的昵称〕。~ ***Browne*** (***belt***) (军官的)皮带,武装带。~ ***Hill***〔美卑〕地狱;魔鬼。***stand*** ~〔俚〕会钞,付(酒)账。***take one's*** ~ ***upon it***〔俚〕保证,敢于承担。***Uncle*** ~ 山姆大叔〔美国、美国人的绰号〕。***upon my*** ~〔英俚〕我敢发誓;我敢断言。

SAM = surface-to-air missile 地对空导[飞]弹。

S. Am., **S. Amer.** = South America.

sam·a·ra [ˈsæmərə, səˈmɑːrə; ˋsæmərə] ***n*.**【植】翅果,翼果〔如榆,枫等果实〕。

Sa·mar·i·a [səˈmɛəriə; səˋmɛrɪə] ***n*.** 撒马利亚〔古代巴勒斯坦与约旦河间一个地区,同名的王国或其首都〕。

Sa·mar·i·tan [səˈmæritən; səˋmærətn̩] ***n*.**, ***a*.** **1.** 撒玛利亚人(的);撒马利亚语(的)。**2.** 乐善好施者(的)。*a good* ~ 乐善好施的人。*a* ~ *fund* 贫民救济基金。*a* ~ *home* 养育院。**-ism** ***n*.** 慈善;乐善好施。

sa·mar·i·um [səˈmɛəriəm; səˋmærɪəm] ***n*.**【化】钐〔稀有金属元素,化学符号为 Sm 或 Sa〕。

sa·mar·skite [səˈmɑːskait, ˈsæməskait; səˋmɑrskaɪt, ˋsæməskaɪt] ***n*.**【矿】铌钇矿。

Sa·ma-Ve·da [ˈsɑːməˈveidə, -viː-; ˋsɑməˋvedə, -vi-] ***n*.** 娑摩吠陀〔古印度亚尔耶民族的赞歌四吠陀之一〕。

sam·ba [ˈsæmbə; ˋsæmbə] **I** ***n*.** 〔美〕桑巴舞〔巴西一种轻快的二拍子舞〕。**II** ***vi*.** 跳桑巴舞。

sam·bar, sam·bur [ˈsɑːmbə, ˈsæm-; ˋsæmbə˞, ˋsæm-] ***n*.** (*pl*. ~(***s***))【动】水鹿,黑鹿(*Cervus Unicolor*)〔产于印度的一种大鹿〕。

sam·bo [ˈsæmbəu; ˋsæmbo] ***n*.** (*pl*. ~***s***, ~***es***) **1.**〔拉丁美洲〕北美印第安人或黑白混血儿与黑人的后裔。**2.**〔S-〕〔美,侮辱性用语〕黑人。

sam·buke [ˈsæmbjuːk; ˋsæmbjuk] ***n*.** 桑布克琴〔一种近似竖琴的三角形古弦乐器名〕。

Sam·dech [ˈsæmdek; ˋsæmdɛk] ***n*.** 〔高棉语〕陛下,殿下〔对国王、亲王、王子、公主等的敬称,放在称号的前面〕。

same [seim; sem] **I** ***a*.** 〔常 the ~〕 **1.** 相同的,同样的,同种的 (*as*); 同一个 (*with*; *that*; *who*; *which*)。**2.** (和以前)一样,没有变化。**3.** 上述的,该,那个〔和 this, these, that, those 等连用,常用轻蔑意〕。**4.**〔不用 the〕〔罕〕单调的,千篇一律的。*eat the* ~ (*sort of*) *food every day* 每天吃同样的东西。*It is the* ~ *old game*. 老是那一套。*It is the* ~ *with me*. 我也是那样。*She has* *been always the* ~ *to me*. 她对我始终如一。*The life is perhaps a little* ~. 那种生活也许有点单调。**~-sex** *a*.〔美〕(性关系、婚姻关系等上)同性的 (*a* ~*-sex family* 由两个男[女]同性恋者组成的"家庭")。

II *pro*. **1.** 同一事[物];[古]同一人〔常可不用 the〕。**2.**【法、商】该人(等)(= he, him, she, her, they, them 等)。**3.** 上述之物,该物。*We have heard from Mr. Jones and have written to* ~.【商】琼斯君有信来,已复讫。

III *ad*. 一样,相同地,不变。*I think the* ~ *of him as you do*. 我对他的看法和你对他的看法一样。***about the*** ~ = much the ~. ***all*** [***just***] ***the*** ~ **1.** 完全一样 (*It's all the* ~ *to me*. 那对我完全一样)。**2.** 然而还是,仍然 (*I like him all the* ~.(虽有缺点)我仍然喜欢他)。***at the*** ~ ***time*** 同时;〔俚〕〔可省去 the〕然而,可是,还是。***much the*** ~ 差不多完全一样;一丘之貉。***not quite the*** ~ 有点两样。***one and the*** ~ (= ***the very*** ~) 完全相同的,同一的;就是那个。~ ***here***〔口〕我也一样。***the*** ~ **1.** 同样地(= in the ~ way, in the ~ manner)。**2.** 同一事物;上述事物;该人,那个人 (*I wish you the* ~. = (*The*) ~ *to you!* 彼此彼此〔对恭贺新禧时的答话〕)。***the very*** ~ 正是这个,完全相同〔加强语气〕。**-ness** *n*.

sa·mekh, sa·mech [ˈsɑːmek, -mək; ˋsæmɛk, -mək] *n*. 希伯来语的第十五个字母。

Sa·m·i·an [ˈseimiən; ˋsemɪən] **I** *a*. **1.** 萨姆斯 (Samos) 岛的。**2.** 萨姆斯岛居民的。**II** *n*. 萨姆斯岛上的居民。

sam·iel [ˈsæmjel; ˋsæmjɛl] *n*. = simoom.

sam·ite [ˈsæmait; ˋsæmaɪt] *n*. (中世纪一种织有金银线的)锦绣[织锦]。

sa·mi·sen [ˈsæmisən; ˋsæmə͵sɛn] *n*.〔Jap.〕日本三弦。

Saml. = Samuel.

sam·let [ˈsæmlit; ˋsæmlɪt] *n*. 幼鲑。

Sam·my [ˈsæmi; ˋsæmɪ] *n*. **1.**〔俚〕美国兵〔第一次世界大战时对美国远征军大兵的称呼,即对 Uncle Sam 的昵称〕。**2.** Samuel 或 Samantha 的昵称。**3.**〔俚〕笨蛋,傻子,蠢货。***stand*** ~ = stand Sam.

Sam Neua [ˈsæm nuə; ˋsæm no] 桑怒〔老挝城市〕。

Sam·nite [ˈsæmnait; ˋsæmnaɪt] **I** *n*. **1.** 撒姆尼 (Samnium) 的。**2.** 撒姆尼人的。**3.** 撒姆尼语的。**II** *n*. **1.** 撒姆尼人〔意大利中部古撒本 (Sabine) 民族的人〕。**2.** 撒姆尼语。

Sa·mo·a [səˈməuə; səˋmoə] *n*. 萨摩亚群岛〔南太平洋中一群岛〕。

Sa·mo·an [səˈməuən; səˋmoən] *n*., *a*. **1.** 萨摩亚岛人(的)。**2.** 萨摩亚语(的)。

Sa·mos [ˈseimɔs; ˋsemɑs] *n*. 萨姆斯岛〔爱琴海〕。

SAMOS = satellite antimissile observation system 卫星反导[飞]弹观察系统。

sam·o·var [ˈsæməuvɑː; ˋsæmə͵vɑr] *n*. (俄国式)茶炊,茶汤壶;水火壶。*Chinese* ~ 火锅。

Sam·oy·ed(e) [ˌsæmɔiˈed; ͵sæməˋjɛd] **I** *n*. **1.** (西伯利亚西北部的)撒摩耶人。**2.** 撒摩耶语。**3.** 撒摩耶种狗。**II** *a*. **1.** 撒摩耶人的。**2.** 撒摩耶语的。

Sam·oy·ed·ic [ˌsæmɔiˈedik; ͵sæməˋjɛdɪk] **I** *a*. 撒摩耶人的。**II** *n*. 撒摩耶语。

samp [sæmp; sæmp] *n*. **1.**〔美〕玉米糁[粗粉]。**2.**〔美〕玉米粥。

sam·pan [ˈsæmpæn; ˋsæmpæn] *n*.〔中〕舢板;小木船 (= sanpan)。

sam·phire [ˈsæmfaiə; ˋsæmfaɪr] *n*.【植】**1.** (欧洲海滨的)一种伞形科植物,海马齿。**2.** 欧洲海蓬子,钾猪毛菜。厚岸草 (= glasswort)。

sam·ple [ˈsɑːmpl; ˋsæmpl] **I** *n*. **1.** 样品,货样。**2.** 标本;榜样,实例。**3.**【统计】典型取样,抽检查。**4.**【讯】信号瞬时值。**5.**【冶】〔*pl*.〕锌华。*That is a fair* ~ *of his manners*. 那就是他的典型态度。*a light* ~ 光脉冲。***up to*** ~ **1.** 和样品一样[相符]。**2.** 可以接受的,可以同意的。**II** *vt*. 从…取样,从…抽样;提供;货样;对…进行抽样检查。~ **card** (衣料等的)样品卡。~ **copy** 样书。~ **fair** 样品展览会。~ **room** **1.** 样品陈列室。**2.** 矿石样品分析室。**3.**〔美方〕酒吧。

sam·pler [ˈsɑːmplə; ˋsæmplɚ] *n*. **1.** 样品检查员;试饮人(等);抽样者。**2.** 取样器,选样器。**3.** 刺绣图案样本,(文学作品等的)范本。

sam·pling [ˈsæmpliŋ; ˋsæmplɪŋ] *n*. **1.** 取样(品),取标(本)〔指行动或程序〕。**2.** 样品,标本。**3.** 剽窃拼凑歌曲。~ **cock** 取样阀。~ **well** 取样井。

sam·sa·ra [səmˈsɑːrə; səmˋsɑrə] *n*.【佛教,印度教】轮回。

Sam·son [ˈsæmsn; ˋsæmsn], **Samp·son** [ˈsæpsn; ˋsæpsn] *n*. **1.** 萨姆森〔男子名〕。**2.**【圣】参孙〔《圣经》旧约中的力大无比的勇士〕。**3.** 大力士。~ **post**【海】(船上的)吊杆柱。

Sam·u·el [ˈsæmjuəl; ˋsæmjuəl] *n*. **1.** 塞缪尔〔男子名〕。**2.** 撒母耳〔《圣经》中人物,希伯来先知和领袖〕。**3.**《撒母耳记》〔《圣经》旧约全书篇名〕。

Sam·u·rai [ˈsæmurai; ˋsæmʊ͵raɪ] *n*.〔Jap.〕**1.** (日本封建时代的)武士,〔*pl*.〕武士阶级。**2.** 日本陆军军官;〔*pl*.〕日本军阀。~ **bond** "武士"债券〔非日本公司以日元面额发行的债券〕。

san [sæn; sɑn] *n*.〔口〕= **1.** sanatorium. **2.** sanitary. **3.** sanitation.

Sa·n'a, Sa·naa [sɑːˈnɑː; sɑˋnɑ] *n*. 沙那(萨那)〔也门首都〕。

san·a·tive [ˈsænətiv; ˋsænətɪv] *a*. **1.** 有疗效的;有益健康的。**2.**〔喻〕起纠正作用的。

san·a·to·ri·um [ˌsænəˈtɔːriəm; ͵sænəˋtɔrɪəm] *n*. (*pl*. ~*s*, *-ria* [-riə; -rɪə])〔主英〕**1.** 疗养院。**2.** (学校等机构中的)隔离病房。**3.** 疗养地,休养地 (=〔美〕sanitarium)。

san·a·to·ry [ˈsænətəri; ˋsænə͵torɪ] *a*. = sanative.

san·be·ni·to [ˌsænbeˈniːtəu; ͵sænbəˋnito] *n*. (*pl*. ~*s*)【宗史】**1.** (黄色的)悔罪服。**2.** (黑色的)地狱服〔被宗教裁判所判处火刑的异端者受刑时所穿〕。

San·cho Pan·za [ˈsæŋkəu ˈpænzə; ˋsæŋko ˋpænzə] 桑科·潘萨〔西班牙作家塞万提斯著名小说《唐吉诃德》中人物,唐吉诃德的仆人,无文化而有实际经验和富于常识,和唐吉诃德的耽于幻想形成对比〕。

San Cle·mente [ˌsæn kliˈmenti; ͵sæn ˋklɪmɛntɪ]〔美〕圣克利门蒂(岛)。

sanc·ti·fi·ca·tion [ˌsæŋktifiˈkeiʃən; ͵sæŋktəfəˋkeʃən] *n*. **1.** 神圣化;净化,奉献。**2.** 圣洁。

sanc·ti·fy [ˈsæŋktifai; ˋsæŋktə͵faɪ] *vt*. (*-fied*) **1.** 使神圣;使净化;把…奉献给神。**2.** 使圣洁;使纯洁。**3.** 使神圣不可侵犯。**4.** 使成为正当;认可;批准。**5.** 崇奉。**6.** 使能产生幸福。*sanctified airs* 神圣不可侵犯的神态;道貌岸然。

sanc·ti·mo·ni·ous [ˌsæŋktiˈməunjəs, -niəs; ͵sæŋktəˋmonɪəs] *a*. 假装神圣[虔诚]的;伪善的。**-ly** *ad*. **-ness** *n*.

sanc·ti·mo·ny [ˈsæŋktiməni; ˋsæŋktə͵monɪ] *n*. 假装神圣[虔诚];伪善。

sanc·tion [ˈsæŋkʃən; ˋsæŋkʃən] **I** *n*. **1.** 批准;准许;承认。**2.** 赏罚;处罚;【法】惩罚。**3.**〔主 *pl*.〕(对侵略者等的)制裁;良心制裁,制裁力,约束力。**4.**【史】法令。*social* ~ 社会的制裁。*moral* ~ 道德制裁。*punitive* [*vindicatory*] ~ 惩罚。***give*** ~ ***to*** 批准,同意。***suffer the last*** ~ ***of the law*** 被处死刑。***take*** ~***s against*** 对…采取制裁手段。**II** *vt*. **1.** 批准;认可;承认。**2.** 支持,赞许。

sanc·ti·ty [ˈsæŋktiti; ˋsæŋktətɪ] *n*. **1.** 神圣,圣洁。**2.** 尊严。**3.**〔*pl*.〕神圣的义务[感情(等)]。*the* ~ *of an*

S

oath 誓言的神圣性。*the sanctities of the home* 对家庭的神圣义务[感情]。

sanc·tu·a·ry [ˈsæŋktjuəri; ˋsæŋktʃʊˏɛrɪ] ***n*.** **1.** 圣所,圣堂;礼拜堂,神殿;至圣所〔犹太神殿内院藏经处〕;(教堂的)内殿。**2.** (罪犯等的)避难所;庇护所。**3.** (中世教堂等特有的)犯人庇护权。**4.** 禁猎期,禁猎区。*break* ~ 侵入教堂逮捕罪犯[行凶]。*take* ~ (逃入教堂)得到庇护。*a bird* ~ 鸟类禁猎地。

sanc·tum [ˈsæŋktəm; ˋsæŋktəm] ***n*.** **1.** 圣所;内殿。**2.** 〔口〕私室,书房。~ ***sanctorum*** **1.** 至圣所。**2.** 〔谑〕密室,私室。

sanc·tus [ˈsæŋktəs; ˋsæŋktəs] ***n*.** 【宗】三圣颂[曲]。~ **bell** (唱三圣颂时的)圣铃,圣钟。

sand [sænd; sænd] **I** ***n*.** **1.** 沙。**2.** 〔*pl*.〕沙滩,沙洲,沙地,沙漠。**3.** 〔*pl*.〕沙粒;(计时用的沙漏中的)细沙。**4.** 光阴,时间,寿命。**5.** 〔美俚〕勇气,毅力,胆量,坚毅。**6.** 【医】砂状结石。**7.** 【地】含石油砂层。**8.** 粗矿石;尾矿;【冶】模砂。**9.** 砂色;带红的黄色。**10.** 〔美俚〕砂糖。*quick* ~ 流沙。*play on the* ~*s* 在沙滩上玩耍。*The* ~*s* [*His* ~*s*] *are running out*. 期限快到[他的命数将尽]。*a man with plenty of* ~ *in him* 坚毅的人,刚强的人。***built on*** ~ 不稳固的;不安定的。***footprints on the*** ~***s of time*** 留在人世变迁的沙滩上的脚印。***have*** ~ ***in one's craw*** 〔美口〕有勇气[决断,毅力]。***knock the*** ~ ***from under*** 〔美〕使失去立足之地;(设法)占上风。***make ropes of*** ~ 用沙结绳;做不可能[徒劳无功]的事。***numberless as the*** ~(*s*) 多如恒河沙数。***number*** [***plough, sow***] ***the*** ~***s*** 白费气力,徒劳。***put*** ~ ***in the wheels*** [***machine***] 捣乱,暗中破坏。
II ***vt*.** **1.** 撒沙于,铺沙于,把…埋进沙里,用沙掺入。**2.** 用沙[砂纸]擦[磨光]。**3.** 使(船)开上沙滩。~ ***up*** 用沙填塞(油井等)。~ **bag** **1.** ***n*.** 沙包,沙袋。**2.** ***vt*.** 用沙包堵塞,堆上[放上]沙包;用沙包打,用沙包把…击昏[倒];〔美〕强迫,强制。**3.** ***vi*.** 〔口〕(体育比赛中)玩猫腻,以作弊手段让弱势方获胜或打平[如踢假球等]。~**-bank** 沙丘;沙洲。~ **bar** 沙洲,沙堤。~ **bath** **1.** 沙浴。**2.**【化】沙浴器。**3.**【地】沙盘〔用于土质分析〕。~**blast** **1.**【机】喷沙。**2.** 喷沙器。**3.** ***vt*.**, ***vi*.** 以喷沙器清洗[打磨]。~**-blind** 〔古〕视力极差的,半盲的,被沙蒙住眼睛的(~*-blind ostriches* 〔喻〕对外界事情视若无睹的人)。~**-box** **1.** (火车机车上的)沙箱。**2.** (翻砂用的)砂型。~ **box tree** 【植】(美洲热带的)沙匣树(*Hura crepitans*)。~**-break** 防沙林。~**-bur(r)**【植】**1.** 蒺藜草属(*Cenchrus*)植物。**2.** 龙葵(*Solanum rostratum*)。~**-casting**【机】沙型铸造。~ **cloud** 沙烟,沙漠热风。~ **crack**【兽医】裂蹄;(热沙上行人的)脚裂。~**culture**【农】沙中培养。~ **dab**【动】(北美洲西海岸)沙鲆。~ **dollar**【动】沙海胆,饼海胆。~ **drift** 流沙。~**-eel**【鱼】玉筋鱼。~**-flea** = sandhopper. ~**-fly**【虫】白蛉。~**-glass** (计时用的)沙漏。~**-grouse**【鸟】沙鸡。~**-hill** 沙丘。~**-hiller** 〔美俚〕(住在 Georgia 州等沙丘松林中的)穷白种人。~**-hog** 〔美俚〕挖沙工,水底工作的工人,隧道工人。~**-hopper**【动】沙蚤,矶蚤。~ **jack**【建】沙箱千斤顶。~ **la(u)nce**【动】= ~-eel. ~ **lily**【植】白文珠兰(*Leucocrinum montanum*)。~**-man** (童话中的)睡魔。~**-painting** "洒沙画符"治病法〔那伐鹤印第安人一种巫术〕;"洒沙符"的图案。~ **paper** **1.** ***n*** 砂纸。**2.** ***vt*.** 用砂纸擦[磨光]。~ **piper** ***n*.**【鸟】(矶)鹬。~**-pump**【机】扬沙泵,抽沙泵。~ **shoe** 〔英〕(沙滩上穿的)橡皮底布鞋。~ **sink** (消除海面油污的)沙沉法。~**-stone**【地】沙岩。~**-storm**【气】沙(风)暴。~ **trap** **1.**【高尔夫球】障碍沙坑。**2.** 集沙器。~ **verbena**【植】叶子花属(*Abronia*)植物,(尤指)黄叶子花,大花粉红叶子花。~ **wave** 砂波,砂浪〔沙漠或海底表面经常会移动的砂脊〕。~ **wort**【植】蚤缀属;鹅不食属(*Arenoria*)植物。

san·dal[1] [ˈsændl; ˋsændl] **I** ***n*.** **1.** 草带鞋;草鞋。**2.** 凉鞋。**3.** 便鞋。**II** ***vt*.** (**-*l*(*l*)-**) 使穿上凉鞋;给鞋上系襻。

san·dal[2] [ˈsændl; ˋsændl] ***n*.**【植】檀香木;白檀。*red* ~ 紫檀。~ **wood** ***n*.** 檀香木。

san·da·rac [ˈsændəræk; ˋsændəˏræk] ***n*.** **1.**【化】山达(树)脂。**2.**【植】北非山达树(*Tetraclinus articulata*),山达木。

sand·er·ling [ˈsændəliŋ; ˋsændəˏlɪŋ] ***n*.**【动】三趾鹬(*Crocethia alba*)。

san·dhi [ˈsɑːndhiː, -di; ˋsændhi, -dɪ] ***n*.**【语音】连音(变读),连接音变(例:"*t*"在 *picture* 中读为 [tʃ];"*am*"在 *I am glad* 中读为 [ˈm])。

Sand·hurst [ˈsændhəːst; ˋsændhɝst] ***n*.** **1.** 桑赫斯特〔英格兰南部一小镇〕。**2.** 英国陆军军官学校〔在桑赫斯特〕。*a* ~ *man* 〔英〕桑赫斯特陆军军官学校的学生[出身者]。

San Di·e·go [sæn di(ː)ˈeigəu; ˏsæn diˋego] ***n*.** 圣地亚哥(或译圣迭戈,圣地牙哥)〔美国 California 州南西海岸一港口,为著名的海军、海运基地〕。

Sand·i·ness [ˈsændinis; ˋsændɪnɪs] ***n*.** **1.** 沙质;多沙。**2.** 沙色。**3.** 流沙,不稳定状态。

san·di·ver [ˈsændivə; ˋsændɪvɚ] ***n*.** 浮沫〔玻璃溶液的浮渣废料如硫酸盐等〕。

sand·lot [ˈsændlɔt; ˋsændˏlɑt] **I** ***n*.** (市郊)空旷沙地〔供儿童进行游戏或运动之用〕。**II** ***a*.** (市郊)空旷沙地的。**-lot·ter** ***n*.** 在空旷沙地上游戏的人。

S and M = Sadism and Masochism 施虐和受虐(色情)狂。

Sand·wich [ˈsænwitʃ, -dʒ; ˋsænwɪtʃ, -dʒ] ***n*.** 三维治〔英国五港之一〕。

sand·wich [ˈsænwidʒ, -witʃ; ˋsændwɪtʃ] **I** ***n*.** 三明治,夹心面包片;三明治层状结构[物]。***ride*** [***sit***] ~ 夹坐二人中间。**II** ***vt*.** **1.** 把…夹[挤]在(两层[者])中间。**2.** 将…做成三明治。~ *an appointment in between two board meetings* 在两个重要会议的中间安排插入一次约会。~ **board** **1.** 挂在身体前后的广告牌。**2.** 胶合板。~ **boat** ***n*.** (牛津及剑桥大学划船赛中)一天中优组中最后,劣组中最前的船。~ **generation** 〔美〕"三明治"式一代〔指上有老下有小均需照顾的一代人〕。~ **man** ***n*.** (*pl*. **-men**) 身体前后挂着广告牌(在街头游行)的广告人。~ **shop** 小吃店。

sand·y [ˈsændi; ˋsændɪ] ***a*.** (**-*i*·*er*; -*i*·*est***) **1.** 沙的,沙质的,多沙的。**2.** 沙状的,(头发等)沙色的。**3.** (感觉等)粗涩的。**4.** 不稳固的,不稳定的。

Sand·y [ˈsændi; ˋsændɪ] ***n*.** **1.** 桑迪〔男子名,Alexander 的昵称〕。**2.** 苏格兰人的绰号。

sane [sein; sen] ***a*.** **1.** 神智清楚的;头脑清楚的;精神健全的(*opp*. insane)。**2.** 明智的;合乎情理的,稳健的。**3.** 〔罕〕健康的。*a* ~ *policy* 明智的政策。**-ly** ***ad*.** **-ness** ***n*.**

San Fair·y Ann [ˈsæn ˈfɛəri ˈæn; ˋsæn ˋfɛrɪ ˋæn] 〔军口〕不要紧,别怕(=〔F.〕*ça ne fait rien* [sɑ nə fɛ rjɛ])。

san·for·ized [ˈsænfəraizd; ˋsænfəˏraɪzd] ***a*.**【纺】(棉布)经过预缩水处理过的〔原为商标名桑福赖,指经机械方法抽缩使缩水率大为降低的〕。

San Fran·cis·co [ˌsæn frənˈsiskəu; ˏsænfrənˋsɪsko] ***n*.** 旧金山,三藩市〔美国港市〕。

sang[1] [sæŋ; sæŋ] sing 的过去式。

sang[2] [sæŋ; sæŋ] ***n*.** 〔美口〕参,人参(= ginseng)。

san·ga·ree [ˌsæŋgəˈriː; ˏsæŋgəˋri] ***n*.** 西班牙式桑格里酒〔用葡萄酒加水、糖、香料的一种冷饮〕。

sang-froid [ˈsɑ̃ːŋˈfrwɑː; sɑ̃ˋfrwɑ] ***n*.** 〔F.〕冷静,沉着,镇定(= cold blood)。

San·graal, -grail, -greal [sænˈgreil; sæŋˋgrel] ***n*.**【宗】圣杯〔传说中耶稣在最后的晚餐时所用的杯〕(= Grail)。

san·gri·a [sɑːnˈgriːɑː; sɑnˋgriɑ] ***n*.** = sangaree.

san·gui·na·ri·a [ˌsæŋgwiˈnɛəriə; ˏsæŋgwɪˋnɛrɪə] ***n*.** **1.**【植】血根草(属)(= bloodroot)。**2.** 美洲血根草〔含生物

碱,医用作催吐剂,祛痰剂〕。

san·gui·nar·y [ˈsæŋgwinəri; ˋsæŋgwɪnˏɛrɪ] ***a*.** **1.** 血腥的,血淋淋的;血迹斑斑的。**2.** 残暴的;嗜血的,好杀的,动辄判死刑的。**3.** (话)粗暴的,难听的(=〔英〕bloody)。*a* ~ *battle* 血战。~ *suppression* 血腥镇压。~ *hands* 沾满鲜血的双手。*a* ~ *fool* 大傻瓜。~ *language* 不堪入耳的话。**-ri·ly *ad*.**

san·guine [ˈsæŋgwin; ˋsæŋgwɪn] **I *a*.** **1.** 血红色的;(脸色等)有血色的,红润的;多血质的。**2.** 乐观的;充满自信[希望]的。**3.** 〔罕〕嗜血的,血腥的;残忍的;流血的。*a* ~ *lip* 红润的嘴唇。*a* ~ *person* 乐观自信的人。*a* ~ *nature* [*disposition*] 乐观开朗的性格。~ *slaughter* 血腥的屠杀。***be* ~ *of*** 自信,对…抱乐观。**II *n*.** **1.** 血红色,自信;抱乐观。**2.** (用氧化铁染色的)红粉笔。**3.** 红粉笔画。

san·guin·e·ous [sæŋˈgwiniəs; sæŋˋgwɪnɪəs] ***a*.** **1.** 血的,含有血的。**2.** 【植】血红色的;(动物)有血的。**3.** 多血的,多血质的。**4.** 乐观的,自信的。**5.** 〔罕〕血腥的,残忍的。

san·guin·in [ˈsæŋgwinin; ˋsæŋgwɪnɪn] ***n*.** 【生化】血素。

san·guin·o·lent [sæŋˈgwinələnt; sæŋˋgwɪnələnt] ***a*.** **1.** 血的,含血的,染上血的。**2.** 残酷的。

San·he·drim [ˈsænidrim; ˋsænɪˏdrɪm], **-hed·rin** [sænˈhedrin; sænˋhɛdrɪn] ***n*.** **1.** 【犹太史】最高法院〔古犹太国的最高法院兼参议会,由 71 人组成,兼管宗教事务〕。**2.** 〔S-〕会议,协议会。

san·i·cle [ˈsænikl; ˋsænɪkḷ] ***n*.** 【植】变豆菜〔原被认为具有愈合伤口的疗效〕。

sa·ni·es [ˈseiniiːz; ˋsenɪˏiz] ***n*.** 〔L.〕【医】稀脓,血脓。**-ni·ous *a*.**

san·i·fy [ˈsænifai; ˋsænəˏfaɪ] ***vt*.** (**-*fied***) **1.** 使卫生化,使健康化。**2.** 使具有卫生设备。

san·i·tar·i·an [ˌsæniˈtɛəriən; ˏsænəˋtɛrɪən] **I *a*.** (公共)卫生的。**II *n*.** (公共)卫生学家;保健专家。

san·i·ta·rist [ˈsænitərist; ˋsænətərɪst] ***n*.** = sanitarian.

san·i·tar·i·um [ˌsæniˈtɛəriəm; ˏsænəˋtɛrɪəm] ***n*.** (*pl*. ~*s*, *-i·a* [-riə; -rɪə]) 〔美〕= sanatorium.

san·i·ta·ry [ˈsænitəri; ˋsænəˏtɛrɪ] **I *a*.** 卫生(上)的。*a* ~ *cup* 卫生纸杯(用过一次就废弃)。*a* ~ *engineer* 卫生技师,卫生工程学家;(厕所等的)管道工人。*a* ~ *inspector* 卫生检查官。~ *regulations* 卫生规则。~ *science* 公共卫生学。*a* ~ *towel* [*napkin*, *belt*] 月经带。**II *n*.** (有卫生设备的)公共厕所。~ **cordon** 防疫地带、传染病流行区边界上布置的防疫警卫人员。~ **engineer** (负责策划和管理供水系统、大气污染标准等的)卫生工程师。~ **engineering** 卫生工程学〔如给水排水〕。**-ri·ly *ad*.** **-ri·ness *n*.**

san·i·ta·tion [ˌsæniˈteiʃən; ˏsænəˋteʃən] ***n*.** **1.** 公共卫生,环境卫生。**2.** 卫生设备,(尤指)下水道设备,卫生状况改善。*environmental* ~ 环境卫生。~ **engineer** 〔婉,美〕环卫师〔指垃圾清洁工等,有别于 sanitary engineer〕。~**man** 〔美〕环境卫生员〔简称 sandman〕。

san·i·tize [ˈsænitaiz; ˋsænəˏtaɪz] ***vt*.** (**-*tiz·ed***; **-*tizing***) **1.** 使卫生〔如以灭菌、消毒方法〕。**2.** 使免除有害的东西,使具有良好外观,使消除不良印象。**-r *n*.** (食物加工设备所用的)消毒杀菌剂。

san·i·ty [ˈsæniti; ˋsænətɪ] ***n*.** **1.** 神志清楚,头脑清楚,精神健全,(*opp*. insanity)。**2.** 明智;合乎情理;稳健。*lose one's* ~ 失去理智,发狂。

san·jak [ˈsændʒæk; ˋsændʒæk] ***n*.** 〔Turk.〕州,行政区。

San Jo·sé [ˌsɑːn həuˈsei; ˏsæn (h)oˋze] ***n*.** 圣约瑟〔哥斯达黎加首都〕。

San Jo·se scale [ˈsænhəuˈzei skeil; ˋsænhoˋze skel] ***n*.** 【动】歎蝗〔一种有害于果树的甲虫〕。

San Juan [sænˈhwɑːn; sænˋ(h)wɑn] ***n*.** 圣胡安〔波多黎各首府,在西印度群岛〕。

sank [sæŋk; sæŋk] sink 的过去式。

San·khya [ˈsɑːŋkjə; ˋsɑŋkjə] ***n*.** 僧佉,数论(派)〔印度哲学六正统派中最古一派〕(= Samkhya)。

San Ma·ri·no [ˌsæn məˈriːnəu; ˏsæn məˋrino] ***n*.** 圣马力诺〔意大利半岛东部的一小国〕。

san·nup [ˈsænʌp; ˋsænʌp] ***n*.** 〔美〕印第安人的已婚男子。

san·pro [ˈsænprəu; ˋsænpro] ***n*.** 〔口〕月经保洁用品〔系 sanitary protection 的缩略〕。

sans[1] [sænz; sænz] ***prep*.** 〔古、诗〕无。~ *teeth*, ~ *eyes*, ~ *taste*, ~ *everything* 无齿,无眼,无味,无一切〔指老人,莎士比亚: *As You Like* It II vii. 166 中用语〕。

sans[2] [sɑ̃; sɑ̃] ***prep*.** 〔F.〕= without 〔主要在下列成语中〕。~ ***cérémonie*** [ˈseremɔniː; ˋsɛrɛmɑni] 不拘礼节,没礼貌地。~ ***doute*** [ˈduːt; ˋdut] 无疑。~ ***façon*** [ˈfæsɔ̃ːŋ; ˋfæsɔ̃ːŋ] 坦率地,不客气地。~ ***gêne*** [ˈʒein; ˋʒɛn] 不拘束。~ ***pareil*** [ˈpæˈrei; ˋpæˋre] 无比的。~ ***peur et*** ~ ***reproche*** [ˈpəː ei rəˈprɔʃ; ˋpɝ e rəˋprɑʃ] 无所畏惧,无可非议〔指骑士的性格〕。~ ***phrase*** [ˈfrɑːz; ˋfræz] 不啰唆地,直截了当地。~ ***souci*** [suːˈsiː; suˋsi] 无忧无虑,逍遥自在。

Sans., **Sansk.** = Sanskrit.

San Sal·va·dor [sæn ˈsælvədɔː; sæn ˋsælvəˏdɔr] ***n*.** 圣萨尔瓦多〔萨尔瓦多首都〕。

sans·cu·lotte [ˌsænzkjuˈlɔt; ˏsænzkjʊˋlɑt] ***n*.** **1.** 【史】无套裤汉〔法国大革命时期贵族阶级对急进的共和主义者的蔑称〕。**2.** 下层阶级的人;缺乏教养的人。**3.** 急进主义者;过激分子。**-tic**, **-tish *a*.**, **-tism *n*.** 急进共和主义。

san·sei, S- [ˈsɑːnsei; ˋsɑnse] ***n*.** (*pl*. ~(*s*)) 〔美〕第三代美籍日人〔其祖父为日本移民〕。

san·ser·if [sænˈserif; sænˋsɛrɪf] ***a*.**, ***n*.** 【印】没有衬线的(铅字)。

san·se·vi·e·ri·a [ˌsænsiˈviəriə, -viˈiːriə; ˏsænsəˋvɪrɪə] ***n*.** 【植】虎尾兰属植物。

San·skrit [ˈsænskrit; ˋsænskrɪt] ***n*.**, ***a*.** 梵语(的),梵文(的)。**-ist *n*.** 梵语学家。**-ic *a*.**

sans·ser·if [sænˈserif; sænˋsɛrɪf] ***n*.** = sanserif.

San·ta **1.** [ˈsæntə; ˋsæntə] 〔美〕= Santa Claus. **2.** [ˈsæntə; ˋsɑntɑ] ***n*.** 〔Sp., It.〕= Saint.

San·ta Claus, **Santa Klaus** [ˌsæntəˈklɔːz; ˋsæntɪˏklɔz] 圣诞老人。

San·ta Cruz de Te·ne·rife [ˌsæntə ˌkruːz də tenəˈriːf; ˋsæntə ˋkruz dəˏtenəˋrif] ***n*.** 圣克鲁斯德特内里费〔西班牙加那利(Canary)群岛中特内里费岛的一海港〕。

San·ta Ger·tru·dis [ˈsætəgə ˈtruːdis; ˋsætəgɚ ˋtrudɪs] ***n*.** 〔美〕【动】圣格特鲁地斯菜牛〔美国德克萨斯州的一种杂交肉用牛,可在炎热而饲料稀少的环境里繁殖〕。

San·ta Is·a·bel [ˈsæntə ˈizəbel; ˋsæntə ˋɪzəbel] ***n*.** 圣伊萨贝尔〔赤道几内亚首都的旧称,现称马拉博(Malabo)〕。

San·ta Ma·ri·a [ˈsætə məˈriə, Sp. ˈsɑːntɑː mɑːˈriːɑː; ˋsæntə məˋriə] **1.** 圣玛利亚号〔1492 年哥伦布航海用的旗舰〕。**2.** 圣玛利亚〔危地马拉西南部的一个活火山〕。

San·tia·go [ˌsæntiˈɑːgəu; ˏsæntɪˋɑgo] ***n*.** 圣地牙[亚]哥〔智利首都〕。

San·to Do·min·go [ˈsæntəu dəˈmiŋgəu; ˋsæntodəˋmɪŋgo] ***n*.** 圣多明各〔多米[明]尼加首都,位于海地岛东部〕。

san·ton [ˈsæntən; ˋsæntən] ***n*.** (伊斯兰教的)修士,隐士。

san·ton·i·ca [sænˈtɔnikə; sænˋtɑnɪkə] ***n*.** 【植】蒿属植物;(尤指)山道年草;山道年花。

san·to·nin [ˈsæntənin; ˋsæntənɪn] ***n*.** 【药】山道年〔驱蛔虫药〕。

São To·mé [sɑ̃u tɔːˈme; ˋsɑ̃ʊn tuˋmɛ] ***n*.** 圣多[图]美〔圣多[图]美和普林西比首都〕。**São Tomé and Prinsipe** [ˈprinsipə; ˋprɪnsɪpə] 圣多[图]美和普林西比〔非洲〕。

sap[1][sæp; sæp] I *n*. 1. 树液,(树皮下的)白木质。2. 体液,生命液;元气,精力,活力。*the ~ of life* 元气,精力。*the ~ of youth* 青年的活力。II *vt*. (*-pp-*) 榨取…的树液;去除…的白木质;使衰弱[衰竭]。~ **green** 暗绿色,一种暗绿色的颜料。~ **sucker** 一种以树汁为食的啄木鸟。~ **wood** (树皮下较软的)白木质,边材〔心材外增生的木质部〕。

sap[2][sæp; sæp] I *n*. 1.【军】(袭击敌人用的)坑道,对壕。2. 坑道的挖掘。3. 暗中的破坏,逐步的损坏,削弱。II *vt*., *vi*. (*-pp-*) 1. (在…下面)挖掘使倒塌;(使)逐渐损坏,(使)逐渐削弱。2. 挖坑道进攻[逼近]。3. (水等)逐渐浸蚀。4. 暗中颠覆。~ *a wall* 挖墙脚。~ *a line of trenches* 挖掘坑道逐渐逼近(敌方)防线。~**head**【军】坑道头。

sap[3][sæp; sæp] I *n*. 1. 〔英学生俚〕用功读书的人;埋头工作的人。2. 〔口〕讨厌的工作,苦活。3. 〔美、俚〕= saphead. 4. 〔美俚〕棍子。*It is such a ~*. 这事真麻烦。II *vt*. (*-pp-*)〔美俚〕用棍子打。— *vi*. 〔英学生俚〕死用功。~**head**〔美口〕傻瓜,笨蛋。

SAP = semi-armour-piercing 半穿甲。

sap·a·jou [ˈsæpədʒuː; ˋsæpədʒu] *n*.【动】卷尾猴 (= capuchin)。

sap·an·wood, sap·pan·wood [ˈsæpənwud; səˋpæn-ˏwʊd] *n*.【植】(可提取红染料的)苏方,苏木。

sap·ful [ˈsæpful; ˋsæpfəl] *a*. 树液多的。

sa·phe·na [səˈfiːnə; səˋfinə] *n*.【解】隐静脉。**-nous** [-nəs] *a*.

sap·id [ˈsæpid; ˋsæpɪd] *a*. 1. (食物等)有味道的,有风味的,滋味好的。2. (书等)有趣味的 (*opp*. insipid)。**-i·ty** *n*. 1. 味道,风味,滋味。2. (书等的)趣味。

sa·pi·ence, -en·cy [ˈseipiəns, -si; ˋsepɪəns, -sɪ] *n*. 〔常讽〕(外表上的)学识丰富;智慧;精明。

sa·pi·ens [ˈsæpiəns; ˋsæpɪəns] *a*. 〔L.〕(类似)现代人的。***homo ~*** 人类。

sa·pi·ent [ˈseipiənt; ˋsepɪənt] I *a*. 〔常讽〕1. (貌似)学识丰富的,有高深知识的。2. 聪明的,明智的;精明的。II *n*. 早期人类,史前人。

sa·pi·en·tial [ˌseipiˈenʃəl; ˏsepɪˋenʃəl] *a*. 〔罕〕智慧的;有智慧的;使人增长智慧的。

sap·less [ˈsæplis; ˋsæplɪs] *a*. 1. 无树液的;枯萎的。2. 没有元气的,没有精力的,没有活力的。3. 乏味的,没趣味的。

sap·ling [ˈsæpliŋ; ˋsæplɪŋ] *n*. 1. (直径 3—4 英寸的)树苗;幼树。2. 年轻人。3.【动】仔灵鶠〔一岁以内的〕。*grow ~s* 培育树苗。

sap·o·dil·la [ˌsæpəˈdilə; ˏsæpəˋdɪlə] I *n*.【植】人心果(树)〔美洲热带所产的一种大常青树〕。II *a*. 山榄科 (*Sapotaceae*) 的。

sap·o·na·ceous [ˈsæpəuˈneiʃəs; ˏsæpəˋneʃəs] *a*. 1. 皂质[状]的。2. 难于捕捉的;善于闪避的,圆滑的。

sa·pon·i·fi·ca·tion [səˌpɔnifiˈkeiʃən; səˏpɑnəfəˋkeʃən] *n*.【化】皂化(作用)。

sa·pon·i·fy [səˈpɔnifai; səˋpɑnəˏfaɪ] *vt*., *vi*. (*-fied*)【化】(使)皂化,(使)碱解。**-i·fi·a·ble** *a*. 可皂化的。**-i·fi·er** *n*. 皂化剂。

sap·o·nin [ˈsæpənin; ˋsæpənɪn] *n*.【化】皂角苷。

sap·o·nite [ˈsæpənait; ˋsæpəˏnaɪt] *n*.【矿】皂石。

sa·por [ˈseipɔː; ˋsepɔr] *n*. 1. (物质中能产生味觉的)滋味;味。2. 风味。亦作 **sa·pour**.

sa·po·ta [səˈpəutə; səˋpotə] *n*. = sapodilla.

sa·po·te [səˈpəutiː; səˋpoti] *n*.【植】1. 美洲几种热带树或其果实。2. 美果榄 (= marmalade tree) 〔产于美洲热带地区〕。3. = sapodilla.

sap·per [ˈsæpə; ˋsæpɚ] *n*. 1. 坑道[地雷]工兵。2. 挖掘者[器]。

Sap·phic [ˈsæfik; ˋsæfɪk] I *a*. 1. 希腊女诗人莎孚 (Sappho) 的;莎孚式(诗体)的。2. 〔亦作 s-〕女性同性恋的。II *n*. 〔*pl*.〕莎孚式诗(体)。~ *vice* = Sapphism.

sap·phire [ˈsæfaiə; ˋsæfaɪr] I *n*. 1.【矿】蓝宝石。2. 天蓝色,蔚蓝色。II *a*. 天蓝色的;蔚蓝色的。

sap·phir·ine [ˈsæfərain; ˋsæfərɪn] I *a*. 1. 像蓝宝石的。2. 蓝宝石色的,天蓝色的。3. 蓝宝石制的。II *n*.【矿】假蓝宝石。

sap·phism [ˈsæfizəm; ˋsæfɪzm] *n*. 女子(间的)同性恋。

Sap·pho [ˈsæfəu; ˋsæfo] *n*. 莎孚〔公元前六世纪前后的希腊女诗人〕。

Sa·ppo·ro [səˈpɔːrəu; ˋsɑpporo] *n*. 札幌〔日本城市〕。

sap·py [ˈsæpi; ˋsæpɪ] *a*. (*-pi·er*; *-pi·est*) 1. 多树液的;似白木质的,含大量白木质的。2. 精力充沛的;年富力壮的。3. 〔俚〕愚蠢的;傻;易于伤感到愚蠢程度的。

sapr- *comb*. *f*. 〔辅[子]音前用 sapro- 〕表示"腐败,死": *sapr*aemia; *sapr*ophagous.

sa·pr(a)e·mi·a [sæˈpriːmiə; səˋprimɪə] *n*.【医】腐血症,脓毒中毒。**sap·r(a)e·mic** *a*.

sapro- *comb*. *f*. 表示"腐(败),死": *sapro*be; *sapro*pel.

sap·robe [ˈsæprəub; ˋsæprob] *n*.【生】污水生物。

sap·ro·bic [sæˈprəubik; səˋprobɪk] *a*.【生】1. 污水生物的。2. 腐生植物的。**-bi·cal·ly** *ad*.

sap·ro·gen·ic [ˌsæprəuˈdʒenik; ˏsæprəˋdʒenɪk] *a*.【植】腐生的 (= saprogenous)。

sap·ro·lite [ˈsæprəulait; ˋsæprəˏlaɪt] *n*.【地】腐泥土。**-lit·ic** [ˌsæprəuˈlitik; ˏsæproˋlɪtɪk] *a*.

sap·ro·pel [ˈsæprəupel; ˋsæprəˏpel] *n*.【地】湖泥(腐植质);腐植泥。**-ic** [-ˈpelik; -ˋpelɪk] *a*.

sa·proph·a·gous [səˈprɔfəgəs; səˋprɑfəgəs] *a*.【动】食腐的。

sap·ro·phyte [ˈsæprəufait; ˋsæproˏfaɪt] *n*.【生】腐生植物;腐生生物;腐生菌。

sap·ro·zo·ic [ˌsæprəuˈzəuik; ˏsæprəˋzoɪk] I *a*.【生】1. 食腐的。2. 腐物寄生的。II *n*. 食腐动物。

sap·sa·go [sæpˈseigəu; ˋsæpsəˏgo] *n*.【美】瑞士(产)绿干酪。

Sar. = 1. Sardinia. 2. Sardinian.

SAR, S.A.R. = 1. Sons of the American Revolution. 2. South African Republic. 3. Special Administrative Region 特别行政区。

sar·a·band [ˈsærəbænd; ˋsærəˏbænd] *n*. 1. (西班牙慢拍子)撒拉本舞。2. 撒拉本舞曲。

Sar·a·cen [ˈsærəsn; ˋsærəsn] I *n*. 撒拉逊人〔原为叙利亚附近一游牧民族,后特指抵抗十字军的伊斯兰教阿拉伯人,现泛指伊斯兰教徒或阿拉伯人〕。II *a*. 撒拉逊人的。~ **corn** [**wheat**] 荞麦。**-ic** [ˌsærəˈsenik; ˏsærəˋsenɪk] *a*.

Sar·ah [ˈsɛərə; ˋsɛrə] *n*. 萨拉〔女子名,昵称 Sadie, Sal〕。

SARAH = search and rescue and homing 搜索救援的归航无线电信标。

Sa·ra·je·vo [ˌsærəˈjeivou; ˏsærəˋjevo] *n*. 萨拉热窝(又译塞拉耶佛)〔南斯拉夫一城市〕。

sa·ran [səˈræn; səˋræn] *n*.【化】萨冉树脂;莎纶〔氯乙烯,二氯乙烯共聚纤维〕。

sa·rape [səˈrɑːpi; səˋræpɪ] *n*. = serape.

Sar·a·to·ga [ˌsærəˈtəugə; ˏsærəˋtogə] *n*. 1. 萨拉托加〔美纽约州东部一村落,附近有温泉疗养地〕。2. 〔美〕女用旅行箱〔= ~ trunk〕。~ **chips** [**potato**]〔美〕油炸马铃薯片。

Sa·ra·wak [səˈrɑːwək; səˋrɑwɑk] *n*. 沙劳越〔马来西亚的一个邦〕。

sarc- *comb*. *f*. 〔用于元[母]音前〕= sarco-.

sar·casm [ˈsɑːkæzəm; ˋsɑrkæzəm] *n*. 1. 讽刺,讥讽,挖苦。2. 讽刺话,挖苦话。*squelch sb*. *with biting ~* 用尖刻的挖苦话压服人。

sar·cas·tic, -ti·cal [sɑːˈkæstik(əl); sɑrˋkæstɪk(l)] *a*. 讽刺的,讥讽的,挖苦的。**-ti·cal·ly** *ad*.

sarce·net [ˈsɑːsnet; ˋsɑrsnɪt] *n*. = sarsenet.

sarco- *comb. f.* 表示"肉": *sarco*carp; *sarco*logy.
sar·co·carp [ˈsɑːkəukɑːp; ˋsarkoˏkarp] ***n.*** 【植】**1.** (桃杏等的)果肉。**2.** 肉(质)果皮。**3.** 多果肉的果子。
sar·code [ˈsɑːkəud; ˋsarkod] ***n.*** 【生】原肉质。**-cod·ic** [ˈsɑːˈkɔdik; ˋsarˋkadɪk] ***a.***
sar·coid [ˈsɑːkɔid; ˋsarkɔɪd] ***a.*** 肉的,肉状的。
sar·coid·o·sis [ˌsɑːkɔiˈdəusis; ˏsarkɔɪˋdosɪs] ***n.*** 【医】肉样瘤病,类肉瘤病。
sar·col·o·gy [sɑːˈkɔlədʒi; sarˋkalədʒɪ] ***n.*** 【医】软组织解剖学;肌肉学。
sar·co·ma [sɑːˈkəumə; sarˋkomə] ***n.*** (*pl.* **~s**, ***-ta*** [-tə; -tə]) 【医】肉瘤。
sar·coph·a·gus [sɑːˈkɔfəgəs; sarˋkafəgəs] ***n.*** (*pl.* ***-gi*** [-gai, -dʒai; -gaɪ, -dʒaɪ], *~es*) (雕花大理石)石棺。
sar·co·sine [ˈsɑːkəsiːn; ˋsarkəsin] ***n.*** 【化】肌氨[胺]酸。
sar·cous [ˈsɑːkəs; ˋsarkəs] ***a.*** 肉的,肌肉(组成)的。
sard [sɑːd; sard] ***n.*** 【矿】肉红玉髓,黄玉髓。
sar·da·na [sɑːˈdɑːnə; sarˋdanə] ***n.*** **1.** 萨达纳舞〔西班牙加泰罗[隆]尼亚的一种民间舞蹈〕。**2.** 萨达纳舞曲。
Sar·da·na·pa·li·an [ˌsɑːdənəˈpeiliən; ˏsardənəˋpelɪən] ***a.*** 亚述 (Assyria) 王沙达那帕鲁斯 (Sardanapalus) 似的,荒淫的;穷奢极欲的。
sar·dine[1] [sɑːˈdiːn; sarˋdin] ***n.*** (*pl.* ~(*s*)) **1.** 【鱼】鳁鱼,沙丁鱼。**2.** 〔俚〕庸碌无能的人。*be packed like ~s* 拥挤不堪。**~-fit** ***a.*** 拥挤不堪的。
sar·dine[2] [ˈsɑːdain; ˋsardɪn] ***n.*** = sard.
Sar·din·ia [sɑːˈdinjə; sarˋdɪnɪə] ***n.*** 撒[萨]丁(岛)〔意大利在地中海上的一大岛〕。
Sar·din·i·an [sɑːˈdiniən; sarˋdɪnɪən] **I** ***a.*** **1.** 撒[萨]丁(岛)的。**2.** 撒[萨]丁(岛)人的。**3.** 撒[萨]丁(岛)语的。**II** ***n.*** **1.** 撒[萨]丁(岛)人。**2.** 撒[萨]丁(岛)语。
sar·di·us [ˈsɑːdiəs; ˋsardɪəs] ***n.*** **1.** = sard. **2.** 【圣】希伯来高级祭司胸饰上的宝石。
sar·don·ic [sɑːˈdɔnik; sarˋdanɪk] ***a.*** 嘲笑的,讥笑的,冷笑的,讥讽的。*a ~ laugh* [*chuckle, smile*] 冷笑。**-al·ly** ***ad.***
sar·do·nyx [ˈsɑːdəniks; ˋsardənɪks] ***n.*** 【矿】缠丝玛瑙。
sar·gas·so [sɑːˈgæsəu; sarˋgæso] ***n.*** (*pl.* ~(*e*)*s*) 【植】果囊马尾藻 (= ~ weed)。
sar·gas·sum [sɑːˈgæsəm; sarˋgæsəm] ***n.*** = sargasso.
sarge [sɑːdʒ; sardʒ] ***n.*** 〔美俚〕= sergeant.
sa·ri, sa·ree [ˈsɑːriː; ˋsari] ***n.*** (*pl.* ***-ris***) (印度女人披在身上的)卷布,莎丽服。
sark [sɑːk; sark] ***n.*** 〔Scot.〕衬衣。
Sar·ma·tian [sɑːˈmɑːʃən; sarˋmaʃən] **I** ***a.*** (古时东欧地区维斯杜拉河和伏尔加河之间的)萨尔马提亚的;萨尔马提亚人的。**II** ***n.*** 萨尔马提亚人。
sar·men·tose [sɑːˈmentəus; sarˋmɛntos] ***a.*** 【植】具长匐茎的。
sa·rod, sa·rode [səˈrəud; səˋrod] ***n.*** 萨洛德琴〔类似琵琶的一种印度乐器〕。
sa·rong [ˈsɑːrɔŋ; səˋrɔŋ] ***n.*** (马来民族男女穿的)围裙,莎笼。
sar·os [ˈsɛərɔs; ˋsɛras] ***n.*** 【天】(日蚀和月蚀的)沙罗周期〔计 18 年又 11½ 天,为日蚀和月蚀关系的反复周期〕。
sar·ra·ce·ni·a [ˌsærəˈsiːniə; ˏsærəˋsinɪə] ***n.*** 【植】美洲瓶子植物。
sar·sa·pa·ril·la [ˌsɑːsəpəˈrilə; ˏsarspəˋrɪlə] ***n.*** **1.** 【植】菝葜;菝葜根〔美洲产的热带植物〕。**2.** 菝葜精(香料)。**3.** 菝葜(为香料所做的)汽水。
sarse·net [ˈsɑːsnit; ˋsarsnɪt] ***n.*** 里子薄绸[素纺,棉布];平纹丝带 (= sarcenet, sarsnet)。
sar·tor [ˈsɑːtə; ˋsartɚ] ***n.*** 裁缝,成衣匠〔文学或幽默用语〕。
sar·to·ri·al [sɑːˈtɔːriəl; sarˋtorɪəl] ***a.*** **1.** 裁缝的;缝纫的;衣服的〔文学或幽默用语〕。**2.** 【解】缝匠肌的。*a ~ triumph* 〔谑〕缝制得极好的衣服。*the ~ art* 〔谑〕裁缝艺术。
sar·to·ri·us [sɑːˈtɔriəs; sarˋtɔrɪəs] ***n.*** 【解】(大腿上的)缝匠肌。
SAS = Scandinavian Airlines System 斯堪的纳维亚航空公司。
sas 〔口〕= sarsaparilla.
SASE = self-addressed stamped envelope 回邮信封。
Sa·se·bo [ˈsɑːsəbɔː; ˋsɑsebo] ***n.*** 佐世保〔日本港市〕。
sash[1] [sæʃ; sæʃ] **I** ***n.*** **1.** (妇女、儿童用的)饰带,腰带。**2.** 【军】肩带,绶带,值星带。**II** ***vt.*** 用饰带装饰;给…系上腰带[饰带]。
sash[2] [sæʃ; sæʃ] **I** ***n.*** 窗框,门框;门窗的框格;吊窗;一组这样的窗框。**II** ***vt.*** 在…上装吊窗;给…装上窗格。~ **cord**, ~ **line** 吊窗绳。~ **pocket** 吊窗锤的滑槽。~ **pulley** 吊窗滑轮。~ **rope**, ~ **tape** = ~ line. ~ **weights** 〔*pl.*〕吊窗锤。~ **window** 吊窗;上下拉动的窗。
sa·shay [sæˈʃei; sæˋʃɚ] ***vi.*** **1.** 〔美口〕走〔特指漫不经心或大摇大摆地〕。**2.** (舞蹈中)用快滑步前进。**3.** 斜向行进[移动]。
sa·shi·mi [sɑːˈʃiːmiː; sɑˋʃimi] ***n.*** 〔*pl.*〕生鱼片〔日本菜肴〕。
sas·ka·toon [ˌsæskəˈtuːn; ˏsæskəˋtun] ***n.*** 〔主加〕= juneberry.
Sas·quatch [ˈsæsˌkwɔtʃ; ˋsæsˏkwatʃ] ***n.*** (传说中的)野人。
sass [sæs; sæs] **I** ***n.*** **1.** 蔬菜;(餐末吃的)煮水果。**2.** 〔美俚〕唐突;顶嘴。**II** ***vt.*** 对…说唐突话,和…顶嘴,对…出言不逊。**~-box** 〔美〕说话唐突的人,冒失鬼〔亦作 savce〕。
sas·sa·by [ˈsæsəbi; ˋsæsəbɪ] ***n.*** (*pl.* ***-bies***) 【动】(南非产的)大羚羊。
sas·sa·fras [ˈsæsəfræs; ˋsæsəˏfræs] ***n.*** **1.** 【植】檫树;黄樟,美洲檫木。**2.** 檫木的根和皮〔含芳香挥发油〕。
Sas·sa·nid [ˈsæsənid; ˋsæsənɪd] ***n.*** (*pl.* **~s**, ***Sas·san·i·dae*** [sæˈsænidiː; sæˋsænɪdi]) 萨珊王(朝)〔公元 226? —641 年间波斯萨珊王朝,或其中任何一个君王〕(= Sassanian, Sasanian)。
Sas·se·nach [ˈsæsənæk; ˋsæsnˏæk] ***n.***, ***a.*** 〔Scot.; Ir. 贬〕撒克逊(血统的)人(的);苏格兰[苏格兰低地]人(的)。
sass·y [ˈsæsi; ˋsæsɪ] ***a.*** (***-i·er***; ***-i·est***) **1.** 〔美方〕莽撞的,冒昧的;脸皮厚的,不顾一切的,唐突的,孟浪的,无礼的。**2.** 漂亮的,时髦的,俊俏的,很帅的(= saucy)。
sas·sy bark 【植】**1.** 基尼格木皮。**2.** 基尼格木 (*Erythrophleum guineense*)〔产于非洲〕(= sassywood)。
Sat. = **1.** Saturday. **2.** Saturn.
sat [sæt; sæt] sit 的过去式及过去分词。
SAT = Scholastic Aptitude Test 学术才能测验。
Sa·tan [ˈseitən; ˋsetn] ***n.*** 撒旦,〔s-〕恶魔,魔王。
sa·tang [sɑːˈtæŋ; sɑˋtæŋ] ***n.*** 〔*sing.*, *pl.*〕萨[撒]当〔泰国货币名,硬币,等于 1/100 铢 (Thai baht)〕。
sa·tan·ic, -i·cal [səˈtænik, -ikəl; seˋtænɪk] ***a.*** **1.** 恶魔的;魔王的。**2.** 似恶魔的;邪恶的;蔑视(宗教)道德的。**3.** 丑恶的,极恶劣的。***His S- Majesty*** 〔谑〕魔王。~ ***energy*** 超人的精力。**-i·cal·ly** ***ad.***
Sa·tan·ism [ˈseitənizəm; ˋsetənɪzm] ***n.*** **1.** 恶魔主义,魔鬼崇拜。**2.** 魔鬼行为;恶魔性格;穷凶极恶。
Sa·tan·ist [ˈseitənist; ˋsetənɪst] ***n.*** **1.** 恶魔主义[崇拜]者。**2.** 本性邪恶者。
S.A.T.B. = soprano, alto, tenor, bass.
satch·el [ˈsætʃəl; ˋsætʃəl] ***n.*** **1.** 小背包;(小学生用的)书包。**2.** 【军】图囊。~ **charges** 【军】炸药包。
satch·el(l)·ed [ˈsætʃəld; ˋsætʃəld] ***a.*** 背[有]着小背包[书包]的。
SATCOM = 〔美〕Satellite Communication Agency (陆军)卫星通信机构。
SATCOMA = Satellite Communications Centre 卫星通

信中心。

sate[1][seit; set] *vt*.〔主用被动语态〕**1.** 使饱,喂饱。**2.** 使心满意足。**3.** 使餍足,使腻。*be ~d with* 吃饱,饱享,吃腻,餍足。~ *oneself with* **1.** 饱餐。**2.** 大量享受。

sate[2][sæt, seit; set] sit 的古体过去式及过去分词(= sat)。

sat·een [sæˈtiːn; sæˋtin] *n*.【纺】棉缎,缎纹布;纬缎;横贡。

sate·less [ˈseitlis; ˋsetlɪs] *a*.〔诗〕**1.** 不知饱的。**2.** 无餍的,不知足的。

sat·el·lite [ˈsætəlait; ˋsætlˏaɪt] **I** *n*. **1.**【天】卫星;人造卫星;〔喻〕卫星国。**2.** 随从,帮闲者,食客。**3.**【生】随体(指染色体);陪簇虫;【地】伴生矿物;伴线。**4.** 附属社区,卫星区,郊区。**5.** 附属品。*an artificial* [*earth*] ~ 人造[地球]卫星。*a multistage* ~ 多级人造卫星。**II** *vt*. 通过通讯卫星播送[传播]。~ **dish** 卫星电视碟形[抛物面形]。~ **dish** 碟状卫星信号接收器,卫星碟。~ **DNA**【生】随体去氧核糖核酸。~ **phone** 卫星电话〔通过卫星通信网络的移动电话〕。~ **town** 卫星城。**-lit·ic** [ˌsætəˈlitik; ˏsætəˋlɪtɪk] *a*. 卫星的。

sat·el·oid [ˈsætələid; ˋsætələɪd] *n*. **1.** (因速度较慢而不能作长时间轨道运行的)太空船。**2.** (一种半飞机、半人造卫星式)有人驾驶的太空船。

sa·tem [ˈsɑːtəm, ˈseit-; ˋsɑtəm, ˋset-] *a*.【语言】咝音语言的〔指原始印欧语中阻塞音已变为咝音的语言,而有别于腭音语言(centum)〕。

sa·ti [səˈtiː; səˋti] *n*. = suttee.

sa·ti·a·ble [ˈseiʃiəbl; ˋseʃɪəbl̩] *a*. 可使饱的,可使餍足的;可使满足的。**-bly** *ad*.

sa·ti·ate [ˈseiʃieit; ˋseʃɪˏet] **I** *vt*. = sate[1]. **II** [ˈseiʃiit; ˋseʃɪɪt] *a*.〔诗〕饱足的,吃饱的;满足的。

sa·ti·a·tion [ˌseiʃiˈeiʃən; ˏseʃɪˋeʃən] *n*. = satiety.

sa·ti·e·ty [səˈtaiəti; səˋtaɪətɪ] *n*. **1.** 饱食;餍足,饱足。**2.** 许多,过多(*of*)。*to* ~ 饱饱地,充分地。

sat·in [ˈsætin; ˋsætɪn] **I** *n*. **1.** 缎子;【纺】缎纹;经缎组织;经面缎纹。**2.**〔俚〕杜松子酒。*the* ~ *of a fine skin* 缎子一样的皮肤。*the* ~ *of the coat of a horse* 缎子一样光滑柔软的马毛。~ *cloth* 有光缎纹细呢。~ *double face* 双面缎。*figured* ~ 花缎。~ *finish* (银器等的)擦光处理。*white* ~〔俚〕杜松子酒。**II** *vt*. 对(纸等)作加光处理〔使具缎状光泽〕。~ **paper** 蜡光纸。~ **stitch** (使现缎子光泽的)缎纹刺绣法。~ **straw** (打草帽用的)柔软麦秸。~ **wood** 缎栋。

sat·i·net, sat·i·nette [ˌsætiˈnet; ˏsætɪˋnɛt] *n*.【纺】**1.** 充缎子;缎纹棉毛呢;棉毛缎。**2.** 全丝薄缎。

sat·in·y [ˈsætini; ˋsætnɪ] *a*. 似缎的;光滑的。

sat·ire [ˈsætaiə; ˋsætaɪr] *n*. **1.** 讽刺诗[文];讽刺作品。**2.** 讽刺。*His action is a* ~ *on his boastful pretension*. 他的行动是对他自我吹嘘[卖弄]的一个讽刺。

sa·tir·ic, -i·cal [səˈtirik, -kəl; səˋtɪrɪk, -kl̩] *a*. 讽刺的。

sat·i·rist [ˈsætirist; ˋsætərɪst] *n*. 讽刺诗[文]作者;善于讽刺的人。

sat·i·rize, sat·i·rise [ˈsætiraiz; ˋsætəˏraɪz] *vt*. **1.** 讽刺,写文章讽刺;挖苦。**2.** 违反。*This detestable custom ~s humanity*. 这个可厌的风俗违反人性。

sat·is [ˈsætis; ˋsætɪs] *n*., *ad*.〔L.〕足够,充分,(考试成绩等)及格。***jam*** [dʒæm; dʒæm] 已够,已及格。~ ***superque*** [sjuːˈpəːkwi; sjuˋpɚkwɪ] 足够并已超过;十二分,及格以上。

sat·is·fac·tion [ˌsætisˈfækʃən; ˏsætɪsˋfækʃən] *n*. **1.** 满足,满意,舒服(*at*; *with*)。**2.** [a ~] 使(欲望等)满足的事物。**3.** 偿还,赔偿,义务的履行(*for*)。**4.** 赔偿物。**5.**【宗】苦行赎罪。**6.** (雪耻,挽回名誉损失的)决斗;报复。*I heard the news with great* [*much*] ~. 我听了这个消息非常满意。*It will be a great* ~ *to you to know that* .... 你如果听到…一定很满意。***demand*** ~ 要求道歉[决斗,赔偿]。***enter*** (***up***) ~ 在法院备案表明已偿清应付款项。***give*** ~ 使满足[满意];赔偿;答应决斗。***in full and complete*** ~ 照数还讫,全数还清。***in*** ~ ***of*** 作为…的赔偿。***make*** ~ ***for*** 赔偿,偿还(~ *for a debt* [*crime*] 还债,赎[罪])。***to sb.'s*** ~ = ***to the*** ~ ***of*** 使…满意地,…得使…满意。

sat·is·fac·to·ry [ˌsætisˈfæktəri; ˏsætɪsˋfæktərɪ] *a*. **1.** 令人满足[满意]的,称心如意的(*to*);圆满的。**2.**【神】赎罪的。*His behaviour is anything but* ~. 他的行为实在不能令人满意。~ *results* 圆满的结果。**-ri·ly** *ad*.

sat·is·fi·a·ble [ˈsætisfaiəbl; ˋsætɪsˏfaɪəbl̩] *a*. **1.** 可使满足[满意]的。**2.** 能偿还[赔偿]的。

sat·is·fy [ˈsætisfai; ˋsætɪsˏfaɪ] *vt*. **1.** 使满足,使满意,使果腹;符合(标准),达到(要求)。**2.** 赔偿,偿清;履行(义务);答应(要求),赎(罪)。**3.** 使确信;消除(恐怖、疑惑等);使安心。**4.**【数】满足…的条件;【化】使饱和。~ *one's desire* [*hunger*] 满足欲望[饥饿]。~ *one's aspirations* 实现抱负。~ *one's creditor* 对债权人清偿欠款。~ *one's fears* [*doubts*] 消除恐怖[疑虑]。***be satisfied*** **1.** 满足,满意,吃饱。**2.** 欢喜(*with*)。**3.** 深信,确信(*of*; *that*)(*I'm satisfied he is the thief*. 我确信他就是贼)。***rest satisfied*** 满足于(*with*)。~ ***oneself*** **1.** 满意。**2.** 查明,证明,确实弄明白(*of*; *that*)。~ ***the examiners*** 考试及格。— *vi*. **1.** 令人满意。**2.**【宗】(基督)为世人赎罪。

sat·is·fy·ing [ˈsætisfaiiŋ; ˋsætɪsˏfaɪɪŋ] *a*. **1.** 使人满足的,令人满意的。**2.** 充分的;可以相信的,确实的。**-ly** *ad*.

sat·rap [ˈsætrəp; ˋsetræp] *n*. **1.** (作为古波斯地方长官的)州长,总督。**2.** (殖民地等的)总督。**3.** 暴吏。

sat·u·ra·ble [ˈsætʃərəbl; ˋsætʃərəbl̩] *a*. 可饱和[浸透]的。

sat·u·rant [ˈsætʃərənt; ˋsætʃərənt] **I** *a*. 使饱和的。**II** *n*. **1.**【化】饱和剂,浸渍剂。**2.**【医】制酸剂。

sat·u·rate [ˈsætʃəreit; ˋsætʃəˏret] **I** *vt*. **1.** 使浸透,使渗透,浸;使渗进,使湿透。**2.** 使满,【化】使饱和。**3.**【军】饱和轰炸。~*d compound* 饱和化合物。***be*** ~***d by*** 被…浸透[湿透]。***be*** ~***d with*** 充分渗透着,充满着。~ ***oneself*** (***in***) 埋头(在…中),精通。**II** [-rit; -rɪt] *a*.〔诗〕浸透的,渗透的,颜色浓[深]的;饱和的。

sat·u·rat·ed [ˈsætʃəreitid; ˋsætʃəˏretɪd] *a*. **1.** 饱和的。**2.** 充满…了的。**3.** 浸透的,湿透的。**4.** (颜色)未被白色弄淡的。**5.**〔美俚〕喝醉了的。~ **rock**【地】饱和岩。~ **colo(u)r** 彰色,饱和色。~ **solution**【化】饱和溶液。~ **steam** 饱和蒸气。~ **steel**【冶】共析钢。

sat·u·ra·tion [ˌsætʃəˈreiʃən; ˏsætʃəˋreʃən] *n*. **1.** 浸透,浸润。**2.** 充满;饱和。**3.**【化】饱和(状态)。**4.** 饱和剂。**5.**【物】磁性饱和。**6.**【色】浓度,章度。**7.**【商】(市场的)饱和供应,足量供应。~ **bombing**【空】饱和轰炸。~ **point** 饱和点。~ **pressure** 饱和压力。

Sat·ur·day [ˈsætədi; ˋsætɚdɪ] *n*. **1.** 星期六。**2.**【犹太教】安息日。~ **night special**〔美俚〕周末特备品〔指手枪,因罪犯常在周末作案〕。**~-to-Monday** *n*., *a*. 周末(的)。**-s** *ad*.〔美〕每星期六。

Sat·urn [ˈsætə(ː)n; ˋsætɚn] *n*. **1.**【古罗马】农神。**2.**【天】土星。**3.**【炼金术】铅。**4.** (美国的)土星运载火箭。*the ~'s ring*【天】土星环。~ **salt**【化】醋酸铅。

Sat·ur·na·li·a [ˌsætəːˈneiljə; ˏsætɚˋneljə] *n*.〔*sing*., *pl*.〕【古罗马】农神节〔十二月中旬〕;〔s-〕〔用作 *sing*.〕放肆欢闹,纵情狂欢。*a s- of crime* 恣意犯罪,无法无天。**-li·an** *a*.

Sa·tur·ni·an [sæˈtəːniən; sæˋtɚnɪən] **I** *a*. **1.**【古罗马】农神的。**2.**【天】土星的。**3.** 黄金时代的,繁荣昌盛的,快乐的,幸福的。**II** *n*. (想像中的)土星居民。~ **age** 农神时代,黄金时代。~ **verse** (未受希腊诗体影响以前的)古拉丁诗体。

sa·tur·nic [sə'tə:nik; sə`tɝnɪk] ***a***. **1.** 铅毒的,铅毒性的。**2.**【医】中了铅毒的。

sa·tur·ni·id [sə'tə:ni:id; sə`tɝnɪɪd] **I *n***.【动】(天蚕蛾科(*Saturniidae*)的)天蚕蛾。**II *a***. 天蚕蛾科的。

sat·ur·nine ['sætə(:)nain; `sætɚ,naɪn] ***a***. **1.** 阴沉的,不愉快的;性情乖僻的;沉默寡言的;忧郁的,严肃的。**2.** 讥诮的,讥讽的。**3.** 铅的,铅中毒的。*a man of ~ temper* 性格阴沉的人。*a ~ patient* 铅中毒病人。*a ~ symptom* 铅中毒症状。**-ly *ad***.

sat·ur·nism ['sætə(:)nizəm; `sætɚnɪzm̩] ***n***.【医】(慢性)铅中毒。

sat·yr ['sætə; `sætɚ] ***n***. **1.**〔常作 S-〕【希神】(淫逸放纵半人半兽的)森林之神〔人形,有马或山羊般的耳朵和尾巴〕。**2.** 淫欲无度的男人,色鬼,色情狂者。**3.**〔罕〕猩猩。**4.**【昆】蛇眼蝶。~ **play**【古希腊】森林之神滑稽短歌剧〔其中合唱队化装成森林之神模样〕。**-ic** [sə'tirik; sə`tɪrɪk] ***a***. **1.** 森林之神的。**2.** 色情狂的。

sat·y·ri·a·sis [ˌsæti'raiəsis; ˏsætɪ`raɪəsɪs] ***n***.【医】男性淫狂,色情狂,求雌狂。

sau [sau; saʊ] ***n***.〔越南语〕分〔越南货币名,等于 1/100 盾〕。

sauce [sɔ:s; sɔs] **I *n*. 1** 调味汁,酱油。**2.** 刺激物,趣味。**3.**〔方〕(鱼肉的)配菜[蔬菜等](= garden-~)。**4.**〔美〕(文火)煮的水果;(果)酱。**5.**〔俚〕冒昧,莽撞,唐突,无礼。**6.**〔美俚〕烈酒。*apple ~* 苹果酱。*mint ~* 薄荷酱。*tomato ~* 番茄酱。*What's ~ for the goose is ~ for the gander*. 可以用到乙方的,也可以用到甲方;害人害自己。*Hunger is the best ~*. 饥饿是最好的调味品。*The ~ is better than the fish*. 配菜比鱼还好;喧宾夺主。*None of your ~! = Give me none of your ~! = Don't come with any of your ~! = I don't want any of your ~!* 不要无礼!说话留神点〔别对我胡说八道〕! ***more ~ than fig*** 十分无礼。***serve the same ~ to*** (*sb*.) = ***serve*** (*sb*.) ***with the same ~*** 即以其人之道还治其人之身。***sweet meat and sour ~*** 美味的肉和酸味的配菜;苦乐相间。**II *vt*. 1** 给…加调味汁[品],给…加滋味。**2.**〔俚〕对…说冒昧话。*a sermon ~d with wit* 有风趣的说教。~ **boat** (船形)调味汁碟。~ **box**〔口〕冒失鬼,〔尤指〕莽撞无礼的孩子。~**pan** 有柄小平底锅。~ **pot** (一般的)煮锅。

sau·cer ['sɔ:sə; `sɔsɚ] ***n***. **1.** 茶杯托,茶碟。**2.** (放花盆的)垫盘(等);茶碟状的器物。**3.** 浅碟形盆地。**4.**〔美〕拳击场。~ **eyes** (睁得)又圆又大的眼睛。~**-eyed *a***. (天生或因惊讶等睁得)大而圆的眼睛的。~**man** 外星人,外太空人。

sau·cy ['sɔ:si; `sɔsɪ] ***a***. (*-ci·er*; *-ci·est*) **1.** 冒失的,莽撞的,没礼貌的,不客气的。**2.**〔俚〕灵活的;愉快的;轻快的;活泼的。**3.** 漂亮的,俊俏的,时髦的。**sau·ci·ly *ad***. **sau·ci·ness *n***.

Sa·u·di A·ra·bi·a ['saudi ə'reibjə; sa`udɪ ə`rebjə] 沙特阿拉伯(又译沙乌地阿拉伯)〔位于阿拉伯半岛,首都 Riyadh〕。**Saudi Arabian** 沙特阿拉伯人。

sau·er·bra·ten ['sauəbrɑ:tn, 'zauə-; `saʊrbrɑtn, `zaʊr-] ***n***.〔美〕洋葱醋渍牛肉〔菜名〕。

sau·er·kraut ['sauəkraut; `saʊr,kraʊt] ***n***.〔G.〕泡(白)菜。

sau·ger ['sɔ:gə; `sɔgɚ] ***n***.〔美〕【动】鰤鲈(*Stizostedion canadense*)〔产于美洲〕。

Sauk [sɔ:k; sɔk] ***n***. **1.** (*pl*. *~s*, *~*) 索克人〔以前居住于密执安[密西根]州一带的北美印第安人〕。**2.** 福克斯人〔以前居住于威斯康星州一带的北美印第安人〕;福克斯人和索克人所操的阿尔衮琴语。

Saul [sɔ:l; sɔl] ***n***. 索尔〔男子名〕。

saul [sɔ:l; sɔl] ***n***. = sal[1].

Sau·mur ['səumjuə; so`myr] ***n***. (法国产)梭缪尔白葡萄酒。

sau·na ['saunə, 'sɔ:nə; `saunɑ] ***n***.〔Finn.〕**1.** (芬兰)蒸气浴。**2.** (芬兰)蒸气浴室。

Saun·dra ['sɔ:ndrə; `sɔndrə] ***n***. 桑德拉〔女子名, Sandra 的异体〕。

saun·ter ['sɔ:ntə; `sɔntɚ] ***n***., ***vi***. 闲逛,闲荡;混日子。~ ***through life*** 闲混一辈子;过闲荡生活。

sau·rel ['sɔ:rəl; `sɔrəl] ***n***.【鱼】竹筴鱼(*Trachurus symmetricus*)〔产于欧、美〕。

sau·ri·an ['sɔ:riən; `sɔrɪən] ***a***., ***n***.【动】蜥蜴类的(动物)。

sau·roid ['sɔ:rɔid; `sɔrɔɪd] ***a***., ***n***. 蜥蜴状的(动物)。

sau·ro·pod ['sɔ:rəpɔd; `sɔrəpɑd] **I *n***. 蜥脚类亚目动物〔如雷龙〕。**II *a***. 蜥脚类亚目的。

sau·ry ['sɔ:ri; `sɔrɪ] ***n***.【鱼】长颌竹刀鱼,针鱼,鱵鱼。~ **pike** 竹刀鱼。

sau·sage ['sɔsidʒ; `sɔsɪdʒ] ***n***. **1.** 香肠,腊肠。**2.**〔军俚〕腊肠形[圆柱形]观测气球(= ~ balloon)。**3.**〔口〕德国人。*a Bologna ~* 大红肠。***not have a ~***〔俚〕不名一文。~ **machine** 做香肠用的绞肉机。~ **meat** 香[腊]肠用肉馅。~ **roll** (裹上湿面粉然后油煎的)香[腊]肠肉馅卷。

sau·té ['səutei; so`te] **I *a***. (*pl*. *~(e)s*)〔F.〕【烹】(嫩)煎的,(油)炸的,炒的。**II *n***. (嫩)煎[炸、炒]的菜肴。**III *vt***. (*-(e)d*, *~ing*) 嫩煎。

Sau·terne [səu'tə:n; so`tɝn] ***n***. (法国 Sauterne 地区产的)一种白葡萄酒。

sauve qui peut [F. səuv ki: pə:; ˏsov ki `pœ]〔F.〕四散溃逃,总崩溃。

sav·a·ble ['seivəbl; `sevəbl̩] ***a***. **1.** 可拯救的。**2.** 可节省的。**3.**【宗】可得救的。

Sav·age ['sævidʒ; `sævɪdʒ] ***n***. 萨维奇〔姓氏〕。

sav·age ['sævidʒ; `sævɪdʒ] **I *a*. 1** 荒野的;野性的。**2.** 野蛮的;未开化的。**3.** 凶猛的;残酷的;粗暴的;猛烈的。**4.**【徽】裸体的。**5.**〔口〕愤怒的;暴躁的。*a ~ beast* 野[猛]兽。*a ~ man* 残暴的人;粗野的人。*~ manners* 粗暴的态度。*a ~ criticism* 粗暴的批评。***as ~ as a meat axe***〔美〕**1.** 暴跳如雷的。**2.** 狼吞虎咽的。***get ~ with*** 向…大发脾气。***make a ~ attack upon*** 猛烈攻击。***make sb*. ~** 使大发脾气,惹怒。**II *n*. 1.** 野蛮人;残暴的人;粗野的人。**2.** 野兽。**3.**〔美〕有拘捕狂的警察。**4.**〔*pl*.〕〔美俚〕雇员。**III *vt***. **1.** (马,狗)乱咬[乱踏]。**2.** 用暴力攻击,痛打,痛骂。**-ly *ad***. **-ness *n***.

sav·age·ry ['sævidʒəri; `sævɪdʒrɪ] ***n***. **1.** 野蛮,残暴,凶猛。**2.** 野蛮状态;蛮荒[蒙昧]状态。**3.** 荒野。**4.**〔集合词〕野蛮人,野兽。

sa·van·na, sa·van·nah [sə'vænə; sə`vænə] ***n***. **1.** (美国东南部无树)大平原。**2.** (亚洲)热带大草原。

sa·vant ['sævənt; sə`vɑnt] ***n***. 学者;(特指)著名大科学家。

sa·vate [sə'vɑ:t; sæ`væt] ***n***.〔F.〕(可以用脚和头的)法式拳击。

save[1] [seiv; sev] **I *vt***. **1.** 救,拯救,救济;保全。**2.** 储蓄;贮存;保留。**3.** 节约;节省。**4.** 不误,赶上。**5.**〔美卑〕杀,干掉。**6.** 救(球),阻碍球赛对方得(分)。**7.**【宗】为…赎罪。*~ sb. from danger* 救某人脱离危险。*~ sb. from drowning* 把某人从水里救出来。*God ~ the King!* 上帝保佑国王;国王万岁。*S- [God ~] me from my friends*. 请别那样做!别管闲事! *A stitch in time ~s nine*. 及时一针抵得事后九针。*~ time* 节省时间。*~ the dinner-hour* 赶上吃饭时间。*~ the gate* 关门前赶回。*~ the train* 赶上火车。~ ***appearance*** [***hono(u)r***] 保全体面,保全面子。~ ***one's bacon*** 见 bacon 条。~ ***one's breath*** 缄默。~ ***one's face*** 保全面子。~ ***one's pains*** 不滥费气力,节省精力。~ ***one's pocket*** 免掉出钱。~ ***one's skin*** 见 skin 条。~ ***oneself*** 偷懒。~ ***oneself trouble*** 省事。~ ***the situation*** 挽回局势,度过难关,化险为夷。~ ***the tide*** 趁潮涨时出[入]港抓住时机。~ ***up*** 贮(蓄)。***S- us***! 哎呀! — ***vi***. **1.** 救,拯救;救济。**2.** 贮存,储蓄。**3.** 节约,节省。**4.** (鱼、水果等)

S

不易坏,搁得住。5.【足球】阻止对方得分。*food that will* ~ 搁置不坏的食物。**II** *n*.【足球等】救球;阻碍对方得分。*a fine* ~ 球救得漂亮。

save[2][seiv; sev] **I** *prep*. 除…以外,除了。*all* ~ *him* 除他以外都。*the last* ~ *one* 倒数第二。*I am well* ~ *that I have a cold*. 除了感冒,我没什么毛病。~ ***and except***〔加强语气〕除了…,除…以外。~ ***errors***【商】有错不在此限。~ **that** 此外。**II** *conj*. 1. 若不是;只是。2. 除去,除了。

save-all [ˈseivɔːl; ˋsevˏɔl] *n*. 1.【机】省费器;承油碟;防溅器;挡雾罩。2.【建】承漏布。3. 节约装置。4.(有插烛钉的)烛碟;烛台底盘。5. 工作服;工装,围裙;罩衫。6. 储蓄箱;扑满。7.【海】附加风帆;脚帆。8.(防止货物落水的)安全网。9.〔方〕极端节省的人;吝啬鬼。

sav·e·loy [ˈsæviloi; ˋsævəˏlɔɪ] *n*.〔英〕(熟的)五香辣味腊肠。

Sa·vels [ˈsævəlz; ˋsævəlz] *n*. 萨弗尔斯〔姓氏〕。

sav·er [ˈseivə; ˋsevɚ] *n*. 1. 救助者,救星。2. 省费器,节约装置。3. 俭省的人。*oil* ~【矿】节油装置。

sav·in, sav·ine [ˈsævin; ˋsævɪn] *n*.【植】1. 新疆圆柏(*Juniperus sabina*)。2. 铅笔柏(= red cedar)。

sav·ing[1][ˈseiviŋ; ˋsevɪŋ] **I** *a*. 1. 救助的,救济的,挽救的,援救的,搭救的,挽救的。2. 可取的;保存的,储蓄的。3. 俭省的,节省的,节约的,俭约的,节俭的。4. 无损失的,不赔不赚的。5.【法】保留的,除外的。6. 补偿的;补不足的。**II** *n*. 1. 救助,救济,挽救,援救,搭救,拯救。2.〔*pl*.〕储蓄(金)。3. 俭省,节省,节约。4.【法】保留,除外。5.【化】滤屑。*He has the* ~ (*grace of*) *modesty*. 他有谦逊这一个可取的地方。***From*** ~ ***comes having***. = ***S- is getting***. 节约就是增加收入。~ **bargain** 不赔不赚的交易。~ **clause** 保留条款。

S

sav·ing[2][ˈseiviŋ; ˋsevɪŋ] *prep*. 除…以外。~ *your reverence* [*presence*]〔古〕恕我冒昧的讲;说句失敬的话,您别多心。

sav·io(u)r [ˈseivjə; ˋsevjɚ] *n*. 1. 救济者,救助者,拯救者。2.〔the S-〕救世主,救星。

sa·voir-faire [ˈsævwɑːˈfɛə; ˋsævwɑrˋfɛr] *n*.〔F.〕机警,圆滑,手腕;处世术。

sa·voir-vi·vre [ˈsævwɑːˈviːvr; ˏsaˋvwarˋvivr] *n*.〔F.〕彬彬有礼,举止得体;善于待人接物,熟悉人情事故;有教养。

sa·vor·y [ˈseivəri; ˋsevərɪ] *n*. 1.【植】香草,木质薄荷〔烹调用〕。2.〔美〕= savoury.

sa·vo(u)r [ˈseivə; ˋsevɚ] **I** *n*. 1. 味,味道,滋味,风味;〔古〕香,香味。2. 气味,一点儿,几分。3. 兴味,趣味。4.〔喻〕特点;意味。5.〔诗〕名声,名气。*a book without* ~ 枯燥无味的书。**II** *vt*. 1.〔罕〕给…增加滋味[趣味],使有味[有趣味]。2.〔古〕赏味;欣赏…的味;玩味;鉴赏。3.〔罕、诗〕有…的气味。— *vi*. 有…味道,有…的气味(*of*)。*conduct ~ing insolence* 蛮横的举动。*The offer ~s of impertinence*. 这个提议有点不客气[无礼]。**-less** *a*. 没有滋味的,没有味道的,不好吃的。

sa·vo(u)r·y [ˈseivəri; ˋsevərɪ] **I** *a*. 1. 有滋味的,好吃的;【烹】咸味的;辣味(而不是甜味)的。2.〔常和否定词连用〕舒适宜人的,令人愉快的;体面的;名声好的。*have to live in a not very* ~ *district* 不得不住在一个不大舒服的地段。*have not a very* ~ *reputation* 名誉不大好。**II** *n*.(饭前或饭后有助胃纳的)美味小盘菜肴。**sa·vo(u)r·i·ly** *ad*. **-i·ness** *n*.

sa·voy [səˈvoi; səˋvɔɪ] *n*.【植】皱叶甘蓝〔一种卷心菜〕。

Sa·voy·ard [səˈvɔiɑːd; səˋvɔɪɚd] **I** *a*.(法国)萨伏依(Savoy)地方的。**II** *n*. 1. 萨伏依人。2. 萨伏依歌剧的演员[导演、爱好者]。

Savoy [səˈvoi; səˋvɔɪ] **Operas** 萨伏依轻歌剧〔指英国 Gilbert 作词、Sullivan 作曲的十多个轰动一时的轻歌剧,因这些歌剧最初在伦敦萨伏依剧场演出而得此名〕。

sav·vy [ˈsævi; ˋsævɪ] **I** *vt*., *vi*. (**-vied**)〔俚〕知道;懂得;领悟。*S-? No* ~. 懂吗? 不懂。**II** *n*.〔俚〕见识;理解力;处事才能,机智;精明;本领,专门技能。**III** *a*. 精明的;能干的;有见识的。

saw[1][sɔː; sɔ] see 的过去式。

saw[2][sɔː; sɔ] *n*. 格言,谚语〔通常冠用 old 或 wise〕。

saw[3][sɔː; sɔ] **I** *n*. 1. 锯,锯机。2.【动】锯齿状器官[部分]。3.〔*pl*.〕(昆虫的)产卵锯。4.〔美俚〕十元钞票。*a circular* ~ 圆锯。*a hand back* ~ 手锯。*a chain* ~ 链锯。*a crosscut* ~ 横割锯;两人对拉的锯。**II** (**~ed**; **~n**) *vt*. 锯,锯开;锯成。— *vi*. 用锯;锯。~ ***a horse's mouth*** 勒紧缰绳。~ ***a log into boards*** = ~ ***boards out of a log*** 把木头锯成木板。~ ***crossways*** [***lengthways, longways***] ***of the grain*** 横[顺]着木理锯。~ ***the air with one's hands*** 用手左右挥动。~ ***up*** 锯断,锯掉。~ ***wood***〔美俚〕(在别人疲塌磨蹭的时候)埋头工作。***S- your timber***!〔卑〕干你的事去。~ **blade** 锯带,锯条。~ **bones**〔谑〕外科医生。~**buck** 1.〔美〕锯台,锯木架。2.〔美〕十年刑期;十块钱,十元钞票。~ **chain** 锯链。~-**doctor** 锯齿制作器[机];= saw set. ~**dust** *n*. 锯屑(*let the ~dust out of* (像弄出布娃娃里面锯屑那样)说出…的缺点,戳穿绣花枕头)。~ **fish**【鱼】锯鳐。~**fly**【动】叶蜂,锯蜂。~ **gin** 锯齿轧棉机。~ **grass**【植】锯齿草;牙买加砖子苗(Cladium jamaicense)。~**horse** = ~-buck. ~ **log**〔美〕锯材。~**mill** 1. 锯木厂。2. 大型锯机。~ **pit**(上下各立一人的)锯木坑。~ **set** 锯钳,锯齿修整器[机]。~**tooth** 锯齿。~-**toothed** *a*. 锯齿状的。

saw·der [ˈsɔːdə; ˋsɔdɚ] *vt*., *n*.〔俚〕奉承,谄媚。

sawed-off [ˈsɔːdɔːf; ˋsɔdˏɔf] *a*. 1.〔美俚〕锯短了的。2. 身材矮小的;受排斥的。*a* ~ *gun*〔美俚〕(匪徒等为了便于隐藏携带)锯短的枪。

sawn [sɔːn; sɔn] saw 的过去分词。

saw·n(e)y [ˈsɔːni; ˋsɔnɪ] *n*. 1.〔俚蔑〕苏格兰人。2.〔s-〕笨人,蠢货,傻瓜。

saw-whet owl [ˈsɔːˌwet aul; ˋsɔˏwɛt aʊl]【动】阿加底亚枭(*Aegolius acadica*)〔产于北美〕。

saw·yer [ˈsɔːjə; ˋsɔjɚ] *n*. 1. 锯木者,锯工。2.〔美〕(在河里擦来擦去的)漂流树[圆木]。3.(幼虫蛀入树木里的)蛀树甲虫。

Saw·yer(s) [ˈsɔːjə(z); ˋsɔjɚ(z)] *n*. 索耶(斯)〔姓氏〕。

sax[1][sæks; sæks] *n*. 1. 石板瓦工用的凿刀。2.〔Scot.〕= six.

sax[2][sæks; sæks] *n*.〔俚〕= saxophone.

Sax. = Saxon; Saxony.

sax·a·tile [ˈsæksətil; ˋsæksətɪl] *a*. = saxicolous.

saxe [sæks; sæks] *n*. 1. 萨克森蓝〔一种鲜艳淡蓝色〕(= ~ blue, Saxon blue, Saxony blue)。2.〔德制〕蛋白照相纸。

sax·horn [ˈsækshɔːn; ˋsæksˏhɔrn] *n*.【乐】萨克斯号。

sax·ic·o·lous [sækˈsikələs; sækˋsɪkələs], **sax·ic·o·line** [sækˈsikəlain; sækˋsɪkəˏlaɪn] *a*.【生,生态】生活[成长]于岩石上[岩石间]的。

sax·i·frage [ˈsæksifridʒ; ˋsæksəfrɪdʒ] *n*.【植】虎耳草。

Sax·on [ˈsæksn; ˋsæksn] *n*., *a*. 1.(原住德国、一部分于 5—6 世纪移居英国的)撒克逊人(的);盎格鲁撒克逊人(的)。2. 英格兰人(的)。3. 苏格兰低地人(的)。4. 撒克逊语(的);盎格鲁撒克逊语(的),纯粹英语(的)。~ **blue = saxe** (**blue**)。

Sax·on·ism [ˈsæksənizəm; ˋsæksnɪzm] *n*. 1. 盎格鲁撒克逊语。2. 盎格鲁撒克逊性格。3. 英国风。4. 英国国粹主义。

Sax·on·ist [ˈsæksənist; ˋsæksənɪst] *n*. 1. 盎格鲁撒克逊语学家。2. 英国国粹主义者。3. 外来语排斥论者。

Sax·on·y [ˈsæksəni; ˋsæksnɪ] *n*. 1. 萨克森〔德国一地区〕。2. 光毛呢。**Lower** ~ 下萨克森〔德国州名〕。

sax·o·phone [ˈsæksəfəun; ˋsæksəˏfon] *n*.【乐】萨克斯管。**-phon·ist** [-ˈfəunist; -ˏfonɪst] *n*. 萨克斯管吹奏者。

Sax·ton [ˈsækstn; ˋsækstn̩] ***n.*** 萨克斯顿〔姓氏〕。

sax·tu·ba [ˈsækstjuːbə; ˋsæks͵tjubə] ***n.*** 【乐】(大型)低音萨克斯号。

say [sei; se] (***said*** [sed; sɛd]; 第三人称单数陈述语气现在时 ***says*** [seiz; sez]) **I** ***vt.***, ***vi.*** **1.** 说,讲;表达;表明,宣示;声明,主张,断定。*Say all you know and ~ it without reserve.* 知无不言,言无不尽。*S- no more.* 别再说了。*Never ~ die!* 不可气馁! *Do you mean what you ~?* 你是说真的吗? 你说的是当真的吗? *I mean what I ~.* 我说了是算数的。*S- what you mean.* 把你的意思说明白。*Do you ~ so?* 那是真的吗? *You don't ~ (so)!* 未必吧! 不至于吧! 真的! *You may well ~ so.* 你那样说可能(固然)对;你不妨那么说。*Who shall I ~, sir?* (传达者问来客)你是哪一位? 请问尊姓? *I'll ~ so.* 〔美俚〕你说得很对;我也同意。*He said "Yes".* = *"Yes," said he.* 他说"是"。**2.** 背诵,背,念,诵读。*to be said or sung* 供诵读或歌唱。~ *one's lessons* 背功课,背书。**3.** 〔祈使句〕假定(说),比如说,就说,姑且说,大约(= *let us ~*)。*a few of them, ~ a dozen* 其中几个人,假定[比如说]一打左右吧。*a couple of hours, ~ from four to six* 两个钟头的时间,比方说从四点到六点。**4.** 〔美口〕= **I say** 〔见下〕。**5.** 〔俚〕反驳。***as much as to ~*** 等于说;好像是说…一样地;像要说…似地。***as to ~*** 〔插入语〕也就是说。***Easier said than done.*** 〔谚〕说着容易做时难。***have nothing to ~ for oneself*** 〔口〕总是不开口;没话可说,一言不发。***have something to ~ for oneself*** 有要辩白的话。***have something*** [***nothing***] ***to ~ to*** [***with***] 要〔不〕对[和]…争辩,有话要说[没话可说],有[没有]关系。***hear ~*** 听说,据说。***I cannot ~.*** 我不知道。***I cannot ~ much for ....*** 对…不以为…怎样好;对…不敢恭维。***I dare ~*** 〔插入语〕大概;许是,我想。I ~ = 〔美口〕;喂;喂喂;哎呀;我是说…〔加强语气〕;哎呀(*I ~, John* = 〔美〕~, *John* 喂,约翰。*I ~, what a beauty!* 哎呀! 好漂亮的人[东西]!) ***I should ~ (that)*** 大概,许是。***I should ~ not*** 我以为不是那样。(***It***) ***goes without ~ing that*** 当然不用说…。***It is said that ....*** 据说,听说。(***let us***) ~ 比如说;大约。***may well ~ that*** …很可以说。***mean what one ~s*** 是当真的。***No sooner said than done.*** 一说就做;说到做到。***not to ~ ...,*** 虽不能说…,即使不说(*It is warm, not to ~ hot.* 虽说不上热,但也很暖和了)。~ ***a good word for*** 替…说好话,替…说情,替…辩护,推奖。***S-away!*** 完全说出来吧;尽量说吧! ~ ***for oneself*** 分辩,争辩。***S- on.*** 说下去,继续说吧。~ ***nay*** 否认;拒绝。~ ***one's prayers*** 祷告。~ ***one's say*** [***word***] 说出自己的想法;把话说完;畅所欲言。~ ***out*** 坦白说出,直说。~ ***over*** [***again***] **1.** 再说,反复说。**2.** 背诵…。~ ***something*** = ~ ***grace*** 饭前后的祷告;即席演说几句。~ ***something of*** 批评。~ ***the word*** (下)命令。~ ***to do*** 〔美俚、英卑〕叫,命(*He said (for me) to tell you not to come.* 他叫(我)告诉你不要来。*They said to telephone.* 他们叫(我)打电话)。~ (***sth.***) ***to oneself*** 暗自思量,心想,心中盘算。★"自言自语"是 talk to oneself. ***so to ~*** 〔插入语〕**1.** 好比,活像是,恰如,正像。**2.** 可以这么说。***That is ~ing a great deal.*** 这可了不得。***that is*** (***to***) ~ 〔插入语〕即,换句话说,(也)就是说;至少。***They ~ ...*** 据说,听说。***There is no saying ....*** 很难说,说不准。***though I ~ it*** (***who should not***) 虽然不应该由我来说;我来说虽然不太好。***to ~ nothing of*** 〔插入语〕更不用说,更不待言,更不必说。***to ~ the least of it*** 至少〔插入语〕可以(这样)说;退一步说。***What do you ~ to*** (*a walk*)? = ***What ~ you to*** (*a walk*)? (去散散步)你说怎么样[以为怎么样]? (散步)好不好? ***What I ~ is ....*** 我的意思是…。***when all is said*** (***and done***) 结果;毕竟。

II ***n.*** **1.** 该说的事情;想说的事情;话;言词。**2.** 〔口〕轮到发言,发言的机会,发言权;〔the ~〕〔美〕最后决定权。**3.** 〔the ~〕〔口〕格言,谚语。*It is now my ~.* 现在该我发言[发表意见]了。***have a*** [***some***] ~ 有发言权。***have the*** ~ 〔美〕要想怎样就怎样,有最后决定权。**-er** ***n.*** 发言人;〔古〕诗人。

Sa·yers [ˈseiəz, seəz; ˋseəz] ***n.*** 塞耶斯〔姓氏〕。

say·est [ˈseiist; ˋseɪst], **sayst** [seist; sest] ***vt.***, ***vi.*** 〔古〕say 的第二人称单数陈述语气现在式。

say·ing [ˈseiiŋ; ˋseɪŋ] ***n.*** **1.** 话;言语。**2.** 格言;谚语。*There is no ~ (what may happen).* 不知道(会发生什么事情)。***As the ~ is*** [***goes***].... 俗话说(得好);谚语说;常言道。***It goes without ~ that ....*** 不用说;不消说;很明显;不言而喻。~ ***and doing*** 言行。

say-so [ˈseisəu; ˋse͵so] ***n.*** 〔美口〕**1.** 无证据的断言。**2.** 最后决定权。**3.** 谣传,道听途说。

say·yid, say·id [ˈsɑːjid; ˋsaɪɪd] ***n.*** 赛义德〔穆斯林的一种尊称,尤用于对穆罕默德的后代〕。

Saz·e·rac [ˈsæzəræk; ˋsæzə͵ræk] ***n.*** 〔美〕〔常用 s-〕萨塞拉克鸡尾酒〔一种有苦味(原加苦艾酒)的威士忌鸡尾酒〕。

S.B., SB = **1.** 〔L.〕*Scientiae Baccalaureus* 理学士(= Bachelor of Science)。**2.** simultaneous broadcast(ing)【无】同时广播。**3.** sales book 销货账簿。**4.** South Britain 〔英〕南不列颠。**5.** Special Branch (of Police)(警察局的)特别科。

Sb = stibium【化】锑(= antimony)。

sb. = **1.** somebody. **2.** substantive.

SBA = Small Business Administration 〔美〕小企业管理局。

S-band S 波段〔一种无线电超高频波段〕。

SbE, S by E = south by east 南偏东。

SBKKV = space-based kinetic kill vehicle 〔美〕太空活动杀伤飞行器〔"星球大战"防御计划中的一种武器系统,由轨道卫星上发射的制导导[飞]弹,用以摧毁敌方刚刚发射的导[飞]弹〕。

sbir·ro [ˈzbirəu; ˋzbɪrro] (*pl.* ***-ri*** [-ri; -rɪ]) ***n.*** 〔It.〕警察。

'sblood [zblʌd; zblʌd] ***int.*** 〔古〕该死的! 糟了! 啐! (= God's blood!)。

SBS = sick building syndrome.

SbW, S by W = south by west 南偏西。

SC, S.C. = **1.** Sanitary Corps【军】环境卫生队。**2.** Signal Corps 〔美〕陆军通信兵。**3.** South Carolina 南卡罗来纳〔美国州名〕。**4.** Supreme Court 最高法院。**5.** Security Council (of the United Nations) (联合国)安全理事会。

s.c. = **1.** small capitals【印】小体大写字母。**2.** supercalendered (纸张)特别光洁的。**3.** special constable 〔英〕临时警察。

sc. = **1.** scale. **2.** scene. **3.** scilicet. **4.** screw. **5.** scruple. **6.** scandium. **7.** sculptor. **8.** special circular.

Sc. = **1.** Scotch. **2.** Scots. **3.** Scottish.

scab [skæb; skæb] **I** ***n.*** **1.** 痂,疮痂。**2.** (羊等的)疥癣〔又叫 ~ rubbers〕。**3.**【植】疮痂病,斑点病,(葡萄)黑豆病,(苹果)黑星病。**4.** 〔俚、原美〕不加入工会的工人;工贼。**5.** 〔俚〕恶棍,无赖。**6.** (金属等材料表面的)结疤;铸件表面黏砂;瑕,疵,孔,眼。**II** ***vi.*** (**-bb-**) **1.** (伤口)生痂,(疮)结疤。**2.** 〔俚〕破坏罢工。~ *on strikers* 出卖罢工工人;当工贼。~**land** 荒瘠不毛的火山地带;表面被洪水冲走的不毛之地。~**wort** ***n.***【植】土木香(= elecampane)。

scab·bard [ˈskæbəd; ˋskæbəd] **I** ***n.*** 鞘,剑鞘。***fling*** [***throw***] ***away the*** ~ 丢开剑鞘,断然处置,决死战斗,奋斗到底。**II** ***vt.*** 把(剑)插进鞘中。~ **fish** (大)刀鱼,安哥拉带鱼。

scab·bed [skæbd, -id; skæbd, -ɪd] ***a.*** **1.** 有痂的;满是疮痂的。**2.** 生疥癣的。**3.**【植】感染斑点病等的〔*cf.* scab〕。

S

4. 不足取的,低劣的,下贱的,卑鄙的。

scab·ble [ˈskæbl; ˋskæbl̩] *vt*. (*-bled*; *-bling*) (对采下的石头)作粗糙修整[使粗具形态]。

scab·by [ˈskæbi; ˋskæbɪ] *a*. (*-bi·er*; *-bi·est*) 1. 结(满)痂的。2. 长(满)疥癣的。3. 〔口〕下贱的,卑鄙的。4. 少得可怜的。5. 【植】感染斑点病等的〔*cf*. *scab*〕。6. 【印】不鲜明的。7. 【翻砂】(表面)有疤的。~ *sixpence* 少得可怜的六个便士。**-bi·ly** *ad*. **-bi·ness** *n*.

sca·bi·es [ˈskeibiiːz; ˋskebɪˏiz] *n*. 【医】疥疮,疥螨病。**-et·ic** [ˌskeibiˈetik; ˏskebɪˋɛtɪk] *a*.

sca·bi·o·sa [ˌskeibiˈəusə; ˏskebɪˋosə] *n*. 山萝卜属(*Scabiosa*)植物〔如:轮锋菊(松虫草)(*Scabiosa atropurpurea*)〕。

sca·bi·ous [ˈskeibiəs; ˋskebɪəs] I *n*. 【植】山萝卜。II *a*. 〔罕〕生疥癣的;结满痂的。

sca·brous [ˈskeibrəs; ˋskebrəs] *a*. 1. 【动、植】粗糙的。2. 多障碍的;困难重重的。3. 有伤风化的,猥亵的;品行恶劣的。**-ly** *ad*.

scad[1] [skæd; skæd] *n*. 【鱼】竹筴鱼;圈纹大眼鲷。

scad[2] [skæd(z); skæd(z)] *n*. 〔美俚〕极大数量,大量,许多〔美语多用复数〕。~*s of money* 大量金钱。

scaf·fold [ˈskæfəld; ˋskæfl̩d] I *n*. 1. 【建】脚手架。2. (临时搭的)台架,支架;陈列台,展览台;露天舞台,看台。3. 绞架,断头台;〔the ~〕死刑。4. 【解】骨骼,骨架。5. (露葬用的)尸架。*a flying* ~ 悬空脚手架。*go to* [*mount*] *the* ~ 被处死刑。*send sb*. *to the* ~ 把某人处死刑。II *vt*. 1. 搭脚手架于(某处);使站在脚手架上。2. 把…绞死,把…处死刑。~**ing** 【建】1. 脚手架;台架。2. 脚手架[台架]材料。3. 储料台。4. 【解】骨骼。

S

scag [skæg; skæg] *n*. 〔美俚〕海洛因。

scagl·io·la [skæˈljəulə; skæˋljolə] *n*. 【建】人造大理石;仿云石。

scal·a·ble [ˈskeiləbl; ˋskeləbl̩] *a*. 1. 可攀登的。2. 可秤的。3. 可剥去鳞片的。

sca·lade [skəˈleid; skəˋled] *n*. 〔古〕用梯子攀登;【军】(用云梯)爬城(=escalade)。

scal·age [ˈskeilidʒ; ˋskelɪdʒ] *n*. 1. 缩减[下降]率。2. (对大圆木的)可用材估量。

sca·lar [ˈskeilə; ˋskelɚ] I *n*. 【数】数量;标量,无向量;实量;纯量(*opp*. vector)。II *a*. 1. 梯阶状的,分等级的。2. 【数】数量的;标量的;无向量的。3. 【生】=scalariform. ~ **product** 数(量)积。

sca·la·re [skəˈlɛəri, -ˈlɑː-; skəˋlɛrɪ, -ˋlɑr-] *n*. 【动】天使鱼属(*Pterophyllum*)的鱼;〔尤指〕天使鱼(*Pterophyllum scalare*)。

sca·lar·i·form [skəˈlærifɔːm; skəˋlærəˏfɔrm] *a*. 【动】梯状的;【植】阶纹的。*a* ~ *vessel* 梯纹导管。

scal·a·wag [ˈskæləwæg; ˋskæləˏwæg] *n*. 1. 〔美口〕流氓,无赖。2. 〔贬〕(美国南北战争后重建时期)参加共和党的南部白人。3. 不中用的牲口,瘦小的家畜。

scald[1] [skɔːld; skɔld] I *n*. 烫伤;晒焦。~*s and burns* 烫伤和烧伤。II *vt*. 1. 烫伤,晒焦。2. 把…放在滚水中过一下,嫩煮;用开水消毒,烫。3. 热(牛奶)。*be* ~*ed to death* 被滚水烫死。*the* ~*ed cream* 用热牛奶提取的奶油。~*ing tears* 热泪,血泪。~ (*out*) *a cup* 烫一烫杯子。

scald[2] [skɔːld; skɔld] *n*. 〔口〕头癣。~**-head** *n*. 〔口〕癞痢头。

scald[3] [skɔːld; skɔld] *n*. (古代北欧的)吟唱诗人。

scale[1] [skeil; skel] I *n*. 1. (尺、秤等上刻划的)分度,度数,标,标度,刻度;尺寸;尺,尺度。2. 【乐】(标度)音阶;音列。3. 等级(表),级别(表),品级。4. 【数】计数法,进位法,换算法。5. 比例;比例尺;缩尺程度。6. 率,税率。7. 规模;大小。8. 阶梯,梯子。*a proportional* [*proportionate*] ~ 比例尺。*a reduced* ~ 缩尺。*an enlarged* ~ 放大尺。*a folding* ~ 折尺。*a calculating* [*sliding*] ~ 计算尺。*the binary* [*ternary*, *decimal*] ~ 【数】二[三,十]进法。*a chromatic* [*diatonic*] ~ 半[全]音阶。*the social* ~ 社会地位(等级)。*rate* ~ 定价,价目表。*visibility* ~ 能见度。*the* ~ *of hardness* 【物】硬度(表)。*a rate* ~ 价目表。*Kelvin temperature* ~ 开氏[绝对]温标。*lower* ~ 低读数;刻度下段。*natural* ~ 实物大小;自然数;自然量;固有量。*oil* ~ 油表。*circular* ~ 刻度盘,图标度。*colour* ~ 彩色温标。*be high* [*low*] *in the* ~ *of civilization* 文化程度高[低]。*full* ~ *test* 【火箭】实物试验。**in** ~ 按照一定尺度,在一定限度[范围]内。**on a large** [**small**] ~ 大[小]规模地。**on an extensive** ~ 广泛地[的]。**play** [**sing**, **run over**] **one's** ~**s** 奏[唱、练习]音阶。**sink in the** ~ 降级。**to a** ~ 按一定比例。II *vt*. 1. 用梯子爬上;爬越,攀登(山等)。2. 用缩尺制图;(用比例尺)设计[测量],按比例排列[绘制,制造]。3. 相机决定[判断];〔美〕大略估计,约略计算(林木的可用材等);(按比例)增减。— *vi*. 变成梯子,成梯形;逐步攀登;逐渐增高。~ *the height of scientific knowledge* 攀登科学知识的高峰。~ **down** 按比例缩小[减少,减低]。~ **up** (按比例)增加,扩大,升高。~**-down** (按比例)缩减,降低;【无】分频。~ **model** 比例模型。

scale[2] [skeil; skel] I *n*. 1. 称盘,天平盘。2. 〔*pl*.〕秤,磅秤,天平〔常说 *a pair of* ~*s* 〕。3. (骑师、拳师等的)体重检查(器)。4. 〔the Scales〕【天】天平座;天平宫(=Libra)。5. 正义,裁判。*a beam and* ~*s* 天平。*a beam* ~ (杆)秤。*a platform* ~ 台秤。*a clerk of the* ~*s* 体重检查员。**go to** ~ 量体重。**go to** ~ **at** 体重(多少)。**hang in the** ~ 未作决定。**hold the** ~**s even** 公平裁判。**throw one's sword into the** ~ 用武力解决。**turn** [**tip**] **the** ~**s** 1. 使平衡(局势)发生变化。2. 起决定作用。3. 扭转局面;转变为有利的情势。**turn the** ~ **at ... pounds** 重(若干)磅,有(若干)磅重。II *vt*. 用秤称;把…过秤。— *vi*. 重(若干),有(若干)重。

scale[3] [skeil; skel] I *n*. 1. 鳞〔有时也用作集合词〕。2. 鳞状物。3. 【植】鳞苞,鳞片;甲鳞;翅瓣。4. 齿垢。5. 水锈,锅垢。6. 氧化铁皮,铁鳞;锈皮。7. 【医】鳞癣。8. (眼睛的)翳,阴翳。9. 皮,梁;薄皮;刀鞘。10. =~ insect. *boiler* ~ 锅炉水垢。*Scales fall from one's eyes*. 眼睛的阴翳消掉,发觉错误,觉醒。*anvil* ~ 锻渣。*forge* ~ 锻铁鳞,氧化皮。*mill* ~ 轧屑;轧钢鳞皮。II *vt*. 1. 剥…鳞。2. 刮掉…的锅垢;给…去锈。3. 【炮】清扫(炮筒)。— *vi*. 1. (鳞一般)剥落(*off*; *away*)。2. 生锅垢。~ **armo(u)r** 鳞甲。~ **board** (玻璃框、镜子等的)背板。~ **deposits** 炉管积垢。~·**insect** 介壳虫。~ **moss** 叶苔科植物,叶苔(=liverwort)。

scaled [skeild; skeld] *a*. 1. (屋瓦)排列成鳞状的。2. 【动】有鳞的,有鳞(状)斑(点)的;(鸟)有鳞羽的。3. 刮去了鳞的,已去鳞的。4. (羽毛等)鳞状排列的。5. 用云梯登城而占领的。

sca·lene [ˈskeiliːn; skeˋlin] *n*., *a*. 1. 【数】不等边(三角形)(的)。2. 【解】斜角肌(的)。

sca·le·nus [skeiˈliːnəs; skeˋlinəs] *n*. 〔L.〕【解】斜角肌。

scal·er [ˈskeilə; ˋskelɚ] *n*. 1. 刮鳞器。2. 【齿】牙垢刮除器。3. 攀登者,爬城士兵。4. 〔美〕测树者,检尺员。5. 【电】定标器;计数器。6. 【物】片剥〔电子从夸克上跳离的放应〕。

scal·ing[1] [ˈskeiliŋ; ˋskelɪŋ] *n*. 1. 〔古〕攀登;升高。2. 测量;推列;绘制。3. 【电】定标;电子法计算电脉冲。~ **circuit** 【电】定标电路。~**-ladder** 1. (攻城用)云梯,爬城梯。2. 消防梯。

scal·ing[2] [ˈskeiliŋ; ˋskelɪŋ] *n*. 1. 起皮;去锈。2. 结成水垢。

scal·la·wag [ˈskæləwæg; ˋskæləˏwæg] *n*. =scalawag.

scal·lion [ˈskæljən; ˋskæljən] *n*. 【植】1. 亚宝基隆葱。2. 韭葱。3. 大葱。

scal·lop [ˈskɔləp; ˋskɑləp] I *n*. 【贝】1. 扇贝[海扇]。2. 扇贝肉。3. 扇贝壳〔又叫 ~ shell, 因从前用作朝拜圣地

的纪念章,所以又叫 pilgrim shell〕。4.(烤贝类和鱼类用的)扇贝壳状平锅;扇贝形盘碟。5. 扇贝状薄肉片。6.〔pl.〕扇(贝)形。**II** *vt*. 1. 使成[切成]扇形;饰以扇形花样。2. 烤,焙〔一种烹调法:和以调料,牛乳和稀薄湿面在烤箱中〕。

scal·lop·ing [ˈskɔləpiŋ; ˋskɑləpɪŋ] *n*. 1. 扇贝采捕业。2. 扇状花样饰物。

scal·ly·wag [ˈskæliwæg; ˋskælɪˏwæg] *n*.〔美〕= scalawag.

sca·lo·gram [ˈskeiləgræm; ˋskeləˏgræm] *n*.〔美〕(进行心理学或社会学调查测验用、问题按难易排列的)程度测验(表)。

scal·op·pi·ne [ˌskɑːləˈpiːni, ˌskæl-; ˏskɑləˋpinɪ, ˏskæl-] *n*. 加酒和香料的煎炒牛肉片。

scalp [skælp; skælp] **I** *n*. 1.(带有头发的)头皮。2. 圆秃秃的山顶。3.(无下颌的)鲸头。4. 胜利品〔源于印第安人把敌人头皮剥下作为战利品〕。5. 做股票小投机所得的微小利润。6.〔俚〕抢帽子。***have the ~ of ...*** 打败(某人),打倒(某人)。***out for ~s*** 去剥头皮;〔喻〕去出征;挑战;寻衅;抨击,决心袭击敌人。***take a ~*** 剥取头皮。***take sb.'s ~s*** 剥掉头皮;战胜某人,向某人报仇。**II** *vt*. 1. 剥取…头皮。2. 倒卖(黄牛票);以(某物)囤积居奇牟取暴利。3. 剥去(表面上的一层,如地面),筛去(矿砂或壳物表面一层质量低劣的部分)。4. 夺取(对方的势力);击败;使屈辱。— *vi*. 1. 炒股票〔进行投机取巧牟利活动〕。2. 倒卖黄牛票。~ **lock** 印第安人故意留在头皮上向敌人挑战的一撮头发。

scal·pel [ˈskælpəl; ˋskælpel] *n*. 外科用小手术刀,解剖刀。

scalp·er [ˈskælpə; ˋskælpɚ] *n*. 1. 剥取头皮者。2.【外】骨锉,刮骨刀,解剖刀〔又叫 scalping iron〕。3. 雕刻刀。4.〔美〕进行投机活动者;(车站、戏院等处的)倒卖黄牛票的人,黄牛。5.【股】抢帽子的人,搞股票小投机的人。6. 筛选机。

scal·y [ˈskeili; ˋskelɪ] *a*. (*-i·er*; *-i·est*) 1. 有鳞的;鳞状的。2.【植】有鳞苞的,有鳞片的。3. 有锅垢的;鳞状剥落的。4. 被介壳虫蛀坏了的。5.〔俚〕卑劣的,吝啬的。~ **anteater** = pangolin. ~ **bum**〔美〕邋遢鬼;卑劣的人。~ **lentinus** 松菌。**-i·ness** *n*.

scam [skæm; skæm] *n*., *vt*.〔美俚〕诓骗,诈骗。

scam·mer [ˈskæmə; ˋskæmə] *n*.〔美俚〕(长于用高明手段逃避法律惩处的)逍遥法外的罪犯。

scam·mo·ny [ˈskæməni; ˋskæmənɪ] *n*. 1.【植】墨牵牛子。2. 墨牵牛子脂〔泻药〕。

scamp[1] [skæmp; skæmp] *n*. 1. 恶棍,无赖;流氓。2. 顽皮的家伙。3.〔古〕拦路强盗。

scamp[2] [skæmp; skæmp] *vt*. 草率地做(工作),胡乱地做,不得当地做。**-er** *n*.

scam·per [ˈskæmpə; ˋskæmpɚ] **I** *vi*. 1.(小孩、小走兽)跳跳蹦蹦(*about*)。2.(受惊的动物)奔逃;惊奔(*off*; *away*)。3. 浏览;涉猎(*through*)。4. 匆匆忙忙旅行[走过]。**II** *n*. 1. 奔跑,疾走。2. 匆匆忙忙旅行[浏览,涉猎]。*a ~ through Europe* [*Dickens*] 匆匆忙忙旅行欧洲[浏览狄更斯的小说]。***be (up) on the ~*** 东奔西走,瞎蹦乱跳。***put sb. to the ~*** 使(某人)东奔西跑。

scam·pi [ˈskæmpi; ˋskæmpɪ] *n*. (*pl*. *~(s)*)【动】食虫虾〔可食用〕。

scamp·ish [ˈskæmpiʃ; ˋskæmpɪʃ] *a*. 无赖的;淘气顽皮的。

scan [skæn; skæn] **I** *vt*. (*-nn-*) 1. 细看,细察;审视。2.〔口〕大略一阅;浏览。3. 按韵节念,按句调读,标出(诗)的格律(指划分音步)。4.【电视】扫描;扫掠;搜索。**II** *vi*. 1.(诗)符合格律,读起来抑扬顿挫。2.【无】扫描。*This line does not ~*. 这一行不合韵律。**III** *n*. 1. 细看;细察。2. 扫视,浏览。3.【电视】扫描;扫掠。4. 眼界;视野。**scan·nable** *a*. 1. 可细察的。2. 可标出的,可扫描[掠]的。

Scan., **Scand.** = Scandinavian.

scan·dal [ˈskændl; ˋskændl] *n*. 1. 丑闻;丑名;丑事,丑行,丢脸的事件;舞弊案件;耻辱。2.(社会上的)反感,物议,诽谤,诋毁。*It is a ~ that such things should be possible*. 竟会有这样的事情真是丢脸。*a case of ~* 毁谤事件。***be a ~ to*** 是…的耻辱。***cause*** [***raise***] ***a ~*** 引起公愤[物议]。***spread about ~*** 传播丑闻〔讲人家的坏话〕;毁谤人。***talk ~*** 传播丑闻;说人坏话。~ **monger** 喜欢传播丑闻的人。~ **power**〔美〕臭名;名声臭的人。~ **sheet**〔俚〕黄色小报。

scan·dal·ize [ˈskændəlaiz; ˋskændlˏaɪz] *vt*. 1. 使…愤慨。2. 使…震惊;使…起反感。3. 中伤,诽谤。4. 使…受耻辱。***be ~d at*** 对…大为愤慨。**-iz·er** *n*. 诽谤者,恶意中伤者。**-iz·ing** *a*.

scan·dal·ous [ˈskændələs; ˋskændləs] *a*. 1. 可耻的,丢脸的;出丑的,令人发生反感的。2. 毁谤的,(恶意)中伤的。**-ly** *ad*.

scan·dent [ˈskændənt; ˋskændənt] *a*. 攀缘的〔如藤〕。

scan·di·a [ˈskændiə; ˋskændɪə] *n*.【化】氧化钪。

Scan·di·an [ˈskændiən; ˋskændɪən] *a*., *n*. = scandinavian.

Scan·di·na·via [ˌskændiˈneivjə, -viə; ˏskændəˋnevɪə, -vjə] *n*. 斯堪的纳维亚(瑞典、挪威、丹麦、冰岛的泛称)。

Scan·di·na·vi·an [ˌskændiˈneivjən; ˏskændəˋnevɪən] *n*., *a*. 1. 斯堪的纳维亚(人)的,北欧(人)的。2. 斯堪的纳维亚语(的),北欧语(的)。

scan·di·um [ˈskændiəm; ˋskændɪəm] *n*.【化】钪〔化学符号为 Sc〕。

scan·ner [ˈskænə; ˋskænɚ] *n*. 1. 细辨诗行韵律的人。2. 细查者。3.【电视】扫描器[设备];扫掠器[设备,机构]。4.【无】扫掠天线。5. 析像器。*a disc ~* 析像圆盘。*a film ~* 电视摄影机。*a follow ~* 跟踪扫掠设备。

scan·ning [ˈskæniŋ; ˋskænɪŋ] *n*. 1. 细看,细察,审视。2.【电视】扫描,扫掠,搜索。~ **agent** 像素,元像。~ **beam** 扫描光线。~ **disk**【电视】扫描盘。~ **electron micrograph**【物】扫描电子显微照相。~ **electronic microscopy**【物】扫描电子显微术。~ **element** 像素,元像。~ **line** 扫描线。~ **yoke** 扫描线圈;致偏磁轭;偏转系统。

scan·sion [ˈskænʃən; ˋskænʃən] *n*. 按(轻重)节奏[韵律]念,节奏[韵律]分析。

scan·so·ri·al [skænˈsɔːriəl; skænˋsɔrɪəl] *a*. 1. 攀爬的,(适于)攀附的。2.【动】攀禽类的。

scant [skænt; skænt] **I** *a*. 1. 缺乏的,不足的,不够的(*of*)。2. 恰好够的。3. 将近的。4. 俭约的,节省的;吝啬的。★英国现在常用的是 scanty. *a ~ attendance* 出席者[听众]稀少。*a ~ supply of food* 食品供应不足。*a ~ halfhour* 恰好[仅仅]半小时。*a ~ five yards* 刚够五码。***be ~ of money*** 钱不够[缺钱]。***fat and ~ of breath*** 胖得喘气。***with ~ courtesy*** 不太礼貌地,有点不客气地。**II** *vt*.〔英古、美〕1. 限制,缩减。2. 克扣;吝惜。3. 不客气地对待。**III** *ad*.〔美方〕好容易才,几乎不[没有]。**-ly** *ad*. **-ness** *n*.

scant·ling [ˈskæntliŋ; ˋskæntlɪŋ] *n*. 1. 小木块,小石料;〔集合〕小块材料。2.(木材的)宽厚度;(石料的)体积。3.【建】标品;量度;建筑尺寸。4. 略图,草图。5.【船】船材尺度,船体各部的尺寸。6. 少量,少许,一点点(*of*)。7. 桶架。8.〔古〕样品,样本。

scant·y [ˈskænti; ˋskæntɪ] *a*. (*-i·er*; *-i·est*) 1. 缺乏的,(数量)不足[不多]的(*opp*. ample)。2. 狭小的,稀疏的。3. 吝啬的,俭省的。*Crops are very ~ this year*. 今年收成极少。***be ~ of*** (*words*; *praise*) 难得(开口),不大(称赞)。**-i·ly** *ad*. **-i·ness** *n*.

SCAP [skæp; skæp] = Supreme Commander of the Allied Powers 盟军最高司令。

SCAPA [ˈskæpə; ˋskæpə] = Society for Checking the Abuses of Public Advertizing 公共广告弊端遏制协会。

Scap·a Flow [ˈskæpə ˈfləu; ˋskæpə ˋflo]〔英〕斯卡帕弗

S

洛〔苏格兰北部 Orkney 群岛间的水域;英国海军基地〕。

scape[1][skeip; skep] ***n*.** **1.**【植】(水仙等的)花葶〔指郁金香等由地面或地面上抽出的花梗〕。**2.**【昆】柄节〔膝形触角的长基节〕;独角根;【动】羽轴。**3.**【建】柱身;柱根特大部分。

scape[2][skeip; skep] ***n*.**, ***vt*.**, ***vi*.** 〔方〕= escape. ~ **wheel**【机】擒纵轮(= escape wheel)。

scape[3][skeip; skep] ***n*.** = landscape.

-scape *suf*. 表示"景": sea*scape* 海景。

scape·goat [ˈskeipgəut; ˋskep͵got] ***n*.** **1.** (古代犹太教祭礼中替人承担罪过的)替罪羊。**2.**〔喻〕替(人负)罪者;代人受过者。***be made the*** ~ ***for*** **1.** 做…的替罪者。**2.** 承担…的罪名,代…受过。

scape·grace [ˈskeipgreis; ˋskep͵gres] ***n*.** **1.** 轻浮的人;莽撞的人。**2.** 无赖,恶棍。**3.** 顽童;淘气鬼。

scaph·oid [ˈskæfɔid; ˋskæfɔɪd] ***a*.** 船形的〔尤指船形骨的〕。

scaph·o·pod [ˈskæfəˌpɔd; ˋskæfə͵pɑd] ***n*.**【动】掘足纲(*Scaphopoda*)软体动物。

scap·o·lite [ˈskæpəˌlait; ˋskæpə͵laɪt] ***n*.**【矿】方柱石。

sca·pose [ˈskeipəus; ˋskepos] ***a*.**【植】具花葶的;有根生花梗的。

s. caps. = small capitals

scap·u·la [ˈskæpjulə; ˋskæpjələ] ***n*.** (*pl*. **-lae** [-liː; -li])【解】肩胛骨;肩板;髆。

scap·u·lar [ˈskæpjulə; ˋskæpjələ˞] **I** ***a*.** 肩胛骨的;肩的。**II** ***n*.** **1.**【解】肩胛(骨)。**2.**【动】肩羽,肩翼;肩衣,肩布。**3.**【医】肩胛绷带。**4.**【宗】肩衣;无袖法衣。**5.** 一种无袖工作服。

SCAR = subcalibre aircraft rocket 机载次口径火箭。

S. Car = Scout Car 巡逻车。

scar[1][skɑː; skɑr] **I** ***n*.** **1.** 创伤;伤痕;疤;痕迹。**2.**〔喻〕(精神上或内心的)创伤。**3.**【植】叶柄痕;瘢痕。**4.** (金属等材料表面的)斑疤;痕。*a vaccination* ~ 牛痘疤。*He jests at* ~*s that never felt a wound*.〔谚〕没有受过伤的人总爱嘲笑别人的伤疤;未经痛苦的人不会同情别人。**II** ***vt*.** (**-*rr*-**) **1.** 使留伤痕。**2.**〔喻〕使留痕迹;弄丑。—***vi*.** 长疤;结疤;成疤,〔伤口〕愈合(*over*)。~ **tissue**【医】瘢痕组织。

scar[2][skɑː; skɑr] ***n*.**〔英〕**1.** 巉岩,露岩;断崖;峭壁。**2.** (海中的)孤岩;暗礁。

scar·ab [ˈskærəb; ˋskærəb] ***n*.** **1.**【动】金龟子科甲虫;圣甲虫。**2.** (古埃及人当做丰饶、再生象征的)甲虫形宝石〔古埃及人作为护符〕。

scar·a·bae·id [ˌskærəˈbiːid; ͵skærəˋbiɪd] **I** ***n*.**【动】金龟子。**II** ***a*.** 金龟子科甲虫的。

Scar·a·mouch [ˈskærəmautʃ; ˋskærə͵maʊtʃ] ***n*.** **1.** (古意大利喜剧中)懦弱而好夸口的丑角。**2.**〔s-〕只会吹牛的胆小鬼〔懦夫〕;无赖(汉)。

scarce [skɛəs; skɛrs] **I** ***a*.** (~***r***; ~***st***) **1.**〔用作表语[主词补语]〕(生活必需品)缺乏,不足(*of*)。**2.** 稀有的,罕见的,珍贵的,难得的。*We are* ~ *of provisions*. 我们缺乏粮食。*a* ~ *book* 珍本;难得的书。~ *metals* 稀有金属。~ *times* 市面萧条,困难时节。***make oneself*** ~〔口〕悄悄走[躲]开;退避;溜掉;不露面。**II** ***ad*.**〔古诗〕= scarcely.

scarce·ly [ˈskɛəsli; ˋskɛrslɪ] **I** ***ad*.** **1.** 简直不[没有],几乎不[没有]。**2.** 好容易;勉强。**3.** 将近,刚刚,才。**4.** 的确没有,不至于;一定不,决不。**5.** (刚)一…就〔与 before 或 when 连用〕。**6.** 不…的几乎没有〔与 but 连用〕。*I* ~ *saw him*. 我简直没看见他。*I* ~ *know him*. 我简直不认识他。*I need* ~ *say*. 用不着说,不必说。*He is* ~ *old enough for the office*. 他担任这个职务稍嫌年轻一点。*He can* ~ *write his own name*. 他勉强能写自己的名字。*He is* ~ *seventeen years old*. 他还不到[将近]十七岁。*He can* ~ *have said so*. 他不至于这样说。*S- had we reached home, before it began raining*. 我们(刚)一到家就下起雨来了。*He had* ~ *escaped when he was recaptured*. 他一逃就被逮住了。*There is* ~ *a man but has his weak side*. 无缺点的人几乎没有。~ ***any*** 简直没有。~ ***ever*** 偶然,极少。~ ***less*** 简直相等,简直一样。

scarce·ment [ˈskɛəsmənt; ˋskɛrsmənt] ***n*.** **1.**【建】(墙上,堤岸上或扶壁上的)壁阶。**2.**【矿】梯架。

scar·ci·ty [ˈskɛəsiti; ˋskɛrsətɪ] ***n*.** **1.** 缺乏,缺少,不足。**2.** 稀罕;少见。**3.**【经】匮乏,萧条。*a* ~ *of rain* 雨水缺乏。*a year of great* ~ 大荒年。~ **price** 缺货市价。~ **value**【经】稀少价值。

scare [skɛə; skɛr] **I** ***vt*.** 吓,吓唬;吓走,吓跑(*away*, *off*)。—***vi*.** 吓,吃惊,惊吓,惶恐。***be more*** ~***d than hurt*** 无事自忧,自找烦恼;虚惊。***be*** (***as***) ~***d as a rabbit*** 吓得要命;惊惶失措。***be*** ~***d stiff*** [***hollow***] 吓一大跳。~ ***the pants off of*** 〔美俚〕吓坏…;把…吓得魂不附体。~ ***up*** [***out***]〔美〕**1.** (将猎物)吓出来;(将钱财)敲诈出来;找出,得到。**2.** 筹措,张罗。**II** ***n*.** 吓唬;恐怖,(商界的)恐慌。***get a*** ~ 吓一跳,吓坏。***throw a*** ~ ***into sb***.〔美〕使…吓一大跳,吓坏…。~**crow** ***n*.** **1.** 稻草人。**2.** 骨瘦如柴的人,衣衫褴褛的人。**3.** 威吓物。~**-head-(ing)** ***n*.** 报纸上的煽动性[耸人听闻]大标题。~ **monger** [**merchant**] ***n*.** 散布恐怖谣言[骇人听闻消息]的人。**scar·er** [ˈskɛərə; ˋskɛrə˞] ***n*.** 吓人的人;吓人的事物。

scared [skɛəd; skɛrd] ***a*.** **1.** 吃惊的,吓坏的。**2.**〔方〕怕,不敢(= afraid)。*a* ~ *look* 吃惊的面孔。*I'd be* ~ *to do that*.〔方〕我怕做那件事。

scared·y-cat [ˈskɛədikæt; ˋskɛrdɪ͵kæt] ***n*.** 易受惊吓的人。

scarf[1][skɑːf; skɑrf] **I** ***n*.** (*pl*. ~***s***,〔英又作〕***scarves***) **1.** 围巾;头巾。**2.** 领巾;领带。领结。**3.** 披巾;腰巾。**4.** 桌巾,台巾。**5.** (高级军政人员的)绶带。*red* ~ 红围巾,红领巾。**II** ***vt*.** **1.** 围(围巾)。**2.** 打(领带)。**3.** 披(披巾)。**4.** 盖(台巾)。**5.** 用围巾[台布]围[盖]。

scarf[2][skɑːf; skɑrf] **I** ***vt*.** **1.** 嵌接(木材、金属、皮革)。**2.** 割取(鲸鱼的)油脂和皮。**II** ***n*.** **1.** (木材、金属、皮革的)嵌接。**2.** 嵌接处;(嵌接的)斜面;截面;切口;接榫。**3.** (刻在木头等上的)槽,凹线。**4.** (在鲸鱼尸体上的)纵向切割。~ **joint** 嵌接。~ **skin**【解】(特指)指甲根上的角质表皮。~ **weld**【机】嵌焊;斜面焊接。

scar·i·fi·ca·tion [ˌskɛərifiˈkeiʃən; ͵skærəfəˋkeʃən] ***n*.** **1.**【医】多次划破(法)。**2.** 刺破,划破。**3.** 划(破的)痕(迹)。**4.** 放血(法)。**5.**【农】松土。**6.** 严厉批评。

scar·i·fi·ca·tor [ˈskɛərifikeitə; ˋskærəfɪ͵ketə˞] ***n*.**【医】刺破器,划痕器,放血器。

scar·i·fi·er [ˈskɛərifaiə; ˋskærə͵faɪə˞] ***n*.** **1.**【医】划痕器,放血器;划皮肤的划刀。**2.** 划破者,放血者。**3.**【农】松土器。**4.** (道路工程用的)翻路机。

scar·i·fy [ˈskɛərifai; ˋskærə͵faɪ] ***vt*.** (**-*fied***) **1.**【医】刺破,多次划破(皮肤)。**2.** 给…放血。**3.**【农】松土;对(硬皮种子)作破皮处理(使易于发芽)。**4.** 严厉批评;〔口〕虐待,欺负,折磨。

scar·la·ti·na [ˌskɑːləˈtiːnə; ͵skɑrləˋtinə˞] ***n*.**【医】(轻症的)猩红热。

scar·let [ˈskɑːlit; ˋskɑrlɪt] **I** ***n*.** **1.** 深红色,猩红,鲜红。**2.** 红布;(大主教、英国高等法院法官、英国队军军官等的)红衣。**3.** 象征罪恶的深红色。**II** ***a*.** **1.** 深红的,猩红的,鲜红的。**2.** 面红耳赤的。**3.** 罪恶昭彰的;淫荡的。***turn*** ~ 变得面红耳赤。***wear*** ~ **1.** 穿深红衣服。**2.** (市长等)穿制服。~ **fever** **1.** 猩红热。**2.**〔谑〕(妇女的)军人热[崇拜]。~ **hat** 红衣主教的帽子[职位]。~ **letter** 红 A 字〔美国殖民时期给被判通奸罪者佩戴的耻辱标记〕。~ **pimpernel** = pimpernel【植】海绿(*Anagallis arvensis*)。~ **rash** 蔷薇疹。~ **runner**【植】红花菜豆〔美洲热带产〕。~ **sage**【植】一串红(*Salvia splendens*)。~ **woman** [**whore**] **1.** 异教的罗马〔源出

《新约》启示录;宗教改革时期新教徒用来指罗马天主教会〕。2. 世俗精神。3. 娼妓,淫妇。

scarp [skɑːp; skɑrp] I *n*. 1. 陡坡;险坡;悬崖。2.【建】(城墙的)内斜坡;(外壕的)内削壁。II *vt*. 1. 使成陡坡。2. 在…设斜坡,在…设内削壁。3. 垂直切断(山腰等)。4.〔俚〕偷。

scar·per [ˈskɑːpə; ˋskɑrpɚ] *vi*. 1.〔英俚〕逃走;溜掉。2. 撤退,撤营。

scarves [skɑːvz; skɑrvz] *n*.〔英〕scarf[1]的复数。

scar·y [ˈskɛəri; ˋskɛrɪ] *a*. (*-i·er*; *-i·est*) 1. (马等)易受惊的,胆怯的。2. 可怕的,吓人的。

scat[1] [skæt; skæt] I *int*.〔口〕嘘!〔赶猫等的呼声〕II *vi*.〔口〕走开〔常用命令式〕。~**back**〔足球俚〕迅速敏捷的后卫。

scat[2] [skæt; skæt] *n*.〔英方〕砰〔枪声、打击声,爆炸声等〕。*go* ~〔俚〕1. 粉碎。2. 破产;完蛋。

scat[3] [skæt; skæt] I *n*. (爵士音乐中)无意义的狂叫。II *vi*. (歌唱中间)作即兴的狂叫。

scathe [skeið; skeð] I *n*. 损害,损伤。***keep from*** ~ 使避免伤害;保护。***without*** ~ 平安地;无损伤地。II *vt*. 1. 严厉批评。2.〔古方〕损害,损伤。3. 使枯萎。**-less** *a*. 无伤的,平安的。

scath·ing [ˈskeiðiŋ; ˋskeðɪŋ] *a*. 1. 伤害(性)的,引起剧痛的。2. (眼光)严厉的;尖刻的,苛刻的;(批评等)严厉的。**-ly** *ad*.

sca·tol·o·gy [skəˈtɔlədʒi; skəˋtɑlədʒɪ] *n*. 1. 粪便研究;【医】粪便诊断。2.【古生】粪石学〔研究粪便化石之学〕。3. 粪便学〔研究古时以粪便占卜疾病的民俗学的一科〕。4. 猥亵描写;对猥亵情节的兴趣。

scat·ter [ˈskætə; ˋskætɚ] I *vt*. 1. 散布,撒(种),散播。2. 使散乱;逐散,驱散,击溃;使化为乌有,摧毁(希望等);消除(恐怖等)。3.【物、军】扩散,散射(光、热等)。4. 挥霍,浪费(财产)。—*vi*. 1. 分散。2. 四散,溃散。3. 扩散;(子弹炮火等)散射。~ *seed* 播种。~ *the crowd* 驱散群众。~ ***about*** 散布,撒布。~ ***to the winds*** 挥霍浪费。II *n*. 1. 撒布;散播。2. 散播物。~**-brain** *n*. 1. 思想不集中的人,思想混乱的人。2. 轻率[浮躁]的人。~**brained** *a*. 轻率的,浮躁的。~**good** *n*. 挥霍无度的人。~**gun**〔美俚〕猎枪;机枪。~ **rug** (铺覆部分地板的)小幅地毯。~ **shot** 1. 大型铅弹。2. (猎枪等)散弹的扩散范围。~**shot** *a*. 1. 扩散很广的。2. 一般的,广泛的。**-a·tion** [ˌskætəˈreiʃən; ˏskætəˋreʃən] *n*.

scat·tered [ˈskætəd; ˋskætɚd] *a*. 1. (人家等)疏疏落落的;分散的,散乱的。2. (思想等)不集中的,散漫的。3.【植】星散的,参差的,散生的。4.【物】(光)散射的。

scat·ter·ing [ˈskætəriŋ; ˋskætərɪŋ] I *a*. 1. 分散在不同方向的,分散在不同范围的。2. 广泛扩散的。3. (选票)数量分散的,不集中的。II *n*. 1. 散乱。2. 在媒介质中的散播。3.【物】散射。~ **layer** 能使声波散射的海中浮游生物层。**-ly** *ad*.

scat·ty [ˈskæti; ˋskætɪ] *a*. (*-ti·er*; *-ti·est*) 1.〔俗〕疯疯癫癫的。2.〔俚〕低能的;意志薄弱的。3. 轻率的,浮躁的,粗心的。

scaup [skɔːp; skɔp] *n*.【鸟】斑背潜鸭 (= ~ duck)。

scaur [skɔː; skɑr] *n*. [Scot.] = scar[2].

scav·enge [ˈskævindʒ; ˋskævɪndʒ] *vt*., *vi*. 1. 清除(污物或杂质),打扫(街道等)。2.【动】吃(腐肉等)。3.【机】排除(内燃机等的)废气;给[从](内燃机汽缸)扫气。4.【冶】清除(杂质);纯化(金属液)。5. (从…中)提取有用物质;在废物中提取(有用物质)。~ **trunk**【冶】吹气管。

scav·en·ger [ˈskævindʒə; ˋskævɪndʒɚ] I *n*. 1. 清道夫;清扫工。2. 食腐动物〔指食腐物腐尸〕。3. (纱厂)花屑清扫人。4. 黄色作家,猥亵文章作者。5. 清除剂,净化剂。6.【矿】选池。7. 吹洗泵,清理泵。II *vi*. 1. 做清道夫。2. 排除废气。~ **hunter** 觅物游戏。~**'s cart** 扫街车。~**'s daughter**【英史】铁箍刑具。

Sc.B. = [L.] Scientiae Baccalaureus 理学士 (= Bachelor of Science)。

Sc.D. = [L.] *Scientiae Doctor* 理学博士 (= Doctor of Science)。

sce·na [ˈʃeinə; ˋʃenə] *n*. [It.] 1. (歌剧的)一场。2. (古代剧场的)舞台。3. (精致的戏剧性的)叙唱,宣叙调[部]〔下接咏叹调〕。

sce·na·ri·o [siˈnɑːriəu; sɪˋnɛrɪˏo] *n*. (*pl*. ~*s*) [It.] 1.【剧】剧情说明。2. 歌剧脚本;电影剧本。3. 方案。*a* ~ *editor* 电影剧本编辑。*a* ~ *writer* 电影剧[脚]本作者。

sce·na·rist [siˈnɑːrist; sɪˋnɛrɪst] *n*. 电影剧[脚]本作者。

sce·nar·ize [ˈsiːnəraiz; ˋsinəraɪz] *vt*. 把(小说等)改编成电影剧本。

scend [send; sɛnd] = send[2].

scene [siːn; sin] *n*. 1. (戏剧中的)一场。2.〔常 *pl*.〕场(舞台的)布景。3.【影】场面;出事地点,现场;〔古〕舞台。4. 事件,史实,插话。5. 吵闹;发脾气。6. 景色,景致,风景。7.〔*pl*.〕光景,实况。Act III, S-ii 第三幕第二场。*moving* ~*s* 激动人心的场面。*a set* ~ 背景;大道具。*a* ~ *of disaster* 肇祸现场[情景]。*a* ~ *of action* 出事地点。*the* ~ *of operations* 军事行动的地点;战场。***a carpenter's*** ~ (换布景时演的)插幕。***be quickly on the*** ~ 立刻到达出事地点。***behind the*** ~*s* 知道内幕;秘密地,暗中。***change of*** ~ 场面的变化;转地。***come on the*** ~ 出现,登场。***have a nice*** ~ ***with*** 和…大吵一场。***lay*** [***place***] ***the*** ~ ***in*** 取…做场面,用…做舞台。***make a*** ~ 吵架 (*Please don't make a* ~. 别吵架)。***make the*** ~〔美俚〕在某地露面;参加某项活动。***on the*** ~ 在出事地点,当场。***paint*** ~*s* 画布景。***quit the*** ~ 退场,离场;离开人间,死。***shift*** [***change***] ***the*** ~*s* 1. 换幕,换景。2. 改变环境,转移地点。~ **dock** (舞台旁边的)布景存放处。~**man** [ˈsiːnmən; ˋsinmən] *n*. (*pl*. ~*men*) = ~shifter. ~ **master** 剧院中控制数条灯光电路的开关。~ **painter** 布景画师,画布景者。~**-shifter**【剧】移置布景者。~ **stealer** 在舞台上抢出风头的配角演员,喧宾夺主的配角。

scen·er·y [ˈsiːnəri; ˋsinərɪ] *n*. 1. 景色,景致,风光,风景。★scene 是局部景色。scenery 是全景。2. 舞台面,~(舞台)布景。3. 背景。4.〔罕〕风景画。*landscape* ~ = ~ *of a landscape* 自然景色。***paint*** ~ 画背景。~ **wagon** (有脚轮的)布景台。

sce·nic [ˈsiːnik; ˋsinɪk] I *a*. 1. 布景的,背景的。2. 舞台的,戏剧的。3. 戏剧性的,(表情等)戏剧式的。4. 画一般的;(画等)表现实景的。5. 风景的,风光明媚的,风景佳美的;景色优美的。~ *persons* 戏剧演员。~ *poets* (特指希腊罗马的)戏剧作者。*a* ~ *railway* (游览区里的)游览小铁路。*a* ~ *bas-relief* 故事性的浮雕作品。II *n*. 1. 风景影片;实景电影。2. 风景照片[图片]。**-i·cal** *a*. = scenic. **-i·cal·ly** *ad*.

sce·no·graph [ˈsiːnəgrɑːf, -græf; ˋsinəˏgræf, -ˏgrɑf] *n*. 透视图。

sce·nog·ra·phy [siːˈnɔgrəfi; siˋnɑgrəfɪ] *n*. 1. 透视(图)法。2.〔尤指〕古希腊舞台布景画法。3. 配景图法;写景术。**-graph·ic** [ˌsiːnəˈgræfik; siˋnɑgræfɪk] *a*.

scent [sent; sɛnt] I *n*. 1. 香,气味,香气。2.〔口〕香水。3. (野兽的)臭迹;遗臭。4. 迹,踪迹;线索〔只用单数〕。5.〔a~〕嗅觉,敏锐的感觉。6. "狗捉兔子"游戏 (hare and hounds) 中兔子撒在地上代表踪迹的纸片。*a dog of good* ~ 嗅觉敏锐的狗。*a burning* ~ (动物走后留下的)强烈的臭迹。*a cold* [*hot*] ~ 微弱的[强烈的]臭迹。*a false* ~ 错误的臭迹,错误的线索。***be off the*** ~ [***get the wrong*** ~] 1.【猎】失去猎物的臭迹;追错方向。2.〔转义〕迷失方向;捉住错误的线索,作错误的判断。***cast about for the*** ~ (猎狗)寻找(猎物等)。***follow up the*** ~ (猎狗)闻着臭迹追赶。***get*** ~ ***of*** 闻出;发觉。***have a keen*** ~ ***for an error*** 有发现错误的敏锐感觉。***have no*** ~ ***for*** 对于…没有敏感。***hunt by*** ~ 凭嗅觉追

赶,循臭迹追猎。***on the right*** [***wrong***] ～ 线索正确[错误],得[不得]法。***on the*** ～ ***of*** 获得…的线索 (*be hot on the* ～ *of an important discovery* 及时抓紧重大发现的线索追查)。***put sb. off the*** ～ (用替身等)使人追错方向而逃逸;使人迷失线索。***put*** [***throw***] ***sb. on the*** ～ (自己做向导)使人跟着追,使人跟踪追赶。***put*** [***throw***] ***sb. on a wrong*** ～ = *put sb. off the* ～. ***recover the*** ～ (猎狗)重新嗅到臭迹。***take the*** ～ ***of*** = ***get*** ～ ***of***. **II** ***vt***. **1.** 闻,嗅,闻出。**2.** 察觉,发觉,看破(阴谋等)。**3.** 使香,使臭;在…上洒香水。～ *spring in the air* 空气中感到春天的气息。*The flower* ～*s the air*. 花散布芳香。～ *one's person* 往身上洒香水。—***vi***. **1.** 闻着气味追赶。**2.** 发出气味;发出香味。～ **bag 1.** 香袋;香囊。**2.**【动】臭腺。～ **bottle 1.** 香水瓶。**2.**〔俚〕厕所。～ **gland**【动】臭腺,麝香分泌腺。

scent·ed [ˈsentid; ˋsɛntɪd] ***a***. **1.** 洒了香水的,加有香料的。**2.** 馥郁的,芳香的。**3.** 有…嗅觉的。～ *soap* 香皂。*keen-* ～ 嗅觉敏锐的。

scent·less [ˈsentlis; ˋsɛntlɪs] ***a***. **1.** 不香的,无香气的;无气味的。**2.** 不臭的。**3.** (行猎时)失去了臭迹的。**4.** 无嗅觉的。

scen·tom·e·ter [sinˈtɔmitə; sɪnˋtɑmɪtɚ] ***n***. (记录空气中尘埃污染物等的)气味计。

scep·sis [ˈskepsis; ˋskɛpsɪs] ***n***. **1.** 怀疑。**2.** 怀疑哲学;怀疑主义。

scep·ter [ˈseptə; ˋsɛptɚ]〔美〕= sceptre.

scep·tic [ˈskeptik; ˋskɛptɪk] **I** ***n***. **1.** 怀疑者;抱怀疑态度者。**2.** 怀疑基督教(真理)的人;怀疑宗教教条者,无神论者。**3.**【哲】怀疑论者,不可知论者。**II** ***a***. = sceptical. **scep·ti·cal** ***a***. **1.** 怀疑(论)的。**2.** 怀疑论者的。**3.**〔口〕怀疑,不相信 (*of*; *about*)。

scep·tic·ism [ˈskeptisizəm; ˋskɛptəˏsɪzəm] ***n***. **1.** 怀疑(态度)。**2.** 怀疑论,怀疑主义。**3.** 怀疑宗教(教条)。

scep·tre, scep·ter [ˈseptə; ˋsɛptɚ] **I** ***n***. **1.** (帝王的)权杖,权标;王节。**2.** 〔the ～〕王权,王位。*lay down the* ～ 退位。*wield the* ～ 掌权,统治。**II** ***vt***. 授…以权杖;授…以王节;授…以王[君]权。

scep·tred, scep·tered [ˈseptəd; ˋsɛptɚd] ***a***. **1.** 成了帝王的;有王权的。**2.** 持王节的。

sch. = **1.** school. **2.** scholar.

scha·den·freu·de [ˈʃɑːdənfrɔidə; ˋʃadənˏfrɔɪdə] ***n***. 〔G.〕幸灾乐祸。

Schanz·e [ˈʃæntsə; ˋʃæntsə] ***n***. 〔G.〕【滑雪】跳台。

schap·pe [ʃæp, ˈʃɑːpə; ˋʃapə] ***n***.【纺】绢丝[废丝]织物。

schat·chen [ˈʃɑːtkən; ˋʃætkən] ***n***. (犹太)媒人。

sched·ule [ˈʃedjuːl, Am. ˈskedʒuːl; ˋskɛdʒʊl] **I** ***n***. **1.** 目录。**2.** 表(格);清单,明细表。**3.**〔美〕程序表,计划表;进度表;时间表。**4.**〔美〕预定日期,预定计划。*a* ～ *of prices* 定价表。*a train* ～ 火车时刻表。*a design* ～ 设计计算表,进度表。***according to*** ～ 按照预定计划[时间表]。***behind*** [***ahead of***] ～ (***time***) 比预定时间晚[早]。***file*** [***give in***] ***one's*** ～ (宣布)破产。***on*** ～ (***time***) **1.** 按时间表,准时。**2.** 按照预定计划。**II** ***vt***. **1.** 为…作目录。**2.** 将…列表,把…记入表格。**3.** 将…列入程序表[计划表,进度表];为…规定时间表[进度计划]。**4.** 排定,安排。*Supper is* ～*d for six o'clock*. 晚餐预定六时开始。***be*** ～***d to*** (*sail today*) 预定(本日开船)。～***d time*** (火车等的)时刻表,预定时间。**Scheduled Caste** [**Class**] (在印度,原先属于"不可接触"贱民阶层的)在册种姓。

scheel·ite [ˈʃiːlait; ˋʃilaɪt] ***n***.【矿】白钨矿。

sche·ma [ˈskiːmə; ˋskimə] ***n***. (*pl*. ～*ta* [-tə; -tə]) **1.** 图解;图表;略图。**2.** 摘要,一览;大要,大意;纲要,要略。**3.**【逻】(三段论法的)格。**4.**【修】词彩;词藻;修辞手段。**5.** (康德哲学的)先验图式。**6.** (东正教教士穿的)法衣。

sche·mat·ic [skiˈmætik, skə-; skɪˋmætɪk, skə-] **I** ***a***. **1.** 要领的;纲要的。**2.** 图解的,(按照)图式[公式]的。**II** ***n***. 简图〔如电路图〕。**-i·cal·ly** ***ad***.

sche·ma·tism [ˈskiːmətizəm; ˋskimətɪzəm] ***n***. **1.** 系统分类(或说明)方案;系统性的组合;(事物的)特定系统性安排。**2.** 设计。

sche·ma·tize [ˈskiːmətaiz; ˋskiməˏtaɪz] ***vi***., ***vt***. (*-tized*, *-tiz·ing*) (使)构成计划;按计划(或方案)安排(工作等)。**-ti·za·tion** [ˌskiːmətaiˈzeiʃən; ˏskimətaɪˋzeɪʃən] ***n***.

scheme [skiːm; skim] **I** ***n***. **1.** 计划;方案;路线;设计。**2.** 系统;配合;组织。**3.** 纲目;表;清单;分类表;大纲。**4.** 谋划,策划;诡计;奸计;阴谋。**5.** 图,图式,图型,图解,图表;图纸,设计图,流程图;示意图;线路图。**6.** 电路。*a* ～ *of distribution*【法】分红表。*a* ～ *of scantling*【造船】船体各部明细表。*a* ～ *of wiring*【电】线路图。*bubble* ～ 空头计划(用空头计划诱人认股,进行诈骗取利)。～ *of a symphony* 交响乐的结构。*under the present* ～ *of society* 在现社会机构下。***contrive*** [***form***, ***lay***] ***a*** ～ 计划,拟方案,策划。***in the*** ～ ***of things*** 在事物发展过程中。***prepare a*** ～ ***of***... 作…的计划。(*a painter's*) ～ ***of colour*** (某画家的)着色法。**II** ***vt***., ***vi***. **1.** 计划;设计。**2.** 策划;阴谋;图谋;策动 (*for*; *to*)。～ ***to do*** [***for***] ***sth***. 策划某事。～ ***for power*** 阴谋夺权。**-er** 计划者;阴谋家,野心家。**-ing** ***a***. **1.** 计划的。**2.** 策划的;诡诈的,诡计多端的。

Schen·gen [ˈʃengən; ˋʃɛngən] ***n***. 申根〔卢森堡一城镇〕。～ **Agreement** 申根协定〔指欧盟德、法、荷、比、卢、葡、西等七国之间的边境开放协定,于 1984 年签订于申根,1995 年 3 月开始实施〕。

scher·zan·do [skeəˈtsændəu; skerˋtsando] **I** ***a***., ***ad***. 〔It.〕【乐】戏谑的[地];玩笑的[地];愉快的[地];诙谐的[地];幽默的[地]。**II** ***n***. 诙谐[幽默]的段落。

scher·zo [ˈskeətsəu; ˋskɛrtso] ***n***. 〔It.〕【乐】诙谐曲。

Schick [ʃik; ʃɪk] **test**【医】锡[希]克氏(白喉免疫性)检验。

Schie·dam [ˈskiːdæm; skiˋdɑm] ***n***. **1.** 斯希丹〔荷兰西南部一城市名〕。**2.** 斯希丹地方所产的杜松子酒。

schil·ling [ˈʃiliŋ; ˋʃɪlɪŋ] ***n***. 先令〔奥地利货币单位,等于 100 格罗申 (*Groschen*)〕。

schip·per·ke [ˈʃipəki, ˈskip-; ˋskɪpɚkɪ, ˋskɪp-] ***n***. 一种无尾小黑狗〔原产于比利时,一种在运河上守卫载货船的守卫犬〕。

schism [ˈsizəm; ˋsɪzəm] ***n***. **1.** 分裂。**2.** (特指教会的)分立;(教会的)分派。**3.** 宗派;派别;派系。**4.**【宗】犯宗派分立罪。

schis·mat·ic [sizˈmætik; sɪzˋmætɪk] **I** ***n***. 教会分立(论)者;分裂宗教者。**II** ***a***. **1.** 分裂的。**2.** 派别的,宗派的。**3.** 教会分立论者的;犯宗派分立罪的。**-i·cal·ly** ***ad***.

schis·ma·tize [ˈsizmətaiz; ˋsɪzməˏtaɪz] ***vt***., ***vi***. (引诱…)从事(宗教)分裂活动。

schist [ʃist; ʃɪst] ***n***.【地】片岩;页岩;板岩。

schis·tose [ˈʃistəus; ˋʃɪstos] ***a***. 页(片)岩的;页(片)岩质的;页(片)岩状的。

schis·to·some [ˈʃistəsəum; ˋʃɪstəˏsom] ***n***. 血吸虫;裂体吸虫。

schis·to·so·mia·sis [ˌʃistəsə*u*ˈmaiəsis; ˏʃɪstəsoˋmaɪəsɪs] ***n***.【医】血吸虫病;裂体吸虫病。

schist·ous [ˈʃistəs; ˋʃɪstəs] ***a***. = schistose.

schiz [skits; skɪts], **schiz·o** [ˈskitsəu; ˋskɪzo] ***n***. 〔美俚〕= schizophrenia(***n***.)。**-(z)y** ***a***.

schizo- *comb. f*. 表示"分裂;裂开;解离": *schizo*genesis.

schiz·o·carp [ˈskizəkɑːp; ˋskɪzəˏkɑrp] ***n***.【植】裂果,分果,分离果。**-car·pous**, **-car·pic** ***a***.

schi·zo·gen·e·sis [ˌskizəuˈdʒenisis; ˏskɪzəˋdʒɛnɪsɪs] ***n***.【生】裂配生殖;直裂增殖。

schi·zog·o·ny [skiˈzɔgəni; skɪˋzɑgənɪ] ***n***.【动】直裂增殖;裂配生殖〔= schizogenesis〕。

Schiz·oid [ˈskizɔid; ˋskɪzɔɪd] **I** ***n***.【医】类精神分裂症患者。**II** ***a***. **1.** 类精神分裂症(患者)的。**2.**〔转义〕支离分裂的;自相矛盾的。

schiz·o·my·cete [ˌskizəumaiˈsiːt; ˏskɪzomaɪˋsit] *n.* 【生】裂殖菌类。

schiz·o·my·co·sis [ˌskizəumaiˈkəusiz; ˏskɪzomaɪˋkosɪs] *n.* 【医】裂殖菌病。

schiz·ont [ˈskizɔnt; ˋskɪzɑnt] *n.* 【生】裂殖体。

schiz·o·phrene [ˈskizəufriːn; ˋskɪzəˏfrin] *n.* 【医】精神分裂症患者。

schiz·o·phre·ni·a [ˌskizəuˈfriːniə; ˏskɪzəˋfrinɪə] *n.* 【医】精神分裂症。

schiz·o·phren·ic [ˌskizəuˈfrenik; ˏskɪzəˋfrɛnɪk] **I** *a.* 【医】患精神分裂症的。**II** *n.* 精神分裂症患者。

schiz·o·phyte [ˈskizəfait; ˋskɪzəˏfaɪt] *n.* 【植】分裂植物；分裂菌（*Schizophyta*）。**-phy·tic** [-fitik; -fɪtɪk] *a.*

schiz·o·pod [ˈskizəpɔd; ˋskɪzəˏpɑd] **I** *n.* 裂足类动物〔磷虾类和糠虾类的总称〕。**II** *a.* 裂足类动物的（= schizopodous）。

schiz·o·thy·mi·a [ˌskizəuˈθaimiə; ˏskɪzəˋθaɪmɪə] *n.* 【心】(濒临精神)分裂气质[状态]〔一种精神分裂情绪状态；没有精神分裂症那样严重〕。**-thy·mic** *a.*, *n.*

schiz·(z)y [ˈskizi; ˋskɪzɪ] *a.* 精神分裂的。

schlep, schlepp [ʃlep; ʃlɛp]〔美俚〕**I** *vt.* (*schlep·ped*; *schlep·ping*) 拖，带，运。—*vi.* 拖曳着走；费力地走。**II** *n.* 不中用[不起作用]的人；无足轻重的人；没有工作效率的人。

schlock [ʃlɔk; ʃlɑk] **I** *n.*〔美俚〕贱货；不值钱的东西；次品，劣等品。**II** *a.* 价贱的；不值钱的；次劣的。

schloss [ʃlɔːs; ʃlɔs] *n.*〔G.〕城堡，堡垒。

schmaltz [ʃmɑːlts; ʃmɑlts] *n.*〔G.〕〔美俚〕**1.** 脆弱的感情；伤感。**2.** 极度伤感[渲染、夸张]的音乐[文艺作品]。**3.** 感伤的风格。**4.** (鸡的)脂肪，油腻。～ **herring**【动】鲱鱼。**-y** *a.*

schmalz [ʃmɔːlts; ʃmɑls]〔G.〕= schmaltz.

schmo [ʃməu; ʃmo] *n.* (*pl.* ～(*e*)*s*)〔美俚〕呆子，笨蛋，傻瓜，愚人。亦作 **schmoe**.

schmooze [ʃmuːz; ʃmuz] **I** *vi.* (*schmooz·ed*, *schmooz·ing*)〔美俚〕聊天，扯皮，说闲话，搬弄是非。**II** *n.* 闲谈，闲话，流言蜚语。亦作 **schmoos** [ʃmuːs; ʃmuz].

schmuck [ʃmʌk; ʃmʌk] *n.*〔美俚〕笨蛋，粗鄙的人，愚人。

Schna·bel [ˈʃnɑːbəl; ˋʃnɑbəl] *n.* 施纳贝尔〔姓氏〕。

schnap(p)s [ʃnæps; ʃnæps] *n.* **1.** 荷兰杜松子酒。**2.** 烈酒。

schnau·zer [ˈʃnauzə; ˋʃnauzɚ] *n.* (德国种)刚毛狸犬。

schnit·zel [ˈʃnitsl; ˋʃnɪtsl̩] *n.* 肉片；炸肉片〔尤指小牛肉片〕。

schnook [ʃnuk; ʃnuk] *n.*〔美俚〕易受骗的人；头脑简单的人；可怜虫。

schnor·kel, schnor·kle [ˈʃnɔːkl; ˋʃnɔrkəl] *n.* = snorkel.

schnor·rer [ˈʃnɔrə; ˋʃnɔrɚ] *n.*〔美俚〕乞丐，叫化子；过寄生生活者，食客。

schnoz·zle [ˈʃnɔzl; ˋʃnɑzəl], **schnoz·zo·la** [ʃnɔˈzəulə; ʃnɑˋzolə] *n.*〔美俚〕鼻子。

Scho·field [ˈskəufiːld; ˋskoˏfild] *n.* 斯科菲尔德〔姓氏〕。

schol. = scholarship.

schol·ar [ˈskɔlə; ˋskɑlɚ] *n.* **1.** 学者；古典学者；〔俚〕有文化的人，有某种文科知识的人。**2.** 公费生，领有奖学金的学生。**3.** 学生；门徒；学习者。*He is no* ～. 他决非学者[有学问的人]。*I am a poor hand as a* ～. = *I am not much of a* ～. 我没有什么文化。*a general* ～ 博学的人。*an apt* ～ 颖悟的学生。～**-bureaucrat** (中国旧时的)士大夫。～ **tyrant** 学阀。**-ly** *a.* **1.** 学者派头的，学究气的。**2.** 有学问的，博学的。**-ship** **1.** 学问，学识。**2.** 学业成绩，学习成就。**3.** 奖学金。

scho·las·tic [skəˈlæstik; skoˋlæstɪk] **I** *a.* **1.** 学校的，(学校)教育的。**2.** (像)学生的。**3.** (像)学者的；学究的；烦琐的；卖弄学问的。**4.** 教师的。**5.** 学术的。**6.**〔常 S-〕经院[烦琐]哲学(派，家)的。～ *attainments* 学业成绩。*a* ～ *attire* 校服。～ *education* 学校教育。*a* ～ *institution* 学校。～ *philosophy* 经院哲学；烦琐哲学。**II** *n.* **1.** 有学者派头的人，卖弄学问的人。**2.** 经院[烦琐]哲学家。**-ti·cal·ly** *ad.*

scho·las·ti·cate [skəˈlæstikeit, -kit; skəˋlæstəkɪt] *n.* 【天主】神学院(尤指耶稣会神学院)。

scho·las·ti·cism [skəˈlæstisizəm; skoˋlæstəˏsɪzəm] *n.* **1.** 经院哲学；烦琐哲学。**2.** 墨守成规。

scho·li·a [ˈskəuliə; ˋskolɪə] *n.* scholium 的复数。

scho·li·ast [ˈskəuliæst; ˋskolɪˏæst] *n.* (古典著作的)注释者，评注者。**-li·as·tic** [ˌskəuliˈæstik; ˏskolɪˋæstɪk] *a.*

scho·li·um [ˈskəuliəm; ˋskolɪəm] *n.* (*pl.* ～*s*, *-li·a*) **1.**〔常 *pl.*〕(对于古典著作的)旁注。**2.** 注释，注解，评注。

school[1] [skuːl; skul] **I** *n.* **1.** 学校；〔美〕(大学的)学部，学院；学系；校舍；讲堂，教室。**2.** 研究所，训练所，养成所。**3.**〔不用冠词〕学，学业；上课；功课；授课(时间)；学期。**4.** 全体学生；全体师生。**5.**〔喻〕经验；锻炼所，修养所；学习[修养]环境。**6.** 学派，(画家等的)流派；派别；(机械等的)型。**7.** (牛津大学等的)学位考试科目；〔*pl.*〕大学毕业考试。**8.** (中世纪大学的)学科；学会；〔the ～s〕〔集合词〕大学，学界。**9.** (哲学家、艺术家等的)门徒。**10.** (大学的)讲堂；〔*pl.*〕(牛津大学等的)考场。**11.** 锻炼；【乐】教授规程；【军】训练(规程)。*a continuation* ～ 职业补习学校；成人学校。*a medical* [*law*] ～ 医[法]学部[学院]。*an artisan* ～ 技工学校。*a trade* [*vocational*] ～ 职业学校。*a national* ～〔英〕公立学校。*the chemistry* ～ 化学教室。*a sixth form* ～〔英〕六年级教室。*S- begins at nine o'clock.* 九点钟开始上课。*The whole* ～ *was punished.* 全校学生都受处罚了。*two* ～*s of aviating apparatus* 飞行机的两大类型。***after*** ～ 下课后，放学后（*I will tell you after* ～. 下课后跟你讲）。***at*** ～ **1.** 在学校。**2.** 在求学。**3.** 在上课。***be dismissed*** [***expelled***] ***from*** ～ 被开除学籍。***begin*** [***start***] ～ 开始求学。***finish*** ～ 完成学业。***go to*** ～ 到校上课；上学去；开始求学。***go to*** ～ ***to*** (*sb.*) 受教于某人，跟某人学习，模仿(某人)。***have no*** ～ ***today*** 今天无课。***in*** ～ 在上[求]学。***in the hard*** ～ ***of adversity*** 经受逆境的艰苦锻炼。***in the*** ～*s* = ***in for one's*** ～*s* (某人)正在考试，正在考(牛津大学)学位考试。***keep a*** ～ 办(私立)学校。***leave*** ～ **1.** 退学。**2.** (毕业)离校。**3.** 放学回家。***old*** ～ ***tie***〔英〕毕业后沿用不舍的母校特殊图案的领带；〔转义〕感情用事的地方[怀旧]观念。***put*** [***send***] ***a child to*** ～ 送孩子进学校。～ ***fee***(***s***) 学费。～ ***pence***〔英〕小学校的每周学费。***stay away from*** ～ 旷课（= cut ～）。***teach*** ～〔古〕教学，教书，当教师〔现普通说作 ***teach in a*** ～〕，***tell tales out of*** ～ 见 tale 条。

II *vt.* **1.**〔罕〕给…上学，把…送进学校；在…学习。**2.** 教，教授；教育，教导，教训；训练，锻炼。**3.** 约束，克制。**4.** 训戒。*a well* ～*ed man* 受过良好教育的人；有教养的人。～ *a horse* 驯马。～ *oneself to patience* 锻炼[养成]忍耐力[性]。*be* ～*ed in war* 受过战争训练；富有战争经验。～ *one's temper* 克制脾气。*He will not be* ～*ed.* 他不听人劝导。～ **aeroplane**【空】教练机，练习机。～ **age** **1.** 入学年龄。**2.** 接受义务教育的年限。～**-ager** 学龄儿童。～ **bag** 书包。～ **board** (地方上管理公立学校的)教育委员会。～**-book** **1.** *n.* 教科书。**2.** *a.*〔美〕教科书式的，过于简略的。～ **boy** (小学，中学的)学生。～ **bus** 校车。～ **commissioner**〔美〕督学。～ **committee**〔美〕(由居民中选出人组成参与管理学校事务的)学校委员会。～ **day** 授课日，上课日。～**-day** 学生时代。～ **edition** 书籍作教科书用的版本。～ **fellow** 同校；校友。～ **girl** (小学、中学的)女(学)生。～ **house** **1.** 校舍；小学教员宿舍。**2.** (S- House)〔英〕(public school 的)校长住宅。**3.** 全体寄宿生。～ **inspector** 视学员；督学。

S

~ **ma'am**, ~ **marm**〔美口〕= schoolmistress **1.** 女教师。**2.** 卖弄学问的女人。**3.** 架子十足[傲慢]的女人。~**man** **1.**〔S-〕经院哲学家;烦琐哲学家。**2.**〔*pl.*〕〔美俚〕教师;学者。~**master** **1.** 教师;(男)教员。**2.** 校长。~**mastering** **1.** 当教员。**2.** 学校教育。~ **masterly** *a*. **1.** 教员派头的,教员似的。**2.** 卖弄学问的。~**-mate** *n*. 同学。~ **miss** **1.** 女学生。**2.** 女学生脾气的姑娘。~ **mistress** *n*. **1.** 女教员。**2.** 女校长。~**-room** 教室,讲堂。~**-ship**【军】教练舰,练习舰,教练船。~**teacher** 教师〔尤指小学教员〕。~**teaching** **1.** 教学。**2.** 职业。~ **time** **1.** (学校的)上课时间。**2.** (家里的)用功时间;自修时间。**3.** 训练时间。**4.** 求学时代,学生时代。~ **voucher** 教育补助金券〔可由家长申请,为子女支付学费〕。~**work** 课堂作业,课外作业。~ **yard** **1.** 校园。**2.** (学校的)运动场。~ **year** 学年。

school²[sku:l; skul] **I** *n*. (鱼、鲸等水族动物的)群;队。*a ~ of dolphins* 一群海豚。**II** *vi*. (鱼)成群结队地游,成群前进。~ ***up*** 成群游进水面;集在水面附近。

school·ing [ˈsku:liŋ; ˋskulɪŋ] *n*. **1.** 学校教育;教育。**2.** 学费。**3.** 训练,锻炼;驯马,练马。*He did not get much ~.* 他没有上过多少学[受过多少学校教育]。*to shorten the length of ~* 缩短学制[学习期限]。*a man with less ~* 文化水平较低的人。*pay for the ~ of one's children* 付孩子的学费。

schoon·er [ˈsku:nə; ˋskunɚ] *n*. **1.** 双桅[三桅、四桅]纵帆船。**2.**〔美〕(拓荒者用的)有篷四轮大马车,大篷车(= prairie)。**3.**〔美〕大啤酒杯。~ **rigged** 有纵帆装置的;纵帆式的。

S

Scho·pen·hau·er [ˈʃəupənhauə; ˋʃopən͵hauɚ] *n*. 叔本华, **Arthur**〔1788—1860,德国厌世主义哲学家〕。

schorl [ʃɔ:l; ʃɔrl] *n*.〔G.〕【地】黑电气石(黑碧晒)。**-a·ceous** [ʃɔ:ˈleiʃəs; ʃɔrˋleʃəs] *a*.

schot·tisch(e) [ʃɔˈti:ʃ, Am. ˈʃɔtiʃ; ˋʃɑtɪʃ] *n*. **1.**【乐】一种类似波尔卡 (polka) 的苏格兰慢步圆舞。**2.** 苏格兰慢步圆舞曲。

schtick, schtik [ʃtik; ʃtɪk] *n*.〔美俚〕= shtick.

schul [ʃu:l; ʃul] *n*. = shul.

Schu·man(n) [ˈʃu:mən; ˋʃumən] *n*. **1.** 舒曼〔姓氏〕。**2.** **Robert** ~ 罗伯特·舒曼〔1810—1856,德国作曲家〕。

Schurz [ʃurts; ʃurts] *n*. 舒尔茨〔姓氏〕。

schuss [ʃus; ʃʊs] **I** *n*.〔G.〕(滑雪)直下。**II** *vi*. (滑雪)全速直下。**-er** *n*. 直线全速滑雪者。

schutz·mine [ˈʃutsmi:nə; ˋʃutsminə] *n*.〔G.〕【军】榴霰地雷。

Schutz·staf·fel [ˈʃutsˈʃtɑ:fəl; ˋʃuts͵ʃtɑfəl] *n*.〔G.〕(纳粹的)党卫队,黑衫队(略 S.S. 或 SS.)。

Schuy·ler [ˈskailə; ˋskaɪlɚ] *n*. 斯凯勒〔姓氏〕。

schwa [ʃwɑ:, G. ʃvɑ:; ʃwɑ] *n*. **1.** (英语弱读音节中的)中性母音〔如 *ago* 中的 *a*, *agent* 的 *e*, *sanity* 中的 *i* 等〕。**2.** 国际音标中的[ə]符号。

Schwa·be [ʃwɑ:b; ʃwɑb] *n*. 施瓦布〔姓氏〕。

Schwann [ʃwɔn; ʃwɑn] *n*. 施沃恩〔姓氏〕。

Schwer·punkt [ˈʃvə:rpuŋkt; ˋʃvɚ͵puŋkt] *n*.〔G.〕【军】重点突破战术。

sci. = science; scientific.

sci·ae·nid [saiˈi:nid; saɪˋinɪd] *n*. 石首鱼科 (*Sciaenidea*) 的鱼〔包括石首鱼,黄花鱼〕。**sci·ae·noid** [-nɔid; -nɔɪd] *a*., *n*.

sci·a·gram [ˈsaiəgræm; ˋsaɪə͵græm] *n*. X 射线照片 (= skiagram)。

sci·a·graph [ˈsaiəgrɑ:f; ˋsaɪə͵græf] **I** *n*. **1.** (特指用 X 射线照射的)投影图,X 射线照片。**2.** 房屋纵断面图。**II** *vt*. 对…作 X 射线摄影;对…摄制投影图。

sci·ag·ra·phy [saiˈægrəfi; saɪ͵ægrəfɪ] *n*. **1.** 投影法;X 线照相术。**2.** 房屋纵断面图。**3.**【天】星影计时法。

sci·am·a·chy [saiˈæməki; saɪˋæməkɪ] *n*. 假想战,模拟战;同想像的敌人作战,同影子作战。

sci·am·e·try [saiˈæmitri; saɪˋæmətrɪ] *n*. **1.**【天】日月蚀的数学理论。**2.**【物】射线的数学研究。

sci·at·ic [saiˈætik; saɪˋætɪk] *a*. **1.**【生理、医】坐骨(神经)的。**2.** 坐骨神经(痛)的。

sci·at·i·ca [saiˈætikə; saɪˋætɪkə] *n*.【医】坐骨神经痛。

SCID, Scid = severe combined immunodeficiency【医】严重免疫力缺乏综合症。

sci·ence [ˈsaiəns; ˋsaɪəns] *n*. **1.** 科学;科学研究。**2.** (一门)科学,学科。**3.** 自然科学。**4.** 学;学问;〔古〕知识。**5.** (拳术、马术等的)技术,专门技巧;〔the ~〕〔卑〕拳术。**6.**〔有时作 S-〕信仰疗法,基督教精神疗法〔又称 Christian S-〕。*the pure ~* 纯理论科学。*the ~ of history* 历史学。*social ~* 社会科学。*the most advanced branches of ~ and technology* 尖端科学技术。*physical ~* 自然科学,物理(科)学。*natural ~* 自然科学。*borderline* [*boundary*] *~* 边缘科学。*~ and learning* [*scholarship*] 自然科学和人文科学;学术;学艺。*the Academy of S-* 科学院。*a man of ~* 科学家。*a bachelor of ~* 理学士。*a doctor of ~* 理学博士。***the noble ~*** (***of defence***) 自卫术,拳术,剑术。~ **fiction** 科学(幻想)小说。

sci·en·ti·a est po·ten·ti·a [ski:ˈentiɑ: est pəuˈtenti:ɑ:; skɪˋɛnti͵ɑ ɛst poˋtɛnti͵ɑ]〔L.〕知识就是力量。

sci·en·tial [saiˈenʃəl; saɪˋɛnʃəl] *a*. **1.** 知识的,学问的。**2.** 有知识的,有学问的;学识丰富的。

sci·en·tif·ic [ˌsaiənˈtifik; ͵saɪənˋtɪfɪk] *a*. **1.** (自然)科学(上)的,学术(上)的,科学性的;从事科学工作的。**2.** 应用科学的。**3.** 精通学理的,有学问的。**4.** 合乎科学的;方法正确的;有系统的。**5.** 有专长的。**6.** 有本事的;技术纯熟的;有技巧的。*~ and learned circles* 学术界。*~ studies* [*~ researches*] 科学研究。*a ~ method* 科学方法。*~ experiments* 科学实验。*a ~ man* 科学家。*~ socialism* 科学社会主义。*~ farming* 科学种田。**-i·cal·ly** *ad*.

sci·en·tism [ˈsaiəntizəm; ˋsaɪəntɪzəm] *n*. **1.** 科学信念;科学态度;科学方法。**2.** 唯科学主义。**sci·en·tis·tic** [ˌsaiənˈtistik; ͵saɪənˋtɪstɪk] *a*.

sci·en·tist [ˈsaiəntist; ˋsaɪəntɪst] *n*. **1.** 科学家,自然科学家,科学工作者。★有人爱用 man of science 来代替此字。**2.**【宗】〔S-〕信仰疗法者,基督教精神疗法者 (= Christian S-)。

sci·en·to·me·trics [ˌsaiəntəuˈmetriks; ͵saɪəntoˋmɛtrɪks] *n*. 科学计量学〔信息科学的一个分支〕。

sci. fa. =〔L.〕*scire facias*.

sci-fi [ˈsaiˈfai; ˋsaɪˋfaɪ] *a*., *n*. = science fiction.

scil. =〔L.〕*scilicet* (= namely)。

sci·li·cet [ˈsailiset; ˋsɪlɪ͵sɛt] *ad*.〔L.〕即,就是,换句话说〔缩写 sc.,或 scil.,或 SS.,或 ss.〕。

Scil·la [ˈsilə; ˋsɪlə] *n*.【希神】(居于意大利墨西拿 (Messina) 海峡岩礁上的)六头女妖;意大利墨西拿海峡上的岩礁 (= Scylla)。

scil·la [ˈsilə; ˋsɪlə] *n*.【植】绵枣儿属 (*Scilla*) 植物;〔尤指〕西伯利亚绵枣儿 (*Scilla sibirica*);海葱 (= squill)。

scim·e·tar, scim·i·tar, -ter [ˈsimitə; ˋsɪmətɚ] *n*. (阿拉伯人的)单刃短弯刀,偃月刀;半月形镰刀。

scin·coid [ˈsiŋkɔid; ˋsɪŋ͵kɔɪd] **I** *a*.【动】**1.** 石龙子科的。**2.** 石龙子科动物状的。**II** *n*. 石龙子,蜥蜴。

scin·ti·gram [ˈsintəgræm; ˋsɪntə͵græm] *n*.【激】闪烁(曲线),闪烁图。

scin·tig·ra·phy [sinˈtigrəfi; sɪnˋtɪgrəfɪ] *n*.【物理】闪烁录像术。

scin·til·la [sinˈtilə; sɪnˋtɪlə] *n*. **1.** 火花;闪烁。**2.** 微分子。**3.**〔通例用于否定〕微量;极少,一点。***not a ~ of*** 一丁点…也没有。

scin·til·lant [ˈsintilənt; ˋsɪntələnt] *a*. 发火花的;闪烁的。

scin·til·late [ˈsintileit; ˋsɪntl͵et] *vi*. **1.** 发(出)火花,发

闪光。2. 闪烁。3. (才气)焕发。—vt. 发(出)(火花等)。*Her eyes ~ anger*. 她的眼睛闪烁着愤怒的光芒。

scin·til·la·tion [ˌsintiˈleiʃən; ˏsɪntḷˋeʃən] *n*. 1. 放射闪光,发出火花。2. 闪光,火花。3.【天、物】闪烁(现象)。4. (才气的)焕发,(天才)横溢。~ **camera** 闪烁摄影机。~ **counter**【物】= scintillometer.

scin·til·la·tor [ˈsintileitə; ˋsɪntḷˏetɚ] *n*. 1. 闪烁者,闪烁物。2.【物】闪烁体,闪烁器。

scin·til·lome·ter [ˌsintiˈlɔmitə; ˏsɪntəˋlɑmətɚ] *n*.【物】闪烁计数器 (= scintillation counter)。

scin·til·lo·scope [sinˈtiləskəup; sɪnˋtɪləˏskop] *n*.【物】闪烁(观察)镜。

scin·ti·scan·ner [ˈsintiˌskænə; ˋsɪntɪˏskænɚ] *n*.【物】闪烁扫描器。

sci·o·cra·cy [ˈsaiəkrəsi; ˋsaɪəkrəsɪ] *n*. 科学民主统治。

sci·o·graph [ˈsaiəgrɑːf; ˋsaɪəˏgræf] *n*. = skiagraph. **-ic** *a*.

sci·o·lism [ˈsaiəlizəm; ˋsaɪəˏlɪzəm] *n*. 一知半解;浅学。**sci·o·list** *n*. 学识肤浅的人,一知半解的人,半瓶醋。**-lis·tic** [ˌsaiəˈlistik; ˏsaɪəˋlɪstɪk] *a*. 学识肤浅(者)的,一知半解(者)的,半瓶醋的。

sciol·to [ˈʃɔltəu; ˋʃolto] *ad*. [It.]【乐】1. 自由地;敏捷地;无拘无束地。2. 断音地;断开地;分开地。

sci·om·a·chy [saiˈɔməki; saɪˋɑməkɪ] *n*. = sciamachy.

sci·o·man·cy [ˈsaiəmənsi; ˋsaɪəmənsɪ] *n*. 扶乩;关亡。

sci·on [ˈsaiən; ˋsaɪən] *n*. 1.【植】接穗;(栽种或接枝用的)幼枝,幼芽。2. (主指贵族等的)小孩;后裔。*a ~ of a noble family* [*royal stock*] 贵族[皇家]家庭的子弟。

sci·op·tic [saiˈɔptik; saɪˋɑptɪk], **sci·op·tric** [saiˈɔptrik; saɪˋɔptrɪk] *a*. 用暗箱(成像)的。

sci·re fa·ci·as [ˈsaiəri ˈfeiʃiæs; ˋsaɪrɪ ˋfeʃɪæs] [L.]【法】请告知;请说明理由〔法院命令关系人说明某项成案何以不执行的书状〕。

scir·rhous [ˈsirəs; ˋsɪrəs] *a*.【医】硬(性)癌的。

scir·rhus [ˈsirəs; ˋsɪrəs] *n*. (*pl*. ***scir·rhi*** [ˈsirai; ˋsɪraɪ], ~*es*)【医】硬(性)癌。

scis·sel [ˈsisəl; ˋsɪsḷ] *n*.【机】1. (金属板[片]的)切屑;截屑。2. (冲压后的)金属板余料。

scis·sile [ˈsisil; ˋsɪsɪl] *a*. 可被切割[分裂](成片)的。

scis·sion [ˈsiʒən, ˈsiʃən; ˋsɪʒən] *n*. 1. 切断,割断;剪断。2. 分离,分裂,裂开。3.【物】裂变。

scis·sor [ˈsizə; ˋsɪzɚ] *vt*. 1. (用剪刀)剪,剪断,剪下〔与 off, up, out 连用〕。2. 删除,削减。~ *out a paragraph from a newspaper* 从报纸上剪下一段新闻。~ *up a newspaper* 把报纸剪碎。~ *off a piece of cloth* 剪下一块布来。*items ~ed* 削除了的项目。**~bill**〔美工俚〕1. 对本阶级利益不关心的工人;不参加工会的工人。2. 庄稼汉;没知识的人。**~-bird** = ~ tail. **~-cut** 剪纸。**~-tail**【鸟】(美西南及墨西哥产的)铗尾鸟。~ **tooth** (食肉动物的)裂齿。

scis·sor·ing [ˈsizəriŋ; ˋsɪzərɪŋ] *n*. 1. 剪。2. 〔*pl*.〕剪下来的东西。

scis·sors [ˈsizəz; ˋsɪzəz] *n*. 〔*pl*.〕1. 〔亦可用作单数〕(一把)剪刀,剪子。2. 〔用作单数〕【体】交叉,两腿前后错跃;【摔跤】= ~ hold. *a pair of ~* 一把剪刀。*I want some ~*. 我要几把剪刀。*The ~ aren't sharp*. 这把剪刀不快。*A ~ was lying on the table*. 一把剪刀放在桌子上。~ **and paste** 剪贴工作,编纂工作;东鳞西爪凑合成的东西。**~bird** = scissortail. ~ **chair** (打开后成X形的)折椅。~ **hold**【摔跤】脚搭勾。~ **kick** (游泳,尤指侧泳的)剪水动作。~ **plane** 剪(翼)式飞机。**~tail** = scissortail.

scis·sure [ˈsiʒə; ˋsɪʒɚ] *n*. 〔现罕〕裂口;(身体上或器官上的)纵切口,裂隙。

sci·u·rid [saiˈjuərid; saɪˋjʊrɪd] *n*. 松鼠科 (*Sciuridae*) 动物〔包括松鼠、黄鼠、土拨鼠等〕。**sci·u·roid** [saiˈjuərɔid; saɪˋjʊrɔɪd] *a*. 1. (似)松鼠的。2. 松鼠尾巴状的。

sclaff [sklæf; sklæf] I *vt*.【高尔夫球】用球棒擦[刮]地,把球棒擦着地面打(球)。II *n*. 1. 用球棒擦地一击。2. 〔Scot.〕轻拍,轻击。

scle·ra [ˈskliərə; ˋsklɪrə] *n*.【解】(眼球的)巩膜。

scle·re·id [ˈskliːriid; ˋsklirud] *n*.【植】石细胞,硬化细胞。

scle·ren·chy·ma [skliəˈreŋkimə; sklɪˋrɛŋkɪmə] *n*. 1.【植】厚壁组织。2.【动】石核组织。

scle·ri·a·sis [skliəˈraiəsis; sklɪˋraɪəsɪs] *n*.【医】1. 硬皮病。2. 睑硬结。

scle·rite [ˈskliərait; ˋsklɪraɪt] *n*.【古生】(骨)片;灰质体。

scle·rit·is [skliˈraitis; sklɪˋraɪtɪs] *n*.【医】巩膜炎〔亦作 sclerotitis〕。

scle·ro- *comb. f*. 表示"硬,厚〔在母音前作 scler-〕": *sclero*ma.

scler·o·der·ma [ˌskliərəuˈdəːmə; ˏsklɪrəˋdɝmə] *n*.【医】硬皮病;皮硬化症。

scler·o·der·ma·tous [ˌskliərəuˈdəːmətəs; ˏsklɪrəˋdɝmətəs] *a*. 1. 硬皮病的;皮硬化症的。2.【动】长着硬皮的〔如角质鳞片〕。

scler·oid [ˈskliərɔid; ˋsklɪrɔɪd] *a*.【生】硬的;硬化的,硬结的。

scle·ro·ma [skliəˈrəumə; sklɪˋromə] *n*. (*pl*. ***-ma·ta*** [-mətə;-mətə])【医】硬结。

scle·rom·e·ter [skliəˈrɔmitə; sklɪˋrɑmətɚ] *n*.【机】硬度计〔测矿的硬度〕。

scle·ro·pro·tein [ˌskliərəuˈprəutiːn; ˏsklɪrəˋprotin] *n*.【生化】硬蛋白。

scle·rosed [ˈskliərəust, skliˈrəust; ˋsklɪrost, sklɪˋrost] *a*.【医】患硬化症的;硬化的,硬结的。

scle·ro·sis [skliəˈrəusis; sklɪˋrosɪs] *n*. (*pl*. ***-ses*** [-siːz; -siz]) 1.【医】硬化(症)。2.【植】细胞壁硬化。**-ro·sal** *a*.

scle·rot·ic [skliəˈrɔtik; sklɪˋrɑtɪk] I *a*. 1. 硬的,厚的;硬性的。2.【解】巩膜的。3.【医】硬化的;硬结的。II *n*. 1.【解】巩膜。2. 硬结药,硬化剂。~ *cells* 石细胞。

scle·ro·ti·tis [ˌskliərəuˈtaitis; ˏsklɪrəˋtaɪtɪs] *n*.【医】巩膜炎。

scle·ro·ti·um [skliˈrəuʃiəm; sklɪˋroʃɪəm] *n*. (*pl*. ***-ti·a*** [-ʃiə; -ʃɪə])【生】硬化体;菌核。**scle·ro·tial** [-ʃiəl; -ʃɪəl] *a*.

scle·rot·o·my [skliˈrɔtəmi; sklɪˋrɑtəmɪ] *n*. (*pl*. ***-mies***)【医】巩膜切开术。

scle·rous [ˈskliərəs; ˋsklɪrəs] *a*. 硬化的;骨的,多骨的;骨质的。

Sc. M. = 〔L.〕*Scientiae Magister* 理学硕士 (= Master of Science)。

scobs [skɔbz; skɑbz] *n*. 〔*sing*., *pl*.〕(角、金属等的)锯屑;锯末;锉屑;刨花。

scoff[1] [skɔf; skɔf] I *n*. 1. (特指对宗教的)嘲笑;嘲弄;冷笑 (*at*)。2. 笑柄 (*of*)。II *vi*., *vt*. 嘲笑;嘲弄;冷笑。**-er** *n*. 嘲笑者。**-ing·ly** *ad*. 嘲笑地。

scoff[2] [skɔf; skɔf] I *vt*., *vi*. 1. 〔俚〕狼吞虎咽地吃;饱食。2. 掠夺,攫取。II *n*. 〔俚〕食物;伙食,饭餐。

scoff·law [ˈskɔːflɔː; ˋskɔfˏlɔ] *n*. 〔美口〕惯犯〔尤指违犯交通规则和禁酒法者〕。

scold [skəuld; skold] I *vt*., *vi*. 责骂;叱责。II *n*. 唠唠叨叨[吵吵嚷嚷,高声]骂人的人[妇女],〔特指〕(好骂人的)泼妇。*a common ~* 整天骂人吵得四邻不安的泼妇。**-er** *n*. 责骂者。

scold·ing [ˈskəuldiŋ; ˋskoldɪŋ] I *n*. 责骂,叱责,斥责。*get* [*receive*] *a good ~* 挨一顿大骂。*give sb. a good ~* 把某人大骂一顿。II *a*. 责骂的,叱责的,斥责的;(女人等)爱骂人的。

scol·e·cite [ˈskɔlisait, ˈskəul-; ˋskɑləˏsaɪt, ˋskolə-] *n*.【地】钙沸石。

sco·lex [ˈskəuleks; ˋskolɛks] *n*. (*pl*. ***sco·le·ces*** [skəuˈliːsiːz; skoˋlisiz])【动】(绦虫的)头节,头结。

scol·i·o·sis [ˌskɔliˈəusis; ˏskoliˋosɪs] *n*.【医】脊柱侧凸。

scol·lop [ˈskɔləp; ˋskɑləp] *n*., *vt*., *vi*. = scallop.

scol·o·pen·dra [ˌskɔləuˈpendrə; ˏskɑləˋpɛndrə] *n*. 1.〔S-〕【动】蜈蚣属。2. 蜈蚣。**-drid** [-drid; -drɪd] *a*.

scol·o·pen·drine [ˌskɔləuˈpendrain; ˏskɑləˋpɛndraɪn] *a*.【动】蜈蚣(属)的。

Scom·ber [ˈskɔmbə; ˋskɑmbɚ] *n*. (*pl*. ***-bri*** [-bri; -brɪ])【动】鲭鱼属。

scom·brid [ˈskɔmbrid; ˋskɑmbrɪd], **scom·broid** [-brɔid; -brɔɪd] *a*., *n*.【动】鲭鱼科(的);鲭鱼(科)。

scon [skɔn; skon] *n*. = scone.

sconce[1] [skɔns; skɑns] **I** *n*. 1. (孤立的)小堡垒。2. 隐身处;保护所;避难处[室]。3. 盔。4.〔口〕头,脑袋。5. 才智,智慧,智力,脑力。6. 人头税;特指牛津大学学生违反席间礼貌[吃饭规矩]时的(轻微)惩罚〔或罚出啤酒钱,或喝啤酒〕。7. 浮冰的碎块。**II** *vt*. 1. 筑堡垒守护。2. 对…征收人头税。3. 对…施以薄惩〔特指牛津大学学生违反席间礼貌[吃饭规矩]时被罚出啤酒钱,或喝啤酒〕。

sconce[2] [skɔns; skɑns] *n*. (钉在墙上的)烛台;灯台。

scone [skɔn, skəun; skon] *n*.〔Scot.〕〔英〕(大麦或燕麦等制的)甜烙饼,烤饼〔圆或扇形的〕。

scoop [skuːp; skup] **I** *n*. 1. 勺,杓;戽斗;大匙;勺状物[工具];【医】匙。2. 铲;铲斗;〔英〕煤斗。3. 捞(鱼)网,挡网 (= scoop-net);【空】收集器。4.【机】洞,穴,口,凹进处。5. 舀子。6. (一)舀(之量),(一)铲(之量)。7.〔俚〕(能给一份报纸产生好处的)(独家)内幕(特快)消息,独家新闻,本报特讯,特稿;秘闻。8.〔口〕(由投机而抢先赚取的)一大笔钱,暴利。9. 汤匙形墁刀。*an air* ~【空】(戽斗式)空气吸入孔,进气孔。***at a*** [***one***] ~ 一勺,一舀,一铲;一下子。***get a*** ~ ***on other papers*** 登出特快消息[特讯]压倒他报。***in*** [***with***] ***one*** ~ 一勺;一舀;一铲;一下子。***make a*** ~ 舀一杓;铲一铲。***make a big*** ~〔口〕发大财;抢先得到新闻。***on the*** ~ 饮酒过度;乐而忘返。

II *vt*. 1. 舀 (*out of*)。2. 挖,掘,淘;淘空,挖空;通过淘挖而做成。3.〔口〕扒进;大赚一笔。4. 比…抢先登出特快消息。~ *a rival paper* 用号外消息压倒一家相竞争的报纸。~ ***in*** 1. 舀进。2.〔口〕赚到。~ ***out***【军】接应〔轰炸机返航时由战斗机接应,击退敌机追击〕。~ **channel** 水槽。~ **full** 一(满)勺之量。~ **neck** (开得较低的)圆领口。~ **net** 捞(鱼)网,挡网。~**-wheel** 斗式挖泥转轮;汲水车;戽水水车。**-er** *n*. 舀[掘、掏]的人;(雕刻用的)凿刀。

scoot [skuːt; skut]〔口〕**I** *vi*., *vt*. 1. (使)迅速跑开。2. (使)溜走。3. (使)射出;(使)喷出。**II** *n*. 迅速跑开;溜走;疾走。

scoot·er[1] [ˈskuːtə; ˋskutɚ] *n*. 1. 踏板车〔儿童一脚踏在板上,一脚在地上撑着跑的玩具车〕。2. (像踏板车似的)小型摩托车,速克达机车。3. 水上冰上两用的平底小帆船。4.〔Scot.〕水枪,喷水器。5.【农】开垄犁。6.【天】急驶风暴云〔指海王星表面上像小型摩托车急驶般的较小风暴云系〕。*a motor* ~〔美〕摩托两用(水上冰上)艇。

scoot·er[2] [ˈskuːtə; ˋskutɚ] *n*. = scoter.

scop [skɔp, skəup; skɑp, skop] *n*. 古代盎格鲁撒克逊的(吟游)诗人。

sco·pa [ˈskəupə; ˋskopə] *n*.【动】(蜂等昆虫足上的)花粉刷[栉]。

scope [skəup; skop] *n*. 1. (活动)范围。2. 眼界,视界;视野;见识。3. 力量,能力。4. 发挥能力的"用武之地",余地;机会。5. 广度,广袤;地域。6.【数】分野,辖域。7. (箭式导弹等的)射程。8.【海】(抛出的)锚缆长度。9. 观测设备;显示器;阴极射线管。10.〔美俚〕潜望镜。11.〔古〕目的。12. (算命用的)星占图,天宫图。***beyond*** [***outside***] ***sb.'s*** ~ 越出某人力量范围之外。***give line and*** ~ 先纵后擒;先给自由后压制。***give*** ~ ***to*** [***for***] 给与…以…的自由;给…以发挥…的机会。***have*** (***an***) ***ample*** [(***a***) ***full***, (***a***) ***large***] ~ (***for***) 有充分发挥能力的机会[活动的余地]。***have*** (***a***) ***free*** ~ 有…的自由。***have no*** ~ ***for the imagination*** 无想像的余地。***of wide*** ~ 广泛的,广大的 (*a mind of wide* ~ 见识广大的人。*an undertaking of wide* ~ 范围广大的事业)。***seek*** ~ ***for*** 寻求发挥…的机会;找…(活动的)机会。***within the*** ~ ***of*** 在…的范围内;在…所及的地方。

-scope *suf*. 表示"看的东西,看的器械,…镜,…指示器": tele*scope*.

sco·pol·am·in(e) [skəuˈpɔləmin, ˌskəupəˈlæmin; skoˋpɑləmin, ˏskopəˋlæmɪn] *n*.【化】莨菪胺。

sco·po·phil·i·a [ˌskəupəuˈfiliə; ˏskopəˋfɪlɪə], **scop·to·phil·i·a** [ˌskɔptəuˈfiliə; ˏskɑptəˋfɪlɪə] *n*.【医】视淫。

scop·u·la [ˈskɔpjulə; ˋskɑpjələ] *n*. (*pl*. ***~s***, ***-lae*** [-liː; -li])【动】毛丛。

-scopy *suf*. 看,观察,看的方法: micro*scopy*.

scor·bu·tic [skɔːˈbjuːtik; skɔrˋbjutɪk] **I** *a*.【医】1. 坏血症的。2. 患坏血症的。**II** *n*. 1. 患坏血症者。2. 坏血症特效药。

scorch [skɔːtʃ; skɔrtʃ] **I** *vt*. 1. 灼伤;晒焦;烘焦;烧焦。2. 使枯萎。3. (军队撤退前)烧光(地面物)。4. 使(心里)着急,使焦急。5. 大骂。6.【化】使(橡胶)过早硫化;焦化。*a ~ed earth policy* 焦土政策(反收购企业反收购的)自毁策略。—*vi*. 1. 焦;萎,枯。2. 令人感到灼痛,挖苦。3.〔俚〕(汽车等)高速疾驰。**II** *n*. 1. 烧焦。2.〔俚〕(汽车等的)高速疾驰。~**-pencil** *n*. 烧书(所用的)笔。

scorch·er [ˈskɔːtʃə; ˋskɔrtʃɚ] *n*. 1. 极热的东西。2.〔口〕像火热一样的大热天。3. 尖酸刻薄的话;严厉之斥责;痛骂。4.〔俚〕触目的人或物。5. 高速驾驶汽车(等)的人。6.〔俚〕特级品,极品,热门货。*a week of ~s* 酷热的一周。

scorch·ing [ˈskɔːtʃiŋ; ˋskɔrtʃɪŋ] **I** *a*. 1. 烧焦似的,灼热的,像烧一般的;非常热的。2. 尖酸刻薄的;苛刻的。*a ~ day* 大热天。**II** *ad*.〔口语〕灼热地;热得灼人。**-ly** *ad*.

score [skɔː, skɔə; skor, skɔr] **I** *n*. 1. 斲痕,截痕,刻痕,划线;痕,抓痕;鞭痕;裂缝;记号。2. 对号筹片。3. 计算;百分数,成份;【运】比数。4. 得分;得分记录。5. (酒馆等的)账目,欠款。6. 旧仇,宿怨。7.〔*sing*., *pl*.〕二十,二十人,二十磅重。8.〔*pl*.〕许多。9.〔俚〕成功,幸运。10. 驳倒别人的议论,打倒别人的动作。11. 受骗者,欺诈的目标。12. 论点,理由,缘故,根据。13. (现实的)真相。14.【运】起步线;(射手站立的)打靶线,起射线。15.【乐】总谱,乐谱;(电影歌舞等的)配乐。16.【造船】(滑车的)带槽。*a clean* ~ 全胜得分。*a team* ~ 团体分。*win by a* ~ *of 10 to 9* 以十比九得胜。*five* ~ *of herring* 一捆鲱鱼[100 尾]。~(*s*) *of times* 几十次,屡次。~(*s*) *of years ago* 几十年前。*He is too fond of making cheap* ~*s*. 他总喜欢投机取巧(压倒别人)。*What's the* ~? 现在几分? 形势怎样? *What a* ~! 真运气! *the* ~ 真情;事实;情况。*from the* ~ 从起步线,从打靶线。*a compressed* [*close*, *shot*] ~ (由高音部和低音部压缩成的声乐的)二段总谱。***by ~s*** 大批地,很多,许多。***clear ~s*** [***a*** ~] 1. 付清账款;还债。2. 报仇,雪耻;泄愤。***Death pays all ~s***.【谚】一死百了。***get of*** [***go off***] ***at*** (***full***) ~ (马)全使向前猛冲;(人)精神十足地开始讲[做]。***have an old*** ~ ***to settle with sb***. 跟某人有老账要算[有宿怨]。***in*** ~【乐】用总谱,以总谱方式排列。***in ~s*** 很多,大批,大群。***keep the*** ~ (比赛等)记分数。***make a good*** ~ 得分很多,大成功。***make a*** ~ ***in*** 在…上划一个记号。***make a*** ~ ***off*** (*an awkward heckler*) 驳倒(难对付的诘问者),说得…没话讲。***make a*** ~ ***off one's own bat*** 独立做,靠自己力量做。***on a new*** ~ 重新。***on that*** ~ 因此,因那理由;在那一点上。***on the same*** ~ 用同样理由。***on the*** ~ ***of*** 因为,为了。***pay off*** [***settle***] ***old ~s*** [***an old*** ~] 1. 报复宿

仇。2. 还清旧账。*pay one's* ~ 清账,还清债务。*play to the* ~ 随机应变,见机行事。*quit* ~*s with sb*. 跟某人结清前账;向某人报复。*run up* (*a*) ~(*s*) *to* 对…负债累累。*settle* ~*s with sb*. 找某人清算。*start at* (*full*) ~ = get of at (full) ~. *three* ~ (*years*) *and ten* (人生)七十年;一辈子。*tie the* ~ 打成平局。*wear off* ~ = *clear* ~.

II *vt*. 1. 在…上作斫痕[截痕、刻痕],打记号于,划线于。2. 用线划掉〔又作 ~ out〕。3. 计算。4. 记…的账。5. 不忘记,记住(怨恨)。6. 记…的数,给…批分数。7. 得到(胜利等);【运】获得(分数等)。8. 〔美口〕刻薄地批评,骂,责备。9. (议论等时)说败,击败。10. 【乐】把…写成总谱,为…配乐。11. 将(马)带到起跑线。*a heart* ~*d by sorrow and remorse* 饱经忧患的人。~ *a game* [*goal*, *point*] 胜一局[进一球,得一分]。—*vi*. 1. 记分数。2. 得分,得胜 (*against*)。3. 成功,得利。4. 划线 (*in*); (马)来到起跑线。5. 借款,赊买。*Who will* ~? 不晓得哪个会赢? ~ *against* = ~ *over*. ~ *off* (*sb*.) 〔俚〕打败;驳倒(某人);羞辱(某人);使丢脸。~ *out* (用线)划掉;删去 (*The name and date have been* ~*d out*. 名字和日期已经划掉了)。~ *over* 打败,击败。~ *under* 在…字下划线;强调。~ *up* 1. 把…(作记号)记下;记账。2. 赊,欠下。~ **board**【运】记分牌;比赛经过记录表;记录。~ **book**【运】记分簿,比赛成绩簿。~ **card**【运】记分卡;参加比赛的运动员登记卡。~ **keeper**【运】记分员;记账员。~**pad** (每页都印有格子的)记分簿。~ **sheet**【棒球】记分单。**-less**【运】未得分的。

scor·er [ˈskɔːrə; ˋskorɚ] *n*. 1. 加斫痕[刻痕]的人。2. 刻线条用的东西。3. 作记号的人。4. 算账的人,账房。5. 【运】记分员,得分者。

sco·ri·a [ˈskɔːriə; ˋskorɪə] *n*. (*pl*. **-ri·ae** [-riiː; -rɪi]) 1. 【冶】矿渣;金属渣;铅析(法)渣。2. 【地】〔常 *pl*.〕火山岩渣,熔岩渣,溶岩灰。**-ri·a·ceous** [ˌskɔːriˈeiʃəs; ˏskorɪˋeʃəs] *a*.

sco·ri·fy [ˈskɔːrifai; ˋskorəˏfaɪ] *vt*. (**-fied**)【冶】(用烧熔试金法)析取,使成矿渣,煅烧,使渣化。**-fi·ca·tion** [ˌskɔːrifiˈkeiʃən; ˏskorəfəˋkeʃən] *n*. 【冶】渣化法,铅析金银法。**-fi·er** *n*. 【冶】煅烧皿;渣化皿;试金坩埚。

scorn [skɔːn; skɔrn] I *n*. 1. 藐视;侮弄;嘲笑。2. 受侮弄[嘲笑]的人,被轻视的东西。3. 笑柄。*feel* [*have*] ~ *for* 对…抱藐视心理。*hold in* ~ 藐视,瞧不起。*laugh sb. to* ~ 嘲笑,挖苦(某人)。*point the finger of* ~ *at sb*. 轻蔑地指点某人,嘲笑某人,轻蔑地批评某人。*think* [*hold*] *it* ~ *to* (*do*) 不屑(做)。*think* ~ *of* 藐视,蔑视,瞧不起。II *vt*., *vi*. 1. 蔑视,嘲笑,侮弄。2. 不屑。~ *lying* [*to tell a lie*] 不屑说谎。

scorn·er [ˈskɔːnə; ˋskɔrnɚ] *n*. 藐视者,轻蔑者,嘲笑者。

scorn·ful [ˈskɔːnful; ˋskɔrnfəl] *a*. 1. 藐视的,嘲笑的;傲慢的。2. 〔罕〕当做笑柄的。~ *remarks* 挖苦话。*be* ~ *of* 藐视。**-ly** *ad*. **-ness** *n*.

scor·pae·nid [skɔːˈpiːnid; skɔrˋpinɪd] *n*. 【动】鲉科 (*Scorpaenidae*) 鱼。**scor·pae·noid** [-nɔid; -nɔɪd] *a*., *n*. 【动】鲉科的(鱼)。

Scor·pi·o [ˈskɔːpiəu, -pjəu; ˋskɔrpɪˏo] *n*. 1. 【动】蝎属。2. 【天】天蝎座,天蝎宫。

scor·pi·oid [ˈskɔːpiɔid; ˋskɔrpɪˏɔɪd] *a*. 【动】1. 似蝎的。2. 蝎科的。3. 末端弯曲如蝎尾的;拳卷的。

scor·pi·on [ˈskɔːpjən, -piən; ˋskɔrpɪən] *n*. 1. 【动】蝎。2. 蝎子般的家伙;黑心肠的人。3. 蝎尾鞭。4. (古代)弩炮。5. 〔S-〕= Scorpio. ~**fish** *n*. 【动】锯鲉。~ **fly**【动】蝎虫类 (*Mecoptera*) 昆虫。**S-'s Heart**【天】天蝎宫的主星。

Scot. = 1. Scotch. 2. Scotland. 3. Scottish.

Scot [skɔt; skɑt] *n*. 1. 苏格兰人。2. 〔*pl*.〕盖尔人〔五世纪时从爱尔兰移居到苏格兰的一个高卢部族〕。

scot[1] [skɔt; skɑt] *n*. 估定的[已缴付的]款项,账款;税金。*pay* (*one's*) ~ *and lot* 缴纳按能力负担的教区税,缴清税款;付清所欠;尽应尽的义务。~ *free* 免予支付;未受损害,未受惩罚。

scot[2], **Scot** [skɔt; skɑt] *n*. 〔误用〕= God. *Great* ~! 真是! 糟糕! 哎呀!

Scotch [skɔtʃ; skɑtʃ] I *a*. 1. 苏格兰(人、语)的。★除 Scotch whisky [fir, tweeds, girl]等常用词组外,苏格兰人自己喜欢用 Scottish 或 Scots, 很少用 Scotch; 英格兰人对苏格兰人说恭维话时用 Scots. 2. 〔美俚〕节约的;俭约的;节俭的;朴素的;小气的。II *n*. 1. 〔the ~〕苏格兰人。2. 苏格兰语;苏格兰土腔。3. 〔口〕苏格兰威士忌酒 (= ~ whisky); 〔美俚〕威士忌酒。*a small* ~ 酒味淡的苏格兰威士忌酒。*broad* ~ 苏格兰土话,粗鄙的苏格兰话。*flying* ~ 开往苏格兰的特别快车。*out of all* ~ 〔卑〕过度地,非常地。~ *and English* (分成两组的)儿童捉人游戏。~ *and soda* 威士忌苏打。~ **blessing**〔方〕严厉的申斥。~ **broth** (用蔬菜、大麦米、牛肉或羊肉做成的)苏格兰浓汤。~ **cap** 苏格兰人戴的无边帽 (= Glengarry)。~ **catch** [**snap**]【乐】(后随一长音符的)重拍短音符。~ **cousin** 远亲。~ **fiddle**〔卑〕疥癣。~ **fir**【植】银松。~ **grain** 苏格兰纹理〔一种制革法〕。~-**Highlander** 苏格兰高地人。~-**Irish** 苏格兰—爱尔兰裔的〔指住在爱尔兰北部的苏格兰低地人后裔,尤指移居美国的这种人的后裔〕。~**man** 苏格兰人。~ **mist**【气】苏格兰雾〔多带细雨〕。~ **pine**【植】欧洲赤松 (*Pinus sylvestris*)。~ **tape** 1. 苏格兰胶带〔一种透明薄胶带,亦其商标名〕。2. *vt*. 用透明胶带封口[贴]。~ **terrier**【动】苏格兰㹴犬 (= Scottish terrier)。~ **thistle**【植】苏格兰刺蓟 (*Onopordum acanthium*)。~ **verdict**【法】苏格兰式判决〔对"未证实"刑事案不判"无罪"而暂判"未证实"〕;〔转义〕非最后的决定,未最后定局的事。~ **whisky** 苏格兰威士忌酒。~ **woman** 苏格兰女人。~ **woodcock** 涂鳀酱的烤面包加鸡蛋的食物。

scotch [skɔtʃ; skɑtʃ] I *n*. 1. 浅刻。2. 擦伤,轻伤。3. 玩儿童跳格游戏 (hopscotch) 时地上划的线。4. 止车楔,垫楔,车辖。II *vt*. 1. 轻轻切。2. 在…上加刻痕。3. 使受微伤;伤及。4. 将(蛇等)弄得半死。5. 压碎;粉碎;打破(阴谋等)。6. 扑灭;消除(谣言等);弹压,镇压(暴动等)。*We have* ~*ed the snake*, *not killed it*. 我们将蛇弄得半死,没有把它完全弄死。

sco·ter [ˈskəutə; ˋskotɚ] *n*. 【动】黑凫。

sco·tia [ˈskəuʃə; ˋskoʃə] *n*. 【建】(柱基的)凹圆线饰[凹形边饰]。

Sco·tia [ˈskəuʃə; ˋskoʃə] 〔诗〕= Scotland〔苏格兰的拉丁名称〕。

Sco·tism [ˈskəutizəm; ˋskotɪzəm] *n*. 【哲】(Duns Scotus 的)斯科塔斯哲学〔主张哲学与神学各不相关〕。

Scot·land [ˈskɔtlənd; ˋskɑtlənd] *n*. 苏格兰。~ **Yard** 1. 伦敦警察厅〔采用旧地址名,现已迁移,改称 New ~ Yard〕。2. 伦敦警察厅侦缉处。3. 伦敦警方 (*call in* ~ *yard* 向伦敦警方报警)。

scot·o·graph [ˈskɔtəugrɑːf; ˋskɑtəˏgræf] *n*. 1. 暗处写字器;盲人写字器。2. X 光线照片。

sco·to·ma [skəˈtəumə; skəˋtomə] *n*. (*pl*. ~**ta** [-tə; -tə]) 【医】(网膜上的)暗点;盲点。**sco·tom·a·tous** [skəˈtɔmətəs; skəˋtɑmətəs] *a*.

scot·o·phil [ˈskɔtəufil; ˋskɑtofɪl] *a*. (植物的生长等)喜暗的;需暗的。**-ic** *a*.

sco·to·pi·a [skəˈtəupiə; skoˋtopɪə] *n*. **sco·to·pic** [-ˈtəupik, -ˈtɔpik; -ˋtɑpɪk] *a*. 【医】1. 暗光适应。2. 暗视力。

Scots [skɔts; skɑts] I *a*. 〔Scot.〕苏格兰(人)的〔*cf*. Scotch〕。*the* ~ *language* 苏格兰(低地英)语。*the* ~ *law* 苏格兰法。*pounds* ~ 苏格兰镑。*a* ~ *mile* 苏格兰英里。~ *greys* 苏格兰龙骑兵第二团。II *n*. 1. 〔the ~〕苏格兰民族。2. 苏格兰(英)语,苏格兰方言。*speak broad* ~ 讲苏格兰土话。~**man** 苏格兰人。~**woman** 苏格兰女人。

Scott [skɔt; skɑt] *n*. **1.** 斯科特(司各脱)〔姓氏,男子名〕。 **2. Robert Falcan** ~ 罗伯特·弗·斯科特〔1868—1912,英国 1912 年到达南极的南极探险家〕。**3. Sir Walter** ~ 瓦尔特·司各脱〔1771—1832,苏格兰诗人及小说家〕。

Scot·(t)i·ce [ˈskɔtisi; ˋskɑtɪsɪ] *ad*. 用苏格兰语;用苏格兰方言。

Scot·(t)i·cism [ˈskɔtisizəm; ˋskɑtə͵sɪzəm] *n*. 苏格兰语(法),苏格兰方言;苏格兰语化;苏格兰发音。

Scot·(t)i·cize [ˈskɔtisaiz; ˋskɑtə͵saɪz] *vi*., *vt*. **1.** (使)(言语、习惯等)苏格兰化。**2.** (把…)翻译成苏格兰语。

Scot·tie, Scot·ty [ˈskɔt; ˋskɑtɪ] *n*. (*pl*. **-ties**) 〔口〕= scottish terrier.

Scot·tish [ˈskɔtiʃ; ˋskɑtɪʃ] *a*., *n*. = Scotch. ~ **Gaelic** 苏格兰高地凯尔特语。~ **rite** 苏格兰仪式〔共济会一种仪式制度〕。

scoun·drel [ˈskaundrəl; ˋskaʊndrəl] **I** *n*. 恶棍,无赖。**II** *a*. 恶棍(般)的,无赖的;卑鄙的。**-ism** *n*. **1.** 卑劣;无赖。**2.** 下流举动;恶棍[无赖]行为。**-ly** *a*. 无赖的,恶棍的;凶横的;卑劣的。

scour[1] [ˈskauə; skaʊr] **I** *vt*., *vi*. **1.** (用沙等)擦亮,擦光;擦掉(锈、污点的)(*off*; *away*; *out*);洗涤。**2.** 肃清(海盗等);扫荡。**3.** 洗刷;冲刷;冲洗(管道等)。**4.** 疏浚(河底等)。**5.** (用泻药)泻;打(虫)。**6.** 【冶】侵蚀,烧蚀。**II** *n*. **1.** 磨擦,去锈。**2.** 洗去。**3.** 疏浚。**4.** 扫除,扫荡。**5.** 〔常 *pl*.〕(家畜的)泻药。**6.** 洗涤剂。*give it a* ~ 洗一洗。~**ing-rush** 【植】木贼;笔管草;锁眼草。~**ing-stock** 漂布机。**-ings 1.** (机床的)切屑;残屑。**2.** 擦洗下来的污垢。**3.** 谷皮。**4.** 社会渣滓。**-er** [ˈskauərə; ˋskaʊrə] *n*. 擦洗者;洗刷器。

scour[2] [ˈskauə; skaʊr] *vt*. (急急忙忙来回)搜寻(*about*)。—*vi*. 飞快地跑过,奔跑,搜寻着跑过(*away*, *off*)。~ **along** 跑过,搜索,出没。~ **the coast** 沿海岸搜索,出没在沿岸(一带)。

scourge [skəːdʒ; skɝdʒ] **I** *n*. **1.** 天罚,天灾,灾难,灾害[瘟疫、战争等]。**2.** 苦难的根源,引起灾害的事物,带来灾害的人。**3.** 鞭,笞。*the* ~ *of Heaven* 灾殃,祸患。*the white* ~ 肺痨。**II** *vt*. **1.** 折磨,磨难,使苦恼;严罚,重惩,重责。**2.** 鞭打;鞭笞。

scouse [skaus; skaʊs] *n*. = lobscouse.

scout[1] [skaut; skaʊt] **I** *n*. **1.** 守望员;侦察员;斥候。**2.** 侦察舰;侦察机;搜索救援机。**3.** 童子军。**4.** 【军】侦察,守望,观察。**5.** (牛津大学的)校工〔剑桥大学称 gyp, 都柏林大学称 skip〕。**6.** 〔古〕【板球】外场守场员。**7.** 【动】海鸟;海鸠;善知鸟。**8.** 〔俚〕家伙。*a good old* ~ 有趣的家伙。**be in** [**on**] **the** ~ 在侦察中。**II** *vi*., *vt*. **1.** 侦察(*about*; *round*)。**2.** 寻找;搜索(*out*; *up*)。~ **bomber** 侦察轰炸机。~ **car** 轻装甲巡逻车。~**craft 1.** 侦察术。**2.** 童子军活动。~ **cruiser** 侦察巡洋舰。~**-hood 1.** 童子军身份。**2.** 童子军的精神[作风]。~ **master 1.** 侦察队长。**2.** 童子军领队;〔S-〕〔美俚〕广告公司经理。~ **plane** 侦察机。

scout[2] [skaut; skaʊt] *vt*., *vi*. **1.** 认为荒唐而拒绝(提议,意见等)。**2.** 讥笑,嘲弄。**3.** 轻视。

scow [skau; skaʊ] **I** *vt*. 〔美〕用敞舱驳船驳运;用方头驳船驳运。**II** *n*. 敞舱驳船,方头驳船,大型平底输送船。

scowl [skaul; skaʊl] **I** *n*. **1.** 愁容;皱着眉头的脸;不高兴的脸;绷着的脸;怒容;不悦之色。**2.** (天空)晦暗;阴沉;就要发生暴风雨的样子。**II** *vi*. **1.** 皱眉头;绷脸;瞪着眼看;怒视(*at*; *on*)。**2.** (天气)变坏;阴沉起来;像要下雨。—*vt*. 用怒容(对人)把…压下去;用怒容表示;皱眉拒绝(*away*);对…绷脸使…。~ *sb*. *into silence* 绷着脸使某人无话可说。~ *down* 瞪眼怒视,瞪着眼睛使沉默。**-ing·ly** *ad*.

SCP = single-cell protein 单细胞蛋白。

SCR = **1.** silicon controlled rectifier 【无】硅[矽]可控整流器,可控硅[矽]。**2.** semiconductor controlled rectifier 半导体可控整流器。

scr. = scruple.

scrab·ble [ˈskræbl; ˋskræbl̩] **I** *vi*., *vt*. **1.** (用爪)扒找,乱扒;匆匆忙忙地扒集。**2.** (为生活)挣扎[争夺]。**3.** 七颠八倒地写;乱写,乱涂。**II** *n*. **1.** (乱)扒。**2.** 争夺;挣扎;奋斗。**3.** 乱写,乱涂。**4.** 胡乱写下来的东西,乱写的字。

scrab·bly [ˈskræbli; ˋskræblɪ] *a*. (**-bli·er**; **-bli·est**) 〔口〕**1.** 有抓刮声的。**2.** 长满矮树丛的。**3.** 矮小的。**4.** 多短硬毛的。**5.** 不足取的,没价值的。**6.** 次要的;不重要的。**7.** 下贱的;贫穷的。

scrag [skræg; skræg] **I** *n*. **1.** 骨瘦如柴的人[动物]。**2.** 矮小枯萎的树木[植物]。**3.** 〔英〕肉类的多骨部分,排骨。**4.** (烧汤用的)羊[小牛]颈肉。**5.** 〔俚〕(人的)颈,脖子。**6.** 糟粕,碎块,碎片,碎屑。**II** *vt*. (**-gg-**) **1.** 〔俚〕掐…脖子,勒…颈,绞死(罪犯等)。**2.** 【橄榄球】抱住(对方队员的)脖子。~**-end** 羊颈肉。

scrag·gly [ˈskrægli; ˋskræglɪ] *a*. (**-gli·er**; **-gli·est**) **1.** 稀疏的,稀少的;短小的。**2.** 不规则的;不整齐的;参差的;散乱的。**3.** 破烂的。*a* ~ *beard* 参差不齐的胡子;稀稀拉拉的胡子。**scrag·gli·ness** *n*.

scrag·gy [ˈskrægi; ˋskrægɪ] *a*. (**-gi·er**; **-gi·est**) **1.** 骨瘦如柴的,瘦削的。**2.** 凹凸不平的,高低不平[齐]的。**-gi·ly** *ad*.

scram [skræm; skræm] **I** *vi*. (**-mm-**) 〔美俚〕快离开;滚(开)〔通用于命令语气〕。**II** *n*. **1.** 急速离开。**2.** 紧急刹车。

scram·ble [ˈskræmbl; ˋskræmbl̩] **I** *vi*. **1.** 爬,爬上去,攀登;攀缘(*about*; *up*; *down*; *through*)。**2.** 争先恐后地抢;互相争夺;竭力搜求(*for*)。**3.** 【空】争先恐后地飞起;紧急起飞(应战)。**4.** (蔓草等)蔓延,繁生。**5.** 【无】扰频;【讯】保密。**6.** 〔美足球俚〕(没有挡截队员保护下)单独带球冲锋陷阵。—*vt*. **1.** 攀登;爬(上)。**2.** 炒[搅拌](鸡蛋、牛奶等)。**3.** 扰乱;把…打乱。**4.** 【无】改变…的频率使不被窃听。**5.** 把…胡乱扔(在一堆);撒(钱等让大家来抢)。**6.** 匆忙凑合,凑拢,收集。**7.** 【空】命令…紧急起飞。~*d egg* 炒鸡蛋。~ **after** 搜求,拼命找。~ **along** [**on**] 爬向前;勉强对付过去。~ **for a living** 勉强度日。~ **for office** 争夺职位;抢官做。~ **into one's clothes** 急急忙忙穿上衣服。~ **the dope** 〔美〕比赛中出现与预料相反的成绩。~ **through** 勉强设法通过。~ **up** 爬上去,扒拢。**II** *n*. **1.** 爬上,攀登;攀缘。**2.** 争取;(互相)争夺。**3.** 【空】紧急起飞。**4.** 混乱的动作[活动]。**5.** 【无】扰频;倒频。*a* ~ *for office* 抢官位;争权。**in a** ~ 急忙;赶忙。**scrambler 1.** 爬行者;攀缘者;争先恐后(抢夺)者;攀缘植物。**2.** 【无】扰频器;倒频器;保密器(scrambler phone 防窃听电话)。

scram·jet [ˈskræmdʒet; ˋskræmdʒɛt] *n*. 超音速冲压式喷气发动机[飞机]。

scran [skræn; skræn] *n*. **1.** 〔俚〕食物,粮食。**2.** (食物)屑;残羹剩饭。**Bad** ~ **to you!** 〔Ir.〕见你的鬼去吧! 去你的! **out on the** ~ 〔卑〕做乞丐,去讨饭。

scran·nel [ˈskrænl; ˋskrænl̩] *a*. 〔英古〕**1.** 细(小的);弱。**2.** 难听的,刺耳的。

scran·ny [ˈskræni; ˋskrænɪ] *a*. 〔英方〕瘦骨嶙峋的(= scraggy)。

scrap[1] [skræp; skræp] **I** *n*. **1.** 小片,小块,破片,切剩剪剩的碎片,碎屑,零头。**2.** 〔集体词〕废料。**3.** 〔*pl*.〕破烂东西;残羹剩饭。**4.** (报纸剪下的)零杂资料;断片;断简;残篇。**5.** 【冶】碎铁,铁屑。**6.** 〔*pl*.〕剩余物;油渣;金属渣。**7.** 少许,一点点。*a* ~ *of cloth* 一小块布。*a few* ~*s of news* (零零碎碎的)两三条消息。*a* ~ *of paper* 一小块碎纸;〔讽〕废纸一样的条约。*dry* ~ (干)鱼渣。*green* ~ 生鱼渣。~*s of Latin* 一点点拉丁语知识。**do not care a** ~ 一点不在乎。**not a** ~ 一点也没有…。**II** *vt*. (**-pp-**) 〔俚〕**1.** 把…作为废料拆毁;撕毁。**2.** 废弃,撕毁。~ **basket** 废纸篓。~**book** 剪贴簿;贴报簿。~ **cake** (饲料用)鱼渣。~ **iron** 废铁。

scrap[2] [skræp; skrep] **I** *n*. 1. 打架(*with*);扭打;争吵;口角。2. 拳赛。**II** *vi*. (*-pp-*) 打架。

scrape [skreip; skrep] **I** *vt*. 1. 刮,削,擦,搔,刮去,削去,擦去(*away*; *off*; *out*);擦过(*against*; *past*)。2. 磨擦,打磨。3. 挖出,挖空(*up*; *out*)。4. 凑,收集;勉强凑拢。5. 搜刮;积攒;一点一点地储蓄(*together*; *up*)。6. (乱)弹拨(弦乐器),使咯吱咯吱地响。7. (行礼时)将(右脚)向后一退。8. 用脚擦地板发声以妨碍(演讲者等)。9. (用平地机)平(地)。~ *one's boots* 刮净鞋底。~ *one's chin* 剃胡子。~ *one's plate* 刮光盘中食物。—*vi*. 1. 刮;削,擦;搔(*against*)。2. 积攒;一点一点地积蓄。3. 乱弹,瞎弹(*on*)。4. 将右脚向后退一下鞠躬。5. (鸡等)刨地。*the scrapings and scourings of the street* 1. 街道上的垃圾。2. 街上的流氓无赖。**bow and** ~ 1. 打躬作揖[屈膝];一面鞠躬一面将脚向后一退。2. 奉承;巴结。**pinch and** ~ = ~ **and screw** 省吃省用地储蓄;节约;俭省。~ **along** 1. 擦过去。2. 勉勉强强过下去。~ (**up**) **an acquaintance with ...** 老着脸皮去接近[结识](某人)。~ **down** 1. 擦掉,刮去;弄平。2. 用脚擦地板轰走(演讲者等)。~ **off** 刮去。~ **out a mark** 擦掉记号。~ **the mug** 〔美俚〕刮胡子。~ **through** 1. 好容易完成。2. (考试)勉强及格。3. 勉强对付过去。4. 勉强通过。~ **together** [**up**] 1. 一点一点地贮蓄。2. 设法凑拢(*I paid the bill scraping up the money we had*. 我把我们所有的钱凑起来付清了账)。

II *n*. 1. 刮;削;擦;括痕;擦伤。2. 括削声;摩擦声;乱弹声。3. 打扦。4. (自己招来的)困难,困境,窘境。5. 刮胡子;修面。6. (在面包上)涂点奶油。*a* ~ *of a pen* 1. 大笔一挥。2. 签字。*bread and* ~ 涂了一点点奶油的面包。*a fine* [*pretty*] ~ 为难的事情,困境。**be in a** ~ 正在困难中,正在为难。**get into a** ~ 陷入困境。**out of all** ~ 脱离困难,脱离窘境。~ **iron**【林】树脂收集器。**-penny** *n*. 吝啬鬼。

scrap·er [ˈskreipə; ˋskrepɚ] *n*. 1. 刮(削)的人,擦的人。2. 擦具;搔具;刮刀;刮削器。3. 刮土器,泥擦。4. 鞋擦。5. 橡皮擦。6.【医】刮器;刮刀。7.【军】(扫除炮口内火药的)通条刮子。8. 〔罕〕吝啬鬼;悭吝人;财迷。9. 〔蔑〕理发匠。

scrap-heap [ˈskræphiːp; ˋskræpˏhip] *n*. 垃圾[废料]堆,废铜烂铁堆。*fit the* ~ 毫无用处的;该废弃的。*go to the* ~ 变成废物,荒废,被废弃,没落。*throw* [*toss*, *cast*] *on the* ~ 废弃。~ **policy** 喜新厌旧[用旧就扔]政策。

scrap·ing [ˈskreipiŋ; ˋskrepɪŋ] *n*. 1. 刮,削,擦。2. 刮声,削声,擦声。3. 〔常用 *pl*.〕刮屑。

scrap·per[1] [ˈskræpə; ˋskræpɚ] *n*. 1. 刮(或擦)的人。2. 刮刀;削刮器,刮土机,铲运机。3. 吝啬鬼,守财奴。

scrap·per[2] [ˈskræpə; ˋskræpɚ] *n*. 〔口〕1. 爱打架[吵架]的人;会打架[吵架]的人。2. (职业)拳击家。

scrap·ple [ˈskræpl; ˋskræpl̩] *n*. 〔美〕【烹】玉米面肉末饼。

scrap·py[1] [ˈskræpi; ˋskræpɪ] *a*. (*-pi·er*; *-pi·est*) 1. 碎料的;剩余的;零碎的。2. 片断的;不连贯的;杂乱无章的。*a* ~ *dinner* 一顿拼拼凑凑的饭菜。**-pi·ly** *ad*.

scrap·py[2] [ˈskræpi; ˋskræpɪ] *a*. 〔俚〕1. 爱吵架的;好打架的。2. 斗志旺盛的。

scratch [skrætʃ; skrætʃ] **I** *vt*., *vi*. 1. (用爪、针等)搔;搔(痒);抓;抓(表面);刨;用爪刨[扒,挖](洞)。2. 抓伤[破];刮坏。3. 刺刺地抓;作刮擦声。4. 潦草地写;涂写;乱画。5. 涂掉,勾消;勾划掉(*out*; *out of*)。6. 停止;丢弃。7. (将马)从名单中勾消掉;(使)退出比赛;〔美〕(把…)从后补人名单中删掉。8. 刨拢在一块,凑合。9. 勉强维持[对付,糊口];〔美俚〕伪造(支票)。10. (说唱乐录音中)(使)做出擦音效果。*S- my back and I will* ~ *yours*. = *S- me and I will* ~ *you*. 〔口、谚〕你捧我我就捧你;互相迎合,互吹互捧。~ *one's head* 搔首;为难(*over*)。~ *a match on a box* 在火柴盒上擦火柴。*My pen* ~*es*. 我的钢笔写起来刮纸。~ **about for** 到处竭力搜寻。~ **for oneself** 〔美〕为自己的利益奔走。~ **one's head** 1. 搔头皮。2. (对某事)迷惑不解(*over*)。~ **the surface of** 1. 搔…的表面。2. 有一些…的肤浅知识。~ **together** [**up**] 刨在一块;凑拢(~ *up some money* 凑点钱)。~ (*sb*.) **where he itches** 1. 给(某人)抓痒。2. 迎合人意。

II *n*. 1. 抓;搔。2. 抓痕;搔痕;划痕。3. 抓伤;擦伤;微伤。4.【地】擦痕;【建】刮痕。5. 搔声;刮擦声。6. 〔口〕拙笔;乱写。7.【台[撞]球】造成罚分的一击;空球(亦要罚分)。8.【运】(不接受让步待遇者的)平赛起步线;平赛起跑时间[开始时间]。9.【运】零分;平局。10.【拳】拳击开始线。11. 〔*pl*.〕马脚葡萄疮。12. 半假发〔又称 ~wig〕。13. 〔美俚〕伪造者;假造的支票[钞票]。14. (说唱乐录音中的)擦音(技术)。*a mere* ~ 一点儿擦伤。*a* ~ *man* 不接受让步待遇的赛跑者。*the Old S-* 恶魔。**bring to the** ~ 使决定;使实行;使决心。**by the** ~ **of a pen** 动一动笔,签一个字(*The business could be settled by the* ~ *of a pen*. 那件事大笔一挥签一个字就可以办成)。**come** (**up**) **to** (**the**) ~ 1. 站到拳击开始线上,走[踏]上起步线。2. 挺身迎敌,决意奋斗,坚决行动。3. 能胜任,称职。**no great** ~ 〔俚〕没有什么了不得。**on the** ~ 在起步线上没有让步地,平等地。**start from** [**at**, **on**] ~ 1. 从起步线跑;从零开始。2. 从头做起;白手起家。**up to** ~ 合格;称职;处于良好状态。

III *a*. 1. 〔俚〕东拼西凑的;(船员、球队等)临时凑成的;凑合的;庞杂的,各种各样的。2. 碰巧的;偶然的。3. 平等比赛的;(赛跑等)无让步的。4. 随便写的;打草稿用的。*a* ~ *race* (无让步条件的)平等比赛。**~-and-sniff** *a*. 一擦即发出香味的(~ *cards* 香味片)。~ **back** (抓痒用的)麻姑爪。~**-block** = scratch-pad. ~ **board** 刮板。~ **brush** 钢丝刷。~ **card** 刮蜡卡〔刮去封蜡后即显示出号码的一种抽奖卡〕。~ **cat** 狠毒的女人;凶狠的小孩。~ **coat**【建】打底子的水泥层;(涂灰)打底。~ **hardness** 擦硬度,刻划硬度。~ **hit**【棒球】触击。~ **line**【运】起跑线,起跳线,投掷线。~ **man** 比赛时让别人的人。~**-pad** 〔美〕便条本;拍纸簿。~**-pad memory** 便笺式存储器;高速暂存存储器。~ **paper** 便条纸。~ **test** 1.【医】抓扰试验〔把能引起过敏反应的物质放在微微扰破的皮肤上,试验病人所产生的反应〕。2. 刮痕[硬度]试验。

scratch·er [ˈskrætʃə; ˋskrætʃɚ] *n*. 1. 抓扒者,抓扒工具。2. 制金属模具工人。3. 树木刮痕器。4.【建】划痕器;拉毛爪子。5. 〔美俚〕伪造者。

scratch·y [ˈskrætʃi; ˋskrætʃɪ] *a*. (*-i·er*; *-i·est*) 1. 草率的;潦草的(书、画等)。2. (钢笔等)会刮纸的;瑟瑟响的。3. 东拼西凑的;(船员、球队等)拼凑成的。4. 使人发痒的;搔人的,扎人的。5. 稀少的。**-i·ly** *ad*. **-i·ness** *n*.

scrawl [skrɔːl; skrɔl] **I** *n*. 1. 潦草书写;乱写;乱涂;瞎画。2. 草草写成的信。**II** *vt*., *vi*. 潦草书写;乱写,乱涂;瞎画。~ *all over the wall* 满墙乱写乱画。**-y** *ad*.

scraw·ny [ˈskrɔːni; ˋskrɔnɪ] *a*. (*-ni·er*; *-ni·est*) 〔美〕骨瘦如柴的,瘦骨嶙嶙的。

screak [skriːk; skrik] **I** *vi*. 尖叫;发出尖锐刺耳声。**II** *n*. 尖叫声;尖锐刺耳声;吱吱嘎嘎声〔因摩擦而发出的尖锐的刺耳声〕。

scream [skriːm; skrim] **I** *n*. 1. (恐怖、苦痛的)尖叫声,惊叫声;拼命的叫喊声;尖(高)声大笑;(枭、汽笛等的)尖叫声。2. 〔俚〕非常可笑的人[事情];笑柄。3. 〔美〕伙伴。4. 〔不用冠词〕花哨,夸张。*a* ~ *of laughter* 哄笑。**II** *vi*. 1. 尖声喊叫,拼命叫喊,绝叫;叫喊;呜呜地叫。2. (颜色)花哨刺眼[不协调]。3. (字)花哨潦草。—*vt*. 1. 喊叫着说出。2. 〔~ oneself〕尖叫得使变…。~ **oneself hoarse** 叫哑嗓子。~ **out** 尖声喊叫,发尖声。~ **with laughter** 格格地大笑。

scream·er [ˈskriːmə; ˋskrimɚ] *n*. 1. (尖声)喊叫的人;尖声怪气说话的人。2. 发尖锐刺耳声音的东西。3. 〔俚〕使人笑破肚皮的话[唱歌](等)。4. 令人惊叹[愕]的东

S

西。**5.** 极标致的女人。**6.** 〔美俚〕(报纸上)耸人听闻的[惊人的]大字标题;横贯全页的大标题。**7.** 恐怖(影)片;恐怖场面。**8.** 〔俚〕花哨刺眼的东西;【印】〔俚〕惊叹号。~ **bomb** 啸声炸弹。

scream·ing [ˈskriːmiŋ; ˋskrimɪŋ] ***a*.** **1.** 尖声怪气地叫的,尖声喊叫的。**2.** 发尖锐刺耳声音的。**3.** 使人笑破肚皮的;非常可笑的。**4.** 令人惊叹[愕]的。**5.** 耸人听闻的。**6.** 花哨刺眼的。~ **meemies** [ˈmiːmiːz; ˋmimiz]〔俚〕神经极度紧张(的状态);歇斯底里。

scream·y [ˈskriːmi; ˋskrimɪ] ***a*.** (***-i·er***; ***-i·est***) 尖叫的;悲鸣的;哀号的;怪叫的;尖声怪气的。**-i·ly** ***ad*.**

scree [skriː; skri] ***n*.**〔常 *pl*.〕〔英〕山脚;岩屑堆;碎石堆。

screech [skriːtʃ; skritʃ] **I** ***n*.** (表示恐怖、苦痛、愤怒等的)尖叫声;尖锐刺耳的声音。**II** ***vt*.** 尖声喊叫出 (*out*)。—***vi*.** 发出尖锐刺耳的声音。~**owl** **1.** 叫声很尖的枭;仓鸮。**2.** 凶事预言者。**-y** ***a*.**

screed [skriːd; skrid] **I** ***n*.** **1.** 【建】样板;(混凝土修正机的)整平板;备条。**2.** 冗长的议论[文章,演讲,书信]。**3.** 〔Scot.〕(a) 裂口,裂缝。(b) 碎片;裂片。**II** ***vt*., *vi*.** 〔Scot.〕**1.** (使)裂开;撕破。**2.** 喋喋不休地讲。

screen [skriːn; skrin] **I** ***n*.** **1.** 屏风;围屏;屏幕;帘;幔;帐(等)。**2.** 矮墙,隔板。**3.** 荧光屏;【电】屏蔽;【物】栅,网,帘栅极。**4.** (电视、电脑等的)屏幕;(电影的)银幕;电视屏;〔the ~〕电影(界)。**5.** 粗筛;煤筛。**6.** 滤网,过滤器。**7.** 【印】网纹玻璃;网屏,网板〔照相制版将银粒浓淡色调转变为网目的工具〕。**8.** 【摄】滤光器;网孔。**9.** 掩蔽物;警戒幕。**10.** 【军】掩护部队;掩护舰;屏护[前卫]部队。**11.** 掩护。**12.** 【气】百叶箱。**13.** (金属,塑料等制成的)纱窗;饰窗,纱门。**14.** 【心】屏隔,屏障〔一种隐蔽或掩饰形式〕。*a folding* ~ 折叠屏风。*a smoke* ~ 烟幕。*a touch* ~ 电脑的触摸屏〔以手触摸特定部位即可使屏幕上显示所需信息〕。*make a* ~ *version of* 将…编成电影(剧本)。*put on a* ~ *of indifference* 假装不知道的样子;假装冷淡。~ *mesh* 筛眼;网孔。~ *play* 电影剧(本)[脚本]。~ *time* 放映时间。*show* [*throw*] *on the* ~ 放映。*silk* ~ *method* 丝网漏印法。*under* ~ *of night* 乘黑;在夜幕掩护下。
II ***vt*.** **1.** 遮;遮蔽;隔开;藏匿;庇护。**2.** 筛选(煤炭等);甄别。**3.** 把(小说)拍成电影;把…放映在银幕上。**4.** 【无】屏蔽。—***vi*.** 拍电影,在银幕上出现。~ ***off*** 用幕(屏)隔开;隔出。~ ***out*** **1.** 筛去。**2.** 筛选;选拔;甄别。~ **actor** 电影演员。~ **ager** (迷恋)荧光屏族〔指整天看电视或者玩电脑游戏机的青少年〕。~ **constant** 【电】屏蔽常数。~ **face** 适于上银幕[演电影]的脸。~ **grid** 【无】帘[屏]栅极。**ground** ~ 地网。**lamp** ~ 灯罩。~**land** 电影界〔美国说法多作 ~**dom**〕。**luminescent** ~ 荧光屏[幕]。~ **memory** 【心】屏隔回忆〔回忆一件有关系而不太痛苦的事来屏隔一件回忆起来令人痛苦的事〕。~ **pass** 【足球】过人短传。~ **riddle** 振动筛。~(-)**saver** 【计】屏幕保护程序〔打开计算机但不工作时,此程序被激活,使电脑屏幕上呈现不断变化的图像〕。~ **test** 【影】试镜头〔测验某人是否适于当电影演员〕,试映片断镜头〔检查已拍的镜头在银幕上的效果〕。~**washer**, ~-**wiper** (汽车挡风玻璃上的)雨刷。~ **writer** 电影编剧人[作者]。

screen·ing [ˈskriːniŋ; ˋskrinɪŋ] ***n*.** **1.** 做窗帘[纱窗]。**2.** 审查;甄别;放映。**3.** 〔*pl*.〕筛屑;筛渣。~ *effect* 【无】屏蔽效应。~ *committee* 考选[甄试]委员会。~ *test* 选拔考试;甄别考试。

screeve [skriːv; skriv] **I** ***vi*.** 〔俚〕在路边画图求乞;告地状。**II** ***n*.** 马路图画。**-r** 〔俚〕马路画家;告地状者。

screw [skruː; skru] **I** ***n*.** **1.** 螺旋;螺钉。**2.** 螺旋桨;暗轮。**3.** 暗轮轮船。**4.** 螺旋状物。**5.** 拔塞器;螺丝钻子。**6.** 螺旋的一拧;螺旋的一转。**7.** 〔英俚〕(力争而得的)薪水;工钱。**8.** 爱出难题的教员;难题。**9.** 压迫;暴力。**10.** 吝啬鬼;守财奴;善于讨论还价的人。**11.** 跑乏了[老弱]的马;驽马。**12.** 〔英〕(烟丝的)卷纸;一卷;(盐、烟草、茶叶等的)一包。**13.** 【几何】螺旋体;螺体。**14.** 【台[撞]球】拧;转;【网球】削;搓。**15.** 〔卑〕钥匙;〔尤指〕万能钥匙。**16.** 〔卑〕监狱看守人。*a female* [*an interior*] ~ 阴螺旋。*a male* [*an external*] ~ 阳螺旋。*a poor* ~ 菲薄的薪水。*draw a* ~ 〔俚〕领薪水。*raise sb.'s* ~ 〔俚〕加薪。***a* ~ *loose*** **1.** 毛病;故障。**2.** 有毛病的东西 (*He has a* ~ *loose*. 他头脑有点不对头)。***apply the* ~ *to*** = put the ~ on. ***give a nut a good* ~** 扭紧螺母。***give another turn to the* ~** = put the ~ on. ***have a* ~ *loose*** 疯疯癫癫的,乖僻;古怪;精神不正常。***put a* ~ *on a tennis ball*** (网球)削球。***put the* ~ *on*** [***put ... under the* ~**] 加以强制;强迫;施加压力;催促;催索(债务)。***tighten the* ~*s*** 拧紧螺丝;加强控制。***turn the* ~*s at sb*.** [***sth*.**] 对某人[某事]施加压力[加强控制]。
II ***vt*.** **1.** 用螺丝拧紧[钉紧];拧紧。**2.** 加强(效率);鼓起(勇气)(*up*)。**3.** 拧;扭;扭歪(嘴,脸等)。**4.** 勒索;强逼;使勉强付出。**5.** 虐待;欺压。**6.** 〔美〕严格考试。**7.** 【撞台[撞]球】拧(球);【网球】搓(球);削(球)。**8.** 〔美俚〕与…发生性关系。*His head is* ~*ed on the right way*. 他头脑清楚。*I am* ~*ed down by fixed rules*. 我被清规戒律束缚住了。~ *up a piece of paper into a ball* 把纸揉成一团。—***vi*.** **1.** 起螺丝的作用;扭转;拧转。**2.** 催促;强逼;勒索。**3.** 拼命俭省。**4.** 严格考试。**5.** 〔美俚〕走掉;离开;出去。**6.** 〔美俚〕性交。*The top* ~*s on* [*off*]. 这个盖子可以拧上[拧下]。~ ***around*** 〔俚〕胡混,鬼混。~ ***down*** **1.** 用螺丝拧紧;用螺钉钉住。**2.** 使减低价钱。~ ***in*** 拧进去。~ ***into*** 很会奉承;巴结。~ ***off*** 拔螺丝。~ ***oneself up to*** (*doing sth*.) 勉强做(某事)。~ ***out*** 勒索;逼出。~ ***up*** **1.** 拧紧;钉上。**2.** 卷成螺丝状。**3.** 扭歪(嘴、脸等)。**4.** 强迫。**5.** 非法抬高(地租等)。**6.** 弄糟。**7.** 鼓起(勇气)。~ ***up discipling*** 严格训练[管教]。~**armer** 〔棒球俚〕左手投球员[投手]。~ **auger** 螺旋锥。~**ball** **1.** ***n*.** 〔美俚〕(棒球的)怪球;〔转义〕怪人;白痴;怪事;怪东西;旋转球。**2.** 古怪的;不合情理的;有怪癖的;不安定的,不能预测的。~ **base** 螺钉脚。~ **bean** 【植】螺丝豆(树)。~ **bolt** 螺栓。~ **cap** 螺丝帽;螺旋盖〔有螺纹的瓶盖〕。~ **coupling** 螺旋联结。~**driver** **1.** 螺丝起子;螺丝刀;改锥。**2.** 〔美俚〕橙汁和伏特加酒的混合饮料[鸡尾酒]。~**drive fectory** "螺丝刀"工厂〔指专门以零部件装配整机的装配厂〕。~ **eye** **1.** 环首木螺钉。**2.** 螺丝眼。~ **gear** **1.** 螺轮。**2.** 螺轮联动装置。~ **gearing** 螺轮联动。~ **hook** 螺丝钩。~ **jack** 螺旋起动机;螺旋千斤顶;绞盘 (= **jack** ~)。~ **key** = ~ wrench. ~**loose** **1.** ***a*.** 脾气古怪的。**2.** ***n*.** 脾气古怪的人。~ **nut** 螺帽。~ **pile** 螺旋桩。~ **pine** 【植】露兜树(属)(*Pandanns*)。~ **press** 螺旋压榨机。~ **propeller** 螺旋桨。~ **thread** 螺纹;螺丝线。~-**topped** ***a*.** (瓶等)有螺旋盖的;口上有螺丝的。~-**up** 〔美俚〕弄糟的事情。~ **worm** 【动】螺旋蛆。~ **wrench** 有螺丝的扳钳;活络扳子。**-ed** ***a*.** **1.** 用螺丝拧紧的。**2.** 有螺纹的。**3.** 扭曲的。**4.** 〔俚〕喝醉了的。

screw·y [ˈskruːi; ˋskruɪ] ***a*.** **1.** 螺旋形的。**2.** 〔美俚〕神经有点不对头的;古怪的;特别的。**3.** 〔俚〕吝啬的。**4.** 〔俚〕喝醉了的;微醉的。**5.** 不中用的;(马)老弱的。**6.** 扭曲的。**7.** 不实际的。**8.** (容易)使人误解的。

scrib·al [ˈskraibəl; ˋskraɪbl] ***a*.** **1.** 笔写的;抄写(者)的。**2.** (犹太)法学家的。*a* ~ *error* 笔误。

scrib·ble[1] [ˈskribl; ˋskrɪbl] **I** ***vt*., *vi*.** **1.** 胡写;乱写;潦草地写。**2.** 滥写(文学作品等)。*No scribbling!* 禁止涂写。*scribbling block* 〔英〕便笺簿 (= scratch-pad)。*scribbling paper* 便条纸。**II** ***n*.** **1.** 胡写;乱写;潦草书写。**2.** 拙劣文字;粗制滥造的文章。**-r** ***n*.** **1.** 乱写[书写潦草]的人。**2.** 拙劣的作者;粗制滥造的作家。

scrib·ble[2] [ˈskribl; ˋskrɪbl] ***vt*.** 【纺】粗梳;预梳;头道梳理(羊毛等)。**-r** ***n*.** 粗[预]梳机。

scribe [skraib; skraɪb] **I** ***n*.** **1.** 能写一笔好字的人;书法家。**2.** 抄写员;书记;文牍员。**3.** 新闻记者。**4.** 【史】书史。**5.** 【犹太史】法学家。**6.** 【谑】作家;〔美〕电影剧本作

S

家。7. = scriber. *a ring* ～〔美〕报导有奖拳赛的新闻记者。**II** ***vi***. 缮写;做抄写员。—***vt***. 用划线器划线;【木工】雕合;使配合。～**-awl**【机】画针。

scrib·er [ˈskraibə; ˋskraɪbɚ] ***n***. **1.**【建】划线[片]器。**2.** 书写者;刻划者。

scrim [skrim; skrɪm] ***n***. (作窗帘等用的)条纹稀棉布[麻布]。

scrim·mage [ˈskrimidʒ; ˋskrɪmɪdʒ] **I** ***n***. **1.** 扭打;混战;小战斗,小冲突。**2.**【橄榄球】扭夺;并列争球。**3.** (分成两队)练球。**II** ***vi***. **1.** 扭打;参加混战。**2.**【橄榄球】投入[加入]扭夺;并列争球。—***vt***.【橄榄球】(练球时)与(对方)对抗。***scrimmager n***. **1.** 扭打者;扭夺者。**2.**【橄榄球】前锋。

scrimp [skrimp; skrɪmp] ***vt***., ***vi***. **1.** 过分缩减。**2.** 节省;俭省。**3.** 吝啬。**4.** 少给;克扣。**-y *a***.

scrim·shank [ˈskrimʃæŋk; ˋskrɪm͵ʃæŋk] ***vi***. 〔英军俚〕玩忽职务;逃避任务;回避责任;偷懒。**-er *n***. 玩忽职守者。

scrim·shaw [ˈskrimʃɔː; ˋskrɪmʃɔ] **I** ***vt***., ***vi***. (在漫长的航程中水手于暇时)在(贝壳;鲸牙等上)做精致手工[雕刻、彩画等]。**II** ***n***. (水手做的这种)精致工艺品。

scrip[1] [skrip; skrɪp] ***n***. **1.** 纸片;纸条。**2.** 字条;收条。**3.** 临时单据;(以备换取正式股票等有价证券的)临时凭证。**4.** (市政府等在非常时期发行的)临时通货;军用券。**5.** 股票,证券。**6.**〔美口〕药方。**7.**〔美俚〕(从前的)辅币。～ **dividend** 日后兑现的股票红利证书。

scrip[2] [skrip; skrɪp] ***n***. 〔英古〕旅行袋,朝香袋。

Scripps [skrips; skrɪps] ***n***. 斯克里普斯[姓氏]。

scrip·sit [ˈskripsit; ˋskrɪpsɪt] ***v***. 〔L.〕(某人)著,撰。

script [skript; skrɪpt] **I** ***n***. **1.** 手写的文件 (*opp*. print); 稿本;手迹;笔迹。**2.**【印】书写体(铅字);【法】原本,正本 (*opp*. copy)。**3.**【影,剧】脚本;(广播节目等的)底稿。**4.**〔英〕考卷。**II** ***vt***. 〔美俚〕把…改编成电影剧本,把…写成广播稿。—***vi***. 写电影脚本[广播稿等]。～ **writer** 剧本[电影脚本,广播剧,广播节目稿]作者。**-er *n***. = ～ writer.

Script. = Scripture.

scrip·to·ri·um [skripˈtɔːriəm; skrɪpˋtorɪəm] ***n***. (*pl*. ～***s***; ***-ri·a*** [-riə; -rɪə]) **1.** (修道院内的)缮写室。**2.** 〔美〕电影剧本作者事务室。

scrip·tur·al [ˈskriptʃərəl; ˋskrɪptʃərəl] ***a***. **1.**〔S-〕圣经的;根据圣经的。**2.** 经文的;经典的。**-ly *ad***. 按照圣经,从圣经上。

scrip·ture [ˈskriptʃə; ˋskrɪptʃɚ] ***n***. **1.**〔S-〕(基督教)圣经〔通常说作 Holy Scripture 或 the Scriptures〕。**2.**〔S-〕〔罕〕圣经的一句[一节]。**3.** 经文;经典;圣典。**4.** 书写的文件;文稿;著作。**5.**〔英古〕铭。*Buddhist* ～*s* 佛经。*a* ～ *text* 采自圣经的一段引文。

scrive·ner [ˈskrivnə; ˋskrɪvnɚ] ***n***. 〔古〕**1.** 代笔人,抄写员。**2.** 公证人。**3.** 掮客;放债者。～**'s cramp** [**palsy**]【医】书写痉挛 (writer's cramp)。

scro·bic·u·late [skrəuˈbikjulit; skroˋbɪkjəlɪt] ***a***. **1.**【生】具粒陷的。**2.** 有小凹的,有浅槽的。

scrod [skrɔd; skrɑd] ***n***. 〔美〕小鳕鱼[特指已切开去骨准备烹调的]。

scrof·u·la [ˈskrɔfjulə; ˋskrɔfjələ] ***n***.【医】淋巴结[节]结核的;瘰疬。

scrof·u·lous [ˈskrɔfjuləs; ˋskrɑfjələs] ***a***. **1.** (生)淋巴结[节]结核的;瘰疬(性)的。**2.** 道德败坏的;腐化堕落的。

scroll [skrəul; skrol] **I** ***n***. **1.** (写在羊皮纸等上的)古代文书手卷;书卷;画卷;卷轴。**2.**〔古〕表;目录;文稿;阅件。**3.** 涡卷形的东西;【建】漩涡;涡卷形装饰[花样];涡卷。**4.**【空】涡形边。**5.**【机】涡形管;盘香牙;平面螺丝。**6.**【乐】(提琴等上的)涡卷形头。**7.**【数】涡卷。**8.** (签名后面的)花押;花字。**9.** 细长的旗。**10.**【解】甲介骨。***on the*** ～ ***of fame*** 名垂史册;留名后世。**II** ***vt***., ***vi***. 〔罕〕〔通例用被动语态〕**1.** 用涡卷花样装饰。**2.** (使)成卷形,(把…)卷成卷轴形。**3.** 在(卷轴)上题字;题记;铭刻。～ **chuck** (车床的)三爪卡盘,三爪自动定心卡盘。～ **head**【海】船头涡卷装饰。～ **painting** 卷轴画。～**saw** 线锯;钢丝锯;云形截锯。～**-shears** 涡形剪床;曲线剪床。～ **wheel** 涡形齿轮。～**-work** 涡卷装饰;云形花样。

scroll·able [ˈskrəuləbl; ˋskroləbḷ] ***a***. 可卷起的;【计】(文本等)可在屏幕上卷动的。

scrooch, scrootch [skrutʃ; skrʊtʃ] ***vi***. 〔口〕蹲下;蜷缩;耸起;挤成一团。

scroop [skruːp; skrʊp] **I** ***n***. 轧轧(的响)声。**II** ***vi***. 作轧轧声;轧轧地响。

scro·tum [ˈskrəutəm; ˋskrotəm] ***n***. (*pl*. ***-ta*** [-tə; -tə], ～***s***)【解】阴囊。

scrouge [skraudʒ; skrudʒ, skraʊdʒ] ***v***., ***n***. 〔口〕压榨;勒索;榨取;剥削。

scrounge [skraun*d*ʒ; skraʊndʒ] ***vi***., ***vt***. 〔口〕**1.** 觅取。**2.** 乞取;乞讨。**3.** 骗取;偷,擅自攫取。～ ***around*** (用不正当的方法)搜寻 (～ *around for sth*. *to eat* 到处找东西吃)。

scrub[1] [skrʌb; skrʌb] **I** ***vt***., ***vi***. (***-bb-***) **1.** 用力擦洗,擦净;擦洗(地板等),擦去(污斑)等;用力摩擦。**2.**【化】(使)(气体)净化;(从气体中)分离出,提出。**3.**〔口〕(临时宣布)取消;废弃;中止;去除,消除。**II** ***n***. **1.** 擦;擦洗。**2.** 擦(洗)者。～(**-**)**brush**〔美〕〔英〕洗衣刷;板刷;硬毛刷;洗船刷 (= scrubbing-brush)。～**bing tower** 涤气塔。～**-up** 彻底擦洗。

scrub[2] [skrʌb; skrʌb] **I** ***n***. **1.** 矮小的树木;灌木;灌丛(地带)。**2.** 瘦小的家畜;杂种(家畜)。**3.** 矮小的人[物];不中用的人。**4.**〔口〕二流运动员;〔*pl*.〕二流球队。**II** ***a***. 〔美〕**1.** 矮小的。**2.** 不中用的,低劣的;次等的。**3.** 由预备队员组成的;二流球队的。

scrub·ber [ˈskrʌbə; ˋskrʌbɚ] ***n***. **1.** 擦洗员;擦洗甲板的水手。**2.** 板刷;刷帚;擦布。**3.**【化】煤气洗净器;涤气器;清洁器;洗涤器;滤清器;【制革】洗皮机。

scrub·by [ˈskrʌbi; ˋskrʌbɪ] ***a***. **1.** 灌丛繁茂的;尽是矮树的;杂木丛生的。**2.** 矮小的;低劣的;次等的。**3.** 难看的;不成样子的。**-bi·ness *n***.

scruff [skrʌf; skrʌf] ***n***. 颈背。***take*** (*sb*.) ***by the*** ～ ***of the neck*** 抓住(某人)颈背。

scruff·y [ˈskrʌfi; ˋskrʌfɪ] ***a***. (***scruff·i·er***; ***scruff·i·est***) **1.** 褴褛的;蓬乱的;邋遢的;杂乱的。**2.** 卑鄙的,可鄙的。**scruff·i·ly *ad***. **scruff·i·ness *n***.

scrum [skrʌm; skrʌm], **scrum·mage** [ˈskrʌmidʒ; ˋskrʌmɪdʒ] ***n***.【橄榄球】= scrimmage.

scrump·tious [ˈskrʌmpʃəs; ˋskrʌmpʃəs] ***a***. 〔俚〕**1.** 极好的;头等的;第一流的。**2.** 吸引人的;令人愉快的;很讨人喜欢的。**3.** 美味的;好吃的。**4.**〔罕〕好挑剔的,吹毛求疵的。

scrunch [skrʌn*t*ʃ; skrʌntʃ] ***v***., ***n***. = crunch.

scru·ple[1] [ˈskruːpl; ˋskrupḷ] **I** ***n***. 〔否定、成语外常用 *pl*.〕(对事情正当与否的)考虑;顾虑;迟疑;犹豫;思量;顾忌;自责;良心的责备。***a man of no*** ～ 肆无忌惮[无所不为]的坏蛋。～*s of conscience* 良心的责备。***do not care a*** ～ 毫不在乎。***do not stick at*** ～***s*** 不加思量,不迟疑。***have little*** ～ ***about doing*** ... 做…毫无顾忌。***have no*** ～***s about*** 毫不踌躇,不惜。***have*** ～***s about*** 对…有所顾忌,对…踌躇。***make no*** ～ ***of doing*** [***to do***] ... 做…毫不迟疑[没有顾忌]… ***stand on*** ～ 有所顾忌,顾虑。***without*** ～ 毫无顾忌地。**II** ***vi***., ***vt***. 顾虑;迟疑;犹豫;思量;顾忌;怀疑;疑心;〔罕〕(对…)感到良心的责备。*Don't* ～ *to ask for anything you want*. 你要什么请尽量讲。～ *at nothing* (*to do*) 肆无忌惮;毫无顾忌。

scru·ple[2] [ˈskruːpl; ˋskrupḷ] ***n***. **1.** 吩(英美药衡单位; = 20 grains; = 1.296g)。**2.** 微量。

scru·pu·los·i·ty [ˌskruːpjuˈlɔsiti; ˏskrupjəˋlɑsətɪ] ***n***. 仔细周到;顾虑;犹豫;踌躇;小心谨慎。

S

scru·pu·lous [ˈskruːpjuləs; ˋskrupjələs] *a*. **1.** 顾虑多的,小心谨慎的,步步留心的。**2.** 谨严的,认真负责的;一丝不苟的;无懈可击的;细心的。**3.** 正确的;彻底的;完全的。*a* ~ *proof-reader* 认真负责[一丝不苟]的校对员。**be ~ about** 对…不马虎;对…很注意。**not over** ~ 不过份客气,不过份拘谨。**pay ~ attention to** 细心注意。**-ly** *ad*.

scru·ta·ble [ˈskruːtəbl; ˋskrutəbl̩] *a*. 可辨认的;可理解的。

scru·ta·tor [skruːˈteitə; skruˋtetɚ] *n*. (精细的)检查者;调查者;观察者。

scru·tin [skrytɛ̃; skrytɛ̃] 〔F.〕投票。~ *d'arrondissement* 对个别候选人投票(法)。~ *de liste* 对成批名单投票(法)。

scru·ti·neer [ˌskruːtiˈniə; ˏskrutəˋnɪr] *n*. 〔英〕检查者;〔特指〕检票人;监票者。

scru·ti·nize [ˈskrutinaiz; ˋskrutn̩ˏaɪz] *vt*., *vi*. **1.** 细看;细读。**2.** 细察;审查;彻查。**-niz·ing·ly** *ad*. 细看地,仔细检查地。

scru·ti·ny [ˈskruːtini; ˋskrutnɪ] *n*. **1.** 细看;细读。**2.** 仔细检查[考察];复查;彻查。**3.** 选票检查[复查]。**demand a** ~ 要求(重新)检查(选票)。**make a ~ into** 细查;彻查。**not bear** ~ 经不住复查。**subject to the ~ of** 可由[有待]…进行复查[彻查、追究]。

scry [skrai; skraɪ] *vi*. (***scried***; ***scry·ing***) 使用水晶球占卜。**-er** *n*. 水晶球占卜师。

SCSI [读作 skʌziː; skʌzi] = small computer system interface【计】小型电脑系统界面[联接装置],SCSI 接口。

S

scu·ba [ˈskuːbə; ˋskubə] *n*. 〔美〕水肺〔潜水者用的水下呼吸器〕。

scud [skʌd; skʌd] **I** *n*. **1.** 飞跑。**2.** 飞云;雨云〔= showery ~〕;(随风移行的)阵雨;(被风吹来的)飞沫[雾,雨,雪]。**3.** 〔学生语〕飞毛腿。**4.**【矿】白云岩。**II** *vi*. (**-dd-**) **1.** 飞跑;疾行;掠过;飞过。**2.**【海】顺风疾驶。~ ***over the sky*** (云等)飞过天空。~ ***under bare poles*** 不张帆顺风行驶。

scuff [skʌf; skʌf] **I** *vi*. **1.** 拖着脚走;(局促不安地)拖脚行走。**2.** 用脚碰触试探。—*vt*. **1.** 拖着(脚)走。**2.** 磨损(鞋底、鞋面、地板等)。**3.** 拳打,打伤;攻击。**II** *n*. **1.** 拖脚行走;拖步。**2.** 拖着脚走的声音。**3.** 拖鞋。**4.** 〔美〕(鞋面上磨损的)疤痕,白瘢。

scuf·fle [ˈskʌfl; ˋskʌfl̩] **I** *vi*. **1.** 扭打,乱斗,混战(*with*)。**2.** 拖脚行走。**II** *n*. **1.** 扭打,混战。**2.** 拖脚行走,拖步;拖着脚走的声音。~ **hoe** 板锄。

scull [skʌl; skʌl] **I** *n*. **1.** 〔美〕(一人或二人用短桨[橹]划的比赛用)轻便小艇;小划艇〔英国称 skuller 或 skiff〕。**2.** 船的尾橹。**3.** 轻便短桨〔又称 ~ing oar〕。**II** *vt*., *vi*. **1.** 用短桨划;划(轻便小艇)。**2.** 用短橹摇(船)。

scull·er [ˈskʌlə; ˋskʌlɚ] *n*. **1.** 用短桨划小船的人。**2.** 〔英〕= scull **1**.

scul·ler·y [ˈskʌləri; ˋskʌlərɪ] *n*. 〔英〕碗碟洗涤室;餐具存放室。~**-maid** 女佣。

scul·lion [ˈskʌljən; ˋskʌljən] *n*. **1.** 〔古〕厨房下手;(大宅厨房中)洗盘碟的帮工。**2.** 地位低微的人。

sculp [skʌlp; skʌlp] *vt*., *vi*. 〔口〕= sculpture.

sculp. = sculptor.

scul·pin [ˈskʌlpin; ˋskʌlpɪn] **I** *n*. (*pl*. ~(*s*)) **1.**【动】杜父鱼;鲉。**2.** 〔美俚〕不中用的人;不成器的家伙。**3.** 不中用的东西。**II** *a*. 〔美〕不中用的。

sculps. = sculpsit.

sculp·se·runt [ˈskʌlˈpsiərʌnt; skʌlpˋsirʌnt] *n*. 〔L.〕某某等人谨刻(= They sculptured)〔一般置于雕刻作品上雕刻作者姓名的后面〕。

sculp·sit [ˈskʌlpsit; ˋskʌlpsɪt] *v*. 〔L.〕他[她]雕刻(此作品),(某某)谨刻(= He [She] sculptured)〔一般置于雕刻作品上雕刻作者姓名的后面〕。

sculpt [skʌlpt; skʌlpt] *vt*., *vi*. **1.** 雕;刻;塑(模型)。**2.** 雕塑(= sculp)。**3.** 做(发式)。

sculp·tor [ˈskʌlptə; ˋskʌlptɚ] (*fem*. ***-tress*** [-tris; -trɪs]) *n*. 雕刻[塑]家[师];雕刻[塑]工人。**-tress** [-tris; -trɪs] 女雕刻[塑]家[工人]。

sculp·tur·al [ˈskʌlptʃərəl; ˋskʌlptʃərəl] *a*. 雕刻[塑]的。**-ly** *ad*.

sculp·ture [ˈskʌlptʃə; ˋskʌlptʃɚ] **I** *n*. **1.** 雕刻(术);雕塑(术)。**2.** 雕像;雕刻[塑]物[品]。**3.**【动、植】(好像雕刻成的)刻纹;【地】刻蚀。*clay* ~*s* 泥塑(像)。*a* ~*d pillar* 雕花柱。**II** *vt*. **1.** 雕刻[塑]。**2.** 〔通例用被动语态〕雕饰。**3.**【地】刻蚀。—*vi*. **1.** 雕刻。**2.** 以雕刻为职业。

sculp·tur·esque [ˌskʌlptʃəˈresk; ˏskʌlptʃəˋrɛsk] *a*. **1.** 像雕刻一般的,有雕刻风味的。**2.** 精致的;肃穆的。**3.** 秀丽的,眉清目秀的。**-ly** *ad*. **-ness** *n*.

scum [skʌm; skʌm] **I** *n*. **1.** (煮沸或发酵时发生的)浮渣,浮垢;沫子;渣滓,碎屑,(清炉)渣块。**2.** 卑贱的人;下贱的人。**3.** 〔美学俚〕(服侍高年级生的)一年级大学生。*the* ~ *of the earth* [*of mankind*] 人类的渣滓。*the* ~ *of society* 社会的渣滓。**II** *vt*. (**-mm-**) 去除(浮渣),撇去(沫子)。—*vi*. 形成泡沫;生浮皮(*over*);变得满是浮渣。

scum·ble [ˈskʌmbl; ˋskʌmbl̩] **I** *vt*.【油画】(薄涂暗色)使(油画等)变柔和暗淡;【铅笔画】(用粉笔涂擦或用指尖轻擦)使(轮廓或线条)柔和。**II** *n*. **1.** (线条的)暗淡[柔和];暗色。**2.** 薄涂(彩色或粉);轻擦。**3.** 薄涂的彩色[粉]。

scum·my [ˈskʌmi; ˋskʌmɪ] *a*. **1.** (***-mi·er***; ***-mi·est***) 生[有]浮渣[浮皮、沫子]的。**2.** 〔美〕卑劣的;卑贱的;无价值的。

scun·ner [ˈskʌnə; ˋskʌnɚ] 〔Scot.〕**I** *vt*., *vi*. (对…)讨厌;厌恶。**II** *n*. 厌恶。**take a ~ against** 对…抱反感;厌恶。

scup [skʌp; skʌp] *n*. 〔美〕【鱼】尖口鲷。

scup·per [ˈskʌpə; ˋskʌpɚ] **I** *n*.【海】(甲板的)排水孔;(屋顶等的)排水口;泄水口;水沟。**II** *vt*. **1.** 〔英俚〕(用袭击办法)杀伤;杀死,击溃。**2.** 使(船)沉没。

scup·per·nong [ˈskʌpənɔŋ; ˋskʌpɚˏnɔŋ] *n*. **1.** 史卡帕农葡萄〔产于美国史卡帕农河流域〕。**2.** 史卡帕农葡萄酒。

scurf [skəːf; skɝf] *n*. **1.** 皮屑;头皮;头垢。**2.** 鳞片状附物;附物的残垢。**3.**【植】粗皮病;糠秕。**-y** *a*. (***-i·er***; ***-i·est***) **1.** 尽是皮屑的;像皮屑的。**2.**【植】糠秕状的;有糠秕的。

scur·ril(e) [ˈskʌril; ˋskɝɪl] *a*. 〔古〕= scurrilous.

scur·ril·i·ty [skʌˈriliti; skəˋrɪlətɪ] *n*. **1.** 粗俗;下流。**2.** 粗话,漫骂;下流行为。**-ril·ous** [ˈskʌriləs; ˋskɝələs] *a*. **-ly** *ad*. **-ness** *n*.

scur·ry [ˈskʌri; ˋskɝɪ] **I** *vi*. (**-ried**) 急匆匆地走;急赶(*away*; *off*)。—*vt*. 使急赶;催促。**II** *n*. **1.** 快步急跑;疾走。**2.** 仓皇奔跑声。**3.** 骤雨;骤雪。**4.** 短距离赛马。

scur·vied [ˈskəːvid; ˋskɝvɪd] *a*. 患坏血病的。

scur·vy [ˈskəːvi; ˋskɝvɪ] **I** *a*. (***-vi·er***; ***-vi·est***) **1.** 〔废〕= scurfy. **2.** 卑鄙的;无耻的;下流的。**II** *n*.【医】坏血病。~ **grass**, ~ **weed** (对坏血病有特效的)辣根菜;坏血病草。**-vi·ly** *ad*. **-vi·ness** *n*.

scut [skʌt; skʌt] *n*. **1.** (兔、鹿的)短尾。**2.** 短尾兽。**3.** 〔俚〕可鄙的人;(卑鄙)小人。

scu·ta [ˈskjuːtə; ˋskjutə] *n*. scutum 的复数。

scu·tate [ˈskjuːteit; ˋskjutet] *a*. **1.**【动】盾形的,有鳞甲[大鳞]的,有盾片的。**2.**【植】(椭圆)盾状的(= peltate)。

scutch [skʌtʃ; skʌtʃ] **I** *vt*. **1.** 〔Scot.〕鞭打。**2.**【纺】(梳)打(棉花、麻等);清(棉);开(布)幅。**II** *n*. **1.**【纺】梳打器;清棉机;打麻机;开幅机(= scutcher)。**2.**【建】砖工锤。

scutch·eon [ˈskʌtʃən; ˋskʌtʃən] *n*. **1.** = escutcheon. **2.** 钥匙孔盖。**3.** 姓名牌子。**4.** 盾形标牌;盾饰。

scutch·er [ˈskʌtʃə; ˋskʌtʃɚ] *n*. 1.【纺】打棉机,展棉机;打麻机;(染整)开幅机。2. 打棉者;打麻者。

scute [skjuːt; skjut] *n*.【动】= scutum.

scu·tel·late [ˈskjuːtəleit; ˋskjutlˏet] *a*.【生】1. 盾状的;小盾片状的。2. 有小鳞片[盾片]覆盖[保护]的。

scu·tel·la·tion [ˌskjuːtəˈleiʃən; ˏskjutəˋleʃən] *n*.【动】(鸟腿,鱼身的)鳞片的排列[性状]。

scu·tel·lum [skjuːˈteləm; skjuˋtɛləm] *n*. (*pl*. **-tel·la** [-ə;-ə]) 1.【植】盾片。2.【动】小盾片;菱状鳞片。

scu·ti·form [ˈskjutiˌfɔːm; ˋskjutɪˏfɔrm] *a*. 盾形的。

scut·ter [ˈskʌtə; ˋskʌtɚ] *vi*.〔英〕= scurry.

scut·tle[1] [ˈskʌtl; ˋskʌtl̩] *n*. 1. 煤桶;煤斗;煤箱〔又作 coalscuttle〕。2. 满煤桶(的分量)。3. 筐〔装谷物、蔬菜等〕。

scut·tle[2] [ˈskʌtl; ˋskʌtl̩] **I** *n*. 1.【船】小舱口;舷窗;船底孔洞。2.【建】天窗;气窗。3. (汽车的)前窗。**II** *vt*. 1. 在(船底)凿孔(使船沉没);凿沉。2. 破坏(计划);毁坏。3. (完全)放弃。~ **butt**, ~ **cosk** 1. (甲板上的)饮用自来水,饮用喷泉;饮水柜台。2.〔美海军俚〕谣言;闲话。

scut·tle[3] [ˈskʌtl;ˋskʌtl̩] **I** *vi*.〔匆匆忙忙地〕快走,〔慌慌张张地〕急奔 (*away*; *off*)。**II** *n*. 疾走;快跑。

scu·tum [ˈskjuːtəm; ˋskjutəm] *n*. (*pl*. **-ta** [-tə; -tə]) 1. 古罗马的长盾。2.【动】鳞甲;盾片,盾板。3.【解】髌骨。4.〔美〕雨衣。5. [S-]【天】盾牌座。

Scuz·zy [ˈskʌzi;ˋskʌzɪ] *n*.【计】SCSI 接口。

Scyl·la [ˈsilə; ˋsɪlə] *n*. 1. (意大利 Messina 海峡中著名大漩涡 Charybdis 对面的)锡拉巨岩。2. (住在锡拉巨岩上的)六头十二手的女怪。***between*** ~ ***and Charybdis*** 进退两难;左右为难;前有虎后有狼;腹背受敌。

scy·phi·form [ˈsaififɔːm; ˋsaɪfɪˏfɔrm] *a*.【植、动】酒杯状的;杯形的。

scy·pho·zo·an [ˌsaifəˈzəuən; ˏsaɪfəˋzoən] *n*., *a*.【动】钵水母纲 (*Scyphozoa*) 动物(的)。

scy·phus [ˈsaifəs; ˋsaɪfəs] *n*. (*pl*. **scy·phi** [-fai; -faɪ]) 1. (古希腊)双耳平底杯。2.【植】(某些花的)杯状部。

scythe [saið; saɪð] **I** *n*. (长柄)大镰刀;(古代装在战车车轮轴上的)战车镰刀。**II** *vt*. 用大镰刀割(草等)。~-**man** 1. 使用大镰刀的人。2. 时间与死亡的拟人化。

Scyth·i·a [ˈsiðiə; ˋsɪθɪə] *n*. 塞西亚〔黑海与里海间东北部一古地名〕。**Scyth·i·an** [ˈsiðiən; ˋsɪθɪən] *a*., *n*. 塞西亚的;塞西亚人[语](的)。

S.D., SD = South Dakota 南达科他〔美国州名〕。

s.d. = several dates; 〔L.〕 *sine die*.

S.D. = 1. Doctor of Science. 2. single decker. 3. sight-draft (即期汇票)。

S/D = sea-damaged.

S. Dak. = South Dakota 南达科他〔美国州名〕。

s.dev. = standard deviation 标准偏差。

SDI = Strategic Defense Initiative 战略防御计划〔即星(球大)战计划 (Star Wars)〕。

SDH = synchronous digital hierarchy【电信】同步数字式程序。

SDR = Special Drawing Rights (国际货币基金组织的)特别提款权。

SDS = Students for a Democratic Society〔美〕学生争取民主社会组织。

S.E., SE, s.e. = southeast; southeastern.

S/E = stock exchange 证券交易所。

Se = selenium【化】硒。

se- *pref*. 表示"离开,离去,分开,不用"。

SEA = Southeast Asia 东南亚。

sea [siː; si] *n*. 1. 海;海洋;内海;大(淡水)湖。2.〔*pl*. 或与不定冠词连用〕海面(状态);浪;波涛;大浪;潮流。3. 很多;大量;茫茫一片。4. 海事;海上生活;航海。*the high* ~*s* 公海 (*opp*. the closed ~ 领海)。*Praise the* ~, *but keep on land*. 隔岸观火。*There are as good fish in the* ~ *as ever came out of it*. 世上富源如鱼虾,日日取用无尽期。(意指失去这个机会还有那个机会)。*The* ~ *gets up* [*goes down*]. 波浪大起来[平静下去]了。*a long* ~ (通常的)波涛滚滚的海。*a high* [*rough, heavy*] ~ 巨浪汹涌[怒涛滔天]的海。*a quarter* ~ 冲上船尾的大浪。*a full* ~ 高潮。*A high* ~ *is running* = *The* ~ *is running high*. (海上)怒涛汹涌。*a* ~ *of trouble* 无限的麻烦。***above the*** ~ 海拔。***across the*** ~*(s)* 远隔重洋;渡过大海;到海外;在海外。***arm of the*** ~ 海湾。***a*** ~ ***of*** ... 大量的。***at full*** ~ 满潮,在高潮上;绝顶;极端。***at*** ~ 1. 在海上;在航海中。2. 迷惑;茫然;不知如何是好。***be*** (***all***) ***at*** ~ 如堕五里雾中;(简直)不晓得怎样才好;茫然。***be buried at*** ~ 葬身海中。***between the devil and the deep*** ~ 腹背受敌;进退两难。***beyond the*** ~*(s)* = across the ~(s). ***by*** ~ 由海路;经海路;乘船。***by the*** ~ 在海边。***command of the*** ~ 制海权。***follow the*** ~ 当海员;做水手。***freedom of the*** ~*s* 海上通航权。***go*** (***down***) ***to the*** ~ 到海边去。***go to*** ~ = ***follow the*** ~ 当海员;做水手。***half*** ~*s* ***over*** 酒喝得太多;有点醉。***head the*** ~ 迎浪行驶。***keep the*** ~ 1. (船)在海中;在继续航行中。2. 保持制海权。***on the*** ~ 1. 在海(岸)上。2. 乘船;在海面的船上。3. 临海;在海岸;在海边。***out to*** ~ 离港。***put*** (***out***) ***to*** ~ 开船出航;离港出海。***over the*** ~*(s)* = across the ~(s). ***ship a*** ~ (小艇)冒浪(前进)。***stand to*** ~ 离陆驶向海中。***take the*** ~ 乘船;在船上服务;出海;开船;下水。***take to*** ~ 启航。***the closed*** ~ 领海。***the high*** ~*s* 公海。***the mistress of the*** ~*(s)* 海上霸主(旧时英国的称号)。***the narrow*** ~*s* 英法海峡。***the seven*** ~*s* (世界)七大洋〔即北冰洋,南冰洋,北大西洋,南大西洋,北太平洋,南太平洋及印度洋〕;全球。***wish sb. at the bottom of the*** ~ 希望某人葬身鱼腹;咒(某人)不得好死。~ **air** 海洋[海上,海边]空气。~-**air** *a*. 海空的。~ **anchor** 海上风暴时用的浮锚;海锚。~ **anemone**【动】海葵。~ **bag** 水手旅行袋。~ **bank** 防波堤;海岸的护堤。~-**bar** 海燕。~ **barrow**【动】(海鳐鱼的)卵壳。~ **bass**【鱼】巴西刺鲈。~ **bathing** 海水浴。~ **bear** 1. 白熊;北极熊。2. 膃肭兽;海狗。~-**beaver** 海獭。~ **bed** 海底。~ **bells**【植】海滨牵牛花。~ **bird** 海鸟。~ **biscuit** [~ **bread**]【海】(可以久藏的)硬饼干;硬面包。~ **board** 海岸;海滨;沿海地方。~ **boat** 1. 远洋轮船;能耐波浪的船。2. (大轮船上的)救生艇。~ **book** 航海图。~ **boots** (海员用的)高统防雨靴。~-**born** *a*. 1.〔诗〕从海里生出来的 (*the* ~-*born city* = Venice. the ~-*born goddess* = Aphrodite)。2. 海中出产的。~-**borne** *a*. 用海轮装运的;海运的;〔船〕浮在海上的 (~-*borne articles* 舶来品。~-*borne commerce* 海上贸易。~-*borne goods* 海运货物)。~ **bream**【动】鲷;棘鬣鱼。~ **breeze** (白天从海面吹到陆上的)海(上和)风。~ **brief** = sea letter. ~ **brown** 海豹皮色的。~ **calf**【动】海豹。~ **captain** 1. 船长;舰长。2. 海军上校。3.〔诗〕大航海者。4. 海上名将。~ **catfish**【动】海鲶。~ **change** 1. (因海的作用而发生的)变形。2. 重大[显著]的变化[转变]。~ **chest** 1. 水手用的贮物箱。2.【船】通海吸水箱。~ **chestnut**【动】海胆。~ **clutter** 海波干扰。~ **coal**【英史】(被海水从沉积物中冲刷出来的)煤;从纽卡塞海运来的煤。~ **coast** 海岸;海边;海滨。~ **cock** 1. (船壳上的)海底阀;通海[船底]旋塞。2.〔谑〕海盗。3.【动】黑腹鹬。~ **cook** 船上厨师〔对新水手的蔑称〕。~ **cow**【动】1. 海牛。2. 海象。3. 河马。~**craft** 1. 航行海上的船只。2. 航海术。~ **craw-fish** [**crayfish**]【动】= spring lobster. ~ **crow**【鸟】海鸥。~ **cucumber**【动】海参。~ **damage** 海损。~ **devil**【鱼】华脐鱼,鮟鱇。~ **dog** 1.【动】海豹;【鱼】棘鲛。2.〔转义〕海盗;老练水手[海员]。~ **drome**【空】海上机场。~ **duck**【海】海鸭。~**dust** 1. 沙漠中的砖红色灰尘;从干旱陆地吹向海上的红尘。2.〔俚〕盐。~ **duty** 出海[海上]勤务。~ **eagle**【动】一种捕食鱼类的鹰;白尾鹰;〔美方〕鹗。~-**ear**【动】鲍属海产贝类;鲍。~ **earth** 海底电

S

缆接地。～ **echo** 海水反射的回波。～ **elephant**【动】海象;大海豹。～ **fan**【动】石帆;海团扇;柳珊瑚。～ **farer**〔诗〕1. 海员;水手。2. 航海者;海上旅行者。～**-faring** *a*., *n*. 1. 航海事业(的)。2. 水手工作(的)(*a ～faring life* 水手生活;航海生活。*a ～-faring man* 水手;海员)。～ **farming** 海产养殖。～ **feather**【动】海鳃;海羊;海羽(=～ pen)。～ **fern**【动】石帆。～ **fight** 海战。～ **floor** 海底;海床。～**-floor spreading**【地】海床扩张〔指海洋地壳由地幔岩浆的上升所造成的扩张〕。～ **flower**【动】= sea anemone. ～ **foam** 1. 海面泡沫。2.【矿】海泡石。～ **food**〔美〕海味;鱼。(*a ～-food caterer* 鱼贩)。～ **force** 海军。～ **fox**【鱼】长尾鲛。～ **fret**〔英〕海雾。～ **front** 1. 海岸;海边。2. 海滨马路。3. 海岸区。4. (都市、房屋的)向海的一面。～ **gauge** 1.【海】吃水[船入水的深度]。2. 气压测探器;自记海深计。～ **girt** *a*. 四面环海的。～**-god** 海神。～**-goddess** 海的女神。～ **going** *a*. 1. (适于)航行远洋的。2. 从事航海业的(*a ～ going vessel* 远洋轮船。*a ～ going hack*〔美〕旧式汽车。*a ～-going pipe line* 海底油管)。～**grape** 1. 马尾藻。2. 乌贼鱼等类海生动物。3. 海葡萄〔美国佛罗里达州沿海的一种结葡萄状果实的植物〕。～**-green** *n*., *a*. 1. 海绿色(的)。2. 潮浸(的)。～ **gull**【鸟】海鸥。～ **hare**【动】海兔;雨虎。～**haul** = ～ lift. ～ **hedgehog**【动】1. 海胆。2. 河豚;鱼虎。～ **hog**【动】海豚。～ **holly**【植】海滨刺芹。～ **horse** 1.【神话】(拖海神战车的)半马半鱼的怪物。2.【动】海马;龙落子;马头鱼;海象。3.〔转义〕白色的浪峰。～**-island (cotton)** 海岛棉。～**jack** 海上劫持。～ **jeep**〔美海军〕水陆两用吉普车。～**-jelly**【动】水母。～ **kale**【植】欧洲海甘蓝。～ **king** (古代北欧的)海盗王。～**lamprey**【动】海七鳃鳗。～ **lane** 航路;海上航线。～ **lavender**【植】匙叶草属植物。～ **lawyer** 1.〔海俚〕好讲歪理的水手[人]。2.【鱼】鲨鱼。～ **legs**〔*pl*.〕1.〔口〕(船颠簸时仍能站稳不晕船的)水手腿。2. 不晕船(*get* [*have*, *find*] *one's ～ legs on* 在船上能不晕船地正常行走。*get* [*have*] *one's ～ legs off* 登陆后能毫无晕船感觉地正常行走)。～ **leopard**【动】(南冰洋)海豹(类)。～ **letter** (海关发给非交战国船只的)中立国船舶证。～ **level** 海(平)面;标准[平均]海面(*above ～ level* 海拔)。～ **lemon** 海牛。～**lift** *n*. 海上运输。～**lily**【动】海百合。～ **line** 1. 水平线;海岸线。2.〔*pl*.〕深海渔业用钓绳。～ **lion** 1.【动】海狮。2.【徽】半狮半鱼的怪物。**S- Lord** 海军大臣〔英〕〔海军部四个海军首长之一〕。～ **maid(en)** 1. 美人鱼。2. 海中女神。～ **mark** 1. 潮汛线。2. 航海标;航标〔如灯塔等〕。～ **mat**【动】藻苔虫。～ **mew**【鸟】海鸥〔特指产于欧洲的一种〕。～ **mile** 海里;浬。～**monster** 1. 海怪。2.【鱼】银鲨鱼。～**mount** 海底山。～ **mouse**【动】海毛虫,鳞沙蚕属动物。～ **needle**【鱼】海针鱼。～ **nettle**【动】刺水母。～ **nymph** 海妖。～ **onion**【植】棉枣儿海葱;(欧洲)春棉枣儿。～ **otter**【动】海獭。～ **pass** = sea letter. ～ **pen**【动】海鳃。～ **pie** 1. (水手吃的)咸肉馅饼。2. 捉蚝者。3.〔英〕【鸟】长嘴鹬。～ **piece** 海景画。～ **pig**【动】海豚;儒艮。～ **pink**【植】海簪。～ **plane** 水上(飞)机。～ **plant** 海草;海藻。～ **port** 海港;海口;商埠。～ **power** 1. 海军力量。2. 制海权。3. 海军强国。～ **purse**【动】(鳐鱼等的)角质卵壳[卵袋]。～ **quake** *n*. 海啸;海底地震。～ **raven**【动】绒林父鱼。～ **return** (雷达)海面(反射)讯号。～ **robin**【鱼】欧鲂鮄。～ **room** 1. 足够行船的水面。2. (足够)自由行动的余地。～ **rover** 1. 海盗。2. 海盗船。～ **salt** 海盐。**Seasat** (美国用以收集海洋表面资料的)海洋卫星。～ **scallop**【动】扇贝。～ **scape** 1. 海景。2. 海景画。～ **scorpion**【动】广鳍类动物。～ **serpent**【动】海蛇。～ **service** 1. 海上勤务。2. 海军。～ **shell** 海软体动物的壳;贝壳;海贝。～ **shore** 1. *n*. 海滨;海岸;【法】满潮线与退潮线间之地。2. *a*. 海滨的。～ **sick** *a*. 晕船的。～ **sickness** 晕船。～**side** *n*., *a*. (特指充作游泳场;休养地等的)海边(的);海滨(的)(*go to the ～side* 到海边去游泳。*a ～side hotel* 海滨旅馆。*a ～side resort* 海水浴场)。～ **sider**〔美〕住在海边的人;去洗海水澡的人。～ **sleeve**【动】乌贼;墨鱼。～**slug**【动】海牛(= nudibranch)。～ **snake**【动】海蛇。**Seaspeak** 海事[航运]术语。～ **spiders**【动】1. 蜘蛛蟹。2. 鳑鱼。3. 海盘车(鱼)〔海蜘蛛类动物〕(= Pycnogonida)。～**squirt**【动】海鞘类(动物)(= *ascidians*)。～ **stock**, ～ **stores** 船上食粮。～ **swallow**【动】海鸥,海燕(= stormy petrel)。～ **tangle**【植】墨角藻;褐色藻。～ **term** 航海用语。～ **train** 1. 运载火车的轮渡。2. 海上运输队。～ **trout**【动】海鳟。～ **trumpet**【植】荒布〔南太平洋的一种海带〕。～ **urchin**【动】海胆。～ **wall** 防波堤;海堤。～ **walnut**【动】栉水母门动物。～ **ware** 海草〔尤指肥田用的〕。～**way**【海】1. 航路;航道;海路。2. 外海;外洋;公海;大海。3. (船冒浪)航行。4. 波涛汹涌的海(面)。(*in a ～-way* 在惊涛骇浪中。*make ～-way* 航行)。～**-weed** 海草;海藻。～ **whale**【动】鲲鲸。～ **whips**【动】海鞭子〔柳珊瑚属动物〕。～ **wife** 濑鱼。～ **worthiness** 适于航海;适航性。～ **worthy** *a*. (船)适于航海的,耐航[风浪]的。～ **wrack** 海藻;海草〔尤指浪潮送上岸来的海藻〕。**-ward** *a*., *n*., *ad*. 朝海(的);向海(的);海那一边(的)。**-wards** *ad*. 向海;向海那一边。

Sea·bee [ˈsiːbiː; ˋsiˌbi] *n*.〔美俚〕1. 海军工程营成员。2.〔*pl*.〕海军工程营〔源于美 1941 年成立的 Construction Battalion 两词词首 C, B 两字母的读音〕。

Sea·borg [ˈsiːbɔːg; ˋsibɔrg] *n*. 西博格〔姓氏〕。

sea·bor·gium [ˈsiːbɔːdʒiəm; ˋsiˌbɔdʒɪm] *n*.【化】𨭎〔第106号元素〕。

S.E.A.C. = Southeast Asia Command〔英旧〕东南亚司令部。

seal[1] [siːl; sil] **I** *n*.〔*sing*., *pl*.〕【动】1. 海豹。2. 海豹毛皮(制品)。3. 海豹皮色〔灰黄深褐色〕。4.〔Seals〕〔美〕海豹突击队〔美国的一支海陆空军突击队〕。*the common* [*harbor*] ～ (斑纹)海豹。*the fur* ～ 膃肭兽,海狗。**II** *vi*. 猎海豹。

seal[2] [siːl; sil] **I** *n*. 1. (打在火漆,铅等上的)火漆封印;封蜡;封铅;封条。2. 捺印;封缄。3. 印;图章;戳记;纪念邮戳。4. 图记;记号。5. 保证;严守秘密的誓约;守秘密的义务。6. 密封;隔离;堵塞。7.【机】密封垫;焊接。8.【物】绝缘。9. 征候;预兆。10. (下水道的)S形防臭弯管(=～pipe)。*the privy* ～ 御玺。*Lord Keeper of the Great* [*Privy*] S- 掌玺大臣。*the ～s* 英国上议院议长[国务大臣]的公章;上议院议长[国务大臣]的官职。*a bond under sb.'s hand and* ～ 有某人签名盖章的字据。*the ～ of love* 爱情的标志[接吻、结婚等]。*the ～ of death* 死的征兆。***a ～ upon sb.'s lips*** 堵嘴钱。***affix*** [***put***, ***set***] ***one's ～ to*** 在…上盖印;对…表示同意;保证…批准。***break the ～*** 开封;拆信。***conduit ～*** 线管壳。***pass the ～s*** 得到批准。***put the ～ upon*** = ***put ... under ～*** 在…封上火漆印[打上封印]。***receive the ～s*** 接印;接任。***set one's ～ to*** 1. = affix one's ～ to. 2. 批准;赞同。***take off the ～*** 拆信;开封。***under*** [***with***] ***a flying ～*** 以开口信。***the great ～*** = ***the ～ of state*** 国玺。***under my hand and ～*** 经我签名盖章。***under ～*** 盖有印鉴(的)。***under the ～ of secrecy*** (约定)保守秘密。**II** *vt*. 1. 盖印于;打印于;在(度量衡器、商品等上)加上检验封印。2.〔常作 ～ up〕在…上打上封印;封;密封(信等)。3. 关进;关闭;密闭(容器、窗等)。4.【电】使(插头与插孔等)紧密接触。5. 用水泥等充填。6. 闭(嘴);缄(口等);守(秘密)。7. 证明。8. 保证(*with*)。9. 决定;确定;注定(命运);解决。10.〔英海军〕接受;采用。11. 在…上划十字;给…施洗礼;(摩门教徒)举行(结婚[过继]仪式)。*The treaty has been signed and ～ed*. 条约已经签字盖章[签订]。*a ～ed letter* 密信。*～ing pliers* 铅印钳。*～ing wire* 铅印铅丝。*My lips are ～ed*. 我的嘴被封住了[我已经不好开口了]。***a ～ed book*** 加上封印[不能打开]的书;谜,不可理解的事

物。*as good as* ~*ed* (命运)是注定了[算完蛋了]。~ *in* 1. 封入。2. 焊死。~ *off* 1. = ~ *up*. 2. 熨开;脱焊。~ *on* 焊上。~ *up* 1. 封;密封。2. 确定。~ **ring** 印章戒指。

Sea·lab [ˈsiːˌlæb; ˋsiˏlæb] *n*.【美海军】海底实验室。

seal·ant [ˈsiːlənt; ˋsilənt] *n*. 封蜡;火漆;密封胶。

seal·er[1] [ˈsiːlə; ˋsilɚ] *n*. 1. 海豹猎船。2. 海豹猎人。

seal·er[2] [ˈsiːlə; ˋsilɚ] *n*. 1. 盖印人;密封人。2. 密封器;封口机。3. 封口机操作者。4. (度量衡器等的)检验员。5. 保护层。

seal·er·y [ˈsiːləri; ˋsilərɪ] *n*. 1. 海豹群集地;海豹猎场。2. 捕海豹业。

seal-fishery [ˈsiːlfiʃəri; ˋsilfɪʃərɪ] *n*. 1. 猎海豹业。2. 海豹猎场。

seal·flow·er [ˈsiːlˈflauə; ˋsɪlˈflaʊr] *n*.【植】荷包牡丹。

seal·ing [ˈsiːliŋ; ˋsilɪŋ] *n*. 猎海豹业。

sealing-wax [ˈsiːliŋwæks; ˋsilɪŋwæks] *n*. 火漆;封蜡。

SEALS = Sea-Air-Land-Soldiers〔美〕陆海空特遣队〔指擅长水下爆破和侦察的美国海军特种兵〕。

seal·skin [siːlskin; ˋsilˏskɪn] *n*. 1. 海豹皮。2. 海豹皮大衣。

seal·wort [ˈsiːlwəːt; ˋsilˏwɝt] *n*.【植】黄精;平铺漆姑草。

seam [siːm; sim] I *n*. 1. 缝;线缝。2. 接口;接缝;接合处;接合线。3. 裂缝。4. (脸上的)皱纹。5. 伤痕。6.【船】(船板间的)缝隙。7.【地,矿】层;矿层;节理;煤层。8. (铸件等的)接痕。9.【解】骨缝。II *vt*. 1. 缝拢;缝合;接合;合拢。2.〔主用被动语态〕使生裂缝[皱纹、伤痕]。3.【编织】在(袜子等上)做棱线。*be* ~*ed with care* [*old age*] 因忧虑[年老]而生了皱纹的。*be* ~*ed with wounds* 有伤痕的。—*vi*. 1. 生裂缝;裂开。2.【编织】做棱线。**-er** 1. 缝纫机。2. 缝纫工。**-less** *a*. 无缝的(*a* ~*less steel pipe* 无缝钢管。*a* ~*less tubing mill* 无缝钢管厂)。

sea·man [ˈsiːmən; ˋsimən] *n*. (*pl*. **-men**) 1. 水手;船员;海员。2. 水兵。*a merchant* ~ 商船船员。*a good* [*poor*] ~ 能干的[不行的]船员。*a leading* ~〔英〕一等水兵。*an able* [*able-bodied*] ~〔英〕二等水兵。*an ordinary* ~〔英〕= *an apprentice* ~〔美〕三等水兵。~ *recruit*〔美〕候补水兵〔低于三等水兵〕。**-like, -ly** *a*. 像水手的。**-ship** *n*. 海员技术;航海技术。

seam·ster [ˈsemstə, ˈsiːm-; ˋsimstɚ, ˋsɛm-] *n*.〔古〕裁缝(= tailor)。

seam·stress [ˈsemstris; ˋsimstrɪs, ˋsɛmstrɪs] *n*. 女裁缝,女缝工。

seam·y [ˈsiːmi; ˋsimɪ] *a*. (**-i·er**; **-i·est**) 1. 有缝的;有裂缝的。2. 粗糙不光洁的;难看的;丑恶的;令人不快的。*the* ~ *side* (衣裳等的)里面;(社会等的)丑恶的一面;阴暗面。**-i·ness** *n*.

Sean [ʃɔːn; ʃɔn] *n*. 肖恩〔男子名,John 的异体〕。

Sean·ad Eir·eann [ˈʃænəðˈɛərən; ˋsænadˋɛrən]〔Ir.〕爱尔兰共和国参议院。

sé·ance [ˈseiɑ̃ːns; ˋseɑns] *n*. [F.] 1. 集会,会议。2. 降神(术)会。

sear[1] [siə; sɪr] I *a*. 〔诗〕干枯的;干瘪的;枯萎的。*the* ~ *and yellow leaf* 〔喻〕老年;老境。II *vt*. 1. 使干枯;使凋萎。2. 烧焦;烧灼。3. 加烙印于。4. 使憔悴。5. 使失去感觉;使麻木。*a countenance* ~*ed by grief and weeping* 因悲伤哭泣而憔悴的脸。*a* ~*ed conscience* 麻木了的良心。—*vi*. 1. 枯萎;凋谢。2. 灼伤。3. 变得麻木不仁。III *n*. 烙印;焦痕。~**ing iron** 烙铁。

sear[2] [siə; sɪr] *n*. 扣机〔枪炮的一种保险装置〕。

search [səːtʃ; sɝtʃ] I *vt*. 1. 搜查;检查(身体、衣袋等);搜索,搜寻;找;寻找。2. 调查;查究;探求;追求;根究(*into*)。3. (冷风等)到处侵入,刺透。4.【军】使(火力)向纵深展开。~ *sb*. 搜查身体。~ *a book* 在一本书里查找材料。~ *one's memory* 竭力回忆。*The shrapnel was* ~*ing every cranny*. 榴霰弹正在四散开来。II *vi*. 1. 搜寻,搜查(*for*);探求。2.【计】觅数,检索。~ *after* [*for*] 寻找;寻求,追求;探求(~ *after health* 讲究健康;保养。~ *a house for papers* 在一座房屋里搜查文件)。~ *into* 调查;研究;根究。*S- me*!〔美〕我不知道。~ *out* 搜出;查出;探出;找出。III *n*. 1. 搜索;搜寻;寻找。2. 探索;探求(*after*; *for*);调查;检查。*in* ~ *of* 寻找;去找;追求;为了寻求;试图发现。*make a* ~ *after* [*for*] (去)找;寻求;追求。~ **coil**【无】搜索线圈;探测线圈。~ **engine**【计】(用以搜索因特网上信息的)电脑搜索程序,搜索引擎。~ **light** *n*. 1. 探照灯(光)。2. = flash light (*play a* ~*-light on* 用探照灯照)。~ **party** 搜索队。~ **warrant** (住宅)搜查证。

search·er [ˈsəːtʃə; ˋsɝtʃɚ] *n*. 1. 搜查者;搜寻者;探求者;调查者,检查者。2. 海关检查员;船舶检查员;囚犯检查员。3.【无】搜索器;大炮检查器。4.【医】探针;膀胱(石)探杆。

search·ing [ˈsəːtʃiŋ; ˋsɝtʃɪŋ] I *a*. 1. 搜查的;搜索的。2. 仔细的;彻底的;严格的。3. (目光等)锐利的。4. (冷风)刺骨的。*a* ~ *examination* 仔细严格的考试。*a* ~ *look* 锐利的眼光。~ *wind* 刺骨寒风。II *n*. 搜寻;搜查;搜索;探索;调查;探究。*the* ~*(s) of heart* 反复扪心自问。~ **gunfire**【军】纵深射击。

Sea·shore [ˈsiːʃɔː; ˋsiˏʃor] *n*. 西肖尔〔姓氏〕。

sea·son [ˈsiːzn; ˋsizn̩] *n*. 1. 季;季节;〔美〕雨季。2. (水果、鱼类等的)旺季;流行季节;时令;活动期。3. 好时机;适当时机。4. 一时;暂时。5. 社交季节;某种活动的季节[期间]。6.〔英口〕(电车等的)季票;月票。7.【林】干材法。*the* (*four*) ~*s* 四季。*a dry* [*wet, rainy*] ~ 旱[雨]季。*the* ~ *of occurrence* (热带的)暴风雨季节。*a close* [*an open*] ~ 禁猎[打猎]期。*rush* ~ 旺季;忙季。*the harvest* ~ 收获期。*the strawberry* ~ 草莓旺季。*a dead* [*a dull, an off*] ~ (*in trade*) (营业的)淡季。*the height of the* ~ (流行的)极盛时期。*There is a* ~ *for work and for play*. 玩也好,工作也好,都有个时候。*the* (*London*) ~ 伦敦社交季节[初夏时期]。***at all*** ~***s*** 一年四季;一年到头。***for a*** ~ 一时;一会儿;暂时。***in due*** ~ 在适当的时候。***good*** ~ 恰好;尽早;及早;及时地。***in*** ~ 1. 时机正好的;恰合时宜的(*a word in* ~ 合时宜的话)。2. 尽早;及早。3. (水果等)正旺;当令;应时。4. (狩猎)在猎期。5. (动物)在发情期中。***in*** ~ ***and out of*** ~ 始终;不断;任何时候;一年到头。***out of*** ~ 1. 过时的。2. 失去时机。3. 过了旺季。4. 在禁猎期。

II *vt*. 1. 使熟练;使(习)惯。2. 风干;晒干(木材);晾干,对…进行干燥处理;使陈化。3. 使适应(气候等)。4. 给…加味[调味]。5. 给…增加趣味。6. 缓和,调和。*a* ~*ed soldier* (有经验的)老兵。~ *tobacco* 晒烟叶。*cattle* ~*ed to diseases* 免疫家畜。*highly* ~*ed dishes* 佐料多味道浓的菜肴。~*ed wood* 干材。*conversation* ~*ed with humour* 有风趣的谈话。—*vi*. 1. 熟练;习惯。2. (木材)变干;陈化。~ ***oneself to*** (*cold*) 练得不怕(寒冷)。~ **opener** 球类赛季的揭幕比赛。

sea·son·a·ble [ˈsiːznəbl; ˋsiznəbl] *a*. 当令的;合时的;及时的。*a* ~ *weather* 合时的气候。*a* ~ *aid* 及时的援助。**-a·bly** *ad*.

sea·son·al [ˈsiːzənl; ˋsiznəl] *a*. 季节(性)的。**-ly** *ad*.

sea·son·ing [ˈsiːzniŋ; ˋsiznɪŋ] *n*. 1. 调味品;调味剂;佐料。2. 调和;缓和。3. 处理(法);气候处理;风干;干燥(处理);木材干燥法;老化。4.【物】(磁控管的)不稳定性;时效。

season-ticket [ˈsiːznˈtikit; ˋsiznˈtɪkɪt] *n*. 月季票;长期票;定期车票(=〔美〕commutation-ticket)。

seat [siːt; sit] I *n*. 1. 座;座位;席位;席次。2. 椅子;凳子。3. (椅子等的)座部;垫子。4. 臀部;裤裆。5. 地位;场所;位置;所在地;中心地。6. 邸宅;别墅。7. 王座;主教座;王权,主教权。8. 议员席。9. (交易所等的)会员资格。10. (马、脚踏车等的)骑法;坐法;骑乘姿势。*S-*

S

must be booked in advance. 座位必须预定。*the* ~ *of disease* 病源;病灶;患部。*the* ~ *of war* 战场。*the county* ~ 县城(行政机构所在地)。*the* ~ *of learning* 学术中心地。*the* ~ *of soul* 神经中枢。*a safe* ~ 稳可当选的选举区。***have a good*** ~ 骑法不错。***have a*** ~ 〔美〕= take a ~. ***keep one's*** ~ 留在原位不动。***lose one's*** ~ 失去原有的位置[席位];落选。***on the anxious*** ~〔美〕提心吊胆。***take a*** ~ 坐下。***take one's*** ~ 就座;入座。***take one's*** ~ ***in the House of Commons*** (当选后)开始充当众议院议员。***vacate*** [***resign***] ***one's*** ~ 辞去议员职。***win a*** ~ ***in Congress*** 获得国会议员席位;当选为议员。**II** *vt*. **1.** 使…坐下,使…就座。**2.** 在…设座位;给…装座位。**3.** 给(机器等)装底座;给…装座子[垫子]。**4.** 给…掉换[修补]垫子[座子]。**5.** 安装;安置。**6.** 安插(职位);派…做议员。**7.** 安牢;使固定。**8.** 住;住定。*Pray be* ~*ed*. 请坐下。*The hall is* ~*ed for 5000*. 这个讲堂坐得下五千人。***be*** ~***ed*** **1.** 坐着。**2.** 坐落在;位于…。~ ***a candidate*** 选举候补人。~ ***oneself*** 坐下;就座;入席。~ ***oneself along*** (*the Mediterranean coast*) 定居于(地中海沿岸)。~ **angle**【机】支座角钢。~**belt** (汽车、飞机上的)座位安全带。~ **clay** 耐火土。~ **earth**【农艺】根土。~ **frame** 座架。~**mate** (飞机、公共车辆等上的)邻座者。~(-)**mile** 客运里程(指一名旅客一英里的旅程)。~**-pack** *a*. 座垫式 (~*-pack parachute* 可作座垫用的降落伞)。~**work** 课堂作业[学生在课堂座位上做的功课]。

seat·ed [ˈsiːtid; ˋsitɪd] ***a***. **1.** (有)…座位的。**2.** (有)…座垫的。**3.** 根深的;固定的。*a deep-* ~ *disease* 痼疾。

S

seat·er [ˈsiːtə; ˋsitɚ] ***n***. 有(若干)座位的飞机[汽车等]。*a Four-* ~ 四座飞机[汽车等]。

seat·ing [ˈsiːtiŋ; ˋsitɪŋ] ***n***. **1.** 座位(设备);座位数。**2.** 椅料;椅垫;椅布。**3.** 骑姿,骑法。*a* ~ *capacity* 座(位)数;容纳量。

SEATO [ˈsiːtəu, si(ː)ˈætəu; ˋsito, sɪˋæto] = Southeast Asia Treaty Organization 东南亚条约组织。

Se·at·tle [siˈætl; sɪˋætl̩] ***n***. 西雅图〔美国华盛顿州港市〕。

se·ba·ceous [siˈbeiʃəs; sɪˋbeʃəs] ***a***. 脂肪(状)的;脂肪多的;分泌脂肪的。~ **cyst**【医】皮脂腺囊肿。~ **gland**【解】皮脂腺。

se·bac·ic [siˈbæsik; sɪˋbæsɪk] ***a***. 含脂的。~ **acid**【化】癸二酸。

Se·bas·tian [siˈbæstjən; sɪˋbæstʃən] ***n***. 塞巴斯蒂安〔男子名〕。

Se·bas·to·pol [siˈbæstəpl; sɪˋbæstəpl̩] ***n***. = Sevastopol.

S.E.bE = South-east by East 东南偏东。

se·bif·er·ous [siˈbifərəs; sɪˋbɪfərəs] ***a***.【生】生脂肪的,分泌脂肪的,多脂肪的 (= sebiparous)。

seb·or·rhe·a, seb·or·rhoe·a [ˌsebəˈriːə; ˏsɛbəˋriə] ***n***.【医】皮脂溢。**-rhe·ic, -rhoe·ic** ***a***.

S.E.bS. = South-east by South 东南偏南。

se·bum [ˈsiːbəm; ˋsibəm] ***n***.【医】(皮脂腺中分泌的)脂肪,皮脂。

sec. = **1.** secant. **2.** second; seconds; secondary. **3.** secretary. **4.** secured; security. **5.** sector; section, sections. **6.** 〔L.〕*secundum*.

S.E.C. = **1.** Supreme Economic Council 〔澳〕最高经济委员会。**2.** Securities and Exchange Commission 〔美〕证券交易委员会。**3.** Social Economic Council 〔荷〕社会经济理事会。

SECAM = *Séquence de Couleurs avec Mémoire* 〔F.〕彩色顺序存储;(法国)"色康"五彩电视系统 (= Colo(u)r Sequence with Memory)。

se·cant [ˈsiːkənt; ˋsikənt] **I** ***a***. 分[交]割的;(横)切的,交叉的。**II** ***n***.【数】正割;割线。*a* ~ *line* 切线;割线。

sec·a·teur [ˈsekətəː; ˏsɛkəˋtɝ] ***n***. 〔常用 *pl*.〕修枝铗[钳];整枝剪[大剪刀]。

sec·co [ˈsekəu; ˋsɛko] **I** ***a***. 〔It.〕**1.**【乐】无伴奏的;简朴的。**2.** 干燥的;无水分的。**II** ***n***. 干(灰泥)壁画[画法]; (= secco painting; tempera)。

se·cede [siˈsiːd; sɪˋsid] ***vi***. (从教会、政党等)退出;脱离 (*from*)。

se·ced·er [siˈsiːdə; sɪˋsidɚ] ***n***. 退出者;脱离者;退党者。

se·cern [siˈsəːn; sɪˋsɝn] ***vt***. 分;区分;鉴别。—***vi***. 分开;分离。**-ment** ***n***.

se·cern·ent [siˈsəːnənt; sɪˋsɝnənt] **I** ***a***.【生】分泌(性)的。**II** ***n***. **1.**【生理】分泌器官;分泌作用。**2.** 分泌促进剂[药物]。

se·ces·sion [siˈseʃən; sɪˋsɛʃən] ***n***. **1.** (从教会、政党等的)脱离;退出;分裂。**2.**【建】直线式;直线派。**3.** 〔S-〕【美史】(1861 年南方十一州的)脱离联邦。***the War of S-*** 〔美〕南北战争。**-ism** ***n***. **1.** 脱离论;分离论;分裂主义。〔常 S-〕【美史】(南北战争时的)分离主义 (*national* ~*ism* 民族分裂主义)。**2.**【建】直线式;分离式。**-ist** ***n***. **1.** 脱离论者;【美史】(南北战争时的)分离主义者;分裂主义者。**2.**【建】直线派建筑家。

Seck·el [ˈsekəl; ˋsɛkl] ***n***. 〔美〕红棕皮小甜梨。

se·clude [siˈkluːd; sɪˋklud] ***vt***. **1.** 使分离;隔离;隔绝(人、场所等)。**2.** 使隐退;使隐居。~ *oneself from the world* 隐退;与世隔绝。

se·clud·ed [siˈkluːdid; sɪˋkludɪd] ***a***. 与世隔绝的;偏僻的;幽静的;隐退的。*a* ~ *place* 与外界隔绝的所在。

se·clu·sion [siˈkluːʒən; sɪˋkluʒən] ***n***. **1.** 隔离;隔绝;隐退。**2.** 偏僻的地方。*a policy of* ~ 闭关自守政策。*live in* ~ 过退隐生活。

se·clu·sive [siˈkluːsiv; sɪˋklusɪv] ***a***. **1.** 爱僻静的;隐居性的;隔离性的。**2.** 退隐的。**-ly** ***ad***.

sec·ond[1] [ˈsekənd; ˋsɛkənd] **I** ***a***. **1.** 第二的;第二次的;二等(的)。**2.** 次等的;较差的;劣于…的 (*to*)。**3.** 〔美〕较年轻的。**4.** 另一(个)的;又一(个)的;别的;类似的。**5.** 次(的);副(的);从属的;辅助的。**6.**【乐】第二度音程的;低音部的。*a* ~ *cabin* 二等舱。*the* ~ (*largest*) *town in the country* 国内第二(大)城市。*a* ~ *time* 再(一次)。*a* ~ *coat* 第二层(油漆等)。*a* ~ *pair of boots* 另一双皮鞋。*a* ~ *helping* (食物)再来的一份。***be the*** ~ ***to come*** 第二个来的。***come in*** ~ (赛跑时)跑得第二。***come*** ~ (***in one's estimation, affection***) 得第二;占第二位。***every*** ~ ***day*** 隔一天;隔日。***in the*** ~ ***place*** 第二(点);其次。***on*** ~ ***thoughts*** 经重新考虑后。~ ***to none*** 不比任何人[东西]差;最好的;第一等的。***Shall*** [***Will***] ***never be*** ~ 决不后人。
II ***n***. **1.** 第二人[物];次一等的人[物];副。**2.** 跑第二的人;第二名。**3.** (某月的)二日;初二;二号;(火车等的)二等车。**4.** 辅助人[者];助手;副手;(决斗的)帮手。**5.** 其他的人[物]。**6.** 〔*pl*.〕【商】二级品;次品;二等货;次等品;次货。**7.** 粗面粉;粗面粉做的面包。**8.**【乐】第二度音程;第二音;二度;低音部(声音);低音部乐器。**9.**【汽车】第二档。**10.**【商】汇票的第二联〔又称 ~ of exchange〕。**11.**【棒球】二垒。*a good* [*poor*] ~ 跟第一件差不多[差得远]的第二件衣服。*the* ~ *in command* 副司令官。*He* [*She*] *will soon take a* ~. 他[她]就要第二次结婚了。***act as a most useful*** ~ 大力支援[辅助];成为左右手。***get into a*** ~ 坐上二等车。
III ***vt***. **1.** 辅助;支援;支持;赞成(提议)。**2.** [siˈkɔnd; sɪˋkɑnd]【英军】暂时调派担任特殊职务。~ *words with deeds* 用行动支持自己的言论。*be* ~*ed for service on the staff* 被暂时调到参谋部工作。—***vi***. 附议;附和。~ **advent** [**S- Advent**] 基督再临。~ **ballot** 决选投票。~ **banana** 〔美俚〕(戏剧、杂耍中的)配角;次要人物。~ **base**【棒球】第二垒。~ **baseman**【棒球】二垒手。~ **chamber** 上(议)院。**S- Chamber** (荷兰)众议院。~ **childhood** 老耄(智力衰退)期。~**-coming-of-Christ head** 〔美新闻〕横贯全页的红字大标题。~ **contact**【天】

蚀既。~ **cousin** 远房堂[表]兄弟姊妹。~**-cut file** 中细锉。~**-degree burn** 二级烧伤。~ **division** 低级文官;(监狱里的)中等待遇。~ **drawer** *a*.〔美口〕次等的,第二流的。**S- Empire** 法兰西第二帝国(1852—1870)。~ **endoderm**【生】后成内胚层。~ **estate** 第二等级[贵族]。~**fiddle** 1.(乐队的)第二小提琴(演奏者)。2. 第二把手;〔美俚〕二等角色。~ **floor**〔美〕二楼;〔英〕三楼。~ **front** 第二战场。~ **growth**【植】次生林。~**-guess** *vi*., *vt*. 1. 事后批评[劝告]。2. 预言;猜测。~**-guesser** 事后聪明的人。**S- International**【史】第二国际。~ **language** 第二语言〔一个国家中除国语而外广泛使用的或被正式承认的第二种语言〕。~ **lieutenant** 少尉[陆军,海军陆战队,〔美〕空军]。~ **mate** [**officer**]【海】二副。~ **mortgage** 二次抵押。~ **nature** 第二天性(*Habit is a* ~ *nature*. 习惯是第二天性)。~ **nerves**【解】视神经。~**-pair back** [**front**]〔英〕三楼后[前]房。~ **papers**〔美〕(外国侨民要求加入美国国籍的)第二次申请书。~ **person**【语法】第二人称。~ **pilot** 副驾驶员。~**-rate** 1. *a*. 第二流的;二等的;次等的。2. *n*. 次等货;次级品;二等战舰;二流人物。~**-rater** 二流人物;二等角色;次等货。~ **reading** (议会中对提案的)二读。**S- Republic** (法兰西)第二共和国(1848—1852)。~ **root** 次生根。~ **self** 第二自我(指心腹朋友等)。~ **sight** 1. 超级视力;千里眼。2. 卓见;预见力。~ **soprano** 次高音。~ **sound**【物】第二声。~ **speed** 二档速度。~ **stor(e)y** = ~ floor. ~**-stor(e)y** *a*. 1. 第二层楼的。2.〔俚〕(贼)从二层楼进屋的。~**-stor(e)y man**〔俚〕(从楼上进屋的)夜盗,窃贼。~**-strike** *a*.(核子武力)反击的;报复的。~**-string** *a*. 1.【体】(指球员)后备的。2.〔转义〕次等的,第二流的。~**-stringer** 后备球员。~ **teeth** 成人齿;永久齿。~ **thoughts** [〔美〕**thought**] 重新考虑;重想。~**-timer** 第二次犯罪的罪犯。~ **wind** 重新振作;精神恢复;恢复元气。**S- World War** 第二次世界大战(1939—1945)。

sec·ond[2] [ˈsekənd; ˋsɛkənd] *n*. 1. 秒(=1/60 分);秒(针)。2. 片刻;一瞬间。3. 弧秒(=1/3600 弧度)。*He was done in a few* ~*s*. 他一会儿就累倒了。*Wait a* ~! 等一下! *in a* ~ 立刻。

sec·ond·a·ri·ly [ˈsekəndərili; ˋsɛkənˏdɛrəlɪ] *ad*. 1. 在第二;其次。2. 从属地,在第二位。

sec·ond·a·ry [ˈsekəndəri; ˋsɛkənˏdɛrɪ] I *a*. 1. 第二(位)的,第二次的;中级的(*opp*. primary)。2. 副(的);从属的;附属的;辅助的;补充的;次要的;次等的;代理的。3.【医】继发(性)的,第二期的。4.【地】中世代的;次生的。5.【电】(产生)感应电流的;次级电流的。6.【化】仲的,次的;副的,二代的。7. 中等教育[学校]的。8.【语】音次重音的。9. 间接的;非原始的。*Of the two contradictory aspects, one must be principal and the other* ~. 矛盾着的两方面中,必有一方面是主要的,他方面是次要的。*a* ~ *cause* 副因。~ *action* 副作用。*a* ~ *product* 副产物。*the S- strata*【地】中世层。*be of* ~ *importance* 不大重要。II *n*. 1. 助手;副手;帮手;代理人;被委任者;次要的人;次要的东西。2.【天】双星中较小较暗的一个;卫星。3. 副低气压。4.【电】次级[二次]绕组[线圈]。5.【动】(鸟的)次级飞羽;腕羽;(昆虫的)后翅。6.【地】中世代。7.【语】次重音。~ **battery** = ~cell. ~ **carbon atom**【化】仲碳原子。~ **cell**【物】蓄电池;副电池。~ **circle**【天】第二圈,副圈。~ **coil**【电】副线圈。~ **colour** 等和色;合成色。~ **contact** 辅助触点。~ **current**【电】二次电流,次级线圈电流。~ **diagonal**【数】次对角线。~ **education** [**school**] 中等教育[学校]。~ **electron**【物】次级电子。~ **emission**【物】次级发射。~ **evidence** 补证。~ **fan**【矿】局部(辅助)扇风机。~ **fever**【医】后热。~ **foci** 共轭焦点。~ **forest**【林】再生林。~ **gas** 精洗煤气。~ **generator** 蓄电池;变压器;变量器。~ **inductance** 二次电路电感。~ **line** 支线。~ **metal** 再用[生]金属。~ **planet**【天】卫星。~ **protection tube**【冶】热电偶护管。~ **radiation**【原】次级辐射。~ **sex characteristic**【生】次要性征。~ **syphilis**【医】二期梅毒。~ **union**【医】二次愈合,化脓愈合。

sec·ond-best [ˈsekəndˈbest; ˋsɛkəndˋbɛst] I *a*. 第二等的,第二流的,第二位的。II *n*. 第二等的东西。*one's* ~ *clothes* 第二件好衣裳。*come off* ~ 输;被击败;被…胜过。

sec·ond-chop [ˈsekəndˈtʃɔp; ˋsɛkəndˋtʃɑp] *n*.〔俚〕二等货;下等货。

sec·ond-class [ˈsekəndˈklɑːs; ˋsɛkəndˋklæs] I *a*. 1.〔英〕第二等的,次级的。2. 第二类的。3. 第二流的。*a* ~ *carriage* 二等(客)车。~ *matter*〔美〕第二类邮件〔新闻纸类、定期刊物等〕。II *ad*. 乘二等车地;坐二等舱地。*travel* [*go*] ~ 坐二等车[舱]旅行。

sec·ond·er [ˈsekəndə; ˋsɛkəndɚ] *n*. 1. 后援者。2.(尤指动议的)附议者;赞成者。

sec·ond-hand[1] [ˈsekəndˈhænd; ˋsɛkəndˋhænd] I *a*. 1. 用过的;旧的;做旧货买卖的。2. 第二手的;间接(得来)的;(由旁人那里)听[借]来的;(学说等)不是独创的。~ *books* [*clothes*] 旧书[衣]。~ *witness* 陈述传闻情况的证人。II *ad*. 从旧货店(买到);从第二手;间接(地)。*buy* ~ 买旧货。III *n*. 旧货。*at* ~ 1. 用旧货。2. 间接(地);辗转(得来地)。~ **smoke** 间接吸烟,被动吸烟。~ **tap**【机】中丝锥;二丝锥。

sec·ond-hand[2] [ˈsekəndˈhænd; ˋsɛkəndˋhænd] *n*.(钟表的)秒针。

sec·ond·ly [ˈsekəndli; ˋsɛkəndlɪ] *ad*. 第二;其次。

se·con·do [seˈkɔndəu; seˋkondo] *n*.〔It.〕【乐】(协奏曲的)第二部〔尤指四手联弹钢琴曲中的较低音部〕。

se·cre·cy [ˈsiːkrisi; ˋsikrəsɪ] *n*. 1. 秘密(状态);隐蔽(状态);守秘密。2. 保密;保密能力。*I can rely on his* ~. 我相信他不会泄漏秘密。*in* [*with*] ~ 秘密地;暗中。*in the* ~ *of one's own heart* 在内心深处。*with the utmost* ~ 极秘密地。

se·cret [ˈsiːkrit; ˋsikrɪt] I *a*. 1. 秘密的;机密的;隐秘的。2. 僻远的。3. 隐藏的;看不见的。4. 神秘的;奥妙的;不可思议的。5. 隐居的。6.〔罕〕沉默寡言的。*a* ~ *code* 密码。*a* ~ *door* 暗门。*a* ~ *errand* 秘密差使。*a* ~ *passage* 秘密通道。*a* ~ *valley* 僻静的山谷,幽谷。*the* ~ *workings of nature* 鬼斧神工。*a* ~ *passion* [*sorrow*]〔美学生语〕意中人。*be* ~ *in one's habits* 有一切喜欢背着人做的习惯。*keep* (*sth*.) ~ 保守(某事)秘密。II *n*. 1. 秘密的事情;秘密;机密。2. 秘诀;隐蔽的真义。3.〔*pl*.〕神秘;奇迹。4.〔*pl*.〕秘处;阴部〔又称 ~ parts〕。*an open* ~ 公开的秘密。*the* ~ *of success* 成功的秘诀。*be in the* ~ 知道秘密;知道内情;参与秘密。*in* ~ 秘密地;偷偷摸摸地。*keep a* [*the*] ~ (保)守秘密。*let out a* ~ 泄漏秘密。*let sb. into the* ~ 告诉秘密;传授秘诀。*make a* [*no*] ~ *of* 隐秘[不隐秘];把[不把]…保守秘密。~ **agent** 特务;间谍。~ **ballot** 无记名投票。~ **ink** 隐显墨水。~ **joint**【机】暗接。~ **nail** 暗钉。~ **police** 秘密警察。~ **process** (虽非专利却受法律保护的)秘密工艺。~ **service** 1. 特务组织;特务机构;情报机关;情报部门。2. 特务工作。3.〔美〕(财政部的)特工处〔缩写为 S. S.〕。~ **society** 秘密会社;帮会。**-ly** *ad*.

sec·re·taire [ˌsekriˈtɛə; səˏkreˋtɛr] *n*. = escritoire.

sec·re·tar·i·al [ˌsekrəˈtɛəriəl; ˏsɛkrəˋtɛrɪəl] *a*. 1. 秘书的;书记的。2. 部长的;大臣的。

sec·re·tar·i·at(e) [ˌsekrəˈtɛəriət; ˏsɛkrəˋtɛrɪət] *n*. 1. 书记[秘书、部长]的职务。2. 秘书长办公室;秘书处,书记处。3. 秘书处[书记处]全体工作人员。*United Nations S-* 联合国秘书处。

sec·re·tar·y [ˈsekrətri; ˋsɛkrəˏtɛrɪ] *n*. 1. 秘书;书记,干事。2.〔S-〕〔美〕部长;〔英〕大臣。3.(上部附有书橱的)写字台。4. 书写体大写铅字。*a private* ~ 秘书。*the*

S

Party S- (共产党)书记。*an honorary* ～ 名誉干事。*the S- of State* 〔美〕国务卿;〔英〕大臣〔也有单称 Minister 的〕。*the S- of Defense* 〔美〕国防部部长。*the S- of State for Home* [*Foreign*] *Affairs* = *the Home* [*Foreign*] *S-* 〔英〕内务[外交]大臣。*a general* ～ 秘书长;总书记。～ **bird** 鹭鹰;(南非产)食蛇鸟。～**-general** 秘书长;书记长;总书记。**-ship** 书记[秘书、部长、大臣]的职位[任期]。

se·crete [siˈkriːt; sɪˋkrit] *vt*. **1.** 藏,隐藏;隐匿〔通常指物〕。**2.** 侵吞。**3.**【生理】分泌。*a secreting cell* 分泌细胞。

se·cre·tin [siˈkriːtn; sɪˋkritɪn] *n*.【生】分泌素。

se·cre·tion [siˈkriːʃən; sɪˋkriʃən] *n*. **1.** 隐匿;藏匿;隐藏。**2.**【生理】分泌。**3.** 分泌物;分泌液。**4.** 树液。

se·cre·tive [siˈkriːtiv; sɪˋkritɪv] *a*. **1.** 遮遮掩掩的;躲躲闪闪的;沉默寡言的;守口如瓶的;秘而不宣的;不坦率的;隐秘的。**2.**【生】(促进)分泌的。**-ly** *ad*. **-ness** *n*.

se·cre·to·ry [siˈkriːtəri; sɪˋkritərɪ] **I** *a*.【生】(促进)分泌的。**II** *n*. 分泌器官。

secs. = **1.** seconds. **2.** sections.

sect [sekt; sɛkt] *n*. **1.** 派(别);宗派;教派〔尤指教义不同的分裂教派〕。**2.** (哲学等的)学派;党派;团体。

sect. = section(al)。

sec·tar·i·an [sekˈtɛəriən; sɛkˋtɛrɪən] **I** *a*. 宗派的;分裂教派的;派系的;学派的;宗派主义的。*Cadres should guard against* ～ *tendencies*. 干部应该防止宗派主义的倾向。**II** *n*. **1.** 宗派主义者。**2.** 某宗派[教派]成员。**-ism** *n*. 宗派主义。

sec·ta·ry [ˈsektəri; ˋsɛktərɪ] *n*. **1.** 〔古〕某宗派成员。**2.**【英史】分裂教派[长老派(等)]信徒。

sec·tile [ˈsektail; ˋsɛktɪl] *a*. (矿物等)可切开的;(云母等)可剖成片的;【植】(叶子)可分的。

sec·tion [ˈsekʃən; ˋsɛkʃən] **I** *n*. **1.** (外科、解剖的)切断;切割;切开。**2.**【外科】切片,【金相】磨石。**3.** (果子的)瓣。**4.**【数】截口。**5.** 截面(图);剖面(图);断面(图)。**6.** 段;断片;部分。**7.** 部件;零件。**8.** 部门;部;处;科;组;股;【工】工段。**9.** 木材的切口。**10.** (文章等的)节[段落];(条文等的)款;条;项。**11.** 轮廓。**12.**【乐】(乐队的)乐器组。**13.** (团体的)派;党;(社会的)阶层;界。**14.** 区域;地段;分区;区划。**15.**【矿】采区;【生】派;亚属。**16.** (铁路的)区间。**17.** 〔美〕一平方英里的面积。**18.**【军】班;(炮兵)排;〔英〕小队;〔美〕小分队。*a vertical* ～ 纵断面。*a cross* [*transverse*] ～ 横断面。*a horizontal* ～ 水平断面。*an oblique* ～ 斜断面。*a microscopic* ～ (显微镜检查用的)切片。*an accounts* ～ 会计科。*a* ～ *leader*【军】班长;(炮兵)排长。***build in*** ～***s*** 分段制造。***convey in*** ～***s*** 拆开搬运。**II** *vt*. 解,拆(船等);把…分(成)节[段、组],区分;作截面图;(做显微镜检查用)将…切(成)片。**body** ～ 机身;床身。～ **crew** = ～ gang. ～ **cutter** 切片机。～ **cutting** 切片法。**S- Eight** 美国陆军条例第八节〔不合军队要求(尤指精神不正常)而开除军籍〕;据此被开除军籍的士兵。～ **gang**【铁路】工务段养路班。～ **hand** [**man**]【铁路】护路工。～ **mark** 分节号[即 §]。～ **paper** (制图用)(方)格纸。～ **plane** 剖面。

sec·tion·al [ˈsekʃənəl; ˋsɛkʃənl̩] *a*. **1.** 部分的;区分的;部门的;段落的;(分)节的;分项的;有区分的;分级的。**2.** 地方性(强)的;地段的;区域的。**3.** 局部的;断面(图)的。～ *quarrels* 派系间的争吵。*a* ～ *chief* 科[股,组]长。*a* ～ *boat* 可以拆开的小船。*a* ～ *plan of a building* 建筑物的断面图。**-ism** *n*. 地方主义;本位主义。**-ly** *ad*.

sec·tion·al·ize [ˈsekʃənəlaiz; ˋsɛkʃənl̩ˏaɪz] *vt*. (*-ized*, *-iz·ing*) **1.** 把…分成段[区];把…划成区〔尤指地理区划〕。**2.** 使具有地方性;使成党派性。**-al·i·za·tion** [-ˈzeiʃən; -ˋzeʃən] *n*.

sec·tor [ˈsektə; ˋsɛktɚ] *n*. **1.**【数】扇形(面)。**2.** 函数尺;两脚规。**3.** 防(御分)区;扇形战区;方面战区;阵线。**4.**【机】扇形齿轮。*a* ～ *of a sphere* 扇形圆锥。～ **gear**【机】扇形齿轮。～ **scan** 监视某一有限地区的雷达扫描。

sec·to·ri·al [sekˈtɔːriəl; sɛkˋtɔrɪəl] **I** *a*. **1.** 扇形的。**2.**【植】扇形嵌合体的。**3.**【动】适于裂食肉类的。**II** *n*. (食肉动物的)裂齿。

sec·u·lar [ˈsekjulə; ˋsɛkjəlɚ] **I** *a*. **1.** 现世的;此世的;尘世的;俗界的;世俗的;非宗教(性)的。**2.**【天主】修道院外的。**3.** 一世纪一次的;一代一次的。**4.** 长期的;长久的;不朽的;〔诗〕古老的。～ *affairs* 俗事;世事。～ *education* 普通教育〔与宗教教育相对〕。*the* ～ *acceleration*【天】长期加速度。～ *arm* [*power*] 俗权。*a* ～ *equation*【数】特征方程。*a* ～ *change* 缓慢变化。～ *depression*【地】缓慢下降。～ *fame* 不朽的名声。*the* ～ *bird* 不死鸟 (= phoenix)。*the* ～ *oaks* 古老的橡树。*a* ～ *phenomenon* 百年一度的奇异现象。**II** *n*. **1.**【宗】俗僧;教区牧师;俗人。**2.** 〔美〕(黑人中间流行的)俗歌 (*opp*. spiritual)。**-ism** *n*. 现世主义;世俗论;宗教与教育分离论。**-ist** *n*. 世俗论者;宗教与教育分离论者。

sec·u·lar·i·ty [ˌsekjuˈlæriti; ˏsɛkjəˋlærətɪ] *n*. **1.** = secularism. **2.** 世俗性,现世性;对于世俗事务的牵挂;俗心;俗事。

sec·u·lar·i·za·tion [ˌsekjuləraiˈzeiʃən; ˏsɛkjələraɪˋzeʃən] *n*. **1.** 世俗化;还俗。**2.** 脱离[不隶属于]教会;使教育与宗教分离。**3.** 改作俗用。

sec·u·lar·ize [ˈsekjuləraiz; ˋsɛkjələˏraɪz] *vt*. **1.** 使世俗化;使还俗。**2.** 使脱离[不隶属于]教会;使(教育)和宗教分离。**3.** 使改作俗用。

se·cund [ˈsiːkʌnd; ˋsikʌnd] *a*.【动、植】偏向一边[侧,方]的;只有一边的;只生在一边的。

sec·un·dines [ˈsekʌndainz; ˋsɛkʌnˏdaɪnz] *n*. *pl*. **1.**【医】胞衣;胎盘;胎膜 (= afterbirth)。**2.**【植】内种皮;(胚珠的)内珠皮[内包皮]。

se·cun·do [siˈkʌndəu; sɪˋkʌndo] *ad*. 〔L.〕其次;第二。

se·cun·dum [siˈkʌndəm; sɪˋkʌndəm] *prep*. 〔L.〕依据;根据。～ ***artem*** [ˈɑːtem; ˋɑrtɛm] 〔L.〕人工地;科学地;技术地;巧妙地。～ ***legem*** [ˈliːdʒem; ˋlidʒɛm] 〔L.〕根据法律;从法律。～ ***naturam*** [nəˈtjuːræm; nəˋtjuræm] 〔L.〕自然地;天然地。～ ***quid*** [kwid; kwɪd] 〔L.〕只在某点上,只在某一方面;不是绝对的;不是一般的;有限制地。～ ***usum*** [ˈjuːsəm; ˋjusəm] 〔L.〕根据惯例。

se·cur·a·ble [siˈkjuərəbl; sɪˋkjurəbl̩] *a*. **1.** 能拿到手的;能获得的。**2.** 可保安全的。

se·cure [siˈkjuə; sɪˋkjur] **I** *a*. (*-cur·er*; *-cur·est*) **1.** 安心的;不必担心的;有把握的。**2.** 可靠的。**3.** 安全的。**4.** 坚固的;牢固的。**5.** 必定的;拿稳的。**6.** 不怕逃走的;关得牢靠的。**7.** 〔古〕过分自信的;自负的。*a* ～ *place* 安全地方。*I have got him* ～. 我牢牢地逮住了他。*a* ～ *fool* 糊涂虫。***be*** ～ ***against*** [***from***] 没有…的危险。***be*** ～ ***of*** 对…有信心的,认为…靠得住的。***feel*** ～ (***about***, ***as to***) (对…)放心;认为不要紧。***have one's mind*** ～ 放下心。***keep*** (*a prisoner*) ～ 把(犯人)关牢。**II** *vt*. **1.** 使确实可靠;把…弄稳当。**2.** 使安全;防护;保卫;妥善保管。**3.** 搞到;把…拿到手;得到;获得。**4.** 吸引住。**5.** 招致;促成。**6.** 紧闭;关牢;关进;绑住 (*to*)。**7.** 保证;担保;保险。**8.** 指定把财产遗赠给… (*to*)。**9.**【海】吩咐…停止工作;使停止(操作)。～ *a vein* (做外科手术时)防止静脉出血。～ *valuables* 将贵重物品收藏妥当。*a fully* ～*d loan* 有十足担保的借款。～ *oneself against* [*from*] *loss* 防止损失。～ *oneself against accidents* 投保人身意外险。～ *oneself against the cold* 作好御寒准备。～ ***arms***!【军】(口令)倒挟枪! (以免雨水淋湿枪机)。～ (*sth*.) ***from sb***. 从(某人处)拿到(某物)。～ ***one's ends*** 达到目的。—*vi*. **1.** 作出保证;承诺保险〔开出保险单〕。**2.**【海】停止工作;值勤完毕。**3.** 抛锚停靠。**-ly** *ad*. **-ness** *n*.

securi- *comb*. *f*. 表示"斧": *securi*form.

se·cu·rit·ize [siˈkjuəritaiz; sɪˋkjurətaɪz] *vt*. 将(资产等)

变为债券。

se·cu·ri·ty [siˈkjuəriti; sɪˋkjʊrətɪ] ***n*.** **1.** 安全(感);安稳;稳妥;平安。**2.** 确实;确信;把握;可靠性;安心。**3.**【军】防御物。**4.** 保护;防护;保卫;防御(*against*; *from*);治安,安全防卫。**5.**【法】保证,担保;抵押。**6.** 担保品;保证金;借用证(*for*)。**7.** 担保人;保证人。**8.**〔*pl*.〕证券;债券;公债;股票。**9.**〔古〕疏忽;大意。*public* ～ 公安。*public* ～ *organs* 保卫机关;公安机关。*What* ～ *can you offer for it*? 你对这件事能拿什么做担保呢? *S- is the greatest enemy*. 疏忽[麻痹大意]是最大的敌人。***give*** ～ ***against*** 保护;使无…之忧。***go*** [***enter into***, ***give***] ～ ***for*** 做…的保人。***in*** ～ 安全。***in*** ～ ***for*** 作…的担保。***on good*** ～ 有可靠的抵押。～ **analyst** 股市分析家。～ **blanket** 安乐毯〔给小孩抓摸使感觉舒适安全的小绒毯〕。～ **clearance** (对参加机密工作的人进行的)安全调查。**S- Council** (联合国的)安全理事会。～ **guard** (多为私人雇佣的)保安(人员)。～ **police** 秘密警察。～ **risk**〔美〕(不适合参加国家机密工作的)不可靠分子。

secy., **sec'y** = secretary.

Se·dan [siˈdæn; sɪˋdæn] ***n*.** 色当〔法国东北部一城市,1870年普法战争战场〕。

se·dan [siˈdæn; sɪˋdæn] ***n*.** **1.** 轿子。**2.**〔美〕轿[汽]车。～ **chair** 轿子。

se·date [siˈdeit; sɪˋdet] **I *a*.** (***-dat·er***; ***-dat·est***) 沉着的;安详的;镇静的;平静的;静肃的(*opp*. excitable)。**II *vt*.** 使服镇静剂而安静下来。**-ly *ad*.**

se·da·tion [siˈdeiʃən; sɪˋdeʃən] ***n*.**【医】**1** 镇静。**2.** 镇静状态。

sed·a·tive [ˈsedətiv; ˋsɛdətɪv] **I *a*.** 镇静的;镇定的;止痛的。**II *n*.**【医】镇静剂;止痛药。

se de·fen·den·do [siː ˌdefənˈdendəu; siˏdɛfɛnˋdɛndo]〔L.〕为了自卫,自卫;正当防卫。

sed·en·ta·ri·ly [ˈsedəntərili; ˋsɛdəntərəlɪ] ***ad*.** **1.** 坐着地;不活动地。**2.** 需要坐着的。**3.** 定居不动地。

sed·en·ta·ri·ness [ˈsedəntərinis; ˋsɛdəntɛrɪnɪs] ***n*.** **1.** 坐着;不活动。**2.** 定居。

sed·en·ta·ry [ˈsedntəri; ˋsɛdnˏtɛrɪ] **I *a*.** **1.** 坐定不动的;坐着做的。**2.** 坐成的;(病)坐出来的。**3.**【动】定居一地的;定栖的(鸟);(贝壳等)固定附着的;(昆虫)静止的。～ *habits* 常坐的习惯。*a* ～ *posture* 坐着的姿势。*a* ～ *statue* 坐像。**II *n*.** **1.** 爱坐的人;坐着工作的人。**2.**【动】坐巢蜘蛛。～ **soil** 原地土壤,原生土。

Se·der [ˈseidə; ˋsedɚ] ***n*.** (*pl*. ***Se·dar·im*** [siˈdɑːrim; sɪˋdɑrɪm] ～*s*)【犹】犹太人出埃及节(祝宴)。

se·de·runt [siˈdiːrənt; sɪˋdirənt] **I *vi*.**〔L.〕(某某等人)出席(= There sat ...)。～ A, B ... 出席人甲,乙(等等)。**II *n*.** 集会;会议;联欢会;座谈会。

sedge [sedʒ; sɛdʒ] ***n*.**【植】苔(草);菅茅;蓑衣草。*the sweet* ～ 菖蒲。*a* ～ *warbler* [*wren*]【动】苇滨雀。

Sedg·wick [ˈsedʒwik; ˋsɛdʒwɪk] ***n*.** 塞奇威克〔姓氏〕。

sedg·y [ˈsedʒi; ˋsɛdʒɪ] ***a*.** (***-i·er***; ***-i·est***) **1.** 薹属植物丛生的。**2.** 似薹的。

se·di·le [seˈdaili; sɛˋdaɪlɪ] ***n*.** (*pl*. ***-dil·ia*** [-ˈdailiə; -daɪlɪə])〔多用 *pl*.〕(教堂南侧的一排座位)祭司席;牧师席。

se·dil·i·a [seˈdailiə; sɪˋdɪlɪə] ***n*.** sedile 的复数。

sed·i·ment [ˈsedimənt; ˋsɛdəmənt] ***n*.** **1.** 沉淀(物);沉渣。**2.**【地】沉积物。

sed·i·men·tal, **sed·i·men·ta·ry** [ˌsediˈmentl, -təri; ˏsɛdəˋmɛntl, -tərɪ] ***a*.** **1.** 沉淀[沉积](物)的;沉淀性的。**2.** 沉淀[沉积]成的;水成的。～ **clay** 沉积黏土。～ **deposit**【地】沉积矿床;成层沉积。～ **rocks**【地】沉积岩;水成岩。

sed·i·men·ta·tion [ˌsedimenˈteiʃən; ˏsɛdəmənˋteʃən] ***n*.** **1.** 沉淀[沉积、沉降](作用)。**2.** 沉积学,沉积法。～ **rate** [**test**] (血液等的)沉降速度[检查]。～ **velocity** 沉降速度。

sed·i·men·tol·o·gy [ˌsedimonˈtɔlədʒi; ˏsɛdəmənˋtɑlədʒɪ] ***n*.**【地】水成岩学;沉积学。

se·di·tion [siˈdiʃən; sɪˋdɪʃən] ***n*.** **1.** 煽动暴乱[闹事]的言论[行动]。**2.** 扰乱治安;暴动;骚乱。*a* ～ *bill* 危害治安煽动取缔法。*stir up a* ～ 煽起暴动。*a speech abounding in* ～ 富有煽动性的演说。

se·di·tion·ar·y [siˈdiʃənəri; sɪˋdɪʃənˏɛrɪ] **I *a*.** = seditious. **II *n*.** (*pl*. ***-ar·ies***) 骚乱煽动者;煽动分子。

se·di·tious [siˈdiʃəs; sɪˋdɪʃəs] ***a*.** 煽动(性)的;扰乱治安的;煽动叛变的。*a* ～ *demagogue* 煽动家。*a* ～ *harangue* 煽动性演说。**-ly *ad*.** **-ness *n*.**

se·duce [siˈdjuːs; sɪˋdjus] ***vt*.** **1.** 诱使…堕落;诱坏;使入歧途。**2.** 勾引;诱奸(妇女);挑唆,诱出(人)。**3.** 使入迷;迷惑;吸引。*The beauty of the evening* ～*d me abroad*. 傍晚的美景把我吸引到户外去了。

se·duce·a·ble [siˈdjuːsəbl; sɪˋdjusəbl], **se·duc·i·ble** [-ibl; -ɪbl] ***a*.** **1.** 可引诱的;可诱惑的。**2.** 易被勾引的;可诱奸的。

se·duce·ment [siˈdjuːsmənt; sɪˋdjusmənt] ***n*.**〔罕〕= seduction.

se·duc·er [siˈdjuːsə; sɪˋdjusɚ] ***n*.** **1.** 诱惑者。**2.** 勾引者;〔特指〕诱奸者。

se·duc·tion [siˈdʌkʃən; sɪˋdʌkʃən] ***n*.** **1.** 引诱;诱惑。**2.** 勾引;诱奸。**3.**〔常 *pl*.〕诱惑物;吸引力;魅力。*the* ～*s of country life* 乡村生活的吸引力。

se·duc·tive [siˈdʌktiv; sɪˋdʌktɪv] ***a*.** **1.** 引诱的;诱惑的。**2.** 勾引的;诱奸的。**3.** 吸引人的,富有魅力的。**-ly *ad*.**

se·duc·tress [siˈdʌktris; sɪˋdʌktrɪs] ***n*.** 有勾引力的女人;勾引男人的女人。

se·du·li·ty [siˈdjuːliti; sɪˋdjulətɪ] ***n*.** 勤勉,勤奋;坚持努力;恒心。

sed·u·lous [ˈsedjuləs; ˋsɛdʒələs] ***a*.** **1.** 勤勉的;孜孜不倦的。**2.** 小心周到的。～ *attention* 密切注意。～ *flattery* 百般奉承。*with* ～ *care* 小心周到地(注意着)。

Se·dum [ˈsiːdəm; ˋsidəm] ***n*.**【植】景天属植物。

see[1] [siː; si] ***n*.**【宗】主教的职位[权力];主教的辖区。*the Apostolic* [*Holy*, *Papal*] *S-* = *S- of Rome* 教皇的职位;罗马教廷;〔有时指〕教皇。

see[2] [siː; si] (***saw*** [sɔː; sɔ]; ***seen*** [siːn; sin]) **I *vt*.** **1.** 看见;看到。**2.** 细看;观察。**3.** 观看;参观。**4.** 查看;检查。**5.** 看出;看破;明白;领会;领悟;认为。**6.** 体验;经历。**7.** 遇见;会见;访问;谒见。**8.** 学懂。**9.** (护)送;陪送。**10.** 留心;留神;注意;考虑;负责;务必使…。**11.** 帮助;设法。**12.**〔美俚〕收买;贿赂。**13.** 让;允许;任凭;听凭。**14.** 看上;喜欢;同意。**15.** (纸牌赌博中)与(对方)下同样赌注(要求对方摊牌);〔转义〕接受…的挑战。*S- p*. 5. 见第五页;参看第五页。*Let us* ～ *a great deal of each other*. 我们以后经常见见面吧。*I have seen nothing of him these days*. 我近来简直没有看见他。*I* ～ *you*.〔美〕我明白你的意思。*Well*, *I'll* ～ *what I can do*. 好的,我想想办法看。*He will never* ～ *fifty again*. 他已五十(岁)出头了。*I am* ～*ing no one today*. 我今天谁都不(会)见。*I saw him as far as the station*. 我一直送他到车站。*I don't* ～ *being made use of*. 我是不愿意受人利用的。*I couldn't* ～ *myself getting home before dark*. 我认为我不可能在天黑之前赶回家〔此种用法多用于否定句〕。—***vi*.** **1.** 看见;看;视。**2.** 查看;检查;想一想。**3.** 明白;懂;理解;看透。**4.** 注意,小心;留神;照顾;监督。*S-*?〔口〕= *Do you* ～? 明白了吧? *You shall* ～. 你不久就会明白的;以后告诉你。*You* ～. 你知道;你说;你想;你看;就这样,是不是。*I* ～. 原来如此;明白了。*Let me* ～. 让我想想看。***as far as I can*** ～ 就我所知;根据我的判断。***as I*** ～ ***it*** 据我看;我以为。***do not*** ～ ***it in that light*** 不那样想。***first*** ～ ***the light*** (***of day***) 呱呱坠地;诞生。***have seen better*** [***best***] ***days*** 过过好日子,过去情况不错(*She must have seen better days*. 她过去生活得不错,现在不行了。

S

He was dressed in an old coat that had seen better days. 他穿着一套本来是很不错的旧西装)。***I'll be ~-ing you***. 〔美俚〕再见。***I will ~ that...*** 一定设法使…。***I will ~ you blowed*** [***damned, hanged***] (***first, before***)... 无论如何这种事情我是不干的。***live to ~ ...*** 活着看到…。~ ***a doctor*** 去看医生。~ ***about*** 注意；查看；查询；留意于；留神。~ ***after*** 照料；照应；照顾。~ ***at a glance*** 一见就知道；一看就明白。~ ***company*** 接见客人。~ (***sb.***) ***coming*** 〔俚〕使某人上当 (*He saw you coming*. 你上他当了)。~ ... ***done*** 监督…(的)完成。~ ***double*** 见 double. ***S- everything clear***!【海】预备〔放小船时的口令〕! ~ ***eye to eye*** 见 eye 条。~ ***fit*** [***good***] (*to do*) 觉得…是适当的[好的]。~ ***for oneself*** 自己去看；亲眼看。~ ***here*** 〔美〕喂喂。~ (*sb.*) ***home*** 送(某人)到家。~ ***if*** [***whether***]... 看看是否。~ ***into*** 1. 调查；检查。2. 看透彻；领会；了解；彻底理解。~ ***it*** 了解；理会；明白。~ ***justice done*** 1. 设法使事情处理得公平合理。2. 报了仇。~ ***life*** 体验生活；见世面。~ ***much*** [***little***] ***of*** 常常[很少]见到某人。~ ***no further than one's nose*** 前头漆黑[看不见]。~ ***sb. off*** 送(某人)启行；为某人送行。~ ***one's way*** (***clear***) ***to do***(***ing***) …有可能[有意思]做…。~ ***out*** 1. 把…送到大门口。2. 看到底；听到底；〔俚〕看穿；看破。3. 做到底；取胜，完成；贯彻。~ ***out of the corners of one's eyes*** 偷看；侧目而视。~ ***over*** 查看；检查；视察。~ ***red*** 见 red 条。~ ***the devil*** 〔卑〕喝醉。~ ***the good of*** 知道…的好处；尝到甜头。~ ***the inspector*** 收买[贿赂]检查员。~ ***the last of*** 赶走…；和…断绝关系。~ ***the red light*** 发现危险在前。~ ***the time when*** 遭遇…。~ ***the use of*** 知道…的用途[价值]。~ ***things*** 发生幻觉。~ ***through*** 1. 看透；看穿；识破。2. 坚持；贯彻 (~ *through a brick wall* [*a millstone*] 眼睛尖；眼光厉害)。~ (***sb.***) ***through*** (*his troubles*) 帮助某人(渡过难关)。~ (***sth.***) ***through*** [***out***] 1. 办好某事；将(某事)做到底。2. 看到底；看完。~ ***to*** 注意；留心；当心，负责；检查 (~ *to one's business* 注意自己的事；照看；照料)。~ (***to it***) ***that*** ... 留心使…，设法使，务必使；注意使；努力使；保证。~ ***visions*** 看见幻景；想像丰富地预想到未来景象；有先见之明，有眼力；未卜先知。~ ***well and good*** 〔口〕觉得好；认为不要紧。~ ***which way the cat jumps*** 见 cat 条。~ ***with*** 同意。~ ***with half an eye*** 一看就明白[了解]。***you ~*** 〔插入语〕是不是；你瞧；你听我说。***S- you later***. 再见。~**-through** 1. ***a***. (物件等)透明的，可以看到内部的；(衣服等)透视的，极薄的。2. ***n***. 透视装，极薄的衣服。

see·catch [ˈsiːkætʃ; ˋsikætʃ] ***n***. 〔美〕【动】(阿拉斯加海域)成年雄海豹 (= seecathie)。

seed [siːd; sid] **I** ***n***. (*pl*. ~(*s*)) 1. 〔集合词〕【植】种；种子。2. 颗粒；晶粒。3. 〔*pl*. 通例 seed〕【生理】精液；鱼精；鱼卵；蚝(等的)卵。4. 子孙；苗裔；后裔；种族。5. 〔*pl*. 通例 ~s〕萌芽；根本；根源。6. (玻璃中的)气泡。*the ~s of disease* 病因；病根。***go*** [***run***] ***to ~*** 1. 花谢结子。2. 消瘦；失去活力；衰颓[落]；〔美〕成为废料。***in ~*** 1. 在结实[结子]时期。2. 播着种的。***raise up ~*** 繁殖子嗣。**II** ***vi***. 1. 播种。2. 结实；结出种子；成熟；脱籽。—***vt***. 1. 播(种)；去…的核；脱…的籽；弄去…的种子。2. 催促发育[成长]；催化；催促加速。3. 用种子花样装饰；把…做成点花底子。4.【运】从(运动员)中挑选种子选手。*~ing stage* 出苗期。*~ing time* 播种期。~ *down* 撒种；播种。~ ***the draw***【运】安排种子选手分布在各组出场。~ **bank** (储藏濒危植物品种的)种子库。~ **bearer** 母树。~**bed** 1. 苗床。2. 〔喻〕发源地；温床。~ **breeding** 良种繁殖。~**cake** 撒有芬香种子(如芝麻)的糕饼。~ **case** 果皮；荚蒴。~**coat** 种皮，果被。~ **coral** (装饰用)珊瑚珠。~**corn** (作种用的)谷种；〔美〕玉米种。~ **crystal** 籽晶；晶种。~ **dressing**【农】拌种。~ **farm** 采种圃。~ **fat** 植物油。~ **fern** 种子蕨。~ **fish** 产卵期的鱼。~ **huller** 去壳机，去皮机。~ **leaf**【植】子叶。~ **manure** 种肥。~ **money** (用以吸引更多资金的)种子基金，股金。~ **oyster** (繁殖用)牡蛎种。~ **pearl** 小粒珍珠；米珠。~ **plant**【植】种子植物 (= spermatophyte)。~ **plot** 苗床；策源地。~ **pod**【植】荚果。~ **production** 种子繁殖。~ **shrimp**【动】= ostracod. ~ **sower** 播种机。~ **subassembly** 1. 种子配件。2. 点火装置。~ **time** 播种时期〔晚春及初夏〕。~ **tuber** 种薯。~ **vessel**【植】(囊)果皮。

seed·er [ˈsiːdə; ˋsidɚ] ***n***. 1. 播种者；播种机。2. 除核器；去核机。

seed·ing-machine [ˈsiːdiŋməʃiːn; ˋsidɪŋməˏʃin] ***n***. 播种机。

seed·less [ˈsiːdlis; ˋsidlɪs] ***a***. 无核的；无子的。

seed·ling [ˈsiːdliŋ; ˋsidlɪŋ] ***n***.【植】1. 种子繁殖。2. 实生苗。

seeds·man [ˈsiːdzmən; ˋsidmən] ***n***. (*pl*. ***-men***) 1. 播种者。2. 卖种子者；种子商。

seed·y [ˈsiːdi; ˋsidɪ] ***a***. (***-i·er***; ***-i·est***) 1. 种子多的。2. 结子的。3. (玻璃)多气泡的。4. (白兰地酒)带草香的。5. 〔口〕消瘦的；憔悴的。6. 破旧的；褴褛的。7. 不很高尚的；下流的；低级的。8. 不愉快的；无精打采的；(脸色等)难看的。**-i·ly** ***ad***. **-i·ness** ***n***.

See·ger [ˈsiːgə; ˋsigɚ] ***n***. 西格〔姓氏〕。

see·ing [ˈsiːiŋ; ˋsiɪŋ] see 的现在分词。**I** ***n***. 视觉；视力；看。*S- is believing*. 百闻不如一见。**II** ***conj***. 因为，既然，鉴于。~ (***that***) 因为…；既然；鉴于；从…一点来看 (~ *his youth and inexperience* 因为他年轻没经验)。**S- Eye** 〔美新泽西州〕1. 能给瞎子带路的狗。2. 能给瞎子领路的狗的训练所名称。

seek [siːk; sik] ***vt***. (***sought*** [sɔːt; sɔt]) 1. 找；寻觅。2. 谋求(名誉等)；图谋；请求；求得。3. 寻求；探求；追求；调查；研究。4. 〔古〕去；赴。—***vi***. 1. 找；搜索；寻觅。2. 寻求；探求；要求。***be not far to ~*** 1. 在近处；就在旁边。2. 很明白；很简单。***be*** (***much***) ***to ~*** 还(很)需要探求；还(非常)不够；(非常)缺乏 (*He is to ~ in intelligence*. 他才智不够)。***be yet to ~*** 还没有，还得找找看。***deliberately ~ all means*** 处心积虑。~ ***a lady's hand in marriage*** 向女人求婚。~ ***after*** [***for***] 求；寻求；探究。~ ***by all means*** 处心积虑。***S- dead***! 去找!〔命令猎狗去找打中的猎物〕。~ ***one's bed*** 就寝。~ ***out*** 找出；寻求；想获得。~ ***safety in flight*** 逃难。~ ***sb.'s life*** 图谋杀害某人。~ ***the truth from facts*** 实事求是。~ ***through*** 找遍。

seek·er [ˈsiːkə; ˋsikɚ] ***n***. 1. 搜索者；探求者。2.【火箭】自导导弹[飞弹]；自动导引的弹头。3. 〔S-〕(英国 17 世纪的)求正教徒。

seel [siːl; sil] ***vt***. 1. 〔古〕拿线缝(鹰的眼睛等)；闭(眼睛)。2. 弄瞎；使眼睛发花。3. 蒙骗。

seem [siːm; sim] ***vi***. 1. 好像；似乎；好像是。2. 〔与人称代词连用〕〔口〕(感到)好像，(觉得)似乎。3. 〔与引导代词 it 连用〕看来好像。*He ~s* (*to be*) *deaf*. 他好像是聋子。*I do not ~ to like him*. 〔口〕不知道什么缘故我总是不喜欢他。*Be what you ~* (*to be*). 表里要一致；言行必须一致。*She ~ed an old woman*. 她看上去像个老太婆。*I ~ed to have seen a dog*. 我好像看到了一条狗。***it ~s*** 据说，据传；好像，似乎。***It ~s to me that*** …我想，我以为，据我看。***it should*** (or ***would***) ~ = it ~s. ★seem 和 appear 在应用上常无差别，但前者似可导致某种结论，后者仅仅显示某一客观现象：He seems to be sick, for he *appears* pale. **-er** ***n***. 装模作样的人，做作的人。

seem·ing [ˈsiːmiŋ; ˋsimɪŋ] **I** ***a***. 表面的；外表上的；外观上的。*with ~ sincerity* 好像很诚实地。**II** ***n***. 外观；表面，外表。*the ~ and the real* 外表和实际。**-ly** ***ad***.

seem·ly [ˈsiːmli; ˋsimlɪ] **I** ***a***. (***-li·er***; ***-li·est***) 1. 合宜的；适当的；得体的。2. 好看的；美貌的。**II** ***ad***. 合宜地；

S

适当地。**-li·ness** *n*.

seen [siːn; sin] see 的过去分词。*a*. 1. 看得见。2. 〔古〕懂得;熟悉的;精通的。*be well* [*ill*] ~ *in music* 精通音乐。

seep[1] [siːp; sip] *vi*. 〔美 Scot.〕渗出;漏出;(观念等)渗入。~**age** *n*. 〔美 Scot.〕1. 漏水;渗流。2. 渗漏;渗出(现象)。3. 【矿】油苗。**-y** *a*. 排水不良的;湿气很重的。

seep[2] [siːp; sip] *n*. 水陆两用吉普车。

se·er [ˈsiːə, siə; sɪr] *n*. 1. 观看者。2. 预言者;先知;幻想家。3. 晶球占卜者。

seer·band [ˈsiəbænd; ˋsɪrˏbænd] *n*. 印度缠头纱。

seer·fish [ˈsiəfiʃ; ˋsɪrfɪʃ] *n*. (印度)鲭鱼。

seer·suck·er [ˈsiəsʌkə; ˋsɪrˏsʌkɚ] *n*. (印度)泡泡纱。

see·saw [ˈsiːˈsɔː, ˈsiːsɔː; ˋsiˏsɔ] I *n*. 1. 跷跷板(戏)。2. 上下动;前后动;动摇;变动。II *ad*., *a*. 上下动地[的];前后动地[的];交互地[的];拉锯性地[的]。III *vi*. 1. 玩跷跷板戏;一上一下地玩;上下动;前后动;动摇。2. 交替;(温度等)升降;涨落。~ **battle** [**game**] 拉锯战。~ **circuit** 【无】跷跷板放大电路。~ **policy** 观望政策。~ **switch** 【电】交互转换开关。

seethe [siːð; sið] *vi*. (~*d* [-d; -d], 〔古〕*sod* [sɔd; sɑd]; ~*d*, 〔古〕*sod·den* [ˈsɔdn; ˋsɑdn]) 1. 煮滚;沸滚。2. 沸腾;激昂。— *vt*. 〔古〕煮;浸(在水等中)。*seething waters* 波涛汹涌的海面。*be sodden to the skin* 浑身湿透。

seg [seg; sɛg] *n*. 〔美俚〕种族隔离主义者。

se·gar [siˈgɑː; sɪˋgɑr] *n*. cigar 的别字。

seg·gie [ˈsegi; ˋsɛgɪ] *n*. 〔美俚〕= seg.

seg·ment [ˈsegmənt; ˋsɛgmənt] I *n*. 1. (自然形成的)段落;断片;部分;分节;段;节。2. 【数】(线)段;弓形。3. 圆缺;球缺。4. 环节;切片。5. 【生】分裂片;体节;环节;【植】细裂片;全裂片。6. 【电】整流子片;【计】程序段;【机】扇形体;弧层;拼合轮缘。*a* ~ *of an orange* 橘子的一片。*the jointed* ~*s of a bamboo stem* 一根竹子的许多节段。*in* ~*s* 成节[段],分节[段]。II *vi*. 【生】分裂。*guide* ~ 弓形座。*mica* ~ 云母片。— *vt*. 分割,分裂;【生】使分裂。*a* ~*ed worm* 环虫。~ **gear** 【机】弓形齿轮。

seg·men·tal, seg·men·ta·ry [segˈmentl, ˈsegməntəri; sɛgˋmɛntl, ˋsɛgmənterɪ] *a*. 1. 节的;段的;分节的;分段的;部分的;线段的;弓形的。2. 圆缺的;球缺的。3. 【生】环节的;体节的;分节的。~ **organ** 【生】环节器官。~ **phonemes** 【语音】分解音素〔指音节中的元音、辅音和半元音〕。

seg·men·ta·tion [ˌsegmənˈteiʃən; ˏsɛgmənˋteʃən] *n*. 1. 分割;切断。2. 【生】(细胞)分裂;(动物)分节;断裂。~ **cavity** 【生】囊胚腔;分裂腔;卵裂腔。

se·gno [ˈsenjəu; ˋsenjə] *n*. 〔It.〕【乐】记号〔尤指再奏部分开始或终了的记号〕。

Se·grè [seˈgre; sɛˋgrɛ], **Emilio** 赛格雷〔1905—,意大利裔美籍物理学家,1959 年诺贝尔物理学奖获得者〕。

seg·re·gate [ˈsegrigeit; ˋsɛgrɪˏget] I *vt*. 1. 分开;分离;隔开,对…实行种族隔离。2. 【生】使分异;使变成其他种属、类别(*from*, *under*)。~ *boys and* [*from*] *girls* 把男孩和女孩分开。*segregating harvest* 【农】分段收割。~*d junction* 中继线分线束。— *vi*. 1. 分开;分离(*from*)。2. 【化】分凝;【物、冶】偏析;熔析;【生】分异;(成熟分裂时等位基因)分离。3. 实行种族隔离。II [-git; -gɪt] *a*. 1. 分离的;隔离(开)的;单独的。2. 实行种族隔离的。3. 【冶】偏析的。

seg·re·ga·tion [ˌsegriˈgeiʃən; ˏsɛgrɪˋgeʃən] *n*. 1. 分离;分开;隔离。2. 【化】分凝;【物、冶】偏析;熔析;【生】分异。【机械】离析性。3. (等位基因)分离。*racial* ~ 种族隔离。**-ist** *n*. (种族)隔离主义者。

seg·re·ga·tive [ˈsegrigeitiv; ˋsɛgrɪˏgetɪv] *a*. 1. 分离的;分开的;易分离的;隔离性的。2. (人)不合群的;不欢喜交际的。

se·gue [ˈsegwei, ˈseigwei; ˋsɛgwe, ˋsegwe] I *vi*. (*-gued*, *-gue·ing*) 【乐】继续如前;延续;连续;不间断;(伴奏者)跟随独奏[独唱]者表情演奏。II *n*. 【乐】继续如前。

se·gui·dil·la [ˌsegəˈdiːljə; ˏsɛgəˋdiljə] *n*. 1. 塞圭地拉舞〔一种有响板伴奏的西班牙舞蹈〕。2. 塞圭地拉舞曲〔歌词、诗节〕。

sei·cen·to [seˈtʃentəu; seˋtʃɛnto] *n*. 〔It.〕〔常 S-〕第十七世纪〔指意大利文艺的一个分期〕。

seiche [seiʃ; seʃ] *n*. 〔Swiss F.〕【地】湖震;假潮;湖面;波动;湖啸。

sei·del [ˈzaidl, ˈsai-; ˋsaɪdl̩] *n*. (*pl*. ~(*s*)) 大啤酒杯〔有时指连盖大啤酒杯〕。

Seid·litz [ˈsedlits; ˋsɛdlɪts] *n*. 塞得利兹〔捷克和斯洛伐克的硷质矿泉地〕。~ **powder** 【化】塞得利兹粉〔一种轻泻剂,也可以用以制成碱质矿泉水〕。

sei·gneur [seiˈnjəː, siːˈnjə; sinˋjɚ] *n*. 封建领主;庄园主;诸侯;贵族;显贵。

sei·gneur·y [ˈseinjəri, ˈsiːn-; ˋsenjərɪ, ˋsin-] *n*. (*pl*. *-gneur·ies*) 1. 领主权。2. 贵族庄园。

seign·ior [ˈseinjə, ˈsiːnjə; ˋsinjɚ] *n*. 1. 君主;封建领主;庄园主;贵族,乡绅。2. (用作尊称)先生(= Sir)。~**age** *n*. 1. 君权;领主权。2. 铸币税。3. 硬币铸造利差。

seign·ior·al [ˈseinjərəl, ˈsiːn-; ˋsenjərəl, ˋsin-] *a*. = seignorial. **sei·gnior·i·al** [-riəl; -rɪəl] *a*. = seignorial.

seign·ior·y [ˈseinjəri, ˈsiːn-; ˋsinjərɪ] *n*. 1. 君权;领主权。2. 领地。3. (中古意大利共和国的)市政议会。

seign·or·al [ˈseinjərəl, ˈsiːn-; ˋsenjərəl, ˋsin-] *a*. = seignorial.

sei·gno·ri·al [seiˈnjɔːriəl, siː-; sinˋjorɪəl] *a*. 1. 君主的;领主的;庄园主的。2. 掌握大权的,有主权的。

Seil [zail; zaɪl] *n*. 〔G.〕(登山运动用)爬山绳索。

seine [sein, siːn; sen] I *n*. (捕鱼用)拖拉大围网;拉网。II *vt*., *vi*. 用拖网捕(鱼)。

Seine [sein; sen] *n*. (流经巴黎的)塞纳河。

sei·ri·a·sis [saiəˈraiəsis; saɪəˋraɪəsɪs] *n*. 【医】日射病。中暑。

seise, sei·sin [siːz, -zin; siz, -zɪn] = seize 2., seizin.

seism [ˈsaizəm; saɪzm] *n*. 地震。

seis·mal [ˈsaizməl; ˋsaɪzml] *a*. 地震(引起)的。

seis·mic, -mi·cal [ˈsaizmik, -ikəl; ˋsaɪzmɪk, -ɪkəl] *a*. 地震(性)的;由地震引起的;易生地震的。*a* ~ *area* 震域;震区。*the* ~ *centre* [*focus*, *origin*, *vertical*] 震源;震中,震央。*a* ~ *detector* 地震检波器。*a* ~ *ray* 地震线。*a* ~ *region* 地震区。~ **shift** 【地】(地震引起的)地壳移动;〔喻〕灾难性的剧变。**-cal·ly** *ad*.

seis·mic·i·ty [saizˈmisiti; saɪzˋmɪsətɪ] *n*. 【地】1. 震态;震状。2. 震级。3. 地震活动性。

seis·mics [ˈsaizmiks; ˋsaɪzmɪks] *n*. 地震探测(法)。

seis·mism [ˈsaizmizm; ˋsaɪzmɪzm] *n*. 【地】地震(现象)。

seismo- *comb*. *f*. 表示"地震": *seismo*gram.

seis·mo·gram [ˈsaizməgræm; ˋsaɪzməˏgræm] *n*. 【地】震波图;地震波曲线。

seis·mo·graph [ˈsaizməgrɑːf; ˋsaɪzməˏgræf] *n*. 地震仪。

seis·mog·ra·pher [saizˈmɔgrəfə; saɪzˋmɑgrəfɚ] *n*. 地震学者,地震检测专家。

seis·mo·graph·ic [ˌsaizməˈgræfik; ˏsaɪzmoˋgræfɪk] *a*. 地震仪的;测震学的。

seis·mog·ra·phy [saizˈmɔgrəfi; saɪzˋmɑgrəfɪ] *n*. 1. 地震测定法。2. 测震学。

seismol. = 1. seismology. 2. seismological.

seis·mo·log·ic, -i·cal [ˌsaizməˈlɔdʒik, -ikəl; ˏsaɪzməˋlɑdʒɪk, -ɪkəl] *a*. 地震学(上)的。**-ly** *ad*.

seis·mol·o·gist [saizˈmɔlədʒist; saɪzˋmɑlədʒɪst] *n*. 地震学家。

seis·mol·o·gy [saizˈmɔlədʒi; saɪzˋmɑlədʒɪ] *n*. 地震学。

seis·mom·e·ter [saizˈmɔmitə; saɪzˋmɑmətɚ] *n*. 【地】

S

(比 seismograph 精密的)测震仪;地震检波器。

seis·mo·met·ric [ˌsaizməˈmetrik; ˏsaɪzməˋmɛtrɪk] ***a***. = seismometrical.

seis·mo·met·ri·cal [ˌsaizməˈmetrikl; ˏsaɪzməˋmɛtrɪkl̩] ***a***. **1.** 地震仪[计,表]的。**2.** 地震检测术的。

seis·mo·scope [ˈsaizməskəup; ˋsaɪzməˏskop] ***n***. 地震波显示仪。

seis·mo·scop·ic [ˌsaizməˈskɔpic; ˏsaɪzməˋskɑpɪk] ***a***. 地震波显示仪的;地震波显示仪记录的。

sei·ty [ˈsiːti; ˋsitɪ] ***n***. 自身;自我;个性。

seiz·a·ble [ˈsiːzəbl; ˋsizəbl̩] ***a***. **1.** 可抓住[捉到,拿到,捕捉,夺取,抢到,劫掠,掠夺;占领]的。**2.** 可没收的。

seize [siːz; siz] ***vt***. **1.** 抓;捉;捕;夺;抢;劫掠;掠夺。**2.** 〔通例用被动语态〕【法】查封;充公;没收;扣押。**3.** 依法占有(终身或世袭领地等)(= seise)。**4.** (心中)明白;了解。**5.** 〔通例用被动语态〕(病等)侵袭。**6.** 【海】(用细索)绑住;捆上(*up*)。~ *the point* 抓要点。~ *an opportunity* = ~ *the occasion* 抓牢机会;乘机。~ *a fortress* 夺取要塞。*the struggle to* ~ *power* 争夺政权的斗争。*I cannot* ~ *your meaning*. 我不明白你的意思。— ***vi***. **1.** 抓住;捉住;夺取(*on*, *upon*)。**2.** 利用;采用(*on*, *upon*)。**3.** (机器因过热或过压而)停止转动;停住(*up*)。***be ~d of*** 占有着…;〔喻〕拥有(情报等);知道(消息等);(很)晓得。***be ~d with*** 被…侵扰;害…患,得(*be ~d with gout* 害痛风症。*be ~d with a panic* 起恐慌。*be ~d with terror* 害怕)。~ ***hold of*** 抓住;捉住;逮住;占领。~ ***on*** [***upon***] 猛扑;袭击;利用;采用(提议)。***stand ~d of*** = be ~d of. ~ ***up*** (机器由于过热、摩擦、压力等)失灵;轧住。~ ***sb***. ***up*** 【海】把某人绑在索具上(以便鞭打)。

S

seiz·er [ˈsiːzə; ˋsizɚ] ***n***. **1.** 抓[捉,捕](…)的人。**2.** 没收者;扣押者。**3.** (捕捉猎物的)猎犬。

sei·zin(e) [ˈsiːzin; ˋsizɪn] ***n***. 【法】**1.** (终身或世袭领地等的)依法占有。**2.** 占有物;所有地;财产。~ ***in deed*** [***fact***] 事实上的占有。

seiz·ing [ˈsiːziŋ; ˋsizɪŋ] ***n***. **1.** 捕捉;强夺。**2.** 所有;占有;强占。**3.** 查封;没收;扣押。**4.** 【海】(用细绳索)捆绑;捆扎;捆结。**5.** 〔*pl*.〕捆(扎用的细绳)索。**6.** 卡住;材料黏附在模子上。

sei·zor [ˈsiːzə; ˋsizɚ] ***n***. 【法】(尤指终身或世袭领地的)占有人;扣押者。

sei·zure [ˈsiːʒə; ˋsiʒɚ] ***n***. **1.** 捉拿;捕捉。**2.** 夺取;占领;掠夺;篡夺。**3.** 查封;没收;充公。**4.** 捕获物;没收物;扣押物。**5.** (疾病的)突然发作;〔特指〕脑溢血。*the* ~ *of power* 夺取政权。*die from a* ~ *of apoplexy* 中风而死。

se·jant [ˈsiːdʒənt; ˋsidʒənt] ***a***. 【徽】(狮子等)前腿伸直地坐着的。

Sejm [seim; sem] ***n***. 波兰议会。

sel. = selected; selection(s); selector.

se·la·chi·an [siˈleikiən; sɪˋlekɪən] **I** ***n***. 【动】鲨类;(亚纲)(*Selachii*)的鱼。**II** ***a***. 鲨类(亚纲)的。

se·la·dang [seiˈlɑːdɑːŋ; səˋlɑdɑŋ] ***n***. 【动】马来犦。

sel·a·gi·nel·la [ˌselədʒiˈnelə; ˏsɛlədʒɪˋnɛlə] ***n***. 【植】卷柏属(*Selaginalla*)植物。

Sel·den [ˈseldən; ˋsɛldən] ***n***. 塞尔登[姓氏]。

sel·dom [ˈseldəm; ˋsɛldəm] **I** ***ad***. 不常;很少;难得…。*He* ~, *if ever*, *goes out*. = *He* ~ *or never goes out*. 他很少出门。*It is* ~ *that a man lives to be a hundred years old*. 人生百岁古来稀。***not*** ~ 往往;时常。~ ***or never*** = ***very*** ~ 很少;简直不。**II** ***a***. 不常的;稀少的。

se·lect [siˈlekt; səˋlɛkt] **I** ***vt***. 选;选择;挑选;选拔。*Her father let her* ~ *her own birthday present*. 她的父亲让她自己挑选生日礼品。— ***vi***. 挑选,选择。**II** ***a***. **1.** 挑选出来的;精选的;极好的。**2.** 〔口〕爱挑三拣四的;挑剔的。**3.** 苛择的;入会条件苛刻的。*a* ~ *crew* 一批精选的水手。*be* ~ *in choosing one's friends* 择友谨慎。~ *wines* 精选的酒。**III** ***n***. **1.** 〔口〕精选品;顶好的货色。**2.** 〔常 *pl*.〕被挑选者。~ **committee** (英国下院受命进行某一特别调查工作的)小型特别委员会。~ **school** (学生经过挑选的)私立学校。~ **society** 上流社会。

se·lect·ed [siˈlektid; sɪˋlɛktɪd] ***a***. 挑选出来的;精选的。~ **clientele** 〔美〕= restricted clientele.

se·lect·ee [ˌselekˈtiː; səˏlɛkˋti] ***n***. 选征合格的士兵;应征兵。

se·lec·tion [siˈlekʃən; səˋlɛkʃən] ***n***. **1.** 选择;挑选;选拔。**2.** 拔萃;选择物;精选物[品];文选。**3.** 【无】分离,(自动电话)拨号。**4.** 【生】选择,淘汰。~*s from great poets* 名家诗选。*mass* ~ 混合选种。*artificial* [*reproductive*, *sexual*] ~ 人为[生殖,雌雄]淘汰。*natural* ~ 自然淘汰。~ **committee** 提案处理委员会。

se·lec·tive [siˈlektiv; səˋlɛktɪv] ***a***. **1.** 选择的;挑选的;有选择性的;淘汰的。**2.** 【无】选择性的。~ **amplifier** 【无】选频放大器。~ **buying** 〔美〕选择性购买(一种抵制形式)。~ **hardening** 【冶】局部淬火;局部硬化;选择硬化。~ **lever** (汽车等的)选速杆。【电】~ **relay** 选择(性)继电器;谐振继电器。**S- Service** 〔美〕选征兵役制。**-ly** ***ad***.

se·lec·tiv·i·ty [silekˈtiviti; səˏlɛkˋtɪvətɪ] ***n***. **1.** 选择;精选。**2.** 【无】选择性;选择度;【物】选择能力;选择率。

se·lect·man [siˈlektmæn; səˋlɛktmən] ***n***. (*pl*. **-men**) 〔美〕〔美国新英格兰(New England)地区除罗得岛(Rhode Island)外各州的〕市政委员。

se·lec·tor [siˈlektə; səˋlɛktɚ] ***n***. **1.** 选择者;挑选者;选拔者;精选者。**2.** 【无】选择器;选波器;调谐旋钮;波段开关。**3.** 【计】选数器;选数管。**4.** 分离机。**5.** 〔澳〕可向政府廉价购买土地的移民。~ **switch** (电话交换机的)自动接线机;(电视机的)选台旋钮。

se·lec·tron [siˈlektrɔn; səˋlɛktrɑn] ***n***. **1.** 【计】选数管。**2.** 【化】聚酯树脂。

sel·e·nate [ˈselineit; ˋsɛləˏnet] ***n***. 【化】硒酸盐。

Se·le·ne [siˈliːni; səˋlini] ***n***. 【希神】(月之女神)塞妮涅。

se·len·ic [siˈlenik; sɪˋlinɪk] ***a***. 【化】**1.** (正)硒的;四价硒的。**2.** 六价硒的。~ **acid** 硒酸。

sel·e·nide [ˈselinaid; ˋsɛlənaɪd] ***n***. 【化】硒化物。

se·le·ni·ous [siˈliːniəs; sɪˋlinɪəs] ***a***. 【化】二价硒的,亚硒的;四价硒的。

sel·e·nite[1] [ˈselinait; ˋsɛləˏnaɪt] ***n***. **1.** 【矿】透明石膏。**2.** 【化】亚硒酸盐。

sel·e·nite[2] [siˈliːnait; ˋsɛləˏnaɪt] ***n***. 〔S-〕(旧时想像中的)月中居民。

se·le·ni·um [siˈliːniəm, -njəm; səˋlinɪəm, -njəm] ***n***. 【化】硒。*a* ~ *cell* 【电】硒光电池,硒光电管。

sel·e·nod·es·ist [ˌseliˈnɔdist; ˏsɛləˋnɑdɪst] ***n***. 月球学家。

sel·e·nod·e·sy [ˌseliˈnɔdisi; ˏsɛləˋnɑdɪsɪ] ***n***. 【天】月面测量学。

se·le·no·graph [siˈliːnəgrɑːf; sɪˋlinəˏgræf] ***n***. 【天】月面图。

sel·e·nog·ra·pher [ˌseliˈnɔgrəfə; ˏsɛləˋnɑgrəfɚ] ***n***. 月面学家。

sel·e·nog·ra·phic [siˌliːnəˈgræfik; siˏlinəˋgræfɪk] ***a***. 月面学的。

se·le·nog·raph·y [ˌseliˈnɔgrəfi; ˏsɛləˋnɑgrəfɪ] ***n***. 【天】月面学。

sel·e·nol·o·gy [ˌseliˈnɔlədʒi; ˏsɛləˋnɑlədʒɪ] ***n***. 【天】月球学。

Se·leu·cid [siˈluːsid; səˋlusɪd] **I** ***n***. (*pl*. ~*s*, **-ci·dae** [-siˌdiː; -səˏdi]) 塞琉古王朝的一代君王。**II** ***a***. 塞琉古王朝的(= seleucidan)。

self [self; sɛlf] **I** ***n***. (*pl*. ***selves*** [selvz; sɛlvz]) **1.** 自己;自身;本身;【哲】自我;我。**2.** 本性;本质。**3.** 私利;私心,私欲。**4.** 〔俗〕我;我自己;本人。**5.** 本身〔某种抽象性

质的体现〕。6.【园艺】单色花；原色花〔未经人工培育变色的〕。7.〔商、谑〕我〔你、他〕自己（= myself, yourself, himself）。*my poor* [*humble*] ～〔自称〕敝人，在下，不才。*one's second* ～ 密友。*our two selves* 我们两个。*our noble selves*！〔谑〕（干杯时）祝各位健康！*your good selves*【商】您；您处；您店。*your honoured selves* 阁下。*Rour Royal S-* 殿下。*S- is a bad guide to happiness*. 利己心带不来幸福。*S- do*, ～ *have*. 自作自受。*a ticket admitting* ～ *and friend* 限本人和朋友用的入场券。*Please accept our thanks to Mr. Jones and* ～. 谢谢您和琼斯。**by one's** ～ 单独。**have no thought of** ～ 没有个人打算。**one's better** ～ 良心；本性中良好的一面。**pay to** ～〔支票用语〕认票不认人。**rise above** ～ 舍己为人。**pity's** ～ 极令人遗憾[怜悯]的(事物或人)。**II** *a*. 1.〔古〕同样的；这；那。2. 纯净的；一样的；单一的；(颜色等)同一的；(弓等)用一根木头做的；同样材料的。*the* ～ *way* 用同样方法。*at that* ～ *moment* 正在那同一时刻。*a* ～ *button* 用与衣料相同的材料制成的钮扣。**III** *vt*. 使近亲繁殖；使同种繁殖；【植】使自花受精。— *vi*.【植】自花受精。

-self *suf*. 自己：my*self*, him*self*.

self- *pref*. 1. 自己；自我。2. 自行；自动：*self*-control, *self*-conscious.

self-a·ban·don [ˈselfəˈbændən; ˏsɛlfəˋbænd] *n*. 自暴自弃；放肆。

self-a·base·ment [ˈselfəˈbeismənt; ˏsɛlfəˋbændənmənt] *n*. 自贬，自卑，自我菲薄。

self-ab·hor·rence [ˈselfəbˈhɔːrəns; ˏsɛlfəbˋhɔrəns] *n*. 自我憎恶。

self-ab·ne·ga·tion [ˈselfəbniˈgeiʃən; ˋsɛlfˏæbnəˋgeʃən] *n*. 克己，自制；自我牺牲。

self-ab·sorbed [ˈselfəbˈsɔːbd; ˏsɛlfəbˋsɔrbd] *a*. 只顾自己的；自私的。

self-ab·sorp·tion [ˈselfəbˈsɔːpʃən; ˏsɛlfəbˋsɔrpʃən] *n*. 1. 只顾自己；自私自利。2.【物】自吸收。

self-a·buse [ˈselfəˈbjuːs; ˏsɛlfəˋbjus] *n*. 1. 自暴自弃。2. 手淫。

self-act·ing [ˈselfˈæktiŋ; ˋsɛlfˋæktɪŋ] *a*. 自动的。

self-ac·tu·al·i·za·tion [ˈselfæktjuəlaiˈzeiʃən; ˋsɛlfˏæktjuəlaɪˋzeʃən] *n*. 充分发展自己的才能；充分实现自己的抱负。

self-ac·tu·al·ize [ˈselfˈæktjuəlaiz; ˋsɛlfˋæktjuəlˏaɪz] *vi*. 充分认识自己的抱负，自我认识；充分发展自己的才能。

self-ad·dressed [ˈselfəˈdrest; ˋsɛlfəˋdrɛst] *a*. 写明发信人自己的地址的。*a* ～ *envelope* 写明发信人姓名地址的信封。

self-ad·just·ing [ˈselfəˈdʒʌstiŋ; ˋsɛlfəˋdʒʌstɪŋ] *a*. 自动调节的。

self-ad·vance·ment [ˈselfədˈvɑːnsmənt; ˏsɛlfədˋvænsmənt] *n*. 对自身利益的促进。

self-af·fec·ted [ˈselfəˈfektid; ˋsɛlfəˋfɛktɪd] *a*. 自负的。

self-af·fir·ma·tion [ˈselfˌæfə(ː)ˈmeiʃən; ˋsɛlfˏæfɚˋmeʃən] *n*. 自己证明；自行断定；自己作主；【心】自我肯定。

self-ag·gran·dize·ment [ˈselfəˈgrændizmənt; ˏsɛlfəˋgrændɪzmənt] *n*. (不择手段地)自我扩张(权势、财富等)。

self-a·nal·y·sis [ˈselfəˈnælisis; ˏsɛlfəˋnæləsɪs] *n*. 自我精神分析。

self-an·ni·hi·la·tion [ˈselfˌənaiəˈleiʃən; ˋsɛlfəˏnaɪəˋleʃən] *n*. 1. 自毁，自杀。2.【神学】自我消融，自我消失〔消失于与神融合的神秘状态中〕。

self-ap·point·ed [ˈselfəˈpɔintid; ˋsɛlfəˋpɔɪntɪd] *a*. 自己作主的；自行推荐[任命]的；自封的。～ *duties* 自己喜欢做的职务。

self-ap·pre·ci·a·tion [selfəˌpriːʃiˈeiʃən; sɛlfəˏpriʃɪˋeʃən] *n*. 自我欣赏。

self-as·ser·tion [ˈselfəˈsəːʃən; ˏsɛlfəˋsɝʃən] *n*. 1. 自作主张；坚持己见；一意孤行。2. 任性；自负；逞能。

self-as·ser·tive [ˈselfəˈsəːtiv; ˏsɛlfəˋsɝtɪv] *a*. 1. 自作主张的；坚持己见的；一意孤行的。2. 任性的；自负的；逞能的。

self-as·sumed [ˈselfəˈsjuːmd; ˏsɛlfəˋsumd] *a*. 独断独行的；专断的；僭越的。

self-as·sur·ance [ˈselfəˈʃuərəns; ˏsɛlfəˋʃurəns] *n*. 1. 自信，自恃。2. 自足；自满。

self-as·sured [ˈselfəˈʃuəd; ˏsɛlfəˋʃurd] *a*. 1. 自信的。2. 自满自足的。

self-be·tray·al [ˈselfbitreiəl; ˏsɛlfbɪˋtreəl] *n*. 自我暴露。

self-bind·er [ˈselfˈbaində; ˋsɛlfˋbaɪndɚ] *n*. 1.【农】自动束禾[草]机。2. 自动装钉器[机]。3. 活页夹。

self-bred [ˈselfˈbred; ˋsɛlfˋbrɛd] *n*.【生】自交系。

self-cen·tred [ˈselfˈsentəd; ˋsɛlfˋsɛntɚd] *a*. 1. 自我本位[中心]的；自私自利的。2. 自给自足的。3. 作为中心而固定不动的。

self-clos·ing [ˈselfˈkləuziŋ; ˋsɛlfˋklozɪŋ] *a*. 自动关闭的。*a* ～ *door* 自动关闭的门。

self-col·lect·ed [ˈselfkəˈlektid; ˏsɛlfkəˋlɛktɪd] *a*. 沉着的；冷静的。

self-col·o(u)red [ˈselfˈkʌləd; ˋsɛlfˋkʌlɚd] *a*. 1. 单色的；纯色的。2. 天然色的；(织物)本色的。

self-com·mand [ˈselfkəˈmɑːnd; ˏsɛlfkəˋmænd] *n*. 自制；克己；沉着，镇定自若。

self-com·pat·i·ble [ˈselfkəmˈpætəbl; ˏsɛlfkəmˋpætəbl̩] *a*.【植】能自花传粉的。

self-com·pla·cen·cy [ˈselfkəmˈpleisnsi; ˏsɛlfkəmˋplesn̩sɪ] *n*. 自我陶醉；自满；自得。

self-com·pla·cent [ˈselfkəmˈpleisnt; ˏsɛlfkəmˋplesn̩t] *a*. 自我陶醉的，自满自得的。

self-com·posed [ˈselfkəmˈpəuzd; ˏsɛlfkəmˋpozd] *a*. 镇定自若的；冷静的。

self-con·ceit [ˈselfkənˈsiːt; ˏsɛlfkənˋsit] *n*. 自负；自大，自夸。**-ed** *a*.

self-con·cept [ˈselfkənˈsept; ˏsɛlfkənˋsɛpt] *n*. = self-image.

self-con·cern [ˈselfkənˈsəːn; sɛlfkənˋsɝn] *n*. 只顾自己，自私自利。**-ed** *a*.

self-con·demned [ˈselfkənˈdemd; ˏsɛlfkənˋdɛmd] *a*. 受良心责备的；自责的。

self-con·fessed [ˈselfkənˈfest; ˏsɛlfkənˋfɛst] *a*. 自(动承)认的。*He is a* ～ *drunkard*. 他自己承认自己是个醉鬼。

self-con·fi·dence [ˈselfˈkɔnfidəns; ˋsɛlfˋkɑnfədəns] *n*. 自信；自恃。

self-con·fi·dent [ˈselfˈkɔnfidənt; ˋsɛlfˋkɑnfədənt] *a*. 自信(力强)的；自恃的。**-ly** *ad*.

self-con·scious [ˈselfˈkɔnʃəs; ˋsɛlfˋkɑnʃəs] *a*. 1. 自觉的。2. 怕难为情的；害羞的。**-ly** *ad*. **-ness** *n*.

self-con·se·quence [ˈselfˈkɔnsikwəns; ˋsɛlfˋkɑnsəˏkwɛns] *n*. 妄自尊大。

self-con·sist·ent [ˈselfkənˈsistənt; ˏsɛlfkənˋsɪstənt] *a*. 前后照应的，首尾一贯的，无自我矛盾现象的。

self-con·sti·tuted [ˈselfˈkɔnstitjuːtid; ˏsɛlfˋkɑnstəˏtjutɪd] *a*. 自定的；自我任命的，(保护人等)自许的；(机构等)自行设立的。

self-con·tained [selfkənˈteind; ˏsɛlfkənˋtend] *a*. 1. 沉默寡言的；不爱说话的。2. 独立的；自恃的；自足的；自治的；自制的。3.【机】(本身)设备齐全的；整套装在一起的；装备在一个容器里的。4. (公寓等)独门独户的；出入各别的。5.〔喻〕独立的。～ *and self-sufficient* 自给自足的。

self-con·tempt [ˈselfkənˈtempt; ˏsɛlfkənˋtɛmpt] *n*. 自我轻蔑。

S

self-con·tent, self-con·tent·ment [ˈselfkənˈtent, -mənt; ˏsɛlfkənˋtɛn, -mənt] *n*. 自满。

self-con·tent·ed [ˈselfkənˈtentid; ˏsɛlfkənˋtɛntɪd] *a*. 自满的。

self-con·tra·dic·tion [ˈselfˌkɔntrəˈdikʃən; ˋsɛlfˏkɑntrəˋdɪkʃən] *n*. 自相矛盾。

self-con·tra·dic·to·ry [ˈselfˌkɔntrəˈdiktəri; ˋsɛlfˏkɑntrəˋdɪktərɪ] *a*. 自相矛盾的;前后矛盾的。

self-con·trol [ˈselfkənˈtrəul; ˏsɛlfkənˋtrol] *n*. 克己;自制。**-ed** *a*.

self-crit·i·cal [ˈselfˈkritikəl; ˋsɛlfˋkrɪtɪkl̩] *a*. 自我批评[判]的。

self-crit·i·cism [ˈselfˈkritisizəm; ˋsɛlfˋkrɪtɪsɪzəm] *n*. 自我批评。

self-cul·ti·va·tion [ˈselfˌkʌltiˈveiʃən; ˋsɛlfˏkʌltəˋveʃən] *n*. 自我修养。

self-cul·ture [ˈselfˈkʌltʃə; ˋsɛlfˋkʌltʃɚ] *n*. 自修;自我修养。

self-de·cep·tion [ˈselfdiˈsepʃən; ˏsɛlfdɪˋsɛpʃən] *n*. 自欺。

self-de·feat·ing [ˈselfdiˈfiːtiŋ; ˏsɛlfdɪˋfitɪŋ] *a*. 弄巧成拙的;自我拆台的,使自己失败的。

self-de·fence, 〔美〕 **self-de·fense** [ˈselfdiˈfens; ˏsɛlfdɪˋfɛns] *n*. 自卫(术);【法】自卫权;正当权利。

self-de·lu·sion [ˈselfdiˈluːʒən; ˏsɛlfdɪˋluʒən] *n*. = self-deception.

self-de·ni·al [ˈselfdiˈnaiəl; ˏsɛlfdɪˋnaɪəl] *n*. 自我牺牲;克己,无私。

S

self-de·ny·ing [ˈselfdiˈnaiiŋ; ˏsɛlfdɪˋnaɪɪŋ] *a*. 克己的;无私的;自我牺牲的。

self-de·pend·ence [ˈselfdiˈpendəns; ˏsɛlfdɪˋpɛndəns] *n*. 依靠自己;自力更生。**-pend·ent** [-ˈpendənt; -ˋpɛndənt] *a*.

self-des·truc·tion [ˈselfdisˈtrʌkʃən; ˏsɛlfdɪˋstrʌkʃən] *n*. 自毁;自杀。

self-de·ter·mi·na·tion [ˈselfdiˌtəːmiˈneiʃən; ˋsɛlfdɪˏtɝməˋneʃən] *n*. 1. 自决。2. 民族自决。3. 【哲】(强调意志自由的)自我决定。

self-de·ter·min·ing [ˈselfdiˈtəːminiŋ; ˋsɛlfdɪˋtɝmɪnɪŋ] *a*. 自决的;民族自决的;自我决定的。

self-de·vo·tion [ˈselfdiˈvəuʃən; ˏsɛlfdɪˋvoʃən] *n*. 自我牺牲;献身。

self-dis·ci·pline [ˈselfˈdisiplin; ˋsɛlfˋdɪsəplɪn] *n*. 自律;自我约束。

self-dis·ci·plined [ˈselfˈdisiplind; ˋsɛlfˋdɪsəplɪnd] *a*. 自律的;自己约束自己的;自动守纪律的。

self-dis·trust [ˈselfdisˈtrʌst; ˏsɛlfdɪsˋtrʌst] *n*. 自疑;无自信 (*opp*. self-confidence)。

self-doubt [ˈselfˈdaut; ˋsɛlfˋdaʊt] *n*. 自疑;对自己缺乏信心。

self-dram·a·ti·za·tion [ˈselfˌdræmətaiˈzeiʃən; ˋsɛlfˏdræmətaɪˋzeʃən] *n*. 装腔作势;自吹自擂;大摇大摆。

self-dram·a·tiz·ing [ˈselfˈdræmətaiziŋ; ˋsɛlfˋdræməˏtaɪzɪŋ] *a*. (像演员般)装腔作势的;自吹自擂的;大摇大摆的。

self-drive [ˈselfˈdraiv; ˋsɛlfˋdraɪv] *a*. 〔英〕租来自己驾驶的。~ **car** 〔英〕出租汽车。

self-driv·en [ˈselfˈdrivn; ˋsɛlfˋdrɪvən] *a*. (车辆等)自动推进的。

self-ed·u·cated [ˈselfˈedjuːkeitid, -ˈedʒu-; ˋsɛlfˋɛdʒəˏketɪd, -ˋɛdʒu-] *a*. 自修的;自学的;自我教育的。

self-ef·face·ment [ˈselfiˈfeismənt; ˏsɛlfɛˋfesmənt] *n*. 谦让,避免出风头。

self-em·ployed [ˈselfimˈplɔid; ˏsɛlfɛmˋplɔɪd] *a*. 1. 自己经营的;不受雇于别人的。2. 不专为某一雇主工作的。

self-en·er·giz·ing [ˈselfˈenədʒaiziŋ; ˋsɛlfˋɛnɚdʒaɪzɪŋ] *a*. 【机,电】自激的;自给供电的;自身增大能量的。

self-en·er·gy [ˈselfˈenədʒi; ˋsɛlfˋɛnɚdʒɪ] *n*. 固有能量。

self-es·teem [ˈselfisˈtiːm; ˏsɛlfəˋstim] *n*. 1. 自重;自尊。2. 自大;自满 (*opp*. diffidence)。

self-ev·i·dent [ˈselfˈevidənt; ˋsɛlfˋɛvədənt] *a*. 自明的,不需证明的;不言而喻的。

self-ex·am·i·na·tion [ˈselfigˌzæmiˈneiʃən; ˋsɛlfɪgˏzæməˋneʃən] *n*. 自我检查,反省。

self-ex·ci·ta·tion [ˈselfˌeksiˈteiʃən; ˋsɛlfˏɛksəˋteʃən] *n*. 【物】自激;自励磁。

self-ex·cit·er [ˈselfikˈsaitə; ˏsɛlfɪkˋsaɪtɚ] *n*. 自激发动机。

self-ex·e·cut·ing [ˈselfˈeksikjutiŋ; ˋsɛlfˋɛksəˏkjutɪŋ] *a*. 【法】(法律条约等在特定条件下)自动生效的。

self-ex·ist·ent [ˈselfigˈzistənt; ˏsɛlfɪgˋzɪstənt] *a*. 自存的,独立存在的。

self-ex·plain·ing, self-ex·plan·a·to·ry [ˈselfikspleiniŋ, -ˈplænətəri; ˏsɛlfɪkˋsplenɪŋ, -ˋsplænəˏtorɪ] *a*. (意义)不解自明的。

self-ex·pres·sion [ˈselfiksˈpreʃən; ˏsɛlfɪkˋsprɛʃən] *n*. 自我表现。

self-faced [ˈselfˈfeist; ˋsɛlfˋfest] *a*. (石面)未加雕凿的,天然的。

self-feed·er [ˈselfˈfiːdə; ˋsɛlfˋfidɚ] *n*. 1. 【机】自动给料机,自给器。2. 【农】(牲畜的)自动喂饲槽。

self-fer·ti·li·za·tion [ˈselfˌfəːtilaiˈzeiʃən; ˋsɛlfˏfɝtl̩əˋzeʃən] *n*. 1. 【植】自花受精[传粉] (*opp*. cross-fertilization)。2. 【动】自体受精。

self-for·get·ful [ˈselffəˈgetful; ˏsɛlffɚˋgɛtfəl] *a*. 忘我的,无私的。

self-ful·fill·ment [ˈselffulˈfilmənt; ˏsɛlffʊlˋfɪlmənt] *n*. 自力完成;自力达到期望[目标];(预言的)自我应验。

self-gen·er·at·ing [ˈselfˈdʒenəreitiŋ; ˋsɛlfˋdʒɛnəˏretɪŋ] *a*. 【生】自生的;自然发生的。

self-giv·en [ˈselfˈgivn; ˋsɛlfˋgɪvn̩] *a*. 1. 出自本身的。2. 自封的。

self-giv·ing [ˈselfˈgiviŋ; ˋsɛlfˋgɪvɪŋ] *a*. 舍己为人的,无私的。

self-glo·ri·fi·ca·tion [ˈselfˌglɔrifiˈkeiʃən; ˏsɛlfˏglorɪfəˋkeʃən] *n*. 自我陶醉,自命不凡,自负。

self-gov·ern·ing [ˈselfˈgʌvəniŋ; ˋsɛlfˋgʌvɚnɪŋ] *a*. 1. 自治的。2. 自制的。*a* ~ *colony* 自治殖民地。*a* ~ *dominion* 自治领。*a* ~ *man* 一个能自我克制的人。

self-gov·ern·ment [ˈselfˈgʌvənmənt; ˋsɛlfˋgʌvɚnmənt] *n*. 1. 自治。2. 自制,克己。

self-grav·i·ty [ˈselfˈgræviti; ˋsɛlfˋgrævɪtɪ] *n*. 【物】自重力。

self-guid·ed [ˈselfˈgaidid; ˋsɛlfˋgaɪdɪd] *a*. 自导的,自动导向的。

self-hard·en·ing [ˈselfˈhɑːdniŋ; ˋsɛlfˋhardnɪŋ] *a*. 自(动)硬(化)的;空气硬化的〔特指钢在空气中自行冷却而硬化〕。

self-hate, self-hatred [ˈselfˈheit, -trid; ˋsɛlfˋhet, -trɪd] *n*. 怨恨自己。

self-heal [ˈselfˈhiːl; ˋsɛlfˋhil] *n*. 有医疗作用的植物〔特指夏枯草〕。

self-help [ˈselfˈhelp; ˋsɛlfˋhɛlp] *n*. 1. 自助,自立。2. 【法】自救行为。

self-hood [ˈselfhud; ˋsɛlfhʊd] *n*. 1. 个性,自我。2. 自我中心,自私。

self-hu·mil·i·a·tion [ˈselfhjuːˌmiliˈeiʃən; ˋsɛlfhjuˏmɪlɪˋeʃən] *n*. 自辱,自我丢丑;自卑。

self-hyp·no·sis [ˈselfhipˈnəusis; ˏsɛlfhɪpˋnosɪs] *n*. 自我催眠。

self-i·den·ti·ty [ˈselfaiˈdentiti; ˋsɛlfaɪˋdɛntətɪ] *n*. 自我同一性,自我同一感。

self-ig·nite [ˈselfigˈnait; ˏsɛlfɪgˋnaɪt] *vi*. 自燃,自动点火。**-ni·tion** [-ˈniʃən; -ˋnɪʃən] *n*.

self-im·age [ˈselfˈimidʒ; ˋsɛlfˋɪmɪdʒ] *n*. 自我形象,对自己的看法[估价]。

self-im·por·tance [ˈselfimˈpɔːtəns; ˏsɛlfɪmˋpɔrtəns] *n*. 妄自尊大。**-tant** [-tənt; -tn̩t] *a*.

self-im·posed [ˈselfimˈpəuzd; ˏsɛlfɪmˋpozd] *a*. 自愿承担的,自己强加的。*a* ～ *task* 自己要做的工作。

self-im·prove·ment [ˈselfimˈpruːvmənt; ˏsɛlfɪmˋpruvmənt] *n*. 自我改进[改善]。

self-in·clu·sive [ˈselfinˈkluːsiv; ˏsɛlfɪnˋklusɪv] *a*. 包括自己在内的;自含的。

self-in·crim·i·na·tion [ˈselfˌinkrimiˈneiʃən; ˏsɛlfˋɪnkrɪməˏneʃən] *n*. (因自己的供词、答词而)牵连;自陷法网;自认犯罪。

self-in·duc·tion [ˈselfinˈdʌkʃən; ˏsɛlfɪnˋdʌkʃən] *n*. 【电】自感应。

self-in·dul·gence [ˈselfinˈdʌldʒəns; ˏsɛlfɪnˋdʌldʒəns] *n*. 自我放纵,任性;纵欲。

self-in·dul·gent [ˈselfinˈdʌldʒənt; ˏsɛlfɪnˋdʌldʒənt] *a*. 自我放纵的,任性的;纵欲的。

self-in·flict·ed [ˈselfinˈfliklid; ˏsɛlfɪnˋflɪktɪd] *a*. 自己造成的,自使蒙受的。

self-in·i·ti·at·ed [ˈselfiniʃiˈeitid; ˏsɛlfɪnˋɪʃɪˏetɪd] *a*. 自己发起的;自创的。

self-in·sur·ance [ˈselfinˈʃuərəns; ˏsɛlfɪnˋfʊrəns] *n*. 自我保险。

self-in·ter·est [ˈselfˈintərist; ˋsɛlfˋɪntərɪst] *n*. **1**. 自身利益。**2**. 私心,自私自利。

self·ish [ˈselfiʃ; ˋsɛlfɪʃ] *a*. 自私自利的,只顾自己的;利己的 (*opp*. atruistic)。**-ly** *ad*. **-ness** *n*.

self-jus·ti·fi·ca·tion [ˈselfˌdʒʌstifiˈkeiʃən; ˏself-ˏdʒʌstəfəˋkeʃən] *n*. 自我证明(正当,合理);自我辩明。

self-know·ing [ˈselfˈnəuiŋ; ˋsɛlfˋnoɪŋ] *a*. 有自知之明的。

self-know·ledge [ˈselfˈnɔledʒ; ˋsɛlfˋnɑlɪdʒ] *a*. 自知之明;自觉。

self·less [ˈselflis; ˋsɛlflɪs] *a*. 忘我的,无私的。*a* ～ *man* 一个无私的人。

self-liq·ui·dat·ing [ˈselfˌlikwiˈdeitiŋ; ˋsɛlfˋlɪkwəˏdetɪŋ] *a*. **1**. 能自行收回成本并产生利润的。**2**. 能使货物迅速变为现款的。

self-load·er [ˈselfˈləudə; ˋsɛlfˋlodæ] *n*. 自动装弹的武器,半自动武器。

self-load·ing [ˈselfˈləudiŋ; ˋsɛlfˋlodɪŋ] *a*. 自动装载的;自动装弹进膛的。

self-love [ˈselfˈlʌv; ˋsɛlfˋlʌv] *n*. **1**. 自我怜爱。**2**. 自负,自大。**3**. 自私。

self-made [ˈselfˈmeid; ˋsɛlfˋmed] *a*. **1**. 独自做的,自己搞的。**2**. 自力更生的,靠自己努力而成功的。

self-mail·er [ˈselfmeilə; ˋsɛlfˋmelɚ] *n*. 邮简(不用信封,填上姓名、住址即可投寄的广告、小册子等)。

self-mas·ter·y [ˈselfˈmɑːstəri; ˋsɛlfˋmæstərɪ] *n*. 自制,约束自己,沉着。

self-mor·ti·fi·ca·tion [ˈselfˌmɔːtifiˈkeiʃən; ˏsɛlfˏmɔrtəfəˋkeʃən] *n*. 禁欲(主义)。

self-mo·tion [ˈselfˈməuʃən; ˋsɛlfˋmoʃən] *n*. 自动。

self-mov·ing [ˈselfˈmuːviŋ; ˋsɛlfˋmuvɪŋ] *a*. 自动的。

self-mur·der [ˈselfˈməːdə; ˋsɛlfˋmɝdɚ] *n*. 自杀;自我毁灭。

self-noise [ˈselfˈnɔiz; ˋsɛlfˋnɔɪz] *n*. (船破浪前进时产生的)自噪声。

self-o·pin·ion·at·ed, self-o·pin·ioned [ˈselfəˈpinijəneitid, -ˈpinjənd; ˏsɛlfəˋpɪnjənˏetɪd, -ˋpɪnjənd] *a*. 固执己见的,刚愎自用的;自负的。

self-or·gan·i·za·tion [ˈselfˌɔːgənaiˈzeiʃən; ˋsɛlfˏɔrgənaɪˋzeʃən] *n*. 组织工会;加入工会。

self-os·cil·lation [ˈselfˌɔsiˈleiʃən; ˋsɛlfˏɑsɪleʃən] *n*. 【物】自生振荡。

self-par·tial·i·ty [ˈselfˌpɑːʃiˈæliti; ˋsɛlfˏpɑrʃɪˋæləti] *n*. **1**. 自视过高。**2**. 徇私,自我偏袒。

self-per·pet·u·a·ting [ˈselfpəˌpetjuˈeitiŋ; ˋsɛlfpɚˋpɛtʃʊˏetɪŋ] *a*. **1**. 使自身长存不废的。**2**. 恋栈的,想尽办法保留自己官职的。

self-pit·y [ˈselfˈpiti; ˋsɛlfˋpɪtɪ] *n*. 自怜。

self-poise [ˈselfˈpɔiz; ˋsɛlfˋpɔɪz] *n*. **1**. 自动平衡。**2**. 镇定。**-d** *a*.

self-pol·li·nate [ˈselfˈpɔlineit; ˋsɛlfˋpɑləˏnet] *vt*., *vi*. 【植】(使)自花授[传]粉的。**-d** *a*.

self-pol·lu·tion [ˈselfpəˈluːʃən; ˏsɛlfpəˋluʃən] *n*. 手淫,自淫。

self-por·trait [ˈselfˈpɔːtreit; ˋsɛlfˋportret] *n*. 自画像;自我描述。

self-pos·sessed [ˈselfpəˈzest; ˏsɛlfpəˋzɛst] *a*. 有自制力的;沉着的,冷静的。

self-pos·ses·sion [ˈselfpəˈzeʃən; ˏsɛlfpəˋzɛʃən] *n*. 沉着,冷静,泰然自若。

self-praise [ˈselfˈpreiz; ˋsɛlfˋprez] *n*. 自我称赞,自我吹嘘。

self-pres·er·va·tion [ˈselfˌprezəˈveiʃən; ˋsɛlfprɛzɚˋveʃən] *n*. 自我保存,自卫本能。

self-pride [ˈselfˈpraid; ˋsɛlfˋpraɪd] *n*. 自负。

self-pro·claimed [ˈselfprəˈkleimd; ˏsɛlfprəˋklemd] *a*. 自称的,自封的。

self-pro·duced [ˈselfprəˈdjuːst; ˏsɛlfprəˋdjust] *a*. 本身产生的。

self-pro·nounc·ing [ˈselfprəˈnaunsiŋ; ˏsɛlfprəˋnaʊnsɪŋ] *a*. 在原词上标注读音符号的。*a* ～ *dictionary* 标音字典。

self-pro·pelled [ˈselfprəˈpeld; ˏsɛlfprəˋpɛld] *a*. **1**. 自动推进的,自己开动的;【军】(火炮)自行的。**2**. 装备有自行火炮的。

self-pro·tec·tion [ˈselfprəˈtekʃən; ˏsɛlfprəˋtɛkʃən] *n*. 自我防护,自卫。*a means of* ～ *against riot* 防备暴乱的自卫手段。

self-ques·tion·ing [ˈselfˈkwesʃəniŋ; ˋsɛlfˋkwɛstʃənɪŋ] *n*. 反省。

self-re·act·ing [ˈselfriːˈæktiŋ; ˋsɛlfriˋæktɪŋ] *a*. 自动适应的,自动调整的。

self-read·ing [ˈselfˈriːdiŋ; ˋsɛlfˋridɪŋ] *a*. 易读的。

self-re·al·i·za·tion [ˈselfˌriəlaiˈzeiʃən; ˋsɛlfˏriələˋzeʃən] *n*. 本人才能的充分发挥。

self-re·cord·ing [ˈselfriˈkɔːdiŋ; ˏsɛlfrɪˋkɔrdɪŋ] *a*. 自动记录的,自记的。

self-re·flec·tion [ˈselfriˈflekʃən; ˋsɛlfrɪˋflɛkʃən] *n*. 反省。

self-ref·er·ence [ˈselfˈrefərəns; ˋsɛlfˋrɛfərəns] *n*. 【逻】自我参考命题,和自身有关的命题。

self-ref·e·ren·tial [ˈselfˌrefəˈrenʃəl; ˋsɛlfˏrɛfəˋrɛnʃəl] *a*. **1**. 【逻】(命题或陈述)自参照的;真假自明的。**2**. 与自己有关的。

self-re·gard [ˈselfriˈgɑːd; ˏsɛlfrɪˋgɑrd] *n*. **1**. 利己,利己心。**2**. 自尊,自尊心。

self-reg·is·ter·ing [ˈselfˈredʒistəriŋ; ˋsɛlfˋrɛdʒɪstərɪŋ] *a*. 自动记录的。*a* ～ *anemometer* (自记)风力计。

self-reg·u·la·tion [ˈselfˌreguˈleiʃən; ˋsɛlfˏrɛgjʊˋleʃən] *n*. 【自】自动调整,自动调节。

self-re·li·ance [ˈselfriˈlaiəns; ˏsɛlfrɪˋlaɪəns] *n*. 依靠自己;自力更生。

self-re·nun·ci·a·tion [ˈselfriˌnʌnʃiˈeiʃən; ˋsɛlfrɪˏnʌnsɪˋeʃən] *n*. 献身;舍己;牺牲自己;大公无私。

self·rep·li·cat·ing [ˈselfˈreplikeitiŋ; ˋsɛlfˋrɛplɪketɪŋ] *a*. 【生】自我复制的。

self-re·proach [ˈselfriˈprəutʃ; ˏsɛlfrɪˋprotʃ] *n*. 自责;后悔。

self-re·spect [ˈselfrisˈpekt; ˏsɛlfrɪˋspɛkt] *n*. 自尊,自尊心;自重。*lose one's* ～ 丧失自尊心。

self-re·straint [ˈselfrisˈtreint; ˌsɛlfrɪˋstrent] ***n*.** 自我克制,自我约束。

self-re·veal·ing [ˈselfriˈviːliŋ; ˋsɛlfrɪˋvilɪŋ] ***a*.** 无意中流露的,自我暴露的。

self-rev·e·a·tion [ˈselfˌreviˈleiʃən; ˋsɛlfˌrɛvəˋleʃən] ***n*.** 无意中的流露;自我暴露。

self-right·eous [ˈselfˈraitʃəs; ˋsɛlfˋraɪtʃəs] ***a*.** 自以为是的;自以为有道德的;伪善的。

self-rule, self-rul·ing [ˈselfˈruːl, -liŋ, ˌsɛlfˋrul, -lɪŋ] ***n*.** = self-government.

self-sac·ri·fice [ˈselfˈsækrifais; ˋsɛlfˋsækrəˌfaɪs] ***n*.** 牺牲自己;自我牺牲。

self-same [ˈselfseim; ˌsɛlfˋsem] ***a*.** 完全相同的,一样的。*We arrived here on the ~ day*. 我们恰好是同天到达这里的。

self-sat·is·fac·tion [ˈselfˌsætisˈfækʃən; ˋsɛlfsætɪsˋfækʃən] ***n*.** 自鸣得意;自满。

self-sat·is·fied [ˈselfˈsætisfaid; ˋsɛlfˋsætɪsˌfaɪd] ***a*.** 自满的,自鸣得意的。

self-seal·ing [ˈselfˈsiːliŋ; ˌsɛlfˋsilɪŋ] ***a*.** 自动封闭的;自行封口的;自固的。~ **tank** 自封式油箱。~ **tire** 自封式轮胎。

self-seek·er [ˈselfˈsiːkə; ˋsɛlfˋsikɚ] ***n*.** 追求私利的人;只求自己享乐的人。

self-seek·ing [ˈselfˈsiːkiŋ; ˋsɛlfˋsikɪŋ] ***a*.** 追求私利的;只求自己享乐的。

self-serv·ice [ˈselfˈsəːvis; ˋsɛlfˋsɝvɪs] ***n*., *a*.** 无人售货(的);顾客自己取用(的)。*a ~ cafeteria* 顾客自己取用食物的餐馆。

self-serv·ing [ˈselfˈsəːviŋ; ˋsɛlfˋsɝvɪŋ] ***a*.** 为个人利益服务的;图私利的。

self-slaugh·ter [ˈselfˈslɔːtə; ˌsɛlfˋslɔtɚ] ***n*.** 自杀。

self-slay·er [ˈselfˈsleiə; ˌsɛlfˋsleɚ] ***n*.** 自杀者。

self-sow [ˈselfˈsəu; ˋsɛlfˋso] ***vi*.** 【植】(植物利用风、水等自然力)自然播种。

self-sown [ˈselfˈsəun; ˋsɛlfˋson] ***a*.** 自然播种的,自然生长的。

self-start·er [ˈselfˈstɑːtə; ˋsɛlfˋstɑrtɚ] ***n*.** **1.** 【机】(内燃机的)自动起动装置。**2.** 〔美口〕工作主动的人,自行发起某项计划等的人。

self-steer·ing [ˈselfˈstiəriŋ; ˋsɛlfˋstɪrɪŋ] ***a*.** (船)自操纵的,自动化驾驶的。

self-stud·y [ˈselfˈstʌdi; ˋsɛlfˋstʌdɪ] ***n*.** **1.** 自我研究。**2.** 自学。

self-styled [ˈselfˈstaild; ˋsɛlfˋstaɪld] ***a*.** 自称的,自封的。*a ~ authority on history* 自封的历史界权威。

self-suf·fi·cient [ˈselfsʌˈfiʃənt; ˌsɛlfsəˋfɪʃənt] ***a*.** **1.** 自给自足的。**2.** 过于自信的;傲慢的。**-cien·cy** [-ʃənsi; -ʃənsɪ] ***n*.**

self-sug·ges·tion [ˈselfsəˈdʒestʃən; ˌsɛlfsəgˋdʒɛstʃən] ***n*.** 【心】自觉暗示,自我暗示。

self-sup·port [ˈselfsəˈpɔːt; ˌsɛlfsəˋport] ***n*.** 自立;自给;自营。

self-sup·port·ing [ˈselfsəˈpɔːtiŋ; ˌsɛlfsəˋportɪŋ] ***a*.** **1.** 自立的,自给的,自谋生活的。**2.** 【建】自承的。*a ~ student* 工读生。

self-sur·ren·der [ˈselfsəˈrendə; ˌsɛlfsəˋrɛndɚ] ***n*.** 自动屈从;沉溺,放任。

self-sus·tain·ing [ˈselfsəsˈteiniŋ; ˌsɛlfsəˋstenɪŋ] ***a*.** **1.** 自给的,自立的。**2.** 【建】自承的。**3.** 自持的。

self-taught [ˈselfˈtaut; ˋsɛlfˋtɔt] ***a*.** 自学的,自修的;自学而获得的。*Japanese Self-Taught*《日语自修读本》。

self-tim·er [ˈselfˈtaimə; ˋsɛlfˋtaɪmɚ] ***n*.** 【摄】自拍器,快门自动关闭装置。

self-tor·ture [ˈselfˈtɔːtʃə; ˋsɛlfˋtɔrtʃɚ] ***n*.** 苦行;自我折磨。

self-ward [ˈselfwəːd; ˋsɛlfwɚd] ***ad*., *a*.** **1.** 向自己地[的];朝着自己地[的]。**2.** 内向地[的]。**-s** ***ad*.**

self-will [ˈselfˈwil; ˋsɛlfˋwɪl] ***n*.** 任性;固执己见。**-ed** ***a*.** 任性的;执拗的。

self-wind·ing [ˈselfˈwaindiŋ; ˋsɛlfˋwaɪndɪŋ] ***a*.** (钟等)自动上发条的。

self-wrong [ˈselfˈrɔːŋ; ˋsɛlfˋrɔŋ] ***n*.** 自作孽;自我戕害。

Sel·juk [selˈdʒuːk; sɛlˋdʒuk] **I** ***n*.** (土耳其的)塞尔柱王朝;塞尔柱朝君主[臣民]。**II** ***a*.** = Seljukian.

sel·juk·i·an [selˈdʒuːkiən; sɛlˋdʒukɪən] ***a*.** 塞尔柱王朝的,塞尔柱王朝时代人的。

sell [sel; sɛl] (***sold*** [səuld; sold]) **I** ***vt*.** **1.** 卖,售(*opp*. buy);促进…的销路,使好卖。**2.** 〔喻〕出卖(朋友,节操),背叛(祖国)。**3.** 〔口〕〔通例用被动语态〕欺骗;使失望。**4.** 〔美〕宣传;推荐;说服;使接受;使赞成。*Do you ~ wine?* 有葡萄酒卖吗? *S- it for what it will bring*. 随市卖出。*The good quality will ~ good*. 高质量会促进货品销路。*Sold again!* 〔俚〕又上了一次当! *~ an idea to the public* 〔美〕对公众宣传某一种主张;使公众接受一种观念。—***vi*.** **1.** 卖出,售出。**2.** 销售(= be sold)。**3.** 〔口〕得到承认[采纳];得到赞同。**4.** 当店员;做推销员。*The book ~s for ten dollars*. 此书售价十美元。*~ by the dozen* 按打出售。*~ at 10 for one yuan* 一块钱十个。*Beef ~s very dear*. 牛肉很贵。*a doctrine that will ~* 一种能被接受的学说。*To S-*. 〔标示〕出售。***be sold on*** 〔美〕热中于…,给…迷住。***made to ~*** (不考究品质地)造来卖的。~ ***a bargain*** 愚弄,欺骗。~ ***a match*** [***game***] 受贿赂故意输掉,出卖比赛。~ (***sb*.**) ***a pup*** 〔美俚〕欺骗(某人)。~ ***at a bargain*** 廉价卖出。~ ***at a Loss*** [***sacrifice***] 亏本卖出。~ ***at a profit*** 赚钱卖出。~ ***by public auction*** 拍卖。~ ***by retail*** 零售。~ (***by***) ***wholesale*** 批发,批售。~ ***down the river*** 〔美谑〕出卖。~ ***high*** 以高价卖出。~ ***like wildfire*** [***hot cakes***, ***T-shirts***] 畅销。~ ***off*** (打折扣)销完;卖清(存货)。~ ***one's life dear***(***ly***) 使敌人蒙受巨大损失而后死。~ ***oneself*** **1.** 卖身;出卖人格。**2.** 〔俚〕自我宣传,自荐。~ ***out*** **1.** 卖完;脱销。**2.** 〔美口〕欺骗。**3.** 〔美俚〕出卖;背叛。~ ***short*** 【交易所】卖空。~ ***time*** 接受播送广告业务。~ ***up*** 拍卖;变卖(债务人的财产以抵债)。~ ***well*** 易于销售,行销。**II** ***n*.** **1.** 卖,销售(术)。**2.** 〔俚〕欺骗;诳骗。**3.** 失望。*What a ~!* 多失望! 上当啦! **~athon, ~-a-thon** 【口】马拉松式推销〔尤指长时期的廉价销售〕。**~-by date** 到期日;终结日,大限之期。~(-)**through** 零售录像带 (= ~(-)through video)。**-a·ble** ***a*.** 可以出售的。

sell·er [ˈselə; ˋsɛlɚ] ***n*.** **1.** 卖主,卖方。**2.** 行销货。*a good ~* 易于销售的货品。*a best ~* 畅销品;畅销书。*a ~s' market* (缺货时)有利于卖方的市场。

sell·ing [ˈseliŋ; ˋsɛlɪŋ] **I** ***n*.** 出售;卖。*a ~ price* 售价。*a ~ agent* 代销商店。*a ~ race* 出售(胜马的)赛马。**II** ***a*.** **1.** 出售的,卖的。**2.** 销路好的。*a low ~ price* 使货物易销的低价。

sell-off [ˈselɔːf; ˋsɛlˌɔf] ***n*.** 廉价抛售;出清存货。

sell·out [ˈselaut; ˋsɛlˌaʊt] ***n*.** 〔美〕**1.** 满座的演出;入场券全数销完的一场戏[比赛](等)。**2.** (商品)售缺,脱销。**3.** 〔美俚〕出卖;背叛;告密。

Sel·ma [ˈselmə; ˋsɛlmə] ***n*.** 塞尔玛〔女子名〕。

sel·syn [ˈselsin; ˋsɛlsɪn] ***n*.** 【电】**1.** 自动同步机,自整角机。**2.** 直流自协调。*~ generator* 自动同步发电机。

Selt·zer [ˈseltsə; ˋsɛltsɚ] ***n*.** 塞尔查水〔一种德国矿泉水,亦作 ~ water〕;〔S-〕仿制的矿泉水。

sel·va [ˈselvə; ˋsɛlvə] ***n*.** (*pl*. ~***s***) (南美亚马逊河流域)热带雨林。

sel·vage, sel·vedge [ˈselvidʒ, ˈselvedʒ; ˋsɛlvɪdʒ, ˋsɛlvɛdʒ] ***n*.** **1.** 【纺】织边;布边;纸边。**2.** 【矿】(包围矿脉的)黏皮。**3.** 【地】断层泥。**4.** 锁的孔板。**5.** 边缘;断片。*make the best use of the ~s of one's time* 尽量利用片断[零碎]的时间。

sel·vaged [ˈselvidʒd; ˋsɛlvɪdʒd] *a*. (织物)有织边的。

sel·va·gee [ˌselvəˈdʒiː; ˏsɛlvəˋdʒi] *n*.【海】(外缠细绳的)束环索。

selves [selvz; sɛlvz] self 的复数。

SEM = scanning electron microscope 扫描电子显微镜。

Sem. = Seminary; Semitic.

sem. = semicolon.

se·man·teme [siˈmæntiːm; səˋmæntim] *n*.【语】义素〔语义单位〕。

se·man·tic [siˈmæntik; səˋmæntɪk] *a*. 语义(学)的。～ **net**【计】语义网〔指电脑存储器中设计成和人类记忆力特征相应的数据信息排列〕。

se·man·ti·cist [siˈmæntisist; səˋmæntəsɪst] *n*. 语义学家。

se·man·tics [siˈmæntiks; səˋmæntɪks] *n*. **1.**【语】语义学。**2.**【哲】语义哲学;语义学派。

sem·a·phore [ˈseməfɔː, -fəə; ˋsɛməˏfor] **I** *n*. **1.** (铁路的)臂板信号(机),信号(灯);信号装置。**2.** (军队的)旗语通信(法)。**II** *vt*. 打信号(机)通知。—*vi*. 打信号;打旗语。

sem·a·phor·ic(al) [ˌseməˈfɔrik(əl); ˏsɛməˋfɑrɪk(əl)] *a*. **1.** 臂板信号(机)的;信号灯的;信号装置的。**2.** 用旗语通信的。**-cal·ly** *ad*.

se·ma·si·ol·o·gy [siˌmeisiˈɔlədʒi; sɪˏmesɪˋɑlədʒɪ] *n*. = semantics **1.**.

se·mat·ic [siˈmætik; sɪˋmætɪk] *a*.【生】(毒蛇等的颜色)预告危险的,有警告作用的;引起其他动物警戒的。～ *colours* [*coloration*] 警戒色。

sem·bla·ble [ˈsembləbl; ˋsɛmbləbl] **I** *a*.〔古〕**1.** 相似的。**2.** 合适的。**3.** 显而易见的;外观上的;外表的;表面的;非真实的。**II** *n*.〔古〕**1.** 类似物。**2.** 相似;类似。

sem·blance [ˈsembləns; ˋsɛmbləns] *n*. **1.** 外观;外貌,外表;样子。**2.** 类似;相似。**3.** 貌似物。**4.** 肖像。**5.** 假装;伪装。***have no*** ～ ***of*** 一点不像…。***have the*** ～ ***of*** 像…。***in*** ～ 外貌是;外表上。***in the*** ～ ***of*** 以…的姿态。***make*** ～ (***that, as if***) 假装。***put on a*** [***make***] ～ ***of*** 装做…(的样子)。***to the*** ～ ***of*** 像…似地。***under the*** ～ ***of*** 装着…(的样子);在…的幌子下。***without even the*** ～ ***of*** 连像…的地方也没有,一点…的味道也没有。

se·mé [ˈsemei; səˋme] *a*.〔F.〕【徽】(星、百合花等)小花纹星罗棋布的;碎花纹的。

se·mei·og·ra·phy [ˌsiːmaiˈɔgrəfi; ˏsimaɪˋɑgrəfɪ] *n*.【医】症状记录。

se·mei·ol·o·gy [ˌsiːmaiˈɔlədʒi; ˏsimaɪˋɑlədʒɪ], **se·mei·ot·ics** [-ˈɔtiks; -ˋɑtɪks] *n*. **1.**【医】症状学。**2.** 符号学。**3.** 手势语言(= semiology)。

sem·eme [ˈsemiːm; ˋsɛmim] *n*.【语】词义要素;义素。

se·men [ˈsiːmen; ˋsimən] *n*. (*pl*. **sem·i·na** [ˈseminə; ˋsɛmɪnə], ～*s*) **1.**【生理】精液。**2.**【植】种子;胚种。

se·mes·ter [siˈmestə; səˋmɛstɚ] *n*. 六个月的时期;(美、德等国学校课程的)半学年;一学期。**-tral** [-trəl; -trəl] *a*.

sem·i [ˈsemi; ˋsɛmɪ] *n*. **1.**〔口〕= semitrailer. **2.**〔英俗〕半独立式住宅。

sem·i- *pref*. **1.** "半";"部分"。**2.** 一半;(一般时期中)出现两次的: *semi*-colony, *semi*monthly.

sem·i-ab·stract [ˈsemiˈæbstrækt; ˏsɛməˋæbstrækt] *a*. (艺术品等)半抽象的。

sem·i·air-cooled [ˈsemiˈɛəkuːld; ˏsɛməˋɛrkuld] *a*. 半气冷的。

sem·i·an·nual [ˈsemiˈænjuəl; ˏsɛmɪˋænjuəl] *a*. 半年一次的,一年两次的。**-ly** *ad*.

sem·i·a·quat·ic [ˈsemiəˈkwætik; ˏsɛmɪəˋkwætɪk] *a*.【植】半水生的;近水生的;【动】半水栖的。

sem·i·ar·id [ˈsemiˈærid; ˏsɛməˋærɪd] *a*. 半干旱的。

sem·i·au·to·mat·ed [ˈsemiˌɔːtəˈmeitid; ˏsɛməˏɔtəˋmetɪd] *a*. = semiautomatic.

sem·i·au·to·mat·ic [ˈsemiˌɔːtəˈmætik; ˏsɛməˏɔtəˋmætɪk] *a*. (机器、武器等)半自动的。

sem·i·breve [ˈsemibriːv; ˋsɛməˏbriv] *n*.【乐】全音符。

sem·i·cen·ten·ni·al [ˈsemisenˈtenjəl; ˏsɛməsɛnˋtɛnɪəl] **I** *a*. **1.** 五十年一度的。**2.** 持续半个世纪的。**II** *n*. 五十周年;五十周年纪念。

sem·i·cen·tu·ry [ˈsemiˈsentʃuri; ˏsemɪˋsɛntʃʊrɪ] *n*. **1.** 半个世纪;五十年。**2.**【板球】五十分。

sem·i·cho·rus [ˈsemiˌkɔːrəs; ˋsɛməˏkorəs] *n*.【音】小合唱〔指部分合唱队员的合唱〕。

sem·i·cir·cle [ˈsemiˌsəːkl; ˋsɛməˏsɝkl̩] *n*. **1.** 半圆。**2.** 半圆形体。*sit in a* ～ 坐成半圆形。

sem·i·cir·cu·lar [ˈsemiˈsəːkjulə; ˏsɛmɪˋsɝkjəlɚ] *a*. 半圆形的。～ **canal**【解】(耳的)半规管。

sem·i·civ·i·lized [ˈsemiˈsivilaizd; ˏsɛməˋsɪvl̩ˏaɪzd] *a*. 半文明的,半开化的。

sem·i·clas·si·cal [ˈsemiˈklæsikəl; ˏsɛməˋklæsɪkl̩] **I** *a*. 半古典的。**II** *n*. 半古典的音乐[作品等]。

sem·i·co·lon [ˈsemiˈkəulən; ˋsɛməˏkolən] *n*. 分号〔即;〕。

sem·i·co·lo·ni·al [ˈsemikəˈləunjəl; ˏsɛməkəˋlonɪəl] *a*. 半殖民地的。

sem·i·col·o·ny [ˈsemiˈkɔləni; ˏsɛmɪˋkɑlənɪ] *n*. 半殖民地。

sem·i·con·duc·tor [ˈsemikənˈdʌktə; ˏsɛməkənˋdʌktɚ] *n*.【物】半导体。

sem·i·con·scious [ˈsemiˈkɔnʃəs; ˏsɛməˋkɑnʃəs] *a*. 半自觉的;半意识的;半知觉的。

sem·i·con·ser·va·tive [ˈsemikənˈsəːvətiv; ˏsɛməkənˋsɝvətɪv] *a*.【遗传】半保留的;半保守的。

sem·i·cyl·in·der [ˈsemiˈsilində; ˏsɛməˋsɪlɪndɚ] *n*. 半圆柱体。

sem·i·dai·ly [ˈsemiˈdeili; ˏsɛməˋdelɪ] *a*., *ad*. 一天两次的[地]。

sem·i-dem·i·sem·i·qua·ver [ˈsemiˈdemisemiˌkweivə; ˏsɛməˋdɛmɪˋsɛməˏkwevɚ] *n*.【乐】六十四分音符。

sem·i·de·tached [ˈsemidiˈtætʃt; ˏsɛmədɪˋtætʃt] *a*. 半分离的;(房屋)一侧与他屋相接的。

sem·i·di·am·e·ter [ˈsemidaiˈæmitə; ˏsɛmɪdaɪˋæmətɚ] *n*. 半径;【天】(天体的)视半径。

sem·i·di·ur·nal [ˈsemidaiˈəːnl; ˏsɛmədaɪˋɝnl] *a*. **1.** 半天的;半天内做完的。**2.** 半天一次的,一天两次的,每隔十二小时的。

sem·i·dome [ˈsemidəum; ˋsɛməˏdom] *n*.【建】半圆屋顶;半圆形天花板。**-d** *a*.

sem·i·dou·ble [ˈsemiˈdʌbl; ˏsɛməˋdʌbl̩] *a*.【植】半重瓣的。

sem·i·el·lip·ti·cal [ˈsemiˈiliptikəl; ˏsɛməɪˋlɪptɪkəl] *a*. 半椭圆(形)的。

sem·i·feu·dal [ˈsemiˈfjuːdl; ˏsɛməˋfjudl̩] *a*. 半封建的。

sem·i·fi·nal [ˈsemiˈfainl; ˏsɛməˋfaɪnl̩] *n*., *a*.【体】半决赛(的)。

sem·i·fi·nal·ist [ˈsemiˈfainəlist; ˏsɛməˋfaɪnl̩ɪst] *n*. 半决赛选手。

sem·i·fin·ished [ˈsemiˈfiniʃt; ˏsɛməˋfɪnɪʃt] *a*. **1.**【机】半加工的;半制的。**2.** 半完成的;半成品的。

sem·i·fin·ishing [ˈsemiˈfiniʃiŋ; ˏsɛməˋfɪnɪʃɪŋ] *n*. 半精加工。

sem·i·for·mal [ˈsemiˈfɔːməl; ˏsɛməˋfɔrml̩] *a*. 半正式的〔指衣着等〕。

sem·i·in·fi·nite [ˈsemiˈinfinit; ˏsɛməˋɪnfɪnɪt] *a*.【数】半无穷的,半无限的。

sem·i·lit·er·ate [ˈsemiˈlitərit; ˏsɛməˋlɪtərɪt] *a*. 半文盲的;略知阅读和书写的;识字而不会书写的。

sem·i·lu·nar [ˈsemiˈljuːnə; ˏsɛməˋlunɚ] *a*. 半月形的。

sem·i·man·u·fac·tures [ˈsemiˌmænjuˈfæktʃəz; ˏsɛməˏmænjʊˋfæktʃɚz] *n*. *pl*. 半成品。

sem·i·met·al [ˈsemiˈmetl;ˏsɛməˋmɛtl̩] ***n.***【物】半金属。

sem·i·me·tal·lic [ˈsemimiˈtælik;ˏsɛməmɪˋtælɪk] ***a.*** 半金属的。

sem·i·month·ly [ˈsemiˈmʌnθli;ˏsɛməˋmʌnθlɪ] **I** ***a.*** ***ad.*** 一月两次的[地]。**II** ***n.*** 半月刊。

sem·i·na [ˈseminə; ˋsɛmɪnə] ***n.*** semen 的复数。

se·mi·nal [ˈsiːminl, ˈse-; ˋsɛmənl] ***a.*** **1.** 精液的。**2.**【生】胚种的,种子的。**3.** 繁殖的,再生的,生殖的;生产(性)的;有力的。**4.** 潜在的;(思想等)含蓄的。**5.** 胚胎的;萌芽状态的;待发育的;将大为发展的。**6.** 根本的,基本的。～ *fluid* [*semen*] 精液。～ *power* 生殖力。*the* ～ *principle* 基本原则。*in a* ～ *state* 在胚胎状态中的;处于待发达状态中的。～ **cup**【昆】卵突杯。～ **duct**【解】输精管。～ **leaf**【植】子叶。～ **receptacle** [**reservoir**]【解】受[贮]精囊。**-ly** ***ad.***

sem·i·nar [ˈseminɑː; ˋsɛməˏnɑr] ***n.*** **1.** (大学的)研究班;研究小组。**2.** 研究室,研究科目。**3.** (专家)研讨会,讲习会。

sem·i·nar·i·an [ˌsemiˈnɛəriən;ˏsɛməˋnɛrɪən] ***n.*** **1.** 研究班[研讨会等]的参加者。**2.** 神学院学生。

sem·i·nar·ist [ˈsemiˌnɛərist; ˋsɛməˏnɛrɪst] ***n.*** = seminarian.

sem·i·na·ry [ˈseminəri; ˋsɛməˏnɛrɪ] ***n.*** **1.** 高等中学;女子中学[学院]。**2.** 神学校[院];养成所。**3.** 发源地;温床。**4.** = seminar. *a* ～ *of revolution* 革命的温床。*a* ～ *of vice* 罪恶的渊薮。

sem·i·na·tion [ˌsemiˈneiʃən; ˏsɛməˋneʃən] ***n.*** = dissemination.

sem·i·nif·er·ous [ˌsemiˈnifərəs;ˏsɛməˋnɪfərəs] ***a.*** **1.**【植】生种子的,结子的。**2.** 生精液的,输精的。～ *tubes* 输精管。

sem·i·niv·o·rous [ˌsemiˈnivərəs;ˏsɛməˋnɪvərəs] ***a.*** 食种子为生的。

Sem·i·nole [ˈseminəul; ˋsɛməˏnol] ***n.*** (*pl.* ～, ～*s*) (印第安人的)塞米诺尔族;塞米诺尔语。

sem·i·no·ma [ˈsemiˈnəumə;ˏsɛməˋnomə] ***n.***【医】睾丸肿瘍。

sem·i·oc·ca·sion·al·ly [ˈsemiəˈkeiʒənlli; ˏsɛmɪəˋkeʒənllɪ] ***ad.*** 〔美口〕偶然地。

sem·i·of·fi·cial [ˈsemiəˈfiʃəl;ˏsɛmɪəˋfɪʃəl] ***a.*** 半官方的。*a* ～ *statement* 半官方的声明。**-ly** ***ad.***

se·mi·ol·o·gy [ˌsemiˈɔlədʒi;ˏsimɪˋɑlədʒɪ] ***n.*** **1.**【医】症状学。**2.** 符号学。**3.** 手势语言。**-o·log·ic** [-əˈlɔdʒik; -əˋlɔdʒɪk], **-o·log·i·cal** ***a.*** **-o·log·ist** ***n.***

se·mi·ot·ic [ˌsemiˈɔtik;ˏsimɪˋɑtɪk] **I** ***n.*** 〔常用复数,动词用单数〕【哲】符号论;符号学。**II** ***a.*** = semiotical.

se·mi·ot·i·cal [ˌsemiˈɔtikəl;ˏsɛmɪˋɑtɪkəl] ***a.*** **1.** 与符号有关的;符号学的。**2.** 症状学的。**-ti·cian** ***n.*** 符号学专家;症状学研究者。

sem·i·o·vip·a·rous [ˈsemiəuˈvipərəs;ˏsɛmɪoˋvɪpərəs] ***a.***【动】半卵生的〔如袋鼠等,未完全发育即出生,因而需在母体袋中生活一段时期〕。

sem·i·pal·mate [ˌsemiˈpælmit;ˏsɛməˋpælmet] ***a.***【动】半蹼足[趾]的。

sem·i·par·a·site [ˌsemiˈpærəsait;ˏsɛməˋpærəsaɪt] ***n.***【动】半寄生 (= hemiparasite)。

sem·i·per·me·a·ble [ˌsemiˈpəːmjəbl;ˏsɛməˋpɝmɪəbl̩] ***a.*** 半渗透的。

sem·i·post·al [ˌsemiˈpəustəl;ˏsɛməˋpostl] **I** ***a.*** 半邮政的。**II** ***n.*** 半邮政邮票〔售价高于票面值,其收益多用于非邮政的公用事业〕。

sem·i·pre·cious [ˌsemiˈpreʃəs;ˏsɛməˋprɛʃəs] ***a.*** (宝石)半珍贵的;不算太珍贵的〔指石榴石,绿松石,蛋白石等〕。

sem·i·pri·vate [ˈsemiˈpraivit;ˏsɛməˋpraɪvɪt] ***a.*** 半私用的;〔尤指〕(医院病房)私人半专用的〔指医院病房的等级,大体分为普通病房,私人半专用病房,私人专用病房〕。

sem·i·pro [ˌsemiˈprəu;ˏsɛməˋpro] ***n.***, ***a.*** 半职业性选手(的)〔semiprofessional 之略〕。

sem·i·pro·duc·tion [ˈsemiprəˈdʌkʃən; ˏsɛməprəˋdʌkʃən] ***n.***【经】中间生产。

sem·i·pro·fes·sion·al [ˌsemiprəˈfeʃənl; ˏsɛməprəˋfɛʃənl] **I** ***a.*** 半职业性的;〔尤指〕(体育等)半职业性活动的;由半职业性运动员从事的。**II** ***n.*** 半职业性运动员。**-ly** ***ad.***

sem·i·pub·lic [ˈsemiˈpʌblik;ˏsɛməˋpʌblɪk] ***a.*** 半公开的。

sem·i·qua·ver [ˈsemiˌkweivə; ˋsɛməˏkwevɚ] ***n.***【乐】十六分音符。

sem·i·re·li·gious [ˈsemiˈrilidʒəs;ˏsɛmɪrɪˋlɪdʒəs] ***a.*** 半宗教性的。

sem·i·re·tired [ˈsemiriˈtaiəd;ˏsɛmɪrɪˋtaɪrd] ***a.*** 半退休的。

sem·i·rev·o·lu·tion [ˈsemiˌrevəˈluːʃən; ˏsɛməˏrɛvəˋluʃən] ***n.*** 半回转。

sem·i·rig·id [ˈsemiˈridʒid;ˏsɛməˋrɪdʒɪd] ***a.*** (飞艇)半硬式的。

sem·i·sav·age [ˈsemiˈsævidʒ;ˏsɛməˋsævɪdʒ] **I** ***a.*** 半野蛮人。**II** ***n.*** 半野蛮人。

sem·i·sil·low [ˈsemiˌsailəu; ˋsɛməˏsaɪlo] ***n.***【农】半休闲。

sem·i·skilled [ˈsemiˈskild;ˏsɛməˋskɪld] ***a.*** (工人)半熟练的;只需有限训练即可操作的。

sem·i·soft [ˈsemiˈsɔft;ˏsɛməˋsɔft] ***a.*** 半软的〔如干酪〕。

sem·i·som·nus [ˈsemiˈsɔmnəs;ˏsɛməˋsɑmnəs] ***n.***【医】半[轻]昏迷;昏睡。

sem·i·star [ˈsemiˈstɑː;ˏsɛməˋstɑr] ***n.*** 〔美俚〕二流电影明星;二流演员。

sem·i·starved [ˈsemiˈstɑːvd;ˏsɛməˋstɑrvd] ***a.*** 半饥饿的。

sem·i·steel [ˈsemiˈstiːl;ˏsɛməˋstil] ***n.***【冶】高级铸铁;钢性铸铁;半钢质。

sem·i·syn·the·tic [ˈsemisinˈθetik; ˏsɛməsɪnˋθɛtɪk] ***a.***【化】半合成的。

Sem·ite [ˈsiːmait, ˈse-; ˋsɛmaɪt, ˋsɛ-] **I** ***n.*** 闪族(人),闪米特族(人)〔古代包括希伯来人、亚述人、腓尼基人、阿拉伯人、巴比伦人等〕;〔今特指〕犹太人。**II** ***a.*** = Semitic.

Se·mit·ic [siˈmitik, seˈm-; səˋmɪtɪk] **I** ***a.*** 闪族(语言)的;〔今特指〕犹太人的。**II** ***n.*** 闪语〔希伯来语、阿拉伯语等〕。

Se·mit·ics [siˈmitiks, seˈm-; səˋmɪtɪks] ***n.*** 〔动词用单数〕闪族学〔研究闪族的文化、语言、文学等的科学〕。

Sem·it·ism [ˈsemitizəm; ˋsɛməˏtɪzəm] ***n.*** **1.** 闪语表达方式。**2.** 闪族人气质;闪族人性格;闪族人思想。**3.** 亲犹太人思想[主义]。

Sem·i·to-Ha·mit·ic [ˈsemitəuhæˈmitik; ˏsɛmətohæˋmɪtɪk] ***a.*** 亚非语系的,闪含语系的 (= Afro-Asiatic)。

sem·i·tone [ˈsemitəun; ˋsɛməˏton] ***n.***【乐】半音;半音程。*a major* [*minor*] ～ 长[短]半音。

sem·i·trail·er [ˈsemiˌtreilə;ˏsɛməˋtrelɚ] ***n.*** 半拖车;单轴拖车;双轮拖车,挂车。

sem·i·trans·par·ent [ˈsemitrænsˈpɛərənt; ˋsɛmətrænsˋpɛrənt] ***a.*** 半透明的。

sem·i·trop·i·c(al) [ˈsemiˈtrɔpikəl;ˏsɛməˋtrɑpɪkl̩] ***a.*** 副热带的;亚热带的。

sem·i·tur·bu·lent [ˈsemiˈtəːbjulənt;ˏsɛməˋtɝbjələnt] ***a.*** 半湍流的。

sem·i·u·ni·form [ˈsemiˈjuːnifɔːm;ˏsɛməˋjunəfɔrm] ***a.*** 半均匀的。

sem·i·vo·cal [ˈsemiˈvəukəl;ˏsɛməˋvokl̩] ***a.***【语音】半元音的。

sem·i·vow·el [ˈsemiˈvauəl; ˋsɛməˏvaʊəl] ***n.***【语音】半元音〔英语 w, y 的发音〕;半元音字母〔指如 w, y〕。

sem·i·week·ly [ˈsemiˈwiːkli;ˏsɛməˋwiklɪ] **I** ***ad.***, ***a.***

每半周一次(的);一周两次(的)。**II** ***n*.** 半周刊;三日刊。

sem·i·works [ˈsemiwəːks; ˏsɛməˋwɝks] ***n*.** *pl*. 〔用作 *sing*. 或 *pl*.〕(试制新产品或试行新工艺的)小规模工厂。

sem·i·year·ly [ˈsemiˈjəːli; ˏsɛməˋjɪrlɪ] **I** ***a*.**, ***ad*.** 一年两次的[地];半年一次的[地]。**II** ***n*.** 半年刊。

sem·o·la [ˈseməlǝ; ˋsɛməlǝ], **sem·o·li·na** [ˌseməˈliːnǝ; ˏsɛməˋlinǝ] ***n*.** (做布丁等用的)粗粒面粉。

sem·per [ˈsempǝ; ˋsɛmpɚ] ***ad*.** 〔L.〕经常;永远。~ *fidelis* [fiˈdeilis; fɪˋdilɪs] 永远忠诚〔美海军陆战队箴言〕。~ *paratus* [pǝˈreitǝs; pǝˋretǝs]永远有准备;时刻准备着〔美海岸警卫队箴言〕。

sem·per·vi·rent [ˌsempǝˈvaiǝrǝnt; ˏsɛmpɚˋraɪrǝnt] ***a*.** (植物)常绿的。

sem·per·vi·vum [ˌsempǝˈvaivǝm; ˏsɛmpɚˋvaɪvǝm] ***n*.** 【植】长生草属 (*Sempervivum*) 植物。

sem·pi·ter·nal [ˈsempiˈtəːnl; ˏsɛmpɪˋtɝnl̩] ***a*.** 〔诗〕永久的;永远的。

sem·pli·ce [ˈsemplitʃi; ˋsɛmplɪtʃe] ***a*.**, ***ad*.** 〔It.〕【乐】单纯的[地];自然的[地];真实的[地];无装饰音的[地]。

sem·pre [ˈsempri; ˋsɛmpre] ***ad*.** 〔It.〕【乐】自始至终(按照指示的色调演奏)。~ ***forte*** 【音】始终强音地。~ ***piano*** 【音】始终柔和地。

semp·stress [ˈsem*p*stris; ˋsɛmpstrɪs] ***n*.** = seamstress.

sen [sen; sɛn] ***n*.** 〔*sing*., *pl*.〕**1.** 钱〔日本辅币的单位,等于1/100日元〕。**2.** 仙〔印度尼西亚等的辅币单位〕。

Sen. = **1.** Senate. **2.** Senator. **3.** Senior.

sen., **senr.** = senior.

se·na·ry [ˈsiːnǝri; ˋsɛnǝrɪ] ***a*.** 六(个)的;六进制的;以六为基础的。~ *division* 六分。~ *scale* 【数】六进制。

sen·ate [ˈsenit; ˋsɛnɪt] ***n*.** **1.** (古罗马的)元老院。**2.** [S-] (美、法等国议会的)参议院;上(议)院。**3.** 立法机构(全体成员);立法程序。**4.** (剑桥大学等的)评议会;理事会。~ **house** **1.** 参议院议事厅。**2.** (剑桥大学等的)评议会办公处 (*a* ~ *house examination* 剑桥大学等的学位考试。*a* ~ *house problem* 上述考试中的数学题)。

sen·a·tor [ˈsenǝtǝ; ˋsɛnǝtɚ] ***n*.** **1.** 参议员;上(议)院议员。**2.** (古罗马)元老院议员;(剑桥等大学的)评议员;理事。**3.** 〔美〕参议员〔对现任或前任参议员的尊称〕。**-ship** ***n*.** 参议员[上议院议员]的地位[职务、任期]。

sen·a·to·ri·al [ˌsenǝˈtɔːriǝl; ˏsɛnǝˋtɔrɪǝl] ***a*.** **1.** 参议院[员]的;上(议)院的。**2.** 元老院(议员)的。**3.** 〔美〕有参议员选择权的。**4.** (大学)评议会的。~ **courtesy** 〔美〕参议院礼貌否决〔当总统任命某州官员受到该州参议员反对时,参议院为对这些参议员表示尊重而对总统任命不予认可〕。~ **district** 〔美〕参议员选举区。**-ly** ***ad*.**

se·na·tus [siˈneitǝs; sɪˋnetǝs] ***n*.** 〔L.〕**1.** (古罗马的)元老院。**2.** (苏格兰某些大学的)评议会。

send[1] [send; sɛnd] ***vt*.** (***sent*** [sent; sɛnt]) **1.** 送;寄。**2.** 打发;派;遣(使者等)。**3.** 发(信)。**4.** 放;投;掷;射(球、箭等)。**5.** 传递(酒等)。**6.** 【电】传导;输送。**7.** (神等)赏;赐;降;施。**8.** 促使;使处于;使陷入;使(变)成…。**9.** 〔美俚〕(尤指奏摇滚乐)使兴奋;使心荡神移。~ *a messenger* 派人送信。*S- help at once!* 请立刻派帮手来! ~ *a person mad* 使人发狂。*These records used to* ~ *her*. 这些唱片过去往往使她听得如醉如痴。*God* ~ *it may* (*not*) *be so!* 但愿(不)是这样。—***vi*.** **1.** 派人;遣人。**2.** 送音讯;寄信;【电】播送。**3.** 〔美俚〕如醉如狂地唱[奏]爵士即兴音乐。*If you want me, please* ~. 假若有事找我,请即告知。~ ***along*** 随即发送;使加紧;促进。~ ***and do*** 派人去做。~ ***away*** **1.** 撵走;开除;解雇。**2.** 把…送到远处;写信[派人]至远方。**3.** 派人去拿[去请] (*for*)。~ ***down*** **1.** 〔英大学俚〕勒令退学;开除。**2.** 使下降;使下落;使减少。**3.** 使到(饭厅)去。~ (***sb*.**) ***flying*** 解雇某人;撵走某人;打走某人;把某人打倒在地。~ ***for*** 派人去叫[请];遣人去拿;乞求 (~ *for a doctor* 派人去请医生。~ *for a book* 派人去拿一本书)。~ ***forth*** [***out***] **1.** 送出;发送。**2.** 发出(香气)。**3.** 长[生]出(芽,枝等)。**4.** 派遣。**5.** 出口。~ ***in*** **1.** 送。**2.** 拿出;提出。**3.** 递(名片)。**4.** 参加展览 (~ *in one's papers* (海陆军人等)提出辞呈;呈请辞职。~ *in one's jacket* 辞职。~ *in one's name* 申请参加(比赛))。~ ***off*** **1.** 寄出;发(信、货等)。**2.** 驱逐,撵走。**3.** 送别(出走、旅行等的人)。**4.** 差遣;辞退。~ ***on*** **1.** 转送;转寄(信等)。**2.** 预送;先送 (*Please* ~ *the letter on to my mother*. 请将此信转送家母)。~ ***one's love*** (*to sb*.) 向(某人)问安。~ ***out*** = ~ *forth*. ~ ***over*** 播送。~ ***packing*** 解雇;撵走;开除 (*He was sent packing for stealing*. 他因盗窃被开除)。~ ***round*** **1.** 传递;使传阅。**2.** 派遣 (*A notice was being sent round among the representatives*. 在代表中传阅一项通知)。~ ***through*** 报告;通知(消息等)。~ (***sb*.**) ***to school*** 〔美俚〕把某人送入感化院。~ ***up*** **1.** 弄上去;使上升。**2.** 提出(报告等)。**3.** 传递(球等)。**4.** 检举。**5.** 〔美口〕把某人送进监牢。**6.** 端出(饭菜)。**7.** 【海】扬(帆)。**8.** 冷笑;〔英〕(采用模仿办法)使显得可笑。~ ***word*** 通知;报知;转告。~**-out** ***n*.** 送出[输出]量。~**-up** (装作严肃的)讽刺性模仿;讽刺。

send[2] [send; sɛnd] **I** ***n*.** 〔海〕**1.** 波浪的推(进)力。**2.** 船的纵摇。**II** ***vi*.** (***sent***) 【海】(船被波浪推着)前进;(纵摇时)船头[船尾]向上翘起。

Sen·dai [ˈsenˈdai; ˋsɛnˋdaɪ] ***n*.** 仙台〔日本城市〕。

sen·dal [ˈsendl; ˋsɛndl] ***n*.** **1.** 森丹绸〔中世纪产的一种薄绸,做衣服、旗帜等用〕。**2.** 森丹绸袍。

send·er [ˈsendǝ; ˋsɛndɚ] ***n*.** **1.** 发送人;送货人。**2.** 【讯】发射机;发送机;发报机;发射器;(电话的)送话器。**3.** (天线)引向器;记发器。**4.** (电报)电键。**5.** 〔美俚〕能使人兴奋若狂的爵士即兴音乐演奏者。*a multi-class* ~ 万用记发器[记录器]。*a* ~ *decoder* 发报机译码器。*the* ~ *of a letter* 发信人。

send·ing [ˈsendiŋ; ˋsɛndɪŋ] ***n*.** **1.** 发送,派遣;【讯】发射。**2.** 信件。**3.** 神赐,天降。~ **set** 发射机。~ **station** 发射台;发信局。

send-off [ˈsendˈɔːf; ˋsɛndˏɔf] ***n*.** **1.** 送别;欢送。**2.** 发动;起动。**3.** 〔美俚〕(开创事业时的)鼓励;(吹捧性质的)推荐;介绍。**4.** 〔美俚〕送葬;葬礼。*a* ~ *party* 欢送会。*give* (*sb*.) *a fine* ~ 〔口〕盛大欢送(某人)。

Sen·e·ca [ˈsenikǝ; ˋsɛnɪkǝ] ***n*.** **1.** 印第安人的塞尼加族。**2. Lucius** ~ 卢修斯·塞尼加〔公元前4?—公元65,罗马政治家,哲学家,作家〕。

sen·e·ga [ˈsenigǝ; ˋsɛnɪgǝ] ***n*.** 【植】美远志;美远志根〔治蛇毒咬伤,亦用作祛痰药〕。

Sen·e·gal [ˌseniˈgɔːl; ˏsɛnɪˋgɔl] ***n*.** **1.** 塞内加尔〔非洲〕。**2.** 〔the ~〕塞内加尔河〔非洲〕。~ **ese** [ˌsenigɔːˈliːz; ˏsɛnɪgɔˋliz] **1.** ***n*.** 塞内加尔人。**2.** ***a*.** 塞内加尔(人)的。

se·nesce [siˈnes; sɪˋnɛs] ***vi*.** 开始衰老。

se·nes·cent [ˈsenisnt; sǝˋnɛsnt] ***a*.** 衰老的;开始衰老的。

sen·es·chal [ˈseniʃǝl; ˋsɛnǝʃǝl] ***n*.** (中世纪贵族的)管家;执事。

se·nhor [seˈnjɔː; seˋnjor] ***n*.** (*pl*. ~*s*, ***se·nho·res*** [seˈnjɔːriːz; seˋnjɔriz]) 〔Pg.〕先生 (= Mr., Sir);绅士。***se·nhor·a*** [seˈnjɔːrǝ; seˋnjorǝ] ***n*.** 〔Pg.〕夫人;太太。***se·nho·ri·ta*** [ˌsenjɔːˈriːtǝ; ˏsenjoˋritǝ] ***n*.** 〔Pg.〕小姐。

se·nile [ˈsiːnail; ˋsinaɪl] ***a*.** **1.** 老年的;因年老发生的;衰老的。**2.** 【地】老年期的。~ *atrophy* 老衰性萎缩。~ *dementia* 老年性痴呆。~ *river* 老年河。

se·nil·i·ty [siˈniliti; sǝˋnɪlǝtɪ] ***n*.** 老迈;衰老;老耄。

Sen·ior [ˈsiːnjǝ; ˋsɪŋjɚ] ***n*.** 西尼尔〔姓氏〕。

sen·ior [ˈsiːnjǝ; ˋsinjɚ] (*opp*. junior) **I** ***a*.** **1.** 年长的;(同名两人中)年纪较大的。★略作 Sen., Senr. 或 Sr., 附在姓名后,以区别父子或两个同姓的人: *John Smith, Sr*. 老[大]约翰·史密斯。**2.** 前辈的;先辈的;资格老的;资深的。**3.** 主席的;上级的;高级的。**4.** 〔美〕(中学)最高年级的;(大学)四年级的;毕业班的;〔英〕高年级的。*a*

～ *statesman* 富有资历的政治家。*a* ～ *officer* 高级军官。*a* ～ *man* 高班(学)生。*a* ～ *citizen* 老年人〔尤指退休老人〕。*a* ～ *counsel* 首席律师。*the* ～ *partner* (股份公司的)董事长;主持人;(商行的)主要合伙人。*the* ～ *branch of a family* 一个家族的嫡系。～ ***in office*** 上级的。***the*** ～ ***service*** 〔英〕海军。**II *n*. 1.** 年长者。**2.** 前辈;上司;上级;资历深者。**3.**〔英〕高班生;〔美〕(中学)最高年级生,(大学)四年级生;毕业班生;〔英〕高年级生。*Paul is his brother's* ～ *by two years*. 保罗比弟弟大两岁。～ **citizen**〔美〕年长〔指已退休者,多为 65 岁以上的老人〕。～ **high school**〔美〕高级中学(10～12 年级)。～ **school**〔英〕高级中学〔招收 14—17 岁学生〕。

sen·i·o·res pri·o·res [ˌsiːniˈɔːriːz praiˈɔːriːz; ˏsiniˋoriz praɪˋoriz] 〔L.〕让年长者居先;先老后小。

sen·i·or·i·ty [ˌsiːniˈɔriti; sinˋjɔrətɪ] ***n*. 1.** 年长;上级,前辈。**2.** 老资格;年资深;资历。*Promotion goes by* ～. 按资历晋升。*the first on the* ～ *list* 资格最老的成员。～ **rule**〔美〕资深通例〔国会中由多数党资历最老议员任委员会主席的规定〕。

sen·na [ˈsenə; ˋsɛnə] ***n*. 1.**【植】山扁豆属植物;番泻树。**2.**【药】番泻叶〔缓泻剂〕。

sen·net [ˈsenit; ˋsɛnɪt] ***n*.**〔古〕(演员上下场的)喇叭奏鸣;号角。

sen·night, se'n·night [ˈsenait; ˋsɛnaɪt] ***n*.**〔古〕一星期。*Tuesday* ～ 一星期前[后]的星期二。

sen·nit [ˈsenit; ˋsɛnɪt] ***n*. 1.**【海】(通常由三根至九根打成的)扁索。**2.** 草帽辫。

S

se·ñor [seˈnjɔː; senˋjɔr] ***n*.** 〔Sp.〕(*pl*. ***se·ñores*** [-ˈnjɔːres; -ˋnjɔres]) **1.** 先生〔与姓氏连用〕。**2.** 绅士。

se·ño·ra [seˈnjɔːrə; senˋjorə] ***n*.** 〔Sp.〕**1.** 太太,夫人〔与姓氏连用〕。**2.** 女士。

se·ño·ri·ta [ˌsenjəˈriːtə; ˏsenjəˋritə] ***n*.** 〔Sp.〕**1.** 小姐〔与姓氏连用〕。**2.** 女士。

sen·sate [ˈsenseit; ˋsɛnset] **I *a*. 1.** 有感觉的;有知觉力的。**2.** 由感官知觉到的,感觉到的。～ *matters* 可感知的物质。**II *vt*., *vi*.** 〔罕〕感觉,感知。**-ly *ad*.**

sen·sa·tion [senˈseiʃən; sɛnˋseʃən] ***n*. 1.** 感觉;知觉。**2.** 兴奋的感情;感动;激动。**3.** 轰动;轰动一时的事物。*a* ～ *of fear* 恐怖感。*a disagreeable* ～ 不愉快的感觉。*create* [*cause, make*] *a* ～ 使感动;动人视听;引起世人注意;引起轰动。*a literary* ～ 轰动文坛的作品。*a* ～ *of the first magnitude* 最为轰动的大事件。*three days'* ～ 一时的轰动;昙花一现的声名。*the latest* ～ (戏剧、事件等)最新的轰动一时的事物。

sen·sa·tion·al [senˈseiʃənəl; sɛnˋseʃənl] ***a*. 1.** 感觉的;感情的;感动的;知觉的;有感觉的。**2.** 使感动的;轰动世间的;惊动社会的;耸人听闻的;令人激动的。**3.** 投合时好的。**4.** 非常的;异常的;(胜利等)巨大的。**5.** 出名的。**6.**【哲】感觉论的。*a* ～ *crime* 骇人听闻的罪行。*a* ～ *victory* 巨大的胜利。*a* ～ *novel* 轰动一时的小说。**-ism *n*. 1.**【哲】感觉论。**2.**【伦】官能主义。**3.** (文艺上)耸人听闻的手法。**4.** 投合时好的行为。**-ist *n*. 1.** 感觉论者;官能主义者。**2.** 采用耸人听闻手法的人。**-ly *ad*.**

sen·sa·tion·al·ize [senˈseiʃənlˌaiz; sɛnˋseʃənlˏaɪz] ***vt*.** (***-ized, -iz·ing***) 使引起轰动;耸人听闻地报导[渲染]。

sense [sens; sɛns] **I *n*. 1.** 感官;官能。**2.** 感觉;知觉;…感;…心。**3.** 意念;观念;意识。**4.** 感觉器;【计】感受;读出。**5.**〔*pl*.〕理智;理性。**6.** 思考;辨别力;判断力;见识。**7.**【数】指向;向旨;方向。**8.** 意味;意义。**9.** 公众意见[情绪];舆论。*the* ～*s* = *the five* ～*s* 五官。*a sixth* ～ = *the muscular* ～ 第六官能,运动觉;〔口〕直觉。*a* ～ *of duty* 责任感。*a* ～ *of honour* 名誉心。*a* ～ *of time* 时间的观念。*the moral* ～ 道德观念。*a man of* ～ 有理智的人。*common* ～ 常识;通情达理。*good* ～ 健全的见识;明智的判断;切合实际的想法;通情达理。～ *of current* 【电】电流方向。～ *of organization* 组织性。***against all*** ～***s*** 荒谬绝伦。***be lost*** [***dead***] ***to all*** ～ ***of shame*** 全不知耻。***bring sb. to his*** ～***s*** 使某人醒悟过来。***come to one's*** ～***s*** 恢复理性;恢复知觉;苏醒过来;醒悟过来。***have a keen*** ～ ***of duty*** 责任心极强。***have more*** ～ ***than to*** = ***have too much*** ～ ***to*** 因为有头脑所以不会做…。***have no*** ～ ***of humour*** 不懂幽默。***have the*** ～ ***to*** (*do*) 有做…的头脑 (*He had not the* ～ *to do so*. 他没有这样做的脑筋)。***in all*** ～***s*** (= in every ～) 在任何一点上;在各种意义上;彻头彻尾。***in a broad*** [***narrow***] ～ 在广[狭]义上。***in a*** ～ 在某种意义上;有一点儿。***in every*** ～ = *in all* ～*s*. ***in no*** ～ 决不是。***in one's*** ～***s*** 精神正常;头脑清醒;有理智。***in some*** ～ 在某种意义上;在某种程度上。***in the direct*** ～ ***of the word*** 按照这个词的原义。***in the true*** ～ 名副其实的。***lose one's*** ～***s*** 昏过去;发痴;发疯。***make*** ～ (话等)有意义;合理;有道理;讲得通 (*What you say doesn't make* ～ *to me*. 你说的话我不能理解)。***make*** ～ ***of*** 了解[弄懂]…的意义 (*Can you make* ～ *of what she says*? 你懂得她说的是什么意思吗?)。***make*** ～ ***out of nonsense*** 弄清糊涂话的意义。***out of one's*** (***right***) ～ (神智)失常;发疯;(醉得)糊里糊涂 (*It almost frightened me out of my* ～*s*. 几乎把我魂都吓掉了)。***speak*** [***talk***] ～ 讲得有理;说有意义的话。***stand to*** ～〔口〕有道理;说得有理。***take leave of one's*** ～***s*** 精神失常;发疯。***take the*** ～ ***of*** 弄明白…的意向 (*take the* ～ *of the meeting* 问清到会群众的意见)。***talk*** ～ = speak ～. ***There is no*** [***some***] ～ ***in doing*** .... 做…是没有[有一些]道理的[意义的] (= It doesn't make ～ to do...)。**II *vt*. 1.** 感觉到;觉得;〔美口〕发觉。**2.** 了解;理会;明白。**3.**【自】自动检测。～ **antenna** 辨向天线。～ **cell** 感觉细胞。～ **centre** 感觉中枢。～ **datum** 感性材料;感性资料。～ **detector** [**finder**]【电】探向器;定向器;单值无线电测向器。～ **organ** 感(觉器)官。～ **perception** 感性知觉。～**-preserving *a*.**【拓】保向的。～ **signal** 探向信号。～ **stress** = sentense stress. ～ **winding** [**wire**]【计】读出线,读出绕组。

sense·less [ˈsenslis; ˋsɛnslɪs] ***a*. 1.** 无知觉的,无感觉的,不省人事的。**2.** 无知的;愚蠢的。**3.** 无意义的。*a* ～ *person* 糊涂虫。*a* ～ *argument* 谬论。***fall*** ～ 晕倒;失去知觉。***knock sb.*** ～ 把某人打得晕过去。**-ly *ad*.**

sen·si·bil·i·ty [ˌsensiˈbiliti; ˏsɛnsəˋbɪlətɪ] ***n*. 1.** 感性,感觉(力)。**2.** 敏感(性);灵敏度。**3.** 感受性;感光性;感光度;感度。**4.**〔常 *pl*.〕感情;(诗歌的)感伤情调。*wound sb.'s sensibilities* 伤人感情。

sen·si·ble [ˈsensəbl, -sibl; ˋsɛnsəbl] ***a*. 1.** 能感觉到的;可觉察的;明显的。**2.** 发觉;觉悟;明白;感知;知道 (*of*)。**3.** 懂事的;有常识的;通情达理的;明智的;合情合理的;有理智的;(人、方法等)聪明的。**4.** 有知觉的。**5.** (计划等)切合实际的;实用的。**6.** (数量等)相当大的。**7.**〔古〕易感的;敏感的 (*to*)。*a* ～ *change for the better* [*worse*] 显著变好[坏]。*He was* ～ *enough to mind his own business*. 他很聪明,不管别人闲事。*I'm very* ～ *of your kindness*. 我深感您的好意。～ *clothing* 实用的衣服。*a* ～ *idea* 明智的意见。*a* ～ *man* 聪明人。*a* ～ *plan* 切合实际的计划。*a* ～ *proposal* 合理的建议。*a* ～ *reduction in price* 大幅度降价。～ **heat**【物】显热 (*opp*. latent heat)。**-ness *n*.** 懂事;明智。

sen·si·bly [ˈsensəbli, -si-; ˋsɛnsəblɪ, -sɪ-] ***ad*. 1.** 能感觉到地。**2.** 显著地;明显地。**3.** 敏感地;易感觉地。**4.** 聪明地,乖巧地。

sens·ing [ˈsensiŋ; ˋsɛnsɪŋ] ***n*. 1.** 感觉。**2.**【无】测向;偏航显示;【计】读出。*remote* ～ 遥感。～ *elements* 灵敏部件。～ *units* 传感器。

sen·si·tive [ˈsensitiv; ˋsɛnsətɪv] ***a*. 1.** 有感觉的。**2.** 敏感的,感觉灵敏的;敏锐的。**3.** 易受伤的。**4.** (神经)过敏的,神经质的。**5.** 易于发生反应的。**6.** (软片等)感光的。**7.** (市场等)易波动的;易受影响的。**8.** 极机密的;极微妙的。**9.**〔罕〕感觉的;感官的。～ *faculty* 感性;感(觉)

官(能)。*a* ～ *position* 一个涉及高度机密而微妙的职位。***be*** ～ ***to*** 对…敏感,易感受…。～ ***about one's appearance*** 关心外表;注意修饰。～ **paper**【摄】感光纸。～ **plant**【植】含羞草。～ **strain**【植】敏感晶系[菌株]。**-ly** ***ad***.

sen·si·tiv·i·ty [ˌsensiˈtiviti; ˏsɛnsəˋtɪvətɪ] ***n***. **1**. 敏感(性);感受性。**2**. (仪器等的)灵敏性。**3**.【摄】感光度。

sen·si·ti·za·tion [ˌsensitaiˈzeiʃən; ˏsɛnsətaɪˋzeʃən] ***n***. **1**.【医】敏感(作用);感受(作用);致敏(感)。**2**.【物】敏化,激活。**3**.【摄】感光。

sen·si·tize [ˈsensitaiz; ˋsɛnsəˏtaɪz] ***vt***., ***vi***. **1**. (使)[变]敏感。**2**.【物】(使)敏化;激活。**3**. (使)(照相底片)具感光力;(使)(照相底片)易于感光。

sen·si·tom·e·ter [ˌsensiˈtɔmitə; ˏsɛnsəˋtɑmətə˞] ***n***.【物,摄】感光计;曝光表。

sen·sor [ˈsensə; ˋsɛnsə˞] ***n***. **1**. = sensory (***n***.). **2**.【自】感受器;传感器;灵敏元件,控制仪板上显示温度、辐射量等变动的装置。

sen·so·ri·al [ˈsenˈsɔːriəl; sɛnˋsorɪəl] ***a***. = sensory (***a***.)

sen·so·ri·mo·tor [ˌsensəriˈməutə; ˏsɛnsərɪˋmotə˞] ***a***.【生理,心】感觉运动的。

sen·so·ri·um [senˈsɔːriəm; sɛnˋsorɪəm] ***n***. (*pl*. ～*s*, *-ri·a* [-riə; -rɪə]) **1**.【解】感觉中枢。**2**.【医】意识;(整个人体的)感官系统。

sen·so·ry [ˈsensəri; ˋsɛnsərɪ] **I** ***a***. **1**. 感觉(上)的。**2**.【生理】感官的;知觉器官的。**II** ***n***. 感觉器官〔又作 ～ organs〕。

sen·su·al [ˈsensjuəl; ˋsɛnʃuəl] ***a***. **1**. 肉体(上)的;官能的。**2**. 肉欲的。**3**. 色情的;淫荡的;肉感的;耽于肉欲的。**4**.【哲】感觉论的。*a* ～ *attraction* [*charm*] 肉欲上的吸引力。～ *appetites* 肉欲。～ *pleasures* 肉体[官能]上的快乐。*a* ～ *person* 好色之徒。**-ism** ***n***. **1**.【哲】感觉论。**2**.【美】官能主义。**3**.【伦】纵欲主义。**4**. 肉欲主义;好色。**-ist** **1**.【哲】感觉论者。**2**. 肉欲主义者;纵欲者;好色者。**-ly** ***ad***. **-ness** ***n***.

sen·su·al·i·ty [ˌsensjuˈæliti; ˏsɛnʃuˋælətɪ] ***n***. **1**. 纵欲;淫荡;好色。**2**. 感觉性;感能。

sen·su·al·ize [ˈsensjuəlaiz; ˋsɛnʃuəlˏaɪz] ***vt***. 使荒淫;使耽于声色。

sen·su·ous [ˈsensjuəs; ˋsɛnʃuəs] ***a***. **1**. 感觉(上)的;感官的。**2**. 敏感的。**3**. 官能享受的;(引起)美感的;审美的。★ 与 sensual 不同之处在于它不含丑恶意义。

sen·sur·round [sensəˈraund; sɛnsəˋraʊnd] ***n***. (一座电影院内的)现场包围音响。

sent [sent; sɛnt] send 的过去式及过去分词。***be*** ～ ***down south***〔美〕被送进监狱。***be*** ～ ***off in disgrace*** 碰一鼻子灰走了。***be*** ～ ***to the showers***〔美〕在比赛中被替换下场。

sen·tence [ˈsentəns; ˋsɛntəns] **I** ***n***. **1**.【法】宣判;判决。**2**. 判刑。**3**.【语法】句(子)。**4**.【逻】命题。**5**.【乐】乐句。**6**.【生化】句〔构成基因的核苷酸三联密码或密码子的序列〕。**7**.〔古〕名言;格言。*a* ～ *of death* 死刑。*a dark* ～ 难懂的文句。***pass*** ～ ***upon*** [***on***] ***sb***. 对某人判刑。***serve a*** ～ 服刑。***under*** ～ ***of*** 被判决;受…宣判。**II** ***vt***. 宣判;判决;处刑。*be* ～*d to death* 被判处死刑。*be* ～*d for theft* 因盗窃罪被判刑。～ **stress** [**accent**] 句子的重音。～ **word** 相当于句子的单词〔Come! Certainly, 等〕。

sen·ten·tial [senˈtenʃəl; sɛnˋtɛnʃl̩] ***a***. **1**.【法】判决的;判断的。**2**.【语法】句子的。*a* ～ *analysis* 句子分析。*a* ～ *pause* 句的停顿。

sen·ten·tious [senˈtenʃəs; sɛnˋtɛnʃəs] ***a***. **1**. 格言(多)的;警句(多)的。**2**. 简洁的。**3**. (故作)庄重的;说教式的。*a* ～ ***essayist*** 爱用警句的杂文家。**-ly** ***ad***. **-ness** ***n***.

sen·tience, -en·cy [ˈsenʃəns, -si; ˋsɛnʃəns, -sɪ] ***n***. **1**. 感觉力[性];知觉(能)力。**2**. 感觉;知觉。**3**. 直觉;单纯的感性。

sen·tient [ˈsenʃənt; ˋsɛnʃənt] **I** ***a***. **1**. 感觉的;知觉的。**2**. 有感觉[知觉]力的。～ *cells* 感觉细胞。**II** ***n***.〔罕〕**1**. 有知觉[感觉(力)]的人[物]。**2**. 意识;心 (= mind)。

sen·ti·ment [ˈsentimənt; ˋsɛntəmənt] ***n***. **1**. (思想)感情;情操。**2**.【艺术】情趣;情感。**3**. 情绪。**4**. 感情上的弱点;感伤。**5**.〔常 *pl*.〕意见;观点。**6**. 感想;简短的致词。*patriotic* ～ 爱国心。*hostile* ～*s* 敌意。*a man of* ～ 感情用事的人。*a man of tender* [*noble*] ～ 多愁善感[情操高尚]的人。*general* ～ 一般意见;舆论。*These are my* ～*s*. =〔谑〕*Them's my* ～*s*. 这就是我的想法。***ascertain sb.'s*** ～***s on*** [***regarding***] …查明(某人)对于…的意见。***free from*** ～ 不带感伤情绪;不夹杂个人好恶。***give*** [***propose***] ***a*** ～ 发表感想。***run to*** ～***s*** 感情用事。

sen·ti·men·tal [ˌsentiˈmentl; ˏsɛntəˋmɛntl̩] ***a***. **1**. 感情的;情绪的;情操的。**2**. 感情用事的;多愁善感的;感伤的;充满柔情的;动情的。*a* ～ *girl* 多愁善感的姑娘。*a* ～ *drunkard* 酒后易动感情的人。～ *considerations* [*motives*] 人情;情面。*a* ～ *patriot* 慷慨悲歌之士。*strike a* ～ *note* (演讲等时)作出感情激动的姿态。～ **damage**【保险】推定损害。**-ism** ***n***. **1**. 感情主义;感伤主义。**2**. 多愁善感;故作多情。**3**. 感情用事的言行;牢骚。**-ist** ***n***. 感情主义者;感伤主义者;多愁善感的人;故作多情的人;感情用事的人。**-ly** ***ad***.

sen·ti·men·tal·i·ty [ˌsentimenˈtæliti; sɛntəmɛnˋtælətɪ] ***n***. **1**. 感伤性;多愁善感;柔情。**2**. 故作多情。

sen·ti·men·tal·ize [ˌsentiˈmentəlaiz; ˏsɛntəˋmɛntl̩ˏaɪz] ***vi***. (*-ized*, *-izing*) 伤感;感伤地想;感伤地行事。～ *over* [*about*] *the past* 思往事而伤感。—***vt***. **1**. 使伤感;使有感情。**2**. 对…伤感;感伤地看待[处理]。**-zation** ***n***.

sen·ti·mo [ˈsentimou; ˋsɛntɪmo] ***n***. **1**. 分〔菲律宾辅币单位〕。**2**. (菲律宾的)一分硬币。

sen·ti·nel [ˈsentinl; ˋsɛntənl̩] **I** ***n***. **1**. 哨兵;步哨。**2**. 看守人。*post* [*station*] *a* ～ 放(步)哨;设看守(人)。***stand*** ～ (***over***) 站岗;放哨;守卫。**II** ***vt***. (*-ll-*) **1**. 在…设岗哨。**2**. 警戒,守卫。

sen·try [ˈsentri; ˋsɛntrɪ] **I** ***n***.【军】**1**. 哨兵;岗哨;步哨。**2**. 看守,警卫。**3**.〔古〕望楼。*a* ～ *on colours* 军旗卫兵。***be on*** ～ 站岗,看守。***come off*** ～ 下岗;交班;退哨。***go on*** ～ 上岗;接班;上哨。***keep*** ～ 警备;***post on*** ～ 放步哨,使上哨。***relieve a*** ～ 换哨;换班;换防。***stand*** ～ 站岗;看守;放哨。**II** ***vt***. (*-tried*) 在…设岗哨。—***vi***. 站岗,放哨。～ **box** **1**. 哨房;岗亭。**2**.【无】调谐部分。～ **duty** 步哨勤务。～ **go** **1**. 步哨勤务;步哨线。**2**. 换哨命令。

Se·nus·si, Se·nu·si [siˈnuːsi; sɪˋnusɪ] ***n***. (*pl*. *-si*) 北非穆斯林的一个战斗性同道会(的会员)。**-si·an** ***a***.

sen·za [ˈsentsə; ˋsɛntsɑ] *prep*.〔It.〕〔略 s.〕【乐】无。～ ***sordino*** 无弱音器。～ ***stromenti*** 无乐器地。～ ***tempo*** 不拘节拍地。

s.e.o.o. =〔F.〕sauf erreur ou omission 错误遗漏不在此限。

Se·oul [səul; sol] ***n***. 汉城〔韩国首都〕。

sep. = **1**. sepal. **2**. separate. **3**. septic.

Sep. = September.

sep·al [ˈsepəl, ˈsiːpl; ˋsipl̩, ˋsɛpl̩] ***n***.【植】萼片。

se·pal·oid [ˈsiːplˌɔid; ˋsipəlˏɔɪd] ***a***.【植】萼片状的 (= sepaline)。

sep·a·ra·bil·i·ty [ˌsepərəˈbiliti; ˏsɛpərəˋbɪlətɪ] ***n***. 可分(离)性。

sep·a·ra·ble [ˈsepərəbl; ˋsɛpərəbl̩] ***a***. 可分(离)的;可分隔的;可分开的(*from*; *into*; *between*)。**-bly** ***ad***.

sep·a·rate[1] [ˈsepəreit; ˋsɛpəˏret] ***vt***. **1**. 分;分开;分离;隔开;隔离;切断;割断。**2**. 区别;分别;识别。**3**. 使脱离关系;使分居。**4**. 开革;开除;遣散;使退役。**5**.【化】离析,从…中提取。～ *milk* 提取奶油。***be*** ～***d by*** 被…隔

S

断。**be ～d from** 和…分离开;和…分散。～ **into** 分离成。—*vi*. 1. 分开;离开;分离;脱离。2. (公司等)解散。3. 分居。4.【化】离析,析出。

sep·a·rate² [ˈseprit; ˋsɛmprɪt] **I** *a*. 1. 分开的;分离的(*from*)。2. 各别的;各自的;各个的;单独的;独立的,不相连的。3. 分别开的;分居的。4. 离开肉体的。*a book in three ～ volumes* 分为三卷的书。～ *houses* 独立式房舍。**II** *n*. 1. (杂志论文的)抽印本;单行本。2. 〔*pl*.〕可以不配套单独穿的妇女服装。3. 分开的事物。～ **estate** [**property**] (妻子的)独有财产。～ **maintenance** (夫妻分居后妻子的)赡养费。～ **school** (加拿大的)非公立学校(尤指天主教学校)。**-ly** *ad*.

sep·a·ra·tion [ˌsepəˈreiʃən; ˏsɛpəˋreʃən] *n*. 1. 分离;分类;分开。2. 隔开;间隔;脱离。3. (夫妇的)分居。4. 分隔物。5.【化】离析;析出;释出。6.【矿】分选。7.【电】(导线的)间距;间隙。8.【海】(装货的)隔票垫料。9.【地】(断层引起的)离距。～ *of powers* (政府)权能的分立。*contact* ～【电】接点间隙。*judicial* ～【法】(法庭判定的)夫妇分居。～ **allowance** (政府给出征军人家属的)分居津贴。～ **centre**【军】复员转业中心。～ **coal** 精选煤。～ **energy**【物】结合能。～ **pay** 遣散费。**-ist** *n*. = separatist.

sep·a·ra·tism [ˈsepərətizəm; ˋsɛpərəˏtɪzəm] *n*. 1. (政治、宗教上的)分离主义;脱离主义。2. 分离;分裂;脱离;隔离。*feudal* ～ 封建割据。**-tist** *n*. 1. 分离主义者。2. 脱离国教的人。3. 主张独立[自治]者。

sep·a·ra·tive [ˈsepərətiv; ˋsɛpəˏretɪv] *a*. 1. 倾向分离的;分离(性)的。2.【动、植】区别性的。3. 区别的;分别的。

sep·a·ra·tor [ˈsepəreitə; ˋsɛpəˏretə] *n*. 1. 分离者。2. 分离器;液体分离器;分液器;离析器;脱脂器。3. (蓄电池的)隔板。4. 分离片;垫圈;隔离物;隔片。5.【矿】分选机。6. (数据项目)分隔标志。*an electric* ～ 滤波器。

sep·a·ra·to·ry [ˈsepərətəri; ˋsɛpərəˏtorɪ] *a*. 使分离的;分离用的;离析用的。*a* ～ *funnel* 分液漏斗。

Se·phard [siˈfɑːd; sɪˋfɑrd] *n*. = Sephardi.

Se·phar·di [seˈfɑːdi; sɪˋfɑrdi] *n*. (*pl*. *-dim* [-dim; -dɪm]) 西班牙[葡萄牙]籍的犹太人(的后裔)。**-dic** *a*.

se·pi·a [ˈsiːpjə; ˋsipɪə] **I** *n*. (*pl*. ～*s*, *-pi·ae* [-piiː; -pɪi]) 1.【动】乌贼;〔S-〕乌贼属。2. 乌贼的墨汁;乌贼墨色;深褐色。3. 用乌贼墨制成的深褐色颜料[墨水];用乌贼墨颜料[墨水]绘制的画。**II** *a*. 乌贼墨的;深棕色的;深褐色的。

se·pi·o·lite [ˈsiːpiəlait; ˋsipɪəˏlaɪt] *n*.【矿】海泡石。

se·poy [ˈsiːpɔi; ˋsipɔɪ] *n*. 旧时英国军队中的印度兵。

sep·pu·ku [seˈpuːkuː; ˏsɛpˋpuku] *n*. 〔日〕切腹自杀。

sep·sis [ˈsepsis; ˋsɛpsɪs] *n*.【医】1. 腐败;腐败作用;败血。2. 脓毒病;败血症。

sept [sept; sɛpt] *n*. 1. 氏族。2. (爱尔兰或苏格兰)氏族。

Sept. = 1. September. 2. Septuagint.

sept-, septa-, septem-, septi- *comb. f*. 七: *sept*angle, *septem*partite.

sep·ta [ˈseptə; ˋsɛptə] *n*. septum 的复数。

sep·tal¹ [ˈseptl; ˋsɛptl̩] *a*. 氏族 (sept) 的。

sep·tal² [ˈseptl; ˋsɛptl̩] *a*.【生】中隔 (septum) 的;隔膜的;芽胞壁的。

sep·tan [ˈseptən; ˋsɛptən] *a*.【医】每七天复发一次的。～ **fever**【医】七日热。

sep·tan·gle [ˈseptæŋgl; ˋsɛpˏtæŋgl̩] *n*. 七角形,七边形。

sep·tan·gu·lar [sepˈtæŋgjulə; sɛpˋtæŋgjələ] *a*. 七角(形)的,七边(形)的。

sep·tar·i·um [sepˈtɛəriəm; sɛpˋtærɪəm] *n*. (*pl*. *-i·a* [-ə; -ə])【矿】龟背石;裂心结核;核桃心结核。**-tar·i·an** *a*.

sep·tate [ˈsepteit; ˋsɛptet] *a*.【生】有中隔[隔膜]的;分隔的。

Sep·tem·ber [sepˈtembə, səp-; sɛpˋtɛmbə] *n*. 九月。

sep·tem·par·ti·te [ˌseptemˈpɑːtait; ˏsɛptɛmˋpɑrtaɪt] *a*. 1. 由七部分组成的;分成七部分的。2.【植】七深裂的;七裂的。

sep·te·na·ry [sepˈtiːnəri; ˋsɛptəˏnɛrɪ] **I** *a*. 1. 七的;七个的;由七个组成的;以七为基础的。2. 乘[除]以七的。3. 七进制的。4. 七年一次的;为期七年的;七年一度的。**II** *n*. 1. 七;七个。2. 七年间。3. 七进制。4. 七个一套;七个一组。5.【诗】七音步的诗行。

sep·ten·nate [sepˈtenit; sɛpˋtɛnet] *n*. 1. 七年;七年期间;为期七年。2. 七年的任期。

sep·ten·ni·al [sepˈtennjəl, -niəl; sɛpˋtɛnɪəl] *a*. 1. 七年的;每七年的;七年一次的。2. 继续七年的。**-ly** *ad*.

sep·ten·tri·o·nal [sepˈtentriənl; sɛpˋtɛntrɪənl] *a*. 〔古〕1. 北方的;北部的。2. 来自北方的。3. 北风的。

Sep·ten·tri·o·nes [septentriˈəuniːz; septɛntrɪˋoniz] *n*. 北斗七星;大熊座。

sep·tette, 〔美〕 **sep·tet** [sepˈtet; sɛpˋtɛt] *n*. 1. 七人小组;七人一组;七个一组。2.【乐】七重奏[唱],七部合奏[唱]曲。

sept·foil [ˈseptfɔil; ˋsɛptˏfɔɪl] *n*. 1. 七叶形饰物〔尤指天主教七种圣物的象征〕。2.【建筑】七叶形。3.【植】直立委陵菜。

sep·tic [ˈseptik; ˋsɛptɪk] **I** *a*.【医】1. 脓毒性的;败血症的。2. 腐败性的;使[致]腐败的;使[致]败血的。**II** *n*. 引起腐败的东西;腐败物。～ **poisoning** 腐败物中毒;败血症。～ **tank** 化粪池。

sep·ti·cae·mi·a, 〔美〕 **-ce·mi·a** [ˌseptiˈsiːmiə; ˏsɛptəˋsimɪə] *n*.【医】败血症。**-cae·mic** *a*.

sep·ti·ci·dal [ˌseptiˈsaidl; ˏsɛptəˋsaɪdl̩] *a*.【植】室间开裂的。**-ly** *ad*.

sep·tif·ra·gal [sepˈtifrəgəl; sɛpˈtɪfrəgəl] *a*.【植】胞轴开裂的。**-ly** *ad*.

sep·ti·lat·er·al [ˌseptiˈlætərəl; ˏsɛptɪˋlætərəl] *a*. 七边(形)的;七面的。

sep·til·lion [sepˈtiljən; sɛpˋtɪljən] *num*. 〔英〕100 万的 7 乘方[7 次幂]〔1 后有 42 个 0 的数〕;〔法,美〕1,000 的 8 乘方[8 次幂]〔1 后有 24 个 0 的数〕。

sep·ti·mal [ˈseptiməl; ˋsɛptɪməl] *a*. 七的。

sep·time [ˈseptiːm; ˋsɛptim] *n*.【剑】(八种防御姿势中的)第七个姿势。

sep·tu·a·ge·nar·i·an [ˌseptjuədʒiˈnɛəriən; ˏsɛptʃuədʒəˋnɛrɪən], **sep·tu·ag·e·na·ry** [-ˈdʒiːnəri; -ˋædʒəˏnɛrɪ] *a*., *n*. 七十岁的(人);七十至八十岁的(人)。

Sep·tu·a·ges·i·ma [ˌseptjuəˈdʒesimə; ˏsɛptʃuəˋdʒɛsəmə] *n*.【宗】四旬斋〔Lent〕前的第三个星期日(亦作 Septuagesima Sunday)。

Sep·tu·a·gint [ˈseptjuədʒint; ˋsɛptʃuəˏdʒɪnt] *n*. 希腊文《旧约全书》〔相传公元前三世纪(270 年)七十二位犹太学者于亚历山大用七十二日译成〕。

sep·tum [ˈseptəm; ˋsɛptəm] *n*. (*pl*. *-ta* [-tə; -tə])【解、动、植】隔壁;中隔;隔膜;芽胞壁;胞片;(珊瑚的)隔片。

sep·tu·ple [ˈseptjupl; ˋsɛptʊpl̩] **I** *n*., *a*. 七倍(的);七的。**II** *vt*. 以七倍之;用七乘;使变成七倍。

sep·tu·plet [sepˈtʌplit, -ˈtjuːplit, -ˈtuː-; sɛpˋtʌplɪt, -ˋtuplɪt, -ˋtu-] *n*. 1. 一胎七个中的一个。2. (同样的)七个一组。3. 七胞胎[用作复数]。

sep·ul·cher [ˈsepəlkə; ˋsɛpəlkə] *n*. 〔美〕= sepulchre.

se·pul·chral [siˈpʌlkrəl; səˋpʌlkrəl] *a*. 1. 坟墓的。2. 葬礼的。3. 阴森的;阴沉的。*a* ～ *monument* 墓碑。*a* ～ *mound* 冢。*a* ～ *stone* 墓石,墓碑。*a* ～ *voice* 阴[低]沉的声音。

sep·ul·chre [ˈsepəlkə; ˋsɛpl̩kə] **I** *n*. (尤指石岩凿成的)坟墓;地下坟墓;冢。*the* ～ *of one's hopes* 〔喻〕绝望。***the whited*** ～ 伪君子;伪善者;虚有其表的人〔见《圣经》"马太福音"〕。***the Holy*** ～【宗】圣墓;耶稣墓。**II** *vt*.

S

埋葬。

sep·ul·ture [ˈsepəltʃə; ˋsɛpl̩tʃɚ] 〔古〕 *n*. 1. 埋葬。2. 坟墓;墓地。

seq. = 1. sequel. 2. sequence. 3. squentes; sequentia 〔L. = the following〕.

se·qua·cious [siˈkweiʃəs; sɪˋkweʃəs] *a*. 1. 随从的;顺从的;盲从的,附和的。2. 缺乏独创精神的。3. 〔喻〕奴性的。4. 〔罕〕(论证等)推论上有条不紊的;合乎逻辑推论的;前后一贯的。**-ly** *ad*. **se·quac·i·ty** [siˈkwæsiti; sɪˋkwæsətɪ] *n*.

se·quel [ˈsiːkwəl; ˋsikwəl] *n*. 1. 继续,后续。2. 后果;结果;结局。3. 续集;续篇。4. 〔罕〕推论。*the ~ of a novel* 小说的续篇。***as a ~ to* [*of*]** 作为…的后果;由于…结果。***in the ~*** 结果;到后来。**-ize** *vi*. (作品等)写续篇;(电影等)拍续集。

se·que·la [siˈkwiːlə; sɪˋkwilə] *n*. (*pl*. *-lae* [-liː; -li]) 1. 〔常 *pl*.〕【医】后遗症;续发症;后发病;遗患。2. 结果;后果。

se·quence [ˈsiːkwəns; ˋsikwəns] *n*. 1. 继续;接续;连续。2. 顺序;程序;次第;关系;关联。3. 后果;结果;接着发生的事;后事;后文。4. 【数】数列;序列;数贯。5. 【无、计】指令序列;定序。6. 【计】顺序机〔将信息项目排成顺序的机器〕。7. 【乐】用不同音调反复演奏一组乐句。8. 【天主】宣讲福音前唱的圣歌。9. 【牌】顺。10. 【影】(描述同一主题的)连续镜头;片断,插曲;场景。*a logical ~* 条理;逻辑顺序。*a causal* [*physical*] *~* 因果关系。*the natural ~ to* [*for*] *folly* 愚笨行为的必然结果。***in rapid ~*** 一个接着一个;紧接着。***in regular ~*** 挨次;按次序;逐一;有条不紊地。***in ~*** 挨次;顺次;逐一。***~ of tenses***【语法】时态的配合[接续,呼应]。**~-controlled** 程序控制的。

se·quent [ˈsiːkwənt; ˋsikwənt] I *a*. 1. 继续的;连续的;随着…而发生的 (*on*; *upon*; *to*)。2. 继起的;继承的。3. 结果的。*a ~ order* 连续的顺序。*a ~ king* 继位的国王。II *n*. 接着发生的事;后果;结果。**-ly** *ad*.

se·quen·tes [siˈkwentiːz; sɪˋkwentiz] ***se·quen·ti·a*** [-ʃiə; -ʃɪə] 〔L.〕以下 (= the following)。★ 略作 Seq. 或 Seqq., 用于引文页数[章数、行数]之后,其前常加用 et (= &): *P*. 10 (*et*) *seq*(*q*) 第十页以下。

se·quen·tial [siˈkwenʃəl; sɪˋkwenʃəl] I *a*. 1. 继续的;连续的;随着…而发生的 (*to*)。2. 结果的。3. 〔美俚〕(避孕丸)按期服食的。II *n*. 〔*pl*.〕〔美俚〕按期服食的避孕丸。**~ analysis**【统计】序列分析。**~ circuit**【电】程序电路。**-ly** *ad*.

se·ques·ter [siˈkwestə; sɪˋkwestɚ] I *vt*. 1. 使分开;使隔离;使退隐。2. 【法】扣押;没收;查封 (= sequestrate)。3. 【国际法】接收;扣押(敌产)。*~ oneself from the world* 退隐。II *vi*. 弃权;【法】(遗孀)放弃(对亡夫财产等的)要求。III *n*. 【化】螯合剂,金属封锁剂。**~ed** *a*. 退隐的;(人、生活孤独的);(房子等)僻静的。

se·ques·trant [siˈkwestrənt; sɪˋkwestrənt] *n*. 【化】多价螯合作用。

se·ques·trate [siˈkwestreit; sɪˋkwɛstret] *vt*. 【法】1. 查封;没收。2. 假扣押,把…暂交第三者保管;暂行保管(有争议物)。3. 〔古〕隔离,分离。**-tra·ble** *a*. 1. 可查封的;可扣押的;可没收的。2. 〔古〕可隔离的;可分离的。

se·ques·tra·tion [siˌkwesˈtreiʃən; sɪˏkwɛsˋtreʃən] *n*. 1. 隐退;隐居。2. 【法】假扣押;假执行;暂时查封;没收;争执物的保管。3. 〔古〕分隔,分开。4. 【化】多价螯合作用。

se·ques·tra·tor [ˈsiːkwestreitə; ˋsikwɛsˏtretɚ] *n*. 1. 【法】财产查封人;没收者。2. 有争议财产的暂行保管人。

se·ques·trum [siˈkwestrəm; sɪˋkwɛstrəm] *n*. (*pl*. ~, *-tra* [-trə; -trə]) 【医】腐骨片;坏骨片;死骨片。

se·quin [ˈsiːkwin; ˋsikwɪn] *n*. 1. 古代威尼斯[马耳他、土耳其]的金币名。2. 装饰衣服用的圆形小金属片。

se·quoi·a [siˈkwɔiə; sɪˋkwɔɪə] *n*. 【植】红杉〔又称 redwood〕; 〔S-〕红杉属。**S- National Park** 美国国家加州红杉公园〔以其高大的红杉著称〕。

ser. = 1. serial. 2. series. 3. service. 4. sermon.

ser [siə; sɪr] *n*. 西阿〔印度重量单位, 2.057 磅〕(= seer)。

se·ra [ˈsiərə; ˋsɪrə] *n*. serum 的复数。

se·rac [ˈseræk; seˋrak] *n*. 〔常 *pl*.〕【地】冰雪柱;冰塔。

se·ragl·io [seˈrɑːliəu; sɪˋræljo] *n*. (*pl*. *~s*) 1. (伊斯兰教国家的)后宫;闺房。2. (一群)妻,妾。3. 〔the (old) S-〕【史】(土耳其)宫廷。

se·ra·i [seˈrɑːi, -ˈrei; səˋraɪ] *n*. (*pl*. *~s*) 1. (伊朗等国家的)旅店;(队商)客栈。2. (土耳其等伊斯兰教国家的)宫殿;后宫。

ser·al [ˈsiərəl; ˋsɪrəl] *a*. 【生态】演替系列的。

ser·al·bu·min [sirəlˈbjumin; sɪrəlˋbjumɪn] *n*. 【生化】血清蛋白。

se·rang [səˈræŋ; səˋræŋ] *n*. 〔英印〕(东印度的)水手长。

se·ra·pe [səˈrɑːpi; seˋrapɪ] *n*. 〔美〕(拉丁美洲人的)披肩毛毯;披身毛毯。

ser·aph [ˈserəf; ˋserəf] *n*. (*pl*. *~s*, *-a·phim* [-im; -ɪm]) 1. 【宗】六翼天使〔最高位天使〕。2. (《圣经》旧约)撒拉弗。**-ic**, **-i·cal** *a*. [seˈræfik(əl); səˋræfɪk(əl)] 天使般的;纯洁的。

Serb [səːb; sɝb] I *a*. 塞尔维亚(人)的;塞尔维亚语的。II *n*. 1. 塞尔维亚人。2. 塞尔维亚语。

Ser·bia [ˈsəːbjə, -biə; ˋsɝbɪə] *n*. 塞尔维亚〔前南斯拉夫一地区〕。

Ser·bi·an [ˈsəːbjən, -biən; ˋsɝbɪən] *a*., *n*. = Serb.

Ser·bo-cro·a·tian [ˌsəːbəukrəuˈeiʃən; ˏsɝbokroˋeʃən] I *n*. 塞尔维亚—克罗地亚语[人]。II *a*. 塞尔维亚—克罗地亚语的;塞尔维亚—克罗地亚人的。

Ser·bo·ni·an [səːˈbəunjən, -niən; sɝˋbonɪən] *a*. 古埃及塞波尼斯 (Serbonis) 大沼泽的。**~ bog** 1. (旧时尼罗河三角洲与苏伊士运河之间的)危险的沼泽。2. 困境;绝境。

sere[1] [siə; sɪr] *a*. 〔诗〕干枯的 (= sear)。

sere[2] [siə; sɪr] *n*. 【生】植生系列;演替系列。

se·rein [səˈræŋ; səˋræŋ] *n*. 〔F.〕【气】(热带地方日落后晴空落下的)晴空雨。

ser·e·nade [ˌseriˈneid; ˏserəˋned] I *n*. 【乐】1. 小夜曲。2. = serenata 2. II *vt*., *vi*. (对…)唱[奏]小夜曲。*~ one's ladylove* 对情人唱[奏]小夜曲。**-r** *n*.

ser·e·na·ta [ˈseriˈnɑːtə; ˏserəˋnatə] *n*. (*pl*. *~s*, *-te* [-te; -te]) 【乐】1. 合唱剧。2. (介乎组曲与交响乐之间的)多乐章器乐曲。

ser·en·dip·i·ty [ˌserənˈdipiti; ˏserənˋdɪpətɪ] *n*. 易于偶然发现珍宝的运气〔源出英国作家 H. Walpole 所著童话 *The Three Princes of Serendip*〕。

se·rene [siˈriːn; səˋrin] I *a*. 1. 清澈的;晴朗的;(天空等)明朗的。2. (海、生活等)宁静的;安定的;(一生等)没有风波的。3. 沉着的;(性情)沉静的;(人、脸色、性格等)安详的。4. 〔S-〕殿下〔欧洲大陆对王公的尊称,说作 *His S- Highness*, *Your S- Highness* 等〕。II *n*. 〔诗、古〕晴朗(天空);平静(的海)。III *vt*. 〔诗〕使(海、脸色等)平静;宁静;使(天空)明朗。***All ~!*** 〔俚〕百事顺利;一切都好。***the ~ drop = the drop ~***【医】黑蒙。

se·ren·i·ty [siˈreniti; səˋrenətɪ] *n*. 1. 晴朗。2. 宁静;平静。3. 安详;从容。4. 〔S-〕殿下。*His S-* = His Serene Highness.

serf [səːf; sɝf] *n*. 1. 农奴。2. 奴隶。3. 像奴隶一样的人。

serf·age [ˈsəːfidʒ; ˋsɝfɪdʒ] *n*. = serfdom.

serf·dom [ˈsəːfdəm; ˋsɝfdəm] *n*. 1. 农奴身分;农奴的境遇[地位]。2. 农奴制。3. 奴役。

serf·hood [ˈsəːfhud; ˋsɝfˏhud] *n*. 1. 〔总称〕农奴;奴隶。2. = serfdom.

Serg(t)【军】= sergeant.

serge [səːdʒ; sɝdʒ] *n*. (粗)哔叽。*~ cloth* 哔叽呢。

ser·gean·cy [ˈsɑːdʒənsi; ˋsardʒənsɪ] *n*. 军士等 (sergeant) 的职位。

ser·geant [ˈsɑːdʒənt; ˋsɑrdʒənt] ***n*.** **1.**【军】军士;(英陆军、空军、海军陆战队;美陆军、海军陆战队)中士。**2.** 警官,巡官。**3.**【英史】(在皇家法庭具有特权的)高级律师。**4.** 〔S-〕〔美〕一种地对地导弹。***colour*** ~ (英海军陆战队)上士。***master*** ~ (美陆军[空军、海军陆战队])军士长。~ ***at arms*** =〔英〕serjeant-at-arms, (议会、法院等的)卫士。***staff*** ~ (英陆军)上士;(美空军)参谋军士。***technical*** ~ (美空军[海军陆战队])技术军士。~**-at-law**【英史】(在皇家法庭具有特权的)高级律师。~ **aviation** (军士级)航空长。~ **first** [**1st**] ***class*** (美陆军)上士。~ **fish**【动】**1.** 军曹鱼(属)。**2.** 军曹鱼(科)。~ **major** 军士长。~**-ship** = sergeancy.

se·ri·al [ˈsiəriəl; ˋsɪrɪəl] **I** ***a*.** **1.** 连续的;一连串的;一系列的。**2.** 按期出版的;(小说等)连载的;连续刊行的;连续广播的。**3.** 分期偿付的。**4.**【计】中行的;串联的。*a* ~ *number* **1.** 序号;编号。**2.**【军】军号;入伍编号。*a* ~ *publication* 陆续出版的成套出版物。*a* ~ *story* 连载小说。~ *rights* 连续刊载的版权。**II** ***n*.** **1.** 连载小说;连续广播;连续电视;连本影片。**2.** 定期刊物。**3.**【军】行军梯队。***in*** ~ ***order*** 顺次。***write in*** ~***s*** 写连载小说(等)。~**-access memory**【计】串行存取存储器。~ **killer** 连续杀人犯;连环杀手。

se·ri·al·ism [ˈsiəriəlizəm; ˋsɪrɪəlɪzəm] ***n*.**【乐】十二音阶体系;十二音阶体系作曲技法;序列音系理论。**se·ri·al·ist** ***n*.**

se·ri·al·ize [ˈsiəriəlaiz; ˋsɪrɪəlˏaɪz] ***vt*.** (***-iz·ed***; ***-iz·ing***) **1.** 使连续。**2.** 连载;连续出版;分集[分期]顺次出版。**-za·tion** [-ˈzeiʃən; -ˋzeʃən] ***n*.**

se·ri·al·ly [ˈsiəriəli; ˋsɪrɪəlɪ] ***ad*.** 顺次;连续(地);连续登载(地)。*The novel will appear* ~. 这篇小说将连续登载。

se·ri·ate [ˈsiəriit; ˋsɪrɪɪt] **I** ***a*.** **1.** 顺序的;连续的。**2.**【植】轮的;列的;层的。**II** [ˈsiərieit; ˋsɪrɪˏet] ***vt*.** (按)顺序排列,使连续。**-ly** ***ad*.**

se·ri·a·tim [ˌsiəriˈeitim; ˏsɪrɪˋetɪm] ***a*.**, ***ad*.** 〔L.〕连续(地);顺次(地);逐一[条](地)。*discuss* ~ 逐条讨论。

se·ri·a·tion [ˌsiəriˈeiʃən; ˏsɪrɪˋeʃən] ***n*.** 顺次排列。

Ser·ic [ˈserik, ˈsiərik; ˋsɛrɪk, ˋsɪrɪk] ***a*.** **1.** 〔古、诗〕= Chinese 2. 〔s-〕**2.** 丝绸的;丝制的。

ser·i·cate, ser·i·cat·ed, se·ri·ceous [ˈserikt, -keitid, siˈriʃəs; ˋsɛrəkɪt, -ketɪd, sɪˋrɪʃəs] ***a*.** **1.** 丝(状)的;像丝的。**2.**【动,植】有丝状柔毛的;有绢毛的;有丝光的。

ser·i·cin [ˈserisin; ˋsɛrəsɪn] ***n*.**【纺】丝胶蛋白。

ser·i·cite [ˈserisait; ˋsɛrɪˏsaɪt] ***n*.**【矿】丝[绢]云母。

ser·i(ci)·cul·tur·al [ˌseri(si)ˈkʌltʃərəl; ˏsɛrɪ(sɪ)ˋkʌltʃərəl] ***a*.** 养蚕的;蚕丝业的。

ser·i·(ci)cul·ture [ˈseri(si)kʌltʃə; ˋsɛrɪ(sɪ)ˏkʌltʃɚ] ***n*.** 养蚕;养蚕业。

ser·i·(ci)cul·tur·ist [ˌseri(si)ˈkʌltʃərist; ˏsɛrɪ(sɪ)ˋkʌltʃərɪst] ***n*.** 养蚕家;蚕丝(业)者。

ser·i·e·ma [ˌseriˈiːmə, -ˈeimə; ˏsɛrɪˋimə, -eˋmə] ***n*.**【动】叫鹤。

se·ries [ˈsiəriːz; ˋsɪrɪz] ***n*.** 〔*sing*., *pl*.〕**1.** 连续;系列。**2.** 套;辑;丛刊;丛书。**3.**【生】区;族。**4.**【植】轮;列;层;系。**5.**【动】列;组。**6.**【数】级数。**7.**【化】系;系列;组。**8.**【电】串联 (*opp*. parallel)。**9.**【地】统;(岩系的)段。**10.**【乐】音列。**11.**【商】货物分类法。**12.**【美体】由同队进行的一连串比赛。**13.**【语音】一组交替元音〔如 *sing*, *sang*, *sung*〕。*a* ~ (*of books*) 丛书。*the first* ~ 第一辑。*a* ~ *of victories* 连战连胜。*a* ~ *of misfortunes* 一连串的不幸。*a* ~ *of years* 连年。*an arithmetical* [*a geometrical*] ~ 等差[等比]级数。*a* ~ *and parallel circuit* 混联电路。*a* ~ *circuit* 串联电路。***a*** ~ ***of*** 一系列;许多。***in*** ~ **1.** 连续;逐次。**2.** 按顺序排列。**3.** 作为丛书。【电】成串联;串联的。***in*** ~ ***with*** 与…串联;与…相连。***round robin*** ~【运】循环赛。~ **aiding** (线线圈等的)正向串联;相助串联。~ **dynamo** [**generator**] 串激发电机。~ **machine** 串行计算机;串激电机。~ **modulation** 串馈式屏极调剂;阳极调剂。~ **motor** 串激电动机。~**-multiple connection** 串并联。~ **opposing** (线圈等的)反向串联。~**-parallel** ***a*.** 串并联的;混联的。~ **reactor** 串联电感器;串联扼流圈。~ **resonance** 串联[电压]谐振。~ **winding** 串联绕组,串联绕法。~**-wound** ***a*.** 串绕的;串联的;串激的。

ser·if [ˈserif; ˋsɛrɪf] ***n*.**【印】衬线〔如字母 I 上下两端的细横线〕〔*cf*. sanserif〕。

ser·i·graph [ˈserigrɑːf, -græf; ˋsɛrɪˏgrɑf, -ˏgræf] ***n*.** **1.**【纺】绢网印花。**2.**【纺】(试验绞丝用的)生丝复式强伸力机。**-er** [siˈrigrəfə; sɪˋrɪgrəfɚ] ***n*.** 绢网印花者。**-y** [siˈrigrəfi; sɪˋrɪgrəfɪ] ***n*.** 绢网印花工艺。

ser·in[1] [ˈserin; ˋsɛrɪn] ***n*.**【动】金丝雀 (*Serinus canarius*)。

ser·in[2] [ˈserin; ˋsɛrɪn] ***n*.** = serine.

ser·ine [ˈsiːriːn; ˋsɛrin] ***n*.**【化】丝胺酸。

se·rin·ga [siˈriŋgə; sɪˋrɪŋgə] ***n*.**【植】三叶胶属 (*Hevea*) 植物〔产于巴西〕。

se·ri·o·com·ic, -i·cal [ˈsiəriəuˈkɔmik, -ikəl; ˏsɪrɪoˋkɑmɪk, -ɪkl] ***a*.** 装作庄重其实是滑稽的;半庄半谐的。**-i·cal·ly** ***ad*.**

se·ri·ous [ˈsiəriəs; ˋsɪrɪəs] ***a*.** **1.** 严肃的;一本正经的;(人、脸等)庄重的。**2.** 认真的;真诚的;恳切的。**3.** 重要的;重大的。**4.** 危险的;严重的。**5.** 〔古〕宗教的;伦理学的;〔谑〕虔诚的。**6.** 热中的,很感兴趣的。*You cannot be* ~. 你是说着玩儿的吧。*Are you* ~? 你(说的)是真的吗? *a* ~ *opponent* 须认真对待的敌手;劲敌。~ *damage* 严重的损害。***and now to be*** ~ 现在来谈正经的〔用作插入语〕。***make a*** ~ ***attempt*** 认真试一试。***pretending to be*** ~ 像煞有其事地。~ ***advice for sb***. 正告某人。~ ***money*** 〔美〕巨款。***take for*** ~ 当真。***think in a*** ~ ***light*** 认真想。

se·ri·ous·ly [ˈsiəriəsli; ˋsɪrɪəslɪ] ***ad*.** 严肃;认真;严重。~ *ill* 害着重病。~ *speaking* 老实讲;认真说来。*Do you* ~ *mean what you say*? 你这话是不是当真的? *be* ~ *offended* [*affected*] 大怒[受重大影响]。***now*** ~ 说正经的。***take*** ~ 重视;认真(想);当真。

se·ri·ous-mind·ed [ˈsiəriəsˈmaindid; ˋsɪrɪəsˋmaɪndɪd] ***a*.** 认真的;严肃的;热诚的;一本正经的。

se·ri·ous·ness [ˈsiəriəsnis; ˋsɪrɪəsnɪs] ***n*.** **1.** 严肃;认真。**2.** 严重;重大。***in all*** ~ 郑重地;十分认真地 (*tell sb*. *in all* ~ 正告某人)。***with affected*** ~ 像煞有其事地。

ser·iph [ˈserif; ˋsɛrɪf] ***n*.** = serif.

ser·jeant [ˈsɑːdʒənt; ˋsɑrdʒənt] ***n*.** 〔英〕= sergeant.

ser·mon [ˈsəːmən; ˋsɝmən] ***n*.** **1.**【宗】布道;讲道;说教。**2.** 训诫;训导。**3.** 唠叨得令人厌烦的长篇演讲。**4.** (受自然界的启发而作的)道德上的反省。*preach* [*deliver*] *a* ~ 讲道。*a lay* ~ 非宗教家的宗教谈。**-ic, -i·cal** [səːˈmɔnik(əl); sɝˋmɑnɪk(əl)] ***a*.**

ser·mon·et(te) [ˌsəːməˈnet; ˏsɝməˋnɛt] ***n*.** 简短的讲道。

ser·mon·ize [ˈsəːmənaiz; ˋsɝmənˏaɪz] ***vi*.** **1.** 讲道,布道;说教。**2.** 写作讲道稿。**3.** 训诫,训导。—***vt*.** **1.** 对…布道。**2.** 训诫,对…说教。**-r** ***n*.** 布道者,训诫者。

sero- *comb*. *f*. 浆液;血清: *sero*sity.

se·rol·o·gy [siəˈrɔlədʒi; sɪˋrɑlədʒɪ] ***n*.**【医】血清学。**-log·i·cal** [ˌsiərəˈlɔdʒikəl; ˏsɪrəˋlɑdʒɪkəl] ***a*.**

se·ro·sa [siˈrəusə, -zə; sɪˋrosə] ***n*.** (*pl*. ~***s***, ***-sae*** [-siː; -si]) **1.**【动】浆膜, (= serous membrane); 绒(毛)膜 (= chorion)。**2.**【动】(昆虫的)胚膜。**-l** ***a*.**

se·ros·i·ty [siˈrɔsiti; sɪˋrɑsətɪ] ***n*.** **1.**【医】浆液;滑液。**2.** 浆液性;浆液状。

se·rot·i·nal [seˈrɔtinæl; sɪˋrɑtənl], **se·rot·i·nous** [siˈrɔtinəs; sɪˋrɑtɪnəs] ***a*.** **1.** 夏末的;晚夏的。**2.**【植】晚熟的;迟季的。

se·ro·to·ner·gic [ˌsiərəutəˈnəːdʒik; ˏsɪrətəˋnɝdʒɪk] ***a*.**

【生化】产生血清素的,血清素激活的。

se·ro·to·nin [ˌsiərəˈtəunin, ˌser-; ˌsɪrəˋtonɪn, ˌsɛr-] ***n.*** 【生化】5-烃色胺[血管收缩素]。

se·ro·type [ˌsiərəˈtaip; ˌsɪrəˋtaɪp] **I** ***n.*** 血清类型。**II** ***vi.*** 按血清类型分类。

se·rous [ˈsiərəs; ˋsɪrəs] ***a.*** **1.** 如水的;稀薄的。**2.**【医】(像)浆液的;血浆(般)的;血清的。~ *fluid* 浆液。~ **cavity** 浆液膜腔。~ **gland**【解】浆液腺。~ **membrane** 浆膜。

ser·ow [ˈserəu; ˋsɛro] ***n.*** 鬣羚属 (*Capricornis*) 动物[产于南亚]。

Ser·pens [ˈsəːpenz; ˋsɝpɛnz] ***n.***【天】巨蛇座。

ser·pent [ˈsəːpənt; ˋsɝpənt] ***n.*** **1.** 大毒蛇。**2.** 奸人;阴险的人。**3.** 蛇状焰火。**4.**【乐】蛇状管,蛇形号。**5.** [the S-]【天】巨蛇座。***the*** (***Old***) ***S-*** 撒旦;恶魔。**S- Bearer** = Serpens. ~**-charmer** (吹笛)耍蛇的人。~ **eater**【动】食蛇鸟。~**'s tongue** ***n.*** **1.** 鲨牙化石。**2.** 双尖剑。**3.**【植】瓶尔小草属 (*Ophioglossum*) 植物。

ser·pen·tar·i·um [ˌsəːpənˈtɛəriəm; ˌsɝpənˋtɛrɪəm] ***n.*** (动物园的)蛇馆;养蛇室。

ser·pen·tine [ˈsəːpəntain; ˋsɝpənˌtin] **I** ***a.*** **1.** 蛇一般的。**2.** 蜿蜒的;弯弯曲曲的;盘旋的;螺旋形的。**3.** 阴险的;奸险的;狡猾的。*a* ~ *pipe* 蛇管。*a* ~ *verse* 头尾词相同的诗。*the* ~ *turnings* [*windings*] (河流、道路的)蜿蜒;曲折。~ ***windings*** 转弯抹角地逢迎[巴结]。**II** ***n.*** **1.**【矿】蛇纹石。**2.** (古代的)蛇形大炮。**3.**【滑冰】S形曲线;蛇形线(同轴上三个圆形)。**4.** [the S-] (伦敦海德公园的)曲折蜿蜒的水池。**5.** 蛇形物。**III** ***vi.*** 蜿蜒地流;迂回曲折前进;缠绕。**-d** ***a.*** **1.** 有蛇(栖息)的。**2.** 蛇形的,弯曲的。

ser·pi·go [səːˈpaigəu; sɝˋpaɪgo] ***n.***【医】匐行疹;圈癣。**-pig·i·nous** [-ˈpidʒinəs; -ˋpɪdʒənəs] ***a.***【医】(皮肤病等)匐行的。

ser·ra·nid [səˈreinid, -ˈræ-, -ˈrɑː-; səˋrenɪd, -ˋræ-, -ˋrɑ-] **I** ***n.*** 鮨科 (*Serranidae*) 的鱼[包括锯鮨]。**II** ***a.*** 鮨科的 (= serranoid)。

ser·ra·noid [ˈserənɔid; ˋsɛrənɔɪd] ***a.***【鱼】鮨科的。

ser·rate [ˈserit; ˋsɛrɪt] **I** ***a.***【生】锯齿形的;有锯齿的。**II** ***vt.*** 使成锯齿状。**III** ***n.***【军】飞机的反截击雷达设备。

ser·ra·tion [seˈreiʃən; sɛˋreʃən] ***n.*** 锯齿(状);锯齿形(突起)。

ser·ried [ˈserid; ˋsɛrɪd] ***a.*** (行列等)密集的;排紧的;拥挤的。

ser·ru·late, -lat·ed [ˈserjuleit, -id; ˋsɛrjuˌlet, -ɪd] ***a.*** 细锯齿形的。

ser·ru·la·tion [ˌserjuˈleiʃən; ˌsɛrjuˋleʃən] ***n.*** **1.** 锯齿状;锯齿形。**2.** 细小锯齿。

ser·tu·lar·ian [ˌsəːtjuˈlɛəriən; ˌsɝtʃuˋlɛrɪən] ***n.***【动】海桧叶属水母[体形分枝如桧叶]。

se·rum [ˈsiərəm; ˋsɪrəm] ***n.*** (*pl.* ~*s*, ***-ra*** [-rə; -rə]) **1.**【医】血清。**2.** 血浆。**3.** 浆液;树液。**4.** 乳清;乳浆。~ **albumin**【生化】血清白蛋白。~ **disease** 血清病。~ **globulin**【生化】血清球蛋白。~ **hepatitis** 血清性肝炎。~ **therapy**【医】血清疗法。

ser·val [ˈsəːvəl; ˋsɝvəl] ***n.***【动】(非洲)长脚山猫;薮猫。

serv·ant [ˈsəːvənt; ˋsɝvənt] ***n.*** **1.** 仆人;佣人;雇工。**2.** [美]奴仆;奴隶。**3.** 随员;献身…的人;追随者;信徒。**4.** 官吏;公务员;服务员;雇员。**5.** 有用之物。*an indoor* ~ 内勤;佣人[厨役等]。*an outdoor* ~ 外勤佣人[园丁等]。*an upper* ~ 管家。*All government officials are* ~*s of the people*. 一切政府官员都是民众的公仆。*Fire and water may be good* ~*s, but bad masters*. 水火是忠仆,但一旦逞凶则危害极大。*a* ~ *of art* 献身艺术的人。*a civil* ~ 文官。*the* ~*s of a railway company* 铁路公司职员。***His*** [***Her***] ***Majesty's*** ~***s*** = ***the king's*** [***queen's***] ~***s*** [英]官吏;公务员;演员。***the*** ~ ***of the*** ~***s*** 上帝最卑下的仆人[罗马教皇的自称]。***Your obedient*** ~ 某某谨启[信函结尾语]。~ **girl**, ~ **maid** ***n.*** 女仆。

serve [səːv; sɝv] **I** ***vt.*** **1.** (为…)服务;为…尽力[效劳]。**2.** 侍候;招待(客等)。**3.** 端上;摆出(食物);斟(酒)。**4.** 服(刑,役);供[奉](职);经历,度过。**5.** 符合;对…有用,对…适用,适合(目的)。**6.** 满足(欲望、食欲;要求;需要);供给。**7.** 分派,分配。**8.** 对待;处理。**9.** 操作;发射(大炮);使用(枪)。**10.** 主演。**11.** 开动。**12.**【海】卷缠(绳索等)。**13.**【法】送达(命令等)。**14.**【网球】开(球);发(球)。**15.** (种马等)与(母畜)交配。*to* ~ *the people heart and soul* 全心全意地为民众服务。~ *coffee hot* 把咖啡趁热端上桌(供饮用)。*First come, first* ~*d*. 先到的先招待。*S- the ladies first*. 女客先得到供应[招待]。*Lunch is* ~*d now*. 现在开午饭了。*Is there anyone to* ~ *me?* [顾客叫服务员]有人(给我)服务吗? *What can we* ~ *you with?* [店员对顾客]给您拿点什么? 您要些什么? —***vi.*** **1.** 服务;服役;供[奉]职。**2.** 有用;合用;可作…用;作为 (*as*, *for*); 足够;适宜。**3.** 侍候;服侍;端菜;斟酒。**4.**【网球】开球;发球。**5.** (举行弥撒时)充当助祭。***as memory*** ~***s*** 每逢想起的时候。***as occasion*** ~***s*** 一有机会。***make the past*** ~ ***the present and foreign works*** ~ ***China*** 古为今用,洋为中用。~ ***a gun*** 炮击。~ ***an attachment*** 送达查封令 (*on*, *upon*)。~ ***sb. a bad turn*** 使人吃苦头。~ ***sb. a trick*** [~ ***a trick on sb.***] 欺骗某人。~ ***at table*** 侍应人吃饭[上菜等]。~ ***behind a counter*** 做店员;站柜台。~ ***for nothing*** 毫不中用。~ ***in the ranks*** 服兵役。~ ***one's apprenticeship*** 当学徒。~ ***one's sentence*** = ~ time. ~ ***one's time*** 做满任期[规定期限];服刑。~ ***sb.'s turn*** [***need***] 对某人合用;够某人用。~ ***oneself of*** 利用。~ ***out*** **1.** 分给;分配(食粮等)。**2.** 端出(饭菜等);斟(酒等)。**3.** 做到期满。~ (***sb.***) ***out*** 使自食其果;给予报复。~ (***sb.***) ***right*** 给(某人)该得的待遇 (*It* ~*s him* [*you*] *right*. 他[你]活该。*He is rightly* [*well*] ~*d*. 他算得到报应了)。~ ***round*** **1.** 挨次分派(食物)。**2.** 捆上。~ ***tables*** 张罗膳食(而忽视精神需要)。~ ***the Devil*** 干坏事;犯罪。~ ***the need*** [***turn***] 有用;合用;够用。~ ***the purpose of*** 可用于;可充当;合乎…的目的。~ ***the time*** 骑墙观望。~ ***time*** 服刑。~ ***under sb.*** 在某人下面工作。~ ***up*** 端出(饭菜等);上(菜)。~ (***sb.***) ***with*** 拿出…给(某人);提供;供给。***when the tide*** ~***s*** 方便的时候。**II** ***n.***【网球】开球;发球。*Whose* ~ *is it?* 该谁发球?

serv·er [ˈsəːvə; ˋsɝvɚ] ***n.*** **1.** 服务者;工作者;侍候者;服役者。**2.**【网球】开球人;发球人。**3.** 上菜用的器具[如托盘,手推小车等];布菜用的火匙、叉子等。**4.** 助祭[做弥撒时神父的助手]。

Ser·vi·an [ˈsəːvjən, -viən; ˋsɝvɪən] ***a.***, ***n.*** = Serbian.

Ser·vice [ˈsəːvis; ˋsɝvɪs] ***n.*** 塞维斯[姓氏]。

serv·ice [ˈsəːvis; ˋsɝvɪs] **I** ***n.*** **1.** 服务;工作;公务;职务;事务;业务;行政部门(人员),服务机构(人员)。**2.** 事业;公用事业;(交通、供水、供电等)公共设施(业务)。**3.** 仪式;(宗教)礼拜仪式(乐曲);【宗】功德,修行[祈祷、行善等]。**4.**【军】勤务;服役;兵役(期间)。**5.** 军种;勤务部队。**6.** 利益;有用。**7.** 照顾;帮助。**8.** [常 *pl.*]贡献,功劳。**9.** (厂方对售出机械等的)维修(服务)。**10.** 服务业;服务公司。**11.** (用膳时的)侍候;招待;上菜;斟酒。**12.** (全套)餐具;茶具。**13.**【海】(防止绳索磨损而进行的)卷缠;缠索材料[纱线、帆布或金属丝]。**14.** 装弹发射(大炮) **15.** (传票等的)送达、执行。**16.**【网球】开球;发球;开球方式[方面]。**17.** 国债利息。**18.** (种马等)与母畜的交配。**19.** = service tree. *public* ~ 公务。*government* ~ 行政事务;政府机关;公务员。*postal* ~ 邮政业务。*There is a good* ~ *of trains*. 火车客运业务良好。*the U.S. Information S-* 美国新闻处。*the secret* ~*s* 特务机关。*the reporting* ~ (会议的)报到处。*a marriage* [*burial*] ~ 婚[丧]礼。*the civil* ~ 文官。*the*

S

(*fighting*) ～*s* 陆海空军。*the united* ～*s* 陆海军。*the junior* [*senior*] ～〔英〕陆[海]军。*Will you do me a* ～? 帮我一个忙好吗? *My* ～ *to you*! 祝你健康;敬你一杯;干一杯吧。*a* ～ *of glass* 一套玻璃茶具。*a table* ～ 一套餐具。*Whose* ～ *is it*? 该谁开球? *Personal* ～【法】直接送达当事人。***at your*** ～ 敬候差遣,请随意(使用)(*I am at your* ～. 您有事请随时吩咐好了。*I am so-and-so at your* ～. 我叫某某,有事请随时吩咐)。***be of*** ～ ***to*** 对…有用[有帮助]。***enter into*** ～ = go into ～. ***break*** ～【网球】接发球胜一局。***enter the*** ～ 入伍。***enter*** [***go***] ***upon*** ～ 参加战斗;上火线;服现役。(***give***) ***my*** ～ ***to*** 请向(某人)致候。***give*** ～ ***to*** 为…效劳。***go into*** ～ = ***go*** (***out***) ***to*** ～ 去帮工;去做仆人。***have seen*** ～ **1.** 上过火线[参加过战斗]。**2.** 已经用旧。***in active*** ～ 在职;在现役。***in*** ～ 在帮工;被雇用着;在军中服役;(车辆等)仍在使用中。***of no*** ～ 无用。***on His*** [***Her***] ***Majesty's S-*** 〔英〕公事〔公文免费邮递印记,略 O. H. M. S.〕。***on*** ～ 在职(的);在役(的)。***out of*** ～ **1.** 退职;退役。**2.** 已不能用的;已作废的。***pay lip*** ～ ***to*** 空口说白话;嘴上说得好听。***place at sb.'s*** ～ 听任某人使用。***present one's*** ～ ***to*** 向…致敬。***put*** (***sth.***) ***into*** ～ 把(某物)投入使用。***render a*** ～ 帮忙;效劳,尽力;贡献。***retire from*** ～ 退役;退职。***see*** ～ 有(作战)经验;(物品)用旧[用完成时态]。～ ***by substitution***【法】代理送达。***take sb. into one's*** ～ 雇用某人。***take*** ～ ***with*** 在…处做事[服务]。***take the*** ～ 发球,开球。**II** ***vt.*** **1.** 为…做后勤[第二线、辅助性]服务工作;满足(顾客)需要。**2.** 检修;维修,保养(车辆、仪器、电视机等)。**3.** 支付(公债等)的利息并提存偿债基金。**4.** (种马等)与(母畜)交配。～ *an automobile* 修理汽车。～ *the needs of customers* 满足许多顾客的需要。**III** ***a.*** **1.** 武装部队的;服现役用的。**2.** 服务性的;为提供后勤[资料等]服务的。**3.** 仆人用的;仆人的。～ **apartment** (兼有住家和旅馆特点的)商务套房〔收费也较低,办公住宿两用〕。～ **area** **1.** 服务区域。**2.** 供水区域。**3.**【无】广播区域。～**berry** 花楸(树)果(实)。～ **book**【宗】祈祷书。～ **break** (网球等)对方发球而己方取胜局。～ **bus** (长途)公共汽车。～ **call**【军】集合号;上班[上操等]号;下班号。～ **cap** 〔美〕军礼帽。～ **car** 〔美婉〕殡仪车。～ **ceiling**【空】实际(上)升限(度)。～ **club** (机关团体的)福利部;【军】军官俱乐部。～ **counter** 服务台。～ **court**【网球】发球时球应落入的地方[内场]。～ **depot** = **1.** ～ station. **2.**【军】后勤仓库。～ **diagram** 行车图表。～ **dress** 军便服 (*opp.* full dress)。～ **elevator** 运货电梯;服务人员电梯。～ **entrance** 服务人员出入处。～ **flat** 〔英〕能包饭的公寓。～ **hatch** 递送饭菜的小窗。～ **industry** 服务性行业〔如餐饮业等〕。～ **interruption** (电话)不通。～ **lift** 运货电梯,服务人员使用的电梯。～ **line** **1.**【电】用户进线。**2.**【网球】发球线。～**man** ***n.*** (*pl.* ***-men***) **1.** 军人。**2.** 维修人员。～ **meter**【电话】通话次数计。～ **module** (太空飞船的)机械舱[包括机械系统和燃料储备等]。～ **parts** 备用零件。～ **pipe** (由总管通入屋内的)自来水[煤气]输送管。～ **plate** 托盘。～ **plaza** (高速公路路边设有加油站;饮食店等的)服务点。～ **record** 服务经历。～ **round** 作战用炮弹、实弹。～ **stairway** (房屋后部)勤杂人员使用的楼梯。～ **station** 服务站;修理站;加油站;(飞机的)停留处。～ **stripe** 〔美〕军龄臂章。～ **telegram**【讯】公电。～ **tree**【植】花楸树;治疝花楸。～ **water** 家用[自来]水。～**-woman** (*pl.* ***-women***) **1.** 女军人。**2.** 女维修工。～ **yard** 后院;杂作场。

serv·ice·a·ble [ˈsəːvisəbl; ˋsɝvɪsəbl] ***a.*** **1.** 合用的;有用的;便利的;适于平时使用的(*to*)。**2.** 经用的;耐用的。**3.** 正常的;能操作的。**-bly** ***ad.***

serv·i·cing [ˈsəːvisiŋ; ˋsɝvɪsɪŋ] ***n.*** 维修。

ser·vi·ette [ˌsəːviˈet; ˏsɝviˋet] ***n.*** 餐巾。

serv·ile [ˈsəːvail; ˋsɝvl̩] **I** ***a.*** **1.** 奴隶的。**2.** 奴性的;奴颜婢膝的;卑屈的;屈从的;隶属的。**3.** 无创造性的;无独立精神的。**4.**【语】附属性的〔指本身不发音,只表示在它之前的元音字母发长音的字母,如 stone 一词中的 e 字母;或指词中表示派生关系[词性变化、语法关系等]的部分。如 mother's, sees, students 等词中的 s.〕。～ *flattery* 卑躬屈膝的奉承。～ *labour* 奴隶般的劳动。**II** ***n.*** 奴隶。～ **letter** 除表示另一字母的发音外别无作用的字母〔如 manage*a*ble, sal*e*able 中的 *e* 等〕。～ **works**【宗】礼拜六禁止做的卑下工作。**-ly** ***ad.*** **-ness** ***n.***

ser·vil·i·ty [səːˈviliti; səˋvɪlətɪ] ***n.*** **1.** 奴隶处境。**2.** 奴颜婢膝;奴性;卑屈;屈从。**3.** 隶属。

ser·ving [ˈsəːviŋ; ˋsɝvɪŋ] **I** ***n.*** **1.** 服务;服侍;伺候;上菜。**2.** (食物的)一份;一客。**II** ***a.*** 用于上菜的。*a* ～ *spoon* 布菜匙;分菜匙。

ser·vi·tor [ˈsəːvitə; ˋsɝvətɚ] ***n.*** **1.** 〔古、诗〕仆从;跟班;侍从。**2.**【史】(牛津大学的)工读生。

ser·vi·tude [ˈsəːvitjuːd; ˋsɝvəˏtjud] ***n.*** **1.** 奴役;奴隶状态;(刑罚)劳役。**2.**【法】地役(权);使用权。*in* ～ *to one's evil passions* 变成邪念的俘虏(为非作歹)。*penal* ～ *for life* 终身劳役;无期徒刑。～ *to by product* 副产物使用权。

ser·vo [ˈsəːvəu; ˋsɝvo] ***n.*** 〔用作定语或前缀〕**1.**【自】伺服。**2.** 伺服系统;随动系统;伺服机械;从动系统。**3.**【空】舵机〔自动驾驶仪附件〕。*an on-off* ～ 继电随动系统。～ **actuator** 伺服执行机构;伺服拖动装置。～ **amplifier** 跟踪系统放大器;伺服放大器。～**-analog computer** 伺服模拟计算机。～ **control** 伺服控制;随动控制。～**-driven** ***a.*** 伺服拖动的。～**-gear** 助力机构;伺服机构;伺服系统。～**-link** 助力传动装置;助力系统;伺服系统。～ **mechanism** 伺服机构;随动系统。～ **modulation** 伺服调剂。～ **motor** 伺服电动机;继动器。～**-positioning** 伺服定位。～ **potentimeter** 伺服电位计。～**-recorder** 伺服记录器。～**-stabilization** 伺服稳定。～**-system** 随动系统,跟踪系统。～ **valve** 伺服(操纵)阀。

SES = socioeconomic status 社会经济地位。

ses·a·me [ˈsesəmi; ˋsɛsəmɪ] ***n.***【植】脂麻;芝麻。～ *oil* 芝麻油;香油。～ *soy* 芝麻酱。***open*** ～ 开门咒〔源于《天方夜谭》〕;(过难关的)秘诀;窍门。

ses·a·min [ˈsesəmin; ˋsɛsəmɪn] ***n.***【生化】芝麻明;脂麻素。

ses·a·moid [ˈsesəmɔid; ˋsɛsəˏmɔɪd] **I** ***a.*** 芝麻(籽)形的;【解】籽骨的。～ *bone* 籽骨。～ *cartilage* 籽软骨。**II** ***n.***【解】籽软骨。

sesqui- *comb. f.* 表示"一个半": *sesqui*oxide.

ses·qui·car·bon·ate [ˌseskwiˈkɑːbənit, -neit; ˏsɛskwɪˋkɑrbənɪt, -net] ***n.***【化】倍半碳酸盐。

ses·qui·cen·ten·ni·al [ˌseskwisenˈteniəl; ˏsɛskwɪsɛnˋtɛnɪəl] ***n.***, ***a.*** 一百五十年纪念(的)。

ses·qui·ox·ide [ˌseskwiˈɔksaid; ˏsɛskwɪˋɑksaɪd] ***n.***【化】倍半氧化物;三氧化二 ....。*nickel* ～ 三氧化二镍。

ses·qui·pe·da·li·an [ˈseskwipiˈdeiliən; ˏsɛskwɪpəˋdelɪən] **I** ***a.*** **1.** 一英尺半(长)的。**2.** (词,语)极长的;多音节的。**3.** 好用长词的。**II** ***n.*** 长词。

ses·sile [ˈsesail; ˋsɛsl̩] ***a.***【生】**1.** 无柄的;无腹柄的。**2.** 固着的;座生的。*a* ～ *leaf* 无柄叶。～ *medusa* 座生水母。

ses·shin [ˈseʃn; ˋsɛʃɪn] ***n.*** 〔Chin.〕(静坐)敛心,闭关,坐关〔佛教禅宗的一种隐居沉思,通常持续 5—7 天〕。

ses·sion [ˈseʃən; ˋsɛʃən] ***n.*** **1.** 会议;会议的一次[一届];开会;(法庭的)开庭。**2.** 开会期;开庭期。**3.** 〔美, Scot.〕学期。**4.** 〔美〕授课时间。**5.** 〔*pl.*〕〔英〕(处理小案件的)治安法庭。**6.**【商】(证券交易等的)市;盘。**7.** (为某项活动或目的集合在一起的)一段时间。**8.** 基督教长老会的地区性执行理事会。**9.** 〔美〕地方刑事法院 (= the court of ～)。*be in* ～ 在开会中;在会议中;在开庭中。*the autumn* ～ (英国国会夏天休会后的)秋季会期。*the plenary* [*full*] ～ 全体会议。*between* ～*s* 休会期间。*the conference now in* ~ 现在召开的会议。*petty* ~*s* 即决审判;即决法庭。*quarter* ~*s*〔英〕(每三月一次的)季审法院〔1972 年由 Crown courts 取代〕。*the morning* ~【商】(交易所的)早市。**-al** *a*.

ses·ter·ti·um [ses'tə:tiəm; sɛs`tɝʃɪəm] *n*. (*pl*. **-ti·a** [-ʃjə;-ʃɪə]) 塞斯特帖姆〔古罗马货币单位,等于 1,000 塞斯特斯 (*sesterce*)〕。

ses·tet [ses'tet; sɛs`tɛt] *n*. **1**.【乐】六重唱(曲);六重奏(曲);六人演出小组。**2**.【诗】十四行诗的最后六行,六行诗节。

ses·ti·na [ses'ti:nə; sɛs`tinə] *n*. (*pl*. ~*s*, **-ne** [-ni; -nɪ]) 六节诗〔一种抒情诗的格式,每节六行,最后另加一节为三行;第一节六行的末一词,按不同次序在其他五节各行的末尾重复之,并出现在最后一节三行的中间及末尾〕。

SET = safe electronic transaction 安全电子交易〔指用信用卡通过因特网支付款项的商业交易〕。

Set [set; sɛt] *n*.【埃神】赛特〔古埃及神话中兽头人身象征邪恶的神〕。

set [set; sɛt] **I** *vt*. (**set**; **set·ting**) **1**. 放;搁;贴;靠。~ *a cup on the table* 把杯子放在桌上。~ *it against the wall* 把它靠在墙上。~ *eyes on* 注视;碰见。**2**. 安置;布置;安排;设置;装置。~ *a guard at the gate* 派卫兵守门。**3**. 使固定。~ *a butterfly* 钉住蝴蝶(做标本)。~ *a cutting tool on a carriage* 把切削刀具固定在刀架上。**4**. 镶;嵌。~ *a jewel* 镶宝石。*an island* ~ *in a sea of silver* 镶在银色海面上的一个岛。**5**. 种植。~ *seeds* [*plants*] 播种;种(植物)。**6**. 扬(帆);扯上;扯开。~ *sail* 张帆;开船。**7**. 设(陷阱);张(罗网)。**8**. 点燃;放(火)。~ *fire to* 放火。**9**. 签(字);盖(章)。~ *seal* [*signature*] *to the deed* 在证书上盖章[签字]。~ *one's hand to a document* 在文件上签字。**10**. 树立(榜样、模范)。~ *an example* 树立榜样;示范;以身作则。~ *the fashion* 树立新型样板;开风气。**11**. 规定;约定;择定(日子等);指定(地点);划定(界限);确定;决定;制定;颁布。~ *a price* 定价钱。~ *the atomic mass of hydrogen at 1 atomic mass unit* 把氢原子量定为一个原子量单位。**12**. 创造(记录)。~ *a new production record* 创造新的生产记录。**13**. 使坚固;使凝结;弄硬;使牢固。~ *the white of an egg by boiling it* 煮蛋使蛋白凝固。*Cold* ~*s jellies*. 果子冻[肉冻]因冷而冻结。**14**. 使(头发)成波浪形;卷(头发)。~ *one's hair* 把头发卷[作]成波浪形。**15**. 接骨;整骨。~ *the broken bone* 正骨。**16**. 锉(锯齿);抢(剃刀);对(钟、表),拨准(钟的指针);校正(仪器);调整。~ *a clock* [*watch*] *by the TV time signal* 按电视台的报时对钟[表]。~ *an alarm clock* (*for five a. m.*) 把闹钟拨到(早晨五点)。**17**.提出(问题,任务);出(题目);指定(作业)。~ *an examination paper* 出考试题目。**18**. 排(铅字)。**19**. 使从事;使…[指定]做某事[某动作]。~ *him to the task* 使[指定]他做那件工作。**20**. 专心;集中;倾注。~ *one's heart on* ... 一心要;迷恋。~ *one's affections on* 爱上;热爱。**21**. 使处于某种状态。~ *his mind at ease* 使他安心。~ *a question at rest* 使问题得到解决。~ *machines in motion* 使机器开动。~ *the bell a-ring* 把钟敲响。~ *right* 矫正;弄正。~ *things going* 使事情进行下去。~ *affairs in order* 使事情就绪。**22**. 为(诗、词)谱曲;改写(乐曲);配(布景)。~ *piano music for the violin* 改钢琴曲成小提琴曲。~ *word to music* 将歌词编成曲子。**23**. 使(母鸡)孵蛋。~ *a hen* 使一母鸡孵蛋。**24**.〔桥牌〕打败(对手)。**25**. 使朝某一方向。~ *one's feet homeward* 朝回家的方向走。**26**. 使移动。~ *a match of fire* 以火柴点火。~ *a pen to paper* 提笔写字,著书立说。**27**.〔方〕使坐下。**28**. 释放。~ *a prisoner free* 释放犯人。**29**. (猎狗)以鼻指着(猎物)以指示其位置。**30**. 使(颜色)固着。—*vi*. **1**. (太阳等)(沉)落;偏西。*The sun has* ~. 太阳落了。*His star has* ~. 他的命运完了。**2**. (液体等)凝固;凝结;固定。*The jelly has* ~. 肉冻凝结起来了。*His character has* ~. 他的性格固定下来了。*His face* ~. 他绷起面孔。*Her eyes* ~. 她的眼睛瞪住了。**3**. 着手;从事。**4**. 开始活动;开始工作。**5**. (水、风等)流向;吹向;(感情、意见等)倾向。*The tide* ~*s in* [*out*]. 潮水涨[退]了。**6**. 结果实;结子儿。**7**. 植树;插树。**8**. (母鸡)孵卵。**9**. (衣服等)合身;适合。*The coat* ~*s badly*. 这件上衣不合身。**10**. (猎犬)站住指示猎物所在。**11**. (跳舞)采取面对面姿势。**12**. (骨)接合;(金属)永久变形。**13**.〔方〕坐。**14**. (头发)卷成波浪形。**15**. 攻击(*upon*)。**16**. (颜色)固着。**be hard** ~ **1**. 处于为难境地(*for*; *to*)。**2**. (蛋)在孵化中。**3**. 感到饥饿。**be sharp** [**keen**] ~ **1**. 很饿。**2**. 渴求。**3**. (脸)表情严肃。~ **a case** 假定。~ **a limit to** (规定)限制;缩减(冗费)。~ **a thief** [**rogue**] **to catch a thief** [**rogue**] 以毒攻毒。~ **about 1**. 开始;下手;着手。**2**.〔口〕攻击。**3**. 散布(谣言)。**4**.〔俚〕连接殴打;乱打。~ **abroad** 散布;推广;宣扬;公开发表。~ **afloat 1**. 落水;使下水。**2**. 着手;开始。~ **against 1**. 比较;对照。**2**. 使对抗;使反对;使猜忌。**3**. 使平衡。**4**. 使不和;离间。**5**. 赌。~ **agoing** [**going**] 使动;开动;使开行。~ **apart 1**. 留出(充当别用)。**2**. 分开;分离。~ **aside** 拨出;搁置;驳回。~ **at** 袭击;嗾使(狗等)。~ **at ease** [**rest**] 使安心;安慰;抚慰。~ **at large** [**liberty**] 释放;解放。~ **at odds**, ~ **at variance** 挑拨离间;使争吵;使打架。~ **back 1**. 阻碍;阻止。**2**. 使挫折;使退步。**3**. 拨慢(钟表的方针)。**4**.〔美口〕使(某人)花钱 (*How much did it* ~ *you back?* 它使你花了多少钱?)。~ **before 1**. 摆在…前面;拿出;盛出(食物);(把酒)斟出。**2**. 告诉(事实等);陈述;说明;劝导。~ **by 1**. 搁在一旁;拿开;搁起;藏起;保留。**2**. 尊重;珍重。~ **by the compass** 按照罗盘测定(方位)。~ **by the heels 1**. 上脚镣。**2**. 拘禁;监禁;逮捕;使不能活动[无能,无用]。**3**. 弄翻;弄倒。~ **down 1**. 搁下;丢下。**2**. 让乘客下车;把东西卸下车。**3**. 记入;登记。**4**. 定;设;制定。**5**. 归于;归功于。**6**. 认为是由于 (*to*);认为;视为;看作 (*as*)。**7**.〔俚〕谴责。**8**.〔美〕着陆;降落。~ **foot** 踏上;进入。~ **forth 1**. 显示;明示。**2**. 排列;陈列。**3**. 公开;发行;公布。**4**. 陈述;宣布;说明。**5**. 表彰;颂扬;赞扬。**6**. 出发。~ **forward 1**. 促进;助长。**2**.提出;宣布;声明。**3**. 出发;启程。**4**.拨快(钟、表)。~ **free 1**. 释放。**2**.【化】使游离。~ **going** 开动;展开。~ **in 1**. 固定;停当。**2**. 涨潮。**3**. 进来;来到。**4**. 开始 (*The rainy season has* ~ *in*. 雨季开始了)。~ **in order** 整顿;整理。~ (*a friend*) **in the world** 提拔(朋友)。~ **little** [**light**] **by** 轻视。~ **loose** 解开;释放。~ **off 1**. 分;分割;划开;区划。**2**. 装饰;使更鲜明;衬托出;使显得更美丽;表扬。**3**. 使爆发;发射(焰火);燃放。**4**. 出发;动身。**5**. 扣除;抵销。**6**. 对照;对比。**7**. 使开始(做某事)。**8**.【印】(墨未干)弄污(次页)。~ **off against** 使和…对抗;使对照;扣除;抵销。~ **on 1**. 前进。**2**. 嗾使;挑唆;挑拨;煽动;鼓动。**3**. 使跟踪追赶。**4**.【火箭】定位;调节。**5**. 置放(在上);端上(桌子)。**6**. 决心要拿到。**7**. 埋头;专心(工作等)。**8**. 攻击;袭击。**9**. 出发;动身。**10**. 着手;开始。~ ... **on foot** 开始;着手。~(**sb.**) **on his feet** 使站立;帮助人独立谋生。~ (**sb.**) **on his way** 送人上路(以免走错)。~ **one's face against** (坚决)反对。~ **one's face to** 正视;决心去做;着手做。~ **one's hand to 1**. 抓住;握住。**2**. 着手做;开始做。~ **one's hand** [**name, signature, seal**] **to a document** 在文件上签名[盖章]。~ **one's hand to the plough** 开始工作;开始做。~ **one's teeth** 咬紧牙关;〔喻〕下定决心(干)。~ **one's wits to another's** 和人闹意见;跟人辩论。~ **oneself against** 反对,与…相对抗。~ **oneself right** 自行改正;表明自己的正当。~ **oneself to do** 竭力设法。~ **oneself up in opposition to** 同…唱对台戏[相对抗]。~ **out 1**.出发;动身。**2**. 开始 (~ *out in business* 动手做事)。**3**. (潮水)退落。**4**. 分派;发布。**5**. 分界,区划;限

S

定。6. 陈列;敍装;准备好使出去。7. 修饰;装饰。8. 表示;申述;陈述。9. 测定(位置)。10.【石工】(把上面的石头)砌出一点。11. 隔开一定距离栽植。12.【印】用完(架上铅字);(把字)排稀。～ **over** 1. 放在…上。2. 支配。3. 定为…的监督人。4. 移交;递交。～ ***people by the ear*** 使争吵。～ ***store*** [***much***] ***by*** 尊重;敬重。～ ***the axe to*** 1. 动手斫倒[破坏]。2.摧毁。～ ***the Thames on fire*** 做不平凡的事。～ ***to*** 1. 认真着手;动手做。2. 打起来。3. 吃起来。～ ***up*** 1. 竖起;摆正。2. 建立;创立;发起;开办 (～ *up for oneself* 独自经营)。3. 供给;供应;预备;准备好拿出;〔美口〕摆(菜等)。4. 提高(声音);喊叫。5. 提出;提议;提倡;主张;提示;揭示。6. 假装。7. 胜过;使获胜 (*over*, *about*); 使掌握权力。8. 使自立。9. 振起精神;恢复(健康);复原。10. 敬(一杯);请吃(酒);使醉。11. 使高兴;使兴高采烈;使扬扬得意。12. 拿出拍卖。13. 排版;拼版;把剥制的标本等拼装;裱装。14. 装置;装备。15.【军】训练;锻炼。16.【海】扯紧索具。〔口〕使受冤枉,使被诬陷。～ ***up against*** 和…对抗。～ ***up for*** 自称为;装作;摆…的架子。～ ***upon*** = ～ on. ～ ***upside down*** 弄颠倒。

II ***a***. 1. 确定的。2. 固定的;不动的;装好的。3. 强硬的;(意见等)坚决的;决心的;急切的。4. 顽固的;固执的;不变的。5. 既定的;预定的;规定的;指定的;正式的。6. 凝结的;凝固的。7. 安好的;装好的;造成的;做成的。8. 准备就绪的;(赛跑等)作好预备姿势的;(拳击等)摆好架子准备出击的。9. (两军)对垒的。～ *eyes* 凝视不动的眼睛。*deep* ～ *eyes* 深陷的眼睛。*a* ～ *battle* 正式的战斗。*a* ～ *discourse* 正式演说,准备过的演说。*a* ～ *distance* 一定的距离。*a* ～ *machine* 安好的机器。*a* ～ *screw* 定位螺钉。*a* ～ *smile* 假笑。***all*** ～〔美俚〕准备妥当;准备就绪。***at the*** ～ ***time*** 在规定时间。***be*** ～ ***in one's opinions*** 意见坚定。***get*** ～〔赛跑口令〕预备 (*On your mark! Get* ～! *Go!* 各就各位! 预备! 跑!)。***in*** ～ ***terms*** 用陈套。***of*** [***on***, ***upon***] ～ ***purpose*** 故意。～ ***form for all cases*** = ～ ***method for different cases*** 千篇一律,以不变应万变。***with*** ～ ***teeth*** 咬紧牙关。

III ***n***. 1.〔诗〕(太阳等的)下沉;日没。2.机组;(成套)设备;电子仪器。3. (餐具等的)套;(同类事物的)批,组,副,对;(由若干卷书组成的)部,集。4.【数】集(合);【运】(网球等竞技比赛的)一局,一盘。5.【物】变定;【机】(弹簧等因使用过度形成的)变形。6. 打印具;练铁完成器;螺旋钳;平起子;附钩螺旋钳;(铆钉的)打头器;(垫在桩头上使间接受力的)桩头垫;钳子;扣子;【木工】敲钉楔;锯齿;锉锯器。7. (墙壁的)末次粉刷。8. (铺路用)花岗石。9. 型;形。10.【园艺】插条;苗木;树苗;幼树;树秧。11. 刚结成的果实;种用小块茎[块根]。12. 一窝(蛋)。13. 同伴;同类的人;党;派;集团;阶层;界。14. (风、潮水等的)方向,进路;倾向,趋势。15.【心】定向。16. 歪斜;弯曲构造;弯曲;转弯。17. 形状;形势;姿势;体态;态度。18.【猎】猎犬发现猎物时的蹲立不动姿势。19. (液体的)凝结;硬化;【捕鲸】戳刺;打进。21.【剧】舞台装置;布景。22.【影】发声装置。23.【无】接收机。24.【矿】巷道支架。25. 锯齿的倾角;铅字宽度。26. 卷做头发。27. 一窝蛋。28.〔英〕(獾的)洞穴。29. 猎狗发现猎物时的蹲立姿势。30. (篮球)远距离投篮。*a dinner* ～ 一套餐具。*a radio* ～ 收音机。*a television* ～ 电视机。*an extension* ～【电话】分机。*a head* ～ 听筒;耳机。*a complete* ～ 全副;全套。*Jones and his* ～ 琼斯和他的同伙。*He is not of my* ～. 他不是我的同道。*the best* ～ 权贵阶层。*the fast* ～ 一伙放荡人物。*a literary* [*political*] ～ 一班文艺界[政治界]人士。***a dead*** ～ 1. 难关;死路;挫折。2. 猛烈的攻击;反对的态度。3. (恋爱中人等的)如痴如迷的态度;死死地纠缠。4.【猎】猎狗发现猎物时的蹲立姿势。～**-aside** ***n***. 1.〔美〕联邦政府下令储备的军用物资。2. 任何储备的物品。～**back** ***n***. 1. 挫折;倒退;(病的)复发;逆流。2. 延迟;阻碍。3. 向后运动;后退;逆转。4.【建】(高楼上层壁面的)缩进;收进;上层壁面逐渐收进的高楼。5. 后棱角。6. 制动器。～ **chisel** 宽刃凿刀。～**down** ***n***. 1. 申斥;斥责;辱骂;反驳;拒绝。2. (电车、火车等的)一段(路);搭乘。～**-fair** 1. ***a***. (天气)晴定了的。2. ***n***. 镘平的灰泥面。～**-in** 1. ***n***. (潮等的)上涨;开始;(冰霜雨雪的)来临,降落。2. ***a***. 套入的;嵌装在里面的;附建在墙壁上的。～**off** ***n***. 1. 扣除;抵销。2.装饰;装饰品;陪衬物 (*to*)。3. (旅行的)出发。4.【建】墙壁的凸出部。5.【印】粘脏(未干油墨粘到另一张印张上)。～ **out** ***n***. 1. 开始 (*at the first* ～ *out* 最初,起头)。2. 出发;动身。3. 准备;预备;布置。4. 设备;装备。5. (餐具等的)一套。6. 开饭;摆桌子。7. 陈列。8.【印】排松[使字母之间有空隙];排完(架上铅字)。～ **phrase** 成语;陈套。～**piece** ***n***. 1. 按传统格式制作的艺术作品。2. 大架焰火;花式焰火[构成较复杂画面的]。3.一套可移动的、立体的舞台布景。4. 精心布置的行动[局势]。～ **scene** 舞台立体布景。～ **screw** 固定[定位]螺丝,弹簧调节螺丝。～ **shot**【篮球】(在发球线处或一角作的)远投,长投,长射。～ **square** 三角板。～ **theory**【数】集(合)论。～**-to** ***n***. (*pl*. ～**-tos**) 殴斗;拳赛;争论;较量。～**-top box**【计】机顶盒,顶置盒[指一种把电视机等家用电器和电脑网络相联接的装置]。～**-up** ***n***. 1. 组织;机构;构造;体制。2. 体格;身体的构造。3.〔美〕(身体的)姿势;姿态。4. 布置好的餐桌[餐具]。5. (科学仪器等的)装置;装配;配置;调整;准备。6. (选定的)摄影机位置;某一位置的胶片拍摄长度。7.〔美俚〕(故意布置得)容易做的工作;布置得一面倒的比赛。8.〔美俚〕本领不行的拳击选手。9.〔美撞球〕易于得分的球。10.〔美俚〕拿烈酒请客;混有威士忌酒的汽水。11. 计划;方案。12.【无】调定。13.【计】运算电路的构成。

se·ta·ceous [siˈteiʃəs; sɪˋteʃəs] ***a***. 1. 具[有]刚毛的。2. 鬃毛状的;鬃状的。**-ly** ***ad***.

SETAF = Southern European Task Force (北大西洋公约组织的)南欧特遣部队。

Seth [seθ; sɛθ] ***n***. 1. 塞斯[男子名]。2. = Set.

SETI *abbr*. search for extraterrestrial intelligence 寻找地球外有智慧生物。

se·tif·er·ous [seˈtifərəs; sɪˋtɪfərəs] ***a***.【生】具刚毛的,生刚毛的。

se·ti·form [ˈsiːtiˌfɔːm; ˋsitɪˏfɔrm] ***a***. 刚毛状的。

se·tig·er·ous [seˈtidʒərəs; sɪˋtɪdʒərəs] ***a***. = setiferous.

se·ton [ˈsiːtn; ˋsitn̩] ***n***.【医】1. 串线(法);泄泄线。2. 排液。

se·tose [ˈsiːtəus; ˋsitos] ***a***. = setaceous.

set·te·cen·to [ˌsetteˈtʃentou; ˏsetteˋtʃɛnto] ***n***.〔It.〕(意大利文艺的)十八世纪(时期)。

set·tee [seˈtiː; sɛˋti] ***n***. 1. 长靠椅;中、小型长沙发。2. 三角帆船。

set·ter [ˈsetə; ˋsɛtɚ] ***n***. 1. 安放者;安装者;嵌镶者;排字者;作曲者。2. 教唆者;嗾使者;为警察作谍报的人;(盗贼的)眼线。3.塞特种猎狗。4.【无】调节器;给定装置。～**-forth** 发行者;说明者。～**-off** 装饰物品。～**-on** 攻击者;教唆者;煽动者。

set·ting [ˈsetiŋ; ˋsɛtɪŋ] ***n***. 1. 安装;装配;装置;安放。2. (机器的)底座。3. 调整。4. 整齿。5. 锉锯子。6. 配乐;谱曲。7. (果树的)坐果。8.【印】排字。9. 镶嵌;镶嵌物;镶嵌(宝石等)的框子。10.【剧,影】剧景;布景;舞台面。11. 背景;(花园的)布置;环境。12. (天体的)没落;(日、月的)沉落。13. (潮水、风等的)方向。14. 凝结;凝固;硬化。15. 炮床。16. 一套餐具。17.【空】定位;【建】下沉。*a* ～ *hen* 伏窝的母鸡。*a circle* ～【测】度盘位置。*a* ～ *of butterflies* 一组蝴蝶标本。*with a sea* ～ 用海作背景。*a* ～ *chamber* 沉淀室。*a* ～ *tank* 澄水池。～ **box** 昆虫标本板。～ **lotion** 卷发水。～**-needle** 制标本用的木柄针。～ **rule**【印】排字尺。～ **stick** 排字托盘。～ **up**【无】调定。～**-up exercises** 徒手体操。

set·tle[1] [ˈsetl; ˋsɛtl̩] ***vt***. 1. 安排;使妥贴;使安定,处理好,

办好;决定;解决,确定。**2.** 使平静;使镇定。**3.** 调停;排解。**4.** 设定;派定;安牢;放牢。**5.** 使就职。**6.** 使坐下。**7.** 使守规矩,使就范。**8.** 使坚固;使坚实;使地干硬。**9.** 使澄清;使沉淀;使降;【地】沉降。**10.** 支付;清算;清偿;结清(款项、账目等)。**11.** 使住定;安顿;使定居。**12.** 殖民(某地)。**13.** 赠予。**14.**【法】指定;授与;让渡;和解。**15.**【动】使受孕。~ *a daughter by marriage* 嫁女儿。*That ~s the matter*. 这样问题就解决了。*The Government is quite ~d in power*. 政权稳固。~ *a claim* 结清债务。—*vi*. **1.** 稳定;固定;平安;平静。**2.** 了结;解决。**3.** 偿付;清算;结算。**4.** 决定;确定。**5.** 安家;成家;安居;定居;侨居。**6.** 栖息。**7.** 变坚固;变结实。**8.** 澄清;沉淀;下沉;沉降。**9.** 和解。**10.**【动】受孕;怀胎。*The weather has ~d at last*. 天气终于稳定下来了。~ *down to dinner* 坐定下来用餐。~ ***an account*** 清算;〔美、运〕雪耻,挣回面子。~ ***down*** **1.** 平静下来;恢复镇静。**2.** 沉淀;沉。**3.** 定居;成家;移居。**4.** 定下心来;定心去做。~ ***for*** 满足于,对…感到满意。~ ***in*** **1.** 搬入(新住所);使某人搬进(新住所)。**2.** 定居;殖民。**3.** 在家从容休息(~ *in London* 长住伦敦)。~ ***into shape*** 逐渐成形,(事情)有了眉目。~ ***on*** [***upon***] **1.** 授与;赠与(财产、遗产等)。**2.** 决定;选定(*They have ~d on you as my successor*. 他们已选定你为我的继承人)。**3.** (鸟等)停在;歇落在。~ ***one's affairs*** (在遗嘱等中)安排自己后事。~ ***oneself*** 成家;择定住处;安家。~ ***oneself*** (***down***) 定心去做。~ ***sb. hash*** 〔美俚〕征服[收拾]某人。~ ***the score*** 〔美运〕挣回面子。~ ***up*** **1.** 决定。**2.** 解决;支付。~ ***with*** **1.** 与…和解。**2.** 决定;讲定。**3.** 收拾。**4.** 付清,算清。**5.** 与…成交。

set·tle[2] [ˈsetl; ˋsɛtl] ***n***. 高背长靠椅〔座位下为柜子〕。

set·tled [ˈsetld; ˋsɛtld] ***a***. **1.** 固定(下来)的;确定不变的;稳定(下来)的。**2.** 根深蒂固的;坚固的;安定的。**3.** 安居在一个地方的;有居民的。**4.** 深切的。**5.** 决定的。**6.** 终身借用的。**7.** 算清了的;已付清的。**8.**【化】沉降的;澄清的。*a ~ abode* 固定的住所。*a ~ melancholy* 深愁。~ *conviction* 确信。*a ~ government* 稳定的政府。~ *weather* 稳定的天气。~ *estate* 终身租地。

set·tle·ment [ˈsetlmənt; ˋsɛtlmənt] ***n***. **1.** 解决。**2.** 决定。**3.** 镇定;安定。**4.** 固定;定着。**5.** 澄清;沉淀;沉淀物;沉积物;【地】沉陷。**6.** 和解。**7.** 整理;清理。**8.** 支付;清算;清偿;结账;决算。**9.** 殖民;殖民地;居留地;租界;(新)住宅区;居民点。**10.** 〔美〕部落;村落。**11.** 殖民团体;(一地的)居民社会。**12.** 居住权。**13.** 成家;有家属。**14.**【法】(财产的)授与;让渡;处理。**15.** (房屋等的)下沉。**16.** (作为慈善事业的)贫民区社会改良团体。*a ~ out of court*【法】(自行)和解。*terms of ~* 和解条件。*the International S-* (昔时上海等处的)公共租界。*a marriage ~*【法】结婚时的财产授与处理。*a social ~* 社会服务处。***come to a*** ~ **1.** 解决。**2.** 决定。**3.** 和解。***make a*** ~ ***on*** [***upon***] 授财产给。***reach a*** ~ = *come to a ~*. ~ **duty** 遗产税。~ **worker** 贫民区社会改良团体工作人员。

set·tler [ˈsetlə; ˋsɛtlɚ] ***n***. **1.** 居留者;定居者。**2.** 移居者;殖民者;开拓者。**3.** 〔口〕决定性打击;定论;最后解决者。**4.** 赠予者;调停者。**5.**【化】澄清器。**6.**【冶】前床;沉积槽。

set·tling [ˈsetliŋ; ˋsɛtlɪŋ] ***n***. **1.** 固定;安置。**2.** 沉淀。**3.** 〔*pl*.〕沉淀物;渣滓。**4.** 决定;解决。**5.** 结账;清算;决算。**6.** 移住;殖民。**7.** 镇静。~ **day** ***n***. 〔英〕(交易所等的)清算日;交割日;结账日。~ **tank** 沉淀槽。

set·tlor [ˈsetlə; ˋsɛtlɚ] ***n***.【法】财产授与人。

Se·vas·to·pol [siˈvæstəpl; sɪˋvæstəpl̩] ***n***. 塞瓦斯托波尔〔欧洲克里米亚半岛西南港市〕。

sev·en [ˈsevn; ˋsɛvən] **I** ***num***. 七,第七(章、卷、页等)。**II** ***n***. **1.** 七个东西。**2.** 七个一组。**3.** 七岁。**4.** 七点钟。**5.** 七个人;第七个人[物]。**6.** 〔喻〕十分,很多。*be frightened out of one's ~ senses* 吓得魂飞魄散。***at sixes and sevens*** 乱七八糟。***seventy times*** ~ 巨额数目(源出《圣经》《马太福音》)。~ **deadly sins**【宗】七大罪〔即 pride, covetousness, lust, anger, gluttony, envy, sloth, 据云犯此等罪者即下地狱〕。~**fold** ***a***., ***ad***. **1.** 七倍的[地];七重的[地];七折的[地]。**2.** 非常的[地]。~**-hilled city** 罗马(的别名)。**S- Hills** 罗马七丘〔罗马城即建于此七座小山丘上及其附近〕。~**night** 七昼夜;一周;一星期。~ **principal virtues** 七美德〔即 faith, hope, charity, prudence, justice, fortitude, temperance〕。**S- Sages** 希腊七贤〔有几种说法,最通常指 Bias, Chilon, Cleobulus, Periander, Pittacus, Solon, Thales〕。~ **seas** 七大洋〔指南、北太平洋、南、北大西洋、印度洋、南、北冰洋〕;全球。**S- Sisters** 七姊妹(指世界七大石油公司,亦可指美国七所有名的女子学院)。~**-up** 七点儿〔二人到四人玩的一种牌戏,七点成局〕。

sev·en·teen [ˈsevnˈtiːn; ˏsɛvənˋtin] **I** ***num***. (基数词)十七;第十七。**II** ***n***. **1.** 十七个。**2.** 十七的数[物、人]。**3.** 十七的记号。**4.** 十七岁。*sweet ~* 十七芳龄,妙龄。~**-year locust**【动】[美]十七年蝉〔幼虫在地下 13~17 年才成虫〕。

sev·en·teenth [ˈsevnˈtiːnθ; ˏsɛvənˋtinθ] **I** ***num***. **1.** 第十七(的)。**2.** 十七号(的)。**3.** 十七分之一(的)。**II** ***n***. 〔the ~〕(月的)十七日。

sev·enth [ˈsevnθ; ˋsɛvənθ] **I** ***num***. **1.** 第七。**2.** 七号。**3.** 七分之一。**II** ***n***. **1.** (月的)七日。**2.**【乐】第七音[程、度];第七和音。*a ~ part* 七分之一。*the ~ of May* 5 月 7 日。**S- Art** 第七艺术〔指电影〕。**S- Avenue** 纽约市第七街;纽约市妇女服装中心。~ **chord**【乐】七和音。~**-day** ***a***. 以星期六为安息日的。~ **heaven** **1.** 七重天。**2.** 极乐世界(*be in the ~ heaven* 欢天喜地地;在无上的幸福中)。~**-inning touch** 〔美〕努力;奋发;使劲。**-ly** ***ad***.

sev·en·ti·eth [ˈsevntiiθ; ˋsɛvəntɪɪθ] ***num***. **1.** 第七十(的)。**2.** 七十号(的);第七十次(的)。**3.** 七十分之一(的)。

sev·en·ty [ˈsevnti; ˋsɛvəntɪ] **I** ***num***. (基数词)七十;第七十(页等);七十个。**II** ***n***. **1.** 七十个东西。**2.** 七十的记号。**3.** 七十多岁。**4.** 〔*pl*.〕(世纪的)七十年代。*the nineteen ~* 1970 年。*the nineteen seventies* 二十世纪七十年代(略 1970's)。**5.** 〔*pl*.〕七十到七十九岁的时期。**6.** 〔俚〕快转速唱片。**the S-** **1.** 翻译希腊文旧约《圣经》的七十二个译者〔常作 LXX〕。**2.** 古犹太的高等参议院。~**-eight** **1.** ***num***. 七十八(个)。**2.** ***n***. 每分钟七十八转的唱片,快转速唱片。~**-five** ***n***.【军】法国的 75 毫米大炮。~ **fold** ***a***., ***ad***. 七十倍的(地)。~**-four** ***n***.【史】装有 74 门大炮的军舰。~**-three** ***n***. 〔美〕祝平安〔Best wishes 的电报记号〕。

sev·er [ˈsevə; ˋsɛvɚ] ***vt***. **1.** 切断;割断。**2.** 断绝;分隔开;使不和;离间。**3.**【法】分割(产业等);分别处理(权益等)。**4.** 区别。~ *diplomatic relations with* 和…断绝外交关系。~ *friends* 离间朋友。—***vi***. **1.** 分离;分裂。**2.** 分开;断。*The rope ~ed under the strain*. 索子拉断了。~ ***one's connection with*** 和…断绝关系。~ ***oneself from*** 退(会);脱离;和…分离。

sev·er·a·ble [ˈsevərəbl; ˋsɛvərəbl̩] ***a***. 可分开的;〔尤指〕【法】权益(或职责范围)可分开的〔指契约〕。**sev·er·a·bili·ty** [ˌsevərəˈbiliti; ˏsɛvərəˋbɪlətɪ] ***n***.

sev·er·al [ˈsevrəl; ˋsɛvərəl] **I** ***a***. **1.** 几个的;(二以上)多个的;数个的。**2.** 各不相同的;种种的。**3.** 各自的,各个的。**4.** 专有的,独占的,个人的。**5.**【法】有连带责任的。**6.** 〔方〕大量的。*Each has his ~ ideal*. 各人有各人的理想。*They went their ~ ways*. 他们各走各的去了。*S- men, ~ minds*. 各人有各人的想法。*three ~ items* 三个各不相同的项目。*a ~ estate* 个人的财产。*a joint and ~ responsibility* 连带责任。*myself and ~ others* 我和其他几个人。***each*** [***every***] ~ 各别的,各个的(*Each ~ ship sank her opponent*. 各舰分别击沉

了敌舰。*each* ～ *part* 各部分)。**for** ～ **days** 好几天。～ **times** 屡次;好几次。**II** ***pron***. 几个,数个;数人。*S- have given their consent*. 有几个人已表示同意。～ *of us* 我们当中的几个人。～**-fold** ***a***., ***ad***. **1**. 有几部分的[地];有几方面的[地]。**2**. 好几倍的[地]。

sev·er·al·ly [ˈsevrəli; ˋsɛvərəlɪ] ***ad***. 各自;分别;个别(地)。*conjunctly* [*jointly*] *and* ～【法】负连带责任地。*The bond was signed jointly and* ～. 证书上有联名签字。*exeunt* ～【剧】分别退场。

sev·er·al·ty [ˈsevərəlti; ˋsɛvrəltɪ] ***n***. (*pl*. ***-ties***) **1**. 各自;各个;单独。**2**. 个人拥有的财产;**3**. 个人拥有财产;(土地的)个人所有权。

sev·er·ance [ˈsevərəns; ˋsɛvərəns] ***n***. **1**. 切断;隔断。**2**. 分离,隔离。**3**. (关系等)断绝。**4**. 区别;差别。～ **pay** (雇主违约辞退工人时的)解雇费;遣散费。

se·vere [siˈviə; səˋvɪr] ***a***. (***-ver·er***; ***-ver·est***) **1**. (面孔等)严肃的;严正的;(训练等)严格的;严厉的;(批评家等)苛刻的。**2**. 猛烈的;剧烈的;(暴风等)凶猛的;凛烈的;厉害的,(疾病等)严重的。**3**. 困难的;艰难的;(工作等)极难的。**4**. (建筑)简朴的;简练的;(文艺作品)严谨的;朴素的;朴实的。**5**.精确的。*a* ～ *pain* 剧痛。*a* ～ *wound* 重伤。*a* ～ *sickness* [*disease*] 重病。**be** ～ **on** [**upon**] 猛烈攻击;严厉对付。

se·vere·ly [siˈviəli; səˋvɪrlɪ] ***ad***. **1**. 猛烈地;剧烈地。**2**. 严密地;严格地。**3**. 严重地。**4**. 严厉地;苛刻地。**5**. 简洁地。**be** ～ **ill** [**wounded**] 患重病[负重伤]。**leave** [**let**] ～ **alone** (因讨厌而)敬而远之。

se·ver·i·ty [siˈveriti; səˋvɛrətɪ] ***n***. **1**. 严肃;严正;严格;严厉;苛刻。**2**. 严重。**3**. 厉害;猛烈。**4**. 严密。**5**. 纯洁。**6**. 简朴;简练。**7**.【机】刚度;硬度。～ **factor** 硬[刚]度系数。

Se·ville [ˈsevil, səˈvil; ˋsɛvɪl, səˋvɪl], **Se·vil·la** [seiˈviːjɑː; seˋvijɑ] ***n***. 塞维利亚〔西班牙城市〕。**vil·li·an** ***a***.

Se·vres [ˈseivr; ˋsɛvrə] ***n***. **1**. 塞夫勒〔法国城市〕。**2**. 塞夫勒(产的)陶器。

sew [səu; so] ***vt***. (～***ed***; ～***ed***, ***sewn*** [səun; son]) **1**. 缝;缝合;缝制;缝做;缝补。**2**. 装钉(书籍)。～ *a garment* 缝外套。～ *a buttonhole* 锁钮扣眼。—***vi***. 缝纫;做针线活。**be** ～**ed up** **1**.【海】搁浅;停顿。**2**. 喝醉。～ **in** 缝进(～ *money in a bag* 把钱缝进袋里)。～ **on** 缝上。～ **up** 1. 缝拢;缝合。2. 把…缝入;缝进。3.〔卑〕使累极。4.〔俚〕使大醉。5. 使(船)搁浅;使无可奈何。6. 欺诈。7.〔美俚〕绝对控制住;垄断;压住。8. 解决,确定;〔美俚〕成功地完成(协商、合约等)。

sew·age [ˈsju(ː)idʒ; ˋsjuɪdʒ] **I** ***n***. **1**. 阴沟污物;污水。**2**. 下水道。**II** ***vt***. **1**. 用污水灌溉[作肥料]。**2**. 装设下水道于(某地)。～**-farm** **1**. 污水利用农场;污水灌溉田。**2**. 污物处理场。～ **tank** 化粪池;污水(沉淀)池。

se·wan [ˈsiːwən; ˋsiwən] ***n***. 西文〔北美阿尔衮琴印第安人所用的贝壳货币〕。

Se·ward [ˈsiːwəd; ˋsjuəd] ***n***. **1**. 西沃德〔姓氏〕。**2**. **W. H**. ～ 威廉·西沃德〔1801-1872, 美国政治家,曾任国务卿〕。～**'s Folly** **1**. 阿拉斯加的别称。**2**. 暂时看来愚蠢、日后显示出极为合算的行为〔源出西沃德用巨款从俄国购买阿拉斯加之举〕。

se·wel·lel [sjuːˈwelel, siˈwelel; sjuˋwɛlɛl, sɪˋwɛlɛl] ***n***.【动】(美国西海岸的)山狸。

sew·er[1] [ˈsəuə; ˋsoə] ***n***. **1**. 缝纫者;缝工;成衣师。**2**. 缝纫机。

sew·er[2] [ˈsjuə; ˋsjuə] **I** ***n***. 阴沟;污水管道;下水道;排水管。*the trunk* ～ 下水干道。**II** ***vt***. **1**. 从…排污水。**2**. 在…开阴沟;装设下水道于。～ **gas**【化】阴沟气;沟道气。～ **rat**【动】褐鼠。

sew·er[3] [ˈsjuːə; ˋsjuə] ***n***. (中世纪贵族宅第中的)司膳管家[家仆]。

sewer·age [ˈsjuəridʒ; ˋsjuərɪdʒ] ***n***. **1**. 污水;污物(= sewage)。**2**. 暗沟工事;下水设备;下水道系统,排水系统;沟渠系统。**3**. 下水处理;污水。**4**. 肮脏思想[言行]。

sew·ing [ˈsəuiŋ; ˋsoɪŋ] ***n***. **1**. 缝纫。**2**. (书的)装订。**3**. 缝纫物;针线活。**4**.〔*pl*.〕(缝纫用)线。～ **circle** 妇女义务缝纫组。～ **cotton** 缝纫棉线。～ **machine** **1**. 缝纫机。**2**.【装钉】穿线订书机。～ **needle** (缝纫用)针。～ **-press**【印】锁线装订机。～ **thread** (缝纫用)线。

sewn [səun; son] sew 的过去分词。～**-up** ***a***. **1**.〔俚〕累极了的。**2**.〔俚〕大醉的。

sex [seks; sɛks] **I** ***n***. **1**. 性;(男女的)性别;〔集合词〕男性,女性。**2**. 性的活动[器官];性交;性欲;色情。*persons of both* ～*es* 男男女女。*the two* ～*es* 男女;雌雄。*without distinction of age or* ～ 不分男女老幼。**have** ～〔美俚〕发生性行为。**the fair** [**gentle**, **softer**, **weaker**] ～ 女性;妇女。**the male** [**rough**, **sterner**, **stronger**] ～ 男性,男人。**the** ～〔谑〕女人。**II** ***vt***. **1**. 区别(小鸡等)的性别。**2**. 增强…的性感;刺激起…的性欲。～ *it up*〔美俚〕两性间的热烈爱抚。～ *up*〔美口〕**1**. 勾引(异性)。**2**. 增加吸引力(～ *up the movie with some fighting scenes* 加几场打斗镜头以加强影片的吸引力)。**III** ***a***. 性的;与性有关的。～ **appeal** 性的吸引力;性感。～**-and-shopping** ***n***.〔美〕(专门描写豪门玉女、艳妇富婆等以逛高级商店购昂贵物品和沉迷于性爱为其生活内容的)低级艳情小说〔时常缩写为 sex'n' shopping〕。～**-blind** ***a***. 无性别差异的;无性别歧视的。～ **cell** 生殖细胞。～ **change** (通过外科手术所作的)性别改变,变性。～ **clinic** 性病诊所。～ **education** 性教育。～ **hormone** 性激素。～ **impulse** 性的冲动。～ **instinct** 性的本能。～ **linkage**【生】伴性(遗传);性连锁。～**linked** ***a***.【生】伴性的;性连锁的。～ **pot**〔美俚〕性感女人。～ **ratio** 男女人口比例。～ **role** 性别作用;性别职责。～ **shop** 色情用品商店。～ **therapy**【医】性心理疗法〔指通过咨询或其他心理疗法来治疗阳痿或性冷淡、性感缺失等〕。～ **typing** 性别分工,男女分工;性别类别。～ **urge** (病态的)性欲。～ **worker**〔婉〕妓女。

sex-, **sexi-** *comb*. *f*. 六: *sex*angle, *sexi*llion.

sex·a·ge·nar·i·an [ˌseksədʒiˈnɛəriən; ˏsɛksədʒəˋnɛrɪən] ***a***., ***n***. 六十至六十九岁的(人);六十多岁的(人)。

sex·ag·e·na·ry [sekˈsædʒinəri; sɛksˋædʒɪˏnɛrɪ] **I** ***n***. **1**. 六十个(东西)。**2**. = sexagenarian (***n***.)。**II** ***a***. **1**.六十的。**2**. = sexagenarian (***a***.)。

Sex·a·ges·i·ma [ˌseksəˈdʒesimə; ˏsɛksəˋdʒɛsəmə] ***n***.【宗】四旬节前第二个星期日〔亦作 S- Sunday〕。

sex·a·ges·i·mal [ˌseksəˈdʒesiməl; ˏsɛksəˋdʒɛsəml] **I** ***a***. 六十的;以六十为基础的;六十进位的。**II** ***n***.【数】六十分数〔以六十为分母的分数〕。

sex·an·gle [ˈseksˌæŋgl; ˋsɛksˏæŋgl] ***n***.【数】六角形。

sex·an·gu·lar [seksˈæŋgjulə; sɛksˋæŋgjələ] ***a***. 六角的。

sex·cen·te·na·ry [ˌsekssenˈtiːnəri; sɛksˋsɛntɪˏnɛrɪ] **I** ***a***. 六百年的。**II** ***n***. 六百年纪念。

sexed [sekst; sɛkst] ***a***. **1**. 性别的;有性别的。**2**. 有性欲的;性感的。～**-up** ***a***.〔美俚〕**1**. 性感的。**2**. 吸引人的。

sex·en·ni·al [sekˈsenjəl, -niəl; sɛksˋɛnɪəl] **I** ***a***. 六年间的;连续六年的;每六年的,六年一次[度]的。**II** ***n***. 六周年纪念。**-ly** ***ad***.

sex·er·cise [ˈseksəsaiz; ˋsɛksəsaɪz] ***n***., ***vi***. (做)性训练〔指从事增强作爱能力、提高个人性吸引力等的训练〕。

sex·foil [ˈseksfɔil; ˋsɛksˏfɔɪl] ***n***.【建】六叶[六瓣花]形(装饰图案);【植】六瓣花,六叶复叶。

sexi- *comb*. *f*. = sex-.

sex·il·lion [sekˈsiljən; sɛksˋɪljən] ***n***. = sextillion.

sex·i·ly [ˈseksili; ˋsɛksəlɪ] ***ad***.〔口〕性感地。

sex·i·ness [ˈseksinis; ˋsɛksənɪs] ***n***.〔口〕性吸引力;性感。

sex·ism [ˈseksizm; ˋsɛksɪzm] ***n***. 性别歧视〔尤指歧视妇女〕。

sex·ist [ˈseksist; ˋsɛksɪst] ***n***. 实行性别歧视的人。

S

sex·i·va·lent [ˈseksiˌveilənt; ˋsɛksəˏvelənt] ***a.*** 【化】六价的。

sex·less [ˈsekslis; ˋsɛkslɪs] ***a.*** 无性别的;无性的;中性的;无性感的。

sex·ol·o·gy [sekˈsɔlədʒi; sɛksˋɑlədʒɪ] ***n.*** 【医】性行为学。**sex·ol·o·gist** ***n.*** 性行为学研究家。

sex·par·tite [seksˈpɑːtait; sɛksˋpartaɪt] ***a.*** **1.** 分成六部(分)的。**2.** 【植】六深裂的。~ **vault** 【建】六肋拱穹。

sex·ploit·a·tion [ˌsekspləiˈteiʃən; ˏsɛksplɔɪˋteʃən] ***n.*** 〔美〕(电影等大肆宣扬色情的)性泛滥。

sex·ploit·er [ˈsekspləitə; ˋsɛksˏplɔɪtɚ] ***n.*** 〔美〕色情电影。

sext [sekst; sɛkst] ***n.*** **1.** 【宗】第六时[正午]祈祷(仪)式。**2.** 【乐】第六度音程。

sex·tan [ˈsekstən; ˋsɛkstən] **I** ***a.*** 隔六天发作一次的。*a ~ fever* 【医】六日热。**II** ***n.*** 【医】六日热。

Sex·tans [ˈsekstənz; ˋsɛkstənz] ***n.*** 【天】六分仪(星)座。

sex·tant [ˈsekstənt; ˋsɛkstənt] ***n.*** **1.** 六分仪。**2.** 【天】〔S-〕六分仪(星)座(=Sextans)。**3.** 〔罕〕圆的六分之一。

sex·tet, sex·tette [seksˈtet; sɛksˋtɛt] ***n.*** **1.** 六人[物]的一组。**2.** 【乐】六重唱;六重奏;六重唱[奏]表演者。**3.** 六行诗节。**4.** 曲棍球队。**5.** 【化】六隅。

sex·tile [ˈsekstl; ˋsɛkstl] **I** ***n.*** 【天】(二天体互距的)六十度之位置。**II** ***a.*** 【天】(二天体互距)六十度之位置的。

sex·til·lion [seksˈtiljən; sɛksˋtɪljən] ***n.*** **1.** 〔英、德〕100万的6次幂[乘方]〔1后有36个0的数〕。**2.** 〔美、法〕1,000的7次幂[乘方]〔1后有21个0的数〕。

sex·to [ˈsekstəu; ˋsɛksto] ***n.*** (*pl.* ~*es*) 六开本(的书)。

sex·to·dec·i·mo [ˈsekstəuˈdesiməu; ˏsɛkstoˋdɛsɪˏmo] ***n.*** (*pl.* ~*s*) 十六开(的书[纸])〔略16 *mo* 或16°,通常读作 sixteenmo〕。

sex·ton [ˈsekstən; ˋsɛkstən] ***n.*** 教堂司事〔担任教堂内外管理、敲钟、墓地等工作〕。

sex·tu·ple [ˈsekstjupl; ˋsɛkstjʊpl] **I** ***a.*** **1.** 六倍的;六重的。**2.** 【乐】六拍子的。**II** ***vt.***, ***vi.*** (使)变成六倍。

sex·tu·plet [seksˈtjuplit, -ˈtuːplit, -ˈtʌplit; sɛksˋtjuplɪt, -ˋtuplɪt, -ˋtʌplɪt, ˋsɛkstʊplɪt] ***n.*** **1.** 一胎六个之一。**2.** (同一类的)六个一组。**3.** 〔*pl.*〕一胎六个。**4.** 【乐】六连音。

sex·tu·plic·ate [seksˈtjuːplikeit; sɛksˈtuplɪˏket] **I** ***vt.*** **1.** 使成六倍。**2.** 把…打印成六份。**II** [seksˈtjuːplikit; sɛksˋtuplɪkɪt] ***a.*** **1.** 重复六次的。**2.** 第六的。**III** ***n.*** **1.** 第六个同类物。**2.** 相同的六份。

sex·u·al [ˈseksjuəl; ˋsɛkʃʊəl] ***a.*** **1.** 性的;有性别的。**2.** 性欲的。**3.** 生殖的;【生】有性的。~ **affinity** 异性间的吸引力。~ **appetite** 性欲。~ **perversion** 变态性欲。~ **intercourse** [**commerce**] 性交。~ **diseases** 性病。~ **generation** 【生】有性世代。~ **harassment** 性骚扰。~ **organs** 性器官;生殖器。~ **orientation** (对同性或异性感兴趣的)性取向,性倾向。~ **politics** 性别政治〔指男女两性之间为争夺支配权等所作的安排或社会秩序〕。~ **reproduction** 【生】有性生殖。~ **selection** 【生】性选择,雌性淘汰。~ **spore** 【植】有性胞子。**-ly** ***ad.***

sex·u·al·i·ty [ˌseksjuˈæliti; ˏsɛkʃʊˋælətɪ] ***n.*** **1.** 性别;有性状态。**2.** 性欲;性生活[行为]。

sex·u·al·ize [ˈseksjuəlaiz; ˋsɛkʃʊəlˏaɪz] ***vt.*** (*-iz·ed*; *-iz·ing*) 给以性的特征;使有性别。

sex·y [ˈseksi; ˋsɛksɪ] ***a.*** (*-i·er*; *-i·est*) 〔美俚〕**1.** 有性的吸引力的;性感的;色情的。**2.** 因加装饰而更为有趣的。**3.** 诱人的,有吸引力的。

Sey·chelles [seiˈʃelz; seˋʃɛlz] ***n.*** 塞舌耳(群岛)〔非洲〕。

Sey·mour [ˈsiːmɔː, ˈseimɔː; ˋsɪmɔr, ˋsemɔr] ***n.*** 西摩〔姓氏,男子名〕。

SEZ = Special Economic Zone (中国深圳等)经济特区。

Sez·you [sezˈjuː; sɛzˋju] (=says you) 〔美俚〕你说你的吧(我可不信)。

sf. =〔It.〕*sforzando*.

S.F. = **1.** San Francisco. **2.** Sinn Fein 〔爱尔兰〕新芬党。

s.f. = **1.** selffeeding 自动送料;自动进给。**2.** sinking fund 减债资金。**3.** square foot. **4.** *sub fine* [*finem*] 〔L.〕(【乐】到末尾)。**5.** semi-finished 半加工的;半完成的。**6.** =square foot 平方英尺。**7.** =science fiction 科幻小说。

Sfax [sfɑːks; sfɑks] ***n.*** 斯法克斯〔突尼斯港市〕。

Sfc = sergeant first class (〔陆军〕上士)。

S.F.C. = specific fuel consumption 单位耗油率。

sfer·ics [ˈsfiəriks, ˌsfer-; ˋsfɛrɪks] ***n.*** 〔动词用单数〕【无】**1.** 低频天电(=atmospherics)。**2.** 低频天电学,天电学。**3.** 远程雷电。**4.** 风暴电子探测器。

sfor·zan·do [sfɔːˈtsɑːndəu; sforˋtsɑndo] 〔It.〕 **I** ***a.***, ***ad.*** 【乐】强调;着重;力;突出。**II** ***n.*** (*pl.* *-dos*) 特强符号 "sf"。

sfor·za·to [sfɔːrˈtsɑːtəu; sforˋtsɑto] 〔It.〕 ***a.***, ***ad.*** = *sforzando*.

sfz =〔It.〕*sforzando*.

s.g. = specific gravity 【物】比重。

SG = sweep generator 扫描[扫频]振荡器。

sg. = signature.

S.G. = **1.** Solicitor-General. **2.** 〔L.〕【海】*salutis gratia* (为安全起见)。**3.** 【海】ship and goods 船货。**4.** screen grid 【电】帘栅(极)。**5.** signal generator 信号发生器。**6.** spark gap 【电】电火隙;火花隙。

sgd. = signed.

s.g.d.g. =〔F.〕*Sans garantie du gouvernment* (〔F.〕=without Government guarantee) 政府不予担保。

sgl. = single 单独的;单一的;纯粹的,单纯的。

SGML = standardized general mark-up language 【计】标准通用置标语言。

SGR = sodium graphite reactor 【核】石墨慢化钠冷反应堆;钠石墨反应堆。

sgraf·fi·to [skræˈfiːtəu, It. zgrɑːfˈfiːtəu; skræˋfito, It. zgrɑfˋfito] ***n.*** (*pl.* ***-fi·ti*** [-tiː; -ti]) 【建】**1.** 五彩拉毛粉饰法。**2.** 五彩拉毛粉饰。**3.** 五彩拉毛粉饰陶瓷。

Sgt., **sgt.** = sergeant.

Sgt. Maj. = Sergeant Major.

sh. =〔美〕**1.** share. **2.** sheet. **3.** shilling. **4.** shunt.

S.H. = School House.

SHA = sideral hour angle 【海】赤经共轭量;恒星时角。

shab·by [ˈʃæbi; ˋʃæbɪ] ***a.*** (***-bi·er***; ***-bi·est***) **1.** (衣衫)褴褛的;破旧的。**2.** 失修的。**3.** 肮脏的。**4.** 卑劣的;卑鄙的。**5.** 吝啬的。**6.** 低劣的;拙劣的;简陋的。*a ~ street* 肮脏的马路。*a ~ fellow* 卑鄙的家伙;小气鬼。~**-genteel** ***a.*** 穷要面子的;摆穷架子的。**-bi·ly** ***ad.*** **-bi·ness** ***n.***

shab·rach, shab·rack [ˈʃæbræk; ˋʃæbræk] ***n.*** (骑兵用的)鞍被[鞍褥]。

Sha·bu·oth [ʃɑːˈvuːəut, ʃəˈvuːəus; fæˋvuot, ʃəˋvuos] ***n.*** = Shavuot.

shack[1] [ʃæk; ʃæk] **I** ***n.*** **1.** 〔美、加〕窝棚;圆木小屋。**2.** (派某种用场的)小室,房间;〔美俚〕无线电收发室。**II** ***vi.*** 居住;暂住。~ **up** **1.** 住下。**2.** 过夜;宿泊。**3.** (与人)姘居;同居。~ **job** 〔美俚〕情妇,姘头。

shack[2] [ʃæk; ʃæk] ***n.*** **1.** 〔美〕游民。**2.** 驽马;废马。**3.** 【铁路】〔美俚〕制动员。~ **fever** 〔美俚〕(游民)想打瞌睡的疲乏。

shack[3] [ʃæk; ʃæk] ***n.*** **1.** 〔方〕落穗;落实。**2.** 收获后茬地上的放牧自由权。

shack[4] [ʃæk; ʃæk] ***vt.*** 〔美口〕追到;拣起并把(球)丢回去;取回来。

shack·le [ˈʃækl; ˋʃækl] **I** ***n.*** **1.** 〔常 *pl.*〕手铐;脚镣;〔*pl.*〕桎梏。**2.** 〔*pl.*〕束缚(物);羁绊(物);阻碍(物);碍手碍脚的东西。**3.** 枷形装饰。**4.** 【机】钩环;【铁路】(车厢间的)钩链。**5.** 【电】绝缘器。**6.** 【海】十五英尺长的缆绳[锚链]。*the ~s of convention* 陈规旧习的束缚。**II**

S

vt. 1. 给…上手铐[上脚镣]。2. 束缚;拘束。3. 妨碍;阻碍。4. 用钩链连结。5.【电】在…装绝缘器。~ **bone** [Scot.] 1. 动物的膝或肘关节。2. 手腕,腕关节。

Shack·le·ton [ˈʃækltən; ˋʃækl̩tən] *n*. 1. 沙克尔顿[姓氏]。2. **Sir Ernest Henry** ~ 沙克尔顿[1874—1922,英国南极探险家]。

shad [ʃæd; ʃæd] *n*.【鱼】(美洲)河鲱。

shad·berry [ˈʃædberi; ˋʃæd͵bɛrɪ], **shad·bush** [ˈʃædbuʃ; ˋʃæd͵bʊʃ] *n*. 1.【植】唐棣属(*Amelanchier*)植物。2. 唐棣果实(又称 shadblow)。

shad·chan, shad·chen [ˈʃɑːtkhən; ˋʃætkhən] *n*. = schatchen.

shad·dock [ˈʃædək; ˋʃædək] *n*.【植】柚子。

shade [ʃeid; ʃed] **I** *n*. 1. 荫;阴处;树阴。2. [*pl*.] 阴暗,幽暗。3. 遮阳;遮棚;天幔;阳伞;灯罩;帘;幕;屏风;挡风物;遮尘物;挡热隔子;玻璃罩。4. [*pl*.] [美俚]太阳眼镜。5. (画的)阴暗部分;朦胧色;晕色;明暗;浓淡;色调。6. [诗][主 *pl*.]阴居处;僻远处。7. 幽灵;阴魂。8. [the ~s][诗]黄泉;冥府;阴间;死;坟墓。9. [*pl*.]酒窖;地下室酒吧间;旅馆的酒吧间。10. 些许;少许。11. 愁容,面色阴郁。12. [美俚]窝赃犯。*the ~ of night* 夜色苍茫。*the same colour in a light ~* 同样颜色浅一点的。*This picture shows fine effects of light and ~.* 这幅画的明暗效果很好。*people of all ~s (of opinions)* (意见)千差万别的人们。***a ~ of*** 少许;微微(*a ~ of difference* 微微一点区别)。***cast into the ~*** 使失色;使相形见绌。***delicate ~s of meaning*** 意义的细微层次。***fall into the ~*** 1. 被夺去光彩;黯然失色。2. 被赐下来。***go down to the ~s*** 死。***in [into] the ~*** 1. 在阴处;在树阴下;在暗处。2. 没落;衰微(*in the ~ of obscurity* 避着人眼;被人遗忘)。***not a ~ of doubt*** 毫不怀疑。***put into the ~*** = *cast into the ~*. ***~s of ...*** 让人联想到(某事物)。***S- of Priscian [Plato, Soyer]!*** 活见鬼! [普里兴、柏拉图、索雅三人各为语法、哲学、烹饪之祖;语法家、哲学家、厨师闹笑话时的叹声]。***the shadow of a ~*** 幻影;虚中之虚。***throw into the ~*** = *cast into the ~*. ***under the ~ of*** (*a tree*) 在(树)阴底下。***without light and ~*** (画)没有明暗的;(文章等)单调的。**II** *vt*. 1. 遮(光);阴蔽;遮蔽;覆盖;隐藏;在…装遮阳篷[天棚](等)。2. 使暗;使失色;使黯淡。3. 在(画上)画阴影;使色彩具有明暗层次。4. 使(意见,方法等)逐渐改变。5. [美]略减(物价)。6. 使(风琴管)音调缓和。~ *one's eyes with one's hand* 用手挡住射向眼睛的直射光。*a ~d lamp* 装有灯罩的灯。~ **density**【林】郁闭度。— *vi*. (色彩、意见、意义等)逐渐变化(*away; off; into*)。

shad·i·ly [ˈʃeidəli; ˋʃedəlɪ] *ad*. 1. 多荫地;阴暗地。2. 暧昧地;可疑地。

shad·i·ness [ˈʃeidinis; ˋʃedɪnɪs] *n*. 1. 多阴;阴暗。2. 暧昧;可疑。

shad·ing [ˈʃeidiŋ; ˋʃedɪŋ] *n*. 1. 阴蔽。2.【绘画】阴影;明暗;浓淡。3. [喻]隐微的渐变;细微差别[层次]。

sha·doof [ʃɑːˈduːf, ʃəˈduːf; ʃɑˋduf] *n*. (中东地区农民用的)汲水吊杆;桔槔。

shad·ow [ˈʃædəu; ˋʃædo] **I** *n*. 1. (阴)影;影像;阴暗;黑暗。2. 影子;形影相随的人。3. 跟着客人来的人;不速之客;食客。4. [美俚]侦探。5. 鬼;幽灵;幻影。6. 迹象;苗头;前兆;预兆。7. 少许;一点点。8. 隐藏处;庇护;保护;隐退(处)。9. (电波传播)静区。10. [美俚][贬]黑人。11. 郁郁寡欢(的神色)。12. 没落,微贱。13. (友谊等的)暂时中断。*Coming events cast their ~s before.* 事未发生,先有苗头。*May your ~ never grow less!* 祝你永远健康! *the ~s of old age* 老态。*the ~ of a name* 虚名。*the ~ of death* 死的前兆。***be afraid of one's own ~*** 风声鹤唳,草木皆兵;胆小,容易受惊。***be the ~ of one's former self*** = ***be worn to a ~*** 瘦成皮包骨头。***cast ~s*** 投影;预兆。***catch [grasp] at ~s, run after ~s*** 捕风捉影;徒劳。***fight with one's own ~*** 和自己的影子作战,进行毫无结果的斗争。***have only the ~ of*** (*freedom*) 获得有名无实的(自由)。***in the ~*** 在阴处;在暗处。***in the ~ of*** 在…的附近[身边];与…很接近。***live in the ~*** 隐姓埋名。***quarrel with one's own ~*** 容易为小事情而发莫名其妙的脾气。***under [in] the ~ of*** 1. 在…的附近[身边]。2. 与…很接近。3. 在…的保护下。***within the ~ of*** 在…的身边。***without a ~ of doubt*** 毫不怀疑地。**II** *vt*. 1. 把影子投在…上;用自身的影子遮住;遮阴;遮暗;遮住;遮蔽;遮盖;隐藏;隐匿。2. 保护;庇护。3. (在画上)画阴影;使朦胧;使阴暗。4. 尾随;跟牢;盯牢;盯梢;(短期培训中教练员、师傅等)陪伴着(实习生、学员等)工作。5. 暗暗表示;预示;成为…的前兆。*He is ~ed by the police.* 他被警察盯住了。~ *forth some future occurrence* 预示将来的事。— *vi*. 渐变;变阴暗。~ **aircraft** 侦察机。~ **angle** 影锥角。~ **area** 投影面积。~ **bands**【无】影带。~ **box** [美](挂在墙上,有玻璃盖的)陈列框。~**box** *vi*. 1. 作拳击练习;与假想的对手作拳斗。2. 避免作出直接的决定行动。~ **cabinet** 1. [英](假拟的由在野党人士组成的)影子内阁。2. 总统[首相]的智囊团。~ **dance** 影舞[不见舞者本人,只见其映在幕布上的影子]。~ **effect**【无】阴影效应;屏蔽效果。~ **factory** 战时可转产军需品的民用工厂。~**land** 1. 鬼世界,阴府。2. 想像中的世界,幻境。~**-manage** *vt*. 幕后操纵。~ **mask** 1. 投影掩模;障板。2. (彩色显像管的)遮蔽屏。~ **play** 影子戏。~ **price**【经】影子价格,尾随价。~ **silk** 闪光绸。~ **tone** 半色调。

shad·ow·graph [ˈʃædəugrɑːf; ˋʃædo͵græf] *n*. 1. (用阴影在墙上作成的)投影画;描影;影像图。2.【摄】(逆光)影像;逆光摄影;阴影摄影。3. 放射线照相(= radiograph); X 光摄影。4. = shadow play.

shad·ow·y [ˈʃædəui; ˋʃædəwɪ] *a*. 1. 多阴影的;多荫的;郁苍的;阴暗的。2. 朦胧的;模糊的。3. 影子一般的;虚幻的。4. 前兆性的;暗中表示的;爱空想的。*a ~ hope* 微薄暗淡的希望。**shad·ow·i·ness** *n*.

shad·y [ˈʃeidi; ˋʃedɪ] *a*. (*-i·er; -i·est*) 1. 多阴影的;有荫的;荫蔽的;成荫的;背阴的;遮阴的。2. (年龄)过了盛年的。3. 不可靠的;不明不白的;可疑的。4. 阴暗的;秘密的;背着人的。*a ~ character* 可疑的人物[性格]。*keep ~* [美]避开人眼;藏匿。***on the ~ side of*** 1. 在…的黑暗一面;在…的背阴方面;在下坡路上。2. [年龄]…多岁;超过;大于(*on the ~ side of forty* 已过四十)。**-i·ly** *ad*. **-i·ness** *n*.

SHAEF = Supreme Headquarters Allied Expeditionary Force (二次大战期间)盟军最高统帅部。

shaft [ʃɑːft; ʃæft] **I** *n*. 1. 箭;箭杆。2. (枪、槌、斧等的)柄;矛。3.【植】秆;茎;柄。4.【动】羽轴;羽干。5. (古生物的)主突起茎。6. [the ~s]辕;车杠;车把。7. 烛台杆;鞭柄;棍棒;旗竿。8.【建】柱身。9. (露出屋面的)烟囱。10. 轴;旋转轴。11.【冶】炉身。12.【矿】矿井;竖坑;通风管道;升降井。13. 光线;电光。14. 柱;柱身。15. [美]纪念标;尖塔。16. [美俚]大腿。~ *excavation* 井筒掘进;竖井。*~s of satire [ridicule, envy]* 尖锐的讽刺[嘲笑,嫉妒]。~ *walls* 炉墙。***get the ~*** [俚]受骗。***give (sb.) the ~*** [俚]欺骗(某人)。***have a ~ left in one's quiver*** 还有本钱,还有计可施。**II** *vt*. 给…装上杆柄(或轴等);撑(船)。— *vi*. 射出…的光线。~ **bearing**【机】轴承。~ **horse** 辕马。~ **house**【矿】(竖坑口升降机器用的)粗架。~ **sinking**【矿】凿井。

Shaftes·bur·y [ˈʃɑːftsbəri; ˋʃæfts͵bɛrɪ] *n*. 沙夫茨伯里[姓氏]。

shaft·ing [ˈʃɑːftiŋ; ˋʃæftɪŋ] *n*.【机】1. 轴系。2. 传动轴。3. 轴材。

shag[1] [ʃæg; ʃæg] *n*. 1. 粗毛。2.【纺】长绒;长绒粗呢。3. 粗烟丝。4. 杂[蓬]乱的一丛[毛发,草丛,灌木等]。

shag[2] [ʃæg; ʃæg] *n*.【动】欧洲鸬鹚[鹈鹕];绿鸬鹚;有冠鸬

鹨。

shag[3] [ʃæg; ʃæg] 〔美〕 *vt*. (*shag·ged*, *shg·ging*) **1**. 追赶;追回。**2**. 钉在…后面;紧跟在后面;推拥。

shag·a·nap·pi [ˈʃægəˌnæpi; ˏʃægəˋnæpɪ] *n*. 生皮带;〔总称〕皮条。

shag·bark [ˈʃægbɑːk; ˋʃægˏbɑrk] *n*. 〔美〕【植】**1**. 小糙皮山核桃树。**2**. 这种树的木材。**3**. 这种树结的核桃。

shagged [ˈʃægid; ˋʃægɪd] *a*. **1**. 〔英口〕累坏了;累垮了。**2**. 有〔似〕粗毛的。**3**. 有粗植物的。**4**. 表面粗糙的。

shag·gy [ˈʃægi; ˋʃægɪ] *a*. (*-gi·er*; *-gi·est*) **1**. 多粗毛的;毛发蓬松的。**2**.【动、植】有绒毛的;草木丛生的。**3**. 粗野的;不整洁的。~ **dog story** **1**. 冗长繁琐叙述后有一个意外结尾的故事。**2**. 以一个会说话动物为主角的故事〔笑话等〕。**-gi·ly** *ad*. **-gi·ness** *n*.

sha·green [ˈʃægriːn; ʃəˋgrin] *n*. **1**. 鲨革。**2**. 表面呈粒状的皮革。

shah [ʃɑː; ʃɑ] *n*. 〔Per.〕王;伊朗国王的称号。~**dom** 伊朗国王的领土;王位。

Sha·hap·ti·an [ʃɑːˈhæptiən; ʃɑˋhæptɪən] *n*. = Sahaptin.

shai·tan [ʃaiˈtɑːn; ʃaɪˋtɑn] *n*. **1**. 魔鬼;〔尤指〕〔常用 S-〕撒旦〔穆斯林用语〕。**2**. 恶人;坏人。

shake [ʃeik; ʃek] (*shook* [ʃuk; ʃʊk]; *shak·en* [ˈʃeikən; ˋʃekən]; *shak·ing*) **I** *vt*. **1**. 摇;摇动;摇撼。**2**. 动摇(信念、决心等);使(人心)动摇。**3**. 挥(拳)。**4**. 摇醒(睡着的人)(*up*)。**5**. 摇落(*from*; *out of*)。**6**. 使战栗;使发抖。**7**. 减损;减少;挫折(勇气等)。**8**.〔俚〕摆脱。**9**.【乐】使发颤声;使抖颤。**10**.〔美俚〕=~ down. *To be shaken before taking*.【药】服前摇匀。*His resolution is not to be shaken by anything*. 他的决心是怎么也动摇不了的。*The ranks were shaken, but not broken*. 队伍动摇了,但未崩溃。—*vi*. **1**. 发抖;抖颤;战栗;震颤。**2**. 动;震动;摇曳;摆动;动摇。**3**.【乐】发颤声。**4**.〔美俗〕〔用命令语气〕握手。***be shaken at*** 被…惊吓。***deserve a good shaking*** 该好好的揍一顿。~ ***a foot*** [***leg***] **1**. 跳舞。**2**.〔美俚〕赶快〔通常用命令语气〕。~ ***a loose leg*** 漫游;闲荡;徘徊。~ ***a stick at*** 〔美俚〕数不清(*There are as many taverns as you can ~ a stick at*. 有无数小酒馆)。~ ***down*** **1**. (将果实从树上)摇下来;摇下去;摇平(米谷等)。**2**. 把(毯子等)做成临时床铺。**3**. 使安定〔稳定〕下来。**4**. 整理使有秩序。**5**. 精简;缩减。**6**.〔美俚〕勒索;敲诈;纳(贿)。**7**.【俚】搜查;搜(身);搜索(武器或钱)。~ ***hands*** 握手。~ ***in one's shoes*** 吓得发抖;战栗。~ ***it up***!〔美俚〕赶快! ~ ***off*** **1**. 抖去;弹去;拍去(灰尘等)。**2**. 医好(疾病)。**3**. 抛弃(坏习惯);摆脱(坏朋友)。**4**. 撵走;断绝关系。**5**. 推开;拆开;消除;避开;巧妙逃避。~ ***on it*** 〔美〕口头约定;致祝辞。~ ***on to*** 承认;答应。~ ***one's bones*** 〔卑〕跳舞。~ ***one's finger at*** 拿食指抖颤地指着〔表示威胁,警告,责备〕。~ ***one's fist*** [***stick***] ***in sb. face*** [***at sb.***] 挥拳〔棍子〕威胁。~ ***one's head*** 摇头〔表示拒绝,否定,谴责,失望〕。~ ***one's sides with laughter*** 捧腹大笑。~ ***oneself free*** [***loose***] ***from*** 摆脱。~ ***oneself together*** 奋发;拿出勇气。~ ***out*** 抖开;展开(旗子等);摊开;晒干(毯子等);抖掉(灰尘)。~ ***sb. by the hand*** 和人握手。~ ***the dust from one's feet*** 愤然离开。~ ***the jinx*** 〔美〕连败后打胜。~ ***up*** **1**. 摇匀;摇动;抖匀(枕头等)。**2**. 摇醒。**3**. 打击;鞭挞。**4**. 震动。**5**. 激起。**II** *n*. **1**. 震动;摇动;动摇。**2**. 握手。**3**. 打击。**4**. 冲动;激动。**5**. 发抖;战栗;震惊;〔口〕地震。**6**. (木材的)轮裂,心裂;裂口;裂缝;(由圆木锯成的)盖屋板。**7**.【乐】颤音。**8**.〔口〕片刻;一刹那;一瞬间。**9**.【物】(精密计时单位)百分之一微秒。**10**.〔美口〕牛奶冰淇淋搅和饮料(=milk~)。**11**. 驱逐;撵走;解雇。**12**.〔the ~s〕〔俚〕发冷,疟疾;酒精中毒性精神病人。**13**.【造纸】抄纸机。**14**.〔美俚〕敲诈,勒索;贿赂。**15**. 命运;运气。***a brace of ~s*** 片刻。***a fair*** ~ 〔美〕正常的交易;公正的处置〔安排,待遇〕。***all of a*** ~ 颤抖,索索发抖。***give*** (***sth.***) ***a good*** ~ 使劲地摇。***give a*** ~ **1**. 摇一摇。**2**. 逐出;撵走。***have the ~s*** 发寒热;发疟疾。***in half a*** ~ 立刻;马上;忽然。***in a brace*** [***couple***] ***of ~s = in the ~ of a lamb's tail = in two ~s = in half a ~*** 〔俚〕忽然;马上;立刻。***no great ~s*** 并不出色;并不重要;平凡。***on the ~*** 〔美俚〕参与犯罪活动(尤指行贿、受贿等)。***put sb. on the ~ = put the ~ on sb.*** 〔美俚〕向某人勒索钱财。

shake·down [ˈʃeikˈdaun; ˋʃekˏdaʊn] *n*. **1**. 摇落。**2**. 临时铺的地铺。**3**.〔美俚〕敲诈,勒索。**4**. 狂舞。

shak·en [ˈʃeikən; ˋʃekən] shake 的过去分词。*a*. **1**. 摇晃的;动摇的。**2**. 受震的。**3**. 颓丧的;虚弱的。**4**. 撞碎了的;开了裂的。

shake·out [ˈʃeikˌaut; ˋʃekˏaʊt] *n*. **1**. 抛售(债券等)。**2**. (行情下跌中赢利微薄行业、产品等的)被淘汰。**3**. 股票的暴跌。

shak·er [ˈʃeikə; ˋʃekɚ] *n*. **1**. 摇的人〔物〕;震动的人〔物〕;〔~s〕〔口〕风云人物,有影响的人物。**2**. 震荡器;【纺】混合器;振动(试验)器。**3**. 打绒机。**4**. 振子;筛。**5**. (盖上有细孔的)细孔瓶,胡椒粉缸,盐缸。**6**.〔S-〕震教徒〔十八世纪基督教的一个教派,做礼拜等时颤抖狂舞〕。*a cocktail* ~ 鸡尾酒混和器。*a pepper* ~ (盖上有小孔的)胡椒瓶。

Shake·speare, **Shak·spear(e)** [ˈʃeikspiə; ˋʃekˏspɪr], **William** 莎士比亚〔1564—1616,英国诗人,戏剧家〕。

Shake·spear·e·an, **-i·an** [ʃeikˈspiəriən; ʃekˋspɪrɪən] **I** *a*. 莎士比亚(时代)的;莎士比亚作的;莎士比亚风格的。**II** *n*. 莎士比亚研究者〔崇拜者〕。**-spear·i·a·na** [ˌʃeikspiərˈɑːnə; ˏʃekspɪrɪˋɑnə] *n*. 莎士比亚文学〔研究文献、言行录〕。~ **sonnet** (按莎士比亚十四行诗格律作的)英国十四行诗。**-spear·i·anism** 莎士比亚语风〔文体〕。

shake-up [ˈʃeikˈʌp; ˋʃekˏʌp] *n*. **1**.〔美口〕动乱;骚动。**2**. 摇动;震动;激动;搅动。**3**.〔俚〕机构的大改组;人员大变动。

shak·o [ˈʃækəu; ˋʃæko] *n*. (*pl*. *~s*) (通常前面有一簇羽毛帽缨的)步兵筒状军帽。

shako·dër [ˈʃkəudə; ˋʃkodɚ] *n*. 斯库台〔阿尔巴尼亚城市〕。

Shak·spere [ˈʃeikspiə; ˋʃekˏspɪr] = Shakespeare.

Shak·ti [ˈʃʌkti; ˋʃʌktɪ] *n*.【印度教】= Sakti. **-tism** *n*. = Saktism.

shak·y [ˈʃeiki; ˋʃekɪ] *a*. **1**. 震动的;摇动的。**2**. (手等)发抖的;震撼的;战栗的。**3**. 有裂口的;龟裂的。**4**. (房子、椅子等)摇摇晃晃的。**5**. (地位、信用等)动摇的;不稳的;不可靠的;靠不住的。**6**. (投票人等)三心二意的。**7**. (老人等)衰弱的;有病的。***feel*** ~ 不舒服。***look*** ~ 脸色不好。**-i·ly** *ad*. **-i·ness** *n*.

shale [ʃeil; ʃel] *n*.【矿】页岩。*oil* ~ 油母页岩。~ *oil* 页岩油。

shall [强 ʃæl, 弱 ʃəl, ʃl; ʃæl, ʃəl] *v*. *aux*. ★在现代英语(尤其在美国英语)中有用 will 代 shall 的趋势;目前在美国(口头语)中第一人称用 will 的也很普通,因此本来是 I will 之略的 I'll 也可视作是 I shall 的缩略形式。*I'll go there tomorrow*. **1**.〔单独未来,用于第一人称单复数〕将要,会。*I ~ arrive by the first train tomorrow*. 我将于明天搭头班车到达。*I ~ be back soon*. 我马上就会回来。*You must do this*. — (*I*) *shan't*. 你必须做这件事。——(我)不干〔句中加强 shall 的语势,有表示决心、意志之意〕。**2**. [ʃæl; ʃæl] 〔意志未来,在陈述句中用于第二人称或第三人称,表示说话者的意志、命令、约定、决心、警告、威胁、预言等〕必须;应该;要;得;给。*You ~ do what you are told*. 叫你做什么你就该做什么。*He shan't have any; he has been most rude*. 什么也不给他,他太没礼貌了。*He ~ be punished*. 他得受处罚。*You ~ die*. (= *I will make you die*.) 我要杀死你。**3**. 疑问句:(a)〔单纯未来〕*S- you* …? (b)

〔单纯未来或问对方的意愿〕S- *I* [*we*] ...? (c)〔问对方的意愿〕S- *he* [*she*, *it*, *they*] ...? (d)〔问意愿〕*Will you* ...? (e)〔问意愿或单纯未来〕*Shall he* [*she*, *they*] ...? …吗;…好吗;叫…好吗;是不是想…;会…吗! S- *you go?* 你去吗? S- *I be in your way?* 我会妨碍你吗? S- *I get you some more tea?* 再来点茶好吗? S- *he make a speech?* 叫[请]他演说好吗? **4.**〔在以 if, when 等词开始的从句中,第一人称表示未来,第二或第三人称表示不能确定〕将;便,就。*When I* ~ *see her*, *I* ~ *give her your message*. 我见到她就把你的信交给她。*If he* ~ *come*, *we* ~ *be saved*. 要是他来,我们就有救了。

shal·loon [ʃəˈluːn; ʃəˋlun] *n*.【纺】二上二下斜纹组织;夏龙绒〔作里子或女服用〕。

shal·lop [ˈʃæləp; ˋʃæləp] *n*. **1.**〔诗〕轻舟;小船。**2.** 小型战船。**3.** (四角帆的)双桅船。

shal·lot [ʃəˈlɔt; ʃəˋlɑt] *n*.【植】冬葱;冻葱;亚实基隆葱。

shal·low [ˈʃæləu; ˋʃælo] **I** *a*. **1.** (~*er*; ~*est*) (水、器物等)浅的。**2.** 薄的。**3.** 肤浅的;表面的;皮毛的。**4.** (呼吸)浅短的。**II** *n*.〔常 *pl*.〕浅处;浅滩。**III** *vt*., *vi*. (使)变浅;(使)变浅薄。~**-brained**, ~**-headed**, ~**-pated** *a*. (知识)肤浅的;浅薄的;头脑简单的;愚蠢的。~**-hearted** *a*. 薄情的。**-ly** *ad*. **-ness** *n*.

sha·lom [ʃɑːˈləum; ʃɑˋlom] *n*., *int*. 舍拉姆〔犹太人传统的招呼、道别语,意为"平安"〕。

shalt [强 ʃælt, 弱 ʃəlt, ʃlt; ʃælt, ʃəlt, ʃl̩t] *v*. *aux*.〔古〕shall 的第二人称单数陈述语气现在时〔主语为 thou 时用〕。

shal·y [ˈʃeili; ˋʃelɪ] *a*.【矿】页岩的;含页岩的;页岩状的。

sham [ʃæm; ʃæm] **I** *n*. **1.** 假冒;虚伪;欺诈。**2.** 虚伪的事;伪(装)物;赝品。**3.** 骗子;欺骗者。**4.** (起床后做装饰用的)枕头套;床单。*a pillow* ~ (作装饰用的)绣花枕套。*a sheet* ~ 装饰性床单。**II** *a*. 假的;虚伪的;仿制的。*a* ~ *fight* 演习战;模拟战。*a* ~ *gentleman* 伪君子。*a* ~ ***plea***【法】(以拖延时间为目的的)虚伪的抗辩。**III** *vt*., *vi*. 假装,冒充。~ *illness* [*ill*] 装病。~ *sleep* [*asleep*] 装睡。*She is not ill*, *she is only shamming*. 她没有病,是在装病。~ ***Abraham*** 装病。

sha·man [ˈʃæmən; ˋʃɑmən] *n*. 萨满教巫师。**-ism** *n*.【宗】(西伯利亚北部等处的)萨满教。**-ist** *n*. 萨满教徒。

sham·ble [ˈʃæmbl; ˋʃæmbl̩] **I** *vi*. 蹒跚;踉踉跄跄地走;拖着脚步走。**II** *n*. 蹒跚;踉跄;蹒跚的脚步。

sham·bles [ˈʃæmblz; ˋʃæmbl̩z] *n*. *pl*.〔用作单或复〕**1.** 屠(宰)场;宰牛场。**2.** 肉铺;肉摊;肉市。**3.** 屠杀场(所)。**4.** (被轰炸后的)废墟。**5.** 大混乱。*Her desk is a* ~. 她的桌子上乱七八糟。

shame [ʃeim; ʃem] **I** *n*. **1.** 耻辱;羞耻;羞愧。**2.** 廉耻心;羞耻心。**3.** 可耻的事[人,物]。**4.** 侮辱;凌辱。**5.** 不贞。**6.**〔口〕太岂有此理的事情;不应该的事情;令人惋惜的事。*flush with* ~ 羞得脸红。*a burning* [*crying*] ~ 奇耻大辱。*a life of* ~ 卖笑生涯。*What a* ~ *to treat you like that!* 那样对待你实在太不应该了。***bring a blush of*** ~ ***to sb.'s cheek*** 使人脸红;使丢脸。***bring sb. to*** ~ 使人脸红;侮辱,欺负。***bring*** ~ ***on*** = ***bring to*** ~ 使丢脸;侮辱。***cannot do it for very*** ~ 不好意思做。***cry*** ~ ***upon*** 指责…可耻。***dead to*** ~ 不知耻;不怕难为情。***Fie for*** ~! = ***For*** ~! ***for*** ~ = ***from*** [***out of***] ~ 知耻而;羞得;红着脸。***For*** ~! 真丢脸;好不要脸;真可耻! ***lost to*** ~ = ***past*** ~. ***past*** ~ 无耻;不要脸。***put to*** ~ 给丢脸! 使脸红! 侮辱。***S- on you!*** = ***For*** ~! ***to the*** ~ ***of*** 自觉惭愧地,很惭愧地。***without*** ~ 无耻。***What a*** ~! 真丢脸! 〔口〕真遗憾。**II** *vt*. **1.** 使羞愧;使害羞;使丢脸;侮辱;凌辱。**2.** 使相形见绌;使黯然失色;〔主用被动语态〕使感觉羞耻而 (*into*; *out of doing*)。*He was* ~*d into working* [*out of his bad habits*]. 他羞愧得开始工作了[改了他的坏习惯了]。~ **culture** (为怕丢面子而行为循规蹈矩的)重视保全脸面的文明。~**faced** *a*. **1.** 害羞的;发怯的。**2.** 可耻的;丢人的。**3.**〔诗〕谦逊的;脸皮薄的。**4.** 不惹眼的,朴素的。~ **reel** *n*.〔Scot.〕婚礼后的跳舞。

shame·ful [ˈʃeimful; ˋʃemfʊl] *a*. **1.** 可耻的;丢脸的。**2.** 猥亵的。**-ly** *ad*. **-ness** *n*.

shame·less [ˈʃeimlis; ˋʃemlɪs] *a*. **1.** 无耻的;不要脸的。**2.** 猥亵的,伤风败俗的。**-ly** *ad*. **-ness** *n*.

sham·mer [ˈʃæmə; ˋʃæmɚ] *n*. 冒充者;骗子;说谎者。

sham·my [ˈʃæmi; ˋʃæmɪ] *n*. = chamois.

Sha·mo [ˈʃɑːməu; ˋʃɑmo] *n*.〔Chin.〕沙漠〔特指大戈壁〕。

sham·oy [ˈʃæmɔi; ˋʃæmɔɪ] = shammy.

sham·poo [ʃæmˈpuː; ʃæmˋpu] **I** *n*. **1.** 洗头;洗发。**2.** 洗发剂。~ *powder* 洗发粉。**II** *vt*. **1.** (用肥皂等)洗(头发)。**2.** 给…洗头发。**3.**〔罕〕给…浴后按摩身体。

sham·rock [ˈʃæmrɔk; ˋʃæmrɑk] *n*.【植】**1.** 白花酢浆草 (= white clover)〔爱尔兰的国花〕。**2.** 三叶苜蓿。**3.** 天蓝苜蓿。

sham·us [ˈʃæməs; ˋʃeməs] *n*. (*pl*. ~*es*)〔美俚〕**1.** 警察。**2.** 私家侦探。

Shan [ʃɑːn, ʃæn; ʃɑn, ʃæn] *n*. **1.** (*pl*. ~(*s*)) (居住在东南亚的)掸人。**2.** 掸语。

shan·dry·dan [ˈʃændridæn; ˋʃændrɪˏdæn] *n*. **1.** 二轮轻马车。**2.** 破旧马车。

shan·dy(gaff) [ˈʃændi(gæf); ˋʃændɪ(ˏgæf)] *n*.〔英〕**1.** 啤酒与姜汁混合饮料。**2.** 啤酒与柠檬汽水混合饮料。

Shang·hai [ˈʃæŋˈhai; ˋʃæŋhaɪ] *n*. **1.** 上海。**2.** (上海产)浦东鸡。

shang·hai [ʃæŋˈhai; ˋʃæŋhaɪ] *vt*. **1.** (用酒或麻醉剂)使…失去知觉而把人劫掠到船上去当水手。**2.**〔美俚〕(以武力或其他卑劣手段)强迫…干苦活。**3.** 拐骗,诱拐;胁迫。**-er** *n*. 拐骗者。

Shan·gri-La Shan·gri·la [ʃæŋgriːˈlɑː; ˋʃæŋgrɪˋlɑ] *n*.〔美〕**1.** 香格里拉;世外桃源。**2.** 二次大战时美国的空军秘密基地。**3.**〔美军俚〕厕所。

shank [ʃæŋk; ʃæŋk] *n*. **1.** 胫,小腿;胫骨。**2.** (鸟的)跗骨;(昆虫的)胫节;(牛羊的)腿肉。**3.** 轴;轮轴;杆;柄;钥匙柄。**4.** 锚身;钉身。**5.** 小刀、凿等插入柄内的部分。**6.** 鞋底的中腰;袜子的统。**7.**【印】铅字身。**8.**【植】秆;花梗;叶柄。**9.**〔美口〕末梢;后部;剩余部分;剩余。**10.** 最后一段时间。**11.**【铸造】浇包手柄。**12.**【矿】钻杆尾;钎尾;钎柄。*a long* [*thin*] ~〔蔑〕长[细]脚杆。***ride*** [***go***] ~***'s*** [~***s'***] ***mare*** [***pony***] 步行;走;骑两脚马去。~***s of the evening***〔口〕黄昏将尽时;夜晚最好时。

shan·ny [ˈʃæni; ˋʃænɪ] *n*. (*pl*. **-nies**, ~)【动】线鳚科(*Stichaeidae*)的鱼〔尤指北线 *Lumpenus maculatus*〕。

sha'n't, shan't [ʃɑːnt; ʃænt]〔口〕= shall not. *I* ~.〔口〕我不干。*Now we* ~ *be long*. 我们马上就好了;不用再等多久了。

shan·tey [ˈʃɑːnti, ˈʃæn-; ˋʃæntɪ] *n*. (*pl*. ~*s*) = chantey.

Shan·tung [ʃænˈtʌŋ; ʃænˋtʌŋ] *n*. **1.** 山东。**2.**〔s-〕(山东)茧绸。

shan·ty[1] [ˈʃænti; ˋʃæntɪ] *n*. **1.**〔美〕简陋的(临时)小屋,棚屋。**2.** 下等酒馆。~**-man**〔美〕**1.** 伐木工。**2.** 乡巴佬。~ **town** **1.** (城市)贫民窟。**2.** 棚户区。

shan·ty[2] [ˈʃænti; ˋʃæntɪ] *n*. = shantey.

shap·able [ˈʃeipəbl; ˋʃepəbl̩] *a*. **1.** 可成形[成型]的;可塑造的。**2.** 样子好(看)的。

SHAPE, Shape = Supreme Headquarters, Allied Powers in Europe (北大西洋公约组织的)欧洲盟军最高司令部。

shape [ʃeip; ʃep] **I** *n*. **1.** 形状;样子;形态;外形;模样。**2.** 形式;定型;模型。**3.** 种类。**4.** (没有实体的)朦胧的形象[人影];轮廓。**5.** 幽灵。**6.** 状态;情况。**7.**【剧】戏剧服装;(用来充抵手脚等形状的)戏装衬垫。**8.** (女人的)姿态身段。**9.**〔口〕造法;做法;成绩。**10.** 具体化;体现;

实现。11.【军】(海上远距离联系用的)锥形信号标。*a hat* ~ 帽型。*a fiend in human* ~ 人形的魔鬼;人面兽心的人。***be in bad*** ~ 混乱;紊乱。***get ... into*** ~ 1. 使成一定形状。2. 整顿;使具体化。***give*** ~ (***to***) 给与一定的形状;弄成一个样子;使…成形;修整;实现。***in any*** ~ ***or form*** 以任何形式[任何种类];不论种类方法如何;无论怎样都;随便哪样的。***in bad*** ~ 处于不佳的状态中。***in good*** ~ 状态良好;完整无损。***in no*** ~ 决不;无论如何不;完全不。***in the*** ~ ***of*** 以…的形状;呈…的形状;以…的形式;作为… (*He has nothing in the* ~ *of money*. 什么钱他都没有)。***keep ... in*** ~ 使…保持原形;不使走样。***lick ... into*** ~ 塑造;使像样;使有效能。***put ... in*** ~ 使…成形。***put ... into*** ~ = ***get ... into*** ~. ***put ... out of*** ~ 使变样;使走样。***settle into*** ~ 开始有头绪;上正轨。***take*** ~ 成形;形成;具体化;有显著发展;实现 (*in*)。***take the*** ~ ***of*** 呈…形状;成…形状。**II** ***vt***. 1. 使成形;使具有某种形状;形成;构成,塑造。2. 使适合;使符合。3. 使具体化;实现。4. 说明;表明。5. 设计;计划;图谋;想像;设想。6. 使朝向;使向一定方向发展。7. (修)刨;把(锯齿)锉匀。~ *one's course* 确定方针[办法]。~ *clay into balls* 把黏土搓成圆球。*The hat is* ~*d to your head*. 这顶帽子你戴正好。~ *a question* 提问题。—***vi***. 1. 形成;成形;成型。2. 有前途;成长;发展;发达;发生。*It is shaping well*. 发展得很好;(形状)长得很好。*Let time* ~. 一切听其自然发展吧。~ ***the destiny of*** 决定…的命运。~ ***up*** = ~ ***out*** 〔美〕1. 发展;成形;具体化;显示…的倾向。2. 进入准备状态。3. 协调;合适;举止得体。***wear to one's*** ~ (衣服)穿过一段时间后变得合身。~ **factor** 波形因数[因子]。~**d brick** 异形砖。~**suit** 形体装〔一种线条型紧身女胸衣,通过束紧腰臀等部位以收到苗条的效果〕。~**wear** = ~suit.

shape·less [ˈʃeiplis; ˋʃeplɪs] ***a***. 1. 无定形的;不成样子的;没样子的。2. 形状丑陋的。**-ly** ***ad***.

shape·li·ness [ˈʃeiplinis; ˋʃeplɪnɪs] ***n***. 相称;漂亮;美。

shape·ly [ˈʃeipli; ˋʃeplɪ] ***a***. (***-li·er***; ***-li·est***) 1. 有样子的;模样儿好的。2. 美观的;井井有条的。

shap·er [ˈʃeipə; ˋʃepɚ] ***n***. 1. 造形者;定形物。2. 整形器;【机】成形机;〔口〕牛头刨床。3. (脉冲)形成电路。*a hydraulic* ~ 液压牛头刨床。*a vertical* ~ 立式牛头刨床。*a gear* ~ 刨齿机。~ **amplifier** 脉冲形成放大器。

shape-up [ˈʃeipʌp; ˋʃepˏʌp] ***n***. 〔美口〕1. (临时每天由工头从聚集在码头上的工人中)选雇码头临时工。2. 健康增进。

Sha·piro [ʃəˈpirəu; ʃəˋpɪro] ***n***. 夏皮罗〔姓氏〕。

shard [ʃɑːd; ʃard] ***n***. 1. 碎陶瓷片。2. 薄硬壳;【动】(昆虫的)甲;鞘翅。*break into* ~*s* 粉碎,砸碎。

share[1] [ʃɛə; ʃɛr] **I** ***n***. 1. 一份;份儿, 2. 份额;分配额;分担量。3. 股;股份。4. 〔*pl*.〕〔主英〕股票。*a fair* ~ 应得的份儿;应负担的部分。*ordinary* [*common*] ~*s* 普通股。*preference* [*preferred*] ~*s* 优先股。*a* ~ *certificate* (*to bearer*) (不记名)股票。***bear*** [***take***] ***one's*** ~ ***of*** 负担…的部分;付…的份。***come in for a*** ~ 得到分配;分得一份。***fall to sb.'s*** ~ 由某人负担。***go*** ~***s*** (***with ...***) 平分;分享;均摊;分担;合伙经营;共同负责。***have*** [***take***] ***a*** [***one's***] ~ ***in*** 分担;参加。***on*** [***upon***] ~***s*** 1. 共负盈亏。2. 利害与共;同甘共苦。***the lion's*** ~ 最大[最好]的一份;绝大部分。**II** ***vt***. 1. 均分;均摊;平分;分配;分派。2. 共有;分[同]享,共负,参加,分担。~ *losses* 共同负担损失。~ *the blame* [*responsibility*] 共负责任;共同负责。—***vi***. 受分配;共享;分享;参与 (*in*)。~ *in the profits* 分享收益。~ *with sb. in distress* 与某人共患难。~ ***and*** ~ ***alike*** 平均分配;平均分担;一切与别人分享。~ ***out*** 分配;分给。~ ***sb.'s joys and sorrows*** 和某人同甘共苦[休戚相关]。~ ***weal and woe*** 同甘共苦。~**broke** 股票经纪人。~ **capital** 股份资本。~ **certificate** 股票。~**crop** ***vi***. 〔美南部〕充当分成制佃农。~ **cropper** 〔美南部〕分成制佃户。~ **economy** (员工以持股分红作为工资的)股份制经济。~ **holder** 〔英〕股东。~ **list** 〔英〕股票行市表。~**-out** ***n***. 分配物;配给品;分摊。~**owner** 〔英〕股东,股票持有人。~**ownership** 〔英〕股权。~**d time** 接受校外生课时〔公立中小学校让教会及私立学校学生来校听某些课程的安排措施〕。~**(-)ware**【计】共用软件〔有版权,临时使用可免费,长期使用则须付费〕。

share[2] [ʃɛə; ʃɛr] ***n***. 犁头;犁铧;(播种机等的)刃 (= plough-~)。~**bone**【解】耻骨。

shar·er [ˈʃɛərə; ˋʃɛrɚ] ***n***. 1. 分配者;分派者;分[共]享者;分担者。2. 参与者;关系人 (*in*; *of*)。

shark[1] [ʃɑːk; ʃark] ***n***.【鱼】鲨鱼;〔喻〕财大气粗地收购[兼并]他人企业的人。~ **sucker**【鱼】鲫鱼 (= remora)。

shark[2] [ʃɑːk; ʃark] **I** ***n***. 1. 贪得无厌的人;骗子。2. 高利贷者。3. 〔口〕海关人员。4. 〔美俚〕老手,专家;〔美学生语〕优秀学生 (in mathematics)。**II** ***vt***. 1. 用不正当手段攫取;榨取;骗取;勒索 (*up*)。2. 狼吞虎咽。—***vi***. 骗;诈欺;诳骗。*He* ~*s for a living*. 他靠诈骗过日子。**-er** ***n***. 骗子。

shark·skin [ˈʃɑːkskin; ˋʃarkˏskɪn] ***n***. 1. 鲨鱼皮;鲨皮革。2.【纺】鲨皮布;雪克斯金细呢。

Sharp [ʃɑːp; ʃarp] ***n***. 夏普〔姓氏〕。

sharp [ʃɑːp; ʃarp] **I** ***a***. 1. 锐利的;锋利。2. 尖锐;成锐角的。3. 陡急的;急转的。4. 敏锐的;聪明的;精明的;机警的;狡黠的;狡猾的。5. 敏捷的;轻快的。6. 剧烈的;猛烈的。7. 尖酸的;刻薄的;苛刻的。8. (严寒)像刀割的;刺骨的;(风等)凛冽的。9. 险峻的;陡峭的。10. 急剧的;激烈的。11.【乐】偏高的,升半音的;婴音的。12.【语音】无声音的;清音的;气音的〔p, t, k 等〕;尖声的。13. 苦涩的;酸;辣。14. 准确的;清晰的;轮廓鲜明的;明显的。15. 瘦削的。16. (衣服等)很讲究的;时髦的;漂亮的。*a* ~ *turn* 急转弯。~ *wine* 酸酒。*a short and* ~ *life* 短促而有为的一生。*a* ~ *remark* 严厉[尖刻]的话。~ *freezer* (食品)速冻室。~ *practice* 诈欺;诳骗。~ *tongue* 语言恶毒[刻薄];利嘴。~ *work* 敏速的工作。***as*** ~ ***as a razor*** 厉害的;机警的。***be*** ~ ***at figures*** 算盘精明;擅长计算。***be*** ~ ***upon*** 苛待。***keep a*** ~ ***look-out*** 严密监视。~ ***as a needle*** 非常锐利。***S- is the word***! 赶快,快点。***S- stomachs make short graces***. 肚饿礼仪差〔饿着肚子,饭前感恩祈祷也说得短〕。***take a*** ~ ***walk*** 快步走。**II** ***ad***. 1.尖锐地;锐利地。2. 机警地。3. 急速地;急剧地;突然地。4. (时间)整;准。5.【乐】偏高地;升半音地。*at three o'clock* ~ 三时整;准三时。***Look*** ~! 赶快! 留神! 当心! 注意! **III** ***n***. 1.【乐】升音,升号(即♯)。2. 〔口〕骗子。3. 〔美谑〕专家。4. 〔*pl*.〕(缝纫用)细长针;(针头、手术刀等)医疗用利器。5. 〔*pl*.〕〔英〕粗面粉。*a political* ~ 政治家。**IV** ***vt***., ***vi***. 1. 〔古、卑〕磨利;磨快;磨。2.【乐】(使)提高音调;(使)提高半音。3. 〔俚〕骗,诈欺。~**-angled** 尖角的;锐角的。~**-cut** ***a***. 1. 用快刀切的。2. 干净利落的;分明的。3. 轮廓鲜明的。~**-cut-off** 〔无〕锐截止。~**-eared** ***a***. 耳灵的,听觉敏锐的。~**-edged** 尖缘的;刀刃锋利的,锐利的。~**-eyed** ***a***. 目光锐利的。~ **frost** 严寒。~**-nosed** ***a***. 1. 有尖鼻的。2. 嗅觉敏锐的。~**-pointed** 削尖的;尖锐的。~ **practice** 不择手段谋利的行为;卑鄙交易。~ **sand** 尖角砂。~**-set** ***a***. 1. 非常饿的。2. 渴望的 (*upon*; *after*)。3. 成锐角的,锐利的。4. 使边缘锋利的。~**-shooter** 1. 神枪手;狙击兵。2.【棒球俚】投球名手。~**-sighted** ***a***. 1. 目光锐利的。2. 观察力敏锐的;机警的;敏捷的。~**-tongued** ***a***. 说话尖酸刻薄的;挖苦的。~ **tuning**【无】锐调(谐)。~**-witted** ***a***. 敏捷的;机灵的;聪明的。

sharp·en [ˈʃɑːpən; ˋʃarpən] ***vt***. 1. 磨锐利;磨快;磨尖;削尖;修尖(铅笔等)。2. 使锐利;使敏锐;磨炼(才智等)。3. 加深;加重;加强(苦痛等);使剧烈;使尖锐。4. 加辣。5.【乐】使提高音调;使提高半音。~ *one's tongue* 磨炼说话的能力。*a ~ing stone* 磨石。*~ing tools* 磨刀器。—***vi***. 变锐利;变尖;变锋利;变尖锐;加剧。~ ***one's knife for sb***. 准备惩罚[攻击]某人。

sharp·en·er [ˈʃɑːpnə; ˋʃɑrpnɚ] ***n***. **1**. 磨的人;削的人;磨削者。**2**. 磨具;磨床;刃磨器;削刀;削具。**3**. 锐化器;锐化电路。*a knife-* ~ 磨刀石;磨刀器。*a pencil-* ~ 修铅笔刀[器]。

sharp·er [ˈʃɑːpə; ˋʃɑrpɚ] ***n***. **1**. 磨具;削具。**2**. 骗子〔尤指以赌博行欺骗者〕。*a knife* ~ 磨刀石,磨刀器。*a pencil* ~ 卷笔刀。*a card* ~ 扑克牌赌棍。

sharp·ie [ˈʃɑːpi; ˋʃɑrpɪ] ***n***. 〔美〕**1**. 三角帆平底船。**2**. 骗子;机灵精明的人;时髦人物。

sharp·ly [ˈʃɑːpli; ˋʃɑrplɪ] ***ad***. **1**. 锐利的。**2**. 高音地;锐声地。**3**. 刀割似地。**4**. 严厉地;严酷地。**5**. 苛刻地;刻薄地。**6**. 厉害地;剧烈地。**7**. 敏捷地;机灵地。**8**. 险峻地。

sharp·ness [ˈʃɑːpnis; ˋʃɑrpnɪs] ***n***. **1**. 锐利;尖锐。**2**. 锐度。**3**. 高音;锐音。**4**. 严厉;剧烈。**5**. 严酷;刻薄。**6**. 敏捷;机灵。

sharp·y [ˈʃɑːpi; ˋʃɑrpɪ] ***n***. 〔美俚〕服装华丽的人〔尤指男子〕。

Shar·(r)on [ˈʃɛərən, ˈʃeərən; ˋʃɛrɑn, ˋʃɛrən] ***n***. 莎伦〔女子名〕。

shash·lik [ˈʃɑːʃlik; ˋʃɑʃlɪk] ***n***. 烤羊肉串。

Shas·ter [ˈʃæstə; ˋʃɑstrə], **Shas·tra** [-trə; -trə] ***n***. 〔Ind.〕神圣的著作;圣典。

shat·ter [ˈʃætə; ˋʃætɚ] **I** ***vt***. **1**. 使四面八方散开;使粉碎;把…打得落花流水。**2**. 破坏;捣毁;破灭(希望等)。**3**. 损害;损伤;糟蹋。*her ~ed hopes* 她那些破灭了的希望。*a ~ing blow* 毁灭性打击。*his ~ed nerves* 他那因心灵受创伤而变得极度衰弱的神经。—***vi***. 破碎;碎裂;粉碎;纷纷散落。**II** ***n***. **1**. 破片;碎片。**2**. 破损;粉碎。**3**. (过早的)落花;落果。~**proof** ***a***. (玻璃等)防碎的;不会四散粉碎的。~ **cones**【地】震裂锥。**-ing** ***n***. 脱粒,落粒(性)。

shave [ʃeiv; ʃev] **I** ***vt***. (*-d*; *-d*, ***shav·en*** [ˈʃeivən; ˋʃevn]; ***shav·ing***) **1**. 剃(头发),刮(脸)。**2**. 削,刨;把…切成薄片。**3**. 擦过;掠过。**4**. 修剪(草坪)。**5**. 骗取;强夺。**6**. 〔口〕削减(价格);杀价买进(期票)。**7**. 〔美俚〕险胜,勉强胜过。**8**. 〔美俚〕减少;减轻。*~n and shorn* 刮了脸,剪了发。*The car ~d a wall*. 车子擦墙开过。~ *the sentence to one year* 把刑期减为一年。—***vi***. **1**. 剃胡须;修面。**2**. 勉强通过;善于讲价。~ ***a note*** 〔美〕杀价收购票据。~ ***off*** 剃掉;削去。~ ***through*** 勉强通过;〔口〕勉强考及格。**II** ***n***. **1**. 刮脸;剃胡子;修面。**2**. 削片;薄片。**3**. 擦过,掠过。**4**. 〔口〕侥幸逃过;幸免。**5**. 票据的杀价收买。**6**. 诈欺。**7**. 剃刀,刮刀,削刀;刨刀。*be a close* ~ 侥幸逃过;九死一生。***by a*** [***close***, ***narrow***] ~ 差一点点;险些儿;几几乎。***clean*** ~ **1**. 剃光胡子。**2**. 〔英〕欺骗。***have a close*** ~ ***of it*** = *be a close* ~. ***take a*** ~ ***off*** 削一下。

shave·ling [ˈʃeivliŋ; ˋʃevlɪŋ] ***n***. **1**. 〔蔑〕剃去(顶部)头发的人;(剃发的)和尚;修士。**2**. 小伙子;青年人。

shav·en [ˈʃeivən; ˋʃevən] **I** shave 的过去分词。**II** ***a***. **1**. 修过脸的;刮过脸的。**2**. 修剪过的。

shav·er [ˈʃeivə; ˋʃevɚ] ***n***. **1**. 剃者;削者;刮者;刨者。**2**. 理发师;剃头者;刮脸者。**3**. 剃具;刮刀。**4**. 〔古〕骗子;掠夺者;〔美〕高利贷者;杀价收买(期货等)的人;善于讲价的人。**5**. 〔口〕年轻人,小伙子。**6**. 家伙。*an electric* ~ 电动剃刀。~ **point** [**socket**] 电动剃刀的插座(多设于卫生间)。

shave·tail [ˈʃeivteil; ˋʃevˏtel] ***n***. **1**. 〔美军俚〕没有驯服的骡子。**2**. 〔美军俚〕(新任职的)陆军少尉。*a ~ general* 〔美军俚〕旅长。

Sha·vi·an [ˈʃeivjən, -viən; ˋʃeviən, -vɪən] ***n***., ***a***. **1**. 英国戏剧家萧伯纳 (Bernard Shaw) 作品风格(的)。**2**. 萧伯纳研究家[崇拜者](的)。

shav·ing [ˈʃeiviŋ; ˋʃevɪŋ] ***n***. **1**. 剃;剃胡子;修面。**2**. 〔*pl*.〕削屑;刮屑;刨花。**3**. 票据的杀价收买;诈欺。*~s of wood* 刨花。~ **board** 刨花板。~ **brush** 修面刷。~ **cream** 刮胡膏。~ **horse** 削架;刨工台。~ **lotion** 修面用的香水。~**-shop** 不可靠的银行。~ **soap** 刮胡皂。

Sha·vu·ot [ʃɑːˈvuːəut, ʃəˈvuːəut; ʃɑˋvuot, ʃəˋvuot] ***n***. 【犹太教】五旬节[犹太历九月的第六,七日]。

Shaw [ʃɔː; ʃɔ] ***n***. **1**. 萧〔姓氏〕。**2**. **George Bernard** ~ 萧伯纳〔1856—1950,英国剧作家,批评家〕。

shaw [ʃɔː; ʃɔ] ***n***. 小树林;丛林。

shawl [ʃɔːl; ʃɔl] ***n***. 披肩;围巾。~ **pattern** ***n***. (东方)披肩花样。

shawm [ʃɔːm; ʃɔm] ***n***. 【乐】古双簧管。

Shaw·nee [ʃɔːˈniː; ʃɔˋni] ***n***. **1**. 肖尼〔美国城市〕。**2**. 肖尼人〔美国印第安人的一族〕。

shay [ʃei; ʃe] ***n***. 〔口〕轻便马车(= chaise)。

Shaw·wal [ʃɔːˈwɔːl; ʃɔˋwɑl] ***n***. (穆斯林历的)十月。

she [ʃiː, 弱 ʃi; ʃi, ʃɪ] **I** ***pro***. 她〔人称代名词、第三人称、阴性、单数;所有格是 her 和 hers, 宾格是 her, 复数是 they〕。★ 船舶、国家、月亮、火车等也常比拟作阴性而说作 she。**II** ***n***. [ʃiː; ʃi] (*pl*. *~s* [ʃiːz; ʃiz]) (*opp*. he). 女人;女子;〔蔑〕女的;〔口〕雌。*Is it a he or a ~?* 这是男是女? 是雄是雌? **III** ***a***. 女的;雌的;母的。*a ~-cat* 雌猫。*a ~-napper* 女侦探。*a ~ stuff* 〔美〕(母牛除外的)母畜。~**devil** 狠毒的女人。~**gal** 〔美口〕温柔的女子。

shea [ʃiː; ʃi] ***n***. 【植】牛油树 (*Butyrospermum parkii*) 〔产于非洲,其籽含油脂,可食用,制皂和蜡烛等〕。

sheaf [ʃiːf; ʃif] **I** ***n***. (*pl*. ***sheaves*** [ʃiːvz; ʃivz]) **1**. (谷类等的)束;捆;扎。**2**.【军】火制正面;射面。*a ~ of papers* 一扎文件。*a ~ of arrows* 一束箭〔通常是 24 枝〕。a ~ *of fire*【军】集束弹道。**II** ***vt***., ***vi***. 捆束;捆扎。

sheal·ing [ˈʃiːliŋ; ˋʃilɪŋ] ***n***. 〔Scot.〕= shieling.

shear [ʃiə; ʃɪr] **I** ***vt***., ***vi***. (*~ed*, 〔古〕***shore*** [ʃɔː; ʃɔr]; ***shorn*** [ʃɔːn; ʃorn], *~ed*) **1**. 剪(羊毛等);修剪(树木);剪(呢绒的)长毛。**2**. 〔诗〕(用剑)斩。**3**.【机】剪断,切断;【矿】截割;【物】(使)切变。**4**. 剥夺;抢夺;骗取。**5**. 〔Scot.〕(用镰刀)收割(庄稼)。**6**. 飞起,如割开一般地越过。~ *sheep* = ~ *wool from a sheep* 剪羊毛。*~ed of one's rights* 被剥夺权利。*a cruiser ~ing through the water* 破浪前进的巡洋舰。***a shorn lamb*** 钱被人骗去的笨人。***come home shorn*** 输[亏蚀]得精光回来。~ ***off*** **1**. 剪下来。**2**. 折断。~ ***off sb.'s plume*** 下掉某人的架子[威风];挫某人的骄气。**II** ***n***. **1**. 剪;切;刈割。**2**. 剪下的东西。**3**.【机】剪断;剪力;剪床。**4**.【物】切变;切力;剪力。**5**. (羊的)剪毛次数;(羊的)年岁。**6**.【矿】截割;直立截槽。*a sheep of two ~s* 两岁(剪过两次毛)的羊。~ **diagram** 剪力图。~**hog** 〔英〕剪过第一次毛的羊。~ **hulk** 起重机船〔亦作 sheer hulk, sheerhulk〕。~**ing force** 剪力。~**ing strain**【物】切应变。~**ing strength**【物】抗剪强度;抗切强度。~**ing stress**【物】切胁力;切应力;剪应力。~ **legs** 〔亦作 sheer legs〕= shears. **3**. ~**-ling** 剪了一次毛的羊;一岁羊。~ **steel** 刃钢;剪钢。~ **wave**【物】切变波;剪力波。~**-water**【鸟】鹱。**-er** [ˈʃiərə; ˋʃɪrɚ] ***n***. **1**. 剪切者;剪切工;剪羊毛者。**2**. 可剪毛的羊。**3**. 剪切机,剪床;【矿】直立槽截煤机。**-ing** [ˈʃiəriŋ; ˋʃɪərɪŋ] ***n***. **1**. 剪羊毛。**2**. 剪断,切断。**3**. 剪下的羊毛。

shears [ʃiəz; ʃɪrz] ***n***. 〔*pl*.〕**1**. 大剪刀。**2**.【机】剪床;剪切机。**3**. 起重三角架;人字起重架;起重机叉柱。*a pair of* ~ 一把大剪刀。

sheat·fish [ˈʃiːtfiʃ; ˋʃitˏfɪʃ] ***n***. 【鱼】一种须鲶。

sheath [ʃiːθ; ʃiθ] **I** ***n***. (*pl*. *~s* [ʃiːðz; ʃiðz]) **1**. (刀剑的)鞘。**2**. 护套;外皮;外壳;包装。**3**.【生,解】鞘;兜。**4**.【植】叶鞘。**5**. 茎衣;箨;萎叶。**6**.【昆】翅鞘。**7**. (电缆的)铠装。**8**.【无】阳极;正电压电极;(电子管的)屏极。**9**. (河边)防泛石堤。**10**. 女式紧身连衣裙。**11**. 〔口〕阴茎套,避孕套。**II** ***vt***. = sheathe. ~**bill**【鸟】鞘嘴鸥。~

knife (海员用)带鞘短刀。

sheathe [ʃiːð; ʃið] *vt*. 1. 把…插入鞘;装…入鞘。2. 覆盖;包;套;藏。3. 把(爪)缩回;把(剑)刺入肉体。~ *the sword* 把剑插回鞘里;讲和。**sheath·er** *n*.

sheath·ing [ˈʃiːðiŋ; ˋʃiðɪŋ] I *n*. 1. 外壳;鞘套;外层覆盖;护板;护套;护皮。2.【电】甲套。3.【建】盖板;望板;(屋顶瓦下的)夹衬板〔亦作 ~ board〕。4.【船】覆材;船底包板。5.【空】(螺旋桨)包端。II *a*. 有外层[外壳,包皮等]覆盖的。

sheave[1] [ʃiːv; ʃiv] *n*.【机】滑车轮;起重滑轮;绳轮;槽轮;绞缆轮;滑车;凸轮盘。

sheave[2] [ʃiːv; ʃiv] *vt*. 捆;束(作物等)。

sheaves [ʃiːvz; ʃivz] sheaf 和 sheave 的复数。

She·ba [ˈʃiːbə; ˋʃibə] *n*. 1.【圣】示巴〔阿拉伯南部一古王国,今也门地区,以经营香料、宝石贸易著称〕。2.〔美口〕美女,情妇。

she·bang [ʃiˈbæŋ; ʃəˋbæŋ] *n*.〔美俚〕1. 小屋;居处;房屋;陋屋;茅屋;店铺。2. 妓院;下等酒吧;赌场。3. 东西;事情;勾当〔常与 whole 连用〕。*I'm sick of the whole* ~. 我对整个这件事发腻了。

She·bat [ʃəˈvɑːt; ʃəˋvæt] *n*. [Heb.] (犹太历)五月。

shed[1] [ʃed; ʃɛd] (*shed*; ~*ding*) I *vt*. 1. 流出;落下;倾注。2. 散发(光、热、香等);放射。3. (屋顶、油布等)把(雨水)排泻掉。4.【生】排出(孢子等)。5. (鸟)脱(毛);(树)落(叶);脱落;(蛇)蜕(皮);褪;(鹿)换(角等)。6. 放弃;摆脱(恶习)。7.【电】减少(负荷)。8.〔英口〕解雇(员工等);解散(公司等)。~ *tears* 流泪。~ *blood* 流血;杀。—*vi*. 1. 流出;溢出。2. 散发。3. 脱毛;脱壳;脱换;脱落;蝉蜕。~ ***light on*** 1. 照亮。2. 阐明;解释;将…弄明白。~ ***one's blood for*** 献身。~ ***the blood of*** 使流血;杀伤;杀死。II *n*. 1. 脱落物;蜕落的皮壳。2. 微量的小雪。3. 分水岭。4.【纺】(织机的)梭口;梭道。~ **dormer** 屋顶窗,老虎窗。~ **rod**【纺】分纱杆。

shed[2] [ʃed; ʃɛd] *n*. 1. 小屋;棚屋。2. 堆房;库房。3. 车房。4.〔美〕有盖汽车。*a cattle* ~ 牛槛。*a locomotive* [*an engine*] ~ 机车库。

she'd [ʃiːd, 弱 ʃid; ʃid, ʃɪd] = she had [would].

shed·der [ˈʃedə; ˋʃɛdɚ] *n*. 1. 脱落者;放射者。2. 流出…的人[物];使流出…的人[物]。3. 脱壳期的虾[蟹]。4. 卸件装置;推[拨、抛]料机。*a* ~ *of blood* 流血者;杀人者。

sheen [ʃiːn; ʃin] I *n*. 1. 光辉;光彩;光泽。2. 华服;有光泽的织物。II *a*.【诗】华丽的;光辉的;有光泽的。III *vi*. 发亮;发光彩;照耀;闪闪发光。

sheen·y[1] [ˈʃiːni; ˋʃinɪ] *a*. 发光的;闪烁的;光亮的;有光泽的。

shee·ny[2] [ˈʃiːni; ˋʃinɪ] *n*.〔俚、蔑〕犹太人。

sheep [ʃiːp; ʃip] *n*. [*sing*., *pl*.] 1. 羊;绵羊。2. 羊皮(革)。3. 怯懦的人;羞怯的人;胆小鬼;蠢人。4.〔谑〕〔总称〕信徒;教友;教区居民。*keep* ~ 养羊。***a black*** ~ 家庭中的不肖子;败类;不肖之徒;害群之马;拒绝参加罢工的工人。***a lost*** ~ 迷途羔羊;迷失正道的人。***a wolf in*** ~***'s clothing*** 披着羊皮的狼;口蜜腹剑的人。***cast*** [***make***] ~***'s eyes at*** 向…送媚眼;向…递秋波。***count*** ~ 数羊〔心里计数以求入睡〕。***follow like*** ~ 盲从。***one may as well be hanged for a*** ~ ***as a lamb*** 一不做,二不休。***return to one's*** ~ [***muttons***] 回到本题。~ ***and goats*** 善人与恶人。~ ***herder*** 牧羊人;〔美〕怀俄明州人〔绰号〕。~ ***that have no shepherd*** 乌合之众。***separate the*** ~ ***from the goats*** 区别好人与坏人。~**berry**【植】荚迷(属);荚迷果;羊莓。~**cot(e)** 羊栏;羊舍;羊圈。~**-dip** 1. *n*. 洗羊药水;羊消毒液。2. *vt*. (为收集情报等)使(军官等)伪装成平民;使潜伏于平民百姓中。~ **dog** 牧羊狗[犬]。~ **fescue**【植】羊茅。~**fold**〔英〕羊栏;羊舍;羊圈。~**herder**〔美〕牧羊人。~**hook** 牧羊杖。~ **ked**【动】羊虱蝇(= ~ tick)。~ **laurel**【植】狭叶山月桂。~ **like** *a*. 1. 温顺的;驯良的。2. 怯懦的。~ **man**〔古英〕= shepherd;〔美〕牧羊业者。~**pen**〔英〕= ~fold。~ **range** 牧羊场。~**-run**〔澳〕大牧羊场。~**'s eyes** 媚眼。~**shank** 1. 羊胫;羊的小腿。2. 纤弱而细的东西。3. 无价值的东西;不重要的东西。4.【海】(将长绳暂时缩短的)缩结。~**shead** [ˈʃiːpshed; ˋʃipsˏhɛd] 1. (食用的)羊头。2.【动】羊鲷;淡水石首鱼;红隆头鱼。3. 愚蠢的人。~**shearer** 剪羊毛的人;剪羊毛机。~**shearing** 1. 剪羊毛。2. 剪羊毛时期。3. 剪羊毛节目。~**skin** 1. 羊皮;羊革。2. 羊皮衣服(等)。3. 羊皮纸。4.〔美〕毕业文凭。~ **sorrel**【植】小酸模。~ **station**〔澳〕牧羊场。~ **tick** = ~ ked. ~**-walk**〔英〕牧羊场。

sheep·ish [ˈʃiːpiʃ; ˋʃipɪʃ] *a*. 1. 羞怯的;腼腆的。2. (像绵羊一样)驯顺的;胆怯的;愚钝的。**-ly** *ad*. **-ness** *n*.

sheer[1] [ʃiə; ʃɪr] I *a*. 1. 纯粹的;十足的;全然的;没有搀杂的;不搀水的;绝对的;真正的。2. 透明的;(纱等)极薄的。3. 险峻的;陡峭的;垂直的。*a* ~ *impossibility* 绝对不可能。~ *silk* 薄绸。~ *nonsense* 胡说八道;完全瞎扯。***by the*** ~ ***force of one's will*** 全靠意志力。II *ad*. 完全;绝对。1. 十足;全然;彻底。2. 垂直地;峻峭地;笔直地。*torn* ~ *out by the root* 连根拔除。*The rock rises* ~ *from the water*. 岩石笔直地从水面矗立起来。*fall 300 feet* ~ 垂直坠落[低落]三百英尺。III *n*. 透明薄纱,透明布料的衣服。

sheer[2] [ʃiə; ʃɪr] I *n*. 1.【海】舷弧。2. 以单锚系泊的船位。3. 偏航;偏荡;转向;避开;弯曲进行。***break*** ~ 抛单锚时船位移动而使锚链绕结。***have little*** [***a straight***] ~ 甲板弧度不大。II *vi*., *vt*.【海】(使)偏航;(使)偏荡;避开;(使)转向。~ ***off***【海】离开;躲开。~ **hulk** = shear hulk. ~ **legs** = shear legs.

sheers [ʃiəz; ʃɪrz] *n*. [*pl*.] = shears.

sheet[1] [ʃiːt; ʃit] I *n*. 1. [常 *pl*.] 被单;褥单。2. 裹尸布。3. (忏悔者穿的)白衣;忏悔服。4. 一张(纸);纸张;(尤指黄色)报纸;[*pl*.] 书页;印刷品。5. 表格;图表;单子;票笺;文件;罪犯的记录单。6. (一)片;(一)块;(一)层;薄片;薄板。7. (烤面包的)铁板。8. (水、雪、冰、火、颜色等的)广大的面;一片(汪洋、原野等)。9.〔诗〕帆。10. 邮票的印张〔美国每一印张有邮票 400 枚〕。11.【地】岩席;岩床;【空】涡面;【数】叶。*a bed* ~ 床单。*a fly* ~ 传单。*an operation* ~ 使用说明书;施工说明书;工艺规范。*a work* ~ 工作单。*a log* ~ 纪录表。*a* ~ *of fire* 一片火海。~*s of rain* 倾盆大雨。***a blank*** ~ 1. 一张白纸。2. 纯洁的心灵。***a clean*** ~ 1. 清白的历史。2. 历史清白的人;品行善良的人。***as white as a*** ~ (脸色)刷白。(***get***) ***between the*** ~***s*** 就寝;(睡)在床上。***in*** ~***s*** 1. 成薄板[薄片]。2.【装订】散页;印好放着不加装订。3. (大雨)倾盆;(大雾)蒙蒙。***pale as a*** ~ (脸色)苍白。***put on a white*** ~ 穿上白色忏悔服,忏悔;悔改。~***s hot from the press*** 刚印好的印刷品。***stand in a white*** ~ = put on a white ~. II *vt*. 1. 给…盖被单;在…上铺被单。2. (用裹尸布)包(死尸);覆盖。3. 把(铁板等)延展成薄片;铺开;展开;伸开;扩展;使成一大片。*The lake was* ~*ed with ice*. 湖面结一层冰。—*vi*. 大片地落下;成片地铺开;大片地流动。~ **erosion** 土壤的整块被水冲走。~ **glass** (薄)玻璃板。~ **ice** 水面的冰层。~ **iron** (薄)铁板。~ **lightning** 片状闪电。~ **metal** (薄)金属板。~ **music** 散页乐谱;单张乐谱。~**-steel mill** 薄板厂。

sheet[2] [ʃiːt; ʃit] I *n*.【海】1. 缭绳;帆脚索。2. [*pl*.] (船头或船尾的)空位。***be*** [***have***] ***a*** ~ [***three*** ~***s***] ***in the wind***(***'s eye***)〔俚〕有点醉[大醉]。***with flowing*** ~***s*** (横风时)放松帆脚索。II *vt*. 用帆脚索扣紧(帆)。~ ***home*** 用帆脚索扣住(风帆)。~ **anchor** 1.【海】(船首的)副锚;紧急备用大锚。2. 紧急时的靠山;最后的依靠;最后手段。~ **bend**【海】单索花〔一种绳结,用于把一条绳系在绳环上〕。

sheet·ing [ˈʃiːtiŋ; ˋʃitɪŋ] *n*. 1. 被单料子;床单布。2. 薄板轧制;[集合词] 金属薄板;(塑料)薄膜;薄片;【建】挡

板;护堤板;护贴板;板栅。3. (用被单)覆盖;铺被单;做护板。

Shef·field [ˈʃefiːld; ˋʃɛfild] ***n.*** 设菲尔德(雪菲耳)〔英国城市〕。

sheik, sheikh [ʃeik, ʃiːk; ʃik] ***n.*** 1. (阿拉伯国家的)家长,村长,族长;酋长。2. 伊斯兰教教主。3. 〔美口〕美男子;使妇女倾倒的男子。~**dom** (阿拉伯)酋长统辖的领土,酋长国。**S- ul** [ul; ʊl] **Islam** (土耳其的)伊斯兰教法典权威。

Shei·la [ˈʃiːlə; ˋʃilə] ***n.*** 希拉〔女子名, Cecilia 的异体〕。

she·kar·ry [ʃiˈkæri; ʃɪˋkɑrɪ] ***n.*** = shikaree, shikari.

shek·el [ˈʃekl; ˋʃɛkl] ***n.*** 1. 锡克尔〔古巴比伦及希伯来的衡量单位,约½盎司〕。2. 重一个锡克尔的古希伯来金币或银币。3. 〔*pl.*〕〔美俚〕钱。

Shel·by [ˈʃelbi; ˋʃɛlbɪ] ***n.*** 谢尔比〔姓氏,男子名〕。

shel·don [ˈʃeldən; ˋʃɛldən] ***n.*** 谢尔登〔姓氏,男子名〕。

Shel·drake [ˈʃeldreik; ˋʃɛlˏdrek] ***n.*** 【鸟】冠鸭;麻鸭;翘鼻麻鸭。

shel·duck [ˈʃeldʌk; ˋʃɛlˏdʌk] ***n.*** sheldrake 的雌性。

shelf [ʃelf; ʃɛlf] ***n.*** (*pl.* ***shelves*** [ʃelvz; ʃɛlvz]) 1. 搁架;搁料架;搁板。2. 沙洲;暗礁。3. 格;层。4. 【矿】平层;锡沙矿基岩;【海】承梁架[材];【地】(大)陆棚,大陆架〔又作 continental ~〕。5. 搁板状物;突出的扁平岩石。6. 〔俚〕(同伙中的)告密者。***off the*** ~ 1. 现货供应 (*All of those parts can be purchased off the* ~. 所有这些零件都有现货供应)。2. 〔俚〕复活。***be on the*** ~ 1. 被搁置;束之高阁;无人问津的;废弃的;闲置的。2. (因年老)而没有人雇用;(妇女无人过问)没有结婚的机会[希望];〔美俚〕退休的,退出体育界的。3. 〔商业用语〕推迟的;(计画等)缓行的。4. 〔古〕在当铺内。5. 〔盗贼俚〕被流放。6. 〔俚〕死了。~ **ice** 陆棚冰 (= ice ~)。~ **life** 储藏寿命;货架寿命〔商品储放不变质的期限〕。

She·lia [ˈʃiːljə; ˋʃiljə] ***n.*** 希莉亚〔女子名, Sheila 的异体〕。

shell [ʃel; ʃɛl] **I** ***n.*** (*pl.* ~*s*, 2 义为 ~) 1. 壳;介壳;甲壳;贝。2. (昆虫的)翅鞘;蛹的蜕皮。3. 【解】种子的外皮;荚。4. 【地】地壳;薄硬岩层。5. 【解】外耳。6. 【机】(汽)锅身。7. 【建】薄壳(屋顶);房屋的框架;内部未竣工的建筑物。8. 船体;骨架。9. 子弹壳;炮弹;猎枪子弹;爆破筒。10. (滑车等的)外框;内棺。11. 外观;外表;外形。12. 单人赛用艇。13. 〔英〕(学校的)中级班〔四、五年级〕。14. 〔诗〕竖琴;七弦琴。15. = ~ jacket. 16. 【物】(原子的)电子壳层。17. (刀剑的)护手。18. (像钻进壳中似的)沉默;冷淡。19. 【计】操作系统外壳,命令解释程序〔如 DOS 等〕。*the* ~ *of an egg* [*a walnut*] 蛋[胡桃]壳。*Beetles have* ~*s*. 甲虫有硬壳。*an illuminating* ~ 照明弹。*a tear* ~ 催泪弹。*the* ~ *of a pipe* 管壁。*You're scarcely out of the* ~ *yet*. 你还乳臭未干。***cast the*** ~ 脱壳;蜕皮。***come out of one's*** ~ 不再羞怯沉默。***go*** [***retire***] ***into one's*** ~ 缄默起来;害羞起来;对人持冷淡态度;保持距离。***in the*** ~ 在萌芽[潜伏]时期。**II** ***vt.*** 1. 由壳中剥出(豌豆等);〔美〕剥(玉米);给…脱粒。2. 用壳体包被;用介壳铺(路)。3. 轰击;炮击[轰]。4. 〔棒球俚〕(投手)使(对方)获得多次安全打或得分。~ *oysters* 去牡蛎壳。—***vi.*** 1. 脱壳;蜕壳;(金属等)剥落;(果实等)脱落。2. 炮击。3. 采集贝壳。***as easy as*** ~***ing peas*** 〔口〕非常容易。~ ***out*** 〔俚〕交出;付出;付款,捐献 (*S- out your money!* 拿出钱来!)。~**back** 〔俚〕老水手;绕越赤道的航海者。~ **bark** = shagbark. ~**ed bean** 去荚而食的豆〔有别于刀豆、豇豆等〕。~ **burst** 炮弹的爆炸。~ **company** (在交易所中成为兼并对象的)控股公司。~**fire** 炮火;炮轰。~**fish** 介壳类水生动物。~ **game** 1. 一种骗人的打赌游戏。2. 欺骗。~ **heap** 贝冢;介壳堆。~ **jacket** 〔美〕(热带的)简单礼服;〔英〕(热带地方穿的)陆军军官的常服;圆领露臂服;背心装。~ **lime** 贝壳灰。~ **mound** = ~ heap. ~**proof** [ˈʃelpruːf; ˋʃɛlˋpruf] ***a.*** 防弹的。~ **road** 贝壳铺的路。~ **shock** 【医】炮弹休克;弹震症。~ **structure** (原子、原子核的)壳层构造。~**suit**, ~ **suit** 双层田径服〔面料为防雨尼龙布、衬里为棉布〕。~ **work** 贝壳工艺品。

she'll [ʃiːl, 弱 ʃil; ʃil] = she will [shall].

shel·lac(k) [ʃəˈlæk; ʃəˋlæk] **I** ***n.*** 1. 紫胶;虫胶;虫漆;洋干漆;漆片。2. 含虫胶的唱片原料;虫胶制剂;虫胶清漆。**II** ***vt.*** 1. 给…涂紫胶;以虫胶处理。2. 〔美俚〕打;揍;大败(对方);彻底击败。**-ed** ***a.*** 1. 〔美俚〕喝醉了的。2. 〔美棒球俚〕大败的。**-ing** 1. 殴打;鞭笞。2. 彻底失败;〔美运〕全盘赛输;大败。

shelled [ʃeld; ʃɛld] ***a.*** 1. 脱壳的;脱皮的。2. 有[带]壳的。~ *egg* 带壳的蛋。

shel·ler [ˈʃelə; ˋʃɛlɚ] ***n.*** 1. 剥壳者;脱粒者。2. 剥壳器;脱粒机。

Shel·ley[1] [ˈʃeli; ˋʃɛlɪ] ***n.*** 1. 谢利〔姓氏〕。2. **Percy Bysshe** ~ 雪莱〔1792—1822, 英国诗人〕。

Shel·ley[2] [ˈʃeli; ˋʃɛlɪ] ***n.*** 谢莉〔女子名〕。

shell·ing [ˈʃeliŋ; ˋʃɛlɪŋ] ***n.*** 1. 去壳;去皮。2. 去壳的谷物;谷壳。3. 用壳荚施肥。4. 贝壳采集。5. 炮击。

shell·y [ˈʃeli; ˋʃɛlɪ] ***a.*** 1. 有壳的;贝壳多的。2. 贝壳一样的。3. 由贝壳铺成[制成]的。

shel·ta [ˈʃeltə; ˋʃɛltɚ] ***n.*** 小炉匠切口〔以爱尔兰语和盖尔语为基础,现今尚在英国、爱尔兰等地的补锅匠、游民间使用〕。

shel·ter [ˈʃeltə; ˋʃɛltɚ] **I** ***n.*** 1. 隐藏所;庇护者;避难所;躲避处;蔽身之处。2. 保护;庇护;隐蔽;遮蔽;屏障。3. 掩护物;遮蔽物;掩蔽部。4. 百叶箱。*an Anderson* ~ 〔英〕(上面盖铁板的)家庭防空壕。*an air-raid* ~ 防空洞。*a bus* ~ 公共汽车站候车亭。*a cabman's* ~ (十字路口上)等候雇客的马车棚。***be a*** ~ ***from*** 成为躲避…的处所。***find*** ~ = ***take*** ~. ***fly to sb. for*** ~ = ***seek*** ~ ***at sb.'s house*** 逃进某人家里避难。***give*** ~ ***to*** 庇护。***lend the*** ~ ***of one's name and position to*** 利用自己的名誉地位庇护(某人)。***take*** ~ 避难;躲避;躲雨。***under the*** ~ ***of*** 在…的庇护下。**II** ***vt.*** 1. 遮蔽;隐蔽;隐匿。2. 保护;包庇;掩护。~ *sb. for the night* 留人住一宿。—***vi.*** 躲避,避难。~***ed trades*** (不受外国竞争影响的)国内受保护行业[建筑业、内地运输业等]。~***ed workshop*** (收容残疾人等的)福利工厂。~ ***oneself behind*** (*a hedge*; *superiors*) 躲在(篱笆,上司)背后。~ **area** 【军】战地宿营地区。~**belt** 防风林带。~ **half** 双人帐篷的半幅〔三角形帆布〕。~ **tent** 军用双人帐篷。~ **trench** 【军】掩蔽壕。**-less** ***a.*** 没有隐藏处的;无处避难的;无依无靠的;无保护的;任风吹雨打的。

shel·tie shel·ty, [ˈʃelti; ˋʃɛltɪ] ***n.*** (*pl.* ***-ties***) = 1. shetland pony. 2. shetland sheepdog.

shelve[1] [ʃelv; ʃɛlv] ***vt.*** 1. 装搁架于。2. 把…放在架[搁板]上。3. 搁置(议案等)。4. 罢免;解雇;使(军官等)退役。

shelve[2] [ʃelv; ʃɛlv] ***vi.*** 逐渐倾斜;成斜坡(尤指海岸)。

shelves [ʃelvz; ʃɛlvz] shelf 的复数。

shelv·ing[1] [ˈʃelviŋ; ˋʃɛlvɪŋ] ***n.*** 1. 【建】架子料。2. 〔总称〕架子;一组搁架。3. 搁置;延误。4. 免职;解职。

shelv·ing[2] [ˈʃelviŋ; ˋʃɛlvɪŋ] ***n.*** (海岸等)的倾斜(度)。

She·ma [ʃəˈmɑː; ʃəˋmɑ] ***n.*** 【犹太教】施玛篇〔晨祷和晚祷中的祷文,申述对上帝的笃信〕。

she·male [ˈʃiːmeil; ˋʃimel] ***n.*** 〔美俚〕女人;女性。

Shem·ite [ˈʃemait; ˋʃɛmaɪt] ***n.*** = Semite.

Shem·it·ic [ʃeˈmitik; ʃɛmˋɪtɪk] ***a.*** = Semetic.

she·nan·i·gan [ʃəˈnænigən; ʃəˋnænəˏgæn] ***n.*** 〔美口〕〔常 *pl.*〕1. 鬼把戏;诡计;欺骗。2. 恶作剧;胡闹。3. 无聊的话;无意义的话;胡说。*Cut out the* ~*s*! 别胡说了!

Shen·stone [ˈʃenstən; ˋʃɛnstən] ***n.*** 申斯通〔姓氏〕。

shent [ʃent; ʃɛnt] ***a.*** 〔古、方〕1. 受辱的;丢脸的;羞愧的。2. 失去的;打败的;失败了的。3. 被伤害的;毁坏的;损坏了的。4. 受斥责的;受谴责的。

she-oak [ˈʃiːəuk; ˋʃiok] ***n.*** 1. 【植】(澳洲)木麻黄属 (*Ca-*

suarina）的一种。2．〔澳俚〕强烈啤酒。

She·ol [ˈʃiːəul; ˋʃiol] *n*. 1.【圣】(希伯来人的)阴间。2.〔s-〕冥府;地狱。

Shep·hard [ˈʃepəd; ˋʃɛpɚd] *n*. 谢泼德〔姓氏〕。

shep·herd [ˈʃepəd; ˋʃɛpɚd] I *n*. 1. 牧羊人;牧羊者。2. 牧羊狗[犬]（= ~ dog)。3. 牧师。4. 保护者;指导者。***S- Kings*** 古埃及希克索["牧人"]王朝的国王。***the (good) S-*** 基督。II *vt*. 1. 牧(羊);放牧。2. 照看。3. 领导,指导。~ **dog** 牧羊狗[犬]。~**ess** 牧羊女;乡下姑娘。~ **god** 牧羊神。~**'s crook** (有钩的)牧羊杖。~**'s pie** 肉馅洋芋饼。~**'s plaid** [**check**] 黑白方格花呢。~**'s-pouch**, ~**'s-purse**【植】荠菜。~**'s trade** 1. 写作田园诗。2.【宗】耶稣的业绩。

sher·bet [ˈʃəːbət; ˋʃɝbɪt] *n*. 〔英〕冰冻果汁水;〔美〕果汁奶冻,果汁雪泥。

sherd [ʃəːd; ʃɑrd] *n*. = shard.

she·reef [ʃeˈriːf; ʃɛˋrif] *n*. 1. 穆罕默德的女儿法蒂玛(Fatima)的后裔。2. (阿拉伯国家的)君主;王公,酋长。3. 麦加的地方[行政]长官。

Sher·i·dan [ˈʃeridn; ˋʃɛrədn̩] *n*. 谢里登〔姓氏,男子名〕。

she·rif [ʃəˈriːf; ʃəˋrif] *n*. = shereef.

sher·iff [ˈʃerif; ˋʃɛrɪf] *n*. 〔英〕(任期一年的)名誉郡长〔正式名称为 High S-〕;(某些城市的)行政司法长官;〔美〕县的行政司法长官。***dance at the ~'s ball*** 被处绞刑。~***'s hotel*** 〔俚〕监狱。~***'s sale*** 强制拍卖。~**hood** [~**-ship**] 郡长等的任期[职权]。~**dom** 郡长等的辖区。~ **wick** = ~dom.

sher·lock [ˈʃəːlɔk; ˋʃɝlɑk] *n*. 〔俚〕1. 私家侦探。2. 善于看破奥秘的人〔亦作 Sherlock〕。

Sher·lock Holmes [həumz; homz] 夏洛克·福尔摩斯〔英国作家柯南道尔 (Conan Doyle) 作品中名侦探〕。

Sher·man [ˈʃəːmən; ˋʃɝmən] *n*. 谢尔曼〔姓氏,男子名〕。

Sher·pa [ˈʃəːpə, ʃɛə-; ˋʃɝpə, ʃɛr-] *n*. (*pl*. ~*s*) 谢尔巴人〔喜马拉雅山区尼泊尔一个部族的成员〕;〔s-〕〔英俚〕搬运工〔因谢尔巴人常从事此项职业〕。

Sher·riff [ˈʃerif; ˋʃɛrɪf] *n*. 谢里夫〔姓氏〕。

Sher·rill [ˈʃeril; ˋʃɛrɪl] *n*. 谢里尔〔姓氏〕。

Sher·rill [ˈʃeril; ˋʃɛrɪl] *n*. 谢丽尔〔女子名〕。

Sher·ring·ton [ˈʃeriŋtn; ˋʃɛrɪŋtən] *n*. 谢灵顿〔姓氏〕。

sher·ris [ˈʃeris; ˋʃɛrɪs] *n*. 〔古〕= sherry.

Sher·ry, Sher·rie [ˈʃeri; ˋʃɛrɪ] *n*. 谢丽〔女子名〕。

sher·ry [ˈʃeri; ˋʃɛrɪ] *n*. 雪利酒〔西班牙南部所产的白葡萄酒〕。*brown* ~ 黑雪利酒。~ **cobbler** (加糖水,柠檬)冰雪利酒。~**-glass** 雪利酒酒杯。

Sher·win [ˈʃəːwin; ˋʃɝwɪn] *n*. 舍温〔姓氏,男子名〕。

Sher·wood [ˈʃəːwud; ˋʃɝwʊd] *n*. 舍伍德〔姓氏,男子名〕。

she's [ʃiːz, 弱 ʃiz; ʃiz] = she is [has].

Shet·land [ˈʃetlənd; ˋʃɛtlənd] *n*. (苏格兰东北部的)设得兰(雪得兰)群岛。~ **pony** 设得兰矮种马。~ **sheepdog** 设得兰牧羊狗。~ **wool** 设得兰产的细羊毛。

She·vu·oth [ʃəˈvuːəut; ʃəˋvuot] *n*. 〔Heb.〕= Shavuot.

shew [ʃəu; ʃo] *v*. 〔英古〕= show. ~**bread** 犹太教徒用作祭品的无酵饼,陈设饼〔见《圣经》《出埃及记》(= show-bread)〕。

shewn [ʃəun; ʃon] *v*. 〔英方〕= shown.

s.h.f., shf = superhigh frequency【无】超高额。

Shi·ah [ˈʃiːə; ˋʃiə] *n*. 〔*sing*., *pl*.〕1.【伊斯兰教】什叶派 (= the Shiites)。2. 什叶派教徒 (= Shiite)。

shi·a·tsu [ʃiːˈɑːtsuː; ʃiˋɑtsu] *n*. 〔Chin.〕指压术[中国的一种手指按摩,以此法治病或消除疲劳]。

shib·bo·leth [ˈʃibəleθ; ˋʃɪbəlɪθ] *n*. 1.【犹太史】(基利德人〔Gileadite〕用来鉴别逃亡的厄弗雷姆人〔Ephraimite〕的)检验用词〔看其能否正确地读出该词音,因厄弗雷姆人发不出 sh 音〕。2. (社团成员间彼此辨认的)切口;对口话;黑话;口令。3. (一阶层、一团体的)特殊语言;习惯;服装(等)。

shick·er [ˈʃikə; ˋʃɪkɚ] I *a*. 喝醉的。II *n*. 醉汉;酒鬼 (= shikker)。

shied [ʃaid; ʃaɪd] shy 的过去式和过去分词。

shield [ʃiːld; ʃild] I *n*. 1. 盾;盾牌。2. 罩;屏;屏蔽。3. 防御物;保护物。4. 防御;保护。5. 保护者;庇护者[人]。6. 盾形物;【徽】盾形徽;〔美〕警察[侦探]徽章。7.【动、植】(甲壳等的)盾状部;背甲;头胸甲;龟甲板。8.【地】地盾。9.【矿】掩护支架。10.【电】屏蔽铠装。11.【炮】钢盾;防盾。12. (机器等的)铠装;(隧道用的)铠框。13. 〔the S-〕【天】盾牌座。*a heat* ~ 热屏。***be sb.'s ~ and buckler*** 充当某人的保护者。***both sides of the ~*** 1. 盾的正反两面。2. 事物的表里。***S- of David*** 大卫王的盾牌〔犹太教的六芒星形标志〕。***the other side of the ~*** 1. 盾的反面。2. 问题[事情]的另一面。II *vt*. 1. 用盾挡住;防护;防御;保护;屏蔽。2. 庇护;掩盖。3. 挡开;避开。~ *a country from invasion* 保护一个国家不受侵犯。*Officials ~ one another*. 官官相护。—*vi*. 1. 起盾的作用;起保护作用;防御。2. 充当保护者。~ **back** (英国十八世纪流行的)盾形背椅子。~ **bearer** 携盾侍从。~ **hand** 〔古〕左手。~ **law** 〔美〕新闻保障法〔保护新闻从业人员可拒绝说出机密消息来源的法律〕;原告[证人]权利保障法(保护检举人或证人的法律)。

shiel·ing [ˈʃiːliŋ; ˋʃilɪŋ] *n*. 1. 〔Scot.〕(夏季)羊棚。2. (山区的)夏季牧场。3. 牧羊人住的小屋。4. 运动员的休息棚。

shi·er [ˈʃaiə; ˋʃaɪɚ] I *a*. shy 的比较级。II *n*. 易受惊的马。

shi·est [ˈʃaiist; ˋʃaɪɪst] *a*. shy 的最高级。

S

shift [ʃift; ʃɪft] I *vt*. 1. 变动;改变;搬移;移动;转移;变换;替换;更换。2. 推卸;转嫁。3. 消除;撤除。4.【语】变换(语音)。5. 〔方〕换(衣);使换衣服 6. 〔汽车〕变(速);换(排挡)。6. 〔英口〕出售,卖。~ *all the blame on others* 把一切错误归于别人。—*vi*. 1. 变;移;动;(风)改变方向;漂移。2. 想种种办法;筹划;策划;设法。3. 瞒骗;强辩;托词闪避。4. 挣生活;糊口。5. 〔口〕走开。6.【机】变速;调挡。7.【语】辅音变换。8. 〔方〕换衣服。~ ***about*** 搬来搬去;屡变位置。~ ***for oneself*** 独立谋生。~ ***off*** 拖延;消除;整顿;逃避;推托(责任等);(用借口等)把…打发走。~ ***oneself*** 换衣服 (= ~ one's clothes)。~ ***one's ground*** 改变论据[立场]。II *n*. 1. 变迁;变化;变换;替换;更换;掉换;更易;转移;代用。2. 谋划;办法;计划;手段;权宜之计。3. 哄骗;欺诈。4. 班;轮[换]班;轮值。5. 轮班职工。6. 轮值时间;轮班工作时间。7. 〔古〕女汗衫。8.【农】轮作;轮作农作物;轮作的农地。9.【矿】断层;断层变位;平移。10.【语】辅音变换。11. 〔方〕换衣服;(常更换的)衬衣。12. 〔足球〕开赛前球员阵势的变动。13. (堆砖瓦的)互接法。14. 汽车排挡。*the ~ of responsibility* 责任的转嫁。*an eight-hour ~* 八小时的工作班。*work in three ~s of eight hours* 每班八小时分三班轮流工作。*the day-~* 日班。***make a ~*** 设法过活,应付;将就使用,凑合用;尽量争取做到。*the night-~* 夜班。***be put [reduced] to the ~s*** 被逼得走投无路。***for a ~*** 出于权宜之计;将就地;为眼前打算。***full of ~s and devices*** 足智多谋。***live by ~(s)*** 东拼西凑过日子。***make (a) ~*** 1. 拼拼凑凑过日子。2. 尽力设法利用[应付] (*with*);安于某事物;(没有…也)勉强对付过去 (*without*)。3. 尽力做到〔与不定式连用〕。***one's (or the) last ~*** 最后的手段[办法]。~ ***of crops*** 轮作。***the ~s and changes of life*** (人生的)祸福荣枯。***try every ~ available*** 想尽办法。~ **key** 〔打字机〕大写字体按键。~ **register**【自】移位寄存器。

shift·er [ˈʃiftə; ˋʃɪftɚ] *n*. 1.【电】移动装置;移相器;倒相器;移带器。2. 开关。3. (印字电报机等的)换行器。4. 搬移工。5. 回避论点者。6. (铁矿中的)领班。7. (煤矿中的)辅助工。*a phase ~*【测】调相器。

shift·ing [ˈʃiftiŋ; ˋʃɪftɪŋ] I *a*. 1. 变动的;移动的;多[易]变的。2. 想尽办法的;尽量设法的。3. 用权谋的;哄骗

的;狡赖的;诡诈的。~ *cultivation* 轮作。~ *sand* 流沙。~ *wind* 方向不定的风。**II** ***n*.** **1.** 转移;移动;移位;偏移。**2.** 变化;转变。**3.** 狡赖;遁词诈术等的使用。*gear* ~ (汽车)变换排挡。*phase* ~ (物理学上的)相位移。~ **arm** 变速臂。~ **ga(u)ge** 画线规;根距。~ **spanner** 活动扳手。

shift·less [ˈʃiftlis; ˋʃɪftlɪs] ***a*.** **1.** 没办法的;走投无路的;无计算的;无计谋生的。**2.** 没用的;不中用的;无能的。**3.** 偷懒的;懒惰的;得过且过的。**-ly** ***ad*.**

shift·y [ˈʃifti; ˋʃɪftɪ] ***a*.** (***-i·er***; ***-i·est***) **1.** 变动的;多变的;不稳定的。**2.** 策略多的;足智多谋的;办法多的;善于应变的。**3.** 会哄骗的;诡诈的;不老实的;不正直的;靠不住的。**-i·ly** ***ad*.** **-i·ness** ***n*.**

shi·gel·la [ʃiˈgelə; ʃɪˋgelə] ***n*.** (*pl*. ***-gel·lae*** [-iː; -i], *~s*)【生】志贺氏菌属。

shi·gel·lo·sis [ˌʃigəˈləusis; ˏʃɪgəˋlosɪs] ***n*.**【医】志贺氏菌痢。

shi·kar [ʃikɑː; ʃɪˋkɑr] ***n*.**〔Ind.〕打猎;狩猎。

shi·kar·ee, shi·kar·i [ʃiˈkɑːri; ʃɪˋkɑrɪ], **shi·kar·ry** [-kæ-; -kæ-] ***n*.**〔Ind.〕猎人;做向导的猎人。

Shi·ko·ku [ʃiˈkəukuː; ʃɪˋkoku] ***n*.** 四国〔日本主要岛屿之一〕。

shill [ʃil; ʃɪl], **shil·la·ber** [ˈʃiləbə; ˋʃɪləbɚ] ***n*.**〔美俚〕(道旁摊贩引诱顾客的)假购物同伙;(勾引赌客入局的)赌棍同伙;囮子,托儿;(貌似公正实为某一集团或部门谋取私利的)代言人,代理人。

shil·la·lah, shil·le·la(g)h [ʃiˈleilə; ʃəˋlelə], **shil·la·ly** [-li; -lɪ] ***n*.** (爱尔兰人鞭笞时用的)橡树棒。

S

shil·ling [ˈʃiliŋ; ˋʃɪlɪŋ] ***n*.** 先令〔旧英国货币单位,一镑的 1/20,十二便士为一先令,略 s., sh.,现已改为十进制〕。*2 ~s 6 pence*〔略 2s. 6d. 或 2/6〕二先令六辨士。***cut off sb. with a ~ = cut off one's heir with a ~*** 取消某人的继承权。***long ~s*** 高额工资;高薪。***pay twenty ~s in the pound*** 全数付清。~ ***shocker***〔英〕一先令一本的黄色[侦探,惊险]小说。***take the King's*** [***Queen's***] ~〔英〕入伍;从军,当兵。***want two-pence in the ~*** 一先令短少两辨士;〔口〕智力不足。~ **mark** 书写[印刷]的斜线分隔"/"记号;先令号(原用来隔开先令和便士)。

Shil·luk [ʃiˈluːk; ʃɪˋluk] ***n*.** **1.** (*pl*. ~(*s*)) 希鲁克人〔苏丹的尼罗特人〕。**2.** 希鲁克语。

shil·ly-shal·ly [ˈʃiliʃæli; ˋʃɪlɪˏʃælɪ] **I** ***n*.**, ***vi*.** 磨蹭;支支吾吾;游移不定;踌躇不决;优柔寡断。**II** ***a*.**, ***ad*.** 踌躇不定的[地];优柔寡断的[地]。

shi·ly [ˈʃaili; ˋʃaɪlɪ] ***ad*.** = shyly.

shim [ʃim; ʃɪm] **I** ***n*.**【机】**1.** 薄垫片;楔形填隙片;衬垫;夹铁。**2.** 补偿棒;粗调棒。**II** ***vt*.** 用薄垫片填入;拿填隙片塞;向…中插夹铁。

shim·mer [ˈʃimə; ˋʃɪmɚ] **I** ***n*.** 微光;闪光。**II** ***vi*.**, ***vt*.** (使)微微发亮[发光];(使)闪烁;(使)发闪光。**-y** ***a*.** 发微光的;闪烁的。

shim·my[1] [ˈʃimi; ˋʃɪmɪ] ***n*.**〔口〕女式无袖衬衫(= chemise)。

shim·my[2] [ˈʃimi; ˋʃɪmɪ] **I** ***n*.** **1.**〔美〕西迷舞〔身体颤动着跳的一种狐步舞〕。**2.**【机】震动;摆动;振动。**3.** (机车前轮的)不正常振动[急剧摇荡]。**II** ***vi*.** (***-mied***) **1.** 跳西迷舞。**2.** (汽车)震颤;震动;摆动。

Shi·mo·no·se·ki [ˌʃiməunəuˈseki; ˏʃɪmonoˋsɛkɪ] ***n*.** 下关〔即马关,日本港市〕。

shin[1] [ʃin; ʃɪn] **I** ***n*.** **1.**【解】胫;【昆】胫节;外胫;脚杆骨;胫骨。**2.** 牛的小腿肉。**II** ***vt*.** (***-nn-***) **1.**〔美〕爬(树等)。**2.** (比球时)踢…的外胫。~ *oneself against a rock* 脚杆骨撞在岩石上。—***vi*.** **1.** 攀爬(*up*)。**2.**〔美〕(为借钱而)到处奔走,跑来跑去(*about*);快步走。~ **bone** 胫骨(= tibia)。~ **guard** (运动员用的)护胫。~ **plaster** **1.**〔美〕贴外胫的膏药。**2.**〔美口〕私营银行发行的钞票。**3.** (旧指)贬值的钞票;滥发的纸币。~**-sock** 半长统袜〔长达小腿中部〕。

shin[2] [ʃiːn; ʃin] ***n*.** 希伯来语的第二十一个字母。

shin·dig [ˈʃindig; ˋʃɪndɪg] ***n*.**〔美俚〕盛大舞会[社交集会]。~ **dancer** (夜总会等处)表演色情舞蹈的舞女,色情舞女。

shin·dy [ˈʃindi; ˋʃɪndɪ] ***n*.** **1.**〔口〕纠纷;吵闹;骚动;喧嚣;喧哗。**2.**〔美俚〕盛大宴会;舞会。***kick up a ~*** 引起骚动。

shine [ʃain; ʃaɪn] (***~d***, ***shone*** [ʃɔn, Am. ʃəun; ʃon]; ***shin·ing***) **I** ***vi*.** **1.** 发光;发亮;照耀;闪耀;(太阳)照耀。**2.** 出众;杰出;出风头。**3.** (情感等)明显流露。*a shining painter* 卓越的画家。*She ~s in dancing*. 她跳舞极好。—***vt*.** **1.** 使发光;使发亮;使照耀。**2.**〔过去式及过去分词 ~d〕〔口〕擦亮(皮鞋等);磨光;以灯等照耀。~ *one's shoes* 擦皮鞋。*S- your light over here*. 把灯朝这里照照。***improve the shining hour*** 抓紧时间。~ ***in society*** 在交际场中出风头。~ ***round*** = ~ ***up to***〔美俚〕竭力[百般]讨好[巴结]某人[异性]。**II** ***n*.** **1.** 阳光;晴天;华丽。**2.** 光;光辉;光亮;〔口〕光泽;光彩。**3.**〔美俚〕爱好;喜爱。**4.**〔常 *pl*.〕恶作剧;鬼把戏;诡计。**5.**〔英俚〕纠纷;骚动;吵闹;混乱。**6.**〔美俚、蔑〕黑人。(***come***) ***rain or ~*** **1.** 不论晴雨。**2.** 不管怎样。***keep up*** [***make***] ***a ~*** 引起(大)风潮,引起(大)骚动。***make no end of a ~***〔口〕大闹。***put a good ~ on*** 将…擦得晶亮。***take a ~ to***〔美俚〕喜爱;爱上;看中。***take the ~ off*** [***out of***] 消除…的光泽;使…黯然无光[失色];使相形见绌;胜过。**-less** ***a*.** 无光泽的。

shin·er [ˈʃainə; ˋʃaɪnɚ] ***n*.** **1.** 发光物;闪耀发亮的东西;发光体〔日、月等〕;丝质礼帽。**2.** 出色[杰出]的人物;衣着漂亮的人。**3.**〔美〕(作饵用)银色小鱼。**4.**〔英俚〕钱币;〔尤指〕一镑金币;〔*pl*.〕钱。**5.**〔俚〕受伤后青肿的黑眼圈;眼睛。**6.** 擦皮鞋者。

shin·gle[1] [ˈʃiŋgl; ˋʃɪŋgl] **I** ***n*.** **1.** 屋顶板;木瓦板。**2.** (女式)短发。**3.**〔美口〕(医师、律师等的)小招牌。***hang out one's ~*** 挂牌;开业。**II** ***vt*.** **1.** 用木瓦板盖(屋顶)。**2.** 把(女子头发)剪短。**3.**【冶】锻;压。**4.**〔美俚〕责打(孩子等)。

shin·gle[2] [ˈʃiŋgl; ˋʃɪŋgl̩] ***n*.**〔*sing*., *pl*.〕扁砾石;砂砾;〔英〕(海滨的)鹅卵石;砂石;砂石海滩。

shin·gles [ˈʃiŋglz; ˋʃɪŋgl̩z] ***n*.**〔*sing*., *pl*.〕【医】带状泡疹;缠腰龙。

shin·gly [ˈʃiŋgli; ˋʃɪŋglɪ] ***a*.** 多砂石的;似海滩圆卵石的;铺满圆卵石的。

shin·i·ness [ˈʃaininis; ˋʃaɪnɪnɪs] ***n*.** 光泽;光彩;闪光。

shin·ing [ˈʃainiŋ; ˋʃaɪnɪŋ] ***a*.** **1.** 发光的;反光的;闪光的;光亮的;照耀的。**2.** 灿烂的;显赫的;杰出的;卓越的;辉煌的。

shin·kan·sen [ˈʃiːnˈkɑːnsen; ˋʃɪnˋkɑnsɛn] ***n*.** (日本的)新干线(一种高速火车)。

shin·leaf [ˈʃinˌliːf; ˋʃɪnˏlif] ***n*.**【植】鹿蹄草属(*Pyrola*)植物。

shin·ny[1], **shin·ney** [ˈʃini; ˋʃɪnɪ] **shin·ty** [-ti; -tɪ] **I** ***n*.**〔美〕**1.** (儿童玩的)简式曲棍球戏。**2.** 曲棍球球棍。**II** ***vi*.** **1.** 玩简式曲棍球。**2.** 击球。

shin·ny[2] [ˈʃini; ˋʃɪnɪ] ***vi*.**〔美俚〕攀爬(树等)(*up*)。

Shin·to [ˈʃintəu; ˋʃɪnto] ***n*.** (日本的)神道;神道教。**-ism** ***n*.** **-ist** ***n*.** ***a*.** **-is·tic** ***a*.**

shin·ty [ˈʃinti; ˋʃɪntɪ] ***n*.** = shinny.

shin·y [ˈʃaini; ˋʃaɪnɪ] ***a*.** (***-i·er***; ***-i·est***) **1.** 晴朗的;发光的;辉煌的;光亮的;闪闪发亮的;有光泽的。**2.** 磨亮的;磨光的;磨损的。**-i·ness** ***n*.**

ship [ʃip; ʃɪp] **I** ***n*.** **1.** 船;大船;海船;舰〔作阴性看,代名词用 she, her〕。**2.** 三桅船;全装帆船。**3.** 船形物。**4.**〔俚〕赛艇。**5.**〔美〕飞船;飞机。**6.** 全体船员。*His Majesty's ~*〔英〕军舰。*a capital ~* 主力舰。*a ~'s company* 全体船员。*a ~'s husband* (在岸上代表船方处理事务的)船舶代理人。*a ~'s lawyer*〔美〕次等律师。*~'s papers* 船证;船照。*a space ~* 太空船。***burn***

one's ～ 破釜沉舟。*clear a* ～ 卸货。*gauge a* ～ 量船的吃水量。*go on board a* ～ 乘船。*heave a* ～ *to*【海】停船。*jump* ～ 1. 弃船潜逃。2. 背弃;潜逃。*launch a* ～ 使船下水。*on board a* ～ 在船上;在[往]船内。*lose* [*spoil*] *the* ～ *for a ha'p'orth* (= halfpennyworth) *of tar* 因小失大。*speak a* ～【海】给别的船打招呼[发信号]。*take* ～〔古〕乘船;搭船。*when one's* ～ *comes home* 如果变成富翁;如果有了钱;当某人时来运转;当某人发财时。*wind a* ～【海】掉转船头。**II** *vt*. (*-pp-*) 1. 装上船;用船运;装货;卸货;(用船、铁路、马车等)装运;运送;送。2. 雇(水手)。3. 装上;安上(船具)。4. 〔口〕解雇;赶走;撵走;摆脱。5. (自船舷侧)灌进(海水)。6. 〔口〕推出(新产品等)。—*vi*. 1. 上船;乘船。2. 在船上工作;做水手[水兵]。～ *as bo'sun* 做水手长。～ *a sea* [*water*] 冒着波浪,波浪打上甲板。～ *oars* 把桨安在桨架上。～ *off* 送往;遣送。～ *out* 1. 坐船到国外去。2. 送(某人上船)到海外去。～ *over*〔美〕重新再进海军服役。～ **airplane** [**aeroplane**] 舰上飞机。～ **biscuit** (船上用的)硬饼干。～**board** 船上,舷侧;船。～ **bread** = ～ biscuit. ～ **breaker** 废船包拆人。～ **breaking** 废船拆卸业。～ **broker** 船舶经纪人;水上掮客。～**builder** 造船技师;造船工人;船匠。～ **building** 1. 造船术[学]。2. 造船业。～ **canal** (可航行海船的)海船运河。～ **chandler** 船具商。～ **chandlery** 1. 船具。2. 船具业。～ **fever**【医】斑疹伤寒,船热病。～**fitter** 1. 造船装配工[安装工]。2. (美海军)下士;安装技工。～ **letter** 交普通船运送的信件。～**load** 1. 船货。2. 一艘船的载货量。～**man** 1. 水手;海员。2. 船长。～**-master** 船长;船主。～**mate** 同船水手;水手同伴。～ **money**【英史】造舰税。～ **of the desert** 沙漠之舟,骆驼。～ **of the line**〔古〕(备有七十五门炮以上的)战列舰。～ **of war** (= ～**-of-war**) 战舰。～ **owner** 船主。～ **plane** 舰载飞机。～ **railway** 移船轨道。～**-rigged** 三桅(上备有)横帆的;有横[方形]帆的。～**'s articles** 雇用船员条例。～**'s bell** (每隔半小时的)船上敲钟。～**'s boat** 救生艇。～**'s boy** 船轮服务员 (= cabin boy)。～**'s company** 全体船员。～**shape** *a*., *ad*. 井然有序的[地]。～**'s husband** 船舶代理人;随船押货人。～ **side** 码头的靠船一侧。～ **station** 船上电台。～**way** 造船台。～ **worm** 凿船虫;船蛆。～**wreck** *n*., *vt*., *vi*. 1. 船只失事;(海滩上的)失事船残骸。2. 灭亡;毁灭;失败;挫折。3. 使(船)失事 (*make* ～ *wreck of* 破坏;糟蹋;把…弄得一塌糊涂)。～ **wright** 造船工;船匠。～**yard** 造船厂;船坞。

-ship *suf*. 〔附在形容词或名词后,作成抽象名词后〕表示状态;情况、性质、资格、身分、职、术等: hard*ship*, leader*ship*, member*ship*, scholar*ship*.

ship·ment [ˈʃipmənt; ˋʃɪpmənt] *n*. 1. 装货;船运;装运。2. 装载的货物;载货。3. 载货量。

ship·pa·ble [ˈʃipəbl; ˋʃɪpəbḷ] *a*. 可以装运的,适于装船的,可以运输的;可船运的。

ship·pen [ˈʃipən; ˋʃɪpən] *n*. 牛棚;马房。

ship·per [ˈʃipə; ˋʃɪpɚ] *n*. 发货人;交运货物者;运货者;托运人;货主。

ship·ping [ˈʃipiŋ; ˋʃɪpɪŋ] *n*. 1. 装货;船运;海运;航运;装运;运输。2. 航行。3. 航运业;运输业。4. 〔集合词〕(某一范围内的)全部船舶。5. 船舶总吨数。*line* ～ 定期航运。～ **agent** 运输[船运]代理商。～ **articles** (*pl*.) 船员雇用合同。～ **bill** [**note**] 舱单;船货清单;(海关颁发的)货物准予装船通知单。**S- Board**〔美〕船务局。～ **clerk** (码头上的)理货员;运务员。～ **room** (工厂等的)发货仓库。

ship·pon [ˈʃipən; ˋʃɪpən] *n*. = shippen.

Shi·raz [ʃiəˈrɑːz; ʃɪˋrɑz] *n*. 设拉子〔伊朗城市〕。

shire [ˈʃaiə; ʃaɪr] *n*. 1. (英国的)郡 (= county)。2. 〔the S-s〕(尤指以猎狐出名的)英国中部各郡地区。3. = ～ horse 英国中部出产的;高大有力的拉车马。*a knight of the* ～【英史】郡选议员。*come from the* ～*s*〔英〕是中部地方的(人)。*get in the* ～ *what one loses in the hundred* 失之东隅,收之桑榆。～ **horse** (英国中部出产的、高大有力的)拉车马;大种马。～ **town** 1. 郡的行政机关所在地;郡的首府。2. 中级法院所在地。

-shire [-ʃiə, -ʃə; -ʃɪr, -ʃɚ] *suf*. 〔英〕…州。Berk*shire*, York*shire*, Lanca*shire*.

shirk [ʃəːk; ʃɝk] **I** *n*. 逃避者;偷懒者。**II** *vi*., *vt*. 逃避;躲避;规避(义务、责任等);怠忽;偷懒 (*from*)。～ *military service* 逃避兵役。～ *off* [*out*] 逃开。**-er** *n*. 逃避者;偷懒者。

shir(r) [ʃəː; ʃɝ]〔美〕**I** *n*. 抽褶;松紧线;橡皮筋。**II** *vt*. 把…抽上褶子;【烹】(把奶油和上面包屑)焙烤(蛋)。

shir·(r)ing [ˈʃəːriŋ; ˋʃɝɪŋ] *n*. 抽褶(饰边)。

Shir·ley [ˈʃəːli; ˋʃɝlɪ] *n*. 雪莉〔女子名〕。

shirt [ʃəːt; ʃɝt] *n*. 1. (男式)衬衫。2. (仿男式的)女用衬衫。3. 内衣;汗衫。*T-* ～ T 恤,短袖圆领衫。*get sb.'s* ～ *out* [*off*]〔俚〕惹怒;使发脾气。*give away the* ～ *off one's back* 送掉身上所有的东西;不顾自己尽力接济[帮助]别人。*give sb. a wet* ～ 使(某)人工作到汗流浃背。*hang onto sb.'s* ～*s* 依靠某人。*have not a* ～ *to one's back* 连衬衫都没有,穷极。*have one's* ～ *out* [*off*] 发脾气。*keep one's* ～ *on*〔俚〕保持冷静;不发脾气。*lose one's* ～〔俚〕失去一切;搞得精光。*put one's* ～ *on* [*upon*] (*a horse*)〔俚〕把全部赌本押在(一匹马上)。*Near* [*Close*] *is my* ～, *but nearer* [*closer*] *is my skin*. 为人不如为己。～ **band** (衬衫的领口或袖口等的)衬布。～**dress** = ～ waist, blouse. ～**front** 衬衫的胸部。～ **hunt**〔美〕捉虱子。～ **jacket**〔美〕衬衫式茄克。～**maker** 1. 制衬衣者。2. 简易妇女上衣。～**-sleeves** 1. *n*. 衬衫袖子 (*in one's* ～*-sleeves* 不穿外衣)。2. *a*. 只穿衬衫(不穿外衣)的,衣着随便的;不拘礼貌的,随便的。～**-suit** 休闲装(= leisure suit)。～**tail** *n*. 1. 衬衣的下摆。2. 〔美新闻语〕排在主要新闻下的小新闻;不重要的小事物。*a*. 1. 〔口〕(亲戚)远房的。2. 小的;短的。3. 幼小的。4. 非正式的;随便的。～ **waist**〔美〕= blouse. ～ **waister** 连衣裙。

shir·ting [ˈʃəːtiŋ; ˋʃɝtɪŋ] *n*. 衬衫料子。

shirt·y [ˈʃəːti; ˋʃɝtɪ] *a*. 〔俚〕脾气不好的;发怒的;被激怒的。

shish ke·bab [ˈʃiʃ kəˌbɑːb; ˋʃɪʃ kəˏbʌb] 烤羊肉串 (= shish kabob)。

shit [ʃit; ʃɪt]〔英卑〕**I** *vi*. (*shit*; ～*ting*) 拉屎;通便。—*vt*. 对…胡言乱语;对…胡作非为。**II** *n*. 1. 粪。2. 通便。3. 假装;伪装。4. 胡说;大话。**III** *int*. 〔俚〕〔表示厌恶、惊奇等〕呸! 放屁! **-ty** *a*. 不舒服。

shit·tah [ˈʃitə; ˋʃɪtə] *n*. (*pl*. *shit·tahs*, *shittim*)【植】塞伊尔相思树 (*Acacia seyal*)〔产于亚洲〕。

shit·tim (wood) [ˈʃitim; ˋʃɪtɪm] *n*. 塞伊尔相思树木。

shiv [ʃiv; ʃɪv] *n*. 〔俚〕刀;剃刀;弹簧刀。

Shiva [ˈʃiːvə; ˋʃivə] *n*. = Siva.

shiv·a·ree [ˌʃivəˈriː; ˏʃɪvəˋri] *n*. 〔美〕= charivari.

shive [ʃaiv; ʃaɪv] *n*. 1. 碎片;断片。2. 亚麻硬外皮。3. 〔*pl*.〕下脚麻。4. (大口瓶的)扁薄软木塞。5. 〔美俚〕剃刀;小刀。6. 布上的线头。

shiv·er[1] [ˈʃivə; ˋʃɪvɚ] **I** *vi*., *vt*. 1. (使)发抖;(使)打颤;(使)迎风飘动。**II** *n*. 发抖;颤抖。*give sb. the* ～*s* 使人不寒而栗;使人毛骨悚然。*the* ～*s* 1. 〔口谑〕发冷;战栗;冷颤。2. 【医】疟疾。

shiv·er[2] [ˈʃivə; ˋʃɪvɚ] **I** *n*. 〔常 *pl*.〕碎块;破片;碎片。**II** *vt*., *vi*. 打碎;敲碎;破碎。*break* [*burst*] *into* ～*s* 粉碎。～ *my timbers*! 粉身碎骨! 他妈的!〔水手骂人的话〕。

shiv·er·ing·ly [ˈʃivəriŋli; ˋʃɪvərɪŋlɪ] *ad*. 发着抖! 颤抖着。

shiv·er·y[1] [ˈʃivəri; ˋʃɪvərɪ] *a*. 1. 颤抖的;战栗的;易发抖的;使人打冷颤的;毛骨悚然的。2. 寒冷的。

shiv·er·y[2] [ˈʃivəri; ˋʃɪvərɪ] *a*. 易碎的;脆弱的。

S

shi·voo [ʃiˈvuː; ʃɪˋvu] ***n.*** 〔澳俚〕兴高采烈[吵吵嚷嚷]的庆祝(宴)会。

Shi·zu·o·ka [ʃiˈzuəukɑː; ˋʃɪzuˋokɑ] ***n.*** 静冈〔日本城市〕。

shlep, shlepp [ʃlep; ʃlɛp] 〔美俚〕***n., vt., vi.*** = schlep.

shmaltz [ʃmɑːts; ʃmɑts] ***n.*** 〔美俚〕= schmaltz. **-y** ***a.***

shmuck [ʃmʌk; ʃmʌk] ***n.*** 〔美俚〕= schmuck.

shnook [ʃnuk; ʃnʊk] ***n.*** 〔美俚〕= schnook.

sho ***a.*** 〔南美、方〕= sure.

Sho·ah [ʃəˈɑː, ˈʃəuə; ʃɑˋɑ; ˋʃoə] ***n.*** 〔Heb.〕(二战中纳粹对犹太人的)大屠杀。

shoal[1] [ʃəul; ʃol] **I** ***n.*** **1.** (尤指潮退时露出的)沙洲;浅滩。**2.** 〔常 *pl.*〕潜在的危险[危机,困难];隐患;陷阱。***the ~s*** 海的浅水部分。**II** ***vi., vt.*** **1.** 变浅;变成浅滩;使浅。**2.** 驶入浅水的地方。**III** ***a.*** (水)浅的;(船)吃水浅的。

shoal[2] [ʃəul; ʃol] **I** ***n.*** **1.** (鱼)群。**2.** 〔*pl.*〕〔口〕大群;大量;许多。***in ~s*** 成群;许多。***~s of*** 许多的;大群的(人);充分的(时间)。**II** ***vi.*** (鱼)成群;(鱼)成群集聚。

shoal·er [ˈʃəulə; ˋʃolɚ] ***n.*** 沿海贸易商船[水手]。

shoal·y [ˈʃəuli; ˋʃolɪ] ***a.*** **1.** 多浅滩的。**2.** 多潜在危险的;隐患重重的;尽是陷阱的。

shoat [ʃəut; ʃot] ***n.*** **1.** 小猪。**2.** 〔美俚〕懒鬼;无用的人。

shock[1] [ʃɔk; ʃɑk] **I** ***n.*** **1.** 冲突;冲撞;冲击;突击。**2.** 震动;冲动;激动。**3.** 感动;愤慨;惊愕;震惊。**4.** 地震。**5.** 【医】休克;震荡。**6.** 【电】电击;电震。**7.** 【物】冲波;激波;突跃波;爆音。**8.** (对信用、安全等的)打击。**9.** 〔口〕晕厥。*the ~ of arms* 军队的冲突。*give a terrible ~ to sb.* 使人非常震惊;给与巨大打击。*electric ~* 电振荡;电震,触电。*expansion ~* 膨胀突跃。**II** ***vt.*** **1.** 冲出;使震动;使震荡;激动。**2.** 使震惊;使惊骇;使毛骨悚然;使愤慨。— ***vi.*** **1.** 冲突;震动。**2.** 震惊;震骇;觉得毛骨悚然。***be ~ed to learn*** 听见…感到震惊[极度愤慨]。**~ absorber** 减震器;缓冲器。**~ action** 突袭。**~ incarceration** 〔美〕震慑监禁〔在短时期监禁中强迫犯人作高强度军事操练或从事重体力劳动,使其心生畏惧而愿意改过自新〕。**~ excitation** 冲击激励;震激。**~ free** 无冲击的;无激波的。**~ front** 【物】激震前沿;【天】激波前沿〔导致产生船首波形激波的太阳风和行星磁场相遇区〕。**~ load** 冲击负载;突加负载。**~ mount** 减震器;防震座。**~-proof** ***a.*** 防震的;不怕震的;防电击的。**~-resistant** 抗震的。**~ stall** 【空】激波失速;激波分离。**~ strength** 抗震强度。**~ tactics** 突击战术。**~ therapy** [**treatment**] 休克疗法。**~ troops** 突击部队。**~ wave** 【物】冲击波;激波。**~-workers** 突击工人;突击手。

shock[2] [ʃɔk; ʃɑk] **I** ***n.*** 禾束堆;〔美〕玉米秆堆;干草堆。**II** ***vt., vi.*** 将…堆成捆堆[堆成禾束堆];捆堆禾束。

shock[3] [ʃɔk; ʃɑk] **I** ***n.*** **1.** 蓬乱的一堆(毛发)。**2.** 长毛蓬松的狗;狮子狗。**II** ***a.*** 蓬乱的;茂密的。**~-head, ~-headed** ***a.*** 头发乱蓬蓬的。

shock·er [ˈʃɔkə; ˋʃɑkɚ] ***n.*** **1.** 使人震惊的东西[人]。**2.** 〔英口〕恶劣的东西;不值钱的惊险小说〔常作 *shilling ~*〕;〔美〕耸人听闻的影片[小说等]。

shock·ing [ˈʃɔkiŋ; ˋʃɑkɪŋ] **I** ***a.*** **1.** 使人震惊的;骇人听闻的;触目惊心的;令人毛骨悚然的。**2.** 〔口〕非常粗陋的,非常坏的(菜、声音等)。**II** ***ad.*** 〔口〕极度[说不出地](坏)。**-ly** ***ad.*** **-ness** ***n.***

Shock·ley [ˈʃɔkli; ˋʃɑklɪ] ***n.*** 肖克利〔姓氏〕。

shod [ʃɔd; ʃɑd] **I** shoe 的过去式及过去分词。**II** ***a.*** 穿着鞋的;装有轮胎[铁蹄]的;有金属包头的。

shod·den [ˈʃɔdn; ˋʃɑdn] shoe 的过去分词。

shod·dy [ˈʃɔdi; ˋʃɑdɪ] **I** ***a.*** **1.** 长弹毛的;软再生毛的。**2.** 劣等的;假的;冒充的;虚有其表的。**II** ***n.*** **1.** (拿旧货重制的)翻造呢绒;回纺绒线。【纺】长弹毛;软再生毛;软再生毛织物。**2.** 冒充物;不值钱的东西;(暴发户等的)虚骄假饰。**~** *clothes* 再生呢绒。*a ~ character* 虚有其表的人物。**-di·ly** ***ad.*** **-di·ness** ***n.***

shoe [ʃuː; ʃu] **I** ***n.*** (*pl.* **~s**, 〔古〕 **shoon**) **1.** 鞋〔一般指鞋帮不到踝骨的鞋子;过踝骨的靴子叫 boots; 在美国也叫鞋子为 low ~s, 叫靴子为 ~s〕。**2.** 鞋形物。**3.** 蹄铁。**4.** (汽车的)轮胎,外胎。**5.** (汽车轮的)制动器,煞车。**6.** 【机】闸瓦。**7.** (手杖等的)金属箍。**8.** (中国从前的)马蹄银(等)。**9.** 【建】桩靴。**10.** 【电】端;靴;管头;触屐。**11.** 【空】尾撑;【火箭】导向板;发射导轨。**12.** 〔*pl.*〕所处的地位[境遇]。*a pair of ~s* 一双鞋子。*high ~s* 长统[高帮]鞋。*The ~ is on the other foot.* 责任在别人身上;情况完全相反了,现在不是这样了。***another pair of ~s*** 另一回事;另一个问题。***cast aside like an old ~*** 弃若敝屣。***die in one's ~s*** 横死;惨死;(尤指)被绞死。***fill sb.'s ~s*** 接替某人;步某人后尘。***in another's ~s*** 处于别人的地位。***in one's ~s*** 穿着鞋子。***know*** [***feel***] ***where the ~ pinches*** (由经验)知道困难[症结]之所在。***lick sb.'s ~s*** 巴结某人。***look after*** [***wait for***] ***dead men's ~s*** 窥伺[等待]遗产。***over ~s over boots*** 一不作,二不休。***over*** [***up to***] ***the ~s*** 深深钻进去;深深陷入。***put the ~ on the right foot*** 责备应该责备的人;责备得当。***shake in one's ~s*** 发抖;害怕;颤栗。***~ of the launcher*** 发射导轨;起动导轨。***stand in sb.'s ~s*** 代替[取得]某人职位,处于某人位置[境遇]。***The ~ is on the other foot.*** 情况安全不同了。***where the ~ pinches*** 症结所在,困难所在,痛苦之处。**II** ***vt.*** (**shod** [ʃɔd; ʃɑd], **shoed**; **shod, shoed, shod·den** [ˈʃɔdn; ˋʃɑdn]) 给…穿鞋;给(马)钉蹄铁;给…装上鞋状物;装金属片包覆。*neatly shod feet* 穿着像样的鞋子的脚。*~ a horse* 给马钉蹄铁。*a staff shod with iron* 端部包上铁皮的棍子。**~black, ~boy** 擦鞋子的(人)。**~-blacking** 黑鞋油。**~box** 鞋盒;鞋盒式建筑物。**~brush** 鞋刷。**~buckle** 鞋扣。**~horn** 鞋拔。**~-lace** 鞋带。**~ leather** **1.** 鞋用皮革。**2.** 〔口〕(集合名词)鞋(*save ~ leather* 节省鞋子,尽量少走路)。**~less** ***a.*** **1.** 没有鞋的;不穿鞋的。**2.** 没有钉蹄铁的。**~ lift** = shoehorn. **~maker** 鞋店;鞋匠。**~making** **1.** 制鞋;补鞋。**2.** 制鞋业。**~pac(k)** 派克高统保温、防水靴。**~ polish** 鞋油。**~shine** **1.** 擦皮鞋。**2.** 擦亮鞋面光泽。**3.** 擦皮鞋者。**~shop** 鞋店。**~ store** = ~ shop. **~-string** **1.** 〔美〕【无】电线。**2.** 鞋带(*on a ~-string* 〔美口〕用很少的本钱。*walk on one's ~-string* 〔美〕陷入贫困)。**~ string potatoes** 拔丝洋芋。**~ tree** 〔美〕鞋楦。

shoe·bill [ˈʃuːbil; ˋʃuˏbɪl] ***n.*** 【动】鹭 (*Balaeniceps rex*) 〔发现于中非白尼罗河沿岸〕。

sho·er [ˈʃuːə; ˋʃuɚ] ***n.*** 钉蹄铁工人;挂掌匠。

sho·far [ˈʃəufə Heb. ʃəuˈfɑː; ˋʃofɚ, ʃoˋfɑr] ***n.*** (*pl.* **-fars**; Heb. **-frot** [-ˈfrəut; -ˋfrot]) (犹太教徒礼拜时用的)羊角号。

sho·ji [ˈʃəudʒi; ˋʃodʒɪ] ***n.*** (*pl.* **sho·ji, -jis**) 〔Jap.〕拉门〔日本式拉动开关的门扇〕(= shoji screen)。

Sho·na [ˈʃəunɑː; ˋʃonɑ] ***n.*** **1.** (*pl.* **Sho·nas, Sho·na**) 修纳人〔罗得西亚与邻近的莫桑比克的农民〕。**2.** 修纳语。

shone [ʃɔn; ʃon] shine 的过去式及过去分词。

shoo [ʃuː; ʃu] **I** ***int.*** 嘘! 〔驱赶禽类的嘘声〕。**II** ***vi., vt.*** 发"嘘!"声驱赶。

shoo·fly [ˈʃuːˌflai; ˋʃuˏflaɪ] ***n.*** 〔美〕**1.** 舒弗莱舞〔曳步舞〕。**2.** (小孩的)动物状摇椅〔如摇动木马等〕。**3.** 糖浆馅饼 (= shoofly pie)。**4.** (铁路的)临时轨道;临时便道。**5.** (印刷机)拨离爪〔使在印的纸离开滚筒转移到纸台的装置〕。

shoo-in [ˈʃuːin; ˋʃuˏɪn] ***n.*** 〔美口〕十拿九稳的取胜者。

shook[1] [ʃuk; ʃʊk] shake 的过去式。

shook[2] [ʃuk; ʃʊk] ***n.*** **1.** 一套装配木桶[木箱等]的木板。**2.** 禾捆。

shoon [ʃuːn; ʃun] ***n.*** 〔古〕shoe 的复数。

shoot [ʃuːt; ʃut] **I** ***vt.*** (**shot** [ʃɔt; ʃɑt]) **1.** 发射;射(箭);开(枪);放(炮);放射(光线)。**2.** 射中;打中;射死;射伤;

打伤;〔喻〕毁坏。3. 投;掷;抛出;倒出;撒(网等)。4. 爆破;使爆炸。5.〔美俚〕递送;传递。6.【纺】投(梭)。7. 发(芽);发出(*forth*; *out*; *up*)。8. 突出;伸出;突入。9. 闩(门);上(门栓);拔出(门栓)。10.【足球】射门;【篮球】投篮;击(球)。11. 掷(骰子)。12. 飞速通过;迅速投送[派遣];迅速推进。13. 拍摄。14. 把…刨光。15.〔通例用 p.p.〕织入异色纬纱。16. 测量(天体的)高度。17. 给…注射[打针]。—*vi*. 1. 射箭;放枪;放炮。2. 射击;(子弹)打中;击中。3. 出猎;拿枪打猎。4. 迅速移动;箭一般地飞行;射出。5.(船)飞也似地开行;(车)疾驰(而过)。6.(光)闪发。7.(牙齿等)感到剧痛;急痛。8.(草木)发芽;生长;长大;发育。9. 高耸(*up*);落下;流下。10. 冲出;突出;伸出。11.〔足球〕射门;〔篮球〕投篮;打球。12. 掷骰子等。13.【纺】投梭。14.〔美〕拍电影,拍照;摄影。15.〔美俚〕讲吧;快讲。~ *out one's tongue* 伸出舌头。~ *rubbish* 倒垃圾。*S- the salt to me*. 把盐递给我。~ *edges* 刨齐边缘。***I'll be shot if*** ... 如果是…的话打死我好了;决不是…。~ ***a bolt*** 拉开[插上]插销。~ ***a covert*** [***an estate***] 在猎场[庄园]打猎。~ ***ahead*** 疾进;超过;追过。~ ***a line***〔俚〕吹牛。~ ***a match*** 参加竞射。~ ***a tie*** 射击比赛比分相同时重行射击。~ ***away*** 1. 继续不停的发射子弹;打光;射完(子弹等)。2. 打掉;击毁。3. 像子弹出膛般飞快离去。~ ***craps***〔美俚〕掷骰子。~ ***disc*** 掷骰子。~ ***down*** 1. 射落;打下来;射倒。2. 击死;打死。3.〔口〕严厉谴责;〔俚〕驳倒。4. 遗弃。~ ***fire***(眼睛)闪闪发光;发亮。~ ***for*** [***at***] 力争;切望。~ ***forth*** 射出;弄出。~ ***into***〔美〕使人相信;想左右某人。~ ***off*** 1.〔及物用法〕发射(子弹);击毁,打掉(腿等);使爆炸。2.〔不及物用法〕像子弹出膛般飞快离去;吹嘘(*about*)。(~ *off firecrackers* 放鞭炮。*have one's leg shot off* 一条腿给打断了。*The driver without a word shot off before he could rightly be seated*. 他还没有坐稳当司机就一言不发驱车飞驶了)。~ ***off one's bazoo***〔美俚〕自夸。~ ***off one's*** [***the***] ***mouth*** [***face***]〔美俚〕像连珠炮似地讲;信口开河;瞎说乱讲;瞎吹牛;夸口。~ ***one's cookies***〔美俚〕呕吐。~ ***one's wad***〔美〕说想说的;做想做的。~ ***oneself in the foot*** 咎由自取,搬起石头砸自己的脚。~ ***out*** 1. 射出;投出;发出。2. 突出;伸出;高耸。3. 用武力解决。~ ***over*** [***to***] ***a dog*** 用狗打猎。~ ***sb. full of daylight***〔美俚〕把某人打得全身都是枪眼。~ ***straight*** 正打中。~ ***the breeze***〔美俚〕说大话;夸大;胡扯;吹牛;畅谈。~ ***the bull***【俚】漫谈;夸张。~ ***the moon***〔英俚〕(为了逃避清偿房租)在夜间带着自己的东西潜逃。~ ***the Niagara*** 冒极大风险,企图做冒险的事。~ ***the sun***【海】用六分仪测太阳高度。~ ***the works***〔美俚〕孤注一掷,〔喻〕倾全力而为;尽人事。~ ***up*** 1. 上冒;喷出;欣欣向荣;猛长;暴腾;猛跳;高耸;涨价。2.〔俚〕注射麻醉剂。3.〔美俚〕乱射;乱放枪;乱放枪吓人。4.〔美卑〕抛弃。***shot between wind and water*** 被击中吃水线附近;击中要害。

II *int*. 哼! 嘘!〔反感,失望声〕。

III *n*. 1. 射击;发射;开枪;放炮;(火箭等的)试射。2.〔棒球俚〕快球的小弯球。3. 打鞭会;狩猎;〔英〕游猎会。4. 游猎地;猎场。5. 迅速的移动[动作]。6. 急流;奔流;喷泉;富矿体。7. 光线;光道。8. 芽;苗;新梢;嫩枝。9.(滑运木材、煤等的)滑水路;滑槽;泻槽;斜槽。10. 垃圾场。11. 摄影;拍电影。12. 推力;(冰块,土块)崩落。13.(划桨时)两划间的间隔时间。*transplant rice ~s* 插秧。*take a* ~〔美〕经由急流航行;抄近路。*the whole* ~ 所有的东西;全部;一切。***be on the*** ~〔美〕预备射击;备战。~**out**【足球】(踢成平局后的)点球决胜负。

shoot·er [ˈʃuːtə; ˋʃutɚ] *n*. 1. 射手;式箭;炮手;猎者;爆破手。2. 流星;火器;枪;〔美〕手枪。*a sharp* ~ 狙击兵。*a six*~ 六响[六发子弹]枪。*a pea* ~(用豆作子弹的)玩具豆子枪。

shoot·ing [ˈʃuːtiŋ; ˋʃutɪŋ] *n*. 1. 发射;射击;射出;发出。2. 射杀;枪杀。3. 打鸟;狩猎;打猎。4. 狩猎权;猎场。5. 摄影。6. 刺痛;剧痛。7.〔美俚〕兴奋;骚动;乱子。8.〔足球〕射门;〔篮球〕投篮。*Why all the* ~?〔美俚〕怎么这样闹法? *trouble* ~ 故障检修。~ **box** 狩猎小屋。~ **gallery** 1.(游艺场所的)打靶场。2.〔美俚〕注射麻醉剂的秘密处所。~ **iron**〔俚〕枪。~ **off**(比分相等时)延长射击比赛。~ **range** 打靶场;射击场。~ **script**(电影)摄影台本;分镜头脚本。~ **star** 1. 流星。2.【植】美国樱草。~ **stick** 猎人手杖〔握手处可拆下当座子〕。~ **war** 实战;热战(*opp*. cold war)。

shoot-the-chute [ˈʃuːtðəˈʃuːt; ˋʃutðəˋʃut] *n*. = chute-the-chute.

shop [ʃɔp; ʃɑp] **I** *n*. 1.〔英〕铺子;店铺;(零售)商店〔美国用 store〕;(大商店里的)特殊部门。2.〔*pl*.〕工厂;工场;车间;修理所。3.(本人的)职业;本行;业务。4.〔俚〕工作;职业。5. 事务所;办事处;机构;场所。6. 家;自己的家。7. 房屋;建筑物。8. 学校;大学(等);〔the S-〕〔英俚〕〔废〕陆军军官学校。*closed* ~〔美〕不得雇用非工会会员的企业。*back* [*repair*] ~*s* 修理厂[车间]。*Shop*!〔在店门口向里面喊〕喂,有没有人! *Cut the* ~! 别讲本行的事! *How are they all at your* ~?〔俚〕府上各位好吗? ***all over the*** ~〔俚〕零乱;杂乱;到处;任意;盲目。***come*** [***go***] ***to the wrong*** ~〔俚〕找错门道,找错了人〔指求助、打听消息等〕。***keep***(***a***)~ 开店;照管店务。***set up*** ~ 开店;开始营业。***shut up*** ~ 1. 停止(工作、游戏等)。2. 歇业;关店;宣告破产。***sink the*** ~ 不谈自己职业上的[本行的,专门的]事情。***smell of the*** ~ 商人气息;行业气息。***talk*** ~ 动不动谈自己职业上的事情;三句话不离本行;说行话。***the other*** ~ 作为竞争劲敌的企业、学校或是其他机构。**II** *vi*.(*-pp-*)1. 买东西(去)。2. 到处寻找。—*vt*. 1.〔俚〕逮捕;投入监狱。2.〔俚〕密告;出卖(某人)。3. 选购(商品);挑选(商品)。4. 送往修理所修理。5.〔美〕解雇。*go ~ping* 去买东西。~ *around* 1. 到处选购;到一家一家店铺访求[买东西]。2.〔美〕找事[好职位]。~ **assistant**〔英〕店员。**-at-home** *a*.〔美〕(通过电话或网上订货等手段)在家购物的。~**-boy**〔英〕店伙计。~**-call**(对厂主不满时的)厂内集会。~ **card** 营业卡;营业证。~ **chairman**, ~ **deputy** = ~ steward. ~ **drawing** 制造图。~ **girl**〔英〕女店员。~ **hours** 营业时间。~ **keeper** 1.〔英〕零售商人;店主,老板。2.〔俚〕冷货;陈货。~**lifter** 店铺扒手。~ **lifting** 入店行窃。~**-made**〔美〕定做的。~**man** 1. 店铺商人;零售商。2. 店员;伙计。~ **steward**(一个工厂的)工人代表。~**talk** 行话;非工作时间谈论本行的谈话。~ **truck** 修理车。~**-union** 工会。~**-walker**〔英〕(百货商店等的)巡视员;招待员。~**window**(商店的)橱窗(*put all one's goods in the ~window = have everything in the ~window* 全部摆出来给人看;浅薄;内容空虚)。~**worn** [ˈʃɔpwɔːn; ˋʃɑpˏworn] 店里摆旧的;滞销的;陈旧的。

sho·phar [ˈʃəufəː, Heb. ʃəuˈfɑː; ˋʃofɚ, ʃoˋfɑr] *n*. = shofar.

shoppe [ʃɔp; ʃɑp] *n*. = shop.

shop·per [ˈʃɔpə; ˋʃɑpɚ] *n*. 1. 买东西的人;顾客。2.(商店雇用的)代客选购货物的人。3.(商店雇用的)打听行情的人。4.〔美〕购物指南〔登载当地各商店广告的传单〕。

shop·ping [ˈʃɔpiŋ; ˋʃɑpɪŋ] *n*. 买东西。*do one's* ~ 买东西。~ **& fucking** = sex-and-shopping. ~ **bag** 购物袋。~**-bag lady**(手持之购物袋为其全部家当的)街头流浪妇女,女无家可归者。~ **centre** 购物中心;市郊商店区。~ **therapy**〔谑〕购物疗法〔指妇女以逛商店购买高档衣物来消遣解闷〕。

shop·py [ˈʃɔpi; ˋʃɑpɪ] *a*. 1. 商人的;生意人(似)的。2. 像零售店的;职业气味的(会话等)。3. 商店多的。4. 三句不离本行的。

sho·ran [ˈʃɔːræn; ˋʃɔræn](= short-range navigation)*n*.【空】1. 近程无线电导航系统;肖兰系统。2. 短程无

S

线电导航法。3. 近距助航仪。

shore[1][ʃɔː, ʃɔə; ʃɔr, ʃor] ***n***. 1. 岸;海岸;滨。2.【法】满潮线和退潮线中间的地区。3.〔常 *pl*.〕陆(地)。*a* ~ *line* 滨线;海岸线。*a* ~ *fish* 近海鱼。~ *to ship service* 水陆联络设备。*one's native* ~(*s*) 故乡;故国。***go on*** ~ 上岸。***in*** ~ 近岸。***off*** ~ 1. 离岸。2. 在离海岸不远处。***on*** ~ 在岸上。***put on*** ~ 使上岸;起(货)上岸。***within these*** ~***s*** 在这个国家内。~**-based** [ˈʃɔːbeist; ˋʃorˏbest] 以陆地为基地的;以海岸为基地的。~ **bird** 水鸟;沙禽;涉禽。~ **dinner**〔美〕海鲜餐。~ **fast** (将船系在岸边的)粗索,大索。~**fly**【昆】水蝇。~ **leave** (船员)上岸假(期)。~ **reef** 裾礁。

shore[2][ʃɔː; ʃor] **I** ***n***. (房屋、树木、修建中房屋等的)支柱;斜撑柱。**II** ***vt***. 用支柱[斜撑]撑住 (*up*)。

shore[3][ʃɔː; ʃor]〔古〕shear 的过去式。

shor·ing [ˈʃɔːriŋ; ˋʃorɪŋ] ***n***.〔集合词〕支柱;斜撑柱。

shorn [ʃɔːn; ʃorn] **I** shear 的过去分词。**II** ***a***. 1. 被剪过的。2. 被拿去的;被夺去的;被剥去的。*shaven and* ~ 修过面剪过发的。*closely* ~ 剪短的(头发等)。~ *of* (*one's money*) 被抢去了(钱)。

Short [ʃɔːt; ʃɔrt] ***n***. 萧特〔姓氏〕。

short [ʃɔːt; ʃɔrt] **I** ***a***. 1. 短的;短暂的。(*opp*. long)。2. 矮的;低的 (*opp*. tall)。3. 短期的。4. 简短的;简略的;缩写的。5.【语音】短音的。6. 不足的;不够的;短少的。7. 不及的;达不到的。8. (见闻等)浅陋的。9. 简慢的;唐突的;无礼的;急性子的;不高兴的;发着脾气的。10.〔口〕不搀水的,强烈的(酒等);〔威士忌〕纯的。11.【商】卖空的;抛空的;无存货的。12.〔金属〕脆的;易裂的;易碎的;松脆的(饼等)。13. 波涛汹涌的(海)。14. (智力等)弱的;(记忆力)差的。*a* ~ *life and a merry one* 短暂光辉的一生。*a* ~ *mile distance* 不到一英里的距离。*In speaking one should be* ~ *and to the point*. 说话要简捷扼要。*He was very* ~ *with me*. 他对我很冷淡。~ *memory* 善忘。*a* ~ *temper* 急性子。*something* ~ 烈酒。***come*** [***drop***, ***fall***] ~ (*of*) 在某方面有所不足;在某方面差一点;有缺陷;辜负期待,达不到目的。***in the*** ~ ***run*** 在短时期里。***little*** ~ ***of*** 几乎;简直 (*It is little* ~ *of a miracle* 简直是奇迹)。***make*** [***let***] ***a long story*** ~ 说得简单些。***make*** ~ ***work of*** 迅速处理[破坏、消费];杀死。***nothing*** ~ ***of*** 完全是;不折不扣的是;简直可以说;除…外;别无…。***run*** ~ (***of***) 缺乏。~ ***and sweet*** 1. (说话)扼要的。2. 短而愉快的。~ ***arm drill***〔美军俚〕花柳病检查。~ ***of*** 缺少;达不到;除了;只要不是 (*be* ~ *of money* 缺少钱)。~ ***of breath*** [***puff***] 喘着气。

II ***ad***. 1. 简短地;简单地。2. 缺乏;不足。3. 脆。4. 突然;忽然。5. 简慢地;唐突地。***be taken*** ~ 忽然想解手[大、小便]。***bring*** [***pull***] ***up*** ~ 忽然停止。***cut*** ~ 突然停止;突然阻止。***sell*** ~ 卖空。***take sb. up*** ~ 阻断(某人)谈话。

III ***n***. 1. 概略;要点;不足;缺乏。2.【语音】短音节;【乐】短音符。3.【商】卖空;(交易所的)空方;空头。4.【棒球】游击手。5.〔*pl*.〕(运动)短裤。6. 不到规定长度的东西[鱼等]。7.〔*pl*.〕短少的数额;【印】短少部数;追加部数。8. 次货;废料;次粉;细麦子。9. (报刊的)短讯;短篇;(电影的)短片 (= ~ piece *or* film)。10.【电】= ~-circuit. 11.〔美俚〕汽车。12.〔*pl*.〕短期票据[债券]。*The long and* ~ *of it is* .... 总而言之;简单地说。***at*** (***the***) ~ 简单地;立即。***for*** ~ 简称[简称人名时用]。***in*** ~ 简单地说;总之。

IV ***vt***. 1. 故意少给;欺骗。2.【电】使短路。3. 卖空(股票)〔亦作 ~ short〕。~**-arm**, ~**-armed** ***a***. 1. 胳臂短的;蜷起手臂的(一击等)。2. 短距离的。~ **bill** 短期票据。~ **bit**〔美〕一角;十分[美元]。~**bread** 松脆的酥饼。~**cake** [ˈʃɔːtkeik; ˋʃɔrtˏkek]〔美〕松饼;脆饼。~ **change** [ˌʃɔːtˈtʃeindʒ; ˏʃɔrtˋtʃendʒ] 1. 故意少给找头。2. 欺骗。~**-circuit** 1.【电】短路;漏电。2. ***vt***., ***vi***. 使短路;漏电。~ **clothes** [**coats**] 童装。~ **coming** [ʃɔːtˈkʌmiŋ; ˋʃɔrtˋkʌmɪŋ] 1. 不足;缺乏。2. (谷类等的)歉收。3. 短处;缺点;忽略;玩忽。~**-common** [ˈʃɔːtˈkɔmən; ˋʃɔrtˋkɑmən]〔*pl*. 作单数用〕缺粮,最低定量。~ **contract**【商】买空卖空。~ **covering**【商】空头补进。~ **crop** 低产。~**cut** 近路;捷径。~**date** (票据等的)短期。~**-dated** ***a***. 1. 短期的。2. 时间很短的。~**-day** ***a***.【植】短日照的。~**-day plant**【植】短日照的植物。~ **division**【数】(不写明演算过程的)简短除法。~ **end** 败局;处于劣势的一方。~**-ender** (竞赛中)没有希望获胜的一方。~**fall** 1. 不足;短缺;亏空。2. 短缺之量。~ **field**〔棒球〕内野二垒与三垒间的地区。~**-fired** ***a***.〔陶器等〕火候不足的。~ **fuse**〔美俚〕火爆性子,急燥脾气。~**hand** 1. 速记;速记法。2. 速记记录文字。~**-handed** [ˈʃɔːtˈhændid; ˋʃɔrtˏhændɪd] ***a***. 人手不足的。~**hand-writer** 速记员。~**head** 1. 短颅人。2. (赛马)险胜。~**horn** [ˈʃɔːthɔːn; ˋʃɔrtˏhɔrn] 1. 短角菜牛。2.〔美〕(特指西部牧场中的)东部的人;新来的人;生手。~**-horned grasshopper**【昆】蝗。~ **iron** 铁头短棒。~**-legged** [ˈʃɔːtˌlegid; ˋʃɔrtˏlɛgɪd] ***a***. 腿短的。~**-life**, ~**-lived** [ˈʃɔːtˈlivd; ˋʃɔrtˋlaɪvd] ***a***. 短命的;一时的;昙花一现的。~ **order** 快餐。~ **position** 1.【商】空头户;做空头。2. 全部售完;售缺。~**-range** 短射程的;短期的。~ **residuum** 浓缩残铀。~ **rib** 假肋骨。~ **robe** 军人职业。~ **round**【军】近弹。~ **sale**【商】卖空。~ **seller**【商】卖空的人;空头。**short** ~**s** (妇女穿在外面的)冬季短裤。~ **shrift** 1. (死刑犯临刑前的)短促忏悔。2. 不耐烦;漠不关心。~**sighted** ***a***. 1. 近视(眼)的。2. 眼光短浅的。~ **snort** (喝酒)一口喝尽;快饮。~**-spoken** [ˈʃɔːtˈspəukən; ˋʃɔrtˋspokən] ***a***. (寒暄等)冷淡的,马马虎虎的;简慢的。~**stop** [ˈʃɔːtstɔp; ˋʃɔrtˏstɑp]【棒球】游击手。~**-stop**【摄】停显液。~ **subject** 正片放映前的短片。~**-tempered** ***a***. 急性子的;暴躁的,易怒的。~ **tennis** (供儿童等玩的)短场网球[场地短、球拍小、球网低]。~**-term** [ˈʃɔːttəːm; ˋʃɔrtˋtɝm] ***a***. 短期的。~ **ton** 短吨,美吨〔= 2000 磅或 0.907 公吨〕。~ **wave** [ˈʃɔːtweiv; ˋʃɔrtˏwev] 1. ***n***. 短波;短波无线电发射机。2. ***vt***. 用短波无线电发射[播送]。~**-winded** [ˈʃɔːtˈwindid; ˋʃɔrtˋwɪndɪd] ***a***. 1. 气促的;喘气的。2. 简短的;短促的。

shor·ti·a [ˈʃɔːtiə; ˋʃɔrtɪə] ***n***.〔美〕【植】杖草叶岩扇 (*Shortia galacifolia*)。

short·ie [ˈʃɔːti; ˋʃɔrtɪ] ***n***.〔口〕= shorty.

short·age [ˈʃɔːtidʒ; ˋʃɔrtɪdʒ] ***n***. 不足,缺少;不足额;〔美〕缺点,缺陷。*owing to* ~ *of staff* 由于人员的缺少。*a* ~ *of 50 tons* 五十吨的短缺额。***cover*** [***make up for***] ***the*** ~ 弥补不足。

short·en [ˈʃɔːtn; ˋʃɔrtn̩] ***vt***. 弄短,缩短;减少;使松脆;收(帆),缩(帆);给(脱去长的婴孩服)改穿短衣。~ *one's arm* [*sword*] 缩回胳臂[剑]。*have a coat* ~*ed* 把上衣改短。~ *the arm of* 限制…的力量。~ *a child* 给孩子改穿短衣。—***vi***. 变短,缩短,缩小。

short·en·ing [ˈʃɔːtniŋ; ˋʃɔrtn̩ɪŋ] ***n***. 1. 缩短;简写;缩略词。2. 起酥油。

short·ly [ˈʃɔːtli; ˋʃɔrtlɪ] ***ad***. 立刻,马上,不久;简单;简短。*answer* ~ 简短地回答。~ *after* …之后立即。~ *before* …之前不久。*to put it* ~ 简言之。

short·ness [ˈʃɔːtnis; ˋʃɔrtnɪs] ***n***. 短;不足,缺少;简单;脆性。~ *of breath* 喘气。***for*** ~ = for short.

short·y [ˈʃɔːti; ˋʃɔrtɪ] ***n***.〔口〕矮子,矮小的动物;小东西;〔俚〕酒。

Sho·sho·ne [ʃəuˈʃəuniː; ʃoˋʃonɪ] ***n***. 1. (*pl*. ***-sho·nes***, ***-sho·ne***) 肖肖尼族人[美国北部的一种印第安人]。2. 肖肖尼语 (= Shoshoni)。

shot[1][ʃɔt; ʃɑt] **I** shoot 的过去式及过去分词。**II** ***a***. 1. 打[发射]出去的;被射中的;发了芽的。2.〔美俚〕坏得不能再使用的;注定要失败的。3.【纺】杂色的,闪光的,色彩幻变的。4.〔俚〕喝醉了的。~ *cloth* 闪光绸。*crimson*

~ *with gold* 闪金光的深红色。*half* ~ 醉得差不多了。~ ***through with*** 充满…的。~ ***to pieces*** 破烂不堪的;毁坏了的。

shot[2][ʃɔt; ʃɑt] **I** ***n***. (*pl*. ~*s*) **1.**〔*pl*. ~〕弹,子弹,炮弹;散弹;【运】铅球。**2.** 射击,打枪,开炮;枪声;炮声;(网的)一撒;〔口〕(烈酒的)一口;〔俚〕(吗啡等的)注射;〔俚〕(酒吧等的)账。**3.** 射程;瞄准;狙击。**4.** 射手,枪手。**5.** 猜测,推测。**6.**【矿】炸破,爆破;炸药;【运】射门;投篮;(网球,台球)一击;【纺】投梭;(电影和摄影的)拍摄距离;拍摄;镜头;照片;〔美〕【无】广播节目。*a* ~ *of distress* 遇难信号炮。*a pot* ~ 容易的狙击。*a bad* ~ 不行的射击手;猜错,搞错。*a dead* ~ 神枪手。*a good* ~ 好枪手,好射手;猜对。*Good* ~! 打得好! 好球! *a crane* [*zoon*] ~【影】俯瞰摄影。*a long* ~ 长射程;远程摄影;远景(镜头);大胆的企图[猜测]。*a mid* ~【影】中景。*a follow* ~【影】跟镜头。*a model* ~【影】模型摄影。*a big* ~〔美俚〕名人。~ *beer* 加有酒精的啤酒。***as a*** ~ 作为猜测 (*As a* ~ *I should say she's about forty*. 看来她怕有四十岁左右了)。***at a*** ~ 一枪就。***get*** [***have***, ***make***] ***a*** ~ ***at*** 射击;推测,猜测。***have a*** ~ ***for*** [***at***] 尝试,试试看。***in*** ~ 在射程内。***like a*** ~〔口〕(像子弹一样)快,立刻。***not ... by a long*** ~ 绝对没有希望的,绝对不行的。***not worth powder and*** ~〔口〕不值得费力。***off like a*** ~ 子弹一样地,立刻。***out of*** ~ 在射程外。***pay*** [***stand***] ***the*** ~〔俚〕付账。***put the*** ~ 掷铅球。***within ear-*** ~ [***rifle-*** ~] 在听得见[子弹打得到]的距离内。***within*** ~ = *in* ~.

II ***vt***. (***-tt-***) 装弹药;装沙子;石子摇洗(瓶子等);用铁锤吊着使沉下,加铅粒使沉重;(用喷射法)使成颗粒。~ **clock**【体】投篮时限钟〔规定进攻方须于45秒内出手投篮的时限〕。~ **effect**【电】散粒效应。~**gun 1.** ***n***. 散弹枪,鸟枪,猎枪。**2.** ***a***.〔美俚〕强制的,用武力的。~**hole** 弹孔,弹痕。~**-proof** ***a***. 防弹的。~**-put(ting)**【运】(掷)铅球。~ **tower** 制弹塔;〔美俚〕厕所。~ **welding**【机】点焊。

shote [ʃəut; ʃot] ***n***. = shoat.

shott [ʃɔt; ʃɑt] ***n***. 北非盐湖盆地。

should [强 ʃud, 弱 ʃəd, ʃd; ˋʃud ʃəd, ʃd] ***aux***. ***v***. shall 的过去式。**1.**〔在间接引语中用作 shall 的过去式〕将,会。*He said he* ~ *succeed in the examination* (= *He said*, "*I shall* succeed in the examination"). 他说了他会考取的。**2.** (a)〔在虚拟语气的现在时条件句中〕万一…的话,如果…的话。*If I* ~ *fail I would try again*. 万一失败我还要试一试。(b)〔在表示与过去事实相反的虚拟语气的主句中〕就会。*If he had said so*, *I* ~ *have been angry*. 他要是这样说了,我就生气了。(c)〔省略虚拟的条件〕也许会,可能。*It is beautiful*, *I* ~ *say*. 啊,真漂亮。*I* ~ *like to go*. (假如有人劝)我也许会去的。*She is under thirty*, *I* ~ *think*. 我想她还不到三十(岁)。*it* ~ *seem* 好像是,总像是〔比 it seems 委婉〕。**3.** (a)〔不问人称,表示义务、责任〕应该,必须。*We* ~ *not do such a thing*. 我们不应该做这种事情。*You* ~ *not speak so loud*; *it is bad manners*. 说话声音别那么大,这没礼貌。*Why in the world* ~ *I go*? 为什么一定要我去。*You are not behaving as you* ~. 你的行为不得当。(b)〔说话者的意志、许诺〕*If the book is in the library*, *it* ~ *be at your service*. 这本书如果在图书馆里,那你就可以拿去看。*You* ~ *do it if you can*. 如果你能做的话,这件事就请你做了。(c)〔确实或可能有的未来或期待〕会。*They* ~ *arrive by one o'clock*, *I think*. 我想他们一点钟以前总会到的。*If the farmers can get continuous sunshine*, *they* ~ *have a satisfactory harvest*. 天气如果继续好下去,农民们就会得到满意的收获了。**4.**〔在表示当然、意外、遗憾等意的句子中〕竟会…(是)。*It is natural* [*proper*, *necessary*] *that he* ~ *do so*. 他这样做是当然[适当,必要]的。*It is surprising that he* ~ *have been so foolish*. 真想不到他会那样愚蠢。*It is a pity that he* ~ *miss such a golden opportunity*. 真可惜,他竟会失去这样一个绝好的机会。*I wonder such a man as he* ~ *have succeeded*. 想不到他那样的人竟会成功。*They* ~ *not have been allowed to come*. 原不该让他们来的。**5.**〔表示踌躇、委婉、谦逊、客气〕可,好像是,倒,大概是。*I* ~ *hardly think so*. 我倒并不那样想。*S- you like tea*? 你喜欢茶吗? **6.**〔和 why, who, how 等连用,表示理由不易了解或吃惊〕*Why* ~ *he resign*? 他为什么要辞职呢? *Who* ~ *do it*? 该叫谁做呀? *Who* ~ *write it but himself*? 你当是谁写的,是他自己呀? **7.** (a)〔在表示意志、提议、意向、决定、命令等的从句中〕*It was proposed that we* ~ *act at once*. 有人提议我们必须立刻行动。*I was determined that he* ~ *write his letters first*. 我已决定让他先写他的信。(b)〔在 lest 后的状语从句中〕*I stayed in lest I* ~ *catch cold*. 我怕伤风,所以待在屋里。**8.**〔在让步状语从句中〕即使。*S- he fail*, *he would try again*. 即使他失败了,他也会再努力一试的。

should·a [ˈʃudə; ˋʃudə]〔美俚〕= should have.

shoul·der [ˈʃəuldə; ˋʃoldɚ] **I** ***n***. **1.** 肩,肩膀;〔*pl*.〕双肩;肩背;〔喻〕担当的能力;【动】(昆虫的)肩角,前角,中胸角,侧角。**2.** 肩胛关节;(牛等连前腿的)肩肉;(衣服、家具等的)肩部;【筑城】(棱堡面与侧面所成的)肩角;【印】(铅字的)字肩;【建】用来支持的凸出部;路肩〔路两侧不铺柏油的部分,用于紧急停车〕。**3.** 掮枪的姿势。**4.**【地】山肩,谷肩;峁;【海】吃水浅的凸出处[弯曲部]。***clap*** [***tap***] ***sb***. ***upon the*** ~ 拍人的肩膀;逮捕。***come to the*** ~ 掮枪。***dislocate*** [***put out***] ***one's*** ~ 肩胛关节脱臼。***give*** [***show***, ***turn***] ***the cold*** ~ ***to*** 冷落某人,对某人表示冷淡;躲避某人,对某人表示讨厌,同某人断绝往来。***have a head upon one's*** ~***s***〔口〕懂事,懂道理。***have broad*** ~***s*** 肩膀阔而强壮;能掮重物;能担负重任。***lay the blame on the right*** ~***s*** 指责应负责任的人。***over the*** ~讥讽,挖苦。***overleap one's*** ~***s***〔美〕大显身手;超越自己的成绩或正常状态。***put on sb***.'***s*** ~***s*** [***put on the*** ~***s of sb***., ***shift on to other*** ~***s***] 叫人家负责任,把责任推给别人。***put an old head on young*** ~***s*** 叫年轻人懂事,使年轻人认真负责。***put*** [***set***] ***one's*** ~ ***to the wheel*** 积极工作,勤奋工作;帮助人。***rub*** ~***s with*** 和…接触;并肩,协力,团结一致。~ ***to*** ~ 密集;并肩;协力,互相帮助。***straight from the*** ~ 直截了当地,不留情地,开诚布公地。***with one's*** ~ ***to collar*** 紧张地(工作),拼命地(干)。**II** ***vt***. 把…掮在肩上,掮,担;掮起。—***vi***. 用肩膀推,使劲推。**III** ***a***. 峰肩的(指航空客运量开始由高峰回落时期等)。~ **belt** 背带;肩带;(司机的)安全带。~ **blade**, ~ **bone** 肩胛骨。~ **brace** 驼背矫正器。~ **girdle**【动】(脊椎动物的)肩带 (= pectoral girdle)。~ **harness** (汽车驾驶者的)安全带。~ **knot** 肩章;肩饰。~ **loop**〔美〕(陆军的)肩章。~ **mark**〔美〕(海军的)肩章。~ **patch**【军】(所属部队)番号臂章。~**-pegged** ***a***. 肩膀强壮的〔指马〕。~ **strap**【军】肩章,(裤子等的)背带;吊带。~**-surfer**〔美〕(以排在他人身后窥视或在远处以望远镜偷看等手段)窃取他人银行存款卡[电话卡等]密码的人,窃号贼。

shoul·dered [ˈʃəuldəd; ˋʃoldɚd] ***a***.〔用以构成复合词〕肩膀…的;着的。

should·est [ˈʃudist; ˋʃudɪst] ***aux***. ***v***.〔古〕= shouldst.

should·n't [ˈʃudnt; ˋʃudnt] = should not.

shouldst ***aux***. ***v***. [强 ʃudst, 弱 ʃədst, ʃdst; ʃudst 弱 ʃədst, ʃdst]〔古〕= should〔主词为 thou 时用〕。

shout [ʃaut; ʃaʊt] **I** ***vi***. 呼喊,叫喊;喝叫 (*at*); 喊,叫 (*to*);〔澳俚〕付请客喝酒的账。—***vt***. 大声讲,呼喊出;高声呼喊使…,喊跑,喊走,呼喊着鼓励,呼喊着助威。*It's all over bar* [*but*] *the* ~*ing*. 场赛终止,只是呼喊声不绝。*Now you're* ~*ing*.〔美俚〕说得真恰当,说得好极了。~ ***for*** 大声叫唤(侍者);〔美政〕竭力支持。~ ***for*** [***with***] ***joy*** 欢呼。~ ***sb***. ***down*** 大声喝倒某人;

S

〔美〕打败某人。～ ***out*** 大声嚷,呼喊。～ ***something rude*** 大骂。～ ***with laughter*** 大声笑。***within ～ing distance*** 在大声喊叫时听得见的距离内。**II** ***n***. 呼喊,叫喊,呐喊;〔澳俚〕付请客账,会钞。*give a ～ of warning* 大喊危险。*It's my ～*.〔口〕我请我请。*the last ～*〔美俚〕最新式样,最时髦的东西。

shout·er [ˈʃautə; ˋʃaʊtɚ] ***n***. 叫喊的人;〔美〕后援者,支持者。

shove [ʃʌv; ʃʌv] **I** ***vt***. 推,推动,推进;使劲猛推;推开;卖掉;〔口〕乱放,乱塞。—***vi***. 推,推进,推出;推挤。*Don't ～ wait your turn*. 别推,顺次等候好了。*S- it in your pocket*. 把它放在你的口袋里。～ ***across***〔美〕杀。～ ***along*** 推着走。～ ***in*** 推进。～ ***off***(拿篙子)把船撑开;〔美俚〕乘船离开;分别,走掉。～ ***on*** 推着往前走。～ ***one's clothes on***〔口〕穿上衣服。～ ***out***(拿篙子)把船撑开。～ ***past*** 推开…往前走。～ ***publicity***〔美运〕指挥宣传。～ ***the queer***(美)付给伪币。**II** ***n***. 推,推出,推开;【地】走向滑移。

shov·el [ˈʃʌvl; ˋʃʌvl] **I** ***n***. 铲,铁锹,(舀糖用的)杓子(= ～ hat)。**II** ***vt***. (***-l(l)-***) 拿铲子铲,拿杓子舀。—***vi***. 用铲子工作。～ ***food into one's mouth*** = ～ ***up*** [***down***] ***food*** 大口大口吃。～ *up* [*in*] *money* 大大赚钱。～**bill**【鸟】阔嘴鸭,琵琶嘴鸭。～**board**(在甲板等上玩的)推盘游戏;作这种游戏场地。～**ful** 满铲。～ **hat**(教士戴的)宽边铲形帽。～ **head**【动】窄头双髻鲛。～**-nosed** ***a***. 宽头的;宽喙的;宽扁鼻的。～**-nosed** [～ nose] **shark**【动】双髻鲨,犁骨鳐。～**-nosed sturgeon**【动】铲鲟。～ **stiff**〔美〕用铁锹的工人;生手工人。～ **ware**【计】铲件[指内容似抄袭的光碟等翻版媒体产品]。

shov·el·ler [ˈʃʌvlə; ˋʃʌvlɚ]〔美〕**shov·el·er** ***n***. **1.** 用铲子铲的人;推土机驾驶员。**2.** = shovel-bill.

show [ʃəu; ʃo] **I** ***vt***. (***～ed***; ***shown*** [ʃəun; ʃon],〔罕〕***～ed***) **1.** 给看,示,出示;显示,显出;陈列,展出,供参观;炫耀,卖弄。**2.** 教,告诉;指示,指出。**3.** 带领,指引,向导,领导参观;说明;证明。**4.** 给与,施与。**5.**【法】陈述,申辩。—***vi***. **1.** 显现;呈现;显眼;〔口〕露脸,出来,跑出来。**2.**〔口〕展览,演出,放映(电影)。**3.**〔美俚〕(赛马)跑第…名。*S- your tickets, please!* 请把票拿出来! *S- me a liar, and I'll ～ you a thief*. 撒谎是做贼的第一步。*It ～s you better*. 这使你格外显眼。*He didn't ～ all day yesterday*.〔美俚〕他昨天整天没露面。～ *that he is no fool* 证明他不笨。***have sth. to ～ for*** 在…方面有可显示的成绩。***I'll ～ you***. 你等着瞧吧(威吓语)。～ ***a leg*** 起床。～ ***sth. the fire*** 把…稍微热一热。～ ***cause*** 讲理由。～ ***daylight*** 有洞,有窟窿。～ ***fight*** 反抗;顽强抵抗。～ ***in*** 领进(客等)。～ ***off*** 卖弄,夸示(学问等);展览,陈列;使显眼。～ ***oneself*** 出现,露面。～ ***oneself off as*** 夸耀,标榜。～ ***one's cards*** [***colours***] 摊牌,公开自己的计划,吐露自己的真实打算。～ ***one's hand*** 摊牌,表明思想[目的]。～ ***one's heels*** 一溜烟地逃走;〔美运〕追过;大显比赛的优越本领。～ ***sb. the door*** 叫人走,逐出,撵跑;〔美〕拒绝要求。～ ***sb. to the door*** 送到门口。～ ***out*** 送出(客人)。～ ***sb. over*** [***round***] 带着[遍处]参观。～ ***the wing***(用飞行访问)显示空军力量。～ ***up*** 显眼;暴露,揭发;嘲笑;〔口〕出席,到场,露面(*He never ～s up at balls*. 他从来不参加舞会)。**II** ***n***. **1.** 表示;显示;展览;展览会;展览物,陈列品;演出;景象,壮观;洋相,丑相;出丑的人;就任(等)游行。**2.** 卖弄,夸示,炫耀;粉饰,盛装,铺张;外观,外貌,装扮,假装;样子;痕迹,征象。**3.**〔俚〕机会;事情,事件;团体,机关。**4.**【医】(临产时)见红;(月经开始时)现血;【矿】初现浮散矿;(矿脉,石油,天然气的)迹象。**5.**〔美赛马俚〕第三名。*an one-horse ～* 小公司,小商店;小事;小东西。*a road ～* 巡回演出;(新影片的)故意提高票价的盛大演出。*variety ～s* 杂耍。*a ～ of gold* 金矿迹象。*He is fond of ～*. 他爱漂亮。*a fine ～ of blossom on the trees this year* 今年花开得很壮观。*I have no ～ of trying*. 我没有干的机会。*The dinner was a dull ～*. 这个宴会乏味。***boss the ～*** 操纵;主持(演出)。***for ～*** 为夸示,为给人家看。***give away the*** (***whole***) ***～*** 露马脚,讲滑了嘴泄漏秘密;失言;叛变;揭穿内幕(等)。***give sb. a fair ～*** 给与表现机会。***have a*** [***the***] ***～ of*** 好像。***in dumb ～*** 打着手势(表示);用手比划着。***in open ～*** 公然。***in ～*** 外表是,外观是,表面是。***make a good ～*** 好看,有看头;大出洋相。***make a ～ of*** 卖弄,夸示,展览,装门面,装样子。***make a ～ of oneself*** 丢丑,弄出笑话。***on ～*** 成为展览物;被陈列着。***put on a ～*** 假装;装病(*He is not really ill she's just putting on a ～*. 他不是真病,他不过是装病罢了)。***put up a good*** [***bad***] ***～*** 演出好[不好],干得(不)好。***run the ～*** 操纵;主持(演出)。～ ***of force*** 炫耀武力。～ ***of hands*** 举手(表决)。～ ***of reason*** 似乎有理。***stand a ～*** 有可能,有希望。～ **bill** 海报,招贴,广告。～**boat**〔美〕演艺船。～ **bread**(犹太教的)供神面包。～ **business** [biz-; bɪz-] 娱乐性行业[指戏院、电影院,电视等]。～ **card** 广告牌;货样纸板。～**case** 陈列箱,陈列橱;〔美俚〕应接室;(试片)影戏院(*a ～-case try*〔美剧〕试片会)。～**down**〔美〕摊牌;〔喻〕最后的较量;公布,暴露;〔美俚〕危机。～**folk**〔总称〕表演业者,娱乐业人士。～**girl** 歌舞团女演员,夜总会歌舞女郎。～**ground** 展览场地。～**man** **1.**(戏剧等的)演出主持人(或经理人)。**2.**〔爱〕出风头的人。～**-manship**(马戏等的)经营术;杂剧演出技巧。～**-off** 夸耀;卖弄;〔美〕自大的人,爱吹牛的人。～**piece** 样品;陈列品,展品。～**-place** 可参观的场所[建筑物],名胜。**S-Sunday**〔英〕节日前夜的星期天。～**room** 货品陈列室。～**up**〔口〕暴露,揭发。～ **window** 橱窗,陈列窗。

show·er[1] [ˈʃauə; ˋʃaʊɚ] **I** ***n***. **1.** 阵雨;(风雪等的)一阵。**2.** 淋浴;(弹)雨(等),阵雨一样涌到的东西(信等);【物】射丛;(美)(为新娘等举行的)送礼会;大批礼物。*a ～ stick*〔美〕雨伞。*be caught in a ～* 遇到阵雨。*Letters come in ～s*. 信件一批一批地涌到。*a labile ～*【物】晶霰。*a meson ～*【物】介子簇射。*send sb. to the ～s*〔美〕拒绝要求;散会。**II** ***vt***. 把…给阵雨淋湿;使湿透;阵雨似地倾注(炮弹等);大量给与(礼物等)(*upon*)。—***vi***. 下阵雨;阵雨似地落下。～ ***affections upon*** 对…倾注爱意。～ **bath** 淋浴(装置);湿透。

show·er[2] [ˈʃəuə; ˋʃoɚ] ***n***. 出示者;表示者;展出者;指示者[器]。

show·er·y [ˈʃauəri; ˋʃaʊərɪ] ***a***. 阵雨般的;多阵雨的。**-i·ness** ***n***.

show·ing [ˈʃəuiŋ; ˋʃoɪŋ] ***n***. 表现;展览(会);〔口〕外观,外表;主张。***make a good*** [***bad***] ***～*** 表现好[不好]。***on one's own ～*** 按照自己主张。

show-me [ˈʃəumi; ˋʃo͵mi] ***a***. 没有证据不相信;需要有证明的。*a ～ attitude* 存疑态度。*Show-me State*〔美〕密苏里州[别名,由美国谚语 I'm from Missouri(不见不信)而来]。

shown [ʃəun; ʃon] show 的过去分词。

show·y [ˈʃəui; ˋʃoɪ] ***a***. 华美的,华丽的;炫耀的;显眼的;好看的。**-i·ly** ***ad***. **-i·ness** ***n***.

shp, SHP = shaft horsepower【机】轴马力。

shpt. = shipment.

shr. = share(s).

shram [ʃræm; ʃræm] ***vt***.〔英方〕使冷得麻木。

shrank [ʃræŋk; ʃræŋk] shrink 的过去式。

shrap·nel [ˈʃræpnəl; ˋʃræpnəl] ***n***.〔*sing*., *pl*.〕**1.** 榴霰弹。**2.**〔集合词〕榴霰弹片。

shred [ʃred; ʃrɛd] **I** ***n***. 裂片;碎片;破布条;少量。*left without a ～ of reputation* 名誉扫地。*not a ～ of evidence* 毫无证据。*without a ～ of clothing on* 一丝不挂。***in ～s and tatters*** 破烂不堪,穿得破破烂烂。***tear to ～s*** 扯碎,扯得稀烂。**II** (***～ded***,〔古〕***shred***; ***～ding***) ***vt***., ***vi***. 撕碎,切碎;切成丝;破碎。

shrew [ʃru:; ʃru] ***n***. 泼妇,悍妇;【动】鼩鼱〔又叫

~-mouse〕。

shrewd [ʃruːd; ʃrud] ***a***. 敏捷的,机灵的,机敏的,精明的;锐利的;〔古〕严酷的,刺骨的,猛烈的(风等);狡猾的,油滑的;〔古〕刻毒的。***do (one) a ~ turn*** 给(某人)吃一个苦头。***have a ~ tongue*** 说话刻薄。**-ly** ***ad***. **-ness** ***n***.

shrew·ish [ˈʃruːiʃ; ˋʃruɪʃ] ***a***. 泼妇似的,爱骂人的;刻薄的。**-ly** ***ad***. **-ness** ***n***.

shriek [ʃriːk; ʃrik] **I** ***n***. 尖锐的喊声[笑声];〔美〕引起人注意的事物;怪有趣的东西。**II** ***vi***. 尖声叫喊,惊喊;引人注意。—***vt***. 尖声讲,令人吃惊地说;动人听闻地报导[描述]。*give* [*utter*] *a ~* 发出尖叫,惊喊。*a ~ing heading* 惊人的标题。*~ out* 尖声哭叫。*~ with laughter* 高声大笑。*~ with pain* 痛得绝叫。*~ curses at sb*. 厉声咒人。

shriev·al·ty [ˈʃriːvəlti; ˋʃrivl̩tɪ] ***n***. sheriff 的职位[任期]。

shrieve [ʃriːv; ʃriv] ***n***. 〔废〕= sheriff.

shrift [ʃrift; ʃrɪft] ***n***. (对牧师所作的)忏悔;认罪。*short ~* 死刑执行前的短暂忏悔时间。*give* [*get*] *short ~* 很快解决掉[处死];不耐烦地摆脱掉;对…简慢无礼[漠不关心]。

shrike [ʃraik; ʃraɪk] ***n***. 【鸟】伯劳,百舌鸟。

shrill [ʃril; ʃrɪl] **I** ***a***. 尖声的,刺耳的;强烈的,刺激的,哀诉的;怒冲冲的;讨厌的,过度的。**II** ***n***. 尖锐的声音。**III** ***vt***., ***vi***. 〔诗〕【修】发尖锐音;尖声锐气地讲[唱] (*out*)。**IV** ***ad***. = **shrilly** ***ad***. 用尖锐的声音。

shrimp [ʃrimp; ʃrɪmp] **I** ***n***. (*pl*. ~*s*, 〔集合词〕~) **1**. 【动】褐虾,河虾。**2**. 〔俚〕矮子;微不足道的人。**II** ***vi***. 捕捉褐虾。~ **plant** 【植】麒麟吐珠。~ **sauce** 虾油。**-er** ***n***. 捕虾者;捕虾器。

shrine [ʃrain; ʃraɪn] **I** ***n***. 神龛;神祠,庙;神殿;圣地。*the ~ of art* 艺术圣地。**II** ***vt***. 〔诗〕安置在神龛里;祀在祠堂里;奉为神圣。

shrink [ʃriŋk; ʃrɪŋk] **I** ***vi***. (***shrank*** [ʃræŋk; ʃræŋk], ***shrunk***; ***shrunk*** [ʃrʌŋk; ʃrʌŋk], 〔罕〕***shrunken*** [ˈʃrʌŋkən; ˋʃrʌŋkən]) **1**. 皱缩;缩短,收缩。**2**. 变小,减小。**3**. 退缩,畏缩,害怕。—***vt***. **1**. 使皱缩,弄皱;使缩短。**2**. 缩进,拉回。~ ***away*** 衰退;退缩,退避。~ ***back*** 退缩,畏缩,害怕。~ ***fit*** 【机】热配合,冷缩配合;烧嵌。~ ***from*** (*do*)*ing* 畏缩不…。~ ***into oneself*** 踌躇。~ ***to nothing*** 渐渐缩小到没有。~ ***up*** 缩拢,缩成一团。~***ing violet*** 非常怕羞的人;谦逊的人。**II** ***n***. **1**. 皱缩;收缩,缩水;畏缩;退缩。**2**. 精简人员,缩编。

shrink·age [ˈfrinkidʒ; ˋʃrɪŋkɪdʒ] ***n***. **1**. 皱缩;缩水;减缩;减少。**2**. 【物】缩误;缩减量;(肉类在运输、加工过程中的)重量的损耗。~ *in the market place* 市场萎缩。~ **theory** 【地】冷缩说。

shrink·ing [ˈʃrinkiŋ; ˋʃrɪŋkɪŋ] ***a***. 畏缩的,退缩的,踌躇的,犹豫不决的。**-ly** ***ad***.

shrive [ʃraiv; ʃraɪv] ***vt***. (~***d***, 〔古〕***shrove*** [ʃrəuv; ʃrov]; ~***d***, 〔古〕***shriven*** [ˈʃrivən; ˋʃrɪvən] ***shriv·ing***) 听忏悔而赦免…的罪。—***vi***. 听忏悔;忏悔赎罪。~ *oneself* 忏悔以求赎罪。

shriv·el [ˈʃrɪvl; ˋʃrɪvl̩] ***vt***., ***vi***. (***shriv·elled***; ***shriv·el·ling*** [ˈʃrivliŋ; ˋʃrɪvlɪŋ]) (使)皱缩;(使)干瘪;(使)枯萎;(使)无能为力,(使)失效。

shriv·en [ˈʃrivən; ˋʃrɪvən] 〔古〕shrive 的过去分词。

shroff [ʃrɔf; ʃrɑf] **I** ***n***. (旧中国、印度的)银钱兑换商;钱兑店;货币鉴定人,收账员。**II** ***vt***. 鉴别(钱币)。

Shrop·shire [ˈʃrɔpʃiə; ˋʃrɑpʃɪr] ***n***. **1**. (英国)什罗郡。**2**. (黑头黑脚白毛无角)肉用羊。

shroud [ʃraud; ʃraʊd] **I** ***n***. **1**. 裹尸布,尸衣。**2**. 覆盖物,屏蔽,掩蔽(物),幕,帐。**3**. 【空】罩,侧板;【机】护罩;套管;(水车的)侧板。**4**. 〔*pl*.〕【海】支桅索;【空】= ~ line 降落伞的吊伞索。*a ~ ring* 【机】覆环。*wrapped in a ~ of mystery* 笼罩着神秘的气氛。**II** ***vt***. 用裹尸布覆盖;覆盖,隐藏。~**-laid** ***a***. 四单股向右绞成的(绳索)。

shrove [ʃrəuv; ʃrov] 〔古〕shrive 的过去式。

Shrove·tide [ˈʃrəuvtaid; ˋʃrov͵taɪd] ***n***. 忏悔节。

shrub[1] [ʃrʌb; ʃrʌb] ***n***. 灌木,灌木丛。

shrub[2] [ʃrʌb; ʃrʌb] ***n***. 果汁甜酒〔果汁加糖及少量 rum 酒等做成的饮料,通常叫 rum-~〕;冰果汁水。

shrub·ber·y [ˈʃrʌbəri; ˋʃrʌbərɪ] ***n***. 〔集合词〕灌木丛;灌木丛生的地方;(公园等中的)灌木丛中的路;〔美俚〕络腮胡。

shrub·by [ˈʃrʌbi; ˋʃrʌbɪ] ***a***. 灌木状的;多灌木的。

shrug [ʃrʌg; ʃrʌg] **I** ***vt***., ***vi***. (***shrugged***, ***shrug·ging***) 耸(肩)。~ *one's shoulders* 耸耸肩膀〔表示不快、绝望、惊讶、疑惑、冷笑等〕。~ ***off*** (耸肩)表示轻蔑[不屑];摆脱;扭身脱掉(衣服)。**II** ***n***. 耸肩。

shrunk [ʃrʌŋk; ʃrʌŋk] **I** shrink 的过去式及过去分词。**II** ***a***. 浸缩过的,缩过水的,不会再缩的(毛织品)。

shrunk·en [ˈʃrʌŋkən; ˋʃrʌŋkən] **I** 〔罕〕shrink 的过去分词。**II** ***a***. 皱缩的。~ *grains* 不饱满的籽粒,瘪籽。

shs. = shares.

SHS = solar home system 家用太阳能系统。

shtet·l [ˈʃtetl; ˋʃtetl̩] ***n***. (*pl*. ***shtet·lach*** [-lɑːkh; -lɑkh], ***shtet·ls*** [-lz; -lz]) (第二次世界大战前东欧的)犹太人小村。

shtg. = shortage.

sh.tn., **sh.ton**. = short ton 短吨。

shtick [ʃtik; ʃtɪk] ***n***. 〔美俚〕**1**. 滑稽场面。**2**. 引人注意的小噱头。**3**. 特别才能,特色。

shuck [ʃʌk; ʃʌk] **I** ***n***. **1**. 壳,皮,荚;贝壳;〔*pl*.〕〔美口〕不值一提的东西。**2**. 骗局。***light a*** ~ 〔美俚〕急匆匆跑掉。***not worth ~s*** 毫无价值。**II** ***vt***. 剥壳,剥皮,剥荚。~ ***off*** 〔美口〕脱掉(上衣等);舍弃;摆脱;无限期拖延。

shucks [ʃʌks; ʃʌks] ***int***. 〔美俚〕呸! 哼! 〔表示藐视、失望、厌恶等〕。

shud·der [ˈʃʌdə; ˋʃʌdɚ] **I** ***vi***. 发抖,打颤,战栗 (*at*; *to do*)。**II** ***n***. 发抖,战栗。~ ***at the thought of*** = ~ ***to think of*** 一想到…就发抖[毛骨悚然]。

shuf·fle [ˈʃʌfl; ˋʃʌfl̩] **I** ***vt***. **1**. (尤指走路时,把脚)在地上拖曳;滑来滑去。**2**. (笨拙地)穿上,披上,脱去;狡猾地进行(某事)。**3**. 混和,搅乱;洗(纸牌);移来移去;反复挪动。**4**. 推诿,推开;〔美〕使火车转轨。—***vi***. **1**. 洗纸牌。**2**. 拖着脚步走[舞蹈];把脚挪来挪去;移动;推诿自己职责,推托,搪塞;蒙混。**3**. 笨拙地穿衣[脱衣]。~ *cards* 洗纸牌。~ *the cards* 〔喻〕改变机构人事;改变政策。~ ***off*** 脱掉,丢弃,抛弃 (~ *off this mortal coil* 死)。~ ***off*** (*a duty*) ***upon*** [***onto***] 把(责任)推给…。~ ***through*** 搪塞过去。**II** ***n***. 拖着脚走;(舞蹈的)拖步;搅乱,混合;洗牌;轮到洗牌;混蒙;推托,敷衍。*double ~* 一脚迅速拖动两次的舞步。~ **board** ***n***. = shovel-board.

shul [ʃuːl; ʃul] ***n***. = synagogue.

Shu·lam·ite [ˈʃuːlə͵mait; ˋʃuləm͵aɪt] ***n***. 书拉密〔《旧约·雅歌》中所赞美的少女〕。

shun [ʃʌn; ʃʌn] ***vt***. 避开,躲开(危险等)。

'shun [ʃʌn; ʃʌn] ***int***. 立正! 〔attention 之略〕。

shune [ʃuːn; ʃun] ***n***. 〔Scot.〕shoe 的复数。

shunt [ʃʌnt; ʃʌnt] **I** ***vt***. **1**. 逃避,躲开,闪开;〔口〕将(工作、义务等)推给别人;拖延,搁置(计划、讨论等)。**2**. 【铁路】把(车)开到岔轨上,调车;【电】在…上装分路器,使分路[流]。—***vi***. 退到旁边,闪开,躲开;(车)转入岔轨;改变话题,把话闪开;改变意思。**II** ***n***. **1**. 【铁路】侧避;调车;调轨;转轨;轨闸;【电】分路[分流]器。**2**. 〔俚〕(汽车)撞车,碰撞。*a ~ing station* 【铁路】调度站。*a ~* (*wound*) *dynamo* 【电】并激发电机。~ **winding** 【电】并激绕组,分流绕组,并联线圈;分线组;分线法。

shunt·er [ˈʃʌntə; ˋʃʌntɚ] ***n***. 【铁路】扳道员,转辙员,扳闸员;道岔机;调车机车;〔俚〕有能力的组织者。

shush [ʃʌʃ; ʃʌʃ] **I** ***int***. 嘘! 别响! 安静。**II** ***vt***. 叫…别出声。

S

Shu·shan [ˈʃuːʃaːn; ˋʃuʃɑn] 苏沙(苏萨) (Susa) 〔伊朗西部废墟古城在圣经里的名称〕。

shut [ʃʌt; ʃʌt] **I** *vt*. (*shut* [ʃʌt; ʃʌt]; ~ *ting*) **1.** 关闭 (*opp*. open); 把…关在门外, 排斥; 关进, 围进 (*in*; *into*); 关上(箱子等), 闭上(嘴等) (*up*); 封闭, 封锁; 停止开放[营业]; 叠拢, 合拢(伞、小刀等); 挟住, 挟进。**2.** 使暗, 隐藏。—*vi*. 关闭; 塞住; (店铺等)关门。*S- the door after you*. 随手关门。~ *the door against sb*. 把某人关在门外。~ *a book* 合上书。*The door* ~ *with a bang*. 门砰地一声关上了。***be*** ~ ***of*** (*sb*.) 〔英俚〕摆脱, 甩开(某人)。~ ***down*** **1.** 关闭; 关拢(窗等); 停业, 停工; 停止, 阻止, 禁止。**2.** (夜色、迷雾等)浓暗下来。~ ***down on*** 〔口语〕禁止, 压制。~ ***in*** **1.** 把…关进去, 监禁; 围住; 遮住。**2.** (夜等)降临, 迫近 (*The night has* ~ *in*. 天黑了)。~ ***off*** 阻断, 关上(自来水、收音机、煤气等); 使不接触, 使隔离, 使隔开。~ ***one's eyes*** [***ears***] ***to*** 假装没有看见[听见]; 拒绝看[听]。~ ***one's face*** [***head***] 〔俚〕默不作声。~ ***one's heart to*** 对…漠不关心。~ ***one's lights*** (***off***) 死。~ ***one's mind to*** 死不答应。~ ***one's mouth*** 闭嘴不响, 不开口 (*S- your mouth* 〔口〕别响。~ *sb*.*'s mouth* 叫某人莫开口)。~ ***one's teeth*** 咬紧牙关。~ ***out*** 不让进来, 关在外头; 遮得看不见; 【棒球】不让得分。~ ***the door in sb.'s face*** 闭门不纳。~ ***the door on*** [***upon***] (***sb***.) 把…关在门外, 限制, 绝对不许…进来[出去]; 完全不把…当做问题, 根本不理睬 (~ *the door on the proposals* 对建议根本不理睬)。~ ***together*** 接合, (尤指)焊合(金属物)。~ ***up*** **1.** 关上, 关住; 监禁; 密封, 密藏; 停止。**2.** 不许开口, 使人哑口无言; 不响 (~ *up shop* 关店。*S- up*! 〔俚〕住嘴! 别说)。**II** *n*. **1.** 〔主持〕关闭, 闭锁, 终止, 完结。**2.** 焊接缝。**3.** 【语音】闭锁音。**4.** 【机】冷塞。**III** *a*. 紧闭的; 声音低沉的。闭锁音 (l, p, t, k, b, d 等)的。~**down** 停工, 停业。~**-eye** 〔美俚〕酒; 睡眠。~**-in** **1.** *a*. 闭居家中的; 孤僻的。**2.** *n*. 病弱不外出的人。~**-off** 中止; 堵塞; 中断; 关闭器〔如阀门〕。~**out** (把某人)排斥在外; 关在外面; 停工, 锁闭厂门; (在比赛等中)不让对方得分。

Shute [ʃuːt; ʃut] *n*. 舒特〔姓氏〕。

shut·ter [ˈʃʌtə; ˋʃʌtɚ] **I** *n*. **1.** 百叶窗; 护窗板; (照相机上的)快门, (光)闸; 光盘; 【火箭】(调节喷气口的)鱼鳞板; 风琴里的关开; 开闭器; 关闭者。**2.** 〔*pl*.〕〔美拳〕眼睛。***put up the*** ~***s*** 关上护窗板; 关铺子。***take down the*** ~***s*** 打开护窗板[百叶窗]。**II** *vt*. **1.** 给…装上百叶窗。**2.** 使关上百叶窗。**3.** 装光闸于(照相机上)。

shut·ter·bug [ˈʃʌtəˌbʌg; ˋʃʌtɚˏbʌg] *n*. 〔美俚〕摄影迷, 摄影爱好者。

shut·tle [ˈʃʌtl; ˋʃʌtl̩] **I** *n*. **1.** (织机的)梭; (缝纫机的)滑梭; (编织用的)梭形针。**2.** 穿梭般来回; 短程来回运输(线, 工具); 【空】穿梭式来回不停的民航运输机[轰炸机]; 【宇航】航天飞机, 太空穿梭机〔由火箭发射进入太空轨道运行若干时日后重新飞回地面, 可反复使用〕。〔美〕短程盘运火车〔又叫 ~-train〕。**3.** 穿梭旅行; 穿梭外交(活动)。**II** *vt*., *vi*. (使)作穿梭式来回运动; (使)前后移动, (使)来回如梭。~ **armature** 【电】梭形电枢。~ **bus** 〔美〕区间(公共汽)车。~**-bombing** 【空】穿梭轰炸。~ **diplomacy** 穿梭外交。~ **service** (火车、飞机、巴士等的)定点往返服务。

shut·tle·cock [ˈʃʌtlkɔk; ˋʃʌtl̩ˏkɑk] **I** *n*. **1.** 羽毛球。**2.** 羽毛球运动。**3.** 争论之点; 犹豫的人。**II** *vt*. 抛来抛去, 打来打去, 往返递送。—*vi*. 来回走动, 穿梭似往返。

s.h.v. = [L.] *sub hac voce* [*hoc verbo*] 在此词下, 参见该词。

shy[1] [ʃai; ʃaɪ] **I** *a*. (~*er*; ~*est*, 〔罕〕 ***shi·er***; ***shi·est***) **1.** 胆小的, 见人就躲避的。**2.** 怕羞的; 羞怯的。**3.** 畏缩的; 存戒心的, 小心的, 谨防…的 (*of*)。**4.** 不易捉摸的; (话题)难懂的, 费解的。**5.** (植物)很少开花结子的; (动物)很少下仔的。**6.** 〔口〕【牌】还没有出赌注的。**7.** 〔俚〕缺少, 不足 (*of*)。*This made him* ~ *of trying it again*. 这使他不敢再试了。*She was* ~ *two months of her nineteenth birthday*. 她差两个月就是十九岁的生日。***fight*** ~ ***of*** 厌恶…, 避开…。***look*** ~ ***at*** [***on***] 怀疑。***of*** ~ ***disposition*** 怯懦的。***once bit*** [***bitten***], ***twice*** ~ 一回遭蛇咬, 二回怕井绳。**II** *n*. (*pl*. *shies*) (马)惊退, 惊逸。**III** *vi*. **1.** 惊退, 惊逸, 畏缩 (*at*)。**2.** 避开 (*away from*)。*He isn't the man to* ~ *at difficulties*. 他不是在困难面前畏缩的人。*Her eyes* ~ *away from mine*. 她一见我盯她就把自己的眼睛避开了。—*vt*. 避开(某人)。*He has shied us lately*. 他近来对我们不理睬了。**-ly** *ad*. **-ness** *n*.

shy[2] [ʃai; ʃaɪ] **I** *n*. **1.** 投扔, 乱丢。**2.** 〔口〕嘲弄。**3.** 〔口〕尝试; 企图; 目标; 机会。*three shies a penny* 一辨士投掷三次。***have a*** ~ ***at*** **1.** 试图投中某物。**2.** 挖苦, 嘲弄。**3.** 想得到, 想(做)。**II** *vt*., *vi*. (用石子、球等)乱投 (*at*)。

-shy [ʃai; ʃaɪ] *comb*. *f*. 怕…的, 讨厌…的: gun-*shy*, work-*shy*.

shy·er [ˈʃaiə; ˋʃaɪɚ] *n*. 畏缩不前的人; 胆小的马, 易受惊的马。

shy·ster [ˈʃaistə; ˋʃaɪstɚ] *n*. 〔美〕讼棍; 手段卑鄙的人[政客]。

si [siː; si] *n*. 【乐】长音阶的第七音。

Si = 【化】 silicon.

S.I. = **1.** Sandwich Islands 〔旧〕桑威奇群岛〔美, 现称 Hawaiian Islands 夏威夷群岛〕。**2.** short interest 短期债券总额。**3.** Staten Island. 〔美〕(纽约大都会的)斯塔屯岛。

SIA = Singapore Airlines 新加坡航空公司。

si·al [ˈsaiæl; ˋsaɪæl] *n*. 【地】矽铝带, 矽铝层。**-ic** *a*.

si·al·a·gogue [saiˈæləˌgɔg; saɪˋæləˏgɑg] *n*. 【化】催涎剂。**-gog·ic** *a*.

si·a·lid, si·al·i·dan [ˈsaiəlid, saiˈælidən; ˋsaɪəlɪd, saɪˋælɪdən] **I** *a*. 【动】蛇蛉蜓科 (*Sialidae*) 的。**II** *n*. 蛇蛉蜓科昆虫。

si·a·loid [ˈsaiəˌlɔid; ˋsaɪəˏlɔɪd] *a*. 似唾液的。

Si·am [ˈsaiæm, saiˈæm; saɪˋæm] *n*. 暹逻〔泰国 (Thailand) 的旧称〕。

si·a·mang [ˈsiːəˌmæŋ; ˋsiəmæŋ] *n*. 【动】合趾猿 (*Symphalangus syndactylus*) 〔产于马来半岛和苏门答腊〕。

Si·a·mese [saiəˈmiːz, ˈsaiə-; ˏsaɪəˋmiz] **I** *a*. **1.** 暹逻的; 暹逻人[语]的。**2.** 孪生的; 相似的; [s-]【建】(管道)二重联接的。**II** *n*. [*sing*., *pl*.] 暹逻人; 暹逻语; 暹逻猫。***the*** ~ ***twins*** 连体双胞胎; 情投意合的朋友, 如胶似漆的朋友。**III** [s-] *vt*. 连接; 结合。*They are* ~*d to France*. 它们同法国相连。

sib [sib; sɪb] 〔英古〕**I** *a*. 有血缘关系的 (*to*); 近亲的。**II** *n*. 血亲; 〔集合词〕亲族; 〔常 *pl*.〕兄弟姊妹; 【人类】氏族; 【生】(同科、属)亲缘动植物; 【选种】同系。

Sib. = Siberia; Siberian.

Si·ber·i·a [saiˈbiəriə; saɪˋbɪrɪə] *n*. 西伯利亚〔俄国一地区〕。

Si·be·ri·an [saiˈbiəriən; saɪˋbɪərɪən] *a*., *n*. 西伯利亚的(人)。~ ***husky*** 爱斯基摩狗。

sib·i·lance, -cy [ˈsibiləns, -si; ˋsɪbl̩əns, -sɪ] *n*. 发咝音; 齿音, 咝音 〔s, ʃ, z, ʒ 等〕。

sib·i·lant [ˈsibilənt; ˋsɪbl̩ənt] **I** *a*. 发咝音的, 作咝咝声的。**II** *n*. 咝音(字)。

sib·i·late [ˈsibileit; ˋsɪbl̩ˏet] *vt*., *vi*. 发咝音; 咝咝地说。

sib·i·la·tion [ˌsibiˈleiʃən; ˏsɪbl̩ˋeʃən] *n*. 发咝音; 咝音; 作咝咝声。

sib·ling [ˈsibliŋ; ˋsɪblɪŋ] *n*. **1.** 〔常 *pl*.〕兄弟姊妹; 同胞。**2.** 【人类】氏族成员; 【生】同科, 同属。

sib·yl [ˈsibil; ˋsɪbl] *n*. (古代的)女巫; 女卜者, 女预言者, 女卫士。**-byl·ic** *a*.

sib·yl·line [siˈbilain; ˋsɪblˏin] *a*. 女巫的; 预言的, 神秘的。~ ***books*** (古罗马)《西坡拉占语集》; 〔转义〕起初不

想买后来反愿出高价收买的东西。

SIC = specific inductive capacity 电容率。

sic[1] [sik; sɪk] ***a***. 〔Scot.〕= such.

sic[2] [sik; sɪk] ***vt***. (~***ced***; ~***cing***) = sick[2].

sic [sik; sɪk] ***ad***. 〔L.〕原文如此〔对引文错误、可疑处的附注〕。~ ***jubeo*** [ˈjuːbiəu; ˋjubɪo] 这是我的意思,这是我的命令。~ ***passim*** [ˈpæsim; ˋpæsɪm] 以下同此[仿此]。~ ***transit gloria mundi*** [ˈtransit glɔuriːə mundiː; ˋtransɪt gloriə mʊndi] 尘世繁华转眼即逝。~ ***volo***, ~ ***vos non vobis*** [ˈvəus nɔn ˈvəubis; ˋvos nɑn ˋvobɪs] 〔L.〕你这样做原来并不是为了自己〔指某人做某事而另一人获得利益〕。

Si·ca·ni·an [siˈkeiniən; sɪˋkenɪən] ***a***. = Sicilian.

sic·ca·tive [ˈsikətiv; ˋsɪkətɪv] **I** ***a***. 促使干燥的。**II** ***n***. (加在油漆中的)干燥剂。

sice[1] [sais; saɪs] ***n***. = syce.

sice[2] [sais; saɪs] ***n***. 〔英俚〕六便士;(骰子的)六点。

Si·cil·i·an [siˈsiljən, -liən; sɪˋsɪlɪən] **I** ***a***. 西西里岛的,西西里岛人的。**II** ***n***. 西西里岛人;西西里方言。

Sic·i·ly [ˈsisili; ˋsɪslɪ] ***n***. 西西里(岛)〔意大利〕。

sick[1] [sik; sɪk] ***a***. **1**. 病的,有病的,身体不舒服;〔美,英古〕虚弱的。**2**. 〔用作表语〕〔英口〕使人作呕的,恶心的;厌倦,厌恶(人生等)(*of*);油腻(*to*);失望(*at*);想望着,怀念着(*for*)。**3**. 不健康的;有病容的;精神不振的,苍白的。**4**. 在月经期中。**5**. (情况)失常的;(船)需要修理的。**6**. 【农】地力变瘠了的,不适于栽种…的;带有病菌的(土地)。**7**. (铁)发脆的;(葡萄酒)变了味的。~ *of love* [*a fever*] 害着相思病[热病]。*the* ~ 病人,病员。*It makes me* ~ *to think of that*. 一想起这件事我就发腻。*He was* ~ *with me for being so late*. 他怪我这样迟。*a boat* ~ *of paint* 需要重行油漆的船。*tomato*-~ 不能栽番茄的。***be*** ~ ***at heart*** 觉得讨厌,心中烦闷,悲观。***be*** ~ ***of doing nothing*** 闲得发腻。***be*** ~ ***to dead of*** 对…腻得要命。***fall*** [***get***] ~ 生病。***feel*** [***turn***] ~ 觉得要呕,作呕,恶心。***go*** [***report***] ~ 请病假。***look*** ~ 给人留下的印象不深;显得逊色。***make sb***. ~ 使人作呕;〔美〕使生病。~ ***as a dog*** 〔美〕病重的。~ ***into death*** 病得要死。~ **bay** (军舰等的)病房。~**bed** 病床。~ **benefit** 疾病补助。~ **building** 病楼〔有通风不良等毛病而会不利于住户健康的楼房〕。~ **building syndrome** 病楼综合症〔"病楼"中的住户因环境不佳而产生头痛、头晕等〕。~ **call** 【军】伤病员集合(准备就诊),伤病员集合号。~ **flag** 检疫旗。~ **headache** 呕吐性头痛。~ **leave** (照领工薪的)病假。~ **list** (尤指陆海军的)病员名单。~**room** 病房。~**-worker** 补缺工人。

sick[2] [sik; sɪk] ***vt***. 追击;攻击;(纵狗)追击;〔美〕嗾使(狗等)去咬[去攻击]。*He* ~*ed the dog on me*. 他嗾狗来咬我。

sick·en [ˈsikn; ˋsɪkən] ***vt***. 使生病;使作呕,使恶心;使厌倦。—***vi***. 患病;觉得要吐,想呕,恶心(*at*);厌倦,厌恶(*of*)。

sick·en·er [ˈsikənə; ˋsɪkənɚ] ***n***. 致病之物;过量的药物;催吐物;呕吐红菇;令人讨厌的东西;厌倦的感觉;〔学生俚〕讨厌的家伙。

sick·er [ˈsikə; ˋsɪkɚ] ***n***. 〔美军俚〕住院病人。

sick·ish [ˈsikiʃ; ˋsɪkɪʃ] ***a***. 像要生病似的,有点不舒服的;像要吐的。**-ly** ***ad***. **-ness** ***n***.

sick·le [ˈsikl; ˋsɪkl] ***n***. 镰刀,小镰刀;装在斗鸡脚上的镰刀形距铁;〔the S-〕【天】(狮子座中的)镰形星群。~ **alfalfa** 黄花苜蓿。~ **bar** (刈草用)切割器。~**bill** 【动】杓鹬。~ **cell** (**anemia** 或 **disease**) 【医】镰形血球(贫血)。~ **feather** (公鸡的)镰形羽尾,鸡翎。~**man** 收割者。~**mia** 【医】镰状血球贫血。

sick·li·ness [ˈsiklinis; ˋsɪklənɪs] ***n***. **1**. 疾病,多病。**2**. 恶心,呕吐。**3**. 苍白;(光色的)暗淡。*There is little* ~ *here this year*. 今年这里的疾病很少。*a sudden* ~ *of disgust* 厌恶得突然呕吐发作。

sick·ly [ˈsikli; ˋsɪklɪ] **I** ***a***. **1**. 有病的,病态的;虚弱的,(面容等)苍白的;多愁善感的。**2**. 令人作呕的;(风土等)有碍健康的;疾病流行的;易引起疾病的。**3**. 令人生厌的,(笑样等)阴沉的。**4**. (光或色)暗淡的,微弱的;惨淡的。*a* ~ *child* 一个多病的孩子。*a* ~ *season* 疾病流行的季节。*a* ~ *moonlight* 暗淡的月光。**II** ***vt***. 使现病容。

sick·ness [ˈsiknis; ˋsɪknɪs] ***n***. 病,疾病;恶心,呕吐。*a ceylon* ~ 脚气病。*a country* ~ 思乡病。*a falling* ~ 癫痫。

sic pas·sim [sikˈpæsim; sɪkˋpæsɪm] ***n***. 〔L.〕全书下同〔注释中有某种特殊规定时的行文用语〕。

Sid = side-impact dummy (试验新汽车侧面碰撞对乘客会有何影响用的)侧撞试验假人。

SIDA [ˈsiːdɑ; ˋsidɑ] = syndrome(d') immunite deficience acqueri 〔F.〕艾滋病。

Sid·dhar·tha [sidˈdɑːtə; sɪˋdɑrtə] ***n***. 悉达多〔佛教始祖释迦牟尼的本名〕。

Sid·dons [ˈsidnz; ˋsɪdnz] ***n***. 西登斯〔姓氏〕。

sid·dur [siˈduə, ˈsiduə; ˋsɪdʊr] ***n***. (*pl*. **-dur·im** [-ˈiːm; -ˋim], **-durs**) 犹太教祈祷书。

side [said; saɪd] **I** ***n***. **1**. (左右上下等的)边,侧面;(事物内外等的)面,方面;(人、物等的)旁,旁边。**2**. 〔数〕(三角形等的)边;(立体的)面。**3**. (身体的)侧边,胁;(牛羊等从脊骨一分为二的)半片;肋肉。**4**. (父方、母方等的)方,血统;(一个集团中的)派别,(敌对的)一方。**5**. 【海】舷侧;【徽】纵线;【台球】侧击转球;【印】页。**6**. 〔俚〕(摆)架子,傲慢,自大。**7**. (比赛的)队。**8**. 〔美俚〕一段[一页,一份]台词。**9**. 河岸,山坡。*the right* [*wrong*] ~ (纸、布等的)正[反]面。*the flat* ~ (刀)背。*the near* [*off*] ~ (马、车的)靠近[远离]路边的一边。*Let's play* ~*s*. 我们来分成两方比赛吧。*No* ~!【橄榄球】比赛完毕! *Which* ~ *are you on*? 你属于哪一派? *The school has a strong* ~. 该校有实力雄厚的一队。*He is English on his mother's* ~. 他的母系是英国血统。*a* ~ *of bacon* 一块熏肋肉。*six* ~*s of dialog* 〔美剧〕六页台词。***by sb.'s*** ~ = ***by the*** ~ ***of*** 在…的旁边;在…的附近;和…比较。***change*** ~***s*** (改变立场)投到对方去。***clear*** ~ 【海】露出在水面上的部分。***from all*** ~***s*** 从各方面;到处;从四面八方。***from*** ~ ***to*** ~ 左右(摇等)。***have lots of*** ~ 架子十足。***have*** [***put on***] ***too much*** ~ 太摆架子,太傲慢。***hold*** [***shake***, ***burst***, ***split***] ***one's*** ~ (***with*** [***for***] ***laughter***) 捧腹大笑。***look on all*** ~***s*** 到处细看。***off*** [***on***] ~ 【橄榄球】违犯规则[合规则]的地位。***on all*** ~***s*** 四方八面,到处。***on one*** ~ 在一旁,在一边;斜着。***on the high*** ~ 相当高。***on the other*** ~ 反对方面的;在对面。***on the right*** ~ = ***on the*** ~ ***of the angels*** 在正对面。***on the right*** [***better***, ***bright***] ~ ***of*** 未过…岁。***on the*** ... ~ 趋向于…,稍微…一点(*Prices were on the high* ~. 物价稍微高一点)。***on the*** ~ 顺便,附带;作为副业;〔美口〕略略添上,稍微加上。***on the*** ~ ***of*** 站在…一边,袒护…,帮着…。***on the small*** ~ 相当小。***on the wrong*** [***shady***] ~ ***of*** 过了…岁。***on the wrong*** ~ ***of the door*** 被关在门外,被拒绝入内。***on this*** ~ ***of*** 在…的这一边;未到(某时日)。***on this*** ~ (***of***) ***the grave*** 在现世。***place*** [***put***] ***on one*** ~ 放到一边;忽视,不当回事。***put on*** ~ **1**. 乱摆架子。**2**. 【台球】侧击使旋转,给球一捻。~ ***by*** ~ 并排着,并肩,连接着(*with*)。~ ***door trade*** 〔美拳〕临时买票入场的观众。***stand by sb.'s*** ~ 站在某人方面,伙同某人。***take*** ~***s*** [***a*** ~] 左袒,偏袒;拥护(某方面)。

II ***a***. **1**. 旁,旁边的,侧面的;横。**2**. 次要的,枝节的,副的;片面的。*a* ~ *mark* 旁注。*a* ~ *issue* 枝节问题。*a* ~ *job* 副业。

III ***vi***. **1**. 支持;偏袒,附和,站在…的一边(*with*)。**2**. 宽度仅有…。**3**. 〔英俚〕摆架子。—***vt***. **1**. 支持;站在…的一边。**2**. (将宰了的猪等)对半切开;刨平(木材等的)

S

侧面;装上侧面;【建】钉上披叠板。3.〔俚〕收拾开;放到一边,推开。*We should* ～ *with the people*. 我们要站在百姓方面。～**arm** 1. *ad*. 由体侧。2. *a*. 体侧的。～**arms** 腰佩武器[刺刀,佩剑,手枪等]。～**band**【无】边(频)带。～**-board** 餐具柜。～**bone** 臀骨;【兽医】环骨肿。～**-burns**〔*pl*.〕〔美〕短连鬓胡子。～**car** 1.(摩托车的)边车;(爱尔兰的)轻便三轮马车。2.〔常 S-〕鸡尾酒。～**chain**【化】侧链。～**check**(马缰绳的)侧勒。～**circuit**【电】实线电路。～**crops** 杂粮。～**dish**【烹】添菜,小菜。～**drum**(军用)小鼓。～**effect**(药物)副作用。～**elevation** 侧视图。～**entrance** 侧门。～**foot** *vt*., *vi*.【足球】用脚的侧面踢(球)。～**kick**〔美俚〕老伙伴,朋友;死党。～**light** 1. 侧面光;边窗;舷窗;舷灯。2.(报刊上的)杂闻;间接的说明(*let in* [*throw*] *a* ～ *light on* [*upon*]... 间接说明,偶然证明)。～**line** 旁线,横线;副业,兼职;(本业以外的)兼售商品。～**long** *ad*., *a*. 倾斜地(的);横向地(的);间接地(的)(*give sb*. *a* ～ *long glance* 斜眼看人,瞟人)。～**-looking** *a*.(雷达、声纳)侧向扫描的,侧视的(指以锐角发射信号以获得侧面图像)。～**man**(爵士音乐)乐队队员,伴奏者。～**meat** 肋肉〔尤指腌的或烟熏过的〕。～**money** 横财。～**note** 旁注。～**piece** 侧部,边件。～**saddle** 女鞍。～**scanning** *a*. =～looking. ～**shaft**【机】侧轴,副轴。～**show** 余兴;枝节问题,小问题,小事件。～**slip** 1. 旁枝;私生子。2. 舞台上首和下首的槽〔大道具出入用〕。3.【空】(机翼)侧滑;沿横轴方向的运动。～**splitter**〔俚〕叫人笑痛肚皮的笑话。～**splitting** *a*. 笑痛肚皮的。～**step** 1. *n*. 向旁边避让一步;(上车下车的)踏板。2. *vt*., *vi*. 向旁边避让;靠向旁边;〔美俚〕逃避,规避。～**stroke** 侧击,横击;侧泳,横泳;附带行动。～**swipe** 1. *vt*., *vi*. 擦边撞击。2. *n*. 擦撞。～**tone** 侧音。～**track** 1. *n*.〔主美〕【铁路】(等候交车的)岔道,侧线。2. *vt*.〔主美〕转入侧线;〔转义〕降到从属地位;避让;扣压,拖延(事件);转变(话题)。～**view** 侧面图;侧面形状。～**walk**〔美〕人行道(=〔英〕*pavement*)。～**walk superintendent**〔美口〕站在路边看拆建房屋的闲人。～**wall** 轮胎壁。～**ward** 1. *a*. 旁,横,侧面的。2. *ad*. =～wards. ～**wards** *ad*. 横,斜,向旁边,从旁边。～**way** 1. *n*. 小路,岔路;人行道。2. *ad*., *a*. =～ways. ～**ways** *ad*., *a*. 旁,横,斜着,从旁边。～**-wheel** *a*. 有明轮的(船)。～**wheeler**〔美〕明轮船。～**whiskers** 络腮胡子。～**wind**〔英〕1. *n*. 侧风;间接的影响[手段、方法]。2. *a*. 间接的。～**winder** *n*.〔美〕1. 响尾蛇(导弹)。2. 横击,侧击。～**wise** *ad*., *a*. =～ways.

sid·er [ˈsaidə; ˋsaɪdɚ] *n*. 帮派成员。

si·de·re·al [saiˈdiəriəl; saɪˋdɪrɪəl] *a*.【天】星的,恒星的;星座的。～ *light* 星光。～ **day** 恒星日〔23 时 56 分〕。～ **hour** 恒星时〔恒星日的 1/24〕。～ **year** 恒星年〔365 日 6 时 9 分 9 秒〕。

sid·er·ite [ˈsidərait; ˋsɪdəˏraɪt] *n*.【矿】菱铁矿;陨铁。

sid·e·rog·ra·phy [ˌsidəˈrɔgrəfi; ˏsɪdəˋrɑgrəfɪ] *n*. 雕钢术;钢板雕刻(复制)术。

sid·er·o·lite [ˈsidərəlait; ˋsɪdərəˏlaɪt] *n*. 铁陨石。

sid·er·o·sis [ˌsidəˈrəusis; ˏsɪdəˋrosɪs] *n*.【医】(因吸进铁粉发生的)铁质沉着病,铁尘肺。

si·des·man [ˈsaidzmən; ˋsaɪdzmən] *n*. 党羽,同党;副教区委员;教会副执事。

si·di [ˈsiːdi; ˋsidɪ] *n*.〔印度和非洲东部用语〕埃塞俄比亚[衣索比亚]人;黑人。

sid·ing [ˈsaidiŋ; ˋsaɪdɪŋ] *n*. 1. 偏袒,附和,支持。2.【铁路】(等候交车等用的)岔道,侧线;〔美〕【建】披叠板;【船】(船材的)边宽;(运河等的)让船处。

si·dle [ˈsaidl; ˋsaɪdḷ] *vi*.(羞怯或偷偷地)侧身而行;侧身挨近(*up*)。

Sid·ney, Syd·ney [ˈsidni; ˋsɪdnɪ] *n*. 西德尼〔姓氏,男子名〕。

Si·don [ˈsaidn; ˋsaɪdṇ] *n*. 希登〔即 Saida 赛达〕〔黎巴嫩港市〕。

sid·y [ˈsaidi; ˋsaɪdɪ] *a*.〔口〕高视阔步的,趾高气扬的,傲慢的。

Sie·bold [ˈziːbɔlt; ˋzibɑlt] **P. F. von** 席博尔特〔1796—1866,德国博物学家〕。

siè·cle [ˈsjekl; ˋsjɛkḷ] *n*.(*pl*. ***-cles*** [-kl; -kḷ])〔F.〕百年,一世纪;年代,时代。

siege [siːdʒ; sidʒ] **I** *n*. 1. 包围,围攻;被围攻;围攻期间。2. 说服,劝诱;强求;长期努力;长期折磨;不断袭击。3. 炉底,炉床。*a regular* ～ 正攻法。*a state of* ～ 戒严。～ *warfare* 包围战。***lay*** ～ ***to*** 包围,围攻。***lay*** ～ ***to a lady's heart*** 千方设法地追求女人。***press*** [***push***] ***the*** ～ 猛烈围攻。***raise the*** ～ ***of*** 解…的围;停止围攻。***stand a*** ～ 抵御围攻。***under heavy*** ～ ***by*** 在…的重重包围之中。***undergo a*** ～ 被围攻。**II** *vt*.〔古〕围攻,包围。～**-basket** 堡篮;弹盾。～ **gun** 攻城炮。～ **money**, ～ **piece**(受围城市临时发行的)应急货币。～ **train** 攻城炮兵连。～**works**〔*pl*.〕攻城设施。

Sieg·fried [ˈsiːgfriːd; ˋsigfrid] *n*. 齐格弗里德〔男子名〕。～ **line**(二战时德国西部边境的)齐格菲防线。

Sieg Heil [ˈziːkˈhail; zikˋhaɪl]〔G.〕胜利〔德国法西斯分子见面时招呼用语〕。

sie·mens [ˈsiːmənz; ˋsimenz] *n*.〔单复同〕【电】西门子(亦作"姆欧",电导单位)。

si·en·na [siˈenə; sɪˋenə] *n*. 浓黄土〔一种矿物颜料〕;赭石;赭色。*raw* ～ 生赭石〔黄色颜料〕。*burnt* ～ 煅赭石〔红黄色颜料〕。

Si·en(n)·ese [ˌsaiəˈniːz, ˌsiː-; ˏsiənˋiz] **I** *a*.(意大利都市)西爱那(Sienna)的。*the* ～ *school*(13、14 世纪的)西爱那画派。**II** *n*.〔*sing*., *pl*.〕西爱那人。

Si·er·ra [ˈsiərə; ˋsɪrə] 通讯中用以代表字母 S 的词。

si·er·ra [ˈsiərə, siˈerə; sɪˋɛrə] *n*. 1.〔美〕【地】锯齿山脊;岭。2.【鱼】马鲛。

Si·er·ra Le·o·ne [ˈsiərə liˈəun; sɪˋɛrə lɪˋonɪ] 塞拉利昂〔旧译塞拉勒窝内〕(非洲)。

si·es·ta [siˈestə; sɪˋɛstə] **I** *n*.(特指西班牙、拉丁美洲等国的)午睡;〔美剧〕闭场(时间)。**II** *vi*. 午睡。

sieur [sjœːr; sjɚ] *n*.〔F.〕〔古〕先生〔相当于 sir 的尊称〕。

sieve [siv; sɪv] **I** *n*. 1.(细眼)筛。2.(约装一 bushel 的)粗筐。3.〔喻〕嘴松的人,守不住秘密的人,嘴不严的人。*a head* [*memory*] *like a* ～ 记性糟透了。*draw water with a* ～ = *pour water into a* ～ 白费气力,徒劳。*as leaky as a* ～ 嘴松,容易泄漏秘密。**II** *vt*. 筛,筛选。～ **tube**【植】筛管。

sif·fleur [siˈfləː; sɪˋflɚ] *n*.(*pl*. ～*s*; *fem*. ***siffleuse***, [-fləːz; -flɚz])〔F.〕口哨音乐家。

sift [sift; sɪft] *vt*. 1. 筛,筛分;精选;细查;清理。2. 在…上撒(胡椒等)(*over*; *upon*)。—*vi*. 1. 被筛下。2. 精选;详查(*into*)。3. 落进。～ *the flour from the bran* 把面粉从麦麸中筛出来。

sift·er [ˈsiftə; ˋsɪftɚ] *n*. 筛者;精选者;细选者;筛子;撒粉器。

sift·ings [ˈsiftiŋz; ˋsɪftɪŋz] *n*.〔*pl*.〕1. 筛出来的东西,似筛下来的东西。2. 筛除物;杂质。

SIG = Signal Corps 通信兵(部队)。

Sig. = Signor; signal; signature.

sigh [sai; saɪ] **I** *n*. 叹气,叹息(声);(风、树的)啸声,呜咽声。*draw* [*fetch*, *heave*] *a* ～ 叹气,抽口气。**II** *vi*. 1. 叹气,叹息。2. 悲叹;渴慕(*for*)。3.(风等)呜咽呼啸。—*vt*. 叹息着说(*forth*; *out*)。

sigh·ing·ly [ˈsaiiŋli; ˋsaɪɪŋlɪ] *ad*. 叹息地;呼啸着;哀鸣着。

sight [sait; saɪt] **I** *n*. 1. 视力,视觉。2. 眼界,视域,视界,视距。3. 观看;壮观;奇观;风景;〔the ～s〕名胜。4. 光景,情景;视察,观察。5. 意见,见解。6. 视门,窥孔;瞄准,照准;(枪、炮的)准星,瞄准器。7.〔a ～〕〔口〕许多,大量。8.〔口语〕机会。9.〔美〕直线,直路。10.〔美〕说笑话逗同伴快活的牧童。*have long* ~ 看得远。*have far* ~ 有远见。*short* ~ [*near* ~] 近视! 眼光短浅,缺乏远见。*Get out of my* ~! 滚开! *I cannot bear the* ~ *of him*. = *I hate the very* ~ *of him*. 我连看也不要看他。*a beautiful* ~ 美景。*a bill payable at long* [*short*] ~ 见票后远期[短期]照付的票据。*a perfect* ~ 实实在在的壮观;十足的笑话。*see* [*do*] *the* ~*s of London* 游览伦敦名胜古迹。*a radar* ~ 雷达瞄准器。***a*(*long*) ~ *better*** 〔口〕比…好得多,远胜。***a ~ for sore eyes*** 看着舒服的东西;佳客,珍品(等)。***a ~ of*** 非常多的。***at first ~*** 一见就;乍看起来(*love at first* ~ 一见倾心)。***at ~*** 一看见就;见(票)即(付)(*play music at* ~ 一看见乐谱就演奏得出。*read at* ~ 读得流利)。***at the ~ of*** 一看见就。***be in ~*** 看得见,在眼前。***catch* [*have*, *gain*, *get*] *~ of*** 发现,看出。***come in ~*** 呈现在眼前;可以望见。***find favour in sb.'s ~*** 受某人欢迎,得某人宠爱,被某人看中。***go* [*get*] *out of ~*** 看不见了。***in full of ~*** 【商】暂时入口申请书。***in one's own ~*** 由自己的眼光看来,照自己的见解。***in sb.'s ~*** 在某人面前;照某人的眼光看来,由某人来看(*Do what is right in your* ~. 你认为该做的就做吧)。***in ~*** 看得见(*Peace is in* ~. 和平不远了)。***in* [*within*] *~ of*** 在看得见…的地方。***in the ~ of*** 由…看来。***keep sth. in ~ = keep ~ of sth.*** 看守物件。***know by ~*** 曾经见过,见过面。***line of ~*** 瞄准线,视线。***lose one's ~*** 失明,成瞎子。***lose ~ of*** 看不见了…,看漏了…;忘了…;失踪了。***make a ~ of oneself*** 打扮得故意使人注意;给人取笑。***not by a long ~*** 远不及。***on ~ = at ~***. ***out of ~*** 1. 在看不见的地方,看不见。2.〔口语〕(瘦得)不成样子。3.〔口〕好到极点,非常出色;无可争辩地,毫无问题地,绝对地(*Out of* ~, *out of mind*. 离久情疏)。***put out of ~*** 藏起;用尽;吃掉,喝掉。~ ***unseen*** 〔美商〕不看现货。***take a ~ of*** 看。***take ~*** 瞄准。***upon ~ = at ~***.

II *a*. 一看就能做[演奏,翻译]的,不必预先准备的;【商】见票即照付的。~ *translation* 看到原文就下笔的翻译。III *vt*. 1. 看见;观测(天体等);熟视。2. 给…装瞄准器。3. 调准瞄准器;瞄准。4. 出示,给看(票据等)。—*vi*. 瞄准;(向某一方向)察看。~***ing board*** 测视牌。~***ing pendant*** 瞄准锤。~***ing shot*** 试射,练射。~ **gag** 哑剧;不说话而充分表示意义的可笑场面。~**line** 【剧】(观众)视线〔剧场中每一座位都能无阻地看清舞台面的线〕。~ **reading** 见谱即奏[唱],见文即译[读,理解]。~**worthy** *a*. 值得看的。

sight·ed [ˈsaitid; ˋsaɪtɪd] *a*. 〔用以构成复合词〕…视的,眼光…的,…视眼的。*near-* [*far-*] ~ 近[远]视的。

sight·less [ˈsaitlis; ˋsaɪtlɪs] *a*. 无视力的,盲,瞎;〔罕、诗〕看不见的。

sight·ly [ˈsaitli; ˋsaɪtlɪ] *a*. 好看的;显眼的;〔美〕可以眺望风景的。

sight·see [ˈsaitsi:; ˋsaɪtˏsi] *vt*. (*-saw*; *-seen*; *-ing*)〔美〕游览,参观。**-r** *n*. 游览者,参观者。

sight·see·ing [ˈsaitsi:iŋ; ˋsaɪtˏsiɪŋ] I *n*. 游览,观光。II *a*. 游览的,参观的。*a* ~ *car* 游览汽车。*a* ~ *party* 参观团。

sig·il [ˈsidʒil, 常读 ˈsig-; ˋsɪdʒəl,ˋsɪg-] *n*. 1. 印,印章。2. 魔符;魔法;魔。

sig·int, SIG·INT [ˈsigint; ˋsɪgɪnt] *n*. 信号情报〔指通过监测无线电通讯或其他电子情报来截获传输的信号〕。

sig·ma [ˈsigmə; ˋsɪgmə] *n*. 希腊字母表的第十八字母〔Σ, σ, s, 相当于英语的 s〕【动、植】S [Σ] 形;【心】千分之一秒。

sig·mate [ˈsigmeit; ˋsɪgmet] I *vt*. 加 s 在…的词尾。II *a*. S形的;Σ形的。

sig·moid [ˈsigmɔid; ˋsɪgmɔɪd] *a*., *n*. S [Σ]形的;【医】乙状的;乙状结肠。*the* ~ *flexure* 【解】乙状弯曲。~**o-scope** 【医】乙状结肠窥镜。

Sig·mund [ˈsigmənd; ˋsɪgmənd] *n*. 西格蒙德〔男子名〕。

sign [sain; saɪn] I *n*. 1. 记号,符号。2. 信号,暗号。3. (示意的)姿势,手势;表示。4. 招牌,广告(牌)。5. 形迹、痕迹〔常与 no 连用〕;〔美〕(野兽的)足迹。6. 证据;预兆;朕兆;性状;【医】症状。7.【圣】奇迹。8.【天】(黄道十二宫的)宫。9.〔罕〕徽章;旗。*deaf-and-dumb* ~*s* 聋哑人的手势;聋哑字母。*talk in* ~*s* 用手势表达想说的话,打手势语。~ *of assent* 同意的表示。*a call* ~ 呼号。~*s and wonders* 奇迹。~ *and countersign* 问答口令;暗语问答,暗号。***bear the ~ of the times*** 带有时代的特征。***give the high ~*** 〔美〕发出信号〔尤指危险的信号〕。***in ~ of*** 作为…的记号。***make a ~ to*** 对…作暗号[打手势]。***make no ~ of*** 没有…的样子[征象]。***show a ~ of*** 现出…的样子或形迹,有…的征兆。~ ***of the cross*** 划押,作为签名的十字记号;用手划的十字。***There are ~s of....*** 有…的征象。

II *vt*. 1. 用信号表示,做姿势通知;预示。2. 签名于,署名于,画押于;签名盖章约定;〔美〕使签名,使订约;(签名)雇用;加记号于。3. 画十字于。—*vi*. 用姿势通知,打手势,使眼色,做暗号;签名;订契约(*on*)。~*ed and sealed* 签了名盖了章。~*ed*, *sealed*, *and delivered* 【法】已签名盖章交还,决定。*The treaty was* ~*ed today*. 条约今天签了字了。*He* ~*ed to me to enter the garden*. 他招手要我进园里。~ **assent** (用动作)表示同意。~ *away* 在证书上签字让与(财产等)。~ **for** 签收。~ **in** (使)签到[报到,登记]。~ **off** 【无】1. 广播完毕,收播。2. 签字发誓戒绝;废除(契约);断绝(关系)。3.〔美俚〕停止讲话,住嘴,停止。4. 签字结束(写信等)。~ **on** 签字聘用[就聘];签字承认;作工作记录。~ **over** = ~ *away*. ~ **up** 〔美口〕签字应征[应聘,受雇];(报名)参加。~**board** 招牌;〔美〕招贴板,布告板。~ **digit** 【电脑】符号数位。~ **language** 手势语,身势语。~ **manual** 1. (国王的)亲笔署名。2. 特征,特性。~ **off** 广播结束(时的用语);停止工作。~ **painter** 写招牌的(人)。~ **post** 1. *n*. 招牌柱,广告柱;路标;明显的表示[线索,症状]。2. *vt*. 在…设置招牌柱[路标等];为…提供方向指示[指导等]。

sig·nal [ˈsignl; ˋsɪgnl] I *n*. 1. 信号,暗号;信号器。2. 动机,导火线(*for*)。3. 预兆,征象。*call* ~ 【无】呼号。*an alarm* ~ 警报(器)。*an information* ~ 〔美〕暴风警报(旗)。*an international code of* ~*s* 国际通用信号。*a* ~ *of distress* = *a distress* ~ 船只失事信号。II *a*. 1. 暗号的,作信号用的。2. 显著的,非常的,优越的。*a* ~ *victory* [*defeat*] 大胜[败]。III *vt*., *vi*. (〔英〕*-ll-*) 发信号[警报]给(人、船等);用信号[警报]通知(暴风、危险等);用动作[手势]示意;预示。*a* ~*ing bomb* 信号弹。~ **book** (尤指陆海军等的)信号[旗语]通信手册。~ **box** (铁路的)信号房。~ **code** 信号密码。~ **corps** 通信队;[S- C-]〔美陆军〕通信兵团。~ **fire** 烽火,烽烟。~ **flag** 信号旗。~ **generator** 发(信)号机。~ **gun** 号炮。~(**s**) **intelligence** 信号[通讯]情报。~ **lamp** 信号灯。~**man** 信号员。~**ment** 特征描述〔如缉捕令中对逃犯的描述〕。~**officer** 【军】通信主任;信号军官。~ **plate** (电视摄像机前的)信号板。~ **rocket** 信号火箭。~ **station** 信号所,望楼。~ **word** 【语】信号词(如连接词、代词、介词、冠词等)。

sig·nal·ize [ˈsignəlaiz; ˋsɪgnəˏlaɪz] *vt*. 1. 用信号通知。2. 使著名;使显眼;表明;显示。3. 在…设置交通信号。~ *a victory by public rejoicing* 万众欢腾庆祝胜利。~ *oneself by* 因…著名。

sig·nal·ly [ˈsignəli; ˋsɪgnlɪ] *ad*. 显著,突出,非常。

sig·na·to·ry [ˈsignətəri; ˋsɪgnəˏtorɪ] I *a*. 签署的,签约的。II *n*. 签字人;签约国,缔盟国。*the* ~ *powers to a treaty* 条约签字国,缔约国。

sig·na·ture [ˈsignitʃə, -nətʃə; ˋsɪgnətʃɚ] *n*. 1. 签名,署名,画押,盖章。2.【乐】记号〔调号或拍子记号〕;【无】(广

S

播节目开始或完毕的)信号曲;【代数】符号差;【印】装钉用折叠号码;【医古】外征;【药】(注明在药瓶上的)用法说明〔略 S, sig.〕;〔古〕象征,特征。*add one's* ～ *to* 在…上签字。*a time* ～【乐】拍子记号。*a key* ～【乐】调号。*bear the* ～ 有署名,签过字。*over sb.'s* ～ 经某人签名,有某人签字为凭。～ **drive** 签名运动。～ **dynamics** 签名动力学〔一种电子测定签名动作全过程的技术〕。～ **loan**【经】无担保贷款。～ **tune** (无线电广播或电影的)信号(歌)曲。

sign·er [ˈsainə; ˋsaɪnɚ] *n*. 签名人;(用手势)示意者;〔S-〕美国独立宣言署名人。

sig·net [ˈsignit; ˋsɪgnɪt] *n*. **1**. 印;图章;〔the ～〕玺。**2**. 〔喻〕痕迹,影像。***writer to the*** ～〔Scot.〕【法】律师。～ **ring** 图章戒指。

sig·nif·i·cance [sigˈnifikəns; sɪgˋnɪfəkəns] *n*. **1**. 有意义,意味深长;意义,旨趣。**2**. 重要(性),紧要,重大;【统】显著性。*a word of great* ～ 意味深长的一个词。***of no*** [***little***] ～ 不重要的,无关紧要的。

sig·nif·i·cant [sigˈnifikənt; sɪgˋnɪfəkənt] *a*. **1**. 有意义的;大有讲究的,意味深长的。**2**. 表明…的 (*of*)。**3**. 重要的,重大的,值得注意的。**4**. 有效的,有影响的。**5**. 非偶然的。**6**.【语】有区别的;有实义的。*a historically* ～ *meeting* 一次有历史意义的会议。*a* ～ *wink* 意味深长的眼色。*a gesture* ～ *of consent* 说明同意的姿态。～ *figures*【数】有效数字。**-ly** *ad*.

sig·ni·fi·ca·tion [ˌsignifiˈkeiʃən; sɪgˏnɪfəˋkeʃən] *n*. 意义,含意;〔罕〕表示;正式通知。*a primary* ～ 本义。

sig·nif·i·ca·tive [sigˈnifikətiv, -keit-; sɪgˋnɪfəˏketɪv] *a*. **1**. 有意义的;意味深长的。**2**. 表示…的 (*of*)。**3**. 为…提供推定证据的。～ *of approval* 表示答应了的。

sig·ni·fy [ˈsignifai; ˋsɪgnəˏfaɪ] *vt*. (***-fied***) **1**. 表示,象征;意味。**2**. 成为预兆,预示。**3**. 〔常用于否定句〕有重大关系[影响]。*Please* ～. 请表示意见。*What does it* ～? 那是什么意思呢? 这有什么关系呢? *What does K. G.* ～? K. G. 是什么意思? —*vi*. **1**. 有重要性,要紧。**2**. 〔美俚〕装模作样,装腔作势。*It does not* ～. 没有什么关系。～ ***little*** 不大重要,没有什么关(*to*)。～ ***much*** 很重要,有很大关系 (*to*)。

si·gnior [ˈsiːnjɔː; ˋsinjɔr] *n*. 〔英〕=〔It.〕*Signor*.

si·gnor [ˈsiːnjɔː; ˋsinjor], ***si·gno·re*** [siːˈnjɔːre; sinˋjorɛ] *n*. 〔It.〕(*pl*. ***signo·ri*** [-ri; -rɪ]) **1**. 〔S-〕= Mr. 或 Sir. **2**. (特指意大利的)贵族,绅士。

Si·gno·ra [siːˈnjɔːrə; sinˋjorə] *n*. (*pl*. ***-re*** [-re; -rɛ]) 〔It.〕夫人,太太〔相当于 Madam, Mrs.〕。

si·gno·re [siːˈnjəure; sinˋjorɛ] *n*. (*pl*. ***si·gno·ri*** [-ri; -rɪ]) **1**. 〔S-〕先生〔意大利尊称呼语,单独使用,不连姓名〕。**2**. 绅士,贵族。

Si·gno·ri·na [ˌsiːnjəˈriːnə; ˏsinjəˋrinə] *n*. 〔It.〕(*pl*. ***-ne*** [-nei; -ne]) **1**. 小姐〔对少女的尊称〕。**2**. 姑娘,少女。

si·gno·ri·no [sinjəuˈriːnəu, E. ˌsinjəˈriːnəu; sɪnjəˋrino, ˏsɪnjəˋrino] *n*. (*pl*. ***-ri·ni*** [-niː; -ni]; E. ***-ri·nos***) **1**. 〔S-〕少爷〔对青年男子的尊称〕。**2**. 青年男子,少年。

sig·no·ry [ˈsiːnjəri; ˋsinjəri] *n*. = seigniory。

Si·grid [ˈsigrid; ˋsɪgrɪd] *n*. 西格丽德〔女子名〕。

Sikh [siːk; sik] **I** *n*. (印度的)锡克教徒。**II** *a*. 锡克教徒的,锡克教徒似的。**-ism** *n*.

Sik·kim [ˈsikim; ˋsɪkɪm] *n*. 锡金〔亚洲〕。

sil [sil; sɪl] *n*. 〔美〕傻子 (= silly person)。

si·lage [ˈsailidʒ; ˋsaɪlɪdʒ] **I** *n*. 青贮饲料。*a* ～ *cutter* 切草机。**II** *vt*. 青贮 (= ensilage)。

Si·las [ˈsailəs; ˋsaɪləs] *n*. 赛拉斯〔男子名〕。

Si·las·tic [siˈlæstik; sɪˋlæstɪk] *n*.【化】矽橡胶〔原为商标名〕。

si·lence [ˈsailəns; ˋsaɪləns] **I** *n*. **1**. 沉默,无言;无表示;无声,沉静,肃静,寂静;【乐】停止。**2**. 忘却,湮没;无表示;无音讯。*a man of* ～ 沉默寡言的人。*S- gives consent*. 沉默即承认,没有表示就是承认。*I beg pardon for my long* ～. 长久没有写信给你,请原谅。*The rest is* ～. 其余就不知道了。***break*** ～ 打破沉默,开口讲话。***buy sb.'s*** ～ 收买某人使不开口[守秘密]。***in*** ～ 沉默着,静静地。***keep*** ～ 保持沉默,不开口。***observe a moment's*** ～ ***in honour of*** 为(某人等)静默一分钟。***pass a matter with*** ～ = ***pass over a matter in*** ～ 不过问某事。***pass into*** ～ 被遗忘。***put to*** ～ = ***reduce to*** ～ 把…驳得哑口无言。**II** *vt*. **1**. 使(嘈杂声音等)静下来;堵住…的嘴,使无言;使(敌人的炮台等)沉默,打哑。**2**. 把…说得无话可对,使哑口无言;使停止;使安静。*a* ～*d gun* 装有消音器的枪。**III** *int*. 请静一静,嘘,喂。～**-cloth** 桌布垫布。

si·lenc·er [ˈsailənsə; ˋsaɪlənsɚ] *n*. **1**. 使沉默的人。**2**.【机】消音装置,消声器;【炮】消音器。**3**. 压倒对方的议论。

si·lent [ˈsailənt; ˋsaɪlənt] *a*. **1**. 沉默的,无言的;寡言的;无声的,寂静的。**2**. 未作记述的,没有提及的;未说出的。**3**. 音讯不通的;静止的,不活动的。**4**.【语音】不发音的。**5**.【商】匿[隐]名的。*a* ～ *thought* [*agreement*] 默想[认]。*a* ～ *film* 默片。*S- waters run deep*. 静流水深。*History is* ～ *about it*. 史书上没有记述这件事情。～ *partner* 〔美〕匿名合伙人。～ ***as the grave*** 没有一点声音。～ **butler** 〔美〕烟灰盒。～ **drama** 哑剧。～ **(earth)quake**【地】无声地震〔指地壳构造板块的滑动或移动〕。**(the) S- Service** 英国海军。～ **service** 〔美〕海军;潜艇部队。**-ly** *ad*. 默然,寂然,不声不响。**-ness** *n*.

Si·le·nus [saiˈliːnəs; saɪˋlinəs] *n*. **1**.【希腊】塞列努斯〔森林神的首领,酒神的养父〕。**2**. 〔S-〕= satyr. **3**. 愉快的醉汉。

Si·le·sia [saiˈliːzjə; saɪˋliʃɪə] *n*. **1**. 西利西亚〔中欧东部一地区〕。**2**. 〔s-〕(作窗帘或衣里用的)一种牢固而轻软的亚麻布[斜纹布]。

si·le·si·a [saiˈliːzjə; səˋliʃə] *n*. 亚麻布;薄斜纹布。

Si·lex [ˈsaileks; ˋsaɪlɛks] *n*. **1**. 〔美〕玻璃咖啡壶〔商标名〕。**2**. [s-] = silica. **3**. 无水矽酸制成的耐热玻璃。

sil·hou·ette [ˌsilu(ː)ˈet; ˏsɪluˋɛt] **I** *n*. 侧面影像,剪影;轮廓,廓影。***in*** ～ = ***on*** ～ 像影画一样,成剪影;呈现轮廓。**II** *vt*. 〔常用被动语态〕给…画侧面影像;使映出影子;使呈现轮廓。

sil·i·ca [ˈsilikə; ˋsɪlɪkə] *n*.【矿】硅石,二氧化硅。～ **gel** (氧化)硅胶。～ **glass** 石英玻璃 (= quartz glass)。

sil·i·cate [ˈsilikit; ˋsɪlɪkɪt] *n*.【化】硅盐酸。

si·li·ceous [siˈliʃəs; sɪˋlɪʃəs] *a*. = silicious.

si·lic·ic [siˈlisik; səˋlɪsɪk] *a*. **1**. 含硅的。**2**. 硅的,像硅的。～ *acid*【化】硅酸。

sil·i·cide [ˈsiliˌsaid; ˋsɪlɪˏsaɪd] *n*.【化】硅化物。

sil·i·cif·er·ous [ˌsiliˈsifərəs; ˏsɪlɪˋsɪfərəs] *a*.【化】含硅的,生硅土的。

si·lic·i·fy [siˈlisifai; sɪˋlɪsəˏfaɪ] *vt*., *vi*. (***-fied***)【化】(使)硅化。

si·li·cious [siˈliʃəs; sɪˋlɪʃəs] *a*. 硅质的,含硅的 (= siliceous)。～ *sand stone* 玻璃砂。

si·li·ci·um [siˈliʃiəm; sɪˋlɪʃɪəm] *n*.【化】硅 (silicon 的旧称)。～ **steel**【冶】硅钢。

sil·i·cle [ˈsilikl; ˋsɪlɪkl] *n*.【植】角,短荚。**-cu·lar** *a*.

sil·i·con [ˈsilikən; ˋsɪlɪkən] *n*. = silicium. **Silicon Alley** 硅巷〔原指电脑业集中的纽约一社区,现可泛指城市中的电脑业集中区,源出 Sikcon Valley〕。～ **carbide**【化】碳化硅(俗称金钢砂)。～ **controlled rectifier** 可控硅整流器。～ **transistor** 硅晶体管。**Silicon Valley** 硅谷〔美国加州南部圣他克拉拉谷地高科技电脑业云集的地区〕。

sil·i·cone [ˈsilikəun; ˋsɪlɪkon] **I** *n*.【化】(聚)硅氧烷;硅有机树脂;(聚)硅酮。**II** *vt*.【美容】用硅胶对(妇女)进行丰乳手术。～ **neuron**【计】模拟神经元硅片〔一种正在试验中的模拟人的神经细胞功能的硅片〕。～ **rubber**

【化】硅(氧)橡胶。

sil·i·co·sis [ˌsiliˈkəusis; ˏsɪlɪˋkosɪs] *n*.【医】石末沉着病,硅肺。

si·lic·u·la [siˈlikjulə; sɪˋlɪkjʊlə] *n*. (*pl*. **-lae** [-ˌliː; -ˏli]) = silicle.

si·lic·u·lose [siˈlikjuˌləus; sɪˋlɪkjʊˏlos] *a*.【植】1. 有短角的。2. 短角形的。

sil·i·qua [ˈsilikwə; ˋsɪlɪkwə] *n*. (*pl*. **-quae** [-kwiː; -kwi]) 1. = silique. 2.【解】长角状包被。

si·lique [siˈliːk; sɪˋlik] *n*.【植】长角(果)〔十字花科的长形果实〕。

silk [silk; sɪlk] *n*. 1. 蚕丝;丝;绸,绢,缎;〔*pl*.〕绸衣〔特指拳师、骑师在比赛时所穿的〕。2. 丝状物。3.〔英〕皇室律师的绸袍;〔口〕皇室律师。4.(宝石等的)绢丝光泽。5. 玉米的须。6. 降落伞。*artificial* ~ (= artificial fibre) 人造丝。*raw* ~ 生丝。*air* ~ 空心丝。***hit the*** ~ 用降落伞降落。***sit among the*** **~*s*** = ***take*** (***the***) ~ 当皇室律师。***thrown*** ~ 丝经,搓好的丝。~ **conditioning** 生丝检查。~ **cotton** (**tree**) 吉贝(树)。~ **gland**【动】丝腺。~ **gown** 皇室律师绸袍。~ **hat** 大礼帽。~ **mill** 丝厂;织绸厂。~ **paper** 薄纸。~**screen** (丝绢网印花用的)丝绢网。~**screen process**【纺】丝绢网印花法。~-**stocking** 1. *n*. 有闲阶级(的人);贵族。2.〔美〕*a*. 穿着长统丝袜的;奢华的;贵族(一样)的。~**weed**【植】马利筋。~**worm** 蚕 (*a ~worm egg raising station* 种蚕场)。

silk·en [ˈsilkən; ˋsɪlkən] *a*. 1. 丝(制)的;丝一样的;绸缎的;〔诗〕柔软的,光滑的,有丝光的;优雅的。2. 穿着绸衣的,奢华的。3. 圆滑的。~ *rustling* 绸衣的簌簌声。*her* ~ *locks* 她的柔软光滑的头发。

silk·y [ˈsilki; ˋsɪlkɪ] *a*. 1. 丝一样的,像绸缎的;光滑的,有丝光的。2. 优雅的,温柔的;善于奉承的,圆滑的。3.(酒)舐着舒服的。**-i·ness** *n*.

sill [sil; sɪl] *n*. 1.【建】基石,基本;踏板;楣,门槛,窗台。2.【地】岩床,岩层,海底山脊;平巷底,矿山巷道的底面;底梁。3.【机】(车体底框的)梁。

sil·la·bub [ˈsiləbʌb; ˋsɪləˏbʌb] *n*. 一种用牛奶与葡萄酒合成的甜饮料;华而不实的东西;空洞无物的话。

sil·ler [ˈsilə; ˋsɪlɚ] *n*.〔Scot.〕银;金钱。

sil·li·man·ite [ˈsilimənait; ˋsɪlɪməˏnaɪt] *n*.〔美〕【地】硅线石 (= **fibrolite**)。

sil·ly [ˈsili; ˋsɪlɪ] **I** *a*. (**-li·er**; **-li·est**) 1. 傻的,愚蠢的;无聊的,无意义的,头昏眼花的,稀里糊涂的。2.【板球】逼近三柱门的。3.〔古〕单纯的,天真的;无知的;不中用的。**II** *n*.〔儿、口〕傻子,蠢货。*a* ~ *laugh* 傻笑。*Don't be* ~! 别傻了。*Don't be a* ~! 别胡说! ***be knocked*** ~ 被打得失去知觉。***go*** ~〔口〕成傻瓜。***the*** ~ ***season***〔新闻用语〕新闻饥荒期〔8,9月〕。~ **Billy** 笨蛋。~ **milk**〔美〕酒。~ **money**〔美〕多得用不完的钱。**-li·ly** *ad*. **-li·ness** *n*.

si·lo [ˈsailəu; ˋsaɪlo] **I** *n*. (*pl*. ~*s*) 青贮塔;【飞弹】井状地下仓库,发射井。*an upright* ~ 青贮塔。**II** *vt*. 用青贮塔贮藏(牧草等)。~**buster**〔美军俚〕攻击敌方导弹发射井的核弹。

si·lox·ane [siˈlɔksein; sɪˋlɑksen] *n*.【化】硅氧烷。

silt [silt; sɪlt] **I** *n*. 泥沙,淤泥(沉积处)。~ *content* 淤泥含量。*the total volume of* ~ 淤泥总量。**II** *vt*., *vi*. (用淤泥)阻塞 (*up*);淤积。**-y** *a*.

Si·lu·ri·an [saiˈljuəriən, si-; səˋlʊriən, sɪ-] *n*., *a*. 1. (Wales 南部古代英国住民)志留 (Silures) 人(的)。留人居住地方。2.【地】志留纪(的),志留系(的)。

si·lu·rid [siˈluərid, sai-; sɪˋljurɪd, saɪ-] **I** *n*.【动】鲇科 (*Siluridae*) 的鱼;鲇鱼,鲶。**II** *a*. 鲇科的。

sil·va, sil·van = sylva, sylvan.

sil·ver [ˈsilvə; ˋsɪlvɚ] **I** *n*. 1. 银;银币;钱。2. 银(白)色的。3. 银器;银丝,银边带。4.〔美〕【摄】银盐;硝酸银。**II** *a*. 1. 银的;银制的;像银的;银白的,(头发等)发银光的。2. 银声的,清亮的;雄辩的。3. 和平的,平静的;寂静的。4. 银本位的。5. 25 周年的。*native* ~ 天然银。*fine* [*pure*, *refined*] ~ 纯银。*a* ~ *tongue* 能言善辩。*a* ~ *jubilee* 二十五周年纪念。***be born with a*** ~ ***spoon in one's mouth*** 生于富有家庭。**III** *vt*. 包银,镀银;使成银白色;涂银,涂锡汞合金(在镜子等上);【摄】涂硝酸银子。—*vi*. 变成银一样;(头发)变白;发银光。~ **age** 白银时代〔神话传说中最幸福的黄金时代后情况稍差的时代;文学史上指:1. 罗马 Augustus 皇帝到 Hadrian 皇帝期间(公元 14—138)的拉丁文学隆盛时代。2. Anne 女皇在位时(1701—15)的英国文学隆盛时代〕。~ **anniversary** 25 周年纪念日。~ **bath**【化】银锅;银浴器;【摄】银箔;银盘溶液;银盐溶液槽。~ **bell**【植】银钟花树(又叫 ~-bell tree)。~ **betty**【植】银果胡颓子。~ **birch**【植】纸皮桦 (= paper birch)。~ **bond** 银色铜管乐器乐队。~ **bromide**【化】溴化银。~ **bullets** 1.〔美〕市民认购的战时公债。2.〔美口〕高招,好主意。~ **certificate**〔美〕银元券〔旧时一种可以兑换现银的纸币〕。~ **chloride**【化】氯化银。~ **fish** *n*.【鱼】银色金鱼;【虫】蠹鱼,西洋衣鱼。~ **foil** 银箔。~ **fox**【动】银狐。~-**gilt** *a*. 镀银的。~-**grey** *n*., *a*. 银灰色(的)。~ **hake**【动】银无须鳕。~ **iodide**【化】碘化银。~ **Latin** 白银时代的拉丁语。~ **leaf** 银箔。~ **lining** (失望或不幸中的)一线希望〔一点慰藉〕。~ **nitrate**【化】硝酸银。~ **paper** 上等薄纸;银箔纸;锡纸;【摄】银感光纸。~ **perch**【动】石首鱼;类石首鱼。~ **plate** 银餐具。~-**plated** *a*. 包银的,镀银的。~ **point** 1. 银笔画。2. 银的熔点。~ **protein**【化】蛋白银。~ **salmon**【动】银大马哈鱼 (= coho)。~ **screen** 银幕;电影界。~ **side** 牛腿肉的最好部分。~**side(s)**【动】银汉鱼。~**smith** 银(器)匠。~ **solder** 银焊条。~-**spoon** *a*. 出生于富贵之家的。~ **standard** (通货制的)银本位。**S- State** 银州〔美国内华达州的别名〕。**S- Streak** 银条纹〔英吉利海峡的别名〕。~-**tail**〔澳俚〕有钱人。~-**tongued** *a*. 口才流利的。~ **thaw** [**frost**]【气】雨淞,冻雨 (= glitter ice)。~**ware** 银器,银制品;〔美运〕优胜杯。~ **wedding** (婚后二十五周年的)银婚礼。~**weed**【植】1. 鹅绒委陵菜。2. 银叶花。

sil·ver·i·ness [ˈsilvərinis; ˋsɪlvərɪnɪs] *n*. 1. 像银,银光,银色,银白。2. 声如银铃,银铃声。

sil·ver·ing [ˈsilvəriŋ; ˋsɪlvərɪŋ] *n*. 1. 镀银,包银。2. 镀上的银层;银色光泽。3.【摄】用硝酸银使感光。

sil·ver·ly [ˈsilvəli; ˋsɪlvɚlɪ] *ad*. 像银一样地。

sil·vern [ˈsilvən; ˋsɪlvɚn] *a*. 1. 银的,银制的;像银的。2. 银铃般的,清脆响亮的。3. 第二位的,次好的。4. 银白的。

sil·ver·y [ˈsilvəri; ˋsɪlvərɪ] *a*. 1. 像银一样的,银色的,银白的。2. 银铃一般的,清脆响亮的。3. 含银的;包银的,镀银的。

Sil·via [ˈsilviə; ˋsɪlvɪə] *n*. 西尔维娅〔女子名〕。

sil·vi·cal [ˈsilvikl; ˋsɪlvɪkl̩] *a*. 森林的;造林学的;森林生态学的。

sil·vic·o·lous [silˈvikələs; sɪlˋvɪkələs] *a*. 生长于林地的。

sil·vics [ˈsilviks; ˋsɪlvɪks] *n*. (作单数用)森林生态学。

sil·vi·cul·ture [ˈsilvikʌltʃə; ˋsɪlvɪˏkʌltʃɚ] *n*. 造林学,造林法。**-turist** *n*. 林学家。

s'il vous plaît [sil vu plɛ; ˏsɪlvʊˋplɛ]〔F.〕(= if you please) 请。

SIM = subscriber identity module【电信】用户识别卡。

Sim [sim; sɪm] *n*. Simeon 和 Simon 的昵称。

sim. =〔It.〕*simile*.

si·ma [ˈsaimə; ˋsaɪmə] *n*.【地】硅镁带,硅镁层。

si·mar [siˈmɑː; sɪˋmɑr] *n*. (中世纪后期妇女穿的)宽长袍。

Sim·birsk [simˈbiəsk; sɪmˋbɪrsk] *n*. 辛比尔斯克〔前苏联乌里扬诺夫斯克 (Ulyanovsk) 的旧称〕。

Sim·fe·ro·pol [ˌsimfiˈrəupl; ˏsɪmfəˋrɔpl̩] *n*. 辛非洛普

(辛菲罗波尔)〔前苏联城市〕。

sim·i·an [ˈsimiən; ˋsɪmɪən] ***n.***, ***a.*** 猿(的),类人猿(的);像猿猴的。

sim·i·lar [ˈsimilə; ˋsɪmələ˞] **I** ***a.*** **1.** 近似的,相似的,类似的(*to*)。**2.**【乐】平行前进的。~ *triangles*【数】相似三角形。~ *permutations*【数】同班排列。***be ~ to*** 像,类似。**II** ***n.*** 类似物;相像的人;相似物。**-ly** ***ad.***

sim·i·lar·i·ty [ˌsimiˈlæriti; ˏsɪməˋlærətɪ] ***n.*** **1.** 类似,相像,相似。**2.** 类似点;类似物,相似物。

sim·i·le [ˈsimili; ˋsɪməˏli] ***n.***【修】直喻,明喻。

sim·i·le [ˈsiːmilei; ˋsiməˏle] ***n.*** 〔It.〕【乐】同样,同上〔略 *sim.*〕。

si·mil·i·tude [siˈmilitjuːd; səˋmɪləˏtjud] ***n.*** **1.** 类似,相似(*between*)。**2.** 类似物,一模一样的人。**3.** 样子。**4.** 外貌;〔罕〕比喻;【数】相似。***assume the ~ of*** 装成…的样子。***in ~s*** 用比喻。***in the ~ of*** 模仿着,以…的姿态。***speak*** [***talk***] ***in ~s*** 用比喻说。

sim·i·lize [ˈsimilaiz; ˋsɪməˏlaɪz] ***vi.***, ***vt.*** 用比喻说明。

sim·i·ous [ˈsimiəs; ˋsɪmɪəs] ***a.*** = simian.

sim·i·tar [ˈsimitə; ˋsɪmɪtə˞] ***n.*** = scimitar.

Sim·la [ˈsimlə; ˋsɪmlə] ***n.*** 西姆拉〔印度城市〕。

sim·mer [ˈsimə; ˋsɪmə˞] **I** ***vi.*** 徐徐沸腾,慢慢烧滚;(危机等)处于酝酿中。—***vt.*** (用文火)炖,煨;拼命忍住(笑);压住(怒火)。~ ***down*** 用文火熬浓;冷掉;平定下来。~ ***with anger*** 怒火中烧。**II** ***n.*** **1.** 徐徐沸腾。**2.** 勉强忍住的笑[积怒]。***at a*** [***on the***] ~ 在文火上慢慢煨着;快要沸腾,快要爆发。***bring*** (*water*) ***to a ~*** 使(水)烧滚。

sim·o·le·on [siˈməuliən; sɪˋmolɪən] ***n.*** 〔美俚〕一美元。

Si·mon [ˈsaimən; ˋsaɪmən] ***n.*** 西蒙〔姓氏,爱称:Sim〕。~ **Pure** 真物,真人(*the real ~ Pure* 真物,真人)。**s-pure** **1.** ***n.*** 〔美俚〕业余选手。**2.** ***a.*** 真正的,道地的,原原本本的;业余的,非职业性的。

sim·o·ny [ˈsaiməni; ˋsaɪmənɪ] ***n.*** 圣职买卖(罪)。

si·moom, si·moon [siˈmuːm, -ˈmuːn; sɪˋmum, -ˋmun] ***n.***【气】西蒙风,带沙风暴〔非洲和阿拉伯地方的干热风〕。

simp [simp; sɪmp] ***n.*** 〔美俚〕= simpleton.

sim·pa·ti·co [simˈpɑːtikəu, -ˈpæt-; sɪmˋpɑtɪko, -ˋpæt-] ***a.*** 同情的,性情随和的;相容的,和谐的;意气相投的。

sim·per [ˈsimpə; ˋsɪmpə˞] **I** ***n.*** 傻笑;假笑。**II** ***vi.*** 假笑;傻笑。—***vt.*** 傻[假]笑着说。

sim·ple [ˈsimpl; ˋsɪmpl̩] **I** ***a.*** (***-pler***; ***-plest***) **1.** 单纯的;简单的,简易的;轻便的。**2.** 质仆的,自然的,天真的;朴素的;率直的,坦白的,露骨的。**3.** 无知的,头脑简单的,愚蠢的。**4.** 普通的,平常的。**5.** 卑贱的,身份低微的,无足轻重的。**6.** 完全的,纯粹的。*a ~* (*mode of*) *life* 简单的生活。~ *diet* 简单的饮食,粗茶淡饭。~ *beauty* 纯朴的美。*Mine is a ~ nothing.* 我的东西实在不像样子[不足一道]。*You must be very ~ to be taken in by such a story.* 你会上这种话的当,太老实了。*a ~ soldier* 普通一兵。*a ~ peasant* 一个普通农民。~ *twist of the wrist* 〔美〕易如反掌的事;轻而易举的办法。***gentle and ~*** 〔方〕贵贱,上下。***pure and ~*** 绝对的,完全的,纯粹的,十足的(*It is a mistake pure and ~.* 这是纯粹的错误)。**II** ***n.*** **1.** 头脑简单的人;单纯之物,单体。**2.** 〔古〕药用植物;药草制剂。~ **equation**【化】一次方程式。~ **harmonic motion**【物】简谐运动〔略 S. H. M.〕。~**-hearted** ***a.*** 纯洁的;天真的。~ **interest**【经】单利。~ **leaf**【植】单叶。~**minded** ***a.*** 轻信的,易上当的,头脑迟钝[简单]的(= ~hearted)。~ **past**【语法】简单过去式。~ **pendulum**【物】单摆。~ **sentence**【语法】简单句。**Simple Simon** **1.** 傻瓜西蒙〔一首儿歌里的人物〕。**2.** 傻瓜,笨人。**-ness** ***n.*** 〔罕〕= simplicity.

sim·ple·ton [ˈsimpltən; ˋsɪmpl̩tən] ***n.*** 笨人,傻子。

sim·plex [ˈsimpleks; ˋsɪmplɛks] **I** ***a.*** 单纯的,单一的。【无】单工的;单缸的。**II** ***n.*** (*pl.* ***-plex·es***, ***-pli·ces*** [-pləsiːz; -pləsiz])【数】单纯形。

sim·pli·ci·ter [simˈplisitə; sɪmˋplɪsɪtə˞] ***ad.*** 〔L.〕绝对地,无条件地,完全地,纯然;普遍地,无限地。

sim·plic·i·ty [simˈplisiti; sɪmˋplɪsətɪ] ***n.*** **1.** 单纯;简单,简易;轻便。**2.** 质朴;天真;朴素;诚实。**3.** 无知,愚钝。**4.** 卑贱。

sim·pli·fi·ca·tion [ˌsimplifiˈkeiʃən; ˏsɪmpləfəˋkeʃən] ***n.*** 简单化;单一化;单纯化。

sim·pli·fy [ˈsimplifai; ˋsɪmpl̩əˏfaɪ] ***vt.*** 简化;使简易;使单纯。

sim·plism [ˈsimplizəm; ˋsɪmplɪzm̩] ***n.*** 过分简单化;(看问题)片面(性)。*an astonishing ~ in dealing with international issues* 在处理国际问题上令人吃惊的片面简单。

sim·plist [ˈsimplist; ˋsɪmplɪst] **I** ***n.*** 简单化者,把问题看得过于简单的人。**II** ***a.*** = simplistic.

sim·plis·tic [simˈplistik; sɪmˋplɪstɪk] ***a.*** 把复杂问题搞得过于简单的,简单化的。**-ly** ***ad.***

sim·ply [ˈsimpli; ˋsɪmplɪ] ***ad.*** **1.** 简单地;明白易懂地;坦白地,露骨地;朴素地;天真地;率直地。**2.** 单单,仅仅。**3.** 〔加强语气〕真正,的确,绝对;非常,极。*It is ~ a question of time.* 这不过是时间的问题罢了。*The cold was ~ awful.* 冷得真厉害。*It is ~ beautiful.* 这个的确是美。

Simp·son [ˈsimpsn; ˋsɪmpsn] ***n.*** 辛普森〔姓氏〕。

sim·u·la·crum [ˌsimjuˈleikrəm; ˏsɪmjəˋlekrəm] ***n.*** (*pl.* ***-cra*** [-krə; -krə]) 像;影,幻影;伪品,假像。

sim·u·lant [ˈsimjulənt; ˋsɪmjʊlənt] ***a.*** **1.** 模拟的;伪装的,看起来像…的。**2.**【生】拟态的。*colouration ~ of surroundings* 保护色。

sim·u·lar [ˈsimjulɑ; ˋsɪmjʊlə˞] ***a.***, ***n.*** 〔古〕= simulant.

sim·u·late [ˈsimjuleit; ˋsɪmjəˏlet] **I** ***vt.*** 假装,冒充,装做;模拟;模化;【生】拟(态),拟(色)。~ *death* 装死。~ *Jove* (演员)装扮作乔夫神。**II** ***a.*** = simulated [-id; -ɪd] 假装的;装成的;模仿的;拟态的。~ *rain* 人工降雨。

sim·u·la·tion [ˌsimjuˈleiʃən; ˏsɪmjəˋleʃən] ***n.*** 假装;模拟;装病,装疯;【生】拟态,拟色。

sim·u·la·tor [ˈsimjuleitə; ˋsɪmjəˏletə˞] ***n.*** **1.** 模仿的人,假装的人。**2.** 模拟器,仿真器,模拟装置[设备];模拟计算机;模拟宇航机。

sim·ul·cast [ˈsiməlkɑːst; ˋsaɪməlˏkæst] ***vi.***, ***vt.***, ***n.*** (广播和电视)同时联播(节目)。

sim·ul·ta·ne·i·ty [ˌsiməltəˈniːti; ˏsaɪml̩təˋniətɪ] ***n.*** 同时,同时性,同时发生[存在]。

sim·ul·ta·ne·ous [ˌsiməlˈteinjəs; ˏsaɪml̩ˋtenɪəs] ***a.*** 同时发生的,同时做的,同时的(*with*)。~ *development of heavy and light industries* 重工业和轻工业同时并举。~ ***broadcast***【无】联(合广)播。~ **equations**【数】联立方程式。**-ly** ***ad.*** 同时,一齐。

sin[1] [sin; sɪn] **I** ***n.*** **1.** (道德上的)罪,罪恶(*against*);过失;违背常情。**2.** 无礼貌,粗鲁。*setting ~s* 容易陷入的罪恶[恶习]。*It is a ~ to be indoors on such a fine day.* 这样好的天气待在家里实在不对[罪过]。***commit a ~*** 犯罪。***for my ~s*** 〔谑〕自作自受,活该。***like ~*** 〔俚〕厉害地,猛烈地(*hate sb. like ~* 恨死某人)。***live in open ~*** 过明目张胆的罪恶生活。***visit the ~s*** [***a ~***] (*upon a sinner*) 使(犯罪者)受报复。**II** ***vi.*** (***-nn-***) 犯罪(*against*);违犯(礼仪、教规等)(*against*)。~ ***in one's ill health*** 因干坏事而招致健康损坏。—***vt.*** 犯(罪恶)。***be more ~ned against than ~ning*** 受到超过应得程度的惩罚。~ ***away one's health*** 因干坏事而损坏健康。~ ***one's mercies*** 对幸运无动于衷[不感激]。~**-offering** 赎罪祭。~ **tax** 〔美口〕罪孽税〔指对烟草、酒、赌博业等征收的税〕。

sin[2] [sain; saɪn] ***n.***【数】= sine[1].

sin[3] [siːn; sin] ***n.*** = shin[2].

Si·nai [ˈsainiai; ˋsaɪnaɪ] *n*. 西奈(半岛)〔埃及〕;(西奈半岛上的)西奈山。

Sin·an·thro·pus [ˌsinænˈθrəupəs; ˏsɪnænˋθropəs] *n*. 〔L.〕【考古】中国猿人(= Peking Man)。

sin·a·pism [ˈsinəpizəm; ˋsɪnəpɪzm] *n*. 【医】芥子泥。

since [sins; sɪns] **I** ***conj***. **1**. …以来,以后,自从…的时候起。★**1**.主句中动词用现在完成式时, since 所引导的子句须用过去式: *We have both changed* ~ *we parted*. 分别以来彼此都变了。**2**.主句主语为 it, 动词用现在[过去]式时, since 引导的子从句须用过去[过去完成]时: *It is two years* ~ *we parted*. 我们分别以来有两年了。*It was two years* ~ *we had parted*. 那时我们已经分别两年了。**2**. 因为,所以,既是。★在表示原因的几个连词中,语气最强的词是 because, 其次是 since, 再其次是 as, for。because 是直接说明问话 why? 的'理由'、'原因'。since 是站在'时间'立场用'既是…就…'的意义去说明事件关系中的自然结果的;表达这一理由的 since 通常放在句首,但在省略句中也可放在句中: *S- force is no remedy, let us try conciliation*. 武力既不中用,就想法和解吧。*That is a useless*, ~ *impossible, proposal*. 既然不可能,那就是一个没用的提议。**II** ***prep***. …以来,以后,…之后,自从。*S- seeing you I have had good news*. 见面以后得到(你的)不少好消息。~ midnight 午夜之后(到此时)。~ ***then*** 其后,从此一直。**III** ***ad***. **1**. 以后,此后,以来。★由前置词惯用短语 ~ *then*, ~ *that* 略去 then (时), that (事)而形成: *I have not seen him* ~ (= ~ *then*). (那时)以后没见过他。**2**. (距今几年)以前;(从那时候起几年)以前。★由 *conj*. **1**. 义转变成的: *It is two years* ~ (*we parted*). = *We parted two years* ~ (= *ago*). 我们是在两年以前分别的。*It was two years* ~ (*we had parted*). = *We had parted two years* ~ (= *before*). 我们是在那以前两年分别的。***ever*** ~ 从那时起,此后一直。***long*** ~ 好久以前,已久。***not long*** ~ 就在不久,未久。

sin·cere [sinˈsiə; sɪnˋsɪr] *a*. (**-cer·er**; **-cer·est**) **1**. 真挚的;真诚的。**2**. 〔古〕纯粹的,不混杂…的 (*of*)。

sin·cere·ly [sinˈsiəli; sɪnˋsɪrlɪ] *ad*. 真挚地,真诚地;诚实地。***Yours*** ~ 谨启〔信的结尾语〕。

sin·cer·i·ty [sinˈseriti; sɪnˋsɛrətɪ] *n*. 真挚,真实;诚实,诚意;纯粹。*meet it in all* ~ 开诚相见。

sin·ci·put [ˈsinsipʌt; ˋsɪnsɪˏpʌt] *n*. 【解】前顶〔颅顶的前半部〕。

Sin·clair [ˈsiŋklɛə; ˋsɪŋklɛr] *n*. 辛克莱〔姓氏〕。

Sind [sind; sɪnd] *n*. 信德(信地)〔巴基斯坦省名〕。

sine [sain; saɪn] *n*. 【数】正弦〔略 sin〕。~ *curve* 正弦曲线。~ *wave* 正弦波。

si·ne [ˈsaini; ˋsaɪnɪ] *prep*. 〔L.〕无。~ ***die*** [ˈdaii:; ˋdaɪɪ] 无限期地,无期;日期不定。~ ***prole*** [ˈprəuli; ˋprolɪ] 【法】无后嗣[子女]的。~ ***qua non*** [kweiˈnɔn; kweˋnɑn] 必要条件[资格]。

si·ne·cure [ˈsainikjuə; ˋsaɪnɪˏkjʊr] *n*. 闲职,挂名差事,〔尤指〕领干薪的牧师职。*hardly a* ~ = *not a* ~ = *no* ~ 繁忙的差事。**-cur·ist** *n*. 冗员;担任挂名差事的人;领干薪的牧师。

sin·ew [ˈsinju:; ˋsɪnju] **I** *n*. **1**. 【解】腱。**2**. 〔*pl*.〕肌肉,筋肌;体力;精力。**3**. 〔常 *pl*.〕中坚,主力,资源,支持的人[或物]。*the* ~*s of war* 军费[军备];军事力量。**II** *vt*. 用腱连结;(好像使用肌筋似的)给…以力量,支持。

sin·ew·y [ˈsinju(:)i; ˋsɪnjəwɪ] *a*. 腱的,腱质的;肌肉发达的;强壮有力的;遒劲的。

sin·fo·ni·a [ˌsinfəˈni(:)ə; ˏsɪnfəˋniə] *n*. 〔It.〕【乐】**1**. = symphony. **2**. 〔古〕器乐曲;(初期意大利歌剧的)序曲。

sin·ful [ˈsinf*u*l; ˋsɪnfʊl] *a*. 有罪的,罪孽深重的;该遭天罚的;不道德的,邪恶的。**-ly** *ad*. **-ness** *n*.

sing [siŋ; sɪŋ] **I** *vi*. (***sang*** [sæŋ; sæŋ], 〔罕,美〕 ***sung*** [sʌŋ; sʌŋ]; ***sung***) **1**. 歌唱;(鸟、虫、风、壶、箭、子弹等)唱歌似的鸣叫;耳鸣;〔诗〕作诗;歌颂,赞美 (*of*)。**2**. 〔美俚〕向警察局自首。~ *in* [*out of*] *tune* 唱得合[不合]调。~ *for the youth* 为青春歌唱。—*vt*. **1**. 唱,歌唱;吟诵。**2**. 唱着使…。**3**. 称赞,歌颂。~ *sb*. *into good humour* 用歌唱使某人心情好转。~ *the harvest home* 唱着歌把庄稼收回家里。*The song has been sung to death*. 这首歌听腻了。***give sb. something to*** ~ ***for*** 惩罚某人,叫人吃吃苦头,使(顽皮小孩)哭出声来。***make sb.'s head*** ~ 把某人脑袋打得发响。~ ***another song*** [***tune***] 〔口〕改变调子[论调、方针、态度(等)];沮丧、变谦恭。~ ***away*** 用唱歌排遣(烦恼等)。~ ***by ear*** 不看谱学唱。~ ***for joy*** 快乐极了。~ ***for one's supper*** 付出力气以取得酬劳;做应做的事情(不是吃白饭)。~***ing the blues*** 〔美运〕垂头丧气。~ ***low*** 谨慎小心地说。~ ***of*** 歌(功),颂(德),唱歌庆贺。~ ***sb.'s praises*** 竭力称赞某人。~ ***out*** 〔俚〕大声说,喊叫 (*S- out if you want anything*. 你要什么就大声说吧)。~ ***small*** 变得垂头丧气,变得低声下气。~ ***the same*** [***old***] ***song*** [***tune***] 翻来覆去老是那一套。~ ***to the piano*** 合着钢琴唱。~ ***up*** 使劲地唱。**II** *n*. **1**. (风、小河、开水壶等的)呜呜声,嗖嗖声。**2**. 〔美口〕歌唱会。***on the*** ~ (开水壶等)呜呜地响。

Sing. = Singapore.

sing. = singular.

sing-a·long [ˈsiŋəˌlɔŋ; ˋsɪŋəˏlɔŋ] *n*. 〔口〕(非正式的)歌诵会。

Sin·ga·pore [ˌsiŋgəˈpɔ:; ˋsɪŋgəˏpor] *n*. **1**. 新加坡〔亚洲〕。**2**. 新加坡〔新加坡首都〕。

singe [sindʒ; sɪndʒ] **I** *vt*. (~***d***; ~***ing***) **1**. 烧焦;燎(猪、布等的)毛,烧茸。**2**. 损害(名誉等)。*I can smell something* ~*ing*. 有东西烧焦了。~*d cat* 〔美〕给人不良印象的人。~ ***hair*** 烧燎毛发的末梢。~ ***one's feathers*** [***wings***] 弄坏名誉;(事业,冒险)失败,亏损。~***sb.'s beard*** 侮辱。—*vi*. 烧焦。**II** *n*. 烧焦;燎毛,烧茸。

Sing·er [ˈsiŋə; ˋsɪŋɚ] *n*. **1**. 辛格〔姓氏〕。**2**. **I.M.** ~ 辛格〔1811—1875,美国发明家〕。

sing·er[1] [ˈsiŋə; ˋsɪŋɚ] *n*. 歌手;鸣禽;诗人。

sing·er[2] [ˈsiŋə; ˋsɪŋɚ] *n*. (屠宰场的)燎毛工人;燎毛器,燎发器。

Sin·gha·lese [ˌsiŋgəˈli:z; ˏsɪŋgəˋliz] *a*., *n*. = Cinhalese.

sing·ing [ˈsiŋiŋ; ˋsɪŋɪŋ] *n*. 唱歌,声乐;鸟鸣;耳鸣;【物,无】振鸣,嘤鸣,啸声。~ **bird** 鸣禽。~ **school** **1**. (特指18世纪美国的)成人音乐教习所。**2**. 〔美俚〕(警察的)拷问;(警察局的)询讯室。~ **voice** 歌声,乐声。

sin·gle [ˈsiŋgl; ˋsɪŋgl] **I** *a*. **1**. 仅只一个的,单独的;单式的;【植】(花等)单瓣的;【无】单工的,单次的。**2**. 独身的,单身的;孤独的;一人用的。**3**. 一人对一人的;单层的。**4**. 纯真的,单纯的;诚实的。**5**. 一次的;唯一的;无比的。**6**. 〔英〕(酒等)味淡的,力弱的。**II** *n*. 一个 (*opp*. double)。【棒球】单打;〔美俚〕一垒手;〔*pl*.〕【网球】单打比赛;〔*pl*.〕多股线;【植】单瓣花;〔英〕单程票;〔主美,加,常作 *pl*.〕单身男人[女子]。*each* ~ *person* 每一个人。*a* ~ *life* 独身生活。*a* ~ *man* 单身汉。*a* ~ *woman* 单身女人;〔婉〕妓女。*a* ~ *bed* 单人床。*a* ~ *flower* 单瓣花。*a* ~ *premium* 一次付清的保险费。*a* ~ *heart* 专一[真诚]的心。~ *devotion* 全心全意的献身精神。~ *ale* 淡啤酒。~*s silk* 多股生丝,缫制生丝。***with a*** ~ ***eye*** 诚心诚意地,一心一意地。***work with a*** ~ ***purpose*** 同心协力地工作。**III** *vt*. 拣出,选拔。~ *out the biggest apples* 拣出最大的苹果。—*vi*. **1**. 【棒球】作一垒手。**2**. (马)单步行进。~**-acting** *a*. 单作用的,单动的。~**-action** *a*. (枪)单发的。~ **blessedness** 〔谑〕独身状态。~**-blind** *a*. 单盲的〔指仅有作试验者了解情况而不让被试验者知情〕。**bond** 【化】单键。~**-breasted** *a*. (上衣等)单排钮的。~ **entry** 单式簿记。~**-eyed** *a*. **1**. 独眼的。**2**. 纯真的,赤诚的,诚实的。~ **file** 单行,一路纵队。~ **foot** 单步〔马的一种步法〕。~**-handed** **1**. *a*.

只有一只手的,单手的;单独的;能使用一只手的;可以单独做的。**2**. *ad*. 只手;单独,独力。~**-hearted** *a*. 有诚意的;诚实的,真心的;一心一意的。~**hood** 单身,未婚。~ **market** 单一市场〔允许成员国之间的商品、资本、人员等自由流动并建立共同货币的市场〕。~**-minded** *a*. = single-hearted. ~ **parent** 单亲〔离异一方一个人抚养子女者〕。~**-phase** *a*.【电】单相的。~**s bar**〔美〕(以单身男性或女子为主要服务对象的)单身酒吧。~ **seater** 单座车[飞机]。~**-sex** *a*.〔英〕单性别的;(学校等)男女分开的。~**-side-band**〔无〕单边带的。~**-space** *vt*. 不空行地打字[抄写]。~ **standard 1**. (尤指男女)应同样遵守的道德标准。**2**. (货币的)单本位制。~**stick** (练习用)剑形木棍;单棍(搏斗);剑术。~**-sticker**〔美口〕单桅帆船。~ **tax** 单一税〔制〕。~ **ticket** 单程车票。~**-track** *a*. 单轨的;单向的;死心眼的。~ **tree** 单驾横木 = whiffle tree. **-ness** *n*. 单一,单独;诚意。

sin·glet [ˈsiŋglit; ˋsɪŋglɪt] *n*. **1**. (男士)汗衫;背心。**2**.【物】单线;独态;单纯。~ *state* 独态。

sin·gle·ton [ˈsiŋgltən; ˋsɪŋgl̩tən] *n*.【牌】(某一花色的)单张;孤张;手拿孤张的人;〔美俚〕只有一个影片的演出;独一无二的(人或物)。

sin·gly [ˈsiŋgli; ˋsɪŋglɪ] *ad*. **1**. 各自地,分别地;单独地;独自地。**2**. 诚实地,真诚地。

sing·song [ˈsiŋsɔŋ; ˋsɪŋˏsɔŋ] **I** *n*. 单调;拙劣的歌唱;声调平板的诗;〔英口〕临时凑成的歌咏会。**II** *a*. 单调的;毫不精彩的,平淡无味的。**III** *vt*., *vi*. 用单调的声音读〔说〕。

sing·spiel [ˈziŋˌʃpiːl; ˋzɪŋˏʃpil] *n*. (*pl*. ***-spiel·en*** [-ən; -ən]) 小歌剧〔德国 18 世纪的一种歌剧〕。

sin·gu·lar [ˈsiŋgjulə; ˋsɪŋgjələ˞] **I** *a*. **1**. 唯一的,独一的,单独的,一人的,一个的;【法】各自的,各个的;【逻】单称的;【语法】单数的。**2**. 奇特的,特别的,异常的;非凡的,卓越的。~ *clothes* 奇装异服。~ *nature* 奇特性。*a most* ~ *phenomenon* 一个最奇特的现象。***all and*** ~ 所有的人;一律;完完全全一个不漏。***be dressed in*** ~ ***fashion*** 穿着奇装异服。**II** *n*.【语法】单数;单数的词。~ **number**【语法】单数。~ **successor**【法】特定继承人。**-ly** *ad*. **1**. 异常;格外。**2**. 单独;个别;【语法】用单数。**-ness** *n*. = singularity. **-y** *a*.【语法】单元的,一元的,不成对的。

sin·gu·lar·i·ty [ˌsiŋgjuˈlæriti; ˏsɪŋgjəˋlærətɪ] *n*. **1**. 奇特;特别,非凡,异常;奇特的东西;怪癖,特性。**2**.〔罕〕独一,单一,独个。**3**.【天】奇点〔宇宙物体收缩至无限大密度和无限小体积的空间的一个假想点〕;【数】奇点。

sin·gu·lar·ize [ˈsiŋgləraiz; ˋsɪŋgjələˏraɪz] *vt*. 使成单数;使奇特。

Sin·ha·lese [ˌsinhəˈliːz; ˏsɪnhəˋliz] *a*., *n*. = Cinhalese.

Sin·i·cism [ˈsinisizəm; ˋsɪnəsɪzm̩] *n*. 中国式,中国风味,中国习惯;中国语(风)。

Sin·i·co-Ja·pan·ese [ˈsinikəuˌdʒæpəˈniːz; ˋsɪnəkoˏdʒæpəˋniz] *n*., *a*. 中日的;日语里面的汉字(的);仿中国古文的日语文体(的)。

sin·is·ter [ˈsinistə; ˋsɪnɪstə˞] *a*. **1**. 不吉的,凶险的,不祥的;有害的;阴险的,险恶的;邪恶的。**2**.〔谑〕左的 (*opp*. dexter)【徽】(盾章)左边的。*a* ~ *design* 阴险的计划,阴谋。**-ly** *ad*.

sin·is·tral [siˈnistrəl; ˋsɪnɪstrəl] *a*. (*opp*. dextral) 向左的,(贝壳等)左旋的;(比目鱼)左边朝上的;用左手的。

sin·is·tro·dex·tral [ˌsinistrəuˈdekstrəl; ˏsɪnəstroˋdɛkstrəl] *a*. 从左向右行的,从左向右指的。

sin·is·trorse [ˈsinisˌtrɔːs, ˈsinisˈtrɔːs; ˋsɪnɪsˏtrɔrs] *a*.【植】左旋的。**-ly** *ad*.

sin·is·trous [ˈsinistrəs; ˋsɪnɪstrəs] *a*. = sinister.

Si·nit·ic [siˈnitik; sɪˋnɪtɪk] **I** *n*. 汉语,中文。**II** *a*. 中国的;中国人的;汉语的,中国文化的。

sink[1] [siŋk; sɪŋk] **I** *vi*. (***sank*** [sæŋk; sæŋk],〔古、美〕***sunk*** [sʌŋk; sʌŋk]; ***sunk***, ***sunken*** [ˈsʌŋkən; ˋsʌŋkən]) **1**. 下沉,沉没。**2**. (日、月等)沉入地平线下;低落;下垂;下沉,坍下去,塌下去,下陷。**3**. (声音等)低落;(火势)减弱;(病人等)衰弱;(精神等)沮丧,消沉;衰颓,沦落,败落,堕落 (*into*; *under*)。**4**. (物价等)跌落,减少,退落。**5**. (水等)沁进,渗下,渗入;(教训等)深入(心里等) (*in*; *into*; *through*)。**6**. (眶、双颊等)凹[陷]下去;(眼睛)低垂;(坡等)斜下去。**7**. (鱼)游入水底深处。*The sun* ~*s in the west*. 太阳落在西方。*The floods are* ~*ing rapidly*. 洪水正在急退中〔水位迅速降低〕。*He is* ~*ing fast*. 他迅速地一天比一天更衰弱〔快要去世〕。*The dye* ~*s in well*. 这个染料容易吃进去[渗进去]。*The war now sank into peace*. 战争平定了。—*vt*. **1**. 弄沉,使沉没;击沉;使下沉。**2**. 使衰弱,使没落,使败落;损害,毁坏(名誉等);使颓然下垂,垂下来。**3**. 使降低;使低落;使…弱;使沮丧,使颓丧。**4**. 掘,凿,挖(井等);(把桩,管子等)向下挖掘,打进,插进,埋入(地下等);(将石头等)嵌入(墙壁等);【铸造】雕,刻。**5**. 减少,减低(力量等),使(股票等)跌价;糟蹋掉,丧失,荡尽(财产等)。**6**. 偿还(国债等);投资给(难以收回成本的事业)。**7**. 使看不见,隐藏。**8**. 不重视,不理,不当做问题。**9**.【印】低行(排)。~ *a ship* 把船弄沉。~ *one's head upon one's breast* 颓丧地垂下头来。~ *a well* 掘井。~ *a stone in the wall* 把石头嵌进墙里。~ *minor differences* 不计较微小的差异。~ *a die* 雕一个印模。***One's heart*** ~***s within one***. 消沉,灰心。~ ***a fact*** 息事宁人。~ ***down*** 沉没;晕过去,昏倒。~ ***in another's estimation*** 声望降低;失去别人(对他)的信任[尊重]。~ ***into absurdity*** 做荒唐事。~ ***into a chair*** 深深地坐进椅子里。~ ***into a faint*** 晕过去。~ ***into oblivion*** 被忘掉。~ ***into the grave*** 死掉。~ ***one's identity*** 隐瞒身分。~ ***oneself*** [***one's own interests***] 舍己为人。~ ***or swim*** 孤注一掷,不管好歹。~ ***out of sight*** 隐没不见。~ ***to the elbow***〔美拳〕打得着实。~ ***tooth into***〔美俚〕吃。~ ***under*** 受不了…而倒下去。**II** *n*. **1**. (厨房的)洗涤槽;水斗,水糟,水池;阴沟;渗水坑;【地】落水洞;〔美俚〕海洋。**2**. 巢窟,藏垢纳污之所。**3**. 洼地,湖沼。**4**.【物】中子吸收剂;变换器,换能器;转发器。**5**.【剧】布景起落口。~ **school**〔英〕污水槽学校〔指教学质量等低劣的末流学校〕。~ **unit = kitchen unit.**

sink·age [ˈsiŋkidʒ; ˋsɪŋkɪdʒ] *n*. **1**. 下沉。**2**. 下沉度。**3**. 下沉地带;低洼地。

sink·er [ˈsiŋkə; ˋsɪŋkə˞] *n*. **1**. 沉下的人[物]。**2**. (钓丝等的)坠子。**3**. 掘井[矿井]的人;开模工(人)。**3**.〔美俚〕银元。**4**.〔美口〕饼干,炸面圈。= doughnut. ~*s and suds*〔美口〕炸面圈和咖啡。***hook***, ***line***, ***and*** ~〔美口〕完全地,全部地。

sink·hole [ˈsiŋkhəul; ˋsɪŋkˏhol] *n*. **1**. 阴沟口;污水池;吸尘孔。**2**. 藏垢纳污之所。**3**.【地】灰岩坑;落水洞。

sink·ing [ˈsiŋkiŋ; ˋsɪŋkɪŋ] *n*. **1**. 沉没;沉下;低陷,塌下,凹下。**2**. 试掘;投资。**3**.【建】孔;凹处。**4**. (饥饿、劳苦等造成的)衰弱。*a* ~ *in the stomach* 空腹时胃的虚脱感。*a* ~ *at the heart* 情绪低落。~ **fund** 偿债基金。

sin·less [ˈsinlis; ˋsɪnlɪs] *a*. 无罪的,无辜的;清白的,圣洁的。**-ly** *ad*. **-ness** *n*.

sin·ner [ˈsinə; ˋsɪnə˞] *n*. **1**. (宗教、道德上的)罪人,有罪的人,罪孽深重的人。**2**. 不信神的人。**3**.〔谑〕坏人,顽皮鬼。*as I am a* ~〔断定时说〕正像我是罪人一样,的确。*a young* ~〔谑〕小家伙。

Sinn Fein [ˈʃinˈfein; ʃɪnˋfen] **1**.〔爱〕新芬党〔1905 年成立,以联合拥护爱尔兰独立为目的〕。**2**. 新芬党党员 (= Sinn Feiner)。

Sino- *comb*. *f*. 表示"中国(的)""中国人(的)","汉语(的)": *Sino*logy, *Sino*-Japanese.

Si·no·gram [ˈsainəugræm; ˋsaɪnoˏgræm] *n*. 汉字。

Si·nol·o·gist, Sin·o·logue [siˈnɔlədʒist, ˈsinəlɔg; saɪˋnɑlədʒɪst, ˋsaɪnəˏlɔg] *n*. **1**. 汉学家。**2**. 中国问题专家。

Si·nol·o·gy [si'nɔlədʒi; saɪ`nɑlədʒɪ] ***n*.** **1.** 汉学〔研究中国语言、文学、历史、风俗习惯等〕。**2.** 中国问题研究。

Si·no·ma·ni·a [ˌsainə'meinjə; ˏsaɪnə`menjə] ***n*.** 中国热。

Sin·o·phile, Sin·o·phil ['sainəfil, 'sinəfail, 'sinəfil; `saɪnəfɪl, `saɪnəˏfaɪl] **I** ***a*.** 喜爱中国的,亲华的。**II** ***n*.** 喜爱中国的人;亲华人士。

Sin·o·phobe ['sinəfəub, 'sain-; `sɪnəfob, `saɪn-] **I** ***a*.** 厌恶中国的;排华的。**II** ***n*.** 厌恶中国的人;排华的人。

sin·o·ple ['sinəpl; `sɪnəpl] ***n*.**【地】铁水铝英石;铁石英;朱砂〔黑海南岸 Sinope 产〕。

Si·no-Ti·bet·an [ˌsainəuti'betn; ˏsaɪnotɪ`bɛtn̩] **I** ***a*.**【语言】汉藏语系的。**II** ***n*.** 汉藏语系〔包括汉语、藏语、缅甸语等〕。

SINS = ship's inertial navigation system 船舰惯性导航系统。

sin·ter ['sintə; `sɪntɚ] **I** ***n*.** **1.**【地】泉华〔矿泉四周沉淀的结晶岩石〕。**2.** 铁的锈皮;【冶】熔渣,烧结物。**II** ***vt*.** 烧结。~ **glass**【化】烧结玻璃;多孔玻璃。~ **process** 烧结法。

sin·u·ate ['sinjuit, -eit; `sɪnjʊˏet, -ɪt] **I** ***a*.** **1.** = sinuous **2.**【植】具弯缘的;具深波状的(指边缘)。**II** ***vi*.** (***-at·ed, -at·ing***) 蜿蜒,弯曲,曲折。*The snake ~ed along the ground*. 那蛇沿着地面蜿蜒爬行。**-ly** ***ad*.**

sin·u·a·tion [ˌsinju'eiʃən; ˏsɪnjʊ`eʃən] ***n*.** 波状,蜿蜒,弯曲,曲折。

Si·nui·ju ['ʃiniːdʒuː; `ʃɪnidʒu] ***n*.** 新义州〔朝鲜民主主义人民共和国城市〕。

sin·u·os·i·ty [ˌsinju'ɔsiti; ˏsɪnjʊ`ɑsətɪ] ***n*.** **1.** 蜿蜒,弯曲,起伏。**2.** (情节等)曲折,错综复杂。**3.** 柔软动作。**4.** 〔常 *pl*.〕(河流、道路的)弯曲处。

sin·u·ous ['sinjuəs; `sɪnjʊəs] ***a*.** **1.** 弯曲的,波状的,蜿蜒的(河流等)。**2.** 曲折的,错综复杂的。**3.** 动作柔软的。**4.** 转弯抹角的,间接的;不老实的。**5.**【植】(叶子)具弯缘的,具深波边缘的。**-ly** ***ad*.**

si·nus ['sainəs; `saɪnəs] ***n*.** (*pl*. ~, ~*es* [-siz; -sɪz]) **1.** 弯曲;湾;穴,凹。**2.**【解】窦,【医】瘘。**3.**【植】弯缺,深裂。**4.**【动】(软体动物的)弯;(腕足类的)中槽,凹。

si·nus·i·tis [ˌsainə'saitis; ˏsaɪnə`saɪtɪs] ***n*.**【医】窦炎。

si·nu·soid ['sainəˌsɔid; `saɪnəsˏɔɪd] ***n*.**【数】正弦曲线(= sine curve)。**-al** ***a*.**

Si·on ['saiən; `saɪən] ***n*.** = Zion.

-sion *comb*. *f*. 表示"行为,状态","性质":expan*sion*.

Siou·an ['suːən; `suən] **I** ***n*.** (*pl*. ~(*s*)) **1.** (印第安人)苏语组。**2.** 说苏语的印第安人,苏族人。**II** ***a*.** 苏语组的;苏族人的。

Sioux [suː; su] **I** ***n*.** (*pl*. ~ [-z; -(z)]) 〔北美〕苏族〔印第安人的一族,自称达可塔 (Dakota) 族〕。**II** ***a*.** 苏族的。

sip [sip; sɪp] **I** ***vi*.** (***-pp-***) 啜饮,一点一点地喝。~ *at one's drink* 细细饮酒。—***vt*.** **1.** 呷,啜饮。**2.** 从…中呷吸。~ *tea* 呷茶,啜茗。**II** ***n*.** 啜,一啜之量。*take a* ~ 吸一口。*drink brandy in ~s* 细饮白兰地。**-per** ***n*.** 吸者;饮者;吸浆管。

si·phon ['saifən; `saɪfən] **I** ***n*.** **1.** 虹吸;吸水管,弯管;虹吸管[瓶]。**2.** 苏打水瓶(= ~ bottle)。**3.**【建】存水弯。**4.**【动】呼吸管;【昆】管形口器;(蚊幼虫)管形突;(头足类)体管;(软体动物)水管;(软体、棘皮动物)虹管。**II** ***vt*.** **1.** 用虹吸管吸,虹吸。**2.** 吮吸(民脂民膏等)(*off*)。—***vi*.** 通过虹吸管。~ **barometer** 虹吸气压计。~ **cup**【机】虹吸上油壶。~ **gauge** 虹吸压力计。~ **recorder** 虹吸(管)记录器;【无】波纹收报机。**-al** ***a*.**

si·phon·age ['saifənidʒ; `saɪfənɪdʒ] ***n*.**【物】虹吸能力,虹吸作用。

si·pho·no·phore [sai'fɔnəˌfɔː, 'saifənə-; `saɪfənəˏfor] ***n*.**【动】管水母目(*Siphonophore*)动物。

si·pho·no·stele [sai'fɔnəˌstiːl, 'saifənə-, saiˌfɔnə'stiːli; saɪ`fɑnəˏstil, `saɪfənə-, saɪˏfɑnə`stil] ***n*.**【植】管状中柱。**-ste·lic** [-'stiːlik; -`stilɪk] ***a*.**

si·phun·cle ['saifʌŋkl; `saɪfʌŋkl̩] ***n*.**【动】体管(指硬体);(蚜虫)腹管。

sip·pet ['sipit; `sɪpɪt] ***n*.** **1.** (浸在汤汁里的)小片炸[烤]面包;〔*pl*.〕浸过肉汁的面包片。**2.** 小片,碎片。

sip·py ['sipi; `sɪpɪ] ***n*.** 夕皮士〔指 55 岁以上且经济较富裕的银发族消费者,系 senior independent pioneers 之缩略,仿 hippy 造的新词〕。

sir [强 səː, 弱 sə; sɚ, sɚ] **I** ***n*.** 先生,阁下,君。**1.** 〔一般对职务或年龄比自己大的男子的尊称〕;议长〔议员对议会主席的称呼〕。**2.** 〔商业信件抬头用语〕先生;〔*pl*.〕各位,执事诸君〔通常用 Gentlemen〕。**3.** 〔S-〕〔英〕爵士〔对爵士 (Knight) 或从男爵 (baronet) 的称呼,用于姓名前或名字前,但不用于姓氏前,如 Sir Henry Smith, 日常招呼时称作 Sir Henry, 不称作 Sir Smith〕。**4.** 〔美口〕不分性别,用以强调肯定或否定〔如 *Yes, sir*; *No, sir*〕。**5.** 〔谑〕喂,老兄!〔挖苦或申斥时用〕。**6.** 〔谑〕大人,先生〔如 ~ critic 评论先生。S- Oracle 神示老爷〕。*Good morning*, ~. 先生,早。*Get out*, ~! 喂! 出去!〔挖苦话〕。*Will you be quiet*, ~! 喂,老兄,静一点!〔挖苦话〕。**II** ***vt*.** 称…为先生。*Don't* ~ *me quite so much*. 别那样先生先生的叫我。

sir·car, sir·kar ['səːkaː; `sɚkɚ] ***n*.** 〔印度英语〕**1.** 政府;政府首脑。**2.** 主人,老爷。**3.** 总管;账房先生。

sir·dar ['səːdaː; sɚ`dɑr] ***n*.** **1.** (印度、巴基斯坦、阿富汗等的)首长,贵族,首领。**2.** 高级军官,将军;(旧时埃及军队中的英国)总司令。**3.** (印度的)达官贵人,居重要职位的人。

sire ['saiə; saɪr] **I** ***n*.** **1.** 〔古〕陛下 = Your majesty. **2.** 〔诗〕父;(男性)祖先。**3.** (四足哺乳动物的)种畜〔尤指种马〕。**II** ***vt*.** **1.** (指种马等雄性动物的)生殖。**2.** 产生;创作,创办。~***d by*** …种的。

siree [səː'riː; sə`ri] ***n*.** = sirree.

si·ren ['saiərin; `saɪrən] **I** ***n*.** **1.** 〔或 S-〕【希神】塞壬〔传说中半人半鸟的海妖,常用歌声诱惑过路的航海者而使航船触礁身死〕。**2.** 歌声美妙的女歌手。**3.** 妖妇,妖女;诱惑者[物]。**4.**【动】土鳗属两栖动物;海牛目动物。**5.** 汽笛,警报器。*an air-raid* ~ 空袭警报器。*an ambulance* (*a fire*) ~ 救护(救火)车上的警报器。*a* ~ *bomb* 啸声(炸)弹。*a* ~ *disk* 验音盘。**II** ***a*.** 海妖一样的,诱惑的,迷人的。**III** ***vi*.** (警车、救火车等)响着警报器驱车前进。

si·re·ni·an [saiə'riːniən; saɪ`rinɪən] ***n*., *a*.**【动】海牛目动物(的)。

si·ri·a·sis [si'raiəsis; sɪ`raɪəsɪs] ***n*.**【医】**1.** 日射病,中暑。**2.** 日光浴。

Sir·i·us ['siriəs; `sɪrɪəs] ***n*.**【天】天狼星。

sir·loin ['səːlɔin; `sɚlɔɪn] ***n*.** 牛的上腰部肉,牛腰肉。

si·roc·co [si'rɔkəu; sə`rako] ***n*.** (*pl*. ~*s*) **1.**【气】西洛可风〔欧洲南部从利比亚沙漠吹来的一种常带沙尘,间或带雨的热风〕。**2.** (泛指从炎热或干旱地区吹来的)热风。

sir·ra(h) ['sirə; `sɪrə] ***n*.** 〔古〕你这家伙,小子,老兄〔气愤时对男人的轻蔑称呼语〕。

sir·ree [sə'riː; sə`ri] ***n*.** 〔美口〕= sir〔用在"yes"或"no"后,加重语气〕。

sir-rev·er·ence [ˌsəː'revərəns; ˏsɚ`rɛvərəns] ***int*.** 〔废〕请原谅;抱歉。

sir·up ['sirəp; `sɪrəp] ***n*.** = syrup.

sir·vent(es) [siə'vent, F. sir'vɑːŋt; sɪr`vɛnt, sɪr`vaŋt] ***n*.** (*pl*. ***-ventes*** [-'vents, F. sir'vɑ̃t; -`vɛnts, F. sɪr`vɑ̃t]) 感兴诗〔12、13 世纪法国普洛温斯抒情诗的一种,常具讽刺性〕。

sis [sis; sɪs] ***n*.** 〔美口〕= sister.

sis·al ['sisəl; `saɪsl] ***n*.** **1.**【植】〔中美〕西沙尔龙舌兰。**2.** 西沙尔麻,波尔麻〔用于制绳、麻袋布等,又叫 ~ grass, ~ hemp〕。

S

sis·kin [ˈsiskin; ˋsɪskɪn] ***n.***【鸟】黄雀。

Sis·ley [ˈsisli; ˋsɪslɪ] ***n.*** 西斯利〔姓氏〕。

sis·si·fied [ˈsisiˌfaid; ˋsɪsɪˏfaɪd] ***a.***〔口〕= sissy.

sis·soo [ˈsisuː; ˋsɪsu] ***n.***【植】印度黄檀。

sis·sy [ˈsisi; ˋsɪsɪ] **I** ***n.***〔美〕**1.**〔口〕女子气的男孩或男子。**2.** 懦弱的人,胆小鬼。**3.** 姊妹,少女。**4.**〔俚〕搞同性恋的人。~ ***beer***〔美〕(酒精成分在 3.2% 以下的)淡啤酒。**II** ***a.***〔美〕女人似的,柔弱的。**-ish** ***a.***

sister [ˈsistə; ˋsɪstɚ] **I** ***n.*** **1.** 姊,妹。**2.** 情同手足的女子;女同事,女伙伴,女同学,女社友,女会友。**3.**〔英〕护士长;(一般)护士。**4.**【天主】修女。**5.**〔喻〕姊妹;同类的事物。**6.** (同一母体出生的)同胞雌性动物。*a full* [*whole*] ~ 同胞姊妹。*a half* ~ 异父[母]姊妹。*elder* [*younger*] ~ 姊姊[妹妹]。~ *arts* (具有某种共同点的)姊妹艺术。~ *ships* (同型的)姊妹船,姊妹舰。*Fatal S-s* [*S-s three, three S-s*]【希神、罗神】命运三女神。*S- of Mercy* 慈善姊妹会〔尤指 1827 年创建于都柏林教育慈善组织〕。***be like ~s*** 像姊妹一样,非常亲密。***waste and its ~ want*** 浪费及其同胞姊妹——匮乏。**II** ***a.*** 姐妹的;同类(型)的。**III** ***vt.*** 如姐妹般相待。**~-german** ***n.*** (*pl.* ~***s-german***) 同胞姊妹,同父母的姊妹。**~-hood** ***n.*** 姊妹关系;妇女团体,妇女会;护士长的职务。~ **hook**【机】双抱钩。**~-in-law** [ˈsistərinlɔ; ˋsɪstərɪnˏlɔ] ***n.*** (*pl.* ***sisters-***) 姑,姨;[配偶的姊妹]嫂,弟媳。~ **uterine** (同母异父的)姐妹。**-ly** ***a.*** 姊妹般的。

sis·tern ***n.*** 〔*pl.*〕〔美方〕= sisters.

Sis·tine [ˈsistain; ˋsɪstin] ***a.*** 罗马教皇西斯廷(特指 Sixtus 四世或五世)的。~ **Chapel** (罗马教廷中的主要教堂)西斯廷教堂。~ **Madonna** (意大利画家 Raphael 画的)西斯廷圣母像。~ **Vulgate** (教皇 Sixtus 五世时代改订的)拉丁语译本圣经。

sis·troid [ˈsistrɔid; ˋsɪstrɔɪd] ***a.***【数】凸边角的。

sis·trum [ˈsistrəm; ˋsɪstrəm], ***n.*** (*pl.* ***-trum, -tra*** [-trə; -trə]) 铁播子〔一种手摇乐器,又称叉铃,古埃及祭祀司繁殖女神爱西丝 (Isis) 时使用〕。

Sis·y·phe·an [ˌsisiˈfiːən; ˏsɪsəˋfiən] ***a.*** 像西绪福斯(Sisyphus) 的;徒劳无益的。

Sis·y·phus [ˈsisifəs; ˋsɪsəfəs] ***n.***【希神】西绪福斯〔希腊古时国王,因作恶多端,死后堕入地狱,被罚推石上山,但推上又滚下,永远如此,劳苦无已〕。*the stone of* ~ 徒劳。

sit [sit; sɪt] ***vi.*** (***sat*** [sæt; sæt], 〔古〕***sate*** [sæt, seit; sæt, set]; ***sat*** [sæt; sæt]; ~***ting***) **1.** 坐,就座。**2.** (鸟等)栖息,憩息,进窝;(鸡等)伏窝,孵蛋。**3.** (房屋等)坐落,位于;【军】扎营,驻扎。**4.** (衣服)合身,适合。**5.** (风)来自,吹来。**6.** 就职,做议员[委员];出席。**7.** 以某一姿势坐定让人画肖像[照相];充当模特儿。**8.** (议会、法庭等)开会,开庭。**9.** 应试 (*for*)。**10.** 临时替人照看(婴孩)。**11.** 被搁置不用。*The coat does not ~ properly across the shoulders.* 上衣不怎样合身。*His principles ~ loosely on him.* 他的原则对己没有约束力。*The law court will ~ to-day.* 法院今天要开庭了。—***vt.*** **1.** 〔~ oneself〕使坐,使就座。**2.** 骑(马);(用身体或桨)调平(小船)。**3.** (车辆等)可供…坐。**4.** (鸡等)孵(卵)。***make sb. ~ up***〔俚〕使大吃一惊;虐待,虐使,折磨。~ ***at home*** 闲居在家。~ ***at one's feet*** 师事(某人),拜某人为师。~ ***back*** 松劲休息;不活动。~ ***by*** 袖手旁观。~ ***down*** 坐下;住定;占有;(坐下来)开始工作(谈判等);结束发言;(飞机等)降落。~ ***down before*** (*a place*)【军】扎营围攻(某地)。~ ***down hard*** (***up***) ***on***〔美俚〕断然反对,痛斥,痛骂。~ ***down under*** 温顺地忍受(侮辱等)。~ ***down with*** 只好满足于,不得不忍受。~ ***for*** **1.** 坐着〔让人画肖像或照相〕。**2.**〔英〕参加(学位、奖学金等)考试;作…候选人。~ ***heavy on*** 重压;(食物)不消化。~ ***her***〔美〕骑稳(牛、马)不要被摔下。~ ***in***〔美〕参加;列席;出席;代理;参加静坐示威[罢工]。~ ***in judgement on*** 审判,裁判;(高高在上地)批评,评断。~ ***in parliament*** 当议员。~ ***lightly on*** (食物等)不滞胃,不使人难受。~ ***like a bump on a log***〔美〕饱食终日无所用心,整天不做事,呆头呆脑。~ ***loosely on*** (主义等)不受人注意。~ ***on*** **1.** 审理(案件等);调查。**2.**〔俚〕拖延,压制;〔口〕责备 (*He wants ~ting on.* 那个家伙得骂一顿才行)。~ ***on a committee*** 充当(委员会的)委员。~ ***on one's hands*** 不鼓掌赞许;(应行动时)袖手旁观。~ ***on one's knees*** 跪下。~ ***on the bench*** 做法官。~ ***on two chairs*** 脚踏两条船。~ ***out*** **1.** 坐一旁不加入(跳舞比赛等)。**2.** (在宴会中)坐到(众人)走完;坐到(戏)完。~ ***over*** (*a player*)【运】(有利地)排在某选手之后;(打桥牌时)坐在某人上手占有利地位;坐着慢慢地捱过[度过,吃喝完等]。~ ***through*** = ~ *out* (~ *through a long sermon* 耐心听完一篇冗长的说教)。~ ***tight*** **1.** 屹然不动;稳守不动。**2.** 固执己见;坚持自己的主张。**3.**〔美〕耐心等候。~ ***to*** 坐着给…画像[拍照]。~ ***under*** 听…的训导;坐在…的下手(如打牌时)。~ ***up*** **1.** 坐起来;(狗)用后脚站起。**2.** 熬夜。**3.** 端坐,坐正。**4.** 吓一跳;奋起 (~ *up all night* 通宵不睡。~ *up at work* 做夜工。~ *up late at night* 熬到深夜)。~ ***up and take notice***〔英口〕(突然)引起兴趣来;〔美俚〕发觉,注意起来,怀疑起来。~ ***upon*** = ~ *on*. ~ ***well on*** (衣服)很合身。**~-in** 占座抗议,静坐示威。~ **up,** **~-up**【运】仰卧起坐。

si·tar [siˈtɑː; sɪˋtɑr] ***n.*** 西塔琴〔印度的一种六弦乐器〕。**-ist** ***n.*** 西塔琴演奏者。

sit·come [ˈsitkʌm; ˋsɪtkʌm] ***n.*** (广播、电视中的)系列幽默剧 (= situation comedy)。

sit-down (strike) [ˈsitdaun; ˋsɪtˏdaʊn] ***n.***〔美〕静坐罢工。**-er** ***n.***

site [sait; saɪt] **I** ***n.*** **1.** 地点;位置;地基。**2.** 场所,现场。**3.** 遗址。**4.**【计】网站,站点〔电脑网络用户的网站地址〕;万维网址 (= Website)。*construction* ~ 建筑工地。*firing* [*launching*] ~ (火箭等)发射场。*historic ~s* 历史遗址。*nuclear test* ~ 核试验场。*the ~ of a battle* 战场。**II** ***vt.*** 给与位置,为…选定地点;安放;使坐落于(某处)。**-ed** [ˈsaitid; ˋsaɪtɪd] ***a.*** 地点[位置]…的 (*a well-~d factory* 地点好的工厂)。

sith [siθ; sɪθ] ***ad.***, ***conj.***, ***prep.*** 〔古〕= since.

sitio-, sito- *comb. f.* 表示"食物": *sito*logy.

si·tol·o·gy [saiˈtɔlədʒi; saɪˋtɑlədʒɪ] ***n.*** 营养学;选址学〔指建筑房屋等时的选择合适自然环境等的学科〕。

si·to·pho·bia [ˌsaitəˈfəubjə; ˏsaɪtoˋfobɪə] ***n.***【医】恐食症。

si·tos·ter·ol [saiˈtɔstərəul, -rɔːl; saɪˋtɑstərol] ***n.***【化】谷甾醇。

sit·ten [ˈsitn; ˋsɪtn̩]【废】sit 的过去分词。

sit·ter [ˈsitə; ˋsɪtɚ] ***n.*** **1.** 坐的人;坐着给人画像[照相]的人,模特儿。**2.** 孵卵鸡。**3.** 栖息不动[容易命中]猎物;糊里糊涂命中的射击;容易的工作。**4.**〔美口〕临时替人照看孩子的人。

sit·ting [ˈsitiŋ; ˋsɪtɪŋ] **I** ***n.*** **1.** 坐,就座,就席,坐的姿势;充当(绘画[摄影]的)模特儿。**2.** 开会,开庭;会期,开庭期间。**3.** (坐)一次,一气,一股劲儿。**4.** 孵卵;孵卵数;孵卵期。*Can you give me six ~s?* 你可以让我画六次吗? *The ~ is open* [*is called to order*]. 现在开会了。*an opening* [*a final*] ~ 开幕[闭幕]会。**II** ***a.*** **1.** 坐着的,就座的。**2.** 孵卵中的(雌鸟)。**3.** 易于命中的。**4.** 租占着田地[房屋]的。***at a*** [***one***] ~ 一气,一口气,一下子。***be holding a*** ~ 在开会。***to be*** ~ 开会。~ **duck**〔美〕易于命中[易受攻击]的目标;容易上钩的对象。~ **pretty**〔美俚〕占着良好位置。~ **room** 起居室。~ **tenant** 现在租占着土地[房屋]的租户。

sit·u·ate [ˈsitjueit; ˋsɪtʃʊˏet] **I** ***a.***〔古〕= situated. **II** ***vt.*** 使某设施等位于[坐落]某地,确定某事发生于某地某时 (*in, at, on*)。使人处于某境地〔多用被动结构,见下条〕。~ *a factory in a suitable site* 把工厂建在一个适

中的地点。*Their apartments were ~d on the first floor*. 他们的住房在二楼。*He can't ~ his recollection in any place or at any time*. 他想不起在什么地方,也想不起在什么时间了。

sit·u·at·ed [ˈsitjueitid; ˋsɪtʃʊˏetɪd] *a*. 1. 位于…的,坐落在…的(*at*; *on*)。2. 处于…地位[境遇、状态]的。*a pleasantly ~ house* 一所地址优美的住宅。*be awkwardly ~* 处于困难的地位,处境尴尬。*thus ~* 在这种状况下。

sit·u·a·tion [ˌsitjuˈeiʃən; ˏsɪtʃʊˋeʃən] *n*. 1. (房屋建筑等的)地点,位置;场所。2. 形势,局面;情况,关系。3. (戏剧等的)紧张场面,危急关头。4. 境遇,处境;在一定时间内作用于生物的内外总刺激。5.【心】情境。6. (特指仆役等的)职业,职位,地位,工作。7.〔古〕健康状况。*the close quarter ~* (同航向或同速度二船间的)最小安全距离。*the domestic ~* 国内形势。*the international ~* 国际形势。*the current ~* 时局。*the political ~* 政局。*the actual ~ at a given time and place* 当时当地的实际情况。*a difficult ~* 困难处境。*a thrilling [tense] ~* 紧张的场面。*cope [do] with the ~* 应付局势,应付当前的情况。*hold a ~* 有职业。*look for a ~* 找事,谋职。*save the ~* 挽回局势,解救危局。*throw up a ~* 放弃职位。~ **comedy**【剧】情景喜剧〔广播、电视中的系列幽默剧,多以故事人物为中心〕。~ **ethics** 境遇伦理学〔主张道德观应依情况而定〕。~**s vacant [wanted]** 事求人[人求事]〔报纸上的招聘[待聘]栏标题〕。**-al** *a*. **-al·ly** *ad*. **-ism** *n*.【心】情境决定行为论。

si·tus [ˈsaitəs; ˋsaɪtəs] *n*. 1. 地点,部位〔尤指动植物器官生来的原位置〕。2.〔军〕位置。*analysis ~*【数】拓朴(学)。

Sit·well [ˈsitwəl; ˋsɪtwəl] *n*. 西特韦尔〔姓氏〕。

Sitz bath [ˈsitsbɑːθ, ˈzits-; ˋsɪtsˏbæθ, sɪts-]【医】坐浴(疗法);坐浴盆。

sitz·krieg [ˈzitskriːk; ˋzɪtsˏkrik] *n*.〔G.〕对峙战,胶着战〔源出第二次世界大战德国在西部战线采取的非进攻性的战术〕。

sitz·mark [ˈsitsˌmɑːk, ˈzits-; ˋsɪtsˏmark, ˋzɪts-] *n*. 滑雪者摔跤后在雪地上留下的痕迹。

Si·va [ˈsivə, ˈsiːvə; ˋsɪvə, ˋsivə] *n*. 湿婆〔印度教三个主神之一,破坏之神〕。**-ism** *n*. 湿婆教。**-is·tic** *a*. 湿婆似的;湿婆教的。**-ite** *n*. 湿婆教徒。

Si·van [siːˈvɑːn, ˈsivən; siˋvɑn, ˋsivən] *n*. (犹太历)九月。

Si·vyer [ˈsiviə; ˋsɪvɪr] *n*. 西维尔〔姓氏〕。

SIW = self-inflicted wound 自伤〔尤指为逃避兵役等的自伤〕。

si·wash [siˈwɔʃ; ˋsaɪwɑʃ] *n*. 1. (阿拉斯加、西北加拿大的)锡沃斯族印第安人。2. 阿拉斯加狗。3. [S-]规模小的内地蹩脚大学。4.〔美俚〕印第安人;〔蔑〕西部的人。

six [siks; sɪks] I *num*. (基数)六;第六(页章等)。II *n*. 1. 六个人[物]。2. 六人一组;由六个单位组成的东西;六个汽缸的发动机[汽车]。3. 六的记号。4. 六点钟。5. 六岁。6.〔英〕六便士;六先令;六点的纸牌;(骰子的)六点。7.〔*pl*.〕一磅重六支装的蜡烛;六分利公债;(手套、鞋子的)六号。~ *and* ~ 六先令六便士。*two and* ~ 二先令六便士。~ *and eight (pence)* 六先令八便士〔英国以前付给律师的一般报酬〕。*It is ~ of one and half-a-dozen of the other*. 半斤八两;难兄难弟。~ *feet above contradiction*〔美〕傲慢的。*a ~ months*〔美剧〕定期半年的契约。~ *ways to [for] Sunday*〔美俚〕在许多方面;完全,彻底。***at ~es and sevens*** 乱七八糟;意见不一致。~ ***to one*** 六比一;优劣悬殊。~**bits**〔美俚〕七角五分(=0.75美元)。~**-by**〔美俚〕大卡车。~**-by-four**〔美军俚〕(有4个驱动轮的六轮卡车,6×4型卡车。~**-by-six**〔美军俚〕(有6个驱动轮的)六轮卡车,6×6型卡车;六轮卡车。~ **chamber** 六响枪。**Six Coanties** 爱尔兰北部六郡。~**fold** *a*., *ad*. 六倍的,六重的,六折的;成六倍;成六重。~**-footer**〔口〕身长六英尺的人;六英尺长的东西。~**-gun**〔美〕六响枪。~**mo** *n*. (纸张)六开。~ **0** ~ 梅毒特效药六〇六(= arsphenamine)。~**-pack** *n*. 六瓶[六罐头]装的食品纸匣。~**pence**〔英〕六便士(银币);微不足道的东西(*It doesn't matter ~ pence*. 这没什么关系。*I don't care (a) ~ pence about it*. 这事我一点儿也不在乎。*the same old ~ pence* 老笨蛋)。~**penny** *a*.〔英〕六便士的;便宜的,不值钱的。~**penny nail** 2英寸长的钉子。~**pennyworth**〔英〕价格六便士的东西;六便士的数量。~**score** *n*., *a*. 一百二十。~**-shooter**〔俚〕六响枪。**-er**【板球】(得)六分(的一)打。

sixte [sikst; sɪkst] *n*.【剑术】第六个招架法。

six·teen [ˈsiksˈtiːn; sɪksˋtin] I *num*. (基数)十六;第十六〔表示章、页第次等时用于该词的后面〕。II *n*. 1. 十六个人[物]。2. 十六的记号。3.【印】十六开。4. 十六岁;十六点钟。*in ~s*【印】以十六开。*in ~ sixties* 在17世纪的60年代〔略作 in 1660's〕。

six·teen·mo [siksˈtiːnməu; sɪksˋtinmo] *n*. (*pl*. ~*s*) = sextodecimo.

six·teenth [ˈsiksˈtiːnθ; sɪksˋtinθ] I *num*. (序数)第十六(的),十六号(的);十六分之一(的)〔常冠于所限定的词之前〕。II *n*. 1. (月的)第十六日。2.【乐】十六分音符。3. 十六分之一。*three ~s* 十六分之三。*the ~* 十六号。

sixth [siksθ; sɪksθ] I *num*. 第六(的),六号(的);六分之一(的)。II *n*. 1. (月的)第六日。2.【乐】六度音程,六度和音;第六音。3. 六年级。4. 六分之一。*the ~ of April* 四月六日。*the ~ hour* 正午。~ ***form***〔英〕(高中)六年级。~***-former*** 六年级学生。~ ***sense*** 第六官能,直觉。**-ly** *ad*.

six·ti·eth [ˈsikstiiθ; ˋsɪkstɪɪθ] *num*. 第六十(的),六十号(的);六十分之一(的)。

Six·tine [ˈsikstiːn, -tin; ˋsɪkstin, -tɪn] *a*. = sistine.

six·ty [ˈsiksti; ˋsɪkstɪ] I *num*. (基数)六十,第六十。II *n*. 1. 六十个人[物]。2. 六十镑。3. 六十的纪号。4. 六十岁;〔*pl*.〕六十到六十九岁的时期。5.〔*pl*.〕(世纪的)60年代。***in eighteen sixties*** 在19世纪60年代〔略作 in 1860's〕。in eighteen ~ 在1860年〔略 in 1860〕。***in the sixties*** 六十多岁(的);在60年代。***like ~***〔美俚〕飞快地,剧烈地,大大地(*run like ~* 飞跑。*ache like ~* 剧痛)。~**-four-mo** *n*. 64开的纸;64开本。~**-four dollar question**〔美俚〕重大问题,难题〔源自40年代无线电问答比赛中所设最高奖为64美元〕。

siz·a·ble [ˈsaizəbl; ˋsaɪzəbl̩] *a*. 相当大的,大的。**-ness** *n*. **-a·bly** *ad*.

siz·ar [ˈsaizə; ˋsaɪzɚ] *n*. (剑桥等大学的)减费生,靠服侍其他学生来津贴学费的学生。

size[1] [saiz; saɪz] I *n*. 1. 大小,尺寸;规模;身材。2. (鞋帽等的)尺码,号;(纸张的)开。3. 巨大,大量;相当大的分量。4.〔口〕实情,真相。5. (人的)能力,才干,身价;(物的)质量,特性。6. 量珠尺,珍珠筛。7.〔口〕体重。8.〔古〕(饭食、酒类的)定量;份饭。*full [natural, real] ~* 如实物大。*life ~* 如真人一般大〔指雕像等〕。*a ~ seven hat* 七(号)大的帽子。*What ~ do you take in gloves?* 您手套尺码要多大? *That's about the ~ of it*.〔口〕实际情况大致就那么样。*a man of a considerable ~* 相当有才干的人。***be of a ~*** 大小相同。***cut down to ~*** 把重要性[威望等]降至合适的程度,还…的本来面目。***for ~*** 试试尺码,试试是否合适;按不同尺码。***of all ~s*** 大小尺码齐全。***be (half, twice) the ~ of*** 如…的(一半,一倍)大小。***of some ~*** 相当大。~ ***and strength*** 大小强弱。***take the ~ of*** 量…的尺寸。II *vt*. 1. 依大小排列;量大小;测量大小;【军】量身段,依身长排列。2. 筛分,分粒。3. 按规定尺寸制作;使…大小合适。—*vi*. 1. (在大小、质量等方面)相同,不相上下(*up to*, *up with*)。2. 领取定食。~ *a company* 按身段高低排列一连士兵。~ *down* 由大到小排列。~ ***up*** 够标准,合

S

尺寸;估量,测量;〔口〕品评,鉴定(人物等)。～ **stick** (鞋匠用的)量脚尺。～**-up** 估量,估计。

size[2] [saiz; saɪz] **I** *n*. (用面粉、树胶、树脂等配制的)胶料,浆糊〔用于给纸张、皮革、织物等浆洗上光〕。**II** *vt*. 给…上胶,对…上浆。*a sizing machine* 浆纱机。

size·a·ble [ˈsaizəbl; ˋsaɪzəbl] *a*. = sizable.

(-)sized [saizd; saɪzd] *a*. 〔构成复合词〕**1**. 有…大小的,…大小的,…号的,…开的。**2**. 依据大小排列的。*small-～* 小型的,小号的。*medium-～* 中等大小的,中型的,中号的。

siz·er [ˈsaizə; ˋsaɪzɚ] *n*. **1**. 分粒器,整粒器;大小分档拣理器。**2**. 〔英俚〕极大的东西。**3**. 【化】上胶器,填料器。*an egg ～* 鸡蛋拣理器。

siz·ing [ˈsaiziŋ; ˋsaɪzɪŋ] *n*. 胶料;填料;上胶,上浆。

siz·ism [ˈsaizizəm; ˋsaɪzɪzəm] *n*. (就业、教育等方面的)身材歧视。

siz·y [ˈsaizi; ˋsaɪzɪ] *a*. 胶水的,浆糊的;胶水[浆糊]般的;胶质的;黏性的。

sizz [siz; sɪz] **I** *n*. 嗞嗞声。**II** *vt*., *vi*. (使)发嗞嗞声。

siz·zard [ˈsizəd; ˋsɪzɚd] *n*. 〔美口〕(夏季的)闷热。

siz·zle [ˈsizl; ˋsɪzl] **I** *vi*. **1**. 〔口〕(油炸时)嘘嘘地响,嗞嗞响。**2**. 表现喜人,进行顺利。**3**. 〔口〕闷热得要命。**4**. 非常愤怒。*The oil lamp ～d softly on his table*. 油灯在他桌上发出轻微的嗞嗞声。*Sales immediately began to ～*. 销售情况立即出现喜人景象。—*vt*. **1**. 把…烧得嗞嗞响;烧之使焦。**2**. 恶言相骂。*They used to ～ each other*. 他们过去常常互相谩骂。**II** *n*. (油炸鱼等时发出的)嘘嘘声,嗞嗞声。

siz·zler [ˈsizlə; ˋsɪzlɚ] *n*. 〔口〕嗞嗞发烫的东西,大热天。

s.j. = *sub judice* 【法】审理中的;在考虑中的 (〔L.〕= under consideration)。

SJ = Society of Jesus.

sjam·bok [ˈʃæmbək; ˋʃæmbɑk] **I** *n*. 〔南非〕犀[河马]皮鞭。**II** *vt*. 用犀皮鞭打。

SJC = Supreme Judicial Court 〔美〕最高法院。

SJD = 〔L.〕 *Scientiae Juridicae Doctor* 法学学博士 (= Doctor of Juridical Science)。

skag [skæg; skæg] *n*. 〔美俚〕烟丝;香烟(头);海洛因。

Skag·er·ra(c)k [ˈskægəræk; ˋskægəˏræk] *n*. 斯卡格拉克海峡〔在丹麦与挪威之间〕。

skald [skɔːld; skɔld] *n*. 古代北欧的诗人 = scald。

skate[1] [skeit; sket] **I** *n*. **1**. (刃式)冰鞋 (= ice ～);(轮式)溜冰鞋 (= roll ～)。**2**. 滑冰,溜冰。**3**. 〔美俚〕足够喝醉的酒量。***have a ～ on*** 〔美俚〕喝醉。**II** *vi*. **1**. 滑冰;溜冰;飞跑。**2**. 掠过,触及 (*over*)。～ ***over*** [***on***] ***thin ice*** 处理难题;巧妙地处理难局。～ **dancing** 冰上舞蹈。～**park** 滑板运动场。

skate[2] [skeit, skit; sket, skɪt] *n*. 【动】鳐鱼。

skate[3] [skeit; sket] *n*. **1**. 〔美俚〕老马,瘦马。**2**. 人;家伙。*cheap ～* 〔美〕吝啬鬼;心肠卑鄙的人。*good ～* 讨人喜欢的人。

skate·board [ˈskeitˌbɔːd; ˋsketˏbɔrd] **I** *n*. 滑板〔小长方木板两端有轮,儿童用以在斜坡上滑着玩的玩具〕。**II** *vi*. (*-boarded*, *-board·ing*) 作滑板运动,滑滑板。**-er** *n*. 玩滑板的人。

skat·er [ˈskeitə; ˋsketɚ] *n*. 滑冰的人,溜冰的人。

skat·ing [ˈskeitiŋ; ˋsketɪŋ] *n*. 滑冰,溜冰。～ **rink** 滑冰场;溜冰场。

skat·ole [ˈskætəul; ˋskætol] *n*. 【化】粪臭素。

ske·an [skiːn; ʃkin] *n*. (古苏格兰和爱尔兰人的)双刃短剑。

Skeat [skiːt; skit] *n*. **1**. 斯基特〔姓氏〕。**2**. **Walter William ～** 沃尔特·威廉·斯基特〔1835—1912,英国语言学家〕。

ske·dad·dle [skiˈdædl; skɪˋdædl] **I** *vi*. 〔口〕仓惶逃走,匆忙离去。**II** *n*. 溃逃,逃走。

skee [ʃiː, skiː; ski] *n*., *vi*. = ski.

skee·sicks [ˈskiːziks; ˋskizɪks] *n*. 〔*pl*.〕〔美俚〕恶棍,流氓;〔对孩子的爱称〕小鬼,小坏蛋。

skeet [skiːt; skit] *n*. 飞靶射击,打飞靶〔从不同角度射击抛掷的泥鸽或泥盘〕。**-er** *n*. 飞靶射击者。

skeet·er [ˈskiːtə; ˋskitɚ] *n*. **1**. 〔美俚〕蚊子。**2**. 小型冰上滑行船。

skeg [skeg; skɛg] *n*. 【船】导流尾鳍。

skein [skein; sken] *n*. **1**. (丝、纱、线等的)(一)束,(一)绞;绞纱,绞丝。**2**. (野禽的)一群。**3**. 纠缠,混乱(的一团)。*the ravelled* [*tangled*] ～ 错综复杂(的一团)。

skel·e·tal [ˈskelitl; ˋskelətəl] *a*. 骨骼的,骸骨的。**-ly** *adv*.

skel·e·ton [ˈskelitən; ˋskɛlətn̩] **I** *n*. **1**. 骨骼,骷髅;(房屋、伞、扇子等的)骨架;残骸;(叶子的)脉络;筋。**2**. 骨瘦如柴的人[动物]。**3**. 梗概,轮廓,概略。**4**. 骨干,基干;【军】(官多兵少的)基干团[连];因战斗伤亡以致缺额极多的部队〔= ～ company, ～ regiment〕。**5**. 不可外扬的丑事。*a mere* [*walking*] ～ 瘦得像骷髅一样的人。*a ～ structure* 骨架,结构。**II** *a*. **1**. 骨骼的。**2**. 只剩骨架的;瘦得皮包骨头的。**3**. 概括的。*a ～ army* 基干部队;官多兵少的部队。*a ～-drill* (人员不足额的)缩员演习。*a ～ hand* 青筋暴起的手。***be reduced to a ～*** (因病)瘦得像骷髅,瘦得只剩一把骨头。***be worn to a ～*** (因生活困苦)瘦得像骷髅。***family ～*** = ～ ***in the cupboard*** [***closet***, ***house***] (不可外扬的)家丑。～ ***at the feast*** [***banquet***] 扫兴的东西。～ **clock** (无外壳而可看到机芯的)骨架钟。～ **crew** 【海】基干船员。～ **crystals** 骸晶。～ **drawing** 【工】草图,骨架图。～ **face** 字体细小的铅字。～ **key** (可以开各种锁的)万能钥匙。～ **staff** (最必需的)基干员工。

skel·e·ton·ize [ˈskelitənaiz; ˋskɛlətnˏaɪz] *vt*. **1**. 使成骨骼,使成骷髅。**2**. 把…节略成为概要。**3**. 大量裁减;把…编成基干部队。～ *a news story* 节略一篇新闻报导。～ *a regiment* 编成基干团。～ *a leaf* 把叶子做成叶脉标本。—*vi*. **1**. 节略,缩略。**2**. 瘦得不像人样。

skel·lum [ˈskeləm; ˋskɛləm] *n*. 〔古〕〔Scot.〕恶棍;无赖,流氓。

skelp [skelp; skɛlp] **I** *vt*. 〔英方〕打,掌击。—*vi*. 赶快走;催促;硬挤过去。**II** *n*. 〔英方〕一击,一巴掌。

Skel·ton [ˈskeltn; ˋskɛltn̩] *n*. 斯克尔顿〔姓氏〕。

skene [skiːn; ʃkin] *n*. = skean.

skep [skep; skɛp] *n*. **1**. 柳条筐(篮)。**2**. (用草辫或柳条编的)蜜蜂箱。

skep·sis [ˈskepsis; ˋskɛpsɪs] *n*. 〔Am.〕= scepsis.

skep·tic [ˈskeptik; ˋskɛptɪk] *n*. 〔Am.〕= sceptic. **-ly** *ad*.

skep·ti·cism [ˈskeptisizəm; ˋskɛptəˏsɪzəm] *n*. 〔Am.〕= scepticism.

sker·ry [ˈskeri; ˋskɛrɪ] *n*. (*pl*. ***-ries***) 〔Scot.〕岩岛,(岩)礁。

sketch [sketʃ; skɛtʃ] **I** *n*. **1**. 草图,粗样,略图;素描,速写;草稿。**2**. 概略,大意,大要,纲领。**3**. 短篇作品,小品文〔如特写、随笔、见闻录等〕。**4**. (滑稽)短剧;独幕剧;短曲、短小器乐曲〔尤指钢琴曲〕。**5**. 滑稽;丑态。*I never saw such a ～*. 从来没有见过这种丑态。***make a ～*** 速写,画草图。**II** *vt*. **1**. 给…绘草图;给…作速写。**2**. 草拟,拟订;记述…的概要,说出…的大意。—*vi*. 绘草图,作速写。～ (***out***) ***a plan*** [***scheme***] 草拟计划。～ **block** *n*. 速写素描簿。～ **book** *n*. 速写簿;小品文集,短文集,随笔集。～ **map** (地形)草图,略图,示意地图。

sketch·y [ˈsketʃi; ˋskɛtʃɪ] *a*. **1**. 速写的,略图似的。**2**. 粗略的,简略的;粗枝大叶的。**3**. 未完成的,不完全的;贫乏的,肤浅的。**-i·ly** *ad*. **-i·ness** *n*.

skew [skjuː; skju] **I** *vi*. **1**. 走偏,斜进,歪斜。**2**. 斜视 (*at*)。—*vt*. **1**. 使歪斜,使偏。**2**. 曲解,歪曲。*～ed statistical data* 歪曲的统计资料。**II** *a*. **1**. 斜的,歪的,偏的;弯曲的。**2**. 误用的;曲解的。**3**. 【数】敧斜的;挠的;非

S

对称的。a ~ *bridge* 斜桥。a ~ *curve* 挠曲线,空间曲线。~ *lines*【物】敧斜(直)线。a ~ *wheel* 歪轮。**III** *n*. 1. 歪斜,扭曲。2.【建】斜砌石;斜交;【机】歪轮;【统】敧斜。***on the ~***〔口〕歪斜地 (*wear one's hat on the ~* 歪戴帽子)。~ **back**【建】拱座,底座,斜块。~**-bald** *a*. 特指马白色与他色夹杂的。~ **polygon** 挠多边形。**-ness** 偏斜,不对称;【统】偏斜度。

skew·er [ˈskjuə; skjuɚ] **I** *n*. 1. 串肉扦,烤肉叉;扦状物,叉状物。2.〔谑〕剑,刀。3. 针状物(如别针)。**II** *vt*. 用串肉扦串起来。

ski [ʃiː, skiː; ski] **I** *n*. (*pl*. ~(*s*)) 1. 滑雪板[鞋,雪橇]。2. (导弹的)推进装置。3. 滑水橇 (= water ~)。**II** *vi*. (~*ed*, ~'*d*) 滑雪;坐雪橇。~**board**, ~**board** 花样滑雪[滑冰]板。~**bob** 单人滑雪车。~ **boot** 滑雪靴。~ **flying** (滑雪运动中的)跳台飞跃〔比谁跳得远〕。~ **joring** 由马或车辆拖曳的滑雪运动。~ **jump** 飞跃滑雪;飞跃滑雪助滑道。~ **lift** (把滑雪者送上高坡的)滑雪运送机。~ **meister** [ˈskiˌmaistə; ˋskɪˏmaɪstɚ] 滑雪能手,职业滑雪运动员;滑雪教练员。~ **mobile** 履带式雪上汽车。~ **mountaineering** 高山滑雪(运动)。~ **pants** 滑雪裤。~**-plane** (能在雪地上降落的)雪上飞机。~ **run** 滑雪坡,滑雪道。~(**-**)**skate** *vi*. 越野滑雪。~ **stick** [**pole**] 滑雪杖。~ **suit** 滑雪服。~ **tow** = ~ lift. ~ **touring** (非比赛的)滑雪旅行。~ **troops** 滑雪部队。

ski·a·gram [ˈskaiəgræm; ˋskaɪəˏgræm] *n*. = sciagram.

ski·a·graph [ˈskaiəgrɑːf; ˋskaɪəˏgræf] *n*. = sciagraph.

ski·ag·ra·phy [skaiˈægrəʃi; skaɪˋægrəfɪ] *n*. = sciagraphy.

ski·a·scope [ˈskaiəˌskəup; ˋskaɪəˏskop] *n*.【医】爱克斯射线透视镜;视网膜镜。

ski·as·co·py [skaiˈæskəpi; ˋskaɪəˏskop] *n*.【医】爱克斯射线透视检查法;视网膜镜检法。

ski·a·tron [sˈkaiətrɔn; ˋskaɪətrɑn] *n*.【电】暗迹管,投映管。

skib·by [ˈskibi; ˋskɪbɪ] *n*.〔美蔑〕日本佬;东方人。

skid [skid; skɪd] **I** *n*. 1. 制动器,煞车 (= ~-pan)。2. (搬移重物用的)滑动垫木,滑道。3. (支承重物的)低平台,垫木。4. (飞机的)起落橇,滑橇;【海】(上下货物时保护船舷的)垫板,护舷木。5. (车辆)高速行驶时或在结冰的道上打滑,溜滑;〔*pl*. 喻〕下坡路。*hit the ~s*〔美俚〕走下坡路;变弱;被打败。*put the ~s under*〔美俚〕使失败,使走下坡路;摆脱,除去。***on the ~s***〔美俚〕快要失败[打败];快要被解雇;正在衰落。**II** *vi*. (**-*dd*-**) 1. (车辆)煞着车滑行,打滑;滑向一侧。2. 在滑材上拖;煞车。3.【空】(飞机转弯时)外滑。4. 急剧下降。5.〔美俚〕败北。*skidding dog*【林】曳运铁钉。—*vt*. 1. 用煞车煞住;使减慢。2. 用垫木支承;用滑材拖。3. 使滑行[打滑]。~ **fin** (飞机的)翼上垂直面。~**-fin antenna**【无】附翼天线,翅形天线。~ **pad**〔美〕试车场。~ **road** 1. 木材滑送道。2. 城镇中伐木工人经常出入的地区。3. = ~ row. ~ **row** (城市中流浪汉、酒鬼等经常出入的)地区〔多小酒店、小旅店和职业介绍所等〕。

skid·dy [ˈskidi; ˋskɪdɪ] *a*. 溜滑(面)的。

ski·doo [skiˈduː; skɪˋdu] *vi*.〔美俚〕出去! 走开!

skid·proof [ˈskidˌpruːf; ˋskɪdˏpruf] *a*. 防滑的,抗滑的。

ski·er [ˈʃiːə, ˈskiːə; ˋʃiɚ, ˋskiɚ] *n*. 滑雪者。

skiff [skif; skɪf] *n*. 小艇,小船。

ski·ing [ˈskiːiŋ; ˋskiɪŋ] *n*. 滑雪术,滑雪运动。

skil·ful [ˈskilfəl; ˋskɪlfəl] *a*. = skillful.

skill[1] [skil; skɪl] *n*. 1. 技巧,技艺,技能。2. 本领;手艺;(专门)技术。3. 巧妙,熟练。4.〔古〕知识,理解力,判断能力。*a specialized ~* 专门技能。*basic ~s* 基本功。*have no ~ in* 没有…的技能。*knowledge and ~* 知识和技能。*language ~s* 掌握语言的能力。

skill[2] [skil; skɪl] *vi*.〔古〕〔常用 it 为主语〕起作用;有助于;有影响。*It ~s not*. 这毫无用处;不起作用。

skilled [skild; skɪld] *a*. 1. = skillful (*in*). 2. 需要技巧的;有技巧的。~ *hands* [*workers*] 熟练工人。~ *labour* 熟练劳动;技工;熟手(工人)。~ *in chemistry* 精于化学。~ *in keeping accounts* 善于管理账目。

skil·let [ˈskilit; ˋskɪlɪt] *n*. 1.〔英〕长柄(矮脚)小锅。2.〔美〕长柄平底锅 (= frying pan)。***put on the ~***〔美〕挨骂,受责备。

skil·ley [ˈskili; ˋskɪlɪ] *n*.〔美俚〕= gravy.

skill·ful [ˈskilful; ˋskɪlfʊl] *a*. 1. 熟练的,灵巧的;擅长于 (*at*; *in*)。2. 制作精巧的。**-ly** *ad*. **-ness** *n*.

skil·ling [ˈskiliŋ; ˋskɪlɪŋ] *n*. 斯吉林〔斯堪的纳维亚旧铜币和货币单位〕。

skil·ly [ˈskili; ˋskɪlɪ] *n*.〔英俚〕稀薄的麦片粥。

skim [skim; skɪm] **I** *vt*. (**-*mm*-**) 1. 撇取(牛奶等的)乳皮[奶油];撇去浮沫;【机】撇渣。2. 使掠过;使擦过,使滑过。3. 略读,快读。4. 使蒙上一层薄膜。5. (为逃税)隐瞒(部分收入)。~ *the cream* (*off milk*) 撇取奶油;〔喻〕提取精华。〔美俚〕为逃税而隐瞒(部分收入)。—*vi*. 1. 掠过,擦过。2. 浏览,略读。3. 结上薄的覆盖层;涂上最后一层(漆、泥灰等)。4.〔美俚〕逃税,漏税。~ *it down*〔美俚〕我可不信! 别吹牛! **II** *a*. 撇去奶油的;用脱脂乳做的。**III** *n*. 撇去浮沫;脱脂乳;(为逃税)隐匿的部分收入。~ **board** 浅水滑水[冲浪]板。~ **gate** 撇渣口;除渣器。~**milk** 脱脂乳。

skim·ble-scam·ble [ˈskimblˌskæmbl; ˋskɪmblˋskæmbl] *a*. 随口说的,杂乱无章的,互不关联的,毫无意义的。

skim·mer [ˈskimə; ˋskɪmɚ] *n*. 1. 撇乳器;撇油器;撇取浮沫的杓子,网杓,漏杓。2. 马马虎虎阅读的人。3.【机】刮路机;铲削器。4. 蜻蜓;【鸟】撇水鸟。5.〔美〕帽子,平顶宽边草帽。

skim·ming [ˈskimiŋ; ˋskɪmɪŋ] *n*. 1. 撇沫,撇取(奶油)。2.〔*pl*.〕浮渣;撇取的奶油;【化】蒸去轻油。3. (赌场的)抽头。~ **dish** 撇取奶油的扁平盘子;平底快船。

skimp [skimp; skɪmp] **I** *vt*. 1.〔口〕马马虎虎做,敷衍了事。2. 少给,克扣;一点一点地[吝啬地]给(食物、金钱等)。—*vi*. 俭省,吝啬。~ *and screw* 吝啬。**II** *a*. 少的,不足的。

skimp·ing·ly [ˈskimpiŋli; ˋskɪmpɪŋlɪ] *ad*. 吝啬地,小气地。

skimp·y [ˈskimpi; ˋskɪmpɪ] *a*. 1. 吝啬的,小气的。2. 勉强够数的;短缺的,不足的;不充分的,不够大的。3. 马马虎虎的,敷衍了事的。**-i·ly** *ad*. **-i·ness** *n*.

skin [skin; skɪn] **I** *n*. 1. (人体的)皮,皮肤。2.〔口〕皮肉;肉体,性命。3. 兽皮,(特指小牛、山羊等小动物的)皮革。【解】真皮。4. 皮制品,(装酒等的)皮囊。5. (果实、葱等的)皮,壳;奶皮。6.【海】(叠起来的)帆的上部;(船体的)外板,壳板。7.〔俚〕骗子;〔美口〕吝啬鬼,小气鬼。8.〔谑〕人,家伙;马,〔尤指〕瘦马。9.〔美俚〕〔*pl*.〕一套鼓〔尤指爵士乐队的〕。10.〔美俚〕一美元。*the true* [*inner*] ~ 真皮。*green* [*raw*, *undressed*] ~ 生皮。*clean ~s*〔澳〕无烙印的野牛。*a bad old ~*〔俚〕老坏蛋。***be in sb.'s ~*** 变做某人。(*I would not be in your ~*. 我无论如何不愿意是你)。***be no ~ off sb.'s back*** [***nose***]〔美口〕与某人无关;对某人没影响。***by*** [***with***] ***the ~ of one's teeth***〔口〕好容易才,幸而。***cast the ~*** 脱皮。***change one's ~*** 改变性格;作风等;改头换面,装出新的面貌。***fly*** [***jump***, ***leap***] ***out of one's ~*** 惊喜若狂;大吃一惊。***get off with a whole ~*** 平安脱险,安然无恙。***get under sb.'s ~*** 抓住某人的心;使某人高兴[发怒、厌烦]。***have a thick*** [***thin***] ***~*** 感觉迟钝[敏锐];面皮厚[薄]。***in a bad ~***〔俚〕情绪不好;发着脾气。***in*** [***with***] ***a whole ~*** 平安无事地。***in one's ~***〔谑〕一丝不挂地。***save one's ~*** 平安逃脱,未受损伤。~ ***and bone***(***s***) (瘦得只剩)皮包骨。***wet***(***ted***) ***to the ~*** 浑身湿透。***wear next to the ~*** 贴身穿着。**II** *vt*. (**-*nn*-**) 1. 剥…的皮;削…的皮;使脱去贴身衣服;(拿皮)覆盖(伤口),使愈合 (*over*);擦伤(皮)。2.〔口〕抢夺,骗取;(严厉)批评;责斥;〔美俚〕(比赛中)击败,胜过。3.〔口〕(用

鞭)驱赶(牲口)。*a* ~*ned rabbit* 瘦鬼。*a* ~*ned diamond* 〔美〕不长草的棒球场。—*vi*. 1. 长皮(*over*);(伤口)愈合,长出新皮。2. 〔美俚〕(考试等时)作弊,夹带。3. 〔口〕攀爬(*up*, *down*);勉强挤过去(*by*, *through*)。4. 〔俚〕逃走,溜掉。***keep one's eyes*** ~***ned*** 〔口〕把眼睛看牢,小心提防。~ ***a flea for its hide*** (***and tallow***)〔口〕非常俭省。~ ***a flint*** 非常吝啬。~ ***a razor*** 做不可能的事情。~ ***a wicked eye*** 〔美〕不怀好意地盯着。~ ***alive*** 〔美俚〕活剥;折磨;严责;使大败。~ ***off*** 脱下(衣服等)。~ ***out*** (猎狗)老远老远地乱跑。~ ***the*** [***a***] ***cat*** 两脚由双手间穿上去翻坐铁杆上。~ ***the lamb*** 全赢,满贯。~**-bound** *a*. 皮绷得紧紧的;【医】患硬皮症的。~**-deep** *a*. 只有一层皮深度的,肤浅的,皮毛的(*Beauty is but* ~*-deep*. 美不过是外表罢了。*a* ~*-deep wound* 擦伤表皮)。~ **disease** 皮肤病。~**-diving** (不穿潜水服而只带面罩、紧身衣、橡皮脚掌等的)潜泳,潜水。~ **effect** 【无】集肤效应。~ **flick** 裸体黄色影片。~**flint** 〔美〕小气鬼,吝啬鬼。~ **friction** 表皮摩擦。~**ful** 满皮囊,满肚子(*have a* ~*ful* 喝饱一肚皮酒)。~**game** 〔美俚〕欺骗。~ **glue** 皮胶。~ **grafting** 【医】表皮移植;植皮术。~**-head** 〔美俚〕光头;剃光头的人;海军陆战队新兵;短发青年暴徒。~ **magazine** 裸体画杂志。~**pop(ping)** 皮下注射麻醉毒品。~**-search** 脱衣[裸体]搜身。~ **test** 【医】皮肤试验。~**tight** *a*. 紧包着身子的。

skink [skiŋk; skɪŋk] *n*. 【动】石龙子科动物。

skinned [skind; skɪnd] *a*. 〔常构成复合词〕1. 有…皮的。2. 没有草皮的。*a* ~*-racetrack* 无草皮的跑道。*dark-*~ 有黝黑皮肤的。

skin·ner [ˈskinə; ˋskɪnɚ] *n*. 1. 剥皮者,皮革工人。2. 皮革商,皮毛商。3. 〔俚〕骗子;〔美〕赶牲口的人。

skin·ny [ˈskini; ˋskɪnɪ] *a*. 1. 皮的;皮状的,皮质的。2. 瘦削的,皮包骨的。3. 不够大的;不够好的;低劣的。4. 〔俚〕吝啬的。~**dip** *n*., *vi*. 裸体游泳。**-ni·ly** *ad*. **-ni·ness** *n*.

skip[1] [skip; skɪp] I *vi*. (***skipped***, ***skip·ping***) 1. (小羊、小孩等)跳,蹦(*about*);跳绳。2. 跳来蹦去;在表面上掠过。3. 跳着读[看];跳过,略过,遗漏。4. 很快地改变(话题、职业等)(*off*; *from*);【乐】急转。5. 回跳,弹回;发跳弹射击。6. 【机】不发火。7. 〔口〕匆匆离开;潜逃,逃亡。8. 〔美〕(学校里)跳级。~ *over* [*across*] *to Japan for a week* 去日本匆匆忙忙旅行一个星期。~ (*over*) *the dull parts of a book* 跳过书中无聊的地方。~ *from golf to theology* 从谈高尔夫球跳到谈神学。—*vt*. 1. 使跳;跳过。2. 跳读,跳看;漏去,省去;忽略。3. 投掷(砖片等)使掠水跳飞。4. 〔常以 it 为宾语〕〔口〕悄悄离开,匆匆离开(某地),逃亡。5. (学校里)使跳级;不出席(学校、教堂、会议等)。~ *two days* 缺席两天。~ ***for joy*** 喜欢得跳。~ ***it*** 〔美俚〕忘掉,不再提起,别提了。~ ***one's bail*** 〔口〕保释中逃亡。~ ***the cinders*** 〔美〕顺着铁路走。II *n*. 1. 轻跳,跳跃。2. 读漏,看漏,遗漏,省略;漏看的东西,略过的东西。3. (计算机的)空白指令;【自】跳跃(进位)。4. 〔俚〕可以跳过不读的部分。~**band** 【无】短波段。~ **bombing** 【军】跳弹轰炸〔一种超低空轰炸〕。~ **distance** 【无】越距,跳跃距离。

skip[2] [skip; skɪp] *n*. (Dublin 大学的)校役,校工。

skip[3] [skip; skɪp] I *n*. = skipper[1]. II *vi*. (***-pp-***) 充当队长〔船长等〕。

skip[4] [skip; skɪp] *n*. 【矿】箕斗,翻斗车,斜井用四轮车,料车;起重箱。~ **park** 翻斗废物场〔配备有翻斗车供存放各种废物〕。

skip·jack [ˈskipdʒæk; ˋskɪpˏdʒæk] *n*. 1. 趾高气扬的纨袴子弟;暴发户。2. 鲣。3. 叩头虫。4. 跳跃玩具。

skip·per[1] [ˈskipə; ˋskɪpɚ] I *n*. 1. (小商船、渔船等的)船长。2. (滚球,冰上溜石等游戏)的队长。3. 〔空军俚〕机长,正驾驶员。~*'s daughters* 高白浪。II *vi*. 充当船长,充当队长。

skip·per[2] [ˈskipə; ˋskɪpɚ] *n*. 1. 跳跃者。2. 【鱼】飞鱼(类);长颌竹刀鱼;【虫】叩头虫;酪蛆;水蝇;弄(花)蝶。

skip·pet [ˈskipit; ˋskɪpɪt] *n*. 封印护套。

skip·ping·ly [ˈskipiŋli; ˋskɪpɪŋlɪ] *ad*. 跳着,蹦着;跳过,漏去,省去。

skip·ping-rope [ˈskipiŋrəup; ˋskɪpɪŋˏrop] *n*. 跳绳用的绳。

skirl [skəːl; skɝl] I *n*. 〔Scot.〕尖锐声;风笛声。II *vi*. (风笛)发尖锐声。—*vt*. 用风笛演奏。

skir·mish [ˈskəːmiʃ; ˋskɝmɪʃ] I *n*. 1. 【军】小接触,小战斗,小冲突。2. 小争论。3. 〔美运〕比赛。II *vi*. 1. 进行小规模战斗;进行小争论。2. 搜索,侦察。*a* ~*(ing) line* 散兵线。

skir·mish·er [ˈskəːmiʃə; ˋskɝmɪʃɚ] *n*. 【军】散兵。

skirr [skəː; skɝ] I *vi*. 〔拟声〕飕飕地动(飞,跑等)。—*vt*. 1. 走遍(某地)搜索。2. 飞越过;使掠过。II *n*. 飕飕声。

skirt [skəːt; skɝt] I *n*. 1. 女裙;(衣服的)裙,下摆。2. 〔俚〕女人,姑娘。3. 物件的裙状部分;套筒;缘,边,端;马鞍两边下垂部分;〔*pl*.〕郊区。4. (牛的)横膈膜。5. 【建】壁脚板。*a divided* ~ (女人骑马用的)裙裤。*on the* ~*s of a city* 在市郊。***clear sb.'s*** ~***s*** 为某人洗去耻辱;表明某人清白无辜。***like a bit of*** ~ 〔口〕喜欢与女人作伴。II *vt*. 1. 用裙子覆盖;使穿裙子。2. 给…装边;给…装防护罩。3. 沿着…边缘;和…接界;绕过…的边缘。4. 避开(危险等);回避(问题等)。—*vi*. 1. 位处边缘;沿边走(*along*, *around*)。~ **chaser** 〔俚〕色情狂者。~ **dancing** [**dance**] (优美地摆着裙子跳的)裙子舞。

skirt·ing [ˈskəːtiŋ; ˋskɝtɪŋ] *n*. 1. 边缘。2. 裙料。3. 〔英〕【建】踢脚板,壁脚板〔又叫 ~-board〕。

skit [skit; skɪt] *n*. 1. 讽刺话[文];讽刺剧,滑稽短剧;幽默故事。2. 〔*pl*.〕〔口〕多数,很多(*of*)。

skitch [skitʃ, skɪtʃ] *vi*. 跟车溜冰〔溜旱冰者抓住行驶中的汽车后杠滑行一段距离后再松手,一种危险且违章的危险运动〕。**-ing** *n*.

skit·ter [ˈskitə; ˋskɪtɚ] *vi*. 1. (水鸟等)轻轻掠过(水面或地面)。2. 轻快地将钓饵在水面上拉动。—*vt*. 使轻轻掠过。

skit·tish [ˈskitiʃ; ˋskɪtɪʃ] *a*. 1. 易惊的(马等)。2. 羞怯的;胆小的。3. (尤指女人)轻佻的。4. 不可靠的,反复无常的。**-ly** *ad*. **-ness** *n*.

skit·tle [ˈskitl; ˋskɪtl] I *n*. 〔英〕九柱戏用的小柱;〔*pl*.〕九柱戏〔类似 ninepins〕。*Life is not all beer and* ~*s*. 人生并不完全是吃喝玩乐。***Knock over like*** ~***s***. 一下子打倒,驳倒。***Skittles***! 别胡说! 胡说! II *vi*. 做九柱戏游戏。—*vt*. 耽误(时机);失误。~ **alley** [**ground**] 九柱戏场。~ **ball** 九柱戏的球。

skiv [skiv; skɪv] *n*. 〔俚〕一镑(金币)。

skive [skaiv; skaɪv] I *vt*. (把皮革等)割成薄片;磨(宝石)。II *n*. (磨宝石用的)钻石轮。

skiv·er [ˈskaivə; ˋskaɪvɚ] *n*. 1. 装订书籍用皮革,帽里子革〔一种切割成薄片羊皮革〕。2. 割革工。3. 割革刀。

skiv·vy [ˈskivi; ˋskɪvɪ] *n*. 1. 〔英口,蔑〕女佣。2. 〔美俚〕(水手等的)短袖内衣;汗衫。

skoal [skəul; skol] *int*. (祝酒词)祝您健康! (一杯酒)。

skoo·kum [ˈskuːkʌm; ˋskukəm] *a*. 〔美俚〕极好的,顶呱呱的;强壮的,有力的。

Sko·p(l)je [ˈskəuplje; ˋskɔpljɛ] *n*. 斯科普里〔前南斯拉夫城市〕。

Skr., **Skt.** = Sanskrit.

sku·a [ˈskjuːə; ˋskjuə] *n*. 1. 【鸟】贼鸥〔挪威产〕。2. 〔S-〕【英空军】大鸥式飞机。

skul(l)·dug·ger·y [skʌlˈdʌgəri; skʌlˋdʌgərɪ] *n*. 〔美口〕欺骗,欺诈,诡计;卑鄙的行为。

skulk [skʌlk; skʌlk] I *vi*. 1. 躲躲闪闪地走(*about*; *through*)。2. 偷偷避开,躲避;躲藏(*behind*);潜逃(*away*)。3. 偷懒;装病;逃避责任。~ ***after*** 躲躲闪闪地跟在后头。II *n*. 1. = ~er 1. 2. 〔古〕狐群。**-er** *n*. 1. 躲藏者。2. 装病者;逃避责任者。**-ing·ly** *ad*. 偷偷摸

摸地；躲躲闪闪地；怯懦地。

skull [skʌl; skʌl] ***n*.** 1. 颅骨，头骨，脑壳，头盖骨。2. 头脑；智能。3.【冶】渣壳；熔铁上的浮渣。*an empty* ～ 头脑空空。*thick* ～ 笨头笨脑。～ ***and crossbones*** 骷髅枯骨图〔由一个骷髅和两根交叉的枯骨组成，作为死的象征；过去为海盗旗标记；现作毒药瓶上的标记〕。～**cap** ***n*.** 1.（无沿绒制室内戴的）便帽。2. 古时的铁盔。3.【植】黄岑属植物，美黄岑，并头草。4.【解】前顶部。～**-drag** ***vi*.**〔美俚〕用功。～**duggery**〔美俚〕= skulduggery. ～ **practice** [**session**] 1.〔俚〕咨询会，交流会，非正式的学术讨论会。2.（运动员）策略研究会议。

skunk [skʌŋk; skʌŋk] **I** ***n*.** 1.【动】臭鼬；臭鼬皮。2.〔俚〕臭名昭彰的卑劣家伙。3.〔美俚〕得零分。***hotter than a*** ～ 烂醉。**II** ***vt*.** 1.〔美俚〕击败〔尤指使对方得零分〕。2. 欺骗。～ **cabbage,** ～**weed** ***n*.**【植】臭菘（属植物）。

sky [skai; skaɪ] **I** ***n*.** 1. 天，天空。2.【宗】天国。3.〔常 *pl*.〕天气；气候，风土。4. 天蓝色。5.〔口〕画展室的顶列画。*a cloudy* ～ 阴云密布的天空。*blue* ～ 蓝天。*If the* ～ *fall(s), we shall catch larks*. 天塌了好捉云雀；不必预先担忧。*He is in the* ～. 他在天上[死了]。～ *piece*〔美俚〕帽子。～ *police*〔美俚〕牧师。～ *scout*〔美军俚〕随军牧师。***be raised to the skies*** 升天了，死了。***in the skies*** 高兴，得意扬扬。***laud sb. to the skies*** 把(某人)捧上天。***out of a clear*** [***blue***] ～ 晴天霹雳一般地，突然。***to the skies*** 无保留地；过分地。***The*** ～ ***is the limit***. 没有限制。***under a foreign*** ～ 在异乡，在异国。***under the open*** ～ 露天，在野外。**II** ***vt*.**（***skied***）将(画)挂在最高一排；【板球】(将球)高打，打上去。～ *one*〔美棒球〕打大飞球。～ **blue** ***a*.** 天蓝色的，蔚蓝的。～**board** 空中(乘风)滑翔板，空中冲浪滑翔板。～**-borne** ***a*.** 空运的；空降的。～**bus** 空中客车〔指乘客毋需预订机票的班机〕。～**-clad** ***a*.**〔古〕(巫婆)一丝不挂的；〔俚〕裸体的。～**diving**【空】(延缓张伞的)跳伞特技表演〔在自由坠落时作表演动作〕。～**-gun** 高射炮。～**-high** ***a*., *ad*.** 极高的；天一样高。～**jack** 1. ***vt*.**〔口〕空中劫持(飞机)。2. ***n*.** 劫机。～**lab**（用火箭发射到太空中的）太空实验室。～**-lark** 1. ***n*.**【鸟】云雀，天鹨，告天子。2. ***n*., *vi*.**〔口〕闹着玩，嬉戏；寻欢作乐。～**larker** ***n*.**〔美〕轻薄子，轻薄女人。～ **lift** ***v*., *n*.** 空运。～**light** 天窗。～**line** 天边，天涯，地平线；(山、大厦等)空中轮廓；展览会场的顶层。～**lounge** 把旅客从城里送往机场的车辆〔有时指连车带人一同送往机场的直升机〕。～**man**〔美俚〕飞行员；伞兵。～ **master** 巨型客机。～ **motel** [ˈskaiməˌtel; ˋskaɪmoˏtɛl]（机场附近的）汽车旅馆。～ **parlor** 阁楼；最上层的房间。～**pilot**〔俚〕(尤指船上的)牧师；【空】飞行员，驾驶员。～**rocket** 1. ***n*.** 流星焰火；高空探测火箭。2. ***vi*., *vt*.** 突然出现；(使)腾空而起；(使)直线上升；(物价)猛涨。～**-sail**【海】第三层帆。～**scape** 天空风景(画)。～**scraper** 1. 摩天楼；非常高的烟囱。2.【海】第三层帆(skysail)上的三角帆。3.〔美棒球〕钻高飞球。～ **screen** "空网"〔一种用来观测飞弹横偏差的光学仪器〕。～**-shot** 朝天拍摄成的镜头[画面]。～**sign**（设在高楼大厦顶上的）空中广告。～**(-)surfing** 空中(乘风)滑翔运动，空中冲浪运动〔运动员脚绑滑翔板从飞机上跳下，然后乘风滑翔于空中直至打开降落伞落地〕。～**sweeper**（装有雷达瞄准设备的）一种口径75毫米的高射炮。～ **train** 空中列车〔由一架飞机牵引一架或数架滑翔机之机组编队〕。**Skytrain**〔商标〕空中列车〔一种廉价的定期穿梭班机〕。～**trooper** 伞兵。～ **truck**〔口〕运输机。～**ward(s)** ***ad*.** 向天空。～ **wave** 天(空电)波。～**way** 高架公路；航线。～ **winder** ***n*.**〔俚〕飞行员，空军。～ **writing**（飞机放烟飞成的）天空文字；空中广告。

Skye [skai; skaɪ] ***n*.** 1. **Isle of** ～ 斯凯岛〔苏格兰西北部〕。2. ～ **terrier**【动】斯凯㹴狗〔一种身长脚短的长毛猎狐狗〕。

sky·ey [ˈskaii; ˋskaɪɪ] ***a*.** 1.〔诗〕天空的，在天上的，从天上来的。2. 像天空的；天蓝色的，蔚蓝的。3. 极高的；高耸云霄的。

sky·o·graph [ˈskaiəgræf; ˋskaɪəˏgræf] ***n*.** 空摄地图。

sl = 1. slightly. 2. slow.

S.L. = 1. Solicitor-at-Law〔英〕初级律师。2. Support Line〔美〕支承线。

SL = 1. sea level 海拔。2. south latitude 南纬。3. lens spectrometer 透镜分光计。

slab[1] [slæb; slæb] **I** ***n*.** 1. 平板，厚板；(圆木解成板时外面两块带皮的)背板。2.（面包等的）片，厚块；铁块；土块。3. 混凝土路面；【地】板层。4.〔棒球俚〕投球员足标，投手板；难看的人。*a* ～ *of marble* 一块云石板。～ *of moo*〔美〕牛排。*a* ～ *milling*【机】平面铣。**II** ***vt*.** 1. 把…分成厚片，使成厚板。2. 铺石板。3. 将(木材)锯去背板。4. 在…涂上一厚层。～**-sided** ***a*.** 1.〔美〕侧面平坦的。2. 细长的，瘦的，高的。～**stone**（铺路）石板。～**top** 石板面(如大理石桌面)。

slab[2] [slæb; slæb] ***a*.**〔古〕浓稠的，黏的，半流体的。～ *porridge* 稠粥。

slab·ber [ˈslæbə; ˋslæbɚ] ***v*., *n*.** = slobber, slaver.

slack[1] [slæk; slæk] **I** ***a*.** 1.（衣服、绳子等）松的，宽松的。2. 行动迟缓的；无精神的，无气力的。3. 马马虎虎的，懒惰的；松弛的，松懈的，不紧张的。4.（商业等）呆滞的，清淡的，萧条的。5. 温的，微热的；(面包等)未烘干的，烤得不透的；(石灰等)熟化的。6.【语音】松弛的，开口音的。7. 不坚实的，软弱的；不完善的。8. 漏水的，透水的。*He is* ～ *in study*. 他学业上不用功。*I feel* ～. 我觉得发软。*a* ～ *market* 呆滞的市场。～ *muscles* 松弛的肌肉。*a* ～ *oven* 微温的烤箱。*at a* ～ *pace* 慢条斯理地。*keep a* ～ *hand* [*rein*] 松着手[缰绳]；宽大统治。～ *lime* 消[熟]石灰。～ *season* [*time*]【商】淡季。～ *water*（停止涨退的）平潮(期)；静流。～ *weather* 使人倦怠的天气。～ ***in stays***【海】(调头时)转得慢的(船)。**II** ***ad*.** 1. 松弛地；缓慢地。2. 无力地，宽松地，不活泼地。3. 不充分地；不透地。4. 呆滞地，清淡地。**III** ***n*.** 1.（绳、带、帆等的）松弛部分。2. 空隙，空间余宽。3. 轨幅，轨间距离。4. 萧条(时期)，淡季。5. 静止；停滞；平潮期。6.〔*pl*.〕(水手等的)宽裤，工装；〔美〕(男女)运动裤，女裤。7.〔口〕闲散，休息。***have a good*** ～ 舒舒服服地休息一下。***pull in*** [***up***] ***the*** ～ 勒紧松弛部分。**IV** ***vi*.** 1. 怠惰，偷懒；松懈，放松。2. 放慢；减少，和缓，减弱，虚弱；停止。3.（石灰）熟化。4.〔口〕休息，懒散。—***vt*.** 1. 放松；松懈，怠忽。2. 使缓慢，放慢；减少，使缓和。3. 熟化(石灰)。～ ***off*** 放松，松劲；偷工，怠工，敷衍了事。～ ***up*** 放慢，慢下来。**-in, -ing** ***n*., *a*.**（牛仔裤）宽松式(的)。**-ly** ***ad*.** **-ness** ***n*.**

slack[2] [slæk; slæk] ***n*.** 煤渣，煤屑。

slack·en [ˈslækən; ˋslækən] ***vt*.** 1. 松弛，松劲，放松。2. 放慢，使慢下来；削弱；减少。—***vi*.** 1.（绳索等）变松弛，松劲。2.（风等）变弱，减弱。3.〔口〕怠惰，休息。

slack·er [ˈslækə; ˋslækɚ] ***n*.** 1. 战时逃避兵役的人。2.〔口〕逃避责任的人；懒鬼，敷衍塞责的人；怠惰的人。3.【林】架空集材机。

slacks [slæks; slæks] ***n*. *pl*.**（宽松的）裤子。

slag [slæg; slæg] **I** ***n*.** 1. 矿渣，铁渣，炉渣，熔渣。2. 火山岩渣。**II** ***vt*., *vi*.**（**-*gg*-**）(使)起溶渣；(使)成熔渣。～ *cement*【地】溶渣水泥。～ **heap** 熔渣堆。～ **wool** 矿渣绵，渣绒〔将熔化的炉渣用蒸气或压缩空气吹散而成，用作防火、隔热、隔音材料〕。**-gy** ***n*.**

slain [slein; slen] slay 的过去分词。

slake [sleik; slek] ***vt*.** 1. 消除，扑灭(火等)，平息(怒气)；解(渴)；满足。2. 熟化，消化(石灰)。～*d lime* 消[熟]石灰。—***vi*.** 1.〔古〕消除，平息；缓和，松，停。2.（石灰）熟化。～ ***one's last of blood*** 满足血腥欲望。

sla·lom [ˈslɑːləm; ˋslɑləm] **I** ***n*.**〔挪威〕障碍滑雪(赛)。**II** ***vi*.** 进行障碍滑雪赛。

SLAM = 1. supersonic low altitude missile 低空超音速导

S

[飞]弹。**2.** strategic low altitude missile 低空战略导[飞]弹。

slam [slæm; slæm] **I** *vt*. (***-mm-***) **1.** 砰地关上(门等),砰地放下;砰地丢下。**2.**〔口〕猛打;猛击;【牌】以满贯击败对方。**3.**〔美口〕侮辱;猛烈抨击。—*vi*. **1.** 发出砰击,砰地关上。**2.** 猛攻;使劲干。**3.**〔美口〕侮辱,猛烈抨击。~ *the door* 砰地一声关上门;〔喻〕断然拒绝[考虑、商讨]。~ *down the lid of a trunk* 砰的一声关上箱盖。~ *the door in sb's face* 把某人砰的一声关在门外;拒绝听取某人的意见。~ *off* 〔美俚〕离去;死。**II** *n*. **1.** 砰的[轰的]声音。**2.** 猛击,猛攻。**3.**【牌戏】满贯。**4.**〔美口〕侮辱,猛烈抨击。*a grand* ~【桥牌】大满贯。*a little* [*small*] ~【桥牌】小满贯。*with a* ~ 轰的一声。~**bang** *ad*., *vt*., *vi*. 砰地(关上)。~ **dance** 碰碰舞〔"重金属"等摇滚乐迷跳的一种摇滚舞,舞伴彼此猛烈碰撞,并疯狂地上下跳跃〕。~**-dunk 1.**【篮球】跳起扣篮,塞篮。**2.**〔美口〕大满贯,大成功。

slan·der [ˈslɑːndə; ˋslændɚ] **I** *n*. **1.** 诽谤,诋毁;【法】毁谤。**2.** (口头)诽谤罪。**II** *vt*. 讲坏话,污蔑,诽谤。**-er** *n*.

slan·der·ous [ˈslɑːndərəs; ˋslændərəs] *a*. 毁谤的,污蔑的,毁坏名誉的;造谣中伤的。**-ly** *ad*.

slang[1] [slæŋ; slæŋ] **I** *n*. 俚语;(盗贼等的)黑话,切口,隐语;行话,专门语。*army* ~ 军队俚语。*art* ~ 艺术上的行话。*back* ~ 倒读隐语。*doctors'* ~ 医生行话。*schoolboy* ~ 学生俚语。**II** *vt*. 用粗话烂骂。—*vi*. 用俚语,用粗俗的话。

slang[2] [slæŋ; slæŋ]〔方,古〕sling 的过去式。

slan·gu·age [ˈslæŋgwidʒ; ˋslæŋgwɪdʒ] *n*.〔谑〕多俚语的话[作品];俚语。

slang·y [ˈslæŋi; ˋslæŋɪ] *a*. 鄙俗的,俚语多的;滥用俚语的。

slank [slæŋk; slæŋk]〔古〕slink 的过去式及过去分词。

slant [slɑːnt; slænt] **I** *a*. 倾斜的,歪斜的。**II** *n*. **1.** 倾斜;歪斜;斜坡;斜线,斜向,斜面;斜线号(/)。**2.** (对某事的)倾向性;观点,态度,意见;偏见,偏向,歪曲。**3.**〔口〕斜眼看。**4.**〔古、美〕挖苦,讽刺。**5.**〔俚〕机会。*I need to get your* ~ *on the situation*. 请说说您对于情况的意见。*on the* [*a*] ~ 倾斜着,倾斜地。***a*** ~ ***of wind***【海】一阵风;顺风。***have a*** ~ ***on***〔美〕喝醉。**III** *vi*. **1.** 倾斜;歪斜;倾向;斜向前进。**2.**〔美俚〕走开。—*vt*. **1.** 使倾斜,弄歪斜。**2.** 使具有倾向性;使带某种色彩;加以歪曲。~ **rhyme** 借押韵,不完全韵[用音韵相近,但不属于同一韵部的词借押,如。lid, lad; wait, made.]。

slan·ten·dic·u·lar, slan·ting·dic·u·lar [ˌslɑːntinˈdikjulə, -iŋ-; ˏslæntnˋdɪkjulɚ] *a*.〔谑〕倾斜的;间接的;拐弯抹角的。

slant·ing [ˈslɑːntiŋ; ˋslæntɪŋ] *a*. 倾斜的;歪斜的。**-ly** *ad*.

slant·ways [ˈslɑːntweiz; ˋslæntˏwaɪz] *ad*. 倾斜地,歪斜地。

slant·wise [ˈslɑːntwaiz; ˋslæntˏwaɪz] *ad*., *a*. 倾斜地[的],歪斜地[的]。

slap [slæp; slæp] **I** *n*. **1.** 一巴掌,一拍;击拍声。**2.** 侮辱;拒绝。**3.**【机】松动(声)。*a* ~ *in the face* 脸上一巴掌,一个耳光;〔喻〕(意外的)拒绝[侮辱、失望、责备等]。**II** *vt*. (***-pp-***) **1.** (用巴掌或其他扁平东西)打,拍;啪的一声关上(门等)。**2.** 啪的一声放下(*down*);猛掷;漫不经心扔掉。**3.** 攻击,侮辱。**4.**〔美口〕任意涂;任意对…罚款[课税]。~ *on* 啪的一声穿上[戴上]。~ (*sb*.) *on the back* 拍拍(某人)脊背[表示赞许等]。~ *a defeat on*〔美运〕打败对手。~ ***down***〔美俚〕粗暴地压制,制止,镇压。—*vi*. (用手掌或其他扁平东西)拍打,掴。~ ***and tickle***〔口〕(男女间的)打闹调情。**III** *ad*. **1.** 啪的一下。**2.** 猛然,突然。**3.** 直接,一直,迎面。*The tail came* ~ *off*. 尾巴忽然掉了下来。***run*** ~ ***into*** 迎面相撞。~**bang 1.** *ad*. 突然;猛然。**2.** *a*. 匆促的,草率的,鲁莽的。~**dash 1.** *a*., *ad*. 匆促的[地],草率的[地],鲁莽的[地]。**2.** *n*. 鲁莽;草率;草率做成的东西。**3.** *vt*. 乱做;瞎做,乱七八糟地涂抹(墙壁等);起草,草拟。~**dashery** *n*. 草率;脏乱。~ **happy** *a*.〔美俚〕(因受击)头昏目眩的;胜利冲昏头脑的,愚蠢的。~**jack** *n*.〔美〕= flapjack; griddlecake. ~ **man**〔美俚〕便衣警官。~**stick** *n*. (滑稽戏里打人时能发出响声的)敲板,击板;低级滑稽戏。*a*. 低级滑稽戏的。~**-up** *a*.〔俚〕第一流的,上等的;最新式的;铺张的。

slap·ping [ˈslæpiŋ; ˋslæpɪŋ] *a*.〔俚〕非常快的;(马、人)魁梧的;极好的。*a* ~ *pace* 快步。*a* ~ *horse* 高大的马。*a* ~ *dinner* 美肴佳餐。

slash [slæʃ; slæʃ] **I** *vt*. **1.** 深深砍入,深深切进;割下,割开;乱砍,乱斩;鞭打。**2.** 严厉的批评[谴责]。**3.** 在(织物上)开裂缝,在(衣服上)开叉。**4.**〔美、俚〕减(薪),减少。**5.** 猛动,猛挥,猛拉。~ ***and burn*** 裁(员),精简(人员)。—*vi*. **1.** 乱砍,乱斩,挥击(*at*)。**2.** 猛进;猛飞;冲;严厉地批评[谴责]。**II** *n*. **1.** 深砍,深切;乱砍,乱斩;刀痕,伤痕,鞭痕。**2.** 衣服上开的叉[缝]。**3.** (树木被砍后的)林中空地;(树林砍伐后留下的)枝桠,废材;〔*pl*.〕长满灌木的洼地。**4.**〔美、俚〕减薪,减少。**5.** 斜线号(/)。~ **pine**〔美〕(佛罗里达产的)坚硬松木;加勒比松。~ **pocket** 斜口插袋。

sla·sher [ˈslæʃə; ˋslæʃɚ] *n*. **1.** 断木机。**2.**〔美俚〕衣裳时髦的花花公子,香喷喷的纨袴子。**3.** (挥刀等)乱砍的人。~ **film** 凶杀影片[录像带,影碟等]。

slash·ing [ˈslæʃiŋ; ˋslæʃɪŋ] **I** *a*. **1.** 乱斩的,猛砍的。**2.** (批评等)不客气的,严厉的,厉害的。**3.** 冲劲十足的;(步子等)飞快的(等)。**4.**〔口〕(财产等)巨大的。**5.** 倾泻的,急降的。**6.** (颜色)鲜明的。*a* ~ *rain* 一阵倾盆大雨。*a* ~ *success* 巨大的战功。**II** *n*.〔美〕伐木区域;〔*pl*.〕废材,残木。

slat[1] [slæt; slæt] **I** *n*. (金属、木材的)板条;狭板;〔俚〕〔*pl*.〕肋骨。**II** *vt*. (***-tt-***) 用板条制作;装上板条。***hit the*** ~***s***〔美俚〕(躺下)睡觉。

slat[2] [slæt; slæt] **I** *vi*. (***-tt-***)〔英,美方〕(帆、索等)劈啪劈啪地碰撞;敲打;猛烈拍动。—*vt*.〔英、美方〕猛投,猛掷;打,击,以拳连接。**II** *n*. 拍打声;猛烈的一击。

S. lat. = south latitude 南纬。

slatch [slætʃ; slætʃ] *n*. (一段时间的)清静;安静无事的间隔。

slate[1] [sleit; slet] **I** *n*. **1.** (建筑用)板石;石板,石板瓦;板岩。**2.** (书写用)石板。**3.** 鼠灰色;石板色,暗蓝灰色。**4.**〔美〕候补人[候选人]名单;内定名单。**5.** (操行等的)记录。*There is a loose* ~ *in his house*. = *He has a* ~ *off*. 他精神有点不对。*a clean* ~ 良好的经历,历史清白。***break*** [***smash***] ***the*** ~〔美〕取消候选人名单。***clean the*** ~ 勾销往事;了脱义务;免除义务。***make up the*** ~〔美〕拟定(候选人)名单。***start with a clean*** ~ (改过)自新;重新开始。***under the same*** ~ 在同一屋顶下,在一家。***wipe off the*** ~ 勾销往事。**II** *vt*. **1.** 用石板瓦盖(屋顶)。**2.**〔美口〕提名…做候补人[候选人]。~ **black** 石板黑。~ **club**〔英〕(每人每星期拿出少数钱组织的)互助会。~**-colo(u)red** 石板色的,暗蓝灰色的。~ **pencil** 石笔。

slate[2] [sleit; slet] *vt*. **1.**〔口〕(在报刊上)抨击,谴责。**2.** 责骂(部下等);痛打,鞭打,拳打。

slat·er [ˈsleitə; ˋsletɚ] *n*. **1.** 石板瓦匠;(用石板作刀口的)刮毛器。**2.** 抨击者。**3.**【动】鼠妇(一种陆栖足类甲虫);水栖等足类动物。

Slat·er [ˈsleitə; ˋsletɚ] *n*. 斯莱特〔姓氏〕。

slath·er [ˈsleiðə, ˈslæðə; ˋslæðɚ] **I** *n*.〔美俚〕大量。**II** *vt*. 大量耗用;挥霍。

slat·ing[1] [ˈsleitiŋ; ˋsletɪŋ] *n*. **1.** 盖石板瓦;石板瓦活。**2.** (盖屋顶用的)石板瓦。

slat·ing[2] [ˈsleitiŋ; ˋsletɪŋ] *n*. 严厉的批评,责骂。

slat·tern [ˈslætə(ː)n; ˋslætɚn] **I** *n*. **1.** 懒散女人,邋遢女

人。2. 行为不检的女人;荡妇,妓女。II *a*. 懒散的;邋遢的,不整洁的。

slat·tern·ly [ˈslætə(:)nli; ˋslætɚnlɪ] *a*., *ad*. 1. 懒散的[地];邋遢的(地),不整洁的(地)。2. (女人)行为放荡的[地]。**-li·ness** *n*.

slat·ting [ˈslætiŋ; ˋslætɪŋ] *n*. 板条料,板条。

slat·y [ˈsleiti; ˋsletɪ] *a*. 1. 板岩(质)的,石板状的。2. 蓝灰色的。

slaugh·ter [ˈslɔːtə; ˋslɔtɚ] I *n*. 1. 屠宰。2. (大)屠杀;杀戮,残杀。3. 大减价,大贱卖。4.〔口〕强烈谴责,猛烈抨击。II *vt*. 1. 屠宰;(大)屠杀。2. 大减价,大贱卖。3.〔口〕强烈谴责,猛烈抨击。~**house** *n*. 屠场。**-er** *n*. 屠夫,屠宰工人;刽子手,屠杀者。

slaugh·ter·ous [ˈslɔːtərəs; ˋslɔtərəs] *a*. 好杀的,凶暴的,残忍的;破坏性的。**-ly** *ad*.

Slav [slɑːv, slæv; slɑv] I *n*. 斯拉夫人;〔the ~s〕斯拉夫民族。II *a*. 斯拉夫民族的;斯拉夫语的。**-ist** *n*.

Slav. = Slavic; Slavonian; Slavonic.

slave [sleiv; slev] I *n*. 1. 奴隶。2. …的奴隶,耽迷于…的人 (*of*; *to*)。3. 奴隶一般工作的人,苦工。4.【动】奴隶蚁 (=~ ant)。5.【机】从动装置。6. 卑劣的人。7.〔*pl*.〕〔美〕职业棒球选手。*a ~ to duty* 拼命尽本分工作的人。*be a ~ of* [*to*] *drink* = *a ~ to the bottle* 酒的奴隶,酒鬼。*a willing ~* 甘心情愿唯命是从的人。*the ~ of one's wife's caprices* 悉听妻子左右的男人。*the ~s of fashion* 拼命赶时髦的人们。II *vi*. (像奴隶一样)拼命工作,牛马似地工作,做苦工。~**-born** *a*. 生于奴隶家庭的。~ **driver** 奴隶监督人;残酷的老板[监工]。~**-grown** *a*. 使用奴隶种植的。~**holder** 蓄奴者,奴隶主。~**-hunter** 捕掳奴隶去贩卖的人。~ **labo(u)r** 奴隶劳动;强迫劳动。~**-making ant**【动】蓄奴蚁。~ **market** 奴隶市场;〔美俚〕职业介绍所。~**-pusher**〔美〕残酷的老板。~**robot** 机器人。~ **ship** 贩奴船。~ **state** (美国南北战争前)实行奴隶制度的州。~ **station** (双曲线导航系统中受主台控制的)辅助电台。~ **tail** 男士小辫〔一种时髦发型,有些青少年在后脑蓄一根小辫,其余部位则剪成短发或平头〕。~ **trade** [**traffic**] 奴隶贩卖。

slav·er[1] [ˈsleivə; ˋslevɚ] *n*. 买卖奴隶者,奴隶贩子;贩奴船。

slav·er[2] [ˈslævə; ˋslævɚ] I *vi*. 1. 淌口水,垂涎。2. 奉承,谄媚。—*vt*. 口水淌湿…;流涎弄脏(衣服等)。II *n*. 1. 口水,唾液,吐沫。2. 奉承,谄媚。

slav·er·y[1] [ˈsleivəri; ˋslevərɪ] *n*. 1. 奴隶身分,奴隶状态。2. 奴隶制;占有奴隶。3. 苦役;奴隶般的劳动。4. 束缚;屈从;耽迷(酒色等) (*to*)。

slav·er·y[2] [ˈslævəri; ˋslævərɪ] *a*. 流口水的;被口水弄脏的。

slav·ey [ˈslɑːvi, ˈsleivi; ˋslevɪ] *n*. 〔英俚〕(做粗笨杂事的)女工。

Slav·ic [ˈslævik, ˈslɑːv-; ˋslævɪk] *a*., *n*. = Slavonic.

Slav·i·cist [ˈslɑːvisist, ˈslævisist; ˋslævəsɪst] *n*. 斯拉夫语言、文化的研究者 (= Slavist)。

Slav·i·cize [ˈslævisaiz; ˋslævəˏsaɪz] *vt*. 使斯拉夫化。

slav·ish [ˈsleiviʃ; ˋslevɪʃ] *a*. 1. 奴隶(一样)的;奴性的,卑屈的。2. 无独创性的;盲从的,模仿的。*a ~ flatterer* 卑躬屈节地奉承者。**-ly** *ad*. **-ness** *n*.

Slav·ism [ˈslɑːvizəm; ˋslævɪzm] *n*. 斯拉夫人特点,斯拉夫式;斯拉夫主义;斯拉夫语风。

slav·oc·ra·cy [sleiˈvɔkrəsi; slevˋɑkrəsɪ] *n*. 〔美〕蓄奴派,蓄奴集团〔美国南北战争前,南方的奴隶主与拥护奴隶制度的统治集团〕。

Sla·vo·ni·a [sləˈvəuniə; sləˋvonɪə] *n*. 斯拉沃尼亚〔前南斯拉夫德拉瓦河 (Drava) 与萨瓦河 (Sava) 二河之间地区〕。**Sla·voni·an** [sləˈvəunjən, -niən; sləˋvonɪən] I *a*. 斯拉沃尼亚的;斯拉沃尼亚人的;斯拉夫民族的;斯拉夫语的。II *n*. 斯拉沃尼亚人;斯拉夫人;斯拉夫语。

Sla·von·ic [sləˈvɔnik; sləˋvɑnɪk] I *a*. 斯拉夫民族的,斯拉夫人[语]的。II *n*. 斯拉夫语。

Slav·o·nize [ˈslævənaiz, ˈslɑː-; ˋslævənaɪz, ˋslɑv-] *vt*. 使斯拉夫化。

Slav·o·phil(e) [ˈslævəfil; ˋslævəfɪl] *n*. 亲斯拉夫人的人;赞赏斯拉夫文化习俗的人。

Slav·oph·i·lism [sləˈvɔfilizm; sləˋvɑfɪlɪzm] *n*. 19 世纪中叶俄国知识分子主张斯拉夫文化,斯拉夫文化优越论。

Slav·o·phobe [ˈslævəfəub; ˋslævəfob] *n*. 憎恨[畏惧]斯拉夫人[文化]的人。

Slav·o·phobi·a [ˈslævəfəubjə; ˋslævəfobjə] *n*. 对斯拉夫人[文化]的憎恨[畏惧]。

slaw [slɔː; slɔ] *n*. 〔美〕= coleslaw.

slay [slei; sle] *vt*. (***slew*** [sluː; slu]; ***slain*** [slein; slen]) 1. 杀死;杀害;毁灭。2.〔美俚〕使(异性)迷恋(自己);给人强烈的好印象;使…发生好感[愉快,喜欢,快乐]。*The slaves slew their master with swords*. 奴隶们用乱刀砍死主人。*Your jokes ~ me*. 你的笑话使我笑破肚皮。*slay'em*〔美俚〕迅速给人强烈好印象的人。—*vi*. 造成死亡。*No other infection so quickly ~s*. 再没有别的疾病会造成如此迅速的死亡。

slay·er [ˈsleiə; ˋsleɚ] *n*. 杀人者,凶手。

SLBM = 1. submarine-launched ballistic missile 潜艇发射的弹道导[飞]弹。2. sea-launched ballistic missile 海上发射的弹道导[飞]弹。3. satellite-launched ballistic missile 人造卫星发射的弹道导[飞]弹。

SLCM = Submarine-launched cruise missile 潜艇发射的巡航导[飞]弹。

sld. = sailed; sealed; sold.

sleave [sliːv; sliv] I *n*. 1. 细丝。2. 乱丝;纠缠。II *vt*. 把(乱丝)解开,理(丝)。*~d silk*【纺】丝吐。—*vi*. 分成细丝。

sleaze [sliːz, sliz] *n*. 低劣的人或物品。

sleaz·y [ˈsliːzi; ˋslizɪ] *a*. 1.【织】质地薄的。2.〔转义〕质量差的;低劣的;卑劣的。3. 不整洁的;破旧的;未修理的。**-zi·ness** *n*.

sled [sled; slɛd] I *n*. 1. (小)雪橇,滑橇,滑板。2.【空】滑轨;空气动力车。3.〔美〕采棉机。II *vt*. (**-dd-**) 1. 用雪橇运。2. 用采棉机采。—*vi*. 乘雪橇。*hard ~ding*〔美〕困难的工作;难局。*smooth ~ding*〔美〕顺利轻松的工作。**-plane** 雪上飞机。**-der** 乘雪橇者;拉雪橇的动物。

sledge[1] [sledʒ; slɛdʒ] I *n*. 雪橇;〔英〕(从前送犯人赴刑场用的)席橇。II *vt*., *vi*. 用雪橇运;坐雪橇走。

sledge[2] [sledʒ; slɛdʒ] = sledgehammer.

sledge·ham·mer [ˈsledʒˌhæmə; ˋslɛdʒˏhæmɚ] I *n*. 1. 用双手抡打的长柄大铁锤。2.〔美〕连续猛击的拳击家。II *vt*. 用大锤连续猛击。—*vi*. 用大锤猛击。III *a*. 用大锤猛击的;猛烈的,重大的,致命的。*a ~ blow* 重大的打击,致命的打击。*a ~ argument* 激烈的争论;驳得对方哑口无言的论点。

sleek [sliːk; slik] I *a*. 1. (毛发等)光滑的,柔滑的;油滑的,有光泽的;整洁的。2. (动植物)喂养得好的,长得好的,健康的。3. 嘴甜的,花言巧语的,圆滑的。4. 非常时髦的,豪华的;兴旺的。*~ dark hair* 柔滑乌黑的头发。*as ~ as a cat*〔喻〕像猫一样圆滑谄媚。II *vt*. 1. 使光滑,使有光泽。2.〔口〕使整洁。—*vi*. 1.〔口〕滑动。2.〔口〕打扮整洁,打扮漂亮 (*up*)。**-ly** *ad*. **-ness** *n*.

sleek·it [ˈsliːkit; ˋslikɪt] *a*. 〔Scot.〕1. 光滑的,柔滑的。2. 圆滑的,诡诈的。3. 手巧的,能干的。

sleek·y [ˈsliːki; ˋslikɪ] *a*. = sleek.

sleep [sliːp; slip] I *vi*. (***slept***; ***slept*** [slept; slɛpt]) 1. 睡,睡眠,睡着。2. 被埋葬着;长眠。3. 麻痹,发麻。4. (陀螺)稳定地飞速旋转。5. 静止,过闲静日子,醉生梦死。6. 过夜,住宿。7. 发生性关系。8.【动】冬眠,蛰伏;【植】(花叶)夜间闭合。—*vt*. 1. 睡(觉)。2. 用睡眠消除。3. 可住,供给…住宿。*~ well* [*badly*] 睡得好[不好]。*~ late* (早晨)起得晚,睡懒觉。*She slept eight* *hours*. 她睡了八小时。*The sails* ～. 风帆被风鼓胀得静止不动。～ *a sound sleep* 熟睡一觉。*This hotel* ～*s 500 guests*. 这旅馆可供五百人住宿。*I shall* ～ *in New York tonight*. 今晚在纽约过夜。*Let* ～*ing dogs lie*. 不要打草惊蛇;不要自惹麻烦。～ ***around*** 〔俚〕到处与人发生性关系。～ ***away*** 1. ＝～ off. 2. 在睡眠中打发日子,把时间浪费在睡眠中。～ ***in*** 1. 〔英〕(佣人)住在东家家里。2. 睡过头。3. 睡懒觉。～ ***off*** 睡过(时候);睡掉(忧愁等),用睡眠治好(头痛等)。～ ***on*** [***upon***, ***over***]... 将…睡着想一晚;将…拖到明天。～ ***one's last*** (***sleep***) 长眠。～ ***out*** 1. (佣工)睡在自己家里,日作夜归。2. 睡过。3. 露宿。～ ***over*** 1. 寄宿别人家;不在家过夜。2. 忽略,不注意。～ ***over one's work*** [***happiness***] 沉醉在工作[幸福]中。～ ***rough*** 在公园[车站等处]过夜。～ ***the clock round*** 一睡十二个钟头。～ ***the sleep of the just*** 〔谑〕酣睡,安心睡眠。～ ***with one's fathers*** 死去。**II** ***n***. 1. 睡眠。2. 长眠,永逝,死。3. 昏迷,麻痹;静止,静寂。4.【动】冬眠,蛰伏;【植】(花、叶)夜间闭合。5. 夜。6. 睡意。*He talks in his* ～. 他说梦话。*a dead* ～ 熟睡。*the beauty* ～ (午夜前入睡的)头觉。*a broken* ～ 不眠不夜。*Not ten* ～*s have passed since the last of our fighting men returned*. 自从我们最后一个战斗员回来至今还不到十天。***be dying with*** ～ 瞌睡得要死。***fall on*** ～ 〔古〕就眠;死。***go to*** ～ 入睡,睡着〔多用于否定句〕。***last*** ～ 死,长眠。***lay sb. to*** ～ 使…入睡;埋葬。***lose*** ～ 失眠。***put*** [***send***] ***to*** ～ 哄(孩子)睡;使麻醉;消除。***the*** ～ ***that knows not breaking*** [***no waking***] 永眠,长逝,死。～ **apnea**【医】(可能由呼吸道梗阻等引起的)睡眠时呼吸暂停。～**-in** ***a***., ***n***. 住宿在雇主家的(佣工)。～**-out** ***a***., ***n***. 不住宿在雇主家的(佣工)。～ **producer** 〔美剧〕使人打瞌睡的戏。～ **strike** (上班时躺倒不干活的)静卧罢工。～**walking** 梦游病。～**wear** 睡衣。

sleep·er [ˈsliːpə; ˋslipɚ] ***n***. 1. 睡眠者;懒人;死人。2. 有(卧)铺(设备的)飞机;【铁路】〔美〕卧车,卧铺;〔英〕枕木;(可翻过来作床铺用的)可卧座位。3. 冬眠动物。4.【建】小阁栅;【船】机座垫。5.〔美〕长期不受人注意而一举受人瞩目的人或物。6.〔常 *pl*.〕小儿睡衣裤。7. 在耳上作了记号而未打烙印的小牛。*a good* ～ 睡眠好的人。*a heavy* ～ 不易惊醒[睡眠酣畅]的人。*a light* ～ 易惊醒[睡眠不酣]的人。～ **agent** (暂时不活动的)潜伏间谍。～ **plane** 设有卧铺的飞机。～ **seat** 可调节的斜靠背坐椅,睡椅。～ **sofa** (翻过沙发面可作床睡的)坐卧两用沙发。

sleep·i·ly [ˈsliːpili; ˋslipəlɪ] ***ad***. 想睡地,瞌睡地;静寂地。

sleep·i·ness [ˈsliːpinis; ˋslipɪnɪs] ***n***. 想睡,困倦。

sleep·ing [ˈsliːpiŋ; ˋslipɪŋ] **I** ***n***. 睡眠;休止,静止。**II** ***a***. 睡着的;睡眠用的。*a* ～ *beauty* 1. (童话中的)睡美人;〔转义〕贪睡的美人,懒美人。2.【植】白花酢浆草 (＝～ clover)。～ **bag**, ～ **sack** 睡袋〔旅行等用〕。～ **car**, ～**-carriage** 卧车。～ **draught** [**pill**, **potion**, **tablet**] 安眠药(片),催眠剂。～**-dropsy**【医】睡眠病。～ **giant** 沉睡的巨人;潜力尚未得到充分发挥的国家[大公司等]。～ **partner** (不参与经营的)匿名合伙人。～ **policeman** 〔英〕减速路坎〔为防止汽车行驶速度过快而在路面上有意铺设的一系列路脊〕。～ **rent** 固定的租金;不依获利多寡而增减的资金。～ **saloon** 〔英〕(高级)卧车。～ **sickness** (热带)嗜眠病;嗜眠性脑炎。～ **suit** 睡衣裤。～ **walker** 梦游病者。～**walking** 梦游(病)。

sleep·less [ˈsliːplis; ˋsliplɪs] ***a***. 1. 不眠的,睡不着的;醒着的。2. 无休止的,不停的;活跃的;警觉的。*a* ～ *night* 不眠之夜。～ *wind* 刮个不停的风。**-ly** ***ad***. **-ness** ***n***.

sleep·y [ˈsliːpi; ˋslipɪ] ***a***. 1. 想睡的,瞌睡的;嗜睡的。2. 困乏的(声音等);懒散的;寂静的。3. 使睡的,催眠的。4. 睡着的,不活动的;感觉迟钝的;水果等(因开始干枯腐烂而变得)乏味的。*a* ～ *song* 催人入眠的歌。*a* ～ *little town* 呆滞的小城镇。*a* ～ *valley* 寂静的山谷。*feel* ～ 想睡。～ *sickness* 〔口〕嗜眠性脑炎。～**head** 贪睡的人;(终日)昏昏欲睡的人;懒鬼。**-i·ly** ***ad***. **-i·ness** ***n***.

sleet [sliːt; slit] **I** ***n***. 1. 冻雨,雨夹雪,霎。2. 雨淞,冰凌。**II** ***vi***. 下雨夹雪;下冻雨。**-y** ***a***. 雨淞一样的。

sleeve [sliːv; sliv] **I** ***n***. 1. 袖子,袖套。2.【机】套筒,套管,套。3. 唱片套。4.【气】风(向)袋。*Every man has a fool in his* ～. 〔谚〕人人都有不够聪明之处。***hang on sb.'s*** ～ 听从某人。***hang*** [***pin***] ***one's judgement*** [***opinion***] (***up***) ***on sb.'s*** ～ 依靠某人给自己出主意。***have a plan*** [***a card***, ***something***] ***up one's*** ～ 别有用心,另有应急计划,另有秘诀。***laugh*** [***smile***] ***in*** [***up***] ***one's*** ～ 暗笑,在肚子里笑。***roll*** [***turn***] ***up one's*** ～***s*** (为工作或搏斗)卷起袖子;磨拳擦掌。***wear one's heart on one's*** ～ 开诚布公,坦率。***work in one's*** ～***s*** 脱去上衣做活,只穿着衬衫工作。**II** ***vt***. 给…装袖子,给…装套筒。～ **button** 袖口钮。～ **dog** 袖笼小犬〔常指可放在衣袖内的小狮子犬〕。～ **emblem** (军队中文职人员佩戴的)袖章。～**-fish**【动】枪鲗,鱿鱼。～ **gun** 袖珍手枪。～**let** 袖套。～ **link** 袖钮。～ **nut**【机】套筒螺母。～ **target**【空】筒形拖靶〔飞机在飞行中拖曳的靶子〕。～ **valve**【机】套阀。**-less** ***a***.

sleigh [slei; sle] **I** ***n***. (马拉的)雪橇,雪车。**II** ***vi***. 坐雪橇(走),用雪橇运送。～ **bells** 雪橇铃〔挂在拉雪橇牲口身上的小铃〕。

sleight [slait; slaɪt] ***n***. 1. 技巧,手法。2.〔古〕诡计,奸诈;〔罕〕手段,策略。～ ***of hand*** 1. (在变魔术时蒙蔽观众的)手法。2. 戏法,花招,特技。***resorted to a*** ～ ***of hand*** 耍了一个花招。***turn out to be a clumsy*** ～ ***of hand*** 弄巧成拙。～**-of-mouth** ***n***. 〔口〕耍嘴皮子。

slen·der [ˈslendə; ˋslɛndɚ] ***a***. 1. 细,细长的,苗条的。2. 柔弱的,纤弱的。3. 狭,窄;微薄的,微小的,不足的。4. 微弱的,薄弱的(基础等)。5.【语音】细弱的。*a* ～ *girl* 身段苗条的少女。*a* ～ *cheque* 小额支票。～ *hopes* 渺茫的希望。～ *means* 小小本钱,小额财产。**-ly** ***ad***.

slen·der·ize [ˈslendəraiz; ˋslɛndəˏraɪz] ***vt***., ***vi***. 使〔变〕细长。

slept [slept; slɛpt] sleep 的过去式及过去分词。

sleuth [sluːθ; sluθ] ***n***. 1.〔古〕(人或兽的)足迹,嗅迹。2. ＝sleuthhound. 3.〔美口〕侦探。

sleuth·hound [ˈsluːθhaund; ˋsluθˏhaʊnd] ***n***. 1. 警犬,嗅觉敏锐的猎狗。2.〔口〕厉害的侦探。

slew[1] [sluː; slu] slay 的过去式。

slew[2], **slue** [sluː; slu] ***n***. 〔美,加拿大〕泥淖;沼地。

slew[3] [sluː; slu] **I** ***vt***. 使回转,使旋转 (*around*, *round*)。—***vi***. 旋转,滑溜。**II** ***n***. 回转,旋转,旋转后的位置。

slew[4] [sluː; slu] ***n***. 〔常 *pl*.〕〔美口〕大量,大批,大群 (*of*)。

slice [slais; slaɪs] **I** ***n***. 1. 薄片,切片,一片;一部分。2. 餐刀,(切薄片用的)菜刀;锅铲;火铲;刮子。3.【印】油墨铲。4.【建】泥板,泥刀。5.【海】进水台用楔。6.【无】限幅,削波。7.【运】(高尔夫球)左[右]曲球,(乒乓球)削球,左旋球。*a* ～ *of bread* 一片面包。*a* ～ *of luck* 幸运。**II** ***vt***. 1. 把…切成薄片。2. 切下,切去;切开,分开 (*away*, *from*, *off*)。3. 用(火铲)铲;用(泥刀)铺。4. (高尔夫球)使球曲向左[右]边;(乒乓球)削球。—***vi***. 1. 切。2. 打左[右]曲球。～ **bar** 炉钎。～**-of-life** ***a***. 栩栩如生地反映实际生活的一个片断的。**-r** ***n***. 切片机。

slick [slik; slɪk] **I** ***a***. 1. 光滑的,滑溜的。2. 熟练的,灵巧的。3. 聪明的,机灵的;圆滑的,口齿伶俐的;狡猾的,诡诈的。4.〔口〕(文体等)华而不实的。5. 陈腐的,老一套的;平凡的,无独创性的。6.〔美俚〕极好的,第一流的;吸引人的,好玩的。7. 纯然的,单纯的。*a* ～ *alibi* 圆滑的托词。*a* ～ *style of writing* 花哨的文体,华而不实的文体。*a story of the* ～ *variety* 老一套的故事。*He did it out of* ～ *perversity*. 他全然是出于不合情理的想法做了这件事的。(***as***) ～ ***as a whistle*** 敏捷地;干净

S

利落地。**II** ***ad*.** **1.** 润滑地(转动);自如地,灵活地。**2.** 熟练地,巧妙地。**3.** 直接地,径直地;正面;恰好地,恰巧地。*go* ~ 运转自如,进行顺利。*run* ~ *into sth*. 迎面撞上某物。**III** ***vt*.** **1.** 使光亮;使滑溜。**2.** 使美观;整顿,使齐整。**3.** 占…的便宜;揩…的油。~ *the flour on a board with a spatula* 用抹刀把擀面板上的面块刮平。*turn out to be* ~*ed* 结果吃了亏。~ **down** 捋平,使平服。—***vi*.** 打扮整洁,打扮漂亮 (*up*)。**IV** ***n*.** **1.** 〔美〕(水上有一层油膜的)平滑面;油膜。**2.** 平滑器;刮刀;修型熳刀。**3.** 〔美俚〕(装潢漂亮、内容浅薄的)通俗杂志〔= ~ paper〕。**4.** 没有花纹的汽车轮胎。~ **chick** 〔美俚〕装束漂亮的女子。~**ed-up** ***a*.** 〔美〕干净的,整洁的,漂亮的。~**-paper** **1.** ***n*.** (印刷通俗杂志的)油光纸。**2.** ***a*.** 印在油光纸上的。

slick·en·side [ˈsliknˌsaid; ˋslɪkən͵saɪd] ***n*.** 〔常用作 *pl*.〕【地】擦痕面,断面擦痕,滑面。

slick·er [ˈslikə; ˋslɪkɚ] ***n*.** **1.** 〔美〕(宽大的)油布雨衣。**2.** 〔美口〕狡猾的骗子。**3.** 【工】刮子,刮刀。**4.** 〔美俚〕衣着讲究、精通世故的城里人。

slide [slaid; slaɪd] **I** ***vi*.** (***slid*** [slid; slɪd]; ***slid***, 〔美〕***slid·den*** [ˈslidn; ˋslɪdn̩]; ***slid·ing***) **1.** 滑;(在雪或冰上)滑动;滑倒,滑掉。**2.** 改变位置,脱离原来位置;不知不觉陷入 (*into*)。**3.** 【棒球】滑垒;【乐】滑动。**4.** 偷偷进入;潜逃,偷偷溜掉。**5.** 流,流逝;放任自流。*The book slid off my knee*. 书由我膝头上滑落。~ *into bad habit* 渐渐养成坏习惯。*The economy slid from recession to depression*. 经济由退缩进入萧条。~ *from grave to gay* 渐渐由严肃中欢闹起来。—***vt*.** **1.** 使滑动;使滑倒;滑溜地进行。**2.** 用滑冰(等)消磨(时间)。**3.** 偷偷[轻轻]放进去,使溜进去 (*in*, *into*)。***let things*** [***it***] ~ 听其自然;放任不管。~ ***away*** 偷偷跑掉,溜掉。~ ***over*** 略过,回避 (*He slid over the delicate subject*. 他对那个困难问题一点而过)。**II** ***n*.** **1.** 滑动;滑道,滑坡,滑轨;滑面。**2.** 土崩,山崩;雪崩。**3.** 【地】(层面)断层;冲断面;褶皱。**4.** 【棒球】滑垒。**5.** 滑动的部分;【机】滑板;滑盖;滑座;【物】滑动片;幻灯片;(显微镜的)载片;【摄】(照相机的)拉盖。**5.** 【乐】滑音,延音;长号的 U 形伸缩管。**6.** (妇女保持头发整齐的)发夹 (= hair ~)。*a nodal* ~【物】测节器。~ **area** 容易产生山体滑坡的地区。~ **bar**【机】滑杆;导杆。~ **block**【机】滑块。~ **carriage**【军】滑动炮架。~ **door** 拉门。~ **fastener** 拉链,拉锁。~ **knot** 止滑结。~ **projector** 幻灯机。~ **rule** 计算尺。~ **trombone** = trombone. ~ **valve**【机】滑阀。~**way** 滑道,滑坡。**-r** **1.** 滑动的人或物;(器械的)滑动部分。**2.** 【棒球】曲线球。

slid·ing [ˈslaidiŋ; ˋslaɪdɪŋ] **I** ***a*.** 滑动的;易变的,不稳定的。**II** ***n*.** 滑动。~ **door** 拉门。~ **rule** 计算尺。~ **scale** **1.** 计算尺。**2.** 【经】(按物价涨落折算工资、税款等的)折价计算法;比例增减法。~ **seat** (赛艇的)滑座。

slight [slait; slaɪt] **I** ***a*.** **1.** 轻微的,细微的;微小的,少量的。**2.** 纤细的,细长的;苗条的,瘦小的。**3.** 不结实的;脆弱的。**4.** 〔罕〕轻蔑的。**5.** 不足取的,(辩解等)无聊的。*a* ~ *cold* 轻微的伤风。*a* ~ *criticism* 无力的批评,轻微的批评。*I have not the* ~*est doubt*. 我没有丝毫怀疑。*She takes offence at the* ~*est thing*. 她极易发怒。***make*** ~ ***of*** 轻视。***not in the*** ~***est*** 一点不 (= not at all)。**II** ***n*.** 轻蔑,怠慢,侮辱;忽视。*suffer* ~*s* 受到怠慢。***put a*** ~ ***on*** [***upon***] ***sb*.** 蔑视某人,瞧不起某人。**III** ***vt*.** **1.** 轻视,蔑视,藐视。**2.** 玩忽;怠慢。~ *one's work* 玩忽职守。*feel* ~*ed* 感觉受到藐视。

slight·ing [ˈslaitiŋ; ˋslaɪtɪŋ] ***a*.** 轻蔑的,无礼的。*a* ~ *remark* 轻蔑的话。**-ly** ***ad*.**

slight·ly [ˈslaitli; ˋslaɪtlɪ] ***ad*.** **1.** 轻微地,轻轻地。**2.** 细长地,苗条地。**3.** 有一点,略;脆弱地。**4.** 〔罕〕轻蔑地。*be* ~ *wounded* 受了轻伤的。*be* ~ *deaf* 有一点聋。*be* ~ *built* (建筑物等)不牢固的;(体格)瘦弱的,细长的。*I knew him* ~. 我略为认识他。

sli·ly [ˈslaili; ˋslaɪlɪ] ***ad*.** = slyly.

slim [slim; slɪm] **I** ***a*.** **1.** 纤细的,苗条的;微弱的。**2.** 不足取的,琐细的,无价值的;(议论等)不充实的,空洞的。**3.** 〔方〕狡猾的,油滑的。*a* ~ *excuse* 理由不充分的借口。*very* ~ *chances of success* 成功的希望很渺茫。*the* ~*mest* (*of*) *evidence* 最不充分的证据。**II** ***vt*.,** ***vi*** (***-mm-***) (使)变细;(使)减肥,(用运动等)减轻体重。*He feels like dieting to* ~ *down*. 他很想节制饮食来减肥。~ **jim** **1.** ***n*.** 瘦高个儿。**2.** ***a*.** 细长的。~**ming diet** 减肥饮食。~**ming exercises** (保持身材苗条的)减肥体操。**-ly** ***ad*.**

slime [slaim; slaɪm] **I** ***n*.** **1.** 软而滑的东西。**2.** 黏土,稀泥。**3.** 黏质;(蜗牛等的)黏液。**4.** 沥青;〔*pl*.〕【矿】矿泥;煤泥。**5.** 〔转义〕令人不愉快的黏腻的东西。**6.** 谄媚;堕落。~ *flux*【林】伤口流液。**II** ***vt*.** **1.** (用稀泥等)涂,糊;(尤指蛇吞蛙等时)分泌黏液使黏滑。**2.** 清除黏液[稀泥等]。**3.** 把(矿石)研磨成矿泥。—***vi*.** **1.** 弄得泥糊糊;变黏滑。**2.** 〔英俚〕滑脱,用狡猾手段脱身溜掉 (*away*; *through etc*.)。~ **mold** [**fungus**]【生】黏菌 (= myxomycete)。~ **pit** **1.** 产沥青的矿井。**2.** 贮矿泥的坑。

slim·ming [ˈslimiŋ; ˋslɪmɪŋ] ***n*.** 减轻体重;减肥;减食疗法。

slim·nas·tics [ˌslimˈnæstiks; ͵slɪmˋnæstɪks] ***n*.** 减肥操,减肥健美操。

slim·sy [ˈslimzi; ˋslɪmzɪ], **slimp·sy** [ˈslimpsi; ˋslɪmpsɪ] ***a*.** 〔美〕脆弱的,薄弱的;不结实的;不耐穿的。

slim·y [ˈslaimi; ˋslaɪmɪ] ***a*.** **1.** 黏糊糊的;(分泌)黏液的;泥泞的。**2.** 〔口〕谄媚的;可鄙的;讨厌的。**-i·ly** ***ad*.** **-i·ness** ***n*.**

sling[1] [sliŋ; slɪŋ] **I** ***n*.** **1.** 投石器;弹弓。**2.** 投掷;打击;一击。**3.** 【医】悬带;【海】钩索,吊锁,吊索,吊链;一吊货,一关;【军】(枪的)背带。**4.** 后跟用带绊住的女鞋。*have* [*carry*] *one's arm in a* ~ 用悬带吊着手臂。**II** ***vt*.** (***slung*** [slʌŋ; slʌŋ], 〔古〕***slang*** [slæŋ; slæŋ]; ***slung***) **1.** 用投石器投;投掷,扔。**2.** 用悬带吊挂;吊起(辘轳等)。~ *a door open* 把门推开。~ *abuse* 〔俚〕谩骂。~ *arms* 把枪用背带挂在肩膀上。~ *a sword from a belt* 把佩刀吊在带子上。~ *type* 排字。—***vi*.** 用投石器投;大踏步走。~ ***chin music*** 〔美〕说(空话)。~ ***one's hook*** 〔俚〕逃走,离去。~ ***ink*** 〔俚〕(卖稿人)赶写(稿件);做新闻记者。~ ***mud at sb*.** 谩骂,毁谤。~ ***over*** 使劲拥抱。~ ***oneself up*** 溜上。~ (***the***) ***woo*** 〔美俚〕= *pitch* (*a*) *woo*. ~ **cart** (装有千斤吊的)吊搬车。~ **dog** 吊钩。~**shot** **1.** 弹弓[玩具]。**2.** 【宇航】弹射[利用某天体的引力突然加速以改变航向等的太空飞行]。**-er** 用投石器者;投掷装置;吊环,吊索;吊装工。**-er ring**【空】防冻液洒射环。

sling[2] [sliŋ; slɪŋ] ***n*.** 〔美〕果汁甜酒〔用烈酒、糖、果子露掺水混合而成的饮料〕。

slink[1] [sliŋk; slɪŋk] **I** ***vi*.** (***slunk*** [slʌŋk; slʌŋk], 〔罕〕***slank*** [slæŋk; slæŋk]; ***slunk***) 偷偷地走进,溜走,潜逃 (*away*; *by*; *off*)。**II** ***n*.** 鬼鬼祟祟的人。**-y** ***a*.** **1.** 偷偷摸摸的,行动诡秘的。**2.** 〔俚〕动作[线条]柔和优美的。

slink[2] [sliŋk; slɪŋk] **I** ***vt*.** (***slunk*** [slʌŋk; slʌŋk], 〔罕〕***slank*** [slæŋk; slæŋk]; ***slunk***) (动物,尤指家畜)早产,流产。**II** ***n*.** 早产的小牛。**III** ***a*.** 早产的,不足月的(小牛等)。

SLIP = Serial Line Internet [Interface] Protocol【计】串线网际协议。

slip[1] [slip; slɪp] **I** ***vi*.** (~***ped***, 〔古〕***slipt*** [slipt; slɪpt]; ~***ped***; ~***ping***) **1.** 滑(动);滑倒,跌跤。**2.** 滑脱,松脱;(骨等)脱节,脱落。**3.** 溜,溜走,潜逃 (*away*, *off*);悄悄走;(时间)不知不觉地过去,逝去 (*by*; *away*)。**4.** 疏忽;遗忘;弄错。**5.** (机会等)被错过,被放走。**6.** 〔口〕(健康)变坏,(质量)下降。**7.** 【空】侧滑。**8.** 〔美俚〕颓丧,垂头丧气。**9.** 匆忙地穿上[脱去] (*into* [*out of*])。*Mind*

S

you don't ～. 当心别滑倒。*He often* ～*s in his grammar*. 他常常犯文法错误。*Mistakes will* ～ *in*. (注意是注意,但)错误难防。—***vt*.** **1.** 使滑动;偷偷放进,偷偷地搁到。**2.** 错过,放走(机会等);解开,脱去(*off*; *down*);放走(狗等);放开。**3.** 省去(某事项等);漏掉,遗漏。**4.** 不留神地说出,漏出(话等)。**5.** (牲畜)早产。**6.** 〔美俚〕付(款);偷偷地塞(钱)。***let*** ～ ***the dogs of war*** 挑起战争。～ ***along*** 〔俚〕急急忙忙地走,飞也似地跑。～ ***down to the wire*** 〔美运〕比赢。～ ***from one's memory*** 遗忘。～ ***into*** 急急穿上;〔俚〕痛殴;竞赛;攻击。～ ***me five*** 〔美俚〕握手。～ ***off*** 急急脱掉;偷偷拿走;偷偷跑掉,溜掉。～ ***on*** 一下子穿上。～ ***out of joint*** 脱节,脱榫。～ ***over*** 对…漫不经心。～ ***sth. over on sb.*** 用欺骗手段把某物塞给他人;用欺骗手段胜过他人(*try to* ～ *sth. over on one's customers by substituting inferior merchandise for that ordered* 将所订购的商品以次品代替企图欺骗顾客)。～ ***the anchor*** 【海】斩断锚链。～ ***the leash*** 〔美〕摆脱束缚,得到自由。～ ***through sb.'s fingers*** 从某人的掌握中逃脱。～ ***up*** 滑一跤;〔美〕弄错;失败。**II *n*.** **1.** 滑动;滑倒,失足,跌跤。**2.** 滑脱;滑落。**3.** 【地】(岩层的)滑距;山崩,断层。**4.** 【船】滑台,滑路;船台;两码头间的水区。**5.** 【机】滑程,滑率;滑动量;润滑性[度];空转;转差。**6.** 【空】侧滑。**7.** 过失,错误;失败;错过,遗漏;意外事故。**8.** 溜走,不告而别。**9.** 〔常 *pl.*〕狗带。**10.** 女人套裙;(幼孩的)外衣,围兜;〔*pl.*〕(男式)游泳裤,枕套。**11.** 〔美〕系船处;停泊处。**12.** 〔俚〕(牲畜)流产。**13.** 【剧】舞台边门。**14.** 【陶器】泥釉,滑泥。**15.** 【鱼】小比目鱼。**16.** 【板球】外场员;〔*pl.*〕外场员防区。～ *of the memory* 遗忘。*a* ～ *of the pen* 写错。*a* ～ *of the tongue* 失言。*a deposit* [*withdrawal*] ～ 存款[取款]单。*There's many a* ～ *between the cup and the lip*. 〔谚〕杯已到口还会失手,往往功败垂成;凡事都难以十拿九稳。*give sb. the* ～ 趁某人不防溜掉,甩掉某人。～ **carriage** 〔英〕滑脱车厢〔快车经过不停的车站时解下的车厢〕。～**case** 书套,唱片套。～ **clay** 易熔土,易滑土。～**cover** **1.** *n*. 椅套,沙发套。**2.** *vt*. 给(椅子,沙发等)罩上套。～ **dress**, ～**dress** 无袖吊带裙。～**hook** (需要时很容易脱落的)滑钩,速脱钩。～**horn** 〔美俚〕= trombone. ～**knot** 滑结,蝶结。～ **noose** 滑结[蝶结]套。～**-on** **1.** *a*. 易穿脱的。**2.** *n*. 无带扣便鞋;套衫,宽松的外套。～**-over** = pullover. ～**page** 【机】滑动(量);滑程;动力传递损耗。～**ped disk** 【医】椎间盘突出〔常引起坐骨神经痛〕。～**-ring** 【电】滑环,汇流[电]环。～ **road** (通向快车道的岔道。～**sheet** 【印】衬纸〔用于防止刚印好的纸页上的湿油墨染污另一页〕。～**shod *a*.** 穿着塌跟鞋的;不齐整的,乱七八糟的,懒散的;潦草的,疏漏的,粗糙草率的。～**shods** 〔美〕鞋子。～**slop** **1.** *n*. 无味的食物、谈话、著作(等)。**2.** *a*. 淡(酒等);无聊的,没有价值的;潦草的。**3.** *vi*. 趴踏趴踏地走;写无聊文章。～**stick** 〔美俚〕= slide rule. ～ **stitch** 【纺】暗针。～**stream** 【空】(由螺旋桨转动产生的)滑流,切向流;向后气流。～**up** 〔口〕失败,错误;不幸事故。～**way** 【船】滑台;下水滑道;船台。

slip[2] [slip; slɪp] **I *n*.** **1.** 【园艺】插条,插穗;幼枝;〔喻〕子孙,后裔。**2.** 木条,纸条,(土地等的)一长条;(条形)传票,便条;【印】长条排样[校样]。**3.** 瘦长的青年人。**4.** 【机】楔形磨石。**5.** 〔美〕条凳座位。*an inventory count* ～ 盘存点料单。*an issue* ～ 领料单。**II *vt*.** (**-*pp*-**) 剪取(插条)。

slip·per [ˈslipə; ˋslɪpɚ] **I *n*.** **1.** 〔常 *pl.*〕拖鞋;(室内)便鞋。**2.** (马车的)煞车;【机】滑动部分;滑展。**3.** (小孩的)围兜;放猎狗的猎人。*a bed-* ～ 床上便器。***take one's*** ～ ***to*** 用拖鞋打…。**II *vt*.** (用拖鞋)打(孩子等)。—***vi*.** 穿着拖鞋走。*She* ～*ed across the room from her bed*. 她下床穿着拖鞋走过房间。～ **bath** 公共浴室。～ **chair** (卧室用的)矮椅。～ **sock** (室内穿的)连袜便鞋。

slip·per·y [ˈslipəri; ˋslɪpərɪ] ***a*.** **1.** 滑,滑溜的。**2.** 易滑脱的。**3.** 狡猾的,不可靠的;易变的。**4.** 含糊的;难以解释的。*a* ～ *customer* 滑头。*a* ～ *situation* 变化不定的形势。～ *as an eel dipped in butter* 狡猾极了的,极不可靠的。～ **elm** 【植】(北美)滑榆(木、皮)。～ **water** 滑溜水〔内含聚合物,流经水管时可减少摩擦力〕。**-per·i·ly *ad*.**

slip·ping [ˈslipiŋ; ˋslɪpɪŋ] ***a*.** **1.** 〔美俚〕渐渐松弛的,渐渐不行了的,渐渐吃不开了的,渐渐变懒的。**2.** 电视图像水平偏移的。

slip·py [ˈslipi; ˋslɪpɪ] ***a*.** 麻利的,手脚灵活的;〔口,方〕= slippery. ～**-ring** 【电】汇电环。

slipt [slipt; slɪpt] 〔古〕slip[1]的过去式。

slit [slit; slɪt] **I *n*.** **1.** 狭长切口;裂缝,狭缝。**2.** (自动售货机的)投钱口。**II *vt*.** (***slit***, ～***ted***; ～***ting***) **1.** 切开,割开;扯裂,剖开,切成长条。**2.** 使成狭缝。*He appears to have two* ～*s for eyes*. 他眯细着眼睛。～ *a hide into thongs* 把兽皮切成皮条。—***vi*.** 纵切,纵裂。～ **trench** 【军】避弹狭壕。**slit·ter *n*.**

slith·er [ˈsliðə; ˋslɪðɚ] **I *vi*.** 滑动;滑行;蜿蜒地滑行。—***vt*.** 使滑动,使滑行。**II *n*.** 滑动;滑行。**-y *a*.**

sliv·er [ˈslivə, ˈslaivə; ˋslɪvɚ] **I *n*.** **1.** 长条,裂片,细片;碎料。**2.** 【纺】条子,梳条,棉条。**3.** (作鱼饵用的)小鱼片。**II *vt*.** **1.** 把…剖成长条,把…切成薄片。**2.** 把(鱼)剖成两半。—***vi*.** 切开;裂开。

sli·vo·vitz [ˈslivəˌvits; ˋslɪvəvɪts] ***n*.** 梅子白兰地〔尤指东欧的〕。

Sloan [sləun; slon] ***n*.** 斯隆〔姓氏〕。

slob [slɔb; slɑb] ***n*.** **1.** 〔英方〕泥,(河底)烂泥。**2.** 〔口〕懒汉;蠢汉,笨蛋,无用的人;邋遢[粗鲁]的人;〔美俚〕大胖子。～ **ice** 〔纽芬兰的〕混杂着雪的浮冰。

slob·ber [ˈslɔbə; ˋslɑbɚ] **I *vi*.** **1.** 淌口水,垂涎。**2.** (说话时)感情迸发,过分伤感。—***vt*.** **1.** 口水淌湿。**2.** 哭诉;过分伤感[令人讨厌]地说[写]。**3.** 将(工作)敷衍了事,马马虎虎做。～ *over sb*. 将人弄得尽是口水,流着口水接吻;拼命宠爱;哭诉。～ *a bibful* 〔美〕倾诉满肚皮牢骚;唠叨一大堆。**II *n*.** 口水;哭诉;唠叨。*all of a* ～ 淌着口水。～**gullious *a*.** 〔美俚〕上好的;美味的。

Slo·cum [ˈsləukəm; ˋslokəm] ***n*.** 斯洛克姆〔姓氏〕。

sloe [sləu; slo] ***n*.** 【植】黑刺李(树或果);〔美〕野梅。～**-eyed** 眼睛黑而大的;长着杏眼的。～ **gin** 野梅红金酒。

slog [slɔg; slɑg] **I *vt*.** (**-*gg*-**) (打板球或拳击等时)猛击。—***vi*.** **1.** 猛击。**2.** 顽强地行进,吃力地走(*on*)。**3.** 拼命工作,苦干(*away*)。**II *n*.** **1.** 乱打,猛击。**2.** 苦干。**3.** 吃力地行进。

slo·gan [ˈsləugən; ˋslogən] ***n*.** **1.** (原为苏格兰高地和爱尔兰氏族号召战斗的)呐喊;集合信号。**2.** 口号,标语。**3.** (商业广告上用的)短语。**-eer** **1.** ***vi*.** 拟定标语口号;使用标语口号。**2.** ***n*.** 标语口号拟制[使用]者。**-istic *a*.** **-ize *vt*.** 使成标语口号;以标语口号方式表达;标语口号化。

slog·ger [ˈslɔgə; ˋslɑgɚ] ***n*.** (棒球等的)猛击者。

sloid [slɔid; slɔɪd] ***n*.** = sloyd.

slo·mo, slo-mo [ˈsləuməu; ˋslomo] ***n*.** 〔口〕慢动作;慢动作重放(装置)〔系 slow motion 的缩略〕。

sloop [slu:p; slup] ***n*.** **1.** 多帆单桅小船。**2.** 【军】海岸炮舰;(尤指二次大战中担任反潜任务的)小型护航舰。*a* ～ *of war* 〔英〕古代的炮舰。

slop[1] [slɔp; slɑp] **I *n*.** **1.** 稀泥;半融化的雪;泥浆。**2.** 泼落的水;弄湿了的地方;水坑。**3.** 〔*pl.*〕(粥等)流体食物;(作饲料的)泔水。**4.** 不值钱的感伤。**5.** (酿造过程中的)釜馏物;废液;废油。**6.** 〔俚〕不整洁的人。**7.** 不含酒精的饮料。**8.** 〔*pl.*〕人体排泄物。*live on* ～*s* 吃稀的过日子。**II *vi*.** (**-*pp*-**) **1.** 泼出,撒出,溢出。**2.** 在泥浆[化了的雪]中走。—***vt*.** **1.** 泼出,撒出;泼脏。**2.** 用泔水喂(猪等)。**3.** 溅污,弄脏。**4.** 咂咂地吃;贪婪地喝。***get*** ～***ped*** 喝醉。～ ***over*** **1.** 泼出,溅出,溢出。**2.** 滔滔不停地说。**3.** 变得极感伤,感情太流露。～***up*** 〔美〕喝(啤)酒。(***be***)

S

~ped over [**up**]〔美〕喝醉了的。(**be**) **~ped to the ear** 喝得烂醉的。~ **basin** [**bowl**]〔英〕(餐桌上)倒剩茶等用的盆。~ **chute** 船后部的垃圾筒。~ **jar** 盛污水[小便]的缸[桶]。~ **pail** 污水桶。~ **sink** 倒泔水或冲洗拖把的水池。

slop[2] [slɔp; slɑp] ***n***. 〔*pl*.〕(宽大的)罩衣[工作服],(价钱低廉的)现成衣服;〔*pl*.〕〔水手用语〕衣服,卧具;〔俚〕裁缝。~ **chest** (船上)准备发给海员的贮藏品。~**-room** (船上的)被服室。~**seller**〔美〕现成服装商。~**shop**〔美〕现成服装店。~**work** 现成衣服缝制工作;现成衣服,便宜衣服;马马虎虎的工作。(*No ~ ever dropped from his pen*. 他从不草率写文章)。

slop[3] [sləup; slɑp] ***n***. 〔英俚〕警察〔由倒读 police 转化而成〕。

slope [sləup; slop] **I** ***n***. **1**. 倾斜,坡度;坡,斜坡,斜面;【印】斜体。**2**.【军】掮枪的姿势。**3**.【数】斜率。**4**.【矿】斜井。**5**. 经济衰退。**6**.〔美军俚〕〔贬〕东方人。*a gentle ~* 缓坡。**II** ***vt***. 弄斜,使倾斜,使成斜坡。—***vi***. **1**. 倾斜,成斜坡。**2**.〔口〕逃亡;来,去。~ ***about***〔俚〕闲荡。***S-arms!***〔口令〕掮枪。~ ***off***〔俚〕离去;逃亡。~ **wash**【地】斜坡冲刷物,坡积物。**-wise** ***ad***. 倾斜着。

slop·ing [ˈsləupiŋ; ˋslopɪŋ] ***a***. 倾斜的,成斜坡的。**-ly** ***ad***. **-ness** ***n***.

slop·pi·ness [ˈslɔpinis; ˋslɑpɪnɪs] ***n***. **1**. 泥泞;潮湿;稀薄。**2**. 懒散;(工作)草率;易伤感;(外表)邋遢。

slop·py [ˈslɔpi; ˋslɑpɪ] ***a***. **1**. 稀薄的,(食品)流质的。**2**. 雨多的(天气);水坑多的;泥泞的;被污水溅污的,满是污水的。**3**. 懒散的;(工作)草率的。**4**. 易伤感的;含泪的。**5**. (外表)邋遢的;喝醉的。~ **joe** 碎牛肉饼。**-pi·ly** ***ad***.

slosh [slɔʃ; slɑʃ] **I** ***n***. =**1**. slush. **2**. 溅泼声。**3**.〔美〕稀薄的食物[饮料]。**4**.〔俚〕胡话。**II** ***vi***. 在水[泥]中挣扎[乱走];到处乱溅;发出液体晃动声。—***vt***. 搅动;溅泼;〔英俚〕打。**-ed** ***a***.〔主英俚〕喝醉了的。

slot[1] [slɔt; slɑt] ***n***. **1**. 狭缝,窄孔;【机】槽沟;自动售货机投钱口。**2**.【空】翼缝。**3**.〔美口〕(集体或系列中的)位置,职位。~ **aerial**【电】槽形天线。~ **car** 遥控电动玩具汽车。~**-drills**【机】铣槽。~ **machine** 自动售货机(等);吃角子老虎[赌具]。~ **man** 负责新闻编排的报纸编辑。~ **television** (投入硬币即可收视的)自动电视机。

slot[2] [slɔt; slɑt] **I** ***n***. (鹿等的)足迹,嗅迹。**II** ***vt***. 跟着足迹追赶。

slot[3] [slɔt; slɑt] ***n***. 〔英方〕门闩;〔方〕条板。

sloth [sləuθ; sloθ] ***n***. **1**. 懒惰,怠惰。**2**.【动】树懒〔产于南美洲的一种哺乳动物,行动迟缓〕。~ **bear**【动】(印度等地的)懒熊。

sloth·ful [ˈsləuθfəl; ˋsloθfəl] ***a***. 偷懒的,懒惰的。

slouch [slautʃ; slautʃ] **I** ***n***. **1**. 没精打采[垂头丧气]的姿态[步调]。**2**. (帽边等的)下垂,耷拉。**3**. 萎靡不振的人;不整洁的人;不中用的人;〔美〕无价值的场所[人、物]。*a ~ hat* 垂边帽,阔软边呢帽。*He is no ~*. 他不是不中用的人。**II** ***vi***. **1**. 没精打采地走[坐,站]。**2**. 耷拉,低垂。—***vt***. 使低垂。**-y** ***a***. **-i·ly** ***ad***. **-i·ness** ***n***.

slough[1] [slau; slaʊ] **I** ***n***. **1**. 低洼泥泞的地方,泥潭,泥坑;泥沼。**2**. 绝望的境地;堕落;道德败坏。**3**. [sluː; slu]〔美、加拿大〕沼泽地中的小溪,叉流,河湾。*the ~ of despond* 失望的泥沼;绝境;异常沮丧的状态。**II** ***vt***. **1**. 使陷入泥沼;〔喻〕使陷入泥坑,使堕落,使沉沦。**2**.〔美俚〕逮捕;监禁 (*up, in*)。—***vi***. 在泥浆中跋涉。

slough[2] [slʌf; slʌf] **I** ***n***. **1**. (蛇等蜕的)皮,壳;(动物身上)定时脱落的外表部份。**2**. 被丢弃的东西(习惯、嗜好,成见等)。**3**.【医】腐肉,痂;脱落。**II** ***vi***. **1**. 长痂,生痂。**2**. (蛇皮等的)脱落;(蛇等)蜕皮。**3**. (标点等)漏掉。**4**. (岩石、河岸等)崩塌。—***vt***. **1**. 脱落(皮等)。**2**. 抛弃,丢弃 (*off*)。**3**.【牌】丢掉(没用的牌)。~ (*off*) *bad habits* 戒掉坏习惯。~ **over** 当作微不足道;轻视。

slough·y[1] [ˈslaui; ˋslaʊɪ] ***a***. 泥泞的;泥沼一样的。

slough·y[2] [ˈslʌfi; ˋslʌfɪ] ***a***. 蛇脱皮似的;腐肉似的,疙痂似的;脱落的。

Slo·vak [ˈsləuvæk; ˋslovæk] **I** ***n***. 斯洛伐克人;斯洛伐克语。**II** ***a***. 斯洛伐克的,斯洛伐克人的,斯洛伐克语的。

Slo·va·ki·a [sləuˈvækiə; sloˋvɑkɪə] ***n***. 斯洛伐克(欧洲一国家名)。

Slo·va·ki·an [sləuˈvækiən; sloˋvɑkɪən] ***n***., ***a***. =Slovak.

slov·en [ˈslʌvən; ˋslʌvən] **I** ***n***. 不修边幅的人,邋遢鬼,懒鬼,字迹[工作]潦草的人。**II** ***a***. =**1**. slovenly. **2**. 未开垦的;未开化的。

Slo·vene [ˈsləuviːn; sloˋvin], **Slo·ve·ni·an** [sləuˈviːnjən; sloˋvinɪən] **I** ***n***. 斯洛文尼亚人,斯洛文尼亚语。**II** ***a***. 斯洛文尼亚的,斯洛文尼亚人的;斯洛文尼亚语的。

Slo·ve·ni·a [sləuˈviːnjə; sloˋvinɪə] ***n***. 斯洛文尼亚〔前南斯拉夫一地区,现已成为独立国家〕。

slov·en·ly [ˈslʌvənli; ˋslʌvənlɪ] ***a***., ***ad***. 邋遢的[地],不修边幅的[地],不整洁的[地];懒散的[地];草率的[地]。

slow [sləu; slo] **I** ***a***. **1**. 慢的,缓慢的 (*opp*. fast; quick; rapid; swift)。**2**. 迟钝的,笨的;没精神的,不活泼的;(表演等)没趣的。**3**. 不激烈的,不尖锐的;温和的,低下的。**4**. 要求很长时间的,逐步的。**5**. 慢于…的,慢了的;晚于…的 (*on*)。**6**. 落后的;落后于时代的。**7**. 作用缓慢的。**8**. (商业)吊滞的。**9**. (路面等)妨碍前进(或行动的);使减速的。*a ~ train* 慢车。*~ poison* 缓效毒药。*~ fire* 文火。*a ~ oven* 火力小的炉灶。*a ~ student* 学得慢的学生。*He was ~ to anger* [*wrath*]. 他不轻易发怒。*His clock is ~*. 他的钟慢。*My watch is five minutes ~*. 我的表慢五分钟。*a ~ convalescence* 缓慢的恢复健康。*~ music* 哀乐。*find life ~ in the country* 觉得乡间生活沉闷。*a ~ town* 没有生气的城镇。*a ~ season* 淡季。*~ in action* 行动缓慢。*~ at account* 不善于算账。~ ***and steady*** [***sure***] 慢而稳,稳步的。~ ***as*** (***cold***) ***molasses*** (***in January***)〔美〕极缓慢的;极迟钝的。~ ***as the seven-year itch***〔美〕极缓慢的。~ ***of speech*** [***wit***] 嘴钝[迟钝]的。**II** ***ad***. 缓慢地;慢慢。*go ~* 慢慢走;慢慢做;耽误;小心地进行。*How ~ you read!* 你读得真慢! **III** ***vt***. 使慢,开慢,拖延 (*down*; *up*; *off*);使呆滞。—***vi***. 放慢,慢起来,减(低)速(度)。~ *down* [*up*] (*a motor-car*) 减低(汽车)速度。~ **burn**〔美俚〕渐渐的发怒。~**coach** 迟钝的人,慢性子的人;时代落伍者。~ **dance** 慢步舞;〔喻〕磨洋工,怠工,装装样子地做事。~**down** 减缓,减速;减退。~ **infection**【医】慢性感染〔往往由慢性病毒引起,多具致命性〕。~ **match** 慢燃引信头[火绳,导火线]。~**-motion** ***a***. 慢动作的;慢镜头的。~**-motion camera** (**picture**)【影】(拍慢镜头的)高速摄影机,用高速摄影机拍摄的(影片)。~**-moving** ***a***. 动作缓慢的,无进展的;(商品等)滞销的。~ **neutron**【物】慢中子。~**poke**〔美俚〕做事慎重的人,慢性子的人。~ **starter**〔美拳〕初防守后猛攻的拳击手。~ **time** **1**.〔口〕(与夏季时间区别的)标准时间。**2**.【军】慢步〔每步 75 厘米每分钟 75 步的步调〕。~ **up** 减缓。~**-witted** ***a***. 迟钝的,笨的。~**worm**【动】蛇蜥。**-ly** ***ad***. **-ness** ***n***.

sloyd [slɔid; slɔɪd] ***n***. 以木雕手工为基础的手工教育 (= sloid)。

S.L.P. = Socialist Labor Party〔美〕社会劳工党。

slub [slʌb; slʌb] **I** ***n***.【纺】头道粗纺的棉纱[羊毛];纱节,大肚纱[疵点]。**II** ***vt***., ***vi***. (**-bb-**)【纺】轻捻,粗纺。

slub·ber [ˈslʌbə; ˋslʌbɚ] **I** ***vt***. **1**. 敷衍了事,马马虎虎做;乱七八糟地做。**2**.〔英方〕弄脏,玷污。**II** ***n***.〔美〕卑鄙的人。

sludge [slʌdʒ; slʌdʒ] **I** ***n***. **1**. 泥,泥浆,烂泥。**2**. (锅炉等的)泥状沉积物。**3**. 半溶的雪;浮冰。**4**.【矿】矿泥;煤泥;淤渣;钻泥。**5**.【油】(油灌底部的)酸渣;碱渣。**6**.【医】血泥,红血球在血管中凝集。**7**.〔美俚〕胡说;脏话;猥亵行为。**II** ***vt***. **1**. 涂上污泥;清除污泥。**2**.【医】使成血泥。

S

～ **worm**【动】正颤蚓。

sludg·y [ˈslʌdʒi; ˋslʌdʒɪ] *a*. 有淤泥的;泥泞的。

slue[1][sluː; slu] **I** *vt*. 使斜向;【海】使转,使回转。—*vi*. 回转。**II** *n*. 回转;回转后的方向。

slue[2][sluː; slu] *n*. =slew[2].

slue[3][sluː; slu] *n*. =slew[4].

slue·foot [ˈsluːfut; ˋslufʊt] *n*. 〔美俚〕侦探。

sluff [slʌf; slʌf] *n*.【地】小雪崩。

slug[1][slʌg; slʌg] **I** *n*. **1**.【动】蛞蝓,蜒蚰,鼻涕虫;蛞蝓状幼虫。**2**. 动作缓慢的人[动物,车,船];懒人。**3**. 金属块[棒];(气枪的)子弹。**4**. (开动自动售货机等的)代硬币的金属片;〔美〕【电话】5 分代币。**5**.【印】大嵌条。**6**.【物】斯勒格,斯(质量单位)。**7**.【无】铁心;波导调配柱;〔美口〕一口[一杯]酒。*a sea* ～ 海参。**II** *vi*. (*-gg-*) **1**. 捕杀蛞蝓。**2**. 偷懒;睡着。**3**. 〔美〕喝一口酒。～ *indoors* 懒散在家里,偷懒在家。—*vt*. 在…中插嵌片。～**abed** *n*. 〔古〕睡懒觉的人。

slug[2][slʌg; slʌg] *v*., *n*. 〔美口〕=slog. ～**-nutty** *a*. 〔美俚〕=punch-drunk.

slug·fest [ˈslʌgfest; ˋslʌg͵fɛst] *n*. 〔美俚〕拳赛。

slug·gard [ˈslʌgəd; ˋslʌgɚd] **I** *n*. 懒人。**II** *a*. =**-ly** 懒人的,懒的。

slug·ger [ˈslʌgə; ˋslʌgɚ] *n*. **1**. 〔美口〕(棒球拳击等的)猛击者。**2**. (不善于自卫的)职业拳击家。

slug·ging [ˈslʌgiŋ; ˋslʌgɪŋ] *n*. 〔美俚〕打得猛的拳击赛[棒球赛]。

slug·gish [ˈslʌgiʃ; ˋslʌgɪʃ] *a*. **1**. 偷懒的,懒惰的(人)。**2**. (流水等)动得缓慢的,停滞的;惰性的;呆钝的,不活泼的。**3**. (市场等)清淡的,萧条的。**-ly** *ad*.

S

sluice [sluːs; slus] **I** *n*. **1**. 水闸,水门,水闸门〔又称～gate, ～valve〕;闸沟,泄水道〔又称～way〕;闸口。**2**. (被闸门拦住或从闸门流出的)蓄水;泄水。**3**.【林】(流放木材的)斜水槽。**4**.【矿】(洗金矿等用的)流矿槽;〔转义〕根本,源泉。*open* [*let loose*] *the* ～*s* 开水闸,让水流出;〔喻〕将想说的话说出来;让感情发泄出来。*have a* ～ 〔俚〕洗澡。**II** *vt*. **1**. 开闸灌溉,开闸放(水)。**2**. 冲洗,好好地洗。—*vi*. 流出,奔流。

slum[1][slʌm; slʌm] **I** *n*. **1**. 〔常 *pl*.〕贫民窟,贫民区。**II** *vi*. (*-mm-*) 到贫民区去[观光,游玩等];在贫民区发展保险业务[从事慈善事业]。～**dweller** 贫民窟居民。～**lord** 〔俚〕贫民窟房东〔尤指勒索高价而不管房屋维修的屋主〕。

slum[2][slʌm; slʌm] *n*. =slumgullion.

slum·ber [ˈslʌmbə; ˋslʌmbɚ] **I** *n*. **1**. 微睡;安眠,熟睡;打盹儿。**2**. 蛰伏[静止]状态。**II** *vi*. **1**. 睡眠,微睡。**2**. 蛰伏;处于静止状态。—*vt*. (用睡眠)消磨(时间)(*away*)。*a* ～(*ing*) *robe* 〔美〕睡衣。*a* ～ *bum* 〔美俚〕夜间看门人。

slum·ber·er [ˈslʌmbərə; ˋslʌmbərɚ] *n*. 睡眠者;微睡者。

slum·ber·ous, slum·brous [ˈslʌmbərəs, -brəs; ˋslʌmbərəs] *a*. **1**. 瞌睡的,昏昏欲睡的。**2**. 催眠的,使人瞌睡的。**3**. 睡着的,打着盹儿的;寂静的。

slum·gul·lion [slʌmˈgʌliən; slʌmˋgʌljən] *n*. **1**. 〔美俚〕淡饮料。**2**. 炖肉;马铃薯洋葱炖肉。**3**. 原油渣。**4**.【矿】洗矿沟中淤积的红泥浆。**5**. (捕鲸船甲板上的)残余血油。**6**. 〔美蔑〕不中用的家伙;仆役。

slum·mer [ˈslʌmə; ˋslʌmɚ] *n*. 贫民区居民;出入贫民区从事慈善事业[发展保险业务]的人。

slum·my [ˈslʌmi; ˋslʌmɪ] *a*. 贫民区的。

slump [slʌmp; slʌmp] **I** *n*. **1**. 〔方〕陷入,掉下;〔方〕沼地。**2**.【商】(物价等的)暴跌;(事业的)衰败,低落;(精神等的)消沉,萎靡。**II** *vi*. **1**. 〔方〕掉下,陷入(泥、雪等中);崩坍。**2**. 失败,挫折。**3**.【商】暴跌;衰败;消沉。**4**.【矿】塌陷,崩塌。～ *into a chair* 倒在椅子里。*hit a* ～ 〔美〕(选手成积)猛落。

slump·fla·tion [slʌmpˈfleiʃən; slʌmpˋfleʃən] *n*.【经】(伴随有失业、商业不景气的)萧条性通(货膨)涨。

slung [slʌŋ; slʌŋ] sling 的过去式及过去分词。～ **shot** 〔美〕(弹弓上用的)石弹。

slunk [slʌŋk; slʌŋk] slink 的过去式及过去分词。

slur [sləː; slɝ] **I** *vt*. 藐视,轻视;忽略,略过(*over*)。**2**. 急促而不清楚地讲[写]。**3**.【乐】圆润地接连唱[演奏];加连接线。**4**. 弄脏,玷污,诬蔑;诽谤;掩饰;隐瞒;假装没看见。**5**.【印】涂污,印模糊。**II** *n*. 污点;耻辱;毁谤,诬蔑,污辱;【乐】连接线;【印】污点,模糊不清。*put a* ～ *upon* =〔美〕*cast* ～*s at* 毁谤,诬蔑。

slurb [sləːb; slɝb] *n*.【俚】市郊贫民区。

slurp [sləːp; slɝp] **I** *vt*., *vi*.【俚】咕噜咕噜地喝;叭嗒叭嗒地吃。**II** *n*. 〔俚〕咕噜[叭嗒]声〔吃喝或吸吮〕。

slur·ry [ˈsləːri; ˋslɝɪ] *n*. **1**. 泥浆;灰泥,水泥浆。**2**. 膏剂;【机】型心粘合液。～ *seed treatment*【农】拌种处理。

slush [slʌʃ; slʌʃ] **I** *n*. **1**. 烂泥;污水。**2**. 半融雪(冰);雪水。**3**. 薄胶泥;搪瓷液料;脂膏。**4**.【机】机油;抗蚀润滑油;白铅石灰,油灰。**5**. 水泥砂浆;纸浆。**6**. 过于感情用事的言语[文字];哭诉;废话。**7**. 〔美俚〕贿赂;伪钞。**II** *vt*. **1**. 使溅上泥浆[雪水],溅污。**2**. 涂润滑油于;给…灌上泥浆;给…嵌上油灰;冲洗(甲板)。—*vi*. **1**. (在泥浆等中)吃力地行走。**2**. 发出溅泼声。**-y** *a*. 泥泞的。**-i·ness** *n*.

slut [slʌt; slʌt] *n*. **1**. 母狗。**2**. 邋遢女人,懒女人。**3**. 放荡的女人,妓女。**4**. 〔谑〕少女,顽皮女孩。**-tish** *a*. **-tish·ly** *ad*. **-tish·ness** *n*.

slut·ter·y [ˈslʌtəri; ˋslʌtərɪ] *n*. 邋遢;龌龊;放荡(=stuttishness)。

sly [slai; slaɪ] *a*. (～*er*, *sli·er*; ～*est*, *sli·est*) **1**. 狡猾的,狡诈的。**2**. 顽皮的;淘气的。**3**. 秘密的,暗中的,偷偷摸摸的。**4**. 〔方〕灵活的,巧妙的。*He is a* ～ *dog*. 他是一个狡猾的家伙。*on* [*upon*] *the* ～ 〔口〕秘密地,偷偷地。～**boots** *n*. 〔*sing*., *pl*.〕顽皮的家伙[小孩、动物等];狡猾的人。**-ly** *ad*. **-ness** *n*.

slype [slaip; slaɪp] *n*. 〔英〕(从教堂通到别院的)走廊。

SM, S.M. =**1**. 〔L.〕*Scientiae Magister* 理科硕士(=master of science)。**2**. Sergeant Major【军】军士长。**3**. Soldier's Medal〔美〕军人奖章(因作战以外的英勇事迹而被授予的奖章)。**4**. strategic missile 战略导〔飞〕弹。**5**. submarine minelayer 布雷潜水艇。**6**. short metre〔诗〕短韵律。**7**. Special Message〔美〕特别咨文。**8**. square metre 平方米;平方公尺。

S-M, s-m =**1**. sado-masochism【医】施虐—受虐狂。**2**. sado-masochist【医】施虐—受虐狂者。

Sm =【化】samarium.

SMA = Surplus Marketing Administration. 〔美〕(军用)剩余物资销售管理局。

smack[1][smæk; smæk] **I** *n*. **1**. 味,滋味,风味;气味。**2**. 遗痕。**3**. 些微,一点点。*a* ～ *of wine to each* 每人一点酒。**II** *vi*. 有味,有…的风味;有…的气味;有点像…的地方(*of*)。*Southern cookery* ～*s of oil*. 南方口味油重。*His gait* ～*s of the sea*. 他走路的样子有点像海员。*a wet* ～ 讨厌的人,使人扫兴的人。

smack[2][smæk; smæk] **I** *n*. **1**. 咂嘴(声);接吻(声);鼓舌(声)。**2**. 用掌拍打(声);鞭声,劈拍声。*get a* ～ *in the eye* 遭受突如其来的打击[挫折];〔喻〕感到出乎意料的失望。*have a* ～ *at* 〔口〕去试,去尝试。*tickets at three dollars a* ～ 三元一张的票。**II** *vt*., *vi*. **1**. 咂(嘴),有声响地吻。**2**. 啪的一声用手掌猛击;(使)劈拍地响。～ *one's lips over* 咂嘴;满足。～ *down* 〔美俚〕(对不守本分的人)责斥,使屈辱。**III** *ad*. **1**. 啪的一下;使劲;猛地。**2**. 准确地,恰好,正好。*hit sb*. ～ *in the face* 啪的打一个耳光。*go* ～ *into the ditch* 啪的一跤摔在沟中。*run* ～ *into* 正好撞在。

smack[3][smæk; smæk] *n*. 单桅小帆船;(有鱼池设备的)渔船。

smack[4][smæk; smæk] *n*. 〔俚〕海洛因。～**head** 吸海洛因

者。

smack·er [ˈsmækə; ˋsmækɚ] ***n*.** **1.** 咂嘴的人;鞭打的人。**2.** 啪的一击;殴打。**3.** 极大的东西;绝好的东西。**4.** 〔美俚〕一元。**5.** 嘴巴,嘴唇;〔口〕大声接吻。

smack·ing [ˈsmækiŋ; ˋsmækɪŋ] ***a*.** 活泼的,精神勃勃的;兴旺的;尖锐的。

smacks·man [ˈsmæksmən; ˋsmæksmən] ***n*.** (有鱼池设备的)渔船的船主[船员]。

small[1] [smɔl; smɔl] **I *a*.** **1.** 小 (*opp*. large); 少 (*opp*. large, numerous); 细小的;窄小的;琐细的;些微的;少额的(收入等);小规模的。**2.** 吝啬的,小器的,小心眼儿的。**3.** 难为情的,觉得羞耻的;低级的,贫穷的;卑劣的。**4.** (雨)细微的;(声音)微弱的;(酒等)清淡的。★ little 含有可怜可爱的意思, small 只照实叙述事实。*a* ~ (*bottle of*) *soda* (*water*) 一小瓶苏打水。*a* ~ *audience* 人数不多的听众[观众]。~ *years* 小时候,幼年。~ *arms* 轻便武器,〔尤指〕步枪。~ *errors* 小过,小错。~ *rain* 细雨。*He has* ~ *French and less German*. 他不大懂法语,德语更不行。*It is* ~ *of you to say so*. 你这样说那就小气了。*a* ~ *nature* 小心眼。~ *cares and worries* 无谓的操心烦恼。~ *punkins* 〔美〕无足轻重的;所谓要人;〔讽〕小要人〔其实是不足道的小人物〕。***and* ~ *blame to him*** 对他没有多少可以责备的地方。***and* ~ *wonder*** 没有什么奇怪的。***and such* ~ *deer*** 其他闲杂人等,其他的人们。***be great in* ~ *matters*** 小事聪明。***by* ~ *and* ~** 慢慢地,一点一点地。***feel* ~** 觉得难为情,觉得羞耻。***in a* ~ *way*** 小规模地;朴素地。***in* ~ *numbers*** 少。***It is* ~ *wonder that*** (这件事)并不足怪。***live in a* ~ *way*** 简朴谨慎地过日子。***look* ~** 显得渺小,自渐形秽。***of no* ~ *consequence*** 重大的。***on the* ~ *side*** 比较小。**II *n*.** **1.** 〔the ~〕细小部分;〔尤指〕腰部。**2.** 小物,琐碎东西;身分低的人。**3.** 〔*pl*.〕小商品;〔英口〕小件洗濯物;〔英牛津大学〕〔*pl*.〕= responsions. (*the*) *great and* (*the*) ~ 身分高高低低的人们。***a* ~ *and early*** 人少而早散的晚会。***in* ~** = 〔罕〕in the ~ 小规模。***Small is beautiful***. 〔谚〕小的就是好的,越小越好。**III *ad*.** 小声地,轻轻地(讲等)。**~-beer** **1.** ***n*.** 淡啤酒。**2.** ***a*.** 无价值的,微不足道的 (*think no* ~*-beer of oneself* 自负)。**~-bore** **1.** 小口径枪的。**2.** 眼界狭窄的。**3.** 〔口〕小辐度的,不惹眼的。**~ calorie** 小卡(热量单位)。**~-cap** 【经】小盘股〔指风险小而收益率高的小资本股票〕。**~ capitals** 【印】小大写字体。**~ change** 找头;无聊话;〔美〕无用的人[东西];琐事。**~clothes** 〔*pl*.〕〔古〕短裤,小件衣服。**~ fry** 小鱼;微不足道的人[物]。**~-fry** ***a*.** 不重要的。**~ game** 小猎物。**~ helm** 【海】小角度转舵。**~holder** (耕地 1—50 英亩的)小自耕农。**~holding** 小自耕农地,小块地,小地产。**~ hours** 夜半后一、两点钟的时间,深更半夜。**~ letter** 小写字母。**~-minded** ***a*.** 气量狭窄的,小心眼的,小气的。**~ money** = ~ change. **~mouth back bass** 【动】小口黑鲈。**~ potatoes** 〔亦可作单数用〕〔美俚〕小人物。**~ pox** 【医】天花。**~ print** 小字体印刷品(租约、保险单等下端的)附属细则〔多载明各种保留条件〕。**~-scale** ***a*.** 小比例尺的(地图);小规模的 (~*-scale business operations* 小规模商业活动)。**~ stores** (船上卖烟等给船员的)小杂货部。**~sword** 轻剑。**~ talk** 闲谈。**~-talk** ***vi*.** 聊天 (*they like to* ~*-talk*. 他们喜欢聊天)。**~ time** **1.** 无关紧要的小事。**2.** 小杂耍团的巡回表演。**~-time** ***a*.** 〔美口〕不重要的,不成功的,不出色的,劣等的 (~*-time stuff* 劣货;笨举;琐事)。**~-timer** 小剧团从业人员;小规模事业组织的从业人员。**~-town** 小市镇的;乡土气的,内地色彩的,朴实的。**~wares** 杂货,小东西;狭幅衣料。**smal·ly** ***ad*.** 小规模地。

small·age [ˈsmɔːlidʒ; ˋsmɔlɪdʒ] ***n*.** 〔罕〕【植】野芹菜 (*Apium graveolens*)。

small·ish [ˈsmɔːliʃ; ˋsmɔlɪʃ] ***a*.** 略小的,有点小的。

small·ness [ˈsmɔːlnis; ˋsmɔlnɪs] ***n*.** 小,少;些微;小规模;低贱;吝啬,小气;卑鄙。

smalt [smɔːlt; smɔlt] ***n*.** **1.** 【化】大青,花绀青,藤紫〔颜料〕。**2.** (用钴、钾碱、矽石制成的)蓝玻璃。**3.** 大青色。

smal·tite [ˈsmɔːltait; ˋsmɔltaɪt], **smal·tine** [-tin; -tɪn] ***n*.** 【矿】砷钴矿。

smal·to [ˈsmɑːltəu, It. ˈzmɑːltəu; ˋzmalto] ***n*.** (*pl*. ***-tos***, ***-ti*** [-tiː; -tɪ]) **1.** 用于镶嵌工艺的色玻璃或搪瓷。**2.** 一块色玻璃,一块搪瓷。

smar·agd [ˈsmæræɡd; ˋsmæræɡd] ***n*.** 〔现罕〕= emerald. **-ine *a*.**

sma·rag·dite [sməˈræɡdait; sməˋræɡdaɪt] ***n*.** 【矿】绿闪石。

smarm·y [ˈsmɑːmi; ˋsmɑrmɪ] 〔英口〕 ***a*.** 满口恭维话的,爱拍马屁的。

smart [smɑːt; smɑrt] **I *a*.** **1.** 灵敏的,灵巧的,敏捷的,聪明的,伶俐的。**2.** 漂亮的,衣冠楚楚的,潇洒的;时髦的。(*opp*. shabby, dingy)。**3.** 精明的,狡猾的。**4.** 刺痛的,厉害的,强烈的,猛烈的,尖锐的;辛辣的;活泼的,有力的;爽快的,痛快的;〔口〕粗鲁的,无礼的。**5.** 〔口〕可观的,相当大[多]的。**6.** 〔口〕(机器等)灵巧的,(炸弹等)激光制导的;电脑化的,智能型的。*a* ~ *saying* 漂亮话。~ *clothes* 漂亮的衣服。~ *dealings* 狡猾的手段。~ *frost* 严霜。*a* ~ *skirmish* 猛烈的小接触。*walking a* ~ *pace* 轻快的步伐行走。*a* ~ *few* 相当多(的)。~ *weapons* 智能化武器,激光制导的武器。***as* ~ *as a new pin*** [***threepence***] 〔口〕非常潇洒的[时髦的]。***as* ~ *as a steel trap*** 〔美俚〕(做生意等)非常精明的。***be* ~** (***about it***) 做得麻利。***make a* ~ *job of it*** 办得巧妙。***right* ~** 〔美口〕极大的,许许多多的 (*a right* ~ *rain* 暴雨)。**~ *as threepence*** 〔英俚〕穿着得漂亮。**II *ad*.** = smartly. **III *vi*.** **1.** 刺痛;作痛。**2.** 痛苦,伤心,悲痛;愤慨 (*under*)。**3.** 受罚,受罪 (*for*)。~ *under an injustice* 因受委曲而感痛心。*The eyes* ~ *with smoke*. 眼睛给烟熏得痛。~ *from an insult* 因受辱而愤慨。~ *with mortification* 因屈辱而痛心。~ *for* 因…受罚,因…吃苦头。**IV *n*.** **1.** 疼痛;苦痛;悲痛;愤慨。**2.** 〔有时用 *pl*.〕〔美、加俚〕才智,聪敏。*feel the* ~ *of one's folly* 痛恨自己愚蠢。**~ alec**, **~-aleck** [-ˈælik; -ˋælɪk], **~-aleckry**, **~-aleckism** 自作聪明,自以为样样都懂;刚愎自用。**~-alecky *a*.** 自作聪明的,自以为样样都懂的。**~ bomb** 激光制导炸弹,灵敏炸弹。**~ card** 万用卡,智能卡〔类似信用卡,但内藏微处理机,储存银行账目,保险财务,病历等多种数据,可与电脑数据库接通〕。**~ chance** 〔美〕绝好的机会;大量。**~ drink** 益智饮料〔果汁或咖啡等饮料中加入维生素、矿物质、草药等,据说能有益智作用〕。**~ ellick** [-ˈelik; -ˋælɪk] ***n*.** 自作聪明的人。**~ money** **1.** 惩罚性赔偿金。**2.** 〔英〕伤兵抚恤金。**3.** (知道内情者投下的)可操胜算的赌注[投资]。**~ set** 〔美〕时髦人士。**~-weed** 【植】蓼车。

smart·en [ˈsmɑːtn; ˋsmɑrtn̩] ***vt*.** **1.** 使漂亮潇洒,打扮 (*up*)。**2.** 使活泼,使轻快。**3.** 使强烈;使清醒[了解情况]。**4.** 使聪明,使精明 (*up*)。—***vi*.** **1.** 变得漂亮潇洒。**2.** 变强烈。~ ***oneself*** (漂漂亮亮地)打扮。~ ***up*** 〔美俚〕劝告;说明。

smart·ie [ˈsmɑːti; ˋsmɑrtɪ] ***n*.** = smarty.

smart·ish [ˈsmɑːtiʃ; ˋsmɑrtɪʃ] **I *a*.** **1.** 相当漂亮的。**2.** 〔口〕相当的。**II *ad*.** 〔口语〕厉害。***a* ~ *few*** 许多。

smart·ly [ˈsmɑːtli; ˋsmɑrtlɪ] ***ad*.** **1.** 华美地,漂亮地。**2.** 一阵一阵刺痛地;厉害地,剧烈地,猛烈地。**3.** 聪明地;精明地;机敏地;伶俐地。

smart·y [ˈsmɑːti; ˋsmɑrtɪ] ***n*.** 自作聪明的人 (= smart aleck)。**~-pants** = smarty.

smash [smæʃ; smæʃ] **I *vt*.** **1.** 打碎,打破,打烂;压碎,捣烂;碰撞。**2.** 使破产,击溃。**3.** 猛击;猛掷;【网球】从上往下猛杀,猛扣。**4.** 使(原子、原子核)发生裂变。~ *up the furniture* 捣毁家具。~ *an egg* 打破蛋。~ *the record* 打破纪录。~ *the jinx* 〔美运〕连败后的胜利,否极泰来。

—*vi*. 1. 碎裂,粉碎;压碎。2. 猛冲,猛撞(*against*, *into*, *through*)。3. 破产,倒闭(*up*);瓦解,垮掉。4. 扣球,杀球。5.〔俚〕使用伪造的货币。～ *in a door* (从外面)打破门户。～ *into a wall* 撞在墙上。**II** *n*. 1. 破碎,粉碎;全部毁灭;破产;(火车等的)猛撞,重击;破碎声,重击声。2.【网球】杀球,扣球。3. 甜酒薄荷水。4.〔美〕大成功。*the* ～ *of two automobiles* 两车相撞。***all to*** ～ (完全)粉碎;全部崩溃。***come*** [***go***] (***to***) ～ 粉碎;破产。***play*** ～〔美〕破产。**III** *ad*. 轰然。***run*** [***go***] ～ ***into*** 和…迎面相撞。～ **hit** 最佳电影;演出极为成功的戏剧。

smashed [smæʃt; smæʃt] *a*.【俚】沉醉的;烂醉如泥的。

smash·er [ˈsmæʃə; ˋsmæʃɚ] *n*. 1. 打碎者,击破器,破碎器。2.〔俚〕猛烈的打击,崩溃;厉害的回答,使人无可答辩的议论。3. 绝好的东西;漂亮的人[物]。4.〔俚〕用假钱的人,赝币,伪币。

smash·ing [ˈsmæʃiŋ; ˋsmæʃɪŋ] *a*. 1. 凶猛的,沉重的,惨重的,粉碎性的(打击等)。2. 活泼的,(商业情况等)兴旺的。3.〔俚〕漂亮的,突出的,不一般的。*a* ～ *success* 极大的成功。*a* ～ *victory* 巨大胜利。*have a* ～ *time* 玩得非常痛快。

smash-up [ˈsmæʃʌp; ˋsmæʃ,ʌp] *n*. 1.〔口〕破碎,粉碎。2.〔美〕(火车等的)猛撞。3. 失败,破产;崩溃,破灭。

smat·ter [ˈsmætə; ˋsmætɚ] **I** *n*.〔美、英古〕肤浅的知识(=smattering)。**II** *vt*. 一知半解地谈论;肤浅地研究,涉猎。—*vi*. 一知半解地瞎说,装懂,充内行。**-er** *n*. 一知半解的人。

S

smat·ter·ing [ˈsmætəriŋ; ˋsmætərɪŋ] *n*. 1. 肤浅的知识,一知半解;半瓶子醋。2. 少数,少量。*to rest content with a* ～ *of knowledge* 满足于一知半解。

smaze [smeiz; smez] *n*.【气】烟霾〔烟和雾的混合物〕。

S.M.C. = spermatocyte; sperm mother-cell【生】精母细胞。

sm.c., **sm. caps.** = small capitals【印】小大写字体。

SME = small and medium-size enterprise 中小型企业。

smear [smiə; smɪr] **I** *vt*. 1. 搽上,涂上,抹上(油、漆等)。2. 涂去,抹掉。3. (油、墨水等)抹脏,涂污,弄得模糊不明,涂得不能辨认。4.〔美〕(尤指政客)诽谤,糟蹋(名誉)。5.〔美俚〕打倒,打垮,击破。～ *the address on a letter* 把信上的地址弄得看不清楚。～ *the record*〔美运〕大胜。～ *a wet signature* 把一个墨迹未干的签名弄得模糊不清。～ *a word* 涂掉一个字。**II** *n*. 1. 油迹,污点,污斑。2.【生】涂片;涂料;釉。3.〔美口〕诽谤,中伤。*a* ～ *camera* 扫描摄影机。～**-bund** 诽谤集团。～**-case**〔美〕乡下干酪。～**-caster**〔美〕诽谤者。

smear·y [ˈsmiəri; ˋsmɪrɪ] *a*. 弄脏的,易涂污的;油污的;涂用的。**-i·ness** *n*.

smec·tic [ˈsmektik; ˋsmɛktɪk] *a*. 1.【化】碟状液晶分子的,近晶的。2. 净化的。

Smed·ley [ˈsmedli; ˋsmɛdlɪ] *n*. 斯梅德利〔姓氏〕。

smeech [smiːtʃ; smitʃ] *n*.〔方〕焦臭;浓烟。

smeg·ma [ˈsmegmə; ˋsmɛgmə] *n*.【医】阴垢;包皮垢。～**-tic** *a*.

smell [smel; smɛl] **I** *vt*. (***smelt***,〔美〕～***ed*** [-d;-d]) 1. 闻,嗅。2. 闻出;发觉,查出(*out*)。3. 发出…的气味。～ *trouble* 觉察出困难。～ *the milk to tell if it's sour* 闻一下牛奶,看是否发酸了。—*vi*. 1. 有嗅觉;有难闻的气味;有某种气味[样子](*of*)。2. 闻闻看(*at*; *of*; *to*);想闻出(*about*)。*You* ～ *wine*. 你身上一股酒味。*You shall* ～ *of the whip*. 要你尝尝鞭子的味儿。*Meat began to* ～. 肉开始发臭了。*a* ～*ing committee*〔美俚〕调查委员。～ ***about*** [***round***] 到处嗅寻,到处打听。～ ***a rat*** 怀疑起来。～ ***of drink*** 有酒臭,有酒气。～ ***of the inkhorn*** 有学究气。～ ***of the lamp*** (人的模样)显然是用功到深夜;(著作上)表现出下过苦工夫。～ ***out*** 1. 闻出,嗅出。2. 细心研究出;察觉,找到。～ ***powder*** 体验实际战斗生活。～ ***the ground***【海】水渐浅,渐渐减低速度。～ ***up*** (使)发散臭气,(使)充满臭气[气味]。**II** *n*. 嗅觉;香,臭,气味;闻,嗅。*What a lot of* ～*s*! 真难闻! ***have a*** ～ ***of*** = ***take a*** ～ ***at*** (将…)闻闻看。～**age**〔集合词〕有香味的植物。～**-feast** 逢人家请客就去大吃的人;食客。～**ing bottle** (装有碳酸铵的)嗅盐瓶。～**ing salts** (从前治昏厥、头痛用的)炭酸铵醒药,嗅盐。**-er** 1. 发出臭气的人[东西]。2.〔俚〕鼻子;〔俚〕间谍。3.〔俚〕(对准鼻子的)猛击。4. (动物的)触角,触须。**-less** *a*. 无臭的,无气味的。**-y** *a*.〔口〕有臭味的,发臭的。

smelt[1] [smelt; smɛlt] smell 的过去式及过去分词。

smelt[2] [smelt; smɛlt] *n*. (*pl*. ～*s*,〔集合词〕～)【鱼】胡瓜鱼(属)。

smelt[3] [smelt; smɛlt] *vt*.【冶】熔炼;提炼;冶炼。—*vi*. 受熔炼。～**ing furnace** 熔炉。**-er** *n*. 1. 熔铸工,冶炼者。2. 冶炼厂;熔炉。

smelt·er·y [ˈsmeltəri; ˋsmɛltərɪ] *n*. 冶炼厂。

smew [smjuː; smju] *n*.【鸟】脖鸦,斑头秋沙鸭。

SMG, **smg** = submachine gun 冲锋枪,轻型自动枪,半自动枪。

smice [smais; smaɪs] *n*. 冰雾。

smidg·en [ˈsmidʒən; ˋsmɪdʒɪn] *n*.〔美口〕一丁点儿(= smidgin, smidgeon)。

smi·lax [ˈsmailæks; ˋsmaɪlæks] *n*.【植】1. [S-] 菝葜属。2. 卵叶天门冬。

smile [smail; smaɪl] **I** *vi*. 1. 微笑(*at*; *on*; *upon*)(*opp*. frown)。2. 讥笑,冷笑(*at*)。3. 眉开眼笑,现笑脸;表示友好态度;(天气等)变晴朗;呈现乐观气象。—*vt*. 1. 做某种笑容;以微笑表示。2. 以微笑促使。*I should* ～.〔美口〕好得很,我很高兴。*She* ～*s her consent*. 她以微笑表示同意。～ *a forced smile* 强作笑容。***come up smiling*** (对失败、灾难等)不屈服地挺身迎接。～ ***sb***. ***into good humor*** 微笑着使人高兴起来。～ ***at*** 看着…微笑;(对威胁等)一笑置之,无视,嘲笑(*She* ～*d at his threats*. 她对他的威胁一笑置之)。～ ***away*** 笑着忘掉;一笑置之。～ ***on*** 向…微笑(*Fortune* ～*d on us*. 好运来了)。～ ***upon*** = ～ *on*. **II** *n*. 1. 微笑;冷笑;笑脸;喜气;友好态度。2.〔美俚〕一杯威士忌酒。*He was all* ～*s when I met him next*. 第二次碰见时他已经满脸笑容[不生气]了。*a forced* ～ 勉强的笑容。*a best Sunday* ～〔口〕非常快乐的笑。*a bitter* ～ 苦笑。*crack a* ～ 展颜微笑。*have a* ～ 喝一杯威士忌。***the*** ～***s of fortune*** 好运。**-r** *n*. **-less** *a*.

smile·age [ˈsmaileidʒ; ˋsmaɪledʒ] *n*.〔美俚〕持久的愉快心情;不绝的微笑。

smile·y [ˈsmaili; ˋsmaɪlɪ] *n*.【计】(用电脑键盘上的圆括号、短线和冒号等拼打出的一个圆形笑脸图像的)笑容符。

smil·ing [ˈsmailiŋ; ˋsmaɪlɪŋ] *a*. 微笑的,含笑的,亲切的;明媚的(风景等);表示好感的;呈现乐观气象的。**-ly** *ad*.

smirch [sməːtʃ; smɝtʃ] **I** *vt*. 玷污,损坏(名誉等)。**II** *n*. 污斑;污点(*on*; *upon*)。

smirk [sməːk; smɝk] **I** *n*. 傻笑;假笑。**II** *vi*. 假笑,嘻嘻地傻笑(*at*; *on*; *upon*)。—*vt*. 假笑着说。

smite [smait; smaɪt] **I** *vt*. (***smote*** [sməut; smot],〔古〕***smit***; ***smitten*** [ˈsmitn; ˋsmɪtn]; ***smote***,〔古〕***smit*** [smit; smɪt]; ***smit·ing***) 1. 打,重击;杀死。2. 破坏,毁灭(*with*);打败;惩罚。3. (疾病等)侵袭,袭击(*with*)。4. 使深深感动;迷住;使心中苦恼。—*vi*. 打,重击,撞;突然来临(*on*; *into*)。～ *a person dead* 打死某人。*My conscience* ～*s me*. 我良心上过意不去。*be smitten by the charms of* 被…的魅力迷住。*be smitten with palsy* 害中风病。～ *on the door* 敲门。*His knees smote together*. 他的双膝互撞。**II** *n*.〔口〕打,打击;【板球】猛击;尝试,企图;一点儿。*It didn't do a* ～ *of good*. 一点儿效果也没有。*have a* ～ *at it* 试试看。

Smith [smiθ; smɪθ] *n*. 1. 史密斯〔姓氏〕。2. **Adam** ～ 亚当·史密斯〔1723—1790,英国经济学家〕。

smith [smiθ; smɪθ] ***n*.** **1.** 铁匠,冶工,锻工;金属工匠。**2.** 〔通常用以构成复合词〕…的制造者。〔*cf*. gold*smith* 金匠,silver*smith*, 银匠; tune*smith* 作曲者〕。

smith·er·eens [ˈsmiðəˈriːnz; ˏsmɪðəˋrinz] ***n*.** 〔*pl*.〕〔口〕碎片,碎粉。*break* [*smash*] *into* [*to*] ~ 粉碎。*It should be smashed to* ~. 应当彻底摧毁。

smith·er·y [ˈsmiθəri; ˋsmɪθərɪ] ***n*.** 锻冶术;铁匠铺,铁工厂,锻工车间;铁匠业。

Smith·field (**Market**) [ˈsmiθfiːld; ˋsmɪθfild] ***n*.** 伦敦肉市场。

Smith·son [ˈsmiθsn; ˋsmɪθsən] ***n*.** 史密森〔姓氏〕。

Smith·so·nian Institution [smiθˈsəunjən; smɪθˋsonɪən] (设在华盛顿的)美国国立博物馆〔因出资创办人史密森得名〕(=S- Institute)。

smith·son·ite[ˈsmiθsəˌnait;ˋsmɪθsənˏaɪt]***n*.**【矿】菱锌矿。

smith·y [ˈsmiði, ˈsmiθi; ˋsmɪθɪ] ***n*.** **1.** 铁匠铺;锻工车间;锻铁炉。**2.** 铁匠,锻工。

smit·ten [ˈsmitn; ˋsmɪtn̩] smite 的过去分词。

S.M.M. =〔L.〕*Sancta Mater Maria* (=Holy Mother Maria)【宗】圣母玛利亚。

smock [smɔk; smɑk] **I** ***n*.** 〔古〕女衬衣;(孩子、妇女、画家等的)罩衫(=smockfrock)。**II** ***vt*.** 给…穿上罩衫;用褶裥装饰。~ **frock** (欧洲农民干活时穿的)长罩衫。

smock·ing [ˈsmɔkiŋ; ˋsmɑkɪŋ] ***n*.** 规则几何图案的抽褶。

smog [smɔg; smɑg] **I** ***n*.** 烟雾〔smoke+fog〕。**II** ***vt*.** 使被包围在烟雾中。**-gy** ***a*.**

smok·a·ble [ˈsməukəbl; ˋsmokəbl] **I** ***a*.** 可吸的;可抽的。**II** ***n*.** 〔*pl*. 集合词〕各种烟(香烟、雪茄烟等)。

smoke [sməuk; smok] **I** ***n*.** **1.** 烟,烟尘,烟柱;雾;水气,蒸气;尘雾。**2.** 没有实体[意义、现实性]的事物;空谈;空虚。**3.** 模糊视线的东西。**4.** 抽烟;香烟、雪茄烟;〔俚〕内含大麻叶毒品的香烟。**5.** 烟色;暗灰色。**6.** 〔美俚〕劣质酒。**7.** 〔俚〕黑人。**8.** 〔俚〕铁道救火员。**9.** 〔俚〕大麻(制品)。*No* ~ [*There is no* ~] *without fire*. 无火不生烟,无风不起浪。*a box of good* ~*s* 〔俚〕一盒上好雪茄烟。*have a* ~ 抽一口烟。***blow*** ~ 〔俚〕吸大麻毒品。***end up in*** ~ 烟消云散,不成功,终成泡影。***from*** ~ ***into smother*** 越来越坏。***go up in*** ~ **1.** 烧尽。**2.** 〔喻〕毫无结果,化为乌有。***like*** (***a***) ~ (***on fire***) 〔俚〕无阻碍地,迅速地,轻易地。***watch my*** ~ 〔美俚〕看我的本领,看我做得多快。~ ***and mirrors*** 像魔术般骗人的东西,为转移人们的注意力而故意制造的假象。**II** ***vi*.** **1.** 烟,熏;冒烟;冒水蒸气;(烟似地)袅袅上升。**2.** 吸烟,抽烟。**3.** 迅速地走(致使尘土飞扬)。**4.** 发火,生气(*against*);〔学生语〕脸红。**5.** 〔古〕受苦,受罚。**6.** 〔美俚〕开枪。**7.** 〔俚〕吸大麻。—***vt*.** **1.** 用烟熏,熏脏,熏黑;熏走,熏死(虫等);熏制。**2.** 吸(烟),抽(烟),抽烟而…。**3.** 〔古〕发觉;怀疑;〔美〕查明,使说出秘密。**4.** 〔古〕嘲弄,欺负,欺骗。**5.** 〔美俚〕开枪打,射击。**6.** 〔俚〕吸(大麻毒品)。*That oil-lamp* ~*s badly*. 那盏油灯烟冒得很厉害。*You must not* ~ *in this carriage*. 车内不可抽烟。~ *oneself sick* 抽烟抽得不舒服。*The milk has been* ~*d*. 牛奶带烟味儿了。*Put that in your pipe and* ~ *it*. 仔细想想(我的话)吧。~ *like a chimmney* 烟瘾很大。*Their swords* ~*d with blood*. 冒血腥气。~ **abatement** (城市的)烟雾消除法。~ **alarm** (防火用的)烟雾报警器。~ **ball** = ~ bomb. ~ **bell** 烟罩。~ **bomb** 烟幕弹。~**box** (汽锅的)烟室,烟箱。~**chaser** 森林灭火员。~ **consumer** 完全燃烧装置。~ **curtain**【军】烟幕。~ **detector** (防火用的)烟雾报警器,烟尘探测器。~**-dry** ***vt*.** 熏干,烟熏。~**-dried** ***a*.** 熏制的。~**-fest** 〔美〕抽烟叙谈会。~**-filled room** (旅馆中)政客们进行商谈的密室。~ **helmet**, ~ **mask** 救火,防毒面具。~ **house** 熏制所;熏肉贮藏所。~ **jack** (借烟囱内气体上升力驱动的)自动旋转烤肉装置。~ **jumper** 空降森林灭火员。~**-oh** = smoko. ~ **pipe** (连接烟囱和炉子的)烟道。~ **point** (油脂、燃油等的)发烟点,发烟最低温度。~ **projector** 烟幕放射器。~ **proof** ***a*.** 不透烟的,防烟的。~ **ring** 吸烟者吐出的烟圈。~ **room** 〔主英〕吸烟室。~**screen**【军】烟幕;障眼法。~ **seasoning** 炉干。~ **shell** 发烟炮弹。~ **signal** 狼烟;征兆,象征。~**stack** 烟囱。~**-stone**【矿】烟晶。~ **tracer** 曳烟弹。~ **tree**【植】黄栌(属)。~**-up** 〔美俚〕广告宣传;学生成绩不及格通知;轰炸。~ **wag(g)on** 〔美俚〕手枪;火车。~ **tobacco** 不冒烟草〔指供烟民咀嚼而非燃吸的烟草〕。

smoke·less [ˈsməuklis; ˋsmoklɪs] ***a*.** 无烟的。~ **area** (城市中的)无烟区。~ **cigaretter** 无烟灰香烟〔燃纯碳,有烟草味,但不含焦油〕。~ **power** 无烟火药。

smok·er [ˈsməukə; ˋsmokɚ] ***n*.** **1.** 熏制(肉类)者。**2.** 吸烟者,吸烟室;〔口〕允许抽烟的车厢;允许吸烟的音乐会;〔美〕男子非正式的聚会。**3.** 冒烟的东西,施放烟幕的船只[飞机]。**4.** 养蜂用熏箱。**5.** 〔学生语〕害羞的人。**6.** 〔美俚〕蒸汽火车头。*a heavy* ~ 烟瘾大的人。~***'s face*** 吸烟过度而使脸部起皱纹。~***'s heart*** [***throat***] 吸烟过度而生的心脏病[喉病]。**-y** ***n*.** 吸烟室。

Smok·ey [ˈsməuki; ˋsmokɪ] ***n*.** 护林熊〔森林防火标志,是一头穿着护林人员制服的漫画熊〕;〔美俚〕警察,(尤指公路上的)巡警〔亦作~ Bear〕。

smok·i·ly [ˈsməukili;ˋsmokəlɪ] ***ad*.** 冒着烟;烟雾弥漫;如烟。

smok·ing [ˈsməukiŋ; ˋsmokɪŋ] **I** ***n*.** **1.** 冒烟;冒气。**2.** 吸烟。**II** ***a*.** **1.** 冒烟的,烟熏的;冒气的。**2.** 吸烟的;〔口〕(证据)凿〔譬喻用法,参见 ~ gun〕。**III** ***ad*.** 冒着气;冒着烟。*No* ~ 禁止吸烟。*a* ~ *steed* 冒汗的马。~ *hot soup* 热气腾腾的汤。~ **bed** 〔口〕(尤指名人)与别人上床(发生性关系)的铁证。~ **cap** 吸烟帽。~ **car** [**carriage, compartment**] (火车等的)吸烟室。~ **concert** 允许吸烟的音乐会。~ **gun** 〔口〕确凿证据,铁证。~ **jacket** (在家平时穿的防烟尘)便服。~ **lamp** (船上的)允许吸烟信号灯。~**-mixture** 混合烟丝。~ **room** 吸烟室。~**-room** ***a*.** 淫秽的,只适合男子的 (*a* ~*-room talk* 避开女人讲的话)。~ **stand** 烟灰缸座。

smo·ko [ˈsməukəu; ˋsmoko]〔Aus.〕***n*.** **1.** 工作休息和抽烟时间;吃茶点时间。**2.** 允许抽烟的音乐会。

smok·y [ˈsməuki; ˋsmokɪ] ***a*.** **1.** 冒烟的;熏的;如烟的;烟雾弥漫的。**2.** 熏黑了的,熏污了的。**3.** 不高兴的,不开心的;〔美俚〕雾深的。~ **quartz**【矿】烟晶。**-i·ly** ***ad*.** **-i·ness** ***n*.**

smol·der [ˈsməuldə; ˋsmoldɚ] ***vi*.**, ***n*.** =smoulder.

Smol·lett [ˈsmɔlit; ˋsmɑlɪt] ***n*.** 斯莫利特〔姓氏〕。

smolt [sməult; smolt] ***n*.** 初次由河入海的小鲑。

smooch[1] [smuːtʃ; smutʃ] ***vi*.** ***n*.** 〔美俚〕接吻;拥抱,爱抚;〔美〕=smutch.

smooch[2][smuːtʃ; smutʃ] **I** ***n*.**, ***vt*.** 弄脏。**II** ***n*.** 污迹。

smooth [smuːð; smuð] **I** ***a*.** **1.** 滑溜的,平滑的,光滑的(表面)(*opp*. rough)。**2.** 流利的,流畅的(文章等);柔嫩的,柔和的,悦耳的(声音、调子等);进行顺利的(事情);口齿伶俐的(人);温和的,圆滑的(态度等)。**3.** 平静的,安稳的(航海等)。**4.** 无毛的,无须的(脸等)。**5.**【语音】不送气的。**6.** 调匀的(液体,浆糊等);易上口的,匀和的,温和的(酒等)。**7.** 〔美俚〕极好的,绝妙的,可爱的,迷人的。*make* ~ 弄平滑;扫除障碍。*run* ~ 进行顺利(*The course of true love never did run* ~. 恋爱无坦途;好事多磨)。**II** ***ad*.** =smoothly. *a* ~ *skin* 光滑的皮肤。*a* ~ *chin* 没有须的下巴。~ *temper* 温和的脾气。~ *manners* 文明礼貌的态度[举止]。*a* ~ *flight* 平稳的飞行。*The way is now* ~. 路平坦了;困难扫除了。*a* ~ *cocktail* 温和可口的鸡尾酒。***get to*** [***reach***] ~ ***water*** 到达平静的海面;度过困难到达顺境。***in*** ~ ***water*** 处身顺境。***speak*** ~ ***words*** 圆滑地搪塞。**III** ***vt*.** **1.** 把…弄平滑[光滑],烫平,垫平,校平 (*away*; *down*; *out*; *over*)。**2.** 抹平,抚平(发等);使流利,使流畅;使容易;消除(障碍等)。**3.** 掩饰,粉饰,遮掩。**4.** 使柔和;缓和,镇定。**5.** 使(文体、举止)高雅,使(面部表情)平和;使

S

(晚年等)平安。—*vi*. 1. 变平滑,变光滑。2. 变平静,变缓和(*down*)。~ *away* [*over*] 使容易,排除,解决(困难等);调解,调停;掩饰,粉饰。~ *the way* 铺平道路,排除障碍,使容易做。IV *n*. 1. [口]光滑部分,平滑的水面[地面];(事情的)平易方面,愉快方面。2. 抚平,抹平。3. [美]平地;草原;一角银币。4. 修光[磨平]的工具。*give a* ~ *to the hair* 把头发抹平。*take the rough with the* ~ 安然自愉,不介意人世苦乐浮沉。~**bore** 滑膛枪,滑膛炮。~ **breathing**【语音】不送气符号[希腊文中做在打头的不送气母音前的"'"];不送气音。~**-dogfish**【动】星鲨。~**-drying** *a*. (指织物)免烫,干后自然平滑不皱的。~ **face** 1. 没胡子的脸。2. 伪善的人,谄媚的人。~**-faced** *a*. 表面平滑的;刮得光滑的(脸),没胡须的,讨人欢喜的,和颜悦色的;装老实的,装谦恭的。~**hound**【动】星鲨属鲨鱼。~**ing**【统】修匀。~**ing iron** 烙铁,熨斗。~ **move** [美]聪明的[爽快的、狡猾的]行动。~ **muscle**【解】平滑肌。~**-paper magazine** [美]高级杂志。~**ing plane** (木匠的)细刨。~**-shaven** *a*. 胡须刮得光光的,不留胡须的。~**-spoken**, ~**-tongued** *a*. 油嘴滑舌的,甜言蜜语的;娓娓动听的,能说会道的。~ **things** 恭维话。**-ly** *ad*. **-ness** *n*.

smooth·en [ˈsmuːðən; ˋsmuðən] *vt*., *vi*. = smooth.

smooth·ie [ˈsmuːði; ˋsmuðɪ] *n*. [美俚]圆滑的人;会迎合人的人;举止文雅的人。

smor·gas·bord [ˈsmɔːgəsbɔːd; ˋsmɔrgəsˏbɔrd] *n*. [Sw.] 1. 瑞典式餐前冷菜;瑞典式冷菜宴会;瑞典式冷菜餐馆。2. 大杂烩。

S

smor·zan·do [smɔːˈtsɑːndəu; smɑrˋtsando] *a*. [It.]【乐】(音响)逐渐消失,减弱音响和减慢速度。

smote [sməut; smot] smite 的过去式。

smoth·er [ˈsmʌðə; ˋsmʌðɚ] I *vt*. 1. 使透不过气来,使窒息;闷死,扼杀;盖熄,闷住(火等)。2. 抑制住(感情),止住;隐蔽,遮掩(罪恶等);扣压(报告等);笼罩,覆盖。3.【烹】蒸,焖,煨。4. 密密地涂上[浇上]。5. [美运]使对方大败。—*vi*. 1. 透不过气来,窒息;闷死。2. 用文火闷烧,微燃,闷燃,熏,冒烟;给包住,隐藏;(事实等)被捂住。3. 被抑制,被忍住。~ *a yawn* 忍住呵欠。~ *a scandal* 掩盖丑事。~ *the patient in blankets* 把病人包在毯子里。~ *a salad with oil* 在生菜上浇满油。~ *sb*. *with* (*kisses*) (吻得)透不过气来。~ *up* 蒙蔽过去,含糊了结;压制。II *n*. 1. 窒息物;窒息状态,被抑制状态。2. 浓烟,浓雾,浓尘;冒烟,冒着烟的火。3. 制止,抑制。4. 一片混乱,一大堆乱七八糟的东西。~*ed mate* (国际象棋)用马将死对方王的一着。**-er** *n*. **-y** *a*.

smo(u)l·der [ˈsməuldə; ˋsmoldɚ] I *vi*. 1. 慢燃;用文火闷烧,熏烧。2. (愤怒等)在心中燃烧;表现出闷在心里的愤怒[仇恨];郁积。II *n*. 慢燃,无焰闷燃。*The* ~ *will soon be a flame*. 闷火很快变为烈焰。

smouse [smaus; smaus] *n*. [俚]犹太人;(南非的)商贩。

s. m. p. = [L.] *sine mascula prole* 无男性后代(= without male issue)。

Smri·ti [ˈsmriti; ˋsmrɪtɪ] *n*. 印度传统的宗教教义。

smudge[1] [smʌdʒ; smʌdʒ] I *n*. 1. 污点,污斑,污迹。2. 模糊的字迹。II *vt*. 1. 弄脏,涂污,玷污。2. 涂去,使模糊。—*vi*. 变脏,被弄脏;变模糊。

smudge[2] [smʌdʒ; smɑdʒ] I *n*. (为驱虫或防止农作物冻伤而生的)冒浓烟的火堆,浓烟。II *vt*. 使冒浓烟;用烟熏(驱虫)。

smudg·y [ˈsmʌdʒi; ˋsmʌdʒɪ] *a*. 弄脏了的;熏黑了的;不鲜明的。**-i·ly** *ad*. **-i·ness** *n*.

smug [smʌg; smʌg] I *a*. 1. 整洁的;体面的。2. 沾沾自喜的,自以为是的(人)。*the* ~ *calculation* 如意算盘。II *n*. 1. 自命不凡的人,沾沾自喜的人。2. [英大学俚]死用功不活动的学生,书呆子。**-ly** *ad*. **-ness** *n*.

smug·gle [ˈsmʌgl; ˋsmʌgl̩] *vt*. 走私,私运,做…的走私生意;夹带,偷偷拿进[拿出](*in*; *out*; *over*)。—*vi*. 走私。~*d goods* 走私货。~ *a clause into the bill* 偷偷在议案上添了一项条款。

smug·gler [ˈsmʌglə; ˋsmʌgl̩ɚ] *n*. 走私者;走私船;私酒酿造者。

smug·gling [ˈsmʌgliŋ; ˋsmʌgl̩ɪŋ] *n*. 走私;秘密买卖。*a* ~ *ring* [*gang*] 走私集团。

smurf [sməːf; smɚf] I *vt*., *vi*. (通过让多人分头去银行购买本票等手段)把(贩毒等非法所得现金)"洗"干净(而成为合法资金),拆分洗(钱)。II *n*. 拆分洗钱者。

smut [smʌt; smʌt] I *n*. 1. 煤灰,煤炱;(含大量泥质的)劣煤。2. 污点;污斑;污物。3.【植】黑穗病,黑粉病。4. 猥亵的言语[文字];[美][*pl*.]猥亵的图片。*covered* (*kernel*) ~ 坚黑穗病。*loose* (*kernel*) ~ 散黑穗病。*long* ~ 角黑穗病。*head* ~ 黑穗病。II *vt*. (-*tt*-) 1. (用煤烟等)弄脏,弄黑。2. 使患黑穗病[黑粉病]。—*vi*. 1. 变黑;弄脏。2. 患黑穗病[黑粉病]。*brother* ~ [卑]你。(*Ditto, brother* ~. 伙计,你也一样[反击口气])。~ **ball**【微】马勃菌科的菌。~ **mill** (清除患黑穗病谷粒的)清谷机。**-ty** *a*.

smutch [smʌtʃ; smʌtʃ] I *n*. 1. 污点,污迹。2. 炭炱;尘垢;污物。II *vi*. [英古、美] = smudge. —*vt*. (用煤烟等)弄脏,弄黑。**-y** *a*.

smut·ty [ˈsmʌti; ˋsmʌtɪ] *a*. 1. 给煤灰弄黑的,熏黑的。2. 患黑穗病[黑粉病]的;猥亵的。**-ti·ly** *ad*. **-ti·ness** *n*.

Smyr·na [ˈsməːnə; ˋsmɚnə] *n*. 士麦那[即 Izmir 伊兹密尔][土耳其港市]。

Smyr·ni·ot(e) [ˈsməːniət; ˋsmɚnɪˏɑt] *a*., *n*. (土耳其西部海港)士麦那的(人)。

Smyth [smiθ, smaiθ; smɪθ, smaɪθ] *n*. 史密斯[姓氏]。

S/N = shipping note 装船通知书。

Sn =【化】stannum (= tin); sanitary.

s. n. = 1. [L.] *secundum naturam* 自然地。2. *sine nomine* 无名称;出版者不详;姓名不详。

snack [snæk; snæk] I *n*. 1. 快餐;小吃;点心。2. 一口;一份。*go* ~*s* [口]均分,分派,摊分。*Snacks*! 平均分呀! II *vi*. 吃快餐[小吃,点心]。~ **bar**, ~ **counter**, ~ **stand** 快餐馆[部、摊]。~ **pellet** (压制成颗粒状的)方便食品。~ **table** 供单人用的折叠式小餐桌。

snack·er·y [ˈsnækəri; ˋsnækərɪ] *n*. 快餐馆,小吃馆。

snack·e·teer [ˈsnækeˈtiːə; ˋsnækɛˋtir] *n*. [美俚]经常急匆匆地吃一顿快餐的人;爱吃零食的人。

snaf·fle[1] [ˈsnæfl; ˋsnæfl̩] I *n*. 圈嚼子[无勒索的轻马衔],轻勒马衔。*ride* (*sb*.) *in* [*on, with*] *the* ~ 轻轻地控制,用温和手段控制。II *vt*. 给(马等)装上圈嚼子;[俚]控制。

snaf·fle[2] [ˈsnæfl; ˋsnæfl̩] *vt*. [英俚]盗用,偷。

sna·fu [snæˈfuː, ˈsnæfuː; snæˋfu] I *n*. [美军俚]情况混乱。II *a*. 混乱的。III *vt*. 搅乱,使混乱。

snag [snæg; snæg] I *n*. 1. 残干,残根;根株;水中隐树,沉树;暗礁;[喻]障碍。2. 暴牙,歪牙;缺牙;牙根。3. 意外的[隐蔽的]阻碍,困难。II *vt*. (-*gg*-) 1. 在沉树上绊住;碰在沉树[暗礁]上撞坏。2. 妨碍,阻挠。3. 清除沉树[其它障碍物]。4. 迅速抓住。5.【织】擦毛,抽丝。6. 偷取,夺取。—*vi*. 撞在沉树上(绊住);形成暗礁,阻碍。*come up against a* ~ = *strike a* ~ 撞上沉树[暗礁]。*run into* ~*s* 碰钉子。~ *a pickup* [美]拦到(而搭上)一辆顺路的(汽车等)。~ *the current* [美俚]了解(情况)。

snag·ged, **snag·gy** [ˈsnægid, ˈsnægi; snægd, ˋsnægɪ] *a*. 根株多的;沉树多的;[美俚]脾气坏的,弯扭的。

snag·gle·tooth [ˈsnægltuːθ; ˋsnæglˏtuθ] *n*. (*pl*. **-teeth**) 不整齐的牙齿;歪牙;破齿。**-ed** *a*.

snail [sneil; snel] *n*. 1.【动】蜗牛。2. 动作缓慢的人[动物],懒人。3.【机】涡形轮。4. [美]肉桂面包卷。~*s and slugs*【动】腹足类。*at a* ~*'s pace* [*gallop*] 慢条斯理地,非常慢地。~ **clover**, ~**-trefoil** *n*.【植】苜蓿属;蜗牛苜蓿。~**mail** 蜗牛式邮件[指与电子邮件 e-mail 相对而言的普通邮件,如平信等]。~**-paced**, ~**-slow**

a. 慢得像蜗牛的。～ **park** 蜗牛养殖场。

snake [sneik; snek] **I** ***n***. **1.** 蛇。**2.** 冷酷阴险的人,卑鄙的人,虚伪的人。**3.** 〔美俚〕西弗吉尼亚 (West Virginia) 人的绰号。**4.** (劣质)威士忌酒;〔*pl*.〕〔美俚〕震颤性酒疯[谵妄]。**5.** 〔美俚〕男阿飞。*a black* ～ 长鞭子;运煤火车。**6.** 〔the S-〕蛇形浮动〔70 年代欧洲的一种外汇联合浮动制度,～in the tunnel 的缩略用法〕。*a poor* ～ 穷人,干苦活的人。*a* ～ *in one's bosom* 恩将仇报的人 (*warm* [*cherish*] *a* ～ *in one's bosom* 爱护忘恩负义的人,养虎贻患)。*a* ～ *in the grass* 潜伏着的危险,隐患;暗藏的敌人。***be above*** ～ 〔美〕活着,生存着。***have*** ～***s in one's boots*** 〔美俚〕烂醉如泥;患震颤性酒狂病[谵妄]。***raise*** [***wake***] ～***s*** 无故惊扰人;惹事,引起不愉快的事。***see*** ～***s*** 喝醉酒;患震颤性酒狂病[谵妄]。**II** ***vi***. **1.** 弯曲;蜿蜒;弯弯曲曲地走。**2.** 偷偷行进,偷偷溜走。—***vt***. **1.** 扭弯;扭转。**2.** 迂回地取(道)。**3.** 〔美〕拖,拉,拖出来。～**bird**【动】蛇鹈。～**bite** (毒)蛇的咬伤。～**boot** (防)蛇靴,高统靴。～ **charmer** 弄蛇人。～**-charming** 弄蛇。～ **dance 1.** 蛇舞〔印第安人的一种宗教仪式〕。**2.** 蜿蜒前进的队伍。～ **doctor** 〔美〕 **1.** 蜻蜓。**2.** 角鱼蛉幼虫。～**-eater**【动】**1.** 獴。**2.** 鹫鹰。～ **feeder** 〔美〕蜻蜓。～ **fence** 〔美〕弯弯曲曲的栅栏。～**fly** ***n***. 蛇蛉亚目昆虫;骆驼虫。～ **gourd** 蛇甜瓜,菜瓜;丝瓜。～**('s)-head**【植】贝母。～ **hips** (男子)苗条的臀部。～**-locked** ***a***. 蛇发的。～**mouth**【植】红朱兰(花)。～ **oil** 蛇油〔江湖医生的一种万应药〕。～ **pit 1.** 蛇窖。**2.** 恐怖和混乱的地方。**3.** 精神病医院。～**root**【植】蛇根草;蛇根草的根〔能治蛇咬伤〕。～**'s eyes** 〔美俚〕一对么〔两粒骰子都是么点〕。～**skin** 蛇皮(皮革)。～**stone**【古生】菊石;蛇石。～**weed**【植】拳参。～**wood**【植】**1.** 蛇(纹)木。**2.** 马钱子(又名番木鳖)。

snak·y [ˈsneiki; ˋsnekɪ] ***a***. **1.** (像)蛇的;蛇多的;弯弯曲曲的,蜿蜒的。**2.** 狡猾的,阴险的;冷酷的,残忍的。*a* ～ *rod* (*Mercury* 神的)蛇杖。～ *locks* [*hair*] (复仇女神 Furies 的)蛇发。**-i·ly** ***ad***.

SNAP = **1.** systems for nuclear auxiliary power 核辅助动力系统。**2.** subsystem for nuclear auxiliary power (原子)核温差电池,核热电池,核热电堆。

snap [snæp; snæp] **I** ***vt***. (***snapped*** [snæpt; snæpt]; ***snap·ping*** [ˈsnæpiŋ; ˋsnæpɪŋ]) **1.** 猛地咬住;猛扑。**2.** 突然折断。**3.** 砰地关上(盖子等) (*down*)。**4.** 使(鞭子等)劈拍地响;弹击。**5.** 〔口〕急速拍摄;急速射击;急速投掷[传球]。**6.** 厉声说,吆喝着说 (*out*)。**7.** 〔美〕突然伸出。—***vi***. **1.** 抢夺,抓住;猛地咬住,猛扑;连声应承住 (*at*),突然折断。**2.** 劈拍地[砰地、格达地]响;(门)咔哒一声关上。**3.** 突然发亮[指眼睛,因忿怒而闪亮]。**4.** 谩骂 (*at*)。～ *a pistol* 咔哒一声扳动手枪的扳机。*He was* ～*ped falling off his horse*. 他正摔下马的时候给照下相来了。*The bolt* ～*ped into its place*. 门闩咔哒一声扣上了。*The door* ～ *ped to*. 门咔哒一声关上了。～ ***at a chance*** 抓住机会。～ ***at an offer*** 抢先答应。～ ***into it*** 〔美俚〕急忙开始[干起来]。～ ***one's fingers at*** 用两个指头叭地一弹[表示不关心,轻蔑]。～ ***sb. head*** [***nose***] ***off*** 怒冲冲地[鲁莽地]打断某人的话;恶狠狠地回答。～ ***out*** 〔美〕起来;精明地干;【火箭】排出,放出。～ ***out of it*** 〔美俚〕突然摆脱某种不好的状态;变更办法;(尤指)停止抱怨[忧虑、悲伤等]而迅速振作起来。～ ***short*** 突然折断;突然打断别人的话;喝阻。～ ***to attention*** (兵士)急忙采取立正姿势。～ ***up*** 咬住;突然插嘴。～ ***up an offer*** 抢着答应。**II** ***n***. **1.** 猛咬,猛扑。**2.** 拍地一下折断;砰地关上;(鞭等的)劈啪声;弹指。**3.** 揿钮,按扣。【无】揿钮接头。**4.** 急促而粗暴的言语。**5.** (天气的)急变;(特指)骤冷;〔口〕【摄】快照;【棒球】急投。**6.** 〔口〕精力,元气,气力。**7.** 脆薄饼干。**8.**【剧】演员的临时雇用;〔美俚〕容易的工作;容易对付的人。*a cold* ～ 〔美〕骤冷。*There is no* ～ *left in him*. 他一点精力都没有了。*a style without much* ～ 不很生动的文章风格。***in a*** ～ 立刻,马上。***not care a*** ～ 毫不在乎。***not worth a*** ～ 毫无价值,毫无用处。***with a*** ～ 啪地一下子,突然。**III** ***a***. 一碰就锁上的(锁等);突然的;〔美俚〕容易的。*a* ～ *lock* 弹簧锁。*a* ～ *division* 临时[当场]表决。*take a* ～ *vote* 举行临时[仓猝的]表决[投票]。*a* ～ *assignment* 容易的工作。**IV** ***ad***. 砰[啪]地一下,突然。*S-! went an oar*. 咔嚓一声,折断了一支桨。～ **action**【电】瞬时作用。～**back 1.** (橄榄球)快速传球。**2.** 很快恢复过来。～ **bean** 云豆,菜豆。～ **bolt** 弹簧门栓。～**-brim 1.** ***n***. 可翻起的帽沿。**2.** ***a***. (帽沿)可以翻起的。～**-brim hat** 帽顶纵摺,前沿下垂的男帽。～**dragon**【植】金鱼草(属);(从燃有白兰地酒的盘子中)抢吃葡萄干等(游戏),这样抢到的食物。～ **fastener** 摁扣。～ **gauge** (外)卡规。～ **hook** (绳索上的)弹簧保险搭扣。～**ping beetle**【动】叩头虫。～**ping turtle**【动】鳄鱼科动物,〔尤指〕啮龟。～**roll**【空】(飞行特技)快滚。～**shoot** ***vt***. 快镜拍摄。～**shooter 1.** 快枪手。**2.** 快镜拍摄者。～**shot** ***n***., ***v***. 仓卒的射击;急射;(拍)快照。

snap·per [ˈsnæpə; ˋsnæpɚ] ***n***. **1.** 咬人的狗[动物];啪啪响的东西。**2.** 偷窃者;爱骂人的人。**3.** 揿钮,按扣〔*cf*. snap 条〕。**4.**【动】啮龟;鳄龟 (= snapping turtle);新西兰真鲷;叩头虫。**5.** 〔俚〕= whopper. **6.** 〔*pl*.〕牙齿。～**-up** (*pl*. ～***s-up***) ***n***. 争夺者。*a* ～*-up of bargains* 争购便宜货者。

snap·pish [ˈsnæpiʃ; ˋsnæpɪʃ] ***a***. **1.** 爱咬人的(狗等)。**2.** 暴躁的,爱骂人的。**-ly** ***ad***. **-ness** ***n***.

snap·py [ˈsnæpi; ˋsnæpɪ] ***a***. **1.** 活泼的,精神饱满的;敏捷的。**2.** 漂亮的,时髦的;聪明的。**3.** (天气)冷飕飕的。**4.** 〔罕〕= snappish. **5.** 发出劈啪声的。*a short*, ～ *article* 简短而有力的文章。*Make it* ～! 〔口〕直截了当地干;快干。

S

snare[1] [snɛə; snɛr] **I** ***n***. **1.** 绊子,圈套,罗网,陷阱。**2.** 诱惑。**3.**【外科】(肿瘤等的)勒除器。*fall into the* ～ 落入圈套,上当。*lay a* ～ 设圈套。**II** ***vt***. 安圈套;(用圈套等)捕捉,套住,绊住,陷害;诱惑。**-r** ***n***.

snare[2] [snɛə; snɛr] ***n***. (绷在小鼓下面的)肠线,响弦。

snarl[1] [snɑːl; snɑrl] **I** ***vi***. (狗等)嗥叫,咆哮;骂 (*at*; *against*)。**II** ***vt***. 咆哮着说,怒喝 (*out*)。**III** ***n***. 嗥叫,咆哮;谩骂。**-ly** ***a***.

snarl[2] [snɑːl; snɑrl] 〔英古、美〕 **I** ***n***. **1.** 缠结,缠乱。**2.** 混乱,纠纷。**3.** 乱糟糟一群。**II** ***vt***. **1.** 使(线、发等)缠结,弄乱。**2.** 使为难,使惶惑。**3.** (在金属薄片上)打出浮凸花纹。—***vi***. 缠结。*a* ～*ed skein* 乱丝;杂乱的工作。～ *traffic* 使交通混乱。*a* ～*ing-iron* 敲花器。***get all*** ～***ed up*** 乱成一团。**-y** ***a***.

snarl·er [ˈsnɑːlə; ˋsnɑrlɚ] ***n***. 嗥叫的狗[动物];乱骂人[咆哮]的人。

snatch [snætʃ; snætʃ] **I** ***vt***. **1.** 抢,抓住;抢去,夺去,攫取 (*away*; *off*; *up*; *down*; *from*)。**2.** 趁机获得;侥幸救出;杀死。**3.** 〔美俚〕诱拐,绑架。—***vi***. 攫取,抢夺,抓住 (*at*)。～ *a hurried meal* 急急忙忙吃饭。～ *an opportunity* 抓住机会。*He was* ～*ed away by premature death*. 他突然夭亡。*The handbag was* ～*ed from its owner*. 手提包从物主手中夺走。*He was* ～*ed from the jaws of death*. 他侥幸得救,从死亡中抢救出来。～ *a kiss* 冷不防接一个吻。～ *a nap* 抓空小睡。～ *at an offer* 抢先答应。～ *at the chance of* 抓住机会。**II** ***n***. **1.** 抢夺,抓住,攫取;【举重】抓举。**2.** 小片,破片;一节,两三句;(膳食的)一口;(工作等的)一阵子,一下工夫。**3.** 〔美俚〕诱拐,绑架。*a* ～ *of sleep* 短短一觉。～*es of song* 断断续续的歌唱。***by*** (***fits and***) ～***es*** = ***in*** ～***es*** 断断续续地。***make a*** ～ ***at*** 动手想攫取。～ **block**【海】扣绳滑轮;凹口滑轮。～ **crop** (只求快速收益而不顾及保养地力的)抢种作物,短期作物。～ **squard** 搜捕小分队。

snatch·er [ˈsnætʃə; ˋsnætʃɚ] ***n***. 〔美俚〕= kidnapper.

snatch·y [ˈsnætʃi; ˋsnætʃɪ] ***a***. 不完全的;不连续的;断断

续续的,间歇的,不定的。-i·ly *ad*.

snath, snathe [snæθ, sneið; snæθ, sneð] *n*. 〔美〕大镰刀的长柄。

snaz·zy [ˈsnæzi; ˋsnæzɪ] *a*. 〔美俚〕漂亮的,时髦的;显眼的;动人的。

SNCC = Student National Coordinating Committee 〔美〕学生全国统一行动委员会。

sneak [sniːk; snik] I *vi*. 1. 偷偷逃走,偷偷跑来(*about*; *away*; *in*; *off*; *out*; *past*; *round*)。2. 行动鬼祟[神秘,卑怯];〔口〕偷窃。3. 〔学俚〕告密,告发。~ ***out of*** (*a room*) 偷偷地溜出(屋子),逃走。~ ***up and down*** 偷偷跑来跑去。—*vt*. 1. 偷偷地做[通过];〔口〕偷窃,隐藏。~ *a look at sth*. 偷看某物。~ *smoke* 偷吸烟。II *n*. 1. 鬼鬼祟祟的人,卑怯的人。2. 小偷;〔英〕〔学俚〕告密的人。3. 溜走,偷偷摸摸的举动。4. 【板球】滚球;〔*pl*.〕橡皮底帆布鞋。III *a*. 不声不响进行的;偷偷的。*a* ~ *attack* 偷袭。~ *raid* 【空】偷袭。~ *raider* 偷袭者。~ **current** 【电】潜行电流,寄生电流。~ **preview** 【影】(用于估计观众反应的)突击试映。~ **thief** (溜进屋去行窃的)小偷。

sneak·er [ˈsniːkə; ˋsnikɚ] *n*. 〔美〕鬼鬼祟祟的人;〔口〕〔*pl*.〕橡皮底帆布鞋。

sneak·ing [ˈsniːkiŋ; ˋsnikɪŋ] *a*. 1. 偷偷逃走[进入]的,潜逃的;偷偷摸摸的。2. 不知不觉在心里产生的;别人不知道的;卑怯的。~ *notion* [*suspicion*] 〔美〕不知不觉在心里产生的想法[疑惑]。*have a* ~ *affection for him* 暗暗爱慕他。*have a* ~ *feeling it is not right* 心里感到不对头。-**ly** *ad*.

S

sneak·y [ˈsniːki; ˋsnikɪ] *a*. 鬼鬼祟祟的;卑怯的。-**i·ly** *ad*. ~ **pete** 〔美俚〕劣等的酒;酒脚。

sneer [sniə; snɪr] I *n*. 1. 嘲笑,冷笑,讥笑。2. 鄙视;冷语。II *vi*. 讥诮,嘲笑;冷笑(*at*)。—*vt*. 轻蔑地笑着说出,冷笑着说;讥诮着予以打消(*away*; *down*);嘲笑得使…。~ *sb*. *out of countenance* 嘲笑得使某人张惶失措。~ *down a proposal* 对提案嗤之以鼻,予以否定。-**er** *n*.

sneer·ing·ly [ˈsniəriŋli; ˋsnɪrɪŋlɪ] *ad*. 嘲笑地,冷笑地,鄙视地。

sneeze [sniːz; sniz] I *n*. 打喷嚏,喷嚏(声);轻视。II *vi*. 打喷嚏。***not to be*** ~***d at*** 不可轻视,相当不错,值得考虑。~**weed** 【植】堆心菊(属)。~**wort** 【植】珠蓍。

snell[1] [snel; snɛl] *a*. 〔方〕1. 活泼的,敏捷的。2. 精明的,伶俐的。3. 厉害的;锐利的;猛烈的。

snell[2] [snel; snɛl] I *n*. 〔美〕(一端系钓钩一端连结在钓丝上的)根线。II *vt*. 把钓钩系在钓丝上。

SNG = synthetic [substitute] natural gas 合成[代用]天然气。

snick [snik; snɪk] I *vt*. 1. 作细刻痕于;微微割开[伤]。2. 猛击。3. 【板球】削(球)。II *n*. 细刻痕;【板球】削球。

snick·er [ˈsnikə; ˋsnɪkɚ] *vi*., *n*. = snigger.

snick·er-snee [ˈsnikəˈsniː; ˋsnɪkɚˏsni] *n*. 短刀,砍刀。

snide [snaid; snaɪd] I *a*. 〔口〕1. 假的,伪造的。2. 劣等的;卑劣的。3. 恶意的,嘲弄的;贬抑的。II *n*. 人造宝石;假钱,伪币。~ *remarks* 暗讽的话。*a* ~ *trick* 狡诈的伎俩。-**ly** *ad*. -**ness** *n*.

snides·man [ˈsnaidzmən; ˋsnaɪdzmən] *n*. 使用假钱的人。

sniff [snif; snɪf] I *vi*. 1. (伤风鼻塞时)呼呼地吸(气);嗅。2. 嗤之以鼻,蔑视,轻视(*at*)。—*vt*. 1. 用力吸;嗅,闻。2. 嗅到,闻出,发觉。~ (*out*) *peril* [*danger*] 发觉危险。~ *at a flower* 嗅花。~ ***up*** 用鼻子吸入,闻。II *n*. 1. 吸,嗅,闻;吸气(声)。2. 嗤之以鼻。3. 从鼻子吸入的东西。*a* ~ *of fresh air* 吸一口新鲜空气。-**er** *n*. 1. 嗅探者;嗅探器。2. 【计】监视软件〔可秘密监视他人网络通信情况〕。

snif·fle [ˈsnifl; ˋsnɪfl̩] *vi*., *n*. = snuffle.

snif·fy [ˈsnifi; ˋsnɪfɪ] *a*. 〔口〕瞧不起人的,傲慢的;〔美〕微臭的。

snift·er [ˈsniftə; ˋsnɪftɚ] I *n*. 1. 〔Scot.〕(用鼻子)嗅,闻,吸(气)。2. 突然的暴风。3. 〔美〕矮脚小口酒杯;〔美俚〕一小杯酒,一口酒。4. 有柯卡因[古柯碱](*cocaine*)瘾的人。5. 〔*pl*.〕伤风鼻塞。II *vi*. 闻,嗅;吸气。

snift [snift; snɪʃt] *vi*., *vt*. 〔方〕= sniff.

snift·ing valve [ˈsniftiŋvælv; ˋsnɪftɪŋvælv] 【机】喷气阀,吸气阀。

snift·y [ˈsnifti; ˋsnɪftɪ] *a*. 1. 傲慢的,轻蔑的。2. 〔俚〕有吸引人的气味的。3. 〔美俚〕下贱的,卑劣的(= nifty)。

snig·ger [ˈsnigə; ˋsnɪgɚ] I *vi*. 嘻皮笑脸地笑,吃吃地笑,窃笑(*at*; *over*)。—*vt*. 嘻皮笑脸地说。II *n*. 窃笑。

snig·gle [ˈsnigl; ˋsnɪgl̩] *vi*., *vt*. (把钓钩放进鳗洞里)钓(鳗)。~ *for eels* 钓鳗。

snip [snip; snɪp] I *vt*. (**-pp-**) 剪,剪断;剪去;剪做。—*vi*. 剪。II *n*. 1. 一剪;剪切声;(剪下的)片断,小片,一份。2. 〔英口〕裁缝。3. 〔美口〕藐小的人;傲慢无礼的人。4. 〔*pl*.〕(剪金属薄片的)大剪;铁丝剪。***go*** ~***s*** 均分;分摊。~**-snap** 喀嚓喀嚓〔剪刀声〕(*Snip-snap went the scissors and her golden locks fell*. 剪刀喀嚓一响她的金发便掉下来了)。

snipe [snaip; snaɪp] I *n*. 〔*sing*., *pl*.〕1. 【鸟】鹬,沙锥鸟。2. 〔美俚〕烟屁股,香烟头;雪茄烟头。3. 狙击。4. 可鄙的人。*a* ~ *hunter* 〔美俚〕被众人开玩笑的人。*a* ~ *shooter* 〔美俚〕拾烟屁股的人。II *vi*. 打沙锥鸟;狙击(*at*);中伤,暗害。—*vt*. 狙击。

snip·er [ˈsnaipə; ˋsnaɪpɚ] *n*. 【军】狙击兵,狙击射手。~**scope** 【军】红外线瞄准镜,夜袭镜〔利用红外线作用能在暗处看见目标〕。

snip·pet [ˈsnipit; ˋsnɪpɪt] *n*. 1. 小片;小片断。2. 〔*pl*.〕(消息,知识等)的片断;摘录,零星的东西。3. 〔美口〕年轻人,不足道的人。~*s of news* 零星消息。

snip·py [ˈsnipi; ˋsnɪpɪ] *a*. 1. 脾气急躁的;言语唐突的。2. 无礼的;骄傲的;摆架子的。3. 零碎的。-**pi·ly** *ad*. -**pi·ness** *n*.

snit [snit; snɪt] *n*. 一阵怒气,怄气。

snitch[1] [snitʃ; snɪtʃ] I *n*. 〔美俚〕贼。II *vt*. 偷,扒。—*vi*. 偷窃。

snitch[2] [snitʃ; snɪtʃ] I *vi*. 〔俚〕告发,告密(*on*)。II *n*. = **snitcher** 〔俚〕告密者,告发者。

sniv·el [ˈsnivl; ˋsnɪvl̩] I *vi*. (***sniv·el***(***l***)***ed*** [ˈsnivəld; ˋsnɪvl̩d], ***sniv·el***(***l***)***ing*** [ˈsnivəliŋ; ˋsnɪvl̩ɪŋ]) 1. 流鼻涕;抽鼻子。2. 啜泣,抽噎地哭,哭鼻子;哭诉。3. 假哭,哭着装后悔[同情,失望]。II *n*. 1. 流鼻涕,吸鼻涕(声)。2. 啜泣;哭鼻子,哭诉。3. 假哭;假话,假作慈悲,装可怜相。4. 〔古〕鼻涕。5. 〔*pl*.〕〔方〕伤风。

sniv·el·(l)er [ˈsnivlə; ˋsnɪvl̩ɚ] *n*. 爱哭的人;哭诉者;假哭者。

S.N.O. = senior naval officer 〔英〕高级海军军官。

snob [snɔb; snɑb] *n*. 1. 假绅士;谄上傲下的人,势利小人;附庸风雅之徒;假内行。2. 〔学俚〕街坊;〔英方〕不参加罢工的工人,工贼。3. 〔古〕身分低贱的人,无教养的人;皮匠,鞋匠。~ **appeal** (商品引起顾客要派头的)吸引力。

snob·ber·y [ˈsnɔbəri; ˋsnɑbərɪ] *n*. 摆绅士架子;势利,谄上傲下;附庸风雅;假充内行;〔*pl*.〕势利行为。

snob·bish [ˈsnɔbiʃ; ˋsnɑbɪʃ] *a*. 谄上傲下的,势利的;假充内行的。

snob·oc·ra·cy [snɔˈbɔkrəsi; snɑˈbɑkrəsɪ] *n*. 〔谑〕俗不可耐的人们,势利的人们。

snood [snuːd; snud] I *n*. 1. 〔Scot.〕(未婚女子用的)束发带,头带。2. 〔美〕袋状发网,袋形帽。3. = snell[2]. ***lose one's silken*** ~ 已非未婚的少女。II *vt*. 用束发带[发网]束(发)。

snook[1] [snuk; snʊk] *n*. (*pl*. ***snook***, ***snooks***) 【动】1. 锯盖鱼科(Centropomidae)的鱼〔尤指锯盖鱼(*Centropomus undecimalis*)产于大西洋热带地区〕。2. 类似锯

盖鱼科的鱼。

snook[2][snuːk, snuk; snuk, snʊk] *n*. 〔俚〕拿拇指按着鼻尖,招动其余四指表示轻蔑的动作。*cock* [*cut*, *make*] ~*s* [*a* ~] *at* 用上述动作表示瞧不起[轻蔑]。*Snooks!* 这有什么了不起! 去你的!

snook·er [ˈsnuːkə; ˋsnukɚ] I *n*. 1. 一种落袋撞球戏〔使用十五个红球,六个其他颜色的球〕。2. 〔英俚〕Woolwich 陆军军官学校的新生。II *vt*. 〔俚〕击败,挫败。

snoop [snuːp; snup] *vi*. 1. 〔美口〕探听,窥探。2. 偷窃,抽偷(货物等);管闲事。-**y** *a*.

snoop·er [ˈsnuːpə; ˋsnupɚ] *n*. 窥探者,探听者;装有雷达的飞机 (= sneak-thief)。~**scope** 红外线夜望镜,夜间探测器。

snoot [snuːt; snut] I *n*. 1. 〔美俚〕(人的)鼻子;脸;愁眉苦相的脸,(表示某种感情的)鬼脸。2. 【火箭】(翼的)前缘,喷嘴,小孔。II *vt*. 轻蔑地对待;对之表示厌恶;讥笑。

snoot·y [ˈsnuːti; ˋsutɪ] *a*. 〔美口〕自大的,傲慢的,势利的。-**ily** *ad*. -**i·ness** *n*.

snooze [snuːz; snuz] 〔口〕I *vi*., *vt*. (尤指在白天)打瞌睡,睡午觉,懒散地混过 (*away*)。II *n*. 打瞌睡,午睡。

snore [snɔː, snɔə; snor] I *n*. 鼾声,呼噜。II *vi*., *vt*. 打鼾,打呼噜;在鼾声中混过 (*away*; *out*)。~ *oneself awake* 打鼾弄醒。-**r** *n*.

snor·kel [ˈsnɔːkl; ˋsnɔrkl] I *n*. 1. (潜艇或潜水者的)通气管;水下呼吸管。2. (救火车上的)液压起重机。II *vi*. 使用通气管潜泳[航]。

snort[1] [snɔːt; snɔrt] I *vi*. 1. (马等)喷响鼻子。2. (表示不同意、轻蔑、惊愕、焦躁等时)哼鼻子,喷鼻息。3. (轻蔑、愤怒时)狂笑,高声大笑。4. (汽锅)喷汽。—*vt*. 1. 喷着鼻息说。2. (喷鼻息似地)喷出。3. 吸入(粉末状毒品)。II *n*. 1. 鼻息,鼻息声;(汽锅)喷气声。2. 〔美俚〕一口酒。

snort[2] [snɔːt; snɔrt] *n*. = snorkel.

snort·er [ˈsnɔːtə; ˋsnɔrtɚ] *n*. 1. 鼻息粗的人[动物];声音吵闹的汽车(等)。2. 〔俚〕暴风。3. 极大的东西;极好的东西;令人咋舌的人[事物],使人捏把汗的表演。4. 〔口〕申斥。5. 〔美〕一小杯酒。6. (装有水下通气管的)潜水艇。

snort·y [ˈsnɔːti; ˋsnɔrtɪ] *a*. 鼻息粗的;轻蔑的;愤怒的;不以为然的。

snot [snɔt; snɑt] *n*. 1. 〔卑〕鼻涕。2. 〔俚〕傲慢无礼的(年轻)人,卑贱的人。3. 〔*pl*.〕蚝。~ **rag** *n*. 〔俚〕手绢儿,手帕。

snot·ty [ˈsnɔti; ˋsnɑtɪ] I *a*. 1. 〔卑〕尽是鼻涕的。2. 无礼的;急躁的。II *n*. 〔英海军俚〕= midshipman.

snout [snaut; snaʊt] I *n*. 1. (猪、象等的)鼻子;猪鼻形的东西;〔蔑〕(人的)大鼻子。2. (断岩的)露头。3. (软管等的)嘴;【动】吻状突起,吸盘;(船的)冲角。4. 〔俚〕烟草。II *vt*. 装管嘴。~ **beetle** 【动】象鼻虫。-**y** *a*.

Snow [snəu; sno] *n*. 斯诺[姓氏]。

snow [snəu; sno] I *n*. 1. 雪;下雪;〔*pl*.〕积雪。2. 雪白色;雪白的[像雪花的]东西;白花;〔*pl*.〕白发;泡沫。3. 〔美俚〕银币;海洛因;柯卡因[古柯碱] (*cocaine*) 粉(等);白布丁。4. 【无】雪花干扰[效应]。*a heavy* (*fall of*) ~ 一场大雪。*a* ~ *flier* 〔美〕冬季到暖和的南方去的流浪者。II *vi*. 下雪;(花瓣等)雪一般地落下来。—*vt*. 1. 使像雪一般地落下来。2. 用雪封住,用雪覆盖。3. 使雪白;使有白发。4. 〔俚〕用花言巧语欺骗。*It* ~*s*. 下雪。*Complaints* [*Congratulations*] *came* ~*ing in*. 抗议[贺电]像雪片似地飞来。*It* ~*ed petitions*. 请愿书纷至沓来。***be*** ~***ed in*** [***up***, ***over***] 1. 被大雪封住;被花言巧语蒙蔽住。2. 〔美俚〕被毒品麻醉。***be*** ~***ed under*** 埋在雪里;〔美〕被彻底打败,被压倒。~**ball** 1. *n*. 雪球;雪战;〔谑〕白发黑人;〔英〕滚雪球募捐法[甲捐后劝乙捐,乙又劝丙捐的方法];【烹】苹果馅稻米布丁;【植】荚蒾属。2. *vi*., *vt*. 扔雪球;打雪仗;(使)滚雪球般迅速增长。~-**balling** *a*. 滚雪球一样(迅速增长)的。~**bank** 堤状大雪堆。~ **banner** (从山顶吹向空中的)旗帜状散雪,"雪旗"。~**bell** 【植】安息香属植物。~ **belt** 多雪地带;〔S-〕(美国北部的)霜冻地带。~**berry** 【植】1. 北美雪球(浆果)。2. 白浆果。~ **bird** 1. = junco. 2. 【动】雪鹀。3. 〔美俚〕有海洛因[柯卡因]瘾的人。~-**blind** *a*. 雪盲的。~ **blindness** 雪盲(症)。~**blink** 【气】雪照云光。~ **blower** 吹雪机,螺桨式除雪机。~**bound** *a*. 给雪围住的,给雪封住的。~-**broth** 1. 雪水,融雪。2. 冰镇酒类。~ **bunny** 初学滑雪的(女)人。~ **bunting** 【动】雪鹀。~ **bush** 【植】山白刺美洲茶。~**cap** 1. (山上的)雪顶。2. (产于中美洲的)白头蜂鸟。~-**cannon** 雪炮〔可喷出小冰晶体制作人工滑雪场〕。~**capped** *a*. 顶上积雪的。~**cat** 雪地履带式车辆,雪地车。~-**clad** *a*. 大雪覆盖的。~ **cruiser** (极地探险用的)大雪车。~**drift** 吹雪;雪堆;【植】香雪球。~**drop** 【植】雪花莲属。~-**fall** 下雪(量)。~-**fence** (铁路的)避雪墙。~ **field** 雪原;万年雪。~**flake** 雪片;【动】雪鹀;【植】雪片莲属;〔俚〕投掷反射带的导弹。~ **gauge** 雪量计。~ **goggles** (滑雪、登山用)墨镜。~ **goose** 【动】雪雁。~ **grouse** 【动】雷鸟属鸟。~ **ice** 冻雪。~-**in-summer** 【植】绒毛卷耳。~ **job** 〔俚〕花言巧语欺骗[劝诱]。~ **leopard** 【动】雪豹。~ **line**, ~ **limit** 雪线。~**man** 雪人。~**mobile** 机动雪车。~ **mold** 【植】雪腐病。~-**on-the-mountain** *n*. 【植】银边翠。~ **plant** 【植】赤雪藻。~-**plough**, ~ **plow** 雪犁,扫雪机;滑雪板制动器。~ **plume** (由山顶吹下来的)雪缕。~**scape** 雪景。~**shed** (保护铁道的)防雪棚。~**shoe** 1. *n*. 雪鞋。2. *vi*. 穿雪鞋走。~**shoe hare** [**rabbit**] 【动】雪兔。~**slide**, ~**slip** 雪崩。~**storm** 雪暴,暴风雪;【无】"雪花"干扰。~**suit** 儿童风雪服。~**surfing** 冲浪式滑雪〔站在大滑雪板的一侧滑雪下山的一种滑雪运动〕。~ **sweeper** 扫雪器。~ **tire** 雪地防滑轮胎。~ **train** 〔美〕(开到冬季运动场去的)雪地专车。~ **tyre** (用于雪地行驶的)防滑轮胎。~ **water** (用雪化成的)雪水。~**white** *a*. 雪白的。

Snow·den [ˈsnəudn; ˋsnodn] *n*. 斯诺登[姓氏]。

SNOWMAX [ˈsnəumæks; ˋsnomæks] *n*. 〔商标〕雪菌〔一种干燥的冷冻菌体,用以制造人工滑雪场上的人造雪〕。

snow·y [ˈsnəui; ˋsnoɪ] *a*. 雪(样)白的;多雪的。-**i·ly** *ad*. -**i·ness** *n*. ~ **egret** 【动】雪鹭。~ **owl** 【动】雪鸮。

SNPO = Space Nuclear Propulsion Office 〔美〕航天核推进办事处。

SNR = supernova remnant 【天】超新星遗迹。

SNSE = Society of Nuclear Scientists and Engineers 〔美〕核子科学家工程师学会。

snub [snʌb; snʌb] I *n*. 1. 故意怠慢;斥责。2. 〔罕〕狮子鼻。II *a*. 狮子鼻的。III *vt*. (-**bb**-) 1. 【海】勒住缆索突然煞住;突然制止(别人发言)。2. 故意怠慢,故意冷落。3. 叱止,断然拒绝;责骂。4. 压熄(香烟等)。*being snubbed* 碰一鼻子灰。~-**nosed** *a*. 狮子鼻的。

snub·ber [ˈsnʌbə; ˋsnʌbɚ] *n*. 1. 突然制止[阻止]的人;断然拒绝的人;责骂人的人。2. 【机】减振器;缓冲器;减声器;【船】锚链制止器。

snub·by [ˈsnʌbi; ˋsnʌbɪ] *a*. 1. 故意怠慢的;好斥责人的。2. (有点像)狮子鼻的,(鼻子)朝天的。

snuck [snʌk; snʌk] 〔美口〕 sneak 的过去式。

snuff[1] [snʌf; snʌf] I *n*. 烛花,灯花。II *vt*. 剪烛花,剪灯花。—*vi*. 死去 (*out*)。***go off like the*** ~ ***of a candle*** 突然死掉。~ ***it*** 〔英俚〕死。~ ***out*** 弄熄,吹熄(蜡烛等);压灭(希望等);消灭,扫除;扑灭,镇压;〔俚〕死。

snuff[2] [snʌf; snʌf] I *vt*. 1. (伤风鼻阻时)呼呼地吸(气);吸入。2. 闻,嗅;闻出,嗅出。—*vi*. 1. (伤风鼻阻时)呼呼地吸气;吸鼻烟;哼鼻子,嗤之以鼻;(狗、马等)喷鼻子。2. 动怒,愤怒。II *n*. 1. 吸鼻子;喷鼻子;闻,嗅。2. 气息,气味。3. 鼻烟;【医】鼻吸药,鼻粉,闻药。4. 动怒,生气。~ *tobacco* 吸鼻烟。*take a* (*pinch of*) ~ 吸(一撮)鼻烟。***beat to*** ~ 打得要死,痛殴。***give sb***. ~ 痛骂。***in high*** ~ 趾高气扬地,傲然。***put*** (***sb***.) ***up to*** ~ 〔俚〕

给(人)出主意。**take it in ～** 动怒,生气,发火。**up to ～**〔俚〕**1.** 精明的,不易受骗的;老油条。**2.**〔美俚〕符合一般标准的,有效力的,万应的。～**-and-butter** *n.*, *a.*〔英〕黄褐色(的);欧洲人和印度人的混血种(的)。～ **box [bottle]** *n.* 鼻烟盒[瓶]。～**-colo(u)red** *a.* 鼻烟色的,黄褐色的。～ **film** 凶杀纪实色情影片。～ **mill**〔苏格兰〕鼻烟盒;碾鼻烟器。～ **stick** 鼻烟勺。～**-taker** 吸鼻烟者。～**-taking** 吸鼻烟。

snuff·er [ˈsnʌfə; ˋsnʌfɚ] *n.* **1.** 剪烛花的人;〔*pl.*〕烛花剪子〔常作 a pair of ～s〕。**2.** 喷鼻子的[动物];吸鼻烟的人。**3.** 海豚。

snuf·fle [ˈsnʌfl; ˋsnʌfl̩] **I** *n.* **1.** 鼻声,鼻音,鼻塞声;抽鼻子;哽咽声。**2.**〔the ～s〕鼻伤风。**3.** 哀诉。**II** *vi.* **1.** 抽鼻子;喷鼻子。**2.** 用鼻音讲[唱](*out*)。**3.** 嗅,闻;嗅寻。**4.**〔罕〕哀诉。—*vt.* **1.** 用鼻音讲[唱](*out*)。**2.** 嗅着去找;抽着鼻子嗅。**-r** *n.* **1.** 抽鼻子的人。**2.** 哀诉的人。

snuff·y [ˈsnʌfi; ˋsnʌfɪ] *a.* **1.** 鼻烟色的;像鼻烟的;给鼻烟弄脏了的;吸鼻烟的。**2.**〔口〕生气的;脾气不好的;不讨人喜欢的;傲慢的,目空一切的。**-i·ness** *n.*

snug [snʌg; snʌg] **I** *a.* **1.** (房屋等)温暖而舒适的,不受寒冷侵袭的。**2.** (衣服等)合身的,恰好的,整洁的。**3.** 温和的(气候);舒服的,畅快的;(人)生活安乐的;(收入,地位)可以温饱的。**4.** (船只)建造得很好,宜于航海的。**5.** 隐密的。*a ～ little cottage* 舒适的小农舍。*a ～ shop* 小巧整洁的商店。**as ～ as a bug in a rug** 非常舒适地,极安乐地。**lie ～ for some time** 暂时躲避着。**lie ～ in bed** 舒舒服服地躺在床上。**II** *vi.* (**-gg-**)〔方〕舒适地蜷伏;偎依。—*vt.* **1.** 弄整洁,弄舒服;使紧贴合身。**2.** 藏好;隐藏。**3.**【海】作好暴风来袭的准备(*down*)。**-ly** *ad.* **-ness** *n.*

S

snug·ger·y [ˈsnʌgəri; ˋsnʌgərɪ] *n.*〔口〕温暖舒服的地方;私室,书房;(旅馆的)酒吧间。

snug·gies [ˈsnʌgiːz; ˋsnʌgiz] *n.*〔*pl.*〕女式保暖长内衣。

snug·gle [ˈsnʌgl; ˋsnʌgl̩] *vi.* **1.** 舒适地蜷伏;偎依。**2.** 挨近,紧靠(*up*; *to*)。—*vt.* **1.** (将孩子等)紧抱。**2.** 使舒服温暖。～ *down in bed* 舒舒服服地睡在床上。～ *up to sb.* 偎依[紧靠]着某人。

snur·fing [ˈsnəːfiŋ; ˋsnɝfɪŋ] *n.*〔美〕冲雪运动〔乘一种特殊冲雪板作雪上冲浪的运动〕。

S.O. = **1.** Stationery Office〔英〕文书局。**2.** Staff Officer 参谋。**3.** suboffice 分局(处,社,公司)。**4.** shipping order【商】运货单。**5.** special order(s) 专门定单;【军】特别命令。

S.O., **s/o** = seller's option 卖主选择权。

so[1] [强 səu, 弱 səu, sə; so, sə] **I** *ad.* **1.**〔表示方式、方法、情况等〕那么,那样;这么,这样。*You will never do it ～.* 你那样做不行。*They may do ～, if they please.* 随他们的便。*Hold the knife ～.* 这样持刀。*He is not a child and should not be treated ～.* 他不是小孩,不要这样对待。**2.**〔表示程度〕到那个程度,那样,那么。*Why are you panting ～?* 你为什么那么喘气? *Don't walk ～ fast.* 别走得那么快。*He didn't expect to live ～ long.* 他没想到会活得那么长命。**3.**〔表示强调〕非常,很,极,十分。*I am ～ glad to see you.* 我看见你非常高兴。*Thank you ～ much.* 多谢多谢。*He is ever ～ angry.* 他气得不得了。**4.**〔代替表语或谓语,使用倒装语序〕也…。*You are young and ～ am I.* 你年轻,我也年轻。*Tom speaks French and ～ does his brother.* 汤姆会讲法语,他的兄弟也会讲法语。**5.**〔语气〕原来,那么。*So you are back again at last!* 那么你终于回来了! *So you are Doctor Smith.* 原来你就是史密斯博士。**6.**〔用作表语〕(a) 那样的。*But it is ～.* 可是倒是那样的。*Is that ～?* 是那样吗? *Not ～.* 不是那样。*How ～?* 怎么会那样呢? *Quite ～.* = *Just ～.* 正是那样。(b) 不错,真的。*You said it was good, and ～ it is.* 你说过它好,它真好呀! *Nineteen fifty? So it is.* 1950 年? 正是。*It was cold yesterday. So it was.* 昨天天气冷。是的。*We have all worked hard. So we have.* 我们都努力工作。是的。**7.**〔代替形容词〕这么,那么。*He is complacent — ～ much so that he does not know what he is worth.* 他很自满——自满得忘乎所以。*They wanted fifty dollars but John could not pay ～ much.* 他们要五十元美金,可是约翰付不起那么多。**8.**〔关联副词〕(a)〔so ... that 结构〕…得…,这样…以便;如此…以致。*We have ～ arranged matters that one of us is always on duty.* 我们已经做了安排,使得我们之中总有一个人在值班。*It ～ happened that I couldn't attend the meeting.* 碰巧我无法参加会议。*He was ～ angry that he couldn't speak.* 他很生气,气得连话也讲不出了。*He was ～ ill that we had to send for a doctor.* 他病得很厉害,我们不得不请了一位医生来。*It is ～ small that you cannot see it.* 小得你看不出来。(b)〔so that 结构,口语常将 that 省略〕以便,为了;所以。*Speak clearly, ～ that they may understand you.* 说话说清楚,以便他们能够听得懂你的意思。*Finish this ～ (that) you can start another.* 把这个做完,好开始另一个。*All precautions have been taken, ～ that we expect to succeed.* 已经采取了各项预防措施,所以我们有希望成功。*Nothing was heard of him, ～ that people thought that he was dead.* 再没有听到关于他的什么消息,所以人们认为他已经死了。(c)〔as ..., so ... 结构〕像…那样;…也…。*As you treat me, ～ will I treat you.* 我像你对待我那样对待你[你怎样对待我,我也怎样对待你]。(d)〔so ... as... 结构〕像…一样。〔not so ... as ... 结构〕没有…那样。*They must ～ walk as he walked.* 他们必须照他的步法走。他怎样走,他们也一定要怎样走。*I am not ～ tall as he.* 我没有他高。*He was not ～ much angry as disappointed.* 生气还是其次,他倒是失望得厉害。*He is not ～ old as you think.* 他的年纪没有你以为的那么大。

II *conj.* **1.**〔古〕只要…,要是,既是。*So it is done, it matters not how.* 只要成功,怎样办都行。**2.**〔口〕那样就…(= so that)。*Turn it from time to time ～ it may be cooked alike on both sides.* 常常翻翻,那样两面就烤得匀了。

III *int.* 好,那样行了;别动;别吵;停住,〔命牛马〕缩!〔又作 soho〕。*A little more to the right, ～!* 再靠右一点儿,行了! *If that will content him, ～.* 倘若那会满足他,那就行了。*If you agreed, ～; if not, ～.* 要是同意,好;要是不同意,也好。

IV *pro.* **1.**〔用作 say, call, speak, tell, think, hope, expect, suppose, imagine, fear, hear, do 等动词的宾词〕。*I think ～.* 我想是这样。*I suppose ～.* = *So I suppose.* 我想大概是那样。*I told you ～.* 我不是跟你说过是这样了吗? *Do you say ～?* = *You don't say ～.* 真的吗〔表示惊奇〕。*So he says.* 他这样说。**2.**〔用在 or 之后〕左右,上下,约。*two hundred or ～* 两百上下。*an hour or ～* 一个钟头左右。*He is forty or ～.* 他大概是四十岁。**and ～**〔英古,美〕所以,从此(就…了);〔古〕其次(*And ～ to dinner*)。**and ～ forth** = **and ～ on** 等等。**even ～**〔古〕确是那样。**ever ～** 非常,很(*He is ever ～ clever.* 他很聪明。*He has ever ～ many children.* 他有不少孩子。*That is ever ～ much better.*〔口〕那个好得多)。**ever [never] ～ bad** 无论怎样坏。**every ～ often**〔美〕时时。**if ～** 要是那样的话。**in ～ far as** 到…的程度,在…范围内;只要(*You will succeed in ～ far as you persevere.* 你能坚持,便会得到相对的成功)。～ **and in no other way** = ～ and ～ only 别无他法。～ **and ～** 某某,这么这么,如此这般〔参看 *so-and-so*〕。～ ... **as to** …得…(*He was ～ angry as to be unable to say.* 他愤怒得话都说不出了)。～ **as to** 为使,以便。～ **be it** 那样也好,算啦;不管喽。～ **far** 就是那么些;到现在为止,到此刻为止,到这

里[那点,这点,那个程度]为止(*So far for today*. 今天就是那么些了。*So far so good*. 到这里为止,一切还好;到那点为止,一切还好)。~ ***far as*** 就…而论,在…的范围内(~ *far as I know* 就我所知。~ *far as I am concerned* 至于我。~ *far as the style goes* 若就文章风格来讲。~ *far as in me lies* 尽我力量所及)。~ ***far from*** 非但不…反而(*So far from loving him, I hate him*. 我非但不爱他,反而恨他)。~ ***goes the story*** 据说。~ ***long***! 〔口〕再见。~ ***long as*** 只要。~ ***many*** 很多(的);和…一样多的,同样多的;全都是(*You have ~ many*. 你有很不少。~ *many apples and ~ many pears* 这么多的苹果和同样多的梨)。~ ***much*** 和…一样多;就只那么多;多少(*It is only ~ much rubbish*. 全是废物。*At ~ much a week* [*a head*] 每礼拜[每人]多少(钱)。~ *much brandy and ~ much water* 一半白兰地一半水)。~ ***much for*** … …的事情[话]就是这么些[至此为止];…不过如此(*So much for him, now about* …. 他的事情就这样好了,下面且说…罢。*So much for his learning*. 〔蔑〕那家伙的学问不过如此)。~ ***much more*** 更加。~ ***much*** ~ ***that*** … 到要…,因为非常…。~ ***much the better*** 反而好。~ ***please you*** 〔古〕= if you please. ~ ~ 〔口〕既不算好也不算坏,勉勉强强,还好(*How are you getting along? Oh, ~ ~*. 近来怎么样? 唉,勉勉强强)。~ ***styled*** [***termed***] 叫做…的,所谓。~ ***that's that*** 〔口〕所以是这样。~ ***then*** 原来如此,那么,所以。~ ***to say*** [***speak***] 好比,如同,可谓。***So what***? 那么又怎样呢? 那怎么样了呢? 结果怎样呢? 那有什么关系呢? 你想怎么样呢? **~-and-~** [ˈsəuənsəu; ˋsoənso] ***n***. 某某人,某某事(*Mr. ~-and-~* 某某先生。*He asked them to do ~-and-~*. 他叫他们做某事)。**~-called** ***a***. 所谓的,号称的〔常含贬义〕。

so[2] [səu; so] ***n***. 【乐】= sol[1].

soak [səuk; sok] **I** ***vt***. **1**. 浸,泡;弄湿,使湿透。**2**. 沉浸在(工作,学习中)(用反身代词)。**3**. 浸出;吸出;吸收(*in*; *up*);〔俚〕使大醉。**4**. 〔口〕向…敲竹杠,敲榨;多要价钱;征重税。**5**. 〔俚〕典当,典押(东西)。**6**. 重击,痛殴。—***vi***. **1**. 浸泡。**2**. 渗透,印进(*into*)。**3**. 〔口〕大喝,狂饮。**4**. 经受长时间热处理。*Blotting paper ~s up ink*. 吸墨纸能吸墨水。~ *the rich* 向富人征重税。**II** ***n***. **1**. 浸,泡;浸液,浸渍。**2**. 〔口〕大雨。**3**. 〔俚〕狂喝滥饮的人,酒鬼;酒宴;狂饮。**4**. 〔俚〕典当。**5**. 殴打。***in*** ~ 〔俚〕(东西)在典押中[当铺里]。~ ***it*** 使为难;〔美〕处罚(*to*)。~ ***oneself in*** 沉浸在,埋头于,专心(研究)。~ ***out*** 浸泡掉,吸出。

soak·age [ˈsəukidʒ; ˋsokɪdʒ] ***n***. **1**. 浸,泡;浸渍;浸湿性,吸水量。**2**. 电容器的静电荷。

soak·er [ˈsəukə; ˋsokɚ] ***n***. 浸渍物;【化】浸渍剂;(石油)裂化反应室;〔俚〕酒鬼;〔口〕倾盆大雨;〔*pl*.〕婴儿用的尿布垫。

so-and-so [ˈsəu*ənd*səu; ˋsoən͵so] **I** ***n***. 某某人;某某东西。**II** ***ad***. 如此这般;相当。*Mr. S-* 某先生。*He says ~ would be offended*. 他说某某人恐怕要生气。

soap [səup; sop] **I** ***n***. **1**. 肥皂。**2**. 【化】脂肪酸盐。**3**. 〔美俚〕钱(尤指贿赂);奉承,假恭维;胡话。**4**. 〔美口〕肥皂剧(= ~ opera)。*a cake* [*cube, tablet*] *of ~* 一块肥皂。*hard ~* 硬肥皂。*marine ~* 海水皂,船用肥皂。*medical ~* 药皂。*soft ~* 软肥皂,钾肥皂;〔俚〕奉承话。*toilet ~* 香皂。***How are you off for*** ~? 〔俚〕你身上有钱吗? ***no*** ~ 〔美俚〕无结果,不成功;不接受(建议,要求等)。***wash one's hands in invisible*** ~ 搓手〔表示忸怩、为难的表情〕。**II** ***vt***. **1**. 用肥皂搓洗,上肥皂。**2**. 〔俚〕拍马屁,奉承。~ ***the ways*** 使事情顺利进行。**~ bark**【植】皂树;皂树皮;金龟树属含皂苷的树。**~ berry** = ~-nut. **~-boiler** 肥皂锅,肥皂制造者。**~-boiling** 肥皂制造(业)。**~box 1**. ***n***. 〔美〕(街头演说用的)肥皂箱。**2**. ***vi***. (站在肥皂箱上)(作)街头演说,煽动。**~boxer** 街头演说家。**~ bubble** 肥皂泡;短暂而空虚的好景。**~ dish** 肥皂缸[碟]。**~ earth**【化】皂石,滑石。**~ flakes** 肥皂片。**~-nut**【植】无患子。**~ opera**〔美〕肥皂剧〔内容常为家务事的日间广播或电视剧;常是肥皂制造商主办,观众为家庭妇女〕。**~ plant** 制皂植物。**~-pod**【植】皂荚。**~ powder** 肥皂粉。**~ stone**【化】皂石。**~ suds**〔*sing*., *pl*.〕(起泡的)肥皂水,肥皂泡。**~ test** 皂试验〔用以测定水的硬度〕。**~-wort** 肥皂草。

soap·y [ˈsəupi; ˋsopɪ] ***a***. **1**. 肥皂状的,肥皂质的;尽是肥皂的。**2**. 〔俚〕满口奉承话的;油滑的。~ *water* 肥皂水。~ *feeling* 滑腻的感觉。**-i·ly** ***ad***. **-i·ness** ***n***. **-less** ***a***.

soar [sɔː, sɔə; sor] **I** ***n***. **1**. 高飞,翱翔,飞升。**2**. 上升高度;高飞范围。**II** ***vi***. **1**. 高飞,翱翔,飞上去。**2**. 耸立,屹立。**3**. (物价)飞涨,暴腾,猛增;(思想等)向上。**4**.【空】滑翔。—***vt***. 〔诗〕飞翔到,高飞到。*beyond the ~ of fancy* 出乎意料之外;想像不到。*The temperature ~-ed to 80°*. 温度猛升到80度。**-er** ***n***.

soar·ing [ˈsɔːriŋ, ˈsɔər-; ˋsorɪŋ] ***a***. 高飞的;翱翔的(鹰等);高耸云霄的(尖塔等);高超的(思想等)。*a ~ eagle* 凌空翱翔的鹰。*a ~ flight* 高空飞行;滑翔飞行。*a ~ plane* 滑翔机。*a ~ ambition* 远大的抱负,雄心壮志。~ *spire* 高入云霄的尖顶。

SOB, S.O.B., s.o.b. [ˈesˌsəuˈbiː; ˋɛ͵soˋbi] ***n***. 〔美俚〕(骂人语)畜生,狗娘养的〔son of a bitch 的缩略〕。

sob [sɔb; sɑb] **I** ***vi***. (**-bb-**) **1**. 抽噎,啜泣;哽咽,呜咽。**2**. (风等)发出呜咽声。—***vt***. **1**. 抽噎着说,哭诉(*out*)。**2**. 哭得使…。**II** ***n***. 抽噎(声),啜泣(声);哽咽,呜咽;(风等的)呜咽声。**~ sister**〔美俚〕写感情文章的女记者;演感伤角色的女演员;感伤而不实际的人。**~ story**〔美俚〕感伤故事。**~ stuff**〔美新闻、剧〕感伤材料,感伤文章[故事]。

sob·bing·ly [ˈsɔbiŋli; ˋsɑbɪŋlɪ] ***ad***. 啜泣地,呜咽地,抽抽噎噎地。

sob·by [ˈsɔbi; ˋsɑbɪ] ***a***., ***n***. 〔美俚〕引人感伤的 = sob sister.

so·ber [ˈsəubə; ˋsobɚ] **I** ***a***. **1**. 没有醉的,清醒的,没有喝酒的;节酒的,饮食有节制的。**2**. 严肃的,认真的,冷静的;稳重的,非极端的;非想像的,不夸张的;神志清醒的。**3**. 朴素的,素净的,不鲜艳的(颜色、衣服等)。*a ~ truth* 不夸大或歪曲的事实真相。*Who are the moderate and ~*? 谁是温和冷静派呢? ***as ~ as a judge*** 挺严肃的。***become*** ~ 酒醒。***in one's ~ senses*** 神志清醒地,冷静地,沉着地。***in ~ earnest*** 非常认真[严肃]地。***in ~ fact*** 事实上。***lead a ~ life*** 认真过日子,不喝酒过日子。**II** ***vt***. 使酒醒;使严肃,使认真;使冷静,使沉着;使忧郁。—***vi***. 酒醒(*up*; *off*);变严肃,变认真;变清醒(*down*)。**~-blooded** ***a***. 严肃的,沉着的。**~-headed, ~minded** ***a***. 沉着的,头脑冷静的。**~sided** ***a***. 稳重的;严肃的。**~sides**〔口〕沉着的人,严肃的人。**~ water**〔谑〕苏打水。**-ly** ***ad***. **-ness** ***n***.

so·ber·ize [ˈsəubəraiz; ˋsobəraɪz] ***vt***. 〔古〕使清醒,使庄重严肃。

sob·fest [ˈsɔbfest; ˋsɑbfɛst] ***n***. 〔美〕伤心落泪的场合;互相倾吐苦情。

so·bri·e·ty [səuˈbraiəti; səˋbraɪətɪ] ***n***. 节酒;清醒;认真;节制;谨严;冷静,沉着,稳健。

so·bri·quet [ˈsəubrikei; ˋsobrɪ͵ke] ***n***. 非正式的名字[头衔];浑名,绰号。

Soc. = **1**. Socialist. **2**. Society.

soc·age [ˈsɔkidʒ; ˋsɑkɪdʒ] ***n***. 无兵役租佃(制)〔英国中世纪一种租佃制度,佃户不对领主服兵役,只缴地租或服其他劳役〕。

so-called [ˈsəuˈkɔːld; ˋsoˋkɔld] ***a***. 所谓的,号称的〔英国习惯常含有不信或轻视之意〕。

soc·cer [ˈsɔkə; ˋsɑkɚ] ***n***. 〔口〕英式足球(= football, association football)。**~mom**〔口〕足球妈咪〔指有年轻孩子的母亲,因青少年一般都爱看足球比赛〕。

S

So·chi [ˈsəutʃi; ˋsotʃɪ] ***n***. 索契〔前苏联港市,为著名休养地〕。

so·cia·bil·i·ty [ˌsəuʃəˈbiliti; ˏsoʃəˋbɪlətɪ] ***n***. **1.** 爱交际;会交际;讨人欢喜,和气。**2.** 社交性格[心理,倾向,气氛]。**3.**【生】群集度。

so·cia·ble [ˈsəuʃəbl; ˋsoʃəbl̩] **I** ***a***. **1.** 爱交际的;会交际的;讨人欢喜的,和气的。**2.** 喜欢群居的;社交性的;宜于交际的。**II** ***n***. **1.**〔美〕恳亲会,联谊会,联欢会。**2.**〔英〕对座四轮马车;双座三轮自行车;(二人座)S 形椅子。**-bly** ***ad***.

so·cial [ˈsəuʃəl; ˋsoʃəl] **I** ***a***. **1.** 社会的,社会上的。**2.** 交际的,社交的;喜欢交际的。**3.** 合群的;【动】群居的;【植】丛生的。**4.**【史】同盟国间的。**5.** 一定社会阶层[地位]的;上流社会的。**6.** 社会性的。～ *customs* 社会习俗。～ *history* 社会历史。～ *investigations* 社会调查。～ *reforms* 社会改革。*her busy* ～ *life* 她繁忙的社交生活。*Man is a* ～ *animal*. 人是群居动物。～ *advancement* 社会地位的提高。*one's* ～ *equals* [*inferiors*, *superiors*] 社会地位与自己相同[比自己低、比自己高]的人们。～ *order* 社会秩序。～ *origin* 出身。～ *politics* 社会政策。～ *problem* 社会问题。～ *rank* 社会等级,社会地位。～ *register* 〔美〕社会名人录。～ *student* 社会学研究家。*the* ～ *evil* 卖淫。**II** ***n***. 社交聚会,联谊会。*a church* ～ 教友联谊会。～ **anthropology** 社会人类学。～ **climber** 向上爬的人,企图进入上流社会的人。～ **column** (报纸上的)社会新闻专栏。～ **contract** [**compact**] 民约,社会契约;〔美〕政府与工会互相妥协协议〔规定工会限制其增薪要求,而政府则制订对工人有利的经济和社会政策〕。～ **dancing** 交际舞,交谊舞。**S-Darwinism** 社会达尔文主义。～ **democracy** 社会民主主义。～ **democrat** 社会民主党人。～ **disease** 性病,花柳病,(肺病等)社会性疾病。～ **engineering** 社会工程。～ **gospel** 社会福音;〔美〕社会福音运动。～ **insurance** 社会保险。～**-minded** ***a***. 关心社会的;热心于社会福利的。～ **psychology** 社会心理学。～ **science** 社会科学。～ **secretary** 交际秘书。～ **security** 社会保障,〔美〕政府的公共福利计划。～ **service** 社会福利事业。～ **studies** 社会学科〔指中学、大学中的历史、地理、经济、人类学、社会学等课程〕。～ **wage** 社会福利工资。～ **welfare** 社会福利;社会福利救济。～ **work** 社会福利工作。～ **worker** 社会福利工作者。**-ly** ***ad***. 社会上;社交上,交际上;和睦地,亲密地。

so·cial·ism [ˈsəuʃəlizəm; ˋsoʃəlˏɪzəm] ***n***. 社会主义。*scientific* ～ 科学社会主义。*utopian* ～ 空想社会主义。*Christian S-* 基督教社会主义〔企图用基督教的教义来实现社会主义〕。

so·cial·ist [ˈsəuʃəlist; ˋsoʃəlɪst] **I** ***n***. 社会主义者。**II** ***a***. **1.** 社会主义的。**2.**〔S-〕社会党的。**S- Party** 社会党。

so·cial·is·tic [ˌsəuʃəˈlistik; ˏsoʃəˋlɪstɪk] ***a***. 社会主义(者)的。

so·cial·ite [ˈsəuʃəlait; ˋsoʃəˏlaɪt] ***n***. 〔美〕社会名流,社交界的知名人士。

so·ci·al·i·ty [ˌsəuʃiˈæliti; ˏsoʃɪˋælətɪ] ***n***. 社会性;爱交际;社会的风俗习惯;群居性。

so·cial·i·za·tion [ˌsəuʃəlaiˈzeiʃən; ˏsoʃələˋzeʃən] ***n***. 社会(主义)化。

so·cial·ize [ˈsəuʃəlaiz; ˋsoʃəˏlaɪz] ***vt***. **1.** 使社会化;使社会主义化。**2.** 使适应社会需要;使适合于过社会生活。**3.** 使参加集体学习,使(学习)组织化。—***vi***. 〔美口〕参加社交活动。～*d medicine* 〔美〕公费医疗制,社会化的医疗制度。

so·ci·e·tal [səˈsaiətl; səˋsaɪətl̩] ***a***. 社会的。～ **parent** 社会父母〔社会上无子女而领养孩子的人〕。**-ly** ***ad***.

so·ci·e·ty [səˈsaiəti; səˋsaɪətɪ] ***n***. **1.** 社会。**2.** 会,社;协会,学会,公会,团体。**3.** 交际,社交;社交界〔特指上流社会〕;社交场所。**4.** 群居,群栖。**5.** 〔美〕教区居民。*primitive* ～ 原始社会。*class* ～ 阶级社会。*slavery* ～ 奴隶社会。*feudalist* ～ 封建社会。*a charitable* ～ 慈善团体。*I enjoy your* ～. 和您交往真高兴。*avoid* [*seek*] *the* ～ *of* 避免[追求]和…来往[相处]。*be quit of sb.'s* ～ 和…断绝来往。*go into* ～ 入交际界;常赴宴会。*live in* ～ 出入交际界。～ **beauty** 交际花。～ **column** (报刊上的)社会新闻专栏。～ **editor** 社会栏编辑。～ **gossip** 社交界的流言蜚语。～ **house** 加入公会的印刷所。～ **lady** 社交界[上流社会]妇女;〔英〕出入宫廷的妇女。**Society of Friends** (基督教)公谊会。**Society of Jesus** (天主教)耶稣会。～ **verse** 社交诗〔一种轻松,有风趣的诗〕。

So·cin·i·an·ism [səuˈsiniənizəm; soˋsɪnɪənɪzəm] ***n***. 索齐尼教义〔16 世纪意大利神学家 Faustus Socinus 所主张,否认三位一体,耶稣的神性等,而以唯理论来解释罪恶和得救〕。

so·ci·o·bi·o·lo·gy [ˌsəusiəubaiˈɔlədʒi; ˏsosɪobaɪˋɑlədʒɪ] ***n***. 社会生物学〔研究生物社会行为基础的学科〕。

so·ci·o·cul·tu·ral [ˌsəusiəuˈkʌltʃərəl; ˏsosɪoˋkʌltʃərəl, -ʃɪ-] ***a***. 社会文化的;涉及社会文化因素的。

so·ci·o·e·co·lo·gy [ˌsəusiəuiːˈkɔlədʒi; ˏsosɪoiˋkɑlədʒɪ] ***n***. 社会生态学〔指受环境影响的社会分工与组织状况〕。

so·ci·o·e·co·nom·ic [ˈsəusiəuˌiːkəˈnɔmik; ˏsosɪoˏikəˋnɑmɪk, -ʃɪ-, -ˏɛkə-] ***a***. 社会经济(学)的。

so·ci·o·gram [ˈsəusiəˌgræm, ˈsəuʃi-; ˋsosɪəˏgræm] ***n***. 【社会学】社会关系分析表[图]。

sociol. = sociology; sociological; sociologist.

so·ci·o·lin·guis·tics [ˌsəusjəuˈliŋgwistiks; ˏsoʃəˋlɪŋgwɪstɪks] ***n***. 社会语言学。

so·ci·o·log·i·cal [ˌsəusjəˈlɔdʒikəl; ˏsoʃɪəˋlɑdʒɪkl̩, ˏsosɪ-] ***a***. 社会学(上)的。**-ly** ***ad***.

so·ci·ol·o·gist [ˌsəusiˈɔlədʒist; ˏsoʃɪˋɑlədʒɪst, ˏsosɪ-] ***n***. 社会学家。

so·ci·ol·o·gy [ˌsəusiˈɔlədʒi; ˏsoʃɪˋɑlədʒɪ, ˏsosɪ-] ***n***. 社会学。

so·ci·om·e·try [ˌsəusiˈɔmitri; ˏsosɪˋɑmətrɪ, -ʃɪ-] ***n***. **1.** 社会关系计量学。**2.** 社会群体心理测定法。**-met·ric** [-ˈmetrik; -ˋmɛtrɪk] ***a***.

so·ci·o·path [ˈsəusiəˌpæθ, -ʃi-; ˋsosɪəˏpæθ, -ʃɪ-] ***n***. 极端反社会的人〔精神病患者的一种类型〕;不爱社交的人。**-ic** ***a***.

so·ci·o·po·lit·i·cal [ˌsəusiəupəˈlitikl; ˏsosɪopəˋlɪtəkəl, -ʃɪ-] ***a***. 社会和政治的。

sock[1] [sɔk; sɑk] **I** ***n***. (*pl*. ～**s**,【商】**sox**) **1.** 短袜。**2.** 鞋内的皮革衬垫。**3.** (古希腊,罗马喜剧演员穿的)轻便软鞋;〔喻〕喜剧;【美剧】大成功。**4.** 〔美俚〕钱袋;银柜;准备金,存款;巨款。**5.** = windsock. *an associate of the* ～ *and buskin* 戏剧演员。***old*** ～***s*** (男子之间的亲热称呼)老兄。***Pull up your*** ～***s***! 〔英俚〕鼓起劲来;加紧努力! ***Put a*** ～ ***in*** [***into***] ***it***! 〔俚〕别讲话! **II** ***vt***. **1.** 给…穿上短袜。**2.** 〔美俚〕储蓄(钱)。～ ***away*** 把钱存放一边。～ ***in*** 关闭(机场);禁止(飞机)起落。

sock[2] [sɔk; sɑk] **I** ***vt***. 〔俚〕用力打击,殴打。～ ***it to sb***. 〔美俚〕猛揍某人。**II** ***n***. 拳打;拳头。～ *peddler* 〔美〕拳击选手。***give sb***. ～(***s***) 痛殴。**III** ***ad***. 正好,对准,迎面。*He hit me* ～ *in the eye*. 他一拳正好打在我的眼睛上。

sock[3] [sɔk; sɑk] **I** ***n***. 〔英学俚〕食品,零食,点心。**II** ***vt***., ***vi***. (请…)吃零食。

sock·dol·a·ger, sock·dol·o·ger [sɔkˈdɔlədʒə; sɑkˋdɑlədʒɚ] ***n***. 〔美俚〕决定性的一击[回答];大成功;异常大的东西。

sock·er [ˈsɔkə; ˋsɑkɚ] ***n***. 〔英俚〕英式足球(= soccer)。～ ***eleven*** = ～ ***team*** 足球队。

sock·er·in·o [sɔkəˈriːnəu; ˏsɑkəˋrino] ***n***. 〔美俚〕大成功。

sock·et [ˈsɔkit; ˋsɑkɪt] **I** ***n***. **1.** (承物或藏物的)孔,洞,窝,凹处,承口。**2.**【解】(眼)窝,腔;(齿)槽;【地】牙槽;

(烛台的)烛窝;轴孔;【机】承窝;座;套节;轴承。3.【电】插口,插座,管座。*the eye* ~ 眼窝。*an electric bulb* ~ 电灯泡插座。*a* ~ *pipe* 套管。*a reducing* ~ 异径管节,大小头。*a screw* ~ 螺丝插口。~ *wrench* 套筒扳手。**II** *vt*. 1. 给…配插座[承口等];使装入插座,用插座固定住。2. 用球棒的后跟击(高尔夫球)。

sock·eye [ˈsɔkˌai; ˋsɑkˏaɪ] *n*.【动】红大麻哈鱼(*Oncorhynchus nerka*)〔产于北太平洋,常用作罐头食品〕。

sock·o [ˈsɔkəu; ˋsɑko] **I** *n*.〔美俚〕1. 大成功〔特指演出等〕。2. 猛击,重拳〔尤指打在下巴上的〕。**II** *vt*. 猛击,使一举成功。**III** *a*., *ad*. 非常成功的(地),极为卖座的(地)。

soc·le [ˈsɔkl; ˋsɑkl, ˋsokl] *n*. 1.【建】(石像、石柱等的)座石,柱脚。2. (电子管的)管脚,管底。

Soc·ra·tes [ˈsɔkrətiːz; ˋsɑkrəˏtiz] *n*. 苏格拉底〔公元前469? —399,古希腊哲学家〕。

So·crat·ic [sɔˈkrætik; soˋkrætɪk] **I** *a*. 苏格拉底的,苏格拉底哲学的;信奉苏格拉底的。**II** *n*. 苏格拉底的信徒。~ **method** 苏格拉底问答法[对话法]。

sod[1] [sɔd; sɑd] **I** *n*. 1. (切成方块的)草皮;草根泥;草地。2. 土地,故乡,本国。*a* ~ *buster* 〔美〕乡下人;农民;农科大学生。*a* ~ *widow* 〔美〕寡妇。*the old* ~ 祖国,故乡。***turn the*** ~ 挖地。***under the*** ~ 在坟墓里,长眠地下。**II** *vt*. (**-dd-**) 铺草皮,用草皮覆盖。

sod[2] [sɔd; sɑd] *n*. 1. 〔卑〕〔谑〕人,家伙〔尤作骂人语〕。2. 〔英俚〕鸡奸者,兽奸者〔系 sodomite 的简写〕。

sod[3] [sɔd; sɑd] 〔古〕seethe 的过去式及过去分词;煮熟的。

so·da [ˈsəudə; ˋsodə] *n*. 1.【化】苏打,碱,碳酸钠;碳酸氢钠;小苏打;氢氧化钠;氧化钠;(化合物中的)钠。2. 苏打水,汽水。*washing* ~ 洗涤用苏打〔使水软化〕。*baking* ~ 烹调用苏打,小苏打。*caustic* ~ 烧碱,苛性钠。~ **ash** 无水碳酸钠,纯碱,苏打灰。~ **biscuit** [**cracker**] 苏打饼干。~ **fountain** (装有龙头的)散装苏打汽水容器[柜台];〔美〕冷饮小卖部〔多半附设在药房中,兼卖冰淇淋、点心等〕。~ **glass** 钠玻璃。~ **jerk** [**jerker, squirt**] 冷饮柜台售货员。~ **lime**【化】碱石灰。~**list** (天主教徒的)慈善会会员。~ **mica** 钠云母。~ **nitrate** 智利硝石。~ **pop** 汽水。~**-water** 苏打水,汽水。

so·da·lite [ˈsəudəˌlait; ˋsodəˏlaɪt] *n*.【矿】方钠石。

so·dal·i·ty [səuˈdæliti; soˋdælətɪ] *n*. 1. 联谊会,兄弟会,团体。2. (罗马天主教徒间宗教性或慈善性的)会社。

sod·den [ˈsɔdn; ˋsɑdn] **I** *a*. 1. 湿润的,发潮的;没有烤透的(面包等);浸透了的,泡胀了的。2. (因沉迷于酒而变得)呆头呆脑的,无表情的,麻木的。~ *ground* 浸透水的土地。~ *features* 呆头呆脑的样子。~ *minds* 迟钝的脑子。**II** *vt*. 1. 浸,泡,弄湿。2. 使呆头呆脑,使(头脑)麻木。—*vi*. 浸透;变软;腐败。**-ly** *ad*. **-ness** *n*.

Sod·y [ˈsɔdi; ˋsɑdɪ] *n*. 索迪〔姓氏〕。

sod·dy[1] [ˈsɔdi; ˋsɑdɪ] *a*. 草皮的;铺满草皮的;草地多的。~ *soil* 生草土。

sod·dy[2] [ˈsɔdi; ˋsɑdɪ] *n*. 〔美西部〕(草泥墙的)窝棚。

so·dic [ˈsəudik; ˋsodɪk] *a*. 钠的,含钠的。

so·di·um [ˈsəudjəm, -diəm; ˋsodɪəm] *n*. 钠。~ **benzoate**【化】苯甲酸钠。安息香酸钠。~ **bicarbonate** 小苏打。【化】碳酸氢钠。~ **borate**【化】硼砂。~ **bromide**【化】溴化钠。~ **carbonate** 纯碱。【化】碳酸钠。~ **chlorate**【化】氯酸钠。~ **chloride** 氯化钠,食盐。~ **cyanide**【化】氰化钠。~ **dichromate**【化】重铬酸钠。~ **fluoroacetate**【化】氟化醋酸钠〔一种毒鼠药〕。~ **hydrosulphite**【化】连二亚硫酸钠。~ **hydroxide** 烧碱。【化】氢氧化钠。~ **nitrate** 硝酸钠,智利硝石。~ **pentothal**【药】喷妥撒钠。~ **perborate**【化】过硼酸钠。~ **phosphate**【化】磷酸钠。~ **propionate**【化】丙酸钠。~ **silicate**【化】矽酸钠,水玻璃。~ **sulfate**【化】硫酸钠。~ **thiosulfate**【化】硫代硫酸钠,大苏打。~**-vapor lamp** 钠蒸气灯。

sod·om·ite [ˈsɔdəmait; ˋsɑdəmˏaɪt] *n*. 1. 鸡奸者,兽奸者。2. 反常的性交。

sod·om·y [ˈsɔdəmi; ˋsɑdəmɪ] *n*. 鸡奸,兽奸。

SOED, S.O.E.D. = Shorter Oxford English Dictionary《简编牛津英语辞典》。

so·ev·er [səuˈevə; soˋɛvɚ, sʊˋɛvɚ] *ad*. 1. 无论〔用于 how 后的形容词之后或最高级形容词之后〕。2. 不论何种,任何,完全(没有)〔用于名词后面,与否定语连用〕。*How great* ~ *he may be*. 无论他怎样伟大。*the most selfish* ~ *in this world* 天下最自私的。*He has no home* ~. 他完全没有家。

SOF = sound on film.

so·fa [ˈsəufə; ˋsofə] *n*. 沙发。*a* ~ *lizard* 〔美〕待在家里不爱参加社交集会的人。~ **bed** (兼可作床的)两用沙发。

so·far [ˈsəufɑː; ˋsofɑr] *n*. (测定水下物体距离的)声发,声波定位(仪)。

Soff [sɔuf; sof] *n*. 索夫〔姓氏〕。

sof·fit [ˈsɔfit; ˋsɑfɪt] *n*. 1.【建】拱腹;楼梯(或柱上楣等的)下部。2.【剧】上部布景,天空布景。

So·fi·a [ˈsəufjə; ˋsofɪə, soˋfiə] *n*. 索非亚〔保加利亚首都〕。

So·fi(sm) [ˈsəufi(zm); ˋsofɪ(zm)] *n*. = Sufi(sm).

So·fos [sɔˈfəuz; sɑˋfoz] *n*. 〔前苏联〕= Sovkhos.

soft [sɔft; sɔft] **I** *a*. 1. 软的,柔软的(*opp*. hard, tough);柔滑的(皮肤,毛发等);悦耳的,好听的,柔和的(声音等);不刺目的(光等);不明亮的,水汪汪的(眼睛等)。2. 温柔的,温和的,和蔼的,厚道的,宽大的(行动、态度等);软弱的,不强健的,不坚强的,吃不了苦的,娇嫩的。3. 平静的,安稳的,平安的,和平的。4. 〔英〕潮湿的,下雨的,解冻的,沉闷的,阴郁的(天气等);线条柔和的,模糊的(轮廓);不陡峭的,坡度小的。5. 愚钝的,痴呆的,低能的。6.【语音】(辅音)带声的,浊的;不送气的;软音的〔gin 的 g, city 的 c〕。7.【化】软化的。8. 无矿盐的(水);不含酒精的(饮料);易消化的(食物);毒性不大的(麻醉品)。9. 〔口〕舒服的,轻松的。10.【商】不稳定的,下跌的(市场,价格等);长期低率的(贷款等);纸币的;黄金后盾不足的,难以兑成外币的(货币)。11.【军】无遮蔽而易受攻击的(军事目标,基地等)。12. 易磁化和消磁的(铁等)。

II *n*. 1. 柔软(部分)。2. 〔口〕拙笨;傻子。3. 〔the ~〕〔美俚〕钱〔尤指纸币〕。*A* ~ *answer turnth away wrath*. 温和的回答可以消解怒气。*S- and fair goes far*. 〔谚〕柔能克刚。~ *breezes* 和风。~ *fire* 文火。~ *hat* 呢帽。~ *manners* 温和的举动。~ *sentence* 宽大的判决。~ *soil* [*ground*] 软土[地]。*as* ~ *as velvet* 像天鹅绒一样柔滑。~ *whispers* 低声的耳语。*in a* ~ *voice* 低声地。~ *nonsense* 傻话。~ *nothings* 情话。~ *things* 恭维话;温柔话,心里话。*a* ~ *tongue* 动听的说话能力。*a* ~ *slope* 缓坡,平坦的斜坡。*I think he is a bit* ~. 我看他有点笨。*a* ~ *job* 轻松的工作。*a* ~ *thing* 〔口〕好差事,舒适而报酬丰厚的工作。~ *market* 〔美俚〕便宜的价钱;疲软的行市。~ *money* 纸币;支票。*an aboveground* ~ *launching site* 地面上易受敌攻击的发射物。~ *iron* 易磁化的铁。~ *X rays* 软性 X 射线。~ *stuff* 〔美俚〕奉承(话)。~ *heel* 〔美俚〕侦探。~ *jack* 〔美俚〕轻易得来的钱财。***appeal to the ~er side of sb.'s character*** 打动某人的慈悲心。***be*** ~ (***up***) ***on sb***. 爱着某人(*He has been* ~ *on her for years*. 多年来他一直爱恋着她)。***go*** ~ 1. 软化。2. 变痴愚,变狂乱(*He's gone* ~. 他变得痴呆[有点狂乱]了)。***have a*** ~ ***place in one's head*** 〔口〕愚笨。***plead guilty to the*** ~ ***impeachment*** 〔口〕自认糊涂。***the*** ~ [***softer***] ***sex*** 女性。**III** *ad*. = softly. *lie* ~ (在柔软的床上)静静地躺着。*Play* [*Speak*] ~*er, please*. 请弹[说]得轻一点。**IV** *int*. 〔古〕别响! *S-! someone comes*. 别响! 有人来了。~**back** 平装书,纸版书。【体】~**ball** 软式棒球,垒球。~**ball squash** 软式壁球〔球心为软性〕。~**-boiled**

S

a. 半熟的(蛋等);心肠软的。～**bound** *a*. 软封面的。～**chancre**【医】软下疳。～ **coal** 烟煤。～**-core** 1. *a*. (作品中的色情描写)比较隐晦的。2. *n*. 比较隐晦的黄色内容。～**cover** = paperback. ～ **currency** 软性通货,不硬挺的通货〔不能兑现或市场价格不高的纸币等〕。～**-dock** (轨道航天器的)软对接(不用机械,而用尼龙绳等来实现)。～ **drinks** 不含酒精的饮料。～ **energy** 软能源(用软技术获得的能源)。～(**-**)**error**【计】软件误差〔指电脑数据在操作中发生的随机差错〕。～**-finned** *a*.【动】软鳍的。～ **fly**【棒球】容易接的飞球。～**-footed** *a*. 脚步轻的。～**goods** 纺织品,非耐用品。～**head** 笨人,蠢人;无主见的人。～**headed** *a*. 笨拙的;无主见的。～**hearted** *a*. 心肠软的,仁慈的。～**-land** *vi*., *vt*. (使)软着陆。～**-lander** 软着陆装置。～**landing**【空】软着陆;【经】软着陆〔指减缓经济增长速度而不引起高失业率和衰退〕。～**line** 温和路线。～**-liner** 温和路线者,温和路线支持[主张]者。～ **loan** 软贷款〔指无条件的低息长期贷款〕。～**money** 1.纸币。2.〔美口〕不受法律约束的竞选捐款,非法政治捐款。～ **nothing** 东拉西扯的软绵绵情话。～**palate** 软腭。～**-pedal** 1. *n*. (用以减弱音量的)钢琴踏板;减弱效果的东西。2. *vt*. 在演奏…时使用减音踏板;降低(意见、批评等)调子;对…不予张扬,秘而不宣;禁止讨论。～**rayed** *a*. (鱼鳍)有软条的。～ **rot**【植】软腐病。～ **rush**【植】灯心草。～ **sawder** *n*. 奉承,谄媚。～**sawder** *vt*. 奉承,谄媚。～ **sell**〔美〕劝诱推销,非强行推销。～**-shell** *a*. 软壳的;脆壳的。～**-shell clam**【动】沙海螂。～**-shelled** *a*. 软壳的。～**-shelled turtle**【动】灶,北美鳖属动物。～**-shoe** *a*. 软鞋踢跶舞。～ **shoulder** (沿公路的)路边软地。～**skills**〔复〕软技术〔指管理与社交才能等〕。～ **snap** 不需花费多少力气的事。～ **soap** 软皂,半液体皂;奉承,拍马屁。～**-soap** *vt*., *vi*. 使用软皂,奉承,阿谀。～**-soaper** 奉承者,拍马者。～ **solder** 软焊料〔用于易熔金属〕。～**-spoken** *a*. 说话温柔的,中听的,会说话的。～ **spot** 性格中易受打动之处,弱点;软弱不振的经济部门[企业]。～ **steel** 软钢〔含碳量低于0.35%〕。～ **sugar** 棉白糖;砂糖。～ **technology** (依靠太阳能、风力等而不用昂贵机械等的)软技术。～ **touch** 耳朵软的人,轻易上当的人;〔美俚〕一打就败的拳击手,可轻易击败的对手。～ **tube**【无】软性(电子)管,低真空管。～ **underbelly** 软弱[易受伤害]的部位。～**ware** (电脑的)软件,软设备;程序设备;语言设备;程度系统;设计电脑方法;计算程序;程序编排手段;方案;资料图纸;【空】软件〔指乘员、载重及燃料等,不包括机械硬件设备〕。～ **water** 软水。～ **wheat** 软麦〔一种低蛋白、软粒心小麦面粉,宜于做糕点〕。～**-witted** *a*. 半痴半呆的,愚蠢的。～ **wood** 软(木)材;针叶树材;针叶树。

sof·ten [ˈsɔːfn; ˋsɔfən] *vt*. 1. 使软化,弄软。2. 减轻,减弱(抵抗或反对)。3. 使(心)变温和;使柔弱;使不闪闪发光;使柔和;使婉转。—*vi*. 1. 变软;变温和,变柔和;变弱,变柔弱。2. 变静,变安稳,融和。～ *water* 使硬水软化成软水。***be ～ed into tears*** 感动得流泪。～ ***up***〔美俚〕(用恭维话等)软化;【军】(进攻前用猛烈轰炸、炮击等)削弱(对方的抵抗力);破坏(对方的士气)。**-er** *n*. 使软化[变柔和]的人[物];软化剂,软水剂。**-ing** *n*.【无】真空恶化;漏气。

soft·ie [ˈsɔːfti; ˋsɔftɪ] *n*.〔口〕软心肠的人;柔弱的人;懦夫;轻信者;笨人。***go*** ～ 爱上,看中。

soft·ish [ˈsɔftiʃ; ˋsɔftɪʃ] *a*. 有点柔软[柔和、仁慈、柔弱]的。

soft·ly [ˈsɔftli; ˋsɔftlɪ] *ad*. 柔软地;轻轻地,低声地,静静地;温和地;宽大地,松弛地。

soft·ness [ˈsɔftnis; ˋsɔftnɪs] *n*. 柔软;温柔;柔和;【农】粉质性。

soft·y [ˈsɔfti; ˋsɔftɪ]〔口〕*n*. = softie.

Sog·di·an [ˈsɔgdiən; ˋsɑgdɪən] *n*. 1. 古索格代亚纳人〔居住在索格代亚纳的伊朗人〕。2. 古索格代亚纳语〔已消亡,属伊朗语〕。

sog·getto [sɔˈdʒətəu; sɑˋdʒəto] *n*.〔It.〕【乐】主题。

sog·gy [ˈsɔgi; ˋsɑgɪ] *a*. 1. 浸水的,湿润的,潮湿的。2. 未烤透的。3. 迟钝的,不活泼的;沉闷的,乏味的。*a ～ lawn* 潮湿的草地。*a ～ bread* 未烤透的面包。～ *prose* 枯燥无味的散文。**-gi·ly** *ad*. **-gi·ness** *n*.

SoHo[1] [ˈsəuhəu; ˋsoho] = south of Houston〔美〕梭荷中心〔纽约市曼哈顿南部一地区,以先锋派艺术、音乐、电影和时装等知名〕。

SOHO[2] = small office/home office 家庭办公室,家庭企业。

so·ho [səuˈhəu; soˋho] *int*. 1. 缩啊!〔命马止步声〕。2. 来啦!〔发现猎物时的叫声〕。

soi-di·sant [ˈswɑːdiːˈzɑ̃ː; swɑdiˋzɑ̃] *a*.〔F.〕所谓的,自称的,冒充的。*a ～ artist* 自命的艺术家。

soi·gné [swɑːˈnjei; swɑˋnje] *a*. (*fem*. ***soignée***)〔F.〕打扮得极考究的;整洁的;时髦的。*a ～ restaurant* 高雅的饭店。

soil[1] [sɔil; sɔɪl] *n*. 1. 泥土,土壤;土质。2. 土地,国土。3. 滋生地,温床。4. 农业生活,务农。*clayey* [*sandy*] ～ 黏[砂]壤。*poor* [*rich*] ～ 瘦[肥]土。*high* ～ 轻质土。*alluvial* ～ 冲积土。*arable* ～ 耕地。*a tiller* [*child*, *son*] *of the* ～ 农民;本地人。*the lord of the* ～ 领主,地主。～ *conservation* 土壤保持。～ *invaders*【农】土壤寄居菌。*on foreign* ～ 在外国。*one's native* [*parent*] ～ 故乡,祖国。～ **bank**〔美〕联邦休耕地补助制。～**binder** 护土植物。～**borne** *a*. (病毒等)由土壤传播的,在土壤中的。～ **conservation** 土壤保持。～ **science** 土壤学。

soil[2] [sɔil; sɔɪl] **I** *n*. 1. 脏东西,污物,污秽,污斑。2. 粪尿,肥料。*a ～ pipe* 污水管。*night ～* 粪便。**II** *vt*. 1. 弄脏,弄污;污染,污损。2. 污辱,败坏。3. 给…上粪[施肥]。—*vi*. 被弄脏,变脏。～ *one's hands with*〔喻〕因…弄脏手;染手。*It ～s easily*. 那东西容易脏。～ *a field* 给田施肥。～*ed clothes* 脏衣服。

soil[3] [sɔil; sɔɪl] *vt*. (给畜舍内畜牲)喂青草[青饲料];(用青饲料给畜牲)通便;催肥。～*ing crops* 青饲料作物。

soil·age [ˈsɔilidʒ; ˋsɔɪlɪdʒ] *n*. 1. 青饲料作物。2. 弄脏,肮脏,污秽。

soil·ure [ˈsɔiljuə; ˋsɔɪljʊr] *n*.〔古语〕1. 污涂,污染。2. 污秽,污斑。

soi·rée [ˈswɑːrei; swɑˋre] *n*. 晚会,晚上举行的聚会。

soi·xante-quinze [F. swɑːsɑ̃ntkɛ̃nz; ˋswɑsɑ̃tˋkɛ̃z] *n*.〔F.〕法国75毫米口径的炮。

so·ja [ˈsəujə, ˈsəudʒə; ˋsodʒə, ˋsojə] *n*.【植】大豆。

so·journ [ˈsɔdʒəːn, ˈsʌdʒəːn; ˋsodʒɝn] **I** *n*. 旅居,侨居;逗留,寄居。**II** [ˈsɔdʒəːn, ˈsʌdʒ-; soˋdʒɝn, ˋsodʒɝn] *vi*. 旅居,逗留。*a ～ in the country* 在乡间逗留。**-er** *n*.

soke [səuk; sok] *n*.【英史】1. 区域审判权。2. 司法管辖区。

so·ko [ˈsəukəu; ˋsoko] *n*. 黑猩猩。

so·kol [ˈsəukɔːl; ˋsokɔl] *n*. 索科尔〔意为"鹰",捷克斯洛伐克的体育运动组织〕。

Sol [sɔl; sɑl, sɔl] *n*. 1. 男子名〔Solomon 的爱称〕。2. 【罗神】太阳神;太阳。3. [s-](炼金术中的)金。

sol[1] [sɔl; sol] *n*.【乐】全音阶第五音。

sol[2] [səul; sol] *n*. (*pl*. ～*s*) 索尔〔秘鲁货币单位〕。

sol[3] [sɔl; sɑl, sol] *n*.【化】溶胶,液胶。

sol[4] [sɔl; sɑl] *n*.【天】火星日〔长24小时37分22秒〕。

Sol. = Solicitor; Solomon.

sol. = solicitor; soluble; solution.

S.O.L.〔美〕倒霉的;为难的 (= short of luck)。

so·la[1] [ˈsəulə; ˋsolə] *n*.【植】(印度合萌属的)合欢草;(用合欢草的轻茎制成的)遮阳帽 (= ～ topi)。

so·la[2] [ˈsəulə; ˋsolə] *a*. solus 的阴性。

sol·ace [ˈsɔləs; ˋsɑlɪs, -əs] **I** *n*. 安慰;安慰物。**II** *vt*. 1. 安慰,抚慰。2. 缓和,减轻。3. 使高兴,使快活。～ ***oneself with*** 拿…来自慰。

so·lan [ˈsəulən; ˋsolən] *n*.【动】塘鹅(=~-goose)。

so·la·nin(e) [ˈsɔləniːn, -nin; ˋsoləˏnin, -nın] *n*.【化】茄碱。

so·lar [ˈsəulə; ˋsolɚ] **I** *a*. 太阳的,根据太阳运行测量的;因太阳作用产生的。**II** *n*. = solarium. *the* ~ *system* 太阳系。*a* ~ *spot* 太阳黑点。~ *light* 日光。~ *energy* 太阳能。*a* ~ *battery* 太阳能电池。~ *heat* 太阳热。~ **calendar** 阴历。~ **collector** 太阳能收集器。~ **constant** 太阳常数〔太阳辐射的基准量〕。~ **corona** 日冕。~ **cycle** 太阳周期〔一般以28年为一个周期,日历上月日和星期的一定排列重复出现〕;太阳活动周〔以11年左右为周期,太阳的一些主要现象重复出现〕。~ **day** 太阳日。~ **eclipse** 日蚀。~ **eyepiece** 太阳目镜。~ **fever** = dengue. ~ **flare** 耀斑。~ **flowers** 只在白天开一个时候的花。~ **furnace** 太阳炉。~ **glass** 茶色玻璃。~ **hour** 太阳时。~ **house** (收集辐射热的)太阳室。~ **month** 太阳月。~ **oil** 太阳油;页岩油。~ **plexus**【解】太阳(神经)丛;〔口〕心窝儿。~ **prominences** 日环。~ **sail** 太阳帆〔星际航行中利用太阳能作为动力的一种设备〕。~ **spectrum** 太阳光谱。~ **time** 太阳时。~ **wind** 太阳风,日射微粒流。~ **year** 太阳年。

so·lar·ism [ˈsəulərizəm; ˋsolərızm̩] *n*. (神话中的)太阳中心说。

so·lar·i·um [səuˈlɛəriəm; soˋlɛrɪəm] *n*. (*pl*. **-ria** [-riə; -rɪə]) 太阳钟,日晷;日光浴室[治疗室]。

so·lar·ize [ˈsəuləraiz; ˋsoləˏraız] *vt*. **1**. 用日光曝晒;使受日光作用。**2**.【摄】使(胶片)曝光过久。—*vi*. (因曝光过久)胶片受损坏。

so·late [ˈsɔleit; ˋsɑlet] *vi*.【化】(凝胶)液化,成为液胶。**-la·tion** *n*.

so·la·ti·um [səuˈleiʃjəm, -ʃiəm; soˋleʃɪəm] *n*. (*pl*. **-tia** [-ʃiə; -ʃɪə]) 赔偿;安慰金。

sold [səuld; sold] sell 的过去式及过去分词。

sold·er [ˈsɔldə; ˋsɑldɚ] **I** *n*. **1**. 焊药,焊剂;焊锡。**2**. 结合物,联接因素。*hard* ~ 硬焊药。*soft* ~ 软焊药。**II** *vt*., *vi*. 焊;接合;锡焊;焊接;(使)结合。~**ing iron** 焊铁,烙铁。~ **paste** 焊药。

sol·dier [ˈsəuldʒə; ˋsoldʒɚ] **I** *n*. **1**. 军人;(陆军)士兵(*opp*. officer); 战士,勇士。**2**. 富有军事经验[军事技术]的人;军事家,军事指挥员。**3**. 为某事业献身的人。**4**.〔口〕偷懒[装病]的人,懒汉。**5**.【动】(群居性昆虫)兵虫;兵蚁;寄居蟹;〔俚〕熏鲱鱼。*a* ~ *of the carpet* 游手好闲,贪图享受的人(=carpet knight)。*the great* ~*s of history* 历史名将。~ *of fortune* 雇用军人;(追求名利的)冒险家。*a great* ~ 勇将。*a militia* ~ 民兵。*a private* [*common*] ~ 兵。*tin* [*toy*] ~*s* 玩具兵。***come the old*** ~ ***over sb***. 拿老资格派头指挥某人,教训某人;欺骗,哄骗。***go for a*** ~ 参军。***no*** ~ 没有指挥能力的军官,没有做军人资格的人。***old*** ~ 老兵;老资格,老手;〔俚〕(酒席等的)空瓶;雪茄烟头[屁股]。***play at*** ~***s*** 玩军队游戏。**II** *vi*. **1**. 当兵。**2**.〔口〕偷懒,装病。—*vt*.〔美〕逃避,规避。*He has* ~*ed all over the world*. 他做军人,走遍了全世界。~**s and sailors** 陆军和海军。~ **ant**【动】兵蚁,澳洲大赤蚁。~ **colour**〔美〕全部清一色。~ **crab**【动】寄居蟹。~**'s heart** 军人病〔一种心脏病〕。~**s' home**〔美〕退伍军人收容所。~**'s medal**〔美〕军人奖章〔对非战斗英勇行动授予的奖章〕。~**'s wind**【海】侧横风。**-like**, **-ly** *a*. 像军人的,像武士的,勇敢的,英勇的。**-ship** *n*. 军人身分[品质];军事才干。

sol·dier·y [ˈsəuldʒəri; ˋsoldʒərı] *n*. **1**.〔集合词〕军人,军队。**2**. 军事训练,军事知识[科学]。

sol·do [ˈsɔldəu; ˋsɑldo, ˋsɔldo] *n*. (*pl*. **-di** [-diː; -di]) 索尔多〔意大利铜币,= $\frac{1}{20}$ lira〕。

sole[1] [səul; sol] **I** *n*. **1**. 脚底,跖;鞋底;鞋底皮;袜底。**2**.【农】犁底;垄沟底;蹄底;【筑城】(炮眼的)底面;【船】底板;(高尔夫球棒的)底部。**II** *vt*. 装鞋底,换鞋底;(高尔夫球)使棒底接触地面。~**bar** 车架纵梁。~**channel** *n*. 鞋底缝线的凹槽。~ **mark**【地】底痕。

sole[2] [səul; sol] *n*. (*pl*. ~*s*,〔集合词〕~)【动】鳎科的鱼;舌鳎;箬鳎鱼,板鱼。

sole[3] [səul; sol] *a*. **1**. 单独的,单一的,唯一的。**2**. 孤独的;独立的;独占的。**3**.【法】未婚的,独身的〔主要用于妇女〕。*She was her mother's* ~ *confident*. 她是母亲唯一信任的人。~ *reason* 唯一的理由。~ *rights to a patent* 专利独享的权利。*a feme* ~ 独身女人。***have*** [***be in***] ~ ***charge of*** 单独掌管,是…的总负责人。***have the*** ~ ***responsibility of*** 单独负…的责任。***have the*** ~ ***right of*** 有…的独占权。***on one's own*** ~ ***responsibility*** 单独负责地。~ **trader** 个体商人;不靠丈夫而独立经商的妻子。**-ness** *n*.

sol·e·cism [ˈsɔlisizəm; ˋsɑləˏsızəm] *n*. **1**. 违反语法;文理不通。**2**. 失礼,无礼。**3**. 误谬,背理。

sol·e·cist [ˈsɔlisist; ˋsɑlısıst] *n*. 违反语法的人;失礼的人,不合情理的人。

sol·e·cis·tic [ˌsɔliˈsistik; ˏsɑlıˋsıstık] *a*. 违反语法的;不通的;无礼貌[不合情理]的。

sole·ly [ˈsəulli; ˋsollı] *ad*. 独自,单独;单只;完全。~ *because* [*on account*] *of* 完全为了。~ *for your sake* 只为了你。

sol·emn [ˈsɔləm; ˋsɑləm] *a*. **1**. 严肃的,庄严的。**2**. 仪式隆重的,庄重的。**3**. 一本正经的,装腔作势的。**4**. 重大的,严重的。**5**. 按照仪式的,合仪式的,神圣的,宗教上的。**6**. 黝暗阴沉的。*a* ~ *feast day* 隆重的节日。*give a* ~ *warning* 提出严重警告。*put on a* ~ *face* 装出一本正经的面孔。*a* ~ *oath*【法】正式的誓约。***in*** ~ ***form*** 正式的[地]。

so·lem·ni·fy [səˈlemniˌfai; səˋlɛmnəˏfaı] *vt*. 使严肃,使庄重。

so·lem·ni·ty [səˈlemniti; səˋlɛmnətı] *n*. **1**. 庄严,严肃,庄重,隆重。**2**. 一本正经,装腔作势。**3**.〔常 *pl*.〕仪式;【法】正式。

sol·em·ni·sa·tion, 〔Am.〕**-za·tion** [ˌsɔləmnaiˈzeiʃən; ˏsɑləmnəˋzeʃən, -naıˋze-] *n*. 庄严化;举行典礼[仪式]。~ *of marriage* 举行婚礼。

sol·em·nize [ˈsɔləmnaiz; ˋsɑləmˏnaız] *vt*. 使庄严;举行…的典礼。~ *a marriage* 举行婚礼。

so·len [ˈsəulən; ˋsolən] *n*.【贝】竹蛏。

so·le·no·cyte [səˈliːnəˌsait; səˋlinəˏsaıt] *n*.【生】火焰细胞,管细胞。

so·le·no·glyph [səˈliːnəˌglif; səˋlinəˏglıf] *n*.【动】管牙类(*Solenoglyha*)毒蛇。

so·le·noid [ˈsəulinɔid; ˋsoləˏnɔıd] *n*.【电】螺线管;圆筒形线圈。

sol-fa [sɔlˈfɑː; solˋfɑ] **I** *n*.【乐】唱名;视唱法。**II** *vt*., *vi*. 视唱〔指用唱名来唱,通常看谱即唱〕。~ **syllables** 七唱名(即 do, re, mi, fa 等)。

sol·fa·ta·ra [ˌsəulfəˈtɑːrə; ˏsolfɑˋtɑrɑ] *n*.【地】硫质喷气孔。

sol·fége [sɔlˈfeʒ; sɑlˋfɛʒ] *n*.【乐】**1**. = solfeggio. **2**. 音乐基础理论教学。

sol·feg·gio [sɔlˈfedʒəu, -dʒiːəu; sɑlˋfɛdʒo, -dʒıˏo] *n*. (*pl*. **-feg·gios**, **-feg·gi** [-ˈfedʒi; -fɛdʒı])【乐】**1**. 视唱练习。**2**. 视唱音阶使用〔尤指看谱视唱〕。

so·li [ˈsəuliː; ˋsoli] solo 的复数。

so·lic·it [səˈlisit; səˋlısıt] *vt*. 恳求,乞求,请求;征求;要求,恳求给予。**2**.【法】教唆;诱惑;(妓女)拉(客);送贿赂请求。**3**. 提起(注意);诱发,引发。—*vi*. **1**. 请求,恳求,征求(*for*)。**2**. (妓女)拉客。~ *sb*. *for a thing* = ~ *a thing of sb*. 向某人乞求一件东西。*We* ~ *you for your favours* [*custom*]. = *We* ~ *favours* [*custom*] *of* [*from*] *you*.【商】敬希[敬请]惠顾。~ *for funds* 征求捐款;募捐。**-ant** *n*. 请求者;征求者。

so·lic·i·ta·tion [səˌlisiˈteiʃən; səˏlısəˋteʃən] *n*. **1**. 恳求,请求,恳请;征求。**2**. 诱惑;【法】教唆(罪);(妓女等

的)拉客。**3.** 诱发,引发。

so·lic·i·tor [sə'lisitə; sə`lɪsətɚ] ***n*.** **1.** 恳求者,催促者;求婚者;〔美〕掮客,推销员;募捐人。**2.** 〔英〕初级律师;〔美〕(为一个城市或部门负责法律事务的)法务官。*a S- of the treasury* 〔美〕财政部法务官。~ **general** 〔英〕【法】副检察长;〔美〕司法部副部长;(若干州的)首席司法官。

so·lic·it·ous [sə'lisitəs; sə`lɪsɪtəs] ***a*.** **1.** 热切要求[希望]…的,渴望[热心]…的 (*to do*; *of*)。**2.** 担心的,挂念的,惦记的。**3.** 非常关心[注意]的,非常考究的。~ *to please* 渴望讨人欢喜。~ *of his help* 渴望得到他的帮助。*be* ~ *about* [*for*, *concerning*] (*sb.'s health*) 挂念(某人健康)。~ *in matters of dress* 非常讲究衣着。*a* ~ *inquiry about his health* 对他健康关切的询问。**-ly** ***ad*.** **-ness** ***n*.**

so·lic·i·tude [sə'lisitju:d; sə`lɪsə,tjud, -,tud] ***n*.** **1.** 切望,热心;挂念,担心,关心,渴望。**2.** 〔*pl*.〕担心的事情。*show the warmest* ~ *for* ...向…表示最亲切的关怀。*with the warm* ~ *of* 在…的亲切关怀下。

sol·id ['sɔlid; `sɑlɪd] **I** ***a*.** **1.** 固体的;实心的,实质的,密实的。**2.** 【数】立体的,立方的,三维的。**3.** 结实的,坚强的,坚固的,牢靠的 (*opp*. flimsy, slender, slight);有力的,强健的,扎扎实实的,非浮浅的(学习);确实的,可靠的,忠实的;稳健的。**4.** 慎重的,严肃的;(财政上)稳固的,有资产的。**5.** 团结的,全体一致的。**6.** 纯粹的,全体同质的,十足的(金、银等);全部一样的,齐一的,没有浓淡的(颜色等)。**7.** 完整的,完全的;连续无间断的。**8.** 【哲】(有)实体的。**9.** 【印】(行间)密排的。**10.** 〔美乐俚〕极好的,表演精彩的。**11.** 〔美口语〕亲密的,融洽的(*with*)。**12.** 〔美口〕〔用于 good 之后以加强语气〕着实的,有力的。*a* ~ *body* 固体。~ *food* 固体食物[面包、肉等]。*a* ~ *figure* 立体形。*a* ~ *bath* 【医】(沙浴等)固体浴。*a* ~ *bulb* 【植】球茎。*a* ~ *bullet* 实心子弹。~ *comfort* 真正的安慰。~ *earth* [*ground*] 大地。*a* ~ *man* 稳健的人;有资产的人。~ *gold* 足赤(金)。~ *ivory* 〔美〕头脑迟钝的人。~ *measure* 体积,容积。*a* ~ *problem* 【数】三次方程式问题,解析几何问题。*a* ~ *vote* 全场一致的投票。*for a* ~ *hour* 整整一小时。*a* ~ *matter* 【印】实排印件。*a good* ~ *blow* 着着实实的一击。**be** [**go**] ~ **for** [**in favour of**] 团结一致援助[拥护、赞成]。**be** ~ **with** 〔美俚〕确实可以得到…的援助[拥护]。**get** ~ **with** 〔美俚〕得到…的宠信。**II** ***n*.** 固体;【火箭】固体燃料,火箭火药;【数】立体。**III** ***ad*.** 一致。~ **angle** 【几】隅角。~ **circuit** 【电子】固态电路。~ **colo(u)r** 单色。~ **compound** 【语】固定复合词。~**-drawn** ***a*.** 【冶】整体拉伸制成的(管子等)。~ **earthing** 【无】固定接地。~ **fuel** [**propellant**] 【火箭】固体[态]燃料。~ **geometry** 立体几何。~**-hoofed** ***a*.** 有奇蹄的。~**-horned** ***a*.** 有实角的。~ **motor** 【机】固体燃料发动机。~**-looking** ***a*.** 看来很富足的 (~*-looking well-fed citizens* 看上去日子过得很富裕的老百姓)。~**-state** ***a*.** 固态的,固态学的;固态元件[器件]的(~*-state physics* 固态物理学。*a* ~*-state circuit* 固体电路)。~ **vote** 完全一致的投票。**-ly** ***ad*.** **-ness** ***n*.**

sol·i·da·go [,sɔli'deigəu; ,sɑlə`dego] ***n*.** (*pl*. **-gos**) 【植】秋麒麟草(=goldenrod)。

sol·i·da·rism ['sɔlidərizəm; `sɑlədərɪzəm] ***n*.** **1.** 团结一致。**2.** 社会连带主义〔一种社会学理论,认为利害相关的社会组织是以社会成员的相互依存为基础的〕。

sol·i·da·rist ['sɔlidərist; `sɑlədərɪst] ***n*.** 社会连带主义者。**-ris·tic** ***a*.**

sol·i·dar·i·ty [,sɔli'dæriti; ,sɑlə`dærətɪ] ***n*.** 团结一致,共同一致;共同责任;休戚相关。**in** ~ **with** 声援。

sol·i·dar·ize ['sɔlidəraiz; `sɑlɪdə,raɪz] ***vi*.** 团结一致。

sol·i·dar·y ['sɔlidəri; `sɑlədərɪ] ***a*.** **1.** 团结一致的。**2.** 休戚相关的。

so·lid·i·fi·a·ble [sə'lidifaiəbl; sə`lɪdəfaɪəbl] ***a*.** 可固化的,能凝固的;能团结一致的。

so·lid·i·fi·ca·tion [,səlidifi'keiʃən; ,səlɪdəfə`keʃən] ***n*.** 团结;凝固;【化】固体化(作用)。

so·lid·i·fy [sə'lidifai; sə`lɪdə,faɪ] ***vt*.** (**-fied**) **1.** 使凝固,固化。**2.** 使硬;使结晶。**3.** 使团结。—***vi*.** **1.** 变硬,结晶。**2.** 凝固。**3.** 团结。*the* ~ *ing point* 【物】(凝)固点。

so·lid·i·ty [sə'liditi; sə`lɪdətɪ] ***n*.** **1.** 固态;固体;【物】硬度,强度;【空】稠度;充实。**2.** 坚固,坚牢;牢靠,稳固;殷实;确实。**3.** 【数】体积。**4.** 完整性,连续性。

sol·i·dus ['sɔlidəs; `sɑlɪdəs] ***n*.** 〔L.〕(*pl*. **-di** [-dai; -daɪ]) **1.** 索里达〔古罗马帝国君士坦丁大帝发行的金币;欧洲后来称之为 bezant, 略 s. 或 S.〕。**2.** (表示 shilling, 分数等的)斜线分隔符号(/)〔原为 s 的长体 ʃ: 7/6=7s. 6d. 2/3=三分之二〕。

sol·i·fid·i·an [,sɔli'fidiən; ,sɑlɪ`fɪdɪən] ***n*.**, ***a*.** 唯信论者(的)。**-ism** ***n*.** 唯信论。

so·lil·o·quist [sə'liləkwist; sə`lɪləkwɪst] ***n*.** **1.** 自言自语者。**2.** 【剧】独白者。

so·lil·o·quize [sə'liləkwaiz; sə`lɪlə,kwaɪz] ***vi*.** 自言自语;【剧】独白。

so·lil·o·quy [sə'liləkwi; sə`lɪləkwɪ] ***n*.** (*pl*. **-quies**) 自言自语,【剧】独白。

sol·i·ped ['sɔliped; `sɑlɪpɛd] **I** ***n*.** 单蹄兽[马等]。**II** ***a*.** 单蹄的。

sol·ip·sism ['sɔlipsizəm; `sɑlɪpsɪzm] ***n*.** 【哲】唯我论。**-sist** ***n*.** 【哲】唯我论者。

sol·i·taire [,sɔli'tɛə; ,sɑlə`tɛr] ***n*.** **1.** 独粒宝石的首饰[戒指,耳环等],独粒宝石[钻石]。**2.** 单人纸牌戏;单人球戏;单人象棋。**3.** 〔罕〕隐士。

sol·i·ta·ri·ly ['sɔlitərili; `sɑlɪtərəlɪ] ***ad*.** 孤独寂寞地;孤立地。

sol·i·ta·ry ['sɔlitəri; `sɑlə,tɛrɪ] **I** ***a*.** **1.** 独个儿的,孤独的;独居的。**2.** 寂寞的;冷落的,僻远的,人烟稀少的。**3.** 孤立的;单独的,唯一的。**4.** 【解、植】分离的,单生的。**5.** 【动】孤栖的 (*opp*. social, gregarious)。~ *confinement* [*imprisonment*] 单独监禁。*a* ~ *life* 孤独生活。*a* ~ *ramble* 独自漫步。*a* ~ *exception* 唯一的例外。*a* ~ *place* 冷僻的地方。**II** ***n*.** 独居者;隐士;单独监禁。**-ri·ly** ***ad*.** **-ri·ness** ***n*.**

sol·i·tude ['sɔlitju:d; `sɑlə,tjud] ***n*.** 孤独,独居;寂寞(的地方),幽静(的地方),荒野。**in** ~ 独个儿;孤独地;寂寞地。

sol·ler·et ['sɔlə,ret, ,sɔlə'ret; `sɑlə,rɛt, ,sɑlə`rɛt] ***n*.** 铁靴〔欧洲中世纪盔甲〕。

sol·mi·za·tion [,sɔlmi'zeiʃən; ,sɑlmɪ`zeʃən] ***n*.** 【乐】= sol-fa.

so·lo ['səuləu; `solo] **I** ***n*.** (*pl*. ~**s**, **-li** [-li:; -li]) **1.** 【乐】独奏(曲);独唱(曲);独唱[奏];单人舞。**2.** 单独表演;【空】单飞。**3.** 单人纸牌戏;一种惠斯特纸牌戏(由一人对抗三人)。**II** ***a*.** 独唱[奏]的;单独的;单人的。**III** ***ad*.** 独,单独。**IV** ***vi*.** 独唱,独奏;放单飞。

so·lo·ist ['səuləuist; `so,loɪst, `soləwɪst] ***n*.** 独奏者;独唱者。

So·lo man ['səuləu; `solo] 梭罗人〔爪哇猿人的一种〕。

Sol·o·mon ['sɔləmən; `sɑləmən] ***n*.** **1.** 所罗门(男子名)(H. =peaceable)〔爱称 Sol〕。**2.** 圣人,贤人。**Solomon Is.** 所罗门群岛。~**'s seal** 六角星形(☆)。~**'s-seal** 【植】萎蕤;黄精属植物。

So·lon ['səulɔn; `solən] ***n*.** **1.** 梭伦〔古雅典的立法者〕。**2.** 〔s-〕贤人;明智的立法家;〔美口〕议员。**-lo·ni·an**, **-lonic** ***a*.**

sol·on·chak [,sɔlən'tʃæk; ,sɑlən`tʃæk] ***n*.** 盐土。

sol·o·nets, sol·o·netz ['sɔ:lə,nets; `sɔlə,nɛts] ***n*.** (*pl*. **-netses**, **-netz**, **-netzes**) 碱土。

so-long ['səu'lɔŋ; `so`lɔŋ] ***int*.** 〔口〕再会,再见。

sol·stice ['sɔlstis; `sɑlstɪs] ***n*.** 【天】至,至点;最高点。*the* *summer* [*winter*] ~ 夏[冬]至。

sol·sti·tial [sɔlˈstiʃəl; sɑlˋstɪʃəl] *a*. 至的,夏至的,冬至的。

sol·u·bil·i·ty [ˌsɔljuˈbiliti; ˏsɑljəˋbɪlətɪ] *n*. **1.**【化】溶(解)度,溶(解)性;(可)溶性。**2.** 可解释性,可解(决)性。

sol·u·ble [ˈsɔljubl; ˋsɑljəbl̩] *a*. **1.** 可溶的,易溶解的(*in*)。**2.** 能解释的,能解决的;【数】可解的。~ *glass*【化】水玻璃,溶性玻璃。~ *oil* 溶性油。~ *tar* 轻木焦油。

so·lus [ˈsəuləs; ˋsoləs] *a*. (*fem*. **sola**) **1.** 独自,单独〔主,舞台指挥用语〕。**2.** (汽油店等)销售独家产品的。*I found myself* ~. 〔谑〕我那时是孤零零一个人。*Enter the king* ~. 国王单独登场。

sol·ute [ˈsɔljuːt; ˋsɑljut, ˋsoljut, ˋsolut] *n*.【化】溶质;溶解物。

so·lu·tion [səˈljuːʃən, -ˈljuː-; səˋluʃən, -ˋlju-] *n*. **1.** 溶解;溶液,溶体,溶剂。**2.** (补轮胎用的)橡胶水;〔美〕药水。**3.** 解决,解答(*of*; *for*; *to*);解释;(数学等的)解法,解式。**4.** 免除,解除。**5.**【医】消散,消退。*a nitrate of silver* ~ 硝酸银溶液。*chemical* ~ 化学溶解。*mechanical* ~ 机械溶解。~ **pressure**【化】溶解压力。~ **set**【数】解集。~ **treatment**【冶】固溶处理法。

so·lu·tion·ist [səˈluːʃənist; səˋluʃənɪst] *n*. (报刊上的)疑难解答专家。

So·lu·tre·an, So·lu·tri·an [səˈluːtriən; səˋlutrɪən] *a*. 索鲁特期的〔指欧洲旧石器时代前期文化,因遗址在法国小村索鲁特而得名〕。

solv·a·ble [ˈsɔlvəbl; ˋsɑlvə bl̩] *a*. **1.** 可解释[解答、解决]的。**2.** 可溶解的。**-bil·i·ty** [ˌsɔlvəˈbiliti; ˏsɑlvəˋbɪlətɪ] *n*. **1.** 可解释[解答、解决]。**2.** 溶解能力,溶剂化度。

sol·vate [ˈsɔlveit; ˋsɑlvet] **I** *n*.【化】溶剂化物。**II** *vt*. 使(分子,离子)变成溶剂化物。**-va·tion** [sɔlˈveiʃən; sɑlˋveʃən] *n*.

Sol·vay process [ˈsɔlvei; ˋsɑlve]【化】苏尔未法〔制苏打的一种方法〕。

solve [sɔlv; sɑlv] *vt*. **1.** 解释,说明,解答,解决;调停。**2.** 清偿(债务)。**3.**〔古〕解开,松开(结子)。

sol·ven·cy [ˈsɔlvənsi; ˋsɑlvənsɪ] *n*. **1.**【化】溶解力。**2.** 偿付能力。

sol·vent [ˈsɔlvənt; ˋsɑlvənt] **I** *a*. **1.** 有溶解力的,可溶解的;〔喻〕使(信仰等)瓦解[削弱]的(*of*)。**2.** 有偿付能力的。**II** *n*. **1.**【化】溶剂,溶媒(*of*; *for*)。**2.** 解释,说明。**3.** 使瓦解[削弱]的东西。~ *action* 溶解作用。*Water is the commonest* ~. 水是最普通的溶剂。*Alcohol is a* ~ *of resinous substances*. 酒精是树脂性物质的溶媒。*science as a* ~ *of superstition* 作为破除迷信手段的科学。

sol·vol·y·sis [sɔlˈvɔlisis; sɑlˋvɑləsɪs] *n*.【化】溶剂分解(作用)。

Som. = Somaliland; Somerset(shire)。

so·ma[1] [ˈsəumə; ˋsomə] *n*. (*pl*. ~**ta** [-tə; -tə])【生】(动植物的)躯体[干];体细胞。

so·ma[2] [ˈsəumə; ˋsomə] *n*. **1.** 苏麻液〔吠陀仪式的文献中提到的能令人致醉的一种植物液汁〕。**2.**【植】苏麻(*Sarcostemma acidum*)〔一种马利筋属植物,据猜测即上述液汁的来源〕。

So·ma·li [səuˈmɑːli; soˋmɑlɪ] *n*. (*pl*. ~, ~**s**) **1.** (非洲)索马里人[语]。**2.** (非洲)索马里。

So·ma·li·a [səuˈmɑːliə; səˋmɑlɪə] *n*. 索马里〔非洲〕。

So·ma·li·land [səˈmɑːlilænd; səˋmɑlɪˏlænd] *n*. 索马里〔非洲国家〕。

so·ma·scope [ˈsəuməskəup; ˋsoməˏskop] *n*.【医】超声波检查仪。

so·mat·ic [səuˈmætik; soˋmætɪk] *a*. **1.** 身体的,肉体的。**2.**【生、解】体的。**3.** 躯体的;体壁的;体细胞的。*a* ~ *cell* 体细胞,营养细胞。~ *anthropology* 人体学。

so·ma·tol·o·gy [ˌsəuməˈtɔlədʒi; ˏsoməˋtɑlədʒɪ] *n*. 人类躯体学。

so·ma·to·plasm [ˈsəumətəˌplæzm, səuˈmætə-; ˋsomətəplæzm] *n*.【生】体质,体细胞。**-plas·tic** *a*.

so·ma·to·pleure [ˈsəumətəˌpluə; ˋsomətəˏplʊr] *n*.【胚胎学】胚体壁。**-pleu·ral** *a*.

so·ma·to·type [ˈsəumətəˌtaip; ˋsomətəˏtaɪp] *n*. 体型;体格。

som·bre, 〔Am.〕 **som·ber** [ˈsɔmbə; ˋsɑmbɚ] *a*. **1.** 昏暗的;浅黑的,幽暗的;阴沉的。**2.** 忧郁的。**3.** 暗淡的,不鲜艳的(颜色等)。*a* ~ *countenance* 忧郁[阴沉]的面容。*a* ~ *sky* 阴沉的天空。*a man of* ~ *character* 性格忧郁的人。~ *clothes* 暗色的衣服。*a* ~ *hue* 暗淡的颜色。

som·bre·ro [sɔmˈbrɛərəu; sɑmˋbrɛro, -ˋbrɪro, -ˋbrero] *n*. (*pl*. ~**s**) 墨西哥阔边帽。

som·brous [ˈsɔmbrəs; ˋsɑmbrəs] *a*. 〔诗〕= sombre.

some [强 sʌm, 弱 səm, sm; ˋsʌm, ˏsʌm, səm, sm] **I** *a*. 〔和表示否定、疑问的 any 对应的肯定词〕**1.** (a) [sʌm; sʌm]〔用于单数普通名词前〕(有)一个(人、物、时间)。*He went to* ~ *place in Africa*. 他到非洲一个地方去了。*S- fool or other has broken it*. 是一个蠢家伙把它弄坏了。*We must find* ~ *way out of it*. 得想一个方法逃脱才行。★ some 是指完全不知道的事物而言, a certain 则是在知道而故意不说时、或轻蔑地说'某一个…'时用。(b) [sʌm; sʌm]〔强调〕了不起的,极好的。*He is* ~ *scholar*. 他是了不起的学者。*I call that* ~ *picture*. 我觉得那是很不错的画。*This is* ~ *war*. 这是很像样的战争。**2.**〔用于复数普通名词或物质、抽象名词前表示数量〕(a)〔一般〕[səm, sm; səm, sm] 若干(的),多少(的),一些(的),几分(的),一点儿(的)。*I want* ~ *money*. 我需要一点钱。*I saw* ~ *people I knew*. 我看见了几个熟人。★表示疑问、条件时虽用 any, 但表示劝导、拜托而期待 yes 时则用 some: *May I give you* ~ *tea*? 您喝茶吗? *Will you buy me* ~ *books*? 请您给我买几本书好吗? (b) [sʌm; sʌm]〔强调〕有的(人、物)。*S- people do not like that sort of thing*. 有的人不喜欢那种事。*All wood is not hard*; ~ *wood is soft*. 木料不一定都硬,也有软的。(c) [sʌm; sʌm] 相当多的,不少的。*I stayed there for* ~ *days*. 我在那儿待了好多天了。*You'll need* ~ *courage to face this*. 应付这件事情得有相当勇气。**3.** (a)〔用于数词前〕大约。~ *40 tons in weight* 约重四十吨。(b)〔用于距离、时间的单数名词前〕左右。~ *mile* [*hour*] *or so* 一英里[一个钟头]左右。***after*** ~ ***time*** 过了一会,不久之后。***in*** ~ ***degree*** 多少,几分。***in*** ~ ***way or other*** 设法,想法子。~ ***day*** 改天,他日;(今后)有一天。~ ***days ago*** 几天前。~ ***few*** [***little***] 少许,一点,少数,几个。~ ***more*** [səˈmɔː; səˋmɔr] 再…一点。~ ***one*** [ˈsʌm wʌn; ˋsʌm wʌn] 有人;[ˈsʌmˈwʌn; ˋsʌmˋwʌn] 某一个(人)。~ ***other day*** 改天,过天。~ ***punkins***〔美〕名流;摆架子的人。~ ***time*** 暂时,一会儿(=~day)。~ ***time ago*** 先前,不久以前。~ ***time or other*** 迟早,早晚。

II *pro*. 有些人;有的东西;若干(数量);若干部分,多少,几分,有些(*of*)。*Some of it is spoiled*. 其中有些已经坏了。***and*** (***then***) ~〔美俚〕(比那个)还要多一些。~ ***of these days*** 近日内。

III *ad*.〔英俚、美口〕几分,稍微;〔美口〕很,非常,相当。*look* ~〔美口〕很不错。*That's going* ~. 〔美口〕那很不错,那个倒好极啦。*Do you like it*? — *Some*! 你喜欢那个吗? ——当然。

-some *comb. f*. 表示 **1.** "易于…的","使人…的","有…倾向的": weari*some*, quarrel*some*. **2.**〔附加数词后〕"…个一组": two*some*, four*some*. **3.** "体","染色体": chromo*some*, mono*some*.

some·bod·y [ˈsʌmbədi; ˋsʌmˏbɑdɪ, -ˏbʌdɪ, ˋsʌmbədɪ] **I**

n. 有相当身分的人,重要人物。*think oneself to be (a) ~* 自以为是个大人物。*nobodies posing as somebodies* 冒充大人物的小人物。**II *pro*.** 某人,有人。*S- has disclosed the secret*. 有人把秘密泄露出去了。*General S-* 某某将军。*Call a taxi, ~!* 什么人去叫部出租车来吧! *~ **else*** 别人;了不起的人物。*~ **or other*** 某一个人〔不知道是哪一个〕。

some·day [ˈsʌmdei; ˋsəmˏde] ***ad***. (今后)有一天,改日,有朝一日。

some·how [ˈsʌmhau; ˋsʌmˏhaʊ] ***ad***. 设法,想办法,想个方法;不知道怎样,不晓得什么缘故。*I must get it finished ~*. 我总得想办法把它做完才行。*He ~ dropped behind*. 他不晓得怎么落后了。*~ **or other*** 设法;想办法,不晓得为什么。

some·one [ˈsʌmwʌn; ˋsʌmˏwʌn] **I *pro***. 有人,某人〔同 somebody,但多用于书面语,特别是疑问句或否定句的场合〕。*S- wants to see you*. 有人想会见你。*Why can't she go to the dance with ~ else?* 她为何不能同别人去参加舞会呢? *Would ~ please tell me what it is?* 这是什么东西,请哪位告诉我一下。**II *n***. 重要人士,知名人物。

some·place [ˈsʌmpleis; ˋsʌmples] ***ad***. 〔美〕= somewhere.

som·er·sault, som·er·set [ˈsʌməsɔːlt, -set; ˋsʌmɚˏsɔlt, -set] **I *n***. **1**. 筋斗。**2**. (意见等的)颠倒;一百八十度的转变。*cut [make, throw, turn] ~s* 翻筋斗。**II *vi***. 翻筋斗。

Som·er·ville [ˈsʌməvil; ˋsʌmɚvɪl] ***n***. 萨默维尔〔姓氏〕。

some·thing [ˈsʌmθiŋ; ˋsʌmθɪŋ] **I *pron***. **1**. 某物,某事。**2**. 若干,几分;某类事物〔表示的是模糊的概念〕。**3**. 实有物 (*opp*. nothing)。**4**. 重要事物;要人,名人,有出息的人。**5**. 〔口〕喝的,吃的。*There is ~ in him*. 他这个人是有些道理的。*Here is ~ for you*. 送你一点东西。*What's his name? Jim something*. 他叫什么名字? 吉姆什么的。*It is ~ to have got so far*. 弄到那个地步,挺什么(了不起)的了。*You've got ~ there*. 〔口〕你的话有点道理;那是一个好主意。*take [have] a drop of ~* 喝一点(酒)。*S- is better than nothing*. 聊胜于无。*He is [has] ~ in the Customs*. 他在海关里有一个差事[有点地位]。*He lost his train or (did) ~*. 他也许没赶上火车或是什么的啦。*I caught the five ~ train*. 我赶上五点多的火车。*Theory is ~, but practice is everything*. 理论虽重要,实践更重要。***be ~ of a [an]*** ...有一点…,有些像…的地方 (*I am ~ of a musician*. 我有一点点音乐知识)。***have ~ of the ... in one*** 有…的天分。***have ~ on one's mind*** 有心事。***know ~ of everything and everything of ~*** 通百艺而专一长。***make ~ of*** 将…训练成相当的人物;利用…。***or ~*** 大概是…之类的 (*He is a scientist or ~*. 他大概是科学家之类的人物。*She's got a cold or ~*. 她大概是受了凉)。***see ~ of*** (*him*) 和(他)有些来往;有点认识(他)。*~ **damp*** 〔俚〕酒。*~ **for nothing*** 不费劲得到的好处;轻易得来的利益。*~ **good*** 好东西;赛马的内幕消息。*~ **of*** 在某种意义(或程度)上。*~ **of the kind*** 类似的事物。*~ **on the hip*** 〔美俚〕酒。*~ **short*** 〔俚〕酒。*~ **to write home about*** 值得大书特书的事情。*~ **tells me*** 〔口〕我认为… (*S- tells me my watch isn't quite right*. 我觉得我的手表走得不准)。***think ~ of oneself*** 自以为了不起,自命不凡。

II *ad*. 〔古〕几分,有点,多少,相当。*~ **like*** 〔口〕大约,约;有几分像…的,有点像…的;〔口〕了不起的,极好的,伟大的 (*It must be ~ like six o'clock*. 现在一定是六点钟模样了。*That's ~ like!* 〔口〕那倒是极好的东西!)。

III *n*., *a*., *vt*. 〔委婉语〕= hell, devilish, damn. *What the ~ are you doing here?* 你究竟在这儿干什么? *You ~ villain!* 你这大坏蛋! *I'll see you ~ed first!* 该死的东西!

some·time [ˈsʌmtaim; ˋsʌmˏtaɪm] **I *ad***. **1**. 改天,哪一天;(今后)有一天。**2**. 〔古〕从前,往昔。**II *a***. 以前的。*He was ~ mayor of* ...他以前是…市长。*(the) ~ professor at* ...前任…教授。*~ **ago*** 先前,不久以前。*~ **or other*** 迟早。

some·times [ˈsʌmtaimz, səmˈtaimz; ˋsʌmˏtaɪmz, səmˈtaɪmz] ***ad***. 常常,往往,有时。*~ rich, ~ poor* 有时富,有时穷。★本词可用在句首、句尾、动词前,助动词及 be, have 后: ~ he seemed depressed; I go there ~; I ~ go; I am ~ late.

some·way(s) [ˈsʌmwei(z); ˋsʌmˏwe(z)] ***ad***. 设法,想办法;不知道什么缘故。

some·what [ˈsʌm*h*wɔt; ˋsʌmˏhwɑt, ˋsʌmhwət] **I *ad***. 一点儿,稍微,有点,多少。*He answered ~ hastily*. 他回答得轻率了一点儿。**II *n***. 少量,某些数量;少许,某种程度。*He is ~ of a connoisseur*. 他多少总是一个鉴定家。

some·when [ˈsʌm*h*wen; ˋsʌmˏhwen] ***a***. 〔罕〕= sometime.

some·where [ˈsʌm*h*wɛə; ˋsʌmˏhwɛr, -ˏhwær] ***ad***. 某处,在[到]某处,不知道在[到]什么地方。***I'll see you ~ (in hell) first!*** 混蛋! 讨厌(等)。*~ **about*** 大约,约略;几乎;在…的附近,在…的时候 (*~ about here* 在这附近。*~ about fifty* 约五十岁)。

some·whith·er [ˈsʌm*h*wiðə; ˋsʌmˏhwɪðɚ] ***ad***. 〔古〕到某处,不知道到什么地方。

some·wise [ˈsʌmˌwaiz; ˋsʌmˏwaɪz] ***ad***. 〔古〕某种程度地,不知怎地〔通常构成词组: *in ~*〕。

so·mite [ˈsəumait; ˋsomaɪt] ***n***. **1**. 【动】礼节,环节。**2**. 【解】原节,原椎,初椎。**-mit·ic** [-ˈmitik; -ˋmɪtɪk], **-mi·tal** [-mitl; -mɪtl] ***a***.

som·me·lier [ˌsʌmilˈjei, F. sɔmˈlje; ˏsʌmɪlˋje, F. sɑmˋljɛ] ***n***. (*pl*. ***-liers*** [-jeiz; -jez]) (饭店的)酒侍者;斟酒服务员。

som·nam·bu·late [sɔmˈnæmbjuleit; sɑmˋnæmbjəˏlet] ***vi***., ***vt***. 梦行,梦游。**-lation *n***. **-lator *n***.

som·nam·bu·lism [sɔmˈnæmbjulizəm; sɑmˋnæmbjəˏlɪzəm] ***n***. **1**. 梦行,梦游(症)。**2**. 梦游者的恍惚状态。*artificial ~* 催眠术。

som·nam·bu·list [sɔmˈnæmbjulist; sɑmˋnæmbjəlɪst] ***n***. 梦游(症)者。

som·ni- *comb. f*. 表示"睡眠": *somni*ferous, *somni*loquy.

som·nif·er·ous [sɔmˈnifərəs; sɑmˋnɪfərəs] ***a***. 使睡眠的,催眠的;麻醉的。

som·nil·o·quence, som·nil·o·quy [ˈsɔmˈniləkwəns, -kwi; ˋsɑmˋnɪləkwəns, -kwɪ] ***n***. 说梦话,梦呓。

som·nil·o·quous [sɔmˈniləkwəs; sɑmˋnɪləkwəs] ***a***. (说)梦话的,梦呓的。

som·no·lence, -cy [ˈsɔmnələns, -si; ˋsɑmnələns, -sɪ] ***n***. **1**. 思睡,困倦。**2**. 嗜眠状态;幻梦;恍惚。**3**. 【医】嗜眠(症)。

som·no·lent [ˈsɔmnələnt; ˋsɑmnələnt] ***a***. **1**. 想睡的,困倦的。**2**. 催眠的。**-ly *ad***.

Som·nus [ˈsɔmnəs; ˋsɑmnəs] ***n***. 【罗神】睡神。

SOMPA [ˈsɔmpə; ˋsɑmpə] 〔缩〕System of Multicultural Pluralistic Assessment 〔美〕多种文化兼容评定法〔测定儿童智力的一种方法〕。

son [sʌn; sʌn] ***n***. **1**. 儿子;〔*pl*.〕后裔,子孙。**2**. 国人,国民,居民。**3**. 女婿,养子。**4**. 一分子,会员,党员;子弟;(某一专业或品质的)继承者,从事…的人。**5**. 〔年长者对年轻人的称呼〕年轻人;朋友。**6**. 〔S-〕(与冠词 the 连用)耶稣基督。*a ~ of China* 中国人。*a ~ of man* 任何人。*the ~s of men [Adam]* 人类。*the ~s of Abraham* 亚伯拉罕的子孙,犹太人。*a ~ of the Muses* 诗人。*a ~ of the Mars* 军人。*my ~* 小伙子。*old ~*

老朋友。*a favourite* ~ 1. 宠儿,爱子。2.〔美俚〕本州代表支持的总统候选人,政界红人。*every mother's* ~ 每一个人,大家。*his father's* ~ (容貌、性格)像父亲的人。~ *and heir* 长子。~ *of a bitch* 〔卑〕狗娘养的,婊子养的。~ *of a gun* 王八蛋,狗崽子;家伙;讨厌的工作,完成不了的任务。*a* ~ *of Bacchus* 酒鬼。*a* ~ *of dripping* 厨子。*a* ~ *of ebony* 黑人。*Son of God* 天使;精神上依附上帝的人。*a* ~ *of Momus* 爱嘲弄的人,滑稽的人。~ *of the morning* 趁早赶路的人,旅客。~ *of the soil* 本地人;农民。~ *of toil* 劳动者,工人。*The Son of God* [*Man*] 耶稣基督。*the Sons of Liberty* 〔美史〕自由子弟会。*the Sons of the Revolution* 〔美〕革命子弟会。~**-in-law** (*pl*. ~*s-in-law*) 女婿。**-less** *a*. 无后嗣的。**-ly** *a*. 儿子般的;孝顺的。

so·nance, -cy [ˈsəunəns, -si; ˋsonəns, -sɪ] *n*. 【语音】有声音;发浊音,发成节音。

so·nant [ˈsəunənt; ˋsonənt] **I** *a*. 【语音】有声音的,浊音的;成(音)节的。**II** *n*. 浊音 (*opp*. surd); 成节音。

so·nar [ˈsəunɑː; ˋsonɑr] (= sound operation navigation and range) *n*. 声呐,声波导航和测距系统,音响定位器;潜艇探察仪。

so·na·ta [səˈnɑːtə; səˋnɑtə] *n*. 【乐】奏鸣曲。

so·na·ti·na [ˌsɔnəˈtiːnə; ˏsɑnəˋtinə, ˏsonɑˋtinɑ] *n*. 【乐】小奏鸣曲。

sonde [sɔnd; sɑnd] *n*. 探测装置;探头;探针。

Son·dra [ˈsɔːndrə; ˋsɔndrə] *n*. 桑德拉〔女子名, Sandra 的异体〕。

SONET = Synchronous Optical Network 【电信】同步光学网络。

son et lu·mière [sɔ̃ne lyˈmjɛːr; sɑ̃ nɛ lyˋmjɛr] 1. 照明配音技巧〔表现历史景象,尤指晚上在纪念碑前用特殊的照明效果和现场或录音的解说,音乐等〕。2. 这种景象。

song [sɔŋ; sɔŋ, sɑŋ] *n*. 1. 歌,声乐,唱歌。2. 歌曲;歌曲集;歌词。3. 诗歌,短诗,抒情诗;韵文。4. 鸟叫声,鸟语。*a folk* ~ 民歌。*a love* ~ 爱情歌曲。*a popular* ~ 流行歌曲。***break*** [***burst forth***] ***into*** ~ 唱出。***for a*** (***mere***) ~ = ***for an old*** ~ 非常便宜地,简直等于白送地。***go for a*** ~ 贱价抛出。***not worth an old*** ~ 毫无价值的,白送也不要的。***nothing to make a*** ~ ***about*** 〔俚〕没价值的东西,不值一顾。***sing the*** ~ ***to death*** 反复唱得腻死人。~ ***and dance*** 〔美〕歌舞表演;〔口〕(对质问的)解释;演说;空洞的废话;通词。~**bird** 鸣鸟,鸣禽;女歌手,歌女。~**book** 歌曲集。~**-plugging** 通过反复广播使歌曲流行。~**smith** 作曲家。~ **sparrow** 【动】歌鹀。~ **thrush** 【动】歌鸫。~**writer** 流行歌曲作家。

song·fest [ˈsɔːŋˌfest; ˋsɔŋfest, ˋsɑŋ-] *n*. 〔美〕民歌演唱联欢会。

song·ster [ˈsɔŋstə; ˋsɔŋstɚ] *n*. (*fem*. ***song·stress*** [-tris; -trɪs]) 1. 歌手;歌女;歌曲作者;诗人。2. 鸣禽。

So·nia, So·nya [ˈsəunjə; ˋsonjə] *n*. 索尼娅〔女子名, Sophia 的昵称〕。

son·ic [ˈsɔnik; ˋsɑnɪk] *a*. 1. 【物】(利用)音波的;声音的;音速的。2. 能发声音的。~ **barrier** 【空】声垒,音障。~ **boom** 【空】声震。~ **depth finder** 音响测深仪。~ **guide** 声响导〔一种超声波发射装置,装于盲人所带眼镜上,可使其察知前方物体〕。~ **mine** 感音水雷。~ **pollution** 噪声污染〔指有损健康的超标准噪声干扰〕。**-i·cal·ly** *ad*.

son·i·cate [ˈsɔniˌkeit; ˋsɑnəˏket] *vt*. (*-cat·ed*, *-cat·ing*) 使(细胞,病毒等)经声波处理。**-ca·tion** *n*. **-ca·tor** *n*.

son·ics [ˈsɔniks; ˋsɑnɪks] *n*. 〔动词用单数〕声能学。

so·nif·er·ous [səuˈnifərəs; soˋnɪfərəs] *a*. 发声音的,有声音的;传声的。

son·net [ˈsɔnit; ˋsɑnɪt] *n*. 十四行诗;短诗,商籁体。

son·net·eer [ˌsɔniˈtiə; ˏsɑnəˋtɪr, -ɪˋtɪr] **I** *n*. 十四行诗人;〔蔑〕拙劣的诗人,歪诗作者。**II** *vi*. 作十四行诗。

son·net·ize [ˈsɔniˌtaiz; ˋsɑnɪtˏaɪz] *vt*., *vi*. 写十四行诗,写小诗,写短诗。

son·ny [ˈsʌni; ˋsʌnɪ] *n*. 〔口〕〔爱称〕宝宝;孩子,年轻人。

son·o·buoy [ˈsɔnəbɔi; ˋsɑnəbɔɪ] *n*. 【军】声纳浮标;航空侦潜仪。*a radar* ~ 雷达声纳浮标。

so·nom·e·ter [səuˈnɔmitə; soˋnɑmətɚ] *n*. 【物】弦音计;振动频率计;【医】听力计。

so·no·rant [səˈnɔːrənt, səu-; səˋnɔrənt] *n*. 【语音】响辅[子]音。

so·no·rif·ic [ˌsəunəˈrifik; ˏsɑnəˋrɪfɪk] *a*. 发声音的。

so·nor·i·ty [səˈnɔriti; səˋnɔrətɪ, -ˋnɑr-] *n*. 1. 洪亮,响亮(度)。2. 洪亮的音调,响亮的语声[声调]。

so·no·rous [səˈnɔːrəs; səˋnɔrəs, -ˋnor-] *a*. 响亮的,洪亮的。**-ly** *ad*. **-ness** *n*.

son·ship [ˈsʌnʃip; ˋsʌnʃɪp] *n*. 为人子,儿子身分。

son·sie, son·sy [ˈsɔnsi; ˋsɑnsɪ] *a*. 〔英方〕1. 来喜(的),致福(的),幸运的。2. 好看的;体态丰满的,胖得圆滚滚的,血色好的。3. 性情温和的,脾气好的。4. 舒服的,惬意的。

Soo·fee, Soo·fee·ism [ˈsuːfi, ˈsuːfiizəm; ˋsufɪ, ˋsufɪɪzəm] = Sufi, Sufism.

soo·gan [ˈsuːgæn; ˋsugæn] *n*. 〔美俚〕毯子,被单。

sook [suːk; suk] *n*. = souk.

sool [suːl; sul] *vt*. 〔Aus.〕1. 嗾(狗)去咬。2. (猎狗)撕咬(猎物)。3. 敦促,力劝。

soon [suːn; sun] *ad*. 1. 立刻,即刻,马上;一会儿,不久,没多时。2. 快,早。3. 高兴地,欣然。4. 宁愿,不如〔用 sooner 形,常和 would, should, had 等连用〕。*You spoke too* ~. 你说得太急了〔忍一下就好了〕。*S- got*, ~ *gone* [*spent*]. 来得容易去得快。*You will* ~ *get the better of that fellow*. 像他那样的家伙你是不难胜过他的。*S- learned*, ~ *forgotten*. 学得快,忘得快。*Winter has come rather* ~ *this year*. 今年冬天来得早。~ *at five o'clock* 一到五点钟就。***as*** ~ ... ***as*** 〔和 would, could 等连用〕要是能…的话就会…,与其…不如…(*He could as* ~ *write an epic as drive a car*. 他要是能开汽车就会写叙事诗啦。*I would just as* ~ *take a walk* (*as stay at home*). 我(与其待在家里)还不如去散步)。***as*** ~ ***as*** 一…就 (*He got there as* ~ *as he graduated*. 他一毕业就去那里了)。***as*** ~ ***as possible*** 尽快。***at the*** ~***est*** 无论怎样快。***none too*** ~ 在恰到好处的时候。***no*** ~***er*** ... ***than*** ... 一…就… (*No* ~*er said than done*. 一说就实行了;风驰电掣地做了)。~***er or later*** = ~ ***or late*** 迟早,早晚。***The*** ~***er the better*** 越快[早]越好! ***would*** ~***er*** ... (***than***) (与其)…不如 (*I would* ~*er die than do it*. 与其做这事,不如死掉好)。

soon·er [ˈsuːnə; ˋsunɚ] *n*. 1. 〔美〕(在政府开放西部前)抢先取得占有权的人;用不正当手段先下手的人。2. 〔*pl*.〕俄克拉荷马 (Oklahoma) 州人的绰号;〔S-〕~ **State** 捷足州〔俄克拉荷马州的别名〕。

soot [sut; sʊt, sut] **I** *n*. 煤烟(灰),烟炱,油烟;锅灰。**II** *vt*. 煤烟弄脏,弄得尽是煤烟。

sooth [suːθ; suθ] **I** *n*. 〔古〕事实,实际。***for*** ~ 事实上,的确。***in*** (***good***) ~ 〔古〕事实上,其实,真实地。~ ***to say*** = ***to tell the*** ~ 老实说,说老实话。**II** *a*. 1. 〔古〕真实的,真正的。2. 〔诗〕抚慰的;光滑的。~**fast** *a*. 〔古〕说实话的,忠实的;真实的。~**say** *vi*. 预言,预示。~ **sayer** *n*. 1. 占卜者,预言者。2. 【虫】螳螂。~ **saying** *n*. 占卜,预言。

soothe [suːð; suð] *vt*. 1. 安慰,劝慰,抚慰;使镇定(神经、感情),使平静。2. 缓和,减轻,减少(痛苦等)。3. 奉承。~ *a crying baby* 哄哭着的孩子。**-er** *n*. 1. 安慰者[物];奉承拍马者。2. (哄婴儿的)橡皮奶嘴。

sooth·ing [ˈsuːðiŋ; ˋsuðɪŋ] *a*. 1. 安慰性的。2. 缓和的,减轻(痛苦)的;起镇定作用的;催眠的。**-ly** *ad*.

soot·i·ness [ˈsutinis; ˋsʊtɪnɪs] *n*. 烟炱,尽是烟垢;烟垢

状,乌黑。

soot·y [ˈsuti, ˈsuːti; ˋsutɪ, ˋsutɪ] *a*. **1**. 煤烟的,煤灰的;(尽是)烟垢的;烟垢状的。**2**. 给煤烟弄脏的;覆盖着烟炱的。**3**. 乌黑的。~ *smoke* 浓黑的乌烟。*a* ~ *tern*【鸟】乌燕鸥。~ **mold**【生】烟霉(菌)。

SOP, S.O.P. = standing [standard] operating procedure【军】标准作战规定;〔美俚〕标准操作规定,标准做法。

sop [sɔp; sɑp] **I** *n*. **1**. (泡在肉汤、牛奶等中的)面包片;湿透的东西。**2**. (出于让步,息事宁人而给与的)东西;贿赂,让步。**3**. 〔英俚〕傻瓜,懦夫;〔美俚〕酒鬼。*The ground is a mere* ~. 地面湿透啦。***give*** [***throw***] ***a*** ~ ***to Cerberus*** 〔喻〕用贿赂收买。~ ***in the pan*** 煎面包;一口好吃的东西,好滋味。**II** *vt*. 把…泡在肉汤[牛奶等]里;使湿透;用贿赂收买 (*up*)。—*vi*. 泡;湿透;(液体)渗透 (*in, into, through*)。

sop. = soprano.

soph [sɔf; sɑf] *n*. 〔美口〕= sophomore.

So·phi·a [səˈfaiə; səˋfaɪə, ˋsofɪə] *n*. 索菲娅〔女子名〕。

So·phie [ˈsəufi; ˋsofɪ] *n*. 索菲〔女子名〕。

soph·ism [ˈsɔfizəm; ˋsɑfɪzəm] *n*. 诡辩。

soph·ist [ˈsɔfist; ˋsɑfɪst] *n*. **1**. 〔常 S-〕(古希腊以教授修辞学、哲学为职业并以善于诡辩出名的)智者;诡辩学者。**2**. 诡辩家;博学者。

soph·ist·er [ˈsɔfistə; ˋsɑfɪstɚ] *n*. **1**. 诡辩家 (= sohpist)。**2**. 大学的二年级学生 (= junior ~);(英国某些大学的)三年级学生 (= senior ~)。

so·phis·tic, -ti·cal [səˈfistik, -tikəl; səˋfɪstɪk, -tɪkəl] *a*. (古希腊)诡辩学派的;诡辩的,强辞夺理的。~ *reasoning* 诡辩式推理。**-ti·cal·ly** ***ad***.

so·phis·ti·cate [səˈfistikeit; səˋfɪstɪˏket] **I** *vt*. **1**. 用诡辩欺骗;使迷惑;强辞夺理,牵强附会,窜改。**2**. 把杂物掺入(酒、烟等)降低品质,掺杂,掺假,掺坏,伪造。**3**. 使(人)世故,使(人)懂事;使失去天真纯朴。**4**. 使复杂,使精致。**5**. 〔古〕使堕落,使腐化。—*vi*. 强辞夺理,诡辩。**II** *n*. 世故深的人。

so·phis·ti·cat·ed [səˈfistikeitid; səˋfɪstɪˏketɪd] *a*. **1**. 非自然状态的;掺杂的,不纯真的;矫揉造作的;伪造的。**2**. 老于世故的,世故深的,富有经验的,老练的。**3**. (技术、产品等)复杂的,尖端的,高级的;微妙的。**4**. (文学作品等)理智上吸引人的,深奥微妙的,精致的。*a* ~ *oil* 掺假的油。~ *electronic devices* 尖端的电子装置。*a* ~ *adolescent* 老于世故的青少年。*a* ~ *columnist* 老练的专栏作家。*a* ~ *novel* 思想内容深奥的小说。

so·phis·ti·ca·tion [səˌfistiˈkeiʃən; səˏfɪstɪˋkeʃən] *n*. **1**. 玩弄诡辩;诡辩;牵强附会。**2**. 丧失天真,变世故。**3**. 伪品;掺杂品;伪造。

so·phis·ti·ca·tor [səˈfistikeitə; səˋfɪstɪketɚ] *n*. **1**. 诡辩者,强辞夺理的人。**2**. 掺杂者。

soph·ist·ry [ˈsɔfistri; ˋsɑfɪstrɪ] *n*. **1**. 诡辩(法)。**2**. 似是而非的推理[论证];诡辩法的应用。

soph·o·more [ˈsɔfəmɔː, -mɔə; ˋsɑfmˏor, -ˏɔr] *n*. **1**. 〔美〕大学[中学]二年级学生。**2**. 第二年的工作人员。**3**. 自以为有学问而实际上幼稚浅薄的人。**-mor·ic, -mor·i·cal** *a*. 〔美〕二年级学生(气派)的;幼稚而自大的。

So·phy [ˈsəufi; ˋsofɪ] *n*. 〔古〕(16—17 世纪)波斯统治者。

-sophy *comb. f*. 表示"知识","学问": philo*sophy*.

so·pite [ˈsəupait; ˋsopaɪt] *vt*. **1**. 使入睡。**2**. 〔古〕结束,解决。

sopor [ˈsəupə; ˋsopɚ, -pɔr] *n*. 〔L.〕【医】迷睡,酣睡。

so·po·rif·er·ous [ˌsəupəˈrifərəs; ˏsopəˋrɪfərəs, ˏsɑpə-] *a*. 引起迷睡[酣睡]的;催眠的。**-ly** ***ad***. **-ness** ***n***.

so·po·rif·ic, -i·cal [səupəˈrifik, -ikl; sopəˋrɪfɪk, -ɪkl] **I** *a*. 催眠的;令人思睡的,嗜眠的;酣睡的,迷睡的。**II** *n*. 安眠药。**-i·cal·ly** ***ad***.

sop·o·rose [ˈsɔpərəus; ˋsopəros, ˋsɑpəˏros] *a*. 迷睡的,酣睡的;嗜眠的。

sop·ping [ˈsɔpiŋ; ˋsɑpɪŋ] **I** *a*. 湿透的,浸透的。**II** ***ad***. 湿透。

sop·py [ˈsɔpi; ˋsɑpɪ] *a*. **1**. 浸湿的,泡湿的;湿透的。**2**. 多雨的,潮湿的(路、天气等)。**3**. 〔英口〕感情柔弱的,易动感情的;易感伤的。***be*** ~ ***on*** 对(女人等)易动情的。

so·pra·ni·no [ˌsəupræˈniːnəu; ˏsoprəˋnino] **I** *a*.【乐】特高音乐器的。**II** *n*. 特高音乐器〔尤指英国八孔笛(*recorder*)〕。

so·pra·no [səˈprɑːnəu; səˋpræno, -ˋprɑno] **I** *n*. (*pl*. ~*s*, **-*ni*** [-niː; -ni]) **1**.【乐】女高音,高音部。**2**. 女高音歌手;唱最高音者。**II** *a*. 女高音的;最高音的。**-pran·ist** *n*. 女高音歌手;唱最高音者。

-sor *comb. f*. = -or.

so·ra [ˈsɔːrə; ˋsorə] *n*. 〔美〕【动】秧鸡 (*Porzana carolina*)〔多见于北美洲沼泽〕(= ~ rail)。

Sorb [sɔːb; sɔrb] *n*. 索布人〔德国境内一少数民族〕;温德人;索布语。

sorb[1] [sɔːb; sɔrb] *n*.【植】**1**. 花楸树,山梨树。**2**. 花楸果,山梨果〔产于欧洲〕。

sorb[2] [sɔːb; sɔrb] *vt*. 吸附,吸收。

sor·bate [ˈsɔːbeit; ˋsɔrbet] *n*. **1**. 吸着物。**2**.【化】山梨酸盐。

sor·be·fa·cient [ˌsɔːbiˈfeiʃənt; ˏsɔrbəˋfeʃənt] **I** *a*.【医】促进吸收的。**II** *n*. 吸收促进药。

sor·bent [ˈsɔːbənt; ˋsɔrbənt] *n*.【化】吸着剂。

sor·bet [ˈsɔːbət; ˋsɔrbət] *n*. 果汁冰水。

Sor·bi·an [ˈsɔːbiən; ˋsɔrbɪən] **I** *a*. 索布人的;索布语的。**II** *n*. 索布人;索布语。

sor·bic acid [ˈsɔːbik; ˋsɔrbɪk] *n*.【化】山梨酸,己二烯酸;己邻隔二烯酸。

sor·bi·tol [ˈsɔːbiˌtɔːl, -ˌtəul; ˋsɔrbəˏtol, -tɑl] *n*.【化】山梨[葡萄]糖醇,葡[花楸]醇。

Sor·bonne [sɔːˈbɔn; sɔrˋbɑn, -ˋbʌn] *n*. (巴黎)索本神学院;(16—17 世纪)巴黎大学神学院;(现在)巴黎大学的文理学院,〔泛指〕巴黎大学。

Sor·bonn·ist [sɔːˈbɔnist; sɔrˋbʌnɪst, ˋsɔrbənɪst] *n*. 巴黎大学的神学家[神学院学生];巴黎大学文理学院毕业生[学生]。

sor·bose [ˈsɔːbəus; ˋsɔrbos] *n*.【化】山梨糖;花楸糖。

sor·cer·er [ˈsɔːsərə; ˋsɔrsərɚ] *n*. (*fem*. **-*ceress*** [-ris; -rɪs]) 巫师,术士。

sor·cer·y [ˈsɔːsəri; ˋsɔrsərɪ] *n*. 巫术;邪术,妖术。

sor·did [ˈsɔːdid; ˋsɔrdɪd] *a*. **1**. 肮脏的,邋遢的,不清洁的;破烂不堪的。**2**. 心地不纯的,卑鄙的;贪鄙的,贪婪的,吝啬的。**3**. 可怜的,悲惨的。**4**.【植、动】泥色的;色彩暗淡的。~ *slum* 污秽的贫民窟。~ *motives* 卑鄙的动机。*live in* ~ *poverty* 生活在贫困中。**-ly** ***ad***. **-ness** ***n***.

sor·dine [ˈsɔːdiːn; ˋsɔrdin] *n*.【乐】弱音器;弱音踏板。

sor·di·no [sɔːˈdiːnəu; sɔrˋdino] *n*. (*pl*. ***sordini*** [-ˈdiːniː; -ˋdini]) 〔It.〕【乐】= sordine.

sor·dor [ˈsɔːdə; ˋsɔrdɚ] *n*. 不幸;悲惨;卑鄙;肮脏;污秽;下贱。

sore [sɔː, sɔə; sor, sɔr] **I** *a*. **1**. 痛的,疼痛发炎的;(一碰就)疼痛的;受了伤的,皮肤擦破了的,发肿的,生着疮的。**2**. 辛苦的,吃力的(工作等);激烈的,猛烈的,厉害的。**3**. 痛心的,伤心的;悲哀的。**4**. 〔俚〕恼怒的,恼火的,动辄发脾气的。**5**. 〔古〕痛切的,迫切的。**II** ***ad***. 〔古、诗〕= sorely. *a* ~ *throat* 喉痛。*a* ~ *subject* 使人难堪的话题。~ *distress* 非常贫困。*a* ~ *loser* 一输就恼火的人。***a sight for*** ~ ***eyes*** 受欢迎的,悦目的人[物、景致(等)]。***be*** ~ ***about*** 对…痛心[发愁,觉得难过,生气,觉得不高兴,觉得厌恶]。***be*** ~ ***up*** 〔美俚〕发怒。***feel*** ~ 痛;生气。***get*** (***sb***.) ~ 〔口〕(使人)生气,动怒。***in*** ~ ***need of*** 极端需要…。***like a bear with a*** ~ ***head*** 脾气极大的,拗性的。**III** *n*. **1**. 一碰就疼的地方,(伤)痛处;疮肿,溃疡。**2**. 一想起来就难过的事情,伤心事。*a hard* ~ 下

疳。*an open* ~ 积弊。*bed* ~*s* 褥疮。*old* ~*s* 旧伤;旧恨,难过的[伤心的]回忆(等)。~ **place** [**point, spot**] 〔主喻〕触及痛处的问题,一提起来就叫人难为情、生气、痛苦、起反感的问题。~ **throat** 咽喉炎。**-ness** *n*.

sore·back [ˈsɔːbæk; ˋsɔr͵bæk] *n*. 〔美〕维吉尼亚州人的绰号。

sore·head [ˈsɔːhed; ˋsor͵hɛd, ˋsɔr-] *n*. 〔美口〕脾气大[牢骚多]的人,〔尤指〕落魄政客。

sore·ly [ˈsɔːli; ˋsorlɪ, ˋsɔr-] *ad*. **1**. 疼痛地;痛苦地。**2**. 严厉地;猛烈地,激烈地,厉害地。**3**. 非常,很。*be* ~ *oppressed* 痛受压迫。

sor·ghum [ˈsɔːgəm; ˋsɔrgəm] *n*. **1**.【植】蜀黍,高粱;[S-]蜀黍(属)。**2**. 高粱糖浆。**3**. 甜得发腻的东西;过度描述柔情;令人肉麻的文字。*sweet* ~ 甜高粱。

sor·go, sor·gho [ˈsɔːgəu; ˋsɔrgo] *n*.【植】芦粟,甜高粱。(=sweet sorghum)。

so·ri [ˈsəurai; ˋsoraɪ, ˋsɔraɪ] *n*. sorus 的复数。

sor·i·cine [ˈsɔːriˌsain, -sin, ˈsɔri-; ˋsɑrɪ͵saɪn, -sɪn, ˋsɔrɪ-] *a*. 鼩鼱的,似鼩鼱的。

so·ri·tes [səuˈraitiːz; səˋraɪtiz] *n*. **1**.【逻】复合三段论。**2**. 诡辩推理。

sorn [sɔːn; sɔrn] *vi*. 〔Scot.〕**1**. 不请自去地赖着吃赖着住 (*on*),强求膳宿。**2**. 乞求,强求。**-er** *n*. 强求膳宿的人。

so·rop·ti·mist [sɔːˈrɔptimist; səˋrɑptəmɪst] *n*. 国际妇女俱乐部成员;职业妇女福利互助会会员。

so·ror·al [səˈrɔːrəl; səˋrɔrəl, -ˋror-] *a*. 姐妹的,姐妹般的。**-ly** *ad*.

so·ro·rate [səˈrɔːrit; ˋsɔrə͵ret, ˋsor-] *n*. 内妹填房的风俗〔妻子不育或死亡,丈夫娶其一个妹或几个妹为妻〕。

so·ror·i·cide [səˈrɔːriˌsaid; səˋrɑrə͵saɪd] *n*. **1**. 杀害亲姐妹的行为。**2**. 杀害亲姐妹者。**-cid·al** *a*.

so·ror·i·ty [səˈrɔriti; səˋrɔrətɪ, -ˋrɑr-] *n*. 妇女社团;〔美〕大学女生联谊会。

so·ro·sis [səˈrəusis; səˋrosɪs] *n*. **1**.【植】聚花果,椹果[凤梨、菠萝、桑果]等。**2**. 妇女俱乐部。

sorp·tion [ˈsɔːpʃən; ˋsɔrpʃən] *n*.【化】吸着(作用)。**-tive** *a*.

sor·ra [ˈsɔrə; ˋsɑrə] *ad*. 〔爱俚〕= not; never.

sor·rel[1] [ˈsɔrəl; ˋsɔrəl, ˋsɑr-] **I** *a*. 红褐色的,栗色的(马等)。**II** *n*. **1**. 红褐色,栗色。**2**. 栗色的动物。**3**. 三岁的雄鹿。

sor·rel[2] [ˈsɔrəl; ˋsɔrəl, ˋsɑr-] *n*. 含酸液的植物〔如酸模、酢浆草等属的植物〕。

sor·row [ˈsɔrəu; ˋsɑro] **I** *n*. **1**. 悲哀,悲痛,伤心;忧伤,哀悼;悲叹;悔恨,惋惜,遗憾,抱歉。**2**. 可悲的事情,伤心事,不幸;魔鬼。**3**. 悲哀的原因,伤心的原故。*S- comes unsent for*. 悲哀不招自来。*the Man of S-s* 耶稣。*the muckle* ~ 〔Scot.〕魔鬼。*He has had many* ~*s*. 他遭遇过种种不幸。**cause much** ~ **to** 使…非常伤心;给…造成许多烦恼。**express one's** ~ **for one's mistake** 对错误表示遗憾。**II** *vi*. 悲痛,悲叹,惋惜,哀掉 (*for*; *at*; *over*)。**III** *ad*. 〔爱口〕〔常作 sorra〕= not; never. ~ **a bit** 一点儿也没有。~ **drowner** 〔美〕酒。**~-striken** *a*. 哀伤的,悲痛的。

sor·row·ful [ˈsɔrəufəl; ˋsɑrofəl] *a*. **1**. 悲伤的,悲叹的;悲惨的。**2**. 可悲的,可怜的;悔恨的,可惜的,抱歉的。**-ly** *ad*. **-ness** *n*.

sor·ry [ˈsɔri; ˋsɔrɪ, ˋsɑrɪ] *a*. **1**. 〔用作 pred.〕可怜的;觉得难过的 (*for*; *to do*; *that* ...);懊悔的,觉得过意不去的 (*for*);抱歉的,对不起的,遗憾的;惋惜的,可惜的。**2**. 拙劣的,卑劣的;不中用的;没价值的;不成样子的,不体面的;可悲的,悲惨的。**3**. 悲哀的,悲伤的。*I am* ~ *for you*. 我很替你难过。*I am* ~ *for it*. 很抱歉,对不起。*I am* ~ *about it*. 那很遗憾。*I am* (*so*) ~. = 〔口〕*So* ~! = *S-*! 对不起。*You will be* ~ *for this some day*. 你有一天要懊悔这件事的。*Say you are* ~ *and I will forgive you*. 你说你错了我便饶你。*I'm* ~ *for him but it's his own fault*. 可惜那是他自己不对(怨谁呢)。*I am* ~ *to say that I cannot come*. 很遗憾,我不能来。*in a* ~ *state* [*plight*] 处在可怜的境地中。*a* ~ *excuse* 卑劣的借口。*a* ~ *end* 可悲的结局。**cut a** ~ **figure** 出丑。**make a** ~ **spectacle of oneself** 出洋相。(**feel**) ~ **for oneself** 〔口〕垂头丧气,灰心失望。**-ri·ly** *ad*. **-ri·ness** *n*.

sort [sɔːt; sɔrt] **I** *n*. **1**. 种类,类别,品种;种。**2**. 品质,本性,性质。**3**. 方法,情形,样子,程度。**4**. 某种人[物]。**5**.【印】〔主 *pl*.〕一套铅字;〔*pl*.〕【纺】并级毛,同型毛。**6**. 〔古〕(一)群,(一)伙。*all* [*several*, *these*, *those*] ~*s of hats* 所有各种[种种,这几种,那几种]帽子。*He is a good* [*bad*] ~ (*of a fellow*). 〔口〕他是好[坏]人。*He is the right* ~. = *He's my* ~. 他倒是挺合适的人,他正是我需要的人。*Queer* ~ (*of a thing*) *this*! 〔口〕这(东西)倒挺妙。*I don't believe anything of the* ~. 我不相信这种事情。*He is not my* ~. 他那种人我不喜欢。*That's your* ~. 就是这个样呀;〔俚〕那样做挺好。*This copy is hard* [*runs*] *on* ~*s*.【印】这件稿子要用几种铅字排。**after** [**in**] **a** ~ 有些,有几分,稍微。**all of a** ~ 差不多,大同小异。**all** ~(*s*) **of** = **of all** ~**s** 一切种类的,各种各样的。**a** ~ **of** 一种;可以说是…的东西〔*cf*. *of a* ~〕。**in any** ~ 无论如何,必须。**in a** ~ **of way** 略为,比较。**in some** ~ 多少,稍微。**no** ~ **of** 毫无。**nothing of the** ~ 根本没有那种事情,决没有那种事情。**of a** ~ 同一种[类];相当的;勉强称得上的,较差的,所谓的 (*a war of a* ~ 所谓的战争。*a poet of a* ~ 蹩脚的诗人)。**of every** ~ **and kind** 各种各样的。**of one's** ~ 和某人同样身分[性质、品性]的。**of** ~**s** 〔口〕**1**. = of a ~. **2**. 各种各样的,未经挑选的。**of the** ~ 那样的。**out of** ~**s** 觉得不舒服;情绪不好;没有精神;【印】铅字不全。~ **of** = ~ **o'** 〔美口〕〔用作副词〕几分,有点,稍微 (~ *of moist* 有点湿。*I* ~ *of expected it*. 我料到几分了。*Now* ~ *of turn round*! 来稍微转动一下吧)。

II *vt*. 分类;整顿,整理;分选,拣 (*out*)。—*vi*. 〔英古〕一致,相配,适合 (*with*)。~ *letters* 拣信。*a* ~*ing room* [*clerk*] (邮局)拣信室[员]。~ *out* 清理。

sort·a [ˈsɔːtə; ˋsɔrtə] *ad*. 〔美俚〕= sort of.

sort·er[1] [ˈsɔːtə; ˋsɔrtɚ] *n*. **1**. 分类者;选别者,分选者;(邮局)拣信员。**2**.【自】分类器;分类装置;清选机,选别机;(纤维长度)分析器。

sort·er[2] [ˈsɔːtə; ˋsɔrtɚ] *ad*. 〔方、俚〕= sort of.

sor·tes [ˈsɔːtiːz; ˋsɔrtiz] *n*. 〔*pl*.〕〔L.〕签,阄;(翻书)占卜。~ *Homericae* [hoˈmerisiː; hoˋmɛrɪsi] 翻荷马诗占卜。

sor·tie [ˈsɔːti(ː); ˋsɔrti, -tɪ] *n*. **1**.【军】出走;突围;出港。**2**. 出击部队。**3**. (飞机出动的)架次。

sor·ti·lege [ˈsɔːtilidʒ; ˋsɔrtl̩ɪdʒ] *n*. **1**. (抽签)占卜,阄占。**2**. 巫术,妖术。

sor·ti·tion [sɔːˈtiʃən; sɔrˋtɪʃən] *n*. 抽签,拈阄。

so·rus [ˈsɔːrəs; ˋsorəs] *n*. (*pl*. ***-ri*** [-rai; -raɪ])【植】孢子堆;(蕨类的)囊群。

-sory *comb. f*. = -ory.

SOS, S.O.S. [ˈesəuˈes; ˋɛs͵oˋɛs] (= Save Our Souls [Ship]; Suspend Other Service)【讯】失事信号,呼救信号;发失事信号;(= Service of Supply)【军】后勤部,供应署;(= silicon on sapphire) 矽[硅]蓝宝石制作技术。

so-so [ˈsəusəu; ˋso͵so] *a*., *ad*. 一般的(地),还过得去(地);不好也不坏的(地),马马虎虎的(地)。~ *reaction* 〔美〕(观众的)不怎样热烈的喝彩。

sos·te·nu·to [ˌsɔsteˈnuːtəu; sɑstəˋnuto] **I** *ad*. 〔It.〕【乐】自制地,沉着地;集中地并且节奏准确地;保持速度〔通常是中速〕。**II** *n*. (*pl*. ~*s*, ***-ti***) 像上述那样演奏[演唱](部分)。

sot [sɔt; sɑt] **I** *n*. 酒鬼。**II** *vi*. 滥喝,拚命喝酒。

S

so·te·ri·ol·o·gy [səuˌtiəriˈɔlədʒi; soˌtɪrɪˋɑlədʒɪ] ***n.*** 【宗】灵魂拯救〔尤指信耶稣灵魂得救〕;灵魂拯救论[学]。**-log·i·cal** [-ˈlɔdʒikl; -ˋlɑdʒɪkl] ***a.***

So·thic [ˈsəuθik; ˋsoθɪk, ˋsɑθɪk] ***a.*** 【天】天狼星的。***S-Cycle*** [***period***] (古埃及历法)天狼星周期〔=1460天狼星年〕。***S- year*** (古埃及历法)天狼星年〔=365 1/4日〕。

So·tho [ˈsəuθəu; ˋsoθo] ***n.*** **1.** (*pl.* ***So·thos, So·tho***) (南非)索托人。**2.** 索托语。

sot·ted [ˈsɔtid; ˋsɑtɪd] ***a.*** 醉得稀里糊涂的,昏昏沉沉的。

sot·tish [ˈsɔtiʃ; ˋsɑtɪʃ] ***a.*** **1.** 酒鬼似的,滥喝酒的。**2.** (因饮酒过多而)愚蠢的,迟钝的,糊涂的。

sot·to vo·ce [ˈsɔtəuˈvəutʃi; ˋsɑtoˋvotʃɪ] 〔It.〕低声地;把声音压住。

sou [suː; su] ***n.*** (*pl.* ~*s*) 苏〔法国旧铜币;合五生丁〕。*He hasn't a* ~. 〔口〕他一个钱也没有。

sou·bise [suːˈbiːz; suˋbiz] ***n.*** 苏比斯调味汁〔主要成分为融化奶油和洋葱〕。

sou·brette [suːˈbret; suˋbrɛt] ***n.*** 〔F.〕**1.** 【剧】喜剧中风骚的女仆或轻佻的女人;饰同上角色的女演员;在喜歌剧中担任配角的女高音演员。**2.** 女仆。

sou·bri·quet [ˈsəubrikei; ˋsubrɪˏke] ***n.*** = sobriquet.

sou·chong [ˈsuːˈʃɔŋ, -tʃɔŋ; ˋsuˋʃɔŋ] ***n.*** 〔Chin.〕小种毛尖[红茶]。

Sou·dan [su(ː)ˈdæn; suˋdæn] ***n.*** = Sudan.

Sou·da·nese [ˌsuːdəˈniːz; ˏsudəˋniz, -ˋnis] ***a.***, ***n.*** = Sudanese.

souf·flé [ˈsuːflei; suˋfle, ˋsufle] ***a.***, ***n.*** 〔F.〕苏法莱,蛋奶酥〔与打松了的蛋白和奶油搅拌在一起而焙烤的点心〕。

S

sough [sau; sʌf, sau] **I** ***n.*** 飕飕,飒飒〔风等的声音〕。**II** ***vi.*** (风)飕飕地响,飒飒地吹。

sought [sɔːt; sɔt] seek 的过去式及过去分词。

souk [suːk; suk] ***n.*** (北非和中东的)露天市场。

soul [səul; sol] **I** ***n.*** **1.** 灵魂,心灵 (*opp.* body);精神;气魄;热情;道义力量。**2.** 精华,精髓,要素。**3.** 化身,典型。**4.** 领唱者,领袖,首脑,中心人物。**5.** 人。**6.** 〔美〕(黑人表演激起的)强烈感情。**7.** (美国)黑人文化的特征;黑人种族的自豪感。*His whole* ~ *revolted from it.* 他十分讨厌它。*Not a* ~ *was to be seen.* 一个人也没有。*Be a good* ~ *and help me.* 好孩子来帮帮我的忙。*There's a good* ~. 好孩子〔安慰小孩子、仆人等的话〕。*a good* ~ 〔口〕好人。*a thirsty* ~ 酒徒。*Poor* ~! 〔插入句〕可怜。**II** ***a.*** 〔美〕黑人的,黑人文化的,黑人控制的。*a* ~ *radio station* 黑人广播电台。***All Souls' Day*** 万灵节。***by my*** ~ 真的,的的确确。***cannot call one's*** ~ ***one's own*** 完全受别人支配。***for my*** ~ = ***for the*** ~ ***of me*** 一定;无论如何也。***have no*** ~ 没有骨气;(作品等)没有感情。***in my*** ~ ***of*** ~***s*** 天地良心。***keep body and*** ~ ***together*** 苟延残喘。***possess one's*** ~ ***in patience*** 忍耐。***sell one's*** ~ ***for*** 为了…出卖灵魂,作出一切牺牲去得到…。~ ***and body*** 热心地。~ ***aviator*** 〔美〕牧师。***the*** ~ ***of hono(u)r*** 诚实的人。***the very life and*** ~ ***of*** …的灵魂[领袖等]。***to save my*** ~ = *for the* ~ *of me*. ***upon*** (*or* ***'pon, on, 'on***) ***my*** ~ = *by my* ~. ***with one's heart and*** ~ 全神贯注;全心全意。~ **brother** 〔美〕黑人男子。~**-destroying** ***a.*** 消磨精神的,毁灭灵魂的。~**-doctor** 〔俚〕牧师;精神病医生。~ **food** 〔口〕美国南部黑人的传统食物〔如小肠,火腿胫,玉米面包,萝卜缨等〕。~ **kiss** (舌接触舌的)接吻,深深的亲吻。~ **mate** 意气相投的朋友;情人。~ **music** 激情的爵士音乐。~**-searching** 反省,内省。~ **sister** 〔美〕黑人女子。

soul·ful [ˈsəulfəl; ˋsolfl] ***a.*** **1.** 精神[灵魂]上的。**2.** 热情的,充满激情的。**-ly** ***ad.***

soul·less [ˈsəullis; ˋsollɪs] ***a.*** **1.** 缺乏高尚精神的,没有灵魂的。**2.** 卑鄙的;残酷的;无情的。**3.** 没有表情的,发呆的。**-ly** ***ad.***

sound[1] [saund; saʊnd] **I** ***a.*** **1.** 健全的;强壮的,正常的;完好的,无疵的,没有腐烂的(船、牙齿等)。**2.** 正确的;正当的,合法的;合理的,见解正确的;合逻辑的。**3.** 坚牢的,坚固的;确实的,安全的,可靠的,稳当的;正派的;正统的。**4.** 有偿付能力的,资金充实的(公司等)。**5.** 严厉的,厉害的;充分的(睡眠等)。**6.** 【法】有效的。**II** ***ad.*** 充分地。*A* ~ *mind in a* ~ *body.* 有健全的身体才有健全的精神。~ *fruit* 完好的水果。~ *argument* 有充分根据的论点。*a* ~ *policy* 健全的政策。*a* ~ *opinion* 合理的意见。*a* ~ *analysis* 中肯的分析。*a* ~ *investment* 稳妥的投资。*I gave him a* ~ *beating.* 我把他痛打了一顿。*The child is* ~ *already.* 〔口〕孩子已经睡熟了。*sleep a* ~ *sleep* 睡一个畅快的觉。***as*** ~ ***as a bull*** [***colt, roach***] 很健全[健康]。~ ***in wind and limb*** 〔口〕身体健全的。

sound[2] [saund; saʊnd] **I** ***n.*** **1.** 音,响,音响;声音;发音。**2.** 噪音,闹声,各种声音。**3.** 音调;语调;笔调,含意。**4.** 听力的范围。**5.** (唱片、电影等的)录音材料。**6.** 音乐风格。**7.** 〔古〕谣传,名声;意义;印象。***out of*** ~ ***of*** 在听不见…的地方。~ ***and fury*** 喧嚣吵嚷。***within*** ~ ***of*** 在听得见…的地方。**II** ***vi.*** **1.** 响;反响,鸣响;发声音,发音;用声音传播;传播;召唤。**2.** 听来像,令人觉得。**3.** 【法】具有…的性质,具有…的要求 (*in*)。*The bugle* ~*s to battle.* 号角召唤去战斗。*His voice* ~*s as if he had a cold.* 他的声音听起来总像是伤了风似的。*His story* ~*s incredible.* 他的故事听起来难以使人置信。*This* ~*s like a fiction.* 这简直像编成的故事一样。*Strange as it may* ~. 也许听起来奇怪。*The plan* ~*s good.* 这个计划听着不错。*How does this proposal* ~ *to you?* 你以为这个提案怎样? *His action* ~*s in damages.* 他的诉讼具有要求赔偿的性质。— ***vt.*** **1.** 弄响(电铃等)。**2.** 吹号命令,吹…号;吹号[打钟](等)通知,吹号庆祝。**3.** (用语言)表达,发表。**4.** 宣告;传布。**5.** 敲(听声音)检(查);【医】敲诊。~ *the charge* [*retreat*] 吹冲锋[退却]号。~ *an alarm* 发出紧急警报。~ *the lungs* 听诊肺音。~ ***sb.'s*** [***one's own***] ***praises*** 夸奖某人[自己]。~ ***off*** **1.** 〔美俚〕大声说;呱啦呱啦地说;说大话;发牢骚。**2.** 【军】依次报数;呼行军口令(一、二、一等);奏序曲。~**-and-light** (舞厅等)音响与灯光变幻配合的;声光表演的。~ **arrester** 隔音装置。~ **barrier** 【空】音障,声垒。~ **bite** (电台或电视台播放的)一小段评论,三言两语的评述;反复播放的,一小段录像。~**-bite** ***vi.*** 三言两语地说,言简意赅地说。~ **box** (乐器的)共鸣匣;留声机唱头。~ **camera** 同步录音摄影机。~ **card** 【计】声卡。~ **detector** 检声器;测音器;【无】伴音信号检波器。~ **effects** (广播、电视节目、电影等的)音响效果。~ **engineer** 音响[声学]工程师。~ **film** **1.** 录音胶片。**2.** 有声电影。~ **locator** 【物】声波定位器。~ **man** 音响效果操作者。~ **pollution** 噪音污染。~ **projector** 有声电影放映机。~**proof** **1.** ***a.*** 防音的,隔音的。**2.** ***vt.*** 防音,隔音;设防音装置。~ **ranging** 音源探测(法);声波测距(法)。~ **recorder** 录音机。~ **recording** 录音。~ **recordist** 〔美〕【影】录音技师。~ **spectrograph** 分音仪。~ **tosser** 〔美〕【无】播音员。~ **track** 【影】音带,声带;声迹。~ **truck** 广播车。~ **wave** 音波;声波。

sound[3] [saund; saʊnd] **I** ***vi.*** **1.** 测水深;探测(上层空气)。**2.** 试探(别人的意见);调查(可能性)。**3.** (鱼或鲸鱼)突然潜入海底。— ***vt.*** **1.** 测量(海深);锤测;探测。**2.** 【外】用探针检查(尿道等)。**3.** 试探(别人的意见) (*out*)。~ (*out*) *sb. on* [*about*] *a question* 打听某人对某一个问题的意见。**II** ***n.*** 【医】探子,探条,探针。

sound[4] [saund; saʊnd] ***n.*** **1.** 港,海峡;海湾。**2.** 【动】气胞,鳔。**3.** 乌贼,鱿鱼。

sound·er [ˈsaundə; ˋsaʊndɚ] ***n.*** **1.** 发声物[者];【电】发声器,(发)声(收)码器。**2.** 测探员;测深器;【外】探针。*an echo* ~ 回声[回波]探测器。~ **key** 【电】发声电钥。

sound·ing[1] [ˈsaundiŋ; ˋsaʊndɪŋ] ***n.*** **1.** 声距测量,测深。

2.【气】探空,测高。3.〔*pl*.〕测锤到达的水底;(测得的)水深;〔*pl*.〕底质[测锤附带上来的泥沙]。4.【医】探通术,探针诊断。5.【影】发声。*air* ~ 大气探测。*rocket* ~ 用火箭探测大气。***be in*** [***come into***] ~***s*** 在测锤到达的地方;在(进入)水浅的地方[指鲸鱼]。***be out of*** [***off***] ~***s*** 在测锤下达不到的地方。***get off*** ~***s*** 到测锤达不到的地方去;碰到不得意的事情。***get on*** ~***s*** 来到测锤能达到的地方;做着得意的事,渐入佳境。***strike*** ~***s*** 测量水深。***take*** ~***s in*** 测…的水深。~ **balloon**【空】探空气球。~ **lead** 测深铅锤。~ **line** 测深索。~ **rocket** 探空火箭。~**-rod** (量水舱用)量水尺。

sound·ing[2] [ˈsaundiŋ; ˋsaʊndɪŋ] ***a***. 1. 作声的,响亮的。2. 夸张的,言过其实的;空洞的,唱高调的。3. 堂堂的,给人深刻印象的。~ *rhetoric* 空洞的言词。~ *promise* 好听的语言。*a* ~ *oratory* 夸张的演说。*a* ~ *title* 堂皇的头衔。~ **board** 1. 共鸣[共振]板。2. (设在舞台上方或后方增加音响洪亮度的)回声结构。3. 用来扩散舆论的人或物,"传声筒"。4. (用来测验外界对某种意见的反应的)反应灵敏的人。

sound·less [ˈsaundlis; ˋsaʊndlɪs] ***a***. 1. 深不可测的,无底的。2. 无声的,寂静的;不响的。**-ly** ***ad***.

sound·ly [ˈsaundli; ˋsaʊndlɪ] ***ad***. 1. 完好的,无疵地;健全地;稳健地;坚固地;壮健地;正确地;正当地;确实地。2. 严厉地,厉害地。3. 酣畅地。*sleep* ~ 酣睡。

sound·ness [ˈsaundnis; ˋsaʊndnɪs] ***n***. 1. 完好;健全;稳健,确实。2. 坚固;公正,正当。3. 坚固性,坚固度。

soup[1] [suːp; sup] ***n***. 1. (浓)汤。2. 浓汤般的东西;浓雾;硝化甘油;显影液。3.【法】〔英俚〕分配给资历较浅的律师承办的刑事案件。4.〔美俚〕电。5.〔口〕不幸的境遇,困境。*eat* ~ 喝汤。*a* ~ *hound* 爱参加宴会做客的人。**in the** ~〔俚〕受困,在困难中。~ **and fish**〔俚〕男式晚礼服。~ **kitchen** (救济贫民的)施食处;〔美俚〕(汽车式)流动食堂。~ **maigre** 菜汤。~ **plate** 汤盘。~ **spoon** 汤匙。

soup[2] [suːp; sup] **I** ***n***. 〔空俚〕(发动机的)马力;加大了的马力[效率]。**II** ***vt***. 加大马力。~ ***up*** 加大马力;加快(飞机)速度。~**ed-up** ***a***. 1. 加大马力的。2. 加工后变得吸引人的。

soup·çon [ˈsuːpˈsuŋ; supˋsuŋ] ***n***. 〔F.〕怀疑,嫌疑;(可疑的)痕迹;少量,一点点 (*of*)。***not a*** ~ ***of*** 一点没有。

soup·er·y [ˈsuːpəri; ˋsupərɪ] ***n***. 〔美〕餐厅,食堂。

soup·fin shark [ˈsuːpfin ʃɑːk; ˋsupfɪnˋʃɑrk] ***n***. 翅鲨〔其翅可作中菜"鱼翅"〕。

soup·y [ˈsuːpi; ˋsupɪ] ***a***. 1. 浓汤似的。2.〔美口〕雾浓的;阴雨的(天气)。3.〔美俚〕故作多情的;过于多愁善感的。

sour [ˈsauə; saʊr] **I** ***a***. 1. 酸的,酸味的;变酸了的,酸腐的。2. 发酵的。3. 乖张的,乖戾的;愁眉不展的,愠怒的,不开心的;尖酸刻薄的;令人厌恶的,乏味的。4. 坏的,错的;敌对的;不再迷恋的。5.【农】酸性土壤的,瘦瘠的,冷湿的,不毛的(土地等)。6. 没有达到一般[预期]标准[品质]的。7. 酸性反应的。*a* ~ *fellow* 脾气乖张的人。~ *looks* 一肚子不高兴的样子。~ *cream* 酸奶油。~ *milk* 酸奶。*be* ~ *on*〔美俚〕嫌恶,憎厌。~ *grapes* 酸葡萄〔可望而不可及之物〕。**II** ***n***. 1. 酸味,酸东西。2. 讨厌的东西;痛苦,苦恼。3.〔美〕酸味饮料;酸味鸡尾酒。*The sweet and* ~ *together*. 有苦有乐。***get in*** ~〔美俚〕不和,失去…的好感;遇到麻烦。***take the sweet with the*** ~ 对人生苦乐满不在乎。***the sweet and*** ~ ***of life*** 人生的苦乐。**III** ***vt***. 1. 弄酸;使酸败;败坏。2. 使性情乖僻,使情绪不好。3. (漂白时)用弱酸处理;使(土地等)冷湿,使不毛。—***vi***. 1. 变酸;酸败。2. 性情变乖僻,情绪不好。~ ***on***〔美〕讨厌;憎恶。~ **ball** 1. (夹心)酸糖球[水果糖]。2.〔俚〕诉苦者;老是口出怨言的人。~ **cherry**【植】(欧洲)酸樱桃(树)。~**crout**, ~**krout** ***n***. = sauerkraut. ~ **gum**〔美〕= black gum【植】多花紫树。~**humus** 粗腐殖质。~ **mash** 酸麦芽汁〔造威士忌酒用〕。~ **orange**【植】酸橙(树)。~ **salt** 酸味盐〔调味等用,如柠檬酸、酒石酸结晶体〕。~**sop**【植】刺果番荔枝(树)。~ **top**〔美俚〕脾气别扭的人。~**-wood** 一种开白花,叶有酸味的欧石南属小树。**-ly** ***ad***. **-ness** ***n***.

source [sɔːs; sors, sɔrs] **I** ***n***. 1. 源头,水源,源泉。2. 根源,本源;来源。3. 原因;出处;原始资料。4. 提供消息的人。5. 血统。*the* ~ *of wealth* 富源。*historical* ~*s* 史料。*a reliable* [*an authoritative*] ~ 可靠[权威]人士。***draw*** [***have***] ***from a good*** ~ 由可靠方面听到[得到]。***take its*** ~ ***at*** 发源于,出自,起于。***trace to its*** ~ 追根寻源。**II** ***vt***. 〔美〕从(他处)获得(原料、零部件等)。~ **book**〔美〕原始资料集,史料集。~ **language** 始发语言 (*opp*. target language)。~**-material** 原始资料。**-d** ***a***. (消息等)有来源的,有出处的。

sour·dine [suəˈdiːn; sʊrˋdin] ***n***. 【乐】弱音器;噪音抑制器。

sour·dough [ˈsauədəu; ˋsaʊrˏdo] ***n***. 1.〔美西北部、加拿大〕〔口〕探矿者;垦荒者;在阿拉斯加过冬的人;老资格,老手。2. 发面底子,酵种,面肥。

sour·puss [ˈsauəpus; ˋsaʊrˏpʊs] ***n***. 〔美俚〕面色阴沉的人;性情乖戾的人。

sou·sa·phone [ˈsuːzəfəun; ˋsuzəˏfon] ***n***. 大号〔一种大型的吹奏乐器。主要用于军乐队〕。

souse[1] [saus; saʊs] **I** ***n***. 1. 盐渍品,腌货;腌猪耳[脚、头]。2. 腌渍用的盐水。3. 腌浸,泡。4. 浸透,湿透。5.〔美俚〕酒鬼,狂饮。*get a thorough* ~ *in a thunderstorm* 在雷雨中淋得浑身湿透。*give* (*sb*.) *a* ~ (把人)浸入水里。**II** ***vt***. 1. 腌,泡在盐水里,浸入水里。2. 使湿透,泼(水)。3.〔俚〕灌醉。—***vi***. 1. 泡在水里;使湿透。2. 喝醉。***be*** ~***d to the skin*** 浑身湿透。~ ***it***〔美俚〕住嘴,不做声。~ ***oneself***〔美〕洗手洗脸。

souse[2] [saus; saʊs] **I** ***vi***. 〔古〕(鹰等)猛扑下来。—***vt***. 扑在…上面,向…飞扑;猛地扑下而撞倒。**II** ***n***. (鹰在拦截鸟时的)猛扑。**III** ***ad***. 扑通一声;飞扑地,倒栽葱地。

soused [saust; saʊst] ***a***. 腌渍的;〔俚〕喝醉了的。

sou·tache [ˈsuːtɑːʃ; suˋtæʃ] ***n***. 〔F.〕(衣服镶边用的)饰带。

sou·tane [suːˈtɑːn; suˋtɑn] ***n***. (天主教)祭司的法衣。

South [sauθ; saʊθ] ***n***. 索斯〔姓氏〕。

south [sauθ; saʊθ] **I** ***n***. 1. 南;南方。2. 南国居民。3.〔诗〕南风。4.〔the S-〕(一国或一地区的)南方,南部;〔美〕南部各州;【美史】南部邦联;地球的南部〔尤指南极地区〕;〔S-〕南〔国际政治上指工业技术和经济不够先进的国家。*North-South dialogue* 北南对话〔指发展中国家和西方发达国家之间的集体贸易谈判〕。**II** ***a***. 1. 南的,南方的。2. 在南的,向南的;自南方的。**III** ***ad***. 向南方;在南方;自南方。*the far* ~ = *the South Pole* 南极。*the* ~ *country* 南英格兰。*the S- Downs* (*of Hampshire and Sussex*) 南方草原。*S- Island* 南岛〔新西兰(纽西兰)两主岛之一〕。*S- Pole* 南极。*the S- Sea* 南太平洋。*the S- Seas* 南洋。*a* ~ *aspect* 南面。*a* ~ *window* 南面的窗子。*down* ~ (向)南部各州;(向)南方边疆地方。**IV** [sauð, sauθ; saʊð, saʊθ] ***vi***. 1. 转向南方。2.【天】(天体)向南走;越过子午线,过南北线。~ **bound** ***a***. 向南走的,往南去的。~ **by east** 南偏东〔正南偏东 11°15′〕。~ **by west** 南偏西〔正南偏西 11°15′〕。~ **land**〔美〕美国南部(各州) = Dixie. ~**paw** ***a***., ***n***. 〔美〕左撇子;【棒球】惯用左手的;左手投手。

South Africa [sauθ ˈæfrikə; saʊθ ˋæfrɪkə] 南非。

South·amp·ton [sauθˈæmptən; saʊθˋhæmptən, saʊˋθæmptən] ***n***. 南安普敦〔英国港市〕。

South China Sea [ˈsauθˈtʃainəsiː; ˋsaʊθˋtʃaɪnəsi] 南海〔中国〕。

South Carolina [ˈsauθ ˌkærəˈlainə; saʊθ ˏkærəˋlaɪnə] 南卡罗来纳〔美国州名〕。

South Dakota [ˈsauθ dəˈkəutə; ˋsaʊθ dəˋkotə] 南达科他〔美国州名〕。

South·down [ˈsauθdaun; ˋsaʊθˏdaʊn] **I** ***a***. 英国南岗

S

(South Downs)的。II *n*. 英国南岗羊;南岗羊肉。

south·east [ˈsauθˈiːst;ˏsaʊθˋist] I *n*. 1. 东南〔泛指东南方向;正东以南 45°;略作 S E〕。2. 〔S-〕(美国)东南部。~ *by east* 东南偏东。~ *by south* 东南偏南。II *a*. 1. 位于东南的;向东南的。2. 来自东南的。III *ad*. 在东南;向东南;从东南。

south·east·er [ˈsauθiːstə;ˏsaʊθˋistɚ] *n*. 东南大风。

south·east·er·ly [sauθˈiːstəli;ˏsaʊθˋistɚlɪ] I *a*. 向[在、自]东南的。~ *gale* 东南烈风。II *ad*. 向[在、自]东南。III *n*. 东南大风。

south·east·ern [sauθˈiːstən;ˏsaʊθˋistɚn] *a*. 1. 向[在、自]东南的。2. 东南部的;〔S-〕美国东南部的。

south·east·ern·most [sauθˈiːstənməust;ˏsaʊθˋistənˏmost] *a*. 东南端的;最东南的。

south·east·ward [sauθˈiːstwəd;ˏsaʊθˋistwɚd] *a*., *ad*. 向东南的[地]。**-ly** *a*., *ad*. 向东南的[地],自东南的[地]。

south·east·wards [sauθˈiːstwədz;ˏsaʊθˋistwɚdz] *ad*. 向东南。

South·end-on-Sea [ˈsauθˈendɔnˈsiː; ˋsaʊθˋendɑnˋsi] *n*. 滨海绍森德〔英国港市〕。

south·er [ˈsauðə;ˋsaʊðɚ] *n*. 南风,南暴风。

south·er·ly [ˈsʌðəli; ˋsʌðɚlɪ] *a*., *ad*. 南,在南(的);向南(的);从南方来(的)。*a* ~ *course* 南方航线。*sail* ~ (船)向南航行。

south·ern [ˈsʌðən; ˋsʌðɚn] I *a*. (*superl*. ~ **most**) 1. 南的,在南的;向南的;从南的。2. 南方的,南部的,南国的。3. 朝南的,南向的。4. 〔S-〕〔美〕南部各州的,从南部各州来的;有南方地区特征的。II *n*. 南方人,南部人;〔S-〕美国南部方言。*a* ~ *aspect* 南向。*a* ~ *course* 南方航线。~ *trade* 南洋贸易。**the S- Cross**【天】南十字座。~ **hemisphere** 南半球。~ **lights** 南极光。~**wood**【植】青蒿。**-er** *n*. 南方人;〔S-〕南部英格兰人;〔美〕南部各州的人。

Southey [ˈsauði, ˈsʌði; ˋsaʊðɪ, ˋsʌðɪ] *n*. 索西〔姓氏〕。

south·ing [ˈsauðiŋ; ˋsaʊðɪŋ] *n*. 1.【海】南向,南进;南航。2.【天】南向纬度差;南中(天);南赤纬。

south·ron [ˈsʌðrən; ˋsʌðrən, ˋsʌðərən] *n*. 南方人;〔S-〕〔Scot. 蔑〕英格兰人;〔美〕南部各州的人。

south-south·east [ˈsauθsauθˈiːst;ˏsaʊθsaʊθˋist] I *n*. 东南南〔正东以南 22°30′;略作 SSE〕。II *ad*., *a*. 1. 在[向]东南南方(的)。2. 来自东南南方(的)。

south-south·west [ˈsauθsauθˈwest;ˏsaʊθsaʊθˋwɛst] I *n*. 西南南〔正南以西 22°30′;略作 SSW〕。II *ad*., *a*. 1. 在[向]西南南方(的)。2. 来自西南南方(的)。

south·ward [ˈsauθwəd; ˋsaʊθwɚd] I *ad*., *a*. 向南方(的)。II *n*. 向南方向,南方地区。**-ly** *ad*., *a*. 向南方(的);来自南方(的)。

south·wards [ˈsauθwədz; ˋsaʊθwɚdz] *ad*. 向南方。

South·well [ˈsauθwəl; ˋsaʊθwəl] *n*. 索斯韦尔〔姓氏〕。

south·west [ˈsauθˈwest;ˏsaʊθˋwest] I *n*. 1. 西南〔泛指西南方向,或指正西以南 45°;略作 SW〕。~ *by south* 西南偏南〔即西南偏南 11°15′;写为 S33°45′W〕。~ *by west* 西南偏西〔即西南偏西 11°45′,写为 S56°15′W〕。2. 〔S-〕一国或一地区的西南部。II *a*. 1. 位于西南的;向西南的。2. 来自西南的。*a* ~ *wind* 西南风。III *ad*. 在西南;向西南;从西南。

South West Africa 西南非洲。

south·west·er [sauθˈwestə;ˏsaʊθˋwestɚ] *n*. 1. 西南大风,西南大风暴。2. 海员用的防水帽。

south·west·er·ly [sauθˈwestəli;ˏsaʊθˋwestɚlɪ] *ad*., *a*. 1. 在(或向)西南(的)。2. 来自西南(的)。

south·west·ern [sauθˈwestən;ˏsaʊθˋwestɚn] *a*. 1. (在)西南的;向西南的。2. 来自西南的。*a* ~ *wind* 西南风。3. 〔S-〕一国或一地区的西南部的。**-er** *n*. 西南人,住在西南部的人;〔S-〕美国西南部人。

south·west·ward [sauθˈwestwəd;ˏsaʊθˋwestwɚd] I *ad*., *a*. 向西南(的)。II *n*. 西南方向;西南地区。**-ly** *ad*., *a*. 向西南(的);来自西南(的)。

south·west·wards [sauθˈwestwədz;ˏsaʊθˋwestwɚdz] *ad*. 向西南。

sou·ve·nir [ˈsuːvəniə;ˏsuvəˋnɪr, ˋsuvəˏnɪr] *n*. 1. 回忆,追忆。2. 纪念品[礼物]。*This year book ekes out* ~ *of my life in the university*. 这本年鉴帮助我追忆大学生活。~**sheet** (印在纸片上的)纪念邮票。

sou'·west [ˈsauˈwest; ˋsaʊˋwest]【海】= southwest.

sou'·west·er [ˈsauˈwestə; ˏsaʊˋwestɚ] *n*. = southwester.

sov., **sovs**. = sovereign(s).

sov·er·eign [ˈsɔvrin; ˋsɑvrɪn, ˋsʌv-] I *a*. 1. 握有主权的,独立自主的。2. 元首的,国王的。3. 拥有最高权力的。4. 最高的,最上的。5. 优秀的,极好的。6. 完全的。7. 有特效的(药)。II *n*. 1. 主权者;君主,元首。2. 主权国,独立国。3. 〔英口〕金镑〔=20 先令〕。*a* ~ *state* 主权国家。~ *authority* [*power*] 主权[最高权力]。*a* ~ *prince* 君主,元首。*a* ~ *remedy* 特效药。*the* ~ *good* 至善。*show a* ~ *contempt for useless formalities* 表现出对无味的形式的完全蔑视。**-ly** *ad*.

sov·er·eign·ty [ˈsɔvrinti; ˋsɑvrɪntɪ, ˋsʌv-] *n*. 1. 主权,宗主权。2. 君权,统治权。3. 主权国家。*S- will not suffer any infringement*. 主权不容侵犯。

so·vi·et [ˈsəuviet; ˋsovɪɪt, ˏsovɪˋet] I *n*. 1. 〔前苏联〕苏维埃,代表会(议)。2. 〔the S-〕= S- Russia. 3. 〔*pl*.〕苏联人。II *a*. 苏维埃的;〔S-〕苏联的。*the S- Government* (1991 年前的)苏联政府。*the S- people* 苏联人民。*The Russian S- Federated Socialist Republic* 俄罗斯苏维埃联邦社会主义共和国〔前苏联一加盟共和国,略作 R. S. F. S. R.;1991 年苏联改制为独立国协[独联体]后成为独立国家,改名"俄罗斯"〕。*S- Union*, *the Union of S- Socialist Republics* 苏维埃社会主义共和国联盟〔略 U.S.S.R. (苏联),1991 年改制为独立国协[独联体]〕。

So·vi·et·ol·o·gist [ˌsəuvieˈtɔlədʒist;ˏsovɪəˋtɑlədʒɪst] *n*. 研究苏维埃制度的专家;苏联问题专家。

sov·khoz [sɔːvˈkɔːz;sɔvˋkɔz] (*pl*. *sovkhozy*, *sovkhozes* [-ˈkɔːzi, -ˈkɔːziz;-ˋkɔzɪ, -ˋkɔzɪz]) *n*. 〔俄〕国营农场。

sov·ran [ˈsɔvrən; ˋsɑvrən, ˋsʌv-] *n*., *a*. 〔诗〕= sovereign.

sow[1] [səu; so] *vt*. (~*ed*; ~*ed*, *sown*) 1. 播,撒;播种,种。2. 散播,传播;惹起。3. 使密布。*Let's* ~ *our field with rice*. 让我们在田里种稻子吧。*Tom handed in a paper sown with grammatical mistakes*. 汤姆交上去一份满是文法错误的读书报告。—*vi*. 播种。*You must reap what you have sown*. = As a man ~s, *so he shall reap*. 种瓜得瓜种豆得豆。~ **discord** 散播不和,挑拨离间。~ **the sand** 白费气力。~ **the seeds of** (*revolution*) 播下(革命)的种子。

sow[2] [sau; saʊ] I *n*. 母猪;【冶】高炉铁水沟;炉底结块;火铸型;沟铁;大型铸铁;【军】攻城掩舍(= ~ bug)。II *a*. 〔美〕雌的。*You cannot make a silk purse out of a* ~*'s ear*. 猪耳朵做不出丝钱袋来。~ *bosom* 〔美〕腌肋肉,咸肉。*a* ~ *cat* 〔美〕母猫。**as drunk as a** (**David's**, **Davy's**) ~ 烂醉如泥的。**get** [**have**, **take**] **the wrong** [**right**] ~ **by the ear** 〔俚〕弄错[弄对]人,拿错[拿对]东西;见解错误[不错],论断错误[不错],解答错误[不错](等)。~**back** 山脊,沙丘。~**belly** 〔口〕碱猪肉。~**bread**【植】野生仙客来。~ **bug**【虫】土鳖,地鳖,蜱蛾。~**-gelder** 〔古〕阉割母猪卵巢的工人;〔英俚〕下流人物,肮脏鬼。~ **thistle**【植】苦苣菜。

so·war [səuˈwɑː; səˋwɑr, -ˋwɔr] *n*. (印度的)骑兵;传令骑兵。

sow·ens [ˈsəuənz, suː-;ˋsoənz, su-] *n*. 〔*pl*.〕〔Scot.〕发酵燕麦麸粥。

sow·er [ˈsəuə; ˋsoɚ] *n*. 1. 播种者;播种机。2. 散布者;

提倡者,发起人,创办人。

sown [səun; son] sow[1]的过去分词。

sox [sɔks; sɑks] *n*. 〔美俚〕短袜(= socks)。

soy [sɔi; sɔɪ] *n*. **1**. 中国酱油。**2**. 大豆,黄豆。~**-bean** 〔美〕= soya-bean. ~**milk** 豆浆。

so·ya(-bean) [ˈsɔiə(biːn); ˋsɔɪə(bin)] *n*. 大豆;〔英〕= soybean. ~ *cake* 豆饼。

So·ya [ˈsəujɑː; ˋsojɑ] **Strait** 宗谷海峡〔连接日本海和鄂霍次克海〕。

so·zin [ˈsəuzin; ˋsozɪn] *n*. 【生化】(动物体内的)抗菌素,抗毒素。

soz·zled [ˈsɔzld; ˋsɑzəld] *a*. 〔俚〕烂醉的。

SP = shore patrol (美国海军或海军陆战队的)岸上宪兵,基地宪兵。

S.P. = **1**. small pica. **2**. supraprotest. **3**. single phase. **4**. stirrup pump 镫式(手摇)灭火泵。

Sp. = Spain; Spaniard; Spanish.

sp. = **1**. special; specialist. **2**. species. **3**. specific. **4**. spell; spelled, spelling. **5**. spirit. **6**. specimen.

s.p. = 〔L.〕 *sine prole* 无子女(= without issue)。

spa [spɑː; spɑ, spɔ] *n*. **1**. 矿泉,温泉;温泉疗养地。**2**. 游乐胜地[豪华旅馆]。**3**. 〔美〕(新英格兰的药房等附设的)冷饮部。~ **cuisine** 保健菜肴〔指有营养的低热量食品〕。

space [speis; spes] **I** *n*. **1**. 空间;太空。**2**. 空隙,空地;场地;(火车轮船飞机中的)座位;余地;篇幅。**3**. 空白;间隔;距离。**4**. (一段)时间;片刻;一会儿。**5**. 【乐】(谱表的)线间空白,线间;区间。**6**. 【印】隔条,衬条,空铅;空铅间隔;印刷物(或书写)的行间空白,打字稿一格或一行的宽度。**7**. 【电】开键。**8**. 电台(电视)为广告节目留出的时间。**9**. 〔美〕一年徒刑。*celestial* ~ 天空。*outer* ~ 外层空间;星际[宇宙]空间,外太空。*leave a* ~ 留空白。*blank* ~ 空白。*an open* ~ 空地。*a dangerous* ~ 危险区域。*a delivery* ~ 扩散器。*a compression* ~ 高压室。*S- forbids*. 限于篇幅。*a long* [*short*] ~ 长[短]时间。*Let us rest a* ~. 休息一会儿吧。*Your luggage occupies too much* ~. 你的行李占地太多了。*The reading room affords an ample* ~ *for 500 people*. 阅览室面积可能容五百人。*Please leave a wider* ~ *between the lines*. 行间的空请留得大一些。*vanish into* ~ 在空中消失。**the** ~ **of** (多少年)之间。**for a** ~ 暂时。**for the** ~ **of a mile** [**two years**] 一英里的距离[两年]间。**in** ~ 片刻就,一会儿就。**II** *vt*., *vi*. 留间隔;【印】行间[字间]衬空铅。*In designing the houses,* ~ *out them from 10 to 12 yards apart*. 在设计房子时,家与家之间留间隔十至十二码。~*d crop* 宽行栽培。~*d emphasis* 加宽字母间间隔所表示的强调。~ *out* 【印】加宽行间[词间]间隔排匀。**S- Age** 宇宙空间[外太空]时代。~**bar** (打字机的)间隔档,空档。~ **barrel** 〔美口〕用于探索外太空计划的拨款。~**borne** 在宇宙空间运行的;由宇宙飞船运载的。~ **charge** 【电子】空间电荷。~ **colony** 空间移民区〔指设想中的巨型空间人造卫星,其上可供大量人口居住〕。~ **craft** 航天器,宇宙飞船。~ **current** 【无】(管内)空间电流。~**faring** *n*., *a*. 外层空间旅行(的);宇宙飞行(的)。~ **fiction** 宇航冒险小说。~**flight** 宇宙飞行,星际飞行。~ **heater** 小型供暖器〔装于室内,供一室用〕。~**lab** 太空实验室,宇宙空间实验室。~ **lattice** 【物】空间晶格[点阵]。~**less** 无限的;无空隙[间隔、余地]的。~**man** 宇宙空间科学工作者,宇航员,太空人。~ **model** 立体模型。~**-out** *a*. 遨游太空的;(因吸毒而)呆若木鸡。~**plane** 航天飞机。~**port** 宇航[太空]站〔飞船装配、试验、发射中心〕。~**probe** 航天探测器。~**-ship** 宇宙飞船[太空船]。~**shuttle** 太空梭,航天飞行,航天飞机。~**-sickness** 宇航病。~**station** [**platform**] 航天站,宇宙空间站,太空站。~**suit** 航天服,宇航服。~ **time** 【数,物】时空(连续体);时空关系。~**walk** *n*., *v*. 太空漫步,空间行走,宇宙行走〔指太空人[宇航员]离开飞船在外活动〕。~ **writer** 按篇幅计算稿酬的记者或撰稿人;〔美〕= ~ **man**.

spac·er [ˈspeisə; ˋspesɚ] *n*. **1**. 留间隔者[器]。**2**. 隔离物。**3**. 垫片,垫圈;衬垫,衬套;撑挡;隔板;(打字机跳格的)间隔档。**4**. 【印】空铅,衬条。**5**. 【影】暗帧。

spa·cial [ˈspeiʃəl; ˋspeʃəl] *a*. = spatial.

spac·ing [ˈspeisiŋ; ˋspesɪŋ] *n*. **1**. (留)间隔,间距。**2**. 【印】(词间、行间等)调节间隔。**3**. 【农】植距。

spa·cious [ˈspeiʃəs; ˋspeʃəs] *a*. **1**. 宽,广阔的,宽敞的。**2**. (知识)广博的;宽裕的。*a* ~ *room* 宽大的房间。*It's quite beyond me to speak on a* ~ *topic like this*. 我实在讲不了这般博大广泛的题目。**-ly** *ad*. **-ness** *n*.

spa·cis·ter [ˈspeiˌsistə; ˋspeˏsɪstɚ] *n*. 【无】空间电荷晶体管,宽阔管。

Spack·le [ˈspækl; ˋspækl] **I** *n*. **1**. 一次抹墙粉的商标名。**2**. 〔s-〕抹墙粉。**II** *vt*. (**-led**, **-ling**) 〔s-〕抹墙粉于…上。

spade[1] [speid; sped] **I** *n*. **1**. 铲;锹;(剖鲸鱼用的)铲刀。**2**. 【军】(杆住炮架,制止它因后座力而移动的)驻锄。**call a** ~ **a** ~ 直言不讳,有啥说啥。**II** *vt*. 拿铲子铲;拿铲刀切开。*Orders came that we should* ~ *the trench in an hour*. 有命令我们必须在一小时之内挖好战壕。~**fish** 【动】细鳞白鲳;白鲟;匙吻鲟。~**foot toad** 【动】锄足蟾(科动物)。~ **husbandry** 深耕细作。~**-warfare** 堑壕战。~**work** **1**. 铲工,铲活。**2**. 需要努力的准备工作。**-r** *n*. 铲具;用铲子的人。

spade[2] [speid; sped] *n*. (纸牌的)黑桃;黑桃牌;〔*pl*.〕一副黑桃。**in** ~ 〔口〕**1**. 肯定地;明确地;非常强烈地;绝对地。**2**. 直率地。*He told me the whole story in* ~*s and there's no doubt about it*. 他明确地把整个经过都对我讲了,一点也不含糊。

spade[3] [speid; sped] **I** *n*. = spado. **II** *vt*. 〔方〕= spay.

spadg·er [ˈspædʒə; ˋspædʒɚ] *n*. 〔英俚〕麻雀;〔美俚〕孩童。

spa·di·ceous [speiˈdiʃəs; speˋdɪʃəs] *a*. **1**. 浅褐色的,栗色的。**2**. 【植】生肉穗花序的,肉穗花序状的。

spa·di·cose [ˈspeidikəus; ˋspedɪkos] *a*. 肉穗花序的。

spa·dix [ˈspeidiks; ˋspedɪks] *n*. (*pl*. **-di·ces** [speiˈdaisiːz; speˋdaɪsiz]) 【植】肉穗[佛焰]花序。

spa·do [ˈspeidəu; ˋspedo] *n*. 〔L.〕(*pl*. ***-dones*** [speiˈdəuniːz; speˋdoniz]) 阉人;阉兽,阉过的马;【法】无生育能力者。

spae [spei; spe] *vi*., *vt*. 〔苏格兰〕预言。~**wife** 女算命者。

spa·ghet·ti [spəˈgeti; spəˋgetɪ] *n*. 〔It.〕**1**. (意大利式)实心面条。**2**. 【电】漆布绝缘管,绝缘套管。**3**. 〔口〕(线或金属等)无法解开的缠结;混乱;紊乱。~ **suit** 水冷套管式太空人内衣。

spa-hi (spa·hee) [ˈspɑːhiː; ˋspɑhi] *n*. 【史】**1**. 土耳其的非正规骑兵。**2**. (过去法国陆军中的)阿尔及利亚骑兵。

Spain [spein; spen] *n*. 西班牙〔欧洲〕。

spake [speik; spek] 〔古〕speak 的过去式。

spald·er [ˈspɔːldə; ˋspɔldɚ] *n*. 击碎(矿)石的工人。

Spal·ding [ˈspɔːldiŋ; ˋspɔldɪŋ] *n*. 斯波尔丁〔姓氏〕。

spall [spɔːl; spɔl] **I** *n*. 碎片,裂片;碎(矿)石。**II** *vt*., *vi*. **1**. 削,劃,(弄)碎。**2**. 粗斫(生矿)。**3**. 实落;裂开。**4**. 【原】分裂,蜕变。**-ation** [spɔˈleiʃən; spɑˋleʃən] *n*. 【原】分裂,蜕变。

spal·peen [spælˈpiːn; ˋspælpin, spælˋpin] *n*. **1**. 〔爱〕短工工人。**2**. 〔爱〕饭桶,懒汉;无赖;恶棍。**3**. 〔爱〕孩童,少年。

Spam, spam [spæm; spæm] *n*. **1**. (美国)罐头猪肉[火腿](= spiced ham)。**2**. 【计】电子垃圾〔指网上的垃圾广告宣传品等〕。

Sp. Am. = Spanish American 通用西班牙语的美洲人。

span[1] [spæn; spæn] **I** *n*. **1**. 一拃〔手指张开时,拇指尖至小指尖的长度,通常九英寸〕。**2**. (常有短的涵义的)一段

S

时间;很小的间隔;片刻,顷刻。**3.** 广度,全长,从一头到一头。**4.** 跨度;(桥礅间的)礅距。**5.**【空】翼展;(气流)宽度。**6.**【海】跨绳。*the ~ of a man's life* 一个人的一生。*the whole ~ of English history* 英国历史的全程。*the ~ of memory* 记忆所及。**II** *vt*. (**-nn-**) **1.** (用拇指和小指)拃,用拃量。**2.** (眼睛)观测,看到。**3.** (记忆等)到,及。**4.** 横跨,跨越,(桥)跨(在河上),架(桥在河上)弥补。**5.**【海】绑住,系住。—*vi*. (在水中)时浮时沉地向前游泳;(尺蠖)段段移进。*His political life ~s half a century*. 他的政治生涯长达半个世纪。*Imagination will ~ the gap in our knowledge*. 想像会弥补知识的不足。*Over there is a small stream ~ned by a wooden bridge*. 那边有一条架着木桥的小溪。~**-clean** *a*. 非常清洁的。~ **dogs** 木材抓起机。~ **loading**【空】翼展载荷。~**-new** *a*. 崭新的。~**roof** 等斜屋顶。

span² [spæn; spæn] **I** *n*. 〔美,南非〕一对共轭牛,共轭马。**II** *vt*. (把两头牲畜)并排套在车上。

span³ [spæn; spæn] 〔古〕spin 的过去式。

span·cel [ˈspænsl; ˋspænsl̩] **I** *n*. 绊脚索。**II** *vt*. (**-celed**, **-celled**; **-cel·ing**, **-cel·ling**) 用绊脚索羁绊。

span·dex [ˈspændiks; ˋspændɪks] *n*.【纺】斯潘德克斯弹性纤维[用于腰带、游泳衣等]。

span·drel [ˈspændrəl; ˋspændrəl], **span·dril** [-dril; -drɪl] *n*.【建】(三角)拱肩,拱上空间;上下层窗空间。

spang [spæŋ; spæŋ] *ad*. **1.** 恰好,笔直,直接;猛然。*It fell ~ into my lap*. 它正好落在我的怀里。**2.** 完全地。*You've poured too much water into the flower pot. It runs ~ full to the edge*. 你往花盆里浇水太多了,都流到盆沿上了。

S

span·gle [ˈspæŋgl; ˋspæŋgl] **I** *n*. 〔常 *pl*.〕**1.** 亮晶晶的东西,(戏装上的)闪光装饰。**2.** (槠树叶子背面的)菌状瘤。**II** *vt*., *vi*. 用亮晶晶的东西装饰;(使)闪闪发光,闪耀。

span·gled [ˈspæŋgld; ˋspæŋgl̩d] *a*. 装饰着…的,…灿烂的。*star-~ heavens* [*skies*] 星光灿烂的天空。*the Star-Spangled Banner* 星条旗(美国国旗);美国国歌。

Span·iard [ˈspænjəd; ˋspænjɚd] *n*. 西班牙人。

span·iel [ˈspænjəl; ˋspænjəl] *n*. **1.** 长毛垂耳狗。**2.** 卑躬屈膝的谄媚者,走狗。**3.** 〔俚〕无线电制导的飞弹。*the field ~* 猎兔(等)长耳猎犬。*the Japanese ~* (日本)哈巴狗。

Span·ish [ˈspæniʃ; ˋspænɪʃ] **I** *n*. **1.** 西班牙语。**2.** 〔the ~〕西班牙人。**3.** 〔美〕新墨西哥 (New Mexico) 州的别名。**II** *a*. 西班牙的;西班牙人[语]的;西班牙式的。***walk ~*** 〔美俚〕踮着脚尖走,鬼头鬼脑地走;提心吊胆地走。~ **America** (讲西班牙语的)拉丁美洲各国。~ **athlete** 〔美〕吹牛者。~ **bayonet**【植】丝兰属植物;千手兰;麟凤兰。~ **catarrh**【医】流行性感冒。~ **coin** 〔卑〕奉承话,假恭维话。~ **fly**【动】斑蝥。~ **Inquisition** (中世纪天主教审判异端的)西班牙宗教法庭。~ **mackerel**【动】(大西洋)马鲛(属)。~ **Main**【史】南美洲北岸[从巴拿马海峡到奥里诺科河间的区域];南美北东部加勒比海沿岸一带。~ **moss** 〔美〕【植】铁兰。~ **needles** 〔美〕【植】鬼针草(籽,果)。~ **trot** 〔美〕缓步。~**white** 硝酸铋。

spank [spæŋk; spæŋk] **I** *vt*. **1.** (用巴掌、拖鞋等)打(屁股等)。**2.** 赶…前进,催打。**3.** (在比赛中)击败。—*vi*. (马、船等)飞跑,急驶 (*along*)。**II** *n*. 拍打,一巴掌。

spank·er [ˈspæŋkə; ˋspæŋkɚ] *n*. **1.** 大踏步急走的人;飞跑的马。**2.**【船】后樯纵帆。**3.** 〔俚〕极好的东西,了不起的人。

spank·ing [ˈspæŋkiŋ; ˋspæŋkɪŋ] **I** *a*. **1.** 急走的,飞跑的。**2.** (风)猛烈的;强烈的。**3.** 〔口〕极好的,最新式的;了不起的。*a ~ pair of horses* 一对飞跑的马。*a house of ~ modernistic conveniences* 一所有最新式的现代化设备的房子。**II** *ad*. 显著地,突出地。**III** *n*. 打屁股,拍打。

span·less [ˈspænlis; ˋspænlɪs] *a*. 不可测量[计量]的。

span·ner [ˈspænə; ˋspænɚ] *n*. **1.** 用指距测量的人。**2.** 〔英〕(螺钉)扳钳,扳子,扳头;【建】(桥梁的)交叉支撑,横拉条。**3.**【动】= spanworm. *a shifting ~* 活络扳头。***throw a ~ in the works*** 捣乱,妨碍或阻挠人家的计画。

span·worm [ˈspænwəːm; ˋspænˏwɝm] *n*.【动】尺蠖。

Spar, **SPAR** [spɑː; spɑr] *n*. 美国海岸警卫队妇女队员。

spar¹ [spɑː; spɑr] **I** *n*. **1.**【船】圆材[桅、桁等]。**2.** 圆木;【空】翼梁。**II** *vt*. (**-rr-**) **1.** 装圆材。**2.** 用圆材使(船)脱离浅滩。~ **buoy**【船】杆状浮标。~ **deck**【船】轻甲板。~ **varnish**【化】桅杆清漆。

spar² [spɑː; spɑr] *n*.【矿】(不含金属成分的)晶石。*calcareous ~* 重晶石。*cube ~* 硬石膏。*fluor* [*Derbyshire*] ~ 萤石。*heavy ~* 重晶石。*Iceland ~* 方解石,冰洲石。*pearl ~* 白云石。*satin ~* 石膏。

spar³ [spɑː; spɑr] **I** *vi*. (**-rr-**) **1.** (鸡)用脚踢斗。**2.** (拳击中)拳斗;拳打。**3.** 争吵。**4.** (小规模)战斗。*The grocer ~red with her outside his store*. 杂货商在店外和她吵起来了。~ *at each other* 对骂。**II** *n*. **1.** 拳斗。**2.** 斗鸡。**3.** 吵嘴。~**mate** = sparring partner.

spar·a·ble [ˈspærəbl; ˋspærəbl̩] *n*. 无头小鞋钉。

spare [speə; spɛr] **I** *vi*. 节省,俭省。—*vt*. **1.** 不用,抽出,省掉。**2.** 出让,割爱,分让。**3.** 宽恕,饶(命);救命;不伤害,不损害;使某人免遭(麻烦等)。*Have you any ticket to ~?* 你有多余的票子出让吗? *I cannot ~ time for it*. 那件事情我匀不出时间来。*We can ~ you for tomorrow*. 明天可以不要你帮忙了。*Can you ~ me a few minutes?* 你能抽几分钟和我谈谈吗?[你能给我几分钟去办点事吗?]。*S- him the trouble*. 别麻烦他吧。*His satiric poem ~d neither the politicians nor the merchants*. 政客们和商人们都未能免于遭受他的诗篇的讽刺。... ***and to ~*** 多余的,剩余的,过多的,很多的 (= enough and to ~) (*There are cases* (*enough*) *and to ~ of such a thing happening*. 有很多情况都可以发生这种事情)。***enough and to ~*** 过多的,很多的。***if one is ~d*** 要是不死的话。***not ~ oneself*** 不宽容自己,严格要求自己;很卖力,狠干,不疲塌。~ ***no efforts*** (~ *no efforts to push ahead with a project* 不遗余力地推进一项计划)。~ ***no expense*** 不惜工本。~ ***sb.'s blushes*** 不使丢脸害羞。~ ***sb.'s feelings*** 不使难过;不惹怒某人。~ ***oneself the trouble*** 不必自找麻烦,不必操心,不必费神 (*He might have ~d himself the trouble*. 他本来可以不用自找麻烦吗。*You may ~ yourself the trouble*. 你不必费神)。***time to ~*** 余暇。**II** *a*. **1.** 多余的,剩下的(钱等),空闲的(时间等);可以出让的。**2.** 预备的,备用的,替换用的。**3.** 薄弱的,简陋的;粗陋的;俭约的;瘦的。*a ~ bed* 客圆,闲圆。*a ~ ticket* (备)退票,多余的票,剩票。~ *cash* 剩款。*a ~ part* 备件,零件。*a ~ room* 闲房。*a ~ tire* 预备轮胎;〔美俚〕讨厌的人。*a ~ man*【运】预备队员。*a ~ crew*【海】预备船员。**III** *n*. **1.** 节省,俭省。**2.** 预备品,替换品。**3.** 准备金,预备房间(等)。**4.** 〔*pl*.〕(机器等的)备件。**5.** 〔美〕〔十柱戏〕(头两个球把十柱打得)全倒。***make ~*** 节省。~ **hand** 替班工人。~ **part** (机器的)备件。~**-set** *a*. 体型瘦细的。~ **time** *a*. 业余的(学校)。*n*. 业余时间。**-ly** *ad*. **-ness** *n*. **-r** *n*.

spare·rib [ˈspeərib; ˋspɛrˏrɪb, ˋspær-] *n*. (猪的)排骨。

spar·ga·no·sis [ˌspɑːgəˈnəusis; ˏspɑrgəˋnosɪs] *n*.【医】裂头蚴病。

spar·ga·num [ˈspɑːgeinəm; ˋspɑrgenəm] *n*.【生】裂头蚴。

sparge [spɑːdʒ; spɑrdʒ] *vt*., *vi*. (**sparged**; **sparg·ing**) **1.** 洒,撒,喷雾(于)。**2.** (用压缩空气经过喷雾器)搅动(液体)。**-r** *n*. **1.** 喷洒器。**2.**【电】配电器。

spar·go·sis [ˈspɑːgəusis; ˋspɑrgosɪs] *n*.【医】象皮肿。

spar·id [ˈspærid; ˋspɛrɪd] *n*.【动】鲷科 (*Sparidae*) 鱼。

spar·ing [ˈspeəriŋ; ˋspɛrɪŋ] *a*. **1.** 节省的;(对…)爱惜,

舍不得(*of*);节制着的。2.(某方面)贫乏[不足]。3.〔古〕慈悲的,宽大的。*Be* ~ *of your epithets*. 不要乱用形容词;不要随便议论人。*This guide to the museum is* ~ *of information*. 这本博物馆指南内容不丰富。**be** ~ ***of oneself*** 不卖力,不肯吃苦,懒惰。**-ly** ***ad***.

spark[1][spɑːk; spark] **I** ***n***. 1. 火花;火星。2.(钻石等的)闪光;(目光的)闪耀。3. 生气,活力,(才智的)焕发。4.〔美〕小钻石;小宝石。5.〔通常用于否定句〕一丝,一分,一点点。6.【电】电花,瞬态放电。7.【机】(内燃机火花塞的)控制放电装置。8.〔*pl*.〕〔口语〕(船上的)无线电技术员。*A single* ~ *can start a prairie fire*. 星星之火可以燎原。*There was a wild* ~ *in his eyes*. 他的两眼炯炯发光。*The vital* ~ *in him makes him an artist*. 他的生气勃勃的活力使得他成为一个艺术家。*fairy* ~*s* 磷光,鬼火。*a* ~ *of wit* 才气的焕发。*the vital* ~ = *the* ~ *of life* 生气。**as the** ~**s fly upward** 合乎道理,的确,不错。**have not a** ~ **of interest** 毫无趣味。***strike*** ~***s out of sb***. 激发某人的聪明才智。~ **arrester** 火花避雷器。~ **chamber**【核】火花室〔一种粒子探测装置〕。~ **coil**【电】点火[发火]线圈。~ **erosion** 火花电蚀法[金属加工之一种电化学方法]。~ **gap**【电】放电器,火花隙。~ **guard**〔美〕火炉围板。~**-plug** ***vt***. 发动;激励。~ **plug** 1. = sparking plug. 2. 鼓励同伴的人,活跃分子;带头人。~ **transmitter**【电】火花式发电机。~ **telegraphy**【电】电花电报。**II** ***vi***., ***vt***. 发火花,飞火星儿;使闪耀,使闪光;用眼神表示(喜悦等);〔美〕鼓舞,激励。*Joseph is a player who can* ~ *his team to victory*. 约瑟是个能激励他的队员取胜的运动员。*The discovery* ~*ed us to further study*. 这个发现鼓舞我们作进一步的研究。

spark[2][spɑːk; spark] **I** ***n***. 愉快的年轻人;翩翩少年;纨绔子弟,花花公子;求爱者;情郎。**II** ***vi***. 讨好女人,追逐女性。—***vt***.〔美〕求爱,求婚。

spark·ing-plug [ˈspɑːkiŋplʌg; sparkɪŋˋplʌg] ***n***.(内燃机的)火花塞。

spar·kle [ˈspɑːkl; ˋsparkl̩] **I** ***n***. 1. 火花,火星;闪光;光彩。2. 生气,活力。3.(酒等的)气泡。4.【化】发泡。**II** ***vt***., ***vi***. 1. 发火花,迸火星;闪亮,闪耀。2.(才智等)焕发;活跃。3. 起泡。*Father's eyes* ~*d with joy*. 父亲的眼中闪烁出喜悦之色。*Dr. Peter's speech at the party* ~*s with wit*. 彼得博士在会上的演说,妙语如珠。

spar·kler [ˈspɑːklə; ˋsparklɚ] ***n***. 闪亮的东西;宝石;才华焕发的人;〔口〕亮晶晶的眼睛。

spark·let [ˈspɑːklit; ˋsparklɪt] ***n***. 1. 小火花,小火星,小闪光。2.(妇女衣服上的)闪光装饰。3.(自制汽水用的)碳酸胶丸,发泡剂。

spar·kling [ˈspɑːkliŋ; ˋsparklɪŋ] ***a***. 1. 发火花的;迸火星的;闪亮的;灿烂的;活泼的。2. 才华焕发的。3. 有气泡的(香槟酒等)。*When I skate, I'm fearful of the* ~ *ice*. 我滑冰的时候很怕那闪亮的冰。*Dr. Johnson was famous for his* ~ *conversation*. 约翰逊博士以其才华焕发的谈话而知名。~ *wine* 香槟酒;汽酒。**-ly** ***ad***.

Sparks [spɑːks; sparks] ***n***. 斯帕克斯〔姓氏〕。

spar·ling [ˈspɑːliŋ; ˋsparlɪŋ] ***n***.(*pl*. ~, ***-lings***)【动】(欧洲)胡瓜鱼(*Osmerus eperlanus*)。

spar·oid [ˈspɛərɔid, ˈspær-; ˋspɛrɔɪd, ˋspær-] **I** ***a***.【动】鲷科的。**II** ***n***. = sparid 鲷科鱼。

spar·ring [ˈspɑːriŋ; ˋsparɪŋ] ***n***. 1. 拳击。2. 争论,辩论。~ **partner**(职业拳击手的)练拳对手。

spar·row [ˈspærəu; ˋspæro] ***n***. 1.【鸟】麻雀。2.〔美〕个子小的人。~**-bill** 无头小鞋钉。~ **grass** ***n***.〔口〕= asparagus. ~ **hawk** 食雀鹰,鹞。~**-tongue**【植】萹蓄。

spar·ry [ˈspɑːri; ˋsparɪ] ***a***. 晶石的,似晶石的,多晶石的。~ **iron** 菱铁矿。

sparse [spɑːs; spars] ***a***. 1.(树木分布等)稀的;(交通车辆等)稀疏的。2.(人口、毛发等)稀少的。3.(雨量)稀缺的;瘦小的。~ *beard* 稀疏的胡须。*a country of* ~ *population* 人口稀少的小国。**-si·ty** [ˈspɑːsiti; ˋsparsətɪ] ***n***. **-ly** ***ad***. **-ness** ***n***.

Spar·ta [ˈspɑːtə; ˋspartə] ***n***. 斯巴达〔古希腊南部一个城邦〕。

Spar·ta·cist [ˈspɑːtəsist; ˋspartəsɪst] ***n***.【史】(德国)斯巴达克同盟成员。

Spar·tan [ˈspɑːtən; ˋspartn̩] **I** ***a***.(希腊)斯巴达的;斯巴达式的〔刻苦耐劳、严于律己、战争中视死如归〕。**II** ***n***. 斯巴达;斯巴达式的人。*a* ~ *dog* 英国种警犬;残忍的人。**-ism** ***n***. 斯巴达主义[精神、方式、性格]。*Didn't you notice a* ~ *brevity in his speech*? 难道你没有注意到他讲话的那种斯巴达式的"简短"吗?

spar·te·ine [ˈspɑːtiːiːn, -tiːin; ˋspartɪˏin, -tɪɪn] ***n***.【化】鹰爪豆碱。

spart·i·cal [ˈspɑːtikəl; ˋspartɪkəl] ***n***.【物】超对称性粒子。

spa·score [ˈspeiskɔː; ˋspeskɔr] ***n***. 人造卫星位置显示屏。

spasm [ˈspæzəm; ˋspæzəm] ***n***. 1. 痉挛,抽搐。2. 一阵(感情发作或一阵动作);(地震等的)一震。*a* ~ *of the stomach* 胃痉挛。*have a* ~ *of grief* 一阵悲伤。*a* ~ *of coughing* 一阵咳嗽。*a* ~ *of pain* 疼痛一阵。

spas·mod·ic, -i·cal [spæzˈmɔdik, -ikəl; spæzˋmɑdɪk, -ɪkəl] ***a***. 1. 痉挛(性)的;抽搐的。2. 阵发性的,一会儿做一会儿停的,间歇的;勤惰无常的。~ *efforts* 时作时止的努力。*a* ~ *worker*(做事)忽冷忽热的工作者。**-i·cal·ly** ***ad***.

spas·tic [ˈspæstik; ˋspæstɪk] **I** ***a***. 1.【医】痉挛(性)的。2. 患大脑性麻痹的。~ *paralysis*【医】痉挛性麻痹。**II** ***n***. 患大脑性麻痹者。

spat[1][spæt; spæt]〔古〕spit 的过去式及过去分词。

spat[2][spæt; spæt] **I** ***n***. 蚝[牡蛎]卵;贝苗;〔集合词〕幼蚝。**II** ***vi***., ***vt***.(蚝等)产卵。

spat[3][spæt; spæt] ***n***.〔常 *pl*.〕鞋罩。

spat[4][spæt; spæt] **I** ***n***. 1. 掌击,拍打,一个巴掌。2. 大雨(等)的声音。3.〔美口〕口斗,争论;小冲突,小争斗。**II** ***vt***., ***vi***.(***spat·ted*** [ˈspætid; ˋspætɪd]; ***spat·ting*** [ˈspætiŋ; ˋspætɪŋ])〔口〕1. 用巴掌打。2.(雨点等)啪啪地落下。3. 小冲突,争吵。*Bullets were* ~*ting the car*. 枪弹像雨点般打在汽车上。*Mary is* ~*ting with mother again*. 玛丽又在和妈妈吵架了。

spatch·cock [ˈspætʃkɔk; ˋspætʃˏkɑk] **I** ***n***. 杀后马上切成小块下锅煮的鸡肉。**II** ***vt***.(把鸡)杀后就下锅;〔口〕把(文句等)增补[插入](*in*; *into*)。*I'm busy* ~*ing more examples into my book*. 我在忙着给我的书增补更多的例句。

spate [speit; spet] ***n***. 1. 洪水,突然泛滥,猛涨;〔苏格兰〕倾盆大雨。2. 大量。*The river is in* ~. 河水猛涨。*Refugees crossed the border in full* ~. 难民大量地越过了边境。

spa·tha·ceous [spəˈθeiʃəs; spəˋθeʃəs] ***a***.【植】1. 有佛焰苞的。2. 佛焰苞质的。

spathe [speið; speð] ***n***.【植】佛焰苞。

spath·ic [ˈspæθik; ˋspæθɪk] ***a***.【矿】像晶石的,方解石状的;薄层状的。

spa·those[1][ˈspeiθəus, ˈspæθəus; ˋspeθos, ˋspæθos] ***a***. = spathaceous.

spath·ose[2][ˈspæθəus; ˋspæθos] ***a***. = spathic.

spath·u·late [ˈspæθjulit; ˋspæθjəlɪt, -let] ***a***.【植】匙形的,抹刀形的。

spa·tial [ˈspeiʃəl; ˋspeʃəl] ***a***. 1. 空间的;在空间中存在[发生,占有位置]的。2. 占大篇幅的。*too* ~ *a theme for a book like this* 要占很大篇幅,不是这本书所能容得下的主题。**-i·ty** [ˌspeiʃiˈæliti; ˏspeʃəˋælətɪ] ***n***. 空间性。**-ly** ***ad***.

spa·tial·ize [ˈspeiʃəlaiz; ˋspeʃəlˏaɪz] ***vt***. 予以形态[形状];使形状化;使空间化。*Man invented writing to* ~, *i.e. preserve language*. 人类发明了文字,才能给予语言以形态,也就是说,才能把语言保存下来。*cogni-*

tive disposition to ~ *everything* 使每一事物都形象化的认识倾向。**-tial·i·za·tion** ***n.***

spa·ti·o- *comb.f.* 空间的,太空的。*spatio*perceptual 空间知觉的。

spa·ti·og·ra·phy [ˌspeiʃiˈɔgrəfi; ˏspeʃɪˋɑgrəfɪ] ***n.*** 太空学。

spa·ti·o·nau·tics [ˌspeiʃiəuˈnɔːtiks; ˏspeʃɪoˋnɔtɪks] ***n.*** 宇宙航行学。

spa·ti·o·tem·po·ral [ˌspeiʃiəuˈtempərəl; ˏspeʃɪoˋtɛmpərəl] ***a.*** **1.** 存在于时间和空间的。**2.** 时空的。**-ly** ***ad.***

spat·ter [ˈspætə; ˋspætɚ] **I** ***vt.*** **1.** 泼,溅,洒。**2.** 泼脏,溅脏。**3.** 诽谤,诋毁。~ *mud on sb.'s clothes* 溅泥在某人衣服上。*mistakes* ~*ed through the whole of the article* 文章中俯拾皆是的错误。—***vi.*** **1.** 溅,洒。**2.** 喷散;喷唾沫,滴下。**3.** (子弹)雨般射来。**4.** 诽谤。*Rain* ~*ed down on the roof*. 雨滴滴嗒嗒地落在屋顶上。**II** ***n.*** **1.** 泼,溅。**2.** (雨等的)滴滴嗒嗒声。**3.** 泼溅的污迹。**4.** 点滴,少量。*When he finished his recitation, there was a* ~ *of applause*. 他朗诵完了以后,有阵稀稀落落的掌声。~**dash** ***n.*** 〔常 *pl.*〕(从前雨天骑马用的)皮绑腿。~**dock**【植】黄花圆叶苹蓬草;睡莲。

spat·u·la [ˈspætjulə; ˋspætʃələ] ***n.*** **1.** 〔L.〕(涂油漆、涂药等用的)抹刀;刮铲。**2.**【医】压舌片;调药刀。**3.**【动】(瘿蚊幼虫的)胸骨;匙突。

spat·u·lar [ˈspætjulə; ˋspætʃəlɚ] ***a.*** 抹刀似的。

spat·u·late [ˈspætjulit; ˋspætʃəlɪt, -ˏlet] ***a.*** **1.** 抹刀形的,刮铲状的。**2.**【植】(树叶等)匙形的。

S

spav·in [ˈspævin; ˋspævɪn] ***n.***【兽医】跗节内肿。**-ed** ***a.*** 跛的;残废的。

spawn [spɔːn; spɔn] **I** ***n.*** **1.** (鱼等的)卵,子。**2.** (裂殖菌类植物的)丝;菌。**3.** 〔蔑〕小子,小鬼。**4.** 产物,结果。**5.**【植】菌种体,菌砖。**II** ***vt.*** **1.** (使)产卵。**2.** 〔蔑〕生(子)。**3.** 用菌砖栽。**4.** 引起,酿成。*Quarrels are often* ~*ed by misunderstanding*. 争吵常常是误会酿成的。—***vi.*** **1.** (鱼)产卵,(卵)产下来。**2.** 大量生育。*shoot* ~ 产卵。*You* ~ *of the devil*! 你这小鬼!

spay [spei; spe] ***vt.*** 割去(牲畜的)卵巢。

spdl. = 【纺】spindle.

S.P.E. = Society for Pure English 〔英〕纯正英语学会。

speak [spiːk; spik] (*spoke* [spəuk; spok], 〔古〕*spake* [speik; spek]; *spo·ken* [ˈspəukn; ˋspokən]) **I** ***vi.*** **1.** 讲,说,说话;谈话 (*to*; *with*)。**2.** 演说,演讲;发言,陈述,声明。**3.** 表明;(以讲话外的方式)表达,表现;辩解 (*for*),驳 (*against*)。**4.** 〔口〕(乐器、枪炮等)响。**5.**【海】(船)发响,冲水,破浪。**6.** 〔英〕(狗)吠。—***vt.*** **1.** 讲,说,说出,(用画面)声明;朗诵。**2.** 宣告。**3.** 〔古〕证明。**4.** (脸、眼睛等)表示,表现(悲哀、感情等)。**5.**【海】(从船上)高声喊,(用旗语等方式)招呼。**6.** 〔古〕向…说话 (= ~ to sb.)。*The child cannot* ~ *yet*. 孩子还不会说话。*I'll* ~ *to the teacher about it*. 这件事我要和教员谈谈。*Professor Wang is going to* ~ *on Old English tomorrow*. 王教授明天要作关于古英语的讲演。*S- of the devil, and he is sure to appear*. = *S- of angels, and you will hear their wings*. 说鬼就见鬼,说曹操曹操就到。*strictly* ~*ing* 严格地讲。*English spoken here*. 本处通用英语〔商店告白等〕用语。*Facts* ~ *louder than words*. 事实胜于雄辩。*The portrait* ~*s*. 这张画十分逼真。*This* ~*s him generous*. 这表明他宽大。*In the poem, Tate is* ~*ing his usual blind optimism*. 在这首诗里,泰特表达出了他通常的那种盲目的乐观主义。*We spoke a ship or two*. 我们(的船)对一两艘船通过话了。~ *sb. fair* 很有礼貌地同某人说话。***as they*** [***men***] ~ 俗语说。***generally*** ~***ing*** 一般地说来。***nothing to*** ~ ***of*** 不值一说,没有说的价值。***not to*** ~ ***of*** (更)不用说,当然。***so to*** ~ 可以说。~ ***a good word for*** 给…说好话;劝解。~ ***about*** 讲起,说到。~ ***against*** 说…的坏话;作不利于…的陈述。~ ***aside*** 向旁边说,独言独语。~ ***at*** 暗讽,指桑骂槐。~ ***by the book*** 正确讲。~ ***for*** 代表…讲话,为…辩护;订购 (~ *for the new farm tool* 订购新式农具);要求得到 (~ *for more cheese* 要求多给点干酪)。~ ***for itself*** 不说自明 (*There is no need for me to praise it; it* ~*s for itself*. 无需我来称赞,那是不说自明的)。~ ***for oneself*** 为自己辩护,陈述自己意见。~ ***highly of*** 称赞。~ ***ill*** [***evil***] ***of*** 诽谤,诋毁,说…坏话。~ ***in meeting*** 〔美〕发表意见。~ ***not a word of*** 全未谈到。~ ***of*** 讲起,谈到;特别推荐说。~ ***on*** 继续讲;演讲(某问题等)。~ ***one's piece*** 〔美〕说想说的话;【拳】在报上宣传。~ ***out*** [***up***] 大声讲;老老实实讲,明白地讲 (*S- out — don't be afraid*. 照直说——别怕。*S- out — we can't hear*. 大声说——我们听不见)。~ ***to*** 向…说;说到 (*He spoke to the point*. 他说到点子上了,一针见血。);招呼;恳求;申斥,忠告;证明 (*I can* ~ *to his honesty*. 我可以证明他是老实的)。~ ***together*** 商量。~ ***under one's breath*** 悄悄地说。~ ***United States*** 说美国话。~ ***up*** 极力辩护;明说;提高声音说 (*We should* ~ *up about each other's mistakes*. 我们要公开讲明彼此的错误)。~ ***upon*** = ~ *on*. ~ ***volumes*** (***for***) 表示重要意义,为…的有力证据。~ ***well for*** 证明;好[有效]。~ ***well of*** 称赞,说…好话。~ ***with*** 和…谈话,和…商量;〔古〕= talk to. ~ ***without book*** 凭记忆讲。~ **box** 门内外对讲机。**-a·ble** ***a.*** 可以交谈的;可以出口的。

speak·eas·y [ˈspiːkiːzi; ˋspikˏizɪ] ***n.*** (*pl.* ***-eas·ies***) 〔美俚〕非法秘密酒店。

speak·er [ˈspiːkə; ˋspikɚ] ***n.*** **1.** 说话人;演说者;雄辩家。**2.** 广播员。**3.** 扩音器,扬声器;喇叭,话筒。**4.** 〔S-〕英国下议院、美国众议院议长〔美国正式叫做 the S- of the House〕。**5.** (会议的)主席。*Blame not the* ~ *but be warned by his words*. 言者无罪,闻者足戒。*a fine* [*no*] ~ 演说漂亮[不行]的人。*Mr. S-!* 〔招呼〕议长先生。*S- of the House* (美国的)众议院议长。~**-phone** 扬声器电话(由电话线连接的对讲装置)。~**ship** 议长的职位、任期。

speak·ies [ˈspiːkiz; ˋspikɪz] ***n.*** 〔*pl.*〕〔美口〕有声电影;话剧。

speak·ing [ˈspiːkiŋ; ˋspikɪŋ] **I** ***a.*** **1.** 发言的,交谈的,说话的。**2.** 栩栩如生的,活现的,逼真的。**3.** 雄辩的,说明问题的,富于表情的。~ *acquaintance* 见面谈几句的朋友,泛泛之交。*a* ~ *look* 富有表情[意味深长]的样子[眼神]。*a* ~ *likeness* [*portrait*] 栩栩如生的画像。***not on*** ~ ***terms*** (***with***) (和…)不是相互交谈的朋友(点头之交);(和…)见了面也不开口,(和…)不和。**II** ***n.*** 谈话;传说;〔*pl.*〕演说,雄辩(术),语言。***at the*** [***this***] ***present*** ~ 〔美〕现在,眼下。~ ***in tongues*** 出神地喃喃作声〔不自觉地发出无确定意义的声音,有人认为是由于宗教体验而造成 (= glossolalia)〕。~ **clock** 电话报时服务。~ **trumpet** 传话筒;扩音器。~ **tube** 通话管。

spear[1] [spiə; spɪr] **I** ***n.*** **1.** 矛,标枪,鱼叉。**2.** 持矛者[兵]。**II** ***vt.*** 用标枪戳,用鱼叉叉鱼;叉;〔美俚〕得到,捕到。*Papa knows how to* ~ *salmon*. 爸爸知道怎样叉鲑鱼。*S- the cake and put it on the plate, Tom*. 汤姆,叉起蛋糕放在盘子上。—***vi.*** 刺,戳。**III** ***a.*** 父系的,右边的。~ *half* = ~ *side* 父系 (*opp.* distaff [spindle] side)。~ *hand* 右手 (*opp.* shield hand)。~ **fish** **1.** ***n.***【动】四鳍旗鱼(属),旗鱼。**2.** ***vi.*** 用鱼叉捕鱼。~ **carrier** 为骑士持矛者;〔喻〕配角,下手。~**grass**【植】针茅(属)。~**man**, ~**sman** ***n.*** (*pl.* ***-men***) 持矛枪的人[兵]。~ **point** **1.** 矛头,枪尖 (~ *point against* ~ *point* 针锋相对的[地])。**2.** 先锋,先头部队。

spear[2] [spiə; spɪr] **I** ***n.*** (植物的)长形的叶片[嫩芽]。**II** ***vi.*** (植物)长出长叶片[嫩芽]。

spear·head [ˈspiəhed; ˋspɪrˏhɛd] **I** ***n.*** 矛头,枪尖;前锋,

尖端,先锋。**II** ***vt*.**〔美口〕带头;当…的先锋。*act as the* ～ *of* 当…的先锋。

spear·mint [ˈspiəmint; ˋspɪr,mɪnt] ***n*.**【植】绿薄荷,留兰香。

spec [spek; spɛk] ***n*.**〔口〕投机(事业)〔speculation 的缩略〕。***on*** ～ 投机,冒险 (*do a thing on* ～ 冒险干)。

spec. = **1**. special; specially. **2**. specification. **3**. specimen.

spe·cial [ˈspeʃəl; ˋspɛʃəl] **I** ***a*.** (*opp*. general, ordinary, usual) **1**. 特别的,特殊的。**2**. 专门的;专用的;特设的。**3**. 额外的,临时附加的。**4**. 特别亲密的(朋友)。**II** ***n*.** **1**. 特别的人,特别警卫员,特使。**2**. 特别考试。**3**. 特别的东西;临时(列)车,专车;新闻号外,特刊,特稿,特别通讯,特约稿;特制影片。**4**.〔美〕选科生;特别生 (*opp*. regular student)。**5**.【医】特别护士。**6**.〔美〕特制品。*a* ～ *case* 特例。～ *duty* 特殊任务。*a* ～ *purpose computer* 专用计算机。～ *anatomy* 解剖学各论。*a* ～ *constable* 临时警察。*in* ～ 格外,特别。*one's* ～ *chair* 专用椅子。～ **agent** **1**. 特别代理人。**2**. 特务。～ **areas**〔英〕萧条地区。～ **assessment** (对房地产征收的)公用事业专用税。～ **correspondent** 特派记者。～ **course** 选科。～ **delivery** [**handling**]〔美〕快递〔英国叫 express delivery〕。～ **edition** 号外,专刊。～ **effects** (影片和电视中的)特技。～ **hospital** 专科医院。～ **pleading**【法】**1**. 不直接答覆对方而另提出事实以抵消的间接答辩法。**2**. 只讲有利之点回避不利之点的诡辩法。～ **privilege** 特权,特典。～ **steel** 特种钢。**-ism** ***n*.** (学科等)专精一门;专业;特例。**-ist** ***n*.** 专家;专科医生 (*a* ～*ist in diseases of the heart* 心脏病专家)。**-ly** ***ad*.** **-ness** ***n*.** 特殊,专门。

spe·cial·is·tic [ˌspeʃiəˈlistik; ˏspɛʃəˋlɪstɪk] ***a*.** 专家的,专门学科的。

spe·ci·al·i·ty [ˌspeʃiˈæliti; ˏspɛʃɪˋælətɪ] ***n*.**〔英〕= specialty.

spe·cial·ize [ˈspeʃəlaiz; ˋspɛʃəl,aɪz] ***vt*.** **1**. (使)特殊化,(使)专门化。**2**. 专门研究;专门从事。**3**. 专用于…;限定(意义范围等),指定(受款人)。**4**. 特别加指明,列举。**5**.【生】分化;(使)特化,(使)专化。—***vi*.** **1**. 专门研究,专攻。**2**. 逐条详述。**3**.【生】分化,特化,专化。*I'll have to ask you to examine the account and* ～ *each item*. 我得请你检查一下账目逐项详列。*any* ～*d skill* 任何业务专长。*We* ～ *in glass making*. 我们专门从事制造玻璃。**-i·za·tion** ***n*.** **1**. 特化,特殊化;专门化。**2**. (意义的)限定,限制。**3**.【生】特化(作用),专化性。**-d** ***n*.** 指定受款人的支票。

spe·cial·ty [ˈspeʃəlti; ˋspɛʃəltɪ] ***n*.**〔美〕(=〔英〕speciality) **1**. 特性,特质。**2**. 专门,专门研究,专业;专长。**3**. 特制品;特级产品;创制品,新出品。**4**.〔*pl*.〕特点;特别事项。**5**.【法】盖印,盖印证书[契约]。**6**. 钢琴伴奏团体合唱歌。*Biochemistry is his* ～. 生物化学是他的专业[专长]。*Walnut is a local* ～ *here*. 核桃是此地的土特产。***in*** ～ 特别,专门。***make a*** ～ ***of*** 以…为专业;专攻某学科。

spe·ci·ate [ˈspiːʃieit; ˋspiʃɪ,et] ***vt*.**【生】生物形成。

spe·ci·a·tion [ˌspiːʃiˈeiʃən, -siː-; ˏspiʃɪˋeʃən, -si-] ***n*.**【生】物种形成。

spe·cie [ˈspiːʃiː; ˋspiʃɪ] ***n*.**〔*sing*., *pl*.〕硬币 (*opp*. paper money)。*in* ～ 用实物;以同样方法;用硬币。～ *held* [*holding*] *abroad* 流出国外的硬币。～ *money* 硬币。～ *par* 法定平价。～ *payment* 硬币支付。～ **point**【经】黄金输出[入]点〔指达到以出口[入口]黄金较为有利的外汇行情〕。～ **reserve** 硬币储备。～ **shipment** 硬币装运。**the S- Bank** (日本的)正金银行。

spe·cies [ˈspiːʃiːz; ˋspiʃɪz, -ʃiz] ***n*.**〔*sing*., *pl*.〕**1**. 种类;【生】(物)种。**2**.【逻】种。**3**.【原】核素。**4**.【法】形式。**5**.【宗】圣餐物。*a* ～ *of folly* 一种愚蠢行为。*the four* ～【数】四则,加减乘除。*The Origin of S-*《物种起源》〔Darwin 的名著〕。*the* [*our*] ～ 人类。～ **being**【哲】类存在物[指人]。～**-poor** ***a*.**【生】物种贫乏的。～**-rich** ***a*.**【生】物种丰富的。

spe·cif. = specific(ally).

spec·i·fi·a·ble [ˈspesiˌfaiəbl; ˋspɛsə,faɪəbl̩] ***a*.** 可列举的,能详细说明的。

spe·cif·ic, -al [spiˈsifik, -əl; spɪˋsɪfɪk, -əl] **I** ***a*.** **1**. 特殊的;特有的;特定的,专门的。**2**. 明确的,具体的。**3**.【生】种的;【细菌】专性的。**4**.【医】有特效的;由特种病菌[病毒]引起的,特异型的。**5**.【商】按数量征税的。**6**.【物】比的。*I want a* ～ *analysis of the problem*. 我要一个对这问题的专门的分析。*This tells you that there is a* ～ *distinction between the right and the wrong*. 这件事告诉你是与非是有明确的区别的。**II** ***n*.** **1**. 特殊用途的事物。**2**. 详论,细节。**3**. 特性。**4**. 特效药 (*for*)。*a* ～ *sum of money* 一定金额。～ **activity**【物】放射性比度。～ **capacity**【电】电离率;【物】比容量。～ **characters**【生】种特性。～ **duty**【商】从量税。～ **gravity**【物】比重。～ **heat**【物】比热。～ **mass**【物】密度。～ **name**【生】种名。～ **performance**【法】照规定严格执行(合同等)。～ **remedy** [**medicine**] 特效药。～ **surface**【化】比表面,单位表面。～ **volume**【物】比容,体积度。

spe·cif·ic·al·ly [speiˈsifikəli; spɪˋsɪfɪkəlɪ] ***ad*.** **1**. 按种别地,按类别地,按特性地。**2**. 特别地,明确地,各别地;尤其。*I told him* ～ *not to miss Professor Chang's lecture*. 我曾特别地嘱咐他不要缺张教授的课。

spec·i·fi·ca·tion [ˌspesifiˈkeiʃən; ˏspɛsəfəˋkeʃən] ***n*.** **1**. 详细说明,逐一登记,详记。**2**.〔*pl*.〕规范,规格。**3**. 清单,明细单。**4**.【法】(申报新发明时的)设计说明书。**5**.【法】用来料加工制成新产品所取得的权利。*Can you send the job* ～ *to me at once*? 你能把工程作业的详细说明马上送来吗? *a signal* ～ 信号规格;信号技术条件。*working* ～*s* 操作规程。***fall short of*** ～***s*** 不合规格。

spec·i·fic·i·ty [ˌspesiˈfisiti; ˏspɛsəˋfɪsətɪ] ***n*.** **1**. 特异性,特征;种别性。**2**. 特效。**3**.【化】专一性。**4**.【生】专化性。

spec·i·fy [ˈspesifai; ˋspɛsə,faɪ] ***vt*.** (***-fied***) **1**. 指定;具体说明,详细说明。**2**. 逐一登记,详列;列入清单;分类;特殊化。*at a time and place to be specified* 在指定的时间地点。*specified weight* 规定重量。～ *those to whom invitations are to be sent* 具体开明应加邀请的人名。

spec·i·men [ˈspesimin, -mən; ˋspɛsəmən] ***n*.** **1**. 样本,样品,实例,例子;标本;雏形。**2**. 供检查用的材料,试料。**3**.〔口〕怪人。*a* ～ *copy* (新书)样本。*a* ～ *page* 样张。～*s in spirits* 泡在酒精中的标本。*stuffed* ～*s*【动】实制标本。*queer* ～ 怪人。*What a* ～! 真是一个怪家伙!

spe·ci·ol·o·gy [ˌspiːʃiˈɔlədʒi; ˏspiʃɪˋɑlədʒɪ] ***n*.**【生】物种学。**-log·i·cal** [-ˈlɔ-; -ˋlɔ-] ***a*.**

spe·ci·os·i·ty [ˌspiːʃiˈɔsiti; ˏspiʃɪˋɑsətɪ] ***n*.** **1**.〔罕〕外表美观[华而不实](的人[物])。**2**. 貌似有理[似是而非](的言行)。

spe·cious [ˈspiːʃəs; ˋspiʃəs] ***adj*** **1**. 外表美观的。**2**. 貌似有理的。*We wouldn't accept his* ～ *claim*. 我们不会接受他那貌似有理的要求的。**-ly** ***ad*.** **-ness** ***n*.**

speck[1] [spek; spɛk] **I** ***n*.** **1**. 斑点;污点;缺点。**2**. (水果的)疵斑。**3**. 微片,微粒。**4**. 有烂斑的东西〔鱼,水果等〕。*You can't eat fish covered with dark* ～*s*. 你可不能吃满是黑斑的鱼。*Now you put a* ～ *of orange juice in the water*. 现在你在水里放一点点橘子汁。**II** ***vt*.**〔常用 *p*. *p*.〕加斑点;玷污。

speck[2] [spek; spɛk] ***n*.**〔美、南非〕(海豹等的)脂肪;肥肉。

speck·le [ˈspekl; ˋspɛkl̩] **I** ***n*.** 斑点;斑纹〔常用 *p*. *p*.〕。**II** ***vt*.** **1**. 加斑点。**2**. 玷污。**3**. 点缀。*a* ～*d group* [*lot*] 驳杂的人群。～*d trout* 斑鲑,斑鳟〔指各种鲑鱼,鳟鱼,因地而异〕。*dark hair* ～*d with gray* 斑白的头

发。

specks, specs [speks; spɛks] ***n.*** 〔*pl.*〕〔口〕眼镜。

spec·ta·cle [ˈspektəkl; ˋspɛktəkl] ***n.*** **1.** 观览物,展览物。**2.** 光景,景象,状况;奇观,壮观。**3.** 惨状,悲惨景况。**4.** 阅兵典礼。**5.** 表演,场面,场面富丽的影片[戏剧]。**6.** 〔*pl.*〕眼镜。**7.** 【铁路】信号灯灯框。*On Sunday, the kids of the kindergarten made a very amusing* ~. 星期日那天,幼稚园的孩子们作了很有意思的表演。*Such a* ~ *has seldom been seen of late years.* 这样的壮观近年来很少见哪。*a pair of* ~*s* 一副眼镜;〔板球俚〕两次吃零分。*I cannot see things through your* ~*s.* 我的看法和你的不一样。***make a*** ~ ***of oneself*** 出洋相;大大出丑。***see all things through rosy*** ~***s*** 事事(过分)乐观。***wear*** [***take off***] ~***s*** 戴上[取下]眼镜。~ **plate** 【机】双孔板。

spec·ta·cled [ˈspektəkld; ˋspɛktəkld] ***a.*** 戴着眼镜的;【动】有眼镜状斑纹的。*a* ~ *bear* 【动】眼镜熊。

spec·tac·u·lar [spekˈtækjulə; spɛkˋtækjələ˞] **I** ***a.*** **1.** 场面富丽的,壮观的;观赏品的,展览物的。**2.** 引人注意的,惊动一时的,惊人的。*a* ~ *play* 一出场面富丽的戏。*a* ~ *display of lights* 蔚为壮观的灯火。*in a* ~ *fashion* 惊人地,壮观地。**II** ***n.*** **1.** 盛大的场面;壮观,展览物。**2.** 〔美〕一小时半以上的大场面电视节目。**3.** 特大霓虹灯广告。**-ly** ***ad.***

spec·tate [ˈspekteit; ˋspɛktet] ***vi.*** 出席观看。

spec·ta·tor [spekˈteitə; ˋspɛktetə˞, spɛkˋtetə˞] **I** ***n.*** (*fem.* ***-tress*** [-tris; -trɪs]) **1.** (看比赛等的)观众;旁观者。**2.** 〔*pl.*〕〔美〕女运动鞋。*The S-* 〔英〕《旁观者》〔期刊名〕。**II** ***a.*** 〔美〕**1.** 能吸引观众的。**2.** 观看用的;运动用的;华美的,漂亮的。*such* ~ *sports as boxing* 像拳斗之类的能吸引观众的运动。~ **frock** 运动(上)衣。

spec·ta·to·rit·is [ˌspekˈteitəraitis; ˏspɛkˋtetəraɪtɪs] ***n.*** 运动不足病。

spec·ter [ˈspektə; ˋspɛktə˞] ***n.*** 〔美〕= spectre.

spec·tra [ˈspektrə; ˋspɛktrə] ***n.*** spectrum 的复数。

spec·tral [ˈspektrəl; ˋspɛktrəl] ***a.*** **1.** 鬼的;鬼怪(似)的。**2.** 【物】光谱的。*a* ~ *apparatus* 分光器。~ *analysis* 光谱分析。~ *colours* 谱色。~ *line* 光谱线。

spec·tre [ˈspektə; ˋspɛktə˞] ***n.*** **1.** 幽灵;鬼影。**2.** 恐怖的根源,(纠缠不去的)心中暗鬼。*There is no denying that the* ~ *of unemployment and want is constantly haunting them.* 失业和贫乏的幽灵一直在对他们作祟是不能否认的。

spectro- *comb. f.* 光谱的: *spectro*scope.

spec·tro·chem·is·try [ˌspektrəˈkemistri; ˏspɛktroˋkɛmɪstrɪ] ***n.*** 光谱化学。**-chem·i·cal** ***a.***

spec·tro·gram [ˈspektrəˌgræm; ˋspɛktrəˏgræm] ***n.*** 【物】光谱图。

spec·tro·graph [ˈspektrəugrɑːf; ˋspɛktrəˏgræf, -ˏgrɑf] ***n.*** 【物】摄谱仪,分光摄谱仪。**-ic** ***a.*** **-i·cal·ly** ***ad.*** **-y** ***n.***

spec·tro·he·li·o·gram [ˌspektrəˈhiːliəgræm; ˏspɛktroˋhilɪəˏgræm] ***n.*** 【天】太阳单色光照片。

spec·tro·he·li·o·graph [ˌspektrəˈhiːliəˌgrɑːf, -ˌgræf; ˏspɛktrəˋhilɪəˏgrɑf, -græf] ***n.*** 【天】太阳单色光照相仪,日射光谱计。

spec·tro·he·li·o·scope [ˌspektrəˈhiːliəˌskəup; ˏspɛktrəˋhilɪəˏskop] ***n.*** 【天】太阳单色光观测镜。

spec·trom·e·ter [spekˈtrɔmitə; spɛkˋtrɑmətə˞] ***n.*** 【物】分光仪,分光计。*a mass* ~ 质谱仪。*a sound* ~ 声频频谱计。

spec·tro·me·tric [spektrəˈmetrik; spɛktrəˋmɛtrɪk] ***a.*** 光谱测定的,度谱的。

spec·tro·pho·to-e·lec·tric [ˌspektrəfəutəuiˈlektrik; ˏspɛktrəfotoɪˋlɛktrɪk] ***a.*** 【物】分光光电作用的。

spec·tro·pho·tom·e·ter [ˌspektrəufəˈtɔmitə; ˏspɛktrofoˋtɑmətə˞] ***n.*** 【天】分光光度计。**-pho·to·met·ric** [-ˈfəutəmeˈtrik; -ˋfotəmɛˋtrɪk] ***a.*** **-pho·tom·e·try** ***n.***

spec·tro·scope [ˈspektrəskəup; ˋspɛktrəˏskop] ***n.*** 【物】分光镜,分光器。**-scop·ic, -i·cal** ***a.*** **-i·cal·ly** ***ad.***

spec·tros·co·py [spekˈtrɔskəpi; spɛkˋtrɑskəpɪ, ˋspɛktrəˏskopɪ] ***n.*** 【物】分光术,光谱学。**-ist** ***n.***

spec·trum [ˈspektrəm; ˋspɛktrəm] ***n.*** (*pl.* ***-tra*** [-trə; -trə]) **1.** 【物】谱,光谱;波谱;能谱,质谱。**2.** 【无】射频频谱;无线电(信号)频谱。**3.** 【心】(眼睛的)余像;残像。**4.** 〔转义〕范围,幅度;(连续的)系列。*an absorption* ~ 吸收(光)谱。*a bright line* ~ 线状光谱。*an optical* ~ 光谱。*a solar* ~ 太阳光谱。***a wide*** ~ ***of opinion*** 意见的不同幅度甚大。~ **analysis** 光谱分析。~ **distribution** 光谱分布。

spec·u·la [ˈspekjulə; ˋspɛkjələ] ***n.*** speculum 的复数。

spec·u·lar [ˈspekjulə; ˋspɛkjələ˞] ***a.*** **1.** 镜子的;镜子似的,反射的。**2.** 【医】用窥器(检查)的,镜检的。~ *cobalt ore* 辉钴矿。~ *iron* 镜铁矿。~ *orb* 眼睛;透镜。~ *reflection* 【物】单向反射。~ *surface* 【物】反射面。~ *stone* 云母。

spec·u·late [ˈspekjuleit; ˋspɛkjəˏlet] ***vi.*** **1.** 沉思,思索;设想,推测 (*about*; *on*; *upon*)。**2.** 投机 (*in*)。~ *about the origin of the universe* 沉思宇宙的起源。~ *in stocks* 做股票投机。~ ***on a rise*** [***fall***] 做多头[空头]投机,赌涨[跌]。

spec·u·la·tion [ˌspekjuˈleiʃən; ˏspɛkjəˋleʃən] ***n.*** **1.** 沉思,思索,考虑。**2.** 推测;空谈。**3.** 投机,投机事业[买卖]。**4.** 一种纸牌戏。***buy sth. as a*** ~ 投机购买某物。***engage in*** ~ 做投机生意。***much given to*** ~ 想入非非。***Much*** ~ ***is rife concerning*** [***as to***] .... 关于…有许多推测。***on*** ~ 投机,碰运气地。***spread the*** ~ ***that*** 散播空气说。

spec·u·la·tive [ˈspekjulətiv, -leit-; ˋspɛkjəˏletɪv] ***a.*** **1.** 思索的;思辨的;推理的;纯理论的;(专事)推测的。**2.** 投机(性质)的;冒风险的。~ **geometry** 理论几何学。~ **market** 投机市场。**-ly** ***ad.*** **-ness** ***n.***

spec·u·la·tor [ˈspekjuleitə; ˋspɛkjəˏletə˞] ***n.*** **1.** 投机者,投机商人;〔美〕垄断收买(戏票)的人。**2.** 思辨者;纯[抽象]理论家,空谈者。

spec·u·lum [ˈspekjuləm; ˋspɛkjələm] ***n.*** (*pl.* ***-la*** [-lə; -lə], ~***s***) **1.** (古代的)金属镜;反射镜。**2.** 【医】窥器,诊察镜;开张器。**3.** 【天】行星相对位置图谱。**4.** 【动】(鸟的)翼斑,翼镜。**5.** (鳞翅目翅的)透明斑;(鳞翅目幼虫的)颈斑。**6.** 【动】灿点,眼状斑。*a nasal* ~ 【医】鼻镜。~ **metal** 镜齐,制镜用(铜锡)合金。

sped [sped; spɛd] speed 的过去式及过去分词。

speech [spiːtʃ; spitʃ] ***n.*** **1.** 言语;说话;谈话;说话能力(或方式)。**2.** 民族语言,方言,专门语言;〔罕〕流言。**3.** 演说,演讲;发言。**4.** 【语】词(类);引语;用语。**5.** (乐器的)音,音色。*Everybody has the right to give* ~ *to his feelings.* 人人有说出他的感情的权力。*Speech is silver, silence is gold.* 〔谚〕畅言是银,沉默是金。*a man of rapid* [*slow*] ~ 口齿流利[迟钝]的人。*an opening* [*a closing*] ~ 开幕[闭幕]辞。*parts of* ~ 【语法】词类。*a* ~ *community* 使用某种特有语言(或方言)的集团。*freedom of* ~ 言论自由。***deliver*** [***make***] ***a*** ~ 演说。***find one's*** ~ 能说话;说得出话。***give*** ~ ***to*** 说出。***have*** ~ ***of*** (***a person***) 和…谈话。***lose*** [***recover***] ***one's*** ~ 丧失[恢复]说话能力。~**amplifier** 音频放大器。~ **centre** 言语中枢。~ **clinic** 言语矫正所。~**day** 〔英〕学校毕业授奖典礼日。~ **disorder** 语言失常[紊乱]。~ **form** 语言形态。~**maker** 演说家。~ **organ** 发言器官。~**reading** 聋哑人的视话法。~**-way** (某民族地区集团)特有的言语方式。~ **recognizer** 言语识别器。~**writer** 讲演稿撰写人。

speech·i·fy [ˈspiːtʃifai; ˋspitʃəˏfaɪ] ***vi.*** (***-fied***) 〔谑、蔑〕(滔滔不绝地)演说,高谈阔论。**-fi·er** ***n.*** 〔谑、蔑〕滔滔不绝的演说者。**-fication** ***n.***

speech·less [ˈspiːtʃlis; ˋspitʃlɪs] *a*. 1. 不会说话的;哑的。2. 说不出话来的。3. 言语表达不出的;无言的。4. 〔英俚〕烂醉的。*A gorilla is just a ~ animal*. 猩猩只不过是一种不会说话的动物。*The fact that she grew pale showed her ~ fright*. 她面无人色说明了她说不出来的恐惧。~ **with** [**from**] **fear** 吓得说不出话来。**-ly** *ad*. **-ness** *n*.

speed [spiːd; spid] **I** *n*. 1. 快,迅速。2. 速率,速度。3. (汽车的)变速器,排挡。4. (胶片,照相纸)感光速度。5. 〔古〕兴隆,成功。6. 〔美〕甲基苯异丙胺(类毒品)。7. 〔美口〕(大音量和强节奏的)"重金属"(电子)摇滚乐(=~-metal)。*More haste, less* [*worse*] ~. 越急越慢,欲速反迟。*The ship has a ~ of 30 knots*. 这条船时速30海里。*Let's accelerate the ~ of our community construction*. 让我们加快我们社区建设的速度。*a top ~* 最大速度。*a ~ of escape* [*escape ~*]【火箭】第二宇宙速度,逃逸速度〔克服地球引力的速度〕。*a horse of ~* 快马。(**at**) **full ~ = at the top of one's ~** 用全速,开足马力。**make ~** 赶快,赶紧,加快。**put on full ~** 用全速,开足马力。**with ~** 迅速,赶快。**wish** (*sb*.) **good ~ =** *wish good ~* (*to sb*.) 祝…成功。**with all ~** 用全速,开足马力。**II** *vt*. (**sped** [sped; spɛd], *~ed*) (常用 *~ed*) 1. 催,使赶快,促进,快速送传。2. 〔古〕使成功,使成就,使兴隆。3. 祝愿成功,祝一路平安。4. 调节速度,使保持一定速度。*Speed our boat forward*. *It's getting dark*. 使我们的小船快速前进,天黑起来了。*It's time we ~ the parting guests*. 现在是我们去向离别的客人们祝福一路平安的时候了。—*vi*. 1. 迅速前进,快行 (*along*; *down*; *up*; *across*)。2. 进行;过日子。3. 〔美〕(汽车司机)用规定以上的速度驾驶。4. 〔古〕成功,兴隆。*The car sped directly to the village*. 汽车一直地疾驶进入村子里。*I should like to know how you ~*. 我很想知道您的好情况。*God ~ you*! 祝成功! ~ **ill** 不顺利。~ **up** 加快(机器等的)速度;使加紧做(*sth*.)(~ *up the work* 加紧工作)。~ **well** 顺利。~**ball** 1. 快速球类运动。2. (俚)掺海洛因、吗啡的柯卡因。~**-baller** *n*.【棒球】快速球投手。~**bird**, ~**boat** 高速快艇。~ **brake**【空】气动减速煞车,减速器。~ **bump** 减速路脊(=sleeping policeman);〔喻〕小小的障碍。~**-change gear**【机】变速齿轮。~**cop**〔美俚〕取缔超速汽车的警察。~**-down** 减速。~**flash** = ~ light. ~**-fiend**, ~**-hog** = speeder 1. ~ **freak** 毒瘾很深的人。~**gun** 手提式车辆估速器。~ **indicator** 速度计。~**ing**〔美〕(违犯规定的)超速行驶。~**light** 闪光管,频闪放电器。~ **limit** 速度限制。~**-merchant** *n*.〔美〕= speeder 1. (违章超速开车的)汽车司机;【棒球】快速球投手。~**-metal** = speed 7. ~ **multiplier**【机】倍速器。~**reading** (跳过一些段落的)快速阅读。~ **scout**【军】高速侦察机。~ **shop** 高速赛车部件店。~**-track** = ~ way. ~ **trap** 汽车超速监视区。~**up** 1. 加快速度;(机械等的)能率促进。2. (火车等的)高速度化。~**way** 1. 摩托车汽车赛跑道。2. 〔美〕高速公路。~**walk** 电动人行道。~**well**【植】(药用)婆婆纳(属)。

speed·er [ˈspiːdə; ˋspidɚ] *n*. 1. 违法超速开车者。2. 【机】调速装置;加速器。

speed·i·ly [ˈspiːdili; ˋspidḷɪ] *ad*. 快,迅速,赶快,赶紧。

speed·i·ness [ˈspiːdinis; ˋspidɪnɪs] *n*. 迅速。

speed·ing [ˈspiːdiŋ; ˋspidɪŋ] *n*. 超速行驶。

speed·om·e·ter [spiːˈdɔmitə; spiˋdɑmətɚ] *n*.【机】示速器;(汽车等的)速度计,里程计。

speed·ster [ˈspiːdstə; ˋspidstɚ] *n*. 1. = speeder. 2. 双人座高速汽车;快艇。

speed·y [ˈspiːdi; ˋspidɪ] *a*. (*-i·er*; *-i·est*) 快的,迅速的;敏捷的。*a ~ answer* 敏捷的回答。*a ~ retribution* 迅速的报应。

speiss [spais; spaɪs] *n*.【冶】硬渣,黄渣。

spe·lae·an, **spe·le·an** [spiˈliən; spɪˋliən] *a*. 1. 洞穴的,洞穴状的。2. 穴居的。

spe·l(a)e·ol·o·gy [ˌspi(ː)liˈɔlədʒi; ˏspilɪˋɑlədʒɪ] *n*. 洞穴学。**-gist** *n*.

spell[1] [spel; spɛl] *vt*. (**spelled** [spelt, -d; spɛld], **spelt**) 1. (用字母)拼写,边拼边读。2. 费力地读出、读懂 (*out*; *over*)。3. 拼作,拼作…而读作…。4. 认真研究出,琢磨 (*out*)。5. 指示,是…的表现,有…的意义;招致,带来,意味。—*vi*. 拼写;读;〔诗〕研究。*How do you ~ your name*? 你的名字是怎样拼的? *You've ~ed this word wrong*. 你把这个字拼错了。*Can you ~ out this word in the manuscript*? 你能认出手稿中的这个字吗? *Our failure is likely to ~ heavy losses*. 我们的失败可能招致重大的损失。~ *danger* 招致[意味着]危险。~ **backward** 倒拼;曲解,误解。~ **down** 在拼字比赛中胜过(某人)。~ **out** 1. 详细说明,清楚地说明。2.【印】正式拼写,全文拼写出来。~ **over** 思考,考虑。~ **short** 随随便便讲,漫不经心地讲。**-able** *a*. 可拼写的。~**down** 拼字比赛〔尤指失误者即被淘汰的比赛〕。

spell[2] [spel; spɛl] **I** *n*. 1. 轮班,换班;替班;服务时间。2. (天气等)一段(持续的)时间,休息一段时间。3. (工作的)一段时间。4. (疾病等的)一次发作时间。5. 〔口〕短距离,暂时。6. 〔美口〕心里不愉快的时候,烦闷的时候。*Each one of them does a six hours' ~ of duty*. 他们每个人值六小时的班。*Let's take a ~ and have some tea*. 咱们休息一会儿喝点茶。*a ~ of coughing* 一阵咳嗽。*a ~ of fine weather* 连日好天气。*a hot ~* 连热不已。*a ~ of service in Hongkong* 在香港工作一段时间。*a ~ of bad luck* 一连串的坏运气。*a breathing ~* 喘息的机会。**by ~s** 轮流,轮班,断断续续地。**for a ~** 暂时。**give a ~** 使换班休息。**have a ~ = keep a ~ = take a ~** 换班,接班(*have a ~ at the oars* 换班划桨)。**take by ~ = take ~ and** [**for**] ~ 轮流。**II** *vt*. 〔英罕,美〕使换班休息。

spell[3] [spel; spɛl] **I** *n*. 1. 符咒,咒语。2. 吸引力,诱惑力,魔力,魅力。**be bound by a ~ = be under the ~** 给符咒镇住;被…迷住。**break a ~** 破除魔力[吸引力,诱惑力]。**cast** [**lay**, **put**] (*sb*.) **under a ~ = cast** [**lay**, **put**] **a ~** (**up**) **on** [**over**] (*sb*.) 迷住;蛊惑。**II** *vt*. (*~ed* [spelt, -d; spɛlt, -d], **spelt** [spelt; spɛlt]) 1. 念咒镇住,用符咒镇服。2. 蛊惑,迷惑。~**bind** *vt*. 迷惑[诱惑]。~**binder**〔美口语〕(使听者入迷的)雄辩家 (*an air ~binder* 广播演说家)。~**binding** *a*. (演讲等)使人入迷的。~**bound** *a*. 1. 被符咒镇住的。2. 被迷住的,着了迷的。

spell·er [ˈspelə; ˋspɛlɚ] *n*. 拼字者;拼写者;〔美〕拼字书。

spell·ing [ˈspeliŋ; ˋspɛlɪŋ] *n*. 拼字;拼写法。*In English there are often several ~s for one sound*. 英语一个音常常有几种拼写法。*Don't make a mistake in your ~*. 不要在拼法上出错。~ **bee** [**-match**] *n*. 〔美〕拼写比赛。**Spelling Ace**〔商标〕"拼写高手"〔一种手提式电脑,内含一部收词80000条并附搭配句型的词典,用于核对拼写并能核对词的搭配用法得当与否〕。~ **book** 拼写课本。~ **checker**【计】拼写检查程序[功能];拼写检查器。~**pronounciation** 拼写读音法〔指按拼写读音,而不是一般公认的读音的误读〕。

spelt[1] [spelt; spɛlt] spell[1]和 spell[3]的过去式及过去分词。

spelt[2] [spelt; spɛlt] *n*.【植】(作饲料用的)斯佩耳特小麦。

spel·ter [ˈspeltə; ˋspɛltɚ] *n*.【商】锌块;锌合金焊料,硬焊料。

spe·lunk·er [spiˈlʌŋkə; spɪˋlʌŋkɚ] *n*. 洞窟学家,洞窟探险家。**-lunk·ing** *n*.

spence, **spense** [spens; spɛns] *n*. 〔主 Scot.〕1. 食品贮藏室。2. (学校等的)食品供应部。3. (乡间的)内室,起居室。

spen·cer[1] [ˈspensə; ˋspɛnsɚ] *n*. (19世纪男女通用的)短大衣;毛线短褂。

spen·cer[2] [ˈspensə; ˋspɛnsɚ] *n*.【船】(风暴时用的)小斜

S

桁帆。

Spen·cer [ˈspensə; ˋspɛnsɚ] ***n*.** **1.** 斯潘塞〔姓氏,男子名〕。**2. Herbert** ～ 斯宾塞〔1820—1903,英国实证主义哲学家〕。

Spen·ce·ri·an [spenˈsiəriən; spɛnˋsɪrɪən] **I** ***a*.** 英国斯宾塞哲学的;美国人罗吉·斯宾塞(Rogers Spencer)体书法的。**II** ***n*.** 斯宾塞派的哲学家;【书法】斯宾塞体。

spend [spend; spɛnd] **I** ***vt*.** (***spent*** [spent; spɛnt]) **1.** 用(钱),花费。**2.** 乱花;浪费;过(日子)。**3.** 消磨(时间),度过,过日子;用光,用尽(子弹、气力、财产等);消耗;使筋疲力尽,使极度衰弱;费(很多心血等)。**4.** 献出(生命等);【海】失去(桅)。*How much have you spent on books this term?* 这学期你在买书上用了多少钱? *Father is going to ～ the winter in New York.* 父亲将要在纽约过冬。*a life honestly spent in the service of one's country* 忠心耿耿地为国家作奉献的一生。—***vi*.** **1.** 用钱,花钱;浪费。**2.** 耗尽,用尽,用完;筋疲力尽,极度衰弱。**3.** (鱼等)产卵,下子。*Don't ～ without the thought of the next day.* 不要只顾眼前不想明天地花钱。～ ***and be spent*** 出钱又出力,尽全力。～ ***itself*** [***oneself***] 耗尽;筋疲力尽,衰弱 (*The storm has spent itself.* 暴风雨已过去了)。～ ***one's blood*** 费尽心血。～ ***one's breath*** [***words***] (***in vain***) 白费唇舌,说也无用。～ ***one's last*** 动用最后存品[存款]。**-able** ***a*.** 可花费的。**-er** ***n*.** 挥霍者,浪费者。

Spen·der [ˈspendə; ˋspɛndɚ] ***n*.** 斯彭德〔姓氏〕。

spend·ing [ˈspendiŋ; ˋspɛndɪŋ] ***n*.** 经费,开销。～ *money* 〔美〕零用钱。

S

spend·thrift [ˈspend*d*θrift; ˋspɛnd,θrɪft, ˋspɛn,θrɪft] **I** ***n*.** 乱花钱的人,浪费者;浪子,败家子。**II** ***a*.** 乱花钱的;挥霍的,浪费的。*no* ～ 〔美〕吝啬(鬼)。

Spen·ser[1] [ˈspensə; ˋspɛnsɚ] ***n*.** **1.** 斯潘赛〔姓氏〕。**2. Edmund** ～ 爱德门·斯宾塞〔1552? —1599,英国诗人〕。

Spen·se·ri·an [spenˈsiəriən; spɛnˋsɪrɪən] **I** ***a*.** (英国诗人)斯宾塞体的。**II** ***n*.** 斯宾塞 (Spenser) 派诗人。～ **stanza** 斯宾塞体〔斯氏在 *Faerie Queene* 中所用的诗体〕。

spent [spent; spɛnt] **I** spend 的过去式及过去分词。**II** ***a*.** **1.** 筋疲力尽的,冲势已完的,衰弱了的;失去效能的。**2.** (鱼)产了卵的。*a* ～ *arrow* 冲力已完的箭。～ *gas* 废气。～ *material* 废料。～ *residue* 废物。

sperm[1] [spəːm; spɝm] ***n*.** 【生】精子;精液。～ **bank** 精子库〔供人工授精用〕。～ **cell** 精细胞。～ **count** 【医】(一次射出的)精子计数。

sperm[2] [spəːm; spɝm] ***n*.** **1.** = ～ whale 抹香鲸。**2.** = ～ oil 鲸蜡;鲸脑(油)。～ **oil** 鲸油。

sperm(a)-, sperm- *comb. f.* 精子,精液: *sperma*duct.

sper·ma·cet·i [ˌspəːməˈseti, -məˈsiːti; ˏspɝməˋsɛtɪ, -ˋsitɪ] ***n*.** 鲸蜡,鲸脑油。

sper·ma·duct [ˈspəːmədʌkt; ˋspɝmə,dʌkt] ***n*.** 【解】输精管。

sper·ma·go·ni·um [ˌspəːməˈgəuniəm; ˏspɝməˋgonɪəm] ***n*.** (*pl*. ***-ni·a*** [-ə; -ə]) 【植】精原细胞。

sper·ma·ry [ˈspəːməri; ˋspɝmərɪ] ***n*.** **1.** 【动】睾丸;精巢。**2.** 【植】雄器,(蕨苔的)精子器;花粉管。

sper·ma·the·ca [ˌspəːməˈθiːkə; ˏspɝməˋθikə] ***n*.** 【动】(雌虫的)受精囊。

sper·mat·ic [spəːˈmætik; spɝˋmætɪk] ***a*.** **1.** 精子[液]的;精囊的,睾丸的;精巢的;生殖的。**2.** 产生的,发生的。～ *fluid* 精液。*a* ～ *duct* 输精管。～ *cord* 【解】精索。

sper·ma·tid [ˈspəːmətid; ˋspɝmətɪd] ***n*.** 【动】精子细胞。

sper·ma·ti·um [spəˈmeiʃiəm; spɝˋmeʃɪəm] ***n*.** (*pl*. ***-ti·a*** [-ə; -ə]) 【植】**1.** 不动精子。**2.** (锈菌)性孢子。

sper·ma·to·blast [ˈspəːmət*ə*ublæst; ˋspɝmətə,blæst] ***n*.** 精子细胞。

sper·mat·o·cyte [spəˈmætəˌsait, ˈspəːmətə-; ˋspɝmətə,saɪt] ***n*.** 【生】精母细胞 (= sperm mother cell)。

sper·mat·o·gen·e·sis [spəmætəˈdʒenisis, ˌspəːmətəu-; ˏspɝmətəˋdʒɛnəsɪs] ***n*.** 精子发生。**-ge·netic** [-dʒiˈnetik; -dʒɪˋnɛtɪk] ***a*.**

sper·ma·tog·e·nous [spəːməˈtɔdʒənəs; ˏspɝməˋtɑdʒənəs] ***a*.** 产生精子[精液]的。**-e·ny** ***n*.** = spermatogenesis.

sper·mat·o·go·ni·um [spəmətəˈgəuniəm; ˏspɝmətəˋgonɪəm] ***n*.** (*pl*. ***-ni·a*** [-ə; -ə]) 【动】精原细胞。**-go·ni·al** ***a*.**

sper·ma·tol·o·gy [ˌspəːməˈtɔlədʒi; ˏspɝməˋtɑlədʒɪ] ***n*.** 精子学。**-log·i·cal** ***a*.** **-o·gist** ***n*.**

sper·ma·to·phore [ˈspəːmətəfɔː, -fɔə; ˋspɝmətə,for] ***n*.** 【生】精子托,精荚,精球;精原细胞;精子包囊;(低等植物的)精子孢蒴。

sper·ma·to·phyte [ˈspəːmətəfait; ˋspɝmətə,faɪt] ***n*.** 【植】种子植物。

sper·ma·tor·rh(o)e·a [ˌspəːmət*ə*uˈriːə; ˏspɝmətəˋriə] ***n*.** 【医】精溢[漏]。

sper·mat·o·zo·id [spəˌmætəˈzəuid, ˌspəːmətə-; spə,mætəˋzoɪd, ˏspɝmətə-] ***n*.** 【植】游动精子。～ **nucleus** 精核。

sper·ma·to·zo·on [ˌspəːmət*ə*uˈzəuɔn; ˏspɝmətəˋzoɑn] ***n*.** (*pl*. ***-zoa*** [-ˈzəuə; -ˋzoə]) 【生】精子。**-zo·al, -zo·an** ***a*.**

sperm·i·cide [ˈspəːmiˌsaid; ˋspɝˋmɪ,saɪd] ***n*.** 【医】杀精子剂。**-i·ci·dal** ***a*.**

sperm·ine [ˈspəːmiːn; ˋspɝmin, -mɪn] ***n*.** 【生化】精胺,精素,精碱〔作补药用〕。

sper·mi·o·gen·e·sis [ˌspəːmiəuˈdʒenisis; ˏspɝmɪoˋdʒɛnəsɪs] ***n*.** 【动】**1.** 精子形成。**2.** = spermatogenesis.

sper·mo·blast [ˈspəːməblæst; ˋspɝmə,blæst] ***n*.** 【生】精子细胞。

sper·mo·go·ni·um [ˌspəːməˈgəuniəm; ˏspɝməˋgonɪəm] ***n*.** (*pl*. ***-ni·a*** [-ə; -ə]) = spermagonium.

sper·mo·lo·gy [spəːˈmɔlədʒi; spɝˋmɑlədʒɪ] ***n*.** **1.** 精子学。**2.** 种子学。**-log·i·cal** ***a*.** **-o·gist** ***n*.**

sper·mo·phile [ˈspəːməˌfail, -fil; ˋspɝmə,faɪl, -fɪl] ***n*.** 【动】欧黄鼠。

sper·mous [ˈspəːməs; ˋspɝməs] ***a*.** 精子的;精子状的。

sper·ry·lite [ˈsperiˌlait; ˋspɛrɪ,laɪt] ***n*.** 【矿】砷铂矿。

spes·sar·tite, spes·sart·ine [ˈspesəˌtait, -tin; ˋspɛsɚ,taɪt, -tɪn] ***n*.** 【地】锰铝榴矿,闪斜煌斑岩。

spew [spjuː; spju] **I** ***vt*.** **1.** 呕吐。**2.** 喷、涌、渗。—***vi*.** **1.** 呕吐。**2.** 涌出。**3.** 渗出。*This is an active volcano which ～s out lava every year.* 这是个每年喷熔岩的活火山。*One of the ways to purify water is to make it ～ slowly from the soil.* 净化水的方法之一是让它从土中慢慢地渗出。**II** ***n*.** 吐[呕]出物;喷出物,渗出物。

SPF = sun-protection factor 【医】防晒系数〔指防晒霜等化妆品防晒作用的等级〕。

sp.gr. = specific gravity 【物】比重。

sphac·e·late [ˈsfæsileit; ˋsfæsə,let] **I** ***vt*., *vi*.** (使)生坏疽;(使)形成腐肉;(使)生枯斑;(使)腐烂,坏死。**II** ***a*.** 【植】枯萎了的。

sphac·e·la·tion [ˌsfæsiˈleiʃən; ˏsfæsəˋleʃən] ***n*.** 【医】(生)坏疽;腐肉形成。

sphac·el·us [ˈsfæsiləs; ˋsfæsələs] ***n*.** 【医】坏疽,坏死组织;腐肉。

sphag·num [ˈsfægnəm; ˋsfægnəm] ***n*.** (*pl*. ***-na*** [-nə; -nə]) 【植】水藓;泥炭藓。

sphal·er·ite [ˈsfeiliˌrait; ˋsfælə,raɪt, ˋsfe-] ***n*.** 【矿】闪锌矿。

sphene [sfiːn; sfin] ***n*.** 【化】榍石。

sphe·no·don [ˈsfiːnəˌdɔn; ˋsfinə,dɑn] ***n*.** 【动】斑点楔齿蜥 (= tuatara)。

sphe·no·gram [ˈsfiːnəugræm; ˋsfino,græm] *n*. 楔形文字。

sphe·nog·ra·phy [sfiːˈnɔgrəfi; sfiˋnɑgrəfɪ] *n*. 〔罕〕1. 楔形文字书写术。2. 楔形文字学。**-ra·pher** *n*. **-ra·phist** *n*. **-graph·ic** *a*.

sphe·noid [ˈsfiːnɔid; ˋsfinɔɪd] **I** *a*. 楔状的;【解】蝶骨的。**II** *n*. 楔状骨,蝶骨;【地】楔;【化】半面晶形。**-al** *a*.

spher·al [ˈsfiərəl; ˋsfɪrəl] *a*. 1. 球的,球状的。2. 球面的;天体的。3. 匀称的,对称的。

sphere [sfiə; sfɪr] **I** *n*. 1. 球;球体,圆体,球面,球形。2. 天体;星,行星。3. 地球仪,天体仪。4.【天】天球;天空。5.(活动)范围,领域;本分,职分。6. 身分,地位。7.〔美俚〕棒球。*the geometry of ~s* 球面几何学。*a ~ of fortress* 要塞地带。*a ~ of influence* 势力范围。*I take up a second foreign language to widen my ~ of knowledge*. 我选修一种第二外语来扩大我的知识面。***be beyond*** [***out of***] ***one's ~*** 在本人的(某种)范围外,越分。***be in one's ~*** 在本人的(某种)范围内,不越分。***remain in one's proper ~*** 守本分,安分守己。**II** *vt*. 1. 使成球形。2. 把…放在球内;使处于天体之间。3. 包围,围住。4.〔诗〕捧上天;极力赞扬。~ *geometry* 球面几何学。*a ~ triangle* 球面[弧]三角形。

spher·i·cal [ˈsferikəl; ˋsfɛrəkl̩] *a*. 球的;球面的;球形的,圆的;天体的;天空的。*a ~ bush*【机】球面衬。*a ~ conic section*【数】球锥曲线。*a ~ sector* 球心角体。~ **angle**【数】球面角。~ **geometry** 球面几何(学)。~ **trigonometry** 球面三角(学)。**-ly** *ad*.

sphe·ric·i·ty [sfeˈrisiti; sfɪˋrɪsətɪ] *n*. 球状;球面;球体;球(形)度。

spher·ics [ˈsferiks; ˋsfɛrɪks] *n*. 1.【数】球面几何学;球面三角学。2.【气】远距离电气测候法;(低频)天电;(低频)天电学(=sferics)。

sphe·roid [ˈsfiərɔid; ˋsfɪrɔɪd] *n*. 1. 扁球体;回转扁圆体。2.〔美〕棒球用球。

sphe·roi·dal [sfiəˈrɔidl; sfɪˋrɔɪdl], **sphe·roi·dic** [sfiəˈrɔidik; sfɪˋrɔɪdɪk] *a*. 扁球体的;回转扁圆体的。~ *state*【物】球腾态。**-roi·dal·ly** *ad*.

sphe·roi·di·city [ˌsfiərɔiˈdisiti; ,sfɪrɔɪˋdɪsətɪ] *n*. 球形,扁球形,椭球形。

sphe·rom·e·ter [sfiəˈrɔmitə; sfɪˋrɑmətɚ] *n*. 球径计,测球仪。

spher·u·lar [ˈsferjulə; ˋsfɛrulɚ] *a*. 小球(状)的,小球似的。

spher·u·late [ˈsferjulit; ˋsfɛrjulɪt] *a*. 布满小球体的。

spher·ule [ˈsferjuːl; ˋsfɛrul] *n*. 小球(体)。

spher·u·lite [ˈsferjuˌlait, ˈsfiər-; ˋsfɛrjʊ,laɪt, -sfɪr-] *n*.【地】球粒。**-lit·ic** [-ˈlitik; -ˋlɪtɪk] *a*. **-lit·ize** *vt*. 使成球粒。

spher·y [ˈsfiəri; ˋsfɪrɪ] *a*. (***spher·i·er***; ***spher·i·est***)【诗】1. 圆体的,似球的。2. 天体的,关于天体的。

sphinc·ter [ˈsfiŋktə; ˋsfɪŋktɚ] *n*.【解】括约肌。~ ***ani*** 肛门括约肌。**-ter·al** *a*.

sphin·gid [ˈsfindʒid; ˋsfɪndʒɪd] *n*. = hawkmoth.

sphin·go·my·e·lin [ˌsfiŋgəuˈmaiəlin; ,sfɪŋgəˋmaɪəlɪn] *n*.【生化】(神经)鞘磷脂。

sphin·go·sine [ˈsfiŋgəusi(ː)n; ˋsfɪŋgə,sin, -sɪn] *n*.【生化】(神经)鞘胺醇。

sphinx [sfiŋks; sfɪŋks] *n*. (*pl*. *~es*, ***sphin·ges*** [ˈsfindʒiːz; ˋsfɪndʒiz]) 1.〔S-〕【希神】斯芬克斯〔有翼的狮身女面怪物〕。2.【古埃及】狮身人面[鹰头,羊头]巨像。3. 莫名其妙的事,谜似的人[物]。4.【动】天蛾;一种非洲狒狒。

sphra·gis·tics [sfrəˈdʒistiks; sfrəˋdʒɪstɪks] *n*. 印章学。

sp. ht. = specific heat 比热。

sphyg·mic [ˈsfigmik; ˋsfɪgmɪk] *a*.【生理】脉搏的。

sphyg·mo·gram [ˈsfigməˌgræm; ˋsfɪgməgræm] *n*.【医】脉搏描记,脉搏曲线。

sphyg·mo·graph [ˈsfigməgrɑːf; ˋsfɪgmə,græf, -,grɑf] *n*.【医】脉搏描记器。**-ic** *a*.

sphyg·mo·gra·phy [sfigˈmɔgrəfi; sfɪgˋmɑgrəfɪ] *n*.【医】脉搏描记法。

sphyg·mo·ma·nom·e·ter [ˌsfigməuməˈnɔmitə; ,sfɪgmoməˋnɑmətɚ] *n*.【医】血压计。**-mo·man·o·met·ric** [-ˈmetrik; -ˋmɛtrɪk] *a*.

sphyg·mom·e·ter [sfigˈmɔmitə; sfɪgˋmɑmətɚ] *n*.【医】脉搏计。

sphyg·mo·phone [ˈsfigməfəun; ˋsfɪgməfon] *n*.【医】脉搏计。

sphyg·mo·scope [ˈsfigməskəup; ˋsfɪgmə,skop] *n*.【医】脉搏检视器。

sphyg·mus [ˈsfigməs; ˋsfɪgməs] *n*.【医】脉搏。

spic, S- [spik; spɪk] *n*.〔美俚〕墨西哥人;拉丁美洲人。

spi·ca [ˈspaikə; ˋspaɪkə] *n*. (*pl*. ***-cae*** [-siː; -si]) 1.【植】(谷类的)穗。2.【医】人字形绷扎法。3.〔S-〕【天】角宿一〔室女座 α 星〕,天门。

spi·cate, -cat·ed [ˈspaikeit, -ted; ˋspaɪket, -tɛd] *a*. 有穗的;穗状排列的,穗状花序的。

spic·ca·to [spiˈkɑːtəu; spɪˋkɑto] **I** *a*.【乐】〔弦乐器演奏术语〕用跳弓演奏的,分开的,断续的。**II** *n*. 跳弓演奏;跳弓技术;须用跳弓演奏的段落。

spice [spais; spaɪs] **I** *n*. 1. 香料,调味料。2. 香气,香味;〔诗〕芳香。3. 情趣,风味。*Please add more ~ to the cake*. 请给蛋糕多加点香料。*Henry's worn-out joke lacks ~ for anyone*. 亨利的老掉牙的笑话谁听起来也乏味。*a ~ of life* 生活的情趣。*a ~ of humour* 幽默味。**II** *vt*. 1. 给…加香料[佐料](*with*)。2. 给…添趣味(*with*)。~**berry**【植】菱叶番樱桃(浆果)。~ **box** 香料盒。~**bush**【植】1. 黄果山胡椒。2. 西美腊梅。

spic·e·ry [ˈspaisəri; ˋspaɪsərɪ] *n*. 1.〔集合名词〕香料,调味品。2. 香辣味,芳香,香味,香气。

spi·ci·form [ˈspaisifɔːm; ˋspaɪsəfɔrm] *a*. 穗状的。

spick [spik; spɪk] *n*.〔美俚〕= spic.

spick-and-span [ˈspikəndˈspæn; ˋspɪkənˋspæn] *a*. 1. 崭新的,新做的(衣服)。2. 漂亮的;干干净净的,整洁的。

spic·u·la [ˈspikjulə; ˋspɪkjələ] *n*. (*pl*. ***spic·u·lae*** [ˈspikjuliː; ˋspɪkjəli]) 1. 针状体,刺。2.【动】(海绵动物的)骨针,(海参的)骨片;(昆虫的)螯刺,针突,产卵器。3.【植】交合刺。**-r** *a*. = spiculate.

spic·u·late [ˈspikjuˌleit; ˋspɪkjə,let] *a*. 1. 针骨状(的),针状的。2. 有针状体覆盖的;有针状体的(= spicular)。

spic·ule [ˈspikjuːl; ˋspɪkjul] *n*. 1. 针状体;【植】交合刺;穗状花序。2.【动】(海绵动物的)骨针;(海参的)骨片;(昆虫的)螯刺;针突,产卵器。

spic·u·lum [ˈspikjuləm; ˋspɪkjələm] *n*. (*pl*. ***-la*** [-lə; -lə]) [L.] 针骨,针状体;〔尤指〕(海盘车鱼等低级动物中的)交接刺。

spic·y [ˈspaisi; ˋspaɪsɪ] *a*. (***-i·er***; ***-i·est***) 1. 加有香料的;香的。2. 出产香料的。3. 辛辣的;痛快的;有风味的;有趣味的。4. 漂亮的(服装等)。5.(故事等)猥亵的,下流的。*The hillside is green, the air ~*. 山坡青碧空气芬芳。*a ~ magazine* 淫秽下流的杂志。**-i·ly** *ad*. **-i·ness** *n*.

spi·der [ˈspaidə; ˋspaɪdɚ] **I** *n*. 1.【动】蜘蛛。2. 带柄三脚平底锅。3. 三脚架。4.【机】星形轮;十字叉;(螺旋桨的)辐射架;星形接头。5.(中耕机的)泥土粉碎器。6. 设圈套者和入圈套者。7.〔美俚〕缫丝工人。8.〔口〕反谍蜘蛛〔指反间谍人员〕。*a ~ and a fly* 设圈套者和落入圈套者。~ **crab**【动】蜘蛛蟹,尖头蟹。~ **hole**【军】狙击手掩蔽体。~ **line**(光学仪器)交叉瞄准线,叉丝。~**man** 高空作业建筑工。~ **mite**【动】叶螨。~ **monkey**【动】蛛猿。~ **wasp**【动】(幼虫食蜘蛛的)黄蜂。~**web** 蜘蛛网,蜘蛛网状的东西。~**-web coil**【电】蛛网形线圈。~**wort**【植】紫露草。**II** *a*. 鸭跖草科的。**-ous** *a*. 蜘蛛似的。

spi·der·y [ˈspaidəri; ˋspaɪdərɪ] *a*. 1. 蜘蛛(网)似的。2.

S

(像蜘蛛脚一样)细长的(腿,轮辐,笔画等)。**3.** 多蜘蛛的。

spie·gel·ei·sen [ˈspiːgˌlaizn; ˋspigəlˏaɪzən] ***n.*** 【矿】镜铁(=spiegel 或 spiegel iron)。

spiel [spiːl; spil] **I** ***n.*** **1.** 〔美俚〕招徕生意的讲话或演说。**2.** 〔美俚〕流利夸张的演说、讲话。**II** ***vi.*** **1.** 演奏音乐。**2.** 流利夸张的说话或演说。—***vt.*** 流利夸张地讲,背得烂熟般地讲。*Henry is ~ing about the same old story—his innovation in techniques.* 亨利在夸夸其谈地唱老调——大谈他对工艺上的革新。~ ***off*** 〔美俚〕像背诵那样滔滔不绝地讲。

spiel·er [ˈspiːlə; ˋspilɚ] ***n.*** **1.** 〔美俚〕能说会道的演说家,讲话者。**2.** 商业宣传员。**3.** 广告播音员。**4.** 〔澳俚〕骗子。

spi·er [ˈspaiə; ˋspaɪɚ] ***n.*** 侦探,间谍。

spiff [spif; spɪf] **I** ***a.*** 〔俚〕整洁的;漂亮的;上等的;时新的。**II** ***n.*** 〔美俚〕推销佣金;〔*pl.*〕额外的钱。**III** ***vt.*** 〔俚〕使整洁[漂亮]。*The parlour has to be ~ed up a bit before the guests arrive.* 客人们来到之前,得把客厅搞得整洁一点。

spif·fy [ˈspifi; ˋspɪfɪ] ***a.*** (***-fi·er***; ***-fi·est***) **1.** 〔俚〕整洁的;漂亮的;时新的;衣冠楚楚的。**2.** 绝妙的。**3.** 喝醉了的。*You're sure ~ in your new dress.* 你穿上这身新衣服真是漂亮。*The ~ thing is to hit the sack at once.* 最妙不过的事是马上睡觉去。

spif(f)·li·cate [ˈspiflikeit; ˋspɪfləket] ***vt.*** **1.** 〔俚〕痛打。**2.** 使惊慌,使混乱,使狼狈。**3.** 粗暴地对待。**4.** 使完蛋,干掉,杀死。**-cation** [ˌspifliˈkeiʃən; ˏspɪfləˋkeʃən] ***n.***

spif·li·cat·ed [ˈspiflikeitid; ˋspɪflɪketɪd] ***a.*** 〔俚〕慌张的,混乱的,为难的;喝得烂醉的。

spig·ot [ˈspigət; ˋspɪgət] ***n.*** **1.** 〔美〕龙头;放液嘴。**2.** (桶等的)塞子。**3.** (管子的)联接器;套管。*a ~ joint* 【机】套管接合,接嘴。

spig·ot·ty, spig·go·ty [ˈspigəti; ˋspɪgətɪ] **I** ***a.*** 〔美俚〕怪有趣的;有点怪的。**II** ***n.*** 〔美俚〕墨西哥人;南欧人;南洋群岛人。

spik [spik; spɪk] ***n.*** 〔美俚〕= spic.

spike[1] [spaik; spaɪk] **I** ***n.*** **1.** (围墙等上尖头向外或向上的)长钉,尖铁(等)。**2.** 有尖端的细长东西;鞋底尖钉;(运动员的)钉鞋;高跟女鞋的细长的跟。**3.** (铁路上的)道钉。**4.** 【火箭】销钉。**5.** 【讯】尖峰信号;测试信号。**6.** 【动】(不到六英寸的)幼鲐。**7.** 【炮】火门栓。**8.** 〔口〕顽固的高教会派。**9.** 〔美俚〕皮下注射用的针头。*a dog ~* 狗头钉。*a jog ~* 鬼钉。*a ~ nail* 小钉。*an antenna ~* 【无】天线杆。*a ~ top* 枯梢。***hang up one's ~s*** 〔口〕退休,退出职业运动界。**II** ***vt.*** **1.** 打上桩子。**2.** 用大钉钉;打上钉子,用尖物刺。**3.** 把头弄尖。**4.** 塞住(大炮)火门。**5.** 阻挡,抑制,挫败。**6.** 【棒球】用鞋底钉伤(人)。**7.** 【排球】在网边跳起猛扣。**8.** 〔美俚〕掺入烈酒;增强…的效果[生气、风味或美观]。**9.** 【橄榄球】摔(球)触地。~ *an attempt* 挫败一企图。*recite a humorous poem to ~ one's lecture* 背一首滑稽诗来使他的演讲有生气。~ *a rumo(u)r* 〔美〕辟谣;制止谣言。*~d beer* 〔美〕加了烈酒的啤酒。~ ***sb.'s gun*** 破坏某人的计划。~ **coat** 燕尾服。~ **heel** 女皮鞋的高后跟。~ **puller** 拔齿钳。~ **team** 〔美〕中间一匹在前、套在一起的三马队。**~-tooth harrow** 钉齿耙,有多排铁齿的整土耙。

spike[2] [spaik; spaɪk] ***n.*** (谷类的)穗;【植】穗状花序。**~-let** 小穗;小穗状花。~ **lavender** 【植】欧洲宽叶熏衣草。**-d** ***a.***

spike·nard [ˈspaiknɑːd; ˋspaɪknɚd, -nɑrd] ***n.*** **1.** 【植】甘松。**2.** 甘松香油。**3.** 美洲楤木。

spik·y [ˈspaiki; ˋspaɪkɪ] ***a.*** **1.** 大钉似的,尖而长的;锐利的。**2.** 打了尖桩[钉]的。**3.** 〔俚〕难应付的,尖刻的。**4.** 〔英口〕顽固的(高教会派)。*a ~ roller* 羊角碾。

spile [spail; spaɪl] **I** ***n.*** **1.** 塞子。**2.** (桶的)气孔塞,木塞,小塞。**3.** 〔美〕(采糖枫汁用的)插管。**4.** (篱笆的)木头桩子;支柱。**II** ***vt.*** **1.** 在…上插塞子。**2.** 在(桶盖上)开小孔。**3.** 装插管于…,用插管引导。**4.** 打桩支承。**~-hole** (桶的)通气孔。

spil·ing [ˈspailiŋ; ˋspaɪlɪŋ] ***n.*** 〔集合词〕木桩,木材;桩基,桩材;打桩。

spill[1] [spil; spɪl] **I** ***vt.*** (~***ed***, ***spilt***) **1.** 使溢出,使溅出,使(血)流出,撒出;倒出。**2.** 〔俚〕泄漏(秘密等)。**3.** 【海】使风从…漏出。**4.** 使(从马鞍、马车上)摔下来,使跌下来。—***vi.*** **1.** 泼出,溢出,泻出,涌流。**2.** 泄漏出。**3.** 倾覆,倾跌,摔下。**4.** 【海】漏风。**5.** 〔卑〕输掉(钱),浪费。*Take care not to ~ a drop of the medicine.* 注意一滴药也不要洒。*You've ~ed ink all over the carpet.* 你把墨水溅在整个的地毯上了。~ ***one's guts*** 把自己知道的一切都说了出去。~ ***over*** 溢出。~ ***the beans*** = ~ ***it*** 〔美俚〕泄漏秘密。~ ***the blood of*** 杀死。~ ***the dope*** 泄漏情报。~ ***the mazuma*** 〔美〕(任意)花钱,挥霍浪费。**II** ***n.*** **1.** 溢出(量);溅出;涌出;撒出,撒落。**2.** 〔口〕滚下,摔下,跌下。**3.** (雨等的)倾盆下注。**4.** 溢洪道,溢水口(=spill way)。**5.** 因某种商品供应不足而引起的对其他商品的需求。~**back** 倒流式交通大堵塞。

spill[2] [spil; spɪl] ***n.*** **1.** 木片。**2.** (引火用)纸捻儿,引柴。**3.** 小塞子。**4.** 金属细棒;销子。**5.** 锥形[圆筒形]纸包。

spill·age [ˈspilidʒ; ˋspɪlɪdʒ] ***n.*** 溢出,溢出量。

spil·ler[1] [ˈspilə; ˋspɪlɚ] ***n.*** 使溢出者,使溅出者。

spil·ler[2] [ˈspilə; ˋspɪlɚ] ***n.*** (从大鱼网中取出鱼的)堕落网。

spil·li·kin [ˈspilikin; ˋspɪlɪkɪn] ***n.*** 〔主英〕**1.** (挑棒游戏用的)游戏棒。**2.** 〔*pl.* 动词用单数〕挑棒游戏(=spilikin)。

spill·o·ver [ˈspilˌəuvə; ˋspɪlˏovɚ] ***n.*** **1.** 溢出,泻出。**2.** 溢出物,泻出物;过多,外流人口。

spill·way [ˈspilwei; ˋspɪlˏwe] ***n.*** (水库的)溢水口,溢洪道;溢洪堰。*a conduit ~* 溢洪道;溢水管。

spi·lo·site [ˈspailəsait; ˋspaɪləˏsaɪt] ***n.*** 【地】绿点板岩。

spilt [spilt; spɪlt] spill 的过去式及过去分词。*It is no use crying over the ~ milk.* 为洒了的牛奶而哀号是无益的;〔喻〕往者不谏;往事已矣,痛苦也无补于事。

spilth [spilθ; spɪlθ] ***n.*** **1.** 泻出(物),溢出(物)。**2.** 过剩物,废物,垃圾。

spin [spin; spɪn] **I** ***vt.*** (***spun*** [spʌn; spʌn], 〔古〕***span*** [spæn; spʌn]; ***spun***; **~*ning***) **1.** 纺。**2.** 使(陀螺等)旋转;使(车轮)打空转[在冰上,沙中]。**3.** (蜘蛛、蚕等)吐(丝),结(网),(蚕)结(茧)。**4.** 转镟床(等)旋制;钻孔。**5.** 编造;讲(故事等)。**6.** 〔俚〕〔常用 *p. p.*〕使过度疲劳。**7.** 〔美俚〕欺骗。**8.** 〔英〕使考不及格。**9.** (通过离心力作用)抛出,丢开(*off*)。*Cotton is spun into thread.* 把棉花纺成线。*Silkworms ~ cocoons.* 蚕作茧。*Old sailors like to ~ yarns.* 老海员们喜欢讲故事。—***vi.*** **1.** 纺,纺织。**2.** (陀螺等)旋转;眼花,眩晕;(车轮)因打滑而空转。**3.** 吐丝,作茧,像丝一般地流出。**4.** 〔口〕(车、船等)飞驶,飞跑。**5.** 〔俚〕考不取。**6.** 【空】(飞机)螺旋下降,旋冲。**7.** 〔美俚〕跳舞。**8.** 【天文】(星体)自转减缓。*My head ~s.* 我头晕。~ ***in*** 〔美俚〕上圆,睡午觉。~ ***out*** **1.** 拉长,拖长,延长,拖延;使(钱等)勉强再维持一段时间。**2.** 磨度过。**3.** 使汽车作回形滑行。~ ***the bottle*** 〔美〕转瓶游戏〔瓶口所向的人须被人亲吻〕。~ ***your wheels*** 〔美空军俚〕劳而无功。**II** ***n.*** **1.** 兜一圈;自旋,自转。**2.** 飞跑,飞过,疾驶;划一划。**3.** 【空】旋冲;螺旋,旋转;【物】自转。**4.** 眩晕,心里乱。**5.** 〔澳〕运气。**6.** 〔美口〕定调子,起导向作用的意见。*isotopic ~* 同位旋。*nuclear ~* 核自旋。*go for a ~ in a car* 坐汽车去兜圈子。*get into a flat ~* 穷下来。**~-cast** ***vi.*** 用匙形诱饵钓鱼。~**casting** 用匙形诱饵钓鱼。~ **doctor** 〔美〕(能控制舆论导向的)公关专家;(公司、商店、政客等的)公共形象塑造者。**~-down** 【天】(星体的)自转减缓。~ **control** 新闻导向控制。~ **doctor** 起导向作用的人。**~-drier** 旋转式脱水机。**~-flip** 【物】自旋转向。~ **off**

1. 母公司收回子公司全部股本使之脱离的做法。2. 有用的副产品(=spinoff)。～**-up**【天】(星体的)自转增快。

spi·na·ceous [spiˈneiʃəs; spɪˋneʃəs] *a*. (像)菠菜的。

spin·ach, spin·age [ˈspinidʒ; ˋspɪnɪdʒ] *n*. 1.【植】菠菜。2.〔俚〕胡说八道;〔美俚〕不加修剪的胡子;杂乱的蔓生物。

spi·nal [ˈspainl; ˋspaɪnl] I *a*. 1.【生】针的,刺的;棘状突起的。2.【解】脊骨的,脊柱的,脊髓的。～ *anaesthesia* 脊髓(椎)麻醉。～ *canal* 脊管,椎管。～ *column* 脊柱。～ *cord* [*marrow*] 脊髓。～ *nerve*【解】(脊)髓神经。II *n*.〔医〕脊髓麻醉(=～ anaesthesia);脊髓麻醉药。**-ly** *ad*. 在脊骨方面,沿着脊骨。

spi·nate(d) [ˈspaineit, -netid; ˋspaɪneɪt, -netɪd] *a*. 1. 刺一样的,有刺的。2. 有脊的。

spin·dle [ˈspindl; ˋspɪndl] I *n*. 1. 锭子,纺锤。2. (机器的)(主)轴;门锁的转轴。3. 细长的人[物];长茎。4.〔美〕松叶。5. 锭〔线长单位,棉纱为45360英尺,麻丝为43200英尺〕。6. (剑)柄。7.【生】纺锤状细胞。8.【解】纺锤状部分,纺锤状器官。9.【数】纺锤状体。10.【生】纺锤体,梭。11.【海】杆状警标。12. (报馆编辑室的)原稿〔校样〕插钉。13. 液体比重计。14. (栏杆的)纺锤形立柱,螺旋扶梯的中柱。*the number of* ～*s*【纺】锭数。*ring* ～*s*【纺】细纱锭。*the* ～*s in operation*【纺】开工锭数。～ *oil*【机】锭子油,轴润滑油。*a live* [*dead*] ～动[死]轴。*the* ～ *side* 母系,母方。II *vi*. 1. 长成细长茎。2. 长(变)得细长。—*vt*. 1. 装锭子于,使成锭子。2. 用纺锤形锉打(眼)[穿(孔)]。III *a*. 1. 像锭子的。2.〔古〕〔家族〕母系的,母方的(the ～ side 母系,母方)。～ **cell**【生】梭状细胞。～ **file** (插放票据等用的)纸插,票插〔底座固定,上有铁扦〕。～ **legs** 腿细长的人。～**-legged**, ～**-shanked** *a*. 腿细长的。～ **oil**【机】锭子油,轴润滑油。～**-shanks** 细长的腿;腿细长的人。～ **side** (一个家族的)母系,女系。～ **tree**【植】卫矛。

spin·dling, spin·dly [ˈspiŋdliŋ, -dli; ˋspɪŋdlɪŋ, -dlɪ] I *a*. 纺锤形的;细长的。II *n*. 细长物;瘦高个子。

spin·drift [ˈspindrift; ˋspɪnˏdrɪft] *n*.【海】(大风吹起的)浪花,浪沫。

spine [spain; spaɪn] *n*. 1.【解】脊骨,脊柱。2.【植】针,刺。3.【动】棘状突起刺,壳针。4. (书)背;(山)脊。5.〔英方〕草地。6.【地】火山栓,熔岩塔。7.〔美〕(由中心和支持因素转为)勇气,骨气,毅力。8.〔美俚〕铁路上货车的平顶。*a man who lacks* ～ *and starch* 一个缺少骨气的人。～**-chiller** 恐怖小说[电影等]。

spi·nel(le) [spiˈnel; spɪˋnɛl, ˋspɪnəl] *n*.【矿】尖晶石。

spine·less [ˈspainlis; ˋspaɪnlɪs] *a*. 1. 无脊骨的。2. 没骨气[勇气]的,优柔寡断的。3.【生】无刺的。**-ly** *ad*. **-ness** *n*.

spi·nes·cent [spaiˈnesnt; spaɪˋnɛsənt] *a*. 1. 有刺的,具刺的,多刺的。2. 成为有刺的;刺状的。

spi·net [spiˈnet; ˋspɪnɪt, -ɛt] *n*.【乐】(16—18世纪的)键琴。

Spin·garn [ˈspingɑːn, ˈspiŋən; ˋspɪŋgɑrn] *n*. 斯平加恩〔姓氏〕。

spini- *comb. f*. 脊,刺:*spini*tis.

spi·nif·er·ous [spaiˈnifərəs; spaɪˋnɪfərəs] *a*. 有刺的。

spin·i·fex [ˈspiniˌfeks; ˋspɪnɪˏfɛks] *n*.【植】鬣刺属(*Spinifex*)植物。

spin·i·ness [ˈspaininis; ˋspaɪnɪnɪs] *n*. 1. 多针,多刺。2. 困难重重。3. 刺状。

spin·i·tis [spiˈnaitis; spɪˋnaɪtɪs] *n*.【医】脊髓炎。

spin·na·ker [ˈspinəkə; ˋspɪnəkɚ] *n*.【赛艇】大三角帆。

spin·ner [ˈspinə; ˋspɪnɚ] *n*. 1. 纺纱工人。2. 纺纱机。3.【空、机】机头罩,螺旋毂盖,桨毂整流罩。4.【钓鱼】旋转(诱鱼)器;旋转匙状诱饵。5.【橄榄球】带球人的旋转动作(急转身假动作)。6.〔方〕蜘蛛(=spinneret)。7.〔美俚〕卡车司机。

spin·ner·et, spin·ner·ette [ˌspinəˈret; ˋspɪnəˏrɛt] *n*. 1.【动】(蜘蛛、蚕等的)吐丝器。2.【纺】喷丝头。

spin·ner·y [ˈspinəri; ˋspɪnərɪ] *n*. 纱厂。

spin·ney [ˈspini; ˋspɪnɪ] *n*.〔英〕树丛,灌木丛[林]。

spin·ning [ˈspiniŋ; ˋspɪnɪŋ] I *n*. 1. 纺;精纺;棉纱。2. 旋转;自旋;旋压。3. 用旋转匙状诱饵钓鱼。4. (原地不动地蹬踏固定式自行车的)健身车运动。II *a*. 纺纱的;旋转的。*a* ～ *electron* 自旋电子。*a* ～ *flight* 螺旋飞行。*a* ～ *roll*【空】螺旋侧滚。～ ***nose dive***【空】垂直螺旋俯冲。～ **time**〔美〕睡觉时间。～ **frame** 精纺机。～ **jenny** (初期的)多轴纺纱机。～ **machine** 纺纱机,纺丝机。～ **mill** 纱厂。～ **mule** 纺棉机。～ **wheel** 纺车。

spin·off [ˈspinˌɔːf; ˋspɪnˏɔf, -ˏɑf] *n*. 1. (母公司把其子公司所有的股份分发给股票持有人的)抽资摆脱(做法)。2. 副产品;附带的发展,附带的利益(=spin-off)。

spi·nor [ˈspinə; ˋspɪnɚ] *n*.【数】旋量。

spi·nose [ˈspainəus; ˋspaɪnos] *a*. 有刺的,多刺的。

spi·nos·i·ty [spaiˈnɔsiti; spaɪˋnɑsətɪ] *n*. 1. 有刺(物),多刺(物)。2. 棘手的问题。3. 尖刻的话。

spi·nous [ˈspinəs; ˋspaɪnəs] *a*. 1. 多刺的;刺状的,尖细如刺的。2. 棘手的。

Spi·no·za [spiˈnəuzə; spɪˋnozə], **Ben·e·dict** 斯宾诺沙〔1632—1677,荷兰哲学家〕。

Spi·no·zism [spiˈnəuzizm; spɪˋnozɪzm] *n*. 斯宾诺沙哲学。**-no·zist** *n*.

spin·ster [ˈspinstə; ˋspɪnstɚ] I *n*. 1. (尤指中年的)未婚女人,老处女。2.〔美〕纺纱妇女。II *a*. 未婚的。**-hood** *n*. 未婚女子(老处女)的身分。

spin·thar·i·scope [spinˈθæriˈskəup; spɪnˋθærəˏskop] *n*.【原】(计算质点数用的)闪烁镜。

spin·to [ˈspiːntəu; ˋspinto] *a*., *n*.〔It.〕【乐】抒情但带有强烈戏剧成分的(歌手,歌喉)。

spi·nule [ˈspainjuːl; ˋspaɪnjul, ˋspɪn-] *n*.【生】小刺。**-u·lose, -u·lous** [-njuləus, -njuləs; -njʊlos, -njʊləs] *a*.

spin·y [ˈspaini; ˋspaɪnɪ] *a*. (*-i·er*; *-i·est*) 1. 有刺的,多刺的,刺状的,细尖如刺的。2. 困难重重的,麻烦的。～**-anteater**【动】针鼹。～ **dogfish**【动】(白斑)角鲨。～**-finned** *a*.【动】棘鳍的。～**-headed worm**【动】棘头网动物。～ **lobster** 龙虾。～**-rayed**【动】有尖硬鳍的。**-i·ness** *n*.

spi·ra·cle [ˈspaiərəkl, ˈspiərə-; ˋspaɪrəkl, ˋspɪrə-] *n*. 1.【动】(昆虫类的)呼吸孔,气门;(鲸类的)喷水孔。2. 通气孔。**-rac·u·lar** [-ˈrækjulə; -ˋrækjələ] *a*.

spi·rae·a [spaiˈriːə, -ˈriə; spaɪˋriə] *n*.【植】绣线菊(属)。

spi·ral [ˈspaiərəl; ˋspaɪrəl] I *a*. 1. 螺旋形的,盘旋的,盘旋上升的。2.【数】螺线的。*Experts watch the* ～ *development in industry with keen interest*. 专家们以很大的兴趣观察工业的螺旋式的发展。II *n*. 1. 螺旋形物。2. 螺簧;【物】螺线。3.【数】螺(旋)线。4.【空】盘旋,盘旋降落〔又叫～ down〕。5. (足球运动的)旋球。6. (物价等)不断加剧上升或下降。*a* ～ *line* 螺线。*a* ～ *spring* 螺(旋弹)簧,蜷簧。*a* ～ *stair* 螺旋梯。*an inflationary* [*a vicious*] ～ 恶性通货膨胀。III *vt*., *vi*. 1. (〔英〕*-ll-*)使成螺旋形。2.【空】盘旋降落[上升]。3. (物价)螺旋上升[跌落]。**-ly** *ad*. ～ **balance** 螺旋弹簧秤。～ **galaxy**【天】螺旋星系。

spi·ral·i·ty [spaiˈræliti; spaɪˋrælətɪ] *n*. 螺旋形,螺状。

spi·rant [ˈspaiərənt; ˋspaɪrənt] *n*., *a*.【语音】摩擦音(的)。

spire[1] [ˈspaiə; spaɪr] I *n*. 1. 塔尖;尖塔;尖峰;锥形体。2.【植】幼叶;幼苗[禾等的]纤茎。*Have you ever seen the beautiful* ～*s of rocks in Guilin*? 你看过桂林的美丽的塔状尖峰吗? II *vt*. 装尖塔。—*vi*. 1. (塔状)耸立。2. 发芽。*Price* ～*s up almost every week*. 物价几乎每周高涨。

spire[2] [spaiə; spaɪr] I *n*. 1. 螺旋,螺线。2.【动】螺旋部;(软体动物的)螺塔。II *vi*. 螺旋形上升。**-d** *a*.

spi·re·a [spaiˈriːə, -ˈriə; spaɪˋriə] *n*. = spiraea.
spire·let [ˈspaiəlit; ˋspaɪrlɪt] *n*. 小尖塔。
spi·reme [ˈspairiːm; ˋspaɪrim] *n*.【生】染色质纽。
spi·rif·er·ous [spaiˈrifərəs; spaɪˋrɪfərəs] *a*.【动】有螺旋部[螺塔]的,螺旋部[螺塔]结构的〔如某些贝壳〕;有螺旋形[螺塔]附属物的〔如腕足纲〕。
Spi·ril·lum [spaiəˈriləm; spaɪˋrɪləm] *n*. (*pl*. ***-ril·la*** [-lə; -lə])【生】螺旋菌。
spir·it [ˈspirit; ˋspɪrɪt] **I** *n*. **1.** 精神,心灵,灵魂 (*opp*. body, flesh)。**2.** 灵,神;天使,妖精,魔鬼(等);鬼怪,幽灵。**3.**〔只用 *sing*.〕元气,志气;气概,气魄;勇气。**4.**〔*pl*.〕情绪,心情,兴致。**5.** (具有突出精神力量的)人物。**6.** (时代)精神,潮流,风气。**7.**〔常 *sing*.〕态度。**8.** (法律、文件等的)精神 (*opp*. letter 文字)。**9.**〔常 *pl*.〕精(华)。**10.**〔常 *pl*.〕酒精,醇。**11.**【医】酯剂,酒剂,药酒。*It is our duty to cultivate the* ~ *of boldness and fearlessness*. 我们的责任是培育大无畏的精神。*The editorial voices the* ~*s of the young people*. 社论表达了年轻人的心情。*a man of* ~ 精神饱满的人。*an unbending* ~ 倔强的人。*a bold* ~ 大胆的人。*a master* ~ 杰出人物。*the leading* ~ 领袖。*a teenager of* ~ 意志坚强的少年。*Leave this to some more inquiring* ~. 把这个交给更有研究的人去干吧。*He never drinks* ~*s*. 他从来不喝烈酒。~(*s*) *and water* 掺水酒精。~(*s*) *of ammonia*【药】氨酊(卤精)〔10%的氨水溶于酒精中〕。~(*s*) *of hartshorn*【化】鹿精〔氢氧化氨的旧称〕;鹿角酒。~(*s*) *of turpentine* 松节油。~(*s*) *of wine* 纯酒精。***be full of animal*** ~***s*** 血气旺盛。***break sb.'s*** ~***s*** 挫折…锐气,使…垂头丧气。***catch sb.'s*** ~ 引起,兴趣。***give up the*** ~ 死。***have a high*** ~ 精神好,有进取心。***in good*** ~***s*** 精神好,高兴,兴致好。***in high*** ~***s*** 情绪极好,兴高采烈,兴致勃勃 (*He is in high* ~*s today*. 他今天很高兴)。***in low*** ~***s*** 意气消沉,垂头丧气,快快不乐。***in*** ~***s*** 愉快地,活泼地。***in*** (***the***) ~ 心中,在内心;在精神上。***keep up one's*** ~***s*** 打起精神。***lead the life of the*** ~ 过崇尚精神的生活。***lose one's*** ~***s*** 气馁,败兴,垂头丧气。***meek in*** ~ 性情温柔。***out of*** ~***s*** 郁郁不乐,气闷。***raise sb.'s*** ~ 发扬…锐气,使…扬眉吐气。***team*** ~ 团队精神。***recover one's*** ~***s*** 恢复精神。***take in a wrong*** ~ 误会 (*He takes criticism in the wrong* ~. 他误会这个批评了)。***the poor in*** ~ 谦虚的人。***to one's*** ~ 到心里。
II *vt*. **1.** 鼓励,鼓舞 (*up*; *on*);使精神振作。**2.** 拐带,诱拐,拐去 (*away*; *off*)。~ ***up*** 打起精神,拿出精神。~ **blue**【化】醇溶青。~ **colours** 醇溶染料。~ **ga(u)ge** 酒精比重计。~ **gum**【剧】化妆发胶。~ **lamp** 酒精灯。~ **level**【物】(气泡)酒精水准器。~**-rapper** (自称能与死者通信息的)招魂术巫师。~**-room**【海】食物贮藏室。~ **stove** (烹饪用的)酒精炉。~ **writing** 被认为是人在神鬼缠身时写出来的东西。
spir·it·ed [ˈspiritid; ˋspɪrɪtɪd] *a*. **1.** 精神饱满的,生气勃勃的,活泼的;勇敢的;猛烈的。**2.**〔构成复合词〕精神…的,有…心的,心地…的。*a* ~ *girl* 活泼的女孩。*a* ~ *attack* 猛攻。*high* [*low*] ~ 精神极好[萎靡]的。*public-* ~ 热心公益的。**-ly** *ad*. **-ness** *n*.
spir·it·ism [ˈspiritizəm; ˋspɪrɪtɪzm] *n*. = spiritualism.
spir·it·ist [ˈspiritist; ˋspɪrɪtɪst] **I** *n*. 信招魂术的人;【哲】唯灵论者。**II** *a*. 招魂术的;【哲】唯灵论的。
spir·it·less [ˈspiritlis; ˋspɪrɪtlɪs] *a*. **1.** 无精打采的,垂头丧气的;灰心的,冷淡的。**2.** 无生命的,死的。**-ly** *ad*. **-ness** *n*.
spi·ri·to·so [ˌspiriˈtəusəu; ˏspɪrɪˋtoso] *a*.〔It.〕【乐】有精神的;热烈的;有兴致的。
spir·it·ous [ˈspiəritəs; ˋspɪrɪtəs] *a*. **1.** = spirituous. **2.**〔废〕活泼的,情绪高昂的。
spir·it·u·al [ˈspiritjuəl; ˋspɪrɪtʃʊəl] **I** *a*. **1.** 精神(上)的;心灵的。**2.** 神的,灵的,神圣的;宗教的,信仰上的,超乎世俗的。**3.** 高尚的,崇高的,崇尚精神的。**4.** 唯灵论的,招魂论的,鬼的。**II** *n*. **1.**〔*pl*.〕教会事务。**2.**〔美〕(黑人的)圣歌。*the* ~ *man* 心灵;为圣灵所嘉佑的人。*a* ~ *corporation* 宗教团体。*the Lords* ~ 英国上院有神职的议员[主教]。*the negro* ~*s* = ~ *songs*〔美〕黑人圣歌。~ **bouquet**【天主】精神花束〔做特定的善事或参加弥撒为别人或死者祈祷〕。**-ly** *ad*.
spir·it·u·al·ism [ˈspiritjuəlizəm; ˋspɪrɪtʃʊəlˏɪzəm] *n*. **1.**【哲】唯灵论。**2.** 招魂术 (= spiritism)。**3.** 观念论;精神至上主义。**-al·is·tic** [ˌspiritjuəˈlistik; ˏspɪrɪtʃʊəˋlɪstɪk] *a*.
spir·it·u·al·ist [ˈspiritjuəlist; ˋspɪrɪtʃʊəlɪst] *n*. **1.** 唯灵论者。**2.** 迷信招魂术者。**3.** 招魂术巫师。
spir·it·u·al·i·ty [ˌspiritjuˈæliti; ˏspɪrɪtʃʊˋæləti] *n*. **1.** 精神(性);灵性。**2.**〔*pl*.〕教堂或教士的事务、权利或收入。**3.**〔总称〕教士。
spir·it·u·al·i·za·tion [ˌspiritjuəlaiˈzeiʃən; ˏspɪrɪtʃʊəlaɪˋzeʃən] *n*. 精神化;赋予精神意义;从精神上解释。
spir·it·u·al·ize [ˈspiritʊəlaiz; ˋspɪrɪtʃʊəlˏaɪz] *vt*. **1.** 使精神化;赋予精神意义;从精神上来解释。**2.** 以精神来鼓舞。
spir·it·u·al·ty [ˌspiritjuˈælti; ˋspɪrɪtʃʊəltɪ] *n*. **1.** 属于教堂的事务。**2.** 教士,牧师。
spi·ri·tu·el *mas*., ***spi·ri·tu·elle*** *fem*. [ˌspiritjuˈel; ˏspɪrɪtʃʊˋel] *a*.〔F.〕优雅而伶俐的;有风趣的。
spir·it·u·o·sity [ˌspiritjuˈɔsiti; ˏspɪrɪtʃʊˋɑsətɪ] *n*. 含酒精性。
spir·it·u·ous [ˈspiritjuəs; ˋspɪrɪtʃʊəs] *a*. 含酒精的,酒精成分高的;蒸馏过的 (*opp*. fermented)。
spir·i·tus as·per [ˈspiəritəsˈæspə; ˋspɪrɪtəsˋæspɚ]〔L.〕= rough breathing〔语音〕送气音。
spir·i·valve [ˈspaiərivælv; ˋspaɪrəvælv] *a*. 有螺状壳的;(壳)螺状的。
spir·ke·ting [ˈspəːkitiŋ; ˋspɚkɪtɪŋ] *n*.【船】内部腰板。
spiro-[1] *comb*. *f*. 螺线形,蜷线形,螺旋形: *spiro*chaetic.
spiro-[2] *comb*. *f*. 呼吸: *spiro*graph.
spi·ro·chae·ta, spi·ro·chae·te, spi·ro·che·te [ˌspaiərəˈkiːtə, -ˈkiːt; ˏspaɪrəˋkitə, -ˋkit] *n*.【微】螺旋体。**-l** *a*. 由螺旋体引起的。
spi·ro·ch(a)etic [ˌspaiərəˈkiːtik; ˏspaɪrəˋkitɪk] *a*.【微】螺旋体的;由螺旋体引起的。
spi·ro·che·to·sis [ˌspairəkiːˈtəusis; ˏspaɪrəkiˋtosɪs] *n*.【医】波体病,螺旋体病。
spi·ro·graph [ˈspairəˌgrɑːf, -ˌgræf; ˋspaɪrəˏgræf, -ˏgrɑf] *n*. 呼吸描记器。**-ic** *a*.
spi·ro·gy·ra [ˌspairəˈdʒairə; ˏspaɪrəˋdʒaɪrə] *n*.【植】水绵属 (*Spirogyra*) 植物。
spi·roid [ˈspairɔid; ˋspaɪrɔɪd] *a*. 螺旋状的,成螺旋形的。
spi·rom·e·ter [spaiəˈrɔmitə; spaɪˋrɑmətɚ] *n*.【医】呼吸量测定器,肺活量计。
spi·rom·e·tric [ˌspaiərəˈmetrik; ˏspaɪrəˋmetrɪk] *a*. (使用)呼吸量测定器的,呼吸量测定法的。
spi·rom·e·try [ˌspaiəˈrɔmitri; spaɪˋrɑmətrɪ] *n*.【医】呼吸量测定法。
spi·ro·phore [ˈspaiərəufɔː; ˋspaɪrəˏfor] *n*.【医】人工呼吸器。
spi·ro·scope [ˈspaiərəuskəup; ˋspaɪrəˏskop] *n*.【医】呼吸量测定器。
spirt [spəːt; spɚt] *v*., *n*. = spurt[1].
spir·u·la [ˈspi(ə)rjulə, -ulə; ˋspɪrjulə, -ʊlə] *n*. (*pl*. ***-lae*** [-ˌliː; -li])【动】团鲗属 (*Spirula*) 动物;团鲗。
spir·y[1] [ˈspaiəri; ˋspaɪrɪ] *a*. 塔尖(形)的。
spir·y[2] [ˈspaiəri; ˋspaɪrɪ] *a*. 螺旋式的。
spit[1] [spit; spɪt] **I** *vt*. (***spat*** [spæt; spæt],〔古〕***spit***; ***spitting***) **1.** 吐(唾沫等),咯(血) (*out*; *forth*; *up*)。**2.** (唾弃地)说,发(牢骚) (*out*)。**3.** (雨、雪)哗啦或霏霏地落下。**4.** (昆虫)产卵。**5.** 点燃(导火线等)。—*vi*. **1.** 吐

唾沫,吐痰。**2.** 唾弃,蔑视。**3.** (猫等)呼噜呼噜地叫。**4.** (雨、雪)哗啦哗啦或霏霏地下。**5.** (沸水)滚腾。**6.** (蜡烛等)喷出火花,枪发出火舌,(发动机等)劈啪地响。*Please don't ~ at random.* 请不要随便吐痰。*No spitting.* (此处)不得吐痰。*I simply spat my contempt and threw the drug back to the quack.* 我愤怒地表示了我的蔑视,把药扔回给那个江湖医生。*The rain spat icily down and we all felt rather chilly.* 雨冰冷地哗啦哗啦地下着,我们都觉得冷飕飕的。~ *blood* 吐血,咯血。~ ***at*** 向…啐唾沫;藐视,侮辱。~ ***and image*** 极相像的人。~ ***and polish*** 〔英口〕极注意整洁;〔英海军俚〕擦洗打扫整理内务。~ ***in sb.'s face*** 啐唾沫在人脸上,唾弃某人。~ ***in*** [***on***] ***one's hands*** 啐唾沫在手掌上,加紧努力。~ ***it out*** 〔俚〕毫无保留地讲;大声说[唱];打败。~ ***on*** [***upon***] 藐视,侮辱 (= ~ at)。~ ***swapping*** 〔美俚〕接吻。~ ***up*** 咳出;呕出。**II** ***n.*** **1.** 涎,唾液,啐唾沫。**2.** (雨、雪等的)哗啦哗啦或霏霏地下降。**3.** (猫)呼噜呼噜地叫。**4.** 喷火式战斗机;【动】(昆虫的)唾状泡沫,吹泡。**5.** 〔口〕极相像的人,一模一样的物。*He's the ~ of his dad.* 他活像他爹。***be the very*** [***the dead***] ~ ***of*** 和…完全一样,和…一模一样。**~-and-polish** ***a.*** 注重表面;整洁的 (*a ~-and-polish band* 仪容整洁的乐队)。**~ball** ***n.*** (小孩用唾沫弄湿后用作抛投物的)纸团;【棒球】(用唾沫濡湿一部分扔投的)唾球。~ **box** 痰匣。~ **devil** 喷火不倒翁[玩具]。~**kit** 〔美〕痰盂。

spit[2] [spit; spɪt] **I** ***n.*** **1.** 烤肉铁签;(海关关员的)查货铁签。**2.** 岬,沙嘴;狭长的暗礁。**II** ***vt.*** (***spit·ted; spit·ting***) 用铁签穿过(肉片等);(以刀矛等)刺,戳。

spit[3] [spit; spɪt] ***n.*** 〔英〕一铲的深度[分量]。

spit·al [ˌspitl; ˋspɪtl] ***n.*** 〔废〕**1.** 病院,医院[尤指为贫民或麻疯病人等开设的医院]。**2.** (旅行者的)道边窝棚。

spitch·cock [ˈspitʃkɔk; ˋspɪtʃˏkɑk] **I** ***n.*** 烤鳝[鳗]。**II** ***vt.*** 剖开后烤(鳗、鳝等)。

spitch·er [ˈspitʃə; ˋspɪtʃɚ] ***vt.*** 〔军俚〕击沉(敌人的潜艇)。

spite [spait; spaɪt] **I** ***n.*** 恶意;怨恨;遗恨。***bear sb. a ~ = have a ~ against sb.*** 怀恨某人。***from ~ = in ~*** 为泄愤。***in ~ of*** =〔罕〕~ ***of*** 不管,不顾;〔古〕无视。***in ~ of oneself*** 不知不觉的,不由的。***in ~ of sb.'s nose*** [***teeth***] 不管某人反对。***in ~ of you*** 对不起…,***out of ~*** 为泄恨,为出气。***owe sb. a ~*** 怀恨某人。***spite*** [***vent***] ***one's ~*** 解恨,出气。***vent personal ~*** 泄私愤。**II** ***vt.*** 欺负,虐待,妨碍,刁难,泄愤。*cut off one's nose to ~ one's face* 为了泄忿[损人]反而害己。~ **fence** 恶篱笆[对邻居不满而恶意设置,以妨碍其出入]。

spite·ful [ˈspaitful; ˋspaɪtfʊl] ***a.*** 怀恨的,怨恨深的;有恶意的,心毒的。**-ly** ***ad.*** **-ness** ***n.***

spit·fire [ˈspitfaiə; ˋspɪtˏfaɪr] ***n.*** **1.** 喷火的东西。**2.** 〔英〕喷火式战斗机。**3.** 【海】船头三角帆。**4.** 〔特指〕大炮。**5.** 〔口〕脾气暴躁的人[尤指女人及小孩]。**6.** 咬人的狗[猫]。

spit·ter[1] [ˈspitə; ˋspɪtɚ] ***n.*** **1.** 啐唾沫的人。**2.** 〔俚〕= spitball.

spit·ter[2] [ˈspitə; ˋspɪtɚ] ***n.*** **1.** 用铁签烤肉的人。**2.** 开始长角的幼鹿。

spit·tle [ˈspitl; ˋspɪtl] ***n.*** **1.** 唾沫,涎沫。**2.** (沫蝉的)泡沫状分泌物。**~bug, ~insect** 【动】沫蝉 (= froghopper)。

spit·toon [spiˈtuːn; spɪˋtun] ***n.*** 痰盂。

spitz, spitz-dog [spits, -dɔg; spɪts, -dɑg] ***n.*** 尖嘴丝毛狗;〔美〕= spitzenberg.

spit·zen·berg, -burg [ˈspitsənbəːg; ˋspɪtsnˏbɝg] ***n.*** 〔美〕红黄色晚熟种尖头苹果。

spiv [spiv; spɪv] ***n.*** 〔英口语〕**1.** 不务正业靠投机取巧度日的人。**2.** 懒汉。

spiz·zer·inc·tum [ˌspizəˈriŋktəm; ˏspɪzəˋrɪŋktəm] ***n.*** 〔美方〕劲儿,雄心。

splanch·nic [ˈsplæŋknik; ˋsplæŋknɪk] ***a.*** 内脏的。

splanch·nol·o·gy [splæŋkˈnɔlədʒi; splæŋkˋnɑlədʒɪ] ***n.*** 内脏学。

splanch·no·tomy [splæŋkˈnɔtəmi; splæŋkˋnɑtəmɪ] ***n.*** 内脏解剖术,内脏解剖学。

splash [splæʃ; splæʃ] **I** ***vt.*** **1.** 溅,泼(水等);(把衣服等)溅污[湿],泼污[湿]。**2.** 趟水走;溅着水[泥]走。**3.** 泼洒得使到处是斑点。**4.** 〔口〕以显著地位刊登;显眼地展示。**5.** 〔美俚〕击落敌机。**6.** 〔俚〕挥霍钱财。—***vi.*** **1.** 溅泼,溅起水[泥];趟着水[泥]前进。**2.** 发出溅泼[拍激]声。**3.** 〔美俚〕洗澡,游泳。~ *a page with ink* = ~ *ink on a page* 书页上溅满墨水斑迹。~ (*one's way*) *through the mud* 溅着泥向前进。~ *through the stream* 趟着水过小河。*Across the surface of the river was ~ed the flaming gold of the sunrise.* 江面之上布满了初升的太阳的熔金之色。*On the wall of the parlour was ~ed his certificate of merit.* 在客厅的墙上高悬着他的奖状。**II** ***n.*** **1.** 溅,泼。**2.** 溅起的泥(水);飞溅声,水的拍激声。**3.** 游泳,玩水。**4.** 溅污的斑点,污迹。**5.** 斑点;色斑,光斑。**6.** 〔口〕引人注目的报道。**7.** 【药】安非他明。**8.** 〔英口〕(掺威士忌用的)少量汽水(等)。**9.** 〔美俚〕被击落的飞机。**10.** 〔美俚〕一杯水,一碗汤。*a ~ dam* 积水坝。*a ~ fan* 〔美〕游泳迷。***make*** [***cut***] ***a ~*** 发出泼溅声;引人注意,引起轰动。***with a ~*** 啪嚓[噗通]一声。**~board** ***n.*** (车的)挡泥板;(水闸或溢洪道的)挡水板。**~down** (太空船在水面上)溅落。~ **guard** (卡车后轮的)防溅板[帘]。~ **headline** (报纸等)显眼的大字标题。~ **pool** 儿童游泳池[戏水池]。~ **zone** (瀑布附近,海边等的)溅水地带。

splash·er [ˈsplæʃə; ˋsplæʃɚ] ***n.*** **1.** 溅泼者。**2.** (车的)挡泥板,轮罩。**3.** (洗脸架的)遮水板。**4.** 【冶】折焰板。**5.** 〔俚〕挥霍者。

splash·y [ˈsplæʃi; ˋsplæʃɪ] ***a.*** **1.** 易溅的;污水多;泥泞的。**2.** 溅泼的,溅泼着通过的。**3.** 有色斑的。**4.** 〔口〕炫耀的,铺张的,惹人注目的。*a ~ wedding* 铺张的婚礼。**-i·ness** ***n.***

splat[1] [splæt; splæt] ***n.*** (椅背的)中靠板。

splat[2] [splæt; splæt] ***n.***, ***int.*** 淅沥声;哗啦哗啦响。

splat·ter [ˈsplætə; ˋsplætɚ] **I** ***vi.***, ***vt.*** **1.** 溅(水等)。**2.** 啪嚓啪嚓[拨拉拨拉]地响,唠叨,急促不清楚地结结巴巴地讲。**3.** 【讯】边带噪声,相邻信道的干扰。**~-dash** 〔口〕嘈杂声,喧闹。**II** ***n.*** 溅泼。

splay [splei; sple] **I** ***vt.***, ***vi.*** **1.** 伸展开;张开(手掌等)。**2.** 【建】(使)斜削,(使)开成八字形。**3.** (把桶等)造成喇叭状。**4.** 使(马的肩骨等)脱节,脱臼。**II** ***a.*** **1.** 向外张开的,八字形的,宽扁的。**2.** 难看的,没样子的,笨重的。**III** ***n.*** **1.** 展开。**2.** 【建】斜削;斜面(度)。**3.** (枪眼等的)喇叭口。**~-foot** ***n.***, ***a.*** 八字脚(的),平跖外翻脚(的)。**~mouth** 大嘴,阔嘴。

spleen [spliːn; splin] ***n.*** **1.** 【解】脾(脏)。**2.** 愤怒,发脾气。**3.** 〔古〕忧郁,愁闷,消沉,颓丧。***in a fit of*** (***the***) ~ 发脾气,发怒。***bear*** [***have, take***] ***a ~ against*** 恨,怨恨。***vent one's ~ upon*** [***on***] 向…发脾气,拿…出气。~ **wort** 【植】(从前用以治忧郁症的)药铁角蕨。**-less** ***a.*** 脾切除的。

spleen·ful [ˈspliːnful; ˋsplinfʊl] ***a.*** 脾气坏的,发脾气的,不高兴的;忧郁的;恶意的;怀恨的。**-ly** ***ad.***

spleen·ish [ˈspliːniʃ; ˋsplinɪʃ] ***a.*** = spleenful.

spleen·y [ˈspliːni; ˋsplinɪ] ***a.*** = spleenful.

sple·nal·gi·a [spliˈnældʒiə; splɪˋnældʒɪə] ***n.*** 【医】脾痛。

sple·nal·gic [spliˈnældʒik; splɪˋnældʒɪk] ***a.*** 【医】脾痛的。

splen·dent [ˈsplendənt; ˋsplendənt] ***a.*** **1.** 发亮的,光亮的,有光泽的(矿物等)。**2.** 豪华的,辉煌的,显著的,宏大的。

splen·did [ˈsplendid; ˋsplɛndɪd] ***a.*** **1.** 发亮的,光亮的,有光彩的,灿烂的。**2.** 华丽的,壮丽的,壮观的,辉煌的。

S

3. 杰出的,显著的,伟大的,名声赫赫的。4.〔口〕极好的,上等的。*What about going there together?* —*Yes,* ~! 一道去怎么样?——不错,很好! ~ *sight* 壮观。*a* ~ *victory* 大胜。*a* ~ *chance* 极好的机会。*a* ~ *figure in history* 历史上的杰出人物。*a* ~ *dish of ice cream* 一杯极好的冰激凌。**-ly** *ad*. **-ness** *n*.

splen·dif·er·ous [splenˈdifərəs; splɛnˋdɪfərəs] *a*.〔口、谑〕极好的,了不起的,壮丽的,豪华的。**-ly** *ad*. **-ness** *n*.

splen·dour, 〔Am.〕**-dor** [ˈsplendə; ˋsplɛndɚ] *n*. 1. 光辉,光耀,光彩。2. 豪华,壮丽。3. (名声等的)杰出,显赫,显著。*the* ~ *of the sunrise* 日出的光辉。*the* ~ *of his achievements* 他的功绩辉煌。

sple·nec·to·my [spliˈnektəmi; splɪˋnɛktəmɪ] *n*.【医】脾切除术。

sple·net·ic(al) [spliˈnetik(əl); splɪˋnɛtɪk(l̩)] I *a*. 1. 脾的;位于脾附近的,脾病的。2. 易发脾气的,脾气坏的。3. 恶意的,怀恨的。*a letter* ~ *in tone* 一封发脾气语调的信。II *n*. 1. 生脾病的人。2. 易发脾气的人,脾气坏的人。3. 脾病药。**-i·cal·ly** *ad*.

sple·ni·al [ˈspliːniəl; ˋsplinɪəl] *a*.【解】夹肌的。

splen·ic, -i·cal [ˈsplenik, -ikəl; ˋsplɛnɪk, -ɪkəl] *a*. 脾脏的。~ **fever**【兽医】= anthrax 炭疽。

sple·ni·tis [spliˈnaitis; splɪˋnaɪtɪs] *n*.【医】脾炎。

sple·ni·us [ˈspliːniəs; ˋsplinɪəs] *n*. (*pl*. **-nii** [-niai; -nɪaɪ])【解】(颈部的)夹肌。

sple·ni·za·tion [ˌspliːnaiˈzeiʃən; ˏsplɛnɪˋzeʃən, ˏsplinɪ-] *n*.【医】脾样变。

sple·noid [ˈspliːnɔid; ˋsplinɔɪd] *a*.【解】脾样的。

sple·no·meg·a·ly [ˌspliːnəˈmegəli, ˌsplenə-; ˏsplino-ˋmɛgəlɪ] *n*.【医】脾大。

sple·no·tomy [spliˈnɔtəmi; ˋsplɪˋnɑtəmɪ] *n*.【医】脾切开术。

splent [splent; splɛnt] *n*. = splint.

spleu·chan [ˈspluːxən; ˋspluxən] *n*.〔Scot., Irish〕钱袋,烟袋。

splice [splais; splaɪs] I *vt*. 1. 拼接,叠接(木板等);黏接;【生】移植(基因);重组。2. 绞接,编接,捻接(绳子等)。3.〔俚〕使结婚。4.【机】接头。*get* ~*d* 结婚。II *n*. 1. 拼[绞、捻、叠]接(处)。2. 接头;接枝。3.〔俚〕结婚。4.〔俚〕食客。*not by a long* ~〔美〕简直不是…。*sit on the* ~〔板球俚〕小心取守势。~ *the main brace*〔海员俚〕喝酒。**splicer** *n*.

spline [splain; splaɪn] I *n*. 1.【机】花键;方栓;止转楔;齿槽,齿条,键槽条。2.【建】塞缝片。3. 活动曲线规。II *vt*. 1. 开键槽于。2. 用花键(或方栓)联接。

splint [splint; splɪnt] I *n*. 1. 薄木条;藤条。2.〔口〕碎片,裂片。3.【医】夹板。4.【解】腓骨〔又叫 ~-bone〕。5.【兽医】掌骨疣。6. (铠甲的)金属叶。7. 烟煤。II *vt*. 用夹板夹。~ **armo(u)r** 百叶锁子甲。~ **coal** 硬烟煤。

splin·ter [ˈsplintə; ˋsplɪntɚ] I *n*. 1. 碎片,裂片;木片;(炮弹的)破片;(碎木片等的)刺。2. 分裂出来的小派别。3. 微末的事物,微不足道的事情。4.〔美俚〕极瘦的人。II *vt*. 1. 劈成碎片。2. 割裂,使分裂,扯裂。—*vi*. 裂开,劈开;分裂。*run a* ~ *into one's thumb* 拇指上扎了根刺。*Opinions are* ~*ed now*. 意见现在纷纭了。~ **group**= ~ party. ~ **bar**〔英〕马车的横档。~ **deck**【军】防弹片甲板。~ **netting** (军舰的)弹片防御网。~ **party**【政】(从政党中分裂出的)小派别。~**proof** 防弹片的。

splin·ter·y [ˈsplintri; ˋsplɪntərɪ] *a*. 裂片(似)的;多片状的;易碎裂的;碎裂的;粗糙的(岩石等)。

Split [split; splɪt] *n*. 斯普利特〔前南斯拉夫港市〕。

split [split; splɪt] I *vt*. (*split*; ~*ting*) 1. 劈开,切开,割裂,扯裂;剖分。2. 使分裂,使分离;分解;分配。3.【海】扯破(帆)。—*vi*. 1. 裂开,劈开;分离,分开。2. (党派等)分裂。3. 分担;分享。4.〔口〕大笑。5.〔口〕逃跑,开小差;走开。6.〔美俚〕分赃。7. 告密。*S- the grapefruit in two*. 把柚子剖成两半。*S- a compound into its elements*. 把一个化合物分解成元素。*Mother said her headache was* ~*ting*. 妈妈说她头痛欲裂。*The club* ~ *on the journey question into two groups*. 俱乐部在外出旅行的问题分裂为两派。**be** ~ **by parties and factions** 分裂成一些派别。~ **a bottle of wine**〔口〕两人分喝一瓶葡萄酒。~ **across** 分裂成二。~ **away** 分离。~ **fair**〔俚〕讲真话。~ **off** 劈开;分开;分裂出来。~ **on**〔俚〕告密,出卖(朋友)。~ **on** [**upon**] **a rock** 搁浅,触礁;遭遇意外灾难;意见分歧,不和。~ **one's infinitives** 在动词原形和 to 之间插入副词〔例: Allow me to heartily congratulate you〕。~ **one's sides** 捧腹大笑。~ **one's vote** [〔美〕**ticket**] 同时投几个党的候选人的票。~ **open** 裂开,劈开,绷破,爆裂。~ **straws** [**words, hairs**] 作过分仔细的烦琐分析[考查];详细区分。~ **the difference** 互相让步,折中;妥协。~ **up** (使)分裂,(使)分离;〔美俚〕吵架,离婚。~ **with sb**.〔俚〕和某人闹翻;同某物决裂。II *a*. 裂开的,劈开的;分离的,分裂的。*a* ~ *second* [*minute*] 片刻,一转眼的功夫。~ *foot* 双层袜底。III *n*. 1. 劈裂,分裂;裂缝;罅隙;裂片,破片,碎片;(劈开的)柳条;薄板;薄皮。2. 分裂,分化;派别。3.〔美俚〕(往往是赃物的)份儿。4.【矿】分裂通气,分裂气流。5.〔俚〕告密者,奸细;便衣警察。6. 半杯酒;半瓶汽水。7.〔*pl*.〕(劈)一字腿(两腿左右成一直线伸开坐下的表演),劈叉。8. 水果片,冰激凌,糖浆等做成的甜食。*That may lead to a serious* ~ *in our class*. 那可能导致我们班的严重分裂。(*at*) **full** ~ 拼命,飞快地。**run like** ~〔美〕飞一样地跑。~ **end**【橄榄球】边锋。~ **gear**【机】拼合[双片]齿轮。~ **gene**【生化】分裂基因。~ **infinitive**【语法】分离不定式〔在 to 和动词原形之间有副词插入的结构〕。~**-level** *a*.【建】错层式的。~ **mind** 精神分裂症。~**-off** 1. 分裂;分裂出去的东西[派别]。2. (母公司向子公司的)部分股本转移。~ **pea**〔美〕剖开的干豌豆。~ **personality**【医,心】分裂人格。~ **pin**【机】开尾销。~ **reel** (一卷中收入两三部短片的)部分影片。~ **shift**〔美〕(中间间歇比通常长久的)两班制。~ **ticket** [**vote**]〔美〕(一部分投给反对党候选人的)分裂选票。~**-up** 1. 分裂;(股本的)分散转移。2.〔美俚〕吵架;离婚。

split·ter [ˈsplitə; ˋsplɪtɚ] *n*. 1. 劈(切、割)的(工)人。2. 爱作无谓的分析的人。3. 劈裂机,分离器,分解器,分裂机。

split·ting [ˈsplitiŋ; ˋsplɪtɪŋ] I *a*. 1. 要爆裂似的;剧烈的(疼痛等)。2.〔口〕飞也似的,极快的。3.〔口〕笑痛肚皮的。II *n*.【物】裂距;分裂。*at a* ~ *pace* 飞也似地。*a* ~ *laugh* 大笑。*a* ~ *attack* 突破攻势。

split·tism [ˈsplitizəm; ˋsplɪtɪzəm] *n*. 分裂主义。

splodge [splɔdʒ; splɑdʒ] *n*., *vt*. = splotch.

splore [splɔː; splor, splɔr] *n*.〔苏格兰〕1. 闹饮;嬉戏。2. 大混乱。

splosh [splɔʃ; splɑʃ] I *n*. 1.〔口〕泼下的大量的水。2.〔俚〕金钱。II *vt*., *vi*. 泼,溅。III *ad*. 劈劈啪啪地。**-y** *a*.

splotch [splɔtʃ; splɑtʃ] I *n*. 污点,斑点。*a* ~ *of blue paint* 蓝色油漆的污迹。II *vt*. 弄脏;沾污。

splotch·y [ˈsplɔtʃi; ˋsplɑtʃɪ] *a*. (*-i·er*; *-i·est*) 弄脏了的,有污点的,有斑点的。

splurge [spləːdʒ; splɝdʒ] I *n*. 夸示,炫耀,卖弄;摆阔;挥霍。II *vi*. 夸示,卖弄,炫耀。—*vt*. 挥霍。~ *it*〔美〕生活奢华;任意挥霍。*The victory meeting should be one without any* ~. 庆功会应该开成一个毫不炫耀摆阔的会。*Billionaires swarmed into Nice to* ~ *millions during the summer holidays*. 暑期休假时,亿万富翁们群趋尼斯挥霍了百万巨款。**-r** *n*.

splut·ter [ˈsplʌtə; ˋsplʌtɚ] *v*., *n*. = sputter.

SPM = suspended particulate matter 悬浮颗粒物〔大气污染物的一种〕。

Spode [spəud; spod] ***n***. 斯波德陶瓷〔得名于英国陶瓷匠 Josiah Spode (1754—1827)〕。

spod·u·mene [ˈspɔdʒuˌmiːn; ˋspɑdʒuˏmin] ***n***.【地】锂辉石。

spof·fish [ˈspɔfiʃ; ˋspɑfɪʃ], **spof·fy** [ˈspɔfi; ˋspɑfɪ] ***a***.〔英俚〕爱管闲事的;大惊小怪的;小题大做的。

spoil [spɔil; spɔɪl] **I** ***vt***. (*~ed*, ***spoilt***) **1**.〔*p. p.* 用 *~ed*〕〔古〕抢劫,掠夺,强夺 (*of*)。**2**. 损坏,弄坏,糟蹋;把(酒、肉等)放坏。**3**. 惯坏,溺爱坏,宠坏(孩子等);奉承。**4**. 妨碍,破坏(兴趣等)。**5**.〔俚〕杀害,伤害。—***vi***. **1**. (食物等)变坏,糟蹋;腐败。**2**. 抢劫,掠夺。*Our holidays were spoilt by bad weather*. 我们的假期给坏天气毁了。~ *a story in the telling* 笨嘴说坏了(好)故事。*a ~ed child* 惯坏了的孩子。*a spoilt child of fortune* 任性的人,唯我独尊的自私者。*The rain ~ed the hay crop*. 这场雨使牧草遭殃了。*Meat will soon ~ in warm weather*. 天热肉会很快地变得腐坏的。***be ~-ing for a fight*** 一心想打架,很想显一显本事。~ ***sb.'s appetite*** 使某人倒胃口。**II** ***n***. **1**. 抢劫,掠夺;强夺。**2**. 掠夺物;〔常 *pl*.〕战利品;猎获物;(搜集家的)获得物。**3**. 〔常 *pl*.〕〔美〕(胜利政党分给党员的)官位,职位。**4**. 弃泥,掘出的泥土。**5**. 废品,次品。*the ~s of war* 战利品。*the ~ of office*〔美〕猎官,追求官职。~**bank** 弃土堆,废石堆,(煤矿上的)矸石堆。~ **ground** 弃土[废石、煤矸石]堆置场。~ **heap** = ~bank. ~**sport** 妨碍人家欢娱的人,扫人兴的人,插嘴阻挠人的人。~**s system**〔美〕(胜利后分与党员、支持者物质利益和职位的)政党分肥制。**-er** **1**. 掠夺者;破坏者;溺爱者。**2**.【火箭】阻流板;(防止非法录制激光唱片的)扰流器。

spoil·age [ˈspɔilidʒ; ˋspɔɪlɪdʒ] ***n***. **1**. 损坏;(食物等)腐坏。**2**. 损坏物;【印】印坏的纸张。**3**. 因损坏所受的损失。

spoils·man [ˈspɔilzmən; ˋspɔɪlzmən] ***n***. **1**. (*pl*. ***-men***)〔美〕为个人利益而为某政党效劳的人。**2**. 赞成政党分肥制的人。

spoils·mon·ger [ˈspɔilzmʌŋgə; ˋspɔɪlzˏmʌŋgɚ] ***n***.〔美〕卖官鬻爵的政党分肥制政客。

spoilt [spɔilt; spɔɪlt] spoil 的过去式及过去分词。

spoke[1] [spəuk; spok] **I** ***n***. **1**. (车轮的)辐条。**2**.【船】舵轮把柄。**3**. 扶梯棍梯级,梯磴。**4**. (下坡时防止车轮猛转的)木棒(等)煞车。***put a ~ in sb.'s wheel***〔口〕阻挠[破坏]某人的计划。**II** ***vt***. **1**. 给…装上辐条。**2**. 用木棒煞车煞住。**3**. 阻挠,妨碍。*We might easily ~ their scheme if we choose*. 我们要是愿意干的话,可以很容易地阻碍他们计划的进行。~**-bone**【解】(前臂的)挠骨。~ **shave**【机】辐刨片;【木工】辐刨。~**wise** ***ad***. 像(车轮上的)辐条一样地,呈辐射状地。

spoke[2] speak 的过去式。

spo·ken [ˈspəukən; ˋspokən] **I** speak 的过去分词。**II** ***a***. **1**. 口头讲的 (*opp*. written); 口语的 (*opp*. literary)。**2**.〔构成复合词〕口头…的,说话…的。*a ~ message* 口信。*pleasant-~* 说话中听的。~ **language** 口语。~ **title**【影】对白字幕。

spoke·shave [ˈspəukʃeiv; ˋspokˏʃev] ***n***. (制造车辐等用的)辐刀;【机】辐刨片。

spokes·man [ˈspəuksmən; ˋspoksmən] ***n***. (*pl*. ***-men***) 发言人;代言人。

spokes·per·son [ˈspəukspəːsn; ˋspoksˏpɝsn̩] ***n***. 发言人,代言人;辩护士。

spokes·wo·man [ˈspəuksˌwumən; ˋspoksˏwʊmən] ***n***. (*pl*. ***spokeswomen***) 女发言人,女代言人。

spo·li·a o·pi·ma [ˈspəuliə əuˈpaimə; ˋspolɪə oˋpaɪmə]〔L.〕古罗马将军单骑与敌将决斗所夺得的武器;〔喻〕无上的成功或荣誉。

spo·li·ate [ˈspəulieit; ˋspolɪˏet] ***vt***., ***vi***. 抢劫,掠夺。

spo·li·a·tion [ˌspəuliˈeiʃən; ˏspolɪˋeʃən] ***n***. **1**. (尤指交战国对中立国船只的)抢劫,掠夺。**2**.【宗】(教堂俸禄的)冒领;〔美〕腐败,腐朽。**3**.【法】(文件、票据等的)销毁,窜改。**-a·tor** ***n***. **-a·tory** ***a***. 抢劫的,掠夺的,毁灭文件票据的,窜改文件票据的。

spon·da·ic [spɔnˈdeiik; spɑnˋdeɪk] ***a***. (诗句)扬扬格的。

spon·dee [ˈspɔndiː; ˋspɑndi] ***n***. (诗句的)扬扬格。

spon·du·lic(k)s, **spondu·lix** [spɔnˈdjuːliks; spɑnˋdjulɪks] ***n***.〔*pl*.〕〔美俚〕钱,钞票。

spon·dyl·ar·thri·tis [ˌspɔndilɑːˈθraitis; ˏspɑdɪlˏɑrˋθraɪtɪs] ***n***.【医】(脊)椎关节炎。

spon·dyl(e) [ˈspɔndil; ˋspɑndɪl] ***n***.【解】脊椎,椎关节。

spon·dy·li·tis [ˌspɔndiˈlaitis; ˏspɑndɪˋlaɪtɪs] ***n***.【医】脊椎炎。

sponge [spʌndʒ; spʌndʒ] **I** ***n***. **1**. 海绵。**2**. 海绵动物;海绵状的东西〔如泡沫塑料等〕;金属绵。**3**. 加有发酵粉的生面包;海绵布丁,蛋糕。**4**.【医】外科用纱布,棉球。**5**. 枪刷。**6**. (擦身用)海绵揩。**7**.〔古、美口〕食客,寄生者,吃闲饭的。**8**. 一堆蟹子。**9**.〔俚〕大量的人。**10**. 知识丰富的人。***have a ~ down*** 洗一个用海绵擦洗的澡。***pass the*** [***a***] ***~ over*** 抹去,勾销;忘却(旧怨),不再提起。***throw*** [***toss***, ***chuck***] ***up the ~***【拳击】扔掉擦身用的海绵认输;〔口〕认输;投降。**II** ***vt***. **1**. 用海绵揩[擦];消除(债务等),忘却(往事等) (*out*; *off*; *away*); 用海绵擦洗 (*over*; *down*); 用海绵弄湿;用海绵吸 (*up*)。**2**. 占…的便宜,厚着脸骗吃(饭等);乞讨,骗取,敲诈。—***vi***. **1**. (海绵等)吸收。**2**. 采集海绵。**3**. 敲诈。**4**. 寄食,依赖他人过日子 (*on*; *upon*)。*Please ~ my back with alcohol*. 请用酒精擦擦我的背。*Every evening Tom would go to the White Bear to ~ drinks*. 每天晚上汤姆都到白熊酒馆去讨酒喝。*A youngman like you shouldn't ~ on your uncle*. 像你这样的小伙子不该寄食在叔叔家里。~**-bag** (旅途中用的)盥洗用品防水袋。~ **bath** (不入水的)海绵擦浴。~ **cake** 海绵(松)蛋糕。~ **cloth** **1**.【纺】松软棉布,揩车布,海绵布。**2**. (熨衣用的)润湿布。~ **cucumber**, ~ **gourd**【植】丝瓜(络)。~ **rubber** 海绵状橡皮。~ **tree**【植】金合欢。

spong·er [ˈspʌŋdʒə; ˋspʌndʒɚ] ***n***. **1**. 用海绵擦洗的人。**2**. 海绵采集人;海绵采集船。**3**. 寄生食客,依赖他人生活的人,吸血鬼;寄生虫。

spong·i·form [ˈspʌŋdʒifɔːm; ˋspʌndʒɪˏfɔrm] ***a***. 海绵组织的,海绵状的。

spon·gin [ˈspʌndʒin; ˋspʌndʒɪn] ***n***.【化】海绵硬蛋白。

spong·i·ness [ˈspʌndʒinis; ˋspʌndʒɪnɪs] ***n***. 海绵状,海绵质。

spong·ing-house [ˈspɔndʒiŋhaus; ˋspandʒɪŋˏhaʊs] ***n***.【英史】负债人拘留所。

spon·gi·o·pi·lin(e) [ˈspɔndʒiəupilin; ˋspandʒɪopɪlɪn] ***n***.【医】(敷药用)海绵毯。

spong·y [ˈspʌndʒi; ˋspʌndʒɪ] ***a***. (***-gi·er***; ***-gi·est***) **1**. 海绵状的,海绵质的。**2**. 多孔的,吸水的。**3**. 松软有弹性的。**-gi·ly** ***ad***. **-gi·ness** ***n***.

spon·sion [ˈspɔnʃən; ˋspɑnʃən] ***n***. **1**.【法】(为他人所作的)担保,保证。**2**.【国际法】未经受权的代表所作的约定[行为]。

spon·son [ˈspɔnsn; ˋspɑnsn̩] ***n***. **1**. (舷侧)突出部。**2**. (军舰,坦克的)突出炮座。**3**. (水上飞机的)翼梢浮筒。

spon·sor [ˈspɔnsə; ˋspɑnsɚ] **I** ***n***. **1**.【宗】教父,教母。**2**. 发起者,主办者,倡议者。**3**. (船只的)命名人;保证人。**4**. 在广播[电视]作广告节目的资助人。*a ~ for a class tea party* 本班茶话会的发起人。**II** ***vt***. **1**. 发起,主办,倡议。**2**. 做…的保人,担保。**3**. 做广告节目的资助人。*The meeting was ~ed by five departments*. 会议是五个系倡议召开的。*a ~ed programme* 插有广告的广播[电视]节目。**-ship** **1**. 教父[母]身分。**2**. 保证人身分。**3**. 发起,主办;支援;倡议。

spon·so·ri·al [spɔnˈsɔːriəl; spɑnˋsɔrɪəl] ***a***. 保证人的;教父的,教母的;主办人的。

spon·ta·ne·i·ty [ˌspɔntəˈniːiti; ˏspɑntəˋniətɪ] ***n***. **1**. 自

S

发(性);自生。2.〔*pl*.〕自发行为[行动]。

spon·ta·ne·ous [spɔnˈteinjəs, -niəs; spɑnˋteniəs] ***a***. 1. 自发的,一时冲动的。2. 天然发生的(电等);自生的,天然产生的(草木等),不依赖人工的。3. 本能的,自动的。4. (文体)自然流畅的。~ *expression of gratitude* 自发的感激的表示。~ *offer of help* 自动提供的帮助。~ *growth of wood* 树木的天然生长。~ *recovery from indigestion* 消化不良症的自然痊愈。*a* ~ *writer* 文笔自然流畅的作家。~ *combustion* 自燃。~ *generation* 自然发生。**-ly** ***ad***. **-ness** ***n***.

spon·toon [spɔnˈtuːn; spɑnˋtun] ***n***. 短矛,戟;〔美方〕警棍。

spoof [spuːf; spuf]〔俚〕**I** ***n***. 1. 玩笑性的哄骗,戏弄。2. 幽默的讽刺诗[文章]。**II** ***a***. 假的,扯谎的,骗人的。**III** ***vt***. 1. 哄骗,戏弄。2. 开…的玩笑。—***vi***. 1. 欺骗,哄骗,开玩笑。2.【计】冒名顶替,假冒友好网站非法侵入他人电脑,行电子分身术。*Nobody likes those clumsy* ~*s of yours*. 谁都不喜欢你那拙笨的玩笑。*Don't let them* ~ *you*. 不要让他们哄骗你了。**-er** ***n***. **-ing** ***n***. 1. 哄骗。2.【军】电子欺骗。

spook [spuːk; spuk, spʊk] **I** ***n***.〔口〕1. 鬼。2.〔美俚〕出没无常行踪古怪的人〔精神病人,密探等〕。3.〔美俚〕代笔者。4.〔美俚〕黑人。**II** ***vt***. 1. 鬼怪般地出没于。2. 惊吓。—***vi***. (因受惊吓而)逃窜。*At night, he would creep out of the house like a* ~. 夜间,他常常像幽灵一般地从家里偷偷地出来。*When our car drove forward, the deer* ~*ed*. 我们的汽车向前开动时,鹿群吓得逃散了。

S

spook·ish, spook·y [ˈspuːkiʃ, -i; ˋspukɪʃ, -ɪ] ***a***. 1. 鬼似的。2. 有点怪的,不可思议的。3. 稍微地有些神经质的,(容易)害怕的。*Did your* ~ *brother take his night stroll yesterday*? 你那个鬼似的哥哥昨天又在夜里散步了吗? *This mule is rather* ~. 这匹骡子很容易受惊。

spool, SPOOL = simultaneous peripheral operation on-line【计】联机同时外部操作,假脱机操作技术。

spool [spuːl; spul] **I** ***n***. 1.【纺】有边筒子,轴线,线管,线板,线框;短管;卷筒。2. (胶片,录音带等的)卷轴;卷轴状物品。3. 卷络的数量[长度]。**II** ***vt***. 绕在卷轴上;【纺】络纱,络筒。*S- the film for use*. 把胶卷卷上待用。~ **cotton** 木纱团,线团。**-er**【纺】络纱机,筒子车;绕卷轴[筒子]工人。**-ing** ***n***.【纺】络纱,络筒。

spoon[1] [spuːn; spun] **I** ***n***. 1. 匙,调羹。2. 一匙的量。3. 匙状物;匙桨。4.【构球】匙棒,三号高尔夫球棒。5. 挖土机,泥铲。6. (钓鱼用)匙状假饵(= ~ bait)。*It takes a long* ~ *to sup with him*. 和他打交道要小心。*a wooden* ~【史】末席。~ *bread*〔美〕(用匙吃的)湿软奶蛋面包。***be born with a silver*** [***wooden***] ~ ***in one's mouth*** 生在富有[贫穷]的人家。***be past the*** ~ 已经不是孩子(是大人了)。***hang up the*** ~〔俚〕死。***make a*** ~ ***or spoil a horn*** 不计成功失败,破釜沉舟,背城借一。***stick one's*** ~ ***in the wall***〔俚〕死。**II** ***vt***., ***vi***. 1. 拿匙舀,舀取(*into*; *off*; *out*; *up*)。2. 将球轻轻向上打去。3. 用匙状假饵钓鱼。4.〔美俚〕面对背地侧身站着睡。*You're to* ~ *the tomatoes into the jars, Mary, and Jack is to* ~ *out bowls of porridge*. 玛丽,你把番茄舀进罐子里,贾克用匙子舀粥。~ **bait** 匙钩,匙状假饵〔附装在钓丝上用以诱鱼游进的金属片〕。~**bill** ***n***.【鸟】篦鹭;阔嘴鸭。~**-fashion** ***ad***. 面对背地,匙一样地(侧身站着)。~**-feed** ***vt***. 用匙子喂;溺爱;给予(产业等)特惠;填鸭式灌输(知识等)。~**-fed** ***a***. 1. (小孩、病人等)用匙喂的。2. 娇养的。3. (产业等)受到补助金等保护的。4. 受填鸭式教育的;无独立思考[行动]能力的,被当做孩子看待的;〔美〕奢华的。~ **food**, ~ **meat** 半流汁食物;汤类;面包粥。~ **net** 捞网。**-ful** ***n***. 一匙的量,一满匙。

spoon[2] [spuːn; spun] **I** ***n***.〔俚〕傻子,呆子;迷恋者,痴情汉。**II** ***vi***., ***vt***. 1. 痴爱,迷恋。2.〔美〕向…求爱。3.〔口〕谈情说爱,动手动脚。***be*** ~***s on*** 痴爱,迷恋。***on the*** ~ 迷恋着。

spoon·drift [ˈspuːndrift; ˋspunˏdrɪft] ***n***. = spindrift.

spoon·er·ism [ˈspuːnərizəm; ˋspunəˏrɪzəm] ***n***. 首音调换法〔如将 well-oiled bicycle 俏皮地改成 well-boiled icicle 之类;有时并非故意而将首音误置〕。

spoon·y, spoon·ey [ˈspuːni; ˋspunɪ] **I** ***a***. (*-i·er*; *-i·est*)〔俚〕1. 傻气的;愚蠢的。2. 过于多愁善感的。3. 痴恋的,迷恋的(*on*; *upon*)。**II** ***n***. 1. 傻子。2. 痴情汉。**-i·ly** ***ad***. **-i·ness** ***n***.

spoor [spuə; spur, spor, spɔr] **I** ***n***. (野兽的)足迹,嗅迹。**II** ***vt***., ***vi***. 跟着足迹[嗅迹]追。**-er** ***n***. 跟踪者。

spo·rad·ic, -i·cal [spəˈrædik, -ikəl; spoˋrædɪk, -ɪkəl] ***a***. 不时[个别]发生的;分散的;零星的;特发的,散发的。*a* ~ *case* 散发病例。*a* ~ *disease* 单发病。~ *fighting* 零星战斗。~ *mutation*【生】自然突变。**-cal·ly** ***ad***. **-cal·ness** ***n***.

spo·ran·gi·al [spɔːˈrændʒiəl; spəˋrændʒɪəl] ***a***.【生】孢子囊的;孢蒴的。

spo·ran·gi·o·phore [spəˈrændʒiəˌfɔː; spəˋrændʒɪəˏfɔr] ***n***. 孢子囊柄。

spo·ran·gi·o·spore [spəˈrændʒiəspɔː; spəˋrændʒɪəˏspɔr] ***n***.【生】孢囊孢子。

spo·ran·gi·um [spəˈrændʒiəm; spəˋrændʒɪəm] ***n***. (*pl*. ***-gia*** [-dʒiə; -dʒɪə])【生】孢子囊;(苔藓植物的)孢蒴。

spore [spɔː, spɔə; spor, spɔr] **I** ***n***. 1.【生】孢子;胚种。2. (事物的)根源,原因。**II** ***vi***. 长孢子。~ **case** 孢子囊;孢蒴。~ **fruit** 子实体;子囊果。~ **plant** 孢子植物。

spo·re·ling [ˈspɔːrliŋ; ˋsporlɪŋ, ˋspɔr-] ***n***. 孢子苗。

spo·ri·ci·dal [ˌspɔːriˈsaidl; ˏsporɪˋsaɪdl] ***a***. 杀孢子的。

spo·ri·cide [ˈspɔːrisaid; ˋsporɪˏsaɪd, ˋspɔr-] ***n***. 杀孢子剂。

spo·rif·er·ous [spɔːˈrifərəs; spoˋrɪfərəs] ***a***.【生】带孢子的。

spork [spɔːk; spɔrk] ***n***.〔美〕匙叉〔有叉齿的塑料匙,可用作餐叉〕。

spo·ro·blast [ˈspɔrəblæst; ˋspɔrəblæst] ***n***. 孢子细胞。

spo·ro·carp [ˈspɔːrəˌkɑːp; ˋsporəˏkɑrp] ***n***.【植】孢子果;子实体。

spo·ro·cyst [ˈspɔːrəˈsist; ˋsporəˋsɪst] ***n***. 1.【植】孢子被。2.【动】孢子囊,胞蚴。**-tic** ***a***.

spo·ro·gen·e·sis [ˌspɔːrəˈdʒenisis; ˏsporəˋdʒɛnɪsɪs] ***n***.【生】1. 孢子发生。2. 孢子形成。**-gen·ic** [-ˈdʒenik; -ˋdʒɛnɪk] ***a***. **-rog·e·nous** [-ˈrɔdʒinəs; -ˋrɑdʒɪnəs] ***a***.

spo·ro·ge·ny [spəˈrɔdʒini; spəˋrɑdʒɪnɪ] ***n***. = sporogenesis.

spo·ro·go·ni·um [ˌspɔːrəˈgəuniəm; ˏsporəˋgonɪəm] ***n***. (*pl*. ***-ni·a*** [-ə; -ə])【植】(苔藓的)孢子体。

spo·rog·o·ny [spɔːˈrɔgəni; spoˋrɑgənɪ] ***n***.【生】孢子发生,孢子生殖,孢子形成。

spo·ro·phore [ˈspɔːrəˌfɔː; ˋsporəˏfor] ***n***.【植】孢囊柱;子实体。**-phor·ic**, **-roph·o·rous** [-ˈfɔrik, -ˈrɔfərəs; -ˋfɑrɪk, -ˋrɑfərəs] ***a***.

spo·ro·phyll [ˈspɔːrəˌfil; ˋsporəfɪl] ***n***.【生】孢子叶。**-phyll·a·ry** [-ˈfiləri; -ˋfɪlərɪ] ***a***.

spo·ro·phyte [ˈspɔːrəˌfait; ˋsporəˏfaɪt] ***n***.【生】孢子体。**-phyt·ic** [-ˈfitik; -ˋfɪtɪk] ***a***.

spo·ro·zo·an [ˌspɔːrəˈzəuən; ˏsporəˋzoən] **I** ***n***.【生】孢子虫(= sporozoon)。**II** ***a***. 孢子虫的(= sporozoic, sporozoal)。

spo·ro·zo·ite [ˌspɔːrəˈzəuait; ˏsporəˋzoaɪt, ˏspɔr-] ***n***.【生】孢子虫,孢子体,子孢子。

spor·ran [ˈspɔrən; ˋspɑrən] ***n***. (苏格兰人系在裙前做装饰的)毛皮袋。

sport [spɔːt; sport, spɔrt] **I** ***n***. 1. 娱乐,消遣;游戏,玩耍。2.〔常 *pl*.〕运动,运动比赛;打猎,赛马,钓鱼,游泳(等)。3.〔*pl*.〕运动会。4. 闹着玩儿,玩笑;戏谑;嘲笑,

嘲笑对象;玩弄品,玩物。5.(=sportsman)有体育道德精神的人;运动员。6.〔美俚〕讨人喜欢的人。7.爱漂亮[吃喝玩乐]的人;好色之徒,赌徒。8.【生】突变;【植】芽变(枝)。9.变态或畸形的人或动植物。*Fishing affords great ~ to us*. 钓鱼使我们有很好的消遣。*I had fine ~ with my new skates*. 我穿着新冰鞋溜冰玩得痛快极了。*It is fine ~ to sail in a boat*. 驾着小舟游览是很好的娱乐。*What ~!* 真有趣呀! *athletic ~s* 体育运动,运动会。*the ~ of kings*〔美〕赛马;打猎。*a ~ of terms* [*wit*, *words*] 双关语,俏皮话。*the ~ of the fortune* 被命运玩弄的人。*the ~ of nature* 突变种,畸形。*He is an old ~*. 他是一个有趣的人[爽快人]。*Be a good ~!* (像运动家一样)努力干。***for*** [***in***] ~ 闹着玩地。***have good*** ~ 打了一次好猎〔猎获甚多〕。***make ~ of*** 戏弄,愚弄。***say in*** ~ 说着玩儿。**II** ***vt***. 1.〔口〕炫耀,夸示。2.【生】突变为,芽变出。3.〔英〕关门〔表示无暇接待来客〕。4.玩过(时候),浪费。—***vi***. 1.运动,打猎(等)。2.玩耍,游戏;嬉戏。3.闹玩儿,开玩笑。4.【生】发生突变;【植】芽变。*James proudly ~s his new watch*. 詹姆斯骄傲地夸示他的新表。~ *a moustache* 捻弄胡子。*Grandpa is ~ing with us*. 爷爷在和我们开玩笑呢。~ *the Union Jack* 挂出英国国旗。~ ***on the cinders***〔美〕赛跑,参加径赛。~ ***one's oak*** [***timber***, ***door***]〔英大学生俚〕锁上门〔谢绝来客〕。~ ***silk*** 穿(骑师)绸衫;做骑师;(骑师或马)参加赛马。**III** ***a***.〔常作~s〕适于户外活动的,运动(比赛)用的,户外穿的(裙子等)。*a ~s shirt* 运动衬衣。*~s requisites* 运动用具。*a ~s editor* 体育栏编辑。*a ~s page* 体育版。**~s car** 跑车〔双座敞篷,车身低矮〕。**~s cast** ***v***., ***n***.〔美〕【无】(播送)体育运动节目。~ **caster** ***n***. 体育节目广播员。**~sdom**〔美〕运动界。**~s jacket** 猎装〔户外活动或非正式场合穿着的粗花呢男上衣〕。**~s medicine** 运动医学。~ **science** 运动科学。**~s shirt** (可作便装穿的)男子运动衫。**~swear** 运动服装。**~s writer** 体育运动专栏作家。

sport·ful [ˈspɔːtful; ˋsportful, -fl̩] ***a***. 1.游戏的,玩耍的。2.有趣的,愉快的,高兴的。3.开玩笑的。**-ly** ***ad***. **-ness** ***n***.

sport·ing [ˈspɔːtiŋ; ˋsportɪŋ, ˋspɔr-] **I** ***a***. 1.运动的,有关体育运动的,像运动家的;喜欢运动的;喜欢打猎的;运动用的。2.有体育道德的,光明正大的,公平的。3.放荡的,好赌的;投机的,赌博性质的。4.【生】突变的;芽变的;畸形的。**II** ***n***. 运动,比赛;打猎。*a ~ section* (报纸的)体育运动栏。*a ~ editor* 体育运动栏新闻编辑。~ *goods*〔美〕体育运动用具。*the ~ world* 体育运动界。*a ~ man* 体育运动家;打猎者;赌徒。~ *conduct* 正大光明的行为。*a ~ scope* 望远镜。*a ~ thing to do* 危险工作。~ **chance** 胜负机会各占一半的冒险。~ **girl** (**woman**) 妓女。~ **house**〔美,口〕妓院;赌场。~ **page** (报纸的)体育版。**-ly** ***ad***.

spor·tive [ˈspɔːtiv; ˋsportɪv] ***a***. 1.嬉戏的;游戏的;闹着玩的;愉快的,高兴的,玩乐的。2.运动[打猎、赛马(等)]的。3.好色的。4.【生】突[芽]变的;〔古〕色情的。**-ly** ***ad***. **-ness** ***n***.

sports·man [ˈspɔːtsmən; ˋsportsmən, ˋsports-] ***n***. (*pl*. ***-men***) 1.运动家,运动员;爱好运动的人(如打猎,钓鱼)。2.有运动员品质[道德]的人;直爽[正大光明]的人。3.〔美〕赌徒。**~like** ***a***. 像运动家的,合乎运动员道德精神的,直爽的。**-ly** ***ad***. **-ship** ***n***. 运动员精神;运动员风格;体育[运动]道德;正大光明,直爽;打猎[赛马(等)]技术。

sports·wom·an [ˈspɔːtswumən; ˋsports͵wumən, ˋspɔr-ts-] ***n***. (*pl*. ***-wom·en***) 女运动员,女运动爱好者,女运动家。

sport·sy [ˈspɔːtsi; ˋsportsɪ] ***a***. 1.运动时穿的。2.运动服般的。

sport·y [ˈspɔːti; ˋsportɪ, ˋsportɪ] ***a***. (***-i·er***; ***-i·est***)〔口〕1.运动员一样的。2.有体育道德精神的,正大光明的,直爽的。3.(服装)花哨的,华美的。**-i·ly** ***ad***. **-i·ness** ***n***.

spor·u·lar [ˈspɔrjulə; ˋspɔrjələ] ***a***. 小孢子的。

spor·u·late [ˈspɔrjuleit; ˋspɔrju͵let] ***vi***. 形成孢子。

spor·u·la·tion [ˌspɔrjuˈleiʃən; ͵spɔrjuˋleʃən] ***n***. 【生】孢子形成。

spor·ule [ˈspɔrjuːl; ˋspɑrjul] ***n***. 【生】(小)孢子。

SPOT [spɔt; spɑt] = satellite positioning and tracking 人造卫星定位及跟踪。

spot [spɔt; spɑt] **I** ***n***. 1.斑点;污点;疵点,缺点。2.地点;场所,现场;部位;位置;职位;地位。3.处境(尤指困境、窘境)。4.一小片,少量,少许;〔口〕一杯酒。5.〔*pl*.〕【交易所】现货。6.〔美俚〕小额纸币〔常与数词连用〕。7.〔美俚〕非法酒店;没有执照的酒吧;夜总会。8.〔美俚〕舞台聚光灯(=spotlight)。9.〔常接数词〕短期徒刑。10.【撞球】〔特指红球〕最初放置处,置球点(=~-ball)。11.〔俚〕目标。12.【鸟】头上有黑斑的黑尾家鸽。13.太阳的黑点,肺部等处的阴影。14.【鱼】黄鲻。15.〔*pl*.〕金钱豹。16.【无】给某一节目指定的时间;广播中插入的简短公告[广告]。*solar ~s* = *~s in the sun* 太阳黑点;〔喻〕白玉微瑕。*John's face was covered with ~s*. 约翰的脸上全是雀斑。*a tender* [*sore*] ~ 容易触痛之处,不愿别人提起的事情[问题]。*the meeting on the ~* 现场会议。*a ~ of leave* 短暂的休假。*Let's take a ~ of lunch*. 吃一点午餐。***have a*** ~ 喝一杯。***hit the high ~s***〔美俚〕走马看花地浏览;提纲挈领,概括要点。***hit the*** ~〔口〕正合要求;恰到好处。***in a*** ~〔美俚〕处在困境中。***in ~s***〔美〕时时;在某几点上,到某程度。***knock the ~s off*** [***out of***]〔俚〕彻底击败,超过,凌驾。***on*** (***upon***) ***the*** ~ 当场,在现场;立刻;【商】用现货[现款];(人)准备妥当,没有疏忽;(射击等)姿势好;〔美俚〕处境危险的;注定要被暗杀的;【运】在困难环境中苦斗的。***price on*** ~ 现货价格;现金售价。***put one's finger on sb.'s weak*** ~ 指出某人(性格等上)的缺点。***put*** (*sb*.) ***on the*** ~〔美俚〕决定暗杀(某人)。***touch the*** (***tender***) ~ 碰到痛处。***upon the*** ~ = on the ~. ***without ~ or stain*** 毫无缺点。

II ***vt***. (***-tt-***) 1.弄上斑点;弄上污点,弄脏,污辱。2.散布,点缀,布置。3.在…上用点子作记号。4.〔口〕认出,发现,找到,预先认准、猜中(谁会在比赛中获胜等),看出,记认(惯犯等)。5.准确地定出…的位置,使准确地打中目标。6.把…置于需要(或指定)的地点上。7.使处于聚光灯下,集中照射。8.把节目排在特定的时间。9.除去污点(*out*)。10.比赛中给对方以礼让(如下棋让二个棋子)。11.〔美俚〕暗杀,杀死。*Lookouts were ~ted all along the coast*. 沿岸一带都布置了监视哨。*I ~ted him at once as an American*. 我一见就看出他是个美国人。*calicoes ~ted with beautiful flowers* 满幅美丽花朵的印花布。*Everybody ~s the Chinese team as the winner*. 人人都猜准中国队会得胜。*We've ~ted the enemy battery position*. 我们已经测定敌炮连阵地。*He knows how to ~ genial smiles on the audience*. 他知道怎样向观众们投送亲切的微笑。*Our performance is ~ted at 10*. 我们的表演排定在十点钟上场。—***vi***. 1.沾上污点;给污点弄脏;易染污点,易脏。2.【军】从空中侦察敌方目标。3.〔口〕下小雨。*This kind of cloth tends to ~ in the rain*. 这种布容易在雨中弄脏。*We spent the whole morning ~ting*. 我们花了整个早上侦察敌方目标。

III ***a***.〔只作定语〕1.现场的。2.现货的;付现的;专做现货生意的。3.插在电台[电视]节目之间播送的。4.局限于某些项目的;任选的;抽样的。~ *coverage of the parliamentary debate* 议会辩论的现场采访。*a ~ transaction* 现货交易(*with*)。~ *cotton* 现货棉花。~ *delivery* 现货交付。*a ~ sensational news* 一件插播在电视节目中广播的耸人听闻的消息。~ **announcement** (**broadcasting**) 插在节目中的公告[广播]。~ **an-**

S

swer 当场作出的回答。~ **ball**【台球】置球点上的球；有黑点的白球。~ **board**（泥瓦工用的）调灰泥板。~ **cash**【商】货到即付的现金。~ **check** 现场检查；抽样调查；抽查（*a* ~ *check on prices* 对物价的抽查）。~-**check** *vt*., *vi*. 现场检查；抽查，抽样。~ **lamp** 聚光灯。~-**light** 1. *n*. 聚光灯；（汽车上的）反光灯，探路灯；【视】点光；〔喻〕（世人的）视听，注意。2. *vt*. 把光线集中在…，使显著（*a* ~*light hunter*〔美剧〕（演剧时）好到舞台中央去[好出风头]的演员）。~ **news** 最新消息。~ **pass**【体】定点长传球。~ **test** 当场试测。~ **welding** 点焊。

spot·less [ˈspɔtlis; ˋspɑtlɪs] *a*. 1. 纯洁的；没有污点的；无瑕疵的。2. 极其清洁的。-**ly** *ad*. -**ness** *n*.

spot·ted [ˈspɔtid; ˋspɑtɪd] *a*. 1. 有斑点的。2. 有污点[缺点]的。3. 削去树皮打上记号的。4.〔口〕受注意的。~ **adder**【动】1. 黑边乳蛇。2. 黄背锦蛇。~ **dog**〔俚〕葡萄干布丁。~ **fever** 脑脊髓膜炎，斑疹伤寒；（落基山）斑疹热。~ **girl**〔美俚〕马戏团里的长颈鹿。~ **sandpiper**【动】斑点矶鹞。-**ness** *n*.

spot·ter [ˈspɔtə; ˋspɑtɚ] *n*. 1.〔美〕（对雇工等的）秘密监视人；私人雇用的侦探。2.【机】测位仪；定心钻。3.【军】监靶员；弹着及爆炸点观测员；弹着观察机[气球]。4.【铁路】检路器。5.【空】观察机，侦察机；敌机监视员。6.【无】搜索雷达，警戒雷达站。7. 把物件放到指定地点上的人[机器]，指定货物放置地点的人。

spot·ti·ness [ˈspɔtinis; ˋspɑtɪnɪs] *n*. 斑点多，污点多，有斑疹。

spot·ting [ˈspɔtiŋ; ˋspɑtɪŋ] *n*. 配置，装设；落弹观测。

spot·ty [ˈspɔti; ˋspɑtɪ] *a*. (-*ti·er*; -*ti·est*) 1. 多斑点的。2. 尽是污点的；（质量）参差不一的，不规则的。*In his youth, Wang received only a* ~ *secondary education*. 王年轻时只受过不正规的中等教育。*Medical care in those hospitals is rather* ~. 那些医院的医疗质量参差不齐。-**i·ly** *ad*.

spous·al [ˈspauzəl; ˋspauzḷ] *n*., *a*.〔常 *pl*.〕结婚，婚礼(的)。

spouse [spauz; spauz] I *n*. 配偶，夫，妻；〔*pl*.〕夫妇。II *vt*.〔古〕嫁，娶，和…结婚。

spout [spaut; spaut] I *vt*. 1. 喷出，(鲸)喷水。2. 滔滔不绝地讲，吟诵，朗诵。3.〔俚〕典押。—*vi*. 1. 喷出，喷射。2. 高谈阔论。*Water* ~*ed from the break of the pipe*. 水从管子的裂口喷出。II *n*. 1. 喷管，喷嘴；喷口；（茶壶等的）嘴；（鲸类的）喷水孔。2. 水柱，喷流。3.（装谷类时用的）架槽，斜槽。4.【冶】斜槽；流出槽。5.【气】龙卷。6.（过去当铺传送东西用的）筒子；〔俚〕当铺。*Little Tony broke the* ~ *off the teapot*. 小唐尼把茶壶嘴打下来了。***put*** [***shove***, ***pop***] ***up the*** ~ 拿去当押。~ ***opinions*** 哇啦哇啦地提意见。***up the*** ~ 在当押中；〔喻〕经济拮据，穷困。-**er** *n*. 喷油井；捕鲸船；说话滔滔不绝的人，照管流出槽的工人。-**less** *a*. 无喷嘴的。

S.P.Q.R. =〔L.〕*Senatus Populusque Romanus* (= the Senate and the People); small profits, quick returns 薄利多得。

SPR = Swimming Pool Reactor 浸没式反应堆。

sprad·dle [ˈsprædl; ˋsprædḷ] *vt*., *vi*. (-*dled*; -*dling*)〔方，口〕叉开腿站立[行走]。

sprag [spræg; spræg] *n*. 1.（防止车轮滑动的）制轮木。2.【矿】煤面防护柱。*bottom* ~ 底部支撑。*face* ~ 工作面斜支柱。

sprain [sprein; spren] I *n*. 扭伤。II *vt*. 扭，扭伤，挟伤。~ *one's wrist* 扭伤手腕。

sprang [spræŋ; spræŋ] spring 的过去式。

sprat [spræt; spræt] I *n*. 1.【鱼】西鲱。2. 瘦子；小个子；年轻人，小人物，小孩子；〔英俚〕= sixpence. ***Jack*** ~ 矮子；侏儒。***throw*** [***fling away***] ***a*** ~ ***to catch a herring*** [***whale***] 用小虾钓大鱼，用小本赚大钱；抛砖引玉。II *vi*. (-*tt*-) 捕西鲱。

Sprat·ly [ˈsprætli; ˋsprætlɪ] **Islands**“斯普拉特利群岛”〔旧日殖民主义者对我国南沙群岛的称谓〕。

sprawl [sprɔːl; sprɔl] I *vt*. 1. 懒散（或拙笨地）伸开（手足）。2. 使蔓生；使散漫地伸开；潦草地书写。—*vi*. 1. 手脚伸开（成大字形）躺[坐]着。2.（难看地）爬行。3.（陆地、蔓藤等）不规则地延伸，蔓延；（建筑物）无计划地延伸；向四面八方散开；不整齐，散漫。*In our garden, bushes are allowed to* ~ *as they will*. 在我们园子里，灌木丛爱怎么蔓延就怎么蔓延。*Father was* ~*ed out in a sofa*. 爸爸手足伸开地躺在沙发上。II *n*. 1. 手脚伸开躺卧（的姿势）。2. 蔓延；散乱。3.〔美〕毅力。***go*** ~***ing*** 爬行。***send sb***. ~***ing*** 打倒在地。~ ***one's last*** 临死作最后挣扎。-**er** *n*.

spray[1] [sprei; spre] I *n*. 1. 浪花，水花，水雾；雾状物。2.【医】喷雾（液）。3. 喷雾器；消毒器。II *vt*. 喷，喷射；使起浪花；喷雾（入咽喉等）。—*vi*. 喷，（像浪花般）溅散。~ *an insecticide upon plants* = ~ *plants with an insecticide* 用杀虫药喷洒作物。~**board**（船头的）防溅板。~ **can** 喷雾壶[罐]。~ **dry** *vt*. 以喷雾法使（牛奶）干燥。~ **fountain** 喷水池。~ **gun** 喷（漆）枪。~**ing car** 喷水车。~ **method** 喷漆法。~ **nozzle** 喷雾嘴。~-**paint** *vt*. 喷漆于…上；喷涂；喷刷。~ **painting** 喷漆；喷涂；喷刷。~ **needle** 喷雾针。~ **nozzle** 喷雾嘴。

spray[2] [sprei; spre] *n*. 1. 小树枝，小花枝。2. 枝状花样[装饰]；枝状物。~ **drain**（以小树枝填在沟槽内，上面覆土而形成的）排水暗沟。

spray·er [ˈspreiə; ˋspreɚ] *n*. 1. 喷雾的人[东西]。2. 喷雾器；喷油机；喷漆器。3. 喷水车。

spread [spred; sprɛd] I *vt*. (**spread**) 1. 伸开，伸长（手臂等），展开，张开（帆等），打开（地图等）；铺开（毯子等），展宽，展延（金属等）。2. 撒，施，敷，涂，被覆；上胶。3. 散布；流传，传播；普及。4. 把…分期，使延长；拖延（时间）。5. 敲平，铆（钉子等）。6. 详细记载，纪录。7. 展出，展示。8. 布置，安排。—*vi*. 1. 伸开，伸长；扩大，扩张；（金属等）展延。2. 传开，传播，蔓延开；拖延，继续。3.（花、叶等）开放。4.（墨水等）渗开，散开；展开。~ *the news* 传播消息。~ *manure over a field* 在田里撒粪肥。~ *butter on bread* = ~ *bread with butter* 在面包上涂奶油。~ *resolutions upon the minutes* 把决议记录在记录(本)里。~ *the matter on the records* 把情况记录下来。~ *tea on the table* 把茶点摆在桌子上。~ *the table* 摆饭桌准备吃饭；开饭。*It is time to* ~ *for dinner*. 是(摆桌子)开饭的时候了。*Coloured banners* ~ *in the wind*. 彩旗迎风招展。*This is a prescribed course which* ~*s over two semesters*. 这是门两个学期学完的必修课。*A scene of rich harvest* ~ *out before us*. 一片丰收景象展现在我们面前。~ *oneself*〔口〕舒展身体四肢（躺下）；竭力去做，努力，奋发；做得过分，滔滔不绝地讲。~ ***oneself thin***〔口〕企图同时做很多事情而分散精力。~ ***out*** 张开，伸开；铺开；扩大，扩张，展开，伸长。~ ***to*** 传到，波及，蔓延到。

II *n*. 1. 伸展，扩展；扩展度[幅度]，（金属的）展宽，延伸；跨距。2.【机】轮距。3. 传播，普及；蔓延，流行。4.（一片）广阔的土地[水域]；〔美〕大牧场；范围。5. 扩散，扩张，展开；展度；（动植物的）分布。6. 展性；【数】展形。7.〔美〕桌布；床单。8.〔口〕（丰盛的）酒席，宴会。9.〔美〕涂味品〔涂面包的奶油、果酱等〕。10.（报上占大量篇幅或整版的）文章[广告]；连占两版的大幅插图。11.〔美商〕原价和卖价的差额，进销价差。*the* ~ *of the great metropolis* 大都市的扩展。*the gradual* ~ *of higher education* 高等教育的逐渐普及。*a* ~ *of 100,000 acres* 十万英亩的一大片土地。*the wide* ~ *of his answer and yours* 他的答案和你的答案的很大的距离。***give*** (*sb*.) ***a regular*** ~ 请（某人）吃酒席。***no end of a*** ~ 各种各样好吃的东西。

III *a*. 1. 扩大的，伸展的，广大的；大幅的。2.（宝石）薄而无光泽的。~ **eagle** *n*. 1.【徽】展翼鹰[美国国徽]。2. 美国人对于本国的自夸自赞；自夸者。3.【股】（在买卖双方间)吃盘子,加码子。4.【溜冰】横一字形。5.【海】将水手绑在索具上处罚。~**-eagle** 1. *a*. 张翼鹰似的;自夸的,沙文主义的。2. *vt*., *vi*. 伸开四肢跳下[跌下、躺下];【海】把四肢作大字形绑起来,绑起四肢鞭打。~**-eaglism** (美国的)自夸自赞的沙文主义;夸耀本国。~**head** (报纸上占两栏以上的)大标题。~**ing factor** 扩散素〔如透明质酸酶〕。~**-over** 〔英〕(根据特殊需要而作的)部分工时调整。~**sheet program**【计】电子数据表程序〔进行数字和预算运算的软件程序〕。

spread·er [ˈspredə; ˋsprɛdɚ] *n*. 1. 散布者,传播者。2. 展延器,展播器;展着剂。3.【电】开隔体,撑挡。4.【化】涂胶机;扩张器。5.【纺】分纱器;分经筘。

sprech·stim·me [ˈʃpreˌʃtimmə; ˋʃpreˏʃtɪmmə] *n*. 〔G.〕(半像说话,半像唱歌)吟唱。

spree [spriː; spri] **I** *n*. 1. 欢闹,狂欢〔尤指狂饮〕。2. 无节制的狂热行为。3. 阵发性的暴力行动。***go on a*** ~ 痛饮,喝得兴高采烈。***be on the*** ~ 在狂欢中,喝得兴高采烈。**II** *vi*. 狂欢,纵乐,喝得兴高采烈〔常作 ~ it〕。~**killer** 杀人狂。

sprig [sprig; sprɪg] **I** *n*. 1. 小(树)枝,幼枝。2. 小枝状花样饰物。3. 〔谑〕子孙。4. 〔主蔑〕小伙子,少年,小家伙。5. 无头钉,扁头钉。6. 嵌玻璃针。**II** *vt*. (*-gg-*) 1. 用小枝装饰,加小枝花样。2. 剪除小枝。3. 使(草)蔓生。4. 钉扁头钉。

sprig·gy [ˈsprigi; ˋsprɪgɪ] *a*. 多小枝的,多嫩枝的;小枝似的。

spright·ful [ˈspraitfʊl; ˋspraɪtfəl] *a*. = sprightly(a). **-ly** *ad*. **-ness** *n*.

spright·li·ness [ˈspraitlinis; ˋspraɪtlɪnɪs] *n*. 活泼,生气勃勃,轻松愉快。

spright·ly [ˈspraitli; ˋspraɪtlɪ] *a*. (*-li·er*; *-li·est*) 活泼的,生气勃勃的,轻快的。

spring [spriŋ; sprɪŋ] **I** *n*. 1. 春季,春天。2. 青春;初期。3. 〔*pl*.〕大潮时期。4. 泉。5. 源头,水源,根源,本源;发生;动机,原动力。6. 跳跃;弹回,反跳。7. 弹力;弹性。8. 发条,弹簧;(汽车的)钢板。9. 活力,精力,元气。10.【船】(桅杆等的)裂缝;缆索;系船索。11. (甲板的)上翘,转向锚索,倒缆。12.【高尔夫球】棒的弯曲。13.【建】起拱点,起拱面。14. 〔美俚〕年轻无经验的人,年轻幼稚的女子。*the ~ of life* 青春(时代)。*hot ~s* 温泉。*the ~s of one's conduct* 行为的动机。*The custom had its ~ in London*. 这种风俗起源于伦敦。*a hair ~* 发丝弹簧。***set every ~ in motion = set all ~s going*** 开动所有发条;尽全力。***with a ~*** 一跳,一骨碌(起来等)。**II** *vi*. (***sprang*** [spræŋ; spræŋ], ***sprung*** [sprʌŋ; sprʌŋ]; ***sprung***) 1. 跳,跃。2. 跳出;涌出[上];发源。3. 起源于,发生;发芽。4. (木板等)弯曲,反翘,歪,裂开;(地雷)炸开。5. 高出,耸立。6.【建】(拱等)开始,升起。7.【海】拚命划船使飞跃向前。8. 出身。—*vt*. 1. 使跳起来;惊起;跳过。2. 使爆炸,使炸裂,使弯曲,使破裂,使折断。3. 弹出,突然提出。4. 〔主用 *p.p.*〕装弹簧。5. 扭伤(腿等);使跛。6.【建】开始砌(拱洞等)。7.【海】用锚缆转变方向。8. 〔美俚〕(从监狱)释放出去,保释出去。*They sprang to the new task*. 他们争先恐后地去做这件新的工作。*The doors ~ open*. 门砰的一声开了。*The lid sprang to*. 盖子砰的一下盖上了。*The dawn began to ~*. 天开始亮了。*The river ~s in the Alps*. 这条河发源于阿尔卑斯山脉。*He ~s from peasant family*. 他是农家出身。*Many new factories have sprung up in my home town*. 我的家乡新建了许多工厂。*A twenty storied building ~s high above the city*. 一座二十层的高楼高耸于城的上空。*The mistake sprang from his absent-mindedness*. 这错误是由于他的心不在焉造成的。*S- ahead hard!*【海】拚命划。*The ship's timbers are sprung*. 船上材料的接头部分松了。*I've sprung my table-tennis bat*. 我把我的乒乓球拍打裂了。*It was Johnson who sprang the new proposal on them*. 是约翰逊突然向他们提出那个新建议的。~ ***a butt***【海】船因动摇致外部接头变松。***get sprung*** 〔口〕大醉。~ ***a blue book*** 〔美〕临时测验。~ ***a leak*** 生漏缝。~ ***a mine***【军】使地雷爆炸。~ ***a mine upon*** 突然袭击。~ ***a somersault*** 翻筋斗。~ ***a surprise on*** 使…吃一惊。~ ***an arch***【建】砌拱洞。~ ***at*** 扑到。~ ***... for a quid*** 勒索一镑。~ ***forth*** 跳出,冲出,突出;涌出,喷出。~ ***into fame*** 一举成名。~ ***off*** 裂开。~ ***on*** 扑向,袭击。~ ***out of*** 跳出,冲出。~ ***over*** 跳过。~ ***to attention*** 跳起来作立正姿势。~ ***to one's feet*** 立即站起。~ ***up*** 跳上来;发生;萌芽,生长;出现。~ ***up like a mushroom*** 有如雨后春笋迅速大量产生。~ ***upon*** = ~ on. ~ **balance** 弹簧秤,磅秤。~ **beam** 大桁,系梁。~ **beauty**【植】春美草。~ **bed** 弹簧床。~ **binder** 弹簧活页夹。~**blade knife** 弹簧折合刀。~**-board** 跳板;出发点,发端。~**bok**, ~**buck** (*pl*. ~*s*, 〔集合词〕~)【动】南非小羚羊。~ **carriage**, ~ **cart** 弹簧马车,装有弹簧的运货马车。~ **chicken** 童子鸡;〔美俚〕年轻人,天真的人。~**-cleaning** 春季大扫除。~ **equinox** 春分(点)。~ **fever** 〔美〕春困〔某些人在春季初暖时出现的困倦状态〕。**S-Gardens** 园林春〔伦敦市议会所在地〕。~ **gun** 弹簧枪,伏击枪。~**halt**【兽医】= stringhalt. ~**head** 源头,水源;车上的弹簧头。~**house** 〔美〕(建筑在泉水、小溪上的)肉类乳品冷藏所。~**like** *a*. 像春天的。~ **lock** 弹簧锁。~ **mattress** 弹簧床垫。~ **onions** 葱,大葱。~ **peeper**【动】〔美〕小雨蛙。~ **roll** 〔主英〕【烹】(中国的)春卷。~ **steel**【冶】弹簧钢。~**tail**【动】弹尾目昆虫。~**-tide** 大潮,子午潮,朔望潮;舆论,趋势;〔诗〕= springtime. ~**time** 春天,春季;青春;初期;早期;全盛期。~ **water** 泉水。**S- Wheat Belt** 春麦带〔美国明尼苏达州的别名〕。~**wood**【植】早材,春材。

spring·al [ˈspriŋəl; ˋsprɪŋəl] *n*. 〔古〕活跃的小伙子,年轻人(= springald)。

springe [sprindʒ; sprɪndʒ] **I** *n*. 圈套,陷阱。**II** *vt*., *vi*. 设圈套[陷阱]捉捕。

spring·er [ˈspriŋə; ˋsprɪŋɚ] *n*. 1. 跳的人,跳的东西。2.【动】猎,能哄起猎获物的长耳小猎犬〔又叫 ~ spaniel〕。3. 逆戟鲸。4.【建】起拱石,拱脚石。5. = spring chicken.

Spring·hall [ˈspriŋhɔːl; ˋsprɪŋhɔl] *n*. 斯普林霍尔〔姓氏〕。

spring·i·ness [ˈspriːŋinis; ˋsprɪŋɪnɪs] *n*. 有弹力,弹性;多泉水,湿润;轻快。

spring·ing [ˈspriŋiŋ; ˋsprɪŋɪŋ] *n*.【建】起拱点。

spring·i·za·tion [ˌspriŋiˈzeiʃən; ˏsprɪŋɪˋzeʃən, -aɪˋze-] *n*. = vernalization.

spring·less [ˈspriŋlis; ˋsprɪŋlɪs] *a*. 无弹簧的;无泉水的。

spring·let [ˈspriŋlit; ˋsprɪŋlɪt] *n*. 小泉,小河,小溪。

spring·y [ˈspriŋi; ˋsprɪŋɪ] *a*. (*-i·er*; *-i·est*) 1. 有弹力[性]的。2. 轻快的。3. 多泉水的;湿润的。*All the kids went up the hill with ~ steps*. 所有的小孩子都以轻快的步伐上了小山。**-i·ly** *ad*.

sprin·kle [ˈspriŋkl; ˋsprɪŋkl̩] **I** *vt*. 1. 洒;撒;喷淋。2. 撒布,使散布。3. 点缀。—*vi*. 1. 洒,喷淋;撒;散布在。2. 〔主语为 it〕下疏稀的雨。~ *salt on a dish* = ~ *a dish with salt* 在菜肴上撒盐。*His coat was ~d with cigarette ashes*. 他的上衣撒满了纸烟灰。**II** *n*. 1. 洒;撒。2. 小雨。3. 少量;疏稀散布的东西。4. 〔常 *pl*.〕撒在面上的一层东西。5. 洒水器。*Let's cover the cakes with chocolate ~s*. 咱们把蛋糕用巧克力末撒上。

sprin·kler [ˈspriŋklə; ˋsprɪŋklɚ] *n*. 1. 洒水车,洒水器,喷壶;洒水装置。2. (草坪、高尔夫球场的)地下灌浇系统。~ *system* 自动喷水消防系统。

sprin·kling [ˈspriŋkliŋ; ˋsprɪŋklɪŋ] *n*. 1. 洒,撒,撒布;喷雾(工作)。2. (雨等的)点滴;少量;零星。*Don't you have a ~ of common sense?* 你难道一点儿常识也没有吗? *a smart ~* 〔美俚〕很多,许多。~**can** 〔美〕= watering-can [-pot]. ～**-cart**〔美〕= watering-cart.

sprint [sprint; sprɪnt] I *vt*., *vi*. 全速奔跑(短距离)。II *n*. 1. 全速疾跑。2. 短距离赛跑 (= ～ race)。3. 短时间的紧张活动;长距离赛跑中的冲刺。4. 不超过一英里的赛马。*Smith's ～ at the finish was really wonderful*. 史密斯的终点冲刺确实是了不起。～ **car** 短程泥路赛车。

sprint·er [ˈsprintə; ˋsprɪntɚ] *n*. 短跑运动员。

sprit [sprit; sprɪt] *n*.【船】(撑帆用)斜杠,横杠,第一斜桅。～**sail** 斜杠帆。

sprite [sprait; spraɪt] *n*. 1. 妖怪,小妖精。2. 捣蛋鬼,爱恶作剧的人。3.〔古〕鬼魂。

spritz [sprits, G. ʃprits; sprɪts, ʃprɪts] I *vt*., *vi*. 喷水。II *n*. 水花,喷雾。

sprock·et [ˈsprɔkit; ˋsprɑkɪt] *n*.【机】链轮齿,扣链齿;链轮〔又叫 ～ wheel〕。

sprout [spraut; spraʊt] I *vi*. 1. 出芽,发芽,萌芽;抽条。2. 很快地生长。—*vt*. 1. 使发芽;使生长。2.〔美方〕摘去(马铃薯等的)芽。II *n*. 1. 幼芽;新梢,嫩枝。2.〔*pl*.〕【植】球芽甘蓝 (= Brussles sprouts)。3. 幼苗状物,年轻人;〔美俚〕后代。*bamboo ～* 竹笋。*bean ～s* 豆芽。*a ～ who isn't old enough to go to school* 一个岁数小还不能上学的娃娃。*The spring rain has ～ed the seeds*. 春雨使种子发了芽。*Peach trees ～ed their new leaves*. 桃树长出新叶来了。～ **fir**【植】云杉;挪威云杉。～ **forest**, ～ **land** 萌芽林。

spruce[1] [spruːs; sprus] *n*.【植】云杉(属),云杉木〔又叫 ～ fir〕。～ **beer** 云杉酒。～ **grouse**【动】云杉鸡。

S

spruce[2] [spruːs; sprus] I *a*. 整洁的,潇洒的;漂亮的。II *vt*., *vi*. (弄)整洁;(把)打扮漂亮 (*up*)。*My study looks ～*. 我的书房看起来挺漂亮。*Mother told us to ～ the parlour for Christmas*. 妈妈要我们把客厅收拾整洁过圣诞节。*You really must ～ up a bit, Albert*. 阿尔培,你可是得把自己搞得整洁一点了。**-ly** *ad*. **-ness** *n*.

sprue[1] [spruː; spru] *n*.【铸造】浇口,注入口;熔渣。

sprue[2] [spruː; spru] *n*.【医】口炎性腹泻。

spruit [spreit, spruːt; spraɪt] *n*. (南非用语)(只有在雨季才有水的)干涸小河。

sprung [sprʌŋ; sprʌŋ] I spring 的过去式及过去分词。II *a*.〔口〕微醉的。

spry [sprai; spraɪ] *a*. (*-er*; *-est or* ***spri·er***; ***spri·est***) 活泼的,生气勃勃的;敏捷的,轻快的。*When Teacher Ma was 70 years old, he was as ～ as a kitten*. 马老师七十岁的时候,还轻快敏捷地像只小猫一般。**-ly** *ad*. **-ness** *n*.

s.p.s. =〔L.〕*sine prole superstite* 无后代,无子孙 (= without surviving issue)。

spt. = seaport.

Sp. Trs. = Special Troops 特种兵。

spud [spʌd; spʌd] I *n*. 1. 除草锄。2. (栎树)剥皮器,剥皮刀。3.〔俚〕马铃薯。4. 短而粗的东西。II *vt*. (***spudded*** [ˈspʌdid; ˋspʌdɪd]; ***spud·ding*** [ˈspʌdiŋ; ˋspʌdɪŋ])用除草锄锄(草等) (*up*; *out*)。

spudder [ˈspʌdə; ˋspʌdɚ] *n*. (剥树皮用的)铲凿;草锄。

spud·dle [ˈspʌdl; ˋspʌdl] *vi*. 轻掘,翻掘。

spud·dy [ˈspʌdi; ˋspʌdɪ] *a*. 粗而短的;矮胖的。

spue [spjuː; spju] *vt*., *vi*. = spew.

spug [spʌg; spʌg] *n*. 1.〔Scot., 英方〕家雀。2.〔美俚〕反对赠送虚伪礼物的人。

spume [spjuːm; spjum] I *n*. 泡沫,浮沫。II *vt*., *vi*. (使)起泡沫。

spu·mes·cence [spjuˈmesns; spjuˋmɛsəns] *n*. 起泡;泡沫状态。**-cent** *a*. 似泡沫的;发出泡沫的。

spu·mo·ne, ***spu·mo·ni*** [spəˈməuni; spuˋmone] *n*. 〔It.〕意大利式多层不同颜色加蜜饯的冰激凌。

spu·mous, **spum·y** [ˈspjuːməs, ˈspjuːmi; ˋspjuməs, ˋspjumɪ] *a*. 泡沫的,多泡沫的,泡沫状的,被泡沫覆盖的。

spun [spʌn; spʌn] I spin 的过去式及过去分词。II *a*. 1. 纺成的,拉成丝状的。2.〔俚〕精疲力尽的。3.【海】细油麻绳(由二至四股绳条捻成)。～ **cotton** 棉纱。～ **glass** 玻璃纤维。～ **gold** 金丝。～ **rayon**【纺织】人造棉纱;人造棉织物。～ **silk** 绢丝纺绸。～ **string**【乐】钢丝弦。～ **sugar** 棉花糖。～ **yarn** 精纺纱,细纱;麻纱。

spunge [spʌndʒ; spʌndʒ] *n*., *v*.〔古〕= sponge.

spunk [spʌŋk; spʌŋk] I *n*. 1.〔口〕精神,生气;勇气,胆量。2. 急躁,愤怒。3. 引火木柴,火绒。4.〔英方〕火星,小火焰。II *vi*. 点着,烧起来。*Grandpa told a story with rare ～ last night*. 昨天晚上祖父极其生动地讲了个故事。*get sb.'s ～ up* 给某人打气,鼓励某人。～ *out*〔美〕被揭穿,为人所知。～ *up*〔美〕打起精神。—*vt*. 鼓励某人 (*up*)。

spunk·y [ˈspʌŋki; ˋspʌŋkɪ] *a*. (*-i·er*; *-i·est*)〔口〕1. 精神十足的,勇气倍增的。2. 易怒的。3.〔英方〕灿烂的。**-i·ly** *ad*. **-i·ness** *n*.

spur [spəː; spɚ] I *n*. 1. 踢马刺,靴刺,马扎子;【史】金踢马刺〔骑士 (knight) 所用〕。2. 刺激物,鼓励品;促进器;教唆,挑拨,煽动,鼓舞,刺激。3. 树根;【动】(鸟类、虫类等的)距;(斗鸡时加于鸡腿上的)距铁;【植】(花)距;短枝;(军舰的)冲角。4. (攀耙用)刺铁;(登山用)铁钉助爬器。5. 山嘴,山鼻子;石嘴,尖坡,悬岩;支脉,横岭;【建】凸壁;支撑物;【铁路】支线;【代】迹(数)。***clap*** [***give***] ***～s to*** = put ～s to. ***need the ～*** 需要用靴刺踢,需加激励。***on*** [***upon***] ***the ～*** 用足速力,飞快地,火急。***on the ～ of the moment*** 一时兴起[冲动];当场,即席。***put*** [***set***] ***～s to*** 用靴刺踢;激励。***win one's ～s*** (由古时因功被封为骑士转为)得到荣誉,飞黄腾达,出名。***with whip and ～*** = ***with ～ and yard*** 快马加鞭地,立刻,马上。II *vt*. (*-rr-*) 1. 用靴刺踢;装靴刺[刺铁等]。2. 刺激,推动,教唆,煽动,鞭策,鼓舞。3. 斗鸡时用距铁踢[踢伤]。—*vi*. 1. 用靴刺踢马,催马前进;驱赶 (*on*)。2. 疾驰。*Professor Smith's new book ～s interest in his course*. 史密斯教授的新书鼓起了大家对他的课的兴趣。***booted and ～red*** 穿了靴子上了靴刺。～ ***sb. up to*** [***on to***, ***into***] ***action*** 激励某人。～**gall** 1. *n*. (马腹的)靴刺伤。2. *vt*.〔古〕用靴刺踢伤;弄伤。～ **gear**【机】正齿轮。～ **line** [**track**]〔美铁路〕短叉道,支路。～ **wheel** = ～ gear.

spurge [spəːdʒ; spɚdʒ] *n*.【植】大戟(属)植物。～ **laurel**【植】桂叶芫花。

spu·ri·ous [ˈspjuəriəs; ˋspjʊrɪəs] *a*. 1. 假的,乱真的,伪造的。2. 欺骗性的;谬误的。3. 私生的。*When you go to the fair, beware of the quacks selling ～ medicinal herbs*. 你赶集的时候,当心卖假草药的江湖医生。*a ～ fruit* (草莓、无花果等的)假果。～ *oscillation*【物】乱真振荡。**-ly** *ad*. **-ness** *n*.

spur·less [ˈspəːlis; ˋspɚlɪs] *a*. 1. 没有踢马刺的(靴跟等)。2. 没有距的(鸡脚等)。3. 没有花距的。

spurn [spəːn; spɚn] I *vi*. 1.〔古〕踢,踢走,赶走,驱逐;一脚踢开。2. 蔑视,唾弃。—*vt*. 1. 践踏;一脚踢开。2. 轻蔑地拒绝,摒弃,唾弃。*As an armyman, I ～ fearlessly at all danger and the enemy*. 作为一个军人,一切危险和敌人丝毫不在我的眼下。*He ～ed my suggestion that he shouldn't go and see the brawl of the hoodlums*. 他冷然地拒绝了我提的不要去看阿飞们吵架的建议。～ ***at sb.***〔罕〕不理睬某人。～ ***sb.'s affection*** 拒绝某人的爱情。～ ***the ground*** 跳起来。II *n*. 1. 踢开。2. 拒绝;唾弃;不理睬;藐视。

spurred [spəːd; spɚd] *a*. 有靴刺的,装上靴刺的;有距的〔指鸟〕。

spur·ri·er [ˈspəːriə; ˋspɚɪɚ] *n*. 踢马刺[距铁等]制造人。

spur·rite [ˈspəːrait; ˋspɚaɪt] *n*.【化】灰矽钙石。

spur·ry, **spur·rey** [ˈspəːri; ˋspɚɪ] *n*.【植】大爪草属

(*Spergula*) 植物；大爪草 (*S. arvensis*)〔产于北美洲〕。

spurt [spəːt; spɝt] **I** ***vt*.** 喷射。—***vi*.** **1.** 喷出，迸出 (*up*; *out*; *down*)。**2.** 突然拚命努力，在赛跑中最后冲刺；突发。**3.** 发芽，生长。**II** ***n*.** **1.** 突然喷出，突发，突然爆发[冲出等]。**2.** 短促突然的爆发或激增，(怒气、精力等的)迸发。**3.** 短时间。**4.** (营业的)突然兴隆。**5.** (赛跑)最后冲刺，最后死拚。

sput·nik [ˈsputnik; ˋspʌtnɪk, ˋsput-] ***n*.** (苏联)人造地球卫星。*a* ～ *spaceship* 卫星式宇宙飞船。

sput·ter [ˈspʌtə; ˋspʌtɚ] **I** ***vi*.**, ***vt*.** **1.** 飞溅唾沫；(食渣等)飞溅。**2.** 唾沫飞溅地说；激动地争吵。**3.** (湿柴)劈劈啪啪地爆裂。**4.** 爆响着停熄掉，停息 (*out*)。**II** ***n*.** **1.** 急语；吵闹，争论。**2.** 喷溅声。**3.** 劈啪声。*Jack ran up to the referee, ～ing protest*. 贾克跑到裁判跟前，唾沫飞溅地提出抗议。*Fat ～s in the frying pan*. 肥油在炸锅里劈啪劈啪地响。*After the talk with his mother, his excitement ～ed out*. 和母亲争吵过以后，他的激动已经消失了。～**-bridget**, ～**-budget**〔美〕动不动就吵闹的人。**-er** ***n*.** **1.** 语无伦次[说话气急败坏]的人。**2.** 发劈啪声的东西。

sput·ter·ing·ly [ˈspʌtəriŋli; ˋspʌtərɪŋlɪ] ***ad*.** **1.** 唾沫飞溅地。**2.** 气急败坏地，语无伦次的。**3.** 劈啪作响地。

spu·tum [ˈspjuːtəm; ˋspjutəm] ***n*.** (*pl*. **-ta** [-tə; -tə]) 唾液；痰。

sp. vol. = specific volume 比容。

spy [spai; spaɪ] **I** ***n*.** 间谍，密探，侦察，侦探；特务。***set spies after*** [***upon***] 派密探监视。**II** ***vt*.** (***spied***) **1.** 侦察，暗中侦察(监视)。**2.** 察见，发现。**3.** 仔细察看。—***vi*.** **1.** 做密探间谍。**2.** 暗中监视，侦查 (*on*, *upon* 某人 *into*)。*I* ～ *strangers*.〔英议会〕请禁止旁听；请举行秘密会议。～ *out the secret of the enemy's special agent* 侦察出敌特的秘密。～ *on* (*upon*) *the movements of the terrorists* 暗中监视恐怖分子的活动。～ *all the exhibits with an artist* 和一位艺术家一起仔细观察全部展览品。～ *into a complicated affair* 侦察一桩复杂离奇的事件。～ **glass** 小望远镜。～**-hole** (房门上的)窥[监]视孔。～ **plane** 间谍飞机。～ **satellite** 间谍卫星。

sq = **1.** sequence. **2.**〔L.〕*sequens* = (the following one). **3.**〔L.〕*sequentia* (= the following ones)。

Sq. = **1.** Squadron. **2.** Square.

sq. = square.

sq. ft. = square foot [feet].

sq. in. = square inch(es).

sq. mi. = square mile(s).

sqn. = squadron.

sq(q). =〔L.〕*sequentes*, *sequentia*.

squab [skwɔb; skwɑb] **I** ***a*.** **1.** (鸟类)还未生毛的，刚出蛋壳的。**2.** (人)矮胖的。**II** ***ad*.**〔口〕沉重地；咕咚地。**III** ***n*.** **1.** 小鸽子，小鸟，雏。**2.**〔美俚〕少女，小姑娘。**3.** 矮胖子。**4.** 厚垫子；沙发。～**-chick** 雏鸡。～ **pie** 羊肉馅饼[用羊肉、葱、苹果等作馅的馅饼]。

squab·ble [ˈskwɔbl; ˋskwɑbl̩] **I** ***n*.** (为小事)口角，争论。*a* ～ *over property right* 关于产权方面的争论。**II** ***vi*.** 争论，争吵。—***vt*.**【印】搅乱(排好的铅字)。～ *with sb. about* [*over*] *sth*. 为了某件事情和人争吵。**-bler** ***n*.**

squab·by [ˈskwɔbi; ˋskwɑbɪ] ***a*.** 矮胖的。

Squac·co [ˈkwɔːkəu; ˋkwɔko] ***n*.** 竖冠池鹭〔产于南欧、非洲等地〕。

squad [skwɔd; skwɑd] **I** ***n*.** **1.**〔军〕班。**2.** 小组，小队。**3.**〔美〕警车，巡逻车。*an awkward* ～ 一小队新兵。*a beef* ～〔美俚〕大力士打手队。*a flying* ～ 紧急任务执行小组〔如警察局的特勤队〕。*a* ～ *car* (装有无线电话的)警备车。*a* ～ *drill* 班教练。*a* ～ *leader* 班长。*a goon* ～〔美俚〕打手队。*a vice* ～〔美〕(取缔卖淫、赌博等的)警察缉捕队。*a* ～ *room*【军】士兵寝室；(警察局点名分配任务的)集合厅。**II** ***vt*.** (**-dd-**) 成立(军队)的建制；把某士兵编入班的建制内；把人员分成小队。

squad·ron [ˈskwɔdrən; ˋskwɑdrən] **I** ***n*.**【军】**1.** 骑兵中队；(各特种兵的)连。**2.** 分舰队。**3.** 空军中队。**4.** 团体，一组，一群。**5.** (旧时军队)方阵。**II** ***vt*.** 把…编成中队[分舰队]。*a detached* ～ 分遣小舰队。*a flying* ～ 游击分舰队。*a standing* ～ 常备舰队。*a missile* ～ 导[飞]弹中队。～ **leader** ***n*.** **1.** 空军中队长。**2.**〔英〕少校。

squa·er·i·al [ˌskwɔˈɛəriəl; ˏskwɑˋɛrɪəl] ***n*.**【电信】(接收卫星电视广播的)矩形天线。

squail [skweil; skwel] **I** ***n*.** **1.**〔英〕(推盘游戏用的)小圆盘。**2.**〔*pl*.〕推盘游戏；九柱戏。**II** ***vi*.**, ***vt*.** **1.** 投掷铅头棒打鸟或击落树上的果子等。**2.**〔英方〕用投掷棒子的方法打击(人、物)。

squail·er [ˈskweilə; ˋskwelɚ] ***n*.**〔英方〕(投击野禽、松鼠等用)铅头棒。

squa·lene [ˈskweiliːn; ˋskwɑlin, ˋskwe-] ***n*.**【化】角鲨烯，三十碳六烯。

squal·id [ˈskwɔlid; ˋskwɑlɪd] ***a*.** **1.** 肮脏的，邋遢的。**2.** (道德品质)卑劣的。**3.** 贫困的，悲惨的，可怜的。～ *dress* 肮脏的衣服。～ *affairs* 伤风败俗的坏事。～ *motive* 卑鄙的动机。**-ly** ***ad*.** **-ness** ***n*.**

squa·lid·i·ty [skwɔˈliditi; skwɑˋlɪdətɪ] ***n*.** 肮脏，邋遢；卑劣；贫困。

squall[1] [skwɔːl; skwɔl] **I** ***vi*.** (因疼痛、害怕而起的)大声喊叫，怪叫；嚎哭。—***vt*.** 刺耳地大声说，尖声锐气地说。**II** ***n*.** 尖叫，怪叫；大声哭泣。*Mother knows how to comfort a* ～*ing baby. Let her do it*. 妈妈知道怎样哄好大声嚎哭的小孩，还是让她做吧。*An old woman rushed out of the house on fire and* ～*ed*. 一个年老妇女从失火的房子里冲了出来大声地喊叫。

squall[2] [skwɔːl; skwɔl] **I** ***n*.** **1.** (带有雨、雪、雹等的)暴风，飑。**2.**〔口〕麻烦，困难，打扰。*a black* ～【气】乌云飑。*a thick* ～ 带雨雪冰雹的狂风。*a white* ～ 无云飑。***Look out for*** ～***s***. 谨防危险，随时警惕。**II** ***vi*.**〔主语为 it〕刮狂风，起风暴[飑]。～ **line**【气】飑线。

squall·y [ˈskwɔːli; ˋskwɔlɪ] ***a*.** (**-i·er**; **-i·est**) **1.** (像要)起风暴的。**2.** 可怕的，厉害的；不安全的。***look*** ～ 像要刮狂风；〔喻〕形势险恶。

squa·loid [ˈskweilɔid; ˋskwelɔɪd] ***a*.** 似鲨鱼的。

squal·or [ˈskwɔlə; ˋskwɑlɚ] ***n*.** **1.** 肮脏，邋遢。**2.** (道德品质等的)卑劣。**3.** 贫困。

squam [skwɔm; skwɑm] ***n*.**〔美〕(渔夫戴的)油布帽子。

squa·ma [ˈskweimə; ˋskwemə] ***n*.** (*pl*. **-mae** [-miː; -mi]) **1.**【植】鳞片；【动】鳞。**2.** (昆虫的)腋瓣；负须叶，鳞形节；刺缘突。

squa·mate [ˈskweimeit; ˋskwemet] ***a*.** 有鳞的，鳞斑的。

squa·ma·tion [skwəˈmeiʃən, ˈskwei-; skwəˋmeʃən] ***n*.** **1.** 有鳞，多鳞。**2.** 鳞列。

squa·mo·sal [skwəˈməusl; skwəˋmosl̩] **I** ***a*.** = squamous. **II** ***n*.**【解】鳞状骨。

squa·mose [ˈskweiməus; ˋskwemos] ***a*.** = squamous. **-ly** ***ad*.** **-ness** ***n*.**

squa·mous [ˈskweiməs; ˋskweməs] ***a*.** **1.** 鳞状的，覆以鳞的，由鳞片组成的。**2.**【解】鳞状骨的。**-ly** ***ad*.**

squam·u·le [ˈskweimjuːli; ˋskwemjulɪ] ***n*.**【生】小鳞片。

squam·u·lose [ˈskwæmjuˌləus, ˈskweimju-; ˋskwæmjʊˏlos, ˋskwemjʊ-] ***a*.** 有细鳞的，覆以细鳞的，由细鳞组成的。

squan·der [ˈskwɔndə; ˋskwɑndɚ] **I** ***vt*.** **1.** 挥霍；浪费；乱用(时间、金钱等)。**2.** 驱散，使散开。—***vi*.** **1.** 浪费。**2.** 浪荡，漂泊。**3.** 四散。～ *one's money in drink* 把金钱浪费在喝酒上。*Don't* ～ *your time in reading those dime novels*. 不要把你的时间浪费在读那些胡编乱造的廉价小说上。*Many of the enemy were* ～*ed*. 多数敌军都被驱散了。**II** ***n*.** 浪费，挥霍。**-er** ***n*.**

S

squan·der·ing·ly [ˈskwɔndəriŋli; ˋskwɑndərɪŋlɪ] *ad*. 浪费地;滥用乱花地。

squan·der·ma·ni·a [ˌskɔndəˈmeinjə; ˏskwɑndəˋmenɪə] *n*. 浪费狂。

square [skwɛə; skwɛr] **I** *n*. **1**. 正方形,四方块,四角;方形物。**2**. (方形)广场;〔美〕(四面都是马路的)方阵建筑;街区;(方阵建筑中任何一面)一排房子的长度。**3**. 画线板;丁字规,直角尺,矩尺。**4**. 【数】平方,二次幂,自乘。**5**. 【军】方阵。**6**. 【天】矩象。**7**. (象棋盘等的)小方格纵横字谜〔每方格填一字母〕。**8**. 一方〔房屋面积单位,一方为一百平方英尺〕。**9**. 含苞未放的棉蕾。**10**. 〔俚〕古板守旧的人。**11**. 〔美俚〕拳击场。**12**. 〔美俚〕丰富的饭菜〔又叫 ~ meal〕。*Trafalgar* ~ 特拉法加广场〔伦敦市内,又名"鸽子广场"〕。*a house a few ~s up* 两三个街区外的一所房屋。*bring six to* ~ 使6自乘。*a set* ~ 三角板。***by the*** ~ 恰好地。***on the*** ~ 成直角;诚实地,规规矩矩地;平等地;同等地;〔美俚〕诚实的,公正的,可靠的。***out of*** ~ 不成直角,斜;没有秩序地,不规则地;不公平地。

II *a*. **1**. 正方形的;四方的,四角的;成直角的,矩形的。**2**. 宽而结实的(体格、肩膀、船等)。**3**. 适合的,正好的。**4**. 规规矩矩的;光明正大的,正直的,公平的(交易等)。**5**. 同高的,同水准的;平等的,同等的;笔直的,平行的,水平的。**6**. 结清贷借的,两讫的。**7**. 坚决的,断然的(拒绝等),干脆的。**8**. 【数】平方的,等边的。**9**. 〔俚〕充实的,令人满意[满足]的,吃得饱的(饭)。**10**. 【海】和龙骨成直角的(帆桁)。**11**. 〔美俚〕古板守旧的,老派朴质的。*a man of ~ frame* 肩膀宽阔的人。*a ~ deal* = *~ dealing* 〔口〕公平的交易[处理]。*a ~ eater* 吃得净光的人。***all*** ~ 两清,彼此不欠;扯平,不分胜负;一切安排妥当,很好,很满意。***call it*** ~ 当作已清账〔不必再提〕。***get*** (*things*) ~ 〔口〕整顿。***get*** ~ ***with*** 〔口〕和…清算;向…报仇[报复]。***keep ...*** ~ ***to*** 使…与…成直角。***make a*** ~ ***meal*** 饱餐一顿。***make accounts*** ~ 结清,付清。~ ***with the world*** 〔美俚〕与人无借贷关系。

III *ad*. **1**. 四四方方地;成直角地;成方形地;笔直地,端正地。**2**. 正直地,公正地,规规矩矩地。**3**. 坚定地,坚实不动的。*stand* ~ 端正地站着。*play fair and* ~ 表现得公公道道。

IV *vt*. **1**. 把…弄成方形;使成直角。**2**. 检验…的平直度。**3**. 抬平(肩膀等)。**4**. 调正,修正。**5**. 把(纸张等)划分成方格。**6**. 使方正,使符合,使一致。**7**. 扯平,使贷借相抵,算清,结清。**8**. 【数】使作自乘。**9**. 【海】使和桅[龙骨]成直角。**10**. 〔口〕笼络,贿赂,收买。—*vi*. **1**. 成直角。**2**. 符合,调和,一致。**3**. 结清。**4**. 【高尔夫球】分数相同。**5**. 【拳】摆的进攻架势。~ *accounts* 清算,结清,付清。~ *one's shoulders* (吵架前等)抬起肩膀。*Your idea and mine do not* ~. 你跟我的意见不一致。~ ***a rap*** 〔美〕贿赂官吏。~ ***away*** **1**. 扬帆顺风驶行。**2**. (拳击中)摆好架势。**3**. 〔口〕准备停当,整理好。~ ***it*** 〔美〕改过自新。~ ***off*** 〔美〕(拳击中)摆好架势。~ ***oneself*** 〔口〕认错,赔不是,赔偿损失。~ ***the circle*** 作面积等于一个圆的正方形;做异想天开的事。~ ***up*** 〔口〕清账;【拳击】摆好进攻架势。~ **bracket** 【印】方括号。~**-built** *a*. 四方的;(肩膀)宽阔的。~ **dance** (四对男女跳的)方舞。~**d circle** 拳击台。~**dom** 〔俚〕守旧,老派作风。~**face** 廉价烈酒。~**head** 〔美〕在美、加拿大的北欧人;〔蔑〕德国人。~ **John** 〔美俚〕守法良民,不吸毒的人。~ **knot** 平结。~ **leg** 【板球】外内场员(位置)。~**man** 石匠,木匠。~ **matrix** 【数】方阵。~ **measure** 平方单位制,面积量度单位。~ **number** 【数】平方数。~ **one** 起点。~**-rigged** *a*. 【海】横帆的。~ **room** 〔美〕最好的房间。~ **root** 【数】平方根。~ **rule** 直角尺。~ **sail** 【海】横帆。~ **shooter** 〔美〕公平正直的人,老实人。~**-shouldered** 平肩的,阔肩的。~**-toed** **1**. (鞋)方头的。**2**. 古板的,守旧的。~**-toes** 古板的人。

squar·er [ˈskwɛərə; ˋskwɛrə˞] *n*. **1**. 锯木方工人,凿石方工人。**2**. 方形剥刀。**3**. 【无】平方电路。

square·ly [ˈskwɛəli; ˋskwɛrlɪ] *ad*. **1**. 成方形。**2**. 规规矩矩地;公正地。**3**. 断然地。**4**. 笔直地,对准地。**5**. 〔俚〕吃得饱饱地。*face the crisis* ~ 正视危机,断然应付危机。*hit sb*. ~ *in the left eye* 正好打在某人的左眼。

square·ness [ˈskwɛənis; ˋskwɛrnɪs] *n*. **1**. 方形;方正。**2**. 正直,公正。

squar·ish [ˈskwɛəriʃ; ˋskwɛrɪʃ] *a*. 近似方形的,有点方的。**-ly** *ad*.

squar·rose [ˈskwærəus, ˈskwɔr-; ˋskwæros, ˋskwɑr-] *a*. **1**. 【生】粗糙的,具有糙鳞的,糠秕状的。**2**. 【植】末梢成直角突出的;开展的,伸展的。**3**. 多皮层的。**-ly** *ad*.

squar·son [ˈskɑːsn; ˋskwɑrsn̩] *n*. 〔英谑〕兼做牧师的地主。

squash[1] [skwɔʃ; skwɑʃ] **I** *vt*. **1**. 压扁;压碎,压烂;压挤进去。**2**. 镇压(叛乱等);压制;压服;〔口〕使缄默,使住口。—*vi*. **1**. 压扁;压碎,压烂;落下砸扁;挤进去 (*into*)。**2**. 发溅泼声,发咯吱声。**II** *n*. **1**. 扁片;易压碎(烂、扁)的东西。**2**. 〔英〕果汁汽水。**3**. 〔口〕拥挤的人群。**4**. (在筑有围墙的场地上玩的,兼有手球和撒球特点的)墙球;短柄墙球球拍。**5**. 趴跶〔重软东西落下声〕,(行走泥沼地的)咯吱声。*Let me* ~ *the mosquito on the wall*. 让我来把墙上的蚊子揿死。*fall ~ing to the ground* 趴跶一声掉在地上。*We all managed to* ~ *into the bus*. 我们都设法挤进了公共汽车。*The crash reduced the car to* ~. 汽车经过这次碰撞变成一堆稀巴烂的东西了。~ **hat** 软呢帽〔可以折叠的宽边呢帽〕。~ **racquets** (有单双打的)小型墙球戏〔墙网球〕。~ **tennis** (仅有单打的)大型墙球戏〔墙网球〕。~**ed generation** = sandwiched generation.

squash[2] [skwɔʃ; skwɑʃ] *n*. 【植】南瓜,倭瓜;荀瓜;西葫芦。~ **bug** 【虫】南瓜虫。

squash·y [ˈskwɔʃi; ˋskwɑʃɪ, ˋskwɔʃɪ] *a*. (*-i·er*; *-i est*) **1**. 易压碎[压扁]的。**2**. 软而湿的。**3**. (道路)泥泞的。**4**. (水果)熟透了的。~ *cantaloupes* 熟透了的甜瓜。**-i·ly** *ad*. **-i·ness** *n*.

squat [skwɔt; skwɑt] **I** *vi*. (*~ted*, *squat*; *~ting*) **1**. 蹲;坐。**2**. 〔美俚〕大便。**3**. (动物)爬在地上,蹲伏。**4**. 〔口〕坐 (*down*, *on*)。**5**. 【海】(高速航行中)船尾下坐。**6**. 〔美〕非法擅自占住空地、空房、公地等。**7**. 〔美〕依法在公地上定居〔以图取得所有权〕。**8**. 〔美商〕违约。**9**. 〔美俚〕被处电刑。— *vt*. **1**. 使蹲下。**2**. 占住,霸占。*Under the shade of a tree, she ~ted down on the ground*. 在树荫之下,她蹲坐在地上。*He ~ted down as a Japanese*. 他像日本人似的蹲坐着。~ **on** 〔美〕停止;拚命反对;责难。~ ***oneself*** 蹲下。~ **hot** 被电刑处死,坐电椅。***take a*** ~ 大便。**II** *a*. **1**. 蹲着的。**2**. 矮胖的。**III** *n*. **1**. 蹲;蹲伏的位置[姿势]。**2**. 矮胖子。*the hot* ~ 〔俚〕电椅。

squat·ter [ˈskwɔtə; ˋskwɑtə˞] *n*. **1**. 蹲着的人[动物]。**2**. 〔美〕擅自占住者;在公地上定住者。**3**. 〔澳〕牧羊场主。~ **sovereignty** 【美史】人民主权论〔南北战争前的一种政治思想,主张各州人民有权处理其内政,并决定是否容许奴隶制 = popular sovereignty〕。

squat·ty [ˈskwɔti; ˋskwɑtɪ, ˋskwɔtɪ] *a*. (*-ti·er*; *-ti-est*) **1**. 蹲着的。**2**. 矮胖的。

squat·ter [ˈskɔtə; ˋskɑtə˞] *vi*. 涉水而行,趟水。

squaw [skwɔː; skwɔ] *n*. **1**. 北美印地安女人,印第安人的妻子。**2**. 〔俚谑〕老婆。**3**. 〔贬〕女子气的男人。**4**. 蹲跪人形靶。*the ~ with the papoose on her back* 背着孩子的印第安女人;(北斗七星中的)开阳双星。~**fish** 【动】**1**. (美国西部河流中的)折唇鱼。**2**. (北美洲太平洋海岸的)海鲫。~ **man** 娶印第安女人做妻子的白人。

squawk [skwɔːk; skwɔk] **I** *n*. **1**. 嘎嘎〔鸟、鸡、鸭等的叫声〕。**2**. 【鸟】黑冠夜苍鹭。**3**. 〔美俚〕粗厉的叫声。**4**. 大声诉苦,抗议。**II** *vi*. **1**. (鸡、鸭、鸟等)嘎嘎地叫。**2**. 〔美俚〕(粗声或大声地)诉苦,发牢骚,抗议。**3**. 〔美俚〕自首;

告密。*This is the third time the tourists ~ed about the service of the hotel*. 这是旅客们第三次对饭店的服务发牢骚了。*The dog barked and the hens ~ed in terror*. 狗吠了,鸡也吓得嘎嘎地叫了起来。—***vt*.** 粗声叫出。~**-box** (供内部联系用的)扬声器,通话盒。~ **sheet** 飞行员关于飞机在飞行时各种不良情况的报告。**-er *n*.**

squawk·ies [ˈskwɔkiːz; ˋskwɑkiz] ***n*.** 〔*pl*.〕〔美谑〕有声电影。

squeak [skwiːk; skwik] **I *vi*. 1.** (鼠等)叽叽的叫;(婴儿)哇哇的哭;发尖锐声,作轧轹声。**2.** 〔俚〕告密。**3.** 非常侥幸成功[获胜]。—***vt*.** 以短促尖锐声发出(报时信号等)。**II *n*. 1.** 叽叽声〔鼠等的叫声〕;刺耳的尖锐声,轧轹声。**2.** 〔口〕困难通过的危机,极难得的机会。**3.** 机会。*When I entered the room, Little Tom gave a startled ~*. 我进屋的时候;小汤姆吓了一跳哇哇地哭了。*a ~ stick* 〔美俚〕= clarinet. *I had a ~ of it*. 我好容易才得救[成功]了。*We've pulled you through a narrow [near, tight] ~*. 我们侥幸地助你通过了难关。**-er *n*.**

squeak·y [ˈskwiːki; ˋskwikɪ] ***a*.** (***-i·er***; ***-i·est***) 发刺耳声的,叽叽叫的,哇哇哭的,发轧轹声的。**-i·ly *ad*. -i·ness *n*.**

squeal [skwiːl; skwil] **I *vi*. 1.** (婴儿等因痛苦、恐怖、发怒、欢喜等)哇哇地叫,尖声呼叫,号叫。**2.** 〔俚〕激烈抗议(*against*)。**3.** 〔俚〕告密。**II *n*. 1.** 尖叫(声)。**2.** 〔美〕抗议。*The kids ~ed with delight at the sight of the Christmas tree*. 娃娃们看到圣诞树喜欢得尖声高叫起来。*The accountant says she's going to ~ on the manager for graft and embezzlement*. 会计说她就要告发经理贪污公款。 ~ **rule** 〔美〕通知中止妊娠法规〔美国卫生教育福利部规定,如有未成年女孩到医院要求中止妊娠,医生必须通知其家长〕。

squeal·er [ˈskwiːlə; ˋskwilɚ] ***n*. 1.** 发尖叫声的动物,雏鸡等。**2.** 〔学生语〕吵闹的初级生。**3.** 〔美俚〕告密者。

squeal·ing [ˈskwiːliŋ; ˋskwilɪŋ] ***n*.** 【无】啸声,振鸣声;号叫(声)。

squeam·ish [ˈskwiːmiʃ; ˋskwimɪʃ] ***a*. 1.** 易呕吐的。**2.** 易受惊的,易生气的,神经质的。**3.** 过分讲究细节的,好吹毛求疵的,过于拘谨的。**-ly *ad*. -ness *n*.**

squee·gee [ˈskwiːdʒiː, ˈskwiːˈdʒiː; ˋskwidʒi, skwiˋdʒi] **I *n*. 1.** (横木上装有橡皮条用以扫甲板、地板上积水,擦玻璃的)橡皮扫帚。**2.** 【摄】(压去相片上水分的)橡皮滚子。**3.** (自命的)重要人物。**II *vt*. 1.** 用橡皮扫帚扫除,拭清。**2.** 【摄】用橡皮滚子压去水分。 ~ **kid** (在十字路口给停下的汽车用橡皮刷清刷挡风玻璃以索取小费的)刷车童。

squeez·a·bil·i·ty [skwiːzəˈbiliti; skwizəˈbɪlətɪ] ***n*. 1.** 可压榨,可榨取。**2.** 可敲诈,可勒索。

squee·zable [ˈskwiːzəbl; ˋskwizəbl̩] ***a*. 1.** 可压榨的,可榨取的。**2.** 可敲诈的,可勒索的。

squeeze [skwiːz; skwiz] **I *vt*. 1.** 挤,压,塞;压出,挤出(*out*; *from*)。**2.** 压迫,压榨,剥削(老百姓);榨取;勒索,敲诈(*from*)。**3.** 握紧(手等);紧抱。**4.** 压进,挤入(*into*)。**5.** 拓印(碑文等)。**6.** 使(利润等)缩减。**7.** 勉强赢得(赚得)。**8.** 压印(硬币等)。**9.** (桥牌中)逼对方出牌。—***vi*. 1.** 压;挤;挤过(*through*);榨。**2.** 压榨。**3.** 勉强通过[赢得]。**4.** 拓印(碑文等)。~ *a lemon dry* 挤干柠檬。*a ~d lemon [orange]* 〔喻〕被榨干后(被抛弃)的人。*S- yourselves a little*. 请各位再挤紧一点。*Can you ~ past?* 你挤得过去吗? ~ *the shorts* 【交易所】杀空头。~*ing bulls [bears]* 忍痛补卖[买]的多头[空头]。~ ***in*** 挤入。~ ***off*** 扣扳机射击。***Squeeze one!*** 〔美俚〕来一瓶橘子汁。~ ***one's waist in*** 勒紧腰杆。~ ***one's way through a crowd*** 在人群中挤过去。~ ***out*** 榨取,挤出,勒索;排斥,排挤。~ ***out a tear*** 干哭,装哭。~ ***the pocketbooks*** 实行财政紧缩政策。~ ***to death*** 压死。**II *n*. 1.** 挤压,压榨;〔口〕压力。**2.** 握紧,抱紧;塞紧;拥挤。**3.** 〔口〕榨取,勒索,敲诈;贿赂。**4.** 榨出的少量东西。**5.** 密集的一群人。**6.** 佣金,回扣。**7.** (桥牌中)被扔出的牌。**8.** (碑铭等的)拓印。*We all got in, but it was a (tight) ~*. 我们都进去了,可是太拥挤了。*a ~ of people on the square* 广场上密集的一群人。***at [upon] a ~*** 在危急中。***be in a tight ~*** 陷入困境。***put a ~ on sb*.** 对某人施加压力。~ **bottle** 软塑料挤瓶〔挤捏之下,内装之物可以挤出来,如塑料胶水瓶等〕。~**box** 〔口〕六角形手风琴。~**d orange** 已被榨干油水的人[物]。~ **play** 【棒球】**1.** (迫使三垒跑者跑回本垒的)触击,轻打战术。**2.** 【桥牌】迫使对方吐出能起重要作用的牌的出法;〔喻〕施加压力。

squeez·er [ˈskwiːzə; ˋskwizɚ] ***n*. 1.** 压榨者;榨取者,剥削者,敲诈者,勒索者。**2.** 压铆机;压榨机。**3.** 【织】轧水机。**4.** 〔*pl*.〕右上角记有花式和点数的纸牌。**5.** 〔美俚〕吝啬者,小气的人。

squeg [skweg; skwɛg] ***vi*.** (***-gg-***) 【无】作非常不规则的振荡。

squelch [skwelʧ; skwɛlʧ] **I *vt*. 1.** 压碎。**2.** 镇压,压服,压制。**3.** 使哑口无言;使不知所措不再作声。**4.** 在泥水中(使)发出格喳声。—***vi*. 1.** 格喳格喳地作响。**2.** 格喳格喳地响着走,涉水而行。*Five proposals were made and each was ~ed by the manager*. 提出了五项建议,每一个都被经理压了回去。*I could hear his broken shoes ~ing in the water*. 我可以听到他的破鞋在水中格喳格喳作响。**II *n*. 1.** 压碎。**2.** 镇压,压制。**3.** 〔口〕压倒对方的议论[回答];反驳得对方不再作声。**4.** 格喳格喳声。**5.** 【无】噪声抑制(电路);无噪声(电路);【空】静音。~ **circuit** 【无】噪声抑制[无噪声]电路。

sque·teague [skwiːˈtiːg; skwiˋtig] ***n*.** (*pl*. ***sque·teague***) = weakfish.

squib [skwib; skwɪb] **I *n*. 1.** 爆筒;导火管;爆竹,甩炮。**2.** 【军】电气导火管;小型点火器。**3.** (讽刺或幽默的)讲话,短文。**4.** 补白。**5.** 胡乱写成的短文。**II *vi*., *vt*.** (***-bb-***) **1.** 扔爆筒;放爆竹。**2.** 发表或作讽刺短文(*against*; *at*; *on*; *upon*)。**3.** 信口地讲,随便地写。*Don't spend your time writing this sort of ~s*. 不要花时间写这类的讽刺短文了。*A newspaperman says they want versified ~s*. 一个报馆人说他们要幽默的讽刺诗。

squid[1] [skwid; skwɪd] **I *n*.** (*pl*. **~s**, 〔集合词〕~) (食用或作饵用)枪乌鲗,柔鱼,鱿鱼。**II *vi*.** (***-dd-***) **1.** (降落伞)成乌鲗状。**2.** 捕乌鲗;用乌鲗作饵捕鱼。

squid[2] [skwid; skwɪd] ***n*.** 反潜多筒迫击炮。

squiffed [skwift; skwɪft] ***a*.** 喝醉了的。

squiff·er [ˈskwifə; ˋskwɪfɚ] ***n*.** 〔英俚〕六角小手风琴。

squif·fy [ˈskwifi; ˋskwɪfɪ] ***a*.** = squiffed.

squig·gle [ˈskwigl; ˋskwɪgl] **I *n*. 1.** 蜿曲线。**2.** (无法辨认的)曲里拐弯的字迹。**II *vt*.** (***-gled***; ***-gling***) **1.** 形成蜿曲线。**2.** 潦草地书写。—***vi*. 1.** 作蜿曲线。**2.** 蜿蜒蠕动。**-gly *a*.**

squil·gee [ˈskwildʒiː, ˌskwilˈdʒiː; ˋskwɪldʒi, skwɪˋdʒi] ***n*., *vt*.** = squeegee.

squill [skwil; skwɪl] ***n*. 1.** 【植】棉枣儿属植物;海葱;海葱根。**2.** 【动】虾蛄。~**-fiis** 【动】虾蛄。

squil·la [ˈskwilə; ˋskwɪlə] ***n*.** (*pl*. ***-las***, ***-lae*** [-iː; -i]) 【动】虾蛄属(*Squilla*)动物。

squinch [skwinʧ; skwɪnʧ] ***n*.** 【建】对角斜拱。

squin·ny [ˈskwini; ˋskwɪnɪ] ***n*., *vi*., *vt*.** (***-nied***; ***-nying***) 〔罕〕= squint.

squint [skwint; skwɪnt] **I *a*.** 斜着眼的;斜视的;细眯着眼看的。**II *n*. 1.** 斜视眼;斜视。**2.** 一瞥,一瞟。**3.** 倾向(某一政策等)(*to*; *towards*)。**4.** 【建】斜孔小窗;窥视窗。**5.** (教会的)圣体遥拜窗。**6.** 【无】斜倾,偏斜〔指天线方向性〕;斜视角,两波束轴间夹角。*have a bad ~* 斜视得厉害。*Let me have a ~ at it*. 让我看一看。*His*

S

speech shows a ~ *to your view*. 他的演说表现出倾向于你的看法。**III** ***vi*. 1.** 斜着眼看,眯着眼看。**2.** 成斜视眼。**3.** 倾向。**4.** 偏斜,偏斜正确方向。~ ***at*** 瞟一瞟,瞟眼偷看一下;看,窥视。*He lost his glasses and had to* ~ *into the dark*. 他把眼镜丢了,不得不眯着眼在黑地上走。**5.** 有间接关系(或意义)。—***vt*.** 斜视,眯眼睛看。~ **eye** 斜眼者,斜视患者。~**-eyed** ***a*. 1.** 斜眼的。**2.** 斜视的。**3.** 侧目而视的,恶意的。~**ing modifier**【语法】歧义修饰语〔指误放位置的副词,解释为修饰不同的两个词都可以〕。**-ing·ly** ***ad*. -y** ***a*.**

squint·er [ˈskwintə; ˋskwɪntɚ] ***n*.** 斜视者;斜视眼。

squire [ˈskwaiə; skwaɪr] **I** ***n*. 1.**〔英〕(地主阶级的)乡绅,老爷(敬称用)。**2.** 殷勤伺候妇女的人;献殷勤以追求妇女的人。**3.** 骑士的随从;扈从。**4.**〔美〕对治安官,法官的敬称,律师,法官。**II** ***vt*. 1.** 在社交场合作为保护者与特定的一个妇女作伴。**2.** 护卫,侍从。~**arch**〔英〕地主。~**archy**〔英〕地主政治;地主势力;〔集合词〕地主阶层。~**let**, ~**ling** 小地主。

squir·een [ˌskwaiəˈriːn; skwaɪˋrin] ***n*.**〔爱〕乡绅;小地主。

squir·ess [ˈskwaires; ˋskwaɪrɪs] ***n*.** 地主夫人,女地主。

squirm [skwəːm; skwɝm] **I** ***vi*. 1.** 蠕动;蠢动。**2.** 折腾;辗转反侧地不安,觉得不好意思。**II** ***n*. 1.** 蠢动,蠕动;折腾。**2.**〔罕〕【海】绳索的扭曲。**-y** ***a*.**

squir·rel [ˈskwirəl; ˋskwɝəl, skwɝl] ***n*.**【动】**1.** 松鼠。**2.** 松鼠毛皮。**3.**〔美俚〕心理学家。**4.** 威士忌酒。**5.** 怪人,疯子。**6.** 乱开车的人。**7.** 跟屁精〔总是追随在一个小集团之后想成为其一份子的人〕。~ **cage** 松鼠笼子;〔喻〕无目的而又无尽头的调单生活[活动]。~ **corn**【植】加拿大荷包牡丹。~ **dew**〔美〕酒。~ **dumplings**〔美俚〕面条。~**fish** 鳂属的鱼。**a** ~ **food**〔美俚〕坚果〔松子,核桃等〕;精神不健全的人。~**-hawk** 捕食松鼠的大鹰。~ **monkey** 鼠猴。**a** ~ **shooter**〔美俚〕(边远地区的)乡下人。

squir·rel·(l)y [ˈskwəːrəli; ˋskwɝrəlɪ] ***a*.**〔美俚〕古怪的,疯狂的,毫无意义的。

squirt [skwəːt; skwɝt] **I** ***vt*.,** ***vi*. 1.** 喷射,喷湿;喷出。**2.** 注射;(使)进出。**II** ***n*. 1.** 喷,细的喷流。**2.** 水枪;注射器。**3.**〔口〕忽然高升的人;傲慢无礼的年轻人。**4.**〔俚〕喷气式飞机。~ **gun** 喷射器,水枪。~**ing cucumber**【植】喷瓜。

squish [skwiʃ; skwɪʃ] **I** ***vt*.**〔方〕= squash[1]. **II** ***n*. 1.** = squash[1]. **2.**〔口〕= marmalade.

squish·y [ˈskwiʃi; ˋskwɪʃɪ] ***a*.**〔美俚〕湿软的;黏糊糊的;易压扁的;发出泥浆的咯吱声的。

sq. yd. = square yard(s)。

S.R. = **1.** solid rocket 固体(燃料)火箭。**2.** Southern Railway〔英〕南方铁路。**3.** Shipping Receipt 船货收据。**4.** specific resistance 电阻率。**5.** star route〔美〕星号邮线。

Sr. = **1.** Senior. **2.** Sir. **3.**〔Pg.〕Senhor. **4.**〔Sp.〕Señor. **5.**【化】strontium.

Sra = **1.**〔Port.〕Senhor. **2.**〔Sp.〕Señora.

SRAAM = short-range air-to-air missile 近程空对空导[飞]弹。

SRAM = short-range attack missile 近程攻击导[飞]弹。

SRBM = short-range ballistic missile 近程弹道导[飞]弹。

Sres. =〔Sp.〕Señores.

Sri Lanka [sri ˈlæŋkə; ˏsrɪ ˋlæŋkə] 斯里兰卡〔亚洲〕。

SRM = specified risk material 高风险食品〔如牛羊的脑和脊髓制品等,此类食品易引起传染病〕。

S.R.N. = State Registered Nurse〔英〕合格护士。

S.R.O. = **1.** standing room only 只有站票〔戏院或车辆售票处用语〕。**2.** Statutory Rules and Orders 成文法令。**3.** single room occupying〔美〕单身单人旅馆服务〔一种廉价服务设施〕。

S.R.S. = Statistics and Reports Section 统计报告部。

Srta = Señorita.

S.S. = **1.** sections. **2.** shortstop. **3.**【处方】*semis* (〔L.〕= a half).

SS., ss. = **1.** scilicet. **2.** Saints. **3.**〔G.〕*Schutzstaffel*.

S.S., SS = **1.** steamship. **2.**〔G.〕*Schutzstaffel*.

S.S. = **1.** Secretary of State〔美〕国务卿。**2.** Secret Service〔英〕特工处。**3.** short stick 短码尺〔1 码 = 35$\frac{1}{2}$ 英寸〕。**4.** simplified spelling 简易拼写法。**5.** Statistical Society〔英〕(皇家)统计学会。**6.** Sunday-school 主日学校。

S/S = steamship.

SSAWS = spring, summer, autumn, winter snow 四季滑雪胜地〔即室内人工滑雪场〕。

SSB(N) = ship, submarine, ballistic (nuclear-powered) (核动力)弹道导[飞]弹潜艇。

SSC = superconducting supercollider【物】超导超对撞机。

SSCAE = Special Senate Committee on Atomic Energy〔美〕参议院原子能特别委员会。

S.S.E., SSE, s.s.e. = south-southeast.

SSgt, SSGT = staff sergeant〔英〕陆军上士;〔美〕空军[海军陆战队]参谋军士。

SSM = **1.** surface-to-surface missile 地对地导[飞]弹。**2.** staff sergeant major 军士长。

SSR = Soviet Socialist Republic (原苏联的)苏维埃社会主义共和国。

SSP =【生】subspecies 亚种。

SST = supersonic transport【空】超音速运输机。

S.S.W., SSW, s.s.w. = south-southwest 南南西。

ST = sulphathiazole.

S.T. = summer time.

St = Saturday.

St.[1] [sənt, sint, snt; sent, sɪnt, sn̩t] = Saint.

St.[2] = **1.** Street. **2.** Strait.

st. = **1.** stanza. **2.**〔L.〕*stet*〔校对符号〕不删。**3.** stone (重量单位)。**4.** strong. **5.** statute.

s.t. = short ton 短吨。

-st *comb. f.*〔在古语和诗作中接在动词后,构成陈述语气第二人称单数〕: did*st*.

STA = station.

S.T.A. = Sail Training Association〔英〕航海训练协会。

sta. = **1.** station(ary). **2.** stator.

stab. = stable.

stab[1] [stæb; stæb] **I** ***vt*.** (***stab·bed*** [stæbd; stæbd], ***stab·bing***) **1.** 刺,戳,刺入,刺伤。**2.** 伤害,刺痛(感情等)。**3.** 用线钉(书)。**4.**【建】把墙面凿粗糙(以涂灰泥)。—***vi*.** 刺,刺伤。*He was ~bed by a terrorist with a sword*. 他被一个恐怖分子用匕首刺伤了。*Mother's scold ~bed her to the heart*. 妈妈的责骂刺伤了她的心。*A sharp pain ~bed at his right knee*. 他的右膝感觉到一阵剧痛。~ ***sb. in the back*** 背后暗害[中伤]某人。~ ***the pill***〔美棒球〕捕接快球。**II** ***n*. 1.** 刺,戳,刺痛,刺伤。**2.** 一种突然强烈的感觉。**3.** 背后骂[害]人,暗害,中伤。**4.** 试图,努力。*I have a sharp* ~ *of pain in the stomach*. 我的胃突然感觉一阵剧痛。***a*** ~ ***in the back*** 背后一刀,伤人的暗箭,中伤,诽谤。***have* [*make*, *take*] *a*** ~ ***at* [*on*] (*sth*.)**〔美俚〕试图做某事,对某事有企图。~**-culture**【医】穿刺培养(物)。

stab[2] [stæb; stæb] ***a*.** 周薪制,时薪制。*a* ~ *hand* 周薪工人。

stab[3] [stæb; stæb]〔俚〕= established; establishment.

Sta·bat Ma·ter [ˈstɑːbæt ˈmɑːtə; ˋstɑbɑt ˋmɑtɚ, ˋstebæt ˋmetɚ]〔L.〕【宗】圣母悼歌。

stab·ber [ˈstæbə; ˋstæbɚ] ***n*. 1.** 穿刺器。**2.** (虱的)口针。**3.** 穿索针,锥。**4.** 刺客。

stab·bing [ˈstæbiŋ; ˋstæbɪŋ] ***a*.** 刺穿的;伤感情的。**-ly** ***ad*.**

sta·bile [ˈsteibl, -bil; ˋstebɪl, ˋstæbɪl] **I** ***a*. 1.** 稳定的,固

定的,空位的。2.【医】抗温热的,稳定性的。**II** *n*. 静态抽象雕塑〔通常为用金属、铁丝、木头等制作的结构〕。

sta·bil·i·ty [stəˈbiliti; stəˋbɪlətɪ] *n*. 1. 稳定,稳定性,稳度。2. (船等的)复原力。3. 巩固;坚定,持久不变。*secure financial* ~ 确保财政上的稳定。

sta·bi·li·za·tion [ˌsteibilaiˈzeiʃən; ˏstebəlaɪˋzeʃən] *n*. 稳定(作用),币值的稳定;坚定,固定。*effect economic* ~ 实现经济的稳定。**-za·tor** *n*. = stabilizer.

sta·bi·lize [ˈsteibilaiz; ˋstebḷˏaɪz] *vt*. 使稳定;使安定;使固定。—*vi*. 稳定,安定。~ *the currency* 稳定货币。*a ~d warfare* 阵地战。*a stabilizing apparatus* 稳定装置。*stabilizing fins*【空】稳定叶片。*Prices have ~d*. 物价已经稳定了。

sta·bi·liz·er [ˈsteibilaizə; ˋstebəˏlaɪzɚ, ˋstæbə-] *n*. 1. 稳定器,平衡器,止摇机。2. (防止火药自然分解的)稳定剂。3.【空】稳定[安定]面。4.【医】安定剂。5. (防止产量增长过快而降低农业补贴等类的)经济稳定机制。

sta·ble[1] [ˈsteibl; ˋstebḷ] *a*. 1. 稳定的;安定的;固定的。2. 意志坚定的,有恒心的。~ *currency* 稳定的通货。*a* ~ *economy* 稳定的经济。~ *equilibrium*【物】稳[安]定平衡,(船的)复原力。~ *opinions* 坚定的意见。**-bly** *ad*. **-ness** *n*.

sta·ble[2] [ˈsteibl; ˋstebḷ] **I** *n*. 1. 厩,马厩,马棚;〔罕〕牛栏,牛棚。2. 〔集合词〕同一个人所有的[一个马厩内的]全部马匹或牛。3. 〔集合词〕同一个经理人掌握的全部运动员[演员,作家等]。4. 〔常 *pl*.〕【军】马厩值勤;马匹的查看(等);〔常用 ~call〕马厩值勤号。5. 〔美俚〕妓院,属于一个鸨头的全部妓女。6. 大学生用的一套解答书。*the whole* ~ 厩内所有马。*a* ~ *police* 〔美军俚〕马房兵。*back the wrong* ~ 赌错马,失算,考虑错。~ *manure* 厩肥。**II** *vt*., *vi*. 关进马厩(或牛棚)里,拴在马厩(牛棚)里;(马、牛)关在棚里。*Lock* [*Shut*] *the* ~ *door when* [*after*] *the horse is stolen*. 〔谚〕贼走关门。*smell of the* ~ (一个人的言行)带有所从事职业的味道。~**-boy** 马夫。~**-companion**, ~**man** 马夫;〔美俚〕同厩的马;同学;俱乐部同仁。~**mate** 1. 同一马主的马。2. 受雇于同一老板的拳击手。3. 同伙;同学;同事;志同道合者。~ **push** 〔美俚〕内幕新闻;来自有影响人士的消息。~**r** *n*. 厩主,棚主。

sta·bling [ˈsteibliŋ; ˋsteblɪŋ, -bḷɪŋ] *n*. 1. 马厩,牛棚。2. 马厩(或牛棚)的设备。

stab·lish [ˈstæbliʃ; ˋstæblɪʃ] *vt*. 〔古〕= establish.

stac·ca·to [stəˈkɑːtəu; stəˋkɑto] **I** *a*. 1. 〔It.〕【乐】断奏的 (*opp*. legato)。2. 断续的,不连贯的。**II** *ad*. 断奏地,奏成断音地,不连贯地。**III** *n*. 1. 断奏。2. 断续的一段音乐。3. 不连贯的东西(如说话,发动机的声音等)。~ *mark* 断音符号。*Maybe I'm a backnumber. I can never enjoy a play of* ~ *scenes*. 也许我是个落伍的人了,我欣赏不了一出场面互不连贯的戏。

stack [stæk; stæk] **I** *n*. 1. (麦杆等的)堆,垛;干草堆。2. 积材,层积,堆积;〔英〕一堆〔木材等的计量单位,= 108 立方英尺〕。3. 〔常 *pl*.〕(图书馆的)许多书架,书库 (= ~ room)。4.【无】迭式存储器。5. 枪架。6. 烟囱;一排[一群]烟囱,车船的烟突。7.【机】管组。8. 〔英〕(突出海面的)浪蚀岩柱,海中孤峰。9. (赌博时的)一堆筹码。10. 〔口〕许多,大量。*a precariously balanced* ~ *of books* 眼看就要倒下来的一堆书。*a* ~ *of postcards* [*old newspapers*, *shoeboxes*] 一大堆明信片[旧报纸、鞋盒]。*a* ~ *of rice straw* 稻草垛。*a considerable* ~ *of evidence* 大量的证明材料。*have ~s of work to do* 有许多工作要做。~ *of arms* 枪架。**II** *vt*. 1. 堆叠,堆垛,堆积,堆起。2.【空】指令飞机作分层盘旋飞行等待依次着陆。3.【军】架(枪)。4. 秘密地预先安排好,内定。5. 〔美俚〕把房间弄得乱七八糟。6.【桥牌】洗牌作弊。*S- arms!*【军】架枪! ***be nicely ~ed up*** 体态丰满匀称的〔指妇女〕。—*vi*. 成堆,堆起来。***blow one's*** ~ 〔俚〕大发脾气 (*When he came in and saw the mess he blew his* ~. 他一进屋里看见那个混乱情况就大发一顿脾气)。***have the cards ~ed against sb***. 把某人的处境弄得极端不利。~ ***the pins*** 〔美,运〕准备下一次比赛。~ ***up*** 1. 总起来,加起来 (*He is all abroad as to how things* ~ *up today*. 他对当前总的形势毫无所知)。2. (飞机)分层盘旋飞行。3. 与某人相称[比较] (*to*);与…较量[争输赢] (*with*, *against*) (*She doesn't* ~ *up to you*. 她不如你)。4. 牵强附会,表面似乎合理 (*Your story just doesn't* ~ *up*. 你讲的简直是胡说八道)。~ ***up the velvet*** 〔美,剧〕赚到钱,营业情况好。~ **funnel** 烟囱内的尖塔形通风设备。~ **room** 书库。~ **up**【空】分层盘旋飞行。~**yard** 干草堆场,堆谷场。~**ed** *a*. 〔俚〕(妇女)身材匀称而丰满的。**-er** *n*. 1. 堆垛者。2. 可升降摄像机台。

stac·te [ˈstækti:; ˋstækti] *n*. (古犹太人制圣香用的)香料。

stac·tom·e·ter [stækˈtɔmitə; stækˋtɑmətɚ] *n*. 滴量计。

stad·dle [ˈstædl; ˋstædl] *n*. 1. 〔古,方〕底部,底撑架;(尤指)草垛的底。2. 根底,基础。

stade [steid; sted] *n*. (古希腊罗马的)赛马场〔长 607 英尺,周围有台阶式看台〕。

stad·hold·er, stad·thold·er [ˈstædˌhəuldə; ˋstædˏholdɚ] *n*.【史】荷兰的省长,荷兰联合省的最高行政长官。

sta·di·a[1] [ˈsteidiə; ˋstedɪə] *n*.【测,土木】视距(测量);视距仪。

sta·di·a[2] [ˈsteidiə; ˋstedɪə] *n*. stadium 的复数。

sta·di·um [ˈsteidiəm; ˋstedɪəm] *n*. (*pl*. **-dia** [-diə; -dɪə]) 1. 斯达地〔古希腊、罗马长度单位,约 = 600 希腊尺,合 607 英尺;赛跑场的跑道以这个长度为准〕。2.【古希腊】赛跑场;(*pl*. ~*s*) (现在的)运动场,体育场。3.【医】(疾病的第…)期。4.【生】龄期(尤指前后两次换羽或脱皮之间的)。*an indoor* ~ 室内体育馆。

staff[1] [stɑːf; stæf, stɑf] **I** *n*. (*pl*. ***staves***, ~***s***) 1. 〔*pl*. 通常作 staves〕棍,棒,杖,竿;旗竿;(枪、戟等的)柄。2. 支柱。3. 权标,权杖,指挥棒。4. (测量或造船用的)标竿,标尺。5.【机】小轴竿。6. 〔*pl*. 通常作 ~*s*〕【铁道】路签。7.【医】导引探子。8.【音】五线谱。9. (全体)职员,干部,工作人员;编辑部。10.【军】参谋(人员);参谋机构。*Bread is the* ~ *of life*. 面包是生活的必需品〔主要支持物〕。*A son should be the* ~ *of his father's old age*. 儿子是父亲年老的依靠。*the editorial* ~ 编辑部(职员)。*the medical* ~ 全体医务人员。*the teaching* ~ 全体教员。*the domestic* ~ 佣人。*a ~-author* = *a ~-writer* 影片公司属下的作家。*the general and his* ~ 将军和他的参谋(部)。*the Headquarters of the General S-* 总参谋部。*the Chief of the General S-* 总参谋长。*a military* [*naval*] ~ *college* 陆[海]军参谋学院。***be on the*** ~ 在职,是职员[部员]。**II** *vt*. 给…调配部员。*What we need is a hospital and a finely ~ed one*. 我们需要一所医院而且是医务人员充实的医院。~ **captain** (客轮上的)安全官。~ **cuts** 裁减人员。~ **locator** 值勤号铃。~ **notation** 五线谱记谱法。~ **nurse** (护士长管理的)普通护士。~ **officer** 参谋。~ **record**【商】工作记录。~ **sergeant** 〔英陆军〕上士;〔美空军〕参谋军士。~**work** 参谋工作;组织,经营。

staff[2] [stæf; stæf] *n*.【建】纤维灰浆。

staff·er [ˈstɑːfə, ˈstæfə; ˋstæfɚ, ˋstɑfɚ] *n*. 职员,工作人员〔如报刊的编辑人员〕。

staff-tree [ˈstɑːfˈtriː; ˋstɑfˋtri] **I** *n*.【植】南蛇藤属 (*Celastrus*) 植物〔包括美洲南蛇藤 (*Celastrus scandens*)〕。**II** *a*. 卫矛科 (*Celastraceae*) 的。

stag [stæg; stæg] **I** *n*. 1. 牡(赤)鹿,雄狐,公火鸡(等)。2. 阉过的雄畜[牛、猪]。3. 刚长大的雄家禽。4.【商】非会员股票经纪人。5. 非真心投资,遇有利机会即行出售股票的认股者。6. 〔美〕不带女伴的舞客;单身出外交际的男人;全是男人的社交集会〔又叫 ~ party (*opp*. hen party), 忌说 cock party]。**7.** 〔苏格兰〕小马。**8.** 〔英〕告密者。**II** *vi*. (*-gg-*) **1.** 不带女伴单身赴会。**2.** 〔商俚〕买进新股(等)见利即抛。**3.** 不带女伴参加舞会。—*vt*. **1.** 〔英〕监视,盯梢;告发。**2.** 截短长裤。**III** *a*. **1.** 全是男人(集会等)的。**2.** 无异性伴侣的。～ *it* 〔美俚〕单身(不带女伴)赴会。*Jack says he goes* ～ *every Saturday night*. 杰克说他每个星期六晚上都去跳舞,但是不带女伴。～ **beetle** 【虫】锹螂;锹形甲虫;鹿角甲虫。～**-evil** 马的破伤风。～ **horn** 公鹿的角;【植】石松;鹿角大珊瑚。～ **hound** 【动】鹿杰〔猎鹿猎狗〕。～ **muck** 〔美俚〕糊涂虫。

stage [steidʒ; stedʒ] **I** *n*. **1.** 讲台;舞台;戏院,剧场;〔the ～〕戏剧,戏剧艺术;戏剧文学;〔the ～〕戏剧业;剧坛。**2.** (活动)舞台;活动范围(场所);注意中心。**3.** (显微镜的)镜台。**4.** (发展的)阶段,时期,程度,步骤。**5.** 【影】室内摄影场。**6.** (建筑用的)脚手架;栈桥,浮码头,趸船。**7.** 站,驿站;一站路的行程;驿马车,公共马车[汽车]。**8.** 【地】(地层的)阶,段,程;(地文的)期。**9.** 浮码头,趸船(=landing ～)。*a* ～ *hog* 〔美〕爱到舞台正面去表现自己的演员。～ *attitude* 表演(艺术)。～ *presentation* 上演,上场。*in the early* ～*s* 在初期。*the larval* ～ 幼虫期。*The proposal has not yet passed the discussion* ～. 这个提案还没有通过讨论阶段。*The disease now occupies the centre of the medical* ～. 这种病现在是医学界的注意中心。***at the*** ～ ***of being*** 暂时,在目前。***be on the*** ～ 过演员生活。***bring on*** [***to***] ***the*** ～ 上演(戏剧);扮演。***come on*** [***upon***] ***the*** ～ 上舞台,进入社会(活动)。***go on the*** ～ 做演员。***hold the*** ～ 继续上演;引人注目。***put on the*** ～ 上演,扮演。***quit the*** ～ 退出舞台;辞职,退出…界。***take to the*** ～ 做演员。***travel by long*** [***easy, short***] ～***s*** 匆匆[从容]旅行;赶着[拖拖拉拉地]做。**II** *vt*. **1.** 演出,搬上舞台,上演。**2.** 〔美〕筹办,举行,发起(某事)。—*vi*. **1.** 坐公共马车旅行。**2.** (剧本)适于上演,上舞台。～ *a comeback* 〔美〕卷土重来,恢复原有地位;再度走红,复辟;(花)重开。*This play* ～*s only one woman character among the armymen*. 这出戏只有一个女角色在男性军人之中。*Teachers of the Arts College are going to* ～ *an exhibition*. 艺术学院的教师们在筹划着要举办一个展览。～ *a meet* 〔美〕举行比赛。～ **box** (舞台旁)特别包厢。～**coach** 公共马车,驿站马车。～**craft** 戏剧作法,编剧法;编剧才能;戏剧演出法。～ **direction** 舞台说明,演出说明[准备]。～ **director** (戏剧)导演。～ **door** 后台口。～ **drive** 驿站马车夫。～ **effect** 舞台效果。～ **fever** (想做戏剧演员的)演员狂,舞台狂。～ **fright** (特指初上舞台时的)怯场。～ **hand** 舞台[布景,道具,照明]管理员。～**house** **1.** 驿站。**2.** 剧场的后门〔供演、职员进出用〕。～ **manage** *vt*. **1.** 舞台监督。**2.** 作戏剧性安排〔尤指背后操纵〕;操纵,控制。～ **manager** 舞台监督;戏剧导演;戏院经理。～ **play** **1.** (话剧)剧本。**2.** 舞台演出。～ **player** (舞台)演员。～ **right** **1.** (面对演员的)舞台右侧。**2.** 〔～ rights〕上演权。～ **setting** 舞台装置。～**struck** *a*. 一心想做戏剧演员的。～**-wait** 冷场事故,僵场〔由演员等的失误造成演出停顿〕。～ **whisper** (舞台上的)低声旁白;故意给人听见的私语。

stag·er [ˈsteidʒə; ˋstedʒɚ] *n*. **1.** 演员。**2.** 公共马车的马。**3.** 经验丰富的人[动物],识途老马,内行。*an old* ～ 老手,内行。

stage·wise[1] [ˈsteidʒwaiz; ˋstedʒwaɪz] *a*. **1.** 有戏剧知识的。**2.** 有戏剧效果的。*a* ～ *director* 善于制造舞台效果的导演。

stage·wise[2] [ˈsteidʒwaiz; ˋstedʒwaɪz] *ad*. 在舞台上;在戏剧方面。

stage·y [ˈsteidʒi; ˋstedʒɪ] *a*. (*stag·i·er*; *stag·i·est*) = stagy.

stag·fla·tion [stægˈfleiʃən; stægˋfleʃən] *n*. 【经济】经济停滞与通货膨胀,停滞膨胀。

stag·gard [ˈstægəd; ˋstægɚd] *n*. 四岁牡鹿。

stag·ger [ˈstægə; ˋstægɚ] **I** *vi*. **1.** 蹒跚,摇摇晃晃。**2.** 逡巡,犹豫,动摇。—*vt*. **1.** 使摇晃。**2.** 犹豫,动摇。**3.** 使吃一惊,使吓一跳。**4.** 使(辐条等)左右交错;使(复翼飞机的上下翼)前后交错。**5.** 〔口〕使(上下班、吃饭时间等)错开(以减轻交通拥挤情况)。*Grandma managed to* ～ *upstairs*. 奶奶好不容易地摇摇晃晃地上了楼。*For a moment I* ～*ed at the price*. 我听了价钱迟疑了一会儿。*I was positively* ～*ed by the news*. 我真给这个消息吓了一跳。～ *office hours* 错开上下班时间。～ *along* 摇摇晃晃地走。～ ***around the lot*** 〔美〕比赛成绩不行。～ ***in*** 〔美〕(特指赛跑)跑得末名;【棒球】(以很少的比分)勉强得胜。～ ***to one's feet*** 摇摇摆摆地站起来。～***ed wings*** 【空】交错翼。**II** *n*. **1.** 蹒跚,摇晃,动摇,摆动;摆动误差。**2.** 〔*pl*.〕眼花,眩晕,酒醉;〔复数用作单数〕(马等的)晕倒症〔又叫 blind ～s〕。**3.** 斜罩,交错;(上下班等的)交错制。**4.** 〔美〕企图,努力。**5.** 【空】(双翼机)斜罩,前伸角。～ **bush** 【植】马氏南烛〔北美洲东部一种灌木,开白色或粉红色花,牲畜食之中毒〕。～ **juice** [**soup**] 〔美俚〕酒。～ **wires** 【空】斜罩线。

stag·ger·er [ˈstægərə; ˋstægərɚ] *n*. **1.** 摆晃[蹒跚,犹豫]的人。**2.** 难题,难关。

stag·ger·ing [ˈstægəriŋ; ˋstægərɪŋ] *a*. **1.** 摇晃的。**2.** (令人)犹豫的。**3.** 令人吃惊的;压倒的;数目大的令人吃惊的。*The external debts of that country are* ～. 那个国家的外债大得惊人。**-ly** *ad*.

stag·gy [ˈstægi; ˋstægɪ] *a*. (雌畜或阉过的雄畜)像成年雄畜的。

stag·ing [ˈsteidʒiŋ; ˋstedʒɪŋ] *n*. **1.** 脚手架。**2.** 【工】构架,台架。**3.** 驿马车旅行。**4.** 驿[公共]马车业。**5.** 【剧】上演。**6.** 【军】(人员或物资的)分段运输,中间集结。**7.** 【宇】宇宙飞船与火箭脱离。～ **area** 【军】集结待命区。～ **base** 【军】飞机中间停留基地,艇舰船中间补给基地;前进基地。～ **post** 【军】**1.** 集结待命地区。**2.** (飞机的)中途机场。**3.** 预备地点。

Stag·i·rite [ˈstædʒirait; ˋstædʒə͵raɪt] *n*. (古希腊马其顿的)斯塔吉利亚 (Stageira) 城的人。*the S-* 亚里斯多德的别称。

stag·nan·cy [ˈstægnənsi; ˋstægnənsɪ] *n*. **1.** 停滞不动,淤积不流,滞止。**2.** 迟钝,呆滞。**3.** 不景气,不振,萧条。

stag·nant [ˈstægnənt; ˋstægnənt] *a*. **1.** 停滞的,不流动的。**2.** (水等因不流动而)污浊的。**3.** 迟钝的,呆笨的。**4.** 萧条的,不景气的。*The room was small and the air* ～. 屋子小空气污浊。*The market is extremely* ～. 市场极为萧条。*Without self reflection, a man will become* ～. 一个人不经常反省,头脑会变得迟钝。**-ly** *ad*.

stag·nate [ˈstægneit; ˋstægnet] *vt*., *vi*. **1.** (使)(水等)停滞不流。**2.** (使)不动,(使)不活动。**3.** (使)迟钝,(使)不活泼。**4.** (使)变萧条。

stag·na·tion [stægˈneiʃən; stægˋneʃən] *n*. **1.** 停滞,不流,不动;滞止。**2.** 萧条。**3.** 迟钝。*a* ～ *point* 【数】静点,驻点。

stag·nico·lous [stægˈnikələs; stægˋnɪkoləs] *a*. 生活于沼泽地的;生活于死水中的。

stag·y [ˈsteidʒi; ˋstedʒɪ] *a*. (*-i·er*; *-i·est*) **1.** 做戏似的。**2.** 戏剧(性)的;舞台的。**3.** 不真实的,做作的,缺乏真实感的。**-i·ly** *ad*. **-i·ness** *n*.

staid [steid; sted] **I** *a*. **1.** 固定的,不动的,稳定的。**2.** 认真的,踏实的,沉着的 (*opp*. frivolous, flighty)。**II** 〔古、美〕stay[1]的过去式及过去分词。*your* ～ *opinion* 你的一贯主张。*a* ～ *person* 一个沉着踏实的人。**-ly** *ad*. **-ness** *n*.

stain [stein; sten] **I** *vt*. **1.** 弄脏,染污 (*with*);沾污,玷污(名誉等)。**2.** 在(玻璃、生物切片等上面)染色。**3.** 在(糊墙纸上等)着色,印上颜色。—*vi*. 变肮脏,染污;生锈。*It is* ～*ed with ink*. 它让墨水弄脏了。*hands* ～*ed with blood* 沾满血的手;凶手。～*ed glass* 彩色玻璃,彩

画玻璃。*This fabric ~s easily*. 这种织品容易弄脏。II ***n*.** 1. 污点;变色;锈;瑕疵(*on*; *upon*; *of*)。2. 色斑。3. 色素,染色剂,着色剂。***without a ~ on one's character*** 性格上没有缺点。~ **fungus** 变色菌。**-able *a*.**

stained [steind; stend] ***a*.** 1. 玷污的;褪色的。*a ~ hat* 一顶褪了色的帽子。2. 着色的,染色的。*a bookcase ~ and waxed* 着色打蜡的书橱。~ **glass** 有色[彩色]玻璃。

stain·er [ˈsteinə; ˋstenɚ] ***n*.** 1. (木材、皮革等的)着[染]色工。2. 上釉工人。3. 染料,色料,着色液。

stain·less [ˈsteinlis; ˋstenlɪs] ***a*.** 1. 不会脏的,不会染污的。2. 不生锈的。3. 无瑕疵的,纯洁的。~ **steel** 不锈钢。**-ly *ad*.**

stair [stεə; stεr] ***n*.** 1. (梯子的)一级。2. 〔常 *pl*.〕楼梯,阶梯。*the top ~ but one* 上面第二磴。*a flight* [*pair*] *of ~s* 一段楼梯。*He lives up two pairs of ~s*. 他住在三层(即再上去二层)楼上。*a winding ~* 回转楼梯。***below*** [***down***] ***~s*** 1. 在房子最下层。2. 在地下室。3. 在仆人房间。4. 做着底下人工作。***up ~s*** 在[向]楼上。***walk up the ~s*** 上楼梯。~ **carpet** 楼梯地毯。**~case** 楼梯;楼梯间[室]。**~head** 楼梯顶端,梯口。**~mastering** 攀梯(健身)运动。**~rod** 楼梯地毯夹条。**~step** 1. ***n*.** 梯级;(年龄或身材方面)如梯级般一级级降低的兄弟[姊妹]。2. ***a*.** 梯级的;如梯级般一级级降低的。3. ***vi*.** 爬楼梯。**~way** 〔美〕= staircase. **~well** 【建】楼梯井。

staith(e) [steiθ; steθ] ***n*.** 〔英〕(尤指煤炭)装卸转运码头。

stake[1] [steik; stek] I ***n*.** 1. (标)桩;竖管,支柱。2. 火刑柱〔人绑在柱上,周围堆满木材烧死〕;〔the ~〕火刑。3. 桩砧,圆头砧,小铁砧。4. (装在车辆四周,防止所装货物散落的)栅柱。*tether a horse to a ~* 把马拴在木桩上。***pull up ~s*** 〔美口〕离开;迁址。II ***vt*.** 1. 用桩撑持。2. 立桩,用桩分开,用桩标出或围住。3. 拴(马)在桩上;拿桩戳。~ ***off*** [***out***] 立标桩分(界)。~ ***off*** [***out***] ***a claim*** 树立标桩表示所有权;提出要求。~ ***out*** (警方对嫌疑犯)布设监视哨;置于监视之下。~ ***up*** [***in***] 设桩圈起来。**~-boat** 航标艇,赛船标志起点的标艇。~ **body** 有栅柱的(平板)车身。**~-net** 挂在桩上的渔网。**~out** (警方对嫌疑犯)布置监视哨;设有监视哨的地区。~ **truck** 有栅柱的卡车。

stake[2] [steik; stek] I ***n*.** 1. 赌博;赌注,赌金。2. 〔*pl*.〕【运】奖金,奖品;有奖赛马。3. 利害关系;风险。4. 下在投机生意上的股本。5. 〔美口〕= grubstake. *enter for the Maiden Stakes* 【赛马】把赌注押在生马上。*My honour is at ~*. 我的声名在危险中。*He has a deep ~ in the business*. 他和这个商店有极大的利害关系。***at ~*** 被赌着;在危险中;利害[生死]攸关。II ***vt*.** 1. 赌。2. 〔美口语〕= grubstake. 3. 〔美俚〕(有偿地)对…给以经济援助。~ *one's future on a single chance* 拿个人前途作孤注一掷。*I ~ my reputation on his honesty*. 我拿名誉担保他诚实。**~holder** 赌金保管者;风险共同承担者,利益共享者,局内人。

Sta·kha·nov [stəˈhɑːnɔːv; stəˋhɑnɔv], **Alexei Grigorievich** 斯达哈诺夫〔苏联煤矿工人,1935 年创始采煤合理化的方法,产量大增,全国推行,在当时形成一个很大的运动〕。

Sta·kha·no·vism [stəˈhɑːnəvizəm; stəˋhɑnəvɪzəm] ***n*.** 〔苏联的〕斯达哈诺夫运动。

Stal·ac·tic(al) [stəˈlæktik(əl); stəˋlæktɪk(əl)] ***a*.** = stalactitic(al). **-cal·ly *ad*.**

sta·lac·ti·form [stəˈlæktiˌfɔːm; stəˋlæktəˏfɔrm] ***a*.** 钟乳石状的。

sta·lac·tite [ˈstæləktait; stəˋlæktaɪt] ***n*.** 【地】钟乳石;钟乳石状物。

stal·ac·tit·ic, -i·cal [ˌstælәkˈtitik(əl); ˏstælәkˋtɪtɪk(əl)] ***a*.** 钟乳石的;钟乳石状的;钟乳石质的。**-i·cal·ly *ad*.**

sta·lag·mite [ˈstæləgmait; stəˋlægmaɪt, ˋstæləgˏmaɪt] ***n*.** 【地】石笋。

stal·ag·mit·ic(al) [ˌstæləgˈmitik(əl); ˏstæləgˋmɪtɪk(əl)] ***a*.** (多)石笋的,石笋状的;石笋质的。**-cal·ly *ad*.**

stal·ag·mom·e·ter [ˌstæləgˈmɔmitə; ˏstæləgˋmɑmətɚ] ***n*.** (表面张力)滴重计。

stale[1] [steil; stel] I ***a*.** 1. 陈旧的;腐败了的,变坏了的;走了气的,走了味的(酒等);干瘪的;霉臭的。2. 不新鲜的;陈腐的(俏皮话等)。3. (因过劳)弄垮了的,泄了气的(学生、运动员等)。4. 停滞的,不流的。5. 冷淡的,萧条的,呆涩的(市场等)。6. 【法】(因不行使权利而)过期失效的。II ***vt*.** 使陈旧;使没有味道,使走气;使失时效,用旧,用坏。—***vi*.** 变陈旧;走气;走味,失时效。*The bread is too ~ to eat*. 面包过期不能吃了。*Nobody likes your ~ jokes*. 谁也不喜欢你那些陈旧的笑话。~ *beer* 走气啤酒。~ *meat* 不新鲜的肉。*a ~ cheque* 过期支票。*get rid of the ~ and take in the fresh* 吐故纳新。***go ~*** 〔美〕(运动员等)筋疲力尽,丧失元气。**-ly *ad*. -ness *n*.**

stale[2] [steil; stel] I ***n*.** (牛马的)尿,畜尿。II ***vi*.** (牛马)撒尿。

stale[3] [steil; stel] ***n*.** 〔英古〕1. 囮子,(猎人做掩蔽用的)假马。2. 笑柄;受人愚弄成为笑谈的人。

stale·mate [ˈsteilmeit; ˋstelˏmet] I ***n*.** 1. 【国际象棋】僵局,王棋受困。2. 僵持,相持,困境。*His tricks will bring us into a ~*. 他的花招会使我们陷入僵局。***break the ~*** 打开僵局。II ***vt*.** 使成僵局,使王棋受困;使束手无策,使相持。

Sta·lin [ˈstɑːlin; ˋstɑlɪn], **Joseph Vissarionovich** [ˈdʒəuzif visɑriəˈnəuvitʃ; ˋdʒozɪf vɪsɑrɪəˋnovɪtʃ] 约瑟夫·维萨里奥诺维奇·斯大林〔1879—1953,苏联国家领导者〕。

Sta·lin·a·bad [stɑːlinɑˈbɑːt; stɑrlɪnɑˋbɑrt] ***n*.** 斯大林纳巴德〔塔吉克斯坦首都,现称杜尚别〕。

Sta·lin·grad [ˈstɑːlingræd; ˋstɑrlɪngræd] ***n*.** 斯大林格勒[现称伏尔加格勒]〔前苏联城市名,二次大战中苏德两军血战之地〕。

stalk[1] [stɔːk; stɔk] ***n*.** 1. 【植】茎,柄,秆,梗,轴。2. 【动】(无脊椎动物的)茎状部,梗节,肉茎,羽毛管。3. 酒杯脚;寒暑表管。4. 【建】叶梗饰。5. (工厂等的)高烟囱。**~-eyed** 【动】有柄眼的。**~let** 小茎。**-y *a*. -i·ness *n*.**

stalk[2] [stɔːk; stɔk] I ***vi*., *vt*.** 1. 高视阔步,大踏步走。2. (疾病等)蔓延,猖獗。3. 偷偷地走,蹑手蹑脚地走;(用东西掩蔽着身体)偷偷走近,偷偷接近。4. 搜索,追踪。*I saw Bob ~ing out from the kitchen*. 我看见伯普蹑手蹑脚从厨房里出来。*The parade ~ed along the highway*. 游行队伍沿着公路阔步前进。*I'm afraid famine will ~ over the land*. 恐怕饥荒要在那个地方蔓延起来。II ***n*.** 1. 高视阔步;猖獗,弥漫。2. 偷偷接近,潜随。3. 狙击。**-er *n*.**

stalk·er·a·zzi [ˈstɔːkəˈrɑːzi; ˋstɔkəˋrɑzɪ] ***n*.** 〔*pl*.〕(为出售照片专门追踪名人偷拍其隐私生活场面的)追踪偷拍者。

stalk·ing-horse [ˈstɔːkiŋhɔːs; ˋstɔkɪŋˏhɔrs] ***n*.** 1. (猎人用作掩护的)掩护马。2. (为掩护主要候选人而推出的)掩护性候选人。3. 借口;掩饰,托词。

stall[1] [stɔːl; stɔl] I ***n*.** 1. 畜舍的一个隔栏;马房,牛棚。2. (房舍内的)分隔小间;〔美〕汽车间。3. 售货摊;棚店;售品陈列台。4. 〔英〕〔常 *pl*.〕(戏院楼下)正厅前座(观众)。5. (教堂里的)牧师席;教徒们的长排坐椅。6. 【矿】矿坑,采煤道;泥窑;敞式矿砂焙烧炉。7. 【空】失速;失举。8. 橡皮手脚指护套。9. 小分隔间 (a shower ~ 淋浴隔间)。II ***vt*.** 1. 把…关进马房[牛栏];把(牲畜)关着养肥。2. 把(畜舍)分成小格。3. 〔美〕使(马、车)陷入泥中[雪中],使进退不得,(使机车等)停顿,停止。4. 【空】使失速。5. 〔古〕授予(职位)。—***vi*.** 1. 住在畜舍内。2. 陷入泥中[雪中]。3. 【空】失速;失举。4. (发动机)发生

S

障碍,停止,停顿。*a ~ed ox* 关着养肥了的牛。*Heavy rain ~ed traffic*. 大雨使交通停顿。~ *down landing* 【空】失速降落。~**-feed** *vt*. 把牲畜关着养肥。~**-fed** *a*. (牲畜)关着养肥的。~**holder** 摊贩。~**-in** 阻塞交通示威。

stall[2][stɔːl; stɔl] **I** *n*. 〔美俚〕**1**. 口实,借口;拖延,搪塞,敷衍;欺骗办法。**2**. (盗贼或扒手的)同党。**II** *vi*., *vt*. **1**. 欺骗;逃避。**2**. 拖延;支吾,敷衍。~ *for a while* 暂时拖一下。~*ing tactics* 缓兵之计。*He knows how to ~ off the applicants for the houses*. 他很晓得怎样敷衍打发申请住房的人。

stall·age [ˈstɔːlidʒ; ˋstɔlɪdʒ] *n*. **1**. (售货摊的)摆摊权。**2**. 摆摊税。**3**. 摆摊场所[位置]。

stal·lion [ˈstæljən; ˋstæljən] *n*. 公马;种马。

stall·o·me·ter [stɔːˈlɔmitə; stɔˋlɑmɪtɚ] *n*. 失速信号器,气流分离指示器。

stal·wart [ˈstɔːlwət; ˋstɔlwɚt] **I** *a*. **1**. 高大强健的,壮健的。**2**. 绝对忠实的,可靠的;坚定的,刚强的。**II** *n*. **1**. 高大健壮的人。**2**. 忠实于…的人,忠实的成员。**-ly** *ad*. **-ness** *n*.

sta·men [ˈsteimen; ˋstemən] *n*. (*pl*. ~*s*, ***stam·ina*** [ˈstæminə; ˋstæmənə])【植】雄蕊。

stam·i·na [ˈstæminə; ˋstæmənə] *n*. 毅力,持久力;精力,体力。*exhibit enough ~ to master Greek and Latin* 表现出掌握希腊语拉丁语的充足的毅力。*a drilling machine with ~ and correctness of design* 一架有持久力设计准确的钻机。

stam·i·nal [ˈstæminəl; ˋstæmɪnəl] *a*. **1**. 雄蕊的。**2**. 有毅力的,有持久力的,有耐力的。

stam·i·nate [ˈstæminit; ˋstæmənɪt, -ˏnet] *a*.【植】有雄蕊的 (*opp*. pistilate)。*a ~ flower* 雄花。

sta·min·e·al [stəˈminjəl; stəˋmɪnɪəl] *a*. 雄蕊的 (= staminal)。

stam·i·nif·er·ous [ˌstæmiˈnifərəs; ˏstæməˋnɪfərəs] *a*. 有雄蕊的。*a ~ plant* 雄株。

stam·i·node [ˈstæmiˌnəud; ˋstæmənod] *n*.【植】退化雄蕊 (= staminodium)。

stam·i·no·dy [ˈstæmiˌnəudi; ˋstæməˏnodɪ] *n*.【植】(花的器官的)雄蕊显著化。

stam·mel [ˈstæml; ˋstæml] *n*. **1**. 中世纪苦行僧所穿用的一种粗毛布。**2**. 染此种布所用的红色。

stam·mer [ˈstæmə; ˋstæmɚ] **I** *vi*.,*vt*. 口吃;结巴着说(*out*)。**II** *n*. 口吃,结巴。*He ~ed out an excuse*. 他结结巴巴的讲了个借口。*He ~s but not so badly as you say*. 他口吃但不像你说的那么厉害。**-er** *n*.

stam·mer·ing [ˈstæməriŋ; ˋstæmərɪŋ] **I** *a*. (患)口吃的。**II** *n*. 口吃。**-ly** *ad*.

stamp [stæmp; stæmp] **I** *n*. **1**. 戳子,图章,戳记,印记。**2**. 邮票,印花(税)。**3**. 〔常用 *sing*.〕标记;特征;记号,痕迹。**4**. 压型器;压断器;杵子;捣击机。**5**. 跺脚,踏脚;【摔角】把势。**6**. 性质,特征;类型;种类。**7**. 〔美俚〕钞票。*Every article bears the ~ of the maker*. 每一种货品上都有制造者标记。*stick a ~ (on a letter)* 贴邮票。*men of that ~* 那种(类型的)人。*bear the ~ of ...* 带有…的特征。*Your ~ of impatience won't give me a scare*. 你那不耐烦的跺脚吓不了我。*put to ~* (交)付印(刷)。**II** *vt*. **1**. 在…上,盖戳,在…上打图章;印刷,压印。**2**. 在…上贴邮票[印花等]。**3**. 跺,踏(脚);踏碎;跺碎;捣碎。**4**. 铭记(心中);使不朽。**5**. 标出,表示。**6**. 压断;压滚。—*vi*. **1**. 捣碎。**2**. 踩踏,踏脚,跺脚;【摔角】摆把势。~ *a document with the address and date* 给文件盖上地址和日戳。~ *one's name on the page of history* 留名青史。~ *one's feet* 跺脚,踏脚。~ *the grass flat* 踏平草地。~ *upstairs* 当当当地上楼梯。*This alone ~s him (as) a swindler*. 这一件事就表明他是一个骗子。***be ~ed with the brand of ...*** 打上…的烙印。~ ***about the room*** 踏着脚在屋里走来走去。~ ***down*** = ~ ***to the ground*** 蹂躏,践踏。~ ***on*** 拒绝。~ ***out*** 踏灭(火);根绝,扑灭(暴动等)。~ ***with rage*** 发怒跺脚。~**album** 集邮簿。~ **collector** 集邮家。~ **duty** [**tax**] 印花税。~**ing ground** 常到的地方,落脚处。~ **machine** 邮票印刷机。~**mill** 捣碎机,捣岩机,碎矿机。~**-note** (海关发的)装货执照。~**-office** 印花税务局。~**-paper** (未撕开的)一版整张邮票。~ **tax** 印花税。

stamp·age [ˈstæmpidʒ; ˋstæmpɪdʒ] *n*. 跺脚;邮资;盖印。

stam·pede [stæmˈpiːd; stæmˋpid] **I** *n*. **1**. (畜群的)惊跑,乱窜;(军队的)总崩溃,溃逃。**2**. 〔美〕(人群)蜂拥上前;(选举中)突然一面倒。**II** *vi*., *vt*. (使)惊逃,(使)争先恐后逃走,(使)溃散;(使)蜂拥上前;(使大群人)突然采取某种行动。*There was a ~ of panic-stricken crowd from the burning hotel*. 从失火的旅馆中跑出来乱窜的惊惶失措的人群。*I won't allow myself to be ~ed by fear*. 我不会容许我自己被恐惧吓跑的。

stamp·er [ˈstæmpə; ˋstæmpɚ] *n*. **1**. 盖章人。**2**. 打印器。**3**. 压模。**4**. 模压工,冲压工。**5**. 捣碎机。**6**. 〔卑〕〔*pl*.〕脚;靴子。*a backed ~* 复制模。*a master ~* 原模。

Stan [stæn; stæn] *n*. 斯坦〔男子名,Stanley 的昵称〕。

stance [stæns; stæns] *n*. **1**. (高尔夫球,板球)击球的姿势;(运动员的)始发姿势。**2**. 站立姿势;安放的姿势[位置];〔Scot.〕(建筑物的)位置。**3**. 姿态,态度,立场,地位。*If I were you, I'd take a moderate ~ towards your brother's affairs*. 要是我是你,我就会对你弟弟的事件采取温和的姿态。

stanch[1][stɑːntʃ; stæntʃ, stɑntʃ] *vt*. **1**. 使伤口止血;止血;使不漏水。**2**. 停住,止住。—*vi*. 血液止住;水停漏。~ *a cut* 使伤口止血。~ *a leak* 堵水漏。**-er** *n*. 止血药。

stanch[2][stɑːntʃ; stɑntʃ] *a*. = staunch.

stan·chion [ˈstɑːnʃən; ˋstænʃən, -tʃən] **I** *n*. **1**. 支柱,柱子;标桩,标柱。**2**. (拴牲畜的)套架,(畜栏中)限制它们活动的枷。**II** *vt*. 用柱子支撑;装上支柱;把(牲畜)拴在套架上[枷上]。

stand [stænd; stænd] **I** *vi*. (***stood*** [stud; stʊd]) **1**. 站立,站起来 (*up*);站住,站定 (*opp*. sit, lie, kneel, couch, squat)。**2**. (房子等)在,坐落(某处),位于。**3**. (高度、价格、温度、数量等)达到,处于(某种程度,情况)。**4**. 固持,固守,坚守,坚持;在实行,(仍然)有效,维持原状,不变更。**5**. 持久,耐久;不剥落,不褪,不变;不倒;不散;不渗开,不阴;不流,不动,停滞;踌躇。**6**. 可代用,帮。**7**. 〔美〕(公马)可作种马。**8**. 〔英〕做候选人[候补者](*for*)。**9**. 向(某方向)行驶;【海】取某一航向。—*vt*. **1**. 竖起,竖立,使立起,使站立;弄直。**2**. 坚持;耐,忍耐;忍受;顶住,接受。**3**. 费用,要(多少钱)。**4**. 〔口〕请客,付账,会钞。**5**. 【军】排成(某种队形)。**6**. 可容纳(若干人)站立。*S- easy!* 稍息! *S- from under!* 注意脚底下! *The thermometer ~s at 80°*. 寒暑表的读数为八十度。*Food ~s higher than ever*. 食品比从前更贵了。*The agreement ~s*. 契约在有效中。*His resolution will ~*. 他的决心不会动摇。*That translation may ~*. 那个译文可靠。*Let the word ~*. 【校刊】此字不改。*let all ~* 【海】装备全部不动。~ *a ladder against the wall* 把梯子靠在墙上。*He ~s his ground*. 他坚持此见。*I cannot ~ great heat*. 我受不住高温。*I will ~ you a dinner*. 我要请你吃一顿饭。*The matter ~s thus*. 事情就是这样。***as affairs*** [***things matters***] ***now ~*** 按照现状,事实上。~ ***a*** (***good***, ***fair***) ***chance*** (很)有希望,(很)有成功可能。~ ***a good deal of wear*** 耐久,经久,持久。~ ***a show*** 有一个(希望不大的)可能。~ ***against*** 抵抗,反抗;靠在。~ ***alone*** 孤立;卓越,无与伦比。~ ***aside*** 站开;避开;不参加。~ ***at*** 犹豫不决,踌躇。~ ***at attention*** [***ease***] 立正[稍息]。~ ***at bay*** 陷入绝境。~ ***away*** 不接近,离着。~ ***back*** 后退,靠后站,缩在后头,位于靠后一点的地方。~ ***behind*** 后援,做后盾。~

by 1. 站在旁边;袖手旁观。2. 待机;等待;【无】(发报台)准备发送信号;(收报台)处于调谐状态;等待下次收听(例: *Please ~ by*.)。3. 站在一起,帮助,援助(例: *~ by one's friends* 支持某人的朋友)。4. 维持,遵守(例: *~ by one's promise* 遵守诺言)。~ ***clear*** 站开,让开,躲开。~ ***convicted of ...*** 罪状明显,被判…。~ ***corrected*** 接受修改,承认错误。~ ***down*** 1.【法】退出证人席位。2. 暂时辞退。3.【军】不在值勤中。~ ***fast*** [***firm***] 固执,固守,坚持不屈。~ ***fire*** 冒炮火;站在攻击的正面。~ ***firmly on*** 确信,深信。~ ***for*** 1. 起立以示对…的尊敬。2. 主张(*We ~ for reform and renovation*. 我们主张改革和革新)。3. 支持,拥护,帮助。4. 担任…的候选人。5.〔口〕忍耐;忍受(*I won't ~ for such nonsense*! 我不能容忍这样的胡言乱语!)。6. 允许。7.【海】驶向。8. 可代…之用,可当…之用(*This box may ~ for a desk*. 这个箱子可当书桌用)。9. 是…的缩写(*WB ~s for the World Bank*. WB 是英语世界银行的缩写)。~ ***for nothing*** 毫无用处。~ ***good*** 依然真实[有效]。~ ***in*** 1. 加入,参加。2.〔口〕使花费(*It stood me in a lot of money*. 花费我不少钱)。3.【影】(在工作人员考虑拍摄办法时)代替名演员站位置(*for*)。~ ***in for the shore*** 驶向海岸。~ ***in the way of*** 妨碍,阻挠。~ ***in with***〔美俚〕帮助;左袒;和…共同行动;分担(*I'll ~ in with you in this expense*. 我和你分担这笔费用)。~ ***off*** 1. 离着,远离。2.【海】离岸行驶。3.〔美〕疏远,避开(债主或攻击者);延期。4.(因市面萧条等)暂时解雇。~ ***off and on***【海】一忽儿接近海岸一忽儿远离海岸航行。~ ***on*** = ~ *upon* 1. 坚持,拘泥。2.【海】向一个方向笔直航行。~ ***on one's hand*** [***head***] 倒立;讲怪话。~ ***sb. in*** (***good***) ***stead*** 紧急时对某人(非常)有用[便利]。~ ***one's friend*** 袒护朋友,帮助朋友。~ ***sb. up***〔美俚〕(失约)使人失望。~ ***or fall*** (*with, together, by*) 共命运,共浮沉。~ ***out*** 1. 突出;浮出,显著,显眼(*Red plums ~ out against the white snow*. 红梅衬着白雪十分醒目)。2. 抵抗到底,坚持到底;支持到底。(*This is the third time we stood out against the enemy attacks*. 这是我们第三次顶住敌人的进犯了)。3.【海】离岸向海中航行。~ ***out*** (***of war***) 不参加战争。~ ***over*** 1.(工作、讨论等)延期,展期(*Payment will ~ over till next month*. 付款延期到下月。*I object to letting the matter ~ over any longer*. 我反对再把这事拖延下去)。2. 密切注意,监督。~ ***pat*** (扑克)不再换牌;反对任何变更;固执既定的政策;坚决不改变主张。~ ***still*** 站住;搁置不动。~ ***to*** 守(约、条件等);坚决主张,坚持〔常用作 ~ to it that〕;(尤指在天亮前或日落后防备敌人进攻)进入阵地;就活动岗位。~ ***to lose*** [***win***] 看来会输[赢]。~ ***to one's colours*** [***guns***] 坚持。~ ***to reason*** 合乎道理,有理。~ ***under*** 忍受。~ ***up*** 站起来,起立;持久;露头角;〔美俚〕背约。~ ***up for*** 拥护,辩护(*~ up for the truth* 坚持真理)。~ ***up on one's hind legs***〔美运〕显示力量[勇气]。~ ***up to*** 勇敢地抵抗,顶住;经得起,受得住。~ ***up with*** 和…双双站起,和…跳舞;(结婚时)陪侍(新郎新娘)。~ ***upon*** 依靠,依赖,信赖;要看…怎样,视…如何而定;不改变;坚持,主张,拘泥(礼貌)。~ ***well with*** 同某人相处得好;得到某人的好感[好评]。~ ***with*** 和…一致;主张,坚持。~ ***without hitching***〔美〕服从命令,全部照办。

II ***n***. 1. 起立,站立;停止,静止。2. 立场,地位;位置;态度。3. 看台;讲坛,音乐坛;台,架,小桌子;〔美〕(法庭的)证人席。4.〔美〕货摊;售货台。5. 停车场,等车处,(鸟的)栖木;(旅行剧团等的)留宿地,上演地。6.(采伐后)留下的幼树,根生树;(一地区上的)林木,林分;庄稼,青苗,植株。7. 一套,一副,一组。8. 抵抗,反抗;防御。*a ~ for flowers* 花插。*a service ~* 工作梯架。*a hat ~* 帽架。*a fruit ~* 水果摊。*a good ~ of wheat* 一块生长良好的麦苗。*approbation of varietal ~* 品种鉴定。***be at a ~*** 停顿,僵持;不知所措。***be brought to a ~*** = ***come to a ~*** 停顿,弄僵。***make a ~*** 站住(*at*);抵抗到底,阻击(*against; for*)。***put*** [***bring***] ***to a ~*** 使停顿;使为难;阻止。***take a*** [***one's***] ~ 困守(城池等);决定态度,立定脚跟。***take a ~ for*** [***against***] 赞成[反对]。~**-alone** ***a***. 独立经营[活动]的;独立自足的;自立门户的。~**away** ***a***.(衣、裙等)不贴住身子的。~**by** 1.(紧急时的)可依靠(的人物),助力。2.【军】一级战斗准备。3. 备用品,备用设备。4. 救援船只。5. 党羽。6.【无】(呼号)准备发报[收报]。~**by shooting** 站立射击〔相对于飞车射击而言〕。~ **camera** 放在三脚架上的摄影机。~**-down** 休止,暂停;停工;临时解雇时期。~**-fast** ***a***. 固执的;坚定的。~**-in** 1.〔美影〕(开拍前)代替名演员站位置的人;替身。2. 有利地位。3.〔美俚〕照顾,偏袒;门路,线索。~**-messenger**〔美〕(服装等的)活人广告。~**off** 1. ***n***. 离岸驶去;离开,疏远;隔开;孤立;支付延期;抵消,平衡;(橄榄球的) half back;〔美运〕不分胜负,和局;〔英〕闲散,停工。2. ***a***.〔口〕冷漠的,冷淡的;有支座托脚的。~**offish** ***a***. 疏远的,有隔阂的,冷淡的;傲慢的。~ **oil**【化】聚合油,厚油,熟油。~**out** ***a***., ***n***. 1. 杰出的(人物);出色的。2.【运】优秀的选手。3.〔口〕坚持己见的人;孤立主义者。~**pat** 1. ***a***.〔美〕不要求换牌的;〔转义〕固执本党政策的,主张维持现状的,顽固的。2. ***n***. = ~patter. ~**patter**〔美〕顽固分子,死硬派。~**pattism** 保守主义,反对变革。~**pipe** 配水塔,竖管,水鹤。~**point** 立场,立脚点;见地,论点,观点。~**still** 1. ***n***. 停止,停顿,搁浅(*come* [*be brought*] *to a ~* 停顿下来)。2. ***a***. 停顿的,停滞的;引起停顿的,造成停滞的(*a ~ strike* 使生产停顿的罢工)。~**-to**〔英〕【军】战斗准备。~**-up** ***a***. 1. 站立的;(衣领)直立的(*opp*. turn-down);站着的(*a ~-up meal* 立餐)。2. 光明正大的,敢说敢干的,坦率正直的,不要手段的,凭真功夫的。3.〔美〕不守会面约言的。

stand·ard [ˈstændəd; ˋstændəd] **I** ***n***. 1. 标准,水准,规格,模范。2. 旗;军旗,队旗;【徽】标帜,标记;旗标,象征。3.【植】旗瓣。4. 金[银]的纯度标准;(硬币的)法定纯度比例;(作为货币价值标准的)本位。5.(度量衡的)原基;原器。6.〔英〕(小学的)学年,年级。7. 直立支柱;灯台;烛台,电杆,垂直的水管(电管)。8.【林】中年木〔胸径 1—2 英尺〕;保残木,第一代上木;【园艺】直立式整枝,嫁接于树干上的灌木。9. 高脚杯,大杯。*the ~ of living* 生活水准[标准]。*conform to the ~s of the present-day society* 合乎当前社会的准则。*the gold* [*silver*] ~ (货币的)金[银]本位制。***below ~*** 标准以下的,不合格的。***come up to the ~*** 够标准。***fall short of the ~*** 不够标准。***join the ~ of*** 加入…的军队。***raise the ~ of revolution*** 举起革命的旗帜。***under the ~ of*** 在…旗下,参加…的军队。***up to ~*** 达到标准的。***up to the ~*** 合格达到标准。**II** ***a***. 1. 标准的,模范的,规范化的。2. 公认为优秀的,权威的。3. 合格的,普通的,一般的。4. 装支柱的。5. 不依附他物生长的。~ *money* 本位货币。~ *English* 标准英语。*a ~ tree* 自然树。*a ~ writer* 标准作家,权威作家。*the ~ model of a bicycle* 普通型的脚踏[自行]车。~**-bearer**【军】旗手;带头者,倡导者,领导者,领袖(*the Republican ~-bearer*〔美〕共和党领袖,共和党的总统候选人)。~ **candle** 标准烛光。~ **deviation**【统】标准(偏)差。~ **error**【统】标准误差,均方差。~ **ga(u)ge** 标准轮距,标准轨距(=1.435 米)。~ **lamp** (支柱可以伸缩的)落地灯。~ **meridian** 本初子午线。~ **solution** 定规液,标准溶液。~ **time** 标准时间。

standard·bred [ˈstændədˈbred; ˋstændədˋbred] ***n***.〔常用 S-〕美洲的良种马〔用于小跑,溜跑,尤其是驾车赛跑者〕。

stand·ard·ize [ˈstændədaiz; ˋstændədˏaɪz] ***vt***. 1. 使合标准;使标准化;使统一;把…作为标准。2. 使与标准比较,用标准校检。~ *English speech* 使英语标准化。*the ~d products* 标准化产品。**-i·za·tion** ***n***. **-iz·er** ***n***.

stand·ee [stænˈdiː; stænˋdi] ***n***.〔美〕1.(戏院中的)站立

看客。**2.** (电车的)站立乘客。

stand·er-by [ˈstændəˈbai; ˋstændəˋbaɪ] ***n.*** (*pl.* ***standers-by***) 旁观者 (= bystander)。

stand·ing [ˈstændiŋ; ˋstændɪŋ] **I** ***a.*** **1.** 直立的;站着的。**2.**【林】未伐的。**3.**【农】尚未收割的。**4.** 停伫的;停滞的,不再运转的,不流动的。**5.** 持续的,长期有效的,标准的,不退的(颜色)。**6.** 常备的,常设的。**7.**【印】已排好的。**8.** 有垫脚的,有脚的(杯子等)。**9.** (由法律习惯)确立的,永久的。*a* ~ *tree* 立木。*a* ~ *factory* 停工的工厂。*a* ~ *order* 长期订单。*a* ~ *committee* 常务委员会。**II** ***n.*** **1.** 起立,站立;站立处。**2.** 持续时间,存在时间。**3.** 立场;地位,身分。*social* ~社会地位。*a man of high* ~ 身分高的人。*an illness of long* ~ 长期疾病。***be in good*** ~身分相当好。~ **corn** 尚未收割的庄稼。~ **dish** (饭馆等的)常备饭菜。~ **jump** 立定跳远。~ **O** 起立鼓掌[O 为 ovation 一词的缩略]。~ **operation procedure**【军】标准操作程序。~ **order 1.** (客户给银行的)长期委托书。**2.** 长期有效的订单。~ **ovation** 起立欢呼。~ **room** (公共汽车、戏院的)站席空位 (*Standing room only*! 本院只有站票出售!)。~ **rules** (团体、机构、企业的)办事[经营]规则。~ **wave**【物】驻波,定波。

Stand·ish [ˈstændiʃ; ˋstændɪʃ] ***n.*** 斯坦迪什[姓氏]。

stand·ish [ˈstændiʃ; ˋstændɪʃ] ***n.*** [古]墨水缸;笔座。

Stand·ley [ˈstændli; ˋstændlɪ] ***n.*** 斯坦德利[姓氏]。

stane [stein; sten] ***n.***, ***a.***, ***vt.*** [苏格兰,英方] = stone.

Stan·ford [ˈstænfəd; ˋstænfəd] ***n.*** 斯坦福[姓氏,男子名]。

stang[1] [stæŋ; stæŋ] [古语] sting 的过去式和过去分词。

stang[2] [stæŋ; stæŋ] ***n.***, ***vt.***, ***vi.*** [苏格兰、英方] = sting.

stan·hope [ˈstænəp; ˋstænhop, ˋstænəp] ***n.*** 无篷高座马车。

stank[1] [stæŋk; stæŋk] stink 的过去式。

stank[2] [stæŋk; stæŋk] ***n.*** **1.** [英方]池塘;水沟。**2.** [英]坝,堰。

Stan·ley [ˈstænli; ˋstænlɪ] ***n.*** **1.** 斯坦利[姓氏,男子名]。**2. Henry Morton** ~ 斯坦利[1841—1904,英国的非洲探险家]。

Stan·ley [ˈstænli; ˋstænlɪ] ***n.*** 斯坦利(史坦莱)港[马尔维纳斯群岛(福克兰群岛)首府]。

stan·na·ry [ˈstænəri; ˋstænərɪ] [英] **I** ***a.*** 锡矿的,采锡的。**II** ***n.*** [常 *pl.*]锡矿,锡矿产地。

stan·nate [ˈstænit; ˋstænet] ***n.***【化】锡酸盐。

stan·nic [ˈstænik; ˋstænɪk] ***a.***【化】(正)锡的;四价锡的。

stan·ni·fer·ous [stæˈnifərəs; stæˋnɪfərəs] ***a.***【化】亚锡的,二价锡的。

stan·nite [ˈstænait; ˋstænaɪt] ***n.***【矿】黄锡矿。

stan·nous [ˈstænəs; ˋstænəs] ***a.***【化】亚锡的;含锡的;二价锡(的)。

stan·num [ˈstænəm; ˋstænəm] ***n.***【化】锡。

St. An·thony's fire [sntˈæntəniz ˈfaiə; sntˋæntənɪzˋfaɪr] 丹毒型皮肤炎。

Stan·ton [ˈstɑːntən, ˈstæntən; ˋstæntən] ***n.*** 斯坦顿[姓氏,男子名]。

STANVAC [缩] Standard Vacuum Oil Company 美孚真空石油公司[美国]。

stan·za [ˈstænzə; ˋstænzə] ***n.*** **1.**【韵】(诗的)节。**2.** [美]运动比赛的段落[如局、盘、场等]。**3.** (戏剧等在某一地点的)演出期[通常为一星期]。*The troupe has agreed to be held over for another* ~. 剧团已经同意续演一期。**-ic** ***a.***

sta·pe·dial [stəˈpiːdiəl; stəˋpidɪəl] ***a.*** 镫骨的,靠近镫骨的。

sta·pes [ˈsteipiːz; ˋstepiz] ***n.*** (*pl.* ***stapes***, ***stapedes*** [stəˈpiːdiːz; stəˋpidiz])【解】镫骨;【医】镫形绷带。

staph [stæf; stæf] ***n.*** staphylococcus 的缩略词。

staph·y·lo·coc·cus [ˌstæfiləuˈkɔkəs; ˏstæfɪləˋkɑkəs] ***n.*** (*pl.* ***-coc·ci*** [-ˈkɔksai; -ˋkɑksaɪ])【微】葡萄球菌。**-coc·cal**, **-coc·cic** ***a.***

staph·y·lo·plas·ty [ˈstæfiləuˌplæsti; ˋstæfɪləˏplæstɪ] ***n.***【医】悬壅垂成形术。**-plas·tic** ***a.***

staph·y·lor·rha·phy [ˌstæfiˈlɔːrəfi; ˏstæfəˋlɔrəfɪ, -ˋlɑr-] ***n.*** (*pl.* ***-phies***)【医】软腭缝术。

sta·ple[1] [ˈsteipl; ˋstepl̩] **I** ***n.*** **1.** 主要产物(或商品),大宗出产,名产;重要商品。**2.** 销路稳定的商品,常用品,广泛采用的东西。**3.** 主要成分;特色;(谈话等的)要项,主题。**4.** 原材料。**5.** (棉、麻、羊毛等的)纤维,(织物的)质地,底子。**6.** 来源地,中心。**7.**【史】(出口商品的)特定市场,贸易中心城镇。*Tea and silk are the* ~*s of East China*. 茶和丝绸是华东的主要商品。*Dry goods are* ~*s of the store*. 织品是这家商店销路稳定的商品。*I'm trying to make an analysis of the* ~*s of his talk*. 我在试行分析他的谈话的要旨。**II** ***a.*** **1.** 主要的,常产的,大宗生产的。**2.** 经常需要的,经常用的。**3.** 纺织纤维的。*cotton of fine* [*short*] ~细[粗]绒棉。**III** ***vt.*** 分拣,分齐(纤维等),(依长短)分类(羊毛等);分级;穿吊眼(结网)。*We'll have to* ~ *synthetic fibre this afternoon*. 今天下午咱们得把合成纤维分分档。~ **commodities** 主要商品。~ **fibre** 人造短纤维,切断纤维。~**goods** 大路货,主要货品。~ **linen** 大宗生产亚麻织品。

sta·ple[2] [steipl; stepl̩] **I** ***n.*** **1.** 卡钉,U 字钉,肘钉,骑马钉;钉书钉。**2.** 钩环,锁环。**3.**【乐】(双簧管等置有簧片的)嘴套。**II** ***vt.*** 用骑马钉钉住。~ **gun** 铁丝钉书机。

sta·pler [ˈsteiplə; ˋsteplə] ***n.*** **1.** 买卖大宗土产的商人;批发商。**2.** 按纤维长短分类的工人。**3.** 纤维切断机,羊毛分选机。**4.**【装订】铁丝钉书机。

star [stɑː; stɑr] **I** ***n.*** **1.** 星;【天】恒星 (*opp.* planet)。**2.** 星状物,星(形勋)章。**3.**【印】星形号[*]。**4.**【占星术】[常 *pl.*]命星;[*pl.*]命运,运气。**5.** 名演员,明星;[口语]著名人物。**6.**【林】梲。**7.**【动】海星。**8.** (马额等的)白斑。**9.** [卑]初次坐牢的犯人。*a falling* [*shooting*] ~流星。*a fixed* ~恒星。*this* ~ [诗]地球。*His* ~ *was in the ascendant*. 他(那时)正在走运。*My* ~*s*! = [谑] *My* ~*s and garters*! 哎呀! 天哪! [表示吃惊]。*The* ~*s were against it*. 那注定要失败的。*the S- Chamber*【英史】星室法庭[以暴虐专横著称]。***be born under a lucky*** [***an unlucky***] ~ 生在幸福[不幸]中。***curse one's*** ~***s*** 怨恨自己不走运。***march by the*** ~***s***【军】看星行进。***see*** ~***s*** [口]眼里冒金星。***all*** ~ ***cast***【剧】全部角色由名演员扮演。***thank one's*** ~***s*** 觉得运气好,觉得幸福。***trust to one's*** ~相信自己的运气。**II** ***vt.*** (***starred***; ***star·ring***) **1.** 用星(形物)装饰;加星号。**2.** 使…成为明星[名演员],使演主角。—***vi.*** **1.** 星一般地辉耀。**2.** 作出杰出成就。**3.** (演员)主演 (*in*);成为明星[名演员]。**4.** (打台球或玩 domino 输掉而失权的人)出钱购买继续游戏的权利。*They* ~*red her for the first time*. 他们第一次以她为主角。*She has* ~*red in many pictures*. 她已主演多部影片。~**-apple**【植】星苹果(树)。~**backs** [美]预订的座位。**S- Chamber**【英史】星室法庭[以残暴著称]。~ **cluster**【天】星团。~**-crossed** ***a.*** 命运不佳的。~**dom 1.** 明星的地位。**2.** 一群明星。~**drift**【天】星流。~**dust** 宇宙尘。~**finch**【鸟】= redstart. ~ **fish**【动】海星,海盘车。~ **flower**【植】**1.** 七瓣莲(属)。**2.** 星形花植物[如伞形虎眼万年青]。~**gaze** ***vi.*** **1.** 凝视星辰。**2.** 想入非非,做白日梦。**3.** [谑]盯着看[指看女明星等]。~**gazer** 占星家;[谑]天文家;空想家,梦想家;【动】眼镜鱼;[谑]专爱看女明星的人。~**gazing** 凝视,空想,心不在焉。~ **grass**【植】星形花草木植物[包括小金梅草属和肺筋草属]。~**king** 红星苹果。~**less** 无星的。~**let** 小星星;小女明星,儿童演员。~**like** 像星那样亮的,星形的。~**light 1.** ***n.*** 星光 **2.** ***a.*** 星光灿烂的,有星光的。~**lit** ***a.*** = ~ light. ~ **man** 初次坐牢的犯人。~ **metal** 精锑,星纹锑。~**-nosed mole**【动】北美星鼻鼹鼠。~**-of-Bethlehem**【植】伞形虎眼万

年青(属)。**Star of David** (犹太教六芒星形标志)大卫之盾。~ **role**〔美运〕名选手。~ **route** 星形邮线〔偏僻地区专门雇用人员邮递的路线〕;〔美〕铁道两旁的路。**Stars and Bars**【美史】1861 年美国南部联邦旗。~**s of the show**〔美〕某一场比赛中出场的名选手。~ **sapphire**【矿】星彩蓝宝石。~ **shell** 照明弹。~**-spangled** 镶有星星的,星印的(*the Star-Spangled Banner* 美国星条旗;美国国歌)。~ **spot** 明星[球星]效应。~ **streaming**【天】星流。~ **studded** 星罗棋布的;星星点缀着的。~ **system** **1.**【天】天河系。**2.** 以少数明星做台柱的明星制度。~ **thistle**【植】矢车菊(属)。~ **turn**〔主英〕**1.** 演出的主要节目;主要演员。**2.** 被他人广为宣传的人。**the S-s and Stripes** 星条旗〔美国国旗〕。~**-warrior** 星球大战计划的鼓吹者。**S- Wars** 星(球大)战计划 [SDI, 美国 Strategic Defense Initiative (战略防御主动性)计划的俗称]。

star·board [ˈstɑːbəd, -bɔːd; ˋstar,bord, -,bord] **I** ***n.***【海、空】(船、飞机的)右舷(*opp.* port[4])。**II** ***a.*** (在)右舷的。**III** ***vt.*** 转向右舷。*sight a steamer to* ~ 在右舷方向看见一艘轮船。*S- (the helm)!* 舵柄转向右!

starch [stɑːtʃ; startʃ] **I** ***n.*** **1.**【化】淀粉;〔*pl.*〕淀粉质食物。**2.** 古板,僵硬,严格,拘泥,形式主义。**3.**〔美俚〕精力,元气。***take the*** ~ ***out of***〔美俚〕压服,使屈服,使气馁;使…不僵硬。**II** ***vt.*** **1.** 给(衣服)上浆,浆硬。**2.** 使僵硬。*a man of ~ed manners* 古板僵硬的人。~ *the shirts* 浆衬衣。~ **blocker** (旨在减肥的)阻止吸收淀粉的制剂。~**-sweet corn** 甜(粉种)玉米。**-less** ***a.*** 不含淀粉的;未上浆的。

starched [ˈstɑːtʃit; startʃt] ***a.*** 浆过的;古板的,僵硬的,拘泥的。**-ly** ***ad.*** **-ness** ***n.***

starch·i·ly [ˈstɑːtʃili; ˋstartʃɪlɪ] ***ad.*** 古板地,僵硬地,拘泥地。

starch·i·ness [ˈstɑːtʃinis; ˋstartʃɪnɪs] ***n.*** 淀粉质,淀粉性;古板,僵硬,拘泥。

starch·y [ˈstɑːtʃi; ˋstartʃɪ] ***a.*** (***-i·er***; ***-i·est***) **1.** 淀粉(质)的;上过浆的,像浆过的。**2.** 古板的,拘泥的,严格的;〔美〕严肃的,高傲的。

stare [stɛə; stɛr] **I** ***vt.***, ***vi.*** **1.** 盯着看,目不转睛地看(*at*),凝视;瞪眼看得…;瞪眼看,张大眼睛看。**2.** (颜色)太显眼(*out*)。**3.** (毛)倒竖。*She ~d thoughtfully into the distance, deliberating the state of affairs.* 她深思地凝视着远方,考虑当前的情况。*The green hat ~s out unpleasantly.* 绿帽子怪惹眼的。~ ***at*** 目不转睛地看,瞪着看,凝视。~ ***sb. down*** = ~ ***sb. out of countenance*** 瞪得人局促不安。~ ***sb. in the face*** 瞪眼看人;(死、不幸等)就在眼前;(事实等)摆在面前,明明白白。~ ***sb. into silence*** 用眼睛瞪得某人哑口无言。~ ***sb. up and down*** 将人浑身上下打量一番。~ ***with surprise*** 吓[惊奇]得目瞪口呆。**II** ***n.*** 凝视。*Having heard what I said, James looked at me with cold* ~. 听了我讲的话以后,詹姆斯冷然地瞪着我。*With an angry* ~, *Mother silenced Mary.* 妈妈生气地瞪了一眼,吓得玛丽不讲话了。

sta·re de·ci·sis [ˈstɑːri diˈsaisis; ˋstarɪ dɪˋsaɪsɪs] ***n.***〔L.〕照章办事。

star·ing [ˈstɛəriŋ; ˋstɛrɪŋ] **I** ***a.*** **1.** 盯着看的,瞪眼看的,凝视的,目不转睛的;太显眼的。**2.** 怪俗气的。**3.** 倒竖的(头发等)。*stark* ~ *mad* 完全发狂的。**II** ***ad.***〔口〕显然,全然,完完全全。*a* ~ *sheet*【工】检验单。**-ly** ***ad.***

stark [stɑːk; stark] ***a.*** **1.** 僵硬的,严格的,顽固不化的,刻板的。**2.** 完全的,全然的,绝对的,真正的。**3.** 一丝不挂的,赤裸裸的。**4.** 荒凉的,不毛的。*There the dead man lay, ~ and stiff.* 那个死人躺在那里,僵硬直挺。*He gave a ~ denial to the rumour.* 他对谣言加以完全的否认。**-ly** ***ad.*** 完全,全然,简直(*~ly naked* 一丝不挂)。

Stark(e) [stɑːk; stark] ***n.*** 斯塔克〔姓氏〕。

star·ling[1] [ˈstɑːliŋ; ˋstarlɪŋ] ***n.***【鸟】燕八哥,高粱头,欧椋鸟,椋鸟科的鸟。

star·ling[2] [ˈstɑːliŋ; ˋstarlɪŋ] ***n.***【建】杀水桩;桥墩尖端。

starred [stɑːd; stard] ***a.***〔构成复合词〕**1.** 用星装饰的;戴着星章的。**2.** 标有星号的。**3.** 成了明星[主角]的,…主演的。**4.** 命运…的。*a five-~-general*〔美〕五星上将,元帅。*a four-~-general*〔美〕四星上将,大将。

star·ry [ˈstɑːri; ˋstarɪ] ***a.*** (***-ri·er***; ***-ri·est***) **1.** 星的;多星的。**2.** 被星照亮的,星一样闪亮的,明亮的;灿烂的。**3.** 星形的。**4.** 高如天上之星的。~ *eyes* 明亮的眼睛。~ *light* 星光。*a ~ night* 星夜。*a ~ program* 许多明星演出的节目。*a wrist-watch ~ with gold and gem* 一只被黄金和宝石照得闪亮的手表。~**-eyed** ***a.***〔美俚〕(看待事物)过分乐观的;不实际的(梦想家)。**-ri·ness** ***n.***

start [stɑːt; start] **I** ***vi.*** **1.**〔美〕出发,动身,起程。**2.** (机器)开动;开始,着手,下手,发生。**3.** 突然出现,涌出;鼓出,突出。**4.** 跳起,惊起,吃惊,吓一跳。**5.** (船材、钉等)松动,翘曲,歪,脱落。**6.** 参加比赛。—***vt.*** **1.** 使出发,使动身,对(比赛者)发出起跑等信号,使参加比赛。**2.** 开动(机器等),开始,创办,开办;着手,下手。**3.** 引起;使从事。**4.** 惊动;惊起,吓出(猎物)。**5.** 突然开始讲;提出(问题等)。**6.** 使脱节,使松动,弄歪,弄翘曲。**7.** 说出(痛苦等)。**8.** 领头(跳舞等),开始雇用某人。**9.**【海】开桶取酒;把酒从桶里倒出。**10.** 生(火)。~ *from Paris* 从巴黎出发。~ *for home* 动身回家。~ *on a journey* 起程旅行。~ *on a task* 着手工作。~ *work(ing)* =〔口〕~ *to work* 开始工作。*Knowledge ~s with practice.* 知识从实践开始。*A screw has ~ed. Tighten it.* 一个螺丝松了,把它拧紧。~ *a newspaper* 创办报纸。*Your advice ~ed me thinking seriously.* 你的意见引起了我的认真考虑。*Mary has ~ed a baby.*〔口〕玛丽已经怀孕。***get the engine to*** ~ 开动机器。~ ***after*** 尾追,追逐,追赶。~ ***another hare*** 赶出另外一只野兔;〔喻〕提出意料不到的事情。~ ***something*** 制造麻烦(骚乱)。~ ***against*** 起来和…竞选,和…对抗。~ ***aside*** 跳往一旁,跳开。~ ***back*** 惊退,畏缩。~ ***for*** 往…出发,起程,动身(*I'm going to ~ for Shanghai.* 我即将动身去上海)。~ ***from scratch***〔美〕赤手空拳地开始。~ ***from taw***〔美〕白手起家。~ ***in***〔口〕开始,动手(*It ~ed in to rain.* 开始下雨了。*He ~ed in on the cake.* 他吃起蛋糕来了)。~ ***in life*** 开始到社会上做事[谋生]。~ ***off*** 出发,动身(*When shall we ~ off?* 我们什么时候出发?)。~ ***off with*** 从…开始,用…开始(*What shall we ~ off with?* 我们从什么谈起?)。~ ***out*** 跳出;开始,着手;〔俚〕企图,计划(*to do*)(*I'll ~ out to write my paper tomorrow.* 我计划明天写读书报告)。~ ***up*** **1.** 惊跳起来(*Suddenly he ~ed up from the chair.* 突然间他从椅子上惊跳起来)。**2.** 突然出现。**3.** 突然发动。**4.** 开始工作。**5.** 开办,开张。~ ***with a bang***〔美俚〕一开始就顺利,旗开得胜。***to*** ~ ***with*** 首先,第一。

II ***n.*** **1.** 出发,动身,起程;起飞,起动;出发点。**2.** 着手,开始。**3.** 惊跳,惊起;吃惊;〔口〕惊人的事。**4.** (赛跑的)起跑(点);起跑信号;〔转义〕先跑权,优先地位,有利条件(*opp.* handicap)。**5.**〔*pl.*〕发作,冲动;努力。**6.** 松动,脱节,弯曲。**7.**〔古〕(思想、感情等的)爆发。*It is a difficult work at the ~.* 那是一件开头困难的工作。*make an early* ~ 早点动身。*What a ~ you gave me!* 你吓了我一跳! *He gave me a ~ of ten yards.* 他让我先跑十码。***a rum*** ~〔口〕惊人事件。***at the*** ~ 开始,当初。***at the very*** ~ 一开始。***awake with a*** ~ 突然醒来,惊醒。***by fits and ~s*** 一阵一阵地,间歇地。***from*** ~ ***to finish*** 自始至终,彻头彻尾。***get a*** ~ 吃惊,吓一跳。***get*** [***have***] ***the*** ~ ***of*** 比…占先,比…先走一着,先发制人。***give sb. a*** ~ ***in life*** 让某人到社会上谋生,给人职业。***give a*** ~ ***of*** 因…而愣了一下,因…而震颤了一下。***make a*** ~ ***on a job*** 开始工作。***make good*** [***bad***] ~ 开头儿好[不好]。***take a fresh*** ~ 重新

开始。～-up, ～up *n*. 创办中的企业[公司等],新办的企业。

START = Strategic Arms Reduction Talks 战略武器削减谈判。

start·er [ˈstɑːtə; ˋstɑrtɚ] *n*. **1**. 出发者;开始者。**2**. 参加赛跑的人(或马)。**3**. (赛跑等的)起跑发号员;(火车等的)开车发号员。**4**. 起动装置,始动杆,起动机(器)。**5**. 〔口〕原因,诱因。**6**. 〔俚〕无花果干。**7**. 【农】催肥饲料。**8**. 酵母。*as a* ～ = *for a* ～ 首先。～ **fertilizer** 基肥,底肥。～ **home** (供财力不足的新婚年轻夫妇购买的)简易房,过渡房〔先住一段时期,以后有钱时再买更佳房屋〕。～ **marriage** (年轻人带有试验性质并不指望相伴终身的)"起步"婚姻,初次婚姻。

start·ing [ˈstɑːtiŋ; ˋstɑrtɪŋ] *n*. 出发;开始;【机】开动,起动;开车。*at* ～ 最初,开头。～ *material* 原材料。～ *motor* 起动电动机。～ **deck**【空】起飞甲板。～ **gate** (赛马的)起跑栅门。～**-point**, ～**-post** 起点,起跑点,出发点,出发标。～ **rail**【空】跑道,起飞道。

star·tle [ˈstɑːtl; ˋstɑrtl] **I** *vi*., *vt*. (使)大吃一惊,(使)震惊,(使)吓一跳,(使)惊跳。*be* ～*d at* 给…吓一跳。～ *from sleep* 惊醒。**II** *n*. 〔美〕吃惊,震惊;惊跳。

star·tler [ˈstɑːtlə; ˋstɑrtlɚ] *n*. 吓人的人,做惊人事情的人;可惊的事物。

star·tling [ˈstɑːtliŋ; ˋstɑrtlɪŋ] *a*. 可惊的,吓人的。*a* ～ *scandal* 一件使人触目惊心的丑闻。～ *news* 惊人的消息。

star·va·tion [stɑːˈveiʃən; stɑrˋveʃən] *n*. 饥饿;饿死;绝食。～ **cure** [**diet**] 绝食疗法;断食疗法。～ **wages** (难以维持温饱的)极低工资。

starve [stɑːv; stɑrv] *vi*. **1**. 饥饿,为饥饿所苦;饿死;绝食。**2**. 〔英罕〕冻死。**3**. 〔口〕饿得要命。**4**. 因缺乏而极需要,渴望(*for*)。—*vt*. **1**. 使饿死;使饥饿。**2**. 使渴望。**3**. 使极度缺乏。**4**. 〔英罕〕使冻死。～ *the enemy into surrender* 使敌人因饥饿而投降。*be* ～*d to death* 饿死。*My hands are starving while I write*. 我写字的时候,手冻得要命。

starve·ling [ˈstɑːvliŋ; ˋstɑrvlɪŋ] **I** *n*. **1**. 饥饿者。**2**. 饿瘦了的人[动物];营养不良的人[动物]。**II** *a*. **1**. 饥饿的。**2**. 营养不良的。**3**. 极贫困的,匮乏的。

stash [stæʃ; stæʃ] **I** *vt*., *vi*. 〔美俚〕**1**. 隐藏;藏匿。**2**. 贮藏。**3**. 〔英〕停止。**II** *n*. 隐[贮]藏物;隐[贮]藏处。*Mother has* ～*ed some money for future use*. 妈妈藏起来一些钱准备将来花用。*It's a slack season and we're going to* ～ *business*. 现在是生意萧条的季节,咱们不久就要停业了。

sta·sis [ˈsteisis; ˋstesɪs, ˋstæsɪs] *n*. (*pl*. **sta·ses** [-siːz; -siz]) **1**. 【医】瘀滞,郁积。**2**. 静态平衡;停滞。

stat. = statics; stationary; statistical; statistics; statuary; statue; statute.

-stat *comb*. *f*. 稳定器[计],固定装置: aero*stat*, thermo*stat*.

state [steit; stet] **I** *n*. **1**. 〔常作 S-〕国,国家;〔通例作 S-〕(美国、澳洲的)州;〔the States〕美国。**2**. 国务,政权,政府。**3**. 身分,地位,资格,社会阶层。**4**. 状况,情形,情况,形势。**5**. 〔口〕难看的样子,邋遢相。**6**. 忧虑,兴奋,激动[状态]。**7**. 优越的生活;盛大的仪式;尊严,气派。**8**. 〔*pl*.〕(Jersey 及 Guernsey 的)议会。**9**. 〔古〕宝座,(宝座上的)华盖;(餐桌的)上席。**10**. 版画制作中的任一阶段。*fight for the* ～ 为国家作战。*affairs of* ～ 国事。*Have you been to the States*? 你到过美国没有? *What's the* ～ *of affairs*? 有什么情况? *the* ～ *of the case* 实情,真相。*What a* ～ *you are in*! 你怎么这样激动[狼狈]。*a visit of* ～ 正式访问。***a* ～ *of siege*** 戒严状态。***a* ～ *of war*** 战争状态。***be in a* ～** 不太好,不振。***be in a* ～ *of grace***【宗】蒙受神恩。***in a good* ～ *of repair*** 修理得很好。***in a great* ～** 威风凛凛。***in a* ～ *of nature*** **1**. 处于原始(未开化)状态。**2**. 一丝不挂地,裸体。**3**.【宗】有罪。***in a terrible* ～** 情况恶劣;非常激动。***in easy* [*great*] ～** 很轻松[严重]的样子。***in* ～** 堂皇地,庄严地,正式地,郑重地。***keep up one's* ～** 保持尊严,摆架子。***live in* ～** 过豪华生活。***lie in* ～** 殡殓后任人瞻仰。***State of the State message*** 〔美〕(总统的)国情咨文。***State of the World message*** 〔美〕(总统的)世界情势咨文[即外交政策报告]。

II *a*. 国家的,国务的,公务的;〔美〕州的,仪式用的;来宾用的;正式的;华丽的,壮丽的。～ *service* 国务,公务。*a* ～ *call* 〔口〕国事访问。*a* ～ *apartment* 大礼堂,大厅;贵宾室。

III *vt*. **1**. 讲,说明,陈述。**2**. 〔常用 *p*. *p*.〕规定,指定(日期、地点、价钱等)。**3**. 【数】用符号或代数式表示(问题、关系等)。～ *one's case* 陈述自己主张[立场]。*I'll* ～. 〔美〕实在是那样。*It is* ～*d that*... 据说。～ *an account* 开账单,算账。～ **aid** 〔美〕州政府对地方公共事业的补助费。～ **bank** 国家(或州立)银行。～ **capitalism** 国家资本主义。**S- Council** (中国)国务院。～**craft** 管理国家的本领。～ **criminal** 政治犯,国事犯。**S- Department** 〔美〕国务院。**S- Dinner** 〔美〕总统邀请的宴会。～ **documents** [**papers**] 公文。**S- flower** (代表某国某州的)州花。～ **functionary** 官吏。～ **funeral** 国葬。**State-house** 〔美〕州议会大楼;州的首府。～ **land** 公地。～ **medicine** 国家公费医疗。～ **ownership** 国有(制)。～ **policy** 国策。～ **prison** 政治犯监狱;〔美〕州立监狱。～ **socialism** 国家社会主义。～ **trial** (由国家起诉的)政治案件审判。～**'s evidence** 公诉人的证据;〔美〕刑事同案犯的证言[证人](*turn* ～*'s evidence* 〔美〕作共犯证言)。**States General** (荷兰及革命前法国的)议会。**State(s') rights** 〔美〕州权。～**wide** *a*. 遍及全州的。*ad*. 遍及全州地。

stat·ed [ˈsteitid; ˋstetɪd] *a*. **1**. 规定的,固定的,一定的,定期的(会议等)。**2**. 被宣称的;作过说明的。**3**. 【数】用符号或代数式表示的。*The* ～ *office hours are from 8 a.m. to 6 p.m.* 规定办公时间是上午八时至下午六时。*These are all* ～ *exceptions*. 这些都是已经说明的例外。*at* ～ *intervals* 定期。～ *clerk* 【宗】(基督教长老会中推选出来的)书记,执事。**-ly** *ad*.

state·less [ˈsteitlis; ˋstetlɪs] *a*. 无国家的;无国籍的;无公民权的。

state·li·ness [ˈsteitlinis; ˋstetlɪnɪs] *n*. 庄严,堂皇,雄壮,华贵。

state·ly [ˈsteitli; ˋstetlɪ] *a*. (建筑等)庄严的,堂皇的;宏伟的,华贵的。*the* ～ *Altar of Heaven* 宏伟堂皇的天坛。**-li·ness** *n*.

state·ment [ˈsteitmənt; ˋstetmənt] *n*. **1**. 陈述,声明,声明书。**2**. 【法】供述;交待。**3**. 【商】贷借对照表;(财务)报告书。*Statements should be based on facts*. 说话要有根据。*prepare an official* ～ 准备一项正式说明。*make a detailed* ～ *of profit and loss* 出具详细的损益计算书。*issue a* ～ 发表一个声明。*a random* ～ 胡乱的供词。*a bank* ～ 银行报告单[结单]。

stat·er[1] [ˈsteitə; ˋstetɚ] *n*. 陈述者。

stat·er[2] [ˈsteitə; ˋstetɚ] *n*. (古希腊、波斯的)金银硬币。

state·room [ˈsteitrum; ˋstetˏrum, -ˏrʊm] *n*. (宫殿、大厦等的)大厅;(轮船的)单间卧舱,特等舱;〔美〕(火车的)单间卧铺,包房。

state·side [ˈsteitsaid; ˋstetˏsaɪd] *a*., *ad*. 〔美〕(不包括阿拉斯加州和夏威夷州在内的)美国国内(的),在美国大陆(的)。

states·man [ˈsteitsmən; ˋstetsmən] *n*. (*pl*. **-men**) **1**. 政治家。**2**. 〔北英〕自耕农。*an elder* ～ 政界元老。～**-like** *a*. 像政治家的,政治家风度的。～**ship** 治理国家的本领[手腕];政治家风度。**-ly** *a*.

stat·ic[1], **-i·cal** [ˈstætik, -ikəl; ˋstætɪk, -ɪkəl] *a*. **1**. 静止的,静态的,静力的。**2**. 【物】天电的,静电的。**3**. 【无】静态特性。**4**. 固定的,不活泼的,变化小的。**5**. 使安静

的。～ **draft**【机】静力通风。～ **electricity** 静电。～ **energy** 静能,位能。～ **population** 固定不变的人口。～ **sensation** 静位觉,平衡感觉。～ **tube** 静压管。**-i·cal·ly** *ad*.

stat·ic² [ˈstætik; ˋstætɪk] *n*. 1.〔美〕【物】天电;静电;天电[静电]干扰。2.〔俚〕恶言,口角,争吵。

stat·i·ce [ˈstætiˌsi; ˋstætɪ͵sɪ] *n*. 1.【植】匙叶草属植物 (= sea lavender)。2.〔Scot.〕营生,工作,活计。

stat·ics [ˈstætiks; ˋstætɪks] *n*.【物】静力学;【无】静电(干扰)。

sta·tion [ˈsteiʃən; ˋsteʃən] I *n*. 1. 站,台,车站;航空站,机场。2. 派出所;署,局,所。3.【无】电台,电视台。4. 驻地,部戍地,根据地,警备区域;基地;〔集合词〕基地全体人员。5. 停泊地;军港;〔美〕空军兵站。6. 部位,位置,场所。7. 地位;身分;职位,岗位。8. 停留,停驻;站立(姿势)。9.【生】= habitat. 10.【宗】耶稣受难十四处之一(或其图画之一幅)。11.【测】测点,测站,标准距离。12.〔澳〕牧场。13.〔美〕邮政局;〔海关用语〕仓库。*a midway* ～ 错车车站。*a* ～ *agent*〔美〕(火车站)站长。*a power* ～ 发电厂。*an atomic* ～ 原子能发电站。*an air* ～ 飞机场。*a broadcasting* ～ 广播电台。*people of* ～ 有地位的人。～ *call letters* 电台呼号。～ *in life*【法】身分。～ *waggon*〔美〕车站接送汽车,客货两用汽车,面包车。***take up a convenient*** ～ 占有利地位。***take up one's appointed*** ～ 各就指定岗位。II *vt*. 驻扎,安置,配置,设置。～ *a guard at the gate* 门口设置一个警卫员。～ **bill** 船上人员应急岗位部署表。～ **break**【无】(电台)播音间歇〔通常指插入商业广告的时间〕。～**-calendar**〔英〕火车出站时刻指示牌。～ **house**〔美〕派出所;车站。～ **indicator** 火车发车到车公告牌;停车车站揭示板。～**master** (火车站)站长;〔美空军口语〕军用机场司令官。～**-pointer**【测】示点器,三脚分度规,三杆分度仪。～**-to-**～ 1. *a*. (长途电话)叫号的。2. *ad*. 按叫号费率(缴费);站到站地。

sta·tion·a·ry [ˈsteiʃənəri; ˋsteʃən͵ɛrɪ] I *a*. 不动的,静止的,不变的;不增不减的,固定的,装定的。II *n*. 1. 不动的人,固定物。2.〔*pl*.〕驻军。～ **air** (呼吸时留在肺中的)静气。～ **engine** 固定式发动机。～ **engineer** 固定动力机技师。～ **parasitism** 永寄生(现象)。～ **radiant**【天】不动辐射点。～ **states**【物】定态。～ **temperature** 不变的温度。～ **troops** 驻军。～ **vibration**【物】驻波,定波;【无】稳定振荡。～ **wave**【物】定波,驻波。**-ar·i·ness** *n*.

stat·ion·er [ˈsteiʃənə; ˋsteʃənɚ, ˋsteʃnɚ] *n*. 1. 文具商。2.〔古〕书商,出版商。***the Stationers' Hall*** 伦敦书籍出版业工会(会所)。***entered at the Stationers' Hall*** 版权登记讫。

sta·tion·er·y [ˈsteiʃənəri; ˋsteʃən͵ɛrɪ] I *n*. 文具;(尤指)信纸。～ ***and envelopes*** 信纸和信封。II *a*. 文具的。*a* ～ *case* 文具盒。**S- Office** (英国政府)文书局〔出版政府文件等〕。

stat·ism [ˈsteitizəm; ˋstetɪzm] *n*. 中央集权下的经济统治;经济的国家统制;国治主义 (*opp*. anarchism),国家主义。

stat·ist [ˈsteitist; ˋstetɪst] *n*. 1. 国治(国家)主义者,主张国家(中央集权下)统治经济者。2. = statistician.

sta·tis·tic, -ti·cal [stəˈtistik, -əl; stəˋtɪstɪk, -əl] I *a*. 统计(上)的,统计学(上)的。～ *data* 统计资料。～ *figures* 统计数字。II *n*.〔仅用作 *sing*.〕1. 统计资料中的一项。2. (对总体具有代表性的)典型统计论。**-ti·cal·ly** *ad*.

stat·is·ti·cian [ˌstætisˈtiʃən; ͵stætəˋstɪʃən] *n*. 统计工作者;统计学家。

sta·tis·tics [stəˈtistiks; stəˋtɪstɪks] *n*. 1. 统计学,统计法〔用作单数〕。2. 统计数字[资料],统计表〔用作复数〕。*Government* ～ *indicate that prices have gone down*. 政府统计指出物价已经下降。*You may consult the* ～ *on population issued by the government*. 你可以查一查政府发表的人口统计。*the vital* ～ (出生、结婚、死亡等)人口动态统计。*collect* [*take*] ～ 进行统计。

stat·i·tron [ˈsteititrɔn; ˋstetɪtrɑn] *n*. 静电加速器[发生器,振荡器]。

stat·o·blast [ˈstætəˌblæst; ˋstæto͵blæst] *n*.【动】休眠芽。

stat·o·cyst [ˈstætəˌsist; ˋstætə͵sɪst] *n*. 1.【植】平衡囊。2.【动】平衡器,(昆虫的)平衡胞。

stat·ol·a·try [steiˈtɔlətri; steˋtɑlətrɪ] *n*. 中央集权论。

stat·o·lith [ˈstætəˌliθ; ˋstætə͵lɪθ] *n*. 1.【植】平衡石。2.【动】耳石,听石。**-ic** *a*.

sta·tor [ˈsteitə; ˋstetɚ] *n*.【电】(固)定子;【空】导向叶片压气机。

stat·o·scope [ˈstætəskəup; ˋstætə͵skop] *n*.【空】微动气压计;灵敏高度表。

stat·u·a·ry [ˈstætjuəri; ˋstætʃʊ͵ɛrɪ] I *n*. 1. 雕像家,塑像家,雕刻家。2. 雕塑艺术。3.〔集合词〕雕像,塑像。II *a*. 雕像的;适合雕像用的(大理石等)。～ **bronze**【冶】雕像青铜。～ **marble** (白色的)雕像大理石。

stat·ue [ˈstætjuː; ˋstætʃu] I *n*. 雕像,铸像,塑像。II *vt*. 1. 用雕像装饰。2.〔古〕为…雕塑。*the Statue of Liberty* (美国纽约的)自由女神铜像。*a* ～*d garden* 用雕像装饰的花园。

stat·u·esque [ˌstætjuˈesk; ͵stætʃʊˋɛsk] *a*. 雕像般的;雕像一样庄严优美的(轮廓)。**-ly** *ad*. **-ness** *n*.

stat·u·ette [ˌstætjuˈet; ͵stætʃʊˋɛt] *n*. 小雕[塑]像。

sta·ture [ˈstætʃə; ˋstætʃɚ] *n*. 1. (特指人的)身长,身材。2. 才干,(道德精神的)器量;发展、成长的状况或高度。*the lofty moral* ～ *of a revolutionary martyr* 一个革命先烈的崇高精神境界。*a scholar of world* ～ 世界性的学者。*be of mean* ～ 个子矮小。*be small in* ～ 身材小。

sta·tus [ˈsteitəs; ˋstetəs] *n*. 1. 情形,状况,状态。2. 地位;资格;【法】身分。3. 重要地位,要人身分。4. (器材的)本性。*the* ～ *of world affairs* 世界形势。*the international* ～ 国际局势。*the* ～ *of a citizen* 市民[公民]的身分。*social* ～ 社会地位。*a* ～ *seeker* 想往上爬的人。*the alert* ～【军】待机状态。～ ***quo*** [kwəu; kwo]〔L.〕现状,维持现状。～ ***quo ante*** [ˈænti; ˋæntɪ]〔L.〕原状,以前状况。～ ***quo ante bellum***〔L.〕战前状况。～ **offender**〔美〕(虽非少年犯但经常旷课、滋事而被置于法院管辖下的)顽劣青少年。～ **symbol** 社会地位象征〔指能表示某种身分的器物、生活作风等〕。

stat·u·ta·ble [ˈstætjutəbl; ˋstætʃʊtəbl̩] *a*. = statutory.

stat·u·ta·bly [ˈstætjutəbli; ˋstætʃʊtəblɪ] *ad*. 依照法令,法令上。

stat·ute [ˈstætjut; ˋstætʃʊt] *n*. 1.【法】法令,法规;成文法。2. (学校,公司等的)规则,章程,条例。*The Academic Council has passed a* ～ *of marking system*. 教务会议已经通过了一项记分制度章程。～**-book** 法令全书。～ **law** 成文法。～ **mile** 法定英里〔= 5280 英尺或 1609.3 米〕。～**s at large** 一般法规,法令全书。

stat·u·to·ry [ˈstætjutəri; ˋstætʃʊ͵torɪ, -͵tɔrɪ] *a*. 1. 法令的,有关法令的。2. 法定的;依照法令的;可依法处罚的。*a* ～ *provision* 法令条款。*a* ～ *meeting* 第一次股东大会。*a* ～ *minimum* 法定最小限度。～ **rape**【法】强奸妇女(罪)。～ **tariffs** 国定税率。

staunch¹ [stɔːntʃ; stɔntʃ, stɑntʃ] *vt*. 制止(出血),止(血)。— *vi*. (血)停止 (= stanch¹)。

staunch² [stɔːntʃ; stɔntʃ] *a*. 1. 坚固的;坚定的;忠实可靠的。2. 不漏水的,耐航的;不漏气的。*a* ～ *defender of peace and democracy* 和平民主的坚定保卫者。*a* ～ *ally* 坚定可靠的同盟者。*a* ～ *cabin* 不漏水的舱。**-ly** *ad*. **-ness** *n*.

stau·ro·lite [ˈstɔːrəˌlait; ˋstɔrə͵laɪt] *n*.【矿】十字石。**-lit·ic** [-ˈlitik; -ˋlɪtɪk] *a*.

S

stau·ro·scope [ˈstɔːrəskəup; ˋstɔrə͵skop] ***n*.** 十字镜〔测定光在晶体中偏振平面方向的仪器〕。

Sta·vang·er [stəˈvæŋə; stəˋvɑŋɚ, stɑ-] ***n*.** 斯塔万格〔挪威港市〕。

stave [steiv; stev] **I** ***n*. 1.** (桶等的)侧板,狭板,桶板。**2.** (车)辐;梯级(横木)横档。**3.** 棒,棍。**4.** 诗句,诗节。**5.** 【乐】五线谱 (= staff)。**II** ***vt*. 1.** 给(桶)装板;给…换桶板;拆去…的桶板;在(桶、船等上)穿孔;敲破(箱匣等)(*in*);装梯级于,装横档于。**2.** 压扁,打坏,压牢。**3.** 挡开,避开,延缓 (*off*)。—***vi*. 1.** 穿孔。**2.** 破碎。**3.** 快步走过。**4.** 〔美俚〕突进,猛冲。~ ***in*** 冲过,冲破;压扁(帽子等);拆散。~ ***it out*** 争[抵抗]到成功为止。~ ***off*** 挡开;避开,勉强阻止(失败、毁灭、暴露等);延宕,拖延(*measures to* ~ *off an attack* 缓兵之计)。*The boat's hull has been* ~*d in by the tremendous seas*. 小船壳让巨浪打穿了。*Glad that you've* ~*d off the trouble*. 很高兴你避开了这件麻烦事儿。

stav·er [ˈsteivə; ˋstevɚ] ***n*.** 〔美俚〕活动家,精力充沛的干将,积极苦干的工作者。

staves [ˈsteivəz; stevz, stævz] ***n*.** staff[1]和 stave 的复数。

staves·a·cre [ˈsteivzˌeikə; ˋstevz͵ekɚ] ***n*. 1.** 【植】斯塔维翠雀,虱草 (*Delphinium staphisagria*)〔产于欧、亚两洲,其籽含生物碱,可作用外敷用防腐剂〕。**2.** 斯塔维雀翠子,虱草子。

stav·ing [ˈsteiviŋ; ˋstevɪŋ] ***a*.** 〔俚〕特大的,特好的。

stay[1] [stei; ste] **I** ***vi*.** (~*ed*, 〔古美〕 ***staid***) **1.** 停留;暂住,逗留。**2.** 保持下去;持久,坚持。**3.** 站住,停止,中止。暂停。**4.** 并驾齐驱 (*with*)。—***vt*. 1.** 阻止,制止,平息,暂时满足一下。**2.** 坚持,停留到…完,等待到(某一刻);留着度过(某一段时间)。**3.** 使(判决等)延期,延缓。**4.** 〔古〕等候。*S- where you are*. 请原位勿动。*I don't live here, I'm only* ~*ing*. 〔口〕我不住在这里,我只是耽搁几天罢了。*My temperature* ~*s around 39°*. 我的体温老在三十九度左右。*Tell him to* ~ *a minute*. 告诉他停一会儿。*He'll try to* ~ *with his rival*. 他曾尽力和他的敌手并驾齐驱的。*The court has decided to* ~ *the proceeding*. 法庭已决定暂缓进行这诉讼程序。*Keep on, Tom! S- the course*. 汤姆,接着干,跑完全程。*Oh, you must* ~ *dinner, Jane*. 简呀,你一定要留下吃饭。***be unable to*** ~ ***to the end of a race*** 不能坚持到比赛完结。***come to*** ~ 稳定下来(*The fine weather has come to* ~. 天气晴定了)。~ ***at home*** = ~ ***in***. ~ ***away*** 不在家里,长时间内不在,离开一个时期。~ ***away from school*** 缺课。~ ***down strike*** (矿工)井内罢工。~ ***in*** 在家里,不外出。~ ***in the clear*** 〔美〕别碰电线。~***in strike*** 留厂罢工。~***ing power*** 耐久力,持久力。~ ***on* 1.** 继续停留,赖着不走。**2.** 保持。~ ***one's*** [***sb.'s***] ***hand*** (使某人)住手不做某事。~ ***one's stomach*** 忍住饥饿。~ ***out* 1.** 在外头,不在家。**2.** 不干涉,不插手。**3.** 坚持到;结束。~ ***overnight*** 住一晚。~ ***put*** 〔美〕安装牢固,原位不动。~ ***the course*** (赛跑的马)跑到终点;坚持到底。~ ***up* 1.** 不去睡觉 (~ *up late* [*all night*] 很晚[终夜]未睡)。**2.** 不倒,不沉。~ ***with it*** 〔美〕忍耐,容忍。

II ***n*. 1.** 停留,逗留(期间)。**2.** 遏制,抑制;妨碍,阻止。**3.** 延缓;【法】延期。**4.** 持久(力);忍耐(力)。*the* ~ *of judgement* 延缓判决。*The horse has good pace but no* ~. 这马脚步倒快就是没有持久力。***make a long*** ~ 长住,长期逗留。***put a*** ~ ***on*** 抑制;妨碍。~**-at-home** ***a*., *n*.** 不爱出门的(人)。**-er** ***n*.** 逗留者,有持久力者;遏制者[物]。

stay[2] [stei; ste] **I** ***n*. 1.** 【海】(船桅的)支索。**2.** 【机】牵条,拉线;牵条,支杆物。**3.** 支柱;倚靠。**4.** 〔*pl*.〕〔英〕(妇女的)紧身褡,胸衣。*the* ~ *of one's old age* 老年时候的依靠。***be in*** ~***s*** 【海】(船)在掉头,正在换掉[换风,转向上风]方向。***be quick*** [***slack***] ***in*** ~***s*** (船头)掉得快[掉不过去]。***miss*** [***lose***] ~***s*** (~***ed***)【海】掉头没有成功。**II** ***vt*.** (~***ed***)【海】**1.** 用支索[支柱]固定。**2.** 把(船)掉过头来(向上风)。**3.** 支持。— ***vi*.** 【海】转向上风。*Your friendship has* ~*ed me*. 你的友谊支持了我。*Grandma put her hand on the chair to* ~ *her from falling*. 奶奶把手放在椅子上杆住自己不致摔倒。~ **bar** [**rod**] 撑杆。~ **bolt** 牵条螺栓。~**-lace** 〔英〕紧身褡的带子。~ **sail** 【海】(用支索拉紧的)长三角帆,支索帆。~ ***tube*** 拉管 。**-er** ***n*.** 支持者,支撑物。

St. Clair [ˈsiŋkleə; sentˋkler, -ˋklær] ***n*.** 圣克莱尔〔姓氏〕。

STD = standard.

Std = standard.

St. Dft. = 【商】sight draft 见票即付的汇票。

Ste. = 〔F.〕Sainte 〔Saint 的女性〕; Stephen.

stead [sted; stɛd] **I** ***n*. 1.** 代替。**2.** 用处,好处,有帮助。*in sb.'s* ~ 代某人。*in* (*the*) ~ *of* = instead of. *stand sb. in good* ~ 对某人很有用,对某人很有帮助。**II** ***vt*.** 对…有用[有利,有帮助]。

stead·fast [ˈstedfəst; ˋstɛd͵fæst, -fəst] ***a*.** 坚定的(信仰),不动摇的,不变的(意志,朋友)。***be*** ~ ***to*** 坚信(某种主义等)。*our* ~ *ally in peace or war* 无论在战争中或和平中都很坚定的盟国。*a* ~ *gaze* 凝视。**-ly** ***ad*.** **-ness** ***n*.**

stead·i·ly [ˈstedili; ˋstɛdəlɪ] ***ad*.** 稳定地;坚定地;坚固地;不断地。

stead·i·ness [ˈstedinis; ˋstɛdɪnɪs] ***n*. 1.** 稳固,稳当。**2.** 坚定,不变;始终如一;有规则。**3.** 【物】定常性;恒定性;均匀。

stead·ing [ˈstediŋ; ˋstɛdɪŋ] ***n*. 1.** 〔英〕小农场。**2.** 〔苏格兰〕农庄,农场的建筑物。

stead·y [ˈstedi; ˋstɛdɪ] **I** ***a*. 1.** 稳固的,平稳的,稳定的,不变的(脚步、努力等)。**2.** 坚定的,扎实的,牢靠的(船等)。**3.** 有规则的,没有激变的(水流、气候等)。**4.** 镇定的,沉着的,从容的;有节制的;稳健的。**5.** (船)不畏风浪依旧前进的。*A young nurse dressed his wounds with* ~ *hands*. 一个年轻护士稳稳当当地扎裹他的伤处。*He is making* ~ *progress in English*. 他在英语学习中取得稳定的进步。*I know she is* ~ *in her purpose*. 我晓得她是意志坚定的。*Slow and* ~ *wins the race*. 慢而稳事必成。*Steady*! 别急! 镇定! 留心! *Steady*! = *Keep her* ~! 【海】(船头)方向照旧。*a* ~ *theatergoer* 戏院常客。~ *hand* 不抖颤的手;稳定的统治,不可动摇的命令。~ *load* 【工】稳恒负载。~ *wind* 持续而方向不变的风。**II** ***vt*., *vi*.** (***stead·ied***) (使)稳固;(使)稳定,(使)坚定;(使)沉着;(使)变稳重;(使)稳定地动,稳定地前进。*Danger steadies some people*. 有的人在危险时候反而沉着。~ ***on* 1.** 停下,慢。**2.** 沉着;镇定。**III** ***ad*.** 经常地;坚定地;持续不变地。***go*** ~ 〔美口〕经常只和某一异性朋友约会出游;(二人)成为情人。**IV** ***n*. 1.** 【机】固定中心架;台,承。**2.** 〔美俚〕未婚夫[妻],(关系确定的)情人。~**-going** ***a*.** 稳定的;扎扎实实的,稳重的(*opp*. easy-going)。~ **state** 【物】恒稳态。~**state** ***a*.** 【物】稳衡态的,稳态的;相对稳定的。~**state theory** 【天】稳恒态学说〔宇宙论的一种,认为随着宇宙的发展和星系的分出,新物质经常不断地在产生〕。

steak [steik; stek] ***n*.** (做牛排等用的)大块肉片;牛排;大块鱼片。~**house** 牛排餐馆。~ **knife** 吃牛排时用的餐刀。~ **tartare** 鞑靼式生拌牛肉末〔加洋葱葱花、生鸡蛋、胡椒粉生拌,配欧芹菜生吃〕。

steal [stiːl; stil] (***stole*** [stəul; stol]; ***sto·len*** [ˈstəulən; ˋstolən]) **I** ***vt*. 1.** 偷,窃取;剽窃(别人文字);【棒球】盗垒。**2.** 偷偷地做;暗暗拉拢,笼络;突然做。**3.** 僭据,侵占。— ***vi*. 1.** 偷东西,做贼。**2.** 偷偷走近[出去],溜(*along*; *by*; *down*; *from*; *into*; *out of*)。**3.** (船、烟等)悄悄地动;(水,泪等)静静地流。**4.** (棒球)盗垒。*The purse has been stolen from my pocket*. 有人从我的口袋里把钱包偷走了。*She stole a glance at George when* *he was writing that letter*. 乔治写那封信时,她偷偷地看了他一眼。*Father was angry and I stole softly out of the room*. 爸爸生气了,我轻轻地溜出了房间。*The years* ~ *by*. 岁月不知不觉地过去了。~ *sb.'s heart* 在不知不觉间抓牢对方爱情。*The feeling* ~*s* (*in*) *upon me*. 我在不知不觉之间发生这种感情。~ ***a march on*** 偷偷抢在…的前头,占先。~ ***away*** 溜掉。~ ***in*** 偷偷跑进,溜进;(将货物)走私运入;偷偷放进(人或物)。~ ***off*** 偷去,拿跑。~ ***on*** **1.** (睡魔,感觉等)袭来。**2.** 不知不觉地跑来(*The winter has stolen on us*. 冬天悄悄地来了)。~ ***sb.'s clothes*** 仿效某人玩弄之手法;接过某人之口号。~ ***sb.'s thunder*** 抢先做某人想做的事[发表论点等];剽窃别人的发明[研究成果等]抢先利用。~ ***one's way*** 偷偷地来[去]。~ ***out*** 偷偷地溜出去。~ ***over*** = ~ *on*. ~ ***round to the back door*** 偷偷地绕到后门。~ ***the glory*** 〔美运〕创最高记录。~ ***the headlines*** 〔美运〕赛得精彩;创光荣记录。~ ***the show*** [***the limelight***] 〔美剧〕把观众的注意力都吸引到自己身上;使旁的演员都黯然失色地一个人取得很大的成功。**II *n*.** **1.** 〔口〕偷窃;赃物。**2.** 意外之财;诈欺。**3.** 不正当的获得[交易]。**4.**【棒球】盗垒。**-er *n*.** **1.** 偷取者,偷干者。**2.** 僭据者。**3.** (棒球)盗垒者。**4.**【船】合并挡板。

steal·ing [ˈstiːliŋ; ˋstilɪŋ] ***n*.** **1.** 偷窃,盗窃;欺骗。**2.**【棒球】偷垒。**3.** 〔*pl*.〕赃物。**-ly *ad*.** 偷偷地,不知不觉地,暗中。

stealth [stelθ; stɛlθ] ***n*.** **1.** 秘密行动,背人的活动,不为人知的活动。**2.** 行窃。**3.** 隐形,"潜入"[指战机、飞弹等利用涂料、设计等手段吸收或干扰雷达以保护自身之一种技术]。***by*** ~ 秘密,鬼祟,暗中(*eat things by* ~ 偷偷吃东西。*do good by* ~ 暗中做好事)。~ **aircraft** [**bomber, missile**] 隐形飞机[轰炸机,导[飞]弹]。

stealth·y [ˈsteilθi; ˋstɛlθɪ] ***a*.** (*-i·er*; *-i·est*) 偷偷的,秘密的;鬼鬼祟祟的;不声不响的;(飞机、潜艇等)"隐形"的。*a* ~ *glance* 偷看。*a* ~ *murder* 暗杀。~ *footsteps* 蹑足。**-i·ly *ad*. -i·ness *n*.**

steam [stiːm; stim] **I *n*.** **1.** 蒸汽,水蒸气,水气,雾,蒸气压力。**2.** 〔口〕精神,精力,气力;怒气。**3.** 轮船,乘轮船旅行。*dry* ~ 干蒸汽。*high* ~ 高压汽。*a* ~ *limit curve* 汽液界线。*In our plant, technical innovation gets up* ~. 我们厂的技术革新的劲头增加了。*Now, Tom, let the* ~ *off and come to an agreement*. 好了,汤姆,吐完了怨气达成协议吧。*Playing football is one of the ways of letting off youthful* ~. 踢足球是青年人散发精力的方法之一。***at full*** ~ 放足蒸气;开足马力,尽力。***by*** ~ 坐轮船。***get up*** ~ 冒水蒸气;振作精神,拿出干劲;愤怒。***have*** ~ ***on*** 冒着水蒸气。***let off*** ~ 发泄多余的精力;发牢骚。***put on*** ~ 拿出精神。***run out of*** ~ 〔口〕泄气,失去势头。***under its*** [***her***] ***own*** ~(指船)依靠本身的蒸汽力。***under*** ~ 被汽力推动着,在航行中;拿出精神。***work off*** ~ 拿出精力[干劲]工作;发泄某种感情。

II *vi*. **1.** 蒸发,凝结蒸汽;冒水汽;出汗;被水汽弄模糊。**2.** 利用汽力开动[行驶,航行]。**3.** 〔口〕大大进步[进展]。**4.** 〔口〕发脾气。**5.** 〔口〕〔英俚〕(青少年等在公共场所)结帮抢劫。— ***vt*.** **1.** 蒸,煮;蒸软(木材)。**2.** 使蒸发;散发。**3.** 用蒸汽力开动。~ *the meat* 蒸肉。*a* ~*ed bun* 馒头。~ *a ship through the strait* 把轮船开进海峡。*The train* ~*ed into the station*. 火车冒着蒸汽开进车站。*That would make him* ~ *again*. 那会使得他又发火了。~ ***along*** [***ahead***] 拼命开。~ **away** 蒸发;(人)去得快;(工作)做得快。~ **up** (玻璃)蒙上蒸汽而模糊;制造蒸汽;〔口〕拿出精神;鼓励;〔美〕喝酒;喝醉;兴奋,愤怒。~ **bath** 蒸汽浴。~**boat** 汽艇,汽船,轮船。~ **boiler** 蒸汽锅炉。~**-box** **1.** = ~-chest. **2.** 蒸笼。~ **brake** 蒸汽制动机,汽闸。~**-chest**【机】汽柜;【化】蒸汽箱。~**-coal** 蒸汽锅炉用煤。~**-cork** 汽管旋塞。~**-colo(u)r** 蒸汽染色。~ **consumption** (蒸)汽(消)耗量。~ **cooling** 蒸汽冷却(法)。~**-crane** 汽力起重机。~**-cylinder** 汽缸。~ **dome** 聚汽室。~ **engine** 蒸汽机(*like a* ~ *engine* 精力充沛,精神勃勃)。~ **fiddle** 〔美俚〕汽笛风琴(= calliope)。~ **fitter** 汽管装配工人。~**-gas** 过热蒸汽。~ **gauge** 汽表,汽压计。~ **hammer** 汽锤。~ **heat** 汽热;蒸汽热量。~**-heated** 用蒸汽加热的,蒸汽取暖的。~ **heater** 蒸汽加热器。~ **heating** 汽热装置。~ **iron** 蒸汽熨斗。~**-jacket** 汽套。~**-launch** 汽艇,小火轮。~ **navvy** 〔英〕汽力挖掘机,蒸汽铲。~ **packet** 定期轮船。~ **plough** 汽锄,汽犁。~**pipe** 蒸汽输送管。~ **port** 汽门,汽口。~ **power** 蒸汽力。~ **pressure** 蒸汽压力。~**radio** 〔口〕"蒸汽"广播(指和电视等相比如蒸汽机车那样显得过时的无线电广播)。~ **rate** 耗汽率;汽率。~**roll** **1.** ***vt*.** 用蒸汽碾路机压平[压碎];施以高压。**2.** ***vi*.** 〔口〕以不可抗拒之势推进。~**roller** **1.** ***n*.** 蒸汽碾路机;高压手段(无可反抗的)压倒的力量,不可抗力。**2.** ***vt*., *vi*.** = ~roll. **3.** ***a*.** 强制(性)的,高压的。~ **room** 蒸汽浴室。~**ship** 轮船。★和船名连用时略作 s.s. (s.s. Queen Mary 玛丽皇后轮)。~**-shovel** = ~ navy. ~**table** 具有用蒸汽或热水保暖设备的餐桌或食品柜;蒸汽表。~**tight *a*.** 不漏汽的,汽密的;防止蒸汽的,耐汽的。~ **train** 蒸汽机车牵引的老式火车。~ **tug** (小)拖轮。~ **turbine** 蒸汽涡轮。~**whistle** 汽笛。~ **winch** 蒸汽绞车,蒸汽起货机。

steam·er [ˈstiːmə; ˋstimɚ] ***n*.** **1.** 汽船,轮船。**2.** 蒸汽汽车;蒸汽机。**3.** 汽锅;蒸锅,蒸笼。**4.** 用蒸汽工作的人;用蒸汽处理的东西;【动】沙海螂(= soft-shell clam)。~ **basket** (由船方赠送的)旅客礼品篮(通常内装水果、糖果等)。~ **chair** 甲板躺椅,帆布躺椅。~ **rug** 甲板躺椅上用的毛毯。~ **trunk** 扁衣箱,轮船衣箱〔宽而扁,原设计供放在船舱铺位下〕。

steam·i·ness [ˈstiːminis; ˋstimɪnɪs] ***n*.** 蒸汽多,冒水气;蒸汽[雾气]弥漫状态。

steam·ing [ˈstiːmiŋ; ˋstimɪŋ] **I *a*.** **1.** 热气腾腾的。**2.** 〔美〕兴奋的;兴致勃勃的。**II *ad*.** 热气腾腾地。*a* ~ *runner* 跑得热气腾腾的人。*The tea is* ~ *hot*. 茶滚烫滚烫地冒着热气。

steam·y [ˈstiːmi; ˋstimɪ] **I *a*.** (*-i·er*; *-i·est*) 蒸汽的,蒸汽似的,蒸汽多的;雾深的,水气蒙蒙的,潮湿的。**II *n*.** 〔美俚〕色情电影。**-i·ly *ad*. -i·ness *n*.**

ste·ap·sin [stiˈæpsin; stɪˋæpsɪn] ***n*.**【生化】胰脂酶。

ste·a·rate [ˈstiəˌreit; ˋstiəˏret] ***n*.**【化】硬脂酸盐,硬脂酸酯。

ste·ar·ic [stiˈærik; stɪˋærɪk, ˋstɪrɪk] ***a*.**【化】(取自)硬脂的;似硬脂的。~ **acid** 硬脂酸。

ste·a·rin(e) [ˈstiərin; ˋstiərɪn, ˋstɪrɪn] ***n*.** 硬脂(精);甘油(三)硬脂酸酯;商用硬脂酸。

ste·a·rop·tene [ˌstiəˈrɔptiːn; ˏstiəˋrɑptin] ***n*.**【化】硬脂萜,硬脂脑。

ste·a·tite [ˈstiətait; ˋstiəˏtaɪt] ***n*.**【矿】块滑石,冻石,皂石。

ste·a·tol·y·sis [ˌstiəˈtɔlisis; ˏstiəˋtɑlɪsɪs] ***n*.**【化】脂肪分解。

ste·a·to·pyg·i·a [ˌstiətəuˈpidʒiə, -ˈpaidʒiə; ˏstiətəˋpaɪdʒɪə] ***n*.** 臀部特别肥突〔尤指妇女由于臀部脂肪层厚所致,如非洲霍顿督妇女〕。**-pyg·ic, -py·gous** [-ˈpaigəs; -ˋpaɪgəs] ***a*.**

ste·at·or·rhe·a, -or·rhoe·a [ˌstiətəˈriːə; ˏstiətəˋriə] ***n*.**【医】脂肪痢,脂溢。

sted·fast [ˈstedfəst; ˋstɛdˏfæst, -fəst] ***a*.** = steadfast.

Steed [stiːd; stid] ***n*.** 斯蒂德〔姓氏〕。

steed [stiːd; stid] ***n*.** **1.** 〔诗〕(骏)马。**2.** 〔谑〕驽马 = nag. **3.** 〔美〕(学生的)解答书。

steek [stiːk; stik, stek] **I *vt*.** **1.** 〔Scot.〕关门[窗];关闭;监禁。**2.** 缝(合)。— ***vi*.** 缝纫。**II *n*.** (缝纫)一针。

steel [stiːl; stil] **I *n*.** **1.** 钢,钢铁。**2.** 钢制品;刀,剑,打火镰;(女人胸衣等中的)松紧钢条[丝];钢磨;〔美〕剃刀,小

S

刀;钢骨。3.【医】铁剂。4. 钢铁般的坚强,坚硬。5. 钢铁工业;〔*pl.*〕钢铁工业股票。**II** *a.* 1. 钢制的,搀有钢的。2. 钢一样的;坚硬的,冷酷的。3. 钢铁业的。***high-grade*** ~ 优质钢。*low* [*mild, soft*] ~ 软钢。*high* [*hard*] ~ 硬钢。*medium* ~中钢。*small* ~ *shape* 小型钢材。*a cold* ~ 利器,刀剑。*a grip of* ~ 牢牢握紧。*muscles of* ~ 结实的肌肉。*a heart of* ~ 铁石心肠,冷酷的心。*off the* ~〔美〕离开铁路线(的)。***a foe worthy of sb.'s*** ~ 需要认真对付的敌人,够格的对手,劲敌。**III** *vt.* 1. 钢化,用钢包上,用钢作(刀的)刃口。2. 使像钢铁一般;锤炼;锻炼,使坚硬,使坚强。3. 使冷酷。4. 〔美俚〕(用刀)刺杀。~ *oneself in a hard time* 在处境艰难时锤炼自己。~ *one's willpower and physical strength* 锻炼一个人的意志和体质。~ **ball** 钢珠。~ **band** 1. 钢带。2. (西印度群岛等地的)铜鼓乐队。~ **bar** 钢条。~ **blue** 钢青色。~ **casting** 铸钢件,铸钢。~-**clad** *a.* 装甲的,披甲的。~ **diaphragm** 钢膜片。~ **engraving**【印】钢板雕刻(术);钢板印刷品。~ **grey** 青灰色。~ **guitar** 夏威夷吉他。~**head**【动】硬头鳟。**S- Helmets** (德国历史的)钢盔团。~ **ingot** 钢锭,钢块。~-**like** *a.* 钢铁般的。~**maker** 钢铁公司[制造厂]。~-**making** 炼钢。~ **mill** 炼钢厂。~ **plate** 钢板。~ **product** [**section**] 钢材。~ **rule** 钢尺。**S- State** 钢州〔美国宾夕法尼亚州的别名〕。~-**trap** *a.* 极快的,机灵的。~-**wire** 钢丝。~ **wool** 钢丝绒〔用以磨光金属制品〕。~ **work** 钢铁工程,钢制品,钢结构。~**worker** 炼钢工人。~**works**〔用作 *sing.*〕炼钢厂。~**yard** 钢秤,提秤。

S

Steele [stiːl; stil] *n.* 斯蒂尔〔姓氏〕。

Steel·op·o·lis [stiːˈlɔpəlis; stiˋlɑpəlɪs] *n.* 钢都〔英国 Sheffield 的别名〕。

steel·y [ˈstiːli; ˋstilɪ] *a.* (*-i·er; -i·est*) 1. 钢的;含钢的,钢制的;钢色的;硬如钢铁的。2. 顽强的;无情的,冷酷的;极严格的。*a* ~ *northwester* 刺骨的西北风。~ *fortitude* 刚强不屈。**-i·ness** *n.*

steen [stiːn; sten] *a.* = um(p)teen.

steen·bok, steen·buck [ˈstiːnbɔk, -bʌk; ˋstinˏbɑk, -bʌk] *n.* (非洲)小羚羊。

steep[1] [stiːp; stip] **I** *a.* 1. 陡急的,峻峭的,险峻的。2. 〔口〕(要求等)过分的,过当的,过高的;夸张的,极端的。3. 〔古〕极高的。4. 急剧升降的,急转直下的。5. 难以接受的,不合理的。*a* ~ *dive*【空】垂直俯冲。*an impassably* ~ *mountain* 一座无路可以攀登的峻峭的山。*a* ~ *fall in market value* 市场价值的急剧下降。*a* ~ *demand* 一个难以接受的要求。**II** *n.* 倾斜〔16°—26°〕,陡坡;绝壁,悬崖。~ **down** *a.* 陡峭的,险峻的。**-ly** *ad.* **-ness** *n.*

steep[2] [stiːp; stip] **I** *vt.* 1. 泡,浸(*in*);浸湿,浸透。2. 使专心一意,使埋头于…。3. (雾、烟、光等)笼罩(山野、树木等)。— *vi.* (在水中)浸泡。**II** *n.* 1. 浸,泡。2. 泡种子的水,浸渍液。~ *tea in boiling water* 泡茶。*Dried vegetable ~s slowly.* 晾干的菜浸渍得慢。***be ~ed in*** 埋头于,专心于。***be ~ed in prejudice*** 偏见很深。

steep·en [ˈstiːpən; ˋstipən] *vt.* 使陡峭,使险峻。— *vi.* 变险峻,越来越险峻。

steep·er [ˈstiːpə; ˋstipɚ] *n.* 浸渍者;浸渍器。

stee·ple [ˈstiːpl; ˋstipl̩] *n.* (特指礼拜堂的)尖塔,尖顶;(女用)尖塔形头巾。*a* ~ *head rivet*【机】尖头铆钉。~**bush**〔美〕【植】绒毛绣线菊。~ **chase** 越野赛马[跑];障碍赛马[赛跑]。~ **chaser** 参加障碍赛马[赛跑]的运动员。~-**crowned** *a.* (帽子等)尖塔形的。~**d** *a.* 有尖顶的,尖塔型的。~**jack** *n.* 尖塔修理工人,烟囱修理工人,高空作业工人。~ **top** *n.* 1. 尖塔状顶部。2. 北极露脊鲸。

steep·y [ˈstiːpi; ˋstipɪ] *a.* 〔诗〕险峻的,陡峭的。

steer[1] [stiə; stɪr] **I** *vt., vi.* 1. 掌(舵);驾驶(船、车)(*for; towards*);〔主口、诗〕(使)向或沿着(某方)行进(*for; to*)。2. 指导,领导;操纵,控制,筹划。3. 〔美俚〕建议,劝告,忠告。4. 〔美俚〕(替赌场[妓院])拉客。~ *one's flight heavenwards* 飞向空中。*We must* ~ *our efforts towards solving the problem.* 我们必须把努力导向解决问题。*Thanks to your help, we've ~ed clear of the difficulties.* 多亏你的帮忙,我们已经避免了困难。*Where are you ~ing for?* 你上哪儿去? ~ **by** = ~ past. ~ ***sb. clear of*** 设法使某人躲开。~ ***clear of*** 机灵地脱身,避开。~ ***a steady course*** 坚定地不断前进。~ ***one's country to*** 领导国家向…方面前进。~ ***one's way to*** 向…方前进。~ ***past*** 避过,躲过。**II** *n.* 1. 关于行路(或驾驶)的指示。2. 〔美俚〕建议,劝告,忠告。~-**able** *a.* 1. 可驾驶的;易操纵的。2. 〔天线等〕易改变位置的。

steer[2] [stiə; stɪr] *n.* 公牛;(食用)阉牛;〔美〕食用牛,菜牛。

steer·age [ˈstiəridʒ; ˋstɪrɪdʒ] *n.* 1. 驾驶,掌舵。2. 操纵,领导。3.【海】舵(的)效(力),舵能;驾驶装置。4. 船尾;(商船的)三等客舱,统舱。5. 〔美〕(军舰的)下级军官室。***have an easy*** [***a bad***] ~ 顺手[不顺手]。***go*** ~ = ***travel*** ~ 搭三等舱走。~ **passenger** 三等舱乘客。~**way**【海】舵效速率〔足够使舵生效的低速〕。

steer·er [ˈstiərə; ˋstɪrɚ] *n.* 1. 舵手,司机。2. 具有某种驾驶性能的船(车)。3. 〔美俚〕(赌场诱人上钩的)囮子;(妓院等处)拉皮条的。

steer·ing [ˈstiəriŋ; ˋstɪrɪŋ] *n.* 1. 掌舵;驾驶;转向。2. 指导,领导;操纵,控制。*a* ~ *handle* 舵把,方向盘。*current* ~ *logic* 电流控制逻辑。~ **committee**〔美〕(团体,机构等的)指导委员会。~ **engine** 转向舵轮。~ **gear**【海】操舵装置。~ **house** 舵室。~ **wheel**【海】舵轮,驾驶盘;(汽车的)方向盘。

steers·man [ˈstiəzmən; ˋstɪrzmən] *n.* (*pl.* **-men**) 舵手;(汽车)司机。

steeve [stiːv; stiv] **I** *n.* 1.【船】斜艏桅仰角。2. 起重杆;吊杆。**II** *vt.* 1. 用起重桅装货。2. 使(斜艏桅)倾斜。— *vi.* (艏斜桅)倾斜。

Stef·ans·son [ˈstefənsn; ˋstɛfənsn̩], **Vilhjalmur** [ˈvilhjaulmə; ˋvɪlhjaulmɚ] 斯蒂芬森〔1879—1962 美国北极探险家〕。

Stef·fens [ˈstefənz; ˋstɛfənz] *n.* 斯蒂芬斯〔姓氏〕。

steg·o·sau·rus [ˌstegəˈsɔːrəs; ˏstɛgəˋsɔrəs] *n.* (*pl.* **-ri** [-ai; -aɪ])〔美〕【动】剑龙〔产于北美〕。

Stein [stain; staɪn] *n.* 斯坦〔姓氏〕。

stein [stain; staɪn] *n.* (陶制有盖)啤酒杯;玻璃等制的啤酒杯;一啤酒杯的容量。

Stein·beck [ˈstainbek; ˋstaɪnbɛk] *n.* 斯坦贝克〔姓氏〕。

Stein·beck [ˈstainbek; ˋstaɪnbɛk], **John Ernest** *n.* 斯坦贝克〔1902—1968,美国作家〕。

stein·bo(c)k [ˈstainbɔk; ˋstaɪnˏbɑk] *n.* = 1. steenbok. 2. ibex.

Stein·metz [ˈstainmets; ˋstaɪnmɛts], **Charles Proteus** 斯坦梅茨〔1865—1923,美国电工学家、发明家〕。

ste·la [ˈstiːlə; ˋstilə] *n.* (*pl.* **-lae** [-liː; -li]) = stele 1.

ste·le [ˈstiːli; ˋstili] *n.* (*pl.* **-lae** [-liː; -li], **~s**) 1.【考古】(刻有文字或图案的)石版,石柱。2.【植】中柱。

Stel·la [ˈstelə; ˋstɛlə] *n.* 斯特拉〔姓氏〕。

stel·lar [ˈstelə; ˋstɛlɚ] *a.* 1. (恒)星的。2. 星似的,星形的,星光灿烂的;星多的。3. 〔美〕主要的,第一流的。4.【影】名演员的,明星的。~ *photography* 天体摄影术。~ *photometry* 星体光度学。~ **wind**【天】恒星风。

stel·lar·a·tor [ˈsteləˌreitə; ˋstɛləˏretɚ] *n.*【物】仿星器〔一种等离子体实验装置〕。

stel·lat·e(d) [ˈsteleit(id); ˋstɛlet(ɪd)] *a.* 像星的,星形的;放射线状的,星状辐射的。~ **diaphragm**【植】星形隔膜。~ *ornament* 星形装饰品。**-ly** *ad.*

stel·len·bosch [ˈstelənbɔʃ; ˋstɛlənbɑʃ] *vt.* 〔英军俚〕把(某人)调充闲职。

stel·lif·er·ous [ˈsteˌlifərəs; stɛˋlɪfərəs] *a.* 〔罕〕有星的,布满星的。

stel·li·form [ˈstelifɔːm; ˋstɛlɪ͵fɔrm] ***a***. 星形的。

stel·li·fy [ˈstelifai; ˋstɛlə͵faɪ] ***vt***. 使成星状,使成明星,把…列入明星群中。

Stel·lite [ˈstelait; ˋstɛlaɪt] ***n***. 司太立特硬质合金,钨铬钴合金。

stel·lu·lar, stel·lu·late [ˈsteljulə, -lit; ˋstɛljʊlɚ, -lɪt] ***a***. 小星形的;星点花样的。

St. Elmo's fire [sntˈelməuz; sntˋɛlmoz] (暴风雨时在桅顶上或教堂尖塔上常见的)放电辉光球〔亦作 St. Elmo's light〕。

STEM = Scanning transmission electron microscope 扫描透射式电子显微镜。

stem[1] [stem; stɛm] **I** ***n***. **1**. (草木的)茎,干,梗;叶柄,花梗,果柄。**2**. (工具的)柄;把,杆。**3**. 高酒杯的酒脚,菸斗柄;鸦片烟枪。**4**. 〔*pl*.〕〔美俚〕腿。**5**. (手表,怀表的)转柄。**6**. 【动】羽轴。**7**. 【语】词干。**8**. 【化】母体。**9**. 〔美俚〕主要大街,干道。**10**. 种族,血统,家系。**11**. 【船】艏柱;艏材;艏,船头。**12**. 【无】电子管心柱;电晶体管座。**13**. 【乐】符尾。*Don't eat the* ~ *of a mushroom*. 不要吃蘑菇的梗。*a terrestrial* [*an aerial*] ~ 【植】地上茎。*a subterranean* [*an underground*] ~ 【植】地下茎。***from*** ~ ***to stern*** **1**. 从船头到船尾,全船,全舰。**2**. 从头到尾,到处,全部。***give the*** ~ 撞击。~ ***for*** ~ 并排;靠拢。~ ***to*** ~ 船头对着船头。**II** ***vt***. (***-mm-***) **1**. 除掉…的梗茎。**2**. 给…装上柄、杆;给(假花等)装上梗柄。— ***vi***. 〔美〕起源于,起因于,(由…)发生,来自(*from*; *out of*)。*Correct decisions* ~ *from correct judgements*. 正确的决心来自于正确的判断。*Our hopes* ~ *from our previous achievements*. 我们的希望源于我们从前的成就。~ **cell** 【生】干细胞。~ **cup** 高脚杯。~**less** ***a***. 【植】无茎[柄、梗]的。~**let** 小茎,小干,小梗。~**like** ***a***. 茎[柄]状的。~**med** ***a***. **1**. 有茎[梗、柄]的。**2**. 去掉茎[梗、柄]的。~ **rot** (瓜等的)茎腐病;引起此病的真菌。~ **rut** (小麦等的)茎锈病;引起此病的真菌。~**son** 【船】副艏材,船头护木。~**ware** 高脚玻璃器皿,高脚杯。~-**winder** **1**. 〔美口〕有转柄或旋钮上发条的表。**2**. 〔俚〕第一流人物[东西]。**3**. 烟斗管。~-**winding** 〔表〕上弦,上发条。

stem[2] [stem; stɛm] **I** ***vt***. (***-mm-***) **1**. (船)逆(风)开行。**2**. 抵抗,反抗,逆(流)而行,顶着水面上。**3**. 闸住,堵住(水等);遏止,防止,压住,**4**. 【滑雪】转动(滑雪屐)以停止滑雪。— ***vi***. **1**. 堵住,止住。**2**. 逆行。**3**. 转动滑雪屐停止滑行。*Debris have* ~*med the current*. 破瓦片之类的东西堵住了水流。*This is the way to* ~ *the flow of the blood*. 这才是制止流血的方法。**II** ***n***. **1**. 堵塞物,坝。**2**. 闸住,堵住,止住。**3**. 转动滑雪屐停止滑动。

stem·ma [ˈstemə; ˋstɛmə] ***n***. (*pl*. ***-mata*** [-mətə; -mətə]) **1**. 世系,家谱。**2**. 【动】(昆虫的)侧单眼,小眼面〔属复眼的一部分〕。

stem·med [stemd; stɛmd] ***a***. 〔常用以构成复合词〕**1**. 有茎[梗]的;装有小柄的。**2**. 去掉茎(或梗)的。*blue-*~ *grass* 蓝色茎的草。

stem·mer [ˈstemə; ˋstɛmɚ] ***n***. **1**. 〔美〕剔除梗子的工人;(烟厂中)抽梗童工。**2**. 抽梗机。**3**. 【矿】炮棍,塞药棒;导火线留孔针。**4**. 〔俚〕在街头行乞的游民。

stem·ple [ˈstempl; ˋstɛmpl̩] ***n***. 【矿】**1**. (用作梯级的)井筒内横木。**2**. 巷道横梁。**3**. (不用柱腿的)嵌入梁。

sten [sten; stɛn] ***n***. 〔英〕轻机关枪(= sten gun)。

stench [stentʃ; stɛntʃ] **I** ***n***. 臭气,恶臭。*The* ~ *of the rotton fish is fearful*. 烂鱼的臭味太难闻了。**II** ***vt***., ***vi***. (使)发恶臭。-**ful** ***a***. 充满恶臭的。-**y** ***a***. 恶臭的。

sten·cil [ˈstensl, -sil; ˋstɛnsəl, -sl] **I** ***n***. **1**. (镂花)模板,型板,漏(字)板。**2**. (油印)蜡纸。**3**. 刷印上的文字[符号等]。**II** ***vt***. (〔英〕***-ll-***)用模板[蜡纸]刷印。*My job is to cut* ~*s and sort up mails*. 我的工作是刻蜡板和把来信分类。~ **paper** 钢板蜡纸。~ **pen** (刻蜡纸的)铁笔。~-**plate** 模板,型板。-(**l**)**er** ***n***. 刻模板者,刻蜡纸者。

steno- *comb*. *f*. 小,少,薄,狭:*steno*graphy.

steno [ˈstenəu; ˋstɛno] ***n***. 〔美口〕= stenographer, stenography.

sten·o·bath [ˈstenə͵bæθ; ˋstɛnə͵bæθ] ***n***. 【生】狭窄水带生物。-**ic** ***a***.

sten·o·chro·my [steˈnɔkrəmi; ˋstɛnə͵kromɪ] ***n***. 一次印成的彩色印刷术。

sten·o·graph [ˈstenəgrɑːf; ˋstɛnə͵græf, -͵grɑf] **I** ***n***. 速记文字〔用速记法写成的文件〕;速记机。**II** ***vt***. 用速记法记录。-**er**, -**ist** ***n***. 速记员。-**y** ***n***. 速记法;用速记法写成的文件。

sten·o·graph·ic, -i·cal [͵stenəˈgræfik, -ikəl; ͵stɛnəˋgræfɪk, -ɪkəl] ***a***. 速记(术)的。-**cal·ly** ***ad***.

sten·o·ha·line [͵stenəˈheilain, -ˈhælain; ͵stɛnəˋhelaɪn, -ˋhælaɪn] ***a***. 【生】狭盐性的;固定盐度生物的。

sten·o·hy·gric [͵stenəˈhaigrik; ͵stɛnəˋhaɪgrɪk] ***a***. 【生】狭湿性的。

ste·no·ky [stəˈnəuki; stəˋnokɪ] ***n***. 【生】狭栖性。-**no·kous** [-kəs; -kəs] ***a***.

ste·noph·a·gous [stəˈnɔfəgəs; stəˋnɑfəgəs] ***a***. 【生】狭食性的。

ste·nosed [stəˈnəust, -ˈnəuzd; stɪˋnost, -ˋnozd] ***a***. 患(器官)狭窄症的。

ste·no·sis [stiˈnəusis; stɪˋnosɪs] ***n***. 【医】(器官)狭窄。-**not·ic** [-ˈnɔtik; -ˋnɑtɪk] ***a***.

sten·o·therm [ˈstənə͵θəːm; ˋstɛnə͵θɚm] ***n***. 【生】狭温性生物。-**al**, -**ous**, -**ic** ***a***.

sten·o·top·ic [͵stenəˈtɔpik; ͵stɛnəˋtrɑpɪk] ***a***. 【生态】窄幅分布的。

sten·o·type [ˈstenətaip; ˋstɛnə͵taɪp] **I** ***n***. **1**. 〔S-〕速记打字机〔商品名〕。**2**. (速记打字机用的)速记符号。**II** ***vt***. 用速记机记录。-**typ·ic** ***a***.

sten·o·typ·y [ˈstenə͵taipi; ˋstɛnə͵taɪpɪ] ***n***. 速记打字。-**typ·ist** ***n***.

stent [stent; stɛnt] ***n***. 【医】(人工植入患者动脉中使其血液流动不致于阻塞的)支撑管。

Sten·tor [ˈstentɔː; ˋstɛntɔr] ***n***. **1**. (荷马叙事诗 *Iliad* 中)声音宏亮的传音使者。**2**. 〔s-〕声音宏亮的人。**3**. 〔s-〕【动】喇叭虫。**4**. 〔s-〕【动】吼猿。

sten·to·ri·an [stenˈtɔːriən; stɛnˋtorɪən, -ˋtɔr-] ***a***. 声音极宏亮的。

sten·to·ro·pho·nic [͵stentərəˈfɔnik; ͵stɛntərəˋfɑnɪk] ***a***. 声音宏亮的。

step [step; stɛp] **I** ***vi***. (***-pp-***) **1**. 走;跨步。**2**. 踩,踏上(*on*)。**3**. 跳舞,轻快地走,合着步调走。**4**. 跨入,踏进。**5**. 走上。— ***vt***. **1**. 跨,踏,踏入;走(…步)。**2**. (用脚)步测(量)(*out*)。**3**. 跳舞。**4**. 使成梯阶,使成梯级状。**5**. 【海】(将桅杆)竖立在桅座上。*S- this way*. 请打这边走。*Will you* ~ *inside*? 请进来。~ *on sb.'s toe* 踩着某人脚趾。~ ***across*** 走过,横穿过。~ **aside** **1**. 走到一旁。**2**. 避到一旁;让给别人,让步。**3**. 走错路;走入邪道(" *Step aside!* " *barked the policeman*. "躲开点!"警察大声喊着说)。~ ***back*** **1**. 后退,后退一步。**2**. 回想,回顾(*Henry remained silent*, *stepping back into the first time he met her*. 亨利继续沉默着,回想他第一次和她相会的时候)。~ ***down*** **1**. 走下,下(车)。**2**. 辞退。**3**. 退出。**4**. 【电】下降(*I'm old enough to* ~ *down from the office*. 我年纪够老该退休了。*a* ~ *down transformer* 【电】降压变压器)。~ ***forth*** = ~ forward 前进;奋起。~ ***high*** (马)飞跑。~ ***in*** **1**. 走进。**2**. 〔命令〕请进。**3**. 调停,排解;介入,干涉;挤进。~ ***into an estate*** 得到财产。~ ***into sb.'s shoes*** 接替某人,接任某人的位置。~ ***it*** **1**. 跳舞。**2**. 走着去。**3**. 〔口〕赶快。~ ***it with*** 和…齐步。~ ***lively*** 急,赶快。~ ***long*** 大踏步走。~ ***off*** 失策;〔俚〕结婚;〔俚〕死。~ ***on it*** 〔口〕赶快。~ ***on the gas*** 〔美〕加快(汽车)马力;〔口〕赶快。~ ***out***

S

1. 走出屋外。2. 下(车)。3. 放大脚步。4. 辞职。5. 用脚步测量。6. 〔美口〕去跳舞[玩耍、游荡]。*What I'd do is ~ out for a moment.* 我想出去溜一溜。~ **out of line** 采取独立行动。~ **outside** 走出,走到外面。~ **over** 横越,跨过。~ **short** 【军】缩小脚步走。~ **up** 走上去;〔美〕促进,加紧;插嘴;提高;【电】升高(电压)(*a ~ up transformer* 升压变压器)。~ **up to** 接近,走近(*~ up to a girl* 追求,求婚。*~ up to town* 上城里去)。~ **upstairs** 上楼去。~ **well together** (舞伴)跳得[(马)走得]合拍。

II *n*. 1. (脚)步。2. 梯级,阶磴儿,台阶踏板。3. 阶层,等级,升级;〔*pl*.〕梯子,楼梯。4. 一步;步调,步伐;发展,阶段。5. 脚声;足迹。6. 走路样子,步态。7. 步骤,手段,措施,办法。8. 舞步;〔口〕跳舞。9. 【船】桅座。10. 【机】轴瓦;级,档。11. 【乐】音级;度。*He ran down the ~s.* 他跑下楼梯来。*Watch your ~s.* 小心走路,留神脚底下。*The director will approve such ~s.* 处长会同意这些措施的。*We've made a big ~ forward in our studies.* 我们在学习中前进了一大步。*Your paper marks a forward ~ in the research.* 你的报告标志着研究工作的向前发展。*Take such ~s as you think best.* 按你认为最好的步骤办吧。*the last [final] ~* (多级火箭的)最末一级。*a ~ in the social scale* 社会阶层中的一个阶层。**break ~** 【军】走乱脚步,用平常脚步。**fall in ~** 顺着(…的)步调走。**get one's ~** 升级。**give sb. a ~** 给(某人)升一级。**in sb.'s ~s** 步人后尘。**in ~** 齐步。**keep ~** 整齐调步(*with*)。**make a great ~ forward in** 在…上有了很大进步[发展]。**make a ~ forward [backward]** 前进[后退]一步。**miss one's ~** 失足。**out of ~** 错了步伐,弄乱步调,不按(…的)步调走。**pick one's ~s** 一步一步小心走,步步留心。**retrace one's ~s** 走回头路,改变主意,变挂。**rise a ~ in sb.'s opinion [estimation]** 在某人的心目中升高了一步。**~ by ~** 一步一步;切切实实。**~ for ~** 用同样步调,并驾齐驱地。**take a bold ~** 采取断然处置。**take a rash ~** 躁急做错,弄错,失策。**take ~s** 设法,采取措施(*You must take ~s to prevent it.* 你得设法防止它)。**tread in the ~s of** 仿效,跟…的脚步走。**turn one's ~s to [towards]** 转向…走去;改变方向而从事…。**Watch one's ~s!** 小心走路,留心脚底下;小心行动。~ **bearing** 【机】立式止推轴承。~ **block** 【机】级形垫铁。**~-by-~** *a*. 逐步的,逐渐的。~ **cone** 【机】级轮,宝塔轮。~ **dance** 踢跶舞。**~-down** *a*. 减缓的,下降的(*~-down transformer* 降压变压器)。**~-family** 有后父[后母]之家庭。~ **function** 【数】阶梯函数。**~-in** 1. *a*. (鞋)一伸脚就穿好的;(衣)一套就穿上身的。2. *n*. 船鞋;上述女衣,女内衣。**~ladder** 梯子。~ **motor** 步进电动机。**~-out** 【无】失调,失步。**S- Pyramid** (斜面呈梯级状的早期)梯级金字塔〔晚期的斜面多为平面〕。~ **rocket** 多级火箭。**~stone** (大门口的)阶台石,石阶。~ **stool** 梯凳〔可兼作小梯用〕。~ **training** 踢跶跳舞健身操。~ **turn** 【滑雪】侧向换步。**~-up** 1. *a*. 加速的;增强的;促进的,上升的;【电】增加电压的。2. *n*. 逐渐增加。

step·broth·er [ˈstepbrʌðə; ˋstɛp͵brʌðɚ] *n*. 异父兄弟,异母兄弟。

step·child [ˈsteptʃaild; ˋstɛp͵tʃaɪld] *n*. 夫[妻]和前妻[前夫]所生的子女。

step·dame [ˈstepdeim; ˋstɛp͵dem] *n*. 〔古〕继母,后娘。

step·daugh·ter [ˈstepˌdɔːtə; ˋstɛp͵dɔtɚ] *n*. 夫[妻]和前妻[前夫]所生的女儿,继女。

step·fa·ther [ˈstepˌfɑːðə; ˋstɛp͵fɑðɚ] *n*. 继父,后夫。

step·fa·ther·land [ˈstepˌfɑːðəlænd; ˋstɛp͵fɑðɚlænd] *n*. 〔美〕归化国。

steph·a·no·tis [ˌstefəˈnəutis; ͵stɛfəˋnotɪs] *n*. 1. 【植】千金子藤花;千金子藤香。2. 〔S-〕千金子藤属。

Ste·phen, Ste·phan [ˈstiːvn; ˋstivən] *n*. 斯蒂芬〔男子名〕。

Ste·phens [ˈstiːvnz; ˋstivənz] *n*. 斯蒂芬斯〔姓氏〕。

Ste·phen·son [ˈstiːvnsn; ˋstivənsən] *n*. 1. 斯蒂芬森〔姓氏〕。2. **George ~** 史蒂芬生〔1781—1848,英国发明家,蒸汽机的发明人〕。

step·moth·er [ˈstepˌmʌðə; ˋstɛp͵mʌðɚ] *n*. 继母,后母,后娘。

step·ney [ˈstepni; ˋstɛpnɪ] *n*. 〔常 S-〕〔英〕(汽车的)备用轮胎〔又叫 ~-wheel〕。

step·par·ent [ˈstepˌpɛərənt; ˋstɛp͵pɛrənt] *n*. 继父母。

steppe [step; stɛp] *n*. 1. 干草原。2. 〔the Steppes〕(尤指东南欧或西伯利亚的)草原地带。

step·per [ˈstepə; ˋstɛpɚ] *n*. 1. 步态好的人[马]。2. 〔美俚〕舞跳得好的人。3. 时间全花在社交上的大学生;【运】跑者。

step·ping-stone [ˈstepiŋstəun; ˋstɛpɪŋ͵ston] *n*. 1. (跨越浅河)供踏脚的石头。2. 上马石;垫脚石。3. 进身的阶梯;(达到目的的)手段,方法。4. 中途歇脚处。**stand on ~s** 小心翼翼地遵照常规行事,拘泥细节。

step·sis·ter [ˈstepˌsistə; ˋstɛp͵sɪstɚ] *n*. 异父[母]姊妹。

step·son [ˈstepsʌn; ˋstɛp͵sʌn] *n*. 继子;妻[夫]和前夫[前妻]所生的儿子。

step·wise [ˈstepwaiz; ˋstɛp͵waɪz] **I** *a*. 1. 逐步的,逐渐的,分段的。2. 【音】转换音级的。**II** *ad*. 按阶段地,逐步地。

ster. = stereotype; sterling.

-ster *suf*. 1. 做…的人。2. 与…有关系的人。3. 某种样子的人〔常含轻蔑意〕。trick*ster*, gang*ster*, young*ster*.

ste·ra·di·an, ste·rad [stiˈreidiən, ˈsteræd; stɪˋredɪən, ˋstɛræd] *n*. 【物】球面度〔立体角单位〕。

ster·co·ra·ceous [ˌstəːkəˈreiʃəs; ͵stɚkəˋreʃəs] *a*. 含粪的;粪状的;有粪质的。

ster·co·ric·o·lous [ˌstəːkəˈrikələs; ͵stɚkəˋrɪkələs] *a*. 【生】粪栖的〔如某些昆虫〕。

ster·cu·li·a [stəːˈkjuːliə; stɚˋkjulɪə] *a*. 【植】梧桐科(*Sterculiaceae*)的〔包括可可,柯拉树〕。

stere [stiə; stɪr] *n*. 立方米(m^3)。

stere- *comb. f*. 〔用于辅音前〕= sterco-.

ster·e·o [ˈstiəriəu; ˋstɛrɪo, ˋstɪrɪo] *n*., *a* 〔口〕1. = stereotype. 2. = stereoscopic. ~ *camera* 立体摄影机。3. 旧闻。4. 立体声系统[装置];立体声。

ster·e·o- *comb. f*. 1. 立体的。2. 实体的,坚固的,实心的: *stereo*chrome.

ster·e·o·bate [ˈsteriəˌbeit, ˈstiər-; ˋstɛrɪə͵bet] *n*. 【建】无柱底基。

ster·e·o·chem·is·try [ˌstiəriəˈkemistri; ͵stɛrɪəˋkɛmɪstrɪ] *n*. 【化】立体化学。

ster·e·o·chrome [ˈstiəriəˌkrəum, ˈsteriə-; ˋstɪrɪə͵krom, ˋstɛrɪə-] *n*. 【绘画】固色壁画。

ster·e·o·chro·my [ˈstiəriəkrəumi; ˋstɪrɪəkromɪ] *n*. 【绘画】固色壁画法。**-chro·mic** *a*.

ster·e·o·gram [ˈstiəriəˌgræm; ˋstɛrɪə͵græm, ˋstɪr-] *n*. 1. 立体图,体视图,极射(赤面投影)图。2. = stereograph.

ster·e·o·graph [ˈstiəriəgrɑːf, -græf, ˈstiər-; ˋstɛrɪə͵græf, -͵grɑf, ˋstɪr-] **I** *n*. 实体画,立体照片;体视照片。**II** *vt*. 1. 把…摄制成立体照片[体视照片]。2. 准备(照片)供体视。3. 把…印成盲文。

ster·e·o·graph·ic, -i·cal [stiəriəuˈgræfik(əl); stɛrɪoˋgræfɪk(əl)] *a*. 立体[实体]画法的;立体[体视]摄影术的。*a ~ projection* 平射投影。**-cal·ly** *ad*.

ster·e·og·ra·phy [stiəriˈɔgrəfi; ͵stɛrɪˋɑgrəfɪ, ͵stɪrɪ-] *n*. 立体画法;立体[体视]摄影(术)。

ster·e·o·i·so·mer [ˌstiəriəuˈaisəmə; ͵stɛrɪoˋaɪsəmɚ, ͵stɪr-] *n*. 【化】立体异构物。**-ic** [-ˈmerik; -ˋmɛrɪk] *a*. **-ism** *n*.

ster·e·o·lo·gy [stiəriˈɔlədʒi; stɛrɪˋɑlədʒɪ] *n*. 体视学,立体测量学。

ster·e·om·e·ter [stiəri'ɔmitə;ˏstɛrɪˋɑmətɚ] ***n***. 体积计；比重计。

ster·e·o·met·ric [ˌstiəriə'metrik;ˏstɛrɪəˋmɛtrɪk] ***a***. 测体积术的（= stereometrical）。

ster·e·om·e·try [ˌstiəri'ɔmitri;ˏstɛrɪˋɑmətrɪ, ˏstɪrɪ-] ***n***. 测（体）积术，立体几何；比重测定法。

stereo·microscope [ˌstiəriəu'maikrəskəup;ˏstɛrɪoˋmaɪkrəˏskop] ***n***. 体视显微镜。

ster·e·o·phone [stiərə'fəun; stɛrəˋfon] ***n***. 立体声耳机。

ster·e·o·phon·ic [ˌstiəriəu'fɔnik;ˏstɛrɪəˋfɑnɪk] ***a***. 立体声的。～ *record* 立体声唱片。**-cal·ly** ***ad***. **-oph·o·ny** ***n***.

ster·e·o·pho·to·gram·me·try [ˌstiəriəuˌfəutə'græmitri;ˏstɛrɪoˏfotəˋgræmətrɪ] ***n***. 立体摄影测量（术）。

ster·e·o·pho·tog·ra·phy [ˌstiəriəufə'tɔgrəfi;ˏstɛrɪofəˋtɑgrəfɪ, ˏstɪr-] ***n***. 立体摄影术；体视照相摄影术。

ster·e·o·pro·jec·tion [ˌstiəriəuprə'dʒekʃən;ˏstɛrɪoprəˋdʒɛkʃən] ***n***. （投射双像以取体视效应的）立体投影。

ster·e·op·sis [ˌstiəri'ɔpsis;ˏstɛrɪˋɑpsɪs] ***n***. 立体视觉。

ster·e·op·ti·con [stiəri'ɔptikən;ˏstɛrɪˋɑptɪkən, ˏstɪrɪ-] ***n***. **1.** （画面可以淡入淡出而叠现的）立体感幻灯机。**2.** 立体感投影仪。

ster·e·op·tics [ˌstiəri'ɔptiks;ˏstɛrɪˋɑptɪks] ***n***. 〔可用作 *pl*., *sing*.〕立体摄影光学，体视光学。

ster·e·o·scope ['steriəskəup; ˋstɛrɪəˏskop, ˋstɪrɪ-] ***n***. 实体镜，体视镜；立体照相机。**-scop·ic** [-'skɔpik; -ˋskɑpɪk]，**-i·cal** ***a***. **-i·cal·ly** ***ad***.

ster·e·os·co·py [ˌstiəri'ɔskəpi;ˏstɛrɪˋɑskəpɪ, ˏstɪrɪ-] ***n***. **1.** 体视学；体视术，体视法。**2.** 体视。

ster·e·o·sonic [stiəriəu'sɔnik;ˏstɛrɪəˋsɑnɪk, ˏstɪrɪ-] ***a***. 立体声的。

ster·e·o·tax·is [ˌstiəriə'tæksis;ˏstɛrɪəˋtæksɪs] ***n***. 【生】向实体运动。**-tac·tic** [-'tæktik; -ˋtæktɪk] ***a***.

ster·e·o·tape [stiərə'teip; stɛrəˋtep] ***n***. 立体声磁带。

ster·e·o·tel·e·vi·sion [ˌstiəriəu'teliviʒən;ˏstɛrɪoˋtɛləvɪʒən] ***n***. 立体电视。

ster·e·ot·o·my [ˌstiəri'ɔtəmi;ˏstɛrɪˋɑtəmɪ, ˏstɪr-] ***n***. 分体学[术]；切体学[术]〔尤指石头切割术〕。

ster·e·ot·ro·pism [ˌstiəri'ɔtrəpizm;ˏstɛrɪˋɑtrəpɪzm, ˏstɪr-] ***n***. 【生】向实体趋性。**-trop·ic** [-'trɔpik; -ˋtrɑpɪk] ***a***.

ster·e·o·type ['stiəriəutaip; ˋstɛrɪəˏtaɪp, ˋstɪrɪə-] **I** ***n***. **1.** 【印】铅版；铅版制版法，铅板印刷。**2.** 旧框框；陈规老套，旧习，成规，定型。～*-metal*（铸铅字用的）铅。**II** ***a***. **1.** 铅板（印刷）的。**2.** 固定不变的，定型的；陈规旧套的。**III** ***vt***. **1.** 把…浇成铅板。**2.** 用铅版印刷；使固定。**3.** 使符合成规旧习，使僵化。*The practice has been ～d into a tradition*. 这种作法已经定型成了个传统了。**-typed** ***a***. **1.** 浇成铅板的。**2.** 用铅板印刷的。**3.** 固定不变的，陈规旧习的，僵化的（～*d ways of doing business* 陈规旧习的办事方法）。**-typ·ist** ***n***. 盲文版印刷工人。

ster·e·o·typ·er ['stiərəutaipə; ˋstɛrəˏtaɪpɚ] ***n***. **1.** 铸版工（= stereotypist）。**2.** 盲文版印刷机。

ster·e·o·typ·ic [ˌstiəriə'tipik, ˌsteriə-;ˏstɛrɪəˋtɪpɪk, stɪrɪə-] ***a***. **1.** 铅版的；铅板制的。**2.** 浇成铅版的；用铅版印刷的（= stereotypical）。

ster·e·o·typ·y ['stiəriəˌtaipi; ˋstɛrɪəˏtaɪpɪ, ˋstɪrɪ-] ***n***. **1.** 铅版印刷，铅版浇铸术，铅版浇铸。**2.** 【医】定型；刻版症；反常性重复〔如动作，语词等〕，痴呆〔常见于精神分裂症患者〕。

ster·ic ['stiərik, 'sterik; ˋstɛrɪk, ˋstɪrɪk] ***a***. 【化】（原子的）空间（排列）的；位的。～ **hindrance**【化】位阻现象。**-cal·ly** ***ad***.

ster·i·lant ['sterilənt; ˋstɛrələnt] ***n***. 杀菌剂[物]，消毒剂。

ster·ile ['sterail; ˋstɛrəl] ***a***. **1.** 不毛的，不肥沃的，收成不好的。**2.** 【动】无生殖力的，不育的（*of*）。**3.** 【植】不结果实的，中性的；不发芽的。**4.** 没有思想的，枯燥无味的；缺乏独创性的（诗文等）。**5.** 无结果的；无益的，无效果的（交涉等）。**6.** 无菌的，消过毒的；〔美〕（政治上）经过安全审查的。*a ～ woman* 不生育的妇女。～ *soil* 贫瘠的土地[土壤]。*a ～ year* 凶年。～ *flowers* 中性花。*a ～ poem* 乏味的诗。～ *gloves* 消过毒的手套。～ *negotiations* 没有结果的谈判。**-ly** ***ad***.

ste·ril·i·ty [ste'riliti; stɛˋrɪlətɪ] ***n***. **1.** 不毛。**2.** 不育，不孕。**3.** 【植】中性，不稔性；秕粒；无菌（状态）。**4.** （思想）贫乏。**5.** 无效，无结果。

ster·i·li·za·tion [sterilai'zeiʃən; stɛrɪlaɪˋzeʃən] ***n***. **1.** 使不毛，使不肥沃。**2.** 绝育。**3.** 消毒，灭菌。

ster·i·lize ['sterilaiz; ˋstɛrəˏlaɪz] ***vt***. **1.** 使（土地）荒瘠。**2.** 使不孕，使绝种。**3.** 使不起作用，使无效果。**4.** 使（思想）贫乏，使（兴味）索然。**5.** 杀菌，消毒；〔美〕（政治上）对…进行安全审查。**6.** 封存（黄金）。**7.** 拆除（某一地区的）建筑物。*An incompetent teacher ～s the young mind*. 一个不称职的教员把青年人的思想弄得贫乏枯竭起来了。*The nurse is sterilizing the surgical instruments*. 护士在把外科手术器具消毒。～*d milk* 消毒牛奶。**-r** ***n***. 消毒器。

ster·let ['stəːlit; ˋstɝlɪt] ***n***. 【动】小体鲟（*Acipenser ruthenus*）〔产于里海〕。

Ster·ling ['stəːliŋ; ˋstɝlɪŋ] ***n***. 斯特林〔姓氏，男子名〕。

ster·ling ['stəːliŋ; ˋstɝlɪŋ] **I** ***n***. **1.** 英国货币。**2.** 标准纯银；〔集合词〕纯银制品。**II** ***a***. **1.** 英国货币的〔写在金额之后，通常略作 *s. or stg*.〕；英镑的。**2.** 用（纯度为92.5%的）标准纯银制成的；纯粹的，真正的。**3.** 有价值的（书等）；有权威的，信用过得去的，靠得住的（人等）。*five pounds ～* 英币五镑正〔略 *£5s*. 或 *£5stg*.〕。*a ～ article* 真品。～ *sense* 可靠的判断力。～ **area** [**bloc**] 英镑集团，用英镑做标准的地区。～ **balance** 英镑结存。～ **bonds** 英镑债券，英镑公债。～ **exchange** 对英汇兑，英汇。～ **shilling** 英国银币。

stern[1] [stəːn; stɝn] ***a***. **1.** 严格的，严厉的，严峻的，粗暴的，苛刻的。**2.** 坚定的（决心等）。*The school is very ～ in its discipline*. 学校在纪律方面很严格。*Our teacher is ～ to the students*. 我们的教师对学生是严厉的。*Only the ～ spirits of yours can overcome the difficulties*. 只有你们的坚强精神才能克服那些困难。*the ～er sex* 男性。**-ly** ***ad***. **-ness** ***n***.

stern[2] [stəːn; stɝn] ***n***. **1.** 船尾，艉。**2.** 臀部。**3.** （狗等的）尾巴；【徽】狼尾。**4.** （任何东西的）尾部，后部。*S- all!* = *S- hard!*【海】向后。***down by the ～*** 后部吃水比前部深的。***from stem to ～*** 船内到处，全船。***sit at the ～ of the state*** 执政。～ ***foremost*** 船尾朝前，倒退；笨拙地。～ ***on*** 船尾向前地。～ **board** 船的后退。～ **chase** 跟着船尾追击。～ **chaser**【海】舰尾炮；（船赛等的）末艇。～**fast** (**line**) 艉缆。～**foremost** ***ad***. = ～ foremost. ～**most** ***a***. 在船尾最后部的。～**post** 船尾柱。～ **sheets** [*pl*.] 小艇尾台。～**son**【船】艉曲材[肘板]〔也作 ～son knee, ～ knee〕。～**ward(s)** ***a***., ***ad***. 向船尾（的）；在船尾（的）。～**way** 船的后退，倒驶。～**-wheel·er** 船尾外轮船。

ster·nal ['stəːnl; ˋstɝnl] ***a***. 【解】胸骨的；胸骨部位的；近胸骨的；（近）腹甲的；（近）腹板的。

Sterne [stəːn; stɝn] ***n***. 斯特恩〔姓氏〕。

stern(o)- *comb. f*. 胸，胸骨，胸骨和（…）：*sterno*costal.

ster·no·cos·tal [ˌstəːnə'kɔstəl;ˏstɝnoˋkɑstl̩] ***a***. 胸骨和肋骨的。

ster·num ['stəːnəm; ˋstɝnəm] ***n***. （*pl*. **-na** [-nə; -nə]，～*s*）**1.** 【解】胸骨。**2.** 【动】（甲壳类的）腹甲，胸板，（棘皮动物，昆虫的）腹板。

ster·nu·ta·tion [stəːnju'teiʃən;ˏstɝnjuˋteʃən] ***n***. 喷嚏，打喷嚏。

ster·nu·ta·tive [stə'njuːtətiv; stɚˋnjutətɪv]，**-tory** [-təri; -ˏtorɪ] **I** ***a***. （催）喷嚏的。**II** ***n***. 催嚏剂。～ *gas*

喷嚏(性)(毒)气。

ster·nu·ta·tor [ˈstəːnjuˌteitə; ˋstɝnju͵tetɚ] ***n*.** 催嚏剂,喷嚏性毒剂。

ster·nu·ta·to·ry [stəˈnjuːtətəri; stɚˋnjutə͵tɔrɪ, -͵torɪ] **I** ***a*.** 催嚏的,喷嚏的。**II** ***n*.** 催嚏剂,喷嚏剂,会引起喷嚏的物质。

ster·oid [ˈstiərɔid, ˈsterɔid; ˋstɛrɔɪd] ***n*.**【生化】甾类化合物,类固醇。**-al** ***a*.** **-ed** ***a*.** **1.**【医】用类固醇作为药物的;含类固醇的。**2.**【计】(电脑程序)经过修订和扩充的,经过强化的。

ster·tor [ˈstəːtə; ˋstɝtɚ] ***n*.**【医】鼾息;鼾声。

ster·to·rous [ˈstəːtərəs; ˋstɝtərəs] ***a*.** 打呼噜的,鼾声如雷的。**-ly** ***ad*.**

stet [stet; stɛt] [L.] **I** ***n*.**【印】不删,保留〔校对用语,略作 st.,在所删字句下打点线,我国用△表示〕。**II** ***vt*.**【印】不删,在(校样)上批上"不删"[保留]字样。

steth·o·scope [ˈsteθəskəup; ˋstɛθə͵skop] **I** ***n*.**【医】听诊器,听筒。**II** ***vt*.** 用听诊器诊察。

steth·o·scop·ic, steth·o·scop·i·cal [ˌsteθəˈskɔpik, -ˈskɔpikl; ͵stɛθəˋskɑpɪk, -ˋskɑpɪkl] ***a*.**【医】听诊(器)的,听筒的;根据听诊器的。**-cal·ly** ***ad*.**

steth·os·co·py [steˈθɔskəpi; stɛˋθɑskəpɪ] ***n*.**【医】听诊(术)。

Stetson [ˈstetsn; ˋstɛtsn] ***n*.** **1.** 斯特森〔商标名〕。**2.**〔常用 s-〕男帽〔尤指美国西部牧童毡帽〕。

Stet·tin [ˈstetin; ˋstɛtɪn] ***n*.** = Szczecin.

Stet·tinius [stəˈtinjəs; stəˋtɪnjəs] ***n*.** 斯特蒂纽斯〔姓氏〕。

Steve [stiːv; stiv] ***n*.** 史蒂夫〔男子名, Steven 的昵称〕。

stev·e·dore [ˈstiːvidɔː; ˋstivə͵dor, -͵dɔr] **I** ***n*.** 装货卸货工人,码头工人,搬运工人。**II** ***vt*.** 装[卸](货)。— ***vi*.** **1.** 装货,卸货。**2.** 当码头工人。**~'s *knot*** 装卸工人结。

Ste·ven [ˈstiːvn; ˋstivn] ***n*.** 史蒂文〔男子名〕。

Ste·vens [ˈstiːvnz; ˋstivənz] ***n*.** 史蒂文斯〔姓氏〕。

Ste·ven·son [ˈstiːvnsn; ˋstivənsn] ***n*.** 史蒂文森〔姓氏〕。

Ste·ven·son [ˈstiːvnsn; ˋstivənsn], **Robert Louis** 史蒂文森〔1850—1894,英国小说家〕。

Ste·ven·son·ian [ˈstiːvnˈsəunjən; ˋstivnˋsonjən] ***a*., *n*.** 史蒂文森的(研究者)。

stew[1] [stjuː; stju] **I** ***vt*.** **1.** 用文火慢慢煨炖。**2.**〔口〕使焦虑,使着急。— ***vi*.** **1.** 用文火煨烂,炖烂。**2.** 焦虑,着急。**3.** (关在房里)闷热得出汗;发昏;〔俚〕死用功,用苦功。*S- the pork with sugar.* 用糖炖猪肉。*The tea was ~ed.* 茶浸泡得过久变得太苦[太浓]。***let sb. ~ in his own juice [grease]*** 让某人自作自受。**~ *oneself into an illness*** 愁出病来,急出病来。**II** ***n*.** **1.** 炖煮的菜肴〔通常肉类和蔬菜混和在一起〕,混合物。**2.**〔口〕忧虑,着急。**3.**〔美俚〕酒鬼。**4.**〔美俚〕硝化甘油,炸油。**5.**【影】噪声。**6.**〔英俚〕死用功的人。**7.**〔美口〕(飞机上的)女[男]服务员,空姐[空哥](= steward)。*Would you like some beef ~?* 你想吃点炖牛肉吗? *Everybody went into a terrible ~ about it.* 每个人都为它着了一通大急。*Irish ~* 马铃薯洋葱炖羊肉。***in a (regular) ~*** 〔俚〕(因忧虑、愤怒等)心乱如麻,着急,急躁。**~bum**〔美〕醉鬼,酒徒。**~pan** = saucepan. **~pot** (有盖的)炖锅。

stew[2] [stjuː; stju] ***n*.** 〔英〕鱼塘,养鱼池;养蚝场。

stew[3] [stjuː; stju] ***n*.** 〔古〕**1.** 公共浴室,热浴室。**2.** 妓院;妓院区〔常作 the ~s〕。

stew·ard [ˈstjuəd; ˋstjuwɚd] ***n*.** (*fem*. **-ess** [-is; -ɪs]) **1.** 管事,管家。**2.** (学校等的)膳务员,财务管理员;(轮船、飞机、旅馆等的)服务员。**3.** (公会、团体赛马等的)干事,理事;(舞会等的)招待员。**4.**〔美〕车间[部门,工厂]的工会代表。*the Lord High Steward (of England)* (英国)加冕礼事务大臣;(审判贵族法庭的)审判长。*the Lord Steward of the Household*〔英〕皇室内务大臣。**-ess** ***n*.** 女服务员。**-ship** ***n*.** steward 的职位;管理,经营,处理。

Stew·art [ˈstjuət; ˋstjuɚt, ˋstu-] ***n*.** **1.** 斯图尔特〔姓氏,男子名〕。**2. Dugald ~** 斯图尔特〔1753—1828,苏格兰哲学家〕。

stewed [stjuːd; stjud, stud] ***a*.** **1.** 用文火煨[炖]的。**2.**〔美俚〕喝醉了的。**3.** 焦急不安的(*up*)。**~ *to the gills*** 〔卑俚〕喝得烂醉的。

St. Ex(ch). = Stock Exchange 证券交易所。

stg. = sterling.

St. George's [sntˈdʒɔːdʒiz; sentˋdʒɔrdʒɪz] ***n*.** 圣乔治〔格林纳达首府〕。

St. George's Channel [sn*t*ˈdʒɔːdʒiz; sen*t*ˋdʒɔrdʒɪz] 圣佐治海峡〔威尔士和爱尔兰之间〕。

St. George Town [sntˈdʒɔːdʒitaun; sentˋdʒɔrdʒɪtaʊn] ***n*.** 圣乔治〔向风群岛首都〕。

sth. = something.

St. Helena [ˌsenthəˈliːnə; ˋsenthəˋlinə] 圣赫勒拿岛。

sthe·ni·a [sθiˈnaiə, ˈsθiːniə; sθɪˋnaɪə, ˋsθinɪə] ***n*.** **1.**【医】有力,强壮。**2.** (病态)亢进,(过度)兴奋。

sthen·ic [ˈsθenik; ˋsθɛnɪk] ***a*.** **1.**【医】有力的,强壮的(心脏等)。**2.** (病态的)亢进的,兴奋的。**3.** 矮而结实的。

stib·ine [ˈstibiːn, -in; ˋstɪbin, -ɪn] ***n*.** **1.**【化】锑化(三)氢。**2.** (…)胂。

stib·i·um [ˈstibiəm; ˋstɪbɪəm] ***n*.**【化】锑〔Sb〕。

stib·nite [ˈstibˌnait; ˋstɪbnaɪt] ***n*.**【矿】辉锑矿。

stich [stik; stɪk] ***n*.**【诗体学】诗行,一首诗。

stich·o·myth·i·a, sti·chom·y·thy [ˌstikəˈmiθiə, -ˈkɔmθi; ͵stɪkəˋmɪθɪə, -ˋkɑmθɪ] ***n*.** 简短轮流对白〔古希腊戏剧中的一种对白〕。**-myth·ic** ***a*.**

stick[1] [stik; stɪk] **I** ***n*.** **1.** 棒,棍;手杖,棒状物。**2.** 枝条,枯枝;柴。**3.** (蔬菜,草木植物的)茎,梗。**4.** 条状物(如炭条等)。**5.**【空】手柄,驾驶杆,操纵杆;(汽车等的)变速杆,换挡杆。**6.** 向同一目标连续投下的炸弹;一批连续投下的伞兵。**7.**【印】排字架,排字盘。**8.**【乐】指挥棒。**9.**〔the ~〕鞭打;刺戳。**10.** 搀在饮料中的酒。**11.**〔口〕呆子,呆头呆脑的人;蹩脚演员。**12.**【船】桅杆;桁。**13.** 一根木料。**14.**〔*pl*.〕一件家具,建筑物的一部分。**15.**【虫】= ~-insect. **16.**〔the ~s〕〔美口〕林地,边远的山区,郊区。**17.**〔美俚〕大麻烟卷。*Father left his hat and ~ in the hall.* 爸爸把帽子和手杖放在过厅里了。*a short ~* 短码尺〔1 码 = 35½英寸〕。*a dip ~* 量油尺。*a ~ of candy* 一根糖棒。*the ~ of celery* 水芹的梗。*a joy ~*【火箭】驾驶杆,远距离操纵杆。*He wants the ~.* 他该打。*He is a regular ~.*【剧】他是一个十足的木头人。*~ of bombs*〔英〕在轰炸目标上投下的一连串炸弹。*a few ~s of furniture* 几件家具。*big ~ (policy)*〔美政〕大棒政策,实力政策。***all on one ~*** 〔美,俚〕都在一起。***at the ~'s end*** 离开一点儿。***be on the ~*** 〔美俚〕警惕的,效率高的。***beat sb. all to ~s*** 〔美俚〕大败,使惨败。***carry the ~*** 〔美〕变成街头流浪者;彷徨。***cut one's ~*** 〔俚〕逃走。***get [have] hold of the wrong end of the ~*** 误解,弄错。***give sb. the ~*** 鞭打某人。***go to ~s and staves*** (捆好的东西等)散开,瓦解,碎掉,变糟,毁掉。***hold (a) ~(s) with (to)*** 和…旗鼓相当地竞争,和…光明正大的竞争。***hop the ~*** 突然离去,死去。***in a cleft ~*** 进退两难,为难。***lean on a ~*** 拄着拐杖。**~ *and stone*** 全部,一切都。**~ *back [forward]*** 【空】驾驶杆拉后[推前]。

II ***vt*.** **1.** (用木棍)撑持(植物等)。**2.**【印】把(铅字)排在排字盘里。**3.** 刺,戳,刺死。**4.** 钉住,插牢,放置。**5.** 伸出。**6.** 迫使偿付(*up*),抢劫。— ***vi*.** 伸出。*S- the needle into the cloth, Jane.* 珍妮,把针插在布上。*Please ~ the book back on the shelf.* 请把书放回架上。*S- out your tongue.* 伸出你的舌头来。**~ball** 棍球〔儿童在街头玩的类似棒球的球戏〕。**~ force**【机】杆力。**~ful**【印】一排字盘(排字量)。**~ grenade** 木柄手榴弹。**~ insect** 竹节虫。**~ler** **1.** 固执己见的人。**2.** 难题。**~man** **1.** (曲棍球的)击球手。**2.**〔美俚〕(赌物中手执小棒)管骰子摊的人。**~pin** 领带别针。**~seed**〔美〕【植】鹤

虱(属)植物。~ **shift**〔美〕手扳变速器。~ **tight**〔美〕【植】1. = bur marigold. 2. = stickseed. ~ **weed**〔美〕【植】北美各种倒刺毛果植物,如豚草,鹤虱。

stick[2][stik; stɪk] (***stuck***) **I** ***vi*.** 1. 粘,贴,粘住,粘着,固着,不分离。2. 坚持,坚守,忠实,不变心;不离开,留住不动。3. 卡住不动;困住,难住,为难;踌躇,犹豫。—***vt*.** 1. 粘住;贴;使固着;安置。2.〔俚〕忍耐,忍受。3.〔口〕困住,难住,使为难,使动弹不得,使进退两难,使停顿。*Stamps ~ together*. 邮票互相粘住了。*Better ~ to the programme*. 还是按照原程序较好。*Friends should ~ together*. 朋友要团结互助才好。*S- no bills!*〔英〕不许招贴!〔美国说 Post no bills!〕。*Don't forget to ~ a stamp on the envelope*. 不要忘记在信封上贴邮票。*The ship has been stuck here for three days by bad weather*. 由于天气恶劣船在此被阻已有三天。*James was stuck by the teacher's question in the oral exam*. 在口试中,詹姆斯被老师的提问难住了。*I simply can't ~ a whole summer in town*. 我决不能整个夏天老待在城市里。***be stuck on***〔美俚〕爱上,给迷住。~ ***a button***〔美〕使大学生加入联谊会。~ ***at a job*** 坚持做一件工作。~ ***at home*** 守在家里。~ ***at nothing*** 对什么事都毫不踌躇。~ ***by*** 忠于,拥护;留在手里,留在记忆里(*We must ~ by our friends*. 我们必须忠于我们的朋友)。~ ***down***〔口〕写下来;放下;(用浆糊)粘好(*S- down these idioms in your notebook*. 把这些习语记在你的笔记本上)。~ ***fast*** 牢记,粘牢;碰钉子,弄僵(*Your advice will ~ fast in my mind*. 你的意见会牢记在我心中的)。~ ***in*** 添注,加一笔。~ ***in one's craw***〔美俚〕令人不快;(食物)味道不好。~ ***in one's gizzard*** [***throat***] 难消化;难下咽;令人不能接受;令人难于容忍;令人讨厌。~ ***in the mud*** 陷入泥中;进退两难;顽固,保守(*The car is stuck in the mud*. 汽车陷在泥里了)。~ ***it on***〔俚〕乱要价,把账开高;夸大地讲。~ ***it*** 1.〔俚〕忍耐,忍受(*He could not ~ it any longer*. 他不能再忍耐了)。2.(在工作或事业上)站住了脚。~ ***on*** 贴在…上;(船)搁浅。~ ***out*** 坚持到底(*You've only a few pages to go. Stick it out*. 你还有几页书就看完了,坚持到底吧);〔俚〕忍耐,忍受。~ ***out a mile*** 明明白白,一目了然。~ ***out for*** 不停地要求,坚持要。~ ***to*** 粘住,不离,不变,坚持,不放,忠于(*We must ~ to the principle*. 我们必须坚持原则)。~ ***to it*** 忍耐。~ ***to nothing*** 对任何事都容易生厌,没有恒心。~ ***to one's colours*** [***guns***] 坚持(己见);不改变目的。~ ***to one's ribs***〔美俚〕吃饱。~ ***up*** 1. 突出,竖立(*hair ~ing up on end* 头发直竖着)。2.〔英俚〕使为难。~ ***up for*** 支持,拥护。~ ***up to*** 不输给,抵抗;〔方〕追求(~ *up to a girl* 追求一个少女)。~ ***with it***〔美〕忍耐。**II** ***n*.** 1. 发黏;卡住不动。2.(证券等的)滞销。~**-at-it** ***n*.**〔口〕坚定的人。~**-in-the-mud** ***a*., *n*.** 守旧的(人),迟钝的(人),慢手慢脚的(人)(*Mr.* [*Mrs.*] ~*-in-the-mud* 某某人[夫人]〔忘记姓名时用〕)。~**-jaw**〔俚〕(粘牙)太妃糖(等)。~**out** 1. ***n*.** 杰出人物[才能]。2. ***a*.** 出色的,显著的。~**-to-itiveness**〔美口〕***n*.** 顽固,坚持。~**-up** ***n*., *a*.** 竖领(的);〔美俚〕强盗,劫贼;抢劫(的)。~**up man**〔俚〕拦路抢劫的歹徒。

stick·a·bil·i·ty [ˌstikəˈbiliti; ˏstɪkəˋbɪlətɪ] ***n*.** 耐力;坚持力;忍受力。**-able** ***a*.**

stick·er [ˈstikə; ˋstɪkɚ] ***n*.** 1. 粘贴者;粘贴物;固执的人,坚持不懈的人;久坐不走的客人。2. 踌躇不决的人。3. 风琴内连接两条杠杆的木棍。4.〔美俚〕陈货。5. 刺戳的人,杀猪的人;杀猪用的尖刀。6.〔口〕难题,使人为难的东西。7. 滞销品。8.【板球】再三努力得分仍然不多的击球手。9.〔美〕邮票(等)。*Mother says she doesn't want any ~ in the house*. 妈妈说她家里不要久坐不走的客人。*Jones proved himself to be a ~ in the experiment*. 琼斯在实验中证明他是个坚持不懈的人。~ **shock** 高标价冲击波〔某项费用或价格之高昂令人瞠目结舌〕。

stick·i·ness [ˈstikinis; ˋstɪkɪnɪs] ***n*.** 黏结;黏胶,黏着性。

stick·ing [ˈstikiŋ; ˋstɪkɪŋ] ***a*.** 黏的,胶黏的。~ **place** 搭脚处;螺丝钉转得不能再转进去的地方;顶点(*screw one's courage to the ~ place* 鼓起浑身的勇气)。~ **plaster** 橡皮膏。

stick·le [ˈstikl; ˋstɪkl] ***vi*.** 1.(对于琐事的)争执;拘泥细节,固执己见。2. 犹豫,踌躇。~**back**【动】刺鱼,棘鱼,丝鱼。

stick·ler [ˈstiklə; ˋstɪklɚ] ***n*.** 1. 争执琐事的人,固执己见的人(*for*)。2. 难题,费解的事物。*a ~ for quaint ceremonies* 拘泥古怪仪式的人。

stick·um [ˈstikəm; ˋstɪkəm] ***n*.**〔美口〕黏性物质。

stick·up [ˈstikʌp; ˋstɪkˏʌp] ***n*.** 1. 竖起物(如立领等)。2. 抢劫。~ **artist** 手法巧妙的强盗。

stick·y [ˈstiki; ˋstɪkɪ] ***a*.** (***-i·er***; ***-i·est***) 1. 黏的,胶黏的,黏腻的,黏性的。2.〔口〕闷热的,湿气大的。3.〔口〕顽固的,(无多少道理地)固执的。4. 麻烦的,困难的,非常不愉快的,极痛苦的;过分多愁善感而令人生厌的。*He'll come to a ~ end*. 他会惹出麻烦来的。*a ~-beak*〔澳〕好管闲事的人。~ *fingers* 手脚不干净的人,小偷。*a ~ end*〔美〕不好的结果。***a ~ wicket***【板球】泥泞的三柱门;〔主英〕困境,尴尬的处境。~**-back** ***n*.**(背面涂有胶水的)小相片,小票据。~ **floor** 粘胶地板;〔喻〕低层低薪女员工等升迁无望的处境。**-i·ly** ***ad*.** **-i·ness** ***n*.**

stiff [stif; stɪf] **I** ***a*.** 1. 硬的,挺的。2.(手足等)僵直的,僵硬的;〔俚〕死而僵硬了的,死了的。3. 坚牢的,紧绷绷的,绷紧了的(索子)。4. 不灵便的,不易动的,黏牢了的(活塞);一动就痛的。5. 局促的,拘泥的,不自然的,不流畅的,生硬的;顽固的,执拗的,倔强的。6. 强烈的(酒);狂暴的,猛烈的(风等)。7. 费力的,困难的;严厉的(处罚)。8.(物价等)昂贵的;(需要)过高的,过多的;高昂的,极高的。9.【海】不易倾斜的(*opp*. crank)。10. 黏的,胶黏的,浓;稠。11.〔口语〕极不合理的,严厉的,不能答应的。12.〔英方〕结实的,健壮的。*a ~ collar* 硬领。*stand straight and ~* 直挺挺地站着不动。*bore a person ~ = scare a person ~* 吓得某人面孔发青。*a ~ bow* 不自然的鞠躬。*a ~ gale* 猛烈的风,狂风。*a ~'un* (=one) 劲敌〔老练的运动家等〕。*That's a bit ~*. 那太厉害了。*You stood ~ in a foolish argument yesterday*. 昨天你倔强地坚持着愚蠢的议论。*Why, they set ~ prices on the bikes*. 嗨,他们把脚踏[自行]车定了这般昂贵的价钱。*Take this, Tom. A ~ dose*. 喝下这个去,汤姆,一副疗效高的药。***carry*** [***have, keep***] ***a ~ upper lip*** 坚定不移,毅然不动。***have a ~ neck*** 脖子痛得不能转动。***keep a ~ face*** [***lip***] 板着严肃的面孔;毅然不动。***keep a ~ rein*** 紧紧拉住缰绳。***take a ~ line*** 采取强硬态度。**II** ***n*.**〔俚〕1. 死尸。2. 笨蛋,傻瓜;呆板人。3. 吝啬鬼;穷光蛋。4. 普通工人,流动工人。5.〔英〕钞票;私人签发的支票。**-ly** ***ad*.** **-ness** ***n*.**【物】劲度。

stiff·en [ˈstifn; ˋstɪfən] ***vt*.** 1. 使硬化,使挺,使僵硬。2. 加强。3. 使绷紧。4. 使猛烈。5. 使生硬呆板。6. 使浓厚。7. 使黏腻。— ***vi*.** 1. 变硬,变挺,变僵硬。2. 变强,加强。3. 变猛烈。4. 变顽固;变不自然,变生硬。5. 变黏,变稠,变浓厚。6.〔口〕(物价等)上涨,(市面)硬。7. 变得费劲。*Your job is to ~ linen with starch*. 你的工作是把亚麻台布浆洗硬了。*He threw the letter on the desk, ~ed with astonishment*. 他把信扔在书桌上,吃惊得紧张极了。~ *one's attitude* 把态度放强硬。*a ~ing plate* 加强(铁)板。*a ~ing order* (海关发给的)底货装载许可证。*Joints ~ with advancing years*. 人一上年纪,关节就变僵硬了。*Having talked with the commander, his resolution ~ed*. 和指挥官谈过一席话后,他的决心加强了。*The tug ~ed when we got into the mud*. 我们陷入泥里时,牵拉更费劲了。

S

stiff·en·er [ˈstifnə; ˋstɪfənɚ] *n*. **1**. 弄硬的人[物]。**2**. 硬化剂。**3**. 加固用衬料。**4**. 纸壳的衬心。**5**. 补药。**6**. 增强(勇气、决心等)的东西。**7**.【建、机】支肋。**8**.【物】加劲杆,加劲角钢。**9**.〔美俚〕打倒的一击。

stiff-necked [ˈstifˈnekt; ˋstɪfˋnɛkt] *a*. 顽固的,倔强的,傲慢的。

sti·fle[1] [ˈstaifl; ˋstaɪfl] *vt*. **1**. 使窒息,闷死。**2**. 镇压,阻止(反叛等)。**3**. 压灭(火等)。**4**. 藏匿,隐蔽,暗中了结(*up*)。**5**.〔美俚〕打垮。— *vi*. **1**. 憋闷;窒息(而死)。**2**. 受抑制。*I rushed out of the room because the oppressive air ~d me*. 我急忙地出了那个屋子,因为闷热的空气使我窒息起来。~ *sobs* [*yawn*] 压住[忍住]哭泣[呵欠]。~ *a rebellion* 镇压叛乱。

sti·fle[2] [ˈstaifl; ˋstaɪfl] *n*. (马、狗的)后腿膝关节(病)。

sti·fling [ˈstaifliŋ; ˋstaɪflɪŋ] *a*. 令人窒息的,气闷的;沉闷的。**-ly** *ad*.

stig·ma [ˈstigmə; ˋstɪgmə] *n*. (*pl*. *~ta* [-tə; -tə], *~s*) **1**. 耻辱,污名。**2**.〔古〕烙印。**3**.【植】柱头。**4**.【动】气孔,气门;翅痣;(卵的)眼点;点斑。**5**.【医】(病的)特征。小斑。**6**.【宗】圣疤。**7**. 记号,符号,标记〔例如本字典中的〔美〕〔口〕等〕。*No ~ rests on* [*attaches to*] *him*. 他清白无瑕。*Her behaviour will leave a ~ upon her family*. 她的行为会使她家声名有了污点。*He has removed the ~ of drug addictions*. 他已经洗去吸毒的污点了。

stig·mas·ter·ol [stigˈmæstəˌrɔːl, -ˌrəul; stɪgˋmæstə͵rol, -͵rɔl] *n*.【化】豆甾醇。

stig·mat·ic [stigˈmætik; stɪgˋmætɪk] *a*. **1**. 耻辱的,污辱的;丑恶的。**2**. 有烙印的;有记号的。**3**.【植】(有)柱头的。**4**.【动】(有)气孔的。**5**.【医】(有)小斑的。**6**.【宗】有圣疤的。

stig·ma·tism [ˈstigmətizm; ˋstɪgmətɪzm] *n*.【医】**1**. 有小斑。**2**.【医】正视,折光正常〔焦点集中,无散光现象〕。**3**.【物】(透镜)无散像现象。

stig·ma·tize [ˈstigmətaiz; ˋstɪgmə͵taɪz] *vt*. **1**. 给…加污名,把…诬蔑为(*as*)。**2**. 给…打上烙印,在…上作记号。**3**.【宗】使生圣疤;(以催眠术等)使生红斑。~ *sb*. *as a rogue* 诬蔑(某人)是无赖。

stig·ma·tose [ˈstigmətəus; ˋstɪgmətos] *a*.【动、植】= stigmatic.

stil·bene [ˈstilbiːn; ˋstɪlbin] *n*.【化】芪;反二苯代乙烯。

stil·bes·trol [stilˈbestrɔl; stɪlˋbɛstrol, -trɔl, -trɑl] *n*.【生化】已烯雌酚,乙芪酚。

stil·bite [ˈstilbait; ˋstɪlbaɪt] *n*.【地】辉沸石。

stile [stail; staɪl] *n*. **1**. (牧场围堤上专门供人进出的)梯磴。**2**. (日晷仪的)晷针。**3**. 横路栅栏,旋转栅门。**4**.【建】窗(边)挺,门(边)挺;竖框。

sti·let·to [stiˈletəu; stɪˋlɛto] **I** *n*. (*pl*. *~s*, *~es*) **1**. 短剑。**2**. (刺绣用的)针眼锥,打眼锥。**II** *vt*. 用短剑刺(死)。~ **heel** (女鞋的)细高跟。

still[1] [stil; stɪl] **I** *a*. **1**. 静止的,平静的,静寂的。**2**. 温柔的,低声的。**3**. 沉默寡言的。**4**. (酒等)不起泡的。**5**. 没有活力的,死气沉沉的。*S- waters run deep*. 流静水深;外表沉静者心里的东西[学识、计谋等]多。*He is ~ of his tongue*. 他沉默寡言。*All sounds are ~*. 万籁俱静。***as ~ as death*** 极安静的;死一般的寂静。***in ~ meditation*** 在沉思中。**II** *ad*. **1**. 还,仍,尚,现在还,至今还;但是还。**2**.〔与比较级连用〕更其,还要,益发。**3**.〔诗〕常,不断地。*I am tired*; (*but*) ~ *I will work*. 累是累了,但是还要工作。*Will you ~ be here when I return*? 我回来的时候你还在这儿吗? *Take the medicine when it is ~ hot*. 趁热把药喝下去。*He is tall enough, but his brother is ~ taller*. 他的个子够高了,可是他兄弟还要高。***~ and all*** (即使如此)仍然(*Even though you dislike us, ~ and all you should be polite*. 就算你不喜欢我们,你仍然应该对我们客气)。***~ less***〔否定〕何况,更不(*If you don't know, ~ less do I*. 你不知道,我更不知道了。*He is not a scholar, ~ less a poet*. 他不是一个学者,更不是一个诗人)。***~ more***〔肯定〕何况,更不用说(*It is difficult to understand his books, ~ more his lectures*. 他写的书很难懂,他的演讲更不用说了)。**III** *n*. **1**.〔诗〕静止,无声,寂静。**2**. 呆照,普通照片(登在报上或电视节目上的)(*opp*. movies)。**3**. 电视室布景;静物摄影照片;〔口〕静物画。**4**.〔美〕(用电话或口传报的)火灾警报〔又叫 ~ alarm〕。*in the ~ of night* 在深更半夜。**IV** *vt*., *vi*. (使)静止;(使)镇静,遏制(情欲等);止住;(使)安静下来。~ *one's appetite* 满足食欲。*This will ~ the pain of the wound*. 这个药可以止伤口疼。*The wind ~s down*. 风住了。**V** ***conj***. 但是,然而。*He is dull, ~ he tries hard*. 虽然笨,可是他很刻苦。**~birth** *n*. 死产。**~born** **1**. 死产的,死胎的,流产的。**2**. 丝毫不能吸引观众的。**~bugle**〔英〕海军军号,要求全体人员在二次号声前保持原地不动。**~fish** *vi*. 抛锚停船捕鱼。**~-hunt** 偷偷追捕猎物。**~-hunt** *vt*., *vi*. 偷袭,伏击。**~life**【美】**1**. (作描画对象的)静物。**2**. 静物画。**~ small voice** 心灵深处的呼声,良心的私语。**-ness** *n*.

still[2] [stil; stɪl] **I** *n*. **1**. 蒸馏器[室],蒸馏锅。**2**. 酿酒场。**II** *vt*.〔古〕烧(酒);蒸馏。~ **room**〔英〕(酒厂的)蒸馏室;酒库,酒窖。

stil·lage [ˈstilidʒ; ˋstɪlɪdʒ] *n*. **1**. 酿酒厂的放桶台。**2**. 釜馏物。

Still(e) [stil; stɪl] *n*. 斯蒂尔〔姓氏〕。

still·y [ˈstili; ˋstɪlɪ] **I** *a*.〔诗〕平静的,寂静的(夜等)。**II** *ad*. [ˈstilli; ˋstɪllɪ]〔罕〕寂静地,平静地。

stilt [stilt; stɪlt] *n*. **1**.〔常 *pl*.〕高跷;〔美〕腿,脚。**2**.【鸟】长脚鹬。**3**. (水上住宅的)桩柱。***on ~s*** **1**. 踩着高跷。**2**. 大言不惭地,骄傲地。**3**. 趾高气扬地,夸张做作。

stilt·ed, stilt·y [ˈstiltid, ˈstilti; ˋstɪltɪd, ˋstɪltɪ] *a*. **1**. 踩着高跷的。**2**. (文体等)夸张的,浮夸的。**3**. 呆板的,做作的,不自然的。*a ~ arch*【建】上心拱。*a ~ style* 夸张的文体。

Stil·ton [ˈstiltən; ˋstɪltən] *n*. (英国)斯蒂尔顿干酪。

Stil·well [ˈstilwel; ˋstɪlwel, -wəl] *n*. 史迪威〔姓氏〕。

Stim·son [ˈstimsn; ˋstɪmsn] *n*. 斯廷森〔姓氏〕。

stim·u·lant [ˈstimjulənt; ˋstɪmjələnt] **I** *a*. 激励[鼓励,鼓舞]…的,刺激(性)的,使兴奋的。**II** *n*. 刺激物,兴奋剂,酒。*take ~s* 服用兴奋剂;(尤指)喝酒。

stim·u·late [ˈstimjuleit; ˋstɪmjə͵let] *vt*. 激励,刺激,使兴奋,鼓励。— *vi*. **1**. 起刺激作用。**2**.〔口〕服兴奋剂,喝酒。*Your encouragement will ~ me to work more hard*. 你的鼓励会激发我进一步地努力。

stim·u·la·tion [ˌstimjuˈleiʃən; ͵stɪmjəˋleʃən] *n*. 刺激(作用),激励,鼓励;兴奋(作用)。

stim·u·la·tive [ˈstimjulətiv; ˋstɪmjə͵letɪv] **I** *a*. 刺激的;鼓励的,激励的,鼓舞的。**II** *n*. 刺激物,兴奋剂;促进因素。

stim·u·la·tor [ˈstimjuleitə; ˋstɪmjəletɚ] *n*. 鼓励者;刺激物。

stim·u·lus [ˈstimjuləs; ˋstɪmjələs] *n*. (*pl*. **-li** [-lai; -laɪ]) **1**. 刺激。**2**. 刺激物;促进因素。**3**.【电】激源。**4**.【植】刺毛。**5**.【昆】针,刺。*basic ~* 衬底色。**~-response** *a*.【心理】刺激—反应的(过程,关系)。

sti·my [ˈstaimi; ˋstaɪmɪ] **I** *n*. **1**.【高尔夫球】被敌球拦阻。**2**.〔喻〕阻碍(物)。**II** *vt*.〔通常用 *p*. *p*.〕(敌球)阻碍自己球路。

sting [stiŋ; stɪŋ] **I** *vt*., *vi*. (***stung*** [stʌŋ; stʌŋ]) **1**. 刺,螫,叮。**2**. 刺疼,使觉得痛;疼;使苦闷。**3**. 激励;刺激(舌等)。**4**.〔主用 *passive*〕〔美俚〕骗,诳骗;敲诈;抢。*be stung by reproaches* 受责(而不快)。*be stung with desire* 被欲望所驱使。*I was stung for a fiver*. 我被骗去了五镑。*My tooth ~s*. 我的牙齿痛。*a ~ing blow* 痛击,痛打。*a ~ing insult* 奇耻大辱。**II** *n*. **1**. (蜂等的)刺,螫,叮;刺伤。**2**. 苦痛;刺激;讽刺。**3**.【动】针,螫,刺;

【植】刺毛。4.【空】支架,探臂支杆。5.〔美俚〕皮夹子,钱袋;赃物,抢劫物。*His words carry a* ~. 他的话中有刺。*feel the* ~ *of remorse* 觉得悔恨难过。*Your visit will take away the* ~ *of her sorrow*. 您的来访会消除她的悲伤难过。***have a* ~ *in the tail*** 尾上有刺;〔喻〕话中有刺。**~ing hair**【植】螫毛。

sting·a·ree [ˈstiŋəriː; ˋstɪŋə͵ri, ͵stɪŋəˋri] ***n***. = sting-ray.

sting·er [ˈstiŋə; ˋstɪŋɚ] ***n***. 1. 刺的人;刺激者;话锋锐利的人;有刺的动物[植物]。2.【动】针,刺,螫。3.〔口〕痛击,痛殴;尖酸刻薄的话。4. 薄荷鸡尾酒〔白兰地加薄荷精、冰水调成〕。5.〔英俚〕威士忌苏打水。6.〔S-〕"毒刺"式导弹〔美国的一种轻型防守导弹,可托在肩上发射〕。

stin·gi·ly [ˈstindʒili; ˋstɪndʒɪlɪ] ***ad***. 吝啬地,小气地。

stin·gi·ness [ˈstiŋdʒinis; ˋstɪŋdʒɪnɪs] ***n***. 吝啬;不足。

sting·(ing) nettle ***n***.【植】荨麻。

stin·go [ˈstiŋgəu; ˋstɪŋgo] ***n***.〔俚〕烈性啤酒。

sting-ray [ˈstiŋrei; ˋstɪŋre] ***n***.【鱼】海鳐鱼,魟鲼鱼。

stin·gy[1] [ˈstiŋi; ˋstɪŋɪ] ***a***. 有刺的;刺人的;尖锐的,刺骨的。

stin·gy[2] [ˈstindʒi; ˋstɪndʒɪ] ***a***. (***-gi·er***; ***-gi·est***) 吝啬的,小气的 (*in*); 缺乏的,不足的,微小的。

stink [stiŋk; stɪŋk] **I** ***vi***. (***stank*** [stæŋk; stæŋk], ***stunk*** [stʌŋk; stʌŋk]; ***stunk***) 1. 恶臭。2. 名声臭。3.〔美俚〕质量等级差。4. 有大量的 (*of*, *with*)。5. 有某种气味 (*of*)。— ***vt***. 1. 用臭气赶出去 (*out*)。2.〔俚〕闻出臭气。*The soup* ~*s of garlic*. 这汤有大蒜气味。*It's time to* ~ *out the mosquitoes*. 到了把蚊子熏出去的时候了。***can* ~ *it a mile off*** 一英里之外也能闻到这股臭味。~ ***in the nostrils of sb***. = ~ ***in sb.'s nostrils*** 受人讨厌。~ ***of money***〔俚〕是著名的有钱人,有铜臭气。~***ing smut*** 光腥黑穗病;黑穗病菌。**II** ***n***. 1. 恶臭,臭气。2.〔*pl*.〕〔英俚〕化学,自然科学。3.〔美俚〕丑事,丑闻(的张扬)。*Don't make a big* ~ *over such trifles*. 不要为这般的小事大吵大闹。**~ard** = stinker. ~ **ball** (过去海战中的)臭弹。~ **bomb** 恶臭炸弹。~**bug**【动】臭虫;臭蝽;椿象科昆虫。~**coal** 碳氢石。~**horn**【植】(气味恶臭的)鬼笔。~ **pot** 便器;讨厌到极点的人,(骂人的)臭话;〔美〕【动】臭龟;〔美俚〕摩托艇。~**stone**【矿】臭石灰岩,臭石。~ **trap** (阴沟的)防臭瓣。~**weed**【植】臭草〔曼陀罗等〕。~**wood**【植】臭木(树)。**-er** ***n***. 1. 恶臭的人[动物]。2.〔俚〕极讨厌的东西[人、工作、问题(等)]。**-ing** 1. ***a***. 有臭味的,臭的;讨厌的;烂醉的;〔美俚〕很有钱。2. ***ad***. 极,非常。

stink·ard [ˈstiŋkəd; ˋstɪŋkɚd] ***n***. 1. 卑鄙的人;讨厌的人。2. 放臭气的动物(如獾等)。

stink·o [ˈstiŋkəu; ˋstɪŋko] ***a***.〔美俚〕1. 喝醉了的。2. 臭的。3. 讨厌的。4. 蹩脚的。

stint [stint; stɪnt] **I** ***vt***., ***vi***. 1. 吝惜;限制,节制(饮食等)。2.〔古〕停止。**II** ***n***. 1. 吝惜;限制。2. 定量,定额 (*of*); 定额的工作。3.【鸟】滨鹬。***do one's daily* ~** 做每天指定的工作。~ ***oneself in*** [***of***] ***food*** 节制饮食。***with no* ~ = *without* ~** 不吝惜地,无限制地,慷慨地。**-ing·ly** ***ad***. **-less** ***a***.

stip. = stipend(iary).

stipe [staip; staɪp], **sti·pes** [ˈstaipiːz; ˋstaɪpiz] ***n***. 1.【植】(羊齿植物的)叶柄;(菌类的)菌柄。2.【虫】茎节;眼柄。**-d** ***a***. 有柄的。

sti·pel [ˈstaipl; ˋstaɪpl̩] ***n***.【植】小托叶。

sti·pend [ˈstaipend; ˋstaɪpɛnd] ***n***. 1. (公务员、教员、牧师等的)俸给,薪水;退休金,定期津贴。2. (学生的)助学金,定期津贴。

sti·pen·dia·ry [ˈstaipendjəri; staɪˋpɛndɪ͵ɛrɪ] **I** ***a***. 1. 领薪水的。2. 有关薪水的。**II** ***n***. 1. 有薪水的人。2.〔英〕大城市中处理违警案件的有薪水的治安法官〔又叫 ~ magistrate〕。

sti·pes [ˈstaipiːz; ˋstaɪpiz] (*pl*. ***stip·i·tes*** [ˈstipətiːz; ˋstɪpɪ͵tiz]) ***n***. 1. = stipe. 2.【动】(昆虫的)茎节。

stip·ple [ˈstipl; ˋstɪpl] **I** ***vt***.【雕刻】点刻,以点刻手法刻;(绘画的)以点画[点彩]手法画。**II** ***n***. = stippling 1. 点刻(法),点画(法),点彩(法)。2. 呈点画(或点刻状)。**~-graver** ***n***. 点刻工具。

stip·u·lar [ˈstipjulə; ˋstɪpjəlɚ] ***a***.【植】托叶(状)的;有托叶的。

stip·u·late[1] [ˈstipjuleit; ˋstɪpjə͵let] ***vt***. 1. 约定,订定;规定,订明。2. 坚持要求以…为协议条件 (*that*)。3. 保证。*It is* ~*d in the contract that the workers be paid by the piece*. 合同上规定工人们应领计件工资。*That is not of the* ~*d quality*. 那不是合同上所约定的品质。*I* ~ *this only* (*nothing further*). 我要的条件只这一点(别的不要)。— ***vi***. 1. (作为协议条件而)要求 (*for*)。2. 规定 (*for*)。*The contract* ~*s for the use of seasoned timber*. 合同上订明用干透的木料。**-la·tion** [ˌstipjuˈleiʃən; ͵stɪpjəˋleʃən] ***n***. 订约,约定;合同,契约;约定条件,规定,条款。**-la·tor** [ˈstipjuleitə; ˋstɪpjəletɚ] ***n***. 订约人,立合同人,立约人。

stip·u·late[2] [ˈstipjuleit; ˋstɪpjəlɪt, -͵let] ***a***.【植】有托叶的。

stip·ule [ˈstipjuːl; ˋstɪpjul] ***n***.【植】托叶。

stir[1] [stəː; stɚ] **I** ***vt***. (***stirred*** [stəːd; stɚd]; ***stir·ring*** [ˈstəːriŋ; ˋstɚɪŋ]) 1. 动,摇动;(液体等)移动。2. 煽动,鼓动;激动;轰动,激起;唤起,惹起(喜、怒、爱、恨等)。3. 搅动,搅拌。— ***vi***. 1. 动;活动,走动,跑来跑去;〔口〕起床。2. 兴奋;奋起。3. (货币、消息等)流通;传布。~ *the fire* 捅一捅火。*Not a breath* ~*red the lake*. 湖水纹丝不动。*The audience was deeply* ~*red*. 听众深为感动[激动]。*Nobody in the house is* ~*ring yet*. 那家还没有人起床。*Your presence at the meeting will* ~ *trouble*. 你出席会议要惹起麻烦。*S- the soup with a spoon, if it's too hot*. 汤要是太热,用匙子搅搅。*He never* ~*s out of the house*. 他从不外出。*If you* ~, *I'll shoot*. 你动一动,我就开枪。***not* ~ *a finger*** 一根指头也不肯动;翻一翻手掌都不肯。***not* ~ *an eyelid*** 睫毛一根不动;动也不动。~ ***one's stumps***〔口〕赶快(走);赶快干。~ ***oneself*** 奋起。~ ***up*** 搅拌;搅起(火等);煽动,激励,唤起,惹起。**II** ***n***. 1. 动;微动;运动,活动;激动,骚动,轰动;混杂,吵闹;刺激,感动。2. 搅拌,拔,冲,推,挤。*Not a* ~ *was there* [*heard*]. 全无动静。*The news created* (*made*) *a great* ~ *in the country*. 消息轰动了全国。*Give the fire a* ~. 捅捅火。

stir[2] [stəː; stɚ] ***n***.〔俚〕监狱。~**bug** ***n***.〔美俚〕因坐牢而发狂的人。**~-crazy** ***a***. 因禁闭而发狂的。

stir·a·bout [ˈstəːrəbaut; ˋstɚə͵baʊt] **I** ***n***.〔英〕麦片粥;忙忙碌碌的人;混乱。**II** ***a***. 吵闹的,忙碌的。

stirk [stəːk; stɚk] ***n***.〔英方,Scot.〕一两岁的牛犊。

stir·less [ˈstəːlis; ˋstɚlɪs] ***a***. 不动的,平静的;沉静的。

stir·pi·cul·ture [ˈstəːpikʌltʃə; ˋstɚpɪ͵kʌltʃɚ] ***n***.【生】优生法,优种繁殖。

stirps [stəːps; stɚps] ***n***. (*pl*. ***stir·pes*** [ˈstəːpiːz; ˋstɚpiz]) 1. 种族,家系。2.【法】祖先。3.【生】(受精卵内的)决定因子总数。4.【动】(相当于总科的)群。5.【植】种族。

stir·rer [ˈstəːrə; ˋstɚrɚ] ***n***. 1. 搅动者;搅动器;煽动者,搅乱者。2. 活动分子。3. 起得早[晚]的人。

stir·ring [ˈstəːriŋ; ˋstɚɪŋ] ***a***. 1. 活跃的,忙碌的;热闹的;吵闹的(城市)。2. 危险的,动摇民心的。3. 激动人心的,使人兴奋的,激励的,鼓舞的。*a* ~ *speech* 激动人心的演说。*a* ~ *incident* 轰动的事件。*the* ~ *Gulf war* 震惊世界的海湾战争。**-ly** ***ad***.

stir·rup [ˈstirəp; ˋstɪrəp, ˋstɚəp] ***n***. 1. 马镫;马镫带。2.【机】镫形具,支持用铁具。3.【建】镫筋,箍筋。4.【海】系索,镫索,镫(形铁)链。5.【解】镫骨。***high up in the* ~*s*** = ***up the* ~*s*** 身份高;富有。***hold the* ~*s*** (***for***) (为某人)扶住马镫;服事,奉承。~ **bar** 悬镫铁条;(镫的)横踏

板。～ **bone**【解】镫骨。～ **cup**〔英〕(古代)马上离别时的饯别酒。～ **iron** 马镫(不连皮带)。～ **leather** 马镫皮带。～**-piece** (木工用的)镫形支架。～**pump**〔英〕消防手摇灭火泵。～ **strap** 马镫皮带。

stish·ov·ite [ˈstiʃəˌvait; ˋstɪʃəvaɪt] ***n***.【地】超石英。

stitch [stitʃ; stɪtʃ] **I** ***n***. **1**. 一针;针脚;缝线。**2**. 针法,缝法,编法。**3**.(常指肋部)突然,剧痛。**4**. 碎布;〔口〕一部分,一点儿;少许衣服。**5**.〔英方〕畦;(二犁沟间的)窄垄。**6**.〔英方〕距离,一段时间。*A ～ in time saves nine*. 及时一针省得以后缝九针;及时处理,事半功倍。***drop a ～*** (编绒线时)织漏一针。***every ～***全身(装束),全付(行头);风帆的各个部分。***have not a ～ on*** 一丝不挂。***have not a dry ～ on*** 全身湿透。***make small*** [***long***] ***～es*** 密[粗]缝。***feel a ～ in one's side*** 觉得胁部一阵剧痛。***not do a ～ of work*** 一点工作不做。***put a ～ in a garment*** 把衣服缝一缝。***rip out ～es = take out ～-es*** 折缝线。***without a ～ of clothing*** = *have not a ～ on*. **II** ***vt***. **1**. 缝,缝缀,连缀;缝饰;钉。**2**. (把田地)弄成畦,起垄。— ***vi***. 缝纫,拿针缝。～ **up** 缝拢,缝补。～**ing horse** (缝皮料用的)压脚,压板。～ **wheel** (缝皮料用的)穿孔齿锥。～**work** 刺绣,缝纫。～ **wort** ***n***.【植】繁缕(属);刺草,复活节钟草。

stitch·ery [ˈstitʃəri; ˋstɪtʃərɪ] ***n***. 刺绣术;〔*pl*.〕刺绣品。

stith·y [ˈstiði; ˋstɪðɪ, ˋstɪθɪ] **I** ***n***. **1**.〔古,方〕铁砧。**2**. 打铁铺;锻冶场。**II** ***vt***.〔古〕打铁。

sti·ver [ˈstaivə; ˋstaɪvɚ] ***n***. **1**. 荷兰旧辅币〔值二十分之一盾〕。**2**. 小钱;一点点,不值钱的东西。***do not care a ～*** 毫不介意。***have not a ～*** 一文钱也没有。***not worth a ～*** 一文不值。

S

stiv·y [ˈstaivi; ˋstaɪvɪ] ***a***. **1**.〔方〕塞满了的。**2**. 憋闷的。

St. John [ˌsntˈdʒɔn; ˏsentˋdʒɑn] ***n***. 圣约翰〔姓氏〕。

St. John's [sntˈdʒɔnz; sentˋdʒɑnz] 圣约翰〔安提瓜岛(英)首府〕。

St. Leger [sntˈledʒə; sentˋlɛdʒɚ] ***n***. 圣莱杰〔姓氏〕。

St. Lou·is [səntˈluis; sentˋluɪs] 圣路易斯〔西非塞内加尔(Senegal)的首都〕。

St. Lu·ci·a [sntˈluːʃiə; sentˋluʃɪə] ***n***. 圣卢西亚〔拉丁美洲〕。

St. Maur [ˈsntmɔː; ˋsentmɔr] ***n***. 圣莫尔〔姓氏〕。

stoa [ˈstəuə; ˋstoə] ***n***. (*pl*. ***stoae*** [ˈstəuiː; ˋstoi], ～***s***) (古希腊神殿的)拱廊,柱廊。

stoat [stəut; stot] ***n***.【动】(特指夏季被棕色毛的)鼬。

stoc·ca·do, stoc·oa·ta [stəˈkɑːdəu, -ˈkɑːtə; stɑˋkado, -ˋkɑtə] ***n***.〔古〕(用刀、矛等)刺、戳。

sto·chas·tic [stəuˈkæstik; stəˋkæstɪk] ***a***. **1**. 机会的;有可能性的;随便的。**2**.【数】随机的。

stock[1] [stɔk; stɑk] ***n***.〔G.〕滑雪手杖。

stock[2] [stɔk; stɑk] **I** ***n***. **1**. (树等的)干,根株,根茎。**2**.【园艺】砧木;苗木;原种。**3**.〔古〕木块,木头。**4**. 桩,柱;株。**5**. 托柄;枪托;刨身;钻柄,把,柄;锚杆。**6**. 祖先;家系,世系,血统;族;种族,民族。**7**.【语】语族,语系。**8**. 原料,材料,备料;(炖肉等所得的)原汁,汤料。**9**. 本钱,资本;股份,股票;〔*pl*.〕〔英〕公债。★公债美国通常叫 bond; 在英国股份叫 share, 作买卖对象的股票叫 stock, 在美国一律叫 stock. **10**. 库存品,存货,贮存;买进的货,进货。**11**.〔总称〕家畜;牲畜;农具。**12**.【生】群体;群落;一群(蜜蜂等);族类。**13**.【动】原种;无性种。**14**. (18世纪男子兼作衣领用的)宽领带。**15**.【植】紫罗兰(属)。**16**.〔*pl*.〕【船】造船架(枕木);〔*pl*.〕(兽医等用的)固马架;夹架。**17**.〔*pl*.〕【史】足枷;优质砖。**18**.【机】台,座;刨台。**19**.【地】岩干。**20**. 估计,估量,信任,相信。**21**. (牌局开始时)没发完的牌。**22**.〔英〕高级砖。**23**. 固定在某一剧院上演的剧团或其轮换剧目。*foundation ～ seeds* 原种。*a breeder's ～ farm* 原主种圃。*the ～ of a rifle* 枪托。*He has £ 50 in the ～s*. 他有五十镑公债票。*a ～ certificate*〔英〕公债证券;〔美〕股票。*an ordinary ～* =〔美〕*a common ～* 普通股。*a preference ～* =〔美〕*a preferred ～* 优先股。*take over a farm with the ～* 买下一个连同牲畜农具在内的农场。*dead ～* 农具。*fat ～* 食用家畜。*live ～* 牲畜。*mixed paper-～* 混合纸料。*a man of Scotish ～* 一个苏格兰血统的男子。*languages of Teutonic ～* 条顿系的语言。*keep a large ～ of dry goods* 存有大量织物货品。*the gold ～* 黄金储备。*put little ～ in sb*. 不大信任某人。*two-ply ～*夹(层)纸。*malm ～* 白垩砖。***be out of ～*** 没有现货,缺货,卖光。***have*** [***keep***] ***a large ～ of information*** 知识广博。(***have*** [***keep***]) ***in ～*** 有货,办有,备有,持有 (*goods in ～* 现货,存货)。***keep all kinds of goods in ～*** 各货齐备。***lay in a ～ of flour*** 购备面粉。***lock, ～, and barrel*** 枪的全部;全体,一切。***on the ～s***【船】建造中;计划中 (*I've got a couple of books on the ～s*. 计划要读的书有两本)。***out of ～*** 售完,脱销,缺货。***take ～*** 清点存货,盘(点存)货;清理,清点;审查,鉴定 (*of*)。***take ～ in*** 买…的股票;和…发生关系,干与;重视;信任。**II** ***vt***. **1**. 给…装托,柄(枪托、钻柄等)。**2**. 购备,贮备。**3**. 给(农场)购置农具[家畜];给(商店)办货。**4**. 播(种)(*with*);放牧。**5**. 放养(鱼类);在…种上牧草;使(牲畜)受孕。**6**. 给(罪犯)上枷。— ***vi***. **1**. 采办 (*up*)。**2**. 长新梢,出新芽,长主茎。*The market is now fully ～ed*. 市场现在货物充足。*Everybody has to ～ his mind with knowledge*. 人人都要使自己的头脑充满着知识。*a well-～ed library* 藏书充实的图书馆。**III** ***a***. **1**. 库存的,现有的,贮有的;常备的。**2**. 主要的,标准的。**3**. 平凡的,陈腐的;繁殖。**4**. (饲养)家畜的,繁殖用的。**5**. 股票[股份]的。**6**.〔英〕公债的。**7**. 为某一剧院常年雇用的;常年属于某剧院的。**8**.〔美〕矮胖的。*a ～ actor* 专任演员。～ *sizes in boots* 鞋子常备的标准尺寸。*a ～ play* 保留节目,常演的戏。*a ～ bull* 公的种牛。*a ～joke* 陈腐的笑话。～ **account** 存货账;股份账。～ **beet** 饲用甜菜。～ **book** 存货簿。～**breeder** 畜牧业者。～**breeding** 牧畜,畜产,良种繁育。～**broker** 股票[证券]经纪人。～**brokerage**, ～**broking** 证券经纪业。～ **car** **1**. (火车)家畜车箱。**2**. 常备的普通式样的汽车。**3**. 比赛用汽车。～ **certificate** 股票。～ **company** **1**. 股份公司。**2**. 固定在某一剧院上演轮换剧目的剧团。**3**.〔美〕(非明星制的)演员专任制剧团。～ **culture** 原种培养,储备培养。～ **dividend** 以增资股票形式发放的红利;股票息。～ **dove**【鸟】野鸽。～ **ewe** 传种母羊。～ **exchange** 证券交易所。～ **farm** 畜牧场。～ **farmer** 畜牧业者。～ **farming** 畜牧业。～**fish** (未加盐的)鳕鱼干(等)。～ **gang** ***n***. (把木料一次锯成木板的)框锯。～**holder** **1**.〔英〕公债持有人。**2**.〔美〕股东〔英国普通叫做 shareholder〕。～ **-in-trade** **1**. 存货。**2**. 营业用具;必需工具。**3**. 老手段,惯用手段。～**jobber** **1**.〔英蔑〕股票投机商。**2**.〔美〕股票经纪人。～**jobbery**, ～**jobbing** 证券投机买卖(业)。～ **list** **1**.〔交易所公布的〕证券行情表。**2**. 存货表。**3**.〔美〕股份表。～**lock** 装牢在门上的锁。～**man** **1**. 牧场主。**2**.〔主澳〕牧场工人,饲养员。**3**. 仓库管理员。～**-map** 林相图。～ **market** **1**. 股票市场。**2**. 股票买卖。**3**. 股票行情。**4**. 牲畜市场。～ **option**〔美〕(股东的)优先认股权。～ **parking** (将股票暂时转移寄存于他人户头上的)股票假卖出〔以此达到逃避纳税和申报真实财产等目的〕。～**pile** **1**. (原料、食品等的)储备;准备急用的备用原料或物资;贮存。**2**. 资源,富源,矿藏量。**3**. (为战争准备的)核武器。～**piling** ***n***. 贮存,堆存,积存。～ **plot** 原种圃。～**pot** **1**. 炖原汁汤的锅。**2**. 什锦锅。**3**. 杂烩汤。～ **rail** (转辙器的)本轨。～ **raising** 畜牧(业),牲畜饲养(业)。～**rider**〔澳〕骑马牧人。～**room** **1**. (物资、商品等的)仓库。**2**. (旅馆内供旅行推销员用的)商品展出室。～**-still** 静止的,不动的 (*stand ～-still* 站着不动)。～**taking** **1**. 盘货,清点存货。**2**. (事业等的)成绩调查[估计]。**3**. 森林调查。～ **ticker** 证券行情自动记录收报机。～ **watering**〔美〕加发股票而未增

资。～**whip** 牧鞭。～**-work** 1. 备售制品。2.【采】网状(矿)脉。～**yard** (预备屠宰、买卖、装运等用的)牲畜围栏;堆料场。

stock·ade [stɔ'keid; stɑk`ed] **I** *n*. 1. 栅栏,围桩。2. 用栅栏围起的一块地方。3. 排桩的防波堤。4.〔美军俚〕(军营)监牢;俘虏营。**II** *vt*. 用栅栏围住;用栅栏防卫。

stock·er ['stɔkə; `stɑkɚ] *n*. 1. 为屠宰而养肥的小公牛。2. 枪托制造者。3. (钢铁厂堆料场的)碎料工,装料工。4.【机】储料器;堆料机;加煤机。

Stock·holm ['stɔkhəum; `stɑk,hom, -,holm] *n*. 斯德哥尔摩〔瑞典首都〕。～ *tar* (造船用)松焦油。

stock·i·ly ['stɔkili; `stɑkɪlɪ] *ad*. 矮胖地,粗壮地。*a* ～ *built plumber* 身材矮胖的管子工。**-i·ness** *n*.

stock·i·net(te) [,stɔki'net; ,stɑkɪn`ɛt] *n*. 1. (内衣等用)松紧织物;弹力织物。2. 隔行正反针织法。

stock·ing ['stɔkiŋ; `stɑkɪŋ] *n*. 1.〔常 *pl*.〕长袜(*opp*. sock)。2. (毛色和身体其他部分不同的)兽脚。*a pair of* ～*s* 一双长统袜。*elastic* ～*s*【医】(外科用)橡皮袜子。～ *yarn* 针织线。*horse with white* ～*s* 白脚马。***in one's*** ～***s*** [～***-feet***] 光着袜底儿,不穿鞋(*He is* [*stands*] *six feet in his* ～*s*. 他不穿鞋身长六英尺)。***wear yellow*** ～***s*** 妒忌,吃醋。～**ed** *a*. 穿袜的。～ **cap** (冬季戴的有绒球或穗的圆锥形)绒线帽。～ **frame**, ～ **loom**, ～ **machine** 织袜机。

stock·ish ['stɔkiʃ; `stɑkɪʃ] *a*. 像木头似的;蠢笨的;呆滞的。**-ly** *ad*.

stock·ist ['stɔkist; `stɑkɪst] *n*. 存货待售的商人。

stock·y ['stɔki; `stɑkɪ] *a*. (**-i·er**; **-i·est**) 矮胖的,结实的。**-i·ly** *ad*. **-i·ness** *n*.

Stod·dard ['stɔdəd; `stɑdɚd] *n*. 斯托达德〔姓氏〕。

stodge [stɔdʒ; stɑdʒ] **I** *vt*. 1. 暴食,贪婪地吃,使塞饱。2. 使充分满足,使感到腻味。3. 搅拌,掺合。*be* ～*d with tea and buns* 塞满茶点。*He often* ～*s himself with his newspapers*. 他经常遍阅报纸。*You shouldn't* ～ *yourself with roast duck and beef stew, John*. 约翰,你不要让烤鸭和炖牛肉把你的胃口吃倒了。— *vi*. 1. 暴食,狼吞虎咽。2. 重步行走,历经艰苦。**II** *n*.〔英俚〕1. 浓厚的、不易消化油腻的食物。2. 贪吃的人,暴食者;盛筵。3. 枯燥难学的东西,学起来令人生厌的东西。

stodg·y ['stɔdʒi; `stɑdʒɪ] *a*. (**-i·er**; **-i·est**) 1. (食物)浓厚的,不易消化的,胀肚子的。2. (书等)内容枯燥的;(文体等)乏味的。3.〔口〕矮胖的,身体笨重的。4. 装得满满的。5. (人)庸俗的,老派的,守旧的。*I want something to read. These volumes are* ～. 我要一些可读的东西,这些书本本枯燥乏味。*The gateman was a* ～ *fellow of 60*. 看门人是个六十岁的矮胖子。**-i·ly** *ad*.

stoep [stu:p; stup] *n*. (南非荷兰式住宅的)屋前游廊;门廊。

sto·gy, sto·gie ['stəugi; `stogɪ] *n*.〔美〕笨重的皮靴;细长的(低级)雪茄烟。

Sto·ic ['stəuik; `sto·ɪk] **I** *a*. 1. 斯多噶学派的。2.〔s-〕= stoical. **II** *n*. 斯多噶学派的人;〔s-〕禁欲(主义)者。

sto·i·cal ['stəuikəl; `sto·ɪkl̩] *a*. 斯多噶学派的;禁欲主义的;不以苦乐为意的;能忍受痛苦[不幸]的;淡泊的。**-ly** *ad*.

stoi·ch(e)i·om·et·ry [,stɔiki'ɔmitri; ,stɔɪkɪ`ɑmətrɪ] *n*. 化学计量学;化学计算法。

Sto·i·cism ['stəuisizəm; `sto·ɪ,sɪzəm] *n*. 斯多噶哲学;〔s-〕禁欲(主义);淡泊,不以苦乐为意,坚忍。

Stoke [stəuk; stok] *n*. 斯托克〔姓氏〕。

stoke[1] [stəuk; stok] *vt*., *vi*. 1. 给(机车等)烧火[加煤,添煤];把(火)拨旺。2. (在车头上等)做司炉。3.〔俚〕狼吞虎咽吃(食物)(*up*)。～**hold**【海】生火间,锅炉舱;炉前。～**hole** 炉膛口,炉前,生火间。

stoke[2] [stəuk; stok] *n*.【物】沲〔动力黏度单位〕。

stok·er ['stəukə; `stokɚ] *n*. 1. 司炉;烧火工人。2. 自动加煤机(= mechanical ～)。

sto·ke·si·a [stəu'ki:ʒiə, 'stəuksiə; sto`kiʒɪə, `stoksɪə] *n*.〔美〕【植】琉璃菊(*Stokesia laevis*)〔产于美国东南部〕。

Stokes mor·tar ['stəuks'mɔ:tə; stoks`mɔrtɚ] 斯多克式迫击炮,大口径迫击炮。

STOL = short take off and landing 短距起落(飞机)。

stole[1] [stəul; stol] *n*. 1.【古罗马】女式长外衣。2. 女用长条披肩。3.【宗】(牧师神父举行仪式时用)圣带,长巾,祭衣。

stole[2] [stəul; stol] steal 的过去式。

sto·len ['stəulən; `stolən] **I** *v*. **steal** 的过去分词。**II** *a*. 偷得的;偷走的。～ *goods* 赃物,贼赃。

stol·id ['stɔlid; `stɑlɪd] *a*. 呆头呆脑的,感觉迟钝的;不易激动的;(抵抗)顽强的。**-lid·i·ty** [stɔ'liditi; ,stɔ`lɪdətɪ] *n*. **-ly** *ad*. **-ness** *n*.

stol·len ['stəulən; `stolən] *n*.〔G.〕果子甜面包。

sto·lon ['stəulɔn; `stolɑn] *n*.【植】匍匐茎[枝];【动】生殖根。**-ic** *a*.

sto·ma ['stəumə; `stomə] *n*. (*pl*. ～**ta**)【植】气孔;【动】口;(昆虫的)气门,呼吸孔。**-tal** *a*.

stom·ach ['stʌmək; `stʌmək] **I** *n*. 1. 胃。2.〔口〕肚子。3. 胃口,食欲;嗜好,欲望;志趣。*She injured her* ～ *by eating too much*. 她吃得太多伤了胃了。*What a* ～ *he has got*! 他的肚子多大! *My* ～ *turns* [*rises*] *at it*. 一看到[一想到]这个就发恶心。*It goes against my* ～. 这个不合我的胃口[兴趣]。*a proud* [*high*] ～ 傲慢。*the coat of the* ～ 胃黏膜。*coats of the* ～ 胃膜,胃的黏膜层。***have a good*** ～ ***for*** 很想吃,渴望。***have a pain in the*** ～ 肚子[胃]痛。***have no*** ～ ***for*** 不想(做某事),(对某事)没有兴趣。***lie*** (***heavy***) ***on sb.'s*** ～ (食物)滞积胃中,不消化。***on a full*** ～ 饭后,肚子饱时。***on an empty*** ～ 空腹时;饿着肚皮,绝食。***pit of the*** ～ 心窝。***sour*** ～ 胸口作呕。***turn sb.'s*** ～ 使人发呕,使人厌恶。**II** *vt*. 1. 吃…吃得津津有味;消化。2. 忍耐,忍受〔多半与否定词连用〕。3.〔古〕对…发怒。*I cannot* ～ *this insult*. 我不能忍受这种侮辱。～**ache** 胃痛,肚子痛。～ **pump**【医】胃唧筒。～ **tooth** (幼儿的)下犬齿。～ **tube**【医】胃管。～ **warmer**〔英〕热水袋。**-ful** *n*. 满胃,满腹(*have a* ～*ful of grievances* 满腹牢骚)。**-less** *a*. 没有胃的;没有胃口[食欲]的。

stom·ach·al ['stʌməkəl; `stʌməkl̩] *n*., *a*. = stomachic.

stom·ach·er ['stʌməkə; `stʌməkɚ, -tʃɚ] *n*. (17 世纪女用)三角胸衣。

sto·mach·ic, -i·cal [stə'mækik, -ikəl; sto`mækɪk, -əkl̩] **I** *a*. 1. 胃的。2. 健胃的,助消化的。**II** *n*. 健胃剂。

sto·ma·chy ['stʌməki; `stʌməkɪ] *a*. 1.〔英方〕易怒的,脾气急躁的。2. 肚子大的。

sto·ma·ta ['stəumətə; `stomətə] *n*. stoma 的复数。

stom·a·tal, sto·mal ['stəumətl, -məl; `stomətl, -məl] *a*.【动】【植】有气孔的;有气门的。

sto·mate ['stəumeit; `stomet] **I** *a*. 1.【植】有气孔的。2.【动】有口的;有气门的。**II** *n*. = stoma.

sto·mat·ic [stə'mætik; sto`mætɪk] **I** *a*. 1. 口的。2.【植】【动】气孔的,呼吸孔的,气门的。**II** *n*. 口(中用)药;【生】= stomate.

sto·ma·ti·tis [,stəumə'taitis; ,stomə`taɪtɪs, ,stɑmə-] *n*.【医】口内炎,口炎。

sto·mat·(o)- *comb*. *f*. 表示"口的","像口的": *stomato*logy.

sto·ma·to·gas·tric [,stəumətəu'gæstrik; ,stomato`gæstrɪk] *a*. 口和胃的。

sto·ma·tol·o·gy [,stəumə'tɔlədʒi; ,stomə`tɑlədʒɪ] *n*.【医】口腔学。**-log·i·cal** [-'lɔdʒikl; -`lɑdʒɪkl̩] *a*. **-o·gist** *n*. 口腔学家。

sto·ma·to·pod [ˈstəumətəpɔd, ˈstɔmətə-; ˋstomətəpɑd, ˋstɑmətə-] ***n.***【动】口脚类（*Stomatopoda*）动物。

sto·ma·to·scope [stəˈmætəskəup; stəˋmætəskop] ***n.***【医】口腔镜。

sto·ma·tous [ˈstəumətəs, ˈstɔmə-; ˋstɑmətəs, ˋstomə-] ***a.*** 有孔的，有气孔的。

sto·mo·dae·um, sto·mo·de·um [ˌstəuməˈdi:əm, ˌstɔmə-; ˏstoməˋdiəm, ˏstɑm-] ***n.*** (*pl.* ***-dae·a***, ***-de·a*** [-diə; -ˋdiə])【解】口道，口凹。

stomp[1] [stɔmp; stɑmp] **I** ***vt.***, ***vi.*** = stamp〔尤指踏伤、踩死〕。**II** ***n.***〔美〕**1.** 节奏活泼、拍子强烈的爵士乐曲调。**2.** 上述乐曲的舞蹈。**3.** 跺脚，重踩。

stomp[2] [stɔmp; stɑmp] ***n.***, ***vt.*** = stump[2].

S'ton = Southampton.

Stone [stəun; ston] ***n.*** 斯通〔姓氏〕。

stone [stəun; ston] **I** ***n.*** **1.** 石，石头，铺石，石料。**2.** 宝石（= precious ~）。**3.** 石碑，界碑，里程碑，纪念碑；墓石。**4.** 磨（刀）石；捣衣石，砧；研（光）石。**5.** 雹，霰。**6.**【医】结石；结石病。**7.**【植】（水果的）硬核。**8.**〔古〕〔常 *pl.*〕睾丸。**9.**【印】整版石台；调墨石台；整纸石台；石印石。**10.**〔英〕〔单复同〕呖〔重量名，照规定是 14 磅（尤以表示体重时常用），但实际上肉类是 8 磅，干酪是 16 磅，麻是 32 磅，玻璃是 5 磅，羊毛是 24 磅；略作 st.〕。*Stones will cry out*.（极大的罪恶等）会使石头也叫唤起来。*A rolling ~ gathers no moss*.〔谚〕滚石不生苔，频频转行不成材。*a ~'s throw* [*cast*] away 近在咫尺。*blue ~* 绿矾。*Cornish ~* 陶土。*the ~ of Sisyphus* 徒劳。*a heart of ~* 铁石心肠，残忍。*~ on the chest*〔美〕肺结核。***break ~s*** 敲碎（铺路用的）石头；干渺小的差事。***cast ~s*** [***a ~***] ***at*** 谴责，攻击。***cast the first ~*** 向…挑衅。***get blood from a ~*** 石中取血；不可能。***give a ~ and a beating to sb.***〔原赛马〕轻而易举地胜过（某人）。***give sb. a ~ for bread*** 拿石头当面包给；表面帮忙实则愚弄（人）。***leave no ~ unturned*** 挖空心思，用尽一切手段（*to do*）。***mark with a white ~***（古罗马人用白垩在日历上把幸福的日子打上记号，转为）作为喜庆的日子特笔大书。***set a ~ rolling*** 滚动石头；做劳而无功的事情。***set ~ out*** 将石块砌成一层比一层稍稍突出状，依次排列。***swim like a ~***〔谑〕沉下去。***throw ~s*** [***a ~***] ***at*** 谴责，攻击。***throw the first ~ at*** 向…挑衅。***trip over a ~*** 被石头绊倒。***within a ~'s throw of*** 在…的左近；离…不远。

II ***vt.*** **1.** 向…投扔石头（而打死）。**2.** 除去…处的石头。**3.** 除去（水果的）核。**4.** 拿石头围住，堆（石头）；筑（石墙），铺（石头）。**5.** 用石头磨（刀），用石头磨光（皮革）。*~ a well* 用石头砌一口井。*~ sb. to death* 用石头甩死（某人）。**S- Age** 石器时代。**~ ax(e)** 石斧。**~-blind** ***a.*** **1.** 全瞎的。**2.**〔美俚〕大醉的。**~ blue** 灰蓝色。**~-boat**〔美〕运石雪橇。**~-brash** 砂石[石子]多的土地，砂土。**~-breaker** ***n.*** 敲碎石头的工人，碎石机。**~-broke** ***a.***〔俚〕不名一文的，穷困不堪的。**~-cast** = stone's-cast. **~chat**【鸟】黑喉石鹏。**~ coal** 白煤，块状无烟煤。**~-cold** ***a.*** 冰冷如石的，冷透的。**~ composition** 石刻品。**~crop**【植】景天（轻泻剂）。**~ curlew**【鸟】石鸻。**~ cutter** 石匠，石工；截石机。**~-dead** ***a.*** 完全断了气的，完全死了的（*Stone-dead has no fellow*. 杀人灭口）。**~-deaf** ***a.*** 完全聋的，一点也听不见的。**~ fence** 石墙；〔美俚〕混合酒。**~fly**【昆】蜻，石蝇。**~ fruit** 有硬核的水果〔如桃、梅等〕。**~-ground** ***a.*** 在磨石作坊里研磨的。**~-horse** ***n.***〔方〕种马。**~jug** 石罐；〔俚〕牢监。**~-leek** 葱。**~ lily**【植】海百合化石。**~man** **1.** 石工，石匠。**2.**（作界标等用）圆锥形石堆。**3.**【印】装版工人。**~ martin** **1.**【动】石貂，榉貂。**2.** 貂皮上衣[围脖]。**~mason** 石匠。**~ mill** **1.** 碎石机，磨石机。**2.** 石粉工场。**~ pine**【植】意大利五针松。**~-pit** 采石场。**~ powder** 石粉。**~-race** 边跑边拾石块的一种游戏。**~ roller**【动】包鳔鱼；裂唇绒口鱼。**~'s cast** = **~'s throw** 一投石的距离〔约 50 到 150 码〕。**~seed**【植】紫草。**~ sledge** 石匠锤。**~-still** ***a.*** 非常寂静的，一动也不动的。**~ wall** **1.** ***n.*** 石墙，难以逾越的障碍。**2.** ***vi.***, ***vt.***〔主英、口语〕抵制；阻碍；阻碍（调查、议事进行等）；【板球】小心地打。**3.** ***a.*** 石墙（一样坚固）的；坚定的。**~walling** ***n.*** **1.**（板球的）慎打。**2.**〔英〕阻碍议事。**3.** 筑石墙；石墙。**~ware** 缸器；粗陶（器）。**~washing**（牛仔服的）浮石打磨法〔使之收到显得陈旧的效果〕。**~work** **1.**（建筑物的）砖石部分。**2.** 石方工程；石雕工艺；石制品。**3.**〔*pl.*〕（作单数用）石制工艺品，石场。**~wort**【植】轮藻纲植物。**-d** ***a.*** 去核的；喝醉的，沉醉的；（吸毒后）处于麻醉状态的。**-r** ***n.*** 投石者；铺石块者；去核者。

Stone·henge [ˈstəunhendʒ; ˋstonˋhɛndʒ] ***n.***（英国 Salisbury 平原上的）史前巨石群。

stonk [stɔŋk; stɑŋk] **I** ***vt.*** 重炮猛轰。**II** ***n.*** 密集的炮火。*loose a good ~ on the enemy* 向敌军发射了一阵猛烈的密集炮火。

ston·y [ˈstəuni; ˋstonɪ] ***a.*** (***-i·er***; ***-i·est***) **1.** 石的，石头的，石质的，像石头（一样硬）的，多石的。**2.** 多核的（水果）。**3.** 冷酷的，残忍的（心等）；变成石头的；不动的；没有表情的。**4.**〔俚〕破产的，不名一文的。*The path was ~*. 小道上石头很多。*Her story should soften the stoniest of hearts*. 她的事情会使心情最冷酷无情的人也为之感动的。*a ~ gaze* [*stare*, *look*] 冷眼凝视。*~ fear* 吓呆了的恐怖。**~-broke** ***a.*** = stone-broke. **~ coral**【动】石珊瑚。**~hearted** ***a.*** 铁石心肠的，冷静的。**-i·ly** ***ad.*** **-i·ness** ***n.***

stood [stud; stʊd] stand 的过去式及过去分词。

stooge [stu:dʒ; studʒ] **I** ***n.*** **1.**〔口、原美〕（提供笑料、帮腔、作笑谑对象的）丑角的配角。**2.**〔口语〕善于逗笑的人；陪衬人物；帮闲；奸细，密探。**3.** 傀儡，唯命是从的人，走狗。**4.**〔英俚〕飞行练习生。**5.**〔美俚〕副驾驶员。*I'd play ~ to him in the performance*. 在表演中我来给他当作配角。**II** ***vi.*** **1.**〔美俚〕给丑角帮腔。**2.** 充当帮手[帮闲]。**3.**〔英空军俚〕盘旋（同一地上）（*over*; *about*; *around*; *etc.*）。*The police will have ~s watching every move of the suspected terrorists*. 警察会派密探注意有恐怖份子嫌疑的人的每一活动。

stook [stuk; stuk, stʊk] **I** ***n.***〔英〕麦[禾]束堆〔通例是 12 束〕。**II** ***vt.***, ***vi.*** 堆（麦束）。

stook·ie, stook·y [ˈstu:ki; ˋstukɪ] ***n.***〔Scot., Ir.〕呆子，傻瓜。

stool [stu:l; stul] **I** ***n.*** **1.** 凳子；搁脚凳。**2.** 座位，席位。**3.** 便桶；厕所；通便；〔常 *pl.*〕大便；（大便一次的）粪便。**4.**（园艺压条用的）根株，母株；根生嫩苗。**5.** 囮子鸟歇息的树枝；〔美〕囮鸽（= ~-pigeon）。**6.**【机】垫凳。**7.**【建】内窗台。**8.**〔美俚〕情报。*a necessary ~* 厕所。*go to ~* 去解大溲。***come to the ground between two ~s*** = ***fall (to the ground) between two ~s*** 两头落空。**II** ***vt.***〔美〕用囮子引诱。— ***vi.*** **1.** 分蘖。**2.**〔古〕去解大溲。**3.**〔美俚〕替警察局作密探，充当囮子。***~ing stage*** 抽茎，分蘖期。***~ball***（旧时英国的）女子板球。**~ pigeon**〔美〕**1.** 囮鸽。**2.**〔俚〕（诱人赌博等的）囮子。**3.**〔俚〕（警察局的）密探。**~ plate**【机】垫板。**~ shoot** 根株萌芽。**-ing** ***n.*** 分蘖力。

stool·ie [ˈstu:li; ˋstulɪ] ***n.*** = stool pigeon.

stoop[1] [stu:p; stup] **I** ***vi.*** **1.** 弯身；弯腰（*down*）。**2.**（树、岩等）倾斜。**3.** 屈服，屈从，屈身，忍辱；降低身分，堕落（做下流事等）。**4.**（鹰等）飞袭，飞扑（*at*, *on*, *upon*）。— ***vt.*** **1.** 屈，弯，曲。**2.** 使屈服，屈从，自贬，压倒。**3.** 降下（帆、旗等）。*She ~ed down to pick a flower*. 她弯下腰去摘了一朵花。*He ~ed to such meanness*. 他堕落得这般卑鄙。**~ *to conquer*** [***win***] 降低身分而取胜，忍辱取得。**~ *to flattery*** 谄媚奉承。**II** ***n.*** **1.** 弯腰，屈身，驼背。**2.** 屈服，自贬。**3.**（猛禽的）下攫，下扑。*He has a shocking ~*. 他的背驼[弯]得很厉害。**~ labour**〔美〕需要经常弯腰的作业[劳动]。

S

stoop[2] [stuːp; stup]〔美〕*n*. 两侧有可坐的低矮栏杆的门前露台;游廊。

stoop[3] [stuːp; stup] *n*. = stoup.

stop [stɔp; stɑp] **I** *vi*. (~*ped* [-t; -t],〔诗〕*stopt*; *stopping* [ˈstɔpiŋ; ˋstɑpɪŋ]) **1**. 停止;停下来做某事(*to do sth*.)。**2**.〔口〕逗留,歇宿,(偶然)过访。**3**. 踌躇。**4**. 被塞住。**5**.【乐】压住弦或孔以改善音调。— *vt*. **1**. 止住,堵住,塞住,填塞,盖。**2**. 阻止,阻拦;截断,断绝。**3**. 停止(工作、吃饭等);妨碍;停付(支票等);扣留,扣除;阻止。**4**. 止住(伤口)出血;打落(飞鸟等)。**5**.【海】系紧(船缆等)。**6**. 加标点。**7**.【乐】压(乐器的弦、孔,以改变音调)。**8**.〔美运〕打败(对手)。**9**.【海】(用绳子)扎住,扎紧。**10**.【园艺】摘心,打顶。~ *to rest* 停下休息。~ *to think* (把某事)停下来,转而进行思考。~ *thinking* 停止思考。*It has* ~*ped raining*. 雨停了。~ *the traffic* 断绝交通。*What is to* ~ *me from coming*? 我为什么不能来? *S- thief*! 截住强盗! *a badly* ~*ped letter* 标点错乱的信。~ *a bottle with a cork* 用软木塞把瓶子盖上。*The bank* ~*ped his check*. 银行拒付他的支票了。*We'll* ~ *at a hotel for the night*. 我们将在旅馆过夜。*I'll* ~ *at no expense to obtain it*. 我将不惜一切花费来得到它。*I'm* ~*ping with my uncle*. 我暂时住在叔父家。~ ***a bullet*** [***shell***]〔俚〕中弹阵亡[受伤]。~ ***a cheque*** (通知银行)止付支票。~ ***a clock*** [***the clock, the train***]〔美俚〕样子不好看[丑陋]。~ ***a gap*** 修补;弥补,补空;代理。~ ***a packet*** 受重伤;挨臭骂。~ ***at*** 住宿(旅店)。~ ***at no*** (*sacrifices*) 不惜(一切牺牲)。~ ***at nothing*** 什么也做得出,肆无忌惮;勇往直前。~ ***at nothing in committing evils*** 无恶不作。~ ***away*** 外宿。~ ***by***〔美〕顺便到(某处)访问(*He'll* ~ *by on his way home*. 回家途中他将前来访问)。~ ***cold***〔美口〕使呆住。~ ***dead*** 突然停止。~ ***down***【摄】把光圈收小。~ ***in*** 顺便过访某人。~ ***off*** 中途下一下车;用砂填塞(铸模的一部);〔英口〕进监牢。~ ***sb.'s breath*** 闷死人。~ ***sb.'s clock***〔美〕杀人。~ ***one's ears*** 塞住耳朵,不听(*to*; *against*)。~ ***sb.'s way*** 拦住某人路;反对某人。~ ***out*** 遮断(风、日光等);外宿;扣除(*The cost was* ~*ped out of my salary*. 那一笔费用已经由我的薪水中扣除了。);【摄】置于停影液中。~ ***over*** 中途下车;暂留,暂住;住在海外(*Many motorists were forced to* ~ *over in that town because of floods*. 由于洪水泛滥,许多汽车驾驶人员不得不在该城镇中途停留)。~ ***short*** 猛然停止,停止;使(谈话等)停止;【剑术】挡住,回击。~ ***short of*** 差点儿,险些儿,几乎。~ ***the show*** (***cold***)〔美剧〕因某一节目演出精彩,观众多次要求重演以致耽误继续表演。~ ***to look at a fence*** (在障碍前,在困难前)踌躇不前。~ ***up*** 醒着,没有睡;熬夜;塞住(洞口)。~ ***with a friend*** 住在朋友处。

II *n*. **1**. 中止,停止,停车。**2**. 停留处,车站,站;飞机场。**3**. 逗留,歇宿,停留,停靠,停泊。**4**. 终结;终止。**5**.〔英〕句号;标点;间断。**6**. 填塞;妨碍,阻碍。**7**.【乐】(以手指压弦、孔)调整音调;〔转义〕说法,语调,调子。**8**.【机】制子,制楔,制动器,档;销;断流阀。**9**.【乐】风琴的音栓;六弦琴的柱。**10**.【语音】闭塞音〔t, d, k, b 等〕。**11**.【摄】光圈;【物】光阑。**12**.【滑雪】遽止。**13**.【建】门闩。**14**.【海】掣,掣索。**15**.【剑术】挡架。*a bus* ~ 公共汽车站,巴士站。*a full* ~ 句点。*You've four* ~*s before you get to the station*. 你到火车站以前还有四个公共汽车站。*I told him to put a* ~ *to the practice*. 我已经告诉他不要搞那个了。*Every sentence should have its proper* ~. 每句话都应有适当的句点。*It's entirely groundless that you put on the sarcastic* ~. 你发出讽刺的调子是毫无根据的。***bring to a*** ~ 使停止,制止。***come to a*** (***full***) ~ (完全)停止。***make a*** ~ 停止,休息,停留。***put a*** ~ ***to*** 使…停止,使…终止。***put on*** [***pull out, turn on***] ***the pathetic*** ~ 用悲伤的语调说。***without a*** ~ 不停,不停留,不停车。~ **bath**【摄】停影液。~**block** 止轮楔。~**cock**【机】管闩,活栓;活塞。~**-collar**【机】限动环。~**-cylinder press** 自动停滚式印刷机。~**drill** (有凸肩可限制深度的)钻头。~**gap** 塞洞口的东西;填补,充数;权宜之计,敷衍,搪塞。~ **key** [**knob**] 风琴音钮。~**light** (交通岗的)红灯,(汽车的)停车灯。~**-loss order** = ~ order. ~**off** 中途停留(地)。~ **order** (要求经纪人在市价达到一定价格时买进或抛售的)规定价格成交命令;中止命令;止付命令。~**-out** *n*. 中途辍学从事其他活动的学生。~**over 1**. *a*. 中途下车的(票、站等)。**2**. *n*.〔美〕中途下车(站);中途下车许可;中途下车票(*a* ~*over satellite station* 人造卫星中间站)。~**page** 阻止;阻塞,闭塞,停止;故障;(职工工资的)扣除,扣除额;(争议中的)停工;锁厂,罢工;便秘。~ **plate**【机】止动片。~ **press**〔英〕报纸付印时插入的最后消息(栏)。~ **street**〔美〕停车交通口〔车辆到此处必须先停车,得到交通信号才能继续行驶〕。~**valve** 断流阀,停汽阀,节流阀;止阀,闭塞阀。~ **volley** (网球中的)吊短球(恰好过网使对方无法接住的轻击)。~**watch** 停表,记秒表。

stope [stəup; stop] **I** *n*.【矿】回采工作面,梯段开采面;采矿场;矿房。**II** *vt*., *vi*. 在回采面开采(矿石等)。

stop·page [ˈstɔpidʒ; ˋstɑpɪdʒ] *n*. **1**. (活动)中止,停止。**2**.【军】故障;阻塞,堵塞。**3**. 停工,罢工。**4**. 停付。**5**. 扣留,扣除(工资)。

stop·per [ˈstɔpə; ˋstɑpɚ] **I** *n*. **1**. 填塞者,阻止者,止住者。**2**. 阻塞物,塞子。**3**.【机】制动器;限制器;闭锁装置。**4**.【矿】伸缩式凿岩机。**5**. (吸烟斗用的)塞烟具。**6**.【海】掣(索)。**7**.〔美俚〕决定性论断[回答,打击等]。**8**. (空袭时用的)耳塞。*put a* ~ *on* 用塞子塞住;压住,制止。*Papa's stare is a conventional* ~ *to our requests*. 爸爸的瞪眼是对我们请求事项的常见的决定性的回答。**II** *vt*. 用塞子塞住;使闭塞。

stop·ping [ˈstɔpiŋ; ˋstɑpɪŋ] **I** *n*. **1**. 阻止;停止;中止;填塞。**2**. 牙齿填塞料。**3**. 标点。**4**.【矿】风障,风墙,隔墙。**II** *a*. 停的,慢车的。~**-place** *n*. 车站。

stop·ple [ˈstɔpl; ˋstɑpl] **I** *n*. 塞子。**II** *vt*. 用塞子塞住。

stopt [stɔpt; stɑpt]【诗】stop 的过去式和过去分词。

stor·a·ble [ˈstɔːrəbl; ˋstorəbl, ˋstɔr-] **I** *a*. 可储藏的,耐贮藏的;可容纳的。**II** *n*.〔常 *pl*.〕耐储藏品〔如小麦、棉花等〕。

stor·age [ˈstɔːridʒ; ˋstorɪdʒ] *n*. **1**. 贮藏(量),存储(量);(仓库)保管;库容量。**2**. 栈房,仓库,贮藏所。**3**. 栈租,栈费。**4**. 贮存器。**5**.【电】蓄电(瓶)。**6**.【自】(计算机的)存储(器);记忆。*cold* ~ 冷藏。*a locker* ~ 密闭仓。*a* ~ *dam* 蓄洪堰。*Pork and mutton should be kept in cold* ~. 猪羊肉应该冷藏。*The reservoir has in* ~ *about five million cubic metres*. 这水库有五百万立方米的储存量。*500 bales of cotton are in* ~. 库内存有五百包棉花。~ **battery** *n*.【电】蓄电池(组)。

sto·rax [ˈstɔːræks; ˋstoræks, ˋstɔr-] **I** *n*. **1**.【药】苏合香。**2**. 药用安息香(*Styrax officinalis*)。**3**. 安息香属(*Styrax*)植物。**II** *a*. 安息香料(*Styracaceae*)植物的。

store [stɔː, stɔə; stor, stɔr] **I** *n*. **1**.〔*sing*., *pl*.〕贮藏,贮存;准备。**2**.〔*sing*.〕【自】(计算机的)存储器。**3**.〔常 *sing*.〕丰富;大量,多量。**4**.〔英〕栈房,仓库。**5**.〔美〕店铺,商店;〔英〕百货店〔通常叫 the ~s =〔美〕department ~〕。**6**.〔*pl*.〕用品,必需品〔粮食、衣服等〕;补给品,备用品。**7**.【商】原料品,贮存品,存货。**8**.〔常 *pl*.〕= ~ cattle. *a* ~ *of food* 许多食物。*a great* ~ *of facts* 许多事实。*a rich* ~ *of learning* 丰富的知识。*with* ~*s of experience* 有丰富的经验。*a* ~ *of strength* 充裕的体力。*a general* ~ 百货店。*a book* ~ 书店。***in*** ~ 准备着,贮藏着(*I don't know what the future has in* ~ *for us*. 不晓得将来究竟怎么样)。***in*** ~ ***for*** 就要落到…;替某人准备着(*I have an hour's talk in* ~ *for you*. 我有一个钟头的话要跟你谈。*I*

S

have a surprise in ～ *for you*. 我有一件要使你吃惊的事情)。**keep a** ～ 开一个店。**lay in** ～**s for** 为…准备着。**set** (**great**) ～ **by** 重视,器重。**set no great** ～ **by** 不重视,轻视。**II** ***a***. **1.** 贮藏的,贮存的;储备的。**2.** 〔美〕现成的。**3.** 畜牧的,畜产的。～ *bread* 店里烤的面包〔区别于家里自做的〕。*a* ～ *tooth* 假牙。*a* ～ *farm* 畜牧农场。**III** ***vt***. **1.** 积蓄,贮藏;储备;把…存入仓库,把…交给栈房。**2.** 供应,供给。**3.** 蓄(电);容纳。*His head is richly* ～*d with knowledge*. 他脑子里知识可渊博啦。*Let's* ～ *the flowers away from frost*. 让我们把盆花入窖过冬。～ ***away*** 把…贮藏起来。～ ***up*** 贮藏;记住(～ *up a saying in one's heart* 把格言记在心里)。～**card** 商店专用赊购卡。～ **cattle** 为养肥而买进的牛,为出售而养肥的牛。～**front** 〔美〕**1.** ***n***. 商店铺面;沿街的店面房间。**2.** ***a***. 沿街的。～**house** **1.** 仓库,栈房。**2.** (知识的)宝库。～**keeper** **1.** 仓库管理人。**2.** 【海】军需主任。**3.** 〔美〕店主,经理。**4.** 〔美〕滞销货。**5.** 【军】军需品管理员。～**room** 贮藏室商品陈列室。～**ship** 【军】军需船。～(**s**)**man** **1.** 零售店店主。**2.** 仓库工人,仓库管理员。～**d-value card** 现金储值卡〔一种内装记载着存款金额的电脑芯片,但毋需接通网络即可实现无现金交易的智能卡〕。～**wide** 〔美〕***a***. 百货店全部或大部柜台的,全店的(*a* ～*wide sale* 全部商品大减价)。

sto·rey [ˈstɔːri; ˋstorɪ, ˋstɔrɪ] ***n***. (*pl*. ～***s***) **1.** 〔英〕(房屋的)层。**2.** 排列的层。*a house of one* ～ 平房。*a house of three* ～*s* 三层楼的房子。*the basement* ～ 楼底,地下层。*the first* ～〔英〕二楼。***the upper*** ～ **1.** 楼上。**2.** 脑,头(*off in his upper* ～, *wrong in the upper* ～ 神经不正常)。**3.** 乔木的上部枝桠。*beehives arranged in* ～*s* 排成一层一层的蜂房。～**-post** 【建】层柱。

-sto·reyed, -sto·ried[1] [ˈstɔːrid; ˋstorɪd, ˋstɔrɪd] ***a***. 〔构成复合词〕…层楼的;【植】分层的,迭生的。*a five-*～ *building* 五层的楼房。

sto·ried[2] [ˈstɔrid; ˋstorɪd] ***a***. **1.** 传说[故事、历史]上有名的。**2.** 用绘画[雕刻]表现传说[故事、历史]的;用历史画[雕刻]装饰的。*a* ～ *castle* 传说上著名的城堡。*a* ～ *wall of the Liao Dynasty* 辽代的历史故事画墙。

sto·ri·ette [ˌstɔːriˈet; ˏstorɪˋɛt, ˏstɔrɪ-] ***n***. 小故事。

sto·ri·ol·o·gy [ˌstɔːriˈɔlədʒi; ˏstorɪˋɑlədʒɪ, ˏstɔr-] ***n***. 传说研究,传说学。

stork [stɔːk; stɔrk] ***n***. 【鸟】鹳。*a common* [*migratory, white*] ～ 白鹳。*a King S-* 〔喻〕暴君。*a visit from the* ～ 婴儿诞生〔因旧时骗孩子,说婴儿是鹳鸟送来的〕。～ **parking** (超市等门前专供孕妇和刚生过孩子的母亲使用的)"鹳鸟"停车场。～**'s-bill** 【植】老鹳草(属),天竺葵;牻牛儿苗(属)。

storm [stɔːm; stɔrm] **I** ***n***. **1.** 暴风雨,暴风雪,大雪雨,大冰雹,狂风暴雨;【海、气】暴风〔风力十一级〕。**2.** (政治、社会上的)骚动,动乱,风潮。**3.** (感情上的)激动,爆发。**4.** 【军】冲击,猛攻。*We ought to face the world and brave the* ～. 我们应该经风雨,见世面。*A* ～ *is gathering* [*brewing*]. 暴风雨快来了[正在酝酿]。*a* ～ *of applause* 暴风雨似的鼓掌喝彩。*a cyclonic* ～ 旋风。*a* ～ *of rain* 大雨。*After a* ～ *comes a calm*. 雨过天晴。*A* ～ *of criticism was raised by his new novel*. 他的小说招致了极其激烈的批评。～ ***in a teacup*** [***puddle***] 因为一点小事而闹得满城风雨;极小的事情。***take by*** ～ 袭取,强夺,使大吃一惊,使神魂颠倒,使大为感动(*He took her by* ～. 他使她神魂颠倒)。***the*** ～ ***and stress*** 狂飙时期〔尤指18世纪后半德国文学家反抗古典派而活动的时代〕;大动荡。**II** ***vt***. **1.** 袭击,猛攻。**2.** 大力迅速攻占。—***vi***. **1.** (天气)起风暴,下暴雨[雪、雹]。**2.** 冲击,冲进。**3.** 暴怒,怒骂 (*at*)。*At dawn, we* ～*ed the enemy's stronghold*. 拂晓时,我们猛攻了敌人的堡垒。*The quack was* ～*ed with questions*. 江湖骗子受到了猛烈的质问。*It* ～*ed all night*. 风暴整夜不息。*The boss* ～*ed into his office*. 老板气冲冲地进了他的办公室。～**-beaten** ***a***. 受暴风雨打击的,饱经风霜的,饱经患难的。～ **belt** 暴风雨带。～**bird** = petrel. ～ **boat** 强击登陆艇。～**bound** ***a***. 因暴风雨不能出港(受阻)的。～**-card** (航行中测绘的)风暴图。～ **cellar** 〔美〕防风窖。～ **centre** 暴风雨的中心;骚动的中心人物[问题]。～**cloud** 暴风雨前的乌云;动乱的预兆。～**cock** 【鸟】鸫。～**cone** 〔英〕(风暴的)警报球。～ **door** (御风雨、寒气的)外层木板门。～ **drum** (表示有特大暴风雨的圆柱形的)信号。～**-finch** 〔英〕= petrel. ～ **glass** 气候变化预测管。～**ing party** ***n***. 【军】强击队。～ **kite** 失事船把索缆送到陆地上的风筝。～ **lantern**, ～ **lamp** 〔主英〕【海】汽灯,防风灯。～ **petrel** = stormy petrel. ～**proof** 耐风暴的,御风暴的。～ **sail** (风暴时用的)较小而牢的帆。～ **sash** 外重窗(= ～ window)。～ **sewer** 雨水管。～ **signal** 风暴信号。～ **tide** 暴风潮(因岸向风而产生的)。～**-tossed** ***a***. 被暴风乱吹的,被狂风播弄的;心绪极烦乱的。～ **track** 风暴(中心)路径。～ **trooper** **1.** 〔S- T-〕纳粹的冲锋队员。**2.** 突击队员。～ **troops** **1.** 〔S- T-〕纳粹的冲锋队员。**2.** 突击队员,强击部队。～ **valve** 【船】排水口止回阀。～ **warning** 风暴警报。～ **wind** 暴风,狂风。～ **window** (御风雨寒气的)外层木板护窗。～ **zone** 风暴带,风暴区。

storm·i·ness [ˈstɔːminis; ˋstɔrmɪnɪs] ***n***. **1.** 风暴度,猛烈。**2.** 骚乱;吵闹。**3.** 急性子;暴躁,粗暴。

Stor·month [ˈstɔːmʌnθ; ˋstɔrmʌnθ] ***n***. 斯托蒙斯〔姓氏〕。

storm·y [ˈstɔːmi; ˋstɔrmɪ] ***a***. **1.** 风暴的。**2.** 暴风雨(似)的;多风波的。**3.** 猛烈的;急性子的,脾气暴躁的,粗暴的。*a man of* ～ *passion* 性子暴躁的人。*a* ～ *debate* 激烈的争论。*a* ～ *life* 颠沛流离的一生。～ **petrel** 〔美〕【动】海燕;带来麻烦[骚乱,纠纷]的人。**-i·ly** ***ad***. **-i·ness** ***n***.

Stor·t(h)ing [ˈstɔːtiŋ; ˋstorˏtɪŋ, ˋstɔr-] ***n***. (挪威的)议会。

Sto·ry [ˈstɔːri; ˋstorɪ] ***n***. 斯托里[姓氏]。

sto·ry[1] [ˈstɔːri; ˋstorɪ] **I** ***n***. **1.** 故事,传说,传奇,轶事;小说;历史,沿革。**2.** 传记,履历,来历,阅历,经历。**3.** 对某事的描述,叙述。**4.** 内情,真情,情况。**5.** 〔口〕假话,谎话。**6.** (剧等的)情节;电影故事,原作。**7.** 〔美新闻〕特写。*the stories of the revolutionary martyrs* 革命烈士的故事。*His* ～ *is by no means convincing*. 他讲的话丝毫不足令人相信。*All tell the same* ～. 大家异口同声地那么讲。*But that is another* ～. 但那是另外一个问题,那是题外的话。*It is another* ～ *now*. 现在情形不同了。*I know her* ～. 我知道她的经历。*It's a* ～. = *'Tis a* ～. 〔口〕这是假话。*idle stories* 傻话,糊涂话。***as the*** ～ ***goes*** 据传,据说。***be in a*** [***one***, ***the same***] ～ 众口一词。***make up the*** ～ 虚构,捏造。***tell on's*** [***its***] ***own*** ～ 讲自己的身世[本身表明,不言而喻]。***tell stories*** 编故事;说谎。***the*** (***same***) ***old*** ～ 老一套;陈词滥调;陈规旧习。***the same*** ～ ***over again*** 翻来覆去始终不改口的话〔不改变的情况〕。***The*** ～ ***goes*** [***runs***] ***that*****....** 据说。***the whole*** ～ 详情,一五一十,始末根由(*So that's the whole* ～. 原来是这么一回事)。***to make a long*** ～ ***short*** 长话短说,总之,简单说来。**II** ***vt***. **1.** 〔古〕讲…的故事[历史];把…作为故事讲述。**2.** 用故事画装饰。— ***vi***. 说假话。*Oh, you* ～! 哦,你说谎! *He storied about his academic career and his professional career*. 他编造了他的学历经历。～ **art** 叙述艺术。～ **book** 故事书,小说。～ **teller** 讲故事的人,说书人;小说作者,小说家;好讲逸话奇闻的人;〔口〕说谎的人。～**-writer** 故事作者,小说家。

sto·ry[2] [ˈstɔːri; ˋstorɪ] ***n***. = storey.

stoss [stɔs, stɔːs, G. ʃtəus; stɑs, stɔs, ʃtos] ***a***. 〔美〕【地】(处于)逆冰川运动方向的;迎风面的。

stot [stɔt; stɑt] ***n***. 〔北英、方〕小(公)牛,牛犊。

sto·tin·ka [stəuˈtiŋkə; stoˋtɪŋkɑ] ***n***. (*pl*. ***-tin·ki***

[-kiː; -ki]) 斯托丁卡〔保加利亚货币名,等于 1/100 列弗〕。

Stough·ton [ˈstɔːtn; ˋstɔtn̩] ***n***. 斯托顿〔姓氏〕。

stound [staund; staʊnd, stund] **I** ***n***. **1.** 〔古或方〕短时间。**2.** 〔废或方〕疼痛;震惊。**II** ***vi***. 〔苏格兰、英方〕疼,痛。

stoup [stuːp; stup] ***n***. **1.** 【宗】圣水钵。**2.** 〔北英〕大酒杯,酒壶。

stour[1] [stuə; stur] ***n***. 〔古英、方〕 **1.** 战斗,冲突。**2.** 骚动。**3.** 风暴。**4.** 〔苏格兰〕浮尘,灰尘。

stour[2] [stuə; stur] ***a***. 〔苏格兰〕 **1.** 强壮的。**2.** 严厉的,苛刻的。

stout [staut; staʊt] **I** ***a***. **1.** 结实的;坚强的;坚牢的。**2.** 坚定的,坚决的,断然的;勇敢的。**3.** 粗大的,厚的,肥壮的,健壮的;强烈的。**4.** 丰富的(食物等)。*Grandma is a ~ old lady*. 祖母是个健壮的老太太。*I want a ~ bike, as the country road is bad*. 我要一辆结实的脚踏车,因为乡下的路不好走。*a ~ heart* 勇气;勇士。*It's the pay day, for he has brought home a ~ volume from a secondhand bookstore*. 今天发工资,所以他从旧书店里抱回来一厚册书。**II** ***n***. **1.** 黑啤酒。**2.** 烈性啤酒。**3.** 特大号衣服。**4.** 身体结实的人。**~-hearted** ***a***. 勇敢的,无畏的。

stove[1] [stəuv; stov] **I** ***n***. **1.** 火炉,电炉,加热器。**2.** 窑。**3.** 干燥室,烘房。**4.** 【园艺】温室。**5.** 〔美俚〕烟斗。**II** ***vt***. **1.** 用火炉烤[烘干]。**2.** 把…放入温室内培育。**~pipe** **1.** 火炉烟囱管。**2.** 〔俚〕大礼帽〔又叫 ~pipe hat〕。**3.** 〔美俚〕闲谈。**4.** 战壕迫击炮;喷气式战斗机。**5.** 〔*pl*.〕〔美〕裤子。**~pipe committee** 〔美俚〕围炉闲谈;在办公室闲谈的人们。**~ plant** 温室植物。

stove[2] [stəuv; stov] stave 的过去式及过去分词。

sto·ver [ˈstəuvə; ˋstovɚ] ***n***. 〔英方〕谷草类干饲料,饲用茎叶。

stow [stəu; sto] ***vt***. **1.** 装进 (*away*; *in*; *into*);装填,装载;堆垛,堆装。**2.** 收藏,隐藏。**3.** 卷起(帆等)。**4.** 使暂留。**5.** 〔俚〕〔常用命令式〕不要,别,停止。*Before climbing, we ~ed a little cabin with supplies of mountaineering*. 爬山以前,我们把需要的物品堆放在一间小屋里。*S- these away from the fire*. 这些东西堆得离火远些。*The doctor says the patient has to be ~ed in the emergency room*. 大夫说病人要暂时留在急诊室里。*S- the chatter!* 别胡扯! **~ away** 收藏,收拾;躲在船里偷渡;〔谑〕吃光,吃得干干净净。**~ down** 装入,装载。**~ larks!** 别开玩笑! 别闹着玩! **~ the hold with cargo** 把货物装进舱里。

stow·age [ˈstəuidʒ; ˋstoɪdʒ] ***n***. **1.** 装载。**2.** 贮藏;装载[贮藏]的处所[物品、方法、数量、费用]。**3.** 食量,食欲。

stow·a·way [ˈstəuəwei; ˋstoə,we] ***n***. 躲在船里偷渡的人。

Stow(e) [stəu; sto] ***n***. 斯托〔姓氏〕。

STP = **1.** standard temperature and pressure 标准温度与压力。**2.** standard temperature and pulse 正常体温与脉搏。**3.** scientifically treated petroleum 放在发动机燃料油中的一种添加剂;一种产生幻觉的药〔性质似墨斯卡林及安非他明〕。

St. Pierre Is. [sntˈpjɛə; sntˋpjɛr] ***n***. 圣皮埃尔岛。

STR = submarine thermal reactor 潜水艇用热中子反应堆。

str. = **1.** steamer. **2.** strainer. **3.** strait. **4.** string(s). **5.** strophe.

stra·bis·mal, stra·bis·mic, -mi·cal [strəˈbizml, -mik(l); strəˋbɪzml̩, -mɪk(l̩)] ***a***. 【医】斜视的,斜眼的。

stra·bis·mus [strəˈbizməs; strəˋbɪzməs] ***n***. 【医】斜视[眼]。

Stra·bo [ˈstreibəu; ˋstrebo] 斯特雷波〔64? B.C. —A.D. 23?,古希腊地理学家〕。

stra·bot·o·my [strəˈbɔtəmi; strəˋbɑtəmɪ] ***n***. 【医】斜视纠正手术。

Stra·chey [ˈstreitʃi; ˋstretʃɪ] ***n***. 斯特雷奇〔姓氏〕。

strad·dle [ˈstrædl; ˋstrædl̩] **I** ***vi***. **1.** 跨立,叉开腿(坐着);叉开腿走。**2.** 不表明态度,骑墙观望。**3.** 【军】为要确定射程而向目标物前后试击,夹叉射击[轰炸]。— ***vt***. **1.** 跨,骑。**2.** 【军】向(目标)作夹叉射击[轰炸]。**3.** 〔美口〕(对政治问题等)采取骑墙观望态度。**4.** 【股】做一手买进一手卖出的交易。**5.** 【扑克】加倍。**II** ***n***. **1.** 跨立,叉开两腿。**2.** 大踏步。**3.** 骑墙,观望。**4.** 【军】夹叉射击[轰炸]。**5.** 【股】一手买进一手卖出的交易。*You shouldn't have ~d when talking with the guests*. 你和客人们谈话的时候,本来不应该叉开腿坐着的。*It's the second time James ~d. Maybe he'll back out*. 这是詹姆斯第二次不表态了,也许他要打退堂鼓。*George made pots of money by straddling*. 乔治一手买进一手卖出地赚了一大笔钱。~*-trench* 【军】战地便坑。**-r** ***n***.

strafe [strɑːf; stref, strɑf] **I** ***vt***. **1.** 炮击。**2.** (飞机)扫射,轰炸。**3.** 猛击;惩罚。**II** ***n***. 低空扫射,猛烈轰炸;惩罚。**-r** ***n***.

Straf·ford [ˈstræfəd; ˋstræfɚd] ***n***. 斯特拉福德〔姓氏〕。

strag·gle [ˈstrægl; ˋstrægl̩] ***vi***. **1.** 迷路;掉队,和大队分离,被丢在后头,落后,落伍;彷徨,流离。**2.** 蔓延,四散;散开,散在;零落,零乱 (*along*)。**3.** (路、河等)纡曲,蜿蜒。*The crowd ~d along*. 一大群人七零八落地走过去。*A wisp of hair ~d across her ear*. 一束头发散落在她耳朵上。*Weeds ~ over the garden*. 花园里野草蔓延。*The path ~s out a mile long*. 小路迂曲一英里长。

strag·gler [ˈstrægləl; ˋstræglɚ] ***n***. **1.** 迷路者;彷徨者;〔美〕荡游者;孤立者。**2.** 【军】掉队者,归队迟到人员,掉队的飞机。**3.** 失群之鸟。**4.** 蔓生的草木。*cut off the ~s* 砍去冗枝。*a ~'s line* 【军】掉队兵收容线。

strag·gling [ˈstræglinŋ; ˋstræglɪŋ, -gl̩ɪŋ] ***a***. **1.** 落后的,掉队的。**2.** 散漫的,零乱的,队伍散乱的。**3.** 乱七八糟伸开的,蔓生的;散在的,零零落落的;断续的,稀落的。**-ly** ***ad***.

strag·gly [ˈstrægli; ˋstræglɪ] ***a***. = straggling.

straight [streit; stret] **I** ***a***. **1.** 直,一直线的 (*opp*. crooked, bent, curved)。**2.** 直挺的,向(目标)直进的。**3.** 直接的,连续的。**4.** 整齐的,规矩的,端正的,有条理的。**5.** 正直的,坦率的,有品德的。**6.** 〔口〕正确的,可靠的,没有错的(账等);不加修改的,原样未改的,依次的。**7.** 〔俚〕不掺杂的,纯净的;〔美口〕纯粹的。**8.** (发动机)汽缸直排式的。**9.** 彻底支持某候选人[政党]的。**10.** 不论买多少,价钱不变的。*a ~ line* 直线。*~ hair* 不卷的头发。*a ~ face* (故意装做的)正经面孔。*a ~ accent* 长音符号。*a ~ top* 【机】平顶。*a ~ report* 可靠的报告。*a ~ comedy* 按照原作未加改动的喜剧。*a ~ thinker* 逻辑性强的思想家。*a whisky ~* 纯威士忌酒。*a ~ Republican* 顽固的共和党人。(***as***) **~ *as an arrow*** 像箭一样直,笔直。***be ~ with the world*** 〔美俚〕了清债务。***get ~*** 〔美〕了解,搞通,办好,弄好。***in ~ succession*** 连续不断。***keep ~*** 行为正直,(女子)守贞操。***make things ~*** 弄直,整顿。***put*** [***set***] ***things ~*** 整顿[收拾]东西。

II ***ad***. **1.** 直,笔直,垂直。**2.** 正确;老实;率直;坦白;〔俚〕不掺水。**3.** 直接,一直;接续不断地。**4.** 立刻。*He will come ~ from Paris*. 他将直接从巴黎来。***go ~*** 笔直走,正正经经做人。***keep ~ on*** 继续快走。***ride ~*** 骑马跳过障碍一直飞跑。***run ~*** 笔直跑;正正经经做人,不做坏事。***shoot*** [***hit***] **~** 瞄准射击,使命中。**~ *off*** 痛痛快快地,立刻,马上。**~ *out*** 坦白,露骨 (*tell ~ out* 直讲)。

III ***n***. **1.** 直,直线。**2.** (赛跑跑道接近终点处的)直线部分。**3.** (纸牌的)五张牌点数连续的顺子。**4.** 【拳击】直击。**5.** 〔俚〕真相。**6.** (赛马)第一名。*They were even as they reached the ~*. 他们快到终点时还不分胜负。

S

Tell the manager the ~ *of it*. 把实情告诉经理吧。***follow the*** ~ ***and narrow*** 安分守己;循规蹈距。***on the*** ~ 笔直,老实地,正正经经地。***out of the*** ~ 歪着,弯着。~ **A**〔美〕成绩极优良的大学生。~**-ahead** ***a***.〔美〕1. 直接的。2. 不偏离标准的。~ **angle**【数】平角。~ **arch**【建】平拱。~**-arm**(橄榄球)伸直手臂挡住对方。~**-arrow** 1. ***a***. 规矩的;坦率的。2. ***n***. 循规蹈矩的人;正直坦率的人。~**away** 直线跑道;陆路(或水路上)的直段。~ **chain**【化】直链。~**-cut**(烟叶)纵切的。~**edge** ***n***. 直尺,标尺。~**eight**(汽车)八汽缸直排式,直八式。~ **eye** 能看出东西是否正或是否直的眼力。~ **fight** 倾注全力的战斗;【政】两候选人的势均力敌的竞争。~ **goods**〔美〕确确实实的消息;事实,真相。~**jacket** ***n***., ***vt***. = straitjacket. ~ **jet**(无螺旋桨的)喷气式飞机。~**-laced** ***a***. = straitlaced. ~**-line** ***a***. 直线的,直排式的。~ **man**〔美运〕被打败的对手;〔美剧〕给喜剧演员作笑料的配角。~ **paper** 由一个人签发的流通票据。~**-out** 1. ***n***. 对某一政党支持到底的人。2. ***a***. 坦率的,彻底的。~ **razor**(一般理发厅用的)折叠式剃刀。~ **shoot**〔美〕直路;最直接的办法。~ **shooter** 坦白正直的人。~ **ticket**〔美政〕某一政党的全部候选人名单(*vote the* ~ *ticket* 把票全投给一个政党的候选人)。~ **time**〔美〕规定工时;规定工时的工资率。~**way** 1. ***ad***. 直接地,立刻,马上。2. ***a***. 畅通无阻的。**-ly** ***ad***. **-ness** ***n***.

straight·en [ˈstreitn; ˋstretn] ***vt***. 1. 弄直;矫正,纠正。2. 整顿,整理。— ***vi***. 变直;变正,变挺。*I've made up my mind to* ~ *out a very complicated subject*. 我已经下决心把一个非常复杂的题目搞清楚。*I'm going to* ~ *up my room*. 我马上整理我的房间去。~ ***one's face***(笑过后)恢复正常面孔。~ ***out*** 弄(得到)澄清;(得到)解决。~ ***up***〔美〕改善;正派地过日子。**-er** ***n***. 矫正者;改正者;整顿者;【空】整流器。

straight·for·ward [streitˈfɔːwəd; ˏstretˋfɔrwəd] **I** ***a***. 1. 一直向前的;直接的。2. 真正的,老实的;坦率的。3. 直截了当的,易懂的。4. 明确的。*The explanation was* ~. 解释直截了当。**II** ***ad***. 坦率地。**-ly** ***ad***. **-ness** ***n***.

straight·for·wards [streitˈfɔːwədz; ˏstretˋfɔrwədz] ***ad***. 坦率地。

strain[1] [strein; stren] **I** ***vt***. 1. 用力拉,拉紧,抽紧,扯紧。2. 使紧张;尽量使用(肌肉等)。3. 强迫,强制;滥用,尽量利用。4. 拉伤,用力过度而弄伤,使工作过度;使用过度而弄坏;扭伤。5. 曲解,牵强附会。6.【机】使变形,扭歪。7. 抱紧。8. 滤(*out*)。— ***vi***. 1. 尽力,拼命努力。2. 拉,拖(*at*)。3. 扭歪,弯曲,快要折断。4. 滤过,渗出。5. 不肯接受。~ *one's ears* 竖起耳朵注意听。~ *one's voice* 拼命呼喊。~ *one's eyes* 睁大眼睛看。~ *one's wit* 绞尽脑汁。~ *oneself* 过劳。~ *one's authority* 滥用权力。~ *sb.'s good temper* 利用某人脾气好。*Mary* ~*ed her baby to the breast*. 玛丽把小孩紧抱在怀里。~ *a rope to the breaking point* 将绳拉紧到快要断的程度。~*ed relations between officers and men* 搞得不好的官兵关系。~ *the law* 曲解法律。*a* ~*ed interpretation* 歪曲的翻译;牵强的解释。*He is* ~*ing under their pressure*. 他是在他们的压力之下苦撑着。*It's the nature of plants to* ~ *upwards to the light*. 植物的本性是向上挺窜争取阳光。*You, too, will* ~ *at such a demand*. 你也会难以接受这样的要求的。~ ***a point*** 逾分,过分,任意(曲解)。~ ***after*** 尽力追求,拼命想得到[做到]。~ ***at*** 为,辛苦[用气力,费神,尽力]。~ ***at a gnat*** 为小事过分操心。~ ***at the oar*** 拼命划。~ ***courtesy*** 太讲礼貌,过分客气。~ ***every nerve*** 倾全力;全神贯注(*to do*)。~ ***under pressure*** 在压迫下拼命挣扎。**II** ***n***. 1. 拉紧;紧张;尽力,出力。2. 过劳,使用过度;滥用,利用。3. 扭筋,脱臼。4.【物】变形,歪曲;应力,张力;胁变,应变。5. 曲解。*put a great* ~ *on sb.'s resources* 使人担负过重的经济负担。*It was a great* ~ *on my resources*. 这在我财力上是一个很大的负担。***at full***[***utmost***] ~ = ***be on the*** ~ 紧张,拼命。***stand the*** ~ 拼命忍受。***under the*** ~ 因紧张;因过劳。~**ing piece**[**beam**]【建】跨腰梁。

strain[2] [strein; stren] ***n***. 1. 血统,家世;族,种;【生】品系,系;菌株;变种,小种。2. 性格,脾气;倾向,气质。3. 语气;笔调,文风;作风。4.〔常 *pl*.〕一段音乐,歌曲;诗歌。5. 一阵子滔滔不绝的言词;一阵子难听的话。*She comes of a peasant* ~. 她出身于世代农家。*The Germany* ~ *in him makes him like philosophy*. 他的德意志民族的血统使得他喜欢研究哲学。*good* ~*s of seed* 良种。*a hybrid* ~ 杂交种。*a meat* ~ 肉用品种。*He has a* ~ *of melancholy in him*. 他有点忧郁。*in the same* ~ 以同样调子[作风]。*It was the commencement day and the head master would talk in a lofty* ~. 那天是开学典礼,是校长高谈阔论的日子。

strained [straind; strend] ***a***. 紧张的;勉强的,不自然的(态度等);牵强附会的(解释等)。*Notice the* ~ *manners of George before strangers*. 你注意乔治在陌生人面前的不自然的样子。*Let's straighten out their* ~ *relations*. 咱们把他们之间的紧张关系和解了吧。

strain·er [ˈstreinə; ˋstrenɚ] ***n***. 1. 用力拉的人,使劲的人,紧张的人[物]。2. 粗滤器,滤网。3.【机】松紧螺旋扣。

strait [streit; stret] **I** ***a***.〔古〕1. 窄,狭,狭隘的,窄小的(地方、衣服等)。2. 艰难的,窘迫的,穷困的(家境等)。3.【圣】严格的,严厉的。*a* ~ *door* 一个狭窄的门。*a* ~ *Catholic sect* 一个严格的天主教教派。**II** ***n***. 1.〔常 *pl*. 作单数用〕海峡。2.〔常 *pl*.〕窘迫,穷困,艰难。3.〔罕〕地峡。4.【解】(狭)口。*the Straits* (a) = the Straits of Gibraltar. (b) the Straits of Malacca 海峡。***in great*** ~***s*** 处境非常困难。***in*** ~***s for*** 缺乏(某物)。***in increasingly dire*** ~***s*** 处境越来越糟。~**jacket** = strait waistcoat. ~**-laced** ***a***. 穿着紧身的衣服的;(极端)严谨的,拘谨的,拘泥的,观念狭隘的。~**-waistcoat**(束缚疯子或狂暴的囚犯用的)紧衣;拘束,束缚。**-ly** ***ad***.〔古〕狭,窄;严格。**-ness** ***n***.〔古〕窄,狭隘;严厉,严格;困难,艰难,窘迫,缺乏(*straitness of mind* 思想狭隘,气量小,小心眼儿)。

strait·en [ˈstreitn; ˋstretn] ***vt***. 把…弄窄;〔古〕限制,使收缩,收紧;〔主用 *p.p.*〕折磨,使窘迫。***be*** ~***ed for*** 缺乏,苦于没有。

strake [streik; strek] ***n***. 1. 轮箍。2.【船】列钣,外钣;船底板。3.(选矿)淘汰盘。4. 条纹;狭长(草)地。

stra·mash [strəˈmæʃ, ˈstræməʃ; strəˋmæʃ, ˋstræməʃ] ***n***.〔Scot.〕骚乱;口角,争吵;击碎,撞毁。

stra·mo·ni·um [strəˈməuniəm; strəˋmonɪəm] ***n***.【植】曼陀罗花;曼陀罗叶[气喘药]。

strand[1] [strænd; strænd] **I** ***n***. 1.〔诗〕(海、湖、河等的)滨,岸,滩。2.〔the S-〕(伦敦的)河滨马路。**II** ***vt***., ***vi***. 1.(使)(船等)触礁;(使)搁浅。2.(使)处于困境;(使)落后。***be*** ~***ed*** 搁浅;窘迫,进退两难;因资金匮缺,处于困境(*There were no jobs and most of them were* ~*ed in an alien environment*. 那儿并没有工作可找;他们中的大多数人都在异国环境里进退两难)。~ **line**(水退前的)海岸水线。

strand[2] [strænd; strænd] **I** ***n***. 1.(绳子的)股,绞;一股绳子;纤维,绳,线;串。2.【电】导线束;多心裸电缆。3.(思想等的)一个组成部分。**II** ***vt***. 1. 使(绳股)被拆开。2. 绞。3. 打(绳子)。~*ed wire* 绞合金属线。**-er** 搓绳者,拆绳者;搓绳机。

stran·dee [strænˈdiː; strænˋdi] ***n***.(因事故而)中途滞留的旅客。

strange [streindʒ; strendʒ] ***a***. 1. 奇怪的,古怪的,不可思议的。2. 不认识的,陌生的;不熟悉的。3. 生疏的;没有经验的,生手的,外行的。4. 疏远的,冷淡的,不亲热的。5. 外国的,异乡的,别处的。*He is still* ~ *to the job*. 他还不太习惯这个工作。~ *fish*〔口〕怪人。*I am*

S

quite ~ here [*to this place*]. 我对这里十分人地生疏。*The newcomer is very ~ in his manner*. 这新来的人举动上很古怪。*I'm ~ at bridge*. 我对桥牌是外行。*Your friends will help you when you're in a ~ land*. 你在国外的时候,你的朋友们会帮你的忙的。***feel ~*** 身体有点不对,觉得不舒服;头晕眼花,发晕;觉得奇怪,觉得不安定。***make oneself ~*** 装做生人;装做不知道,装做惊奇的样子。~ ***as it may sound*** 听[说]起来也许奇怪。~ ***to say*** [***tell***] 说也奇怪。**-ly** ***ad***. **-ness** ***n***. 【物】(量子数的)奇异性。

stran·ger [ˈstreindʒə; ˋstrendʒɚ] ***n***. **1**. 陌生人,不认识的人;新来的人;客人;异乡人;外国人。**2**. 局外人,门外汉,没有经验的人,不熟悉的人。**3**. 【法】第三者,非当事人。**4**. 〔美〕先生〔= sir, 在乡下对陌生人打招呼用的称呼〕。*the little ~* 〔俚〕小孩子。*He is a ~ to me*. 我不认识他。*You are quite a ~*. 〔口〕好久不见了。*a ~ in a strange land* 住在异乡的外国人。*I see* [*spy*] *~s*. 【英下院】要求禁止旁听,要求旁听者退场。***a ~ to ...*** 不知道,不懂得;陌生,不习惯于 (*He is a ~ to fear*. 他不晓得害怕)。***be shy in the presence of ~s*** 怕生,(小孩子)认生。***make a ~ of*** 冷淡对待。***make no ~ of*** 亲热对待。***make oneself a ~*** 装规矩;拘礼。***no ~ to*** (***sorrow***, ***poverty***) 饱经(忧患、贫困)。

stran·gle [ˈstræŋgl; ˋstræŋgl] ***vt***. **1**. 扼死,勒死,绞死。**2**. 闷住,塞住呼吸;(硬领等)扼住(脖子);闭住(呼吸)。**3**. 压住;压制。~ *a bill* 压住议案。— ***vi***. **1**. 扼[勒,绞]死。**2**. 窒息而死。*It is said that he was ~ed to death by gas*. 据说他是被煤气熏死的。*When I attended his lecture, I always tried hard to ~ yawnings*. 我上他的课时,总是竭力地制止自己打呵欠。~**hold** ***n***. **1**. 【摔跤】勒颈;压制。**2**. 束缚,压制。

stran·gler [ˈstræŋglə; ˋstræŋglɚ] ***n***. **1**. 扼杀者,压制者。**2**. 〔英〕【机】阻气门,阻塞门。

stran·gles [ˈstræŋglz; ˋstræŋglz] ***n***. 〔作单数用〕【兽医】腺疫,传染性卡他。

stran·gu·late [ˈstræŋgjuleit; ˋstræŋgjəˏlet] ***vt***. 勒死,绞死;使窒息;【医】绞扼,绞窄(肠子等)。— ***vi***. 【医】绞扼,绞窄。

stran·gu·la·tion [ˌstræŋgjuˈleiʃən; ˏstræŋgjəˋleʃən] ***n***. 绞窄;窒息。

stran·gu·ry [ˈstræŋgjuri; ˋstræŋgjərɪ] ***n***. 【医】痛性尿淋沥。

strap [stræp; stræp] **I** ***n***. **1**. 带,皮[布、铁]带,铁皮条,(电车等的)拉手吊带。**2**. 磨刀皮带。**3**. (表示军阶等的)肩章。**4**. 搭扣鞋。**5**. 〔the ~〕鞭打。**6**. 【机】狭[带]条,套带,带圈。**7**. 【医】橡皮膏。**8**. 【海】(滑车的)带索。**9**. 【植】小舌片。**10**. 〔俚〕信用,赊。**11**. 【电】捷接,母线。**12**. 〔爱尔兰〕轻佻女子;娼妓。***on*** (***the***) ~ 凭信用,赊。**II** ***vt***. (***-pp-***) **1**. 用带子捆扎,用皮带捆。**2**. 用皮带抽打。**3**. 用皮带磨。**4**. 【医】给…贴上橡皮膏 (*up*; *down*)。— ***vi***. **1**. 拼命工作。**2**. 被捆缚。*The nurse will ~ up your wound*. 护士会绑扎你的伤口。*She works with a baby ~ped to her back*. 她工作时把小孩用带子捆扎在背上。~ ***at*** [***to***] ***one's work*** 拼命工作。~ **brake** 【机】带闸。~**hanger** (电车上)拉着吊带站着的乘客。~ **hinge** 束带式铰链;铁板铰。~**-laid** ***a***. 用两条三股绳平列缝合的。~**less** 无带的,无肩带的 (*~less bra* 无肩带乳罩)。~**-oil** 〔俚〕鞭打。~**work** 用窄带摺叠(或交织)而成的装饰图案。~**wort** 【植】海滨寇秋罗。

strappa·do [strəˈpeidəu; strəˋpedo, -ˋpɑdo] **I** ***n***. (*pl*. *~es*) **1**. (从前的)吊坠刑〔将犯人用绳吊起然后坠下〕,吊坠刑具。**II** ***vt***. 把…处以吊坠刑。

strapped [stræpt; stræpt] ***a***. **1**. 用皮带捆住的,勒有皮带的;用皮带装饰的。**2**. 〔美俚〕资金短少的,身无分文的。

strap·per [ˈstræpə; ˋstræpɚ] ***n***. **1**. 用皮带捆绑的人。**2**. 用磨刀皮带磨刀的人。**3**. 马夫。**4**. 〔口〕粗大东西;身材魁梧的人,彪形大汉。

strap·ping [ˈstræpiŋ; ˋstræpɪŋ] **I** ***a***. 〔口〕魁梧的,强壮的,高大而匀称的。**II** ***n***. 皮带材料;橡皮膏;贴膏法。

Stras·bourg, Strass·burg [ˈstræzbəːg; ˋstræsbɝg, ˋstræz-] ***n***. 斯特拉斯堡〔法国城市〕。

strass [stræs; stræs] ***n***. 施特拉斯铅玻璃〔一种极闪亮的铅玻璃,用以造假宝石,得名于发明者德国人约瑟夫·施特拉斯〕。

stra·ta [ˈstreitə; ˋstretə, ˋstrætə] ***n***. stratum 的复数。

stra·ta·gem [ˈstrætidʒəm; ˋstrætədʒəm] ***n***. 战略,策略;谋略;计策,诡计。

stra·tal [ˈstreitl; ˋstretḷ] ***a***. 【地】成层的,有层次的;地层的。

stra·te·gic(al) [strəˈtiːdʒik(əl); strəˋtidʒɪk(əl)] ***a***. **1**. 战略(上)的;(战略上)重要的。**2**. 为战略计划用的。*one's ~ goal* 战略目标。~ *bombardment* 战略轰炸。~ *bombers* 战略轰炸机。~ *materials* 战略物资。~ *points* 战略据点。~ *retreat* 战略退却。*Strategic Defense Initiate = Star Wars*.

stra·te·gi·cal·ly [strəˈtiːdʒikəli; strəˋtidʒɪkəlɪ] ***ad***. 战略上,颇为策略地。

stra·te·gics [strəˈtiːdʒiks; strəˋtidʒɪks] ***n***. 战略(学);兵法。

strat·e·gist [ˈstrætidʒist; ˋstrætədʒɪst] ***n***. 战略家。*a military ~* 军事家。

strat·e·gy [ˈstrætidʒi; ˋstrætədʒɪ] ***n***. **1**. 战略(学)。**2**. 策略,作战方针〔*cf*. tactics〕。~ *and tactics* 战略与战术。*I know his conception of political ~*. 我晓得他的政治策略的概念。~ *of trading space for time* 用空间换取时间的战略。

Strat·ford-on-Avon [ˈstrætfədənˈeivən; ˋstrætfɚdənˋevən, -ən-] ***n***. 斯特拉特福〔英国市镇,在埃冯河畔,莎士比亚的故乡〕。

strath [stræθ; stræθ] ***n***. 〔Scot.〕老谷底,平底河谷。

strath·spey [stræθˈspei; stræθˋspe, ˋstræθˏspe] ***n***. (苏格兰)斯特拉斯贝舞[曲]。

strat·i [ˈstreitai; ˋstretaɪ] ***n***. stratus 的复数。

strat·i·cu·late [strəˈtikjulit; strəˋtɪkjəlet, -lɪt] ***a***. 【地】薄层的;成薄层的,分层的。**-la·tion** [-ˌtikjuˈleiʃən; -tɪkjəˋleʃən] ***n***.

strat·i·fi·ca·tion [ˌstrætifiˈkeiʃən; ˏstrætəfəˋkeʃən] ***n***. **1**. 【地】层理;分层,层叠形成,成层作用[现象]。**2**. 【园艺】砂藏。

strat·i·form [ˈstrætiˌfɔːm; ˋstrætəˏfɔrm] ***a***. 成层状的;显出层理的;层状的〔如云层〕。

strat·i·fy [ˈstrætifai; ˋstrætəˏfaɪ] ***vt***. (***-fied***) **1**. 使成层,使分层。**2**. 【园艺】以层积法保藏。*stratified alluvium* 成层冲积岩。*a stratified-charge engine* 【机】分层进气发动机。*stratified rock* 成层岩。*stratified sampling* 【统】分层抽样。— ***vi***. 成层;分层。

stra·tig·ra·pher [strəˈtigrəfə; strəˋtɪgrəfɚ] ***n***. 地层学家。

strat·i·graph·ic(al) [ˌstrætiˈgræfik(əl); ˏstrætɪˋgræfɪk(əl)] ***a***. 【地】地层学的。**-cal·ly** ***ad***.

stra·tig·ra·phy [strəˈtigrəfi; strəˋtɪgrəfɪ] ***n***. **1**. 地层。**2**. 地层学。**-pher** ***n***. **-graph·ic** [-ˈgræfik; -ˋgræfɪk] ***a***.

strato- *comb. f*. 表示"层": *strato*cumulus.

stra·to-cham·ber [ˈstrætəuˌtʃeimbə; ˋstrætoˏtʃembɚ] ***n***. 同温研究室。

stra·to·cir·rus [ˌstrætəuˈsirəs; ˏstretoˋsɪrəs] ***n***. 【气】低浓层卷云。

stra·toc·ra·cy [strəˈtɔkrəsi; strəˋtɑkrəsɪ] ***n***. 军人政治,军阀政治。

stra·to·cruis·er [ˈstreitəukruːzə; ˋstrætəˏkruzɚ] ***n***. 同温层飞机。

stra·to·cu·mu·lus [ˌstrætəuˈkjuːmjuləs; ˏstretoˋkjumjələs] ***n***. 【气】层积云。

stra·to-liner [ˈstrætəuˌlainə; ˋstrætə͵laɪnɚ] ***n.*** 同温层客机[班机]。

stra·to·plane [ˈstrætəuplein; ˋstrætə͵plen] ***n.*** 同温层飞机。

strat·o·sphere [ˈstrætəusfiə; ˋstrætə͵sfɪr, ˋstretə-] ***n.*** **1.**【气】平流层,同温层。**2.** 最上层,最高栏,最高部位。**3.** 艰深的学科领域。*a* ~ *Joe*〔美空军口〕高个子,长人。*a* ~ *plane* = stratoplane.

strat·o·spher·ic [ˌstrætəuˈsferik; ͵strætəˋsfɛrɪk] ***a.*** 同温层的。

strat·o·vi·sion [ˈstrætəuˌviʒən; ˋstrætə͵vɪʒən] ***n.***【无】同温层;(通过飞机)转播电视。

stra·tum [ˈstreitəm, ˈstrætəm; ˋstretəm, ˋstrætəm] ***n.*** (*pl.* ***-ta***) **1.** 地层;层。**2.** 阶层。*the field* ~ 地面植被层。*the privileged* ~ 特权阶层。*in all social strata* 社会各阶层的。

stra·tus [ˈstreitəs; ˋstretəs] ***n.*** (*pl.* ***-ti*** [-tai; -taɪ])【气】层云。

Straus(s) [straus; straʊs] ***n.*** 斯特劳斯〔姓氏〕。

stra·vage [strəˈveig; strəˋveg] ***vi.*** (***-vaged***; ***-vag·ing***)〔Scot.〕漫游;游荡(= stravaig)。

straw [strɔː; strɔ] **I** ***n.*** **1.** 稻草,麦秆。**2.** (用稻草,麦秆做成的)东西,(吸冷饮用)麦秆状吸管;草帽〔又叫 ~ hat〕。**3.** 不值钱的东西,琐细无聊的事情;一点点。**4.**〔美俚〕头子;帮手,助理。**5.** 稻草色,浅黄色。**II** ***a.*** **1.** 稻草的,麦秆的。**2.** 稻草[麦秆]做的。**3.**〔口〕不值钱的,无用的,琐细的。**4.** (作为替身的)稻草人般的;假的〔如作为民意测验的假投票〕;假想的。*A* ~ *shows which way the wind blows.* 草动知风向;观微知著。*They suck soda water through* ~*s* (*tube*). 他们用(麦秆状)吸管喝汽水。*Cover the heap of* ~ *when it rains.* 下雨时要把草堆盖上。(***a***) ~(***s***) ***in the wind*** 风向指标,舆论指标,显示大动向的小事,由微知著的征兆。***as a last*** ~ (不断吃亏[遭殃])终于,到了最后。***catch*** (***clutch***, ***grasp***) ***at a*** ~ (落水的人)抓住稻草,抓住靠不住的东西不放。***draw*** ~***s*** 抓(稻草)阄。***gather*** [***pick***] ~***s*** 想睡。***in the*** ~〔古〕(产妇)做月子。***make bricks without*** ~ 想做不能做的事情。***man of*** ~ 稻草人;没财产的人;靠不住的人;假想敌。***not care a*** ~ [***two*** ~***s***, ***three*** ~***s***] 一点儿也不介意。***not worth a*** ~ 毫无价值。***One's eyes draw*** [***gather***, ***pick***] ~***s***. 昏昏欲睡。***out of the*** ~ 分娩之后。***split*** ~***s*** 为一些小事而争吵。***the last*** ~ (一系列打击中)终于使人不能忍受的最后一击[最后因素]。***throw*** ~***s against the wind*** 扬草抵风,螳臂挡车。~ **bail**〔美〕无资力的保人。~ **board** 纸板,马粪纸。~ **bond**〔美俚〕假证券。~**boss**〔口〕工头助手。~**colo(u)r** 稻草色,淡黄色。~ **dicer**〔美〕麦秸草帽。~**-flower** 终年不谢的野花。~**hat theatre** 夏季剧院。~ **in the boots**〔美〕财产。~ **man** **1.** 稻草人。**2.** 无足轻重的人物。**3.** (为了制造取胜的假像而假设的)易于击败的敌对论点。**4.** 被用来作挡箭牌的人。~ **plait** 草帽缏。~ **poll**〔英〕= ~ vote. ~ **rope** 草绳。~ **vote** (考验候选人威望的)测验投票。~ **stem** 一种细脚酒杯。~ **wine** 稻草葡萄酒〔在酿制前,葡萄先放在稻草垫上晒干,故名〕。~ **worm** **1.** 毛翅目昆虫的幼虫(水栖,用为鱼饵)。**2.** 膜翅目昆虫的幼虫(有害麦类)。~ **yellow** 淡黄色。

straw·ber·ry [ˈstrɔːbəri; ˋstrɔ͵bɛrɪ, -bərɪ] ***n.***【植】草莓。*a* ~ *blonde*〔美俚〕红发女郎。~ *leaves*〔英〕公爵的爵位象征〔因为用草莓叶做冠饰〕;公爵。*We grow strawberries in our garden.* 我们的园子里种草莓。~ **bass**【动】(黑色)北美日鲈。~ **bush**【植】美洲卫茅。~ **mark** (草莓状)红色胎记,莓状痣。~ **roan** 枣红色[红棕色]的马。~ **shrub**【植】洋腊梅(属)。~ **tomato**【植】酸浆属植物。~ **tree**【植】**1.** 莓实树。**2.** 美洲卫茅。

straw·y [ˈstrɔːi; ˋstrɔ·ɪ] ***a.*** (***-i·er***; ***-i·est***) 稻草[麦秸]的,稻草[麦秸]做的;稻草[麦秸]形的。

stray [strei; stre] **I** ***vi.*** **1.** 迷路,走失,失败。**2.** 误入歧途,堕落;(议论)离题;(思想)迷失方向。**3.** 仿徨,游荡,漂泊。*Be careful not to* ~ *from* [*off*] *the right path of duty.* 注意不要偏离应尽职责的正道。*Don't* ~ *from the main point of the question.* 不要离开问题的主要之点。**II** ***a.*** **1.** 迷了路的,走失了的,离了群的,失散了的。**2.** 意外的,零落的,偶然见到的(例子等);偶然跑来的(客人等)。*a* ~ *child* 迷路的孩子。*a* ~ *customer* 偶然的顾客。*a* ~ *bullet* 流弹。**III** ***n.*** **1.** 迷路者,迷路(离群的)家畜;无家可归的人;迷路的孩子。**2.**〔英〕〔*pl.*〕因无人继承而归公的遗产。**3.**〔*pl.*〕【无】天电,杂电。**4.**【地】(石油钻探中)偶然出现的间层,杂层。~ *capacity*【电】杂散电容。~ *light* 散射光,漫射光。**-er** 迷路者;流浪者;不走正路的人。

streak [striːk; strik] **I** ***n.*** **1.** 纹理,条纹,斑纹,条痕,条层,色条,色线。**2.**【矿】矿脉,矿层;矿物痕[粉]色。**3.**【微】划线,条斑。**4.** 倾向;气味(性格上不太显著的)特色。**5.**〔口〕一连串,一系列。**6.**〔美口〕短时期,暂时。~*s of red light in the east* 东方上空的红光条纹。*He has a* ~ *of obstinacy in him.* 他有一点儿固执。*a* ~ *of lightning* 一道闪电。*She has had a long* ~ *of bad luck.* 她遭遇了一连串的不幸。*I'll hit a* ~ *someday.* 有一天我会走段好运。***go like a*** ~〔美俚〕飞跑。***have a*** ~ ***of*** 有…的气味。(***off***) ***like a*** ~ (***of lightning***) (闪电一样)迅速,风驰电掣地。***the silver*** ~〔英〕英吉利海峡。**II** ***vt.***〔通例用 *p.p.*〕加纹理于,加条纹于。— ***vi.*** **1.** 成条纹。**2.**〔常作 ~ **it**〕像闪电一样发光。**3.** (在公共场合)裸体飞跑。~ **camera** 扫描照相机。~ **disease**【植】条死病。**-er** ***n.*** 裸跑者。

streak·ed [striːkt; strikt, ˋstrikɪd] ***a.*** 有纹理的,有条纹的;〔美〕狼狈的,慌张的,不安的。**-ly** ***ad.***

streak·ing [ˈstriːkiŋ; ˋstrikɪŋ] ***n.***〔美〕裸奔,裸体飞跑。

streak·y [ˈstriːki; ˋstrikɪ] ***a.*** (***-i·er***; ***-i·est***) **1.** 有纹理的,有条纹的。**2.**〔口〕不均匀的,混杂的,多变的。**3.**〔俚〕易怒的,脾气坏的。**4.** 忧虑的,担心的,不安的。*Wash your dirty* ~ *face, Johnny.* 洗你那脏的有了泥条的脸去,琼尼。*He is always nervous and* ~ *about the final exam.* 他对大考总是感到放心不下的。**-i·ly** ***ad.*** **-i·ness** ***n.***

stream [striːm; strim] **I** ***n.*** **1.** 河流,小河;川,溪。**2.** 流出,流注;一连串,(人物等的)辈出。**3.** (事件等的)连续;(财富等的)滚滚而来。**4.** 趋势,倾向,潮流。**5.**〔英〕(一个年级学生中按智力划分的)班组。*A bridge is being built over the foaming* ~. 正在这条怒流滚滚的河上建造一座桥。*The accident delayed a long* ~ *of cars, buses and bicycles.* 这一交通事故阻碍了一条汽车、公共汽车和脚踏车的长流。*a* ~ *of lava* 熔岩流。*sun* ~*s* 太阳光线。*the* ~ *of time* [*times*] 时代趋势。*the* ~ *of popular opinion* 舆论趋势。*the* ~ *of thought* 思潮。***against the*** ~ 逆流;违反时势。***down*** (***the***) ~ 顺流,向下游。***go by in a*** ~ 一连串陆续通过。***in*** ~***s*** [***a*** ~] 连续,陆续,接连,川流不息地。***in the*** ~ 在河的中流。***up*** (***the***) ~ 逆流,向上游。***with the*** ~ 顺流;顺应时势。**II** ***vi.*** **1.** 流,流动;(泪等)流出;(光线等)射出。**2.** 蜂拥而进,鱼贯而行,川流不息地通过。**3.** (旗等)飘扬,招展;(头发)飘动。— ***vt.*** **1.** 使流,使流出,倾注。**2.** 使飘扬;展开(旗帜等)。**3.** 把(学生)按智力等分班。*Students are now* ~*ing back to their dormitories.* 现在学生们川流不息地回到宿舍去。*I turned off the light and let the moonlight* ~ *in through the window.* 我关上电灯,让月光从窗间照射进来。*The flag is* ~*ing in the wind.* 旗帜在风中飘扬。*a* ~*ing cold* 流鼻涕淌眼泪的感冒。*a* ~*ing umbrella* 淌着雨水的伞。*crowd* ~*ing past* 接连不断走过的群众。*Her eyes* ~*ed tears.* 她的眼睛流泪。*The honeysuckle was* ~*ing scent.* 忍冬花放出香气。*The school* ~*s pupils into three classes.* 学校按智力把学生分成三班。~**line** **1.** ***n.***【物】流线。**2**

a. 流线型的。3. *vt*. 把…做成流线型;调整(机构等)使现代化或提高效率(*a ~lined method* 流水作业法。*a ~lined car* 流线型汽车)。~ **liner** 流线型火车[飞机(等)]。~ **of consciousness** 意识流。~ **time** 连续开工时间,工作周期。**-d** *a*. 1. = ~line. 2. 最新式的。

stream·er [ˈstriːmə; ˋstrimɚ] *n*. 1. 飘扬的旗幡(作装饰的)飘带(等)。2. 测风带。3. 横幅标语。4.〔新闻语〕横贯全版的大标题。5.【气】光幂;〔*pl*.〕北极光。6.【电】流光,射光;(电子雪崩产生的)电子流。*a paper* ~ 五彩纸带[开船时送别用(等)]。

stream·ing [ˈstriːmiŋ; ˋstrimɪŋ] *n*. 1. 流动。2.【生】胞质环流。3.〔主英〕学生编班制。4.【计】(可使音频视频不用下载而快速为用户所享受的)流动或接收法。

stream·let [ˈstriːmlit; ˋstrimlɪt] *n*. 小河,细流,小溪。

stream·y [ˈstriːmi; ˋstrimɪ] *a*. 1. 河流多的。2. 流水般的。3. 发光的。

street [striːt; strit] *n*. 1. 街,街道,马路;〔美〕(东西向的)纬路。2. 车道(*opp*. sidewalk)。3. 街区;街区居民。4. 〔the S-〕〔英口〕= Lombard S-, Fleet S-;〔美口〕= Wall S-. 5.〔美俚〕释放出狱,自由。*I met him in* [〔美〕*on*] *the* ~. 我在街上碰见他。*a main* [*side*] ~ 大[背]街。***be dressed for the*** ~ 穿着上街的服装。***beat the ~s*** 巡街。(***go***) ***on the ~s*** 漂泊在街上;在街头做妓女。***in the open*** ~ 在街上,公然。***in the*** ~ 在户外,在屋外。***live in the*** ~ 老是在外头,老是不在家。***not in the same*** ~ ***with*** 〔口语〕(能力)不能与…相比。***not the length of a*** ~ 相差不远。***take to the ~s*** 睡在街上,走上街头[游行]等。***walk the ~s*** (在街头)作妓女。~ **Arab** [**arab, urchin**] 流浪儿。~ **booking office** 市内车票售票处。~**car**〔美〕市内有轨电车。~ **cred** 〔口〕街头信誉〔指在穿着打扮的时髦性等方面被一般青少年所认同,系 ~ credibility 的缩略〕。~ **cries** (小贩)叫卖声。~ **door** 临街大门。~ **fighting** 巷战。~ **girl** 妓女。~**-legal** *a*. 允许在街头出售[经营、进行活动等]的。~**-map** (~**-plan**) 街道图。~ **market**【交易所】场外市场[交易]。~ **orderly**〔英〕街道清扫工。~ **paper** 短期支票。~ **people** 街头颓废派。~ **price** (交易所)场外行情。~ **sweeper** 1. 扫街车,清道机。2. 街道清洁工。~ **value** (非法市场上出售的毒品等的)马路价值。~**-walker** 妓女。~**walking** 卖淫。~ **yarn**〔美〕道听途说,无稽之谈。

strem·ma [ˈstremə; ˋstrɛmæ, ˋstrɛmə] *n*.【医】关节脱臼。

strength [streŋkθ; strɛŋθ, strɛŋkθ] *n*. 1. 力,力量,体力。2. 强度,浓度;长处;(要塞等的)抵抗力。3. 实力;兵力;全体人数,额定人数,编制。4. 笔力;文势。5. (证券等的)市价坚挺。6.〔美俚〕(可能有的)利润。*have not the* ~ *to do it* 没有气力做这个。*That will add* ~ *to your argument*. 那会增加你的辩论的力量的。*Take part in the physical exercises and build up your* ~. 参加体育活动增强体力。*the* ~ *of will* 意志力。*the* ~ *of the alcohol* 这酒精的浓度。*fighting* ~ 战斗力。*mobilized* ~ 战时编制。*effective* ~ 实额,实际人数。*a policy of* ~ 实力政策。*What is your* ~? 你们一共有多少人? *a tower of* ~ 金城铁壁。*the breaking* [*shock*, *tensile*] ~ 抗断[抗冲、抗拉]强度。*the working* ~ 资用强度。~ *of draught*【机】通风强度。~ *of material* 材料力学。~ *of structure* 构造力学。***be*** [***be taken***] ***on the*** ~【军】编入编制内。***below*** ~ 不够编制。***by main*** ~ 奋力。***in full*** ~ 全体动员。***in*** (***great***) ~ 人多势众地,用巨大力量。***on the*** ~〔英口语〕在士兵名册上。***on*** [***upon***] ***the*** ~ ***of*** 依赖,靠着。***up to*** ~ 够编制。***with all one's*** ~ 尽力。

strength·en [ˈstreŋθən; ˋstrɛŋθən] *vt*. 1. 加强,巩固,使强壮,使坚强有力;使增强实力。2. 勉励;激励。3. 增加…的艺术效果。— *vi*. 1. 实力增强;变强。2. (价格)上涨,坚挺。*The enemy has ~ed their defensive position*. 敌人已经加强了他们的防御阵地。*Criticism and self-criticism* ~ *unity*. 批评与自我批评能增进团结。~ ***sb.'s hand*** 增加某人的资本(实力)。~ ***sb.'s hands*** 使某人得以采取强有力的行动。

stren·u·ous [ˈstrenjuəs; ˋstrɛnjʊəs] *a*. 勤奋的,用力的,费劲的,紧张的;热心的;热烈的。*a* ~ *job* 一樁费劲的活儿。*a* ~ *examination* 紧张的考试。*make* ~ *efforts* 鼓足干劲,尽力。**-ly** *ad*. 拚命地。**-ness** *n*.

strep [strep; strɛp] streptococcus 的缩略形式。

Streph·on [ˈstrefɔn; ˋstrɛfɑn] *n*. 苦恋的男子〔Sidney 叙事诗中的主人翁,牧童〕。~ **and Chloe** [ˈkləui; ˋkloɪ] 一对恋人。

strep·i·to·so [strepiˈtəusəu; ˏstrɛpɪˋtoso] *ad*.〔It.〕【乐】喧闹地。

strep·to·coc·cus [ˌstreptəuˈkɔkəs; ˏstrɛptəˋkɑkəs] *n*. (*pl*. **-coc·ci** [-ˈkɔksai; -ˋkɑksaɪ]) 链球菌。**-coc·cic, -coc·cal** *a*.

strep·to·ki·nase [ˌstreptəˈkaineis, -ˈkineis; ˏstrɛptəˋkaɪnes, -kɪnes] *n*.【生化】链激酶。

strep·to·my·ces [ˌstreptəˈmaisiːz; ˏstrɛptəˋmaɪsiz] *n*. (*pl*. ~)【生】链丝菌属(*Streptomyces*)菌。

strep·to·my·cin [streptəuˈmaisin; ˏstrɛptəˋmaɪsɪn] *n*.【药】链霉素。

strep·to·thri·cin [ˈstreptəθraisin; ˏstrɛptəˋθraɪsɪn] *n*.【生化】链丝菌素,紫放线菌素。

stress [stres; strɛs] I *n*. 1. 压力,压迫,紧迫,紧张。2.【语音】重音;重读;【诗】扬音;语势,着重点。3. 重要(性),重点,强调。4.【物】应力;胁强,重力。*The landlord has imposed a severe* ~ *on the poor tenants*. 房东给贫苦的房客们加了很大的压力。*We must lay* ~ *on self reliance*. 我们必须强调自立更生。*Give* ~ *to the 2nd syllable*. 重读第二音节。~ *diagram*【工】应力图。*moisture* ~ 缺水。*tensile* ~【材】抗张应力。***be ~ed out*** (因心理压力过重而)精疲力尽的。***driven by*** ~ ***of*** = *under* ~ *of*. ***in times of*** ~ 在紧张[繁忙,困难]的时候。***lay*** [***place***, ***put***] ~ ***on*** 强调,用力干,着重于。***under*** ~ ***of*** 被…逼迫着,在…强制下,由于,因为。II *vt*. 1. 着重,强调,加重语气说。2. 用重音读。3. 加压力[应力]于,压,压迫。~**-om·e·ter** [-ˈsɔmitə; -ˋsɑmɪtɚ] *n*.【物】应力计。~ **mark** 重读符号。~ **test** 1.【物】应力测验。2.(检验心脏活动能力的)紧张状态测验〔紧张运动后的心血管压力测试〕。**-ful** *a*. **-less** *a*.

stretch [stretʃ; strɛtʃ] I *vt*. 1. 伸展,伸出;展开,铺开,扩张;张,绷,拉直;拉长,拉扯。2. 使(精神,肌肉等)紧张,倾注全力;睁大(两眼等)。3. 勉强解释,曲解;充分利用;乱用,滥用(法律等);夸大(地讲)。4.〔俚〕把…打倒在地。5.〔俚〕吊死;绞死;为…作装殓[埋葬]准备。— *vi*. 1. 伸展,伸长,扩张;(时间)继续,拖长,延长到;伸手(脚),伸懒腰;能伸长扩张。2. 夸大地讲,吹牛。3.【海】张帆航行;前进;努力。4. 做吃饭时的侍应员。5.〔俚〕被吊死;绞死。~ *a carpet* 铺开地毯。~ *an umbrella* 撑开伞。~ *out a helping hand* 伸出援助的手,假以援手。*She ~ed herself to provide for the family*. 她竭尽全力养家活口。*yawn and* ~ (*oneself*) 打呵欠伸懒腰。*He lay ~ed on the lawn*. 他伸开四肢躺在草地上。*The forest ~es for miles*. 森林绵延数英里。*His memory ~es back to his early childhood*. 他回想起自己的童年。~ *a point* 勉强让步,例外办理[应允]。~ *for the impossible* 勉强去做那些做不到的事情。~ *one's credit* 滥用信用。~ *one's powers* 滥用权力。~ ***one's legs*** (久坐后)伸腿,散步。~ ***out*** 伸手;开始大踏步走。~ ***to the oar*** [***stroke***] 用力划。II *n*. 1. 伸,伸开,伸出,伸长,延亘,连绵。2. 紧张;过度伸张,延伸。3. 持续的一段时间,一段路程,一口气;【海】一气航行的距离。4. (赛马场两边的)直线跑道,最后阶段。5. 滥用;越权。6. 夸张,夸张话。7.〔俚〕徒刑,(尤指)一年徒刑。8. 弹性。*There is a* ~ *of hills near the village*. 在村子

S

附近有一片连绵的小山。*To impose a penalty on smoking in the street is a ~ of the law*. 对在街上吸烟罚款是对法律的滥用。*a long ~ of time* 一段长时间。*a ~ of sea* 一段海滩。*a ~ of road* [*open country, water*] 一段道路[一片原野,一片汪洋]。***all the ~ was gone*** 拉长到不能再拉。***at a ~*** 一口气,不休息地(*work for six hours at a ~* 一口气工作六个钟头)。***beyond the ~ of*** 超乎…范围以外。***bring to the ~*** 尽力,紧张。***by a ~ of imagination*** 想入非非。***link up into a single ~*** 连成一片。***on a ~*** = at a ~. ***on*** [***upon***] ***the ~*** 紧张着。***put*** [***set***] ***upon the*** (***full***) ***~*** 使极度紧张,倾注全力。***to the utmost*** [***furthest***] ***~*** 极度,到极点。***with a ~ and a yawn*** 伸着懒腰打着呵欠。**III** ***a***. 弹性的,有弹力的。~ *woven fabrics* 弹性织物。~ *hosiery* 弹力袜。*a ~ limousine* 多门多座的超长豪华车。

stretch·a·bil·i·ty [ˌstretʃəˈbiliti; ˏstrɛtʃəˋbɪlətɪ] ***n***. 伸张,铺开,拉长;紧张;曲解,夸大。

stretch·er [ˈstretʃə; ˋstrɛtʃɚ] ***n***. **1**. 伸张者;拉伸机,延伸器,伸张器;绷开用具,鞋绷,帽绷,绷画布的框子(等)。**2**. 担架。**3**. 【建】顺(砌)砖,顺边砖,横砌石。**4**. (桌椅腿之间的)横档;划手的蹬脚板。**5**. (钓鱼用的)蚊钩。**6**. 〔俚〕夸张话,谎话。*a pulse ~* 脉冲展宽器。*a ~ bearer* 担架手。*a ~ case* 重伤。~ *bond* 【建】顺砖砌合。~*-party* 担架队。

stretch-out [ˈstretʃaut; ˋstrɛtʃˏaʊt] ***n***. 〔美口〕(增加工作量而不加或不按比例增加工资的)加紧劳动强度的工业管理制度;少花钱多办事的节约措施。

S

stretch·y [ˈstretʃi; ˋstrɛtʃɪ] ***a***. **1**. 能伸长的,有弹性的;易伸长的。**2**. 想伸伸懒腰的。~ *nylon* 弹性尼纶。

streu·sel [ˈstruːzl, ˈstrɔi-, G. ˈʃtrɔizəl; ˋstruzl̩, ˋstrɔɪ-, ˋʃtrɔɪzəl] ***n***. (撒在糕点上的)糖粉奶油细末。

strew [struː; stru] ***vt***. (~***ed***; ~***ed***, ***strewn*** [struːn; strun]) **1**. 撒(沙、花等)在…上;播;散播。**2**. 点缀(*with*);铺盖。*The table is strewn with books*. 桌子铺满了书。*Their custom is to ~ flowers over the graves*. 他们的风俗是在坟墓上撒花。

stri·a [ˈstraiə; ˋstraɪə] ***n***. (*pl*. ***striae*** [ˈstraiiː; ˋstraii]) **1**. 【解、动、植】线条,(条)纹,壳纹;壳线间隙;(昆虫的)陷痕。**2**. 【地】条痕,擦痕。**3**. 【建】柱沟。

stri·ate [ˈstraieit; ˋstraɪet, -ɪt] ***vt***. 加条纹,(条痕)于…上。

stri·at·e(d) [ˈstraieit(id); ˋstraɪet(ɪd)] ***a***. 有条纹的,有细槽[壳纹]的。**-ly** ***ad***.

stri·a·tion, stri·a·ture [straiˈeiʃən, -ˈeitʃə; straɪˋeʃən, ˋstraɪətʃɚ] ***n***. (有)条纹,(有)条痕;擦痕;【物】辉纹。

strick [strik; strɪk] ***n***. 【纺】(绢纺的)切丝;(拣麻后的)小麻把。

strick·en [ˈstrikən; ˋstrɪkən] **I** 〔古〕strike 的过去分词。**II** ***a***. **1**. 被打伤的,受了伤的(鹿);被侵害的;受了创伤的;用斗刮刮平了的。**2**. 〔构成复合词〕受…灾的,患…病的,为…苦恼着的。*a ~ deer* 负了伤的鹿。*a ~ field* 〔古〕大决战;战场。*a famine-~ area* 饥馑地区。*poverty-~* ***a***. 贫困的。***be ~ with*** 被…折磨,患(…病等)。***be well ~ in years*** 相当上了年纪,衰老。~ ***hour*** 整整一小时。

strick·le [ˈstrikl; ˋstrɪkl̩] ***n***. **1**. 斗刮。**2**. 【机】元刮板;刮型器,铸型棍。**3**. 【机】磨石;油石。**4**. 磨镰刀器。

strict [strikt; strɪkt] ***a***. **1**. 严格的;严厉的。**2**. 精确的,精密的;严谨的;严密的。**3**. 【植】笔直的。**4**. 〔古〕紧密的,亲密的。*You seem too ~ with your young ones*. 你对小孩子们似乎太严厉了。*He is very ~ in observing the regulations*. 他在遵守规章方面很严格。~ *discipline* 严格的纪律。*a ~ observer of rules* 严守规则的人。***in ~ confidence*** 十分秘密。***in the ~ sense of the word*** 严格地讲。***live in ~ seclusion*** 完全隐居。**-ness** ***n***.

stric·tion [ˈstrikʃən; ˋstrɪkʃən] ***n***. 收紧,收缩,压缩。

strict·ly [ˈstriktli; ˋstrɪktlɪ] ***ad***. **1**. 严格地。**2**. 精密地;严密地。**3**. 断然;全然。**4**. 〔美俚〕的确,确实。*He is ~ an honest man*. 他的确是一个老实人。~ *speaking* 严格地讲。

stric·ture [ˈstriktʃə; ˋstrɪktʃɚ] ***n***. **1**. 束紧;束缚,限制。**2**. 【医】狭窄。**3**. 〔常 *pl*.〕酷评,谴责,非难。***pass ~s on*** 攻击,责杂;弹劾。

strid(den) [ˈstrid(n); ˋstrɪdn̩] stride 的过去分词。

stride [straid; straɪd] **I** ***vi***. (***strode*** [strəud; strod]; 〔罕〕 ***strid*** [strid; strɪd], ***strid·den*** [ˈstridn; ˋstrɪdn̩]; ***strid·ing***) **1**. 迈步,大踏步走,迈进。**2**. 跨过(*over*);〔罕〕= straddle. — ***vt***. **1**. 跨过(水沟等);跨,骑。**2**. 大踏步走过。*We are striding forward both in English and in mathematics*. 我们的英语和数学都在大幅度地取得进展。**II** ***n***. **1**. 大步,阔步。**2**. 一跨(的宽度)。**3**. 迈进。**4**. 〔*pl*.〕〔俚〕裤子。***at*** [***in***] ***a ~*** 一跨,一步(就几尺等)。***get into one's ~*** 开始(顺利,正常,有劲地)进行。***have a fine ~*** 大踏步悠然自得地走。***hit one's ~*** = *get into one's ~*. ***make a big ~, make great*** [***rapid***] ***~s*** 大有进步,进展迅速。***strike one's ~*** = *get into one's ~*. ***take in one's ~*** 一跨而过;轻而易举地解决(困难)(*take obstacles in one's ~* 一跨而过障碍;轻而易举地克服困难)。***with big ~s*** 迈步,大踏步。

stri·dent [ˈstraidnt; ˋstraɪdn̩t] ***a***. 轧轧叫的,唧唧叫的,刺耳的。**-ly** ***ad***. **-dence, -cy** ***n***.

stri·dor [ˈstraidə; ˋstraɪdɚ] ***n***. **1**. 尖锐刺耳的声响。**2**. 【医】喘鸣。

strid·u·late [ˈstridjuleit; ˋstrɪdʒəˏlet] ***vi***. (蝉、蟋蟀等)唧唧地叫,轧轧地叫;发粗锐声;摩擦发音。**-lant** ***a***. **-la·tion** ***n***. **-la·to·ry** ***a***.

strid·u·lous [ˈstridjuləs; ˋstrɪdʒələs] ***a***. 发刺耳声的,作唧唧声的(= stridulant)。

strife [straif; straɪf] ***n***. **1**. 竞争,倾轧,吵架,斗争,战争。**2**. 努力奋斗。***internal ~*** 内讧。***at ~*** 不和,相争。

strig·il [ˈstridʒəl; ˋstrɪdʒɪl] ***n***. (古希腊、罗马人浴后,擦去身上水分的)擦身器。

stri·gose [ˈstraigəus; ˋstraɪgos, strɪˋgos], **strigous** [ˈstraigəs; ˋstraɪgəs] ***a***. **1**. 【植】有糙伏毛的,有鳞片的。**2**. 【动】有硬鬃的。**3**. 有细密槽纹的。

strike [straik; straɪk] **I** ***vt***. (***struck*** [strʌk; strʌk]; ***struck***, 〔古〕 ***strick·en*** [ˈstrikn; ˋstrɪkən]; ***striking***) **1**. 打,敲,击,殴;碰,撞,攻击,冲击。**2**. (用尖刀等)刺穿,戳进,咬,抓。**3**. 碰到,到达,发现,找到。**4**. 打制,铸造,打出;擦,压。**5**. 拉下,扯下,收起,叠起。**6**. 使突然发生,使得病,突然使。**7**. 给(人)留下印象,使感动,打劫,使想起。**8**. 采取(…态度),装出,摆出。**9**. (钟)报(时)。**10**. 商定,决定(市价),结算。**11**. 用刮斗器刮平。**12**. 使(植物)扎根。**13**. 装嘴子(在桶上)。**14**. (木匠)在…上打墨线。**15**. 缔结(契约),订(合同)。**16**. (船)触(礁等);(光)照在…上。**17**. 勾销,取消。**18**. 到达,进入。**19**. 弹奏。**20**. (昆虫)产卵于。**21**. 组成(陪审团)。~ *the table with one's fist* 拿拳头捶桌子。~ *sb. a violent blow* 猛击,痛殴。~ *one's head against the lintel* 把头撞在门楣上。*be struck by lightning* 被雷打。*The ship struck a rock*. 船触礁。~ *sb. with a dagger* 拿尖刀戳某人。*Unfortunately he was struck by a snake*. 很不幸他让蛇咬伤了。*We shall ~ the main road beyond the wood*. 我们过了森林就会找到大路的。~ *oil* 发现石油;〔口〕得到意外收获,发横财。~ *an agreement* 订合同。~ *a medal* 冲压而制出纪念章。~ *a match* 擦火柴。~ *a false* [*right*] *note* 作出错误[正确]的表示。~ *a sail* 下帆。~ *one's flag* 下旗;〔喻〕投降。~ *a camp* 收帐篷。~ *the tents* 拔营。~ *sb. all of a heap* 〔口〕使吃惊。*be struck dumb* 愕住,目瞪口呆。~ *terror into every heart* 使大家恐怖。*How does his play-*

ing ~ *you*? 他的演出你觉得怎么样? ~ *sb*. *as ridiculous* 使某人觉得好笑。*An idea has struck me*. 我想起了一个念头。*It* ~*s me that* …觉得;想起。*be struck by her beauty* 对她的美丽产生深刻印象。~ *a graceful attitude* 装正经。*It has just struck four*. 刚敲过四点钟。~ *bargains* 做成几笔买卖。~ *a balance* 结账。*The young pines have struck roots*. 小松树都扎根了。*This item must be struck out*. 此项条款必须勾掉。*Only a few musicians know how to* ~ *a lyre*. 只有少数的音乐家会弹七弦琴了。

—*vi*. **1.** 打,敲,殴,攻击,冲击;碰,撞,触;(船)触礁,搁浅,下帆。**2.** (蛇兽等)抓咬。**3.** 罢工,罢课,罢市。**4.** (心脏)搏动,(光)落下,(声音)被听到,(蚝)贴附。**5.** (时钟)敲,鸣。**6.** 擦(打)火。**7.** 刺透,穿透。**8.** 打动,给以印象,突然想到。**9.** 开始,朝某方向前进。**10.** 勾销。**11.** 扎根发芽。**12.** 降旗。**13.** 鱼上钩,拉住钩的鱼。**14.** 触发电弧,(雷电)闪击。**15.** 努力,力争。*S- while the iron's hot*. 趁热打铁,趁机行事。*The match wouldn't* ~. 火柴擦不着。~ *to the left* 向左走。*Cold* ~*s into one's marrow*. 冷透骨髓。*The disease struck inwards*. 疾病内攻。*The damp* ~*s through the walls*. 湿气透入墙壁。*A ship* ~*s*. 船投降了。*His hour has struck*. 他的死期来到了。*The hour has struck for* .... 应该…的时候到了。*The ship struck on a reef*. 船触礁了。*What* ~*s at a first reading is its vivid images*. 初读时它给人的印象是形象生动。*The lightning struck again*. 又打闪了。*The root of the young tree has struck deep into earth*. 小树的根已经深深地扎入土里。*I've struck on a novel means of doing the job*. 我突然想到干这个活的一个新奇的方法。~ ***a bad patch*** 经历一个倒霉时期。~ ***a blow for*** ... 拼命要得到…。~ ***a line*** [***path***] 找到门路。~ ***a mine*** 【海】触水雷。~ ***against*** 为反对…而罢工 (~ *against long hours* 为反对工作时间过长而罢工)。~ ***aside*** 闪开,躲开(刀尖)。~ ***at*** 企图打破,袭击,打击,攻打。~ ***at the root of*** 要毁掉…,想根绝…。~ ***back*** 打回来;反射过来。~ ***down*** 打倒,击灭;杀;(将鱼)装桶保藏;(病)侵入(人身),使生(病);(太阳)晒得受不了。~ ***for*** 为要求…而罢工 (~ *for higher wages* 为要求提高工资而罢工)。~ ***hands*** 〔古〕订买卖契约。~ ***home*** 使受致命伤;击中要害,取得预期效果 (*His interpretation struck home*. 他的解释得当)。~ ***in*** 突然插嘴;干涉;(疾病)内攻 (*Here someone struck in with a question*. 这儿忽然有人提出一个问题来)。~ ***into*** 突然,开始 (~ *into a gallop* 忽然跑起来),(忽然)跑,逃(进);打,扎(进)。~ ***it rich*** 〔美口〕发现矿产[油田];发横财,走运。~ ***off*** 斩去;删去,涂去;扣除,除去(利息等);印刷 (~ *off a book*); 当场画[写];显眼。~ ***out*** 打去;打出(火花等) (*of*); 删去,涂去;想出,创出,拟出;使发挥;使一下子发生(某结果);用手脚划水游泳;跳出;蹶起;(天才等)发挥;一下子发生;【棒球】使三击不中而出局 (~ *out a plan* 拟出一个计划。~ *the name out* 删去名字。~ *out of a track* 失掉踪迹。~ *out for the midstream* 奋力游向中流)。~ ***through*** 删去;刺穿。~ ***up*** 挡起(敌手、刀剑);(在金属上)浮雕;开始弹奏,开始唱;定(约等);和人开始…,结(交)(~ *up an acquaintance* 突然[偶然]做起朋友来)。~ ***up with*** 〔美〕偶然碰见(某人)。~ ***upon an idea*** 忽然想起一个主意来。

II *n*. **1.** 打击,殴打。**2.** 【军】(集中)攻击;空袭;进行一次空袭的一群飞机。**3.** (钟)报时;钟声。**4.** 罢工,罢课(等)。**5.** 【棒球】(击球员的)击球失败;(投手投出的)正球,好球 (*opp*. fall);【滚木球】第一球撞倒全部木柱(的分数)。**6.** 【地】走向。**7.** 〔美俚〕(石油、金矿等的)发现;大发横财,走红运;讹诈,勒索,恐吓。**8.** (一次的)铸币额。**9.** (鱼的)上钩。**10.** = strickle. **11.** (酒类的)品级;烈度。**12.** 不利条件;缺点。**13.** (畜牧的)皮毛蝇蛆病。**14.** 【植】植根。*carry out an air* ~ *against* …对…进行空袭。*ten* ~*s from the station clock* 车站的十点钟钟鸣。*a general* ~ 总罢工。***break up a*** ~ 破坏罢工。***call a*** ~ 发动罢工。***call off a*** ~ 停止罢工。***go on*** ~ 实行罢工。***have two*** ~***s against one*** 三击中有二击不中;〔美口语〕处境不利,形势不利。~ **benefit**, ~ **pay** (工会拿出的)罢工津贴。~**bound** *a*. 因罢工而停业的;罢工所造成的(困难等)。~ **breaker** 破坏罢工的工人,工贼,代替罢工者工作的工人。~ **breaking** 破坏罢工。~**-clause** 罢工条件。~ **fault** 【地】走向断层。~ **fund** 罢工基金。~ **measure** 斗刮量法。~ **order** 罢工命令。~**out** 【棒球】(三击不中)击球员出局。~ **zone** 【棒球】好球区。

strik·er [ˈstraikə; ˋstraɪkɚ] *n*. **1.** 打击者,打手,爱打人的人。**2.** 打铁工匠。**3.** 罢工者。**4.** (时钟报点的)锤,报点时钟。**5.** 斗刮。**6.** 鱼叉。**7.** 叉鱼人。**8.** 撞针。**9.** 〔英〕(网球的)接球人 (*opp*. server)。**10.** 〔美〕(陆军军官的)勤务兵等。

strik·ing [ˈstraikiŋ; ˋstraɪkɪŋ] *a*. **1.** 打击的;攻击的,突击的。**2.** 显著的,明显的,触目的,惊人的。**3.** 罢工中的。*a* ~ *force* 【军】突击部队。~ *dockers* 罢工中的码头工人。~ *suits* 引人注目的成套衣服。~ *velocity* 弹着速度,命中速度。~ **distance** 打得到的距离[范围] (*within* ~ *distance of* 在…打得到的距离内)。**-ly** *ad*.

string [striŋ; strɪŋ] **I** *n*. **1.** 线,带,绳子;〔美〕鞋带〔又作 shoe-~,〔英〕称 shoe-lace〕。(穿线、数珠等的)串线,串绳;穿在线上的东西,一串东西;一连串,一系列。**2.** 一串;一行,一排,一列。**3.** 〔集合词〕(训练中的)(常属于一个马主的)一群赛跑的马,牛群,马队;一群。**4.** (弓)弦;(乐器的)弦;〔the ~s〕弦乐器(演奏者)。**5.** 纤维;卷须;(豆荚壳等的)筋,腱。**6.** 【台球】得分数;计分器。**7.** 〔*pl*.〕〔美口〕(附带)条件,限制。**8.** 〔美俚〕谎话。**9.** 【建】束带层;短梯基。*a piece of* ~ 一根绳子,一条带子。*shoe* ~ 鞋带。*a* ~ *of questions* 一连串问题[质问]。*a* ~ *of buses* 一长列公共汽车。*a* ~ *of houses* 一排房屋。***a second*** ~ ***to one's bow*** 另一种手段,第二套办法。***by the*** ~ ***rather than the bow*** 〔口〕直接了当地。***harp on one*** [***the same***] ~ 反复讲同一事件。***have sb***. ***on a*** ~ 任意操纵某人。***have two*** ~***s to one's bow*** 备有两手,备有两套办法。***in a long*** ~ 排成一长串。***no*** ~***s*** 〔美运〕时间没有限制。***no*** ~***s attached*** 没有附带条件。***on the*** ~ 〔美〕有希望。***pull every*** ~ 竭力,拼命。***pull the*** ~***s*** 在背后拉线,在幕后操纵。~ ***tied to it*** (个中)条件,缘故。***the first*** [***second***] ~ 第一[第二]靠得住的人[物];第一[第二]个办法。***touch a*** ~ 〔喻〕触动心弦。***touch the*** ~***s*** 奏弦乐。**II** *vt*. (***strung*** [strʌŋ; strʌŋ]) **1.** 用绳、线、带子(等)捆、扎、挂。**2.** 〔常用 *p*. *p*.〕使紧张,使作好准备;使兴奋。**3.** 把…用线串起来。**4.** 使(弓)上弦;调(乐器)弦,抽(豆荚等的)筋。**5.** 使成一串排列起来,使排成一列 (*up*; *out*)。**6.** 拉直,使伸展,扩张,延长;〔口〕引伸。**7.** 〔美俚〕欺骗,愚弄,戏弄。— *vi*. **1.** (人等)排成一串,蜿蜒排列;成线状;列成一行前进。**2.** 〔美俚〕欺骗,撒谎,戏弄。~ *out scouts along the road* 沿路布置警戒。~ *beans* 掐去菜豆的筋。*He is highly strung for the game*. 他对比赛非常紧张。*I'm strung up to do the job*. 我已经准备好可以干这件工作了。~ ***along with*** 〔美俚〕陪伴,信任(某人);同意(某事)。~ ***sb***. ***along*** 〔美俚〕骗人,使人等待,吊人胃口。~ ***oneself up*** 兴奋紧张;打起精神来想做…。~ ***out*** (使)节目拖长;行列长达;(日期)延长到 (*The program was strung out too long*. 节目拖得太长。) ~ ***together*** (把事实)连贯起来。~ ***up*** 〔口〕勒死,吊,挂起。~ **bag** 网线袋。~ **band** 弦乐队。~ **bark** = stringy bark. ~ **bean** 〔美〕菜豆;豆荚;〔口〕瘦长条子。~**board** 【建】楼基盖板。~ **course** 【建】蛇腹层,束带层。~ **electrometer** 【无】弦线静电计。~ **halt** = springhalt. ~ **piece** 【建】纵梁,楼梯基。~ **quartet(te)** 【乐】弦乐器部合奏(曲)。~ **tie** (蝶形)领结。

S

stringed [striŋd; strɪŋd] ***a*.** **1.** 有弦(乐器)的。**2.** 有蔓的,有卷须的。*a ~ instrument* 弦乐器。

strin·gen·cy [ˈstrindʒənsi; ˋstrɪndʒənsɪ] ***n*.** **1.** 紧急,迫切,逼迫。**2.** (货币、信用等)紧缩,短缺。**3.** 严格,严重,严厉。**4.** 说服力,魄力。*Bankers say financial ~ constitutes a serious threat to the country*. 银行家们说信用紧缩对国家构成了严重的威胁。

strin·gen·do [strinˈdʒendəu; strɪnˋdʒendo] ***a*., *ad*.** 〔It.〕【乐】逐步加紧(的);渐快(的)。

strin·gent [ˈstrindʒənt; ˋstrɪndʒənt] ***a*.** **1.** 紧急的,迫切的;紧迫的。**2.** (货币等)紧缩的,缺乏的。**3.** 严格的,严重的,严厉的;有说服力的。~ *necessity* 紧急需要。**-ly** ***ad*.** **-ness** ***n*.**

string·er [ˈstriŋə; ˋstrɪŋɚ] ***n*.** **1.** 上弦工人,弦匠。**2.**【铁路】纵向轨枕。**3.**【建】纵梁;楼梯基。**4.**【船】纵材。**5.**【地】脉道。**6.** 〔*pl*.〕〔俚〕手铐。

string·y [ˈstriŋi; ˋstrɪŋɪ] ***a*.** (***-i·er***; ***-i·est***) **1.** 线的,带子的;纤维质的,纤维多的,多筋的(肉等)。**2.** 黏性的。**3.** 〔美〕拖遢的。*a ~ throat* (瘦得)青筋暴露的喉咙。**-i·ness** ***n*.**

strip[1] [strip; strɪp] **I** ***vt*.** (***~ped***, 〔罕〕***stript***, ***stripping*** [ˈstripiŋ; ˋstrɪpɪŋ]) **1.** 剥;剥去衣服;剥光;除去,取去(*of*)。**2.** 夺,抢去;剥夺,褫夺(*of*)。**3.** 拆卸,拆除(附属物等);卸去(船上)索具。**4.** 挤干(牛)奶,挤出(鱼卵)。**5.** 去(烟叶的)梗。**6.** 从…中删去不必要的东西。**7.**【矿】剥离(矿层或矿脉上的泥土);使露出;采(锡)。**8.**【化】去除(纤维的)颜色,去色;除去挥发性成分。**9.** 把…撕成带形,切成细条。**10.** 用纸条粘住(书面等)。**11.** 精洗(原料丝绸)。**12.** 折断(齿轮的)齿,磨损(螺丝钉的)螺纹;由于膛速过高擦去子弹的皮。—***vi*.** **1.** 脱去衣服;表演脱衣舞;剥落。**2.** (螺丝钉的)螺纹剥落。**3.**【炮】(炮弹)不旋转地打出去,擦去弹皮。~ *a tree of its bark* = ~ *the bark from a tree* 剥去树皮。*He ~ped off his coat*. 他脱去上衣。~ *a person of his honours* [*wealth*] 剥夺人之荣誉[财产]。~ *the house of everything valuable* 抢去屋内每一件贵重的东西。~ *sb. naked* 剥光人的衣服。~ *tobacco* 去烟梗。~ *for a bath* 脱衣洗澡。~ **bare** 剥光(*Winter stripped bare all the trees*. 冬天落尽了所有的树叶)。~ ***sb*. *of*** (***money***) 抢去某人的(钱)。**II** ***a*.** 脱衣舞的。**a ~ show** 脱衣舞表演。**~-search** 对(嫌疑者)作脱光衣服搜查。

strip[2] [strip; strɪp] ***n*.** **1.** 条带,长条;条板;带状地。**2.** 条状侦察照片;连环漫画。**3.** 支板;插座条。**4.**【空】跑道;简易机场。**5.**【冶】带钢。**6.**【矿】露天剥采。**7.** 捣矿机排矿沉淀槽。**8.** 集邮簿上的一行邮票。**9.** 无茎无梗的烟叶。*film ~s* 电影胶卷。*a runway* ~【空】跑道。*leave a* ~ 〔美俚〕突然停车,急煞车。~ **cartoon** 连环漫画。~ **cell** "小号子"〔专门关押顽劣犯人的生活设施简陋的狭窄小囚室〕。~ **center** (沿公路一字排开,由多家商店组成的路弯购物中心)。~ **cropping** [**planting**] (山坡上防止水土流失的)条植法。~ **film** 幻灯片(带)。~ **leaf** (去茎和梗的)烟叶。~ **light** (舞台照明的)长条状灯。~ **log** 片条钻探剖面。~ **mail** 零售中心,零售商场区。~ **mine** 露天矿。~ **mining** 〔美〕【矿】露天剥采。

stripe [straip; straɪp] **I** ***n*.** **1.** 条纹,条子。**2.** (人的)类型;类别。**3.** 〔*pl*.〕【军】军服上表示等级的条纹。**4.** 犯人穿的横条囚衣;(一道)鞭痕,鞭伤;鞭打。**5.** 条纹衣料,条纹布。**6.** 长方形长条洗矿槽。**7.** 〔*pl*.〕〔口,马戏团用语〕老虎。~ *rust* 条锈病。*the Stars and Stripes* 星条旗〔美国国旗〕。*people of the same* ~ 同一类型的人。*politicians of the Democratic* ~ 民主党一派的政客们。***get one's ~s*** 升级。***lose one's ~s*** 降级。***wear the ~s*** 〔美〕进监牢。**II** ***vt*.** 使…成条纹状,在…上划条纹。**-r**【军俚】带袖章的〔指挥官〕。

striped [stript; straɪpt] ***a*.** **1.** 有条纹的。**2.** 喝醉了的。**~-pants** ***a*.** (在礼仪,社交活动等方面)过于注重形式的。

strip·ling [ˈstripliŋ; ˋstrɪplɪŋ] ***n*.** **1.** 年轻人,小伙子。**2.** 苗木修剪。

strip·per [ˈstripə; ˋstrɪpɚ] ***n*.** **1.** 剥(烟茎烟梗)的人。**2.** 剥毛梳;刮毛器;剥皮器;拆卸器。**3.** 脱光衣服的人;脱衣舞舞女。**4.** 〔俚〕停奶牛。**5.**【化】汽提塔。**6.**【机】冲孔模板。**7.**【油】枯竭井,低产井。**8.** 露天矿矿工。

strip·tease [ˈstriptiːz; ˋstrɪpˏtiz] 〔美〕 **I** ***n*.** 脱衣舞。**II** ***vi*.** 表演脱衣舞。**-r** ***n*.** 〔俚〕表演脱衣舞的女人,脱衣舞娘。

stripy [ˈstraipi; ˋstraɪpɪ] ***a*.** 有条纹的;条纹状的。**-i·ness** ***n*.**

strive [straiv; straɪv] ***vi*.** (***strove*** [strəuv; strov]; ***striven*** [ˈstrivn; ˋstrɪvən]; ***striv·ing***) **1.** 力求,努力(*to do*; *for*; *after*)。**2.** 竞争,斗争(*with*);反抗(*against*)。~ *hard to make greater progress* 力争取得更大的进步。~ *for accuracy* 力争确切。~ *for victory* 争取胜利。~ *with* [*against*] *a temptation* [*difficulty*] 和诱惑[困难]作挣扎。**-r** ***n*.** 努力者;奋斗者;竞争者。

striv·en [ˈstrivn; ˋstrɪvən] strive 的过去分词。

strobe [strəub; strob] **I** ***n*.** 〔缩〕 **1.**【物】频闪观测器(= stroboscope)。**2.** (照相和剧场用的)闪光灯(= strobe light)。**3.**【物】频闪放电管(= strobotron)。**4.**【无】闸门;选通脉冲。**II** ***a*.** = stroboscopic.

stro·bi·la [strəuˈbailə; strəˋbaɪlə] ***n*.** (*pl*. ***-lae*** [-liː; -li])【动】**1.** 横裂体;节裂体。**2.** 水母叠生体。**-r** ***a*.** **-lation** [-ˈleiʃən; -ˋleʃən] ***n*.**

stro·bile, stro·bil [ˈstrəubail, -bil; ˋstrɑbɪl, -bl̩] ***n*.**【植】毬果;球穗花序;孢子叶球。

stro·bi·lus [strəuˈbailəs; ˋstrɑbələs] ***n*.** (*pl*. ***-li*** [-lai; -laɪ]) **1.**【植】毬果,毬花。**2.** = strobila.

strob·o·scope [ˈstrəubəskəup; ˋstrobəˏskop, ˋstrɑbɚ] ***n*.** 圆筒动画镜,万花筒,动态镜;【物】频闪观测器;闪光仪。**-scop·ic, -scop·i·cal** ***a*.** **-scop·i·cal·ly** ***ad*.**

strob·o·tron [ˈstrɔbətrɔn; ˋstrɑbətrɑn] ***n*.** 频闪放电管。

strode [strəud; strod] stride 的过去式。

stro·ga·noff [ˈstrəugənɔːf, ˈstrɔː-; ˋstrogəˏnɔf, ˋstrɔ-] ***a*.** 以酸奶油、肉汤、蘑菇等烹调的。

stroke[1] [strəuk; strok] **I** ***n*.** **1.** 一击,一敲;打,打击;一振,一动;(字的)一笔;一举;一划;(游泳的)一爬;一触;一闪;一刀。**2.** (钟的)鸣声,敲击声;雷打;落雷;(心脏的)跳动,脉搏。**3.** 飞来横祸,意外的打击,意外的幸运。**4.** (疾病的)发作;中风。**5.** 手腕,手法;政策;功劳,成功。**6.** (板球等的)打法;游泳方法[方式];(船的)划法;(坐舵手对面指挥全艇划桨快慢的)尾桨手。**7.** 笔划。**8.** 风格。**9.** 工作量。**10.**【机】冲程,行程,动程。*a thick* [*fine*, *thin*] ~ 粗[细]笔划。*Little ~s fell great oaks*. 〔谚〕水滴石穿。*a finishing* ~ 最后加工;(决定性的)最后一击;最后一笔。*The clock was on the ~ of twelve*. 钟敲十二点。*a ~ of apoplexy* 脑溢血。*a great ~ of diplomacy* 外交上的大成功。*a ~ of genius* 天才的手法。*a fine* ~ 大成功,好成绩。*a ~ of state* = coup d'etat. *He has not done a ~ of work*. 他一点儿工作也没有做。*back* ~ 仰泳。*breast* ~ 俯泳,蛙式(游泳)。*over arm* ~ 自由式(游泳)。*side* ~ 侧泳。~ *of piston* 活塞行程。***a ~ above*** 〔口〕高出一头,高明一些(*She was a ~ above the other girls*. 她比别的女孩子高明些)。***at a*** [***one***] ~ 一举;一笔。***be full of ~s from the life*** 充满写实手法[笔调]。***give the ~ = set the ~*. *have a ~*** 中风,脑溢血。***keep ~*** 整齐一致地划桨。***pull ~*** 划尾桨(指挥快慢)。***pull ~ to another boat*** 和着别的船整齐一致地划。***row ~ = pull ~*. *set the ~*** 确定划桨的方法[速度]。~ ***and strife*** 大闹,搅乱。***with a ~ of the pen*** 大笔一挥(*You could do it with a ~ of the pen*. 你只要大笔一挥[签个字],这事就办成了)。***with measured ~s*** 有步骤地。**II** ***vt*.** **1.** (用笔)在…上划线,勾消。**2.** (划船比赛

中)为…担任尾桨划手,使划尾桨。~ *an average of 28* 一分钟划二十八下。~ **oar** 尾桨(手)。~ **(oar)sman** 尾桨手。

stroke[2] [strəuk; strok] **I** *vt*. 抚,摩;【裁缝】弄伸皱褶。~ ***sb. down*** 平息某人的怒气。~ ***sb.*** [***sb.'s hair***] ***up*** (***the wrong way***) 倒摺(动物等的)毛发;逗恼人,触怒某人。**II** *n*. 抚摩,一抹。**-r** *n*. **1.** 抚摩者。**2.**【印】推纸器。**3.** 谄媚者。

stroke[3] [strəuk; strok] strike 的过去式。

strok·ing·ly [ˈstrəukiŋli; ˋstrokɪŋlɪ] *ad*. 抚摩地;安抚地。

stroll [strəul; strol] **I** *n*. 散步,漫步,溜跶;闲逛;游荡;徘徊;流浪;巡回演出。*a ~ing player* 流浪演员。*a ~-ing company* 流动剧团。**take** [**have**, **go for**] **a** ~ 闲逛,散步,漫步。**II** *vi*. 慢慢地走,散步,闲逛,游荡 (*away*; *off*; *over*; *through*; *along*; *about*);流动演出。— *vt*. 在…游荡。

stroll·er [ˈstrəulə; ˋstrolɚ] *n*. 散步的人;游荡的人,巡回[流动]演员,江湖艺人;流浪者;流氓;〔美〕(折叠式)婴孩车。

stro·ma [ˈstrəumə; ˋstromə] *n*. (*pl*. **-ma·ta** [-tə; -tə]) **1.**【解】基质。**2.**【植】基质;子座。**-l**, **-mat·ic** [-ˈmætik; -ˋmætɪk] *a*.

Strong [strɔŋ; strɔŋ] *n*. 斯特朗[姓氏]。

strong [strɔŋ; strɔŋ] **I** *a*. **1.** 强壮的,有力的,有膂力的;强健的;巩固的,坚牢的,坚固的;坚强的(性格等);强烈的,猛烈的(感情、风等)。**2.** 富有的,有财力的,资力雄厚的;有势力的;强大的,优势的;(兵员)总数达…的。**3.** 强硬的,热心的;效力强的;烈性的,厉害的,浓烈的(饮料);刺鼻的。**4.** 不易消化的(食物等),麸质多的;黏土多的;【农】土质肥沃的。**5.**【商】坚挺的,上涨的;【语法】强变化的 (*opp*. *weak*)。**6.** 能力强的,擅长的。*a ~ case* 有力的主张。*a ~ man* 强壮的人;果断[有魄力]的人。*the ~* 强者;健康的人。*the ~er sex* 男性。*How many ~ are you?* 你们有多少人? *I have a ~ hold over it*. 我紧紧把握着它。*an army 10000 ~* 一万人的一支军队。*a ~ situation* (文艺作品中)动人的情节。~ *language* (咒)骂人的粗话。~ *meat* 难消化的肉。*Markets are ~*. 行情坚挺。*How ~ are you?* 〔美〕你有多少钱? **be ~ against** 坚决反对。**be ~ in** 擅长。**be ~ under** 在…下坚定不移。**by the ~ arm** [**hand**] 用极大的力量,靠力量,用暴力。**have a ~ head** 酒量大。***many millions ~*** 千百万。***one's ~ point*** 一个人的特长,优点。~ ***for*** 〔美俚〕坚决赞成。***take a ~ root*** 把根扎牢。**II** *ad*. 坚强地,有力地,大大地,猛烈地。***come it ~*** = ***go it ~*** 〔俚〕大干,盲干,拼命干 (*That is coming it rather ~*. 太过分;非分要求)。***go ~*** 〔口〕健康;旺盛;吃香;强硬。***put it ~*** 骂,说得刻薄。~**-arm 1.** *vt*. 〔美俚〕殴打,殴打后抢去。**2.** *a*. 用暴力的,狂暴的。**3.** *n*. 暴力,强硬手段。~**box** 保险箱。~ **boy** (重体量的)拳击选手。~ **breeze** 强风(六级风)。~**-brown** 坚牢的牛皮纸。~ **drinks** = 〔古〕~ **waters** 烈性酒。~ **gale** 烈风(九级风)。~**hold** 要塞;据点,根据地;中心点。~ **man** 大力士;有影响的掌权者,红人;独裁者。~ **measure** 强硬手段。~**-minded** *a*. 意志坚强的,果断的,好胜的,有丈夫气概的(女人等)。~**-room** 〔英〕金库,保险库。~ **sand** 黏合砂。~ **suit 1.** (牌戏)张数多而包含大牌的花色。**2.** 优点,长处。~ **wheat** 优质小麦。**-ly** *ad*.

stron·gyl(e) [ˈstrɔndʒil; ˋstrandʒɪl] *n*.【动】圆线虫属寄生虫。

stron·gy·lid [ˈstrɔndʒilid; ˋstrandʒɪlɪd] *n*., *a*.【动】圆线科寄生虫(的)。

stron·gy·lo·sis [ˈstrɔndʒiˈləusis; ˏstrandʒəˋlosɪs] *n*.【医】圆线虫病。

stron·ti·a [ˈstrɔnʃiə, -ʃə; ˋstranʃɪə] *n*.【化】**1.** 氧化锶。**2.** 氢氧化锶。

stron·ti·an [ˈstrɔnʃiən; ˋstranʃɪən] *n*. = strontium.

stron·ti·an·ite [ˈstrɔnʃiənˌnait; ˋstranʃɪənˏaɪt] *n*.【矿】菱锶矿。

stron·tic [ˈstrɔntik; ˋstrantɪk] *a*. 锶的。

stron·ti·um [ˈstrɔnʃiəm; ˋstranʃɪəm] *n*.【化】锶〔Sr.〕**-tic** *a*.

strook [struk; strʊk]〔废〕strike 的过去分词。

strop [strɔp; strap] **I** *n*. (磨剃刀的)皮带;【船】滑车的带索。**II** *vt*. (在皮带上磨刮)使锋利。

stro·phan·thin [strəuˈfænθin; stroˋfænθɪn] *n*.【医】毒毛旋花子苷〔从毒毛旋花中提取的一种强化剂〕;羊角拗质。

stro·phe [ˈstrəufi; ˋstrofɪ] *n*. (古希腊戏剧中歌咏队)向左方舞动唱歌;向左方舞动时唱的歌词;(诗的)节。**-ph·ic**, **-i·cal** *a*. **-cal·ly** *ad*.

strove [strəuv; strov] strive 的过去式。

strow [strəu; stro] *vt*. 〔古〕= strew.

stroy [strɔi; strɔɪ] *vt*. 〔废〕= destroy.

struck [strʌk; strʌk] **I** strike 的过去式,过去分词。**II** *a*. 〔美〕罢工中的,受罢工影响的。*a ~ factory* 因罢工而关闭的工厂。~ **joint**【建】斜刮缝。~ **jury**【法】特选陪审团〔共 12 人〕。~ **measure** (尤指使用刮子的)谷量计量单位(如升、斗、斛等)。

struc·tur·al [ˈstrʌktʃərəl; ˋstrʌktʃərəl] *a*. 构造上的,结构上的,组织上的。~ **botany** 组织植物学。~ **disease**【医】脏器病。~ **unemployment**【经】(因采用先进技术、国外经济影响、人口转移等经济结构变化导致的)结构性失业。~ **engineering** 建筑工程学;结构工程。~ **formula**【化】结构式。~ **geology** 地层学。~ **linguistics**【语】结构语言学。~ **psychology** 结构心理学。~ **resistance**【空】前面阻力。~ **steel** 结构钢,建筑用钢。~ **weight** 机体重量。**-ly** *ad*.

S

struc·tur·al·ist [ˈstrʌktʃərəlist; ˋstrʌktʃərəlɪst] **I** *n*. (社会学、经济学、语言学的)结构论者,结构主义者。**II** *a*. 结构论者的;结构主义者的,结构论的。**-al·ism** *n*.

struc·tur·al·i·ze [ˈstrʌktʃərəlaiz; ˋstrʌktʃərəlaɪz] *vt*. 使(某种机能)体现在组织结构中;使结构化;将…纳入结构中。**-za·tion** *n*.

struc·ture [ˈstrʌktʃə; ˋstrʌktʃɚ] *n*. **1.** 构造,结构;组织;石理,石纹。**2.** 建造物。**3.**【化】化学结构。**4.**【心】(直接经验中显现的)结构性,整体性;整体结构。*military ~s* 工事。**-d** *a*. **-less** *a*.

stru·del [ˈstruːdl, G. ˈʃtruːdəl; ˋʃtrudəl, ˋstrudəl] *n*. 果馅奶酪卷。

strug·gle [ˈstrʌgl; ˋstrʌgl̩] **I** *vi*. 挣扎;努力,奋斗;同…斗争 (*against*; *with*; *for*);挤过去,设法通过 (*along*; *through*; *in*; *on*; *up*);〔美俚〕跳舞。~ *against superior numbers* 和优势兵力战斗。~ ***for breath*** 困难地呼吸。~ ***on*** 拼命活下去,竭力支持下去;继续努力。~ ***to one's feet*** 挣扎着站起来。~ ***with the waves*** 跟波浪搏斗。**II** *n*. **1.** 奋斗;努力;拼搏。**2.** 格斗,斗争,战争。**3.** 努力奋斗的目标,要认真对待的事,麻烦事。**4.**【哲】斗争性。*a death bed* [*last-ditch*] ~垂死挣扎。*desperate ~* 垂死挣扎。*It was something of a ~ to find the money to pay*. 当时要筹一笔支付款项在某种意义上讲是一件麻烦事。***put up a last-ditch ~*** 负隅顽抗。~ ***for existence*** 生存奋斗。~ **buggy** 〔美〕汽车。

strug·gler [ˈstrʌglə; ˋstrʌglɚ] *n*. 挣扎的人;努力者,奋斗者;竞争者,斗争者。

strug·gling·ly [ˈstrʌgliŋli; ˋstrʌglɪŋlɪ] *ad*. 斗志昂扬地;艰苦奋斗地。

strum [strʌm; strʌm] **I** *vt*. (***-mm-***) 拙劣地[胡乱地]弹奏。(弦乐器等) — *vi*. 乱弹,乱奏 (on)。**II** *n*. 胡乱弹的声音。*the ~ of typewriters* 打字机的嗒嗒声。**-mer** *n*.

stru·ma [ˈstruːmə; ˋstrumə] *n*. (*pl*. ***-mae*** [-miː; -mi]) 【医】腺病;甲状腺肿;【植】瘤状突起,小叶节。**-mose**, **-mous** [-məus, -məs; -mos, -məs] *a*.

strum·pet [ˈstrʌmpit; ˋstrʌmpɪt] *n*. 〔古〕妓女。

strung [strʌŋ; strʌŋ] string 的过去式,过去分词。～ **out** 有吸毒瘾(因而虚弱)的。

strut[1] [strʌt; strʌt] **I** *vi*. (*-tt-*) 肿胀,鼓起,膨胀;大摇大摆地走,趾高气扬地走;(孔雀等)展屏或竖着尾巴走;装模作样地走。**II** *n*. 高视阔步。～ ***around*** 招摇过市。～ ***one's frame*** 〔美运〕出场比赛。～ ***one's stuff*** 〔美俚〕炫耀;自负。**-ling** *a*. 肿胀的,自负的,趾高气扬的。

strut[2] [strʌt; strʌt] **I** *n*. 支柱,支杆;抗压构件;轨撑;【空】(双翼机的)翼间支柱。**II** *vt*. (*-tt-*) (用支柱等)支持,撑住。

stru·thi·ous [ˈstru:θiəs; ˋstruθɪəs] *a*. 【动】鸵鸟类(*Struthioniformes*)的。

Strutt [strʌt; strʌt] *n*. 斯特拉特〔姓氏〕。

strut·ter [ˈstrʌtə; ˋstrʌtə˞] *n*. 高视阔步的人;有翼间支柱的飞机。

stru·vite [ˈstru:vait; ˋstruvaɪt] *n*. 【矿】鸟粪石。

strych·ni·a, strych·nin(e) [ˈstrikniə, -ni:n; ˋstrɪknɪə, -nin] *n*. 【化】马钱子碱,士的宁。**-nic** *a*.

strych·nin·ism [ˈstrikninizm; ˋstrɪknɪnɪzm̩] *n*. 【医】士的宁中毒,马钱子碱中毒。

Sts. = Saints.

S.T.T.L. = 〔L.〕*Sit tibi terra levis* 【宗】愿你安眠于地下〔墓碑题铭〕。

Stu. = Stuart.

Stu·art [ˈstjuət; ˋstjuə˞t] *n*. 斯图尔特〔姓氏〕。

Stuart [ˈstjuət; ˋstjuə˞t, ˋstu-] *n*. ***the*** ～***s*** = ***the House of*** ～ (英国)斯图亚特王朝〔1603—1649, 1660—1714〕。

stub [stʌb; stʌb] **I** *n*. **1**. 树桩;残材。**2**. 短(截)线;(铅笔、雪茄烟等的)剩余部分。**3**. (残齿的)根;〔美〕(支票的)存根,票根。**II** *a*. 粗短的。**III** *vt*. (***stubbed*** [ˈstʌbid, stʌbd; ˋstʌbɪd, stʌbd], ***stub·bing*** [ˈstʌbiŋ; ˋstʌbɪŋ]) 挖去树桩;连根拔除,根除 (*up*); 踩熄(烟蒂) (*out*); 树桩[石头等]绊(脚)。～**bed** *a*. 树桩多的;树桩状的,粗短的。～ **land** 残谷地 ～**mortise** 【建】短粗榫眼。～ **nail** 断钉;破损马掌钉。～ **pen** 笔尖短粗的钢笔。～**-tenon** 【建】短粗榫。～**wing** 【空】短翼;稳定浮翼。

stub·ble [ˈstʌbl; ˋstʌbl] *n*. **1**. 〔常 *pl*.〕(稻麦的)残桩;〔集合词〕谷茬,麦茬,茬地。**2**. 短发,短胡子。

stub·bled [stʌbld; stʌbld], **stub·bly** [-bli; -blɪ] *a*. (***-bli·er***; ***-bli·est***) 尽是谷茬[麦茬]的,茬多的,茬地的;满脸短胡子的。～ **root** 宿根。

stub·born [ˈstʌbən; ˋstʌbə˞n] *a*. 顽固的;倔强的;顽强的;难驾驭的,不听话的;难熔化的(金属等)。*a* ～ *resistance* 顽强的抵抗。～ *facts* 不容抹煞的事实。*a* ～ *illness* 顽疾。***as*** ～ ***as a mule*** 非常固执的。**-ly** *ad*. **-ness** *n*.

Stubbs [stʌbz; stʌbz] *n*. 斯塔布斯〔姓氏〕。

stub·by [ˈstʌbi; ˋstʌbɪ] *a*. (***-bi·er***; ***-bi·est***) 多树桩的;树桩似的,粗短的。～ **pencil** 秃铅笔头。**-bi·ness** *n*.

stuc·co [ˈstʌkəu; ˋstʌko] **I** *n*. (*pl*. ～*es*, ～*s*) 【建】拉毛水泥,拉毛粉饰,灰墁。**II** *vt*. 粉刷,墁上(灰泥),用拉毛粉饰法粉饰。～ **pattern** 拉毛粉饰型板。～ **work** 拉毛粉饰(活儿),灰墁,灰泥。

stuck [stʌk; stʌk] stick 的过去式及过去分词。～ ***on*** 眷恋;爱上。～***-up*** *a*. 〔口〕骄傲的,自高自大的,自以为了不起的;自私的。

stud[1] [stʌd; stʌd] **I** *n*. **1**. 大头钉;饰钉;【机】双头螺栓,柱(头)螺栓 (= ～ bolt); 轴;端轴颈;销子,中介轴;(装硬领的)金属扣,(衣袖等的)饰钮;(钟表等的)键钮;【建】壁骨;墙筋;中间柱。**2**. 〔美〕四明一暗扑克牌戏〔又叫 ～ poker〕。**II** *vt*. (***stud·ded*** [ˈstʌdid; ˋstʌdɪd], ***stud·ding*** [ˈstʌdiŋ; ˋstʌdɪŋ]) 加饰钉;用饰钮装饰;散饰,散布,点缀;用壁骨支撑。～***ded with*** 散布着…的,点缀着…的,星罗棋布的。

stud[2] [stʌd; stʌd] *n*. (专为繁殖、打猎、赛马等饲养的)马,马群;〔美〕种马;种(公)畜;养马场。*a* ～ *farm* 种马农场,配种站。～**book** (马、犬等的)血统记录簿。～**horse** 种马。

stud. = student.

stud·ding [ˈstʌdiŋ; ˋstʌdɪŋ] *n*. 【建】壁骨(用料);房间净高度。～**sail** 【海】补助帆,翼帆。

stude [stju:d, stu:d; stjud, stud] *n*. 〔美俚〕= student.

student [ˈstju:dənt; ˋstjudn̩t] *n*. **1**. (大)学生〔美国也指中学生〕;(大学、研究院的)研究生;(牛津大学 Christ Church 的)公费研究生。**2**. 研究者;学者。*a* ～ *of life* 研究生命问题的学者。**3**. 〔美俚〕初学者,初学吸毒的人。*a law* ～ 法科学生。～ **assistant** 助教。～ **council** (大学与中学中之)学生会。～ **government** 学生自治会。～ **interpreter** 见习翻译员。～ **lamp** 〔美〕(可随意调节高低的)台灯。～ **teacher** 〔美〕实习教员。～**ship** *n*. 学生的身分;〔英〕奖学金。～ **union** 〔美〕(大学生)学生活动大楼。

stud·ied [ˈstʌdid; ˋstʌdɪd] *a*. 故意的,有意的,有计划的;深思熟虑的;有知识的,精通的 (*in*)。*a* ～ *négligé* 故意不修边幅。*a* ～ *lecture* 反复推敲过的演讲。*a style which is too* ～ 雕琢太过的文体。**-ly** *ad*. **-ness** *n*.

stu·di·o [ˈstju:diəu; ˋstjudɪ,o] *n*. (美术家、照相馆等的)工作室,画室,雕刻室;照相室;〔*pl*.〕电影制片厂;(广播电台的)播音室;【电视】演播室。～ **apartment** 〔美〕以一个房间为单元的公寓。～ **couch** 〔美〕可以作床用的长沙发;三用沙发。～ **theatre** 实验剧场。

stu·di·ous [ˈstju:djəs; ˋstjudɪəs] *a*. **1**. 好学的,勤勉的,用功的;热心的,专心的;慎重的,谨慎的,小心的。**2**. 有意的,故意的。***be*** ～ ***of*** 努力,热心,专心。***be*** ～ ***of doing sth***. 非常想做某事。***be*** ～ ***to do sth***. 热心[细心]做某事。～ ***to please*** 刻意讨好。**-ly** *ad*. **-ness** *n*.

stud·y [ˈstʌdi; ˋstʌdɪ] **I** *n*. **1**. 用功,勤学;〔常 *pl*.〕学习;研究 (*of*); 研究对象;研究项目;值得研究的问题;学问,学业,学科;专题论文;调查。**2**. 书房,书斋;研究室;(个人)工作室。**3**. 〔古〕沉思默想。**4**. 试作;【美】习作;【乐】练习曲。**5**. 【剧】背台词;读台词,背台词的演员。*His face was a perfect* ～. 他的面孔真有意思。*To write correctly is my* ～. 我的努力目标是写得正确。*a quick* [*slow*] ～ 台词记得快[慢]的演员。*quit studies* 罢课。***in a brown*** ～ 呆想,默想,深思。***make a*** ～ ***of*** 研究。**II** *vt*. (***stud·ied***) **1**. 学习;研究;记诵(台词等),练习。**2**. 用心,考虑,图谋;注意看,仔细端详。— *vi*. 用功,学习,练习;研究;努力,留心;默想。～ *sb.'s face* 仔细端详某人面貌。～ *one's own interests* 图谋自己利益。～ *to avoid disagreeable topics* 努力避免不愉快的话题。～ *to wrong no man* 留心不误伤别人。～ ***for the bar*** 为了预备做律师而学习。～ ***one's part*** 【剧】记诵自己的台词。～ ***out*** 想出;解(谜等)。～ ***to be wise*** 努力学聪明。～ ***up*** 用功预备(考试等)。～ ***up on*** 〔口〕认真研究,调查,考查。～ **circle** 专题研究组。～ **hall** 〔美〕自修室;指定在自修室进行的课时。～**-in** *n*. 〔美〕听课抗议[示威]。

stuff [stʌf; stʌf] **I** *n*. **1**. 材料,原料,资料;〔美剧〕脚本,台词。**2**. 要素;本质,品质。**3**. 织物;〔特指〕毛织品,呢绒。**4**. 所有物,家具;【海】(焦油,松节油等构成,木船防腐用的)混合涂料。**5**. 枪弹,炮弹。**6**. 〔俚〕〔the ～〕钱,现金;〔美俚〕真材实质,优良特征。**7**. 废物,屑;拙劣的作品;梦话;废话。**8**. 〔美俚〕毒品,麻醉剂;走私货物,走私威士忌酒,赃物。**9**. 〔美空军口〕云;天气。*green* [*garden*] ～ 蔬菜。*sweet* ～ 糖果,糕点。*doctor's* ～ 〔口〕药品。～ *goods* 呢绒。*thick* ～ 四英寸以上的厚木料。*That's the* (*sort of*) ～ *to give them* [*'em, the troops*]. 〔俚〕对那些家伙处置得正好。当然了! 不错! *He is made of sterner* ～ *than his father*. 他的性格比他父亲更严厉。*None of your* ～! 别说废话! *S-* (*and nonsense*)! 胡说! 废话! *All* ～! 完全是胡说! *This book is good* [*poor*] ～. 这本书是好[坏]书。***be great*** ～ 是好家伙[东西]。***be not afraid of such*** ～ 不怕那

一套。*do* [*strut*] *one's* ～〔美俚〕采取行动；承当难局；拿出自己本领，显出拿手好戏；做自己要做[拿手]的事。*Do your* ～！〔美俚〕干你自己的事(别管闲事)！*little* ～〔蔑〕小人物。II *vt*. 1. 填充，塞满；塞入填料；装满；塞住。2. 剥制。3.〔美〕(在票箱中)投入大量假选票。4.〔俚〕诓骗。5.〔美〕把(篮球)扣入篮内，盖帽式投(球)。— *vi*. 狼吞虎咽，吃饱。～ *his fingers into his ears* 拿手指塞住耳朵。～ *a cushion with feathers* 用羽毛装垫子。～ *a box with old clothes* 拿旧衣服塞满箱子。～ *a child with food* 把孩子喂得过饱。*a* ～*ed bird* 剥制的鸟标本。*a* ～*ed shirt*〔美俚〕摆架子的人，神气十足的小人；有钱[有地位]的人。～ *oneself* 吃得过饱。～ *one's head with* 满脑袋的…。III *a*. 毛织品做的，呢绒做的。**-er** *n*. 1. 填充者；填充物；填塞工人。2. (和信件等一同装在信封里的广告之类的)附寄物。3.〔俚〕贩卖假货的人。～ **gown**〔英〕(资历浅的律师所穿的)毛料礼服。

stuff·ing [ˈstʌfiŋ; ˋstʌfɪŋ] *n*. 填充物，填料〔装进枕头、被子、垫子等的羽毛、棉花等；填在八宝鸡之类里面的配料〕(报纸杂志的)补白；剥制。～ **box**【机】填充[填料]函。

stuff·y [ˈstʌfi; ˋstʌfɪ] *a*. (*-i·er*; *-i·est*) 闷热的，气闷的；鼻子不通气的；沉闷乏味的；古板的，保守的；一本正经的；架子十足的。**-i·ly** *ad*. **-i·ness** *n*.

stug·gy [ˈstʌgi; ˋstʌgɪ] *a*.〔英方〕矮胖的，强壮的。

Stu·ka [ˈʃtuːkə, ˈstuːkə; ˋstukə, ˋʃtukɑ] *n*.〔G.〕(德国)俯冲轰炸机。

stull [stʌl; stʌl] *n*.【矿】横梁，横撑；支柱。

stul·ti·fi·ca·tion [ˌstʌltifiˈkeiʃən; ˏstʌltəfəˋkeʃən] *n*. (使)显得愚蠢；愚弄；(使)归于无效；【法】声明精神错乱。

stul·ti·fy [ˈstʌltifai; ˋstʌltəˏfaɪ] *vt*. (*-fied*) 使显得愚蠢；愚弄；使自相矛盾；(由于其后的矛盾行为)使归于无效；【法】声明(某人)精神错乱。～ *oneself* 显得愚蠢，陷入自相矛盾中，做前后矛盾的事情，取消前言；【法】自己声明精神错乱。**-fi·er** *n*.

stum [stʌm; stʌm] I *n*. 未[半]发酵的葡萄汁。II *vt*. (*-mm-*) 1. 使(葡萄酒)重新发酵。2. 使(新葡萄酒)停止发酵。

stum·ble [ˈstʌmbl; ˋstʌmbl̩] I *vi*. 1. 绊倒，摔倒 (*at*; *over*)；东倒西歪地走。2. 弄错，搞错，犯错误，犯(道德上的)罪过；失足。3. 说不出话来，结巴；踌躇。4. 偶然碰见 (*on*, *upon*; *across*)。— *vt*. 使绊倒，使失足；使为难；使踌躇莫决。～ *over a stone* 给石头绊倒。～ *through a speech* 结结巴巴地演说。～ *over one's words* 结结巴巴地说。～ *upon a rare book in the library* 在图书馆中偶然发现一本少见的书。～ *along* 东倒西歪地走。～ *at a straw* 动辄为小事发愁。II *n*. 绊倒；失足；差错，失误，过失；失败。～**bum** *n*.〔美俚〕笨手笨脚的人(牲畜)；穷醉鬼；喝醉酒的(或蹩脚的)拳击手。**-r** *n*. 跌跤者；失错者；犯过失者；蹒跚行走者；结结巴巴演说者。

stum·bling block [ˈstʌmbliŋ blɔk; ˋstʌmblɪŋ blɑk] *n*. 绊脚石；障碍。

stu·mer, stu·mour [ˈstjuːmə; ˋstjumɚ] *n*. 1.〔俚〕假支票，假钱；伪钞。2. (赛马中预先安排好不会赢的)马；打不出的子弹。3. 大错。

stump¹ [stʌmp; stʌmp] I *n*. 1. 树桩，残株，残树株。2. 残肢；牙根；(铅笔、扫帚等的)残部；(吸剩的)烟头。3. (美国竞选时在新开垦地区站在树桩上讲的)树桩演说(场)；竞选演说。4. 假腿；〔*pl*.〕〔谑〕腿，脚；【板球】柱。5.〔美国〕挑衅；挑战，考验。*stir one's* ～*s* 快走；出动。*go on* [*take*] *the* ～ 作巡回政治演说。～ *on* [*up*] *a* ～〔美口〕为难，不知道怎么办才好。*on the* ～ 在进行竞选活动。*wear to the* ～*s* 糟蹋(笔、帚)等；使枯死。II *vt*. 1. 砍伐，砍成树桩；掘去树桩。2. (将脚等)碰在石头上；绊，绊倒。3.〔主用 *p.p.*〕妨害，阻碍；使为难。4.〔美口〕挑衅，抵抗；旅行各地进行竞选演说。5.【板球】撞倒柱子退场。6. 当场付款(*up*)。— *vi*. 用假腿走，迈着沉重步子走 (*across*; *along*; *etc*.)；〔美口〕旅行各地作政治演说。*That* ～*s me*. 那把我难住了。～ *it* 逃走；旅行竞选演说。～ *up* 拔去树桩；〔英俚〕付清(应付款项)。～ *gun*, ～**-jumper**〔美〕庄稼汉；树桩演说家。～ **orator** (站在树桩上竞选的)演说家。～ **oratory**〔美〕树桩演说(术)，政治演说(术)。～ **plant** 插条；萌条。～ **speech**〔美〕树桩演说，竞选演说。～ **word** 缩语〔如 bus (<omnibus), exam (<*exam*ination)〕。

stump² [stʌmp; stʌmp] I *n*. (画炭画铅笔画时用纸等卷成圆锥形做成的)擦笔。II *vt*. 用擦笔把…涂出阴影。

stump·age [ˈstʌmpidʒ; ˋstʌmpɪdʒ] *n*. 1. 立木，未伐倒的树木。2. 立木蓄积，立木价值。3.【林】(立木)采伐权。

stump·er [ˈstʌmpə; ˋstʌmpɚ] *n*. 1. 砍伐树桩者。2.〔英俚〕= wicketkeeper；〔美口〕= *stump* orator. 3.〔口〕使人为难的事物，难题，困难的工作。

stump·ster [ˈstʌmpstə; ˋstʌmpstɚ] *n*.〔美〕政治演说家。

stump·y [ˈstʌmpi; ˋstʌmpɪ] I *a*. (*-i·er*; *-i·est*) 树桩多的；树桩状的，粗而短的(铅笔、尾巴、人等)。II *n*. 1. 矮胖子。2.〔美俚〕钱。**-i·ly** *ad*. **-i·ness** *n*.

stun [stʌn; stʌn] I *vt*. 1. 把…打昏过去。2. (打鼓等)使震聋耳朵。3. 使发愣，使目瞪口呆，使大吃一惊。II *n*. 震惊；晕眩；〔美〕胡桃。～ **gas** (防暴用)致晕毒气。～ **gun** (防暴用)致晕枪。

Stund·ism [ˈstundizm; ˋstʊndɪzm] *n*.【宗】斯登教〔1860年农民间信仰新约的一派基督教〕。**-ist** *n*.

stung [stʌŋ; stʌŋ] I sting 的过去式及过去分词。II *a*.〔美俚〕受骗上当的。

stunk [stʌŋk; stʌŋk] stink 的过去式及过去分词。

stun·ner [ˈstʌnə; ˋstʌnɚ] *n*. 打昏人的人〔物〕；把人打昏的一击；〔口〕极好的东西，惊人的东西；〔口〕了不起的人物；极漂亮的人〔尤指女人〕；〔美俚〕第一流的故事。

stun·ning [ˈstʌniŋ; ˋstʌnɪŋ] *a*. 令人晕倒[吃惊]的；震耳欲聋的；〔口〕极好的，极漂亮的；了不起的。**-ly** *ad*.

stun·sail, stun·s'l [ˈstʌnsl; ˋstʌnsl] *n*. = studdingsail.

stunt¹ [stʌnt; stʌnt] I *vt*. 阻碍…的发育，使发育不良；阻碍(生长、发育)。*a* ～*ed tree* 发育不良的树。II *n*. 阻碍发育，发育不全[迟缓]；发育不良的动物，生长不良的植物。

stunt² [stʌnt; stʌnt] I *n*. 1.〔口〕特技，绝技；惊人的技艺；特技飞行 (= ～ flying)；惊人的行为；惊人的手段。2. 花招，噱头。II *vi*., *vt*. (以…动作)作绝技表演[特技飞行]。～**-drive** *vi*. 作汽车特技表演。～**man**【影】特技演员〔专门代替演员作惊险特技动作者〕。

stunt·fest [ˈstʌntfest; ˋstʌntfest] *n*.〔美〕有种种杂耍做余兴的集会。

stunt·ster [ˈstʌntstə; ˋstʌntstɚ] *n*.〔美〕特技表演者。

stu·pa [ˈstuːpə; ˋstupə] *n*.〔Ind.〕卒堵婆，印度塔，浮屠，舍利塔。

stupe¹ [stjuːp; stjup, stʊp] I *n*.【医】热[冷]敷布。II *vt*. 热敷，热罨。

stupe² [stjuːp; stjup] *n*.〔俚〕傻瓜，笨蛋。

stu·pe·fa·cient [ˌstjuːpiˈfeiʃənt; ˏstjupəˋfeʃənt, stu-] I *a*. (*-fied*) 使麻醉的。II *n*.【医】麻醉剂。

stu·pe·fac·tion [ˌstjuːpiˈfækʃən; ˏstjupəˋfækʃən] *n*. (被)麻醉；麻木状态；昏迷；恍惚，茫然。

stu·pe·fac·tive [ˌstjuːpiˈfæktiv; ˏstjupəˋfæktɪv] *a*. 麻醉的，使失去知觉的，致昏迷的。

stu·pe·fy [ˈstjuːpifai; ˋstjupəˏfaɪ] *vt*. (*-fied*) 使麻醉；使失去知觉；使茫然，使发呆。**-fi·er** *n*.

stu·pen·dous [stju(ː)ˈpendəs; stjuˋpɛndəs] *a*. 惊人的，了不起的；大的。**-ly** *ad*. **-ness** *n*.

stu·pid [ˈstjuːpid; ˋstjupɪd] I *a*. 1. 愚蠢的；头脑糊涂的。2. 无聊的(书)，乏味的。3. 感觉迟钝的，麻痹的，昏迷不醒的。II *n*.〔口〕傻瓜，笨蛋。**-ly** *ad*. **-ness** *n*.

stu·pid·i·ty [stju(ː)ˈpiditi; stjuˋpɪdətɪ] *n*. 愚笨，愚钝，糊涂。

stu·por [ˈstjuːpə; ˋstjupɚ] *n*. 无感觉，人事不省，麻木，麻

S

痹，昏迷；茫然若失，恍惚。**-ous** *a*.

stur·died [ˈstəːdid; ˋstɝdɪd] *a*. (羊的)晕倒病的。

stur·dy[1] [ˈstəːdi; ˋstɝdɪ] *a*. 健壮的；坚定的；坚强的，不屈的，刚毅的；生长力强的，耐寒的。*a* ～ *opponent* 顽强的敌手。～ *cloths* 牢的布。～ *knowledge* 真才实学。～ *patriotism* 坚定的爱国精神。**-i·ly** *ad*. **-i·ness** *n*.

stur·dy[2] [ˈstəːdi; ˋstɝdɪ] *n*. (羊的)晕倒病。

stur·geon [ˈstəːdʒən; ˋstɝdʒən] *n*.【鱼】鲟鱼。

Sturmabteilung [ˈʃturmˌɑptailuŋ; ˋʃtʊrmˋɑptaɪluŋ] *n*. 〔G.〕(纳粹的)冲锋队。

Sturm und Drang [ˈʃturm untˈdraŋ; ˏʃtʊrm ʊntˋdrɑŋ] *n*. 〔G.〕1. 狂飙运动 (= the Storm and Stress)。2. 动荡不安。

sturt [stəːt; stɝt] **I** *n*. 激烈的争论；吵架。**II** *vi*. 争吵。— *vt*. 骚扰。

stut·ter [ˈstʌtə; ˋstʌtɚ] **I** *vt*. 结结巴巴地说出。～ (*out*) *an apology* 结结巴巴地道歉。— *vi*. 结结巴巴地说话，口吃地说话。**II** *n*. 结巴，口吃。**-er** *n*. **-ing·ly** *ad*.

Stutt·gart [ˈstutgɑːt; ˋstʌtgɑrt, -gɝt] *n*. 斯图加特〔德国城市〕。

sty[1] [stai; staɪ] **I** *n*. 猪圈 (= pig-sty)；猪圈一样(脏)的房子[睡处]；藏垢纳污之所；妓院。**II** *vt*., *vi*. (*stied*) (把…)关在猪圈里。

sty[2], **stye** [stai; staɪ] *n*.【医】睑腺炎；麦粒肿。*have a* ～ *in one's eye* 患麦粒肿。

Styg·i·an [ˈstidʒiən; ˋstɪdʒɪən] *a*.【希神】冥河 (*Styx*) 的；阴间的，地狱的；阴暗的，阴郁的；不可违背的，不可摆脱的(誓约)。～ *gloom* 漆黑。

sty·lar [ˈstailə; ˋstaɪlɚ] *a*. 笔尖的，像笔尖的，有尖的描画工具的。

style[1] [stail; staɪl] **I** *n*. 1. 风格，作风；体裁；式样，型；种类。2. 文体；说话的态度，语调。3. 模样，仪表，态度，风采；品位，品格。4. 时式，时样，时尚。5. 名称，称呼，尊称。6. 历法。7. (在蜡板上写字用的)铁笔；〔诗〕笔；铅笔；雕刻刀；日晷仪的针；蚀刻针；唱针。8.【植】花柱；【动】尾片，节芒，尾须；铗下器；产卵器。*She has an elegant* ～. 她具有优雅的风格。*live in* (*grand*) ～ 过豪华的生活。*the* ～ *of study* [*writing*] 学[文]风。*a concise* ～ 简洁的文体。*democratic* ～ *of work* 民主作风。*give his full* ～ 把他的头衔详细说出。*My* ～ *is plain John Smith*。我的名字就叫约翰·史密斯。*the Old* [*New*] *S-* 旧[新]历。***in*** ～ 有样子，很时新。***in the*** ～ ***of*** 仿…式。***out of*** ～ 没有样子，不时新。***the*** [***that***] ～ ***of thing*** 那样的事，说法，做法，事件 (*I've had quite enough of that* ～ *of thing*. 那种事我已经受够了)。**II** *vt*. 1. 称，给…命名；把…叫做。2. (按照新款式)设计(服装)，使符合流行式样；为…造型。～ *oneself an old sailor* 自称老海员。～**book** *n*. 1. 文字体例样本。2. 时装图样；书。～ **sheet** (印刷厂等用的)排印体例说明表。

style[2] [stail; staɪl] *n*. = stile.

sty·let [ˈstailit; ˋstaɪlɪt] *n*. 1. 小剑，匕首。2.【外】探针；通管丝；管心针；锥刺；【植】小花柱；【虫】螯针，口针。

sty·li [ˈstailai; ˋstaɪlaɪ] stylus 的复数。

sty·li·form [ˈstailiˌfɔːm; ˋstaɪləfɔrm] *a*. 尖笔状的；尖形的；刺状的；茎状的；针形的。

styl·ish [ˈstailiʃ; ˋstaɪlɪʃ] *a*. 时髦的，时式的，时样的；漂亮的。**-ly** *ad*. **-ness** *n*.

styl·ist [ˈstailist; ˋstaɪlɪst] *n*. 文体家；文体批评家；(家具等的)设计人；动作、风度优美的人〔如运动员〕。

sty·lis·tic(al) [staiˈlistik(əl); staɪˋlɪstɪk(əl)] *a*. 文体(家)的；风格上的。**-cal·ly** *ad*. **-s** *n*. 文体论；文体修辞学。

sty·l·ite [ˈstailait; ˋstaɪlaɪt] *n*.【宗】(古代住在高柱上的)柱上苦行者。

styl·i·ze [ˈstailaiz; ˋstaɪˏlaɪz] *vt*. 〔常用 *p.p.*〕使(图画等)具有某种风格；使风格化，使程式化。**-za·tion** [ˌstailaiˈzeiʃən; ˏstaɪlaɪˋzeʃən] *n*.

sty·lo [ˈstailəu; ˋstaɪlo] *n*. (*pl*. ～*s*) 〔口〕= stylograph.

stylo- *comb. f*. 表示"柱"，"杆"，"管"：*stylo*bate.

sty·lo·bate [ˈstailəbeit; ˋstaɪləbet] *n*.【建】柱座。

sty·lo·graph [ˈstailəgrɑːf; ˋstaɪləˏgræf, -ˏgrɑf] *n*. 针尖式自来水笔。**-ic** *a*. 针尖式自来水笔的；铁笔[尖笔]书写(用)的。**-i·cal·ly** *ad*.

sty·log·ra·phy [staiˈlɔgrəfi; staɪˋlɑgrəfɪ] *n*. 尖笔书(或画)法。

sty·lo·hy·oid [ˌstailəˈhaiˌɔid; ˏstaɪləˋhaɪˏɔɪd] *n*.【解】茎突舌骨。

sty·loid [ˈstailɔid; ˋstaɪlɔɪd] *a*. 茎状突起的，尖笔形的；【解】柱状的。

sty·lo·lite [ˈstailəˌlait; ˋstaɪləlaɪt] *n*. 石笔杆〔石灰岩和灰页岩中的小柱状构造〕。

sty·lo·po·di·um [ˌstailəˈpəudiəm; ˏstaɪləˋpodɪəm] *n*. (*pl*. *-di·a* [-ə; -ə]) 【植】(花的)柱茎。

sty·lus [ˈstailəs; ˋstaɪləs] *n*. (*pl*. ***sty·li*** [ˈstailai; ˋstaɪlaɪ]) 1. 铁笔，尖笔；(留声机的)唱针；描画针；记录针；日晷指针。2.【解】笔状突起；花柱；针突；生殖器鞘；产卵管。3.【计】光笔。

sty·mie, sty·my [ˈstaimi; ˋstaɪmɪ] *n*., *vt*. (*-mied*, *-mie·ing*) 妨碍(计划等) (= stimy) 阻碍。

sty·mied [ˈstaimiːd; ˋstaɪmɪd] *a*. 〔美〕被袭击的，被侵入的。

styp·sis [ˈstipsis; ˋstɪpsɪs] *n*. 止血剂效用，止血剂的使用。

styp·tic [ˈstiptik; ˋstɪptɪk] **I** *a*.【医】止血的。**II** *n*. 止血药。～ **pencil** (用明矾等止血药制成的，用来止住刮脸后出血等小创口的)止血笔。

styp·tic·al [ˈstiptikəl; ˋstɪptɪkəl] *a*. = styptic.

styp·tici·ty [stipˈtisiti; stɪpˋtɪsətɪ] *n*. 止血作用，收敛性。

sty·rax [ˈstaiəræks; ˋstaɪræks] *n*.【化】苏合香脂；【植】安息香。

sty·rene, sty·rol [ˈstaiəriːn, -rɔl; ˋstaɪrin, -rɑl] *n*.【化】苯乙烯。

sty·ro·foam [ˈstairəfəum; ˋstaɪrəfom] *n*.【商标】(聚苯乙烯)泡沫塑料，保丽龙。

sty·ron [ˈstairɔn; ˋstaɪrɑn], **sty·rone** [ˈstairəun; ˋstaɪron] *n*.【化】肉桂醇；【商标】斯蒂龙〔一种聚苯乙烯商品〕。

Styx [stiks; stɪks] *n*.【希神】(围绕地狱的)冥河。*black as the* ～ 漆黑。*cross the* ～ 死。

SU = strontium unit.

S.U. = set up.

su·a·bil·i·ty [sju(ː)əˈbiliti; ˏsjuəˋbɪlətɪ] *n*. 可控告[起诉]，应控告[起诉]。

su·a·ble [ˈsju(ː)əbl; ˋsju(ʊ)əbl̩] *a*. 可起诉的。**-a·bly** *ad*.

sua·sion [ˈsweiʒən; ˋsweʒən] *n*. 说服，劝告。*moral* ～ 道义上的劝告。

sua·sive [ˈsweisiv; ˋswesɪv] *a*. 劝告性的；有说服力的。**-ly** *ad*. **-ness** *n*.

suave [sweiv; swɑv, swev] *a*. 温和的，和蔼的；殷勤讨好的(人、态度等)；适口的，平和的(酒、药等)。**-ly** *ad*. **-ness** *n*.

sua·vi·lo·quence [ˈswæviləkwəns; ˋswævɪləkwəns] *n*. 〔美〕谦和的大话。

sua·vi·ter in mo·do, for·ti·ter in re [ˈswævitə in ˈməudəu, ˈfɔːtitə in ˈriː; ˋswævɪtɚɪn ˋmodo, ˋfɔrtɪtɚɪn ˋri] 〔L.〕态度柔和而行为果断；外柔内刚。

suav·i·ty [ˈswæv̩əti; ˋswævətɪ, ˋswɑv-] *n*. 温和，和蔼，谦和；适口，和淡；愉快。

sub[1] [sʌb; sʌb] *a*. 附属的，辅助的，补充的。*a* ～ *post office* 邮政支局。

sub[2] [sʌb; sʌb] **I** *n*. 代替物；代替者；〔美〕候补队员 (= substitute)。**II** *vi*. (*-bb-*) 做补充[候补]人员；〔口〕做替工 (for)。— *vt*. 〔美俚〕替…进行比赛。

sub[3] [sʌb; sʌb] ***n*.** 潜水艇。

sub[4] [sʌb; sʌb] ***n*.** 〔美俚〕低能者。

sub[5] [sʌb; sʌb] ***n*.** 订户 (= subscriber); 订购 (= subscription)。

sub[6] [sʌb; sʌb] ***prep*.** 〔L.〕在…的下面,…的下面的。~ ***finem*** [ˈfainəm; ˋfaɪnəm] 参看本章末〔略 s. f.〕。~ ***judice*** [ˈdʒuːdisi; ˋdʒudɪsɪ] 审理中的,未决的。~ ***rosa*** [ˈrəuzei; ˋroze] 秘密地。~ ***silentio*** [siˈlenʃiəu; sɪˋlɛnʃɪo] 暗中,偷偷地。~ ***voce*** [ˈvəusi; ˋvosɪ] 在该词下,参看该词〔略 s. v.〕。

sub. = subaltern; subject; sublieutenant; submarine boat; subscriber; subscription; substitute; suburb (an); subway.

sub- *pref*. ★如在以 c, f, g, m, p, r 等字母为首的从拉丁语来的词之前,则往往因同化作用分别变成 suc-, suf-, sug-, sum-, sup-, 在 c, p, t 等字母前又常变为 sus-. **1.** 在…之下,在下: *sub*sternal, *sub*way. **2.** 次级的;局部的;副;再,分,子, *sub*prefect, *sub*heading, *sub*species, *sub*divide, *sub*let, *sub*program. **3.** 稍微,接近,近乎;次,亚,逊: *sub*acid, *sub*alpine, *sub*aquatic, *sub*atom, *sub*tropical, *sub*cylindrical, *sub*delirium, *sub*erect, *sub*human. **4.** 〔附加在倍数形容词前表示该数的倒数〕: *sub*double = 1:2 [double = 2:1], *sub*triple = 1:3 [triple = 3:1]。

sub·ac·e·tate [sʌbˈæsiˌteit; sʌbˋæsətet] ***n*.** 【化】碱式醋酸盐。

sub·ac·id [ˈsʌbˈæsid; sʌbˋæsɪd] ***a*.** 带酸味的;(言语等)有点刺人的;【化】微酸(性)的。**-a·cid·i·ty** [sʌbæˈsiditi; sʌbæˋsɪdətɪ] ***n*.** **-ly** ***ad*.** **-ness** ***n*.**

sub·a·cute [ˌsʌbəˈkjuːt; ˏsʌbəˋkjut] ***a*.** **1.** 稍微尖锐的。**2.** 亚急性的。**-ly** ***ad*.**

Sub·ad·ult [ˈsʌbˈædʌlt, ˈsʌbəˈdʌlt; ˏsʌbəˋdʌlt, sʌbˋædʌlt] ***a*.** 接近成年的。

sub·aeri·al [sʌbˈɛəriəl; sʌbˋɛrɪəl] ***a*.** 地面上的,地面上发生的;接近地面的。

sub·a·gent [ˈsʌbˈeidʒənt; sʌbˋedʒənt] ***n*.** 副代理人。**-gency** ***n*.** 分销处。

sub·al·pine [ˌsʌbˈælpain; sʌbˋælpaɪn] ***a*.** **1.** 阿尔卑斯山脉山麓的。**2.** 在山区林线下(4—6 千英尺之间)生长的;亚高山的。

sub·al·tern [ˈsʌbltən; səbˋɔltɚn] **I** ***a*.** 下,次,副,部下的,属下的;〔英军〕陆军中的;【逻】特称的。~ *opposition* 【逻】大小对当。**II** ***n*.** 副官,部下,僚属;〔英军〕陆军中尉;【逻】特称命题;特称判断 (= ~ proposition)。

sub·al·ter·nate [səbˈɔːltənit; səbˋɔltɚnɪt, -ˋæl-] **I** ***a*.** **1.** 循次序的;连续的。**2.** 【植】近互生的。**II** ***n*.** 【哲】特称命题。**-ly** ***ad*.** **-tion** ***n*.**

sub·ant·arc·tic [ˌsʌbæntˈɑːktik; ˏsʌbæntˋɑrktɪk, -ˋɑrtɪk] ***a*.** 环绕南极圈地区的,副南极地区的。

Sub·a·pi·cal [ˈsʌbˈæpikəl; ˏsʌbˋæpɪkəl] ***a*.** 在顶点下的;接近顶点的。

sub·a·quat·ic [ˈsʌbəˈkwætik; ˏsʌbəˋkwætɪk, -əˋkwɑtɪk] ***a*.** **1.** 【生】半水栖的,半水生的。**2.** = subaqueous.

sub·a·que·ous [ˈsʌbˈeikwiəs; sʌbˋekwɪəs, -ˋækwɪ-] ***a*.** 水下的,水下发生的;水下用的。

sub·arc·tic [sʌbˈɑːktik; sʌbˋɑrktɪk] ***a*.** 近北极的,亚极带的。

sub·ar·ea [ˈsʌbˈɛəriə; sʌbˋɛrɪə] ***n*.** 分区。

sub·ar·id [ˈsʌbˈærid; sʌbˋærɪd] ***a*.** 亚干燥的。*a ~ region* 亚干燥地区。

sub·as·sem·bler [ˈsʌbəˈsembləː; ˏsʌbəˋsɛmblɚ] ***n*.** 部件装配工。

sub·as·sem·bly [sʌbəˈsembli; ˏsʌbəˋsɛmblɪ] ***n*.** 【机】局部装配;配件,组件,部件。

sub·as·tral [sʌbˈæstrəl; sʌbˋæstrəl] ***a*.** 星下的,天下的,地上的。

sub·at·mos·pher·ic [ˈsʌbˌætməsˈferik; ˋsʌbˏætməsˋfɛrɪk] ***a*.** 低于大气层的;低[次]于大气压的。

sub·at·om [sʌbˈætəm; sʌbˋætəm] ***n*.** 次原子。**-ic** ***a*.** 次原子的,比原子小的;在原子内的。**-ics** ***n*.** 次原子学。

sub·au·di [sʌbˈɔːdai; sʌbˋɔdaɪ] ***vt*.**, ***vi*.** 〔L.〕〔用于祈使语气〕根据领会补充(所需词语)。

sub·au·di·tion [ˈsʌbɔːdiʃən; ˏsʌbɔˋdɪʃən] ***n*.** 领会言外意义;言外之意。

sub·au·ric·u·lar [ˈsʌbɔːˈrikjuːlə; ˏsʌbɔˋrɪkjʊlɚ] ***a*.** 【解】耳廓下的。

sub·av·er·age [ˈsʌbˈævəridʒ; sʌbˋævərɪdʒ] ***a*.** 低于一般水平的。

sub·base [ˈsʌbˌbeis; ˋsʌbˏbes] ***n*.** 【建】副基层,下基层。

sub·base·ment [ˈsʌbˌbeismənt; ˋsʌbˏbesmənt] ***n*.** 【建】副地下层,副地下室。

sub·bass [ˈsʌbˈbeis; ˋsʌbˏbes] ***n*.** 【乐】(管风琴中发出最低音的)最低音踏瓣[音栓]。

sub·bing [ˈsʌbiŋ; ˋsʌbɪŋ] ***n*.** **1.** 做代替人;做替工。**2.** 地下灌溉。**3.** 【摄】胶层。

sub·branch [ˈsʌbˌbræntʃ; ˋsʌbˏbræntʃ, -ˏbrɑntʃ] **I** ***n*.** 小分支;支店,次级分店。**II** ***vi*.** 分成小分支。

sub·breed [ˈsʌbbriːd; ˋsʌbbrid] ***n*.** 【生】亚品种。

sub·cabi·net [ˈsʌbˈkæbinit; ˋsʌbˋkæbɪnɪt] ***n*.** (美国总统自选的)非正式顾问团。

sub·cal·i·ber, sub·cal·i·bre [sʌbˈkælibə; sʌbˋkælɪbɚ] ***a*.** **1.** 小口径的,次口径的。**2.** 发射小口径枪子弹的。

sub·car·ti·lag·i·nous [sʌbˈkɑːtiˈlædʒinəs; sʌbˋkɑrtɪˋlædʒɪnəs] ***a*.** 【解】**1.** 在软骨下的。**2.** 半软骨的。

sub·ce·les·tial [ˌsʌbsiˈlestʃəl; ˏsʌbsəˋlɛstʃəl] ***a*.** 天下的;天顶下的;地球(上)的;世俗的。

sub·cel·lar [ˈsʌbselə; ˋsʌbˏsɛlɚ] ***n*.** 地下室下的地下室,下层地窖。

sub·cen·tral [ˌsʌbˈsentrəl; sʌbˋsɛntrəl] ***a*.** 近中心的,在中心之下的。**-ly** ***ad*.**

sub·cer·e·bral [ˈsʌbˈseribrəl; ˏsʌbˋsɛrɪbrəl] ***a*.** 大脑下面的。

sub·chas·er [ˈsʌbtʃeisə; ˋsʌbˏtʃesɚ] ***n*.** 〔美〕猎潜舰[艇] (= submarine chaser)。

sub·chlo·ride [sʌbˈklɔːraid; sʌbˋklɔraɪd] ***n*.** 【化】低[次]氯化物,氯化低价物。

sub·class [ˈsʌbklɑːs; ˋsʌbˏklæs, -ˏklɑs] ***n*.** 【生】亚纲;【数】子集(合)。

sub·cla·vi·an [sʌbˈkleiviən; sʌbˋklevɪən] 【解】**I** ***a*.** 在锁骨下的。**II** ***n*.** 锁骨下静脉,锁骨下动脉。

sub·clim·ax [sʌbˈklaimæks; sʌbˋklaɪmæks] ***n*.** 【生态学】亚顶级[颠峰](植物)群落,亚演替顶极。

sub·clin·i·cal [sʌbˈklinikl; sʌbˋklɪnəkl] ***a*.** 【医】无明显临床症候的。**-ly** ***ad*.**

sub-cloud [ˈsʌbˈklaud; sʌbˋklaud] ***a*.** 云下的。~ *car* 【空】(飞艇上的)云下观测吊篮(可放到云层以下)。

sub·col·le·gi·ate, sub·col·lege [ˌsʌbkəˈliːdʒiit, ˈsʌbˈkɔlidʒ; ˏsʌbkəˋlidʒɪɪt, ˏsʌbˋkɑlɪdʒ] ***a*.** 准大学程度的;为学力不足(或无意入正式大学)的学生设置的。

sub·com·mis·sion·er [ˈsʌbkəˈmiʃənə; ˋsʌbkəˋmɪʃənɚ] ***n*.** (委员会所属的)小组委员。

sub·com·mit·tee [ˈsʌbkəmiti; ˋsʌbkəˏmɪtɪ] ***n*.** 小组委员会。

sub·com·pact [ˈsʌbˈkɔmpækt; sʌbˋkɑmpækt] ***n*.** (比小型汽车更小的)超小型汽车。

sub·con·scious [ˈsʌbˈkɔnʃəs; sʌbˋkɑnʃəs] ***a*.** 下意识的;潜意识的,半自觉的。**-ly** ***ad*.** **-ness** ***n*.**

sub·con·ti·nent [ˌsʌbˈkɔntinənt; sʌbˋkɑntənənt] ***n*.** 次大陆。

sub·con·tract [sʌbˈkɔntrækt; sʌbˋkɑntrækt] ***n*.**, ***v*.** 转订的契约[合同],转包[分包]合同;转包工程。**-trac·tor** ***n*.** 分包者,转包人。

sub·con·tra·ry [sʌbˈkɔntrəri; sʌbˋkɑntrɛərɪ, -trərɪ]

a., *n.*【逻】小[下]反对关系的[判断]。

sub·cool [ˈsʌbˈkuːl; sʌbˋkul] *vt.* 使过冷,使低温冷却。

sub·cool·ing [sʌbˈkuːliŋ; sʌbˋkulɪŋ] *n.* **1.** 低温冷却,局部冷却。**2.** 欠火候,加热不足。

sub·cos·tal [sʌbˈkɔstl; sʌbˋkɑstl̩] **I** *a.*【解】肋下的。**II** *n.* 肋下肌。

sub·crit·i·cal [sʌbˈkritikl; sʌbˋkrɪtɪkl̩] *a.* **1.** 近乎危急的。**2.** (原子)次临界的。

sub·cry·stal·line [ˈsʌbˈkristəlain; ˋsʌbˋkrɪstəlaɪn] *a.* 部分结晶的,结晶不清楚的。

sub·cul·ture [ˈsʌbˌkʌltʃə; ˋsʌbˏkʌltʃɚ] *n.* **1.** 亚[次]文化群〔年龄、地位、观念等相当的一伙同道者〕。**2.**【生】再次培养。**-tur·al** *a.*

sub·cu·ta·ne·ous [ˈsʌbkjuːˈteiniəs; ˏsʌbkjuˋtenɪəs] *a.* 皮下的。~ *injection* 皮下注射。**-ly** *ad.*

sub·dea·con [ˈsʌbˈdiːkən; sʌbˋdikən] *n.*【宗】(基督教圣公会、天主教会等的)副助祭;副执事。

sub·dean [ˈsʌbˈdiːn; sʌbˋdin, ˋsʌbˏdin] *n.* **1.** (英国教会或天主教的)副教长。**2.** (大学的)副院长;副系主任;副教务长。

sub·deb [sʌbˈdeb; sʌbˋdɛb, ˋsʌbˏdɛb] *n.*, *a.*〔美口〕= subdebutante.

sub·deb·u·tante [ˈsʌbˈdebjuˈtɑ̃ːnt; sʌbˏdɛbjʊˋtɑnt, sʌbˋdɛbɪəˏtænt] *a.*, *n.*〔美口〕快要进入社交界的年龄不到 20 岁的(少女)。

sub·de·lir·i·um [ˈsʌbdiˈliriəm; ˏsʌbdɪˋlɪrɪəm] *n.*【医】轻谵妄。

sub·di·rec·to·ry [ˈsʌbdiˈrektəri; ˋsʌbdəˋrɛktərɪ] *n.*【计】子目录。

sub·dis·ci·pline [ˈsʌbˈdisiplin; ˋsʌbˋdɪsəplɪn] *n.* 学科的分支。

sub·dis·trict [ˈsʌbˌdistrikt; ˋsʌbˏdɪstrɪkt] *n.* 分区。

sub·di·vide [ˈsʌbdiˈvaid; ˏsʌbdəˋvaɪd] *vt.*, *vi.* 再分;细分。**-rid·able** *a.*

sub·di·vis·i·ble [ˈsʌbdiˈvizəbl; ˏsʌbdəˋvɪzəbl̩] *a.* 可再分[细分]的。

sub·di·vi·sion [ˈsʌbdiviʒən; ˏsʌbdəˋvɪʒən, ˋsʌbdəˏvɪʒən] *n.* 再分;细分;再分之下的部分;(供出售的)小块土地,分装的商品;【军】半个师,半个连。**-al** *a.*

sub·dom·i·nant [ˈsʌbˈdɔminənt; sʌbˋdɑmənənt] *n.*, *a.* 第二位优势(的);【生】亚优势种(的);【乐】次属音(的)。

sub·dou·ble [sʌbˈdʌbl; sʌbˋdʌbl̩] *a.* 二分之一的。

sub·du·a·ble [səbˈdjuːəbl; səbˋdjuəbl̩] *a.* 可征服的;可抑制的。

sub·dual [səbˈdju(ː)əl; səbˋdjuəl, -ˋdu-] *n.* 征服,屈服,屈从;抑制;缓和。

sub·duce [səbˈdjuːs; səbˋdjus] *vt.* 减去,取回,扣除。

sub·duct [səbˈdʌkt; səbˋdʌkt] *vt.* **1.** 减去,取回,扣除。**2.**【地】使潜没;使下潜。

sub·duc·tion [səbˈdʌkʃən; səbˋdʌkʃən] *n.* **1.** 减去,取回,扣除;【数】减法。**2.**【地】潜没(使一个地壳板块下降到另一板块之下)。

sub·due [səbˈdjuː; səbˋdju] *vt.* **1.** 使屈从,打败,征服(敌国等)。**2.** 镇压,压制(情欲),克制(怒气等);驯养,驯伏。**3.** 开辟,开拓(土地);根除(杂草等)。**4.** 放低(声音等),弄低;弄淡,减淡(颜色),减弱(光线);减轻(炎症)。~ *a rough land* 开荒。*a ~d voice* 低声。*a ~d light* 柔(和的)光(线)。

sub·dued [səbˈdjuːd; səbˋdjud] *a.* **1.** 被征服的。**2.** 被抑制的。**3.** 缓和的,柔和的。

sub·du·pli·cate [ˈsʌbˈdjuːplikit; sʌbˋdjupləkɪt] *a.*【数】用平方根得出的;用平方根表示的。

sub·ed·it [ˈsʌbˈedit; sʌbˋɛdɪt] *vt.*〔英〕**1.** 充当…的助编。**2.** 以助编身份对(稿件)进行编辑加工(例如做整理稿件等技术工作;画版样,批格式等)。

sub·ed·i·tor [ˈsʌbˈeditə; sʌbˋɛdɪtɚ] *n.* 副主笔;助理编辑。

sub·em·ployed [ˌsʌbˈimplɔid; ˏsʌbˋɪmplɔɪd] *a.* 就业不足的。

sub·ep·i·der·mal [ˈsʌbˌepiˈdəːməl; ˏsʌbɛpɪˋdɝməl] *a.*【解】表皮下的。

sub·e·qual [sʌbˈiːkwəl; sʌbˋikwəl] *a.* 差不多相等的。

su·ber [ˈsjuːbə; ˋsjubɚ] *n.*【植】木栓(组织);软木槲;软木。

sub·e·rect [ˌsʌbiˈrekt; ˏsʌbɪˋrɛkt] *a.* 几乎直立的;几乎笔直向上生长的。

su·be·re·ous [suˈbiəriəs; sʊˋbɪrɪəs] *a.*【植】似软木的;软木质的。

su·ber·ic [*su*ˈberik; sʊˋbɛrɪk] *a.* 软木的,木栓的。~ *acid*【化】辛二酸。

su·ber·in, su·ber·ine [ˈsjuːbərin, ˈsuːbərin; ˋsjubərɪn] *n.*【化】软木脂。

su·ber·i·za·tion [ˌsjuːbəraiˈzeiʃən; ˏsjubəraɪˋzeʃən] *n.*【植】栓化(作用)。

su·ber·ize [ˈsjuːbəˌraiz, ˈsuː-; ˋsubəˏraɪz] *vt.*【植】使栓化。

su·ber·ose, su·ber·ous [ˈsjuːbərəus, -rəs; ˋsjubəˏros, -rəs] *a.*【植】木栓状的,软木质的。

sub·ex·change [ˈsʌbikstʃeindʒ; ˋsʌbɪkstʃendʒ] *n.* (电话)支局,分局。

sub·fam·i·ly [ˈsʌbfæmili; sʌbˋfæməlɪ, -ˋfæməlɪ] *n.*【生】亚科。

sub·floor [ˈsʌbˌflɔː; ˋsʌbˏflɔr, -ˏflɔr] *n.* 底层地板,毛地板,副地板。

sub·form [ˈsʌbfɔːm; ˋsʌbfɔrm] *n.* 从属形式,派生形式。

sub·for·ma·tion [sʌbfɔːˈmeiʃən; sʌbfɔrˋmeʃən] *n.* 从属形态;【空】单编队。

sub·freez·ing [ˈsʌbˈfriːziŋ; sʌbˋfrizɪŋ] *a.* (水的)冰点以下的;凝固点以下的。

sub·frig·id [sʌbˈfridʒid; sʌbˋfrɪdʒɪd] *a.* 亚寒带的。~ *zone* 亚寒带。

sub·fusc [ˈsʌbfʌsk; sʌbˋfʌsk], **sub·fus·cous** [-ˈfʌskəs; -ˋfʌskəs] *a.*〔主英〕暗黑的,带黑色的,黑黝黝的。

sub·ge·nus [ˈsʌbˈdʒiːnəs; sʌbˋdʒinəs] *n.* (*pl.* ***-genera*** [-dʒenərə; -dʒɛnərə], ***~es***)【生】亚属。

sub·gla·cial [sʌbˈgleiʃəl; sʌbˋgleʃəl] *a.* 冰河底的,在冰河下的。*a ~ deposit* 冰下沉积。**-ly** *ad.*

sub·grade [ˈsʌbgreid; ˋsʌbgred] *n.* 路基;地基。

sub·group [ˈsʌbgruːp; ˋsʌbˏgrup] *n.*【化】(周期表的)族;副族,*B* 族;【生】亚群,子群;【数】簇,子群。

sub·gum [ˈsʌbˈgʌm; ˋsʌbˋgʌm] *a.*【烹】(多种蔬菜)什锦的。

sub·heading [ˈsʌbhediŋ; ˋsʌbˏhɛdɪŋ] *n.* 小标题;细目。

sub·hu·man [ˈsʌbˈhjuːmən; sʌbˋhjumən] *a.* **1.** (发展上)次于人类的;低于人类的。**2.** 近于人类的。

Su·bic [ˈsuːbik; ˋsubɪk] **Bay** 苏比克湾〔菲律宾〕。

sub·in·dex [sʌbˈindeks; sʌbˋɪndɛks] *n.* (*pl.* ***-di·ces*** [-diˌsiːz; -dɪsiz]) **1.** 分目(录)。**2.**【数】分指数。

sub·in·feu·da·tion [ˈsʌbinfjuˈdeiʃən; sʌbˏɪnfjʊˋdeʃən] *n.* **1.** (封建制度的)分赐采邑,分封。**2.** 分封土地所有制。**3.** 封地,采邑。

sub·in·ter·val [ˈsʌbˈintəvəl; sʌbˋɪntəvəl] *n.*【乐】小音程;【数】子区间。

sub·ir·ri·gate [sʌbˈiriˌgeit; sʌbˋɪrəget] *vt.* 用地下管道灌溉(土地)。**-ga·tion** *n.* 地下灌溉。

su·bi·to [ˈsuːbiˌtəu; ˋsubɪˏto] *ad.*〔It.〕【乐】突然地,立刻地。

subj. = **1.** subject. **2.** subjective. **3.** subjunctive.

sub·ja·cen·cy [sʌbˈdʒeisnsi; sʌbˋdʒesn̩sɪ] *n.* **1.** 基座,基层。**2.** 毗连于下面的部分。

sub·ja·cent [sʌbˈdʒeisənt; sʌbˋdʒesn̩t] *a.* 在下面的;下层的;较低处的;形成基础的。

sub·ject [ˈsʌbdʒikt; ˋsʌbdʒɪkt] **I** *a.* **1.** 受…支配的,附属

的,从属的,受支配的。**2.** 易受…的,易遭…的,动不动就…的,易患…的(*to*)。**3.** 有关本题目的,有关本科目的。**4.** 以…为条件[转移]的,必须得到…的(*to*)。*Such conduct is ~ to criticism.* 这种行为容易受到批评。*a person ~ to attacks of fever* 容易发寒热的人。*The treaty is ~ to ratification.* 本条约须经批准。*~ to damage* 易遭损害的。*~ to check* 须加核对的。*~ to sale* 以出售为条件的;供出售的。**II** *n.* **1.** (君主国的)臣民,国民。**2.** 主题,问题;论题,话题;主因,原因,起因;科目,学科;主旨;主人翁。**3.**【语法】主语;【哲】主观;我,自我,主体(*opp.* object);【逻】主位,主辞(*opp.* attribute);【乐】主题,乐旨,主旋律;【文艺】主题。**4.** 对象;被催眠者,解剖用尸体;被实验者,实验材料;病人,患者;…质的人,…性质的人。*a British ~* 一个英国国籍的人。*the English ~* (集合词)英国国民。*the ~ of a story* 故事的主题。*a serious ~* 重大问题。*a ~ for laughter* 笑柄。*a medical* [*surgical*] *~* 内科[外科]病人。*a good* [*bad*] *~* 有[没有]希望医好的病人。*a hysterical ~* 歇斯底里患者。*a plethoric ~* 多血质的人。**III** [səbˈdʒekt; səbˋdʒɛkt] *vt.* **1.** 使隶属,使服从,使附属,在…下面(*to*)。**2.** 使受…,使患…,使遭受…;加(*to*)。**3.** 提供,提出,呈核,委托,交给(*to*)。*~ one's plans to another's consideration* 把计划提交别人斟酌。**be ~ed to** 受到,容易受到,遭受,处于;被…折磨。**~ oneself to** 蒙,受。**~ catalogue** 按学科分类的图书目录。**~ index** 内容[主题]索引。**~ matter** 题目,论题,话题;题材,内容。**~-raising**【语】主语上升(转换语法用语,如把 It is likely that he will do it. 句型换为 He is likely to do it.) **-less** *a.* 无题的;无主题的。

sub·jec·tion [səbˈdʒekʃən; səbˋdʒɛkʃən] *n.* 征服;服从,屈从。**bring under ~** 征服;使服从。**in ~** 服从。

sub·jec·tive [sʌbˈdʒektiv; səbˋdʒɛktɪv] **I** *a.*【哲】主观的(*opp.* objective);【语法】主格的。**II** *n.*【语法】主格。**-ly** *ad.*

sub·jec·tive·ness [səbˈdʒektivnis; səbˋdʒɛktɪvnɪs] *n.* 主观,主观性。

sub·jec·tiv·ism [sʌbˈdʒektivizəm; səbˋdʒɛktɪvɪzm̩] *n.*【哲】主观主义。

sub·jec·ti·vist [səbˈdʒektivist; səbˋdʒɛktɪvɪst] **I** *a.* 主观主义的。**II** *n.* 主观主义者。**-tic** *a.* **-ti·cal·ly** *ad.*

sub·jec·tiv·i·ty [ˌsʌbdʒekˈtiviti; ˏsʌbdʒɛkˋtɪvətɪ] *n.* 主观性;主观,主观主义。*In studying a problem, we must shun ~.* 研究问题,忌带主观性。

sub·join [ˈsʌbˈdʒɔin; səbˋdʒɔɪn] *vt.* 添加,增补,追加。

sub·ju·ga·ble [ˈsʌbdʒəgəbl; ˋsʌbdʒəgəbl̩] *a.* 可征服的,可制服的。

sub·ju·gate [ˈsʌbdʒugeit; ˋsʌbdʒəˏget] *vt.* 征服,制服,使服从;镇压,压住,抑制(感情等)。

sub·ju·ga·tion [ˌsʌbdʒuˈgeiʃən; ˏsʌbdʒəˋgeʃən] *n.* 征服;镇压。*the danger of national ~* 亡国的危险。**-ist** *n.* 亡国论者。

sub·ju·ga·tor [ˈsʌbdʒugeitə; ˋsʌbdʒəgetɚ] *n.* 征服者;镇压者。

sub·junc·tive [səbˈdʒʌŋktiv; səbˋdʒʌŋktɪv] **I** *a.*【语法】虚拟的,假设的。*the ~ mood* 假设语气。**II** *n.* 虚拟语气;(动词的)虚拟态。**-ly** *ad.*

sub·king·dom [ˈsʌbˈkiŋdəm; sʌbˋkɪŋdəm, ˋsʌbˏkɪŋdəm] *n.*【生】门,亚界。

sub·lap·sar·i·an [ˌsʌblæpˈseriən, -ˈsær-; ˏsʌblæpˋsɛrɪən, -ˋsær-] *n.*, *a.*【宗】= infralapsarian. **-ism** *n.*

sub·late [səbˈleit; səbˋlet] *vt.* **1.**【逻,哲】否定;与…相矛盾;扬弃。**2.** 消除,勾销。

sub·la·tion [sʌbˈleiʃən; sʌbˋleʃən] *n.* 否认;消除;【逻】否定;【哲】扬弃。

sub·lease [ˈsʌbˈliːs; ˋsʌbˏlis] *n.*, *vt.* (土地的)转租,分租。**sub·les·see** [ˈsʌbleˈsiː; ˏsʌblɛˋsi] *n.* 转租租户。**sub·les·sor** [-ˈsɔː; -ˋsɔr] 转租人。

sub·let [ˈsʌbˈlet; sʌbˋlet] *vt.*, *vi.* (*sublet*; *subletting*), *n.* 转租;分租;转包。

sub·le·thal [sʌbˈliːθəl; sʌbˋliθəl] *a.* (毒药的量等)不足以致命的。

sub·li·brar·ian [ˈsʌblaiˈbreəriən; ˏsʌblaɪˋbrɛrɪən] *n.* 图书馆副馆长[副管理员]。

sub·lieu·ten·ant [ˈsʌbleˈtenənt, Am. ˌsʌbluːˈtenənt; ˏsʌbluˋtɛnənt] *n.* [英海军]中尉。*an acting ~* [英海军]少尉。

sub·li·mate [ˈsʌblimeit; ˋsʌbləˏmet] **I** *vt.*【化】使升华,提纯;提高,使高尚,纯化;理想化。— *vi.* 升华,纯化。**II** [-mit; -mɪt] *a.* 升华的;纯化的;高尚的。**III** *n.*【化】升华物;升汞(= corrosive ~)。

sub·li·ma·tion [ˌsʌbliˈmeiʃən; ˏsʌbləˋmeʃən] *n.*【化】升华,提纯;使高尚,纯化。

sub·lime [səˈblaim; səˋblaɪm] **I** *a.* **1.** 崇高的,庄严的,(地位)高贵的;雄伟的;卓越的;超群的;壮烈的;【化】升华的;[诗]崇高的,高尚的。**2.** 傲慢的。**3.** [谑]极端的,无比的。**4.**【解】接近表面的,体表的。*a ~ commander* 卓越的指挥员。*~ courage* 英勇出众。*~ impudence* 极端无耻。*~ nerves* 体表神经。*his ~ highness* [古]殿下。**II** *n.* [the ~]庄严,崇高;壮美;宏伟;至高无上,极点(*of*)。*Your answer is the ~ of stupidity.* 你的回答是极端愚昧的。**III** *vt.*, *vi.* **1.** 提高,(使)变得高尚[纯化,理想化]。**2.**【化】(使)升华,精炼。**-ly** *ad.* **-r** *n.*

sub·lim·i·nal [sʌbˈliminl; sʌbˋlɪmənl, -ˋlaɪmə-] *a.*【心】阈下的;潜在的。*the ~ self* 阈下[潜在]自我。**-ly** *ad.*

sub·lim·it [səbˈlimit; səbˋlɪmɪt] *n.* (略低于最高限额的)次高限额。

sub·lim·i·ty [səˈblimiti; səˋblɪmətɪ] *n.* **1.** 崇高(性),雄伟(性)。**2.** 庄严的东西;崇高的人。**3.** 极致,极点。**4.** 精华。

sub·lin·gual [sʌbˈliŋgwəl; sʌbˋlɪŋgwəl] *a.*【解】舌下的,舌下腺的。*~ gland* 舌下腺。

sub·lu·na·r, -na·ry [sʌbˈluːnə(ri); sʌbˋlunɚ(rɪ)] *a.* 月下的;地上的;现世的。

sub·ma·chine·gun [ˈsʌbməˈʃiːngʌn; ˏsʌbməˋʃingʌn] *n.* 手提机关枪。

sub·man [ˈsʌbmæn; ˋsʌbˏmæn] *n.* (*pl.* **-men**) 低能者(*opp.* superman);人面兽心的人。

sub·mar·gin·al [sʌbˈmɑːdʒinəl; sʌbˋmɑrdʒɪnl̩] *a.*【生】亚缘的,近边缘的;【植】近叶缘的;【经】限界以下的,边际以下的,得不偿失的。**-ly** *ad.*

sub·ma·rine [ˈsʌbməriːn; ˏsʌbməˋrin] **I** *a.* 水下的,海中的,海底的,海生的。*a ~ armour* 潜水服。*a ~ boat* 潜艇。*a ~ cable* 海底电线。*a ~ volcano* 海底火山。**II** *n.* 潜艇;海底动物[植物];[美] = hero sandwich;[*pl.*][美俚]脚。*an A ~ = an atomic ~* 核子潜艇。**III** *vt.* (用潜艇)击沉,袭击。**~ pipe line** 海底电缆[管道]。**~ warfare** 潜艇战。**~ sandwich** = hero sandwich. **-r** *n.* 潜艇兵,潜艇人员。

sub·max·il·la [ˌsʌbmækˈsilə; ˏsʌbmækˋsɪlə] *n.* (*pl.* **-lae** [-iː; -i], **-las**)【解】下颌;下颌骨。

sub·max·il·lar·y [sʌbˈmæksiˌleri; sʌbˋmæksəˏlɛrɪ, ˏsʌbmækˋsɪlərɪ] *a.*【解】颌下的。

sub·me·di·ant [ˌsʌbˈmiːdiənt; sʌbˋmidɪənt] *n.*【乐】全音阶的第六度;次中和弦;次中音。

sub·me·nu [səbˈmenjuː; səbˋmenju] *n.*【计】子菜单,子选项单。

sub·merge [səbˈməːdʒ; səbˋmɝdʒ] *vt.* **1.** 使浸在水中,把…放在水中,使沉入水中;淹没,使泛滥;使沉溺。**2.** 使落到贫穷境地。— *vi.* 潜水;沉没,淹没;消失。*The factory is ~d with orders.* 工厂因订单过多而穷于应付。*be ~d* 被水淹没,遭水灾。*~d displacement* 排水量。*~d houses* 被水淹没的房屋。*the ~d tenth* (占英国人口 1/

10 的贫困不堪的)底层阶级。~**d reef** 暗礁。~**d speed** (潜艇的)潜航速度。

sub·mer·gence [sʌbˈməːdʒəns; səbˋmɝdʒəns] *n*. 沉没,浸入;淹没,泛滥;潜水,潜航。

sub·mer·gi·ble [sʌbˈməːdʒəbl; səbˋmɝdʒəbl̩] **I** *a*. 能沉入水中的;能潜航的。**II** *n*. 潜艇。

sub·merse [səbˈməːs; səbˋmɝs] *vt*. = submerge.

sub·mersed [sʌbˈməːst; səbˋmɝst] *a*. 没入水中的;生长在水下的。

sub·mers·i·ble [sʌbˈməːsəbl; səbˋmɝsəbl̩] *a*. = submergible. **-bil·i·ty** *n*. 潜航性能,潜航力。

sub·mer·sion [sʌbˈməːʃən; səbˋmɝʃən, -ʒən] *n*. = submergence.

sub·mi·cro·scop·ic [ˌsʌbmaikrəˈskɔpik; ˏsʌbmaɪkrəˋskɑpɪk] *a*. 超微观的,普通显微镜下看不见的。

sub·min·i·a·ture [sʌbˈminiətʃə; sʌbˋmɪnɪətʃɚ, -ˋmɪnə-] **I** *a*. (照相机等的)超小型的。*a* ~ *camera* 超小型照相机;袖珍照相机。**II** *n*. 袖珍照相机。

sub·min·i·a·tur·ize [sʌbˈminiətʃəraiz; sʌbˋmɪnɪətʃəˏraɪz] *vt*. 微型化。**-za·tion** *n*.

sub·miss [səbˈmis; səbˋmɪs] *a*. 〔古〕恭顺的;卑下的。

sub·mis·sion [səbˈmiʃən; səbˋmɪʃən] *n*. **1**. 屈服,服从,归顺,投降;谦恭,柔顺。**2**.【法】提交公断;提交物;意见,看法;建议。**3**. 提交;呈递。**4**. 认过,自白,自白书。*I demand the ~ of the signature to an expert*. 本人要求把签名提交专家鉴定。***be frightened into ~*** 吓倒。***My ~ is that ....*** = I submit that .... 我的意见是…,我认为…。***with all due ~*** 必恭必敬地。

S

sub·mis·sive [sʌbˈmisiv; səbˋmɪsɪv] *a*. 服从的;顺从的,柔顺的,谦恭的。**-ly** *ad*. **-ness** *n*.

sub·mit [səbˈmit; səbˋmɪt] *vt*. (**-mm-**) **1**. 使服从,使顺从;使屈服。**2**. 提交;委托,提出,提供;请求判断。**3**. 认为(*that*)。— *vi*. 服从,顺从;屈服,投降;甘受(*to*)。*All important problems must be ~ted to the committee for discussion*. 一切重要问题均须提交委员会讨论。*I ~ that he is mistaken*. 我认为他是错了。*I ~ that this should be allowed*. 我想这是可以允许的。*I ~ to being parted from you*. 我只好忍痛跟你分别了。*The minority should ~ to the majority*. 少数应服从多数。***~ oneself to*** 甘受,服从。***~ willingly*** 心悦诚服。

sub·mit·tal [səbˈmitəl; səbˋmɪtl̩] *n*. 服从,顺从,屈服。

sub·mon·tane [sʌbˈmɔntein; sʌbˋmɑnten] *a*. 山麓的,山脚下的。

sub·mul·ti·ple [ˈsʌbˈmʌltipl; sʌbˋmʌltəpl̩] *n*.【数】因数,约数;次倍量;【电】分谐波。

sub·nar·cotic [ˈsʌbnɑːˈkɔtik; ˏsʌbnɑrˋkɑtɪk] *n*. 轻度麻醉性的。

sub·nor·mal [ˈsʌbˈnɔːməl; sʌbˋnɔrml̩] **I** *a*. 正常以下的,低能的;逊常的,异常的。**II** *n*. 低能者;【数】次法距;次法线。**-ly** *ad*. **-i·ty** [-ˈmæliti; -ˋmælətɪ] *n*.

sub·note·book [ˈsʌbˈnəutbuk; ˋsʌbˋnotbuk] *n*.【计】小型笔记本电脑。

sub·o·ce·an·ic [ˌsʌbəuʃiˈænik; ˏsʌboʃɪˋænɪk] *a*.【地】位于[发生于]大洋下的,洋底的。

sub·oc·u·lar [ˈsʌbˈɔkjulə; sʌbˋɑkjulɚ] *a*.【解】眼下的。

sub·of·fice [ˈsʌbˈɔfis; ˋsʌbˏɑfɪs] *n*. 支局,分局,分办事处。

sub·op·tim·ize [səbˈɔptimaiz; səbˋɔptɪmaɪz] *vi*. 次优化,局部最优化,最佳利用某系统的某一部分。

sub·or·bit·al [sʌbˈɔːbitl; sʌbˋɔrbɪtl̩] *a*. **1**.【航】(宇宙[太空]航行的)小轨迹飞行的。**2**. 在眼眶之下的。

sub·or·der [ˈsʌbɔːdə; sʌbˋɔrdɚ, ˋsʌbˏɔrdɚ] *n*.【生】亚目。

sub·or·di·nal [sʌbˈɔːdinl; səˋbɔrdɪnl̩] *a*.【生】亚目的。

sub·or·di·nate [səˈbɔːdinit; səˋbɔrdnɪt] **I** *a*. 下级的,次级的,副职的;从属的;服从的(*to*)。*a ~ clause*【语法】从句。*~ crops* 补播作物。*a ~ officer* 部属,部下。*a ~ volcano* 单成火山。**II** *n*. 部属,部下,下级;从句。**III** [səˈbɔːdəneit; səˋbɔrdnˏet] *vt*. 使在次级,使被放在…下,使从属,使服从;轻视。***be ~d to the state plans*** 被纳入[服从]国家计划。**-ly** *ad*. **-ness** *n*.

sub·or·di·nat·ing [səˈbɔːdineitiŋ; səˋbɔrdnˏetɪŋ] *a*. 从属的。~ *conjunction*【语法】从属[主从]连词(= subordinate conjunction)。

sub·or·di·na·tion [səˌbɔːdiˈneiʃən; səˏbɔrdnˋeʃən] *n*. 被放在次级,使从属;次级,次等;服从,从属,从属关系。

sub·or·di·na·tion·ism [səbɔːdiˈneiʃənizm; səˏbɔrdəˋneʃənɪzm] *n*.【神】(三位一体中的第二位第三位从属于第一位的)从属说。

sub·or·di·na·tive [səˈbɔːdinətiv; səˋbɔrdəˏnetɪv, -nətɪv] *a*. 从属的,表示从属关系的。

sub·orn [sʌˈbɔːn; səˋbɔrn, sʌ-] *vt*. (用收买办法等)使发假誓,使作假证明;唆使,收买。**-er** *n*.

sub·or·na·tion [ˌsʌbɔːˈneiʃən; ˏsəbɔrˋneʃən] *n*. 贿赂人发假誓[做伪证];贿人犯罪,唆使。

sub·or·na·tive [səˈbɔːnətiv; səˋbɔrnətɪv] *a*. 发假誓的;使做假证明的;唆使的,收买的,教唆的。

sub·ox·ide [sʌbˈɔksaid; sʌbˋɑksaɪd, -sɪd] *n*.【化】低[次]氧化物。

sub·pack·age [ˈsʌbˈpækidʒ; sʌbˋpækɪdʒ] *n*., *vt*. 分装,分包。

sub·phy·lum [sʌbˈfailəm; sʌbˋfaɪləm] *n*. (*pl*. **-la** [-lə; -lə])【生】亚门。

sub·plot [ˈsʌbplɔt; ˋsʌbˏplɑt] *n*. (小说、剧本的)次要情节。

sub·p(o)e·na [səbˈpiːnə, səˈpiː-; səbˋpinə, səˋpi-] **I** *n*.【法】传票。**II** *vt*. (~**ed**, ~**'d**) 用传票传唤[索取],传讯,把…传到案。

sub·po·lar [ˈsʌbˈpəulə; sʌbˋpolɚ] *a*. 近(南、北)极的,近极地的;【天】极下的;【气】副极地的。

sub·pre·fect [ˈsʌbˈpriːfekt; sʌbˋprifɛkt] *n*. **1**. 副长官。**2**. 县长;(法国城市的)区长。

sub·pre·fec·ture [sʌbˈpriːfektʃə; sʌbˋprifɛktʃɚ] *n*. 县;区;县[区]长的职位[权限]。

sub·prin·ci·pal [sʌbˈprinsipl; sʌbˋprɪnsəpl̩] *n*. **1**. 副院长,副校长。**2**. (建筑)次要承重构件。**3**.【乐】(风琴的)八音的最低音[基本音]。

sub·prior [ˈsʌbˈpraiə; ˋsʌbˏpraɪɚ] *n*. 修道院副院长。

sub·quad·rate [ˈsʌbˈkwɔdrit; sʌbˋkwɑdrɪt] *a*. 近正方形的;正方形而有圆角的。

sub·re·gion [ˈsʌbˌriːdʒən; ˋsʌbˏridʒən] *n*.【生】亚区;分区;【数】子区域;分压。**-al** *a*.

sub·rep·tion [səbˈrepʃən; sʌbˋrɛpʃən] *n*. **1**. 用蒙骗手段获取利益〔尤指骗取教会捐赠〕。**2**. 隐瞒真相虚报事实。**3**. 由虚伪事实所引出的推断。**-rep·ti·tious** [-repˈtiʃəs; -rɛpˋtɪʃəs] *a*. **-ly** *ad*.

sub·ro·gate [ˈsʌbrəˌgeit; ˋsʌbrəˏget] *vt*. **1**. (人员)取代,接替。**2**.【法】取代〔代债务人清偿债务而接替原债权人地位享受其一切权利〕。

sub·ro·ga·tion [ˌsʌbrəˈgeiʃən; ˏsʌbrəˋgeʃən] *n*.【法】代替;取代;接替。

sub·ro·sa [sʌbˈrəuzə; sʌbˋrozə] *ad*. 秘密地;私下地;机密地。

sub·rou·tine [ˌsʌbruːˈtiːn; ˏsʌbruˋtin] *n*.【电子学】子程序。

subs. = subscription; subsidiary.

sub·sat·el·lite [ˈsʌbˈsætəlait; sʌbˋsætəlaɪt] *n*. (由人造卫星[太空船]带进轨道后放出的)子卫星。

subs·cap = subscribed capital 应募资金。

sub·scap·u·lar [sʌbˈskæpjulə; sʌbˋskæpjulɚ] *a*.【解】在肩胛下的。

sub·scribe [səbˈskraib; səbˋskraɪb] *vt*. **1**. 捐纳,捐助;认捐;签名(认捐等)。**2**. 订购,订阅,预定;征求订户,征求定购者。**3**. 签名,署名。—*vi*. **1**. 认捐,捐助;赞成,同

意。2. 预约,预定;订阅(*for*, *to*)。3. 签名,署名(*to*)。～ *to a fund* 对某一种基金认捐。～ *for a book* 订购书籍。*Some one has* ～*d a motto*. 有人写下了一句座右铭。*The* ～*d names carry weight*. 签名者的一些姓名起着很大作用。

sub·scrib·er [sʌbsˈkraibə; sʌbsˋkraɪbɚ] ***n*.** 1. 捐助人,捐款人。2. 预约者,订购者;订户。3. 〔the ～〕签名人。4. 用户。*a telephone* ～ 电话用户。*a* ～ *list* 电话簿。

sub·script [ˈsʌbskript; ˋsʌbskrɪpt] **I *a*.** 写在下面的(*opp*. adscript)。**II *n*.** 添标,下标,下角数码〔如 H_2O 的 2〕。

sub·scrip·tion [səbˈskripʃən; səbˋskrɪpʃən] ***n*.** 1. 认捐,捐款;预约,预定。2. 订费,预约费;(书籍等的)预约,订购;订阅。3. (医生的)(处方下的)调剂附注。4. 署名,签名。***open* [*close*] *the* ～ *lists*** 开始[截止]募捐[预订,认股(等)]。***solicit* ～*s*** 募捐。～ **blank**【商】认股单。～ **book** 认捐簿;预订登记簿;订购的书;(入场券等的)联票本。～ **liberary** 收费图书馆。～ **price** 订费,预约费。

subsec. = subsection (*pl*. ***subsecs***).

sub·sec·tion [ˈsʌbˌsekʃən; sʌbˋsɛkʃən, ˋsʌbˏsɛk-] ***n*.** 小节,小组,小区分;细目;(炮兵)分队。

sub·se·quence [ˈsʌbsikwəns; ˋsʌbsɪˏkwɛns, -kwəns] ***n*.** 接续;紧随…之后;随后发生的事情;后果。

sub·se·quent [ˈsʌbsikwənt; ˋsʌbsɪˏkwɛnt] ***a*.** 其后的,其次的;作为结果而发生的,附随的(*to*)。～ *events* 随后发生的事情。～ *to his death* 在他死后。～ *upon* 作为…的结果而发生的,接着…发生的。**-ly *ad*.** 其后,其次,接着。

sub·sere [ˈsʌbˌsiə; ˋsʌbˏsɪr] ***n*.**【生】次生演替系列。

sub·serve [səbˈsəːv; səbˋsɝv] ***vt*.** 帮助,补助;对…有用,对…有帮助;促进。

sub·ser·vi·ent [sʌbˈsəːviənt; səbˋsɝvɪənt] ***a*.** 充当下手的,充当工具(的);从属的;有帮助的,有用的,有贡献的;卑躬屈节的。***be* ～ *to*** 追随,屈从。**-ence, -ency *n*. -ly *ad*.**

sub·set [ˈsʌbset; ˋsʌbˏsɛt] ***n*.** 小集团;【数】子集(合)。

sub·sex·tu·ple [sʌbˈsekstjupl; sʌbˋsɛkstjupl̩] ***a*.** 六分之一的。

sub·share [ˈsʌbʃeə; ˋsʌbˏʃɛr] ***n*.** 利息单,股息券。

sub·shell [ˈsʌbʃel; ˋsʌbˏʃɛl] ***n*.**【原】支壳层。

sub·shrub [ˈsʌbˌʃrʌb; ˋsʌbˏʃrʌb] ***n*.**【植】半灌木。

sub·side [səbˈsaid; səbˋsaɪd] ***vi*.** 1. (船)下沉,沉下去;沉到底,沉淀;(地等)凹下去,下陷。2. (风雨、骚动、冲动等)平静下来,平息;(洪水等)退去,减退;(肿、热度等)消退,退烧。3. 〔主、谑〕(像沉下去似的)坐下,跪下,躺下。*Her grief* ～*d*. 她的悲伤消退了。*The floods have* ～*d*. 洪水退了。

sub·sid·ence [ˈsʌbsidəns; səbˋsaɪdns, ˋsʌbsədəns] ***n*.** 1. 沉淀;沉下,陷下。2. 平静,平息;减退,衰耗。

sub·sider [sʌ́bˈsaidə; sʌbˋsaɪdɚ] ***n*.**【化】沉降槽。

sub·sid·ia·ry [səbˈsidjəri; səbˋsɪdɪˏɛrɪ] **I *a*.** 1. 辅助的,帮助的。2. 次要的,附属的。3. 补足的(*to*);(指雇佣兵)为另一国所雇佣的。～ *coins* 辅币。*a* ～ *craft* 辅助舰。～ *payments* 补助金。～ *business* 业余工作;副业。～ *foodstuffs* 副食品。*a* ～ *stream* 支流。*a* ～ *treaty* 军事援助协定。～ *troops* 雇佣部队。**II *n*.** 1. 补给品。2. 附属者,附属品。3. 子公司〔= ～ company〕。4. 【乐】副主题。

sub·si·di·za·tion [ˌsʌbsidiˈzeiʃən; ˏsʌbsɪdɪˋzeʃən] ***n*.** 补助,津贴,给奖。

sub·si·dize [ˈsʌbsidaiz; ˋsʌbsəˏdaɪz] ***vt*.** 1. 给…补助金,给…津贴,向…发放奖金。2. 用贿赂拉拢,收买。

sub·si·dy [ˈsʌbsidi; ˋsʌbsədɪ] ***n*.** 助学金,补助金,津贴;奖金;(国家间的)财政援助;【英史】(给国王的)特别津贴。

sub·sist [səbˈsist; səbˋsɪst] ***vi*.** 1. 生存;活下去,维持生命,维持生活(*on*; *upon*)。2. 存在;继续存在;【哲】(逻辑上、理论上)存在;抽象地存在。—***vt*.** 〔罕〕供给…粮食,供养。*We are unable to* ～ *without air and water*. 没有空气和水我们就活不下去。～ *by begging* 靠讨饭维持生活。

sub·sist·ence [sʌbˈsistəns; səbˋsɪstəns] ***n*.** 1. 生存;存在。2. 生计;生活费;口粮;给养。3. 【哲】存在;存在物,实体。***gain one's* ～** 活得下去。***labour for* ～** 做工过日子。～ **agriculture** (仅供维持自家生活的)生存农业。～ **department**〔美〕粮食部,兵站部。～ **diet** 维持生命所需要的最小限度食物。～ **economy** 自给经济(往往仅足以维持生存)。～ **farm** [**homestead**]〔美〕(为失业工人办的)自耕自给农场。～ **farming** = ～ agriculture. ～ **level** (勉强维持生活的)低生活水平。～ **money** 生活费。～ **rates**〔美〕(船客的)膳费。～ **stores**〔美〕粮食,(军人的)粮饷。～ **wages** 仅够维持生活的最低工资。

sub·sist·ent [səbˈsistənt; səbˋsɪstənt] ***a*.** 生存的;现存的,存在的;生计的;给养的;附着的,固有的。

sub·soil [ˈsʌbsɔil; ˋsʌbˏsɔɪl] **I *n*.**【农】下层土,心土,底土;【建】天然地基。**II *vt*.** 翻起…的底土,深耕。

sub·so·lar [sʌbˈsəulə; sʌbˋsolɚ] ***a*.** 1. 太阳正下面的;赤道的。2. 日光下的,现世的。

sub·son·ic [ˈsʌbˈsɔnik; sʌbˋsɑnɪk] **I *a*.** 亚音(速)的。**II *n*.** 亚音速飞机。

sub·space [ˈsʌbˌspeis; ˋsʌbˏspes] ***n*.**【数】子空间。

sub·spe·ci·e [sʌbˈspiʃiː; subˋspɪʃi]〔L.〕在…的状态下,以…形式。

sub·spe·ci·e ae·ter·ni·ta·tis [sʌbˈspiʃiːaiˌtəniˈtɑːtis; sʌbˋspɪʃiaɪˏtɚˋnɪtɑtɪs]〔L.〕在永恒的状态下,以永恒的形式。

sub·spe·cies [ˈsʌbspiːʃiːz; sʌbˋspiʃɪz, ˋsʌbˏspiʃɪz, -ʃiz] ***n*.**【生】亚种。

sub·spe·ci·fic [ˌsʌbspiˈsifik; ˏsʌbspɪˋsɪfɪk] ***a*.**【生】亚种的。

subst. = substantive; substitute.

sub·stance [ˈsʌbstəns; ˋsʌbstəns] ***n*.** 1. 物质,材料;【哲】实体,本体,本质(*opp*. appearance)。2. 实质,内容;(故事等的)要旨,要领,大意,梗概。3. 财产,资产,资力。4. 【神】灵,(三位一体的)体。5. (织品的)质地。*The* ～ *is usually more important than the form*. 内容总是比形式重要。*I can tell you the* ～. 我可以讲大意给你听。*a porous* ～ 多孔体。*a man of* ～ 资产家,财主。***in* ～** 实体上,本质上;大体上。***sacrifice the* ～ *for the shadow*** 只图虚名不求实效,舍本逐末。***waste one's* ～** 浪费财产。～ **abuse** (对烟、酒、毒品等的)难戒除的瘾,恶瘾。～ **P**【生化】P 物质,肽物质(分布于中枢神经系统,据说与痛觉有关)。

sub·stand·ard [səbˈstændəd; sʌbˋstændɚd, ˋsʌbˏs-] ***a*.** 1. 标准以下的。2. 〔美〕【法】(食品、药品成分)法定标准以下的。3. 【语】非标准语的;非规范化的。

sub·stan·tial [səbˈstænʃəl; səbˋstænʃəl] ***a*.** 1. 实质的,真正的;【哲】实在的,实体的,本体的,本质的。2. 有财产的,有资产的;有真价的,有信用的,可靠的。3. 富裕的;有实力的。4. 有内容的,充实的;有价值的;质地好的,坚固的,坚牢的,结实的。5. 相当的,多额的,很多的;紧要的。6. 大体上的,事实上的(一致、成功等)。*a* ～ *hope* 可靠的希望。*a* ～ *farmer* 富裕的农民。*a man of* ～ *build* 体格结实的人。*a* ～ *house* 坚固的房子。*a* ～ *concession* 相当大的让步。*a* ～ *improvement* 显著的进步。*a* ～ *point* 重要的地点。**-ism *n*.**【哲】实体论。**-ist *n*.** 实体论者。**-ness *n*.**

sub·stan·tial·i·ty [səbˌstænʃiˈæliti; səbˏstænʃɪˋælətɪ] ***n*.** (有)实质,(有)内容;(有)实体,(有)形体;坚固。

sub·stan·tial·ize [səbˈstænʃəlaiz; səbˋstænʃəlˏaɪz] ***vt*., *vi*.** (使)实体化;(使)实质化,(使)成为真实。

sub·stan·tial·ly [səbˈstænʃəli; səbˋstænʃəlɪ] ***ad*.** 1. 实体上,本质上,实质上;大体上。2. 坚强地,坚固地。3. 充分地,丰富地。

S

sub·stan·tials [səbsˈtænʃəlz; səbsˋtænʃəlz] ***n***. 〔*pl*.〕 **1**. 实质性部分;重要部分。**2**. 纲要,要领,大意。

sub·stan·tiate [sʌbsˈtæʃieit; səbˋstænʃɪˏet] ***vt***. **1**. 使具体[实体]化。**2**. 证实,证明某事有根据。

sub·stan·ti·a·tion [səbˌstænʃiˈeiʃən; səbˏstænʃɪˋeʃən] ***n***. 具体化;证实。

sub·stan·ti·a·tive [səbˈstænʃiˌeitiv; səbˋstænʃɪˏetɪv] ***a***. **1**. 表示存在的,表示实在的。**2**. 独立的;有实体的;变为实体的;具体的。**3**. 证实的,确认的。

sub·stan·ti·a·tor [səbˈstænʃieitə; səbˋstænʃɪˏetɚ] ***n***. 证明人,证人。

sub·stan·ti·val [sʌbstənˈtaivəl; ˏsʌbstənˋtaɪvl̩] ***a***. 【语法】实词的,名词性的。**-ly** ***ad***.

sub·stan·tive [ˈsʌbstəntiv; ˋsʌbstəntɪv] **I** ***a***. **1**. 实体的;真实的。**2**. 独立的,自立的。**3**. 坚固的;实质的;本质的。**4**. 【语法】实词的,名词的;表示存在的。**5**. 【法】实体的,规定权利与义务的。**II** ***n***. 【语法】实词,名词。~ *colours* 直接染料。~ *enactment* 明文规定。~ *major* 领正薪的少校。~ *motion* 正式动议。~ *right* 基本人权〔指法律规定权利之外的生存权等〕。**-ly** ***ad***.

sub·stan·ti·vize [ˈsʌbstəntivaiz; ˋsʌbstəntɪvˏaɪz] ***vt***. 【语法】使名词化。

sub·sta·tion [ˈsʌbsteiʃən; ˋsʌbˏsteʃən] ***n***. 分站;变压所;支局,分局,派出所。*a power* ~ 变电所。

sub·stit·u·ent [sʌbˈstitjuənt; sʌbˋstɪtʃuənt] ***n***. 代替者,取代者;【化】取代基。

sub·sti·tute [ˈsʌbstitjuːt; ˋsʌbstəˏtjut] **I** ***n***. **1**. 代替者[物],代用品;候补员;后补选手;收入(数)。**2**. 【语法】代用词[语]。**3**. 【矿】转接器,短节。*There's no* ~ *for parents*. 父母亲是没有别人可以代替的。**II** ***vt***. 以…代替,用…代替(*for*);【化】取代。~ *A for B*. 用A代B。~ *margarine for butter* 用人造奶油代替奶油。~ *sb*. *by* [*with*] *another* 用别人接替某人。— ***vi***. 作…代理者,〔美〕代替;【化】取代。*John will* ~ *for his father*. 约翰将作为他父亲的代理人。

sub·sti·tu·tion [ˈsʌbstitjuːʃən; ˏsʌbstəˋtjuʃən] ***n***. **1**. 代,代用,代替,更替,置换。**2**. 【化】取代;【数】代换;代入;【法】预定继承人;【语法】词的代用。**-al** ***a***. **-ary** ***a***.

sub·sti·tu·tive [ˈsʌbstitjuːtiv; ˋsʌbstəˏtjutɪv] ***a***. 代替的,代用的;取代的;补充的。~ **tooth** 永久齿。

sub·sti·tu·tor [sʌbsˈtitjuːtə; sʌbsˋtɪtjutɚ] ***n***. 替手;代用品。

sub·storm [səbˈstɔːm; səbˋstɔrm] ***n***. 【物】磁层亚暴〔地球磁层中的一种扰乱〕。

sub·strate [ˈsʌbstreit; ˋsʌbstret] ***n***. **1**. 底层,地层。**2**. 【无】(半导体工艺中的)衬底,基底。**3**. 【生】(生态学中的)基层;【生化】受质;被酶作用物。

sub·strat·o·sphere [sʌbˈstrætəsfiə; sʌbˋstrætəsfɪr, -ˋstre-] ***n***. 【空】亚[副]平流层;亚[副]同温层。

sub·stra·tum [ˌsʌbˈstrɑːtəm, ˌsʌbˈstreitəm; sʌbˋstretəm, -ˋstræt-] ***n***. (*pl*. *-ta* [-tə; -tə]) **1**. 下层;基础;【生】(生态学中的)基层;根本。**2**. 【生化】培养基;基质;【农】下层土;底土,心土;【摄】(胶片片基与乳剂间的)胶层。**3**. 〔*pl*.〕〔美〕下层社会。

sub·struc·ture, sub·struc·tion [ˈsʌbˈstrʌktʃə, -ʃən; sʌbˋstrʌktʃɚ, -ʃən] ***n***. **1**. 【建】下部结构,下层建筑,基础工程,地下建筑。**2**. 基础,根基,根底。**-tur·al** ***a***.

sub·sume [sʌbˈsjuːm; səbˋsum, -ˋsɪum] ***vt***. 【逻】包摄,包含。

sub·sump·tion [sʌbˈsʌmpʃən; səbˋsʌmpʃən] ***n***. 【逻】包摄,包含;包容;(三段论法的)小前提。

sub·sur·face [ˈsʌbˈsəːfis; sʌbˋsɝfɪs] **I** ***a***. 表面下的,液面下的;地下的,水面下的。**II** ***n***. 地面下[水面下]的部分〔岩石,土壤,水层等〕。

sub·syn·chron·ous [ˈsʌbˈsiŋkrənəs; sʌbˋsɪŋkrənəs] ***a***. 【电】次同步的,亚同步的。

sub·sys·tem [ˈsʌbˌsistim; ˋsʌbˏsɪstəm, ˏsʌbˋsɪs-] ***n***. (系统的)分部;分体系,支系统。

sub·tan·gent [ˈsʌbˈtændʒənt; sʌbˋtændʒənt] ***n***. 【数】次切线[距]。

sub·teen [ˈsʌbˈtiːn; ˋsʌbtin] ***n***. 〔美〕将近十三岁的儿童。

sub·tem·per·ate [ˈsʌbˈtempərit; sʌbˋtɛmpərɪt] ***a***. 亚温带的。

sub·ten·an·cy [ˈsʌbˈtenənsi; sʌbˋtɛnənsɪ] ***n***. (房、地等)转借,转租。

sub·ten·ant [sʌbˈtenənt; sʌbˋtɛnənt] ***n***. (房屋、土地的)转租租户。

sub·tend [səbˈtend; səbˋtɛnd] ***vt***. **1**. 【数】(弦、边)对(弧、角)。**2**. 【植】衬托,把…包在叶腋内。**3**. 包插,包含。

sub·ten·der [ˌsʌbˈtendə; ˏsʌbˋtɛndɚ] ***n***. 【军】潜艇供应船(= submarine tender)。

sub·tense [səbˈtens; səbˋtɛns] **I** ***n***. 【数】弦,对边。**II** ***a***. 根据所对角度测量的。~ **method** 【测】视测法。

sub·ter- *pref*. 下;在下;少于,次于;私下: *subter*natural.

sub·ter·fuge [ˈsʌbtəfjuːdʒ; ˋsʌbtɚˏfjudʒ] ***n***. 遁辞,托辞,口实;欺骗,诡计;规避。

sub·ter·human [ˌsʌbtəˈhjuːmən; ˏsʌbtəˋhjumən] ***a***. 低于人类的。

sub·ter·min·al [ˈsʌbˈtəːminl; sʌbˋtɝmɪnl̩] ***a***. 几乎在末端的。

sub·ter·nat·u·ral [ˌsʌbtəˈnætʃərəl; ˏsʌbtɚˋnætʃərəl] ***a***. 逊于天然的;不十分自然的。

sub·ter·rane [ˈsʌbtərein; ˋsʌbtəˏren] ***n***. 下层;洞穴,地下室;【地】表层下基岩。

sub·ter·ra·ne·an, -ne·ous [sʌbtəˈreinjən, -niəs; sʌbtəˋrenɪən, -nɪəs] ***a***. **1**. 地下的,地中的。**2**. 隐藏的,秘密的。*a* ~ *railroad* 地下铁路。*a* ~ *line* 地下线。*a* ~ *dwelling* 地下住所。~ *pupa* 动埋蛹。~ *river* 【地】伏流,地下河。**-ly** ***ad***.

sub·text [ˈsʌbtekst; ˋsʌbtɛkst] ***n***. 言外之意,潜台词。

sub·thresh·old [ˈsʌbˈθreʃhəuld; sʌbˋθrɛʃhold] ***a***. (药剂量)次于最低限度的,不足以起作用的。

sub·til(e) [ˈsʌtl; ˋsʌtl̩, ˋsʌbtɪl] ***a***. (*-til·er*; *-til·est*) 〔古〕= subtle.

sub·ti·lin [ˈsʌbtilin; ˋsʌbtɪlɪn] ***n***. 【生化】枯草菌素。

sub·til·ty, sub·til·i·ty [ˈsʌbtəlti, -tiliti; ˋsʌbtəltɪ, -ˋtɪlətɪ] ***n***. 〔古〕= subtlety.

sub·til·i·za·tion [ˌsʌtlaiˈzeiʃən; ˏsʌtl̩aɪˋzeʃən] ***n***. 稀薄化;纤细化;微妙化;精细化。

sub·til·ize [ˈsʌtilaiz; ˋsʌtl̩ˏaɪz, ˋsʌb-] ***vt***. **1**. 使稀薄;使纤细。**2**. 使有细微区别;使微妙,使精细。**3**. 精细地讨论;穿凿附会。— ***vi***. **1**. 趋于精细[微妙]。**2**. 详细讨论。**3**. 过分精细。

sub·til·ty [ˈsʌtəlti; ˋsʌtl̩tɪ] 〔古〕= subtlety.

sub·ti·lysin [sʌbtiˈlaisin; sʌbtɪˋlaɪsɪn] ***n***. 【生化】枯草菌溶素。

sub·ti·tle [ˈsʌbtaitl; ˋsʌbˏtaɪtl] **I** ***n***. (书籍的)副题;小标题;【影】说明字幕;对白字幕。**II** ***vt***. 加副标题于…;为…加说明[对白]字幕。

sub·tle [ˈsʌtl; ˋsʌtl̩] ***a***. (*-tler*; *-tlest*) **1**. 精细的;巧妙的,精巧的,敏感的,敏锐的。**2**. 微妙的,难于捉摸的,难解的。**3**. 狡猾的,阴险的(敌人)。**4**. 〔古〕稀薄的。~ *intellect* 睿智。*a* ~ *observer* 敏锐的观察者。~ *fingers* 灵巧的手指。*a* ~ *power* 神秘不可思议的力量。*a* ~ *perfume* 幽雅的香味。**-ness** ***n***.

sub·tle·ty [ˈsʌtlti; ˋsʌtl̩tɪ] ***n***. **1**. 精妙;巧妙,纤巧;敏锐,敏感;细微的区别;微妙,难捉摸。**2**. 狡猾,阴险。**3**. 稀薄。

sub·tly [ˈsʌtli; ˋsʌtlɪ] ***ad***. 巧妙地;细微地,微妙地;难解地;狡猾地。

sub·ton·ic [sʌbˈtɔnik; sʌbˋtɑnɪk] ***n***. 【乐】全音阶的第七个音,下主音。

sub·to·pi·a [sʌbˈtəupjə, -ˈtɔpjə; sʌbˋtopɪə] ***n***. 〔英〕〔蔑〕城市化的乡村地区;城乡一律化丧失自然美景的趋

势〔该词由 sub 加 (u)topia 构成〕。**-n** ***a***.

sub·to·pic [ˈsʌbˌtɔpik; ˋsʌbˏtɑpɪk, sʌbˋtɑp-] ***n***. (主题的)分题。

sub·to·tal [ˈsʌbˌtəutl; sʌbˋtotl, ˋsʌbˏt-] **I *n***. 部分和,小计。**II *vt*., *vi***. 求(…的)部分和[小计]。

sub·tract [səbˈtrækt; səbˋtrækt] ***vt***., ***vi***. 减去,扣除(*from*)。*That ~s nothing from his merit*. 那丝毫没有减损他的功绩。**-or**, 〔美〕**-er *n***. 减少者,减去者;【数】减数。

sub·trac·tion [sʌbˈtrækʃən; səbˋtrækʃən] ***n***. 减去,扣除(*from*);【数】减法。

sub·trac·tive [sʌbˈtræktiv; səbˋtræktɪv] ***a***. 减少的;【数】(应)减去的,带有减号[负号]的。

sub·tra·hend [ˈsʌbtrəhend; ˋsʌbtrəˏhɛnd] ***n***.【数】减数。

sub·trans·par·ent [ˈsʌbtrænsˈpɛərənt; sʌbtrænsˋpɛrənt] ***a***. 半透明的。

sub·treas·ur·y [sʌbˈtreʒəri; ˋsʌbˏtrɛʒərɪ, sʌbˋtrɛʒərɪ] ***n***. 〔美〕国[金]库分库。

sub·tribe [ˈsʌbtraib; ˋsʌbˏtraɪb] ***n***.【生】亚族。

sub·trop·ic, -i·cal [ˈsʌbˈtrɔpik(əl); sʌbˋtrɑpɪk(əl)] ***a***. 亚热带的。**-ics *n***. *pl*. 亚热带。

su·bu·late [ˈsjuːbjulit; ˋsjubjuˏlet, -lɪt] ***a***.【植】钻状的;锥形的。

sub·um·brel·la [ˌsʌbʌmˈbrelə; ˏsʌbʌmˋbrɛlə] ***n***.【动】(水母的)下伞(面)。

sub·urb [ˈsʌbəːb; ˋsʌbɝb] ***n***. **1.** 〔常 *pl*.〕郊区,城郊,市郊,近郊。**2.** 〔*pl*.〕附近,周围。***in the ~s*** 在郊区。***the ~s of sorrow*** 悲哀的境遇。

sub·ur·ban [səˈbəːbən; səˋbɝbən] **I *a***. **1.** 郊区的,住在城郊的。**2.** 〔英〕土气的;偏狭的。*a ~ point of view* 偏狭的观点。**II *n***. 〔美〕郊区居民。~ **neurosis** 市郊神经官能症〔指妇女僻居市郊,整天忙于家务产生的精神不适〕。

sub·ur·ban·ite [səˈbəːbənait; səˋbɝbənˏaɪt] ***n***. 郊区居民。

sub·ur·ban·ize [səˈbəːbənaiz; səˋbɝbənˏaɪz] ***vt***., ***vi***. (使)变为市郊,(使)市郊化。**-i·za·tion *n***.

sub·ur·bi·a [səˈbəːbiə; səˋbɝbɪə] ***n***. 郊区;〔集合词〕郊区居民;郊区居民风习。

sub·ur·bi·car·i·an [səˌbəːbiˈkeriən; səˏbɝbɪˋkɛrɪən] ***a***. 在罗马市郊的;〔尤指〕【天主】教皇的第七管区的。

sub·ur·sine [sʌbˈəːsain; sʌbˋɝsaɪn] ***a***. 有点像熊的。

sub·va·ri·e·ty [ˈsʌbvəraiəti; ˏsʌbvəˋraɪətɪ] ***n***.【生】亚变种。

sub·vene [səbˈviːn; səbˋvin] ***vi***. 〔罕〕进行帮助,来补救,干预。

sub·ven·tion [səbˈvenʃən; səbˋvɛnʃən] ***n***. (政府的)补助金;津贴;援助。**-ary *a***.

sub ver·bo [sʌbˈvəːbəu; sʌbˋvɝbo] 〔L.〕(辞典,索引等中)见某词条。

sub·ver·sion [sʌbˈvəːʃən; səbˋvɝʃən, -ʒən] ***n***. 颠覆(活动);破坏;覆灭,瓦解。*protect one's country from ~ by external enemies*. 防御国家外部敌人的颠覆活动。**-ary *a***.

sub·ver·sive [sʌbˈvəːsiv; səbˋvɝsɪv] **I *a***. 颠覆(性)的,破坏(性)的。**II *n***. 颠覆分子。**-ly *ad***. **-ness *n***.

sub·vert [səbˈvəːt; səbˋvɝt] ***vt***. 颠覆,推翻,破坏(国家等);搅乱(人心),败坏(风化),腐蚀(思想)。**-er *n***.

sub·vit·re·ous [ˈsʌbvitriəs; ˋsʌbvɪtrɪəs] ***a***. **1.** 光泽不及玻璃的。**2.**【物】亚琉态的。

sub·vo·cal [ˈsʌbˈvəukəl; sʌbˋvokl̩] ***a***. 默读的。**-ize *vi***. 默读。

sub·way [ˈsʌbwei; ˋsʌbˏwe] ***n***. **1.** (过马路的)地道(=〔美〕underpass)。**2.** 〔美〕地下铁道[列车]。

sub·ze·ro [sʌbˈziərəu; ˏsʌbˋzɪro] ***n***., ***a***. 零下(的);负(的);严寒(的)。

suc- *pref*. 〔用于 c 前〕= sub-.

suc·cades [səˈkeidz; səˋkedz] ***n***. 〔*pl*.〕蜜饯糖果。

suc·ce·da·ne·um [sʌksiˈdeiniəm; ˏsʌksɪˋdenɪəm] ***n***. (*pl*. ~*s*, ***-nea*** [-niə; -nɪə]) 代用品〔如牙医代替贵重金属的合金〕;代用药;代理人,替手。**-da·ne·ous** [-ˈdeiniəs; -ˋdenɪəs] ***a***.

suc·ceed [səkˈsiːd; səkˋsid] ***vt***. 继…之后,继续;接着…发生;〔诗〕使成功。—***vi***. **1.** 成功,获得成效;(计划等)顺利进行。**2.** 继承,承受;接连,接着发生(*to*)。*Summer ~s spring*. 春去夏来。*~ sb. as Premier* 接替某人担任总理。*Nothing ~s like success*. 一事成功事事顺利。*~ in doing sth*. 做某事成功。*~ in examination* 考试及格。*His plans ~ed*. 他的计划成功了。~ ***in life*** 发迹。~ ***oneself*** 〔美〕再度当选;连任,留任。***~ing years*** 接连的几年。★“继承”意义的 ***n***., ***a***. 分别为 succession, successive. “成功”意义的 ***n***., ***a***. 分别为 success, successful. **-ent *a***.

suc·cen·tor [səkˈsentə; səkˋsɛntɚ] ***n***. (教堂)唱诗班代理指挥[副指挥];唱诗班的低音领唱人。

suc·cès de scan·dale [sukˈsei də skɑ̃ːnˈdɑl; sykˋse də skɑ̃ nˋdɑl] ***n***. 〔F.〕(文艺作品等)因内容丑恶而轰动的臭名声;臭名远扬的作品。

suc·cès d'es·time [sukˈsei desˈtiːm; ˏsykˋsɛˏdɛsˋtim] ***n***. 〔F.〕(对不大成功的演员、作者的)礼貌上的欢迎[称赞]。

suc·cès fou [sukˈseiˌfuː; sykˋseˏfu] ***n***. 〔F.〕令人趋之若狂的大成功。

suc·cess [səkˈses; səkˋsɛs] ***n***. **1.** 成功,成就;好结果,好成绩;成功者;考试及格者。**2.** 〔方、罕〕结果,成绩。*a good ~* 好结果,成功。*an ill [a bad] ~* 坏结果,失败。*have great ~ in life* 大大发迹了。*He was a great ~ as an actor*. 他的演员生涯是非常成功的。*My holiday in Switzerland was a great ~*. 我在瑞士度过的假期是一次大成功。*The evening was a ~*. 那晚(的宴会)很是热闹愉快。***drink ~ to*** 为祝…成功而干杯。***make a ~ of ...*** 把…做得很成功。***make*** (*conferences*) ***a ~*** 开好(会议)。***meet with ~*** 成功。~ **story** 发迹史,发迹者;大获成功之事例。~ **worker** 对国家有重大贡献的工人[工作者]。

suc·cess·ful [sʌkˈsesful; səkˋsɛsfəl] ***a***. 成功的;结果好的;有成绩[成就]的;及格的;(会等)盛大的;幸运的;出了头的。*a ~ play* 成功的戏剧。*a ~ candidate* 及格者;当选者。*a ~ man* 一帆风顺的人。***be ~ in*** 在…上成功。**-ly *ad***. **-ness *n***.

suc·ces·sion [səkˈseʃən; səkˋsɛʃən] ***n***. **1.** 接连发生,继起,接续;继承性;(计算技术的)逐次性。**2.** 继承;继承权;继承顺序;继任;后继。**3.**【生】系列;世系,系统;演替;【农】轮栽。*a ~ of disasters* 灾连祸接。*He is not in the ~*. 他没有继承权。***by ~*** 按照继承顺序。***in due ~*** 按自然的次序。***in ~*** 接连,接着。***in ~ to*** 继…之后(担任)。~ **duty** 继承税。~ **state** (由一国分裂出之)继承国,后继国。

suc·ces·sion·al [sʌkˈseʃənəl; səkˋsɛʃənəl] ***a***. 相继的,连续的。

suc·ces·sive [sʌkˈsesiv; səkˋsɛsɪv] ***a***. 接连的,相继的,连绵的,继续的,连续的;逐次的。**-ly *ad***. 接连,相继,依次。

suc·ces·sor [sʌkˈsesə; səkˋsɛsɚ] ***n***. 继承人;继任者,接班人;后继者(*opp*. predecessor);顶替者(*to*)。*unworthy ~s* 不肖子孙。*~s to a cause of ...* 某一事业之后继者。

suc·ci [ˈsʌkai, ˈsʌksai; ˋsʌkaɪ, ˋsʌksaɪ] succus 的复数。

suc·ci·nate [ˈsʌksiˌneit; ˋsʌksɪˏnet] ***n***.【化】琥珀酸盐(或酯);丁二酸盐(或酯)。

suc·cinct [səkˈsiŋkt; səkˋsɪŋkt] ***a***. **1.** 简洁的,简明的。**2.** 〔古〕紧束的,紧贴在身上的;卷起的。**-ly *ad***. **-ness *n***.

suc·cin·ic [səkˈsinik; səkˋsɪnɪk] ***a***. ~ **acid** 琥珀酸,丁

二酸。

suc·cin·ite [ˈsʌksinait; ˋsʌksɪnˏaɪt] ***n.*** 琥珀(色)。

suc·cor [ˈsʌkə; ˋsʌkɚ] ***n.*** 〔美〕= succour.

suc·co·ry [ˈsʌkəri; ˋsʌkərɪ] ***n.*** 【植】菊苣(= chicory)。

suc·co·tash [ˈsʌkətæʃ; ˋsʌkəˏtæʃ] ***n.*** 〔美〕豆煮玉米〔常加有腊肉〕。

suc·co(u)r [ˈsʌkə; ˋsʌkɚ] **I** ***n.*** 援助,救援;援助者,支援物品;〔*pl.*〕〔古〕援军。**II** ***vt.*** 帮助,救济,支援。

suc·cu·bus [ˈsʌkjubəs; ˋsʌkjəbəs] ***n.*** (*pl.* ***-bi*** [-bai; -ˏbaɪ]) 女妖;妖魔;娼妓。

suc·cu·lence, -cy [ˈsʌkjuləns(i); ˋsʌkjələns(ɪ)] ***n.*** **1.** 多汁(性);【植】肉质性。**2.** 青饲料。

suc·cu·lent [ˈsʌkjulənt; ˋsʌkjələnt] **I** ***a.*** **1.** 多汁的,多液的。**2.** 极有兴趣的,津津有味的;有活力的。**II** ***n.*** 肉质植物。~ **fodder** 青饲料。**-ly** ***ad.***

suc·cumb [səˈkʌm; səˋkʌm] ***vi.*** 屈服;死 (*to*)。~ *to curiosity* 被好奇心所驱使。~ *to temptation* 经受不住诱惑。~ *to one's enemies* 被敌人打败,向敌人屈服。~ *to superior numbers* 被优势压倒。~ *to disease* 病死。

suc·cus [ˈsʌkəs; ˋsʌkəs] ***n.*** 分泌液;液汁;植物液剂。

suc·cuss [səˈkʌs; səˋkʌs] ***vt.*** 猛摇(病人)以确定体腔内有无积液。

suc·cus·sa·tory [səˈkʌsətəri; səˋkʌsəˏtorɪ, -ˏtɔrɪ] ***a.*** (地震)上下振动振幅小的。

suc·cus·sion [səˈkʌʃən; səˋkʌʃən] ***n.*** 猛摇;【医】振荡(法)。

suc·cus·sive [səˈkʌsiv; səˋkʌsɪv] ***a.*** 强烈摇动的;〔原尤指〕【医】振荡的〔猛摇(病人)以诊察体腔内有无积液〕。

S

such [sʌtʃ; 弱音 sətʃ; sʌtʃ, sətʃ] **I** ***a.*** 〔无比较级及最高级。在句中可用作定语、表语;有时为避免形容词的重复出现可作代用词;与 all, any, many, no, one, few, some 一起修饰名词时,放在这些词的后面;引出形容词从句修饰名词时,一般放在名词的前面,如放在后面,则含有轻蔑意味;与另一形容词一起修饰单数名词时位于不定冠词 a(n) 之前,如 such a big table〕。**1.** (a) 那样的,这样的,那种,这种。~ *a man* 那样的人。~ *men* 那样的人们。*all* ~ *men* 所有那一类人。*any* [*some*] ~ *man* [*thing*] 一个这样的人[东西]。*no* ~ *thing* 那种事情不会有! 不会! ~ *a*(*n*) *one* 〔雅〕那样的人;〔古〕某人。*He is not well off, only he seems* ~. 他并不富裕,只是像富裕罢了。*Long may he continue* ~! 希望他永远那样! *You may use my car,* ~ *as it is*. 这样一部汽车,请将就用吧。*S- is life* [*the world*]! 人生就是这样! *S- master,* ~ *servant*. 有其主必有其仆。(b)〔用作关连词,与 as 相呼应〕像…那样的。~ *things as iron, silver, and gold* 铁、银、金这一类东西。*I said no* ~ *thing* (*as that*). 我没说那种事。*Children* ~ *as these will never learn anything*. 这样的孩子是学不到什么东西的。*I am not* ~ *a fool* (= so foolish) *as to believe that*. 我不是连那种事都会相信的笨蛋。*His illness was not* (*one*) ~ *as to cause anxiety*. 他的病不是那种令人着急的病。(c)〔用作关连词,与 that 相呼应〕如此…以致。*She had* ~ *a fright that she fainted*. 她吓得昏倒了。*S- was the force of the explosion that all the windows were broken*. 爆炸力大得把所有的窗子都震破了。**2.** (a)〔和形容词连用〕那样,这样;〔口〕非常。*I have never met* ~ *a good man*. 我从来没有碰见过那样好的人。~ *a big stick* 那样大的手杖。*We had* ~ *a pleasant time* (= so pleasant a time). 〔口〕我们那时候真是开心极了。(b)〔不连接形容词,直接连接名词〕那样好的,漂亮的,了不得的,伟大的,厉害的,这样坏的。*Did you ever see* ~ *weather?* 你见过这样坏[好]的天气没有? *We had* ~ *sport!* 我们(那时)玩得有趣极了! *We never had* ~ *sport*. 我们从来没有那样快活过。*He cannot come too often, he gives* ~ *pleasure*. 他这样有趣,可惜他不常来。*Don't be in* ~ *a hurry*. 别这样慌呀。**3.**〔法律条文或商业文件用语〕上述的,上开的,此类的。*Whoever shall make* ~ *return* .... 作上述报告者…。**4.**〔不定意义〕如此这般的,这样的,某某。*We know that on* ~ *a date he lived at number so and so of* ~ *and* ~ *a street*. 我们知道他在这个时期是住在这样一条街的某某号里。*S- and* ~ *results will follow from* ~ *and* ~ *causes*. 有如此这般的原因就有如此这般的结果。**II** ***pro.*** **1.** 这样的人[物]〔通常指复数〕。*I dislike* ~. 我不欢喜那种东西。**2.** …的人们[东西]〔~ *person*(*s*) 或 ~ *thing*(*s*) 之意〕。~ *as believe me* 相信我的人们。**3.**〔卑,商〕那样的事情,刚才所说的事情[东西],那,这,他们。*S- can be easily done*. 那容易做。**III** ***adv.*** 这样地,如此地,那么。***all*** ~ 大家,人人,人们(*So peace to all* ~. 祝大家平安。*all* ~ *as have erred* 有错的人们)。***and*** ~ 〔口〕等等(*tools, machines, and* ~ 工具、机器等等)。***another*** ~ 再一个那样的人[物],同样的一个人[物]。***as*** ~ 本身;以那个资格[身分],名符其实地(*Wealth, as* ~, *doesn't matter much* 财富本身算不了什么。*In country places strangers are welcome as* ~. 在乡间,外乡人是名符其实作为外乡人受到欢迎的)。~ ***as it is*** 品质不好的,没有什么价值的(东西)(*He won't refuse to give you his help,* ~ *as it is*. 他不会拒绝帮助你的,尽管对你帮助不大)。

such-and-such [ˈsʌtʃənsʌtʃ; ˋsʌtʃənsʌtʃ] ***a.*** 某某;这样那样的。*the payment of* ~ *sums to* ~ *persons* 把某些钱付给某些人。

such·like [ˈsʌtʃlaik; ˋsʌtʃˏlaɪk] **I** ***a.*** 这样的,诸如此类的,这种。**II** ***pro.*** 这样的人[东西],这种人[东西]。*Avoid pork and* ~ *indigestible food*. 忌吃猪肉和这一类不消化的东西。

suck [sʌk; sʌk] **I** ***vt.*** **1.** 吮吸,咂(奶头、指头等);吸进,吞进,吃(奶)。**2.** 吸收(水分、知识等) (*in*); 得到(利益等) (*from; out of*)。—***vi.*** 吮吸;吃奶;(水泵)抽吸。~ ***a rich teat*** 〔美〕得到肥缺。~ ***around*** 〔美俚〕(为得到好处)老在(某人、某处)四周打转。~ ***at*** 吸,抽(*He sat ~ing at his pipe*. 他坐着抽烟斗)。~ ***in*** 吸进去;吸收(知识);(漩涡等)卷进去。~ ***in to*** 〔英学生俚〕拍马屁。~ ***in your guts*** 〔美〕别响! ~ ***one's teeth*** 啧啧地不胜羡慕。~ ***out*** 吸出。~ ***the blood of*** 吸取…的血;榨取膏血。~ ***the breast of*** 吃…的奶。~ ***the monkey*** 〔俚〕拿瓶子喝。~ ***up*** 吸,吃(水、奶等)吸收;吸取。~ ***up*** (***to***)〔英学生俚〕= ~ in to. **II** ***n.*** **1.** 吮吸,咂,吸入;吃奶;卷入。**2.** 一口,一杯。**3.**〔俚〕(奶瓶等的)奶头;〔俚〕酒;〔英学生俚〕〔*pl.*〕糖果。**4.**〔英学生俚〕欺骗;失望,失败。*Sucks!* = *What a* ~! 真是大失所望!〔看见很像有把握的对手失败时说的玩笑话〕。*a child at* ~ 奶娃娃,乳儿。***be at*** ~ 吃着奶。***give*** ~ ***to*** 给…吃奶。***take a*** ~ ***at*** 吸一吸,吸一口。~**fish** ***n.*** 鲫鱼。~**-in** ***n.*** 〔英俚〕失望;失败;欺骗。~ **off 1.** ***a.*** 卑鄙的。**2.** ***n.*** 马屁精。~**-up** ***n.*** 〔俚〕拍马屁的人。

suck·er [ˈsʌkə; ˋsʌkɚ] **I** ***n.*** **1.** 吮吸者;吃奶的孩子;(尚未断乳的)仔猪,仔鲸(等)。**2.** 吸管;吸皮〔小孩玩具〕;(唧筒的)吸子;〔口〕棒棒糖。**3.**【植】徒长枝,腋芽,根出条;(寄生植物的)吸器,吸根;【动】吸盘;【鱼】(有吸盘的)胭脂鱼类。**4.**〔美俚〕傻瓜,笨蛋;生手;没有经验的人,初出茅庐,不懂事的人;容易上当的人;马戏团观众。**5.**〔美俚〕食客,寄生虫;酒量好的人。**6.** 不正当的经纪人;诈欺取财的人。*an ice* ~ 冰棒。*a* ~ *trap* 〔美〕骗人的手段[方法]。***play for a*** ~ 〔美俚〕骗;骗去别人的钱。***S-State*** 〔美〕伊利诺斯 (***Illinois***) 州的别名。**II** ***vt.*** 摘去(植物等)的徒长枝[腋芽]。—***vi.***【植】生出徒长枝[腋芽];成为吸根。~ **bomb** 〔俚〕诱饵炸弹〔先爆炸一颗小炸弹以引来救援或围观的更多人,再爆炸更大的炸弹〕。~**fish**【鱼】= remora. ~ **list** 〔美俚〕有希望成为顾客或捐献者的人的名单,容易上当受骗的傻瓜名单。

suck·ing [ˈsʌkiŋ; ˋsʌkɪŋ] ***a.*** 吮吸的;吃奶的,没有断奶

的;〔口〕不熟练的,不懂事的。~ **louse** 虱。~**-pig** (整只烤用的)乳猪。~ **stomach**【动】吸胃。

suck·le [ˈsʌkl; ˋsʌkl] *vt*. **1**. 给…喂奶[哺乳];抚育,养育。**2**. 吮吸,吸取。**-r** *n*. **1**. 哺乳动物。**2**. 乳儿;幼兽。

suck·ling [ˈsʌkliŋ; ˋsʌklɪŋ] *n*. 乳儿,乳兽;乳臭未干的小伙子,生手。*babies and ~s* 全是娃娃。

su·crase [ˈsuːkreis; ˋsukres] *n*.【生化】蔗糖酶;转化酶(=invertase)。

su·crate [ˈsuːkreit; ˋsukret] *n*.【化】蔗糖合物。

Su·cre [ˈsuːkrei; ˋsukre] *n*. **1**. 苏克雷〔玻利维亚法定首都〕。**2**. **A. J. de ~** 苏克雷〔1795—1830,南美厄瓜多尔和玻利维亚的解放者,玻利维亚第一任大总统〕。**3**. 〔s-〕苏克雷〔厄瓜多尔货币单位〕。

su·crose [ˈsjuːkrəus; ˋsukros] *n*.【化】蔗糖。

suc·tion [ˈsʌkʃən; ˋsʌkʃən] *n*. **1**. 吸,吸引,吸入;吸力。**2**. 吸气,吸气通风;【物】空吸。**3**. 〔英〕喝酒。**4**. 吸水管。~ **cup** 吸杯。~ **fan** 吸风机。~ **gas** 煤气。~ **head** 吸引高度。~ **lift** 吸引升力。~ **machine** 吸尘器。~ **pipe** 吸入管,吸水管。~ **plate**【机】吸板;【医】吸附假牙床。~ **pump** 抽水机,真空泵。~ **stroke**【机】吸入(冲)程;吸气冲程。

suc·to·ri·al [sʌkˈtɔːriəl; sʌkˋtorɪəl, -ˋtɔr-] *a*.【动】吸的,吸附的;适于吸的;有吸盘的,吸附生活的;吸血为生的。

Su·dan [suːˈdæn; suˋdæn] *n*. 苏丹〔非洲北部,撒哈拉(Sahara)沙漠南部、大西洋与红海间辽阔地区的总名称〕。***The S-*** 苏丹(国名)。~ **grass**【植】苏丹草〔一种一年生牧草〕。**-ic 1**. *a*. 苏丹的;苏丹语的。**2**. *n*. 苏丹人。

Su·da·nese [suːdəˈniːz; ˏsudəˋniz] **I** *a*. 苏丹(Sudan)的。**II** *n*. 〔*sing*., *pl*.〕苏丹人。

su·dar·i·um [sjuˈdeəriəm; suˋderɪəm] *n*. (*pl*. ***-ria*** [-riə; -rɪə]) **1**. 在上面奇迹地留有耶稣面容的手帕。**2**. 〔泛指〕奇迹一样显现的耶稣像。**3**. 盖过耶稣的头的手巾。

su·da·tion [sjuːˈdeiʃən; suˋdeʃən] *n*. 出汗,发汗。

su·da·to·ri·um [sjuːdəˈtɔːriəm; ˏsjudəˋtorɪəm, ˏsudəˋtorɪəm] *n*. (*pl*. ***-ria*** [-riə; -rɪə]) 发汗浴,蒸气浴;热气浴室。

su·da·to·ry [ˈsjuːdətəri; ˋsudəˏtorɪ, ˋsɪu-, -ˏtɔrɪ] **I** *a*. 促进发汗的;发汗的。**II** *n*. 发汗剂;发汗浴;热气浴室(=sudatorium)。

sudd [sʌd; sʌd] *n*. 〔Ar.〕水面植物堆集。

sud·den [ˈsʌdn; ˋsʌdn̩] **I** *a*. 突然的,忽然的,意想不到的,急剧的。*a ~ load*【工】骤加载荷。*be ~ in one's action* 行动唐突。*~ death* 暴死;(不分胜负时增加的)最后一次决赛时间。**II** *n*. 突然,忽然。(***all***) ***of a ~***, ***on a*** [***the***] ~, ***all on a ~*** 突然,忽然。**-ly** *ad*. **-ness** *n*.

su·dor·if·er·ous [ˌsjuːdəˈrifərəs; ˏsudəˋrɪfərəs] *a*. 分泌汗的。

su·dor·if·ic [ˈsjuːdəˈrifik; ˏsudəˋrɪfɪk, ˏsɪu-] **I** *a*. 发汗的;促进发汗的。**II** *n*. 发汗药。

Su·dra [ˈsuːdrə; ˋsudrə] *n*. 首陀罗〔印度四种姓中的最下等级,即奴隶〕。

suds [sʌdz; sʌdz] *n*. 〔*pl*.〕肥皂液(=soap-~);肥皂泡;泡沫;〔美俚〕啤酒;钱。***in the ~*** 〔俚〕在困难中;穷困;沮丧。**-y** *a*.

sue [sjuː, suː; su, sɪu] *vt*. **1**. 控告,控诉,和…打官司。**2**. 请求。**3**. 〔古〕求婚。—*vi*. 起诉。~ *at* (*the*) *law* 打官司,起诉。~ *for a breach of promise* 控告违约。~ *for peace* 求和。~ ***and labour clause*** 损害防止条款〔海上保险用语〕。~ ***out***【法】**1**. 请求法院给予(赦免等)。**2**. 提起(诉讼)要求判决。

Sue [sjuː, suː; su] *n*. Susan, Susanna, Susannah (女子名)的昵称。

sude [sweid; swed] *n*. (里面经过柔软加工的做手套等用)小山羊皮(=~ leather)。**-d** *a*. 仿麂皮的。

Suel·len [suːˈelin; suˋɛlɪn] *n*. 苏埃琳〔女子名〕。

su·et [ˈsjuit, ˈsuit; ˋsuɪt, ˋsjuɪt] *n*. (牛羊等腰部的)板油。~ **pudding** 羊油布丁。**-y** *a*.

Su·ez [ˈsju(ː)iz; ˋsuɛz, suˋɛz, ˋsɪu-] *n*. 苏伊士〔埃及港市〕。*the ~ Canal* 苏伊士运河〔埃及〕。

suf- *pref*. 〔用于 *f* 前〕=sub-.

suf. =suffix.

suff. =suffix; sufficient.

suf·fer [ˈsʌfə; ˋsʌfɚ] *vt*. **1**. 遭受,蒙受;经受;体验到(痛苦等)。**2**. 〔常与否定词连用〕忍受,忍耐,忍住。**3**. 宽恕,原谅;允许,容忍,听任。~ *a loss* 遭受损失。~ *death* 死。~ *punishments* 受罚。*I will not ~ such conduct*. 我不能容忍这种行为。*She could not ~ criticism*. 她受不了批评。*I will not ~ fools gladly*. 我对这类糊涂事看不下去。*I cannot ~ you to be idle*. 我不能让你偷懒。~ *sb. to come* 允许某人来。— *vi*. **1**. 受苦。**2**. 受害,受损失,吃亏。**3**. (因某事而)受罚(*for*)。**4**. 患病(*from*)。*We all have to ~ at some time in our lives*. 在我们一生中都免不了有受苦的时候。*Our work will ~ greatly if we are careless*. 我们如不小心,工作就会受到很大损失。*He will ~ for his folly*. 他会因自己的蠢行而受到惩罚。*The child ~s from measles*. 这小孩得了麻疹。~ *a great deal* 吃大亏。

suf·fer·a·ble [ˈsʌfərəbl; ˋsʌfərəbl̩, ˋsʌfrəbl̩] *a*. 忍受得了的,忍得下去的;可以容许的。**-ness** *n*. **-bly** *ad*.

suf·fer·ance [ˈsʌfərəns; ˋsʌfrəns, ˋsʌfərəns] *n*. **1**. 容许,宽容,默许;忍耐(力),耐性;〔英古〕服从,苦难。**2**. (海关的)落货许可,起货许可。***be beyond ~*** 不能忍受。***on*** (***by***, ***through***) ~ 经默许;在勉强容忍的情况下。~ **wharf** [**quay**] 公许码头,指定码头。

suf·fer·er [ˈsʌfərə; ˋsʌfərɚ] *n*. **1**. 受苦的人,苦恼的人;受难者;遭难者,受害者。**2**. 病人,患者。

suf·fer·ing [ˈsʌfəriŋ; ˋsʌfrɪŋ, ˋsʌfərɪŋ] **I** *n*. 痛苦,苦恼,苦难;〔常 *pl*.〕灾害,损害。*air one's ~s* 诉苦。**II** *a*. 痛苦的,苦恼的,患病的。

suf·fice [səˈfais; səˋfaɪs, -ˋfaɪz] *vt*. 满足…的需要,使满足。—*vi*. 足够。*Half-a-dozen ~d him*. 半打就使他满足了。*That ~s to prove it*. 那足够证明这个了。***S- it to say that...*** 说…就够了。

suf·fi·cien·cy [səˈfiʃənsi; səˋfɪʃənsɪ] *n*. 充足,满足;充分的财力;自满,自负;〔古〕能力,资格。

suf·fi·cient [səˈfiʃənt; səˋfɪʃənt] **I** *a*. **1**. 充分的,足够的。**2**. 〔古〕有能力的,能胜任的,够资格的。~ *food* 充足的食物。*Not ~*!【银行】存款不足〔略 *N/S*〕。*have not ~ courage for it* 没有做这事的充分勇气。***S- unto the day is the evil thereof*** (=sufficient for the day is its evil)【圣】今日之忧患已够今日打发(不能再为明天忧虑了)。*It is ~ to feed a hundred men*. 这足够供养一百个人的。**II** *n*. 〔主、卑〕足够(的量)。*Have you had ~*? 你(吃)够了吗? **-ly** *ad*.

suf·fic·ing·ly [sʌˈfaisiŋli; sʌˋfaɪsɪŋlɪ] *ad*. 足够地。

suf·fix I [ˈsʌfiks; ˋsʌfɪks] *n*. 词尾;附加器[物];【数】下标;添标,尾标。**II** [sʌˈfiks; səˋfɪks, ˋsʌfɪks] *vt*. 加…作后缀;把…附在后头。*a dummy ~*【物】傀标。**-al** *a*.

suf·fix·a·tion [sʌfikˈseiʃən; sʌfɪkˋseʃən] *n*. 加后缀,加词尾。

suf·flate [səˈfleit; səˋflet] *vt*. 〔废〕使膨胀,给…打气(=inflate)。**-fla·tion** *n*.

suf·fo·cate [ˈsʌfəkeit; ˋsʌfəˏket] *vt*. 使窒息,使不能呼吸;闷死,闷坏;闷熄(火等)。—*vi*. 呼吸闭塞,窒息,受阻;发展不了。***be ~d by*** 被…闭住呼吸,被…闷死(*He is ~d by grief*. 他悲痛欲绝)。

suf·fo·cat·ing [ˌsʌfəˈkeitiŋ; ˋsʌfəˏketɪŋ] *a*. 令人窒息的,憋气的。**-ly** *ad*.

suf·fo·ca·tion [sʌfəˈkeiʃən; ˏsʌfəˋkeʃən] *n*. 窒息。

suf·fo·ca·tive [ˈsʌfəkeitiv; ˋsʌfəˏketɪv] *a*. 憋气的,要窒息的。~ **catarrh**【医】毛细气管炎。

S

suf·fo·ca·tor [sʌfəˈkeitə; ˋsʌfə͵ketɚ] ***n*.** 令人窒息的东西。

Suf·folk [ˈsʌfək; ˋsʌfək] ***n*.** **1.** 沙福克〔英国东部一郡〕。**2.** (无角、黑头黑脚的)英国肉用羊。**3.** = ~ punch (栗毛短脚的)英国挽马。**4.** 英国小黑猪。

suf·fra·gan [ˈsʌfrəgən; ˋsʌfrəgən] **I** ***n*.**【宗】副监督,副主教。**II** ***a*.** 辅助的;副主教的。*a* ~ *bishop* = *a bishop* ~ 副主教。*a* ~ *see* 副主教辖区。

suf·frage [ˈsʌfridʒ; ˋsʌfrɪdʒ] ***n*.** **1.** 投票;投票权,选举权,参政权。**2.** 投票赞成;同意,赞成,赞同。**3.**〔常 *pl*.〕【宗】应祷;代祷。*household* ~ 户主选举权。*manhood* (*woman*) ~ 成年男子(妇女)选举权。*universal* [*popular*] ~ 普选(制)。***give one's*** ~ ***to*** [***for***] 投…的票〔对…投赞成票〕。

suf·fra·gette [sʌfrəˈdʒet; ͵sʌfrəˋdʒɛt] ***n*.** 从事妇女参政运动的妇女。

suf·fra·get·tism [ˌsʌfrəˈdʒetizm; ͵sʌfrəˋdʒɛtɪzm] ***n*.** 妇女有选举权的主张,妇女参政主义。

suf·fra·gist [ˈsʌfrədʒist; ˋsʌfrədʒɪst] ***n*.** 主张扩大参政权者,妇女参政主义者。

suf·fru·ti·cose, suf·fru·tes·cent [sʌˈfruːtiˌkəus, -fruːˈtesnt; sʌˋfrutɪ͵kos, -fruˋtɛsn̩t] ***a*.**【植】半灌木状的。

suf·fu·mi·gate [səˈfjuːmiˈgeit; səˋfjumə͵get] ***vt*.** 从下面熏蒸。**-gation** ***n*.**

suf·fuse [səˈfjuːz; səˋfjuz] ***vt*.**〔常用 p. p.〕(泪,光等)充满,弥漫。*skies* ~*d with amethyst* 一片紫色的天空。~*d eyes* 泪眼。***be*** ~***d with*** 充满,弥漫。

suf·fu·sion [səˈfjuːʒən; səˋfjuʒən] ***n*.** 充溢,弥漫;(脸等)涨红。

suf·fu·sive [səˈfjuːsiv; səˋfjusɪv] ***a*.** 充满的,洋溢的,弥漫的。

Su·fi [ˈsuːfi; ˋsufɪ] ***n*.**【宗】**1.** 苏非派(伊斯兰教的神秘主义派别)。**2.** 苏非派信徒。**-fism** ***n*.** 苏非派。

sug- *pref*. =sub-.

sug [ʃug; ʃʊg] **I** ***n*.**〔美〕漂亮,可爱的姑娘。**II** ***vt*.**〔英〕(打着进行市场调研的幌子)对…作诈骗性推销。

sug·an [ˈsʌgən; ˋsugən, ˋsʌgən] ***n*.** **1.**〔美俚〕= soogan. **2.**〔爱尔兰〕手搓的草绳;粗毯子。

sug·ar [ˈʃugə; ˋʃugɚ] **I** ***n*.** **1.** 糖;【化】糖。**2.** 甜言蜜语,阿谀奉承。**3.**〔俚〕钱,贿金。**4.**〔美俚〕麻醉品;心爱的人。*block* [*cube*, *cut*] ~ 方糖。*confectioner's* ~ 最好白糖。*raw* [*brown muscovado*] ~ 红糖,黑糖。~ *of lead* 铅糖;二醋酸铅。~ *of milk* 乳糖。**II** ***vt*.** **1.** 撒糖于,加糖于,把…弄甜,给…裹上糖衣。**2.** 甜甜蜜蜜地讲,用甜言蜜语哄骗(引诱);〔美俚〕用钱收买。**3.**〔俚〕〔用被动语态〕该死(= damn)。—***vi*.** **1.** 糖化;制造枫糖;变成糖状颗粒。**2.**〔英俚〕(工人)偷懒。*Liars be* ~*ed!* 你们这些撒谎的家伙真该死! ~ ***off***〔美俚〕偷偷跑掉,溜掉。~ ***the pill*** 把药丸加上糖衣,把令人痛苦的事情说得委婉些;把痛苦的事弄成易于接受的。~ **apple**【植】番荔枝。~ **bag**〔澳〕有蜜的蜂巢。~ **baker** 制糖业者。~ **basin**〔英〕(餐桌上的)糖缸(= ~ bowl)。~**bean** 棉豆,香豆,雪豆,金甲豆。~ **beet**【植】甜菜。~**berry**【植】朴属植物;朴树,朴果。~**bird** 吸花蜜的鸟。~**bush**〔美〕糖枫林。~ **camp**〔美〕枫糖制造厂。~ **candy**〔英〕冰糖;〔美〕(冰糖做的)上等糖果;甜品;讨人喜欢的人[物]。~ **cane**【植】甘蔗。~**coat** ***vt*.** 使甜蜜;在…上包糖衣。~ **corn** 甜玉蜀黍。~ **crops** 糖料作物。~**-cured** ***a*.** 用糖、盐和硝加工过的。~**-daddy**〔美〕老荒唐〔与年轻女孩厮混的不正派老头〕。~ **diabetes**【医】糖尿病。~ **gum** 糖桉树。~**house** 糖厂。~**loaf** 棒棒糖,塔糖;锥形丘。~ **maple**【植】糖槭。~ **mill** 糖厂,糖坊。~ **palm** 桄榔。~ **pine**【植】兰伯氏松,糖松。~**plum** 小糖果;甜言蜜语。~**-refinery** 炼糖厂。~ **report**〔美俚〕(尤指寄给士兵的)情书。~ **spoon** 糖匙〔比茶匙更圆更深〕。~**-tit** 糖奶头〔用布包糖成奶头状哄婴孩用〕。~ **tongs**〔*pl*.〕方糖钳子。

sug·ar·er [ˈʃugərə; ˋʃugərɚ] ***n*.** 工作偷懒的人。

sug·ar·i·ness [ˈʃugərinis; ˋʃugərənɪs] ***n*.** **1.** 糖状,糖质,甜味;甜性;甜度。**2.** 奉承,甜言蜜语。

sug·ar·y [ˈʃugəri; ˋʃugərɪ, ˋʃugrɪ] ***a*.** 糖状的,含糖的,糖质的,甜的;甜言蜜语的。

sug·gest [səˈdʒest; səgˋdʒɛst, səˋdʒɛst] ***vt*.** **1.** 暗示,绕着弯儿讲。**2.** 建议,提议,提出(计划等)。**3.** 使想起,使联想到;表明;提醒,指点,启发。~ *some idea to sb*. 示意某人。*It is* ~*ed that*.... 有人提议…。*Can you* ~ *any means to do it*? 你能不能给我想个什么办法做这件事? ***I*** ~ ***that*** .... 我觉得,我认为。~ ***itself to*** 浮现在…的心中。

sug·gest·i·ble [səˈdʒestibl; səgˋdʒɛstəbl̩, səˋdʒɛst-] ***a*.** 可暗示的;可提议的;【催眠术】易受暗示的。**-i·bil·i·ty** [səˌdʒestiˈbiliti; sə(g)͵dʒɛstəˋbɪlətɪ] ***n*.**

sug·ges·ti·o fal·si [səˈdʒestiəu ˈfælsai; səgˋdʒɛstʃɪoˋfælsaɪ]〔L.〕虚伪的暗示。

sug·ges·tion [səˈdʒestʃən; səgˋdʒɛstʃən, səˋdʒɛs-] ***n*.** **1.** 暗示;指点,启发;联想。**2.** 提议,建议,方案,发言。**3.** (猥亵的)挑逗。**4.** 样子,模样,气味;微量,迹象。*no* ~ *of provincial accent in sb*.*'s speech* 听不出某人的话里有任何乡下口音。*blue with a* ~ *of green* 略带绿色的蓝色。***make*** [***offer***] ***a*** ~ 提议,建议。***on the*** ~ ***of*** 在…的建议下。~ ***of the past*** 联想到过去。

sug·ges·tive [səˈdʒestiv; səgˋdʒɛstɪv, səˋdʒɛs-] ***a*.** **1.** 暗示…的,提醒…的,引起对…的联想的 (*of*)。**2.** 富于暗示的,可作参考的。**3.** 挑逗性的,猥亵的。*be* ~ *of a thief* 使人联想到小偷。~ *medicine* 暗示疗法,催眠疗法。**-ly** ***ad*.** **-ness** ***n*.**

sui·cid·al [sjuiˈsaidl; ͵suəˋsaɪdl̩, ͵sɪu-] ***a*.** 自杀(性)的;自灭的。*a* ~ *policy* 自杀政策。**-ly** ***ad*.**

sui·cide [ˈsjuisaid; ˋsuə͵saɪd, ˋsɪu-] **I** ***n*.** 自杀;自杀者;自灭(行为)。*commit* ~ 自杀,自尽。*a* ~ *squad* 敢死队。**II** ***vt*.**〔~ oneself〕自杀。—***vi*.**〔口〕自杀。**III** ***a*.** 自杀的;自杀性的。~ **bombing** 自杀性爆炸。~ **gene**【生】自杀基因〔指某些细菌具有的终止其自身生命的自灭基因〕。

su·i ge·ne·ris [ˈsjuːaiˈdʒenəris; ˋsjuɪˋdʒɛnərɪs, ˋsɪu-]〔L.〕独特的;自成一类的;特殊的。

su·i ju·r·is [ˈsjuˈdʒuəris; ˋsuaɪˋdʒʊrɪs]〔L.〕【法】成年,到法定年龄;有权处理自己的事务。

suil·line [ˈsjuːilain; ˋsuəlaɪn, -lɪn] ***a*.**【动】属猪科的。

su·int [ˈsjuːint, swint; ˋsjuɪnt, swɪnt] ***n*.** **1.** 羊毛汗,脂汗。**2.**【化】羊毛粗脂。

suisse [swiːs; swis] ***n*.** (*fem*. ***suissesse***)〔F.〕〔古〕看门人;门警。

suit [sjuːt; sut, sɪut, sjut] **I** ***n*.** **1.** 申诉,起诉,诉讼;控告;讼案。**2.** 请求,恳求;求婚,求爱。**3.** 一套房间;一套衣服,一套马具,(纸牌的)同样花式的一组牌。**4.**〔the ~〕〔美俚〕军装。*a civil* [*criminal*] ~ 民事[刑事]诉讼。*a* ~ *of black* 一套黑衣服[丧服]。*a two-piece* ~ 由两件组成的一套衣服〔如一件上衣和一条裤子的男服,一件上衣和一条裙子的女服〕。*a business* ~〔美〕一套日常衣服。***a dress*** ~ 一套晚礼服。***a long*** ~ 同样花式四张以上的一组牌;〔喻〕胜人之处。*one's strong* ~ 优点,长处。*a short* ~ 同样花式不到四张的牌。*a* ~ *of dittos* 同一料子的一套衣服。***all of one*** ~ 清一色。***bring a*** ~ ***against sb*.** 控告某人。***fail in one's*** ~ 求婚失败。***follow*** ~ 跟牌…仿效别人。***have a*** ~ ***to*** 向…有所请求。***in one's birthday*** ~ 赤裸裸地,一丝不挂地。***institute a*** ~ ***against sb*.** 控告某人。***make*** ~ 请求,乞求。***man in*** (***dark*** [***gray***]) ~***s*** 匿名大官;元老。***out of*** ~***s*** 不和睦。***press*** [***push***] ***one's*** ~ 哀求,死乞白赖地求婚。***prosper in one's*** ~ 求婚成功。***get*** [***put on***] ***the*** ~ 从军,投军。**II** ***vt*.** **1.** 适合;相配。**2.** 使适合,使适宜 (*to*)。**3.**〔英古,美〕供给…一套衣服。**4.** 讨好(某人)。*The date* ~*s me well*. 这个日子对我很适

宜。*The role does not* ~ *him*. 这个角色不适合他演。*It* ~*s me to put up with him*. 宽容他正合我的心意。~ ***all tastes*** 人人中意(*No book* ~*s all tastes*. 没有人人中意的书)。~ ***sb. down to the ground*** 对…十分合宜。~ ***sb.'s book*** 正合某人要求。~ ***the action to the word*** 使言行一致,说到做到。***S- yourself***. 随你的便。— ***vi***. **1.** 与…相称,对…合适(*with*)。**2.** 合适,适当,可行。*The job* ~*s with his abilities*. 这工作他做合适。*Red does not* ~ *with her complexion*. 红色与她的肤色不相称。*Which date* ~*s best*? 哪个日期最合适?

suit·a·bil·i·ty [sjutəˈbiliti; sjutəˋbɪlətɪ] ***n***. 适合,适当,合宜,相配。

suit·able [ˈsjuːtəbl; ˋsutəbl, ˋsɪu-, ˋsju-] ***a***. 合适的;适宜的,适当的;相当的(*to*; *for*)。*This wine is not* ~ *to my taste*. 这酒不合我的胃口。*a problem* ~ *for class discussion* 适于作课堂讨论的问题。**-bly *ad***. **-ness *n***.

suit·case [ˈsjuːtkeis; ˋsut͵kes, ˋsjut-] ***n***. 手提箱。~ **war** 手提箱战争〔指恐怖份子暗藏炸药于手提箱内进行的破坏活动〕。

suite [swiːt; swit] ***n***. **1.** 随员。**2.** (房间、器具等的)一套,一副;【乐】组曲。**3.**【计】(软件的)套件。*a* ~ *of rooms* 一套房间。

suit·ing [ˈsjuːtiŋ; ˋsutɪŋ, ˋsjutɪŋ] ***n***. **1.**【商】〔常 *pl*.〕(上等的,做成套衣服用的)套头料。**2.** 一套[身]衣服。

suit·or [ˈsjuːtə; ˋsutɚ] ***n***. (*fem*. ***suitress*** [-ris; -rɪs]) **1.**【法】起诉人,原告。**2.** 请愿者,请求者。**3.** 求婚者,求爱者。

su·key, sukie, suky [ˈsuːki; ˋsukɪ] ***n***. 〔方〕开水壶。

su·ki·ya·ki [sukiːˈjaːkiː; ˋsukiˋjɑki, ˋsʊkɪˋjɑkɪ] ***n***. 〔日〕寿喜烧,鸡素烧,日本式火锅。

Suk·kot, Suk·kos, Suk·koth [suˈkəut, ˈsukəus; suˋkot, ˋsʊkos] ***n***. 犹太结茅节〔犹太历1月15—22日〕。

sul·cate, sul·cat·ed [ˈsʌlkeit, -id; ˋsʌlket, -ɪd] ***a***.【植,解】有槽的,有沟的,有纵沟的。

sul·cus [ˈsʌlkəs; ˋsʌlkəs] ***n***. (*pl*. ***-ci*** [-sai; -saɪ]) 沟,纵沟,〔尤指〕【解】脑回转间的裂槽。

sul·fa, sul·pha [ˈsʌlfə; ˋsʌlfə] **I *a***. 磺胺的。**II *n***. 〔*pl*.〕= ~ drugs 碲胺制剂。

sulfa- *comb. f*. 〔美〕= sulpha-.

sul·fa·di·a·zine, sul·fa·di·a·zin [͵sʌlfəˈdaiəziːn, -zin; ͵sʌlfəˋdaɪə͵zin, -zɪn] ***n***. 〔美〕【药】磺胺嘧啶。

sul·fa·guan·i·dine; sul·fa·guan·i·din [͵sʌlfəˈgwæniːdiːn, -ˈgwɑːni-, -din; ͵sʌlfəˋgwænɪ͵din, -dɪn] ***n***. 〔美〕【药】磺胺胍〔肠胃消炎片〕(= sulphaguanidin(e))。

sul·fal·de·hyde [sʌlˈfældihaid; sʌlˋfældɪhaɪd] ***n***.【化】硫醛。

sul·fa·mer·a·zin(e) [͵sʌlfəˈmerəzi(ː)n; ͵sʌlfəˋmɛrə͵zin] ***n***. 〔美〕【药】磺胺甲基嘧啶(= sulphamerazin(e))。

sul·fa·me·thoxy·pyri·da·zine [͵sʌlfəmiˈθɔksipirədæziːn; ͵sʌlfəmɪˋθɑksɪpɪrədæzin] ***n***.【药】磺胺甲氧嗪[长效磺胺]〔略作 SMP〕。

sul·fa·nil·a·mide [͵sʌlfəˈniləmaid; ͵sʌlfəˋnɪlə͵maɪd] ***n***. 〔美〕【药】磺胺,胺苯磺胺,对氨基苯磺醯胺(= sulphanilamide)。

sul·fa·nil·ic acid [͵sʌlfəˈnilik; ͵sʌlfəˋnɪlɪk]【化】磺胺酸,对氨基苯磺酸。

sul·fa·nil·yl·guan·i·dine [͵sʌlfənililˈgwænidiːn; ͵sʌlfənɪlɪlˋgwænɪdin] ***n***. = sulfaguanidine.

sul·fa·pyr·a·zin(e) [͵sʌlfəˈpirəziːn; ͵sʌlfəˋpɪrəzin, -zɪn] ***n***. 〔美〕【药】磺胺吡嗪(= sulphapyrazine)。

sul·fa·pyr·i·din(e) [͵sʌlfəˈpiridi(ː)n; ͵sʌlfəˋpɪrɪ͵din, -dɪn] ***n***. 〔美〕磺胺吡啶(= sulphapyridine)。

sulf·ar·se·nide [sʌlˈfɑːsi͵naid; sʌlˋfɑsɪ͵naɪd] ***n***.【化】硫砷化物。

sul·fa·sux·i·din(e) [͵sʌlfəˈsʌksidi(ː)n; ͵sʌlfəˋsʌksə͵din, -dɪn] ***n***. 〔美〕【药】磺胺杀克啶;琥珀醯磺胺噻唑(= sulphasuxidine)。

sul·fate [ˈsʌlfeit; ˋsʌlfet] ***n***. 〔美〕= sulphate.

sul·fa·thi·a·zole [͵sʌlfəˈθaiəzəul; ͵sʌlfəˋθaɪə͵zol] ***n***. 〔美〕= sulphathiazole.

sul·fa·tize [ˈsʌlfətaiz; ˋsʌlfət͵aɪz] ***vt***. = sulphatize.

sul·fid·al [ˈsʌlfidl; ˋsʌlfɪdl̩] ***n***.【化】胶状硫。

sul·fid(e) [ˈsʌlf(a)id; ˋsʌlfaɪd, -fɪd] ***n***. 〔美〕= sulphid(e)。

sul·fi·nyl [ˈsʌlfinil; ˋsʌlfənl̩] ***n***. 〔美〕= sulphinyl.

sul·fi·te [ˈsʌlfait; ˋsʌlfaɪt] ***n***. 〔美〕= sulphite.

sul·f(o)- *comb. f*. 〔美〕= sulph(o)-.

sul·fo·acid [ˈsʌlfəuæsid; ˋsʌlfoæsɪd] ***n***.【化】磺酸,硫代酸。

sul·fo·acy·la·tion [ˈsʌlfəu͵æsiˈleiʃən; ˋsʌlfo͵æsɪˋleʃən] ***n***.【化】磺基乙酰[醯]化作用。

sul·fo·car·bon·ate [sʌlfəuˈkɑːbənit; sʌlfoˋkɑbənɪt] ***n***.【化】硫代碳酸盐[酯]。

sul·fo·nal [ˈsʌlfənl; ˋsʌlfə͵næl, ͵sʌlfəˋnæl] ***n***. 〔美〕= sulphonal.

sul·fon·a·mide [͵sʌlˈfɔnəmid; sʌlˋfɑnəmaɪd, ͵sʌlfəˋnæmaɪd, -mɪd] ***n***. 〔美〕= sulphonamide.

sul·fo·nate [ˈsʌlfəneit; ˋsʌlfə͵net] 〔美〕= sulphonate.

sul·fone 〔美〕= sulphone.

sul·fon·ic [sʌlˈfɔnik; səlˋfɑnɪk] 〔美〕= sulphonic.

sul·fo·ni·um [sʌlˈfəuniəm; sʌlˋfonɪəm] 〔美〕= sulphonium.

sul·fon·meth·ane [͵sʌlfəunˈmeθein; ͵sʌlfonˋmɛθen, -fɔn-] (〔美〕= sulphonmethane). ***n***.【药】双乙磺丙烷,二乙眠砜〔安眠药〕。

sul·fo·nyl [ˈsʌlfənil; ˋsʌlfənl̩, -nil] 〔美〕= sulphonyl.

sulf·ox·ide [sʌlˈfɔksaid; sʌlˋfɑksaɪd] 〔美〕= sulphoxide.

sul·fur [ˈsʌlfə; ˋsʌlfɚ] ***n***. 〔美〕= sulphur.

sul·fu·rate [ˈsʌlfju͵reit, -fjuə-; ˋsʌlfə͵ret, -fjə-] 〔美〕= sulphurate.

sul·fur-bot·tom [ˈsʌlfəˈbɔtəm; ˋsʌlfɚ͵bɑtəm] ***n***.【动】白长须鲸(= blue whale)。

sul·fu·reous [sʌlˈfjuriəs; sʌlˋfjʊrɪəs] 〔美〕= sulphureous.

sul·fu·ret [ˈsʌlfjuret; ˋsʌlfjə͵rɛt] ***n***., ***vt***. 〔美〕= sulphuret.

sul·fu·ric [sʌlˈfjurik; sʌlˋfjʊrɪk] 〔美〕= sulphuric.

sul·fu·rize [ˈsʌlfju͵raiz, -fə-; ˋsʌlfjə͵raɪz] ***vt***. 〔美〕= sulphurize.

sul·fu·rous [ˈsʌlfərəs, sʌlˈfjuərəs; ˋsʌlfərəs, sʌlˋfjərəs] ***a***. 〔美〕= sulphurous. **-ly *ad***. **-ness *n***.

sul·fur·y [ˈsʌlfəri; ˋsʌlfərɪ, -frɪ] ***a***. = sulphury.

sul·fur·yl [ˈsʌlfəril, -fjuril; ˋsʌlfərəl, -fjər-, -ril] ***n***. = sulfonyl.

sulk [sʌlk; sʌlk] **I *n***. 〔常 *pl*.〕绷脸;愠怒;生气;不高兴;愠怒[生气]的人。***in a*** ~, ***in the*** ~***s*** 生气。***have the*** ~***s*** 绷着脸,心里不高兴。**II *vi***. 生气,绷脸。

sulk·y [ˈsʌlki; ˋsʌlkɪ] **I *a***. (*-i·er*; *-i·est*) **1.** 含怒的,不高兴的,生气的,绷着脸的。**2.** 阴沉的,阴郁的(天气等);【植】萎缩的,蔫萎的。**II *n***. 单座二轮马车。~ *plough* 双铧犁。**-i·ly *ad***. **-i·ness *n***.

sul·lage [ˈsʌlidʒ; ˋsʌlɪdʒ] ***n***. 废物,垃圾;污水;淤泥;【冶】勺内熔化金属的熔渣。

sul·len [ˈsʌlən; ˋsʌlɪn, -ən] **I *a***. **1.** 不高兴的,愁眉不展的,绷着脸的,阴郁的。**2.** (天气、天空等)阴沉的,昏暗的。**3.** 悲哀的,悲惨的,伤心的。**4.** 行动缓慢的,死气沉沉的。**II *n***. 〔*pl*.〕〔口〕不高兴,绷脸;忧郁。***in the*** ~***s*** 在不愉快中,情绪不好。**-ly *ad***. **-ness *n***.

Sul·li·van [ˈsʌlivən; ˋsʌləvən] ***n***. 沙利文〔姓氏,男子名〕。

Sul·ly [ˈsʌli; ˋsʌlɪ] ***n***. 萨利〔姓氏〕。

sul·ly [ˈsʌli; ˋsʌlɪ] **I *vt***. 弄脏;玷污,污腐,糟蹋(名誉等),

S

毁损。II *n*.〔古〕污点,污斑。

sul·pha- *comb. f*. 磺胺(=sulfa-): *sulpha*diazine.

sul·pha·di·a·zine, -a·zin [ˌsʌlfəˈdaiəziːn, -zin; ˏsʌlfəˋdaɪəzin, -zɪn] *n*. [药]磺胺嘧啶。

sul·pha·mate [ˈsʌlfəmeit; ˋsʌlfəmet] *n*.【化】氨基磺酸盐[酯]。

sul·pha·meth·yl·thi·a·zole [ˈsʌlfəˌmeθilˈθaiəzəul; ˋsʌlfəˏmɛθɪlˋθaɪəzol] *n*.【药】磺胺甲基噻唑。

sul·pha·pyr·i·dine [ˌsʌlfəˈpiridiːn; ˏsʌlfəˋpɪrɪdin] *n*.【药】磺胺吡啶。

sul·pha·quin·ox·a·line [ˌsʌlfəkwiˈnɔksəliːn; ˏsʌlfəkwɪˋnɑksəlin] *n*.【药】磺胺喹沙啉。

sul·phate [ˈsʌlfeit; ˋsʌlfet] I *n*.【化】硫酸盐;硫酸酯。*ammonium* ~硫酸铵。*calcium* ~石膏。*copper* ~硫酸铜,胆矾。*iron* ~硫酸铁,绿矾。*magnesium* ~硫酸镁,泻盐。II *vt*. 用硫酸[硫酸盐]处理;使与硫酸(盐)化合;使成硫酸盐;【电】使(蓄电池极板上)硫酸铅化合物沉积。—*vi*. 硫酸盐化;【电】(蓄电池极板)被硫酸铅沉淀覆盖。~ **ion** 硫酸根离子。~ **paper** 硫酸盐纸(如牛皮纸)。

sul·pha·thi·a·zole [ˌsʌlfəˈθaiəzəul; ˏsʌlfəˋθaɪəˏzol] *n*.【药】磺胺噻唑。

sul·pha·ting [ˈsʌlfeitiŋ; ˋsʌlfetɪŋ] *n*. 硫酸垢。

sul·pha·tion [ˈsʌlfeiʃən; ˋsʌlfeʃən] *n*.【电】硫酸化。

sul·pha·tize [ˈsʌlfətaiz; ˋsʌlfətaɪz] *vt*. 使成硫酸盐。

sul·phide [ˈsʌlfaid; ˋsʌlfaɪd, -fɪd] *n*.【化】硫化物;硫醚。*arsenious* ~ 雄黄,石黄。*copper* ~硫化铜。*iron* ~黄铁矿。*mercury* ~辰砂,银朱。

S

sul·phi·nyl [ˈsʌlfinil; ˋsʌlfɪnɪl] *n*.【化】亚硫酰基,亚磺酰。

sul·phite [ˈsʌlfait; ˋsʌlfaɪt] *n*. **1**.【化】亚硫酸盐[酯]。**2**.〔美俚〕(思想、谈话等)有独创性的人。

sul·ph(o)- *comb. f*. 硫代,磺基: *sulpho*nate, *sulpho*nyl.

sul·pho·cyan·ic [ˌsʌlfəusaiˈænik; ˏsʌlfosaɪˋænɪk] *a*. ~ **acid**【化】硫氰酸,硫代氰酸。~ **ester**【化】硫氰酸酯。

sul·pho·nal [ˈsʌlfənæl; ˋsʌlfəˏnæl, ˏsʌlfəˋnæl], **sul·phonmeth·ane** [-fəunˈmeθein; ˏsʌlfonˋmɛθen, -fɑn-] *n*.【药】索佛那,二乙眠砜甲烷〔催眠药〕;眠砜甲烷。

sul·phon·a·mide [ˌsʌlˈfɔnəmid; ˏsʌlˋfɑnəmɪd] *n*.【药】磺胺,磺胺类药物。

sul·pho·nate [ˈsʌlfəˌneit; ˋsʌlfənet] I *n*.【化】磺酸盐。II *vt*. 使磺化。

sul·pho·ne [ˈsʌlfəun; ˋsʌlfon] *n*.【化】砜。

sul·phon·ic [sʌlˈfɔnik; sʌlˋfɑnɪk] *a*. 磺酸的。~ **acid group**【化】磺(酸)基。~ **derivatives** 磺基衍生物。

sul·pho·ni·um [sʌlˈfəuniəm; sʌlˋfonɪəm] *n*.【化】锍,一价阴性基。

sul·pho·nyl [ˈsʌlfənil; ˋsʌlfənḷ, -nil] *n*.【化】磺酰,硫酰。

sul·pho·vin·ic [sʌlfəuˈvainik; sʌlfoˋvaɪnɪk] *a*. ~ **acid**【化】烃(换)硫酸,乙(换)硫酸。

sulph·ox·ide [sʌlˈfɔksaid; sʌlˋfɑksaɪd] *n*.【化】亚砜。

sul·phur [ˈsʌlfə; ˋsʌlfɚ] I *n*.【化】硫(磺);硫磺色,黄绿色,【动】粉蝶科蝶,螠虫。*flowers of* ~硫粉,硫磺华。*milk of* ~硫磺乳,白色硫磺华。*roll* [*stick*] ~精制硫磺,棒状硫磺。~ *and molasses*〔美〕硫磺糖水〔水儿解毒剂〕。II *vt*. 用硫磺熏;用硫磺处理;用亚硫酸盐处理;在…中加硫磺。~**-bottom (whale)**【动】长箦鲸。~ **butterfly**【动】粉蝶。~**-spring** 硫磺温泉。~**-weed**, ~ **wort** *n*.【植】药用前胡。

sul·phu·rate [ˈsʌlfjureit; ˋsʌlfəret] *vt*.【化】使硫化;用硫磺处理。

sul·phu·ra·tion [ˌsʌlfjuˈreiʃən; ˏsʌlfəˋreʃən] *n*.【化】硫化作用。

sul·phu·ra·tor [ˈsʌlfjureitə; ˋsʌlfəretɚ] *n*. 硫磺熏蒸器[漂白器]。

sul·phu·re·ous [sʌlˈfjuəriəs; sʌlˋfjʊrɪəs] *a*. 硫磺(质)的,含硫磺的,硫磺臭的;【植】硫磺色的。

sul·phu·ret I [ˈsʌlfjurit; ˋsʌlfjʊrɪt] *n*.【化】硫化物,硫醚(=sulphide)。II [-ret; -rɛt] *vt*. 使硫化;用硫处理。

sul·phur·et·ted [ˈsʌlfjuretid; ˋsʌlfjʊrɛtɪd] *a*.【化】硫化的,含硫磺的。~ **hydrogen** 硫化氢。

sul·phu·ric [sʌlˈfjuərik; sʌlˋfjʊrɪk] *a*.【化】(正)硫的。~ **acid** 硫酸。~**anhydride** 三氧化硫,硫(酸)酐。

sul·phu·rize [ˈsʌlfjuəraiz; ˋsʌlfjʊraɪz] *vt*. (=sulphurate)用二氧化硫烟雾处理[漂白、消毒]。

sul·phur·ous [ˈsʌlfərəs; ˋsʌlfərəs, -fjərəs, sʌlˋfjʊrəs] *a*. **1**.【化】亚硫的,有硫磺臭味的;硫磺色的。**2**.〔喻〕地狱似的,凶恶的。**3**. 吵闹到极点的;狂热的,紧张的。~ **acid** 亚硫酸。~ **anhydride** [**oxide**] 二氧化硫,亚硫酐。

sul·phur·y [ˈsʌlfəri; ˋsʌlfərɪ] *a*. (似)硫磺的。

sul·phur·yl [ˈsʌlfəril, -fjuril; ˋsʌlfərəl, -fjə-, -ril] *n*.【化】=sulphonyl.

sul·tan [ˈsʌltən; ˋsʌltṇ] *n*. **1**. 苏丹〔某些伊斯兰国家统治者〕。**2**.【史】〔S-〕土耳其皇帝。**3**. 土耳其种小白鸡。*the sweet* [*yellow*] ~【植】紫[黄]矢车菊。

sul·ta·na [sʌlˈtɑːnə; sʌlˋtænə, -tɑnə] *n*. **1**. 苏丹之妻[女儿、姊妹、母]。**2**. 王妃。**3**. [səlˈtɑːnə; səlˋtɑnə]〔英〕淡黄葡萄干。**4**.【动】苏丹鸟〔一种小涉禽〕。

sul·tan·ate [ˈsʌltənit; ˋsʌltṇɪt, -ˏet] *n*. 苏丹(sultan)的领地;职位;苏丹统治的国家。

sul·tan·ess [ˈsʌltənis; ˋsʌltənɪs] *n*. =sultana 1.

sul·try [ˈsʌltri; ˋsʌltrɪ] *a*. (*-tri·er*; *-tri·est*) 闷热的,酷热的;情绪激动的,狂热的,狂暴的;(言语等)激烈的,粗暴的;淫乱的,猥亵的。**-tri·ly** *ad*. **-tri·ness** *n*.

Su·lu [ˈsuːluː; ˋsulu] *n*. 苏禄人〔菲律宾的苏禄群岛人,属莫洛部族〕。**-an** *a*.

su·lu [ˈsuːluː; ˋsulu] *n*. 苏鲁〔斐济岛人的衣服,像纱龙〕。

SUM= surface-to-underwater missile 舰对水下导弹[飞弹]。

sum [sʌm; sʌm] I *n*. **1**. 总数,总计,总额;【数】和。**2**. 〔the ~〕概略,大要,要点。**3**. 款项,金额。**4**. 算术(题);运算,计算。**5**.【诗】顶点,绝顶,极点。~ *remainder, product, quotient* 和,差,积,商。*a* ~ *total* 总计,合计。*the* ~ *of his opinions* 他的意见的要点。*a good* [*considerable, round*] ~一大[整]笔钱。*a large* [*small*] ~ *of* 巨[小]额的,大[小]量的。***be good at*** **~s** 算术好。**do** [***work, make***] **a** ~(*s*) 计算,做算术题。**in** ~大体上,一言以蔽之,总之。***the*** ~ (***and substance***) 要点。***the*** ~ ***of things*** (最高的)公共利益;宇宙。II *vt*. (*-mm-*) 合计,总计;总结,总括,概括。—*vi*. 总计(*into, to*);(法官听原告、被告陈述后)概括要点(*up*)。*Contributions* ~*s to several thousand dollars*. 捐款总计达数千美元。~ *up* 总计,总结;总起来说。~ *up experiences* 总结经验。~ **up**〔口〕概括;总结。

sum- *pref*. 〔用于 m 前〕=sub-.

su·mac(h) [ˈsuːmæk, ˈsjuː-, ˈʃuː-; ˋʃumæk, ˋʃɪu-, ˋsu-, ˋsju-] *n*. **1**.【植】漆树属。**2**. 苏模;苏模叶,苏模鞣料。*the Japanese* ~漆树。

Su·ma·tra [su(ː)ˈmɑːtrə; suˋmɑtrə, -ˋme-] *n*. 苏门答腊(岛)〔印度尼西亚〕。

Su·ma·tran [suˈmɑːtrən; suˋmɑtrən, -ˋme-] I *a*. 苏门答腊岛(人)的。II *n*. 苏门答腊岛人。

sum·bal, sum·bul [ˈsʌmbæl -bʌl, -bul; ˋsʌmbæl -bʌl, -bul] *n*. **1**. 五福花阿魏根,麝香根,苏布(根)。**2**. 缬草。

Su·mer·i·an [suːˈmiəriən, -ˈmer-; suˋmɪrɪən, sju-] I *a*. **1**. 苏美尔的。**2**. 苏美尔人的。II *n*. **1**. 苏美尔人〔古代幼发拉底河下游地区的居民〕。**2**. 苏美尔语。

Su·me·rol·o·gy [ˌsjuːməˈrɔlədʒi; ˏsuməˋrɑlədʒɪ] *n*. 苏美尔文史语言研究。

su·mi [ˈsuːmi; ˋsumɪ] *n*. 〔Jap.〕墨,墨汁。

sum·less [ˈsʌmlis; ˋsʌmlɪs] *a*. 无数的,无限的;估计不出的。

sum·ma [ˈsumə; ˋsʊmə, ˋsʌmə] ***n***.〔L.〕(*pl*. ***-mae*** [-iː; -i]) **1**. 综合性论文〔中世纪学者所作〕。**2**. 综合性事物。

sum·ma cum lau·de [ˈsʌməˈkʌm ˈlɔːdi; ˋsʌmə͵kʌm ˋlɔdɪ,ˋsʊmə͵kʊmˋlaʊdɪ]〔L.〕享有最高荣誉;按最优等级;以最优学业成绩(毕业)。

sum·ma·ri·ly [ˈsʌmərili; ˋsʌmərəlɪ, səˋmɛr-] ***ad***. **1**. 概括地,扼要地,简单地。**2**. 立刻,马上。

sum·ma·ri·ness [ˈsʌmərinis; ˋsʌmərɪnɪs] ***n***. **1**. 摘要,简要,简略,简便。**2**. 速成,迅速,即刻,速决。

sum·ma·rist [ˈsʌmərist; ˋsʌmərɪst] ***n***. 概括者,摘要者。

sum·ma·rize [ˈsʌməraiz; ˋsʌmə͵raɪz] ***vt***. 概括,扼要讲;总结;做…的摘要。**-za·tion *n***. 总结。

sum·ma·ry [ˈsʌməri; ˋsʌmərɪ] **I *a***. 概括的,扼要的,摘要的;【法】简单(化)的,即决的;当场的,立刻的,马上的。**II *n***. 概要;摘要,总结,一览;梗概。~ *reports* 简报。~ **jurisdiction** 即决裁判权。~ **justice** 即决裁判。~ **punishment** 即刻处罚。~ **court-martial**【军】军纪法庭〔只审理一般性小过失〕。

sum·ma sum·ma·rum [ˈsʌmə sʌˈmeirəm; ˋsʌmə sʌˋmerəm]〔L.〕总计,合计。

sum·ma·tion [sʌˈmeiʃən; sʌmˋeʃən] ***n***. 总结;总数;【数】加法,求和;【法】(双方论据的)辩论总结。**-al *a***.

sum·ma·tor [sʌˈmeitə; sʌmˋetɚ] ***n***.【自】加法器,相加器。

sum·mer[1] [ˈsʌmə; ˋsʌmɚ] **I *n***. **1**. 夏季。**2**. 壮年时期;最盛期。**3**. 年岁,年龄〔通常附带数词而用复数〕。*the ~ of life* 壮年时期。*a young woman of some twenty ~s* 二十来岁的年轻女人。*Indian* ~〔美〕小阳春,风和日丽的天气。*St. Lake's* ~〔英〕(在十月十八日前后出现的)暖和天气。*St. Martin's* ~〔英〕(在十一月十一日前后出现的)暖和天气。~ ***and winter*** 不论冬夏,(爱情等)始终不渝。**II *a***. 夏季的。*a ~ bonnet* 夏季女帽。*spend one's ~ vacation* [*holidays*] 度暑假。**III *vi***. 度过夏季,避暑 (*at*; *in*)。—***vt***. 使度过夏季;夏季放牧(家畜)。~ ***over the sugar***〔美〕把糖贮存起来度过夏季。~ **cypress**【植】地肤。~ **house** (花园中的)凉亭;〔美〕避暑别墅。~ **lightning** (距离极远的听不见雷声的)闪电。~ **resort** 避暑地。~ **sausage** 夏季香肠〔干硬不易变质的〕。~ **school** 暑期学校。~ **solstice** 夏至。~**squash**【植】欧洲南瓜,西葫芦。~ **suit** 夏装。~**tide**, ~**-time *n***. 夏季。~ **time**〔英〕(将钟点拨快一小时的)夏季时间〔略 S.T.; =〔美〕daylight-saving time〕。**S-White House**〔美〕总统避暑别墅。~**wood** 晚材,秋材。

sum·mer[2] [ˈsʌmə; ˋsʌmɚ] ***n***.【建】大梁,檩条;楣;柱顶石。

sum·mer[3] [ˈsʌmə; ˋsʌmɚ] ***n***.【自】加法器。

Sum·mer [ˈsʌmə; ˋsʌmɚ] ***n***. 萨默〔姓氏〕。

sum·mer·ing [ˈsʌməriŋ; ˋsʌmərɪŋ] ***n***. **1**. 夏令牧场〔放牧〕。**2**. 早熟苹果。**3**. 暑假;度夏,避暑。

sum·mer·ly, **sum·mer·y** [ˈsʌməli, -ri; ˋsʌmɚlɪ, -rɪ] ***a***. 夏(天)的,像夏天的。

sum·mer·sault, **sum·mer·set** [ˈsʌməsɔːlt, -set; ˋsʌmə͵sɔlt, -sɛt] ***n***. = somersault.

sum·ming-up [ˈsʌmiŋˈʌp; ˋsʌmɪŋˋʌp] ***n***. 总结。*a scientific ~ of the work movement* 对该项工作的科学总结。

sum·mit [ˈsʌmit; ˋsʌmɪt] ***n***. **1**. 顶,绝顶;最高级级位;峰会,最高级会议〔会谈〕;【几】顶点。**2**. 极点,极度。***at the ~*** 最高层的。~ ***conference*** 最高级会议,峰会。**-ry *n***. 最高级会议(外交)。

sum·mon [ˈsʌmən; ˋsʌmən] ***vt***. **1**. 召唤;传唤(被告等);召集(议会);号召。**2**.【军】劝降,招降。**3**. 振起,鼓起(勇气等)。~ *a servant* 把仆人叫来。~ ***up*** 鼓起(勇气等)(*to do*; *for*)。**-er *n***.

sum·mons [ˈsʌmənz; ˋsʌmənz] **I *n***. (*pl*. ~***es***) 召唤,召集;【法】传唤;传票;【军】招降劝告。*answer sb.'s* ~应某人之召。*receive a* ~接到传票,被传。*serve a ~ on* [*upon*] *sb*. = *serve sb. with a* ~把传票送给某人。**II *vt***.〔口〕传到,传唤。

sum·mum bo·num [ˈsʌməm ˈbəunəm; ˋsʌməmˋbonəm]〔L.〕最高善,至善。

Sum·ner [ˈsʌmnə; ˋsʌmnɚ] ***n***. 萨姆纳〔姓氏〕。

su·mo (**wrestling**) [ˈsuːməu; ˋsumo] ***n***.〔Jap.〕相扑〔一种摔跤运动〕。

su·mo·to·ri [ˈsəuməuˈtəuriː;ˋsomoˋtori] ***n***.〔Jap.〕相扑运动员。

sump [sʌmp; sʌmp] ***n***. 唧筒井;水坑;污水坑;油池;盐田;【矿】水仓,水窝;【机】油盘;油柄箱;(汽车的)润滑油壶。~ **pump** 水仓泵,润滑油泵。

sumph [sʌmf; sʌmf] ***n***.〔英方〕软弱自卑的人;窝囊废。

sump·ter [ˈsʌm*p*tə; ˋsʌmptɚ] ***n***. 驮马;驮东西的牲口。~**-horse** 驮马。

sump·tion [ˈsʌm*p*ʃən; ˋsʌmpʃən] ***n***.【逻】大前提。

sump·tu·a·ry [ˈsʌm*p*tjuəri; ˋsʌmptʃʊ͵ɛrɪ] ***a***. 限定费用的;(法令等)取缔挥霍浪费的。

sump·tu·ous [ˈsʌm*p*tjuəs; ˋsʌmptʃʊəs] ***a***. 奢侈的,豪华的;高价的。**-ly *ad***. **-ness *n***.

sun[1] [sʌn; sʌn] **I *n***. **1**. 太阳;阳光;〔古〕日出,日落。**2**. (有卫星的)恒星。**3**. 像太阳的东西;中心人物;荣耀;权力。**4**.〔诗〕日;年。**5**. (旧式用煤气点燃的)簇灯〔= ~-burner〕。***a place in the ~*** 顺境;显要的地位。***adore*** [***hail***] ***against the ~*** 从右向左,反时针方向。***from ~ to ~*** 从日出到日落,一天到晚。***have the ~ in one's eyes*** 太阳耀眼睛。***hold the candle in the ~*** 白费,徒劳。***in the ~*** 在阳光下;〔美〕喝醉。***keep out of the ~*** 放在阴处,避晒。***One's ~ is set***. 全盛时期已经过去。***rise with the ~*** 早起。***see the ~*** 生出,诞生;活着。***shoot the ~***〔俚〕= take the ~。***take the ~*** **1**.【海】测量太阳的高度。**2**. 进行日光浴。***the rising ~*** 依附新发迹的权势人物。***under the ~*** **1**. 在天底下,在地上,在这个世上。**2**. 究竟,到底。***with the ~*** 从左向右,顺时针方向。**II *vt***. (**-nn-**) 晒,曝,晾。—***vi***. 晒太阳,做日光浴。~ ***one's moccasins***〔美俚〕死。~ ***oneself*** 晒太阳;受(宠)。~**baked *a***. 太阳晒干[晒裂]的。~**-bath**, ~**bathing** 日光浴,日光(浴)疗法。~**beam** 日光;〔口〕爽朗的孩子(等);〔*pl*.〕〔美俚〕金币。~**belt**〔美〕阳光地带〔指美国南部地区〕。~**bird**【动】**1**. 太阳鸟。**2**. = ~-grebe. ~**bittern**【动】**1**. 太阳鹭鸶。**2**. = ~-**grebe**. ~**blind**〔英〕窗帘,百叶窗。~ **block** 防晒乳膏。~**bonnet** 遮阳(女,童)帽。~**bow** 虹。~**burn *vi*.**, ***n***. 晒黑,晒焦,晒干;晒斑。~**burner** 旧式煤气簇灯。~**burnt** 晒黑的,晒焦的。~**burst** (云隙间)入射的阳光;〔美〕(大钻石周围用小钻石镶成光芒状的)旭日形首饰。~**-cured *a***. 晒干的,晒制的(肉、鱼等)(~*-cured tobacco* 晒烟)。~**-deck** 日光浴甲板[走廊]。~**dew**【植】茅膏菜属。~**dial** 日晷。~ **disk** 日轮〔埃及太阳神象征〕。~**dog**【气】幻日;(出现在地平线不高处的)小虹。~**down 1**. ***n***. 日落,日没;〔美〕阔边女帽。**2**. ***vi***. (因处在陌生环境中而)产生夜间幻觉。~**downer**〔澳〕傍晚时到牧场中借住的无业游民;〔美海俚〕要船员在日落时就回舰的军官。~**dress** 背心裙〔一种低领口之无袖连衣裙〕。~**-dried *a***. 晒干的。~**drops**【植】日见草属。~**fast *a***. 久晒不变[不褪色]的,耐晒的。~ **fever** 骨痛热;日射病热。~**fish**【鱼】太阳鱼;翻车鱼。~**flower**【植】向日葵。〔S-〕〔美〕堪萨斯(Kansas)州的别名。~**glasses**〔*pl*.〕墨镜,太阳眼镜。~**glow** 朝霞,晚霞;太阳白冕。~ **god** 日神,太阳神。**Sun Gan** (电影摄影用的)便携式强光照明灯〔商标名〕。~**-grebe**【动】日鹏。~ **helmet** (男子用)硬壳太阳帽。~**kissed *a***. **1**. 太阳照到的(山顶)。**2**. 太阳晒得透熟的(果实)。~**kist *a***.〔美商〕= sunkissed **2**. ~**lamp** (医疗用)太阳灯;【影】使光线作抛物线反射的大电灯。~**light** 日光。~**lit *a***. 太阳照着的,太阳晒着的。~**lounge** (=〔美〕~ *parlor*, ~ *porch*)(有长玻璃窗的),日光

S

(浴)室。~-powered *a*. 以太阳能为动力的。~proof *a*. 不透日光的;耐光性的,久晒不变的。~-pump【物】日光泵。~rays【医】太阳光线。~rise 日出(时);黎明;〔诗〕日出的地方,东方。~rise industry 朝阳产业〔如电脑芯片制作、生物化学产品研制等高科技行业〕。~job 有发展前途的职业〔如电脑程序设计师等〕。~room 日光(浴)室。~scald, ~-scorch 晒伤,日灼病。~seeker 冬日去日暖地区之旅游者。~set 日落,日没;傍晚;晚霞;日落的地方,西方;晚年,末尾,末路。〔S-〕〔美〕亚利桑那(*Arizona*)州的别名。~set clause〔美〕"日落"条款〔合同或协议中规定的合约到期时须兑现的条件或待遇〕。~set industry 夕阳产业〔旧的制造业等〕。~set law〔美〕"日落法"〔定期审查政府机构工作以便决定是否保留该机构或其工作计划之法律〕。~shade 阳伞;遮阳,天棚;阔边帽;(女帽的)遮阳;【物】物镜遮阳罩。~shine 阳光,日光;太阳晒着的地方;〔美〕黄金;晴天;欢快(*Sunshine State*〔美〕新墨西哥(New Mexico)州的别名)。~shine law〔美〕"阳光法"〔要求政府机构工作加强公开性之法律〕。~shiny *a*. 日光一样的;阳光照耀的;愉快的,温暖的,添加生气的。~star【动】海星,海盘车。~spot(太阳)黑子;【医】雀斑;【影】光线强烈的大电灯。~stone【矿】日长石;太阳石;猫眼石,金绿石。~stroke【医】日射病,中暑。~struck *a*. 中暑的。~suit 日光服〔由短裤和两根背带组成的童装〕。~tan 晒红,晒黑;晒斑。~-tanned *a*. 太阳晒黑的。~trap 阳光异常充足的地方。~up〔美方〕= sunrise. ~ward(s) *a*., *ad*. 向太阳地。~wise *ad*., *a*. 从左向右的,顺时针方向地(的)。~worship 太阳崇拜。-less *a*. 没有太阳的,晒不到太阳的,阴暗的;没趣的,寂寞的。

S

sun[2], **sunn** [sʌn; sʌn] *n*.【植】印度麻,菽麻;印度麻纤维(=~ hemp)。

Sun. = Sunday.

sun·dae, sun·day [ˈsʌndei; ˋsʌndɪ] *n*.〔美〕圣代〔冰淇淋加水果奶油等〕。

Sunda Islands [ˈsʌndə ˈailəndz; ˋsʌndə ˋaɪləndz] 巽他群岛〔亚洲〕。

Sun·da·nese [sʌndəˈni:z; ˏsʌndəˋniz, -ˋnis] *n*.〔*sing*., *pl*.〕巽他人,巽他语。

Sunda Strait (Sumatra 岛与 Java 岛间的)异他海峡。

Sun·day [ˈsʌndi; ˋsʌndɪ] **I** *n*. 星期日;(基督教国家的)礼拜日,安息日,主日。*last* ~ = *on* ~ *last* (在)上一个星期日。*next* ~ (在)下一个星期日。*on* ~ 在星期日。*on* ~*s* 每到星期日。*this* ~ (在)本星期日。*Mid-Lent* ~ = *Mothering* [*Refreshment*] ~. *Show* ~〔牛津大学〕校庆日前的星期日。*Low* ~ 复活节后的星期日。**II** *a*. 业余的,星期日举行的;(服饰等)星期天出门穿的,最佳的。**III** *vi*. 过星期日。***a week*** [***month***] ***of*** ~*s* 许多时日。***look two ways to find*** ~ 斜着眼看。~ **best** [**clothes**] (节假日穿的)本人最好的衣着。~**-go-to-meeting** *a*. (服装,举止等)〔俚〕最好的,最上品的,最漂亮的。~ **letter** = dominical letter. ~ **punch**〔美拳〕猛击;〔转义〕(对付敌手的)强有力手段。~ **run**〔美俚〕长距离。~ **school** 主日学校(的师生);〔美俚〕扑克牌戏。~ **school truth** 尽人皆知的道理[事实]。~ **school words**〔美俚〕谩骂,咀咒;发誓。**Sundays** *ad*. 在每星期天(go swimming ~ 每星期天都去游泳)。

sun·der [ˈsʌndə; ˋsʌndɚ] *vt*., *vi*. (使)分离,分开,切开。*in* ~ 分开着。

sun·dries [ˈsʌndriz; ˋsʌndrɪz] *n*.〔*pl*.〕杂品,杂货;杂事;杂费;【簿】杂项。

sun·dry [ˈsʌndri; ˋsʌndrɪ] *a*. 各种各样的,种种的,杂多的。***all and*** ~ 全部;所有的人。***talk of*** ~ ***matters*** 谈种种事情。~ **goods** 杂货。

SUNFED = Special United Nations Fund for Economic Development 联合国经济发展特别基金会。

sung [sʌŋ; sʌŋ] sing 的过去式及过去分词。

sunk [sʌŋk; sʌŋk] **I** sink 的过去式及过去分词。**II** *a*. = sunken;〔俚〕失败了,完蛋了。*Now we're* ~.〔口〕完了。~ **fence** 隐篱,伏栅,矮墙。~ **screw**【机】埋[沉]头螺钉。

sunk·en [ˈsʌŋkən; ˋsʌŋkən] **I** *v*. sink 的过去分词。**II** *a*. 沉没的,沉下去的;凹下去的;内陷的;水中的,水底的;埋着的,地中的;消瘦的。~ *cheeks* 下陷[消瘦]的脸颊。~ *eyes* 凹陷的眼睛。~ *battery* 潜伏炮台。~ *rocks* 暗礁。~ *tubs* (埋入地面的)低浴缸。

sun·ket [ˈsʌŋkit, ˈsuŋ-; ˋsʌŋkɪt, ˋsuŋ-] *n*.〔英方〕食物;美味。

Sun·na, Sun·nah [ˈsunə; ˋsunə] *n*. (伊斯兰教)传统教规〔以穆罕默德言行为根据的伊斯兰教规;《可兰经》的附经〕。

Sun·ni [ˈsuni:; ˋsunɪ] *n*. (*pl*. ***Sun·ni***) = Sunnite.

Sun·nite [ˈsunˌait; ˋsunaɪt] *n*. (伊斯兰教)逊尼派教徒。**Sun·nism** *n*.

sun·ny [ˈsʌni; ˋsʌnɪ] *a*. (***-ni·er***; ***-ni·est***) 太阳(般)的;阳光照耀的;向阳的,和煦的;愉快的,快乐的;快活的(性情等)。~ *days* 大晴天。~ ***side up***〔美俚〕单煎一面蛋黄在上的煎鸡蛋。***the*** ~ ***side*** 向阳的方面;光明面;不满(…岁)(*be on the* ~ *side of forty* 没有到四十岁。*look on the* ~ *side of things* 对事情抱乐观态度)。**sun·i·ly** *ad*. **sun·ni·ness** *n*.

sun·ny·a·se(e) [sʌˈnja:si; sʌˋnjɑsɪ] *n*.〔印〕托钵僧。

Sun·shin·ers [ˈsʌnʃainəz; ˋsʌnˏʃaɪnəz] *n*.〔美〕新墨西哥(New Mexico)州人的别名。

su·o ju·re [ˈsu:əu ˈdʒuri; ˋsuo ˋdʒurɪ]〔L.〕凭本身的资格,根据本身的权利。

su·o lo·co [ˈsu:əuˈləu kəu; ˋsuoˋloko]〔L.〕处于本身的地位,位置得当。

sup[1] [sʌp; sʌp] **I** *vt*. (***-pp-***) **1**. 啜(茶、汤等)。**2**. 经验,尝。—*vi*. 啜,用匙喝。~ *sorrows by the ladleful* 尝尽悲伤的滋味。*He that* ~*s with the devil needs a long spoon*. 跟恶魔喝汤调羹要长,对坏人必须提防。**II** *n*. 啜一口。*take neither bit* [*bite*] *nor* ~ *of the food* 东西一口也不吃。

sup[2] [sʌp; sʌp] (***supped*** [sʌpt; sʌpt], ***sup·ping*** [ˈsʌpiŋ; ˋsʌpɪŋ]) *vi*. 供给晚饭。~ ***on*** 吃…当晚饭,晚饭吃…。~ ***out*** 在外面吃晚饭。—*vt*. 晚上喂(动物)(*up*)。

sup. = **1**. superior. **2**. superlative. **3**. supplement; supplementary. **4**. supply.

sup- *pref*.〔用于 P 前〕= sub-.

Sup. Ct. = **1**. Superior Court 上级法院。**2**. Supreme Court〔美〕联邦最高法院。

supe [su:p; sup] *n*.〔俚〕**1**.〔美〕= supernumerary. **2**.【空】(发动机的)马力。

su·per [ˈsju:pə; ˋsupɚ, ˋsɪu-, ˋsju-] **I** *n*. **1**.〔口〕= supernumerary. **2**.〔口〕= superintendent. **3**.〔口〕【商】特级品,特大号商品;超级市场;【影】特制影片 = superfilm. **4**.〔盗贼俚〕表。**5**.【印】(书背内的)上浆纱布。**II** *a*.〔口〕**1**. 面积的,平方的。**2**. 超级的,极度的;过分的;超等的,极好的。**III** *ad*. 非常;过分地。**IV** *vt*. 用上浆纱布装(书脊)。—*vi*. 担任跑龙套角色。

su·per- *pref*. 在…之上;从上;再;特别;极,过度;超;总;次,副:~*-conductor* 超导体。

super. = superintendent; supernumerary.

su·per·a·ble [ˈsju:pərəbl; ˋsupərəbl, ˋsju-] *a*. 可胜过的,可凌驾的,可超越的。**-bly** *ad*. **-ness** *n*.

su·per·a·bound [ˌsju:pəˈbaund; ˏsupərəˋbaund, ˏsju-] *vi*. 过多,有余;极多。

su·per·a·bun·dance [ˌsju:pərəˈbʌndəns; ˏsupərəˋbʌndəns, ˏsju-] *n*. 过度,过多剩余;极丰富,极多。

su·per·a·bun·dant [ˌsju:pərəˈbʌndənt; ˏsupərəˋbʌndənt, ˏsju-] *a*. 过多的,多余的;极多的。**-ly** *ad*.

su·per·add [ˈsju:pərˈæd; ˏsupɚˋæd, ˏsju-] *vt*. (在…)外加,再添上,添加;附带说。

su·per·ad·di·tion [ˈsjuːpərəˈdiʃən; ˏsupɚəˋdɪʃən, ˏsju-] *n*. 外加,再添;附加(物),添加(物)。

su·per·al·loy [sjuːpəˈælɔi; ˏsupɚˋælɔɪ] *n*. 超级合金〔防氧化,耐高温及高压的合金〕。

su·per·an·nu·ate [sjuːpəˈrænjueit; ˏsupɚˋænjuˏet, ˏsju-] *vt*. 认为(某人)过于年老[旧式]而辞退[淘汰];给养老金使退休;认为(某生)年龄太大[成绩太差]而勒令退学。

su·per·an·nu·at·ed [sjuːpəˈrænjueitid; ˏsupɚˋænjuˏetɪd] *a*. 领受养老金而退休的;过了服务年龄的,过时的,废弃了的。*a ~ vessel* 老舰,废舰。**-ly** *ad*. **-ness** *n*.

su·per·an·nu·a·tion [ˌsjuːpərˌænjuˈeiʃən; ˏsupɚˏænjuˋeʃən, ˏsju-] *n*. 年老退休;淘汰,废弃,退休金。

su·per·a·que·ous [sjuːpəˈeikwiəs; sjupɚˋekwɪəs] *a*. 水上的。

su·per·a·tom·ic bomb [ˌsjuːpərəˈtɔmik; ˏsupərəˋtɑmɪk] 超原子弹,氢弹。

su·perb [sjuːˈpəːb; suˋpɝb, sə-] *a*. **1**. 宏伟的,壮丽的;(色彩)美丽的,华美的。**2**. 〔口〕极好的,超等的,无上的。*a ~ binding* 极好的装订。*a ~ view* 壮观,绝景。*a ~ courage* 极大的勇气。**-ly** *ad*. **-ness** *n*.

su·per·bi·par·tient [ˈsjuːpəbaiˈpɑːʃiənt; ˋsjupɚbaɪˋpɑrʃɪənt] *a*. 三对五的。

su·per·bi·quin·tal [ˌsjuːpəbaiˈkwintl; ˏsjupɚbaɪˋkwɪntl̩] *a*. 五对七的。

su·per·bi·ter·tial [ˌsjuːpəbaiˈtəːʃəl; ˏsjupɚbaɪˋtɝʃəl] *a*. 三对五的。

su·per·bolt [ˌsjuːpəˈbault; ˏsupɚˋbolt] *n*. 超雷电〔可释放巨大光能〕。

su·per·bomb·er [ˌsjuːpəˈbɔmə; ˏsupɚˋbɑmɚ, ˏsju-] *n*. 超级轰炸机。

su·per·cal·en·der [ˌsjuːpəˈkæləndə; ˏsupɚˋkæləndɚ, ˋsupɚˏ-, ˏsju-] **I** *n*. 【造纸】超级研光机。**II** *vt*. 用超级研光机研光。

su·per·cal·en·dered [sjuːpəˈkælindəd; ˏsupɚˋkæləndɚd] *a*. 特别光洁的(纸类等)。

su·per·car·go [ˈsjuːpəkɑːgəu; ˏsupɚˋkɑrgo, ˏsju-] *n*. (*pl*. *~es*, *~s*) (商船)货物经管员〔代表船主处理一切营业事务〕。

su·per·car·ri·er [ˈsjuːpəkæriə; ˋsupɚˏkærɪɚ] *n*. 超级航空母舰。

su·per·charge [ˌsjupəˈtʃɑːdʒ; ˏsupɚˋtʃɑrdʒ, ˏsju-] *vt*., *vi*. 增加(…的)负荷;【机】(使)增压。**-er** *n*. 增压器。

su·per·cil·i·a·ry [sjuːpəˈsiliəri; ˏsupɚˋsɪlɪˏɛrɪ, ˏsju-] *a*. 眼睛上面的;眉毛的。

su·per·cil·i·ous [sjuːpəˈsiliəs; ˏsupɚˋsɪlɪəs, ˏsju-] *a*. 目空一切的,傲慢的,自大的。**-ly** *ad*. **-ness** *n*.

su·per·cit·y [ˈsjuːpəˌsiti; ˋsjupɚˏsətɪ] *n*. = megalopolis.

su·per·class [ˈsjuːpəˌklɑːs, -klæs; ˋsupɚˏklæs, ˋsju-] *n*. 【生】总纲。

su·per·col·lid·er [sjuːpəkəˈlaidə; ˏsupɚkəˋlaɪdɚ] *n*. 【物】超级(电子)对撞机。

su·per·co·los·sal [ˌsjuːpəkəˈlɔsl; ˏsupɚkəˋlɑsl̩] *a*. 极巨大的。

su·per·co·lum·ni·a·tion [ˌsjupəkəˌlʌmniˈeiʃən; ˏsupɚkəˏlʌmnɪˋeʃən, ˏsju-] *n*. 【建】重列柱。**-co·lum·nar** [ˌsjuːpəkəˈlʌmnə; ˏsjupɚkəˋlʌmnɚ] *a*.

su·per·con·duc·tiv·i·ty [ˌsjupəˌkɔndəkˈtiviti; ˏsjupɚˏkɑndəkˋtɪvətɪ] *n*. 【物】超导电性 (superconduction)。**-duct·ing**, **-duc·tive** *a*. **-duc·tor** *n*.

su·per·con·scious [ˌsjupəːˈkɔnʃəs; ˏsupɚˋkɑnʃəs, ˏsju-] *a*. 超意识的,知觉异常灵敏的。

su·per·cool [ˌsjuːpəˈkuːl; ˏsupɚˋkul, ˏsju-] *vt*. 使过度冷却〔指冷却到凝固点以下而不凝结〕。— *vi*. 过度冷却。

su·per·cooled [ˌsjupəˈkuːld; ˏsjupɚˋkuld] *a*. 【化】过冷(的),(不凝结而)冷却到冰点以下的。

su·per·crat [ˈsjuːpəkræt; ˋsjupɚˏkræt] *n*. 〔美口〕(部长级的)高级官员,大官,大员。

su·per·cres·cent [ˌsjuːpəˈkresnt; ˏsupɚˋkrɛsnt, ˏsju-] *a*. 寄生的。

su·per·crim·i·nal [sjuːpəˈkriminl; sjupɚˋkrɪmɪnl̩] *n*. 〔美〕罪魁。

su·per·crit·i·cal [ˌsjuːpəˈkritikəl; ˏsupɚˋkrɪtəkl̩] *a*. 吹毛求疵的。

su·per·dom·i·nant [ˌsjuːpəˈdɔminənt; ˏsupɚˋdɑmənənt, ˏsju] *n*. 【乐】全音阶的第六度;次中和弦,次中音 (= submediant)。

su·per·dread·nought [ˌsjuːpəˈdrednɔːt; ˏsupɚˋdrɛdˏnɔt, ˏsju-] *n*. 超级无畏战舰。

su·per·du·per [ˌsjuːpəˈdjuːpə; ˋsupɚˋdupɚ] *a*., *n*. 〔美俚〕极大的,极好的(东西);了不起的。

su·per·e·go [sjuːpərˈegəu; ˏsupɚˋigo, -ˋɛgo, ˏsju-] *n*. 【心】超我。

su·per·el·e·va·tion [ˌsjuːpəˌeliˈveiʃən; ˏsupɚˏɛləˋveʃən] *n*. 【交】(铁路或公路的)超高。

su·per·emi·nent [ˌsjuːpəˈeminənt; ˏsupɚˋɛmənənt, ˏsju-] *a*. 卓绝的,卓越的,优越的,超群地,异常突出的。**-ence** *n*. **-ly** *ad*.

su·per·em·pir·ic·al [sjuːpəremˈpirikəl; sjupərɛmˋpɪrɪkəl] *a*. 超经验的。

su·per·er·o·ga·tion [ˌsjuːpərerəˈgeiʃən; ˏsupɚˏɛrəˋgeʃən, ˏsju-] *n*. 职责以外的工作,额外工作;【宗】余功。

su·per·er·o·ga·to·ry [ˌsjuːpereˈrɔgətəri; ˏsupərəˋrɑgəˏtorɪ, ˏsju-] *a*. 职责以外的,额外的;【宗】余功的。

su·per·ette [ˈsjuːpərit, ˌsjuːpəˈret; ˏsupɚˋɛt] *n*. 小型自动售货杂货店。

su·per·ex·cel·lence [sjuːpərˈeksələns; ˏsupɚˋɛksələns, ˏsju-] *n*. 极其精美[优良],卓绝,至高无上。

su·per·ex·cel·lent [sjuːpəˈreksələnt; ˏsupɚˋɛksələnt, ˏsju-] *a*. 极其精美的,极其优良的,卓越的;〔口〕极好的,超高级的,无上的。

su·per·ex·ci·ta·tion [ˌsjuːpəreksiˈteiʃən; ˏsjupərɛksɪˋteʃən] *n*. 过度兴奋[刺激]。

su·per·ex·ploit [sjuːpəriksˈplɔit; sjupərɪksˋplɔɪt] *vt*. 过度剥削。**-ation** *n*.

su·per·ex·ploit·ed [sjuːpəriksˈplɔitid; sjupərɪksˋplɔɪtɪd] *a*. 遭受过度剥削的。

su·per·fam·i·ly [ˈsjuːpəˌfæmili; sjupɚˋfæməlɪ] *n*. (*pl*. **-lies**)【生】总科。

su·per·fat·ted [sjuːpəˈfætid; ˏsupɚˋfætɪd, ˏsju-] *a*. (肥皂)含脂过多的。

su·per·fe·cun·da·tion [ˌsjuːpəˌfiːkənˈdeiʃən, -ˌfekən-; ˏsupɚˏfikənˋdeʃən] *n*. 【生】同期复孕。

su·per·fe·ta·tion [ˌsjuːpəfiːˈteiʃən; ˏsupɚfɪˋteʃən] *n*. 【生】异期复孕。

su·per·fi·cial [sjuːpəˈfiʃəl; ˏsupɚˋfɪʃəl, ˏsju-] *a*. **1**. 表面的;面积的,平方的。**2**. 肤浅的,浅薄的,一知半解的。*~ water* 地面水。*a ~ wound* 表皮上的伤。*81 ~ feet* 八十一平方英尺。*a ~ writer* 浅薄的作家。**-ly** *ad*.

su·per·fi·ci·al·i·ty [sjuːpəfiʃiˈæliti; ˏsupɚˏfɪʃɪˋælətɪ, ˏsju-] *n*. 肤浅,浅薄;表面性;表面现象。

su·per·fi·ci·a·ry [sjuːpəˈfiʃiəri; ˌsupɚˋfɪʃɪˏɛrɪ, ˏsju-] *n*. 【法】有地上权者,租地造屋者。

su·per·fi·ci·es [ˌsjuːpəˈfiʃiiːz; ˏsupɚˋfɪʃɪˏiz, ˏsjupɚˋfɪʃiz] *n*. 〔*sing*., *pl*.〕表面;面积;表面现象,外观;【法】地上物件;地上权。

su·per·film [ˈsjuːpəfilm; ˋsjupɚfɪlm] *n*. 【影】特制影片。

su·per·fine [ˈsjuːpəˈfain; ˏsupɚˋfaɪn] *a*. 【商】特级的,最好的;过分精细的,特别精细的。

su·per·fix [ˈsjuːpəˌfiks; ˋsjupɚˏfɪks] *n*. 【语】语法功能重音〔为了分别词性对同一词标注的不同重音,如 ˈinsert

表示名词，in'sert 表示动词〕。

su·per·flare [ˈsjuːpəflɛə; ˋsjupəflɛr] *n.*【天】超耀斑。

su·per·flu·id·i·ty [ˌsjuːpəfluˈiditi; ˏsupəˏfluˋɪdətɪ] *n.*【物】超流性。**-flu·id** [-ˈfluːid; -ˋfluɪd] *n.*, *a.*

su·per·flu·i·ty [ˌsjuːpəˈfluiti; ˏsupəˋfluətɪ, ˏsju-] *n.* 太多，过剩，多余；奢侈(品)；〔常 *pl.*〕不必要的东西，过剩的东西。

su·per·flu·ous [ˌsjuːˈpəːfluəs; suˋpɝfluəs, sə-] *a.* 过多的，多余的。*It may be ~ to say that....* 说…也许是多余的。**-ly** *ad.* **-ness** *n.*

su·per·for·t(ress) [ˈsjuːpəˌfɔːtris; ˋsjupəˏfɔrtrɪs, -trəs] *n.*〔美〕超级空中堡垒。

su·per·fuse [ˌsjuːpəˈfjuːz; ˏsupəˋfjuz, ˏsju-] *vt.* **1.**〔罕〕倾注，浇盖。**2.** = supercool. **-fu·sion** [-ˈfjuːʒən; -ˋfjuʒən] *n.*

su·per·gi·ant [ˈsjuːpəˌdʒaiənt; ˋsupəˏdʒaɪənt] *n.*【天】超巨星。

su·per·glob·slop·ti·ous, su·per·gob·o·slop·ti·ous [ˌsjuːpˈglɔbslɔpʃəs, -ˈgɔbɔ-; ˏsjupˋglɑbslɑpʃəs, -ˋgɑbɑ-] *a.*〔美〕非常漂亮的，非常好的。

su·per·hawk [ˈsjuːpəhɔːk; ˋsjupəhɔk] *n.* 强硬鹰派。

su·per·heat [sjuːpəˈhiːt; ˏsupəˋhit, ˏsju-] *vt.* 使过(度加)热；【化】使(液体不蒸发而)加热到沸点以上。**-er** *n.* 过热器。

su·per·he·ro [ˈsjuːpəˌhiərəu; ˋsjupəhɪəro] *n.* **1.** 奇才；超级明星。**2.**(作品、影片等中虚构的具有超常本领并专门惩恶扶弱的)超英雄。

su·per·het·e·ro·dyne [ˈsjuːpəˈhetərədain; ˏsupəˋhɛtərəˏdaɪn, ˏsju-] **I** *n.*【无】超外差式(收音机)。**II** *a.* 超外差的。

su·per·high [ˈsjuːpəˈhai; ˋsjupəˋhaɪ] *a.* 超高的。~ **frequency**【无】超高频率。

su·per·high·way [ˌsjuːpəˈhaiˌwei; ˏsupəˋhaɪˏwe, ˏsju-] *n.*〔美〕高速公路(=expressway)。

su·per·hu·man [sjuːpəˈhjuːmən; ˏsupəˋhjumən, ˏsju-] *a.* 超人的；神灵的；超过常人的。**-ly** *ad.*

su·per·im·pose [sjuːpərimˈpəuz; ˏsupərɪmˋpoz, ˏsju-] *vt.*(把…)加在…的上面；附加，添加(*on*; *upon*)。**-si·tion** *n.*

su·per·im·preg·na·tion [ˌsjuːpərimpregˈneiʃən; ˋsjupərɪmpregˋneʃən] *n.*【生】异期复孕，重孕。

su·per·in·cum·bent [ˌsjuːpərinˈkʌmbənt; ˏsupərɪnˋkʌmbənt, ˏsju-] *a.* **1.** 横在上面的；搁[架]在上面的；(压力的)自上而下的。**2.** 拱立的，高悬的，悬空的。~**-bed**【地】复层，叠层。**-cum·bence, -cum·ben·cy** *n.* **-ly** *ad.*

su·per·in·duce [ˌsjuːpərinˈdjuːs; ˏsupərɪnˋdjus, ˏsju-] *vt.* 再加，添加；另立…为承继人；另娶；(在已有的状态、效果等上)使另有增加〔如在某种疾病之上使并发另一种疾病〕。

su·per·in·duc·tion [ˌsjuːpərinˈdʌkʃən; ˏsjupərɪnˋdʌkʃən] *n.* 添加，附加；影响。

su·per·in·tend [ˌsjuːpərinˈtend; ˏsuprɪnˋtɛnd] *vt.*, *vi.* 管理，监督，指挥。

su·per·in·tend·ence, su·per·in·ten·den·cy [sjuːpərinˈtendəns, -dənsi; sjupərɪnˋtɛndəns, -dənsɪ] *n.* 管理；监督(权)。

su·per·in·tend·ent [sjuːpərinˈtendənt; ˏsuprɪnˋtɛndənt] *n.* 管理人，监督人，指挥人；(某一部门的)主管，负责人；(陆海军学校等的)校长；厂长，所长。

su·per·in·var [sjuːpərinˈvɑː; sjupərɪnˋvɑr] *n.*【冶】超殷钢〔一种铁镍合金〕。

Su·pe·ri·or Lake [sjuːˈpiəriə leik; sjuˋpɪrɪə lek] *n.* 苏必利尔湖〔位于美国和加拿大之间〕。

su·pe·ri·or [sjuːˈpiəriə; səˋpɪrɪə, sʊ-] **I** *a.*(*opp.* inferior) **1.** 在上的，上部的，比…高的，上级的，高级的。**2.** 优良的，上等的，优秀的。**3.** 优势的，比…多的；比…好的；比…强的，胜过…的(*to*; *in*)。**4.** 超越…的，不为…所动的(*to*)。**5.** 傲慢的，高人一等的。**6.**【植】(萼)在子房上的，(子房)在萼上的，上生的；【印】位于右上角的；较一行中其他铅字略高的。*a ~ person* 有教养的人士；〔常谑〕自以为了不起的人。*a ~ figure* [*letter*]上角数码或字母〔如 X^2 的 2〕。***be absolutely ~ in every specific campaign*** 在每一个具体战役上，是绝对的优势。***be ~ to*** 胜过，强过，比…好；超然于，不为…所动(*He felt ~ in mathematics to John.* 他觉得自己的数学比约翰强。*be ~ to difficulties* 不屈服于艰难困苦。*be ~ to bribery* 不为贿赂所动)。***rise ~ to*** 超越…，超然于，不为…所影响。(*They were resolved to rise ~ to every obstacle.* 他们决心战胜一切障碍)。***with a ~ air*** 骄傲地。**II** *n.* 长辈，上级，前辈；优越者；优胜者；〔S-〕修道院长；【印】上角字码。~ **court** 上级法院。~ **limit**【数、机】上限，最大尺寸。~ **numbers**(兵力、人数或数量上的)多数，优势。~ **planet**【天】地(轨)外行星。**-ly** *ad.*

su·pe·ri·or·i·ty [sjuːpiəriˈɔriti; səˏpɪrɪˋɔrətɪ, sʊ-, -ˋɑr-] *n.* 优越(性)，超越，优秀，优势(*to*; *over*)；傲慢(*to*; *over*)。~ *in strength* [*ability*, *intelect*] 实力[能力、智力]方面的优势。*sense of ~* 优越感。~ *to bribery* [*temptation*] 拒绝贿赂[不受诱惑]的超越精神。*assume an air of ~* 摆架子。~ **complex**【心】优越感，优越情结。

su·per·ja·cent [ˌsjuːpəˈdʒeisnt; ˏsupəˋdʒɛsnt, ˏsju-] *a.* 压[搁，悬]在上面的。

su·per·jet [ˈsjuːpədʒet; ˋsjupədʒɛt] *n.* 超音速喷气式飞机。

su·per·jum·bo [ˌsjuːpəˈdʒʌmbəu; ˏsupəˋdʒʌmbo] *n.* 超级巨型飞机。

su·per·jun·ket [ˈsjuːpədʒʌŋkit; ˋsjupədʒʌŋkɪt] *n.*〔美〕大宴会。

su·per·kid [ˈsjuːpəkid; ˋsjupəkɪd] *n.* **1.** 神童。**2.** 接受超前教育的儿童。

superl. = superlative.

su·per·la·tive [sjuːˈpəːlətiv; səˋpɝlətɪv, sʊ-] **I** *a.* 最上的，最高的；【语法】最高级的。*the ~ degree*【语法】最高级。**II** *n.*【语法】最高级；最高级词[形式]。***full of ~s***(话等)夸张的。***speak in ~s*** 夸大其词地讲。**-ly** *ad.* **-ness** *n.*

su·per·lat·tice [sjuːpəˈlætis; sjupəˋlætɪs] *n.*【物】超点阵，超(结)晶格。

su·per·lin·er [sjuːpəˈlainə; ˋsupəˏlaɪnə, ˋsju-] *n.* 超级客轮[机]。

su·per·lob·gosh·i·ous [sjuːpəˈlɔbgɔʃiəs; sjupəˋlɑbgɑʃɪəs] *a.*〔美〕第一流的；吹毛求疵的。

su·per·lu·nar [sjuːpəˈljuːnə; ˏsupəˋlunə, -ˋlɪunə] *a.* 月亮上头的，月亮外的，天上的，非现世的(= superlunary)。

su·per·mal·loy [sjuːpəˈmælɔi; sjupəˋmælɔɪ] *n.* 超透磁合金。

su·per·man [ˈsjuːpəmæn; ˋsupəˏmæn] *n.* 超人。

su·per·man·ish [ˈsjuːpəmæniʃ; ˋsupəˏmænɪʃ, ˋsju-] *a.*〔美〕自大的，骄傲的。

su·per·mar·ket [ˈsjuːpəˌmɑːkit; ˋsupəˏmɑrkɪt] *n.* 自动售货商店，超级市场；自选商品店。~ **TV**(超市内廉价货品般的)质量低劣之电视节目。

su·per·mo·del [sjuːpəˈmɔdl; supəˋmɑdl̩] *n.* 超级名模。

su·per·mun·dane [sjuːpəˈmʌndein; ˏsupəˋmʌnden, ˏsju-] *a.* 超脱俗界的，超现世的。

su·per·nac·u·lum [sjuːpəˈnækjuləm; ˏsupəˋnækjələm, ˏsju-] **I** *n.*(应该喝得一滴不剩的)美酒。**II** *ad.* 干杯；(喝得)一滴不剩。*drink ~* 喝光。

su·per·nal [sjuːˈpəːnl; suˋpɝnl̩, sju-] *a.* 崇高的，神圣的；〔诗〕天上的；超凡的。~ *beings*(住在天上的)神仙，

天使。～ *melodies* 仙乐。**-ly** *ad*.

su·per·na·tant [sjuːpəˈneitənt; ˌsupɚˋnetənt, ˌsju-] **I** *a*. 浮在表层的。**II** *n*. 浮在表层的东西;【化】上层清液。

su·per·na·tion·al [sjuːpəˈnæʃənl; ˌsupɚˋnæʃənl] *a*. 由若干国家组成的;控制几个国家的。

su·per·nat·u·ral [sjuːpəˈnætʃərəl; ˌsupɚˋnætʃrəl] **I** *a*. 超自然的;不可思议的,怪异的;神乎其神的,神妙的。**II** *n*. 超自然现象[作用]。**-ism** *n*. 超自然的力[作用,现象];超自然主义。**-ist** *n*. 超自然主义者。**-ly** *ad*. **-ist·ic** *a*.

su·per·nat·u·ral·ize [ˌsjuːpəˈnætʃərəˌlaiz; ˌsupɚˋnætʃərəlˌaɪz, ˌsju-] *vt*. **1**. 使超自然化。**2**. 把…看作超自然的。

su·per·nor·mal [ˈsjuːpəˈnɔːməl; ˌsupɚˋnɔrməl, ˌsju-] *a*. 超常态的;异常的。

su·per·no·va [ˌsjuːpəˈnəuvə; ˌsupɚˋnovə] *n*. (*pl*. **-vae** [-viː; -vi]; **-vas**)【天】超新星。～ **remnant**【天】超新星遗迹〔指超新星存在过程的最后阶段,可缩略为 SNR〕。

su·per·nu·mer·ar·y [sjupəˈnjuːmərəri; ˌsupɚˋnjumərˌɛrɪ, -ˋnu-, ˌsju-] **I** *a*. 额外的,外加的;补充的,代理的;多余的。**II** *n*. 额外人员,冗员;临时雇员;跑龙套的小配角;临时演员;杂工,冗物。

su·per·nu·tri·tion [ˌsjuːpənjuːˈtriʃən; ˌsupɚnjuˋtrɪʃən, ˌsju-] *n*. 营养过多。

su·per·or·der [ˈsjuːpəˌɔːdə; ˌsupɚˋɔrdɚ, ˌsju-] *n*.【生】总目。

su·per·or·di·nate [ˌsjuːpəˈɔːdinit, -ˌeit; ˌsupɚˋɔrdɪnɪt, -et] *a*. 高级的;高官阶的,地位高的。

su·per·or·gan·ic [sjuːpərɔːˈgænik; ˌsupɚɔrˋgænɪk, ˌsju-] **I** *a*. 超机体的。**II** *n*. 〔the ～〕超机体现象。

su·per·or·gan·ism [ˌsjuːpəˈɔːgənizm; ˌsjupɚˋɔrgənɪzm̩] *n*. 超有机体〔一群相互依赖、共同行为成为一个单位的有机体,如群居昆虫〕。

su·per·par·a·site [ˌsjuːpəˈpærəˌsait; ˌsupɚˋpærəˌsaɪt, ˌsju-] *n*.【生】(寄生于寄生物上之)复寄生物。**super·par·a·sit·ism** *n*. 〔*pl*.〕复寄生现象。

su·per·pa·tri·ot [ˌsjuːpəˈpeitriət; ˌsupɚˋpetrɪət, -ˋpæt-] *n*. 爱国狂。**-ic** *a*. **-ism** *n*.

su·per·phos·phate [sjuːpəˈfɔsfeit; ˌsupɚˋfɑsfet, ˌsju-] *n*.【化】过磷酸盐,酸性磷酸盐;过磷酸钙〔肥料〕。

su·per·phys·i·cal [ˌsjuːpəˈfizikl; ˌsupɚˋfɪzɪkl̩, ˌsju-] *a*. 超物质的;超出已知物理定律所能解释的。

su·per·plas·tic·i·ty [ˌsjuːpəplæsˈtisiti; ˌsjupɚplæsˋtɪsətɪ] *n*. 超塑性,超黏性。**-plas·tic** *a*., *n*.

su·per·pol [ˈsjuːpəpɔl; ˋsjupɚpɑl] *n*. 政党头面人物。

su·per·pos·a·ble [ˌsjuːpəˈpəuzəbl; sjupɚˋpozbl̩] *a*. 可置于上面的;【数】可重合的,可叠合的。

su·per·pose [sjuːpəˈpəuz; ˌsupɚˋpoz, ˌsju-] *vt*. (把…)置于…的上面,叠上(*on*; *upon*);使重合。

su·per·posed [ˌsjuːpəˈpəuzd; sjupɚˋpozd] *a*.【植】叠生的。

su·per·po·si·tion [ˌsjuːpəpəˈziʃən; ˌsupɚpəˋzɪʃən, ˌsju-] *n*. 叠加,重合。

su·per·pow·er [sjuːpəˈpauə; ˌsupɚˋpauɚ, sju-] *n*. **1**. 超等的巨大力量;超级大国。**2**.【电】(一地区的)联合发电总量。**3**. 超国家政治实体(指管强国的国际组织)。

su·per·pro·fit [sjuːpəˈprɔfit; sjupɚˋprɑfɪt] *n*. 超额利润。

su·per·pro·ton [sjuːpəˈprəutɔn; sjupɚˋprotɑn] *n*.【物】超质子。

super·qua·dri·par·tient [sjuːpəkwɔdriˈpɑːʃiənt; sjupɚkwɑdrɪˋpɑrʃɪənt] *a*. 九对五的。

su·per·ra·di·ance [sjuːpəˈreidjəns; sjupɚˋredjəns] *n*.【物】超发光。

su·per·ra·di·a·tion [sjuːpəˈreidiˈeiʃən; sjupɚˋredɪˋeʃən] *n*.【物】超辐射。

su·per·re·al·ism [sjuːpəˈriəlizəm; ˌsupɚˋriəlˌɪzm̩, ˌsju-] *n*. ＝surrealism.

su·per·re·gen·er·a·tion [ˌsjuːpəriˈdʒenəˈreiʃən; ˌsupɚrɪˌdʒɛnəˋreʃən, ˌsju-] *n*.【无】超再生,超回授。**-a·tive** *a*.

super·rum·dif·fer·ous [ˌsjuːpəˈrʌmdifərəs; ˌsjupɚˋrʌmdɪfərəs] *a*. 〔美〕非常有趣的。

su·per·sat·u·rate [sjuːpəˈsætʃəreit; ˌsupɚˋsætʃəˌret, ˌsju-] *vt*.【化】使过饱和。**-ra·tion** *n*. 过饱和。

su·per·scope [ˈsjuːpəskəup; ˋsjupɚˌskop] *n*. 超宽银幕。

super·scout [ˈsjuːpəskaut; ˋsjupɚˌskaʊt] *n*. 空中侦察。

su·per·scribe [sjuːpəˈskraib; ˌsupɚˋskraɪb, ˌsju-] *vt*. (将姓名等)写[刻]在…的上面;在(信封等上)写姓名住址。

su·per·script [ˈsjuːpəskript; ˋsupɚˌskrɪpt] **I** *a*. 写在右上角的(如 a^2 的 2)。**II** *n*.【数】上标。

su·per·scrip·tion [ˌsjuːpəˈskripʃən; ˌsupɚˋskrɪpʃən, ˌsju-] *n*. 写[刻]上;(信封等上的)姓名住址;题名,标题,铭题;(处方上部的)拉丁词 recipe (服用)等字样。

su·per·se·cret [ˌsjuːpəˈsiːkrit; ˌsupɚˋsikrɪt] *a*. 绝密的。

su·per·sede [ˌsjuːpəˈsiːd; ˌsupɚˋsid, ˌsju-] *vt*. **1**. 代替;接替;更替;继任。**2**. 将…免职,撤换。**3**. 废除,废弃。**-sed·ence** *n*. **-r** *n*.

su·per·se·de·as [ˌsjuːpəˈsiːdiæs; ˌsupɚˋsidɪˌæs, ˌsju-] *n*.【法】中止[暂缓]执行状。

su·per·se·dure [ˌsjuːpəˈsiːdʒə; ˌsupɚˋsidʒɚ, ˌsju-] *n*. **1**. 替代;接替。**2**. 废弃(＝supersedence)。

su·per·sen·si·ble [ˌsjuːpəˈsensibl; ˌsupɚˋsɛnsəbl̩] *a*. 超越感觉的。**-si·bly** *ad*.

su·per·sen·si·tive [ˌsjuːpəˈsensitiv; ˌsupɚˋsɛnsətɪv, ˌsju-] *a*. **1**. 过于敏感的,过敏的。**2**.【摄】感光特快的。**-ness**, **-ti·vi·ty** *n*.

su·per·sen·so·ry [ˌsjuːpəˈsensəri; ˌsupɚˋsɛnsərɪ, ˌsju-] *a*. ＝supersensible.

su·per·sen·su·al [ˌsjuːpəˈsenʃuəl; ˌsupɚˋsɛnʃuəl, ˌsju-] *a*. ＝ **1**. supersensible. **2**. ＝spiritual.

su·per·sen·su·ous [ˌsjuːpəˈsensjuəs; ˌsjupɚˋsɛnsjuəs] *a*. ＝supersensual.

super·ses·qui·alter·al [ˌsjuːpəseskwiˈɔːltərəl; ˌsjupɚsɛskwɪˋɔltərəl] *a*. 五对二的。

super·ses·qui·ter·tial [ˌsjuːpəseskwiˈtəːʃəl; ˌsjupɚsɛskwɪˋtɝʃəl] *a*. 七对三的。

su·per·ses·sion [ˌsjuːpəˈseʃən; ˌsupɚˋsɛʃən, ˌsju-] *n*. 代替;接替;更替;撤换;废弃。**-sive** *a*.

su·per·ship [ˈsjuːpəʃip; ˋsjuːpəʃɪp] *n*. 超级油轮。

super·sleuth [ˈsjuːpəsluːθ; ˋsjupɚsluθ] *n*. 〔美〕＝G-man.

su·per·sol·id [sjuːpəˈsɔlid; ˋsupɚˌsɑlɪd, ˋsju-] *n*. 超立体,多次体。

su·per·son·ic [ˌsjuːpəˈsɔnik; ˌsupɚˋsɑnɪk, ˌsju-] **I** *a*.【物】超声波的;【空】超音速的。**II** *n*. **1**. 超声波[频]。**2**. 〔口〕超音速飞机。～ *waves* 超声波。～ *aircraft* [*transport*] 超音速飞机。**-s** *n*. 超声学;超音速学。

su·per·sound [ˈsjuːpəsaund; ˋsupɚˌsaʊnd, ˋsju-] *n*.【物】超声。

su·per·star [ˈsjuːpəstɑː; ˋsupɚˌstɑr] *n*. **1**. (影视界等的)超级明星。**2**.【天】超星体。

su·per·state [ˈsjuːpəˌsteit; ˋsupɚˌstet] *n*. 超级(大)国,"老子"国〔欺压小国的大国〕。

super·stish [ˈsjuːpəstiʃ; ˋsjupɚstɪʃ] *a*. 〔美〕迷信的。

su·per·sti·tion [ˌsjuːpəˈstiʃən; ˌsupɚˋstɪʃən] *n*. 迷信;迷信习惯[行为];〔古〕邪教,异教,异端。***break down*** **～*s*** 破除迷信。

su·per·sti·tious [ˈsjuːpəˈstiʃəs; ˌsupɚˋstɪʃəs] *a*. 迷信(上)的。**-ly** *ad*. **-ness** *n*.

su·per·stra·tum [ˌsjuːpəˈstreitəm, -ˈtrɑː-; ˌsupɚˋstretəm, ˌsju-] *n*. (*pl*. **-ta** [-tə; -tə]) 上层;覆盖层。

su·per-string [ˈsjuːpəstriŋ;ˋsjupəstrɪŋ] ***n.*** 【物】超弦〔一种关于物质构造的理论假设〕。

su·per·struc·ture [ˈsjuːpəˌstrʌktʃə; ˋsupəˏstrʌktʃə, ˋsju-] ***n.*** (对下层基础而言的)上部建筑(*opp.* substructure),(船舶的)上部构造,(对经济基础而言的)上层建筑。*the reaction of the* ~ *on the economic base* 上层建筑对于经济基础的反作用。**-tur·al** ***a.***

su·per·sub·ma·rine [ˈsjuːpəˈsʌbməriːn; ˏsupəˋsʌbməˏrin, ˏsju-] ***n.*** 超级潜水艇。

su·per·sub·stan·tial [ˌsjuːpəsəbˈstænʃəl; ˏsupəsəbˋstænʃəl, ˏsju-] ***a.*** 超物质的。

su·per·sub·tle [ˌsjuːpəˈsʌtl; ˏsupəˋsʌtl, ˏsju-] ***a.*** 过分精细的,过分微妙的。

su·per·tank·er [ˈsjuːpəˈtæŋkə; ˋsupəˏtæŋkə] ***n.*** 超级油轮。

su·per·tax [ˈsjuːpətæks; ˋsupəˏtæks, ˋsju-] **I** ***n.*** 附加(累进所得)税;特别附加税。**II** ***vt.*** 对…征收附加税。

su·per·ter·ra·ne·an [ˌsjuːpətiˈreiniən; ˏsupətəˋrenɪən, ˏsju-] ***a.*** 地球表面上的。

super·ter·rene [ˌsjuːpətəˈriːn; ˏsjupətəˋrin] ***a.*** = superterrestrial.

su·per·ter·res·tri·al [ˌsjuːpətəˈrestriəl; ˏsupətəˋrɛstrɪəl, ˏsju-] ***a.*** 地面上的。

su·per·ton·ic [ˈsjuːpəˈtɔnik; ˏsupəˋtɑnɪk, ˏsju-] ***n.*** 【乐】(音阶的)第二音,上主音。

super·tri·par·tient [ˌsjuːpətraiˈpɑːʃiənt; ˏsjupətraɪˋpɑrʃɪənt] ***a.*** 七对四的。

S

Super Tuesday 〔美〕超级星期二〔总统竞选初选日,指选举年3月份的第二个星期二〕。

su·per·va·ca·ne·ous [ˌsjuːpəvəˈkeiniəs; ˏsupəvəˋkenɪəs] ***a.*** 多余的,不需要的。

su·per·vene [ˌsjuːpəˈviːn; ˏsupəˋvin, ˏsju-] ***vi.*** 接着发生,意外发生,附带发生,并发;添加,附加。—***vt.*** 取代;在…之后发生。**-ven·tion** [-ˈvenʃən; -vɛnʃən] ***n.*** 意外发生,附带发生(事件);附加,添加;续发,并发;取代。

su·per·ven·ient [ˌsjuːpəˈviːnjənt; ˏsjupəˋvinjənt] ***a.*** 意外发生的,节外生枝的,附加的;接踵而至的。

su·per·vise [ˈsjuːpəvaiz; ˏsupəˋvaɪz] ***vt.***, ***vi.*** 监督;管理。

su·per·vi·sion [ˌsjuːpəˈviʒən; ˏsupəˋvɪʒən] ***n.*** 监督;管理。***under the*** ~ ***of*** 在…监督下。

su·per·vi·sor [ˈsjuːpəvaizə; ˏsjupəˋvaɪzə] ***n.*** 监督人;管理人;(书的)审订者;〔英〕铁道线路检查员;〔美〕(选举的)镇行政官员;〔美〕督学员。**-ship** ***n.*** 监督(管理)人的职位。

su·per·vi·so·ry [ˌsjuːpəˈvaizəri, ˈsjuːpəvaizəri; ˏsupəˋvaɪzərɪ, ˏsju-] ***a.*** 监督的,管理的。

su·pi·nate [ˈsjuːpiˌneit; ˋsupəˏnet] ***vt.***, ***vi.*** 【解】(使)(前肱、足等)旋转向上(或向外)。

su·pi·na·tion [sjuːpiˈneiʃən; ˏsupəˋneʃən, ˏsju-] ***n.*** (手脚的)转动(作用),旋后(作用),外转(作用)(*opp.* pronation);仰卧。

su·pi·na·tor [ˈsjuːpiˌneitə; ˋsupəˏnetə] ***n.*** 【解】旋后肌。

su·pine[1] [sjuːˈpain; suˋpaɪn, sɪu-] ***a.*** **1.** 仰卧的,仰天的;掌心向上[朝外]的。**2.** 懒惰的,因循的,苟安的。**-ly** ***ad.*** **-ness** ***n.***

su·pine[2] [ˈsjuːpain; ˋsupaɪn, ˋsɪu-] ***n.*** **1.** (拉丁语法中的)动名词。**2.** (动词不定式的)目的式。

SUPO = superpower water boiler 超功率沸腾式反应堆(水锅炉)。

supp., **suppl.** = supplement; supplementary.

sup·per [ˈsʌpə; ˋsʌpə] ***n.*** 晚餐;(夜间娱乐后的)宵夜。*have* [*take*] ~ 吃晚饭。*What is there for* ~? 晚饭吃什么? *At what time is* ~? 什么时候开晚饭? *We sat down to a good* ~. 我们坐下来吃一顿丰盛的晚饭。*the Last S-* 【宗】(耶稣被钉死在十字架前夕与十二门徒一同吃的)最后晚餐。*the Lord's S-* 【宗】最后晚餐;圣餐(仪式)。~ **club** 高级夜总会。

sup·plant [səˈplɑːnt; səˋplænt] ***vt.*** (用策略、阴谋手段等)排挤掉;取…而代之;代替;移换。**-a·tion** [-ˌlɑːnˈteiʃən; -ˏlænˋteʃən] ***n.*** **-er** ***n.***

sup·ple [ˈsʌpl; ˋsʌpl] **I** ***a.*** (***-pler***; ***-plest***) **1.** 柔软的;易弯曲的;(动作)轻快的;柔和的。**2.** 柔顺的,顺从的,唯唯诺诺的;巴结的,迎合人意的。**3.** (思想等)反应灵活的。**II** ***vt.*** 使柔软;使柔顺,使顺从;驯(马)。—***vi.*** 变柔软;变柔和。~**jack** 软韧的藤杖;【植】一些木质藤类植物的通称;〔喻〕〔美〕傀儡。**-ly** ***ad.*** **-ness** ***n.***

sup·ple·ment [ˈsʌplimənt; ˋsʌpləmənt] **I** ***n.*** 增补;补足,追加;(书报的)补遗,附录;增刊;【数】补角;补码。**II** [-ment; -mɛnt] ***vt.*** 补足,增补。**-ta·tion** [-ˈteiʃən; -ˋteʃən] ***n.***

sup·ple·men·tal [sʌpliˈmentl; ˏsʌpləˋmɛntl] ***a.*** = supplementary.

sup·ple·men·ta·ry [ˌsʌpliˈmentəri; ˏsʌpləˋmɛntərɪ] **I** ***a.*** 增补的,追加的;【数】补角的。**II** ***n.*** (*pl.* ***-ries***) 增补者,增补物。

sup·ple·tion [səˈpliːʃən; səˋpliʃən] ***n.*** 【语】异干互补,替补(作用)。〔例:went 原先是 wend 的过去式,现在是 go 的过去式的替补形式〕。**-tive** [-tiv; -tɪv] ***a.***

sup·ple·to·ry [ˈsʌpliˌtɔri; ˋsʌpləˏtorɪ, -ˏtɔr-] ***a.*** = supplementary.

sup·pli·ance [ˈsʌpliəns; ˋsʌplɪəns] ***n.*** 恳求,哀求。

sup·pli·ant [ˈsʌpliənt; ˋsʌplɪənt] ***a.***, ***n.*** 恳求的[人]。**-ly** ***ad.***

sup·pli·cant [ˈsʌplikənt; ˋsʌplɪkənt] **I** ***a.*** 恳请的,祈求的。**II** ***n.*** 祈求者,恳请者。

sup·pli·cate [ˈsʌplikeit; ˋsʌplɪˏket] ***vt.*** 恳求,哀求;祈求。—***vi.*** 恳求,祈求(*to sb.*; *for sth.*)。**-cat·ing·ly** ***ad.*** 死气白赖地。

sup·pli·ca·tion [sʌpliˈkeiʃən; ˏsʌplɪˋkeʃən] ***n.*** 恳求,哀求(*to*; *for*);【宗】祈求。

sup·pli·ca·to·ry [ˈsʌplikətəri; ˋsʌplɪkəˏtorɪ, -ˏtɔrɪ] ***a.*** 恳求的,哀求的。

sup·pli·er [səˈplaiə; səˋplaɪə] ***n.*** 供应者,供给者;补充者;厂商。

sup·ply[1] [səˈplai; səˋplaɪ] **I** ***vt.*** (***-plied***) 供给;供应;配给;补充,填补,弥补(不足、损失等)。*Cows* ~ *us* (*with*) *milk.* 母牛供给我们牛奶。*The cow supplies milk.* 这头牛有奶。~ *the market* 供应市场。~ *a demand* 满足要求。~ *a want* 弥补不足。~ *an office* 代理职务。~ *the place of* 代替。**II** ***n.*** **1.** 供给;供应,给养;军需;补充;〔常 *pl.*〕供给物,供应品;生活用品;补给品;存货;贮藏(量);(储备)物资。**2.** 〔废〕代理者,代课教员,代理牧师。**3.** 〔*pl.*〕粮食,口粮;〔*pl.*〕经费,(个人)开支[生活费]。*His father cut off the* ~. 他父亲停止了他的生活费。*a* ~ *and marketing cooperative* 供销合作社。*an inexhaustible* ~ *of coal* 无穷的煤贮藏量。*the Committee of S-* (英国下院的)预算委员会。*economize the household supplies* 节省家用。***have a good*** ~ ***of*** 备有许多…。***in short*** ~ 供应不足。***line of*** ~ 【军】供应线,补给线。***short*** ~ 供不应求。***tension in*** ~ 供应不济,供应紧张。***the free*** ~ ***system and the wage system*** 供给制和工资制。***the law of*** ~ ***and demand*** 【经济】供求规律。~ **base** 兵站,补给基地。~ **department** 供应处;军需处。~ **wire** 供电线。

sup·ply[2] [ˈsʌpli; ˋsʌplɪ] ***ad.*** = supplely.

sup·port [səˈpɔːt; səˋport, -ˋpɔrt] **I** ***vt.*** **1.** 支承,支撑;支持;支援,维护。**2.** 援助;拥护,赞助。**3.** 扶养,赡养(家属);资助,维持。**4.** 鼓舞,激励。**5.** 忍受,忍耐。**6.** 证明,证实。**7.** 【剧】扮演(角色);配,为…担任配角;【乐】为…伴奏。~ *towns with electricity to* 向城镇供电。*I can't* ~ *this heat.* 我忍受不了这样的热度。*The* *speaker was ~ed on the platform by the mayor*. 演讲人在讲台上有市长陪着。~ *a family* 养家活口。~ ***oneself*** 自谋生计。**II** ***n*.** **1.** 支持,维持;支持者;支柱,支座,撑体;桁架。**2.** 扶助,援助;鼓励;拥护;赞成,赞助。**3.** 抚养,赡养;生计,活计,衣食;赡养费。**4.**【军】支援部队,预备队;【乐】伴奏(部);【剧】助演(者),配角。*a ~ of the state* 国家的栋梁。*Price ~s*〔美〕(政府给农民的)补助金。***enlist the ~ of*** 争取(某人的)支持。***give ~ to*** 支持,支援。***in ~ of*** 支持;支援;拥护。**-less** ***a*.**

sup·port·a·ble [səˈpɔːtəbl; səˋportəbḷ, ˋpɔrt-] ***a*.** 可支持的;可忍受的;可援助的,可拥护的;可赞成的;可抚养的。**-bly** ***ad*.**

sup·port·er [səˈpɔːtə; səˋportɚ, -ˋpɔr-] ***n*.** **1.** 支持者;援助者;拥护者,赞成者,赞助者,后盾,后台老板;后援者;〔谑〕腿。**2.** 抚养者,赡养者。**3.** 支持物,支架;托器;【外】绷带,绷带;腹带;护身〔运动时保护下体的松紧三角带〕。**4.**【化】载体,担体。

sup·port·ing [səˈpɔːtiŋ; səˋportɪŋ, -ˋpɔrt-] ***a*.** **1.** 起支持[支撑]作用的。**2.** 协助[配合、支援]的;起配角作用的。**3.** 可提供证据的,证实的。*a ~ actor* 男配角。~ **angle iron** 角铁托。~ **cast** 助演阵容。~ **fire**【军】支援射击。~ **force** 承力,支力。~ **plate** 底板。~ **resistance**【物】支承阻力。

sup·port·ive [səˈpɔːtiv; səˋportɪv, -ˋpɔr-] ***a*.** 支持的,支援的,赞许的。~ **therapy** [**treatment**] **1.**【医】谈话疗法。**2.** 辅助疗法。

sup·pos·a·ble [səˈpəuzəbl; səˋpozəbḷ] ***a*.** 可设想的,可假设的。**-bly** ***ad*.**

sup·pos·al [səˈpəuzl; səˋpozḷ] ***n*.** 想像;假定(= supposition)。

sup·pose [səˈpəuz; səˋpoz] ***vt*.** **1.** 设想,推测;猜想某事[某人]如何 (*to do*; *to be*)。**2.** 假定〔证题时用语,和 given, provided 通用〕。**3.** 意味着;必须先假定,以…为必需条件。**4.**〔现在分词或祈使语气〕如果…好不好。**5.**〔口〕如果(= if)。*I ~ you are right*. 我想你说得对。*I should ~ him to be about fifty*. 我可也猜他是五十岁左右。*Supposing* [*Suppose*] *you miss your tiger, he is not likely to miss you*. 你如果打不着老虎,老虎不见得吃不着你。*Purpose ~s foresight*. 目的就意味着预见。*S- we try*. 去试试吧。*S- we go to bed*. 咱们去睡吧。***be ~d to*** (*do*) **1.** …(在职务上)要,应该(*You are ~d to be here at eight every day*. 你应该每天八点钟到这里)。**2.**〔用于否定句〕〔口〕不许,不准 (*You're not ~d to smoke here*. 不许你在这儿吸烟)。—***vi*.** 推测,料想。*I ~ so*. 我想是的。

sup·posed [səˈpəuzd; səˋpozd] ***a*.** 假设的;想像上的;假定的。*a ~ case* 一个假设的情况。

sup·pos·ed·ly [səˈpəuzidli; səˋpozɪdlɪ] ***ad*.** 想像上,大概,恐怕,想必。~ *written by* ... 被认为是…写的。

sup·po·si·tion [ˌsʌpəˈziʃən; ˏsʌpəˋzɪʃən] ***n*.** 想像,推测;假定。***on the ~ that*** 假定…。

sup·po·si·tion·al [ˌsʌpəˈziʃənəl; ˏsʌpəˋzɪʃənḷ] ***a*.** 想像上的;假定的,推测的。**-ly** ***ad*.**

sup·pos·i·tious [ˌsʌpəˈziʃəs; ˏsʌpəˋzɪʃəs] ***a*.** = supposititious.

sup·pos·i·ti·tious [səˌpɔziˈtiʃəs; səˏpɑzəˋtɪʃəs] ***a*.** 顶替的,冒充的,假的;〔罕〕想像的,推测的。*a ~ child* 一个冒充的孩子。~ *writings* 伪书。**-ly** ***ad*.** **-ness** ***n*.**

sup·pos·i·tive [səˈpɔzitiv; səˋpɑzɪtɪv] **I** ***a*.** 想像的,假定的,推测的。**II** ***n*.**【语法】假设连词〔如 *if*, *assuming*, *provided* 等〕。

sup·pos·i·to·ry [səˈpɔzitəri; səˋpɑzəˏtorɪ, -ˏtɔrɪ] ***n*.**【医】坐药,栓剂,塞剂。

sup·press [səˈpres; səˋprɛs] ***vt*.** **1.** 镇压,压制;扑灭(火等)。**2.** 止住,忍住(泪,欲望等);隐瞒(证据等)。**3.** 禁止(书等的)发卖,禁止发行;删掉。~ *a yawn* 忍住呵欠。*with laughter ~ed* 忍住笑。**-er** ***n*.**〔美〕= suppersor.

sup·pressed [səˈprest; səˋprɛst] ***a*.** **1.** (病)症状不显明的。**2.** 被抑制的,忍住的。**3.** 被删去的。*a ~ desire*〔美〕(瞒着不说的)意中人。*sounds of ~ laughter* 抑压住的笑声。*a ~ passage* 删去的一节。

sup·press·i·ble [səˈpresibl; səˋprɛsəbḷ] ***a*.** 可镇压的,可禁止的,可制止的。

sup·pres·sion [səˈpreʃən; səˋprɛʃən] ***n*.** **1.** 镇压,扑灭。**2.** 抑制;隐匿;含蓄。**3.** 制止;禁止;删除;【医】闭止;萎缩。*the ~ of a rising* 镇压一次起事。~ *of facts* 隐瞒事实。

sup·pres·sio ve·ri [səˈpresiəuˈviərai; səˋprɛsɪoˋvɛraɪ]〔L.〕隐瞒事实[真象]。

sup·pres·sive [səˈpresiv; səˋprɛsɪv] ***a*.** 镇压的;压制的;隐蔽的;抑制的;禁止的;删去的。

sup·pres·sor [səˈpresə; səˋprɛsɚ] ***n*.** 镇压者;隐蔽者;禁止者;删除者;抑制因子;【物】消声器;【无】抑制栅极。

sup·pu·rate [ˈsʌpjuəreit; ˋsʌpjəˏret] ***vi*.**【医】酿脓,化脓。

sup·pu·ra·tion [ˌsʌpjuəˈreiʃən; ˏsʌpjəˋreʃən] ***n*.** 化脓;脓。

sup·pu·ra·tive [ˈsʌpjurətiv; ˋsʌpjəˏretɪv] **I** ***a*.** 酿脓的,化脓(性)的。**II** ***n*.** 化脓剂,催脓剂。

supr. = supreme.

su·pra [ˈsjuːprə; ˋsuprə, ˋsju-] ***ad*.**〔L.〕在上,在前 (*opp*. infra)。***vide ~*** 见上。

su·pra- *pref*. 上,超越,前。*supra*conductivity. ★在解剖学用语中与 super- 同义。

su·pra·con·duc·tiv·i·ty [ˈsjuːprəkɔndʌkˈtiviti; ˋsjuprəkɑndʌkˋtɪvətɪ] ***n*.**【物】超导电性。

su·pra·lap·sar·i·an [ˌsjuːprəlæpˈseriən, -ˈsɛər-; ˏsjuprəlæpˋsɛrɪən, -ˋsɛr-] **I** ***n*.**【宗】堕落前拯救论者〔加尔文教派的一个分支,声称上帝在人类堕落前就预定拯救的计划〕。**II** ***a*.** 堕落前拯救论者的。**-ism** ***n*.**

su·pra·lim·i·nal [ˌsjuːprəˈliminl; ˏsuprəˋlɪmənḷ] ***a*.**【心】阈上的。**-ly** ***ad*.**

su·pra·mo·lec·u·lar [ˌsjuːprəməˈlekjulə; ˏsuprəməˋlɛkjəlɚ] ***a*.**【化】超分子的;许多分子组成的。

su·pra·mun·dane [ˈsjuːprəˈmʌndein; ˏsuprəˋmʌnden, ˏsju-] ***a*.** 超越现世的。

su·pra·na·tion·al [ˌsjuːprəˈnæʃənl; ˏsuprəˋnæʃənḷ] ***a*.** 超国家的。~ *authority* 超国家的权威。**-ism** ***n*.**

su·pra·nat·u·ral [ˌsjuːprəˈnætʃərəl; ˏsuprəˋnætʃərəl] ***a*.** 超自然的。

su·pra·or·bit·al [ˌsjuːprəˈɔːbitl; ˏsuprəˋɔrbɪtḷ, ˏsju-] ***a*.**【解】眼上的;眶上的。

su·pra·pol·i·tics [ˈsjuːprəˈpɔlitiks; ˋsjuprəˋpɑlɪtɪks] ***a*.** 超政治的。

su·pra·pro·test [sjuːprəˈprəutest; ˏsuprəˋprotɛst, ˏsju-] ***n*.**【商,法】参助承兑〔付款人拒绝付款时第三者为维持出票人信誉而出面承兑〕。

su·pra·re·nal [ˌsjuːprəˈriːnl; ˏsuprəˋrinəl, ˏsju-] **I** ***a*.** 肾上的,肾上腺的。**II** ***n*.** 肾上腺(= ~ gland)。

su·pra·spi·nal [ˈsjuːprəˈspainl; ˋsjuprəˋspaɪnḷ] ***a*.**【解】脊棘上的,刺突上的。

su·prem·a·cist [səˈpreməsist, sju-; səˋprɛməsɪst, su-] ***n*.** (某一)种族优越论者,种族霸权论者。*a white ~* 白人优越论者[至上主义者]。

su·prem·a·cy [sjuˈpreməsi; səˋprɛməsɪ, su-] ***n*.** 至高;优越性[地位];最高地位;无上权威;霸权。*naval ~* 制海权;海上霸权。*an oath* [*act*] *of ~*〔英〕确认英王对国教有管辖权而否认罗马教皇管辖权的宣誓[法令]。

su·preme [sjuːˈpriːm; səˋprim, su-] ***a*.** 最上的,最高的,极上的,无上的,非常的,极度的,最优秀的,最重要的。*the S- (Being)* 上帝。*the S- Pontiff* 罗马教皇。*a ~ measure* 死刑。*the ~ end* 最终[最主要的]目的。***the ~ moment*** [***hour***] 最关紧要的一刹那,生死关头,决定性时刻。***make the ~ sacrifice*** 献出崇高的生命,光荣

S

牺牲。*S- being* 上帝;至高无上者。~ **commander** 最高统帅。**S- Court**〔美〕(全国的或州的)最高法院。**S- Court of Judicature**〔英〕最高法院。~ **good** [**end**] 至善。~ **power** 最高权力。**S- Soviet** (苏联)最高苏维埃。**S- Truth** = Aum Shinrikyo 奥姆真理教〔日本的一种邪教〕。~ **wallop**〔美〕极大的乐趣。**-ness** *n*.

Su·pre·mo [səˈpriːməu; səˋprimo] *n*. 总裁,首脑。

supt. = 1. superintendent. 2. support.

sur. = 1. surplus. 2. surcharged. 3. surface.

sur-[1] *pref*.〔用于 r 前〕= sub-.

sur-[2] *pref*. 1. 在来自古法语的英语中与 super- 同义: *sur*render, *sur*charge, *sur*face. 2. 在科学术语中与 super-, supra- 同义: *sur*renal = suprarenal.

su·ra[1] [ˈsuərə; ˋsurə] *n*. (伊斯兰教经典的)章;棕榈酒。

su·ra[2] [ˈsjuərə; ˋsjurə] *n*.【医】腓肠。

Su·ra·ba·ja, Su·ra·ba·ya [ˌsuːrəˈbɑːjə; ˏsurəˋbɑjə] *n*. 苏腊巴亚〔即泗水,印度尼西亚港市〕。

su·rah[1] [ˈsuərə; ˋsjurə] *n*. = sura[1].

su·rah[2] [ˈsjuərə; ˋsurə, ˋsjurə] *n*. 斜纹软绸(= ~ silk)。

su·ral [ˈsjuərəl; ˋsjurəl] *a*.【解】小腿腹的。

sur·base [ˈsəːbeis; ˋsɝˏbes] *n*.【建】台基上缘装饰线脚。

sur·based [ˈsəːˌbeist; ˋsɝˏbest] *a*.【建】1. 有台基上部线脚的。2. 扁拱形的。

sur·cease [səːˈsiːs; sɝˋsis] I *n*.〔古〕停止,终止。II *vt*. 完全停止。—*vi*. 停止。

sur·charge I [ˈsəːtʃɑːdʒ; ˋsɝˏtʃɑrdʒ] *n*. 1. 过重,装货过多,超载;装填过多;负荷过重;充电过度。2. 过高的要价。3. 附加费;(对纳税人的)虚报罚款;(邮票、印花等的)欠资罚款;(邮票上的)改价印记。4. 指出对方账目漏记一笔贷方款项。5.【化】总误差。II [səːˈtʃɑːdʒ; sɝˋtʃɑrdʒ] *vt*. 1. 使超载,使装得过多;使(火药)装填过度;使负荷过重;使充电过度。2. 对…收取附加费;对…征收虚报罚款[欠资罚款],在…上盖改价印记。3. 使要价过高。4. 指出对方在(账上)漏记贷方款项。

sur·cin·gle [ˈsəːsiŋgl; ˋsɝsɪŋgl̩] I *n*. (马的)肚带;(教士长袍上的)腰带。II *vt*. (用肚带)勒紧(马腹等)。

sur·coat [ˈsəːkəut; ˋsɝˏkot] *n*. 上衣;(中世纪的)女外衣;武士铠甲上穿的外衣。

sur·cu·lose, sur·cu·lous [ˈsəːkjuləus, -ləs; ˋsɝkjəˏlos, -ləs] *a*.【植】有根出条[吸根]的。

surd [səːd; sɝd] I *a*.【数】不尽根的,无理数的;【语音】无声的,清音的。II *n*.【数】不尽根,无理数;【语音】无声音,清音〔p, f, s, t, k 等〕。

surd·i·mut·ism [səːdiˈmjuːtizm; ˏsɝdɪˋmjutɪzm̩] *n*. 聋哑。

sur·do·mute [ˈsəːdəmjuːt; ˋsɝdəˏmjut] *n*. 又聋又哑的人。

sure [ʃuə, ʃɔː; ʃur] I *a*. 1.〔用作表语〕(主观觉得)确实的;深信,确信;(对…)有信心,有把握(*of*; *that*);肯定(要),一定(会)(*to do*; *to be*)。2.〔用作定语〕(客观上)无疑问的,真实的,实在的;不可避免的,必然要发生的;(方法、效果等)正确的;可靠的;稳妥的,牢靠的,坚固的;(立场)坚定的。*Are you ~ (of it)?* 你认为确实的吗?真的吗? *I am not so ~ of that*. 我不太清楚。*Don't be too ~*. 别太肯定。*Fight no battle you are not ~ of winning*. 不打无把握之仗。*I'm not ~ if I can do it*. 我不敢肯定我能做。*It's ~ to be wet*. 肯定要下雨。*a ~ proof* 确凿的证据。*slow and ~* 稳步的。*a ~ draw* 一定可以打出狐狸来的矮树丛;一定可以套出实情来的话。*a ~ hand* 可靠的人。*a ~ poison*〔美棒球俚〕优秀投手。*a ~ shot*〔美俚〕神枪手,百发百中的射击员。***be ~ of*** [***that***] 确信,深信(*He is ~ of success*. 他深信他会成功。*You may be ~ of his honesty*. 你可以相信他的诚实)。***be*** [***feel***] ***~ of oneself*** 自信。***be ~ to*** (*do*) 必定,一定(*His work is ~ to succeed*. 他的工作必定获得成功。*Be ~ to tell me*. 别忘记一定讲给我听)。***feel ~*** (***of***, ***that ...***) = *be ~* (*of*, *that ...*)。***for ~*** 一定要,必须;必然,当然,毫无疑问(*Be there by six o'clock for ~*. 你一定要在六点钟以前到那里)。***I am ~*** 的确,真的;一定(*I'm ~ I don't know*. = *I'm ~ I can't tell*. 我真的不知道)。***make assurance double*** [***doubly***] ***~*** 要稳而又稳,要加倍小心[注意]。***make ~*** 弄明白,查明白,小心一点;确信(*I believe the line is from 'Lycidas', but you had better make ~*. 我相信这一句诗是"李西达斯"里面的,然而你最好是查查看。*I make ~ it would rain, but it didn't*. 我确信要下雨的,可是没下)。***make ~ of*** 将,弄明白,查明白;将…拿到手;叮嘱明白。***make ~*** (***that***) 务必;务请(*Please make ~ you understand this point*. 务请你们体谅这一点)。***S- thing!***〔美俚〕真的!当然(*Shall you be at the dance? — S- thing!* 你参加舞会吗?——当然参加!) ***to be ~*** 1.〔让步〕自然,固然。2.〔感叹〕哎呀!真的!一点不假(*So it is, to be ~!* 一点不假就是那样啦! *Well, To be ~!* 哼,好!啊!) ***Well, I am ~!*** = To be ~! II *ad*. 的确,一定;〔美〕当然!好。*Are you coming? — S-!* 你去吗?——当然去。***as ~ as a gun, as ~ as eggs are eggs, as ~ as death*** [***fate***], ***as ~ as nails, as ~ as you live***〔口〕的的确确。~ ***enough*** 果真(*I said it would be, and ~ enough it is*. 果然被我说中了)。~**enough** *a*.〔美口〕真正的;确实的。~**fire** *a*.〔美口〕不错的,确实的(方法),可靠的,必成的。~**footed** *a*. 脚步稳的(马);踏实的;不会失错的;稳当的,可靠的。**-ness** *n*.

sure·ly [ˈʃuəli; ˋʃurlɪ] *ad*. 的确,确实,无疑;必定,一定;稳当地,安全地;(回答)当然,好;〔古〕是的,是那样的;不致于,未必。*Should you be willing to try? — S-*. 你愿意试一试吗?——好。*You ~ don't mean to be cruel*. 我想你总不致于要做残暴的事吧。***as ~ as*** = as sure as. ***slowly but ~*** 稳扎稳打地,明确不移地。

Sure·té [syrte; syrtɛ], ***La n***.〔F.〕巴黎警察厅。

sure·ty [ˈʃuəti, ˈʃɔː-; ˋʃurtɪ, ˋʃurətɪ] *n*. 保证(人),担保(人);保释金;〔古〕安全,牢靠;确实。***of a ~***〔古〕的确,必定。***stand ~ for*** 做…的保证人。**-ship** *n*. 保证人的地位[资格,责任]。

surf [səːf; sɝf] I *n*. 1. 拍岸碎浪[涛声],迎头碎浪,海滨浪花。2.【计】(网上)浏览,漫游。II *vt*. 1. 在…冲浪。2.【计】在(电脑上)冲浪〔指在电脑中漫游,搜索想要的信息〕。~***ing the Net***【计】网上冲浪〔在网上浏览漫游〕。~**bird**【鸟】滨浪鹬。~**board** (冲浪运动的)冲浪板。~**boat**【海】冲浪艇。~**-bum** 冲浪运动迷。~**-cast** *vi*. 冲浪捕鱼。~ **clam**【动】碎浪蛤蜊。~ **fish**【动】1. 海鲫鱼科鱼。2. 石首鱼科鱼。~**man** 冲浪艇员;〔美〕海岸警备队救生员。~**perch** 海鲫鱼科鱼。~**ride** *vi*. 冲浪,驾冲浪板作冲浪运动。~**riding** 冲浪运动。~ **scotor**【动】黑凫;斑头海番鸭。**-er** *n*. 冲浪运动员。**-ing** *n*. 冲浪运动。

sur·face [ˈsəːfis; ˋsɝfɪs] I *n*. 1. 表面;地面;水面;广场,空地。2. 外观,外表,皮毛。3.【几】面;切口;【空】翼面。II *a*. 表面的;地面的,水面的;外观的,外表上的;(对高架及地下铁路说的)平地上的;(对矿井内说的)矿井外的。*an adjusting ~*【空】调节板。*a supporting ~*【空】支持面积。*a plane ~* 平面。*~s in contact* = *rubbing ~s* 摩擦面。*look at the ~ only* 只看外表。*One never gets below the ~ with him*. 人们无法看透他的内心。*a ~ raider* 海上突击舰。***look below*** [***beneath***] ***the ~ of things*** 看到事物的内部。***of the ~*** 外观上的,表面的。***on the ~*** 表面上,外表上。III *vt*. 为…装面[配面],对…作表面处理;使成平面;掘开…的地面;铺(路面);使(潜艇)浮出水面。— *vi*. 地面采掘,井外劳动;浮出水面。~**-active** *a*.【化】表面活性的。~**car**〔美〕地面车辆。~ **colo(u)r** 表面色;凸板印刷用的颜料。~ **conductance**【电】表面电导。~ **crystallization** 表面结晶。~ **displacement**【海】(水上)排水量。~**-ef-**

fect ship〔美〕气垫船。~**-field**【电】近面电场。~ **flow** 表流,径流。~ **force** 地[水]面部队;水面舰艇。~ **gauge**【机】划平面针盘。~ **mail** 普通邮件〔与航空邮件相对〕。~**man**【矿】井上[地面]工人;【铁道】护路工人。~ **noise** (唱片上的)杂音。~**plate** (检验表面平正度的)平板。~ **printing** 凸版印刷;凸板印染。~ **tension**【物】表面张力。~**-to-air** *a*. (导弹)地对空的。~**-to-**~ *a*. (导弹)地对地的。~**-to-underwater** (导弹)地对水下的;水面舰艇和水下潜艇之间的。~ **transportation** 陆上运输。~ **water** 地面水,淤水。~ **wave** (地震的)面波;【电】表面电波,地表电波。

sur·fac·tant [sə:ˈfæktənt; sɚˋfæktənt] *n*.【化】表面活化剂。

sur·fe·it [ˈsə:fit; ˋsɚfɪt] **I** *n*. (饮食)过度;过量;放纵;(饮食过度引起的)不适,恶心。**II** *vi*. 吃[喝]得太多(*of*; *on*; *upon*);放纵。—*vt*. 给…吃[喝]得太多,使胸中作恶;使沉溺于(*with*)。

sur·fi·cial [sə:ˈfiʃəl; sɚˋfɪʃəl] *a*.【地】地表的,地面的。

surf·y [ˈsə:fi; ˋsɚfɪ] *a*. 多碎浪的,浪花似的。

surg. = surgeon; surgery; surgical.

surge [sə:dʒ; sɚdʒ] **I** *n*. 大浪,波涛;波涛汹涌的大海;(人群、感情等的)汹涌,洋溢,起伏,高涨;〔诗〕海;【机】波动,浪涌,喘振;【电】电流急冲,电涌;【海】缆绳滑脱;急速松缆;(绞盘急速松缆的)锥形部。**II** *vi*. 起大浪,(人群、感情等)汹涌,高涨;蜂拥而来,迈进;【电】电涌;振荡,【海】缆绳滑脱;松缆。—*vt*.【海】急放(锚链,缆索等)。*a* ~ *current* 冲激电流。*surging crowds* 蜂拥而来的人群。

sur·geon [ˈsə:dʒən; ˋsɚdʒən] *n*. 外科医生;【军】军医;船医。~ **dentist** 牙医。~**fish**【动】刺尾鱼科鱼。~ **general**〔美〕军医总监(*Surgion-General's Department* 军医总监部);〔美〕公共卫生局医务长官。~**'s knot**【医】手术结,外科结。**-cy** *n*. 外科医生[军医]之职位[资格、职责等]。

sur·ger·y [ˈsə:dʒəri; ˋsɚdʒərɪ] *n*. **1**. 外科(学);外科手术。**2**. 外科手术[实验]室;〔英〕医院;诊所。*the clinical* ~ 临床外科。*the plastic* ~ 整形外科。

sur·gi·cal [ˈsə:dʒikəl; ˋsɚdʒɪkl̩] *a*. 外科的;外科医术的;外科用的,外科手术的。*a* ~ *operation* 外科手术。~ **strike**【军】外科手术式的打击,范围有限制的打击〔尤指用于政治目的之空袭〕。**-ly** *ad*. 用外科手术,在外科上。

surg·y [ˈsə:dʒi; ˋsɚdʒɪ] *a*. (*-i·er*; *-i·est*) 波涛汹涌的。

su·ri·cate [ˈsuriˌkeit; ˋsurɪˏket] *n*. 沼狸〔产于非洲南部〕。

Su·ri·nam [ˌsuəriˈnæm; ˏsurɪˋnɑm, -ˋnæm], **Su·ri·name** [ˌsuəriˈnɑ:mə; ˏsurɪˋnæmə] *n*. 苏里南〔拉丁美洲〕。

sur·lo·in [ˈsə:lɔin; ˋsɚˏlɔɪn] *n*. = sirloin.

sur·ly [ˈsə:li; ˋsɚlɪ] *a*. (*-li·er*; *-li·est*) 心眼儿坏的;粗暴的;脾气大的;险恶的(天气等)。**-li·ly** *ad*. **-li·ness** *n*.

sur·mis·a·ble [sə:ˈmaizəbl; sɚˋmaɪzəbl̩] *a*. 可推测的。

sur·mise I [ˈsə:maiz; sɚˋmaɪz, ˋsɚmaɪz] *n*. 推测,猜测;猜疑。**II** [sə:ˈmaiz, ˈsə:mis; sɚˋmaɪz, ˋsɚmɪs] *vt*. 推测,猜测。

sur·mount [sə:ˈmaunt; sɚˋmaunt] *vt*. 登上,越过;克服,打破(困难等);〔常用 p.p.〕顶上覆盖着,顶上戴着(*by*; *with*)。*a peak* ~*ed with snow* 顶上盖满白雪的峰顶。

sur·mount·a·ble [sə:ˈmauntəbl; sɚˋmauntəbl̩] *a*. 可登越的,可越过的;可克服的。

sur·mul·let [sə:ˈmʌlit; sɚˋmʌlɛt] *n*.【鱼】一种鲱鲤(= red mullet)。

sur·name [ˈsə:neim; ˋsɚˏnem] **I** *n*. 姓,氏;别号,别名,绰号。**II** *vt*. 加上姓[别号],用姓[别号]称呼。

sur·pass [sə:ˈpɑ:s; sɚˋpæs, -ˋpɑs] *vt*. 超过;优于,胜过。~ ***oneself*** 超越自我,取得前所未有的好成绩。

sur·pass·ing [sə:ˈpɑ:siŋ; sɚˋpæsɪŋ, -ˋpɑs-] *a*. 出人头地的,卓越的;极优越的。**-ly** *ad*.

sur·plice [ˈsə:pləs; ˋsɚplɪs] *n*.【宗】白色法衣。~**-fee**〔英〕(主持婚丧喜事的)牧师费。**-d** *a*. 穿白色法衣的。

sur·plus [ˈsə:pləs; ˋsɚplʌs] **I** *n*. 剩余,过剩;【会计】结余;【商】盈余;公职;〔美〕(特指政府为了维持价格而贮存的)剩余农产品。**II** *a*. 过剩的,多余的,剩余的。~ *food stamps*〔美〕剩余粮食购买券。~ *funds* 剩余基金。~ *labo(u)r* 剩余劳动力。~ **population** 过剩人口。~ **value**【经】剩余价值。~ **valve**【机】溢阀。

sur·plus·age [ˈsə:pləsidʒ; ˋsɚplʌsɪdʒ] *n*. 剩余,过剩;冗词;废话;【法】(诉状中不必要的或与案情无关的)枝节问题。

sur·plus·itis [sə:pləˈsaitis; sɚpləˋsaɪtɪs] *n*.〔美〕生产过剩病。

sur·print [ˈsə:ˌprint; ˋsɚˏprɪnt] *vt*., *n*.【印】添印,复印;【摄】(使)晒印过度。

sur·pris·al [səˈpraizəl; səˋpraɪzl̩] *n*.〔罕〕= surprise.

sur·prise [səˈpraiz; səˋpraɪz] **I** *vt*. **1**. 使吃惊,使惊奇,使觉得意外。**2**. 出其不意地袭击[捉住];突袭占领。**3**. 乘对方不备使其做某事[交待,承认],从其得到某信息等。**4**. 当场逮捕;忽然发现。*The news greatly* ~*d us*. 这消息使我们大为吃惊。*They* ~*d the burglar while he was still trying to open the safe*. 当窃犯还在设法开保险柜的时候,他们出其不意地把他捉住了。~ *a confession from sb*. 在某人不备时使其供认。~ *a witness into telling the truth* 使证人不知不觉中说出真实情况。*I should not be* ~*d if* ... [*to learn*] 即使…我也不会惊奇。*They* ~*d him in the act*. 他们冷不防地当场抓住了他。**II** *n*. **1**. 惊奇,吃惊。**2**. 可惊的事情,意外事情。**3**. 奇袭,偷袭。*His arrival was a great* ~. 他的到达真是个意外。*I have a* ~ *for you*. 我有一个意想不到的东西给你看[消息跟你讲]。***What a*** ~! 真想不到! ***be taken by*** ~ 冷不防竟被…吓一跳。***to my great*** ~ 使我非常惊奇的是。**III** *a*. 出乎意料的;令人惊奇的。*a* ~ *visit* 事先没有通知的访问。~ **muster**【军】紧急集合。~ **packet**〔英〕(如硬币夹心糖等的)有奖糖果袋,意想不到之物。~ **party** 奇袭队,令人惊奇的事。〔美〕各人自带食品突然到某朋友家里的聚会。~ **roll-call**【军】紧急点名。

S

sur·pris·ed·ly [səpˈraizdli; səpˋraɪzdlɪ] *ad*. 惊奇地,诧异地。

sur·pris·ing [səpˈraiziŋ; səˋpraɪzɪŋ] *a*. 可惊的,惊人的,意外的,奇怪的,不可思议的。**-ly** *ad*.

sur·prize [səˈpraiz; səˋpraɪz] *vt*., *n*. = surprise.

sur·qued·ous, -qui- [ˈsə:kwidəs; ˋsɚkwɪdəs] *a*. 傲慢的。

sur·que·dry, sur·quid·ry [ˈsə:kwidri; ˋsɚkwɪdrɪ]〔Scot.〕*n*. 傲慢。

surr. = surrender(ed); surrogate.

sur·ra [ˈsʌrə, ˈsu:rə; ˋsʌrə, ˋsurə] *n*. (牛马等的)恶性贫血症。

sur·re·al [səˈriəl; səˋriəl] *a*. 超现实的(= surrealistic)。

sur·re·al·ism [səˈriəlizəm; səˋriəlˏɪzm̩] *n*. 超现实主义。

sur·re·al·ist [səˈriəlist; səˋriəlɪst] *n*. 超现实主义者。**-ic** *a*. **-ical·ly** *ad*.

sur·re·but [sʌriˈbʌt; ˏsɚ·rɪˋbʌt] *vi*.【法】(原告)对被告第三次答辩进行驳斥。

sur·re·but·tal [ˌsə:riˈbʌtl; ˏsɚrɪˋbʌtl̩] *n*.【法】(原告对被告第三次辩驳)提出证据。

sur·re·but·ter [səriˈbʌtə; ˏsɚ·rɪˋbʌtɚ] *n*.【法】(原告的)第三次驳辩。

sur·re·join [sʌriˈdʒɔin; ˏsɚ·rɪˋdʒɔɪn] *vi*.【法】(原告)驳斥被告的第二次答辩。

sur·re·join·der [sʌriˈdʒɔində; ˏsɚ·rɪˋdʒɔɪndɚ] *n*.【法】(原告对被告的)第二次驳斥。

sur·ren·der [sə'rendə; sə`rɛndɚ] **I** *vt.* (被迫)交出,引渡;让渡;放弃;辞(职);(为退回一部分保险费)撤消(保险契约),退保;使…听摆布〔~ oneself〕;按官价供应(产品)。~ ***oneself to*** 向…投降;沉迷在,沉醉在,听任…摆布(~ *oneself to despair* 悲观绝望而不思自拔)。~ ***oneself to justice*** 向法院自首。—*vi.* 屈服,自首,投降;(要塞)陷落。~ *and confess ones crimes* 自首认罪。~ *at discretion* 无条件投降。~ ***to one's bail*** (犯人)交保期满后自动归押。**II** *n.* 让渡,交出;屈服,投降;让与;(保险的)解约;(生产单位)额定供应物品。~ ***of a fugitive*** 【国际法】逃犯的引渡。~ **value** (被保险人解除保险时)退保金额;当做废品处理的价钱。**-er** *n.*

sur·rep·ti·tious [ˌsʌrəp'tiʃəs; ˏsɝəp`tɪʃəs] *a.* 秘密的;偷偷的。*a ~ glance* 偷看。**-ly** *ad.* **-ness** *n.*

Sur·rey ['sʌri; `sɝɪ] *n.* 萨里[姓氏]。

sur·rey ['sʌri; `sɝɪ] *n.* 〔美〕双人四轮游览马车[汽车]。

sur·ro·gate I ['sʌrəgit; `sɝəgɪt] *n.* **1.** 代理人,代表,委员;〔英〕(宗教法庭上)主教代表。**2.** 〔美〕遗嘱检验法庭[法官]。**3.** 代用品,代替,代理 (*for*; *of*);代孕者〔指代人怀孕的母亲或精子捐赠者〕;【心】代用人物〔例如在感情上可代替自己的父母的人〕。**II** [-geit; -ˏget] *vt.* **1.** 代理。**2.** 【法】代替,代替…的地位。~ **mother** 代孕母亲。~ **parent** 代行职责家长〔指通常由社会名流担任的青少年精神指路人〕。

sur·round [sə'raund; sə`raʊnd] **I** *vt.* 围住,围绕,环绕;【军】包围。***be ~ed with*** [***by***] 被…环绕着。**II** *n.* 外围物;铺在地毯周围的东西;围猎。**~-sound** 〔英〕包围声〔具有包围收听者效果的一种高保真度放声〕。

sur·round·ing [sə'raundiŋ; sə`raʊndɪŋ] **I** *n.* 〔*pl.*〕周围的事物[情形],环境;附近。*picturesque ~s* 画一样美丽的环境。*social ~s* 社会环境。**II** *a.* 包围着的;周围的。*the ~ country* 附近,近郊。

sur·sum cor·da ['səːsəm'kɔːdə; `sɝsəm`kɔrdə] 〔L.〕鼓起勇气来,别气馁。

sur·tax ['səːtæks; `sɝˏtæks] *n.*, *vt.* (对…征收)附加税,(将…征收)超额累进所得税。

Sur·tees ['səːtiːz; `sɝtiz] *n.* 瑟蒂斯[姓氏]。

sur·ti·tle ['səːtaitl; `sɝtaɪtl] **I** *n.* (演出歌剧等时打出的)舞台上方字幕。**II** *vt.* 为(歌剧等)配字幕。

sur·tout ['səːtuː, səː'tuː; sɚ`tut, -`tu] *n.* 男用外套;女用有帽斗篷。

surv. = surveying; surveyor.

sur·veil·lance [səː'veiləns; sɚ`veləns, -`veljəns] *n.* 【法】监视,管制。***under ~*** 在管制[监视]下。

sur·veil·lant [səː'veilənt; sɚ`velənt, -`veljənt] *n.* 监视者;密探。

sur·vey I [səː'vei; sɚ`ve] *vt.* **1.** 眺望,俯瞰,环顾。**2.** 审视;通盘考虑[考察],观察(形势);概括,综合评述。**3.** 测量(土地),勘查,踏勘;检查,调查,鉴定。—*vi.* 测量(土地)。**II** ['səvei; `sɝve, sɚ`ve] *n.* **1.** 环顾。**2.** 概观;检查,鉴定书。**3.** 调查(表);调查所;测量;测量部;测量图。*a ~ of English literature* 英国文学概观。***make a ~ of*** 测量;考察;调查,检查。~ **course** (入门的)概论课。~ **line** 【测】测线。

sur·vey·ing [sə'veiiŋ; sɚ`veɪŋ] *n.* 测量(学、术),勘测。*a ~ reporter* 测量员。*a ~ ship* 测量舰。

sur·vey·or [səː'veiə; sɚ`veɚ] *n.* 测量员,勘测员,测地员;检查员;调查员;〔英〕(度量衡等的)检查官 (*of*);〔美〕(入口货的)检验官;鉴定人。~ **general** 总监督官;测量主任。~**'s level** (矿坑)测量水准器。~**'s measure** 测量长度[以链计算。一链 = 20.1168 米]。

sur·viv·a·ble [sə'vaivəbl; sɚ`vaɪvəbl] *a.* 可长存的,可存活的,不易破坏[损坏]的。**-a·bil·i·ty** *n.*

sur·viv·al [sə'vaivəl; sɚ`vaɪvl] *n.* 生存;残存;幸存;残存者;成活(植株);残余,残存物,遗物,遗风。*the ~ of the fittest* 适者生存。*philosophy of ~* 保命哲学。~ **guilt** 幸存者的内疚感。~ **kit** 救生包〔飞行员等用〕。**-ism** (恶劣环境下的)求生技能练习。

sur·vive [sə'vaiv; sɚ`vaɪv] *vt.* 在…之后还活着,比…长命;经受得住;得免于(难),从(灾难等)中得救;经历(灾难后)还活着。—*vi.* 还活着,活下去,未死;残存。*He ~d his wife.* 他比妻子活得久。*His mental faculties ~d his physical powers.* 他身体虽坏精神还好。*The custom still ~s.* 这个风俗还残留着。~ *one's usefulness* 虽已无所作为但还活着。*Only five of the crew ~d the shipwreck.* 在这次海难中只有五名船员幸免于死。~ *all perils* 历经万险而幸存。

sur·vi·vor [sə'raivə; sɚ`vaɪvɚ] *n.* **1.** (灾难中)未死的人,幸存者,残存者。**2.** 遗族;残存物,遗物。**3.** 〔经受住生活挫折如犯罪、破产等之后〕重新正常生活的人。**-ship** *n.* 未死,尚在,残存;【法】生存者对共有财产中死者所有部分的享有权。

Sus. = Sussex (shire).

sus- *pref.* 〔用于 c, p, t 前〕= sub-.

Su·sa ['suːsə; `susə] *n.* 古代波斯王朝设有夏宫的都市。

Su·san, Su·zan ['suːzn; `suzn̩, `sju-] *n.* 苏珊〔女子名,Susanna(h) 的昵称〕。

Su·san·na(h) [suː'zænə; su`zænə] *n.* 苏珊娜[女子名]。

sus·cep·tance [sə'septəns; sə`sɛptəns] *n.* 【电】电纳。

sus·cep·ti·bil·i·ty [səseptə'biliti; səˏsɛptə`bɪlətɪ] *n.* **1.** 感受性,易感性,敏感性 (*to*);敏感度,灵敏度;【医】感病性;感药性;〔*pl.*〕敏感之处,感情。**2.** 【物】磁化系数;磁化率。*wound* [*offend*] *sb.'s susceptibilities* 伤害某人的感情。

sus·cep·ti·ble [sə'septəbl; sə`sɛptəbl̩] *a.* **1.** 易感的,敏感的;易受影响的;易感染的,易害(某病)的 (*to*);多情善感的。**2.** 〔用作表语〕容许…的,能…的 (*of*)。*wood ~ of a high polish* 一擦就光亮的木材。***be ~ of*** (*proof*) 能(证明)的。***be ~ to*** 对…敏感,易感受…,易害…,易被…吸引的(*be ~ to cold* 容易伤风)。**-ti·bly** *ad.* **-ness** *n.*

sus·cep·tive [sə'septiv; sə`sɛptɪv] *a.* 易感的,敏感的 (*of*);易于接受(影响)的;许可…的,能…的 (*of*)。**-ness** *n.* **-tiv·i·ty** [ˌsʌsep'tiviti; ˏsʌsɛp`tɪvətɪ] *n.*

su·shi ['suːʃi; `suʃɪ] *n.* 〔Jap.〕生鱼片冷饭团。

Su·si ['suːsi; `susɪ] *n.* (东印度)丝十锦条纹棉布。

Su·sie, Su·sy ['suːzi; `suzɪ] *n.* 苏西〔女子名,Susan 的昵称〕。

sus·lik ['sʌslik; `sʌslɪk] *n.* 【动】**1.** 欧黄鼠 (*Gitellus citellus*)〔产于欧亚大陆北部和中部〕。**2.** 欧黄鼠皮。

sus·pect I [səs'pekt; sə`spɛkt] *vt.* **1.** 怀疑,觉得…可疑,觉得(人、约定等)靠不住。**2.** 猜疑。**3.** (有点)感觉到,(有点)知道,(有点)发觉(危险、阴谋等)。—*vi.* 有怀疑,怀疑,觉得可疑。~ *sb. of a crime* 怀疑某人犯了罪。*a ~ed case* 疑病患者。*I ~ he is ill.* 我感到他是病了。*You, I ~, don't care.* 我想,你不在乎罢[并不喜欢]。**II** ['sʌspekt; `sʌspɛkt] *n.* 嫌疑犯,被怀疑的人。**III** *a.* 〔用作表语〕可疑的。*The statement of an interested party is naturally ~.* 当事人的陈述是当然可疑的。

sus·pect·a·ble [səs'pektəbl; sə`spɛktəbl̩] *a.* 可(怀)疑的。

sus·pend [səs'pend; sə`spɛnd] *vt.* **1.** 吊起,悬挂。**2.** 停止;使停职,使停学;除名,开除。**3.** 使悬而未决;保留(承诺、判断等)。**4.** 中止,暂时停止,暂时作废。**5.** 【化】使悬浮(液中)。—*vi.* **1.** 暂停,中止。**2.** 悬空;悬宕;悬浮。**3.** 【商】无力支付,宣布破产。~ *a bird-cage from the ceiling* 把鸟笼吊在天花板上。~ *payment(s)* 停止支付。~ *a motor licence* 暂时吊销汽车执照。*~ed particles of dust* 悬浮的尘埃微粒。~**ed animation** 不省人事,假死。

sus·pend·er [səs'pendə; səs`pɛndɚ] *n.* 〔常 *pl.*〕吊杆,吊索;吊材;挂钩;挂篮;〔英〕吊袜带;〔美〕(裤子的)背带;【制革】吊鞣池。

sus·pense [səsˈpens; səˋspɛns] *n*. **1.** 悬挂,悬吊。**2.** 中止,暂停,停止。**3.** 悬而未决,含糊不定;悬虑;【法】权利停止。*hold one's judgement in* ~ 暂时不加判断。*keep* (*sb.*) *in* ~ 不告诉(某人)结果,让(人)悬虑不安。~ **account**【簿】悬账,暂记账。**-r** *n*.〔口〕悬念电影,惊醒电影。

sus·pense·ful [səˈspensfᴜl; səˋspɛnsfəl] *a*. **1.** 犹豫不决的。**2.** 焦急不安的。**3.** 热切的。**4.**〔罕〕(正当权益的)中止的。

sus·pen·si·ble [səsˈpensəbl; səˋspɛnsəbl] *a*. 可吊挂的,可悬浮的;可中止的;可以暂搁的。**-bil·i·ty** *n*.

sus·pen·sion [səsˈpenʃən; səˋspɛnʃən] *n*. **1.** 悬吊,悬挂;悬垂;悬架吊架。**2.** 中止,停止;停止支付[宣判,处刑];停职,停学,停权。**3.** 悬置,保留,未决。**4.**【化】悬浮(液);悬胶(体);【乐】悬留法;悬留音;【修】悬疑法〔以引起读者的好奇心,关心下文〕;【商】停止[无力]支付。~ *of arms* [*hostilities*] 停战。~ *of business* 停业。~ *of publication* 暂停刊行。~ **bridge** 悬桥,吊桥。~ **points**, ~**periods**【语】省略号[…]。~ **railway** 高架铁路。~ **switch** (电灯的)吊装开关。~ **transport** 悬浮搬运。

sus·pen·si·o per col·lum [səsˈpensiəupəːˈkɔləm; səsˋpɛnsɪopɚˋkɑləm]〔L.〕绞刑〔通常略作 ***sus. per coll.*** [ˈsʌspəːˈkɔl; ˋsʌspɚˋkɑl]〕。

sus·pen·sive [səsˈpensiv; səˋspɛnsɪv] *a*. **1.** 中止的,休止的,暂停的;有停止权的。**2.** 悬而未决的;悬念的;不安的。*a* ~ *novel* 情节紧张的小说。**-ly** *ad*.

sus·pen·soid [səsˈpensɔid; səˋspɛnsɔɪd] *n*.【化】悬胶(体)。

sus·pen·sor [səsˈpensə; səˋspɛnsɚ] *n*.【医】悬带,吊绷带;【植】胚柄,囊柄。

sus·pen·so·ry [səsˈpensəri; səˋspɛnsərɪ] **I** *a*. 悬吊的,悬挂的;中止的。**II** *n*. 悬吊物;【医】悬带;吊绷带;【解】悬肌。*a* ~ *bandage* 悬带。~ **ligament**【解】悬韧带〔尤指眼球水晶体悬韧带〕。

sus·per col(l). =〔L.〕*suspensio per collum* (= hanging by the neck)。

sus·pi·cion [səsˈpiʃən; səˋspɪʃən] **I** *n*. **1.** 怀疑,疑心,猜疑;嫌疑。**2.**〔口〕一点儿。*a* ~ *of arrogance* [*brandy*] 有点骄傲[白兰地味]。***above*** ~ 无可怀疑。***have a*** ~ ***of*** 具有少许…风味。***on*** (***the***) ~ ***of*** 因…的嫌疑。***under*** ~ 被怀疑,有嫌疑。***with*** ~ 怀疑,疑心。**II** *vt*.〔美俚〕怀疑。**-less** *a*. 不怀疑的。

sus·pi·cious [səsˈpiʃəs; səˋspɪʃəs] *a*. **1.** 可疑的。**2.** 多疑的,疑惧的;对…起疑心 (*of*; *about*)。*a* ~ *character* 可疑的人物。*a* ~ *nature* 多疑的天性。*There is something* ~ *about it*. 那有点儿可疑。**-ly** *ad*. **-ness** *n*.

sus·pi·ra·tion [ˌsʌspiˈreiʃən; ˏsʌspəˋreʃən] *n*.〔罕〕叹息,一声长叹。

sus·pire [səsˈpaiə; səˋspaɪr] *vi*.〔诗〕叹息。

Sus·sex [ˈsʌsiks; ˋsʌseks, -ɪks] *n*. **1.** 南萨克斯〔传说中英国古代一王国〕。**2.** 索赛克斯〔英国一郡〕。

sus·tain [səsˈtein; səˋsten] *vt*. **1.** 支撑,支持。**2.** 补养;维持;加强,鼓舞;使…持续;养(家)。**3.** 遭受;忍受,忍耐。**4.** 证明,证实;(法庭等)确认,承认,认可;准许。**5.** 能胜任;能扮演(角色),善于表演(性格)。**6.** 抵挡。*food sufficient to* ~ *life* 足够维持生活的食物。~ *a defeat* 吃败仗;受挫折。~ *an injury* 负伤。~ *a great loss* 蒙受重大损失。~ *comparison with another* 能和别人相比而无逊色。~ *the objection* 容纳异议。~ *one's rôle* 能扮演所担任的角色。*The sea wall* ~*s the shock of the waves*. 海堤能抵挡海浪的冲击。**-ment** *n*.

sus·tain·able [səˈteinəbl; səsˋtenəbl] *a*. 可支撑的,可持续的。~ **agriculture** 可持续发展的农业〔指增产不足靠破坏地力与环境等〕。~ **development** 可持续发展〔指在资源、环境等诸多方面能保证一个地区能长期发展而非竭泽而渔式的对资源、环境等进行掠夺式的开发〕。**Sus·tain·a·bil·i·ty** [səsˌteinəˈbiliti; səsˏtenəˋbɪlɪtɪ] *n*. (发展的)可持续性。

sus·tained [səsˈteind; səˋstend] *a*. 持续的;持久(不变)的;被支持的。*make* ~ *efforts* 再接再厉。~ *efforts* 持续不懈的努力。~ *flight* 稳定持久的飞行;【火箭】巡航飞行。~ *note*【物】持续音[符]。~ **yield** (木材等可再生资源之)持续产量。

sus·tain·er [səsˈteinə; səsˋtenɚ] *n*. 支持者;维持者;持续者;【火箭】主级发动机;〔美〕= sustaining program(me).

sus·tain·ing [səsˈteiniŋ; səˋstenɪŋ] *a*. 支持的;持续的,持久的,维持着的;补身的,滋补的,增加气力的(食物等);赞助的。~ **pedal** (钢琴的)延音踏板。~ **power**【机】持久力。~ **program(me)**〔美〕(电台、电视台)非营业性独立节目。

sus·te·nance [ˈsʌstinəns; ˋsʌstənəns] *n*. **1.** 食物,粮食,给养;营养;生计;支持(物)。**2.** 维持,持久,耐久。*How shall we get* ~? 我们怎样维持生活呢? *There is no* ~ *in it*. 这里面没有营养。

sus·ten·tac·u·lum [ˌsʌstenˈtækjuləm; ˏsʌstɛnˋtækjələm] *n*. (*pl*. **-la** [-lə; -lə])【解】支持性组织。**-tac·u·lar** *a*.

sus·ten·ta·tion [sʌstenˈteiʃən; ˏsʌstɛnˋteʃən] *n*. 支持(物);维持;供养;扶养,生活的维持;粮食,食物。~ **fund** (基督教会为接济教士所设的)资助基金。

sus·ten·ta·tive [ˈsʌstenteitiv, səsˈtentətiv; ˋsʌstɛnˏtetɪv, səˋstɛntətɪv] **I** *a*. 支持的;受到支持的;维持的,保存的。**II** *n*. 支持物,维持物。

sus·ten·tion [səˈstenʃən; səˋstɛnʃən] *n*. 支撑,被支撑;维持,得到维持。

Su·su [suːˈsuː; suˋsu] *n*. **1.** (*pl*. ***Su·su(s)***) 苏苏人〔一西非游牧部族,分布在几内亚等地〕。**2.** 苏苏语。

su·sur·rant [suˈsəːrənt; sjuˋsɝənt] *a*. 耳语的,喃喃低语的,窸窣作响的(= susurrous)。

su·sur·rate [suˈsəːreit; sjuˋsɝet] *vi*. 耳语,喃喃低语,沙沙作响,窸窣作响。**-ra·tion** *n*.

su·sur·rus [suˈsəːrəs; sjuˋsɝəs] *n*. **1.** 低语声,喃喃低语声,窃窃私语声。**2.** 沙声,沙沙声淙淙,潺潺声。

sut·ler [ˈsʌtlə; ˋsʌtlɚ] *n*. 随军酒食小贩。

Su·tra [ˈsuːtrə; ˋsutrə] *n*.〔Sans.〕(婆罗门教,佛教等的)箴言(集);经文,经典;(佛教的)修多罗经(= Sutta)。

sut·tee [ˈsʌtiː, sʌˈtiː; sʌˋti, ˋsʌti] *n*.〔Sans.〕殉夫自焚的寡妇;殉节风俗。**-ism** *n*. 殉节风俗。

sut·tle [ˈsʌtl; ˋsʌtl̩] *n*.【商】净重。

su·tur·al [ˈsjuːtʃərəl; ˋsutʃərəl, ˋsju-] *a*.【医】缝合的,位于接缝处的。

su·ture [ˈsjuːtʃə; ˋsutʃɚ, ˋsju-] **I** *n*.【医】缝合(术);缝线;【植、动】接缝;【解】缝,骨缝。**II** *vt*. 缝合,缝拢,连接。**-ra·tion** *n*.

SUV = sport-utility vehicle 多用途(箱式)跑车。

Su·va [ˈsuːvə; ˋsuvə] *n*. 苏瓦〔斐济首都〕。

Su·zann(e) [suːˈzæn; ˋsuzæn] *n*. 苏珊〔女子名, Susan 的异体〕。

su·ze·rain [ˈsjuːzərein; ˋsuzərɪn, -ˏren, ˋsju-] **I** *n*. 宗主国;【史】封建主,藩王。**II** *a*. 有宗主权的。

su·ze·rain·ty [ˈsjuːzəreinti; ˋsuzərɪntɪ, -ˏren-, ˋsju-] *n*. 宗主权;封建主的权力[地位]。

SV = **1.**〔L.〕*Sancta Virgo*【基督】圣母(= Holy Virgin)。**2.** sailing vessel 帆船。**3.** surface vessel 水面舰船。**4.** stop valve【机】断流阀,停汽阀,节流阀。**5.** sluice valve【机】闸水阀。**6.** safety valve 安全阀。

S.V. = **1.**〔L.〕*Sanctitas Vestra* (= Your Holiness) 陛下(对罗马教皇的尊称)。**2.** *Sons of Veterans* 退伍军人子弟会。**3.** specific volume【物】比容。

s.v. =〔L.〕*sub voce* [*sub verbo*] (字典等中表示参看的用语)参看在,词条,在某词下(= *under the word*)。

S

Sva·raj [svaːˈraːdʒ; svaˋradʒ] ***n.*** =swaraj.

SVD =swine vesicular disease【兽医】猪水疱病。

svelte [svelt; svɛlt] ***a.*** 〔F.〕细长的,身材苗条的,文雅的,柔和的;(指美术作品)线条明快的,流畅的。

S.W., SW, s.w. =southwest; southwestern.

swab [swɔb; swab] **I** ***n.*** **1.** (擦洗甲板等用的)拖把,拖帚,墩布;枪炮刷,炮帚。**2.** 〔俚〕海军军官的肩章;〔海俚〕粗人,蠢货。**3.** 〔美俚〕(商船上的)水手。**4.**【医】(裹有药棉用以擦洗、敷药等的)拭子,药签;用拭子取下的化验标本。**II** ***vt.*** (***-bb-***) 擦抹,揩拭 (*up*);(拿拖帚等)擦洗 (*down*);抹药。~ (***down***) ***the decks*** 用拖帚擦甲板。~ ***up*** 用拖帚把水拖干。~ ***down*** 擦洗甲板;洗澡。~ **downs** (海员的)肩饰。

swab·ber [ˈswɔbə; ˋswabɚ] ***n.*** **1.** 使用墩布拖擦的人;墩布。**2.** 〔俚〕粗人,蠢材。**3.** 水手;装管工。

swab·bie, swab·by [ˈswaːbi; ˋswabɪ] ***n.*** 〔俚〕水手;〔美俚〕美海军兵士〔常用作称呼〕。

swacked [swækt; swækt] ***a.*** 〔俚〕醉迷糊的,醉醉的。

swad·dle [ˈswɔdl; ˋswadl] **I** ***vt.*** **1.** (尤指用被包、襁褓等)包裹,包缠。**2.** 束缚,限制。***swaddling bands*** [***clothes***] 被包,襁褓;〔喻〕束缚自由的东西(*still in* [*hardly out of*] *swaddling clothes* 还在襁褓中,还是一个没解包的孩子)。**II** ***n.*** 襁褓。

Swa·de·shi [swaːˈdeiʃi; swəˋdeʃɪ] ***n.*** 〔印〕抵制英[外]货运动。

S.W.Afr. =South-West Africa 西南非洲。

swag [swæg; swæg] **I** ***n.*** **1.** 摇晃,倾侧。**2.** 〔俚〕掠夺来的物品,赃物;用不正当手段得来的东西。**3.** 〔澳〕(流动工人、流浪者的)背包。**4.** 悬垂的花枝[花环];【建】垂花饰;水潭,洼地。**II** ***vi.*** (***-gg-***) **1.** 摇晃,倾侧。**2.** 〔澳〕背着背包旅行。**3.** 垂下,沉下。

swage [sweidʒ; swedʒ] **I** ***n.***【机】(锻工用)陷型模,铁模。**II** ***vt.*** 型锻;(用陷型模)使成形。~ **block**【机】型砧。

swag·ger [ˈswægə; ˋswægɚ] **I** ***vi.*** 大摇大摆地走 (*about*; *in*; *out*);摆架子,装模作样;傲慢;吹牛,说大话 (*about*)。—***vt.*** 吹牛恫吓。*strut and* ~装腔作势。~ *sb. into concession* 说大话吓人让步。**II** ***n.*** 昂首阔步;摆架子;傲慢态度。**III** ***a.*** 〔口〕漂亮的,(衣服等)时髦的。~ **cane** 〔英〕轻便手杖。~ **coat** 宽式女短大衣。~ **stick** (军官用的)轻便手杖。**-er** ***n.*** 昂首阔步的人;狂妄自大的人;吹牛者。

swag·ger·ing·ly [ˈswægəriŋli; ˋswægərɪŋlɪ] ***ad.*** 架子十足地,傲慢地,大摇大摆地。

swag·man [ˈswægmən; ˋswægmən] ***n.*** 〔澳口〕无业游民,〔美俚〕收买贼赃的人。

Swa·hi·li [swaːˈhiːli; swaˋhilɪ] ***n.*** **1.** (*pl.* ***-lis***, ***-li***) (东非的)斯瓦希里人。**2.** 斯瓦希里语。

swain [swein; swen] ***n.*** 乡下的年轻人;(牧歌中的)乡下情郎;〔谑〕情人,求婚者;崇拜者。

swain·ish [ˈsweiniʃ; ˋswenɪʃ] ***a.*** 〔诗或古〕**1.** 乡村少年的。**2.** 乡村情郎的。**3.** 情人的。**-ness** ***n.***

S.W.A.K., SWAK, swak = sealed with a kiss 一吻而封〔爱人、小孩等的信封用语〕。

swale [sweil; swel] **I** ***vt., vi.*** 〔方〕放火烧(树林等);(使)被烧光;(使)(蜡烛)烧完。**II** ***n.*** 〔英方、美〕沼地,洼地;滩槽。

swal·low[1] [ˈswɔləu; ˋswalo] ***n.***【鸟】燕子。*One* ~ *does not make a summer*. 一只燕子不成夏天,不可光凭偶然现象就下断语。~ *dive* 燕式跳水。~ *coat* 燕尾服。~*'s nest* 燕子的窝;燕窝;高处的东西;高地炮兵阵地,高地射击队[便衣队]。~**tail** ***n.*** **1.** 燕尾;〔口〕燕尾服。**2.** 燕尾旗的末端;【动】凤蝶;燕尾鸢;【木工】燕尾榫,鸽尾榫;【筑城】燕尾外障,(炮台外面的)燕尾形外堡;有倒钩的箭头。~**-tailed** ***a.*** 燕尾形的。

swal·low[2] [ˈswɔləu; ˋswalo] **I** ***vt.*** **1.** 吞,咽 (*down*; *up*; *in*)。**2.** 轻信,囫囵吞枣地不加考虑。**3.** 淹没 (*up*)。**4.** 忍耐,忍受(侮辱)。**5.** 收回(前言)。**6.** 耗尽,用尽,消尽。—***vi.*** 吞,咽。*Such stories are rather hard to* ~. 这种故事很难相信。~ *hook, line, and sinker* 〔美俚〕轻信。*The expenses* ~ *up most of the profits*. 花费大而利润少。~ ***a camel*** 吞下骆驼〔隐忍无法无天的事情等〕。~ ***one's teeth*** 〔美〕, ~ ***one's words*** 收回前言,认错道歉。~ ***the anchor*** 永远脱离航海生活;〔美俚〕离开美国海军。~ ***the bait*** 上钩,上当。~ ***up*** 吞下去;卷进去;耗尽。**II** ***n.*** **1.** 吞咽;一咽,一吞。**2.** 胃管,食道;咽喉,喉咙。**3.** 吸孔。**4.**【海】(滑车等的)通索孔。***at one*** ~ 一口就。***have a small*** ~食道狭窄。***take a*** ~ ***of*** 吞[喝]一口。~ **hole** 〔地〕灰岩坑。**-able** ***a.*** 可吞食的。

swal·low·er [ˈswɔləuə; ˋswaloɚ] ***n.*** 吞咽者;贪吃的人。

swal·low·wort [ˈswɔləuˌwəːt; ˋswaloˏwɝt] ***n.***【植】**1.** 白屈菜。**2.** 牛皮消属植物,药用白前〔(*Cynanchum nigrum*),产于美国东部〕。

swam [swæm; swæm] swim 的过去式。

swamp [swɔmp; swamp] **I** ***n.*** 沼泽,沼地,湿地;【矿】煤层聚水洼。**II** ***vt.*** 陷入沼泽;淹没,使浸在水中;使(小舟)沉没,使翻掉;使吃苦头,糟蹋;使陷入困难(不得脱身)。—***vi.*** 满;沉没,翻掉;吃苦头,糟蹋掉。***be*** ~***ed with*** (*invitations*) 忙于(种种应酬)。~ *boat* 浅水平底船。~ **buggy** 〔军口〕水陆坦克;水陆两用平底军车;螺旋桨平底快艇。~ **fever**【医】疟疾。~ **land** 沼泽地。~ **glider** =~ boat. ~ **seed** 〔美俚〕稻米。

swamp·er [ˈswɔːmpə; ˋswampɚ] ***n.*** **1.** 沼泽地居民。**2.** 帮手;清洁工。**3.** 〔美俚〕卡车司机的帮手,搬运工。

swamp·ish [ˈswɔːmpiʃ; ˋswampɪʃ] ***a.*** 沼泽地似的,沼泽似的。

swamp·root [ˈswɔmprəut; ˋswamprot] ***n.*** 〔美〕威士忌酒。

swamp·y [ˈswɔmpi; ˋswampɪ, ˋswɔmpɪ] ***a.*** (***-i·er***; ***-i·est***) 沼泽的;多沼泽的;潮湿的。

swan[1] [swɔn; swan] ***n.*** **1.**【鸟】天鹅。**2.** (杰出的)歌手,诗人;〔S-〕【天】天鹅座。*a black* ~(澳洲产)黑天鹅;珍品。~ **dive** 〔美〕=swallow dive. ~**herd** 天鹅饲养者。~**'s-down** 天鹅绒;起毛厚软呢。~**'s neck** 天鹅颈形曲线,浅S形曲线〔用于装饰〕。~ **shot** 打天鹅等用的巨弹。~**skin** 天鹅皮;厚密法兰绒。~ **song** 传说中天鹅临终时的美妙歌声;最后的诗[乐曲],绝笔,最后的功业。~**-upping** ***n.*** 〔英〕天鹅嘴上刻标记〔在捕获的小天鹅嘴上刻画记号作为捕获人的标记〕。

swan[2] [swɔn; swan] ***vi.*** **1.** 闲逛,随意旅行。**2.** (车辆等)蜿蜒行驶。

swan[3] [swɔn; swan] ***vi.*** 〔方、美俚〕发誓。***I*** ~! 老天!〔表示吃惊、着急等〕。

swang [swæŋ; swæŋ] 〔古、方〕swing[1]的过去式。

swank [swæŋk; swæŋk] **I** ***n.*** **1.** 〔口〕炫耀(服饰);虚张声势;摆排场;夸嘴,吹牛。**2.** 优雅;漂亮。**II** ***vi.*** 吹牛,炫耀。**III** ***a.*** =swanky.

swank·er [ˈswænkə; ˋswænkɚ] ***n.*** 〔主英〕说大话的人;摆排场的人。

swank·y [ˈswæŋk; ˋswæŋk] ***a.*** (***-i·er***; ***-i·est***) 〔口〕虚夸的,吹牛的,自大的;爱出风头的;时髦的。**-i·ly** ***ad.*** **-i·ness** ***n.***

swan·ner·y [ˈswɔnəri; ˋswanərɪ] ***n.*** 天鹅饲养所。

Swan·sea [ˈswɔnzi; ˋswansɪ, -zɪ] ***n.*** 斯旺西〔英国港市〕。

Swan·son [ˈswɔnsn; ˋswansn̩] ***n.*** 斯旺森〔姓氏〕。

swap [swɔp; swap, swɔp] ***vt., vi., n.*** =swop. ~ **credits** (股票市场中的)互惠信贷。~ **meet** (交换物品的)集市,易货市场。

swap·per [ˈswɔpə; ˋswapɚ] ***n.*** (物物)交换者;以货易货者;集市交易者。

swa·raj [swəˈraːdʒ; swəˋradʒ] ***n.*** 〔印地〕**1.** 自治,独立。**2.** 〔S-〕(英国殖民统治时期争取自治的)印度自治党。**-ist** ***n.*** 印度自治党人,主张印度自治者。

sward [swɔːd; swɔrd] **I** ***n.*** 草地;草皮。**II** ***vt., vi.*** (给…)铺上草皮。

sware [swɛə; swɛr]〔古〕swear 的过去式。

swarm[1] [swɔːm; swɔrm] **I** ***n*.** **1.** (昆虫的)群,蜂群;【生】浮游单细胞(生物)群,游走孢子。**2.** 大群;大堆。*a ~ of sightseers* 大群游客。*a ~ of letters* 一大堆信。***in ~s*** = ***in a ~*** 成群;大批。**II** ***vi*.** **1.** 蜂拥成群(而去);(蜜蜂)成群离巢,分群;【生】(细胞等)成群裂出[浮游]。**2.** 密集;群集;被挤满;充满。**3.** 攀缘,攀登。*The garden ~s with bees*. 花园里有许多蜜蜂飞来飞去。*The mosquitoes ~ed about us*. 蚊子成群地环绕着我们。*People ~ed into the cinema*. 人们蜂拥而进入电影院。*The swamp ~s with mosquitoes and other insects*. 沼泽地到处都有蚊子和小昆虫。—***vt*.** **1.** 攀缘。**2.** 挤满。*~ (up) a rope* 攀缘绳索。*be ~ed with (rats)* 充满着(老鼠)。~ **spore**【生】游动孢子。~ **theory**【物】(液晶)攒动说。**-ing**【虫】婚飞;分群;群游。

swarm[2] [swɔːm; swɔrm] ***vi*., *vt*.** (抱着)爬(树等)。

swarm·er [ˈswɔːmə; ˋswɔrmɚ] ***n*.** **1.**【动】蜂涌子,蜂群。**2.** 一大群。**3.** 云集者。

swart [swɔːt; swɔrt] ***a*.**〔古〕= swarthy.

swarth [swɔːθ; swɔrθ] **I** ***n*.**〔方〕= sward. **II** ***a*.** = sworth.

swarth·y [ˈswɔːði; ˋswɔrðɪ, -θɪ] ***a*.** (脸)黑黝黝的;晒黑了的;黝暗的。**-i·ly** ***ad*.** **-i·ness** ***n*.**

swash [swɔʃ; swɑʃ] **I** ***n*.** **1.** (水的)泼散,激溅,冲刷;奔流声;哗啦哗啦[水声];冲击。**2.** 虚张声势。**3.** 猪饲料。**4.** 湍急的流水;(河口)浅滩;〔美〕为海潮冲刷的沙洲。**II** ***vi*.** 泼散(水),(浪)冲激,发出哗啦哗啦的声音;奔流;虚夸;虚张声势;寻衅闹事;恃强凌弱;摆空架子(*with*);猛击。—***vt*.** 晃动(水等);洗,拨(水)。*a ~ing blow* 痛击。~**buckler** ***n*.** 虚张声势;寻衅滋事的人;暴徒,流氓。~**-buckling**, ~**bucklering** ***n*., *a*.** 虚张声势(的);寻衅滋事(的),恃强凌弱(的)。~ **buckle head** (船的)缓冲舱壁。~ **letter** 花饰斜体(大写)字母。~ **plate**【机】旋转斜盘。

swas·ti·ka, swas·ti·ca [ˈswɔstikə, ˈswæs-; ˋswɑstɪkə, ˋswæs-] ***n*.** **1.** 万字饰,卍字饰(相传为象征太阳、吉祥等的标志)。**2.** 卐字〔德国纳粹党党徽〕。

SWAT, S.W.A.T. = Special Weapons Attack Team 特种警察突击队〔接受过使用特种武器训练的军事警察部队〕。

swat [swɔt; swɑt] ***n*., *vt*.**〔美口〕拍,打(蝇等);猛击。~ **fest**〔美俚〕不高明的高尔夫球赛;激烈的拳击比赛;【棒球】击球后上垒次数多的比赛。

swatch [swɔtʃ; swɑtʃ] ***n*.** (小块)布样,皮样,样片,样品;一小束,一小簇。~**-book** 样品本。

swath [swɔːθ; swɑθ, swɔθ] ***n*.** (*pl*. *~s*) 割下的一行草[麦];(一镰刀的)刈幅;(镰刀的)一挥;(刈后的)一条刈迹;一行。***cut a (wide) ~***〔美〕夸耀;自以为了不起。~ **harvesting** 分段收割。

swathe [sweið; sweð] **I** ***n*.** 包扎绷带,包布。**II** ***vt*.** 绑,缠裹;包围,封住。

swa·ther [ˈswɔːθə; ˋswɔθɚ] ***n*.** 割谷机。

swat·ter [ˈswɔtə; ˋswɑtɚ] ***n*.** (蝇)拍(= fly ~);拍打者。

sway [swei; swe] **I** ***vi*.** **1.** 摇摆,摇动,动摇;歪,倾斜,偏向一边;转向。**2.** 有权力,占支配地位,得势;统治。—***vt*.** **1.** 摇,摇动,使动摇;弄歪,使倾斜;使偏向一边。**2.** 支配,操纵,统治。**3.** 挥(剑);【海】扯起(帆桁)(*up*)。*Branches ~ in the wind*. 树枝在风里摇晃。*He is not ~ed by arguments*. 他不为议论所动。*~ the scepter* 挥舞权杖,掌握大权。*~ the realm* 统治[独霸]一方。**II** ***n*.** **1.** 摇动;动摇;倾斜,偏向,偏重;(武器等的)挥舞。**2.** 权势,势力;影响;统治。*one's complete ~* 独霸。***hold [bear] ~*** 掌握全权,有支配…的力量(*over*)。***own love's ~*** 自认被爱情所支配。***under the ~ of*** 受着…的支配,在…的支配下。~**back** ***n*.** (马的)特别下凹的背部。~**backed** ***a*.** 背部特凹的(马)。~ **bar**〔美〕(汽车的)防倾侧杆。**-er** ***n*.**

Swa·zi [ˈswɑːziː; ˋswɑzɪ] ***n*.** (*pl*. ***Swa·zis***, ***Swa·zi***) **1.** (非洲东南部的)斯威士人。**2.** 斯威士语。

Swa·zi·land [ˈswɑːzilænd; ˋswɑzɪˏlænd] ***n*.** 斯威士兰〔非洲〕。

SWbS, SW by S = southwest by south 西南偏南。

SWbW, SW by W = southwest by west 西南偏西。

swc = special weapons center〔美〕特种武器中心。

sweal [sweil; swil] = swale.

swear [swɛə; swɛr] (***swore*** [swɔː; swor, swɔr],〔古〕***sware*** [swɛə; swɛr]; ***sworn*** [swɔːn; sworn, swɔrn]) **I** ***vi*.** **1.** 立誓,发誓,宣誓(*by*; *on*; *upon*);〔口〕断言。**2.** 咒骂,臭骂(*at*)。—***vt*.** 立誓,起誓,发誓;〔口〕郑重申言,断言;使宣誓。*I'll be sworn*.〔口〕一定的。***not enough to ~ by*** 真正一点点。***~ a charge [an accusation] against*** 发誓控告[弹劾](某人)。***~ an oath*** 发誓;大骂。***~ at*** 臭骂;〔俚〕(颜色)和…完全不调和。***~ before*** = ***~ by*** 对…发誓;〔口〕非常信赖(*He ~s by his doctor*. 他极信任他的医生)。***~ black is white*** 颠倒黑白;强辩。***~ by the name of*** 拿…的名字来发誓。***~ for*** 保证,担保。***~ in*** 使宣誓就职。***~ like a pirate [trooper]*** 大骂。***~ off***〔口〕发誓戒(酒等),发誓不再。***~ on one's sword [the Bible]*** 指着剑[把手搁在圣经上]发誓。***~ out***〔美〕通过发誓而获得(对被告的拘捕证)。***~ the peace against sb*.** 发誓控告某人要杀害他。***~ (to)*** 保证(*I believe that is true, but I can't ~ (to) it*. 我想那是真的然而我不能绝对肯定)。***~ to oneself*** 暗自发誓。**II** ***n*.**〔口语〕誓言;发誓,宣誓;咒骂;骂人话。*hard ~s* 伪证,伪誓。~ **word** 咒骂;骂人话;宣誓;怒骂。**-er** ***n*.** **-ing** ***n*.** 发誓。

sweat [swet; swɛt] **I** ***n*.** **1.** 汗;出汗。**2.** 水气,气汗。**3.**〔口〕吃力的工作;苦差;〔口〕不安,焦急;赶紧;【赛马】赛前练跑;〔俚〕兵。*cold ~* 冷汗。*night(ly) ~s* 盗汗。*They will not take the ~*. 他们是不肯出力的。*Compiling a dictionary is an awful ~*. 编字典是一种吃力的苦工。*an old ~* 老兵;老手。***all of a ~*** = in a ~. ***be running [dripping] ~*** 流着大汗。***by [in] the ~ of one's brow [face]*** 额上出着汗,靠自己辛勤劳动。***cannot stand the ~ of it*** 受不了那个辛苦。***in a cold ~*** 捏一把冷汗;提心吊胆地。***no ~***〔美俚〕没有麻烦,没问题;好办。***in a ~*** 流着大汗;担着心,着急地;赶紧。**II** (*~ed*, ***sweat***) ***vi*.** **1.** 出汗;结露水;(烟草等)发酵,发汗。**2.** 流着汗工作;努力;累得流汗;被剥削。**3.** 不安;焦虑,烦恼。—***vt*.** **1.** 使出汗;〔口〕被汗弄脏,弄得尽是汗;使流出,使排出。**2.** (在苛刻的条件下)残酷剥削,吸(人)血汗,榨取(劳力、金钱)。**3.** 使(烟叶、皮等)发酵;把(汗)揩干,把(湿气)弄干。**4.** 把(金银硬币)放在袋里摩擦以收集(金银粉末);【冶】加热提炼;热析,熔焊。**5.**〔俚〕勒索;〔美俚〕拷问。*~ at night* 出盗汗。*The doctor ~s his patient*. 医生使病人发汗。*~ed clothes* 用极低工价制成的衣服。*~ed labo(u)r* 被残酷剥削的劳动,血汗劳动。*He shall ~ for it*. 他要后悔的。***~ away at one's job*** 努力工作。***~ down***〔美俚〕大大压缩。***~ it*** 感到烦恼。***~ it out***〔美〕束手无策地[紧张地、流着汗地]等待或忍受(到最后)。***~ like a trooper***〔美〕汗流得浑身都是,汗流浃背。***~ off*** = ***~ out*** 发汗祛除[如医治感冒,减轻体重];〔美俚〕辛苦地支持到最后,忍受到最后。***~ the game***〔美〕干着急地旁观胜负。***~ with fear*** 吓得出冷汗。~**band** (帽子的)防汗衬圈。~**-bath** 蒸汽浴。~ **blood**〔美〕极度紧张的劳动[焦急心情]。~**box** 监狱中的单独牢房,烟叶[生皮]发酵槽;〔美俚〕拷问;〔学生语〕考场。~**-duct [gland]** 汗腺。~ **equity**〔美〕血汗股权〔房客等因对房屋修缮所作的服务而获得的对该房屋的部份股权〕。~**ing system** (残酷剥削人的)血汗工资制。~ **pants** 运动长裤。~ **shirt** = T-~长袖无领衫。~**shop** 血汗工厂〔残酷剥削工人的工厂〕。~ **suit** 运动服。

S

sweat·er [ˈswetə; ˋswɛtɚ] ***n*.** **1.** 出汗(过多)的人[物]; 发汗剂;发汗[发酵]器。**2.** 血汗工人;榨取工人血汗的雇主,包工工头,裁缝包工头。**3.** 厚运动衫;圆领绒衣或毛衣。**4.**【化】石蜡发汗室;(烟叶、生皮等的)发汗器。**5.** 〔美〕在远离牧场办事处的小屋找饭吃的外路人。

sweat·y [ˈsweti; ˋswɛtɪ] ***a*.** (*-i·er*; *-i·est*) **1.** 尽是汗的,汗湿透的;发汗臭的。**2.** 汗似的。**3.** 流汗的,辛苦的,吃力的。**-i·ly** ***ad*.** **-i·ness** ***n*.**

Swed. = Sweden, Swedish.

Swede [swiːd; swid] ***n*.** **1.** 瑞典人。**2.** 〔~, s-〕〔英〕= rutabaga.【植】芜菁甘蓝,瑞典芜菁,芸苔。

Swe·den [ˈswiːdn; ˋswidn] ***n*.** 瑞典〔欧洲〕。

Swe·den·bor·gi·an [ˌswiːdnˈbɔːdʒiən, -gi-; ˏswidnˋbɔrdʒɪən, -gɪ-] **I** ***n*.** 斯韦登博格〔瑞典神秘主义宗教家,自称能与鬼魂交往〕信徒,〔尤指〕新耶路撒冷教会教徒。**II** ***a*.** 斯韦登博格的;斯韦登博格教义的;斯韦登博格信徒的。**-ism, -borg·ism** [-ˌbɔːg-; -bɔrg-] ***n*.**

Swed·ish [ˈswiːdiʃ; ˋswidɪʃ] **I** ***a*.** 瑞典(式)的;瑞典人[语]的。**II** ***n*.** 瑞典语;〔the ~〕〔集合词〕瑞典人。~ **massage**【医】瑞典式按摩(疗法)。~ **movements**【医】瑞典式按摩手法。~ **turnip**【植】= **rutabaga** 芜菁甘蓝,瑞典芜菁,芸苔。

swee·ny [ˈswiːni; ˋswinɪ] ***n*.** 〔美〕(特指马肩的)肌肉萎缩(症);傲慢。

sweep [swiːp; swip] **I** ***vt*.** (*swept* [swept; swɛpt]) **1.** 扫(房间等),扫除,打扫;刷,掸(灰尘等)。**2.** (像扫一样)吹去,刮去,冲去(*along*; *away*; *down*; *off*);完全消灭,把…一扫而光,疏浚(河底);拉(网等);【军】扫射;扫(雷);扫荡;肃清,消灭。**3.** 完全胜过。**4.** 扫过,擦过,掠过;拖过;〔主诗〕用手指弹(乐器)。**5.** 四下眺望,周览,环视,扫视;【电视】扫描。**6.** 描绘…的轮廓。**7.**【铸造】刮(模型)。—***vi*.** **1.** 用扫帚扫;拿刷子刷;打扫。**2.** 掠过,扫过;扫视;飞快地滑过;吹去,刮去;飞来,袭来。**3.** 衣裙曳地地走;大摇大摆地通过。**4.**【军】扫荡;扫射;扫雷;(飞机、军舰等)长驱直入;游弋。**5.** 延伸。**6.** (鲸鱼等)摇尾巴。*A new broom ~s clean*. 新笤帚扫得干净,新官上任三把火。~ *a constituency* 独占选举区内多数选票(取得全胜)。*be swept along in the crowd* 被人群推动着往前走。*be swept off one's feet* 被(波浪)冲击而站不住脚,被感情所支配不由自主。~ ***across the length and breadth of the country*** 席卷全国。~ ***away*** 扫清;迅速消灭,肃清;冲走。~ ***everything*** [***the enemy***] ***before*** (***one***) 以破竹之势前进,摧枯拉朽地扫荡敌人。~ ***off*** 扫清;(疫疠等)杀死(不少人);吹走。~ ***one's audience along with one*** (演讲人)紧紧抓牢听众心理。~ ***over*** 风靡;向…扩展;眺望,环视;袭击;狂刮;将…一扫而光。~ ***the board*** 扫盘子[赢得全部赌注];〔喻〕独占鳌头。~ ***the deck*** (波浪)冲洗甲板;扫射甲板。~ ***the seas*** 在海上横冲直撞;扫海;扫荡海上敌人。**II** ***n*.** **1.** 打扫,扫除。**2.** (风的)刮,吹,扫掠,(水的)冲刷;(波浪的)冲激;【军】扫荡;扫射;扫雷;(飞机,军舰等)游弋;长驱直入;肃清,清除;(手等的)一挥;〔喻〕迅速进步[发展]。**3.** (土地的)延伸,扩张;区域,范围;眺望,环视;天体观测;【电视】扫描。**4.** 弯曲;弯路;弯流;偏差。**5.** 大胜(指选举等)。**6.** 清扫员;(特指)扫烟囱工人(= chimney ~);〔俚〕不干净的人,卑劣的人,讨厌的人。**7.**【海】船侧弯曲部;扫海索;长桨;【火箭】后掠翼行,箭形。**8.** (桔槔的)秤杆。**9.** 〔*pl*.〕机枪队。**10.** 〔常 *pl*.〕〔口〕= sweepstakes. **11.** 〔常 *pl*.〕扫集物(= sweepings)。*a ~ of mountain country* 山国风光一瞥。*as black as a ~* (像扫烟囱的人一样)漆黑的,脏的。*a regular little ~* 肮脏的孩子。*You dirty ~!* 你这坏蛋! ***at one ~*** 一举[挥,扫]。***beyond the ~ of*** 达不到的地方,在可达到的范围以外。~ ***of*** 扫清;完全撤换。***make a ~ to the left*** 向左拐,向左弯斜。~**back**【空】后掠形;后掠角;(离心压缩机叶片的)后倾,后弯。~ **circuit**【电】扫描电路。~ **(second) hand** (钟表的)长秒针。~ **net** 大拖网;捕虫网。~**up** 大扫除。

sweep·er [ˈswiːpə; ˋswipɚ] ***n*.** **1.** 清扫工人,清扫员。**2.** 清扫机。**3.** 扫海船,扫雷艇。

sweep·ing [ˈswiːpiŋ; ˋswipɪŋ] **I** ***a*.** **1.** 扫清的;扫荡的;一扫而光的;一网打尽的。**2.** 势如破竹的,势不可挡的,厉害的。**3.** 包括无遗的;彻底的;概括的,笼统的(陈述等)。**4.** 彻底的,大大的。**5.** 延伸的,弯弯曲曲似的。**II** ***n*.** **1.** 扫除,扫清,扫荡;扫海。**2.** 〔*pl*.〕扫集物;一堆垃圾。**3.** 底层的人们。~ *changes* 巨变,大变。~ **brush** 扫帚。~ [**sweep**] **circuit**【电】扫描电路。~ [**sweep**] **net** (渔船用的)大拖网,捕虫网。**-ly** ***ad*.** **-ness** ***n*.**

sweep·stake(s) [ˈswiːpsteik(s); ˋswipˏstek(s)] ***n*.** 〔*sing*., *pl*.〕一人或数人赢得赌金的赛马[彩票],〔泛指〕彩票(赌博)。

Sweet [swiːt; swit] ***n*.** **1.** 斯威特〔姓氏〕。**2.** **Henry ~** 斯威特〔1845—1912,英国语音学家,语言学家〕。

sweet [swiːt; swit] **I** ***a*.** **1.** 甜(蜜)的(*opp*. bitter, sour);滋味好的;芳香的;醇美的(*opp*. dry);(音调)甜美的。**2.** 〔口〕可爱的;好看的。**3.** 愉快的,快乐的;畅快的。**4.** 无恶味的;不咸的(水);新鲜的(*opp*. stale, rancid, sour)。**5.** 温柔的,亲切的。**6.** 轻快的;轻便的,灵活的;容易驾驶的。**7.**【石油】脱硫的,香化的。**8.** 非酸性的,适于耕作的(土地)(*opp*. sour)。~ *chatter* = ~ *line* = ~ *patter* 〔美〕花言巧语。*the ~ chow-chow* 糖果蜜饯(等)。*a ~ man* 〔美〕情郎。~ *flowers* 香花。*a ~ mamma* 〔美〕甜姐儿。~ *music* 美妙的音乐。*a ~ little dog* 可爱的小狗。*a ~ motor* 滑溜无声的发动机。~ *running* 顺畅的运行。~ *air* 新鲜空气。*keep the room clean and ~* 使屋子保持整洁[宜人,合乎卫生]。*You will have a ~ time putting that machine together again*. 〔口〕〔反〕要把那部机器装还原样可是个「美差啊」(是很费工夫的)。***at one's own ~ will*** 任意,随意。***be ~ on*** [***upon***] 〔口〕迷恋;爱上。***have a ~ tooth*** 爱吃甜品。~ ***and twenty*** 二十岁的美人。~ ***nothings*** 情侣之间的悄悄话[多为内容重复、空洞之甜言蜜语]。***too ~*** 〔美〕马上,立刻;巴不得。**II** ***n*.** **1.** 甜味;好吃的东西;糖果,甜食;餐后的甜点心;甜酒。**2.** 〔常 *pl*.〕愉快的事;称心的东西。**3.** 〔主、称呼〕亲爱的人(= darling)。**4.** 〔常 *pl*.〕〔诗〕芳香。**5.** 〔美口〕= ~ potato. **6.** 〔美音乐俚〕旋律优美的缓慢的跳舞音乐。*the ~ and the bitter* [*the ~s and bitters*] *of life* 人生的苦乐。*the ~s of the year* 一年里头的快乐季节。~ **alyssum**【植】香雪球。~ **basil**【植】紫花罗勒。~ **bay**【植】月桂树;维吉尼亚木兰。~**-bough** 〔美〕苹果树。~ **bread** (小牛、小羊等的)胰脏,胰脏或胸腺〔被认为是一种美味〕。~**briar**, ~**brier**【植】多花蔷薇。~ **cherry**【植】欧洲甜樱桃(树)。~ **clover**【植】草木犀属植物。~ **cider** 尚未发酵之苹果酒。~ **corn** 〔美〕**1.** 甜玉米。**2.** (做菜用的)嫩玉米。~ **fern** 香蕨木。~ **flag**【植】白菖蒲。~ **gale**【植】香杨梅。~ **gas** (不含硫化氢之)脱臭气,无硫天然气〔可作燃料〕。~ **going** 舒适顺利的愉快旅行。~ **gum**【植】枫香属(树脂),胶皮糖香树(木);苏合香。~**heart** **1.** ***n*.** 爱人;情人;十分讨人欢喜的人[物]。**2.** ***vt*.**, ***vi*.** 〔口〕谈恋爱;求爱。~ **heart contract** [**deal**] 有利于业主的秘密劳资协定。~ **John**【植】狭叶美洲石竹。~ **majoram**【植】薄荷属植物〔尤指莱乔栾那,叶可作烹调香料〕。~ **man** 〔美俚〕情夫;男妓。~**-meat** 〔常 *pl*.〕糖果,甜食;蜜饯。~**mouth** ***vt*.** 〔美俚〕奉承,讨好。~ **oil** 橄榄油;菜油。~ **one** 狠狠一击;〔称呼〕= darling. ~ **patootie** 甜姐儿。~ **pea**【植】香豌豆(花)。~ **pepper**【植】灯笼椒。~ **potato** 甘薯。~**root**【植】黄杨叶念珠藤;菖蒲。~**-scented** ***a*.** 香,香味好的,有芳香的。~ **shop** 〔英〕糖果铺。~ **sixteen** 〔美〕可爱的十六岁小姑娘。~ **spot** (球拍等上的)最有效击球点。~**-sop**【植】番荔枝。~ **sultan**【植】香芙蓉。~ **take** 〔美拳击〕售票成绩好。~ **talk** 甜言蜜语。~**-talk** ***vi*.**, ***vt*.** (向…)说甜言蜜语,奉承巴结。~**-tempered** ***a*.** 心地温

S

和的。～ **toil** 自己乐意干的苦差事。～ **violet**【植】香堇菜。～ **water** 淡水,饮用水;糖水;[化](脂肪水解时产生之)甜水。～ **william** [亦作]【植】美洲石竹。～**wood**【植】=～ bay.

sweet·en [ˈswiːtn; ˋswitn] *vt*. **1.** 把…弄甜,给…加糖;把…弄香,给…去臭;使减低酸性;【石油】使脱硫;〔美俚〕用威士忌酒加浓;使(声音)美妙,使(音调)好听。**2.** 使愉快。**3.** 使温和,使温柔;减轻(悲伤),缓和。**4.** 把…弄清洁,使新鲜,给…消毒。**5.** 增加(担保品;扑克赌注)。～ *one's life* 使生活愉快。～ *a room* 把房间消毒[搞好房间里的清洁卫生]。～ ***the deal*** 为促使交易成功而提供种种优惠条件〔有时甚至是贿赂等〕。—*vi*. 变甜;变香;变悦耳;变得令人愉快;变清洁;变美丽;变清新舒服。

sweet·er·ia, sweeter·y [swiːˈtiəriə, -ˈtiəri; swiˋtɪrɪə, -ˋtɪrɪ] *n*. 〔美〕糖果店。

sweet·ie [ˈswiːti; ˋswitɪ] *n*. **1.** 〔常 *pl*.〕〔儿语〕= sweetmeat. **2.** 〔美口〕情人 = sweetheart. ～**pie** 情人。

sweet·ing [ˈswiːtiŋ; ˋswitɪŋ] *n*. 香苹果;〔古,称呼〕= darling.

sweet·ish [ˈswiːtiʃ; ˋswitɪʃ] *a*. 有甜味的;甜甜的;可爱的。**-ly** *ad*.

sweet·ly [ˈswiːtli; ˋswitlɪ] *ad*. 甜(蜜)地,芬芳地;(音调)美妙;可爱,亲切。*reply* ～ 回答得亲切。*speak* ～ 话说得亲切[愉快;轻快,温和]。*The saw cuts* ～. 这把锯子好锯。*The bicycle runs* ～. 这辆自行车好骑。

sweet·ness [ˈswiːtnis; ˋswitnɪs] *n*. 甜蜜;甜味,美味;甜度;新鲜;芳香;美音,佳调;可爱;愉快;温和,温柔,亲切。

sweet·ums [ˈswiːtəmz; ˋswitəmz] *n*. 〔美〕甜姐儿。

sweet·y [ˈswiːti; ˋswitɪ] *n*. = sweetmeat.

swell [swel; swɛl] (*~ed*; ***swollen*** [ˈswɔːln; ˋswolən], 〔古〕 ***swoln***, 〔罕〕 *~ed*) **I** *vi*. **1.** 膨胀;肿大;变大,增大,增长,壮大;(土地)隆起。**2.** (声音等)变高。**3.** (河水)上涨;起浪。**4.** 骄傲,自负,趾高气扬 (*with*);(感情)激昂,紧张,兴奋。—*vt*. **1.** 使膨胀;使鼓起;使肿大;增大,增加(支出等);使高涨;使增长,使壮大。**2.** 使自负,使自大,使趾高气扬,使得意扬扬。**3.**【乐】使增强。*The injured wrist ~ed* (*up*). 受伤的手腕肿起来了。*the ~ing tide* 正在上涨的潮水。*a swollen budget* 庞大的预算。～ *a note* 增强乐音。***have a ~ed head*** 〔俚〕得意忘形,自高自大(*have* [*suffer from*] *a ~ed head* 〔俚〕自以为了不得)。～ ***the chorus of admiration*** 加入赞美者[崇拜者]之列。～ ***the ranks of*** 加入,参加。～ ***the total*** 使总数增大;滥竽充数。***swollen with indignation*** 怒火填膺。**II** *n*. **1.** 膨胀;肿胀,肿大;增大,增加;加强;强大;情绪高涨。**2.** 浪涛汹涌。**3.**【地】海涌。**4.**【乐】渐强到渐弱(的符号)〔〈〉〕。**5.** (土地的)隆起;(手臂等的)鼓包,隆起(部分)。**6.** 〔口〕名人;名手,名家;服装时髦的人;〔口〕自夸的人,妄自尊大的人。*a* ～ *in politics* 政界名人。*a* ～ *at tennis* 网球名手。*What a* ～ *you are*! 你多么漂亮啊! **III** *a*. 〔口〕漂亮的,(音乐家等)高超的;高级的,时髦的。*He looks* ～. 他很时髦。*a* ～ *pianist* 了不起的名钢琴家。*a* ～ *dame* 〔美〕时髦、漂亮的女子。～ **box**【乐】(风琴的)音响调节箱[器]。～**-differous** *a*. 〔美〕有趣的,舒服的;优雅的;华丽的。～**-fish**【鱼】圆鲀;东方鲀。～**-front** *a*. 正面鼓起的。～**-head**〔美俚〕自高自大的人。～ **mob** 〔英〕打扮成绅士的一伙扒手。～**mobman** 〔英〕打扮成绅士的扒手。～ **organ** 有音响调节器的风琴。

swell·dom [ˈsweldəm; ˋswɛldəm] *n*. 〔俚〕上流社会,时髦人物的圈子。

swel·le·gance [ˈsweliːgəns; ˋswɛligəns] *n*. 〔美〕非常优雅。

swel·le·gant [ˈsweləgənt; ˋswɛləgənt] *a*. 〔美〕非常优雅的。

swell·el·e·gous [ˈsweləligəs; ˋswɛləlɪgəs] *a*. 〔美〕优雅的;漂亮的;过分华丽的。

swell·ing [ˈsweliŋ; ˋswɛlɪŋ] *n*. 肿胀;增大;肿瘤;隆起,膨胀;隆起部。

swell·ish [ˈsweliʃ; ˋswɛlɪʃ] *a*. 〔俚〕漂亮的,时髦的。

swelp [swelp; swɛlp] **I** *int*. 〔美俚〕= So help (me God). 我敢发誓。**II** *n*. 可怜的抗议者。

swel·ter [ˈsweltə; ˋswɛltɚ] **I** *vi*., *vt*. (使)中暑,(使)热得发昏,(使)热得没气力。**II** *n*. **1.** 闷热的空气,酷热,炎暑。**2.** 满身大汗,非常紧张的心情。**3.** 混乱。

swel·ter·ing [ˈsweltəriŋ; ˋswɛltərɪŋ, ˋswɛltrɪŋ] *a*. 酷热的;使人热得发昏的。**-ly** *ad*.

Swensky [ˈswenski; ˋswɛnskɪ] *n*. 〔美〕瑞典人。

swept [swept; swɛpt] sweep 的过去式及过去分词。～**-out** *a*. 〔英〕流线形的。～**-up** *a*. (头发)向上梳的,向头顶梳的。

swept·back [ˈsweptˌbæk; ˋswɛptˏbæk] *a*. **1.** 有后掠形(箭形)的〔指机翼〕。**2.** (飞机)有后掠翼的。

swept·wing [ˈsweptˌwiŋ; ˋswɛptˏwɪŋ] *a*.【空】有后掠机翼的,有箭形机翼的。

swerve [swəːv; swɝv] **I** *vi*. 转弯;偏斜;突然改变方向;滑出;闪避;逸出常轨 (*from*)。—*vt*. 使转弯,使改变方向;使滑出;使离正轨。**II** *n*. 转向,偏斜(的程度);滑出;逸出;背离;【板球】曲球。～ *from the path of duty* 不守本分,不负责任。**-less** *a*. 坚定不移的。

swev·en [ˈswevn; ˋswɛvn] *n*. 〔古〕梦;幻影。

S.W.G., SWG = standard wire ga(u)ge【电】标准线规。

Swi·a·ge·cats [ˈswiːidʒkæts; ˋswiɪdʒkæts] *n*. 〔美〕南达科塔(South Dakota)州和该州居民的别名。

swick·y [ˈswiːki; ˋswikɪ] *n*. 〔美〕威士忌酒。

Swift [swift; swɪft] *n*. **1.** 斯威夫特〔姓氏〕。**2. Gustavus Franklin** ～ 斯威夫特〔1839—1903,美国企业家,铁路冷藏车之发明人〕。**3. Jonathan** ～ 斯威夫特〔1667—1745,英国讽刺作家,*Gulliver's Travels* 的作者〕。

swift [swift; swɪft] **I** *a*. **1.** 飞快的,迅速的,敏捷的;即时的,立刻的(答复等);突然发生的。**2.** 易…的,动不动就…的 (*to do*)。**3.** 时间极短的(苦痛等)。*a* ～ *wit* 急智。***as*** ～ ***as thought*** 立刻,马上,一转眼。**II** *n*. **1.**【动】褐雨燕;蝾螈;一种小蜥蜴;蝙蝠蛾,鬼蛾。**2.** (纺织机等的)大滚筒;纺车,卷线车。**3.** 急流,急湍。**4.** 〔口〕手脚快速的排字工人。**III** *ad*. 迅速地;敏捷地。～**-footed** *a*. 走得快的。～**-handed** *a*. 手快的;行动[操作]敏捷的。～ **fox**【动】(北美的)小狐〔简称 ～〕。～**let**【鸟】金丝雀。～**-winged** *a*. 飞得快的。**-ly** *ad*. **-ness** *n*.

swift·er [ˈswiftə; ˋswɪftɚ] *n*.【海】低桅前支索,下前支索;绞盘加固索〔用来连接各绞盘棒末端〕。

swift·y [ˈswifti; ˋswɪftɪ] *a*. 〔美〕极引人注意的。

swig [swig; swɪg] *n*., *vi*., *vt*. 〔口〕大口喝,痛饮。

swill [swil; swɪl] **I** *vt*. **1.** 大口喝,痛饮。**2.** 冲洗 (*out*)。—*vi*. 大口喝,痛饮。**II** *n*. **1.** 大喝;痛饮,狂饮;劣酒。**2.** 冲涮,洗涤。**3.** 馊水,残汤剩菜[猪饲料]。**4.** 过分打扮的人。*swell* ～ 〔美俚〕油水足的残汤剩菜〔意指奢侈的生活〕;奢侈的饮食。

swim [swim; swɪm] (***swam*** [swæm; swæm]; ***swum*** [swʌm; swʌm]; ***swim·ming***) **I** *vi*. **1.** 游水,游泳。**2.** 浮游,漂浮,漂流。**3.** 充溢,充斥,充满;浸,泡 (*in*; *with*)。**4.** 浮动,滑动;打转;浮现,恍然出现;眼花,眩晕。—*vt*. 游过;与…比赛游泳;使(狗等)游泳;使(船等)浮起;泡(在水中)。*I cannot* ～ *a stroke*. 我一点也不会游泳。～ *to the bottom* = ～ *like a stone* [*tailor's goose*] 〔谑〕(不会水)沉下。～*ming eyes* = *eyes that* ～ *with tears* 眼泪汪汪的眼睛。～ *a race* 参加游泳比赛。*I will* ～ *you 100 yards*. 我要跟你赛游 100 码。～ *wheat to select seed* 浸麦选种。***sink or*** ～ 好歹试试看,不管是沉是浮。～ ***against the tide*** [***stream***] 溯流游泳;违反时势[潮流]。～ ***between two waters*** 驶行中流;取中庸之道。～ ***on one's back*** 仰泳。～ ***with the tide*** [***stream***] 顺着潮流,顺水推舟。**II** *n*. **1.** 游泳;浮动,浮现;滑走。**2.** 潮流,时势,(事件的)趋势。**3.** 眩晕。

S

4. 深渊。**be in the** ~ 熟悉内情;顺应潮流,与目前形势一致。**have** [**take**] **a** ~ 游泳。**out of the** ~ 不明内情;脱离当前形势;不合潮流。~ **bladder** (鱼)鳔。~-**feeder** (淡水捕鱼用的)水下给饵器。~ **fin**〔美〕(潜水蛙人用的)橡皮脚蹼。~ **meet** = swimeet. ~ **pool** 游泳池。~ **ring** 救生圈。~**suit** [**wear**] 游泳衣。

swi·meet [ˈswimiːt; ˋswɪmit] **n.**〔美〕游泳比赛。

swim·ma·ble [ˈswiməbl; ˋswɪməbl̩] **a.** 1. 可游泳的。2. 游泳活动期的。3. 游泳距离的。

swim-man-do [swimˈmɑːndəu; swɪmˋmɑndo] **n.**【军】河川突击队。

swim·mer [ˈswimə; ˋswɪmə] **n.** 游泳者;鳔。

swim·mer·et(te) [ˈswimərət; ˋswɪmər͵ɛt] **n.**【动】(甲壳类的)桡肢,游泳足。

swim·ming [ˈswimiŋ; ˋswɪmɪŋ] **n.** 1. 游泳。2. 眩晕。*go* ~ 去游泳。*I have a* ~ *in my head.* 我头晕。~ **bath** (室内)游泳池。~-**bell**【动】(水母等的)气胞囊。~-**belt** 救生圈。~ **bladder** 鱼鳔。~ **costume** 游泳衣。~ **gala** 水上运动会。~ **hole**〔美〕(河湾等处可供游泳的)游泳水塘。~ **pool** 游泳池。~ **trunks** *n. pl.* 男游泳裤。-**ly** *ad.* (进行)顺利,顺畅(*go* ~*ly* 一帆风顺)。

swim·mist [ˈswimist; ˋswɪmɪst] **n.**〔美〕游泳家。

swim·my [ˈswimi; ˋswɪmɪ] **a.** 有点儿头晕的;引起头晕的,模糊的。-**i·ly** *ad.* -**i·ness** *n.*

Swin·burn(e) [ˈswinbəːn; ˋswɪndɚn] **n.** 斯温伯恩〔姓氏〕。

swin·dle [ˈswindl; ˋswɪndl̩] I *vt.*, *vi.* 诈取,骗取,欺骗,诓骗。II *n.* 1. 欺骗。2. 冒牌货,冒名顶替者。-**r** *n.* 骗子,诈骗犯。

swin·dling·ly [ˈswindliŋli; ˋswɪndlɪŋlɪ] **ad.** 用诈骗手段。

swine [swain; swaɪn] **n.** (*sing.*, *pl.*)猪,卑鄙下流的家伙。*some sheep and several* ~ 几只羊和几头猪。~-**herd** 猪倌,牧猪人,养猪人。~ **plague**【医】猪肺疫。~-**pox**【医】水痘。

swin·er·y [ˈswainəri; ˋswaɪnərɪ] **n.** 1. 猪栏;猪群。2. 粗野,卑鄙下流的行为。

swing [swiŋ; swɪŋ] I *vi.* (**swung** [swʌŋ; swʌŋ], **swang** [swæŋ]; **swung**) 1. 摆动,摇摆,摇动,挥动,摇荡。2. (人、马车等)大摇大摆地走(*along*; *past*; *by*),〔摆动着手臂〕轻松地走[跑]。3. 荡秋千。4. 悬挂着(*from*);〔口〕被处绞刑,被吊死。5. 回旋;转动,转身;转变方向。【海】(船停泊时因风或潮水)旋转。6. 挥手打击。7. (指音乐)具有激荡人心的韵调;演奏[唱]摇摆舞音乐。8.〔美俚〕出风头;赶时髦;非常活跃〔特指追求逸乐〕。—*vt.* 1. 使摆动,摇摆,摇动,(往复)摇荡;挥舞(棍棒等);回转,转动。2. 使(一排兵等)转向;使以弧线前进。3. 吊起,悬挂。4.〔美口〕使办成功;经营,办理;处理,支配。5. 演奏[唱](摇摆舞音乐)。*Their mind swung as one to home.* 他们不约而同地想念起家乡来。~ *by one arm from a branch* 用一只胳膊(把自己)吊在树枝上。*The door swung shut.* 门关上了。*I swung over to the subject of the pictures.* 我转到了有关电影的话题上。*He could not* ~ *the enterprise.*〔口〕他主持不了那个企业。~ *the door open* [*shut*] 把门打开[关上]。~ *a catgut*〔美〕撒网。**no room to** ~ **a cat** (*in*) 狭窄。**a** ~ **around** [〔英〕**round**] **on one's heel** 掉转身子。~ (**a**)**round the circle**〔美〕(总统候选人等的)竞选旅行。~ **at**〔美〕挥拳打,对准…打过去。~ **clear of** (船)掉转方向躲避。~ **for it** 因(…)而被处绞刑。~ **in with** 加入;与…合作。~ **into line** (军队等)转成横队。~ **one's weight** 运用自己的影响力。~ **round** 掉转方向。~ **the lead**〔军俚〕假病,逃职。~ **to** (门)(砰的一声)关上。

II *n.* 1. 摆动,摇动,摇摆;挥动;摆幅,振幅,摆动量;大摇大摆的步伐。2. 秋千。3. 自由活动范围,行动自由。4. 趋势,倾向;推动力。5.〔只用 *sing.*〕韵律,音律,旋律。6.【摄】(暗箱的)转动;【拳击】横击,挥击。7.【滑雪】旋转;【滑冰】犹豫摆动。8.〔口〕一阵工作;进行,开展。9. (巡回)旅行。10. 摇摆舞音乐。11.【商】行情涨落。12.〔美〕(态度等的)周期性交替。*the* ~ *of the pendulum* 钟摆的摆动;势力的盛衰交替;党派间的政权交替。*have a* ~ 荡秋千。**get into** (**the**) ~ **of one's work** 工作起劲起来,工作顺利展开。**give full** [**free**] ~ **to it** 听其自然,放任自流。**go with a** ~ (音调)流利;(事情)顺利。**have one's full** ~ 自由行动,自由掌握。**in full** ~ 正起劲,正在紧张时候,正在积极进行(*The work is in full* ~. 工作正顺利全速推行)。**let it have its** ~ = *give full* ~ *to it.* **What you lose on the** ~**s you make** [**gain**] **on the roundabouts** 失之东隅,收之桑榆。**take a** ~ **at**〔美〕= ~ *at.* **take one's full** ~ = *have one's full* ~. **the** ~**s** 秋千族〔指摇摆不定的人,尤指在多元化社会中对多种选择拿不定主意的年轻人〕。III *a.* 1. 摇摆乐的。2. 悬挂的;(门等)可绕轴心旋转的。3. (在选举中)举足轻重的。~**around**〔宇〕绕行星返地轨道。~**back** (原来的观点习惯等之)恢复。~**boat** 船形荡千。~ **bridge** 平转[旋]桥,旋(开)桥。~**by**【宇】(航天器)绕行星变轨。~ **chair** 转椅(= rocking chair)。~(**ing**) **door** 转门。~ **gateer**〔美〕摇摆音乐家。~-**around**【宇航】绕行星返地轨道〔利用某行星的重力场改变飞行方向的太空船轨道〕。~ **jack** 横式起重机。~ **link**【机】摆杆。~ **music** 摇摆舞音乐。~-**over** 大转变,大急转〔指思想、态度等〕;(杂技动作中的)单臂悬垂旋转。~ **room**〔美〕(工厂工人)吸烟室,休息室。~ **shift**〔美〕(下午四点到半夜的)中班工作,中班工人。~ **span**〔美〕旋开桥,跳桥。~ **vote** 决定票。~-**wing**【空】(可变)后掠翼。

swinge [swindʒ; swɪndʒ] *vt.*〔古〕打,猛打;惩戒;〔方〕把…烧焦。

swing(e)·ing [ˈswiŋdʒiŋ; ˋswɪndʒɪŋ] I *a.* 重,凶猛的(打击等);〔口〕极大的,巨大的;了不得的(损失);极好的,优等的。II *ad.* 极大地,非常地。

swing·er[1] [ˈswiŋə; ˋswɪŋɚ] **n.** 1. 时髦人物。2.〔俚〕浪荡公子。

swing·er[2] [ˈswiŋə; ˋswɪŋɚ] **n.** 1.〔废〕彪形大汉。2.〔英口〕庞然大物。

swin·ge·roo [͵swiŋdʒəˈruː; ͵swɪŋdʒəˋru] **n.**〔美〕= swing music.

swing·ing [ˈswiŋiŋ; ˋswɪŋɪŋ] **a.** 1. 摆动的,摇摆的。2. 一挥(摇)而成的。3.〔美俚〕活跃的,极时髦的。-**ly** *ad.*

swin·gle [ˈswiŋgl; ˋswɪŋgl̩] I *n.* 1. 打麻器,打麻棍;(连枷的)打禾棍。2.〔美俚〕风流的独身者。II *vt.* 用打麻器打[打制]。~**bar**, ~**tree** (兽力车;犁等的)轭,曲木。

swing·ster [ˈswiŋstə; ˋswɪŋstɚ] **n.**〔美〕摇摆舞乐师。

swin·ish [ˈswainiʃ; ˋswaɪnɪʃ] **a.** 猪的;猪似的;粗鲁的;贪婪的,下流的。-**ly** *ad.* -**ness** *n.*

swink [swiŋk; swɪŋk] I *vi.* (**swank**, **swonk**; **swonken**)〔英古〕辛苦,辛辛苦苦地工作。II *n.* 辛苦,苦工。

Swin·ner·ton [ˈswinətən; ˋswɪnɚtən] **n.** 斯温纳顿〔姓氏〕。

swipe [swaip; swaɪp] I *n.* 1.〔口〕柄;握杆。2. (板球等的)猛打,重击;猛击,摩擦(人、马的)身体。3. 马夫;〔美俚〕贼。II *vt.*, *vi.* 1. 猛击,猛打。2. 大口喝,牛饮。3. 刷(卡)〔指让机器读取信用卡、身份证卡、车票卡等中的磁码信息〕,将(信用卡等)插入槽内刮擦;〔美俚〕乘机偷。-**r** *n.* 1. 猛击者。2. 酒鬼。3. 刷卡者。4.〔美俚〕偷窃者。

swipes [swaips; swaɪps] **n.** (*pl.*)〔英〕(低级)啤酒;杯中喝剩的啤酒。

swi·ple, swip·ple [ˈswipl; ˋswɪpl̩] **n.** 连枷头,连枷上的短棒。

swirl [swəːl; swɚl] I *n.* 1. (水、风等的)旋转,漩涡。2. 卷状的东西;卷曲的形状;(雪的)纷飞。3. 纷乱。4.〔美〕弯曲,围绕。5. 鱼跃。II *vi.* 1. 打转。2. (头)晕。3. 弯

曲盘旋,(雪)纷飞。～ **skirt** 旋动式女裙。**-er** *n*.【空】涡旋式喷嘴,离心式喷嘴。**-y** *a*. 1. 成涡旋形的。2.〔Scot.〕纠缠的。

swish [swiʃ; swɪʃ] I *n*. 1. (鞭子在空中挥动,衣裙在走动时的)嗖嗖声,沙沙声。2. 飒飒声。3. (鞭棒的)挥动。4. 漂亮,时髦。5.〔美俚〕搞同性恋的男子。II *a*. 1. 漂亮的,时髦的。2.〔美俚〕搞同性恋的。***in the*** ～ 见闻广博,熟悉内情。III *vi*. 嗖嗖地挥动;作沙沙声。—*vt*. 把(鞭子)挥动得嗖嗖地响;唰地甩动(尾巴);用(棍子)抽断(树枝等),沙沙地削去(*off*);用(鞭子)抽打。～**-swash**〔俚〕啤酒。**-er** *n*. 衣着时髦的人。

swish·y [ˈswiʃi; ˋswɪʃɪ] *a*. (***swish·i·er***; ***swish·i·est***) 1. 发嗖嗖声的,作窸窣响的。2.〔俚〕搞同性恋的(= swish)。～-～ *a*.〔美〕三心二意的,靠不住的。

Swiss [swis; swɪs] I *n*. 1.〔*sing*., *pl*.〕瑞士(Switzerland)人;瑞士语,(特指)瑞士的德国语。2. (瑞士)卫兵;看门。II *a*. 瑞士的;瑞士人的。～ **chard**【植】牛皮菜,瑞士甜菜,唐万苣(= chard)。～ **Guards** (从前法国和现在罗马教皇雇用的)瑞士卫兵。～ **roll** (有果酱的)面包卷。

SWISSAIR = Swiss Air Transport Company 瑞士航空公司。

Swit. = Switzerland.

switch [switʃ; swɪtʃ] I *n*. 1. (树上折下的)细树枝;软鞭子;鞭打。2. 假发;(尾巴上的)毛簇。3.〔美〕【铁道】道岔扳子,轨闸转辙器;侧线。4.【电】开关;电闸;电键;转换器;【电话】接线台。5.【军】斜行壕。6. (思想等的)大转变。7.〔美〕(金融机构和销售店的)电脑化联网。*a change-over* ～ 转换开关,转向开关。*a pull* ～ 拉线开关。*a three wire* ～ 双联开关。*a time* ～ 定时断路器。*a clock* ～ 定时开关。*a line* ～ (自动电话的)寻线机,预选器;线路开关。II *vt*. 1. 鞭打;摆动;摇(尾);猛然抢去。2. 挂断(…的电话)(～ *sb*. *off*);关闭(电流),关(电灯)(*off*; *out*)。4. 通(电流),接通(电话给某人),开(电灯)(*on*)。5. 改变,转变(思想、谈话等);【铁道】给扳道岔;调配(车厢)。—*vi*. 1. 鞭打。2.【铁道】扳道岔;调车。3. 挂断电话(*off*)。4. 转换,转变。～ *an electric light on* [*off*] 开[关]灯。～ *off to another like of thought* 改变想法[思路]。*Let's* ～.〔美〕走吧;开动吧。***I'll be*** ～***ed***.〔美口〕〔表示否定、惊讶〕(*I'll be* ～*ed if you do*. 你要是能的话我就把头砍掉)。～ ***off*** [***on***] 不收听[收听](某一广播)。～ ***through***【电信】转接。～**back** (游乐园里乘着玩的)惊险小铁路;【铁路】之字形爬山铁路;【影】倒叙往事的镜头。～ **base** 开关座〔一般为电木板〕。～**blade knife** (按钮后会自动打开的)弹簧折刀。～**board**【电】配电盘;(电信、电话)交换机,交换台;配电盘。～ **box** 配电箱,开关盒。～ **cane**【植】软条青篱竹。～ **gear** 开关设备。～**hitter** 左右手都能击球的棒球运动员。〔美俚〕多才多艺的人。～ **lever** 开关杆,转辙杆。～**-man** 扳道工人;调车助手。～ **mugger**〔美〕电话接线生。～ **over** 转换转变。～ **room** 配电室;电话交换室。～ **selling** 换货诱售〔用廉价品作广告诱来顾客后再出售高价货物〕。～**-signal** 转辙信号。～**tower**〔美〕信号房。～ **trading** 转手贸易。～**yard** (铁路的)调车场;编组站。

switche·roo [ˌswitʃəˈruː; ˏswɪtʃəˋru, ˋswɪtʃəˏru] *n*.〔俚〕突然变化,大转变,可怕的巨变。

swith [swiθ; swɪθ] *ad*.〔方〕立即,迅速地。

swith·er [ˈswiðə; ˋswɪðɚ] *vi*., *n*.〔Scot.〕疑惑;踌躇,拿不定主意。

Switz. = Switzerland.

Switz·er [ˈswitsə; ˋswɪtsɚ] *n*.〔古〕瑞士人;瑞士雇佣兵;(罗马教皇的)瑞士卫兵。

Switz·er·land [ˈswitsələnd; ˋswɪtsɚlənd] *n*. 瑞士〔欧洲〕。

swiv·el [ˈswivl; ˋswɪvl] I *n*.【机】转环,转节;旋转接头;旋轴;活节;回旋炮;旋桥;(旋椅的)底座。II *vi*., *vt*. (**-ll-**) 旋转,回转;用转节固定[支住]。～ **chair** 转椅(*a* ～*-chair man*〔美〕高级职员)。～**-eye** 斜视眼。～**-eyed** *a*. (眼)斜视的。～ **gun** 回旋炮。～**-hip** *vi*. 扭着臀部走路。～ **hook** 转动钩。～**-led** *a*. 装了转环[活节]的。～ **loom** 绣花机。～ **plough** 双向犁。～ **table**【机】转台。～ **weaving**【纺】挖花织造。～ **wing**【航】(飞机的)回转翼〔指机翼既能后倾又能前倾〕。

swiv·et [ˈswivət; ˋswɪvɪt] *n*.〔方,口〕烦躁不安,极度激动;不安。

swiz(z) [swiz; swɪz] *n*. (*pl*. ***swizzes***)〔方〕欺骗,诈取。

swiz·zle [ˈswizl; ˋswɪzl̩] I *n*.〔口〕碎冰鸡尾酒。II *vt*. 用搅酒棒搅和。—*vi*. (过量地)喝酒。～ **stick** 搅酒棒〔搅和鸡尾酒等用的玻璃棒〕。

swob [swɔb; swɑb] *n*., *vt*. = swab.

swob·ble [ˈswɔbl; ˋswɑbl̩] *vt*., *vi*.〔美俚〕大口大口地吞;急急忙忙地吃。

swol·len [ˈswəulən; ˋswolən] I swell 的过去分词。II *a*. 1. 肿起的;膨胀的;涨了水的。2. 浮夸的;骄傲的。～ **cranium**〔美〕自负;自我主义。～**-headed** *a*. 骄傲的,自高自大的。

swoon [swuːn; swun] I *n*. 昏厥,晕倒;神魂颠倒。***fall into a*** ～ 晕过去,昏倒。II *vi*. 1. 晕过去,昏倒;神魂颠倒。2. (乐声等)渐渐微弱,渐渐消失。

swoop [swuːp; swup] I *vi*. (鹰)飞下猛扑;突然袭击(*down*; *on*; *upon*)。～ *down upon an enemy* 突袭敌人。—*vt*. 攫去;〔口〕抢去(*up*)。II *n*. 飞扑;从上攫取;抢夺;【空】下扑。***at a single*** ～ 一下子,一举。***at one fell*** ～ (灾难的)迅速而恐怖地袭来;一下子。***make a*** ～ ***at*** 突袭,飞扑。***with a*** ～ 一抓;一下子。**-ing** *a*. 飞下猛扑的;(表面)陡斜的。

swoosh [swuːʃ; swuʃ] I *vi*., *vt*. (使)哗哗地流;(使)嗖嗖地动[发射]。II *n*. 哗哗声,嗖嗖声。

swop [swɔp; swɑp] I *n*.〔俚〕交换。*Shall we try a* ～? 咱们交换交换好吗? *take a* ～〔商俚〕交易未成反而被顾客骂一顿。II *vt*., *vi*.〔俚〕交换,互换。*Never* ～ *horses while crossing the stream*. 过河莫换马,阵前不换将〔困难局面中不可随便采取人事等变动〕。

sword [sɔːd; sord, sɔrd] *n*. 1. 剑,刀;〔军俚〕刺刀。2.〔the ～〕武力;兵权;权力;杀戮,战争。*the* ～ *and the purse* 武力和财力。*the* ～ *of justice* 司法权。*the* ～ *of the Spirit* 上帝的话。*the fire and* ～ (侵略军的)烧杀;强暴的军事手段。*the* ～ *of State* [*honour*] 国剑〔大节日在英王前所捧的宝剑〕。***at the point of the*** ～ 被迫,在威胁下。***be at*** ～***'s points*** (***with each other***)(彼此)不和。***cross*** ～***s*** 交锋,决斗;争论(*with*)。***draw the*** ～ 拔剑;发动战争。***measure*** ～***s*** (决斗前)检查剑长;决斗,战斗(*with*)。***put to the*** ～ 杀死。***put up*** [***sheathe***] ***the*** ～ 收剑,把剑插进鞘里;停止战争,讲和。***throw one's*** ～ ***into the scale*** 采取使用武力的办法。***wear the*** ～ 当兵。***worry the*** ～ (比赛击剑时)不断地快刺以乱对手阵脚。～ **arm** 右臂。～ **bayonet** (枪上的)刺刀。～ **bean** 刀豆。～**bearer** 捧剑侍从〔帝王、武士的侍从〕。～ **belt** 剑带,刀带。～**bill**【动】长嘴蜂雀。～ **cane** 藏有刀剑的手杖。～**craft** 剑术;〔现罕〕军事力量[技巧]。～**-cut** 刀伤。～ **dance** 舞剑;剑舞。～ **fern**【植】耳蕨,肾蕨。～**fish**【鱼】箭鱼,旗鱼〔有剑状大上颚的一种大海鱼〕。〔S-〕【天】旗鱼座;剑鱼座;〔S-〕〔英〕双翼海上飞机。～**-flag**【植】黄菖蒲。～ **grass**【植】刀状或齿状叶草。～**-guard** (刀剑的)护手。～**-hand** 右手。～ **knot** 剑柄带结。～**-law** 强权政治;军事管制,戒严令。～**like** *a*. 似刀剑的。～ **lily**【植】剑兰,唐菖蒲,水仙菖蒲。～**man**〔古〕= swordsman. ～**play** 剑术;舞剑;激烈的争论;唇枪舌剑。～**proof** 刀剑不入的。～ **smith** 刀剑匠。～**stick** = sword cane. ～**tail**【动】剑尾鱼。

swords·man [ˈsɔːdzmən; ˋsordzmən] *n*. 剑客;〔古〕军人,武士。～**-ship** *n*. 剑术。

swore [swɔː, swɔə; swor] swear 的过去式。

sworn [swɔːn; sworn] I *v*. swear 的过去分词。II *a*. 盟

S

誓的。~ *brothers* 结拜弟兄;死党。~ *friends* 莫逆(朋友)。~ *enemies* [*foes*] 死敌,不共戴天之仇。~ *evidence* 经过发誓的证据[证言]。

swot[1] [swɔt; swɑt] **I** ***vt***. (*-tt-*)〔英学生俚〕下苦功学;临时(抱佛脚地)攻读(功课) (*up*)。—***vi***. 死用功,用功学习。~ ***at a subject*** = ~ (***a subject***) ***up*** 匆匆忙忙用功学习(某一功课)。**II** ***n***. (尤指数学的)刻苦用功;辛苦;吃力的工作;用功的人。*What a* ~! 真吃力;好苦。

swot[2] [swɔt; swɑt] ***vt***., ***n***. = swat.

swound [swaund; swaʊnd, swund, saʊnd] ***vi***., ***n***. 〔古〕= swoon.

'swounds [zwaund*z*; zwaʊndz, zaʊndz] ***int***. 〔古〕畜牲!该死的家伙!〔为 God's wounds 的缩简形式 = zounds〕。

Swtz. = Switzerland.

swum [swʌm; swʌm] swim 的过去分词。

swung [swʌŋ; swʌŋ] swing 的过去式及过去分词。~ **dash** (波形)代字号〔~〕。

swuz·zy [ˈswʌzi; ˋswʌzɪ] ***a***. 〔美〕可爱的,有吸引力的;有趣的。

swy [ˈswai; ˋswaɪ] ***n***. 〔澳俚〕两个,二先令硬币;二年徒刑,抛双币打赌。~ **game** 抛双币打赌。

S. Y. = steam yacht 蒸气机快艇(游艇)。

SY = square yard 平方码。

sy- *pref*. 〔用于 s + 辅音之前或 z 前,为 syn- 的变体〕: *sy*stem, *sy*zygy.

Syb·a·rite [ˈsibərait; ˋsɪbə͵raɪt] **I** ***n***. 希巴利(***Sybaris***)〔意大利一古都〕人;〔or s-〕爱奢侈享乐的人,纵情逸乐的人。**II** ***a***. = Sybaritic.

Syb·a·rit·ic, -rit·i·cal [sibəˈritik, -əl; sɪbəˋrɪtɪk, -əl] ***a***. 希巴利人的;纵情逸乐的。**-i·cal·ly** ***ad***.

syb·a·rit·ism [ˈsibəraitizəm; ˋsɪbəraɪ͵tɪzm̩] ***n***. 奢侈享乐;骄奢淫逸。

Syb·il [ˈsibil; ˋsɪbl̩, -ɪl] ***n***. 希宝〔女子名〕。

syb·il [ˈsibil; ˋsɪbl̩, -ɪl] ***n***. sybyl 的变体。

syc·a·mine [ˈsikəmain; ˋsɪkəmɪn, -͵maɪn] ***n***. 【圣】黑子桑〔见新约圣经「路加福音」第 17 章 6 节〕。

syc·a·more [ˈsikəmɔ:, -mɔə; ˋsɪkə͵mor, -͵mɔr] ***n***. 【植】**1.** 埃及无花果树。**2.** 美国梧桐。**3.** 假挪威槭〔一种枫树〕。

syce [sais; saɪs] ***n***. 〔印〕马夫。

sy·cee [saiˈsi:; saɪˋsi] ***n***. (旧时中国使用的)银锭(= ~ silver)。

sy·chno·carp·ous [ˌsiknəˈkɑ:pəs; ͵sɪknəˋkɑrpəs] ***a***. 【植】多年生的,多次结果的。

sy·co·ni·um [saiˈkəuniəm; saɪˋkonɪəm] ***n***. (*pl*. ***-ni·a*** [-niə; -nɪə])【植】隐头花序。

syc·o·phan·cy [ˈsikəfənsi; ˋsɪkəfənsɪ] ***n***. 谄媚,拍马。

syc·o·phant [ˈsikəfənt; ˋsɪkəfənt] **I** ***n***. 谄媚者。**II** ***a***. 谄媚的。**-ly** ***ad***. **-ism** = sycophancy.

syc·o·phan·tic, syc·o·phan·tish [sikəˈfæntik, -ˈfæntiʃ; sɪkəˋfæntɪk, -ˋfæntɪʃ] ***a***. 谄媚的。

sy·co·sis [saiˈkəusis; saɪˋkosɪs] ***n***. 【医】须疮。

Syd·ney [ˈsidni; ˋsɪdnɪ] ***n***. 悉尼〔澳大利亚港市〕。

sy·e·nite [ˈsaiənait; ˋsaɪə͵naɪt] ***n***. 【地】正长岩。**-nit·ic** [-ˈnitik; -ˋnɪtɪk] ***a***.

Sykes [saiks; saɪks] ***n***. 赛克斯〔姓氏〕。

syl- *pref*. 〔用于 l 前〕= syn: *syl*logism.

syll. = syllable(s)。

syl·la·bar·i·um [ˌsiləˈbæriəm; ͵sɪləˋbɛrɪəm] ***n***. 〔L.〕(*pl*. ***syl·la·bar·a*** [-riə; -rɪə]) (= syllabary)。

syl·la·ba·ry [ˈsiləbəri; ˋsɪlə͵bɛrɪ] ***n***. 音节表;字音表。*the Japanese* ~ 日本语五十音图,假名表。

syl·la·bi [ˈsiləbai; ˋsɪlə͵baɪ] ***n***. syllabus 的复数。

syl·lab·ic [siˈlæbik; sɪˋlæbɪk] **I** ***a***. 音节的,拼音的;表示音节的;构成音节的;音节分明的;按音节的;(诗体)以音节数为格律的。**II** ***n***. 构成音节的声音,浊音;有声字;〔*pl*.〕以音节数为格律的诗。**-i·cal·ly** ***ad***.

syl·lab·i·cate [siˈlæbikeit; sɪˋlæbɪ͵ket] ***vt***. 把…分成音节;使构成音节。

syl·lab·i·(fi)·ca·tion [ˈsilˌæbi(fi)ˈkeiʃən; sɪ͵læbə(fə)ˋkeʃən] ***n***. 构成音节,区分音节。

syl·lab·i·cit·y [silæˈbisiti; sɪlæˋbɪsətɪ] ***n***. 成音节,可构成音节。

syl·lab·i·fy, syl·la·bize [siˈlæbifai, ˈsiləbaiz; sɪˋlæbə͵faɪ, ˋsɪlə͵baɪz] ***vt***. = syllabicate.

syl·la·bism [ˈsiləbizm; ˋsɪləbɪzm̩] ***n***. **1.** 音节法。**2.** 音节划分。

syl·la·ble [ˈsiləbl; ˋsɪləbl̩] **I** ***n***. **1.** 音节。**2.** 一言半字。*Not a* ~! 半个字也不说。**II** ***vt***. 把…分成音节;使分成音节发音[读出,说出];〔诗〕说出(名字、话),讲! ~**d** 〔构成复合词〕有…音节的。*a three-*~*d word* 三音节的词。

syl·la·bub [ˈsiləbʌb; ˋsɪlə͵bʌb] ***n***. = sillabub.

syl·la·bus [ˈsiləbəs; ˋsɪləbəs] ***n***. (*pl*. ***-bi*** [-bai; -baɪ], ~***es***) (讲义等的)摘要,提纲;课程提纲,教学大纲;【法】(判例前的)判决要旨。

syl·lep·sis [siˈlepsis; sɪˋlɛpsɪs] ***n***. (*pl*. ***-ses*** [-si:z; -siz])【语法,修】共轭法,一笔双叙法〔如 *Either they or I am wrong*. 句中的谓语 am wrong 一肩双挑 they 和 I 两个主语〕。**-lep·tic·(al)** ***a***.

syl·lo·gism [ˈsilədʒizəm; ˋsɪlə͵dʒɪzəm] ***n***. **1.** 【逻】推论式,三段论(法)。**2.** 演绎法。**3.** 巧妙的推论,诡辩。

syl·lo·gis·tic, -ti·cal [siləˈdʒistik, -tikl; sɪləˋdʒɪstɪk, -tɪkl] ***a***. 三段论法的;演绎的。**-ti·cal·ly** ***ad***. 用三段论法;演绎地。

syl·lo·gize [ˈsilədʒaiz; ˋsɪlə͵dʒaɪz] ***vi***., ***vt***. 用三段论法推论。

sylph [silf; sɪlf] ***n***. **1.** (15 至 16 世纪德国医学家 Paracelsus 学说中指生存在空气里没有灵魂而有生死的)"空气中之精灵"。**2.** 身材苗条的妇女。**3.** 【鸟】长尾蜂鸟。~**-like** [-laik; -laɪk] ***a***. 窈窕的。

sylph·id [ˈsilfid; ˋsɪlfɪd] ***n***. **1.** 小"气精"(*cf*. sylph 条)。**2.** 身材苗条的女孩。**-id·ine** [-din, -ˌdain; -dɪn, -͵daɪn] ***a***.

syl·va [ˈsilvə; ˋsɪlvə] ***n***. (*pl*. ~***s***, ***-vae*** [-vi:; -vi]) 森林;林木;林木志。

syl·van [ˈsilvən; ˋsɪlvən] **I** ***a***. 森林(多)的;林栖的。**II** ***n***. 森林女妖;林中居民,林栖鸟兽。

syl·van·ite [ˈsilvəˌnait; ˋsɪlvən͵aɪt] ***n***. 【矿】针碲金银矿。

syl·vat·ic [silˈveitik; sɪlˋvætɪk] ***a***. **1.** 森林的,森林中的。**2.** 伤害森林动物的。~ *plague* 森林瘟疫〔南北美洲西部森林中伤害野生动物的一种瘟疫,啮齿动物及其跳蚤是病菌的媒介〕。

Syl·ves·ter [silˈvestə; sɪlˋvɛstɚ] ***n***. 西尔威斯特〔男子名〕。

Syl·vi·a [ˈsilviə; ˋsɪlvɪə] ***n***. 西尔维娅〔女子名〕。

syl·vi·cul·ture [ˈsilvikəltʃə; ˋsɪlvɪ͵kʌltʃɚ] ***n***. 造林(学)。

syl·vite [ˈsilvait; ˋsɪlvaɪt], **syl·vin(e)** [ˈsilvin; ˋsɪlvɪn] ***n***. 【化】钾盐石〔一种可作肥料之天然氯化钾〕。

sym- *pref*. 〔用于 b, p, m 前〕= syn-.

sym. = symbol, symbolic【化】symmetrical; symphony.

sym·bi·ont [ˈsimbaiɔnt; ˋsɪmbaɪ͵ɑnt, ˋsɪmbɪ-] ***n***. **1.** 共栖生物。**2.** 共生者;[体]共生成分。**-tic** ***a***.

sym·bi·o·sis [simbaiˈəusis; ͵sɪmbaɪˋosɪs, ͵sɪmbɪ-] ***n***. 【生】共生(现象),共栖。*antagonistic* ~ 对抗性共生〔如藓苔等〕。

sym·bi·ot·i·cal [ˌsimbaiˈɔtikl; ͵sɪmbaɪˋɑtɪkl̩] ***a***. 【生】共生的。**-cal·ly** ***ad***.

sym·bol [ˈsimbəl; ˋsɪmbl̩] **I** ***n***. **1.** 记号,符号。**2.** 象征,表征。**3.** 【宗】信条。*a chemical* ~ 化学符号。*White is the* ~ *of purity*. 白是纯洁的象征。**II** ***vt***., ***vi***.

(*-l*(*l*)-)〔罕〕= symbolize.

sym·bol·ic, -i·cal [sim'bɔlik, -ikl; sɪm`bɑlɪk, -ɪkl] ***a***. 记号的,符号的;象征的。~ **address**【电脑】符号地址。~ **books**【宗】(基督教的)信条书〔尤指新教各派之基本教义汇编等〕。~ **logic**【数】符号逻辑,数理逻辑。

sym·bol·ics [sim'bɔliks; sɪm`bɑlɪks] ***n***.【宗】信条神学,宗教象征论;【人类学】古代宗教仪式学;符号象征学。

sym·bol·ism ['simbəlizəm; `sɪmbl͵ɪzəm] ***n***. **1**. 记号表示,符号使用;象征的表现;象征意义,象征性;【语】表象;【哲】符号论。**2**. (特指文艺方面的)象征主义。**3**.【宗】符号象征〔如以十字架象征基督受难〕。

sym·bol·ist ['simbəlist; `sɪmblɪst] ***n***. (象征)符号使用者,象征派诗人[画家],象征主义者;符号论者;符号象征学学者。**-is·tic** [ˌsimbə'listik; ͵sɪmbə`lɪstɪk] ***a***.

sym·bol·ize ['simbəlaiz; `sɪmbl͵aɪz] ***vt***. 用符号表示,是…的符号;象征,代表。**-i·za·tion** [ˌsimbəlai'zeiʃən; ͵sɪmbəlaɪ`zeʃən] ***n***.

sym·bol·o·gy [sim'bɔlədʒi; sɪm`bɑlədʒɪ] ***n***. 符号表示法;表号学,象征学;符号论。

Sy·ming·ton ['saimiŋtən; `saɪmɪŋtən] ***n***. 赛明顿〔姓氏〕。

sym·met·al·lism [sim'metəlizəm; sɪm`mɛtəlɪzm] ***n***.【经】金银混合本位,金银复体位制。

sym·met·ric, -ri·cal [si'metrik, -rikəl; sɪ`mɛtrɪk, -rɪkl] ***a***. 对称的,匀称的,相称的,平衡的。**-ri·cal·ly** ***ad***.

sym·me·trize ['simitraiz; `sɪmɪ͵traɪz] ***vt***. 使对称;使匀称,使相称,使平衡。**-tri·za·tion** [ˌsimitrai'zeiʃən; ͵sɪmɪtraɪ`zeʃən] ***n***.

sym·me·try ['simitri; `sɪmɪtrɪ] ***n***. 对称;匀称;调和;匀称美。*bilateral* ~ 左右对称。*radial* ~ 辐射对称。

Sym·onds ['saiməndz, 'simənd*z*; `saɪməndz, `sɪməndz, -nz] ***n***. 西蒙兹〔姓氏〕。

Sy·mons ['saimənz, 'simənz; `saɪmənz] ***n***. 西蒙斯〔姓氏〕。

sym·pa·thec·to·my [ˌsimpə'θektəmi; ͵sɪmpə`θɛktəmɪ] ***n***. (*pl*. *-mies*)【医】交感神经切除术。

sym·pa·thet·ic [simpə'θetik; ͵sɪmpə`θɛtɪk] **I** ***a***. **1**. 同情的,有同情心的,表示同情的。**2**. 相投合的;称心的,满意的。**3**.〔口〕抱好感的;抱同感的。**4**.【生理】交感(神经)的。**5**.【物】共鸣的,共振的。*a* ~ *strike* 同情罢工。**II** ***n***.【解】交感神经系;(对催眠术等)易感受的人。~ **ink**【化】(起初无色后来经过某种作用才现色的)隐显墨水。~ **nerve**【解】交感神经。~ **vibrations**【物】共振。**-i·cal·ly** ***ad***.

sym·pa·thin ['simpəθin; `sɪmpəθɪn] ***n***.【生化】交感(神经)素。

sym·pa·thize ['simpəθaiz; `sɪmpə͵θaɪz] ***vi***. 表示同情;相怜;同感;共鸣;同意,赞成;一致,调和 (*with*);吊慰,安慰。~ *with sb. in his grief* 对某人的悲痛表示同情。

sym·pa·thiz·er ['simpəθaizə; `sɪmpə͵θaɪzɚ] ***n***. 同情者;同感者;支持者,赞助者。

sym·pa·tho·lyt·ic [ˌsimpəθəu'litik; ͵sɪmpəθo`lɪtɪk] ***a***. 有减少交感神经系统活动作用的〔指药品,化学品等〕。

sym·pa·tho·mi·met·ic [ˌsimpəθəumi'metik; ͵sɪmpəθomɪ`mɛtɪk] ***n***. 模仿交感神经作用的〔指药品,化学品等〕。

sym·pa·thy ['simpəθi; `sɪmpəθɪ] ***n***. **1**. 同情(心);怜悯。**2**. 同感,同意,赞成;一致,协调。**3**. 慰问,吊慰。**4**.【物】共振,共鸣;【生理】交感;感应;引力。*You have my sympathies*. 你得到我的同情。***express*** ~ ***for*** 慰问。***feel*** ~ ***for***, ***have*** ~ ***for*** 同情。***in*** ~ ***with*** 同情;赞成;跟着,和…一致(*Prices are low in* ~ *with the general depression*. 物价是随着市面的普遍萧条而低落的)。***out of*** ~ 出于同情。***out of*** ~ ***with*** 对…不同情;不赞成,对…没有同感;和…不一致。***win*** ~ ***of*** 博得…的同情。~ **strike** 同情罢工〔指为声援他厂、他行业或他处之罢工工人而举行者〕。

sym·pat·ric [sim'pætrik; sɪm`pætrɪk] ***a***.【生,生态】分布区重叠的。**-pat·ri·cal·ly** ***ad***. **-pat·ry** ***n***.

sym·pet·al·ous [sim'petləs; sɪm`pɛtələs] ***a***.【植】合瓣的(= gamopetalous)。

sym·phon·ic [sim'fɔnik; sɪm`fɑnɪk] ***a***.【乐】交响乐(式)的;谐音的,调和的。~ **ballet** (有)交响乐(伴奏的)芭蕾舞。~ **dance** 交响乐舞曲。~ **poem**【乐】交响诗。**-i·cal·ly** ***ad***.

sym·pho·ni·ous [sim'fəuniəs; sɪm`fonɪəs] ***a***. 谐音的,调和的。**-ly** ***ad***.

sym·pho·nist ['simfənist; `sɪmfənɪst] ***n***. 交响乐作曲家。

sym·pho·ny ['simfəni; `sɪmfənɪ] ***n***. **1**.【乐】交响乐,交响曲。〔口〕交响音乐会。**2**.〔古〕和音,谐音,协音;(色彩等的)调和。~ **orchestra** 交响乐团[队]。

sym·phyl·lous ['simfiləs; `sɪmfɪləs] ***a***.【植】联生叶的。

sym·phys·ial [ˌsim'fiziəl; ͵sɪm`fɪzɪəl] ***a***. **1**.【解,动】联合的。**2**.【植】合生的(= symphyseal)。

sym·phy·sis ['simfisis; `sɪmfəsɪs] ***n***. (*pl*. **-ses** [-siːz; -siz])【解】(骨的)联合(线);【虫】膜连;【植】合生,拼生。

sym·po·di·um [sim'pəudiəm; sɪm`podɪəm] ***n***. (*pl*. ***-di·a*** [-diə; -dɪə])【植】假轴,假枝条,合轴。**-di·al** ***a***.

sym·po·si·ac [sim'pəuziˌæk; sɪm`pozɪ͵æk] ***a***. **1**. (古希腊)酒会的,宴会的。**2**. 座谈会的;讨论会的。**3**. 专题文集的。

sym·po·si·arch [sim'pəuziɑːk; sɪm`pozɪɑrk] ***n***. 宴会[酒会]的主人;(宴席上的)中心人物;专题讨论会上的主席。

sym·po·si·ast [sim'pəuziˌæst; sɪm`pozɪæst] ***n***. 座谈会、酒会等的参加者。

sym·po·si·um [ˌsim'pəuziəm, -'pɔ-; sɪm`pozɪəm] ***n***. (*pl*. ***-sia*** [-ziə; -zɪə]) **1**. (古代希腊的)酒会,宴会。**2**. 专题讨论会,座谈会,学术报告会。**3**. 专题论集,论业。

symp·tom ['sim*p*təm; `sɪmptəm] ***n***. 症状,征候;征兆。*an objective* [*a subjective*] ~ 客观[主观]症状;医生所能看出的外征〔病人感到的内征〕。**-less** ***a***.

symp·tom·at·ic, -i·cal [simptə'mætik, -ikəl; sɪmptə`mætɪk, -ɪkl] ***a***. 有症状的,有症候的;有征兆的;根据症状的;表征的。**-cal·ly** ***ad***.

symp·tom·a·tize ['simptəməˌtaiz; `sɪmptəmə͵taɪz] ***vt***. 表现出…的症状,有…的表征(= symptomize)。

symp·tom·a·tol·o·gy [simptəmə'tɔlədʒi; ͵sɪmptəmə`tɑlədʒɪ] ***n***.【医】症状学,征候学;(一种病的)总症状,全部症状;症候群。

syn. = synonym; synonymous; synonymy.

syn- *pref*. 〔在 l 前作 syl-, 在 b, m, p 前作 sym-, 在 r 前作 syr-, 在 s 前作 sys- 或 sy-〕共,合,同,与,连,类。

syn·aer·e·sis, syn·er·e·sis [si'niərisis; sɪ`nɛrɪsɪs] ***n***. **1**.【语音】(二)元音融合,元音缩合。**2**.【生】凝线;【化】胶体脱水收缩(作用)。**3**. 凝块,凝胶。

syn·aes·the·si·a, syn·es·the·sia [sinəs'θiːziə; ͵sɪnəs`θiʒɪə, -ʒə] ***n***.【生理】伴生感觉,联觉。**-thet·ic** ***a***.

syn·a·gog(ue) ['sinəgɔg; `sɪnə͵gɔg, -͵gɑg] ***n***. 犹太教会堂;犹太教徒的集会。**-gog·al, -gog·ic, -gog·i·cal** ***a***.

syn·a·loe·pha, syn·a·le·pha [ˌsinə'liːfə; ͵sɪnə`lifə] ***n***. 元音融合,融合音节〔两个相邻元音通常是通过省略而融合为一个音节。如: *th' eagle for the eagle*, *the eagle* 融合成 *th' eagle*〕。

syn·an·thous [si'nænθəs; sɪ`nænθəs] ***a***.【植】花和叶同时出现的。

syn·apse [si'næps; sɪ`næps] ***n***.【解】突触,(神经元的)触处。

syn·ap·sis [sin'æpsis; sɪ`næpsɪs] ***n***. (*pl*. **-ses** [-siːz; -siz])【生】染色体结合;联合;【解】突会,(神经元的)触处。**-ap·tic** ***a***.

syn·ar·thro·di·al [ˌsinɑː'θrəudiəl; ͵sɪnɑr`θrodɪəl] ***a***.【解】不动关节的。

S

syn·ar·thro·sis [sinɑːˈθrəusis; ˌsɪnɑrˋθrosɪs] ***n***. (*pl*. *-ses* [-siːz; -siz])【解】不动关节。

sync, synch [siŋk; sɪŋk] **I** ***vt*.**, ***vi***. synchronize 的缩略词。**II** ***n***. ***synchronization*** 的缩略词。

syn·caine [siŋˈkein; sɪŋˋken] ***n***.【化】盐酸即普鲁卡因。

syn·carp [ˈsinkɑːp; ˋsɪnkɑrp] ***n***. **1.**【植】复果,聚花果(= multiple fruit)。**2.** 合心皮果。

syn·car·pous [sinˈkɑːpəs; sɪnˋkɑrpəs] ***a***.【植】**1.** 合心皮的。**2.** 合心皮果的。**-car·py** ***n***.

syn·chon·dro·sis [ˌsiŋkənˈdrəusis; ˌsɪŋkɑnˋdrosɪs] (*pl*. *-ses* [-siːz; -siz]) ***n***.【解】软骨结合。

syn·chro [ˈsiŋkrəu; ˋsɪŋkro] **I** ***n***.【电】(自动)同步机。**II** ***a***. 同步的。

synchro- *comb*. *f*. 表示"同步": *synchro*mesh, *synchro*nous.

syn·chro-cy·clo·tron [ˈsiŋkrəuˈsaiklətrɔn; ˌsɪŋkroˋsaɪklətrɑn, -ˋsɪklə-] ***n***.【原】稳相[同步回旋]加速器。

syn·chro·flash [ˈsiŋkrəuflæʃ; ˋsɪŋkrəˌflæʃ] ***a***.【摄】用闪光和快门同步装置的。

syn·c(h)ro·mesh [ˈsiŋkrəmeʃ; ˋsɪŋkrəˌmɛʃ, ˋsɪn-] ***n***., ***a***.【机】同步啮合(的)。~ *gear*【机】同步齿轮。

syn·chro·nal [ˈsiŋkrənəl; ˋsɪŋkrənḷ, ˋsɪn-] ***a***. = synchronous.

syn·chron·ic, -i·cal [siŋˈkrɔnik, -ikəl; sɪŋˋkrɑnɪk, -ɪkəl] ***a***. **1.** = synchronous. **2.** 只涉及某一特定时期(而不考虑历史演变)的;【语言】共时性的。~ **linguistics** 共时语言学。

syn·chro·nism [ˈsiŋkrənizəm; ˋsɪŋkrəˌnɪzəm, ˋsɪn-] ***n***. **1.**【物】同步(性),并发,同时性,【电】同期。**2.** (历史事件的)同时处理,综合对照表示,对照历史年表;【绘画】异时事迹的同幅表现;【影】同步画面与声音。

syn·chro·nis·tic [siŋkrəˈnistik; ˌsɪŋkrəˋnɪstɪk] ***a***. = synchronous.

syn·chro·ni·za·tion [ˌsiŋkrənaiˈzeiʃən; ˌsɪŋkrənaɪˋzeʃən] ***n***. 同时;同时性;【物】同步,同期;【影】同期[步]录音,配音译制。

syn·chro·nize [ˈsiŋkrənaiz; ˋsɪŋkrəˌnaɪz, ˋsɪn-] ***vi***. 同时化,同时发生[举行](*with*);(几个钟表)指示同一时刻;【物】同步,整步;【影】声、像同步化,同步录音。— ***vt***. **1.** 使同时;【物】使同[整]步。**2.** 校准,对准(钟表)。**3.** 同时处理,综合对照表示(历史事件);【影、电视】使声像一致;作同时[步]录音处理。~**d sleep**【医】同步睡眠〔很少做梦之一种睡眠状态〕。

syn·chro·niz·er [ˈsiŋkrənaizə; ˋsɪŋkrəˌnaɪzɚ] ***n***.【电】同步器;整步器;协调器。~ **gear** 同步齿轮。

syn·chro·nous [ˈsiŋkrənəs; ˋsɪŋkrənəs, ˋsɪn-] ***a***. 同时的,同期的;【物】同步的。~ **converter**【电】同步变流机。~ **discharger**【电】同步放电器。~ **machine**【电】同步电机。~ **motor**【电】同步电动机。~ **orbit**【宇】同步轨道。~ **satellite** 地球同步卫星。~ **vibration**【物】同步振动。**-ly** ***ad***.

syn·chro·ny [ˈsiŋkrəni; ˋsɪŋkrənɪ] ***n***.【物】同步;同步性。

syn·chro·scope [ˈsiŋkrəˌskəup; ˋsɪŋkrəˌskop] ***n***.【电】同步指示仪,同步示波器。

syn·chro·tron [ˈsiŋkrətrən; ˋsɪŋkrəˌtrɑn] ***n***.【原】同步加速器。

syn·clas·tic [sinˈklæstik; sɪnˋklæstɪk] ***a***.【数】【物】(曲面)同方向的。~ **curvature** 同向曲率。~ **surface** 同向曲面。

syn·cli·nal [siŋˈklainl, sin-; sɪnˋklaɪnḷ, ˋsɪŋklɪnḷ] **I** ***a***.【地】向斜的。**II** ***n***.【地】向斜(层)。~ **axis** 向斜轴。~ **valley** 向斜谷。

syn·cline [ˈsiŋklain; ˋsɪŋklaɪn, ˋsɪn-] ***n***.【地】向斜(层)。

syn·cli·no·ri·um [ˌsiŋkləˈnɔːriəm; ˌsɪŋkləˋnorɪəm] ***n***. (*pl*. *-ri·a* [-ə; -ə])【地】复向斜。

syn·com [ˈsɪŋkɔm; ˋsɪŋkɑm] ***n***.〔口〕同步通讯卫星。

syn·con [ˈsiŋkɔn; ˋsɪŋkɑn] ***n***.〔口〕电话会议,电视会议。

syn·co·pal [ˈsiŋkəpl; ˋsɪŋkəpl] ***a***. **1.**【语】词中略去字母或音节的,如 *Gloucester* 略成 *Gloster*. **2.** 假死的;昏厥的。

syn·co·pate [ˈsiŋkəpeit; ˋsɪŋkəˌpet, ˋsɪn-] ***vt***.【语】词中省略,中略〔省去中间字母或音节;如将 never 省略成 ne'er〕;【乐】切分。**-pa·tion** [ˌsiŋkəˈpeiʃən; ˌsɪŋkəˋpeʃən] ***n***.

syn·co·pe [ˈsiŋkəpi; ˋsɪŋkəpɪ, ˋsɪn-, -ˌpi] ***n***.【语】词中省略,中略(语);【乐】切分;【医】昏厥。

syn·cre·tism [ˈsiŋkritizəm; ˋsɪŋkrɪˌtɪzəm, ˋsɪn-] ***n***. (哲学上、宗教上的)诸说混合;【语】不同变化形式的合并。**-tic** ***a***. **-ist** ***n***., ***a***. (宗教)信仰诸说混合论者(的)。

syn·cre·tize [ˈsiŋkrəˌtaiz; ˋsɪŋkrɪˌtaɪz, ˋsɪn-] ***vt***., ***vi***. (使)混合,(使)融合,(使)调合。

syn·crom·esh ***n***., ***a***. = synchromesh.

syn·cy·ti·um [sinˈsiʃiəm; sɪnˋsɪʃɪəm] ***n***. (*pl*. *-ti·a* [-ə; -ə])【动】多核体;含胞体。**-cy·ti·al** [-əl; -əl] ***a***.

synd. = syndicate.

syn·dac·tyl(e) [sinˈdæktl; sɪnˋdæktɪl] **I** ***a***. 并趾的,并指的。**II** ***n***. 并趾哺乳动物(或鸟)。**-ism** ***n***.

syn·de·sis [ˈsindisis; ˋsɪndəsɪs, sɪnˋdi-] ***n***. (*pl*. *-ses* [-siːz;-ˌsiz]) **1.** 捆扎,联结。**2.**【遗】染色体结合(= synapsis)。

syn·des·mo·sis [ˌsindesˈməusis; ˌsɪndɛsˋmosɪs] ***n***. (*pl*. *-ses* [-siːz; -siz])【解】韧带联合。**-mot·ic** [-ˈmɔtik; -ˋmɑtɪk] ***a***.

syndet = synthetic detergent 合成洗涤剂。

syn·det·ic [ˌsinˈdetik; sɪnˋdɛtɪk] ***a***.【语法】连结的,(用连接词)连接的。**-i·cal·ly** ***ad***.

syn·dic [ˈsindik; ˋsɪndɪk] ***n***. **1.** 地方行政长官。**2.**【法】经理,理事。**3.** (特指剑桥(Cambridge)大学委员会的)委员。**4.**〔美〕破产管财人。

syn·di·cal [ˈsindikl; ˋsɪndɪkḷ] ***a***. **1.** 市政官的,大学理事的;商业代理人(或经理)的。**2.** 工团主义的。

syn·di·cal·ism [ˈsindikəlizəm; ˋsɪndɪkḷˌɪzəm] ***n***. 工团[工联]主义。**-cal·ist** ***n***. 工团主义者,工联派。**-is·tic** ***a***.

syn·di·cat [sɛ̃ndiˈkɑː; sɛ̃ndɪˋkɑ] ***n***.〔F.〕工会。

syn·di·cate I [ˈsindikit; ˋsɪndɪkɪt] ***n***. **1.** 大学委员会的职务;理事会;(特指剑桥大学的)委员会。**2.** 辛迪加〔企业的联合组织〕。**3.**〔美〕报业辛迪加〔向各报刊同时出售稿件,供同时发表的企业〕。**4.** 罪犯辛迪加,操纵犯罪集团的组织。**II** [-keit; -ˌket] ***vt***., ***vi***. (使)组成组织辛迪加;由辛迪加承办;通过报业[杂志业]辛迪加在多家报刊上同时发表。~ **columnist** (多家报纸同时发表其文章的)特约专栏作家。**-ca·tion** [ˌsindiˈkeiʃən; ˌsɪndɪˋkeʃən] ***n***.

syn·di·ca·tor [ˈsindiˌkeitə; ˋsɪndɪˌketə] ***n***. 辛迪加组织者[经营者,参加者]。

syn·drome [ˈsindrəum; ˋsɪndrəˌmi] ***n***. **1.**【医】综合症,症候群。**2.** (某一事物的)全部特征;特征群;(具有某种共同性的不同事物的)集合。

syn·drom·ic [sinˈdrəumik, -ˈdrɔmik; sɪnˋdromɪk, -ˋdrɑmɪk] ***a***. 综合病症的,症候群的。

syne [sain; saɪn] ***ad***., ***prep***., ***conj***.〔Scot.〕= since; 曾经,以前。*auld lang* ~ 以往,往昔,从前。

syn·ec·do·che [siˈnekdəki; sɪˋnɛkdəkɪ] ***n***.【修】提喻法;举隅法〔以局部代表全部和以全部喻指部分,例如用 roof 表示整个 house,用 the army 表示某一个 soldier〕。**-chic, -chic·al** ***a***. **-cal·ly** ***ad***.

syn·ec·tics [siˈnektiks; sɪˋnɛktɪks] ***n***. 群体[环境]生态。

syn·e·col·o·gy [ˌsiniˈkɔlədʒi; ˌsɪnəˋkɑlədʒɪ] ***n***.【生】群落生态学。

syn·e·phrine [siˈnefriːn; sɪˋnɛfrin] ***n***.【化】交感醇。

syn·er·e·sis [siˈniərəsis; sɪˋnɛrɪsɪs] ***n***. **1.** = synaeresis. **2.** = synizesis.

syn·er·get·ic [ˌsinəˈdʒetik; ˏsɪnɚˋdʒɛtɪk] ***a*.** 合作的，协作的。**-cal·ly** ***ad*.**

syn·er·gid [siˈnəːdʒid, ˈsinə-; sɪˋnɝˋdʒɪd, ˋsɪnə-] ***n*.** 【生】助细胞。

syn·er·gism [ˈsinədʒizm; ˋsɪnɚdʒɪzm] ***n*. 1.** 配合作用〔尤指药物〕。**2.** (人体各器官各部位如肌肉的)协同作用。**-gis·tic** ***a*.** **-gis·ti·cal·ly** ***ad*.**

syn·er·gist [ˈsinədʒist; ˋsɪnɚdʒɪst] ***n*. 1.** 【生理】协同器官；【药】配合剂，增强剂，增效剂，协助药，佐药。**2.** 【宗】神人协力论者。

syn·er·gy [ˈsinədʒi; ˋsɪnɚdʒɪ] ***n*.** 协同，配合(= synergism)。**-gic** [siˈnədʒik; sɪˋnɝdʒɪk] ***a*.**

syn·e·sis [ˈsinisis; ˋsɪnɪsɪs] ***n*.** 【语法】意义明确而不合语法的结构〔如 Neither of them are present〕。

syn·es·the·si·a [ˌsinisˈθiːʒiə, -ʒiə; ˏsɪnəsˋθidʒɪə, -ʒə] ***n*.** 【生理】【心】联觉，牵边感觉，共同感觉。**-thet·ic** [-ˈθetik; -ˋθɛtɪk] ***a*.**

syn·fuel [ˈsinˌfjuːəl; ˋsɪnˏfjuəl] ***n*.** 合成燃料。

syn·ga·my [ˈsiŋgəmi; ˋsɪŋgəmɪ] ***n*.** 【生】配子配合；两性生殖。**-mic, -mous** ***a*.**

syn·gas [ˈsiŋgæs; ˋsɪŋgæs] ***n*.** 合成气〔尤指用低级煤生产的可燃气〕。

Synge [siŋ; sɪŋ] ***n*. 1.** 辛〔姓氏〕。**2. John Millington ～** 辛·米宁顿(1871—1909，爱尔兰诗人，剧作家)。

syn·gen·e·sis [sinˈdʒenisis; sɪnˋdʒɛnəsɪs] ***n*.** 【生】有性生殖；群落发生；群落演替。**-ge·net·ic** [-ˈdʒenitik; -ˋdʒɛnɪtɪk] ***a*.**

syng·na·thous [ˈsiŋnəθəs; ˋsɪŋnəθəs] ***a*.** (鱼)颌部向外伸成管状吻部的。

syn·i·ze·sis [ˌsiniˈziːsis; ˏsɪnəˋzisɪs] ***n*. 1.** 【语音】元音缩[融]合〔两相邻元音缩合而成一音节，但不构成双元音〕。**2.** 【生】凝线。

syn·kar·y·on [sinˈkæriˌɔn, -ən; sɪnˋkærɪˏɑn, -ən] ***n*.** 【生】合核体；结合核(= syncaryon)。

syn·od [ˈsinəd; ˋsɪnəd] ***n*.** 【宗】宗教会议；[转义]讨论会，会议；【天】会合。**-al** ***a*.**

syn·od·ic, -i·cal [siˈnɔdik(əl); sɪˋnɑdɪk(l)] ***a*. 1.** = synodal. **2.** 【天】会合的，相合的。～ **month** 【天】朔望月。**-ly** ***ad*.**

syn·oe·cious [siˈniːʃəs; sɪˋniʃəs] ***a*.** 【植】**1.** 雌雄混生同苞的。**2.** 精子器与颈卵器同簇的。**-ly** ***ad*.**

syn·oi·cous [siˈnɔikəs; sɪˋnɔɪkəs] ***a*.** = synoecious.

syn·o·nym [ˈsinənim; ˋsɪnəˏnɪm] ***n*. 1.** 同义字，同义词，类语(*opp*. antonym)；〔口〕类似物；【生物】(同物)异名。**2.** 【生化】同义密码子。**-i·ty** [sinəˈnimiti; ˏsɪnəˋnɪmətɪ] ***n*.** 同意义。**-ic** ***a*.**

syn·o·nym·ist [siˈnɔnimist; sɪˋnɑnəmɪst] ***n*.** 同义词研究者。

syn·on·y·mize [siˈnɔniˌmaiz; sɪˋnɑnəˏmaɪz] ***vt*.** 举出…的各个同义词，分析…的同义词。

syn·on·y·mous [siˈnɔniməs; sɪˋnɑnəməs] ***a*.** 同义词的，类语的；同义的(*with*)。**-ly** ***ad*.**

syn·on·y·my [siˈnɔnimi; sɪˋnɑnəmɪ] ***n*.** 同义(词)；同义词研究；(为加强意义的)同义词叠用。

synop. = synopsis.

syn·op·sis [siˈnɔpsis; sɪˋnɑpsɪs] ***n*.** (*pl*. ***-ses*** [-siːz; -siz]) 提要，提纲，梗概，大意；对照表，一览；说明书。

syn·op·size [siˈnɔpsaiz; sɪˋnɑpsaɪz] ***vt*.** 作…的提要，总结，作…的摘要。

syn·op·tic, -ti·cal [siˈnɔptik, -tikəl; sɪˋnɑptɪk, -tɪkl] **I** ***n*.** 〔常 S-〕以共同观点叙述的福音书(作者)。〔指圣经新约的前三部福音书及其作者〕。**II** ***a*.** 提要的，大意的；以共同观点叙述的(福音书的)。*a* ～ *chart* 【气】天气概要图。**S- Gospels** 【宗】对观福音书〔指马太福音书马可福音书和路加福音书〕。**-cal·ly** ***ad*.**

syn·op·tist [siˈnɔptist; sɪˋnɑptɪst] ***n*.** 以共同观点叙述的福音书作者。

syn·os·te·ol·o·gy [sinɔstiˈɔlədʒi; sɪˏnɑstɪˋɑlədʒɪ] ***n*.** 【医】关节学。

syn·os·te·o·sis [ˌsinɔstiˈəusis; sɪˏnɑstɪˋosɪs], **syn·osto·sis** [ˌsinəˈstəusis; ˏsɪnəˋstosɪs] ***n*.** 【解】骨性结合。**syn·os·to·tic** [ˌsinəˈstɔtik; ˏsɪnəˋstɑtɪk] ***a*.**

syn·o·vi·a [siˈnəuviə; sɪˋnovɪə] ***n*.** 【解】滑液。

syn·o·vi·al [siˈnəuviəl; sɪˋnovɪəl] ***a*.** 滑液的；滑膜的。

syn·o·vi·tis [sinəˈvaitis; sɪnəˋvaɪtɪs] ***n*.** 【医】滑膜炎。

syn·sep·al·ous [sinˈsepləs; sɪnˋsɛpləs] ***a*.** 【植】合萼的(= gamosepalous)。

syn·tac·tic, -ti·cal [sinˈtæktik, -tikəl; sɪnˋtæktɪk, -tɪkl] ***a*.** 句法的。**-ti·cal·ly** ***ad*.** **-tac·tics** ***n*.** 〔*pl*.〕【语】句法学；【数】错列组合论；【逻】句法学；符号关系学，符号组合学。

syn·tax [ˈsintæks; ˋsɪntæks] ***n*.** 【语法】**1.** 句法；句子结构学。**2.** 措辞法，字句排列法。

syn·the·sis [ˈsinθisis; ˋsɪnθəsɪs] ***n*.** (*pl*. ***-ses*** [-siːz; -siz]) 综合，【化】合成；【逻】综合(法)；【语】综合(性)；语词的合成；【医】接合；【物】合成综合。～ **gas** 【化】合成气〔多指以劣煤生产之可燃气〕。

syn·the·sist [ˈsinθisist; ˋsɪnθəsɪst] ***n*.** 综合者；合成法使用者。

syn·the·size [ˈsinθisaiz; ˋsɪnθəˏsaɪz] ***vt*.** 综合；用综合法处理；人工合成。—***vi*.** 综合；合成。

syn·the·siz·er [ˈsinθiˌsaizə; ˋsɪnθəˏsaɪzɚ] ***n*.** 合成者，合成物；〔尤指〕【电】合成器，综合器。

syn·thet·ic, -i·cal [sinˈθetik, -ikəl; sɪnˋθɛtɪk, -ɪkl] **I** ***a*. 1.** 综合的；合成的；(橡胶等)人造的。**2.** 代用的；摹拟的，假想的；虚构的；【语】综合(性)的。**II** ***n*.** 化学合成物；合成纤维(织物)；合成剂[品]。～ *detergent* 合成洗涤剂。～ *fertilizer* 人造肥料。～ *gasoline* 人造汽油，合成汽油。～ **geometry** 【数】综合几何。～ **philosophy** (H. Spence 提倡的)综合哲学。～ **resin** 【化】合成[人造]树脂。～ **rubber** 【化】合成橡胶。**-cal·ly** ***ad*.** **-thet·ics** ***n*.** 〔*pl*.〕合成品。

syn·the·tize [ˈsiŋθitaiz; ˋsɪnθəˏtaɪz] ***vt*.** = synthesize.

syn·thon [ˈsinθɔn; ˋsɪnθɑn] ***n*.** 合成纤维。

synth·pop [ˈsiŋθpɔp; ˋsɪŋθpɑp] ***n*.** 合成流行乐〔指用电子合成器(synthesizer)演奏的流行音乐〕。

syn·to·my·cin, syn·tho·my·cin [sintəˈmaisin, -θɔ-; sɪntɑˋmaɪsɪn, -θɑ-] ***n*.** 【药】合霉素。

syn·ton·ic [sinˈtɔnik; sɪnˋtɑnɪk] ***a*.** 【无】谐振[调]的；〔心〕情绪平静的，与环境相适应的。～ **circuit** 【无】谐振电路。**-i·cal·ly** ***ad*.**

syn·to·ni·za·tion [ˌsintənaiˈzeiʃən; ˏsɪntənaɪˋzeʃən] ***n*.** 【无】谐振法；同步，同期。

syn·to·nize [ˈsintənaiz; ˋsɪntəˏnaɪz] ***vt*.** 【无】使调谐，使谐振。**-r** ***n*.** 【无】共振器。

syn·to·nous [ˈsintənəs; ˋsɪntənəs] ***a*.** 【无】谐振的。

syn·to·ny [ˈsintəni; ˋsɪntənɪ] ***n*.** 【无】谐振，共振，调谐。

syph·i·lis [ˈsifilis; ˋsɪflɪs] ***n*.** 【医】梅毒。*primary* [*secondary*, *tertiary*] ～ 第一[二、三]期梅毒。～ *insontium* 先天性梅毒。

syph·i·lise, syph·i·lize [ˈsifilaiz; ˋsɪfəlaɪz] ***vt*. 1.** 使感染梅毒。**2.** 【医】以梅毒为…作预防注射。**-li·sa·tion** ***n*.**

syph·i·lit·ic [sifiˈlitik; ˏsɪfəˋlɪtɪk] **I** ***a*.** 梅毒的，梅毒性的，患梅毒的。**II** ***n*.** 梅毒病患者。

syph·i·loid [ˈsifiˌlɔid; ˋsɪfəˏlɔɪd] ***a*.** 【医】类梅毒的。

syph·i·lol·o·gy [ˌsifiˈlɔlədʒi; ˏsɪfəˋlɑlədʒɪ] ***n*.** 【医】梅毒学。**-o·gist** ***n*.**

syph·i·lo·ma [ˌsifiˈləumə; ˏsɪfɪˋlomə] ***n*.** 〔医〕梅毒瘤。

sy·phon [ˈsaifən; ˋsaɪfən, -fɑn] ***n*., *vt*., *vi*.** = siphon.

syr. = syrup.

Syr·a·cuse [ˈsaiərəkjuːz; ˋsaɪrəkjuz] ***n*. 1.** 叙拉古库斯〔意大利语作 Siracusa，西西里岛东南一港口〕。**2.** 锡拉丘兹〔美国纽约州中部城市〕。

sy·ren [ˈsaiərən; ˋsaɪrən, -rɪn] ***n*.** = siren.

S

Syr·ette [si'ret; sɪ`rɛt] *n*. 〔美〕西来皮下注射针管〔商标名〕。

Syr·i·a ['siriə; `sɪrɪə] *n*. 叙利亚〔亚洲〕。

Syr·i·ac ['siriæk; `sɪrɪ,æk] **I** *a*. 叙利亚的;古叙利亚语的;〔罕〕叙利亚的。**II** *n*. 古叙利亚语。

Syr·i·a·cism ['siriəsizəm; `sɪrɪəsɪzm] *n*. 叙利亚语风。

Syr·i·an ['siriən; `sɪrɪən] **I** *a*. (现代或古代)叙利亚的;叙利亚人的。**II** *n*. 叙利亚人。~ **Desert** 叙利亚大沙漠〔阿拉伯半岛北部〕。

Sy·rin·ga [si'riŋgə; sə`rɪŋgə] *n*. 【植】**1**. 丁香花(属)。**2**. 〔s-〕山梅花;紫丁香花。

syr·inge ['sirindʒ; `sɪrɪndʒ] **I** *n*. 注射器;水枪,注水器;注油器;洗涤器;灌肠器。*a hypodermic* ~ 皮下注射器。**II** *vt*. 注射;(用注水器)灌溉,浇(草木等);洗涤。

sy·rin·ge·al [si'rindʒiəl; sə`rɪndʒɪəl] *a*. 【动】(鸟的)鸣管的。

sy·rin·go·my·e·li·a [si,riŋgəumai'iːliə; sə,rɪŋgomaɪ`ilɪə] *n*. 【医】脊髓空洞症,脊髓神经胶瘤病。

syr·inx ['siriŋks; `sɪrɪŋks] *n*. (*pl*. ~*es*, *sy·rin·ges* [si'rindʒiːz; sɪ`rɪndʒiz]) **1**. 牧神排管芦笛。**2**. (鸟的)鸣管。**3**. 【解】耳咽管;欧氏管。**4**. 【医】瘘管,瘘。**5**. 【考古】(古埃及金字塔中通往墓穴的)曲折起伏的隧道。

syr·phid ['səːfid; `sɝfɪd] *n*., *a*. 【动】食蚜虻科(*Syrphidae*)昆虫(的)。

syr·tis ['səːtis; `sɝtɪs] *n*. (非洲北海岸的)流沙,浮沙。

syr·up ['sirəp; `sɪrəp] *n*. **1**. 糖浆。**2**. 甜蜜的情感。**3**. 〔俚〕金钱。*cough* ~ 咳嗽糖浆。*golden* ~ 【商】(餐桌上用的)高级金黄糖浆。

syr·up·y ['sirəpi; `sɪrəpɪ, `sɝ-] *a*. 糖浆状的;(音乐等)甜蜜的。

sys- *pref*. 〔用于 s 前〕= syn-.

sys(t). = system.

sy·sop ['sisɔp;`sɪsɑp] *n*. 【计】系统管理员(= system operator)。

sys·sar·co·sis [,sisɑː'kəusis;,sɪsɑr`kosɪs] *n*. 【解】肌性结合,肌性联合。

sys·tal·tic [sis'tæltik; sɪs`tæltɪk] *a*. 【医】(心脏等)收缩舒张交替的。

sys·tem ['sistim; `sɪstəm] **I** *n*. **1**. 体系,系统;分类法;组织;设备,装置。**2**. 方式;方法;作业方法。**3**. 制度;主义。**4**. 次序,规律。**5**. 世界,宇宙。**6**. 〔the ~〕身体,全身;机体。**7**. 【天】系;说。**8**. 【乐】总谱表。*a ideological* ~ 思想体系。*a* ~ *of philosophy* 哲学体系。*a refrigerating* ~ 致冷装置。*a water regulating* ~ 分水闸。*a* ~ *of management* 一整套管理方法。*a clear cutting* ~ 【林】皆伐作业。*a* ~ *of rating* 定额法。*the sales* ~ 销货法。*What* ~ *do you go upon* [*on*]? 你用什么方法进行呢? *social* ~*s* 社会制度。*the feudal* ~ 封建制度。*the great* ~ 宇宙。*the Ptolemaic* ~ 托勒密天动说。*the Copernican* ~ 哥白尼地动说。*the solar* ~ 太阳系。*Too much tea is bad for the* ~. 喝茶过多有害身体。***have one's* ~ *out of order*** 身体不好。~**s analysis** 【信息】系统分析法。~**s dynamics** 系统动力学。~**s engineering** 【信息】系统工程学。~**s software** 【电脑】系统软件。**-less** *a*.

sys·tem·at·ic [sisti'mætik;,sɪstə`mætɪk] *a*. **1**. 有系统的,成体系的;有组织的;有条不紊的,有步骤的。**2**. 【博】分类(学)的。**3**. 存心的,蓄意的;一贯的,惯常的。*a* ~ *worker* 有条不紊地工作[有一套办法]的工人。*a* ~ *liar* 一贯撒谎的人。~ *intrigues* 有计划有组织的阴谋。~ *botany* [*zoology*] 植物[动物]分类学。**-i·cal** *a*. **-i·cal·ly** *ad*.

sys·tem·a·tics [,sisti'mætiks;,sɪstə`mætɪks] *n*. 〔作单数用〕分类学,分类(法)(= taxonomy)。

sys·tem·a·tism ['sistimətizm; `sɪstəmə,tɪzm] *n*. 分门别类;制度化;体系化。

sys·tem·a·tist ['sistimətist; `sɪstəmətɪst] *n*. **1**. 照章办事者,按照系统行事者,履行制度者。**2**. 分类学者。

sys·tem·a·ti·za·tion ['sistimətai'zeiʃən; `sɪstəmətaɪ`zeʃən] *n*. 组织化;系统化,体系化;分类。

sys·tem·a·tize ['sistimətaiz; `sɪstəmə,taɪz] *vt*. 使组织起来,使组织化,使体系化,定…的次序,使有系统;把…分类。

sys·tem·a·ti·zer ['sistimətaizə; `sɪstəmə,taɪzɚ] *n*. 使系统化者;组织者;分类者;【商】组织业者,承包业者。

sys·tem·a·tol·o·gy [,sistimə'tɔlədʒi;,sɪstəmə`tɑlədʒɪ] *n*. 体系学[论],系统学[论]。

sys·tem·ic [sis'temik; sɪs`tɛmɪk] *a*. 系统的,体系的;【生理】全身的;【生】内吸收的;【农药】散发的,内吸的。~ *circulation* 全身循环。~ **insecticide** 内吸杀虫剂。~ **painting** (抽象艺术的)系统派绘画(作品)。**-i·cal·ly** *ad*.

sys·tem·ize ['sistimaiz; `sɪstəm,aɪz] *vt*. = systematize. **-i·za·tion** [,sistimətai'zeiʃən;,sɪstəmətaɪ`zeʃən] *n*.

sys·to·le ['sistəli; `sɪstə,li, -lɪ] *n*. 【生理】心脏收缩;(希腊、拉丁语诗律)长音节的缩短。**-tol·ic** [sis'tɔlik; sɪs`tɑlɪk] *a*.

sys·tyle ['sistail; `sɪstaɪl] *a*. 【建】相邻二柱间距离等于柱直径之二倍的,柱间较狭的。

sys·ty·lous ['sistiləs; `sɪstɪləs] *a*. 〔植〕合花柱的。

sy·zy·gi·al [si'zidʒiəl; sɪ`zɪdʒɪəl] *a*. 【天】朔望的。

syz·y·gy ['sizidʒi; `sɪzədʒɪ] *n*. 〔常 *pl*.〕**1**. 【天】对点[合点,望点];朔望。**2**. (相反的或有关系之)一对事物。**3**. (希腊或拉丁诗歌的)二韵脚。**-y·gal**, **syz·y·get·ic**, **sy·zyg·i·al** ['sizəgəl, 'sizidʒiəl, -'dʒetik; `sɪzəgəl, `sɪzɪdʒɪəl, -`dʒɛtɪk] *a*.

Szcze·cin [Pol. ʃtʃe'tsin; ʃtʃɛ`tsɪn] *n*. 什切青〔波兰北部港市〕。

Sze·ged ['seged; `sɛged] *n*. 塞格德〔匈牙利城市〕。

T

T, t [tiː; ti] (*pl*. **T's**, **t's** [tiːz; tiz]) **1**. 英语字母表第二十个字母。**2**. T 字形物,丁字物。*a T bandage* 丁字形绷带。***be marked with a T*** 〔英〕(犯人拇指上)被盖上 T 字烙印;是有名的盗贼。***cross one's* [*the*] *t's*** 不忘给字母 t 划上短横;点横不漏;细致入微;着重[细讲]某点(*cf*. i's)。***to a T*** 〔口〕精确,恰好,正好(*You hit it off to a T*. 你猜得恰好)。**T-shirt** 短袖圆领男汗衫。**T square** 丁字尺。

T [tiː; ti] 中世纪罗马数字的 160。$\bar{T}$ = 160,000。

t' [t; t] **1**. 〔古〕〔在动词原形前〕= to: *t'attempt* = *to attempt*

tempt. 2. 〔方〕〔在名词前〕= the: *t'bottle*.

't [t; t] **1.** 〔诗〕= it: *'tis* = it is. *do't* = do it. *on't* = on it. **2.** 〔口〕= not: *can't* = cannot.

T., t. = **1.** tenor. **2.** territory; territorial. **3.** 〔L.〕 *tomus* (= volume). **4.** ton(s). **5.** tablespoon(s). **6.** Testament. **7.** Tuesday. **8.** Turkish. **9.** tare. **10.** target. **11.** teaspoon(s). **12.** telephone. **13.** temperature. **14.** 〔It.〕 *tempo*. **15.** tome. **16.** town(ship). **17.** transit. **18.** transitive. **19.** troy.

T.A. = **1.** teaching assistant 助教。**2.** telegraphic address 电报挂号。**3.** Territorial Army 〔英〕本土军。

Ta =【化】tantalum.

ta [tɑ:; tɑ] 〔俚、儿〕谢谢。*You must say* ~. 你要说声谢谢。*Ta muchly*. 多谢。

TA = transactional analysis【心】(行为科学中的)相互作用分析。

TAA = Technical Assistance Administration (UN) (联合国)技术援助局。

Taal, taal [tɑl; tɑl] ***n.*** 塔尔语(早期的南非荷兰语)。

taa·ta [ˈtɑːtɑ:; ˋtɑtɑ] ***n.*** 〔东非英语〕(儿语)爸爸。

TAB = **1.** Technical Assistance Board (of the United Nations) (联合国)技术援助委员会。**2.** *Technical Abstract Bulletin* (US Dept. of Defense Publication)《科技简报》〔美国国防部刊物〕。

Tab [tæb; tæb] ***n.*** 〔英俚〕〔Can*tab*(rigian)之略〕剑桥大学学生[毕业生]。

tab [tæb; tæb] **I** ***n.*** **1.** (附属在衣服等上的)垂片,荷叶边;(附属在物件上用来拉动、悬挂的)拉手,耳片,扣环,带子;(帽子的)护耳;鞋带,鞋带头包铁;(卡片、纸张边上供写标签、编号用的)凸出部。**2.**【火箭】调整片,薄片,阻力板。**3.** 〔口〕账单;全部费用。**4.**【军】参谋的领章。**5.** 〔美〕小报;【剧】短剧 (= tabloid); 药片 (= tablet)。**6.** 表格;制表人 (= tabulator)。**7.** 平板;【机】工作台。***go*** ~ 〔美〕把戏剧缩短。***keep* (*a*) ~ [~*s*] *on*** 〔美〕看守,检查,监督(*He is keeping ~s on the boys*. 他看守着孩子们)。**II** ***vt.*** (**-bb-**) 〔口〕**1.** 做上耳片等。**2.** 选择,选取。**3.** 制…的一览表;记录。~ **show** 〔美〕傻瓜。

tab·a·nid [ˈtæbənid; ˋtæbənɪd] ***n.***【动】虻科 (*Tabanidae*) 动物〔包括马虻和鹿虻〕。

tab·ard [ˈtæbəd; ˋtæbəd] ***n.*** (中世纪武士穿在铠甲外面绣有纹章的)战袍;侍从武官制服;(中世纪农民穿的)粗呢宽外衣。

ta·bar·dil·lo [tɑ:bɑ:ˈdi:ljəu; tɑbɑrˋdiljo] ***n.*** 〔Sp.〕墨西哥斑疹伤寒。

tab·a·ret [ˈtæbərit; ˋtæbərɪt] ***n.***【纺】塔巴勒绸〔异色波纹和缎纹条子间隔排列〕。

Ta·bas·co, t- [təˈbæskəu; təˋbæsko] ***n.*** **1.** 塔巴斯哥(墨西哥州名)。**2.** 塔巴斯哥辣沙司。

taba·sheer, taba·shir [ˈtæbəʃiə; ˋtæbəʃɪr] ***n.*** 竹黄〔印度人用以治疗痔疮等病的药材〕。

tab·bi·net, tab·by·net [ˈtæbinet; ˋtæbɪnet] ***n.***【纺】波纹塔夫绸[毛葛]。

tab·by [ˈtæbi; ˋtæbɪ] **I** ***n.*** **1.**【纺】平纹绸[织物]。**2.** 斑猫 (= ~ cat); 雌猫; 斑蛾 (= ~ moth)。**3.** 〔主英〕老处女,爱搬弄是非的妇女。**4.**【建】(沙土及碎石混合的)土质混凝土,灰砂。**II** ***a.*** 斑纹的;有平纹的。**III** ***vt.*** 加上平纹。

tab·e·fac·tion [ˌtæbiˈfækʃən; ˌtæbəˋfækʃən] ***n.***【医】病瘦,憔悴,衰弱。

tab·er·na·cle [ˈtæbə(:)nækl, ˋtæbəˌnækl] **I** ***n.*** **1.** 临时住房;帐篷。**2.** 〔T-〕圣幕〔古犹太的移动式神堂〕;犹太神堂。**3.** (非国教徒的)礼拜堂,教堂,会堂;〔T-〕〔美〕(摩门教) Mormon 大会堂。**4.**【宗】(安置圣徒像等的)圣龛;圣室;圣柜。**5.** (作为灵魂的临时住所的)躯壳。**6.**【海】(木船的)桅座。**II** ***vi.*** 暂时栖身,灵魂附体。—***vt.*** 使居住…,置于圣龛中。**-nac·u·lar** ***a.***

ta·bes [ˈteibi:z; ˋtebiz] ***n.***【医】**1.** 消瘦,消耗,痨瘵。**2.** 脊髓痨 (= *dorsal* ~ 或 ~ *dorsalis*)。

ta·bes·cent [təˈbesnt; təˋbɛsn̩t] ***a.*** 造成浪费的,消耗性的,摧毁性的。**-cence** ***n.***

tabes dor·sa·lis [ˈteibi:z dɔ:ˈseilis; ˋtebiz dɔrˋselɪs]【医】脊髓痨。

ta·bet [ˈteibit; ˋtebɪt] ***n.*** 〔Scot.〕感觉,感触。

ta·bet·ic [təˈbetik; təˋbɛtɪk, -ˋbitɪk], **tab·id** [ˈtæbid; ˋtæbɪd] **I** ***a.***【医】脊髓痨的;脊髓梅毒性的。**II** ***n.*** 脊髓痨患者;脊髓梅毒病患者。

tab·i·net [ˈtæbinit; ˋtæbɪnɪt] ***n.*** = tabbinet.

tab·la [ˈtɑ:blɑ:; ˋtɑblɑ] ***n.***【乐】(音高可以调整的)对鼓〔尤指印度的手鼓〕。

tab·la·ture [ˈtæblətʃə; ˋtæbləˌtʃʊr, -tʃɚ] ***n.*** 桌状面;【乐】(弦乐器用的)弦线标谱(法);〔古〕想像中的景象,生动的描述;【考古】载有题铭、绘画、图案的平面[版片];碑版。

ta·ble [ˈteibl; ˋtebl̩] **I** ***n.*** **1.** 桌子;饭桌,餐台。**2.** 手术台;工作台;游戏台;赌台;写字台。**3.** (饭桌上的)食物,酒菜,伙食;一桌人〔指进餐者、玩牌者〕。**4.** 平面;平板,平盘;书板,画板;板画;碑版。**5.** 表,目录;〔*pl*.〕(古代刻有法典的)铜表;法典。**6.**【地】高原,台地。**7.** (手相)掌,手掌;【乐】共鸣板;【解】(头盖的)骨板。**8.**【建】上楣,花檐,装饰板;镶板;束带层。*the pleasures of the* ~ 饮食之乐。~ *manners* 餐桌[吃饭]礼仪,吃相。*a humble* [*poor*] ~ 简陋的饭食。*a liberal* [*bountiful*] ~ 丰盛的饮食。*the high* ~ (英大学)校长餐桌。*a* ~ *finisher* 〔美〕食量大的人。*a green* ~ (铺着绿呢桌布的)赌台,棋桌。*an operating* ~ 手术台。*the logarithmic* ~ 对数表。*the multiplication* ~ 乘法表。*a* ~ *of contents* 目次,目录。*water* ~ 潜水面,地下水面[水位]。***at*** ~ 在吃饭。(***be***) ***upon the*** ~ 尽人皆知,公开讨论的。***keep a good*** ~ 经常吃得好。***keep an open*** ~ (摆饭桌)欢迎客人。***lay*** (*a measure*) ***on the*** ~ 将(议案)延期讨论。***lay*** [***set, spread***] ***the*** ~ 摆饭桌。***learn one's*** ~***s*** 学习乘法表。***lie on the*** ~ (议案等)搁置。***on the*** ~ 公开地;摆在桌面上。***put sb. under the*** ~ 〔美〕打败(人);灌醉,使醉。***set the*** ~ ***in a roar*** 使满座的人哄笑起来。***sit*** (***down***) ***at*** (***the***) ~ 入席,就座用膳。***turn the*** ~***s*** 扭转形势;转败为胜(*The* ~*s are turned*. 形势[局面]扭转过来了)。***under the*** ~ **1.** 昏头昏脑;酒醉。**2.** 作为贿赂,私下,走后门(*put sb. under the* ~ 使人头昏脑胀。*drink sb. under the* ~ 灌醉某人。*give money under the table to get a position* 为谋求职位花钱贿赂)。***upon the*** ~ 尽人皆知。〔英〕***wait at*** ~ = 〔美〕 ***wait on*** ~ 伺候进餐。

II ***vt.*** 放在桌子上;提交讨论[考虑];〔美〕搁置(议案);支付;嵌接(木材);制表,记入表内;缝上宽边加强(风帆)。~ **bell** 桌铃。~ **book** 数学计算表手册〔如对数表等〕;桌上摆设书本〔通常为画册〕。~**cloth** 桌布,台布。~**-cut** ***a.*** (宝石)顶面磨平了的。~**-dance** ***vi.*** (半裸着身子)在桌面上跳舞,跳桌面舞。~**-flap** (折叠式桌面的)折板。~**-glass** (餐桌上的)玻璃器皿。~**-hop** ***vi.*** (在餐馆、舞场中)周旋于餐桌之间。~**-inking**【印】调墨板。~ **knife** 餐刀。~**land**【地】高原,台地。~ **linen** 餐桌用布类(桌布,餐巾等)。~ **look-up**【计】查表。~**mate** 同席进餐者,餐桌同座。~ **money** 俱乐部的餐费;(贴补高级军官的)交际津贴;~**mount** 平顶海底山;桌状山 (= guyot)。~ **planing machine** 龙门刨床。~ **salt** (精制)食盐。~**scape** 桌面景观〔指书架、钢琴架或其它桌面上的装饰品和摆设〕。~**-service** 成套餐具。~ **setter** (饭前在桌上)摆放餐具的人;〔喻〕(棒球的)一、二棒击球手〔先设法上垒,为后几棒铺路〕。~ **shore** 平低岸。~ **spoon** 汤匙,大调羹。~ **talk** 餐桌谈话;座谈,茶话。~ **talker** 吃饭时能说会道的人。~ **tennis** 乒乓球。**The T-s of the Law** (基督教)摩西十诫。~**-topped** ***a.*** 顶上平的。~**ware** 餐具。~**-water** 餐用矿泉水。~ **wine** 开胃酒〔含酒精 8-13%〕。

T

tab·leau [ˈtæbləu; ˋtæblo, tæbˋlo] ***n***. (*pl*. ~***x*** [-z; -z], ~***s***) **1**. 动人的场面,景色。**2**. 舞台造型〔由活人扮演的动人场面〕;戏剧性场面。***Tableau***! 想像一下这种情景!〔电影舞台倒叙等用语〕(= Curtain!)。~ ***vivant*** [ˈviːvɑ̃ːŋ; ˋvivɑ̃ŋ] 活画。

table d'hôte [ˈtɑːblˈdəut; ˋtæblˋdot, ˋtɑblˋdot] (*pl*. ***tables d'hote***) 〔F.〕(规定价格和菜肴供应的)客饭,份饭;(旅馆等的)公共餐桌。

tab·let [ˈtæblit; ˋtæblɪt] ***n***. **1**. (木、石等的)平板;牌子;匾额;门牌。**2**. 书板〔古代人在上写字的木质、象牙、金属薄板〕;〔常 *pl*.〕便条簿,信纸簿,图画纸簿(等)。**3**. (开火车时交司机的)开车牌,开车灯;【医】药片,片剂;(糖、肥皂等的)小块,片;【建】笠石,顶层。**4**.【计】图形输入板。*a memorial* ~ 纪念碑。

ta·bling [ˈteibliŋ; ˋteblɪŋ] ***n***. **1**. 桌布,餐巾。**2**. 制表;造册。**3**.【建】盖顶,墙帽;束带层。**4**. (木工)嵌合。**5**.【海】(帆的加固)阔边。

tab·loid [ˈtæblɔid; ˋtæblɔɪd] **I** ***n***. **1**. 〔T-〕药片。**2**. (文简图多的)小报。**3**. 文摘。**II** ***a***. 摘要的,缩编的。*a* ~ *journalism* [*newspaper*] 小报。*a* ~ *play* 短剧。***in*** ~ ***form*** 以扼要压缩形式。~ **journalism** 黄色小报,媚俗小报。~ **television** 媚俗的电视节目〔就像小报上迎合庸俗趣味的内容一样〕。

tab·loid·ish [ˈtæblɔidiʃ; ˋtæblɔɪdɪʃ] ***a***. 〔美〕小报的;简约的;非正式的。

ta·boo [təˈbuː; təˋbu] **I** ***n***. **1**.【宗】禁忌;戒律。**2**. 视为禁忌的习俗;禁止接近〔使用,交际〕。**3**.【语】禁忌语。***put the*** ~ ***on sth***., ***put sth***. ***under*** ~ 严禁。**II** ***vt***. 列为禁忌;禁止。

tabo(u)r [ˈteibə, -bɔː; ˋtebɚ] **I** ***n***. 手鼓。**II** ***vi***. 敲手鼓。

tab·o(u)·ret [ˈtæbərit; ˏtæbəˋrɛt, ˋtæbərɪt] ***n***. 矮凳;绣框,锈架;(小)手鼓。

tab·o·rin [ˈtæbərin; ˏtæbəˋrin, ˋtæbəˏrin] ***n***.【乐】(用一根鼓棒打的)小鼓(= taborine)。

Ta·briz [tɑːˈbriːz; təˋbriz] ***n***. 大布里士〔伊朗城市〕。

ta·bu [təˈbuː; təˋbu] ***n***., ***vt***. = taboo.

tab·u·la [ˈtæbjulə; ˋtæbjələ] ***n***. 〔L.〕(*pl*. ***-læ*** [-liː; -li]) 牌子,平板;书板;【解】骨板;【解】(腔肠动物的)横隔板;【古生】横板。~ ***rasa*** [ˈreisə, ˋresə] 干净(无字)的书板,白纸状态,白纸一样纯洁的心。

tab·u·lar [ˈtæbjulə; ˋtæbjəlɚ] ***a***. **1**. 板(状)的;扁平的;薄板做成的;薄层的。**2**. 表(格)的,按表格计算的。~ *spar*【矿】矽灰石。*arrange in* ~ *form* 排列成表格(形式)。*a* ~ *cash-book* 多桁[表格]式现金出纳簿。*the* ~ *standard* 按物价指数计算的币值标准表。**-ly** ***ad***.

tab·u·late [ˈtæbjuleit; ˋtæbjəˏlet] **I** ***vt***. **1**. 使成板[片]状,使成平面。**2**. 制成表格,制…的一览表。*the* ~*d quotation* 行情表。**II** [-it; -ɪt] ***a***. 平面的,板状的;【动】有横隔板的。

tab·u·la·tion [ˌtæbjuˈleiʃən; ˏtæbjʊˋleʃən] ***n***. 制表,造册,表格。

tab·u·la·tor [ˈtæbjuleitə; ˋtæbjəˏletɚ] ***n***. 制表人;(打字机的)制表键;制表机。

TAC = **1**. Technical Assistance Committee (of the Economic and Social Council of the United Nations) (联合国经济及社会理事会)技术援助委员会。**2**. Tactical Air Command 〔美〕战术空军司令部。**3**. Thai Airways Company 泰国航空公司。

tac·a·ma·hac [ˈtækəməˌhæk; ˋtækəməˏhæk] ***n***.【植】**1**. 大叶钻天杨树脂。**2**. 大叶钻天杨 (*Populus balsamifera*) (= tacamahaca, tacmahack)。

tac·au·tac [ˈtækəuˈtæk; ˋtækoˋtæk] ***n***.【剑】格刺;快速连续的挡架和攻击。

ta·ce [ˈteisiː; ˋtesi] ***vi***. 〔L.〕别说话! *T- is Latin for a candle*. 〔谑〕别漏嘴! 别开口!

tace [tæs, teis; tæs, tes] ***n***. tasse [变体]。

ta·cet [ˈteiset, ˈtæ-; ˋtesɛt] ***n***., ***vi***. 〔L.〕【乐】静默,休止。

tach(e) [tætʃ; tætʃ] ***n***. 〔古〕钩,环,扣。

tache [tɑːʃ, tæʃ; tɑʃ, tæʃ] ***n***. **1**.【医】斑点;雀斑,痣。**2**. 〔Scot.〕瑕疵,缺点。

tach·isme [ˈtæʃizəm, F. tɑːˈʃism; ˋtæʃɪzm̩, tɑˋʃɪsm] ***n***.【绘】(把颜料泼于画布上的)泼色画法。**-iste** ***a***.

tachisto-, **tacho-**, **tachy-** *comb*. *f*. 〔Gr.〕急,速: *tachy*metry.

ta·chis·to·scope [təˈkistəˌskəup; təˋkɪstəˏskop] ***n***. 速示器。**-scop·ic** [-ˈskɔpik; -ˋskɔpɪk] ***a***.

ta·chom·e·ter [tæˈkɔmitə; təˋkɑmətɚ, tæ-] ***n***. 转速计,旋速计;(飞机等的)速度计;流速计;【生理】血流计。

ta·chom·e·try [tæˈkɔmitri; təˋkɑmətrɪ] ***n***. 转速测定法。

tach·o·scope [ˈtækəuskəup; ˋtækoˏskop] ***n***. 转速表。

tachy- *comb*. *f*. 急,速。

tach·y·car·di·a [ˌtækiˈkɑːdiə; ˏtækɪˋkɑrdɪə] ***n***.【医】心搏[动]过速。

tach·y·graph [ˈtækiˌgrɑːf, -ˌgræf; ˋtækəˏgrɑf, -ˏgræf] ***n***. **1**. 速记。**2**. 速记者。

ta·chyg·ra·pher [tæˈkigrəfə, tə-; tæˋkɪgrəfɚ, tə-] ***n***. 速记者。

tach·y·graph·ic, **-i·cal** [ˌtækiˈgræfik(ə)l; ˏtækɪˋgræfɪk(ə)l] ***a***. 速记术的。

ta·chyg·ra·phy [ˌtækiˈgræfi; tæˋkɪgrəfɪ] ***n***. 速记术。**-phist** ***n***.

tach·y·la·li·a [ˌtækiˈleiliə; ˏtækɪˋlelɪə] ***n***.【语】语言急速;速语癖。

tach·y·lyte, **-lite** [ˈtækilait; ˋtækɪlaɪt] ***n***.【矿】玄武玻璃。

ta·chym·e·ter [tæˈkimitə; tæˋkɪmətɚ] ***n***.【测】(供快速测定距离、方位等用的)速测仪,视距计。

ta·chym·e·try [tæˈkimitri; tæˋkɪmətrɪ] ***n***. 视距快速测量(法),速测法。

tach·y·on [ˈtækiːɔn; ˋtækiˏɑn] ***n***. 速子。

ta·chys·ter·ol [tæˈkistəˌrəul, tə-; təˋkɪstərɑl] ***n***.【化】速甾醇。

tac·it [ˈtæsit; ˋtæsɪt] ***a***. **1**. 缄默的;不发表意见的;心照不宣的;暗中的。*a* ~ *agreement* [*understanding*] 默契。~ *approval* 默许。~ *consent* 默认[许]。**2**.【法】因法律的执行而引起的。~ *declaration*【法】默示。*the* ~ *law* 习惯法。**-ly** ***ad***. **-ness** ***n***.

tac·i·turn [ˈtæsitəːn; ˋtæsɪˏtɚn] ***a***. 无言的,沉默寡言的。**-tur·ni·ty** [ˌtæsiˈtəːniti; ˏtæsəˋtɚnətɪ] ***n***.

tack[1] [tæk; tæk] **I** ***n***. **1**. 平头钉;图钉。**2**. (裁缝)暂缝,粗缝,假缝。**3**. (英议会随财政法案提出的)附带条款。**4**.【海】纵帆当风面的上下角索;横帆当风面的上下角;(视帆向而定的)航向;同一航向的一个航程;逆风换抢,抢风行驶;〔转义〕曲折前进。**5**. 方针;方法;策略。**6**. 〔Scot.〕贷借契约,借地契约;租得的牧地。**7**. (半干油漆等的)黏着性。*a thumb* ~ 图钉。*try another* ~ 改变方针。***be on the right*** [***wrong***] ~ 航向正确[错误],方针对头[错误]。***be on the*** ~ 〔口〕戒酒。***come*** [***get***] ***down to*** (***brass***) ~***s*** 〔美〕直截了当地说,谈实际问题。***sail on the port*** [***starboard***] ~【海】左舷[右舷]抢风航行。~ ***and*** ~【海】接二连三地抢风调向。**II** ***vt***. **1**. (用平头钉)钉 (*down*)。**2**. 附加,添 (*to*; *on to*)。**3**. 暂时缝上,假缝,粗缝 (*together*; *to*)。**4**. (英议会在财政法案上)附加没有关系的条款。**5**.【海】使抢风掉向。— ***vi***.【海】抢风掉向;改变方针[政策]。

tack[2] [tæk; tæk] ***n***. **1**.【海】食物。**2**. 劣质材料;赝品;华丽而不值钱的小玩意;破烂物品。*hard* ~ (航海用的)硬面包;粗劣的食品。*soft* ~ 软面包;较精美的食品。~ **room** (牲口棚旁的)饲料间。

tack·i·fy [ˈtækifai; ˋtækɪˏfaɪ] ***vt***. 使发黏了。**-fier** ***n***.【化】增黏剂。

tack·le [ˈtækl; ˋtækl] **I** ***n***. **1.**〔复〕滑车;【海】[ˈteikl; ˋtekl] 帆的滑车索具。**2.** 用具,装备。**3.**【橄榄球】抱住(对方抱[带]球奔跑的球员)。**II** ***vt***. **1.** 用滑车拉上;用滑车固定。**2.** (给马)配上马具。**3.** 抓住,捉住,扭住;【橄榄球】抱住(对方抱[带]球奔跑的球员)。**4.** 就某事向某人交涉[争论] (*sb. on sth.*)。**5.** 应付,处理(工作等)。— ***vi***. 认真开始 (*to*)。*I ~d him on this question*. 我跟他在这个问题上展开争论。~**-fall** ***n***. 复滑车的通索。**-r** ***n***.

tack·ling [ˈtækliŋ; ˋtæklɪŋ, ˋtækl̩ɪŋ] ***n***. 扭住;复滑车装置;〔古〕(船的)索具。

tack·y[1] [ˈtæki; ˋtækɪ] ***a***. 发黏的,胶黏的。

tack·y[2] [ˈtæki; ˋtækɪ] ***a***. 〔美口〕**1.** 邋遢的;褴褛的,破旧不堪的。**2.** 俗气的,不雅观的,寒酸的。

TACMAR [ˈtækmɑː; ˋtækmɑr] (= tactical multifunction array radar) 战术多功能相控阵雷达。

ta·co [ˈtɑːkəu; ˋtɑko] ***n***. (*pl*. ***-cos***) (墨西哥)炸玉米卷〔夹有肉末和莴苣丝〕。

Ta·co·ma [təˈkəumə; təˋkomə] ***n***. 塔科马〔美国港市〕。

tac·on·ite [ˈtækəˌnait; ˋtækəˏnaɪt] ***n***. 【矿】铁燧石,矽铁矿。

tact [tækt; tækt] ***n***. 机智,机敏;得体;老练,圆滑;【乐】拍子;〔罕〕触觉。

tact·ful [ˈtæktf*u*l; ˋtæktfəl] ***a***. 机智的,机敏的;得体的;老练的,圆滑的。**-ly** ***ad***. **-ness** ***n***.

tac·tic [ˈtæktik; ˋtæktɪk] **I** ***n***. = tactics. **II** ***a***. **1.** 顺序的,依次排列的。**2.**【化】有规结构的;【生】(有)趋性的。

tac·ti·cal [ˈtæktikəl; ˋtæktɪkl] ***a***. 战术(上)的;策略(高明)的,善于机变的。*a ~ diameter*【海】回转直径。*a ~ flagship*【美海】作战旗舰。*a ~ march* 战备行军。*~ obstacles* 战斗障碍物。*~ situation* 战况。**-ly** ***ad***.

tac·ti·cian [tækˈtiʃən; tækˋtɪʃən] ***n***. 战术家;战略家;策略家。

tac·tics [ˈtæktiks; ˋtæktɪks] ***n***. **1.** 战术〔*cf*. strategy〕;策略。*grand* [*minor*] ~ 高等[小]战术。*the two ~* 两种策略;两手。*customary ~* 惯用的伎俩。**2.**【语】法素学;序素学。

tact·ile [ˈtæktail; ˋtæktɪl] ***a***. 触觉的,有触觉的,能触知的;【绘】表现[具有]实体感觉的。*~ hairs*【生】触毛。*a ~ organ* 触觉器官。*~ values* 触觉值。*~ corpuscle* 触觉小体。

tac·til·i·ty [tækˈtiliti; tækˋtɪlətɪ] ***n***. 感触性。

tac·tion [ˈtækʃən; ˋtækʃən] ***n***. 〔罕〕接触。

tact·less [ˈtæktlis; ˋtæktlɪs] ***a***. 无机智的,不机敏的;不圆滑的;笨拙的。

tac·tom·e·ter [ˈtæktɔˈmitə; tækˋtɑmətɚ] ***n***. 触觉计。

tac·tu·al [ˈtæktjuəl; ˋtæktʃuəl] ***a***. 触觉的,触觉器官的。**-ly** ***ad***. 用触觉。

TACV = tracked air cushion vehicle 履带式气垫车〔在混凝土轨道上开行的高速气垫列车〕。

tad[1] [tæd; tæd] ***n***. 〔美俚〕小(男)孩。

tad[2] [tæd; tæd] ***n***. 少量。

tad·pole [ˈtædpəul; ˋtædˏpol] ***n***. 【动】蝌蚪;〔*pl*.〕〔美谑〕Mississippi 人的别名;〔美〕法国小孩。*~'s shimmy*〔美〕适当的东西。~ **galaxy**【天】蝌蚪星系〔一群其结构伸长如蝌蚪状的射电星系〕。

Ta·dzhik·i·stan [tɑːˈdʒikistɑːn; təˋdʒɪkɪˏstæn, -ˏstɑn] ***n***. 塔吉克。

taedi·um vi·tae [ˈtiːdiəmˈvaitiː; ˋtidɪəmˋvaɪti] 〔L.〕厌世观。

tael [teil, ˈteiəl; tel] ***n***. 两〔中国从前的衡量和货币单位;印度、印度支那等的重量单位,约 = $1\frac{1}{3}$ 盎斯〕。

tae kwon do [ˈteiˈkwɔnˈdəu; ˋteˋkwɑnˋdo] ***n***. 【体】跆拳道〔一种可以拳打脚踢的徒手格斗术〕。

ta'en [tein; ten] 〔方、诗〕= taken.

tae·ni·a [ˈtiːniə; ˋtinɪə] ***n***. (*pl*. ***-niæ*** [-niiː; -nɪi]) (古希腊、罗马的)头带;【解】带状结构;【建】(多利斯建筑的)束带饰;【动】条虫(属)。~**cide**【医】杀条虫剂。~**cidal** ***a***. 杀条虫的。**-sis**【医】条虫病。

tae·ni·oid [ˈtiːniɔid; ˋtinɪˏɔɪd] ***a***. 带状的;(像)条虫的。

TAF = Tactical Air Force〔美〕战术空军。

T.A.F. = tumour angiogenesis factor 肿瘤生成因子。

taf·fer·el, taff·rail [ˈtæfərəl, ˈtæfreil; ˋtæfərəl, ˋtæfrel] ***n***. 【船】船尾上部;船尾栏杆。

taf·fe·ta, taf·fe·ty [ˈtæfitə, ˈtæfiti; ˋtæfɪtə, ˋtæfɪtɪ] ***n***. 塔夫绸,平纹绸,府绸。

taf·fy [ˈtæfi; ˋtæfɪ] ***n***. **1.** = toffee 太妃糖。**2.**〔美俚〕拍马屁,奉承。~ **pull**〔美〕拍马奉承的交际集会。

taf·ia, taf·fi·a [ˈtæfiə; ˋtæfɪə] ***n***. 塔非亚酒〔西印度群岛用甘蔗制的一种甜酒〕。

Taft [tæft, tɑːft; tæft] ***n***. 塔夫脱〔姓氏〕。

tag[1] [tæg; tæg] **I** ***n***. **1.** (衣服上的)垂下物,附属物;带端的金属箍[包头]。**2.** 标签;附笺,贴纸;(系在被监控的人或物上的)电子跟踪标签。**3.** (动物的)尾;(衣服等的)边,饰缝;(电缆等的)终端。**4.** (文章、演说终了时的)结束语;陈套语,(诗歌末尾的)叠句;(戏剧的)收场白。**5.** 卑劣人物;下层平民。**6.** 卷发,卷毛;(羊的)缠结纷乱的毛。**7.** (花体字的)拖长的尾巴;〔美俚〕花笔涂画的留名〔用漆喷涂在公共场所墙上等的个人代号〕。**8.**〔美俚〕浑名。*a parts ~* 零件牌。*a price ~* 价目标签。~ ***and rag*** = ~, ***rag and bobtail*** = tagrag 下层社会。**II** ***vt***. (**-gg-**) **1.** 装金属箍(在带端);标记;加标签;加上(附加物),添加 (*to*; *on to*);接连 (*together*);押韵。**2.** 剪(羊的)缠结难分的乱毛。**3.**〔口〕尾随。**4.**〔口〕给…起诨名,把…叫做。**5.**【原】(用同位素)作标记,示踪。**6.**〔美口〕(对车辆)放上一张停车票;(对开车者)给一张犯规通知。**7.**〔美俚〕在(公共场所墙上等)喷涂留名;以花笔涂画装饰(场所等)。— ***vi***. 〔口〕紧跟在后头,钉在后头,追随,尾随 (*at sb.'s heels, after sb.*)。*~ged atom* 示踪原子,标记原子。~ **board** 作货运标签等用的硬纸。~ **day**〔美〕慈善事业街头募捐日(对捐款者赠以小标签)。~ **end** 末端;残余。~**line**〔美俚〕(高潮下的)结尾语。~ **question**【语法】附加疑问〔例: You're ready, *aren't you*?〕。~**rag** 跟在后面瞎哄乱嚷的人们;下层社会;(破烂衣服上垂挂着的)破布,褴褛。~ **sale**〔美〕(宅前)标价出售(清宅旧货)〔亦作 garage sale〕。~**tail**〔美〕食客,帮闲。~ **team** 互助合作小组。~**-team** ***vt***. 和…搭档。~**-team match** 车轮式比赛;团体对抗赛。~ **up**【棒球】返垒。

tag[2] [tæg; tæg] **I** ***n***. 捉迷藏。**II** ***vt***. (玩捉迷藏时)捉住。

Ta·ga·log [tɑːˈgɑːlɔg, ˈtægəlɔg; ˋtægəˏlɑg, tɑˋgɑlɑg] ***n***. **1.** (*pl*. ***-logs, -log***) 他加禄人〔菲律宾岛上的马来亚人〕。**2.** 他加禄语〔1962 年定为菲律宾国语〕。

tag·ger [ˈtægə; ˋtægɚ] ***n***. **1.** 垂下物;附随者。**2.** 装(金属箍等)的人;加贴标签的人。**3.** 剪乱羊毛的器具。**4.**〔*pl*.〕极薄的铁片。**5.** (捉迷藏中的)捉人者。

tag·meme [ˈtægmiːm; ˋtægmim] ***n***. 【语】法位〔语法单位〕,序位;语法功能段。**-me·mic** [-ˈmiːmik; -ˋmimɪk] ***a***.

tag·me·mics [tægˈmiːmiks; tægˋmimɪks] ***n***. 〔*pl*.,作单数用〕【语】法位学,序位学。

Ta·hi·ti [tɑːˈhiːti; tɑˋhitɪ, -ti] ***n***. 塔希提岛〔南太平洋〕。

Ta·hi·ti·an [təˈhiːʃən, tɑː-, -tiən; tɑˋhitɪən] **I** ***a***. 塔希提岛的,塔希提人的,塔希提语的。**II** ***n***. **1.** 塔希提人〔尤指塔希提岛的波利尼西亚人〕。**2.** 塔希提语〔指波利尼西亚语〕。

TAI = **1.**〔F.〕*Transports Aériens Intercontinentaux*〔法〕洲际航空运输公司。**2.** Thai Airway International 泰国国际航空公司。

tai·ga [ˈtaigə; ˋtaɪgə] ***n***. (北部亚寒带的)针叶林带;泰加群落〔森林〕;针叶树大森林。

tail[1] [teil; tel] **I** ***n***. **1.** 尾巴。**2.** 尾状物,垂下物;(西服的)垂尾,燕尾;〔*pl*.〕燕尾服。**3.** 辫子;风筝尾巴。**4.** 末端;结尾,后部;〔俚〕屁股。**5.** 随员,扈从;【军】军属队伍;属

T

员,跟在后面的人,晚辈;〔美俚〕尾随的侦探;(等候购物等)排成一行的人们,长蛇阵。**6.** 钱币的反面。**7.**【建】(瓦、石板等露出的)下部;【乐】符尾;【空】尾翼;尾面;【天】彗星尾;【印】(书页的)地脚。**8.**〔*pl*.〕渣滓,(剩下的)尾脚。*the* ~ *of the eye* 外眼角。*She wears her hair in a* ~. 她梳着辫子。*a* ~ *gate* 下闸门。*a* ~ *wind* 由后面吹来的风。*a* ~ *fin* 尾鳍。***at the* ~ *of*** 在末尾,在最后。***cannot make head or* ~ *of*** 不知道是什么事情。***close on sb.'s* ~** 迫近某人后头,就在某人后头。***get one's* ~ *down*** 畏缩,害怕,丧失勇气。***get* [*keep*] *one's* ~ *up*** 情绪很高,振奋,有勇气,有精神。***go into* ~*s*** 穿燕尾服(等)。***have one's* ~ *up* [*down*]** 情绪好[不好]。***keep the* ~ *in waters*** 〔口〕兴隆,走运。***out of the* ~ *of the eye*** 斜瞅。***play* (*at*) *heads and* ~*s*** 扔钱猜正面还是反面。**~*s up*** (人)精神好;〔喻〕跃跃欲试。***turn* ~** 退走,掉头,逃走。***twist the* ~ *of*** 做出使…讨厌的事情;触犯…。***with the* ~ *between the legs*** 夹着尾巴;〔喻〕惊恐,垂头丧气,畏缩。***with the* ~ *of the eye*** 斜瞅。

II *vt*. 装上(风筝)尾巴;添上,接上,连结上 (*on*; *on to*);跟踪,尾随;〔口〕切去尾巴,切去末端;(狗等)拖着尾巴;【建】(把材料的一端)嵌入 (*in*; *into*; *on*)。—***vi*.** 尾巴似地垂下,拖着尾巴;尾巴似的[分散地]拖在后面;跟在后头,排成队;船尾搁浅(在暗礁上);(停泊时)把船尾掉向顺风[顺流]方面;(鱼)把尾巴露出水面。~ ***after*** 尾随,排在…的后头(*Some fifteen boys* ~*ed after the parade*. 十五六个男孩尾随在游行队伍之后)。~ ***away* [*off*]** 零零落落地落在后头,弄得零零落落;渐渐变细,渐渐减少,渐渐消失(*The path* ~*s off into the woods*. 小径逐渐消失在树林中)。~ ***out*** 〔美〕逃走;走。~ ***to the tide*** = ~ ***up and down the stream*** (停泊的船)使船尾顺着潮流[河流]。~ ***up*** 〔美〕使病牛站起。~**back** **1.**【橄榄球】(置于发球线后方的)尾后卫。**2.**〔英〕(因交通堵塞引起的)汽车长蛇阵。~**board** (卡车,装货马车等的)后箱板。~**bone** 尾骶骨。~**coat** 燕尾服。~**covert**【动】尾部覆羽。~**dive**【空】尾坠。~**-down *ad*., *a*.**【空】机尾朝下(的)。~**drop**【空】尾坠。~**end** 尾端;末尾;〔*pl*.〕(谷类的)屑。~**fan**【动】扇尾鳍。~**fin *n*.** 尾鳍;【空】直尾翼;垂直安定面。~**gate** **1.** = ~board. **2.** ***vi*., *vt*.** 紧跟前车行驶。~**-heavy *a*.**【空】尾部重的;后头重的。~**light**(= ~ **lamp**) (汽车等的)尾灯。~**margin**【印】(书页的)地脚。~**piece** 尾片;附属物;【建】半端梁;【机】尾端件;【印】补白图案;(提琴等的)系弦板。~**pipe** (汽车等的)排气尾管;(烟斗的)吸管。~**plane**【空】横尾翼,水平安定面。~**race** (水车的)泄水道。~**skid**【空】尾橇。~**-slide**【空】尾冲。~**spin**【空】尾旋,螺旋;〔转义〕失去控制;混乱。~**stock**【机】尾座[架];顶针[尖]座(= foot stock)。~**-turret**【空】机尾炮塔。~**-wagging** (滑雪中)高速转身;【空】摆尾〔一种特技飞行〕。~**wind** 顺风。**-ee *n*.** 被盯梢的人。**-ing *n*.** 装尾巴;【建】嵌入墙壁内的砖石凸出部;屑,糟,渣滓,矿渣。**-ism *n*.** 尾巴主义。

tail[2] [teil; tel] **I *n*. 1.**【法】限定继嗣;限定继承权;限嗣继承财产。**2.**【印】(书籍页面的)地脚;底边空白。*an estate in* ~ 限嗣继承财产。*an heir in* ~ 限定继承人。**II *a*.** 限定继承的。

tail·end·er [ˈteilendə; ˋtelˋɛndɚ] ***n*.** 占倒数第一名者。

tail·gate[1] [ˈteilˌgeit; ˋtelˏget] **I *n*. 1.** (车辆后部的)尾板,后挡板。**2.** (运河的)下闸门。**II *vt*., *vi*.** 紧跟前面的车辆之后行驶。

tail·gate[2] [ˈteilgeit; ˋtelˏget] ***n*.** 〔美〕狂热的爵士音乐演奏。**-r *n*.**

taille [teil, F. ˈtɑːjə; tel, ˋtɑjə] ***n*. 1.** (法国国王或领主征收的)封建税〔指人头税或代役税〕。**2.**〔罕〕妇女胸部的形状,或妇女背心的式样。

tai·lor [ˈteilə; ˋtelɚ] **I *n*.** (*fem*. ~*ess* [-ris; -rɪs]) 裁缝,缝工,成衣工;【军】缝纫兵。*The* ~ *makes the man*. 〔谚〕佛靠金装人靠衣裳。~*'s clippings* 衣料样本。***ride like a* ~** 不善骑马。***sit* ~ *fashion*** 盘腿坐。**II *vi*.** 开服装店;做裁缝,做衣服。— ***vt*.** 缝制(衣服);供应服装。*He is well* ~*ed*. 他的衣服做得好。~**-bird** 长尾缝叶莺。~**-made *a*. 1.** 缝制得讲究的;服装讲究、大方的。**2.** 定做的。**3.** 香烟机卷的〔自卷之对〕。

tai·lor·ed [ˈteiləd; ˋteləd] ***a*. 1.** (女式服装)线条简单、腰身合体的。**2.**〔美〕简单明了的,干净利落的。

tai·lor·ing [ˈteiləriŋ; ˋtelərɪŋ] ***n*. 1.** 裁缝业,成衣业。**2.** 裁缝法,缝工。

tain [tein; ten] ***n*.** 薄锡板,锡箔。

Taine [tein; ten, tɛn], **H. A.** 泰纳〔1828—1893,法国的批评家,历史家〕。

Tai·no [ˈtainəu; ˋtaɪno] ***n*. 1.** (*pl*. ***-nos, -no***) 泰诺人〔西印度群岛的一支已绝种的印第安人〕。**2.** 泰诺语〔属阿拉瓦语〕。

taint [teint; tent] **I *vt*.** 弄脏,污染;使感染(病毒等);毒化(思想,感情等),使腐败;使坠落。— ***vi*.** 沾染;感染;腐败,坠落。*His character is* ~*ed by selfseeking*. 他的性格带有利己的缺点。~*ed family* 有遗传病的家族。~*ed goods* 非工会会员制造或经手的商品,来历不明的商品。~*ed meat* 腐肉。~*ed money* 肮脏钱。*Meat will readily* ~ *in close weather*. 肉在闷热天气容易腐败。**II *n*. 1.** 污点;污名。**2.** 传染;腐败。**3.**〔废〕气味,痕迹。

'tain't [teint; tent] = it ain't.

taj [tɑːdʒ; tɑdʒ] ***n*.** (伊斯兰教徒的)圆锥形高帽。**T-Mahal** [məˈhɑːl; məˋhɑl] (印度 Agra 的)泰姬陵。

Ta·jik [ˈtɑːdʒik; ˋtɑdʒɪk] ***n*. 1.** (*pl*. ***-jiks, -jik***) 塔吉克人[族]。**2.** = Tajiki.

Ta·jik·i [ˈtɑːdʒiki, tɑːˈdʒiːki; ˋtɑdʒɪkɪ, tɑˋdʒikɪ] ***n*.** 塔吉克语〔塔吉克人说的波斯方言〕。

Ta·jik·i·stan [ˈtɑːdʒikistæn; ˋtɑdʒɪkɪstæn] ***n*.** 塔吉克斯坦〔中亚一国家名〕。

take [teik; tek] **I *vt*.** (***took*** [tuk; tʊk]; ***taken*** [ˈteikən; ˋtekən]) **1.** (用手)拿,取,抓,握,捕,捉,逮捕;俘虏;攻取,占领;【牌】吃掉,胜过。~ (*sb.*) *in the act* 当场逮捕。~ *sb. in one's arms* [*heart, breast*] 抱住某人,拥抱某人;爱上某人。~ *sb. by the nose* 捏住某人鼻子。~ *a fortress by storm* 用猛攻夺下要塞。~ *sth. up with one's fingers* 用手指拿起某物。~ *sth. on one's shoulder* 掮起某物。**2.** 取得;获得,拿到;(从某处)得到,取出;发源于。~ *a degree* 取得学位。*He* ~*s 100 dollars a month*. 他拿一百块钱的月薪。*What will you* ~ *for this bicycle*? 这部自行车你要(卖)多少钱? *I will not* ~ *a cent less*. 一分钱也不能少。~ *a name from the inventor* 得名于它的发明者。*The river* ~*s its rise from a lake*. 这条河发源于一个湖。**3.** 携带;带去;带领参观;搬移。~ *sb. about a town* 领人参观城市。~ *sb. through a book* 指导某人读一本书。*Will this road* ~ *me to the station*? 这条路能到车站吗? ~ *the dog out for a walk* 带领狗出去散散步。**4.** 买;预订(座位等);订阅;租借(房子)。*I'll* ~ *the book for two yuan*. 这书要是卖两元我就买了。*Which newspapers do you* ~? 你订阅哪几份报纸? ~ *a cottage at the seaside for* (*the*) *summer* 在海边租一所小房子过夏。**5.** 接受(礼物等);娶(妻);收(房客等);采用,选取;接纳(新会员等)。~ *things as they come* 来什么接受什么。~ *medical advice* 受医生诊断。~ *a wife* 娶妻。~ *a woman to wife* 娶一个女人做妻子。~ *lodgers* 收房客。**6.** 理解,领悟(言语、行动的意义);认为,想像,当做。*I* ~ *it that* … 我以为…。*Do you* ~ *me*? 你懂我的意思吗? *How would you* ~ *this passage*? 这一节你怎么解释? ~ *something well* [*in good part*] 往好的方面解释某事,把…当做好意。~ *something ill* [*amiss, in ill part*] 往坏的方面解释某事,把…当做恶意。*Must not* ~ *ill of him*. 不要怪他。**7.** 听

从(忠告);甘受,忍受(侮辱等);担负(责任);答应(请求等);担任(职位);执行(任务等)。*T- my word for it*. = *You may* ~ *it from me*. 你相信我的话好了。你可以相信那是真的。~ *the blame* 担负过失的责任。~ *orders* 接受命令[任命]。~ *the throne* [*crown*] 接受王位;即位。**8.** 耗费(时间等);需要(多少时间等)。*These things* ~ *time*. 这些事情需要花费时间。*It* ~*s an hour to go there*. 到那里需要一个钟头。**9.** 搭乘,骑;进去,隐藏;越过,渡过。~ *a train* 坐火车。~ *ship* 坐船。~ *a hurdle* 跳过栏去。~ *a bus to town* 乘公共汽车进城。**10.** 拿走,取走,消除;减去。~ *sb.'s life* 杀死。~ *3 from 5* 五减三。**11.** 记录,记下;描画;拍摄;量(尺寸等)。~ *notes* 做记录。~ *a speech* (听报告)做笔记。~ *measurements* 量尺寸。~ *sb.'s measure* 量某人身长;〔喻〕看穿某人。~ *sb.'s temperature* 量某人的体温。**12.** 采取(某一行动);发生(某种感情等),经验。~ *action* 采取行动。~ *comfort* 得到安慰。~ *delight* (*in*) 对…感觉愉快[快乐],欢喜…。~ *a trip* 旅行。~ *a walk* 散步。~ *a rest* 休息。*A disease* ~*s its course*. 病加重。**13.** 吃;喝;吸入;服用。~ *a cup of tea* 喝一杯茶。~ *a meal* 吃饭。~ *a deep breath* 行深呼吸。~ *too much* 吃得[喝得]太多。*die by taking poison* 服毒死亡。**14.** (病)侵袭;(火)着起来,烧到;吸收(染料等)。*be taken ill* [*bad*] 生病。~ *fire* 着火;发怒,生气。**15.** 打中,击中;出其不意地袭击;吸引,迷住;欺骗;〔美俚〕打败,打垮。~ *sb. by surprise* 突然袭击某人。*be much taken with* [*by*] *a girl* 深深地爱上一个姑娘。~ *sb.'s fancy* 占有某人的心。~ *a fancy to sb*. 爱上某人。*He took his readers with him*. 他把他的读者吸引住。*I was badly taken*. 我大大受骗了。**16.** 采取(形状、态度、意见、主义等);发(誓)。~ *an oath* 发誓。**17.**【乐】奏,弹,唱。— ***vi*. 1.** 拿,取,获得;获得财产。**2.** 拿去,除去;减去;损失(价值等);扣除。**3.** (鱼鸟等)被捕,被捉。*Fish always* ~ *best after rain*. 雨后鱼最好钓。**4.** (药)奏效;(牛痘等)发;〔罕〕烧着;【化】凝结,凝固;(墨水在纸上)吃得牢,不容易褪色。*Dry fuel* ~*s readily*. 干燥的燃料极易着火。**5.** 欢喜,爱好 (*to*);开始 (*to*)。**6.** 受欢迎,博得喝彩。**7.** (相)照得(好或不好)。*She* ~*s better standing*. 她的相是站着照较好。**8.** 去,前进,赴,到 (*across fields, to the wood*)。~ *down the mountain on a run* 一口气跑下山。**9.** 〔口〕得(病),(病)传染。~ *ill* 〔口、方〕= be taken ill. **10.** 生根;发芽。**11.** 〔美〕(立刻)采取行动而…〔用 ~ *and* ... 的形式,差不多没有增加什么意义〕。*If you do so I will* ~ *and tell father*. 你要是这样做我就告诉父亲。***be taken in one's prime*** 夭亡,短命而死。***be taken prisoner*** 被俘,成俘虏。***be taking a beating*** 挨打。~ ***a back seat*** 〔美俚〕让别人领头,谦逊。~ ***a bow*** 〔美俚〕鞠躬答谢喝彩;〔美〕值得赞美。~ ***a brief*** 【法】受理案件。~ ***a brodie*** 〔美俚〕得不到喝彩;跌倒;(演出)失败;(名誉等)迅速败坏。~ ***a bush*** 逃进树林里。~ ***a challenge lying down*** 〔美俚〕拒绝挑战,不参加比赛。~***a chance*** 〔美〕冒险,做做看。~ ***a corner*** 拐弯。~ ***a cottage course*** 〔美〕(大学生)在毕业前结婚。~ ***a fall*** 〔美俚〕跌倒;(被)打败;受挫折。~ ***a flier*** 做投机买卖。~ ***a gander at*** 〔美口语〕看,瞧,仔细检查。~ ***a hot squat*** 〔美俚〕被执行死刑。~ ***a knock*** 〔美〕被监禁。~ ***a licking*** 〔美俚〕失败;弄糟;赔本。~ ***a poke at*** 〔美俚〕打,殴,正面攻击人;讽刺人。~ ***a pot shot*** 〔美俚〕乱打(枪);瞎猜。~ ***a program*** 〔美俚〕顺从,照办。~ ***a punch at*** 〔美俚〕打算。~ ***a risk*** 【商】承受保险。~ ***a*** (***run-out***) ***powder*** 〔美俚〕逃掉,跑掉。~ ***a shot at*** 〔美俚〕抓牢机会;试一试。~ ***a slope*** 上坡。~ ***a swap*** [***swop***] 售物者挨顾客一顿骂。~ ***a turn*** (***on the beach***) (在岸上)散步。~ ***a whirl at*** 〔美俚〕企图。~ ***after*** 尾随;仿效;像。~ ***an account of stock*** 【商】清点存货,盘货。~ ***an opponent over the sticks*** 【美体】打败对手。~ ***away*** 拿走;剥夺;减;收拾饭桌。~ ***back*** 拿回,收回;取消(约定等),承认说了错话。~ ***coolly*** 泰然处之。~ ***cover*** 躲避,躲藏。~ ***down*** 拿下,扯下,降下,卸下;卷起;记下;卸下;拆,拆毁(房子),拆散(头发),分开;挫其骄气;吞下去,咽下去。~ ***down one's*** (***back***) ***hair*** [~ ***one's*** (***back***) ***hair down***] 〔美俚〕坦白地说;推心置腹。~ ***earth*** (狐)逃进洞里;隐藏。~ ***for*** 认为,以为;当做;误认,弄错(*I was taken for my sister*. 人家把我错认做我的妹妹了。*What do you* ~ *me for*? 你把我当作什么人? 你以为我是做什么的?)。~ ***for a ride*** 〔美匪俚〕绑去杀死,欺骗。~ ***from*** 减少(…的重量、价值等)(~ *from the pleasure* 减少兴趣。*The size of her hat* ~*s from her height*. 因为帽子大她的身段就显得矮了)。~ ***in*** **1.** 收进;收容,留宿;装入(货物);带进(房间等)。**2.** 接收(钱);在自己家里承接(洗衣、缝纫等);〔英〕订阅(报纸等)。**3.** 包括,包容,加以考虑;〔美〕访问,参观。**4.** 缩小,弄窄(衣服等);卷(帆),收帆。**5.** 理会,了解。**6.** 欺骗(*I was nicely taken in*. 我上了大当)。~ (*a boy*) ***in charge*** 收养(孩子)。~ ***in tow*** 【海】牵船;牵航。~ ***in your washing***!【海】收护舷物,收索端。~ ***into account*** [***consideration***] 考虑到。~ ***into camp sb***. 骗过,瞒过;使某人上当。~ ***into*** (*one's*) ***confidence*** 信任。~ ***into one's head*** [***mind***] 忽然想起[想到]。~ ***it*** 相信;〔口〕受罚;〔美俚〕甘心受批评[奚落];勇敢地忍受不幸(等)。~ ***it and like it*** 〔美俚〕不大甘心地忍受批评[嘲笑、不幸(等)]。~ ***it away*** 〔美俚〕去干吧。~ ***it easy*** 轻松点! ~ ***it hard*** 关心,担心;悲伤。~ ***it on the chin*** 〔美俚〕赛输;考不上,失败。~ ***it on the lam*** 〔美俚〕仓皇逃走。~ ***it out of*** 向…报仇[泄恨];使失势;使疲乏;虐待,剥削,榨取…的血汗。~ ***it out on*** (*sb*.) 拿(别人)出气(*They were taking it out on one another because of their hopeless dissatisfaction*. 他们由于没有希望获得满足而彼此以恶言相敬来出气)。~ ***it that*** 相信,信以为,认为。~ ***it*** (***up***) ***on one*** (***self***) (*to do*) = ~ upon one (self). ~ ***off*** **1.** ***vt***. 取出,拿走;脱去(帽子、衣服等),剥;放(手等);移,移送;带走,带去;免除(~ *off a heavy tax* 免除重税);杀死,弄死(*be taken off by cholera* 患霍乱丧命);免职;减(价);喝干;抄写,印;学(人家的样),学样取笑。**2.** ***vi***. 动身,起程;走掉;退职;跳出;【空】起飞;(潮)退落;(风)停息。~ ***on*** **1.** ***vt***. 承接,担任(工作等);较量(~ *sb. on at golf* 和某人比赛高尔夫球);装(某种样子);呈现(形势);长(肉);雇用,给加入,给入伙;〔美〕打败人。**2.** ***vi***. 〔口〕愤激,激昂,悲伤欲绝(*Don't* ~ *on so*! 别这样悲伤);受欢迎,得人心。~ ***on a cargo of this*** 〔美〕请细心听这件事吧。~ ***one's life in one's hand*** 冒极大危险。~ ***one's life upon a thing*** 拚着性命去做某事。~ ***oneself away*** [***off***] 走掉,离开。~ ***out*** 取出;带到,带出(散步等);拔(牙等),除去(污点等);取得(专卖权等),拿到(执照等);借出(书籍等);摘出(要点);(桥牌)表示不同意伙伴所叫的花色而改叫。~ ***out of*** 取出,除去;要赔偿;报仇(*That* ~*s all the fun out of it*. 那扫兴极了。~ *a leaf out of sb.'s book* 仿效某人)。~ ***over*** 接收,接手,接办,接管;继承。~ ***sb. by the hand*** 握住[牵着]某人的手。~ ***sb. for all in all*** 无论从哪一点来看,各方面都。~ ***sth. lying down*** 甘心容忍[屈服](*He doesn't* ~ *such an insult lying down*. 他不能忍受这样的侮辱)。~ ***the air*** 升空,飞行。~ ***the cake*** 〔美俚〕赢得奖赏;胜过别人,出人头地;获得成功。~ ***the count*** 〔美俚〕被打昏过去,死掉。~ ***the field*** 出征。~ ***the measure of sb.'s foot*** 看出某人弱点。~ ***the rap*** 〔美俚〕挨骂,受罚,被打败,失败。(*You must*) ~ ***the rough with the smooth*** (你必须)了解快乐就有痛苦。~ ***the water*** 跳入水中(逃走)。~ ***to*** 爱,喜欢,嗜好;开始,开始做;参加;逃入;沉迷在;…起来(~ *to smoking* 抽起烟来。*He took to studying English*. 他开始学习英语。~ *to the air with* 开始播

送)。～ *to be* = ～ for. ～ *to the boat* 改乘小船。～ *to the timber* 〔美〕躲起来。～ *to the woods* 【美政】逃避责任;弃权。～ *up* 1. 拿起;举起;拾起;给搭(火车等),(汽车等)接纳(乘客),(船)承装(货物);收做(徒弟等);保护。2. 逮捕。3. 吸收(水分等),耗费(时间),占(地位);吸引(注意等)。4. 打断人家的话,打岔;责备。5. 开始,动手(工作等),从事;提出,处理(问题);继续(中断的话),接下去讲。6. 承接(定货);接受(挑战、打赌),应征;承兑(期票),支付。7. 定居(住处)。～ *up the chant* 人云亦云。～ *up with* 甘受;忍受(虐待等);采用;遵奉(某说);信奉(学说);和…亲近;与…同居;向…求婚。～ *upon one(self)* 1. 负担,承担(责任等)。2. 毅然,大胆(～ (*it*) *upon one(self) to say sth.* 毅然说出某事)。II *n*. 1. 捕获;收获;捕获量,收获量;〔俚〕利益,盈益;(入场券的)售得金额。2.【印】(排字工人)一次所排的原稿;【影】(一次拍摄的)镜头。3.〔美口〕观点,看法(*on*)。*a great* ～ *of salmon* 鲑鱼的大量捕获。*make a large* ～ 大量猎获。～ **away** *a*.〔英〕(饭菜)外卖的,买回去的。～**down** *a*., *n*. 可拆散的(机器);可拆下的部分;〔口〕叫人受气的人[事],欺人的人[事]。～-**home pay** 〔美〕(扣去捐税等后的)净薪。～-**in** 〔口〕欺骗。～-**it-or-leave-it** *a*. 要求作出断然抉择的,不容讨价还价,模棱两可或觅取妥协办法的。～-**off** 缺点;(滑稽的)摹仿;讽刺画;起点;起跳点;【空】起飞(点),离水(点)(～-*off run* 起飞滑行距离)。～**out** 1. *n*. 取出,拿出;〔美〕(餐馆)外卖菜。2. *a*. 卖外卖菜的(餐馆);【桥牌】暗示改叫花色的加倍。～**over** 接收,接管(政权等)。～**up** 提升,拉紧,绷紧;拉紧装置;(缝纫机上提针线上升的)提升装置;【影】卷片装置;纠正。

taken [ˈteikən; ˋtekən] take 的过去分词。～ *altogether* 总括起来说;总之。

tak·er [ˈteikə; ˋtekɚ] *n*. 取者;捕获者;接受者;收取者;购买者;打赌者。*a ticket* ～ 收票员。

T

tak·er-in [ˈteikəin; ˋtekɚˏɪn] *n*.【纺】(梳棉机的)刺毛辊〔亦作 licker-in〕。

takin [ˈtɑːkin, ˈtei-; ˋtɑkɪn, ˋte-] *n*.【动】扭角羚 (*Budorcas taxicolor*)〔栖于喜马拉雅山的森林中〕。

tak·ing [ˈteikiŋ; ˋtekɪŋ] I *a* 1. 迷人的,可爱的。2. 会传染的。II *n*. 1. 捕获;捕获物;捕获总量。2.〔*pl*.〕售得金额,所得,收入。3.〔口〕激动,兴奋;烦恼。*in a* ～ 1. 在激动中。2. 在困难中(*in a great* ～ 心烦意乱)。～-**off** 除去;【空】起飞。-**ly** *ad*. -**ness** *n*.

tak·y [ˈteiki; ˋtekɪ] *a*.〔口〕= taking.

tal·a·poin [ˈtæləpoin; ˋtæləˏpɔɪn] *n*. (斯里兰卡及泰国等地的)和尚;【动】小长尾猴〔产于西非〕。

ta·lar·i·a [təˈlɛəriə; təˋlɛrɪə] *n*.〔*pl*.〕〔L.〕【希神、罗神】(Mercury, Iris 等的)脚翼;翼靴。

talc [tælk; tælk] I *n*.【矿】滑石;云母。II *vt*. (*talcked*, *talced*; *talck·ing*, *talc·ing*) 用滑石处理。～ *powder* 滑石粉,爽身粉。～ *spar* 菱锰矿。

tal·cite [ˈtælsait; ˋtælsaɪt] *n*.【地】1. 滑块石。2. 变白云母。

talck·y [ˈtælki; ˋtælkɪ] *a*. = talcose.

talc·ose, talc·ous [ˈtælkəus, -kəs; ˋtælkos, -kəs] *a*. (含)滑石的。

talcum [ˈtælkəm; ˋtælkəm] *n*. 1. = talc. 2. 滑石粉,爽身粉(= ～ powder)。

tale [teil; tel] *n*. 1. 故事,传说。2. 坏话;谣言;谎话。3.〔古〕计算;总计。*a fairy* ～ 神仙故事,童话。*traveler's* ～*s* 大话,牛皮。*old wives'* ～*s* 荒唐故事。*a* ～ *of a tub* 无稽之谈。*a* ～ *of nought* 〔废〕无聊琐事。*a* ～ *of a roasted horse* 弥天大谎。*Thereby hangs a* ～. 其中大有文章。*The shepherd tells his* ～.〔古〕牧羊人清点他的羊数。*The* ～ *is complete*.〔古〕数目不错,并无短缺。*His* ～ *is told* [*has been told*]. 他已经完了[运数尽了]。***a*** ～ ***that is told*** 废话;陈腐话。***bring*** ～*s* = *carry* ～*s* = *tell* ～*s*. ***if all*** ～***s be true*** 据说。***in a*** [*the same*] ～ 同一,一致。***jump in one*** ～ 一致。***one and the same*** ～ 同一事件。***tell its own*** ～ 自白来历;不说自明。***tell one's*** ～ 自述;说本人要[应]说的话;(使者)陈述所负使命。***tell*** ～***s*** (***out of school***) 讲坏话,说小话,搬弄是非。～**bearer** 说人隐私的人;搬弄是非的人。～**bearing** 搬弄是非。～**teller** 说人隐私的人;搬弄是非的人;讲故事的人。

tal·ent [ˈtælənt; ˋtælənt] *n*. 1. 天资;才能,才干,本事。2.〔集合词〕人才。3.〔俚〕〔集合词〕【赛马】老赌手;【商】内行。4. 古希腊[希伯来]的重量及货币名。***hide one's*** ～***s in a napkin*** 埋没自己的才能,不好好利用自己的才能。～ **scout** 物色人才者。

tal·ent·ed [ˈtæləntid; ˋtæləntɪd] *a*. 有才能的;能干的。

tal·ent·less [ˈtæləntlis; ˋtæləntlɪs] *a*. 没有天资的;无能的。

ta·ler [ˈtɑːlə; ˋtɑlɚ] *n*. (*pl*. *ta·ler*) 泰勒〔德国旧时一种银币〕。

ta·les [ˈteiliːz; ˋteliz] *n*.〔L.〕【法】候补陪审员(名册);候补陪审员召集令。～**man** *n*. 候补陪审员。

tali [ˈteilai; ˋtelaɪ] *n*. talus[1]的复数。

Tal·i·a·cotian [tæliəˈkəuʃən; tælɪəˋkoʃən] *n*. 隆鼻术,美鼻术。

tal·i·on [ˈtæliən; ˋtælɪən] *n*.【法】同态惩罚(法);同态报复(法);以牙还牙;反坐。

tal·i·ped [ˈtæliˌped; ˋtælɪˏpɛd] I *a*. 畸形足的,拐脚的。II *n*. 拐脚的人,拐脚的动物。

tal·i·pes [ˈtæliˌpiːz; ˋtælɪˏpiz] *n*.【医】畸形足(= clubfoot)。

tal·i·pot [ˈtælipɔt; ˋtælɪˏpɑt] *n*. 1.【植】扇形棕榈。2. 从扇形棕榈提炼的淀粉。

tal·is·man [ˈtælizmən; ˋtælɪsmən, ˋtælɪz-] *n*. (*pl*. ～*s*) 护符,避邪物;法宝。*a protective* ～ 护身符。*cherish as a* ～ 奉为至宝。-**ic(al)** *a*. 护符的;有神奇魔力的。

talk [tɔːk; tɔk] I *vi*. 谈话,商谈,(用动作等)表示意思;(用无线电)通信;饶舌,唠叨;空谈;(开水壶)嚷叫,发响。— *vt*. 讲,谈;谈着消磨(光阴);谈论;讲着话使…(*into*; *out of*)。*Let's sit down and* ～. 让我们坐下来谈谈。～ *in English* 用英语讲。～ *English* 讲英语。～ *politics* 谈政治。～ *a child to sleep* 用话哄孩子睡。(*He would*) ～ *a horse's* [*a donkey's*] *hind leg off* = ～ *the bark off a tree* 〔美〕讲个不停,滔滔不绝地讲。～ *oneself hoarse* (*out of breath*) 讲得声音嘶哑(喘不过气来)。～ *in one's sleep* 说梦话。*People will* ～. 人家会说闲话的,人言可畏。***Money*** ～***s***. 金钱万能。～ ***a leg off*** = ～ ***an arm off*** 〔美〕说个不停,刺刺不休。～ ***about*** 讲(某事),谈论(*What are you talking about?* 你们在谈论什么? *I do not want to be* ～*ed about*. 我不愿意给人议论)。*The accused begins to* ～. 被告开始交代了。～ ***against time*** 说话消磨时间。～ ***at*** 暗指着…说,影射某人。～ ***away*** 说着话消磨(时间);靠讲话来忘记(恐怖等)。～ ***baby*** 用对小孩子讲话的口气说(*to*)。～ ***back*** 反唇相讥,回嘴。～ ***big*** [*tall*]〔俚〕夸口,吹牛。～ ***business*** 谈正经事。～ (***cold***) ***turkey*** 〔美〕照实说,老老实实说;正正经经讨论,讨论基本问题。～ ***down*** 驳倒;放低嗓子说;放大声音盖过其他声音;【空】(用无线电)引导着陆。～ ***from the point*** 离题,说得不着边际。～ (*sb*.) ***into*** [***out of***] 说服(某人)做[停止做]…。～ ***of*** 讲,谈论;说要(*T- of the devil, and he will appear* 说到曹操,曹操就到。*He is* ～*ing of going abroad*. 他说要出国去。*Talking of*... 说到,讲到)。～ ***one's head off*** 〔美〕= ～ ***a leg off*** 说个没完。～ ***out*** 尽量谈;彻底说,说完;〔英〕将(议案的)讨论拖到闭会而悬置不决。～ ***out of turn*** 〔美俚〕弄错;干涉,阻碍。～ ***over*** 1. *vi*. 商谈,商量。2. *vt*. 说服。～ ***round*** 1. *vi*. 转弯抹角地讲。2. *vt*. 说服;说得使回心转意。～ ***shop*** 讲自己的本行话[事情]。～ ***the*** ～ 〔美口〕只说

不做。～ ***the*** ～, ***walk the walk*** 说到做到。～ ***through one's hat*** = ～ ***through*** (***the back of***) ***one's neck*** 〔口〕夸张,吹牛;乱说。～ ***to*** 向…谈;〔口〕申斥,劝谏(*I'll* ～ *to him*. 要说他一顿了)。～ ***to hear one's teeth rattle*** 〔美〕胡说。～ ***to oneself*** 自言自语。～ ***together*** 商量,谈判。～ ***United States*** 〔美〕说明美国公民的意见;讲英语;讲美国话。～ ***up*** 大声讲,明白地讲;〔美〕讨论。**II** ***n***. 谈话;商谈,商议,谈判;讲演;谣传;话题,话柄;空话;隐语,黑话;方言;语调,口气。*big* ～〔美口〕大话。*an idle* ～ 无聊话,闲扯,山海经。*small* ～ 闲谈。*tall* ～ 大话。*I heard it in* ～. 我是听人传说的。*He is all* ～. 他只会说(不会做)。*It will end in* ～. 还不过是空话[传闻]罢了。*That's the* ～. 〔美〕好,洗耳恭听。***all*** ～ ***and no cider*** 议而不决,空谈而无结果。***make a*** ～ 造成口实,使人议论。***make*** ～ 一味空谈;闲聊。～**-back** 对讲电话。～**-in** 演讲示威;座谈;讨论。～ **radio** 谈话广播节目。～ **show** (广播中的)谈话节目,脱口秀。

talk·a·thon [ˈtɔːkəθɔn; ˋtɔkəθɑn] ***n***. 〔美〕(议会中为拖延时间而进行的)冗长的讨论;冗长的演说;候选人的长篇广播[电视]竞选答问。

talk·a·tive [ˈtɔːkətiv; ˋtɔkətɪv] ***a***. 喜欢说话的,多嘴的,健谈的(*opp*. taciturn)。**-ly** ***ad***. **-ness** ***n***.

talk·ee-talk·ee [ˈtɔːkiˈtɔːki; ˋtɔkɪˋtɔkɪ] ***n***. **1.** 闲话;唠叨话。**2.** (黑人等的)蹩脚英语。**3.** 〔美〕爱说话的人。

talk·er [ˈtɔːkə; ˋtɔkɚ] ***n***. **1.** 谈话人。**2.** 饶舌者。**3.** 空谈家。**4.** 〔美〕有声电影。*a good* ～ 健谈的人。

talk·ie [ˈtɔːki; ˋtɔkɪ] ***n***. 有声电影。

talk·i·ness [ˈtɔːkinis; ˋtɔkɪnɪs] ***n***. **1.** 喜欢说话;多嘴。**2.** 对话多。

talk·ing [ˈtɔːkiŋ; ˋtɔkɪŋ] ***a***. (会)说话的;多嘴的;富于表情的(眼睛等)。*a* ～ *doll* 会叫的洋娃娃。*a* ～ *iron* 〔美俚〕手枪。～ **book** (盲人用)书刊录音唱片[带]。～ **date** (情侣间只以交谈为乐而不涉及性活动的)清谈幽会。～**-down system** 【空】无线电导航(着陆)装置。～ **machine** 留声机。～ **point** 论点。～ **shop** 〔英〕空谈俱乐部。～**-to** 〔口〕责备,责斥。

talk·y [ˈtɔːki; ˋtɔkɪ] ***a***. = talkative. ***talky-talky*** 〔口〕对话(过)多的。

tall [tɔːl; tɔl] **I** ***a***. **1.** 身材高的,高大的。**2.** 〔美口〕(数量)大的。**3.** 〔俚〕过分的,夸张的。*a* ～ *chimney* 高烟囱。*He is 6 feet* ～. 身高六英尺。*a* ～ *price* 高价。*a* ～ *dinner* 丰盛的饭菜[宴席]。*a* ～ *story* 大谎话。～ *talk* 大话。*a* ～ *order* 苛刻的要求,难办的差使。～ *grass country* 〔美〕西部草原地带。～ *hat* 大礼帽。～ *timber* [*uncut*] 〔美〕深山野地。～ *water man* [*sailor*] 远洋海员。**II** ***ad***. 〔口〕夸大地;趾高气扬地。**-ness** ***n***.

tal·lage [ˈtælidʒ; ˋtælɪdʒ] ***n***. 〔古英〕(封建领主向佃户征收的)地租。

tall·boy [ˈtɔːlbɔi; ˋtɔlˏbɔɪ] ***n***. **1.** 〔英〕高脚橱柜。**2.** (烟囱顶部的)通风管。**3.** 高脚杯。

Tal·lin(n) [ˈtælin; ˋtælɪn] ***n***. 塔林〔爱沙尼亚城市〕。

tal·low [ˈtæləu; ˋtælo] **I** ***n***. 牛[羊]脂,兽脂。～ *candle* (牛)脂烛。**II** ***vt***. 涂兽脂;把(牲畜)养肥。**beef** [**mutton**] ～ 牛[羊]脂。～**-chandler** (牛)脂烛制造人,卖脂烛的商人。～**-faced** ***a***. 脸色苍白的。

tal·low·y [ˈtæləui; ˋtælo·ɪ] ***a***. 兽脂质的;牛脂似的;油腻的;苍白的。

tal·ly [ˈtæli; ˋtælɪ] **I** ***n***. **1.** 符木,符节,符契;计数的签筹,货签,筹码;(符契上的)刻记;符合物,对中之一;一模一样的东西。**2.** 〔罕〕账;计算;得分;(货物计算上的)单位数〔如一打,一百等,交点货物如说 8, 10, tally 时,这 tally 就指 12 或一打;如说 96, 98, tally 时,这 tally 就指一百〕。**3.** 【海】理货,点数。**4.** 木牌,铜牌;标签。*a hand* ～ 计数器。*a* ～ *card* 〔美〕计数卡片。(***sell goods***) ***by the*** ～ 按打[按捆](出售货物)。***live*** (***on***) ～ = ***live*** ～ ***with*** (***a woman***) 〔俚〕姘居。***make*** [***earn***] ***a*** ～ ***in a game*** 在比赛中得分。***strike*** ～ 符合;行动一致。**II** ***vt***. 刻在符木上;计算,总结(*up*);记录;使符合;(上货卸货时)点数;【海】(向船尾方向)拉(帆脚索)。— ***vi***. 符合,吻合(*with*)。*The two stories do not* ～. 两种说法对不上。*It tallies with the facts*. 合乎事实。～ **clerk 1.** (选举的)检票员。**2.** = tallyman. ～**-man 1.** 分期付款赊卖人;拿样品卖货的人。**2.** (船上的)理货员,司签员。**3.** 〔俚〕姘夫。～**-register** 计数器。～ **sheet** 账单;〔美〕(选举的)票数记录纸。～ **shop** 〔英〕分期付款赊卖店。～ **system,** ～ **trade** 〔英〕分期付款赊销法。～**-woman** 姘妇。

tal·ly·ho [tæliˈhəu, ˈtælihəu; tælɪˏho, ˏtælɪˋho] **I** ***int***. 嗬嗬〔猎人嗾狗声〕。**II** ***n***. (*pl*. ～***s***) **1.** "嗬"声。**2.** 〔美〕四马马车〔雪橇〕。**III** ***vi***. 发出"嗬"声。— ***vt***. 嗬嗬地嗾(狗)。

tal·ma [ˈtælmə; ˋtælmə] ***n***. (19 世纪前半期的)塔尔马式披肩。

tal·mi gold [ˈtælmigəuld; ˏtɑlˋmigold, ˋtɑlmɪgold] 镀金黄铜。

Tal·mud [ˈtælmud, -məd; ˋtælmʌd, -məd] ***n***. 犹太圣法经传。**-ic** [tælˈmʌdik; tælˋmʌdɪk], **-i·cal** ***a***. **-ist** ***n***.

tal·on [ˈtælən; ˋtælən] ***n***. 〔常 *pl*.〕(猛禽,猛兽的)爪;爪形手;魔爪;【建】爪饰;【牌】分剩的牌;锁键上受到钥匙推压的部分;剑柄的根部;(债券、股票等上的)息票。

tal·qual. = 〔L.〕*talis qualis* (= of ordinary or average quality) 普通的,寻常质量的。

ta·lus¹ [ˈteiləs; ˋteləs] ***n***. (*pl*. ***-li***) 【解】距骨;踝。

talus² [ˈteiləs; ˋteləs] ***n***. 斜面;斜坡;(城墙的)斜面;【地】(断崖下的)塌磊,山麓堆积。

Tam. = Tamil.

tam [tæm; tæm] ***n***. = tam-o'-shanter.

tam·a·bil·i·ty [ˌteiməˈbiliti; ˏteməˋbɪlətɪ] ***n***. 可驯养性。

tam·a·ble [ˈteiməbl; ˋteməbl̩] ***a***. 可驯养的。

ta·mal, ta·ma·le [təˈmɑːli; təˋmɑlɪ] ***n***. (墨西哥的)玉米面包卷的辣味肉饼〔蒸或烤的〕。

ta·man·dua [ˌtɑːmɑːnˈdwɑː; ˏtɑmɑnˋdwɑ] ***n***. 【动】小食蚁兽 (*Tamandua tetradactyla*)〔产于热带美洲〕。

Ta·ma·ra [təˈmærə; təˋmærə] ***n***. 塔玛拉〔女子名〕。

tam·a·rack [ˈtæməræk; ˋtæməˏræk] ***n***. 【植】**1.** 美洲落叶松。**2.** 美洲落叶松木材。

tam·a·rin [ˈtæmərin; ˋtæmərɪn] ***n***. 【动】绢毛猴〔南美洲产〕。

tam·a·rind [ˈtæmərind; ˋtæməˏrɪnd] ***n***. 【植】罗望子树〔豆科常绿乔木〕;罗望子果,酸荚〔做清凉饮料等用〕。*bastard* ～ 合欢。

tam·a·risk [ˈtæmərisk; ˋtæməˏrɪsk] ***n***. 【植】柽柳属植物。

ta·ma·sha [təˈmɑːʃə; təˋmɑʃə] ***n***. (印度的)展览;演出,娱乐节目;典礼。

Ta·ma·tave [ˌtæməˈtɑːv; ˏtæməˋtɑv] ***n***. 塔马达夫〔马达加斯加省省会〕。

tam·bac [ˈtæmbæk; ˋtæmbæk] ***n***. 【植】沉香。

tam·bour [ˈtæmbuə; ˋtæmbʊr] **I** ***n***. (低音)鼓;(圆形)绣花绷架;绷架上做的绣品;【筑城】(出入口前的)圆堡;【建】鼓形柱。**II** ***vt***., ***vi***. (用绷架)绣,装饰。

tam·bour·a, tam·bur·a [tɑːmˈburə; tɑmˋbʊrə] ***n***. 【乐】塔姆布拉〔类似吉他的印度古老乐器,在东方流行〕。

tam·bou·rine [tæmbəˈriːn; ˏtæmbəˋrin] ***n***. (周围有发声金属片的)手鼓;铃鼓;(法国南部的)手鼓舞(曲);【动】一种非洲野鸽。

tam·bu·rit·za [tæmˈburitsə; tæmˋbʊrɪtsə] ***n***. 【乐】塔姆布里扎流特琴一类的古老乐器,在斯拉夫地区南部流行〕。

tame [teim; tem] **I** ***a***. **1.** 驯养了的(*opp*. wild)。**2.** 栽

培的(植物);开垦的(土地)。**3.** 驯服的,温顺的;没有骨气的。**4.** 单调的,平淡的,沉闷的(景色等)。**5.** 没有精神的,无精打采的,不活泼的。*a ~ cat* 家猫;食客。*a ~ description* 单调的描写。**II** *vt*. **1.** 驯养(禽兽)。**2.** 驯服,制服。**3.** 使没精神,抑制(热情等)。**4.** 把(色彩等)弄柔和。

tame·a·ble [ˈteiməbl; ˋteməbl̩] *a*. = tamable.

tame·less [ˈteimlis; ˋtemlɪs] *a*. 难驯养的;野性的,暴烈的。

tame·ly [ˈteimli; ˋtemlɪ] *ad*. 驯熟地;柔顺地;乖乖地,没有骨气地。

tame·ness [ˈteimnis; ˋtemnɪs] *n*. 驯熟;温柔,无气力;平凡,沉闷。

tam·er [ˈteimə; ˋtemɚ] *n*. 驯(养)…的人。*a ~ of lion* = *a lion ~* 驯狮人。

Tam·er·lane [ˈtæməlein; ˋtæmɚˏlen] *n*. 〔Timour 或 Timur 的别名,意为"跛帖木儿"〕帖木儿〔1336—1405〕。

Tam·il [ˈtæmil; ˋtæml̩, ˋtæmɪl] *n*. (南亚的)泰米尔人;泰米尔语。

Tam·ma·ny [ˈtæməni; ˋtæmənɪ] **I** *n*. 〔美〕坦慕尼协会〔= ~-Society, 纽约市民主党组织〕。**II** *a*. 坦慕尼协会成员的;坦慕尼协会式的。~ **Hall** 坦慕尼厅。**-ism** *n*. **-nyite** *n*.

tam·my [ˈtæmi; ˋtæmɪ] *n*. = tam-o'-shanter.

tam-o'-shan·ter [tæməˈʃæntə; ˏtæməˋʃæntɚ] *n*. (苏格兰)宽顶无沿圆帽。

tamp [tæmp; tæmp] *vt*. **1.** 用黏土等填塞(装有炸药的洞口)。**2.** 捣固,砸牢(路基等)。*a ~ing bar* 【铁道】砸道棒。

tam·pal·a [tæmˈpælə; tæmˋpælə] *n*. 【植】雁来红(*Amaranthus gangeticus*)。

tam·per[1] [ˈtæmpə; ˋtæmpɚ] *vi*. 干扰,损害,削弱;窜改(遗嘱、稿件等);贿赂。~ *with an illness* (医生)故意瞎医使病拖长。~ *with voters* 收买投票人。

tamper[2] [ˈtæmpə; ˋtæmpɚ] *n*. **1.** (爆破孔)填塞人;捣固者。**2.** 夯,夯具。**3.** (中子)反射器;(中子)反射剂。

Tam·pe·re [ˈtɑːmpere; ˋtɑmpɛrɛ] *n*. 坦佩雷〔芬兰城市〕。

Tam·pi·co [tæmˈpiːkəu; tæmˋpiko, ˋtæmpɪˏko] *n*. 坦皮科〔墨西哥港市〕。

tam·pi·on [ˈtæmpiən; ˋtæmpɪən] *n*. 塞子;炮口塞;【乐】风琴管上端的塞子。

tam·pon [ˈtæmpən; ˋtæmpɑn] **I** *n*. **1.** 【医】(塞伤口用的)棉塞,止血塞。**2.** (塞在头发里的)假发。**II** *vt*. 用棉塞塞住(伤口)。

tam·pon·ade [ˈtæmpənid; ˋtæmpənɪd], **tam·ponage** [-idʒ; -ɪdʒ], **tam·pon·ment** [-mənt; -mənt] *n*. 棉塞填入法;填塞(法)。

tam-tam [ˈtʌmtʌm; ˋtʌmˏtʌm] *n*. **1.** 锣。**2.** = tom-tom.

tan[1] [tæn; tæn] **I** *vt*. (*-nn-*) **1.** 鞣(革),硝(皮)。**2.** 使晒成棕褐色。**3.** 〔俚〕鞭打。— *vi*. 变柔软,晒成棕褐色。~ *sb.'s hide* 〔美俚〕鞭打(某人)。**II** *n*. **1.** 鞣料树皮;(鞣皮后的)鞣料渣〔又叫 spent ~, 铺路等用〕。**2.** 黄褐色,棕黄色,晒黑的皮色;〔*pl*.〕棕黄色皮鞋〔衣着〕。*kiss the ~* 〔俚〕从马上掉下来。*the ~* 〔俚〕马戏团。**III** *a*. 黄褐色的,棕黄色的。~**bark** 鞣料树皮。~**yard** 制革厂。

tan[2] [tæn; tæn] *n*. = tangent.

ta·na [ˈtɑːnə; ˋtɑnə] *n*. = thana.

tan·a·ger [ˈtænədʒə; ˋtænədʒɚ] *n*. 【鸟】(中南美)莺类。

Ta·na·na·rive [tɑnɑnɑˈriːv; ˏtɑnɑnɑˋriv] *n*. 塔那那利佛〔马达加斯加首都〕。

tan·dem [ˈtændəm; ˋtændəm] **I** *a*., *ad*. (两匹马)前后纵列;串联,串列 (*opp*. abreast)。*a ~ bus* [*trolley-bus*] 联挂公共汽车[无轨电车]。*a ~ bicycle* 双人自行车。*a ~ sender* 转接记发器。*drive ~* 将马前后串联着驾驶。**II** *n*. 两匹[数匹]前后串联在马车上的马;双马串联马车;双人自行车;串翼型飞机。

tang[1] [tæŋ; tæŋ] **I** *n*. **1.** (刀剑等插入柄中的)柄脚。**2.** 强烈的气味[臭味]。**3.** 气息,意味;风味。*wine with a ~ of the cask* 带有桶味的酒。*be seasoned with the ~ of humour* 带有幽默的意味。**II** *vt*. 使其有…气味。

tang[2] [tæŋ; tæŋ] **I** *n*. 响亮而有余音的声音;当的一声。**II** *vt*., *vi*. (敲金属物等)使铛铛地响,使鸣响。

tang[3] [tæŋ; tæŋ] *n*. 【植】墨角藻。

Tan·ga [ˈtæŋgə; ˋtæŋgə] *n*. 坦噶〔坦桑尼亚港市〕。

Tan·gan·yi·ka [ˌtæŋgəˈnjiːkə; ˏtæŋgənˋjikə, ˏtæŋgæn-] *n*. 坦噶尼喀〔坦桑尼亚一地区〕。

tan·gen·cy [ˈtændʒənsi; ˋtændʒənsɪ] *n*. 接触。

tan·gent [ˈtændʒənt; ˋtændʒənt] **I** *a*. **1.** 接触的。**2.** 【数】切线的,相切的;正切的。**3.** 离题的。**II** *n*. 【数】切线;切面;正切(线);正切尺,瞄准表尺;〔美口〕(铁路的)直线区间。~ *elevation* 瞄准角。*a ~ scale* [*sight*] 正切尺,瞄准表尺。***fly*** [***go***] ***off at*** [***in***, ***on***, ***upon***] ***a ~*** (思想)忽然转变;突然越出本题;突然改变话题[做法]。*fly off at a ~ into outside matters* 突然离开本题说些不相干的题外话。

tan·gen·tal [ˈtændʒəntəl; tænˋdʒɛntl̩], **-tial** [tænˈdʒenʃəl; tænˋdʒɛnʃəl] *a*. **1.** 【数】切线的;切的;正切的。**2.** 稍微有点关系的;肤浅的,离开本题的;突然越出常态的。*a ~ angle* 切角。~ *coordinates* 切线座标。~ *movement* 水平运动,切向运动。**-tial·ly** *ad*.

Tan·ge·rine [ˈtændʒəˈriːn; ˏtændʒəˋrin] **I** *a*. (摩洛哥国)丹吉尔的。**II** *n*. 丹吉尔人。

tan·ge·rine [ˌtændʒəˈriːn; ˏtændʒəˋrin] *n*. **1.** (欧洲)红橘,柑橘。**2.** 橘红色。**3.** 〔美〕(内部处于四分五裂状态的)"橘瓣公司"。

tan·gi·ble [ˈtændʒəbl; ˋtændʒəbl̩] *a*. 可触知的,有实质的,实在的;确实的;【法】有形的。~ *material benefits* 看得见的物质利益。~ *assets* 有形财产。**-ness** *n*. **-bly** *ad*. **-bili·ty** *n*.

Tan·gier [tænˈdʒiə; tænˋdʒɪr, ˋtændʒɪr] *n*. 丹吉尔〔摩洛哥港市〕。

tan·gle [ˈtæŋgl; ˋtæŋgl] **I** *vt*., *vi*. (使)缠结,弄乱,(使)纷乱,(使)纠缠;笼络;诱陷;(使)受牵累;〔美俚〕吵闹,打架;竞争 (*with*)。**II** *n*. **1.** 缠结,纠缠,纠纷;混乱。**2.** 〔美俚〕吵闹,打架;拳赛。**3.** 海底动植物采集器;海带(类)。*His thoughts were in a ~.* 他的思想陷于紊乱。~**foot** 黏虫胶;〔美俚〕威士忌酒。~**some** *a*. 紊乱的;复杂的。**-r** *n*.

tan·gly [ˈtæŋgli; ˋtæŋglɪ] *a*. 缠结的,紊乱的。

tan·go [ˈtæŋgəu; ˋtæŋgo] **I** *n*. (*pl*. *~s*) 探戈舞(曲)。**II** *vi*. 跳探戈舞。*a ~ tea* 探戈舞茶会。

tan·gram [ˈtæŋgrəm; ˋtæŋgrəm] *n*. (中国的)七巧板。

tangy [ˈtæŋi; ˋtæŋɪ] *a*. (*-i·er*; *-i·est*) 有浓烈气味[滋味]的;怪臭的。**-i·ness** *n*.

tan·ist [ˈtænist; ˋtænɪst] *n*. (古爱尔兰)选妥的(凯尔特酋长)继承人〔当酋长活着时便在亲属中选出〕。

tank [tæŋk; tæŋk] **I** *n*. **1.** 罐,槽;箱;柜〔盛液体或气体的大容器〕;(火车头的)水柜;(船上的)液体舱;〔美、英方〕水堰,贮水池;游泳池;【船】模型试航池;【电】储能电路。**2.** 【军】战车,坦克。**3.** 〔美俚〕小镇市,小村庄;酒量大的人;(拘禁新犯人)的牢房。**II** *vt*. 装满槽[柜];贮存在槽[柜]里。*an air ~* 【火箭】压缩空气瓶。*a heavy* [*light*] *~* = *a male* [*female*] *~* 重[轻]坦克。*a ~ crew* 坦克手。*a ~ circuit* 储能电路。~ *farming* 无土[槽式]栽培法。~**buster** 防坦克飞机。~ **car** 运油[水]汽车[车厢];油[水]槽车。~**man** 坦克手。~**ship** 油船。~ **station** 给水站。~ **suit** 〔美〕(有肩带的)女式泳装。~ **top** 〔美〕背心装。~ **town** (尤指火车停车加煤水的)小镇。**-er** *n*. 油船;【空】加油车;油罐。

tan·ka [ˈtɑːŋkə; ˋtæŋkə] *n*. 〔Jap.〕短歌〔三十一音节字的日本诗体〕。

T

tank·age [ˈtæŋkidʒ; ˋtæŋkɪdʒ] *n*. (油等的)罐贮过程[措施];罐贮费用;罐容量;罐贮量;(用碎肉、内脏等脱脂后制成的)桶装下脚〔肥田用〕。*animal* ～ 骨肉粉。

tank·ard [ˈtæŋkəd; ˋtæŋkɚd] *n*. (有柄)大(啤酒)杯;一大杯。*cool* ～ 冷饮,清凉饮料。

tankette [tæŋˈket; tæŋkˋɛt] *n*. 小坦克。

tank·ful [ˈtæŋkful; ˋtæŋkfʊl] *n*. (*pl*. *-fuls*) 一罐之量。

tan·na = thana.

tan·na·ble [ˈtænəbl; ˋtænəbl̩] *a*. 可鞣的,可硝制的。

tan·nage [ˈtænidʒ; ˋtænɪdʒ] *n*. 鞣皮;制革(法)。

tan·nate [ˈtæneit; ˋtænet] *n*. 【化】鞣酸盐,单宁酸盐。

tan·ner[1] [ˈtænə; ˋtænɚ] *n*. 制革工人,鞣皮工人。

tanner[2] [ˈtænə; ˋtænɚ] *n*. 〔英俚〕六辨士(旧)硬币。

tan·ner·y [ˈtænəri; ˋtænərɪ] *n*. 制革[鞣皮]厂;〔罕〕鞣皮法。

tan·nic [ˈtænik; ˋtænɪk] *a*. 鞣质的,丹宁的;由鞣酸皮得到的。～ **acid** 【化】鞣酸,单宁酸。

tan·nin [ˈtænin; ˋtænɪn] *n*. 鞣质,单宁;单宁酸。

tan·ning [ˈtæniŋ; ˋtænɪŋ] *n*. 鞣皮(法),制革(法);(皮肤)晒黑;〔俚〕鞭打,责打。～ **agent** 鞣剂。～ **bed** (利用太阳灯)把皮肤晒成棕黑色的健身床。

tan·noy [ˈtænɔi; ˋtænɔɪ] *n*. 〔英〕声重放和扩大系统〔一种有线广播或扩音系统〕。

Ta·no·an [ˈtɑːnəuən; ˋtɑnoən] *n*. 塔努安语〔北美种印第安语语系,包括基奥瓦语和目前新墨西哥一些村庄中说的三种语言〕。

tan·rec [ˈtænrək; ˋtænrək] *n*. = tenrec.

tan·sy [ˈtænzi; ˋtænzɪ] *n*. 【植】艾菊。

tan·ta·late [ˈtæntəˌleit; ˋtæntəlet] *n*. 【化】钽酸盐。

tan·tal·ic [tænˈtælik; tænˋtælɪk] *a*. 【化】含钽的;五价钽的;正钽的。

tan·ta·lite [ˈtæntəˌlait; ˋtæntəlaɪt] *n*. 【化】钽铁矿。

tan·ta·li·za·tion [ˌtæntəlaiˈzeiʃən; ˏtæntələˋzeʃən] *n*. 令人着急;逗人。

tan·ta·lize [ˈtæntəlaiz; ˋtæntlˏaɪz] *vt*. 使看到拿不到而焦急[难受],要给不给地逗弄,逗惹,愚弄。*The sight is most tantalizing*. 这光景真惹人着急。**-liz·ing** *a*. **-liz·ing·ly** *ad*. …得令人着急。

tan·ta·lous [ˈtæntələs; ˋtæntələs] *a*. 【化】亚钽的,三价钽的。

tan·ta·lum [ˈtæntələm; ˋtæntl̩əm] *n*. 【化】钽〔Ta〕。

tan·ta·lus [ˈtæntələs; ˋtæntl̩əs] *n*. 〔英〕(初看似可随意取用、实则有暗锁的)玻璃酒柜。

tan·ta·mount [ˈtæntəmaunt; ˋtæntəˏmaʊnt] *a*. 同等价值[效力]的,与…相等的 (*to*)。*Such an explanation is* ～ *to a confession*. 这样一种解释等于一篇自白。

tan·ta·ra [tænˈtɑːrə; ˋtæntərə, tænˋtærə, -ˋtɑrə] *n*. 喇叭声,角笛声。

tan·tiv·y [tænˈtivi; tænˋtɪvɪ] **I** *n*. 〔古〕疾驰;快跑;【猎】催促赶快向前的叫声。**II** *ad*. 快,迅速,疾驱。**III** *a*. 快的,突进的,猛冲的。

tan·to [ˈtæntəu; ˋtɑntə] *ad*. 〔It.〕【乐】太;甚。*allegro non* ～ 急速但不太快地。

tan·trum [ˈtæntrəm; ˋtæntrəm] *n*. 〔口〕发脾气。***be in one's*** ～***s*** 在发脾气。***fly*** [***get***, ***go***] ***into one's*** ～(*s*) 发脾气。

Ta·nya [ˈtænjə; ˋtænjə] *n*. 塔尼娅〔女子名, Tatiana 的昵称〕。

Tan·za·ni·a [ˌtænzəˈniːə; ˏtænzəˋniə] *n*. 坦桑尼亚(坦尚尼亚)〔非洲〕。

Tao [tɑːəu, tau; tɑo, taʊ] *n*. 〔汉〕道〔道家学说〕;〔t-〕(儒家的)道。

Ta·o·ism [ˈtɑːəuizəm; ˋtaʊɪzəm, ˋdaʊɪzəm] *n*. (中国的)道教;道家学说。

Ta·o·ist [ˈtɑːəuist, ˈtauist; ˋtaʊɪst, ˋdaʊɪst] *n*., *a*. 道家(的);道教徒(的),道士(的)。**-ic** *a*.

tap[1] [tæp; tæp] **I** *vt*. (*-pp-*) **1.** 轻打[拍,敲]。**2.** 补鞋底,打鞋掌;打(着做)出〔如用发报机打出电讯〕。**3.** 选举,选择。— *vi*. **1.** 轻敲,轻打 (*at*; *on*)。～ *the door with a stick* = ～ *a stick against the door* 用手杖轻轻叩门。～ *at* [*on*] *the door* 敲门。**II** *n*. 轻打,轻敲;轻敲声;(装在踢跶舞鞋底尖上的)铁片;(补鞋底的)掌子;〔*pl*.〕【英军】吃饭号(声);【美军】熄灯号(声)。*I hear a* ～ *at* [*on*] *the door*. 我听见门上敲了一下。～**-dance** (跳)踢跶舞。

tap[2] [tæp; tæp] **I** *n*. (酒桶等的)流出口,嘴子;(水管的)分支,支管;〔英〕旋塞,龙头,活嘴;【电】分接头,抽头;〔英〕酒吧间;【机】螺丝攻,阴螺模;(电话线上)搭线窃听;(各种流出口的)流出物。*liquor of the same* ～ 同样品质的酒。***in*** [***on***] ～ 随时能取用的(酒);随时能买到的(债券的);〔美俚〕手边的,随时可得到的,现成的。***turn the*** ～ ***on*** [***off***] 放开[关上]龙头。**II** *vt*. (*-pp-*) **1.** 装嘴子;从嘴子里放酒(等)出来,开桶;(在树等上)作切口采取树液;【医】(腹部等开洞)放出液体。**2.** 开辟,开发(矿山等)。**3.** 【电】分接(电流);分接头;(从总管)分接(自来水等);搭线窃听(电话等)。**4.** 〔喻〕提倡(新学说等);开拓(新领域)。**5.** 〔俚〕求取,借取(捐款、小账等)。**6.** 【机】(用螺丝攻)刻螺母。～ *the admiral* 〔海俚〕偷桶里的酒。*a* ～*ped coil* 多(接)头线圈。～ **bolt** 【机】(带头)螺栓。～ **bond** 〔美〕国库债券。～ **borer** 开塞锥;【机】螺孔钻。～ **hole** 放液口。～**-house** 〔英〕小酒馆;酒吧;小旅店。～**ped-out** *a*. 财源枯竭的。～**room** 酒吧间,酒室。～ **root** 【植】直根,主根。～**-water** 自来水。

ta·pa, tap·pa [ˈtɑːpə; ˋtɑpɑ] *n*. 塔帕〔太平洋某些岛上居民用来做衣服的构树皮〕(又叫 ～ cloth)。

tape [teip; tep] **I** *n*. 狭带,棉线带;卷尺;带尺;电报收报纸带;磁带,录音带;【电】绝缘胶布;【运】决胜线上的细绳;【机】传动带;【动】条虫;〔俚〕烈酒;〔美俚〕舌头。*red* ～ (扎公文文件的)红带,官样文章,文牍主义;〔Red T-〕威士忌酒商标。*breast the* ～ 赛跑得第一名。**II** *vt*. 用带捆扎;钉上带子;用胶带粘住;【装订】穿线钉(书);用卷尺测量;用磁带录音;〔俚〕估量,判断(某人)。*a* ～*d window* 贴上纸条的玻璃窗。*I have* (*got*) *him* ～*d*. 我看出他是个什么人了。～ **deck** 〔美俚〕简化的磁带录音放音盘。～ **grass** 【植】苦草。～ **line**, ～ **measure** 卷尺,带尺。～ **machine** (股票行市)自动收报机、磁带录音机。～ **recorder** 磁带录音机。～ **transport** (录音机的)磁带传送系统。～**worm** 【动】条虫。

ta·per [ˈteipə; ˋtepɚ] **I** *n*. **1.** 细小的蜡烛;蜡烛心。**2.** 〔诗〕微光;(形体、力量)逐渐缩减,逐渐缩减。**3.** 尖塔形;锥形;锥度,斜度。**4.** 【机】拔梢。**II** *a*. **1.** 渐细的,锥形的;斜的。**2.** 依次递减的。**III** *vi*. 渐细,变尖 (*away*; *off*; *down*);渐少,递减。— *vt*. **1.** 使渐细,使尖。**2.** 依次递减,逐渐减少。**-ed** *a*. **-ing** *a*. **-ing·ly** *ad*.

tap·es·try [ˈtæpistri; ˋtæpɪstrɪ] **I** *n*. 壁毡,挂毡;家具的绣[织]花罩毯。**II** *vt*. 用壁毡装饰;罩上绣[织]花罩毯。

ta·pe·tum [təˈpiːtəm; təˋpitəm] *n*. (*pl*. *-pe·ta* [-ə; -ə]) **1.** 【解、动】毯〔尤指照膜;反光组织;反光色素层;纤维毯〕。**2.** 【植】绒毡层。**-pe·tal** *a*.

tap·i·o·ca [ˌtæpiˈəukə; ˏtæpiˋokə] *n*. (用 cassava 根制成的)木薯淀粉,珍珠粉。

ta·pir [ˈteipə; ˋtepɚ] *n*. 【动】貘。

tap·is [ˈtæpi(ː); ˋtæpi, ˋtæpɪs] *n*. 织花帷幕,挂毯,(尤指议事桌上的)桌毯。***on*** [***upon***] ***the*** ～ 在审议中,在商讨中。

ta·pote·ment [təˈpəutmənt; ˏtaˏpotˋmɑ̃] *n*. 【医】叩抚法,轻叩按摩法。

tap·per [ˈtæpə; ˋtæpɚ] *n*. 轻敲者;〔方〕啄木鸟;轻击锤;(发报机的)电键;散屑器;树液采集器。

tap·pet [ˈtæpit; ˋtæpɪt] *n*. 【机】挺杆。

TAPPI = Technical Association of the Pulp and Paper Industry 〔美〕纸浆与造纸工业技术协会。

tap·ping[1] [ˈtæpiŋ; ˋtæpɪŋ] *n*. 轻敲(声)。

T

tap·ping[2] [ˈtæpiŋ; ˋtæpɪŋ] ***n*.** **1.** (开孔)导出液体。**2.** 【医】穿刺抽液;放腹水。**3.** 【冶】出钢;出铁;出渣。**4.** 【电】抽头,分支,分流。**5.** 【机】攻螺丝。

tap·ster [ˈtæpstə; ˋtæpstɚ] ***n*.** 酒吧间招待员。

tapu [təˈpuː; təˋpu] ***n*.** = tabu, taboo.

ta·que·ri·a [ˈtɑːkəriːə; ˋtɑkəriə] ***n*.** 墨西哥快餐店〔出售炸玉米粉圆饼、煎玉米卷等〕。

tar[1] [tɑː; tɑr] **I *n*.** **1.** 焦油;柏油,煤焦油沥青。**2.** 〔美俚〕黑咖啡。**II *vt*.** (***-rr-***) 涂柏油;〔喻〕弄污。~ *boilers* [*heels*] 〔美〕北卡罗来纳(North Carolina) 州人的别名。*He was ~red with profiteering brush*. 他因谋取不正当的利益而声名狼藉。***be tarred with the same brush*** [***stick***] 都有同样的缺点;都做着同样的坏事,一丘之貉。~ ***and feather*** 将人浑身涂满柏油再粘上羽毛〔一种私刑〕;严加惩罚(*be ~red and featherd for what one has done* 因所作所为而受到严惩)。~ **boy** 〔澳口〕(给被剪毛受伤的羊的伤口涂焦油的)涂焦油工。**~brush** 柏油刷(*a knight of the ~brush* 水手)。~**macadam** 柏油碎石(路面)。

tar[2] [tɑː; tɑr] ***n*.** 〔口〕水手,水兵。*a Jack T-* 水手。*an old ~* 老水手。

tar·a·did·dle [ˈtærədidl; ˋtærəˏdɪdl̩] ***n*.** 〔口〕谎话。

tar·an·tara [ˌtærənˈtɑːrə; ˏtærənˋtɑrə] ***n*.** 喇叭声,角笛声。

ta·ran·tass [ˌtærənˈtæs; ˏtærənˋtæs] ***n*.** 俄式四轮马车。

tar·an·tel·la [ˌtærənˈtelə; ˏtærənˋtɛlə], **-telle** [-ˈtel; -ˋtɛl] ***n*.** 塔兰台拉舞(曲)〔意大利那不勒斯(Naples)地区的一种轻快的民间舞(曲)〕。

tar·ant·ism [ˈtærəntizəm; ˋtærəntɪzm] ***n*.** 【医】塔兰台拉毒蛛病,跳舞病〔一种臆病,过去认为系受塔兰台拉毒蜘蛛所致,可以跳舞来医治〕。★易与 chorea 混同。

Ta·ran·to [təˈræntəu; ˋtarɑnto, təˋrænto] ***n*.** 塔兰托〔意大利的海军基地〕。

ta·ran·tu·la [təˈræntjulə; təˋræntʃələ] ***n*.** (*pl*. ***~s***, ***-lae*** [-liː; -li]) 【虫】(南欧的)多毛毒蜘蛛,塔兰台拉毒蛛。

tar·a·tan·ta·ra [ˈtærətænˈtɑːrə; ˏtærəˋtæntərə, -tænˋtærə] ***n*.** 喇叭声,角笛声。

Ta·ra·wa [tɑːˈrɑːwɑː; tɑˋrɑwɑ] ***n*.** 塔拉瓦岛〔西太平洋岛国吉尔伯特群岛首府〕。

ta·rax·a·cum [təˈræksəkəm; təˋræksəkəm] ***n*.** 【植】蒲公英(属);蒲公英(制剂)。

tar·boosh [tɑːˈbuːʃ; tɑrˋbuʃ] ***n*.** 〔Ar.〕土耳其帽〔通常带有红色穗子〕。

tar·da·men·te [ˌtɑːdəˈmente; ˏtɑrdɑˋmɛntɛ] ***ad*.** 〔It.〕【乐】缓慢地。

tardi·grade [ˈtɑːdigreid; ˋtɑrdɪˏgred] ***a*., *n*.** 迟钝(的);【动】缓步类(动物)(的)。

tar·di·ly [ˈtɑːdili; ˋtɑrdɪlɪ] ***ad*.** 缓慢地;迟缓地;不愿意地;拖拉地。

tar·di·ness [ˈtɑːdinis; ˋtɑrdɪnɪs] ***n*.** 缓慢;迟缓;拖拉。

tar·do [ˈtɑːdəu; ˋtɑrdo] ***a*., *ad*.** 〔It.〕【乐】徐缓的[地]。

tar·dy [ˈtɑːdi; ˋtɑrdɪ] ***a*.** (***-di·er***; ***-di·est***) 缓慢的;迟延的,迟到的 (*in*);磨蹭的,拖拉的。*make a ~ appearance* 迟到。*a ~ reform* [*amendment*] 为时已晚的改革[补救]。*a ~ consent* 勉强的答应。

tar·dy·on [ˈtɑːdiːˌɔn; ˋtadiˏɑn] ***n*.** 【物】亚光(速粒)子,慢子。

tare[1] [teə; tɛr] ***n*.** **1.** 【植】巢菜〔救荒野豌豆〕;小巢菜〔硬毛果野豌豆〕。**2.** 稗子,莠草。**3.** 坏影响,不良成分。

tare[2] [teə; tɛr] **I *n*.** **1.** (货物的)皮重。**2.** 车身自重〔燃料等除外〕。**3.** 【化】容器的重量;配衡体。~ ***and tret*** 皮重估定法。**II *vt*.** 量皮重;【物】校准。

tar·fu(bar) [ˈtɑːfjuː(bɑː); ˋtɑrfju(bɑr)] 〔美海俚〕= things are really fouled up (beyond all recognition) 搞得面目全非。

targe [tɑːdʒ; tɑrdʒ] ***n*.** 〔古〕小圆盾。

tar·get [ˈtɑːgit; ˋtɑrgɪt] ***n*.** 靶子,标的;目标;(嘲笑等的)对象;笑柄 (*for*);(储蓄,贸易等的)定额,指标;小羊的颈胸肉;【物】(X 射线管中的)对阴极;【测】标杆,标板;【铁路】圆板信号机;〔古〕小圆盾。*a ~ area* 轰炸目标地区。*a ~ ship* 靶舰。*a ~ buster* 〔美俚〕打飞靶的人。*~ practice* 打靶,射击演习。***hit a ~*** 达到定额[指标]。***one's ~ for tonight*** 〔英军俚〕女友。**~-card** (打靶用的)记分卡。~ **date** 预定日期。~ **language** 归宿语言 (*opp*. source language 始发语言)。~ **tuner** 预设单频小收音机。

Tar·gum [ˈtɑːgəm; ˋtɑrgʌm] ***n*.** (*pl*. ***~s***; ***~im***) 阿拉米亚(Aramaic)语译的《旧约圣经》。**-ist *n*.** Targum 的译者,研究者。

Tar·heel [ˈtɑːˌhiːl; ˋtɑrˏhil] ***n*.** 〔美口〕北卡罗来纳州人〔北卡罗来纳州的别称〕。

tar·iff [ˈtærif; ˋtærɪf] **I *n*.** **1.** 关税(表),税率(表),税则。**2.** 〔英〕(旅馆、铁路等的)价目表,收费表;(电话等的)计价,收费。*conventional* [*statutory*] *~s* 协定[国定]税率。*preferential* [*retaliatory*] *~s* 特惠[报复]税率。*~ rates* 税率,(保险等的)协定率。*a ~ scale* 税率表;工资等级表;运费[收费]表。**II *vt*.** 征收关税;定税率;定收费标准。~ **wall** 关税壁垒。

tar·la·tan [ˈtɑːlətən; ˋtɑrlətn], **tar·letan** [-le-; -lɛ-] ***n*.** 【纺】塔拉丹[达尔拉顿]薄纱。

Tarmac, t- [ˈtɑːmæk; ˋtɑrˏmæk] ***n*.** **1.** 铺路柏油〔商标名〕。**2.** 〔英〕= tarmacadam 碎石柏油路。

tarn[1] [tɑːn; tɑrn] ***n*.** 【地】冰斗湖,山中小湖。

tarn[2] [tɑːn; tɑrn] ***n*.** = tern[1].

tar·nal [ˈtɑːnəl; ˋtɑrnl̩] ***a*., *ad*.** 〔美俚〕真正(的),十足(的);极度(的)〔eternal 的别字,用来加强语气〕。**-ly *ad*.**

tar·na·tion [tɑːˈneiʃən; tɑrˋneʃən] **I *n*.** 〔美俚〕诅咒,咒骂 (= damnation)。**II *int*.** 〔方、俚〕该死! 讨厌! **III *a*.** 该死的,讨厌的。*Why are you in such a ~ hurry?* 你为什么这样瞎忙?

tar·nish [ˈtɑːniʃ; ˋtɑrnɪʃ] **I *vt*.** **1.** 使晦暗,使丧失光泽。**2.** 使生锈,使变色。**3.** 玷污,败坏(名誉等)。— ***vi*.** 变晦暗,(丧)失(光)泽,生锈,变色。**II *n*.** 晦暗,锈;表面变色;污点。**-a·ble *a*.**

ta·ro [ˈtɑːrəu; ˋtɑro] ***n*.** (*pl*. ***~s***) 【植】(野)芋;芋头。

tar·ot [ˈtærəuət, tæˈrəu-; ˋtæroət, tæˋto-] ***n*.** 〔常用 T-〕(算命用的)有图纸牌。

tarp [tɑːp; tɑrp] ***n*.** 〔口〕tarpaulin.

tar·pan [ˈtɑːpæn; ˋtɑrpæn] ***n*.** (18 世纪时绝种的)欧洲野马。

tar·pau·lin [tɑːˈpɔːlin; tɑrˋpɔlɪn] **I *n*.** **1.** (防水)柏油[焦油]帆布;盖舱板的油布。**2.** (船员用的)雨衣,雨帽。**3.** 〔古、口〕水手,船员。**II *a*.** 油布做的。

tar·pon [ˈtɑːpɔn; ˋtɑrpɑn] ***n*.** 【动】(美国南海岸及西印度群岛一带产)大海鲢。

tarra·did·dle [ˈtærədidl; ˋtærəˏdɪdl̩] ***n*.** = taradiddle.

tar·ra·gon [ˈtærəgən; ˋtærəˏgɑn] ***n*.** 【植】(西伯利亚的)龙蒿,(作调味作料用的)龙蒿叶,茵陈蒿。

tar·ra·go·na [ˌtærəˈgəunə; ˏtærəˋgonə] ***n*.** (西班牙)塔拉贡纳甜酒。

tarred [tɑːd; tɑrd] ***a*.** 涂有柏油的。*~ cloth* 黑油布。*~ roofing felt* 油毛毡,沥青纸板。

tar·ri·ance [ˈtæriəns; ˋtærɪəns] ***n*.** 〔古〕**1.** 耽搁;迟延。**2.** 旅居,逗留。

tar·ri·er [ˈtæriə; ˋtærɪɚ] ***n*.** 拖延者,逗留者。

tar·ri·ness [ˈtɑːrinis; ˋtɑrɪnɪs] ***n*.** 涂柏油,柏油(质)。

Tar·ring [ˈtæriŋ; ˋtærɪŋ] ***n*.** 塔灵〔姓氏〕。

tar·ry[1] [ˈtæri; ˋtærɪ] **I *vi*.** (***-ried***) **1.** 逗留,暂住,旅居。**2.** 〔美口〕迟延,耽搁,踌躇,犹豫;等待。*~ a few day in New York* 在纽约逗留几天。*~ on the way* 在路上耽搁。*~ for sb*. 等待某人。*Why do you ~ so long?* 你为何耽搁这么久? — ***vt*.** 〔古〕等待。*~ a reply* 等待

答复。II *n*.〔美〕逗留。*during his* ~ 在他逗留期间。

tarry[2]['tɑːri; `tɑrɪ] *a*. 柏油(质)的;涂柏油的;给柏油弄脏的。

tar·sal ['tɑːsəl; `tɑrsl] I *a*.【解】跗骨的,跗节的;睑板的。II *n*. 跗骨(关节)。

tar·si·a ['tɑːsiə; `tɑrsɪə] *n*. (15世纪意大利流行的)嵌木制品。

tar·si·er ['tɑːsiə; `tɑrsɪɚ] *n*.【动】(东印度)眼镜猴。

tar·so·met·a·tar·sus [ˌtɑːsəuˌmetə'tɑːsəs; `tɑrso,metə`tɑrsəs] *n*.【动】跗蹠骨。

Tar·sus ['tɑːsəs; `tɑrsəs] *n*. 塔索斯〔古城名,在今土耳其南部,为圣保罗之故乡〕。

tar·sus ['tɑːsəs; `tɑrsəs] *n*. (*pl*. *-si* [-sai; -saɪ])【解】跗骨;睑板;鸟胫骨;(昆虫的)跗节;蹠节。

tart[1][tɑːt; tɑrt] *a*. 1. 酸的,辛辣的。2. 尖酸刻薄的;严厉的。*a* ~ *flavour* 酸味。*a* ~ *reply to our letter* 对我们函件尖刻的答复。**-ly** *ad*. **-ness** *n*.

tart[2][tɑːt; tɑrt] *n*. 1.〔英〕(果)馅饼;〔美〕上有牛奶蛋糊或果酱的馅饼。2.(原系表示亲爱的用词,现在通常用指轻佻的)少女,女人;妓女。~ **up** *vi*.〔主英俚〕打扮得花哨〔尤指用价廉的服饰〕。

tar·tan[1]['tɑːtən; `tɑrtn̩] I *n*. 1. 格子花呢(服)。2.(穿格子花呢衣服的)苏格兰高地人[苏格兰高地联队的士兵]。II *a*. 格子花呢的。

tartan[2]['tɑːtən; `tɑrtn̩] *n*. (航行于地中海沿岸的)独桅三角帆船。

Tar·tar ['tɑːtə; `tɑrtɚ] I *n*. 1. 鞑靼人,鞑靼语;塔塔尔族,塔塔尔人。2.〔常作 t-〕剽悍的人,强暴的人,难对付的人。3. 悍妇。II *a*. 鞑靼(人)的。*catch a* ~ 碰到劲敌,骑虎难下。*a young* ~ 强横的孩子。

tar·tar(e) ['tɑːtə; `tɑrtɚ] *n*. 1.【化】酒石;酒石酸氢钾。2.【医】牙垢;牙石。*cream of* ~ 酒石(英)。~ *emetic* 催吐酒石,酒石酸氧锑钾。~ *sauce* (也作 tartare sauce)酸泡菜调味酱〔由蛋黄酱、碎酸泡菜、油橄榄、香葱搅和制成,食海味时用〕。

Tar·tar·e·an [tɑː'teəriən; tɑr`terɪən] *a*. 地狱(般)的。

Tar·tar·i·an [tɑː'teriən; tɑr`terɪən] *a*. 鞑靼的,鞑靼人的。

tar·tar·ic [tɑː'tærik; tɑr`tærɪk, -`tɑrɪk] *a*. 酒石(酸)的,含酒石(酸)的。~ *acid* 酒石酸。

tar·tar·ize ['tɑːtəraiz; `tɑrtər,aɪz] *vt*. 酒石化;用酒石处理。**-i·za·tion** *n*.

tar·tar·ous ['tɑːtərəs; `tɑrtərəs] *a*. 酒石的,酒石性的,像酒石的,含酒石的。

Tar·ta·rus ['tɑːtərəs; `tɑrtərəs] *n*. 1.【希神】大恶人死后受罪罚之处的极深层地狱。2. 冥府,地狱。

Tar·ta·ry ['tɑːtəri; `tɑrtərɪ] *n*. 鞑靼(地方)。

tart·let ['tɑːtlit; `tɑrtlɪt] *n*. 小(果)馅饼。

tar·trate ['tɑːtreit; `tɑrtret] *n*.【化】酒石酸盐。**-d** 从酒石中提取的,含酒石(酸盐)的。

Tar·tuffe [tɑː'tuf; tɑr`tuf] *n*. 1. 塔图夫〔法国17世纪喜剧作家莫里哀所作同名喜剧的主人翁〕。2.〔t-〕伪君子,伪善人,假信徒。

TAS = 1. telephone answering service 电话应答服务。2. true airspeed【空】实际空速,真空速。

tas·e·om·e·ter [ˌtæsi'ɔmitə; ˌtæsɪ`ɑmɪtɚ] *n*. 应力计。

Tash·kent [tæʃ'kent; ˌtæʃ`kent] *n*. 塔什干〔乌兹别克城市〕。

ta·sim·e·ter [tə'simitə; tə`sɪmətɚ] *n*. 微压计。**-e·try** *n*. 微压测定。**-met·ric** *a*.

task [tɑːsk; tæsk, tɑsk] I *n*. 1.(派定的)工作,任务,功课。2. 艰苦的工作,苦差使。3.〔废〕租税,税款。*set* (*sb*.) *a* ~ 派(某人)一个任务。*be at one's* ~ 在做着工作。*It's quite a task to figure out 10 problems in an hour*. 一小时内算出十道习题可是个艰苦的工作。***bring*** [***call***, ***take***] ***sb***. ***to*** ~ (*for doing sth*.) (为…)责备(某人)。***take a*** ~ ***upon oneself*** 接受任务。II *vt*. 1. 派给工作。2. 虐待,使作苦工。3.〔废〕课税。~ *one's energies* 尽全力。~**bar**【计】(通常显示于电脑屏幕底部的)任务栏。~ **force**【军】特混(特遣)部队或舰队;〔转义〕专门工作组。~**master** (*fem*. ~**mistress**) 工头;监工;虐待者,严厉的主人。~ **wages** 包工工资。~**work** 派定的工作,包工,吃重的工作。

Tas·man ['tæzmən; `tɑsmɑn, `tæzmən] 塔斯曼〔1602? —1959,荷兰航海家,大洋洲的塔斯马尼亚岛及新西兰的发现者〕。

Tas·ma·nia [tæz'meinjə; tæz`menɪə, -`menjə] *n*.〔略 Tasm.〕(大洋洲东南的)塔斯马尼亚岛。**Tas·ma·nian** [tæz'meinjən; tæz`menɪən] *a*., *n*. (大洋洲东南)塔斯马尼亚的(人)。~ **devil** 袋熊。~ **wolf** 袋狼。

Tass, TASS [tæs; tæs, tɑs] =〔Russ.〕*Telegrafnoye Agentvo Sovyetskovo Soyuza*〔苏联〕塔斯社(= Telegraph Agency of the Soviet Union)。

tass [tɑːs, tæs; tæs, tɑs] *n*.〔Scot.〕1. 小酒杯或有足无柄的小杯。2. 一杯的量,一口的量。

tasse [tæs; tæs] *n*. 盔甲的腿甲,腿罩。

tasse [tɑs; tɑs] *n*.〔F.〕杯子。

tas·sel[1]['tæsl; `tæsl] I *n*. 1. 缨,绶,流苏。2. 垂花,穗状花序。3. 丝带书签。4.〔美〕玉米的穗状雄花。5.【建】承梁木。II *vt*. (〔英〕 *-l*(*l*)-) 1. 装上缨绶[流苏]。2. 使抽穗;(为了使作物苗长)摘去穗状雄花。— *vi*. 抽穗,(玉米)长穗须。*a golden-~ed silk banner* 金穗锦旗。

tas·sel[2]['tæsl; `tæsl̩] *n*.〔废〕= tercel.

tast·a·ble ['teistəbl; `testəbl̩] *a*. = tasteable 可尝的;可口的,滋味好的。

taste [teist; test] I *vt*. 1. 尝,尝味,品(尝)味道;吃出…的味道;〔通例用于否定句〕饮食,吃。2. 经验,享受;体会(双关语等);〔古〕爱好。— *vi*. 1. 尝味,辨味。2. 有…的味道,有…的滋味(*of*);有…的气味(*of*)。3.〔古〕吃一口,喝一口;〔古〕尝,经验(*of*)。~ *tea* 品茶。*The wounded soldier has not ~d food for two days*. 这伤员两天来什么也没吃。*He has ~d the sweets and bitters of life*. 他尝遍了人生的酸甜苦辣。*It ~s sour*. 这东西有酸味。*It ~s of mint*. 这东西有薄荷味。*Good medicine ~s bitter to the mouth*. 良药苦口。*The valiant never ~s of death but once*. 勇士舍生取义只经历一次死的痛苦。***on tasting*** (商店中的食品、糖果样品等)供公众品尝的。II *n*. 1. 滋味;味觉。2. 尝味;(贫穷等的)滋味,经验。3. 一口;一点点,些微。4. 爱好,兴趣;审美力,鉴别力,欣赏力。5. 风味;风格。*It is bitter to the* ~. 这个味苦。*A cold dulls sb.'s* ~. 伤风使某人吃东西没味道[使失去辨别滋味的能力]。*Tastes differ* [*vary*]. 口味人各不同。*the English* ~ 英国人的爱好[口味]。***a bad*** ~ ***in the mouth*** 令人不快的余味,坏印象。***a matter of*** ~ 爱好[口味]问题。***be in bad*** ~ 很俗气,样子不好,不雅致。***be in good*** [***excellent***, ***admirable***] ~ 很有风味,很雅致。***be out of*** ~ 没有审美力,粗俗;没眼光。***give*** (*sb*.) ***a*** ~ ***of*** 给尝,使经验。***have a*** (***small***) ~ ***of*** 尝一口…看看。***have a*** ~ ***for*** 爱好;对…具有兴趣。***man of*** ~ 有欣赏力的人。***to sb.'s*** ~ 合乎某人的口味。***to*** ~ 酌量,…到适合口味(*add pepper to* ~)。***to the king's*** [***queen's***] ~ 很好,毫无问题,很有水准。~**bud**【生理】味蕾。~**maker** 时髦风尚的带头人。

taste·ful ['teistful; `testfəl] *a*. 1. 有鉴赏力的,有欣赏力的。2. 雅致大方的。3. 美观的。4. 美味的。**-ly** *ad*. **-ness** *n*.

taste·less ['teistlis; `testlɪs] *a*. 1. 没有味道的,不好吃的。2. 没有趣味的,乏味的。3. 不雅致的,粗俗的,煞风景的;无鉴别力[欣赏力]的。~ *beer* 淡而无味的啤酒。*a* ~ *melodrama* 一出索然无味的情节剧。*a set of* ~ *furniture* 一套俗气的家具。

tast·er ['teistə; `testɚ] *n*. 1. 以尝味来鉴定质量为职业的试味员。2.【史】封建帝王贵族为防下毒而设的试食

T

员。3. 尝味器〔长柄匙,小杯等〕。4.【化】吸移管,吸量管,吸管。5.【动】触须,触肢。6. (出版社的)审稿员。7.〔口〕碟装冰淇淋。*a wine* ~ 品酒人。

tast·y [ˈteisti; ˋtestɪ] ***a***. (*-i·er*; *-i·est*) **1.**〔口〕美味的,可口的,好吃的。**2.**〔口〕有风味的,雅致的,大方的(服装等)。*a* ~ *hors d'œuvre* 美味的餐前小吃。**-i·ly** ***ad***. **-i·ness** ***n***.

TAT = thematic apperception test【心】主题理解测验。

tat[1] [tæt; tæt] ***n***. **1.** 轻打。**2.**〔口〕(只有 4,5,6 三数的)骰子。*tit for* ~ 一报还一报地,针锋相对地。

tat[2] [tæt; tæt] ***vi***., ***vt***. (*tat·ted*, *tat·ting*) 梭织;用梭织法编织。

tat[3] [tɑːt; tɑt] ***n***. 粗麻布。

tat[4] [tɑːt; tæt] ***n***. (印度英语)矮种马,小马。

ta-ta [ˈtæˈtɑː; ˋtɑˏtɑ, ˋtæ-] **I** ***int***.〔口、儿〕再会! **II** ***n***.〔美俚〕机关枪。

ta·ta·mi [təˈtɑːmi; tɑˋtɑmɪ] ***n***. (*pl*. *-mi*, *-mis*)〔Jap.〕(日本人铺在房屋地板上的)草垫,草席,榻榻米。

Ta·tar [ˈtɑːtə; ˋtɑtɚ] ***n***., ***a***. = Tartar. **Ta·tari·an**, **Ta·taric** ***a***.

Ta·ta·ry [ˈtɑːtəri; ˋtɑtərɪ] = Tartary.

Tate [teit; tet] ***n***. 泰特〔姓氏〕。

Tate Gal·ler·y [ˈteitˈgæləri; ˋtetˋgælərɪ] 泰特绘画陈列馆〔英国美术馆的俗称,得名于最初捐赠所藏美术品的泰特〕。

ta·ter [ˈteitə; ˋtetɚ] ***n***.〔口〕= potato 马铃薯。

Ta·tia·na [ˌtætiˈɑːnə; ˏtætɪˋɑnə] ***n***. 塔蒂亚娜〔女子名〕。

ta·tou·(ay) [ˈtɑːtuː(ai); ˋtætuˏe, ˏtɑtuˋaɪ] ***n***.【动】犰狳(= armadillo)。

tat·ter[1] [ˈtætə; ˋtætɚ] **I** ***n***.〔常 *pl*.〕破布条,碎布,碎纸片,破衣服。***in*** (***rags and***) ***~s*** 破烂,褴褛。***tear to ~s*** 扯得稀烂,扯碎;驳得体无完肤,痛驳。**II** ***vt***. 扯碎,撕碎。

tatter[2] [ˈtætə; ˋtætɚ] ***n***. 梭编者。

tat·ter·de·ma·lion [ˌtætədəˈmeiljən; ˏtætɚdɪˋmeljən, -ˋmæljən] ***n***. 衣服褴褛的人。

tat·tered [ˈtætəd; ˋtætɚd] ***a***. (衣服等)破碎的,破烂的;衣服褴褛的。

tat·ter·sall [ˈtætəˌsɔːl; ˋtætɚˏsɔl] **I** ***n***. 浅色衬底上的深色方格图案。**II** ***a***. 有浅色衬纸上的深色方格图案的。

Tat·ter·sall's [ˈtætəsɔːlz; ˋtætɚˏsɔlz] ***n***. (伦敦)塔特赛尔马市场。*He knows his* ~ *better than his Greek Testament*.〔英〕他不爱功课专爱赛马。

tat·ter·y [ˈtætəri; ˋtætərɪ] ***a***. (衣服等)破烂的;褴褛的。

tat·ting [ˈtætiŋ; ˋtætɪŋ] ***n***. **1.** 梭编法。**2.** 用梭编法编的花边。

tat·tle [ˈtætl; ˋtætl] **I** ***n***. **1.** 闲谈,空话。**2.** 饶舌。**3.** 谈论别人的隐私。*a* ~ *basket* = ~ *box*〔美〕搬弄是非的人;传闻。**II** ***vi***., ***vt***. **1.** 闲谈,空谈。**2.** 饶舌。**3.** 乱讲(别人的私事等)(*about*);泄露秘密。~ *about the squabbles of the family next door* 乱讲隔壁那户人家的口角。**III** ***a***. 饶舌的,乱搬弄是非的。~**tale** 乱讲别人私事的人,乱搬弄是非的人。

tat·tler [ˈtætlə; ˋtætlɚ] ***n***. **1.** 爱说闲话的人。**2.** 喜欢谈论别人隐私的人。**3.**【鸟】鹬类。

tat·too[1] [təˈtuː, tæˈt-; tæˋtu] **I** ***n***. (*pl*. *~s*) **1.**【军】归营信号(号声或鼓声)。**2.** 门规。**3.** 冬冬连敲声。**4.**〔英〕(配有军乐作为娱乐的)归营行军。***beat the devil's*** ~ (焦躁或沉思等时候)用手指得得地敲桌子,脚跟着地脚尖敲出嗒嗒声。**II** ***vi***. **1.** 吹归营号。**2.** 得得地敲。

tat·too[2] [təˈtuː; təˋtu] ***n***., ***vt***. 纹身,刺花。**-er** ***n***. 纹身师。**-ist** ***n***. 纹身的人。

tat·too·ing [tæˈtuːiŋ; tæˋtuɪŋ] ***n***. **1.** 刺字,纹身。**2.** 皮肤所刺的花纹。

tat·ty[1] [ˈtæti; ˋtætɪ] ***n***. (印度用于阻挡户外热气或防臭的)湿香帘。

tat·ty[2] [ˈtæti; ˋtætɪ] ***a***.〔英口〕**1.** 衣衫褴褛的,破旧的,不整洁的。**2.** 低劣的。**3.** 不调合的。**-ti·ly** ***ad***. **-i·ness** ***n***.

Ta·tum [ˈteitəm; ˋtetəm] ***n***. 泰特姆〔姓氏〕。

tau [tɔː, tau; tɔ, taʊ] ***n***. **1.** 希腊语的第十九个字母〔T. τ 相当于拉丁字母的 t〕。**2.** T 字形。**3.** T 字形物。~ *cross* T 字形十字架。**4.**【物】τ 介子〔一种弱相互作用的基本粒子〕。

Tauch·nitz [ˈtauknits; ˋtaʊknɪks] ***n***. 陶赫尼次版〔德国 Tauchnitz 书店翻印的廉价本英语书籍〕。

taught [tɔːt; tɔnt] teach 的过去式及过去分词。

taunt[1] [tɔːnt; tɔnt] **I** ***n***. **1.** 辱骂,奚落,嘲弄。**2.** 反激。**3.** 嘲弄的对象,笑柄。~ *sb*. *with his conduct* 责骂某人的行为。*endure the ~s of one's classmates* 忍受同班学生的嘲弄。**II** ***vt***. **1.** 辱骂,嘲弄。~ *Little Tom with being a newcomer* 嘲弄小汤姆是个新手。**2.** 用嘲笑刺激。**-er** ***n***. **-ing·ly** ***ad***.

taunt[2] [tɔːnt; tɔnt] **I** ***a***.【海】很高的(桅等)。**II** ***ad***. 扯满风帆。

taupe [təup; top] ***n***. 灰褐色。

tau·rine[1] [ˈtɔːrain; ˋtɔraɪn] ***a***. **1.** 像公牛的。**2.** 牛类的。**3.**【天】金牛座的。

tau·rine[2] [ˈtɔːriːn; ˋtɔrin] ***n***.【化】牛磺酸,氨基乙磺酸,牛胆碱。

tau·ro·cho·licacid [ˌtɔːrəˈkəulik; ˏtɔrəˋkolɪk, -ˋkɑl-]【化】牛磺胆酸。

tau·rom·a·chy [tɔːˈrɔməki; tɔˋrɑməkɪ] ***n***. 斗牛戏。

Tau·rus [ˈtɔːrəs; ˋtɔrəs] ***n***.【天】金牛座;金牛宫。

Taus·sig [ˈtausig; ˋtaʊsɪg] ***n***. 陶西路〔姓氏〕。

taut [tɔːt; tɔt] ***a***. **1.**【海】(绳子等)拉紧的,绷紧的。**2.** (肌肉、神经)紧张的。**3.** (服装、器具等)整齐的,整洁的;秩序井然的。**4.** 纪律严明的,严格的,严峻的。*a* ~ *hand*【海】严格的军官。*a* ~ *helm* 船逆风开驶时的舵。**-ly** ***ad***. **-ness** ***n***.

taut·en [ˈtɔːtn; ˋtɔtn̩] ***vt***., ***vi***. 拉紧,绷紧。

tauto- *comb*. *f*. 相同: *tauto*logical.

tau·to·chrone [ˈtɔːtəkrəun; ˋtɔtəkron] ***n***.【物】等时降落轨迹。

tau·to·chro·nism [tɔːˈtɔkrənizəm; tɔˋtɑkrənɪzm̩] ***n***.【物】等时性。

tau·tog [tɔːˈtɔg; ˋtɔtɑg] ***n***.【动】(美国大西洋岸的)蚝隆头鱼(*Tautogaonitis*)。

tau·to·log·i·c(al) [ˌtɔːtəˈlɔdʒik(əl); ˏtɔtəˋlɑdʒɪkl̩] ***a***. **1.** 同义反复的,重言式的,类语叠用的。**2.** 重复的,赘述的。**-ly** ***ad***.

tau·tol·o·gism [tɔːˈtɔlədʒizm; tɔˋtɑlədʒɪzm̩] ***n***. 重言式,同义重复,赘述。

tau·tol·o·gist [tɔːˈtɔlədʒist; tɔˋtɑlədʒɪst] ***n***. 爱叠用类语的人;说话啰唆的人。

tau·tol·o·gize [tɔːˈtɔlədʒaiz; tɔˋtɑləˏdʒaɪz] ***vi***. 叠用类语,同义重复。

tau·tol·o·gous [tɔːˈtɔləgəs; tɔˋtɑləgəs] ***a***. **1.** = tautological. **2.** 分解的,分析的。**-ly** ***ad***.

tau·tol·o·gy [tɔːˈtɔlədʒi; tɔˋtɑlədʒɪ] ***n***. **1.** 重言(式),同义重复,类语叠用〔如: in sorrowful〕。**2.** 重复,赘述。

tau·to·mer [ˈtɔːtəmə; ˋtɔtəmɚ] ***n***.【化】互变(异构)体。

tau·tom·eri·sm [tɔːˈtɔmərizəm; tɔˋtɑməˏrɪzm̩] ***n***.【化】互变(异构)现象。

tau·to·nym [ˈtɔːtəˌnim; ˋtɔtəˏnɪm] ***n***.【生】重名,属种同名。**-ic** [-ˈtɔnimik; -ˋtɑnɪmɪk] ***a***. **-y** [-ˈtɔnimi; -ˋtɑnəmɪ] ***n***.

tau·toph·o·ny [tɔːˈtɔfəni; tɔˋtɑfənɪ] ***n***. 同音重复。

tav [tɑːf, tɔːv; tɑf, tɔv] ***n***. 希伯来语第二十三个字母(= taw)。

tav·ern [ˈtævə(ː)n; ˋtævɚn] ***n***. **1.** 酒馆,酒店。**2.** 小旅馆,客栈。**-er** 酒店主。

taw[1] [tɔː; tɔ] ***vt***. **1.** (不用单宁而用明矾和盐的溶液)鞣制(生皮),硝(皮)。**2.**〔方〕鞭打。

taw^{2}[tɔː; tɔ] ***n*.** **1.** 弹石游戏。**2.** 弹石。**3.** 弹石游戏的基线。*come* [*bring*] *to* ～【连】(使)站在起步线上,(使到)预定的位置。

taw·dry [ˈtɔːdri; ˋtɔdrɪ] **I** ***a*.** (*-dri·er*; *-dri·est*) 价廉而花哨的,俗气的。～ *clothing* 价廉而花哨俗气的衣服。**II** ***n*.** 价廉而花哨的东西。**-i·ly** ***ad*.** **-i·ness** ***n*.**

taw·ny [ˈtɔːni; ˋtɔnɪ] ***n*.**, ***a*.** 黄褐色(的),茶色(的)。

taws(e) [tɔːz; tɔz, tɑz] **I** ***n*.** 〔*sing*., *pl*.〕〔Scot.〕(抽打纺锤使旋转的,打孩子用的)细小皮鞭。**II** ***vt*.** 鞭打。

tax [tæks; tæks] **I** ***n*.** **1.** 税,租税,租款(*on*; *upon*)。**2.** 〔美〕会费。**3.** 负担。**4.** (*pl*. *-es*)〔英口〕收税官。*an additional* ～ 附加税。*a business* ～ 营业税。*a housing and land* ～ 房地产税。*an income* ～ 所得税。*an import* (*export*) ～ 进(出)口税。*a poll* (*capitation*) ～ 人头税。*free of* ～ 免税。～*-free imports* 免税进口货。～ *in kind* 用实物缴纳的税。*a heavy* ～ *upon one's health* 有害健康的繁重负担。**II** ***vt*.** **1.** 对…抽税,征税。**2.** 使负重担,虐待;绞(脑汁);竭(力等)。**3.** 责备,谴责,非难。**4.** 〔美〕讨(价);要人支付。**5.**【法】评定(损失赔偿金,诉讼费等)。～ *one's ingenuity* 用尽心机。～ *sb*. *with a fault* 责备某人的过失。*How much did they* ～ *you for that hat*?〔美〕那顶帽子他们要你多少钱? ～ **bearer** 纳税人。～ **break** 减税优惠。～ [～**ed**] **cart** 〔英〕(免税的)农[商]用二轮单马运货车。～ **collector** 〔古〕, ～**-gatherer** 收税官。～**-deductible** ***a*.** 计算所得税时可扣除的。～ **disc** 〔英〕"税盘"〔一种圆形小张贴物,贴在汽车挡风玻璃上,表示已缴纳养路税〕。～ **duplicate** **1.** 不动产估税证书。**2.** (按估税证书开票的)核税根据单。～ **dodger** 偷税人。～**evasion** 逃税。～**-exempt** ***a*.** 免税的。～ **farmer** 包税人。～**-free** ***a*.** 免税的,无税的;上过税的。～ **haven** 逃税场所(指税率很低的国家或地区)。～**mobile** 〔美〕流动收税车。～**-payer** 纳税人。～ **stamp** 纳税印花。～ **therapist** 〔美口〕(为委托人提供咨询的)税单填写专家〔美国填写每年的退税单有最终时限,且内容复杂,令人头痛,故而须请专家协助〕。～ **title**【法】〔美〕(购买公开拍卖的不动产的不纳税的)买主所有权。

tax·a [ˈtæksə; ˋtæksə] ***n*.** taxon 的复数。

tax·a·ble [ˈtæksəbl; ˋtæksəbḷ] ***a*.** **1.** 应征税的,有税的。**2.**【法】当然可要求的。**-ness** ***n*.** **-bil·i·ty** [ˌtæksəˈbiliti; ˏtæksəˋbɪlətɪ] ***n*.** **-bly** ***ad*.**

tax·a·tion [tækˈseiʃən; tæksˋeʃən] ***n*.** **1.** 征税,抽税。**2.** 税制。**3.** 税额(款)。**4.** 税收(额)。**5.** 清算诉讼费用。*a* ～ *bureau* [*office*] 税务局[署]。*progressive* ～ 累进税率。***be subject to*** ～ 应纳税。***be exempt from*** ～ 免税。

tax·eme [ˈtæksiːm; ˋtæksim] ***n*.**【语言】语法元素;语法元素分类标志。**-e·mic** [tækˈsiːmik; tækˋsimɪk] ***a*.**

tax·i [ˈtæksi; ˋtæksɪ] **I** ***n*.** **1.** 出租汽车,计程车(= ～-cab)。**2.** = taximeter. **3.** = taxiplane. **II** ***vi*.** (～*ed*; *tax·i·ing*, *tax·y·ing*) **1.** 〔口〕搭乘出租汽车。**2.**【空】滑行。—***vt*.** **1.** 用出租汽车接送。**2.** 使(飞机)滑行。～**cab** = taxi. ～**-coach** 〔罕〕大型出租汽车。～ **dancer** 舞女。～**-flying**【空】滑走飞行。～**man** 出租汽车司机。～**meter** (乘出租汽车等的)车费计算表,计程器。～**plane** 出租飞机。～ **rank** [**stand**] 出租汽车站[停车处]。～**way**【空】滑行道。

tax·i·der·mal, **tax·i·der·mic** [ˌtæksiˈdəːməl, -mik; ˏtæksəˋdɝml, -mɪk] ***a*.** 动物标本剥制(术)的。

tax·i·der·mist [ˈtæksidəːmist; ˋtæksɪdɝmɪst] ***n*.** (动物标本)剥制师。

tax·i·der·my [ˈtæksidəːmi; ˋtæksəˏdɝmɪ] ***n*.** (动物标本)剥制术。

tax·ing [ˈtæksiŋ; ˋtæksɪŋ] ***a*.** 繁重的,费力的,使疲劳的。

tax·is^{1} [ˈtæksis; ˋtæksɪs] ***n*.** **1.**【语法】排列,次序。**2.**【医】(脱肠等的)整复(术)。**3.**【动】分类(法)。**4.**【生】移性,趋(向)性。**5.** 〔古希腊〕(军队的)队,分队。

tax·is^{2} [ˈtæksis; ˋtæksɪs] ***n*.** taxi 的复数。

-taxis *comb*. *f*. 排列: para*taxis*.

tax·ite [ˈtækˌsait; ˋtækˏsaɪt] ***n*.**【地】斑杂岩。**-it·ic** [-ˈsitik; -ˋsɪtɪk] ***a*.**

tax·ol·o·gy [tækˈsɔlədʒi; tækˋsɔlədʒɪ] = taxonomy.

tax·on [ˈtæksɔn; ˋtæksɑn] ***n*.** (*pl*. ***tax·a*** [-sə; -sə]) 分类单位[类别,项目]。

tax·o·nom·ic(al) [ˌtæksəˈnɔmik(əl); ˏtæksəˋnɑmɪk(əl)] ***a*.** 分类学的,分类的。

tax·on·o·mist [tækˈsɔnəmist; tæksˋɑnəmɪst] ***n*.** 分类学者。

tax·on·o·my [tækˈsɔnəmi; tæksˋɑnəmɪ] ***n*.** **1.** (尤指动植物)分类。**2.** 分类学,分类法。

tax·us [ˈtæksəs; ˋtæksəs] ***n*.** (*pl*. ***tax·us***)【植】紫杉属(*Taxus*)植物。

tax·y·ing [ˈtæksiiŋ; ˋtæksɪɪŋ] taxi 的现在分词。*The airliner was* ～ *for a takeoff*. 班机正在滑行准备起飞。

Tay·lor [ˈteilə; ˋtelɚ] ***n*.** 泰勒〔姓氏〕。

TAZARA = Tanzania-Zambia Railway 坦赞铁路。

taz·za [ˈtɑːtsə; ˋtɑtsə] ***n*.** 浅杯,扁花瓶〔常带垫座,作装饰用〕。

TB, **T.B.** = **1.** torpedo boat 鱼雷(快)艇。**2.** tubercle bacillus 结核杆菌。**3.** tuberculosis 肺结核。

T / B = trial balance (会计)试算表。

Tb =【化】terbium.

T / BA = Tables of Basic Allowance【军】基准津贴表。

T-bar [ˈtiːˌbɑː; ˋtiˏbɑr] ***n*.** T形滑杆〔挂在用电来带动的很长的钢缆上,拉两个滑雪者上山〕。

TBD, **T.B.D.** = torpedo-boat destroyer 舰队,驱逐舰〔旧称〕。

Tbi·li·si [ˈtpilisi; ˋtpɪlɪsɪ] ***n*.** 第比利斯〔格鲁吉亚城市〕。

TBM = tactical ballistic missile 战术弹道导弹。

T-bone steak [ˈtiːbəun; ˋtibon] 带T形骨的腰部嫩肉片。

tbs., **tbsp.** = tablespoon; tablespoonful.

TC = Trusteeship Council (UN) (联合国)托管理事会。

T.C. = **1.** Tank Corps 〔英〕坦克部队。**2.** temporary constable 临时警察。**3.** Town Councillor 〔英〕镇议员。

Tc【化】= technetium.

TCA = Trans-Canada Airlines 全加拿大航空公司。

TCAS = traffic collision avoidance system 空中防碰撞系统〔即空中交通系统〕。

TCBM = transcontinental ballistic missile 洲际弹道导弹。

T.C.D. = Trinity College, Dublin 〔爱〕都伯林圣三一学院。

tchick [tʃik; tʃɪk] **I** ***n*.** 乞!〔赶马的声音〕。**II** ***vi*.** (赶马时)发乞乞声。

TCP/IP【计】传输控制协议/网际协议〔合称为 Transmission Control Protocol/Internet Protocol〕。

TD = **1.** tank destroyer 自行防坦克炮。**2.** = tractor-drawn 牵引车牵引。

T.D. = **1.** Telegraph Department 电报局[处]。**2.** 〔L.〕*ter die* (= three times a day)【处方】每日三次。**3.** Territorial Decoration 〔英〕本土军服役勋章。

TDMA【电信】时分多址(技术)〔系 time-division multiple access 之缩略〕。

T.D.N., **t.d.n.** = total digestible nutrients 完全可以消化的养分。

T.E. = Topographical Engineer 测绘工程师。

Te =【化】tellurium.

tea [tiː; ti] **I** ***n*.** **1.** 茶;茶叶。**2.** 茶树。**3.** 茶水;茶汤。**4.** 〔英〕午后茶点,午后小吃;茶会。**5.** 〔美俚〕大麻(叶),大麻香烟。*black* ～ 红茶。*green* ～ 绿茶。*brick* [*tile*] ～ 茶砖。*strong* [*weak*] ～ 浓[淡]茶。*cold* ～ 冷茶;〔口〕酒。*the first infusion* (*of*) ～ 刚泡出的茶,头遍茶。*early* ～ 早茶。*afternoon* ～ = *five o'clock* ～ 午后茶点。*high* ～ = *meat* ～ 茶点便餐〔比一般午后

茶点晚一点有肉食冷盆的正式茶点〕。***come*** [***go***] ***to*** ~ ***with*** 和…吃茶点去。***make*** ~ 泡茶。***take*** ~ ***with sb.*** 与某人打交道;与某人发生冲突。**II** ***vi.*** 吃午后茶点;拿出午后茶点。*We* ~ *at 4.* 我们在四点钟吃茶点。— ***vt.*** ~ *a guest* 请客人喝茶。~ **bag** 袋装茶叶,茶袋〔沏茶时连袋泡在水里〕。~ **ball** 滤茶器。~ **berry**【植】平铺白珠树(果实),冬青油,冬绿油。~ **biscuit** 茶点。~ **board** 茶盘。~ **boat**〔美俚〕一杯茶。~ **bread** (吃茶点时的)软面包。~ **caddy** 茶叶罐。~ **cake**〔英〕午后吃茶时的点心。~ **canister**〔美俚〕头。~ **cart** = ~ wag(g)on. ~ **chest** 茶叶箱。~ **cloth** 吃茶点用的小台布;(茶器等的)擦布。~ **cosy** 茶壶保温罩。~ **cult** (**ceremony**) 日本的茶道,品茗会。~**cup** 茶杯,一茶杯的量(*storm in a* ~ *cup* 茶杯里的风波;因小事而争吵)。~**-cupful** 一茶杯的量。~**dance** 有茶点的傍晚舞会。~**-dealer** 茶商。~**-fight**〔口〕= tea party. ~**-garden** 茶园,茶圃,有茶室的花园。~ **gossip** 茶话。~ **gown** (女人的)茶会服,访问服。~ **grounds** 茶渣。~ **grove** 茶山。~**house** (中国、日本等的)茶馆,茶室。~ **jar** 茶叶瓶,茶叶缸。~**kettle** 开水壶。~ **leaf** 茶叶,〔*pl.*〕茶渣。~ **of heaven** 甜茶。~ **oil** 茶子油。~ **olive**【植】木犀,桂花。~ **pad**〔美俚〕大麻毒窟。~ **party** 茶会,茶话会。~**-plant** 茶树。~ **plantation** 茶园。~**pot** 茶壶。~**poy** (三脚)茶几。~**room** 茶馆。~ **rose** 香水月季。~ **service** = ~ **set** 一套茶具。~ **shop** = tea place 茶馆,〔英〕便餐馆。~ **spoon** 茶匙。~ **stall** 茶摊,茶馆。~ **stirrer** 搅茶器。~ **table** 茶桌。~**-table** ***a.*** 像在茶桌前喝茶似的。~ **taster** (鉴别茶叶质量的)品茶员。~**things** = tea set. ~**time** 喝茶(吃茶点)的时候。~ **tray** 茶盘。~ **tree** 茶树。~**-urn** 开水壶。~ **wag(g)on** (有轮的)茶具台。

teach [tiːtʃ; titʃ] (***taught*** [tɔːt; tɔt]) ***vt.*** **1.** (向某人)教、讲授(某课程);使某人学会做某事 (*to do sth.*)。**2.** (以某事或某经验教训)教育、教导某人 (*that*)。**3.**〔口〕(如对方做某事则予以)教训;告诫某人别做某事。**4.** 使…学习;做…的教师。~ *a child to read* 教孩子识字[阅读]。~ *physics to the students* 教学生物理。*I taught him how to swim.* 我曾教他游泳。*T- your granny to suck eggs!* = *T- a dog to bark!*〔谚〕班门弄斧。*This will* ~ *you to speak the truth.* 这就是给你的教训,教你别再撒谎。*The practice of science* ~*es us that knowledge is power.* 科学的实践使我们认识到知识就是力量。~ *oneself* 自学。~ *school* 当教员。— ***vi.*** **1.** (进行)教书、教学、讲授(活动)。**2.** (学科)可以讲授;(课程)教起来(如何如何)。*She* ~*es at a primary school.* 她在小学教书。*I've been* ~*ing four periods this morning.* 今天上午我已教了四节课。*a course that* ~*es easily* 一门容易教的课。*I will* ~ *you to meddle in my affairs.* 你再管我的事我就要教训你了。~**ware** 教学用视听材料。

teach·a·ble [ˈtiːtʃəbl; ˋtitʃəbl] ***a.*** **1.** 可教的;受教的,肯听教训(学)的,驯顺的。**2.** 适合教学的,便于讲授的。

teach·er [ˈtiːtʃə; ˋtitʃɚ] ***n.*** **1.** 教师,教员,老师,先生。**2.**【空】教练机。*a bomb* ~ 轰炸预习机。***be one's own*** ~ 自学。*a* ~ *of mathematics in a secondary school* 中学的数学教员。*a lady* [*woman*] *teacher* 女教师。*a* ~*'s college* 师范学院。~ ***by negative example*** 反面教员。

teach·er·age [ˈtiːtʃəridʒ; ˋtitʃərɪdʒ] ***n.***〔美西部〕教员住宅(区)。

teach-in [ˈtiːtʃin; ˋtitʃˏɪn] ***n.*** (大学师生对引起争论的问题进行讨论或辩论的)宣讲会〔尤指为反对某一政策而举办的宣讲会〕。

teach·ing [ˈtiːtʃiŋ; ˋtitʃɪŋ] ***n.*** **1.** 教学,讲授。**2.**〔常 *pl.*〕教导,教训,教义,学说。*methods of* ~ 教学方法。~ **fellow** 兼任教职的研究生。~ **machine** (装有电子计算机自动配合学生学习进度的)电子教学机。

Teague [tiːg; tig] ***n.***〔蔑〕爱尔兰人〔因爱尔兰人爱用 Tadhg [tæg, tiːg, taig; tæg, tig, taɪg] 这个字做名字〕。

teak [tiːk; tik] ***n.***【植】柚树(木) (= ~-wood)。

teal [tiːl; til] ***n.*** (*pl.* ~*s*,〔集合词〕~)【鸟】短颈野鸭;小凫;水鸭。*mandarin* ~ 鸳鸯。~ *blue* 青凫。

team [tiːm; tim] **I** ***n.*** **1.** (运动比赛的)队,团;工作队,工作组,作业班;一班[一组]工人。**2.** (一起拖车子的)一队牲口,联畜,联兽。**3.** (野鸭等的)群,同胎仔,一窝的雏。**4.** 牲口和所拉的车。*a basket-ball* ~ 篮球队。*a* ~ *race* 团体赛跑。*a* ~ *event* 团体赛。*a football* ~ 足球队。*an inspection* ~ 视察小组。**II** ***vi.*** 协同工作,赶联畜;驾驶卡车。— ***vt.*** 把(牛马等)联套在车上;用联畜运;〔美〕(将工作)交给承包人;使转包工作。~ ***up with***〔美〕和…协作。~**mate** 同队队员。~ **player** 通力合作者。~**-teach** ***vi.***〔美〕进行[参加]小组教学。~**-teaching** 小组教学〔若干教师分任专题,共同完成一项教学任务〕。~**wise** ***ad.*** 像联畜一样成组[成一行]。~ **work** 合作,协同工作。

team·ster [ˈtiːmstə; ˋtimstɚ] ***n.*** **1.**〔美〕联畜驾驭者。**2.** 联畜中的一匹[一只]。**3.**〔美〕卡车司机。

tear¹ [tiə; tɪr] ***n.*** **1.** 泪。**2.** 滴,水珠,露珠,玻璃珠,树脂珠(等)。**3.**〔*pl.*〕〔美俚〕珍珠。~*s of Eos* 朝露。~*s of joy* 快乐的眼泪。~*s of strong wine* 烈酒汽化而结在杯边上的酒珠。*Job's* ~*s* 薏苡。***draw*** ~***s from*** 引出眼泪。***drop a*** ~ ***over*** 哀悼。***in*** ~***s*** 流着泪,含泪,哭着。***laugh away one's*** ~***s*** 笑着把眼泪掩饰过去。***laugh till the*** ~***s come*** 笑到淌眼泪。***move sb. to*** ~***s*** 使感动得流泪 (*He is easily moved to* ~*s.* 他爱淌眼泪)。***shed*** ~***s*** 流泪。***squeeze out a*** ~ 勉强淌一滴眼泪。***with*** ~***s*** 哭着,含泪 (*Her eyes swim with* ~*s.* 她眼泪汪汪)。***without*** ~***s*** 轻松地;不必(因受苦而)流泪。~ **bomb** 催泪弹。~**drop** **1.** ***n.*** 泪(珠)。**2.** ***a.*** 泪珠状的。~**-duct** 泪腺[管]。~**gas** ***n.***, ***vt.*** (用)催泪毒气(袭击)。~**jerker**〔美俚〕使人流泪的戏剧[电影]。~ **shell** = ~ bomb. ~**-smoke** 催泪毒气。~**-stained** ***a.*** 有泪痕的。

tear² [teə; tɛr] **I** ***vt.*** (***tore*** [tɔː; tɔr]; ***torn*** [tɔːn; tɔrn]) **1.** 撕,撕开,撕裂 (*in two*; *to pieces*; *apart*; *asunder*)。**2.** 扯(头发等);刺破,刺伤,划破,抓破(皮肤等)。**3.** 抢去,夺去,扯掉 (*away*; *down*; *from*; *off*; *out*; *up*)。**4.** 使分裂(国家等)。**5.** 使烦恼[激动],使精神不安。~ *down a poster* 扯下一张招贴画。*A nail tore a hole in her overcoat.* 钉子把她的大衣戳了个洞。~ *a child from sb.'s arms* 把某人抱着的孩子夺过去。~ *a leaf from a calendar* 从日历牌上撕下一页。~ *up a tree by the root* 把一棵树连根拔起。~ *off several pages* 扯掉好几页。*The club is torn by factions.* 俱乐部因派系而分裂。*Her heart is torn by conflicting emotions.* 矛盾的感情使她心胸极为烦闷。~ *'em out of their chairs*【美剧】引起观众热烈喝彩。— ***vi.*** 撕,扯 (*at*); 裂开,拉破,猛冲,飞跑,狂奔 (*about*; *along*)。*This brown paper* ~*s easily.* 这牛皮纸一撕就破。*The cover of the parcel won't* ~. 这包裹的封皮撕不开。~ *at the cover of a postal parcel* 扯邮包的封皮。*children* ~*ing about in the courtyard* 在院子里飞跑的孩子。~ *up the staircase two steps at a time* 两级一步地飞跑奔上楼梯。***be torn with grief*** 悲痛欲绝。***feel torn between two choices*** 难为取舍。~ ***away*** 撕掉;扯开;飞跑。~ ***down*** 扯下;拆毁;猛冲(~ *down a hill* 飞跑下山)。~ ***in pieces*** 撕得粉碎。~ ***it***〔口〕打破计划[希望等](*That's torn it.* 那就糟了,那就完蛋了)。~ ***into*** 跑进。~ ***off*** 扯掉,扯开;飞跑;〔美俚〕急急忙忙做成某事(*He tore off some sleep.* 他匆匆忙忙睡一会儿)。~ ***oneself away from*** 忍痛离开…而去,和…忍痛分离;挣开,甩开(讨厌的人)。~ ***one's hair*** 因悲哀或发怒)扯头发。~ ***one's way*** 猛进。~ ***out*** 撕下,扯

T

下。～ *out of* 跑出。～ *out one's hairs* = ～ one's hairs. ～ *round* [*around*]〔美〕到处奔忙;过放纵生活。～ *through* 飞快地穿过[横贯]。～ *to pieces* 撕碎,扯碎;催毁,彻底揭发,驳得体无完肤。～ *up* 撕碎,扯碎;拔出,连根拔起;使离散,扰乱;跑上。～ *up jack* 引起骚动。**II** *n*. 裂缝,绽线的地方;撕裂;狂奔,激怒;〔美〕狂闹,闹饮。*stand wear and* ～ 耐穿耐用。～ *and wear* 磨损;损伤;损失。～**down** 待拆房屋。～ **sheet** 报刊中某部分的单印页〔特指交给广告投登人的广告样张〕。～ **strip** 拉开包装用的狭带。

tear·ful [ˈtiəful; ˋtɪrful, -fl] *a*. **1**. 流泪的,含泪的,泪汪汪的。**2**. 使人泪流的,悲痛的(消息等)。*grandpa's* ～ *face* 祖父的老泪纵横的脸。～ *voice* 哭声。～ *news* 悲痛的消息。**-ly** *ad*. **-ness** *n*.

tear·ing [ˈteəriŋ; ˋterɪŋ] *a*. **1**. 撕裂的。**2**. 把心撕裂似的,令人痛苦的。**3**.〔口〕激烈的(宣传)。**4**. 猛烈的(风);狂奔的,狂冲的。**5**.〔主英〕了不起的。*a* ～ *toothache* 剧烈的牙痛。*proceed at a* ～ *pace* 疾步前进。*a* ～ *wind* 极其猛烈的风。*a* ～ *success* 了不起的成就。

tear·less [ˈtiəlis; ˋtɪrlɪs] *a*. 没有泪的。

tear·y [ˈtiəri; ˋtɪrɪ] *a*. (*-i·er*; *-i·est*) = tearful.

Teas·dale [ˈtiːzdeil; ˋtizˏdel] *n*. 蒂斯代尔〔姓氏〕。

tease [tiːz; tiz] **I** *vt*. **1**. 逗弄;取笑,戏弄。**2**. 强求,勒索。**3**. 梳理(羊毛等);起(呢绒的)毛,起绒,拉绒。～ *a boy about his curly hair* 戏弄一个小男孩长的打卷的头发。～ *Grandma for money* 缠着祖母要钱。～ *sb. with jest* 和某人开玩笑逗弄他。**II** *n*. 逗惹,戏弄;〔口〕爱戏弄人的人。

tea·sel [ˈtiːzl; ˋtizl] **I** *n*. **1**.【植】川续断,起绒草。**2**.【纺】起绒刺果;起绒机。*fuller's* ～【植】起绒草。**II** *vt*. (〔英〕*-l(l)-*)(用起绒刺果)使(布)起绒。**-er**【纺】起绒机;拉毛工人。

teas·er [ˈtiːzə; ˋtizɚ] *n*. **1**. (爱)惹恼人的人。**2**. 强求者,勒索者。**3**.〔口〕令人烦恼的事物;难题。**4**.〔商口〕含蓄而容易引起人好奇心的广告。*It doesn't pay to invite a* ～ *like that*. 犯不上招引那样的头痛的事儿。

teat [tiːt; tit] *n*. 乳头;乳房;橡皮奶嘴;(机械上的)小突。

teazel, teazle [ˈtiːzl; ˋtizl] *n*., *vt*. = teasel.

Te·bet, Te·vet [ˈteiˈveit, ˈteivəs; teˋvet, ˋtevəs] *n*. 〔Heb.〕犹太历的第四月。

tec [tek; tɛk] *n*.〔俚〕= detective.

tech. = technical; technology.

tec(h) [tek; tɛk] *n*.〔俚〕技术学校。

teched [tetʃt; tɛtʃt] *a*. 神经不正常的。

tech·head [ˈtekhed; ˋtɛkhɛd] *n*.〔口〕技术迷。

tech·i·ly [ˈtetʃili; ˋtɛtʃɪlɪ] *ad*. 恼怒地;情绪不佳地。

tech(n). = technical(ly); technology.

tech·net·i·des [ˈtekniˈtaidis; ˋtɛknɪˋtaɪdɪs] *n*.〔*pl*.〕【化】锝[锘]系元素。

tech·ne·ti·um [tekˈniːʃiəm; tɛkˋniʃɪəm] *n*.【化】锝(Tc)〔旧名 masurium 钨〕。

tech·ne·tron·ic [ˌtekniˈtrɔnik; ˏtɛknɪˋtranɪk]〔美〕*a*. 使用电子技术(解决各种问题为特征)的。*a* ～ *society* 使用电子技术的社会。

tech·nic [ˈteknik; ˋtɛknɪk] **I** *n*. **1**. 专门术语;专门技术。**2**.〔常 *pl*.〕技巧。**3**. = technics. **II** *a*. = technical.

tech·ni·cal [ˈteknikl; ˋtɛknɪkl] *a*. **1**. 技术(性)的,工艺的;学术(上)的;专门(技术)的。**2**.【法】根据法律的,法律上的。**3**.【商】人造的;用工业方法制造的,由市场内部因素(如投机等)引起的。**4**.〔美俚〕外表的,表面上的,浅薄的。～ *skill* 专门技能,技术水平。*a* ～ *expert* 技术专家。*a* ～ *adviser* 技术顾问。*a* ～ *book* 专门性的画。*a* ～ *difficulty* 技术[法律、手续]上的困难。～ **analysis** 技术[工艺]分析。～ **assault** (根据法律而成立的)人身攻击。～ **school** 技术学校。～ **sergeant**〔美军〕(空军或海军陆战队的)技术军士;陆军上士的旧称〔现称 sergeant first class〕。～ **terms** 术语,专门名词。

tech·ni·cal·i·ty [ˌtekniˈkæliti; ˏtɛknɪˋkælətɪ] *n*. 技术性,专门性,学术性;学术性事项,专门事项;专门术语。

tech·ni·cal·ly [ˈteknikəli; ˋtɛknɪkəlɪ] *ad*. 技术上,学术上,专业上。

tech·ni·cian [tekˈniʃən; tɛkˋnɪʃən], **tech·ni·cist** [ˈteknisist; ˋtɛknɪsɪst] *n*. 技术员,技师;专家。

tech·ni·cism [tekˈnisizəm; tɛkˋnɪsɪzm] *n*. 技术主义〔指过份强调技术性和规程,过份依靠机械等〕。

tech·ni·col·our [ˈtekniˌkʌlə; ˋtɛknɪˏkʌlɚ] **I** *n*.【影】彩色印片法;彩色电影[电视]。**II** *a*. 彩色(印片法)的;色彩鲜艳的。

teck·ni·con [ˈteknikɔn; ˋtɛknɪˏkan] *n*.【乐】弹奏技巧练习器。

tech·nics [ˈtekniks; ˋtɛknɪks] *n*.〔*pl*.〕**1**. (专门)技术;工艺;技巧,手法。**2**. 术语,专门用语。**3**. 学术上[专业性]的事项。

tech·nik [ˈteknik; ˋtɛknɪk] *n*.〔口〕(尤指电脑行业的)技术人员〔亦作 techie〕。

tech·ni·phone [ˈteknifəun; ˋtɛknɪˏfon] *n*. (练习指法用的)无声钢琴。

tech·nique [tekˈniːk; tɛkˋnik] *n*. **1**. (专门)技术;(艺术上的)技巧,技能。**2**. 手法〔如画法,演奏法等〕。**3**. 方法。*advanced cinematic* ～ 高级电影技巧。*a newly-developed* ～ 一项新发展的技能。*a statistic* ～ 一种统计方法。

techno- *comb. f*. 技术,工艺;技巧。

tech·noc·ra·cy [tekˈnɔkrəsi; tɛkˋnakrəsɪ] *n*. 专家政治(论),技术统治(论)〔主张一切工作,从生产到国家行政,全部由专家管理的学说〕。

tech·no·crat [ˈteknəkræt; ˋtɛknəˏkræt] *n*. **1**. 专家治国论者,技术统治论者。**2**. (高级)技术人员。

tech·nog·ra·phy [tekˈnɔgrəfi; tɛkˋnagrəfɪ] *n*. 技术发展史。

tech·noid [ˈteknɔid; ˋtɛknɔɪd] *n*. 电脑技术迷,喜爱摆弄电脑上瘾的人。

technol. = technology; technological.

tech·no·la·try [tekˈnɔlətri; tɛkˋnalətrɪ] *n*. 技术崇拜。

tech·no·log·ic, tech·no·log·i·cal [ˌteknəˈlɔdʒik, -kəl; ˏtɛknəˋladʒɪk, -kl] *a*. **1**. 技术[工程](上)的,技术学的。**2**. 因工艺技术高度发展而引起的。*a* ～ *school* 技术学校。～ *unemployment* 技术失业,因技术高度发展所造成的失业。

tech·nol·o·gist [tekˈnɔlədʒist; tɛkˋnalədʒɪst] *n*. 技术员,工艺师,(工程技术)专家。

tech·nol·o·gy [tekˈnɔlədʒi; tɛkˋnalədʒɪ] *n*. **1**. 技术,工程,工艺。**2**. 制造学,工艺学。**3**. 术语(汇编)。*science and* ～ 科学和技术。*the* ～ *of sugar* 制糖法。～ **transfer** 技术转让。

tech·no·phobe [ˈteknəfəub; ˋtɛknəfob] *n*. 害怕高新技术(如电脑等)的人。

tech·nop·o·lis [tekˈnɔpəlis; tɛkˋnapəlɪs] *n*. 专家政治,专家体制。

tech·no·stress [ˌteknəˈstres; ˏtɛknəˋstrɛs] *n*. 高新技术紧张症〔因不适应使用电脑等高新技术设备而产生的神经紧张〕。

tech·no·struc·ture [ˌteknəˈstrʌktʃə; ˏtɛknəˋstrʌktʃɚ] *n*. 技术专家体制;〔集合词〕技术专家。

techy [ˈtetʃi; ˋtɛtʃɪ] *a*. = tetchy.

teck [tek; tɛk] *n*.〔美俚〕= detective.

tec·nol·o·gy [tekˈnɔlədʒi; tɛkˋnalədʒɪ] *n*. 儿童学 (= pedology[2])。

tec·to·gene [ˈtektədʒiːn; ˋtɛktədʒin] *n*.【地】深地槽,海渊。

tec·tol·o·gy [tekˈtɔlədʒi; tɛkˋtalədʒɪ] *n*.【生】组织形态学。

tec·ton·ic [tekˈtɔnik; tɛkˋtanɪk] *a*. **1**. 构造的;建筑的。**2**.【生】构造的。**3**.【地】地壳构造上的,起因于地壳运动

T

的。

tec·ton·ics [tekˈtɔniks; tɛkˋtɑnɪks] ***n*. 1.**【建】筑造学,构造学。**2.**【地】构造地质学,大地构造学。

tec·ton·ism [ˈtektənizm; ˋtɛktənɪzm̩] ***n*.**【地】地壳运动(= diastrophism)。

tec·to·rial [tekˈtɔːriəl; tɛkˋtorɪəl] ***a*.** 构成覆盖物的。~ *membrane*【解】耳蜗覆膜。

tec·trix [ˈtektriks; ˋtɛktrɪks] ***n*.** (*pl*. ***-tri·ces*** [-trəˌsiːz; -trəˏsiz])【动】覆羽。

tec·tum [ˈtektəm; ˋtɛktəm] ***n*.** (*pl*. ***tec·ta*** [-tə; -tə])【解、动】**1.** 盖。**2.** 致密层。**-tal** ***a*.**

Ted [ted; tɛd] ***n*.** 特德〔男子名,Edward 或 Theodore 的昵称〕。

ted [ted; tɛd] ***vt*.** (**-dd-**) 摊晒(干草等);撒,散开。

Ted·der [ˈtedə; ˋtɛdɚ] ***n*.** 特德〔姓氏〕。

ted·der [ˈtedə; ˋtɛdɚ] ***n*.** 摊晒干草的人,干草撒散机。

Ted·dy [ˈtedi; ˋtɛdɪ] ***n*.** 特迪〔男子名, Edward 或 Theodore 的昵称〕。~ *Football*〔美〕(拟人语)足球先生。~ **bear** 玩具熊。~ **boy** (英国六十年代的)无赖青年。~ **girl** 无赖女青年。

ted·dy [ˈtedi; ˋtɛdɪ] ***n*.** (常用 *pl*. **-dies**)〔美〕妇女连衫衬裤〔尤指 20 世纪 20 年代流行的一种内衣〕。

Te *De·um* [teiˈdeium, tiːˈdiːəm; teˋdeum, tiˋdiəm]〔L.〕感恩赞美诗,感恩赞美诗的音乐。

te·di·ous [ˈtiːdiəs; ˋtidɪəs, ˋtidʒəs] ***a*.** 单调沉闷的,令人生厌的,冗长乏味的。*a* ~ *speech* 一个冗长乏味的讲演。*Too many abstract statements made his paper very* ~ *to me*. 他的读书报告抽象的讲法太多使我生厌。**-ly** ***ad*.** **-ness** ***n*.**

te·di·um [ˈtiːdiəm, -djəm; ˋtidɪəm] ***n*.** 沉闷,单调,冗长乏味。

tee[1] [tiː; ti] ***n*. 1.** 英语字母 T. **2.** T 字[丁字]形物;T(形)管,三通;丁字铁。*a* ~*-piece* 丁字接头。***to a*** ~ 恰好地,丝毫不差地。~ **shirt** 圆领短袖汗衫。

tee[2] [tiː; ti] **I *n*. 1.** (高尔夫球发球时放球的)球座。**2.** 发球点〔美式足球开球时的发球点〕。**3.** (套圈等游戏中的)目标。*dead from the* ~ 发球时未打中球。*a* ~ *top-notcher*〔美〕高尔夫球名手。**II *vt*., *vi*. 1.** 放(球)在球座上。**2.** 准备。*Joe* ~*ed the ball up for the final hole*. 乔把高尔夫球放在球座上准备打向最后的球穴。~ ***off*** 从球座发球;开始;〔美俚〕严厉责备,痛骂(*on*);触怒,使不快。

tee[3] [tiː; ti] ***n*.** (塔顶的)笠状顶饰。

tee-hee [ˈtiːˈhiː; tiˋhi] **I *int*.** 嘻,嘿(窃笑声)。**II *n*.** 窃笑声。**III *vi*.** = tehee 窃笑,小声笑。

teel [tiːl; til] ***n*. 1.** = sesame. **2.** 麻油。

teem[1] [tiːm; tim] ***vi*. 1.** 充满;富于,有很多(*with*)。**2.**〔古〕产崽仔,结实。*That book* ~*s with blunders*. 那本书错误不少。*Fish* ~ *in the Chinese waters*. = *the Chinese waters* ~ *with fish* 中国近海鱼产丰富。— ***vt*.**〔古〕产,生。

teem[2] [tiːm; tim] ***vt*. 1.**〔古〕把…倒空;倒出。**2.**【冶】把(钢水等)…注入模具。— ***vi*.** (雨水等)倾注。

teem·ing [ˈtiːmiŋ; ˋtimɪŋ] ***a*.** 多产的;充满的,丰富的;很多的。*a* ~ *brain* (思想)丰富的头脑。

teen[1] [tiːn; tin] ***n*. 1.**〔古、方〕悲哀,痛苦。**2.** 不幸。**3.** 损害,伤害。**4.**〔苏格兰〕愤怒。

teen[2] [tiːn; tin] **I *n*. 1.** = teen-ager 13—19 岁。**2.** 13—19 世纪。**II *a*.** 十几岁的;13—19 岁的。

-teen *suf*. 十〔基数词 13—19 的后缀〕: six*teen*.

teen-age [ˈtiːneidʒ; ˋtinɪdʒ] ***n*., *a*.** (~d)少年[13—19 岁]时代(的)。

teen-ag·er [ˈtiːnˌeidʒə; ˋtinˏedʒɚ] ***n*.** (13—19 岁的)少年,少女。

teener [ˈtiːnə; ˋtinɚ] ***n*.** = teen-ager.

teens [tiːnz; tinz] ***n*.** 〔*pl*.〕十多岁[13—19 岁]。***enter one's*** ~ 刚 13 岁。***in one's*** ~ 十多岁时,在少年时代。***out of one's*** ~ = ***pass one's*** ~ (刚)过了少年时代。

teen·ster [ˈtiːnztə; ˋtinztɚ] ***n*.**〔美〕= teen-ager.

teen·sy [ˈtiːnsi; ˋtinzɪ] ***a*.**〔口〕= tiny.

tee·ny [ˈtiːni; ˋtinɪ] ***a*.** (***-ni·er***; ***ni·est***)〔方、口;主儿〕tiny 的变体。~**-weeny**〔口〕小小的;小额的。

teen·y-bop·per [ˈtiːniˌbɔpə; ˋtinɪˏbɑpɚ] ***n*.**〔美俚〕摹嬉士〔20 世纪 60 年代学嬉皮士那一套的青少年;尤指女子〕。

tee·pee [ˈtiːpi; ˋtipɪ] ***n*.** (北美印地安人的)圆锥形帐篷。

tee·ter [ˈtiːtə; ˋtitɚ] **I *vi*., *vt*.**〔美口〕**1.** (使)蹒跚。**2.** 颠簸。**3.** 摇摆。**4.** 跷跷板。*Look! There's a drunken man* ~*ing at the head of the stairs*. 看,有个醉汉在楼梯顶那里摇摇欲坠呢。**II *n*. 1.** 蹒跚。**2.** 颠簸。**3.** 摇摆。**4.** 跷跷板。~ **board** 跷跷板。~**-totter** 跷跷板。

teeth [tiːθ; tiθ] ***n*.** tooth 的复数。

teethe [tiːð; tið] ***vi*.** 出乳牙,生牙。

teeth·ing [ˈtiːðiŋ; ˋtiðɪŋ] ***n*.** 出乳牙,出牙期。~ *ring* (供出牙期婴儿咬的)橡皮环。~ *troubles* 生牙期的疼痛;〔喻〕事情开始期的暂时困难。

teeth·ridge [ˈtiːθˌridʒ; ˋtiθˏrɪdʒ] ***n*.**【医】上齿龈前部的内壁;牙嵴。

tee·to·tal [tiːˈtəutl; tiˋtotl̩] ***a*.** 主张戒酒的,绝对戒酒的;〔口〕完全的,绝对的,彻底的。~ *drink* 不含酒精的饮料。*His Majesty's* ~ *hotel*〔俚〕监狱。**-ism** ***n*.** 绝对戒酒主义。**-er**〔英〕**-tal·ler** ***n*.** 绝对戒酒(主义)者。

tee·to·tum [tiːˈtəutəm; tiˋtotəm] ***n*.** (用手指捻转的)四方[六方]陀螺,捻转儿。*like a* ~ 旋转着。

tef·lon [ˈteflɔn; ˋtɛflɑn] ***n*.**【化】(商标名)特氟纶,聚四氟乙烯〔由美国杜邦公司生产的一种绝缘塑料,涂于锅内可使食物不粘锅〕;〔美口〕(使某人的形象或声誉不受损害的)"特氟纶"式保护膜〔出了事可推卸责任等〕。~ **President**〔美〕"特氟纶"式总统〔指总是诿过于人而自己推卸掉责任的总统〕。

TEG, teg, t.e.g. = top edge(s) gilt 顶端烫金〔指书籍〕。

teg(g) [teg; tɛg] ***n*.** 两岁的羊。

teg·men [ˈtegmən; ˋtɛgmɛn] ***n*.** (*pl*. ***teg·mi·na*** [ˈtegminə; ˋtɛgmɪnə]) **1.** 外皮,被覆;壳。**2.**【植】内种皮。**3.**【动】(昆虫的)覆翅;阳(茎)基。**-mi·nal** [-minəl; -mɪnəl] ***a*.**

Te·gu·ci·gal·pa [teˌguːsiˈgælpə; təˏgusɪˋgælpə] ***n*.** 特古西加尔巴〔洪都拉斯首都〕。

tegu·lar [ˈtegjulə; ˋtɛgjələ] ***a*.** 瓦的,像瓦的,瓦状(排列)的。

teg·u·ment [ˈtegjumənt; ˋtɛgjəmənt] ***n*.**【动、植】皮,外皮,被膜;壳。

te·hee [tiːˈhiː; tiˋhi] **I *int*.** 嘻,嘿(窃笑声)。**II *n*.** 窃笑声。**III *vi*.** 窃笑,小声笑。

Teh·ran, Te·he·ran [tiəˈrɑːn, ˌtehəˈrɑːn; ˏtɪəˋrɑn, ˏtɛhəˋrɑn, tɛˋrɑn] ***n*.** 德黑兰〔伊朗首都〕。

Te·huel·che [teˈweltʃi; tɛˋwɛltʃɪ] ***n*.** (*pl*. ***-ches***, ***-che***) 德卫尔彻人〔南美巴塔哥尼亚的主要土著民族,以身躯高大著称〕。

te·ig·i·tur [teiˈidʒiˌtuə; teˋɪdʒɪˏtʊr] ***n*.**【天主】"因此你…"〔弥撒主祷文的开始二词〕。

teil (**-tree**) [tiːl; til] ***n*.**【植】(欧洲)菩提树。

tek·tite [ˈtekˌtait; ˋtɛkˏtaɪt] ***n*.**【矿】熔融石,玻殒石,雷公墨。

tel. = telegram; telegraph(ic); telephone.

tel, tell [tel; tɛl] ***n*.**【考古】(层层覆盖古代遗址的)人工丘阜。

te·laes·the·sia [ˌtelisˈθiːziə; ˏtɛləsˋθiʒə, -ʒɪə, -zɪ-] ***n*.** = telesthesia.

tel-[1] *comb*. *f*. = tele-[1].

tel-[2] *comb*. *f*. = tete-[2].

tel·a·mon [ˈteləmən; ˋtɛləmən] ***n*.** (*pl*. ***telamones*** [teləˈməuniːz; tɛləˋmoniz])【建】男像柱。

tel·an·gi·ec·ta·sis, tel·an·gi·ec·ta·sia [telændʒi-

ˈektəsis, -ˈteiʒiə; tɛlˏændʒɪˋɛktəsɪs, -ˋteʒɪə] *n*. (*pl*. *-ses* [-ˌsiːz; -ˏsiz])【医】毛细管扩张。**-tat·ic** [-ˈtætik; -ˋtætɪk] *a*.

tel·au·to·gram [teˈlɔːtəgræm; tɛlˋɔtəˏgræm] *n*. 传真电报。

tel·au·to·graph [teˈlɔːtəgrɑːf; tɛlˋɔtəˏgræf] *n*. 传真电报(机)。

tel·au·tog·ra·phy [ˌteləːˈtɔgrəfi; ˏtɛləˋtɑgrəfɪ] *n*. 传真电报学[术]。

tel·au·to·mat·ics [teˈlɔtəmətiks; tɛˋlɑtəmətɪks] *n*. **1**.【无、自】自动遥控机械学。**2**.【力学】自动遥控装置。

Tel A·viv [tel əˈviːv; ˋtɛl əˋviv] 特拉维夫〔以色列港市〕。

tel·co [ˈtelkəu; ˋtɛlko] *n*.〔口〕电信公司。

tele-[1] *comb*. *f*. 远,远距离,遥控;电视;电信;电传:*tele*meter; *tele*vision.

tele-[2] *comb*. *f*. 目的,末端:*tele*ology.

tel·e [ˈteli; ˋtɛlɪ] *n*. 电视 (= television)。

tel·e·arch·ics [teˈliɑːkiks; tɛˋləɑkɪks] *n*. 无线电飞机操纵术。

tel·e·ba·rom·e·ter [telibəˈrɔmitə; tɛləbəˋrɑmɪtɚ] *n*. 远距气压计。

tel·e·bet [teliˈbet; tɛlɪˋbɛt] *n*. **1**. 电话赌赛马〔用电话通过彩票代理商对赛马下赌注〕。**2**. (赛马场外的)闭路电视彩票经营部。

tel·e·bit [teliˈbit; tɛləˋbɪt] *n*. 二进制遥测系统。

tel·e·book [teliˈbuk; tɛlɪˋbʊk] *n*. 电视剧剧情说明书。

tel·e·came·ra [ˈteliˌkæmərə; ˋtɛləˏkæmərə] *n*. 电视摄像机,远距离摄影机。

tel·e·cast [ˈtelikɑːst; ˋtɛləˏkæst, -ˏkɑst] **I** *n*.〔口〕**1**. 电视广播。**2**. 电视节目。**II** *vt*., *vi*. (~, *~ed*) 用电视广播,作电视广播。**-er** *n*. 电视广播员。

tel·e·cen·tric [ˈteliˌsentrik; ˋtɛləˏsɛntrɪk] *a*.【物】焦阑的,远心的。

tel·e·cin·e [ˈtelisini; ˋtɛləsɪnɪ] *n*. **1**. 电视(传送)电影。**2**. 电视电影演播室。**3**. 电视电影传送装置。

tel·e·com·mu·ni·ca·tion [ˈtelikəˌmjuːniˈkeiʃən; ˏtɛləkəˏmjunəˋkeʃən] *n*. **1**. 电信。**2**. 〔*pl*.〕电信学〔口语中可缩略为 telecomms〕。

tel·e·con [ˈtelikɔn; ˋtɛləkɑn] *n*. 电话会议 (= teleconference)。

tel·e·con·fer·ence [teliˈkɔnfərəns; tɛləˋkɑnfərəns] **I** *n*. (通过电话、电视等的)电信会议;远距离通讯会议。**II** *vi*. 参加[召开]电信会议。

tel·e·con·trol [ˈtelikənˈtrəul; ˋtɛləkənˋtrol] **I** *n*. 遥控。**II** *vt*. **-trol·led** 遥控。**III** *a*. 遥控的。

tel·e·cop·ter [ˈteliˈkɔptə; ˋtɛlɪˋkɑptɚ] *n*. 空中电视台〔装有摄像机和现场播放设备的直升机〕。

tel·e·course [ˈtelikɔːs; ˋtɛləˏkors] *n*. 电视讲座,电视(传授的)课程。

te·le·diag·no·sis [ˈteliˌdaiəgˈnəusis; ˋtɛləˏdaɪəgˋnosɪs] *n*. (医生与病人通过电视进行的)电视诊断。

tel·e·dish [teliˈdiʃ; tɛlɪˋdɪʃ] *n*. (接收卫星电视的)碟形天线,抛物面天线。

tel·e·du [ˈteliduː; ˋtɛləˏdu] *n*.【动】马来獾。

tel·e·fac·sim·i·le [ˈtelifæksimili; ˋtɛləfæksɪmɪlɪ] *n*. 电报传真。

tel·e·film [ˈtelifilm; ˋtɛləˏfɪlm] **I** *n*. 电视影片。**II** *vt*. 把…摄成电视影片。

teleg. = telegram; telegraph(y)。

te·le·ga [teˈlegɑː; tɛˋlɛgə] *n*. (俄国的)运货马车。

tel·e·gauge [teliˈgeidʒ; tɛləˋgedʒ] *n*. 遥测仪。

tel·e·gen·ic [teliˈdʒenik; ˏtɛlɪˋdʒɛnɪk, ˏtɛlə-] *a*. 适于拍摄电视的。

telego·ni·o·meter [ˈteligəuniˈɔmitə; ˋtɛləgonɪˋɑmɪtɚ] *n*. 方向针,遥远测角计,无线电测向仪。

te·leg·o·ny [tiˈlegəni; tɪˋlɛgənɪ] *n*.【生】感应遗传,前父遗传〔认为先前父兽的特性能遗传给同一母兽与其他公兽所生的后代,这一动物遗传的假想现已被证明不确切〕。**tel·e·gon·ic** [ˌteliˈgɔnik; ˏtɛləˋgɑnɪk] *a*.

tel·e·gram [ˈteligræm; ˋtɛləˏgræm] *n*. 电报。*a ~ in cipher* [*plain*] *language* 密码[明码]电报。*a ~ in code language* 号码[密码]电报。*a ~ form* [〔美〕*blank*]电报纸。*by ~* 用电报。*milk* [*tap*] *a ~* 偷电报。*send a ~* 拍发电报。

tel·e·graph [ˈteligrɑːf, -græf; ˋtɛləˏgræf, -ˏgrɑf] **I** *n*. **1**. 电报机。**2**. 电报。**3**. 信号机。**4**. (船上驾驶台与轮机之间的)传令钟。**5**. (运动比赛等的)报分牌 (= ~-board)。**6**. 电讯〔报纸名,如 *The Daily T-*〕。*a ~ office* [*station*] 电报局。*a ~ slip* 电报纸。*a ~ restante* 留局待领电报。*by ~* 用电报。*submarine ~* 海底电报。**II** *vt*. **1**. 打电报,用电报通知[传送信息],电告。**2**. 电汇。**3**. 在揭示板上示出(比分等)。**4**. 无意中流露。*~ sb*. *a message* 给某人打电报。*~ sb*. *the score of the game* 把球赛比分电告某人。*a smile that ~ed consent* 流露出同意的微笑。— *vi*. 打电报。*Shall I ~*? 我可以打电报吗? *~ to her at once* 立刻给她打电报。*~ for sb*. [*to sb*. *to come*] 电邀某人。~ **board** (运动比赛时得分)揭示板。~ **cable** 电报电缆。~ **code** 电码。~ **key** 电报发报键,电钥。~ **line** 电报线路。~ **operator** 报务员。~ **plant**【植】舞萩〔印度豆科灌木〕。~ **pole** [**post**] 电线杆。~ **printer** 打[印]字电报机。~ **receiver** 收报机。~ **register** 收报机。~ **repeater** 电报转发机[中继机]。~ **stamp** 电报费收讫章。~ **transmitter** 发报机。~**-wire** 电报电线。

te·leg·ra·pher [tiˈlegrəfə; təˋlɛgrəfɚ] *n*. 报务员。

tel·e·graph·ese [ˈteligrɑːfiːz; ˏtɛləgræˋfiz] *n*., *a*. 电报体裁(的)。

tel·e·graph·ic, tel·e·graph·i·cal [ˌteliˈgræfik, -əl; ˏtɛləˋgræfɪk, -l̩] *a*. **1**. 电报的,电信的。**2**. 电报机的。**3**. 电送的。**4**. 电报体裁的,简洁的。*a ~ message* 电报。*a ~ money order* 电汇。*a ~ picture* 电传图片。**-cal·ly** *ad*.

te·leg·ra·phist [tiˈlegrəfist; təˋlɛgrəfɪst] *n*. 〔英〕电信技术员;〔英军〕通信兵;电信技术家。

te·leg·ra·phone [tiˈlegrəfəun; təˋlɛgrəˏfon] *n*. 录音电话机。

te·leg·ra·phy [tiˈlegrəfi; təˋlɛgrəfɪ] *n*. 电信技术[工程];电报学;电报。*electric wave ~ = Hertzian* [*wireless*] *~* 无线电报(术)。*line ~* 有线电报(术)。*facsimile* (*picture*) *~* 传真电报(术)。*submarine ~* 海底电报(术)。

tel·e·ki·ne·sis [ˌtelikiˈniːsis; ˏtɛləkɪˋnisɪs] *n*.【心灵学】心灵遥感(现象)。**-net·ic** [-ˈnetik; -ˋnɛtɪk] *a*.

tel·e·lec·ture [ˈteliˈlektʃə; ˋtɛləˋlɛktʃɚ] *n*. **1**. 电话扬声器。**2**. 电话讲课,电话讲演。

tel·e·mark [ˈtelimɑːk; ˋtɛləˏmɑrk, ˋtɛlə-] *n*.【滑雪】屈膝旋转法,旋转停止法。

tel·e·me·chan·ics [telimiˈkæniks; ˏtɛlɪməˋkænɪks, ˏtɛlə-] *n*. 遥控机械学;遥控力学。

tel·e·me·ter [ˈtelimiːtə, tiˈlemitə; təˋlɛmətɚ] **I** *n*. **1**. 遥测计[仪],遥测发射器。**2**. 测远仪,测深仪,测距仪。**II** *vt*., *vi*. 遥测;用遥测发射器传送。*data ~ed from a spaceship* 从太空船传来的数据。

tel·e·me·ter·ing [ˈtelimiːtəriŋ; ˋtɛləˏmitərɪŋ, təˋlɛm-] *n*. 遥测;沿无线电遥测线路传送(信息)。

te·lem·e·try [tiˈlemitri; təˋlɛmətrɪ] *n*. 遥测学;遥测术,测距术。**-met·ric** *a*. **-ri·cal·ly** *ad*.

tel·e·mi·cro·scope [teliˈmaikrəskəup; tɛləˋmaɪkrəˏskop] *n*. 望远显微镜。

tel·e·mo·tion [teliˈməuʃən; tɛləˋmoʃən] *n*. 无线电操纵,遥控(操纵)。

te·le·mo·tor [ˈtelimautə; ˋtɛləmotɚ] *n*. **1**. (使用电力、水力或机力等的)动力遥控装置。**2**.【电】遥控电动机。**3**.【船】油压操舵器。

T

tel·en·ceph·a·lon [ˌtelenˈsefəˌlɔn; ˏtɛlɛnˋsɛfəlɑn] ***n.*** (*pl*. ***-la*** [-lə; -lə])【解】端脑, 终脑;【生】(胚胎)前脑胞。**-ce·phal·ic** [-siˈfælik; -sɪˋfælɪk] ***a.***

teleo- *comb. f.* 目的, 末端 (= tele²-)。

tel·e·ol·o·gy [ˌteliˈɔlədʒi; ˏtɛlɪˋɑlədʒɪ, ˏtilɪ-] ***n.***【哲】目的论。**-log·ic, -log·i·cal** ***a.*** **-olo·gist** ***n.*** 目的论者。

tel·e-op·er·a·ted [teliˈɔpəreitid; tɛlɪˋɑpəretɪd] ***a.*** 遥控的。

Tel·e·o·sau·rus [ˌteliəˈsɔːrəs; ˏtɛlɪəˋsɔrəs] ***n.***【古生】完龙。

tel·e·ost; tel·e·os·te·an [ˈteliɔst, ˈtiːli-, -ˈɔstiən; ˋtɛlɪˏɑst, ˋtilɪ-, ˏtɛlɪˋɑstɪən] **I** ***n.***【动】新鳍类 (*Neopterygii*) 或真骨类 (*Teleostei*) 鱼。**II** ***a.*** 新鳍类或真骨类鱼的。

te·le·pa·per [ˈteliˌpeipə; ˋtɛləˏpepɚ] ***n.*** 电视传真报纸(或文件)。

tel·e·path·ic [ˌteliˈpæθik; ˏtɛlɪˋpæθɪk, ˏtɛlə-] ***a.*** 心灵感应的, 以心传心的。

te·lep·a·thy [tiˈlepəθi; təˋlɛpəθɪ] ***n.*** 心灵感应(术), 传心术。

teleph. = telephone; telephony.

tel·e·phone [ˈtelifəun; ˋtɛləˏfon] **I** ***n.*** 电话(机)。*a dial* ~ 自动电话。*a public* ~ 公用电话。*a* ~ *booth* [*box*] (公用)电话亭。*a* ~ *directory* [*book*] 电话用户号码簿。*a* ~ *operator* 话务员。*a* ~ *receiver* (电话)听筒。*a* ~ *set* 电话机。*a* ~ *subscriber* 电话用户。*a* ~ *transmitter* (电话)话筒。*speak to sb. over the* ~ 和某人通电话。*You are wanted on the* ~. 请你去接电话。***by*** ~ 用电话。***call*** (*sb.*) ***on the*** ~ 给(某人)打电话。***call sb. to the*** ~ 叫某人听电话。***talk on*** [***over***] ***the*** ~ 打电话, 通电话。**II** ***vt.*** 打电话给某人, 把某事用电话通知某人。— ***vi.*** 给某人打电话 (*to*)。~ *the secretary* 打电话给秘书。~ *a message to sb.* 打电话给某人告诉他一项消息。*He* ~*d that he would come in the afternoon.* 他打电话来说他下午来。~ **tag** 〔美口〕电话捉迷藏游戏〔甲打电话给乙, 乙不在; 等到乙回电话给甲, 甲又不在等〕。

tel·e·phon·ee [ˌtelifəuˈniː; ˏtɛləfoˋni] ***n.*** 接电话的人。

tel·e·phon·er [ˈtelifəunə; ˋtɛləfonɚ] ***n.*** 打电话的人。

tel·e·phon·ic [ˌteliˈfɔnik; ˏtɛləˋfɑnɪk] ***a.*** 电话的, 用电话传送的, 电话机的。**-i·cal·ly** ***ad.***

te·leph·o·nist [tiˈlefənist; təˋlɛfənɪst] ***n.*** 〔主英〕话务员; 电话接线生。

tele·pho·no·graph [ˌteliˈfəunəgrɑːf; ˏtɛləˋfonəgræf, -grɑf] ***n.*** 电话录音机。

te·leph·o·ny [tiˈlefəni; təˋlɛfənɪ] ***n.*** 电话技术。*rural* ~ 乡村电话。*secret* ~ 保密电话。*toll* ~ 长途电话(技术)。*wireless* ~ 无线电话(术)。

tel·e·phote [ˈtelifəut; ˋtɛlɪfot, ˋtɛləf-] ***n.*** **1.** 传真电报机。**2.** 远距照相机。

tel·e·pho·to [ˈteliˈfəutəu; ˋtɛlɪˏfoto] **I** ***a.*** **1.** 远距照相的。**2.** 传真照相的。*a* ~ *camera* 远距照相机。*a* ~ *lens* 远距照相镜头, 摄远镜头。**II** ***n.*** **1.** 远距照相(术), 远距摄影(术)。**2.** 传真电报, 传真照片。**3.** 摄远镜头 (= ~ lens)。

tel·e·pho·to·graph [ˈteliˈfəutəgrɑːf, -græf; ˏtɛləˋfotəˏgræf, -ˏgrɑf] **I** ***n.*** 远距摄影照片; 电传照片。**II** ***vt., vi.*** 用远摄镜头拍摄; 用电传照片发送。**-ic** ***a.*** **-i·cal·ly** ***ad.***

tel·e·pho·tog·ra·phy [ˈtelifəˈtɔgrəfi; ˏtɛləfoˋtɑgrəfɪ] ***n.*** 远距摄影(术); 电报传真术。

tele·pho·to·me·ter [ˌtelifəuˈtɔmitə; ˏtɛləfoˋtɑmətɚ] ***n.*** 远距光度计。

tel·e·play [ˈteliplei; ˋtɛlɪˏple] ***n.*** 电视广播剧。

tel·e·por [ˈtelipɔː; ˋtɛləˏpor] ***vt.*** 远距传物〔将物质转变为能, 传送到目的地后重新转变为物质〕。**-ta·tion** [-ˈteiʃən; -ˋteʃən] ***n.***

tel·e·pre·sence [ˈtelipresəns; ˋtɛlɪprɛsəns] ***n.***【计】远程监控。

tel·e·print·er [ˈteliprintə; ˋtɛləˏprɪntɚ] ***n.*** 电传打字电报机。

tel·e·promp·ter [ˈteliˌprɔmptə; ˋtɛlɪˏprɑmptɚ] ***n.*** (在电视演说者面前将讲稿逐行现出的)讲词提示器〔原商标名〕。

tel·e·pu·ter [ˈtelipjuːtə; ˋtɛlɪpjutɚ] ***n.***【计】(可与因特网联通的)联网电视机。

tel·e·ran [ˈteliræn; ˋtɛləræn] ***n.*** 电视雷达导航仪 (*tele*vision, *r*adar, *a*ir 和 *n*avigation 的缩合词)。

tele·re·ceiv·er [ˌteliriˈsiːvə; ˋtɛlərɪˏsivɚ] ***n.*** 〔美〕电视(接收)机。

tel·e·re·cord [ˈteliriˌkɔːd; ˋtɛlərɪˏkɔrd] ***vt.*** 将为…摄制为电视片, 录像。**-ing** ***n.*** 电视录像, 电视片摄制; 电视片放映, 电视片。

tel·er·gy [ˈtelədʒi; ˋtɛlɚdʒɪ] ***n.*** **1.** 透视力, 视觉特异功能。**2.**【心】远隔精神作用。

tel·e·sat [ˈtelisæt; ˋtɛləˏsæt] ***n.*** 通信卫星〔系 telecommunications satellite 的缩合词〕。

tel·e·scope [ˈteliskəup; ˋtɛləˏskop] **I** ***n.*** **1.** 望远镜。**2.**【天】远镜座。*an astronomical* ~ 天文望远镜。*a binocular* ~ 双筒望远镜。*an equatorial* ~ 赤道仪。*a radio* ~ 射电望远镜。*a reflecting* ~ 反射式望远镜。*a relief* ~ 体视望远镜。*a sighting* ~ 瞄准望远镜。**II** ***vi.*** 嵌进, 套叠; (列车等)相碰撞而嵌在一起。*The two cars collided and* ~*d.* 两节车相撞嵌在一起了。— ***vt.*** 嵌进, (使)套入, (使)(依次)叠进; (使)缩短。~ **bag** (旅行用)伸缩皮包。~ **fish** 数眼金鱼。~ **level** 水准仪。

tel·e·scop·ic [ˌteliˈskɔpik; ˏtɛləˋskɑpɪk] ***a.*** **1.** 望远镜的; 用望远镜看的, 只能用望远镜看见的。**2.** 能看见远处的, 远视的。**3.** 套筒的, 套管的; 伸缩自如的。*a* ~ *chimney* 伸缩烟囱。~ *joint* 套叠接合。*a* ~ *object* 只有用望远镜才能看到的物体。*a* ~ *screw* 套叠螺旋。*a* ~ *sight* (大炮上的)望远瞄准器。*a* ~ *tube* 套叠管。**-i·cal·ly** ***ad.***

tel·e·scop·i·form [ˌtelisˈkɔpifɔːm; ˏtɛlɪsˋkɑpɪfɔrm] ***a.*** 望远镜形的; 套叠的; 可伸缩的。

tel·e·sco·pist [tiˈleskəpist; təˋlɛskəpɪst] ***n.*** (善于)使用望远镜的人。

te·les·co·py [tiˈleskəpi; təˋlɛskəpɪ] ***n.*** 望远镜使用法; 望远镜制造法。

tel·e·script [ˈteliskript; ˋtɛlɪskrɪpt] ***n.*** **1.** 电视广播稿。**2.** 电视剧本。

tel·e·scrip·tor [ˌtelisˈkriptə; ˏtɛlɪˋskrɪptɚ] ***n.*** = teletypewriter.

tel·e·seism [ˈtelisaizəm; ˋtɛləˏsaɪzm̩] ***n.***【地】远震。

tel·e·seme [ˈtelisiːm; ˋtɛlɪˏsim, ˋtɛlə-] ***n.*** (旅馆等的)电铃; 信号机。

tel·e·set [ˈteliset; ˋtɛləsɛt] ***n.*** 电视(接收)机。

tel·e·sis [ˈtelisis; ˋtɛləsɪs] ***n.*** (自然和社会力量)有目的使用; 有计划的发展。

tel·e·spec·tro·scope [ˌteliˈspektrəˌskəup; ˏtɛlɪˋspɛktrəˏskop] ***n.*** 远距分光镜。

tel·e·ster·e·o·scope [ˌteliˈsteriəskəup; ˏtɛləˋstɛrɪəskop, -ˋstɪr-] ***n.*** 体视望远镜。

tel·es·the·si·a [ˌtelisˈθiːʒə, -ziə; ˏtɛlɪsˋθiʒə] ***n.***【心】超阈限感觉。**-thet·ic** [-ˈθetik; -ˋθɛtɪk] ***a.***

te·les·tic, te·les·tich [ˈtelistik, tiˈle-; təˋlɛstɪk, ˋtɛləˏstɪk] ***n.*** 各行最后一字母可以拼成一[几]个词的诗。

tel·e·switch [ˈteliswitʃ; ˋtɛlɪˏswɪtʃ] ***n.*** 遥控键, 遥控开关。

tel·e·ther·mom·e·ter [ˌteliθəˈmɔmitə; ˏtɛlɪθɚˋmɑmətɚ, ˏtɛlə-] ***n.***【物】遥测温度计。

tel·e·thon [ˈteliθɔn; ˋtɛlɪθɑn] ***n.*** 〔美〕(马拉松式)长时间电视节目。

tel·e·type [ˈteliˌtaip; ˋtɛlɪˏtaɪp, ˋtɛlə-] **I** ***n.*** 〔美〕**1.** 电

传打字电报机。**2.** 电传打字电报。**3.** 电传打字电报术。**II** ***vt***., ***vi***. (*-typed*, *-typ·ing*) 用电传打字机发送(电报)。**-typ·ist** ***n***. 电传打字电报员。

tel·e·type·set·ter [ˌteliˈtaipˌsetə; ˌtɛləˋtaɪpˌsɛtɚ] ***n***. 〔美〕电传排字机。

tel·e·type·writ·er [ˌteliˈtaipraitə; ˌtɛləˋtaɪpˌraɪtɚ] ***n***. 〔美〕电传打字电报机。

te·leu·to·spore [təˈluːtəˌspɔː; təˋlutəˌspɔr] ***n***. 【生】冬孢子 (= teliospore)。**-spor·ic** ***a***.

tel·e·view [ˈtelivjuː; ˋtɛlɪˌvju, ˋtɛlə-] ***vt***., ***vi***. 用电视机收看;看电视。**-er** ***n***. 看电视的人。

tel·e·vise [ˈtelivaiz; ˋtɛləˌvaɪz] ***vt***. **1.** 电视播送,实况播送。**2.** 摄制成电视节目;(用电视机)收看。*The tennis final will be ~d live*. 网球决赛实况将由电视转播。*a ~d panel discussion* 由电视广播的问题公开讨论会。

tel·e·vi·sion [ˈteliˌviʒən; ˋtɛləˌvɪʒən] ***n***. 电视。*black-and-white ~* 黑白电视。*closed-circuit* [*industrial*] *~* 内部闭路[工业]电视。*colour ~* 彩色电视。*combat ~* 指挥作战用的电视。*commercial* [*sponsored*] *~* 商业电视。*the two-way ~* 双向电视。*I won't allow Little Mary to watch ~ till midnight*. 我不会让小玛丽看电视到午夜的。*That's the third time the varsity team appeared on ~ this season*. 那是我们校队本季第三次在电视上出现。~ **camera** 电视摄像机。~ **engineer** 电视工程师。~ **network** 电视(广播)网。~ **picture** 电视图像。**-al**, **-ary** ***a***.

tel·e·vi·sor [ˈtelivaizə; ˋtɛlɪˌvaɪzɚ, ˋtɛlə-] ***n***. 电视播送[接收]机;电视播送者;电视机观看者。

tel·e·vis·u·al [ˌteliˈvizjuəl, -ʒuəl; ˌtɛləˋvɪʒuəl] ***a***. **1.** 电视的。**2.** 适于上电视镜头的。*a ~ scene* 一个适于拍电视的场面。

tel·e·vox [ˈtelivɔks; ˋtɛləˌvɑks] ***n***. (由声音操纵的)机器人。

tel·e·writ·er [ˈteliˌraitə; ˋtɛləˌraɪtɚ] ***n***. 电传打字机。

tel·ex [ˈteleks; ˋtɛlɛks] **I** ***n***. **1.** (与电话线路接通的)电报用户直通电路。**2.** 用户直通电报。**II** ***vt***. 发用户直通电报。

tel·fer ***n***. 〔美〕= telpher.

telg. = telegram.

tel·har·mo·ni·um [ˌtelhɑːˈməuniəm; ˌtɛlhɑrˋmonɪəm] ***n***. 音乐电传机。

te·li·al [ˈtiːliəl, ˈteliəl; ˋtilɪəl, ˋtɛlɪəl] ***a***. 【生】**1.** 冬孢子堆的。**2.** 后期锈菌的。

te·lic [ˈtiːlik, ˈtelik; ˋtɛlɪk] ***a***. 抱有某种目的的,有目的的。*~ movements* 有目的的行动。

te·li·o·spore [ˈtiːliəˌspɔː, ˈteliə-; ˋtilɪəˌspɔr, ˋtɛlɪə-] ***n***. 【生】冬孢子。**-spor·ic** [-ˈspɔrik; -ˋspɔrɪk] ***a***.

te·li·um [ˈtiːliəm, ˈteliəm; ˋtilɪəm, ˋtɛlɪəm] ***n***. (*pl*. *-li·a* [-liə; -lɪə]) 【生】冬孢子堆。

tell [tel; tɛl] **I** ***vt***. (*told* [təuld; told]) **1.** 讲;说。**2.** 告诉,吩咐,命令(某人做某事)(*to do sth*.);指示(*where*; *that*; *how*; *what*)。**3.** 泄漏(秘密等),明白说出,吐露。**4.** 断定说,保证。**5.** 辨别,区别(*from*);决定;知道,明白,了解。**6.** 点数。*I'm ~ing you*. 〔美俚〕注意听我说(这是很重要的)。*T- (sb.) good-bye*. 〔美〕道别。*Let me ~ the good news to everybody*. 让我把好消息告诉大家。*The old peasant told us of (about) his sufferings*. 老农民给我们讲述他所受的苦。*I told him to go on*. 我吩咐他继续说下去。*T- us how you fixed up the machine*. 告诉我们你是怎样修好这架机器的。*His face told (that) he was satisfied with the speech*. 他脸上显示出他对演讲感到满意。*It is very important that one should be able to ~ the true friends from the false ones*. 能辨别真假朋友是非常重要的。*I can ~ you that it's not easy*. 我敢断定地告诉你这事不易。*Let's ~ the noses and call it a day*. 咱们计算一下人数收工吧。*I can ~ you*. = *I ~ you*. = *Let me ~ you*. 的确,真的。*No, I ~ you*. 真的不可以。*I'll ~ you what*. 讲给你听,告诉给你,有话跟你讲。*Never ~ me* = *Don't ~ me*. 不至于吧;不见得吧;我不信[表示惊讶,不快或恐惧等]。*You're ~ing me!* 〔美俚〕这事不用你说,我全知道了。— ***vi***. **1.** 讲,报告(*about*; *of*);〔口〕搬弄是非,说坏话;〔儿〕告发;〔英方〕嚼舌头(*on*; *of*)。**2.** 奏效,产生效果;影响;命中,打中,击中。**3.** 证明;(颜色、声音等)显明,表明。**4.** 〔古〕计数;数票,检票。*I told you so!* = *Did I not ~ you so?* 我不是跟你讲过了吗? *The story ~s of the life of a famous poet*. 这故事讲的是一个著名诗人的生平。*Tom is the man that ~s on sb. whenever there's sth. wrong*. 汤姆是个一出毛病就告发别人的家伙。*Smoking will ~ on you when you're getting old*. 你上年纪时就会感受到吸烟的影响了。*How can I ~?* 我怎么说得上来呢? *Who (can) ~?* 谁知道? 谁也不知道。*You can never ~*. 谁也不知道。*It is the man behind the gun that ~s*. 重要的不是枪而是开枪的人,胜败在人不在武器。*Every shot told*. 百发百中。*The colour of the ink ~s of the fraud*. 墨水的颜色说明是作弊。**do ~** 不见得吧,不至于吧。~ **a tale** 讲故事;泄露内中原因。~ **against the motion** 宣布提案(因只有少数票)不能成立。~ **all** 〔美俚〕自白,说出秘密,说出真话。~ **apart** 辨别,识别(*~ things apart* 辨明情况)。~ **away** 念咒文驱除(病痛等)。~ **down** 〔口〕付(钱)。~ **it to sweeney** [**the marines**] 〔美〕没有那样的事。~ **noses** 〔口〕点人数。~ **off** 数清;分派(工作);【罕】编号;谴责。~ **on** [**upon**] 告密,告发;对…有效,影响到。~ **one's prayers** 祈祷。~ **out** **1.** 数钱付账。**2.** = *~ away*. ~ **over one's hoard** 数积蓄的钱。~ **the tale** 〔俚〕编造假话;讲述可怜的遭遇博取同情。~ **the world** 〔美〕公开讲,扬言。~ (*so many*) **years** 〔口〕显出有(几)岁了[一般指显老]。**II** ***n***. 〔方〕话,传闻。*I've a ~ for you*. 我有一句话要跟你说。*according to their ~* 〔美卑〕据说。

T

Tel·ler [ˈtelə; ˋtɛlɚ] ***n***. 特勒[姓氏]。

tell·er [ˈtelə; ˋtɛlɚ] ***n***. **1.** 讲述者,讲故事的人。**2.** (银行的)出纳员。**3.** 计算者,(投票的)点票员。**4.** 【军】防空情报报告员。*a frequency ~* 频率指示器。*a deposit ~* 存款员。*a paying (receiving) ~* 付[收]款员。**-ship** ***n***. teller 的职位。

tell·ing [ˈteliŋ; ˋtɛlɪŋ] **I** ***a***. **1.** 有效的,有力的。**2.** 生动的;透露真情的,说明问题的。**with ~ effect** 有显著效验。*a ~ blow* 有效的打击。*a ~ stanza in the poem* 那首诗中生动的一节。*That's ~*. = *That would be ~*. 〔口〕说这种话就要露马脚了。**II** ***n***. 讲,可讲的事。*There is no ~*. 难说;不知道。*take a ~* 〔口〕听劝告。**-ly** ***ad***.

tell·tale [ˈtelteil; ˋtɛlˌtel] **I** ***n***. **1.** 告密的人,搬弄是非的人。**2.** 泄露内情的事物,证据。**3.** 【机】指示器,登记机;(指示油罐充油程度等的)警告器。**4.** 【海】舵位指示器;挂罗针仪。**5.** (考勤卡上记录职工上下班时间的)考勤钟。**II** ***a***. 告密的,搬弄是非的;泄露内情的;起警告作用的。*a ~ blush* 泄露隐情的脸红。*a ~ signal* 【电】警告讯号。

tel·lu·ral [teˈljuərəl; tɛˋlʊrəl, -ˋljʊ-] ***a***. 地球的,地上的;地球居民的。

tel·lu·rate [ˈteljureit; ˋtɛljʊˌret] ***n***. 【化】碲酸盐;碲酸酯。

tel·lu·ri·an[1] [teˈljuəriən; tɛˋlʊrɪən, -ˋljʊ-] **I** ***a***. 地球的,地球上的;住在地球上的。**II** ***n***. **1.** 地球居民。**2.** 地球仪。

tel·lu·ri·an[2] [teˈljuəriən; tɛˋlʊrɪən, -ˋljʊ-] ***n***. = tellurion.

tel·lu·ric[1] [teˈljuərik; tɛˋlʊrɪk, -ˋljʊrɪk] ***a***. 地球的,源出于地球的,陆生的。

tel·lu·ric[2] [teˈljuərik; tɛˋlʊrɪk, -ˋljʊrɪk] ***n***. 【化】(正)碲

的。～ *acid* 碲酸。

tel·lu·ride [ˈteljuraid; ˋtɛljʊˏraɪd, -rɪd] ***n***.【化】碲化物,碲醚,碲根。

tel·lu·ri·on [teˈljuəriɔn; tɛˋlʊrɪˏɑn, -ˋlɪʊ-] ***n***.(表示地球公转、自转的)地球仪。

tel·lu·rite [ˈteljuˌrait; ˋtɛljʊˏraɪt] ***n***. **1.**【化】亚碲酸盐。**2.**【矿】黄碲矿。

tel·lu·ri·um [teˈljuəriəm; tɛˋlʊrɪəm, -ˋlɪʊ-] ***n***.【化】碲(Te)。

tel·lu·rize [ˈteljuˌraiz; ˋtɛljʊˏraɪz] ***vt***. (***-rized***; ***-rizing***)【化】使碲化,使与碲结合,使含碲。

tel·lu·rous [ˈteljurəs, teˈlju-; ˋtɛljʊrəs, tɛˋljʊ-] ***a***.【化】亚碲(的)。

Tel·lus [ˈteləs; ˋtɛləs] ***n***.【罗神】特勒斯(大地女神)。

tel·ly [ˈteli; ˋtɛlɪ] ***n***.〔英口〕电视;电视机。

Tel·net [ˈtelnet; ˋtɛlnɛt] ***vi***., ***n***.【计】远程登录(服务)。

telo-[1] *comb*. *f*. = tele-[1].

telo-[2] *comb*. *f*. = tele-[2].

tel·o·dy·namic [ˌtelədaiˈnæmik; ˏtɛlədaɪˋnæmɪk] ***a***. 远程传送动力的。～ *transmission* 远程传送[输电]。

te·lome [ˈtiːləum; ˋtilom] ***n***.【植】顶枝。

tel·o·mer [ˈteləmə; ˋtɛləmɚ] ***n***.【化】调聚物。

te·lome·ter [tiˈlɔmitə; tɪˋlɑmɪtɚ] ***n***. = telemeter.

tel·o·phase [ˈteləfeiz; ˋtɛləˏfez] ***n***.【生】(细胞分裂的)末期。

tel·o·type [ˈtelətaip; ˋtɛləˏtaɪp] ***n***. **1.** 电传打字电报机。**2.**(一份)电传打字电报。

tel·pher [ˈtelfə; ˋtɛlfɚ] **I** ***n***., ***a***. 电动缆车(的);高架电动索道(的)。*a* ～ *railway* 高架索道。**II** ***vt***. 用电动缆车(电动索道)运输。～ **age** [-ridʒ; -rɪdʒ] ***n***. 索道,高架[电动缆车]运输。

tel·son [ˈtelsn; ˋtɛlsn] ***n***.【动】尾节。

T

Tel·star, tel·star [ˈtelˌstɑː; ˋtɛlˏstɑr] ***n***.〔美〕通信卫星〔商标名〕。

Tel·u·gu [ˈteləˌguː; ˋtɛləˏgu] **I** ***n***. **1.** 泰卢固语〔印度东部德拉维人语言〕。**2.** (*pl*. ***-gus***, ***-gu***)(印度)泰卢固人。**II** ***a***. 泰卢固语的;泰卢固人的 (= Telegu)。

telvsn. = television.

tem·blor [temˈblɔː; tɛmˋblɔr] ***n***. (*pl*. ***~s***, ***-blor·es*** [-ˈblɔːreis; -ˋblɔres])〔美〕地震。

tem·er·ar·i·ous [ˌteməˈreəriəs; ˏtɛməˋrɛrɪəs] ***a***. 不顾前后的,鲁莽的,轻率的,蛮勇的。*a* ～ *crossing of the Pacific by a small sailing boat* 乘一艘小帆船轻率的横渡太平洋。**-ly** ***ad***.

te·mer·i·ty [tiˈmeriti; təˋmɛrətɪ] ***n***. 鲁莽,轻率,蛮勇。

temp. = **1.** temperature. **2.** temporal. **3.** temporary. **4.** 〔L.〕 *tempore* (= in the time of).

temp [temp; tɛmp] **I** ***n***.〔口〕临时工,临时雇员。**II** ***vi***.〔口〕做临时工,当临时雇员。

Tem·pe [ˈtempi; ˋtɛmpɪ] ***n***. **1.** 潭蓓谷〔(古希腊)塞沙利(Thessaly)地方的溪谷〕。**2.**〔转义〕风光明媚的溪谷。

Tem·pe·an [temˈpiːən; tɛmˋpiən] ***a***. 潭蓓谷的;风光明媚的。

Tem·pel·hof [ˈtempəlhəuf; ˋtɛmpəlhof] ***n***. 柏林郊外的国际飞机场。

tem·per [ˈtempə; ˋtɛmpɚ] **I** ***n***. **1.** 气质;性情,脾气。**2.** 情绪,心情;激动的情绪,激愤,暴躁。**3.** 特征,倾向。**4.**(黏土的)黏度;(灰泥的)稠度;(钢等的)锻炼;淬硬,回火;淬火度;含碳量;硬度;韧度。**5.** 中和剂;调和剂;增效剂。**6.**〔古〕适中,中庸,中和。*an equal* [*even*, *a calm*] ～ 性情平和。*a hot* [*quick*, *short*, *fiery*] ～ 急躁的脾气。(***be***) ***in a*** (***bad***) ～ 发着脾气,生着气。(***be***) ***in a good*** ～ 心情好。***get*** [***go***, ***fly***] ***into*** [***in***] ***a*** ～ 发怒,发脾气。(***get***) ***out of*** ～ 动气,发怒。***in a fit of*** ～ 在发怒中。***in a good*** [***bad***] ～ 在平静[不快]的心情中。***keep*** [***control***] ***one's*** ～ 忍气。***lose one's*** ～ 发脾气,动怒。***lost*** ～ 退火[减低硬度]。***put sb. out of*** ～ 惹怒某人。***show*** ～ = get out of ～. *the* ～ *of the modern Chinese painting* 近代中国绘画的倾向。**II** ***vt***. **1.** 调和,使缓和,调节;减轻,镇定。**2.** 揉和(黏土等);【冶】使回火;硬化(玻璃);〔转〕锻炼;【乐】(按平均律)调音。～ *justice with mercy* 恩威并施。*~ed* [～-*ing*] *steel* 回火钢。*a well-～ed sword* 锻造得极好的剑。— ***vi***. 变柔软;(金属)经回火后具有适当韧度。

tem·pe·ra [ˈtempərə; ˋtɛmpərə] ***n***.(用蛋黄调和颜料的)蛋黄彩画(法);蛋黄颜料;招贴画颜料。

tem·per·a·ble [ˈtempərəbl; ˋtɛmpərəbl̩] ***a***. **1.** 可回火的;可锻炼的。**2.**(灰泥等)可调和的,可揉和的。

tem·per·a·ment [ˈtempərəmənt; ˋtɛmprəmənt, -pərə-] ***n***. **1.** 气质,性情,脾气。**2.**(中世纪生理学中的)质〔分为多血、黏液、胆汁、忧郁等四质〕。**3.**(性情)暴躁,喜怒无常,易激动。**4.**【乐】平均律。*a nervous* ～ 神经质。*be excitable* [*placid*] *by* ～ 性情易激动[冷静]。*a scale of equal* ～ 等程音阶。

tem·per·a·men·tal [ˌtempərəˈmentl; ˏtɛmprəˋmɛntl, -pərə-] ***a***. 气质的,性情的;性情暴躁[浮躁]的;神经质的;多变的,变幻无常的。*a* ～ *dislike for music* 对音乐方面生性不喜欢。*a* ～ *weather* 变幻无常的天气。**-ly** ***ad***.

tem·per·ance [ˈtempərəns; ˋtɛmprəns] ***n***. **1.** 节制,节欲;适中,稳健;〔古〕自制,克己。**2.** 节酒,戒酒。*practise* ～ *in diet* 节制饮食。*a* ～ *hotel* 不卖酒的旅馆。～ *drinks* 无酒精的饮料。

tem·per·ate [ˈtempərit; ˋtɛmprɪt] ***a***. **1.** 有节制的,节欲的;适中的,不过分的,稳健的。**2.** 节酒的,戒酒的。**3.**(气候等)温和的。*a man of* ～ *habits* 有节制的人。*a* ～ *statement* 稳健的说明。*the north* ～ *zone* 北温带。**-ly** ***ad***. **-ness** ***n***.

tem·per·a·ture [ˈtempəritʃə; ˋtɛmprətʃɚ] ***n***. **1.** 温度,气温。**2.** 体温。**3.**〔口〕发烧,高烧。***have*** [***run***] ***a*** ～〔口〕(体温)比正常高,发烧。***take one's*** ～ 量体温。～ **curve** (病人的)体温曲线;温度曲线。～ **gauge** 温度计。～ **gradient** 气温(变化)陡度〔尤指高度增加下的变化〕。

tem·pered [ˈtempəd; ˋtɛmpɚd] ***a***. **1.** 回火的,经过锻炼的。**2.** 调合的;温和的。**3.** 性情…的,脾气…的。**4.**【乐】调正的〔尤指调成平均律的〕。～ *steel* 回火钢。*bad*-～ 脾气坏的。

tem·pest [ˈtempist; ˋtɛmpɪst] **I** ***n***. **1.** 大风暴,暴风雨,暴风雪。**2.** 骚动,动乱,风潮,暴动。*The wind grew to a* ～. 风势加剧成了风暴。*a* ～ *of applause* 暴风雨般的掌声。*a* ～ *in a teapot* 小事引起的大风波;小题大作。**II** ***vt***., ***vi***. 使骚动;狂暴。～**-beaten** ***a***. 受暴风雨袭击的。～**-swept** ***a***. 为暴风雨席卷的。～**-tossed** [-tost] ***a***.(受暴风雨振荡)飘摇不定的。

tem·pes·tu·ous [temˈpestjuəs; tɛmˋpɛstʃuəs] ***a***. 大风暴的,暴风雨[雪]的;骚动的,动乱的。*a* ～ *state* 动乱状态。**-ly** ***ad***.

tempi [ˈtempiː; ˋtɛmpi] ***n***. tempo 的复数。

Tem·plar [ˈtemplə; ˋtɛmplɚ] ***n***. **1.**〔基督教〕圣殿骑士,圣殿骑士团团员。**2.**〔T- or t-〕(属于伦敦 Inner Temple 或 Middle Temple 法学协会的)律师,法学家。**3.**〔美〕圣殿骑士互济会会员。*Knights* ～*s* 1118 年为保护耶路撒冷耶稣墓及朝拜基督教圣地而在该城组织的基督教信徒。*Good* ～*s* 戒酒会。

tem·plate [ˈtemplit; ˋtɛmplɪt] ***n***. **1.** = templet. **2.**【计】模板。

Tem·ple [ˈtempl; ˋtɛmpl] ***n***. 坦普尔〔姓氏〕。

tem·ple[1] [ˈtempl; ˋtɛmpl̩] ***n***. **1.** 庙,寺,圣堂,神殿。**2.**(基督教的)教堂;礼拜堂,大厦。**3.** 某些老人互助会的地方分会。**4.**〔美〕专供某种活动之用的场所。**5.**〔美卑〕厕所,化妆室,电影院;〔the T-〕伦敦圣殿骑士团的圣殿〔现为法学协会 (Inns of Court) 的两个会所,即 Inner Temple 和 Middle Temple〕。*a* ～ *of luxury and beauty* 玉殿金阙。

tem·ple[2] [ˈtempl; ˋtɛmpl] ***n*.** **1.** 太阳穴,鬓角,颞。**2.**【虫】后颊。**3.** (眼镜的)柄脚。

tem·ple[3] [ˈtempl; ˋtɛmpl] ***n*.**【纺】(织机的)边撑,伸幅器。

tem·plet [ˈtemplit; ˋtɛmplɪt] ***n*.** **1.** (切金属、石、木等时用的)样板,模板。**2.** (供描摹用的)透明图样。**3.**【建】垫石[木];(墙中的)承梁。**4.**【船】船架的楔。

tem·po [ˈtempəu; ˋtɛmpo] ***n*.** (*pl*. ~*s*, ***tempi*** [ˈtempi:; ˋtɛmpi]) 〔It.〕 **1.**【乐】速度,拍子。**2.** 〔喻〕(局势等的)发展速度,步调。**3.** (下棋的)一着,一步。*slow* ~ 缓缓的拍子。*We won't let any unreasonable delay upset the* ~ *of production*. 我们决不容许任何毫无道理的迟延捣乱了生产的发展速度。

tem·po·ral[1] [ˈtempərəl; ˋtɛmpərəl] **I** ***a*.** **1.** 暂时的,一时的,转瞬间的(*opp*. eternal)。**2.** 此世的,现世的;世俗的(*opp*. spiritual)。**3.** 时的,时间的 (*opp*. spatial);【语法】表示时间的,时态的。**II** ***n*.** **1.** 一时的事物[权力等];俗事,世事。**2.** 世俗的权力〔多指教会的财产和收入〕。*a* ~ *death* 假死。~ *aims* 世俗的目标。~ *conjunctions* 时间连接词(如 when, while 等)。~ *matters* 世俗的事物。~ *peers* = *lords* ~ 不居僧职的上院议员。**-ly** ***ad*.**

tem·po·ral[2] [ˈtempərəl; ˋtɛmpərəl] **I** ***n*.** 太阳穴,颞部;颞骨[肌,动脉等]。**II** ***a*.** 颞的。*the* ~ *bone* 颞骨。

tem·po·ral·i·ty [ˌtempəˈræliti; ˏtɛmpəˋrælətɪ] ***n*.** **1.** 一时,暂时,无常。**2.** 世事,俗利,俗人;俗界。**3.** 〔*pl*.〕宗教团体的财产[收入]。

tem·po·ra·ry [ˈtempərəri; ˋtɛmpəˏrɛrɪ] **I** ***a*.** **1.** 一时的,暂时的,临时的 (*opp*. lasting)。**2.** 昙花一现的,无常的 (*opp*. permanent)。*a* ~ *receipt* 临时收据。~ *needs* 临时需要。~ *planting* 假植。~ *punishment* 有期徒刑。~ *workers* 临时工。**II** ***n*.** 临时工 (= ~ worker)。**-i·ly** ***ad*.** **-i·ness** ***n*.**

tem·po·rize [ˈtempəraiz; ˋtɛmpəˏraɪz] ***vi*.** **1.** 顺应时势,迎合潮流;两面讨好,骑墙。**2.** 采取权宜手段。**3.** 因循,拖延。**4.** 妥协,姑息。*temporizing measures* 权宜手段,临时办法。~ *between the section chief and the head clerk* 为组长和管理员之间谋求妥协。**-za·tion** [-ˈzeiʃən; -ˋzeʃən] ***n*.**

tem·po·riz·er [ˈtempəraizə; ˋtɛmpəˏraɪzɚ] ***n*.** 顺应时势的人,迎合潮流的人,两面讨好的人,骑墙主义者;因循姑息的人,一味临时应付的人。

tem·po·riz·ing·ly [ˈtempəraiziŋli; ˋtɛmpəˏraɪzɪŋlɪ] ***ad*.** 姑息地,因循地,暂时应付地。

tempt [tem*p*t; tɛmpt] ***vt*.** **1.** 诱惑,教唆;引起(食欲等);引诱;怂恿。**2.** 诱导;使发生兴趣。**3.** 冒…的风险。**4.** 〔古〕试探,尝试,试验;〔古〕蔑视;激怒。~ *sb. to sin* 诱人犯罪。*I am* ~*ed to have a look at it*. 总想去看一看。*Can't I* ~ *you to have another helping*? 再吃一点好吗? ~ *the storm* 冒着暴风雨的危险。**-able** ***a*.** 易被引诱的,可诱惑的。**-a·bil·i·ty** ***n*.** 可诱惑性。

temp·ta·tion [tempˈteiʃən; tɛmpˋteʃən] ***n*.** 诱惑;诱惑物;魔道;〔古〕考验。*resist* ~ 抵制诱惑。***fall into*** [***give way to***, ***yield to***] ~ 受诱惑。***lead*** (*sb*.) ***into*** ~ 使人入迷。

temp·ta·tious [tem*p*ˈteiʃəs; tɛm*p*ˋteʃəs] ***a*.** 〔美〕诱惑性的。

tempt·er [ˈtemptə; ˋtɛmptɚ] ***n*.** (*fem*. ***temptress*** [-ris; -rɪs]) 诱惑者,诱惑物;〔the T-〕魔鬼。

tempt·ing [ˈtemptiŋ; ˋtɛmptɪŋ] ***a*.** 诱惑的,迷人的。*This orange looks very* ~. 这个橘子看来很吸引人。*a* ~ *market* 吸引人的市面。**-ly** ***ad*.**

tempt·ress [ˈtemptris; ˋtɛmptrɪs] ***n*.** 引诱人的女人,妖妇。

tem·pu·ra [ˈtempuˌrɑ:, temˈpurə; ˋtɛmpʊˏrɑ, tɛmˋpurə] ***n*.** 干炸鱼虾〔一种日本菜,将鱼、虾及蔬菜等蘸上鸡蛋、牛奶面糊炸熟〕。

tem·pus fu·git [ˈtempəsˈfju:dʒit; ˋtɛmpəsˋfjudʒɪt] 〔L.〕光阴似箭。

ten [ten; tɛn] **I** ***num*.** (基数)十,十个;第十(页、章等)。**II** ***n*.** **1.** 十个人。**2.** 十件东西。**3.** 十的记号。**4.** 十元纸币。**5.** (早晨或晚上的)十点钟。**6.** 十岁。*the second paragraph on page* ~ 第十页第二段。*Please give me five* ~*s and* ~ *fives for this hundred*. 这张百元券请兑换给我五张十元券和十张五元券。~***s of thousands*** 好几万。***the upper*** ~ (***thousand***) 贵族阶层,上流社会。★ ten 和 twenty, hundred, thousand 等一样,常用以泛指'多'义。例: *He is* ~ *times the man you are*. 他比你高明得多。*I'd* ~ *times rather stay here*. 我极愿待在这里。~ *times as easy* 容易得多。~**-gallon hat** 〔美俚〕宽边高顶帽。~**-minute man** 〔美〕精力充沛的人。~**-percenter** 〔美俚〕演员、作家、职业运动员等的代理人(抽百分之十佣金的人)。~**-space hitch** 〔美俚〕十年徒刑。~**-spot** **1.** 十元一张的纸币。**2.** 〔美俚〕十年的刑期。~**-strike** 〔美〕〔十柱戏〕十柱全倒;大量,侥幸的意外;大胜利,大成功;优异成绩。~ **to one** 十比一,十之八九 (*T- to one it'll clear up in an hour or so*. 一个小时左右后,天准会放晴)。~**-twenty-thirty** 〔美俚〕只会演老套戏的小剧团或剧场;微不足道的(剧团)。~**-yards** 〔美俚〕一千元。

ten. = tenement; tenor; 〔It.〕 *tenuto*.

ten·a·ble [ˈtenəbl, ˈti:n-; ˋtɛnəbl] ***a*.** **1.** 守得住的(城市、阵地、堡垒等),可防守的。**2.** 站得住的(意见等)。**3.** 有条理的(学说等)。**4.** 能保持[继续]的。*a* ~ *analysis of* 站得住的分析。*a* ~ *scholarship at a university for a period of three years* 可保持三年的大学奖学金。**-bil·i·ty** [ˌtenəˈbiliti; ˏtɛnəˋbɪlətɪ] ***n*.** **-ness** ***n*.**

ten·ace [ˈteneis; ˋtɛnes] ***n*.**【桥牌】同花但不完全连续的几张大牌〔如 A, Q 间无 K〕。

te·na·cious [tiˈneiʃəs; tɪˋneʃəs] ***a*.** **1.** 固执的,顽固的,执拗的。**2.** 抓牢不放的;强韧的,牢靠的(记忆等)。**3.** 黏(性)的,黏着力强的。*be* ~ *in defense* 坚守。*be* ~ *of life* 生命力强的〔指动物〕。*be* ~ *of one's opinion* 固持己见。*have a* ~ *memory for dates* 对年月日记忆力强。~ **clay** 黏土。**-ly** ***ad*.**

te·nac·i·ty [tiˈnæsiti; tɪˋnæsətɪ] ***n*.** **1.** 固执,坚持,顽强,不屈不挠,顽固。**2.** 紧握。**3.** 坚韧,(记忆力)强。**4.** 黏性。**5.**【物】韧性,韧度。*adhere to the principle with an unremitting* ~ 不屈不挠地坚持原则。~ *of purpose* 不屈不挠的志愿。

te·nac·u·lum [tiˈnækjuləm; tɪˋnækjuləm] ***n*.** (*pl*. **-la** [-lə; -lə]) 【医】(外科手术用的)持钩,挟钩。

te·naille, te·nail [təˈneil; təˋnel] ***n*.**【筑城】钳堡,凹角堡。

ten·an·cy [ˈtenənsi; ˋtɛnənsɪ] ***n*.** **1.** (土地、房屋的)租佃,租用。**2.** 租借权。**3.** 租期。**4.** (职位、处所等的)占据,据有。*His* ~ *of the office won't be long to run*. 他的办公室的租期即将届满。

ten·ant [ˈtenənt; ˋtɛnənt] **I** ***n*.** **1.** 租地人,佃户;租屋人,房客;凭借人,租户。**2.** 居住者,住户,占用者。**3.**【法】(不动产诉讼的)被告;不动产占有人。~*s of the woods* [*trees*] 林间居民〔指鸟类〕。*a* ~ *by courtesy*【法】继承亡妻遗产的男人。*a* ~ *in dower*【法】继承亡夫遗产的女人。*the* ~ *of the grave* 死人。**II** ***vt*.** 租借;租用(房子,土地)。— ***vi*.** 居住。~ **farmer** (**-peasent**) 佃户,佃农。~ **farming** 佃耕。~**-right** 租地权,佃耕权。**-able** ***a*.** 可租的,可借的,可住的。**-less** ***a*.** 没有人借的;没有人住的,空(地)。**-ry** ***n*.** 〔集合词〕租地人,佃户,房客,租户。

tench [tentʃ; tɛntʃ] ***n*.** (*pl*. ~***es***, 〔集合词〕~)【鱼】欧洲鲤,丁鲹鱼。

tend[1] [tend; tɛnd] ***vt*.** **1.** 看管(牛羊等),照料,照管,管理(植物等)。**2.** 护理。**3.**【海】守望,照料(船身随潮水转动时锚索不绕乱)。~ *a flock of sheep* 看一群羊。*James* ~*s a drug store for his uncle*. 詹姆士替他叔父照料着

一家药店。～ *the wounded* 护理伤员。— ***vi*. 1.** 服侍,招待(*on*; *upon*)。**2.** 注意,照看;办理(*to*)。～ *on* (*upon*) *the distinguished guests* 招待贵宾。～ *to one's affairs* 办理(某人自己的)事务。**-ing *n*.** 田间管理。

tend[2][tend; tɛnd] ***vi*. 1.** 趋向(于),倾向(于)〔后接介词 *to*, *towards*〕。**2.** 对…有帮助,有助于〔后接不定式 *to*...〕。**3.** 有…倾向〔后接不定式 *to*...〕。*It* ～*s to the same conclusion*. 趋向于同一结论。*His religious philosophy* ～*s towards pantheism*. 他的宗教思想倾向于泛神论。*Prices are* ～*ing upward*. 物价趋涨。*measures* ～*ing to increase the annual output* 有助于提高年产量的种种设施。*She* ～*s to be sad*. 她动不动就伤感。

tend·ance [ˈtendəns; ˋtɛndəns] ***n*.** 服侍,照料,看护;关心,注意;〔古,集合词〕侍从人员。

ten·dencious, -tious [tenˈdenʃəs; tɛnˋdɛnʃəs] ***a*.** 有倾向性的。～ *novel* 倾向性小说〔提出并且阐述某一鲜明主题的小说,即 thesis novel〕。**-ly *ad*. -ness *n*.**

tend·en·cy [ˈtendənsi; ˋtɛndənsɪ] ***n*. 1.** 倾向,趋势。**2.** 性情,偏好(*to*; *toward*)。**3.** (话或作品等的)旨趣,意向,倾向性。*correct criminal* ～ 矫正犯罪倾向。***have a*** ～ ***to*** [***towards***] 有…的倾向,渐趋。*show a* ～ *to fall behind with his studies* (他)显示出功课跟不上的倾向。

ten·der[1][ˈtendə; ˋtɛndɚ] ***a*. 1.** 嫩,软(*opp*. tough)。**2.** 幼弱的,柔弱的。**3.** 敏感的,易受损伤的;易受感动的;容易疼痛的。**4.** 温柔的;慈悲的;亲切的。**5.** 未成熟的,不懂世故的。**6.** 柔和的(色、光等)。**7.** 需要慎重对待的,微妙的,难处理的(问题等)。**8.** 胆小的,对…顾虑多的,小心的,慎重对待…的(*of*; *for*)。**9.**【海】易倾侧的,稳度小的。～ *green* 嫩绿。*a* ～ *beefsteak* 嫩牛排。*He is* ～ *to weakness*. 他和善到柔弱的地步。*a* ～ *conscience* 慈悲的心肠。*a* ～ *plant* 幼树,难培育的树;难对付的人。*a* ～ *shoot* 嫩芽。*a* ～ *spot* 痛处,弱点。***be*** ～ ***for sb.'s honour*** 顾虑某人面子。***be*** ～ ***of hurting sb.'s feelings*** 生怕伤害人家感情。***grow*** ～ ***of sb***. 爱上,钟情于。***of*** ～ ***age*** 年纪还小。～**foot *n*.** (*pl*. ***-foots***; ***-feet***)〔美俚〕新来的人,生手;(童子军的)新团员。～**hearted *a*.** 心地温和的,慈善的。～**loin**〔美〕里脊肉,脊肉;〔T- *or* t-〕(纽约等大城市内)罪恶活动区,警察人员便于榨取贿赂的油水肥厚区。**-ly *ad*. -ness *n*.**

tend·er[2][ˈtendə; ˋtɛndɚ] ***n*. 1.** 照看者;看管者。**2.** 附属船,供应船,联络船。**3.**【铁路】煤水车;(附属在墩布等上的)小给水器。

ten·der[3][ˈtendə; ˋtɛndɚ] **I *vt*. 1.** (正式)提出,提供。**2.**【法】清偿,偿付,赔出(赔偿费)。**3.**〔美〕给与(接见等)。— ***vi*.** 估价,投标(*for*)。～ *one's resignation* 提出辞呈。～ *one's thanks* 致谢。～ (*him*) *a reception* 给予接见;给予欢迎[开欢迎会]。～ *for the construction of three new dormitories* 投标承建三所新宿舍。**II *n*. 1.** 提出,提供。**2.**【法】清偿,偿付,赔交;赔偿费;提供物;投标;估价单,投标书。**3.** 法定货币(= legal ～)。*call for* ～*s for a building* 建造新楼投标。*put in* [*make*, *send in*] *a* ～ *for sth*. 参加对…的投标。～ *bidding* 投标。～ *offer* 招标。

ten·der·ome·ter [ˌtendəˈrɔmitə; ˏtɛndəˋrɑmɪtɚ] ***n*.**【农】(测定水果和蔬菜嫩度的)嫩度计。

ten·di·ni·tis [ˌtendiˈnaitis; ˏtɛndɪˋnaɪtɪs] ***n*.**【医】腱炎。

ten·di·nous [ˈtendinəs; ˋtɛndənəs] ***a*.**【解】腱的;腱质[状]的。

ten·don [ˈtendən; ˋtɛndən] ***n*.**【解】腱。

ten·drac [ˈtendræk; ˋtɛndræk] ***n*.** = tenrec.

ten·dril [ˈtendril; ˋtɛndrɪl] ***n*.**【植】卷须。*a* ～ *of hair* 卷发。

tend·some [ˈtendsəm; ˋtɛndsəm] ***a*.**【医】需要看护的。

ten·e·brif·ic [ˌteniˈbrifik; ˏtɛnɪˋbrɪfɪk] ***a*.** 产生黑暗的;阴暗的。

ten·e·brifi·cate [ˌteniˈbrifikeit; ˏtɛnɪˋbrɪfɪket] ***vt*.** 使阴暗[阴郁]的。

ten·e·brous [ˈtenibrəs; ˋtɛnəbrəs] ***a*.**〔古〕黑暗的,阴暗的,阴沉的,阴郁的;难解的,晦涩的。*a* ～ *chamber* 一个阴暗的房间。*a* ～ *saying* 晦涩的话。

ten-eight·y, 1080 [ˈtenˈeiti; ˋtɛnˋetɪ] ***n*.**〔美〕1080 灭鼠药。

ten·e·ment [ˈtenimənt; ˋtɛnəmənt] ***n*. 1.** 占有[保有,享有]物(土地、房屋、爵位等);租用地;租住的房子。**2.** 房屋,住房,公寓;(公寓中的)一套房间;(几户合住的低级)公共住宅(= ～-house)。～ *of clay* = *the soul's* ～〔诗〕肉体。**-al, -a·ry *a*.**

te·nesmus [tiˈnezməs, -ˈnes-; tɪˋnɛzməs, -ˋnɛs-] ***n*.**【医】里急后重;下坠,后坠。

te·net [ˈtiːnet, ˈtenit; ˋtɛnɪt, ˋtinɪt] ***n*.** 教义,教条,信条;原则。*I hold to the* ～ *that theory should be united with practice*. 我坚持理论和实践必须相结合的原则。

ten·fold [ˈtenfəuld; ˋtɛnˋfold, -ˏfold] **I *a*.** 十倍的,十重的。**II *ad*.** 十倍地,十重地。

Tenn. = Tennessee.

ten·ner [ˈtenə; ˋtɛnɚ] ***n*.**〔英〕十镑纸币;〔美〕十元纸币。

Ten·nes·se·an [ˌtenəˈsiən; ˏtɛnəˋsiən] ***n*., *a*.** (美国)田纳西州的;田纳西州人。

Ten·nes·see [ˌteneˈsiː, -nə-; ˏtɛnəˋsi, ˋtɛnəˏsi] ***n*.**〔美〕田纳西州。*the* ～ *Valley Authority* 田纳西流域(水利工程)管理局〔略 TVA〕。

ten·nis [ˈtenis; ˋtɛnɪs] ***n*.** 网球。*a* ～ *ball* [*court*] 网球[场]。～ *sets* 网球用具。～ **flannels** 法兰绒运动裤。～ **net** 网球球网。～ **racket** 网球拍。

ten·nist [ˈtenist; ˋtɛnɪst] ***n*.**〔美〕网球运动员。

Ten·ny·son [ˈtenisn; ˋtɛnəsn̩] ***n*.** 坦尼森〔姓氏〕。

ten·on [ˈtenən; ˋtɛnən] **I *n*.**【木工】雄榫,榫舌,凸榫。**II *vt*.** 接榫;造榫。**-er *n*.** 接榫者,制榫机。

ten·or[1][ˈtenə; ˋtɛnɚ] ***n*. 1.** (生活等的)进程,方向,趋向。**2.** 要旨,大意;性质。**3.**【法】(法律文件的)正确文本;誊本。**4.** (支票的)限期。**5.**【矿】(矿石的)金属含量,品位。*the* ～ *of a lecture* 演讲的大意。*the even* ～ *of one's life* 平凡的生平经历。

ten·or[2][ˈtenə; ˋtɛnɚ] **I *n*. 1.** 男高音,男高音歌手。**2.** 次中音部;次中音乐器。**3.**〔乐曲〕(一组钟里的)最低音钟。**II *a*. 1.** 男高音的。**2.** 次中音部的。**3.** (一组钟里)最低音的。～ **clef** 次中音谱号。

ten·o·rite [ˈtenəˌrait; ˋtɛnəraɪt] ***n*.**【矿】黑铜矿。

te·nor·rha·phy [təˈnɔːrəfi, -ˈnɔ-; təˋnɔrəfɪ, -ˋnɑ-] ***n*.** (*pl*. ***-phies***)【医】腱缝术。

te·not·o·my [tiˈnɔtəmi; tɪˋnɑtəmɪ] ***n*.**【医】腱切断术。

ten·pen·ny [ˈtenpəni; ˋtɛnˏpɛnɪ, -pənɪ] **I *a*.** (价格)十辨士的。**II *n*.** (每百根十辨士的)3 寸大钉(或其长度)。

ten·pin [ˈtenpin; ˋtɛnpɪn] ***n*.**〔美〕(十柱戏的)柱子。

ten·pins [ˈtenpinz; ˋtɛnˏpɪnz] ***n*.**〔美〕**1.**〔作单数用〕十柱戏。**2.**〔作复数用〕十柱戏的十根木柱。

ten-pounder [ˈtenˈpaundə; ˋtɛnˋpaʊndɚ] ***n*. 1.** 十磅重的东西;十磅炮弹。**2.** 价值十镑的东西,十镑纸币。**3.**【英史】一年支付租金十镑而享有选举权的市民。**4.**【动】海鲢。

ten·rec, ten·drac [ˈtenrek, -dræk; ˋtɛnrɛk, -dræk] ***n*.**【动】无尾猬〔非洲马达加斯加岛产〕。

tense[1][tens; tɛns] ***n*. 1.**【语法】时,时态。**2.**〔L.〕〔古〕时间。*the perfect* ～ 完成时。*the progressive* [*continuous*] ～ 进行时。***at prime*** ～ 最初,起初;立即。

tense[2][tens; tɛns] **I *a*. 1.** 拉紧的,抽紧的(绳子)(*opp*. lax, loose)。**2.** 紧张的。**3.**【语音】紧的。*a* ～ *atmosphere* 紧张的气氛。*a* ～ *vowel* 紧元音。～ *muscles* 绷紧的肌肉。～ *nerves* 紧张的神经。*He read the letter with a* ～ *anxiety*. 他紧张焦虑地看那封信。**II**

vt., *vi*. (使)绷紧,(使)紧张。**-ly** *ad*. **-ness** *n*.

ten·si·ble [ˈtensibl; ˋtɛnsəbl] *a*. 能拉长的,能伸展的。**-bil·i·ty** [ˌtensiˈbiliti; ˏtɛnsɪˋbɪlətɪ] *n*. 可伸长性。**-ly** *ad*.

ten·sile [ˈtensail; ˋtɛnsl, -sɪl] *a*. 张力[拉力]的;抗张的;能伸长的。～ *force*【物】张力。～ *strain*【物】张应变。～ *strength*【物】抗张强度,拉力。～ *stress*【物】张应力,拉应力。*a* ～ *test* 拉力试验。**-sil·i·ty** [-ˈsiliti; -ˋsɪlətɪ] *n*.

ten·sim·e·ter [tenˈsimitə; tɛnˋsɪmətɚ] *n*. (气体)张力计。

ten·si·om·e·ter [ˌtensiˈɔmitə; ˏtɛnsɪˋɑmətɚ] *n*. 张力计,表面张力计。

ten·sion [ˈtenʃən; ˋtɛnʃən] I *n*. 1. 拉紧;伸张。2. (精神、局势等)紧张。3.【物】张力,拉力,牵力;(弹性体的)应力;(蒸气等的)膨胀力,压力。4.【电】电压,拉伸力,拉紧[绷紧]装置,绷子。*create* [*ease*, *reduce*] *the international* ～ 制造[缓和]国际紧张局势。*reduce* [*relieve*] *the* ～ *of the market* 缓和市场紧张情况。*T- runs high*. 形势极为紧张。*surface* ～ 表面张力。*vapor* ～ 蒸气张力。*a high* ～ *current* 高压电流。～ *failure* 伸张破坏。II *vt*. 张紧,使紧张。**-al** *a*.

ten·si·ty [ˈtensiti; ˋtɛnsətɪ] *n*. 紧张(度);张力。

ten·son [tənˈsəun; tənˋson] *n*. 〔古,罕〕顶嘴诗,对吟争论诗(=tenzon)。

ten·sor [ˈtensə; ˋtɛnsɚ, -sɔr] *n*. 1.【解】张肌。2.【数】张量。～ **lamp**, ～ **light** 伸展灯〔装在有铰链的轴上,能伸向各种位置的强光灯〕。

ten-spot [ˈtenspɔt; ˋtɛnˏspɑt] *n*. 〔美俚〕十点(纸牌)。

ten-strike [ˈtenstraik; ˋtɛnˏstraɪk] *n*. 1.【十柱戏】十柱全倒。2.〔美口〕大成功。

tent[1] [tent; tɛnt] I *n*. 1. 帐篷;帐篷状东西。2. 寓所,住处。3.【摄】携带暗室(=dark ～)。4.【医】(防止气体散发用的)帷罩。*pitch a* ～ 搭帐棚。*strike a* ～ 拆帐棚。II *vt*. 1. 用帐篷遮盖。2. (使)住在帐篷里。— *vi*. 1. 住帐篷;宿营。2. 暂居。*We're going to* ～ *in the Golden Hill for a week*. 我们将在金山宿营一周。～-**bed** (能调节温度、湿度的)帐篷式卧床;行军床。～ **caterpillar**【昆】黄褐天幕毛虫。～ **club** (印度的)长矛猎猪俱乐部。～ **fly** 帐棚盖。～ **guy** 帐棚支索。～ **peg** 帐棚桩子。～-**pegging** 跑马拔桩戏。～ **pole** 帐篷支柱。～ **pole movie** 支柱影片,叫座影片,创收影片。～ **show** 帐篷下的户外演出。～ **stitch** (刺绣)斜向平行针脚。～ **trailer** 帐篷拖车。

tent[2] [tent; tɛnt] I *n*.【医】塞条。II *vt*. 将塞条嵌进伤口,插入塞条。

tent[3] [tent; tɛnt] *n*. (西班牙产)深红葡萄酒。

tent[4] [tent; tɛnt] *n*., *vt*. 〔Scot.〕1. 注意。2. 看护,照料。3. 观察。

ten·ta·cle [ˈtentəkl; ˋtɛntəkl] *n*. 1.【动】触器,触手,触须,触角;【植】触丝,触毛。2.〔喻〕像触手的东西。*cut off the ～s of the aggressors* 斩断侵略者的魔爪。**～d** *a*. 有触器的。

ten·tac·u·lar [tenˈtækjulə; tɛnˋtækjələ] *a*. 触手(状)的。～ **cirri** 触须。

ten·tac·u·late [tenˈtækjuleit; tɛnˋtækjulet, -lɪt] *a*. 1.【动】具触手(触角,触须)的。2.【植】具触毛的。**～d** *a*. 具触手[触角,触须,触毛]的。

ten·tac·u·li·ferous [tenˌtækjuˈlifərəs; tɛnˏtækjuˋlɪfərəs] *a*. 具触手的。

ten·tac·u·li·form [tenˈtækjulifɔːm; tɛnˋtækjulɪˏfɔrm] *a*. 触手状的。

ten·tage [ˈtentidʒ; ˋtɛntɪdʒ] *n*. 〔总称〕帐篷,宿营装备。

ten·ta·tive [ˈtentətiv; ˋtɛntətɪv] I *a*. 1. 试验(性质)的;尝试的;暂时的。2. 踌躇(莫决)的,不确定的;无把握的。*a* ～ *suggestion* 试探性建议。*a* ～ *agenda* 暂定议程。II *n*. 1. 试验;试验性提案,假说。2.【法】未遂罪。**-ly** *ad*. **-ness** *n*.

tente d'abri [tɑnt dɑbri; tɑnt dɑbri] 〔F.〕轻帐篷。

ten·ter[1] [ˈtentə; ˋtɛntɚ] I *n*. 1.【纺】拉幅机,绷布机,绷布架。2.〔古〕拉幅钩,张布钩。II *vt*., *vi*. 用绷布机绷(布),(把)布绷紧。*be on* (*the*) *～s* 〔古〕= *be on* ～-*hooks* 提心吊胆,焦虑不安。～ **frame**【纺】拉幅机;张布架。～-**hook** 拉幅钩;张布钩。

tent·er[2] [ˈtentə; ˋtɛntɚ] *n*. 〔英〕(尤指工厂看机器的)看守人,看管人。

tenth [tenθ; tɛnθ] I *num*. 第十(的);十分之一(的)。II *n*. 〔the ～〕1. (月中的)十日,十号。2. 十分之一。3.【乐】第十音;十度音程。4.【空】(妨碍视线的)云层〔由于厚度分为十级〕。5.【史】什一税。*a* ～ *part* 十分之一。*There was ten ～s cloud at that time*. 当时云层厚度是十度。～-*rate* 最劣等的。**-ly** *ad*.

ten·ty [ˈtenti; ˋtɛntɪ] *a*. 〔Scot.〕注意的,提防的。

ten·u·is [ˈtenjuis; ˋtɛnjuɪs] *n*. (*pl*. *tenues* [-iːz; -iz])【语】清爆破音([k], [t], [p])。

te·nu·i·ty [təˈnjuːiti; tɛnˋjuətɪ, tɪˋnɪuətɪ] *n*. 1. 细,薄。2. (空气、流体等的)稀薄,稀薄度。3. (光声等)微弱,无力。4. 薄弱;无力;贫乏。*the* ～ *of one's style of writing* 文体平淡。

ten·u·ous [ˈtenjuəs; ˋtɛnjuəs] *a*. 1.〔罕〕细的,薄的。2. 稀薄的。3. 微细的,精细的,烦琐的。4. 贫乏的;空洞无力的。*a* ～ *fog* 薄雾。～ *wires* 细电线。*ideas too* ～ *to be adopted* 太空洞不值得采纳的想法。

ten·ure [ˈtenjuə; ˋtɛnjɚ] *n*. 1. (财产、职位等的)占有,保有,享有。2. 占有期间。3. 占有条件。4. (土地的)使用(权,期),所有权。*collective land* ～ 土地的集体所有权。*during his* ～ *of office* 他在职期间。*one's* ～ *of life* 寿命。*He holds his life on a precarious* ～. 他过着朝不保夕的生活。*On what* ～ *does he hold the house*. 他占用这所房子凭着什么条件?

ten·u·ri·al [teˈnjuəriəl; tɛnˋjurɪəl] *a*. 土地占有[使用]的;依赖于保有权的;任职期的。*This* ～ *reformation never degenerated into a scrabble for land*. 这个土地改革从未沦为土地的抢夺。**-ly** *ad*.

te·nu·to [teˈnuːtəu; tɛˋnuto] I *a*. 〔It.〕【乐】持续,保持原有时值或音量〔在音符上写 ten. 或画横线表示〕。II *n*. (*pl*. *～s*, *-ti* [-tiː; -ti]) 持续号,保持号。

tenzon [ˈtenzn; ˋtɛnzn] *n*. 对吟争论诗,顶嘴诗〔11至13世纪法国南部及意大利北部的抒情浪漫诗人对吟的一问一答抒情诗〕。

te·o·cal·li [ˌtiːəuˈkæli, teɔːˈkɑjiː; ˏtioˋkælɪ, ˏteoˋkɑji] *n*. (*pl*. *-cal·lis* [-iːz, Sp. -jiːz; -iz, Sp. -jiz]) (中美洲等地的)古代神庙。

te·o·sin·te [ˌtiəˈsinti; ˏtɪəˋsɪntɪ] *n*.【植】墨西哥类蜀黍(*Euchlaena mexicana*)。

te·pee [ˈtiːpiː; ˋtipi] *n*. = teepee.

tep·e·fac·tion [ˌtepəˈfækʃən; ˏtɛpəˋfækʃən] *n*. 微温;温热。

tep·e·fy [ˈtepifai; ˋtɛpəˏfaɪ] *vt*. (*-fied*) 使微热,使温。— *vi*. 变微热,变温。

te·phi·gram [ˈtiːfigræm; ˋtifɪˏgræm] *n*.【气】温熵图。

teph·ra [ˈtefrə; ˋtɛfrə] *n*. 〔*pl*.〕〔动词用单数或复数〕【地】火山灰,火山碎屑。～**chronology**【地】火山灰年代学。

teph·rite [ˈtefrait; ˋtɛfraɪt] *n*.【地】碱玄岩。**-rit·ic** [-ˈritik; -ˋrɪtɪk] *a*.

tep·id [ˈtepid; ˋtɛpɪd] *a*. 1. 不冷不热的,微热的;温热的。2. 不大热心的(招待、赞扬等)。3.〔美剧〕(收入)平常的。～ *tea* 温热的茶。*a* ～ *evening* 不冷不热的晚上。*a* ～ *reception* 不大热情的招待。**-ly** *ad*. **-i·ty**, **-ness** *n*.

tep·i·dar·i·um [ˌtepiˈdeəriəm; ˏtɛpəˋdɛrɪəm] *n*. (*pl*. *-dari·a* [-riə; -rɪə]) (古罗马澡堂的)温水浴室。

te·poy [ˈtiːpɔi; ˋtipɔɪ] *n*. = teapoy.

te·qui·la [tə'ki:lə, tei'ki:lɑ:; tə`kilə, te`kilɑ] ***n***. 〔美〕 **1.** 龙舌兰酒。**2.**【植】墨西哥龙舌兰。

ter [tə:; tɚ] ***ad***. 〔It.〕 **1.**【音】三度。**2.**【医】三次。

ter. = terrace; territory.

ter- *comb. f.* 三度,三次,三倍: *ter*nate.

tera- *comb. f.* 垓,万亿,兆兆 (= 10^{12})。*tera*volt【电】垓电子伏(特)。*tera*watt【电】垓瓦(特)。

te·ra·byte ['terəbait; `tɛrəbaɪt] ***n***.【计】兆兆字节。

te·ra·flops ['terəflɔps; `tɛrəflɑps] ***n***.【计】每秒万亿次浮点运算。

te·rai [tə'rai; tə`raɪ] ***n***. (在亚热带戴的)阔边毡帽。

ter·aph ['terəf; `tɛrəf] ***n***. (*pl*. ***teraphim*** ['terəfim; `tɛrəfɪm]) (古希伯莱的)家神像。

ter·a·tism ['terətizm; `tɛrətɪzm] ***n***. **1.**【医】畸(形)胎,怪胎,异形,畸形。**2.** 恶魔崇拜。**3.** 好奇癖。

terato- *comb. f.* 畸形,怪物。

ter·a·to·gen ['terətədʒən; `tɛrətədʒən] ***n***.【医】畸形因素〔如化学原因或疾病等〕。**-geny** [-dʒəni; -dʒənɪ] ***n***.【医】畸形发生,畸胎形成。**-gen·ic** [-'dʒenik; -`dʒɛnɪk] ***a***.

tera·toid ['terətɔid; `tɛrə,tɔɪd] ***a***.【生】奇形怪状的,畸形的。

ter·a·tol·o·gy [,terə'tɔlədʒi; ,tɛrə`tɑlədʒɪ] ***n***. **1.**【生】畸形学;畸胎学。**2.** 怪物研究,怪物故事讲述,怪物故事集。**-log·i·c** [-rətə'lɔdʒik; -rətə`lɑdʒɪk], **-log·i·cal** ***a***.

ter·bi·a ['tə:biə; `tɚbɪə] ***n***.【化】氧化铽。

ter·bi·um ['tə:biəm; `tɚbɪəm] ***n***.【化】铽〔Tb〕。~ *metals* 稀土族金属。

terce [tə:s; tɚs] ***n***. = tierce.

ter·cel ['tə:sl; `tɚsl], **tercelet** ['tə:slit; `tɚslɪt] ***n***. (鹰猎用的)雄鹰,雄隼。

ter·cen·te·na·ry, ter·cen·ten·ni·al [,tə:sen'ti:nəri, -'tenjəl; tɚ`sɛntə,nɛrɪ, ,tɚsɛn`tɛnɪəl] ***n***., ***a***. 三百年(间)(的);三百年纪念日(的),三百年纪念日的庆祝(的)。

ter·cet ['tə:sit; `tɚsɪt, tɚ`sɛt] ***n***. **1.**【乐】(二拍中的连奏)三连音符。**2.** 三拍子;【韵】同押一韵的连续三行诗。

Ter·com ['tɛəkɔm; `tɛrkɑm] ***n***.【军】地形匹配系统〔巡航导弹内部按照地形起伏控制飞行路线的电脑制导系统,系 terrain contour matching 的缩略〕。

ter·e·bene [terə'bi:n; `tɛrə,bin] ***n***.【化】萜,特惹萜,芸香烯。

ter·e·bic [te'rebik; tɛ`rɛbɪk] ***n***.【化】芸香酸 (= ~ acid)。

ter·e·binth ['terəbinθ; `tɛrə,bɪnθ] ***n***.【植】笃薅香(树)。*oil of* ~ 松节油。

ter·e·bin·thine [,terə'binθain; ,tɛrə`bɪnθɪn] ***a***. 笃薅香的,萜(质)的。

te·re·do [tə'ri:dəu; tə`rido] ***n***. (*pl*. **~s, *-di·nes*** [-dini:z; -dɪniz])【动】鉴船虫(属),船蛆。

Ter·ence, Ter·rance, Ter·rence ['terəns; `tɛrəns] ***n***. 特伦斯〔男子名〕。

te·reph·thalic ['te,ref'θælik; ,tɛrɛf`θælɪk] ***a***. ~ *acid*【化】对苯二酸,对酞酸。

Te·re·sa [tə'ri:zə; tə`rizə] ***n***. 特丽萨〔女子名,Theresa 的异体〕。

te·rete [tə'ri:t, 'teri:t; tə`rit, `tɛrit] ***a***.【生】圆柱状的,圆筒形的。

ter·gal ['tə:gəl; `tɚgəl] ***a***.【解】背的,背板的。

ter·gem·i·nate [tə:'dʒeminit; tɚ`dʒɛmənɪt] ***a***.【植】三次双生的。

ter·gi·ver·sate ['tə:dʒivə:seit; `tɚdʒɪvɚ,set] ***vi***. **1.** 变节,背叛。**2.** (以言词)支吾,搪塞,有意改变或曲解词义。**-sa·tion** [,tə:dʒivə:seiʃən; ,tɚdʒəvɚ`seʃən] ***n***. **-sator** ***n***.

ter·gum ['tə:gəm; `tɚgəm] ***n***. (*pl*. ***-ga*** [-gə; -gə]) 〔L.〕【动】背甲;(昆虫的)背板。

ter·i·ya·ki [,teri'jɑ:ki; ,tɛrɪ`jɑkɪ] ***n***. 〔Jap.〕蘸糖色烤〔日本式烤肉或鱼,将肉或鱼在酱油里腌泡过或蘸过后烤熟〕。

term [tə:m; tɚm] **I** ***n***. **1.** 期限,期间。**2.** 学期,任期;(支付)结算期;【法】开庭期,(权利的)有效期间;定期租借(地产)。**3.** 字眼,词语;术语,专门名词;〔*pl*.〕措词,说法。**4.**【数,物】项;条;【逻】项;名词。**5.** 〔*pl*.〕交谊,关系,地位。**6.** 〔*pl*.〕(契约、谈判等的)条件,条款,约定,协定;要求额,价钱;费用。**7.** 界石,界标;界限;极限,尽头,终点。**8.**【海】船尾栏杆两端的装饰。**9.**【建】胸像柱。**10.** (正常的)分娩期。*accept* [*reject*] *sb.'s* ~*s* 接受[拒绝]某人条件。*a derogatory* ~ 贬义词。*a long* [*short*] ~ 长[短]期。*the major* [*middle, minor*] ~【逻】大[中、小]项。*technical* [*scientific*] ~*s* 专门[科学]术语。*Terms cash*. 条件为现金支付。*Terms, two dollars a week*. 学费每周两元。~*s for peace* 媾和条件。***be born at full ~s*** (小孩)足月生。***be in ~s*** 在谈判[交涉、商量]中。***bring*** (*sb*.) ***to ~s*** 使某人接受条件,使某人就范[投降]。***come to ~s*** 达成协议,谈判成功;投降,让步。***during one's ~ of office*** 在任期内。***extreme ~*** (数)外项。***for a ~ of five years*** 限期五年。***force sb. to come to ~s*** 迫使…就范。***in any ~*** 无论如何,在任何条件下。***in black and white ~s*** 白纸黑字,毫不含糊。***in*** (***good***) ***set ~s*** 明确地。***in high ~s*** 极力称赞。***in plain ~s*** 简单说。***in ~s of*** 依…,据…;从…方面;用…特有的字眼(*in* ~*s of approval* [*reproach*] 赞成[谴责])。***keep a ~*** 上一个学期的课。***keep on good*** [***friendly***] ***~s*** 保持良好[友好]关系。***keep ~s with*** 和…继续谈判[交涉]。***make ~s with*** 和…谈妥[妥协]。***not*** (***up***) ***on any ~s*** 决不。***not on borrowing ~s*** 不友好,无交情。***on bad ~s*** 不和,不睦(*with*)。***on easy ~*** 以宽大的条件。***on equal ~s*** 处于平等的地位。***on even ~s*** (和…)不相上下(*with*)。***on one's own ~s*** 按照自己的条件(价钱)。***on speaking ~s*** 泛泛之交(*with*)。***on visiting*** [***familiar, first-name, intimate, writing***] ~ ***s with*** 和…有往来[很熟、通信]的朋友关系。***sales ~s*** 售货条件。***set a ~ to*** 对…加以限制,给…规定期限。***set ~s*** 定条件。***upon no ~s*** 决不。**II** ***vt***. 把…叫做,把…称为。*He ~ed this gas argon*. 他把这种气体叫做氩气。*He has no right to ~ himself an expert*. 他没有权力自封为专家。*I would ~ it a case of treason*. 我想称之为一起叛国案。~ **day** 支付日,租金等〔苏格兰〕法定季度结账日;【律】开庭日,科学工作的观察日。~ **deposit** 定期存款。~ **insurance** 定期人寿保险。~ **of public summons**【法】公告期间。~ **of redemption**【法】偿还期限。~ **of validity**【法】有效期间。~ **paper** 学期论文。~ **policy** 定期人寿保险契约(保单)。~**s of reference** 权限;受权调查范围。

term. = terminal; termination.

ter·ma·gan·cy ['tə:məgənsi; `tɚməgənsɪ] ***n***. (女人的)凶悍,暴躁。

ter·ma·gant ['tə:məgənt; `tɚməgənt] **I** ***a***. 好骂人的,好争吵的,凶悍的,暴躁的。**II** ***n***. 好争吵[骂人]的女人,悍妇,泼妇。

term·er ['tə:mə; `tɚmɚ] ***n***. 服徒刑的罪犯。*a life* ~ 服无期徒刑的罪犯。

ter·mi·na·ble ['tə:minəbl; `tɚmɪnəbl] ***a***. 可终止的,有限期的。**-bil·i·ty** ***n***. 限期性。**-ness** ***n***. **-bly** ***ad***.

ter·mi·nal ['tə:minl; `tɚmənl] **I** ***a***. **1.** 终端的,终点的,结尾的;极限的。**2.** 定期的,每期[季]的;每学期的,学期终[末]的。**3.** 期终的;末期的;【植】顶生的;【解、动】末梢的;分界处的,端的。**4.**【逻】名辞的。*a* ~ *landmark* 界标。*the* ~ *stage* 末期。*the* ~ *station* 终点站。**II** ***n***. **1.** 末尾,末端。**2.**【语言】词尾〔最后的音节,字母,音素,音节等,结尾的词〕。**3.**【电】电极,(电池的)端;接头,

端子;线端。4.〔美〕终点(站)。5.〔*pl*.〕卸货(等)车站用费。6.【建】端饰;胸像柱。7. 学期考试, 大考。～ **charges** 上货[卸货]费。～ **check valve**【机】管端止回阀。～ **juncture**【语言】停顿时刻。～ **leave**〔美〕(老兵退役前的)末次假期。～ **market** (农产品)集散的中心市场。～ **nose-dive**【空】极限垂直俯冲。～ **parenchyma**【植】轮界薄壁组织。～ **sequencer** (火箭的)终端序列发生器〔发射前由电脑控制倒计时读数的一种电子装置〕。～ **velocity**【物】收尾速度。

ter·mi·nal·ly [ˈtəːminəli; ˋtɝmɪnḷɪ] ***ad***. 在末端, 在终点;每期, 每季;在学期末尾。

ter·mi·nate [ˈtəːmineit; ˋtɝməˏnet] **I** ***vt***. **1**. 使结束, 使停止, 使终止。**2**. 解除(契约等);结束。**3**. 限定, 定界。— ***vi***. 终止, 结束, 归于, 以…告终(*in*);达到尽头;满期。**II** [ˈtəːminit; ˋtɝmənɪt] ***a***. 终止的;有限的(小数等)。*It is said that the General Motors is going to ～ your contract*. 据说通用汽车公司要解除和你订的契约。*What's the meaning of the word that ～s the sentence?* 那句话结尾的词意思是什么? *Her appeal has ～d favourably*. 她的上诉胜诉了。*Murphy's unhappy martial life ～d in divorce*. 墨菲的不幸的婚姻以离婚告终。

ter·mi·na·tion [ˌtəːmiˈneiʃən; ˏtɝməˋneʃən] ***n***. **1**. 末端, 终点;终止, 终结;结局, 结束。**2**. 限定, 界限, 限度。**3**.【语法】词尾。*the ～ of an agreement* 契约满期日。*the ～ of our trip* 我们旅行的终点。*a ～ slip*〔美〕解雇通知书。***bring to a ～*** 使了结, 结束。***put a ～ to sth***. 结束某事。**-al** ***a***.

ter·mi·na·tive [ˈtəːminətiv; ˋtɝməˏnetɪv, -nətɪv] **I** ***a***. **1**. 结尾的, 终止的;限定的。**2**.【语】结尾的, (动词等)表示动作完成的。**II** ***n***.【语】词尾。**-ly** ***ad***.

ter·mi·na·tor [ˈtəːmineitə; ˋtɝməˏnetɚ] ***n***. **1**. 限定者[物];终止者[物]。**2**.【化】(链的)终止剂;【生化】终止符。**3**.【天】(月、星表面上的)明暗界线。

termi·ner [ˈtəːminə; ˋtɝmɪnɚ] ***n***.【法】判决 (*cf*. oyer)。

termi·ni [ˈtəːminai; ˋtɝməˏnaɪ] ***n***. terminus 的复数。

ter·mi·nism [ˈtəːminizəm; ˋtɝmənɪzəm] ***n***.【神】忏悔期限论;【哲】= nominalism.

ter·mi·no·log·i·cal [ˌtəːminəˈlɔdʒikəl; ˏtɝmɪnəˋlɑdʒɪkḷ] ***a***. 术语的, 用语上的;术语学(上)的。*a ～ inexactitude* 谎言, 假话。

ter·mi·nol·o·gy [ˌtəːmiˈnɔlədʒi; ˏtɝməˋnɑlədʒɪ] ***n***. **1**.〔集合词〕专门名词, 术语。**2**. 术语学;名词学。**-gist** ***n***. 术语学家。

ter·mi·nus [ˈtəːminəs; ˋtɝmənəs] ***n***. (*pl*. *～es*, *-ni*) **1**. (铁路, 汽车, 航路等的)终点。**2**.〔英〕终点站〔美国叫 terminal〕。**3**. 界限, 极限。**4**.〔T-〕(古罗马的)守界神。**5**. 界桩, 界标, 界柱。

ter·mi·nus ad quem [ˈtəːminəs ædˈkwem; ˋtɝmɪnəs ædˋkwɛm]〔L.〕(辩论等的)归结点, 目标;结论;(契约的)终止期。

terminus a quo [ˈtəːminəs ei ˈkwəu; ˏtɝmɪnəs e ˋkwo]〔L.〕(辩论等的)出发点;(契约的)开始期。

ter·mi·tar·i·um [təːmiˈtɛəriəm; ˏtɝmɪˋtɛrɪəm] ***n***. (*pl*. ***termitaria***) 螱窠;人工白蚁巢, 白蚁养殖器。

ter·mi·ta·ry [ˈtəːmitəri; ˋtɝmɪˏtɛrɪ] ***n***. (*pl*. ***-ries***) = termitarium.

ter·mite [ˈtəːmait; ˋtɝmaɪt] ***n***.【虫】白蚁。*a ～ hill* [*heap*] 白蚁的窠。

term·less [ˈtəːmlis; ˋtɝmlɪs] ***a***. 无限的, 无期限的;无条件的;〔诗、古〕难于形容的。

term·ly [ˈtəːmli; ˋtɝmlɪ] ***a***., ***ad***. (指事物发生、款项支付等)定期的(地)。

term·or [ˈtəːmə; ˋtɝmɚ] ***n***.【法】定期租户, 终身租户。

tern[1] [təːn; tɝn] ***n***.【鸟】燕鸥。

tern[2] [təːn; tɝn] **I** ***n***. **1**. 三个一套, 三个一组, 三重。**2**.〔美〕三桅帆船 (= ～ schooner);中彩的三个号码;中彩三个号码的奖。**II** ***a***. = ternate.

ter·na·ry [ˈtəːnəri; ˋtɝnərɪ] ***a***. **1**. 三个的, 三个组成的, 三重的。**2**. 第三的。**3**.【化】三元[成分]的;【数】三元的, 三变数的, 三进位的。～ **alloy(s)** 三元合金。～ **scale** 三进记数法。～ **set**【数】三分点集。

ter·nate [ˈtəːneit; ˋtɝnɪt, -net] ***a***. **1**. 三个的。**2**.【植】三出的。*a ～ leaf* 三裂叶。**-ly** ***ad***.

terne, terne·plate [təːn, ˈtəːnˌpleit; tɝn, ˋtɝnˏplet] ***n***. (镀铅锡)薄钢板, 白铁板。

ter·ni·on [ˈtəːniən; ˋtɝnɪən] ***n***. **1**.〔现罕〕三个一套;三合一;三人(事物或思想等)的组合。**2**. 三价原子, 三价基。**3**.【乐】三和弦。

ter·pene [ˈtəːpiːn; ˋtɝpin] ***n***.【化】萜烯, 萜(烃)。

ter·pin·e·ol [təˈpiniˌəul; tɝˋpɪnɪol] ***n***.【化】萜品醇。

Terp·sich·o·re [təːpˈsikəri; tɝpˋsɪkərɪ, -ˏri] ***n***.【希神】特普丝歌利〔司歌舞的女神〕。

Terp·si·cho·re·an [ˌtəːpsikəˈriːən; ˏtɝpsɪkəˋriən] **I** ***a***. **1**. 特普丝歌利的。**2**.〔t-〕舞蹈的。**II** ***n***.〔t-〕〔谑〕跳舞的人;舞蹈家。

ter(r). = terrace; territory.

ter·ra [ˈterə; ˋtɛrə, ˋtɛrɑ] ***n***.〔L.〕**1**. 地;土。**2**.〔T-〕土地(神)。～ **alba** 管土, 白土〔如石膏粉, 瓷土, 镁氧〕。～ **cariosa** 矽藻土。**terrae filius** (*pl*. ***terrae filii***) 小百姓。～ **firma** 大地, 陆地;稳固的地位。～ **incognita** [inˈkɔgnitə; ɪnˋkɑgnɪtə] (*pl*. ***terrae incognitae*** [ˈteriːinˈkɔgnitiː; ˋtɛriɪnˋkɑgnɪtɪ]) 未知的土地;未知的领域。～ **Japonica** = gambier. ～ **nera** [ˈneirə; ˋnɛrə] (古代画家做颜料用的)黑土。～ **rossa** (石灰石风化而成的)红土。～ **verde** [ˈvɛədei; ˋvɛrde] = ～ **verte** [vert; vɛrt] 绿土;绿土颜料。

ter·race [ˈterəs; ˋtɛrɪs, -əs] **I** ***n***. **1**. 台地, 阶地, 梯田;坛, 坪;有花坛(等)的庭园。**2**. (房屋前面的)平台;露台, 阳台。**3**. 柱廊, (东方式)平屋顶。**4**.〔美〕(马路中央的)小公园。**5**. 高台街〔高于街道的一排房屋, 有这样房屋的街道〕。**6**.【地】(海岸等的)阶丘。**II** ***vt***. 使成台地, 使成坛, 筑坛建造成平顶。*a ～d roof* 平的屋顶。*～d fields* 梯田。

ter·ra·cot·ta [ˈterəˈkɔtə; ˋtɛrəˋkɑtə] ***n***. **1**. 制陶赤土, 赤土陶器。**2**. 赤褐色。**3**. 空心砖, 琉璃砖。**4**. 一种褐色的柑子。

ter·rain [ˈterein; tɛˋren, ˋtɛren] ***n***. **1**. 地面;地带;地区。**2**. (知识的)领域范围。**3**.【军】地形, 地势。**4**.【地】岩层, 岩群;地质建造。*a difficult ～ for a counterattack* 不利于反攻的地形。*the whole ～ of home economics* 家政学的整个领域。～ **following radar** 地形调整雷达〔飞机或导弹上装设的一种雷达系统, 能根据地形自动调整飞行高度, 从而可保护贴近地面飞行〕。

ter·ra·ma·re [ˌterəˈmaːri; ˏtɛrəˋmarɪ] ***n***. 〔*pl*.〕(*sing*. ***ter·ra·ma·ra*** [ˌterəˈmaːrə; ˏtɛrəˋmarə]) 土性沉积物;(南欧)史前沉积。

ter·ra·mycin [terəˈmaisin; ˏtɛrəˋmaɪsɪn] ***n***. 土霉素, 氧四环素, 地霉素。

ter·rane [təˈrein, ˈterein; tɛˋren, ˋtɛren] ***n***.【地】= terrain.

ter·ran·eous [teˈreiniəs; təˋrenɪəs] ***a***.【植】地上生长的, 陆生的。

ter·ra·pin [ˈterəpin; ˋtɛrəpɪn] ***n***.【动】龟鳖类爬行动物〔如泥龟, 甲鱼〕。

ter·ra·que·ous [teˈreikwiəs; tɛˋrekwɪəs] ***a***. 由水陆形成的, 水陆的。

ter·rar·i·um [teˈrɛəriəm; təˋrɛrɪəm] ***n***. (*pl*. *～s*, ***-raria*** [-iə; -ɪə]) 陆地动物饲养场。

ter·raz·zo [təˈræzəu, teˈrɑːtsəu; təˋræzo, tɛˋrɑtso] ***n***. 〔It.〕【建】水磨石(地板)。

Ter·rell [ˈterəl; ˋtɛrəl] ***n***. 特雷尔〔姓氏, 男子名〕。

ter·rene [teˈriːn; tɛˋrin] **I** ***a***. **1**. 土质的;陆地的, 地球的。**2**. 尘世的, 世俗的。**II** ***n***. **1**. 地球, 陆地。**2**.【地】地表。

ter·re·plein [ˈtɛəplein; ˋtɛr͵plen] ***n*.**【军】垒道〔炮台上安炮处〕。

ter·res·tri·al [tiˈrestriəl; təˋrɛstrɪəl] **I *a*. 1.** 地球(上)的。**2.** 地上的(生活等),人间的 (*opp*. celestial),现世的。**3.** 陆地的,陆生的,陆栖的(动植物)。**II *n*. 1.** 地球居民。**2.** 〔*pl*.〕陆生动[植]物,陆栖动物。**3.** 〔罕〕地球。*the* [*this*] ~ *globe* [*ball*] 地球。*a* ~ *globe* 地球仪。*a* ~ *journey* 陆地旅行。~ *aims* [*interests*] 名利心。~ *planets* 类地行星。

terret [ˈterit; ˋtɛrɪt] ***n*.** (笼头上套住缰绳的)铁环;(系链条,皮带等的)扣环。

terre-verte [ˈteə͵vət; ˋtɛr͵vɛrt] ***n*.**【地】绿色土。

ter·ri·ble [ˈterəbl, -ribl; ˋtɛrəbl] **I *a*. 1.** 可怕的,骇人的。**2.** 〔口〕非常的,厉害的,极度的。**3.** 〔口〕极坏的。*a* ~ *accident* 一桩可怕的意外事件。*a* ~ *winter* 极冷的冬天。*in a* ~ *hurry* 慌慌忙忙地。*a* ~ *performance* 极坏的演出。*It's* ~! 糟得很! **II *ad*.** 〔口〕非常,很,极。*The weather was* ~ (= terribly) *hot*. 天气热极了。**III *n*.** 〔主 *pl*.〕可怕的人[东西]。**-ness *n*.**

ter·ri·bly [ˈteribli; ˋtɛrəblɪ] ***ad*. 1.** 可怕地。**2.** 〔口〕厉害,很,极。*He speaks Chinese* ~ *well*. 他的中国话讲得非常好。*It's* ~ *late*. 太晚了。

ter·ric·o·lous [teˈrikələs; tɛˋrɪkələs] ***a*.**【生】陆栖的,陆生的。

ter·ri·er[1] [ˈteriə; ˋtɛrɪɚ] ***n*. 1.** 㹴〔灵敏的小猎狗〕。**2.** 〔英俚〕本土军士兵。*a bull* [*fox*] ~ 短毛㹴。*an Irish* [*Scotch*, *Skye*, *Yorkshire*] ~ 长毛㹴。*a Maltese* [*toy*] ~ 玩赏㹴。

ter·ri·er[2] [ˈteriə; ˋtɛrɪɚ] ***n*.**【法】地产册,地籍簿。

ter·rif·ic [təˈrifik; təˋrɪfɪk] ***a*. 1.** 可怕的,凄惨的。**2.** 〔口〕极大的,非常的,猛烈的。**3.** 〔美俚〕了不起的,极好的。*drive at a* ~ *speed* 以极高的速度开车。*think oneself* ~ 自以为了不起。*He weathered a* ~ *storm*. 他度过了一场可怕的暴风雨。**-rif·i·cal·ly *ad*.**

ter·ri·fy [ˈterifai; ˋtɛrə͵faɪ] ***vt*.** (**-*fied***) 使恐怖,吓唬,威胁。*You* ~ *me*! 吓我一跳! ***be terrified at*** [***by***, ***of***, ***with***] 给…吓一跳。***be terrified out of one's senses*** (***wits***) 吓得魂不附体。~ (*sb*.) ***into doing*** 威胁(某人)做某事。

ter·rig·e·nous [teˈridʒinəs; tɛˋrɪdʒɪnəs] ***a*.**【地】**1.** 陆源(沉积)的。**2.** 陆生的。~ **deposit** 陆源沉积。

Ter·rill [ˈteril; ˋtɛrɪl] ***n*.** 特里尔〔姓氏,男子名〕。

ter·rine [teˈriːn; tɛˋrin] ***n*.** 〔F.〕(连同内装食品卖的)陶罐。

ter·ri·to·ri·al [͵teriˈtɔːriəl; ͵tɛrəˋtorɪəl] **I *a*. 1.** 领土的。**2.** 土地的。**3.** 区域的,地方的。**4.** 〔T-〕〔美〕准州的,领土(或领地)的。**II *n*. 1.** 〔T-〕〔英〕本土军士兵。**2.** 地方部队的士兵。~ *air* [*sky*, *waters*, *seas*] 领空[海]。~ *ambitions* 领土野心。~ *expansion* 领土扩张。~ *industry* 地方工业。~ *integrity* 领土完整。*T- laws* 美国领地的法律。~ *limit* 国界。~ *sovereignty* 领土主权。**-ly *ad*.**

ter·ri·to·ri·al·ism [͵teriˈtɔːriəlizəm; ͵tɛrəˋtorɪəlɪzm, -ˋtorɪ-] ***n*. 1.** 地主阶级统治制。**2.** 地方政府权力高于教会的制度。**3.** 〔常 T-〕犹太人居住地自治主义[运动]。**4.** 【史】(神圣罗马帝国的)领地居民信奉当地宗教的规定。

ter·ri·to·ri·al·ist [ˈteriˈtɔːriəlist; ͵tɛrɪˋtorɪəlɪst] ***n*.** (地方)政府权力高于教会制度的鼓吹者,主张地方政府权力高于教会制度的人。

ter·ri·to·ri·al·i·ty [͵teri͵tɔːriˈæliti; ͵tɛrə͵torɪˋælətɪ] ***n*. 1.** 地区性。**2.**【人性学】(动物的)地盘性,地区性。

ter·ri·to·ri·al·ize, -ise [͵teriˈtɔːriəlaiz; ͵tɛrəˋtorɪəl͵aɪz, -ˋtorɪ-] ***vt*. 1.** 扩张领土。**2.** (通过扩张)使成为领土;(通过扩张)使成为领地。**3.** 按地区分配。**-al·i·zation *n*.**

ter·ri·to·ry [ˈteritəri; ˋtɛrə͵torɪ, -͵torɪ] ***n*. 1.** 领土,版图,领地。**2.** 地区。**3.** (科学知识、行动等的)领域,范围。**4.**【商】势力范围。**5.** (野鸟的)生活范围。**6.** 〔T-〕(美国)准州,(加拿大)地区。*a leased* ~ 租借地。*in the* ~ [*sphere*, *field*, *domain*] *of physics* 在物理学的领域内。***take in too much*** ~ 走极端;说得过分;牵涉过多。

ter·ror [ˈterə; ˋtɛrɚ] ***n*. 1.** 恐怖。**2.** 恐怖的原因。**3.** 可怕的人[物]。**4.** 〔口〕极可憎的人。**5.** 〔the T-〕= the Reign of T-. *a holy* ~ 难对付的家伙。*a perfect* ~ 讨厌到极点的家伙。***be a*** ~ 〔口〕做使人为难的事情,捣蛋的人。***be a*** ~ ***to*** 对…是一个恐怖,使…畏惧[害怕]。***be in*** ~ ***of*** 害怕…。***have a*** ~ ***of sth***. 对某事害怕。***flee in*** ~ 非常惊慌地逃跑。***strike*** ~ ***into sb.'s heart*** 使某人恐怖,吓坏。***the king of*** ~***s*** 死。***the Reign of T- = the*** (***Red***) ***T-***【法史】恐怖时代〔指法国革命中 1793 年 5 月到翌年 7 月一段时期〕。***the White T-*** 白色恐怖〔特指 1795 年保王党员对革命党的残酷报复〕。

ter·ror·ism [ˈterərizəm; ˋtɛrə͵rɪzəm] ***n*. 1.** 恐怖主义[手段,政治]。**2.** 威吓,胁迫。

ter·ror·ist [ˈterərist; ˋtɛrərɪst] ***n*.** 恐怖主义者,恐怖分子。

ter·ror·ize [ˈterəraiz; ˋtɛrə͵raɪz] ***vt*.**, ***vi*. 1.** (使)恐怖;采取恐怖手段,胁迫。**2.** 实行恐怖统治。**-i·za·tion *n*.**

ter·ror·i·zer [ˈterəraizə; ˋtɛrəraɪzɚ] ***n*. 1.** 采取恐怖手段的人。**2.** 〔美〕【影】恐怖片。

ter·ror-strick·en, -struck [ˈterəstrikən, -strʌk; ˋtɛrə͵strɪkn, -strʌk] ***a*.** 受了惊吓的,吓破了胆的。

Ter·ry [ˈteri; ˋtɛrɪ] ***n*. 1.** 特里〔姓氏,男子名,Terence 的昵称〕。**2.** 特丽〔女子名,Theresa 的昵称〕。

ter·ry [ˈteri; ˋtɛrɪ] ***n*. 1.**【纺】起毛毛圈,毛圈织物。**2.** 〔俚〕无线电(雷达自动)测高计。

terse [təːs; tɝs] ***a*.** (言谈,文笔等)简练的,简洁的,简短的。*a* ~ *and vigorous style* 简洁有力的文体。*a* ~ *note of dismissal with no explanation* 一封没有说明理由的简短的辞退信。**-ly *ad*. -ness *n*.**

ter·tial [ˈtəːʃəl; ˋtɝʃəl] **I *a*.** 第三列的〔指鸟翼基部关节上所生的拨风羽〕。**II *n*. 1.** 第三列拨风羽,臂翼。**2.**【语法】状语词,第三级成分。

ter·tian [ˈtəːʃən; ˋtɝʃən] **I *a*.** 隔一天发生的,间日的。**II *n*.**【医】间日热,三日热。~ *malaria* 间日疟。

ter·ti·a·ry [ˈtəːʃəri, -ʃiə-; ˋtɝʃɪ͵ɛrɪ, -ʃərɪ] **I *a*. 1.** 第三的,第三位的,第三级的。**2.**【化】特的,叔的,三代的。**3.**【医】第三期的。**4.** 〔T-〕【地】第三纪的;第三系的。*the T- period* [*system*]【地】第三纪[系]。~ *alcohol* 叔醇。~ *phosphate* 三代磷酸盐。**5.**【语】第三的。*a* ~ *stress* 第三重音。**II *n*. 1.** 〔T-〕【地】第三纪,第三系,第三纪层。**2.**【宗】第三级教士。**3.**【动】第三列拨风羽,臂翼。**4.**【医】〔*pl*.〕第三期梅毒的症状。~ **college** 〔英〕高等院校。~ **industry** 第三产业。~ **syphilis**【医】三期梅素。

ter·tio [ˈtəːʃiəu; ˋtɝʃɪo] ***ad*.** 〔L.〕第三。

ter·ti·um quid [ˈtəːʃiəmˈkwid; ˋtɝʃɪəmˋkwɪd] 〔L.〕**1.** (模棱两可,地位暧昧的)第三者。**2.** 中间物。**3.** 〔谑〕三角关系中的第三者。

ter·tius [ˈtəːʃjəs, -ʃiəs; ˋtɝʃɪəs] ***a*.** 〔L.〕第三的,(三者中)年纪[年级]最小的。*Jones* ~ 三个琼斯中年纪[年级]最小的(那个)。~ ***gaudens*** [ˈgɔːdənz; ˋgɔdənz] 得渔翁之利的第三者。

ter·va·lent [təˈveilənt; tɝˋvelənt] ***a*. 1.**【化】三价的。**2.**【生】三价染色体 (= trivalent)。

ter·y·lene [ˈteri͵liːn; ˋtɛrəlin] ***n*.**【纺】涤纶〔原商标名〕。

ter·za ri·ma [ˈtəːtsəˈriːmə; ˋtɛrtsəˋrimɑ] (*pl*. ***terze rime*** [ˈteətseiˈriːmei; ˋtɛrtseˋrime]) 〔It.〕(像但丁《神曲》中所用的)三行诗隔句押韵法〔韵律为 aba, bcb, cdc...〕。

ter·zet·to [təːtsetəu; tɛrˋtsɛtto] ***n*.** 〔It.〕【乐】三重奏

[唱];三声中部。

TESA = testicular sperm aspiration【医】睾丸精子激发术。

TESL [ˈtesəl; ˋtɛsl] = teaching English as a second language 非母语英语教学。

Tes·la [ˈteslə; ˋtɛslə], **Nikola** 泰斯拉〔1857—1943,美国电机工程师〕。~ **coil** 泰斯拉(空心)变压器。

tes·la [ˈteslə; ˋtɛslə] ***n.***【电】泰斯拉〔磁束密度 MKS 单位〕。

TESOL [ˈtiːsəl; ˋtisəl] = teaching English to speakers of other languages 对说外国语的人进行英语教学的教师。

tes·sel·lar [ˈtesələ; ˋtɛsələ˞] ***a.*** **1.** 似小(长)方形镶嵌物的。**2.** 用小(长)方形镶嵌物嵌成的。

tes·sel·late [ˈtesileit; ˋtɛsl͵et] ***vt.*** (把路面等)镶嵌作花纹状。**-d** ***a.*** **1.** 嵌成花纹的,镶嵌细工的。**2.**【植】具方格斑纹的;【动】棋盘格形的(*a ~d pavement* 嵌装图案的人行道)。

tes·sel·la·tion [ˌtesəˈleiʃən;͵tɛsəˋleʃən] ***n.*** 嵌石装饰,棋盘形布置〔嵌石装饰〕。

tes·se·ra [ˈtesərə; ˋtɛsərə] ***n.*** (*pl.* ***-rae*** [-riː; -ri]) **1.** 镶嵌物〔玻璃、象牙、大理石等作成的小方块〕。**2.**【古罗马】(骨、象牙、木头等做的)入场券[证];骰子;标记。

tes·se·ral [ˈtesərəl; ˋtɛsərəl] ***a.*** **1.** 镶嵌物(似)的。**2.**【物】等轴(晶系)的。

tes·si·tura [ˌtesiˈtjuərə;͵tɛsɪˋturɑ] ***n.*** 〔It.〕【乐】(应用)声域,音域。

Test. = Testament.

test[1] [test; tɛst] **I** ***n.*** **1.** 检验,检查;考查;测验;考试;考验。**2.** 检验用品;试金石;【化】试药;(判断的)标准。**3.**【化】化验;(用试剂检查出来的)检查结果;【冶】(分析用)灰皿,烤钵,提银盘。**4.**〔口〕= ~match. **5.**【英史】宣誓。*an acceptance* ~ 验收。*an achievement* ~ 成绩测验。*a blood* ~ 血液检查。*a live* ~【火箭】载人试验。*a performance* ~ 性能试验。*a service* ~ 运行试验,使用试验。*a strength* ~ 强度试验。*a* ~ *in physics* 物理测验(考试)。*a* ~ *object* (显微镜的)检验物。*the supreme* ~ 最高标准。*the* ~ *of practice* 实践的检验。***put to the*** ~ 试验,检验。***stand*** [***bear, pass***] ***the*** ~ 试验合格。***take the*** ~ 就职宣誓。**II** ***vt.*** **1.** 考查,测验,试验,检验,考验。**2.**【化】(用试药)检验,化验。**3.**【冶】精炼(金银)。*A game like that ~ed our strength.* 像那样的一场球赛考验了我们的力量。*I'll have my blood ~ed.* 我要检查一下血。~ *ore for gold* 检验矿砂的含金成分。— ***vi.*** **1.** 受试验,受测验。**2.** 测得结果。**3.** (为鉴定而)进行测验(*for*)。*Let's use another method to* ~ *for its pulling force.* 让我们用另外一种方法来测验它的拉力。~ **ban** 禁止核试验协定。~**bed** 试验台,试验机器用的支架。~**-drive** ***vt.*** 试验;尝试。~ **field** 试验场地。~**lying** (执法人员的)说谎;(警员等执法中的)舞弊。~ **match** (国际)板球决赛。~ **mixer** 试验混合器。~ **paper** **1.** 试纸。**2.** 测验题目纸[试卷]。**3.**〔美〕鉴定笔迹用的文件。~ **pattern**【电视】测试图。~ **pilot** 试飞员。~ **tube** 试管。~**-tube baby** 试管婴儿〔从母体内取出卵子使其在实验室试管内受精,然后再植入子宫正常发育〕。~ **types**〔*pl.*〕试力鉴定表。~**-working** (机器的)试车,试开。**the** ~ **act** **1.** 宣誓书。**2.**〔T- A-〕〔英史〕审查条例。**-a·ble** ***a.*** **1.** 可试验的。**2.**【法】有资格作证[立遗嘱]的,可根据遗嘱处理的。**-ed** ***a.*** 经过考验的。

test[2] [test; tɛst] ***n.***【动】(软体类的)介壳,甲壳;【植】(外)种皮。

testa [ˈtestə; ˋtɛstə] ***n.*** (*pl.* ***-tae*** [-tiː; -ti])【植】(外)种皮。

tes·ta·cean [tesˈteiʃən; tɛsˋteʃən] **I** ***a.***【动】介壳类的,有介壳的根足虫类的。**II** ***n.*** 介壳类动物。

tes·ta·ce·o·lo·gy [ˌtesˌteisiˈɔlədʒi; ˋtɛs͵tesɪˋɑlədʒɪ] ***n.*** 贝类学;介类学。

tes·ta·ceous [tesˈteiʃəs; tɛsˋteʃəs] ***a.*** **1.** 介壳的;有介壳的;介壳质的。**2.**【生】红砖色的,黄褐色的。

tes·ta·cy [ˈtestəsi; ˋtɛstəsɪ] ***n.***【法】留有遗嘱。

tes·ta·ment [ˈtestəmənt; ˋtɛstəmənt] ***n.*** **1.** 契约;誓约。**2.**〔T-〕【宗】(基督教)圣约书,旧约全书或新约全书。**3.**〔口〕一部新约全书。**4.**【法】遗言,遗嘱。**5.** 确实的证明。**6.** 信仰的宣告、声明。*the New* [*Old*] *T-* 新[旧]约全书。*one's last will and* ~【法】(处理身后财产的)遗嘱。*make one's* ~ 立遗嘱。*a military* ~ 军人遗嘱;口头遗嘱。**-tal** (根据)遗嘱的。

tes·ta·men·ta·ry [ˌtestəˈmentəri;͵tɛstəˋmɛntərɪ] ***a.*** (根据)遗嘱的;遗嘱中写明的。

tes·ta·mur [tesˈteimə; tɛsˋtemə˞] ***n.*** (英国大学的)试验及格证。

tes·tate [ˈtesteit; ˋtɛstet] **I** ***a.*** 留有遗嘱的。**II** ***n.***【法】留有遗嘱而死的人;立遗嘱人。

tes·ta·tor [tesˈteitə; ˋtɛstetə˞, tɛsˋtetə˞] ***n.*** (*fem.* ***-trix*** [-triks; -trɪks], *pl.* ***-tri·ces*** [-trisiːz;-trɪ͵siz]) 立有[留有]遗嘱的人。

test·ee [tesˈtiː; tɛsˋti] ***n.*** 受测验者;测验对象。

test·er[1] [ˈtestə; ˋtɛstə˞] ***n.*** **1.** 试验者,检验者,化验者。**2.** 检验器,化验装置。**3.** (试验用的)对照物。*a* ~ *strain*【生】测交品系。*a carpet* ~〔俚〕射频脉冲发生器。

tes·ter[2] [ˈtestə; ˋtɛstə˞] ***n.*** (床,布道坛等上的)天盖,华盖。

tes·ter[3] [ˈtestə; ˋtɛstə˞] ***n.*** (一面有头像的)古银币;〔古、谑〕六辨士。

tes·tes [ˈtestiːz; ˋtɛstiz] ***n.*** testis 的复数。

tes·ti·cle [ˈtestikl; ˋtɛstɪkl̩] ***n.***【解】睾丸;精巢。**-tic·u·lar** ***a.*** 睾丸的,睾丸状的。

tes·tic·u·late [tesˈtikjuleit; tɛsˋtɪkjʊlɪt] ***n.***【植】**1.** 睾丸状的。**2.** 双丸状的。

tes·ti·fy [ˈtestifai; ˋtɛstə͵faɪ] ***vi.*** 证明;证实(*to*);证言;作证(*to*)。— ***vt.*** 证明,证言;(事物)成为证据,证实;表明,声明。~ *against sb.* 作不利于某人的证言。~ *to sb.'s honesty* 证明某人诚实。~ *one's regret* 表示歉意,说对不起。~ *under oath that* 发誓证明(声明)。**-fi·ca·tion** [ˌtestifiˈkeiʃən;͵tɛstɪfɪˋkeʃən] ***n.*** 证明;证言,证据。**-fi·er** ***n.*** 证明人。

tes·ti·mo·ni·al [ˌtestiˈməunjəl, -niəl;͵tɛstəˋmonɪəl] **I** ***n.*** **1.** (人品、能力、资格等的)证明书;鉴定书,推荐书。**2.** 奖状,奖品,感谢信,表扬信,纪念品。**II** ***a.*** **1.** 有关证明(鉴定)书的。**2.** 褒奖的,表扬的。**-ize** [**-ise**] ***vt.*** **1.** 给…开证明书。**2.** 赠送…奖品。

tes·ti·mo·ny [ˈtestiməni; ˋtɛstə͵monɪ] ***n.*** **1.** 证据;证明,证言。**2.** 声明,宣言。**3.** 表示,表明。**4.**〔the ~〕〔古〕(基督教)十诫;〔*pl.*〕神的箴言。**5.**〔古〕抗议(*against*)。*give* ~ *as to ...* 关于…作证。*give false* ~ 作伪证。*His smile was* ~ *of his consent.* 他的微笑表明他同意了。*I can bear* ~ *to his good character.* 我可以证明他的品德良好。~ *of witness*【法】人证。***call sb. in*** ~ 传某人作证。***produce*** ~ ***to*** [***of***] 提出…的证据。

tes·ti·ness [ˈtestinis; ˋtɛstɪnɪs] ***n.*** 易怒,暴躁。

tes·tis [ˈtestis; ˋtɛstɪs] ***n.*** (*pl.* ***testes*** [-tiːz; -tiz])【解】= testicle.

tes·ti·tis [tesˈtaitis; tɛsˋtaɪtɪs] ***n.***【医】睾丸炎。

tes·ton, tes·toon [ˈtestən, -ˈtuːn; ˋtɛstn, tɛsˋtun] ***n.*** 头像银币〔正面有人头的欧洲古银币;尤指 16 世纪法国的一种银币。铸有亨利八世头像的英国硬币〕。

tes·tos·ter·one [tesˈtɔstərəun; tɛsˋtɑstə͵ron] ***n.***【生化】睾丸素〔睾(甾)酮〕。

test-tube [ˈtesˈtjuːb, ˈtesˈtuːb; ˋtɛst͵tjub, -͵tɪub, -͵tub] ***a.*** **1.** 在试管中培养(或生长)的。**2.** 由人工授精而生产的。**3.** 化学合成的。*a* ~ *body* 试管婴儿,人工受胎婴儿,人授精儿。

tes·tu·di·nal [tesˈtjuːdinəl, -tuː-; tɛsˋtudənl̩, -tju-] ***a.*** 龟的;龟甲的,如龟的。

T

tes·tu·di·nar·i·ous [ˌtestjuːdiˈnɛəriəs; tɛsˏtudəˋnɛrɪəs, -ˏtju-] *a*. 玳瑁形的。

tes·tu·di·nate [tesˈtjuːdineit; tɛsˋtudəˏnet, -nɪt, -ˋtju-] **I** *a*. **1.** 龟甲形的。**2.** 龟的。**II** *n*. 龟。

tes·tu·di·neous [ˌtestjuːˈdiniəs; ˏtɛstjuˋdɪnɪəs] *a*. 如龟甲形的。

tes·tu·do [tesˈtjuːdəu; tɛsˋtjudo, -ˋtu-] *n*. (*pl*. ~*s*, *-dines* [-diniːz; -dɪniz]) **1.**【古罗马】攻城用龟甲形掩蔽物。**2.**〔T-〕【动】陆龟(属)。

tes·ty [ˈtesti; ˋtɛstɪ] *a*. (*-ti·er*; *-ti·est*) **1.** 性急的,易怒的,暴躁的。**2.** (话等)气恼的,烦躁的。*grow more and more* ~ *with age* 随着年纪大而变得越来越性急。*the* ~ *manager* 暴躁的经理。*one's* ~ *remarks* 某人的气话。**-ti·ly** *ad*.

Tet [tet; tɛt] *n*. (越南的)春节。

te·tan·ic [tiˈtænik; tɪˋtænɪk] **I** *a*.【医】破伤风性的,强直性痉挛的。**II** *n*.【药】痉挛诱起剂;强直剂。

tet·a·nize [ˈtetənaiz; ˋtɛtəˏnaɪz] *vt*. (*-nized*, *-nizing*)【医】引起强直性痉挛,使强直。**-za·tion** [ˌtetənaiˈzeiʃən; ˏtɛtənaɪˋzeʃən] *n*.

tet·a·nus [ˈtetənəs; ˋtɛtənəs] *n*.【医】**1.** 破伤风;破伤风菌。**2.** 强直(性痉挛);肌强直。

tet·a·ny [ˈtetəni; ˋtɛtənɪ] *n*.【医】手足搐搦;强直。

te·tar·to·he·dral [tiˌtɑːtəuˈhiːdrəl; tɪˏtɑrtoˋhidrəl] *a*.【物】四分面的〔一种晶形,它仅显出晶系的对称所需完面数的四分之一的〕。

tetched [tetʃt; tɛtʃt] *a*. **1.** 被触动的,受触犯的。**2.** 精神有点失常的。

te(t)ch·y [ˈtetʃi; ˋtɛtʃɪ] *a*. 易怒的,脾气乖戾的。**-i·ly** *ad*. **-i·ness** *n*.

tête-á-tête [ˈteitɑːˈteit; ˋtetəˋtet] **I** *ad*.〔F.〕仅仅两人地,面对面地,两人私下地。**II** *n*. 促膝谈心;对谈,相对密谈;(两人之间谈的)心腹话;对坐的两人;面对面式的双人椅[沙发]。**III** *a*. 仅两人的,面对面的,两人私下的。*have a* ~ (*talk*) *with sb*. 和某人密谈。*dine* ~ *with sb*. (单独或私下)同某人一起进餐。

tête-bêche [ˈtetˈbeʃ; ˏtɛtˋbɛʃ] *a*. (两张邮票)图案一正一反的。

teth, tet [tet; tɛt] *n*. 希伯来文的第九个字母。

teth·er [ˈteðə; ˋtɛðɚ] **I** *n*. **1.** (拴牛马等的)系绳,系链。**2.** (知识、力量、权限等的)限度、范围。***at the end of one's*** ~ 智穷才尽,用尽方法,穷途末路;忍无可忍地。***beyond one's*** ~ 为某人力所不及;在某人权限外。**II** *vt*. **1.** (用绳,铁链)拴系。**2.** 拘束,束缚。*a horse ~ed to a tree* 一匹拴在树上的马。

teth·er·ball [ˈteðəˌbɔːl; ˋtɛðɚˏbɔl] *n*. **1.** 绳球(游戏)〔用绳将一小球系在木杆上,两人用手或木棒反向击球,看谁先将绳完全绕在木杆上〕。**2.** (绳球游戏用的)小球。

Te·ton [ˈtiːtɔn; ˋtitɑn] *n*. **1.** (*pl*. *-tons*, *-ton*) 提顿族人〔美国达科他的印第安人〕。**2.** 提顿语。

tetr- *comb. f*.〔用于元音前〕四:*tetr*ode.

tetra- *comb. f*.〔用于辅音前〕四:*tetra*gon.

tet·ra [ˈtetrə; ˋtɛtrə] *n*.【动】脂鲤〔一种热带鱼〕。

tet·ra·bas·ic [ˌtetrəˈbeisik; ˏtɛtrəˋbesɪk] *a*.【化】四碱价的;四元的;四代的。

tet·ra·brach [ˈtetrəˌbræk; ˋtɛtrəˏbræk] *n*.【韵、诗】有四个短音节的词或音步。

tet·ra·bran·chi·ate [ˌtetrəˈbræŋkiˌeit, -it; ˏtɛtrəˋbræŋkɪˏet] *a*.【动】四鳃类(*Tetrabranchia*)动物〔包括鹦鹉螺;缸鱼〕。

tet·ra·chlo·ride [ˌtetrəˈklɔːraid; ˏtɛtrəˋkloraɪd] *n*.【化】四氯化物。

tet·ra·chord [ˈtetrəkɔːd; ˋtɛtrəˏkɔrd] *n*.【乐】**1.** 四度音阶。**2.** (古代的)四弦乐器。**-al** *a*.

te·trac·id [teˈtræsid; tɛˋtræsɪd] *n*.【化】**1.** 四酸。**2.** 具有四个氢氧基的醇类。

tet·ra·cyclic [ˌtetrəˈsaiklik; ˏtɛtrəˋsaɪklɪk] *a*.【植】四轮列的,四轮花的。

tet·ra·cy·cline [ˈtetrəˈsaiklin, -lain; ˏtɛtrəˋsaɪklɪn, -laɪn] *n*.【药】四环素。

tet·rad [ˈtetræd; ˋtɛtræd] *n*. **1.** 四个;四个一组的东西。**2.**【生】四合子,四分体。**3.**【化】四价元素。**4.**【几】拼四小组。**-ic** *a*.

tet·ra·dac·tyl(e) [ˌtetrəˈdæktil; ˏtɛtrəˋdæktɪl] *a*., *n*. 四趾的(动物)。**-tyl·ous** *a*.

te·trad·y·mite [təˈtrædimait; təˋtrædəmaɪt] *n*.【矿】辉碲铋矿。

tet·ra·eth·yl [ˌtetrəˈeθl; ˏtɛtrəˋɛθəl] **lead**【化】四乙铅。

tet·ra·gon [ˈtetrəgən; ˋtɛtrəˏgɑn] *n*. **1.**【几】四角[边]形。**2.**【物】四重轴。

tet·ra·gon·al [teˈtrægənl; tɛˋtrægənl̩] *a*. **1.** 四角[边]形的。**2.**【物】正方晶的。~ *prism* 正方柱。

tet·ra·gram [ˈtetrəgræm; ˋtɛtrəgræm] *n*. 由四个字母组成的词,四文字符号。

tet·ra·hed·ral [ˌtetrəˈhedrəl; ˏtɛtrəˋhidrəl] *a*. **1.** 有四面的。**2.**【几】四面(体)的;【植】四分同裂的。~ *complex* 四面线丛。

tet·ra·he·drite [ˌtetrəˈhiːdrait; ˏtɛtrəˋhidraɪt] *n*.【矿】黝铜矿。

tet·ra·hed·ron [ˌtetrəˈhedrən; ˏtɛtrəˋhidrən] *n*. (*pl*. ~*s*, *-dra* [-drə; -drə]) **1.**【几】四面体。**2.**【植】四分体形。**-dral** *a*.

tet·ra·hy·dro·can·na·bi·nol [ˌtetrəˌhaidrəuˈkænəbiˌnɔl; ˏtɛtrəˏhaɪdroˋkænəbɪˏnɑl] *n*.【药】四氢大麻酚。

tet·ral·o·gy [teˈtrælədʒi; tɛˋtrælədʒɪ] *n*. **1.** (戏剧、歌剧、小说等的)四部曲。**2.**【古希腊】四部剧〔由三部悲剧一部喜剧组成〕。

te·tram·er·ous [teˈtræmərəs; tɛˋtræmərəs] *a*.【生】四跗节的;(花的部分,好花轮)四个一组的;四复的,四重的(=4-merous)。

tet·ram·e·ter [teˈtræmitə; tɛˋtræmətɚ] *n*. 四音步句[诗]。

Tet·ra Pak [ˈtetrəpæk; ˋtɛtrəpæk]〔美〕(包装牛奶或饮料的)四面体纸板盒(亦作 Tetra pack)。

tet·ra·pet·a·lous [ˌtetrəˈpetələs; ˏtɛtrəˋpɛtələs] *a*.【植】四花瓣的。

tet·ra·phyl·lous [ˌtetrəˈfiləs; ˏtɛtrəˋfɪləs] *a*.【植】四叶的。

tetra·ploid [ˈtetrəplɔid; ˋtɛtrəˏplɔɪd] *n*., *a*.【生】四倍体(的)。**-y** *n*.

tet·ra·pod [ˈtetrəpɔd; ˋtɛtrəˏpɑd] *n*., *a*. **1.**【动】四脚动物(的)。**2.** 四脚体〔四脚从一个中心以放射状伸出,互成 120°角;三脚支在一个平面上站立时,一脚向上〕。

tet·rapo·dy [teˈtræpɔdi; tɛˋtræpədɪ] *n*. = tetrameter.

te·trap·ter·ous [teˈtræptərəs; tɛˋtræptərəs] *a*. **1.**【动】四翅的,四翼的。**2.**【植】四翅(状)的。

te·trarch [ˈtiːtrɑːk, ˈtet-; ˋtitrɑrk, ˋtɛt-] *n*. **1.** 四分之一统治者;四分之一长官〔古罗马行省的四分之一的地区长官〕。**2.** 从属小君主,小诸侯等权力较小的统治者。**3.** 共同掌权的四人(四个官吏)。**4.**〔古希腊军队〕方阵的小队长。**5.**【植】四原型。

te·trarch·ate, te·trach·y [ˈtiːtrɑːkeit, -ki; ˋtitrɑrkˏet, -kɪ] *n*. **1.** (罗马帝国行省)四分之一地区的长官职位;四分之一辖区或职权。**2.** 四头统治,四头统治集团。

tet·ra·spo·ran·gi·um [ˌtetrəspɔːˈrændʒiəm; ˏtɛtrəspoˋrændʒɪəm] *n*. (*pl*. *-gia* [-ə; -ə])【植】四分孢子囊。

tet·ra·spore [ˈtetrəˌspɔː; ˋtɛtrəˏspor] *n*.【植】四分孢子。

tet·ra·stich [ˈtetrəˌstik; ˋtɛtrəˏstɪk, tɛˋtræstɪk] *n*. 四行一节的诗,四行诗。**-ic** *a*.

te·tras·ti·chous [teˈtræstikəs; tɛˋtræstɪkəs] *a*.【植】四列的。

tet·ra·syl·lab·ic [ˈtetrəsiˈlæbik; ˏtɛtrəsɪˋlæbɪk] *a*. 四音节的。

tet·ra·syl·la·ble [ˈtetrəsiləbl; ˏtɛtrəˋsɪləbl̩] *n*. 四音节

词。

tet·ra·tom·ic [ˌtetrəˈtɔmik; ˌtɛtrəˋtɑmɪk] ***a***.【化】**1.** 四原子的。**2.** 四羟基的。

tet·ra·va·lent [ˌtetrəˈveilənt; ˌtɛtrəˋvelənt, tɛˋtrævə-] ***a***.【化】**1.** 四价的。**2.** 有四种原子价的 (= quadrivalent)。

tet·rode [ˈtetrəud; ˋtɛtrod] ***n***.【电】四极管。

tet·ro·do·tox·in [ˌtetrədəuˈtɔksin; ˌtɛtrədoˋtɑksɪn] ***n***. 河豚毒。

te·trox·ide [teˈtrɔksaid, -sid; tɛˋtrɑksɪd] ***n***.【化】四氧化物。

tet·ryl [ˈtetril; ˋtɛtrəl] ***n***.【化】特屈儿,三硝基苯甲硝胺。

tet·ter [ˈtetə; ˋtɛtɚ] ***n***.【医】水泡疹,皮疹,湿疹。*moist* ~ = *humid* ~ 湿疹。*scaly* ~ 鳞屑癣。

TEU = twentyfoot equivalent unit 标准箱(长 20 英尺为标准集装箱)。

Teut. = Teuton; Teutonic.

Teu·to·ma·ni·a [tjuːtəˈmeiniə; tjutəˋmenɪə] ***n***. 亲条顿狂;亲德。

Teu·to·ma·ni·ac [tjuːtəˈmeiniæk; tjutəˋmenɪˌæk] ***n***. 亲条顿狂者;亲德者[派]。

Teu·ton [ˈtjuːtən; ˋtjutn, ˋtu-] **I** ***n***. 条顿人〔指:**1.** 古代条顿族的成员。**2.** 现代条顿系民族的成员,尤指德国人;又称日耳曼人〕。**II** ***a***. = Teutonic.

Teu·to·nes [ˈtjuːtnˌiːz, ˈtuːtnˌiːz; ˋtjutnˌiz, ˋtutnˌiz] ***n***. 〔*pl*.〕条顿族〔居住在易北河北的一个古代民族〕。

Teu·ton·ic [tjuːˈtɔnik; tjuˋtɑnɪk] **I** ***a***. **1.** 条顿民族的;北欧民族的;德国民族的。**2.** 条顿[日耳曼]语的。**II** ***n***. 条顿语,日耳曼语。~ **Order** 条顿骑士团〔中世纪十字军中的一个组织〕。

Teu·ton·i·cism, Teu·ton·ism [tjuːˈtɔnisizəm, ˈtjuːtənizəm; tjuˋtɑnɪsɪzm, ˋtjutənɪzm] ***n***. **1.** 条顿(语)风,条顿腔。**2.** 外国语中的德语成分。**3.** 条顿(或德国)文化。**4.** 条顿[日耳曼]主义。**5.** 条顿[日耳曼]民族优越论。

Teu·ton·ist [ˈtjuːtnist, ˈtuː-; ˋtjutənɪst, ˋtu-] ***n***. **1.** 条顿民族优越论者〔尤指日耳曼民族优越论者〕。**2.** 赞同条顿[日耳曼]风俗(生活等)者。**3.** 条顿或日耳曼(语)学家。

Teu·ton·i·za·tion [ˌtjuːtənaiˈzeiʃən; ˌtjutnɪˋzeʃən, ˌtu-] ***n***. 条顿化,日耳曼化。

Teu·ton·ize [ˈtjuːtənaiz; ˋtjutnˌaɪz, ˋtu-] ***vt***. 条顿化[日耳曼化]。

Teu·to·phile [ˈtjuːtəufail; ˋtjutofaɪl] ***a***., ***n***. 亲条顿(的),亲德派(的)。

Teu·to·pho·be [ˈtjuːtəfəub; ˋtjutəfob, ˋtu-] ***n***., ***a***. 恐惧条顿者(的);恐日耳曼派(的)。**-bia** ***n***. 恐条顿病;恐德病。

TEW = tactical early warning 战术预先警报,战术远程警戒。

Te·wa [ˈteiwə; ˋtewə] ***n***. **1.** (*pl*. *-was*, *-wa*) 特瓦人〔居住在新墨西哥印第安人村庄的六个印第安种部族中任何一族的成员〕。**2.** 特瓦语。

Tex. = Texan; Texas.

tex [teks; tɛks] ***n***.【纱】特克斯支数制〔每千米克数〕。

Tex·an [ˈteksən; ˋtɛksn, ˋtɛksən] ***a***., ***n***. 〔美〕德克萨斯州的(人)。

Tex·as [ˈteksəs; ˋtɛksəs] ***n***. **1.** 德克萨斯〔美国州名〕。**2.** 〔美〕(内河轮船的)最高甲板舱。~ **fever** 〔美〕德克萨斯牛瘟。~ **Ranger** 〔美〕德克萨斯州骑警队。~ **tower** 〔美〕海上雷达站〔在海上建起平台,上设雷达,用于监视来自空中的袭击〕。

tex·as [ˈteksəs; ˋtɛksəs] ***n***. 〔美〕(内河轮船的)最高甲板舱。

text [tekst; tɛkst] ***n***. **1.** 原文,本文,正文;(文艺学等所说的)文本。**2.** 课文,课本,教科书。**3.** 基督教圣经经文,经句〔常引作说教题目〕。**4.** 主题,论题。**5.** (歌谱的)歌词。**6.** 版本。**7.** = ~ hand. *a full* ~ 全文,正文。*a* ~ *in physics* 物理课本。***stick to one's*** ~ (谈话)不离本题。~**book** 教科书,课本。*a* ~ *book example* 极好的例子。~**bookish**, ~ **booky** ***a***. 〔口〕教科书式的,像教科书一样呆板无味的。~ **edition** 供教学用的版本。~ **hand** 粗体正楷字。~ **letter** 黑体字。~**-to-speech** ***a***. (为供盲人收听而)将文字转换成语言的。

tex·tile [ˈtekstail; ˋtɛkstl, -tɪl, -taɪl] **I** ***n***. 〔常 *pl*.〕纺织品;纺织原料。**II** ***a***. 纺织(品)的。~ *fabrics* 纺织品,纺织物。~ *fibres* 纺织纤维。~ *glass* 纺织玻璃纤维。~ **machinery** 纺织机器。

tex·to·lite [ˈtekstəlait; ˋtɛkstəˌlaɪt] ***n***. 层压胶布板,织物酚醛塑胶,夹布胶木。

text. rec. = 〔L.〕*textus receptus* (= the received *or accepted text*) 通用文本。

tex·tu·al [ˈtekstjuəl; ˋtɛkstʃuəl] ***a***. 原文的,本文的;按照原文的,原原本本的;教科书的。~ **criticism** (古籍的)校勘。**-ism** 严守原文〔尤指基督教圣经经文〕,校勘学。**-ist** ***n***. 墨守(或精通)原文的人〔尤指基督教圣经经文〕。**-ly** ***ad***.

tex·tu·ar·y [ˈtekstjuəri; ˋtɛkstʃuˌɛrɪ] **I** ***a***. = textual. **II** ***n***. (*pl*. *-aries*) = textualist.

tex·tur·al [ˈtekstʃərəl; ˋtɛkstʃərəl] ***a***. 织物的;组织上的。

tex·ture [ˈtekstʃə; ˋtɛkstʃɚ] **I** ***n***. **1.** (织物的)组织,结构,质地,织法。**2.** 织品,织物。**3.** (皮肤的)肌理;(岩石、木材等的)纹理。**4.**【生】组织。**5.** (文艺作品等的)结构,组织。**6.** 气质,性格,本质,实质,特征。*cloth of* (*a*) *coarse* [(*an*) *open*] ~ 粗纹织物。*cloth of* (*with*) (*a*) *close* ~ 密纹织物。*the* ~ *of the culture of the Tang Dynasty* 唐代文化的特征。**II** ***vt***. 使具有某种结构或特征。**-less** ***a***. 无明显结构的,无定形的。

T.F. = **1.** task force 特遣部队。**2.** Territorial Force 〔英〕本土军部队。**3.** time factor 时间因数。

Tg = type genus【生】标准属,模式属。

tg = **1.** telegram. **2.** telegraph.

T-group [ˈtiːgruːp; ˋtɪgrup] ***n***. 训练小组〔现代美国的一种所谓精神治疗法,受治疗者在专门训练员的指导下,在小组内不受约束地用言语表达内心感情〕。

TGSM = terminally guided sub-munition【军】终点制导子导弹。

Th. = **1.**【化】thorium. **2.** Theodore. **3.** Thomas. **4.** Thursday.

th. = thermal.

-th[1] *suf*. **1.** 作 four 以上序数词的后缀: four*th*, sixti*eth*. **2.** 表示分母: three-fif*ths* 五分之三。

-th[2] *suf*. 由形容词、动词构成抽象名词: tru*th*, grow*th*.

-th[3] *suf*. 〔古〕构成动词陈述语气现在第三人称单数〔相当于现在的 -s, -es〕: do*th* (= does), ha*th* (= has).

Thack·er·ay [ˈθækəri; ˋθækərɪ, ˋθækrɪ] ***n***. 撒克里〔姓氏〕。

Thad [θæd; θæd] ***n***. 撒德〔男子名, Thaddeus 的昵称〕。

Thad·deus [θæˈdi(ː)əs; θæˋdɪəs] ***n***. 撒迪厄斯〔男子名〕。

Tha·i [ˈtɑːi(ː); ˋtɑ·i, taɪ] ***n***., ***a***. 泰国语[人](的)。

Thai·land [ˈtailænd; ˋtaɪlənd] ***n***. 泰国〔亚洲〕。**-er** ***n***. 泰国人。

thal·a·men·ceph·a·lon [ˌθæləmenˈsefəˌlɔn; ˌθæləmenˋsɛfəˌlɑn] ***n***. (*pl*. *-la* [-lə; -lə])【医】间脑 (= diencephalon)。**-ce·phal·ic** [-siˈfælik; -sɪˋfælɪk] ***a***.

tha·lam·ic [θəˈlæmik; θəˋlæmɪk] ***a***.【解】丘脑的;【植】花托的。

thal·a·mus [ˈθæləməs; ˋθæləməs] ***n***. (*pl*. *-mi* [-mai; -maɪ]) **1.**【解】丘脑;室,床。**2.**【植】(柱状)花托。**3.** (古希腊的)闺房,内室。*optic thalami*【解】视神经床,视丘。

tha·las·sic [θəˈlæsik; θəˋlæsɪk] ***a***. **1.** (关于)海洋的,深海的。**2.** (关于)海湾的,内海的。

thal·as·soc·ra·cy [ˌθælɑˈsɔkrəsi; ˌθæləˋsɑkrəsɪ] ***n***. 制

海权。**-las·soc·rat** [-ˈlæsəkræt; -ˋlæsəkræt] ***n.*** 拥有制海权者。

thal·as·sog·ra·phy [ˌθæləˈsɔgrəfi; ˏθæləˋsɑgrəfɪ] ***n.*** 海洋学。**-pher** ***n.***

t(h)a·ler [ˈtɑːlə; ˋtɑlɚ] ***n.*** 〔*sing.*, *pl.*〕德国旧银币名。

Tha·les [ˈθeiliːz; ˋθeliz] ***n.*** 泰勒斯〔640? —546? B.C., 希腊哲学家〕。

Tha·li·a [θəˈlaiə; θəˋlaɪə] ***n.*** 【希神】**1.** 萨拉亚〔司喜剧, 田园诗的女神〕。**2.** (赐人美丽和欢乐的)三女神 (the Graces) 之一。**-li·an** ***a.***

tha·lid·o·mide [θəˈlidəˌmaid; θəˋlɪdəˏmaɪd] ***n.*** 【药】擦里多米德〔镇静药,会引起婴儿畸形〕。

thal·lic [ˈθælik; ˋθælɪk] ***a.*** 【化】(正)铊的;三价铊的;含(正)铊的。

thal·li·um [ˈθæliəm; ˋθælɪəm] ***n.*** 【化】铊〔Tl〕。

thal·loid [ˈθælɔid; ˋθælɔɪd] ***a.*** 【植】似叶状体的。

thallo·phyte [ˈθæləfait; ˋθæləˏfaɪt] ***n.*** 【植】菌藻植物。**-phyt·ic** ***a.***

thal·lous [ˈθæləs; ˋθæləs] ***a.*** 【化】亚铊的;一价铊的。

thal·lus [ˈθæləs; ˋθæləs] ***n.*** (*pl.* ***thal·luses*** [-ləsiz; -ləsɪz], ***thalli*** [-lai; -laɪ])【植】叶状体;菌体。

thal·weg [ˈtɑːlveg; ˋtɑlveg] ***n.*** **1.**【地】河流谷底线。**2.**【法】(国际法)河道分界线。

Thames [temz; tɛmz] ***n.*** (英国)泰晤士河。***set the ~ on fire*** 作惊人之举;成为杰出的人物;大显身手。

than [强 ðæn, 弱 ðən, ðn; ðæn, ðən, ðn] **I** ***conj.*** **1.** 〔用于形容词、副词比较级之后〕比,比较。*Health is better ~ money.* 健康胜于金钱。*He is taller ~ I (am).* 他比我高〔现在口语常作 ~ me〕。*You love him more ~ I.* 你爱他胜过我爱他。*That morning I got up later ~ usual.* 那天早上我比平常起床晚些。*You love him more ~ me.* 你爱他胜过爱我。*He is more of a teacher ~ a scholar.* 他是一位教师,不是什么学者。*Something is better ~ nothing.* 聊胜于无。**2.** 〔用于 *rather*, *sooner* 等之后〕与其…(毋宁、宁愿、不如、索性)。*I would rather* [*sooner*] *die ~ disgrace myself.* 与其受辱不如死了好。**3.** 〔用于 hardly; scarely, barely 之后〕(刚刚…)就 (= when)。*Hardly had she heard the news ~ she began to cry.* 她一听到那个消息就开始大哭。*We barely arrived ~ it was time to leave.* 我们刚刚到达,就到了应该离开的时间了。**4.** 〔用于 other, else, anywhere, different 等之后〕除…(以外),除…(以外的)。*He has no other friend ~ you.* 他除你以外没有朋友。*He is otherwise ~ I thought.* 他不是我所想像的那样人。*You won't find such friendship anywhere ~ in this country.* 除了在这个国家,你在别处是得不到这种友谊的。*It was none other ~ the principal.* 不是别人,是校长本人。**II** ***prep.*** **1.** 比〔用于 ~ whom, ~ which〕。*Here is my new teacher, ~ whom a better does not exist.* 这就是我的新教员,谁也比不上他。**2.** 〔后接计量数目〕超过。*Her car goes faster ~ 110 miles per hour.* 她的汽车的时速超过 110 英里。***no more ~*** 仅仅,只是 (*It's no more ~ a misunderstanding.* 这只是个误会)。***no other ~*** **1.** 只有。**2.** 正是,就是(*It is no other ~ his mother.* 那就是他母亲)。

tha·na [ˈtɑːnə; ˋtɑnə] ***n.*** **1.** 〔印英〕警察局。**2.** 军事基地。

than·age [ˈθeinidʒ; ˋθenɪdʒ] ***n.*** 【英史】大乡绅 (thane) 的身分[地位、领地]。

thanat(o)- *comb. f.* 死: *thanato*logy.

than·a·toid [ˈθænətɔid; ˋθænəˏtɔɪd] ***a.*** **1.** 像死的,死一般的。**2.** 致死的,致命的。

than·a·to·lo·gy [θænəˈtɔlədʒi; ˏθænəˋtɑlədʒɪ] ***n.*** 死亡学,死因学。

than·a·to·phi·di·a [ˈθænətəˈfidiə; ˏθænətəˋfɪdɪə] ***n.*** 〔*pl.*〕毒蛇。

than·a·to·pho·bi·a [ˌθænətəˈfəubiə; ˏθænətəˋfobɪə] ***n.*** 死亡恐怖[畏惧];(病态的)畏死。

than·a·top·sis [ˌθænəˈtɔpsis; ˏθænəˋtɑpsɪs] ***n.*** 对于死的见解[思考]。

thane [θein; θen] ***n.*** **1.**【英史】(因服兵役而领有封地的)大乡绅,相当于后来的骑士、男爵等。**2.**【苏格兰史】(有封地的)氏族长。**-dom** ***n.*** = thanage. **-hood** ***n.*** **1.** 〔总称〕大乡绅,领主。**2.** 大乡绅的地位[职权]。**-ship** ***n.*** = thanage.

thank [θæŋk; θæŋk] **I** ***vt.*** **1.** 感谢,道谢。**2.** 劳驾。~ *sb. for a thing* 为某事感谢人。*T- you!* 谢谢〔偶然也说 I ~ you!〕。*T- you for that ball!* 劳您驾拿那个球给我! *No more, ~ you.* 够了,谢谢你。*No, ~ you.* 不,谢谢(你)〔表示拒绝时说的客气话〕。*T- God* [*Heaven*]! 谢天谢地。*T- you for nothing!* (表示蔑视的拒绝)算了,别瞎起劲;别管闲事! *Thanking you in anticipation.* (承蒙…)谨先致谢〔请托信中套语〕。***have*** (***only***) ***oneself to ~ for*** = ***~ oneself for*** 〔谑〕真是活该,真是自作自受,只能怪自己(*You have only yourself to ~ for that.* = *You may ~ yourself for that.* 你真是活该,你真是自作自受)。***I will ~ you to*** (*do*). 请你,劳驾;〔反、谑〕(还是请)…好(*I will ~ you to shut the door.* 劳驾把门关上。*I will ~ you to be a little more polite.* 还是文明礼貌点儿好)。**II** ***n.*** 〔*pl.*〕谢意,谢忱,感谢,谢辞,谢礼。*express one's ~s* 道谢。*Thanks!* 谢谢! (= Thank you!) *No, ~s.* 不,谢谢。*Thanks for your kindness.* 谢谢你的好意! *A thousand ~s.* = (*Many*, 〔古〕 *Much*) *~s.* = (*Please accept*) *my best ~s.* 多谢多谢。*Small* [〔谑〕 *Much*] *~s I got for it.* 人家并不领情[感谢]! 〔谑〕感谢得很[其实不感谢]! ***bow one's ~s*** 鞠躬致谢。***give*** [***return***] ***~s to*** 感谢。***No ~s!*** 别管闲事! (*No ~s to him though.* 可是请他别管闲事吧)。***~s a million*** 〔美俚〕= ~ *you.* ***~s to*** 幸亏,由于(*~s to my foresight* 幸亏我有先见之明)。~ **offering** 【宗】感恩的供品,谢恩的奉献。**-er** ***n.*** 感谢者。**-ee, -y, -ye** [ˈθæŋkjiː; ˋθæŋkji] ***int.*** 谢谢。

thank·ful [ˈθæŋkfəl; ˋθæŋkfəl] ***a.*** **1.** 感谢的,感激的,感恩不尽的(*to* sb.; *for* a thing)。**2.** 感到欣慰,非常高兴 (*that*)。*We are ~ to you for all your assistance.* 我们感谢您们的一切协助。*You should be ~ that your son has won the scholarship.* 你应该为你的儿子获得奖学金感到高兴。**-ly** ***ad.*** **-ness** ***n.***

thank·less [ˈθæŋklis; ˋθæŋklɪs] ***a.*** **1.** 不感激的,忘恩负义的。**2.** 不受人感谢的,不受人注意的;不讨好的,不合算的,徒劳的,无利的(工作等)。*a ~ task* 一项徒劳无益的任务。**-ly** ***ad.*** **-ness** ***n.***

thanks·giv·ing [θæŋksˈgiviŋ; ˏθæŋksˋgɪvɪŋ] ***n.*** **1.** 感谢,感恩,谢恩;谢恩祈祷。**2.** 〔T-〕(基督教)感恩节〔在美国是十一月的最后一个星期四,在加拿大是十月的第二个星期一〕。

thank·worth·y [ˈθæŋkˌwəːði; ˋθæŋkˏwɝðɪ] ***a.*** 〔古〕应该感谢的,可感谢的。

thank-you-ma'am, -mam, -marm [ˈθæŋkjumaːm; ˋθæŋkjuˏmæm, -ˏmɑm] ***n.*** 〔美俚〕(使车子震动的)横贯路中的小沟;道路的凹凸不平处。

than·a·tol·o·gy [ˌθænəˈtɔlədʒiː; ˏθænəˋtɑlədʒi] ***n.*** 【医】临终学〔研究人临死前之心理及其安抚疗法等的学科〕。

thar [tɑː; tɑr] ***n.*** 【动】(尼泊尔产)一种羚羊。

tharm [θɑːm; θɑrm] ***n.*** 〔Scot.〕肠;〔美〕肚子;(做琴弦用的)肠线。

that[1] [ðæt; ðət] **I** ***pro.*** (*pl.* ***those*** [ðəuz; ðoz]) **1.** 〔指示代名词〕(a)〔指眼前的、说过的事物或人,又指比较 this 稍微远一点的〕那;那个东西;那件事情;那个人。*What is ~?* 那是什么? *T- is what I want to know.* 那就是我想知道的事情。*Who is ~ in the parlour?* 客厅里的那个人是谁? *Which will you have, this or*

～? 你要哪个,这个还是那个? (b)〔用作关系代名词的先行词,该关系代名词为宾格时常省略〕(…的)事物;(…的)人。*All those* (～) *I saw were inadequate*. 我所看见的都不行。(c)〔用来代替前面已提到的名词,以免重复〕*The area of New York is larger than* ～ *of London*. 纽约的面积比伦敦的(面积)大。*After* ～ *we had a quiz*. 随后我们考了个小测验。(d)〔指前述二物中的〕前者(*opp*. this 后者)。**2.**〔关系代名词〕[ðət] (a)〔引出修饰先行词的定语从句,口语中宾格的 that 常省去〕…的。*those* ～ *love us* 爱我们的人们。*those* (～) *we love* 我们所爱的人们。*His article contains much* ～ *is useful*. 他的文章里有很多有用的东西。*Is this the book* (～) *you were looking for*? 你要找的书是这本吗? (b)〔用作关系副词承接表示时间等的名词〕…的(时候、样子、方法等,常省略)。*the last time* ～ *I saw you* 上次见你的时候。*the way* ～ *he did it* 他做这事的方法。(c)〔在从句中用于不加冠词的,表示某种特性的词后,作表语〕*Newcomer* ～ *he is, he knows what's the right thing to do*. 尽管他是个新手,他却知道应该做些什么。***and all*** ～ 以及这类的东西[事情];…等。***and*** ～ 而且(*He makes mistakes, and* ～ *very often*. 他犯了错误,而且是常常犯)。***and at*** ～ **1.** 虽然如此还是;〔口〕而且(*The price of the tea was 500 dollars, and not a very good tea at* ～. 茶叶要五佰块钱一斤,而且不是很好的茶。*It was a dull play but at* ～ *Jack enjoyed it*. 那是出枯燥无味的戏,可是杰克还真喜欢它)。**2.**〔美俚〕真正,实在。***Come out of*** ～! 〔俚〕走开,出去;滚蛋! ***for all*** ～ 然而仍旧。***like*** ～ 那样地。***only*** ～ 就只那么多。***So*** ～*'s* ～. ***= That's*** ～. 完了,就是这样〔发言完毕时的话〕(*I won't go and* ～*'s* ～. 说不去就不去)。～ ***being so*** 因为那个缘故,因此。～ ***is*** (***to say***) 这就是说,即。***That's it***. 对啦,正是如此。***That's so***! ***= That's right***! 好;是的;〔美〕赞成! ***T-*** [***those***] ***will do***. 那正好[正合适],行了。***upon*** ～ 于是,于是马上。***with*** ～ 于是;这样说着。

II ***a***.〔指示形容词,后接复数名词时用 these〕[ðæt] **1.** 那,那个。(a)〔指面前看得见的〕: *Can you see those trees*? 你看得见那些树吗? ～ *man there* (看)那个人。(b)〔指不详细说也知道的东西〕: *What was* ～ *noise*? 那声音是什么? (c)〔用指远处的一切东西或过去的时候〕: *from* ～ *day on* 从那天起。*in* ～ *country* 在那个国家。*in those days* 在那时候。～ *day* 那一天。～ *once* 那一次。(d)〔和 *this* 搭配应用〕: *He went to this doctor and* ～. 他看过好些医生〔这个和那个等等医生〕。**2.** 那,那个,那种。～ *sonorous voice which we know so well* 我们所熟悉的那种洪亮的声音。～ *horse of yours* 你那匹马。～ *courage which you boast of* 你所夸耀的那种勇气。**3.**〔和连词 that 同用〕那样的。*He has* ～ *confidence in his theory that he would put it into practice tomorrow*. 他对自己理论抱有那样的自信简直明天就要拿去实行一样。*He was angry to* ～ *degree that he foamed at the mouth*. 他气得嘴边沫子直冒。～ ***kind***〔美俚〕那种(没价值),不愉快的[东西、人]。

III [强 ðæt; 弱 ðət; ðæt; ðət] ***conj***. **1.**〔引导名词从句,本身无词汇意义,常可省去〕*I know* (～) *it was so*. 我知道当时是那样的。*It is certain* ～ *he was there*. 他当时在那里,这是确实的。*He said* (～) *he was there*. 他说当时他在那里。**2.**〔引导包含 may, might, should 等情态动词的状语从句,表示目的〕为…。*We eat* ～ *we may live*. 我们是为了活下去而吃饭的。**3.**〔在 so, such 之后引出表示结果的状语从句〕*I am so tired* (～) *I cannot stand*. 我累得站不住。**4.**〔引出表示理由或原因的状语从句〕因为。*I am glad* ～ *he came*. (因为)他来了我很高兴。*Not* ～ *I'm unwilling to do the job, but I'm unequal to it*. 不是因为我不愿意干这个工作,而是我干不了。**5.**〔引出表示判断的标准的状语从句〕*Are you mad* ～ *you speak so wild*? 你疯了吗? 那样乱讲! **6.**〔引导表示愿望、惊愕、愤恨等的从句,主语常可省略〕要是…多好;想不到…;希望。*T-* [*Would* ～] *I had never been born*! 我要是没有生下来那多好。*T- it should ever come to this*! 想不到会到这个地步。*O* [*Would*] ～ *it might be the last*. 希望这是最后一次[希望不要再有这种事]。***in*** ～〔古、书面语〕以…的理由,因为(*in* ～ *they are men* 因为他们是男人)。***not*** ～ (…之事)并非如此(*not* ～ *I know of* 据我所知并非如此)。***now*** ～ 既然,由于(*Now* ～ *you mention it, I do remember*. 你这样一说,我想起来了)。***seeing*** ～ 因为。

IV [ðæt; ðæt] ***ad***.〔口〕那样,那么。*He wasn't* ～ *angry*. 他没有那么生气。*He knows only* ～ *much*. 他就知道那么多。*Can she walk* ～ *far*? 她能走得那么远吗? *I stayed in your house for a week when you were* ～ *high*. 你才那么高的时候,我在你家住过一个星期。

thatch [θætʃ; θætʃ] **I** ***n***. **1.** 盖屋顶的材料〔稻草、茅草、棕榈〕。**2.** 草屋顶。**3.**〔口、谑〕(长在头上的)头发。**4.** (作物下的地面上的)杂草。**II** ***vt***. (用稻草等)盖(屋顶);像用茅草盖屋顶般覆盖。**-er** ***n***. 盖屋顶者。**-y** ***a***.

Thatch·er [ˈθætʃə; ˋθætʃɚ], **Margaret** (**Hilda**) 撒切尔夫人(1925 –),英国政治家,1979 – 1990 年任英国首相。**-ism** ***n***. 撒切尔主义〔指她奉行的强硬政治路线〕。

thatch·ing [ˈθætʃiŋ; ˋθætʃɪŋ] ***n***. **1.** 葺屋顶,盖屋顶。**2.** 葺屋顶的材料,葺屋稻草[茅草]。

thau·ma·tol·o·gy [ˌθɔːməˈtɔlədʒi; ˏθɔməˋtɑlədʒɪ] ***n***. (研究神奇事物的)神奇学。

thau·ma·trope [ˈθɔːmətrəup; ˋθɔməˏtrop] ***n***. 幻影转盘〔一种玩具,圆盘的一面画鸟笼,另一面画鸟,旋转时好像鸟在笼中〕。

thau·ma·turge [ˈθɔːmətəːdʒ; ˋθɔməˏtɝdʒ] ***n***. 奇术师;魔术师,术士。**-tur·gic, -tur·gi·cal** ***a***.

thau·ma·tur·gist [ˈθɔːmətəːdʒist; ˋθɔməˏtɝdʒɪst] ***n***. = thaumaturge.

thau·ma·tur·gy [ˈθɔːmətəːdʒi; ˋθɔməˏtɝdʒɪ] ***n***. 魔术;奇术;幻术。

thaw [θɔː; θɔ] **I** ***vi***. **1.** (冰、雪等)解冻,融化。**2.**〔口〕(冰冷的身体)渐渐温暖起来。**3.** (态度、感情等)缓和起来。*It* ～*s*. = *It is* ～*ing*. 解冻了。*The ground has* ～*ed out*. 雪已经融化了。*After the talk, he began to* ～. 谈话之后,他的态度开始缓和下来。—***vt***. 使融化;使暖和。～ *out the frozen assets* 解除对资产的冻结。～ (*out*) *the guests* 使客人们不再拘束。**II** ***n***. **1.** 融雪,融霜;解冻。**2.** 缓和。**3.** 融雪[融霜]的温暖气候。*a silver* ～ 树冰,雾冰。*A* ～ *has set in*. 融雪的气候[解冻的时节]到了。*a* ～ *point* 露点。**-less** ***a***. (永)不融化的。

thaw·y [ˈθɔːi; ˋθɔ·ɪ] ***a***. 融雪的,融霜的;解冻的。

ThB = thorium B 钍B〔铅的同位素 Pb^{212}〕。

THC = tetrahydrocannabinol【药】四氢大麻酚。

Thc = thorium C 钍C〔铋的同位素 Bi^{212}〕。

THD = thread.

ThD = thorium D 钍D〔铅的同位素 Pb^{208}〕。

the [强 ðiː; (元音之前)弱 ði, (辅音之前)弱 ðə, ð; ði, ðɪ, ðə, ð] **I** ***art***.〔特定用法〕这(个),那(个);这种,那种;这一类,那一类的〔限定意义很轻,通常不必译出〕。**1.**〔指只说出名称对方就知道是什么的事物〕。(a)〔表示已被确认、提到,遇到,正在谈到,熟悉的实际存在的人或事物,意义相当于"这(些)","那(些)",以区别于 a, an"一个","某个"〕: ～ *mountain* 这(个)山〔区别于 a mountain〕。*Shut* ～ *door, please*. 请关上门。*We keep a horse and are all fond of* ～ *horse*. 我们养着一匹马,我们大家都喜欢那匹马。(b)〔独特的、独一无二的事物〕; ～ *sun* 太阳。～ *earth* 地球。～ *world* 世界。～ *universe* 宇宙。～ *House* (*of Commons*) 英国的下议院。～ *Channel* 英吉利海峡。(c)〔季节,自然现象,方位等(特别当这些名词前不用形容词时)〕: (～) *spring*

〔春夏秋冬前不用冠词也行〕。~ *day* 白天。~ *night* 黑夜。~ *wind* 风。~ *cold* 冷(空气等)。~ *east* 东方。(d)〔病名(现除口语及俚语中古复数形式的名词前尚保留外,其余通常省略)〕:(~) *smallpox* 天花。(~) *measles* 麻疹。(~) *gout* 痛风。~ *blues* 忧郁。~ *drink* 〔俚〕酒癖。(e)〔指身体的一部分,为物主代词的代用语〕:*I took him by ~ hand*. 我牵住他的手〔*cf*. I took his hand.〕。(f)〔用于乐器名称前〕:*play ~ violin* 拉小提琴。**2.**〔用于专有名词前〕(a)〔复数形式的山(脉),地区,国家〕:~ *Alps* 阿尔卑斯山(脉)。~ *Balkans* 巴尔干的国家。~ *United States* 美利坚合众国。(b)〔河流、运河、半岛、沙漠〕:~ *Thames* 泰晤士河。~ *Panama* (*Canal*) 巴拿马运河。~ *Crimea* 克里米亚半岛。~ *Sahara* 撒哈拉沙漠。(c)〔习惯上使用定冠词的某些场所、街道、城市、国家等〕:~ *Oxford Road* 牛津路。~ *Congo* 刚果。~ *Argentine* 阿根廷。*T- Hague* 海牙。(d)〔船名、飞机名、铁路名〕:~ *Queen Mary* 〔常作 S.S. Queen Mary〕玛丽女王号。~ *Stockton and Darlington Railway* 斯达克敦一达灵敦铁路。(e)〔某些旅馆,剧院等建筑物〕:~ *Imperial Hotel* 帝国旅馆。~ *Capital* 首都剧院。(f)〔语言名〕:~ *English*. (g)〔某些书、报、杂志名〕:~ *Times*《时报》。~ *New York Times*《纽约时报》。★用人名做书名时不加 the: Robinson Crusoe. (h)〔称号、爵位等之前〕:~ *Duke of Wellington* 威灵顿公爵。~ *Right Honourable George Gordon Byron* 乔治·戈登拜伦阁下。*Alfred ~ Great* 艾尔弗雷德大帝〔其后接姓名时不用 the: King George〕。(i)〔爱尔兰、苏格兰等族长姓氏前〕:~ *Macnab*, ~ *Fitz-Gerald*. **3.**〔表示一定前后关系〕(a)〔用于被限制性的名词或定语从句修饰的名词前〕:~ *pencil in my hand* 我手中的(那)支笔。~ *book you lost* 你丢失的那本书。(b)〔附加在形容词最高级或序数词前〕:~ *greatest possible victory* 最大最大的胜利。~ *hundredth time* 第一百次。~ *last but not ~ least* 最后的但并不是最不重要的。(c)〔普通名词前=such〔such a〕;抽象名词前=such= so=enough〕:*He is not ~ man to betray a friend*. 他不是出卖朋友的人(=... not such a man as will betray...)。*He had ~ kindness to show me the way*. 承他好意给我指路。*T- impudence of the fellow*! 那家伙真无耻! **4.**〔加强语气的用法〕出色的,典型的,无双的(等)。*Caesar was ~ general of Rome*. 凯撒是罗马唯一的将军。*Do you mean ~ Gorky*? 你是说(大文豪)高尔基吗?〔通常用斜体字表现,发音[ðiː; ði]〕。**5.**〔英〕〔计量单位名词前〕:*at one dollar ~ pound* [*yard*] 每磅[码]一元钱。*hire by ~ week* 按周雇用。*so much by ~ day* 一日若干钱。*8 minutes to ~ mile* 八分钟跑一英里。

II〔代表用法〕…那样的东西,…那种东西。**1.**〔用单数普通名词代表它的一类时(所谓代表的单数)〕(a)〔表示动植物等的种类,种属〕:*T- horse is useful to man*. ★man 和 woman 除与 child, boy, girl 等对照应用外,代表单数不用 the: Man has tamed the horse. (b)〔the+单数普通名词,则指出其功能,属性等使具抽象性〕:*pleasant to ~ eye* (=sight) 看着舒服。*keep ~ wolf from the door* 免于饥饿。*The pen is mightier than ~ sword*. 文的比武的力量大。(c)〔the+形容词=抽象名词或具体名词〕:~ *sublime* = *sublimity* 崇高(的事物)。~ *beautiful* = *beauty*〔美〕. ~ *unexpected* 意料不到的事。~ *old and ~ young* 老年和青年。**2.**〔复数名词前〕〔用在人民、阶级、人群或家族姓名等的名词前,表示集体或全体〕:~ *Clives* 克来弗一家(的人们)。*those renowned among ~ Chinese* 中国人中的有名的人们。*a plant not yet known to ~ botanists* 植物学家们还不知道的一种植物。

III[ðə, ði; ðə, ðɪ] ***ad*. 1.**〔加在形容词、副词比较级前,用作指示副词〕更,越发;反而。*He worked ~ harder, because he had been encouraged*. 他因为受了鼓励,工作越发努力了。*I like him all ~ better for his criticism on me*. 他批评了我,我反而更喜欢他。**2.**〔加在形容词副词前作关连副词用〕愈…愈…。*T- sooner*, ~ *better*. 愈早愈好。★**1.**前头的 the 是关连副词,后头的 the 是指示副词。**2.** 关连副词从句也可以放在后面: One wants, ~ more one has. = T- more one has, ~ more one wants. 越有越贪。***so much ~ better*** [***worse***] 那样更好[坏]。

the·an·dric [θiˈændrik; θɪˋændrɪk] ***a*.** 神人两性的;神人的。

the·an·throp·ic, -throp·i·cal [θiːænˈθrɔpik, -kəl; ˏθiænˋθrɑpɪk, -kəl] ***a*.** 具有神人两性的;把神性体现在人身上的,神人同形的。

the·an·thro·pism [θiˈænθrəpizm; θɪˋænθrəpɪzm] ***n*. 1.** 神人一体。**2.** 神人一体说〔尤指耶稣基督〕。**-pist *n*.**

the·ar·chy [ˈθiːɑːki; ˋθiɑrkɪ] ***n*.** 神的统治;神治国;神权政治;(统治的)神们。

theat(r) = theatre; theatrical(ly).

the·a·tre,〔美〕**the·a·ter** [ˈθiətə; ˋθiətɚ, ˋθɪə-] ***n*. 1.** 剧场,戏院。**2.**〔the ~〕戏,戏剧;〔集合词〕(某一国、某一作家的)戏剧作品,戏剧文学。**3.** 戏剧效果;表现手法。**4.** (阶梯式)讲堂,会场;手术教室。**5.** 活动场所,(发生重要事件的)场所;【军】战区;战场。*a patent ~*〔英〕钦许剧场。*a picture ~* 电影院。*do a ~ = go to the ~* 看戏去。*the modern ~* 近代剧。*the ~ of Lao She*〔总称〕老舍的剧作。*the ~ of the absurd* 荒诞派戏剧。*the ~ of war* 战场。*The opera was good ~*. 这出歌剧的舞台效果好。~ **goer** 经常(或爱)看戏的人。~ **going** 看戏。~**-in-the-round** (表演场地设于中心,观众围着观看的)圆形剧场。**the living ~** 舞台剧(与电影及电视剧相对而言)。

the·at·ric [θiˈætrik; θɪˋætrɪk] ***a*.** = theatrical.

the·at·ri·cal [θiˈætrikəl; θɪˋætrɪkl] **I *a*. 1.** 剧场的,戏院的。**2.** 戏剧(式)的,戏剧性的;做戏似的,夸张的。~ *effect* 戏剧效果。~ *scenery* 剧景。~ *way of speaking* 做戏似的讲话方式。**II *n*. 1.**〔*pl*.〕戏剧(表演)〔尤指业余演出〕。**2.**〔*pl*.〕戏剧表演艺术;做戏似的动作。**3.** 戏剧演员。*private* [*amateur*] ~*s* 业余戏剧[演出]。**-ism *n*.** 戏剧演出法,戏剧行为[派头],夸张作风。**-i·ty** [θiˌætriˈkæliti; θɪˏætrɪˋkælətɪ] ***n*.** 戏剧性[行为、派头、作风]。**-ly *ad*.** 用戏剧;做戏似地。

the·at·ri·cal·ize [θiˈætrikəˌlaiz; θɪˋætrɪklˏaɪz] ***vt*. 1.** 使适合于演出。**2.** 把…戏剧化,夸张。**-i·za·tion *n*.**

the·at·rics [θiˈætriks; θɪˋætrɪks] ***n*.**〔*pl*.〕〔作单数用〕戏剧演出(法);舞台表演艺术;戏剧[舞台]效果;戏剧化的言行。

the·ba·ine [ˈθiːbəˌiːn, θiˈbeiin; ˋθibəˏin, θɪˋbe·ɪn] ***n*.**【化】蒂巴因。

Thebes [θiːbz; θibz] ***n*. 1.** 底比斯〔埃及尼罗河畔的古城〕。**2.** 底比斯〔希腊古城〕。**-ban** [ˈθiːbən; ˋθibən] ***a*.**

the·ca [ˈθiːkə; ˋθikə] ***n*.** (*pl*. **-cae** [-siː; -si]) **1.**【植】药室;孢蒴。**2.**【动,解】鞘;壳;囊;膜;(珊瑚的)外壁。**-l *a*.**

the·cate [ˈθiːkit; ˋθikɪt, -ket] ***a*.** 有膜的,有鞘的。

thé dan·sant [ˌtei dɑ̃nˈsɑ̃ŋ; ˏteˏdɑ̃nˋsɑ̃ŋ]〔F.〕(*pl*. ***thés dan·sants*** [dɑ̃sɑ̃ŋ; dɑ̃sɑ̃ŋ]) (午后茶点时间的)茶舞(=tea dance)。

thee [ðiː, 弱 ði; ði, ðɪ] ***pro*.**〔thou 的宾格〕你。***Get ~ gone***! 走开! ★教友会教徒作 thou 用,并且接第三人称形式的动词。Thee does (=You do) not understand. 你不懂。

thee·lin [ˈθiːlin; ˋθilɪn] ***n*.**〔废〕【医】= estrone.

thee·lol [ˈθiːlɔːl, -ləul; ˋθilol, -lɑl] ***n*.**〔废〕【医】= estriol.

theft [θeft; θɛft] ***n*. 1.** 偷窃(罪),盗窃(罪)。**2.** 被盗,失窃。**3.**〔罕〕赃物。*commit a ~* 做盗窃案。~*s from a museum* 从博物馆盗窃的赃品。~**less** 非盗窃的;不会失窃的。~**proof** 防盗的。

thegn [θein; θen] ***n.*** 〔古〕= thane.

the·ic [ˈθiːik; ˋθiɪk] ***n.*** 喝茶过多的人,嗜茶成癖的人。

the·in(e) [ˈθiːi(ː)n; ˋθi·in, -ɪn] ***n.*** 【化】茶碱,咖啡因。

their [ðɛə, (元音之前)弱 ðər; ðɛr, ðər] ***pro.*** **1.** 〔they 的所有格〕他们的。**2.** 〔泛指,用以代替不确定的单数先行词〕他的,她的 (= his, her)。*Our thanks to any one who will support us after* ~ *deliberation.* 对经过深思熟虑愿意支持我们的任何人表示感谢。*I don't think the house is* ~ *own.* 我想那房子不是他们自己的。

theirn [ðɛən; ðɛrn] ***pro.*** 〔方〕= theirs; their own.

theirs [ðɛəz; ðɛrz] ***pro.*** 〔they 的物主代词,既可指代上文提过的东西,也可指代下文提到的事物〕**1.** 他们的东西,他[她]们的亲属[或有关的人]。**2.** 〔泛指用以代替不确定的单数先行词〕他(她)的 = his, hers. *These books are* ~. 这些书是他们的。*That's not the custom of* ~. 那不是他们的习俗。*T- is the largest house on the block.* 他们的住宅是该街区最大的住宅。*Are you a friend of* ~? 你是他的朋友吗? *I have my book, does each student have* ~? 我已有书本了,是不是每位同学都有了? *I will do my part if everybody else will do* ~. 要是大家都做那我也做。

the·ism[1] [ˈθiːizəm; ˋθiɪzəm] ***n.*** 有神论 (*opp.* atheism); 一神论。**the·ist** ***n.*** **-is·tic, -is·ti·cal** ***a.***

the·ism[2] [ˈθiːizəm; ˋθiɪzəm] ***n.*** 【医】茶(碱)中毒。

Thel·ma [ˈθelmə; ˋθɛlmə] ***n.*** 塞尔玛〔女子名〕。

them [强 ðem, 弱 ðəm; ðɛm, ðəm] **I** ***pro.*** **1.** 〔they 的宾格,用作宾语,口语中也用作表语〕他们,她们,它们。*The books are new; take care of* ~. 这些书是新的,对它们当心保存。*It was very kind of* ~. 他们太客气了。*That's* ~. 就是他们。**II** ***a.*** 〔非标准用法〕〔= those〕: *He doesn't want* ~ *books.* 他不要那些书。

the·mat·ic, -mat·i·cal [θiːˈmætik(əl); θiˋmætɪk(əl)] ***a.*** **1.** 主题[论题]的。**2.** 【语言】词干的,构干的。**3.** 【乐】主旋律的。*a* ~ *vowel* 构干元音。**-i·cal·ly** ***ad.***

theme [θiːm; θim] ***n.*** **1.** (文章,讨论的)主题;论题;话题。**2.** (学生的)作文,论文,作文题。**3.** 【语言】词干;【乐】主题,主旋律。**4.** 【无】= signature; 【无】信号曲[调]。**5.** (某人的)口头禅;爱谈的话题。*a favourite* ~ *for poetry (of, with) (the poets)* 诗(诗人们)喜欢用的主题。~ *song* 主题歌。~ **park** 主题公园〔以自然、童话、文化等主题布置的公园〕。~ **restaurant** (在建筑造型、室内布置、就餐文化氛围等方面独具某种特色的)主题饭店。

The·mis [ˈθiːmis, ˈθemis; ˋθimɪs] ***n.*** 【希神】特弥斯〔司法律、正义的女神〕;〔人格化〕法律,正义。

them·selves [ðəmˈselvz; ðəmˋsɛlvz] ***pro.*** 〔*pl.*〕**1.** 〔强义〕他[她、它]们亲自[自己]。**2.** 〔反身〕他[她,它]们自己。**3.** 〔泛指〕用以代替不确定的单数先行词他(她)自己 = himself 或 herself. *They did it* ~. 那是他们自己做的。*They are deceiving* ~. 他们在欺骗自己。

then [ðen; ðɛn] **I** ***ad.***, ***conj.*** **1.** 〔指过去或未来的一个特定时间〕那时,当时。**2.** 〔表示顺序〕(a) 〔时间〕然后,其次。(b) 〔序列〕此外,加上,加之,而且。(c) 〔推理〕既然这样,那么;因此。*Things were different* ~. 那时一切都和现在不同。*First comes spring,* ~ *summer.* 先到的是春天,然后是夏天。*And* ~ *she had such a fine head of hair.* 而且她有一头非常美丽的头发。*T- it is useless to go on.* 那么继续下去也没用。*Let's begin, then.* 那么,咱们就开始吧。***but*** ~ 但是;但是另一方面。***now ...*** ~ ***...*** 有时…有时…。***now*** ~ 〔抗议、警告〕可是,喂! (*Now* ~, *a little less noise there.* 喂喂,静一点! *Now* ~, *what are you doing?* 慢着,你在干什么呢? *Now* ~, *don't hit me in the eye!* 当心,别打着我的眼睛)。~ ***and not till*** ~ 那时候才开始。~ ***and there = there and*** ~ 当时,当场。即时。***well*** ~ 既然这样。***what*** ~ [~ ***what***] (下一步)怎么办,又怎么样呢。**II** ***a.*** 当时的。*the* ~ *conditions* 当时的情况。*the* ~ *ruler* 当时的统治者。**III** ***n.*** 那时。*before* ~ 那时以前。*by* ~ 到那时,那时。*from* ~ *on* 从那时起。*since* ~ 那时以来,以后。*till* ~ 到那时,那时以前。***every now and*** ~ 时时。

the·nar [ˈθiːnɑː; ˋθinɑr] **I** ***n.*** **1.** 手掌;足底。**2.** 鱼际〔大拇指根部掌上突出的肌肉〕拇指球。**II** ***a.*** 手掌的;足底的;鱼际的。

thence [ðens; ðɛns] ***ad.*** 因此;〔古〕从那里;〔罕〕从那时起(自那以后)。*It* ~ *appears that* 由此看来显然是。*T- it follows that* 所以就…了。*I would suggest that we (should) go to the New York and* ~ *to Boston.* 我建议去纽约,然后从那里去波士顿。~ **forth,** ~ **forward** ***ad.*** 从那时,其后;从那里。

the·o- *comb. f.* 神: *theo*logy, *theo*phany.

The·o·bald [ˈθiəbɔːld; ˋθiə͵bɔld] ***n.*** 西奥博尔德〔男子名〕。

the·o·bro·mine [ˌθiəˈbrəumiːn, -min; ͵θiəˋbromin, -mɪn] ***n.*** 【化】可可碱。

the·o·cen·tric [ˌθiəˈsentrik; ͵θioˋsɛntrɪk] ***a.*** 【神】以神为中心的。**-cal·ly** ***ad.*** **-i·ty** [-ˈtrisiti; -ˋtrɪsətɪ] ***n.*** **-tri·sm** [-trizm; -trɪzm] ***n.***

the·oc·ra·cy[1] [θiˈɔkrəsi; θiˋɑkrəsɪ] ***n.*** **1.** 神权政治,(尤指古犹太的)僧侣[祭司]政治。**2.** 神权国家。**3.** 占统治地位的(掌握政权的)僧侣集团。

the·oc·ra·cy[2] [θiˈɔkrəsi; θiˋɑkrəsɪ] ***n.*** **1.** 泛神崇拜〔如既信奉基督教又拜佛像〕。**2.** 通过冥想使心灵与上帝贯通融合。

the·o·crat [ˈθiːəkræt; ˋθiə͵kræt] ***n.*** 神权主义者,神权政治中的统治者。

the·od·o·lite [θiˈɔdəlait; θɪˋɑdəl͵aɪt] ***n.*** 【测】经纬仪。**-ic** ***a.***

The·o·dore [ˈθiədɔː; ˋθiə͵dɔr, -͵dor] ***n.*** 西奥多〔男子名〕。

the·og·o·ny [θiˈɔgəni; θiˋɑgənɪ] ***n.*** 神谱;叙述神统的史诗;神统系谱学。**-nic** ***a.***

theol. = theologian; theological; theology.

the·o·lo·gi·an [θiəˈləudʒjən; ͵θiəˋlodʒən, -dʒɪən] ***n.*** 神学家,神学研究者。

the·o·log·i·cal [θiəˈlɔdʒikəl; ͵θiəˋlɑdʒɪkl] ***a.*** 神学(上)的;神学性质的;根据圣经的,作为神言来看的。**-gist** ***n.*** **-ly** ***ad.***

the·ol·o·giz·e [θiˈɔlədʒaiz; θiˋɑlə͵dʒaɪz] ***vt.*** 使神学化。— ***vi.*** 作神学理论上的阐述。**-r** ***n.*** 神学理论的阐述者。

the·o·log(ue) [ˈθiːəlɔg; ˋθiə͵lɔg, -͵lɑg] ***n.*** 〔美口〕神学院学生,神学家。

the·ol·o·gy [θiˈɔlədʒi; θiˋɑlədʒɪ] ***n.*** 神学。

the·om·a·chy [θiˈɔməki; θiˋɑməkɪ] ***n.*** 诸神间的战争;对诸神的战争。

the·o·mor·phic [ˌθiəˈmɔːfik; ͵θiəˋmɔrfɪk] ***a.*** 神形的,有神的形象的。**-phism** ***n.***

the·on·o·mous [θiˈɔnəməs; θɪˋɑnəməs] ***a.*** 神统治的,神控制的。**-ly** ***ad.*** **-o·my** ***n.***

the·op·a·thy [θiˈɔpəθi; θɪˋɑpəθɪ] ***n.*** (*pl.* ***-thies***) (宗教信仰的)虔诚。

the·oph·a·ny [θiˈɔfəni; θɪˋɑfənɪ] ***n.*** 神的显现。

The·o·phras·tus [θi(ː)əˈfræstəs; ͵θiəˋfræstəs] ***n.*** 西奥弗拉斯塔〔372? —287 B.C., 希腊的哲学家〕。

the·o·phyl·line [ˌθiəˈfiliːn, -in; ͵θiəˋfɪlin, -ɪn] ***n.*** 【化】茶碱。

theor. = theorem.

the·or·bo [θiˈɔːbəu; θiˋɔrbo] ***n.*** (*pl.* ~*s*) (17 世纪琵琶状)双首琴。

the·o·rem [ˈθiərəm; ˋθiərəm] ***n.*** **1.** (能证明的)一般原理,公理,定律,法则。**2.** 【数】定理。**-mat·ic** [-ˈmætik; -ˋmætɪk], **-mat·ical** ***a.*** **-i·cal·ly** ***ad.***

T

the·o·ret·ic [θiəˈretik; ˏθiəˋretɪk] ***a***. = theoretical.

the·o·ret·i·cal [θiəˈretikəl; ˏθiəˋretɪkl] ***a***. **1.** 理论(上)的,学理上的 (*opp*. applied)。**2.** 假设(性)的;纯理论的,推理的。**3.** 空论的 (*opp*. practical)。～ *physics* 理论物理学。～ *prepossession* 脱离实际预先形成的印象。**-ly** ***ad***.

the·o·re·ti·cian [ˌθiərəˈtiʃən; ˏθiərəˋtɪʃən] ***n***. 理论家。

the·o·ret·ics [θiəˈretiks; ˏθiəˋretɪks] ***n***. 〔*pl*. 作单数用〕(某一学科的)理论(内容)。

the·o·rist [ˈθiərist; ˋθiəˏrɪst] ***n***. 理论家;学说创立人;空论家。

the·o·rize [ˈθiəraiz; ˋθiəˏraɪz] ***vi***. **1.** 创立学说。**2.** 建立理论,理论化。**3.** 作理论上讨论,推理。**-riz·er** ***n***.

the·o·ry [ˈθiəri; ˋθiərɪ, ˋθɪərɪ] ***n***. **1.** 理论,学理,原理。**2.** 学说,论说 (*opp*. hypothesis)。**3.** 推测,揣度。**4.** 〔口〕见解,意见。*the* ～ *of two points* 两点论。*Darwin's* ～ *of evolution* 达尔文的进化论。～ *of equations* 【数】方程论。～ *of everything* 【物】(把相对论、量子论和宇宙大爆炸理论都包括在内的)万用理论。～ *of relativity* 【物】相对论。*the atomic* ～ 原子说。*Our scheme is good both in* ～ *and in practice*. 我们的方案在理论上和实施上都是好的。*combine* [*separate*] ～ *with* [*from*] *practice* 理论结合[脱离]实际。*My* ～ *is that we must bring new blood into the Institute through appointment of younger men to important positions*. 我的意见是我们学院应该通过重用年轻一些的人来注入新的血液。～ *of games* 博弈论,对策论,权衡利弊得失的形势分析。

the·o·soph [θiəˈsɔf; ˋθiəsɑf], **the·os·o·pher** [θiˈɔsəfə; θɪˋɑsəfɚ], **-phist** [-fist; -fɪst] ***n***. 通神论者;接神论者。

the·os·ophy [θiˈɔsəfi; θɪˋɑsəfɪ] ***n***. **1.** 【宗】神智学,通神论。**2.** 〔常 T-〕(万物轮回,人可以通过修持获得神性的)接神论。

T

ther·a·p· = therapeutics.

ther·a·peu·tic, -ti·cal [θerəˈpjuːtik, -tikəl; ˏθɛrəˋpjutɪk, -tɪkəl] ***a***. 治疗(学)的,疗法(上)的。**-ti·cal·ly** ***ad***.

ther·a·peu·tics [ˌθerəˈpjuːtiks; ˏθɛrəˋpjutɪks] ***n***. 【医】治疗学;疗法论。

ther·a·peu·tist [ˌθerəˈpjutist; ˏθɛrəˋpjutɪst] ***n***. = therapist.

ther·a·pist [ˈθerəpist; ˋθɛrəpɪst] ***n***. 【医】治疗学家。

ther·a·py [ˈθerəpi; ˋθɛrəpɪ] ***n***. 【医】疗法;疗效。*new acupuncture* ～ 新针疗法。*radio* ～ 放射疗法。

-therapy *suf*. 治疗,疗法: radio*therapy*.

ther·blig [ˈθəːblig; ˋθɝblɪg] ***n***. (工业生产中)操作动作的基本单位(记号)。

there [ðɛə; ðɛr] **I** ***ad***. **1.** 在那里,到那里,在那个地方。**2.** 在那一点上。**3.** [强 ðɛə, 弱 ðə; ðɛr, ðə]〔无场所观念,用于 be, come, go 等动词之前。主语除人称代词外应置于后面,以加强语气引起注意;与 be 连用时表示"有"的意思〕。**4.** 与 seem, appear 等动词连用。*I see a bird* ～. 我看见一只鸟在那里。*I am now on my way* ～. 我正在往那里去。*You are right* ～. 在那一点上你说得对。*T- you go again*. 你又来这一套了。*Is* ～ *a telephone in your house*? 你家有电话吗? *T- is no one there*. 那里一个人也没有。*T- comes the bus at last*. 公共汽车可来啦。*T- seems* (*to be*) *something wrong about the teletype*. 电传打字电报机好像有点毛病。*T- goes the bell*. 钟响了。*T- he goes*! 看,他做[说]那样的事! *T- it goes*! 哎呀,掉下来了[坏了,不见了,等等]。***Are you*** ～ ?〔电话用语〕喂喂?***... as*** ～ ***is*** 如果说有…。***be all*** ～〔口〕(能力,精神)很正常,一切很好(*He is all* ～ *as a teacher*. 他当老师很好)。***get*** ～〔俚〕达到目的,成功。***have been*** ～ ***before***〔口〕到过那里(所以很熟习)。***here and*** ～ 这里那里。***neither here nor*** ～ 不得要领;不相干;没有关系。***then and*** ～ 在当时当地。～ ***is no ... ing*** 很难…,无法…,不能…(*T- is no telling when he will arrive*. 很难说他什么时候会来)。***T- it is***! 就在那里。～ ***or thereabouts***〔场所、价格、数目或时间等〕大约,大致那样。***There's a good boy***. 真是乖孩子〔哄孩子时说的话〕。***T- you are***! 原来你在这儿! 你这才来! 就是这个,就在这儿;就是这样嘛;这就是你要的,拿去吧! 完了,就是这些,目的达到了。***You have me*** ～. 这就输给你了;这一下让你抓住了。**II** ***pro***.〔用于介词之后〕那里。***from*** ～ 从那里,(***live***) ***near*** ～ (住)在那附近。***up to*** ～ 到那里。**III** ***int***. 那! 唷! 哎呀! 你瞧! 好啦!〔表示确信、胜利、失望、鼓励、安慰、挑衅、唆使等,引起注意,加强语气〕。*T-*! ～! *Never mind*. 好啦! 好啦! 不要紧的。*T- now*! 你瞧! 你看多好! *You* ～! 喂。*I think I've a say in the matter, so* ～! 我认为我有发言权,就是这样。

there·a·bout(s) [ˈðɛərəbaut(s), ˌðɛərəˈb-; ˏðɛrəˋbaʊt(s)] ***ad***. **1.** (表示地点)附近。**2.** (表示数量,时间,程度等)左右;大约,上下。*from the year 1963 or* ～ 从1963年前后。*in three years or* ～ 三年左右。

there·aft·er [ðɛərˈɑːftə; ðɛrˋæftɚ, -ˋɑf-] ***ad***. **1.**〔书面语〕此后。**2.**〔罕〕据此。

there·a·gainst [ˌðɛərəˈgeinst; ðɛrəˋgɛnst] ***ad***. 相反,反对;对立地。

there·a·nent [ˌðɛərəˈnent; ˏðɛrəˋnɛnt] ***ad***.〔Scot.〕关于那。

there·at [ðɛərˈæt; ðɛrˋæt] ***ad***.〔古〕在那里[那时];因此;据此。

there·by [ˈðɛəbai; ðɛrˋbaɪ] ***ad***. **1.** 因此,所以。**2.**〔古〕在那附近 = thereabout(s). *T- hangs a tale*. 其中有点蹊跷[必有原因]。

there·for [ðɛəˈfɔː; ðɛrˋfɔr] ***ad***.〔古〕因此;为此;由于这样。

there·fore [ˈðɛəfɔː, -fɔə; ˋðɛrˏfor, -ˏfɔr] ***ad***., ***conj***. 因此,为此,所以。*The new yacht is smaller and* ～ *cheaper*. 这艘新游艇比较小,因此就比较便宜。*It rained*; ～ *the track and field meet was put off*. 天下雨,因此运动会延期。

there·from [ðɛəˈfrɔm; ðɛrˋfrɑm] ***ad***.〔古〕从那里。

there·in [ðɛərˈin; ðɛrˋɪn]〔古〕***ad***. 其中;在那里;在那点上。

there·in·aft·er [ˌðɛərinˈɑːftə; ˏðɛrɪnˋæftɚ, -ˋɑf-] ***ad***. 【法】在下(文)。

there·in·be·fore [ˌðɛərinbiˈfɔː, -biˈfɔə; ˏðɛrɪnbɪˋfor, -ˋfɔr] ***ad***. **1.** 【法】在上(文)。**2.** (文章或讲话等)在前的一部分中,在上文中。

there·in·to [ðɛərˈintuː, -tu; ðɛrˋɪntu, -tʊ, ˏðɛrɪnˋtu] ***ad***.〔古〕往那里面,往其中。

ther·e·min [ˈθerəmin; ˋθɛrəmɪn] ***n***. 铁耳明式电子乐器。

there·of [ðɛərˈɔv, -ˈɔf; ðɛrˋɑv] ***ad***.〔古、谑〕(把)它;将它;它的;由此。*Do not eat* ～. 不要吃它。*an evil and the remedy* ～ 一项弊端及其匡正办法。*Excess in drinking is the evil* ～. 饮酒过度由此而生祸害。

there·on [ðɛəˈɔn; ðɛrˋɑn] ***ad***.〔古〕**1.** 在其上,在那上面。**2.** = thereupon. *the latest news and our commentary* ～ 最新消息以及我们关于它的述评。

there·out [ðɛəˈaut; ðɛrˋaʊt] ***ad***.〔古〕从那(里面);在…外面。

there's [强 ðɛəz, 弱 ðəz; ðɛrz] = there is [has].

The·re·sa [tiˈriːzə, təˈriːzə; tɪˋrizə, təˋrizə] ***n***. 特丽萨〔女子名〕。

there·to [ðɛəˈtuː; ðɛrˋtu] ***ad***.〔古〕到那里;〔古、诗〕此外,又。

there·to·fore [ðɛətəˈfɔː; ˏðɛrtəˋfor, -ˋfɔr] ***ad***. 那时以前,直到那时。

there·under [ðɛərˈʌndə; ðɛrˋʌndɚ] ***ad***. 在其下;在那一

项目[条款]下。*a word and the examples given* ～ 一个词及其下面所举的例句。

there·un·to [ðɛər'ʌntu:;ˏðɛrʌn`tu, ðɛr`ʌntu] **ad.** 〔古〕= thereto.

there·up·on [ˌðɛərə'pɔn;ˏðɛrə`pɑn] **ad.** 于是,因此;于是立刻;[古]在那上面。

there·with [ðɛə'wiθ, -'wið; ðɛr`wɪð, -`wɪθ] 〔古〕 **ad.** 以那,以这;于是;立刻,同时。*every person connected* ～ 每一个与之有关的人。

there·with·al [ˌðɛəwi'ðɔ:l;ˏðɛrwɪð`ɔl] **ad.** 〔古〕于是;此外,又,同时。

the·ri·ac ['θiəriæk; `θɪrɪˏæk] **n.** **1.** 糖浆。**2.** (蛇毒的)解毒剂。**3.** 万灵药。

the·ri·an·throp·ic [ˌθiəriæn'θrɔpik;ˏθɪrɪæn`θrɑpɪk] **a.** 半人半兽的。

the·ri·o·mor·phic [ˌθiəriə'mɔ:fik;ˏθɪrɪə`mɔrfɪk] **n.** 兽形的〔指某些神而言〕。

therm. = thermometer.

therm- *comb. f.* = 热;热电 (= therm-)。

therm(e) [θə:m; θɝm] **n.** **1.**【物】克卡〔即小卡 = 4.2×10^7 erg〕。**2.** 大卡,千卡。**3.** 煤气热量单位〔在英国 = 100,000 B.T.U.; 在美国 = 1,000 千卡〕。

thermae ['θə:mi:; `θɝmi] **n.** 〔*pl.*〕〔L.〕【古希腊、罗马】温泉;公共浴室,大澡堂。

ther·mal ['θə:məl; `θɝml] **I** **a.** **1.** 热的,热量的,温热的;由热造成的。**2.** 温泉的。～ *barrier*【空】热障。～ *capacity* 热容量。～ *conductivity*【物】导热性;导热系数。*a* ～ *power station* 热电站,火力发电站。*a* ～ *unit* 热量单位。～ *springs* 温泉。**II** **n.**【空】上升暖气流。～ **pulse**【物】热脉冲〔核爆炸后产生的热量扩散波〕。**-ing** **n.**【体】气流滑翔〔借助上升暖气流在空中滑翔〕。**-ly** **ad.**

therm·al·loy ['θə:məlɔi; `θɝməlɔɪ] **n.**【冶】热合金,耐热耐蚀合金,镍铜合金。

therm·an·(a)es·the·si·a [ˌθə:mænəs'θi:ʒə, -ʒiə, -ziə;ˏθɝmənɛs`θiʒə] **n.** 无冷热感觉(力);冷热感麻木。

ther·mate ['θə:meit; `θɝmet] **n.**【军】混合燃烧剂〔燃烧弹及榴弹中所用的混合剂,由铝热剂及其他物质混合制成〕。

ther·mel ['θə:mel; `θɝmɛl] **n.** (装有热电偶的)热电温度计。

therm·(a)es·the·si·a [ˌθə:mes'θi:ʒə, -ʒiə, -ziə;ˏθɝmɛs`θiʒɪə, -`θiʒə] **n.** 冷热敏感性,冷热感觉(力)。

ther·mic ['θə:mik; `θɝmɪk] **a.** 热的,由于热的。～ *rays* 热线。～ *fever* 日射病。

Ther·mi·dor ['θə:miˌdɔ:, F. tɛrmi'dɔ:r; `θɝməˏdɔr, tɛrmi`dɔr] **n.** 热月〔法国资产阶级革命时期共和历的第十一月,相当于公历七月十九日到八月十七日〕。**-ean, -ian** **a.** 热月的;热月政变式的,热月党人的。

therm·i·on ['θə:maiən; `θɝmɪən, `θɝmˏaɪən] **n.**【物】热离子。

therm·i·on·ic [ˌθə:mi'ɔnik;ˏθɝmɪ`ɑnɪk, -maɪ-] **n.**【物】热离子的。*a* ～ *tube* [*valve*] 热离子管。～ *current* 热离子[电子]电流。～ *emission* 热离子放射。**-s** **n.** 热离子学。

ther·mistor [θə:'mistə; θɝ`mɪstɚ] **n.**【电】热敏电阻;热控管;热(变电)阻器,测温电阻器。

ther·mit ['θə:mit; `θɝmɪt], **-mite** [-mait; -maɪt] **n.**【冶、化】铝粉焊接剂;铝热剂。～ *bomb* 铝热剂燃烧弹。～ *iron* 铝热还原铁。～ *method* [*process*]铝热(剂)法。～ *welding* 火焊。

thermo- *comb. f.* 〔用于辅音前〕热;热电: *thermo*nuclear, *thermo*phone.

ther·mo·am·me·ter ['θə:məu'æmitə, -'æmmi:tə;ˏθɝmə`æmˏmitɚ] **n.**【电】热电偶安培计。

ther·mo·ba·rom·e·ter [ˌθə:məubə'rɔmitə;ˏθɝmobə`rɑmətɚ] **n.** **1.** 温度气压计。**2.** 虹吸气压表。

ther·mo·bat·ter·y [ˌθə:məu'bætəri;ˏθɝmo`bætərɪ] **n.**【电】温差电池组。

ther·mo·chem·i·cal [ˌθə:mə'kemikl;ˏθɝmo`kɛmɪkl̩] **a.** 热化学的。

ther·mo·chem·is·try ['θə:məu'kemistri;ˏθɝmo`kɛmɪstrɪ] **n.**【化】热化学。

ther·mo·cline ['θə:məˌklain; `θɝməˏklaɪn] **n.** 温水层〔较热的水面区与较冷的深水区之间的水层〕。

ther·mo·colo(u)r ['θə:məuˌkʌlə; `θɝmoˏkʌlɚ] **n.** 热敏油漆,示温涂料,色温标示。

ther·mo·cou·ple ['θə:məuˌkʌpl; `θɝmoˏkʌpl̩] **n.**【物】热电偶,温差电偶(= thermoelectric couple)。

ther·mo·cut·out [ˌθə:məu'kʌtaut;ˏθɝmo`kʌtaʊt] **n.** 热保险装置,热断流器。

ther·mo·duric [θə:məu'djuərik;ˏθɝmo`djurɪk] **a.**【菌】耐热的,不能用巴氏灭菌法杀灭的。

ther·mo·dy·nam·ic ['θə:məudai'næmik;ˏθɝmodaɪ`næmɪk] **a.** 热力的。*a* ～ *cycle* 热力循环。**-s** **n.** 热力学。

ther·mo·e·lec·tric(al) [θə:məui'lektrik(l);ˏθɝmo·ɪ`lɛktrɪk(l̩)] **a.**【物】热[温差]电的。*a* ～ *current* 温差电流,热电流。*a* ～ *pyrometer* 热电(偶)高温计。～ *couple* 温差电偶,热电偶。*a* ～ *thermometer* 热电偶温度计。

ther·mo·e·lec·tric·i·ty ['θə:məuiˌlek'trisiti;ˏθɝmo·ɪˏlɛk`trɪsətɪ] **n.**【物】温差电,热电。

ther·mo·e·lec·trom·e·ter [ˌθə:məuiˌlek'trɔmitə;ˏθɝmo·ɪˏlɛk`trɑmətɚ] **n.**【电】热电计。

ther·mo·e·lec·tro·mo·tive [ˌθəməuiˌlektrə'məutiv;ˏθɝmo·ɪˏlɛktro`motɪv] **a.**【物】热电动的,温差电的。

ther·mo·e·lec·tron [ˌθə:məui'lektrɔn;ˏθɝmo·ɪ`lɛktrɑn] **n.**【物】热电子。～ *tube* 热电子管。

ther·mo·el·e·ment [ˌθə:məu'elimənt;ˏθɝmo`ɛlɪmənt] **n.**【物】温差电偶,热电偶,热电元件,温差电元件。

ther·mo·gen·e·sis [θə:məu'dʒenisis;ˏθɝmo`dʒɛnɪsɪs] **n.**【生理】生热(作用)。**-ge·net·ic** **a.** 生热的,生热作用的。**-gen·ic** **a.** 生热的,产热的。

ther·mo·gram ['θə:məgræm; `θɝməˏgræm] **n.** 自记温度图(曲线);温谱图。

ther·mo·graph ['θə:məgrɑ:f, -græf; `θɝməˏgræf, -ˏgrɑf] **n.** 温度(自动)记录器;记录温度计。

ther·mog·ra·phy [θə:'mɔgrəfi; θɝ`mɑgrəfɪ] **n.** **1.** 温度记录,发热记录;自记温度。**2.** 热写法;炙出写法。

ther·mo·la·bile [ˌθə:məu'leibil;ˏθɝmo`lebɪl, -bl̩] **a.**【生化】感热的,非耐热性的(*opp.* thermostable)。

ther·mol·o·gy [θə:'mɔlədʒi; θɝ`mɑlədʒɪ] **n.** 热学。

ther·mo·lu·mi·nes·cence [ˌθə:məuˌlu:mi'nesəns;ˏθɝmoˏlumə`nɛsns] **n.** 热发光(现象)。**-nes·cent** **a.**

ther·mol·y·sis [θə'mɔlisis; θɝ`mɑləsɪs] **n.**【化】热(分)解(作用);【生理】散热(作用)。**-lyt·ic** **a.**

ther·mo·mag·net·ic [ˌθə:məumæg'netik;ˏθɝmomæg`nɛtɪk] **a.**【物】热磁的。～ *effect* 热磁效应。

ther·mom·e·ter [θə'mɔmitə; θɝ`mɑmətɚ] **n.** 寒暑表,温度计;体温表(= clinical ～)。*a combination* ～ (三氏)对照寒暑表。*a maximum* [*minimum*] ～ 最高[最低]温度计。***a centigrade*** [***Celsius***] ～ 摄氏温度计〔略 C〕。***a Fahrenheit*** ～ 华氏温度计〔略 F〕。***a Reaumur*** ～ 列氏温度计〔略 R〕。

ther·mo·met·ric, -ri·cal [ˌθə:mə'metrik, -rikəl;ˏθɝmə`mɛtrɪk, -rɪkl] **a.** 温度计的,寒暑表的,测温的,据温度计测得的。

ther·mom·e·try [θə:'mɔmitri; θɝ`mɑmətrɪ] **n.** **1.** 检温,温度测量。**2.** 计温学,测温法,计温术。

ther·mom·o·dule [ˌθə:məu'mɔdjul; θɝmo`mɑdjul] **n.**【物】热电微型组件。

ther·mo·mo·tor [ˌθə:mə'məutə;ˏθɝmə`motɚ] **n.** 热力机〔尤指蒸汽机〕。

T

ther·mo·nu·cle·ar [ˌθəːməuˈnjuːkliə; ˏθɝmoˋnuklɪɚ, -ˋnju-] ***a***. 【原】热核(反应)的。*a* ~ *bomb* 热核炸弹。*a* ~ *reaction* 热核反应。*a* ~ *weapon* 热核子武器。*a* ~ *war* 热核战争。

ther·mo·nu·cle·o·nics [ˌθəːməuˈnjuːkliˈɔniks; ˏθɝmoˋnjuklɪˋɑnɪks] ***n***. 【原】热核子学;热核技术。

ther·mo·nuke [ˈθəːmənjuːk; ˋθɝməˏnjuk, -ˏnuk] ***n***. 【物】〔美口〕核子武器。

ther·mo·paint [ˈθəːməupeint; ˋθɝmopent] ***n***. 示温涂料;彩色温标示漆,测温漆。

ther·mo·pen·e·tra·tion [ˈθəːməuˌpeniˈtreiʃən; ˏθɝmoˏpɛnɪˋtreʃən] ***n***. 【医】内科透热法。

ther·mo·pe·ri·od·ism [ˌθəːməuˌpiəriˈɔdizəm; θɝmoˏpɪrɪˋɑdɪzəm] ***n***. 【生】温周期现象。**-pe·ri·o·dic·i·ty** ***n***.

ther·mo·phase [ˈθəːməufeis; ˋθɝmoˏfes] ***n***. 【植】温期。

ther·mo·phile [ˈθəːməˌfail; ˋθɝməˏfaɪl, -fɪl] ***n***. 【医】嗜热性。

ther·moph·i·lic [ˌθəːməˈfilik; θɝˋmɑfɪlɪk, ˏθɝmoˋfɪlɪk] ***a***. 【生】嗜热性的,适温的,喜温的。~ *bacteria* 适温细菌。

ther·mo·phone [ˈθəːməfəun; ˋθɝməˏfon] ***n***. **1.** 【讯】热线式受话器,温热发声器。**2.** 传声温度计(或器)。

ther·mo·phore [ˈθəːməufɔː, -fɔə; ˋθɝməˏfor, -ˏfɔr] ***n***. 蓄热器。

ther·mo·pile [ˈθəːməupail; ˋθɝməˏpaɪl] ***n***. 【物】温差电堆,热电堆。

ther·mo·plas·tic [ˌθəːməuˈplæstik; ˏθɝmoˋplæstɪk] **I** ***n***. 热塑塑料;热塑性物质。**II** ***a***. 热塑性的(*opp*. thermosetting)。**-i·ty** ***n***. 热塑性。

ther·mo·reg·u·la·tion [ˌθəːməuˌregjuˈleiʃən; ˏθɝməˋrɛgjəˋleʃən] ***n***. **1.** 温度调节。**2.** 【生理】体温调节。

ther·mo·reg·u·la·tor [ˌθəːməˈregjuleitə; ˏθɝməˋrɛgjuˏletɚ] ***n***. 温度调节器。

ther·mo·run·away [ˈθəːməuˈrʌnəwei; ˋθɝmoˋrʌnəˏwe] ***n***. 【物】热致击穿,热致破坏。

ther·mos (bottle [flask]) [ˈθəːmɔs; ˋθɝməs, ˋθɝ-] ***n***. 热水瓶,暖瓶。

ther·mo·scope [ˈθəːməskəup; ˋθɝməˏskop] ***n***. 验温器,测温器[锥]。**-scop·i·c(al)** ***a***.

ther·mo·set [ˈθəːməset; ˋθɝməset] **I** ***n***. 【化】热固性,热硬性。**II** ***a***. 热固(硬)性的,热变定的。

ther·mo·set·ting [ˌθəːməuˈsetiŋ; ˋθɝmoˏsɛtɪŋ] ***a***., ***n***. 【化】热固(的),热硬性(的),热后就坚硬化(的)(*opp*. thermoplastic)。

ther·mo·si·phon [θəːməuˈsaifən; ˏθɝmoˋsaɪfən, -fɑn] ***n***. 热虹吸管;温差环流系统。

ther·mo·sphere [ˈθəːməsfiə; ˋθɝməsfɪr] ***n***. 【气】热(成)层〔大气中间层以上部份,温度随高度增高〕。

ther·mo·stable [θəːməuˈsteibl; ˏθɝmoˋstebl̩] ***a***. 【生化】耐热性的(*opp*. thermolabile)。

ther·mo·stage [ˈθəːməusteidʒ; ˋθɝmoˏstedʒ] ***n***. 【植】春化阶段;温期阶段。

ther·mo·stat [ˈθəːməstæt; ˋθɝməˏstæt] ***n***. **1.** 恒温器。**2.** (灭火设备等)温变自动启闭装置。*a* ~ *blade* 温变断流器。**-ic** ***a***. **-i·cal·ly** ***ad***.

ther·mo·statics [ˌθəːməˈstætiks; ˏθɝməˋstætɪks] ***n***. 【物】静热力学。

ther·mo·tax·is [ˌθəːməˈtæksis; ˏθɝməˋtæksɪs] ***n***. **1.** 【生】向热性,趋温性。**2.** 【生理】体温调节。**-tax·ic**, **-tac·tic** [-tik; -tɪk] ***a***.

ther·mo·ten·sile [ˌθəːməˈtensɪl; ˏθɝməˋtɛnsɪl, -saɪl] ***a***. 有热抗张强度的。

ther·mo·ther·a·py [ˌθəːməuˈθerəpi; ˏθɝmoˋθɛrəpɪ] ***n***. 【医】温热疗(法)。

ther·mot·ics [θəˈmɔtiks; θɚˋmɑtɪks] ***n***. 〔复数作单数用〕【物】热学。

ther·mot·ro·pism [θə(ː)ˈmɔtrəpizəm; θɚˋmɑtrəpɪzm] ***n***. 【生】向热[温]性,趋热性。*negative* ~ 背热性,负向热性。*positive* ~ 向热性,正向热性。**ther·mo·trop·ic** ***a***.

the·roid [ˈθiərɔid; ˋθɪrɔɪd] ***a***. 野兽似的,兽性的。

the·rol·o·gy [θiəˈrɔlədʒi; θɪˋrɑlədʒɪ] ***n***. 【动】哺乳动物学。

The·ron [ˈθirən; ˋθɪrən] ***n***. 西伦〔男子名〕。

the·ro·pod [ˈθiərəˈpɔd; ˋθɪrəˏpɑd] ***n***. 【古生】兽脚亚目(*Theropoda*)动物〔如恐龙〕。

ther·sit·i·cal [θəˈsitikl; θɚˋsɪtɪkl̩] ***a***. 大声的,辱骂的,庸俗下流的,满口下流话的。

the·sau·rus [θi(ː)ˈsɔːrəs; θɪˋsɔrəs] ***n***. (*pl*. ***-sau·ri*** [-ˈsɔːrai; -ˋsɔraɪ]) **1.** 宝库;知识的宝库。**2.** (尤指同义词等的)辞典,百科全书;(分类)词汇集,(词语、资料等的)汇编,文选。

these [ðiːz; ðiz] ***pro***., ***a***. 〔this 的复数〕这些。*in* ~ *days* 近来。~ *days* 近来。~ *times* 现时。*We have been working the case* ~ *ten days*. 近十天来我们一直搞这个案子。***one of*** ~ ***days*** 两三天内。★ ***one of*** ~ 〔常带轻蔑意〕一个这种人:*He's one of* ~ *artist chaps*. 他是一个不三不四的艺术家。

these [ˈteːzə; ˋtezə] ***n***. 〔G.〕纲领;提纲。

The·seus [ˈθiːsiəs, ˈθiːsjuːs; ˋθisjus, ˋθisus, ˋθisɪəs] ***n***. 【希神】提修斯〔雅典王子,曾除灭盗贼立功,并进入克里特岛迷宫斩妖除怪〕。

the·sis [ˈθiːsis; ˋθisɪs] ***n***. (*pl*. ***theses*** [ˈθiːsiːz; ˋθisiz]) **1.** 论点,论题;【逻】命题,假设。**2.** 作文;毕业论文,学位论文。**3.** [ˈθesis; ˋθɛsɪs] 【韵】(现代诗韵中的)抑音节,弱音节(*opp*. arsis);(古希腊、罗马诗中的)扬音节;【乐】强声部。*sb.'s principal theses* 某人的主要论点。*scientific theses* 科学论断。~ *novel* (= tendentious novel) 阐明某一鲜明主题的主题小说。

Thes·pi·an [ˈθespiən, -pjən; ˋθɛspɪən] **I** ***a***. **1.** (古希腊诗人)狄斯比斯(Thespis)的。**2.** 悲剧(性)的;戏剧的〔尤指悲剧的〕。**II** ***n***. 演员;悲剧演员。*the* ~ *art* 戏剧。

Thes·sa·lo·ni·an [ˌθesəˈləuniən; ˏθɛsəˋlonɪən] **I** ***a***. (Thessalonica) 萨洛尼卡的,萨洛尼卡人的。**II** ***n***. 萨洛尼卡人。

the·ta [ˈθiːtə; ˋθetə, ˋθitə] ***n***. 希腊字母表的第八个字母〔Θ、θ、相当于英语的 th〕。~ **wave** 【生】θ 波〔人轻度睡眠时频率为 4–7 周/秒的脑电波〕。

thet·ic, thet·i·cal [ˈθetik(əl); ˋθɛtɪk(l)] ***a***. **1.** 武断的,规定的。**2.** 【诗】以抑音节开始的;以抑音节组成的。**-i·cal·ly** ***ad***.

the·ur·gy [ˈθiːəːdʒi; ˋθiɝdʒɪ] ***n***. 妖术;法术;神通。**-gic**, **-gi·cal** [θiˈəːdʒik(ə)l; θɪˋɝdʒɪkəl] ***a***. **-gist** ***n***. 术士,施妖术者,法师。

thew [θjuː; θju, θu] ***n***. 〔常用 *pl*.〕**1.** 肌肉。**2.** 筋力,体力,膂力,活力。**3.** 〔古〕精神[道德]的素质。

thew·less [ˈθjuːlis; ˋθjulɪs, ˋθu-] ***a***. 〔主苏格兰〕**1.** 无活力的,无精神的。**2.** 肌肉不发达的,体力虚弱的。

thew·y [ˈθjuːi; ˋθjuɪ] ***a***. (***thew·i·er***; ***thew·i·est***) 肌肉发达的,强壮有力的,精力充沛的。

they [常音 ðei, 弱 ðe; ðe, ðɛ] ***pro***. 〔*pl*.〕〔人称代词、第三人称、复数、主格;所有格 their, 宾格 them, 物主代词 theirs〕**1.** 他们,她们,它们。**2.** 众人,人们。*T- say* 据说。

they'd [ðeid; ðed] **1.** = they had. **2.** = they would.

they'll [ðeil; ðel] = they will; they shall.

they're [ðeiə; ðer] = they are.

they've [ðeiv; ðev] = they have.

thi- *comb*. *f*. 〔用于元音前〕硫:*thi*azine *thi*azole.

thi·a·min(e) [ˈθaiəmi(ː)n; ˋθaɪəˏmin, -mɪn] ***n***. 【生化】硫胺素〔即维生素 B_1〕。

thi·a·za·mide [θaiˈæzəmaid; θaɪˋæzəmaɪd] ***n***. 【药】磺胺噻唑。

thi·a·zine [ˈθaiəˌziːn, -zin; ˋθaɪəˏzin, -zɪn] ***n*.**【化】噻嗪,硫氮杂苯。

thi·a·zole [ˈθaiəˌzəul; ˋθaɪəˏzol] ***n*.1.**【化】噻唑,间氮硫茂。**2.** 噻嗪衍生物。

Thi·bet [tiˈbet; tɪˋbɛt] ***n*.** = Tibet.

thick [θik; θɪk] **I *a*. 1.** (*opp*. thin)厚的;(树枝)粗大的。**2.** 浓厚的,黏稠的;混浊的。**3.** 不透明的;不清晰的(声音沙哑,口齿不清等)。**4.** 阴霾的,有浓雾的。**5.** (树林等)茂密的;(毛发)浓密的;密集的,挤满人的;充满…的。**6.** 频频的,接连不停的(指雨,雪等)。**7.** 混杂的(*with*);众多的;丰富的(*with*)。**8.** (器官,头脑)迟钝的。**9.**〔口〕亲密的,知己的,友好的(*with*)。**10.**〔英俚〕太过分的。**11.** 显著的。*The ice is 3 inches* ~. 冰厚3英尺。*spread the butter* ~ 奶油涂得厚。*a* ~ *mist* [*fog*] 浓雾。~ *clouds* 密云。~ *of hearing* 听觉不灵。~ *speech* 口齿不清的讲话。~ *syrup* 黏稠的糖浆。*trees* ~ *with leaves* 叶子茂密的树。*the air* ~ *with snow* 大雪密集的天空。*The car is* ~ *with people*. 车子挤满了人。*The conditions are a bit too* ~. 条件太过分了。*The river looks* ~ *after the rain*. 雨后河水浑浊。***as* ~ *as thieves*** 非常亲密。***rather* [*a little too, a bit*] ~**〔英俚〕(行为、要求等)太过分,太不要脸,受不了。***get a* ~ *ear***〔英俚〕被打肿了耳朵。***give* (*sb*.) *a* ~ *ear***〔英俚〕把(某人)打肿耳朵。**II *n*. 1.** 最厚[粗]的部分,最浓部分,最活跃的部分,密茂处,最激烈处,最紧张时。**2.**〔口〕笨蛋,傻子。**3.**〔俚〕可可粉。***in the* ~ *of*** 在…的最激烈时,处在…的深处,在…的最紧张时刻。***through* ~ *and thin*** 在任何情形下,不顾艰难困苦;不避艰险,赴汤蹈火。**III *ad*. 1.** 厚;浓;密;深。**2.** 频频地,时常。**3.** (声音)浊;不清晰地。**4.**〔口〕太过分,过度。*The heart beats* ~. 心跳得厉害。***lay it on* ~** 乱恭维。~ **and fast** 纷至沓来,频频地,密集地。~**-and-thin *a*.** 不辞水火的,始终不变的,忠实的。~**-brained *a*.** 头脑迟钝的,低能的。~**head** 笨人,呆子。~**leafed *a*.** 树叶密的;叶厚的。~**set 1. *a*.** 矮胖的,粗而短的;繁茂的;浓密的;质地厚实的。**2. *n*.** 丛林;密篱;厚灯芯绒。~**-skinned *a*.** 厚皮的;脸皮厚的;感觉迟钝的。~**-skulled**, ~**-witted *a*.** 愚钝的。

thick·en [ˈθikən; ˋθɪkən] ***vt*. 1.** 使厚;使粗大;使浓;使浊;稠化。**2.** 使繁茂,使密。**3.** 使深;加多;加强;加牢。—***vi*. 1.** 变厚,变粗大,变浓,变浊。**2.** 变模糊,变暗。**3.** 变厉害,增多,变复杂。**4.** 变坚牢,变结实。*Night* ~*s*. 夜渐深。*If you want to* ~ *the soup, add some flour*. 如果你想使汤浓些,加一点面粉。*Use the paper to* ~ *your notebook*. 用这些纸加厚你的笔记本。*The plot* ~*s*. 情节复杂起来。*The soup* ~*s by boiling*. 汤煮开就变稠了。**-er** 增稠器[剂]。**-ing *n*. 1.** 增浓(粗、密、厚),稠化,增浓过程,稠化过程。**2.** 增稠剂。**3.** 被加厚[加浓等]的东西[部分]。

thicket [ˈθikit; ˋθɪkɪt] ***n*. 1.** 灌木丛。**2.** 丛状物,密集的东西。**3.**【植】植丛,乱丛棵子、薮。**4.**【物】障。

thick·et·ed [ˈθikitid; ˋθɪkətɪd] ***a*.** 灌木丛的,成丛状的;密集的。

thick·ly [ˈθikli; ˋθɪklɪ] ***ad*.** = thick.

thick·ness [ˈθiknis; ˋθɪknɪs] ***n*. 1.** 厚;粗;厚度;粗大。**2.** 浓度,浓厚,黏稠。**3.** 密度;稠密。**4.** 模糊不清,多烟雾,混浊。**5.** 愚笨;迟钝。**6.** 最厚[粗,密,浓]处。**7.** (有一定厚度的东西的)一张,一层。**8.** 亲密。*coal seams of less* ~ *than five feet* 厚度不及五英尺的煤层。*the* ~ *of population in New York* 纽约的人口密度。*wood of different* ~ 厚度不同的木头。*five* ~*es of cardboard* 五层纸板。

thick'un [ˈθikən; ˋθɪkən] ***n*.**〔英俚〕一镑金币;五先令银币。

thief [θiːf; θif] ***n*.** (*pl*. ***thieves*** [θiːvz; θivz]) **1.** 贼,小偷。**2.**〔口〕(使蜡外流的)蜡烛心结的烛花。*Beware of thieves!* 谨防小偷! *to arrest, catch, chase, take up a* ~ 捉(追)贼。***thieves' Latin*** 盗贼黑话。~ **ant**【昆】窃叶蚁。~ **knot** 平结。~ **tube** (从液体容器中取样的)取样管。

thieve [θiːv; θiv] **I *vt*., *vi*.** 偷;行窃。**II *n*.** 小偷。

thiev·er·y [ˈθiːvəri; ˋθivərɪ] ***n*.** 偷窃;贼赃。

thiev·ish [ˈθiːviʃ; ˋθivɪʃ] ***a*.** 爱偷窃的;贼(似)的,偷偷摸摸的;不正当的。**-ly *ad*. -ness *n*.**

thigh [θai; θaɪ] ***n*.**【解】大腿,大腿骨;【虫】股节。~**-bone *n*.** 大腿骨,股骨。~**-high**〔口〕长统袜。

thig·mo·tax·is [ˌθigməˈtæksis; ˏθɪgməˋtæksɪs] ***n*.**【医】向实体运动(= stereotaxis)。**-tac·tic *a*.**

thig·mot·ro·pism [ˈθigˈmɔtrəpizm; θɪgˋmɑtrəpɪzm] ***n*.**【医】向实体趋性(= stereotropism)。**-trop·ic** [-ˈtrɔpik; -ˋtrɑpɪk] ***a*.**

thill [θil; θɪl] ***n*.** (车的)杠,辕。**-er *n*.** 驾辕马(= ~ horse)。

thim·ble [ˈθimbl; ˋθɪmbl] ***n*. 1.** (缝纫用)顶针。**2.** 隐豆戏法用杯子(参阅 thimblerig 条)。**3.** = thimbleful. **4.**〔盗贼俚〕手表。**5.**【机】套筒,套管,外接头,联轴器;离合器;封底管道,盲管道。*a* ~ *knight*〔美〕裁缝。~**-berry**【植】糙莓(= black raspberry)。~ **coupling** [**joint**] 套筒联轴节。~**weed**【植】**1.** 银莲花(属)〔如长果银莲花,河岸银莲花,维吉尼亚银莲花等〕。**2.** 金光菊(属);黄雏菊。

thim·ble·ful [ˈθimblˌful; ˋθɪmblˏful] ***n*.** (酒等的)少量。*a* ~ *of whiskey* 少量的威士忌酒。*He has just a* ~ *of insight into human behaviour*. 他对人们的行为只有一点点见识。

thim·ble·rig [ˈθimblrig; ˋθɪmblˏrɪg] **I *n*.** 隐豆戏法〔用三只杯子和一粒豆表演的快手戏法〕。**II *vi*.** 表演隐豆戏法;变戏法,欺骗。**-ger *n*.** 骗子。

Thim·bu [ˈθimbuː; ˋθɪmbu], **Thim·phu**, **Thim·pu *n*.** 廷布〔不丹首都〕。

thi·mer·o·sal [θaiˈmerəˌsæl, -ˈməː-; θaɪˋmɛrəˏsæl, -ˋmɝ-] ***n*.**【药】噻汞撒。

thin [θin; θɪn] **I *a*.** (~***ner***; ~***nest***) **1.** 薄的(*opp*. thick);瘦的(*opp*. fat, stout);细小的;【印】细体的。**2.** 稀少的,稀疏的(*opp*. dense)。**3.** 稀薄的,淡薄的(液体、气体等)(*opp*. thick);浅薄的,空洞的,没有什么内容的,不充实的。**4.** 显而易见的,易看破的。**5.**〔美口〕手头缺钱;简陋的,微少的(供给等)。**6.**〔美俚〕无聊的,不舒服的,不愉快的。**7.**〔美俚〕将要垮掉的,守不住的。**8.**【摄】(照片、底版)衬度弱的。*a* ~ *board* 薄板。*a* ~ *cat* 瘦猫;〔喻〕无权无势的人。*a* ~ *house* 观众稀少的戏院。*a* ~ *meeting* 来人稀少的集会。*a* ~ *slice of bolony*〔美〕极夸大的要求;傻话;露骨的虚伪;瞎说乱讲的人。*a* ~ *soup* 淡而无味的汤。*a* ~ *story* 内容空洞的故事。~ *green* 淡绿。~ *hair* 稀疏的头发。~ *one*〔美〕十分银币。*That's* (*a lot*) *too* ~.〔口〕太露骨,显而易见。***be* ~ *in the face*** 脸瘦。***have a* ~ *time* (*of it*)** 碰到不愉快事。***look* ~ *after illness*** 病后显得清瘦。**II *ad*.**〔诗〕稀薄,淡,细,疏,稀疏,微。**III *n*.** 细小部分,稀薄部分。**IV *vt*.** 使薄,使细,使稀薄,使淡,使稀疏;【农】间苗;使瘦。*Famine and war have* ~*ned the population*. 灾荒和战争使人口减少了。— ***vi*.** 变薄;变细;变稀薄;变淡;变稀疏;变瘦。*When the crowd* ~*ned, we left the square*. 人群散开的时候,我们离开了广场。~ ***down*** 弄细;变细。~ ***out*** 间(苗),疏(果);(听众)减少;变薄。**-ly *ad*. -ness *n*.**

thine [ðain; ðaɪn] ***pro*.**〔古、诗〕**1.**〔thou 的物主代词〕你[您]的东西。**2.**〔作为 thou 的所有格,用于首字母是元音或 h 音的名词前〕= thy:~ *eyes, heart, etc*.

thing[1] [θiŋ; θɪŋ] ***n*. 1.** (有形或无形的)东西,物;事物。**2.** 事,事件,局面,消息;〔*pl*.〕情形,形势,事态。**3.**〔*pl*.〕个人所有物,衣饰,服装,随身物品;用具,家具,财产。**4.**【法】〔*pl*.〕动产(或不动产)。**5.** 题目,主题。**6.** 细节,要点。**7.** (带感情色彩)家伙,东西〔指人或动物,表示轻蔑,

T

爱情,怜悯]。**8.** 事业,行为,成就,成果。**9.** 举动,行动,目标。**10.**(艺术的)作品;歌曲。**11.**〔the ~〕正适合(需要)的东西[事情];最流行的东西。**12.**〔*pl.*〕文物〔后接形容词〕。*all ~s* 万物,宇宙。*a living ~* 生物。*dumb ~s* 牲畜。*a pretty young ~*〔俚〕漂亮的小姑娘〔也有说作 a P.Y.T.的〕。*You stupid ~!* 你这蠢东西! *He takes ~s too seriously.* 他把事情看得太认真了。*Things have changed greatly.* 情形大大不同了。*~s Chinese* 中国的文物。*tea ~s* 茶具。*a little ~ of mine* 拙作。*That is just the ~ for me.* 那正合我的心意,那对我正好。*I am not quite the ~ this morning.* 今早身体不大舒服。*It is not (quite) the ~.* 有点不对,有点不好的地方。*How are ~s going at the Institute?* 学院里的情况怎么样? *Take your ~s upstairs.* 把你的衣物拿到楼上去。*I've a lot of ~s to do this morning.* 我今天上午有许多事要做。*He spoke of many ~s at the meeting.* 他在会上讲了很多的问题。*In designing the machine, not a ~ is to be overlooked.* 在设计这架机器时一点细节也不要忽略。*This is just the ~ I want.* 这正是我所要的。*At fifty, he would be a man to accomplish great ~s.* 他到五十岁时会有很大的成就。*The ~ now is to see the president at once.* 现在要做的是立刻去见董事长。***among other ~s*** 其中;尤其,格外。***... and ~s*** 〔口语〕…等。***as ~s are*** [***stand***] 据目前形势[情形]。***do the handsome ~ by*** 宽大对待。***for another ~*** 二则,其次。***for one ~...*** (, ***for another ...***) 一方面…(,另一方面);一则…(,再则…);首先…(,其次…)。***get ~s done*** 完成工作任务。***in all ~s*** 无论在什么问题上。***know*** [***be up to***] ***a ~ or two*** 〔口〕机敏,精明,不落空。***learn a ~ or two*** 学得一点东西。***make a good ~ of*** (因)…赚到钱[获利]。***no such ~*** 哪里会,没有这样的事。***of all ~s*** 偏偏(有这种事)。***one ~... another*** 一样一样,各方面;…是一回事…又是一回事,…和…是不同的(*taking one ~ with another* 一样一样[前前后后]想一想。*A man of talent is one ~, and a pedant another.* 有才能的人和卖弄学问的人是不一样的)。***Poor ~!*** 可怜! ***see ~s*** 发生幻觉,见神见鬼。***take ~s as they are*** 随遇而安,对一切事情都处之泰然。***the latest ~ in*** (*hats*)(帽子的)最新式样,最时髦的(帽子)。***The ~ is ...*** 目前的问题是,目前最要紧的是。***~ in itself*** 【哲】自在之物,物自体。***~ of naught*** [***nothing***] 不足道的东西[事情]。***~s have long been in a bad way*** (***for sb.***) 某人的日子很不好过,情况很坏。**~s mortgaged**【法】抵押品。**~s personal** [**real**]【法】动产[不动产]。

thing² [θiŋ; θɪŋ] ***n.*** (斯堪的那维亚各国的)议会[司法机构](=ting)。

thing·a·my, thing·a·ma·bob [ˈθiŋəmi, -əˈmɑːbɔb; ˋθɪŋəmɪ, -əˋmɑbɑb]; **thing·um·a·jig** [-əmidʒig; -əməˏdʒɪg], **thingum·bob** [-əmbɔb; -əmbɑb], **thingummy** [-əmi; -əmɪ] ***n.*** 〔口〕**1.** (对叫不出名字或暂时忘记的人或物的代称)那么个东西[人]。**2.** 机件装置;零件。

thing·ness [ˈθiŋnis; ˋθɪŋnɪs] ***n.*** **1.** 物体属性(或状态)。**2.** (事物的)客观实在性。

thing·y [ˈθiŋi; ˋθɪŋɪ] ***a.*** 物(体)的,物质的;实际的。

think [θiŋk; θɪŋk] **I** ***vt.*** (***thought*** [θɔːt; θɔt]) **1.** 想,思索,构思;考虑。**2.** 想出,想起。**3.** 认为,以为。**4.** 猜想,想像。**5.** 想要,打算。**6.** 使想。**7.** 感到。*I ~ I shall meet him today.* 我想[认为]今天会遇见他。*I don't ~ it's five o'clock yet.* 我看还不到五点。*I ~ him (to be) honest.* 我认为他(是)老实(的)。*I'll ~ the matter over.* 这事我得细细考虑考虑。*We should always use our brains and ~ everything over carefully.* 凡事应该用脑筋好好想一想。*I can't ~ how she could figure out all the problems in an hour.* 我想不出她怎么在一个小时之内算出所有的习题的。*Let's go and have a walk in the garden. You will ~ yourself silly.* 咱们出去在花园里散散步吧,你用脑过度,再不出去散散步就要变傻了。*I thought to finish these letters before ten o'clock.* 我原来打算十点钟以前把这些信都写好了。*I thought to find you in the library.* 我原来猜想会在图书馆里找到你。*Who would have thought that they could win the game.* 谁会想到他们竟能赢得那场球呢。*I ~ no harm in paying a visit to the Jones.* 我感到拜访琼斯家没有害处。— ***vi.*** **1.** 想。**2.** 想像,思索,思考,考虑(*over*; *about*; *of*; *on*)。**3.** 想出,想起(*of*; *on*)。**4.** 企图,想要,打算(*of*)。**5.** 料想。*Only ~!* 嗳,你想想看! *~ evil* 想干坏事。*Please ~ again.* 请再想想。*A university student should learn to ~.* 一个大学生应该学会思考。*I don't ~ so.* 我认为不是那样。*I'm thinking about the plan we're going to lay out.* 我在考虑我们要提出的计划。*T- over what I've said.* 把我所讲的话细细地想想。*What do you ~ of the idea?* 你认为这个想法怎么样? *That's a useful book to people who ~ of literary life.* 那是一本对想要从事文学生活的人有用的书。*I've thought deeply on our difficulties and the ways to get out of them.* 我深思了我们的困难及其解决办法。***I don't ~.*** 〔俚〕我倒有点不相信〔添加在反话,讥刺话等后面〕(*You are a pattern of tact, I don't ~.* 你的手腕了不起,我倒有点不相信)。***I ~*** 是…吧〔插句或句尾〕。***I ~ not.*** 我以为不是那样。***~ and ~*** 想了又想,细想。***~ aloud*** 自言自语,边想边说。***~ away*** 想开了(如不信神了);想得忘了(如牙齿痛)。***~ better of ...*** 改变…的念头;对某人有较高的评价。***~ fit*** [***good, proper, right***] ***to*** (*do*) 认为…适当(*I ~ fit to refuse.* 我以为拒绝的好)。***~ harm to*** 想害…,企图加害。***~ highly*** [***no end, well***] ***of*** 看重某人(某事),评价极高。***~ little*** [***nothing***] ***of*** 看不起,轻视;满不在乎(*~ nothing of walking 30 miles a day* 一天 30 英里也满不在乎)。***~ much of*** 重视,看重;赞美,夸奖。***~ of*** **1.** 想起;想出(*I cannot ~ of the right word*)。**2.** 想,企图(*He is ~ing of...*)。**3.** 细想(*T- of what I told you.*)。***~ oneself into a dilemma*** 想得无所适从。***~ oneself into a fever*** 想得头脑发热[兴奋不已]。***~ out*** 想透;想出。***~ out loud*** 〔美〕=~ aloud. ***~ sense*** 通情达理地设想。***~ shame*** 以为耻辱,羞愧。***~ through*** =~ *out*. ***~ to oneself*** 暗暗地自言自语;在心中想[打算,思量]。***~ twice*** 踌躇。***~ up*** 〔美〕想出,想起;〔口〕发明。***~ well*** [***ill***] ***of*** 认为好[坏]。***~ with*** 和…意见相同。

II ***n.*** 〔方、口〕思考;想法;念头。*Give it another ~.* 再想想吧。*Let's exchange ~s.* 咱们交换交换想法。***have a hard ~*** 苦思冥想。

III ***a.*** 思想(方面)的;供思考的。*a ~ teleplay* 引人思索的电视剧。**~-in** 〔口〕座谈会,专题讨论会。**~ piece** 〔美新闻语〕署名的评论文章[背景资料等]。**~ centre** [**tank, factory**] 智囊团[班子],智囊[谋划]中心。**~-tanker** 智囊(人物)。

think·a·ble [ˈθiŋkəbl; ˋθɪŋkəbl̩] ***a.*** 可想像的;可能的。*I'm sorry to say her idea is hardly ~.* 对不起,她的想法是几乎不可想像的。**-ness** ***n.*** **-a·bly** ***ad.***

think·er [ˈθiŋkə; ˋθɪŋkɚ] ***n.*** 思想家;思考者。*a deep ~* 深刻的思想家。

think·ing [ˈθiŋkiŋ; ˋθɪŋkɪŋ] **I** ***n.*** **1.** 思考,思索,考虑。**2.** 思想,观点,见解,想法。*plain living and high ~* 朴素的生活与崇高的思想。*It is man's social being that determines his ~.* 人们的社会存在,决定人们的思想。*There is nothing either good or bad but ~ makes it so.* 无所谓好坏,只是有那种想法才弄成这样子。*He is of my way of ~.* 他和我意见[想法]相同。***to my ~*** 我以为。**II** ***a.*** 思想的;有思想的;通情达理的;深思熟虑

的。*a* ～ *part* (戏剧里)不说话的角色。***all*** ～ ***men*** 凡是有头脑的人都(这样说等)。～**-box** 书房。～ **cap** 思考。～ **distance** 思考距离。～**-machine** 电子计算机。**the** ～ **public** 思想界。**-ly** ***ad***. **-ness** ***n***.

think·so [ˈθiŋksəu; ˋθɪŋk,so] ***n***.〔口〕单纯的初步意见。

thin·ner [ˈθinə; ˋθɪnɚ] ***n***. 稀释剂,冲淡剂,稀料;对…进行稀释(或冲淡)的人。

thinning [ˈθiniŋ; ˋθɪnɪŋ] ***n***.【农,园艺】间苗;蔬花,蔬果。

thin·nish [ˈθiniʃ; ˋθɪnɪʃ] ***a***. 有点薄[细,瘦,稀疏]的。*His new novel is tinged with* ～ *humour*. 他的新小说略带诙谐。

thin-skinned [ˈθinˈskind; ˋθɪnˋskɪnd] ***a***. 薄皮的;敏感的,神经过敏的;易怒的。

thi(o)- *comb. f*. 硫,硫代:*thio*ntimonate.

thi·o [ˈθaiəu; ˋθaɪo] ***a***.【化】硫的,含硫的。～ **acid** 硫代酸。

thi·o·al·de·hyde [ˈθaiə*u*ˈældəhaid; ,θaɪoˋældə,haɪd] ***n***.【化】硫醛;乙硫醛。

thi·o·an·ti·mo·nate, -mo·ni·ate [ˌθaiəuˈæntiməˌneit, -ˈməuniˌeit; ,θaɪoˋæntəmə,net, -ˋmonɪ,et] ***n***.【化】硫代锑酸盐,全硫锑酸盐。

thi·o·an·ti·mo·ni·te [ˌθaiəuˈæntiməˌnait; ,θaɪoˋæntəmə,naɪt] ***n***.【化】硫代亚锑酸盐。

thi·o·ar·se·nate [ˌθaiəuˈɑːsiˌneit, -snit; ,θaɪoˋɑrsɪn,et] ***n***.【化】硫代砷酸盐。

thi·o·ar·se·nite [ˌθaiəuˈɑːsiˌnait; ,θaɪoˋɑrsɪ,naɪt] ***n***.【化】硫代亚砷酸盐。

thi·o·bac·te·ri·a [ˌθaiəubækˈtiəriə; ,θaɪobækˋtɪrɪə] ***n***.〔*pl*.〕(*sing*. ***-ri·um*** [-əm; -əm])【化】硫细(杆)菌。

thi·o·car·ba·mide [ˌθaiəuˈkɑːbəˌmaid; ,θaɪokɑrˋbæmaɪd] ***n***.【化】硫脲(= thiourea)。

thi·o·cy·a·nate [ˌθaiəuˈsaiəˌneit; ,θaɪoˋsaɪənet] ***n***.【化】硫氰酸盐(或酯)。

thi·o·gly·col·(l)ic [ˌθaiəuglaiˈkɔlik; ,θaɪoglaɪˋkɑlɪk] ***a***.【化】～ *acid* 巯基乙酸,氢硫基乙酸。

thi·o·kol [ˈθaiəkəul; ˋθaɪə,kɑl] ***n***. 聚硫橡胶,乙硫橡胶〔商标名〕。

thi·ol [ˈθaiəul, -ɔːl; ˋθaɪol, -ɑl] ***n***.【化】硫醇(类) = mercaptan.

thi·o·nate [ˈθaiəˌneit; ˋθaɪə,net] ***n***.【化】硫代硫酸盐。

thi·onic [θaiˈɔnik; θaɪˋɑnɪk] ***a***.【化】硫的;含硫的。～ *acid* 连硫酸,硫逐酸。

thi·o·nine [ˈθaiəˌniːn, -nin; ˋθaɪə,nin, -nɪn] ***n***.【化】硫堇;劳氏紫。

thi·o·nyl [ˈθaiənil; ˋθaɪənəl] ***n***.【化】亚硫酰。

thi·o·pen·tal (sodium) [ˌθaiəˈpentæl, -tɔːl, -tl; θaɪəˋpentæl, -təl, -tl]【药】硫喷妥钠〔麻醉剂〕。

thi·o·phene [ˈθaiəˌfiːn; ˋθaɪə,fin] ***n***.【化】噻吩。

thi·o·phos [θaiˈɔfəus; θaɪˋɑfos] ***n***. = parathion.

thi·o·phos·phate [ˌθaiəuˈfɔsfeit; ,θaɪoˋfɑsfet] ***n***.【化】硫代磷酸盐(或脂)。

thi·o·sin·am·ine [ˌθaiəusinˈæmiːn, -ˌsinəˈmiːn; ,θaɪosɪnˋæmɪn] ***n***.【化】基硫脲烯丙。

thi·o·sul·fate [ˌθaiəuˈsʌlfeit; ,θaɪoˋsʌlfet] ***n***.【化】硫代硫酸盐(或酯)。

thi·o·u·ra·cil [ˌθaiəuˈjurəsil; ,θaɪoˋjʊrəsəl] ***n***.【药】硫脲嘧啶〔抗甲亢、心绞痛等的药物〕。

thi·o·u·re·a [ˌθaiə*u*juəˈriə; ,θaɪojʊˋrɪə] ***n***.【化】硫脲。

thi·ram [ˈθairæm; ˋθaɪræm] ***n***.【药】二硫四甲秋兰姆,双硫胺甲酰。

third [θəːd; θɝd] **I** ***num***. **1**. 第三〔略 3rd.〕。**2**. 三分之一(的)。**II** ***n***. **1**.〔the ～〕第三。**2**. 第三者〔指人〕。**3**. (时间或角度的)一秒的六十分之一。**4**.〔the ～〕(某月的)三日。**5**.〔*pl*.〕【法】归遗孀所有的亡夫遗产的三分之一。**6**.【乐】第三音;三度音程;三度和音。**7**. (汽车的)第三档(速度)。*one* ～ *of the total* 全体的三分之一。*two* ～*s* 三分之二。*No* ～ *ever joined our conferences*. 没有第三者曾参加我们的会议。*a major* ～【乐】大三度。*a* ～ *sex* 不男不女的人;搞同性关系的人;阉人。**III** ***ad***. 坐三等车(舱)。～ **age** 第三年龄〔指位于中年之后的老年〕。～ **base** (= the ～).【体】(棒球)第三垒。～**-class** ***a***. **1**. 三等,三级,三等品,三等舱。**2**.〔美〕三类邮件(书,广告信等)。～ **degree**〔美〕逼供,疲劳讯问;拷问。～**-degree burn**【医】三级烧伤。～ **dimension warfare** 立体战。～**-dimensional** ***a***. 第三维的,有深(厚)度的,栩栩如生的。～ **ear**〔美俚〕告密者。～ **estate** (法国革命前的)第三等级,平民等。～ **eyelid**【解】瞬膜。～ **floor**〔英〕四楼,〔美〕三楼。～ **force** 第三种力量;起平衡作用的力量。～ **house**〔美俚〕(国会的)第三院〔院外活动集团〕。**T- International** 第三国际。～ **kingdom**【生】第三界〔某些生物学家建议的一种分类界别,指不同于动、植物界,包括原始细菌在内的一类有机体〕。～ **market** 第三市场,证券市场。～ **party**【法】第三党。～ **person** 第三者;【语法】第三人称。～ **rail** 电动机车的输电轨;〔美俚〕酒。～**-rate** ***a***. 三等的,第三流的,低劣的,下等的。～**-rater** ***n***. 低等(下等)的人物。**T- Reich** 第三帝国〔1933—1945 年间希特勒统治下的德国〕。**T- Republic** 法兰西第三共和国(1870—1940)。**T- Sea Lord**〔英〕海军部第三把手副部长,海军军需长。～ **service** 航空。～ **stream**【乐】第三乐派〔将爵士音乐即兴技术与古典音乐技术结合起来的乐派〕。～ **ventricle**【解】第三脑室。**T- Wave** 第三次浪潮〔指信息技术的出现将掀起继农业革命和工业革命之后的第三次发展浪潮,系由美国未来学家 Alvin Toffler 提出〕。**T- World** 第三世界〔指亚、非、拉美的发展中国家〕。

third·ly [ˈθəːdli; ˋθɝdlɪ] ***ad***. 第三。

thirl [θəːl; θɝl] ***vt***., ***vi***.〔英方〕**1**. 钻孔,穿孔。**2**. = thrill.

thirst [θəːst; θɝst] **I** ***n***. **1**. 渴。**2**. 渴望,热望 (*after*; *for*; *of*)。**3**. (土地等的)干燥,干旱。**4**.〔口〕酒瘾,想喝酒。*have a* ～〔口〕想喝一杯。*feel* (*quench*, *relieve*, *slake*) ～ 感觉(止)渴。*awaken one's* ～ *for further study* 唤起某人作进一步研究的热望。**II** ***vi***. 渴望 (*after*; *for*);〔古〕渴。*All the students of our class* ～ *after knowledge* [*to learn*]. 我们班的所有的同学都渴望知识[学习]。

thirst·i·ly [ˈθəːstili; ˋθɝstɪlɪ] ***ad***. 口渴地;渴望着。

thirst·i·ness [ˈθəːstinis; ˋθɝstɪnɪs] ***n***. 渴;渴望;干旱。

thirst·y [ˈθəːsti; ˋθɝstɪ] ***a***. (***-i·er***; ***-i·est***) **1**. 口渴的。**2**. 耗油的。**3**. 渴望的 (*for*)。**4**. 干燥的,干旱的。**5**. 使人口渴的。*Young man should be* ～ *for knowledge*. 青年人应该渴望知识。

thir·teen [ˈθəːˈtiːn; θɝˋtin] ***num***., ***n***. (基数)十三,十三个;十三个人[东西];十三岁;十三的记号。*the* ～ *superstition* 以十三为不吉的迷信。

thir·teenth [ˈθəːˈtiːnθ; ˋθɝˋtinθ] ***num***., ***n***. 第十三;十三分之一(的);(月的)十三日。*a* ～ *juryman*〔美俚〕不公正的法官。**-ly** ***ad***.

thir·ti·eth [ˈθəːtiiθ; ˋθɝtɪɪθ] ***num***., ***n***. 第三十,三十分之一(的);(月的)三十日。

thir·tish [ˈθəːtiʃ; ˋθɝtɪʃ] ***a***. 三十岁的,三十岁左右的。

thir·ty [ˈθəːti; ˋθɝtɪ] **I** ***num***. (基数)三十,三十个(的)。**II** ***n***. 三十的记号;【网球】得两分时的称呼;〔*pl*.〕〔the ～〕三十多岁,〔*pl*. thirties〕三十年代;〔美新闻语〕完,终〔原稿末页记上"30",表示"完"〕;死。***in the nineteen thirties*** 在 20 世纪 30 年代〔略 in 1930's〕。***in nineteen*** ～ 在 1930 年。***in the thirties*** (年龄)三十多岁(的);在(某一世纪的)三十年代(的);(温度表)三十多度(的)。～ **cents**〔美〕不良的;劣质的。～**fold** ***a***., ***ad***. 三十倍的;成三十倍地。～**-second note**【乐】三十二分音符 (= demisemiquaver)。～ **something**〔美口〕三十多岁的人〔源自美国一部同名电视剧〕。～**-twomo** ***n***. (*pl*. ***-mos***)【印】三十二开本〔略 32mo〕;三十二开纸。

this [ðis; ðɪs] (*pl*. ***these***) **I** ***pro***.〔指示代词〕**1**. 这,这

T

个,这事,这人。2. 这时;这里。3. 下面所说的事,刚才(以上)所说的事。4. (前述二物中的)后者(*opp*. that 前者)。*What is all* ～? 这是怎么回事? *T- is Mr. Wang speaking*. 我是小王〔打电话用语〕。*T- is Mr. Smith*. 这位是史密斯先生。*It was Miss Mary* ～ *and Miss Mary that*. 这也是玛丽小姐那也是玛丽小姐〔风头十足〕。*Get out of* ～! (从这里)滚出去! *The reason is* ～. 理由是这样。*Of the two plans,* ～ *is perhaps more practical*. 两个计划中,后者比前者也许更切合实际一些。*T- is the latest news from the front*. 下面是前线报导的最新消息。**at** ～ 这里。**by** ～ 这时。**for all** ～ 尽管如此。**like** ～ 这样的;像这样。**put** ～ **and that together** 把二者综合起来(一想)。～ **here** [ˈereˈ]〔俚、方〕= this. ～, **that, and the other** 一切东西,种种东西[人]。**with** ～ 一面这样说(一面就…),说完这个(就…)。**II** *a*. 1. 这,这个。2. 今…,本…。3. 〔与表示时间的词组连用〕刚过去的,即将来到的。～ *fountain pen of yours* 你的这支自来水笔。～ *year* 今年。～ *month* 本月。～ *day month* 上一个月[下一个月]的今天。～ *morning* 早晨。～ *day* 今天。～ *time* 这次;这时候。**for** ～ **once** = **for** ～ **time** 只这一次。**to** ～ **day** 到今天。**III** *ad*. 就是这样,这样地。～ **early** 这样早。～ **high** (就)只这样高,到这样的高度。～ **much** 就只这些,到此为止。

thisa and thata [ˈðisə ænd ðətə; ˋðɪsəˏænd ðətə]〔美俚〕各种有趣的玩意儿。

this·ness [ˈðisnis; ˋðɪsnɪs] *n*.【哲】"此"性;现实性。

this·tle [ˈθisl; ˋθɪsl] *n*. 1.【植】蓟。2.〔英〕〔the T-〕蓟花勋位[勋章]。**grasp the** ～ **firmly** 毅然解决棘手局面。～ **digger**〔美〕土头土脑的人。～**down** 蓟的种子[冠毛];轻物。～ **finch** 金翅雀。

this·tly [ˈθisly; ˋθɪslɪ] *a*. 多蓟的,蓟繁茂的;像蓟的;有刺的,会刺的。

T

thith·er [ˈðiðə; ˋθɪðɚ, ˋðɪðɚ] **I** *ad*.〔古〕到那里,到那边。**II** *a*. 对过的,对岸的,那边的。*the* ～ *side of the stream* 河对岸。*on the* ～ *side of forty* 四十(岁)开外。**hither and** ～ 到处,向各处,忽此忽彼。～**to** *ad*. 直到那时。～**ward(s)** *ad*. 到那里,到那边。

thix·ot·ro·py [θikˈsɔtrəpi; θɪkˋsɑtrəpɪ] *n*.【医】触变性,摇溶(现象)。**-trop·ic** [-ˈtrɔpik; -ˋtrɑpɪk] *a*.

Th. M. = Master of Theology 神学硕士。

tho, tho' [ðəu, 弱 ðo; ðo] *ad*., *conj*. = though.

Tho. = Thomas.

thole[1] [θəul; θol] *vt*.〔英方,苏格兰〕1. 忍受,遭受(苦痛等)。2. 接受;允许。

thole[2] [θəul; θol] *n*. 桨座,桨架,桨脚;镰柄(= tholepin)。

Thom·as [ˈtɔməs; ˋtɑməs] *n*. 汤马斯〔姓氏,男子名〕。

Tho·mism [ˈtəumizəm, ˈθəu-; ˋtomɪzm, ˋθo-] *n*.【宗,哲】托马斯主义〔指托马斯阿奎那神学及其现代流派〕。**-mist** *n*., *a*. 托马斯主义者[的];托马斯神学的。**-mis·tic** *a*.

Thomp·son [ˈtɔmpsn; ˋtɑmpsn, ˋtɑmsn] *n*. 汤普森〔姓氏〕。

Thom·son [ˈtɔmsn; ˋtɑmsn] *n*. 汤姆森〔姓氏〕。

thong [θɔŋ; θɔŋ, θɑŋ] **I** *n*. 皮带,皮条,皮鞭,鞭梢。**II** *vt*. 装皮带;用皮带系结;用皮带(鞭)打。

Thon·ga [ˈθɔŋgə; ˋθɔŋgə] *n*. 1. (*pl*. **-gas, -ga**) 桑格人〔指莫桑比克农民〕。2. 桑格语〔属班图语〕。

Thor [θɔː; θɔr] *n*.【北欧神】雷神〔司雷雨、战争、农业〕。

tho·rac·ic [θɔːˈræsik; θoˋræsɪk] *a*.【解】胸(廓)的,胸部的。～ *cavity* 胸腔。～ *duct* 胸导管。

thoracico-, thorac(o)- *comb. f*.【医】胸,胸廓: *thoraco*plasty.

tho·ra·co·lum·bar [ˌθɔːrəkəuˈlʌmbə; θoˏrækoˋlʌmbɚ] *a*.【解】1. 胸腰部的。2. 交感神经的。

tho·ra·co·plas·ty [ˈθɔːrəkəuˌplæsti; ˋθorækoˏplæstɪ] *n*. (*pl*. **-ties**)【医】胸廓成形术。

tho·ra·cot·o·my [ˌθɔːrəˈkɔtəmi; ˏθorəˋkɑtəmɪ] *n*. (*pl*. **-mies**)【医】胸廓切开术。

tho·rax [ˈθɔːræks; ˋθoræks] *n*. (*pl*. **～es, thoraces** [θɔːˈreisiːz; θoˋresiz]) 1.【解】胸,胸腔,胸廓,胸部(昆虫体三部分的中间部分)。2.【古希腊】胸甲,胸板。

Tho·ra·zine [ˈθɔːrəˌziːn; ˋθorəˏzin] *n*.【药】氯丙嗪〔chlorpromazine 的商标名〕。

Thor·eau [ˈθɔːrəu; ˋθoro] *n*. 索罗〔姓氏〕。

tho·ri·a [ˈθɔːriə; ˋθorɪə] *n*.【化】氧化钍。

thori·a·nite [ˈθɔːriənait; ˋθorɪəˏnaɪt] *n*.【矿】方钍石〔含放射能〕。

tho·rite [ˈθɔːrait; ˋθoraɪt] *n*.【矿】钍石。

tho·ri·um [ˈθɔːriəm; ˋθorɪəm] *n*.【化】钍。

thorn [θɔːn; θɔrn] *n*. 1. 刺;荆棘。2.【动】壳针。3. 苦恼、忧虑的原因。4. 古代英语字母的 p (= th)。*Roses have* ～*s*. 玫瑰多刺,有快乐就有苦恼。*a* ～ *in one's side* [*flesh*] 不断使人苦恼的东西。**be** [**sit, stand, walk**] (**up**) **on** ～**s** 如坐针毡,焦虑不安。～ **forest** 热带旱生林。～ **apple**【植】1. 白花蔓陀罗。2. 山楂果。～**-back**【鱼】鳐鱼。～ **bush** 有刺灌木;刺丛。**-less** *a*. 无刺的。**-like** *a*. 像刺一样的。

Thorn·dike [ˈθɔːndaik; ˋθɔrnˏdaɪk] *n*. 桑代克〔姓氏〕。

Thorn·ton [ˈθɔːntən; ˋθɔrntn, -tən] *n*. 桑顿〔姓氏〕。

thorn·y [ˈθɔːni; ˋθɔrnɪ] *a*. (**-i·er**; **-i·est**) 1. 多刺的,有针的;像刺的。2. 刺丛繁茂的。3. 棘手的,困难多的;痛苦的。*a* ～ *path* 荆刺丛生的小路,难走的道路。*a* ～ *subject* 争论多的题目,难题。**-i·ly** *ad*.

thoro [ˈθʌrə; ˋθɝo, ˋθɝə] *a*., *ad*., *prep*., *n*.〔废〕= thorough.

thoron [ˈθɔːrɔn; ˋθorɑn] *n*.【化】钍射气(略 Tn)〔射气同位素,Em[220]〕。

thor·ough [ˈθʌrə; ˋθɝo, -ə] **I** *a*. 1. 彻底的,全面的,充分的,彻头彻尾的,根本的,详尽的,严密的。2. 绝对的,完善的。3. 非常精确的,(对细节)不厌其烦的。*a* ～ *reform* 彻底的改革。～ *investigation* 周密的调查。*a* ～ *rest* 绝对的安静。*a* ～ *description of the game* 对该球赛的详尽的描述。*be* ～ *in one's work* 工作严谨认真。*a* ～ *person* 一丝不苟的人。*a* ～ *insulator* 套管绝缘子。**II** *prep*., *ad*.〔古〕= through. **III** *n*.〔T-〕【英史】(如英王查理一世实行的)专横政策(= a policy of ～)。～**-bass**【乐】通奏低音(记谱法);和声法;和声学。～**-brace** 勒在马车车身下起弹簧作用的皮带。～**-bred** 1. *a*. 纯种的(动物);〔T-, t-〕纯种的(马犬等),精神奕奕的(人),受过严格训练的,优美的,第一流的,高尚的。2. *n*. 纯种动物;〔T-〕纯种马。3. 有教养的人,受过严格训练的人。4. 最好的车子(等)。～**fare** 通道,大街,大路(*opp*. *cul-de-sac*, private road);水路;通行(*No* ～ *fare*! 禁止通行!)。～**going** *a*. 完全的,彻底的,十足的。～**paced** *a*. 训练得十分好的(马等);完全的,彻底的,彻头彻尾的(坏蛋等)。～**pin** (马的)跗关节肿胀。～**-wort**【植】贯叶泽兰(= boneset)。

thorp(e) [θɔːp; θɔrp] *n*.〔古〕村庄。★现仅用于英国北部地名。

Thos. = Thomas.

those [ðəuz; ðoz] **I** *pro*.〔that 的复数〕那些东西[人];人们。*There are* ～ *who say* ... 也有说…的人们。**II** *a*. 那些。**in** ～ **days** 那时,当时。

Thoth [θəuθ, tənt; θoθ, tot] *n*. 古埃及的智慧和魔术的神〔鹭头人身〕。

thou[1] [ðau; ðaʊ] **I** *pro*. (*pl*. **ye**)〔人称代名词、第二人称、单数,主格;所有格为 thy 或 thine,宾格为 thee,物主代词为 thine〕〔古〕你,汝。★现仅用于祈祷、诗、方言(基督教公谊会教徒(Quakers)常用以代 you 但有时也用 thee 代)。**II** *vi*., *vt*. (不说 you 而)用 thou 称呼。

thou[2] [θau; ðaʊ] *n*.〔俚〕〔thousand 的缩语〕一千,〔英〕一千镑;〔美〕一千元。

though [ðəu, 弱 ðə; ðo, ðə] **I** *ad*. 可是,但是,然而,不过

还是;话虽这样说。*The grapes*, ~, *may be sour*. 可是,葡萄也许是酸的。*I wish you had told me*, ~. 话虽这样说,你告诉我就好了。*He said he would write to her*. *He didn't*, ~. 他说他要写信给她,可是,他没有写。*I've a bit of headache*. *It's nothing much*, ~. 我有一点头痛,不过并不厉害。**II** ***conj***. 虽然,虽则,尽管,即使,纵然。*T- it was late*, *we decided to set out*. 虽然已经晚了,我们还是决定动身了。*T- he was a professor* [*Professor* ~ *he was*], *he took an active part in politics*. 虽然他是个大学教授,他在政治上很活跃。***as*** ~ …恰如,好像。***even*** ~ 即使,纵然。***What*** ~ …? 即使…有什么要紧[关系]? 怕什么?

thought[1] [θɔːt; θɔt] ***n***. **1**. 思想。**2**. 思维;思考;推理能力,思想活动。**3**. 思潮,思想方式。**4**. 〔除否定外常 *pl*.〕(想做某事的)想法,意图,观念,意向,打算。**5**. 关心,挂念,忧虑,顾虑。**6**. 〔与不定冠词 a 连用作状语〕一点,些许,稍微。*What is the central* ~ *of this article*? 这篇文章的中心思想是什么? *Keep quiet*. *Father is deep in* ~. 安静些,爸爸在沉思。*Professor Wang is going to open a course in modern literary* ~. 王教授将开一门现代文艺思潮的课。*Don't keep your* ~*s to yourself*. 不要把你的想法闷在心里。*He never gives a* ~ *to his studies*. 他从来不把功课放在心上。*You are much in my* ~*s*. 我常常想念你。*Please be a* ~ *more straightforward*. 请稍许坦率一点。*I have* ~*s of singing*. 我想唱歌。*That's a happy* [*striking*] ~. 那是个好主意[好想法]。***after much*** [***serious***] ~ 仔细考虑后。***as quick as*** ~ 立刻,马上。***at the*** ~ ***of*** 一想到。***be lost*** [***sunk***, ***absorbed***, ***buried***] ***in*** ~ 在呆呆地默想。***bestow a*** ~ ***on*** = ***give a*** ~ ***to*** 考虑一下,想一想。***beyond*** ~ 意想不到的。***in*** ~ 左思右想。***on second*** ~***s*** 再次考虑后,重新考虑后。***take*** ~ 担忧,担心(*Take no* ~ *for the future*. 不要担心将来)。***two schools of*** ~ 〔美俚〕两个意见,两种可能。***upon*** [***with***] ***a*** ~ 立刻,马上。***without a moment's*** ~ 立刻,当场。***without*** ~ 不加考虑就…,贸然。~ **control** 思想控制。~ **disorder** 【医】思维障碍。~**-out** ***a***. 思虑周到的;经过仔细考虑的。~**-provoking** ***a***. 令人深思的,发人深省的。~**-reader** 读心术者;善于揣摩别人思想的人。~**-reading** 【心】测心术。~ **-stream** 【心】思想流。~ **transference** 【心】思想传递。~ **way** 思想方法。

thought[2] [θɔːt; θɔt] think 的过去式及过去分词。

thought·ful [ˈθɔːtful; ˋθɔtfəl] ***a***. **1**. 认真思考的,不轻率的;细心的,沉思的,若有所思的。**2**. 体贴人的,亲切的;对…关心的;对…忧虑的 (*of*)。**3**. 思想丰富的,富有思想的,经过认真考虑的,有创见的。*For about ten minutes*, *he didn't say anything and was* ~. 有十分钟的功夫,他没有讲话,在沉思着。*How* ~ *of you*! 考虑得真周到! ***be*** ~ ***of one's safety*** 关心[注意]自己的安全。***be*** ~ ***of others*** 考虑到[关心]别人。**-ly** ***ad***. **-ness** ***n***.

thought·less [ˈθɔːtlis; ˋθɔtlɪs] ***a***. **1**. 无思想的。**2**. 轻率的;粗心的,缺乏考虑的。**3**. 不体贴人的,自私的。*Maybe it's* ~ *of me*. 也许是我粗心了。*It's quite natural that a boy of nine is* ~ *of future*. 九岁的小孩子当然不会考虑到将来的事。**-ly** ***ad***. **-ness** ***n***.

thou·sand [ˈθauzənd; ˋθauznd] **I** ***a***. **1**. 千,千个的。**2**. 无数的,很多的。*a* ~ *times* 几千次;好多次,屡次。*a* ~ *times easier* 容易得多(一千倍)。*A* ~ *thanks* [*pardons*, *apologies*]. 万分感谢[对不起]。**(*a*)** ~ ***and one*** 无数的,很多很多的。***different in a*** ~ ***and one ways*** 千差万别。***for the*** ~ ***and first time*** 无数次,三番二次。***in the upper ten*** ~ 〔古、口〕属于上层贵族阶级。**II** ***n***., ***num***. **1**. 千,一千个[人,东西];千的记号。**2**. 〔*pl*.〕无数,许多。*a* ~ = *one* ~ 一千。*three* ~ 三千。*a hundred* ~ 十万。~*s of people* 数千人。***a*** ~ ***to one*** =〔口语〕***a*** ~ ***nuts to an orange pip*** 千对一,几乎绝对的。***by the*** ~ 论千,按千(出售等)。***by*** ~***s*** 好几千。***one in a*** ~ 千里挑一的人物,罕有[杰出]人物;例外。***tens of*** ~***s of men*** 几万人。~***s and tens of*** ~***s*** 千千万万。

thou·sand·fold [ˈθauzəndfəuld; ˋθauzṇd͵fold] **I** ***a***. 千倍的。**II** ***ad***. 成千倍。

thou·sandth [ˈθauzəndθ; ˋθauzṇdθ] ***n***. (*pl*. ~***s***), ***a***. 第一千(的);千分之一(的);微小的。

THQ = Theatre Headquarters 战区司令部。

thr = through.

Thra·cian [ˈθreiʃən; ˋθreʃən] **I** ***a***. 色雷斯〔巴尔干半岛东半部〕的,色雷斯人的。**II** ***n***. **1**. 色雷斯人。**2**. 色雷斯语〔现已灭绝,属印欧语系〕。

thral(l)·dom [ˈθrɔːldəm; ˋθrɔldəm] ***n***. 奴隶的身分[地位,状态];奴役;束缚。

thrall [θrɔːl; θrɔl] **I** ***n***. 奴隶 (*of*; *to*); 奴役;奴隶状态[地位];束缚,被束缚的身体。**II** ***a***. 〔古〕被奴役的,被束缚的;拘泥于…的;变成奴隶的 (*to*)。***in*** ~ 受奴役。***in*** ~ ***to*** 被…束缚着;拘泥于…。*We wouldn't allow you to make yourself a* ~ *to such an evil person as James*. 我们不会听任你给像詹姆士那样的坏人当奴隶的。*At the concert*, *I was held in* ~ *by the music*. 在音乐会上,我让音乐给迷住了。**III** ***vt***. 使成奴隶;迷惑住;使神魂颠倒 (*to*)。**-dom** ***n***. = thral(l)dom.

thrash [θræʃ; θræʃ] **I** ***vt***. **1**. 打(谷),使脱粒。**2**. (用棍、鞭等)痛打;猛烈摆动。**3**. 〔美口,运〕击败,胜过。**4**. 反复进行;千锤百炼;仔细研讨,搞清楚 (*out*)。**5**. 【海】使(船)逆风破浪前进。*Let's* ~ *the matter over before putting it on the agenda*. 这件事我们要反复研究之后再把它列入议事日程。*It's time to* ~ *out all the problems*. 是把所有的问题都搞得一清二楚的时候了。—***vi***. **1**. 打谷,打禾,脱粒;打,击。**2**. 翻来覆去;东撞西碰;(腿脚)乱跌;(手臂)乱挥。**3**. 逆风前进。*The patient* ~*ed about with pain*. 病人痛得直翻腾。**II** ***n***. 打击;击败;【泳】(自由式用脚、手)打水。

thrash·er [ˈθræʃə; ˋθræʃɚ] ***n***. **1**. 打谷者;打谷机,脱粒机。**2**. 【鱼】长尾鲨鱼。**3**. 〔美〕美洲一种鸫属鸣禽。*brown* ~ 【动】褐噪鸫。

thrash·ing [ˈθræʃiŋ; ˋθræʃɪŋ] ***n***. 脱粒,打谷;鞭打,笞打。~ **floor** 打谷场。~ **machine** 打谷机。

thra·son·i·cal [θrəˈsɔnikəl; θreˋsɑnɪkḷ] ***a***. 自负的,夸口的。

thrawn [θrɔːn; θrɔn] ***a***. 〔Scot〕**1**. 弯曲的,扭弯的。**2**. 倔强的,邪恶的,不法的,不正当的,违反常情的,任性的。

thread [θred; θrɛd] **I** ***n***. **1**. 线;细丝;〔英〕麻纱,〔美〕棉纱;纤维。**2**. 细线,细流,细矿脉。**3**. (议论等的)思路,条理,线索,情节;【计】(公告板上讨论的)话题,题材。**4**. 螺齿,螺丝。**5**. 〔*pl*.〕〔美〕衣服。*a piece of* ~ 一根线。*a* ~ *of light* 细细的一线亮光。*the* ~ *of one's argument* 争办的头绪。***be worn to a*** ~ (衣服由于长久地穿着)磨得快要破烂。***cut one's mortal*** ~ 割断命脉,自杀。***gather up the*** ~***s*** 综合(分别处理的问题、部分等)。***hang by*** [(***up***) ***on***] ***a*** ~ 朝不保夕;千钧一发。***have not a dry*** ~ ***on one*** 浑身湿透。***resume*** [***pick up***, ***take up***] ***the*** ~ ***of a story*** (回到正题)言归正传。~ ***and thrum*** (好好歹歹)扫数,尽都,全都。~ ***of life*** 生命线,命脉,生命。**II** ***vt***. **1**. 穿线(入针眼等);拿线穿(珠粒等)。**2**. 为照相机装胶片。**3**. 穿过,挤过。**4**. 车螺纹。~ *a camera* 为照相机装胶片。~ *a needle* 穿针。~ *one's way through the crowd* 穿过人丛。*a* ~*ed mandrel* 【机】螺纹心轴。— ***vi***. **1**. 通过,穿透过。**2**. (糖浆等)滴下成丝状。*They* ~*ed carefully along the narrow pass*. 他们沿着狭窄的小路小心翼翼地鱼贯而行。~**bare** ***a***. (衣服由于长久穿着而)露出底子的织线的;破旧的;陈腐的,陈旧的(议论等)。~**fin** 【动】马鲅科的鱼。~ **lace** 织线花边。~**like** 细长的。~ **mark** (纸币纸上的)彩色丝纹。~**-needle** 穿线游戏〔大家拉手排成一

T

行,由一头的人挨次穿过另一头的两人间〕。～ **paper** **1.** 裹线束的纸条。**2.** 瘦子,细长的人。～**worm**【动】蛲虫(= pinworm)。

thread·y [ˈθredi; ˋθrɛdɪ] *a*. **1.** 线(做)的,纤维(或丝状物)构成的。**2.** 线状的,丝状的。**3.** 纤细的;微弱的(脉搏)。**4.** 能形成一丝一丝的。**-i·ness** *n*.

threap [θriːp; θrip] *vt*. **1.** 责骂,吵架。**2.** 顽固地坚持,执拗。

threat [θret; θrɛt] **I** *n*. **1.** 恐吓,威吓,威胁。**2.** 凶兆,(…的)样子,(…的)危险。*There is a* ～ *of rain*. 像要下雨。*The* ～ *of flood has been relieved*. 洪水的威胁解除了。*I won't be intimidated by a* ～ *against my life*. 对生命的威胁是吓不倒我的。**II** *vt*., *vi*.〔古、方〕= threaten.

threat·en [ˈθretn; ˋθrɛtn] *vt*. **1.** 恐吓,恫吓,威胁。**2.** 预示凶兆,有…的危险。— *vi*. 像要发生;快要来临。*It will greatly* ～ *the security of this country*. 它将会极大地威胁本国的安全。～ *him with death* 用死威胁他。*The company is* ～*ed with bankruptcy*. 这家公司有破产的危险。*Do you mean to* ～? 你是想恫吓吗? *It* ～*s to rain*. 好像就要下雨了。★用于"威胁某人"的含义,threaten 主要意在通过威胁达到威胁者的目的;menace 除有书面语的意味外,侧重威胁者是怀有敌意的。**-ed** *a*. **1.** 受到威胁的。**2.** (某些野生动、植物品种)濒危的,濒临灭绝危险的。**-er** *n*.

threat·en·ing [ˈθretəniŋ; ˋθrɛtənɪŋ] *a*. 恐吓的,威胁的;危险的,险恶的。**-ly** *ad*.

three [θriː; θri] **I** *num*. (基数)三,三个;第三(章、页等)。～ *days of grace*【法】三天内付款的宽限期。～ *foot three* 三英尺三英寸。*the* ～ *C's*〔美〕三大产物〔Copper, Corn 及 Cotton〕。*the* ～ *K's*〔英〕国王、宪法、教会。*the* ～ *L's*【海】了望、测铅、纬度 (= Look-out, Lead and Latitude)。*a* ～ *Op. packet*【海】有三名无线电通讯员的客船。～ *parts* 四分之三;大部分;八九成,几乎。～ *quarters* 四分之三;九个月〔一年的四分之三〕。～ *services* 三军〔海陆空军〕。*give sb*. ～ *cheers* [～ *times* ～] 对某人欢呼三次[九次]。**II** *n*. **1.** 三个人[东西]。**2.** 三岁,三时。**3.**【板球】3字型。～ ***and six***〔英〕三先令六便士〔3s. 6d.〕。～ ***ten***〔英〕三镑十先令〔£3 10s.〕。*a child of* ～ 三岁的孩子。*the One in T- = the T- in One*【宗】(上帝的)三位一体。***by*** [***in***] ～*s* = ～ ***by*** ～ 每三个(人);三个三个地。～**-address** *a*.【计】三地址的。～**-axis** *a*. 三轴的,三自由度的。～**-bagger**〔棒球俚〕三垒打(= three-base hit)。～**-body** *a*.【数,物】三体的。～**-bottle** *a*. 能一次喝三瓶葡萄酒的,酒量大的。～**-colo(u)r** *a*. 三色的(～*colour process* 三(原)色版印刷[照相]术。～*colour printing* 三色版)。～**-corner** *a*. 三棱的。～**-cornered** *a*. 三角的;由三个竞争者形成的(～*-corner relation* 三角关系)。～**-D** (= ～ dimensions) *n*., *a*. 三维(的),三度空间(的);【影】立体电影。～**-decker** (从前的)三层甲板都装有炮的军舰;三层楼房;三卷本小说(或书),三层夹心面包。～**fold** **1.** *a*. 三倍的,三重的。**2.** *ad*. 成三倍,成三重。～**half-pence** 一便士半[1½d.]。～**-handed** *a*. 三只手的;(游戏)三人玩的。～ **handkerchief**〔美俚〕(引人落泪不止的)伤感剧。～**-in-one**【宗】三位一体。～ **k's** 脏、难、险的低薪工种〔源自日语〕。～**-lane** *a*. (道路)三车道的。～**-legged** *a*. 有三条腿的(～*legged race* 二人三脚竞走)。～**-martini lunch** 丰盛午餐。～**-master** 三桅船;〔特指〕三桅纵帆船。～**-mile limit**【法】(沿岸三海里内的)领海。～**-monthly** *a*., *n*. 三个月出版一次的;季刊。～**-pair**〔英〕四层楼上的房间;住在四楼的人。～**-peat** *n*., *vi*. (赢得)三连冠。～ **pence** [ˈθrepəns, ˈθrip-; ˋθrɛpəns, ˋθrɪp-] 三便士硬币;三便士(金额)。～**penny** [ˈθrepəni, ˈθrip-; ˋθrɛpənɪ, ˋθrɪp-] *a*. 三便士的;不足道的,廉价的(*a* ～*-penny bit* [*piece*] 三便士硬币)。～**-percent** **1.** *a*. 百分之三的;利息三厘的。**2.** *n*.〔*pl*.〕〔英〕三厘公债。～**-phase** *a*.【电】三相的。～**-piece** *a*. 三件一套的(西服)。～**-pile** *a*., *n*. 有三层绒毛的(毛毯),特级毛毯。～**-ply** **1.** *a*. 三重的,三股头的(线等)。**2.** *n*. 三夹板,三合板。～**-pointer**〔军俚〕**1.** = ～-point landing. **2.** 绝对正确的事物。～**-point landing**【空】主轮尾轮三轮同时着陆法。～**-quarter**, ～**-quarters** **1.** *a*. 四分之三的;【摄】大半身的;脸的四分之三的〔正面与侧面之间〕。**2.** 四分之三;【橄榄球】(half-back 和 full-back 之间的)中后卫〔threequarter back 之略〕。～**-ring circus** 三个场地可同时表演的大马戏场;热闹的场面[演出](*Their family reunions are always* ～*-ring circuses*. 他们全家团聚的场面热闹非凡)。～ **R's** **1.** 读,写,算。**2.** 基本功,基础知识;要害。～**score** *n*., *a*. 六十(的),六十岁(的)。～**-seater** 三人座(的飞机、汽车等)。～**some**【高尔夫球】三人比赛;〔美俚〕三个一组,三个一队。～**-square** *a*. 截面成等边三角形的。～**-star** *a*. (美军将官)三星级的(*a* ～*-star general* 中将)。～**-thirty**〔美军俚〕限制活动三个月并罚款三十元的惩罚。～**-two**〔美俚〕啤酒。～**-way** *a*. 三向的;三路的。～**-wheeler** 三轮汽车[摩托车]。

3W = World Wide Wet【计】万维网。

threm·ma·tol·o·gy [ˌθreməˈtɔlədʒi; ˏθrɛməˋtɑlədʒɪ] *n*. 动植物养育学,饲育学。*plant* ～ 育种学。

thre·net·ic, -i·cal [θriˈnetik, -ikəl; θrɪˋnɛtɪk, -ɪkl̩] *a*. 悲哀的,哀悼的,哀歌的。

thre·no·de, thre·no·dy [ˈθriːnəud, -nədi; ˋθrinod, ˋθrɛnod, -nədɪ] *n*. **1.** 悲歌,哀歌;挽歌。**2.** 悲哀,哀悼。**-nod·ic, -i·cal** *a*. **-ist** *n*.

thre·o·nine [ˈθriːəni(ː)n; ˋθriəˏnin, -nɪn] *n*.【生化】苏氨[胺]酸。

threp·sol·o·gy [θrepˈsɔlədʒi; θrɛpˋsɑlədʒɪ] *n*. 营养学。

thresh [θreʃ; θrɛʃ] **I** *vt*., *vi*. = thrash. **II** *n*. 脱粒。～***ing floor*** 打谷场,脱粒场。～***ing machine*** 打谷机,脱粒机。**-er** *n*. **1.** 打谷机,脱粒机,打谷者。**2.**【动】长尾鲨。

thresh·old [ˈθreʃhəuld; ˋθrɛʃold, ˋθrɛʃhold] *n*. **1.** 门槛;入口,门口。**2.**【心】阈限。**3.** 界限,限度。**4.**【物】临界值,阈。**5.** 入门,开始,开端。*Seniors of the* ～ *of the diplomatic career are expected to take this course*. 希望即将从事外交工作的四年级生选修本课程。***at the*** ～ ***of*** 在…的开始,就要开始的时候。***cross sb.'s*** ～ 走进某人家里。***cross the*** ～ 跨进门内。***on the*** ～ 在门口。***on the*** ～ ***of*** 在…的开头,就要…。～ **of consciousness**【心】识阈。

threw [θruː; θru] throw 的过去式。

thrice [θrais; θraɪs] *ad*. **1.** 三次,三度,三倍。**2.** 屡次,再三;十分,非常。～ *blessed* [*happy*, *-favo*(*u*)*red*] 极幸福的。

thrid [θrid; θrɪd] *vt*. (**-dd-**)〔古、方〕= thread;〔特指〕穿过。

thrift [θrift; θrɪft] *n*. **1.** 节约,节俭。**2.** 兴旺,繁荣;健壮。**3.**〔Scot.〕繁荣的手段,工作,劳动,(植物的)繁茂,有利可图的职业。**4.**【植】海石竹。*To practice* ～ *is a virtue*. 节俭是美德。～ **shop** 节俭商店〔出售人们丢弃的旧衣着什物,尤指将出售所得用于慈善目的〕。

thrift·less [ˈθriftlis; ˋθrɪftlɪs] *a*. **1.** 不节俭的,浪费的。**2.** 不兴旺的。**3.** 不健壮的,不繁茂的。**4.** 无价值的。**-ly** *ad*. **-ness** *n*.

thrift·y [ˈθrifti; ˋθrɪftɪ] *a*. (*-i·er*; *-i·est*) **1.** 节约的,俭省的。**2.** 兴旺的,繁茂的,健壮的,繁荣的。*We will bring in a measure to be* ～ *with raw materials*. 我们要提出一项节约原材料的措施。**-i·ly** *ad*. **-i·ness** *n*.

thrill [θril; θrɪl] **I** *n*. **1.** 一阵毛骨悚然的感觉,一阵激动的感觉;(由于恐怖或快感的)紧张感。**2.** 战栗,发抖,震颤,颤动。**3.** 心跳,脉搏;【医】(心脏的)震颤(音)。**4.** (电影,电视剧,小说的)刺激性,紧张感。**5.** 惊险小说 (= thriller)。*We got* (*felt*, *experienced*) *a* ～ *of surprised pleasure out of the mountain-climbing*. 在那次

爬山中我们感觉到一种意想不到的快乐。*The news sent a ～ of joy to my heart*. 这消息使我心中感到一阵激动的欢乐。*a ～ killing* 一宗单纯为追求刺激而杀人的案子。**II** *vt*. **1.** 使毛骨悚然,使紧张,使激动,使心里怦怦地跳;使热血沸腾。**2.** 使颤动,使发抖,使震颤。— *vi*. **1.** 受激动,心里怦怦地跳。**2.** 颤动,发抖(*with*)。**3.** (感情等)闪过(*along*; *through*; *over*)。*Little Tom was so ～ed at going to the movie*. 小汤姆去看电影是那么地激动。*His voice ～s with terror*. 他恐怖得声音发抖。*Fear ～ed through my veins*. 我毛骨悚然地感到一阵害怕。

thrill·er [ˈθrilə; ˋθrɪlɚ] *n*. 〔口〕使人激动的东西[人物];使毛骨悚然[战栗]的东西;〔特指〕惊险小说[电影,戏剧]。

thrill·ing [ˈθriliŋ; ˋθrɪlɪŋ] *a*. **1.** 毛骨悚然的;惊心动魄的,动人的,使人激动的。**2.** 颤动的,抖动的。**3.** 刺骨的。"*How ～!*", *he cried*. 他大声说道,"多么令人激动啊!" *Put on your overcoat. The wind's ～*. 寒风刺骨,穿上你的大衣。**-ly** *ad*.

thrips [θrips; θrɪps] *n*. 【虫】蓟马〔谷类害虫〕。

thrive [θraiv; θraɪv] *vi*. (**throve** [θrəuv; θrov], 〔罕〕**thrived** [θrivd; θrɪvd]; **thriven** [ˈθrivən; ˋθrɪvən] 〔罕〕**thrived**) **1.** 兴旺,繁荣;成功;致富。**2.** 茁壮成长,(动物)上膘,发胖,(植物)繁茂,蔓延。*The markets is ～ing*. 市场繁荣。*Tropical plants ～ in a greenhouse*. 热带植物在温室里茁壮生长。

thriv·en [ˈθrivən; ˋθrɪvən] thrive 的过去分词。

thro', thro [θruː; θru] *prep*., *ad*., *a*. 〔美〕= through.

throat [θrəut; θrot] **I** *n*. **1.** 【解】咽喉,喉咙;喉头;颈前。**2.** 嗓子,嗓音。**3.** (器物的)咽喉状部分;窄路,出入口。**4.** 【火箭】(喷管的)临界截面。～ *latch* 〔美俚〕喉(头);会厌;(马笼头上的)喉勒。*a sore ～* 咽喉炎[痛]。*a clergyman's sore ～* 慢性喉炎。*a ～ of brass* 尖锐的嗓音。***at the top of one's ～*** 尽量放大嗓子。***clear one's ～*** (说话前)清嗓子。***cut one another's ～s*** 采取两败俱伤的政策,相互残杀。***cut one's (own) ～*** 抹脖子,自刎;自招灭亡。***cut the ～ of*** 杀死;使灭亡。***fly at sb.'s ～*** **1.** (狗等)扑向某人。**2.** 攻击,袭击。***full (up) to the ～*** 吃得很饱。***give sb. the lie in his ～*** 面责某人说谎,揭破谎话。***have a bone in one's ～*** 难于启齿。***jump down sb.'s ～*** 〔美俚〕突然反唇回击,打断某人讲话,使某人无话可说,突然猛烈攻击[批评]。***lie in one's ～*** 扯大谎。***pour [send] down the ～*** 把(金钱等)花在饮食上;喝酒。***stick in one's ～*** 骨梗在喉;(话)要说说不出。***take [catch, have, hold, seize] by the ～*** 扼住喉咙。***thrust [cram, force, push, ram] sth. down sb.'s ～*** 逼人接受[向人强行灌输](意见等)。**II** *vt*. **1.** 用喉音说唱,沙哑地说唱。**2.** 掘(沟);开槽。～ **lozenge** 【药】润喉片。～ **microphone**, ～ **mike** 喉式传声器。

throat·y [ˈθrəuti; ˋθrotɪ] *a*. (*-i·er*; *-i·est*) **1.** (声音)喉部发出的。**2.** 喉音的,嘎声的,沙哑的。**-i·ly** *ad*. **-i·ness** *n*. 嗓音沙哑;粗声粗气。

throb [θrɔb; θrɑb] **I** *n*. **1.** (心等的)跳动,悸动,搏动。**2.** (有规律的)颤动。**II** *vi*. (**throbbed**; **throb·bing**) (心脏,脉搏等的)跳动,悸动,抽动,(有规律地)颤动;激动;(轮船)噗噗地颤动。*My heart is ～bing violently*. 我的心在剧烈地跳动着。*Being a rural district 15 years ago, the city is now ～bing with the pulse of modern industry*. 这个城十五年前还是个农业地区,现在有了现代工业在顺利地活跃着。**～bing** *a*. 跳动的;抽动的;震动的。**～bing·ly** *ad*.

throe [θrəu; θro] **I** *n*. **1.** 〔常 *pl*.〕剧痛,痛苦,苦闷;死亡前的挣扎。**2.** 〔*pl*.〕(分娩时的)产痛,阵痛;(新事物等)产生前的挣扎[困难]。*the ～ of composition* 创作的阵痛[构思的艰苦]。***in the ～s of...*** 在产生…之前的挣扎中。**II** *vi*. 非常受痛苦,苦闷。

Throg·mor·ton Street [θrɔgˈmɔːtən; θrɑgˋmɔrtən] *n*. 盔街〔伦敦商业中心〕;伦敦股票交易所;〔集合词〕伦敦股票交易(经纪人);股票市场。

throm·bin [ˈθrɔmbin; ˋθrɑmbɪn] *n*. 【生化】凝血酶。

throm·bo·cyte [ˈθrɔmbəˌsait; ˋθrɑmbəˏsaɪt] *n*. 【医】血小板,凝血细胞(= plateler)。**-cyt·ic** [-ˈsitik; -ˋsɪtɪk] *a*.

throm·bo·em·bo·lism [ˌθrɔmbəuˈembəlizm; ˏθrɑmboˋɛmbəlɪzm̩] *n*. 【医】血栓栓塞。

throm·bo·gen [ˈθrɔmbədʒən, -ˌdʒen; ˋθrɑmbədʒən, -ˏdʒen] *n*. 【医】凝血酶原(= prothrombin)。

throm·bo·ki·nase [ˌθrɔmbəuˈkaineis, -ˈkineis; ˏθrɑmbəˋkaɪnes, -ˋkɪnes] *n*. 【医】凝血(酶)致活酶(= thromboplastin)。

throm·bo·pe·ni·a [ˌθrɔmbəuˈpiːniə; ˏθrɑmboˋpinɪə] *n*. 【医】凝血酶减少症。

throm·bo·phle·bi·tis [ˌθrɔmbəufliˈbaitis; ˏθrɑmboflɪˋbaɪtɪs] *n*. 【医】血栓(性)静脉炎。

throm·bo·plastic [ˌθrɔmbəuˈplæstik; ˏθrɑmboˋplæstɪk] *a*. **1.** 血栓形成的。**2.** 凝血的。**-cal·ly** *ad*.

throm·bo·plas·tin [ˌθrɔmbəuˈplæstin; ˏθrɑmbəˋplæstɪn] *n*. 凝血激酶;【药】(止血的)凝血质。

throm·bo·sis [ˌθrɔmˈbəusis; θrɑmˋbosɪs] *n*. 【医】血栓形成。

throm·bot·ic [θrɔmˈbɔtik; θrɑmˋbɑtɪk] *a*. 血栓形成的。

thrombus [ˈθrɔmbəs; ˋθrɑmbəs] *n*. 【医】血栓。

throne [θrəun; θron] **I** *n*. **1.** (帝王的)宝座;王[帝]位;王权。**2.** 国王,皇帝。**3.** 教皇座,主教座;教皇[主教]的地位。**4.** 【宗】〔T-〕〔*pl*.〕九级天使中的第三级。***come to [mount] the ～*** 即位。**II** *vt*. 〔诗〕使即王位,使登基。～**room** (设有宝座的)正式观见室;权势的所在地方[中枢]。

throng [θrɔŋ; θrɔŋ] **I** *n*. **1.** 大群;人群;一大群人。**2.** 事务纷集[紧迫]。**3.** 众多,大量。*a ～ of people* 一大群人。*He was ～ed by the multitude*. 他被一大群人所包围。*On the square there was a wildly cheering ～*. 广场上有一大群欢呼雷动的人群。**II** *vi*., *vt*. 群集,拥塞,挤满(*about*; *round*);蜂拥而至。*These thoughts ～ed on my mind*. 这些想法纷然地杂集在我的心头之上;(我)浮想联翩。

thros·tle [ˈθrɔsl; ˋθrɑsl̩] *n*. **1.** 【鸟】画眉 = song thrush. **2.** 【纺】翼锭精纺机〔又叫 ～-frame〕。

throt·tle [ˈθrɔtl; ˋθrɑtl̩] **I** *n*. **1.** 〔方〕喉咙,气管。**2.** 【机】风门,节气阀,节流阀〔又叫 ～ valve〕;风门杆,节流杆〔又叫 ～ lever〕。**3.** 【无】扼流圈。***at full ～*** = ***with the ～ against the stop*** 全速地,开足马力。**II** *vt*. **1.** 掐喉咙,扼杀,缢死,使窒息。**2.** 压制,抑压,抑制(讨论、贸易等)。**3.** 【机】(用节汽阀等)调节;使节流;使减速。— *vi*. **1.** 窒息。**2.** 【机】节流,减速。*High tariffs ～ trade between nations*. 高的关税抑制着国与国之间的贸易。～**hold** 扼杀;压制,抑制。～ **jockey** 〔俚〕(船舶的)引航员;(飞机等的)驾驶员。

through [θruː; θru] **I** *prep*. **1.** 通过,穿过,贯穿。**2.** 从(洞孔等)中间,透过。**3.** 〔时间〕从…的开始到末了,从头到尾;〔场所〕到处,全面。**4.** 〔指方法、手段等〕经由,通过,以…。**5.** 〔指原因、理由〕由于,因为;多亏。**6.** 做完,用尽。*The river flows ～ the city*. 这条河贯穿这个城。*May I ～ you ask the delegate of ... to ...* 可否通过你代为请求某代表…。*The sun breaks ～ the clouds*. 日光从云缝中穿漏出来。～ *the winter* 整个冬天,一冬。～ *life* 一生中,毕生。～ *long years* 长年间。*be famous ～ the world* 闻名全世界。*go ～ an operation* 做完手术。*go ～ college* 修完大学课程。*pass ～ crisis [tribulation]* 度过危机[历尽千辛万苦]。～ *carelessness* 由于疏忽。*to fulfill the task ～ your help* 完成任务多亏你帮忙。***be on display ～ April 30***

T

展览至四月三十日截止。*be ~ one's task* 做完工作[课题]。*see ~ a brick wall* [*a millstone*] 能透过一道砖墙看见;〔转义〕眼光敏锐(*One can't see ~ a brick wall*. 不可能的事情就是不可能)。~ ***all ages*** 永远。~ ***the cabin window*** (海军军官)靠人情升官。~ ***the hawse-pipe*** 水兵升成军官。~ ***thick and thin*** 遍历艰苦。***unity ~ struggle*** 以奋斗求团结。**II** ***ad***. **1**. 穿过,通过,经历;从头到尾,完全,全部;到最后,到底,彻底;透;完毕。**2**. 出来。*pierce a thing ~* 刺穿一件东西。*come ~* 〔美俚〕取得成功;取胜。*all the night ~* 通宵,彻夜。*read the book ~* 将书看完。*This train goes ~ to New York*. 这一列车直达纽约。*Is he ~?* 〔口〕他(考试)及格了吗? *I am ~ now*. 〔口〕我已经做好了。*The enemy is trying to break ~*. 敌人企图突围。***all ~*** 一直,从来就。***be ~ with*** 〔口〕做好(工作等);和…绝交;和…分手(*I am ~ with that fellow*. 我和那个家伙断绝关系了)。~ ***and ~*** 完完全全;彻头彻尾(*wet ~ and ~* 浑身湿透)。**III** ***a***. **1**. 直通的,直达的。**2**. (道路)可以通行的。**3**. 穿过的,有洞的。**4**. 〔英〕(电话)接通;〔美〕通话完毕。*a ~ street* 直通街道,干道。~ *transport by land and water* 水陆联运。*a ~ ticket* 联运票,全程票。*a ~ train* 直达车。*Jack's trousers are ~ at the knees*. 杰克的裤子膝盖处破了洞了。*You are ~*. 你要的电话接通了。*He is almost ~*. 他的电话快打完了。~ **bolt**【机】贯穿螺栓。~ **cock**【机】直旋塞。~**-put** 生产量[能力],生产率;通过量;容许能力。~**-station** 中间站。~**-stone**【建】系石。~**way**〔美〕(=expressway) **1**. 高速公路。**2**. 直通街道。

through·ly [ˈθruːli; ˋθrulɪ] ***ad***. 〔古、圣〕=thoroughly.

through·out [θruːˈaut; θruˋaʊt] **I** ***prep***. 从一头贯通到另一头;从头贯穿到底;完完全全;从头到尾;自始至终;到处,全面,彻头彻尾。~ *the day* 终日,整天。~ *one's life* 毕生,整个一生中。~ *the country* 全国。**II** ***ad***. 任何部分,任何地方,到处;全部;彻头彻尾;自始至终。*The house is well built ~*. 这房子整个儿都造得好。*be of one piece ~* 完全一样。

throve [θrəuv; θrov] thrive 的过去式。

throw [θrəu; θro] **I** ***vt***. (***threw*** [θruː; θru]; ***thrown*** [θrəun; θron]) **1**. 扔,抛,投,摔,掷,丢。**2**. 摔倒,使翻倒;(将船等)冲上(暗礁等);(马)把…摔下来。**3**. 匆匆穿上或披上(大衣等)(*on*; *over*);匆匆脱掉(*off*);(蛇)蜕(皮)。**4**. 伸(四肢),挺(胸)仰(首),挥(拳)。**5**. 使挨(骂等)。**6**. 丢弃,放弃;摆脱;发出,射出(光线等);发射(炮弹等)。**7**. 出(纸牌),掷(骰子)。**8**. (家畜)产仔。**9**. 捻(生丝);旋制陶坯。**10**. 突然变动(身体的一部分姿势);转动,推动,打开,关闭(离合器等机件)。**11**. 推(入某状态),使陷于,使…化。**12**. 〔美〕故意输掉(比赛等)。**13**. 〔俚〕开办,举行(舞会等)。

—***vi***. 扔,摔,投,掷 (*at*);投球,扔球;掷骰子。*Who threw a stone over the fence?* 是谁把块石头扔过篱笆的? *At last I threw Tony to the ground*. 我终于把汤尼摔倒在地上。*Knowing it was late, he threw on his overcoat and went to school*. 他晓得晚了,匆忙地穿上大衣上学去了。*Take care! Fish is able to ~ the hook*. 当心! 鱼儿是能挣脱鱼钩的。*The engineer's advice threw light on the scheme*. 工程师的意见有助于我们对计划的理解。*You'll have to ~ your chests out when marching in parade*. 在游行时要挺起胸来。*The door was thrown open*. 门突然大开。*The country has been thrown into an upheaval*. 这个国家已经陷入动乱之中。*Don't ~ off your own responsibility*. 不要把你的职责卸脱了。*This kind of watch has been thrown out of the market*. 这种表已被排挤出市场外了。*The ship was thrown on the coast*. 那艘船被(浪)打到岸上去了。***be thrown into confusion*** 陷入混乱。~ ***a fit*** 〔美〕狂怒。~ ***a monkey wrench into the transmission*** 〔美俚〕妨碍;干涉;破坏。~ ***a party*** 〔美口〕举行舞会。~ ***sb. into the shade*** 使相形见绌。~ ***a scare into*** 〔美〕威胁;吓坏。~ ***a veil over*** 掩蔽,遮蔽,隐藏。~ ***a vote*** 投票。~ ***about*** 到处抛扔;挥舞(手臂);使…回转(~ *money about* 挥金如土。~ *one's arms about* 挥舞手臂)。~ ***away*** 抛弃;白费,浪费(*upon*);拒绝(劝告);失去(机会)(*Kindness is thrown away upon him*. 对他好是白费)。~ ***back*** **1**. 使后退,拒绝。**2**. 反射。**3**. 拉回,阻止。**4**.【遗传】呈返祖现象。~ ***by*** 废弃,抛弃。~ ***cold water on*** 泼冷水,打击别人的热情。~ ***down*** **1**. 摔倒,打倒,推翻,拆毁。**2**. 扔下,贬;使沉淀;〔俚〕拒绝(~ *down one's arms* 放下武器,投降,屈服。~ *down one's brief* (律师)拒绝接受案件。~ *down one's tools* 丢下工具罢工)。~ ***for large stakes*** 下大注。~ ***good money after bad*** 想捞回损失而损失更大。~ ***in*** **1**. 投入,扔进。**2**. 发边界球。**3**. 注入;插入;使(齿轮等)咬合,接合;【电】接通;添加(~ *in a word* 插嘴)。~ ***in one's hand*** 丢弃(不要的牌);(从争执中)抽身。~ ***into*** 使热烈从事,使投身于,使专门从事。~ ***into shape*** 使具雏形;整理。~ ***into the bargain*** 添加,再加。~ ***it with*** 〔美〕和某人合伙做。~ ***light on*** (*a matter*) 说明,弄明白。~ ***off*** **1**. 抛弃,丢弃。**2**. 脱掉(衣服)。**3**. 摆脱(习惯、拘束等)。**4**. 切断(电路等)。**5**. 推翻。**6**. 一气写成,即席作成(诗等)。**7**. 甩掉,脱离(追踪者等)。**8**. 开始,(猎狗)开始出猎,跳出,咬起来。~ ***sb. off his guard*** 使(某人)不留心。~ ***oneself at the head of*** 公然表示亲热[指女性对男性];(不得体地)竭力讨好。~ ***oneself down*** 躺下。~ ***oneself into*** 开始热心做(某事),起劲地投身于某事(*You must ~ yourself eagerly into the work*. 你必须热诚地、竭力地投入工作)。~ ***oneself into the arms of*** 投入…怀抱;成为…的妻子。~ ***oneself*** (***up***)***on*** 依靠;求助于;完全依赖于;猛扑,突袭。~ ***one's hat into the ring*** 〔美俚〕加入比赛,参加竞争。~ ***open*** 推开;猛然打开;开放(*to*)(~ *open the door to* 使…成为可能,打开…的门路)。~ ***out*** **1**. 投出,扔出。**2**. 派出。**3**. 突出。**4**. 增建(侧房)。**5**. 发出(热、光等)。**6**. 萌(芽等)。**7**. 逐出,撵出。**8**. 显示。**9**. 转弯抹角地说。**10**. 拒绝;否决(议案)。**11**. 跑过(人)。**12**.【棒球】使出局。**13**. 使(离合器等)分离,脱开。~ ***out of work*** 使失业。~ ***over*** **1**. 抛弃(难友等);放弃,毁弃(合同等)。**2**. 转换,变换。~ ***together*** (*artificially*)(勉强)凑成,(勉强或偶然)凑集。~ ***up*** **1**. 抛上,举起,抬起,推上(窗)。**2**. 急造。**3**. 丢弃,辞(职等)。**4**. 呕吐。**5**. 使显眼(~ *up one's arms* 举起双手;投降。~ *one's eyes up* 抬起眼睛;因恐怖或惊呆睁大眼睛)。~ ***up one's toenails*** 〔美〕剧烈[大量]呕吐。

II ***n***. **1**. 扔,丢,摔,投,掷,抛。**2**. 投距,射程。**3**. (银幕,扩音器等的)距离。**4**. 投球。**5**. (摔跤中)将对方摔倒(的方法)。**6**. 掷骰;掷出的点数。**7**. 冒险。**8**. (女用)围巾。**9**. (沙发,卧床等的)罩单。**10**. (钓鱼)投钓丝。**11**.【机】冲程;行程;摆度。**12**. (陶工的)车床,镟床。**13**.【地】断层垂直位移,落差。**14**.【测】冲掷(幅)。*a good ~* 好球。***at a stone's ~*** 在一投石之遥,在近处。~ ***of money*** 资产;很多钱。~**away** **1**. ***n***. 〔俚〕广告传单。**2**. ***a***. 可扔掉的。~**away line** 即兴的台词。~**back** 后退;阻止;返祖遗传(现象)。~**-down** 〔澳新〕爆竹。~**-net** 撒网,投网。~**off** (打猎、赛跑的)起步,出发,机会(*at the first ~off* 在刚开始时;*one's last ~off* 最后的机会)。~**-out** 被抛弃的人[东西];废品,次货。~ **rug** 小块地毯(=scatter rug)。~ **weight** (导[飞]弹的)有效载荷。**-er** ***n***. 喷射器。

thrown [θrəun; θron] **I** throw 的过去分词。**II** ***a***. 捻了的。~ *silk* 捻丝。

throw·ster [ˈθrəustə; ˋθrostɚ] ***n***. **1**. 掷骰子的人。**2**. 捻丝人,捻丝工。

thru [θruː; θru] 〔美〕=through. ~**way** ***n***. 〔美〕高速公路。

thrum[1] [θrʌm; θrʌm] ***n*. 1.**【纺】织边,绒边;机头。**2.** 〔*pl*., *sing*.〕粗乱纱头,线头;乱丝头,接头纱。**3.** 碎屑;【海】〔*pl*.〕绳屑。**4.** 缨子,穗子。**5.**【植】雄蕊;花丝,花药。***not to care a*** ~ 一点也不介意。***thread and*** ~ 好好歹歹。

thrum[2] [θrʌm; θrʌm] **I *vi*., *vt*.** (***-mm-***) **1.** 单调地[拙劣地]弹拨,随便地弹拨(弦乐器)。**2.** 用指头敲(桌子等)。**3.** 单调乏味地讲述。~ *a guitar out of tune* 弹吉他弹得不搭调。**II *n*.** 弹拨(声);得得声,轧轧声。

thru·out [θruːˈaut; θruˋaʊt] ***ad*., *prep*.** 〔美〕= throughout.

thrush[1] [θrʌʃ; θrʌʃ] ***n*.**【鸟】鸫属的鸟;画眉。*the song* ~ (欧洲)画眉鸟。

thrush[2] [θrʌʃ; θrʌʃ] ***n*.**【医】鹅口疮;真菌性口炎;【兽医】蹄叉腐疽。

thrust [θrʌst; θrʌst] **I *vt*.** (***thrust***) **1.** 猛推,冲;猛掀,冲入,插入,推入(出),突出,伸出,塞,刺,戳,戳穿。**2.** 逼迫,把[将]…强加于…(*into*)。**3.** 突然提出,不恰当地插进(插嘴等)。— ***vi*. 1.** 推,冲;强行推入,冲入;强行推进,突进;冲过去。**2.** 挺伸,延伸。~ *one's hand into one's pocket* 将手插进口袋里。~ *one's way through a crowd* 冲过人群。*It's not time for you to* ~ *in a question now*. 现在轮不到你插嘴提问题。*It was John who* ~ *a person aside*. 是约翰把一个人猛推在一旁的。*Unexpected events* ~ *themselves continually athwart our path*. 在我们工作的进程中,出乎意料的事层出不穷。*After he invented the new drilling machine, honours were* ~ *upon him*. 他发明了新的钻机之后,许多荣耀都加在他的身上了。*He showed great reluctance to accept the responsibility* ~ *upon him*. 对强加给他的责任,他不乐于承担。~ *at sb. with a dagger* 以匕首戳人。~ *on one's gloves* 急忙带上手套。~ *through* 挤过。***be*** ~ ***into fame*** 突然出名。~ ***a hand in*** 插手,干预。~ ***aside*** 推开。~ ***home*** 把(短刀等)深深刺入。~ (*sth*.) (***up***) ***on*** (*sb*.) (将东西)推给(某人);强卖给(某人)。~ ***oneself forward*** = ~ ***oneself in*** = ~ ***one's nose in*** 探听;插嘴;出头,干涉。~ ***one's way*** 向前推进,勉强挤过。~ ***out*** 推出;逐出,赶出;挤出,排出;发射。**II *n*. 1.** 推,冲;刺。**2.** 攻击;苛评,讥刺。**3.**【军】突入,突击,冲锋;【机】推力,侧向压力;【地】逆断层;冲断层;【矿】煤柱压裂。*a reactive* ~ 反冲力。*make a* ~ *with a dagger* 用匕首冲刺。*the* ~ *and parry of A and B* 甲乙两人间唇枪舌剑的激烈辩论[攻击]。~ **hoe** 推锄。~ **point**【军】推力点;突破战术。~ **stage 1.** 三面对着观众的舞台。**2.** 戏场内向前伸出很远的舞台前台。

thruster [ˈθrʌstə; ˋθrʌstɚ] ***n*. 1.** 冲的人;戳的人。**2.** 向上钻营者。**3.**〔口语〕插嘴的人。**4.** 推冲器,起飞加速器。

thrust·ing [ˈθrʌstiŋ; ˋθrʌstɪŋ] ***a*.** 自作主张的,盛气凌人的,无情的。**-ly *ad*.**

thruway [ˈθruːwei; ˋθruˏwe] ***n*.** 〔美〕= throughway.

thud [θʌd; θʌd] **I *n*. 1.** 砰的一声,啪嚓一声〔重物坠落等声音〕。**2.** 砰然一声。*The tree fell to the ground with a* ~. 树轰隆一声倒在地上。**II *vt*., *vi*.** (***-dd-***) 砰的一声重击;砰的一声落下(倒下);发出轰的一声。*a thudding fist* 强有力的拳头。

thug [θʌg; θʌg] ***n*. 1.** 〔常 T-〕谋杀教团团员〔印度旧时,因崇拜破坏女神,以杀人抢劫为业的宗教组织成员〕。**2.** 凶手,暴徒。

thug·gee [ˈθʌgiː; ˋθʌgi], **thug·ger·y** [ˈθʌgəri; ˋθʌgərɪ], **thug·gism** [ˈθʌgizm; ˋθʌgɪzm̩] ***n*.** 谋杀,谋财害命。**-gish *a*.**

thuja [ˈθjuːdʒə; ˋθudʒə, ˋθju-] ***n*.**【植】侧柏,金钟柏(= arborvitae 1.)。

Thu·le [ˈθjuːli(:); ˋθjulɪ, ˋθu-, -li] ***n*. 1.** (古代航海家所谓的)北极。**2.** 神秘地区;世界尽头。**3.**〔t-〕遥远的目标。*the ultima* ~ 世界的尽头;天涯海角;最远点;绝顶,极点;最终目的。

thu·li·a [ˈθjuːliə; ˋθjulɪə] ***n*.**【化】氧化铥。

thu·li·um [ˈθjuːliəm; ˋθjulɪəm] ***n*.**【化】铥(Tm 或 Tu)。

thumb [θʌm; θʌm] **I *n*. 1.** 拇指。**2.**【建】馒形饰。*Put your* ~*s up*! 〔俚〕使劲! *Thumbs down*! 差劲儿! *Thumbs up*! 〔俚〕好! 顶好! *a golden* ~ = *a* ~ *of gold* = *a miller's* ~ 摇钱树。*a* ~ *nail* 〔美〕一块钱。*a* ~ *pusher* 〔美〕在路上要求搭乘别人汽车的人。**II *vt*. 1.** 翻阅,用拇指翻脏[翻坏](书页等);反复读。**2.** 笨手笨脚地做;拙劣地弹(钢琴等)。**3.** 〔美口〕翘起拇指要求搭乘。*He* ~*ed his way to Boston*. 他搭乘别人顺路的车去波士顿。***be all*** ~***s*** 手笨(*His fingers are all* ~*s*. 他手笨脚笨)。***bite the*** ~***s at*** 蔑视。***by rule of*** ~ 单凭不多的经验,根据粗浅的常识。***count one's*** ~***s*** 消磨时间。***turn up*** [***down***] ***the*** ~ 表示赞成[反对],表示称赞[贬低],表示满意[不满]。***turn*** ~***s down to*** 反对(*We turned* ~*s down to that suggestion*. 我们反对这个建议)。***turn*** ~***s up*** [***on***] 赞成。***twiddle*** [***twirl***] ***one's*** ~***s*** 抚弄大拇指,无聊。***under sb.'s*** ~ 受人支配,仰人鼻息。~***ed pic*** 〔美〕禁止上演的影片。~ ***it*** (要求)搭乘顺路的车。~ ***one's nose at*** 〔美〕嗤之以鼻。~ ***the nose at*** 〔美俚〕打败敌手。~ ***through*** 翻查一过。~**s-down *n*.** 责备,不赞成。~ **index** [**notch**] (书边)指标索引。~**mark** (尤指留在书页上的)拇指痕。~**nail 1. *n*.** 拇指甲;极小的东西,简短的文字,简明的提要[略图]。**2. *a*.** 极小的,微型的;简短的(论文等)。~**-nut** 蝶形螺母。~ **piano** 拇指琴〔一种非洲拨弦乐器〕。~ **pick**【乐】拇指拨子。~ **pin** 〔美〕图钉。~**print** 拇指印纹;〔美俚〕个人性格特征。~**-screw**【机】指拧螺旋;蝶形螺钉;(古时的)拇指夹刑具。~**stall** 拇指套。~**tack** 〔美〕= ~ pin.

thumb·er [ˈθʌmə; ˋθʌmɚ] ***n*.** (要求)搭坐顺路汽车旅行的人。

thump [θʌmp; θʌmp] **I *n*. 1.** 砰,咚〔用拳头、棍子等重击的声音〕。**2.** 重击。**3.** (电话中的)电报噪音。**4.**【无】键击[低音]噪音。*He threw the box on the table with a* ~. 他砰的一声把匣子扔在桌子上。**II *vt*.** (砰地)重击;(用拳头等)捶打。— ***vi*.** 重击,捶击(*at*, *on*),咚咚地走,脚步沉重地走;(心脏等)扑扑地跳,悸动。*Getting very angry, the boss* ~*ed the desk with his fist*. 老板生气了,用拳头重捶桌子。*There is a man* ~*ing at the door*. 有个人捶门哪。*On hearing the news, my heart* ~*ed with excitement*. 听到这消息,我兴奋得心砰砰地跳。~ ***the*** [***a***] ***cushion*** (牧师讲道时)敲着讲坛垫子用力地讲。

thump·er [ˈθʌmpə; ˋθʌmpɚ] ***n*. 1.** 敲打的人[物]。**2.** 〔口〕巨大的人[物]。**3.** 极大的谎话。

thump·ing [ˈθʌmpiŋ; ˋθʌmpɪŋ] **I *a*. 1.** 〔口〕非常的,巨大的;极好的;极大的(谎话等)。**2.** 尺码大的。**3.** 极好的。*She gave birth to a* ~ *ten-catty baby last night*. 昨天夜里,她生了个好大的十斤重的婴儿。**II *ad*.** 非常地。

thun·der [ˈθʌndə; ˋθʌndɚ] **I *n*. 1.** 雷,雷声。**2.** 轰响。**3.** 〔*pl*.〕怒喝,谴责,威吓,恐吓,弹劾。**4.** 〔古〕霹雳。**5.** 〔在惊恐、愤怒、强调时加强语气〕究竟,到底。~*s* [*a* ~*s*] *of applause* 雷鸣般的喝彩声[掌声]。*the* ~ *of News-Times* 新闻时报上的激烈抨击。*What in* ~ [*What the* ~] *is that*? 那究竟是怎么件事情? *Where in* ~ *did he lose the money*? 他的钱到底是在什么地方丢的? **II *vi*. 1.** 打雷。**2.** 轰响。**3.** 大声叫。**4.** 怒喝,骂,谴责(*against*)。—***vt*. 1.** 像打雷一样地讲[谴责,恫吓,发射等]。**2.** 大声说出,吼叫。*It* ~ *s*. 打雷,雷鸣。~ *at the door* 像打雷一样地敲门。*Guns* ~*ed a salute*. 礼炮轰鸣。~ *into the stretch* 〔美〕开始赛马。***By*** ~! 哎! 真的! 岂有此理! ***run away with sb.'s*** ~ = ***steal sb.'s*** ~ 先声夺人,抢先讲某人要讲的话;窃取某人的方案[发明等]抢先发表[利用]。~**-and-light-**

ning 1. *n*. 雷电,谴责,攻击。2. 由截然相反的色彩配在一起,夺目的彩色。~**bird** (北美印第安人神话中)引起雷雨的巨鸟。~**bolt** 雷电,霹雳,落雷;恐吓,怒喝;意外的事情,意外打击;闪电苏岩;【古生】箭石(*This information was a ~bolt to her*. 这消息对她真是一个晴天霹雳。*with the power of a ~-bolt* 以雷霆万钧之势)。~-**clap** *n*. 霹雳;晴天霹雳(似的消息[事件])。~-**cloud** 雷云。~-**gust** 伴有大风的暴雷雨。~**head**【气】(雷雨前的)雷雨[雷暴]云砧。~ **peal** = ~ clap. ~-**shower** 雷阵雨。~**squll** 雷飑。~**stone** (旧时以为是雷电发射下来的)飞来石〔实际为化石,古代石器等〕。~-**storm** *n*. 雷雨。~**stricken**, ~**struck** *a*. 被雷霹的;吓坏了的,大吃一惊的。

thun·der·a·tion [ˈθʌndəˈreiʃən; ˌθʌndəˋreʃən] *n*. 雷电,霹雳;意外的事件,晴天霹雳。

thun·der·er [ˈθʌndərə; ˋθʌndərɚ] *n*. 怒喝的人,咆哮如雷的人。***the T-*** 1. =【罗神】朱庇特(Jupiter)。2. 〔英谑〕伦敦泰晤士报(*The Times*)的外号。

thun·der·ing [ˈθʌndəriŋ; ˋθʌndərɪŋ] **I** *a*. 1. 雷鸣的,打雷的;雷一样响亮的。2. 〔口〕非常的,极大的(谎话、错误、坏蛋等)。*a ~ great fellow* 非常高大的家伙。*a ~ error* 极大的错误。**II** *ad*. 〔口〕非常,异常。-**ly** *ad*.

thun·der·ous [ˈθʌndərəs; ˋθʌndərəs, -drəs] *a*. 1. 雷的;雷鸣似的,轰隆轰隆响的。2. 多雷的,形成雷的。3. 可怕的。

thun·der·y [ˈθʌndəri; ˋθʌndərɪ] *a*. 打雷似的;将要打雷似的;形势不稳的。

Thur. = Thursday.

Thur·ber [ˈθəːbə; ˋθɝbɚ] *n*. 瑟伯〔姓氏〕。

thu·ri·ble [ˈθjuəribl; ˋθjʊrəbl] *n*. 【天主教】香炉。

thu·ri·fer [ˈθjurifə, ˈθur-; ˋθjʊrəfɚ, ˋθʊr-] *n*. 【天主教】祭坛侍僧[僧童]〔祭坛上捧香炉的侍僧或僧童〕。

thu·ri·fi·ca·tion [ˌθjuərifiˈkeiʃən; ˌθjʊrəfɪˋkeʃən] *n*. 焚香。

thu·ri·fy [ˈθjurifai; ˋθjʊrəˌfaɪ] *vt*. (-*fied*) 在…前[附近]烧香;用香熏。

Thur·man [ˈθəːmən; ˋθɝmən] *n*. 瑟曼〔姓氏,男子名〕。

Thur(s). = Thursday.

Thurs·day [ˈθəːzdi; ˋθɝzdɪ] *n*. 星期四(略 Thur., Thurs.)。*Holy ~* (基督教) 1. 升天节(复活节后四十天的星期四)。2. 复活节前三天的星期四(= Maundy [ˈmɔːndi; ˋmɔndɪ] ~)。-**s** *ad*. 〔美〕每星期四,在任何星期四。

Thurs·ton [ˈθəːstən; ˋθɝstən] *n*. 瑟斯顿〔男子名〕。

thus [ðʌs; ðʌs] *ad*. 1. 如此,这样,像这样,例如。2. 到这程度,到这地步,这么 3. 如下。4. 于是,因此。*T- it goes on*. 如此继续下去。*It ~ appears that* ... 因此看起来好像…。~ ***and so*** 〔美〕= *so*. ~ ***and*** ~ 云云,这样这样,如此这般。~ ***far*** 至今,迄今,到现在为止,至此,到这里为止。~ ***much*** 这么多,到这里为止(*T- much at least is clear*. 至少这一些是明白的)。-**ly** *ad*. = thus.

thus·ness [ˈðʌsnis; ˋðʌsnɪs] *n*. 〔谑〕这个样子。*Why this ~ ?* 为什么会这样?

thwack [θwæk; θwæk] *n*., *vt*., *vi*. 〔拟声词〕啪地一声打;重击(= whack)。

thwaite [θweit; θwet] *n*. 〔英〕新开地,开垦地。

thwart [θwɔːt; θwɔrt] **I** *vt*. 1. 反对;阻挠;挫败(对方意图等)。2. 〔古〕横过,穿过。**II** *a*. 横着的,穿过的;不利的。**III** *ad*., *prep*. 横跨,横过。**IV** [θɔːt; θɔt] *n*. (横贯小艇的)坐板。*I don't think that will ~ our purposes*. 我认为那不会使我们的目的受到挫折。*It's only too natural that he will be ~ed in his ambitions*. 他的图谋将遭到挫败是很自然的事。~**ship** *a*. 横贯船身的。~**ships** *ad*.

T.H.W.M. = Trinity House high water mark 〔英〕海务局高潮水位标志。

ThX = thorium X 钍X〔即 Ra[224] 镭[224]〕。

thy [ðai; ðaɪ] *pro*. 〔古〕〔thou 的所有格〕你的。

Thy·es·te·an [θaiˈestiən; θaɪˋɛstɪən] *a*. 吃人肉的〔希腊神话,Thyestes 与其弟妹 Atrens 通奸,遭怨恨,食间,后者杀前者儿子供餐,前者不知食之,故有此意〕。

thy·la·cine [ˈθailəˌsain, -sin; ˋθaɪləˌsaɪn, -sɪn] *n*. 【动】袋狼(= tasmanian wolf)。

thyme [taim; taɪm] *n*. 【植】百里香(属),麝香草。

thy·mic[1] [ˈθaimik; ˋθaɪmɪk] *a*. 【解】胸腺的。

thy·mic[2] [ˈtaimik; ˋtaɪmɪk] *a*. 【植】百里香的;麝香草的。

thy·mi·dine [ˈθaimiˌdiːn, -din; ˋθaɪmɪˌdin, -dɪn] *n*. 【药】胸(腺嘧啶脱氧核)苷。

thy·mine [ˈθaimiːn, -min; ˋθaɪmin, -mɪn] *n*. 【药】胸腺嘧啶。

thy·mol [ˈθaimɔl; ˋθaɪmol, -mɑl] *n*. 【化】百里(香)酚,麝香草酚。

thy·mus [ˈθaiməs; ˋθaɪməs] *n*. 1. 【解】胸腺 2. 麝香草。~ **gland** 胸腺。

thym·y [ˈtaimi; ˋtaɪmɪ] *a*. 多百里香的,有麝香草香的。

thy·ra·tron [ˈθairətrɔn; ˋθaɪrəˌtrɑn] *n*. 【无】闸流管。

thy·ris·tor [θaiˈristə; θaɪˋrɪstɚ] *n*. 【无】闸流晶体管;半导体闸流管;半导体开关元件。

thy·rite [ˈθairait; ˋθaɪraɪt] *n*. 1. 几利〔砂砾陶,一种非线性电阻〕。2. 泰利〔电阻值随所加电压而变的一种材料〕。

thy·rode [ˈθairəud; ˋθaɪrod] *n*. 1. 泰罗〔一种计数器用电子管〕。2. 矽可控整流器。

thy·roid [ˈθaiərɔid; ˋθaɪrɔɪd] **I** *a*. 1. 盾状的。2. 【解】甲状(软骨)的;甲状腺的。~ *cartilage* 甲状软骨。~ *gland* [*body*] 甲状腺。**II** *n*. 1. 【解】甲状腺;甲状软骨。2. 【药】甲状腺剂。~ **body**【解】甲状腺。~ **cartilage**【解】甲状软骨。

thy·ro·ad·e·ni·tis [ˈθairəuˌædˈnaitis; ˋθaɪroˌædˋnaɪtɪs] *n*. 【医】= thyroiditis.

thy·roid·ec·to·my [ˌθairɔiˈdektəmi; ˌθaɪrɔɪˋdɛktəmɪ] *n*. (*pl*. -*mies*)【医】甲状腺切除术。

thy·roid·i·tis [ˌθairɔiˈdaitis; ˌθaɪrɔɪˋdaɪtɪs] *n*. 【医】甲状腺炎。

thy·ro·tox·i·co·sis [ˌθairəuˌtɔksiˈkəusis; ˌθaɪroˌtɑksəˋkosɪs] *n*. 【医】甲状腺机能亢进,甲状腺毒症(= hyperthyroidism)。

thy·rot·ro·phin, **-ro·pin** [θairəuˈtrəufin, -pin; θaɪroˋtrofɪn, -pɪn] *n*. 【医】促甲状腺激素。

thy·rox·in(e) [θaiˈrɔksi(ː)n; θaɪˋrɑksɪn] *n*. 【生化】甲状腺素。

thyr·soid, **-soi·dal** [ˈθəːsɔid, -ˈsɔidəl; ˋθɝsɔɪd, -ˋsɔɪdəl] *a*. 【植】聚伞圆锥花序的。

thyr·sus [ˈθəːsəs; ˋθɝsəs] *n*. (*pl*. -*si* [-sai; -saɪ]) 1. 【希神】酒神杖〔酒神(Racchus)所执的顶端为松果形的手杖〕。2. 【植】聚伞圆锥花序。

thy·sa·nu·ran [ˌθaiseˈnjurən, ˌθise-; -ˈnur-; ˌθaɪsɛˋnjurən, ˌθɪsɛ-; -ˋnʊr-] *n*. 【动】缨尾目(*Thysanura*)动物〔包括衣鱼〕。-**nu·rous** *a*.

thy·self [ðaiˈself; ðaɪˋsɛlf] *pro*. 1. 你自己〔thou 的反身代词〕。2. 〔加强语气用〕你本人,你亲自。

Ti =【化】titanium.

ti[1] [tiː; ti] *n*. 【乐】长音阶七唱名的第七音(= si)。

ti[2] [tiː; ti] *n*. 【植】铁树(*Cordyline terminalis*)〔产于玻里尼西亚和澳大利亚〕。

tia·mat [ˈtaiəmæt; ˋtaɪəmæt] *n*. 〔美空军〕试验用的无人驾驶火箭飞机。

ti·a·ra [tiˈɑːrə, taiˈerə; taɪˋɛrə, tɪˋɑrə] *n*. 1. 古波斯人的头巾;古波斯王的王冕。2. 罗马教皇的三重冕〔象征现世、灵界、地狱三者〕。3. 罗马教皇的职权。4. 女式冕状头饰。

Tib·bett [ˈtibit; ˋtɪbɪt] *n*. 蒂贝特〔姓氏〕。

Ti·ber [ˈtaibə; ˋtaɪbɚ] *n*. 第伯尔河〔横贯罗马市的河

名]。

Ti·be·ri·us [taiˈbiəriəs; taɪˋbɪrɪəs] *n*. 台比留[42B.C.—37A.D., 全名为 ~ Claudius Nero Caesar, 公元1世纪14—37年间为罗马皇帝]。

Ti·bet [tiˈbet; tɪˋbet] *n*. 西藏(中国)。

Ti·bet·an [tiˈbetən; tɪˋbetn̩, ˋtɪbɪt-] *a*., *n*. 西藏的(人);西藏语。

Ti·bet·o-Bur·man [tiˌbetəuˈbəːmən; tɪˏbetoˋbɝmən] **I** *n*. 藏缅语[汉藏语系的一支,包括藏语和缅语]。**II** *a*. 藏缅语的。

tib·i·a [ˈtibiə; ˋtɪbɪə] *n*. (*pl*. **-ae** [ˈtibiiː; ˋtɪbɪˏi]) **1**.【解】胫骨;【动】(昆虫的)胫节;鸡脚的下节。**2**. (原由动物胫骨制成的)胫笛。**-l** *a*.

Tibione [ˈtiːˈbiːwʌn; ˋtiˋbiwʌn] *n*.【医】替比昂[抑制结核杆菌和麻疯杆菌药,即 TB_1]。

tic [tik; tɪk] *n*.【医】**1**. (颜面)痉挛,痉挛性颜面神经痛。**2**. (局部肌肉小)抽搐。~ *douloureux* 三叉神经痛 (= trigeminal neuralgia)。

tic·ca [ˈtikə; ˋtɪkə] *a*. [印](车等)出租的。*a* ~ *gharry* 出租马车。

ti·cal [tiˈkɑːl, -ˈkɔːl; tɪˋkɑl, -ˋkɔl] *n*. **1**. 泰国旧货币单位[现为 *baht* 铢]。**2**. 泰国旧重量单位。

TICK = two-income couple with kids 提克族[指有孩子的双职工夫妻,相对于"丁克"族而言]。

tick[1] [tik; tɪk] **I** *vi*. **1**. (钟表)滴嗒滴嗒响[走]。**2**. 一步一步推移;[口](像钟表般地)持续活动。*Don't worry. After the operation, he'll* ~ *along fine*. 不用担心,手术后他会活得很好。*What makes it* ~? 什么使它这样地动作? — *vt*. **1**. 打点,作记号 (*off*)。**2**. 滴嗒滴嗒记录时间[发出信息] (*out*); 把时间滴滴嗒嗒地打发掉。*The teletype is* ~*ing out messages*. 电传打字电报机滴嗒滴嗒地打出电报来。(*the clock*) ~ ***away*** [***off***] ***the time*** (*of*) 随着滴嗒的钟声,…的时间过去了。~ ***off*** **1**. 打上记号。**2**. [英俚]斥责,责骂。**3**. [口]证明是同一东西;核实无误。**4**. [俚]激怒。**5**. 简略地描述。~ ***out*** (电报机)发出(消息)。~ ***over*** (内燃机等)慢车转动着,松开传动装置;[喻]接近停滞,踌躇,吞吞吐吐。***what makes a person*** [***a thing***] ~ 使人[事]持续活动的动力 (*That's what makes the world* ~. 使世界持续活动的动力,就在于此)。**II** *n*. **1**. 滴嗒(声)。**2**. 一点,一划,查讫号[√]。**3**.【物】标记(器);【无】无线电信号 **4**. [英口]一会儿,一刹那间。*I'll be with you in half a* ~. 稍等片刻,我就来陪你。*come in a* ~ 马上就来。*radio* ~ 无线电报时信号。*time* ~ 计时器。***to*** [***on***] ***the*** ~ 极为准时地 (*get there at five on the* ~ 五时正到达那里)。

tick[2] [tik; tɪk] *n*. **1**. 褥套,枕套[指中间填塞羽毛等物的内套];(做褥套等用的)条纹棉布或麻布;褥面。**2**. (弹簧椅等的)面子。***tight as a*** ~ [美俚]喝得烂醉的。

tick[3] [tik; tɪk] *n*.【动】扁虱,蜱,壁虱。~ *fever*【医】蜱热。

tick[4] [tik; tɪk] **I** *n*. [口] **1**. 信用,赊欠,放债。**2**. 赊(销)。**II** *vi*. 赊销;赊购。—*vt*. 赊销(购)(货物);赊给(某人)。***buy*** [***get***] ***sth***. ***on*** ~ 赊购。***give tick*** 赊销。***go*** (***on***) ~ = ***run on*** ~ 赊购;借款。

tick·er [ˈtikə; ˋtɪkɚ] *n*. **1**. 滴嗒滴嗒响的东西。**2**. 蜂音器,振动子。**3**. (钟表的)摆。**4**. [美俚]挂表,座钟。**5**. [美俚]心脏。**6**. (电报的)收报机;股票行市自动收录机。**7**.【无】断续装置;断续器。~ **tape 1**. (收报机等用的)纸带。**2**. (庆祝,欢迎,送行等抛扔用的)彩色纸带。~**-tape** *a*. 抛彩带的,热烈的 (*get a* ~*-tape reception* [*welcome*, *parade*] 受到抛彩带的盛大欢迎)。

tick·et [ˈtikit; ˋtɪkɪt] **I** *n*. **1**. 票,入场券,车票,票证。**2**. 标签,标价牌,价目签。**3**. 招租帖。**4**. (给违反交通规则者等的)传票。**5**. [英军俚]解除军职命令。**6**. [美]候选人名单;列有候选人名单的选举票;[喻](政党的)政见,政纲;计划,规划。**7**. (资格)证明书;许可证;(飞行员等)执照。**8**. [the ~][口]适当[所需]的东西;当然的事情,正好的事情;计划,方针。*a platform* ~ 月台票。*a season* ~ 月[季]票。*a single* [*return*] ~ 单程[来回]票[美国英语 ~作"来回票"解]。*a price* ~ 价目标签。*cash* ~*s* 门市发票。*vote a straight* ~ [美]所有票数均投选某一政党的候选人。*split a* ~ = *vote a split* ~ [美]兼投另一政党候选人的票。*The whole* ~ *was returned*. 候选人全部当选。*the Democratic* ~ [美]民主党的政纲。*That's the* ~. [口]那正好,那才对。*What's the* ~? [口]怎样才好? 结果怎样? **II** *vt*. **1**. 加标签,附上标价牌。**2**. [美]卖票。***admit by*** ~ ***alone*** 凭券入场。***carry a*** ~ [美]使本党候选人全部当选。***cut a*** ~ [美口]涂掉选票上候选人的名字,投反对票。***get one's*** ~【军】被解除军职。***given a*** ~ [美剧]被辞退。***not quite the*** ~ 有点不适合[不对头]。***vote the split*** ~ [美]兼投一党以上的候选人的票。***vote the straight*** ~ [美]只投某一政党全部候选人的票。***work one's*** ~ [军口](装病等)退役。***write one's own*** ~ 自行计划,自行决定。~ **agent** [美]售票员。~ **broker** [婉]票贩子,"黄牛"。~ **chopper** 剪票员。~ **day** (交易所的)决算日。~ **inspector** 查票员。~ **night** 演员照各自推销票数分配得款的演出日。~ **of leave** *n*. 假释许可证。~**-of-leave man** 假释犯。~ **office** [美]售票处,票房。~**-porter** [英](车站内的)搬运员。~**-punch** 轧票钳。~ **scalper** [美俚](套卖戏票的)黄牛党。

tick·et·y-boo [ˈtikitiˌbuː; ˋtɪkɪtɪˋbu] *a*. [英俚]很好,没问题,行。

tick·ing[1] [ˈtikiŋ; ˋtɪkɪŋ] *n*. 滴嗒声。

tick·ing[2] [ˈtikiŋ; ˋtɪkɪŋ] *n*. 褥套料[做褥套等用的厚底棉布]。*an art* ~ 印花[织花]褥套料。

tick·le [ˈtikl; ˋtɪkl] **I** *vt*. **1**. 搔触(使觉得痒),呵(痒);撩拨。**2**. 逗笑;使高兴,使快乐;使满足。**3**. 用手抓住(鳟鱼等)。— *vi*. 觉得痒,(东西)使人发痒。*He* ~*d me in the ribs*. 他搔触我的肋骨。*I was greatly* ~*d at the joke*. 想起这个笑话感到有趣得了不得。*My ear* ~*s*. 我耳朵痒。*The rough sheets* ~。粗床单使人发痒。~ ***sb.'s palm*** 给某人赏钱[贿赂]。~ ***sb.'s vanity*** 满足某人的虚荣心。~ ***the fancy*** 迎合所好。~ ***the ivories*** [美]弹钢琴。~ ***to death*** 使笑破肚皮 (*I was* ~*d to death at the joke*. 听了那笑话,我的肚皮都笑破了)。**II** *n*. **1**. 搔痒。**2**. 使人发痒[高兴]的东西[事物]。**3**. 愉快的情绪。~**d pink** *a*. [美俚]非常开心,高兴 (*He was* ~*d pink that somebody had remembered his birthday*. 他非常高兴,因为还有人记得他的生日)。

tick·ler [ˈtiklə; ˋtɪklɚ] *n*. **1**. 使感到痒[高兴]的人[物]。**2**. [口]难事,难题。**3**. [美]记事本,备忘录。**4**. [美口]小瓶;(威士忌酒等的)一杯。**5**.【无】屏极回授线圈;【机】初给器。*He's meeting the* ~ *successfully*. 他在顺利地处理着这难题。

tick·lish [ˈtikliʃ; ˋtɪklɪʃ] *a*. **1**. 怕痒的。**2**. 易变的。**3**. 摇晃不稳的;棘手的,难对付的(人、物)。**4**. 易怒的。*a* ~ *situation* 难对付的形势。*The news is quite* ~ *to the ear*. 这消息听起来使人觉得有些难办。

tick·seed [ˈtikˌsiːd; ˋtɪkˏsid] *n*.【植】**1**. 金鸡菊 (= coreopsis)。**2**. 鬼针草属植物 [bur marigold 的俗称]。

tic(k)·tac(k), **tic(k)·tic(k)**, **tick·tock** [ˈtikˈtæk, -tik, -tɔk; ˋtɪkˏtæk, -ˈtɪk, -ˋtɔk] *n*. **1**. 滴嗒滴嗒[钟表声]。**2**. [儿语]钟。**3**. 扑扑[心脏的鼓动等],悸动。**4**. (儿童恶作剧用的)遥控敲门装置。**5**. [英俚]给赛马赌博者提供情报的人 (= ~ man); 提供这种情报时打的手势。

tick-tack-toe [ˌtiktækˈtəu; ˏtɪktækˋto], **tick-tack-too** [-ˈtuː; -ˋtu] *n*. **1**. 三连棋。**2**. (儿童)使用遥控敲门装置的恶作剧。

tick·y tack·y, **ticky-tacky** [ˈtiki ˈtæki; ˋtɪkɪ ˋtækɪ] *a*. (房屋等)用劣质材料制成的;(一排排简陋房屋)看上去单调的,一模一样的。

t.i.d., TID =〔L.〕*ter in die* 每日三次〔药剂处方用语〕(= three times a day)。

tid·al [ˈtaidl; ˋtaɪdl] ***a*.** **1.** 潮汐的;潮水(似)的。**2.** 由于潮水作用的,定时涨落的;开船时间视潮汐而变动的(客船班次)。*His speech caused a ~ wave of indignation throughout the country*. 他的演说在全国掀起了怒潮。~ **air** = ~ **breath** 每一呼吸进出肺部的空气。~ **boat** 开航时间视潮汐而变动的客船。~ **current** 潮流。~ **forest** 潮湿林。~ **harbour** 潮汐港。~ **river** 潮汐河。~ **train** 临港列车。~ **wave** **1.** 潮浪,潮汐波。**2.** 海啸。**3.** (喻)(情绪上的)大波动,(人事上的)大变动。

tid·bit [ˈtidbit; ˋtɪd,bɪt] ***n*.**〔美〕= titbit.

tiddl(e)y [ˈtidli; ˋtɪdlɪ] **I** ***n*.**〔主英俚〕酒。**II** ***a*.** **1.** 喝醉的,步履不稳的。**2.**〔口〕很小的,微不足道的。

tid·dl(e)y·wink [ˈtidliwiŋk; ˋtɪdlɪ,wɪŋk] ***n*.** **1.**〔英俚〕没有执照的酒吧[当铺],下等酒吧。**2.**〔美〕〔*pl*.〕投圆形小筹码进入桌中央杯碟中的游戏。

tide [taid; taɪd] **I** ***n*.** **1.** 潮,潮汐,涨潮时。**2.** 消长,盛衰。**3.** 潮流,趋势,倾向,形势,时机,机运。**4.**【矿山】班,十二个钟头。**5.** 时期,季节。**6.** (宗教上的)节期〔通例用作复合词〕。*Christmas* ~ 圣诞节节期。*at high* [*low*] ~ 处于高[低]潮。*ebb* [*flood*] ~ 落[涨]潮。*the flowing* [*rising*] ~ 涨潮。*the ebbing* [*falling*] ~ 退潮。*spring* [*neap*] ~ 大[小]潮。*The* ~ *is in* [*out or down* 或 *coming in, going out*] 现在是涨潮[落潮]。*The* ~ *is making* [*ebbing*]. 潮正在涨[落]。***attempt to go against the* ~ *of history*** 倒行逆施。***catch the* ~** 抓住时机,趁机。***full* ~ *of pleasure*** 欢乐的绝顶。***go with the* ~** 随大流,赶潮流,顺应潮流。***roll back the* ~ *of war*** 击退侵略。***save the* ~** 趁涨潮进出港口。***swim with the* ~** 随大流,随波逐流。***tail to the* ~** (船只停泊中)随潮起伏。***take fortune at the* ~ = *take the* ~ *at the flood*** 及时利用时机,因利乘便。***The* ~ *turns*.** 形势经常在变化(*The* ~ *turned to* [*against*] *him*. 形势变得对他有利[不利])。***work double* ~*s*** 昼夜工作,日夜苦干。**II** ***vi*.** **1.** 顺应潮水航行。**2.** 像潮水般汹涌(高涨,奔流)。— ***vt*.** **1.** 使随潮水漂行。**2.** 克服。*The General Meigs is tiding into* (*out of*) *the harbor*. 梅格斯将军号在趁潮进港(出港)。*The money is enough to* ~ *him over the difficulties*. 这笔钱足够他度过难关了。~ **gauge** 测潮计。~**land** (随潮水涨落而出没的)潮淹区;〔*pl*.〕领海底地。~**-lock** 潮闸。~ **mark** 潮标。~**rip** 潮流冲激成的大浪。~ **rock** 随潮水起落出没的礁石。~ **table** 潮汐表。~**waiter** **1.** 海关水上稽查员。**2.** 机会主义者,观潮派。~**water**〔美〕**1.** 潮水。**2.** 受潮水涨落影响的水区和地区。~**way** **1.** 潮路;潮流 **2.** (河流的)受潮汐影响的部分。

ti·dings [ˈtaidiŋz; ˋtaɪdɪŋz] ***n*.**〔*pl*.〕消息,音信〔动词单复数通用〕。*glad* ~ 喜讯。*good* [*evil*] ~ 好[坏]消息。*That's the best* ~ *for the future*. 那对前途说来是最好的消息。*When the sad* ~ *of his death were* (*was*) *received, we all wept*. 听到他去世的噩耗时,我们都哭了。

ti·dy [ˈtaidi; ˋtaɪdɪ] **I** ***a*.** (***-di·er***; ***-di·est***) **1.** 整洁的,整齐的,爱整洁的。**2.**〔口〕相当好的,相当大的(款项)。**3.**〔口〕健康的。**II** ***n*.** **1.** 沙发,椅背,扶手等的罩布。**2.** 装零碎东西的容器[袋子、筐子等]。*a* ~ *room* 整洁的房间。*a street* ~ 街道上的废物箱。**III** ***vt*.** (***-died***) 弄整洁,整理,收拾 (*up*)。*It's your turn to* ~ (*up*) *the room*. 这回该你收拾房间了。*Wait a minue. I have to* ~ *myself* (*up*) *a bit*. 等一会儿,我梳理一下。**-i·ly** ***ad*.** **-i·ness** ***n*.**

tie [tai; taɪ] **I** ***vt*.** (***tied***; ***ty·ing***) **1.** (用绳带等)扎,系,绑;用带子束紧(帽、鞋等);打(结、领结等);束缚,绑住。**2.** 约束,限制。**3.** 连接;〔口〕使结为夫妇。**4.**【乐】用连接符连接;【铁路】固定铁轨;铺设枕木。**5.**【运】与…打成平局。~ *one's tie* 打领结。~ *one's shoes* 结鞋带。*My tongue is* ~*d*. 我不能说。*Never fear! The dog is* ~*d up*. 不要怕!狗拴着呢。*I am much* ~*d*. 我被工作拖住,一点空闲没有。*See that the boat is securely* ~*d*. 注意要把小船拴牢了。*a* ~*d house* (专供本企业职工租用的)企业宿舍;(专销某家酒的)特约酒店。— ***vi*.** **1.** 结合,连接,结住。**2.** 打结。**3.** 打成平局,不分胜负;势均力敌。~ *with one's competitor* 跟对手不分胜负。*This* ~*s up with what I've told you*. 这和我对你讲过的有关。**II** ***n*.** **1.** 结扎,结子,结儿。**2.** 带子,绳子,领带;毛皮的颈饰;鞋带;〔美〕〔*pl*.〕= Oxford shoes. **3.** 联系,关系,缘分。**4.** 束缚,牵累。**5.**【运】平局,不分胜负,淘汰赛,平局后决胜负的决赛。**6.**【建】连系材。**7.**【乐】连接线[符号]。**8.**〔美〕铁路枕木。**9.**【统】相持。*draw close the* ~*s between the civil and the military* 密切军民关系。*It tends to a stronger* ~ *of friendship between us*. 这有助加强我们之间的朋友关系。*Children are a great* ~. 小孩子们是很大的拖累。***be* ~*d to time*** 被时间束缚着,必须在一定时间内做好。***get* ~*d up*** 结婚。***hit the* ~*s***〔美俚〕顺铁路徒步旅行。***play*** [***run, shoot***] ***off the* ~** 平局后再举行决胜负的决赛。***ride and* ~** 两人轮流骑一马旅行。~ ***off*** (为了止血)缚住血管。~ ***one down*** 使不能起立地绑住某人;束缚,牵制。~ ***sb.'s tongue*** 使某人缄默,堵住某人的嘴。~ ***the knot***〔美〕结婚。~ ***to***〔美俚〕信赖,倚靠;迷恋。~ ***up*** **1.** 绑;系;包扎,包装。**2.** (船只)系泊。**3.** (使)拮据[穷困]。**4.** (罢工中)使交通停顿 (*The accident* ~*d up traffic the entire day*. 那个意外事件使交通整天停顿)。**5.** 冻结(遗产、资本)。**6.**〔美〕联合行动;合伙。~ ***up with*** 和…有(密切)关系。~***d to a tree***〔美〕被打败。~**back** 拴窗帘、帷幕的绳带;〔常 *pl*.〕带有系带的帘幕。~ **bar** [**clasp, clip**] 领带夹。~ **beam**【建】系梁,小屋梁。~**-break** (网球)平局决胜制。~**-breaker**【体】决胜局。~**-dye** ***n*., *vt*.** 扎染(法);扎染的布。~**-in** ***n*., *a*.** 搭配在一起出售的[货品];关系,联系。~ **line**【电】联络线(路);直接接连线;拉线;直接通信线路。~ **peeler**, ~ **whacker**〔美〕(森林中)解制枕木的工人。~**pin** = stickpin. ~ **rod** 系杆,拉杆。~ **tack** 领带别针。~**-up** 关系,牵连;〔美〕(交通工作等)断绝,停顿;(船的)系泊处;〔美方〕拴系牲畜的地方。

tie·mann·ite [ˈtiːmənait; ˋtimə,naɪt] ***n*.**【矿】硒汞矿。

tier. = tierce.

tier[1] [tiə; tɪr] **I** ***n*.** **1.** (阶式看台等的)(一)排,(一)行,(一)层。**2.** (衣服等上的)一行褶裥。**3.**【电】定向天线。**4.** 等级。*seats arranged in* ~*s* 排成一层一层的座位。*the highest* ~ *of society* 社会的最上层。**II** ***vt*., *vi*.** 成层堆积[排列];层层上升。~ *building* 多层房屋。~ *table* 宝塔桌(有两张或更多的相互重叠的圆桌面小桌)。

tier[2] [ˈtaiə; ˋtaɪɚ] ***n*.** **1.** 捆扎者(或工具),包扎工。**2.**〔美方〕(儿用)围涎,胸围。

tierce [tiəs; trɪs] ***n*.** **1.** (装 42 个美国加仑的)中号酒桶;42 加仑的量。**2.**【乐】(音阶的)第三音。**3.**【天主】白天的第三时〔午前九时〕,第三课(第三时作的祈祷)。**4.**【剑术】第三姿势。**5.** [təːs; tɝs]【牌戏】三张同花顺。~ *and quarts* 剑术。

tier·cel [ˈtiəsl; ˋtɪrsḷ] ***n*.** 雄鹰 (= tercel)。

Tier·ra del Fuego [tiˈerrəˌdelˈfweɡəu; tɪˋɛrə,dɛlfuˋego] ***n*.** (南美南端的)火地岛。

tiers é·tat [ˈtjeəzeiˈtɑː; ,tjɛr,zeˋtɑ]〔F.〕(区别于贵族和教士阶级的)第三等级,平民。

tiff [tif; tɪf] **I** ***n*.** **1.** (一杯)酒,(一口)酒。**2.** 小争执,小口角。*a labour* ~ 劳资纠纷。**II** ***vt*.**〔英〕喝一杯。— ***vi*.** **1.** 生气,动怒。**2.** 口角,争吵。**3.**〔印〕吃午饭。*have a* ~ *with one's classmate* 和同班同学发生小口角。

tif·fa·ny [ˈtifəni; ˋtɪfənɪ] ***n*.** **1.** 丝纱罗。**2.** 上浆亚麻薄布。

tif·fin [ˈtifin; ˋtɪfɪn]〔印〕**I** ***n*.** 午饭。**II** ***vi*.** 吃午饭。

Tiflis, Tbilisi [ˈtiflis, tifˈliːs; ˋtɪflɪs, tɪfˋlis] ***n*.** 第比利斯

〔格鲁吉亚首都〕。

tig[1][tig; tɪg] *n*., *vt*. (**-gg-**) 触摸;捉迷藏;〔口〕吵架。

tig[2][tig; tɪg] *n*. 一种旧式带把酒杯。

ti·ger [ˈtaigə; ˋtaɪgɚ] *n*. **1.**【动】虎。**2.** 凶汉,凶性,残性,暴徒。**3.** (穿着制服的)少年马夫。**4.**〔英口〕(网球等比赛的)劲敌 (*opp*. rabbit)。**5.**〔美〕(欢呼三声后)加喊的欢呼〔喝彩声〕,喝彩尾声 (*three cheers and a* ～)。*a red* ～ =cougar. *an American* ～ 美洲虎 (=jaguar)。*the* (*Tammany*) *T-* 〔美〕= Tammany Hall. ***the four ～s of Asia*** 亚洲经济"四小龙"〔"四小龙"是俗称,英语原文其实是"虎"〕。***work like a*** ～ 生龙活虎地工作。～ **beetle**【虫】斑蝥。～ **cat**【动】虎猫,薮猫。～**eye**, ～**'s-eye**【矿】虎眼石。～ **flower**【植】虎斑草。～ **grass**【植】棕叶芦。～ **lily**【植】卷丹。～**man**〔美〕摔跤选手。～ **moth**【虫】灯蛾。～ **salamander**【动】虎纹钝口螈。～ **sweat**〔美俚〕威士忌酒。**-ish** *a*. 虎一般凶猛残忍的,虎纹的。**-ism** *n*. 狞猛,残忍凶暴。

tight [tait; taɪt] **I** *a*. **1.** 坚实的;坚固的,坚牢的,紧的,不松动的。**2.** 紧密的;密封的,气密的;不漏的。**3.** 紧张的,绷紧的 (*opp*. slack, loose)。**4.** 严格的,严厉的。**5.** 紧贴的,正合身的(衣服等);装紧的,密集的。**6.** 麻烦的,棘手的,困难的;危险的。**7.** 整洁的(少女等)。**8.**〔美口〕吝啬的,啬刻的。**9.**【商】供应紧张的。**10.** (比赛等)势均力敌的。**11.** (文字,作品等)紧凑的,精炼的,排得紧的。**12.**〔俚〕醉醺醺的。*The stopper is too* ～ *that it can't be withdrawn*. 瓶塞太紧拔不出来了。*These shoes are painfully* ～. 这双鞋紧得难受。*Fill the cases so that they are* ～. 把这些匣子装得满满的。*I know you're in a* ～ *place again*. 我晓得你又处于困境了。*An armyman must be under* ～ *discipline*. 军人应守严格纪律。*Money is* ～. 银根紧。*a* ～ *squeeze* 紧紧的握手;〔口〕下不得台的情形;〔美〕九死一生;难分胜负的战斗。**II** *n*. 〔*pl*.〕紧身衣。**III** *ad*. 紧,紧紧地。*sit* ～ 坐稳,固执,坚持。***be in a*** ～ ***place*** 处境困难〔窘迫〕。***get*** ～〔俚〕大醉。***keep a*** ～ ***rein*** [***hand***] ***on*** 严厉控制,抓紧。***perform on the*** ～ ***rope*** 走钢丝。～ ***as a mink***〔美〕喝得烂醉的。～ ***corner*** [***spot***] 穷境。～**fisted** *a*. 吝啬的。～**fitting** *a*. 紧身的。～**knit** *a*. 紧密编织的,紧险的。～**-laced** *a*. 穿着紧腰衣的;严格的。～**lipped** *a*. 闭紧嘴的,嘴紧的,话少的。～ **money market** 银根紧的金融市场。～ **riveting**【机】紧密铆合。～**rope** (杂技中走索用的)紧绷索。～**-wad**〔美俚〕吝啬鬼。**-ly** *ad*. **-ness** *n*.

tight·en [ˈtaitn; ˋtaɪtn̩] *vt*., *vi*. 收紧,拉紧,抽紧;绷紧;固定。～ ***one's belt***〔谑〕束紧裤带;节省支出。

ti·glon [ˈtaiglən; ˋtaɪglɑn, -glən], **ti·gon** [ˈtaigən; ˋtaɪgon] *n*. 虎狮〔公虎与母狮杂交的后代〕。

ti·gress [ˈtaigris; ˋtaɪgrɪs] *n*.【动】母老虎;凶恶泼辣的女人。

ti·grine [ˈtaigrain; ˋtaɪgrɪn, -graɪn] *a*. 虎(似)的,虎纹的。

Ti·gri·nya [tiˈgriːnjə; tiˋgrinjə] *n*. 现代埃塞俄比亚语。

Ti·gris [ˈtaigris; ˋtaɪgrɪs] *n*. 〔the ～〕底格里斯河(亚洲)。

tigrish [ˈtaigriʃ; ˋtaɪgrɪʃ] *a*. = *tiger*ish.

T.I.H. = Their Imperial Highnesses〔英〕殿下们。

tike, tyke [taik; taɪk] *n*. **1.** 野狗,杂种狗;小孩子。**2.**〔口〕顽皮的孩子。**3.**〔Scot.〕乡下佬。*a Yorkshire* ～ 约克佬〔无轻蔑意〕。

tik·ker [ˈtikə; ˋtɪkɚ] *n*.【无】= ticker.

til [til, tiːl; tɪl, til] *n*. = teel.

til·ak [ˈtilək; ˋtɪlək] *n*. (印度人)用红化妆油点在前额上的圆点。

til·bu·ry [ˈtilbəri; ˋtɪlˏberɪ, -bərɪ] *n*. 双人坐的二轮轻便马车。

tilde [tild, ˈtildi; ˋtɪldə, -dɪ] *n*. **1.**〔Sp.〕腭鼻音符号(即西班牙字母 n 上加的发音符号〔señor 的'～'〕)。**2.** 代字号〔～〕(又叫 swung dash)。**3.**【数,逻】否定号〔～〕。

Til·den [ˈtildin, ˈtidən; ˋtɪldən] *n*. 蒂尔登〔姓氏〕。

tile [tail; taɪl] **I** *n*. **1.** 瓦;【建】瓷砖,花砖,(软木,橡胶等制的)弹性地砖,贴砖,铺瓦,瓦片,瓦面,瓦管。**2.**〔口语〕礼帽,高顶帽。**3.** (中国麻将牌的)牌。*a Dutch* ～ 彩砖,花砖,画砖。～ *floor* 砖地。～ *roofing* 瓦屋顶。**II** *vt*. **1.** 用瓦盖,铺瓦,砌瓷砖。**2.** (秘密结社集会时)派人守望,使发誓守秘密,严守秘密。***be*** (***out***) ***on the*** ～***s***〔俚〕寻欢作乐,花天酒地。***fly a*** ～〔俚〕把帽子打掉。***have a*** ～ ***loose***〔俚〕有点疯,神志有点错乱。～ **stone**【建】石瓦,石板。～**-tea** 茶砖。

til·er [ˈtailə; ˋtaɪlɚ] *n*. 制瓦工人;瓦匠;秘密结社守望人。

til·er·y [ˈtailəri; ˋtaɪlərɪ] *n*. **1.** 瓦厂。**2.** 装饰性砖瓦铺贴术。

til·ing [ˈtailiŋ; ˋtaɪlɪŋ] *n*. **1.** 盖瓦;铺瓷砖。**2.**〔集合词〕(屋)瓦,瓦类,瓷砖,花砖。**3.** 瓦屋顶,瓦面,砖面,砖瓦结构。

till[1][til; tɪl] **I** ***prep***. 〔基本上与 until 相同,但句首一般不用 till,而用 until〕**1.** 直到…为止。**2.**〔在否定句中〕直到…才…;在…前(不…)。*Wait* ～ *tomorrow*. 等到明天。*serve the people* ～ *death* 为民众服务到死为止〔一生〕。*He did not return* ～ *ten*. 他到十点钟才回。*It was not* ～ *evening that I knew the fact*. 到黄昏时我才知道那件事。**II** ***conj***. **1.** 直到…为止。**2.**〔在否定句后〕在…之前,直到…的时候才…。*We lived in London* ～ *I was twenty*. 我们住在伦敦直到我二十岁。*People do not know the value of health* ～ *they lose it*. 失去健康时,人们才知道健康的价值。～ ***all's blue*** 到极点。**"*T- Called For*"**【铁路】留站(待领);【邮局】留局(待领)。～ ***the cows come home***〔美〕将长时期地;永久地。

till[2][til; tɪl] *n*. **1.** (账桌中)放钱的抽斗,抽屉。**2.** (橱柜中)放贵重物的格子或抽屉。**3.** 钱柜,钱箱。～ *money* 备用现金。

till[3][til; tɪl] *n*.【地】冰碛土(物)。

till[4][til; tɪl] *vt*., *vi*. 耕种,翻耕,耕作。*We've five tractors to* ～ *the land*. 我们有五架拖拉机耕地。～*ed crops* 中耕作物。

till·a·ble [ˈtiləbl; ˋtɪləbl̩] *a*. 适于耕种的。

till·age [ˈtilidʒ; ˋtɪlɪdʒ] *n*. **1.** 耕种,耕作,整地。**2.** 耕作(地);耕地上的作物。

til·land·si·a [tiˈlændziə; tɪˋlændzɪə] *n*.【植】铁兰属(*Tillandsia*)植物〔尤指铁兰〕。

till·er[1][ˈtilə; ˋtɪlɚ] *n*. 耕作者,农夫。*land to the* ～ 耕者有其田。

till·er[2][ˈtilə; ˋtɪlɚ] *n*.【船】舵柄。～**-chain** *n*. 转舵链。～**-rope** *n*. 转舵索。

till·er[3][ˈtilə; ˋtɪlɚ] **I** *n*.【植】分蘖,(树桩上长出的)萌蘖。**II** *vi*. 萌蘖,生新芽,长嫩苗。

till·ite [ˈtilait; ˋtɪlaɪt] *n*.【地】冰碛岩。

tilt[1][tilt; tɪlt] **I** *vi*. **1.** 倾斜(侧),歪斜;翘起。**2.** (在马上)拿枪扎;马上刺枪比赛;〔喻〕抨击,攻击 (*at*; *against*);战斗。**3.**〔美〕有倾向性,偏袒(*toward*)。— *vt*. **1.** 使倾侧;使歪斜,使翘起。**2.** (拿枪)扎,戳,戳过去;〔喻〕攻击;驳,抨击。**3.** 用跳动锤锻打。*He likes to* ～ *his head forward*. 他喜欢把头往前倾。*Don't* ～ *your hat sideways*. 不要歪戴帽子。*In the class meeting, Jack* ～*ed at John*. 班会上,杰克猛烈地抨击了约翰。*The table* ～*ed* (*over*) *and the thermos slid off it to the ground*. 桌子歪了,热水瓶从上面滑到地上。**II** *n*. **1.** 偏倾,歪斜,倾侧;斜坡,坡度。**2.** 马上刺枪比赛;〔喻〕激烈的竞争,争论。**3.**〔美〕比赛;拳赛;竞争;争论。**4.** 跳动锤,落锤。**5.** 跷跷板。(***at***) ***full*** ～ 开足速力,用全速力;猛冲,拼命(冲过去等)。***give a*** ～ 使倾斜。***have a*** ～ ***at*** **1.** 偏向,向…歪。**2.** 攻击,驳斥。***on the*** ～ 倾斜着,歪着。～ ***of wave front***【物】波前倾斜。～**hammer** *n*. 跳动锤 (=clinometer)。～**-meter** 测斜器。～ **rotor**

T

斜旋翼飞机。～-**top** 可调节桌面[顶板]倾斜度的。～-**yard** *n*.(中世纪的)马上冲刺比赛场。-**ed** *a*. 倾斜的,翘起的。

tilt[2][tilt; tɪlt] **I** *n*.(小舟、车辆、地摊等的)帐篷,遮阳;车盖。**II** *vt*. 用帐篷遮盖,搭帐篷。

tilth [tilθ; tɪlθ] *n*. **1**. 耕种,耕作(深度),翻耕。**2**. 耕作地,已耕地[土层];整地。

Tim [tim; tɪm] *n*. 帝姆〔男子名, Timothy 的昵称〕。

Tim. = Timothy.

tim·bal, tim·bul [ˈtimbəl; ˋtɪmbl̩] *n*. **1**. 铜鼓 (= kettledrum)。**2**.【动】(蝉等的)鼓膜,鼓室,鸣腔。

tim·bale [tæmˈbɑːl, ˈtimbəl; ˋtɪmbəl, ˏtɛ̃ˋbɑl] *n*. **1**. 香烤三味〔用鸡、虾、鱼、加大量作料,于鼓形容器内烘烤〕。**2**. 炸(烤)馅饼 (= timbale case)。

tim·ber [ˈtimbə; ˋtɪmbɚ] **I** *n*. **1**. 原木,木材,木料。**2**. (可作木材的)树木;森林;〔美〕森林地,林场。**3**. 横木,栋木;【船】船骨,肋材。**4**. 品质;素质;〔美〕才能,才干。**5**. 〔英〕【猎】木造障碍物[围栏等],(猎狐时用的)木栅栏,木门。**6**.〔板球俚〕三柱门。*cut down* (*fell*) ～ 伐木。*We must safeguard forest* ～. 我们必须保护林木。*Fire destroyed thousand acres of* ～. 火焚毁了千亩林木。*He is a statesman of the highest* ～. 他是个高尚的政治家。*My* ～*s*! = *Shiver* [*Dash*] *my* ～*s*!〔海俚〕混蛋! 可恶! 讨厌!〔水手最普通的骂人话〕。**II** *int*. (伐木工在木倒时喊)倒啦! **III** *vt*. 备以木材;用木料支撑。～-**beast**〔美〕森林工人,伐木工人。～-**cart** 运木车。～ **connector** 木结构。～ **dealer** 木材商。～-**headed** *a*. 〔俚〕笨的。～ **hitch** (套吊圆材的)绳结,8 字结。～ **jack** 〔美〕伐木人。～**land**〔美〕林场,森林。～-**line** 树木线。～ **mill** 锯木厂,木工厂。～ **rattlesnake**【动】林响蛇。～ **right**【法】采伐权(不包括林地所有权)。～ **skipper** = ～ topper〔美〕跳栏运动员。～ **stand improvement**【林】疏伐。～-**toes**〔口〕装有木头假脚的人。～ **wolf** 大灰狼;〔俚〕伐木人。～-**work** 木结构,木材料,木料工厂。～**yard**〔英〕木材堆置场;〔板球俚〕(击球员的)三柱门。

tim·bered [ˈtimbəd; ˋtɪmbɚd] *a*. **1**. 木制的。**2**. 森林的,多树木的。**3**. 露出栋木的〔如墙〕。

tim·ber·ing [ˈtimbəriŋ; ˋtɪmbərɪŋ] *n*. **1**.〔集合词〕木材。**2**. 结构材,木结构。

tim·bre [tɛ̃ːmbr, ˈtæmbə; ˋtɪmbɚ] *n*. 〔F.〕【乐】音色,音质。

tim·brel [ˈtimbrəl; ˋtɪmbrəl] *n*. = tambourine.

Tim·buk·tu, Tim·buc·too [ˌtimbʌkˈtuː; ˏtɪmbʌkˋtu, tɪmˋbʌktu] *n*. 廷巴克图〔马里城市〕。

time [taim; taɪm] **I** *n*. **1**. 时,时间,时日,岁月。**2**. 时候,时刻;期间;时节,季节;〔常 *pl*.〕时期,年代,时代;〔the ～〕当代,现代。**3**. 怀孕期,分娩期;修业期,服役期,学徒期间;(规定的)工作时间,占用时间,所需时间;〔口〕刑期;死期,临终;一生;闲暇,余暇。**4**. 时机,机会;时局,形势。**5**. 次,度,回;倍。**6**.【运】开始! 停!〔裁判员的口令〕。**7**.【乐】拍子,进行速度,节奏。**8**.【军】步伐。**9**.【地】纪。*T- flies*. 光阴似箭。*The new scheme will save both* ～ *and labour*. 新方案既省时间又省劳力。*Have you* ～ *to help us with the job*? 你有时间帮我们干干活儿吗? *nap* ～〔美〕睡觉时间。*dead* ～【火箭】滞后时间,迟滞。*What* ～ *is it*? 现在几点钟? *Have you the* ～? 现在几点? *ancient* ～*s* 古代。*men of the* ～ 现代的人。*We have to remould our world outlook, since* ～*s are different*. 我们必须改变世界观,因为时代不同了。*hard* [*bad*] ～*s* 萧条,不景气。*What a* ～ *you have been*! 相当费工夫了吧! *Now is your* ～! 现在正是你的好机会! *Mary is near her* ～. 玛丽快要分娩了。*I learned much while sewing my* ～. 我当学徒时,学了不少的东西。*We were pressed for* ～. 我们时间很紧迫。*Each* ～ *I spelt the word, I made the same mistake*. 我每次拼写这个词,总是犯同样的错误。*Six* ～*s five is thirty*. 五乘六得三十。*beat* ～ 打拍子。*Time and tide wait for no man*. 岁月不等人。～ *of effect*【商】有效期间。～ *of grace*【法】禁猎期。**II** *vt*. 为…选择时机;安排…时间;测定(赛跑等的)时间;校准(钟表);使合拍。— *vi*. 合拍;一致,调和;【剑术】乘隙进攻。～ *the speed* 计算速度。～ *a watch* 对表。*The remark was not well* ～*d*. 这话说得不是时候。*The plane is* ～*d to take off at 5 a.m*. 飞机定于上午五时起飞。*There's no hurry. One must* ～ *one's blows*. 不要忙,我们要伺机予以打击。***abreast of the*** ～***s*** 赶上时代,不落后于时代;最新式的;熟悉现况的。***against*** ～ 尽快地,分秒必争地,力争及时完成地。***ahead of*** ～ 提早,比原定提前地。***all in good*** ～ 时机一到。***all the*** ～ 始终;〔美〕老是。***and about*** ～ ***too***! 正是时候,正合时机。***as*** ～ ***goes on*** 随着时代的推移。***as*** ～***s go*** 在现在这个时势,在现在这个时节。***at a set*** ～ 在约定的时候。***at a*** ～ 一次(多少);同时;曾经;连续 (*Take two pills at a* ～. 一次吃两粒(药)。*for weeks at a* ～ 连续好几个星期)。***at all*** ～***s*** 不论什么时候;老是。***at no*** ～ 在任何时候都不,从来没有,决不。***at one and the same*** ～ 在同时,一面…一面又。***at one*** ～ 同时;有一个星期,曾经。***at other*** ～***s*** 往常,平素。***at the same*** ～ 同时;但还是。***at this*** ～ ***of*** (***the***) ***day*** 这个时候,到这个时候,这样早[迟]。***at this*** ～ ***of the year*** 在这个时节。***at*** ～***s*** 时时。***be behind*** [***ahead of***] ***the*** [***one's***] ～(***s***) 落后[先进]。***be doing*** ～ ***at ...*** 在…服徒刑中。***be pressed for*** ～ 忙,没工夫。***before one's*** ～ **1**. 提前,不足月(而生)。**2**. 在某人出世前。**3**. 早衰,夭折。***before the*** [***one's***] ～***s*** (跑)在时代前头。***behind*** ～ 迟(到)。***between*** ～***s*** 时时,偶尔,间或。***bid one's*** ～ 等待时机。***buy*** ～ 拖延时间,赢得时间。***by the*** ～ 到…的时候。***by this*** ～ 在这个时候以前;快到这个时候。***call*** ～ (裁判员)宣布时间已到。***can see the*** ～ 可指日以待。***can tell the*** ～ 会看钟;知道现在是几点钟。***come to*** ～ 履行义务。***do*** ～ 服徒刑。***down*** ～【计算机】停机时间。***find*** ～ 有工夫,有空。***for a*** ～ 暂时 (*It will last for a* ～. 暂时还经得住)。***for the*** ～ ***being*** 暂时,在目前。***from one*** ～ ***to the next*** 每一次。***from*** ～ ***to*** ～ 时时。***give sb. the*** ～ ***of his life*** 见 ～ of one's life. ***give*** (***sb.***) ～ 宽限时间,给与考虑的时间。***half the*** ～ **1**. 一半时间 (*We fulfilled the quota in half the* ～. 我们只用一半时间就完成了定额)。**2**. (几乎)经常。***has done*** [***served***] ***its*** ～ (物品)已经用得不能再用了。***have a good*** [***royal***] ～ (***of it***) 很愉快 (*I have had a good* [*bad*] ～ *of it*. (今天)愉快[倒霉]极了)。***have a hard*** ～ = ***have a tough*** (***rough***) ～ ***of it*** 日子不好过。***have the*** ～ ***of one's life*** 快活[痛苦]已极。***Have I*** ～ (***to...***)? 有…的工夫吗? 赶得上…吗? ***have no*** ～ ***to spare*** 没有空,忙得很 ***have oneself a*** ～ 过得快乐。***have*** ～ ***to burn*** 有用不完的时间。***in a week's*** ～ 一星期后。***in good*** [***bad***] ～ 按[误]时,及[不及]时。***in jig*** ～〔口〕极快地。***in*** (***less than***) ***no*** ～〔口〕立刻。***in one's own good*** ～ 在有便的时候。***in one's own*** ～ 在有空的时候。***in one's*** ～ 在…年轻的时候。***in slow*** [***true***] ～ 用缓慢的[正常的]节拍。***in*** (***the***) ***course of*** ～ 最后,经过一段时间。***in the mean*** ～ 在那个时间中;同时。***in the nick of*** ～ 正是时候,正在关键时刻。***in*** ～ **1**. 在恰好的时候,及时,赶上。**2**. 经过一段时间以后;早晚,总有一天。**3**. 和…合拍 (*with*)。***keep good*** [***bad***] ～ (钟)准[不准]。***keep*** ～ 使(脚)合拍子(*with*)。***kill*** ～ 消磨时间。***know the*** ～ ***of day*** **1**. 消息灵通,有经验。**2**. 处事机警,能见机行事。***lose no*** ～ ***in...*** 赶紧…,立刻…。***lose*** ～ (钟表)慢;耽搁。***make*** ～ **1**. 腾出时间做(某事) (*Could you make* ～ *to type this out*? 你能腾出时间把这个打出来吗?)。**2**. (以某种速度)进行。***many a*** ～ [或 ***many*** ～***s***] 多次,常常。***many a*** ～ ***and of*** (或 ***many and many a*** ～)〔诗〕许多次。***mark*** ～ **1**.【军】原地踏步。**2**. (转义)停

滞不前,没有进展。***near one's*** ~ 快死;(产妇)快生。***of the*** ~ 当时的〔尤指当今的,现在的〕。***on*** ~ 按时,准时。***on full*** ~ 全日制的,专任的。***on one's own*** ~ 在规定工作时间以外。***on short*** ~ 开工时间不足,以部分时间开工。***once upon a*** ~ 从前〔故事开头用语〕。***one*** ~ ***with another*** 先后合起来(*He was president one* ~ *with another for ten years*. 他先后一共当了十年校长)。***out of*** ~ 过迟;不合时宜;不合拍的。***pass the*** ~ ***of day*** (*with sb*.) (与某人)打招呼(如说"你早"之类)。***play for*** ~ 拖延着以争取时间。***serve one's*** ~ 做满学徒期间。***some*** ~ ***or other*** 早晚,迟早。***take a long*** ~ 费时间。***So that's the*** ~ ***of day***!〔俚〕情况原来如此!(或原来是你要的花招!)。***straight*** ~ 正规的工作时间(不包括请假或加班等时间)。***take all one's*** ~ 相当麻烦。***take one's*** ~ (***in***) 从容,慢慢干,不急。***take*** ~ 需要时日,费时间。***talk against*** ~ **1**. 在规定时间内尽快讲完。**2**. 用谈话(讨论)消磨时间(以阻挠议案通过等)。***the good old*** ~***s*** 往昔。***There are*** ~***s when*** …有时常会…。***There is a*** ~ ***for everything***. 做事要当其时。***Those were*** (***fine***) ~ ***s***! 好快活的岁月呀! ~ ***about***〔Scot.〕轮流。~ ***after*** ~ = ~ ***and*** (~) ***again*** 反复,再三再四。~ ***and a half*** 超过原工资标准一半的加班工资。~ ***and tide*** 时候,岁月。~ ***enough*** 有充分时间。***Time hangs heavily on sb.'s hands***. 某人感到时间难以打发。***Time is money***.〔谚〕一寸光阴一寸金。~ ***is up*** 时间已到。(***the***) ~ ***of day*** **1**. 时刻(*at this* ~ *of day* 这个时候) **2**. 情况,形势,事态(*He knows the* ~ *of day*. 他知道情况)。(***the***) ~ ***of one's life***〔俚〕一生中特别愉快〔激动〕的一段时间(*have the* ~ *of one's life* 快活〔痛苦〕已极)。~ ***out of mind*** [~ ***immemorial***] 自从很早很早以来;很久以前。~ ***to run***【商】扣除日;经过日数。~ ***to spare*** 余暇。~***s out of*** (或 ***without***) ***number*** 数不清的再三再四,无数次。***Times Square*** **1**. (纽约市 Broadway 与 42 号街交叉处的)纽约时报广场。**2**.〔美〕纽约方言。***T- was when***.... 事情发生在从前…的时候。***to*** ~〔英〕=〔美〕on ~. ***up to*** ~ 准时。***watch one's*** ~ 伺机。***work against*** ~ 以最大的速度工作。***with*** ~ 随着时间的经过。~ **alarm** 定时警报。~ **and a half** 相当于原工资一倍半的加班费。~ **ball** 报时球。~**-bargain**【商】期货交易。~ **base** **1**. 时间坐标;【无】时基,时轴。**2**. 扫描。~ **bill** **1**.〔英〕(火车的)时间表。**2**.【商】(定)期(付现支)票。~ **bomb** **1**. 定时炸弹。**2**. 潜在的爆炸性局势。~ **book** **1**. 出勤记录簿。**2**. = ~ table. ~**card** 出勤[工作]时间记录卡片。~ **capsule** 当代文物史料储放器〔埋藏起来供后人了解当时情况〕。~ **clock** 生产[出勤]记录钟;【无】时钟脉冲。~ **constant** (电子)时间常数。~**-consuming** ***a***. 花费大量时间的。~ **deposit** 定期存款。~ **difference** 时差。~ **discount**【商】贴现。~ **draft**【商】期票。~**-expired** ***a***.【军】满服役期的。~ **exposure**【摄】时间曝光〔半秒钟以上〕;时间曝光相片。~ **factor** 时间因素。~ **fuse** 定时信管(~ *fuse bomb* 定时炸弹)。~ **frame**〔美〕时间框架,一段时间。~ **gun** 午炮,报时炮。~ **immemorial** ***a***. **1**. 太古的;久远的。**2**.【英法】有史以前的〔法令规定为 1189 年,理查一世统治时为界〕。~**- interval** 时间(间隔)。~**keeper** 钟表;工作时间记录员;(运动比赛等的)计时员(*a good* [*bad*] ~*keeper* 时间准确[不准确]的钟表[人])。~ **killer** **1**. 消磨时间的人。**2**. 消遣物。~ **lag** (一事和另一事之间的)时间间隔;【物】时滞。~**-lapse** ***a***.【影】微速摄影的〔以低速摄影,用正当速度放映,用来显示植物的缓慢生长过程〕。~ **limit** 期限,限期。~ **loan** (**money**) 定期贷款。~ **lock** 定时锁。~**-out** 休息时间;不算在工作时间内的时间;【运】暂停时间。~**-piece** **1**. = chronometer. **2**. 钟表。~**rate** 计时工资制。~**-saving** ***a***. 节约时间的。~**server** 趋炎附势的人。~**-serving** ***n***., ***a***. 随波逐流(的);无节操(的)。~ **sharing**【自】分时,时间分割[划分]。~ **sheet** 工作时间记录单,考勤单。~**-shell**【军】曳火弹,空炸炮弹。~(**-**)**shift** 定时移位录像(尤指人不在时由录像机自行录电视节目)。~ **signal** 报时信号。~ **signature**【乐】拍子记号。~ **slot** **1**.【计】时间片。**2**.【电视,无】广播时隙 ~ **space** 时空,四维空间。~ **spirit** 时代精神。~**-table** 时间表。~**-tested** ***a***. 经过时间检验的;为时间所证明了的。~ **unit** 时间单位;准时器,测时计。~ **warp**【物】时间翘曲〔相对论中假想的时流之不连续性或扭曲〕。~**work** 计时工作。~**worn** ***a***. 陈旧的。~ **zone**【天】时区。

time·less [ˈtaimlis; ˋtaɪmlɪs] ***a***. **1**. 超时间的,无限的,永久的,长期有效的,不定期的,不定时的。**2**. 不是时候的,不合时宜的。**-ly** ***ad***.

time·li·ness [ˈtaimlinis; ˋtaɪmlɪnɪs] ***n***. 合乎时机,适时,及时。

time·ly [ˈtaimli; ˋtaɪmlɪ] ***a***. (***-li·er***; ***-li·est***) 及的,适时的,合时的,正好的。~ *help* 及时的帮助。*a* ~ *joke* 正合时机的笑话。

tim·er [ˈtaimə; ˋtaɪmɚ] ***n***. **1**. 时计,跑表。**2**. 记时员。**3**. 定时继电器;程序调节器,定时(延迟)调节器,定时装置,自动定时仪。**4**. (内燃机的)发火定时器。**5**. (汽车的)时速表。**6**. 按时计酬的工人。*a first* ~ *in the office* 初次到职工作的人。*a half* ~〔英〕半工半读的学龄儿童。*an old* ~〔美〕老资格,老手;守旧的人。

time·ous [ˈtaiməs; ˋtaɪməs] ***a***.〔Scot.〕= timely.

Times [taimz; taɪmz], ***The*** (英国)泰晤士报。*write to The* ~ 给泰晤士报投稿;向报社写信。

tim·id [ˈtimid; ˋtɪmɪd] ***a***. **1**. 胆小的,羞怯的,提心吊胆的。**2**.〔用作表语〕对…害怕(*of*);(对生人)难为情(*with*);(对事)缩手缩脚(*about*)。*Jane is* ~ *of the bull dog*. 珍害怕那条叭喇狗。***as*** ~ ***as a hare*** 胆子极小的。**-ly** ***ad***. **-ness** ***n***.

ti·mid·i·ty [tiˈmiditi; tɪˋmɪdətɪ] ***n***. 胆小,羞怯。*Wang shows an almost childlike* ~ *in talking with strangers*. 王和生人谈话简直像小孩子般地羞怯。

tim·ing [ˈtaimiŋ; ˋtaɪmɪŋ] ***n***. **1**. 时间选择。**2**. 定时,校时,计时,调速。**3**.【自】同步;时限。*The* ~ *of our statement is very opportune*. 我们发表声明选择的时机很恰当。*pulse* ~ 脉冲同步,脉冲计时。*a* ~ *dial* (收音机的)电眼。*a* ~ *generator* 定时信号发生器。~ *devices* 定时装置。

ti·moc·ra·cy [taiˈmɔkrəsi; taɪˋmɑkrəsɪ] ***n***. **1**. (柏拉图〔Plato〕著作中)荣誉政治。**2**. (亚里士多德〔Aristotle〕著作中)财权政治。**-crat·ic** [ˌtaiməˈkrætik; ˏtaɪməˋkrætɪk] ***a***.

Ti·mon [ˈtaimən; ˋtaɪmən] ***n***. **1**. 泰门〔希腊哲学家〕。**2**.〔t-〕愤世嫉俗的人。

Timor [ˈtiːmɔː; ˋtimɔr, tɪˋmɔr] ***n***. 帝汶岛〔马来群岛之一〕。

tim·or·ous [ˈtimərəs; ˋtɪmərəs, ˋtɪmrəs] ***a***. = timid. *Don't think I'm a* ~ *teacher who can't control the children*. 不要认为我是个胆子小不敢管小学生的老师。**-ness** ***n***.

Tim·o·thy [ˈtiməθi; ˋtɪməθɪ] ***n***. 蒂莫西〔男子名〕。

tim·o·thy [ˈtiməθi; ˋtɪməθɪ] ***n***.【植】梯牧草,猫尾草。

Ti·m(o)ur [tiˈmuə; tɪˋmʊr] ***n***. 帖木儿(= Tamerlane)。

tim·pa·no [ˈtimpənəu; ˋtɪmpəˏno] ***n***. (*pl*. ***-ni*** [-niː; -nɪ])【乐】定音鼓。**-pa·nist** ***n***. 鼓手。

tim·pan·ol·o·gy [ˌtimpæˈnɔlədʒi; ˏtɪmpæˋnɑlədʒɪ] ***n***.【乐】打鼓学。

tin [tin; tɪn] **I** ***n***. **1**. 锡。**2**. 镀锡薄钢板,马口铁,白铁。**3**. 锡器;罐头;(容量)〔英〕一罐[听](=〔美〕can)。**4**.〔美俚〕警察的徽章;警察。**5**.〔俚〕钱。*stream* ~ 砂锡。*wood* ~ 纤锡矿,木锡石。*a* ~ *of biscuits* 一听饼干。**II** ***a***. **1**. 锡制的;马口铁制的。**2**. 无价值的,蹩脚的;假冒的。*a* ~ *beard* 假胡须。*a little* ~ *god* 自以为了不起的小人物;小爬虫。**III** ***vt***. (***-nn-***) **1**. 镀锡,包锡,包白铁。**2**.〔美〕做成罐头食品。***not on your*** ~ ***type***〔美

俚〕决不。**put the ～ hat on** 结束，制止。～ **can** 1. 锡杯，锡罐。2. 罐头；洋铁罐。3.〔美俚〕老式汽车。4.〔美海军俚〕小驱逐舰，潜艇，深水炸弹。～ **clad** *n*.〔谑〕装甲舰。～ **cow**〔美俚〕罐头牛奶。～ **ear**〔美俚〕1. 聋耳朵；受伤后畸形的耳朵；重听 2. 缺乏乐感的人，缺乏乐感。～ **fish**〔美俚〕鱼雷。～ **foil** *n*. 1. 锡箔；锡纸。2. *vt*. 包上锡箔，用锡纸包。～ **hat** 钢盔；〔*pl*.〕【海俚】醉鬼。～**horn** *a*.，*n*.〔美俚〕不值钱的，吹牛的；无聊人物，浅薄的花花公子，赌金少的赌徒。～**-lined pipe**【机】衬锡管。～ **liquor**【化】二氯化锡液。～ **lizzie**〔或 L-〕老式汽车；价钱便宜的汽车[飞机]。～ **man** *n*. = tinsmith. ～ **opener** 开罐头的刀。～ **pants**〔美俚〕(石蜡处理过的)防水帆布裤。～ **parachute** 低额遣散费(制度)。～**-plate** 马口铁，镀锡铁皮。～ **pot** 1. 锡罐，锡壶，马口铁罐。2. 镀锡时用的镕锡器皿。～**-pot** *a*. 低劣的，微不足道的。～**smith** 白铁匠。～ **solder** 锡焊，软焊锡，软焊料。～**star**〔美俚〕私家侦探。～**stone**【矿】锡石。～**ware** 白铁工艺品（*hand out the* ～ *ware*〔美〕道贺；奖赏；褒奖）。～**work** 锡器，白铁制品；〔*pl*.〕锡器厂，白铁制品厂。

Ti·na [ˈtiːnə; ˋtinə] *n*. 蒂娜〔女子名〕。

tin·a·mou [ˈtinəmuː; ˋtɪnəˏmu] *n*.【鸟】(南美产的)一种鹪科鸟。

tin·cal, tin·kal [ˈtiŋkəl, -kɔl; ˋtɪŋkɑl, -kəl] *n*.【矿】原[粗]硼砂。

tinct. = tincture.

tinct [tiŋkt; tɪŋkt] I *n*. 颜色；色调；染料。II *a*. 着色的，染色的。

tinc·tion [ˈtiŋkʃən; ˋtɪŋkʃən] *n*. 着色，染色。

tinc·to·ri·al [tiŋkˈtɔːriəl; tɪŋkˋtorɪəl] *a*. 颜色的，生色的，着色的，染色的。*a* ～ *pattern* 色样。

tinc·ture [ˈtiŋktʃə; ˋtɪŋktʃɚ] I *n*. 1. 色，色彩；色泽，色调。2. 染料，颜料。3.（染上的）色；迹象；气息，气味，特征。4.【徽】(金属、彩色、毛皮等的)颜色。5.【医】酊剂，药酒。*a* ～ *of red* 红的色调。*a* ～ *of French manners* 法国人的气质。*I'd say he is a man who has the least* ～ *of learning*. 我认为他是个最没有学术气味的人。～ *of iodine* 碘酒。II *vt*. 1. 着色，染。2. 使有某种风味；使带某种气味[色彩]。*be* ～*d with prejudice* 带有偏见。*Your cigar* ～*s the room with an awful smell*. 你吸雪茄烟弄得满屋子都是臭味。

tin·der [ˈtində; ˋtɪndɚ] *n*. 1. 火绒，火种，引火物。2. 导火线。*burn like* ～ 易燃。～**box** 1. 火绒箱。2. 易燃的物品(建筑，场所)。3. 脾气暴躁的人。～ **ore** 羽毛矿。

tin·der·y [ˈtindəri; ˋtɪndərɪ] *a*. 火绒似的，易燃烧的。

tine [tain; taɪn] *n*.（叉、鹿角等的)尖齿，叉。～ **test**【医】结核菌素穿刺试验。

tin·e·a [ˈtiniə; ˋtɪnɪə] *n*.【医】癣。

tined [taind; taɪnd] *a*. 有齿的，有叉的。*a three-* ～ *fork* 三齿叉。

tin·e·id [ˈtiniːid; ˋtɪnɪɪd] I *n*.【动】谷蛾科（*Tineidae*）动物〔包括衣蛾（*Tinea Pellionella*）〕。II *a*. 谷蛾科的。

ting[1] [tiŋ; tɪŋ] I *n*. 玎玲声，铃声。II *vt*.，*vi*.（使)玎玲玎玲响。

ting[2] [tiŋ; tɪŋ] *n*. = thing[2].

ting-a-ling [ˈtiŋəliŋ; ˋtɪŋəˏlɪŋ] *n*.，*ad*. 铃声；玎玲玎玲地(响)。

tinge [tindʒ; tɪndʒ] I *n*. 1.（较淡的)色彩，色调。2. 迹象，味道，气味。3. 微量；少许。II *vt*.（*ting*(*e*)·*ing*）1. 染，着色于。2. 使具有某种气味。*This dish has a strong* ～ *of Chinese cuisine*. 这道菜很有些中国菜的风味。*have a* ～ *of hypocrisy* 有点伪善气。*There is a slight* ～ *of humour in it*. 这里边有点幽默气味。*These are words* ～*d with cynicism*. 这是些有挑毛病意味的字眼。*Now the maple leaves are* ～*d with autumn red*. 现在枫叶微带秋天的红色。

tin·gle [ˈtiŋgl; ˋtɪŋgl] I *n*. 1. 刺痛；(耳等的)鸣响。2. 震颤。3. 激动，兴奋。II *vi*. 1.（身体因寒冷、打击等)刺痛。2.（耳等)鸣叫。3. 震颤，激动，兴奋。*Don't make such a harsh noise*. *My ears are tingling*. 别这样刺耳地吵，我都震聋了。

ti·ni·ness [ˈtaininis; ˋtaɪnənɪs] *n*. 极小，微小。

tin·kal [ˈtiŋkəl; ˋtɪŋkl] *n*. = tincal.

tink·er [ˈtiŋkə; ˋtɪŋkɚ] I *n*. 1.〔英〕小炉匠；补锅匠；修补匠；补锅；修补。2. 拙劣的工人；粗劣的修补。3.〔美〕杂活工人，打杂工。4.〔苏，爱〕吉卜赛人；流浪工人；流浪者；乞丐。5. 小臼炮。6.〔美〕小鲐鱼。II *vi*.，*vt*. 做补锅匠；拙劣地修补。**have a** ～ **at** ... 笨拙地设法修理。**not care a** ～**'s damn** [**curse, cuss**] 一点不在乎。**not worth a** ～**'s cuss** (**curse, damn**) 毫无价值。**T- toy**〔美〕(原商标名)结构玩具〔一套各种形状的零件，儿童可用螺栓等接合零件自由地结合成房屋，车辆等结构〕。**-ly** *a*. 补锅匠似的；粗笨的，拙劣的。

tin·kle [ˈtiŋkl; ˋtɪŋkl] I *n*. 1. 玎玲(声)。2.〔俚〕电话。*give sb*. *a* ～ 给某人打电话。II *vi*.，*vt*. 1.（使)玎玲玎玲响。2.〔美，儿〕撒尿。～ *a bell* 摇铃。

tin·kler [ˈtiŋklə; ˋtɪŋklɚ] *n*. 1. 玎玲玎玲响的东西[人]。2.〔俚〕铃铛。**-kling** *a*. 玎玲玎玲响的。

tinned [tind; tɪnd] *a*. 1. 镀锡的，包锡[包白铁]的。2.〔英〕罐头的（=〔美〕canned)。～ *iron* [*plate*] 白铁皮，马口铁。～ air【海】人工通风。～ *salmon* 罐头鲑鱼。～ **dog**〔澳俚〕罐装肉，听装肉。

tin·ner [ˈtinə; ˋtɪnɚ] *n*. 1. 白铁匠。2.〔英〕罐头商，罐头食品工人。3. 锡矿矿工。

tin·ner·y [ˈtinəri; ˋtɪnərɪ] *n*. 白铁厂；锡厂；罐头食品厂。

tin·ni·ness [ˈtininis; ˋtɪnɪnɪs] *n*. 1. 含锡成分，似锡。2. 光亮而不值钱；(声音)细弱无力；(文章等)空洞无味。

tinning [ˈtiniŋ; ˋtɪnɪŋ] *n*. 锡器[白铁器皿]制造(业)；罐头。

tin·ni·tus [tiˈnaitəs; tɪˋnaɪtəs] *n*.【医】耳鸣。

tin·ny [ˈtini; ˋtɪnɪ] *a*.（*-ni·er*; *-ni·est*）1. 锡的，多锡的，含锡的，产锡的。2. 像锡的；(声音)不响亮的；不耐久的，光亮不值钱的，细弱无力的，空洞无内容的。

tin-pan, tin-pan·ny [tinˈpæn; ˋtɪnˏpæn] *a*. 像敲白铁罐那样的，噪音的，嘈杂的。***Tin-Pan Alley***〔美俚〕流行歌曲作家和发行人的集中地；〔总称〕流行歌曲作家和发行人；流行歌曲。

tin·sel [ˈtinsəl; ˋtɪnsl] I *n*. 1.（做节日衣饰等；闪闪发光的)金属箔，金属丝；闪亮的装饰。2. 金银丝织品。3. 华丽而不值钱的东西，俗丽的东西。II *a*. 1. 金银丝(箔)制的，闪亮的。2. 华丽而不值钱的，俗丽的，虚饰的。III *vt*.（*-l*(*l*)*-*）用金属箔丝等装饰；装饰得烂烂华丽。**-ly** *a*.

Tin·sel·town [ˈtinsəltaun; ˋtɪnsltaʊn] *n*.〔美口〕浮华城〔指好莱坞〕。

tint [tint; tɪnt] I *n*. 1. 色彩，色调，色泽，色度；着色。2. 气息，迹象，痕迹。3.【物】色辉。4.【镌版】线晕〔用平行线表现的阴影〕。5.【印】淡色，(支票等上用柾网线构成的)底色。*autumnal* ～*s* 秋色，金黄色，红叶。*in all* ～*s of red* 用种种浓淡不同的红色。*red of* [*with*] *a blue* ～ 带蓝的红色。*crossed* [*ruled*] ～ 网线[花纹]版。**flat** ～ 制服。II *vt*. 给…着(染)色；作线晕。～**-block**【印】(印底色用的)底色版。～**less** *a*. 无色的。～**tool** 刻线刀。**-er** *n*. 1. 着(染)色者，着(染)色器。2.（作衬底的)素色幻灯片。

tin·tin·nab·u·lar, -ula·ry [ˌtintiˈnæbjulə, -ləri; ˏtɪntɪˋnæbjələ, -ˏlɛrɪ] *a*. 玎玲玎玲响的(铃等)，铃似的。**-lation** *n*. 玎玲声。

tin·tin·nab·u·lous [ˌtintiˈnæbjuləs; ˏtɪntɪˋnæbjələs] *a*. 玎玲玎玲响的。

tin·tin·nab·u·lum [ˌtiŋtiˈnæbjuləm; ˏtɪntɪˋnæbjələm] *n*.（*pl*. **-la** [-lə; -lə]）1. 铃，(小金属所构成的)响器。

2. 铃声。

tin·tom·e·ter [tinˈtɔmitə; tɪnˋtɑmətɚ] ***n.***【物】色辉计,比色计。

ti·ny [ˈtaini; ˋtaɪnɪ] **I** ***a.*** (***-ni·er***; ***-ni·est***) 极小的。**II** ***n.*** **1.** 小孩子。**2.**【医】癣。*little* ～＝～ *little*〔口〕怪小的,小得可怜的。

-tion〔来自动词的名词后缀〕动作,状态,结果〔*cf*. -ation, -cion, -ion, -sion, -xion〕: addi*tion*, tempta*tion*.

-tious〔来自 -tion 型名词的形容词后缀〕…的,有…的: ambi*tious*, ficti*tious*.

tip[1] [tip; tɪp] **I** ***n.*** **1.** (塔、手指、尾巴等的)尖,尖端,顶端,末端,梢。**2.** 装在末端的东西,加固末端的金属环[箍];鞋尖。**3.** 香烟的过滤嘴。**4.** 镀金用毛刷。**5.** (鸟或飞机的)翼尖(梢)。*a mountain* ～ 山顶。**II** ***vt.*** (***-pp-***) **1.** 装尖头。**2.** (用金属箍等)包上尖头。**3.** 割去顶梢。**4.** 剪(发)。***from*** ～ ***to*** ～ (张开的翼的)从这一翼尖到那一翼尖。***from*** ～ ***to toe*** 彻头彻尾,完完全全。***have at the*** ～***s of one's fingers*** 精通;(在手头)随时可以使用。***on*** [***at***] ***the*** ～ ***of one's tongue*** (想说的话)已到舌尖,险些要说出。～ ***in*** (装订时)插入图片页。***to the*** ～***s of one's fingers*** 彻底,彻头彻尾。***walk on the*** ～***s of one's toes*** 踮着脚走。

tip[2] [tip; tɪp] **I** ***vt.*** (***-pp-***) **1.** 使倾;翻倒,使倾覆;扔出;推倒(人)。**2.** 倒出,倒光,倒掉(沙砾、垃圾等)。**3.** 脱(帽)打招呼。—***vi.*** 倾斜;翻倒;翻转。～ *the scale(s)* 使天平倾斜;起决定作用,举足轻重;扭转局势;占优势。*He got so angry that he* ～*ped the table up*. 他气得把桌子推翻了。*Don't* ～ *your tea into the saucer*. 不要把茶倒进茶碟里。*The ship* ～*ped over at 10 a.m*. 船是上午十时翻的。**II** ***n.*** **1.** 倾斜。**2.** (垃圾等的)弃置场。*The lamp post has a slight* ～ to the west. 灯杆稍微有点向西歪。～ ***off*** 倒出;〔俚、方〕死;杀死。～ ***out*** 倒光;翻倒;(被)扔出;〔俚、方〕死。～ ***over*** **1.** 翻倒。**2.**〔美俚〕死。**3.**〔美俚〕抢劫,搜查。～ ***over the perch***〔美俚〕死。～ ***up*** 倾,歪,翻倒。～**-box** 倾卸箱。～**car**, ～**cart**, ～**-lorry** 自动卸货车,倾倒车。

tip[3] [tip; tɪp] **I** ***vi.*** (***-pp-***) **1.** 给小费。**2.**〔口〕(赌赙等)暗通消息。— ***vt.*** **1.** 轻触,轻击。**2.** 给(小费),赏(酒钱)。**3.**〔口〕暗中通知,秘密报知,提醒。*Don't* ～ *freely*. 不要乱给小费。*T- us a signal, if you can*. 有可能时,给我们个信号。*T- us a song*.〔口〕唱一个歌给我们听听吧。～ *fives*〔美〕握手。～ *grand*〔美〕跑;溜掉。～ *one*〔美〕干一杯(酒)。～ *one's mitt*〔美〕握手;泄漏自己的计划。**II** ***n.*** **1.** 轻击;【棒球】擦球(立即往垒上跑)。**2.** 赏钱,酒钱,小费。**3.** 暗示;(行情等的)秘密消息,特别消息,预测。**4.** 妙法,秘诀;警告。*the straight* ～ 可靠的秘密消息。*Take my* ～. 照我的话去做。*the* ～ *for extracting greasespots* 去油迹的秘诀。***get the*** ～ ***to*** 接到关于怎样做某事的秘密通知。***give the*** ～ ***to*** 暗中关照去做某事。***miss one's*** ～〔口〕打错主意,失策。～ ***off***〔俚〕忠告,警告,提醒,给…递点子。～ ***sb. the wink*** (向某人)使眼色。～**-and-ran** **1.** ***n.***【棒球】触球即跑。**2.** ***a.*** 打了就跑的 (*a* ～*-and-run raid* 打了就跑的袭击)。～ **sheet** (股票等的)内情通报。

tip-off [ˈtipɔːf; ˋtɪpˏɔf] ***n.*** **1.** 警告。**2.** 预先告诉的消息,暗示。**3.** (篮球赛开始时的)跳球。

tip·pet [ˈtipit; ˋtɪpɪt] ***n.*** **1.** (女用)斗篷;披肩。**2.** (法官、教士的)无袖罩裳。

tip·ple[1] [ˈtipl; ˋtɪpl̩] **I** ***vt.*** 一点点地喝(烈酒),品(酒)。—***vi.*** 饮烈酒,酗酒。**II** ***n.*** 酒,〔尤指致醉的〕烈酒。**-pler** ***n.*** 饮烈酒者;酒徒。

tipple[2] [ˈtipl; ˋtɪpl̩] ***n.*** **1.**〔美〕倒煤场,筛煤场(等)。**2.** 翻斗机;自动倾卸装置;翻锭机。

tip·py[1] [ˈtipi; ˋtɪpɪ] ***a.*** **1.** 毛尖多的(茶)。**2.**〔美口〕易歪向一边的,易倾斜的,摇晃的。

tip·py[2] [ˈtipi; ˋtɪpɪ] ***a.*** 易倾斜的,倾斜的;摇摇晃晃的。

tip·py-toe, tip·py·toe [ˈtipiˌtəu; ˋtɪpɪˏto] ***n.***, ***vi.***, ***a.***, ***ad.***〔口〕= tiptoe.

tip·si·fy [ˈtipsifai; ˋtɪpsɪˏfaɪ] ***vt.*** (***-fied***) 使喝醉。

tip·staff [ˈtipstɑːf; ˋtɪpˏstæf, -stɑf] ***n.*** (***pl.*** ***-staves*** [-teivz; -tevz], ～***s***) **1.** 铁头杖。**2.** 随身携带铁头杖行走的人[巡警等]。

tip·ster [ˈtipstə; ˋtɪpstɚ] ***n.***〔口〕提供(赛马等)消息[内情、行情]的人。*a* ～ *sheet*〔美〕由华尔街透露出来的秘密消息。

tip·sy [ˈtipsi; ˋtɪpsɪ] ***a.*** (***-si·er***; ***-si·est***) **1.** 喝醉了的;微醉的。**2.** 摇摇晃晃的,步履不稳的。**3.** 东歪西倒的。*a* ～ *lurch* 摇摇晃晃的步伐。*On my day off, I'll fix the* ～ *fence*. 我歇班那天就修理歪了的篱笆。～ **cake** (浸葡萄酒的)醉蛋糕,醉饼。**-i·ly** ***ad.*** **-i·ness** ***n.***

tip·toe [ˈtiptəu; ˋtɪpˏto] **I** ***n.*** 脚尖。*Your cap is on the table, Tom. Stand on* ～ *and get it*. 你的帽子在桌子上,汤姆,踮起脚来够它吧。*Don't make any noise. Steal a* ～ *to the door*. 别作声,踮着脚儿走到门口那儿。***be on the*** ～ ***of expectation*** 伸长脖子[殷切]等待,翘首而望[企盼]。***be on*** ～ ***of excitement*** 非常兴奋。***on*** ～ 踮着脚(站立、走路等);小心地,蹑手蹑脚地;悄悄地;伸长脖子。**II** ***a.*** 踮着脚走[站着]的;殷切期待的;偷偷摸摸的,蹑手蹑脚的。**III** ***ad.*** 踮着脚;翘首盼望着;蹑手蹑脚地;悄悄,偷偷。**IV** ***vi.*** 踮着脚(走),蹑手蹑脚地行进。

tip·top [ˈtipˈtɔp; ˋtɪpˋtɑp] **I** ***n.*** **1.** 绝顶。**2.**〔口〕极上,最上,极盛。**II** ***a.*** **1.** 绝顶的。**2.**〔口〕极上的,极好的,头等的。**3.** 有趣的。**III** ***ad.*** 非常,极,至高无上。

TIR = International Road Transport 国际陆路货运(协定)。

ti·rade [taiˈreid, tiˈrɑːd; ˋtaɪred, təˋred] ***n.*** **1.** 长篇议论[攻击](等),激烈言论,激烈演说。**2.** 长文,长诗。**3.**【乐】全音阶的插入音。

ti·rail·leur [ˌtiraiˈləː; tiraˋjoer] ***n.*** 〔F〕【军】散兵;狙击兵。

Ti·ra·na, Ti·ra·në [tiˈrɑːnə; tɪˋrɑnɑ] ***n.*** 地拉那〔阿尔巴尼亚首都〕。

tire[1] [ˈtaiə; taɪr] ***vi.*** 疲倦,累 (*with*); 厌倦 (*of*)。—***vt.*** 使疲倦;使厌倦。*Walking soon* ～*s me*. 我一走路就累。*She never* ～*s of speaking English*. 她讲起英语来从不厌倦。～ ***down*** 把…追赶到跑不动,使疲惫到精疲力尽,逐渐微弱。～ ***out*** = ～ ***to death*** 使疲倦到极度 (*I am* ～*d out*. 我累得要死,十分疲倦)。

tire[2], **tyre** [ˈtaiə; taɪr] **I** ***n.*** 轮箍;轮胎。*a pneumatic* ～ 橡皮轮胎。～ *chain* 轮胎防滑链。**II** ***vt.*** 装轮胎。

tire[3] [taiə; taɪr] **I** ***n.*** **1.**〔古〕(女用)头装,头饰。**2.** 衣装。**3.**〔美〕围裙。**II** ***vt.*** **1.**〔古〕打扮,装饰。**2.** 梳头。

tired [ˈtaiəd; taɪrd] ***a.*** **1.** 疲乏,累 (*with*); (对…感到)厌倦 (*of*)。**2.**〔口语〕生气。**3.** 破旧的,陈腐的。*be* [*get*] ～ *with walking* [*reading*] 走路[读书]累了。*be* ～ *out*. 累得要死,累极了。*I'll take turns with you at the wheel, when you get* ～. 你要是累了,我来替你换着开车。*be* ～ *of the same food every day* 每天吃同样的东西吃腻味了。*get* ～ *from long overwork* 长期过分劳动后感到疲倦。～ ***as a dog***〔美〕累极了。**T-Tim** = **T- Timothy** 懒鬼,懒虫。**-ness** ***n.***

tire·less[1] [ˈtaiəlis; ˋtaɪrlɪs] ***a.*** 不疲倦的;不累的;孜孜不倦的;不屈不挠的,坚忍的。**-ly** ***ad.***

tire·less[2] [ˈtaiəlis; ˋtaɪrlɪs] ***a.*** 无轮箍[轮胎]的。

Ti·re·si·as [taiəˈriːsiæs; taɪəˋrisɪæs] ***n.***【希神】蒂利希阿斯〔因看智慧女神洗澡而致双目失明的、懂鸟语的底庇斯卜卦者〕。

tire·some [ˈtaiəsəm; ˋtaɪrsəm] ***a.*** 令人厌倦[生厌]的,沉闷的,没趣的;麻烦的,讨厌的。*How* ～! *I have left my watch behind*. 真讨厌! 我忘了带表了。*Nobody likes to attend the* ～ *lecture*. 谁也不愿意上那个令人生倦的课。

T

tire·wom·an [ˈtaiəwumən; ˋtaɪrˏwʊmən] *n*. 〔古〕梳妆侍女;(剧场的)女化妆助手。

tir·ing [ˈtaiəriŋ; ˋtaɪərɪŋ] *a*. 使人疲倦[厌倦]的;麻烦的。~ **house** (剧院的)化装间。~ **room** (戏院的)剧装室,化妆室。

tiro [ˈtaiərəu; ˋtaɪro] *n*. (*pl*. ~*s*) = tyro.

ti·ro·cin·ium [ˌtaiərəuˈsiniəm; ˏtaɪroˋsɪnɪəm] *n*. (*pl*. ***ti·ro·cin·i·a*** [ˌtaiərəuˈsiniə; ˏtaɪroˋsɪnɪə]) **1**. 学徒期限,学徒身分。**2**. 技艺入门。

TIROS = television infrared observation satellite 电视红外线观察卫星。

Ti·ros [ˈtairəus; ˋtaɪros] *n*. 电视红外线观测卫星,泰罗斯卫星 (= television infrared observation satellite)。

tir·ra·lir·ra [ˈtirəˌlirə; ˋtɪrəˏlɪrə] *n*., *ad*. 云雀叫声;快活地。

T.I.S. = Technical Information Service 〔美〕技术情报服务处。

'tis [tiz; tɪz]〔诗、方〕= it is.

ti·sane [tiˈzæn, *F*. tiˈzan; tɪˋzæn] *n*. = ptisan.

Tisb·ahb'Ab [tiːˈʃɑːbəˈɑːv, ˈtiʃəˌbɔːv; tiˋʃɑbəˋɑv, ˋtɪʃəˏbɔv] (为纪念犹太圣殿被毁的)犹太斋戒日〔即犹太历五月九日〕。

Tish·ri [tiʃˈriː, ˈtiʃriː; tɪʃˋri, ˋtɪʃri] *n*. 〔Heb.〕(犹太历)元月。

tis·sue [ˈtisjuː; ˋtɪʃʊ] *n*. **1**. 薄绢,薄纱罗(等织物)。**2**. 薄纸,棉纸 (= ~-paper)。**3**. (编造的谎话等的)一套,一连串。**4**.【摄】碳素印像纸。**5**.【生】组织。*toilet* ~ 手纸,卫生纸。*the muscular* ~ 肌肉组织。*the nervous* ~ 神经组织。~ **culture**【医】组织培养;培养出来的组织。~ **paper** 薄绉纸,纱纸。

tit[1] [tit; tɪt] *n*. **1**.【鸟】山雀。**2**.〔古〕小马,瘦马。**3**.〔古、蔑〕小丫头。

tit[2] [tit; tɪt] *n*. 奶头。

tit[3] [tit; tɪt] *n*. 轻打。~ ***for tat*** 一报还一报;用同一方式报复;针锋相对。*give* [*pay*] ~ *for fat* 针锋相对。*a* ~-*for-tat struggle* 针锋相对的斗争。

tit. = title.

Ti·tan [ˈtaitən; ˋtaɪtn] *n*. (*fem*. ***-ess*** [ˈtaitənis; ˋtaɪtənɪs]) **1**.【希神】泰坦巨人族〔*Uranus* (= heaven) 和 *Gaea* (= *earth*)的子女们〕之一;〔~ *or* t-〕巨人。**2**. 力大无比的人;(学界、政界等的)巨头。**3**.【军】大力神导弹。**4**.〔诗〕日神。*a* ~ *crane* (自动)巨型起重机。*the weary* ~ 老大帝国[如英国]。

ti·tan·ate [ˈtaitəneit; ˋtaɪtəˏnet] *n*.【化】钛酸盐,钛酸酯。

Ti·tan·ic [taiˈtænik; taɪˋtænɪk] *a*. **1**.【希神】泰坦巨人族的。**2**.〔常作 t-〕巨大的,力大无比的;伟大的。

ti·tanic [taiˈtænik; taɪˋtænɪk] *n*.【化】钛的,得自钛的。

ti·tan·if·er·ous [ˌtaitniˈifərəs; ˏtaɪtəˋnɪfərəs] *a*. 含钛的。

Ti·tan·ism [ˈtaitnzəm; ˋtaɪtənˏɪzm] *n*. 〔也作 t-〕泰坦精神;(对社会习俗等方面的)造反精神。

ti·ta·nite [ˈtaitˌnait; ˋtaɪtəˏnaɪt] *n*.【化】木屑石 (= sphene)。

ti·ta·ni·um [taiˈteinjəm, ti-; taɪˋtenɪəm, tɪ-] *n*.【化】钛 (Ti)。~ *dioxide* [*white*] 二氧化钛 (= titanic oxide)。

titan·o·saur [ˈtaitənəsɔː; ˋtaɪtənəˏsɔr], **Ti·tan·o·saurus** [ˌtaitənəˈsɔːrəs; ˏtaɪtənəˋsɔrəs] *n*.【古生】(南美白垩纪的)雷龙。

ti·tan·ous [taiˈtænəs, -ti-, ˈtaitnəs; taɪˋtænəs, -tɪ-, ˋtaɪtənəs] *a*.【化】三价钛的,亚钛的。

tit·bit [ˈtitbit; ˋtɪtˏbɪt] *n*. (好吃的东西的)一口,少量;有趣的新闻,珍闻。

ti·ter [ˈtaitə; ˋtaɪtɚ, ˋtitɚ] *n*. **1**.【化】滴定量;滴定(浓)度,滴定率;效价;脂酸冻点(测定)。**2**.【纺】纤度。

tith·a·ble [ˈtaiðəbl; ˋtaɪðəbl] *a*. 可征收什一税的;应缴什一税的。

tithe [taið; taɪð] **I** *n*. **1**. (以产品缴纳的)什一税;〔常 *pl*.〕十分之一的教区税。**2**. 十分之一;小部分;一点点。*great* [*coarse*, *large*] ~ 主要收获的什一税〔小麦、干草、柴、水果等〕。*mixed* ~*s* 农产品的什一税〔乳酪、牛奶、小家畜等的十分之一〕。*personal* [*predial*] ~*s* 个人劳动所得[土地收益]的什一税。*I don't know a* ~ *of it*. 我一点儿不知道。**II** *vt*. 向…征收[缴纳]什一税。— *vi*. 缴纳什一税。~ **barn** 储放什一税农产品的仓库。~ **pig** 作为什一税缴纳的猪。

tith·er [ˈtaiθə; ˋtaɪðɚ] *n*. (= tithe)。

tith·ing [ˈtaiðiŋ; ˋtaɪðɪŋ] *n*. **1**. (征收)什一税。**2**.【英古法】(负联保责任的)十户,十人。**3**. (英国部分地区仍保持的行政单位)十户区。

Ti·tho·nus [tiˈθəunəs; tɪˋθonəs] *n*.【希神】蒂索诺斯〔为特洛伊王子,受曙光女神之宠,并许以永远不死,但事被女神遗忘,终于日见衰老,最后化为蝉〕。

ti·ti [tiˈtiː; tɪˋti] *n*.【动】**1**. 狨(绢毛猴) (*Callithrix jacchus*)〔产于巴西和玻利维亚〕。**2**. 伶猴属 (*Callicebus*) 动物〔产于南美〕。

ti·tian [ˈtiʃiən, ˈtiʃən; ˋtɪʃən, ˋtɪʃɪən] *n*. (妇女头发的)金黄色,赤黄色;〔美〕红发女。

tit·il·late [ˈtitileit; ˋtɪtlˏet] *vt*. **1**. 呵痒。**2**. 使高兴,使兴奋,使兴趣、想像等活跃。*Scientific stories* ~ *the fancy of the school boys*. 科学故事使小学生们的想像力活跃起来。*The news* ~*d the curiosity of the public*. 这桩新闻引起了群众的好奇心。**-la·tion** [ˌtitiˈleiʃən; ˏtɪtəˋleʃən] *n*. **-tive** *a*. **-r** *n*.

tit·(t)i·vate [ˈtitiveit; ˋtɪtəˏvet] *vt*., *vi*. 〔口〕打扮,妆饰。**-tion** [ˌtitiˈveiʃən; ˏtɪtəˋveʃən] *n*.

tit·lark [ˈtitlɑːk; ˋtɪtˏlɑrk] *n*.【鸟】鹨(属)(如水鹨,草地鹨等)。

ti·tle [ˈtaitl; ˋtaɪtl] **I** *n*. **1**. (书籍、诗歌、乐曲等的)标题,题目,题;篇名,书名。**2**. (书的)标题页,扉页。**3**.【影】字幕。**4**. 称号;尊称,头衔,爵位,学位。**5**. 权利,资格。**6**.【法】土地财产所有权;地契。**7**.【运】冠军,锦标。**8**. (用 carat 表示的)金子的纯度[成色]。**9**.【宗】圣职就任资格;(天主教的)教区及该教区内的教堂。*a man of* ~ 有头衔的人,贵族。*John said he would give a good* ~ *to his new book*. 约翰说他要给他的新书起个好书名。*His services give him a* ~ *to our gratitude*. 他工作勤恳,有资格受到我们的感谢。*He has many* ~*s to distinction*. 他有好多资格使他知名。*quiet* ~【法】判决产权属谁。*regal* ~ 王的称号。*Has Jones any* ~ *to the land*? 琼斯有这块土地的产权吗? **II** *vt*. **1**. 加标题于;【影】附加字幕。**2**. 授头衔[爵位等]。**3**. 用头衔[尊称]称呼。~ **deed**【法】地契。~**holder** 选手权保持者,(冠军)称号保持者。~ **match** 锦标赛。~ **page** 书名页,扉页,内封面。~**-part** = ~ **rôle**【剧】(名字作为剧名的)剧名角色,片名角色。~ **piece** 书名篇(文集、戏剧、诗集中被用作书名的文章、剧本、诗篇等)。**-d** *a*. 有爵位的,有贵族头衔的。

ti·tler [ˈtaitlə; ˋtaɪtlɚ] *n*.【影】字幕摄录装置。

tit·ling[1] [ˈtitliŋ; ˋtɪtlɪŋ] *n*. = titlark; = titmouse 1.

ti·tling[2] [ˈtaitliŋ; ˋtaɪtlɪŋ] *n*. 书脊烫金;烫在书脊上的标题;烫金工序。

ti·tlist [ˈtaitlist; ˋtaɪtlɪst] *n*. 冠军称号保持者。

tit·mouse [ˈtitmaus; ˋtɪtˏmaus] *n*. (*pl*. ***-mice*** [-mais; -maɪs]) **1**.【鸟】山雀(属);银喉长尾山雀;花雀。**2**. 小气鬼。**3**. 小东西;小男孩,小女孩。*tufted* ~ 黑额冠山雀。

titrant [ˈtaitrænt; ˋtaɪtrənt] *n*.【化】滴定剂,滴定标准液。

ti·trate [ˈtaitreit; ˋtaɪtret, ˋtɪtret] *vt*.【化】滴定(法)。

ti·tra·tion [ˈtaitreiʃən; taɪˋtreʃən] *n*.【化】滴定(法)。

titre [ˈtaitə; ˋtaɪtɚ, ˋtitɚ] *n*. = titer.

tit-tat-toe [ˌtittætˈtəu; ˏtɪttætˋto, -ˋtu] *n*. = tick-tack-toe.

tit·ter [ˈtitə; ˋtɪtɚ] **I** *n*. **1**. 嗤嗤地笑,傻笑;窃笑。**2**.

〔美〕(不懂事的)小姑娘。**II** ***vi*.** 噗嗤一笑,吃吃地窃笑。

tit·tie [ˈtiti; ˋtɪtɪ] ***n*.** 〔苏格兰〕姐妹 (= titty)。

titti·vate [ˈtitiveit; ˋtɪtəˏvet] ***v*.** = titivate.

tit·tle [ˈtitl; ˋtɪtl̩] **I** ***n*.** **1.** 一点点。**2.** 文字上的小点,小符号。*I don't care one jot or one ~ of what he says*. 他所说的我一点也不在乎。***to a ~*** 准确地,一丝不苟地,丝毫不差地。**II** ***vi*.** 闲谈,杂谈;讲闲话。**~-tattle** ***n*.** 荒唐话,无聊闲谈,杂谈。

tit·tup [ˈtitəp; ˋtɪtəp] **I** ***n*.** **1.** 活泼的动作[举止]。**2.** 轻佻的行为。**3.** (马等的)慢跑。**4.** (船等的)摇摆;不稳重。**II** ***vi*.** (**-*p*(*p*)-**) **1.** 举动活泼;跳跳蹦蹦 (*along*)。**2.** (马)缓跑,小跑。**3.** (船等)摇摆。**4.** 【海俚】掷钱赌酒。*The children ~ed all day on the beach*. 小孩子们在海滩上跳跳蹦蹦了一整天。

tit·tup·py [ˈtitəpi; ˋtɪtəpɪ] ***a*.** 愉快的,活泼的,轻佻的;摇摆的。

tit·ty [ˈtiti; ˋtɪtɪ] ***n*.** (*pl*. ***-ties***) 〔废,俚〕奶头,乳房。

tit·u·ba·tion [ˌtitjuˈbeiʃən; ˏtɪtʃʊˋbeʃən] ***n*.** 摇摇晃晃,蹒跚(步行)。

tit·u·lar [ˈtitjulə; ˋtɪtʃələ˞] **I** ***a*.** **1.** 享有所有权的,有正当权利的,有资格的。**2.** 名义上的,挂名的,有名无实的。**3.** (有)头衔[称号、尊称]的。**4.** 标题的,被用做题名的。*O'Connor gave up his ~ possessions and conducted business in America*. 欧康纳放弃了他有权得到的财产而去美国经商。*a ~ distinction* 头衔显赫。*a ~ rank* 爵位。*a ~ character* (名字作为作品题名的)主题人物。**II** ***n*.** **1.** 有头衔[官阶、称号]的人。**2.** 只有名义的人,挂名的人。**3.** = ~ saint (以其名为教堂名的)教堂的守护圣徒。**-ly** ***ad*.** 名义上,有名无实地;头衔上,标题上。

titu·la·ry [ˈtitjuləri; ˋtɪtʃəˏlɛrɪ] ***a*., *n*.** = titular.

Ti·tus [ˈtaitəs; ˋtaɪtəs] ***n*.** 泰特斯〔男子名〕。

Tiu [ˈtiːuː; ˋtiu] ***n*.** 蒂尤〔日耳曼神话中司天空与战争的神〕。

T.I.V. = thermal-insulating value 绝热值,热隔绝值。

tiz·zy [ˈtizi; ˋtɪzɪ] ***n*.** **1.** 〔英俚〕六辨士。**2.** 〔俚〕战栗;极度兴奋狂乱的心境〔尤指对于小事〕。

t.j., T.J. = talk jockey 〔美口〕(广播电台的)电话访谈节目主持人。

T.J. = turbo jet 涡轮喷气发动机。

TK = tank.

TKO = technical knockout (拳击中的)技术性击倒[被击倒]。

Tl = 【化】 thallium.

tlac [tlɑːk; tlɑk] ***n*.** 〔美俚〕钱。

Tlin·git [ˈtliŋgit; ˋtlɪŋgɪt] ***n*.** **1.** (*pl*. ***Tlin·gits, Tlingit***) 特里吉特人〔阿拉斯加南部和英属哥伦比亚北部沿海地区以航海为职业的美洲印第安人〕。**2.** 特里吉特语。

T.L.O., TLO = total loss only 【商】(保险业)仅负完全损失之责。

TLP = transient lunar phenomena 月球瞬变现象。

TM = **1.** trademark 商标。**2.** tactical missile 战术导[飞]弹。**3.** training manual 〔美〕训练手册。**4.** trench mortar 迫击炮。

T.M. = twist multiplier 【纺】黏(度)系数。

Tm = 【化】 thulium.

T-man [ˈtiːmæn; ˋtiˏmæn] ***n*.** (*pl*. ***-men***) 〔口〕美国财政部特派员。

TMD = Theater Missile Defence 〔美〕战区导[飞]弹防御圈〔美国全球战略防御计划(即"星球大战")的一部分,以防御核攻击为目的〕。

tme·sis [ˈtmiːsis; ˋtmisɪs, təˋmisɪs] ***n*.** 【语法】插词法(为要插入其他一词在复合词和短语中间);whatsoever → *what* place *soever*; absolutely → *abso*-blooming-*lutely*; Yourselves → *your* good *selves*.

T.M.O. = telegraph money order 电汇。

TMV = tobacco mosaic virus 烟草花叶病毒。

T.N. = true north.

Tn = 【化】thoron; train.

tn = ton.

tns = tons.

TNT, T.N.T. [ˈtiːenˈtiː; ˋtiɛnˋti] ***n*.** 【化】梯恩梯(即三硝基甲苯)〔trinitrotoluene 的缩略〕。

T.O. = **1.** technical order 技术说明。**2.** Telegraph Office 电报局。**3.** Transport Officer 运输军官。**4.** turn over 见背面。

T/O = Tables of Organization 〔美〕编制表。

to [在句的末尾强 tuː, 元音前弱 tu, 辅音前弱 tə; tu, tʊ, tə] **I** ***prep*.** **1.** 〔运动的方向〕向,到,去 (*opp*. from)。*turn ~ the left* 向左转。*from east ~ west* 由东到西。*get ~ London* 到达伦敦。*have been ~* …去过,到过,到,回来。*To arms*! 取武器! *To horse*! 上马! **2.** 〔状态的变化〕向,到。*change* [*go, turn*] *from bad ~ worse* 日益恶化。*reclaim a lost child ~ virtue* 挽救一个误入歧途的儿童回到正道上来。*stand ~ attention* 采取立正姿势。*put ~ death* 处死。**3.** 〔范围、程度〕到,达到;…到,…得。*from six ~ nine* 六到九。*This apple is rotten ~ the core*. 这个苹果烂透心了。*an Englishman ~ the core* 一个道地的英国人。*The room was hot ~ suffocation*. 房间热得闷人。*~ the best of my ability* 尽我所能。*~ his name be it said* (虽说是敌人然而)真是名不虚传。*~ a certain degree* [*extent*] 在某种程度上。**4.** 〔时间〕到;缺(…分)。*~ this day* 到今天。*from six ~ nine* 六点到九点。*a quarter ~ nine* 九点差一刻。**5.** 〔目的〕为。*~ that end* 为那个目的。*come ~ the rescue* 来援救。*He was brought up ~ joinery*. 被训练成细木工。*drink ~ sb.'s health* 为某人的健康干杯。**6.** 〔比较〕和…比较,和…比起来;比;对;每,一。*This is nothing ~ that*. 和那个比起来这不算什么。*The score was 4 ~ 1*. 比分是四比一。*ten ~ one* 十对一;什九。*He is far superior ~ me*. 他比我高明得多。*four shillings ~ the pound* 四先令一镑。**7.** 〔依后面名词和前面动词而表示〕:(a)〔结果〕致,致使。*He was flattered ~ his ruin*. 他由于受人吹捧,结果是一败涂地。*~ no purpose* 徒然,白白。(b)〔对立〕对。*face ~ face* 面对面。*fight hand ~ hand* 肉搏。(c)〔适合、协调〕按,应,合。*boots made ~ any foot* 做得谁都合穿的靴子。*quite ~ my taste* 很合我的脾胃。(d)〔随伴〕跟着;配合。*sing ~ the piano* 跟着钢琴唱。(e)〔接触〕在。*hold ~ one's heart* 抱在怀里。(f)〔附加〕在,加在。*add ~* …加在。*That's all there is ~ it*. 那件事情不过如此罢了。*There's nothing ~ him*. 他不过是那样一个人罢了。*Wisdom he has, and ~ his wisdom, courage*. 他聪明,不但聪明,而且勇敢。(g)〔所属〕的。*porch ~ the house* 那房子的门廊。(h)〔古〕作为 (= as)。*He took her ~ wife*. 他娶她为妻。*call ~ witness* 传来作证人。(i)〔在 confess, swear, testify, witness 等动词的后面时〕是…,承认。*confess ~ crime* 承认犯罪。*He swore ~ the miracle* 他发誓说这是奇迹。(j)〔选择〕而不。*prefer death ~ surrender* 宁死不降。**8.** 〔表示接受动作的人或物〕:*Give this book ~ him*. 把这本书给他。*do harm ~ sb.* 损害某人。*drink ~ him* 给他干杯,敬他一杯。*keep* [*have, get*] *the room ~ oneself* 独用房间。**9.** 〔构成动词不定式〕:*To err is human*. 过失为人之常〔用作名词〕。*a house ~ let* 出租的房子〔作定语〕。*I have come ~ see you*. 我来看你〔用作状语〕。★在知觉动词 (see, hear, feel 等),使役动词 (let, make, have)及 please, help 等后不定式 to 常略去(美语即使在其他动词后的 to 也常略去),但在被动结构中则不略去:*She helped me* (~) *compile the dictionary*. *I saw him run*. *He was seen ~ run*. **10.** 〔方、美〕= at. *You can get this article ~ Brown's*. 这个东西可以在布朗商店买到。**11.** *T- you*. 〔古〕知道了。**12.** 作为不定

T

式的代用词：*We didn't want to go but we had* ～. 我们不想去，但我们不得不去〔此处 to 代替 to go〕。**II** [tuː; tu] ***ad.*** 到某种状态；〔特指〕到停止状态；关闭。★也常和动词结合，略去其后宾语，而构成成语：*The door is* ～. 门关着。*push* [*shut*] *the door* ～ 把门关上。***bring sb.*** ～ 使苏醒。***bring*** (*a ship*) ～ 命令(停船)。***come*** ～ (*oneself*) 苏醒。***fall*** ～ 开始；开始吃；开始攻击敌人。***go*** ～〔古〕喂喂；别胡说！***heave*** ～ 停船。

toad [təud; tod] ***n.*** **1.**【动】蟾蜍，癞蛤蟆。**2.** 讨厌的家伙；〔古、谑〕家伙，小家伙〔常作小孩的爱称〕。***eat sb.'s*** ～***s*** 拍某人的马屁。***the biggest*** ～ ***in the puddle*** (在政治方面或其他集团中)众所公认的头子，要人。～ ***under a harrow*** 受压迫[迫害]的人。～**eater** 谄媚者，拍马者。～**eating** 谄媚，奉承，拍马屁。～**fish**【鱼】蟾鱼科的鱼；河豚。～**flax**【植】柳穿鱼。～**-in-the-hole** (裹有湿面的)烤牛排。～ **skin** **1.**【医】蟾皮病。**2.**〔美俚〕钞票。～ **spit**, ～ **spittle** = cuckoospit. ～**-stabber**, ～**-sticker**〔美〕小刀。～**stone**【地】蟾蜍岩；玄武斑岩。～**stool**【植】伞菌科菌，牛肝菌科菌；(尤指)毒菌。

toad·y [ˈtəudi; ˋtodɪ] **I** ***n.*** 拍马屁的人。**II** ***vt.***, ***vi.*** (***toad·ied***) 奉承，拍马屁。**-ism** ***n.*** 谄媚，奉承，拍马屁。

to-and-fro [ˈtu(ː)-ənd-ˈfrəu; ˋtuənˋfro] **I** ***a.*** 往复的，走来走去的；来回的；动摇的。**II** ***n.*** (*pl.* ***tos-and-fros***) 走来走去，来回，往复；交互运动，波动，动摇。**III** ***ad.*** 往复地，来回。

toast[1] [təust; tost] **I** ***n.*** 烤面包片。*buttered* [*dry*] ～ 涂有[不涂]奶油的烤面包。～ *and water* = ～-water. ***as warm as a*** ～〔口〕暖烘烘，很暖。**II** ***vt.***, ***vi.*** **1.** 烘烤(面包片等)。**2.**〔口〕烤暖(脚等)，烤火。～ *oneself* (*before the fire*) 烤火。～ **rack** (餐桌上可放几片烤面包片的)面包架。～ **water** 泡过烤面包片的水〔病人喝的清凉饮料〕。～**-wich**〔美〕夹肉烤面包片。

toast[2] [təust; tost] **I** ***n.*** **1.** 祝酒，干杯；祝酒词。**2.** 被举杯祝贺的人[物；女人]。**3.** 有名的人。*The* ～ *was duly drunk.* 宾主照例祝酒干杯。***have sb. on*** ～〔俚〕自由摆布某人，欺骗某人，愚弄某人。***propose a*** ～ 建议举杯祝酒。***propose the*** ～ ***of*** 建议为…干杯。**II** ***vt.***, ***vi.*** 祝(…健康)干杯，敬…一杯。～ *the poet* 敬诗人一杯。～ **list** 祝酒名单。～ **master** (宴会上)讲祝酒词的人，宴会的主持人。～ **mistress** 宴会的女主持人。～**ee** ***n.*** 被祝酒的人。

toast·er[1] [ˈtəustə; ˋtostɚ] ***n.*** 烤面包片机[小电炉]。

toast·er[2] [ˈtəustə; ˋtostɚ] ***n.*** 祝酒者；致祝酒词的人；奉承女人的人。

toast·y [ˈtəusti; ˋtostɪ] ***a.*** (***toast·i·er***, ***toast·i·est***) **1.** 祝酒的。**2.** 温暖，舒畅，舒适的。

Tob. = Tobias; Tobit.

to·bac·co [təˈbækəu; təˋbæko] ***n.*** (*pl.* ～*s*, ～*es*)【植】烟草；烟叶；烟丝，卷烟，纸烟，嚼烟。*flue-cured* ～ 烤烟。*sun-cured* ～ 晒烟。*smoking* ～ 板丝烟。***T-Road***〔美〕南部种植烟草的地区。～ **cutter** 切烟机，切烟人。～ **heart**【医】烟毒性心脏(病)。～ **pipe** 烟斗，烟管。～ **plant**【植】烟草。～ **pouch** 烟丝袋。**T**～ **Road**, ～ **road** 污秽贫困的乡村地区。～ **worm** [**moth**]【动】烟草天蛾。**-nize** ***vt.***, ***vi*** 用烟叶薰；抽烟卷。

to·bac·co·nist [təˈbækənist; təˋbækənɪst] ***n.*** 烟草商(店)；香烟[烟丝]制造人；〔废〕抽烟的人。

to-be [təˈbiː; tʊˋbi] **I** ***a.*** 〔常用在名词后面〕未来的。*His father-in-law* ～ 他的未来岳父。**II** ***n.*** [the ～] 未来。*Some people only think of the* ～. 有些人总是为未来的事设想。

To·bi·as [təˈbaiəs; toˋbaɪəs] ***n.*** 托拜厄斯〔男子名〕。

to·bin [ˈtəubin; ˋtobɪn] ***n.*** 托宾式室内通风机 (= ～*'s tube*, ～*'s ventilator*)。

To·bit [ˈtəubit; ˋtobɪt]【宗】托比特书〔《旧约》中的《外典》之一〕。

to·bog·gan [təˈbɔgən; təˋbɑgən] **I** ***n.*** 平底雪橇；突然下降[跌价]。**II** ***vi.*** 坐平底雪橇滑下山坡；(股票等)突然跌价，猛跌。～**shoot**, ～ **slide** 平底雪橇滑行场。**-er**, **-ist** 坐平底雪橇的人。

To·bruk, Tu·bruq [ˈtəubruk; ˋtobrʊk] ***n.*** 图卜鲁格〔利比亚港市〕。

To·by [ˈtəubi; ˋtobɪ] ***n.*** 托比〔男子名，女子名，Tobias 的昵称〕。

to·by [ˈtəubi; ˋtobɪ] ***n.*** **1.** 胖老人形啤酒杯 (= Toby jug 或作 T- jug)。**2.**〔美卑〕下等雪茄烟。～ **collar** 有褶宽领

toc·ca·ta [təˈkɑːtə; təˋkɑtə] ***n.*** 〔It.〕【乐】托卡塔曲〔表现键盘乐器演奏者技巧的即兴曲〕。

To·char·i·an, To·khar·i·an [təuˈkeəriən, -ˈkær-; toˋkɛrɪən, -ˋkær-, -ˋkɑr-] **I** ***n.*** **1.** 吐火罗人〔约在公元1000年前住在中亚〕。**2.** 吐火罗语〔现已绝灭的一种印欧语，包括两大方言，最早的记载见纪元前七世纪的文件中〕。**II** ***a.*** 吐火罗的，吐火罗语的。

toch·er [ˈtɔxə; ˋtɑxɚ] ***n.*** 〔Scot.〕嫁妆。

tochka [ˈtɔtʃkɑː; ˋtɑtʃkɑ] ***n.*** 〔Russ.〕小地堡，火力点。

to·co, to·ko [ˈtəukəu; ˋtoko] ***n.*** 〔英俚〕责打，惩罚；痛苦。*catch* [*get*] ～ 挨打，受罚。

to·col·o·gist [təuˈkɔlədʒist; toˋkɑlədʒɪst] ***n.***【医】产科学者，产科医师。

to·col·o·gy [təˈkɔlədʒi; təˋkɑlədʒɪ] ***n.***【医】产科学。

to·copher·ol [təuˈkɔfərəul; toˋkɑfəˏrol, -ˏrɑl] ***n.***【生化】生育酚；抗不育维生素，维生素 E。

toc·sin [ˈtɔksin; ˋtɑksɪn] ***n.*** 警钟；警报，警戒信号。

tod [tɔd; tɑd] ***n.*** **1.** 〔Scot.〕狐；狡猾的人。**2.**〔古〕树丛，薮；(尤指常春藤叶的)繁茂处。**3.**【纺】托德〔羊毛重量单位，通常为 28 磅〕。

to·day, to-day [təˈdei, tuˈdei; təˋde] **I** ***n.*** 今日，今天；现代，现今，当代。*science of* ～ 现代科学。*the writers of* ～ 现代作家。～*s and yesterdays* 现在和过去。**II** ***ad.*** 在今天；现代，现今，当代。*a week ago* ～ 上一个星期的今天。～ *week* [*a week* ～] 下星期的今天。

Todd [tɔd; tɑd] ***n.*** 托德〔姓氏，男子名〕。

tod·dle [ˈtɔdl; ˋtɑdl] **I** ***vi.*** (刚学走的小孩子等)蹒跚；〔谑〕散步；闲荡；〔美〕跳舞。**II** ***n.*** 晃晃荡荡的步子；〔口〕一瘸一瘸走路的小孩；散步。*We must be toddling.* 我们要走了。

tod·dler [ˈtɔdlə; ˋtɑdlɚ] ***n.*** 晃晃荡荡走路的人，晃晃荡荡走路的小孩；〔谑〕散步的人。

tod·dy [ˈtɔdi; ˋtɑdɪ] ***n.*** 棕榈汁[酒]；威士忌[白兰地等]；热饮料〔加柠檬、砂糖用开水调成的甜酒〕。

to-do [təˈduː, tuˈduː; təˋdu] ***n.*** (*pl.* ～***s***) 〔口〕吵闹，骚扰；混乱。*make a terrible* ～ *about losing sb.'s luggage* 因某人丢了行李而闹得天翻地覆。

to·dy [ˈtəudi; ˋtodɪ] ***n.***【鸟】(西印度)翡翠。

toe [təu; to] ***n.*** 脚趾，脚尖；〔口〕脚；(鞋、袜等的)尖；蹄尖；蹄铁尖；工具的尖端；【高尔夫球】球棒尖；(铁轨的)轨端；【建】坡脚；(木工的)斜钉；【机】轴踵。*the big* [*great*] ～ (脚的)拇趾。*the little* ～ (脚的)小趾。*the light fantastic* ～〔谑〕跳舞。***on one's*** ～***s***〔喻〕精神振作，活跃；机警；热心；在活动 (*This job kept John on his* ～*s.* 这工作使约翰忙个不停)。***toast one's*** ～***s***〔口〕烘脚。〔美〕～ ***and heel*** (*it*) 跳舞。～***s up***〔俚〕死。～ ***to*** ～〔美拳〕旗鼓相当地。***tread*** [***step***] ***on sb.'s*** ～***s*** 踩某人的脚尖；得罪某人。***turn one's*** ～***s in*** [***out***] 脚尖朝内[外]走路。***turn up one's*** ～***s***〔俚〕死。**II** ***vt.*** 用脚趾踩，用脚趾钩；装[修补]鞋尖[袜尖等]；用脚尖踢；【高尔夫球】用棒尖打(球)；【木工】斜钉(钉子)。— ***vi.*** 动脚尖；脚尖朝…(方面)。～ *sb. out of the room* 将某人踢出房外。～ ***in*** [***out***] 脚尖朝内[外]走路。～ ***the line*** [***mark***, ***scratch***] (赛跑等时)将脚尖抵在起步线上站着；服从规定[政纲]，服从命令。～ ***the line of*** 和…一鼻孔出气，追随。～**cap** 鞋尖装饰，鞋尖饰皮。～ **crack** (马的)蹄裂病。～ **dance** = ～**-dancing** 脚尖舞。～**hold** 立

足点,基础;实力。~-**in** 前轮内倾;车轮内向。~ **nail** 脚趾甲。~**shoe**, ~ **slipper** 芭蕾舞鞋。~ **smithing**〔美〕跳舞。

toed [təud; tod] ***a*.** **1.** 有(若干)趾的。**2.** 斜钉的,以斜钉固定的。

TOEFL = Test(ing) of English as a Foreign Language 托福考试(作为外国语的英语测验)。

toff [tɔf; tɔf, tɑf]〔英俚〕***n*.** (自以为的)上流社会人物;花花公子,爱打扮的人。*He came out no end of a* ~. 他打扮得怪漂亮地出来了。*the* ~*s* 上层社会。

tof·fee, tof·fy [ˈtɔfi; ˋtɑfɪ, ˋtɔfɪ] ***n*.** 奶油太妃糖。***can't shoot for*** ~〔俚〕怎么打[射击]也打不好,枪法不高明。***not for*** ~〔俚〕绝对不,决不…。

T. of Opns. = Theatre of Operations 战区。

toft [tɔft; tɔft, tɑft]〔英方〕***n*.**【法】宅地,屋基;小丘。~ *and croft* 宅地和宅旁耕地(全部)。

tog [tɔg; tɑg] **I** ***n*.** 上衣;〔常 *pl*.〕〔口〕(一套)衣服。*long* ~*s*【海、俚】上岸穿的外衣。**II** ***vt*.** (**-gg-**) 给穿上,打扮 (*out*; *up*)。~*ged out in full uniform* 穿着礼服[正式制服]。

to·ga [ˈtəugə; ˋtogə] ***n*.** (*pl*. ~**s**, ***togae*** [ˈtəudʒiː; ˋtodʒi]) (古罗马市民穿的)宽大长袍〔= ~ virilis [viˈrailis; vɪˋraɪlɪs]〕;(法官,议员等的)长袍,制服;〔美〕参议员的职位。

to·gat·ed [ˈtəugeitid; ˋtogetɪd] ***n*.** **1.** 和平景色的。**2.** 威严的,神气的;穿外袍的。

to·geth·er [təˈgeðə; təˋgeðɚ] **I** ***ad*.** **1.** 一同,共同;并合,合起来;混合;互相。**2.** 同时,一齐;连续,不停地。*go* ~ 一块儿去。*rent a house* ~ 合租房子。*compare* ~ 放在一起互相比较。*fight* ~ 互打。*Both* ~ *exclaimed*. 两人同时叫了起来。*for hours* ~ 连续好几个钟头。***belong*** ~ 合成一体。***get*** ~ 集合;编纂,汇齐。***hang*** ~ **1.** 结合[纠结]在一起。**2.** 符合。***put two and two*** ~ 综合起来考虑。***taken*** [***taking***] ~ 合起来看。~ ***with*** 和…一起[合起来]。**II** ***a*.**〔美俚〕头脑清楚的;稳当可靠的。

to·geth·er·ness [təˈgeðənis; təˋgeðənɪʃ] ***n*.** 家庭聚会〔家庭亲属间经常进行社交或来往以增进和稳定亲属关系〕。

tog·ger·y [ˈtɔgəri; ˋtɑgərɪ] ***n*.**〔口〕〔集合词〕衣服,(特种)服装。

tog·gle [ˈtɔgl; ˋtɑgḷ] **I** ***n*.**【海】挂索桩,绳针,套索钉;【机】肘节〔=~joint〕套环;肘环套接;【无】反复电路。**II** ***vt*.** 用绳针系紧,拴牢;配备套环[肘节];打开肘节开关(投弹)。~ **flip-flop** 反转触发器。~ **iron** (刃部可移动的)捕鲸标枪。~ **press**【机】肘杆式冲床[压力机]。~ **switch**【电】肘节开关。

To·go [ˈtəugəu; ˋtogo] ***n*.** 多哥〔非洲〕。

TOHO = tiny office home office 袖珍家庭企业〔字面为"很小的家庭办公室"〕。

toil[1] [tɔil; tɔɪl] **I** ***n*.** 苦工,苦役;难事;劳苦,辛苦。**II** ***vi*.** 辛苦工作,劳动 (*at*; *for*);辛苦行进 (*up*; *through*; *along* 等)。

toil[2] [tɔil; tɔɪl] ***n*.**〔常 *pl*.〕圈套,罗纲,网,魔力,迷惑力;阴谋。***be taken in the*** ~***s*** 落网;上圈套,被迷住。

toile [twɑːl; twɑl] ***n*.**〔F.〕薄亚麻织物;麻布。

toil·er [ˈtɔilə; ˋtɔɪlə] ***n*.** 辛苦工作的人。

toi·let [ˈtɔilit; ˋtɔɪlɪt] **I** ***n*.** 梳洗,打扮,化妆;化妆用具;梳妆台;妆饰,服装;厕所,浴室,盥洗室;【医】(手术前后的)洗涤。**II** ***vt*.** 给…穿衣[打扮];照料小孩上厕所。— ***vi*.** 梳妆,打扮;上厕所,上盥洗室。***go down the*** ~ 全功尽弃,一败涂地。***make one's*** ~ 打扮。~ **bowl** 抽水马桶。~ **cover** 梳妆台布。~ **cream** 雪花膏。~ **paper**, ~ **tissue** 手纸,草纸;桑皮纸。~ **powder** 扑粉。~ **roll** 卫生卷纸。~ **room** 化妆室;厕所,盥洗室。~**set** (一套)化妆用具。~ **soap** 香皂。~ **table** 梳妆台。~ **training** 训练小孩大小便。~ **vinegar** 加在洗手水里的香料。~ **water** 花露水。

toi·let·ry [ˈtɔilitri; ˋtɔɪlɪtrɪ] ***n*.** (一套)化妆用具;〔美〕化妆品。

toi·lette [twɑːˈlet; tɔɪˋlet, twɑˋlet] ***n*.** (女人的)化妆,梳妆;服装,装束;礼服,盛装。

toil·ful [ˈtɔilfəl; ˋtɔɪlfəl] ***a*.** 辛苦的,劳苦的。

toil·less [ˈtɔilis; ˋtɔɪlɪs] ***a*.** 不费力的,容易的。

toil·some [ˈtɔilsəm; ˋtɔɪlsəm] ***a*.** 辛苦的,劳累的。**-ly** ***ad*.**

toil·worn [ˈtɔilwɔːn; ˋtɔɪlˏwɔrn] ***a*.** 工作疲乏的,做累了的。

To·jo [ˈtəudʒəu; ˋtodʒo], **Hideki** 东条(英机)〔1885—1948,日本军人,政治家,以侵略中国战犯罪被判处绞刑〕。

To·kay [təuˈkei; toˋke] ***n*.** 妥凯白[紫]葡萄;妥凯葡萄酒〔匈牙利妥凯 (Tokay) 地方产的〕。

toke [təuk; tok] **I** ***n*.**〔英俚〕食物,(尤指)干面包;〔美俚〕吸香烟〔尤指大麻香烟〕一口。**II** ***vt*.**〔美俚〕吸一口(烟)。

Toke·lau Is. [təukəˈlau ˈailənd; ˏtokəˋlaʊ ˋaɪlənd] ***n*.** 托克劳群岛。

to·ken [ˈtəukən; ˋtokən] **I** ***n*.** 象征,记号,标记;表示物,证物;纪念品;代币,代价券;【语】语言符号;【英史】私铸货币;【圣】前兆;暗号。**II** ***a*.** 作为标志的;象征性的。*a* ~ *of love* 爱的象征。***as a*** ~ ***of*** = *in* ~ *of*. ***by*** (***the same***) ~ 据此看来;而且,还有;更加,越发。***by this*** [***that***] ~ 照这个[那个]看来。***in*** ~ ***of*** 作为…的标志〔表示,证物,象征,纪念品〕。***more by*** ~〔古〕= *by the same* ~. ***reduce ... down to*** ~ ***contingents*** 把…裁减[缩减]到象征性的限额。~ **economy** 象征性经济,代币性经济〔发给可调换成有预定价值(如食品、休假等)的代币作为奖励手段〕。~ **forces** 有名无实[象征性]的部队。~ **import**【贸易】(为将来正式输入开路的;小额的)试样输入。~ **money**〔英史〕(商店发行的)代币。~ **payment** 部分偿付。~ **raid** [**resistance**] 象征性空袭[抵抗]。~ **vote**〔英〕(会议)原则同意的象征拨款决议〔实际金额总数不须再行讨论〕。

To·ken·house Yard [ˈtəukənhaus ˈjɑːd; ˋtokənhaʊs ˋjɑrd] ***n*.** (伦敦)土地拍卖市场〔因所在地命名〕。

to·ken·ism [ˈtəuknizm; ˋtokənˏɪzm] ***n*.** 装门面;表面文章。

to·ko [ˈtəukəu; ˋtoko] = toco.

to·kus [ˈtʌkəs; ˋtʌkəs, ˋtokəs, ˋtokəs] ***n*.**〔俚〕屁股。

To·ky·o [ˈtəukjəu; ˋtokɪˏo, -kjo] ***n*.** 东京〔日本首都〕。~ *Bay* 东京湾〔日本〕。

to·la [ˈtəulə; ˋtolɑ] ***n*.** 托拉〔印度金银重量单位,1 金托拉 = 180 grain 或 11.664 gram.〕。

to·lan [ˈtəulæn; ˋtolæn] ***n*.**【化】二苯(基)乙炔。

To·land [ˈtəulənd; ˋtolənd] ***n*.** 托兰〔姓氏〕。

tol·booth [ˈtəulˌbuːθ; ˋtolˏbuθ, -buð] ***n*.**〔Scot.〕牢狱。

tol·bu·ta·mide [təlˈbjuːtəˌmaid; tɑlˋbjutəmaɪd] ***n*.**【药】甲苯磺丁脲,甲糖宁。

told [təuld; told] tell 的过去式及过去分词。

tole[1] [təul; tol] ***vt*.**〔古、方〕引诱,诱惑,诱使,怂恿。

tole[2] [təul; tol] ***n*.** 金属薄片,镀锡铁皮。

To·le·do ***n*.** **1.** [təˈliːdəu; təˋlido] 托利多〔美国港市〕。**2.** [tɔˈleidəu; tɑˋledo] 托莱多〔西班牙城市〕。**3.** [tɔˈleidəu; tɑˋledo] 托莱多宝剑〔西班牙托莱多城精炼的好剑〕。

tol·er·a·bil·i·ty [ˌtɔlərəˈbiliti; ˏtɑlərəˋbɪlətɪ] ***n*.** 可忍受度;勉强,凑和;(健康)尚可。

tol·er·a·ble [ˈtɔlərəbl; ˋtɑlərəbḷ] ***a*.** 可忍受的;可容忍的;可原谅的;过得去的;〔口〕可算得健康的。**-a·bly** ***ad*.**

tol·er·ance [ˈtɔlərəns; ˋtɑlərəns] ***n*.** 忍受;容忍;宽容;耐性;【物】容限;【医】耐受[药]性,耐(药)力;耐(药)量;【植】耐阴性;耐量;【造币、机】公差,容许量。~ *deviation* 容许偏差。~ *on fit* 配合公差。~ *unit* 公差单位。

tol·er·ant [ˈtɔlərənt; ˋtɑlərənt] ***a*.** **1.** 忍受的;容忍的,原谅的,宽大的。**2.** 有耐药性[力]的。***be*** ~ ***of*** [***to-***

ward]对…能容忍。～ ***and understanding with each other*** 互相宽容并互相谅解。

tol·er·ate [ˈtɔləreit; ˋtɑlə͵ret] ***vt***. 忍受;容忍;宽容,默认,容许;有耐药性[力]。*to ～ only praise and no criticism* 只让人表扬,不让人批评。***cannot supinely*** ～ 不能置之不理。**-er** ***n***.

tol·er·a·tion [ˌtɔləˈreiʃən; ͵tɑləˋreʃən] ***n***. 忍受;宽容,默认,默许;信仰自由;容忍异端[教]。**-tive** ***a***.

tol·i·dine [ˈtɔliˌdiːn, -din; ˋtɑlə͵din, -dɪn] ***n***.【化】联甲苯胺。

toll[1] [təul; tol] **I** ***n***. **1**. 税,通行税,过境税;过桥税,渡河费。**2**. 租费,港口税;市场税,摊税;运费;(用所磨谷类一部分作酬的)磨费;长途电话(费)。**3**. (各种使用费的)收费权。**4**. (常用单数)代价;牺牲,死伤人数。*a death* ～ 死亡人数。*a heavy ～ of lives* 死伤惨重。***take ～ of*** 扣去…的一部分;夺去;使…遭受伤亡。**II** ***vt***., ***vi***. 缴纳[征收]通行税[欠费]。～ **bar** (通行税征收处的)关木,关闸。～**bar**【计】工具栏。～ **board**【电话】长途交换台。～ **broadcasting**〔美〕收费的无线电广播。～ **bridge** 收费桥。～ **cable** 长途电话电缆。～ **call** 长途电话。～ **central office** 长途电话总局。～ **gate** 通行税征收卡。～ **house** (过桥费等的)征收所。～ **in gate**【法】入城税。～ **keeper** 收税[费]人。～**-man** 收税[费]人。～ **road** 收费道路。～ **thorough**【法】通行税,过桥税。～ **traverse**【法】私有地通行费。～ **turn**〔英〕【法】牲畜市场税,征收所。**-age** ***n***. 捐税,税收;纳税[费],收税[费]。**-er** ***n***. 收税员,收费员。

toll[2] [təul; tol] **I** ***vt***. 鸣(钟);(鸣钟)宣告[召唤];(鸣钟)报丧。— ***vi***. 鸣钟;(钟)响,鸣。*For whom the bell ～s?* 丧钟为谁而鸣?**II** ***n***. 钟声。～ *the hour* 鸣钟报时。～ *in the people* 敲钟召集群众。

tol-lol, tol-lol·ish [tɔlˈlɔl, -iʃ; ͵tɑlˋlɑl, -ɪʃ] ***a***.〔俚〕相当的,中等的,过得去的。

T

tol·ly [ˈtɔli; ˋtɑlɪ]〔英俚〕**I** ***n***. 蜡烛;棍,杖;塔尖。**II** ***vi***. (在熄灯后)点蜡烛。

Tol·tec [ˈtɔltek; ˋtɑltɛk] ***n***. (古代居住于墨西哥,受马雅文化影响的一支印第安人)托尔铁克人。

Tol·tec·an [ˈtɔltekn, ˈtəu-; ˋtɑltɛkn, ˋto-] ***a***. 托尔铁克人的,托尔铁克文化的。

tol·u(balsam) [təˈljuː; toˋlu] ***n***. (南美)妥卢香脂[胶](= ～ balsam)。～ **tree**【植】妥卢胶树。

tol·u·ate [ˈtɔljuˌeit; ˋtɑljʊ͵et] ***n***.【化】甲苯酸盐或[酯]。

tol·u·ene, tol·uol [ˈtɔljuiːn, ˈtɔljuɔl; ˋtɑljʊin, ˋtɑljʊəl] ***n***.【化】甲苯。

tol·u·ide, to·lu·i·dide [ˈtɔljuˌwaid, -ˈluːdaid; ˋtɑljʊ͵waɪd, -ˋludaɪd] ***n***.【化】N-某酰基甲苯胺。

tol·u·yl [ˈtɔljuː; ˋtɑljʊəl] ***n***.【化】甲苯甲酰。

tolyl [ˈtɔlil; ˋtɑləl] ***n***.【化】甲苯基。

Tom [tɔm; tɑm] ***n***. 汤姆〔男子名,Thomas 的昵称〕。

tom [tɔm; tɑm] **I** ***n***. **1**. 〔T-〕Thomas 的爱称;大钟。**2**. 雄性动物;(特指)雄猫(= ～-cat)。**3**. 大傻瓜(= T-Fool)。**4**.【矿】倾斜粗洗淘金槽;【海】主炮。**5**.〔俚〕= tomato. **II** ***vi***.〔T-〕(***Tommed***; ***Tom·ming***)〔美口〕(像汤姆叔一样)逆来顺受。*Blind T-* 捉迷藏。*Old T-* 强烈的杜松子酒。**T- and Jerry**〔美〕吃喝玩乐的浪荡子;奶蛋热甜酒。**T- Bowiing**【海】海员。～ **boy** 爱玩爱吵的姑娘。**T- Collins**〔美〕冰冻柠檬糖汁汽水杜松子酒。**T-, Dick, and Harry**〔口〕普通人。**T- Farthing**[**Fool**] 傻子,笨蛋(*There's more* [*More people*] *knows T-Fool than T- Fool knows*. 臭名声并不光彩〔蠢人的蠢事别人都看在眼里〕)。**T- Long** 老长个子;讲话冗长的人。～ **nobody** 笨人,傻子。**T- O' Bedlam** 狂人,疯子。**T- Show**《汤姆叔叔的小屋》的(巡回)演出。**T- Thumb** (英国童话里的小人儿)大拇指;矮小的人[东西]。**T-Tiddler's ground** 宝山,金山;〔儿童游戏〕占金山。**T- Tyler** [**Tiler**] 怕老婆的人。

tom·a·hawk [ˈtɔməbɔːk; ˋtɑmə͵hɔk, ˋtɑmɪ-] **I** ***n***. (北美印第安人的)战斧,钺,〔澳〕斧子;〔T-〕(美国)战斧式驱逐机。***bury*** [***lay aside***] ***the*** ～ 停战讲和。***dig up*** [***raise, take up***] ***the*** ～ 宣战。**II** ***vt***. 用战斧斩[杀];激烈批评[抨击]。

tom·al·ley [ˈtɔmˌæli; ˋtɑm͵ælɪ] ***n***. 龙虾肝。

to·man [ˈtəuˈmɑːn; toˋmɑn] ***n***. 托曼〔伊朗金币,值十里亚尔〕;【史】蒙古军队的一师〔10,000 人〕。

to·mat·in [təˈmeitin; təˋmætɪn] ***n***.【生化】番茄素。

to·ma·to [təˈmɑːtəu; təˋmeto, təˋmɑto] ***n***. (*pl*. ***-toes***) **1**.【植】番茄,西红柿。**2**.〔美俚〕姑娘;男人;脸。**3**. 不行的拳击师;棒球用球。～ *worm moth* 番茄天蛾。

tomb [tuːm; tum] **I** ***n***. 坟墓;墓穴;墓碑;〔the ～〕死。**II** ***vt***. 埋葬。***The Tombs***〔美〕纽约市监狱。～**stone** ***n***. 墓石,墓碑;〔*pl*.〕〔美俚〕牙齿;〔美〕(华尔街的)新上市股票[证券]发行公告〔指如同墓碑上文字一样简单的介绍而无细节说明〕。

tom·bac, tom·bak [ˈtɔmbæk; ˋtɑmbæk] ***n***. 顿巴黄铜,人造金,德国黄铜〔铜与锌的合金〕。

tom·bo·lo [ˈtɔmbəˌləu; ˋtɑmbə͵lo] ***n***. (*pl*. ***-los***)【地】沙颈岬,陆连岛,连岛沙洲。

tom·boy·ish [ˈtɔmˌbɔiiʃ; ˋtɑm͵bɔɪɪʃ] ***a***. 男孩子气的女孩的,顽皮的女孩的。**-ly** ***ad***. **-ness** ***n***.

tom-cat [ˈtɔmkæt; ˋtɑm͵kæt] ***n***. 公猫。

tom·cod [ˈtɔmˌkɔd; ˋtɑm͵kɑd] ***n***.【动】**1**. 大西洋霜鳕(*Microgadus tomcod*)。**2**. 太平洋霜鳕(*Microgadus proximus*)。

tome [təum; tom] ***n***. (书的)一卷,一册;(一本)大书,大部头的书,一本巨著。

-tome, -tomo, -tomy *comb. f*. **1**. 一节,一段。**2**.【医】切割器,切开:micro*tome*, thyro*tome*, hepatec*tomy*.

to·men·tose [təuˈmentəus; təˋmɛntos, ˋtomɛn͵tos] ***a***.【动、植】被有棉毛[绒毛]的。

to·men·tum [təuˈmentəm; toˋmɛntəm] ***n***. (*pl*. ***-ta*** [-tə; -tə])【动】棉毛;【植】绒毛;【解】软脑膜的毛状膜裹。

tom·fool·er·y [ˈtɔmfuləri; ͵tɑmˋfulərɪ] ***n***. 愚蠢举动[言语];小丑姿态;恶俗的妆饰;愚蠢而无聊的玩笑。

Tom·lin·son [ˈtɔmlinsn; ˋtɑmlɪnsən] ***n***. 汤姆林森〔姓氏〕。

Tom·my, Tom·mie [ˈtɔmi; ˋtɑmɪ] ***n***. 汤米〔男子名,Thomas 的昵称〕。

tom·my [ˈtɔmi; ˋtɑmɪ] ***n***. **1**. (尤指抵作工资的)面包或食物;实物工资制;〔英〕工人带着上班的食物。**2**.〔常 T-〕〔俚〕英国兵;〔集合词〕英国军队。**3**.【机】螺丝旋棒[杆](= ～-bar)。*soft* ～ 软面包。**T- Atkins** 英国兵。**T- cooker** 轻便火油灯。**T- Gee**〔美俚〕机关枪手;犯罪恶汉。～ **gun**〔美口〕冲锋枪。～**rot**〔俚〕荒唐事,蠢事;大话。～ **screw**【机】贯头螺丝。～**-shop** 实行实物工资制的工厂;厂内使用工资代价券的商店;面包店。

tomo·gram [ˈtəuməgræm; ˋtomə͵græm] ***n***.〔*pl*.〕【医】层面 X 线相片。**-graphy** 层面 X 线照相术。

to·mor·row, to-mor·row [təˈmɔrəu, tuˈmɔ-; təˋmɔro] **I** ***n***. 明日,明天;来日,未来。～ *week* 下星期的明天(八天后)。*the day after* ～ 后天;*He will start ～ morning*. 他明天早上动身。*T- never comes*. 切莫依赖明天。*Never put off till ～ what you can do today*. 今天能做的事不要拖到明天;今日事今日毕。*the world's* ～ 世界的未来。**II** ***ad***. 在明天、未来某一时候。*See you* ～. 明天见。*People ～ will have different ideas about this*. 将来的人们对此会有不同的想法。**-er** ***n***. 做事拖延的人。

tom·pi·on [ˈtɔmpiən; ˋtɑmpɪən] ***n***. = tampion.

Tomp·king [ˈtɔmpkinz; ˋtɑmpkɪnz] ***n***. 汤普金斯〔姓氏〕。

tom·tit [ˈtɔmˈtit; ˋtɑm͵tɪt] ***n***.〔英〕【鸟】山雀科小鸟;山雀,青山雀。

tom·tom [ˈtɔmtɔm; ˋtɑm͵tɑm] **I** ***n***. (印度等地用手拍击

的)长筒鼓(鼓声);锣。**II** ***vi***. 拍击长筒鼓。

-tomy ***n***. *suf*.【医】切割,切开,切除:ana*tomy*.

ton [tʌn; tʌn] ***n***. **1**. 吨〔(a)重量单位,英吨 = 2,240 磅(= long ～ = gross ～),美吨 = 2,000 磅(= short ～),中国通用的公吨 = 1,000 公斤(= metric ～)。(b)商船注册的容积单位 = 100 立方英尺(= register ～ = net ～)。(c)特定货物装载单位:木材(等) = 40 立方英尺,石料 = 16 立方英尺,煤 = 49 bushels, 小麦 = 20 bushels, 盐 = 42 bushels, 葡萄酒 = 252 wine gallons 等。(d)船舰排水单位[排水吨](= 海水 35 立方英尺 = displacement ～)。(e)一般货物装载单位(尺码吨或水脚吨) = 40 立方英尺(= freight ～ = shipping ～)〕。**2**. 〔*pl*.〕〔口〕沉重的重量;许多,大量;〔俚〕每小时一百英里的速度。*five* ～(*s*) *of coal* 五吨煤。*a deadweight* ～【海】重量吨,英吨。*This box of yours weights a* ～. 你这只箱子真沉重。*a* ～ *of books* 许多书。～*s of times* 屡次,许多次。*That is* ～*s better*. 〔口〕那个好得多。～ ***for*** ～ ***and man for man***【海】把捕获奖金公平分给友船。***hit like a*** ～ ***of bricks***〔美俚〕让人吓呆。～**-mile** ***n***. 吨英里〔吨数与英里数之积;铁路、飞机运输量单位〕。

ton [tɔ̃ː; tõ] ***n***. 〔F.〕时兴,时髦,流行。***in the*** ～合乎时髦式样。

-ton *suf*. 都市,城市:Hamp*ton*.

ton·al [ˈtəunəl; ˋtonl] ***a***. 音调的,调子的,音色的,声音的;【乐】调性的;【绘画】色调的。～ **density** 色调密度;音品密度。～ **paper** 扩音纸。

to·na·li·ty [təuˈnæliti; toˋnælətɪ] ***n***. **1**. 音调,(音乐的)调性,音色。**2**.【绘画】色调。

to·name [ˈtuːneim; ˋtuˏnem] ***n***. 〔方〕(区别同姓同名用的)别名,外号;姓。

ton·dino [təunˈdiːnəu; tonˋdino] ***n***. 圆盘形图画[浮雕];【建】半圆形装饰。

ton·do [ˈtɔndəu; ˋtɑndə] ***n***. (*pl*. ***tondi*** [ˈtɔndi; ˋtɑndɪ]) 圆形意大利瓷盘;圆盘形图画[浮雕]。

Tone [təun; ton] ***n***. 托恩〔姓氏〕。

tone [təun; ton] **I** ***n***. **1**. 调子,音调;音色;音乐。**2**. 语调,语气;(报刊等的)论调。**3**. 格调,风格;风气,气氛,情调;常态;情况;行情;思想状态。**4**.【乐】乐音(*opp*. noise);全音,全音程;【无】可听音;【医】(正常的)健康状态;【语音】声调,语调;音的高低,抑扬;【绘画】色调,色泽,明暗。*a* ～ *of command* 命令的口气。*in an angry* ～ 用发怒的口气。*raise the* ～ *of the school* [*army*] 提高校风[军纪]。*the* ～ *of a market* 市场情况,市况。*He took a high* ～. 他语气很傲慢。*recover* ～ 恢复健康。*the four* ～*s* (华语的)四声。*the oblique* [*deflected*] ～ 仄声。*the upper* [*lower*, *even*] ～ 上[下,平]声。***in a*** ～ 一致。**II** ***vt***. 抑扬顿挫地说,用一种声调说;装腔作势地说;加上调子,调整(乐器的)调子;柔和色调;【摄】调色;使有…的风格。— ***vi***. 具有某种色调;(颜色)调和(*with*)。*a red hat with a coat to* ～ 红帽子和一件色调相配的外衣。～ ***down*** 使柔和;变柔和。～ (***in***) ***with*** (使)调和。～ ***up*** 提高,加强;变强(*Exercise* ～*s up the muscles*. 运动能使肌肉发达)。～ **arm** 留声机的拾音臂。～ **cluster**【乐】音群。～ **colour** 音色;【文艺】风格。～ **control** 音调控制,音色调节。～**-deaf** ***a***. 不善于辨别音高的。～ **language**【语言】声调语言。～**pad**【计】音频传送器〔可通过电话线把数据传送到中央电脑的一种装置〕。～ **painting**【乐】音画(尤指标题音乐的印象主义乐曲的作曲技法)。～ **poem**【乐】音诗〔不拘泥形式的旧乐曲〕。～ **quality** 音品,音色。～ **row** [**series**]【乐】= 音体系。～ **wheel** 音轮。

toned [təund; tond] ***a***. **1**. (语言)有声调的。**2**. 有…音质的〔常构成复合词〕。**3**. 年久变色的〔指纸张等〕。

tone·less [ˈtəunlis; ˋtonlɪs] ***a***. 单调的,平板的;无声调[色调]的。

ton·er [ˈtəunə; ˋtonɚ] ***n***. 调色剂,增色剂;上色剂。

to·net·ic [təuˈnetik; toˋnetɪk] ***a***. 声调语言的,与声调语音有关的。**-i·cal·ly** ***ad***.

to·net·ics [təuˈnetiks; toˋnetɪks] ***n***. 声调学。

tong [tɔŋ; tɑŋ] **I** ***n***. 〔用 *pl*.〕夹子,钳子。*fire* ～*s* 火钳。*a pair of* ～*s* = *a* ～*s* 一把钳子。***would not touch with a pair of*** ～***s*** 碰也不想碰,实在讨厌。**II** ***vt***., ***vi***. 用钳子(夹)。

ton·ga [ˈtɔŋgə; ˋtɑŋgə] ***n***. (印度的)双轮小马车。

Ton·ga [ˈtɔŋgə; ˋtɑŋgə] ***n***. 汤加〔西太平洋〕。

tongue [tʌŋ; tʌŋ] **I** ***n***. **1**. 舌;口条〔食用的牛舌等〕。**2**. 口才,说法;语言;国语;方言;国民。**3**. 舌状物;(环扣的)针;岬,湾;火舌;(皮鞋钮扣下面的)舌皮;铃舌;【建,机】雄榫,榫舌;舌饰;【电】衔铁,舌簧;(继电器的)舌片;【铁路】尖轨;留在舌上的余味〔多指不愉快的余味〕。**4**. 〔美俚〕律师。*a coated* [*dirty*, *furred*] ～【医】长了舌苔的舌头。*Good brandy leaves no* ～ *in the morning*. 好白兰地不会使人第二天感到嘴里不舒服。*one's mother* ～ 家乡话,本国话。*the Chinese* ～ 中国话。***all*** ～***s*** 所有国民。***bite the*** ～ 保持沉默。***find one's*** ～ (张口结舌等之后)能说话了,能开口了。***give*** ～ (猎狗发现猎获物)咬,吠;(人)叫喊。***have a bitter*** [***spiteful***] ～ 嘴毒,说话刻薄。***have a ready*** [***fluent***] ～ 口齿伶俐,口才好。***have a rough*** ～ 说话粗鲁。***hold one's*** ～ 保持沉默。***keep a civil*** ～ ***in one's head*** 措辞谨慎。***lose one's*** ～ (因害臊等)说不出话来。***oil one's*** ～ 说恭维话。***on the tip of one's*** ～ 险些讲出。***on the*** ～***s of men*** 被人谈论。***put out one's*** ～ 伸舌头;〔转义〕(表示某种情绪)做鬼脸。***stick*** [***put***, ***thrust***] ***one's*** ～ ***in one's cheek*** 用舌头顶起脸颊〔侮蔑相〕。***throw*** ～ = *give* ～. ***wag one's*** ～ 不断地唠叨。***with one's*** ～ ***in one's cheek*** 不老实地,讽刺地,挖苦地(*speak with one's* ～ *in cheek about peace* 空谈和平)。**II** ***vt***., ***vi***. 用舌头控制着吹奏;吹奏时用舌头;舔;做舌榫(在板上);(将板等)做成雌雄榫[企口接缝,舌槽]接上〔= ～ and groove〕;〔诗〕讲,说;〔口〕申斥,谴责。～**-and-groove joint** 企口接缝,舌槽榫,雌雄榫。～**-bit** 有阻舌片的马嚼子。～ **bone**【解】舌骨。～ **graft** (园艺学用语)舌接。～**-lashing** 〔口〕辱骂;训斥。～ **let** 小舌,舌状突起。～**-shy** 羞得说不出话来。～**-tie** **1**. ***n***. 短舌。**2**. ***vt***. 使说不出话。～**-tied** 舌头短的;张口结舌的。～ **twister** 绕口令〔如:Peter Piper picked a peck of pickled pepper〕。**-less** ***a***. 没有舌头的;缄默的;哑的。

To·ni [ˈtəuni; ˋtonɪ] ***n***. 托妮〔女子名, Antonia 的昵称〕。

ton·ic [ˈtɔnik; ˋtɑnɪk] **I** ***a***. 滋补的,强身的;增强的,使精神振作的,鼓励的;【医】强直的,僵硬性的;【乐】主音的;【语音】声调的;主重音的;声调语言的。**II** ***n***. 补药,强壮剂;增强剂;兴奋剂;鼓舞物;【乐】主音;【语音】浊音;主重音音节。*hair*-～ 生发油[水]。～ *medicine* 补药。～ *action* 紧张动作。～ *spasm*【医】强直性痉挛。*a* ～ *chord*【乐】主和音。～ **sol-fa** (用唱名 do, re, mi, fa, sol, la, ti 表示的)唱名记谱法[教唱法]。

to·nic·i·ty [təuˈnisiti; toˋnɪsətɪ] ***n***. 强壮;(肌肉组织的)紧张力,强壮度;(溶液的)张性;(体液的)浸透压。

to·night, **to-night** [təˈnait, tu-; təˋnaɪt] **I** ***n***. 今夜,今晚。**II** ***ad***. 在今晚。

to·nite [ˈtəunait; ˋtonaɪt] ***n***.【化】徒那特〔一种猛烈的棉火药〕。

tonk [tɔŋk; tɑŋk] ***vt***. 〔英俚〕猛打;彻底击败;【高尔夫球】把球击得飞起。

ton·ka bean [ˈtɔŋkəbiːn; ˋtʌŋkəbin]【植】零陵香豆。

tonkin [ˈtɔnkin; ˋtɑnˋkɪn] ***n***. (越南产)硬竹〔作钓杆等用〕。a ～ *cane* 青篱竹。

tonn. = tonnage.

ton·nage [ˈtʌnidʒ; ˋtʌnɪdʒ] ***n***. 吨数;(船的)装载吨数,吨位〔每吨按 100 立方英尺计算〕;(特指一国、一个港口的商船的)总吨数;(船、货的)吨税。*gross* ～ 总吨数;〔按吨计算的〕运费。*net* [*registered*] ～ 登记吨数[位]。

T

displacement ～（军舰的）排水量［吨数］。～（*and poundage*）【英史】港税。

tonne [tʌn; tʌn] ***n.*** 公吨（= metric ton）。

ton·neau [ˈtɔnəu; təˋno, tʌ-] ***n.***（*pl.* ～*s*, ～*x* [-z; -z]）［F.］（旧式汽车的）后部座席；（这种旧式汽车的）车身；（法国）二轮轻马车。

-ton·ner [ˈtʌnə; ˋtʌnɚ] ***n.*** *suf.* …吨的船。*a ten-* ～ 十吨的船。

to·nom·e·ter [təuˈnɔmitə; toˋnɑmətɚ] ***n.***【物】音调计；准音器；【物，化】汽压计；【医】眼压计；张力计；血压计。**-e·tric** [ˌtɔnəˈmetrik; ˏtɑnəˋmɛtrɪk] ***a.***

to·nom·e·try [təuˈnɔmitri; toˋnɑmɪtrɪ] ***n.*** **1.** 音调测量学。**2.** 张力测定法。

ton·o·scope [ˈtɔnəskəup; ˋtɑnəˏskop] ***n.***【物】音高镜。

tono·tron [ˈtɔnətrɔn; ˋtɑnəˏtrɑn] ***n.***【无】雷达显示管。

ton·sil [ˈtɔnsil; ˋtɑnsḷ, -sɪl] ***n.***【解】扁桃体［腺］。～ *bath*〔美俚〕酒，一杯酒。

ton·sil·lar [ˈtɔnsilə; ˋtɑnsḷɚ] ***a.*** 扁桃体［腺］的。

ton·sil·lec·to·my [ˌtɔnsiˈlektəmi; ˏtɑnsḷˋɛktəmɪ] ***n.***（*pl.* ***-mies***）【医】扁桃体切除术。

ton·sil·li·tis [tɔnsiˈlaitis; ˏtɑnsḷˋaɪtɪs] ***n.***【医】扁桃体［腺］炎。

ton·sil·lot·o·my [ˌtɔnsiˈlɔtəmi; ˏtɑnsḷˋɑtəmɪ] ***n.***（*pl.* ***-mies***）【医】扁桃体切开术。

ton·so·ri·al [tɔnˈsɔːriəl; tɑnˋsorɪəl, -ˋsɔr-] ***a.***〔谑〕理发师的；理发的。*a* ～ *artist*［*parlour*］〔谑〕理发师［店］。**-ist** ***n.***〔美谑〕理发师。

ton·sure [ˈtɔnʃə; ˋtɑnʃɚ] **I** ***n.*** 削发（仪式）；剃光的圆顶，剃去头发的部分；出家；僧职。**II** ***vt.*** 剃（头）；为…举行剃发式。

ton·tine [tɔnˈtiːn; ˋtɑntin, -nˋtin] ***n.***（17世纪意大利银行家 Tonti 氏倡导的）聚金养老法；［集合词］聚金养老会会员；聚金养老会的基金会员所得的养老金。

to·nus [ˈtəunəs; ˋtonəs] ***n.***【医】紧张〔正常肌肉处于休息状态时的轻微收缩〕。

To·ny [ˈtəuni; ˋtonɪ] ***n.*** **1.** 托尼〔男子名，Ant(h)ony 的昵称〕。**2.**〔美俚〕（有关戏剧艺术的任何一种）年度奖金。

ton·y [ˈtəuni; ˋtonɪ] ***a.***〔美俚〕漂亮的，时髦的，豪华的〔常含讥讽意思〕。

too [tuː; tu] ***ad.*** **1.** 太。**2.** 很，非常，极。**3.** 也，还，同样；又，而且，而又，加之。**4.**〔口〕（不）还是，真的。*This house is* ～ *large for me.* 这房子我住太大了。*We cannot be* ～ *careful.* 无论怎么小心也不算太过；愈小心愈好；不怕过分小心。*I'm going,* ～. 我也去。*She is wise, and active* ～. 她又聪明，又活泼。*I mean to do it* ～.（不单是说）是真要干的。*You are not going.* —*Yes, I am,* ～. 你不去啦。——不，还是要去的。★ **3. 4.** 意之 too 美语有用在句首的：*Too, there were rumours of his resignation.*〔美〕又有他辞职的谣传了。**all** ～ 太（*The holidays ended all* ～ *soon.* 假期过得太快了）。**but** ～（*true*）不幸（是事实）。**none** ～（*pleasant*）一点也不（快乐）。**only** ～ **1.** = but ～. **2.** 非常，极，很（*I am only* ～ *pleased.* 那我是高兴极了）。**quite** ～ = too too（*This is quite* ～. 简直太好了）。～ **bad**〔美〕真不幸，真抱歉。～（**bloody**）**Irish**［**right**］！〔军俚〕当然！～ **... for** 太…不合［不配］。～ **little** 不够。(**...**) ～ **many** 多…个（*You have given me two* ～ many. 你多给了我两个）。**one** ～ **many for sb.** 胜过（某人），比（某人）聪明（*She is one* ～ *many for me.* 她比我强）。～ **much for sb.** 比（某人）强；对…来说太困难了（*This task is* ～ *much for him.* 这任务对他来说太难了）。～ **much**（**of a good thing**）令人受不了（*This was* ～ *much for him.* 这个他受不了）。～ **previous**〔美〕慌忙。～ **... to ...** 太…以致不能（*I went* ～ *late to see him.* 我去得太迟，没有见到他）。～ ～ 非常，很；极好（～ ～ *apparent* 很明白。*This is* ～ ～. 好极了〔后略去 delightful 等形容词，表示假意感激或十二分感激的口气〕）。***very nice*** ～ 非常赞成。

toodle-oo [tuːdlˈuː; ˋtudḷˋu] ***int.***〔谑〕再会〔模仿汽车喇叭声的拟声词〕。

took [tuk; tʊk] take 的过去式。

tool [tuːl; tul] **I** ***n.*** **1.** 工具，用具，器具；【机】刀具；工具母机（= machine ～）。**2.** 爪牙，傀儡，走狗；〔美俚〕扒手。**3.**【装钉】压印机。**4.**［*pl.*］〔美俚〕刀叉（等）。*Books are the* ～*s of a scholar.* 书籍是学者的工具。～ *steel* 工具钢。*a broad* ～（石工的）宽刃凿。*an edge(d)* ～ 刀。*literary* ～*s* 文具。*a poor* ～ 不行的工人。***throw down one's*** ～***s*** = ***down*** ～***s*** 罢工。**II** ***vt.***, ***vi.*** **1.** 用工具加工，用工具制造，用凿刀修整（石头）；【装订】压印。**2.**〔英口〕开车；乘车；〔美俚〕闲逛，闲荡。*Let me* ～ *you down to the station.* 我用车送你上车站吧。*blind* ～ *ing*【印】（硬封面上的）本色压印。

tool·er [ˈtuːlə; ˋtulɚ] ***n.*** 石工用的宽凿。

tool·ing [ˈtuːliŋ; ˋtulɪŋ] ***n.*** **1.** 凿出的装饰。**2.**（工厂投入生产前的）机床安装。**3.** 书籍封面上烫压成的装饰。

tool·mak·er [ˈtuːlˌmeikə; ˋtulˏmekɚ] ***n.*** 制造，维修，校准机床的机工。**-mak·ing** ***n.***

toom [tuːm; tum] **I** ***a.***〔Scot.〕空虚的。*A* ～ *purse makes an oblate merchant.* 口袋一文不名，会使商人烦闷。**II** ***vt.*** 喝干。

'toon [tuːn; tun] ***n.***〔口〕= cartoon. ～ **characters** 卡通片中的人物。

toon [tuːn; tun] ***n.***【植】印度桃花心木。

toot[1] [tuːt; tut] **I** ***n.*** 嘟嘟〔喇叭、笛子等的声音〕；〔美〕闹饮；庆祝。**II** ***vt.*** 吹（喇叭、笛子等），使嘟嘟叫。—***vi.*** 吹喇叭［笛子］嘟嘟地叫；（松鸡等）叫。*Don't* ～. 勿揿喇叭。～ ***one's own horn***〔美口〕自夸，自傲。～ ***the ringer***［***ding-dong***］〔美口〕按门铃。

toot[2] [tuːt; tut] ***n.*** 酒宴；痛饮。

toot·er [ˈtuːtə; ˋtutɚ] ***n.***〔美〕宣传员，广告员。

tooth [tuːθ; tuθ] **I** ***n.***（*pl.* ***teeth***）**1.** 牙齿。**2.** 齿状突出，轮齿，锯齿，耙齿（等）。**3.** 嗜好。**4.**〔常 *pl.*〕（像牙齿那样能咬人的）威力，猛力，（正面）迎击。**5.**〔海口〕［*pl.*］船上的大炮。*a canine* ～ 犬齿。*a false*［*an artificial*］～ 假牙。*a milk* ～ 乳牙。*a molar* ～ 臼齿。*a wisdom* ～ 智齿。*I have a sweet* ～. 我喜欢吃甜东西。*the* ～ *of the wind* 风的威力。***armed to the teeth*** 武装到牙齿，全副武装。***between the teeth*** 低声地。***cast***［***throw***］***sth. in sb.'s teeth***（引用某事）遣责某人。***clench one's teeth*** = *set one's teeth.* ***cut a*** ～ 出牙齿。***cut one's wisdom teeth***（***eyeteeth***）开始懂事。***draw***［***pull***］***sb.'s teeth*** 消除某人不平［烦恼］的根由；拔除某人的爪牙（使无能为害）。***escape by***［***with***］***the skin of one's teeth***〔口〕幸免于难。***from one's teeth*** = ***from the teeth outwards***［***forwards***］怀恨在心地，无诚意的。***grind one's teeth*** 咬牙切齿；生闷气。***have a great*** ～ ***for***（*fruit*）很爱吃（水果）。***in spite of sb.'s teeth*** 不顾某人反对。***in the teeth*** 反抗；公然。***in the teeth of*** 不管，不顾；冒着…；正面受着…。***long in the*** ～ 年纪大（*She is a bit long in the* ～ *to play the part of a young girl.* 她扮演少女的角色年龄太大了一点）。***lose a handful of teeth***〔美拳击〕下巴受猛击。***put teeth in***［***into***］***a new law*** 给与新法律的强制性威力。***set one's teeth*** 咬紧牙关，拼命忍耐。***set sb.'s*** ～ ***on edge*** 使牙齿发酥［发涩］，使腻烦［恼怒］。***show one's teeth*** 张牙露齿，怒视，威吓。***to sb.'s teeth*** 当面，大胆地。～ ***and nail*** 拼命（战斗、反对等）（*They fought* ～ *and nail but lost.* 他们竭尽全力拼搏，结果还是输了）。**II** ***vt.*** 使具齿状；给…装牙齿；刻齿，锉齿（在锯条上等）；（用牙齿）咬（住）。—***vi.***（齿轮等）咬合。～**ache** 牙痛。～**brush** 牙刷。～ **carpenter**〔美俚〕牙医。～**comb** 细（齿）梳。～**-let** 小齿（状突起。）～ **outline** = ～**profile**【机】齿廓，齿形。～**paste** 牙膏。～**pick** 牙签；〔军俚〕刺刀。～**-pow-**

der 牙粉。~ **shell**【动】掘足纲动物。~**some** *a*. 美味可口的。~**-to-tail ratio**【军】前线士兵和后备力量的比率。~**-wash** 刷牙水。~**wort**【植】石芥花(属)。**-ful** *n*. 〔俚〕(白兰地酒等的)一滴,一点点,一小口。**-less** *a*. 没有牙齿的;无力的。

toothed [tu:θt, tu:ðd; tuθt, tuðd] *a*. (装)有牙齿的;锯齿状的。*a* ~ *wheel* 齿轮。~ *whale* 齿鲸亚目动物。

tooth·ful [ˈtu:θful; ˋtuθfʊl] *n*. (酒等)少量,一小口。

tooth·y [ˈtu:θi; ˋtuθɪ] *a*. 露出牙齿的,有凸牙的。

toot·in', toot·ing [ˈtu:tin, -tiŋ; ˋtutɪn, -tɪŋ] *a*. 〔美俚〕说得中肯的,说得有道理的;夸口的,吹牛的。*You're darn* ~. 你的话的确很对。

too·tle [ˈtu:tl; ˋtutl] **I** *vi*. 轻轻吹,反复吹(笛子等);(鸟)嘟嘟叫;(鸡)喔喔叫;空谈,讲废话,写无聊文章。**II** *n*. 吹笛声;空谈,废话;无聊文章。

too-too[1] [ˈtu:tu:; ˋtuˏtu] **I** *ad*. 极,非常,很。**II** *a*. **1**. 过度的,过分的;矫揉造作的。**2**. 〔英〕极好的。*The movie was simply* ~. 这个电影矫揉造作。

too-too[2] [tu:ˈtu:; tuˋtu] *vi*. 嘟嘟地作声〔指吹笛子,哼唱歌等〕。

toots [tu:ts; tuts] *n*. 〔美俚〕宝贝儿,亲亲〔对女孩等的亲热称呼〕。

toot·sy, toot·sie [ˈtu:tsi; ˋtutsɪ] *n*. (尤指儿童或妇女的)脚;〔俚〕= toots; 少女,女人。~**-wootsy** = toots.

Top. = topographic.

top[1] [tɔp; tɑp] **I** *n*. (*opp*. bottom, foot) **1**. 顶,顶部,顶端。**2**. 头,头顶;尖端;树梢,树顶;(事物的)上层部分。**3**. 最高位,首席;艇首的第一号划手。**4**. 极致,绝顶;最好的部分。**5**. 〔常 *pl*.〕(根菜类的)叶子 (*opp*. bottom); 顶芽。**6**. (地、桌子等的)上面,上边;(书页等的)上栏;书顶。**7**. 盖;车盖,车顶;顶篷;壕沟胸壁的顶。**8**. 〔汽车、俚〕高速;剧院最高票价;【机】末档齿轮 (= ~ gear);(香水瓶等的)塞子。**9**. 【纺】束〔= 一磅半;毛条,纤维等的计量单位〕;毛条;化纤束。**10**. 【海】桅楼。**11**. 〔*pl*.〕表面镀金的钮扣;(长筒靴的)筒子;〔*pl*.〕长筒靴,马靴。**12**. 〔美俚〕(尤指马戏团的)大帐篷。**13**. 【化,油】蒸馏出来的轻馏分,蒸馏时的最初挥发成分。**14**. 〔*pl*.〕〔英俚〕上流社会;贵族。**15**. 【桥牌】最大的牌。*the gilt* ~ (书的)天头金边。*the fighting* [*military*] ~ 战斗桅楼。*big* ~ 〔美口〕马戏团的大帐篷。***at the*** ~ ***of*** 在…最高地位;用最高[最大]的(速度、声音等)。***come out*** (***at the***) ~ 得头名,占首位。***come out on*** ~ 赛赢,比赛得头名;获得大成就,出人头地,取得很高的社会地位。***come to the*** ~ 得到名誉;出人头地。***from*** ~ ***to bottom*** [***toe, tail***] 从头到脚,完全;内部;结果,事实上;绝对。(***go***) ***over the*** ~ 跳出壕沟进攻;采取最后手段,采取断然处置;〔美〕赛赢。***on*** (***the***) ~ ***of*** 在…之上,在…的上面;逼近;胜任(工作等);掌握(情况等)。***on*** ~ 在上;〔英〕在(双层公共车辆的)顶座;成功;占优势。***on*** (***the***) ~ 〔英〕〔汽车〕开足马力。***on*** ~ ***of the world*** 〔口〕满意到极点。***on*** ~ ***of that*** 到了最后,最后终于。***over the*** ~ 过份,过度。***take the*** ~ ***of the table*** 坐上座;做主人;做主席。***talk off the*** ~ ***of one's head*** 即席谈话;假充内行谈外行话。***the*** ~ ***of the milk*** 最好[最精彩的]部分;精华。***the*** ~ ***of the tide*** 满潮;情况最好的时候,正当高潮时候。***the*** ~ ***of the tree*** [***ladder***] 最高地位,(某一范围的)最上层,顶尖儿。***to the*** ~ ***of one's bent*** 极力。~ ***and tail*** 全体,全部;结果,事实上;彻头彻尾。~ ***heavy*** 〔美〕喝得烂醉的。***the*** ~ ***of the morning*** (***to you***) 〔方〕早,你早。~ ***or tail*** 〔否定式中〕全然 (*I could not make* ~ *or tail of it*. 我完全弄不懂)。~ ***to bottom*** 倒,逆;从头到脚,完全。

II *a*. 最高的,主要的,第一名的。*the* ~ *layer* 最上层。~ *honours* 极大的荣誉。~ *quality* 最好品质。***at*** ~ ***speed*** 用最高速度。***come out*** ~ ***dog*** 占上风;取胜。***the*** ~ ***notch of*** 〔美〕最高(度)。(***the***) ~***s*** 〔俚〕最好的;最精干的;最受欢迎的。

III *vt*. (**-pp-**) **1**. 戴上,盖上;装顶部。**2**. 到…的顶上,高过,比…高;胜过,超过;得头名。**3**. 高过;高度为(多少)。**4**. 面施,铺施(肥料在地面上);去(树)梢,打顶,摘心;剪(蜡烛的)芯;【染】末染;【高尔夫球】打球顶;【海】使(桅桁等)倾斜。**5**. 〔美俚〕绞死。— *vi*. 完成;结束 (*off, out, up*); 取胜;拔尖。~ *a fence* 跳过篱笆。*He* ~*s six feet*. 他身高六英尺。*He* ~*s his father by half a head*. 他比他父亲高出半个头。*a deer that topped 300 pounds* 三百多磅重的一只鹿。~ ***off*** 完成;结束;〔美〕暗杀 (~ *off one's dinner with liqueur* 用酒结束晚餐)。~ ***one's part*** 【剧】出色地完成…演出任务。~ ***the standing*** 〔美拳〕占第一位。~ ***up*** 装满,加满。***T- your boom***! 别闹! 滚出去! ~ **banana** 主要演员,喜剧主角;主要人物。~ **billing** 〔美剧〕主角。~ **boots** 〔*pl*.〕马靴。~ **bracket** 〔美俚〕主要角色。~ **brass** 要员,高级官员[军官]。~ **coat** 大衣,外套。~ **cross**【生】顶交。~ **dog** 〔俚〕优胜者;〔美俚〕团体的领袖,老板。~**-drawer** *a*. 最重要的,第一位的。~ **-dress** *vt*. 施顶肥,铺肥。~ **end** 顶端,(较细一头的)尖儿 (*opp*. butt end)。~**flight** *a*. 〔口〕高级的,最好的。~ **fruit** 乔性果,乔木果。~ **gear**【机】高速(挡);末挡齿轮;【海】缆索和帆桁等。~ **gun** 〔口〕一流飞行员;〔喻〕精英。~**hamper** 大树树干上部;【海】中桅以上的帆、索具(等);甲板上的重物〔炮塔、救生艇等,多余的笨重东西〕。~ **hand** 〔美〕精通牧场工作的牧童。~ **hat** 大礼帽。~**-heavy** *a*. 头重脚轻的;不稳定的,不平衡的;资本过大的。~**-hole 1**. *a*. 〔英俚〕极好的,头等的。**2**. *n*. 【冶】出钢口。~ **horse** 〔美〕最好的马。~**kick** 〔美俚〕军士长。~**-knot** 鸟的冠毛;鸟冠;顶髻;蝴蝶结〔17世纪妇女的头饰〕;〔口〕头;【鱼】比目鱼类。~ **lantern** = ~ **light**【海】桅头灯。~**-level** *a*. 尖[顶]端的 (~*-level stuff* 尖端材料);最高级(人士、官员)的。~ **line** 报纸标题。~**-line** *a*. **1**. 可上头条新闻的;最重要的 (~*-line news* 头条新闻)。**2**. 第一流的,最优秀的 (~*-line hotel* 第一流的旅馆)。~ **liner** 〔英口〕主要的人[物];主要演员。~ **line jobs** 最重要的工作。~**lofty** *a*. 骄傲的,傲慢的。~ **man** = ~-sawyer, ~ sman. ~**mast**【海】中桅。~**most** *a*. 最上的,最高的,绝顶的。~ **news** 时事新闻。~**notch** *a*. 〔口〕最高的,第一流的。~ **price(s)** 高价。~ **quark**【物】顶夸克〔基本粒子之一〕。~ **removal** 摘心,打顶。~**sail**【海】中桅帆。~**sawyer** (锯木坑的)上锯人;〔古〕在上的人,上司。~**secret** 绝密。~ **sergeant**【军】司务长;军士长。~**side 1**. 〔美〕二楼,楼上;〔常 *pl*.〕(水线以上的)船舷;(军舰的)上甲板。**2**. *ad*. 上面,上边〔多指船上甲板上〕。~**sman**【海】桅楼员。~**soil** 表土;耕作层土壤。~ **talks** 最高级会谈。**-full** *a*. 满满的。**-less** *a*. 无顶的;(衣服)无上身的[袒胸露臂的];高得看不见顶的(*a* ~*less bar* (由不穿上衣的女侍应生招待客人的)无上装酒吧)。

top[2] [tɔp; tɑp] *n*. 陀螺。*The* ~ *sleeps*. 陀螺飞速旋转得好像定住一样。***an old*** ~ 〔俚〕老朋友。***sleep like a*** ~ 睡得很熟。

top- *comb*. *f*. 〔用于元音前〕= topo-.

to·paz [ˈtəupæz; ˋtopæz] *n*. 【矿】黄玉;黄晶;【动】南美蜂鸟。*false* [*common*] ~ 黄水晶。

to·paz·o·lite [təuˈpæzəˌlait; təˋpæzəˏlaɪt] *n*. 【矿】黄榴石。

tope[1] [təup; top] *n*. 座佛状圆顶塔,浮屠;印度塔;庙,陵。

tope[2] [təup; top] *n*. (印度的)芒果林,树林;灌木林;园林。

tope[3] [təup; top] *n*. (欧洲沿岸的)星鲨,角鲛。

tope[4] [təup; top] *n*. 【海】中国小木船。

tope[5] [təup; top] *vi*., *vt*. 狂欢,纵酒。

to·pec·to·my [təˈpektəmi; təˋpɛktəmɪ] *n*. 【医】脑皮质的部分切除。

top·er [ˈtəupə; ˋtopɚ] *n*. 酒徒,酒鬼;醉汉。

top·gal·lant [tɔpˈgælənt; ˏtɑpˋgælənt] **I** *n*. 【海】上桅(帆)。**II** *a*. 上桅(帆)的;最高[上]的。

To·phet, Topheth [ˈtəufet; ˋtofɪt, -fɛt] *n*. (耶路撒冷

的)垃圾焚化场〔从前是犹太人供凶神 Moloch 的地方〕;(灼热)地狱。

to·phus [ˈtəufəs; ˋtofəs] ***n.*** (*pl.* ***tophi*** [ˈtəufai; ˋtofaɪ])【医】痛风石。

to·pi·a·ry [ˈtəupiəri, -pjə-; ˋtopɪˏɛrɪ] **I** ***a.*** 修剪成装饰性质的(篱树等),修剪得美观的。**II** ***n.*** 装饰性树木修剪法。~ **art** 林木修剪术。~ **work** 树木整形[修剪]。

top·ic [ˈtɔpik; ˋtɑpɪk] **I** ***n.*** **1.** 论题,题目;话题;标题,细目。**2.** (节,段的)主题。**3.** 原理,原则;【逻,修】总论,概论。**4.**【医】局部药。*a* ~ *sentence* 段落主题提示句。*current* ~*s* 今天的话题。**II** ***a.***【医】局部的。

top·i·cal [ˈtɔpikəl; ˋtɑpɪkl] ***a.*** **1.** 题目的,论题的;条分缕析的。**2.** 有关时事的。**3.** 地方的。**4.**【医】局部的。**5.** 原理的,原则的。*in* ~ *form* 分列标题,有提纲细目地。*a* ~ *caricature* 时事漫画。*a* ~ *anaesthetic* 局部麻醉剂。**-ly** ***ad.***

top·i·cal·i·ty [ˌtɔpiˈkæliti; ˏtɑpɪˋkælətɪ] ***n.*** 地区性,主题性,时事性,【医】局部性。

top·min·now [ˈtɔpˌminəu; ˋtɑpˏmɪno] ***n.***【动】**1.** 花鳉科 (*Poeciliidae*) 鱼〔如食蚊鱼 (*Gambusia offinis*)〕。**2.** 鳉科 (*Cyprinodontidae*) 鱼。

topo- *comb. f.* 场所;地方: *topo*graphy, *topo*logy.

to·pog. = topographical; topography.

to·pog·ra·pher [təˈpɔgrəfə; toˋpɑgrəfɚ, tə-], **-phist** [-fist; -fɪst] ***n.*** 地志作者,地志学者;地形测量员。

top·o·graph·ic, -i·cal [ˌtɔpəˈgræfik, -ikəl; ˏtɑpəˋgræfɪk, -ɪkl] ***a.*** 地志的,地形(学上)的;地形测量的。*a* ~ *drawing* 地形图。*a* ~ ***machine***【空】歪斜矫正机。

to·pog·ra·phy [təˈpɔgrəfi; toˋpɑgrəfɪ] ***n.*** 地志;地形(测量)学;地形,地势;地势图;(物产的)分布状况;【解】局部解剖学。

to·pol·o·gy [təˈpɔlədʒi; toˋpɑlədʒɪ] ***n.*** 地学志;【数】拓扑学;拓扑(结构);【解】局部解剖学。**-i·cal** ***a.***

to·pon·o·my [təˈpɔnəmi; toˋpɑnəmɪ], **to·pon·y·my** [-nimi; -nɪmɪ] ***n.*** 地名志;地名研究;【解】局部[部位]命名法。

top·o·nym [ˈtɔpəˌnim; ˋtɑpoˏnɪm] ***n.*** **1.** 地名。**2.** 表明起源、地点的名称〔如在动物词汇手册中〕。

top·per [ˈtɔpə; ˋtɑpɚ] ***n.*** 上层的东西;【商】(水果等商品的)盖面货;高档货,尖儿货;高浪;〔俚〕高顶大礼帽;〔英俚〕第一流人物;女式宽大短外衣。

top·ping [ˈtɔpiŋ; ˋtɑpɪŋ] **I** ***a.*** 高耸的,屹然的;〔美〕傲慢的;〔罕〕第一流的;上等的;愉快的,健康的。**II** ***n.*** 顶部,上层;〔*pl.*〕剪下来的小枝;【油】拔顶;〔美俚〕〔*pl.*〕饭后的点心。*a* ~ *axe* 修枝斧。~ *cove*〔俚〕刽子手。~ *lift*【海】千斤索,吊扣索。

top·ple [ˈtɔpl; ˋtɑpl] ***vi.***, ***vt.*** (高的东西)摇摆,摇摇欲坠,倒塌;摇动,推倒,推翻。~ *old idols* 破除古老的偏见[迷信]。~ **down** (使)垮下来。~ **over** 推倒,摇倒。

tops [tɔps; tɑps] **I** ***a.*** 〔用作表语〕(能力、技巧、智力、品质等)极好,最好,首屈一指,无与伦比,呱呱叫;最高级的,第一流的,高档的。*His work is* ~. 他的作品是第一流的。*That car is* ~. 那辆车质量最高。**II** ***n.*** 〔俚〕〔常作 the ~,为 top[1] 的复数形式〕第一流人物,最佳产品。*He's the* ~. 他是第一流人物。

top·sy·tur·vy [ˈtɔpsiˈtəːvi; ˋtɑpsɪˋtɝvɪ] **I** ***ad.***, ***a.*** 颠倒地[的];乱七八糟地[的]。**II** ***n.*** 颠倒;混乱。**III** ***vt.*** 弄颠倒;弄得乱七八糟。**-dom** ***n.*** 〔谑〕颠倒[混乱]状态。

toque [təuk; tok] ***n.*** 无檐女帽;【动】头巾猿(= tuque)。

tor [tɔː; tɔr] ***n.*** 多岩石小山;【地】(特指英国 Dartmoor 的)突岩。

to·rah, to·ra [ˈtɔːrə; ˋtorə, ˋtɔrə] ***n.*** (*pl.* ***-roth*** [-rəuθ; -roθ])〔H.〕【犹太教】**1.** 经学,律法,教导。**2.** = pentateuch. **3.** 旧约全书。**4.** 全部经典〔包括旧约和圣法经传〕。

torc [tɔːk; tɔrk] ***n.*** = torque 1.

torch [tɔːtʃ; tɔrtʃ] ***n.*** 火炬,火把;【机】气炬,喷灯;〔英〕手电筒;知识的光[源泉];〔美俚〕手枪。*the* ~ *of Hymen* 恋情。*the inverted* ~ 倒火炬,死的象征。*an electric* ~ 手电筒。***carry a*** [***the***] ~ ***for*** 迷恋,单恋;热烈赞助。***hand on the*** ~ 把知识[文化]的火把传给后代。~-**bearer** 执火炬者;传授文化[知识]者;某一运动的首倡者[领导者]。~ **fishing** 灯光捉鱼法。~**light** 火炬(的光)(*a* ~*light procession* [*parade*] 火炬游行)。~ **race**【古希腊】火炬接力赛跑。~ **song**〔美俚〕单恋之歌。~ **welding**【机】气炬焊接。~**wood** (多树脂的)火炬木。

torch·ier, torch·iere [tɔːˈtʃiə; tɔrˋtʃɪr] ***n.*** (可在地上移动的)落地灯,脚灯〔没有灯罩而有一个反射盘,使光线向上射,形成间接照明〕。

tor·chon [ˈtɔːʃən; ˋtɔrʃən] ***n.*** 〔F.〕拭布〔擦拭器皿和家具等用〕。~ **lace** 镶边花边,饰带花边。~ **paper** 粗面水彩画纸。

torch·y [ˈtɔːtʃi; ˋtɔrtʃɪ] ***a.*** 伤感恋歌式的。

tore[1] [tɔː; tor, tɔr] ***n.***【建】座盘饰;【几】环形圆纹曲面;管环,环面。

tore[2] [tɔː, təə; tor, tɔr] tear 的过去式。

tor·e·a·dor [ˈtɔriədɔː; ˋtɔrɪəˏdɔr, ˏtoreaˋðor] ***n.*** 〔Sp.〕(骑马)斗牛士。~ *pants* 紧身半长女运动裤。

to·re·ro [təuˈreərəu; toˋrero] ***n.*** 〔Sp.〕徒步的斗牛士。

to·reu·tic [təuˈruːtik; toˋrutɪk] ***a.*** 雕金术,(金属)浮雕术。~**s** 〔*pl.*〕〔用作单〕金属浮雕工艺。

to·ri [ˈtɔːrai; ˋtoraɪ, ˋtɔr-] ***n.*** torus 的复数。

tor·ic [ˈtɔːrik; ˋtɔrɪk, ˋtɑr-] ***a.*** 花托的,花托状的;座盘饰的;环形圆纹曲面的。

To·ri·no [tɔˈriːnɔ; tɑˋrinɑ] ***n.*** 托里诺〔意大利城市,即都灵 Turin〕。

tor·ment **I** [ˈtɔːment; ˋtɔrmɛnt] ***n.*** 苦痛,苦恼,苛责,拷问;讨厌[麻烦]的东西;〔古〕拷问台。*The child is a positive* ~. 〔口〕这孩子讨厌极啦。**II** [tɔːˈment; tɔrˋmɛnt] ***vt.*** 使苦恼,使痛苦,折磨;使混乱;欺负,虐待;拷问。**-er** ***n.***

tor·men·t·il [ˈtɔːmentil; ˋtɔrmɛnˏtɪl] ***n.***【植】直立委陵菜〔根部可用于硝皮或作染料〕。

tor·men·tor, tor·menter [tɔːˈmentə; tɔrˋmɛntɚ] ***n.*** (*fem.* ***-tress***) 使苦痛的人[物],折磨者;【农】轮耙;【海】长肉叉;舞台两侧的固定幕布;(摄声片时的)回声防止幕;【法】死刑执行人。

tormi·na [ˈtɔːminə; ˋtɔrmɪnə] ***n.*** 〔*pl.*〕【医】肠绞痛;剧烈腹痛。

torn [tɔːn; torn, tɔrn] tear 的过去分词。

tor·na·do [tɔːˈneidəu; tɔrˋnedo] ***n.*** (*pl.* ~*es*, ~*s*) **1.**【气】陆龙卷,大旋风,龙卷风。**2.** 〔喻〕(喝彩、责骂声、子弹等的)爆发,大批袭来。~ **cellar** 〔美〕防风窖。**-dic** [tɔˈnædik; tɑˋnædɪk] ***a.***

to·roid [ˈtɔːrɔid; ˋtorɔɪd, ˋtɔr-] ***n.*** **1.**【电】环,环形线。**2.**【机】超环面。**-al** ***a.***

To·ron·to [təˈrɔntəu; təˋrɑnto] ***n.*** 多伦多〔加拿大港市〕。

to·rose [ˈtɔːrəus, tɔːˈrəus; ˋtoros, təˋros] ***a.*** **1.** 膨涨的,鼓起的。**2.**【植】节状的 (= torous)。

tor·pe·do [tɔːˈpiːdəu; tɔrˋpido] **I** ***n.*** (*pl.* ~*es*) 鱼雷,水雷;(油井)爆破筒;【铁路】(警报用)信号雷管;掼炮;鱼雷形汽车;【鱼】电鲼,鲟;〔美俚〕(被雇用的)刺客。*a guided* ~ 制导鱼雷。*an aerial* ~ 空雷;遥控滑翔导弹。*a* ~ *battery* 鱼[水]雷炮台。*a diving* ~ 深水炸弹。*a ground* ~ 海底水雷。*a* ~ *shop* 鱼雷工厂。**II** ***vt.***, ***vi.*** 用鱼雷[空雷]袭击;发射鱼雷;敷设水雷;(在油井内)装置爆破筒;破坏(政策、制度、计划等);使失去(活动能力等)。~ **boat** 鱼雷艇 (*a* ~ *boat catcher* = *a* ~ *boat destroyer* 舰队驱逐舰〔略作 t. b. d.,正式名叫 destroyer〕)。~ **bomber** 鱼雷轰炸机。~ **catcher** 水雷捕捉网,鱼雷艇捕捉舰。~ **gunboat** 水雷炮舰〔正式名称叫 *torpedo-boat*〕。~-**net**, ~-**netting** 鱼雷防御网。~

plane【空】鱼雷轰炸机。～ **planter**【海】水敷雷舰。～ **station** 鱼雷艇根据地。～ **tube** 鱼雷发射管。

Torpex [ˈtɔːpeks; ˋtɔrpɛks] *n*.【海军】(爆炸能力为 TNT 1.5 倍的)铝蜡炸药。

tor·pid [ˈtɔːpid; ˋtɔrpɪd] **I** *a*. 麻痹的;不活泼的;迟钝的;(动物)冬眠的。**II** *n*.〔英〕**1**.〔*pl*.〕(牛津大学)四旬节艇赛。**2**. 四旬节艇赛选手[用艇]。**-ly** *ad*. **-ness** *n*.

tor·pid·i·ty [tɔːˈpiditi; tɔrˋpɪdətɪ] *n*. 麻痹,迟钝;冬眠,蛰伏。

tor·pi·fy [ˈtɔːpifai; ˋtɔrpəˏfaɪ] *vt*. (**-fied**) 使麻痹,使失去知觉;使迟钝。

tor·por [ˈtɔːpə; ˋtɔrpɚ] *n*. 麻痹;迟钝;冬眠。

tor·por·if·ic [ˌtɔːpəˈrifik; ˏtɔrpəˋrɪfɪk] *a*. 使麻痹的,有麻痹性的,使迟钝的。

torps [tɔːps; tɔrps] *n*.〔海军俚〕水雷军官。

tor·quate [ˈtɔːkweit; ˋtɔrkwet] *a*. **1**. (动物颈部)有异色毛圈的。**2**. 有颈圈的,戴项链的;具环的。

torque [tɔːk; tɔrk] *n*. **1**. (古代条顿人、高卢人戴的)金丝项圈。**2**.【物】扭(力)矩,转(力)矩。～ **converter** 转矩变换器,液力变扭器。～**meter** 扭力表,转矩计。～ **switch**【空】(陀螺仪)校正马达开关。**-s**【动】(动物颈部等的)异色毛皮[羽毛]圈。～ **wrench**【机】转矩扳手。

torr [tɔː; tɔr] *n*.【电】托[真空单位]。

tor·re·fac·tion [ˌtɔriˈfækʃən; ˏtɑrɪˋfækʃən] *n*. 烘,烤,焙;干炒。

tor·re·fy [ˈtɔrifai; ˋtɑrɪˏfaɪ] *vt*. (**-fied**) 烘,烤,焙;干炒。

tor·ren·ize [ˈtɔːrəˌnaiz, ˈtɔ-; ˋtɔrəˏnaɪz, ˋtɑ-] *vt*. 按托伦斯法登记(财产)。

Tor·rens law [ˈtɔːrənz lɔː, ˈtɔr-; ˋtɔrənz lɔ, ˋtɑr-] 托伦斯法[在政府登记土地所有权,由政府发给所有证的各种法令]。

tor·rent [ˈtɔrənt; ˋtɔrənt, ˋtɑr-] *n*. 急流,湍流,洪流;(质问等的)连发,(感情等的)爆发,迸发。*a* ～ *of lava* 熔岩的奔流。*a* ～ *of abuse* 连珠炮一样的谩骂。*It rains in* ～*s*. 大雨倾盆。～*s of rain* 倾盆大雨。～*s of water* 奔流。***stem the*** ～ 抵制;阻止。～ **-regulation** *n*. 防洪工事,防砂工事。

tor·ren·tial [tɔˈrenʃəl; tɔˋrɛnʃəl, tɑ-] *a*. 奔流的,急流的;汹涌的,猛烈的,奔放的。*a* ～ *rain* 倾盆大雨。

Tor·ri·cel·li [ˌtɔriˈtʃeli; ˏtɔrɪˋtʃɛlɪ], **E**. 托里切利〔1608—1647,意大利数学家、物理学家,晴雨表创制者〕。

tor·rid [ˈtɔrid; ˋtɔrɪd, ˋtɑr-] *a*. 晒热的;酷热的,灼热的;热烈的。～ *heat* 炎热。*the T- Zone* 热带。**-i·ty** *n*.

torri·fy [ˈtɔrifai; ˋtɔrəˏfaɪ, ˋtor-] *vt*. = torrefy.

tor·sade [tɔːˈseid; tɔrˋsed] *n*. **1**. 带条。**2**. 饰带。

tor·sel [ˈtɔːsəl; ˋtɔrsl] *n*.【建】承梁木;漩涡饰。

tor·si·bil·i·ty [ˌtɔːsiˈbiliti; ˏtɔrsəˋbɪlətɪ] *n*. 耐扭力,抗扭力。

tor·sion [ˈtɔːʃən; ˋtɔrʃən] *n*. 扭转;扭(转)力;【物】扭(力)矩,转(力)矩;【医】捩转。～ *pairing* 扭曲配对。～ **balance** 扭秤。～ **bar** 扭条,捻杆。～ **meter** 扭力计。～ **pendulum**【物】扭摆。

tor·sion·al [ˈtɔːʃənəl; ˋtɔrʃənl] *a*. 扭的,扭转的。～ **moment**【物】扭(力)矩。～ **pendulum** 扭摆。～ **strength** 抗扭强度。

torsk [tɔːsk; tɔrsk] *n*. (*pl*. **torsk**, **torsks**)【动】鳕科(*Gadidae*)鱼。

tor·so [ˈtɔːsəu; ˋtɔrso] *n*. (*pl*. ～**s**, **-si** [-siː; -si])〔It.〕(人体的)躯干;【雕刻】(断头缺肢的)躯干;雕像;残破不完整的东西;未完成的作品。～**-tosser** *n*.〔美俚〕舞女〔尤指滑稽戏中的〕。

tort [tɔːt; tɔrt] *n*.【法】侵权行为。

torte [ˈtɔːtə, tɔːt; tɔrtə, tɔrt] *n*. (*pl*. **tortes**, *G*. **tor-ten** [ˈtəutən; ˋtortən]) 圆形(果仁)大蛋糕。

tort-fea·sor [ˈtɔːtˈfiːzə; ˋtɔrtˋfizɚ, -zɔr, -ˏfi-] *n*.【法】有民事侵权行为的人,犯民事侵权罪的人。

tor·ti·col·lis [ˌtɔːtiˈkɔlis; ˏtɔrtɪˋkɑlɪs] *n*.【医】斜颈,捩颈,歪头。

tor·tile [ˈtɔːtail, -til; ˋtɔrtɪl] *a*. 扭转的,扭弯的;卷曲的;【植】扭卷的。

tor·til·la [tɔːˈtilə, -ˈtiːljə; tɔrˋtijɑ] *n*.〔Sp.〕(墨西哥的)玉米面饼[面包]。

tor·tious [ˈtɔːʃəs; ˋtɔrʃəs] *a*.【法】民事侵权行为的。

tor·toise [ˈtɔːtəs; ˋtɔrtəs, -tɪs] *n*. 龟 (= testudo); 迟钝的人[东西]。～ **beetle** 龟甲虫[龟状小甲虫的通称]。～**-eater**〔英空军俚〕(能从空中打坦克的)飞行大炮。～**-shell** 龟甲,鳖甲。～**-shell** *a*. 玳瑁(色)的 (*a* ～*-shell cat* 玳瑁色的猫。*a* ～*-shell turtle*【动】玳瑁)。

tor·to·ni [tɔːˈtəuni; tɔrˋtonɪ] *n*. 意大利式冰淇淋[加有樱桃,杏仁等配料]。

tor·tri·cid [ˈtɔːtrisid; tɔrˋtrɪsɪd] *n*.【昆】卷叶蛾。

tor·tu·os·i·ty [ˌtɔːtjuˈɔsiti; ˏtɔrtʃʊˋɑsətɪ] *n*. **1**. 弯扭,曲折。**2**. 不正当。**3**. 委婉。

tor·tu·ous [ˈtɔːtjuəs; ˋtɔrtʃʊəs] *a*. **1**. 弯扭的,曲折的(路、河等),盘旋的。**2**. 不正派的,不正当的,骗人的(政策等)。**3**. 委婉的(话)。**-ly** *ad*. **-ness** *n*.

tor·ture [ˈtɔːtʃə; ˋtɔrtʃɚ] **I** *n*. **1**. 拷问,拷打。**2**.〔常 *pl*.〕折磨;痛苦,苦恼。***put sb. to*** (***the***) ～ 拷问。～ ***of animals***【法】动物虐待。**II** *vt*. 拷问,拷打;折磨;使痛苦;曲解(法律条文等) (*out of*; *into*); 扭弯,扭折。

tor·u·la [ˈtɔrulə; ˋtɑrulə] *n*. (*pl*. **-lae** [-liː;-li], **-las**) 酿母,串状酿母菌属,串菌属。

toru·lin [ˈtɔrjulin; ˋtɑrjulɪn] *n*.【化】维生素 B_1。

to·rus [ˈtɔːrəs; ˋtorəs, ˋtɔr-] *n*. (*pl*. **-ri** [-rai; -raɪ])【植】花托;【解】隆凸[起],圆凸;【建】座盘饰;【机】环形曲面(体)。

To·ry [ˈtɔːri; ˋtorɪ, ˋtɔrɪ] **I** *n*.【英史】托利党党员;【美史】(独立战争时的)亲英派,保王派;〔主 t-〕保守党党员,保守派。**II** *a*. 托利党(党员)的;〔主 t-〕保守党(党员)的,保守派的。**-ism** *n*. 保王主义[行为];〔主 t-〕保守主义;保守行为。

-tory *suf*. = -ory.

tosh[1] [tɔʃ; tɑʃ] *n*.〔主英俚〕胡说,废话;【板球、网球】(容易接的)慢球。

tosh[2] [tɔʃ; tɑʃ] **I** *a*., *ad*.〔Scot.〕整齐,漂亮;舒服;友善,亲切。**II** *vt*. 弄整齐,收拾打扮,装饰。

tosh·er [ˈtɔʃə; ˋtɑʃɚ] *n*.〔英俚〕(综合大学中)不隶属任何学院的学生。

toss [tɔs; tɔs] (〔诗〕 **tost**) **I** *vt*. **1**. (轻)扔,(轻)投,抛;(轻)拌;【网球】把(球)打高;(马)摔落(骑手) (*off*); (公牛用角)将(人等)挑上去;忽然抬起(头等)。**2**. (风、浪等)使动荡,使摇摆,使颠簸;给与精神上的动摇。**3**. 掷钱(等)决定事情。**4**. 打扰;扰乱;使不安。**5**.【矿】摇选(锡矿等)。**6**.〔美俚〕在(某人身上翻来覆去地搜寻毒品等)。— *vi*. 颠簸,摇摆;翻来翻去;摇动;掷钱;〔美剧〕停止。*The ship was* ～*ed by the waves*. 船被浪打得东摇西晃。～ *a pancake* (拿着锅把里面的饼抛起)翻煎饼。*a* ～*ing sea* 波涛汹涌的海。～ ***a dinner***〔美俚〕举行宴会;请客。～ ***about all night*** 整夜翻来覆去。～ ***aside*** 扔弃;搁置不管。～ ***cold water on***〔美运〕照规则禁止。～ ***down*** (倾杯)一口喝下。～ ***hay about*** 翻(晒)干草。～***oars*** 举桨(致敬)。～ ***off*** 一口喝干(酒);敏捷地做好。～ ***one's head*** 把头往后一扬[摆架子或有点不耐烦时的动作]。～ ***the platter***〔美运〕掷铁饼。～ ***to and fro*** 辗转反侧。～ ***up*** 一下子做好[烧好](菜等);掷钱(*Let us* ～ *up for first choice*. 让我们掷钱决定谁先取吧)。**II** *n*. **1**. 抛扔。**2**. 掷钱[猜正反面];掷钱决定;双方各有一半的机会。**3**. 落马;(头等的)猛抬。**4**. 摇摇,兴奋。**5**. 投掷距离。**6**.〔美俚〕翻来覆去的搜身。*the* ～ *of a ball* 投球。*It is quite a* ～ [～*-up*] *whether he comes or not*. 他来不来的可能性各占一半。***take a*** ～〔俚〕从马上摔下来。***win*** [***lose***] ***the*** ～ 掷钱猜赢[猜输];顺利[不顺利]。***within the*** ～ ***of a ball*** 在球所能

投到的距离内。~**pot** 酒徒。~**up** 用掷钱看正反面的办法决定;双方[是否]各有一半的机会;碰运气的事(*At ten o'clock this morning it was still a ~-up whether we should be able to get here*. 今天早上十点钟的时候还很难说我们是否能够到达这里)。

tost [tɔst; tɑst]〔诗〕toss 的过去式及过去分词。

tos·ta·da, tos·ta·do [tɔusˈtɑːdə, -dəu; tɔsˋtɑdə, -do] *n*.〔美〕脆玉米饼。

tot[1] [tɔt; tɑt] *n*.〔口〕〔爱称〕小娃娃,小宝宝;小东西;小杯子;(酒等的)一杯,一口;少量。

tot[2] [tɔt; tɑt] **I** *n*.〔口〕合计;总数,总和。*long ~s* 巨大数目的计算。**II** *vt*., *vi*. 加起来(*up*);总共…(*up*)。

to't [tut; tut, tʊt]〔方、俚〕= to it.

to·tal [ˈtəutl;ˋtotl] **I** *a*. 总计的(金额等);全部的;完全的(失明等),绝对的(禁酒等)。*a ~ history* 通史,全史。*a ~ war* 全面战争。*~ defence* 全面防御。*the sum ~* 总额。*~ output* 总产量。*~ weight* 总重(量)。*~ color blindness* 全色盲。*~ abstinence* 绝对禁酒。*a ~ recall*〔美〕完整的回忆(能力)。**II** *n*. 总数,全体;合计,总计〔常叫 grand ~〕。**III** *vt*.(〔英〕*-ll-*)**1**. 总计达,计算…的总数。**2**.〔美俚〕完全摧毁;向…清算,向…报复。*The visitors ~led 151*. 来访者共计 151 人。— *vi*. 合计;计算总数;总数达到[计有](*to*; *up to*)。*His debts had ~led to $5000*. 当时他的债务总数达到 5000 美元。

to·tal·i·sa·tor [ˈtəutəlaizeitə; ˋtotəlaɪzetɚ] *n*. = totalizator. **-ly** *ad*.

to·tal·is·tic, to·tal·ist [ˌtəutˈlistik, ˈtəutlist; ˏtotˋlɪstɪk, ˋtotlɪst] *a*. = totalitarian. **-tal·ism** *n*.

to·tal·i·tar·i·an [ˌtəutæliˈtɛəriən; toˏtæləˋtɛrɪən] *a*., *n*. 极权主义的;极权主义者。*a ~ state* 极权国家〔如纳粹统治下的德国〕。**-ism** *n*. 极权主义。

to·tal·i·ty [təuˈtæliti; toˋtælətɪ] *n*. 完全,完备;全体,总数;【天】全蚀(时间)。***without viewing things in their ~*** 不看事情的全体。

to·tal·i·za·tor [ˈtəutəlaizeitə; ˋtotl̩əˏzetɚ] *n*. 总额计算机;(赛马等赌博的)赌金计算机。

to·tal·ize [ˈtəutəlaiz; ˋtotl̩ˏaɪz] *vt*. 加起来,总计。— *vi*. 用计算机计算总数。*a ~d war* 总体战。

to·tal·iz·er [ˈtəutəlaizə; ˋtotəlˏaɪzɚ] *n*. 计算总数的人,加法计算器〔尤指赌金计算机〕。

to·ta·quine [ˈtəutəˌkwiːn, -kwin; ˋtotəˏkwin, -kwɪn, -ˏkin, -kɪn] *n*.【药】金鸡纳全碱,金奎宁。

tote[1] [təut; tot] **I** *vt*.〔美口〕携带;运,搬,运输;抱,背;〔美俚〕以…武装,带(枪)。**II** *n*. 装运物。~ **bag** (布制或草编的)大手提包。

tote[2] [təut; tot] **I** *n*.〔英口〕= totalizator;〔方〕总额;〔方〕绝对戒酒的人。**II** *vt*. 计算(总数);总数为…。~ **board** 赌金结算揭示牌。

to·tem [ˈtəutəm; ˋtotəm] *n*. **1**. 图腾〔原始民族崇奉为自己祖先的某种天然物,如鹿、狼、龟等〕。**2**. 图腾像。**3**.〔喻〕崇拜对象。~ **post** [**pole**] (刻有图腾像的)图腾柱。**-ic, -is·tic** [ˌtəutəˈmistik; ˏtotəˋmɪstɪk] *a*.

to·tem·ism [ˈtəutəmizəm; ˋtotəmɪzm̩] *n*. 图腾崇拜,图腾制度。

to·tem·ist [ˈtəutəmist; ˋtotəmɪst] *n*. 图腾制种族成员;图腾制研究者。

t'oth·er, toth·er [ˈtʌðə; ˋtʌðɚ] *pro*., *a*.〔方、口、俚〕另一个,别的。***tell ~ from which***〔谑〕= ***tell one from ~*** 把一个同另一个区别开来。

to·ti·dem ver·bis [ˈtɔtidem ˈvəːbis; ˋtɑtɪdɛm ˋvɝbɪs]〔L.〕(原文)就是这几个词。

tot·i·es quot·i·es [ˈtɔtiiːzˈkwɔtiiːz; ˋtoʃɪˏiz ˋkwoʃɪˏiz]〔L.〕每次。

to·ti·pal·mate [ˌtəutiˈpælmeit; ˏtotɪˋpælmet] *a*.【动】全蹼的〔如鸭;鹈等〕。**-ma·tion** *n*.

to·tip·o·tent [təuˈtipətənt; toˋtɪpətənt] *a*.【动】能由(分)裂球变成胚胎的。**-ten·cy** [-tənsi; -tənsɪ] *n*.

to·to cae·lo [ˈtəutəu ˈsiːləu; ˋtoto ˋsilo]〔L.〕天那样大;极度;完全。***differ toto caelo*** 有天壤之别。

Totten·ham pudding [ˈtɔtənəm; ˋtɑtənəm]〔俚〕(用厨房废料做成的)猪饲料。

tot·ter [ˈtɔtə; ˋtɑtɚ] **I** *vi*. 蹒跚,摇摆,翅翅趄趄地走;摇动;摇摇欲坠。**II** *n*. 蹒跚;摇摆,动摇。*a ~ing government* 动摇不稳的政府。

tot·ter·ing·ly [ˈtɔtəriŋli; ˋtɑtərɪŋlɪ] *ad*. 蹒跚地;摇摇欲坠地。

tot·ter·y [ˈtɔtəri; ˋtɑtərɪ] *a*. 蹒跚的;动摇的,摇摇欲坠的。

tou·can [ˈtuːkæn; ˋtukæn, tuˋkɑn] *n*.【鸟】鵎鵼,巨嘴鸟;〔T-〕【天】巨嘴鸟座。

touch [tʌtʃ; tʌtʃ] **I** *vt*. **1**. 触,碰,摩,摸;触知;【医】触诊;【宗】摸治(瘰疬);用试金石试。**2**. 接触;邻接,毗邻;【几】(直线)切(圆等)。**3**. 使(二物)接触。**4**. 感动;触犯,触怒。**5**. (在物质上)给与影响;害,伤,(精神上)伤害;〔用 p. p.〕使发疯,使发狂;触痛隐私。**6**. 到,及,达;〔用于否定句〕(能力等)匹敌,相等。**7**. 按,撳(铃等);弹,奏(乐器)。**8**. 画,写;添画,修改;略加颜色;完成,修整。**9**.〔用于否定句〕吃,喝;插手,发生关系;涉及。**10**. 提到,谈到,论及。**11**.〔俚〕告借(钱),讨(钱);(用不正当手段)弄(钱);偷;侵占。— *vi*. **1**. 触,碰;接触;【几】切。**2**. (触到时)有…的感觉。**3**.【医】触诊;【宗】摸治(有瘰疬的)病人。**4**. 接近,将近,将达(*at*; *to*; *on*; *upon*)。**5**. (兵士)密集。**6**. 提及,论及,同…有关(*on*; *upon*)。**7**. (船)停靠(*at*)。*The sad story ~ed his heart*. 那个悲惨的故事触动了他的心弦。*He is a little ~ed*. 他有点儿感动。*You ~ me there*. 你的话我受不了[扎耳朵]。*The plants were ~ed with frost*. 这植物被霜冻伤了。*He ~ed his 20*. 他已经到二十岁了。*I couldn't ~ the algebra paper*. 我啃不动[做不出]代数问题。*Nothing will ~ these stains*. 没有什么东西能消除这些斑点。*The abuse does not ~ me*. 那种话骂不着我。*I never ~ a drop*. 我一滴酒都不沾。*clouds ~ed with rose* 带玫瑰色的云彩。*The law can't ~ him*. 法律干涉不了他。*There is nothing to ~ mountain air for giving you an appetite*. 没有任何东西能比得上山间的空气更能促进你的食欲。***as ~ing*** 关于。~ ***at*** 停靠(某一港埠);接近。~ ***down*** = *~-down*. ~ ***elbows*** 紧接;亲密。~ (*sb*.) ***for*** (*a fiver*)〔俚〕(向某人)借[讨](五块钱)。~ (*sb*.) ***home*** [***to the quick***] 触怒,触犯;触及痛处。~ ***in*** 增改,添画(细微部分)。~ ***it off to the nines*** 好好干。~ (*sb*.) ***nearly*** (与某人)有密切关系。~ (*sb*.) ***off*** 超过(某人)。~ ***off*** 正确地表现;草草写;添画;发射;使(炸药)爆发;使开始;挂断电话。~ ***on*** 说到,接近(*~ on the matter lightly* 轻描淡写的说一说)。~ ***one's hat to ...*** 用手触帽行礼。~ ***out***【棒球】触杀;〔俚〕碰到好运气,弄得好。~ ***pitch*** 参加干坏事;接近坏人。~ ***success*** 终于成功。~ ***the spot***〔口〕奏效。~ ***the wind***【海】开足马力。~ ***up*** 润色;完成;用鞭等轻轻打(马);轻轻打痛;唤起(回忆等)。~ ***upon*** = ~ ***on***.

II *n*. **1**. 触,碰;摸,摩;接触;联系。**2**. 触感,触觉。**3**. 一触,一碰;修饰,添画,润色;一笔;笔触;技巧,手腕。**4**. 精神接触,感动;同情,同感;一致。**5**. 痕迹,微量;一点点;小毛病。**6**. 特性,性质;气质,风味。**7**. 论到,提到,说到;暗示。**8**. (金银的)纯度;(纯度)检验戳记;验证;标准;试验;试金石;【物】接触磁化;【乐】弹奏(法);【医】触诊;【橄榄球】触地;(边线与球门线间的)可触地得分的地区。**9**.〔儿戏〕捉迷藏。**10**.〔俚〕告借;侵吞;偷。~ *of nature* 自然的感情;人情味。~ *of the sun* 轻微的中暑[日射病]。*finishing ~es* (绘画等时)最后修饰的几笔;完成。*a characteristic ~* (话等的)特色。*a shilling ~*〔口〕一先令上下。*the Nelson ~* (对付难局的)奈尔逊式的果断手腕。*a ~ of irony* 一点讽刺意味。*want a ~ of salt* 咸味不够;不够味。*This piano is wanting in*

～. 这架钢琴键盘不好[声音不好]。***a near*** ～ 九死一生。***at a*** ～ 稍微一触就,一碰就(*at a* ～ *he yielded* 才一接触他就让步了)。***bring to the*** ～ 试验。***have a*** ～ ***of the tar-brush*** 〔卑〕带有一点儿黑人的血统。***in*** ～ ***of*** 在…能达到的地方,在…的附近。***in*** ～ ***with*** 取得[保持]联系;同情,一致。***keep*** [***lose***] ～ ***with*** 同…保持[失去]联系;知道[不知道]…的情况。***out of*** ～ ***with*** 和…没有通信,和…失去联系,不表同情;和…不一致。***put to the*** ～ 试验。***true as*** ～ 的的确确,一点没错。***within*** ～ ***of*** 在…的附近。～**-and-go** ***n.***, ***a.*** (稍微接触就跑掉的)快速(行动);轻率(的);简略(的);一触即发的(不稳局面)。～ **body**, ～ **corpuscle**【解】触觉体。～ **dancing** 触身舞蹈。～ **football** 触身式橄榄球。～**-down**【橄榄球】触地得分;【空】着陆;着陆过程中的一部分;着陆时间。～**hole** (旧式炮的)火门。～**-last** 捉迷藏。～**-line**【足球】边线。～**-menot**【植】凤仙花(属),苍白凤仙花;喷瓜;【医】狼疮;碰不得的人[事物]。～**pad**【计】触摸式控制板,触摸板。～ **paper** 导火纸。～ **screen**【计】触摸式显示屏,触摸屏〔通过以手触摸即可进行电脑功能选择〕。～**stone** 试金石;〔喻〕检查标准。～ **system** 打字的指法。～**-type** ***vi.*** 按固定指法打字。～**wood** 火绒;易着火的东西;暴躁的人;(一碰到树就不能捉的)捉猫游戏。

touch·a·ble [ˈtʌtʃəbl; ˋtʌtʃəbḷ] ***a.*** 可触知的;可食用的。**-a·bil·i·ty** ***n.***

tou·ché [tuːˈʃei; tuˋʃe] ***int.*** 〔击剑〕击中〔对方击中得分〕;〔转喻〕言中!〔承认争论中对方论点正中要害〕。

touched [tʌtʃt; tʌtʃt] ***a.*** **1.** 激动的,感动的。**2.** 有点发痴的,精神轻微失常的(= touched in the head)。

touch·er [ˈtʌtʃə; ˋtʌtʃɚ] ***n.*** 触摸的人[物];神枪手;〔俚〕一触即发[千钧一发]的危急状况。***as near as a*** ～〔俚〕差一点,快要,险些儿。

touch·ing [ˈtʌtʃiŋ; ˋtʌtʃɪŋ] **I** ***a.*** 动人的;令人感动的。**II** ***prep.*** 关于,提到(= as ～)。

touch·y [ˈtʌtʃi; ˋtʌtʃɪ] ***a.*** (***-i·er***; ***-i·est***) 易怒的,暴躁的;麻烦的,棘手的,难办的(工作等);过分敏感的;易燃烧的。**-i·ly** ***ad.*** **-i·ness** ***n.***

tough [tʌf; tʌf] **I** ***a.*** **1.** 强韧的,弯折不断的;胶黏的。**2.** 硬,嚼不动的(肉等);强健的;〔口〕强硬的(政策等)。**3.** 不屈不挠的,坚强的;顽固的,固执的。**4.** 〔美〕无法无天的,暴戾的,凶恶的。**5.** 难办的,费力的,棘手的(工作等);〔口〕困苦的(命运等)。**6.** 〔美俚〕极好的。**II** ***n.*** 〔美俚〕恶棍,无赖。*a* ～ *customer* 〔口〕粗鲁的家伙。*a* ～ *guy* 〔美〕无赖。*Things are* ～. 生活艰难。*a* ～ *story* 难以相信的故事。***Tough***! 〔俚〕不见得吧! ***get*** ～〔美俚〕凶恶起来;行动勇敢。***have a*** ～ ***time of it*** 日子不好过。～ ***luck*** 〔美俚〕时运不佳;不幸。～ ***on the suckers*** 〔美〕笨人需要花很多钱才能得到的经验。**III** ***vi.*** 〔美俚〕忍耐困难。～ *it out* 忍耐过去。～**-break** 〔美俚〕小小的不幸。～ **love** (父母对子女)严加管教中体现的爱,慈爱家庭气氛中的严格管教。～**-minded** ***a.*** (态度,思想)现实的,讲究实际的;意志坚强的;顽强的。～ **racket** 〔美〕困难的工作。～ **rubber** 硬橡皮。～ **wood** 韧木。**-ness** 韧度,韧性。

tough·en [ˈtʌfn; ˋtʌfn] ***vt.***, ***vi.*** 使[变]强韧;使[变]硬;使[变]强健;使[变]坚强,使[变]顽固;使[变]困难。

tough·ie, tough·y [ˈtʌfi; ˋtʌfɪ] ***n.*** (***pl.*** ***-ies***)〔口〕**1.** 暴徒,流氓,恶棍。**2.** 难题;困境。

Tou·lon [tuːˈlɔ̃ːŋ; tuˋlɑn, tuˋlõ] ***n.*** 土伦〔法国港市〕。

tou·pee, ***tou·pet*** [ˈtuːpei; tuˋpe, -ˋpi] ***n.*** 〔F.〕(尤指头顶上的)一绺头发;(遮住秃顶的)男用假发。

tour [tuə; tʊr] **I** ***n.*** 漫游,游览,周游;旅行;(剧团的)巡回演出;巡回医疗;【军】(在海外基地为时2—3年的)服役期(=～ of duty);(轮值的)班。*a* ～ *of inspection* 视察旅行,巡视。*a* ～ *of the country* = *a provincial* ～ 外地巡回演出。***go on a*** ～ 漫游,巡回,周游。***make a*** ～ ***of the world*** 周游世界。***on*** ～ 漫游中,周游中,巡回中。***the grand*** ～【史】(旧时英国大学生毕业前的)大陆旅行。**II** ***vi.***, ***vt.*** 周游,游览,旅行;参观(画展等);(使)巡回演出[医疗];(车)慢慢开行。～ *France and Italy* 周游法国和意大利。～**ing car** (一般指能坐5—6人的)游览(汽)车。～**ing company** 巡回剧团。

tou·ra·co [tuːrəˈkəu; ˏturɑˋko, ˏturəˋko] ***n.***【鸟】(非洲)大杜鹃。

tour·bil·lion [tuəˈbiljən; tʊrˋbɪljən] ***n.*** **1.** 旋风,旋风涡。**2.** 回旋烟火。

tour de force [ˈtuədəˈfɔːs; ˏtʊrdəˋfors, -ˋfɔrs; ˏtʊr-] 〔F.〕壮举,绝技;(艺术上的)力作。

tour·er [ˈtuərə; ˋtʊrɚ] ***n.*** 旅游者,游客;游览车[飞机]。

tourism [ˈtuərizəm; ˋtʊrɪzṃ] ***n.*** **1.** 旅游,游览旅行。**2.** = tourist industry.

tour·ist [ˈtuərist; ˋtʊrɪst] ***n.*** 漫游者;旅游者,观光者,游客;〔美〕冬季到南部做工的流动工人。～ **agency** 旅行社。～ **attraction** 旅游胜地;吸引游客的事物。～ **bureau** 旅行社;旅游招待所。～ **class** 〔美〕(轮船的)经济舱,(火车,飞机的)经济座[舱]。～ **court** = motel. ～ **industry** 旅游事业。～ **guide** **1.** 导游。**2.** 旅游指南。～ **home** 有房间租给旅客的私人住宅。～ **party** 游览参观团。～ **sleeper** 〔美〕(软席)卧车[客舱]。～ **ticket** 旅游经济票。～ **track** **1.** 旅游路线。**2.** (新西兰)林间小道。～ **trap** 敲竹杠的旅馆、饭店、商店等。

tour·ma·lin(e) [ˈtuəməliːn; ˋtʊrməlɪn] ***n.***【矿】电气石,碧晒。

tour·na·ment [ˈtuənəmənt; ˋtɝnəmənt, ˋtʊr-] ***n.*** (中世纪武士的)马上比武大会;比赛,锦标赛。*a chess* ～ 象棋比赛。*a league* ～ 联赛。

tour·nay [ˈtuəˈnei; ˏtʊrˋne] ***n.*** (家具装饰用)陶奈印花细呢。

tour·ne·dos [tuəniˈdəu; tʊrnɪˋdo] ***n.*** 〔F.〕(***pl.*** ***-dos*** [-ˈdəu; -ˋdo]) 酱汁嫩牛排。

tour·ney [ˈtuəni; ˋtɝnɪ, ˋtʊrnɪ] **I** ***n.*** = tournament. **II** ***vi.*** 参加马上比武;参加比赛。

tour·ni·quet [ˈtuəniket; ˋtʊrnɪˏkɛt, -ˏke] ***n.***【医】止血带,压脉器。

tour·nure [ˈtuənjuə; ˏtʊrˋnjʊr] ***n.*** 〔F.〕轮廓;身材;(张裙)腰架;(女服的)臀部。

Tours [tuə; tʊr] ***n.*** 图尔斯〔姓氏〕。

tou·sle, tou·zle [ˈtauzl; ˋtaʊzḷ] **I** ***vt.*** 〔口〕搅乱,弄乱(头发等);搞乱。**II** ***n.*** 乱发;蓬头散发;纷乱状态。

tou·sy [ˈtauzi; ˋtaʊzɪ] ***a.*** **1.** 蓬头散发的,乱套的。**2.** 简陋的,不讲究的。

Tout [taut; taʊt] ***n.*** 陶特〔姓氏〕。

tout [taut; taʊt] **I** ***vi.*** 招徕,兜售;死乞白赖地劝诱;〔美〕拉选票(*for*);秘密打听(赛马)情报(*round*)。—***vt.*** **1.** 竭力称许[推荐];招徕,兜售。**2.** 打听有关…的消息;暗通。**3.** 提供赛马情报;〔美〕供给(赛马)情报;做(赛马)情报员。**II** ***n.*** 劝诱;招揽;招揽员;(赛马)情报员,暗通消息的人;〔口〕替盗贼把风的人。

tout à fait [ˌtuːtɑːˈfei; ˏtutɑˋfɛ] 〔F.〕完全,全然。

tout court [tuːˈkuːə; ˏtuˋkur] 〔F.〕简单地,简短地。*He called me Jones tout court*. 他简单地叫我琼斯。

tout en·sem·ble [ˌtuːtɔŋˈsɔŋblə; tutɑŋˋsɑŋbl] 〔F.〕整体;概观;整体效果。

tout le monde [ˌtuːləˈmuŋd; ˏtuləˋmuŋd] 〔F.〕全世界;所有的人。

tou·zle [ˈtauzl; ˋtaʊzḷ] ***n.***, ***vt.*** = tousle.

To·vey [ˈtəuvi, ˈtʌvi; ˋtovɪ, ˋtʌvɪ] ***n.*** 托维〔姓氏〕。

TOW = **1.** tube-launched optically-tracked wire-guided (anti-tank missile) "陶"式反坦克导弹〔一种用纯管式发射器发射的光学跟踪有线制导反坦克导弹〕。**2.** take-off weight 起飞全重。

tow[1] [təu; to] **I** ***vt.*** (人、马等沿岸)拉(纤等);(一船用绳子)拖(其他的船);用绳子牵(牛等);拖着走,拉着(孩子)走;在水面上拉(标本采集网)。*a* ～*ed target* 拖靶。*a*

T

～*ing airplane* 拖靶飞机。**II** ***n*.** 用绳拖曳;拖绳;拖船;拖车。*a number of admirers in* ～ 身后跟着一大群赞赏[崇拜]他的人[影迷、戏迷等]。***have in*** ～ = ***take in*** ～ 拉纤,拖航;指导,照顾;拖带,身后跟着。～**boat** 拖轮,拖驳。～**line** 拖缆,纤。～**net** (采集用)拖网。～**-path** 纤路。～**rope** 拖缆,拖索。～ **truck** 拖曳车〔用来拖走抛锚或停放在禁止停放地点的车辆〕。

tow[2] [təu; to] ***n*.** **1.**【纺】落纤;短麻屑;亚麻短缆维,丝束,纤维束。**2.** 亚麻色头发。～ *cloth* 粗麻布。～**head** 亚麻色头发;头发淡黄的人。

tow·age [ˈtəuidʒ; ˋtoɪdʒ] ***n*.** 牵引;拖船;拖船费。

to·ward, to·wards [təˈwɔːd, -ˈwɔːdz; tord(z), tɔrd(z), təˋwɔrd] **I** ***prep*.** **1.**〔运动、方向、位置〕朝,向;走向。*set out* ～ *the town* 向镇上出发。*a tendency* ～ *co-operation* (走向)合作的趋势。*The house looks* ～ *the sea*. 房子朝着海。*get* ～ 靠近(*cf*. *get to*)。*I look* ～ *you*.〔谑〕= *Here's* ～ (普通 *to*) *you*. 敬您一杯。**2.**〔时间〕近…,左右。～*s evening* 天快黑时。～ *five o'clock* 五点钟模样。～ *sixty years of age* 快近 60 岁。**3.**〔数〕近,约。*There were* ～ *a thousand of them*. 来了一千人左右。**4.**〔目的〕为,有助于,可用于。*I saved something* ～ *his education*. 我为了他的教育储蓄了一些钱。*This money goes* ～ *the debts*. 这钱预备用来还债。*go far* ～ 大有助于。**5.**〔关系〕对…。*I felt kindly* ～ *him*. 我对他产生了好感。*their attitude* ～ *the new republic* 他们对新共和国的态度。**II** [ˈtəuəd; tord, tɔrd] ***a*.** **1.**〔古〕〔用作 *pred*.〕迫近的,就要发生[举行]的。**2.** 前途有望的(青年等)。**3.**〔英古〕温顺的,听话的(*opp*. *forward*)。**4.** 正在进行中。*There is some work* ～. 有的工作正在进行中。**-ly** ***ad*.**

tow·el [ˈtauəl, taul; taʊl, ˋtaʊəl] **I** ***n*.** 毛巾;〔美〕擦脸[手]纸(= paper ～)。***a lead*** ～〔俚〕子弹。***an oaken*** ～〔古、俚〕棍棒。***throw*** [***toss***] ***in the*** ～【拳击】承认打败;认输,投降。**II** ***vt*.**, ***vi*.** (〔英〕***-ll-***) 用毛巾擦;〔俚〕殴打。～ *away at one's face* 拿毛巾擦脸。～ *oneself* 拿毛巾擦身体。～ **gourd** 丝瓜。～**-horse**, ～ **rack** 毛巾架。～**-rail** (钉在墙上的)毛巾架。

towel·ling, 〔美〕**tow·el·ing** [ˈtauəliŋ; ˋtaʊəlɪŋ] ***n*.** 毛巾布[料];用毛巾擦。

tow·er [ˈtauə; ˋtaʊɚ] **I** ***n*.** 塔,楼塔;城堡;碉堡;要害地;〔罕〕(负伤鸟的)笔直向上飞;〔美〕铁路信号所。*a bell* ～ 钟楼。*a keep* ～ 城楼。*a martello* ～【史】海岸圆炮塔。*a watch* ～ 望楼。*a water* ～ 给水塔;(水库泄水口的)水塔。*the T-* (*of London*) 伦敦塔。～ *and town* 〔诗〕有人家的地方。～ *of ivory* 象牙塔。～ *of strength* 非常可靠的人;干城,柱石。**II** ***vi*.** 高耸(*above*);胜过;(鹰等)翱翔;(负伤的鸟)笔直飞上去。～ **clock** 屋顶钟,楼钟。～ **house** 中世纪的城堡。～**-man**, ～**-operator**〔美〕信号员,守望员。

tow·ered [ˈtauəd; ˋtaʊɚd] ***a*.** 高耸云霄的;有塔的。

tow·er·ing [ˈtauəriŋ; ˋtaʊərɪŋ] ***a*.** 高耸的,屹立的;突出的;高傲的;激烈的。～ *crimes* 滔天罪行。

Tow·er(s) [ˈtauə(z); ˋtaʊɚ(z)] ***n*.** 托尔(斯)〔姓氏〕。

tow·er·y [ˈtauəri; ˋtaʊərɪ] ***a*.** 有塔的;高耸的。

tow·head [ˈtəuˌhed; ˋtoˏhɛd] ***n*.** **1.** 浅黄头发。**2.** 浅黄头发的人。**-ed** ***a*.**

tow·hee [ˈtauhiː, ˈtəu-; ˋtaʊhi, ˋtohi, toˋhi] ***n*.**〔美〕【动】(北美)雀科的鸟。

town [taun; taʊn] ***n*.** **1.** 镇,市镇,城镇〔狭义:大于 village (村)而非 city(市)的地方。广义:和 country (乡村)相对而言时,不独 city 和 borough (自治市),连 urban district 市(区)亦可称为 ～。有 market 或 fair (市集)的小于 urban district 的村落,亦称为～。美国 New England 各州把相当于 city,无行政机关,仅有 ～ meeting 的自治市称为～;其他各州的 ～ 则相当于 ～ship 的 2. 义〕。**2.**〔the ～〕城镇居民;全体居民。**3.**〔不用冠词〕城市;市区,商业中心区。**4.**〔Scot.〕小农场内的房屋;〔方〕村,小村庄;土拨鼠的巢。*a* county ～ 县城。*the* ～ (附近的)市镇;镇民,市民。*The whole* ～ *knows of it*. 镇上的人没有一个不知道。***woman of the*** ～ 妓女。***a man about*** ～ (尤指伦敦的)在俱乐部、剧场等处闲混日子的人,高等游民。***carry a*** ～ 洗劫市镇。***come to*** ～ 到京里[城里]来;出现,登场;入伙;发迹,成功。***come upon the*** ～ 变成都市里的高等游民;变成娼妓[盗贼]。***go down*** ～〔美〕到商业区去,买东西去;〔俚〕成功。***go to*** ～ **1.** 进京,上省,进城。**2.**〔美〕去市区买东西;过浮华生活;会活动;有声望。***hit*** ～ 到达。***in*** ～ 在京城里,在省上[城里],〔英〕在伦敦。***jump the*** ～ 逃亡。***on*** [= upon] ***the*** ～ 过着高等游民的生活;过着娼妓[盗贼]的生活;〔美〕受城里慈善机构的救济。***out of*** ～ 已离京[城市],〔英〕不在伦敦;已到乡下。～ **and gown** (英国牛津和剑桥的)市民和大学里的人。～ **centre** 市中心。～ **clerk** 镇公所秘书长。～ **council** 镇议会。～ **councillor** 镇议会议员。～ **crier** 到处宣读新颁规则等的镇公务员;公告传报员。～ **dweller** = townsman. ～ **farm**〔美〕养老院。～ **gas** 城市煤气;民用煤气。～ **girl** 城镇女郎;妓女。～ **hall** 市政厅,镇公所。～ **house**〔英〕**1.** 城市住宅,英国贵族的伦敦住宅(*opp*. country seat, country house)。**2.** = ～ hall. ～**let** 小城镇。～ **mains** 城市(煤气)总管道。**T- Major**【军】(市镇)驻军军官。～ **marshal**〔美〕市警察局长。～ **meeting**〔美〕市民大会;(尤指新英格兰诸州行使地方政府权力的)镇选民大会。～ **planning** 都市规划。～**ship** **1.**【英史】= parish. **2.**〔美〕区〔县下的行政区划〕(New England 地区的)自治市。**3.**〔澳〕(计划中的)市区。～**sman** 市民;镇民代表。～ **talk** 街谈巷议。～ **woman** 城市女居民。

Town(e) [taun; taʊn] ***n*.** 汤〔姓氏〕。

town·ee, town·ie [tauˈniː; taʊˋni] ***n*.** 城市[市镇]居民。

Townes [taunz; taʊnz] ***n*.** 汤斯〔姓氏〕。

towns·folk, towns·people [ˈtaunzfəuk; ˋtaʊnzˏfok] ***n*.**〔*pl*.〕都市[城镇]居民。

towns·man [ˈtaunzmən; ˋtaʊnzˏmən] ***n*.** 市民,镇民;同市镇的人。*a fellow* ～同乡。

tow·ser [ˈtauzə; ˋtaʊzɚ] ***n*.** **1.** 大狗。**2.**〔口〕高大粗犷的男人;精明强悍的人。*He is a* ～ *for work and perfect for job*. 他工作扎扎实实,对业务精益求精。

tow·y [ˈtəui; ˋtoɪ] ***a*.** 麻屑(色一样)的;淡黄头发的。

tox- = toxic.

tox·al·bu·min [ˌtɔksælˈbjuːmin; ˏtɑksælˋbjumɪn] ***n*.**【化】毒白蛋白。

toxa·phene [ˈtɔksəfin; ˋtɑksəfɪn] ***n*.**【化】毒杀芬,氯化莰〔有机氯杀虫剂〕。

tox·(a)e·mi·a [tɔkˈsiːmiə; tɑksˋimɪə] ***n*.**【医】毒血症。

tox·e·mic [tɔkˈsimik; tɑksˋimɪk] ***a*.**【医】毒血症的。

tox·ic [ˈtɔksik; ˋtɑksɪk] ***a*.** 有毒的;中毒的。～ *symptoms* 中毒症状。～ *smoke* [*gases*] 毒烟,毒气。～ **anaemia** 中毒性贫血。～ **value** 毒效。～ **waste** 毒性废料。**-i·cal·ly** ***ad*.**

tox·i·cant [ˈtɔksikənt; ˋtɑksɪkənt] **I** ***a*.** 有毒性的。**II** ***n*.** 毒;毒物,毒药;毒素。

tox·i·ca·tion [ˌtɔksiˈkeiʃən; ˏtɑksɪˋkeʃən] ***n*.** 中毒。

toxico- *comb*. *f*. 表示"有毒,中毒": *toxico*genic, *toxico*logy.

tox·i·co·gen·ic [ˌtɔksikəuˈdʒenik; ˏtɑksɪkoˋdʒɛnɪk] ***a*.** 产生有毒物质的。

tox·i·coid [ˈtɔksiˌkɔid; ˋtɑksɪˏkɔɪd] ***n*.** 有毒物〔指任何有毒的化学物质〕。

tox·i·co·log·ic, -log·i·cal [ˌtɔksikəˈlɔdʒik, -lɔdʒikəl; ˏtɑksɪkəˋlɑdʒɪk, -lɑdʒɪkəl] ***a*.** 毒物学的。

tox·i·col·o·gy [ˌtɔksiˈkɔlədʒi; ˏtɑksɪˋkɑlədʒɪ] ***n*.** 毒理学,毒物学。**-o·gist** ***n*.** 毒物学家。

tox·i·co·sis [ˌtɔksiˈkəusis; ˏtɑksɪˋkosɪs] ***n*.**【医】中毒。

tox·in(e) [ˈtɔksin; ˋtɑksɪn] ***n*.** 毒素,毒质。

tox·in·an·ti·tox·in [ˈtɔksinˌæntiˈtɔksin; ˋtɑksɪnˏæntɪ-

ˋtɑksɪn] *n*. 【药】毒素抗毒素合剂。

tox·oid [ˈtɔksɔid; ˋtɑksɔɪd] *n*. 类毒素。

tox·o·ly·sin [ˈtɔksəlaisin; ˋtɑksɑlaɪsɪn] *n*. 解毒素。

tox·oph·i·lite [tɔkˈsɔfilait; tɑkˋsɑfə͵laɪt] *n*. 箭术研究家,爱好箭术的人。**-lit·ic** *a*.

tox·y [ˈtɔksi; ˋtɑksɪ] *a*. 〔Scot.〕〔俚〕喝醉了的。

toy [tɔi; tɔɪ] **I** *n*. 玩具;玩物;儿戏一样的事情;游戏;消遣;像玩具一样的小东西;矮小的人;小动物;无实用价值的东西;小装饰品;〔古〕废话;滑稽文章,无聊文章;双关语,诙谐,戏谑;〔美〕怪人。**II** *a*. 玩具的,模型的;玩具一样的。*a* ~ *dog* 养着玩的小狗。*a* ~ *soldier* (铅制的)玩具兵。*a* ~ *drama* 木偶戏剧本。***make a ~ of*** 当做玩具[消遣],玩弄,不认真做;(小孩子)做…玩。**III** *vi*. 玩耍;玩弄,当做玩具;玩弄,调戏,戏弄(*with*)。~**-box** 玩具箱;〔海俚〕船上的轮机室。~ **boy** (受年长妇女供养的)英俊男子;男妓。~ **food** (其原料预先量好并调制好,分装于有号码袋内的)半成品成套配菜〔供顾客购回家自行做熟〕。~ **shop** 玩具店。~ **theatre** 木偶戏剧场;小剧场。

To·ya·ma [təuˈjɑːmə; tojɑˋmɑ] *n*. 富山〔日本城市〕。

toy·man [ˈtɔimən; ˋtɔɪmən] *n*. 玩具商;玩具制作者。

Toyn·bee [ˈtɔinbi; ˋtɔɪnbɪ] *n*. 托因比〔姓氏〕。

to·yon [ˈtəujən; ˋtoɪən] *n*. 【植】柳叶石楠(*Heteromeles arbutifolia*)〔产于加利福尼亚州〕。

tp. = telephone; township; troop.

t.p. = title page.

t.p.i. = twists per inch【纺】每英寸捻数。

TPN = Triphospho-pyridine nucleotide【生化】三磷酸吡啶核甙酸。

tpr. = trooper.

TPR = temperature, pulse, respiration【医】体温、脉搏、呼吸。

tps. = townships.

TQC = total quality control 全面质量管理(法)。

TR = **1.** Treasury Receipt (美国财政部发行的)国库券。**2.** Training Regulations 操典。

Tr. = **1.** Treasurer. **2.** Troop. **3.** Trust. **4.** Trustee.

tr = **1.** tare. **2.** tower. **3.** trace. **4.** train. **5.** transactions. **6.** transition. **7.** transitive. **8.** translated. **9.** translator. **10.** transport(ation). **11.** treasurer. **12.** tributary. **13.** trill. **14.** trust(ee).

Tr(s) = troops.

tra- *pref*. = trans-.

tra·be·at·ed [ˈtreibiˌeitid; ˋtrebɪ͵etɪd] *a*. 有横梁的。

tra·be·a·tion [ˌtreibiˈeiʃən; ͵trebɪˋeʃən] *n*. 【建】横梁式结构;柱顶盘。

tra·bec·u·la [trəˈbekjulə; trəˋbɛkjələ] *n*. (*pl*. ***-lae*** [-liː; -li]或***-las***) **1.** 【解、动】(昆虫的)蕈体柄;梁,桁,柱;(古生物的)羽楣。**2.** 【植】横条;横隔片。**-r, -te** *a*.

trace[1] [treis; tres] **I** *n*. **1.** 迹,足迹,踪迹,去向。**2.** 痕迹;证迹,线索,结果;【心】记忆痕;【植】(脉)迹。**3.** 微量,【化】痕量;一点点。**4.** 迹线,图形,图样;【筑城】示意图,略图;(自记仪器的)记录图像;(示波器上的)扫描(行程),扫迹。**5.** 【几】交点,交线;接触线;描迹;描绘;【军】经始线;【气象】小到不能计量的雨量[略作 T]。*a* ~ *of fear* 微微有点害怕。(***hot***) ***on the ~s of*** 追踪,追近。**II** *vt*. **1.** 跟踪,追踪;侦探,探索,查找。**2.** 顺着去,跟着…去;追溯由来,追究。**3.** 描绘,画轮廓,打图样;【军】画出(军事设施的)经始线;(用心)写;〔喻〕计划。**4.** 描摹,映描;复写。**5.** 【建】用花窗格装饰。~ ***back*** 追溯 (*The report has been ~d back to you*. 这个谣言追究到你这里来了)。~ ***beans*** 〔美俚〕非常好奇。~ ***out*** 探寻踪迹;描摹,映写;计划 (~(*out*) *a plan* 映绘平面图。~(*out*) *a policy* 草拟一项政策)。—*vi*. **1.** 沿路走;沿路线走。**2.** 追溯到(*to*)。~ **element** 痕量[微量]元素。~ **lighting** (使用带电金属条或轨道提供光源的)轨道照明。

trace[2] [treis; tres] *n*. (马车等的)挽绳,挽车的皮带;【机】连动杆;【植】(脉)迹。***in the ~s*** 上着挽绳;负担日常工作。***jump the ~s*** 挣脱羁绊;〔喻〕摆脱束缚。***kick over the ~s*** 挣脱羁绊;〔喻〕不受驾驭,反抗。

trace·a·ble [ˈtreisəbl; ˋtresəbl̩] *a*. 可追踪的;可追溯的;起源于…的;证迹明白的;可映摹的;可描画的,可摹写的。**-bly** *ad*. **-ness, -bil·i·ty** *n*.

trace·less [ˈtreislis; ˋtreslɪs] *a*. 无痕迹的。**-ly** *ad*.

trac·er [ˈtreisə; ˋtresə] *n*. 追踪者;追踪物,示迹剂;描摹者;描图员;描记器;画线笔,尖笔;航迹自画器;失物追查员;失单;【物】示迹物;曳光剂;【军】曳光弹;【医】探针。*a* ~ *atom* 示迹原子。~ **bullet** [~ **shell**]【军】曳光弹。~ **chemistry**【化】示踪化学。

trac·er·y [ˈtreisəri; ˋtresərɪ] *n*. **1.** 【建】(哥德式建筑的)花窗格。**2.** (刺绣、雕刻等的)网眼工艺。

tra·che·a [trəˈkiːə; ˋtrekɪə, trəˋkiə] *n*. (*pl*. ~***s***, ***-cheae*** [-kiiː; -kii])【解】气管;【植】导管;(昆虫的)呼吸管。

tra·che·ate [ˈtrəkiˌeit; ˋtrekɪ͵et, trəˋkiɪt] *a*. 【动】通过气管呼吸的。

tra·che·id [ˈtreikiːid; ˋtrekɪɪd] *n*. 【植】管胞。**-al** *a*.

trach·e·i·tis [trækiˈaitis; ͵trekɪˋaɪtɪs] *n*. 【医】气管炎。

tracheo- *comb. f*. 气管,导管: *tracheo*tomy, *tracheo*phyte.

tra·che·o·bron·chi·al [ˌtreikiəuˈbrɔŋkiəl; ͵trekɪo-ˋbrɑŋkɪəl] *a*. 【解】气管支气管的。

tra·che·ole [ˈtreikiˌəul; ˋtrekɪ͵ol] *n*. 【动】(昆虫的)小气管。

tra·che·o·phyte [ˈtreikiəuˌfit; ˋtrekɪo͵fɪt] *n*. 【植】导管植物。

trach·e·ot·o·my [ˌtrækiˈɔtəmi; ͵trekɪˋɑtəmɪ] *n*. 【医】气管切开术。

tra·cho·ma [trəˈkəumə; trəˋkomə] *n*. 【医】颗粒性结膜炎,沙眼。**-tous** *a*.

tra·chyte [ˈtreikait, ˈtrækait; ˋtrekaɪt, ˋtrækaɪt] *n*. 【地】粗面岩。

tra·chyt·ic [trəˈkitik; ˋtrekɪtɪk] *a*. 粗面的。

trac·ing [ˈtreisiŋ; ˋtresɪŋ] *n*. 追踪,追溯,追查;描摹,映写,复写;摹图;映写图,透写物;示踪,显迹;【物】线路图寻迹;自动仪表的记录图像。~ **cloth** = ~ **linen** 描图布。~ **paper** 透明描图纸。

track[1] [træk; træk] *vt*. 用纤拉船。—*vi*. 拉纤行驶。~ **road** 纤道。**-age** *n*. 拉纤。**-er** *n*. 拉纤的人。

track[2] [træk; træk] **I** *n*. **1.** 轨迹,轮迹,航迹,痕迹;〔*pl*.〕足迹。**2.** 小路,小径;【物】径迹;历程,路程;行程;行动路线;思路。**3.** (阴谋等的)形迹,线索;跟踪目标;导向装置。**4.** 【运】跑道;径赛[田赛]运动;〔美〕铁道路线,轨道;(录音磁带的)音轨;【机】履带,环带;跨距;(两轮间的)轮距;【地】开合脉。*the beaten* ~ 踏出来的路;常规,惯例。*a single* [*double*] ~ 单[双]轨。***clear the*** ~ 让路;〔命令〕走开! 让开! ***cover*** (***up***) ***one's ~s*** 隐匿行踪;隐藏自己的企图[计划等]。***in one's ~s*** 〔俚〕就在那里,就那样;〔美〕当场;立刻。***in the ~ of*** 仿…的例,学…的样;在…的中途,正在…。***jump*** [***leave***] ***the*** ~ 〔美〕出轨。***keep ~ of*** 追踪;记录;保持联系;密切注意…的动向。***lay ~s*** 铺轨。***lose ~ of*** 〔喻〕忘记,失去联系。***make ~s*** 走开;跑掉,逃走;追(*for*)。***off the*** ~ 出轨;出岔子;(话)离题;(猎狗)失去嗅迹,失去(犯人的)线索。***on the ~ of*** 跟踪追赶,尾追;没有出轨;未出岔子;话未离题;得到…的线索。***put sb. on the ~ of*** 使追踪。***throw off the*** ~ 摆脱(追踪者)。**II** *vt*. 跟踪追赶(*down*);踏成(道路);践踏,踏脏,踏平(等);通过(荒漠);铺设铁路[铁轨];顺着走(旧辙);探索(*out*);拖(船)。—*vi*. 追踪;留下行迹;铺设铁路[铁轨];(车)顺着一定线路走;(车轮)具有一定轮距;〔美口〕走小路,前进;(船)被拖着走。~ *mud through a house* 踏得一屋子泥。~ **athletics** [**events**]【运】径赛。~**(-)ball**【计】跟踪球〔可用以操纵电脑显示屏上光标移动的位置,该球

T

装在盒内,可用手自由转动)。~ **clearer** (机车、雪车等前方的)排障器;(机车的)排雪装置。~ **gauge** 轨距;轨距规。~**ing station** 雷达跟踪站。~**layer** 〔美〕铺轨工人。~**-laying** 铺轨。~ **line** 架空线。~**man** 〔美〕铁路护路员,田径运动员。~ **master** 【铁路】护路员。~ **meet** 〔美〕田径运动会。~**-pad** 【计】触式控制板。~ **record** 成绩纪录。~ **road** 纤道。~ **system** 按学生测验成绩编班制。~**walker** 〔美〕护路员。~**way** 轨道。**-age** 拖船;〔集合词〕轨道;铁道路线;铁道路线全长里数;铁道使用权[使用费]。**-er** *n*. 追踪者;【无】跟踪系统;跟踪器;【军】跟踪标定仪;搜索者;纤夫。**-ing** *n*. 跟踪,跟踪目标;【影】跟踪摄影 (*aided* [*automatic*] *tracking* 半自动[自动]跟踪)。

track·less [ˈtræklis; ˋtræklɪs] *a*. 没有足迹的;人迹未到的;没有路的;不留痕迹的;没有轨道的 (*trackless trams* [*trolley*] 无轨电车)。

tract[1] [trækt; trækt] *n*. **1.** 广阔的地面;(一大段)土地[森林],地带;地域;广阔海面[天空]。**2.** 〔古〕一段时间,长时间。**3.** 【解】管,道,系统;(神经纤维的)束。*a wooded* ~ 一大片森林。*digestive* ~ 消化道。*the optic* ~ 视(神经)束。*the motor* ~ 运动神经索。

tract[2] [trækt; trækt] *n*. (政治、宗教的)短论;小册子;传单;【天主】续唱。

tract·a·ble [ˈtræktəbl; ˋtræktəbl] *a*. 温顺的,驯良的,易驾驭的;易处理的,易加工的。**-bly** *ad*. **-bil·i·ty** *n*.

Trac·tar·i·an [trækˈtɛəriən; trækˋtɛrɪən] **I** *a*. (19世纪30年代鼓吹复兴天主教的)牛津运动的。**II** *n*. 牛津运动者;牛津运动论文作者。**-ism** [-izəm; -ɪzəm] *n*. = Oxford movement.

trac·tate [ˈtræktei t; ˋtræktet] *n*. (专题)论文;小册子。

trac·tile [ˈtræktail; ˋtræktḷ, -tɪl] *a*. 可拉长的;可牵引的。

trac·tion [ˈtrækʃən; ˋtrækʃən] *n*. 拖曳,拖拉,牵引;牵引力;〔喻〕吸力,魅力;【医】(对于肌肉等的)牵引(术);〔美〕市内铁路,有轨电车。*force of* ~ 拖力。*animal* ~ 畜力。*motor* [*steam*] ~ 汽车[铁路]运输。~ **engine** 牵引机。~ **wheel** (火车头的)动轨。**-al** *a*.

trac·tive [ˈtræktiv; ˋtræktɪv] *a*. 拖的,牵引的。~ *effort* [*force*, *power*] 牵引力。~ *resistance* 牵引阻力。

trac·tor [ˈtræktə; ˋtræktɚ] *n*. 拖拉机;牵引车;【空】牵引式飞机 (*opp*. pusher);【医】牵引器。*a farm* ~ 农用拖拉机。~ **beam** **1.** (科幻小说中的)牵引波束〔一种被描写为可将人扯来拉去的能源波束〕。**2.** 被人牵着鼻子走的事;无法摆脱的诱惑。~**-trailer** 拖拉机拖车。

trac·to·rette [ˌtræktəˈret; ˏtræktəˋrɛt] *n*. 〔美〕拖拉机女驾驶员。

Tracy [ˈtreisi; ˋtresɪ] *n*. 特蕾西[姓氏,女子名]。

trade [treid; tred] **I** *n*. **1.** 贸易;商业,交易;零售商。**2.** 职业;行业;(铁匠、木匠等的)手艺。**3.** 〔the ~ 〕〔集合词〕同业,同行;〔口〕酒品制造商人,酒商;〔美〕〔集合词〕顾客,主顾。**4.** 〔美〕(政党间的)妥协,政治交易。**5.** 〔the ~s〕【气象】贸易风;〔英军俚〕潜艇部队。**6.** 〔古〕小道;常习。*domestic* [*home*] ~ 国内贸易。*foreign* [*international*] ~ 对外[国际]贸易。*fair* ~ 互惠贸易。*free* ~ 自由贸易;〔古〕走私。*balance of* ~ 贸易差额。*the* ~ *of war* 军人的职业。*a* ~ *test* 技能考试,技术考试。*service* ~*s* 服务(性)行业。*every man for his own* ~ [*every one to his* ~] 各专其业。***be in*** ~ 是零售商,做小买卖。***by*** ~ 职业是。***drive*** [***do***, ***make***] ***a roaring*** ~ 生意兴隆。

II *vi*. **1.** 贸易,做买卖。**2.** 买东西 (*at*)。**3.** 对换;做正当或不正当交易 (*in*; *with*; *for*)。~ *in salt* 做盐生意。~ *at a store* 在商店买东西。—*vt*. **1.** 从事(证券等)交易。**2.** 以某物换取他物 (~ *sth*. *for sth*. *else*);同某人交换某物 (~ *sth*. *with sb*.)。~ ***away*** 卖掉。~ ***in*** 用交换方式购入。~ ***off*** 卖出。~ (***up***) ***on*** (*sb*.'*s reputation*) 利用(某人的)名声。~ **acceptance** 商业承兑汇票。~ **agreement** (职业等的)雇佣合同。~ **association** 同业公会。~ **board** 劳资协商会议。~ **book** [**edition**] 普及版。~ **books** 商业账簿。~ **circular** 传单;回单;报单。~ **craft** 〔口〕做间谍必备的知识和技能。~ **cycle** 【商】(景气的)周期性。~ **discount** 同行折扣。~ **guild** [**organization**] 同业公会。~ **hall** 工会会所。~**-in** **1.** *n*. 折价物;作价提交的货品;夹有折价物的交易;折价价格。**2.** *a*. 作价提交的。~ **journal** 行业杂志[公报]。~**-last** 交换的好消息〔希望换取对方把听到赞扬自己的话告诉自己,而告诉对方的自己所听到的赞扬对方的话〕(*I have a* ~*-last for you*. 我听到有人称赞你啦)。~**-mark** **1.** *n*. 商标。**2.** *vt*. 贴上商标;登记…的商标。~**sman** (小)商人,零售商人;〔方〕工匠,熟练工人。~ **name** 商号;商品的业内名称。~**-off** 交易。~**speople** 商人们;〔集合词〕零售商贩;零售商贩的家属。~ **première** 【影】(内部)试映。~ **price** 批发价,同行价。~ **route** 商队路线,商船航线。~ **school** 中等职业学校。~ **secret** 厂商的制造秘密。~ **show** 【影】试映。~**s union** 〔主英〕= trade union〔美国叫 labor union〕. ~**s-woman** 女零售商人。~ **union** 工会。~ **unionism** 工会主义。~ **unionist** 工会会员;工会主义者。~ **waste** 工业废液。~ **wind** 【气】信风,贸易风。

trad·er [ˈtreidə; ˋtredɚ] *n*. **1.** 商人。**2.** 〔美〕证券交易所中以自己做买卖为主的经纪人。**3.** 商船。

trad·es·can·ti·a [ˌtrædisˈkænʃiə; ˏtrædɛsˋkænʃɪə] *n*. 【植】紫露草属植物 (= spiderwort)。

Trades Union Congress 英国职工大会(或英国工会联盟)。

trad·ing [ˈtreidiŋ; ˋtredɪŋ] *a*. 从事商业的。~ **estate** (计划性的)商业区。~ **post** (欧美贸易商在非洲等处内地设立的与当地人交易的)贸易站。~ **stamp** 〔美〕赠品兑换券。

tra·di·tion [trəˈdiʃən; trəˋdɪʃən] *n*. **1.** 传说,口碑。**2.** 传统;惯例。**3.** 【宗】经外传说。**4.** 【法】移交,引渡。*break* ~ 打破惯例。*stage* ~ 舞台惯例。***by*** ~ 照传统;据口传。***handed down by*** ~ 口头相传。***T- says*** [***runs***] ***that*** ~据历代传说。***true to*** ~ 名不虚传地。

tra·di·tion·al, tra·di·tion·a·ry [trəˈdiʃənəl, -ʃənəri; trəˋdɪʃənl, -ʃənˏɛrɪ] *a*. 口头传说的;传统的,惯例的,因袭的。~ *Chinese medicine* 中药。

tra·di·tion·al·ism [trəˈdiʃənəlizəm; trəˋdɪʃənḷɪzṃ] *n*. 传统主义;因袭[墨守]惯例。

tra·di·tion·al·ist [trəˈdiʃənlist; trəˋdɪʃənḷɪst] *n*. 传统主义者,因循守旧者。**-is·tic** *a*.

tra·di·tion·al·ly, tra·di·tion·ar·i·ly [trəˈdiʃənəli, -ʃənərili; trəˋdɪʃənəlɪ, -ʃənərɪlɪ] *ad*. 传说上;传统上,照惯例。

tra·di·tion·ist [trəˈdiʃənist; trəˋdɪʃənɪst] *n*. **1.** 传统拥护者。**2.** 研究(纪录、传播)传统习惯的人。

trad·i·tive [ˈtræditiv; ˋtrædətɪv] *a*. 〔罕〕= traditional.

trad·i·tor [ˈtræditə; ˋtrædətɚ] *n*. (*pl*. ***trad·i·to·res*** [-tɔːriːz; -toriz])【史】(在受到罗马人迫害时)基督徒中的叛变者。

tra·duce [trəˈdjuːs; trəˋdjus, -ˋdus] *vt*. 诽谤,中伤,诋毁。**-ment** *n*. 诽谤,诋毁。

tra·duc·er [trəˈdjuːsə; trəˋdjusɚ] *n*. 诽谤者。

tra·du·cian·ism [trəˈdjuːʃənizəm, -ˈduː-; trəˋdjuʃənˏɪzm, -ˋdu-] *n*. 【神】灵魂遗传论〔认为灵魂和肉体一样,也是父母传下来的〕。**-cian·ist** *n*.

traf·fic [ˈtræfik; ˋtræfɪk] **I** *n*. **1.** 交通,(人、车、船、飞机的)来往;交通量;运输;运输量;运输业;旅客,货物。**2.** 交易,贸易 (*in*); 交往;交流。**3.** 电信(业务),通信量,通话量。~ *in rice* 大米交易。*ships of* ~ 商船。*little* ~ 交通[行人]稀少。*heavy* ~ 交通[行人]拥挤。*the* ~ *department* [*section*] 【铁路】运输科[局]。**II** *vt*. (*-ficked*; *-fick·ing*) 在…上通行;以…作交易;出卖[牺牲](名誉等)。— *vi*. 交易,买卖;做肮脏生意 (*in*; *with*; *for*, *away*)。***be open to*** [***for***] ~ 开放;通车。

~ **circle**（十字路的）环状交叉口。~ **constable** = ~ **cop**〔美〕交通警察。~ **island** 交通岛，安全岛。~ **jam** 交通拥挤。~ **load** 交通载荷。~ **manager** 运输经理，运输科长。~ **pattern**【空】起落航线。~ **policeman** 交通警察。~ **regulation** 交通规则。~ **returns** 运输（统计）报告。~ **ship**【军】联络舰。~ **signal** [**light**] 交通信号（灯）。~ **volume** 交通量。

traf·fi·ca·tor [ˈtræfikeitə; ˋtræfɪˏketɚ] ***n.***（汽车的）方向指示器。

traf·fick·er [ˈtræfikə; ˋtræfɪkɚ] ***n.*** 奸商（*in*）；出卖（秘密等）的人。

trag·a·canth [ˈtrægəkænθ; ˋtrægəˏkænθ] ***n.***【植】胶黄耆；【化】黄蓍胶。

tra·ge·di·an [trəˈdʒiːdiən, -djən; trəˋdʒidɪən] ***n.*** 悲剧演员；悲剧作者。

tra·ge·di·enne [trəʒiːdiˈen; trəˏdʒidɪˋɛn] ***n.***〔F.〕悲剧女演员。

trag·e·dy [ˈtrædʒidi; ˋtrædʒədɪ] ***n.*** 悲剧（*opp.* comedy）；惨剧，悲惨事件。*a* ~ *king* [*queen*] 著名悲剧演员[女演员]。*The* ~ *of it*! 真是悲剧！

trag·ic [ˈtrædʒik; ˋtrædʒɪk] ***a.*** 悲剧的；悲剧性的，悲惨的。*a* ~ *tale*（*scene*）悲惨的故事（景色）。~ *drama* 悲剧。~ *flaw*（悲剧主角性格中的）悲剧性缺点。*the* ~ *lesson* 惨痛教训。*the* ~ *stage* 悲剧。*the* ~（人生、文学中的）悲剧性，悲惨因素

trag·i·cal [ˈtrædʒikəl; ˋtrædʒɪkḷ] ***a.***〔罕〕= tragic. **-ly** ***ad.*** **-ness** ***n.***

trag·i·com·e·dy [trædʒiˈkɔmidi; ˏtrædʒɪˋkɑmədɪ] ***n.*** 悲喜剧；又悲又喜的事情[场合]。**-com·ic**, **-com·i·cal** ***a.***

trag·o·pan [ˈtrægəpæn; ˋtrægəpæn] ***n.***【鸟】（亚洲）角雉（属）；红胸角雉。

tra·gus [ˈtreigəs; ˋtregəs] ***n.***（*pl.* **-gi** [-dʒai; -dʒaɪ]）【解】耳屏。

trail [treil; trel] **I** ***vt.*** **1.** 拖曳（衣脚等），拖着走；拖带着；提（枪）。**2.** 跟踪追赶；〔美俚〕落后于。**3.** 拉长声音讲（话）。**4.**〔美〕踏出路来，开辟道路。**5.**〔口〕在电影预告片中为…做广告；预告；预示。—***vi.*** **1.** 拖曳；（发等）拖着；（植物）爬在地上；（蛇）慢慢爬行；拖着尾巴；（云霞、烟雾等）飘。**2.** 拖着脚走（*along*）；落在（队伍）后面；（队伍）四散。**3.**（道路）伸展；（议论）离题。**4.**（猎犬等）追踪猎物。**5.** 减低、变弱（*away*, *off*）。~ *an oar* 拖着桨。~ *mud into the house* 把污泥带进屋内。~ *a stranger to see a friend* 带着一个陌生人去看朋友。~ *the grass* 在草地上踩出一条路。*T- arms* 提枪！~*ing antenna*【无】拖尾天线。~ *off*（声音）逐渐消失。~ *on* 拖延下去。~ *with*〔美俚〕老和…作伴；和…合作。**II** ***n.*** **1.** 痕迹，足迹，踏成的路，小路；长长地拖垂后头的东西；（流星等的）尾；衣裙；（云霞等的）尾迹；（炮架的）架尾，车尾。**2.** 线索，形迹；猎兽的臭迹；（暴风雨等的）余波。**3.**【军】提枪（的姿势）。**4.**〔美俚〕邋遢人，〔尤指〕邋遢女人。***at the*** ~【军】取提枪姿势。***be hot on sb.'s*** ~ 紧追某人。***blaze a*** ~ 开路；带头。***hit the*** ~ 出发；立即走开。***off the*** ~ 失去臭迹[线索]；迷失。***on the*** ~ 找到臭迹[线索]。***on the*** ~ ***of*** 跟踪追赶。~ ***after*** 追随。~ ***one's coat*** [***coattails***] 故意挑衅。~ **bike** 爬山车。**-able** ***a.*** 可用拖车运送的。

trail·er [ˈtreilə; ˋtrelɚ] ***n.*** 拖曳者；拉车牲口；追踪者，追猎者；拖车；拖挂的车辆；蔓草；【影】预告片；〔美口〕〔*pl.*〕跟着马戏班（等）跑的闲人们；〔美〕拖车式活动房屋；（图书编目的）篇身片，片尾。~ **bus** 带拖车的公共汽车。~ **card**（图书编目的）缩微卡片篇身片。~ **net** 拖网。~ **park** [**camp**, **court**] 拖车式活动房屋集中地。~ **pump** 装在拖车上的消防泵。

trail·er·ite [ˈtreilərait; ˋtreləˏraɪt] ***n.***〔美〕住拖车式活动房屋的人。

train [trein; tren] **I** ***vt.*** **1.** 训练；培养，养成；锻炼（身体）；【园艺】使向一定方向生长，整形，整枝（*up*; *over*）。**2.** 瞄准，对准（炮等）（*on*; *upon*）。**3.**〔罕〕拖，曳。**4.**〔古〕引诱，吸引（*away*; *from*）。—***vi.*** **1.** 接受训练；练习；锻炼身体（*for*）。**2.**〔口〕坐火车旅行；〔美俚〕交际，来往；〔美俚〕跳来跳去。*At school we should* ~ *young children*（*how*）*to be good citizens.* 我们在初等学校应当训练青少年（如何）当好优秀公民。*half-* ~*ed* 训练[锻炼]不够的。*over-* ~*ed* 训练[锻炼]过度的。*under-* ~*ed* 训练[锻炼]差的。~ *fine* 严格训练[锻炼]。*He was* ~*ed to be a doctor but later on he decided to become an actor instead.* 他接受的是医生的训练，可是后来却决定做演员了。*Every morning he spends two hours* ~*ing for race.* 他每天早晨花两个小时锻炼赛跑。~ ***down***（选手）练轻体重。〔口〕~ ***it*** 坐火车去。~ ***off*** 用锻炼减轻[减肥]；（子弹）打歪，没打中。~ ***on*** 练好。~ ***with***〔美〕交往；合作[联合]。**II** ***n.*** **1.** 列车，火车。**2.** 队伍；一行，排，列；系列；〔集合词〕随从，随员。**3.** 链，（思想等的）连续；一连串（事件）；接着发生的事件，后事，结果。**4.** 次序；状态。**5.** 拖在后头的东西；衣裙；【军】辎重队；后勤部队；（炮架的）架尾；彗星的尾；鸟尾；导火线；（重而长的）大雪橇。**6.**【机】（传动的）轮列，轮系；齿轮组。*a down* [*an up*] ~ 下行[上行]列车。*a funeral* ~ 送丧的队伍。*a long* ~ *of sightseers* 一大批游客。*an accommodation* [*express*] ~ 普通[特快]列车。*a through* ~ 直达列车。*All is now in*（*good*）~. 完全停当了，全好了。*Everything fell into its old* ~ *again.* 一切又恢复原状了。~ *of mechanism*【机】机构系。~ *of powder*【军】导火线。***by*** ~ 坐火车。***catch*** [***make***] ***one's*** ~ 正赶上火车。***in***（***good***）~ 准备妥当。***in the*** ~ ***of*** 接着，继…之后。***miss one's*** ~ 没赶上火车。***put on a special*** ~ 挂临时加车。***put things in*** ~ 安排妥贴。***ride the gravy*** ~ 获得赚钱好机会；干不费劲的活儿。***take*** ~ ***to*** ... 坐火车去…。~ ***de luxe*** 花车。~**band**【史】民团。~**bearer**（举行婚礼时替新娘等）拉长衣裙的人。~**butcher**〔美〕火车里卖东西的人。~**crew**（列车的）全体乘务员；司炉。~ **dispatcher**〔美〕列车调度员。~ **ferry** 列车渡船。~**-jumper**（美）乘火车逃票者。~**man**〔美〕列车乘务员；（尤指）制动手。~ **master** 货运列车车长；铁路段段长。~**mile** 列车英里。~ **oil** 鲸油。~**sick** ***a.*** 晕车的。~ **sickness** 晕车。

trai·nee [treiˈniː; trenˋi] ***n.*** 受训练的人[动物]。~**ship**（受）训练，（受）军训。

train·er [ˈtreinə; ˋtrenɚ] ***n.*** 训练者，教员；教练（员）；调马师；〔美海军〕（炮的）瞄准手；〔英空军〕教练机；教练设备；【园艺】枝架。

train·ing [ˈtreiniŋ; ˋtrenɪŋ] ***n.*** 训练，教练，练习；锻炼；（马等的）调驯；（枪炮、摄影机等的）瞄准，对准；【园艺】整枝法。***be in*** [***out of***] ~ 练习得好[不好]。***go into*** ~ 开始练习。~ **bit**（烈马用的）马衔。~ **camp** **1.** 军训营。**2.**（运动员的）集训营。~ **college**〔英〕职业学院；（旧时）师范学院。~ **school** **1.**〔英〕= ~-college. **2.**〔美〕少年犯教养所（*a* ~ *school for nurses* 护士职业学校）。~**ship** 练习舰[船]。~ **table** 体育锻炼人员的膳食[食堂]。

traipse [treips; treps] ***n.***〔方，口〕= trapes.

trait [treit; tret] ***n.*** **1.** 特色，特点，特征；性格；脾气；容貌。**2.** 一触，一笔，一画。**3.**〔罕〕一点点，少许（*of*）。*a new* ~ 新品质[特点]。*marked Japanese* ~*s* 日本人的显著特点。*national* ~*s* 国民性。*a bad* ~ 不好的特点。*a* ~ *of humour* 有点幽默感。**4.**【生】性状（= character）。

trai·tor [ˈtreitə; ˋtretɚ]（*fem.* **-tress** [-tris; -trɪs]）***n.*** 卖国贼；叛徒（*of*）。*a hidden* ~ 内奸。~ *and spy* 奸细。*turn* ~ *to one's country* 变成叛国分子。

trai·tor·ous [ˈtreitərəs; ˋtretɚəs, -trəs] ***a.*** 反叛的；叛逆罪的；出卖朋友的；不忠的。*a* ~ *action* 反叛行为。*a* ~ *scheme* 奸计。~ *clique* 卖国[叛徒]集团。**-ly** ***ad.*** **-ness** ***n.***

T

trai·tress [ˈtreitris; ˋtretrɪs] *n*. 女叛徒;女叛逆者;女卖国贼。

tra·ject [trəˈdʒekt; trəˋdʒɛkt] *vt*. 〔现罕〕传导,传达,输送,运送。**-jec·tion** *n*.

traj·ec·to·ry [ˈtrædʒiktəri, trəˈdʒektəri; trəˋdʒɛktərɪ, -trɪ] *n*. (抛射体的)轨道,弹道;流轨;【几】轨线。*a curved* [*direct-fire, flat, highangle fire, low*] ~ 曲射[直射、平射、高射、低射]弹道。

tra·la [trəˈlɑː; trəˋlɑ], **tra·la·la** [-lɑːˈlɑː; -lɑˋlɑ] *int*. 脱啦(啦)〔模拟吹奏乐器,表示欢快的呼声〕。

tram[1] [træm; træm] **I** *n*. **1**. 〔英〕(车轨)电车,有轨电车轨道;〔*pl*.〕电车路线。**2**. = tramcar; tramroad; tramway. **3**. 煤车,矿车。**4**. (索道的)吊兜,吊车。*by* ~ 坐电车。**II** *vt*. (*-mm-*) 用电车(等)运。—*vi*. 坐[开]电车。~**car** 电车;煤车。~**line** = ~way;〔*pl*.〕〔口〕网球场周围的铁丝。~**rail** 轨条;〔*pl*.〕电车轨道;索道。~**road** (电[矿]车)轨道;货车[手摇车]轨道。~**service** (有轨)电车交通。~**stop** 电车站。~**way 1**. = ~road. **2**. 电车轨道;电车。**3**. 〔美〕索道。

tram[2], **trame** [træm; træm] *n*. (丝织品的)纬线。

tram[3] [træm; træm] **I** *n*. **1**. = trammel. **2**. 正确的调整;正确的位置。**II** *vt*., *vi*. (*-mm-*) (用调整装置或椭圆规)调整。

tram·mel [ˈtræməl; ˋtræml] **I** *n*. **1**. 马梏。**2**. 〔常 *pl*.〕(习惯、礼仪等的)拘束,束缚,妨害。**3**. (捕鱼、鱼等的)细网(= ~ net)。**4**. 〔*pl*.〕椭圆规,长径规,梁规。**5**. 【机】横木规。**6**. 锅钩。~*s of examinations* 考试的束缚。**II** *vt*. (〔英〕*-ll-*) 拘束,束缚,妨害;用网捕(鱼等)。*a cross-trammelled horse* 对角两脚有白斑的马。

tra·mon·tane [trəˈmɔntein; trəˋmɑnten, ˋtræmənˏten] **I** *a*. (从意大利方面说)(阿尔卑斯)山外边的;外国的;野蛮的。**II** *n*. 山外边的人,外国人,野蛮人。

T

tramp [træmp; træmp] **I** *vi*. 踩,践踏 (*on*; *upon*);用沉重的脚步走;慢慢走,徒步旅行〔尤指长途〕;漂泊,流浪;(货船)不定期航行。—*vt*. 步行,徒步走;踩洗(衣服等);使(货船)不定期航行。~ ***down*** 踏坏,踩碎。~ ***under one's foot*** [***feet***] 践踏;蹂躏。**II** *n*. 艰苦的长途徒步旅行;徒步旅行者;流动工匠;流浪者;妓女,淫妇;候鸟;(军队行进等的)脚步声;(保护鞋底的)底铁;(在冰上防滑的)鞋底钉;不定期货船;【机】吹火器。*an ocean* ~ 远洋不定期货船。*a* ~ [*steamer*] 不定期货船。***go on a*** ~ 乘不定期货船去。***on the*** ~ 到处流浪。***take a long*** ~ ***to*** 长途跋涉到。**-er** 流浪者;流动工匠;不定期货船。

tram·ple [ˈtræmpl; ˋtræmpl̩] **I** *vt*., *vi*. 踩(烂、碎);踏(坏、倒);蹂躏,摧残;蔑视,轻视,看不起 (*on*; *upon*)。~ ***down*** [***under foot***] 践踏;蹂躏,摧残。**II** *n*. 践踏;践踏声。

tram·po·line [ˈtræmpəˌliːn, -lin; ˏtræmpəˋlin, ˋtræmpəlɪn] *n*. 蹦床〔杂技表演中翻筋斗用〕。**-lin·er**, **-lin·ist** *n*.

tran *pref*. 〔用于 s 前〕= trans-.

trance [trɑːns; træns, trɑns] **I** *n*. 出神;恍惚;【医】迷睡;神志昏迷,昏睡状态;催眠状态。***fall into a*** ~ 精神恍惚;出神。**II** *vt*. = entrance.

trank [træŋk; træŋk] *n*. 〔美口〕安定药,镇定药。

tran·quil [ˈtræŋkwil; ˋtrænkwɪl, ˋtræŋ-] *a*. (~***er***; ~***est***; 〔英〕~***ler***; ~***lest***) 平静的;安静的,镇静的;稳定的。**-ly** *ad*. **-ness** *n*.

tran·quil·(l)i·ty [træŋˈkwiliti; trænˋkwɪlətɪ, træŋ-] *n*. 平静,镇定;稳定。

tran·quil·(l)ize [ˈtræŋkwilaiz; ˋtræŋkwɪˏlaɪz] *vt*., *vi*. (变)镇定,(变)安定。**-(l)ization** *n*.

tran·quil·(l)iz·er [ˈtræŋkwilaizə; ˋtræŋkwɪˏlaɪzɚ] *n*. **1**. 使镇定的人[物]。**2**. 镇静剂;镇定剂;止痛药。

trans. = transaction(s); transfer(red); transitive; translated; translation; transportation; transpose.

trans- *pref*. **1**. 横断,横过: *trans*atlantic. **2**. 贯通;穿通,彻底,完全: *trans*fix. **3**. 超越: *trans*cend. **4**. 变化,移转: *trans*form; *tran*slate. **5**. 外,在[到]那一边: *transal*pine.

trans·act [trænˈzækt, -ˈsækt; trænsˋækt, trænzˋækt] *vt*. 办理;处理,执行(事务等),进行(谈判等)。—*vi*. 办事,处理事务;交易,谈判;协议。**-or** *n*.

trans·ac·tion [trænˈzækʃən; trænsˋækʃən, trænzˋækʃən] *n*. 办理,处理;交易;业务,事务。**2**. 【法】和解。**3**. 〔*pl*.〕(学会等的)会议记录;学报。**4**. 【心】相互影响。*cash* ~*s* 现金交易。~ *for account* 记账交易。~ *for money* 现金交易。~ *on credit* 赊赈交易。*the* ~*s tax* 营业税。**-al** *a*. **-al analysis** 人与人关系的心理分析。

trans·al·pine [ˈtrænzˈælpain; trænsˋælpɪn, trænz-, -paɪn] *a*., *n*. (从意大利那边说)阿尔卑斯山外[北]边的(人)。

trans·am·i·nase [trænsˈæmineis, -zæmineiz; trænsˋæmənes] *n*. 【生化】转氨酶。

trans·am·i·na·tion [trænsˌæmiˈneiʃən, -ˈzæmi-; trænsˏæməˋneʃən] *n*. 【生化】转氨作用。

trans·at·lan·tic [ˈtrænzətˈlæntik; ˏtrænsətˋlæntɪk, ˏtrænz-] **I** *a*. 大西洋彼岸的;隔着大西洋的;〔英〕美洲的;美国的;横渡大西洋的(轮船、航线等)。~ *humour* 〔英〕(使人大笑多于微笑的)美国式幽默。**II** *n*. 大西洋那边的人[物];美国[洲]人;横渡大西洋的轮船。

trans·ca·lent [trænsˈkeilənt; trænsˋkelənt] *a*. 透热的,传热的。**-len·cy** *n*.

Trans·cau·ca·si·a [trænskɔːˈkeiziə; ˏtrænskɔˋkeʒə, -ˋkæ-, -ʃə] *n*. 外高加索〔包括 Armenia, Azerbaijan 及 Georgia〕。**-n** *a*., *n*. 外高加索的[人]。

trans·ceiv·er [trænsˈsiːvə; trænsˋsivɚ] *n*. 【无】收发两用机。

tran·scend [trænˈsend; trænˋsɛnd] *vt*., *vi*. 超出,超过(经验、理性、信念、理解力等);【哲、宗】超越(宇宙、物质世界等);胜过,凌驾。~ *description* 没法形容。

tran·scend·ence, **-en·cy** [trænˈsendəns, -si; trænˋsɛndəns, -sɪ] *n*. 超越,超绝,卓绝;【神】超然存在,先在。

tran·scend·ent [trænˈsendənt; trænˋsɛndənt] **I** *a*. 出类拔萃的,卓越的,超群的;〔经院哲学〕超越亚里士多德的范畴的;【康德哲学】超验的;【神】超越宇宙的。**II** *n*. 卓越的人,尤物;【康德哲学】超越认识的事物。

tran·scen·den·tal [trænsenˈdentl; ˏtrænsɛnˋdɛntl] **I** *a*. 卓越的;〔口〕暧昧的,玄妙的,空幻的;【康德哲学】超验的,直觉的,由直觉得到的(知识等);【数】超越的。**II** *n*. 【数】超越数;〔*pl*.〕〔经院哲学〕超越物〔真、善、美等〕;抽象的普遍概念。~ *curve* 超越曲线。~ *function* 超越函数。**-ly** *ad*. **-ism** *n*. 【哲】超验论,超验哲学;超越主义;(Emerson 的)超越论。**-ist** *n*.

trans·con·duct·ance [ˌtrænskənˈdʌktəns; ˏtrænskənˋdʌktəns] *n*. 【电子】互导,跨导。

trans·con·ti·nen·tal [ˈtrænzˌkɔntiˈnentəl; ˏtrænskɑntəˋnɛntl] **I** *a*. 横贯大陆的;大陆那边[另一端]的。**II** *n*. 〔*pl*.〕〔美〕横贯大陆中西部通到太平洋岸的铁路。

tran·scribe [trænsˈkraib; trænˋskraɪb] *vt*. 誊写,抄录,记录(演说词等);转写,翻译;(将速记符号等)改写成文字;【乐】改作,改编;【无】转录;播送录音。—*vi*. 播放录音。**-er** *n*. 誊写者;抄录器;读数器;信息转换器。

tran·script [ˈtrænskript; ˋtrænˏskrɪpt] *n*. 誊本,抄本,缮本;副本;记录;正式文本;肄业证书;(以另一种形式)转述,改写本。

tran·scrip·tion [trænsˈkripʃən; trænˋskrɪpʃən] *n*. 誊写,抄写;转录;抄本,缮本,副本;转写,翻译;【乐】乐曲改作;【无】录音;录音广播;(广播用)唱片[磁带等]。*phonetic* ~*s* 音标;用音标写成的文字。~ **machine** 录音机。**-al** *a*.

tran·scrip·tive [trænsˈkriptiv; trænsˋkrɪptɪv] *a*. 誊写

的,抄写的;爱抄写的;好模仿的。**-ly** ***ad***.

trans·cur·rent [træns'kʌrənt; træns`kɜənt] ***a***. 横贯的;横延的。

trans·cu·ta·ne·ous [ˌtrænskju(:)'teinjəs;ˏtrænskju(ʊ)-`tenjəs] ***a***.【医】经皮的,由皮的。

trans·duc·er [trænz'djuːsə; træns`djusə] ***n***.【无】转换器;换流器,变频器;换能器,转换装置;发送器;传感器。

trans·duc·tion [træns'dʌkʃən; træns`dʌkʃən] ***n***. **1.**【物】能量转换。**2.**【生】转导(作用)。

tran·sect [træn'sekt; træn`sɛkt] **I** ***vt***. 横切,横断。**II** ***n***.【林】样条。*a belt* ～ 样带。

tran·sec·tion [træn'sekʃən; træn`sɛkʃən] ***n***. 横切;横断面。

tran·sept ['trænsept; `trænsɛpt] ***n***.【建】(教堂的)交叉甬道,十字(形)耳堂。**-al** ***a***.

transf. = transferred.

trans·fer[1] ['trænsfəː; `trænsfɜ] ***n***. **1**. 移转,转送;调职;调任[转学]证书;变换。**2**. (财产;权利等的)转让,让与(证书),移转,授受;(股票等的)过户凭单。**3**. 〔美〕划拨,汇划,汇兑,换算。**4**. (用船载列车乘客的)渡轮码头;(车辆、火车等的)渡轮。**5**. 转车车票(= ～ ticket)。**6**. (供)转印的图画[图案]。**7**.【军】转队兵;转学生;【医】(病物的)迁移。*a* ～ *company* 转运公司。*a* ～ *line* 输送管,传递线。*a telegraphic* ～ 电汇。*a* ～ *slip* 划款条,拨款单。～**-book** 过户总账。～ **case** **1**. 材料传送袋。**2**. (汽车的)分动箱。～ **cell**【植】传递细胞。～ **company** (美)转运公司。～ **factor**【生】(白血球中的)转移因子。～ **day** 〔英〕(公债等的)过户日〔星期1—5〕～ **ink**【印】转写墨。～ **paper** 复写用纸;(制图、美术等用)转写用纸;【印】复制图片等用的纸。～ **payments** 〔美〕(失业救济等)开支。

trans·fer[2] [træns'fəː; træns`fɜ] ***vt***. (***trans·ferred*** ['trænsfəːd; `trænsfɜd]; ***trans·fer·ring*** [-fəriŋ; -fɜrɪŋ]) **1**. 转移;传递,转送;调动,调任,转学;移置;移栽。**2**. 改变,变换。**3**. 交付,转让,让与(财产等)。**4**. 转印;(壁画等的)临摹。—***vi***. **1**. 转移;调职,转学(*to*)。**2**. 换车[船],转车。

trans·fer·(r)a·ble [træns'fəːrəbl, -fərəbl; træns`fɜəbl] ***a***. 能转移[传送,调任]的。**-bil·i·ty** [trænsˌfəːrə'biliti; trænsˏfɜrə`bɪlətɪ] ***n***.

trans·fer·ase ['trænsfəˌreis, -ˌeis; `trænsfəˏres, -ˏez] ***n***.【生化】转移酶。

trans·fer·ee ['trænsfəː'riː;ˏtrænsfə`ri] ***n***. 买者,承买人;受让人;被调动的人。

trans·fer·ence ['trænsfərəns; træns`fɜəns] ***n***. 转移,移动;职务调动;搬运;转送,(财产等的)转卖,让与,交付;权利转移;【心】移情(作用);【电】输电。**-fer·en·tial** ***a***.

trans·fer·or, trans·fer·rer [træns'fəːrə; træns`fɜrə] ***n***. 移交人,转让[让与]人;转印者。

trans·fer·rin [træns'ferin;ˏtræns`fɛrɪn] ***n***.【生化】铁传递蛋白。

trans·fig·u·ra·tion [ˌtrænsfigjuəˌreiʃən;ˏtrænsfɪgjə-`reʃən] ***n***. 变形,改观;美化;〔T-〕(耶稣的)变容,变容节。

trans·fig·ure [træns'figə; træns`fɪgjə] ***vt***. 改变…的形状[容貌],使变形;使改观;美化,理想化,神圣化。

trans·fi·nite [ˌtræns'fainait; træns`faɪnaɪt] ***a***. **1**. 无限的。**2**.【数】超穷的,超限的。～ *cardinal* (*number*) 超穷基数。～ *ordinal* (*number*) 超穷序数。

trans·fix [træns'fiks; træns`fɪks] ***vt***. 戳穿,刺穿;钉住;〔喻〕(恐怖等)把(人)吓得不能动弹;使大吃一惊。～ *sb.'s heart with a spear* 拿标枪戳穿某人心脏。*He was* ～*ed at its sight*. 他看见这个光景就吓呆了。

trans·fix·ion [træns'fikʃən; træns`fɪkʃən] ***n***. 刺穿;钉住;【医】贯穿固定(术)。

trans·form [træns'fɔːm; træns`fɔrm] **I** ***vt***. (使)变形;(使)变化[转化,转变];变态,改变(性质、机能等),改造,改革;【数】变换;【电】变换;转换;变压。—***vi***. 变形,变化,转化;变态。*A caterpillar is* ～*ed into a butterfly*. 毛虫变成蝴蝶。**II** ***n***.【数】变换式;【化】反式。**-able** ***a***.

trans·for·ma·tion [ˌtrænsfə'meiʃən;ˏtrænsfə`meʃən] ***n***. 转变,变化;变形;【生】(尤指昆虫的)转化,变态,改造,改革;变质;【数】变换;【电】变压;【化】(原子结构等)蜕变;〔商店用语〕(女用)假发。*socialist* ～ 社会主义改造。**-ist** ***n***. = transformist.

trans·for·ma·tion·al [ˌtrænsfə'meiʃənl;ˏtrænsfə-`meʃənl] ***a***. **1**. 变形的,变态的。**2**. 〔现罕〕(女人用的)假发的。**3**.【语法】转换(生成)的,转换(派生)的。**4**.【数】变换的。**-ist** ***n***. 转换语法学家。

trans·form·a·tive [træns'fɔːmətiv; træns`fɔrmətɪv] ***a***. 有改革能力的,起改造作用的。

trans·for·ma·tor [træns'fɔːmeitə; `trænsfɔrˏmetə],

trans·form·er [træns'fɔːmə; træns`fɔrmə] ***n***. 使变化的人[东西];【电】变压器;变换器;互感器。*polarity of* ～ 变压器绕线方向。

trans·form·ism [træns'fɔːmizəm, trɑːns-; træns-`fɔrmɪzm] ***n***.【生】变种说,物种演变(论);演化论;演化。**-ist** ***n***. 变种论者;演化论者。

trans·fron·tier [træns'frʌntjə, trɑːns-; træns`frʌntjɪr; trɑns-] ***a***. 国境外的。

trans·fuse [træns'fjuːz; træns`fjuz] ***vt***. 移注(液体);注入;转输;渗入,渗透,灌输;【医】输血;输液,注射(食盐水等)。*He* ～*d his own courage into his men*. 他用自己的勇气鼓舞了部下。

trans·fu·sion [træns'fjuːʒən; træns`fjuʒən] ***n***. 移注;渗入,渗透;灌输;【医】输血(法);输液(法)。

trans·gene [træns'dʒiːn; træs`dʒin] ***n***.【生化】转基因。

trans·gen·ic [træns'dʒenik; træns`dʒɛnɪk] ***a***.【生化】转基因的,(物种)通过转基因培育的。

trans·gress [træns'gres; træns`grɛs] ***vt***. 侵越;超过(界限等);违犯(法律等)。—***vi***. 侵越,越界;犯法,犯规,违法乱纪。**-gres·sion** ***n***. 侵越;违犯;超过;【地】海侵,海进。**-ive** ***a***. **-or** ***n***. 犯法者;违背者;(宗教、道德上的)罪人。

tran·ship [træn'ʃip; træn`ʃɪp] ***vt***. = trans-ship.

trans·hu·mance [træns'hjuːməns; træns`hjuməns] ***n***. 季节性迁移放牧〔牧民和牲畜随季节在山地和洼地之间的迁移放牧〕。**-hu·mant** ***a***.

tran·si·ence, -sien·cy ['trænziəns(i); `trænʃəns(ɪ)] ***n***. 短暂,暂时性,无常。*the* ～ *of human life* 人生朝露。

tran·si·ent ['trænziənt; `trænʃənt] **I** ***a***. 短暂的,一时的;过渡的;匆匆而过的;易逝的;虚幻的,无常的(*opp*. lasting, permanent);【物】瞬变的;〔美口〕过路的,留一会儿就走的(客人等)。～ *guest* 暂住的客人。～ *current* 瞬变电流。～ *pleasures* 片刻的快乐。*snatch a* ～ *glance of* 匆匆瞅了一眼。*a* ～ *note*【乐】经过音。**II** ***n***. 暂时性的东西[人];候鸟;过渡状态;【物】暂态值,瞬变值;【无】瞬变现象[过程],瞬态;过渡现象;〔美〕过客,短期住客。～ **equilibrium**【核】过渡平衡。**-ly** ***ad***. **-ness** ***n***.

tran·si·gent ['trænsidʒənt; `trænsɪdʒənt] **I** ***n***. 妥协者。**II** ***a***. 动摇的,犹豫不决的;妥协的。

transili·ent [træn'siliənt; træn`sɪlɪənt] ***a***. (飞快地)跳跃而过的;跳动不居的,跳动地改变的。

trans·il·lu·mi·nate [ˌtrænsi'luːmiˌneit, ˌtrænz-; ˏtrænsɪ`ljumәˏnet] ***vt***.【医】透照。

trans·il·lu·mi·na·tion ['trænsiˌljuːmi'neiʃən;ˏtrænsɪ-ˏljumə`neʃən] ***n***.【医】透照(法)。

tran·si·re [træn'zaiəri; træn`saɪri] ***n***. 〔L.〕【商】(海关发给船主的)货物通行单。

tran·sis·tance [træn'sistəns; træn`sɪstəns] ***n***.【电】晶体管作用;晶体管效应。

tran·sis·tor [træn'zistə; træn`zɪstə, -`sɪs-] ***n***.【无】晶体(三极)管;晶体管[半导体]收音机。*a* ～ *radio* 晶体管

阱;圈套,诡计。2. 靶鸽发射器;射球戏;(射球戏用的)鞋形射球器。3.【机】防臭瓣,凝汽瓣;汽水阀;(下水道的)存水弯;放泄弯管。4.【宇】(固体火箭发动机的)火药柱挡板;吸尘罩;陷波电路。5.〔英〕二轮轻便马车;〔澳俚〕警察;〔美俚〕嘴;〔美俚〕(车船中)私货藏置处;〔俚〕造伪币的模子。6. = trap-door. 7.〔常 *pl.*〕(爵士音乐的)打击乐器。*a box* ~ 陷笼。*a wave* ~【物】陷波器[电路]。***be caught in a*** ~ = ***fall into a*** ~ 落入陷阱,落入圈套。***be up to*** ~ 不好欺负;精明;狡猾。***land in sb.'s deadly*** ~ 中某人毒计。***lay*** [***set***] ***a*** ~ ***for*** 安捕机捕捉;设计诱陷。***understand*** ~ 懂得自己的利益,精明。**II** *vt.* (**-pp-**) 安捕兽机捕捉,设陷阱捕捉,诱捕;设圈套诱陷,设计诱陷;安防臭瓣,安凝汽瓣;发射(泥鸽);设地板门(在舞台上);【棒球】假捉。—*vi.* 装捕兽机,设陷阱(*for*);充当(矿坑)通风口的值班。~**ball** *n.* 射球戏。~**-circuit**【电】陷扰电路。~ **crop** 诱虫作物。~**door** (舞台等的)地板门,活板门,坠门;(房顶的)天窗;【采】通气门;(衣服等的)钩破缝(*a* ~*door spider*【动】螲蟷)。~**lamp** 诱虫灯。~ **log** = ~ **tree** 饵木,诱虫树。~**shooting** 靶鸽[飞靶]射击。

trap[2] [træp; træp] **I** *n.* 〔*pl.*〕〔口〕随身物品[行李]。**II** *vt.* 给(马)穿马衣[配上装饰品]。

trap[3] [træp; træp] *n.* 〔*pl.*〕梯子。

trap[4] [træp; træp] *n.*【矿】暗色(火成)岩。~**rock** 暗色岩。

tra·pan [trəˈpæn; trəˋpæn] *n.*, *vt.* 〔古〕= trepan.

trapes [treips; treps] **I** *n.* 1. 邋遢[懒]女人。2. 闲荡;跋涉;无目的地步行。**II** *vi.* (尤指女人)闲荡;跋涉;无目的地长时间步行。

tra·peze [trəˈpiːz; træˋpiz, trə-] *n.* 1.【几何】= trapezium. 2. (杂技及体操用的)吊架,高秋千。*a* ~ *acrobat* (杂技)空中飞人。*a* ~ *bar*【机】吊架;吊杆。

tra·pezi·form [trəˈpiːzifɔːm; trəˋpizə͵fɔrm] *a.* 不规则四边形的。

tra·pe·zi·um [trəˈpiːzjəm, -ziəm; trəˋpiziəm] *n.* (*pl.* ~*s*, *-zia* [-zjə, -ziə; -zjə, -zɪə]) 【数】不规则四边形;梯形;【解】大多角骨。

trap·e·zo·he·dron [ˌtræpizəuˈhiːdrən; trə͵pizəˋhidrən, ͵træpə-] *n.*【数】梯面体;偏方二十四面体。

trap·e·zoid [ˈtræpizɔid; ˋtræpəzɔɪd] *n.*, *a.* 1.〔英〕不规则四边形(的)。2.〔美〕梯形(的);【解】小多角骨。**-al** *a.* (***trapezoidal thread***【机】梯形螺纹)。

trap·per [ˈtræpə; ˋtræpɚ] *n.* (特指为取得毛皮)用捕兽机捕兽的人;【电】陷波器;【矿】(矿坑)通风口值班工人。

trap·pings [ˈtræpiŋz; ˋtræpɪŋz] *n.* 〔*pl.*〕装饰;礼服;马饰,(装饰性的)马具。

Trap·pist [ˈtræpist; ˋtræpɪst] *n.* (严肃沉默的)特拉比斯特派修道士。

Trappist·ine [ˈtræpistin, -tain; ˋtræpɪstɪn, -taɪn] *n.* 1. 特拉比斯特派修道女。2. 〔t-〕(法国)特拉比斯特甜酒。

trap·py [ˈtræpi; ˋtræpɪ] *a.* (**-pi·er**; **-pi·est**)〔口〕有圈套的,危险的;欺骗性的。

trap·rock [ˈtræpˌrɔk; ˋtræp͵rɑk] *n.*【地】暗色岩〔圆柱形的黑色火成岩〕。

traps [træps; træps] *n.* 〔*pl.*〕1. 随身携带物;行李。2. 家具。3. 什物。

trapt [træpt; træpt]〔古〕trap 的过去式和过去分词。

tra·pun·to [trəˈpuntəu; trəˋpunto] *n.* (*pl.* **-tos**) 贴绣品。

trash [træʃ; træʃ] **I** *n.* 废料;垃圾;碎屑,修剪下来的枝叶;落叶;玉米秸(等);废烟叶;渣滓;不值钱的东西;劣货;粗制滥造的作品,无聊作品;废话;流氓无赖,社会渣滓。*the white* ~〔美〕南部的贫穷白种人。**II** *vt.* 摘(甘蔗的)叶;除去废料;〔美西部〕擦去;(表示反抗或反叛)捣毁,杀死,消灭。~ **can** 垃圾筒。~ **ice** (混杂着水的)碎冰。~ **television** = tabloid television. ~**-to-energy system** 垃圾能源发电厂。**-er** *n.* 捣毁者。

trash·er·y [ˈtræʃəri; ˋtræʃərɪ] *n.* 废物,垃圾,残屑。

trash·y [ˈtræʃi; ˋtræʃɪ] *a.* 垃圾似的;无价值的。

trass [træs; træs] *n.*【地】火山土;粗面凝灰岩。

trat·to·ria [ˌtrætəˈriːə; ͵trætəˋriə] *n.* 〔It.〕(意大利的)饮食店,饭馆。

trau·ma [ˈtrɔːmə; ˋtrɔmə, ˋtraʊmə] *n.* (*pl.* ~*ta*, ~*s*)【医】外伤,损伤,创伤;外伤症状[原因];【心】(精神)创伤。

trau·mat·ic [trɔːˈmætik; trɔˋmætɪk] **I** *a.* 外伤的,损伤的,创伤的;治外伤的。**II** *n.* 外伤药。

trau·mat·ism [ˈtrɔːmətizəm; ˋtrɔmə͵tɪzəm] *n.*【医】损伤(病),创伤(病);重外伤。

trau·ma·tize [ˈtraumətaiz; ˋtrɔmə͵taɪz] *vt.* 1.【医】使受外伤。2.【心】使受精神创伤。

trau·ma·tol·o·gy [ˌtrɔːməˈtɔlədʒi; ͵trɔməˋtɑlədʒɪ] *n.*【医】外伤学。

trav. = travel; traveller.

trav·ail [ˈtræveil; ˋtrævel, -vḷ] **I** *n.* 1. 辛苦,劳苦;苦工;劳动,工作。2. 分娩;阵痛。*in* ~ 在阵痛中。**II** *vi.* 辛苦工作;发生[感到]阵痛。

trave [treiv; trev] *n.* 〔现罕〕1. 横木,横梁;天花板格。2. 挂掌架,钉蹄铁架〔给牲畜钉铁掌用〕。

trav·el [ˈtrævl; ˋtrævḷ] **I** *vi.* (〔英〕**-ll-**) 1. 旅行〔尤指到外国或远地〕。2. 到外地推销。3. (火车等)行驶;行进;(声、光)传播;(机件等)走动,移动;依次看去,依次想去。4. 与…交往[常在一起]。5. (牲口)一面吃草一面向前走;〔美口〕飞快地走,飞跑;【篮球】带球走。—*vt.* 旅行;赶(畜群等),使移动。~ *second* [*third*] *class* 乘软[硬]席车旅行。~ *for a firm* 代表商行到外地去推销[出差]。*Light* ~*s faster than sound.* 光比声音传播得快。*We have* ~*led far from those days.* 从那时候到现在已经过了很多日子。*The car is* ~*ling.* 汽车飞快地跑着。*Her mind* ~*led over recent events.* 她反复想着最近发生的事情。*Keep* ~*ling!* 〔美口〕去! ~ ***along*** 〔口〕(快步)走! ~ ***it*** 步行,(徒步)旅行。~ ***on steel runners*** 乘雪橇旅行。~ ***out of the record*** 谈到题外(枝节问题)。~ ***through the air*** 乘飞机旅行。**II** *n.* 1. 〔常 *pl.*〕(特指远程的)旅行;旅行记,游记。2. 往来,交通。3.【机】行程,动程,冲程;(彗星、光、音等的)进行,移动,传播。*space* ~*s* 太空飞行[航行]。*go on a* ~ 旅行。~ *of valve*【机】阀行程。~*s in the blue* 沉思冥想。~ **agency** [~ **bureau**] 旅行社。~ **agent** (旅行社的)旅行代理人。~ **brochure** 旅行指南。~ **document** 旅游证件。~**-stained** [~**-soiled**] *a.* 旅行中弄脏的,风尘仆仆的。~**-worn** *a.* 满面风尘的;旅行中用旧的。

trav·el(l)ed [ˈtrævld; ˋtrævḷd] *a.* 旅行过许多地方的,旅行经验多的,见闻广的;旅客多的;【地】漂积的。

trav·el·(l)er [ˈtrævlə; ˋtrævlɚ] *n.* 1. 旅行者,旅客。2. 旅行推销员(= commercial ~)。3.【机】移动式起重机;【船】(铁杆或缆索上的)活环;带有活环的铁杆。4. 〔前用形容词修饰〕走得…的马[车(等)]。*This horse is a fast* ~. 这匹马是一匹走得快的马。***play the*** ~ ***upon*** (*sb.*) = ***tip*** (*sb.*) ***the*** ~ 骗(某人)。~**'s cheque** 旅行支票。~**'s joy**【植】葡萄叶铁线莲。~**'s tale** 旅行见闻谈;无稽之谈。~**'s-tree** 旅人蕉〔马达加斯加(Madagascar)产叶柄基部所贮汁水可供旅行者解渴〕。

trav·el·(l)ing [ˈtrævliŋ; ˋtrævlɪŋ, ˋtrævlɪŋ] **I** *a.* 旅行的,游历的;流动的,移动的。**II** *n.* 旅行,游历;流动(剧团);移动;滑走。~ *expenses* 旅费,盘费。~ **allowance** 旅行津贴。~ **companion** 旅伴。~ **crane** 横动起重机。~ **dress** 旅游服;休闲服。~ **library** 〔美〕流动图书馆。~ **stock**【铁路】车辆;〔澳〕赶送中的畜群。~ **trolley** [**crab**]【机】滑车。~**-wave tube**【无】行波管。

trav·e·log(ue) [ˈtrævəlɔg; ˋtrævə͵lɔg, -͵lɑg] *n.* (同时放映幻灯、电影的)旅行报告(会);旅行记录片。

trav·ers·a·ble [ˈtrævəːsəbl; ˋtrævɚsəbḷ, trəˋvɝ-] *a.* 能横过的,能越过的;可拒绝的;【法】可否认[反驳]的。

trav·ers·al [træˈvəːsl; ˋtrævɚsəl, trəˋvɚ-] *n*. **1.** 横过,横越,横断物,(横向)往返移动。**2.** (城墙,壕沟的)护墙,障碍物;【登山】Z字形攀登。

trav·erse [ˈtrævəːs; ˋtrævɚs, ˋtrævɚs, trəˋvɚs] **I** *vt*. **1.** 横越,横切,横贯;通过;横卧,横放。**2.** 〔罕〕(用东西)阻住;遮断(道路)。**3.** 跋涉,游历;经历。**4.** 〔喻〕详细考察,详论(问题);测定。**5.** 【木工】横刨,横削;【法】否认,反驳;【炮】转动(炮口)。—*vi*. 横越,横切,横断;转动,摆动;(马等)走离正道;【爬山】作Z字形爬登;【测】导线测量。**II** *n*. 横越(旅行);横断物;横木,隔板;阻碍,障碍(物);【建】横梁;(两建筑物之间的)通廊;【筑城】(有盖通路的)横墙;避弹障;【海】Z字形航行;【爬山】Z字形爬登(处);【数】横截线;【机】横动;【计算机】穿程;【法】否认,反驳,抗辩;【炮】炮口的转动。**III** *a*. 横断的,横越的,横贯的。~ *sailing* Z字形航行。

trav·ers·er [ˈtrævəsə; ˋtrævɚsɚ, trəˋvɚ-] *n*. 横越者,横过物;【法】否认者,反驳者,抗辩者;【铁路】转盘,转[移]车台。

trav·erse·table [ˈtrævəsteibl; ˋtrævɚstebl̩] *n*. 【铁路】转盘,转[移]车台;【海】经纬表,方位表。

trav·er·tin(e) [ˈtrævətin; ˋtrævɚtɪn] *n*. 【矿】拟灰石,石灰华,钙华。

trav·es·ty [ˈtrævisti; ˋtrævɪstɪ] **I** *n*. 滑稽模仿;谐摹诗[文];拙劣的做法[演出];牵强附会,曲解。**II** *vt*. 滑稽化;拙劣地表演。~ *sb.'s manner* 滑稽地摹仿某人的举止。~ **role**【剧】反串角色。

Tra·vis [ˈtrævis; ˋtrævɪs] *n*. 特拉维斯(姓氏,男子名)。

tra·vois [trəˈvɔi; trəˋvɔɪ] *n*. (*pl*. *-vois*, *-vois·es*) 马拉雪橇;狗拉雪橇;〔北美印第安人所用的一种雪橇〕(= travoise).

trawl [trɔːl; trɔl] **I** *n*. 拖网;〔美〕(主绳特长而分钩众多的)排钩(钓丝)(= ~-line)。**II** *vi*., *vt*. 拖网;用拖网捕鱼,从事拖网渔业。~**boat** 拖网渔船。~ **net** 拖网。

trawl·er [ˈtrɔːlə; ˋtrɔlɚ] *n*. 拖网渔船,拖网渔夫。

tray [trei; tre] *n*. 盘子,托盘;(博物标本等用的)浅盘,浅箱;(书桌上的)公文格;(皮箱内的)隔底匣;【无】发射箱[架];【火箭】发射架;〔美俚〕三;〔澳俚〕三便士硬币。*a developing* ~【摄】显影盘。*a tea* ~ 茶盘。*an ash* ~ 烟灰碟。*a pen* ~ 钢笔盒。~ **bone**〔美俚〕好极了的;极亲切的。~ **agriculture** = hydroponics. ~ **lunch(eon)** 盘装午餐。~ **table** (可折拢的)托盘桌。

tray·ful [ˈtreiful; ˋtrefʊl] *n*. 满盘,一盘子。

T.R.C. = Thames Rowing Club〔英〕泰晤士河划船俱乐部。

Tr.Co = Trust Company〔美〕信托公司。

treach·er·ous [ˈtretʃərəs; ˋtrɛtʃərəs] *a*. 叛逆的,背叛的,不忠的(*to*);奸诈的,靠不住的。*a* ~ *act* 叛逆行为。~ *weather* 靠不住的天气。~ *ice* (看起来坚固而)踏上去会破裂的冰。*a* ~ *horse* 外表好看的劣马。*a* ~ *smile* 奸笑。~ *memory* 不可靠的记忆。**-ly** *ad*. **-ness** *n*.

treach·er·y [ˈtretʃəri; ˋtrɛtʃərɪ] *n*. 叛逆,谋反,反叛,变节,不忠,背信。

trea·cle [ˈtriːkl; ˋtrikl̩] *n*. 糖浆,糖蜜(=〔美〕molasses);解毒剂;妙药。~ **mustard**【植】桂竹香糖芥。~ **sleep**〔口〕酣睡。

trea·cly [ˈtriːkli; ˋtriklɪ] *a*. 糖蜜似的;糖蜜般甜的;甜蜜的。

tread [tred; trɛd] **I** *vi*. (*trod* [trɔd; trɑd], 〔古〕*trode*; *trodden* [ˈtrɔdn; ˋtrɑdn̩], *trod*) **1.** 踩,踏;走。**2.** 踩碎,踏扁;蹂躏(*on*; *upon*)。**3.** (雄鸟)交尾(*with*)。—*vt*. **1.** 踩,踏;在…上走;踩实,踩出(道路等);践踏,蹂躏。**2.** (雄鸟)交尾。**3.** 跳。~ *grapes* 踩葡萄(榨汁)。~ *wine* 踩取葡萄汁做酒。~ *a measure* (合着音乐)跳一个舞。~ ***away*** 弄错,失败。~ ***down*** 踩结实;踩碎,践踏;压制(感情等);压服。~ ***in*** 用脚把…踩入(地里)。~ ***in sb.'s steps*** 仿效某人;跟某人跑。~ ***lightly*** [***warily***] 轻轻走;小心处理。~ ***on sb.'s corns*** [***toes***] 踩痛某人脚趾;〔喻〕伤人感情;得罪某人。~ ***on air*** 欢天喜地。~ (***as***) ***on eggs*** 如履薄冰。~ ***on sb.'s heels*** 踩着某人鞋后跟;跟着某人到来。~ ***on one's own tail*** 踩自己尾巴;〔喻〕想打人反而打伤自己。~ ***on the gas*** 踏动汽车的加速器;加速,赶紧。~ ***on the heels of*** (人)接踵而至;(事件)接连发生。~ ***on the neck of*** 骑在…头上;蹂躏;压迫。~ ***one's shoe away*** (妇女)失去节操,堕落。~ ***out*** 踩灭(火等);扑灭(叛乱等);踩榨(葡萄汁等);踩出(麦等的)谷粒。~ ***shoe leather*** = ~ ***this earth*** 活着。~ ***the boards*** [***stage***] 登上舞台,做演员。~ ***the deck*** 上船,做水手。~ ***the ground*** 走路,散步。~ ***the paths of exile*** 亡命。~ ***under foot*** 践踏,蹂躏。~ ***water*** 踩水,立泳;〔喻〕原地踏步,停滞不再前进。**II** *n*. **1.** 踩,踏,踏行,步行;步态;脚步声;(雄鸟)交尾。**2.** 【建】(楼梯的)踏板,梯级;级宽;【筑城】(踏垛的)垛顶;【机】轮距[左右轮距离];轮(触轨)面,轮底,轨顶;轨条接触轮底的部分;(车胎的)花纹。**3.** (鞋、雪车滑行部的)底。**4.** 自行车两踏板间的距离;【兽医】(蹄的)践伤;【生】卵的胚点,卵黄系带。*approach with cautious* ~ 轻轻走近。~**-board** (楼梯的)踏板。~**-mill** (从前罚囚犯踩踏的)踏车;单调的工作。~**wheel** 踏车。

trea·dle [ˈtredl; ˋtrɛdl̩] **I** *n*. (纺车等的)踏板(= ~ pedal)。**II** *vi*., *vt*. 踩踏板,踏动踏板;踩踏板开动(缝纫机等)。

Treas. = Treasurer; Treasury.

trea·son [ˈtriːzn; ˋtrizn̩] *n*. 谋反,叛逆(罪),叛国罪;不忠,背信(*to*)。~ **felony**〔英〕【法】叛逆罪。

trea·son·a·ble, trea·son·ous [ˈtriːznəbl, -əs; ˋtriznəbl̩, -əs] *a*. 谋反的,叛逆的,卖国的,不忠的。

treas·ure [ˈtreʒə; ˋtrɛʒɚ] **I** *n*. **1.** 财富,金银财宝,珍宝;珍藏,宝藏。**2.** 最亲爱的人,爱儿,宝贝;宝贵的人材。*a* ~ *day*〔剧俚〕发薪日。*buried* ~ 地财。*a* ~ *room* (船等的)贵重物品保管室。*T- State*〔美〕Montana州的别名。~*s of art* = *art* ~*s* 珍贵美术品[名画、名雕刻等]。*My* ~. 〔尤指呼唤孩子〕宝贝,心肝儿。***spend blood and*** ~ 牺牲生命财产。**II** *vt*. 当做珍宝保存,珍藏;珍重;爱护,爱惜;热爱;铭记(*up*)。~ *up stamps* 集邮。~ **house** 宝库,宝藏。~ **hunt** 寻找藏物游戏。~ **trove**【法】地财〔窖藏金银等〕。

trea·sur·er [ˈtreʒərə; ˋtrɛʒərɚ] *n*. 司库,财务员,出纳员;(美)财政部出纳局长。*Lord High T-* (英国从前的)财政大臣。*T- of the Household* 英国皇室财务主管。**-ship** *n*. 财务员、出纳等的职位。

treas·ur·y [ˈtreʒəri; ˋtrɛʒərɪ] *n*. **1.** 宝库,宝藏。**2.** 金库;〔the T-〕英国财政部;国库;国库券,公债券。**3.** 贮藏所,库房。**4.** 宝典,宝鉴;知识宝库〔指人或书籍〕。**5.** 〔剧、俚〕剧团团员的周薪。**T- Bench** (英国下院议长右边的)内阁阁员席。~ **bill** (美国或英国的)短期国库券。**T- Board** = ***Lords*** (***Commissioners***) ***of the T-***〔英〕财政委员会。~ **bond** (美国的)长期国库券。~ **certificate** (美国的)中期国库券。**T- Department**〔美〕财政部。~ **note**〔英〕代替一镑(或十先令)金币的纸币;〔美〕中期国库券。~ **solicitor**【法】无遗嘱遗产管理人。~ **stock**【商】未发行股份。**T- warrant** 国库支付命令书。

treat [triːt; trit] **I** *vt*. **1.** 对待,待遇;处置;处理。**2.** 款待,请(客)(*to*);招待。**3.** 探讨,论述。**4.** 【化,医】处理(药品等);涂(药等);医治,治疗。—*vi*. 款待,请客;商议,谈判,交涉,协商(*with*);讨论(*of*; *upon*)。*I'll* ~ *you to a bottle of beer*. 我请你喝一瓶啤酒。~ *a disease* 治病。*a* ~*ing plant* 净化(处理)设备。*The book* ~*s of this question*. 这本书是讨论这个问题的。*Whose turn is it to* ~ *next?* 下次该谁请客? ~ ***oneself to*** 舍得(吃、穿等)。**II** *n*. 款待,请客;轮到请客的人;〔口〕愉快的事情,快乐的事情;(为学生举办的)娱乐[集会,远足等]。*It is my* ~ *now*. 这次轮到我请客了。***get on a fair*** ~ 〔英俚〕进步很快。***stand*** ~ 请客,作

T

东。-er *n*. 谈判者;用化学药品处理物品者;【化】处理器,提纯器,精制器。

trea·tise [ˈtriːtiz, -tis; ˋtritɪs] *n*. 论文(*on*)。

treat·ment [ˈtriːtmənt; ˋtritmənt] *n*. 待遇;作业;处理,处置;讨论,论述;【医】治疗,疗法;(种子的)消毒(处理)。*preferential* ~ 优待。*hard* ~ 虐待。*heat* ~ 热处理。*mechanical* ~ 机械加工。*water* ~ 水的净化。***under medical*** ~ 治疗中。

trea·ty [ˈtriːti; ˋtritɪ] *n*. (国家间的)条约,协定;(个人间的)约定;协商,谈判,交涉。***in*** ~ ***with*** 和…交涉中。~ **port** (条约规定的)通商口岸。~ **powers** 缔约各国。

tre·ble [ˈtrebl; ˋtrɛbl̩] I *a*., *n*. 三倍(的),三重(的);【乐】最高音部(的);尖锐刺耳(的);高音(的)。II *vt*., *vi*. (使)成为三倍,增加两倍。~ **clef**【乐】高音符号;高音部。

tre·bly [ˈtrebli; ˋtrɛblɪ] *ad*. 三倍地,三重地。

treb·u·chet [ˈtrebjuʃei, -ʃet; ˋtrɛbjuˏʃe, -ʃet] *n*. 抛石机〔中古兵器〕;分析天平;(捕小鸟等的)捕机,活套儿。

treb·uck·et [ˈtrebjukit; ˋtrɛbjukɪt] *n*. = trebuchet.

tre·cen·tist [treiˈtʃentist; treˋtʃɛntɪst] *n*. 14 世纪的意大利文学家[美术家];14 世纪意大利文艺模仿者[研究者]。

tre·cen·to [treiˈtʃentəu; treˋtʃɛnto] *n*. 〔It.〕(意大利文艺的)14 世纪。

tre·chom·e·tre [triˈkɔmitə; triˋkɑmətɚ] *n*. 车程计,轮转计。

Tree [triː; tri] *n*. 特里〔姓氏〕。

tree [triː; tri] I *n*. 1. 树〔主要指乔木,也可指较大的灌木〕。★玫瑰可以称为 bush, 也可以称为 tree. 2. 木料,木材;木构件;〔古〕绞首台;〔the ~〕(钉死耶稣的)十字架;鞋楦。3. 树形(物),世系图,家系 (= family ~);【数】树(形);【化】树状晶体。*a banana* ~ 香蕉树。*an axle-*~ 心棒,轴料。*a boot-*~ 靴楦[型]。*a saddle-*~ 鞍架。***at the top of the*** ~ 在最高地位。~ ***of Buddha*** 菩提树。~ ***of heaven*** 臭椿。~ ***of knowledge*** (***of good and evil***)【圣】知道善恶的树,智慧之树。~ ***of life*** 生命之树,生命力的源泉;【植】金钟柏。***up a*** ~〔口〕进退两难,不知所措。II *vt*. 赶(猎兽等)上树躲避;〔口〕使处于困境;穷追;把鞋型[楦]插入(鞋内)。~ **agate**【矿】苔纹玛瑙。~**bank** 树籽库。~ **calf** (做书面用的)木纹小牛皮。~ **creeper**【鸟】旋木雀。~ **ear** 木耳。~ **fern**【植】桫椤。~ **frog**【动】雨蛙。~ **heath**【植】欧石南。~ **hopper**【动】角蝉。~ **house** 造在树上的小屋。~ **kangaroo**【动】树袋鼠。~ **lawn** 街心绿化带。~**less** *a*. 无树的。~ **line** 树木线。~ **milk** 树乳〔可饮用〕。~**nail** 木钉[栓]。~ **peony**【植】牡丹。~ **percent** 成苗率。~ **ring** 年轮。~ **shears** 修枝剪。~ **shrew**【动】树鼩。~ **squirrel**【动】松鼠(属)。~ **surgery** 树外科学。~ **toad**【动】雨蛙。~**top** 树顶,树梢。

treed [triːd; trid] *a*. 育林的,植树的。

tref [treif; tref] *a*. 【犹太教】(根据饮食律法)不干净的,不可食的。

tre·foil [ˈtrefɔil, ˈtriːf-; ˋtrifɔɪl] *n*. 【植】三叶草,车轴草;三叶植物;【建】三叶形[饰]。*yellow* ~【植】天兰。~ *knot* 三叶结。

tre·ha·lose [ˈtriːhəˌləus, triˈhɑːləus; ˋtriheˏlos] *n*. 【化】海藻糖。

treil·lage [ˈtreilidʒ; ˋtrelɪdʒ] *n*. 葡萄架;【建】格构。

trek [trek; trɛk] I *vi*. (*-kk-*)〔南非英语〕(坐牛车)旅行;(坐牛车)(集体)迁移;(牛)拉货车;〔口〕旅行〔尤指艰苦步行〕。— *vt*. (牛)拉(车)。II *n*. 〔南非英语〕牛车旅行;集体迁移;牛车一段旅程;〔口〕旅行,跋涉,步行。-**ker** *n*.

trek·kie [ˈtreki; ˋtrɛkɪ] *n*. (科幻片)《星球旅行》影迷。

trel·lis [ˈtrelis; ˋtrɛlɪs] I *n*. 格子;格子墙[篱];格子凉亭;(葡萄等的)棚架;【建】格(子结)构。II *vt*. 装格子(在窗上);用棚架支撑。~**work** 格子;格子结构。

trem·a·tode [ˈtreməˌtəud, ˈtriːmə-; ˋtrɛməˏtod, ˋtrimə-] I *n*. 【动】吸虫网(*Trematoda*)动物。II *a*. 吸虫网的。

trem·ble [ˈtrembl; ˋtrɛmbl̩] I *vi*. 1. 发抖,打颤;(地等)震动;(树叶等)摇晃;(声音)震颤。2. (因恐怖、忧虑等)战栗,焦虑,担心(*at*; *for*)。— *vt*. 使发抖,使战栗,使震动。*I* ~ *at the thought*. 我一想到这个就发抖。*I* ~ *for his safety*. 我非常担心他的安全。*Hear and* ~! 听了别害怕(现在要讲啦)! 好,你记着(我会报复你的)! ~ ***in one's shoes*** 害怕得发抖。~ ***in the balance*** 处于危急[紧要]关头。~ ***out*** 颤抖着说。II *n*. 发抖,震颤,战栗;〔*pl*.〕(牛马的)中毒性震颤病;(人饮用震颤病牛的乳而起的)乳毒病。(***all***) ***in a*** ~ = ***all of a*** ~ = ***on the*** ~〔口〕浑身颤抖着。

trem·bler [ˈtremblə; ˋtrɛmblɚ] *n*. 发抖的人,震颤的东西;【电】自动震动器;电铃;继续器,蜂鸣器。

trem·bling [ˈtrembliŋ; ˋtrɛmblɪŋ] I *n*. 发抖,震颤,战栗;【医】羊虱毒病。***in fear and*** ~ 浑身颤抖着。II *a*. 发抖的,震颤的,战栗的;颤抖的。~ **poplar**【植】欧洲山杨。-**ly** *ad*.

trem·bly [ˈtrembli; ˋtrɛmblɪ] *a*. 〔口〕震颤的,颤抖的。

tre·men·dous [triˈmendəs; trɪˋmɛndəs] I *a*. 可怕的,惊人的;〔口〕巨大的;〔俚〕极好的,非常巧妙的(手段等)。*It means a* ~ *lot to him*. 那对他非常重要。II *ad*. 〔俚〕极,非常。*a* ~ *long way* 一段非常远的路程。-**ly** *ad*. -**ness** *n*.

trem·o·lan·do [treməˈlɑːndəu; ˏtremoˋlɑndo] *ad*. 〔It.〕【乐】用颤音,用碎音。

trem·o·lite [ˈtreməˌlait; ˋtrɛməˏlaɪt] *n*. 【矿】透闪石。

trem·o·lo [ˈtreməlau; ˋtrɛməˏlo] *n*. 〔It.〕【乐】碎音,颤声;风琴的颤音装置。

trem·or [ˈtremə; ˋtrɛmɚ] *n*. 震颤;战栗,发抖;惊恐;颤音;震动,地震。-**ous** *a*.

trem·u·lant [ˈtremjulənt; ˋtrɛmjələnt] *a*. = tremulous.

trem·u·lous [ˈtremjuləs; ˋtrɛmjələs] *a*. 发抖的,颤抖的;吓得打颤的,胆小的;好像发抖一样的(快乐等);颤抖着写的;神经过敏的。-**ly** *ad*. -**ness** *n*.

tre·nail [ˈtriːneil, ˈtrenl; ˋtriˏnel, ˋtrɛnl̩, ˋtrʌnl̩] *n*. = treenail.

Trench [trentʃ; trɛntʃ] *n*. 特伦奇〔姓氏〕。

trench [trentʃ; trɛntʃ] I *vt*. 掘沟,开畦沟;掘翻(田地),深耕;【军】掘壕沟,用战壕防守;【木工】作沟槽;切断,切开。— *vi*. 【军】挖战壕,掘壕前进(*down*; *along*);切断;侵犯,侵占(权利、土地等)(*on*; *upon*);接近(*on*; *upon*)。II *n*. 沟,渠;【军】战壕,壕沟;【林】防火线。*a cover* ~ 掩蔽壕。*a fire* ~ 散兵壕。***mount the ~es*** 进战壕布防。***open the ~es*** 掘战壕,开沟。***relieve the ~es*** 和战壕里的兵换班。***search the ~es*** (用开花弹等)攻击战壕 ~ **back**【医】战壕背痛。~ **cart** 战壕手推车。~ **cavalier**【筑城】斜堤上造的高胸墙。~ **coat** 战壕雨衣。~ **digger** 开沟机。~ **fever**【医】战壕热。~ **foot** 战壕足痛。~ **gun** [**mortar**] 迫击炮。~ **knife**【军】(白刃战用)双刃短刀。~ **mouth**【医】战壕口炎。~ **warfare** 阵地战。

trench·ant [ˈtrentʃənt; ˋtrɛntʃənt] *a*. 1. 〔古诗〕锐利的,犀利的,锋利的。2. (话等)尖锐的,有力的;严厉的,激烈的。3. 清晰的,鲜明的(轮廓等)。-**ly** *ad*. -**chan·cy** *n*.

trench·er [ˈtrentʃə; ˋtrɛntʃɚ] *n*. 1. 掘沟人;挖战壕的士兵;开沟机。2. 〔古〕木盘,木碟;(餐桌上切面包用的)垫板;〔古、喻〕食物;饮食,饮食之乐。~ *companions* 酒肉朋友。~ **cap** (大学的)方帽。~-**fed** *a*. (猎人自己家里)亲自饲养的(猎狗)。~**man** 食者(*a good* [*poor*] ~-*man* 食量大[小]的人);食客,寄食者。

trend [trend; trɛnd] I *n*. (路、河、海岸、山脉等的)走向;方向,方位;倾向,趋势,动向。*the* ~ *of events* 形势。II *vi*. 走向,伸向,转向,侧向;倾向,趋向(*towards*)。-**y** *a*. 最流行[时髦]的;合乎潮流的。

Trent [trent; trɛnt] ***n***. 特伦特〔姓氏,男子名〕。

tren·tal [ˈtrentl; ˋtrɛntl̩] ***n***. 【天主】(给死者做的)三十日连续弥撒。

tre·pan[1] [triˈpæn; trɪˋpæn] **I** ***n***. 【医】环钻,环锯〔新式的叫 trephine〕;凿井器,【矿】钻(矿)机。**II** ***vt***. (**-nn-**) 【医】用环锯[钻](在颅骨上)穿孔;开孔,(在毛刷把上)打眼;(从金属板等上)切出圆盘形物;钻出(岩心)。

tre·pan[2] [triˈpæn; trɪˋpæn] ***vt***. (**-nn-**) 诱捕;诱人圈套,设计诱陷,引诱 (*into*; *from*)。

trep·a·na·tion [ˌtrepəˈneiʃən; ˏtrɛpəˋneʃən] ***n***. 【医】环钻术,环锯术。

tre·pang [triˈpæŋ; trɪˋpæŋ] ***n***. 【动】海参。

treph·i·na·tion [ˌtrefiˈneiʃən; ˏtrɛfəˋneʃən] ***n***. 【医】环钻术,环锯法。

tre·phine [triˈfiːn, -ˈfain; trɪˋfaɪn, -ˋfin] **I** ***n***. 【医】环钻,环锯。**II** ***vt***. 用环钻(在颅骨上)施手术[开圆孔]。

trep·i·da·tion [trepiˈdeiʃən; ˏtrɛpəˋdeʃən] ***n***. (手足的)发抖,颤抖,痉挛;黄道的震动;战栗,恐怖;(心的)动摇。

trep·o·ne·ma [ˌtrepəˈniːmə; ˏtrɛpəˋnimə] ***n***. (*pl*. ***-mas***, ***-ma·ta*** [-mətə; -mətə]) 【微】回线属,密旋体属。**-l**, **-tous** [-mətəs; -mətəs] ***a***.

tres·pass [ˈtrespəs; ˋtrɛspəs] **I** ***n***. 侵入;【体】非法侵入[犯];侵入(私人)房屋[土地];侵害诉讼;(宗教道德上的)干犯,罪过;叨扰,打扰 (*on*; *upon*)。*One* ~ *more I must make on your patience*. 还有一件事要叨扰。*timber* ~ 木材盗伐。**II** ***vi***. **1**. 侵占,侵入(土地等);侵犯,侵害(权利等)(*on*; *upon*);〔古〕干犯天理[道];违犯,犯罪 (*against*)。**2**. 〔客气话〕叨扰,打扰,妨碍 (*on*; *upon*). **3**. 〔古〕罪。— ***vt***. 违犯;破坏。*I shall* ~ *on your hospitality*. 我要来叨扰你了。*May I* ~ *on you for that book?* 请你拿[借]那本书给我好吗? **-er** ***n***. trespass 的人 (*Trespassers will be prosecuted*. (告白)侵入者扭交法办)。

tress [tres; trɛs] **I** ***n***. (女人的)一束长发,卷发;辫子;〔*pl*.〕〔诗谑〕(女人的)松散的长发;〔罕〕花束。**II** ***vt***. 〔常用 *p.p*.〕卷(头发),梳成一束,打成辫子。

-tress *comb. f*. 加在名词之后表示阴性: *waitress*.

tressed [trest; trɛst] ***a***. 梳[结]成发髻的,梳[结]成辫子的。

tressel [ˈtresl; ˋtrɛsl̩] ***n***. = trestle.

tressy [ˈtresi; ˋtrɛsɪ] ***a***. (***-i·er***; ***-iest***) 头发松散的。

tres·tle [ˈtresl; ˋtrɛsl] ***n***. 支架;台架;【建】高架桥,栈桥〔又叫 ~ bridge〕;栈架。~**-core** 【机】转心架。~ **table** 搁板桌。~**tree** 【船】桅顶纵桁。~**work** 栈架结构;栈桥。

tret [tret; trɛt] ***n***. 【商】(为弥补运输时损耗而给买主每百磅加四磅的)饶头,添头。

Tre·vel·yan [triˈviljən, triˈveljən; trɪˋvɛljən, -ˋvɪl-] ***n***. 特里维廉〔姓氏〕。

trevet ***n***. = trivet.

trews [truːz; truz] ***n***. 〔*pl*.〕〔Scot.〕紧身格子呢裤。

T-rex [ˈtiːˈreks; ˋtiˋrɛks] ***n***. "霸王龙"〔美国电影《侏罗纪公园》中一只凶猛的恐龙〕。

trey [trei; tre] ***n***. (牌,骰子上的)三点;三点的纸[骨]牌;〔美运〕三;〔美俚〕三块钱。

T.R.H., **TRH** = Their Royal Highnesses (对王族的尊称)殿下〔间接提及一人以上时用〕。

tri- *comb. f*. 三,三重,三倍。

tri·a·ble [ˈtraiəbl; ˋtraɪəbl̩] ***a***. 可试的,可试验的;【法】应审问的,应审判的。**-ness** ***n***.

tri·ac [ˈtraiæk; ˋtraɪæk] ***n***. 【电子学】三端双向可控矽开关元件。

tri·ac·e·tate [traiˈæsiˌteit; traɪˋæsəˏtet] ***n***. 【化】三醋酸酯,甘油三酸酯。

tri·ac·id [traiˈæsid; traɪˋæsɪd] ***a***. 【化】**1**. 三(酸)价的。**2**. 三元酸。

tri·ad [ˈtraiəd; ˋtraɪæd, -əd] ***n***. 三人一组,三个一组,三种事物[思想]的组合,三合一;【乐】三和弦;【植】三分体,三分细胞;【化】三价原子,三价基;(古 Wales 诗形的)三组配合;〔美〕(战略核力量的)三元体系〔由陆基导弹、潜艇发射的导弹和远程巡航轰炸机三部分组成〕。**-ic** ***a***.

tri·age [triˈɑːʒ; ˋtraɪɪdʒ] ***n***. 【医】治疗类选法〔根据紧迫性和救活的可能性等在战场上决定哪些人优先治疗的方法〕。

tri·al[1] [ˈtraiəl; ˋtraɪəl] ***n***. **1**. (好坏、性能等的)试验;(人或物的)试用;试车。**2**. 【运】选拔赛,预赛。**3**. 考验,磨难,困难,患难;讨厌的人[东西];【法】审问;审判。*a firing* ~ 【火箭】起动试验,发射试验。*a* ~ *and error method* 反复试验法。*a* ~ *balloon* 风向试探气球;舆论[人心]的试探。*a* ~ *match* 【运】预赛。~*s of life* 生活的磨炼。*a criminal* ~ 刑事审判。*the first* ~ 初审。*a new* ~ 复审。*an open* ~ = *a public* ~ 公审。**bring** (*sb*.) **to** ~ 告发,检举;交付审问。**by way of** ~ 试试。**give a** ~ 试用。**make** (**a**) ~ **of** 试,试验。**make the** ~ 试一试,费一点工夫;努力。**on** ~ 试验性质,暂时;试验后,看试验的结果(采用等);在受审 (*take* [*have*, *employ*] *sb*. [*sth*.] *on* ~ 试用某人[物])。**put** (*sb*.) **to** ~ = bring (sb.) to ~ . **run a** ~ 试开。**stand one's** ~ = **take** [**undergo**] **one's** ~ 受审。~ **of the pyx** 硬币样品检查。~ **and error** 【心】尝试—错误,试错法;反复试验。~ **balance** 【会计】试算表。~ **balloon** **1**. 测风气球。**2**. 〔喻〕试探气球。~ **boring** 试钻;【机】钻验。~ **court** 初审法庭。~ **cruise** 试航。~ **eights** 赛艇预选选手。~ **flight** 试飞。~ **horse** 同强手对阵的练习对手。~ **jury** 【法】小陪审团 (= petit jury)。~ **run** [**trip**] 试运转,试车[航]。~ **test** 探索性试验。

tri·al[2] [ˈtraiəl; ˋtraɪəl] ***a***. = trinal.

tri·an·gle [ˈtraiæŋgl; ˋtraɪˏæŋgl̩] ***n***. 【几】三角形;三角形的东西;三角板;【乐】三角铁;〔T-〕【天】三角座;〔常 *pl*.〕【军】(英国从前的)三戟刑具;【船】三圆材起重机;三角关系。*an equilateral* [*isosceles*] ~ 等边[等腰]三角形。*obtuse* ~ 钝角三角形。*scalene* ~ 不规则三角形。

tri·an·gu·lar [traiˈæŋgjulə; traɪˋæŋgjələ] ***a***. 三角(形)的;由三个部分构成的,三重的;三方面的(斗争等);三国间的(条约等)。~ *compasses* 三脚规。~ *numbers* 【数】三角数。~ *crap* 【动】三角蟹。*a* ~ *situation* 三角关系。*a* ~ *treaty* 三国条约。

tri·an·gu·late **I** [traiˈæŋgjuleit; traɪˋæŋgjəˏlet] ***vt***. 使成[分成]三角形;作三角测量;弄成三角(形)。**II** [-lit; -let] ***a***. 三角形的;由三角形形成的,有三角形花样的。

tri·an·gu·la·tion [traiˌæŋgjuˈleiʃən; ˏtraɪæŋgjəˋleʃən, traɪˏæŋ-] ***n***. 三角测量;三角部分。*a net of* ~ 三角网。

tri·arch·y [ˈtraiɑːki; ˋtraɪɑrkɪ] ***n***. 三头政治[国家]。

Tri·as [ˈtraiəs; ˋtraɪəs] ***n***., ***a***. 【地】三叠纪[系](的)。

Tri·as·sic [traiˈæsik; traɪˋæsɪk] **I** ***a***. 【地】三叠纪[系]的 **II** ***n***. 三叠纪[系] (= ~ Period [System])。

tri·at·ic [traiˈætik; trɑɪˋætɪk] ***a***. 由三部形成的。~ *stay* 【海】(两桅头间的)水平支索,桅间索。

tri·a·tom·ic [traiəˈtɔmik; ˏtraɪəˋtɑmɪk] ***a***. 【化】含三原子的;三代的;三羟(基)的。~ *acid* 三价酸。~ *alcohol* 三元醇。~ *molecule* 三原子分子。

tri·ax·i·al [traiˈæksiəl; traɪˋæksɪəl] ***n***. 有三轴的。

tri·a·zine [ˈtraiəˌziːn, -zin, traiˈæziːn; ˋtraɪəˏzin, -zɪn, traɪˋæzin] ***n***. 【化】三嗪三氮杂萘。

tri·a·zole [ˈtraiəˌzəul, traiˈæzəul; ˋtraɪəˏzol, traɪˋæzol] ***n***. 【化】三唑。

trib·a·dism [ˈtribədizəm; ˋtrɪbədɪzm̩] ***n***. 女子同性恋。

trib·al [ˈtraibəl; ˋtraɪbl̩] ***a***. 部落的,部族的。

trib·al·ism [ˈtraibəlizəm; ˋtraɪbl̩ɪzm] ***n***. **1**. 部族制;部族文化,部族组织[生活]。**2**. 对宗族[党派]的忠诚。**-ist** ***a***.

tri·bas·ic [traiˈbeisik; traɪˋbesɪk] ***a***. 【化】三碱(价)的,三元的,三代的。

tribe [traib; traɪb] ***n***. 部落,部族;种族;〔蔑〕一帮,一伙;家族;【古罗马】三部族(后为三十五部族)之一;【生】族;

群,一群;〔*pl.*〕许多;〔美俚〕棒球队。*the dog* ~ 犬族 *Mongol* ~*s* 蒙古各部族。*the scribbling* ~〔口〕文士们。*the whole* ~ *of alarmists* 那批大惊小怪的家伙。

tribes·man [ˈtraibzmən; ˋtraɪbzmən] ***n.*** 部族(男)成员;同族人。

tribes·wom·an [ˈtraibzˌwumən; ˋtraɪbzˏwʊmən] ***n.*** 部族女成员。

trib·let [ˈtriblit; ˋtrɪblɪt] ***n.***【机】心轴,心棒(制管、环、螺帽等用)。

tri·bo·e·lec·tric·i·ty [ˌtraibəuiˌlekˈtrisiti; ˏtrɪboɪˏlɛk-ˋtrɪsətɪ, ˏtraɪ-, -ˏilak-] ***n.***【物】摩擦电。**-elec·tric** ***a.***

tri·bol·o·gy [traiˈbɔlədʒi; traɪˋbɑlədʒɪ] ***n.*** 摩损学。

tri·bo·lu·mi·nes·cence [ˌtraibəuˌlumiˈnesns; ˏtrɪbo-ˏljuməˋnɛsn̩s, ˏtraɪ-] ***n.*** 摩擦发光。**-mi·nes·cent** ***a.***

tri·bom·e·ter [traiˈbɔmitə, tri-; traɪˋbɑmətɚ] ***n.***【物】摩擦计。

tri·bo·phys·ic [ˌtraibəuˈfiziks; ˏtraɪboˋfɪzɪks] ***n.***〔*pl.*〕〔单复数同〕摩擦物理学。

trib·rach [ˈtribræk; ˋtraɪbræk, ˋtrɪb-] ***n.***【韵】三短节音步(⏑⏑⏑)。

tri·bro·mide [traiˈbrəumaid; traɪˋbromaɪd] ***n.***【化】三溴化合物。

tri·bro·mo·eth·a·nol [traiˌbrəuməuˈeθəˌnəul, -ˌnɔːl; traɪˏbroməˋɛθəˏnol, -ˏnɑl] ***n.***【化】三溴化合物。

trib·u·la·tion [ˌtribjuˈleiʃən; ˏtrɪbjəˋleʃən] ***n.*** 苦难,磨难,灾难;艰辛,困苦。

tri·bu·nal [triˈbjuːnl, trai-; trɪˋbjunl, traɪ-] ***n.*** **1.** 审判员席,法官席;法庭。**2.** 制裁,裁判;〔英〕(第一次大战中的)兵役免除审查局。*a military* ~ 军事法庭。*the Hague T-* 海牙国际法庭。*before the* ~ *of public opinion* 在舆论制裁下。

trib·u·na·r·y [ˈtribjunəri; ˋtrɪbjʊˏnɛrɪ, -nərɪ] ***a.*** (古罗马)护民官的。

trib·u·nate [ˈtribjunit; ˋtrɪbjənɪt, -ˏnet] ***n.*** (古罗马)护民官的职位。

trib·une[1] [ˈtribjuːn; ˋtrɪbjun] ***n.*** **1.**【古罗马】护民官〔由平民中选出,原为二名,后增至十名〕;军团司令官〔共六名,一年中每名轮流指挥两个月〕。**2.** 民众领袖;民众的保护人。**-ship** ***n*** 护民官职位[任期]。

trib·une[2] [ˈtribjuːn; ˋtrɪbjun] ***n.*** 讲坛;论坛;〔T-〕〔作报刊名称用〕《论坛报》;(大教堂中的)主教席;(古罗马公会堂的)执政官席位;(赛马场的)看台。

trib·u·ta·ry [ˈtribjutəri; ˋtrɪbjəˏtɛrɪ] **I** ***a.*** 纳贡的;从属的,附庸的(国等);补助的,进贡的;支流的。**II** ***n.*** 纳贡者;属国,附庸国;支流。~ *states* 属国。~ *tears at the tomb* 在坟墓前流下来的眼泪。*a* ~ *river* 支流。

trib·ute [ˈtribjuːt; ˋtrɪbjut] ***n.*** 贡物[金],贡品;纳贡义务[地位];勒索款;赠品,礼物;赞辞,颂辞;〔英〕【采】(给矿工的)份子。*a silent* ~ 默哀。*floral* ~*s* 献花;(丧礼的)供花。*a* ~ *of praise* 赞辞。~ *silk* (中国的)贡缎。***lay a*** ~ ***on***... = ***lay***... ***under*** ~ 使进贡。***pay (a) (high)*** ~ ***to*** 赞颂。***pay the last*** ~ ***to*** 向…最后告别。***pay warm*** ~ ***to*** 热烈赞扬。***the*** ~ ***of a tear*** 一把同情的眼泪。~ ***to sb.'s memory*** 悼辞。***work on*** ~ = ***work the*** ~ ***system*** 按照交纳一定贡物的办法工作。

Tri·cap [ˈtraikæp; ˋtraɪkæp]〔美〕三能师〔美国 70 年代的一种陆军师建制,其坦克、机械化步兵和机动空中支持力量相互配合作战〕。

tri·car [ˈtraikɑː; ˋtraɪˏkɑr] ***n.*** 三轮摩托车。

tri·car·box·yl·ic [traiˌkɑːbɔkˈsilik; traɪˏkɑrbɑkˋsɪlɪk] ***a.***【生化】三羧基(的)。~ **acid**【化】三羧酸。~ **acid cycle**【生化】三羧酸循环。

tri·car·pel·lar·y [traiˈkɑːpiləri; traɪˋkɑrpəˏlɛrɪ] ***a.***【植】三心皮的;三果片的。

trice[1] [trais; traɪs] ***vt.***【海】(用绳索或绞辘)吊起;拉起并捆住(*up*)。

trice[2] [trais; traɪs] ***n.*** 瞬间,顷刻。***in a*** ~ 转瞬间。

tricel [ˈtrisl; ˋtrɪsl̩] ***n.***【纺】特列赛尔〔三醋酯纤维织物,商标名〕。

tri·cen·te·na·ry [traisenˈtiːnəri; traɪˋsɛntɪˏnɛrɪ] ***a.***, ***n.*** = tercentenary.

tri·cen·ten·ni·al [ˌtraisenˈteniəl; ˏtraɪsɛnˋtɛnɪəl] **I** ***a.*** **1.** 三百年才出现一次的。**2.** 延续三百年的。**II** ***n.*** 三百周年纪念日,三百周年的庆祝活动。

tri·ceps [ˈtraiseps; ˋtraɪsɛps] ***n.***【解】三头肌。

tri·cer·a·tops [traiˈserəˌtɔps; traɪˋsɛrəˏtɑps] ***n.***【古生】三觭龙。

-trices, -trix 的复数。

trich- *comb. f.* = tricho-.

trich·i [ˈtriki; ˋtrɪkɪ] ***n.***〔口〕= trichinopoli.

tri·chi·a·sis [triˈkaiəsis; trɪˋkaɪəsɪs] ***n.***【医】倒睫;倒生毛。

tri·chi·na [triˈkainə; trɪˋkaɪnɚ] ***n.*** (*pl. -nae* [-niː; -ni])【动】毛线虫,旋毛形线虫。

trich·i·nize [ˈtrikiˌnaiz; ˋtrɪkɪˏnaɪz] ***vt.***【医】使患旋毛虫(毛线虫)病。

trich·i·nop·o·li, -ly [ˌtritʃiˈnɔpəli; ˏtrɪtʃɪˋnɑpəlɪ] ***n.*** 印度平头雪茄烟〔略 trichi〕。

trich·i·no·sis [trikiˈnəusis; ˏtrɪkəˋnosɪs] ***n.***【医】毛线虫病,旋毛虫病。

trich·i·nous [ˈtrikinəs, triˈkainəs; ˋtrɪkənəs, trɪˋkaɪnəs] ***a.***【医】**1.** 旋毛虫感染病的。**2.** 有旋毛虫病的,旋毛虫病的。

trich·ite [ˈtrikait; ˋtrɪkaɪt] ***n.***【地】发雏晶,晶发。

tri·chlo·ride [traiˈklɔːraid; traɪˋklɔraɪd, -rɪd, -ˋklor-] ***n.***【化】三氯化物。

tri·chlo·ro·eth·yl·ene [traiˌklɔːrəuˈeθiˌliːn; traɪˏkloro-ˋɛθəˏlin] ***n.***【化】三氯乙烯。

tricho- *comb. f.* 头发。

trich·o·cyst [ˈtrikəˌsist; ˋtrɪkəsɪst] ***n.***【动】(刺)丝胞。**-ic** ***a.***

trichogen [ˈtrikədʒən; ˋtrɪkədʒən] ***n.***【药】生发药。

trich·o·gyne [ˈtrikəˌdʒain, -dʒin; ˋtrɪkədʒɪn, -ˏdʒaɪn] ***n.***【生】受精丝。**-gyn·i·al** [-dʒiniəl; -dʒɪnɪəl], **-gyn·ic** ***a.***

tri·choid [ˈtrikɔid; ˋtrɪkɔɪd] ***a.*** 毛状的,发状的。

tri·chol·o·gy [triˈkɔlədʒi; trɪˋkɑlədʒɪ] ***n.*** 毛发学。**-o·gist** ***n.*** 毛发学家;〔美俚〕〔广告用语〕理发专家[名家]。

tri·chome [ˈtraikəum, ˈtrikəum; ˋtraɪkom, ˋtrɪkom] ***n.*** **1.**【植】(表皮)毛状体。**2.** 藻丝。**-chom·ic** [-ˈkɔmik, -ˈkəumik; -ˋkɑmɪk, -ˋkomɪk] ***a.***

trich·o·mon·ad [ˌtrikəˈmɔnæd, -ˈməunæd; trɪkəˋmɑnæd, -ˋmonæd] ***n.***【动】毛滴虫属(*Trichomonas*)动物。

trich·o·mo·ni·a·sis [ˌtrikəməˈnaiəsis; ˏtrɪkoməˋnaɪəsɪs] ***n.***【医】毛滴虫病;〔尤指〕阴道毛滴虫病;引起母牛消瘦和流产的滴虫病。

trichomycin [ˌtrikəˈmaisin; ˏtrɪkəˋmaɪsɪn] ***n.***【药】抗滴虫霉素。

trichopathy [triˈkɔpəθi; trɪˋkɑpəθɪ] ***n.***【医】(毛)发病;(毛)发病治疗。

tri·chord [ˈtraikɔːd; ˋtraɪˏkɔrd] **I** ***n.*** 三弦乐器,三弦琴。**II** ***a.*** 三弦的。

tri·cho·sis [triˈkəusis; trɪˋkosɪs] ***n.***【医】(毛)发病。

tri·chot·o·mize [traiˈkɔtəmaiz; traɪˋkɑtəˏmaɪz] ***vt.*** 分成三部分,分成三类,分成三组。

tri·chot·o·my [traiˈkɔtəmi; traɪˋkɑtəmɪ] ***n.*** 三分(法);【逻】三断法;【神】(把人分为肉体、精神、灵魂)三相法。

tri·chro·ism [ˈtraikrəuizm; ˋtraɪkroɪzm̩] ***n.*** 三色性。**-chro·ic** ***a.***

tri·chro·mat [ˈtraikrəuˌmæt; ˋtraɪkroˏmæt, -krə-] ***n.*** 有三色视觉的人。

tri·chro·mat·ic [traikrəuˈmætik; ˏtraɪkroˋmætɪk], **tri-**

chromic [-mik;-mɪk] *a*. 三(原)色的;三色版的;能正常辨别三原色的。~ *photography* 天然色照相(术)。~ *printing* 三色版印刷。

trick [trik; trɪk] **I** *n*. **1.** 奸计,诡计,骗术;欺骗。**2.** 戏法;快手把戏,幻术;【影】特技(表现法);(狗等的)把戏;〔常贬〕秘诀,诀窍,手法,手腕;手艺。**3.** 恶作剧,鬼把戏,卑鄙手段。**4.** (态度、讲话等的)习惯,怪癖。**5.** 〔美〕无聊的装饰;玩具;〔*pl*.〕杂货。**6.** 舵手的一班(通常二小时),值班时间,班。**7.** 【桥牌戏】一墩。**8.** 〔口〕漂亮的姑娘[小孩]。**9.** 〔美俚〕犯罪。*conjurer's ~s* 戏法。*(the) ~s of fortune* 意外的侥幸,命运的恶作剧。*a dirty [nasty, shabby, dog's] ~* 卑鄙手段。*None of your ~s with me*! 不上你的鬼当! *He is at his ~s again*. 他又在玩鬼把戏了。*the night ~* 夜班。***do the ~*** 〔俚〕达到目的,顺遂。***in ~*** 【徽】用线画,线画的。***know a ~ or two*** 相当精明,相当有办法。***know a ~ worth two of that*** 知道比那好得多的方法。***play a ~ on = play [serve] sb. a ~*** 跟(某人)开玩笑;欺骗。***the whole bag of ~s*** 全部,统统。~ ***flying [riding]*** 特技飞行[马术]。~ ***of senses*** = ~ ***of the imagination*** 错觉。~***s of the memory*** 记错。***turn the*** ~〔俚〕= do the ~。**II** *vt*. 骗,诈欺;装饰,打扮 (*off*; *out*; *up*)。~ *sb. out of his money* 诈骗某人的钱财。*be ~ed into buying a poor car* 受骗买一部次品汽车。*be ~ed out in jewels* 打扮得珠光宝气。— *vi*. 骗人;变戏法;玩鬼把戏,开玩笑 (*with*)。**III** *a*. **1.** 有诀窍的;特技的。**2.** 弄虚作假的,欺诈的。**3.** 漂亮的,能干的。**4.** 靠不住的;(关节等)突然撑不住的。~ ***or treat***! 不请客就捣乱〔万圣节前夕孩子们挨户要礼物时用语〕。~ ***sb. into [out of]*** 骗人去…[骗取…]。~ **cycling** 车技。~ **photography** 特技摄影。~ **scene** 旋转舞台。~ **shot** 【影】特技镜头。~-**track** 俄国双六戏。

trick·er [ˈtrikə; ˋtrɪkɚ] *n*. 耍诡计者;骗子。

trick·er·y [ˈtrikəri; ˋtrɪkərɪ] *n*. 欺骗,诈欺;奸计,诡计,手段,圈套。

trick·i·ly [ˈtrikili; ˋtrɪkəlɪ] *ad*. 用欺骗手法,用诡计。

trick·i·ness [ˈtrikinis; ˋtrɪkɪnɪs] *n*. 欺骗;(工作、问题等的)繁难,复杂。

trick·ish [ˈtrikiʃ; ˋtrɪkɪʃ] *a*. 欺骗的;狡猾的;诡计多端的。

trick·le [ˈtrikl; ˋtrɪkl̩] **I** *vi*. 滴下,淋下,滴滴嗒嗒流[落] (*down*; *out*; *along*); 稀稀落落地来[去、前进];(秘密等)慢慢泄漏 (*out*)。~ ***up*** 一点一点地从一个层次上升到另一个层次。—*vt*. 使滴下;使淌下,使一滴一滴地流。*Tears ~d down her cheeks*. 泪水从她的面颊一滴一滴地流下。*The brook ~d through the valley*. 小溪在峡谷间潺潺流过去。*He ~d the water into the container*. 他将水徐徐注入容器中。**II** *n*. 滴,滴下;细流,涓流;稀稀落落地[去、前进]的人。*a ~ of visitors* 稀稀落落的访客[参观者]。~-**charger** 【电】涓流充电器。~-**down** *a*. 〔美〕积极投资的。~-**down theory** 【经】利益扩散理论。~ **irrigation** 【农】滴灌〔以小直径穿孔软管置于土壤中,每隔一段时间缓慢给水的一种灌溉法〕。

trickly [ˈtrikli; ˋtrɪklɪ] *a*. 滴滴嗒嗒滴[流、落]的。

trick·ster [ˈtrikstə; ˋtrɪkstɚ] *n*. 骗子;要诡计的人;狡猾的人。

trick·sy [ˈtriksi; ˋtrɪksɪ] *a*. (*-si·er*; *-si·est*) 欺骗的,狡猾的;恶作剧的,顽皮的;漂亮的;(工作、问题等)繁难的。**-si·ness** *n*.

trick·track [ˈtriktræk; ˋtrɪk͵træk] = trictrac.

trick·y [ˈtriki; ˋtrɪkɪ] *a*. (*-i·er*; *-i·est*) 狡猾的;机智的;巧妙的;不易处理的,需要技巧的(工作等),错综复杂的。

tri·clin·ic [traiˈklinik; traɪˋklɪnɪk] *a*. 【物】三斜的,三斜晶系的。

tri·clin·i·um [traiˈkliniəm, tri-; traɪˋklɪnɪəm; trɪ-] *n*. (*pl*. ***-nia*** [-njə; -nɪə]) 【古罗马】(围在餐桌三面的)躺椅;设有躺椅餐桌的餐厅。

tri·co·line [ˈtrikəlin; ˋtrɪkəlɪn] *n*. 特里可绫〔丝光棉府绸的一种〕。

tri·col·our [ˈtraikələ; ˋtraɪ͵kʌlɚ] **I** *a*. 〔美〕三色的。**II** *n*. 三色旗〔特指法国国旗〕。**T- Banner** 法国国旗。~ **camera** 三色照相机。

tri·con [ˈtraikɔːn; ˋtraɪkɔn] *n*. 【空】有三个地面台的雷达导航系统。

tri·corn(e) [ˈtraikɔːn; ˋtraɪkɔrn] **I** *n*. 三角帽。**II** *a*. 有三个角的。

tri·cos·tate [traiˈkɔsteit; traɪˋkɑstet] *a*. 【植、动】有三中脉的;有三肋的。

tri·cot [ˈtrikəu; ˋtriko] *n*. 〔F.〕【纺】绒线织品;经编针织物;(芭蕾舞用的)紧身衣;大纹仿毛织品。*a ~ machine* 经编机。

tric·o·tine [trikəˈtiːn; ͵trɪkəˋtin] *n*. 【纺】巧克丁;针织细绸;急斜纹精纺细毛哔叽;条子细棉府绸。

tri·cro [ˈtrikrɔ; ˋtrɪkrɔ] *n*. 万亿〔10^{12}〕。

tri·crot·ic [traiˈkrɔtik; traɪˋkrɑtɪk] *a*. 【生理】三重搏的。**-cro·tism** *n*.

tric·trac [ˈtriktræk; ˋtrɪk͵træk] *n*. 十五子游戏〔一种双方各有十五枚棋子,掷骰子决定行棋格数的游戏,尤指既用木签又用棋子的那一种〕。

tri·cus·pid [traiˈkʌspid; traɪˋkʌspɪd] **I** *a*. 三尖的;【解】三尖瓣的。*a ~ tooth* 三尖齿。**II** *n*. 【解】三尖瓣 (= ~ valve);三尖牙。

tri·cus·pi·date [traiˈkʌspiˌdeit; traɪˋkʌspɪ͵det] *a*. 有三个尖头的。

tri·cy·cle [ˈtraisikl; ˋtraɪsɪkl] **I** *n*. 三轮(脚踏)车;〔美车夫语〕三轮摩托车。**II** *vi*. 骑三轮(脚踏)车。

tri·cy·clic [traiˈsaiklik, -ˈsiklik; traɪˋsaɪklɪk, -ˋsɪklɪk] *a*. 【化】三环的。

trid =〔拉〕*triduum* (处方用语)三日 (= three days)。

tri·dac·tyl, tri·dac·tyl·ous [traiˈdæktil, -əs; traɪˋdæktɪl] *a*. 三指的,三趾的。

tri·dent [ˈtraidənt; ˋtraɪdnt] **I** *n*. **1.** (海神 Neptune 的)三叉戟。**2.** 三齿鱼叉。**3.** 制海权。**4.** 【几】三叉曲线。**5.** 〔T-〕(美国的)三叉戟(式)核潜艇;三叉戟式导[飞]弹。**II** *a*. 三齿的。

tri·den·tate [traiˈdenteit; traɪˋdɛntet] *a*. 三齿的,三尖的,有三叉的。

Tri·den·tine [traiˈdentain, tri-, -tin; traɪˋdɛntɪn, trɪ-, -taɪn] **I** *a*. 意大利北部特伦托 (Trent)的;特伦托宗教会议的;遵守特伦托宗教会议所规定的教义的。**II** *n*. 天主教徒。

tri·di·men·sion·al [ˌtraidiˈmenʃənl; ͵traɪdəˋmɛnʃənl̩] *a*. (长、宽、高)三度的,立体的。

tried [traid; traɪd] **I** try 的过去式及过去分词。**II** *a*. 试验过的;经过考验的;确实的,可靠的(朋友等)。~ *recipe* 验方。***old and*** ~ 完全可靠的。

tri·en·ni·al [traiˈenjəl, -niəl; traɪˋɛnɪəl] **I** *a*. 继续三年的;每三年的,三年一次的;【植】三年生的。**II** *n*. 每三年举行一次的纪念节(等);【植】三年生植物。**-ly** *ad*.

tri·en·ni·um [traiˈeniəm; traɪˋɛnɪəm] *n*. (*pl*. *~s*, ***-enni·a*** [-ˈeniə; -ˋɛnɪə]) 三年(期间)。

Trier [triə; trɪr] *n*. 特里尔〔德国城市〕。

tri·er [ˈtraiə; ˋtraɪɚ] *n*. **1.** 试验者;试验物,试料;试验机。**2.** 试图者,尽力尝试者。**3.** 审问者,法官;审查员。

tri·er·arch [ˈtraiəˌrɑːk; ˋtraɪɚ͵ark] *n*. **1.** (古希腊)三层桨(座)战船之司令官。**2.** 雅典三层桨(座)战船的修造人。

tri·er·arch·y [ˈtraiəˌrɑːki; ˋtraɪɚ͵arkɪ] *n*. (*pl*. ***-archies***) **1.** (古希腊)三层桨(座)战船司令官的职务。**2.** 三层桨(座)战船司令官之统称。**3.** 为国家建造、维修三层桨(座)战船的制度。

tri·eth·yl [traiˈeθl; traɪˋɛθl] *a*. 【化】三乙(烷)基。

tri·fa·cial [traiˈfeiʃəl; traɪˋfeʃəl] *a*., *n*. = trigeminal.

tri·fid [ˈtraifid; ˋtraɪfɪd] *a*.【植】三(尖)裂的。

tri·fle [ˈtraifl; ˋtraɪfl] **I** *n*. **1.** 小事,琐事;琐碎东西;无聊话。**2.** 少量,些许;零钱。**3.** 葡萄酒蛋糕;白镴;〔*pl*.〕白镴制品。*He doesn't stick at* ~*s*. 他不拘小节[不多考虑细故]。***a*** ~ 稍微,有点,一点(*He seems a* ~ *angry*. 他好像有点生气)。***stand upon*** ~***s*** 拘泥小节。**II** *vi*. 说着玩儿,闹着玩儿地讲[行动];玩弄,小看,轻视,愚弄(*with*);做无聊事,讲无聊话;闲混;玩忽(*with*)。*You should not* ~ *with your health*. 不要糟蹋了身体。~ *over a light meal* 吃一点儿点心。*in no mood for trifling* 不是开玩笑的样子。— *vt*. 白费(时间、金钱等)(*away*)。~ **ring** 益智环。

tri·fler [ˈtraiflə; ˋtraɪflɚ] *n*. 闹玩儿的人,开玩笑的人,轻浮的人;做无聊事的人,讲无聊话的人;吊儿郎当的人。

tri·fling [ˈtraifliŋ; ˋtraɪflɪŋ] *a*. 少许的,不足道的,琐碎的;无聊的;轻浮的,轻薄的;吊儿郎当混日子的。*a* ~ *gift* 薄礼。*of* ~ *value* 价值很小的。~ *talk* 无聊的谈话。**-ly** *ad*.

tri·fo·cal [traiˈfəukl; traɪˋfokḷ] **I** *a*.【物】三焦距的。**II** [ˈtraiˌfəukl; ˋtraɪˏfokḷ] *n*. **1.** 三焦距透镜。**2.**〔*pl*.〕有三焦距的眼镜。

tri·fo·li·ate [traiˈfəuliit; traɪˋfolɪɪt, -lɪˏet] *a*.【植】有三叶的。

tri·fo·li·o·late [traiˈfəuliəleit; traɪˋfolɪəˏlet] *a*.【植】有三小叶的。~ **orange**【植】臭枳。

tri·fo·li·um [traiˈfəuliəm; traɪˋfolɪəm] *n*.【植】车轴草属[三叶草属]植物;红车轴草;白车轴草[白三叶草](= clover)。

tri·fo·ri·um [traiˈfɔːriəm; traɪˋforɪəm] *n*. (*pl*. ***-ria*** [-riə; -rɪə])【建】教堂拱门上面的拱廊。

tri·form(ed) [ˈtraifɔːm(d); ˋtraɪfɔrm(d)] *a*. (有)三种形态[式]的;由三部形成的。

tri·fur·cate [traiˈfəːkeit; traɪˋfɝkɪt, -ket] *a*. 三叉的。**-d** *a*. **-ca·tion** *n*.

trig[1] [trig; trɪg] **I** *n*.〔英〕(放在车轮下的)制轮棒[石]。**II** *vt*. (**-gg-**) 煞住,制住(车轮)(*up*)。

trig[2] [trig; trɪg] **I** *a*. 漂亮的,潇洒的,整洁的;精确的;坚牢的;健全的;诚实的。**II** *vt*. (**-gg-**)〔英〕使整洁,修饰,打扮(*out*; *up*)。

trig[3] [trig; trɪg] *n*.〔学生话〕三角。

trig. = trigonometric; trigonometry.

trig·a·mist [ˈtrigəmist; ˋtrɪgəmɪst] *n*. 结过三次婚的人;有三妻[三夫]的人。

trig·a·mous [ˈtrigəməs; ˋtrɪgəməs] *a*. 结过三次婚的;有三夫[三妻]的;【植】有雄、雌、雌雄三种花的。

trig·a·my [ˈtrigəmi; ˋtrɪgəmɪ] *n*. 三次结婚;一妻三夫,一夫三妻。

tri·gem·i·nal [traiˈdʒeminl; traɪˋdʒɛmənḷ] **I** *a*.【解】三叉神经的。**II** *n*. 三叉神经。

trig·ger [ˈtrigə; ˋtrɪgɚ] **I** *n*. (枪上的)扳机;【机】扳柄;闸柄;制轮(机),制滑器;【物】触发器,引爆器;【化】(连锁反应)引起物;〔转〕触发物;【电】起动线路;起动装置。***pull*** [***press***] ***the*** ~ 扳扳机,射击。***quick on the*** ~ 打得快的;〔口〕动不动就开枪的;敏速的;〔美俚〕性急的;三心两意的。**II** *vt*. 扳动扳机射击;触发,激起(*off*)。— *vi*. 松开扳柄。~**-crazy** 杀人不眨眼的。~ **finger** 右手的食指。~**fish**【动】(热带)鳞鲀。~**-happy** 动辄开枪的,好乱开枪的;好战的,轻易发动战争的。

tri·glot [ˈtraiglɔt; ˋtraɪglɑt] *a*. 用三种语文写的[对照的]。

tri·glyc·er·ide [traiˈglisəˌraid; traɪˋglɪsəˏraɪd, -ərɪd] *n*.【化】甘油三酸酯。

tri·glyph [ˈtraiglif; ˋtraɪglɪf] *n*.【建】(陶立克柱式的)三陇板,三角槽排档。**-ic** *a*.

tri·gon [ˈtraigən; ˋtraɪgɑn] *n*.【几】三角形;三角日晷;【古希腊】三角琴;三人球戏;【占星】(十二宫中)互隔 120 度的三宫;三分一对座〔二行星相隔 120 度时的天象,被视为吉兆〕。

trigon. = trigonometric; trigonometry.

trig·o·nal [ˈtrigənl; ˋtrɪgənəl] *a*. 三角(形)的。~ **system**【物】三角晶系。

trig·o·nom·e·ter [ˌtrigəˈnɔmitə; ˏtrɪgəˋnɑmətɚ] *n*. 直角三角计;三角学家;三角测量者。

trig·o·no·met·ric, -i·cal [triˈgənəˈmetrik, -ikəl; ˏtrɪgənəˋmɛtrɪk, -ɪkl] *a*.【数】三角学的;(用)三角法的。~ **function** 三角函数。

trig·o·nom·e·try [ˌtrigəˈnɔmitri; ˏtrɪgəˋnɑmətrɪ] *n*.【数】三角法,三角学;关于三角学的论文[教科书]。

trig·o·nous [ˈtrigənəs; ˋtrɪgənəs] *a*. 三角形的,有三个角的。

tri·graph [ˈtraigrɑːf; ˋtraɪgræf, -grɑf] *n*.【语言】三字母一音。

tri·hed·ral [traiˈhedrəl; traɪˋhidrəl] **I** *a*. 有三面的,三面体的;三面角的。**II** *n*. 三面体。

tri·hed·ron [traiˈhedrən; traɪˋhidrən] *n*. (*pl*. ~*s*, ***-dra*** [drə; drə])【数】三面体。

tri·hy·drate [traiˈhaidreit; traɪˋhaɪdret] *n*.【化】三水合物。**-d** *a*.

tri·hy·drox·y [ˌtraihaiˈdrɔksi; ˏtraɪhaɪˋdrɑksɪ] *a*.【化】三羟(基)的。

tri·i·o·do·thy·ro·nine [traiˌaiədəuˈθairəˌnin; traɪˏaɪədoˋθaɪrəˏnɪn] *n*.【化】三碘化甲腺胺酸。

tri·jet [ˈtraiˈdʒet; ˋtraɪˋdʒɛt] **I** *a*. (有)三个喷气发动机的。**II** *n*. 三喷气发动机飞机。

tri·ju·gate, tri·ju·gous [ˈtraidʒugeit, -gəs; ˋtraɪdʒuˏget, traɪˋdʒuget, -gəs] *a*.【植】有三对小叶的。

trike [traik; traɪk] *n*., *v*.〔口〕(乘)三轮(脚踏)车(= tricycle)。

tri·lat·er·al [traiˈlætərəl; traɪˋlætərəl] **I** *a*.【几】三边的。**II** *n*. 三边形,三角形 。**-ism** *n*.(主张三方合作的)三边主义[作法]。**-ly** *ad*.

tril·by [ˈtrilbi; ˋtrɪlbɪ] *n*.〔英口〕特里比式软毡帽〔又叫 T- hat〕。

tri·lin·e·ar [traiˈliniə; traɪˋlɪnɪɚ] *a*.【数】三线的。

tri·lin·gual [traiˈliŋgwəl; traɪˋlɪŋgwəl] *a*. (懂得)三国语言的。

tri·lit·er·al [traiˈlitərəl; traɪˋlɪtərəl] *a*., *n*. 三(辅音)字母的;三字母词(根)。~ *languages* 三字母词根语言〔词根用三个辅音字母组成的闪族语等〕。**-ism** 三个(辅音)字母组成的词。

tri·lith, tri·li·thon [ˈtrailiθ, -ɔn; ˋtraɪlɪθ, -ɑn] *n*.【考古】(在二直立巨石上搭一块巨石的)三巨石结构。

trill [tril; trɪl] **I** *n*. 抖动声,颤声;【乐】颤音;【语音】(r 的)卷舌音;(鸟的)啼啭。**II** *vt*., *vi*. 用颤音发声[歌唱];(字母 r)发卷舌音;(鸟)啼啭。**-er** *n*.

tril·ling [ˈtriliŋ; ˋtrɪlɪŋ] *n*. 三胞胎中一个;【地】三连晶。

tril·lion [ˈtriljən; ˋtrɪljən] *n*., *a*.〔美、法〕万亿,兆〔百万的二乘方〕;〔英、德〕百亿亿,百万兆〔百万的三乘方〕;大量。**-th 1.** *a*. (第)万亿[百亿亿]的。**2.** *n*. 万亿[百亿亿]分之一。

tril·li·um [ˈtriliəm; ˋtrɪlɪəm] *n*. (*pl*. ~*s*)【植】延龄草(属)。

tri·lo·bate [traiˈləubeit; traɪˋlobet, ˋtraɪlə-] *a*.【植】三裂(片)的(= trilobated, tribobed)。

tri·lo·bite [ˈtrailəbait; ˋtraɪləˏbaɪt] *n*.【古生】三叶虫。

tri·lo·bit·ic [ˌtrailəˈbitik; ˏtraɪləˋbɪtɪk] *a*.【古生】三叶虫纲(*Trilobita*)的。

tri·loc·u·lar [traiˈlɔkjulə; traɪˋlɑkjʊlɚ] *a*.【生】有三室[房、腔]的。

tril·o·gy [ˈtrilədʒi; ˋtrɪlədʒɪ] *n*. (古希腊)连演的三部悲剧;三部曲。

trim [trim; trɪm] **I** *a*. (~*mer*; ~*mest*) 整齐的,整洁的;漂亮的。**II** *ad*. 整齐[整洁]地。**III** *n*. **1.** 调整,整顿,整齐(状态);准备,预备;服装;装饰;(轮船、汽车的)

内部装修;(健康等的)情形,状态。2. 修剪;修剪下来的东西。3.【空】配平;【无】微调,垫整;【军】潜艇的浮力;【海】吃水差;(船的)平衡;(风帆的)受风状况;【建】贴面。*a* ~ *stone* 镶边石。***in fighting*** ~ (军舰等)在备战状态中。***in*** (***good, proper***) ~ 准备好;整齐;情形好;【海】很平衡匀称。***in hunting*** ~ 穿着猎装。***in sailing*** ~ 做好开船准备。***into*** ~ 成适宜的状态。***out of*** ~ 未准备妥当,情形不好,有毛病;不整齐;(船)一边过重。~ ***by the bow*** [***stern***]【空】头[尾]重。**IV** ***vt.*** (***-mm-***) **1.** 调整,整理,整顿,收拾;使整洁,使洁净;布置,装饰(*with*)。**2.** 修剪(头发、指甲等);剪断,剪掉(*away; off*);剪(灯心);刨平,刨去(木料的角)。**3.**【海】装备,(整理舱货等)使(船身)平衡;(将货物等)装进船舱;卸货时搬到舱口;搬匀(船舱内的煤炭);【空】使(飞机)配平。**4.** (鱼群)游近(海岸)。**5.**〔口〕责备,谴责;鞭打,打。**6.**〔卑〕骗取;〔美俚〕欺骗,打垮,打败。~ *one's nails* 剪指甲。~ *off the edges of a photograph* 切齐相片(四边)。—***vi.*** **1.** (政客等)两面讨好,随风转舵,骑墙(*between*)。**2.** (船)平衡;调整帆篷。**3.** 整理,整顿;修剪。~ ***by*** [***on***] ***a wind*** 尽可能扯着帆顺风开行。~ ***in*** 把(木板等)刨整齐嵌入[镶入]。~ ***one's course*** (船)顺风扯帆前进;顺着大势前进。~ ***one's sail*** 见风转舵,随机应变。~ ***oneself up*** 打扮。~ ***sb.'s jacket*** 〔俚〕殴打某人。~ **size** 实际尺寸。**-ly** ***ad.***

trim. = trimetric. 斜方(晶)的。

tri·ma·ran [ˈtraiməˌræn; ˏtraɪməˋræn] ***n.*** 三体艇。

tri·mer [ˈtraimə; ˋtraɪmɚ] ***n.***【化】**1.** 一种三分子的缩合物。**2.** 三聚物。**-ic** ***a.***

trim·er·ous [ˈtrimərəs; ˋtrɪmərəs] ***a.*** **1.**【植】(花)三基数的 (= 3-merous)。**2.**【动】(昆虫)三跗节的。

tri·mes·ter [traiˈmestə; traɪˋmɛstɚ] ***n.*** (约)三个月;(一年三学期制的)学期。

trim·e·ter [ˈtrimitə; ˋtrɪmətɚ] ***n.***, ***a.***【韵】三音格的(诗句),三音步(的)。

tri·meth·a·di·one [traiˌmeθəˈdaiəun; traɪˏmɛθəˋdaɪon] ***n.***【药】三甲环二酮。

tri·met·ric [traiˈmetrik; traɪˋmɛtrɪk] ***a.*** **1.** 三音格[步]的。**2.**【结晶】斜方晶系的 (= orthorhombic)。~ **projection** 三度投影 (= trimetrical)。

tri·met·ro·gon [traiˈmetrəˌgɔn; traɪˋmɛtrəˏgɑn] ***n.***【测】三镜空中摄影法;【军】垂直倾斜混合空中照相。~ **mapping** 垂直倾斜混合空中照相制图。

trim·mer [ˈtrimə; ˋtrɪmɚ] ***n.*** **1.** 调整者,整顿者;整理者;装饰者;修剪人,修理人。**2.**【机】修剪器;(船上的)堆煤机;【空】调整器;配平器;【无】微调电容器;【建】托梁,承接梁;修木器,修整器,剪切具〔灯心铗、剪刀等〕。**3.** 两面讨好的人,随风转舵的人,机会主义者。**4.**〔口〕责备者,殴打者;装货工人。~ **arch** (壁)炉前拱。

trim·ming [ˈtrimiŋ; ˋtrɪmɪŋ] ***n.*** **1.** 整顿,整理;调整,平衡。**2.** 修剪,修理;〔*pl.*〕切屑,碎料。**3.**〔*pl.*〕装饰(品);婉转的措词。**4.**〔*pl.*〕〔口〕配料,配药;〔美〕加入茶中的糖和牛乳。**5.**〔口〕申斥;殴打;败;输;诈骗。**6.** 两面讨好,骑墙,随风转舵。~ **condenser**【无】微调电容器。

tri·mo·lec·u·lar [ˌtraiməuˈlekjulə; ˏtraɪmoˋlɛkjulɚ] ***a.***【化】三分子的。

tri·month·ly [traiˈmʌnθli; traɪˋmʌnθlɪ] ***a.*** 每三个月一次的。

tri·morph [ˈtraimɔːf; ˋtraɪmɔrf] ***n.***【矿】三异晶体同质矿物〔可结成三种不同晶体的矿物〕。

tri·mor·phism [traiˈmɔːfizəm; traɪˋmɔrfɪzm] ***n.*** **1.**【结晶学】三晶(现象)。**2.**【植】三形性。**3.**【动】三态(现象)。**-phic, -phous** ***a.***

tri·mo·tor [ˈtraiˌməutə; ˋtraɪˏmotɚ] ***a.*** 三引擎(发动的)飞机。

Tri·mur·ti [triˈmuəti; trɪˋmurtɪ] 印度教之三神 (*Brahma, Vishnu* 和 *Siva*) 一体〔创造者,维持者,破坏者与再造者的合称〕。

tri·nal, tri·na·ry [ˈtrainl, -nəri; ˋtraɪnḷ, -nərɪ] ***a.*** 三倍的,三重的,三层的,由三个部分形成的。

Trin·co·ma·lee, Trin·co·ma·li [ˈtriŋkəuməˈliː; ˋtrɪŋkoməˋlɪ] ***n.*** 亭可马里〔斯里兰卡港市〕。

trine [train; traɪn] **I** ***a.*** 三倍的,三重的,三层的,三部分组成的;【占星】三分一对座的。**II** ***n.*** 三个一组;【占星】三分一对座〔两行星相距 120 度的天象,被视为吉兆〕;〔the T-〕三位一体。

trin·gle [ˈtriŋgl; ˋtrɪŋgḷ] ***n.*** **1.** 帐杆〔包括挂帘子和悬帷帐等的横木〕。**2.**【建】狭直条饰,方角花边。**3.** (炮座端的)制动棒〔缓和后座力〕。

Trinidad and Tobago [ˈtrinidæd ənd təˈbeigəu; ˋtrɪnɪdæd ənd təˋbego] 特立尼达和多巴哥〔拉丁美洲〕。

trin·i·scope [ˈtrainiskəup; ˋtraɪnɪˏskop] ***n.*** (彩色电视用的)阴极射线管。

Trin·i·tar·i·an [triniˈtɛəriən; ˏtrɪnəˋtɛrɪən] ***a.***, ***n.***【宗】三位一体(说)的;信三位一体的(人);〔t-〕有三个部分的;三倍的。**-ism** ***n.*** 三位一体说[信仰]。

tri·ni·tro·cre·sol [traiˌnaitrəuˈkrisəul, -sɔːl; traɪˏnaɪtroˋkrisol, -sɑl] ***n.***【化】三硝基甲酚[24]。

tri·ni·tro·glyc·er·in [traiˌnaitrəuˈglisərin; traɪˏnaɪtroˋglɪsərɪn] ***n.***【化】硝化甘油,甘油三硝酸酯 (= nitroglycerin)。

tri·ni·tro·tol·u·ene, tri·ni·tro·tol·u·ol [traiˈnaitrəuˈtɔljuiːn, -ˈtɔljuəul; traɪˏnaɪtroˋtɑljʊˏin, -ˋtɑljuol] ***n.***【化,军】三硝基甲苯〔猛烈茶褐炸药,略 TNT〕。

trin·i·ty [ˈtriniti; ˋtrɪnətɪ] ***n.*** **1.**〔the T-〕【宗】三位一体;三位一体的象征。**2.** 三人一组,三个一套的东西;〔俚〕(烟斗等)三件烟具。**3.** = T- Sunday. **T- Brethren** Trinity House 的会员。**T- House**〔英〕领港公会〔掌管领港员的考试、灯塔的建设等〕,海务局。**T- sittings** 高等法院第四期开庭期。**T- Sunday** 三一节,复活主日〔Whitsunday 的下个礼拜天〕。**T- term** **1.** = T- sittings. **2.** (英国牛津大学)紧接 Easter term 之后的学期。

trin·ket [ˈtriŋkit; ˋtrɪŋkɪt] ***n.*** (戒指等)小装饰品,零碎小物件。**-ry** ***n.***〔集合名词〕小装饰品,小物件。

tri·no·mi·al [traiˈnəumiəl; traɪˋnomɪəl] **I** ***a.***【数】三项(式)的;【动、植】三名法的。**II** ***n.***【数】三项式;【动、植】(属名、种名与亚种名)三名(法)。**-ism** ***n.*** 三名法。

tri·nomi·nal [traiˈnɔminl; traɪˋnɑmɪnḷ] ***a.***【动、植】= trinomial.

tri·o [ˈtriːəu; ˋtrio, ˋtraɪo] ***n.*** (*pl.* ~***s***) 三人(一组),三人演出小组;三个一套;【儿】拼三小组;【乐】三重奏[唱];三部合奏[唱]曲;进行曲的中央乐部;(piquet 牌戏) king, queen, jack, ace 各三张的一付牌。*the scenic* ~ *of Shanghai* 上海三景。

tri·ode [ˈtraiəud; ˋtraɪod] ***n.***, ***a.***【无】三极管(的)。

tri·oe·cious [traiˈiːʃəs; traɪˋiʃəs] ***a.***【植】雌花雄花两性花异株的,单全异株的。

tri·ol [ˈtraiɔːl, -əul; ˋtraɪɔl, -ol] ***n.***【化】三醇。

tri·ole [ˈtriəul; ˋtriol] ***n.***【乐】三连音符。

tri·o·let [ˈtri(ː)əulet, ˈtrai-; ˋtraɪəlɪt] ***n.***【韵】二韵脚八句诗。

Tri·o·nes [traiˈəuniːz; traɪˋoniz] ***n.***〔*pl.*〕【天】北斗七星。

tri·or [ˈtraiə; ˋtraɪɚ] ***n.***【法】= trier.

tri·ose [ˈtraiəus; ˋtraɪos] ***n.***【化】丙醣。

tri·ox·ide [traiˈɔksaid; traɪˋɑksaɪd, -sɪd] ***n.***【化】三氧化物。

trip [trip; trɪp] **I** ***n.*** **1.** (短程)旅行,短程行程,航行。**2.** 摔倒,绊倒;失足,失脚;过失;失言,说错。**3.**【机、电】解扣;跳闸。**4.** 轻快的步子。**5.**〔俚〕(服麻醉品者的)迷幻感觉;迷幻麻醉品。**6.** 出渔一次的捕获量(或其利益)。*a round* ~ 往返的行程;周游。**II** ***vi.*** (***tripped*** [tript; trɪpt], ***trip·ping*** [ˈtripiŋ; ˋtrɪpɪŋ]) **1.** 轻快地跑[走];轻轻跳跃。**2.** 绊倒,失脚 (*on; over*);弄错,做错;犯过失;失言,讲错;说不出话。**3.**【机】(擒纵机件的)走动。

T

4. 旅行。— *vt*. **1.** 绊倒,使失脚;勾脚摔倒(*up*)。**2.** 找错,挑错(*up*);使犯错误,使失败。**3.**【海】卷起(锚);竖直(帆桁)。**4.**【机】解扣,松开棘爪而开动。**5.** 产生迷幻感觉。*Such people are bound to* ~ *and fall*. 这样的人是没有不跌倒的。***be*** ~***ped by a difficult question*** 被一个困难问题难倒。***catch sb.*** ~***ping in sb.'s...*** 挑某人…的错处。***go*** ~***ping*** 顺利进行。~ ***it*** 跳舞。~ ***off*** 跳开。~ ***over the root of a tree*** [***on a stone***] 绊倒在树根上[石头上]。~ ***the light fantastic***〔美〕跳舞。~ **circuit**【电】解扣电路。~ **dog**【机】跳档。~ **flare** 绊索照明弹。~ **gear** 跳动装置。~**hammer**【机】杵锤。~ **pass** 旅行免费车票。~**wire** 绊网,地雷拉发线。

TRIP = transformation-induced plasticity【冶】高强度及高延性。

tri·pal·mi·tin [traiˈpælmitin; traɪˋpælmɪtɪn] *n*. 三棕榈精,甘油三个棕榈酸酯。

tri·par·tite [ˈtraiˈpɑːtait; traɪˋpɑrtaɪt] *a*. 分成三部的;三个一组的,三个一副的;一式三份的;【法】三者间的;【植】(叶)三深裂的。*a* ~ *indenture* 三方契约,三联合同。*a* ~ *treaty* 三国条约。**-ti·tion** *n*.

tripe [traip; traɪp] *n*. **1.**【烹】(反刍动物的)肚子。**2.**〔*pl*.〕〔古、卑〕内脏,肚腹。**3.**〔英俚〕没有价值的[可厌的]东西;废话。~*s and keister*〔美俗〕(路边小贩的)三脚架和手提包。

tri·per·son·al [traiˈpəːsnəl; traɪˋpɝsn̩l] *a*.【神】三人的,三人组成的〔指上帝、圣子、圣灵三位一体而言〕。

tri·pet·al·ous [traiˈpetləs; traɪˋpɛtələs] *a*.【植】三花瓣的。

trip·ham·mer [ˈtripˌhæmə; ˋtrɪpˏhæmɚ] *n*. 杵锤(= trip hammer)。

tri·phase [ˈtraifeiz; ˋtraɪfez] *a*.【电】三相的。

tri·phen·yl·meth·ane [traiˌfenlˈmeθein, -finl-; traɪˏfɛnlˋmɛθen, -fɪnl-] *n*.【化】三苯甲烷。

tri·phib·i·an [traiˈfibiən; traɪˋfɪbɪən] **I** *n*. **1.** 水陆空三用飞机。**2.** 海陆空联合作战指挥官。**II** *a*. **1.** 海陆空联合作战的。**2.** 海陆空三栖的。**3.** 能在[从]陆上、水上、雪地或冰上开动[起飞]的。

tri·phib·i·ous [traiˈfibiəs; traɪˋfɪbɪəs] *a*. = triphibian (*a*.).

triph·thong [ˈtrifθɔŋ; ˋtrɪfθɔŋ, ˋtrɪp-] *n*.【语言】三合元音。**-al** *a*.

triph·y·lite [ˈtrifiˌlait; ˋtrɪfɪˏlaɪt] *n*.【矿】磷酸锂铁矿。

tri·pin·nate [traiˈpineit; traɪˋpɪnet] *a*.【植】三回羽状的。**-ly** *ad*.

Tri·pi·takas [traipiˈtɑːkəs; traɪpɪˋtækəs] *n*.【宗】(佛教的)三藏经。

tri·plane [ˈtraiplein; ˋtraɪˏplen] *n*.【空】三翼(飞)机。

tri·ple [ˈtripl; ˋtrɪpl] **I** *a*. 三倍的,三重的,三层的;三部分的;【法】三者间的。**II** *n*. 三倍的数[量];三个一组;【棒球】三垒安打。**III** *vi*. 增至三倍。~ **bond**【化】三键。~ **concerto**【音】三重协奏曲。~ **cross** 涉及三方的叛卖行为。~ **écran**【影】三倍大的银幕。~ **jump** 三级跳远。~**-digit** *a*. 三位数的。~ **measure** = ~ time. ~**-nerved**【植】离基三出脉的。~**-space** *vt*. 空两行打印。~ **tail**【动】松鲷。~ **thread**【机】三线螺纹。~ **threat** 三面手〔有三种特长的足球运动员〕。~ **time**【乐】三拍子。

trip·let [ˈtriplit; ˋtrɪplɪt] *n*. 三个一组,三个一副;三份;【韵】押韵的三句;【乐】三连音符;【物】三重线;三合(透)镜;〔口〕三胞胎中的一个;〔*pl*.〕三胞胎,三人脚踏车;【船】三炼环。

trip·lex [ˈtripleks; ˋtrɪplɛks] **I** *a*. 三部分的;三倍的;三重的;三层的;生三种效果的。**II** *n*. 由三部分组成的东西;【音】三拍子;三部合奏[唱]曲。*a* ~ *building* 三套住房成一单元的房屋。~ **glass** 夹层玻璃。

trip·li·cate [ˈtriplikit; ˋtrɪplɪkɪt] **I** *a*. 三倍的,三重的;三乘的;三个一副的;三份的,一式三份的。*a* ~ *agreement* 一式三份的协定书。**II** *n*. 三个一副中之一;三份中之一;三个一副;三份。*be drawn up in* ~ 作成三份(的文件等)。**III** [-keit; -ˏket] *vt*. 使成三倍;作成三份。~**ratio**【数】三乘比。

trip·li·ca·tion [ˌtripliˈkeiʃən; ˏtrɪpləˋkeʃən] *n*. 三倍;增加成三倍的东西;作三份。

Tri·pli·ce [ˈtriplitʃei; ˋtrɪplɪtʃe] *n*.〔It.〕(1882—1883年德、奥、意)三国同盟。

trip·lic·i·ty [triˈplisiti; trɪˋplɪsətɪ] *n*. 三倍,三重;三个一副;三位一体;【占星】十二宫中相距各120度的三宫。

trip·lite [ˈtriplait; ˋtrɪplaɪt] *n*.【矿】磷铁锰矿。

trip·lo·blas·tic [ˌtripləuˈblæstik; ˏtrɪploˋblæstɪk] *a*.【动】三胚层的。

trip·loid [ˈtriplɔid; ˋtrɪplɔɪd] **I** *a*.【生】三倍体的。**II** *n*. 三倍体。**-y** *n*.

tri·ply [ˈtripli; ˋtrɪplɪ] *ad*. 三倍,三重,三层。

tri·pod [ˈtraipɔd; ˋtraɪpɑd] *n*. 三脚台,三脚桌子[凳子];三脚架;(三足)鼎,三脚香炉;【古希腊】Delphi 的青铜三脚祭坛;Delphi 祭坛模型。~ ***of life*** = ***vital*** ~ 心脏、肺脏和脑髓。~ **landing gear**【空】三轮起落架。**-al, -ic** *a*.

trip·o·dy [ˈtripədi; ˋtrɪpədɪ] *n*. (*pl*. **-dies**) 三音步诗,三音诗句。

Trip·o·li [ˈtripəli; ˋtrɪpəlɪ] *n*. **1.** 的黎波里〔利比亚首都〕。**2.** 的黎波里〔黎巴嫩港市〕。

trip·o·li [ˈtripəli; ˋtrɪpəlɪ] *n*.【矿】风化硅石,硅藻土。~ *earth* 板状硅藻土。

trip·o·lite [ˈtripəˌlait; ˋtrɪpəˏlaɪt] *n*.【矿】硅藻土。

tri·pos [ˈtraipɔs; ˋtraɪpɑs] *n*. (剑桥大学的)荣誉学位考试。

trip·per [ˈtripə; ˋtrɪpɚ] *n*. **1.** 轻快地走[跳]的人。**2.**〔英口〕(当日来回的)游客。**3.** (使)绊倒者;勾脚使绊倒者;【机】钩杆,自动解扣装置;倾卸装置;(铁路上)信号发送装置。

trip·pet [ˈtripit; ˋtrɪpɪt] *n*.【机】(有规律地撞击他物的)凸轮(或其他机械部件)。

trip·ping [ˈtripiŋ; ˋtrɪpɪŋ] **I** *a*. **1.** 轻快地走路的,脚步轻快的。**2.**〔古〕犯过失的;失足犯罪的。**II** *n*. 轻快的跳舞。~ **bar**【机】钩杆,跳动杆。~ **bracket**【海】防颠肘板。~ **device**【机】解装置。**-ly** *ad*. 轻快地;流畅地(讲话等)。

trip·tane [ˈtriptein; ˋtrɪpten] *n*.【化】三甲基丁烷。

trip·ter·ous [ˈtriptərəs; ˋtrɪptərəs] *a*.【植】三翅的。

trip·tych [ˈtriptik; ˋtrɪptɪk] *n*. 三幅一联的图画,三件一组的雕刻;三折写字板。

trip·wire [ˈtripˌwaiə; ˋtrɪpˏwaɪr] *n*. 绊网。

tri·que·trous [traiˈkwiːtrəs, -ˈkwetrəs; traɪˋkwitrəs, -ˋkwɛtrəs] *a*. **1.** 三角形的,三面形的。**2.** 具有三角形横断面的。**3.**【植】三棱的。**-ly** *ad*.

tri·ra·di·ate [traiˈreidiːit, -ˌeit; traɪˋredɪˏet] *a*. 三射的,有三辐射线的。**-ly** *ad*.

trir·eme [ˈtrairiːm; ˋtraɪrim] *n*.【古希腊】三层浆战船。

tri·sac·cha·ride [traiˈsækəˌraid; traɪˋsækəˏraɪd, -rɪd] *n*.【化】三糖。

tri·sect [traiˈsekt; traɪˋsɛkt] *vt*. 三分,三截;【数】三等分。

tri·sec·tion [traiˈsekʃən; traɪˋsɛkʃən] *n*. 三分;【数】三等分。

tri·sec·tor [traiˈsektə; traɪˋsɛktɚ] *n*. 三分;三截;【几】三等分。

tri·sep·tate [traiˈsepteit; traɪˋsɛptet] *a*.【生】具三隔膜的。

tri·shaw, tri·sha [ˈtraiˌʃɔː; ˋtraɪʃɔ] *n*. 三轮车(= pedicab)。

tris·kai·dek·a·pho·bi·a [ˌtriskaiˌdekəˈfəubiə; ˏtrɪskaɪˏdɛkəˋfobɪə] *n*. 对数字13的迷信忌讳,对13的憎恶。

tris·kel·i·on [trisˈkeliɔn, trai-; trɪsˋkɛlɪɑn, -ən] *n*.

(*pl*. -i·a [-ə; -ə]) 三枝(腿,臂)所成的幅射状图形(= triskele)。

tris·mic [ˈtrizmik, ˈtris-; ˋtrɪzmɪk, ˋtrɪs-] *a*. 牙关紧闭的。

tris·mus [ˈtrizməs; ˋtrɪzməs, ˋtrɪs-] *n*. 【医】牙关紧闭。

tris·oc·ta·he·dron [trisˌɔktəˈhi:drən; trɪsˏɑktəˋhidrən] *n*. 三八[二十四]面体。*trigonal* ~ 三方八面体,三角面二十四面体。*tetragonal* ~ 偏方三八面体(= trapezohedron)。**-he·dral** *a*.

tri·so·di·um [traiˈsəudiəm; traɪˋsodɪəm] *a*. 【化】三钠(化的)。

tri·some [ˈtraisəum; ˋtraɪsom] *n*. 【生】三体生物细胞。

tri·so·mic [traiˈsəumik; traɪˋsomɪk] I *a*. 【生】三体生物的。II *n*. 三体生物细胞,三体生物机体。**-so·my** [ˈtraisəumi; ˋtraɪsomɪ] *n*.

triste [tri:st; trist] *a*. 〔F.〕悲哀的,悲惨的,忧愁的;沉闷的。

tris·tesse [tri:sˈtes; trisˋtɛs] *n*. 〔F.〕悲伤,忧郁。

trist·ful [ˈtristful; ˋtrɪstful, -fl] *a*. 〔古〕悲哀的,阴郁的。

tris·tich [ˈtristik; ˋtrɪstɪk] *n*. 【诗】(押韵的)三行诗。

tris·tich·ous [ˈtristikəs; ˋtrɪstɪkəs] *a*. 成三行的,三列的〔尤指成三纵列的植物叶〕。

tri·sub·sti·tut·ed [traiˈsʌbstiˌtju:tid, -ˌtu:tid; traɪˋsʌbstɪˏtjutɪd, -ˏtutɪd] *a*. 【化】三代的,三元取代的。

tri·sul·fide [traiˈsʌlfaid; traɪˋsʌlfaɪd, -fɪd] *n*. 【化】三硫化合物。

tri·syl·lab·ic [ˈtraisiˈlæbik; ˏtrɪsɪˋlæbɪk, ˏtraɪs-] *a*. 三音节的。

tris·yl·la·ble [ˈtraiˈsiləbl; trɪˋsɪləbl̩, traɪ-, ˋtrɪsɪl-, ˋtraɪ-] *n*. 三音节词。

tri·tag·o·nist [traiˈtægənist, tri-; traɪˋtægənɪst, trɪ-] *n*. 【古希腊剧】第三演员。

trite [trait; traɪt] *a*. 用旧了的;陈腐的(字句、观念等)。**-ly** *ad*. **-ness** *n*.

tri·the·ism [ˈtraiθi:izəm; ˋtraɪθɪɪzm̩] *n*. 【宗】三位异体说,三神论。**-the·ist** *n*. 三神论者。

tri·ti·at·ed [ˈtritiˌeitid, ˈtriʃ-; ˋtrɪtɪˏetɪd, ˋtrɪʃ-] *a*. 【化】含氚的;氚化了的。

trit·i·um [ˈtritiəm; ˋtrɪtɪəm, ˋtrɪʃɪəm] *n*. 【化】氚,超重氢〔H^3 或 T〕。

trit·o·ma [ˈtritəmə; ˋtrɪtəmə] *n*. 【植】剑叶兰属(*Kniphofia*)植物〔产于非洲〕。

Tri·ton [ˈtraitn; ˋtraɪtn̩] *n*. 【希神】半人半鱼的海神;〔t-〕【动】蝾螈;梭尾螺(壳)。*a T- among* [*of*] *the minnows* 鹤立鸡群。

triton [ˈtraitn, ˈtraitɔn; ˋtraɪtn] *n*. 【化、物】氚核。

tri·tone [ˈtraiˌtəun; ˋtraɪˏton] *n*. 【乐】三全音音程。

tri·to·ri·um [traiˈtɔ:riəm; traɪˋtorɪəm] *n*. 分液器。

trit·u·rate [ˈtritjureit; ˋtrɪtʃəˏret] I *vt*. 1. 研成粉,磨碎,捣碎。2. 【生理】咀嚼。II *n*. 【药】研制剂。

trit·u·ra·tion [ˌtritjuˈreiʃən; ˏtrɪtʃəˋreʃən] *n*. 研碎,磨碎,【药】研制(法),研磨(法),研制剂〔尤指和有乳糖的〕。

trit·u·ra·tor [ˌtritjuˈreitə; ˋtrɪtʃəˏretə] *n*. 捣[研]碎的人,磨粉人;捣碎器,研钵。

tri·umph [ˈtraiəmf; ˋtraɪəmf, -mpf] I *n*. 1. 【古罗马】凯旋式。2. 凯旋;胜利,征服(*over*);大成功,功绩;胜利[成功]的喜悦,得意洋洋的样子;最好的例子。*His life was a ~ over ill health*. 他的一生是克服疾病的一个最好范例。*a ~ of architecture* 建筑术上的大成功。*the ~ of ugliness* 丑恶无比。***in*** ~ 耀武扬威地,扬扬得意地。***with ill-dissembled*** ~ 带着无可隐藏的得意样子。II *vi*. 欢庆胜利,得胜而狂欢;得胜,战胜,打败,成功(*over*);【古罗马】举行凯旋式。*The forces representing the advanced ideas are bound to ~ sooner or later*. 代表先进思想的势力总有一天会要成功的。

tri·um·phal [traiˈʌmfəl; traɪˋʌmfl] *a*. 凯旋(式)的,祝捷的,庆祝胜利的;胜利的(歌曲等)。*a ~ arch* 凯旋门。*a ~ car* 【古罗马】凯旋车。*a ~ entry* 凯旋入城式。*a ~ feast* 庆功宴。*a ~ progress* 胜利游行。*a ~ return* 凯旋。

tri·um·phant [traiˈʌmfənt; traɪˋʌmfənt] *a*. 得到胜利的,战胜的;成功的;耀武扬威的,得意洋洋的。**-ly** *ad*.

tri·um·vir [traiˈʌmvə; traɪˋʌmvə] *n*. (*pl*. ~*s*, *-vi·ri* [-virai; -vɪraɪ]) 【古罗马】三执政之一。

tri·um·vi·ral [traiˈʌmvərəl; traɪˋʌmvərəl] *a*. (古罗马)三执政之一的,三头政治中的执政者之一的;三执政的,三头政治的,三人一组的。

tri·um·vi·rate [traiˈʌmvirit; traɪˋʌmvərɪt] *n*. 1. 【古罗马】三头政治;三执政官的职位。2. 三人组,三人同盟。*a ~ of friends* (常在一起的)三个朋友。

tri·une [ˈtraiju:n; ˋtraɪjun, traɪˋjun] I *a*. 三位一体的。II *n*. 三人一组,三个一套;【宗】〔the T-〕三位一体。

tri·uni·ty [traiˈju:niti; traɪˋjunətɪ] *n*. = trinity.

tri·va·lence [traiˈveiləns, ˈtrivə-; traɪˋveləns, ˋtrɪvə-] *n*. 【化】三价(= trivalency)。

tri·va·lent [traiˈveilənt; traɪˋvelənt, ˋtrɪvələnt] *a*. 【化】三价的。

tri·valve [ˈtraivælv; ˋtraɪvælv] 【动】I *a*. (贝壳)三瓣的。II *n*. 三瓣贝壳。

triv·et [ˈtrivit; ˋtrɪvɪt] *n*. 三脚架;(火炉上的)三脚铁架。***as right as a*** ~ 〔罕〕正好,十分正确,完全顺利,非常健康。~ ***table*** 三脚桌。

triv·i·a[1] [ˈtriviə; ˋtrɪvɪə] *n*. 〔*pl*.〕〔动词常用单数〕平凡的事情;琐碎的事情;琐事。

triv·ia[2] [ˈtriviə; ˋtrɪvɪə] trivium 的复数。

triv·i·al [ˈtriviəl; ˋtrɪvɪəl] *a*. 1. 琐细的,轻微的;浅薄的,无价值的;平常的,平凡的;(名称)通俗的。2. 【生】种的(*opp*. generic)。~ *matters* 琐事。*T- formalities have been done away with*. 废除烦琐的礼节。*a ~ man* 轻薄的人。*the ~ round of daily life* 平凡的日常生活。*a ~ name* 俗名。*a ~ term* 【生】种名。**Trivial Pursuit** 常识问答游戏。**-ism** *n*. = triviality. **-ly** *ad*. **-ness** *n*.

triv·i·al·i·ty [triviˈæliti; ˏtrɪvɪˋælətɪ] *n*. 小事,琐事;不足道的东西;(人的)浅薄,轻浮;寻常;平凡;一点儿。

triv·i·al·ize [ˈtriviəlaiz; ˋtrɪvɪəlˏaɪz] *vt*. 使琐碎;平凡化;使浅薄[轻浮],轻视。**-i·za·tion** *n*.

triv·i·um [ˈtriviəm; ˋtrɪvɪəm] *n*. (*pl*. *-i·a* [-iə; -ɪə]) (中世纪学校的)三学科〔语法、逻辑、修辞〕;【动】三道体区。

tri·week·ly [ˈtraiˈwi:kli; traɪˋviklɪ] I *a*., *ad*. 三星期一次(的);一星期三次(的)。II *n*. 三周刊;一星期三次的出版物。

-trix *suf*. -(t)or 的女性后缀:aviat*rix*;【数】表示"点";"线";"面":genera*trix*.

Trk = truck.

troat [trəut; trot] *vi*., *n*. (公鹿等)叫春(声)。

tro·car [ˈtrəukɑ:; ˋtrokɑr] *n*. 【医】套(管)针。

tro·cha·ic [trəuˈkeiik; troˋke·ɪk] I *a*. 【韵】扬抑[长短,强弱]格的。II *n*. = trochee.

tro·chal [ˈtrəukl; ˋtrokl̩] *a*. 【动】轮状的。

tro·chan·ter [trəuˈkæntə; troˋkæntə] *n*. 【解】(股骨的)转子,粗隆;(昆虫腿上的)转节。

tro·char [ˈtrəukɑ:; ˋtrokɑr] *n*. 【医】(外科用)套针。

troche [trəuʃ, ˈtrəuki; ˋtrokɪ] *n*. 【药】片剂,锭剂;糖锭。

tro·chee [ˈtrəuki:; ˋtroki] *n*. 【韵】长短格,强弱格,扬抑格。

troch·el·minth [ˈtrɔklˌminθ; ˋtrɑklˏmɪnθ] *n*. 【动】担轮动物门(*Trochelminthes*)动物〔包括腹毛纲〕。

troch·i·lus [ˈtrɔkiləs; ˋtrɑkɪləs] *n*. (*pl*. *-ili* [-ilai; -ɪlaɪ]) (传说中的)鳄鸟;【鸟】蜂鸟。

troch·le·a [ˈtrɔkliə; ˋtrɑklɪə] *n*. (*pl*. *-leae* [-lii:; -lɪi])

T

【解】滑车;(蜂的)翅厚基;【植】滑车形的。

troch·le·ar [ˈtrɔkliə; ˋtrɑkliɚ] *a*. 【解】滑车状的;【植】滑车形的。~ **nerve**【解】滑车神经。

tro·choid [ˈtrəukɔid; ˋtrokɔɪd] **I** *n*. 【数】长短辐旋轮线,次摆线,余摆线;转迹线;【解】滑车[枢轴]关节;【贝】蝾螺类。**II** *a*. 轮子一样动的,用轴旋转的;滑车形的,陀螺形的,圆锥形的(贝)。~ **wave**【物】摆动波。**-al** *a*.

tro·chom·e·ter [trəuˈkɔmitə; troˋkɑmətɚ] *n*. = trechometer.

troch·o·phore [ˈtrɔkəˌfɔː; ˋtrɑkəˏfɔr] *n*. 【动】担轮幼虫。

trochotron [ˈtrəukətrɔn; ˋtrokətrɑn] *n*. 【电】电子转换器;摆线管;余摆管;磁旋管。

trod [trɔd; trɑd] tread 的过去式及过去分词。

trod·den [ˈtrɔdn; ˋtrɑdn] tread 的过去分词。

trode [trəud; trod] *v*. 〔古〕tread 的过去式。

trof·fer [ˈtrɔfə; ˋtrɑfɚ] *n*. 〔美〕天花板凹槽〔供装荧光灯用〕。

trog·lo·dyte [ˈtrɔglədait; ˋtrɑgləˏdaɪt] *n*. (史前的)穴居人;隐居者;不喜欢与人交往的人;粗野堕落的人;【动】类人猿;鹪鹩。**-dyt·ic**, **-dyt·i·cal** *a*.

tro·gon [ˈtrəugɔn; ˋtrogɑn] *n*. 【动】咬鹃〔产于热带〕。

troi·ka [ˈtrɔikə; ˋtrɔɪkə] *n*. 〔俄〕**1**. 三驾马车[雪橇];并驾拉车的三匹马。**2**. 紧密结合在一起的三个人[三件东西];三巨头,三人执政。

trois-temps [trwɑːˈtɔŋ; ˏtrwɑˋtɑŋ] *n*. 〔F.〕三拍子华尔兹舞 (= ~ waltz)。

Tro·jan [ˈtrəudʒən; ˋtrodʒən] **I** *a*. 特洛伊 (Troy) 城[人]的。**II** *n*. **1**. 特洛伊人。**2**. 〔口〕勤勉的人;拳击家,勇士;〔口〕愉快的人,有趣的人,酒友。**3**. 【计】特洛伊木马式病毒〔此种电脑程序貌似正常而实际上起破坏作用〕。*like a* ~ 勇敢地,坚强地,辛苦的。~ **horse**【神话】特洛伊木马〔特洛伊战争时希腊人把战士藏在里面混进特洛伊城〕;〔喻〕内部的破坏集团;【计】特洛伊木马式病毒;【计】特洛伊木马式电脑侦破程序〔以貌似合法的程序偷偷潜入他人网站进行窃密等破坏活动〕。~ **War** (古希腊传说中的)特洛伊战争,荷马史诗《伊利亚特》(*Iliad*) 即以此战争为中心内容。

troll[1] [trəul; trol] **I** *n*. **1**. 轮唱;轮唱歌曲;反复。**2**. 钓丝的卷车;拟饵钩。**II** *vt*., *vi*. **1**. 轮唱;(一面工作一面)用愉快的声音唱[说]。**2**. (用拟饵钩)拖钓。**3**. 〔古〕传递(酒等)。**-er** *n*. 轮唱者。

troll[2] [trəul; trol] *n*. 【北欧神】洞窟巨人,爱恶作剧而态度友好的侏儒。

trol·ley [ˈtrɔli; ˋtrɑlɪ] **I** *n*. **1**. 手推车;〔英〕(装有脚轮,用来送食物的)小台。**2**. (铁路上的)手摇车;空中吊运车。**3**. (电车上的)触轮;〔英〕无轨电车。(= trackless ~ bus);〔美〕(有轨)电车 *a bow* ~ (电车上的)弓形滑接线。***off one's*** ~ 〔美俚〕神经失常,发疯。**II** *vi*., *vt*. 搭乘(电车,手摇车等);用电车,手推车等运载。~ **bus** 〔英〕无轨电车。~ **car** 〔美〕电车。~ **line** (有轨、无轨)电车路线。~ **pilot** 〔美〕电车司机。~ **pole** 触轮杆。~ **shop** (医院里的)手推售货车。~**wheel** 触轮。~ **wire** (电车的)触轮线,架空线。**-man** 电车司机[售票员]。

trol·lop [ˈtrɔləp; ˋtrɑləp] *n*. 邋遢女人,懒妇;堕落的女人;妓女。**-ish** *a*.

Trol·lope [ˈtrɔləp; ˋtrɑləp] *n*. 特罗洛普〔姓氏〕。

trol·ly [ˈtrɔli; ˋtrɑlɪ] *n*., *vi*., *vt*. (**-lied**) = trolley.

trom·ba [ˈtrɔmbə; ˋtrɑmbə] *n*. 〔It.〕【乐】小号。

trom·bi·di·a·sis [ˌtrɔmbiˈdaiəsis; ˏtrɑmbəˋdaɪəsɪs] *n*. 【医】恙螨病 (= trombidiosis)。

trom·bone [trɔmˈbəun; ˋtrɑmbon, trɑmˋbon] *n*. 【乐】长号,拉管。

trom·bon·ist [trɔmˈbəunist; ˋtrɑmbonɪst, trɑmˋbonɪst] *n*. 长号吹奏者。

trom·mel [ˈtrɔməl; ˋtrɑml̩] *n*. 【矿】滚筒筛;洗矿筒。

tro·mom·e·ter [trɔˈmɔmitə; troˋmɑmətɚ] *n*. (地震)微震计。

tromp [trɔmp; trɑmp] *vt*., *vi*. = tramp.

trompe [trɔmp; trɑmp] *n*. (熔矿炉的)水风筒。

-tron *suf*. 表示"工具","仪器","装置"等(尤指真空管,迹原子操纵装置等设备,如 magnetron 磁控电子管, cyclotron 回旋加速器等)。

tro·na [ˈtrəunə; ˋtronə] *n*. 【化】天然碱。

Trond·heim [ˈtrɔnheim; ˋtrɑnhem] *n*. 特隆赫姆〔挪威港市〕。

troop [truːp; trup] **I** *n*. **1**. 〔*pl*.〕军队;部队。**2**. (在行动中的)大群(人);(动物等的)群;一队,一组;(戏剧演员等的)一团。**3**. 【军】骑兵连。**4**. 进军鼓。*a* ~ *of boys* 一队儿童。*regular* ~*s* 常备军。*shock* ~*s* 突击队。*the* ~*s* 〔军口〕我们部队〔I 或 me 的代用语〕。~ *disposition* 军队部署。***despatch*** ~***s*** 出兵,派兵。***get one's*** ~ 升任骑兵连长。***withdraw*** ~***s*** 撤兵。**II** *vi*. **1**. 集合,聚拢,群集 (*up*; *together*)。**2**. 成群结队地走,排着队前进 (*along*; *in*; *out*; *to*)。**3**. 若干人匆匆走掉 (*off*; *away*)。— *vt*. **1**. 编成(队伍,骑兵连)。**2**. 运输(军队) *They came* ~*ing in*. 他们成群结队地进来了。~ *the colour*(*s*) 行军旗敬礼分列式;举行军旗授与典礼。~ **carrier** 部队运送机(车、船)。~**horse** 战马。~**ship** 军队运输船。

troop·er [ˈtruːpə; ˋtrupɚ] *n*. **1**. 骑兵,伞兵;骑警;战马。**2**. 运兵船。**3**. 〔美口〕州警察。***swear like a*** ~ 大骂,痛骂。

troost·ite [ˈtruːstait; ˋtrustaɪt] *n*. 【矿】锰硅锌矿。

trop. = tropic(al)。

trop [trəu; tro] *ad*. 〔F.〕太,太多,过分,非常,很。

tro·pae·o·lin, **tro·pae·o·line** [trəuˈpiəlin; troˋpiəlɪn] *n*. 【染】金莲橙 (= tropeolin, tropeoline)。

tro·pae·o·lum [trəuˈpiːələm; troˋpiələm] *n*. 【植】旱金莲属植物。

trope [trəup; trop] *n*. **1**. 【修】转义;比喻。**2**. 【数】奇异切面。

troph·al·lax·is [ˌtrɔfəˈlæksis; ˏtrɑfəˋlæksɪs] *n*. (*pl*. **-lax·es** [-siːz; -siz]) 【动】交哺现象。**troph·al·lac·tic** [-ˈlæktik; -ˋlæktɪk] *a*.

troph·ic [ˈtrɔfik; ˋtrɑfɪk] *a*. (司)营养的;口器的。~ **behaviour** 趋食行为。~ **disturbance** 营养失调。

tro·phied [ˈtrəufid; ˋtrofɪd] *a*. 用战利品装饰的。

troph·o·blast [ˈtrɔfəˌblæst; ˋtrɑfəˏblæst] *n*. 【生】滋养层。**-ic** *a*.

tro·pholo·gy [trɔˈfɔlədʒi; troˋfɑlədʒɪ] *n*. 营养学。

troph·o·neu·ro·sis [ˌtrɔfəunjuəˈrəusis; ˏtrɑfojuˋrosɪs] *n*. 【医】神经性营养不良。

troph·o·plasm [ˈtrɔfəplæzm; ˋtrɑfəplæzm̩] *n*. 【生】滋养质。

troph·o·thera·py [trɔfəˈθerəpi; trɑfəˋθɛrəpɪ] *n*. 【医】营养疗法。

troph·o·zo·ite [ˌtrɔfəˈzəuit; ˏtrɑfəˋzoaɪt] *n*. 【生】滋养体。

tro·phy [ˈtrəufi; ˋtrofɪ] **I** *n*. **1**. 战利品;胜利纪念物;战利品装饰[图案];奖品[银杯等]纪念品。**2**. (古希腊、罗马的)胜利纪念碑。*a* ~ *belt* 〔美运〕优胜纪录。**II** *a*. 显示身份或地位的,提高身价的。*a* ~ *home* 显示身份地位的住宅。*a* ~ *wife* 足以作为炫耀资本的年轻貌美的妻子。

-trophy *suf*. 营养: hyper*trophy*.

trop·ic[1] [ˈtrɔpik; ˋtrɑpɪk] **I** *n*. **1**. 【天】回归线。**2**. 〔the ~s〕热带(地区)。**II** *a*. 热带(地区)的。*T- of Cancer* [*Capricorn*] 北[南]回归线,夏[冬]至线。

trop·ic[2] [ˈtrɔpik; ˋtrɑpɪk] *a*. 【生】向性的。~ **behaviour** 向性行为。~ **hormone** 促激素。

trop·i·cal [ˈtrɔpikl; ˋtrɑpɪkl] *a*. **1**. 热带(地区)的,回归线下的。**2**. 非常热的;热情的,热烈的,激烈的。**3**. 〔罕〕比喻的;转义的。~ **cyclone** 热带气旋。~ **fish** 热带鱼。

~ **suiting** 夏季衣料。~ **year**【天】太阳年,回归年。~ **zone** 热带。

tro·pine [ˈtrəupiːn; ˋtropin, -pɪn] ***n.***【化】托品碱。

trop·ism [ˈtrəupizəm; ˋtropɪzəm] ***n.***【生】向性。

tro·pist [ˈtrəupist; ˋtropɪst] ***n.*** 作比喻者,用比喻者。

tro·pis·tic [trəuˈpistik; troˋpɪstɪk] ***a.***【生】向性的。

tro·po·col·la·gen [ˌtrəupəˈkɔlədʒən; ˏtropəˋkɑlədʒən] ***n.***【生】原胶原,原胶原蛋白〔形成结蒂组织、骨骼等的胶原纤维的蛋白质〕。

trop·o·log·i·cal [ˌtrɔpəˈlɔdʒikl; ˏtrɑpəˋlɑdʒɪkḷ] ***a.*** 比喻的。**-ly *ad.***

tro·pol·o·gy [trəuˈpɔlədʒi; troˋpɑlədʒɪ] ***n.*** **1.** 比喻的使用。**2.** (圣经中的)比喻的解释。**3.** 比喻语言的论文;比喻语的编纂。

trop·o·pause [ˈtrɔpəpɔːz; ˋtrɑpəˏpɔz] ***n.***【气】对流层顶。

tro·poph·i·lous [trəuˈpɔfiləs; troˋpɑfələs] ***a.***【植】湿旱生的。

trop·o·phyte [ˈtrɔpəufait, ˈtrəupəu-; ˋtrɑpəˏfaɪt, ˋtropo-] ***n.***【植】湿旱生植物。**trop·o·phyt·ic** [-ˈfitik; -ˋfɪtɪk] ***a.***

trop·o·scat·ter [ˈtrɔpəuskætə; ˋtrɑpoˏskætɚ] ***n.***【气】对流层散射 (= tropospheric scatter)。

trop·o·sphere [ˈtrɔpəusfiə; ˋtrɑpəˏsfɪr] ***n.***【气】对流层。

trop·o·spher·ic [ˌtrɔpəuˈsferik, -ˈsfiər-; ˏtrɑpoˋsfɛrɪk, -ˋsfɪr-] ***a.***【气】对流层的。

trop·po [ˈtrɔpəu; ˋtrɑpo, ˋtrɔppo] ***ad.*** 〔It.〕【乐】过度,过甚。*allegro ma non* ~ 轻快但不过甚。*andante ma non* ~ 温和而适度地。

trot [trɔt; trɑt] **I *vi.*** (***trot·ted*** [ˈtrɔtid; ˋtrɑtɪd]; ***trot·ting*** [ˈtrɔtiŋ; ˋtrɑtɪŋ]) **1.** (马)小跑;(人)小跑着走,急匆匆地走。**2.** 〔谑〕走着去。— ***vt.*** **1.** 使(马)小跑;快步走过;搁在膝上颠(小孩等)。**2.** 〔口〕带着走,领着走 (*round*; *to*)。**3.** 〔美俚〕使用现成的译本(做课外作业)。**4.** 〔美〕跳舞。*The child ~ted along after his mother.* 小孩跟在母亲后面很快地往前走。~ *the hills and valleys* 翻山越谷。~ ***a child on the knee*** 使小孩子骑在膝头上颠。~ ***sb. off his legs*** 叫人走得脚软腿酸。~ ***along*** 〔口〕快点去。~ ***away from the pole*** 〔美〕话离题。~ ***in double harness*** 〔美〕已结婚。~ ***out*** 牵马出来得意扬扬地给人看步伐;〔口〕给人看,供人展览;讲(笑话);〔俚〕带着女(人)走路;愚弄。~ ***round*** 〔口〕领着到处串 (*I will ~ you round London.* 我要领着你逛伦敦)。**II *n.*** **1.** (马交互举起前右脚与后左脚或前左脚与后右脚而快走的)小跑;驾车赛马。**2.** (人的)慢跑;散步。**3.** 〔英口〕摇摇摆摆走路的[刚学走的]小孩。**4.** (为工作的)奔走。**5.** 〔美俚〕(做课外作业时用来作弊的)现成译本。**6.** 〔蔑〕老太婆。**7.** 〔俚〕〔*pl.*〕腹泻。**8.** = trotline. (***always***) ***on the*** ~ 一刻不停,席不暇暖,忙忙碌碌。***go for a*** ~ 去散步。***keep*** (***sb.***) ***on the*** ~ 使一刻不停地忙碌奔波。~**-boat *n.*** (往返于码头和锚泊地船只间接送旅客及运送货物的)交通艇。

troth [trəuθ, trɔθ; trɔθ, troθ] ***n.*** 〔古〕**1.** 忠诚。**2.** 真实。**3.** 誓言;婚约。***by*** [***upon***] ***my*** ~ 发誓,一定。(***in***) ~ 〔古〕实在,的确。***plight one's*** ~ 盟誓,(尤指订婚)山盟海誓。~**plight** 〔古〕订婚。

trot·line [ˈtrɔtˌlain; ˋtrɑtˏlaɪn] ***n.*** (钓鱼用的)滚钓线。

Trot·sky·ist [ˈtrɔtskiist; ˋtrɑtskɪɪst], **Trot·sky·ite** [-ait; -aɪt] ***n.***, ***a.*** 托(洛茨基)派(分子)(的)。

trot·ter [ˈtrɔtə; ˋtrɑtɚ] ***n.*** **1.** 小跑的马;走得快的人,工作机敏的人。**2.** 〔*pl.*〕【烹】猪(等的)脚,猪爪;〔口、谑〕(尤指孩子、少女的)脚。

trot·toir [ˈtrɔtwɑː; troˋtwaɪ] ***n.*** 〔F.〕人行道,步行道。

tro·tyl [ˈtrəutil; ˋtrotɪl] ***n.***【化】三硝基甲苯 (= trinitrotoluene)。

trou [trau; traʊ] ***n.*** 〔美俚〕裤子 (= trousers)。

trou·ba·dour [ˈtruːbəduə; ˋtrubəˏdʊr, -ˏdor, -ˏdɔr] ***n.*** **1.** (11—13 世纪法国南部及意大利北部等地的)抒情诗人,行吟诗人。**2.** 〔转〕民谣歌手,民谣曲乐师。

trou·ble [ˈtrʌbl; ˋtrʌbḷ] **I *n.*** **1.** 苦恼,烦恼;麻烦;困难,艰难;灾难。**2.** 苦恼的原因;使烦恼的人,麻烦家伙;疾病;生产,怀孕。**3.** (政局等的)风潮,纠纷,骚动,纷扰。**4.** 故障,事故,干扰。**5.**【矿】断层。*Thank you for your ~.* 麻烦您了,多谢多谢。*It is too much ~.* 麻烦死了。*What is the ~?* 怎么不好啦? 那里不舒服? *The ~ is that ....* 麻烦的是…。*digestive ~(s)* 胃弱。*heart ~* 心脏病。*engine ~* 机器上的毛病。*labour ~(s)* 劳资纠纷。*political ~* 政治风潮。*a ~ man = a ~ shooter* (电路、煤气管等的)检修员。***ask for*** ~ 〔口〕自讨苦吃。***be a*** ~ ***to*** 对…是一个麻烦。***be at the*** ~ ***of doing*** 特意…。***be in*** ~(*s*) ***with*** 和…闹纠纷。***get into*** ~ 招致麻烦,卷入纠纷;受责备;未结婚而怀孕。***get sb. into*** ~ 给某人造成麻烦。***get sb. out of*** ~ 帮助某人解除困难。***get out of*** ~ 摆脱麻烦事;免罚。***give sb.*** ~ 麻烦人,打扰人。***go to the*** ~ ***of ... ing*** 特意…;不辞劳苦…。***have a*** ~ ***with*** 和…闹纠纷[搅不清]。***have*** ~ ***to*** (*do*) 做…很费事。***in*** ~ 为难,窘困;被捕;未婚怀孕。***look for*** ~ = *ask for ~.* ***make*** ~ 捣乱,吵闹。***make*** ~ ***for sb.*** 给某人制造麻烦。***put sb. to*** ~ 麻烦人,使人受累。***save sb.*** ~ 免去某人麻烦,不必某人费事[操心]。***spare sb.*** ~ 不打搅[不麻烦]某人 (*You may spare yourself the ~.* 你不必费神[费事])。***stir up*** ~ 兴风作浪,惹是生非。***take the*** ~ ***to*** (*do*) 不怕麻烦去…,不辞…之劳。***take*** ~ 不辞劳苦,费力,忍苦耐劳 (*He dislikes to take ~.* 他怕麻烦)。**II *vt.*** **1.** 扰乱;搅浑。**2.** 使烦恼,使困苦,使为难,使受累;麻烦,烦扰;请求 (*for*);(病等)折磨。— ***vi.*** 费力,费神;担心,忧虑;激动。***be*** ~***d about*** [***with***] ***money matters*** 为钱操心。***I will*** ~ ***you to*** (*do*) 我要麻烦你去…。***May I*** ~ ***you for*** [***to*** (***do***)] 麻烦你…好吗? ***Pray don't*** ~. 请不要费事。~ ***sb. for money*** 问…要钱。~ ***oneself about*** 担心,害怕。~ ***oneself to*** (*do*) 不辞劳苦地(做)…,特意…。~ **clerk** 故障记录员。~**-free *a.*** 可靠的,无故障的。~ **lamp** 故障探查灯。~**-maker** 惹是生非的人;闹事者,捣乱者。~ **making** 制造麻烦,闹事。~ **man** (机器等的)检修工。~**shooter** 故障检修员;排解纠纷者。

trou·bled [ˈtrʌbld; ˋtrʌbḷd] ***a.*** 为难的,不安的,困惑的;骚乱的,不宁的。~ ***times*** 乱世。~ ***waters*** 波涛汹涌的海;混乱状态 (*to fish in ~ waters* 〔喻〕浑水摸鱼,趁火打劫)。

trou·ble·some [ˈtrʌblsəm; ˋtrʌblsəm] ***a.*** 讨厌的;麻烦的,困难的;(孩子等)难管的,吵闹的。**-ly *ad.*** **-ness *n.***

trou·blous [ˈtrʌbləs; ˋtrʌbləs] ***a.*** 〔古〕**1.** 动乱的,骚乱的。**2.** = troublesome. ~ *times* 乱世。

trou-de-loup [truːdəˈluː; ˏtrudəˋlu] ***n.*** (*pl.* ***trous-*** [truː-; tru-]) 〔F.〕【军】(阻敌进攻的)狼阱。

trough [trɔf, trɔːf; trɔf] ***n.*** **1.** 木盆;马槽,猪槽;承溜;水笕;洗矿槽。**2.** [trau; traʊ] (面包店的)揉面盆,面钵。**3.**【海】(深 6000 米以上的)深海渚;【电】电槽 (= ~ battery);【物】波谷;【数】凹点;【气】槽形低气压。**4.** 〔美剧〕脚光。*a pneumatic ~* 集气槽。*a ~ truck* 油槽车。

trounce [trauns; traʊns] ***vt.*** **1.** 痛打;严责,痛骂。**2.** 〔口〕打败(对手)。

troupe [truːp; trup] **I *n.*** **1.** 剧团,戏班子;马戏团。**2.** 一团,一班,一伙。**II *vi.*** (参加戏班子)巡回演出。

troup·er [ˈtruːpə; ˋtrupɚ] ***n.*** (剧团、马戏团等的)演员,团员;〔口〕有经验的演员。

troup·i·al [ˈtruːpiəl; ˋtrupɪəl] ***n.***【动】拟椋鸟。

trou·ser [ˈtrauzə; ˋtraʊzɚ] **I *n.*** 〔*pl.*〕裤子。*a pair* [*three pairs*] *of ~s* 一条[三条]裤子。★〔口〕〔用单数〕: *Here is a smart ~.* 这是一条漂亮的裤子。***wear the ~s*** (女人)欺压丈夫。**II *a.*** 裤子的。~(**s**)**-pocket**

T

裤兜。～ **stretcher** 撑裤器〔使保持挺拔〕。～ **suit**〔英〕(上衣与裤子相配的)女衫裤套装 (= pantsuit)。

trou·sered [ˈtrauzəd; ˋtraʊzəd] *a*. 穿着裤子的;〔喻〕男的。

trou·ser·ing [ˈtrauzəriŋ; ˋtraʊzərɪŋ] *n*. 裤料。

trous·seau [ˈtruːsəu; truˋso, ˋtruso] *n*. (*pl*. ～*s*, ～*x* [-z; -z]) 嫁妆。

trout [traut; traʊt] **I** *n*. (*pl*. ～*s*〔集合词〕)【鱼】鲑鱼(属);红点鲑鱼(属);真鳟。**II** *vi*. 钓[捕]鳟鱼。～-**coloured** *a*. (马)白毛黑花的。～ **lily**【植】美洲赤莲,犬齿赤莲。～-**perch**【动】鲑鲈。

trout·let, trout·ling [ˈtrautlit, -liŋ; ˋtraʊtlɪt, -lɪŋ] *n*. 小鳟鱼。

trout·y [ˈtrauti; ˋtraʊtɪ] *a*. 多鳟鱼的;像鳟鱼的。

trou·vaille [ˈtruːvail; truˋvaɪl] *n*. 〔F.〕意外的收获,挖到的地财。

trou·vère [truːˈveə; truˋver] *n*. 〔F.〕(11—14 世纪间活跃于法国北部的)行吟诗人。

trove [trəuv; trov] *n*. = treasure-trove.

tro·ver [ˈtrəuvə; ˋtrovə] *n*.【法】要求赔偿被侵占所受损失的诉讼。

trow [trəu; tro] *vi*., *vt*. 〔古〕想;〔附在疑问句后用〕不知道…。*What ails him*, (*I*) ～? 不知道他什么不舒服?

trow·el [ˈtrauəl; ˋtraʊəl] **I** *n*. (泥水匠等的)泥刀,泥铲儿,抹子;【园艺】移植手铲。***lay it on with a*** ～ 用泥铲儿涂抹;大事渲染;竭力阿谀。**II** *vt*. 用泥铲儿涂抹。

Troy[1] [trɔi; trɔɪ] *n*. 特罗伊〔姓氏,男子名〕。

Troy[2] [trɔi; trɔɪ] *n*. 特洛伊〔小亚细亚的古城〕。

troy (weight) [trɔi; trɔɪ] *n*. 金衡〔金、银、宝石的衡制〕。

trs = trustees.

trs. = transpose.

tru·an·cy [ˈtruːənsi; ˋtruənsɪ] *n*. 玩忽职守;(尤指学生的)旷课,逃学。

tru·ant [ˈtruːənt; ˋtruənt] **I** *n*. 玩忽职守者,偷懒者;无故旷课者,逃学者。**II** *a*. 偷懒的,无故缺席的,逃学的;混日子的。**play** ～ 逃学,赖学。**III** *vi*. 玩忽职守;偷懒;无故旷课,赖学,逃学。～ **officer** 训导主任。～ **school**〔英史〕流浪儿学校。-**ry** *n*. 玩忽职守,偷懒;逃学。

Truben·ize [ˈtruːbinaiz; ˋtrubənaɪz] *vt*.【纺】〔商标〕托律本硬挺整理。

truce [truːs; trus] *n*. **1**. 休战,停战(协定)。**2**. 暂时,休止,中止。*a flag of* ～ 停战旗。*a general* [*special*] ～ 全面[局部]停战。*an industrial* ～ 劳资和解。*A* ～ *to* [*with*] *jesting*! 别再开玩笑了! *A* ～ *to nonsense*! 别讲废话! **tru·cial** *a*.

truck[1] [trʌk; trʌk] **I** *n*. **1**. 〔美〕运货汽车,卡车;货车(=〔英〕lorry)。**2**. (铁路上的)手摇车;手推车,(车站上的)电动搬运车;〔英〕无盖货车;转向车;(铁路车辆等的)车架。**3**. 桅杆帽,旗杆帽(等)。**4**.【机】转向架。**5**. 〔罕〕小车轮。*an air* ～ 运货飞机。*a sound* ～ 广播车。**II** *vt*. 把…装上卡车(等);用卡车(等)运。— *vi*. 用卡车运输;充当卡车司机。～**driver**, ～**man** 卡车司机;卡车运输业者。～**load** 一卡车的装载量;一卡车的运费。～ **spring** 车架弹簧。～ **tractor** 货运拖曳汽车。～ **trailer** 货运拖挂车。

truck[2] [trʌk; trʌk] **I** *n*. **1**. 交易,物物交换;买卖。**2**. 交易品;零星货物。**3**. 实物工资(制)。**4**. 〔美〕(作商品出卖的)菜蔬;〔口〕垃圾,废物;废话。***have no*** ～ ***with*** 不和…交易,不和…来往。***stand no*** ～ 不要妥协(等);不能讲废话。～ **crops** 蔬菜作物。～ **farm** [**farmer**]〔美〕菜圃[农]。～ **garden**〔美〕菜[果]园。～ **system** 实物工资制。**II** *vt*., *vi*. **1**. 物物交换。**2**. 沿街叫卖。**3**. 交易,打交道。

truck·age [ˈtrʌkidʒ; ˋtrʌkɪdʒ] *n*. 货车运费;货车租费;卡车运输。

truck·er[1] [ˈtrʌkə; ˋtrʌkə] *n*. 卡车司机,手车搬运员;卡车运输业者。

truck·er[2] [ˈtrʌkə; ˋtrʌkə] *n*. **1**. 物物交易者。**2**. 小贩。**3**. 〔美〕菜农。

truck·le[1] [ˈtrʌkl; ˋtrʌkl] *n*. **1**. 小轮;滑车(轮)。**2**. 有脚轮的矮脚卧床〔不用时可以推入其他床下,又叫～-bed〕。**3**. 〔英方〕小圆筒形乳酪。

truck·le[2] [ˈtrʌkl; ˋtrʌkl] *vi*. 屈从,谄媚 (*to*; *for*)。

truc·u·lence, -len·cy [ˈtrʌkjuləns, -lənsi; ˋtrʌkjələns, -lənsɪ] *n*. 残暴,野蛮,横蛮无理。**truc·u·lent** *a*. 残暴的,凶恶的,蛮横无理的,嚣张的。

Trud·dy [ˈtruːdi; ˋtrudɪ] *n*. 特鲁迪〔女子名,Gertrude 的昵称〕。

trudge [trʌdʒ; trʌdʒ] **I** *vi*., *vt*. 沉重地跋涉,艰苦疲累地走 (*along*)。**II** *n*. **1**. 徒步跋涉。**2**. 沉重的脚步;沉重疲累地走着的人。-**er** 跋涉[步行]者。

trudg·en, trudg·eon [ˈtrʌdʒən; ˋtrʌdʒən] *n*.【泳】特拉真式游泳法〔头面向下两手交互前伸,两腿剪水,又叫 ～ stroke〕。

true [truː; tru] **I** *a*. **1**. 真实的,真正的 (*opp*. false);正当的。**2**. (朋友等)忠实的,诚实的。**3**. 正确的,没有错的;丝毫不差的,逼真的。**4**. 纯正的,(动植物等)纯种的。**5**. (声音等)音调正确的。**6**. (车轮等)位置正确的。*a* ～ *story* 真实情况[叙述]。～ *gold* 真金。*the* ～ *time* 正确的时间。***as*** ～ ***as steel*** [***flint, touch***] 绝对忠实可靠的。***come*** ～ (预言等)成事实;实现;(作物)不变种地发芽生长。***good men and*** ～ 正直人士;陪审员。***hold*** ～ 有效;适用。(***It is***) ～, ***but*** ... 果然不错,但是…。***out of*** (***the***) ～ 不准确,(机械的一部分等)有毛病。***the*** ～ 真理,真实。～ ***as I stand here*** 绝对真实,一点不假。～ ***to life*** 逼真,和原物一模一样,惟妙惟肖。～ ***to nature*** 逼真。～ ***to one's colours*** 忠于自己的信念[主义(等)]。～ ***to one's name*** 名副其实。～ ***to oneself*** 安分守己的,忠实的,老实的。～ ***to the original*** 忠于原文的(翻译等)。～ ***to type*** 典型的。～ ***value of seeds*** 种子利用率。

II *ad*. **1**. 真正地,确实地。**2**. 正当地。**3**. 正确地。*Tell me* ～ 老老实实跟我说吧。*aim* ～ 瞄得准。*breed* ～ *to type* (优良杂种)育成定型纯种。

III *vt*. 配准,配齐(工具、车轮等);校准;整形。*truing up* 校准。～ **absorption**【物】真吸收。～ **bill**【法】陪审员的罪证审定背签;受理起诉状;真实的叙述 (*bring in a* ～ *bill* 认为有罪而予以起诉)。～ **blue 1**. 不褪色的蓝。**2**. (对主义等)绝对忠诚坚定的人。**3**. (十七世纪苏格兰的)长老会教徒。～-**blue 1**. *a*. (对党派)非常忠诚的。**2**. *n*. 忠实的人。～**born** *a*. 嫡出的;道地的,真正的。～**bred** *a*. 纯种的;受过良好教育的 (*a* ～-*breeding hybrid* 不分离杂种)。～ **fly** 苍蝇。～ **fruit**【植】真果。～-**hearted** *a*. 诚实的,忠实的。～ **length** 实长。～ **level** 真水平,标准水平。～**love 1**. 意中人,情人。**2**. 擅羽草 (～*love* [～*lover's*] *knot* 同心结〔象征爱情的蝴蝶结〕)。～**penny 1**. *n*. 〔古〕老实人。**2**. *a*. 〔口〕真正的,纯粹的。～ **ribs**【解】真肋。～-**to-life** *a*. 写实的;反映真实情况的。～ **weight** 实重。-**ness** *n*. 真实;纯粹,纯正;忠实,诚实;认真;正确。

truf·fle [ˈtrʌfl; ˋtrʌfl, ˋtrufl] *n*.【植】块菌(属)〔味鲜美,调味用〕。-**d** *a*. 加有块菌的,用块菌调味的。

trug [trʌg; trʌg, trug] *n*. 〔方〕**1**. 浅底牛奶桶。**2**. (装水果等用的)浅底篮。**3**. = trull.

tru·ism [ˈtruːizəm; ˋtruɪzəm] *n*. **1**. 自明之理;明明白白的事情,起码的常识。**2**. 陈词滥调,老套语。

tru·is·tic [ˈtruːistik; truˋɪstɪk] *a*. **1**. 自明之理的;平凡的。**2**. 陈词滥调的。

trull [trʌl; trʌl] *n*. 〔古〕妓女。

tru·ly [ˈtruːli; ˋtrulɪ] *ad*. **1**. 真正;确实。**2**. 精确地,正确地。**3**. 忠实地,诚实地;老实说。**4**. 正当地,合法地。*Why*, ～, *I cannot say*. 嗯,老实说,我不能告诉你。*Yours* ～ [*Truly yours*] 忠实于您的人〔信末签名前的

客套话〕;〔谑〕本人,鄙人(= myself)。

Tru·man [ˈtruːmən; ˋtrumən] *n*. 杜鲁门〔姓氏,男子名〕。

trump[1] [trʌmp; trʌmp] **I** *n*. **1.** 王牌;有效办法,最后的手段。**2.**〔口〕老实人,好人。*All his cards are ~s*. 〔口〕有利条件都在他一边;他事事顺遂。***hold some ~s*** 手里还有王牌;胸有成竹,有必胜把握。***play a ~*** 拿出王牌;做出惊人之举。***put sb. to his ~s*** 使人打出王牌,逼得人使出最后办法。***turn up ~s***〔口〕意外顺遂;碰上好运。**II** *vt*. **1.** 出王牌吃掉(对手的牌)。**2.** 胜过。— *vi*. 出王牌;拿出有效办法[最后手段]。~ **card** 王牌;有利条件,最后手段(*play one's ~ card* 打出王牌;使出绝招)。

trump[2] [trʌmp; trʌmp] *vt*. 捏造。~ *up a charge against sb*. 冤枉[诬陷]某人。~**ed-up** *a*. 捏造的,诬告的,虚构的;欺诈的。

trump[3] [trʌmp; trʌmp] **I** *n*. 〔古,诗〕喇叭;喇叭声,号声。**II** *vi*., *vt*. 吹喇叭(宣告)。***the last ~***【宗】最后审判日的喇叭声。

trump·er·y [ˈtrʌmpəri; ˋtrʌmpərɪ] **I** *n*. **1.** 中看不中用的东西;废物,废料。**2.** 无聊话,胡话。**II** *a*. 中看不中用的;不足取的;肤浅的。

trump·et [ˈtrʌmpit; ˋtrʌmpɪt] **I** *n*. **1.** 喇叭;【乐】小号;喇叭声,小号声;喇叭般的声音〔如象的吼声等〕。**2.**【乐】(风琴的)小号音栓。**3.** 喇叭形物;【解】喇叭管;【机】漏斗状筒;传声筒;【贝】法螺贝。**4.**〔古〕号手;自夸自赞的人。*blow one's own ~* 自夸,自负,自吹自擂。*the Feast of Trumpets* 犹太人的新年。**II** *vt*. **1.** 吹喇叭通知。**2.** 到处宣扬;鼓吹,极力吹嘘[称赞]。— *vi*. **1.** 吹喇叭。**2.** (象等)发出喇叭似的声音。~ **call** 集合号;要求,命令;激励。~ **conch**, ~ **creeper**【植】美洲凌霄花;中国凌霄花;紫葳。~ **flower** 喇叭花〔美洲凌霄花等喇叭形花〕。~ **honeysucker**【植】贯叶忍冬。~ **major** (骑兵团的)号兵长。~ **shell**【具】法螺(壳)。~ **vine**【植】美洲凌霄花。~**weed**【植】泽兰(属);贯叶泽兰;斑茎泽兰;粉绿茎泽兰。

trump·et·er [ˈtrʌmpitə; ˋtrʌmpɪtɚ] *n*. **1.** 喇叭手,号手,号兵。**2.** 吹鼓手,吹嘘者;自夸自赞的人。**3.** 高声鸣禽〔如鹤、白天鹅等〕。*be one's own ~* 自夸,自吹自赞。***Your ~'s dead!***〔口〕这倒吹得活像!

trun·cal [ˈtrʌŋkəl; ˋtrʌŋkḷ] *a*. 树干的;躯干的。

trun·cate [ˈtrʌŋkeit; ˋtrʌŋket] **I** *vt*. **1.** 截去(圆锥等的)尖端,修剪(树等)。**2.** 删简(冗长的引语等)。**3.**【结晶】截(棱)成平面。**4.**【数】舍位,舍项。**II** *a*. **1.** 截平的,平头的。**2.** 删简了的,断章取义的。**3.**【动,植】(羽,叶)截平的,平头的。

trun·cated [ˈtrʌŋkeitid; ˋtrʌŋketɪd] *a*. **1.** 截短的;截平的,平头的;截成平面的;【几】截去尖端的。**2.** 删简了的,不完全的,断章取义的。

trun·ca·tion [trʌŋˈkeiʃən; trʌŋˋkeʃən] *n*. **1.** 切断,剪断,截去。**2.**【植】切干萌芽。

trun·cheon [ˈtrʌntʃən; ˋtrʌntʃən] **I** *n*. **1.** 短棍;〔英〕警棍。**2.** (作权威标记拿着的)权杖,元帅杖,指挥棍。**II** *vt*. 拿短棒打。

trun·dle [ˈtrʌndl; ˋtrʌndl] **I** *n*. **1.** 小轮,矮轮;(床等的)脚轮。**2.**【机】灯笼式小齿轮,转轴颈。**3.** 滚动(声)。**4.**〔罕〕手推车。**5.** = ~-bed. **II** *vi*. **1.** 靠矮轮动;滚动,旋转。**2.** 走开。**3.**【板球】扔球。— *vt*. **1.** 用矮轮推动;推(手推车);转动,滚动(球等)。**2.** 撵走,打发走。**3.**【板球】扔(球)。~ **bed** (可推入大床下的)带脚轮矮床。~-**tail**〔古〕卷尾狗。

trunk [trʌŋk; trʌŋk] **I** *n*. **1.** 树干(*opp*. branch);躯干,身躯。**2.** 本体,主要部分;(河的)主流;(铁道等的)干线;大血管,大神经(等);【计算机】信息通路;【建】柱身。**3.** 象的长鼻;(鸟虫的)长喙。**4.** (旅行用)大衣箱;汽车后部的行李箱。**5.** 槽,【矿】洗矿槽;总管,筒;筒形唧子;【机】管杆。**6.**【讯】中继(线);〔*pl*.〕〔英〕长途电话。**7.**【船】半显舱室;凸起舱口;围壁洞道。**8.**〔*pl*.〕男用运动裤;〔美〕游泳裤。**9.** = ~ hose. **10.**〔美俚〕行李。*the clear ~*【林】(树干的)枝下高。***live in one's ~s*** 老穿着旅行服装。**II** *vt*.【矿】(铅矿等)在槽中洗选。~ **airline** 航空干线。**III** *a*. 躯干的;主要的;干线的;箱形的;有筒管的。~ **call**〔英〕长途电话(呼叫)(=〔美〕long distance call)。~ **curl** 仰卧起坐。~ **dial(l)ing**〔英〕长途电话拨号。~ **drawers**【商】短裤。~ **engine**【机】筒状活塞发动机。~ **exchange** 长途电话局。~**fish**【动】箱鲀。~ **hose** **1.** *n*. (16—17 世纪时的)大脚短裤。**2.** *a*. 古式的。~ **line** (铁路的)干线;(电话的)干线,中继线,长途线。~ **main**【电】中继干线。~-**nail** (皮箱等用的)饰钉。~ **piston**【机】筒状活塞。~ **relay**【自】中继线替续器。~ **road** 干道,大路;〔美〕(铁路)干线。~ **room** (行李的)贮存室。~ **show**〔美〕(专为大款顾客安排的)不公开的时装表演。

trun·nel [ˈtrʌnl; ˋtrʌnḷ] *n*. 定缝销钉,木钉(= treenail)。

trun·nion [ˈtrʌnjən, -niən; ˋtrʌnjən] *n*.【炮】炮耳;【机】耳轴;空枢。-**ed** *a*. 有炮耳的;有耳轴的。

truss [trʌs; trʌs] **I** *n*. **1.** (干草等的)捆,把,束,一束干草〔老干草 56 磅,新干草 60 磅,稻草 36 磅〕。**2.**【医】疝带。**3.**【植】伞形花,穗状花;花束;果穗。**4.**【船】维系帆桁中段在桅杆上的铁具[绳索]。**5.**【工】构架,桁架,钢梁。*a ~ dam* 草包堤。*a bridge ~* 桥的构架。**II** *vt*. **1.**【烹】将(鸡、鸭的)翅膀[脚]扎在身上;将(人的)两手绑在身体上。**2.** 用桁架支持(屋顶、桥等)。**3.**〔古〕扎紧,捆牢(衣服等)。**4.** 把…处绞刑(*up*)。~ **bridge** 桁架桥,钢梁桥。-**ing** *n*. **1.** 桁架;梁,桁条。**2.** 用桁架支撑[加固];捆紧,扎紧。

trust [trʌst; trʌst] **I** *n*. **1.** 信任,信赖(*in*)。**2.** 责任,义务。**3.** 确信,希望;所倚靠的人[物]。**4.** 委托;保管;委托物;【法】信托;信托财产;【商】赊赈,赊卖。**5.**【经】托拉斯,企业联合。***fulfil one's ~*** 尽责。***have*** [***put***, ***repose***] ***~ in sb***. 信任某人。***hold*** [***be in***] ***a position of ~*** 居于负责地位。***investment ~*** 投资信托公司。***leave in ~*** 委托。***on ~*** 信任着,不看证据地;赊账。***take a ~ on oneself*** 负起责任。***take everything on ~*** 轻信。**II** *vt*. **1.** 信任,信用,信赖。**2.** 委任,委托,信托,托付,交(*to*; *with*);说出(秘密)(*with*)。**3.** 赊卖(*for*)。**4.** 确信,希望,期待(*that*; *to do*)。~ *sb. with a charge* 把任务委托某人。~ *sb. with a secret* 对某人说出秘密,把秘密告诉某人。~ *sb. for wheat* 赊卖小麦给某人。*I ~ that he will come*. 我相信他会来的。— *vi*. **1.** 相信(*in*);信赖(*on*);信赖而托付,恃,靠(*to*);期待(*for*)。**2.** 赊卖。~ *to chance* 交给命运,碰运气。~ **account** 托管财产;信托账户。~**buster**〔美〕反托拉斯官员。~ **company** 信托公司。~ **deed**【商】委托书。~ **fund** 托管基金。~ **money** 委托[托管]金。~ **territory** 托管地,托管领土。~**worthiness** 可信赖,可靠,确实。~**worthy** *a*. 可靠的。-**less** *a*. 不可信托的;不相信别人的。

trus·tee [trʌsˈtiː; trʌsˋti] **I** *n*. 受信托人,受托人;保管人;受托管国;保管委员;(大学等的)评议员,理事。**II** *vt*. **1.** 移交(财产)给受托[保管]人。**2.**〔美〕【法】扣押。-**ship** *n*. 受托人的职责[地位];(受托管国对被托管地的)托管(制度);托管状态。

trust·ful [ˈtrʌstfəl; ˋtrʌstfəl] *a*. 信任的,深信不疑的。-**ly** *ad*. -**ness** *n*.

trust·i·fy [trʌsˈtifai; ˋtrʌstəˏfaɪ] *vt*. (-*fied*) 组成托拉斯。

trust·ing [ˈtrʌstiŋ; ˋtrʌstɪŋ] *a*. 信任的,相信的。-**ly** *ad*.

trust·wor·thy [ˈtrʌstˌwəːði; ˋtrʌstˏwɝðɪ] *a*. 值得信任的,可靠的,确实。-**i·ness** *n*.

trust·y [ˈtrʌsti; ˋtrʌstɪ] **I** *a*. (-*i·er*; -*i·est*) 应相信的,可信赖的,可靠的,忠实的。**II** *n*. 可[受]信任的人[物];〔美〕(得到信任的)受优待囚犯。-**i·ly** *ad*. -**i·ness** *n*.

truth [truːθ; truθ] ***n***. (*pl*. **~s** [truːðz, truːθs; truðz, truθs]) **1.** 真理;真实;真相,事实 (*opp*. lie)。**2.** 真实性。**3.** 诚实,老实。**4.** (机械的)精确度。*To seek ~ from facts*. 实事求是。*There is no ~ in him*. 那家伙一点也不老实。*T- is* [*lies*] *at the bottom of a well*. 真理潜伏在井底[极难发现]。*home ~s* 关于自己的逆耳之言。~ ***to life*** [***nature***] 逼真。***in*** ~ = 〔古〕 ***of a*** ~ 真正,实在;说实在话,老实说。***out of*** ~ (机器)安装得有毛病。***The ~ is that ....*** 实际是…。***tell*** [***speak***] ***the*** ~ 说实话。***to tell the*** ~ = ~ ***to tell*** 实际是,说实在话。~ **drug** [**serum**] (使人吐露真情的)诱供麻醉药。

truth·ful [ˈtruːθ *f*ul; ˋtruθfəl] ***a***. (人等)诚实的,老实的;真实的,真正的。**-ly** ***ad***. **-ness** ***n***.

truth·less [ˈtruːθlis; ˋtruθlɪs] ***a***. 不诚实的;不真实的,虚伪的。**-ness** ***n***.

try [trai; traɪ] **I** ***vt***. (***tried***) **1.** 试,尝试,试行;努力。**2.** 试验,考验;试用,试穿。**3.**【法】审问,审判。**4.** 〔罕〕(问题等)解决。**5.** 折磨;使过劳,过度使用。**6.** 精制,精炼 (*out*);炼(油);榨(油);最后刨光 (*up*)。~ *one's best to win success* 努力争取胜利。~ *each car before selling it* 每辆车试验过后再出售。~ *a new pen* 试用新笔。~ *a jump* 跳跳看。*Do ~ more*! 再吃[喝]一点。*He has been sorely tried*. 他受尽了折磨[考验]。*This malady tries me so much*. 这个病使我非常痛苦。*The lard was tried in a big kettle*. 这猪油是在大锅里炼出来的。— ***vi***. **1.** 尝试;试验;努力。**2.** 〔同 and 和另一种动词原形结构用〕争取,尽力。*T- again*. 再试一遍。~ *at a somersault* 试翻斤斗。~ *for the first prize* 争取得头奖。*He is ~ing to solve the problem*. 他正在努力解决这个问题。*It's hard, but I will try*. 这不容易办,但我要试试看。*T- and finish the work in three days*. 要力争在三天之内把这工作搞完。~ ***a fall with*** 〔美运〕测验技能。~ ***and*** (***do*** 或 ***be***)... 〔口〕尽量,竭力… (*Try and* [*Try to*] *be punctual*. 竭力遵守时间)。~ ***back*** **1.** (回来)再试一试。**2.**【海】放松(绳索等)。~***-ing by hook or by crook*** 千方百计。~ ***for*** 求;企图达到;立志要。~ ***hard*** 拼命试试看 (~ *hard to dupe the public opinion* 竭尽混淆视听之能事)。~ ***it on*** **1.** (老着面皮)试试看。**2.** 摆架子。~ ***it on the dog*** 〔口〕拿食物给狗吃吃看;〔美口〕新戏先在乡下演出以试探效果。~ ***on*** 试穿(衣服);试试看。~ ***one's best*** [***hardest***] 尽全力。~ ***one's hand at*** 试行,做来看看。~ ***one's luck*** 碰碰运气试一试。~ ***one's weight*** 量体重。~ ***out*** (采用前)严密试验;筛矿;量(金属的)纯度。~ ***over*** 试演(戏剧等)。~ ***sb***. ***for*** [***on***] ***murder*** 以杀人罪审判某人。~ ***sb***. ***for his life*** 判决某人死罪。~ ***sb.'s patience*** (使)某人生气[着急](*This boy tries my patience*. 这个孩子真急人)。**II** ***n***. **1.** 试,尝试,试验。**2.**【橄榄球】触球;(因触球获得的)向球门踢球的权利。***have a ~ at it*** [***for it***] 试试看。~**-on** 〔口〕尝试,试验;(特指)诈骗;(假缝服装等的)试穿。~**-out** 〔俚〕试验,尝试;【剧】试演;〔美口〕选拔赛,选拔表演 (*give the play a ~ at Paris* 给这出戏在巴黎来一次试探演出)。~**sail**【海】斜桁纵帆〔风暴时用〕。~ **square** 曲尺,验方角尺。

try·ing [ˈtraiiŋ; ˋtraɪɪŋ] **I** ***a***. **1.** 令人难于忍受的;难堪的;艰难的;令人气愤的。**2.** 试验的。*How very ~ this is*! 这就叫人为难了! **II** ***n***.【裁缝】假缝。~ **plane** (木工的)长刨。~ **square** = try square.

tryp·a·no·some [ˈtripənəsəum; ˋtrɪpənəˏsom], **-so·ma** [-ˈsəumə; -ˋsomə] ***n***.【动】锥虫属。

tryp·a·no·so·mi·a·sis [ˌtripəˌnəusəuˈmaiəsis; ˏtrɪpənəsoˋmaɪəsɪs] ***n***.【医】锥虫病。

tryp·ars·a·mide [tripˈɑːsəmaid; trɪpˋɑrsəmaɪd] ***n***.【药】锥虫胂胺。

tryp·sin [ˈtripsin; ˋtrɪpsɪn] ***n***.【生化】胰朊酶,胰蛋白酶。

tryp·sin·o·gen [tripˈsinədʒən; trɪpˋsɪnədʒən] ***n***. 胰蛋白酶原。

tryp·tic [ˈtriptik; ˋtrɪptɪk] ***a***.【生化】胰蛋白酶的。

tryp·to·phan(e) [ˈtriptəfæn; ˋtrɪptəfen] ***n***.【生化】色氨酸。

tryst [traist, trist; trɪst, traɪst] **I** ***n***. 〔古〕约会,幽会;约会处,幽会处 (= ~ing place)。*a lover's ~* 情人的幽会。***keep*** [***break***] ~ 遵守[不遵守]约会。**II** ***vt***. 和(人)约定;定(约会时间或地点);与…订婚。*the ~ing place* 约会地点。— ***vi***. 约会;赴约。

TS = tensile strength【物】抗张强度,抗拉强度。

tsa·di [ˈtsɑːdi; ˋtsɑdɪ] ***n***. 希伯来语第十八个字母。

tsat. = temperature of saturation 饱和温度。

Tsar [zɑː, tsɑː; zɑr, tsɑr] ***n***. **1.** 沙皇。**2.** 大权独揽者。**-i·na** ***n***. 女沙皇;沙皇皇后。**-ism** ***n***. **-ist** ***n***.

TSE = transmissible spongiform encephalopathy【兽医】疯牛病,传染性海绵状脑病。

tset·se, tset·se-fly [ˈtsetsi; ˋtsɛtsɪ] ***n***.【虫】舌蝇,采采蝇。

T/Sgt., T.Sgt. = **Technical Sergeant** 〔美〕空军[海军陆战队]技术军士。

T.S.H. = Their Serene Highness 尊贵的殿下。

Tshi [tʃwiː; tʃwi] ***n***. = Twi.

Tshi·lu·ba [tʃiˈluːbə; tʃɪˋlubə] ***n***. 齐鲁巴语〔属班图语系,为刚果广大地区的一种混合语〕。

T-shirt [ˈtiːˌʃəːt; ˋtiˏʃɝt] ***n***. 〔美〕**1.** 短袖圆领汗衫。**2.** 圆领运动衫。

tsi = tons per square inch 每平方英寸吨数。

tsim·mes [ˈtsiməs; ˋtsɪməs] ***n***. 骚乱,暴动;大惊小怪;嚷闹,骚扰。

tsk [tisk; tɪsk] **I** ***int***., ***n***. 啧啧声〔表示不同意、同情或假同情等所发的声音〕。**II** ***vt***. 发啧啧声。

T.S.O. = Town Suboffice 〔英〕市镇支行(支局,分局)。

tsor·is [ˈtsɔːris, ˈtsuər-; ˋtsɔrɪs, ˋtsʊər-] ***n***. 烦恼,麻烦,苦恼,悲哀 (= tsores, tsorriss, tsooris)。

tsp. = teaspoon.

T-strap [ˈtiːstræp; ˋtiˏstræp] ***n***. 〔美〕**1.** 丁字形鞋面。**2.** (妇女或女孩穿的)丁字鞋。

Tsu·ga·ru [ˈtsuːgəruː; ˋtsuˋgɑrʊ] ***n***. 津轻海峡〔日本北海道与本州岛之间〕(= ~ Strait)。

tsu·na·mi [tsjuːˈnɑːmi; tsuˋnɑmi] ***n***. 〔日〕海啸,海震。**-c** ***a***.

Tsu·shi·ma [ˈtsuːʃimə, tsu(ː)ˈʃiːmə; tsəˋʃimə, ˋtsʊʃɪˏmɑ] ***n***. 对马(岛)〔日本〕。~ **Strait** 对马海峡。

TT = telegraphic transfer 电汇。

T.T. = **1.** teetotaller 绝对戒酒(主义)者。**2.** tourist trophy 旅游者纪念品。**3.** tuberculintested (牛奶)已作结核菌素检验。

T-time [ˈtiːˈtaim; ˏtiˋtaɪm] ***n***. (火箭、导弹等的)试验发射时间 (= time for test-firing)。

TTL = to take leave 告别。

TTR = **1.** target-tracking radar 目标跟踪雷达。**2.** thermal test reactor 热中子试验反应堆。

TU = **1.** trade union 工会。**2.** training unit 训练单位。

Tu =【化】**1.** thulium. **2.** tungsten.

Tu. = Tuesday.

tu·an [tuːˈɑːn; tʊˋɑn] ***n***. 〔马来西亚敬称〕先生,老板。

Tua·reg [ˈtwɑːreg; ˋtwɑrɛg] ***n***. (*pl*. ~(*s*)) 西撒哈拉和中撒哈拉的柏柏尔人;柏柏尔语。

tu·a·ta·ra [ˌtuːəˈtɑːrə; ˏtuəˋtɑrə] ***n***.【动】斑点楔齿蜥 (*Sphenodon punctatum*) 〔新西兰产〕。

tub [tʌb; tʌb] **I** ***n***. **1.** 桶,木盆;满桶,一桶(的分量)。**2.** 澡盆,浴盆;〔口谑〕洗澡。**3.** 〔蔑〕(说教、讲道的)讲坛。**4.** 〔蔑〕木盆一样的小船;练习用赛艇。**5.**【矿】矿车;(运矿)吊桶;(矿井的)桶框。**6.** 〔美俚〕(行进速度迟慢的)旧船。***a big*** ~ 〔美俚〕低音大鼓。***Every ~ must*** [***Let every ~***] ***stand on its own bottom*** 人须自立,人贵自助。***a tale of a*** ~ 无稽之谈。***in the*** ~ 〔美俚〕破产。***take a cold*** ~ 洗冷水澡。***throw out a ~ to the whale***

转移对方的注意力(以便乘机脱险)。～ ***of guts*** 〔美〕肥胖笨拙的人;庸俗的人;不足取的人。**II** ***vt***. (***-bb-***) **1**. 使入浴;(在浴缸里)为…洗澡。**2**. 使…用练赛艇练习。**3**. 把…种在木盆里;把…装进桶里。**4**.【矿】用铁板等在矿井内作侧壁。— ***vi***. **1**. 洗盆浴。**2**. (衣服等)被放在桶里洗。～ **eight** 八人坐的练习用赛艇。～ **pair** 两人坐的练习赛艇。～ **thumper** 慷慨激昂的讲道师[演讲者]。～**-thumping 1**. ***n***. 慷慨激昂的演讲(姿势);〔美〕【无】大吹大擂的广播广告。**2**. ***a***. 慷慨激昂的;大吹大擂的。

tu·ba [ˈtjuːbə; ˋtjubə, ˋtubə] ***n***. (*pl*. ***-s***, ***-bae*** [-biː; -bi]) **1**.【乐】大号,低音大喇叭;(风琴的)低音大号音栓。**2**. (古罗马的)喇叭。

tub·al [ˈtjuːbl, ˈtuːbl; ˋtjubl̩, ˋtubl̩] ***a***. 管的〔尤指输卵管的〕。～ **ligation**【医】输卵管结扎〔一种女性绝育术〕。～ **pregnancy**【医】管孕,输卵管怀孕[妊娠]。

tu·bate [ˈtjuːbeit, ˈtuː-; ˋtjubet, ˋtu-] ***a***. 有管的;成管的;管的,管形的。

tub·ba·ble [ˈtʌbəbl; ˋtʌbəbl̩] ***a***. 可放在桶里洗的;可沐浴的。

tub·ber [ˈtʌbə, ˋtʌbɚ] ***n***. 沐浴者。

tub·bing [ˈtʌbiŋ; ˋtʌbɪŋ] ***n***. **1**. 制桶;制桶材料。**2**.【矿】丘宾洞,井壁。

tub·bish [ˈtʌbiʃ; ˋtʌbɪʃ] ***a***. **1**. 桶状的。**2**. 肥胖(像木桶似)的。

tub·by [ˈtʌbi; ˋtʌbɪ] ***a***. (***-bi·er***; ***-bi·est***) 桶状的;空桶敲击声似的,(乐器等)钝音的;(人等)矮胖的。

tube [tjuːb; tjub] **I** ***n***. **1**. 管,筒;颜料管。**2**. 管状地下隧道;〔口〕(伦敦的)地下铁道。**3**.【炮】炮身;【汽锅】锅管;【解】管;管乐器;轮胎内胎。**4**. 〔美〕真空管,电子管;电视映像管;电视(机)。*an optic* ～ 望远镜。*a wheel* [*an inner*] ～ 内轮胎。*a photoelectric* ～ 光电管。*a display* ～ (雷达)显示管;(电视)显像管。*a pick-up* [*picture*] ～ 摄像[显像]管。*a pilot* ～ 指示灯。**go by** ～ 〔口〕坐(伦敦)地下铁道车去。**II** ***vt***. **1**. 把…装上管;把…弄成管状。**2**. 使通过管子;〔英〕坐地下铁道车去。～ **colo(u)rs** 〔*pl*.〕管装颜料。～ **culture** (细菌的)试管培养。～ **foot**【动】(棘皮动物的)管足。～ **like** ***a***. 管状的。～ **sock** 无跟圆筒短袜。～ **top** (妇女用的)筒状弹力胸围。～**-well** 管井。

tu·ber [ˈtjuːbə; ˋtjubɚ, ˋtu-] ***n***. **1**.【植】块茎,球根。**2**.【解】结节。**3**. 〔T-〕【植】块菌属。～ **crops**【植】块茎作物。

tu·ber·cle [ˈtjuːbəːkl; ˋtjubɚkl, ˋtu-] ***n***. **1**.【植】小块茎;根瘤;小突。**2**.【解,医】结节,小结;结核(节)。～ **bacillus** 结核菌[略 T.B.]。

tu·ber·cled [ˈtjuːbəːkld; ˋtjubɚkl̩d] ***a***. **1**. (有)根瘤[小突等]的。**2**. 结核菌[病]的。

tu·ber·cu·la [tju(ː)ˈbəːkjulə; tjuˋbɚkjəlɚ, tu-] ***n***. (*pl*.) tuberculum 的复数。

tu·ber·cu·lar [tjuːˈbəːkjulə; tjuˋbɚkjələ] **I** ***a***. = tuberculous. **II** ***n***. 结核病病人。**-ize**, **-ise** ***vt***. = tuberculize.

tu·ber·cu·late [tju(ː)ˈbəːkjulit; tjuˋbɚkjəlɪt], **tu·ber·culat·ed** [-leitid; -lertɪd] ***a***. **1**. 有结节的,有小瘤的。**2**. 结核性的,结核病的。**tuberculation** ***n***.

tu·ber·cule [ˈtjuːbəːkjuːl; ˋtjubɚˏkjul] ***n***. = tubercle.

tu·ber·cu·lin [tjuːˈbəːkjulin; tjuˋbɚkjəlɪn] ***n***. 结核菌素,结核菌苗。

tu·ber·cu·lize [tjuːˈbəːkjulaiz; tjuˋbɚkjəˏlaɪz] ***vt***. 使生瘤;使生结核(病)。

tu·ber·cu·loid [tjuːˈbəːkjuˌlɔid; tjuˋbɚkjəˏlɔɪd] ***a***. 结核节状的;结核病状的。

tu·ber·cu·lo·sis [tjuːˌbəːkjuˈləusis; tjuˏbɚkjəˋlosɪs] ***n***.【医】结核病;〔特指〕肺结核〔略 TB, t.b.〕。*pulmonary* ～ 肺结核。

tu·ber·cu·lous [tjuːˈbəːkjuləs; tjuˋbɚkjələs] ***a***. **1**. 结节(状)的。**2**. 结核(性)的;结核病的。

tu·ber·cu·lum [tjuːˈbəːkjuləm; tjuˋbɚkjələm] ***n***. (*pl*. ***tubercula*** [-lə; -lə])【解】结节,小结。

tu·ber·ose [ˈtjuːbərəus; ˋtjubəros] **I** ***a***. = tuberous. **II** ***n***.【植】晚香玉。

tu·ber·os·i·ty [tjuːbəˈrɔsiti; ˏtjubəˋrɑsətɪ] ***n***. **1**. 有块茎(状态);块茎状;结节状[性]。**2**.【解】粗隆;(骨的)结节。

tu·ber·ous [ˈtjuːbərəs; ˋtjubərəs, ˋtu-] ***a***. 有块茎的;结节性的。～**root** 块根。

tub·fast [ˈtʌbfɑːst; ˋtʌbˏfæst] ***a***. (布等)耐洗的。～ *cottons* 耐洗的棉布。

tubi- *comb*. *f*. 表示"管子","管道","管状"。

tu·bi·fex [ˈtjuːbəˌfeks, ˈtuː-; ˋtjubəˏfɛks, ˋtu-] ***n***. (*pl*. ***-fex·es***, ***-fex***)【动】颤蚓。

tu·bi·form [ˈtjuːbifɔːm; ˋtjubɪˏfɔrm] ***a***. 管状的。

tub·ing [ˈtjuːbiŋ; ˋtjubɪŋ] ***n***. **1**. 装管,配管,制管。**2**. 管道(系统);管料。**3**. 管的一部分。**4**. 〔集合词〕管类。

tu·boid [ˈtjuːbɔid; ˋtjubɔɪd] ***a***. 似管的,管状的。

tu·bu·lar [ˈtjuːbjulə; ˋtjubjəlɚ, ˋtu-] ***a***. **1**. 管系组织的;管状的。**2**. 管子做的;有管的。**3**. 发吹管般声音的。*a* ～ *frame* 管架。～ *furniture* 钢管家具[铁床等]。**-i·ty** ***n***.

tu·bu·late [ˈtjuːbjuˌleit, -lit; ˋtjubjəˏlet, -lɪt] **I** ***a***. = tubular. **II** ***vt***. **-la·tion** ***n***.

tu·bule [ˈtjuːbjuːl; ˋtjubjul, ˋtubjul] ***n***. 小管;【解】细管。

tu·bu·li·flo·rous [ˌtjuːbjuliˈflɔːrəs, tuː-; ˏtjubjəlɪˋflorəs, tu-] ***a***.【植】管状小花的。

tu·bu·lose [ˈtjuːbjuləus; ˋtjubjəlos], **tu·bu·lous** [-ləs; -ləs] ***a***. **1**. 管状的;有小管的。**2**.【植】有管筒状花的。*a tubulous boiler* 管式锅炉。

tu·bu·lure [ˈtjuːbjuˌluə, ˈtuː-; ˋtjubjəljər, ˋtu-] ***n***. (曲颈瓶,蒸馏器的)短管口。

TUC = Trades Union Congress 〔英〕职工大会。

tuck[1] [tʌk; tʌk] **I** ***n***. **1**. (袖子等上的)缝褶,横褶,横裥;折起[折进]部分。**2**. (伸到大网中取鱼用的)网兜儿。**3**.【海】船尾突出部下方[两侧外板接合处]。**4**. 〔英俚〕食品,糕点,酒席。**5**.【运动】折叠式姿势[两手抱住小腿,膝部贴住前胸]。**II** ***vt***. **1**. 在(袖等上)打横褶,打裥;翻折,卷[折]起(袖子等)(*up*)。**2**. 包起,裹起,卷紧。**3**. 把…挤进[塞进],(收)藏起(*in*; *into*; *away*)。**4**. 〔英俚〕吃,喝,拼命吃(*in*; *away*)。**5**. 用网兜儿从大网中把(鱼)捞出。**6**. 〔俚〕勒死(*up*)。— ***vi***. **1**. 打横褶;缩拢。**2**. 〔俚〕狼吞虎咽地吃,拼命吃(*in*; *away*)。～ ***away*** 藏起(*The village is* ～*ed away in a quiet valley*. 村子隐藏在一个幽静的山谷中)。～ ***in*** 把一端折进[塞进];〔口〕耙进;尽量吃(*at* food)。～ ***into*** 藏进;〔口〕把(食物)塞进肚子里。～ ***on*** 〔俚〕乱讨价,瞎要(价钱)。～ ***oneself up in bed*** 裹在被窝里。～ ***up*** 折起一头,卷起;包;〔口〕绞死(犯人)(～ *up one's sleeves* 卷起袖子)。～**-in**, ～**-out** 〔俚〕饱吃。～ **net**, ～ **seine** 网兜儿。～**-shop** 〔英学生语〕糖果食品店。

tuck[2] [tʌk; tʌk] ***n***. 〔Scot.〕鼓声;〔古〕喇叭声。

tuck[3] [tʌk; tʌk] ***n***. 活力,精力。

tuck[4] [tʌk; tʌk] ***n***. 〔古〕一种细长的剑。

tuck[5] [tʌk; tʌk] ***n***. tuxedo 的缩略词。

tuck·a·hoe [ˈtʌkəˌhəu; ˋtʌkəˏho] ***n***. **1**.【植】茯苓(*Poria cocos*)。**2**. 茯苓根和块茎。

tuck·er [ˈtʌkə; ˋtʌkɚ] **I** ***n***. **1**. 打横褶的人,作褶裥的人;缝褶机;(装上去的)衣领;(17、18 世纪时的女用)领布。**2**. 〔澳俚〕食物。**3**. 〔美口〕疲倦。***make*** [***earn***] ***one's*** ～ 勉强糊口。***one's best bib and*** ～ (个人所有的衣服中)最好的一件[套]。**II** ***vt***. 〔美口〕使疲倦,使精疲力尽(*out*)。

tuck·et [ˈtʌkit; ˋtʌkɪt] ***n***. 〔古〕响亮的喇叭声。

Tuc·son [tuːˈsɔn; tuˋsɑn, ˋtusɑn] ***n***. 图森〔美国城市〕。

-tude *suf*. 与形容词、过去分词构成表示性质、状态的抽象名词: alti*tude*, magni*tude*, soli*tude*.

Tu·dor [ˈtjuːdə; ˋtjudɚ, ˋtu-] ***a***., ***n***. 英国都铎王室[朝]

T

的(人);【建】都铎朝式样(的)。*the ~s = the House of ~* 都铎王室。~ **arch** 四心拱。~ **flower** 都铎式花样。~ **rose** 都铎王室蔷薇徽。

Tues. = Tuesday.

Tues·day [ˈtjuːzdi; ˋtjuzdɪ] **I** ***n.*** 星期二。**II** ***ad.*** 在星期二。**-s** ***ad.*** 在每星期二。

tufa [ˈtjuːfə; ˋtjufə, ˋtufə] ***n.*** 【地】华;石灰华,泉华。**-ceous** ***a.***

tuff[1] [tʌf; tʌf] ***n.*** 【地】凝灰岩。**-aceous** [tʌˈfeiʃəs; tʌˋfeʃəs] ***a.***

tuff[2] [tʌf; tʌf] ***a.*** 〔俚〕极佳的。

tuf·fet [ˈtʌfit; ˋtʌfɪt] ***n.*** **1.** 草丛。**2.** 矮凳。

tuft [tʌft; tʌft] **I** ***n.*** **1.** (头发、羽毛等的)簇,丛,束。**2.** 树林;乱丛棵子。**3.** 【织】毛撮,毛绒束;〔美俚〕(下巴上的)山羊胡子。**4.** 【解】丛脉;(细血管)丛。**5.** (坐垫等边上的)饰缝;帽缝;有帽缝的贵族人物。**II** ***vt.*** **1.** 给…饰上饰缝,用饰缝装饰。**2.** 使成簇[丛、球];簇生,丛生。~**-hunter** 〔古〕拍权贵马屁的人。**-ed** ***a.*** 簇状的;有一簇毛发的(*a ~ed duck* 冠凫,凤头鸭)。

tuft·y [ˈtʌfti; ˋtʌftɪ] ***a.*** 成簇[丛]的;多簇[丛]的;簇生的,丛生的。

tug [tʌg; tʌg] **I** ***vt.*** (***tugged*** [tʌgd; tʌgd]; ***tug·ging*** [ˈtʌgiŋ; ˋtʌgɪŋ]) (吃力地)拉,拖(船);用拖船拖曳。—***vi.*** **1.** 用力拖(*at*)。**2.** 尽力,努力,挣扎。~ *a boat onto shore* 把船拖到岸上。~ ***at the*** [***an***] ***oar*** 拼命划船;拚命苦干。~ ***in a subject*** 勉强穿插上一段情节。**II** ***n.*** **1.** 拖,拉,曳引。**2.** 尽力,努力,挣扎,奋斗;激战,搏斗。**3.** 拖轮;(曳引用的)绳索,链条;(马具的)曳革;【矿】装有滑车的铁钩。**4.** 〔俚〕(英国 Eton 学校的)公费生。*We felt a great ~ at parting.* 离别时真难受。~**boat** 拖船。~**-of-love** ***a.*** (离婚双方)争夺子女监护权的。~**-of-war** 拔河(游戏);激战。

tu·grik [ˈtuːgrik; ˋtugrɪk] ***n.*** 图格里克〔蒙古的货币单位〕。

tu·i [ˈtuːi; ˋtuɪ] ***n.*** 【动】(新西兰)蜜雀(*Prosthemadera novaeseelandiae*)。

tuille [twiːl; twil] ***n.*** (铠甲的)腿裙,腰甲。

tu·i·tion [tjuːˈiʃən; tjuˋɪʃən] ***n.*** **1.** 教诲。**2.** 学费。**-al** ***a.*** **1.** 教诲的。**2.** 学费的。

tu·la·r(a)e·mi·a [ˌtuːləˈriːmiə; ˏtuləˋrimɪə] ***n.*** 〔美〕【医】兔热病,土拉(伦斯)菌病。**-re·mic** ***a.***

tu·le [ˈtjuːli; ˋtjulɪ] ***n.*** 〔美〕【植】锐藨草(*Scirpus acutus*);软茎藨草(*Scirpus validus*)〔美国西南部产〕。

tu·lip [ˈtjuːlip; ˋtjuləp, ˋtu-, -ɪp] ***n.*** **1.** 【植】郁金香(属);山慈姑。**2.** 【炮】炮口带。~ **tree** [**poplar**] ***n.*** 【植】鹅掌楸属;美国鹅掌楸。~**wood** 鹅掌楸木。

tulle [tjuːl; tjul, tul] ***n.*** 面纱;薄纱,绢。

tul·li·bee [ˈtʌliˌbiː; ˋtʌlɪˏbi] ***n.*** 【动】湖白鲑。

tum·ble [ˈtʌmbl; ˋtʌmbl] **I** ***vi.*** **1.** 跌倒,摔倒;倒塌;滚下。**2.** 打滚,翻滚。**3.** 翻斤斗。**4.** 〔口〕跌跌撞撞地来[去],慌慌张张地来[去](*to*; *up*; *down*);滚进(*into*);一翻身跳出(*out of*)。**5.** (市价)猛跌。**6.** 无意中遇到,碰见(*into*; *on*)。**7.** 〔俚〕(突然)察觉,恍然大悟(*to*)。**8.** 〔俚〕同意(*to*)。— ***vt.*** **1.** 摔翻,摔倒(*down*);使倒摔下来。**2.** 扔出,扔散(衣服等);弄乱,搅乱。**3.** 把…放入磨箱里磨光。**4.** 打中(鸟兽等)。~ *down* [*up*] *the stairs* 东倒西歪地下(上)楼梯。~ *off a horse* 摔下马来。~ *over a stone* 在石头上绊倒。*It was a long time before she tumbled (to what I mean).* 好长时间她才(对我的意思)恍然大悟。*I ~d on him there.* 我在那里无意中遇见了他。~ ***and toss*** 乱翻乱滚,遍地打滚(*He ~d and tossed from pain.* 他痛得打滚)。~ ***down the sink*** 〔美〕牛饮。~ ***home*** 【海】(舷侧上部)向内弯曲。~ ***in*** 【木工】嵌进;〔俚〕(上床倒下就)睡;【海】= ~home. **II** ***n.*** 跌倒;滚落;翻滚;混乱,乱七八糟。***all in a*** ~ 混乱到极点。***give*** [***get***] ***a*** ~ 〔口〕给予[得到]好评。***have a slight*** [***nasty***] ~ 跌了轻轻一跤[一大跤]。~ **bug** 【虫】金龟子(科甲虫),蜣螂。~**-down** ***a.*** (房子等)摇摇欲坠的,破烂的。~**weed** 【植】风滚草;丝石竹;苋属,广布苋。

tum·bler [ˈtʌmblə; ˋtʌmblɚ] ***n.*** **1.** (平底)玻璃酒杯。**2.** 摔倒的人,打滚的人;翻斤斗的人;杂技演员;不倒翁;(会在空中翻斤斗的人)翻飞鸽。**3.** 衣服干燥机。**4.** (机枪的)机心;(锁里的)制动栓。**5.** 【机】转臂;转筒;摆动换向齿轮,转向轮。**6.** 〔英方〕运肥[粪]车。~ **gears** 【机】三星牙。~ **switch** 倒扳[起倒]开关。**-ful** ***n.*** 一平底玻璃杯之量。

tumbling barrel [**box**] 【机】研磨滚筒,滚转筒。

tum·brel, tum·bril [ˈtʌmbrəl, -bril; ˋtʌmbrəl] ***n.*** **1.** 〔英〕粪车,肥料车。**2.** 【军】二轮弹药车。**3.** (法国革命时代的)死刑犯押送车。

tu·me·fa·cient [ˌtjuːmiˈfeiʃənt, tuː-; ˏtjumɪˋfeʃənt] ***a.*** 【医】引起肿胀的;肿胀的。

tu·me·fac·tion [tjuːmiˈfækʃən; ˏtjuməˋfækʃən, ˏtu-] ***n.*** 【医】肿大,肿胀;疙瘩,疮。

tu·me·fy [ˈtjuːmifai; ˋtjuməˏfaɪ, ˋtu-] ***vt.***, ***vi.*** (使)肿起,(使)肿胀,(使)胀大。

tu·mesce [tuːˈmes; tuˋmɛs] ***vt.*** 使(性器官)发胀。—***vi.*** 体会性器官发胀。

tu·mes·cence [tjuˈmesns, tuː-; tjuˋmɛsns] ***n.*** **1.** 肿胀,肿大。**2.** 肿胀部分。

tu·mes·cent [tjuːˈmesnt; tjuˋmɛsnt] ***a.*** 肿大的,肿胀的。

tu·mid [ˈtjuːmid; ˋtjumɪd, ˋtu-] ***a.*** 肿胀的;涨满的;(文风等)浮夸的,夸张的。

tu·mid·i·ty [tjuːˈmiditi; tjuˋmɪdətɪ, tu-] ***n.*** 肿大,肿起;浮夸,夸张。

tum·my [ˈtʌmi; ˋtʌmɪ] ***n.*** 〔儿〕肚子。~**ache** 肚子痛。~ **bug** 胃病。

tumo(u)r [ˈtjuːmə; ˋtjumɚ, ˋtu-] ***n.*** 【医】肿瘤,癌,疙瘩,赘疣。*a benign* [*malignant*] ~ 良[恶]性肿瘤。**-ous** ***a.*** 肿瘤的;夸张的(*tumourous growth* 【农】陡长)。

tump [tʌmp; tʌmp] ***n.*** 〔英方〕**1.** 小岗,小丘。**2.** 丛〔如草丛〕。

tump·line [ˈtʌmplain; ˋtʌmpˏlaɪn] ***n.*** 〔美〕背物带〔经过前额后转到肩后,使重物正好背在背上〕。

tu·mu·lar [ˈtjuːmjulə, ˈtuː-; ˋtjumjəlɚ, ˋtu-] ***a.*** 土墩的;坟堆的。

tu·mu·li [ˈtjuːmjuli, -lai; ˋtjumjəˏlɪ, -laɪ] ***n.*** 〔*pl.*〕tumulus 的复数。

tu·mu·lose [ˈtjuːmjuˌləus, ˈtuː-; ˋtjumjəlos] ***a.*** 丘陵地的(= tumulous)。

tu·mult [ˈtjuːmʌlt; ˋtjumʌlt] ***n.*** 骚动;暴动;吵闹,喧嚣;激动,烦乱。*His mind was in a ~.* 他心烦意乱。

tu·mul·tu·a·ry [tjuːˈmʌltjuəri; tjuˋmʌltʃʊˏɛrɪ] ***a.*** **1.** 吵闹的,喧嚣的,激动的;不稳的,混乱的。**2.** (军队等)没有纪律的,乌合之众的。

tu·mul·tu·ous [tjuˈmʌltjuəs; tjuˋmʌltʃʊəs, tu-] ***a.*** 吵闹的,喧嚣的;动乱的,纷乱的;激动的。*a roaring and ~ river* 汹涌澎湃的河流。**-ly** ***ad.*** **-ness** ***n.***

tu·mu·lus [ˈtjuːmjuləs; ˋtjumjələs, ˋtu-] ***n.*** (*pl.* ***-es***, ***-li*** [-lai; -laɪ]) 冢,古坟。

tun [tʌn; tʌn] **I** ***n.*** **1.** 大(酒)桶,(酿造用)发酵桶。**2.** 桶〔252 加仑的液量〕。**II** ***vt.*** (***-nn-***) 把(酒)装入大桶。

tu·na [ˈtjuːnə; ˋtunə] ***n.*** 〔美〕【鱼】金枪鱼(科)(= tunny);金枪鱼罐头。~ **clipper** 金枪鱼捕捞船。

tun·a·ble [ˈtjuːnəbl; ˋtjunəbl] ***a.*** **1.** 可调音的。**2.** 能合调的;能发出和声的;和谐的,音调优美的;悦耳的。**3.** 【无】可调谐的。

tun·dish [ˈtʌndiʃ; ˋtʌndɪʃ] ***n.*** 【冶】浇口杯,中间漏槽。

tun·dra [ˈtʌndrə; ˋtʌndrə] ***n.*** 【地】苔原,冻原,冻土带,寒漠。

tune [tjuːn; tjun] **I** ***n.*** **1.** 曲调,调子;语调;态度。**2.** 和谐,调谐,调和。**3.** 情绪;正常状态。**4.** 程度;数量。*the*

~ *the* (*old*) *cat* [*cow*] *died of* 〔口〕刺耳的音乐[歌唱]。*I am not in* ~ *for talk*. 我不想说话。***call one's own*** ~ = ***call the*** ~ 点戏,点唱;任意指挥,发号施令。***change one's*** ~ = ***sing another*** (= *a different*) ~ 改变调子;改变态度。***in*** ~ 合调;和谐,和睦(*with*)。*His ideas are in* ~ *with the times*. 他的思想适合时代潮流。***keep... in*** ~ 使…保持正常状态。***out of*** ~ 不合调;失调。*The piano is out of* ~. 钢琴走调;不和谐,不和睦(*with*)。***to the*** ~ ***of*** (**£5**) 达(5镑)之多。**II** ***vt***. **1.** 校准(乐器的)音调,调准。**2.** 调整,使调和,使一致(*to*)。**3.** 〔诗〕唱,奏。**4.**【无】调谐;调整(频率);收听。— ***vi***. **1.** 协调(*with*)。**2.**【无】调谐,调好频率;收听。~ ***in***【无】调谐,调准;收听;〔美〕开始(~ *in to the news* 收听新闻节目)。~ ***off***【无】中途断绝。~ ***out***【无】**1.** 调准收音机使无(杂音);解谐,失谐。**2.** 〔美〕无视,注意到别处。~ ***up*** **1.** 开始演奏,开始唱;调音,调谐;〔谑〕(孩子)哭起来;(猎狗)咬起来;使发挥全部能力;〔美〕练习(运动比赛)。**2.** 用化学溶剂清除发动机中沉积物。~***d amplifier***【无】调谐放大器。~**smith** (流行歌曲的)作曲者。~**up**, ~**-up** **1.** 调正,调节,调谐。**2.** (运动前的)准备动作。

tune·a·ble [ˈtjuːnəbl; ˋtjunəbḷ] *a*. = tunable.

tune·ful [ˈtjuːnfəl; ˋtjunfʊl] *a*. 转和谐的,音调优美的。**-ly** *ad*. **-ness** *n*.

tune·less [ˈtjuːnlis; ˋtjunlɪs] *a*. **1.** 不合调子的,不合谐的;无韵律的,非乐音的。**2.** (乐器)无声的。**-ness** *n*.

tun·er [ˈtjuːnə; ˋtjunɚ] *n*. 调音的人,调音师;调音器;【无】调谐器。

tung [tʌŋ; tʌŋ] *n*. 〔Chi.〕桐。~ **oil** 桐油。~ **tree**【植】油桐树。

tung·ar [ˈtʌŋgə; ˋtʌŋgɚ] *n*.【无】(二极)钨氩(整流)管。

tung·state [ˈtʌŋsteit; ˋtʌŋstet] *n*.【化】钨酸盐。

tung·sten [ˈtʌŋstən; ˋtʌŋstən] *n*.【化】钨〔w〕。~ **filament** 钨丝。~ **steel**【冶】钨钢。**-ic** [tʌŋsˈtenik; tʌŋˋstɛnɪk] *a*.

tung·stic [ˈtʌŋstik; ˋtʌŋstɪk] *a*.【化】六价钨的,(正)钨的;五价钨的。~ **ocher**【矿】= tungstite.

tung·stite [ˈtʌŋstait; ˋtʌŋstaɪt] *n*.【矿】钨华(= tungstic ocher)。

Tun·gus [tunˈguz; tʊnˋguz] **I** *n*. **1.** (*pl*. ***-gus·es***, ***-gus***) 通古斯人。**2.** 通古斯语。**II** *a*. 通古斯人的;通古斯语的;通古斯文化的(= Tunguz)。

Tun·gus·ic [tunˈguzik; tʊnˋguzɪk] **I** *n*. 通古斯语〔属于阿尔泰语系的一语族,为亚洲中部和东北部人说的,包括通古斯语和满语〕。**II** *a*. **1.** 通古斯人的。**2.** 通古斯语的。

tu·nic [ˈtjuːnik; ˋtjunɪk] *n*. **1.** (古罗马、古希腊人的)长达膝盖的外衣;古时穿在铠甲上的战袍。**2.** (现代妇女运动、舞蹈用的)束腰外衣;〔英〕平常军[警]服[制服]上衣。**3.**【植】种皮;鳞茎皮;膜被;原套;【动】膜;被囊;【解,动】膜;层。**4.**【天主】= tunicle.

tu·ni·ca [ˈtjuːnikə, ˈtuː-; ˋtjunɪkə, ˋtu-] *n*. (*pl*. ***-cae*** [-siː; -si])【解,动】膜;被囊。

tu·ni·cate [ˈtjuːnikeit; ˋtjunɪˏket] **I** *a*.【植】具外皮[鳞茎皮]的,具膜被的;【动】叠套的;被囊类的。**II** *n*.【动】被囊类动物。

tu·ni·cle [ˈtjuːnikl; ˋtjunɪkl, ˋtu-] *n*. **1.**【天主】助祭(穿的)祭服;〔*pl*.〕主教穿的轻绸衣〔身长袖宽〕。**2.**【动、植】薄被膜。

tun·ing [ˈtjuːniŋ; ˋtjunɪŋ] *n*. **1.**【乐】调音[弦]。**2.**【无】调谐;收听。~ **crook** 调音曲管。~ **fork**【乐】音叉。~ **hammer** 调音锤。~ **key** 调音键。~ **peg**, ~ **pin** (弦乐器的)弦轴,弦栓。

Tu·nis [ˈtjuːnis; ˋtjunɪs, ˋtu-] *n*. 突尼斯〔突尼斯首都〕。

Tu·ni·sia [tjuːˈniziə; tjuˋnɪʃɪə, -ˋnɪʃə] *n*. 突尼斯〔非洲〕。~**n** *n*., *a*. 突尼斯人[的]。

tun·nage [ˈtʌnidʒ; ˋtʌnɪdʒ] *n*. = tonnage.

tun·nel [ˈtʌnl; ˋtʌnḷ] **I** *n*. 隧道;地道;坑道;管道,烟道,风洞;【矿】石巷,平峒。~ *warfare* 地道战。**II** *vt*. (〔英〕***-ll-***) **1.** 在…凿隧道[掘坑道]。**2.** 凿隧道通过。~ *one's way* (*through*; *into*) 挖隧道[巷道](穿过;进到)。— *vi*. **1.** 凿隧道[掘坑道]。**2.** 运过坑道(*through*);进隧道(*into*)。~ **borer** 隧道挖凿机。~**-net** (捕鱼用的)袋网。~ **diode**【无】隧道二极管。~ **disease**【医】坑道病,潜涵病。~ **vision** **1.**【军】坑道视界。**2.** 一孔之见,目光短浅。**-er**, **-ler** 隧道(掘进)工;隧道掘进机。

tun·ny [ˈtʌni; ˋtʌnɪ] *n*.【鱼】金枪鱼(类)。

tu·no·scope [ˈtuːnəuskəup; ˋtunoˏskop] *n*. (无线电收音机上调谐用的)电眼,调谐指示器。

tun·y [ˈtjuːni; ˋtjunɪ] *a*. 音调和谐的,音调优美的;【乐】曲调明朗的;易唱的。

tup [tʌp; tʌp] *n*. **1.** 〔英方〕公羊。**2.**【机】冲锤;动力锤的头部;冲面。

tupe·lo [ˈtuːpələu; ˋtupəˏlo] *n*.【植】(多花)紫树(= black gum);紫树木料。

Tu·pi [tuːˈpiː, ˈtuːpi; tuˋpi, ˋtupɪ] *n*. **1.** (*pl*. ***Tu·pis***; ***Tu·pi***) 图皮族〔南美印地安人的一种,居住在巴西和巴拉圭的某些地区〕。**2.** 图皮语〔图皮族人说的图皮—拉瓜尼语的方言,以前为亚马逊地区说的一种混合方言〕。**3.** 南美印地安语系〔包括图皮—拉瓜尼语和南美广大地区所说的其他三十多种语言〕。

Tu·pi-Gua·ra·ni [tuːˈpiːgwɑːrɑːˈniː, ˈtuːpi-; tuˋpiˏgwɑrɑˋni, ˋtupɪ-] *n*. **1.** 图皮—拉瓜尼语。**2.** = tupi.

tup·pence [ˈtʌpəns; ˋtʌpəns] *n*. 〔英口〕= twopence.

tuque [tjuːk; tjuk] *n*. (有鸭舌帽檐的)绒丝帽。

tu quo·que [ˈtjuːˈkwəukwi; tjuˋkwokwɪ] 〔L.〕("你也一样"式的)反驳;(彼此彼此式的)应酬话。*a tu quoque reply* 旗鼓相当的回答;照样回敬一句。

tu·ra·cou, **tu·ra·ko** [ˈtuərəkəu; ˋturəko] *n*. = touraco.

Tu·ra·ni·an [tjuəˈreinjən, -niən; tjʊˋrenɪən, tʊ-] **I** *a*. 都兰语族的,乌拉尔阿尔泰(Ural-Altai)语族的。**II** *n*. 都兰语族;说都兰语族语言的人。

tur·ban [ˈtəːbən; ˋtɝbən] *n*. **1.** (穆斯林的)缠头巾。**2.** 缠头巾式女帽。**3.** (卷贝的)涡纹,螺旋。~ **lily**【植】头巾百合。**-ed** *a*. 缠头巾的;戴缠头巾式女帽的。

tur·ba·ry [ˈtəːbəri; ˋtɝbərɪ] *n*. (*pl*. ***-ries***) **1.** 泥炭采掘场。**2.**【英法】(在他人土地上的)泥炭采掘权。

tur·bel·lar·i·an [ˌtəːbiˈlɛəriən; ˏtɝbɪˋlɛrɪən] **I** *n*.【动】涡虫纲(*Turbellaria*)动物。**II** *a*. 涡虫纲的。

tur·bid [ˈtəːbid; ˋtɝbɪd] *a*. 浑浊的;烟雾浓密的,不透明的;混乱的,一团糟的。**-ly** *ad*. **-ness** *n*.

tur·bi·dim·e·ter [ˌtəːbiˈdimitə; ˏtɝbɪˋdɪmətɚ] *n*. 浊度计。**tur·bi·di·met·ric** [ˌtəbidiˈmetrik; ˏtɝbɪdəˋmɛtrɪk] *a*. **tur·bi·dim·e·try** *n*. 浊度。

tur·bi·dite [ˈtəːbiˌdait; ˋtɝbɪˏdaɪt] *n*.【地】浊积物,浊流岩。

tur·bid·i·ty [təːˈbiditi; tɝˋbɪdətɪ] *n*. 浑浊,浊度;不透明;混乱。~ **current**【地】浊流。

tur·bid·ness [ˈtəːbidnis; ˋtɝbɪdnɪs] *n*. **1.** 混浊;多泥。**2.** 浊;(云,烟的)浓密;暗黑。**3.** 混乱。

tur·bi·nal [ˈtəːbinl; ˋtɝbɪnḷ] **I** *a*. = turbinate. **II** *n*.【解】鼻甲(骨)。

tur·bi·nate [ˈtəːbinit; ˋtɝbənɪt, -ˏnet] **I** *a*. **1.** 陀螺似[形]的;倒圆锥形的。**2.**【解】鼻甲(骨)的。**3.** 像陀螺般转的;螺旋状的。**II** *n*. 螺旋贝壳;【解】鼻甲骨。

tur·bi·nat·ed [ˈtəːbiˌneitid, -nitid; ˋtɝbəˏnetɪd] *a*. **1.** 陀螺状的,阔锥状的。**2.**【解,动】鼻甲的。

tur·bi·na·tion [təːbiˈneiʃən; ˏtɝbɪˋneʃən] *n*. 倒圆锥形;陀螺状旋转[螺旋]。

tur·bine [ˈtəːbin, -bain; ˋtɝbɪn, -baɪn] *n*.【机】(涡)轮机,叶轮机,汽轮机,透平机。*a hydraulic* [*water*] ~ 水轮机。*a steam* ~ 汽轮机。*a* ~ *steamer* 涡轮汽

T

船。～ *boat* 汽轮机船。
tur·bit [ˈtəːbit; ˋtɚbɪt] ***n.***【动】(冠毛卷如螺贝的)浮羽鸽。
tur·bo [ˈtəːbəu; ˋtɚbo] ***n.*** **1.** 透平机,涡轮机。**2.** = turbosuper charger.
tur·bo- *comb. f.* 意为“涡轮”
tur·bo·car [ˈtəːbəukɑː; ˋtɚbo͵kɑr] ***n.*** 涡轮汽车。
tur·bo·charge [ˈtəːbəutʃɑːdʒ; ˋtɚbotʃɑdʒ] ***vt.***【计】增强(功能),加快(应用程序的工作速度等)。
tur·bo·cop·ter [ˈtəːbəukɔptə; ˋtɚbo͵kɑptɚ] ***n.*** 涡轮直升机。
tur·bo-ex·haus·ter [͵təːbəuigˈzɔːstə; ͵tɚboɪgˋzɔstɚ] ***n.*** 涡轮排气机。
tur·bo·fan [ˈtəːbəu͵fæn; ˋtɚbo͵fæn] ***n.*** **1.** 涡轮通风器(= turbofan engine)。**2.** 涡轮风扇。
tur·bo·gen·er·a·tor [ˈtəːbəuˈdʒenəreitə; ͵tɚboˋdʒenə͵retɚ] ***n.*** 涡轮发电机,透平发电机。
tur·bo·jet [ˈtəːbəudʒet; ˋtɚbo͵dʒet]【空】涡轮喷气发动机(= turbojet engine);涡轮喷气飞机。
tur·bo·lin·er [ˈtəːbəu͵lainə; ˋtɚbo͵laɪnə] ***n.*** 燃气轮机火车。
tur·bo·pause [ˈtəːbəu͵pɔːz; ˋtɚbo͵pɔz] ***n.***【气】湍流层顶〔大气湍流停息的区域,在热大气层底部〕。
tur·bo·prop [ˈtəːbəuprɔp; ˋtɚbo͵prɑp] ***n.*** **1.** 涡轮螺桨发动机(= turboprop engine)。**2.** 涡轮螺桨飞机。
tur·bo-pro·pel·ler en·gine [ˈtəːbəuprəˈpelə; ˋtɚboprəˋpelɚ] 涡轮螺桨发动机。
tur·bo-ram-jet [ˈtəːbəuˈræmdʒet; ˋtɚboˋræmdʒet] ***n.*** 涡轮冲压式喷气发动机[飞机]。
tur·bo·su·per·charg·er [͵təːbəusjuːpəˈtʃɑːdʒə; ͵tɚbosjupɚˋtʃɑrdʒɚ] ***n.***【空】涡轮增压器。
tur·bot [ˈtəːbət; ˋtɚbət] ***n.*** (*pl.* ~*s*,〔集合词〕～)【动】大菱鲆;鳞鲀。
tur·bo·train [ˈtəːbəutrein; ˋtɚbo͵tren] ***n.*** 涡轮火车〔时速可达 170 英里〕
tur·bu·lence, -len·cy [ˈtəːbjuləns, -lənsi; ˋtɚbjələns, -lənsɪ] ***n.*** **1.** (风等的)狂暴;激流(现象)。**2.** 骚乱,动乱;强横。**3.**【气】乱流。*a* ～ *amplifier* 紊流型放大器。
tur·bu·lent [ˈtəːbjulənt; ˋtɚbjələnt] ***a.*** **1.** 激流的;湍流的。**2.** 骚乱的;强横的。～ **flow**【物】涡流。
Turco- *comb. f.* = Turkish: *Turco*phil 爱好土耳其(风俗、习惯)的人。*Turco*phobia 憎恶土耳其(风俗、习惯)的人。
Tur·co·man [ˈtəːkəmən; ˋtɚkəmən] ***n.*** = Turkoman.
turd [təːd; tɚd] ***n.***〔俗〕粪块。
tu·reen [təˈriːn; tuˋrin, tju-] ***n.***〔盛汤用〕有盖的陶瓷大盘。
turf [təːf; tɚf] **I** ***n.*** (*pl.* **-s**;〔罕〕***turves*** [təːvz; tɚvz]) **1.** 草皮,草根土;草地。**2.**〔Am.、Scot.〕泥煤。**3.**〔the ～〕赛马场;赛马。**4.**〔美俚〕(流氓集团的)地盘,势力范围。***on the*** ～ **1.** 以赛马为主。**2.** 卖淫。**3.** 穷得身无分文。**II** ***vt.*** **1.** 把(地面)铺上草皮。**2.** 赶出,驱逐。～ ***it***〔美〕徒步旅行。～ ***out***〔俚〕抛出(东西),赶出(人)。～**-bound** ***a.*** 铺有草皮的。～ **court** 草地网球场。～ **peat** 泥煤。
turf·ite, turf·man [ˈtəːfait, ˈtəːfmən; ˋtɚfaɪt, ˋtɚfmən] ***n.*** 喜欢赛马的人;赛马迷〔尤指自己养马或驯马的〕。
turf·y [ˈtəːfi; ˋtɚfɪ] ***a.*** **1.** 草地的,铺着草皮的;草地似的。**2.** 赛马场的,赛马的。**3.** 泥煤的。～ **soil** 生草土。
tur·gent [ˈtəːdʒənt; ˋtɚdʒənt] ***a.***〔现罕〕肿的,肿胀的。
tur·ges·cence, -cen·cy [təːˈdʒesns, -snsi; tɚˋdʒesns, -snsɪ] ***n.*** **1.** 肿,肿胀。**2.**【植物】紧涨,膨压。**3.** 夸张。**-cent** ***a.***
tur·gid [ˈtəːdʒid; ˋtɚdʒɪd] ***a.*** **1.** 肿胀的。**2.** 浮夸的,夸张的。**-ness** ***n.***
tur·gid·i·ty [təːˈdʒiditi; tɚˋdʒɪdətɪ] ***n.*** **1.** 肿胀,肿大。**2.**【植物生理】紧张度。**3.** 浮夸,夸张。
tur·gite [ˈtəːdʒait; ˋtɚdʒaɪt] ***n.***【矿】水赤铁矿。
tur·gor [ˈtəːgə; ˋtɚgɚ, -gɔr] ***n.*** **1.** 肿胀,胀大。**2.** 紧张(现象),膨压。
Tu·rin [tjuˈrin; ˋtjurɪn, tjuˋrɪn] ***n.*** 都灵〔意大利城市,即 Torino 托里诺市〕。
tu·ri·on [ˈtjuəriən; ˋtjurɪən] ***n.***【植】有鳞芽的根出条。**-i·fer·ous** [-ˈnifərəs; -ˋnɪfərəs] ***a.***
Turk [təːk; tɚk] ***n.*** **1.** 土耳其人;突厥人;(尤指)土耳其的穆斯林。**2.** 土耳其马。**3.** 强暴的人,残忍的人。**4.** 淘气鬼,顽童。**5.**〔美〕爱尔兰人。*the Grand* [*Great*] ～【史】土耳其皇帝。*the Young* ～ 青年土耳其党。*a young* [*little*] ～ 淘气鬼,顽童。～**'s cap** ***n.***【植】**1.** 舟形乌头。**2.** = ～'s head 1. ～**'s-cap lily**【植】头巾百合。～**'s head**【海】(绳索上的)饰结。
Turk. = Turkey; Turkish.
Turk- *comb. f.* 表示:**1.** 突厥(人)的,突厥语的。**2.** 土耳其(人,语)的。
Tur·ke·stan [təːkisˈtæn, -ˈtɑːn; ͵tɚkɪˋstæn, -ˋstɑn] ***n.*** 土耳其斯坦。
Tur·key [ˈtəːki; ˋtɚkɪ] ***n.*** 土耳其〔亚洲〕。～ **red** 土耳其红〔一种涂料〕。
tur·key [ˈtəːki; ˋtɚkɪ] ***n.*** **1.**【鸟】火鸡,吐绶鸡。**2.**〔美俚〕劣等货品[作品];演出失败,失败的广播节目。**3.**〔美俚〕(装模作样)摆臭架子的人。**4.**〔美俚〕五角银币;随身携带的卧具;装器具的帆布袋。**5.**〔美俚〕懦夫。*boned* ～【烹】(美国西部的)兔肉。***have a*** ～ ***on one's back***〔美俚〕酒醉;吸毒成瘾。***say*** ～ ***to one and buzzard to another***.〔美俚〕厚此薄彼。***talk*** (***cold***) ～〔美口〕照实说,直说。～ **buzzard**【动】(南美)兀鹰。～ **cock** 雄火鸡;摆臭架子的人。(*as red as a* ～*cock* (因生气等)面孔通红)。～**trot** 火鸡舞。～ **vulture** = ～ buzzard.
Tur·ki [ˈtuəkiː, ˈtəː-; ˋturkɪ] **I** ***n.*** **1.** 中亚突厥语〔尤指现代维吾尔语〕。**2.** 突厥人。**II** ***a.*** 中亚突厥语的,中亚突厥人的。
Tur·kic [ˈtəːkik; ˋtɚkɪk] **I** ***a.*** **1.** 突厥语族的〔属阿尔泰语系,包括土耳其语,阿塞尔拜疆语,鞑靼语,维吾尔语,乌兹别克语和土库曼语〕。**2.** 突厥语民族的。**II** ***n.*** 突厥语族。
Turk·ish [ˈtəːkiʃ; ˋtɚkɪʃ] **I** ***a.*** 土耳其(人)的;土耳其式的;土耳其语的。**II** ***n.*** 土耳其语;土耳其卷烟;土耳其糖果。～ *bath* 土耳其浴,蒸汽浴;〔*pl.*〕土耳其[蒸汽]浴室。*a* ～ *delight* 橡皮糖。*a* ～ *pound* 土耳其镑〔通常写作 £ T〕。*a* ～ *towel* 土耳其毛巾[浴巾]。～ **delight** 土耳其软糖。～ **slipper** 土耳其拖鞋。～ **tobacco** 土耳其烟草。～ **towel** 土耳其毛巾。
Turk·ism [ˈtəːkizəm; ˋtɚkɪzm̩] ***n.*** 土耳其文化;土耳其风俗;土耳其的宗教信仰等。
Tur·ki·stan [təːkiˈstæn; ͵tɚkɪˋstæn, -ˋstɑn] ***n.*** = Turkestan.
Turk·man [ˈtəːkmən; ˋtɚkmən] ***n.*** (*pl.* **-men**) **1.** 土库曼人。**2.** 土库曼语。～ **carpet** 土库曼地毯。
Turk·men [ˈtəːkmən; ˋtɚkmen, -mən] **I** ***n.*** 土库曼语。**II** ***a.*** 土库曼的;土库曼人的;土库曼语的。
Tur·kmen·i·stan [͵təːkmeniˈstɑːn; ͵tɚkmenɪˋstæn, -ˋstɑn] ***n.*** 土库曼斯坦〔亚洲国名〕。
Turko·man [ˈtəːkəmən; ˋtɚkəmən] ***n.*** (*pl.* ～***s***) 土库曼人,土库曼语。
Turks and Caicos Islands 特克斯和凯科斯群岛〔美洲〕。
Tur·ku [ˈtuəku; ˋturku] ***n.*** 图尔库〔芬兰港市〕。
turma·lin(e) [ˈtəːməlin; ˋtɚməlɪn, -͵lin] ***n.*** = tourmalin(e).
tur·mer·ic [ˈtəːmərik; ˋtɚmərɪk] ***n.*** **1.**【植】姜黄(属);郁金。**2.** 郁金根粉〔用作染料、刺激剂、调味料等〕。～**-paper**【化】姜黄(试)纸。
tur·moil [ˈtəːmɔil; ˋtɚmɔɪl] ***n.*** 骚动,喧嚷,混乱。*His mind was in a* ～. 他心里七上八下。

turn [tə:n; tɝn] **I** ***vt*. 1.** 转,转动,旋转,使转弯;移动,拨动,触动。~ *a wheel* 转动轮子。~ *the tap* 拧塞子,旋龙头。*He will not* ~ *a finger to help*. 他不会略费力气帮一点忙。**2.** 转过去,绕过去;【军】迂回(敌人侧面)。~ *the corner* 转弯,拐弯儿。**3.** 翻转过来做(衣服等);翻(书页);折(边等);弄卷(刀口);挖翻(土地);倒转,翻倒,倒置,颠倒;【印】倒植。~ *an old garment* 翻做旧衣。~ *things upside down* 颠倒是非,混淆黑白。**4.** 转向,朝向,指向;〔喻〕集中(注意、努力等);用于,抵充(用途),利用;改变路线。*T- your face this way*. 请把脸转到这边。~ *one's attention to business* 把注意力集中到事务上。~ *the conversation to something else* 把话岔到别的事情上。**5.** 使变化,改变;使变成(…的状态);(货币的)兑换;翻译;使变质,使变坏;使(脑子)错乱;使恶心。~ *English into Chinese* 把英语译成汉语。*Hot weather* ~*s milk*. 天热会使牛奶变坏。*His head is* ~*ed*. 他神经错乱了。*Success has* ~*ed his head*. 成功冲昏了他的头脑。~ *sb.'s stomach* 使人作呕。**6.** 用镟床镟;〔喻〕做得好看(美观、圆满),弄得像样;表现得好。~ *wooden vessels* 用镟床做木碗(等)。*He was perfectly well* ~*ed for trade*. 他做生意最适宜。~ *a period well* 圆满地构造长句。*well-*~*ed sentences* 构造得精致的句子。**7.** 越过,超过(年龄、时刻等)。*He has just* ~*ed 50*. 他刚过五十(岁)。*He is* ~*ed of boy*. 他已经不是小孩子了。*It's just* ~*ed 3 o'clock*. 刚过三点。**8.** 赶走。~ *sb. out* (*from one's door*) 把某人赶出去。— ***vi*. 1.** 转,旋转;打滚,折腾,翻腾;翻倒。*A wheel* ~*s on its axis*. 轮子在轴上旋转。~ *in bed* [*in one's sleep*] 睡眠中翻身。**2.** 转向;回头;转弯;弯曲;(刀刃)卷口;倾斜;注意。*T- to the left*. 向左转(弯)。*It is time to* ~ *now*. 现在该折回了。**3.** 变;改变;(形势)倒转;变成…,变质;转(业);(头)晕;发恶心,想呕。*The milk has* ~*ed* (*sour*). 牛奶变酸了。*My stomach* ~*s*. 我直恶心。**4.** (镟床工艺)被镟,做成。**5.** 转过身来做出反应;反抗。*A worm will* ~. 虫也会反抗的。***as it*** ~***ed out*** 偶尔(是…),碰巧(是…)。~ ***about*** 回头;转向,调向。~ ***against*** 背叛,反抗;使对抗;厌恶。~ ***and rend sb***. 突然袭击[辱骂]某人。~ ***and*** ~ ***about*** 轮流地。~ ***around* 1.** 转身,回头。**2.**〔美〕使向好的方向转变,使变好。~ ***aside* 1. *vt*.** 架开,避开。**2. *vi*.** 脱出,迷失;背过脸去,把脸避开。~ ***away* 1. *vt*.** (把脸)转(过去);避开;驱逐,轰出;防止(灾祸等);解雇。**2. *vi*.** 转过脸去;表示轻蔑[不赞成]。**3. *n*.**〔美〕拥挤在场外的群众。~ ***back* 1. *vi*.** 折回,回来。**2. *vt*.** 逐回,赶回去;拨慢(钟表);折起(衣服)。~ ***down*** 翻下(衣领等),折(纸);扭小(灯火等)(*T- that radio down at once!* 马上把收音机开得小一些!)拒绝考虑,否决,推翻(提案等);拒绝(某人)。*He asked Jane to marry him but she* ~*ed him down*. 他向珍妮求婚但她拒绝了他。~ ***in* 1. *vi*.** 向里(弯曲);转身进去;(把杂草、肥料等)翻入地内;〔美〕带进,拿进;走近。**2. *vt*.** 折进;使向里;上交,递入。(*T- in everything captured*. 一切缴获要归公)。〔口〕上床睡觉。~ ***in all standing*** 和衣睡着。~ (***sth***.) ***inside out*** 把…翻到外面来。~ *one's pockets inside out* 把口袋里子翻出来。~ ***loose*** 释放,解放(~ *loose upon the world* 使…自由生活)。~ ***off* 1. *vt*.** 解雇,逐出;叉开,引开(不愉快的话题等);完成,制成,生产;关掉(自来水、收音机、电灯等);使失掉兴趣(*Popular music really* ~*s me off*. 流行音乐确实使我厌烦);〔俚〕处绞刑;〔俚〕举行婚礼。**2. *vi*.** (人)走入旁路(*We* ~*ed off into a side street*. 我们拐入一条横街);(路)分歧。~ ***on* 1.** 转向,对准;对…进行突击。(*The dog* ~*ed on me and bit me in the leg*. 那只狗向我扑上来,在我腿上咬了一口);反抗;要看…而定,关键就在(*The question* ~*s on this point*. 问题关键就在这一点上)。**2.** 开(电灯、收音机、自来水);【电】接通(电路);〔口〕使人开始(某事)(*to do*);朝向;(突然或自然而然地)显示。(~ *on the power* (突然)显示出力量)。~ ***one's hand to*** 试,试试看。~ ***out* 1. *vi*.** 向外弯曲,向外;罢工;【电】切断;〔口〕起床;(消防队、军队等)出动;结果变成;结果弄清楚是…,原来是…(*The rumour has* ~*ed out* (*to be*) *false*. 谣言原来是假的)。**2. *vt*.** 驱逐,逐出,撵出(~ *sb. out of the room*);欢送(毕业生);(把牛、羊等)放出牧场;倒出,翻出(容器、房间里的东西);翻转,翻过来;暴露;制出,造出;培养;打扮;关断(煤气等),熄(灯等)。~ ***over* 1. *vi*.** 翻滚,打滚;翻身。**2. *vt*.** 使翻倒,倾覆;交付,移交;翻(书页);耕翻(土地);使生活一新;处理;做(多少钱的)买卖,卖得…,〔喻〕熟思,再三考虑(~ *the matter over in one's mind* 心里再三考虑这件事。~ *over £ 500 a week* 每星期卖得五百镑)。~ ***over a new leaf*** 翻开新的一页,重新开始[做人],洗心革面。~ ***ridicule on*** 嘲笑。~ ***round* 1. *vi*.** 旋转;回头;调向,转向;变计;叛变;反对,反抗;【海】停靠(某港)(*He* ~*s round to oppress the common people*. 他反过来压迫老百姓)。**2. *vt*.** 使旋转;朝向;改变(政策);使叛变。~ ***sb. round one's*** (***little***) ***finger*** 任意驱使[玩弄]某人。~ ***the corner*** 度过危机;情形好转。~ ***the edge of*** 锉…锐气,弄钝…的锋芒。~ ***the hands to*** 【海】使全体船员各就岗位。~ ***the hands up*** 【海】把全体船员集中在甲板上。~ ***the point of*** = ~ the edge of. ~ ***the route*** (特指赛马)跑一定距离。~ ***the trick*** 〔美运〕赛赢。~ ***to*** 变成;请求(~ *to sb. for help* 求人帮助);着手工作,使着手工作。~ ... ***to account*** 利用。~ ***up* 1. *vi*.** 向上;朝天;出来,来到;出现,出席;被找到,突然发生(*They are ready to* ~ *up for interrogation whenever they are wanted*. 他们随叫随到,接受讯问);证明是(= ~ out to be)。**2. *vt*.** 扭大(灯火等);向上弯曲;朝向上面;翻开(牌);掘起;找出;〔口〕使作呕(~ *up one's nose at* 轻视…)。~ ***up one's toes*** 〔口〕死亡。~ ***up the sleeves*** 卷起衣袖;〔喻〕准备行动[工作]。***wait for something to*** ~ ***up*** 期待发生变化;抱观望[骑墙]态度。~ ***upon*** = ~ *on* 1.

II ***n*. 1.** 旋转(运动);转身;(杠上运动的)小翻滚;(溜冰的)曲线转折;改变方向,调转方向;转向,转弯;【军】迂回。**2.** 弯曲;转角,转弯处,屈折部。**3.** 变化,变动;机会;转折点,关键。**4.** 倾向,性情,癖性;气质;特殊才能。**5.** 一个回合;走一圈,散步;(恶意或善意的)行为。**6.**〔英〕(杂技)演员。**7.** 说法,口吻。**8.** 轮流,轮班。**9.** 形状,样子。**10.** 一卷,一圈;线匝;圈数,匝数。**11.** 吃惊,意外。**12.**〔*pl*.〕月经。**13.**【乐】回音;【印】(无本字时暂用的)倒头铅字;【机】车床;(转动把手而开关的)门扣。**14.**〔美俚〕(杂耍、广播等的)一个节目。**15.**〔古〕必要,需要。*the* ~ [*a* ~] *of the tide* 潮汐的转变;形势的转变。*Right* [*Left*] ~! 向右[左]转! *a shallow* ~ 慢转弯,大转弯。*a sharp* [*steep*] ~ 急转弯,小转弯。*Matters have taken a bad* ~. 事情恶化了。*He is of a humo*(*u*)*rous* ~. 他性情幽默。*take a* ~ *round the garden* 在园子里走一圈(散步)。*a beautiful* ~ *of words* 漂亮的说法。*It is your* ~ *to sing*. 这次轮到你唱了。*The news gave me a* ~. 这消息使我吃了一惊。***at every*** ~ 在每一个关键时刻;在每一个角落;到处;老是,常常。***by*** ~***s*** 轮流。***come to a critical*** ~ 到危险关头,到关键时刻。***do sb. a good*** [***an ill***] ~ 对…做好事[坏事],待人好[不好]。***give a new*** ~ ***to*** 对…给与新的变化[看法]。***in one's*** ~ 接替,值班。***in the*** ~ ***of a hand*** 反掌之间,立刻。***in*** ~ 挨次,依次。***on the*** ~ 正在变化,就要转变;(牛奶)快要变酸。***make a*** ~ ***for the better*** [***worse***] 使好转[恶化]。***out of*** ~ 次序混乱;在倒霉的时候;不合时宜;〔口〕狂妄自大(*talk out of one's* ~ 说冒昧话)。***serve one's*** ~ 合用,有用。***take a*** ~ (轮流)干一阵子(*take a* ~ *at the oars* 划一阵桨。*take a* ~ *of work* 做一阵工作)。***take a favo***(***u***)***rable*** ~ 好转。***take a*** ~ ***for the better*** [***worse***] 好转[变坏]。***take*** ~***s*** 替换,换班。***take one's***

~(*to do*)轮流接替。*the* ~ *of life* 绝经期,更年期。*to a* ~〔尤指食物〕(煮得)恰到好处。~ *of speed* 速力。~ *of the market* 买卖差价。~ **about** 转身;立场改变;叛变;叛徒;急进主义者;〔美〕旋转木马。~**-about-face** 改变立场。~**-and-bank**[~**-and-slip**] **indicator**【空】转弯倾斜仪,侧滑指示器。~**around** 1. 车辆调头处;(思想、立场的)转变。2. 回航[卸货、加油、检修、上货]所需时日;来回。3. 小修,预防处理。~ **around time** (完成某事〔某项工程等〕所需的)周转时间。~ **bridge** 旋开桥。~**buckle**【机】松紧螺丝扣;【空】紧线器(*a* ~*buckle screw* 松紧螺套)。~**cap** (烟囱的)旋转帽。~**coat** 叛徒。~**cock** 水龙头开关管理员。~**down** 1. *a*. 翻下的(衣领等);折叠式的(卧铺)。2. *n*. 翻领;〔俚〕拒绝。~ **indicator**【海】转向指示计。~**key** (监狱的)看守。~**off** 岔开,避开;岔道;产品;成品。~**-on** 刺激(因素)。~**out** 1. 走出屋外的人群;(集会的)出席者,到会者;外貌;服装;装备。2. 生产(量)。3.〔英〕罢工(者)。4. 临时召集;〔口〕起床(时间)。5. 马车的全套配备和人员。6.【铁路】让车岔道。~**over** 1. (车等的)翻倒;翻折;翻折的东西;半圆煎饼;转换;转让;转页新闻。2. (一定时间内的)补充工人数;补充工人对工人总平均数的比率;(转给另一厂主的)转雇学徒;(一期间的)营业额,周转(额);临时投资额;工程维持费。~**pike**【史】征收通行税的路;通行税征收所,收税栅;通行大路;〔美〕收税高速公路。~**plate**〔英〕= turntable. ~**-round** (轮船的)停泊〔船的入港、卸货、装货和离港〕。~**screw** 螺丝钻,改锥。~**sole**【植】向日葵。~**spit** (旧时训练好会用踏车转动烤肉叉的)转叉狗;旋转烤肉叉的人;旋转式烤肉叉。~ **stile** (能统计出入人数的)旋转栅门。~**-stone**【鸟】翻石鹬(属)。~**table** 转盘式餐桌;(转换机车方向的)转车台,旋车盘;(唱机上的)转盘;(广播用)录音转播机。~**up** 1.〔口〕突然出现的人;突发事件;骚动。2. 斗殴;打架;拳击比赛。3. 卷起的部分;(裤脚的)卷边。

Tur·ner [ˈtəːnə; ˋtɝnɚ] *n*. 特纳〔姓氏〕。

turn·er[1] [ˈtəːnə; ˋtɝnɚ] *n*. 1. 镟(床)工(人),车工。2.〔英〕翻飞鸽。

turn·er[2] [ˈtəːnə; ˋtɝnɚ] *n*.〔美〕翻斤斗的杂技演员,体育运动员;体育俱乐部会员。

turn·er·y [ˈtəːnəri; ˋtɝnərɪ] *n*. 镟制[镟磨]工艺;镟制[镟磨]法;镟制[镟磨]品;车削车间。

turn·ing [ˈtəːniŋ; ˋtɝnɪŋ] *n*. 旋转,转动;转向;弯曲;转弯处;镟制[车削]工艺;镟坯;〔*pl*.〕镟屑;制作。*take the first* ~ *to the right* 由第一个转角处向右拐。*the* ~ *of verses* 作诗。~ **point** 转折点;关键时刻。(*the* ~ *point of a disease* 病势的转折点)。~**saw** = compass saw.

tur·nip [ˈtəːnip; ˋtɝnɪp] *n*. 1.【植】芜菁,萝卜。2.〔俚〕大怀表。*get blood from a* ~ 从大头菜中榨血,做不可能的事。~ **radish** (圆)萝卜。~ **tops**〔*pl*.〕芜菁叶。

Turn·ver·ein [ˈtunfɛəˌain, F. ˈtəːnfəˌrain; ˋturnfɛr-ˏaɪn]〔G.〕*n*. 体育[体操运动员]协会。

tur·pen·tine [ˈtəːpəntain; ˋtɝpənˏtaɪn] I *n*. 松脂(精);松节油〔= oil of ~〕. II *vt*. 涂松节油;制松节油;采松脂。**T- State**〔美〕北卡罗来纳州〔别名〕。**-ti·nous** *a*.

tur·pi·tude [ˈtəːpitjuːd; ˋtɝpəˏtjud, -ˏtud] *n*. 奸恶,卑鄙,卑劣(行为)。

turps [təːps; tɝps] *n*.〔俚〕松节油。

tur·quoise [ˈtəːkwɑːz, -kwɔiz; ˋtɝkwɔɪz, -kɔɪz] *n*. 1.【矿】绿松石。2. 青绿色,天蓝色。~ *blue* 湖蓝,翠蓝。

tur·ret [ˈtʌrit; ˋtɝɪt, ˋturɪt] *n*. 1.【建】塔楼,角塔。2.【古军】(攻城用)移动塔楼。3.【军】(飞机、坦克、军舰的)炮塔,转塔。4.【机】= ~-head. *a* ~ *lathe* 六角车床。~ **captain**〔美〕炮塔长。~ **gun** 炮塔炮。~**head**【机】六角转头;转台。~ **ship** 旋转炮塔舰。

tur·ric·u·late [təˈrikjuˌleit, -lit; təˋrɪkjəˏlet] *a*. 有小角塔的,形似小角塔的(= turriculated)。

tur·tle[1] [ˈtəːtl; ˋtɝtl] I *n*.【动】龟,(特指)青蠵龟,海龟,海鳖;海龟汤〔= ~-soup,美国的 ~-soup 多指甲鱼(terrapin)汤〕。*a green* ~ 海龟。*a snapping* [*mud*] ~ 鳖,甲鱼。*a hawk's-bill* ~ 玳瑁。***Teenage Mutant Ninja Turtles*** (儿童科幻小说中的)忍者神龟〔一群深陷在纽约下水道放射性黏泥中的少年,突变为神通广大的英雄〕;忍者神龟式的英雄人物;忍者神龟的英雄故事〔玩具、电子游戏节目等〕。*turn* ~ 把海龟翻转身来加以捕捉;〔海口语〕(把船等)翻掉;(使)无活动能力。II *vi*. 捉海龟为业。~**back**【船】鲸背甲板。~**-head**【植】龟头花(属);白龟头花。~**neck** 圆翻领(服装)。

tur·tle[2] [ˈtəːtl; ˋtɝtl] *n*.〔古〕= turtledove. ~**-dove** *n*. 斑鸠(*a pair of* ~*-doves* 一对情人)。

turves [təːvs; tɝvz]〔古〕turf 的复数。

Tus·can [ˈtʌskən; ˋtʌskən] I *a*. 托斯卡纳(Tuscany〔意大利中西部地名〕)的;(帽子等)托斯卡纳麦秆的;【建】托斯卡纳式的。II *n*. 托斯卡纳人[语]。

Tus·ca·ro·ra [ˌtʌskəˈrɔːrə; ˏtʌskəˋrɔrə] *n*. 1. (*pl*. *-ras*, *-ra*) 塔斯卡洛拉族人〔印第安的一个部落,原居于美国维吉尼亚和北卡罗来纳州,1722 年参加了易洛魁联盟后移居到纽约和加拿大安大略省〕。2. 塔斯卡洛拉语〔易洛魁语的一种方言〕。

tush[1] [tʌʃ; tʌʃ] I *int*., *n*.〔古〕啐!〔表示申斥、轻蔑等〕。II *vi*. 说一声啐。

tush[2] [tʌʃ; tʌʃ] *n*. (马等的)犬齿;(象、猪等的)长牙。

tush·er·y [ˈtʌʃəri; ˋtʌʃərɪ] *n*. 爱用啐声骂人的习惯[人,文章]。

tusk [tʌsk; tʌsk] I *n*. 1. (象、猪等的)长牙。2.〔谑〕(人的)犬牙,獠牙,暴牙。3. 獠牙似的东西,尖物,(犁等的)尖头。II *vt*. 用长牙齿掘[刺,咬]。~**like** 獠牙[长牙]状的。**-ed** *a*. 有长牙[獠牙]的。

tusk·er [ˈtʌskə; ˋtʌskɚ] *n*. 有长牙的动物;象,野猪(等)。

tus·sah, tus·seh, tus·ser [ˈtʌsə; ˋtʌsə] *n*. 1.【动】柞蚕。2. 柞蚕丝;柞绸。~**-silk** *n*. 柞蚕丝;柞绸。

Tus·saud [ˈtuːsəu; ˋtuso] *n*. 图索〔姓氏〕。

Tus·saud's [təˈsəuz; təˋsoz] (伦敦的)特索氏蜡人馆。

tus·sis [ˈtʌsis; ˋtʌsɪs] *n*.【医】咳,咳嗽。**tus·sive** [-iv; -ɪv] *a*.

tus·sle [ˈtʌsl; ˋtʌsl] *n*., *vi*. 1. 扭打。2. 争论;奋斗(*with*);〔美运〕比赛;争胜。

tus·sock [ˈtʌsək; ˋtʌsək] *n*. 1. 草丛;沼泽上的草丛丘阜。2.〔罕〕丛,簇。3.【植】= ~ *grass* 生草丛,高丛早熟禾草。~ **moth**【动】毒蛾。**-y** *a*.

tus·sor(e) [ˈtʌsɔː, -sə; ˋtʌsor, -sɔr], **tus·sur** [ˈtʌsə; ˋtʌsɚ] *n*. = tussah.

tut[1] [tʌt; tʌt] I *int*., *n*. 嘘! 啧!〔表示不耐烦、轻蔑、指责〕。II *vi*. (**-tt-**) '啧!'〔表示轻蔑等〕(= tut-tut)。

tut[2] [tʌt; tʌt] *n*., *vi*. (**-tt-**)【矿】计件制(工作)。

tu·tee [tjuːˈtiː, tuː-; tjuˋti, tu-] *n*.〔美〕受监护者;受教导者,受指导者。

tu·te·lage [ˈtjuːtilidʒ; ˋtutlɪdʒ, ˋtju-] *n*. 1. 保护,监护;教育,教导,指导。2. 受保护。3. 导师或监护人的职责。

tu·te·lar, tu·te·la·ry [ˈtjuːtələ, -ri; ˋtutlɚ, ˋtju-, ˋtutlˏɛrɪ] *a*. 保护(人)的,监护(人)的。

tu·te·nag [ˈtjuːtinæg; ˋtjutɪˏnæg] *n*. 中国白铜;生锌;锌铜镍合金。

tu·tor [ˈtjuːtə; ˋtutɚ, ˋtju-] I *n*. 1. 私人教师,家庭教师;师傅;〔英大学〕导师;〔美〕助教;(考试)辅导员。2.【法】监护人。II *vt*., *vi*. 1. 做私人[家庭]教师(教);辅导(学生);教练,训斥。2. 监护。3. 抑制(感情等)。4.〔美〕接受单独训练。

tu·tor·age [ˈtjuːtəridʒ; ˋtutərɪdʒ, ˋtju-] *n*. 1. 家庭教师[监护人]的地位[职务];辅导。2. (家庭教师的)酬金。

tu·tor·ess [ˈtjuːtəris; ˋtutərɪs, ˋtju-] *n*. tutor 的女性。

tu·to·ri·al [tjuːˈtɔːriəl; tjuˋtɔrɪəl] I *a*. (大学)导师的;家

庭教师的;辅导的;监护人的。**II** ***n***. 个人辅导时间;受大学教育时间。*the* ~ *system* 导师制。

tu·tor·ship [ˈtjuːtəʃip; ˋtutə͵ʃɪp, ˋtju-] ***n***. tutor 的职务[身份]。

tu·toy·er [ˌtuːtwɑːˈjei, F. tytwaˈje; ͵tutwɑˋje, tytwaˋjɛ] ***vt***. 以亲切而随便的口吻交谈〔如在法语中用“你”(tu 或 toi)而不用“您”(vous)〕。

tu·tress [ˈtjuːtris; ˋtjutrɪs] ***n***. = tutoress.

tut·ti [ˈtutiː; ˋtutɪ, ˋtutti] **I** ***a***.〔It.〕【乐】全体的。**II** ***n***. 合奏;齐唱;(独奏者以外的)全体演奏者。

tut·ti·frut·ti [ˈtuːtiˈfruti; ˋtutɪˋfrutɪ] ***n***.〔美〕**1.** 加有糖渍水果的冰淇淋(或糖果)。**2.** 具有多种水果味的香料。

Tut·tle [ˈtʌtl; ˋtʌtl̩] ***n***. 塔特尔〔姓氏〕。

tut-tut [ˈtʌtˈtʌt; ˋtʌtˋtʌt] ***int***., ***n***. 嘘嘘! 啧啧!〔表示不耐烦、轻蔑、责难〕。

tut·ty [ˈtʌti; ˋtʌtɪ] ***n***. 不纯锌华[氧化锌]。

tu·tu [ˈtuːtuː; ˋtutu] ***n***.〔F.〕(芭蕾舞的)短裙。

Tu·tu·i·la [ˌtuːtuˈiːlɑː; ͵tutʊˋilɑ] ***n***. 土土伊拉岛〔萨摩亚(Samoa)群岛中最大岛〕。

tu·um [ˈtuːəm; ˋtuəm, ˋtju-] ***pron***.〔L.〕你的(东西,财产等)〔拉丁语物主代名词单数第二人称的中性,常指所有物,所有权〕。

Tuvalu [ˈtuːvəlu; ˋtuvəlu] ***n***. 图瓦卢〔大洋洲〕。

tu-whit, tu-whoo [tuˈ*h*wit, tuˈ*h*wuː; tʊˋ*h*wɪt, tʊˋ*h*wu] **I** ***vi***. (*-tt-*)(猫头鹰)嘀嘀地叫。**II** ***n***. 嘀嘀的叫声。

tux [tʌks; tʌks] ***n***.〔美口〕= tuxedo.

tux·e·do [tʌkˈsiːdəu; tʌkˋsido, -də] ***n***. (*pl*. ~*s*)〔美〕夜会便服,无尾晚礼服,小晚礼服〔略 tux〕,〔美俚〕(精神病患者穿的)紧身衣。

tu·y·ère [ˈtwiːjɛə; twiˋjɛr, twɪr] ***n***.〔F.〕【冶】(熔矿炉的)吹风管嘴;风口。

TV, T. V. = television. **TV dinner** 盒装电视便餐〔一种速冻餐,吃前稍热即可〕。★美国 1997 年电视节目分级,在电视屏幕上打出给家长的告示以便他们控制子女的收看范围。这些分级有:**TV-14**,14 岁以下儿童不宜;**TV-G**,老少咸宜;**TV-M**,只适合成人收看,17 岁以下青少年不宜;**TV-PG**,节目中可能有部分儿童不宜的内容;**TV-Y** 适合所有青少年收看;**TV-Y7**,适合 7 岁及 7 岁以上儿童收看。

TVA = Tennessee Valley Authority〔美〕田纳西流域管理局。

TVP = textured vegetable protein 结构性植物蛋白。

TWA = Trans World Airlines〔美〕环球航空公司。

twa [twɑː; twɑ] ***a***., ***n***.〔Scot.〕two 的变体。

twad·dell [ˈtwɔdl; ˋtwɑdl̩] ***n***. 特沃德耳比重计〔用以测量比水重的液体〕。

twad·dle [ˈtwɔdl; ˋtwɑdl̩] **I** ***n***. 闲聊;无聊的废话,讲[写]蠢话。*ignorant* ~ 无知妄说。**II** ***vi***. 聊天。**-r** ***n***. 爱说[写]废话的人。

twain [twein; twen] ***n***., ***a***.〔古〕二,两,双,一对。*cut in* ~ 切成两个,一分为二。

twang[1] [twæŋ; twæŋ] **I** ***n***. **1.** (拨)弦声。**2.** 鼻音;带鼻音的(方言)口音。**3.** (突然的一阵)痛苦。**II** ***vt***., ***vi***. **1.** (使)当地响;当地一声从弓弦上射出。**2.**〔罕〕用鼻音讲。**-y** ***a***. **1.** 似弦声的。**2.** 带鼻音的。

twang[2] [twæŋ; twæŋ] ***n***. **1.** 长久不散的气味,强烈的气味。**2.** 遗迹,痕迹,迹象;含意。

twan·gle [ˈtwæŋgl; ˋtwæŋgl̩] ***vt***. **1.**【罕】使发拨弦声。**2.** 带鼻音讲。**3.** (使)当地(射)出去。

TWAS = (The) Third World Academy of Sciences 第三世界科学学院。

'twas [强 twɔz; 弱 twəz; twɑz]〔方〕= it was.

twat·tle [ˈtwɑːtl; ˋtwɑtl̩] ***n***., ***vi***., ***vt***. = twaddle.

tway·blade [ˈtweiˌbleid; ˋtwe͵bled] ***n***.【植】羊耳蒜属(*Liparis*)植物;双叶兰(*Listera cordata*)。

tweak [twiːk, twik] **I** ***n***. **1.** 拧,捏,扭;力扯。**2.**〔俚〕好办法,妙计。**II** ***vt***. 拧(面颊,耳鼻等),扭,抓住拉;用力拉。—***vi***. (吸毒者发毒瘾时)神经质地抽搐。

twee [twiː; twi] ***a***.〔英口〕装成聪明(优雅)的样子的;装出讨人喜欢的样子的。

Tweed [twiːd; twid] ***n***. 特威德〔姓氏〕。

tweed [twiːd; twid] ***n***. (粗)花呢;〔*pl*.〕花呢衣服。**-y** ***a***. **1.** (粗)花呢的;常常穿着漂亮花呢衣服的。**2.** 爱好户外生活[运动]的;好游乐的。

twee·dle [ˈtwiːdl; ˋtwidl̩] **I** ***n***. (乐器等的)尖锐声。**II** ***vt***., ***vi***. **1.** (吹奏,歌唱)(使)发出尖细的声音。**2.** = wheedle.

twee·dle·dum and twee·dle·dee [ˌtwiːdlˈdʌm ənˌtwiːdlˈdiː; ͵twidl̩ˋdʌmən͵twidl̩ˋdi] 难以区别的[极相似的]两个人[物]。

Tweeds·muir [ˈtwiːdzmjuə; ˋtwidzmjʊr] ***n***. 特威兹缪尔〔姓氏〕。

'tween [twiːn; twin] ***prep***.〔诗〕= between. ~ **deck**【海】(主甲板下的任何一层)中甲板。

tween·er [ˈtwiːnə; ˋtwinə] ***n***.〔口〕无法归类的人,另类。

tween·y [ˈtwiːni; ˋtwinɪ] ***n***. **1.**〔古〕(帮助烧饭和做杂务的)年轻女仆。(= betweenmaid)。**2.** 小雪茄烟。

tweet [twiːt; twit] **I** ***vi***. (小鸟)吱吱地叫,啾鸣。**II** ***n***. 小鸟叫声,啾啾声。**-er**【无】高频扬声器;高音重发器。

tweeze [twiːz; twiz] ***vt***.〔口〕用镊子拔(毛等)。

tweez·er [ˈtwiːzə; ˋtwizɚ] **I** ***n***. 镊子,小钳〔用复数,常作 *a pair of* ~*s*〕。**II** ***vt***. 用镊子钳[拔](毛等)。

twelfth [twelfθ; twɛlfθ] **I** ***num***. **1.** 第十二,第十二号。**2.** 十二分之一(的)。**II** ***n***. **1.** (某月的)十二日。**2.**【乐】第十二音,十二分音,十二度音程。***the*** ~〔英〕八月十二日〔松鸡猎期开始日〕。**Twelfth-cake** ***n***. 主显节的糕饼。**Twelfthday**【宗】主显节〔圣诞节后第十二日,= Epiphany〕。**Twelfthnight** 主显节的前夜;主显节的夜晚。

twelve [twelv; twɛlv] **I** ***num***. (基数)十二;〔用于章、节、行、页等词后〕第十二。**II** ***n***. **1.** 十二,十二个。**2.** 十二个东西[人];十二的记号;十二点钟;十二岁;十二英寸炮。**3.** 十三世纪。**4.**〔the T-〕【宗】= the T- Apostles. ***in*** ~***s***【印】十二开本。***strike*** ~ ***the first time*** [***all at once***] 一开头就显出全副本领[获得大成功]。~**mo** [-məu; -mo] ***a***., ***n***. (*pl*. ***-mos***) = duodecimo〔略 12 mo〕。~**month**〔英〕十二个月,一年(*this day* ~*-month* 明年[去年]的今天)。~**penny** ***a***.〔英〕十二便士的;价廉的。~**tone** ***a***.【乐】十二音体系的。

twen·ti·eth [ˈtwentiiθ; ˋtwɛntɪɪθ] **I** ***num***. **1.** 第二十,第二十号。**2.** 二十分之一。**II** ***n***. (某月的)二十日。*a* ~ *part* 二十分之一。

twen·ty [ˈtwenti; ˋtwɛntɪ] **I** ***num***. (基数)二十;〔用于名词后表示顺序〕第二十。~ ***times*** 二十次;层次,再三,多次。~ ***and*** ~ 许许多多,不计其数。**II** ***n***. **1.** 二十,二十个。**2.** 二十个东西[人];二十的记号。**3.** 许多,大量。**4.**〔*pl*.〕二十年代〔略 '20s〕。**5.**〔*pl*.〕二十多岁。*And* ~ *of these puny lies I'll tell*. 这种毫无价值的瞎话要多少我都可以造出来。***in nineteen*** ~ 在 1920 年。***in the nineteen twenties*** 在二十世纪二十年代〔略 1920's〕。***in the twenties*** 二十多岁(的);在二十年代(的);二十多度(的)。~**-five**【橄榄球、曲棍球】距(球门)25 码界线(以内)。~**fold** ***a***. 二十倍的。~**-four**【印】〔*pl*.〕24 开(本)。~**-fourmo** (*pl*. ~*s*) 24 开本(的书)〔略 24 mo〕。~**-twenty** ***a***.【眼科】20/20 的,视力正常的〔或写作 20/20〕。

'twere [强 twəː, 弱 twə; twɚ]〔诗〕= it were.

twerp [twəːp; twɚp] ***n***.〔俚〕无足轻重的人;可鄙可笑的人。

TWI, T. W. I. = Training within Industry 企业内(不脱产)训练。

twi- *pref*. 二,双重,两倍,两次: twibill, twifold, twi-forked, twi-formed.

T

Twi [tʃwiː, twiː, tʃiː; twi, tʃwi, tʃi] ***n***. **1**. 契维语〔属于克瓦 (kwa) 语支,主要在加纳通用〕。**2**. (*pl*. ***Twis***, ***Twi***) 说契维语的人。

twi·bil(l) [ˈtwaibil; ˋtwaɪˏbɪl] ***n***. 双刃战斧;阔刀;双刃丁字锄〔一刃与柄平行,一刃与柄垂直〕;镰刀。

twice [twais; twaɪs] ***ad***. 两次;两倍。*It is ~ as good*. 加倍地好。~ *as much* 两倍(的份量)。*He is ~ the man he was*. = *He has ~ the strength he had*. = *He is ~ as strong as he was*. 他比从前加倍强壮了。*T- two is four*. 二二得四。***in*** ~ 〔口〕分两次。***once or*** ~ 一两次。***think*** ~ 重新考虑,仔细考虑 (*do not think ~ about* 不再考虑,断然…;不再想起,忘掉,忽视)。~ ***or thrice*** 两三次。~**-laid** ***a***. 再生的〔用旧绳搓成的绳,用旧料做的东西〕。~**-told** ***a***. 讲过两次〔好几次〕的;(话等)陈腐的。**-r** 再度做某事的人,做某事两次的人〔如做两次礼拜〕;兼做两件事的人〔如排字兼印刷工人〕;双倍的结果;〔主英〕骗子。

twid·dle [ˈtwidl; ˋtwɪdl̩] **I** ***vt***. 捻弄。— ***vi***. **1**. 玩弄 (*with*)。**2**. 花式弹奏。**3**. 〔英方〕忙于琐事。**II** ***n***. **1**. 捻。**2**. 波状线,波纹。~ [***twirl***] ***one's thumbs***, 见 twirl 条。**twiddly** ***a***.

twig[1] [twig; twɪg] **I** ***n***. **1**. 桠枝,细枝。**2**. 深矿杖。**3**. 卜杖。**4**. 【解】(血管等的)枝脉;【电】枝线。***hop the*** ~ 逃掉,躲开;突然离去;突然死去。**II** ***vt***. (**-gg-**) 【美俚】用细枝打。**-gy** ***a***.

twig[2] [twig; twɪg] 〔英口〕 ***vt***., ***vi***. (**-gg-**) 懂得,明白,了解;注目,注意,认出,看出,发现。

twi·light [ˈtwailait; ˋtwaɪˏlaɪt] **I** ***n***. **1**. 黎明;薄暮,黄昏;微明;朦胧;【天】晨昏蒙影,曙暮光。**2**. 懵懂;(意义的)模糊。**3**. 衰退没落阶级[状态]。**4**. 〔美俗〕厕所,盥洗室。**II** ***a***. 微明的,幽暗的,朦胧的,有微光的。**III** ***vt***. 使微明,朦胧地照亮。~ **home** **1**. 养老院。**2**. 年老动物收容所。~ **house** 年久失修的房子。~ **sleep** 【医】(无痛分娩法的)半麻醉。~ **zone** 【无】半阴影区。

twi·lit [ˈtwailit; ˋtwaɪˏlɪt] ***a***. 沉浸在柔和的微光中的。

twill [twil; twɪl] **I** ***n***. 斜纹织物[组织、图案] (= ~ weave)。*artillery* ~ 斜纹马裤呢。**II** ***vt***. 把…织成斜纹。

'twill [twil; twɪl] 〔诗〕 = it will.

TWIMC = to whom it may concern (正式信件等的开头)敬启者。

twin [twin; twɪn] **I** ***a***. **1**. 孪生的。**2**. 成对的,酷似的。**3**. 【植】双生[对生]的。*a ~ amplifier* 孪放大器。~ *brothers* 孪生兄弟。~ *crystal* 【物】孪晶。~ *elements* 【化】孪元素。*a ~ engine* 双发动机。~ *triode* 【无】双三极管。*a ~ volume* 两卷一部的书籍中的一册。*a ~ vase* 一对花瓶的一个。**II** ***n***. **1**. 孪生儿之一;〔*pl*.〕孪生儿,双胎,联胎。**2**. 相像的人[物],一对中的一方;〔*pl*.〕对。**3**. 【结晶】孪[双]晶。**4**. 〔T-〕〔*pl*.〕【天】双子座;双子宫。***Siamese*** ~***s*** 【医】暹罗双胎,剑突联胎〔身体相联的双胎〕。**III** ***vt***., ***vi***. (**-nn-**) **1**. (使)生孪生儿。**2**. (同…)成对 (*with*)。**3**. 【物】(使)成双晶。~**-berry** 【植】总苞忍冬;蔓虎刺(树,果)。~ **bill** **1**. 放映两部影片的一场电影。**2**. (同一对球队)一天两场的比赛。~**born** ***a***. 孪生的。~**-engined** 【空】双发动机的。~**-flower** 【植】林奈花(属)。~**-screw** 【船】双轴的。~**-track** ***a***. (核裁军建议)双向的,彼此相对应的。

twine [twain; twaɪn] **I** ***n***. **1**. 二股(以上的)线,捻线,细绳;麻线[绳]。**2**. 搓捻;盘绕;缠绕;纠缠。**II** ***vt***., ***vi***. **1**. 捻,搓;织,编。**2**. (使)缠绕,绕住;缠住;卷。**3**. 蜿蜒。~ *one's arms round* 两臂抱着前胸。**-r** **1**. 捻[织、编等]的人;捻[搓、编]成物,缠绕物。**2**. 缠绕植物〔如扁豆藤〕。

twinge [twindʒ; twɪndʒ] **I** ***n***. **1**. 刺痛,阵痛,剧痛。**2**. 痛心,内疚。**II** ***vt***., ***vi***. (使)刺疼,(使)一阵一阵地疼。

twi-night, **twi·night** [ˈtwaiˌnait; ˋtwaɪˏnaɪt] ***a***. 【美棒球】(傍晚开始而)连赛两场比赛的。

twin·kle [ˈtwiŋkl; ˋtwɪŋkl] **I** ***vi***. **1**. (星等)闪烁。**2**. 眨眼;(眼睛)闪亮。**3**. (舞蹈者的腿等)轻快有节奏地一闪一闪摆动。— ***vt***. 使闪烁,使闪亮;眨(眼)。**II** ***n***. **1**. 闪烁,闪光。**2**. 眨眼;瞬间,霎时间,一刹那。**3**. 一闪一闪有节奏的活动。***in a*** ~ = ***in the*** ~ ***of an eye*** 一眨眼工夫。**-r** ***n***. 闪闪发光体[物]。**-rs** 〔美〕眼睛。

twin·kling [ˈtwiŋkliŋ; ˋtwɪŋklɪŋ] **I** ***a***. 闪烁的,闪亮的,(星等)闪闪发光的。**II** ***n***. **1**. 闪烁。**2**. 眨眼;瞬间,转眼间。***in a*** ~ = ***in the*** ~ ***of an eye*** = ***in the*** ~ ***of a bed post*** 一眨眼工夫,转瞬间。

twirl [twəːl; twɝl] **I** ***vt***. **1**. 使滴溜溜地旋转。**2**. 挥转(手杖等)。**3**. 捻;捻转。**4**. 【美棒球】扔(球)。~ [*twiddle*] *one's thumbs* 闲极无聊中两手的拇指互相捻弄;无所事事,无事可做。~ *one's moustache* 捻胡子。— ***vi***. **1**. 滴溜溜地旋转。**2**. 【美棒球】扔球,投球。**II** ***n***. **1**. 旋转;回旋。**2**. 捻弄。**3**. (花体字的)拉长的笔道。**4**. 〔美俚〕万能钥匙。

twirp [twəːp; twɝp] ***n***. = twerp.

twist [twist; twɪst] **I** ***vt***. **1**. 拧,扭,绞。**2**. 捻,搓;编,织,作,造。**3**. 缠绕,卷。**4**. 扭弯,扭歪;扭伤。**5**. 曲解,牵强附会;抢夺;折磨;扰乱。**6**. 弯弯曲曲地通过(*through*; *along*)。**7**. 使(球)旋转,拧转(球)。~ *threads into a string* 把几根线拧成一条绳。~ *a towel* 绞毛巾。~ *a garland* 编花圈。~ *a fine story* 编造一个巧妙的故事。*He ~ed it out of my hand*. 他从我手中抢去了。~ *one's way through the crowd* 弯弯曲曲地在人群中穿过去。— ***vi***. **1**. 挠曲,扭转;转身;扭伤。**2**. 捻上,搓上;缠上,卷住;盘绕;编花圈。**3**. 成旋涡形;成螺旋形;(球)旋转着前进。**4**. 曲曲弯弯地穿过去。**5**. 跳扭摆舞。***turn***, ~ ***and wind sb***. = ~ ***sb***. ***round one's*** (***little***) ***finger*** 任意驱使[摆弄]某人。~ ***off*** 拧断,扭断,拧开。~ ***one's features*** (痛得)皱眉蹙脸。~ ***the tail*** 〔美〕使汽车开动。~ ***up*** 捻,搓;卷。**II** ***n***. **1**. 一拧,一捻,一扭,一搓;捻转,扭转,扭歪;缠绕,缠乱。**2**. 怪癖;别扭。**3**. 曲解,牵强。**4**. 捻合线,绳子。**5**. 绞花面包;捻卷烟;混合酒。**6**. 〔口〕食欲,胃口。**7**. 弯拐,曲折;螺旋状;【纺】经纱;捻度;【炮】膛线的缠绕度;拧球,旋球;扭摆舞;【造船】转线。**8**. 〔美俚〕(轻浮的)姑娘;妇人。*gin* ~ 白兰地杜松子(混合)酒。*a ~ drill* 麻花钻。***a*** ~ ***in one's nature*** 怪癖,拗脾气。***a*** ~ ***in one's tongue*** 发音[口齿]不清。***a*** ~ ***of the wrist*** 〔喻〕熟练,诀窍。~***s and turns*** 迂回曲折;〔喻〕曲折复杂的情况。

twist·a·ble [ˈtwistəbl; ˋtwɪstəbl̩] ***a***. 可拧扭[搓捻,缠绕,旋转等]的。**-a·bil·i·ty** [ˌtwistəˈbiliti; ˏtwɪstəˋbɪlətɪ] ***n***.

twist·er [ˈtwistə; ˋtwɪstɚ] ***n***. **1**. 扭转的人。**2**. 绞扭器。**3**. 【纺】捻接工人;捻线机。**4**. 【气象】旋风,陆[水]龙卷;沙柱;尘旋。**5**. 【运】旋球。**6**. 〔口〕歪曲事实的人,说谎的人;不正派的人,谎话。**7**. 难事,难题;拗口令 (= tongue ~)。**8**. (杂技中的)空中扭身斤斗。

twist·y [ˈtwisti; ˋtwɪstɪ] ***a***. **1**. 弯弯曲曲的,扭曲的。**2**. 不正直的。**-i·ly** ***ad***. **-i·ness** ***n***.

twit[1] [twit; twɪt] ***vt***., ***n***. (**-tt-**) **1**. 责备。**2**. 挖苦,嘲笑。

twit[2] [twit; twɪt] ***n***. 〔英俚〕傻瓜;可鄙的人。~ **filter** 【计】垃圾函件过滤器〔一种电脑软件,可切断除指定通讯者以外的一切电子邮件〕。

twit[3] [twit; twɪt] ***n***. 颤搐〔一种神经激动的状态〕。

twitch [twitʃ; twɪtʃ] **I** ***vt***., ***vi***. **1**. 急抽,猛拉;抢去 (*off*)。**2**. 抽动;(使)痉挛,抽搐。**3**. (使)发生剧痛。**II** ***n***. **1**. 猛拉,猛抽。**2**. 痉挛,抽筋,抽搐。**3**. 【兽医】捻鼻器。

twite [twait; twaɪt] ***n***. 【鸟】黄嘴朱顶雀 〔= ~-finch〕。

twit·ter [ˈtwitə; ˋtwɪtɚ] **I** ***vi***. **1**. (燕子等)喊喊喳喳地叫。**2**. (激动得)打颤;吃吃地笑。— ***vt***. **1**. 〔口〕(人)喊喊喳喳地讲。**2**. 抖动。**II** ***n***. **1**. 啭鸣,喊喊喳喳的鸣叫声[说话声],吃吃笑声。**2**. 兴奋,抖颤。**3**. 〔方〕忍笑,偷笑。***in a*** ~ 激动中,抖颤着。**-y** ***a***.

'twixt [twikst; twɪkst] ***prep.*** 〔诗、方〕 = betwixt.

two [tuː; tu] **I** ***num.*** **1.** 〔基数〕二;〔从数量上限定表示事物或人的名词〕两个;〔用于表示章节等词之后〕第二。**II** ***n.*** (*pl.* ~*s*) **1.** 两人;两个东西,一对。**2.** 二的记号。**3.** 两点钟。**4.** 两岁。*a total of* ~ 总数两个。*one or* ~ 一两个,少数。*Two heads are better than one.* 三个臭皮匠胜过诸葛亮。~ *bits* 〔美俚〕两角五分。*T- of a trade seldom agree.* 同行是冤家。*Two's company, three's none.* 两好三别扭。*That's a game that* ~ *can play.* = *T- can play at that game.* 互不相让;一个能打一个能还;一报还一报。***a day or*** ~ 一两日。***at*** ~ 在两点钟。***by*** **~*s and threes*** 三三两两;零星地。***in*** ~ 为俩。***in*** ~ **~*s*** 〔口〕立刻,一转眼 (*The business was over in* ~ ~*s.* 工作一转眼之间就好了)。***put*** ~ ***and*** ~ ***together*** 根据情况推论。~ ***and*** ~ = ~ ***by*** 两个两个。~ ***by four*** = ~-by-four. ~-***fifty grand*** 〔美〕二十五万元。~ ***party line*** 【电】两户合用线。~***-to-one shop*** 当铺。~ ***whoop and a holler*** 〔美〕不远的地方,很短的距离。~**-and-one-half-striper** 〔美俚〕海军少校。~**-base hit**, 〔俚〕 ~**-bagger** 【美棒球】二垒打〔击球者能顺利进入二垒的〕。~**-bit** ***a.*** 〔美口〕两角五分的;〔俚〕不值钱的;劣等的,不足道的。~**-by-four** ***a.***, ***n.*** 厚 2 英寸宽 4 英寸的(木材);〔美俚〕极微末的,不足道的。~**-cleft** ***a.*** 【植】二裂的。~**-cycle** 【机】二程循环的。~**-decker** 有两层甲板的船,二层战舰;双层电车[公共汽车]。~**-edged** ***a.*** 双刃的;有两种作用的;暧昧的。~**-faced** ***a.*** = double-faced. ~**-fer** 〔美口〕〔常 *pl.*〕买一送一的货品〔尤指戏票〕。~**-fisted** ***a.*** 〔美口〕双拳并用的;强壮有力的。~**fold** **1.** ***a.*** 两个部分的,两件事的;两倍的,两重的。**2.** ***ad.*** 成两个部分;成两倍,成两重。~**-four** ***a.*** 【乐】四分之二拍子的。**2, 4-D** 【化】2, 4-二氯苯氧醋酸〔一种除草剂〕。**2, 4, 5-T** 【化】三氯苯氧基醋酸〔一种除草剂〕。~**-handed** ***a.*** 有两只手的;双手拿的(剑等);双手都能操作的;两人操作的;两人玩的。~**-input** ***a.*** 【自】有两个输入的 (*a* ~*-input adder* 半加法器)。~**-legged** ***a.*** 两条腿的。~**-line** 【印】两行宽的,比普通型号大一倍的(铅字)。~**-name** ***a.*** (出票人及背书人)两重署名的。~**pence** [ˈtʌpəns; ˋtʌpəns] 〔英〕两便士;两便士银币 (*not care* ~*pence* 一点也不在乎。~*pence coloured* 价廉物美的)。~**penny** [ˈtʌpni; ˋtʌpnɪ] 〔英〕 **1.** ***a.*** 两便士的;不值钱的,低廉的。**2.** ***n.*** 两便士铜币;(1 quart 卖两便士的)廉价啤酒;少量,一点儿。~**penny-halfpenny** ***a.*** 〔英〕不足道的,低廉的。~**-phase** ***a.*** 【电】二相的。~**-piece** ***a.*** 两件一套的。~**-ply** ***a.*** 织成两层的;双重的;双股的(线)。~**-seater** 双人坐的飞机[汽车]。~**-sided** ***a.*** 有两面的,两面派的,怀贰心的。~**some** 两人玩的游戏[舞蹈](等);【高尔夫球】双人比赛;〔美俚〕一对,一双。~**-speed** ***a.*** 【机】双速的。~**-star** ***a.*** 【美军】二星(少将级)的。~**-step** 二拍子圆舞(曲);〔美俚〕小鸡。~**-time** ***vt.***, ***vi.*** 〔美俚〕背叛,欺骗,出卖。~**-time loser** 两次坐牢者;两次失败者;两次离婚者;两度破产者。~**-timer** 〔美俚〕叛徒;骗人[出卖人]的人。~**-tongued** ***a.*** 说假话的;骗人的。~**-twenty** ***n.***, ***a.*** 〔美〕二百二十(的)。~**-way** ***a.*** 双向的;两路的 (*a* ~*-way cock* 【机】双通[双向]龙头。*a* ~*-way radio* 收发两用无线电设备。*a* ~*-way repeater* 【电】双向转发器,双向增音器。*a* ~*-way traffic* 双向交通。*a* ~*-way switch* 双向[路]开关);正反两用的。**-ness** ***n.***

'twould [强 twud, 弱 twəd, təd; twud] 〔诗〕 = it would.

T. W. U. = Transport Workers' Union 〔美〕运输工人联合会。

TWX = teletypewriter exchange 电传打字电报交换(台)。

twy- *pref.* = twi-.

twyer [ˈtwaiə; ˋtwaɪə˞] ***n.*** = tuyère.

tx. = tax(es)。

Ty. = Territory.

-ty[1] *suf.* 十:twen*ty*.

-ty[2] *suf.* 表示性质、状态的名词后缀:loyal*ty*, safe*ty*.

Ty·burn [ˈtaibəːn; ˋtaɪbə˞n] ***n.*** 【史】伦敦死刑场。*a* ~ *tippet* 〔英〕绞索。*the* ~ *tree* 〔英〕绞刑架。

T. Y. C. = Thames Yacht Club 〔英〕泰晤士河游艇俱乐部。

Tyche [ˈtaiki; ˋtaɪkɪ] ***n.*** 【希神】=【罗神】 Fortuna.

ty·coon [taiˈkuːn; taɪˋkun] ***n.*** 〔Jap.〕 **1.** 【史】大君,将军〔日本德川幕府时代的将军〕。**2.** 〔美口〕(实业界、政界的)巨头。

ty·ing [ˈtaiiŋ; ˋtaɪɪŋ] ***n.*** 结子,结儿;系结。

tyke [taik; taɪk] ***n.*** **1.** 野狗,杂种狗。**2.** 〔Scot.〕乡下人;粗野的人。**3.** 小孩;〔口〕顽皮孩子。*a Yorkshire* ~ 约克郡乡下人。

Ty·ler [ˈtailə; ˋtaɪlə˞] ***n.*** 泰勒〔姓氏〕。

tyl·er [ˈtailə; ˋtaɪlə˞] ***n.*** 共济会秘密会所守门人。

ty·lo·pod [ˈtailəpɔd; ˋtaɪləˏpɑd] ***a.***, ***n.*** 【动】有肉趾的(动物);骆驼类[亚目]动物。**-ous** ***a.***

ty·lo·sis [taiˈləusis; taɪˋlosɪs] ***n.*** **1.** 【医】胼胝症。**2.** 【植】(导管内的)侵填体。

tym·bal [ˈtimbl; ˋtɪmbḷ] ***n.*** = timbal.

tym·pan [ˈtimpən; ˋtɪmpən] ***n.*** **1.** 鼓。**2.** (印刷机的)压纸格;衬垫。**3.** 鼓膜(状物)。**4.** 【解、建】 = tympanum.

tym·pa·na [ˈtimpənə; ˋtɪmpənə] ***n.*** tympanum 的复数。

tym·pa·ni [ˈtimpənai; ˋtɪmpənɪ] ***n.*** 〔*pl.*〕【乐】定音鼓。

tym·pan·ic [timˈpænik; tɪmˋpænɪk] ***a.*** **1.** 鼓皮似的,有鼓皮一样作用的。**2.** 【解】鼓膜的;鼓室的,中耳的。~ **bone** 【解,动】鼓骨。~ **membrane** 【解】鼓膜。

tym·pa·nist [ˈtimpənist; ˋtɪmpənɪst] ***n.*** 【乐】鼓手。

tym·pa·ni·tes [timpəˈnaitiːz; ˏtɪmpəˋnaɪtiz] ***n.*** 【医】(腹部)臌胀,气臌。

tym·pa·ni·tis [timpəˈnaitis; ˏtɪmpəˋnaɪtɪs] ***n.*** 【医】中耳炎,鼓室炎。

tym·pa·num [ˈtimpənəm; ˋtɪmpənəm] ***n.*** (*pl.* ~*s*, ***-na*** [-nə; -nə]) **1.** 鼓。**2.** 【解】耳膜,鼓膜;鼓室,中耳;(电话机的)振动膜;【动】颈侧气囊,鸣腔。**3.** 【建】山墙的三角面部分,门楣中心。**4.** 【机】溜槽水车,鼓形水车。

tym·pa·ny [ˈtimpəni; ˋtɪmpənɪ] ***n.*** (*pl.* ***-nies***) 【医】 **1.** 气鼓,鼓胀;鼓响。**2.** 夸张,浮夸,自负。

Tyn·dale [ˈtindl; ˋtɪndḷ] ***n.*** 廷代尔〔姓氏〕。

Tyndall [ˈtindl; ˋtɪndḷ] ***n.*** **1.** 廷德尔〔姓氏〕。**2. J.** ~ 丁铎尔〔1820—1893,英国物理学家〕。**T- effect** 【物】丁铎尔效应。

Tyn·wald [ˈtinwɔld; ˋtɪnwɑld] ***n.*** 马恩岛 (Isle of Man) 的议会。

typ. = **1.** typographer. **2.** typographical. **3.** typography.

typ·al [ˈtaipl; ˋtaɪpḷ] ***a.*** **1.** 标本的,模型的。**2.** 典型的,模范的,代表性的。

typ·a·ble, type·a·ble [ˈtaipəbl; ˋtaɪpəbḷ] ***a.*** 可(用打字机)打字的。

type [taip; taɪp] **I** ***n.*** **1.** 型,类型,(工业产品的)品种;风格,型式。**2.** 典型,榜样,样本,样板,模范,范本;典型人物;具有某种显著特性的人[物、事件]。**3.** 记号,符号;表征,象征。**4.** 【宗】预示。**5.** 【化】(典)型,类型;【生】型,类型,模式标本。**6.** 【印】铅字,活字〔也可作集合词〕;印刷文字,字体。★ **1.** 书籍杂志正文所用铅字通常有三种:roman (罗马体)[正体], italic (斜体), bold (黑体)。每种均有 capital (大写), small capital (小大写)和 lower-case [small] letter 小写。**2.** 字体主要有 Gothic 哥德体(美国叫 Text 或 Black Letter), Old Style 旧体, Modern 新体, Egyptian 埃及体(美国叫 Antique 古体), Sansserif 滑体(美国叫 Gothic), Script 手写体,草体等。**3.** 按宽度可分为:Condensed 狭身, Standard 常身, Ex-

T

tended 阔身。**4.** 按笔画粗细可分为 Lightface 细长体, Medium [Standard] 正常体, Boldface 粗黑体。**5.** 按铅字大小可分为:3 点 (excelsior), 3.5 点 (brilliant), 4.5 点 (diamond), 5 点 (pearl), 5.5 点(〔英〕 ruby, or 〔美〕 agate), 6 点 (nonpareil), 6.5 点 (emerald), 7 点 (minion), 8 点 (brevier), 9 点 (bourgeois), 10 点 (long primer), 11 点 (small pica), 12 点 (pica), 14 点 (English), 16 点 (columbian), 18 点 (great primer), 48 点 (canon) 等〔点即 point, 有音译为磅的〕。*blood* ~ 血型。*a woman of a certain* ~ 〔婉〕某一类型的女人[妓女]。*the* ~ *genus* 【植】(一科中的)代表属。*wooden* ~ 印刷木板。***appear in*** ~ 出版。***in*** ~ 用铅字排成(的)。***set*** ~ 排字。***true to*** ~ 典型的。**II** ***vt*. 1.** 代表,成为…的典型;(是…的)象征。**2.** 付排,用打字机等。**3.** 【医】鉴定(血型)。**4.** 使归属为某一类型;分配(演员)演不同类型的角色。**5.** 浅铸(铅字)。~ ***out*** (以相貌不合适等为理由)拒聘(演员)。—***vi*.** 打字 (= typewrite)。~**bar** 铸成一条的一行铅字。~**cast 1.** ***vt*.** 按类型分配角色;分配给(演员)非常合适的角色。**2.** ***vt*., *vi*.** 铸字,浇字。~ **cutter** 刻铜模的工人。~**face** 铅字面,铅字印出的字样。~ **founder** 铸字厂老板;铸字工人。~ **foundry** 铸字厂。~ **genus** 【生】模式属。~-**high** ***a*.** (木刻板)(厚度)跟铅字高度一样的。~ **metal** 铅字合金。~ **page** 【印】(书页的)版心。~**script** 用打字机打的原稿[文件],打印本。~**set** ***vt*.** 排字,排版。~**setter** 排字工人;排字机。~**setting** 排字。~ **species** 【生】原种。~ **specimen** 【生】模式标本。~ **wash** 【印】去油墨剂。~ **wheel** (某些打字机、电报机上的)活字轮。

-type *suf*. = type: proto*type*, ferro*type*.

typ·er [ˈtaipə; ˋtaɪpɚ] ***n*. 1.** 〔口〕 = typist. **2.** 〔美俚〕机关枪。

Type T (复数为 Type T's) T 型性格(的人),爱冒险和追求刺激(的人)。

type·write [ˈtaiprait; ˋtaɪp͵raɪt] ***vt*.** (*-wrote* [-rəut; -rot]; *-writ·ten* [-ritn; -rɪtn̩]) (用打字机)打印。

type·writ·er [ˈtaipraitə; ˋtaɪp͵raɪtɚ] ***n*. 1.** 打字机。**2.** 〔罕〕 = typist. **3.** 〔美俚〕机关枪。

type·writ·ten [ˈtaipritn; ˋtaɪp͵rɪtn̩] ***a*.** 用打字机打印的。

typh·lit·ic [tifˈlitik; tɪfˋlɪtɪk] ***a*.** 【医】阑尾炎的。

typh·li·tis [tifˈlaitis; tɪfˋlaɪtɪs] ***n*.** 【医】阑尾炎。

Ty·pho·eus [taiˈfəujuːs; taɪˋfojus] ***n*.** 【希神】百头巨怪。

ty·pho·gen·ic [ˌtaifəuˈdʒenik; ͵taɪfəˋdʒɛnɪk] ***a*.** 【医】引起(斑疹)伤寒的;引起肠热病的。

ty·phoid [ˈtaifɔid; ˋtaɪfɔɪd] **I** ***a*.** 【医】伤寒性的。**II** ***n*.** 【医】伤寒 (= ~fever)。**T- Mary** 伤寒病患者[带菌者];传染病患者。**-al** ***a*.**

ty·pho·ma·ni·a [ˌtaifəuˈmeinjə; ͵taɪfoˋmenɪə] ***n*.** 【医】伤寒性谵妄(症候)。

Ty·phon [ˈtaifɔn; ˋtaɪfɑn] ***n*.** 【希神】**1.** = Typhoeus. **2.** Typhoeus 之子。

ty·phon·ic [taiˈfɔnik; taɪˋfɑnɪk] ***a*.** 台风(似)的。

ty·phoon [taiˈfuːn; taɪˋfun] ***n*.** 台风。

ty·phous [ˈtaifəs; ˋtaɪfəs] ***a*.** 【医】斑疹伤寒(性)的。

ty·phus [ˈtaifəs; ˋtaɪfəs] ***n*.** 【医】斑疹伤寒 (= ~ fever)。*malignant* [*simple*] ~ 恶性[轻]斑疹伤寒。

typ·ic [ˈtipik; ˋtɪpɪk] ***a*. 1.** 典型的,定型的,有代表性的。**2.** 正常的,正规的。

typ·i·cal [ˈtipikl; ˋtɪpɪkl̩] ***a*. 1.** 代表的,典型的。**2.** 模范的,成为标本的。**3.** 特有的,独特的。**4.** 象征的。*be* ~ ***of*** ... 代表;象征。**-ly** ***ad*.** **-ness, -ty** ***n*.**

typ·i·fy [ˈtipifai; ˋtɪpə͵faɪ] ***vt*.** (*-fied*) **1.** 成为…的典型;象征;代表;具有…的特质。**2.** 【宗】预示。**-fi·er** ***n*.** 典型代表者,有代表性的事物。**-fi·ca·tion** ***n*.** 典型化。

typ·ing [ˈtaipiŋ; ˋtaɪpɪŋ] ***n*. 1.** 打字;打字术;打字机使用法。**2.** 打印本,打印稿,打印文件。

typ·ist [ˈtaipist; ˋtaɪpɪst] ***n*.** 打字员,打字者。

ty·po [ˈtaipəu; ˋtaɪpo] ***n*.** (*pl*. *~s*) **1.** 〔口〕印刷工人;排字工人。**2.** 〔美口〕排印错误,打字错误。

typo- *comb*. *f*. = type〔元音前用 typ-〕。

typo(g). = typ.

ty·pog·ra·pher [tiˈpɔgrəfə; taɪˋpɑgrəfɚ, tɪ-] ***n*. 1.** 印刷工人。**2.** 印刷术专家。**3.** 印刷业者。

ty·po·graph·ic, -i·cal [ˌtaipəˈgræfik, -ikəl; ͵taɪpəˋgræfɪk, ͵tɪpə-, -ɪkl̩] ***a*.** 印刷(术)上的。*a* ~ *error* 排印上的错误。**-cal·ly** ***ad*.**

ty·pog·ra·phy [taiˈpɔgrəfi; taɪˋpɑgrəfɪ, tɪ-] ***n*. 1.** 印刷(术)。**2.** 印刷品。**3.** 排字式样,印刷体裁。*The* ~ *is clear*. 印刷清晰。

ty·pol·o·gy [taiˈpɔlədʒi; taɪˋpɑlədʒɪ] ***n*. 1.** 【宗】预示论,象征论。**2.** 预兆。**3.** 【哲,语言,生】类型学。**-log·i·cal** [-ˈlɔdʒikəl; -ˋlɑdʒɪkəl] ***a*.**

ty·po·nym [ˈtaipənim; ˋtaɪpənɪm] ***n*.** 【生】**1.** 类型名称,模式名称〔按类型、模式命名的名称〕。**2.** 同名式异名。**-al, -ic** ***a*.**

ty·po·script [ˈtaipəskript; ˋtaɪpəskrɪpt] ***n*.** = typescript.

ty·poth·e·tae [taiˈpɔθiˌtiː; taɪˋpɑθə͵ti, ͵taɪpəˋθiti] ***n*.** 〔*pl*.〕**1.** 〔动词用单数〕印刷业公会。**2.** 印刷商。

typo·tron [ˈtaipətrɔn; ˋtaɪpətrɑn] ***n*.** (高速)字标管,显字管。

TYPP, t. y. p. p. = 【纺】thousands of yards per pound 千码/磅。

typ·tol·o·gy [tipˈtɔlədʒi; tɪp͵tɑlədʒɪ] ***n*.** 敲击显灵招魂术〔一种江湖骗术,说是鬼魂会用敲击办法与人交通〕。

Tyr [tiə; tɪr] ***n*.** 【北欧神话】战神蒂尔。

ty·ra·mine [ˈtairəˌmiːn, -min; ˋtaɪrə͵min, -mɪn] ***n*.** 【化】酪胺。

ty·rannic, -ni·cal [tiˈrænik, -nikəl; tɪˋrænɪk, taɪ-, -nɪkl̩] ***a*.** 暴君的;专制的;暴虐的。**ty·ran·ni·cal·ly** ***ad*.**

ty·ran·ni·cide [tiˈrænisaid; tɪˋrænə͵saɪd, taɪ-] ***n*.** 诛戮暴君(者)。**-ci·dal** [-ˈsaidl; -ˋsaɪdl̩] ***a*.**

tyr·an·nize [ˈtirənaiz; ˋtɪrə͵naɪz] ***vi*., *vt*.** (对…)施行暴政,压制,强横霸道 (*over*)。

ty·ran·no·saur [tiˈrænəˌsɔː, tai-; tɪˋrænə͵sɔr, taɪ-] ***n*.** 【动】恐龙 (= tyrannosaurus)。

tyr·an·nous [ˈtirənəs; ˋtɪrənəs] ***a*.** 暴政的,暴虐的,专横的。**-ly** ***ad*.**

tyr·an·ny [ˈtirəni; ˋtɪrənɪ] ***n*. 1.** 暴政;专制政治,高压政治。**2.** 暴虐,残暴,专横。**3.** 【希腊史】僭主政治。

ty·rant [ˈtaiərənt; ˋtaɪrənt] ***n*. 1.** 暴君;专制君主。**2.** 暴虐专横的人。**3.** 【希腊史】僭主,霸主。*a local* ~ 恶霸,土豪。*scholar* ~*s* 学阀。

Tyre [ˈtaiə; taɪr] ***n*.** 提尔〔古代腓尼基 (Phoenicia) 的有名港口,现属黎巴嫩〕。

tyre[1] [ˈtaiə; taɪr] ***n*., *vt*.** 〔英〕 = tire[2].

tyre[2] [ˈtaiə; taɪr] ***n*.** 〔印度英语〕凝乳。

Tyr·i·an [ˈtiriən; ˋtɪrɪən] ***a*., *n*.** 提尔 (Tyre) 的(人)。~ **purple** 提尔红紫〔染料或染织品〕。

ty·ro [ˈtaiərəu; ˋtaɪro] ***n*.** (*pl*. *~s*) 初生者,生手,新手 (= tiro)。

ty·ro·ci·dine [ˌtairəˈsaidn, -saidiːn; ͵taɪrəˋsaɪdin, -dɪn] ***n*.** 【化】短杆菌酪素。

Tyr·o·lese [tirəˈliːz; ͵tɪrəˋliz, -ˋlis] **I** ***n*.** 〔*sing*., *pl*.〕(奥地利)蒂罗尔 (Tyrol) 人。**II** ***a*.** 蒂罗尔(人)的。

Ty·ro·lienne [tirəuliˈen; tɪroˋljɛn] ***n*.** 〔F.〕蒂罗尔民间舞(曲)。

Ty·rone [tiˈrəun; tɪˋron] ***n*.** 蒂龙〔男子名〕。

tyro·sin(e) [ˈtirəsiːn; ˋtɪrə͵sin] ***n*.** 【生化】酪胺酸;3-对羟苯基丙氨酸。

ty·ro·si·nase [ˈtairəusineis, ˈtirəu-; ˋtaɪrosɪ͵nes, ˋtɪro-] ***n*.** 【化】酪氨酸酶。

ty·ro·thri·cin [ˌtairəˈθraisin, -ˈθrisin; ͵taɪrəˋθraɪsɪn,

-θrɪsɪn] *n*.【化】短杆菌素。

tyr·o·tox·i·con [ˌtaiərəˈtɔksikɔn; ˏtaɪrəˋtɑksɪˏkɑn, ˏtirə-] *n*.【生化】干酪毒。

Tyr·rhene, Tyr·rhe·ni·an [ˈtiriːn, tiˈriːniən, -njən; ˋtɪrin, tɪˋrinɪən, -njən] *a*., *n*. = Etruscan. **Turrhenian Sea** (意大利西面的)第勒尼安海。

Ty·rwhitt [ˈtirit; ˋtɪrɪt] *n*. 蒂里特〔姓氏〕。

tythe [taið; taɪð] *n*., *v*.〔英〕= tithe.

Tyu·men [tjuːˈmen; tjuˋmɛn] *n*. 秋明〔西伯利亚城市〕。

tyu·ya·mu·nite [ˌtjujəˈmuːnait; ˏtjujəˋmunaɪt] *n*.【矿】钙钒铀矿。

Tzar [zɑː; zɑr] *n*. 俄国沙皇(= Tsar)。

Tza·ri·na [zɑːˈriːnə; zɑˋrinə] *n*. 俄国女沙皇;俄国沙皇皇后(= Tsarina)。

T-ze·ro [ˈtiˈziərəu; ˋtiˋzɪro] *n*.〔Russ.〕【宇】(人造卫星等的)发射时间。

tzet·ze [ˈtsetsi; ˋtsɛtsɪ] *n*. = tsetse.

tzi·gane [tsiˈgɑːn; tsɪˋgɑn], **-ga·ny** [-ni; -nɪ] *n*., *a*. 茨冈人(的),吉普赛人(的)。

U

U, u [juː; ju] (*pl*. ***U's***, ***u's*** [juːz; juz]) **1**. 英文字母表第二十一字母。**2**. U 字形的东西。**3**.〔U〕铀的符号(= uranium)。*U-bolt* U 形[马蹄]螺栓。*U-tube* U 字管。**4**.〔U〕〔口〕上流社会的,上层阶级的。**5**.〔U〕〔英〕(影片等的) U 级〔表示老少咸宜,美国的对应分级符号为 G〕。

U., u. = **1**. Uncle. **2**. Union. **3**. University. **4**. unit. **5**. upper. **6**. you. **7**. universal. **8**. uncle.

U./a., u. a. = underwriting account 保险账户[账目]。

UAAC = Un-American Activities Committee〔美〕非美活动调查委员会。

U. A. B. = Unemployment Assistance Board〔英〕失业救济委员会。

UAE = United Arab Emirates 阿拉伯联合大公国(阿拉伯联合酋长国)〔亚洲〕。

UAM = underwater-to-air missile 水下对空导弹。

UAT = 〔F.〕*Union Aéromaritime de Transport*〔法〕联合海空运输公司。

UAW = United Auto, Aircraft and Agricultural Implements Workers of America 美国汽车、飞机、农业机械工人联合会。

UBA = Union of Burma Airways 缅甸联邦航空公司。

U-bahn [ˈjuːbɑːn; ˋubɑn] *n*.〔G.〕地下铁道。

Ub·be·lohde [ˈʌbələud; ˋʌbəlod] *n*. 厄布洛德〔姓氏〕。

Ü·ber·mensch [ˈjuːbəˌmenʃ; ˋybɚˏmɛnʃ] *n*. (*pl*. ***-mensch·en*** [-ən; -ən])〔G.〕**1**. 超人。**2**. 具有超过常人力量的人。

u·bi·e·ty [juːˈbaiəti; juˋbaɪətɪ] *n*.【哲】在一定的场所;所在;位置,位置关系。

u·bi in·fra [ˈjuːbiˈinfrə; ˋjubɪˋɪnfrə]〔L.〕在下面提及之处,见下。

u·biq·ui·tous [juːˈbikwitəs; juˋbɪkwətəs] *a*. 无所不在的,遍在的;〔谑〕(人)到处看见其踪影的。*The struggle between opposites is* ～. 对立的斗争无所不在。**-ly** *ad*. **-ness** *n*.

u·biq·ui·ty [ju(ː)ˈbikwiti; juˋbɪkwətɪ] *n*. (同时)无所不在(性),遍在(性)。

u·bi su·pra [ˈuːbiˈsuːprə, ˈjuː-; ˋjubaɪˋsuprə]〔L.〕在上面提及之处,见上。

U-boat [ˈjuːbəut; ˋjuˏbot] *n*. (德国)潜水艇。

U-bomb [ˈjuːbɔm; ˋjuˏbɑm] *n*. 铀原子弹。

U. C. = **1**. University College〔英〕大学学院。**2**. Upper Canada 上加拿大〔现称安大略省〕。

U / C = **1**. undercharged 装料不足。**2**. unclassified 不保密的。

u. c. = **1**.〔It.〕*una corda*【乐】(钢琴)用弱音踏板(的)。**2**. upper case【印】大写字母(盘)。

U. C. L. = University College, London〔英〕伦敦大学学院。

U. D. = the Underground (Railway London) 伦敦地铁。

U·dall [ˈjuːdəl; ˋjudl̩] *n*. 尤德尔〔姓氏〕。

U. D. C. = **1**. Union of Democratic Control〔美〕民主管理协会。**2**. Urban District Council〔英〕城镇(区)议会。

ud·der [ˈʌdə; ˋʌdɚ] *n*. (牛、羊等的)乳房;乳腺。

ud·dered [ˈʌdəd; ˋʌdɚd] *a*.〔多用以构成复合词〕乳房…的,有(…的)乳房的。*heavy-～ cows* 乳房沉甸甸的母牛。

ud·dre·less [ˈʌdəlis; ˋʌdɚlɪs] *a*. 没有乳房的;没有母乳的;(小羊等)没有母羊的。

u·do [ˈuːdəu; ˋudo] *n*. (*pl*. ～*s*)〔Jap.〕【植】土当归。

u·dom·e·ter [ju(ː)ˈdɔmitə; juˋdɑmətɚ] *n*. 雨量计。

UE, UEW = United Electrical, Radio and Machine Workers of America 美国电器、无线电和机器工人联合会。

UEA = Universal Esperanto Association 国际世界语协会。

UFO [ˈjuːfəu, ˌjuːefˈəu; ˋjufo, ˏjuɛfˋo] *n*. (*pl*. ***UFOs***, ***UFO's***) = unidentified flying object 不明飞行物,真象未明的太空飞行物〔尤指 1947 年以来看到的在太空不同高度以不同速度飞行的东西,亦称飞碟〕。

u·fol·o·gist [juːˈfɔlədʒist; juˋfɑlədʒɪst] *n*. "飞碟"研究者,爱好研究真象未明的太空飞行物者。

u·fol·o·gy [juːˈfɔlədʒi; juˋfɑlədʒɪ] *n*. "飞碟"学,不明飞行物研究。

U·gan·da [ju(ː)ˈgændə, uːˈgændɑː; juˋgændə, uˋgɑndɑ] *n*. 乌干达〔非洲〕。

U·gan·dan [juːgændən; juˋgændən] **I** *a*. 乌干达人的。**II** *n*. 乌干达人。

U·ga·rit·ic [ˌjuːgəˈritik, ˈuː-; ˏjugəˋrɪtɪk, ˋu-] **I** *n*. 乌嘎利特语〔接近古希伯来语的一种已消亡的闪语〕。**II** *a*. 乌嘎利特语的;乌嘎利特人的。

ugh [əːx, ʌx, uh; ux, ʌ, ʊ, ʌx] *int*. 嘿! 呸! 啊!〔表示憎厌、恐怖等〕。

ug·li·fi·ca·tion [ˌʌglifiˈkeiʃən; ˏʌgləfɪˋkeʃən] *n*. 丑化(*opp*. beautification)。

ug·li·fi·er [ˈʌglifaiə; ˋʌglɪˏfaɪɚ] *n*. 破坏美观者,使丑化的人[物]。

ug·li·fy [ˈʌglifai; ˋʌglɪˏfaɪ] *vt*. (**-fied**)〔口〕弄丑,丑化,使丑陋;糟蹋(美等)。

ug·ly [ˈʌgli; ˋʌglɪ] **I** *a*. (**-li·er**; **-li·est**) **1**. 丑的,丑陋的,难看的。**2**. (道德上)丑恶的,邪恶的;丢脸的,(传说的)难听的;不愉快的,(工作等)讨厌的。**3**. 〔口〕爱吵架的,性情别扭的;险恶的;(天气等)像要刮风下雨的。*an* ～ *deed* 丑行。*an* ～ *word* 难听的话。*an* ～ *task* 讨厌的工作。*The sky has an* ～ *look*. 天气靠不住[阴沉]。**as** ～ **as sin** 极丑,极难看;极恶劣。**cut up** ～ 发脾气,发怒。～ **as a mud fence**〔美〕非常粗野的。～ **customer**〔口〕讨厌的人,难对付的家伙。～ **duckling** 丑小鸭;〔喻〕小时不好看,长大后变得出人头地[变美]的女孩子。**II** *n*.〔口〕**1**. 丑陋的人[东西]。**2**. (十九世纪流行的)女帽(上的丝质)遮阳。**-li·ness** *n*.

U·gri·an [ˈjuːgriən, ˈuː-; ˋjugrɪən, ˋu-] **I** *a*. **1**. (西伯利亚以西的或匈牙利(包括马扎尔)的)芬兰-乌戈尔族人的。**2**. 乌戈尔语支〔包括匈牙利语(马扎尔语),佛古尔语和奥斯提雅克语在内的芬兰-乌戈尔语族的一个语支〕。**II** *n*. **1**. 乌戈尔族人。**2**. 乌戈尔语。

U·gric [ˈjuːgrik, ˈuː-; ˋjugrɪk, ˋu-] *n*., *a*. = Ugrian.

U. G. R. R. = Underground Railroad〔英〕地下铁道。

ug·some [ˈʌgsəm, ˈug-; ˋʌgsəm, ˋʊg-] *a*. 可怕的,恐怖的。

UGT, ugt = urgent〔美〕〔电报用语〕急电。

uh [ʌ, ʌn; ʌ, ʌn] *int*. **1**. = huh. **2**. 嗯〔讲话时思索一个词儿或凝思时所发出的声音〕。

UHF, uhf = ultrahigh frequency【无】超高频。

uh-huh [ˈʌˈhʌ; ˋʌˋhʌ] **I** *int*. **1**. 嗯嗯 (= yes)。**2**.〔读时带重鼻音〕嗯 (= no)。**II** *vi*.〔美俚〕求爱。

uh·lan [ˈuːlɑːn; ˋulɑn] *n*.【德史】枪骑兵。

u·hu·ru [uːˈhuruː; uˋhʊru] *n*., *int*.〔Swahili〕乌呼噜,自由。

u. i. =〔L.〕*ut infra* 如下所述,如下所示 (= as below)。

Ui·g(h)ur [ˈwiːguə; ˋwigur] *n*., *a*. (*pl*. ～(*s*)) **1**. 维吾尔(族)人(的)。**2**. 维吾尔语(的)。

u·in·ta·ite, u·in·tah·ite [juˈintəait; jʊˋɪntəˏaɪt] *n*.【矿】〔美〕硬沥青。

uit [ɔit; ɔɪt] ***prep***.〔Afrik.〕外的 (= out)。

uit·land·er [ˈɔitlændə; ˋaɪtˏlændɚ, ˋetˏlændɚ]〔或作 U-〕*n*.〔Afrik.〕外国人,外侨〔尤指布尔战争前居住在(南非)德兰士瓦省非荷兰血统的外国人〕。

U. J. D. =〔L.〕*Utriusque Juris Doctor* (= Doctor of both, 即 Civil & Canon Laws) 民法及教会法规博士。

UK, U. K. = United Kingdom 联合王国。

UKAEA = United Kingdom Atomic Energy Authority 联合王国原子能委员会。

u·kase [juːˈkeiz; ˋjukes, juˋkez] *n*.〔Russ.〕**1**. (沙皇的)圣旨;(沙皇政府的)敕令。**2**. 专横的(官方)命令[通令]。

uki·yo·(y)e [uˈkiːjəujei; ʊˋkijoje] *n*.〔Jap.〕浮世绘。

Ukr. = Ukraine.

U·kraine [ju(ː)ˈkrein; ˋjukren, juˋkren, -ˋkraɪn] *n*. 乌克兰〔欧洲国家名〕。

U·krain·i·an [ju(ː)ˈkreinjən; juˋkrenɪən, -ˋkraɪn-] **I** *n*. **1**. 乌克兰人。**2**. 乌克兰语。**II** *a*. **1**. 乌克兰的。**2**. 乌克兰人的。**3**. 乌克兰语的。

u·ku·le·le [juːkəˈleili; ˏjukəˋlelɪ] *n*.【乐】尤克里里〔夏威夷的四弦乐器,像小型的吉他〕。

u·la·ma [ˈuːləˈmɑː, ˌuːləˈmɑː; ˋuləˋmɑ, ˏuləˋmɑ] *n*.〔*pl*.〕= ulema.

u·lan [ˈjuːlən, ˈuːlɑːn; ˋulɑn, ˋjulən] *n*. = uhlan.

U·lan Ba·tor [ˈuːlɑːn ˈbɑːtɔː; ˋulɑnˋbɑtɔr] 乌兰巴托〔蒙古人民共和国首都〕。

-ular *suf*. 构成形容词,表示"…的","似…的": crevic*ular*.

ULCC = ultra-large crude carrier (载重量在 40 万吨以上的)超大型(原)油轮。

ul·cer [ˈʌlsə; ˋʌlsɚ] *n*.【医】溃疡;〔喻〕积弊,病;症结。*a gastric* ～ 胃溃疡。*a* ～ *gulch*〔美俚〕下等餐馆。

ul·cer·ate [ˈʌlsəreit; ˋʌlsəˏret] *vi*., *vt*.〔作 *vt*. 时主用被动语态〕(使)生溃疡;(使)溃烂;(使)(道德)败坏。

ul·cer·a·tion [ˌʌlsəˈreiʃən; ˏʌlsəˋreʃən] *n*. 溃烂;糜烂;腐败。

ul·cer·a·tive [ˈʌlsərətiv; ˋʌlsərˏetɪv, -ətɪv] *a*. 使生溃疡的;使腐败的。

ul·cer·ous [ˈʌlsərəs; ˋʌlsərəs] *a*. 溃疡(性)的;生溃疡的,溃烂的。*an* ～ *hatred* 痛恨。**-ly** *ad*.

ul·cer·o·gen·ic [ˌʌlsərəˈdʒenik; ˏʌlsərəˋdʒɛnɪk] *a*. 产生溃疡的,致溃疡的。

-ule *suf*. 用以构成名词,表示"小": glob*ule*, pust*ule*.

u·le·ma [ˈuːlimɑː; ˏuləˋmɑ] *n*. *pl*. **1**. 乌力马〔穆斯林的学者或宗教、法律的权威,尤指在土耳其的〕。**2**.〔作单数用〕乌力马委员会[学会];乌力马学会的成员。

u·ler·y·the·ma [juːˌleəriˈθiːmə; juˏlɛrɪˋθimə] *n*. 红斑狼疮。

ULF, ulf = ultra-low frequency【无】超低频。

ul·lage [ˈʌlidʒ; ˋʌlɪdʒ] *n*. **1**. (容器的)缺量;(桶装液体等的)漏损(量);折耗,损耗。**2**. (桶内)油品体积的测定。**3**.〔*pl*.〕〔英俚〕杯中剩酒;残渣。*estimate 2% for* ～ 折耗估计百分之二。**on** ～ 并非满满的。～ **rule** (不浸入油内的)测油尺。

ul·min [ˈʌlmin; ˋʌlmɪn] *n*.【化】棕腐质;赤榆树脂。**ul·mic, ul·min·ic** [ʌlˈminik; ˏʌlˋmɪnɪk] *a*. 棕腐质的 (*ulmic acid*【化】赤榆酸,棕腐酸)。

ULMS = underwater long-range missile system 水下远程导[飞]弹系统〔从潜艇上发的弹道导[飞]弹,射程约为 7000 – 10000 公里〕。

ul·na [ˈʌlnə; ˋʌlnə] *n*. (*pl*. **-nae** [-niː; -ni])【解】尺骨。**-r** *a*.

-ulose *suf*.〔构成名词〕含有酮基的…糖: lev*ulose*

u·lot·ri·chous [juˈlɔtrikəs; jʊˋlɑtrɪkəs] *a*. 毛发卷缩(紧)的。

-ulous *suf*.〔构成形容词〕有…倾向的,充满…特点的: pop*ulous*.

Ul·ster [ˈʌlstə; ˋʌlstɚ] *n*. **1**. 阿尔斯太〔昔时为爱尔兰一地区,今为北爱尔兰及爱尔兰共和国分割〕。**2**. (爱尔兰共和国的)北爱尔兰省。**3**.〔口〕北爱尔兰。**4**.〔u-〕一种有带的粗呢宽大衣。

ult. = ultimate(ly).

ult. =〔L.〕*ultimo*.

ul·te·ri·or [ʌlˈtiəriə; ʌlˋtɪrɪɚ] *a*. **1**. 那一边的。**2**. (计划等)以后的,将来的。**3**. 藏在背后的;不可告人的;心里的。*the* ～ *consequences of one's act* 某人行为的后果。*a man with* ～ *motives* 别有用心的人。*for the sake of* ～ *ends* 别有用心。*have an* ～ *object in view* 心里有鬼,别有用心。*the* ～ *region* 边远地区。**-ly** *ad*.

ul·ti·ma [ˈʌltimə; ˋʌltəmə] **I** *a*.〔L.〕终末的,末尾的,最后的;最远的。**II** *n*.【语音】末音节。～ ***ratio*** 最后的争辩[制裁,手段]。～ ***ratio regum*** (路易十四刻在大炮上的铭文)王者的最后论据[最后手段],武力,战争。～ ***Thule*** [ˈθjuːliː; ˋθjuli] 天涯海角,极限;最后目的。

ul·ti·mate [ˈʌltimit; ˋʌltəmɪt] **I** *a*. **1**. 最后的,最终的,极限的,结局的。**2**. 根本的,首要的,基本的。**3**. 最远的;终极的;【力学】最大的。*the* ～ *end of life* 人生的终极目的。*to the* ～ *ends of the world* 到天涯海角。**II** *n*. 终极;顶点;最后结果;基本事实,基本原理。**in the** ～ 到最后,终于。～ **analysis**【化】元素分析,最终分析。～ **cause** 终极原因。～ **constituent**【语】最终成分,(基本)构成要素。～ **element** 元素。～ **particle**【物】基本粒子。～ **production** 总产量。～ **stage**【林】安定期。～ **strength**【工】极限强度。～ **stress** 极限应力,极限胁强。～ **yield** (加工后产品的)最终收率。**-ly** *ad*. **-ness**

U

n.

ul·ti·ma·tum [ˌʌltiˈmeitəm; ˏʌltəˋmetəm] *n*. (*pl*. ~s, **-ta** [-tə; -tə]) **1.** 最后要求[陈述],最后通牒,哀的美敦书;最后条件。**2.** 最后结论,基本意义[原理]。

ul·ti·mo [ˈʌltiməu; ˋʌltəˏmo] *a*. 〔L.〕上月的〔常略作 ult., ulto.〕。*the 10th ult*. 上月十日。

ul·ti·mo·gen·i·ture [ʌltiməuˈdʒenitʃə; ˏʌltəmoˋdʒɛnətʃɚ] *n*. 【法】幼子继承(制)。

ulto. = *ultimo*.

ul·tra [ˈʌltrə; ˋʌltrə] **I** *a*. 过度的,过激的,极端的。**II** *n*. **1.** 过激论者,极端分子,急进分子,激烈分子。**2.** 〔美口〕高消费顾客,专买高档商品者。**-ism** *n*. 过激论;极端主义。**-ist** *n*., *a*. 极端主义者(的)。

ultra- *comb*. *f*. 极端,超:*ultra*-right; *ultra*micro.

ul·tra-a·cous·tics [ˈʌltrə-əˈku:stiks; ˋʌltrə-əˋkustɪks] *n*. 〔作单数或复数用〕【物】超声学。

ul·tra-audion [ˈʌltrəˈɔdiən; ˋʌltrəˋɔdɪən] *n*. 【无】超三极管。

ul·tra·ba·sic [ˈʌltrəˈbeisik; ˋʌltrəˋbesɪk] *a*. 【化】超碱的,超基性的。~ **rock** 超碱岩,超基性岩。

ul·tra·cen·tri·fuge [ˌʌltrəˈsentrəfju:dʒ; ˏʌltrəˋsɛntrɪfjudʒ] **I** *n*. 超速离心机。**II** *vt*. 用超速离心机分离。

ul·tra·con·ser·va·tive [ˈʌltrəkənˈsə:vətiv; ˏʌltrəkənˋsɝvətɪv] *a*. 极端保守(主义)的。**-ser·va·tism** *n*.

ul·tra-de·moc·ra·cy [ˈʌltrədiˈmɔkrəsi; ˋʌltrədɪˋmɑkrəsɪ] *n*. 极端民主化。

ul·tra·dian [əlˈtreidi:ən; əlˋtrediən] *a*. 次昼夜的,(生物节律或循环)每日重复发生一次以上的。

ul·tra·fash·ion·a·ble [ˈʌltrəˈfæʃənəbl; ˏʌltrəˋfæʃənəbḷ, -ˋfæʃnə-] *a*. 极端时髦的,极其流行的。

ul·tra·fax [ˈʌltrəfæks; ˋʌltrəfæks] *n*. 【无】电视传真电报。

ul·tra·fiche [ˈʌltrəfi:ʃ; ˋʌltrəfiʃ] *n*. 超微缩胶片。

ul·tra·high [ˈʌltrəhai; ˋʌltrəˋhaɪ] *a*. 超高的。~ **frequency** 【无】超高频。

ul·tra·is·tic [ˌʌltrəˈistik; ˏʌltrəˋɪstɪk] *a*. 过激论的,极端主义的。

ul·tra-left [ˈʌltrəˈleft; ˋʌltrəˋlɛft] *a*. 极"左"的。**-ist** *n*. 极"左"分子。

ul·tra·ma·rine[1] [ˌʌltrəməˈri:n; ˏʌltrəməˋrin] *a*. 海外的,海那边的。~ *trade* 海外贸易。

ul·tra·ma·rine[2] [ˌʌltrəməˈri:n; ˏʌltrəməˋrin] *n*., *a*. 佛青色(的),群青色(的);深蓝色(的)。

ul·tra·mi·cro [ˌʌltrəˈmaikrəu; ˏʌltrəˋmaɪkro] *a*. 超微的,小于百万分之一的。

ul·tra·mi·cro·chem·is·try [ˈʌltrəˌmaikrəuˈkemistri; ˏʌltrəˏmaɪkroˋkɛməstrɪ] *n*. 【化】超微(量)化学。

ul·tra·mi·cro·fiche [ˈʌltrəˈmaikrəufiʃ; ˋʌltrəˋmaɪkrofɪʃ] *n*. 超微缩照片。

ul·tra·mi·crom·e·ter [ˈʌltrəmaiˈkrɔmitə; ˋʌltrəmaɪˋkrɑmɪtɚ] *n*. 超测微计。

ul·tra·mi·cro·scope [ˌʌltrəˈmaikrəskəup; ˏʌltrəˋmaɪkrəˏskop] *n*. 超显微镜,超倍显微镜。

ul·tra·mi·cro·scop·ic [ˌʌltrəˌmaikrəˈskɔpik; ˏʌltrəˏmaɪkrəˋskɑpɪk] *a*. **1.** 超出普通显微镜可见度范围的。**2.** 超显微镜的,超倍显微镜的。

ul·tra·mi·cros·co·py [ˌʌltrəmaiˈkrɔskəupi; ˏʌltrəmaɪˋkrɑskəpɪ] *n*. 超显微术,超倍显微镜的应用。

ul·tra·mod·ern [ˈʌltrəˈmɔdən; ˏʌltrəˋmɑdɚn] *a*. 超[过于]现代化的;最新式的。

ul·tra·mon·tane [ˌʌltrəˈmɔntein; ˏʌltrəˋmɑnten] *a*., *n*. **1.** 山那边的(人);阿尔卑斯山以南的(人)。**2.** 〔U-〕【史】信奉教皇至上主义的(人)。

ul·tra·mon·ta·nism [ˌʌltrəˈmɔntinizəm; ˏʌltrəˋmɑntənɪzm] *n*. 【史】教皇至上主义。**-ta·nist** *n*. 信奉教皇至上主义者。

ul·tra·mun·dane [ˈʌltrəˈmʌndein; ˏʌltrəˋmʌnden] *a*. 世界之外的,太阳系外的;超俗世的,超世间的。

ul·tra·nation·al·ism [ˈʌltrəˈnæʃənəlizəm; ˏʌltrəˋnæʃənḷɪzm] *n*. 极端民族主义。**-ist** *n*., *a*. 狭隘民族主义者(的)。

Ul·tra·phone [ˈʌltrəfəun; ˋʌltrəfon] *n*. 〔商标〕(利用数码通信技术的)数控无线电话。

ul·tra·pho·tom·e·ter [ˈʌltrəfəˈtɔmitə; ˋʌltrəfəˋtɑmɪtɚ] *n*. 【物】超光度计。

ul·tra·phys·i·cal [ˌʌltrəˈfizikl; ˏʌltrəˋfɪzəkḷ] *a*. 超物质的。

ul·tra·ra·pid [ˈʌltrəˈræpid; ˋʌltrəˋræpɪd] *a*. (电影拍摄中胶片运行)超速的。~ **picture** (用超速摄影法拍成的)慢动作镜头。

ul·tra·ray [ˈʌltrərei; ˋʌltrəre] *n*. 宇宙线。

ul·tra-re·ac·tion·ar·y [ˈʌltrəriˈækʃənəri; ˋʌltrərɪˋækʃənɛrɪ] *a*. 极端反动的。

ul·tra·red [ˈʌltrəˈred; ˏʌltrəˋrɛd] *a*. 【物】红外线的。

ul·tra-right [ˈʌltrəˈrait; ˋʌltrəˋraɪt] *a*. 极右的。**-ist** *n*. 极右分子。

ul·tra·short [ˈʌltrəˈʃɔ:t; ˏʌltrəˋʃɔrt] *a*. 【物】超短波的。

ul·tra·son·ic [ˈʌltrəˈsɔnik; ˏʌltrəˋsɑnɪk] **I** *a*. 超音的,超音速的。~ *wave* 超声波。**II** *n*. 超声波。

ul·tra·son·ics [ˌʌltrəˈsɔniks; ˏʌltrəˋsɑnɪks] *n*. 〔*pl*.〕〔作单数用〕【物】超声波学。

ul·tra·son·o·graph [ˈʌltrəsəˈnɔgrəf; ˋʌltrəˋsɑnəgræf] *n*. 【医】超声波探病仪。

ul·tra·sound [ˈʌltrəˈsaund; ˋʌltrəˏsaʊnd] *n*. 超声波〔用于医学上诊断、治疗和外科手术等方面〕。

ul·tra·struc·ture [ˈʌltrəˈstrʌktʃə; ˋʌltrəˏstrʌktʃɚ] *n*. 超(显)微结构,亚显微结构。**-struc·tur·al** *a*.

ul·tra·vi·o·let [ˈʌltrəˈvaiəlit; ˏʌltrəˋvaɪəlɪt] **I** *a*. 【物】紫外的;紫外线的;产生[应用]紫外线的。**II** *n*. 紫外线辐射。~ **index** 【气】紫外线指数〔标示地球表面紫外线辐射量的程度〕。~ **light** [**rays**] 紫外线。~ **astronomy** 【天】紫外线天文学〔研究紫外光谱区恒星和星云的学科,多通过轨道人造卫星进行研究〕。

ul·tra vi·res [ˈʌltrə ˈvaiəri:z; ˏʌltrə ˋvaɪriz] 〔L.〕超出(个人、公司等的)法定权限。

ul·tra·vi·rus [ˈʌltrəˈvairəs; ˏʌltrəˋvaɪrəs] *n*. 【医】超病毒;超显微病毒。

u·lu [ˈu:lu:; ˋulu] *n*. (爱斯基摩妇女用的)圆叶刀。

ul·u·lant [ˈju:ljulənt; ˋjuljələnt] *a*. 嗥嗥叫的,嗬嗬地叫的;哀鸣的。

u·lu·late [ˈju:ljuleit; ˋjuljəˏlet] *vi*. **1.** (狗,狼等)嗥吠,吼;(猫头鹰等)嗬嗬地叫。**2.** 哀鸣;悲泣。**-la·tion** [-ˈleiʃən; -ˋleʃən] *n*.

Ul·ya·novsk [u:ˈljɑ:nɔfsk; uˋljɑnɑfsk] *n*. 乌里扬诺夫斯克〔旧称 Simbirsk 辛比尔斯克,俄罗斯城市〕。

U·lys·ses [ju(:)ˈlisi:z; juˋlɪsiz] *n*. **1.** 尤利塞斯〔男子名〕。**2.** 【罗神】尤利西斯〔即希腊神话中的奥德修斯(Odyssus);曾参加围攻特洛伊(Troy)城,智勇双全,亦为荷马史诗《奥德塞》(Odyssey)的主人翁〕。

um. = unmarried.

u. m. = under-mentioned.

um·bel [ˈʌmbəl; ˋʌmbḷ] *n*. 【植】伞形花(序)。

um·bel·lar, um·bel·late [ˈʌmbələ, ˈʌmbəleit; ˋʌmblɚ, ˋʌmbəlɪt, -let] *a*. 【植】伞形花(序)的。

um·bel·lat·ed [ˈʌmbəlitid, -ˌeit-; ˋʌmbəˏletɪd] *a*. 【植】伞形的。

um·bel·lif·er·ous [ˌʌmbeˈlifərəs; ˏʌmbəˋlɪfərəs] *a*. 【植】有伞形花(序)的,伞形花科的。

um·bel·lule [ˈʌmblju:l, əmˈbelju:l; ˋʌmbḷˏjul, ʌmˋbɛljul] *n*. 【植】小伞(形花序)。**-lu·late** *a*.

um·ber [ˈʌmbə; ˋʌmbɚ] **I** *n*. 【化】赭土,棕土,焦茶色,暗褐色。*burnt* ~ 煅赭土〔颜料〕。*raw* ~ 生赭土〔颜料〕。**II** *a*. 赭色的,焦茶色的。**III** *vt*. 把…涂[染]成赭

色。

um·bili·cal [ˌʌmbiˈlaikəl; ʌmˋbɪlɪkl] *a*. 1. 肚脐的;脐侧的;脐状的。2.〔古〕中心的。3. 似以脐带联系的,(关系)密切的;〔罕〕母系的,女系的。～ **ancestor** 母系祖先。～ **cord** 1.【解】脐带;【动】卵黄囊蒂;【植】珠柄。2.【军】(导弹发射前检验内部装置的)操纵缆;【宇】(与舱外工作太空人联系并提供氧气等的)空间生命线。～ **hernia**【医】脐疝。

um·bil·i·cate [ʌmˈbilikit; ʌmˋbɪlɪˏkɪt] *a*. 1. 肚脐状的,中凹的。2. 有肚脐的。

um·bil·i·cat·ed [ʌmˈbilikitid, -ˌkeitid; ʌmˋbɪləˏketɪd] = umbilicate.

um·bil·i·ca·tion [ʌmˌbiliˈkeiʃən; ʌmˏbɪləˋkeʃən] *n*. 1. 脐状。2. 脐形涡〔如小脓疱〕。

um·bil·ic·u·lar [ˌʌmbiˈlikjulə; ˏʌmbɪˋləkjuləˋ] *a*. 脐(状)的。～ *contemplation* (佛教徒)(意守脐下的)坐禅。

um·bil·i·cus [ʌmˈbilikəs; ʌmˋbɪlɪkəs, ˏʌmbɪˋlaɪkəs] *n*. (*pl*. *-ci* [-sai; -saɪ]) 1.【解】脐;【植】种脐;【动】(单瓣贝的)涡孔;【数】脐点。2.〔转〕中心,核心。

um·bil·i·form [ʌmˈbilifɔːm; ʌmˋbɪləˏfɔrm] *a*. 脐形的。

um·bles [ˈʌmblz; ˋʌmbl̩z] *n*. *pl*. 兽类的内脏。

um·bo [ˈʌmbəu; ˋʌmbo] *n*. (*pl*. ～*s*, *um·bo·nes* [ʌmˈbəuniːz; ʌmˋboniz]) 1. 盾心浮雕。2.【动】(两瓣贝的)壳顶;盾顶;【解】(中央)凸,鼓膜凸;【植】(菌盖的)中心突起。

um·bo·nal, -bo·nate, -bon·ic [ˈʌmbənl, -neit, -ˈbɔnik; ˋʌmbonl, ʌmˋbonl, ˋʌmbonɪt, -net, -ˋbɑnɪk] *a*. 具鳞脐的;具脐状突起的;具凸结的。

um·bra [ˈʌmbrə; ˋʌmbrə] *n*. (*pl*. *-brae* [-briː; -bri]) 1. 阴影;【无】本影;暗影;(太阳黑子的)中央暗黑部。2. (古罗马)随客来的不速之客;〔罕〕幽灵。**-l** *a*.

um·brage [ˈʌmbridʒ; ˋʌmbrɪdʒ] *n*. 1. 树阴;叶丛;〔诗〕荫处,阴影。2. 不快;愤怒;悔恨,遗憾。3.〔罕〕痕迹;痕量,微少。4. 怀疑,疑念。***give*** ～ (***to***) 使不愉快,惹怒。***take*** ～ (***at***) 对(…)感觉不快,见怪;生气。

um·bra·geous [ʌmˈbreidʒəs; ʌmˋbredʒəs] *a*. 1. 成荫的,多荫的。2.〔罕〕多疑的,易怒的。**-ly** *ad*. **-ness** *n*.

um·brel·la [ʌmˈbrelə; ʌmˋbrɛlə] **I** *n*. 1. 伞,雨伞;〔罕〕(遮)阳伞〔通常称 sunshade 或 paraso〕。2.〔喻〕保护,保护伞。3.【军】(由战斗机构成的)空中掩护幕;(防止敌机的)掩护火力网 (= ～ barrage)。4.【动】水母[海蜇]的伞膜;伞具 (= ～-shell)。5.【船】烟囱顶罩。**II** *a*. 1. 伞状的,似伞的。2. 包罗众多的,机构庞大的。**III** *vt*. 1. 用伞遮覆。2. 以战斗机队保护伞保护;掩护。*an air* ～【军】空中掩护幕。～ **antenna**【无】伞形天线。～ **arch**【建】道护拱。～ **bird**〔南美〕伞鸟。～ **grass**【植】澳洲稷。～ **leaf**【植】山荷叶。～**man** 摊贩。～ **pine**【植】金松。～ **plant**【植】1. 风车草。2. 盾鬼血。～ **stand** 伞架。～ **tree**【植】(北美)伞木兰;〔口〕伞形树。

um·brette [ʌmˈbret; ʌmˋbrɛt] *n*.【鸟】(非洲)短颈鹭。

Um·bri·an [ˈʌmbriən; ˋʌmbrɪən] **I** *a*. (意大利中部)翁布里亚(地区)的;翁布里亚人的。**II** *n*. 1. 翁布里亚人。2. 已消亡的奥斯肯-翁布里亚语。

um·brif·er·ous [ʌmˈbrifərəs; ʌmˋbrɪfərəs] *a*. 成阴的,有阴影的。**-ly** *ad*.

u·mi·ak [ˈuːmiæk; ˋumɪˏæk] *n*. (爱斯基摩女子划的)木框皮艇。

um·laut [ˈumlaut; ˋumlaʊt] **I** *n*. [G.]【语音】1. 曲音,元音变化〔如德语的 mann, 复数变为 männer;英语的 man, 复数变为 men, foot 变为 feet〕。2. 变音的元音。3. (加在 a, o, u 上的)变音符号(¨)。**II** *vt*. 1. 使(元音)变音。2. 在(元音字母上)加变音符号。

UMP =【化】uridine monophosphate 一磷酸尿苷,尿苷酸 (= uridylic acid)。

ump [ʌmp; ʌmp] **I** *n*. 裁判员。**II** *vi*. 当裁判,当裁判〔umpire 的缩略词〕。

umph[1] [əm(f), mh; ʌmf] *int*. = humph.

umph[2] [uːmf; umf] *n*.〔美俚〕= oomph.

um·pir·age [ˈʌmpaiəridʒ; ˋʌmpaɪrɪdʒ, ˋʌmpərɪdʒ] *n*. 1. 公断人[仲裁人,裁判员]的地位[职务];公断权。2. 公断人的裁决。

um·pire [ˈʌmpaiə; ˋʌmpaɪr] **I** *n*. 1. 公断人,仲裁人;(运动的)裁判员;【军】演习讲评教官;【法】裁定人。2. 决定性的事物。**II** *vt*. 公断,仲裁,裁判,裁定。— *vi*. 任公断人,当裁判。～**ship** *n*. = umpirage.

um(p)·teen [ˈʌm(p)tiːn; ˋʌm(p)ˋtin] *a*.〔俚〕许多的,大量的;无数的。**-th** *a*.〔俚〕(经过无数次后)又一次的。

ump·ty [ˈʌmpti; ˋʌmptɪ] *a*.〔俚〕几十的〔20, 30…90〕,若干的。

umpty-umpth [ˈʌmptiˈʌmpθ; ˋʌmptɪˋʌmpθ] *n*., *a*. 1.〔俚〕很多(的),几十几(的)〔如 20, 21…99〕。2.〔美〕又一个[次](的)。***for the*** ～ ***time*** 几十次。

UMT = Universal Military Training〔美〕普遍军训。

um·teen [ˈʌmtiːn; ˋʌmˋtin] = umpteen.

UMW = United Mine Workers of America 美国联合矿工工会。

UN, U. N. = United Nations 联合国。

un, 'un [ən; ʌn, ən] *pro*.〔俚〕家伙,人;东西 (= one)。*a little* ～ 小家伙,小孩子。*He's a tough 'un*. 他是个厉害家伙。*That's a good 'un*. 妙极〔指双关语、谎话等〕。*you* [*we*] *'uns*〔美南部〕你们[我们]全体。*a red 'un*〔俚〕金币,金挂表。***a stiff 'un***〔俚〕1. 老运动员。2. (赛马中)一定要输的马。3. 尸体。***a wrong 'un***〔俚〕1. 坏人。2. 伪币。

un- [ʌn; ʌn, ən] *pref*. 1. 构成动词表示下列意义:相反动作,如 *un*bend, *un*coil;使丧失,夺去,废止,如 *un*sex, *un*man;由…解放出,由…取出,如 *un*earth, *un*horse;彻底,如 *un*loose, *un*rip. 2. 加在形容词、副词、名词前表示:不,无,非,未;如 *un*happy, *un*happily, *un*happiness, *un*rest.

U·na [ˈjuːnə; ˋjunə] *n*. 尤纳〔女子名〕(亦作 Ona, OOna, Oonagh)。

un·a·bashed [ˈʌnəˈbæʃt; ˏʌnəˋbæʃt] *a*. 不脸红的,不害臊的,不怕难为情的,脸厚的,满不在乎的;沉着的。

un·a·bat·ed [ˈʌnəˈbeitid; ˏʌnəˋbetɪd] *a*. 不减少的;不减退的。

un·ab·bre·vi·at·ed [ˈʌnəˈbriːvieitid; ˏʌnəˋbrivɪˋetɪd] *a*. 不省略的;不删节的;未经压缩的;全文拼写的。

un·a·ble [ˈʌnˈeibl; ʌnˋebl̩] *a*. 不能,不会;〔罕、诗〕弱,无力的。*I am* ～ *to walk*. 我不能走路。

unabr. = unabridged.

un·a·bridged [ˈʌnəˈbridʒd; ˏʌnəˋbrɪdʒd] *a*. 没有省略的;没有删节的,完全的。*an* ～ *edition* 足本。

un·ac·cent·ed [ˈʌnækˈsentid; ʌnˋæksentɪd, ˏʌnækˋsentɪd] *a*.【语音】非重音的。*an* ～ *part*【乐】弱音部。*an* ～ *syllable* 不发重音的音节。

un·ac·cept·a·ble [ˈʌnəkˈseptəbl; ˏʌnəkˋsɛptəbl̩] *a*. 不能接受的;难以承认的,难答应的;不受欢迎的;不称心的,不中意的。

un·ac·com·mo·dat·ed [ˈʌnəˈkɔməˌdeitid; ˏʌnəˋkɑməˏdetɪd] *a*. 1. 不适应的,不适合的。2. 缺乏必需品的;无(膳宿等)设备的。

un·ac·com·mo·dat·ing [ˈʌnəˈkɔmədeitiŋ; ˏʌnəˋkɑməˏdetɪŋ] *a*. 1. 不应允的,不与人方便的,不肯通融的。2. 不亲切的,不随和的;没人情的。

un·ac·com·pa·nied [ˈʌnəˈkʌmpənid; ˏʌnəˋkʌmpənɪd] *a*. 1. 没有伴的;无人伴随的 (*by*; *with*)。2.【乐】无伴奏的。

un·ac·com·plished [ˈʌnəˈkɔmpliʃt; ˏʌnəˋkɑmplɪʃt] *a*. 1. 未完成的,无成就的。2. 无技术的,无能的。*an* ～ *offence*【法】未遂罪行。

un·ac·count·a·bil·i·ty [ˈʌnəˌkauntəˈbiliti; ˋʌnə-

ˏkaʊntəˋbɪlətɪ] **n.** **1.** 无法解释;莫名其妙;奇怪。**2.** 没有责任;不负责任(= unaccountableness)。

un·ac·count·a·ble [ˈʌnəˈkauntəbl; ˏʌnəˋkaʊntəbḷ] **a.** **1.** 无法解释的;莫名其妙的。**2.** 没有责任的,不负责的(*for*)。**-bly** *ad.*

un·ac·count·ed(-for) [ˈʌnəˈkauntid(fɔː); ʌnəˋkaʊntɪd-(fɔr)] **a.** 未予说明的,未予解释清楚的。

un·ac·cred·it·ed [ˌʌnəˈkreditid; ˏʌnəˋkrɛdətɪd] **a.** 未经授权的;未被接受的;未呈递国书的。

un·ac·cus·tomed [ˈʌnəˈkʌstəmd; ˏʌnəˋkʌstəmd] **a.** **1.** 不习惯…的(*to*)。**2.** 不平常的;没有看惯的;珍奇的,奇异的。*I am ~ to public speaking.* 我不习惯在公众面前讲话。

un·ac·knowl·edged [ˈʌnəkˈnɔlidʒd; ˏʌnəkˋnɑlɪdʒd] **a.** **1.** (地位等)不被人承认的。**2.** (错误等)未公开承认的。**3.** (信件等)未得答复的。**4.** (致意等)未得回敬的。

una cor·da [ˈuːnəˈkɔːdə; ˋunəˋkɔrdə] [It.]【乐】用柔音踏板(的);用独弦(的)。**una corda pedal** (钢琴的)弱音踏板。

un·ac·quaint·ed [ˈʌnəˈkweintid; ˏʌnəˋkwentɪd] **a.** **1.** 不知道的,不懂的,不熟悉的(*with*)。**2.** 不认识的,不熟识的,陌生的;不接近的(*with*)。

un·act·a·ble [ˈʌnˈæktəbl; ʌnˋæktəbḷ] **a.** 不能上演的,不适合于演出的。

un·act·ed [ˈʌnˈæktid; ʌnˋæktɪd] **a.** **1.** 未演出的。**2.** 未付诸行动的。**3.** 未受影响的。

un·ac·tu·at·ed [ˈʌnˈæktjueitid; ˋʌnˋæktjʊetɪd] **a.** **1.** (机器等)未开动的。**2.** 未推动的,未经激励的,不受驱使的。

un·a·dapt·a·ble [ˈʌnəˈdæptəbl; ˏʌnəˋdæptəbḷ] **a.** **1.** 不能适应的。**2.** 不能改编的。

un·a·dapt·ed [ˈʌnəˈdæptid; ˏʌnəˋdæptɪd] **a.** **1.** 不适应的;不适合的。**2.** 未经改编的。

un·ad·dressed [ˈʌnəˈdrest; ˏʌnəˋdrest] **a.** (信件)无地址的。

un·ad·mit·ted [ˈʌnədˈmitid; ˋʌnədˋmɪtɪd] **a.** **1.** 不让进入的。**2.** 未被承认的。

un·a·dopt·ed [ˈʌnəˈdɔptid; ˏʌnəˋdɑptɪd] **a.** [英]未被采用的;(尤指新设道路)未为地方当局接手维持的。

un·a·dorned [ˈʌnəˈdɔːnd; ˏʌnəˋdɔrnd] **a.** 没有装饰的;不加渲染的;原来的,自然的,朴素的。

un·a·dul·ter·at·ed [ˌʌnəˈdʌltəreited; ˏʌnəˋdʌltəˏretɪd] **a.** 没有掺杂的,纯粹的;真正的,地道的。**-ly** *ad.*

un·ad·vis·a·ble [ˈʌnədˈvaizəbl; ˏʌnədˋvaɪzəbḷ] **a.** **1.** 不可取的,不适宜的,不智的;不好的,没有好处的。**2.** 不接受劝告的。

un·ad·vised [ˈʌnədˈvaizd; ˏʌnədˋvaɪzd] **a.** 未作过商量[咨询]的;愚蠢的,轻率的,鲁莽的;未接受忠告的。**-ly** [ˌʌnədˈvaizidli; ˏʌnədˋvaɪzədlɪ] *ad.*

UNAEC = United Nations Atomic Energy Commission 联合国原子能委员会。

un·af·fect·ed [ˌʌnəˈfektid; ˏʌnəˋfɛktɪd] **a.** **1.** 不矫揉造作的,自然的;不装扮的,无装饰的,不虚伪的;真心的,真实的。**2.** [ˈʌnəˈfektid; ˋʌnəˋfɛktɪd] 未受影响的,未被感动的;未变动的。**-ly** *ad.* **-ness** *n.*

un·a·fraid [ˈʌnəˈfreid; ˏʌnəˋfred] **a.** 不怕的,不畏惧的。

un·aid·ed [ˈʌnˈeidid; ʌnˋedɪd] **a.** 未受[无人]帮助的;独力的。*observe with an ~ eye* 以肉眼观察。

un·aired [ˈʌnˈɛəd; ʌnˋɛrd] **a.** 不通风的;潮湿的。

un·a·ligned [ˈʌnəˈlaind; ˏʌnəˋlaɪnd] **a.** 不结盟的。~ *countries* [*nations*] 不结盟国家。

unal·lied [ˈʌnəˈlaid; ˏʌnəˋlaɪd] **a.** **1.** 非同盟的。**2.** 无关系的,无所属的。~ *species* 互不相关的种。

un·al·low·a·ble [ˈʌnəˈlauəbl; ˏʌnəˋlaʊəbl] **a.** 不能允许的,禁止的;不能承认的。

un·al·loyed [ˈʌnəˈlɔid; ˏʌnəˋlɔɪd] **a.** **1.** 非合金的。**2.** 没有杂物的,(金属)纯粹的;(幸福)完全的,真正的。

un·al·ter·a·ble [ʌnˈɔːltərəbl; ʌnˋɔltərəbḷ] **a.** 不能变更的,不可改变的,不变的。

un·al·tered [ˈʌnˈɔːltəd; ˋʌnˋɔltɚd] **a.** 不变的,依然如故的。

un·am·big·u·ous [ˈʌnæmˈbigjuəs; ˏʌnæmˋbɪgjʊəs] **a.** 不含糊的,显明的,明确的。

un·am·bi·tious [ˈʌnæmˈbiʃəs; ˏʌnæmˋbɪʃəs] **a.** 无奢望的,没有野心的;谨小慎微的;不显眼的,朴实的。**-ly** *ad.*

un-A·mer·i·can [ˈʌnəˈmerikən; ˏʌnəˋmɛrəkən] **a.** **1.** 不合美国派头的,(风俗、习惯等)非美国式的。**2.** 反美的,非美的。~ *activities* 非美活动(指所谓违反美国利益的活动)。

un·a·mi·a·ble [ˈʌnˈeimjəbl; ʌnˋemɪəbḷ] **a.** 不和蔼的,难亲近的,不友好的。**-a·bly** *ad.*

un·an·chor [ˈʌnˈæŋkə; ˏʌnˋæŋkɚ] **vt.** 使不安定,使不安。

un·a·neled [ˈʌnəˈniːld; ˏʌnəˋnild] **a.**【宗】[古]不涂油的;未受临终涂油礼的。

u·na·nimi·ter [ˌjuːnəˈnimitə; ˏjunəˋnɪmətɚ] **ad.** [L.]【法】= unanimously.

u·na·nim·i·ty [ˌjuːnəˈnimiti; ˏjunəˋnɪmətɪ] **n.** 无异议;全体一致。*the ~ of the Cabinet* 全体阁员意见一致。*the ~ of the applause* 全场拍掌叫好。

u·nan·i·mous [ju(ː)ˈnæniməs; jʊˋnænəməs] **a.** 一致同意的;无异议的,全体一致的。*be ~ in protesting* 齐声抗议。*be greeted with ~ applause* 受全场拍掌欢迎。

un·an·nealed [ˈʌnəˈniːld; ˋʌnəˋnild] **a.** **1.**【冶】未退火的。**2.** [喻]未经锻炼的。

un·an·nounced [ˈʌnəˈnaunst; ˋʌnəˋnaʊnst] **a.** 未经宣布的;未经通报姓名的。

un·an·swer·a·ble [ʌnˈɑːnsərəbl; ʌnˋænsərəbḷ] **a.** 不能回答的,(议论等)不能辩驳的;没有责任的(*for*)。**-a·bly** *ad.*

un·an·swered [ʌnˈɑːnsəd; ʌnˋænsɚd, ʌnˋɑn-] **a.** 无回答的;无反响的。~ *love* 单恋。

un·ap·peal·a·ble [ˈʌnəˈpiːləbl; ˏʌnəˋpiləbḷ] **a.**【法】(判决等)不可上诉的。

un·ap·peal·ing [ˈʌnəˈpiːliŋ; ˋʌnəˋpilɪŋ] **a.** 无吸引力的,不能打动人的。

un·ap·peas·a·ble [ˈʌnəˈpiːzəbl; ˏʌnəˋpizəbl] **a.** 无法平息的,(愤怒)压制不住的,(饥饿)忍受不住的;不能满足的。

un·ap·pe·tiz·ing [ˈʌnˈæpitaiziŋ; ˏʌnˋæpəˏtaɪzɪŋ] **a.** 引不起食欲[兴趣]的。

un·ap·pre·ci·at·ed [ˈʌnəˈpriːʃieitid; ˏʌnəˋpriʃɪˏetɪd] **a.** 未受赏赐的;不被领情的。

un·ap·pre·hend·ed [ˈʌnˌæpriˈhendid; ˏʌnæprɪˋhɛndɪd] **a.** **1.** 未被理解的。**2.** 未被逮捕的。

un·ap·pre·hen·sive [ˈʌnˌæpriˈhensiv; ˏʌnæprɪˋhɛnsɪv] **a.** **1.** 理解力差的。**2.** 不怀疑的;不忧惧的。

un·ap·proach·a·ble [ˌʌnəˈprəutʃəbl; ˏʌnəˋprotʃəbḷ] **a.** **1.** 难接近的。**2.** 无可匹敌的;难企及的。~ *eloquence* 无比的口才。**-a·bly** *ad.* **-ness**, **-a·bil·i·ty** *n.*

un·ap·pro·pri·at·ed [ˌʌnəˈprəuprieitid; ˏʌnəˋproprɪˏetɪd] **a.** 未占用的,(尤指)不属于或未分配给任何人的;非专用的。

un·ap·proved [ˈʌnəˈpruːvd; ˏʌnəˋpruvd] **a.** 未经承认的,未经允许的,未准的。

un·apt [ˈʌnˈæpt; ʌnˋæpt] **a.** **1.** 不相称的,不适当的。**2.** 迟钝的,笨拙的(*to do*; *at*)。**2.** 不易于…的,没有…倾向的;不惯于…的(*to do*)。**-ly** *ad.*

un·ar·gu·a·ble [ˈʌnˈɑːgjuəbl; ʌnˋɑrgjʊəbḷ] **a.** **1.** 不可论证的。**2.** 无可争辩的。

un·arm [ˈʌnˈɑːm; ʌnˋɑrm] **vt.** 解除…的武装,缴…的械,夺去…的武器;使无害。— **vi.** 抛弃武器;放下武器。

un·armed [ˈʌnˈɑːmd; ʌnˋɑrmd] **a.** **1.** 没有武装的,徒手的。**2.**【动、植】没有(角、刺等)防御器官的。

un·ar·mo(u)red [ˈʌnˈɑːməd; ʌnˋarmɚd] *a*. 不穿铠甲的;(舰船等)非装甲的。

un·art·ful [ˈʌnˈɑːtfəl; ʌnˋartfəl] *a*. **1**. 天真的,朴实的;不狡猾的。**2**. 无技巧的,笨拙的。

un·ar·ti·fi·cial [ˈʌnɑːtiˈfiʃəl; ˋʌnartɪˋfɪʃəl] *a*. 非人工的;非人为的;自然的,单纯的。

u·na·ry [ˈjuːnəri; ˋjunərɪ] *a*. 【数】单元的,一元的。

un·a·shamed [ˈʌnəˈʃeimd; ˏʌnəˋʃemd] *a*. **1**. 不知羞耻的,无耻的,恬不知耻的。**2**. 问心无愧的。

un·asked [ˈʌnˈɑːskt; ʌnˋæskt, -ˋɑskt] *a*. 未受请托的;未受请求的,未经要求的;主动提出的。*He came* ~. 他不请自来。

un·as·sail·a·ble [ʌnəˈseiləbl; ˏʌnəˋseləbl̩] *a*. **1**. 攻不破的,防守坚固的。**2**. 没有争论[批评]余地的,无懈可击的。**-a·bly** *ad*.

un·as·ser·tive [ˈʌnəˈsəːtiv; ˋʌnəˋsɝtɪv] *a*. 不武断的;不过分自信的;谦逊的。

un·as·sist·ed [ˈʌnəˈsistid; ˏʌnəˋsɪstɪd] *a*. = unaided.

un·as·sum·ing [ˈʌnəˈsjuːmiŋ; ˏʌnəˋsumɪŋ, -ˋsjum-] *a*. 不摆架子的,谦逊的。**-ly** *ad*.

un·as·sured [ˈʌnəˈʃuəd; ˏʌnəˋʃʊrd] *a*. **1**. 不确定的,无把握的;无自信的。**2**. 未得保证的,不安全的。**3**. 【商】未经保险的;无保险单的。

un·at·tached [ˈʌnəˈtætʃt; ˏʌnəˋtætʃt] *a*. **1**. 无所属的;自由的;中立的。**2**. 尚未订婚[结婚]的。**3**. 【军】待分配的。**4**. 〔英〕(大学中有学籍而)不专属于某一学院的。**5**. 【法】未被逮捕的,未被扣押的。*an* ~ *young lady* 〔口〕还没有订婚的年轻女人。*place sb. on the* ~ *list* 使等待分配。

un·at·tain·a·ble [ˈʌnəˈteinəbl; ˏʌnəˋtenəbl̩] *a*. 难得到的;难达到的,难完成的。

un·at·tend·ed [ˈʌnəˈtendid; ˏʌnəˋtɛndɪd] *a*. **1**. 没有随从的,没有人伴随的。**2**. 没人照顾的,没人管的。**3**. (伤口)没有扎绷带的。**4**. (会议等)无人出席的。

un·at·trac·tive [ˌʌnəˈtræktiv; ˏʌnəˋtræktɪv] *n*. **1**. 不引人注意的,无吸引力的;枯燥乏味的。**2**. 不美的。**-ly** *ad*. **-ness** *n*.

u·nau [juˈnɔː, uˈnau; juˋnɔ, uˋnaʊ] *n*. 【动】(南美洲)两趾树懒。

un·au·then·tic [ʌnɔːˈθentik; ˏʌnɔˋθɛntɪk] *a*. 来路不明的,无根据的,难信的,不可靠的;不是真品的。

un·au·thor·ized [ˈʌnˈɔːθəraizd; ʌnˋɔθəˏraɪzd] *a*. 未被授权的;越权的;未经许可的,未经批准的;没有根据的。*make an* ~ *change* 擅自更改[修改]。

un·a·vail·a·ble [ˈʌnəˈveiləbl; ˏʌnəˋveləbl̩] *a*. **1**. 不可得到的。**2**. 没用的,没有效果的;不能利用的。*Your manuscript is* ~. 〔美〕尊稿不拟采用。~ **energy** 【物】无用能。~ **water** 无效水(分)。

un·a·vail·ing [ˈʌnəˈveiliŋ; ˏʌnəˋvelɪŋ] *a*. 无益的,无用的,无效的。**-ly** *ad*.

un·a·void·a·ble [ʌnəˈvɔidəbl; ˏʌnəˋvɔɪdəbl̩] *a*. **1**. 不能避免的,不得已的。**2**. 不能废除的,不能取消的。**-a·bly** *ad*.

un·a·ware [ˈʌnəˈweə; ˏʌnəˋwɛr] **I** *a*. 〔用作表语〕没有觉察[注意]到的,不知道的 (*of*; *that*)。*be* ~ *of the danger* 未察觉危险。*I am not* ~ *that* ... 我不是不知道…。**II** *ad*., *n*. = unawares. *They may involve themselves* ~. 他们可能不知不觉使自己卷了进去。*at* ~ = *at unawares*. **-ness** *n*.

un·a·wares [ˈʌnəˈweəz; ˏʌnəˋwɛrz] *ad*. 没想到,不料,忽然,突然,无意中,不知不觉间,一个不留神。***be taken*** ~ ***by sb.'s question*** 冷不防被人质问。***at*** ~ 忽然,突然,出其不意。***catch sb.*** ~ = ***take sb.*** ~ 冷不防地捉住某人,出其不意地袭击。

un·backed [ˈʌnˈbækt; ʌnˋbækt] *a*. **1**. (马)无人骑过的,没有驯服的。**2**. 无人支援的,无后援的。**3**. (赛跑的马)无人买票[下赌注]的。

unbaked [ˈʌnˈbeikt; ʌnˋbekt] *a*. (面包)没有烤过的;未熟的;生硬的。

un·bal·ance [ˈʌnˈbæləns; ʌnˋbæləns] **I** *vt*. (***-anced***, ***-anc·ing***) **1**. 使…失去平衡[均衡]。**2**. 扰乱了…的机能;使(心情)紊乱。~ ***sb.'s mind*** 使某人心情紊乱。~ *the budget* 使预算失去平衡。**II** *n*. **1**. (精神、心情的)紊乱状态。**2**. 失去平衡;不对称。**3**. 【物】失衡。

un·bal·anced [ˈʌnˈbælənst; ʌnˋbælənst] *a*. **1**. 失去平衡的;不稳定的。**2**. (心等)紊乱的。**3**. 【商】未决算的。*His reason is* ~. 他理智紊乱了。*an* ~ *type of character* 不稳定的性格。~ *books* 未决算账簿。

un·bal·last·ed [ˈʌnˈbæləstid; ʌnˋbæləstɪd] *a*. **1**. (船)没有压舱物的,卸去底货的。**2**. (路基)未铺沙石的。**3**. 未经稳定化的。

un·ban [ˈʌnˈbæn; ˋʌnˋbæn] *vt*. (**-*nn*-**) 使…合法化,解除对(政党、组织、活动等)的禁令。

un·bap·tized [ˈʌnbæpˈtaizd; ˏʌnbæpˋtaɪzd] *a*. 未受洗礼的,异教徒的,非基督教的。

un·bar [ˈʌnˈbɑː; ʌnˋbɑr] *vt*. (**-*rr*-**) **1**. 卸除…的横木;拔掉…的门闩;开放。**2**. 清除…的障碍。**3**. 挖毁(堤防)。

un·barbed [ˈʌnˈbɑːbd; ʌnˋbɑrbd] *a*. 拆除了有刺铁丝网的。

un·bat·ed [ʌnˈbeitid; ʌnˋbetɪd] *a*. **1**. 〔诗〕未减轻的,未减少的。**2**. 〔古〕不钝的。

un·bear·a·ble [ʌnˈbeərəbl; ʌnˋbɛrəbl] *a*. 难堪的,难受的,不能忍受的,不能容忍的;承受不住的。**-a·bly** *ad*.

un·beat·a·ble [ˈʌnˈbiːtəbl; ʌnˋbitəbl̩] *a*. 打不垮的,不可摧毁的。

un·beat·en [ˈʌnˈbiːtn; ʌnˋbitn̩] *a*. **1**. 未被打过的,未捣碎的。**2**. 未踩过的;未走过的。**3**. 未被击败的;未被超越的。~ *paths* 人迹未至的小径。~ *records* 未被打破的纪录。

un·be·com·ing [ˈʌnbiˈkʌmiŋ; ˏʌnbɪˋkʌmɪŋ] *a*. **1**. 不相称的,不适当的 (*to*; *for*)。**2**. 不体面的,不好看的,不像样子的;不谨慎的,失礼的,(演说等)岂有此理的。**3**. (衣服等)不相配的,不合身的。**-ly** *ad*. **-ness** *n*.

un·be·fit·ting [ˈʌnbiˈfitiŋ; ˏʌnbɪˋfɪtɪŋ] *a*. 不适合的,不相配的,不合适的;不相称的。

un·be·known [ˈʌnbiˈnəun; ˏʌnbɪˋnon] **I** *a*. 〔口〕未知的,不得而知的(*to*)。**II** *ad*. 瞒着。*He did it* ~ *to me*. 他瞒着我干那件事。

un·be·knownst [ˈʌnbiˈnəunst; ˏʌnbɪˋnonst] *a*., *ad*. 〔方〕= unbeknown.

un·be·lief [ˈʌnbiˈliːf; ˏʌnbɪˋlif] *n*. 怀疑;不信;无(宗教)信仰。

un·be·liev·a·ble [ˈʌnbiˈliːvəbl; ˏʌnbɪˋlivəbl̩] *a*. 不可信的。

un·be·liev·er [ˈʌnbiˈliːvə; ˏʌnbəˋlivɚ] *n*. **1**. 不信教的人,异教徒。**2**. 怀疑(论)者。

un·be·liev·ing [ˈʌnbiˈliːviŋ; ˏʌnbəˋlivɪŋ] *a*. **1**. 多疑的;怀疑的;没有信心的。**2**. 不信教的。**-ly** *ad*.

un·belt [ˈʌnˈbelt; ʌnˋbɛlt] *vt*. **1**. 解下…的带子。**2**. 解开带子拔出(刀剑)。

un·bend [ˈʌnˈbend; ʌnˋbɛnd] *vt*. (***un·bent*** [ˈʌnˈbent; ˋʌnˋbɛnt], ~***ed***) **1**. 弄直,伸直(弯曲的东西)。**2**. 放松,弄宽舒,宽解,使休息。**3**. 【海】解下,卸下(帆篷),放松(绳索等),解开(结子等)。~ *a bow* (解下弓弦)使弓松弛。— *vi*. 伸直;松弛;宽舒;舒畅。*He only* ~*s in the family circle*. 他只在家中才感到舒服。

un·bend·ing [ˈʌnˈbendiŋ; ʌnˋbɛndɪŋ] *a*. **1**. 不弯曲的,坚硬的;不屈不挠的,(精神等)坚定的;固执的,顽固的。**2**. 〔罕〕松弛的,不拘束的。

un·bent [ˈʌnˈbent; ʌnˋbɛnt] **I** unbend 的过去式及过去分词。**II** *a*. **1**. 不弯的;(弓等)松弛的。**2**. 不屈服的。

un·be·ru·fen [ˈunbəˈruːfən; ˋunbəˋrufən] *a*. [G.] 罪过!恕我多嘴!〔一种迷信习惯,在说了自夸或过分自信的话之后,以为这样说一声可免除受恶报〕。

un·be·seem·ing [ˈʌnbiˈsiːmiŋ; ˌʌnbɪˋsimɪŋ] *a*. = unbecoming.

un·be·spoken [ˈʌnbiˈspəukən; ˋʌnbɪˋspokən] *a*. 不预定的,不接受预约的。

un·bi·as(s)ed [ˈʌnˈbaiəst; ʌnˋbaɪəst] *a*. 没有偏见的,不偏不倚的,公平的。

un·bid [ʌnˈbid; ʌnˋbɪd] *a*. = unbidden.

un·bid·den [ˈʌnˈbidn; ʌnˋbɪdn] *a*. **1**. 没有受命令的,没有被指使的,自愿的,自动的,自发的。**2**. (客人等)未受邀请的。

un·bind [ˈʌnˈbaind; ʌnˋbaɪnd] *vt*. (*un·bound* [ˈʌnˈbaund; ˋʌnˋbaʊnd]) 解开(结子等);为…解开束缚,解放,释放。

un·bit·ted [ʌnˈbitid; ʌnˋbɪtɪd] *a*. (马)无嚼子的,无缰的。**2**. 不受约束的;不受控制的;无管理的。

un·blank·ing [ˈʌnˈblæŋkiŋ; ˋʌnˋblæŋkɪŋ] *n*. **1**. 【无】增辉。**2**. (信号)开启;开锁。

un·bleached [ˈʌnˈbliːtʃt; ʌnˋblitʃt] *a*. 没有漂白过的;原色的。~ *wax* 生蜡。

un·blem·ished [ʌnˈblemiʃt; ʌnˋblɛmɪʃt] *a*. 无疵的,没有缺点的;清白无瑕的。

un·blenched [ʌnˈblentʃt; ʌnˋblɛntʃt] *a*. **1**. 不退缩的,坚定的。**2**. 未被染污的。

un·blessed, un·blest [ʌnˈblest; ʌnˋblɛst] *a*. 【宗】**1**. 未得神佑的。**2**. 未受祝福的。**3**. 被诅咒的;邪恶的。**4**. 可怜的;不幸的。**5**. 缺少某种好处的。*a hut* ~ *with electricity* 没有电力供应的简陋小屋。

un·blood·ed [ʌnˈblʌdid; ʌnˋblʌdɪd] *a*. **1**. 非纯种的。**2**. 尚未入门的[指打猎等]。

un·blush·ing [ʌnˈblʌʃiŋ; ʌnˋblʌʃɪŋ] *a*. 不脸红的,不害臊的,厚颜无耻的。**-ly** *ad*.

un·bod·ied [ˈʌnˈbɔdid; ʌnˋbɑdɪd] *a*. **1**. 无实体或体形的;非物质的;无定形的。**2**. 脱离开肉体的;脱离现实的。

un·bolt [ˈʌnˈbəult; ʌnˋbolt] *vt*. 拔开(门上的)闩;拔出(窗户等的)插销,打开。

un·bolt·ed[1] [ˈʌnˈbəultid; ʌnˋboltɪd] *a*. 未上栓的,未拴上的。

un·bolt·ed[2] [ˈʌnˈbəultid; ʌnˋboltɪd] *a*. 粗的,未筛过的〔如面粉〕。

un·bon·net [ˈʌnˈbɔnit; ʌnˋbɑnɪt] *vi*. 脱帽,摘去头巾。— *vt*. 从…上取下帽子。**-ed** *a*.

un·bon·ny [ˈʌnˈbɔni; ʌnˋbɑnɪ] *a*. 〔Scot.〕丑的,不健康的。

un·born [ˈʌnˈbɔːn; ʌnˋbɔrn] *a*. **1**. 未出生的;后代的,未来的。**2**. 无开始的,原来就存在的。*an* ~ *child* 未出生的孩子。~ *generations* 未来的人们。

un·bos·om [ˈʌnˈbuzəm; ʌnˋbuzəm] *vt*. 吐露(心事),说出(秘密),剖明(心迹)。~ *oneself* (*to*) (对…)吐露心事,表明心迹。

un·bound[1] [ˈʌnˈbaund; ʌnˋbaʊnd] **I** unbind 的过去式及过去分词。**II** *a*. 解除绑缚的,得到了自由的。*Prometheus* ~ 被释放了的普罗米修斯。

un·bound[2] [ˈʌnˈbaund; ʌnˋbaʊnd] *a*. **1**. 未装订(成书)的。**2**. 【化】非结合的。~ **water** 【化】非结合水。

un·bound·ed [ʌnˈbaundid; ʌnˋbaʊndɪd] *a*. **1**. 无边的,无涯的,无限制的。**2**. 无限的,无节制的,不受控制的。*the* ~ *ocean* 无边无际的海洋。*be received with* ~ *enthusiasm* 获得极热烈的欢迎。**-ly** *ad*.

un·bowed [ˈʌnˈbaud; ʌnˋbaʊd] *a*. **1**. 不躬身的,不弯腰的。**2**. 不屈服的;未被征服的。

un·brace [ˈʌnˈbreis; ʌnˋbres] *vt*. **1**. 放松,解开。**2**. 使松懈;减弱。

un·bred [ˈʌnˈbred; ʌnˋbrɛd] *a*. **1**. 没有教育的,粗鲁的,不知礼仪的。**2**. 未受训练的。**3**. (牲畜)未交配过的。

un·bridge·a·ble [ˈʌnˈbridʒəbl; ʌnˋbrɪdʒəbl̩] *a*. 不能架桥的;不可逾越的。

un·bri·dled [ʌnˈbraidld; ʌnˋbraɪdl̩d] *a*. 没有缰绳的;没有拘束的;肆无忌惮的,放肆的;猖獗的;激烈的,猛烈的。

un·bro·ken [ˈʌnˈbrəukən; ʌnˋbrokən] *a*. **1**. 没有破损的,完好的,完整的;未受挫折的,不沮丧的。**2**. 未受阻碍的,继续不断的。**3**. (马等)未驯服的。**4**. 未开垦的。**5**. (条约等)没有受到破坏的;(纪录等)没有被打破的;(队伍)没有受到扰乱的,未涣散的,整齐的。

un·buck·le [ˈʌnˈbʌkl; ʌnˋbʌkl̩] *vt*. 解开(鞋扣等);把(剑等)从带子上解下。— *vi*. **1**. 解开带扣。**2**. 变得不拘束。

un·build [ˈʌnˈbild; ʌnˋbɪld] *vt*. **1**. 拆毁,摧毁;夷平。**2**. 【物】减低性质[磁性]。

un·built [ˈʌnˈbilt; ʌnˋbɪlt] *a*. **1**. 未建造的,建筑前的。**2**. 无建筑物的。

un·bundle [ˈʌnˈbʌndl; ˋʌnˋbʌndl] *vt*. **1**. 把(不同产品、服务等的价目)作分门别类的处理;对(产品、劳务等)分类定价。**2**. 分割(公司、资产等)出售。

un·bur·den [ʌnˈbəːdn; ʌnˋbɝdn] *vt*. 使卸除负荷,使放下担子;〔喻〕倾诉(压在心理的话)。~ *a mule* 卸下骡子的负荷。~ *oneself to sb*. 对别人倾吐自己的心事。

un·bur·ied [ˈʌnˈberid; ʌnˋbɛrɪd] *a*. **1**. 尚未埋葬的,没有埋葬的。**2**. 被(从坟里)掘出的。

un·but·ton [ˈʌnˈbʌtn; ʌnˋbʌtn̩] *vt*. **1**. 解开…的钮扣;使舒畅,使松弛。**2**. 打开(装甲车等的)顶盖。

un·but·toned [ʌnˈbʌtnd; ʌnˋbʌtnd] *a*. **1**. 钮扣解开的。**2**. 随便的;漫不经心的;不拘礼节的;无拘束的。

unc [ʌŋk; ʌŋk] 〔俚〕unconscious 的缩略字。

un·cage [ˈʌnˈkeidʒ; ʌnˋkedʒ] *vt*. 把(鸟等)从笼里释放,放出。

un·cal·cu·lat·ed [ˈʌnˈkælkjuleitid; ʌnˋkælkjəˌletɪd] *a*. 未经事先筹划[考虑]的。

un·called [ˈʌnˈkɔːld; ʌnˋkɔld] *a*. 没有被召唤的,未受邀请的;未被请求的,未被要求的(*for*)。*come* ~ 不请自来。~ **capital** 【商】未缴资金,未缴股款。**~-for** *a*. 多余的,不必要的;唐突的,多此一举的;不适当的,没有理由的,无缘无故的(*His exhibition of temper was quite* ~*-for*. 他发脾气实在没理由)。

un·can·ni·ness [ʌnˈkæninis; ʌnˋkænɪnɪs] *n*. **1**. 神秘〔尤指可怕,离奇〕。**2**. 不可思议。**3**. 〔Scot.〕危险;严重。

un·can·ny [ʌnˈkæni; ʌnˋkænɪ] *a*. (*-ni·er*; *-ni·est*) **1**. 可怕的,令人毛骨悚然的;不可思议的,神秘的。**2**. 〔Scot.〕危险的;厉害的,严重的。

un·ca·non·i·cal [ˈʌnkəˈnɔnikəl; ˋʌnkəˋnɑnəkl̩] *a*. 不合教规的。*an* ~ *marriage* 不合教规的婚姻。

un·cap [ˈʌnˈkæp; ʌnˋkæp] *vt*., *vi*. (*-pp-*) **1**. 脱(帽);打开(覆盖物)。**2**. 透露,揭示。**3**. 取消对…的上限,对…上不封顶。

un·cared-for [ˈʌnˈkɛədfɔː; ʌnˋkɛrdˌfɔr] *a*. 没人照顾的,没人理睬的,被遗忘的;被遗弃的。

un·cart [ˈʌnˈkɑːt; ʌnˋkɑrt] *vt*. 从车上卸下。

un·case [ˈʌnˈkeis; ʌnˋkes] *vt*. 从(匣子等中)拿出;使公开;使露出,显示。~ *the colours* 挂出军旗。

un·cast [ˈʌnˈkɑːst; ˋʌnˋkɑst] *a*. 演员未选定的,未定角色的。

un·cat·a·logued [ˈʌnˈkætəlɔgd; ʌnˋkætl̩ˌɔgd] *a*. 未列入目录的。

un·caused [ʌnˈkɔːzd; ʌnˋkɔzd] *a*. 无前因的;非创造的;自存的。*a first great cause which is itself* ~ 【哲】本身无前因的始初巨因。

UNCDF = United Nations Capital Development Fund 联合国资本开发基金会。

un·ceas·ing [ʌnˈsiːsiŋ; ʌnˋsisɪŋ] *a*. 不断的,不绝的,不停的。**-ly** *ad*.

un·cen·sored [ˈʌnˈsensəd; ʌnˋsɛnsɚd] *a*. **1**. (书刊等)未经审查的;(书信)未经检查的。**2**. (新闻等)不受限制的;不拘束的。

un·cer·e·mo·ni·ous [ˈʌnˌseriˈməunjəs, -niəs; ˌʌnsɛrə-

ˋmonɪəs] *a*. 1. 不拘仪式[形式]的,随便的。2. 没礼貌的。-**ly** *ad*. -**ness** *n*.

un·cer·tain [ʌnˈsəːtn; ʌnˋsɝtn, -ˋsɝtɪn] *a*. 1. (行动)不定的,含糊的;不确定的,易变的;不可靠的。2. 不能断定的,不明的,未定的。3. 忽明忽暗的,闪烁不定的。*walk with ~ steps* 脚步不稳地走。*be ~ of the facts* 不确实知道事实。*a lady of ~ age* 年龄难于估计的中年女人。*the ~ flicker of a candle* 烛光摇曳。~ **region** 【物】不可辨区。-**ly** *ad*.

un·cer·tain·ty [ʌnˈsəːtnti; ʌnˋsɝtntɪ] *n*. 1. 不确定,不确实,易变;不可靠;含糊。2. 不确实知道,半信半疑。3. 【物】测不准性。*the ~ of life* 人生的无常。***void for ~*** 【法】(遗嘱、证书等)因辞句含糊而无效。~ **principle** 【物】测不准原理。

un·chain [ˈʌnˈtʃein; ʌnˋtʃen] *vt*. 给…解除锁链;解放,释放。

un·chal·lenged [ˈʌnˈtʃælindʒd; ʌnˋtʃælɪndʒd] *a*. 不成为问题的;(问题等)没有引起争论的;无异议的;无人挑战的。*go ~* (陈述等)无问题通过。

un·chanc·y [ˈʌnˈtʃɑːnsi; ʌnˋtʃænsɪ, -ˋtʃɑn-] *a*. 〔Scot.〕不走运的;危险的。

un·change·a·ble [ʌnˈtʃeindʒəbl; ʌnˋtʃendʒəbḷ] *a*. 不可改变的。*~ of purpose* 意志坚定的。-**ness** *n*.

un·changed [ˈʌnˈtʃeindʒd; ʌnˋtʃendʒd] *a*. 不变的,没有变化的,依然如故的。

un·chang·ing [ʌnˈtʃeindʒiŋ; ʌnˋtʃendʒɪŋ] *a*. 不变的。

un·chap·e·roned [ʌnˈʃæpərəund; ʌnˋʃæpərond] *a*. (少女在社交场合)无年长女伴的,无监护人的。

un·charge [ˈʌnˈtʃɑːdʒ; ʌnˋtʃɑrdʒ] *v*. 〔罕〕= unload.

un·charged [ˈʌnˈtʃɑːdʒd; ʌnˋtʃɑrdʒd] *a*. 1. 没有负荷的。2. 未装弹药的。3. 不付费用的。4. 未被正式控告的。5. 【电】无电荷的,不带电荷的。

un·char·i·ta·ble [ʌnˈtʃæritəbl; ʌnˋtʃærətəbḷ] *a*. 没有慈悲心的;不宽恕的;严厉的;无情的。-**ta·bly** *ad*. -**ness** *n*.

un·chart·ed [ˈʌnˈtʃɑːtid; ʌnˋtʃɑrtɪd] *a*. 1. (岛屿等)海洋图上没有(标记)的;(区域)未经测绘的。2. 未知的。

un·chaste [ˈʌnˈtʃeist; ʌnˋtʃest] *a*. 不贞节的,不正经的;淫荡的;(嗜好等)下流的。

un·chas·ti·ty [ˈʌnˈtʃæstiti; ʌnˋtʃæstətɪ] *n*. 不贞节;不正经;淫荡;下流。

UNCHE = United Nations Conference on the Human Environment 联合国人类环境会议。

un·checked [ˈʌnˈtʃekt; ʌnˋtʃɛkt] *a*. 1. 未受抑制的。2. 未经检查的。

un·chris·tian [ˈʌnˈkristjən, ˈʌnˈkristʃən; ʌnˋkrɪstʃən] *a*. 1. 不信奉基督教的。2. 违反基督教教义的。3. 与基督教教徒不相称的。4. 〔口〕令人不能容忍的;糟透的。

un·church [ˈʌnˈtʃəːtʃ; ʌnˋtʃɝtʃ] *vt*. 1. 把(某人)逐出教会。2. 把(某教派)开除出教会;剥夺(某教派)教会资格[权利]。

un·churched [ˈʌnˈtʃəːtʃt; ʌnˋtʃɝtʃt] *a*. 1. 不属于任何教会的;与任何教会无关的;不到任何教堂去的。2. 被逐出教会的。*the vast masses of ~ people* 不属于任何教会的广大群众。

un·ci·al [ˈʌnsiəl, ˈʌnʃəl; ˋʌnʃɪəl, -ʃəl] I *n*. 安色尔字体〔古代用于抄本的一种圆体字〕;用安色尔字体写的抄本。II *a*. 安色尔字体的。

un·ci·form [ˈʌnsifɔːm; ˋʌnsɪˏfɔrm] I *a*. 钩形的;【解】钩骨的。II *n*. 【解】钩骨。

un·ci·na·ri·a·sis [ˌʌnsinəˈraiəsis; ˏʌnsɪnəˋraɪəsɪs] *n*. 【医】钩虫病 (= hookworm disease)。

un·ci·nate [ˈʌnsinit; ˋʌnsɪnɪt] *a*. 钩状的;钩曲的。

U. N. C. I. O. = United Nations Conference on International Organization 联合国国际组织会议。

un·cir·cum·cised [ˈʌnˈsəːkəmsaizd; ʌnˋsɝkəmˏsaɪzd] *a*. 【宗】未受割礼的;不是犹太人的;【圣】异邦人的;异端的;精神上不获重生的。

un·cir·cum·ci·sion [ˈʌnˌsəːkʌmˈsiʒən; ˏʌnsɝkəmˋsɪʒən] *n*. 1. 【宗】无割礼。2. 【圣】〔the ~〕〔集合词〕不受割礼的人,非犹太人,异教徒。

un·cir·cum·stan·tial [ˈʌnˌsəːkəmˈstænʃəl; ˋʌnˏsɝkəmˋstænʃəl] *a*. 不详尽的;非细节的。

un·civ·il [ˈʌnˈsivil; ʌnˋsɪvḷ] *a*. 不文明的,没礼貌的;粗野的;〔古〕野蛮的,未开化的。-**ness** *n*.

un·civ·i·lized [ˈʌnˈsivilaizd; ʌnˋsɪvḷˏaɪzd] *a*. 未开化的,野蛮的。

un·clad [ʌnˈklæd; ʌnˋklæd] I *v*. unclothe 的过去式及过去分词的另一种写法。II *a*. 不穿衣的;赤身裸体的,一丝不挂的。

un·claimed [ˈʌnˈkleimd; ʌnˋklemd] *a*. 无人认领的,没人来取的。*an ~ baggage* 〔美〕没人来取的行李。*an ~ balance* 不来提取的存款余额。*~ goods* 无人提取(认领)的货物。

un·clasp [ˈʌnˈklɑːsp; ʌnˋklæsp] *vt*. 解开…的扣子;放开(抓住的手)。— *vi*. 放开;松开。

un·classed [ˈʌnˈklɑːst; ˋʌnˋklæst] *a*. 1. 未归类的。2. (比赛等)未进入前三名的。

un·clas·si·cal [ˈʌnˈklæsikəl; ʌnˋklæsəkḷ] *a*. 1. 非古典的,反古典的。2. 【物】(定律等)不能用牛顿物理学来说明的。

un·clas·si·fied [ʌnˈklæsifaid; ʌnˋklæsəˏfaɪd] *a*. 1. 未分类[分级]的。2. 非保密的。

un·cle [ˈʌŋkl; ˋʌŋkḷ] *n*. 1. 叔伯;舅父;姑父,姨父。2. 〔口〕〔对年长者的客气,亲切称呼〕大叔,大伯。3. 援助者,支持者;忠告者。4. 〔俚〕开当铺者。5. 〔自称〕老子。*U- Three-balls* 当铺。***at* (*one's*) *~'s*** 在当铺里典押中。***cry* [*say*] *~*** 〔美俚〕投降;承认失败。***talk like a Dutch ~*** 严厉训诫(人)〔见 *Dutch* 条〕。***U- Benny*** 〔美口〕当铺(老板)。***U- Dudley*** 〔美口〕= *your ~*. ***~ on maternal side*** 舅父。***~ on paternal side*** 叔父,伯父。***U- Sam*** 山姆叔叔〔美国政府;美国人的绰号〕。***U- Tom*** 汤姆叔叔〔美国女作家斯陀所著长篇小说 U- Tom's Cabin 中的主角〕;〔有时作 u- Tom〕逆来顺受的人。***U-Tomism*** (黑人的)逆来顺受主义。***Your ~* (*Dudley*)** 〔谑〕我老子〔自称〕。

un·clean [ˈʌnˈkliːn; ʌnˋklin] *a*. 不清洁的,污秽的;行为不正的,不贞洁的;下流的。*~ spirit* 邪鬼〔尤指人心中的邪念〕。-**ly** *ad*.

un·clear [ˈʌnˈkliə; ʌnˋklɪr] *a*. 不清楚的;难懂的;不明白的。

un·clench [ˈʌnˈklentʃ; ʌnˋklɛntʃ], **un·clinch** [ˈʌnˈklintʃ; ʌnˋklɪntʃ] *vt*. 使松开,弄开,撬开。— *vi*. 松开。

un·cloak [ˈʌnkləuk; ʌnˋklok] *vt*. 脱去(外套);揭开(伪装),暴露。— *vi*. 脱去外套。

un·close [ˈʌnˈkləuz; ʌnˋkloz] *vt*., *vi*. 打开;(使)露出。

un·closed [ˈʌnˈkləuzd; ʌnˋklozd] *a*. 1. (门)开着的;(眼界)开阔的。2. 没有结束的,未完的。

un·clothe [ˈʌnˈkləuð; ʌnˋkloð] *vt*. (*-d*, 〔古〕***un·clad*** [ˈʌnˈklæd; ˋʌnˋklæd]) 拾去[剥去]…的衣服;剥光;暴露;揭露。

un·cloud·ed [ˈʌnˈklaudid; ʌnˋklaudɪd] *a*. 没有云的,晴朗的;开朗的,(思路)清晰的。

un·club·ba·ble, un·club·a·ble [ˈʌnˈklʌbəbl; ʌnˋklʌbəbḷ] *a*. 不善于[不爱]交际的。

un·co, un·co' [ˈʌŋkəu; ˋʌŋko] I *a*. 〔Scot.〕1. 不熟知的,陌生的。2. 奇怪的,可怕的。3. 值得注意的,显著的。*an ~ sight* 奇异的景象。***the ~ guid*** 自命清高的人,过分古板的教徒。II *n*. 1. 稀奇的人[物]。2. 〔*pl*.〕特讯,新闻。III *ad*. 很,极,非常。

un·coil [ˈʌnˈkɔil; ʌnˋkɔɪl] *vt*., *vi*. (使)(卷着的东西)展开。*The snake slowly ~ed*. 蛇慢慢伸开(盘着的)身体。

un·col·oured, 〔美〕**un·col·ored** [ˈʌnˈkʌləd; ʌnˋkʌləd] ***a.*** 无色的;未染色[着色]的,本色的;没有修饰的,原样的,(话等)不夸张的。

un·combed [ˈʌnˈkəumd; ʌnˋkomd] ***a.*** (头发等)没有梳过的;蓬乱的。

un·com·bined [ˈʌnkəmˈbaind; ˏʌnkəmˋbaɪnd] ***a.*** **1.** 没有结合的;未联合的。**2.**【化】未化合的;分离的。

un-come-at-a·ble [ˈʌnkʌmˈætəbl; ˏʌnkʌmˋætəbl̩] ***a.*** 〔口〕**1.** 难得到的。**2.** 难接近的。

un·come·ly [ˈʌnˈkʌmli; ʌnˋkʌmlɪ] ***a.*** **1.** 不优美的,不漂亮的,丑陋的。**2.** 不体面的;没礼貌的;不恰当的。

un·com·fort·a·ble [ʌnˈkʌmfətəbl; ʌnˋkʌmfətəbl̩] ***a.*** 不舒适的,不安的,不自在的。*be in an ~ predicament* 处境困难。**-a·bly** ***ad.*** **-ness** ***n.***

un·com·mer·cial [ˈʌnkəˈməːʃəl; ˏʌnkəˋmɝʃəl] ***a.*** **1.** 非商业(性质)的;非营利的。**2.** 违反商业道德的。

un·com·mit·ted [ˈʌnkəˈmitid; ˏʌnkəˋmɪtɪd] ***a.*** **1.** (犯罪等)未遂的。**2.** 不承担义务的,不受(诺言)约束的。**3.** 尚未提交委员会的。**4.** 未监禁的;未送入疯人院的。**5.** 未被授权的,未受委托的。*an ~ crime* 未遂罪。*the ~ unit*【军】未投入战斗的部队。

un·com·mon [ʌnˈkɔmən; ʌnˋkɑmən] **I** ***a.*** 不平常的,不常见的;难得的,非常的,非凡的,珍奇的。**II** ***ad.*** 〔卑口〕= uncommonly.

un·com·mon·ly [ʌnˈkɔmənli; ʌnˋkɑmənlɪ] ***ad.*** 难得;非常,极其。*~ cold* 极冷。

un·com·mu·ni·ca·tive [ˈʌnkəˈmjuːnikətiv; ˏʌnkəˋmjunəˏketɪv, -kətɪv] ***a.*** 不爱说话的,沉默寡言的,拘谨的。**-ness** ***n.***

un·com·pan·ion·a·ble [ˈʌnkəmˈpænjənəbl; ˏʌnkəmˋpænjənəbl̩] ***a.*** 难相处的;不爱交际的。

un·com·plain·ing [ˈʌnkəmˈpleiniŋ; ˏʌnkəmˋplenɪŋ] ***a.*** 没有怨言的,不诉苦的,不发牢骚的;坚忍的,有耐心的。**-ly** ***ad.***

un·com·pli·men·ta·ry [ˈʌnˌkɔmpliˈmentəri; ˏʌnkɑmpləˋmentərɪ] ***a.*** 非赞美性的,贬抑的。

un·com·pro·mis·ing [ˈʌnˈkɔmprəmaiziŋ; ʌnˋkɑmprəˏmaɪzɪŋ] ***a.*** 不让步的,不妥协的,不肯通融的;强硬的;坚决的;不屈的;严厉的。**-ly** ***ad.***

un·con·cern [ˈʌnkənˈsəːn; ˏʌnkənˋsɝn] ***n.*** 漫不经心,不关心,冷淡,不在乎,不介意。*with complete ~* 十分冷淡,满不在乎。

un·con·cerned [ˈʌnkənˈsəːnd; ˏʌnkənˋsɝnd] ***a.*** **1.** 漫不经心的,不关心的,冷淡的,满不在乎的(*about*)。**2.** 与…没有关系的(*in*; *with*)。**3.** 无私心的。**-ly** ***ad.*** **-ness** ***n.***

un·con·di·tion·al [ˈʌnkənˈdiʃənəl; ˏʌnkənˋdɪʃənəl] ***a.*** 无条件的;无限制的;无保留的;绝对的。*an ~ surrender* 无条件投降。**-ly** ***ad.***

un·con·di·tioned [ˈʌnkənˈdiʃənd; ˏʌnkənˋdɪʃənd] ***a.*** **1.** 无条件的,无限制的,绝对的。**2.** 无条件入学的。***the U-***【哲】绝对者。*~* **reflex**【生】无条件反射。

un·con·fessed [ˈʌn-kənˈfest; ˏʌnkənˋfɛst] ***a.*** 未认罪忏悔的;未供认的。

un·con·fined [ˈʌn-kənˈfaind; ˏʌnkənˋfaɪnd] ***a.*** **1.** 无拘束的;自由的;无限制的。**2.** (头发等)松散的。

un·con·firmed [ˈʌn-kənˈfəːmd; ˏʌnkənˋfɝmd] ***a.*** **1.** 未最后确定的。**2.** 未证实的;未确证的;未经认可的。**3.**【宗】未受坚信礼的。

un·con·form·a·ble [ˈʌn-kənˈfɔːməbl; ˏʌnkənˋfɔrməbl̩] ***a.*** **1.** 不顺从的,不服从的。**2.** 不适合的;不一致的。**3.**【地】不整合的。**-a·bly** ***ad.***

un·con·form·i·ty [ˈʌn-kənˈfɔːmiti; ˏʌnkənˋfɔrmətɪ] ***n.*** (*pl.* ***-ties***) **1.** 不相符;不一致;不相称;不顺从。**2.**【地】不整合;不整合面。

un·con·geal [ˈʌnkənˈdʒiːl; ˏʌnkənˋdʒil] ***vt.*** 使溶解,使解冻。

un·con·nect·ed [ˈʌn-kəˈnektid; ˏʌnkəˋnɛktɪd] ***a.*** **1.** 不连结的;分开的。**2.** 不相关联的;不连贯的。**3.** 无亲属关系的。

un·con·quer·a·ble [ʌnˈkɔŋkərəbl; ʌnˋkɑŋkərəbl̩] ***a.*** 不可克服[征服]的;难压制的,遏制不了的。

un·con·scion·a·ble [ʌnˈkɔnʃənəbl; ʌnˋkɑnʃənəbl̩] ***a.*** **1.** 不受良心控制的,肆无忌惮的。**2.** 无节制的,过度的。**3.** 不合理的,不公平的,【法】不正当的。*an ~ bargain*【法】不正当的契约。**-a·bly** ***ad.***

un·con·scious [ʌnˈkɔnʃəs; ʌnˋkɑnʃəs] **I** ***a.*** **1.** 无意识的;失去知觉的,不省人事的。**2.** 不知道的,未发觉的(*of*)。**3.** 无意的,不自觉的。*He was blissfully ~ of it all.* 他本人幸亏一点不晓得。**II** ***n.***【心】无意识〔人不自觉的思想、欲望、行动等〕。**-ly** ***ad.*** 无意识地,无意中,不知不觉,不留神。**-ness** ***n.***

un·con·sid·ered [ˈʌn-kənˈsidəd; ˏʌnkənˋsɪdəd] ***a.*** **1.** 不考虑的;未加考虑的。**2.** 轻率的;未经深思熟虑的。*a hasty, ~ remark* 脱口而出的莽撞话。

un·con·stant [ˈʌnˈkɔnstənt; ʌnˋkɑnstənt] ***a.*** = inconstant.

un·con·sti·tu·tion·al [ˈʌnkɔnstiˈtjuːʃənəl; ˏʌnkɑnstəˋtjuʃənl̩, -ˋtu-] ***a.*** 违反宪法的。**-ly** ***ad.*** **-i·ty** [ˈʌnˌkɔnstiˌtjuːʃəˈnæliti; ˋʌnˏkɑnstəˏtjuʃəˋnælətɪ] ***n.*** 违(反)宪(法)。

un·con·strained [ˈʌn-kənˈstreind; ˏʌnkənˋstrend] ***a.*** **1.** 不受强制的,自由的。**2.** 非强迫的,自发的,自动的。**3.** (态度)不勉强的,从容的。**-ly** [ˈʌn-kənˈstreinidli; ˋʌnkənˋstrenədlɪ] ***ad.***

un·con·straint [ˈʌn-kənˈstreint; ˏʌnkənˋstrent] ***n.*** 无拘束,不受强制,自由,自愿。

un·con·tam·i·nat·ed [ˈʌn-kənˈtæmineitid; ˋʌnkənˋtæmənetɪd] ***a.*** 没有被污染的;未沾染的。

un·con·tem·plat·ed [ˈʌnˈkɔntempleitid; ˋʌnˋkɑntɛmpletɪd] ***a.*** **1.** 未料想到的,意外的。**2.** 未经思考的。

un·con·test·ed [ˈʌnkənˈtestid; ˏʌnkɑnˋtɛstɪd] ***a.*** **1.** 无竞争者的,无竞争的。**2.** 无异议的;明白的,无议论余地的。

un·con·trived [ˈʌn-kənˈtraivd; ˏʌnkənˋtraɪvd] ***a.*** **1.** 事先未计划的,未预谋的。**2.** 自然的,天真的,真诚的。

un·con·trol·la·ble [ˌʌn-kənˈtrəuləbl; ˏʌnkənˋtroləbl̩] ***a.*** 不能控制的,(孩子)无法管束的;〔美〕(聚众闹事者等)难以驾驭的,桀骜不驯的。

un·con·trolled [ˈʌn-kənˈtrəuld; ˏʌnkənˋtrold] ***a.*** 未受控制的,无人管束的,自由的,无拘束的。**-ly** ***ad.***

un·con·ven·tion·al [ˈʌn-kənˈvenʃənəl; ˏʌnkənˋvɛnʃənl̩, -ʃnəl] ***a.*** 非常规的;不按照习惯[惯例]的;不落陈套的。**-ly** ***ad.*** **-i·ty** [ˈʌn-kənˌvenʃəˈnæliti; ˋʌnkənˏvɛnʃəˋnælətɪ] ***n.***

un·con·vert·ed [ˈʌn-kənˈvəːtid; ˏʌnkənˋvɝtɪd] ***a.*** **1.** (形态、作用等)无变化的。**2.** 未改变信仰的。

un·con·vert·i·ble [ˈʌn-kənˈvəːtəbl; ˏʌnkənˋvɝtəbl̩] ***a.*** 不能改变的,难变换的;不能兑换[兑现]的。**-bly** ***ad.***

un·cooked [ˈʌnˈkukt; ʌnˋkukt] ***a.*** 未煮过的,生的。*eat ~* 生吃。

un·cool [ˈʌnˈkuːl; ˋʌnˋkul] ***a.*** 〔俚〕**1.** 极易激动的。**2.** 打扰人的,使人不愉快的,粗野的。

un·co·op·er·a·tive [ˈʌn-kəuˈɔpərətiv; ˏʌnkoˋɑpəˏretɪv, -ˋɑprə-] ***a.*** 不合作的;不配合的。

un·co·or·di·nat·ed [ˈʌn-kəuˈɔːdineitid; ˏʌnkoˋɔrdəˏnetɪd] ***a.*** **1.** 不协调的。**2.** 不同等的;不对等的。

un·cord [ˈʌnˈkɔːd; ʌnˋkɔrd] ***vt.*** 解开…的绳索;拆下(弓上的)弦。

un·cork [ˈʌnˈkɔːk; ʌnˋkɔrk] ***vt.*** 拔去…的塞子[瓶塞];〔口〕吐露,说出(感情等)。**-ed** ***a.***

un·cor·rect·able [ˈʌn-kəˈrektəbl; ˋʌnkəˋrɛktəbl̩] ***a.*** 不可挽回的,不可弥补的。

U

un·cor·rect·ed [ˈʌn-kəˈrektid; ˏʌnkəˋrɛktɪd] *a*. **1**. 未经改正的;未修改的。**2**. 未加管教的,未受谴责的。**3**. 未调整的。

un·cor·rupt [ˈʌn-kəˈrʌpt; ˏʌnkəˋrʌpt] *a*. = uncorrupted.

un·cor·rupt·ed [ˈʌnkəˈrʌptid; ˏʌnkəˋrʌptɪd] *a*. 未腐败的;未堕落的;收买不动的,廉洁的。

un·cor·rupt·i·ble [ˈʌn-kəˈrʌptəbl; ˏʌnkəˋrʌptəbl̩] *a*. 不会腐败的;不能收买的 (= incorruptible)。

un·count·a·ble [ˈʌnˈkauntəbl; ʌnˋkaʊntəbl̩] **I** *a*. **1**. 不可数的。**2**. 数不清的;无法估量的。**3**. 无数的。**II** *n*. 【语法】不可数名词。

un·count·ed [ˈʌnˈkauntid; ʌnˋkaʊntɪd] *a*. **1**. 没有数过的。**2**. 无数的。*a stack of* ~ *bills* 一叠没有数过的钞票。

un·coup·le [ˈʌnˈkʌpl; ʌnˋkʌpl̩] *vt*. 解开(车辆等的)连结挂钩;解开(把狗系在一起的)皮条;拆散,分离开。~ *railway trucks* 使车皮脱钩分开。*an* ~*d axle*【机】不联轴。*an* ~*d wheel* 活轮。— *vi*. 分开,脱开。*The glider* ~*d from the two plane*. 滑翔机与拖机脱开。

un·cour·te·ous [ˈʌnˈkəːtiəs; ʌnˋkɝtɪəs] *a*. 没礼貌的,粗野的。

un·couth [ʌnˈkuːθ; ʌnˋkuθ] *a*. **1**. 笨拙的,粗野的,粗鲁的,不文明的。**2**. 〔古〕陌生的,没有见惯的;〔书〕(地方等)荒凉的;古怪的,怪异的。**-ly** *ad*. **-ness** *n*.

un·cov·e·nant·ed [ʌnˈkʌvənəntid; ʌnˋkʌvənəntɪd] *a*. **1**. 无契约许可[保证、承认]的。**2**. 无契约条款约束[规定]的。

un·cov·er [ʌnˈkʌvə; ʌnˋkʌvɚ] *vt*. **1**. 去除…的遮盖物,打开…的盖子。**2**. 拿下(头上)戴的东西,脱(帽)。**3**. 使露出,揭露;使知道;【军】暴露;除去…的掩护。**4**. 将(狐)赶出。~ *the head* = ~ *oneself* 脱帽表示敬意。~ *one's heart to sb*. 对某人吐露心事。— *vi*. **1**. 揭去盖子,拿掉覆盖物,掀开盖子。**2**. 脱帽致敬。

un·cov·ered [ʌnˈkʌvəd; ʌnˋkʌvɚd] *a*. **1**. 无遮盖的;暴露的;无掩护的。**2**. 未经保险的;无附加担保的。**3**. 不戴帽的。**4**. 不包括在服务范围之内的。*an* ~ *shed* 无遮盖的小棚。~ *legs* 裸露的腿。

U

un·cracked [ʌnˈkrækt; ʌnˋkrækt] *a*. 未裂开的;无裂缝的。~ *asphalt* 未裂化沥青。

un·krate [ˈʌnˈkreit; ˋʌnˋkret] *vt*. 拆箱取出(货物)。

un·cre·at·ed [ˈʌnkriˈeitid; ˏʌnkrɪˋetɪd] *a*. **1**. 尚未创造出来的;不存在的。**2**.【神学】永生的,永存的;自存的。

un·crit·i·cal [ˈʌnˈkritikəl; ʌnˋkrɪtɪkl] *a*. **1**. 无批判力的;批评不当的。**2**. 不加批判的;不加鉴别的。

un·cropped [ˈʌnˈkrɔpt; ʌnˋkrɑpt] *a*. **1**. 未收割的;未采摘的。**2**. (头发、毛等)未修剪的;未剪短的。**3**. (土地)未种植的;无收获的。

un·cross [ʌnˈkrɔːs; ʌnˋkrɔs, -ˋkrɑs] *vt*. 使不交叉。~ *one's leg* 把交叉的腿分开。**-ed** *a*. **1**. 未遇妨碍的,未受挫折的。**2**. 〔英〕(支票)未划线的。**3**. 未被划掉[取消]的。

un·crown [ˈʌnˈkraun; ʌnˋkraʊn] *vt*. = dethrone.

un·crush·a·ble [ˈʌnˈkrʌʃəbl; ˋʌnˋkrʌʃəbl̩] *a*. **1**. 压不碎的;压不住的。**2**. 揉不皱的。

UNCTAD = United Nations Conference on Trade and Development 联合国会议和发展会议。

unc·tion [ˈʌŋkʃən; ˋʌŋkʃən] *n*. **1**.【宗】涂油礼;【医】药膏涂布。**2**. 涂油礼用的油;油膏;〔喻〕安慰物,甜言蜜语。**3**. (宗教性的)热情,感激。**4**. (做作出来的)感动,同情。**5**. 热心;兴趣。*Lay not that flattering* ~ *to your soul*. 不要在你的灵魂上涂抹那种使你感到自慰的香膏吧。*give the dying man extreme* ~ (神父)给临终的人行涂油礼。

unc·tu·os·i·ty [ˌʌŋktjuˈɔsiti; ˏʌŋktʃʊˋɑsətɪ] *n*. **1**. 油性,油滑。**2**. (某些矿石给予触觉的)油滑感。**3**. (土壤的)松软肥沃。**4**. 可塑性。**5**. 油腔滑调。

unc·tu·ous [ˈʌŋktjuəs; ˋʌŋktʃʊəs] *a*. **1**. 油性的,油质的;油腻的;滑溜的;(土壤)松软的。**2**. 塑性的。**3**. 甜言蜜语的;(装作)虔诚的,热忱的,假殷勤的,虚情假意的。**-ly** *ad*. **-ness** *n*.

un·cul·ti·vat·ed [ˈʌnˈkʌltiveitid; ʌnˋkʌltəˏvetɪd] *a*. **1**. 未经耕作的,未开垦的。**2**. 未经磨炼的;没有教养的,粗野的,未开化的。

un·curl [ˈʌnˈkəːl; ʌnˋkɝl] *vt*. 把(卷发等)弄直;展开。~*ed hair* 不卷曲的头发。*lie* ~*ed on the bed* 直挺挺地躺在床上。— *vi*. 变直,伸直;伸开;展开。

un·cus [ˈʌŋkəs; ˋʌŋkəs] *n*. (*pl*. *un·ci* [-sai; -saɪ]) 【解】(昆虫的)爪形突。

un·cut [ˈʌnˈkʌt; ʌnˋkʌt] *a*. **1**. 未切割[修剪]的。**2**. (宝石等)未琢磨的。**3**. (书)尚未切边的,毛边的,未删削的。

un·cy·ber·nat·ed [ˈʌnˌsaibəˈneitid; ˋʌnˏsaɪbəˋnetɪd] *a*. 非电子化的。

un·damped [ʌnˈdæmpt; ʌnˋdæmpt] *a*. **1**. 不潮湿的;不沮丧的;不气馁的。**2**.【电】无衰减的,无阻尼的,等幅的。

un·dat·ed [ʌnˈdeitid; ʌnˋdetɪd] *a*. **1**. 没有注明日期的。**2**. 日期[期限]不一定的。**3**. (一生)无突出事件的。

un·daunt·ed [ʌnˈdɔːntid; ʌnˋdɔntɪd] *a*. 无畏的,勇敢的;刚毅的。**-ly** *ad*. **-ness** *n*.

UNDC = United Nations Disarmament Commission 联合国裁军委员会。

un·dé, un·dée [ˈʌndei; ˋʌnde] *a*.【纹】波状的。

un·dec·a·gon [ʌnˈdekəˈgɔn; ʌnˋdɛkəgɑn] *n*. 十一边形;十一角形。

un·de·ceive [ˈʌndiˈsiːv; ˏʌndɪˋsiv] *vt*. 使不再受骗,使醒悟,打破…的迷梦。~ *sb*. *of his mistakes* 使某人明白自己的错误。*be* ~*d* 醒悟过来;不再抱幻想。

un·de·cid·a·bil·i·ty [ˌʌndiˌsaidəˈbiliti; ˏʌndɪˏsaɪdəˋbɪlɪtɪ] *n*.【逻】【数】不可决定性〔指以某系统的公理既不能证明某命题的成立,又不能证明其不成立的情况〕。

un·de·cid·ed [ˈʌndiˈsaidid; ˏʌndɪˋsaɪdɪd] *a*. **1**. 未决的,未定的。**2**. (天气等)不稳定的。**3**. 优柔寡断的。**4**. (形状等)不明确的,模糊的。**-ness** *n*.

un·de·clared [ˈʌndiˈklɛəd; ˏʌndɪˋklɛrd] *a*. **1**. 未经宣布的。**2**. 不公开的。**3**. 未向海关申报的。

un·de·clined [ˈʌndiˈklaind; ˏʌndɪˋklaɪnd] *a*.【语】无字尾变化的。

un·dec·y·le·nic [ʌndesiˈliːnik, -ˈlenik; ˏʌndɛsəˋlinɪk, -ˋlɛnɪk] **acid**【化】十一碳烯酸。

un·de·fend·ed [ˈʌndiˈfendid; ˏʌndɪˋfɛndɪd] *a*. **1**. 未设防的。**2**. 无充分论据[理由]的。**3**. 无人为之辩护的;无辩护的。*an* ~ *city* 不设防城市。

un·de·filed [ˈʌndiˈfaild; ˏʌndɪˋfaɪld] *a*. 没有弄脏的,未玷污的;纯洁的;纯粹的。

un·de·fined [ˈʌndiˈfaind; ˏʌndɪˋfaɪnd] *a*. **1**. 未下定义的,不用定义解释的。**2**. 不明确规定的;模糊的。

un·de·lete, un-de·lete [ˌʌndiˈliːt; ˏʌndɪˋlit] **I** *n*.【计】复位功能〔一种电脑程序功能,可使文件中被擦洗掉的部分复归原位〕。**II** *vt*., *vi*. (使)存储器上被擦除的数据复位,恢复(被删除的信息)。

un·dem·o·crat·ic [ˈʌndeməˈkrætik; ˏʌndɛməˋkrætɪk] *a*. 不[非]民主的。

un·de·mon·stra·ble [ˈʌnˈdemənstrəbl; ˏʌndɪˋmɑnstrəbl̩] *a*. 无法表明的;不可论证的。

un·de·mon·stra·tive [ˈʌndiˈmɔnstrətiv; ˏʌndɪˋmɑnstrətɪv] *a*. 不露声色的,克制的,谨慎的。**-ly** *ad*. **-ness** *n*.

un·de·ni·a·ble [ʌndiˈnaiəbl; ˏʌndɪˋnaɪəbl] *a*. **1**. 不可否认的,无法抵赖的,无可争辩的;不可否定的。**2**. 无可疵议的,优秀的。**-a·bly** *ad*.

un·de·nom·i·na·tion·al [ˈʌndiˌnɔmiˈneiʃənəl; ˏʌndɪˏnɑməˋneʃənl̩] *a*. 不属于任何宗派[教派]的;无宗教[教派]拘束的;非宗派的。

un·der [ˈʌndə; ˋʌndɚ] **I** *prep*. **1**. 〔位置〕在…下;在表面

之下,在…内部;被…遮蔽着;在…脚下,在…底下。~ *a tree* 在树下。~ *the skin* 在皮下。~ *cover* 在掩蔽之下。*a field* ~ *grass* 长满了草的田地。~ *water* 在水下。~ *a hill* 在山脚下。~ *the sun* 在阳光下;天下,在世界上。2.〔从属关系〕(a) 隶属[从属、指导]之下。~ *the British government* 隶属在英国政府之下。*study* ~ *Dr. Eliot* 在埃利奥特博士指导下研究。(b) 附属…之下,归属于。*come* ~ *this head* 包含在本项目中。~ *Article 43* 在第四十三条下。3.〔处在某种作用、条件、状态等下或某一期间、过程中〕*groan* ~ *tyranny* 在残暴压制下呻吟。~ *medical treatment* 在治疗中。*land* ~ *the plough* = *land* ~ *cultivation* 耕地。~ *the influence of drink* 酒醉。*He tottered* ~ *a heavy load*. 他在重担下摇摇晃晃地走。*It is forbidden* ~ *pain of death*. 违犯者处死。*I am* ~ *an engagement to go*. 我有约会要去。4.〔程度、量值、等级〕(地位)低于…,比…低级的;(年龄、时间、价格、数量等)在…以下(的),未满…(的),不足…(的)。~ *cooling* 过冷。~ *the hour* 在该时间内。*No one* ~ *a captain can hold the post*. 海军上校以下不能担任此职。*children* ~ *twelve years of age* 未满十二岁的儿童。5. 在某种名义、口实下;以…为代表。~ *a false name* 用假名。~ *the mask of friendship* 借友谊为名,在友谊的伪装下。~ *a new name* 换用新名字。6. 根据,依据,按照。~ *the law* 根据法律。~ **age** 未成年。~ **sb.'s hand and seal** 经某人签名盖章。~ **arms** 武装着,手执武器。~ **avow** 发过誓,在誓言下。~ **favour** 如果允许(这样说)的话〔多作插入句〕。~ **fire** 在弹雨下,冒着炮火(*land* ~ *fire* 在炮火下登陆)。~ **foot** 地上(*It was wet* ~ *foot* 地上潮湿);在脚下(踩着)。~ **night** 〔Scot.〕在夜间。~ **one's breath** 小声,低声。~ **sb.'s (very) eye** 在某人眼皮底下,显而易见。~ **the line** 【海】在赤道下。**with a good meal** ~ **one's belt** 饱餐一顿。**II** *ad*. 1. 在下,从属着,服从着。*bring* ~, *get* ~, *keep* ~ 等〔参看各该动词条〕。*The ship went* ~. 船下沉了。2. 在下文中。*See* ~ *for further information*. 更详尽资料见下文。3. 少于,低于。*five dollars or* ~ 五美元或五美元以下。**III** *a*. 1. 下面的,下部的(*opp*. upper);附属的;从属的。2. 较次的;低劣的。3. 过少的,过小的,不足的。*the* ~ *lip* 下唇。~ *servants* 仆役的下手。~ *grazing* 轻度放牧。

under- *comb. f.* 表示:1. "在以下","下面[下方]的":*under*ground. 2. "次于","低于":*under*secretary, *under*graduate. 3. "不足","不够","不充分":*under*act, *under*develop.

un·der·a·chieve [ˈʌndərəˈtʃiːv; ˌʌndərəˋtʃiv] *vi*. (*-chiev·ed*; *-chiev·ing*) 学校学习成绩低于智力测验所得的分数。**-ment** *n*. **-r** *n*. 学校学习成绩低于智力商数的学生。

un·der·act [ˈʌndərˈækt; ˋʌndɚˋækt] *vt*., *vi*. 表演(角色)不足[不充分],表演得含蓄。

un·der·ad·ver·tis·ing [ˈʌndəˈrædvətaiziŋ, ˋʌndɚˋædvɚtaɪzɪŋ] *n*. 宣传不够;广告做得不够。

un·der·age[1] [ˈʌndəˈeidʒ; ˋʌndɚˋedʒ] *a*. 1. 未成年的。2. 未到法定年龄的。

un·der·age[2] [ˈʌndəridʒ; ˋʌndərɪdʒ] *n*. 短少;不足。

un·der·arm [ˈʌndərɑːm; ˋʌndɚˌɑrm] **I** *ad*. 【板球、网球】用低手,手在肩下部动作(= underhand)。**II** *a*. 1. 手臂下的,腋下的。2.【板球,网球】低手击出[扔出]的。

un·der·armed [ˈʌndəˈɑːmd; ˌʌndɚˋɑrmd] *a*. 武器装备不足的;武装得不充分的。

un·der·bel·ly [ˈʌndəbeli; ˋʌndɚˌbɛlɪ] *n*. 1. 下腹部。2.〔喻〕薄弱部位;易受攻击的区域。

un·der·bid [ˈʌndəˈbid; ˌʌndɚˋbɪd] *vt*. (~; *un·der·bid·den* [ˈʌndəˈbidn; ˋʌndɚˋbɪdn], ~; *~ding*) 1. (投标时)出价低于(他人)。2.【牌】以低于可能的得分叫牌。3. 愿以较低报酬做(某事);以低价售出。— *vi*. 1. (投标时)出价不足;出价过低。2.【桥牌】叫牌过低。

un·der·bod·y [ˈʌndəˌbɔdi; ˋʌndɚˌbɑdɪ] *n*. 1. 动物下体。2. 车身底板。3. 船体水下部分。

un·der·boss [ˈʌndəbɔs; ˋʌndɚbɑs] *n*.〔美口〕(黑手党等下层社会组织的)二老板,老二〔地位仅次于"老大"〕。

un·der·bought [ˈʌndəˈbɔːt; ˋʌndɚˈbɔt] underbuy 的过去式和过去分词。

un·der·bred [ˈʌndəˈbred; ˋʌndɚˋbrɛd, ˌʌn-] *a*. 1. 缺乏教养的,没有礼貌的,粗野不文的。2. (马)不是纯种的。

un·der·brush, **un·der·bush** [ˈʌndəbrʌʃ, -buʃ; ˋʌndɚˌbrʌʃ; -bʊʃ] *n*. (树林内的)下层林丛,矮树丛,乱丛棵子。

un·der·bud [ˈʌndəbʌd; ˋʌndɚˌbʌd] *n*. 未入社交界的少女。

un·der·buy [ˈʌndəˈbai; ˋʌndɚˋbaɪ] (*-bought* [-bɔːt; -bɔt]) *vt*. 买得比市价[别人]便宜。

un·der·cap·i·tal·ize [ˈʌndəˈkæpitəlaiz; ˌʌndɚˋkæpɪtḷˌaɪz] *vt*., *vi*. (*-iz·ed*; *-iz·ing*) (对…)投资不足。**-tal·i·za·tion** *n*.

un·der·car·riage [ˈʌndəkæridʒ; ˋʌndɚˌkærɪdʒ] *n*. 1. (车辆,重武器的)下部构造,底架,下架,底盘。2. 飞机脚架,起落架。

un·der·charge [ˈʌndəˈtʃɑːdʒ; ˋʌndɚˋtʃɑrdʒ] *vt*. 1. 对(买方)少要[少算]价钱。2. 给…充电不足;给…少填火药。

un·der·class·man [ˌʌndəˈklɑːsmən; ˌʌndɚˋklæsmən, -ˋklɑs-] *n*. (*pl*. *-men*) (大学的)低年级〔一、二年级〕。

un·der·clay [ˈʌndəklei; ˋʌndɚkle] *n*.【矿】底黏土,煤屑底黏土层。

un·der·clerk [ˈʌndəˈklɑːk; ˋʌndɚˌklɝk] *n*. 下级职员[办事员],助理办事员。

un·der·cliff [ˈʌndəklif; ˋʌndɚˌklɪf] *n*.【地】(因滑坡或坍塌而形成的)副崖,阶地。

un·der·clothed [ˈʌndəˈkləuðd; ˋʌndɚˋkloðd] *a*. 穿得单薄的。

un·der·clothes [ˈʌndəkləuðz, -kləuz; ˋʌndɚˌkloðz] *n*.〔*pl*.〕内衣裤,衬衣裤;汗衫,贴身衣。★可用 many 修饰,但不可与数字连用。

un·der·clothing [ˈʌndəkləuðiŋ; ˋʌndɚˌkloðɪŋ] *n*. = underclothes.

un·der·coat [ˈʌndəkəut; ˋʌndɚˌkot] **I** *n*. 1. 大衣内的上衣。2.〔口〕(女用)衬裙。3. (动物长毛下面的)浓密的绒毛。4. (涂在车辆底部的)底部防锈层;(上漆之前的)内涂层。**II** *vt*. 给…加内涂层。

un·der·cool [ˈʌndəˈkuːl; ˋʌndɚˋkul] *vt*., *vi*. (使)过度冷却(= supercool)。

un·der·cover [ˌʌndəˈkʌvə, ˈʌndəˌkʌvə; ˌʌndɚˋkʌvɚ] *a*. 秘密的,暗中进行的,隐蔽的,掩蔽下的。*an* ~ *scheme* 密谋。

un·der·croft [ˈʌndə-krɔft; ˋʌndɚˌkrɔft] *n*. 地下室,地穴〔尤指教堂的墓穴〕。

un·der·cur·rent [ˈʌndəˌkʌrənt; ˋʌndɚˌkɝənt] *n*. 1. (水流等的)底流,潜流。2. (时势等的)暗流,潜在倾向,潜伏的情绪。3.【电】电流不足。4.【矿】(宽平的)分支洗金槽。

un·der·cut [ˈʌndəkʌt; ˌʌndɚˋkʌt] **I** *n*. 1.〔英〕(牛、猪的)里脊肉。2.〔美〕(伐木的)砍伐切口;伐采不足量。3.【焊】咬边;下陷。4. (网球等)下旋球;【高尔夫球】逆削打法;【拳击】由下上击。**II** [ˈʌndəˈkʌt; ˋʌndɚˌkʌt] *vt*., *vi*. (*-cut*; *~ting*) 1. 从下切割[砍伐];切去(…的)下部;砍进,挖。2. (网球等)用下旋手法击(球);【高尔夫】用逆削法打(球);【商】削低(商品)价格;削价与(竞争者等)抢生意;愿领较低报酬和(他人)抢做某工作。**III** *a*. 下部被削去[切去、挖掉、凿去]的。

un·der·de·vel·op [ˈʌndədiˈveləp; ˌʌndɚdɪˋvɛləp] *vt*., *vi*. 1. (使)发展不充分。2.【摄】(使)显影不足。

un·der·de·vel·oped [ˈʌndədiˈveləpt; ˌʌndɚdɪˋvɛləpt]

U

a. 1. 发展不充分的,不发达的〔尤指经济和工业不够发达,以致生活水准相对低下的〕。2.【摄】显影不足的。～ *nations* 不发达国家。

un·der·do [ˈʌndəˈduː; ˋʌndɚˋdu] *vt*., *vi*. (*-did* [-ˈdid; -ˋdɪd]; *-done* [-ˈdʌn; -ˋdʌn]) 1. 嫩煮,嫩烤(肉等)。2. 不尽全力地做,少做;(使)做得不够。

un·der·dog [ˈʌndədɔg; ˋʌndɚ͵dɔg] *n*. 1. 斗输了的狗;失败者;打败了的选手。2. 退居下风的人;〔美〕地位低的人,受压迫的人。**-ger** *n*. 支持失败者[劣势者等]的人。

un·der·done [ˈʌndəˈdʌn; ͵ʌndɚˋdʌn] *a*. 〔英〕烤[煮]得嫩的;半生不熟的。

un·der·dose [ˈʌndədəus; ˋʌndɚ͵dos] I *vt*. 使服少量[低于通常剂量]的药。II *n*. 小药量,不足的剂量。

un·der·drain [ˈʌndədrein; ˋʌndɚ͵dren] I *n*. 阴沟,暗渠,地下沟道。II [ˈʌndəˈdrein; ˋʌndəˋdren] *vt*. 用暗渠排去(…处)的水。**-age** *n*. 地下排水。

un·der·draw [ˈʌndəˈdrɔː; ͵ʌndɚˋdrɔ] *vt*. (*-drew* [-ˈdruː; -ˋdru]; *-drawn* [-ˈdrɔːn; -ˋdrɔn]) 1. 描画[描写]不充分。2. 在…下划线。**-ing** *n*. 底稿。

un·der·draw·ers [ˈʌndədrɔːəz; ˋʌndɚ͵drɔrz] *n*. 〔*pl*.〕衬裤。

un·der·dress [ˈʌndəˈdres; ͵ʌndɚˋdrɛs] I *vt*., *vi*. (使)穿着得不够郑重,(使)穿过分朴素的服装;(使)穿单薄的衣服。II [ˈʌndədres; ˋʌndɚdrɛs] *n*. = underclothes.

un·der·em·ployed [ˌʌndəimˈplɔid; ͵ʌndɚɛmˋplɔɪd] *a*. 1. 未充分就业的〔尤指非全日性雇佣,以致生活水准低下的〕。2. 未按专长雇佣的〔本是技工,干的是技术性很低的工作,故工资低微〕。

un·der·em·ploy·ment [ˌʌndəimˈplɔimənt; ͵ʌndɚɪmˋplɔɪmənt] *n*. 1. 未充分就业。2. 未按专长就业。

un·der·es·ti·mate [ˈʌndərˈestimeit; ˋʌndɚˋɛstə͵met] I *vt*. 低估;把…的价值估计过低;看轻;估计不足。II *n*. 过低估价,过低评价;轻视;估计不足(= underestimation)。

un·der·ex·pose [ˈʌndərikˈspəuz; ˋʌndərɪkˋspoz, -ɛkˋspoz] *vt*. (*-posed*; *-pos·ing*)【摄】使(底片等)曝光不足。**-ex·po·sure** [-ˈspəuʒə; -ˋspoʒɚ] *n*.

un·der·fed [ˈʌndəˈfed; ͵ʌndɚˋfɛd] I *v*. underfeed 的过去式和过去分词。II *a*. 没有喂饱[吃饱]的;营养不良的。

un·der·feed [ˈʌndəˈfiːd; ˋʌndɚˋfid] *vt*. (*-fed* [-ˈfed; -ˋfɛd]) 1. 不给…充分的食物,不喂饱。2. 不供给…充分的燃料。3. 从下部给…进料。— *vi*. 减食,吃得不够。

un·der·fired[1] [ˌʌndəˈfaiəd; ͵ʌndɚˋfaɪrd] *a*. (陶器)烧得不够的。

un·der·fired[2] [ˈʌndəˌfaiəd; ͵ʌndɚˋfaɪrd] *a*. (锅炉等的)从下生火[加热]的。

un·der·flow [ˈʌndəfləu; ˋʌndɚˋflo] *n*. = undercurrent.

un·der·foot [ˌʌndəˈfut; ͵ʌndɚˋfʊt] I *ad*. 1. 在脚下;践踏,蹂躏;贱视。2. 〔美口〕挡道,妨碍人,碍手碍脚。II *a*. 1. 在脚下的,在地上的。2. 〔美口〕碍事的。

un·der·fund [ˌʌndəˈfʌnd; ͵ʌndɚˋfʌnd] *vt*. 为…提供的资金不足,没有为…提供足够的资金。

un·der·fur [ˈʌndəfəː; ˋʌndɚ͵fɝ] *n*. (河狸、海豹等长毛下面的)细软绒毛。

un·der·gar·ment [ˈʌndəgaːmənt; ˋʌndɚ͵gɑrmənt] *n*. 衬衣,内衣。

un·der·gird [ˈʌndəˈgəːd; ͵ʌndɚˋgɝd] *vt*. (*-gird·ed* [-ˈgəːdid; -ˋgɝdɪd], *-girt* [-ˈgəːt; -gɝt]) 1. (用绳索等)从底层捆牢[加固]。2. 对…给予支持[提供雄厚基础]。

un·der·glaze [ˈʌndəgleiz; ˋʌndɚ͵glez] I *a*. 【制陶】(陶瓷的花样、色彩等)上釉之前画[着色]的,釉底的。II *n*. 釉下画;釉底色彩。

un·der·go [ʌndəˈgəu; ͵ʌndɚˋgo] *vt*. (*-went* [-ˈwent; -ˋwɛnt]; *-gone* [-ˈgɔn; -ˋgɔn]) 经受(检阅、考验等);经验,经历(变迁等);遭受(苦难等)。

un·der·grad [ˌʌndəˈgræd; ˋʌndɚ͵græd] *n*., *a*. 〔口〕= undergraduate.

un·der·grad·u·ate [ˌʌndəˈgrædjuit; ͵ʌndɚˋgrædʒʊɪt, -͵ɛt] *n*., *a*. (肄业中的)大学生(的)。

un·der·grad·u·ette [ʌndəgrædjuˈet; ͵ʌndɚˋgrædʒʊ͵ɛt] *n*. 〔谑〕大学女生。

un·der·ground [ˈʌndəgraund; ˋʌndɚˋgraʊnd] I *a*. 1. 地(面)下的。2. 隐蔽的,秘密的。3. (电影,报刊等)标新立异的,试刊的,试验性而非正式的。4. 反传统的,反现存体制的,激进的,(艺术等)先锋派的。II *n*. 地面下层;地下空间,地道;〔英〕地下铁道(=〔美〕subway);〔the ～〕地下活动,地下组织。*an* ～ *cellar* 地下室,地窖。～ *water* 地下水。～ *intrigues* 阴谋。～ *movement* 地下活动。～ *party* 地下团体,秘密组织。III [ʌndəˈgraund; ͵ʌndɚˋgraʊnd] *ad*. 在地下;秘密地;偷偷地。*go* ～ 潜入地下。～ **railway** (=〔美〕～ **railroad, subway**) 地下铁道;【美史】〔常作 U- R-〕(反蓄奴组织帮助黑人逃亡到非蓄奴州或加拿大去的)地下渠道[组织]。～ **savages** 〔海俚〕轮机室工作人员。

un·der·grown [ˈʌndəˈgrəun; ˋʌndɚ͵gron] *a*. 发育不全的,未长足的。

un·der·growth [ˈʌndəgrəuθ; ˋʌndɚ͵groθ] *n*. 1. 林下植物,下层林丛,矮树丛,乱丛棵子。2. (兽毛下的)绒毛。3. 发育不全。

un·der·hand [ˈʌndəhænd; ˋʌndɚ͵hænd] *a*., *ad*. 1. 【板球、网球】低位手的[地]〔手的位置在肩或肘的水平线下〕;低手扔[打]的[地];(射箭)瞄准时目标见于左手下方的[地]。2. 秘密的[地];不光明正大的[地],阴险的[地],卑鄙的[地]。

un·der·hand·ed [ˈʌndəhændid; ˋʌndɚˋhændɪd] *a*. 1. 秘密的,暗中的,不光明正大的。2. 人手不足的。**-ly** *ad*. **-ness** *n*.

un·der·hung [ˈʌndəˈhʌŋ; ͵ʌndɚˋhʌŋ] *a*. 1. 下颌突出的。2.【木工】自下承接的;(拉门)靠轮子拉动的;在轨道上滑动的。*an* ～ *spring* 悬簧。

un·der·kill [ˈʌndəkil; ˋʌndɚkɪl] *n*. 核杀伤力不足;不足以达到特定目的的活动。

un·der·laid [ˈʌndəˈleid; ͵ʌndɚˋled] *a*. 1. 放置于下的;【矿】向下延伸的。2. 有垫层的,有底基层的,有下支撑物的。

un·der·lap [ˌʌndəˈlæp; ͵ʌndɚˋlæp] *vt*. (*-lapped*; *-lapping*) 使(某物)局部置于[延伸于](另一物)之下;(伸展时)使部分重叠。

un·der·lay [ˌʌndəˈlei; ͵ʌndɚˋle] (*-laid* [-ˈleid; -ˋled]) I *vt*. (以某物)铺在…的下面;【印】衬垫。— *vi*. 【矿】(矿脉等)向下延伸。II [ˈʌndəlei; ˋʌndɚ͵le] *n*. 1. 【印】下衬。2. (垫在地毯下的)油纸、油布(等)。3. 【矿】向下延伸矿体。

un·der·lease [ˈʌndəˈliːs; ˋʌndɚ͵lis] *n*. 【法】转租,转借。

un·der·let [ˈʌndəˈlet; ͵ʌndɚˋlɛt] *vt*. (～; *～ting*) 廉价租出;转租;转借。

un·der·lie [ˌʌndəˈlai; ͵ʌndɚˋlaɪ] *vt*. (*-lay* [-ˈlei; -ˋle]; *-lain* [-ˈlein; -ˋlen]; *-lying*) 1. 位处在…下面;成为…的基础。2. 【经】拥有优先于…的权利,作为优先于…的担保[抵押品]。3. 【语】成为(派生语的)语根。

un·der·life [ˈʌndəlaif; ˋʌndɚ͵laɪf] *n*. (与表面生活方式不同的)私生活。

un·der·line[1] [ˌʌndəˈlain; ͵ʌndɚˋlaɪn] I *vt*. 1. 划线于…下面,给…划字下线;加强,强调;使突出。2. 在(戏单下面)预告下期节目。II [ˈʌndəlain; ˋʌndɚ͵laɪn] *n*. 1. 字下线。2. (戏单下面的)下期预告。3. 图下说明文字。

un·der·line[2] [ˌʌndəˈlain; ͵ʌndɚˋlaɪn] *vt*. 作…的衬里;衬在…下面。

un·der·lin·en [ˈʌndəlinin; ˋʌndɚ͵lɪnɪn] *n*. (麻布)衬衣,内衣。

un·der·ling [ˈʌndəliŋ; ˋʌndɚlɪŋ] *n*. 〔蔑〕下属,下手。

un·der·lin·ing [ˌʌndəˈlainiŋ; ˋʌndɚ͵laɪnɪŋ] *n*. (衣服

的)里子,衬料。

un·der·lip [ˈʌndəˈlip; ˏʌndəˋlɪp] *n*. 下唇。

un·der·ly·ing [ˈʌndəˈlaiiŋ; ˋʌndəˋlaɪɪŋ] *a*. **1**. 在下的,下层的。**2**. 基础的。**3**. 隐晦的;潜在的。**4**. 【法】(债券)优先的;【经】第一的,(担保、权利等)主要的。*the* ~ *mortgage* 第一担保[抵押]。

un·der·man [ˈʌndəˈmæn; ˋʌndəˏmæn] *vt*. (**-nn-**)给(船只等)配备人员过少。

un·der·manned [ˈʌndəˈmænd; ˋʌndəˋmænd] *a*. 人员[手]不足的。

un·der·men·tion·ed [ˈʌndəˈmenʃənd; ˋʌndəˋmɛnʃənd] *a*. 下述的。

un·der·mine [ˌʌndəˈmain; ˏʌndəˋmaɪn] *vt*. 掘…的下面,在…下面掘地道,暗掘;冲蚀;削弱…的基础;用阴险手段毁损,暗中破坏(名声等);伤害(健康等)。~ *a fortress* 挖地道破坏堡垒。**-r** *n*.

un·der·most [ˈʌndəməust; ˋʌndəˏmost] *a*., *ad*. 最下(位)的[地],最低的[地]。

un·der·neath [ˈʌndəˈniːθ; ˏʌndəˋniθ, -ˋnið] **I** *ad*. **1**. 在下面[底下]。**2**. 在下部[下层]。*wear wool* ~ (外衣)里面穿着毛线衫。*a house rotten* ~ 底部已经坍坏的房屋。*He got* ~ *the skin of his audience*. 他深入了听众的内心。**II** *prep*. **1**. 在…的下面[下部]。**2**. 在…的支配下,隶属于…。**3**. 〔古〕在…的形式下,在…的幌子下。*the river flowing* ~ *the bridge* 在桥下流过的河。*sit* ~ *a tree* 坐在树下。~ *the yoke of* ... 在…的枷锁下。**III** *a*. **1**. 下面的;底层的;较低的。**2**. 潜在的,字里行间的。~ *meanings* 字里行间的意义,弦外之音。**IV** *n*. 下部,下面。*Someone was pushing up from* ~. 有人在下面往上推。

un·der·nour·ish [ˈʌndəˈnʌriʃ; ˋʌndəˋnɝɪʃ] *vt*. 使营养不足;使吃不饱。**-ed** *a*. 营养不足的。**-ment** *n*. 营养不足。

un·der·pants [ˈʌndəˌpænts; ˋʌndəˏpænts] *n*. 〔*pl*.〕衬裤。

un·der·part [ˈʌndəpɑːt; ˋʌndəˏpɑrt] *n*. **1**. (动物的)下体;(飞机机身的)腹部。**2**. 附属地位;次要角色。

un·der·pass [ˈʌndəpɑːs; ˋʌndəˏpæs, -ˏpɑs] *n*. 〔美〕(在铁路等下面通过的)地道;地下通道;下穿交叉道;高架桥下通道。

un·der·pay [ˈʌndəˈpei; ˋʌndəˋpe] *vt*. (**-*paid*** [-peid; -ped]) **1**. 付得太少,付得不足。**2**. 少付…工资,扣付…工资。**-ment** *n*.

un·der·pin [ˌʌndəˈpin; ˏʌndəˋpɪn] *vt*. (**-nn-**) 从下方支持,用东西支撑(建筑物等);加固,使坚固;支援,支持。**-pin·ning** *n*. **1**. 加支柱;支柱,支持物;支承结构,支承基础,墙基;支援。**2**. 〔口〕〔常作 *pl*.〕腿。

un·der·play [ˈʌndəˈplei; ˏʌndəˋple] **I** *vt*., *vi*. **1**. 表演得不充分;故意地不作充分表演。**2**. 【牌戏】扣着(大牌)不出而出小牌;未充分发挥(手中大牌)的威力。**II** [ˈʌndəplei; ˋʌndəˏple] *n*. 含蓄克制的表演;暗中活动;出小牌。

un·der·plot [ˈʌndəplɔt; ˋʌndəˏplɑt] *n*. **1**. (小说、戏剧等的)次要情节,穿插。**2**. 阴谋诡计。

un·der·price [ˌʌndəˈprais; ˏʌndəˋpraɪs] *vt* **1**. 将…的定价低于货物的实际价值。**2**. 削价竞售。

un·der·priv·i·leged [ˈʌndəˈprivilidʒd; ˋʌndəˋprɪvəlɪdʒd] **I** *n*. 〔the ~〕〔总称〕部分基本权利被剥夺的阶层;〔婉〕社会地位低下的阶层。**II** *a*. 享受不到正当权利的;贫困的;社会地位低下的,在社会下层的。

un·der·pro·duc·tion [ˈʌndə-prəˈdʌkʃən; ˋʌndə-prəˋdʌkʃən] *n*. 生产不足(以满足需求)。

under·proof(ed) [ˌʌndəˈpruːf(d); ˋʌndəˋpruf(d)] *a*. 含酒精成分在标准强度以下的。~ *spirit* 纯度低于标准的酒精。

un·der·prop [ˌʌndəˈprɔp; ˏʌndəˋprɑp] *vt*. (**-*pp-***) 支撑于下;支撑;支持。

un·der·quote [ˈʌndəˈkwəut; ˏʌndəˋkwot] *vt*. (**-*quot·ed***; **-*quot·ing***) **1**. 对(货物)报价过低;报价低于(别的价格);报价低于(市场价格)。**2**. 报价低于(其他售者)。

un·der·rate [ˌʌndəˈreit; ˋʌndəˋret] *vt*. 估低,贬低;看轻,轻视。

un·der·run [ˈʌndəˈrʌn; ˏʌndəˋrʌn] **I** *vt*. (**-*ran*** [-ˈræn; -ræn]; ~; **-*run·ning***) **1**. 在…下通过[跑过,穿过,伸展]。**2**. 【海】拉起(缆绳等)从头到尾检查,乘小船沿(缆绳)下方检查。*The boat underran the bridge*. 那艘船从桥下驶过。**II** *n*. **1**. 在下通过的东西;暗流。**2**. 低于估计的产量。

un·der·score [ˌʌndəˈskɔː; ˏʌndəˋskor, -ˋskɔr] **I** *vt*. 在…下面划线;强调。**II** *n*. [ˈʌndəskɔː; ˋʌndəˏskɔr] 字下线。

un·der·sea [ˌʌndəˈsiː; ˋʌndəˋsi] *a*., *ad*. 海面以下,海底的[地]。*ad*. 也作 **un·der·seas**.

un·der·sec·re·ta·ry [ˈʌndəˈsekritəri; ˏʌndəˋsɛkrəˏtɛrɪ] *n*. 副部长,次长。*Under-Secretary of State* 〔美〕副国务卿。

un·der·sell [ˈʌndəˈsel; ˏʌndəˋsɛl] *vt*. (**-*sold*** [-ˈsəuld; -ˋsold]) 以低于别人的价格出售;廉价出售。

un·der·set[1] [ˈʌndəˈset; ˏʌndəˋsɛt] *vt*. (~; **-*set·ting***) **1**. 支撑;支持;放在…下面。**2**. 〔英〕转租,转借。

un·der·set[2] [ˈʌndəset; ˋʌndəˏsɛt] *n*. (和海面风向或流向相反的)底流;【矿】下部矿脉。

un·der·sexed [ˈʌndəˈsekst; ˏʌndəˋsɛkst] *a*. 性欲不强的,性欲冷淡的。

un·der·sher·iff [ˈʌndəˌʃerif; ˋʌndəˏʃɛrɪf] *n*. 副郡长,县副警长。

un·der·shirt [ˈʌndəʃəːt; ˋʌndəˏʃɝt] *n*. (衬衫里面的)汗衫,贴身内衣。

un·der·shoot [ˌʌndəˈʃuːt; ˏʌndəˋʃut] *vt*. (**-*shot*** [-ˈʃɔt; -ˋʃɑt]) **1**. (发射炮弹、射箭等)因角度太低而脱(靶),因射程太短而未达(目标)。**2**. (飞机因失速等)降落未达(跑道、着路场)。— *vi*. 脱靶,未达目标。

un·der·shorts [ˈʌndəˌʃɔːts; ˋʌndəˏʃɔrts] *n*. 〔*pl*.〕(男人和儿童穿的)裤衩。

un·der·shot [ˈʌndəʃɔt; ˋʌndəˏʃɑt] *a*. 下射的,(水轮)下击的;下部[下半部]突出的。

un·der·shrub [ˈʌndəʃrʌb; ˋʌndəˏʃrʌb] *n*. 小灌木(丛)。

un·der·side [ˈʌndəsaid; ˋʌndəˏsaɪd] *n*. 下面;内面;小腹。

un·der·sign [ˌʌndəˈsain; ˏʌndəˋsaɪn] *vt*. 在(文件、信等)的下面[后面]签名。*the* ~***ed*** [ˈʌndəsaind; ˏʌndəˋsaɪnd] 在下面签名者〔用作单或复〕。

un·der·size(d) [ˈʌndəˈsaiz(d); ˋʌndəˋsaɪz(d)] *a*. **1**. 比普通小的,小型的;个子小的;不够大的。**2**. (矿砂等)经过一定规格筛孔中筛下的。

un·der·skirt [ˈʌndəˈskəːt; ˋʌndəˏskɝt] *n*. 衬裙。

un·der·slung [ˈʌndəˈslʌŋ; ˏʌndəˋslʌŋ] *a*. **1**. (汽车底盘)装附于车轴弹簧上的。**2**. 重心在底部的,下大上小的。**3**. (嘴合拢后)下齿突出于上齿外的,突下颌的。

un·der·soil [ˈʌndəsoil; ˋʌndəˏsɔɪl] *n*. 心土,底土,地面下的土壤。

un·der·song [ˈʌndəˌsɔŋ; ˋʌndəˏsɔŋ] *n*. 【乐】(歌曲的)伴唱附歌;〔喻〕言外之意。

un·der·spin [ˈʌndəspin; ˋʌndəˏspɪn] *n*. 球的朝后方旋转。

un·der·staffed [ˈʌndəˈstɑːft, -ˈstæft; ˏʌndəˋstæft, -ˋstɑft] *a*. 人员减少的;人手不足的。

un·der·stand [ˌʌndəˈstænd; ˏʌndəˋstænd] *vt*. (**-*stood*** [-ˈstud; -ˋstʊd]; **-*stood***, 〔古〕**~*ed***) **1**. 懂得;了解,明白,理解,领悟,领会(真意等);熟悉,通晓(学问等);知道,晓得对付(孩子、马等)。**2**. 听说,获悉。**3**. 推测,推定,以为;以为当然。**4**. 〔常用被动语态〕隐含,不言而喻地省略(话等)。*Do you* ~ *me*? 你懂我的意思吗? *He*

U

~*s French*. 他懂法语。*I fail to* ~ *the reason*. 我不了解那个理由。*Am I to* ~ *that you refuse*? 你是说不愿意吗? *Please* ~ *me, I absolutely refuse*. 请你不要弄错,我是绝对拒绝的。*I* ~ *him to say that* ... 我以为他是说…。*Do I* ~ (*you to say*) *that* ...? 那么你是说…吗? *In this case the verb may be understood*. 这种情形动词可以省掉。— ***vi***. **1**. 懂得,了解,明白,理解;有理解力。**2**. 谅解。**3**. 听说。*When you speak Japanese she cannot* ~. 你讲日语她不懂。*Do animals* ~? 动物有理解力吗? *He is ill, I* ~. 我听说他生病了。***a tongue not understood by the people*** 异邦之言,外国语。***give sb. to*** ~ ***that*** 通知某人…,告诉某人…;使某人领会… (*He gave me to* ~ *that* ... 他说…)。***It is understood that*** ... 当然…;不用说…。***It must be understood that*** ... 话得说明白…。***make oneself understood*** 使自己的意思为人了解,说明自己的意思 (*Can you make yourself understood in English*? 你能用英语说明你的意思吗?)。***Now***, ~ ***me***! 喂,听着! 〔常表示惊恐或警告〕。~ ***one another*** 互相了解,互相谅解,互相同情(而要好起来)。**-a·ble** ***a***. 可懂的,可理解的。

un·der·stand·ing [ˌʌndəˈstændiŋ; ˏʌndɚˋstændɪŋ] **I** ***n***. **1**. 认识,了解,理解,领悟,理会。**2**. 悟性,理解力,智力;【哲】知性 〔*opp*. reason〕。**3**. 谅解;同情;默契;协议;约定;条件。**4**. 〔*pl*.〕〔英俚、谑〕鞋;脚。*It is a matter of* ~. 那是认识问题。*a man of* ~ 头脑清楚的人。*a man without* ~ 头脑不清楚的人。*a tacit* ~ 默契。***arrive at*** [***come to***] ***an*** ~ ***with*** ... 和…取得谅解,和…达成(非正式的)协议。***have*** [***keep***] ***a good*** ~ ***with*** ... 和…意见一致。***on the*** ~ ***that*** ... 给…为条件。***on this*** ~ = ***with this*** ~ 以这条件,在这一谅解之下。**II** ***a***. **1**. 能体谅别人的,通情达理的。**2**. 明智的,聪明的,颖悟的。*an* ~ *man* 通情达理的人。

un·der·state [ˈʌndəˈsteit; ˋʌndɚˋstet] ***vt***. 打着折扣说,有意识地轻描淡写;少报(损失等),少说(能力、要求等) (*opp*. exaggerate)。

un·der·state·ment [ˈʌndəˈsteitmənt; ˋʌndɚˏstetmənt, ˏʌndɚˋstet-] ***n***. **1**. 掩饰;轻描淡写。**2**. 有节制的陈述。

un·der·stock[1] [ˈʌndəˈstɔk; ˏʌndɚˋstɑk] **I** ***vt***. **1**. 不充分供应,使存货不充足。**2**. 不充分供应(农场等)牲畜。**II** [ˈʌndəstɔk; ˋʌndɚstɑk] ***n***. 存货不足。

un·der·stock[2] [ˈʌndəstɔk; ˋʌndɚˏstɑk] ***n***. 【植】(嫁接用的)砧木。

un·der·stood [ˌʌndəˈstud; ˏʌndɚˋstʊd] **I** understand 的过去式及过去分词。**II** ***a***. **1**. 得到充分理解的。**2**. 取得同意的。**3**. 不言自明的。

un·der·strap·per [ˈʌndəstræpə; ˋʌndɚˏstræpɚ] ***n***. 〔口〕= underling.

un·der·stra·tum [ˈʌndəˈstreitəm; ˋʌndɚˏstretəm] ***n***. (*pl*. ~***s***, ***-ta*** [-tə; -tə]) = substratum.

un·der·strength [ˈʌndəˈstreŋθ; ˋʌndɚˏstrɛŋθ] ***a***. **1**. 力量不足的,强度不够的。**2**. 兵员不足的。

un·der·struc·ture [ˈʌndəˌstrʌktʃə; ˋʌndɚˏstrʌktʃɚ] ***n***. 基础,下层结构。

un·der·stud·y [ˈʌndəstʌdi; ˋʌndɚˏstʌdɪ] **I** ***vt***. **1**. 【剧】练习做(临时替角);临时代替(某演员)演出。**2**. 实地研习,实习(某工作)。**II** ***n***. **1**. 垫角,临时替角,候补演员;〔美运〕后补队员。**2**. 候补人员;生力军。

un·der·sur·face [ˈʌndəˈsəːfis; ˋʌndɚˏsɝfɪs] **I** ***n***. 底面。**II** ***a***. 水面下的;表面下的。*an* ~ *craft* 潜水艇。

un·der·take [ˌʌndəˈteik; ˏʌndɚˋtek] ***vt***. (***-took*** [-ˈtuk; -ˋtʊk]; ***-ta·ken*** [-ˈteikən; -ˋtekən]) **1**. 承担;承办;答应,约定 (*to do sth*.)。**2**. 担保,保证 (*that*)。**3**. 断言 (*that*)。**4**. 着手,从事。**5**. 〔古〕向…挑战。*He undertook to be here at ten o'clock*. 他答应十点钟到这儿来。~ *a dangerous task* 承担一件危险任务。— ***vi***. **1**. 〔古〕担保,保证,负责,做证人 (*for*);应承,约定。**2**. [ˈʌndəteik; ˋʌndɚtek] 〔口〕承办丧事。*He undertook for her security*. 他保证她的安全。

un·der·tak·er [ˌʌndəˈteikə; ˏʌndɚˋtekɚ] ***n***. **1**. 承担人,承办人;计划者,营业者。**2**. [ˈʌndəteikə; ˋʌndɚtekɚ] 殡仪事业经营人。

un·der·tak·ing [ˌʌndəˈteikiŋ; ˏʌndɚˋtekɪŋ] ***n***. **1**. 计划,企图;承办,承包;事业,企业;工作。**2**. 担保,保证,应承,约定。**3**. [ˈʌndəteikiŋ; ˋʌndɚtekɪŋ] 殡仪事业。*welfare* ~*s* 生活福利事业。

un·der·ten·ant [ˈʌndəˈtenənt; ˋʌndɚˏtɛnənt] ***n***. 转租的承租人。

under-the-counter [ˈʌndəðəˈkauntə; ˋʌndɚðəˋkaʊntɚ] ***a***. 〔口〕**1**. 秘密(出售)的;走后门的;非法的。**2**. 稀罕的,贵重的。

under-the-table [ˈʌndəðəˈteibl; ˋʌndɚðəˋtebl] ***a***. 秘密的,暗中进行的。~ **payment** (为达到逃税等目的而用现金进行的)秘密付款,账外付款。

un·der·things [ˈʌndəθiŋz; ˋʌndɚˏθɪŋz] ***n***. 〔*pl*.〕(女用)内衣裤。

un·der·tint [ˈʌndətint; ˋʌndɚˋtɪnt] ***n***. 淡色;浅色;柔和的颜色。

un·der·tone [ˈʌndətəun; ˋʌndɚˏton] ***n***. **1**. 低音;小声。**2**. 潜在性质[成分,意义];(市场的)潜在趋势。**3**. 浅色,淡色;底色。

un·der·took [ˌʌndəˈtuk; ˏʌndɚˋtʊk] undertake 的过去式。

un·der·tow [ˈʌndətəu; ˋʌndɚˏto] ***n***. **1**. 从岸边退回去的浪,退浪。**2**. 【地】底流,下层逆流。

un·der·trick [ˈʌndətrik; ˋʌndɚtrɪk] ***n***. 【桥牌】未完成定约的任一墩(牌)。

un·der·val·u·a·tion [ˈʌndəˌvæljuˈeiʃən; ˋʌndɚˏvæljʊˋeʃən] ***n***. 低估价值,过低评价;轻视。

un·der·val·ue [ˌʌndəˈvæljuː; ˋʌndɚˋvælju] ***vt***. **1**. 把…的价值估低[评价过低];看轻,小看,轻视。**2**. 降低…的价值。

un·der·vest [ˈʌndəˈvest; ˋʌndɚˋvɛst] ***n***. 〔英〕汗衫,贴身衣 (=〔美〕undershirt)。

un·der·waist [ˈʌndəweist; ˋʌndɚˏwest] ***n***. 〔美〕穿在罩衫下的内衫;小孩的内衣。

un·der·wa·ter [ˈʌndəˈwɔːtə; ˋʌndɚˏwɔtɚ, -ˏwɑtɚ] **I** ***a***. **1**. 在水下的,水中的。**2**. 用于水下的。**3**. 【船】吃水线以下的。*an* ~ *boat* 潜水艇。**II** ***ad***. **1**. 在水下。**2**. 【船】在吃水线以下。**III** ***n***. (海洋等)水面下的水;水下,水底。

un·der·way [ˈʌndəˈwei; ˏʌndɚˋwe] **I** ***a***. **1**. 【海】在航行中的。**2**. 在旅途[行进]中(发生、进行、使用)的;正在进行[工作]中的。**II** ***ad***. 进行中(= under way)。

un·der·wear [ˈʌndəwɛə; ˋʌndɚˏwɛr] ***n***. 〔集合词〕衬衣,内衣。

un·der·weight [ˈʌndəˈweit, 形容词读作 ˌʌndəˈweit; ˋʌndɚˋwet, ˏʌndɚˋwet] ***n***., ***a***. 重量不足(的)。

un·der·went [ˌʌndəˈwent; ˏʌndɚˋwɛnt] undergo 的过去式。

un·der·wing [ˈʌndəwiŋ; ˋʌndɚˏwɪŋ] ***n***. (昆虫的)后翅。

Un·der·wood [ˈʌndəwud; ˋʌndɚwʊd] ***n***. 安德伍德〔姓氏〕。

un·der·wood [ˈʌndəwud; ˋʌndɚˏwʊd] ***n***. = undergrowth.

un·der·work [ˈʌndəˈwəːk; ˏʌndɚˋwɝk] **I** ***vt***. (***-worked***; 〔古〕***-wrought*** [-ˈrɔːt; -ˋrɔt]) **1**. 对…付出的劳力不够;对…未尽力工作;未完成。**2**. 未充分使用;不使(牛马等)尽力劳动。**3**. 拿低于…的工资工作。— ***vi***. 不尽力劳动[工作],劳动[工作]得不够。**II** [ˈʌndəwəːk; ˋʌndɚˏwɝk] ***n***. **1**. 附属工作,杂务。**2**. 松松散散的工作。**3**. 【建】支持结构,下层结构,根基。

un·der·world [ˈʌndəwəːld; ˋʌndɚˏwɝld] ***n***. **1**. 下界,地狱,阴间。**2**. (地球另一面的)对跖点。**3**. 下层社会,社

会的底层〔尤指从事卖淫、盗窃等罪恶活动的社会集团〕。**4**.〔古〕地上;地球。

un·der·write [ˈʌndərait; ˌʌndəˋraɪt] *vt*. (*-wrote* [-rəut; -rot]; *-writ·ten* [-ˌritn; -ˌrɪtn]) **1**.〔除过去分词外不常用〕写在下面,署名。**2**. 签名承认[担保],签名接受(保险);签名承受,认购,认捐;赞同。*the under-written signatures* [*names*] 签名人。— *vi*. 经营(海上)保险业。

un·der·writ·er [ˈʌndəraitə; ˋʌndəˌraɪtə] *n*. **1**. 保险商;(特指)水险商。**2**. (股份、公债等的)承购人。**3**. 承诺支付者。

un·der·writ·ing [ˈʌndəraitiŋ; ˋʌndəˌraɪtɪŋ] *n*. **1**. 保险业;水险业。**2**. (股份等的)签名承受。*an U- Member* 〔英〕伦敦劳埃德 (Lloyd) 船舶协会的正式会员。

un·der·wrought [ˈʌndəˈrɔːt; ˌʌndəˋrɔt] underwork 的过去式及过去分词。

un·de·scrib·a·ble [ˈʌndisˈkraibəbl; ˌʌndɪˋskraɪbəbl̩] *a*. 无法描写的,难用笔墨形容的。

un·de·served [ˈʌndiˈzəːvd; ˌʌndɪˋzɝvd] *a*. **1**. 不该受的,不应得的,不当的。**2**. 冤枉的。**-ly** [-ˈsəːvidli; -ˋsɝvɪdlɪ] *ad*.

un·de·serv·ing [ˈʌndiˈzəːviŋ; ˌʌndɪˋzɝvɪŋ] *a*. 不配…的,不值得…的 (*of*)。*Such trifles are* ~ *of attention*. 这类鸡毛蒜皮的小事不值得注意。

un·de·signed [ˈʌndiˈzaind; ˌʌndɪˋzaɪnd] *a*. 不是故意的,非预谋的;无意中做的,偶然的。**-ly** *ad*. 无意中,偶然。

un·de·sign·ing [ˈʌndiˈzainiŋ; ˌʌndɪˋzaɪnɪŋ] *a*. 无欺的;直爽的;诚实的;不狡诈的;不卑劣的。

un·de·sir·a·bil·i·ty [ˈʌndiˌzaiərəˈbiliti; ˌʌndɪˌzaɪrəˋbɪlətɪ] *n*. 不受欢迎,讨厌,不愉快;不合需要。

un·de·sir·a·ble [ˈʌndiˈzaiərəbl; ˌʌndɪˋzaɪrəbl̩] **I** *a*. 不合要求的,不受欢迎的,不良的,讨厌的,不愉快的,不方便的。~ *aliens* 不受欢迎的外国人。*at a most* ~ *moment* 在最不巧的时候。**II** *n*. **1**. 不受欢迎的人[东西]。**2**. 不良份子。**-a·bly** *ad*.

un·de·tect·ed [ˈʌndiˈtektid; ˌʌndɪˋtɛktɪd] *a*. 没有被发现的,没有被识破的。

un·de·ter·mined [ˈʌndiˈtəːmind; ˌʌndɪˋtɝmɪnd] *a*. **1**. 未确定的,尚待确定的。**2**. 优柔寡断的,没有决断力的。

un·de·vel·oped [ˈʌndiˈveləpt; ˌʌndɪˋvɛləpt] *a*. 不发达的,未发展的;(土地等)未开发的。

un·de·vi·at·ing [ʌnˈdiːvieitiŋ; ʌnˋdivɪˌetɪŋ] *a*. 未离正道的,没有迷失正路[方向]的。**-ly** *ad*.

un·de·vout [ˈʌndiˈvaut; ˌʌndɪˋvaʊt] *a*. 没有敬神念头的,不虔诚的。**-ly** *ad*.

un·did [ʌnˈdid; ʌnˋdɪd] undo 的过去式。

un·dies [ˈʌndiz; ˋʌndɪz] *n*.〔*pl*.〕〔俚〕女用内衣。

un·dif·fer·en·ti·at·ed [ˈʌnˌdifəˈrenʃieitid; ˌʌndɪfəˋrɛnʃɪˌetɪd] *a*. 无差别的;一致的。

un·dig·ni·fied [ʌnˈdignifaid; ʌnˋdɪgnəˌfaɪd] *a*. 不尊严的,不庄重的;有损尊严的,不体面的,不像样的。

un·di·lut·ed [ˈʌndaiˈljuːtid; ˌʌndɪˋlutɪd] *a*. 没有冲淡的,没有搀杂的,未稀释的;纯粹的。

un·di·min·ished [ˈʌndiˈminiʃt; ˌʌndəˋmɪnɪʃt] *a*. 没有减少的,没有衰落的,没有降低的。

un·dine[1] [ˈʌndiːn; ˋʌndin] *n*. 女水仙,水中精灵〔据说须和凡人结婚后才能具有灵魂和生孩子〕。

un·dine[2] [ˈʌndain; ˋʌndaɪn] *n*.【医】洗鼻器;洗眼壶。

un·di·rect·ed [ˈʌndiˈrektid; ˌʌndəˋrɛktɪd] *a*. **1**. 未受指导的;不受指引的。**2**. (信等)未写姓名住址的,无通讯处的。

un·dis·cern·ing [ˈʌndiˈsəːniŋ, -ˈzəː-; ˌʌndɪˋzɝnɪŋ] *a*. 没有识别力的;感觉迟钝的。

un·dis·charged [ˈʌndisˈtʃɑːdʒd; ˌʌndɪsˋtʃɑrdʒd] *a*. **1**. (货等)未卸下的。**2**. (水等)未放[排]出的,(炮弹等)未引发的,未射出的。**3**. (人员等)未遣散的。**4**. (职责等)未履行的;(债务等)未偿清的。

un·dis·ci·plined [ʌnˈdisiplind; ʌnˋdɪsəˌplɪnd] *a*. **1**. 没有训练的,训练不足的。**2**. 没有修养的;散漫的,(军队等)无纪律的。

un·dis·closed [ˈʌndisˈkləuzd; ˌʌndɪsˋklozd] *a*. **1**. 未让人知的,未泄露的。**2**. 没有指名的;身分不明的。

un·dis·cov·ered [ˈʌndisˈkʌvəd; ˌʌndɪˋskʌvɚd] *a*. 未被发现的;未知的;隐藏的。

un·dis·crim·i·nat·ing [ˈʌndisˈkrimineitiŋ; ˌʌndɪˋskrɪməˌnetɪŋ] *a*. **1**. 不加区别的;不分青红皂白的;一视同仁的。**2**. 无鉴别力的。

un·dis·guised [ˈʌndisˈgaizd; ˌʌndɪsˋgaɪzd] *a*. 没有伪装的;不掩饰的;露骨的,公然的,赤裸裸的。**-ly** *ad*.

un·dis·mayed [ˈʌndisˈmeid; ˌʌndɪsˋmed] *a*. 不沮丧的,不气馁的;镇定自若的,不害怕的。*be* ~ *by failure* 不为失败所吓倒。

un·dis·posed [ˈʌndisˈpəuzd; ˌʌndɪˋspozd] *a*. **1**. 未处理的,未卖出的。**2**. (身体)不适的,不爽的。**3**. 不乐意的,不想的 (*to do sth*.)。

un·dis·put·ed [ˈʌndisˈpjuːtid; ˌʌndɪˋspjutɪd] *a*. 无争议的,无疑的,确实的,当然的。

un·dis·so·ci·at·ed [ˈʌndiˈsəuʃieitid; ˌʌndɪˋsoʃɪetɪd] *a*.【化】未离解的。

un·dis·tin·guish·a·ble [ˈʌndisˈtiŋgwiʃəbl; ˌʌndɪˋstɪŋgwɪʃəbl̩] *a*. 不能区别的,分别不清的;紊乱的。

un·dis·tin·guished [ˈʌndisˈtiŋgwiʃt; ˌʌndɪˋstɪŋgwɪʃt] *a*. **1**. 未区别开的,不加分别的。**2**. 听[看]不清楚的。**3**. 不特别显眼的;不著名的,平凡的。

un·dis·tort·ed [ˈʌndisˈtɔːtid; ˌʌndɪsˋtɔrtɪd] *a*. **1**. 未失真的。**2**. 不偏激的,不极端的。

un·dis·turbed [ˈʌndisˈtəːbd; ˌʌndɪˋstɝbd] *a*. 没有受到搅乱[干扰、妨碍]的;镇静的;泰然自若的。

un·di·ver·si·fied [ˈʌndaiˈvəːsifaid; ˌʌndəˋvɝsɪˌfaɪd] *a*. 没有变化的,千篇一律的;单一的。

un·di·vid·ed [ˈʌndiˈvaidid; ˌʌndəˋvaɪdɪd] *a*. **1**. 没有分开的;(利润等)未分配的。**2**. 连绵不断的;完整的。**3**. 专心的,专一的。~ *attention* 专心。

un·do [ʌnˈduː; ʌnˋdu] *vt*. (*-did* [-ˈdid; -ˋdɪd]; *-done* [-ˈdʌn; -ˋdʌn]) **1**. 使恢复原状,使复旧;取消,废除。**2**. 脱去,拆去,解开,打开,放松。**3**.〔古〕解释,说明,解(谜等)。**4**. 破坏;毁灭;糟蹋;败坏;使落魄,使破落。**5**. 勾引,诱奸。*What's done cannot be undone*. 覆水难收。*It is better for the doer to* ~ *what he has done*. 解铃还需系铃人。~ *a match* 解除婚约。~ *a parcel* 打开包裹。~ *a knot* 解开结子。

un·dock [ʌnˈdɔk; ʌnˋdɑk] *vt*., *vi*. **1**.【海】(使)(船)驶出船坞[驶离码头]。**2**.【宇】(使)(会合后的宇宙飞船)在宇宙空间中相脱离。

un·do·er [ʌnˈduːə; ˌʌnˋduɚ] *n*. **1**. 取消者。**2**. 解开…的人。**3**. 败坏者,毁掉(别人)的人,诱惑者。

un·do·ing [ʌnˈduːiŋ; ʌnˋduɪŋ] *n*. **1**. 复旧,取消。**2**. 解开。**3**. 毁灭,败坏,破落;祸根。*Drink will be his* ~. 喝酒将使他毁灭。

un·do·mes·ti·cated [ˈʌndəˈmestikeitid; ˌʌndəˋmɛstɪˌketɪd] *a*. **1**. 不适于[不惯于]家庭生活的(人)。**2**. (动物)未驯服的。

un·done[1] [ʌnˈdʌn; ʌnˋdʌn] **I** undo 的过去分词。**II** *a*. **1**. 脱去的,解开的,放松的。**2**. 毁灭的,败坏的,破落的。*The package came* ~. 行李解开了。*I am* ~. 我已经不行啦[完啦]!

undone[2] [ˈʌndʌn; ˋʌndʌn] *a*. 没有做的,未做完的。*leave* (*things*) ~ (把事情)放着不做,搁起来。*remain* ~ 未做。

un·dou·ble [ʌnˈdʌbl; ʌnˋdʌbl̩] *vt*. (*-bled*; *-bling*) **1**. 使之不再成倍。**2**. 展开,摊开,使挺直。

un·doubt·ed [ʌnˈdautid; ʌnˋdaʊtɪd] *a*. 没有疑问的,肯定的,确实的,真正的。**-ly** *ad*.

un·doubt·ing [ʌnˈdautiŋ; ʌnˋdaʊtɪŋ] *a*. 不怀疑的;信

任的。

UNDP = United Nations Development Program(me) 联合国发展方案〔或译联合国发展计划署,系联合国管理援助或支援发展中国家的各种基金的一个机构〕。

un·dra·mat·ic [ˈʌndrəˈmætik; ˌʌndrəˋmætɪk] *a*. 1. 缺乏戏剧性的,平淡无奇的,非戏剧化的。2. 不适合于戏剧[舞台]的。

un·drape [ˈʌnˈdreip; ʌnˋdrep] *vt*. 1. 使脱去衣服。2. 揭开,打开。**-d** *a*. 1. 没有用布盖着的。2. 没有穿衣服的,裸体的。

un·draw [ˈʌndrɔː; ʌnˋdrɔ] *vt*., *vi*. (**-drew** [-ˈdruː; -ˋdru]; **-drawn** [-ˈdrɔːn; -ˋdrɔn]) 拉回来,拉向旁边,拉开(帐幕等)。

un·dreamed-of, un·dreamt-of [ʌnˈdremtɔv; ʌnˋdrimdɑv] *a*. 梦想不到的,意外的。

un·dress [ˈʌnˈdres; ʌnˋdrɛs] **I** *vt*. 1. 使脱去[脱光]衣服。2. 使卸下装饰。3. 暴露,剥除…的伪装。4.【医】解掉…的绷带。~ *oneself* 脱衣服。— *vi*. 脱衣服。**II** *n*. (家常)便服;【军】军便服。

un·dressed[1] [ˈʌnˈdrest; ʌnˋdrɛst] *a*. 1. 没有穿衣服的,裸体的。2. 穿着家常便服的;未穿与当时情况所要求的服装的。

un·dressed[2] [ˈʌndrest; ˋʌndrɛst] *a*. 1. 没有扎绷带的。2. 没有加调料[配料]的,未加工的;没有整理好的;(皮等)未鞣的。~ *meat* 未加调味品的肉。~ *leather* 生皮。~ *ore* 原矿。

un·due [ˈʌnˈdjuː; ʌnˋdju] *a*. 1. 过度的,过分的,不相称的。2. 非常的。3. 不正当的,非法的。4.【商】(期票等)未到期的。*Don't treat the matter with ~ haste*. 不要过急的处理那个问题。~ ***influence***【法】不当压迫,威胁手段。

un·du·lant [ˈʌndjulənt; ˋʌndjələnt, -də-] *a*. 波状的,波动的。~ **fever**【医】波状热,布鲁氏杆菌病。

un·du·late [ˈʌndjuleit; ˋʌndjəˌlet] **I** *vi*. (水面、风中的麦田等)波动,起浪;(土地等)起伏。— *vt*. 使波动,使起伏。**II** [ˈʌndjulit; ˋʌndjəlɪt] *a*. 波状的,波动起伏的(= undulated)。**-lat·ing** *a*. **-lat·ing·ly** *ad*.

un·du·la·tion [ˌʌndjuˈleiʃən; ˌʌndjəˋleʃən] *n*. 波动;波状起伏;【物】波动,振动;【医】搏动,心跳。

un·du·la·to·ry [ˈʌndjulətəri; ˋʌndjələˌtorɪ] *a*. 波动的;起伏的;波浪形的。*the ~ theory* (*of light*)【物】(光的)波动说。

un·du·ly [ˈʌnˈdjuːli; ʌnˋdjulɪ, -ˋdulɪ] *ad*. 不相称地;不适[正]当地;过度。

un·du·pli·cat·ed [ʌnˈdjuːplikeitid; ʌnˋdjupləˌketɪd] *a*. 1. 未复制的。2. 无匹敌的;无法模拟的。

un·du·ti·ful [ˈʌnˈdjuːtifəl; ʌnˋdjutɪfəl, -ˋdu-] *a*. 不顺从的,不忠的;不尽责的。**-ly** *ad*.

un·dy·ing [ʌnˈdaiiŋ; ʌnˋdaɪɪŋ] *a*. 不死的,不朽的,永恒的;不绝的,无休止的。**-ly** *ad*.

un·earned [ˈʌnˈəːnd; ʌnˋɝnd] *a*. (收入等)不劳而获的;分外的。~ *income* 不劳所得。~ *increment* (土地的)自然增值。

un·earth [ˈʌnˈəːθ; ʌnˋɝθ] *vt*. 1. (从地中)掘出;从洞中赶出(狐等)。2. 发现;揭露,揭发(阴谋等)。

un·earth·ly [ʌnˈəːθli; ʌnˋɝθlɪ] *a*. 1. 不是这个世界的,非尘世的,超自然的。2. 神秘的;可怕的,令人毛骨悚然的,奇怪的。3. 〔口〕荒谬的。*Why call me at this ~ hour*? 怎么在这个时候叫醒我? **-li·ness** *n*.

un·eas·y [ʌnˈiːzi; ʌnˋizɪ] *a*. 1. 不安的;忧虑的,担心的。2. 不舒服的,不自在的,不适意的,拘束的。3. 〔罕〕不容易的,困难的。*feel ~ about the result* 对将来结果忧虑不安。*feel ~ in tight clothes* 衣服紧,觉得不舒服。~ *manners* 不自然的态度。**-i·ly** *ad*. **-i·ness** *n*.

un·e·co·nom·ic, -i·cal [ˈʌnˌiːkəˈnɔmik, -əl; ˌʌnikəˋnɑmɪk, -əl] *a*. 不经济的;浪费的。

UNEDA = United Nations Economic Development Administration 联合国经济开发署。

un·ed·i·fy·ing [ˈʌnˈedifaiiŋ; ʌnˋɛdəˌfaɪɪŋ] *a*. 1. 不起启发[开导]作用的。2. (道德上)不体面的,不光彩的。

un·ed·it·ed [ˈʌnˈeditid; ʌnˋɛdɪtɪd] *a*. 1. 未作过编辑加工的。2. 未刊行的。3. (新闻等)未经审查的;【影】未剪辑的。

un·ed·u·cat·ed [ˈʌnˈedjukeitid; ʌnˋɛdʒəˌketɪd] *a*. 没受教育的,失学的,没有知识的。

UNEF = United Nations Emergency Force 联合国紧急部队。

un·e·mo·tion·al [ˈʌniˈməuʃənl; ˌʌnɪˋmoʃənl̩, -ʃnəl] *a*. 不易激动的;缺乏感情的;冷漠的。

un·em·ploy·a·ble [ˈʌnimˈplɔiəbl; ˌʌnɪmˋplɔɪəbl̩] **I** *a*. 不适于[不能被]雇用的。**II** *n*. 不能被雇用的人。

un·em·ployed [ˈʌnimˈplɔid; ˌʌnɪmˋplɔɪd] **I** *a*. 1. 没有受雇用的,失业的。2. 不用的,未加利用的,闲置的;空闲的。**II** *n*. 〔the ~〕〔集合词〕失业者。~ **capital**【商】游资。

un·em·ploy·ment [ˈʌnimˈplɔimənt; ˌʌnɪmˋplɔɪmənt] *n*. 失业;失业状况。~ **benefit** [**compensation**] 失业救济。~ **dole** 失业津贴。~ **insurance** 失业保险。~ **pay** 失业补贴。

un·en·closed [ˈʌninˈkləuzd; ˌʌnɪnˋklozd] *a*. 1. 没有(用墙、篱等)围起来的;公共的。2. (修道院等)没有被围墙与世隔绝的;(修女等)不住在修道院内的。

un·en·cum·bered [ˈʌninˈkʌmbəd; ˌʌnɪnˋkʌmbɚd] *a*. 不受妨碍的;没有(债务、子女等)负担的。

un·end·ing [ʌnˈendiŋ; ʌnˋɛndɪŋ] *a*. 1. 无尽的,不停的,不断的。2. 无穷的,永久的。

un·en·dorsed [ˈʌninˈdɔːst; ˌʌnɪnˋdɔrst] *a*. 1. 未背书的。2. 未认可的;未准许的。

un·en·dur·a·ble [ˈʌninˈdjuərəbl; ˌʌnɪnˋdjʊrəbl̩, -ˋdʊr-] *a*. 不可容忍的,难忍受的。

un·en·gaged [ˈʌninˈgeidʒd; ˌʌnɪnˋgedʒd] *a*. 1. 没有约定的;未定婚的。2. 没有占用的;有空的,闲着无事的。

un-Eng·lish [ˈʌnˈiŋgliʃ; ʌnˋɪŋglɪʃ] *a*. 非英国式的;不像英国人的;不符合英语习惯的。

un·en·light·ened [ˈʌninˈlaitnd; ˌʌnɪnˋlaɪtnd] *a*. 1. 〔古〕未照亮的。2. 落后的;无知的,未经启蒙的。

un·en·tan·gle [ˈʌninˈtæŋgl; ˌʌnɪnˋtæŋgl̩] *vt*. 解开(结等);排解(纠纷等)。

un·en·ter·pris·ing [ˈʌnˈentəpraiziŋ; ʌnˋɛntɚˌpraɪzɪŋ] *a*. 1. 无事业心的;没有冒险精神的。2. 疲沓的;保守的。

un·en·vi·a·ble [ˈʌnˈenviəbl; ʌnˋɛnvɪəbl̩] *a*. 不值得羡慕的。**-a·bly** *ad*.

un·en·vi·ous [ˈʌnˈenviəs; ʌnˋɛnvɪəs] *a*. 1. 不妒忌的;无恶意的。2. 不吝惜的。

UNEP [ˈjuːnep; ˋjunɛp] *n*. 联合国环境规划署〔成立于1972年,系 United Nations Environment Program 之缩略〕。

un·eq·ua·ble [ˈʌnˈekwəbl; ʌnˋɛkwəbl, -ˋikwə-] *a*. 1. (气候等)不调匀的,不温和的。2. 不稳定的;无规律的。3. 易怒的。

un·e·qual [ˈʌnˈiːkwəl; ʌnˋikwəl] *a*. 1. (大小、轻重、长短等)不等的。2. 不齐的,不平均的;不平等的;不对称的。3. (品质、价格)不一样的,不同的,不均一的。4. 不适合的,不胜任的,不充分的 (*to*)。~ *treaties* 不平等条约。*an ~ contest* 双方实力不相等的比赛。~ *pulsations* 跳动不均匀的脉搏。*be ~ to the duty* 不能胜任。~ **stops**【机】不对称触止。**-ly** *ad*.

un·e·qualled, 〔美〕**un·e·qualed** [ˈʌnˈiːkwəld; ʌnˋikwəld] *a*. 1. 不等同的。2. 无敌的,无比的,无双的;极好的。

un·e·quiv·o·cal [ˈʌniˈkwivəkəl; ˌʌnɪˋkwɪvəkl̩] *a*. 不含糊的,明确的;直率的,坦白的。**-ly** *ad*.

un·e·rase [ˈʌniˈreiz; ˋʌnɪˋrez] = undelete.

un·err·ing [ˈʌnˈəːriŋ; ʌnˋɝɪŋ, -ˋɛrɪŋ] *a*. 没有错的,没有过失的;准确的,正确的。

UNESCO, U·nes·co [ju(:)ˈneskəu; juˋnɛsko] = United Nations Educational, Scientific and Cultural Organization 联合国教育科学及文化组织〔简称"教科文组织"〕。

un·es·cort·ed [ˈʌnesˈkɔːtid; ˏʌnɪsˋkɔrtɪd] *a*. 无人伴送的,无护送的;无护航的。

un·es·sen·tial [ˈʌniˈsenʃəl; ˏʌnəˋsɛnʃəl] **I** *a*. 非本质的;不是主要的;不必要的。**II** *n*. 不必要之物。

un·e·ven [ˈʌnˈiːvən; ʌnˋivən] *a*. **1.** 不平坦的,凹凸不平的。**2.** 不一律的,参差不齐的;品质不匀的。**3.** 不势均力敌的,不平衡的。**4.**【数】奇数的。*of* ~ *temper* 喜怒无常的,三心二意的。*an* ~ *contest* 力量悬殊的竞争。~ *numbers* 奇数。~ **bars**【体】高低杠〔女子体操比赛项目之一〕。**-ly** *ad*.

un·e·vent·ful [ˌʌniˈventfʊl; ˏʌnɪˋvɛntfəl, -fl̩] *a*. 无重大事故的;过程平凡的;平淡无事的。**-ly** *ad*.

un·ex·am·pled [ˌʌnigˈzɑːmpld; ˏʌnɪgˋzæmpl̩d, -ˋzɑm-] *a*. 无先例的,前所未有的,空前的,无比的;例外的。

un·ex·cep·tion·a·ble [ˌʌnikˈsepʃənəbl; ˏʌnɪkˋsɛpʃənəbl̩] *a*. 无懈可击的,无从指摘的,极好的,完美的。**-a·bly** *ad*.

un·ex·cep·tion·al [ˌʌnikˈsepʃənl; ˏʌnɪkˋsɛpʃənl̩] *a*. **1.** 非例外的;平常的。**2.** 不许有例外的。

un·ex·e·cut·ed [ˈʌnˈeksikjuːtid; ʌnˋɛksɪˏkjutɪd] *a*. 没有实行的,未执行的;未根据条款履行的。

un·ex·haust·ed [ˈʌnigˈzɔːstid; ˏʌnɪgˋzɔstɪd] *a*. **1.** 未(用)尽的。**2.** 取用不完的。**3.** (对问题的研究等)尚不彻底的;研究不完的。**4.** 不会疲倦的。**5.** (罐中煤气等)未完全排出的。

un·ex·pect·ed [ˈʌniksˈpektid; ˏʌnɪkˋspɛktɪd] *a*. 想不到的,料不到的,意外的,忽然的,突然的。**-ly** *ad*. **-ness** *n*.

un·ex·posed [ˈʌniksˈpəuzd; ˏʌnɪkˋspozd] *a*. **1.** 未曝光的。**2.** 未揭露的;未公开的。

un·ex·pressed [ˈʌniksˈprest; ˏʌnɪkˋsprɛst] *a*. 不明说的;未表达的。

un·ex·press·ive [ˈʌnikˈspresiv; ˏʌnɪkˋsprɛsɪv] *a*. **1.** 未能表达原意的。**2.** 无表情的;沉默的。**3.** 〔废〕无法表达的;不可表达的。

un·ex·pur·gat·ed [ˈʌnˈekspəːgeitid; ʌnˋɛkspɚˏgetɪd, ˏʌnɛksˋpɝgetɪd] *a*. 未删节的〔指淫秽处未加删除的书籍〕。

un·fad·ing [ʌnˈfeidiŋ; ʌnˋfedɪŋ] *a*. 不褪色的;不凋萎的;不衰的,不朽的。~ *glory* 不朽的荣誉。**-ly** *ad*.

un·fail·ing [ʌnˈfeiliŋ; ʌnˋfelɪŋ] *a*. **1.** 无尽的,无穷的。**2.** 可靠的,不会出错的,确实的。**-ly** *ad*.

un·fair [ˈʌnˈfɛə; ʌnˋfɛr] *a*. 不公平的,不公正的,有偏私的;不光明正大的,不正直的。~ *means* 卑劣手段。**-ly** *ad*. **-ness** *n*.

un·faith·ful [ˈʌnˈfeiθfʊl; ʌnˋfeθfəl] *a*. **1.** 不忠实的;不正直的;不贞洁的。**2.** (翻译等)不可靠的,不正确的。**-ly** *ad*. **-ness** *n*.

un·fal·ter·ing [ʌnˈfɔːltəriŋ; ʌnˋfɔltərɪŋ] *a*. 坚定的;不犹豫的。

un·fa·mil·iar [ˈʌnfəˈmiljə; ˏʌnfəˋmɪljɚ] *a*. **1.** 不熟知的;不熟悉的,生疏的;没有经验的 (*with*; *to*)。**2.** 新奇的,陌生的。*I am* ~ *with the Greek language*. 我对希腊语不怎么熟悉。**-ly** *ad*.

UNFAO = United Nations Food and Agriculture Organization 联合国粮食及农业组织。

un·fash·ion·a·ble [ˈʌnˈfæʃənəbl; ʌnˋfæʃənəbl, -ˋfæʃnə-] *a*. 不流行的,不时髦的,过时的,旧式的。**-a·bly** *ad*.

un·fash·ioned [ˈʌnˈfæʃənd; ʌnˋfæʃənd] *a*. 未成形的;未加工的。

un·fast·en [ˈʌnˈfɑːsn; ʌnˋfæsn̩] *vt*., *vi*. 放松;解开;松开。

un·fa·thered [ˈʌnˈfɑːðəd; ʌnˋfɑðɚd] *a*. **1.** 〔诗〕无父的;〔喻〕不认识父亲的,私生的。**2.** 原著者[学说创立者(等)]不明的,出处不明的。

un·fa·ther·ly [ˈʌnˈfɑːðəli; ʌnˋfɑðɚlɪ] *a*. 不像父亲的;无慈父之情的。

un·fath·om·a·ble [ʌnˈfæðəməbl; ʌnˋfæðəməbl̩] *a*. **1.** 深不可测的,无底的。**2.** 深奥的,难解的。

un·fath·omed [ˈʌnˈfæðəmd; ʌnˋfæðəmd] *a*. **1.** (深度)还没有探测清楚的。**2.** (事件、性格等)难理解的。**3.** (刑事案件等)尚未侦破的,没有得到解决的。

un·fa·vour·a·ble, 〔美〕**-vor-** [ˈʌnˈfeivərəbl; ʌnˋfevrəbl] *a*. **1.** 不适宜的,不顺利的,不利的。**2.** 〔古〕(容貌)丑陋的。**3.** 不吉的,不祥的。**4.** 否定的,相反的。**5.** 令人不快的。*the* ~ *balance of trade* 贸易逆差,入超。***make allowance for*** ~ ***occurrences*** 留有余地以备出现不利情况。**-a·bly** *ad*. **-ness** *n*.

un·fea·si·ble [ˈʌnˈfiːzəbl; ʌnˋfizəbl̩] *a*. 不能实行[实施]的。

un·fed [ˈʌnˈfed; ʌnˋfɛd] *a*. **1.** 得不到食物的,饥饿的。**2.** 没有加燃料的。**3.** 没有得到支持的。

un·feed [ˈʌnˈfiːd; ʌnˋfid] *a*. 未得到工资[小费]的,无报酬的。

un·feel·ing [ʌnˈfiːliŋ; ʌnˋfilɪŋ] *a*. **1.** 没有感觉的。**2.** 无情的,残酷的,冷酷的。**-ly** *ad*.

un·feigned [ʌnˈfeind; ʌnˋfend] *a*. 不是伪装的,真实的,诚实的。**-ly** [ʌnˈfeinidli; ʌnˋfenɪdlɪ] *ad*.

un·felt [ˈʌnˈfelt; ʌnˋfɛlt] *a*. 未感觉到的。

un·fem·i·nine [ˈʌnˈfeminin; ʌnˋfɛmənɪn] *a*. 不适合女性的;不像女性的;不温柔的。

un·fenced [ˈʌnˈfenst; ʌnˋfɛnst] *a*. 没有篱笆[土墙、木栅]的;没有防御的。

un·fer·ti·lized [ˈʌnˈfəːtilaizd; ʌnˋfɝtl̩ˏaɪzd] *a*. **1.** (土地)不肥沃的。**2.** 未施肥的。**3.**【生】未受精的。

un·fet·ter [ˈʌnˈfetə; ʌnˋfɛtɚ] *vt*. 打开…的脚镣;释放,使自由。

un·fet·tered [ˈʌnˈfetəd; ʌnˋfɛtɚd] *a*. 解去脚镣的;没有受到拘束的,自由的。*the* ~ *press* 自由出版(权)。

un·fil·i·al [ˈʌnˈfiliəl; ʌnˋfɪlɪəl, -ˋfɪljəl] *a*. 不像儿子的,不孝的。

un·filled [ˈʌnˈfild; ʌnˋfɪld] *a*. **1.** 未填充的,空的。**2.** (定货等)未供应的。

un·fil·ter·a·ble [ˈʌnˈfiltərəbl; ʌnˋfɪltərəbl̩] *a*.【生】(病原菌)非滤过性的。

un·fin·ished [ˈʌnˈfiniʃt; ʌnˋfɪnɪʃt] *a*. **1.** 未完成的,没有做好的。**2.** 未加琢磨的,没有完成最后加工的〔如抛光、修整等〕。**3.**【纺】未整理过的;未漂白[染色]的。

un·fired [ʌnˈfaiəd; ʌnˋfaɪrd] *a*. **1.** 未燃的,未烧焙的。**2.** 未发射的。

un·fit [ʌnˈfit; ʌnˋfɪt] **I** *a*. **1.** 不适当的,不适宜的,不适任的。**2.** (身体、精神)不健全的人。*a house* ~ *for human habitation* 不适宜人住的房子。**II** [ʌnˈfit; ʌnˋfɪt] *vt*. (**-tt-**) 使不适当,使不适宜 (*for*);未供应某种装备。*houses unfitted with baths* 无浴室设备的房子。**III** *n*. 〔the ~〕**1.** 不适宜[不称职]的人们。**2.** (身体、精神)不健全的人。**-ness** *n*.

un·fix [ˈʌnˈfiks; ʌnˋfɪks] *vt*. **1.** 解下,拆下,摘下,拔去;放松。**2.** 使(人心等)动摇;使不固定,使不稳定。*U-bayonets*!【军】〔口令〕下刺刀!

un·fixed [ˈʌnˈfikst; ʌnˋfɪkst] *a*. **1.** 被解下的,被摘下的,被拔下的;被放松的。**2.** 不固定的,动摇的;未确定的。

un·flag·ging [ʌnˈflægiŋ; ʌnˋflægɪŋ] *a*. 不减弱[松懈]的;不垂头丧气的,不倦的。**-ly** *ad*.

un·flap·pa·ble [ˈʌnˈflæpəbl; ʌnˋflæpəbl] *a*. 〔口〕不易激动的;不易手足失措的;镇定自若的。**-pa·bil·i·ty** [ʌnˌflæpəˈbiliti; ʌnˏflæpəˋbɪlətɪ] *n*.

U

un·fledged [ˈʌnˈfledʒd; ʌnˋflɛdʒd] *a*. 未生羽毛的,羽毛未丰的;未十分发达的,未成熟的,乳臭未干的。

un·flinch·ing [ʌnˈflintʃiŋ; ʌnˋflɪntʃɪŋ] *a*. 不畏缩的,不退缩的;果敢的。**-ly** *ad*.

un·fo·cus(s)ed [ʌnˈfəukəst; ʌnˋfokəst] *a*. **1.** 无焦点的,不集中于一点的。**2.** 不专心的。

un·fold[1] [ʌnˈfəuld; ʌnˋfold] *vt*. **1.** 打开,张开,摊开,铺开(折叠的东西等)。**2.** 展开;开展,发展。**3.** 逐渐表露;说明。~ *a newspaper* 打开报纸。~ *one's intentions* (逐渐)表露意图。— *vi*. **1.** (运动等)展开。**2.** 显露;呈现。**3.** (蓓蕾等)张开。*Buds* ~ *into flowers*. 蓓蕾开成花朵。

un·fold[2] [ˈʌnˈfəuld; ʌnˋfold] *vt*. 将(羊等)放出栏外。

un·forced [ˈʌnˈfɔːst; ʌnˋforst, -ˋfɔrst] *a*. **1.** 非强迫的,自愿的。**2.** 不勉强的,自然的,不费力的。

un·fore·seen [ˈʌnfɔːˈsiːn; ˏʌnforˋsin] *a*. 未预见到的,意外的;偶然的。*the* ~ 未预见到的事情,意外的事情。

un·for·get·ta·ble [ˈʌnfəˈgetəbl; ˏʌnfəˋgɛtəbḷ] *a*. 难忘的;铭刻肺腑的。**-ta·bly** *ad*.

un·for·giv·a·ble [ˈʌnfəˈgivəbl; ˏʌnfəˋgɪvəbḷ] *a*. 不可原谅[饶恕]的。

un·for·giv·ing [ˈʌnfəˈgiviŋ; ˏʌnfəˋgɪvɪŋ] *a*. **1.** 不宽恕的,不原谅人的。**2.** 爱记仇的;无情的。

un·formed [ʌnˈfɔːmd; ʌnˋfɔrmd] *a*. **1.** 无定形的;不成形的。**2.** 未形成的;未发展起来的。**3.** 未作成的;未创造出来的。

un·for·ti·fied [ˈʌnˈfɔːtifaid; ʌnˋfɔrtəˏfaɪd] *a*. **1.** (城市等)未设防的。**2.** 〔转义〕未加强的。**3.** 信念不足的;不稳定的。

un·for·tu·nate [ʌnˈfɔːtʃənit; ʌnˋfɔrtʃənɪt] **I** *a*. **1.** 不幸的;运气不好的,倒霉的。**2.** 不成功的,不恰好的,效果不好的。**3.** 使人遗憾的;可叹的。**II** *n*. 不幸的人;被社会遗弃的人。**-ly** *ad*. **-ness** *n*.

un·found·ed [ˈʌnˈfaundid; ʌnˋfaʊndɪd] *a*. **1.** 没有根据[理由]的,(谣言等)无稽的。**2.** 没有创立的。~ *hopes* 虚幻的希望。**-ly** *ad*. **-ness** *n*.

un·freeze [ˈʌnˈfriːz; ʌnˋfriz] *vt*. (*-froze* [-ˈfrəuz; -ˋfroz], *-froz·en* [-ˈfrəuzn; -ˋfrozn], *-freez·ing*) **1.** 使融化。**2.** 解除(对价格、物资等控制的)冻结。

un·fre·quent [ʌnˈfriːkwənt; ʌnˋfrikwənt] *a*. 不常出现的;难得的,珍奇的。

un·fre·quent·ed [ˈʌnfriˈkwentid; ˏʌnfrɪˋkwɛntɪd] *a*. 人迹罕到的,行人稀少的,冷落的。

un·friend·ed [ʌnˈfrendid; ʌnˋfrɛndɪd] *a*. 没有朋友[伙伴]的;孤立无援的。

un·friend·ly [ˈʌnˈfrendli; ʌnˋfrɛndlɪ] *a*. **1.** 不友好的,有敌意的。**2.** (气候)不宜人的,不利的,不顺利的 (*to*; *for*) 〔常用于构成复合形容词,如 environment-~ (污染环境的),ozone-~ (破坏臭氧层的), user-~ (不方便使用者操作的)等〕。

un·frock [ˈʌnˈfrɔk; ʌnˋfrɑk] *vt*. **1.** 脱去…法衣,免去…的圣职。**2.** 剥夺…的职权;开除,罢黜,把…除名。

un·froze [ˈʌnˈfrəuz; ʌnˋfroz] unfreeze 的过去式。

un·fro·zen [ˈʌnˈfrəuzn; ʌnˋfrozn] **I** unfreeze 的过去分词。**II** *a*. 不冻的,不冷的;未凝结的。

un·fruit·ful [ˈʌnˈfruːtful; ʌnˋfrutfəl, -fʊl] *a*. **1.** 不结果实的;不毛的,贫瘠的;(动物等)不产子的。**2.** 没有结果的,无效的,(努力等)徒然的。

un·fund·ed [ˈʌnˈfʌndid; ʌnˋfʌndɪd] *a*. **1.** 未备基金的,没有经费的。**2.** 暂时借入的,(公债)短期的。*the* ~ *debt* 暂借款。

un·fun·ny [ˈʌnˈfʌni; ʌnˋfʌnɪ] *a*. 不滑稽的。

un·furl [ʌnˈfəːl; ʌnˋfɝl] *vt*., *vi*. 展开(旗、帆等);打开(雨伞等);展示,揭示,公开。

un·fur·nished [ˈʌnˈfəːniʃt; ʌnˋfɝnɪʃt] *a*. 无装备的,无供应的;(房间等)没有家具等设备的。

UNGA = United Nations General Assembly 联合国大会。

un·gain·ly [ʌnˈgeinli; ʌnˋgenlɪ] *a*., *ad*. **1.** 笨拙的[地]。**2.** 难看的[地];粗俗的[地]。**3.** 拙劣的[地]。**-i·ness** *n*.

un·gar·bled [ˈʌnˈgɑːbld; ʌnˋgɑrbḷd] *a*. **1.** 〔古〕未经拣选的;未经筛分的。**2.** 不歪曲的;没窜改的。**3.** 清楚的;明白的,率直的。

un·gat·ed [ʌnˈgeitid; ʌnˋgetɪd] *a*. 无(大)门的;闭塞的。~ *level crossing* 无道口拦木的公路与铁路交叉。

un·gear [ˈʌnˈgiə; ʌnˋgɪr] *vt*. **1.** 把(齿轮等)脱开。**2.** 使脱节。**3.** 卸下(马具等)。

un·gen·er·ous [ˈʌnˈdʒenərəs; ʌnˋdʒɛnərəs, -ˋdʒɛnrəs] *a*. 不慷慨的,不大度的;胸襟狭窄的,小气的;吝啬的。

un·gen·tle·man·ly [ʌnˈdʒentlmənli; ʌnˋdʒɛntḷmənlɪ] *a*. 没有绅士风度的;缺乏教养的,粗鄙的。

un·get-at-able [ˈʌngetˈætəbl; ʌngɛtˋætəbḷ] *a*. 不容易到达[接近]的。

un·gift·ed [ˈʌnˈgiftid; ʌnˋgɪftɪd] *a*. **1.** 缺乏才能的。**2.** 〔古〕空手的,无所获的。

un·gird [ˈʌnˈgəːd; ʌnˋgɝd] *vt*. (*-girded*, *-girt* [-ˈgəːt; -ˋgɝt]) 解开…的带。

un·girt [ˈʌnˈgəːt; ʌnˋgɝt] **I** ungird 的过去式和过去分词。**II** *a*. **1.** 不缚带的;带子松的。**2.** 缺乏纪律的;松弛的。

un·glazed [ˈʌnˈgleizd; ʌnˋglezd] *a*. **1.** (陶瓷器等)没有上釉的,素烧的。**2.** (纸张)无光的;没有上矾水的。**3.** 没有镶玻璃的,没有玻璃窗的。

un·gloved [ˈʌnˈglʌvd; ʌnˋglʌvd] *a*. 没有带手套的。

un·glued [ˈʌnˈgluːd; ʌnˋglud] *a*. 脱粘的,脱开的;拆开的。*a stamp* ~ *from an envelope* 从信封上揭下的邮票。*come* ~ 〔俚〕情急心躁。

un·god·ly [ʌnˈgɔdli; ʌnˋgɑdlɪ] *a*. **1.** 不信神的,不怕神的。**2.** 邪恶的,罪孽深重的;无法无天的。**3.** 〔口〕荒唐的;不可容忍的。**-li·ness** *n*.

un·gov·ern·a·ble [ʌnˈgʌvənəbl; ʌnˋgʌvənə bḷ] *a*. **1.** 难治理的,难控制的。**2.** 放肆的;激烈的。

un·grace·ful [ˈʌnˈgreisful; ʌnˋgresfəl] *a*. 不优美的,不雅致的;粗鄙的,没礼貌的;难看的,没样子的。**-ly** *ad*. **-ness** *n*.

un·gra·cious [ˈʌnˈgreiʃəs; ʌnˋgreʃəs] *a*. **1.** 不亲切的,冷淡的。**2.** 没礼貌的,粗野的。**3.** 令人不快的,讨厌的。**-ly** *ad*. **-ness** *n*.

un·gram·mat·i·cal [ˈʌngrəˈmætikəl; ˏʌngrəˋmætɪ kḷ] *a*. 不合[违反]语法的;(文字)不通的。

un·grate·ful [ʌnˈgreitful; ʌnˋgretfəl] *a*. **1.** 不感恩的,忘恩负义的。**2.** 徒劳的,白费气力的。**3.** 讨厌的,不愉快的。*an* ~ *food* 令人厌恶的食物。**-ly** *ad*. **-ness** *n*.

un·green [ˈʌnˈgriːn; ˋʌnˋgrin] *a*. **1.** (人)不关心环境保护的。**2.** (产品、活动等)污染环境的,破坏生态平衡的。

un·ground·ed [ˈʌnˈgraundid; ʌnˋgraʊndɪd] *a*. **1.** 没有根据[理由]的,不从事实出发的。**2.** 不真实的,捏造的。**3.** 【无】不接地的。

un·grudg·ing [ˈʌnˈgrʌdʒiŋ; ʌnˋgrʌdʒɪŋ] *a*. **1.** 不吝惜的,慷慨的。**2.** 自愿的。*give sb*. ~ *praise* 满口称赞某人。**-ly** *ad*. 慷慨;欣然。

ungt. *n*. 【处方】软膏,油膏(= ointment)。

un·gual [ˈʌŋgwəl; ˋʌŋgwəl] *a*. 爪[距、蹄](似)的;有爪[距、蹄]的。

un·guard·ed [ˈʌnˈgɑːdid; ʌnˋgɑrdɪd] *a*. **1.** 不留神的,不谨慎的。**2.** 没有防备的。***in an*** ~ ***moment*** 一个不留神;一不小心。**-ly** *ad*.

un·guent [ˈʌŋgwənt; ˋʌŋgwənt] *n*. **1.** 药膏。**2.** (机器的)润滑油。**-ary** *a*.

un·gui·bus et ros·tro [***ore***] [ˈʌŋgwibəs et ˈrɔstrəu ˈɔre; ˋʌŋgwɪbəs ɛt ˋrostro ˋorɛ] 〔L.〕用爪和嘴;用全力;拚命。

un·guic·u·late [ʌŋˈgwikjuleit; ʌŋˋgwɪkjʊˏlet, -lɪt] **I**

a.【动】有爪的;【植】花瓣有爪状底部的。**II** *n*. 有爪动物。亦作 **-d.**

un·gui·form [ˈʌŋgwifɔːm; ˋʌŋgwɪfɔrm] *a*. 爪[蹄]状的。

un·guis [ˈʌŋgwis; ˋʌŋgwɪs] *n*. (*pl*. ***un·gues*** [-gwiːz; -gwɪz])【动】爪,距,蹄;【植】(某些花的花瓣的)爪状底部。

un·gu·la [ˈʌŋgjulə; ˋʌŋgjələ] *n*. (*pl*. ***-lae*** [-liː; -li]) **1.**【几】蹄状体。**2.**【植】(某些花的花瓣的)爪状底部。

un·gu·lar [ˈʌŋgjulə; ˋʌŋgjələ˞] *a*. = ungual.

un·gu·late [ˈʌŋgjuleit; ˋʌŋgjəlɪt, -ˏlet] **I** *a*. 蹄状的;有蹄的;有蹄类的。**II** *n*. 有蹄动物。

Unh【化】元素𬭶的符号(= unnilhexium)。

un·hack·neyed [ʌnˈhæknid; ʌnˋhæknɪd] *a*. **1.** 未陈旧的;不陈腐的;还新鲜的;崭新的;有创造性的。**2.**〔古〕不熟练的;没有经验的。

un·hair [ˈʌnˈhɛə; ʌnˋhɛr] *vt*., *vi*. 拔除…的毛[发];使无毛〔如革鞣制前〕。

un·hal·low [ʌnˈhæləu; ʌnˋhælo] *vt*. 亵渎,污渎。**-ed** *a*. 亵渎神明的。

un·hand [ʌnˈhænd; ʌnˋhænd] *vt*. 把手从…放开;放掉。

un·han·dled [ˈʌnˈhændld; ʌnˋhændld] *a*. **1.** 未经手触过的;未经处理过的;未讨论过的。**2.** 未经驯服的。

un·hand·some [ˈʌnˈhænsəm; ʌnˋhænsəm] *a*. **1.** 不美丽的,不漂亮的,难看的。**2.** 没礼貌的。**3.** 吝啬的,小气的。**-ly** *ad*.

un·hand·y [ˈʌnˈhændi; ʌnˋhændɪ] *a*. **1.** 笨拙的。**2.** 难处理[使用]的,不便的。**3.** 不在手边的。**-i·ly** *ad*. **-i·ness** *n*.

un·hap·pi·ly [ʌnˈhæpili; ʌnˋhæpɪlɪ] *ad*. **1.** 不幸福地;悲惨地,愁苦地,不快乐地。**2.** 不幸,偏巧,可惜。**3.** 不适当地,拙劣地。

un·hap·py [ʌnˈhæpi; ʌnˋhæpɪ] *a*. **1.** 不幸的;悲惨的,不快乐的;不吉利的。**2.** 不凑巧的。**3.** (讲法等)不恰当的。**-i·ness** *n*.

un·harmed [ˈʌnˈhɑːmd; ʌnˋhɑrmd] *a*. 没有受损害的,没有受伤的;平安无事的,无恙的。

un·harm·ful [ˈʌnˈhɑːmful; ʌnˋhɑrmfəl] *a*. 无害的。**-ly** *ad*.

un·harm·ing [ˈʌnˈhɑːmiŋ; ʌnˋhɑrmɪŋ] *a*. 不伤人的;无害的。

un·har·ness [ˈʌnˈhɑːnis; ʌnˋhɑrnɪs] *vt*. **1.** 解下(马等的)马具。**2.** 解下…的铠甲。**-ed** *a*. 解下了马具的;(瀑布、风等)不能利用作动力的。

un·hat [ʌnˈhæt; ʌnˋhæt] *vi*. (*-tt-*)〔古〕脱帽致敬。

un·hatched [ˈʌnˈhætʃt; ʌnˋhætʃt] *a*. **1.** 未孵化的;未充分孵化的。**2.** 未准备就绪的;没实现的。

un·haunt·ed [ʌnˈhɔːntid; ʌnˋhɔntɪd] *a*. **1.** 无(某物)出没的。**2.** 不受扰乱的,不受干扰的。

UNHCR = United Nations High Commissioner for Refugees 联合国难民事务高级专员办事处。

un·health·ful [ˈʌnˈhelθful; ʌnˋhɛlθfəl] *a*. 有害身体的,不卫生的;不健康的。**-ly** *ad*.

un·health·y [ʌnˈhelθi; ʌnˋhɛlθɪ] *a*. **1.** 不健康的,病弱的。**2.** 有害健康的,(风土等)有害的。**3.** (精神上)不健全的,不良的。**-i·ly** *ad*. **-i·ness** *n*.

un·heard [ˈʌnˈhəːd; ʌnˋhɝd] *a*. **1.** 未被听到的。**2.** 不被倾听的;(案件等)未予审问的;未被给予申述机会的。**3.**〔古〕前所未闻的。

un·heard-of [ʌnˈhəːdɔv; ʌnˋhɝdˏɑv] *a*. 从未听见过的,前所未闻的,空前的。*on an ~ scale* 以空前的规模。

un·heed·ed [ʌnˈhiːdid; ʌnˋhidɪd] *a*. 没有受到注意的,没人理睬的,没人注意的。

un·heed·ing [ˈʌnˈhiːdiŋ; ʌnˋhidɪŋ] *a*. 不注意的,不留心的;疏忽的。**-ly** *ad*.

un·help·ful [ˈʌnˈhelpful; ʌnˋhɛlpfəl] *a*. **1.** 无用的,无益的。**2.** 不予帮助的,不予合作的。

un·hemmed [ˈʌnˈhemd; ʌnˋhɛmd] *a*. 没有褶边[卷边]的。

un-he·ro [ʌnˈhiərəu; ʌnˋhiro] *n*. "反英雄",非传统派主角〔新流派文艺作品中的主人公,多为平凡委琐怯懦的小人物,即所谓"反英雄"〕。**-ic** *a*. 不是英雄的,怯懦的。

un·hes·i·tat·ing [ʌnˈheziteitiŋ; ʌnˋhɛzəˏtetɪŋ] *a*. 不踌躇[犹豫]的;即时的,迅速的。**-ly** *ad*.

un·hewn [ˈʌnˈhjuːn; ʌnˋhjun] *a*. 未经刀斧斫削成形的;粗糙的;粗野的。

un·hinge [ʌnˈhindʒ; ʌnˋhɪndʒ] *vt*. **1.** 取下…的铰链;把…从铰链上摘下。**2.** 使分开,使裂开。**3.** 使(精神等)发狂,动摇,搅乱,扰乱。*~ a door* 摘下一扇门。*Her mind was ~d*. 她精神失常了。

un·hip [ˈʌnˈhip; ʌnˋhɪp] *a*.〔美口〕无时代感的,不流行的。

un·his·tor·ic, -tor·i·cal [ˈʌnhisˈtɔːrik, -ˈtɔrikəl; ˏʌnhɪsˋtɔrɪk, -ˋtɔrɪkl] *a*. **1.** 非历史的;仅属传说的,未真正发生过的;〔尤指〕【语】无历史根据的。**2.** 不熟悉历史的。**3.** 偶然的,例外的。

un·hitch [ˈʌnˈhitʃ; ʌnˋhɪtʃ] *vt*. 解下(拴着的马等),解开。

un·ho·ly [ʌnˈhəuli; ʌnˋholɪ] *a*. (*-li·er*; *-li·est*) **1.** 不神圣的,不洁净的。**2.** 不信神的,不虔敬的。**3.** 邪恶的。**4.**〔口〕厉害的,可怕的。**5.**〔口〕不合理的。*They were kicking up an ~ row*. 他们正引起一场大闹。**-li·ly** *ad*. **-li·ness** *n*.

un·hon·oured,〔美〕**-ho·nored** [ˈʌnˈɔnəd; ʌnˋɑnə˞d] *a*. **1.** 没有受到尊敬的。**2.** (支票)被拒绝接受[支付]的。

un·hook [ˈʌnˈhuk; ʌnˋhʊk] *vt*. **1.** 把…从钩上取下。**2.** 解开(衣服等的)搭钩。

un·hoped(-for) [ʌnˈhəupt(fɔː); ʌnˋhopt(fɔr)] *a*. 意外的,没想到的。*get unhoped-for success* 得到意外的成功。

un·horse [ˈʌnˈhɔːs; ʌnˋhɔrs] *vt*. **1.** 把…拉下马来,使摔下马来。**2.** 赶…下台;推翻。**3.** 卸去(驾车的)马。

un·house [ˈʌnˈhauz; ʌnˋhauz] *vt*. **1.** 把…撵出去,把…赶出屋外,使无家可归[无处居住]。**2.**【商】由仓库中提出。

un·hu·man [ˈʌnˈhjuːmən; ʌnˋhjumən] *a*. **1.** 非人类的。**2.** 超人类的,非人间的。**3.**〔罕〕残酷的,不近人情的。

un·hung [ˈʌnˈhʌŋ; ʌnˋhʌŋ] unhang 的过去式和过去分词。

un·hur·ried [ʌnˈhʌrid; ʌnˋhɝɪd] *a*. 不匆忙的;从容不迫的;悠闲的。

un·hurt [ˈʌnˈhəːt; ʌnˋhɝt] *a*. 没有受伤的;未受损害的。

un·hus·band·ed [ʌnˈhʌzbəndid; ʌnˋhʌsbəndɪd] *a*. **1.** 无丈夫的,未嫁的。**2.** (土地)未耕耘的。

un·husk [ʌnˈhʌsk; ʌnˋhʌsk] *vt*. 剥去(稻谷等的)外壳;〔喻〕揭露。

un·hy·phen·at·ed [ʌnˈhaifəneitid; ʌnˋhaɪfəˏnetɪd] *a*. **1.** 未附加连字符的。**2.** (人种)纯粹的。

u·ni- *comb. f*. 一,单;一个;一边;一方: *uni*florous, *uni*lateral.

U·ni·ate, U·ni·at [ˈjuːniət, -ˌeit; ˋjunɪət, -ˏet] *n*., *a*. 合并教派的(教徒)〔主张与罗马天主教会合并的东正教教徒〕。

u·ni·ax·i·al [ˈjuniˈæksiəl; ˏjunɪˋæksɪəl] *a*. 单轴的。~ **crystal**【物】单轴结晶体。

u·ni·cam·er·al [ˈjuːniˈkæmərəl; ˏjunɪˋkæmərəl] *a*. (议会)一院制的。

UNICEF [ˈjuːnisef; ˋjunɪsɛf] = United Nations International Children's Emergency Fund, 现名 United Nations Children's Fund 联合国儿童基金会。

u·ni·cel·lu·lar [ˈjuːniˈseljulə; ˏjunɪˋsɛljələ˞] *a*.【生】单细胞的。~ *animals* 单细胞动物。

u·ni·corn [ˈjuːnikɔːn; ˋjunɪˏkɔrn] *n*. **1.** 独角兽〔传说中

身体似马、头中央有一螺旋状独角的怪兽〕;【怪】独角野牛。2.【动】独角鲸;独角甲虫;有甲状棘的贝类。3.〔the U-〕【天】麒麟座。4. 三马马车;三马马车的一套马。*a Chinese* ~ 麒麟。

u·ni·cos·tate [ˌjuːniˈkɔsteit; ˌjunɪˋkɑstet] *a*. 单肋的;【植】单叶肋的,中脉显明的〔指叶〕。

u·ni·cy·cle [ˈjuːnisaikl; ˋjunɪˏsaɪ kl̩] *n*. (杂技表演用)独轮脚踏车。

un·i·de·a'd, -de·aed [ˈʌnaiˈdiəd; ˏʌnaɪˋdiəd] *a*. 无思想的;无头脑的,愚钝的。

un·i·de·al [ˈʌnaiˈdiəl; ˏʌnaɪˋdiəl] *a*. 1. 非唯心的。2. 非理想的;非想像的。3. 不理想的;不完美的;平淡无味的。

un·i·den·ti·fied [ˈʌnaiˈdentifaid; ˏʌnaɪˋdɛntɪˏfaɪd] *a*. 不能辨认的,来路[身分]不明的。*an* ~ *plane* 国籍不明的飞机。*an* ~ *flying object* 飞碟,不明飞行物。

u·ni·di·men·sion·al [ˈjuːnidiˈmenʃənl; ˋjunɪdəˋmɛnʃənl] *a*. 一维的,一度的;线性的。

u·ni·di·rec·tion·al [ˈjuːnidiˈrekʃənl; ˏjunɪdəˋrɛkʃə nl̩] *a*. 单向的。

UNIDO = United Nations Industrial Development Organization 联合国工业发展组织。

u·ni·fi·a·ble [ˈjuːnifaiəbl; ˈjunəˏfaɪə bl̩] *a*. 可统一的;可联合的;能一致的。

u·ni·fi·ca·tion [ˌjuːnifiˈkeiʃən; ˏjunəfəˋkeʃən] *n*. 统一,合一,联合;一致。

u·ni·fi·er [ˈjuːnifaiə; ˋjunəfaɪɚ] *n*. 统一物;联合者;使一致的人[物]。

u·ni·fi·lar [ˈjuːniˈfailə; ˏjunɪˋfaɪlɚ] *a*. 单线的,仅有一条线的,单丝的。

u·ni·flo·rous [ˈjuːniˈflɔːrəs; ˏjunɪˋflorəs] *a*. 【植】单花的。

u·ni·fo·li·ate [ˈjuːniˈfəuliit; ˏjunɪˋfolɪˏet] *a*. 【植】1. 单叶的。2. = unifoliolate.

u·ni·fo·li·o·late [ˈjuːniˈfəuliəleit, -lit; ˏjunɪˋfolɪəlet, -lɪt] *a*. (复叶)具一小叶的。

u·ni·form [ˈjuːnifɔːm; ˋjunəˏfɔrm] I *a*. 1. (形状、性质等)一样的,同一的;一致的;相同的。2. 一贯不变的;始终如一的。3. 规格一致的,均匀的,齐一的。*be* ~ *in size* [*shape*] 大小[形状]一律。II *n*. 1. 制服;军服;〔the ~〕军人。2. 通讯中用以代表字母 u 的词。*an undress* ~ 军便服。*a full-dress* ~ 军礼服。***in full*** ~ 全副军装。***out of*** ~ (未穿制服而)穿着便服。III *vt*. 使规格一律,使均一;使穿制服。~ **acceleration** 匀加速(度)。~ **crop**【林】同龄林。~ **function**【数】单值函数。~ **motion**【机】匀速运动。~ **system**【林】伞伐作业。**-ly** *ad*.

u·ni·formed [ˈjuːnifɔːmd; ˋjunəˏfɔrmd] *a*. 穿军服的;穿制服的。

u·ni·form·i·tar·i·an [ˌjuːniˌfɔːmiˈtɛəriən; ˏjunəˏfɔrməˋtɛrɪən] I *a*. 1.【地】均变说的;持均变说的。2. 坚持某种均等一致说的。II *n*.【地】均变论者;坚持某种均等一致说者。

u·ni·form·i·tar·i·an·ism [ˌjuːniˌfɔːməˈtɛəriənizəm; ˏjunəˏfɔrməˋtɛrɪənɪzm] *n*.【地】均变说〔认为地质纪元中一切地质变化都可用浸蚀、沉积、火山作用等现有物理和化学作用来解释〕。

u·ni·form·i·ty [juːniˈfɔːmiti; ˏjunəˋfɔrmətɪ] *n*. 1. 一样,一律,一式,划一,一致。2. 均匀;无变化,单调。

u·ni·fy [ˈjuːnifai; ˋjunəˏfaɪ] *vt*. 使成一体,合一;统一,使一致,使一元化。

u·nij·u·gate [juˈnidʒəgeit, ˌjuːniˈdʒuːgit; juˋnɪdʒəget] *a*.【植】具一对(小叶)的。

u·ni·lat·er·al [ˈjuːniˈlætərəl; ˏjunɪˋlætərəl] *a*. 1. 一方的,一侧的,单边的,单方的,片面的。2. 单系的〔指父系或母系一方〕。3.【植】单侧的。4.【语音】单边音的。~ **conduction**【电】单向导电。~ **contract**【法】单方(承担义务)契约。~ **relative** 单侧亲缘。~ **winding**【电】单向绕法,单向绕组。**-ly** *ad*.

u·ni·lat·er·al·ism [ˈjuːniˈlætərəlizəm; ˏjunɪˋlætərəlɪzm] *n*. 单方,单向,片面,单系(现象);【植】单侧(状态)。

u·ni·lay·er [ˈjuːniˈleiə; ˏjunɪˋleɚ] *n*.【物】单分子层。

u·ni·lin·e·ar [ˈjuːniˈliniə; ˏjunɪˋlɪnɪr] *a*. 1. 始终遵循一条发展(或前进)道路的;一条路线贯穿始终的;单线的。2. 分阶段发展的。

u·ni·loc·u·lar [ˈjuːniˈlɔkjulə; ˏjunɪˋlɑkjəlɚ] *a*.【生】单室的;单房的。

un·i·m·ag·in·a·ble [ˌʌniˈmædʒinəbl; ˏʌnɪˋmædʒɪnə bl̩, -ˋmædʒnə bl̩] *a*. 不能想像的;想不到的;无法理解的。**-a·bly** *ad*.

u·ni·mod·al [ˈjuːniˈməudl; ˏjunɪˋmo dl̩] *a*.【统计】(曲线)单峰的。

u·ni·mod·u·lar [ˈjuːniˈmɔdjulə; ˏjunɪˋmɑdjʊlɚ] *a*.【数】单位模的。

u·ni·mog [ˈjuːniˈmɔg; ˋjunɪˋmɑg] *n*. (能抽吸垃圾、铲雪、撒盐等的)多功能清扫机[车]。

un·im·paired [ˈʌnimˈpɛəd; ˏʌnɪmˋpɛrd] *a*. 未受损伤的;未削弱的;没有减少的。

un·im·pas·sioned [ˈʌnimˈpæʃənd; ˏʌnɪmˋpæʃənd] *a*. 没有热情的;不动感情的。**-ly** *ad*.

un·im·peach·a·ble [ˌʌnimˈpiːtʃəbl; ˏʌnɪmˋpitʃə bl̩] *a*. 无可怀疑的;无可指摘的;无懈可击的;无过失的,无罪的。**-a·bly** *ad*.

un·im·por·tant [ˈʌnimˈpɔːtənt; ˏʌnɪmˋpɔrtn̩t] *a*. 不重要的;琐细的,平凡的。

un·im·pos·ing [ˈʌnimˈpəuziŋ; ˏʌnɪmˋpozɪŋ] *a*. 1. 给人印象不深刻的,不引人注目的;没有威严的。2. (工作等)不是非做不可的。

un·im·press [ˈʌnimˈpres; ˋʌnɪmˋprɛs] *vt*. 未能给(某人、观众、读者等)留下深刻印象。

un·im·pressed [ˈʌnimˈprest; ˏʌnɪmˋprɛst] *a*. 无印记的;没有印象的;未受感动的。

un·im·pres·sive [ˈʌnimˈpresiv; ˏʌnɪmˋprɛsɪv] *a*. 给人印象不深的;不令人信服的。

un·im·proved [ˈʌnimˈpruːvd; ˏʌnɪmˋpruvd] *a*. 1. 没有改善[改良]的;没有得到增进的。2. (土地)没有耕作的。3. (机会等)没有充分利用的。4. (牛羊等)未经选种的。5. (道路)没有坚实路面的。

un·in·cor·po·rat·ed [ˈʌninˈkɔːpəreitid; ˏʌnɪnˋkɔrpəretɪd] *a*. 1. 未组成社团的。2. 未被承认为自治组织的;未包含[合并]在内的。*an* ~ *village* 非自治村落。

un·in·flu·enced [ˈʌnˈinfluənst; ʌnˋɪnfluənst] *a*. 不为他人所动的,不受影响的,不受感化的;没有偏见的,公平的。

un·in·flu·en·tial [ˈʌninfluˈenʃəl; ʌnˏɪnfluˋɛnʃəl] *a*. 不发生影响的;没有左右别人的力量的。

un·in·form·a·tive [ˈʌninˈfɔːmətiv; ˏʌnɪnˋfɔrmətɪv] *a*. 不提供情报的。

un·in·formed [ˈʌninˈfɔːmd; ˏʌnɪnˋfɔrmd] *a*. 1. 没有得到通知[情报]的。2. 无知识的;蒙昧的。

un·in·hab·it·a·ble [ˈʌninˈhæbitəbl; ˏʌnɪnˋhæbɪtə bl̩] *a*. 不适于居住的。

un·in·hab·it·ed [ˈʌninˈhæbitid; ˏʌnɪnˋhæbɪtɪd] *a*. 没有人住的,(岛等)无人的。

un·in·hib·it·ed [ˈʌninˈhibitid; ˏʌnɪnˋhɪbətɪd] *a*. 放纵不羁的,不受抑制的〔尤指言行等不受通常的社会制约或心理上的约束〕。

un·in·jured [ˈʌnˈindʒəd; ʌnˋɪndʒɚd] *a*. 没有受损伤的。

un·in·spired [ˈʌninˈspaiəd; ˏʌnɪnˋspaɪrd] *a*. 未受鼓舞的,思想感情不活跃的;无独创性的;庸庸碌碌的。

un·in·struct·ed [ˈʌninˈstrʌktid; ˏʌnɪnˋstrʌktɪd] *a*. 1.

U

未受教育的,无知的。**2.** 未获指示如何投票的,未决定投谁的票的。

un·in·tel·li·gent [ˈʌninˈtelidʒənt; ˏʌnɪnˋtɛlədʒənt] ***a.*** 无知的;缺乏智力的,愚蠢的。**-gence** ***n.*** **-ly** ***ad.***

un·in·tel·li·gi·ble [ˈʌninˈtelidʒəbl; ˏʌnɪnˋtɛlədʒə bl̩] ***a.*** 难理解的,莫名其妙的。**-bly** ***ad.*** **-bil·i·ty** [ˈʌninˌtelidʒəˈbiliti; ʌnɪnˏtɛlɪdʒəˋbɪlətɪ] ***n.***

un·in·tend·ed [ˈʌninˈtendid; ˏʌnɪnˋtɛndɪd] ***a.*** 非故意的,不是存心的。

un·in·ten·tion·al [ˈʌninˈtenʃənəl; ˏʌnɪnˋtɛnʃənl̩] ***a.*** 不是故意的,无意的,无心的。**-ly** ***ad.***

un·in·ter·est·ed [ˈʌnˈintristid; ʌnˋɪntərɪstɪd] ***a.*** **1.** 没有(利害)关系的;公平的。**2.** 不感觉兴趣的,不注意的,漠不关心的,冷淡的。

un·in·ter·est·ing [ˈʌnˈintristiŋ; ʌnˋɪntərɪstɪŋ] ***a.*** 无趣的,乏味的,令人厌倦的。**-ly** ***ad.***

un·in·ter·rupt·ed [ˈʌnintəˈrʌptid; ˏʌnɪntəˋrʌptɪd] ***a.*** **1.** 不停的,不断的,连续的。**2.** 未受干扰的。**-ly** ***ad.*** **-ness** ***n.***

u·ni·nu·cle·ate [ˈjuːniˈnjuːkliit; ˏjunɪˋnjuklɪɪt, -nu-] ***a.***【原】单核的。

un·in·vit·ed [ˈʌninˈvaitid; ˏʌnɪnˋvaɪtɪd] ***a.*** 没有被邀请的;多此一举的,多余的;冒昧的。

un·in·vit·ing [ˈʌninˈvaitiŋ; ˏʌnɪnˋvaɪtɪŋ] ***a.*** 不吸引人的,无吸引力的。**-ly** ***ad.***

U·ni·o [ˈjuːniəu; ˋjunɪˏo] ***n.*** **1.**【动】珠蚌(属)。**2.**〔u-〕蛤蜊;蚝。

u·nion [ˈjuːnjən; ˋjunjən] ***n.*** **1.** 联合,结合,合并;团结,融洽,一致。**2.** 同盟,联盟。**3.** 公会,协会;工会;〔U-〕大学生俱乐部。**4.** 结婚,婚姻。**5.**〔the U-〕联邦。**6.**〔英〕联合教会。**7.**〔英〕教区间的救济工作联合会;联合救济院。**8.** 联邦旗,(特指)英国国旗。**9.**【纺】(棉和麻等的)混纺织物;交织织物。**10.**【机】联接,管接,管套接。**11.**【数】并集;逻辑和。**12.**【医】愈合。*peasants'* ～ 农会。*U- is strength.* 团结就是力量。*a three-way* ～ 三通管接头。***fly a flag*** ～ ***down***【海】挂倒旗〔遭难信号〕。***in*** ～ 共同,一同。***the Union*** 1. 1707 年英吉利和苏格兰的合并;1801 年大不列颠和爱尔兰的合并。2. 美利坚合众国。***the Soviet U-*** (前)苏联。***the U- flag*** = ***the U- Jack*** 英国国旗。～ ***by*** (***the***) ***first intention***【医】第一期愈合。～ ***by*** (***the***) ***second intention***【医】第二期愈合〔化脓后愈合〕。～**-busting** ***n.***, ***a.*** 打击工会(的)。～ **card** 工会会员证。～ **catalogue** 联合图书目录。～ **colour** 统一染料,万用染料。～ **hours**〔美棒球〕九回。**U- House** = ～ **workhouse**〔英〕联合救济院。～ **jack** (国旗上)象征联合的部分;联合象征旗。～ **link**【机】联环。～ **man** (= ～ **member**)〔美〕工会会员。～ **nut** 接合螺母。～ **shop** 须按资方与工会协定条件雇用工人的工厂。～ **suit**〔美〕连衫裤。～ **three-way cock**【机】三通旋塞。～ **wages** 工会规定的工资率。

u·nion·ism [ˈjuːnjənizəm; ˋjunjənɪzm] ***n.*** **1.** 联合主义,联合原则。**2.** 工会主义;工联主义。**3.**【美史】〔the U-〕(南北战争时反对南北分裂的)联邦主义。**4.** 统一主义〔北爱尔兰统一党的原则和做法〕。

u·nion·ist [ˈjuːnjənist; ˋjunjənɪst] ***n.*** **1.** 联合主义者。**2.**〔U-〕【美史】(南北战争时的)联邦主义者;【英史】(反对爱尔兰自治案的)统一党党员。**3.** 工会会员;工会[工联]主义者。**-ic** [ˌjuːnjəˈnistik; ˏjunjəˋnɪstɪk] ***a.***

u·nion·i·za·tion [ˌjuːnjənaiˈzeiʃən; ˏjunjənɪˋzeʃən, -naɪ-] ***n.*** **1.** 组织成工会。**2.** 使符合工会会章。

u·nion·ize [ˈjuːnjənaiz; ˋjunjənˏaɪz] ***vt.*** **1.** 联合。**2.** 使成为工会;使加入工会;使遵守工会规章。— ***vi.*** **1.** 联合。**2.** 加入工会;加入联合组织。

un·i·on·ized [ʌnˈaiənaizd; ʌnˋaɪənaɪzd] ***a.***【物,化】未电离的。

u·nip·a·rous [juˈnipərəs; juˋnɪpərəs] ***a.*** **1.**【植】每一分枝只生一茎轴的,单梗的〔如聚伞花序〕。**2.**【动】每次产一个卵的;每胎生一子的;只生过一子的。

u·ni·par·tite [ˌjuːniˈpɑːtait; ˏjunɪˋpɑrtaɪt] ***a.*** 未分裂的;不能分割的。

u·ni·ped [ˈjuːniped; ˋjunɪpɛd] ***a.*** 单足的,独脚的。

u·ni·per·son·al [ˌjuːniˈpəːsənl; ˏjunɪˋpɝsə nl̩] ***a.*** **1.** 仅作为个人存在的;仅包含一个人的;仅以个人形式表现出来的。**2.**【语法】(动词)仅用于单一人称的〔尤指第三人称单数〕。

u·ni·pet·al·ous [ˌjuːniˈpetləs; ˏjunɪˋpɛtələs] ***a.***【植】单(花)瓣的,仅有一花瓣的。

u·ni·pla·nar [ˌjuːniˈpleinə; ˏjunɪˋplenɚ] ***a.*** 单面延展的;在同一平面的。

u·ni·pod [ˈjuːnipɔd; ˋjunɪˏpɑd] ***n.*** 独脚(支撑)架。

u·ni·po·lar [ˈjuːniˈpəulə; ˏjunɪˋpolɚ] ***a.***【电】单极的;【生】单尾的,(细胞等)单极的。

u·ni·po·lar·i·ty [ˌjuːnipəuˈlæriti; ˏjunɪpoˋlærətɪ] ***n.*** **1.**【电】单极性。**2.**【动】单极体。

u·nip·o·tent [ju(ː)ˈnipətənt; juˋnɪpətənt] ***a.*** **1.** 只能向一个方向发展的,只有一个结果的。**2.**【生】偏能的。

u·nique [juːˈniːk; juˋnik] **I** ***a.*** **1.** 唯一的;无双的;无比的;独特的。**2.**〔口〕珍奇的,极好的。**3.**【数,物】单价的;单值的。**II** ***n.*** 独一无二的人[物、事实]。**-ly** ***ad.*** **-ness** ***n.***

u·ni·ra·mous [ˌjuːniˈreiməs; ˏjunɪˋreməs] ***a.*** 有单枝的。

u·ni·sex [ˈjuːniseks; ˋjunɪsɛks] ***a.***〔口〕(服装、发式等)不分男女的。

u·ni·sex·u·al [ˈjuːniˈseksjuəl; ˏjunɪˋsɛkʃuəl] ***a.*** **1.**【生】单性的;雌雄异体的。**2.** 限于一种性别的,非男女同校的。**-i·ty** [ˈjuːniˌseksjuˈæliti; ˋjunɪˏsɛkʃuˋælətɪ] ***n.***

u·ni·son [ˈjuːnizn, -sn; ˋjunəsn, -zn] ***n.*** **1.** 调和,一致。**2.**【乐】同音,同度;齐唱,齐奏。***in*** ～ 一齐(唱等);一致(行动等)。**-al** ***a.***

u·ni·so·nant [ˈjuːniˈsəunənt; ˋjunɪˋsaunənt] ***a.*** 一致的;【乐】同音的,同度的。

u·ni·so·nous [ˈjuːniˈsəunəs; juˋnɪsənəs] ***a.*** = unisonant.

u·nit [ˈjuːnit; ˋjunɪt] ***n.*** **1.** 个体,一个,一人。**2.** (计值、组织、机构)单位;单元;小组,分部;【军】部队;分队。**3.**【机】机组,装置;元件,部件,附件;一组用具[设备]。**4.**【数】单位数;最小整数;基数。*the guerrilla* ～*s* 游击队。*army* ～*s* 陆军部队。*international electrical* ～*s* 国际电力单位〔volt, ohm 等〕。*the C. G. S. system of* ～*s* 厘米、克、秒单位制。*a line* ～【电】接线盒。*the remote control* ～ 遥控装置。*the drive* ～ 传动装置。*a point* ～ 质点。*a missile-borne* ～ 导弹附件。*an infrared detection* ～【火箭】热探头。***be a*** ～〔美〕一致(*We were a* ～ *on the question.* 我们在这个问题上是一致的)。～ **area** 单位面积。～ **cell**【物,无】(单位)晶胞;单位粒子。～ **character**【遗】单位性状。～ **factor**【生】单一因子。～ **holder** 联合托拉斯股票持有人。～ **(magnetic) pole**【物】单位磁极。～ **price** 单价。～ **rule**〔美〕单位投制〔一个代表团可不顾其中少数人的意见,作为一个单位投票〕。～ **school**【军】随营学校。～ **train** 专列货车。～ **trust** 联合托拉斯〔共同投资的企业、互惠基金等〕。

u·nit·age [ˈjuːnitidʒ; ˋjunətɪdʒ] ***n.*** 计量单位(的规定)。

UNITAR = United Nations Institute for Training and Research 联合国训练研究所。

U·ni·ta·ri·an [juːniˈtɛəriən; ˏjunəˋtɛrɪən] **I** ***n.*** **1.**【宗】(基督教的)唯一神教派教徒。**2.**〔u-〕一神论者;一元论者;单一政府主义者,中央集权主义者。**II** ***a.***【宗】唯一神教派的;〔u-〕单一的,一元的。**-ism** ***n.*** 唯一神教派。

u·ni·ta·ry [ˈjuːnitəri; ˋjunəˏtɛrɪ] ***a.*** **1.** 一个的,单一的,单元的。**2.** 整体的,一致的。**3.** 中央集权主义的。**4.**【数】单式的。**5.**【哲】一元论的。*a* ～ *operator* 幺正算符。～ *space* 单式空间。

u·nite[1] [ju(ː)ˈnait; juˋnaɪt] ***vt.*** **1.** 使合成一体,结合;接

U

合;使联合,合并。2. 使混合,粘合。3. 使结婚。4. 兼备(各种性质)。~ *one with another* 合并[结合]甲和乙。~ *bricks with cement* 用水泥砌砖。— ***vi***. 成为一体,合一,联合,团结;混合,一致,协力。*People all over the world* ~! 全世界人民联合起来!

u·nite[2] [ˈjuːnait, juˈnait; ˋjunaɪt] ***n***. 由奈特〔英国詹姆斯一世时的金币,等于二十先令〕。

u·nit·ed [juˈnaitid; jʊˋnaɪtɪd] ***a***. 1. 联合起来的;合并在一起的,统一的。2. 一体同心的,团结一致的,协力的。3.【植】连生的。*a* ~ *effort* 共同努力。*a* ~ *action* 一致行动。*U- we stand, divided we fall*. 团结顶得住,分裂必垮台。*break into a* ~ *laugh* 一起哄笑起来。*in one* ~ *body* 成一体。***the U- Arab Emirates*** [eˈmiərits; ɛˋmɪərɪts] 阿拉伯联合酋长国。***the U- Kingdom*** (大不列颠和北爱尔兰的)联合王国〔略 U. K.〕。***the U- States*** (***of America***) 美利坚合众国〔略 U. S. (A.)〕。**U- Nations** 联合国〔略 UN〕。**U- Nations Organization** 〔略 UNO〕联合国组织。**U- Nations Security Council** 联合国安全理事会。**U- Press (International)** (美国)合众(国际)社。**-ly** ***ad***. 联合,一致,协力。

u·ni·tive [ˈjuːnitiv; ˋjunətɪv] ***a***. 1. 统一的。2. 趋于统一的。

u·nit·ize [ˈjuːnitaiz; ˋjunətaɪz] ***vt***. (*-iz·ed*, *-iz·ing*) 使成为一单位或一整体。**-i·za·tion** [ˌjuːnitaiˈzeiʃən; ˏjunətaɪˋzeʃən] ***n***.

u·ni·ty [ˈjuːniti; ˋjunətɪ] ***n***. 1. 单一,唯一;个体,整体,统一体。2. 团结,一致,和睦,调和。3. 同质,同式,同样;不变性,一贯性。4. 统一;合一。5.【数】一,单位元素。6.【法】共同租地权,共有。~ *and multiplicity* 一和多。*the dramatic unities* = *the unities of time, place, and action* 戏剧上时间、场所、情节的一致,三一律。*family* ~ 家庭融洽。*national* ~ 全国一致。***live at*** [***in***] ~ 融洽过日子,和睦相处 (*with*)。~ **coupling**【机】完整耦合。~ **dividend**【政】统一红利〔指国家重新统一可给各方带来的好处〕。

Univ. = Universalist;〔英〕University.

univ. = 1. universal(ly). 2. university.

UNIVAC = universal automatic computer 通用电子计算机。

u·ni·va·lence [ˌjuːniˈveiləns; ˏjunəˋveləns], **-len·cy** [-lənsi; -lənsɪ] ***n***.【生】单价;【化】一价,独价。

u·ni·va·lent [ˌjuːniˈveilənt, juˈnivələnt; ˏjunəˋvelənt, jʊˋnɪvələnt] ***a***. 1.【生】(染色体)单价的,单独的。2.【化】单一价的〔指只有一种价的元素〕。

u·ni·valve [ˈjuːnivælv; ˋjunəˏvælv] **I** ***n***.【动】单壳(软体动物)〔如蜗牛〕。**II** ***a***. 1. 单壳(的)。2. (介壳虫的)单盖瓣(的)。**-d** ***a***.

u·ni·ver·sal [ˌjuːniˈvəːsəl; ˏjunəˋvɝ sl] **I** ***a***. 1. 宇宙的,万有的,万物的;完全的,绝对的;全世界的。2. 人类全体的,万人的;全面的,普及的,普通的。3. 一般的,普遍的;【机】通用的,万能的;【逻】全称的。4. 万般的;多方面的;多才多艺的。*a* ~ *peace* 世界和平。*a* ~ *language* 世界通用语言。~ *brotherhood* 四海同胞。*a* ~ *maid* 打杂女佣工。*a* ~ *agent* 总代理人,全权代理人。~ **algebra** 泛代数(学)。**II** ***n***.【逻】全称命题;【哲】一般(性),普遍(性);共相。~ **arithmetic** 一般算术。~ **boiler graphite**【机】洗锅用铅粉。~ **chuck**【机】自动卡盘。~ **constant**【数】普适常数[恒量]。**U- Coordinated Time** 协调世界时〔以原子钟在若干个记时站测定的标准时间,等于格林威治时的平太阳时〕。~ **coupling**【机】万向(联轴)节,万向接头(= ~ joint)。~ **gravitation**【物】万有引力。~ **instrument**【天】万能仪。~ **joint**【机】万向接头。~ **joint knuckle**【解】自由关节。~ **mill**【机】万能铣床。**U- Product Code**〔美〕统一商品代码〔印在包装上的一系列编码线、空格和数字,可供商店结账处用光学扫描器读出定价等〕。~ **suffage** 普选(权)。~ **time**【天】世界时。~ **validity**【哲】普遍有效[正确]性。

u·ni·ver·sal·ism [ˌjuːniˈvəːsəlizəm; ˏjunəˋvɝsəlɪzm] ***n***. 1.〔U-〕【宗】宇宙神教;普济主义。2. = universality.

U·ni·ver·sal·ist [ˌjuːniˈvəːsəlist; ˏjunəˋvɝslɪst] **I** ***n***. 宇宙神教徒。**II** ***a***. = universalistic.

u·ni·ver·sal·is·tic [ˌjuːniˌvəːsəˈlistik; ˏjunəˏvɝsəˋlɪstɪk] ***a***. 1.〔U-〕【宗】宇宙神教(徒)的。2. 普遍的,一般的。

u·ni·ver·sal·i·ty [ˌjuːnivəˈsæliti; ˏjunəvɝˋsælətɪ] ***n***. 一般性,普遍性,无所不包性。*the* ~ *of contradiction* 矛盾的普遍性。

u·ni·ver·sal·i·za·tion [ˌjuːniˌvəːsəlaiˈzeiʃən; ˏjunəˏvɝsəlaɪˋzeʃən] ***n***. 一般化,普遍化,普及。

u·ni·ver·sal·ize [ˌjuːniˈvəːsəlaiz; ˏjunəˋvɝslˏaɪz] ***vt***. 使一般化,使普遍化。

u·ni·ver·sal·ly [ˌjuːniˈvəːsəli; ˏjunəˋvɝslɪ] ***ad***. 1. 一般地,全面地。2. 普遍地。

u·ni·ver·sal·ness [ˌjuːniˈvəːsəlnis; ˏjunəˋvɝslnɪs] ***n***. 1. 宇宙性,万有。2. 普遍性。3. 整体,全体。4. 全面;多面。5. 通用。6. 广用。7.【逻】全称性。

u·ni·verse [ˈjuːnivəːs; ˋjunəˏvɝs] ***n***. 1. 宇宙;万有,天地万物,森罗万象;全世界;全人类。2. 全领域;【统】全域;【逻】整体。3.【天】银河系;恒星与星辰系。*the fundamental law of the* ~ 宇宙的根本规律。~ ***of discourse***【逻】论域。

u·ni·ver·si·ade [ˌjuːniˈvəːsiæd; ˏjunəˋvɝsɪæd] ***n***.〔口〕世界大学生运动会 (= the World University Games)。

u·ni·ver·si·ty [ˌjuːniˈvəːsiti; ˏjunəˋvɝsətɪ] ***n***. 1. (综合)大学。2. 大学当局。3.〔集合词〕大学人员。4.〔口〕【体】大学选手,大学队。*The* ~ *carried the day*. 大学队得胜了。~ **extention** 大学教育普及运动〔如成人业余教育,夜大学等〕。~ **man** 大学生;受过大学教育的人。

u·ni·ver·sol·o·gy [ˌjuːnivəˈsɔlədʒi; ˏjunəvɝˋsɑlədʒɪ] ***n***. 宇宙学。

u·niv·o·cal [ˌjuːniˈvəukəl; juˋnɪvəkḷ] ***a***. 一意的,单意的;不含糊的。

U·nix [ˈjuːniks; ˋjunɪks] ***n***.【商标】【计】Unix (电脑)操作系统。

un·joint [ʌnˈdʒɔint; ʌnˋjɔɪnt] ***vt***. 1. 使分开,使脱节。2. 把(关节)拆离。

un·just [ˈʌnˈdʒʌst; ʌnˋdʒʌst] ***a***. 1. 不义的,不正当的,不法的。2. 不公平的,不公道的。~ *enrichment* 不正利得,横财。*the* ~ 不正当的人们。**-ly** ***ad***.

un·jus·ti·fi·a·ble [ʌnˈdʒʌstifaiəbl; ʌnˋdʒʌstəˏfaɪəbḷ] ***a***. 不能认为合理的,不能认为正当的,不能为之辩护的,无理的。**-a·bly** ***ad***.

un·kempt [ˈʌnˈkem*p*t; ʌnˋkɛmpt] ***a***. 1. 不整洁的,乱七八糟的;(服装等)邋遢的。2. (头发)未梳的,蓬乱的。3. (言语等)粗野的,生硬的。**-ness** ***n***.

un·kenned [ʌnˈkend; ʌnˋkɛnd] ***a***.〔Scot.〕不知道的;奇异的。

un·ken·nel [ʌnˈkenl; ʌnˋkɛnəl], ***vt***. (*-neled*, *-nelled*; *-nel·ing*) 1. 把(狐等)从洞穴中逐出;放(犬)出窝。2. 暴露;揭开;揭发。— ***vi***. (狐等)出洞;(犬)出窝。

un·kept [ˈʌnˈkept; ʌnˋkɛpt] ***a***. 1. 被忽略的,被忽视的。2. 未加防御的。3. 未被存储的。

un·key [ˈʌŋki; ˋʌŋkɪ] ***n***.〔美俚〕黑人老头子。

un·kill·able [ʌnˈkiləbl; ʌnˋkɪləbl] ***a***. 1. 不死的,长生的;毁灭的。2. 永久的,永恒的;持久的;不朽的。3. 无法超越的;不可战胜的。

un·kind [ʌnˈkaind; ʌnˋkaɪnd] ***a***. 不和善的;不亲切的;冷酷的。**-ness** ***n***.

un·kind·ly [ʌnˈkaindli; ʌnˋkaɪndlɪ] **I** ***a***. = unkind. **II** ***ad***. 不和善地,不亲切地;冷酷地。

un·knit [ʌnˈnit; ʌnˋnɪt] ***vt***. (~, *~ted* [ʌnˈnitid; ʌnˋnɪtɪd]; *~ting*) 拆(编织物);解(结);平整(皱褶);〔喻〕

展开(皱起的眉头)。

un·knot [ʌn'nɔt; ʌn`nɑt] *vt*. (***un·knot·ted*** [ʌn'nɔtid; ʌn`nɑtɪd]; ***-knot·ting***) **1**. 解(结)。**2**. 解决(难题、困难)。

un·know·a·ble ['ʌn'nəuəbl; ʌn`noəbl] **I** *a*. 不可知道的;【哲】不可知的。**II** *n*. 〔the U-〕【哲】不可知物。

un·know·ing [ʌn'nəuiŋ; ʌn`noɪŋ] *a*. **1**. 不知道的,没察觉…的 (*of*)。**2**. 无知的。~ *aid to enemy* 无知的[自己不知道的]利敌行为。**-ly** ***ad***.

un·known ['ʌn'nəun; ʌn`non] **I** *a*. **1**. 未知的,未详的;未被发觉的。**2**. 数不清的,无数的。*a man* ~ *to me* 我不知道[认识]的人。~ *wealth* 巨富。~ ***to*** …所不知道的;〔作副词用〕没有给…知道,不给…晓得 (*He did it* ~ *to me*. 他没有让我知道就做了那件事了)。**II** *n*. 未[不]认识的人[物];【数】未知数[量,元]。***the Great U-*** 伟大的匿名作家〔Sir Walter Scott 的历史小说《威弗利》匿名出版时,人们对该书作者的尊称〕。***the U-Warrior*** [〔美〕***Soldier***] 无名战士〔其遗体被选出作为阵亡将士的代表接受国葬〕。***venture into the*** ~ 闯进未知世界中,大胆地探索未知的世界。

un·la·boured ['ʌn'leibəd; ʌn`lebɚd] *a*. **1**. 未经耕作的。**2**. (似乎)不费力的。**3**. 自然的,流利的。

un·lace ['ʌn'leis; ʌn`les] *vt*. **1**. 解开(鞋等的)带子。**2**. 【猎】把(打到的野兽)切成块。

un·lade ['ʌn'leid; ʌn`led] *vt*. (***-lad·ed***; ***-lad·ed***, ***-lad·en***; ***-lad·ing***)给…卸货;卸(货)。— ***vi***. 卸货。

un·laid ['ʌn'leid; ʌn`led] unlay 的过去式和过去分词。

un·la·ment·ed ['ʌnlə'mentid; ˏʌnlə`mɛntɪd] *a*. 没有人悲悼的,没有人叹息的,没有人惋惜的。

un·lash [ʌn'læʃ; ʌn`læʃ] *vt*. 解开(绑着的东西)。

un·latch ['ʌn'lætʃ; ʌn`lætʃ] *vt*. 拉开(门窗的)闩;开(门上的)暗锁;解开(鞋)扣。

un·law·ful ['ʌn'lɔːful; ʌn`lɔfəl] *a*. **1**. 不法的,违法的,非法的,不正当的。**2**. 私生的。*an* ~ *assembly* 非法集会。**-ly** ***ad***. **-ness** ***n***.

un·lax [ʌn'læks; ʌn`læks] *vi*., *vt*. 〔美〕= relax.

un·lay ['ʌn'lei; ʌn`le] *vt*. (***-laid*** [-'leid; -`led])【海】退缠(缠绕着的绳缆等),拧散(绳线的股)。

un·lead·ed [ʌn'ledid; ʌn`lɛdɪd] *a*. **1**. 没有用铅包的,未用铅来增加重量的。**2**. 【印】在间隔中未插铅条的。

un·learn ['ʌn'ləːn; ʌn`lɝn] *vt*., *vi*. (~***ed***, ***-learnt*** [-'ləːnt; -`lɝnt]) (使)忘掉(学过的东西);(使)抛弃(谬见、坏习惯等)。

un·learn·ed[1] [ʌn'ləːnid; ʌn`lɝnɪd] **I** *a*. 无学识的;无文化的;未受教育的。**II** *n*. 〔the ~〕蒙昧无知的人们。**-ly** ***ad***.

un·learned[2] [ʌn'ləːnt, -ləːnd; ʌn`lɝnt, -lɝnd] *a*. **1**. 不是学来的,不学就知道的。**2**. 未学过的,未学会的。

un·learnt [ʌn'ləːnt; ʌn`lɝnt] **I** unlearn 的过去式和过去分词。**II** *a*. = unlearned[2].

un·leash ['ʌn'liːʃ; ʌn`liʃ] *vt*. **1**. 解开…的皮带[链索]。**2**. 〔喻〕解放,使自由;放纵;发动。~ *one's desire* 纵欲。~ *a war* 发动战争。—***vi***. 不受约束;自由自在(地寻欢作乐);随随便便。

un·leav·ened ['ʌn'levnd; ʌn`lɛvənd] *a*. **1**. 不含酵素的,未予发酵的。**2**. 没有受到影响[感化]的。

un·less [ən'les, ʌn'les; ən`lɛs, ʌn`lɛs] **I** ***conj***. 如果不,要是不,除非。*We shall go* ~ *it rains*. 如果不下雨我们就去。*U- you work harder, you will not pass the examination*. 如果不加紧用功,你就不能通过考试。*U- absolutely compelled, I shall not go*. 除非万不得已,我是不去的。~ ***and until*** = until 〔unless and 是冗语〕。**II** ***prep***. 除…之外。*U- a miracle, he'll not be back in time*. 除非发生奇迹,他不会及时赶回来。★此种用法隐含着一个动词被省略,即相当于 U- a miracle (happens) ....

un·let·tered ['ʌn'letəd; ʌn`lɛtɚd] *a*. **1**. 不是用文字写成的;无字的;没有字母等记号的。**2**. 没有学识的;目不识丁的。

un·li·censed ['ʌn'laisənst; ʌn`laɪsənst] *a*. **1**. 没有执照[许可证]的。**2**. 无节制的,放纵的。*an* ~ *physician* 没有执照的医生,未经许可的医生。

un·licked ['ʌn'likt; ʌn`lɪkt] *a*. **1**. (仔兽)没有经过母兽舐干净的。**2**. 不像样的;撒野的,没礼貌的。*an* ~ *cub* 撒野的小兽;撒野的小伙子[小姑娘]。

un·like ['ʌn'laik; ʌn`laɪk] **I** *a*. 不同的,不相似的,相异的。~*signs* 不同的符号。**II** ***prep***. 不像…,和…不同。*The picture is quite* ~ *him*. 这张照片完全不像他。*How* ~ *you to forget your dinner*! 你怎么也会忘记吃饭!

un·like·ly [ʌn'laikli; ʌn`laɪklɪ] *a*. **1**. 未必有的,不像是真的,不一定有希望的。**2**. 〔后接不定式,可用作表语〕未必可能的,不大可能的,不一定有把握的。*What he tells us is* ~ *to happen*. 他告诉我们的,不像是真事。*A victory is* ~ *but not impossible*. 胜利不一定有希望但也不一定不可能。*He is* ~ *to come*. 他未必会来。*It is not* ~ *that a huge wave has overturned his boat*. 一阵大浪把他的船打翻了,这种情况不是不可能的。***in the*** ~ ***event of*** 万一。**-i·hood**, **-i·ness** ***n***.

un·lim·ber[1] [ʌn'limbə; ʌn`lɪmbɚ] **I** *a*. 不易弯曲的;僵硬的。**II** *vt*., *vi*. (使)变得柔软;(使)柔软。

un·lim·ber[2] [ʌn'limbə; ʌn`lɪmbɚ] *vt*., *vi*. 卸下(炮的)牵引车准备(开炮);(使)准备行动。

un·lim·it·ed [ʌn'limitid; ʌn`lɪmɪtɪd] *a*. **1**. 无边的,无限的;没有限制的;没有限定的,不定的。**2**. 极大的;过多的,过度的。~ *liability* 无限责任。*an* ~ *company* 无限公司。~ *exposure* 长时间曝光。*drink* ~ *coffee* 喝过多的咖啡。**-ly** ***ad***.

un·link ['ʌn'liŋk; ʌn`lɪŋk] *vt*., *vi*. 解开(链环);拆散。

un·liq·ui·dat·ed ['ʌn'likwideitid; ʌn`lɪkwəˏdetɪd] *a*. 未清算的,未决算的;未偿还的,支付的。

un·list·ed [ʌn'listid; ʌn`lɪstɪd] *a*. **1**. 未登上名册的。**2**. 非公开登记的;内部安排的。**3**. (证券)未上证券市场的。

un·lit ['ʌn'lit; ʌn`lɪt] *a*. 未点燃的;未点亮的。

un·liv·a·ble ['ʌn'livəbl; ʌn`lɪvəbl̩] *a*. 不宜居住的;不舒适的〔指居住条件〕。

un·live ['ʌn'liv; ʌn`lɪv] *vt*. 抹除[忘却](过去的生活经历);(以新的生活)消除(过去经历的后果)。*History cannot be* ~*d*. 历史是不能抹掉[忘却]的。*He wishes to* ~ *the crimes he has committed*. 他希望(以新的生活)消解他所犯的罪行。

un·load ['ʌn'ləud; ʌn`lod] *vt*. **1**. 从…卸下货载;卸下(货载)。**2**. 解除…的负担;摆脱(身上的负担);倾吐(压在心里的思想)。**3**. 退出(枪膛里的)子弹。**4**. 【商】抛售(证券)。— ***vi***. **1**. 卸货,起货。**2**. 退出枪弹。**-er** ***n***. 卸货人;卸载机。

un·lock ['ʌn'lɔk; ʌn`lɑk] *vt*. **1**. 开(门、箱等的)锁。**2**. 使张开;使开启。**3**. 表白(心迹)。**4**. 揭露(秘密);破译;解读。**5**. 释放出。— ***vi***. 开启着,被解开;不受羁绊。

un·looked-for [ʌn'luktfɔː; ʌn`lʊktˏfɔr] *a*. 未予寻求过的;没有预料到的,想不到的,意外的。

un·loose ['ʌn'luːs; ʌn`lus], **un·loos·en** [-n; -n̩] *vt*. 解开,放松;释放。**-loos·a·ble** ***a***.

un·love·ly ['ʌn'lʌvli; ʌn`lʌvlɪ] *a*. 不可爱的,不美的;可厌的。

un·lov·ing ['ʌn'lʌviŋ; ʌn`lʌvɪŋ] *a*. 无爱意的,无情的,冷酷的。

un·luck·i·ly [ʌn'lʌkili; ʌn`lʌkɪlɪ] ***ad***. 不幸;偏巧,偏偏。

un·luck·y [ʌn'lʌki; ʌn`lʌkɪ] *a*. (***-i·er***; ***-i·est***) **1**. 不幸的,倒霉的。**2**. 不凑巧的;令人遗憾的。**3**. 不顺利的,不成功的。**4**. 不吉利的,不祥的。***in an*** ~ ***hour*** 偏偏,偏巧。**-i·ly** ***ad***.

unm. = unmarried.

U

un·make [ˈʌnˈmeik; ʌnˋmek] *vt*. (*-made* [-ˈmeid; -ˋmed]) 1. 破坏,毁坏;使消失。2. 使变形,使变质。3. 废除(国王等)。4. 改变(决定等)。

un·man [ˈʌnˈmæn; ʌnˋmæn] *vt*. (*-nn-*) 1. 使失去男子汉气概,使落魄[沮丧]。2. 阉割,给…去势。3. 撤去…的人员[船员]。

un·man·age·a·ble [ʌnˈmænidʒəbl; ʌnˋmænɪdʒəbl] *a*. 无法处理的,难办理的,难收拾的;难管理的,难应付的,难弄的;(孩子)不听话的。*the* ~ *situation* 难收拾的局势。*an* ~ *horse* 劣马。**-a·bly** *ad*.

un·man·ly [ˈʌnˈmænli; ʌnˋmænlɪ] *a*. (*-li·er*; *-li·est*) 不像男子汉的;娇气的;没胆量的,懦弱的。

un·manned [ʌnˈmænd; ʌnˋmænd] *a*. 1. 无人驾驶[操作]的,遥控的。2. 无人居住的,荒废的。3. 失去男子气概的。4. 被阉割过的。

un·man·ner·ly [ʌnˈmænəli; ʌnˋmænəlɪ] *a*., *ad*. 没礼貌的[地],粗野的[地]。

un·marked [ˈʌnˈmɑːkt; ʌnˋmɑrkt] *a*. 1. 未做记号的。2. 没被注意到的。

un·marred [ˈʌnˈmɑːd; ʌnˋmɑrd] *a*. 未玷污的;未损伤的,未损坏的。

un·mar·ried [ˈʌnˈmærid; ʌnˋmærɪd] *a*. 未婚的;独身的。

un·mask [ˈʌnˈmɑːsk; ʌnˋmæsk] *vi*. 脱去假面具,现出本来面目。— *vt*. 撕下…的假面具;暴露;揭露;【军】(开炮佯射)使(敌方炮位)暴露。

un·match·a·ble [ˈʌnˈmætʃəbl; ʌnˋmætʃəbl] *a*. 1. 难匹敌的,无可比拟的,不能对抗的。2. 不能相配的。

un·matched [ˈʌnˈmætʃt; ʌnˋmætʃt] *a*. 1. 无敌的,无比的。2. (颜色等)不相配[衬]的。

un·mean·ing [ʌnˈmiːniŋ; ʌnˋminɪŋ] *a*. 1. 没有意义的。2. (面孔等)呆板的,没表情的。**-ly** *ad*.

un·meant [ʌnˈment; ʌnˋmɛnt] *a*. 不是故意的。

un·meas·ured [ʌnˈmeʒəd; ʌnˋmɛʒəd] *a*. 1. 不可测量的。2. 无边无际的;没有界限的。3. 【韵】不按照韵律的。

un·meet [ʌnˈmiːt; ʌnˋmit] *a*. = unfit.

un·men·tion·a·ble [ʌnˈmenʃənəbl; ʌnˋmɛnʃənəbl] I *a*. 说不出口的,难于出口的。II *n*. 〔*pl*.〕1. 难于说出口的事物。2. 〔谑〕裤子;内衣。

un·mer·ci·ful [ʌnˈməːsiful; ʌnˋməsɪfəl] *a*. 1. 无慈悲心的,无情的,残忍的。2. 过分的,过大的。**-ly** *ad*.

un·mer·it·ed [ˈʌnˈmeritid; ʌnˋmɛrɪtɪd] *a*. 无功而得的,不该得的;不配的,(赏罚)不当的。

un·me·thod·i·cal [ˈʌnmiˈθɔdikəl; ˌʌnmɪˋθɑdɪkl] *a*. 没有什么方法的,不讲究方式的;没有组织的,没有条理的,胡乱的。**-ly** *ad*.

un·met·ri·cal [ˈʌnˈmetrikəl; ʌnˋmɛtrɪkl] *a*. 不按照音律的。

un·mil·i·ta·ry [ˈʌnˈmilitəri; ʌnˋmɪləˌtɛrɪ] *a*. 1. 非军事的。2. 违反军队训练[规律]的。3. 不像军人的。

un·mind·ful [ʌnˈmaindful; ʌnˋmaɪndfəl, -ˋmaɪnfəl] *a*. 不注意的,漫不经心的;易忘的 (*of*; *that*)。**-ly** *ad*.

un·mis·tak·a·ble [ˈʌnmisˈteikəbl; ˌʌnməˋstekəbl] *a*. 不会弄错的,不可能发生误解的,明白的。*The slogans are* ~. 口号明确。**-a·bly** *ad*.

un·mit·i·gat·ed [ʌnˈmitigeitid; ʌnˋmɪtəˌgetɪd] *a*. 1. 没有和缓的,没有减轻的。2. 十足的,纯粹的。*an* ~ *lie* 纯粹的骗人话。*an* ~ *ass* 大傻瓜。**-ly** *ad*.

un·mixed, -mixt [ˈʌnˈmikst; ʌnˋmɪkst] *a*. 没有掺杂的,纯粹的。*not an* ~ *blessing* 不是纯粹的幸福。

un·mo·lested [ˈʌnməuˈlestid; ˌʌnməˋlɛstɪd] *a*. 未受到烦扰的;平静的。

un·moor [ˈʌnˈmuə; ʌnˋmʊr] *vt*., *vi*. 【海】1. (使)拔锚,(使)解缆。2. (使)改泊单锚。

un·mor·al [ˈʌnˈmɔrəl; ʌnˋmɔrəl, -ˋmɑrəl] *a*. 1. 非道德的;和道德无关的,不涉及道德的。2. 没有道德观念的;不道德的。**-ly** *ad*.

un·mount·ed [ˈʌnˈmauntid; ʌnˋmaʊntɪd] *a*. 1. (图画、照片等)没有镶边框的。2. 未上炮架的。3. 不骑马的。

un·moved [ˈʌnˈmuːvd; ʌnˋmuvd] *a*. 1. (决心等)坚定的。2. 不动心的,冷静的,镇定的。

un·muf·fle [ʌnˈmʌfl; ʌnˋmʌfəl] *vt*. (*-fled*; *fling*) 1. 揭去(脸上、头上等的)遮盖物。2. 脱去(桨、鼓等)套子。— *vi*. 除去覆盖物。

un·mur·mur·ing [ˈʌnˈməːməriŋ; ˋʌnˋmɝmərɪŋ] *a*. 不嘟囔的;不发牢骚的。**-ly** *ad*.

un·mu·si·cal [ˈʌnˈmjuːzikəl; ʌnˋmjuzɪkl] *a*. 1. 非音乐的;不悦耳的,不合调子的,难听的。2. 不懂音乐的,没有音乐修养的;对音乐没有兴趣的;没有音乐技巧的。

un·muz·zle [ˈʌnˈmʌzl; ʌnˋmʌzl] *vt*. 1. 拿下(狗等的)口罩。2. 〔喻〕对…解除束缚言论自由的法令。

un·nam(e)·a·ble [ˈʌnˈneiməbl; ʌnˋneməbl] *a*. 叫不出名字来的;(恐怖等)不可名状的。

un·named [ˈʌnˈneimd; ʌnˋnemd] *a*. 没有名称的;未指名的;没有明确指定[说明]的。

un·nat·u·ral [ʌnˈnætʃərəl; ʌnˋnætʃərəl] *a*. 1. 不合自然规律的,不应有的。2. 不自然的;做作的,勉强的。3. 不合人情[人道]的;变态的;残忍的。4. 奇异的,奇怪的。*die an* ~ *death* 横死;死于非命。*an* ~ *smile* 假笑。~ **crime** [**vice, act**] 鸡奸。**-ly** *ad*. **-ness** *n*.

un·nec·es·sa·ri·ly [ʌnˈnesisərili; ʌnˋnɛsəˌsɛrəlɪ] *ad*. 不必要地,多余地,无用地,徒然,无谓。

un·nec·es·sa·ry [ʌnˈnesisəri; ʌnˋnɛsəˌsɛrɪ] I *a*. 不必要的,多余的,无用的,无益的。*with* ~ *care* 怀着不必要的顾虑。II *n*. 〔罕〕〔常 *pl*.〕不必要[多余]的东西。

un·neigh·bour·ly, 〔美〕**-bor·ly** [ˈʌnˈneibəli; ʌnˋnebəlɪ] *a*. 不像邻人的,没有邻舍情谊的;不懂交际的,不友好的;不亲切的。

un·nerve [ˈʌnˈnəːv; ʌnˋnɝv] *vt*. 使失去意志力,使丧失勇气;使身心交疲。

un·neu·rot·ic [ˌʌnnjuˈrɔtik; ˌʌnnjuˋrɑtɪk] *a*. 神经正常的。

un·nil·hex·i·um [ˌjuːnəlˈheksiəm; ˌjunəlˋhɛksiəm] *n*. 【化】钅喜。

un·nil·pen·ti·um [ˌjuːnəlˈpentiəm; ˌjunəlˋpɛntiəm] *n*. 【化】钅杜。

un·nil·qua·di·um [ˌjuːnəlˈkwædiəm; ˌjunəlˋkwædiəm] *n*. 【化】钅卢。

un·no·ticed [ˈʌnˈnəutist; ʌnˋnotɪst] *a*. 不受人注意的;没有受到注意的;不触目的;没人理睬的。*pass* ~ 被忽略过去;被遗漏。

un·num·bered [ˈʌnˈnʌmbəd; ʌnˋnʌmbəd] *a*. 1. 没有数的。2. 数不清的,无数的。3. 未编号的。

UNO [ˈjuːnəu; ˋjuno] = United Nations Organization 联合国组织。

uno ani·mo [ˈjuːnəu ˈænimәu; ˋjuno ˋænɪmo] 〔L.〕一致地,无异议地。

un·ob·jec·tion·a·ble [ˈʌnəbˈdʒekʃənəbl; ˌʌnəbˋdʒɛkʃənəbl, -ˋdʒɛkʃnə-] *a*. 1. 难反对的,不能指摘的,无可非议的。2. 不致引起反感的;婉转的。

un·ob·serv·ant [ˈʌnəbˈzəːvənt; ˌʌnəbˋzɝvənt] *a*. 1. 不注意[留心]的;没有观察力的。2. 不遵守(规章等)的(*of*)。

un·ob·served [ˈʌnəbˈsəːvd; ˌʌnəbˋzɝvd] *a*. 1. 没有观察到的,没有受到注意的。2. (规章等)未受人遵守的。

un·ob·tru·sive [ˈʌnəbˈtruːsiv; ˌʌnəbˋtrusɪv] *a*. 不突出的,不触目的,不冒昧的,谦逊的。**-ly** *ad*.

un·oc·cu·pied [ˈʌnˈɔkjupaid; ʌnˋɑkjəˌpaɪd] *a*. 1. (房子等)没人住的,空着的。2. 【军】未被占领的,无人占领的。3. 空闲的,无事的。

un·of·fend·ed [ˈʌnəˈfendid; ʌnəˋfɛndɪd] *a*. 没被冒犯的,没被得罪的;不生气的。

un·of·fend·ing [ˈʌnəˈfendiŋ; ˌʌnəˋfɛndɪŋ] *a*. 1. 不侵犯人的,不冲撞人的。2. 无害的,无罪的。

un·of·fi·cial [ˈʌnəˈfiʃəl; ˏʌnəˋfɪʃəl] ***a*.** 非官方的,非正式的;非法定的。*an* ～ *candidate* 非正式候补人。**-ly** ***ad*.**

un·o·pened [ˈʌnˈəupənd; ʌnˋopənd] ***a*. 1.** 没有打开过的;没有拆开的,封着的。**2.** (书页)未裁开的。**3.** (港口等)不开放的。

un·or·gan·ized [ˈʌnˈɔːgənaizd; ʌnˋɔrgənˏaɪzd] ***a*. 1.** 未加组织的;未编成的;无组织的。**2.**【生】无细胞结构的。**3.**〔美〕没有加入工会组织的。～ **ferment** 非生(物)酶,抗热酶,非机体酵素。

un·o·rig·i·nal [ˈʌnəˈridʒənəl; ˏʌnəˋrɪdʒənl̩] ***a*. 1.** 无独创性的。**2.** 非原先的。

un·or·tho·dox [ˈʌnˈɔːθədɔks; ʌnˋɔrθəˏdɑks] ***a*.** 非正统的;异端的。**-ly** ***ad*.**

un·os·ten·ta·tious [ˈʌnˌɔstenˈteiʃəs; ˏʌnɑstənˋteʃəs] ***a*.** 不虚饰门面的;不自大的,不傲慢的;朴素的。**-ly** ***ad*.**

Unp【化】元素铕的符号(= unnilpentium)。

un·pack [ˈʌnˈpæk; ʌnˋpæk] ***vt*.** 打开(包裹等),解开;从(包裹等)中拿出;从(车、马上)卸下货物。— ***vt*.** 打开包裹[行李(等)]。

un·paged [ʌnˈpeidʒd; ʌnˋpedʒd] ***a*.** (书等)未标页码的。

un·paid [ˈʌnˈpeid; ʌnˋped] ***a*. 1.** 未付的,(债等)未还的,未缴纳的。**2.** 不受酬的,名誉上的;没薪水的;无报酬的。*letters posted* ～ 欠资信件。***the*** (***great***) ～〔主英〕无薪法官。～ **workers**〔美〕无薪劳动者〔指操持家务的家庭主妇、慈善事业的志愿工作者等〕。

un·paired [ˈʌnˈpɛəd; ʌnˋpɛrd, -ˋpærd] ***a*. 1.** 未配对的;无配偶的。**2.** (鱼)奇(鳍)的。

un·pal·at·a·ble [ʌnˈpælətəbl; ʌnˋpælətəbl, -lɪtə-] ***a*.** 味道不好的;不好吃的;没味的;可厌的。**-a·bly** ***ad*.**

un·par·al·leled [ʌnˈpærəleld; ʌnˋpærəˏlɛld] ***a*.** 无比的,无双的;空前的。*an* ～ *victory* 空前大胜。～ *in history* 史无前例的。

un·par·don·a·ble [ʌnˈpɑːdnəbl; ʌnˋpɑrdn̩əbl̩] ***a*.** 不能宽恕的,不能原谅的。**-a·bly** ***ad*.**

un·par·lia·men·ta·ry [ˈʌnˌpɑːləˈmentəri; ˏʌnpɑrləˋmɛntərɪ] ***a*.** 违反议会法[议会惯例]的;议会内所不许的。～ *language* 不谨慎的话,气愤话。**-i·ly** ***ad*.**

un·pat·ent·ed [ˈʌnˈpeitəntid; ʌnˋpetəntɪd] ***a*.** 未获得专利权的,非专利的。

un·pa·tri·ot·ic [ˈʌnpætriˈɔtik; ˏʌnpætrɪˋɑtɪk] ***a*.** 不爱国的,没有爱国心的。**-i·cal·ly** ***ad*.**

un·paved [ˈʌnˈpeivd; ʌnˋpevd] ***a*.** 没有铺砌的,没有铺路的。

un·peg [ʌnˈpeg; ʌnˋpɛg] ***vt*.** (***-gg-***) **1.** 从…拔去木栓。**2.** 拔去[除去]木栓以松开。**3.** 使(证券等)解冻。

un·peo·ple [ˈʌnˈpiːpl; ʌnˋpi pl] ***vt*.** 消灭(某地)的居民,把(某地)弄成无人居住之地。**-d** ***a*.** 无居民的,无人的。

un·per·ceived [ˈʌnpəˈsiːvd; ˏʌnpəˋsivd] ***a*.** 未被发觉的,没有给人看见[被人注意]的。

un·per·fect [ˈʌnˈpəːfikt; ʌnˋpɝfɪkt] ***a*.** = imperfect.

un·per·son [ˈʌnˈpəːsn; ʌnˋpɝsn̩] **I** ***n*.** 退出一切公开场合的人,被完全忘却[像不存在一样]的人,没落人物〔指失去影响的政治家、知名人士等〕。**II** ***vt*.** 使变成没落人物。

un·per·suad·a·ble [ˈʌnpəˈsweidəbl; ˏʌnpəˋswedəbl̩] ***a*.** 不能说服的;坚定不移的,固执的。

un·per·turbed [ˈʌnpəˈtəːbd; ˏʌnpəˋtɝbd] ***a*.** 没有受到扰乱的;平静的,镇定的。

un·pick [ˈʌnˈpik; ʌnˋpɪk] ***vt*. 1.** 拔开,割开。**2.** 拆开(针脚);拆开(衣服等的)针脚。

un·picked[1] [ˈʌnˈpikt; ʌnˋpɪkt] ***a*.** 拆开针脚的,拆缝的。

un·picked[2] [ˈʌnˈpikt; ʌnˋpɪkt] ***a*. 1.** 未经挑选的,未拣过的。**2.** (花等)未摘的。

un·pin [ˈʌnˈpin; ʌnˋpɪn] ***vt*.** (***-nn-***) (从衣服等上)拔去别针;拔去别针拆开;拔掉(门)闩,拔去(插销)。

un·pit·ied [ˈʌnˈpitid; ʌnˋpɪtɪd] ***a*.** 没人怜悯的,没人同情的。

un·placed [ˈʌnˈpleist; ʌnˋplest] ***a*. 1.** 未得到安置的;没有固定位置[职位]的。**2.**【赛马】未获得前三名的。

un·planned [ˈʌnˈplænd; ʌnˋplænd] ***a*. 1.** 无计划的;未经筹划的。**2.** 意外的。

un·play·a·ble [ˈʌnˈpleiəbl; ʌnˋpleəbl̩] ***a*. 1.** 无法用乐器演奏的。**2.** (高尔夫球等)无法击出的。

un·pleas·ant [ʌnˈpleznt; ʌnˋplɛznt̩] ***a*.** 令人不愉快的,不舒服的,可厌的。**-ly** ***ad*.**

un·pleas·ant·ness [ʌnˈplezntnis; ʌnˋplɛzntnɪs] ***n*. 1.** 不愉快,不快,煞风景,无趣。**2.** 不和,倾轧。***have a slight*** ～ ***with sb*.** 和某人有点不痛快。***the late*** [***recent***] ～〔美谑〕南北战争〔又指南北战争后的美西战争、世界大战等〕。

un·pleas·ing [ˈʌnˈpliːziŋ; ʌnˋplizɪŋ] ***a*.** 令人不愉快的;可厌的;没趣的。

un·plug [ˈʌnˈplʌg; ʌnˋplʌg] ***vt*.** (***-gg-***) 拔去…的塞子[插头];去掉…的障碍物。**-ed** ***a*.**〔口〕(演奏)不使用电声乐器和音响设备的。

un·plumbed [ʌnˈplʌmd; ʌnˋplʌmd] ***a*. 1.** 未用铅锤线测量过垂直度的。**2.** 未查明的;不完全懂的。**3.** 无煤气、水管、下水道等设备的。**4.** 未加铅封的。

un·pol·ished [ˈʌnˈpɔliʃt; ʌnˋpɑlɪʃt] ***a*. 1.** 没有磨光的,没有擦亮的,没有光泽的。**2.** 未经润饰的。**3.** 不文雅的,粗鲁的,没礼貌的。

un·po·lit·i·cal [ˈʌnpəˈlitikəl; ˏʌnpəˋlɪtɪkl̩] ***a*. 1.** 无政治意义的;非政治的。**2.** 不关心政治的。

un·polled [ʌnˈpəuld; ʌnˋpold] ***a*. 1.** 未记名的,(选票)未登记的;未投票的,未点票的。**2.** 未作过民意测验[意见调查]的。

un·pop·u·lar [ˈʌnˈpɔpjulə; ʌnˋpɑpjələ] ***a*.** 无人望的,不受欢迎的;不流行的。*become more and more* ～ 越来越不得人心。

un·pop·u·lar·i·ty [ˈʌnˌpɔpjuˈlæriti; ʌnˏpɑpjəˋlærətɪ] ***n*.** 无人望,不受欢迎;不流行。

un·post·ed[1] [ʌnˈpəustid; ʌnˋpostɪd] ***a*.** 未悬挂"不得侵入"的告示的。

un·post·ed[2] [ʌnˈpəustid; ʌnˋpostɪd] ***a*.** (职位)无固定的。

un·post·ed[3] [ʌnˈpəustid; ʌnˋpostɪd] ***a*. 1.** 未付邮的,未投邮的。**2.** 未接到通知的。

un·prac·ti·cal [ˈʌnˈpræktikəl; ʌnˋpræktɪkl̩] ***a*.** 没有实践的,不切实际的;不实用的。

un·prac·tised,〔美〕**-ticed** [ʌnˈpræktist; ʌnˋpræktɪst] ***a*. 1.** 练习不足的;不熟练的;缺少经验的。**2.** 未实行的;未实际应用的,未使用的。

un·prec·e·dent·ed [ʌnˈpresidəntid; ʌnˋprɛsəˏdɛntɪd] ***a*. 1.** 没有前例的,空前的;无比的。**2.** 新奇的;崭新的。*an* ～ *success* 空前的成功。**-ly** ***ad*.**

un·pre·dict·a·ble [ˈʌn-priˈdiktəbl; ˏʌnprɪˋdɪktəbl̩] ***a*.** 无法预言的。**-a·bly** ***ad*.**

un·prej·u·diced [ʌnˈpredʒudist; ʌnˋprɛdʒədɪst] ***a*. 1.** 没有偏见[成见]的,公平的。**2.** (权利等)没有受到损害的。

un·pre·med·i·tat·ed [ˈʌnpriˈmediteitid; ˏʌnprɪˋmɛdəˏtetɪd] ***a*.** 非预谋的,不是故意的,没有预先考虑过的。～ *homicide* 非预谋杀人。**-ly** ***ad*.**

un·pre·pared [ˈʌnpriˈpɛəd; ˏʌnprɪˋpɛrd] ***a*. 1.** 没有预备[准备]的;临时的,(演说)即席的。**2.** 还没有决心[准备好]的 (*for*)。*Fight no battle* ～. 不打无准备之仗。*You caught me* ～. 你钻了我的空子。**-ly** ***ad*.**

un·pre·pos·sess·ing [ˈʌnˌpriːpəˈzesiŋ; ˏʌnpripəˋzɛsɪŋ] ***a*.** 不讨人喜欢的,不吸引人的。

un·pre·sent·a·ble [ˈʌn-priˈzentəbl; ˏʌnprɪˋzɛntəbl] ***a*.** 见不得人的;不像样的,拿不出去的。

un·pre·tend·ing [ˈʌnpriˈtendiŋ; ˏʌnprɪˋtɛndɪŋ], **un·pre·ten·tious** [-tenʃəs; -tɛnʃəs] ***a*.** 不装腔作势的,不

U

骄傲的,谦逊的。-ly *ad*.

un·prin·ci·pled [ʌn'prinsəpld; ʌn`prɪnsə pld] *a*. 无原则的,无节操的,无耻的,无道德的;蛮横无理的。

un·print·a·ble [ʌn'printəbl; ʌn`prɪntəbl] *a*. (因淫猥等)不能付印的,不适于付印的。

un·priv·i·leged ['ʌn'privilidʒd; ʌn`prɪvəlɪdʒd] *a*. 没有特权的,享受不到特权的;〔美〕处在社会下层的。

un·pro·duc·tive ['ʌnprə'dʌktiv; ˏʌnprə`dʌktɪv] *a*. 1. 没有出产物的,不毛的;没有收益的。2. 非生产性的。3. 没有效果的,徒然的。-ly *ad*.

un·pro·fessed ['ʌn-prə'fest; `ʌnprə`fest] *a*. 不公开宣称的。

un·pro·fes·sion·al ['ʌnprə'feʃənəl; ˏʌnprə`fɛʃənl] *a*. 1. 不是专家的;不是本行的;不在行的。2. 违反职业上习惯[道德、行规]的。3. 非职业性的,业余的。4. 与专门职业无关的。-ly *ad*.

un·prof·it·a·ble [ʌn'prɔfitəbl; ʌn`prɑfɪtəbl] *a*. 没有利润的,赚不到钱的;无益的,无效的,没用的。-a·bly *ad*.

un·prom·is·ing ['ʌn'prɔmisiŋ; ʌn`prɑmɪsɪŋ] *a*. 没有希望的,前途无望的;结果未必良好的。

un·prompt·ed ['ʌn'prɔm*p*tid; ʌn`prɑmptɪd] *a*. 未经提示的;未经敦促的,自发的。

un·pro·nounce·a·ble ['ʌnprə'naunsəbl; ˏʌnprə`naʊnsəbl] *a*. 不能发音的;难发音的。

un·pro·pi·tious ['ʌnprə'piʃəs; ˏʌnprə`pɪʃəs] *a*. 不吉利的,不祥的,背时的,倒霉的。-ly *ad*.

un·pro·tect·ed ['ʌnprə'tektid; ˏʌnprə`tɛktɪd] *a*. 1. 没有防卫的,不设防的。2. 无装甲的。3. 没有得到关税保护的。4. 无保护(人)的。

un·proved ['ʌn'pru:vd; ʌn`pruvd] *a*. 未被证明的;未经检验的。

un·pro·vid·ed ['ʌn-prə'vaidid; ˏʌnprə`vaɪdɪd] *a*. 1. 无供给的,无生活来源的。2. 未作准备的。

un·pro·voked ['ʌn-prə'vəukt; ˏʌnprə`vokt] *a*. 无缘无故的,非因触犯而发生的。

un·pub·lished ['ʌn'pʌbliʃt; ʌn`pʌblɪʃt] *a*. 未发表过的;未公开出版的。

un·pun·ished ['ʌn'pʌniʃt; ʌn`pʌnɪʃt] *a*. 未受处罚的,得免刑罚的;逍遥法外的。

un·pu·ri·fied ['ʌn'pjuərifaid; `ʌn`pjurɪfaɪd] *a*. 未纯化的,未精制的。

Unq. 【化】元素𨧀的符号(= unnilquadium)。

un·qual·i·fied ['ʌn'kwɔlifaid; ʌn`kwɑləˏfaɪd] *a*. 1. 不够格的,没有资格的;不适任[适当]的。2. [ʌn'kwɔlifaid; ʌn`kwɑləfaɪd] 无条件[限制]的,绝对的;〔口〕十足的,彻底的。*an* ~ *fool* 大傻瓜。-ly *ad*.

un·quench·a·ble [ʌn'kwentʃəbl; ʌn`kwentʃəbl] *a*. 不能熄灭的;(热情)压制不住的;止不住的。-a·bly *ad*.

un·ques·tion·a·ble [ʌn'kwestʃənəbl; ʌn`kwestʃənəbl] *a*. 无疑问的,不成问题的;无可非议的;确实的,当然的,明确的。-a·bly *ad*.

un·ques·tioned [ʌn'kwestʃənd; ʌn`kwestʃənd] *a*. 1. 不成为问题的。2. 未受调查[审问]的。3. 无人争辩[怀疑]的,无异议的。

un·ques·tion·ing [ʌn'kwestʃəniŋ; ʌn`kwestʃənɪŋ] *a*. 不提问题[质问]的,没有疑问的;毫不迟疑[踌躇]的;无条件的,绝对的。

un·qui·et ['ʌn'kwaiət; ʌn`kwaɪət] I *a*. 1. 不平静的;动摇的,不稳的。2. 不安的。II *n*. 1. 动荡。2. 焦虑,不安。-ly *ad*. -ness *n*.

un·quot·a·ble ['ʌn'kwəutəbl; ʌn`kwotə bl] *a*. 不能引用的,无引用价值的。

un·quote ['ʌn'kwəut; ʌn`kwot] *int*. 〔美〕〔口授用语〕引语结束!

un·rav·el [ʌn'rævəl; ʌn`rævl] *vt*. (-*l*(*l*)-) 1. 解开,拆散,拆开(毛线、绳索等)。2. 解明,阐明,解决。— *vi*. 散开,松线。

un·read ['ʌn'red; ʌn`red] *a*. 1. (书等)未读的;尚未审阅的。2. 不读书的,无教育的;无学识的。

un·read·a·ble [ʌn'ri:dəbl; ʌn`ridəbl] *a*. 1. 不能读的;不能辨认的。2. 难读的;不值得读的。

un·read·y ['ʌn'redi; ʌn`rɛdɪ] *a*. 1. 没有预备[准备]的。2. 不敏捷的。3. 〔古、方〕拖沓的,衣着不讲究的。-i·ly *ad*. -i·ness *n*.

un·re·al ['ʌn'riəl, 'ʌn'ri:əl; ʌn`riəl, ʌn`ril] *a*. 不实在的;非现实的;不真实的。-ly *ad*.

un·re·al·is·tic ['ʌnriə'listik; ˏʌnrɪə`lɪstɪk] *a*. 不现实的;不实际的;空想的。-cal·ly *ad*.

un·re·al·i·ty ['ʌnri'æliti; ˏʌnrɪ`ælətɪ] *n*. (*pl*. -*ties*) 1. 不真实,不实在。2. 幻想。3. 虚构;不切实际。

un·rea·son ['ʌn'ri:zn; ʌn`rizn] *n*. 无理,缺乏理性;不合理;背理。

un·rea·son·a·ble [ʌn'ri:znəbl; ʌn`riznə bl, -znə bl] *a*. 1. 无理性的,不懂道理的,不讲理的。2. 不合理的,荒唐的;过度的,(价格等)过高的,(收费等)不当的。-a·bly *ad*.

un·rea·soned [ʌn'ri:znd; ʌn`rizənd] *a*. 不合理的,无理的。

un·rea·son·ing [ʌn'rizniŋ; ʌn`riznɪŋ] *a*. 无理性的;不加考虑的;不懂[不讲]道理的。-ly *ad*.

un·re·claimed ['ʌnri'kleimd; ˏʌnrɪ`klemd] *a*. 1. (人)未改造好的,未改邪归正的。2. (土地)未开垦的。3. (物品)未收回的。

un·rec·og·nized ['ʌn'rekəgnaizd; ʌn`rɛkəgˏnaɪzd] *a*. 1. 未被认识的,未认出的,没人认识的。2. 未被承认的。

un·re·con·struct·ed ['ʌnˌri:kən'strʌktid; ˏʌnrikən`strʌktɪd] *a*. 〔美〕1. 未重建的,未改造的。2. 坚持早已过时的做法或观点的〔尤指反对美国南北战争后南部各州改组〕。

un·re·deemed ['ʌnri'di:md; ˏʌnrɪ`dimd] *a*. 1. 未实现的,未履行的。2. 未赎回的。3. 未缓和的,未减轻的。4. 未收复的,未恢复的。5. 未偿还的。

un·reel ['ʌn'ri:l; ʌn`ril] *vt*., *vi*. = unwind.

un·reeve ['ʌn'ri:v; ʌn`riv] (-*rove* [-'rəuv; -`rov], -*reeved*) *vt*. 从(滑车等)拉回(绳子)。

un·re·fined ['ʌnri'faind; ˏʌnrɪ`faɪnd] *a*. 1. 未经炼的,非精制的。2. 粗俗的,下流的。

un·re·flect·ing ['ʌnri'flektiŋ; ˏʌnrɪ`flɛktɪŋ] *a*. 1. 不反省的,不顾前后的,轻率的。2. 不反射的。-ly *ad*.

un·re·gard·ed [ʌnri'gɑ:did; ˏʌnrɪ`gɑrdɪd] *a*. 不受注意的,无人理睬的,被轻视的,被疏忽的。

un·re·gen·er·ate, -ated ['ʌnri'dʒenərit, -itid; ˏʌnrɪ`dʒɛnərɪt, -ɪtɪd] *a*. 【宗】灵魂不得再生的〔尤指改变信仰精神上得到再生的〕;不改过自新的;不悔改的;罪孽深重的。

un·re·lent·ing ['ʌnri'lentiŋ; ˏʌnrɪ`lɛntɪŋ] *a*. 1. 不宽恕的,铁面无私的,冷酷无情的。2. 坚定的;毫不松懈的,不屈不挠的。-ly *ad*.

un·re·li·a·ble ['ʌnri'laiəbl; ˏʌnrɪ`laɪə bl] *a*. 不能信任的;不可靠的。-a·bly *ad*. -bil·i·ty ['ʌnˌrilaiə'biliti; `ʌnˏrɪlaɪə`bɪlətɪ] *n*.

un·re·lieved ['ʌnri'li:vd; ˏʌnrɪ`livd] *a*. 1. 未得缓和的;(病痛,疾苦等)未经解除的;(贫民)未受救济的。2. 无变化的;单调的。

un·re·li·gious ['ʌnri'lidʒəs; ˏʌnrɪ`lɪdʒəs] *a*. 1. 无宗教的,无宗教信仰的;漠视[反对]宗教的;违反宗教原则的,亵渎的,不虔诚的。2. 与宗教无牵连的;非宗教的。

un·re·mark·a·ble ['ʌnri'mɑ:kəbl; `ʌnrɪ`mɑrkə bl] *a*. 不值得注意的;不显著的;平凡的。

un·re·mit·ting [ˌʌnri'mitiŋ; ˏʌnrɪ`mɪtɪŋ] *a*. 不断的,不停的;坚持不懈的,坚忍的。*an* ~ *struggle* 坚持不懈的斗争。-ly *ad*.

un·re·mu·ner·a·tive ['ʌnri'mju:nərətiv; ˏʌnrɪ`mjunə-

ˏretiv, -nərətɪv] *a*. 不合算的,无利可获的,无报酬的。

un·re·pent·ant [ˈʌnriˈpentənt; ˏʌnrɪˋpentənt] *a*. **1.** 不悔改的。**2.** 顽固不化的。

un·re·quit·ed [ˈʌnriˈkwaitid; ˏʌnrɪˋkwaɪtɪd] *a*. **1.** 无报答的;(工作)得不到报酬的。**2.** 有仇未报复的。~ *love* [*affection*] 单恋。

un·re·serve [ˈʌnriˈzəːv; ˏʌnrɪˋzɝv] *a*. 不保留,坦率。

un·re·served [ˈʌnriˈzəːvd; ˏʌnrɪˋzɝvd] *a*. **1.** 无保留的,坦白的,无隐瞒的,率直的。**2.** 不加克制的。**3.** 无限制的,无条件的,完全的。**4.** (座位等)没有人预定的。**-ly** *ad*. **-ness** *n*.

un·re·solved [ˈʌnriˈzɔlvd; ˏʌnrɪˋzɑlvd] *n*. **1.** 不坚决的,无决心的。**2.** 未解决的;未议决的;未澄清的。**3.** 未分解的,未加分析的。

un·res·pon·sive [ˈʌnrisˈpɔnsiv; ˏʌnrɪˋspɑnsɪv] *a*. 无反应[答覆]的,迟钝的;冷淡的。**-ly** *ad*.

un·rest [ˈʌnˈrest; ʌnˋrɛst] *n*. 不稳;不安;骚乱。

un·re·strained [ˈʌnriˈstreind; ˏʌnrɪˋstrend] *a*. 无限制的,不受约束的;自由的。**-ly** *ad*.

un·re·straint [ˈʌnriˈstreint; ˏʌnrɪˋstrent] *n*. 无限制,无拘束,放纵,放肆,猖獗。

un·re·strict·ed [ˈʌnrisˈtriktid; ˏʌnrɪˋstrɪktɪd] *n*. 不受限制的;不受约束的;无管制的;自由的。

un·rid·dle [ˈʌnˈridl; ʌnˋrɪdl] *vt*. 解(谜);说明。

un·rig [ˈʌnˈrig; ʌnˋrɪg] *vt*. (**-gg-**)【海】解去(船的)索具;拆去…的装备;〔口〕剥去…的衣服。

un·right·eous [ʌnˈraitʃəs; ʌnˋraɪtʃəs] *a*. 不公正的,不正当的;不义的,罪恶的。*the* ~ 歹徒。**-ly** *ad*. **-ness** *n*.

un·rip [ʌnˈrip; ʌnˋrɪp] *vt*. (**-pp-**) **1.** 割开,扯开;劈开;剖开。**2.** 〔现罕〕使…知道,揭示。

un·ripe [ˈʌnˈraip; ʌnˋraɪp] *a*. 未(成)熟的;时机未熟[未到]的,过早的;年轻的。

un·ri·valled, 〔美〕 **-valed** [ʌnˈraivəld; ʌnˋraɪvḷd] *a*. 无敌的,没有竞争对手的,无比的,无双的。

un·robe [ˈʌnˈrəub; ʌnˋrob] *vt*., *vi*. (使)脱去长袍,(使)脱去衣服。

un·roll [ˈʌnˈrəul; ʌnˋrol] *vt*., *vi*. 解开(卷物),打开,铺开;展开,(使)现出。

un·roof [ˈʌnˈruːf; ʌnˋruf] *vt*. 拆去…的屋顶[覆盖]。

un·root [ˈʌnˈruːt; ʌnˋrut, -ˋrʊt] *vt*. = uproot.

un·round [ʌnˈraund; ʌnˋraʊnd] *vt*.【语音】**1.** 不圆唇发出(某母音)。**2.** 使(唇)保持不圆形〔如发 she 的母音〕。**-ed** *a*.

un·rove [ʌnˈrəuv; ʌnˋrov] unreeve 的过去式及过去分词。

UNRRA, U. N. R. R. A. [ˈʌnrɑː; ˋʌnrə] = United Nations Relief and Rehabilitation Administration 联合国善后救济总署,联总。

un·ruf·fled [ˈʌnˈrʌfld; ʌnˋrʌfḷd] *a*. **1.** 不骚动的,不混乱的;稳定的,沉着的,平静的。**2.** 不起皱的。

un·ruled [ˈʌnˈruːld; ʌnˋruld] *a*. **1.** 不受支配[统治]的,调皮捣蛋的。**2.** (纸)没有画格子的。

un·ru·ly [ʌnˈruːli; ʌnˋrulɪ] *a*. (***-li·er***; ***-li·est***) 不受拘束的;不守规矩的;难驾驭的,横蛮的,任性的。*to be* ~ *in word or deed* 乱说乱动。***an*** ~ ***member*** 舌头。**-li·ness** *n*.

UNRWA = United Nations Relief and Works Agency 联合国难民救济及工程局。

un·sad·dle [ˈʌnˈsædl; ʌnˋsædḷ] *vt*. **1.** 卸下(马等的)鞍。**2.** 使从鞍上摔下来,使坠马。— *vi*. 卸鞍。

un·safe [ˈʌnˈseif; ʌnˋsef] *a*. 不安全的,不安稳的,危险的。

un·said [ˈʌnˈsed; ʌnˋsɛd] **I** unsay 的过去式及过去分词。**II** *a*. 未说出口的。*leave it* ~ 搁置不提。

un·sal(e)·a·ble [ˈʌnˈseiləbl; ʌnˋseləbḷ] *a*. 不能出卖的;卖不掉的;没有销路的。

un·sal·a·ried [ˈʌnˈsælərid; ʌnˋsælərɪd] *a*. 不拿薪金的;没有报酬的。

un·sanc·tioned [ˈʌnˈsæŋkʃənd; ʌnˋsæŋkʃənd] *a*. 未经认可的,未批准的;不可接受的。

un·san·i·ta·ry [ˈʌnˈsænitəri; ʌnˋsænəˏtɛrɪ] *a*. 不卫生的,有碍健康的。

un·sat·is·fac·to·ry [ˈʌnsætisˈfæktəri; ˏʌnsætɪsˋfæktrɪ, -tərɪ] *a*. 不能令人满意的;不合要求的;不充分的。

un·sat·is·fied [ˈʌnˈsætisfaid; ʌnˋsætɪsfaɪd] *a*. 未满足的;不满意的。

un·sat·u·rat·ed [ˈʌnˈsætʃəreitid; ʌnˋsætʃəˏretɪd] *a*. 未饱和的;不饱和的。~ *compounds* 不饱和化合物。~ *steam* 未饱和蒸汽。

un·sa·vour·y, -vor·y [ˈʌnˈseivəri; ʌnˋsevərɪ] *a*. **1.** 不好吃的,味道不好的。**2.** 可厌的;令人不快的;(名誉等)不好的。**-i·ly** *ad*. **-i·ness** *n*.

un·say [ˈʌnˈsei; ʌnˋse] *vt*. (***-said*** [-ˈsed; -ˋsɛd]) 取消,收回,撤回(前言)。

UNSC = **1.** United Nations Security Council 联合国安全理事会。**2.** United Nations Social Commission 联合国社会委员会。

un·scal·a·ble [ˈʌnˈskeiləbl; ʌnˋskeləbḷ] *a*. 爬不上的,无法攀登的。

un·scared [ˈʌnˈskeəd; ʌnˋskɛrd] *a*. 未吓倒的,不害怕的。

un·scathed [ˈʌnˈskeiðd; ʌnˋskeðd] *a*. (身、心等)没有受损伤的。

UNSCCUR = United Nations Scientific Conference on the Conservation and Utilization of Resources 联合国保存与运用资源科学会议。

un·schol·ar·ly [ˈʌnˈskɔləli; ʌnˋskɑlə·lɪ] *a*. 没有学问的,没有学识的;不像学者的。

un·schooled [ˈʌnˈskuːld; ʌnˋskuld] *a*. **1.** 没有受过学校教育的,没有受过训练的;没有经验的。**2.** 非后天的,未受教育影响的;天赋的。**3.** (某地)没有学校的。

un·sci·en·tif·ic [ˈʌnsaiənˈtifik; ˋʌnsaɪənˋtɪfɪk] *a*. **1.** 非科学的;非学术的;不科学的。**2.** 不按照科学方法的。**3.** 无科学知识的。**-i·cal·ly** *ad*.

UNSCOP = United Nations Special Commission on Palestine 联合国巴勒斯坦特别调查委员会〔曾于1947年9月成立过的一个联合国机构〕。

un·scram·ble [ʌnˈskræmbl; ʌnˋskræmbḷ] *vt*. (***-bled***; ***-bling***) 〔口〕**1.** 使不再混乱;整理,清理。**2.** 分解(集成物)使恢复原状。**3.** 使(收音机排除杂音干扰而)收听清晰;使(电视等)图像变清楚;破解(密码)。~ ***an omelet*** 想把鸡蛋卷重新摊开复原,想做办不到的事。

un·screened [ʌnˈskriːnd; ʌnˋskrind] *a*. **1.** 无屏障的,无保护的。**2.** 未筛过的。**3.** 没有改编或拍成电影的。

un·screw [ˈʌnˈskruː; ʌnˋskru] *vt*., *vi*. 起[扭松](…的)螺丝;取下(螺丝)。

un·scru·pu·lous [ʌnˈskruːpjuləs; ʌnˋskrupjələs] *a*. 毫无顾忌的;不择手段的;无所不为的;肆无忌惮的;没有节操的,无耻的。~ *and vicious* 穷凶恶极的。**-ly** *ad*. **-ness** *n*.

un·seal [ˈʌnˈsiːl; ʌnˋsil] *vt*. **1.** 打开…的封印,拆封。**2.** 使解除束缚;打开(封住的情况)。

un·seam [ˈʌnˈsiːm; ʌnˋsim] *vt*. 拆(缝);使开缝;使裂开。

un·search·a·ble [ʌnˈsəːtʃəbl; ʌnˋsɝtʃəbḷ] *a*. 不能探寻的;神秘的;不可测的。**-a·bly** *ad*.

un·sea·son·a·ble [ʌnˈsiːznəbl; ʌnˋsiznəbḷ] *a*. **1.** 不合时令的,季候不顺的,(气候等)反常的。**2.** 过时的,不合时宜的。**3.** 不适于某种场合的,不得当的。**-a·bly** *ad*. **-ness** *n*.

un·sea·soned [ˈʌnˈsiːznd; ʌnˋsiznd] *a*. **1.** 没有调味的,未加佐料的。**2.** 未成熟的;没有经验的。**3.** 未干的。**4.** 不习惯于某地风土[气候]的,不服水土的。~ *timbers* 还没有干的木料。~ *wood* 新砍倒的木材。

un·seat [ˈʌnˈsiːt; ʌnˋsit] *vt*. **1.** 使从座位上摔下,把…拉下马来。**2.** 使失去座位;夺去(议员的)议席,使失去资格;使离职。

un·sea·wor·thy [ˈʌnˈsiːwəːði; ʌnˋsi͵wɝðɪ] *a*. 经不住海上风浪的,(船)不适于航海的。

un·se·cured [ˈʌnsiˈkjuəd; ͵ʌnsɪˋkjʊrd] *a*. **1.** 不安全的,不稳当的;未固定的。**2.** 无保证的,无担保的。*an* ～ *loan* 没有担保的贷款。

un·seem·ly [ˈʌnˈsiːmli; ʌnˋsimlɪ] *a*., *ad*. 不体面,不好看;不相称;不适当。**-i·ness** *n*.

un·seen [ˈʌnˈsiːn; ʌnˋsin] **I** *a*. **1.** 看不见的。**2.** 未被看到的。**3.** 未见过的。**4.** 未事先过目的,不用参考材料的,即席的。**5.** 毋需事先研究就能看懂的。**II** *n*. 即席翻译;即席翻译的章节。*the* ～ 看不见的东西;灵魂世界。*an* ～ (*translation*) 即席翻译(一段章节)。*an* ～ *passage* 考试时让考生即席翻译[讲解]的一段文字。

un·seg·re·gat·ed [ˈʌnˈsegrigeitid; ʌnˋsɛgrə͵getɪd] *a*. 打成一片的;未实行种族隔离的。

un·sel·dom [ˈʌnˈseldəm; ˋʌnˋsɛldəm] *ad*. 屡见不鲜;常常。*not* ～〔误用〕= unseldom.

un·self·ish [ˈʌnˈselfiʃ; ʌnˋsɛlfɪʃ] *a*. 不利己的,大公无私的,没私心的,无我的。**-ly** *ad*. **-ness** *n*.

un·sell [ˈʌnˈsel; ʌnˋsɛl] *vt*. (**un·*sold*** [ˈʌnˈsəuld; ˋʌnˋsold]) 劝(某人)打消(某种念头),动摇(某人)对(某事的支持等)。～ *the public on its faith in sth*. 劝说公众不要对某事表示信心。～ *sb*. *on the idea of doing sth*. 劝说某人放弃做某事。

un·serv·ice·a·ble [ˈʌnˈsəːvisəbl; ʌnˋsɝvɪsəbl̩] *a*. 无用的,不能(再)使用的;不能胜任[作战]的。

un·set [ˈʌnˈset; ʌnˋsɛt] *a*. **1.** 未安装上的,未镶上的。**2.** (水泥、沥青等)尚未凝固的。**3.** (太阳)尚未落山的。

un·set·tle [ˈʌnˈsetl; ʌnˋsɛtl̩] *vt*. 搅乱,动摇;使不安定;使不能稳定。— *vi*. 动乱不定;离开固定位置。**-ment** *n*.

un·set·tled [ˈʌnˈsetld; ʌnˋsɛtl̩d] *a*. **1.** 易变的,(天气等)不稳定的;(意见等)动摇的;不安定的,(状态等)动乱的。**2.** 未付清的,未清算的。**3.** 未定的;(问题等)未决的。**4.** 未定居的;(岛上)无居民的。*an* ～ *market* 动荡的市面。

un·set·tling [ˈʌnˈsetliŋ; ˋʌnˋsɛtlɪŋ] *a*. 使人不安的;(消息)混乱的。

un·sex [ˈʌnˈseks; ʌnˋsɛks] *vt*. **1.** 使失去性的特征(尤指女性特征);使男性化。**2.** 使失去性功能。

un·shack·le [ˈʌnˈʃækl; ʌnˋʃækl̩] *vt*. 解去…的枷锁;释放。

un·shack·led [ˈʌnˈʃækld; ˋʌnˋʃækl̩d] *a*. 被解去枷锁的;不受束缚的。

un·shad·ed [ˈʌnˈʃeidid; ʌnˋʃedɪd] *a*. **1.** (光线)未被遮住的,(窗等)无遮蔽的。**2.** (图画)未画阴影的;(照片)无光度差别的。**3.** (声调)无变化的。

un·shad·owed [ˈʌnˈʃædəud; ʌnˋʃædod] *a*. 无暗影的;没被阴影笼罩的。

un·shak·a·ble [ʌnˈʃeikəbl; ʌnˋʃekəbl̩] *a*. 不可动摇的;坚定不移的。

un·shak·en [ˈʌnˈʃeikən; ʌnˋʃekən] *a*. 不动摇的;坚定的。

un·shaped [ˈʌnˈʃeipt; ʌnˋʃept] *a*. **1.** 未成形的。**2.** 畸形的,难看的,不成样子的。**3.** 粗制的;粗糙的。

un·shape·ly [ˈʌnˈʃeipli; ʌnˋʃeplɪ] *a*. 不好看的,样子不好的;不匀称的;畸形的。

un·shap·en [ʌnˈʃeipən; ʌnˋʃepən] *a*. **1.** 无[未]定型的;不成形的。**2.** 畸形的;破相的;丑陋的 (= unshaped)。

un·shav·en [ˈʌnˈʃeivn; ʌnˋʃevən] *a*. 未剃须的,未修面的。

un·sheathe [ˈʌnˈʃiːð; ʌnˋʃið] *vt*. **1.** 拔(剑等)出鞘。**2.** 揭开覆盖物;脱去(衣服)。～ *the sword* 拔剑;宣战,开战。

un·shel·tered [ˈʌnˈʃeltəd; ʌnˋʃɛltɚd] *a*. 无遮蔽的,暴露的;无保护的。

un·ship [ˈʌnˈʃip; ʌnˋʃɪp] *vt*., *vi*. (**-*pp*-**) **1.** 从船中起出(货),卸(货);使(船客等)下船。**2.**【海】解下(桨、船具等)。**3.**〔口〕取去,除去。

un·shod [ˈʌnˈʃɔd; ʌnˋʃɑd] *a*. **1.** 没有穿鞋的,赤脚的。**2.** (马)没有钉蹄铁的,蹄铁脱落的。**3.** 没有轮缘的;没有轮胎[外胎]的。**4.** (杖等)无铁包头的。

un·shrink·a·ble [ˈʌnˈʃriŋkəbl; ʌnˋʃrɪŋkəbl̩] *a*. 不会收缩[缩小]的;防缩的。

un·shrink·ing [ʌnˈʃriŋkiŋ; ʌnˋʃrɪŋkɪŋ] *a*. 不退缩的,不畏缩的,不踌躇的。

un·sift·ed [ˈʌnˈsiftid; ʌnˋsɪftɪd] *a*. **1.** 没有筛过的。**2.** 未经仔细审查过的。

un·sight·ed [ˈʌnˈsaitid; ʌnˋsaɪtɪd] *a*. **1.** 未看见的;看不见的。**2.** 未经检查的,未审视的。**3.** 无瞄准器的;不用瞄准器的。*buy sth*. ～ 看也不看就买下某物。**-ly** *ad*.

un·sight·ly [ʌnˈsaitli; ʌnˋsaɪtlɪ] *a*. (***-li·er***; ***-li·est***) 不好看的;不美观的,难看的。**-li·ness** *n*.

un·skil·ful, un·skill·ful [ˈʌnˈskilfʊl; ʌnˋskɪlfəl] *a*. 不熟练的;不灵活自如的。**-ly** *ad*. **-ness** *n*.

un·skilled [ˈʌnˈskild; ʌnˋskɪld] *a*. **1.** 不熟练的;笨劣的(*in*)。**2.** 不需要熟练技能的。～ *labour* 粗活。*the* ～ 生手工人。

un·slaked [ˈʌnˈsleikt; ʌnˋslekt] *a*. **1.** 未满足的;未安抚的。**2.** 未放松的,依然紧张的。**3.** (石灰)未消毒或沸化的。

un·sling [ˈʌnˈsliŋ; ʌnˋslɪŋ] *vt*. (***-slung*** [-ˈslʌŋ; -ˋslʌŋ]) **1.** 把挂着的(步枪等)取下来。**2.**【海】取下…的吊索;自吊索上放下。

un·snap [ʌnˈsnæp; ʌnˋsnæp] *vt*. (**-*pp*-**) **1.** (犬等)松(咬)。**2.** 解开(衣服上的)钮扣,拉开(皮包等的)揿钮。

un·snarl [ʌnˈsnɑːl; ʌnˋsnɑrl] *vt*. 解开…的纠缠;解决(纠纷)。

un·so·cia·ble [ʌnˈsəuʃəbl; ʌnˋsoʃəbl] *a*. **1.** 不爱[善]交际的;孤僻的。**2.** 简慢的,不和气的;不亲切的。**3.** 不能并存的;水火不相容的。**-bly** *ad*. **-ness**, **-bil·i·ty** [ˈʌnˌsəuʃəˈbiliti; ˋʌn͵soʃəˋbɪlətɪ] *n*.

un·so·cial [ˈʌnˈsəuʃəl; ʌnˋsoʃəl] *a*. **1.** 非社会的。**2.** 不合群的;不爱[善]交际的;孤僻的。**3.** 反社会的。**4.** (个人时间安排上)不用于社交的。～ **hours**〔英〕非社交时间〔指个人正常工作以外的工作时间〕。**-ly** *ad*.

un·soiled [ˈʌnˈsɔild; ʌnˋsɔɪld] *a*. **1.** 没有弄脏的;洁净的。**2.** 未玷污的;清白的。

un·sold·er [ˈʌnˈsɔldə; ʌnˋsɑldɚ] *vt*. **1.** 拆焊,拆开(焊接物)。**2.** 使分开,分离。

un·so·lic·it·ed [ˈʌn-səˈlisitid; ͵ʌnsəˋlɪsɪtɪd] *a*. 未经请求[恳求]的;主动提供的;自发的;无缘无故的,没来由的;多余的。～ *testimonials* (未经请求)顾客主动寄来的表扬信。

un·solv·a·ble [ˈʌnˈsɔlvəbl; ˋʌnˋsɑlvəbl] *a*. **1.** 无法解释[解答,解决]的。**2.** 不能溶解的。**3.**【数】不可解的。

un·solved [ˈʌnˈsɔlvd; ʌnˋsɑlvd] *a*. 未解释的;未解决的。

un·son·sy [ʌnˈsɔnsi; ʌnˋsɑnsɪ] *a*.〔Scot.〕带来厄运的,显出厄运的;不祥的。

un·so·phis·ti·cat·ed [ˈʌnsəˈfistikeitid; ͵ʌnsəˋfɪstɪ͵ketɪd] *a*. **1.** 不老练的;单纯的,思想不复杂的,天真烂漫的。**2.** 简单易懂的。**3.** 不掺假的,真正的,纯正的。**-ly** *ad*. **-ness** *n*.

un·sort·ed [ˈʌnˈsɔːtid; ʌnˋsɔrtɪd] *a*. 未分级的,未分选的。～ *coal* 原煤。

un·sought [ˈʌnˈsɔːt; ʌnˋsɔt] *a*. 未经谋求(而得到)的;意外获得的。

un·sound [ˈʌnˈsaund; ʌnˋsaʊnd] *a*. **1.** 不健全的,有病的。**2.** 腐烂了的,(商品等)已坏的。**3.** 根据不足的;理由不充分的。**4.** 不安全的,不坚固的;没有信用的,(商店等)不可靠的。**5.** (睡眠)不沉的,不酣的。*a person of* ～ *mind* 精神不健全的人。～ *slumber* 不深的微睡。

-ly *ad*. -ness *n*.

un·sound·ed[1] [ˈʌnˈsaundid; ˋʌnˋsaundɪd] *a*. 未经探测的,深度未明的。

un·sound·ed[2] [ˈʌnˈsaundid; ˋʌnˋsaundɪd] *a*. 1. 未说出的。2. (字母等)不发音的。

un·spar·ing [ʌnˈspɛəriŋ; ʌnˋspɛrɪŋ] *a*. 1. 大方的,不吝惜的,慷慨的。2. 不宽恕的,不客气的,(批评)严厉的。*be ~ in one's efforts* 拚命努力。*be ~ of* [*in*] *praise* 竭力表扬。*give with ~ hand* 慷慨给与。-ly *ad*.

un·speak [ˈʌnˈspiːk; ʌnˋspik] *vt*. (*-spoke* [-ˈspəuk; -ˋspok]; *-spok·en* [-ˈspəukən; -ˋspokən])〔废〕取消(前言)。

un·speak·a·ble [ʌnˈspiːkəbl; ʌnˋspikəbl] *a*. 1. 说不出的,形容不出的。2. 恶劣透顶的,坏不堪言的。3. 不能说的,不可说的,怕说的,一说就讨厌[恐惧]的;〔美〕不愿说的。*His manners are ~*. 〔口〕他的举动是说不出的令人讨厌。-a·bly *ad*.

un·spe·cial·ized, -ised [ˈʌnˈspeʃəlaizd; ˋʌnˋspɛʃəlaɪzd] *a*. 1. 非专门化的。2.【生】(机体)非特殊化的;无特定功能的。

un·spec·i·fied [ˈʌnˈspesifaid; ʌnˋspɛsəˏfaɪd] *a*. 1. 未指定的;未加规定的。2. 未特别指定[规定]的;未详细说明的。

un·spent [ˈʌnˈspent; ʌnˋspɛnt] *a*. 没有用完的,未耗尽的。

un·sphere [ʌnˈsfiə; ʌnˋsfɪr] *vt*. (*-spher·ed*, *-sphering*)〔古〕使(星辰等)离开某一范围;使失势。

un·spo·ken [ˈʌnˈspəukən; ʌnˋspokən] I unspeak 的过去分词。II *a*. 1. 不说出口的,未说的。2. 无言的。3. 无人与之交谈的 (*to*)。4. 不言而喻的,意在不言中的。

un·sports·man·like [ˈʌnˈspɔːtsmənlaik; ʌnˋsportsmənˏlaɪk] *a*. 1. 不像运动员[猎人]的,违反[缺少]运动员精神的。2. 不公正[光明正大]的。

un·spot·ted [ˈʌnˈspɔtid; ˋʌnˋspɑtɪd] *a*. 没有斑点[污点、瑕疵]的;纯洁的,清白的。~ ***from the world*** 没有染上社会恶习的。

un·sprung [ˈʌnˈsprʌŋ; ʌnˋsprʌŋ] *a*. (车、椅等)没有装弹簧的。

un·sta·ble [ˈʌnˈsteibl; ʌnˋste bl] *a*. 1. 不稳定的,不牢固的。2. 不坚定的,动摇的,易变的,反复无常的。

un·stained [ˈʌnˈsteind; ʌnˋstend] *a*. 没有被染污的;清白的,没有瑕疵的。~ *friendship* 纯洁的友谊。

un·state [ˈʌnˈsteit; ʌnˋstet] *vt*. 〔古〕使失去尊严[地位]。

un·stead·y [ˈʌnˈstedi; ʌnˋstɛdɪ] I *a*. 1. 不稳固的。2. 不坚定的;动摇的;易变的,反复无常的,不可靠的。3. 行为古怪的;品行不好的。***be ~ of purpose*** 拿不定主意。II *vt*. 使不稳定,使动荡。-i·ly *ad*. -i·ness *n*.

un·steel [ˈʌnˈstiːl; ʌnˋstil] *vt*. 1. 使失去坚硬性。2. 解除…的武装。3. 使软下来;使回心转意[改变决定]。

un·step [ˈʌnˈstep; ʌnˋstɛp] *vt*. (*-pp-*)【海】把桅杆(从桅座上)取下来。

un·stick [ˈʌnˈstik; ʌnˋstɪk] *vt*. (***un·stuck*** [ˈʌnˈstʌk; ˋʌnˋstʌk]) 1. 使不粘着,使脱胶;扯开(粘着的东西)。2. 〔口〕使(飞机)离地。***come unstuck***〔俚〕弄糟,失败。

un·stint·ing [ˈʌnˈstintiŋ; ˋʌnˋstɪntɪŋ] *a*. 没有限制的;慷慨的。-ly *ad*.

un·stop [ˈʌnˈstɔp; ʌnˋstɑp] *vt*. (*-pp-*) 1. 拔去…的塞子;打开(风琴的)音栓。2. 排除(管道等的)障碍[阻塞]。

un·sto·ried [ˈʌnˈstɔːrid; ʌnˋstorɪd, -ˋstɔr-] *a*. 未载入史册的;未记进故事的。

un·strained [ʌnˈstreind; ʌnˋstrend] *a*. 1. 未滤净的。2. 不勉强的,不牵强附会的,自然的。

un·strap [ˈʌnˈstræp; ʌnˋstræp] *vt*. (*-pp-*) 解开…的皮带。

un·stressed [ˈʌnˈstrest; ʌnˋstrɛst] *a*. 1. 不强调的,不着重说的;放松了的;不加强语势的。2.【语音】不重读的;非重音的。3.【物】无应力的,无应变的。

un·string [ˈʌnˈstriŋ; ʌnˋstrɪŋ] *vt*. (***un·strung*** [ˈʌnˈstrʌŋ; ˋʌnˋstrʌŋ]) 1. 把(弦)解下[放松];解开(绳索、带子);从线上退下(珠子等)。2. 〔常用被动语态〕使(神经等)衰弱[混乱];使不安。

un·struc·tured [ʌnˈstrʌktʃəd; ʌnˋstrʌktʃɚd] *a*. 非正式[有系统地]组织起来的;松散的;自由的;开放的。

un·strung [ʌnˈstrʌŋ; ʌnˋstrʌŋ] I *v*. unstring 的过去式和过去分词。II *a*. 1. 神经质的,精神失常的;不安的;丧失勇气的。2. (弓)弦松的,(球拍等)网绳松的。

un·stuck [ʌnˈstʌk; ʌnˋstʌk] I *v*. unstick 的过去式和过去分词。II *a*. 1. 松开的;(附着的东西)脱开的;未粘住的。2. 紊乱的;失灵的,受到挫折的。

un·stud·ied [ʌnˈstʌdid; ʌnˋstʌdɪd] *a*. 1. 非学到的,非由自觉努力而获得的。2. 自发的;自然的;不装腔作势的。3. 未曾学习过的;不熟习的;不精通的 (*in*)。4. 随便的,即席作成的。

un·sub·dued [ˈʌnsəbˈdjuːd; ˏʌnsəbˋdjud] *a*. 1. 没有被征服的。2. 未能克制的。3. 未减轻的;未缓和的。

un·sub·si·dized [ˈʌnˈsʌbsidaizd; ˋʌnˋsʌbsədaɪzd] *a*. 没有补助的;不受津贴[资助]的。

un·sub·stan·tial [ˈʌnsəbˈstænʃəl; ˏʌnsəbˋstænʃəl] *a*. 1. 无实质的,无实体的;(房屋等)不结实的;单薄的,(饭菜等)不丰盛的,内容不充实的。2. 非现实的,空想的。-ly *ad*. -ti·al·i·ty [ˈʌnsəbˌstænʃiˈæliti; ˋʌnsəbˏstænʃɪˋælətɪ] *n*.

un·sub·stan·ti·at·ed [ˈʌnsəbˈstænʃieitid; ˏʌnsəbˋstænʃɪˏetɪd] *a*. 无确实根据[证据]的。

un·suc·cess·ful [ˈʌnsəkˈsesful; ˏʌnsəkˋsɛsfəl] *a*. 不成功的,失败的。-ly *ad*. -ness *n*.

un·suit·a·ble [ˈʌnˈsjuːtəbl; ʌnˋsjutə bl] *a*. 不合适的,不适宜的;不相适应的,不相称的。-a·bly *ad*. -bil·i·ty *n*.

un·suit·ed [ˈʌnˈsjuːtid; ʌnˋsjutɪd] *a*. 不适宜的;不适当的,不合适的 (*for*; *to*);不相称的,不相容的。

un·sul·lied [ˈʌnˈsʌlid; ʌnˋsʌlɪd] *a*. 1. 没弄脏的。2. 没有污点的,洁白的,清白的。

un·sung [ˈʌnˈsʌŋ; ʌnˋsʌŋ] *a*. 1. (歌)未唱出的。2. 未被诗人礼赞的,未被诗歌中歌颂的。

un·sunned [ˈʌnˈsʌnd; ʌnˋsʌnd] *a*. 1. 晒不到太阳的;未受日晒的;未晒黑的。2. 没有公开的。3. 阴郁的,闷闷不乐的。

un·sup·port·ed [ˈʌnsəˈpɔːtid; ˏʌnsəˋportɪd, -ˋpɔrt-] *a*. 1. 没有支撑的。2. 没有受到支持[支援,证实]的。

un·sure [ˈʌnˈʃuə; ʌnˋʃur] *a*. 1. 缺乏信心的;没有把握的。2. 不确知的。3. 不稳定的;不安全的。4. 不可靠的。

un·sur·passed [ˈʌnsə(ː)ˈpɑːst; ˏʌnsɚˋpæst] *a*. 未被人胜过的;无比的,卓绝的,(同类中)最优的。

un·sus·pect·ed [ˈʌn-səsˈpektid; ˏʌnsəˋspɛktɪd] *a*. 1. 无嫌疑的;不受怀疑的。2. 不知其存在的;意外的。*an ~ danger* 未曾料想到的危险。

un·sus·pect·ing [ˈʌnsəsˈpektiŋ; ˏʌnsəˋspɛktɪŋ] *a*. 1. 不怀疑的;不猜疑的;相信的。2. 没有料想到…的 (*of*)。-ly *ad*.

un·sus·pi·cious [ˈʌnsəsˈpiʃəs; ˏʌnsəˋspɪʃəs] *a*. 不怀疑[猜疑]的。-ly *ad*. -ness *n*.

un·swathe [ˈʌnˈsweið; ʌnˋsweð] *vt*. 解开…的裹布[绷带等]。

un·swayed [ˈʌnˈsweid; ʌnˋswed] *a*. 不为所动的;不受影响的。

un·swear [ˈʌnˈswɛə; ʌnˋswɛr] *vt*. (***un·swore*** [ˈʌnˈswɔː; ˋʌnˋswɔr], ***un·sworn*** [ˈʌnˈswɔːn; ˋʌnˋswɔrn]) (发新誓)取消(前誓);违背(誓言)。— *vi*. 违背誓言;食言。

un·sweet [ˈʌnˈswiːt; ˋʌnˋswit] *a*. 1. 不甜的;不可口的。2. 难闻的,臭的。3. 难听的。4. 令人不快的,令人厌恶的。

un·swept [ˈʌnˈswept; ʌnˋswɛpt] *a*. 未扫(清)的。

un·swerv·ing [ʌnˈswəːviŋ; ʌnˋswɝvɪŋ] *a*. **1.** 没有(走)歪的;不偏离的。**2.** 〔喻〕忠贞的,坚定的。**-ly** *ad*. **-ness** *n*.

un·swore [ˈʌnˈswɔː; ˋʌnˋswɔr] unswear 的过去式。

un·sworn [ˈʌnˈswɔːn; ʌnˋsworn, -ˋswɔrn] unswear 的过去分词。

un·sym·met·ri·cal [ˈʌnsiˈmetrikəl; ˏʌnsɪˋmɛtrɪ kl̩] *a*. 不对称的,不匀称的。**-ly** *ad*.

un·sym·pa·thet·ic [ˈʌnsimpəˈθetik; ˏʌnsɪmpəˋθɛtɪk] *a*. **1.** 不同情的;无同情心的,无情的,冷淡的。**2.** 不抱好感的,抱有反感的。**-i·cal·ly** *ad*.

un·sys·tem·at·ic [ˈʌnsistiˈmætik; ˏʌnsɪstəˋmætɪk] *a*. 无系统的,不规则的;无组织的。**-i·cal·ly** *ad*.

UNTAA = United Nations Technical Assistance Administration 联合国技术援助局。

un·taint·ed [ˈʌnˈteintid; ʌnˋtentɪd] *a*. 未染污的;(品德)没有污点的,清白的。

un·tamed [ˈʌnˈteimd; ʌnˋtemd] *a*. **1.** 未驯养的,野性的。**2.** 未受抑制[控制]的;奔放不羁的。

un·tan·gle [ˈʌnˈtæŋgl; ʌnˋtæŋgl̩] *vt*. **1.** 解开(乱结)。**2.** 清理;解决(纠纷等)。

un·tanned [ˈʌnˈtænd; ʌnˋtænd] *a*. **1.** (皮革)未鞣的。**2.** (皮肤)没有晒黑的。

un·taught [ˈʌnˈtɔːt; ʌnˋtɔt] **I** unteach 的过去式及过去分词。**II** *a*. **1.** 无教育的,无知识的。**2.** 不教自会的;没有人教过的,非习得的;天生的,自然的。~ *modesty* 天生的谦逊。

un·taxed [ˈʌnˈtækst; ˋʌnˋtækst] *a*. 免税的;未完税的;负担不过重的。

un·teach [ˈʌnˈtiːtʃ; ʌnˋtitʃ] *vt*. (*-taught* [-ˈtɔːt; -ˋtɔt]) **1.** 使忘记[抛弃](学过的东西);使不相信。**2.** 进行与…相反的教育,使改变想法。

un·teach·a·ble [ˈʌnˈtiːtʃəbl; ʌnˋtitʃə bl̩] *a*. **1.** 不可教的,难教导的;不听话的。**2.** 无法传授的。

un·tem·pered [ˈʌnˈtempəd; ʌnˋtɛmpɚd] *a*. **1.** 【冶】未回火的;〔喻〕未经锻炼的。**2.** (石灰等)未拌和[调和]的。**3.** 未减轻[缓和]的;不加节制的。

un·ten·a·ble [ˈʌnˈtenəbl, -ˈtiːn-; ʌnˋtɛnə bl̩, -ˋtinə-] *a*. **1.** 维持[支持]不住的;(论点等)站不住的。**2.** 守不住的。**3.** 不能租赁[占用]的。**-a·bly** *ad*.

un·tend·ed [ˈʌnˈtendid; ˋʌnˋtɛndɪd] *a*. 被忽略了的;未受到照顾的。

un·thank·ful [ˈʌnˈθæŋkful; ʌnˋθæŋkful, -fəl] *a*. **1.** 不感谢的 (*to*; *for*);忘恩负义的。**2.** 不令人感激的;没有什么好处的;令人不快的。*She was ~ to her boy friend for his gift*. 她并不感谢男朋友送东西给她。*an ~ task* 吃力不讨好的工作。**-ly** *ad*. **-ness** *n*.

un·think [ˈʌnˈθiŋk; ʌnˋθɪŋk] *vt*. (*un·thought* [ˈʌnˈθɔːt; ˋʌnˋθɔt]) 打消(某个念头);不再想…;对…改变想法。— *vi*. 放弃想法,停止思考。

un·think·a·ble [ˈʌnˈθiŋkəbl; ʌnˋθɪŋkəbl̩] *a*. **1.** 不能想像的,想像不出的。**2.** 〔口〕绝不可能的;荒谬不经的,不可相信的。**3.** 不能考虑的;不必加以考虑的。

un·think·ing [ˈʌnˈθiŋkiŋ; ʌnˋθɪŋkɪŋ] *a*. **1.** 无思想的;无思考能力的。**2.** 不经心的,轻率的。**3.** 未作思考的。**-ly** *ad*.

un·thought-of [ʌnˈθɔːtɔv; ʌnˋθɔtˏɑv, -ˏʌv] *a*. 没有想到的;意外的。

un·thread [ˈʌnˈθred; ʌnˋθrɛd] *vt*. **1.** 从(针上等)把线抽下。**2.** 摆脱(缠缚)。**3.** 曲折地走出(迷宫等);解(谜)。

un·thrift·y [ˈʌnˈθrifti; ʌnˋθrɪftɪ] *a*. **1.** 不俭省的,浪费的,奢侈的。**2.** 不经济的;无利可图的。**3.** 不繁茂的;不兴隆的。

un·throne [ʌnˈθrəun; ʌnˋθron] *vt*. 废去…的王位 (= dethrone)。**-ment** *n*.

un·ti·dy [ʌnˈtaidi; ʌnˋtaɪdɪ] **I** *a*. **1.** 不整齐的,邋遢的;杂乱的,乱七八糟的。**2.** 不合适的,不适宜的。**3.** 不干净利落的,不简练的。**II** *vt*. 使不整洁,使杂乱无章。**-di·ly** *ad*. **-di·ness** *n*.

un·tie [ˈʌnˈtai; ʌnˋtaɪ] *vt*. (*-ty·ing*, *-tie·ing*) **1.** 解开。**2.** 使解去束缚,使解除约束,解放。**3.** 解决(困难等)。**4.** 允许私营公司竞争(国营企业的生意)。— *vi*. 解开,松开。

un·til [ənˈtil, ʌnˈtil; ənˋtɪl, ʌnˋtɪl] **I** *prep*. 〔时间〕**1.** 直到…为止;到。**2.** 在…以前;不到…(不)〔用在否定句中〕。*Wait ~ four o'clock*. 等到四点钟。*It was not ~ yesterday that I learned it*. 到昨天我才知道。**II** *conj*. **1.** 直到…为止;到(…的时候)。**2.** 在…以前;不到…(不)〔用在否定句中〕。*Wait here ~ I come*. 在这儿一直等到我来。*He didn't come back ~ the sun had set*. 他直到太阳落山以后才回来。★ till 与 until 同义,但在主句之前的从句或短语中,通常用 until: Until he returns, nothing can be done. 他不回来什么也不能做。*unless and ~* = until.

un·time·ly [ʌnˈtaimli; ʌnˋtaɪmlɪ] **I** *a*. **1.** 不到时候的,不合时令的;过早的,未成熟的。**2.** 不凑巧的,不合时宜的。**II** *ad*. **1.** 不合时令地;过早地。**2.** 不凑巧。**-li·ness** *n*.

un·time·ous [ʌnˈtaiməs; ʌnˋtaɪməs] *a*. 〔Scot.〕= untimely.

un·tipped[1] [ʌnˈtipt; ʌnˋtɪpt] *a*. 没有装头的,没有装过滤嘴的。

un·tipped[2] *a*. 没有付小费的。

un·tir·ing [ʌnˈtaiəriŋ; ʌnˋtaɪrɪŋ] *a*. 不(知)疲倦的,不屈不挠的。**-ly** *ad*.

un·ti·tled [ˈʌnˈtaitld; ʌnˋtaɪ tld] *a*. **1.** 没有称号[头衔]的。**2.** 没有标题的。**3.** 没有权利[资格]的。

un·to [元音前 ˈʌntu, 辅音前 ˈʌntə, 句尾、孤立时 ˈʌntuː, ˋʌntu, ˋʌntə, ˋʌntu] *prep*. 〔古〕**1.** 到;对。★与 to 同,但不能用作不定式的符号。**2.** 直到;到…时为止 (= until)。*The soldier was faithful ~ death*. 战士至死忠贞不渝。

un·told [ˈʌnˈtəuld; ʌnˋtold] *a*. **1.** 未叙述的,没有说到的,没有泄漏的,没有传出去的。**2.** 说不尽的;数不清的,无数的;极大的,(痛苦等)说不出的。~ *wealth* 不知其数的财富。

un·tomb [ˈʌnˈtuːm; ʌnˋtum] *vt*. 从(墓中)掘出;发掘。

un·touch·a·ble [ʌnˈtʌtʃəbl; ʌnˋtʌtʃə bl̩] **I** *a*. **1.** 不可触摸的,碰不得的。**2.** 碰不到的,不可及的。**3.** 不可捉摸的,无形的。**4.** (因肮脏,使人厌恶等)不可接触的。**II** *n*. **1.** 不可接触者,贱民〔印度的最低社会阶层〕。**2.** 被遗弃的人。**3.** 棘手的事。**4.** 无可疵议的人。

un·touched [ˈʌnˈtʌtʃt; ʌnˋtʌtʃt] *a*. **1.** 没有碰过的,没有动过的;原原本本的。**2.** 不受感动的,不动心的。**3.** 没有谈论到的,没有提到的。*The subject remains ~*. 这个题目仍然没有触及。

un·to·ward [ʌnˈtəuəd; ʌnˋtord] *a*. **1.** 〔古〕不听话的,倔强的。**2.** 不顺利的;麻烦的;(境遇等)不幸的。**3.** 不适当的;不合宜的。*an ~ event* 麻烦事。~ *circumstances* 逆境。**-ly** *ad*. **-ness** *n*.

un·trace·a·ble [ʌnˈtreisəbl; ʌnˋtresəbl̩] *a*. **1.** 难摹写的。**2.** 难追查的;难寻觅的。

un·tram·melled, 〔美〕**-meled** [ˈʌnˈtræməld; ʌnˋtræml̩d] *a*. 没有上脚镣[手铐]的;没有受到阻碍[束缚]的;自由的。

un·trans·fer·a·ble [ˈʌn-trænsˈfəːrəbl; ˏʌntrænsˋfɝə bl̩] *a*. 不可转移的;不可让与的。

un·trans·lat·a·ble [ˈʌntrænsˈleitəbl; ˏʌntrænsˋletə bl̩] *a*. 不可翻译的;不宜译的。

un·trav·elled, **un·trav·eled** [ʌnˈtrævld; ʌnˋtrævl̩d] *a*. **1.** 不见人迹的〔指道路等〕。**2.** 不大旅行的〔尤指远行〕。

un·tread [ˈʌnˈtred; ʌnˋtrɛd] *vt*. (*un·trod* [ˈʌnˈtrɔd;

ˋʌnˋtrɑd]; ***un·trod·den*** [ˈʌnˈtrɔdn; ˋʌnˋtrɑdn̩], ***untrod***) 折回(原路),返回(= retrace)。

un·treat·ed [ˈʌnˈtriːtid; ˋʌnˋtritɪd] ***a***. 未处理的;未加工的,未浸渍的。~ *rubber* 生橡胶。

un·tried [ˈʌnˈtraid; ʌnˋtraɪd] ***a***. **1**. 未试过的,未验过的,还没实验过的;未试用过的;没有经验的。**2**.【法】尚未审问的。*leave nothing* [*no means*] ~ 没有一种办法未试过;用尽手段。

un·trod(den) [ˈʌnˈtrɔd(n); ʌnˋtrɑd(n)] **I** untread 的过去分词。**II** ***a***. 未受践踏的;人迹未到的。

un·trou·bled [ˈʌnˈtrʌbld; ʌnˋtrʌ bl̩d] ***a***. **1**. 未受烦扰的,没有忧虑的。**2**. (湖面)平静的。

un·true [ˈʌnˈtruː; ʌnˋtru] ***a***. **1**. 不真实的,虚伪的,假的。**2**. 不忠实的;不贞洁的;不诚实的。**3**. 不合标准[型号、尺寸]的;不正的,不准的。**4**. 不正当的。**-tru·ly** ***ad***.

un·truss [ʌnˈtrʌs; ʌnˋtrʌs] ***vt***. **1**. 解掉…的束缚。**2**. 〔废〕使脱衣。

un·trust·wor·thy [ˈʌnˈtrʌstwəːði; ʌnˋtrʌstˏwɝðɪ] ***a***. 不能信任[信赖]的,靠不住的。

un·truth [ˈʌnˈtruːθ; ʌnˋtruθ] ***n***. (*pl*. ~**s** [-ðz, -θs; -ðz, -θs]) **1**. 不真实;虚假;虚伪;虚妄。**2**. 谎话。

un·truth·ful [ˈʌnˈtruːθful; ʌnˋtruθfʊl, -fəl] ***a***. **1**. 不真实的,虚伪的;不正确的。**2**. 不诚实的,说谎的。**-ly** ***ad***. **-ness** ***n***.

un·tuck [ˈʌnˈtʌk; ʌnˋtʌk] ***vt***. 拆散(褶子等);展开。~ *the rug* 展平地毯。~ *one's legs* 把腿分开。

un·turned [ˈʌnˈtəːnd; ʌnˋtɝnd] ***a***. 没有翻转的,没有颠倒的;没有掘翻的。***leave no stone*** ~ 用尽一切手段;千方百计。

un·tu·tored [ˈʌnˈtjuːtəd; ʌnˋtjutɚd, -ˋtu-] ***a***. **1**. 没有教育的;粗野的;无知的。**2**. 单纯的,纯朴的,天真的。

un·twine [ˈʌnˈtwain; ʌnˋtwaɪn] ***vt***., ***vi***. 解开(缠绕的东西),拆开,解开。~ *two climbers* 把缠绕在一起的两根蔓藤分开。

un·twist [ˈʌnˈtwist; ʌnˋtwɪst] ***vt***., ***vi***. 拆开,解开(搓合的绳、线等)。

un·used [ˈʌnˈjuːzd; ʌnˋjuzd] ***a***. **1**. 未用过的;不用的,空着的;未消耗的。**2**. [ˈʌnˈjuːst; ˋʌnˋjust] 不习惯的,无经验的 (*to*)。*hands* ~ *to toil* 不习惯劳动的手。

un·u·su·al [ʌnˈjuːʒuəl; ʌnˋjuʒuəl] ***a***. **1**. 不常见的,不普通的,难得的。**2**. 例外的;奇异的。**-ly** ***ad***. **-ness** ***n***.

un·ut·ter·a·ble [ʌnˈʌtərəbl; ʌnˋʌtərə bl̩] **I** ***a***. **1**. (快乐、苦痛等)说不出的;形容不出的。**2**. 十足的,彻底的,极端的。**3**.【语音】无法发音的。**II** ***n***. 〔*pl*.〕〔谑〕裤子。**-a·bly** ***ad***.

un·val·ued [ˈʌnˈvæljuːd; ʌnˋvæljud] ***a***. **1**. 不受重视的,没有价值的。**2**. 价值未经估定的,未估价的。*an* ~ *policy* 未估价的保险单。

un·va·ried [ʌnˈveərid; ʌnˋverɪd] ***a***. **1**. 经常一贯的,不变的。**2**. 单调乏味的,千篇一律的。

un·var·nished [ˈʌnˈvɑːniʃt; ʌnˋvɑrnɪʃt] ***a***. **1**. 没有涂(清)漆的。**2**. [ʌnˈvɑːniʃt; ʌnˋvɑrnɪʃt] 〔喻〕未加装饰的;未加修饰的;原样的,直率的。

un·var·y·ing [ʌnˈveəriiŋ; ʌnˋverɪɪŋ] ***a***. 无变化的;不改变的;恒定的。**-ly** ***ad***.

un·veil [ʌnˈveil; ʌnˋvel] ***vt***. **1**. 除去…的面纱;除去…的覆盖物;(举行揭幕礼时)揭开…的幕;〔美剧〕使(戏)开幕。**2**. 使现出本来面目;揭露(秘密等)。~ *a statue* 举行雕像揭幕礼。— ***vi***. **1**. 除去面纱[幕布]。**2**. 显露。**-ing** ***n***. 揭幕式。

un·ver·i·fi·able [ˈʌnˈverɪfaiəbl; ʌnˋvɛrɪfaɪəbl̩] ***a***. 不能证实的;无可考证的;无法检验的。

un·versed [ˈʌnˈvəːst; ʌnˋvɝst] ***a***. 不精通的;不熟练的;无知的;没有经验的。

un·vo·cal [ʌnˈvəukl; ʌnˋvo kl̩] ***a***. **1**. 不多说话的;沉默的。**2**. 不悦耳的。**3**. (声音等)不流畅的。

un·voice [ʌnˈvɔis; ʌnˋvɔɪs] ***vt***.【语音】把(某浊辅音)读作(其对应的)清辅音,把…发成清辅音。

un·voiced [ˈʌnˈvɔist; ʌnˋvɔɪst] ***a***. **1**. 未表示的;未说的;未说出的。**2**.【语音】读成清辅音的;发清辅音的,无声的。

un·want·ed [ˈʌnˈwɔntid; ʌnˋwɑntɪd] ***a***. **1**. 不需要的;无用的;多余的。**2**. 讨厌的;有缺点的。

un·war·like [ˈʌnˈwɔːlaik; ʌnˋwɔrˏlaɪk] ***a***. 不好战的。

un·warned [ˈʌnˈwɔːnd; ʌnˋwɔrnd] ***a***. 没有受警告[告诫]的;没有预先通知的,出其不意的。

un·war·rant·a·ble [ʌnˈwɔrəntəbl; ʌnˋwɑrəntəbl̩, -ˋwɔr-] ***a***. **1**. 难保证的;不能承认的;难允许的。**2**. 无法辩护的;不可原谅的;不应当的。**-a·bly** ***ad***.

un·war·rant·ed [ˈʌnˈwɔrəntid; ʌnˋwɔrəntɪd, -ˋwɑr-] ***a***. **1**. 没有保证的。**2**. [ʌnˈw-; ʌnˋw-] 未经授权的;不能承认的;不许可的;没有根据的;不应当的。*an* ~ *action* 不许可的行为。

un·war·y [ˈʌnˈweəri; ʌnˋwerɪ] ***a***. 不注意的,不审慎的,疏忽的;轻率的。**-i·ly** ***ad***. **-i·ness** ***n***.

un·washed [ˈʌnˈwɔʃt; ˋʌnˋwɑʃt] **I** ***a***. **1**. 没有洗的,不清洁的。**2**. 不是沿海[沿河]的。**3**. 无知的,地位卑下的,群氓的。**II** ***n***. 〔the ~〕〔集合词〕无知和地位卑下的大众,低下的社会阶层,群氓。***the great*** ~ 群氓。

un·wast·ed [ʌnˈweistid; ʌnˋwestɪd] ***a***. **1**. 未浪费的。**2**. 未蚀耗或减少的。**3**. 未遭蹂躏破坏的。**4**. 未因病瘦弱的。

un·wa·ver·ing [ʌnˈweivəriŋ; ʌnˋwevrɪŋ, -ˋwevərɪŋ] ***a***. 不动摇的;不犹豫的,坚定的,毅然的。**-ly** ***ad***.

un·wea·ried [ʌnˈwiərid; ʌnˋwɪrɪd] ***a***. 不疲劳的;不倦的;不屈不挠的。**-ly** ***ad***.

un·wea·ry·ing [ʌnˈwiəriiŋ; ʌnˋwɪrɪɪŋ] ***a***. **1**. 不会疲倦的;坚持不懈的。**2**. 不使人疲倦的;不令人厌烦的。

un·weave [ˈʌnˈwiːv; ʌnˋwiv] ***vt***. (***un·wove*** [ˈʌnˈwəuv; ˋʌnˋwov]; ***un·wo·ven*** [ˈʌnˈwəuvən; ˋʌnˋwovən]) 拆散(织物)。

un·weight·ed [ʌnˈweitid; ʌnˋwetɪd] ***a***. **1**. 没有心理上的负担的。**2**. 被认为不重要的。

un·wel·come [ʌnˈwelkəm; ʌnˋwɛlkəm] **I** ***a***. **1**. (客人等)不受欢迎的 (= unwelcomed)。**2**. (消息等)不愉快的,讨厌的。**II** ***n***. 冷淡。**III** ***vt***. 冷淡地对待[接受]。**-ly** ***ad***. **-ness** ***n***.

un·well [ˈʌnˈwel; ʌnˋwɛl] ***a***. **1**. 不舒服的,病弱的;有病的。**2**. 〔婉〕月经期中。

un·wept [ˈʌnˈwept; ʌnˋwɛpt] ***a***. **1**. 不被人哀悼的。**2**. (泪)不流下的。

un·whole·some [ˈʌnˈhəulsəm; ʌnˋholsəm] ***a***. **1**. 不卫生的,有碍健康的;对身心有害的;腐败的。**2**. (像)有病的。**3**. (气味、滋味等)令人不快的,讨厌的。**-ly** ***ad***. **-ness** ***n***.

un·wield·y [ʌnˈwiːldi; ʌnˋwildɪ] ***a***. **1**. 使用不便的,不便利的。**2**. 笨重的。**3**. 笨拙的。**-i·ly** ***ad***. **-i·ness** ***n***.

un·will [ʌnˈwil; ʌnˋwɪl] ***vt***. 打消(原有意图);改变(主意,意图,期望)。

un·willed [ˈʌnˈwild; ʌnˋwɪld] ***a***. 不是故意的;无意识的。

un·will·ing [ˈʌnˈwiliŋ; ʌnˋwɪlɪŋ] ***a***. **1**. 不愿意的,不情愿的;厌恶的。**2**. 勉强做[说、给]的。*be* ~ *to do* 不愿意做。~ *admiration* 勉强的赞美。**-ly** ***ad***. **-ness** ***n***.

un·wind [ˈʌnˈwaind; ʌnˋwaɪnd] ***vt***., ***vi***. (***un·wound*** [ˈʌnˈwaund; ˋʌnˋwaund]) **1**. 解开,展开(卷绕的东西)。**2**. 放松;伸直。**~ing protein**【生化】解链蛋白,解链酶〔亦作 unwindase〕。

un·wis·dom [ˈʌnˈwizdəm; ʌnˋwɪzdəm] ***n***. 愚蠢(行为);蠢话。

un·wise [ˈʌnˈwaiz; ʌnˋwaɪz] ***a***. 不聪明的,不明智的,愚蠢的;不适当的。**-ly** ***ad***.

un·wish [ʌnˈwiʃ; ʌnˋwɪʃ] ***vt***. **1**. 放弃(希望);不再希望。**2**. 〔废〕祈愿除去。

U

un·wished-for [ʌnˈwiʃtfɔː; ʌnˋwɪʃt,fɔr] *a*. 非所希望的,不欢迎的。

un·wit·nessed [ˈʌnˈwitnist; ʌnˋwɪtnɪst] *a*. **1.** 未被觉察到的。**2.** 无证人签署的。

un·wit·ting [ʌnˈwitiŋ; ʌnˋwɪtɪŋ] *a*. 不知不觉的,无意的,无心的。**-ly** *ad*.

un·wom·an·ly [ʌnˈwumənli; ʌnˋwumənlɪ, -ˋwumənlɪ] *a*. 不像女人的;女人不应有的。

un·wont·ed [ʌnˈwəuntid; ʌnˋwʌntɪd, -ˋwon-] *a*. **1.** 不常有的,罕有的,异常的。**2.** 〔罕〕不习惯的,不熟悉的(*to*)。**-ly** *ad*. **-ness** *n*.

un·work·a·ble [ˈʌnˈwəːkəbl; ʌnˋwɝkəbl] *a*. 无法工作[使用、开动、处理、实行等]的。

un·worked [ˈʌnˈwəːkt; ʌnˋwɝkt] *a*. **1.** 未制成形的;粗糙的。**2.** 未使用的。

un·world·ly [ʌnˈwəːldli; ʌnˋwɝldlɪ] *a*. **1.** 非尘世的;非世俗的,超脱名利之外的;精神世界的,出世的。**2.** 没有社会经验的。*the* ～(*-minded*) *people* 无俗念[名利心]的人们。**-li·ness** *n*.

un·worn [ˈʌnˈwɔːn; ʌnˋworn, -ˋwɔrn] *a*. **1.** 没有磨损的,没有擦破的。**2.** 没有用旧的;没有穿旧的;不常穿的。**3.** 〔喻〕(精神、感觉等)没有受损伤的;清新的。

un·wor·thi·ness [ʌnˈwəːðinis; ʌnˋwɝðɪnɪs] *n*. 无价值,不相称;卑鄙。

un·wor·thy [ʌnˈwəːði; ʌnˋwɝðɪ] *a*. **1.** 没有价值[优点]的;不足取的,卑劣的。**2.** 不值的,不配的,辜负(*of*);…所不应有的(*of*)。*an* ～ *son* 不肖之子。～ *of praise* 不配受表扬。*a conduct* ～ *of an artist* 艺术家所不应有的行为。**-thi·ness** *n*.

un·wound [ˈʌnˈwaund; ʌnˋwaund] **I** *v*. unwind 的过去式和过去分词。**II** *a*. **1.** (钟、表等)没有上发条的。**2.** (从卷绕状态)松散的。

un·wound·ed [ˈʌnˈwuːndid; ʌnˋwundɪd] *a*. 未受伤的;完好无损的。

un·wove [ˈʌnˈwəuv; ˋʌnˋwov] unweave 的过去式。

un·wo·ven [ˈʌnˈwəuvən; ˋʌnˋwovn] unweave 的过去分词。

un·wrap [ˈʌnˈræp; ʌnˋræp] *vt*. (*-pp-*)打开,解开(包扎等)。— *vi*. 散开。

un·writ·ten [ˈʌnˈritn; ʌnˋrɪtn] *a*. **1.** 没有写下的,没有记录的。**2.** 口头的,口传的;未成文的。**3.** 白纸一张的,没有写着字的。～ **constitution** 【法】不成文宪法。～ **law** 【法】不成文法,习惯法。

un·wrought [ˈʌnˈrɔːt; ʌnˋrɔt] *a*. **1.** 没有制造的;未最后成形的;没有做成功的。**2.** 没有加工的;未开发的;(矿山等)没有开采的。～ *materials* 原料。

un·yield·ing [ʌnˈjiːldiŋ; ʌnˋjildɪŋ] *a*. **1.** 不屈服的;顽强的,坚强的。**2.** 坚硬的,弯曲不了的。**-ly** *ad*. **-ness** *n*.

un·yoke [ˈʌnˈjəuk; ʌnˋjok] *vt*. 解(轭);解除(束缚);解开,分开。— *vi*. 卸去轭;〔喻〕停止工作。

un·zip [ʌnˈzip; ʌnˋzɪp] *vt*., *vi*. (*-pp-*) **1.** 拉开(拉链)。**2.** 拉开(…的)拉链(以敞开衣襟等)。

un·zoned [ˈʌnˈzəund; ˋʌnˋzond] *a*. 没有划分区域的;不受限制的。

up [ʌp; ʌp] (*opp*. down) **I** *ad*. (*superl*. **up·per·most** [ˈʌpəməust; ˋʌpə-most]) **1.** 向[在]上,向[在]上面;向[在]被认为处于上方的地方或方面〔如河流的源头,首都,上级机构,北方等〕。*go* ～ *to the top of a hill* 走上山顶。*Come* ～ *here*. 上这儿来;到上边来。*I'm going* ～ *to Shenyang*. 我上沈阳去。**2.** (站)起;(坐)起,(从床上)起身。*She was already* ～. 她已经起床了。*be* [*stay*] ～ *all night* 通夜未睡。**3.** 〔数量等〕以上;〔时间等〕以后,…以来。*from $ 50* ～ 五十美元以上,从50美元起。*from my youth* ～ 我年轻时代以后[以来]。**4.** 上涨,升高;上升;高声;猛然;奋起;激昂;(开始活动)起来;发迹。*Prices have gone* ～. 物价全涨了。*sing* ～ 高声唱。*The country was* ～. 全国人民发动起来了。*All the town is* ～. 全市生气蓬勃。*The hunt is* ～. 围猎正在开始。*The beer is very much* ～. 这啤酒泡沫很多〔比较:*Beer is* ～. 啤酒正在涨价〕。*His temper is* ～. 他正在发脾气。*He has gone* ～ *in my opinion*. 他在我的心目中的地位已经上升。*start* ～ *the engine* 把机器开动起来。**5.** (问题)提起,出现;(事情)发生。*The question came* ～ *in conversation*. 这个问题在谈话中提出了。*Is anything* ～? 有什么事情发生吗? *What's* ～ (*with you*)? (你)怎么啦? (你)出了什么事? **6.** (全部)完毕。*eat* ～ *everything* 吃得干干净净。*The time is* ～. 时间到了;时间没有了。*The game is* ～. 一切完了。*The House is* ～. 议会闭会了。*It is all* ～ (=〔俚〕*It is all U. P.* [ˈjuːˈpiː; ˋjuˋpi]) *with him*. 那个人已经没有希望了。*Your chance is* ～. 你的机会已经完了。**7.** 赶上,跟上;胜过。*She worked hard to catch* ～ *with the rest of the class*. 她努力用功以求赶上班上其余的人。*Never fall behind, keep* ～! 不要落后,要跟上(时代)! **8.** (收藏)起来;(收集)起来;(加)起来;(扎)起来。*save* ～ *money* 把钱贮存起来。*add* ～ *these figures* 把这些数目加起来。*tie* ～ *the package* 把这包东西扎起来。**9.** 〔省略动词〕…起来,…上来。*Up with it!* 竖起来! 抬起来! *Up with you!* 站起来! 上来! *Up!* 起来! 上来。**10.** 【海】迎风,向风。*Up helm!* 【海】迎风转舵! **11.** 【棒球】任打击手,处于进攻一方;【高尔夫球】以(若干穴数)胜过;【网球】以(若干分)超过;【体】〔美、加〕双方各得(…分),平。*The golfer was two strokes* ～ *on his opponent*. 该高尔夫球选手胜对手两穴。*She was two* ～ *on her opponent*. 她胜过对手两分。*The score is 10* ～. 比分为十平。**12.** 〔构成动词短语,大致有三种情况〕:(a) 改变原动词的意义,构成新义,如 *look* ～ 寻找; *turn* ～ 出现。(b) 加强原动词的语气,如 *dress* ～; *clean* ～. (c) 并不增加任何意义,这常在口语中出现,如 *write* ～ *a story*. **be not** ～ **too much** 不是怎样了不起的(好)东西。**be not** ～ **to one's job** 承当[干]不了…的工作。～ **against** 〔口〕面临;遭遇(障碍等)。～ **against it** 〔美俚〕面临(经济)困难,处境困难。**be** ～ **and about** (病人)已经起床走动了。**be** ～ **and doing** 工作积极;非常活跃。**be** ～ **for** (*an examination*) 正在(考试)。**be** ～ **in** [**on**] (*art*) 擅长(艺术)。～ **and at** 〔美〕攻击;承受。～ **and down** **1.** 上上下下,忽上忽下。**2.** 升降浮沉。**3.** 各处,到处;来来去去(*run* ～ *and down* 跑来跑去)。～ **in arms** 武装起义;采取敌对态度。～ **in the air** 〔美〕狼狈的,惊慌的;激昂的。～ **on one's toes** 〔美〕机敏热心的。～ **there** 在那里;〔美俚〕天堂。～ **to** **1.** 到,一直到(*from a pauper* ～ *to a prince* 从乞丐一直到王子。～ *to the present day* 直到现在)。**2.** 〔口〕做(着),干(着),计划(着)(*What are you* ～ *to now?* 你现在在做什么? *He is* ～ *to no good*. 他净干坏事)。**3.** 胜任,适于(*be* ～ *to the needs of an emergency* 紧急时可用)。**4.** 〔原美〕…的责任,轮到…;靠(*It is* ～ *to me to* ..., …是我的责任[义务]。*It is* ～ *to us to organize the people*. 民众靠我们去组织)。～ **to** [**with**] **1.** 和…并排(*I could not get* [*catch*] ～ *to him*. 我追不上他。*Slow down a bit and let me come* ～ *with you*. 跑慢一点让我赶上吧)。**2.** (功绩、成功等)不相上下,可以相比,相近(*He is* ～ *to his father as a scholar*. 他是一个和他父亲不相上下的学者)。～ **to snuff** 见 snuff. ～ **to the gills** 〔美俚〕烂醉的。～ **to the handle** 〔美俚〕完全。**well** ～ **in** (*mathematics*) 精通,擅长(数学)。**II** *prep*. **1.** (从低处、低位置等)向[在]高处,向[在]…的上面,向[在]上面。**2.** 向[在](河的)上游,溯(流)。**3.** 顺着(路等)。**4.** (离海)向[在](内地);向内部。*live* ～ *a mountain* 住在山上。*work one's way* ～ *a form* 向上一级升进。*travel* ～ (*the*) *country* 向内地旅行[进行]。～ **a tree** 〔美俚〕进退两难。～ **hill and down dale** 翻山越谷;不

U

顾一切,彻底。～ ***one's alley***〔美俚〕适合某人的才能[能力、素养]。～ ***the pole*** 1. 进退两难。2. 醉醺醺;发着疯。～ ***the river***〔美俚〕在坐牢,吃着官司。**III** ***a***. (***up·per*** [ˈʌpə; ˋʌpɚ]; ***up·most*** [ˈʌpməust; ˋʌpmost], ***up·per·most*** [ˈʌpəməust; ˋʌpɚmost]) 上面的,向上面的,向上头的;【海】(舵)转向上风头的。*an* ～ *train* 上行车;〔英〕(到伦敦去的)上行车。*the* ～ *line*【铁路】上行线;【电讯】上行线路。*an* ～ *platform* 上行线月台。*an* ～ *stroke* 往上写的笔划。**IV** ***n***. 1. 上面,上头;高处,高地;上坡路。2. 繁荣,兴盛。3. 正在逐步上升的人,有名望的人。4. 上行车。5.〔美俚〕〔*pl*.〕刺激性毒品。***on the*** ～ ***and*** ～〔美俚〕光明正大地,正直地。～***s and downs***(人生等的)盛衰,浮沉;(土地等的)高低,起伏(*a house full of* ～*s and downs* 楼梯多的房子。*He has had his* ～*s and downs in life*. 他现在已体验到生活中的酸甜苦辣了)。**V** ***vt***. (***-pp-***)〔口、方〕举起,拿起(*with*);抬高,提高(价格),增加(产量)。*try to* ～ *output* 设法提高产量。*an upped sail* 扬起的风帆。— ***vi***. 1.〔口、方〕举起,拿起(*with*)。2.〔口、卑〕站起来,起来,突然跳起来,突然开口,突然做某事。3.〔美俚〕服用兴奋剂。*He* ～*ped with his fist* [*stick*]. 他举起了他的拳头[拿起了他的手杖]。*He* ～*s and says*. 他突然开口说。*He* ～*ped and struck me*. 他突然跳起来打我。

up- *comb*. *f*. = up. 1. 带有副词的意义,加用于动词(主要为被动语态)及动名词前:*up*lifted, *up*bringing. 2. 带有前置词的意义,构成副词、形容词及名词:*up*hill, *up*country. 3. 添加形容词的意义:*up*land, *up*stroke.

U. P., UP = United Press〔美〕合众国际社。

u. p. = underproof(酒精含量)低于标准,在标准以下。

U. P. [ˈjuːˈpiː; ˋjuˋpi] ***ad***.〔口〕完了(= up)。*All is U. P. with her*. 她一切全完了,她完蛋了。

up. = 1. upper. 2. underproof.

up·a·long [ˌʌpəˈlɔŋ; ˏʌpəˋlɔŋ] ***ad***.〔方〕向上,朝上;向东方,从西部。

up-and-about [ˈʌpənd əˈbɔt; ˋʌpəndəˋbɑt] ***a***. 1.(病人)已起床走动。2. 非常活跃的。

up-and-coming [ˈʌpəndˈkʌmiŋ; ˋʌpəndˋkʌmɪŋ] ***a***.【美】精力饱满的,奋发有为的,进取的,积极努力的;新起的。

up-and-down [ˈʌpənˈdaun; ˋʌpənˋdaʊn] ***a***. 1.〔俚〕一上一下的,(运动)往复的;(道路)起伏不平的。2.(命运等)盛衰无定的。3.〔美〕(答复等)直率的;断然的;(谎话等)十足的。*an* ～ *life* 命运多变的生活。*an* ～, *cheerful girl* 直爽快活的女孩。～ **dial** 附有显示发条松紧程度指示针的钟表面。

up-and-up [ˈʌpəndˈʌp; ˋʌpəndˋʌp] ***n***. 1.〔美俚〕日益向上[进步]。2. 诚实,光明磊落。*on the* ～ 进行顺利,繁荣;诚实地,公平地。

U·pani·shad [uːˈpæniʃəd; uˋpænɪˏʃæd] ***n***.《奥义书》〔印度《吠陀》圣典的最后部分〕。

u·pas [ˈjuːpəs; ˋjupəs] ***n***. 1.【植】见血封喉树〔一种毒树〕。2. 见血封喉树的毒液。3.(道德上的)有害影响,毒害。

up·beat [ˈʌpbiːt; ˋʌpˏbit] **I** ***n***. 1. 向上的趋势;向上摆动。2.【乐】弱拍;(指挥棒)向上挥舞(以示弱拍)。**II** ***a***. 活泼的;愉快的,高兴的,乐观的。

up·blaze [ʌpˈbleiz; ʌpˋblez] ***vi***. 燃烧起来。

up·borne [ʌpˈbɔːn; ʌpˋbɔrn] ***a***. 1. 被高举的,被抬高的,升高了的。2. 被支持着的。

up·bow [ˈʌpˌbəu; ˋʌpˏbo] ***n***.(小提琴、大提琴等的)上弓,全弓奏〔记号是 V〕。

up·braid [ʌpˈbreid; ʌpˋbred] ***vt***. 责备,谴责。～ *sb*. *with his ingratitude* [*for being ungrateful*] 责备某人忘恩负义。**-er** ***n***. 责备者。**-ing** ***n***., ***a***. 责备(的)。

up·bring·ing [ˈʌpbriŋiŋ; ˋʌpˏbrɪŋɪŋ] ***n***. 抚养,养育;教育,培养。

up·build [ʌpˈbild; ʌpˋbɪld] ***vt***. (***up·built*** [ʌpˈbilt; ʌpˋbɪlt], ***up·build·ing*** [ʌpˈbildiŋ; ʌpˋbɪldɪŋ]) 建立;组织;振兴。**-er** ***n***. 建立者;组织者;振兴者。

UPC = Universal Product Code.

up·cast [ˈʌpkɑːst; ˋʌpˏkæst, -ˏkɑst] **I** ***a***. 向上扔的,向上投掷的;向上的;朝上的。**II** ***n***. 上投,上抛;向上扔的东西;【矿】上风井,上风口。**III** ***vt***. 把…向上抛。

up·chuck [ˈʌptʃʌk; ˋʌpˏtʃʌk] ***vi***., ***vt***., ***n***.〔美口〕呕吐。

up·com·ing [ˈʌpˌkʌmiŋ; ˋʌpˏkʌmɪŋ] ***a***. 即将到来的。

up·coun·try [ˈʌpˈkʌntri; ˋʌpˋkʌntrɪ] **I** ***n***.(远离海岸线的)内地。**II** ***a***. 1.〔蔑〕乡下的;内地的。2. 单独的,纯朴的。**III** [ʌpˈk-; ʌpˋk-] ***ad***.〔口〕向内地,在内地。*travel* ～ 在内地旅行。

up·date [ʌpˈdeit; ʌpˋdet] **I** ***vt***.〔美〕(通过修订、增补)使(书等)成为最新式的[现代化的],使(书等)与(当前条件)相适应。**II** ***n***.【自】(供电子计算机使用的)最新情报。

up·do [ˈʌpduː; ˋʌpdu] ***n***. (*pl*. ***-dos***) 高发髻〔头发向上梳的一种发型〕。

up·draft [ˈʌpdrɑːft; ˋʌpdræft] **I** ***n***.【气】上曳气流,上升气流。**II** ***a***. 向上通风的。

up·end [ʌpˈend; ʌpˋɛnd] ***vt***., ***vi***.(使)颠倒,(使)倒竖,倒置,倒转。

up·front [ʌpˈfrʌnt; ʌpˋfrʌnt] ***a***.〔美口〕1. 最前面的;首要的。2. 预先到来的;预先做的。3. 正直的;坦率的,无拘束的。

up·grade [ˈʌpgreid; ˋʌpˋgred] **I** ***n***., ***a***.〔美〕上坡(的);上升(的)。**II** ***ad***. 往山上,上坡。**III** ***vt***. 提升(…级别);提高(重要性、质量等);使升级。

up·growth [ˈʌpgrəuθ; ˋʌpˏgroθ] ***n***. 1. 成长,发育,发展。2. 发展的结果,成长物。

up·heav·al [ʌpˈhiːvəl; ʌpˋhivl] ***n***. 1. 鼓起,举起,抬起;【地】隆起。2. 骚扰,动乱;激变,剧变。

up·heave [ʌpˈhiːv; ʌpˋhiv] ***vt***., ***vi***. (***-heaved***, ***-hove*** [ʌpˈhəuv; ʌpˋhov]) 鼓起;举起,顶起,抬起;(因火山、地震等)(使)隆起。

up·held [ʌpˈheld; ʌpˋhɛld] uphold 的过去式和过去分词。

up·hill [ˈʌpˈhil; ˋʌpˋhɪl] **I** ***a***. 1. 上坡的;上升的。2. 费力的,辛苦的,艰难的。3. 高处的。*It is an* ～ *road all the way*. 这条路一直是上坡路。*an* ～ *work* 费力的工作。**II** ***ad***. 上山;上坡;艰难地。**III** ***n***. 向上的斜坡。

up·hold [ʌpˈhəuld; ʌpˋhold] ***vt***. (***up·held*** [ʌpˈheld; ʌpˋhɛld]) 1. 抬高,举起。2. 支持,支援;鼓励。3. 赞同,拥护;【法】确认,批准(判决等)。4.〔英〕= upholster. ～ *justice* 伸张正义。**-er** ***n***. 抬高者,举起者;支持者;确认者。

up·hol·ster [ʌpˈhəulstə; ʌpˋholstɚ] ***vt***. 1.(用家具)布置,(用地毯、帷帘等)装饰。2. 给(沙发等)做软垫[布面等]。*an* ～*ed chair* 装有软垫[皮面垫子]的椅子。

up·hol·ster·ed [ʌpˈhəulstəd; ʌpˋholstɚd] ***a***. 1.(房间)经过布置的。2.(沙发等)装软垫的。3.〔美俚〕肥胖的;稳重的。～ **mittens**〔美俚〕拳击用皮手套。

up·hol·ster·er [ʌpˈhəulstərə; ʌpˋholstɚrɚ] ***n***. 室内装饰商,家具商。

up·hol·ster·y [upˈhəulstəri; ʌpˋholstərɪ] ***n***. 1. 室内装饰品〔帷帘、地毯等〕。2. 室内装饰业,家具业。

up·hove [ʌpˈhəuv; ʌpˋhov] upheave 的过去式及过去分词。

UPI = United Press International〔美〕合众国际社(= UP)。

up·keep [ˈʌpkiːp; ˋʌpˏkip] ***n***. 1. 维修,保养。2. 维修费,保养费。

up·land [ˈʌplənd; ˋʌplənd] **I** ***n***.〔*sing*., *pl*.〕高地,山地,台地;〔*pl*.〕高地地区,旱地。**II** ***a***. 高地的,山地的。～ **cotton**(短纤维)陆地棉。～ **rice** 旱地稻。～ **plover**【动】高原鹬。

U

up·lift [ʌpˈlift; ʌpˋlɪft] I *vt*. 1. 举起,提起。2. 打起(精神),发扬(优良品德),鼓起(干劲)。3. 提高(社会地位)。4.【地】使(地面)上升。II [ˈʌplift; ˋʌpˏlɪft] *n*. 1. 举起,抬起。2.【地】隆起。3.〔美〕(优良品德的)发扬,(精神的)高涨,(感情的)激发;进步。4.〔口〕(使胸部鼓起的)乳罩(= ~ brassiere)。*an* ~ *worker* 热心社会工作的人。**-er** *n*.

up·link [ʌpˈliŋk; ʌpˋlɪŋk] I *n*.【宇航】(从地面向航天器或卫星传送数据或信号的)上行线路。II *vt*. (从地面)向上传送(数据、信号等给飞行器或卫星)。

up·load [ʌpˈləud; ʌpˋlod] *vi*., *vt*.【计】上载(文件),把(文件)传给他人〔与下载(download)传送信息的方向正相反〕。

up·man·ship [ˈʌpmənˌʃip; ˋʌpmənˏʃɪp] *n*. one-upmanship 胜人一筹的本事(的缩略词)。

up·mar·ket [ˈʌpmɑːkit; ˋʌpmɑkɪt] *a*.〔英〕(为)高收入消费者的;高档的,高级的,高质量的。

up·most [ˈʌpməust; ˋʌpˏmost] *a*., *ad*. = uppermost.

up·on [强 əˈpɔn; əˋpɑn; 弱 əpən; əpən] *prep*. = on (*prep*.)。★ upon 和 on 意义相同,一般可互相调换;但 1. 日期前只用 on。2. 口语中多用 on。3. upon 语气较强,与动词连用或在句末,多用 upon, 如:*I have not enough to live* ~. 我收入不够生活。4. 在某些习语中, on 与 upon 不能互换,如:*once upon a time* 等习语用 upon, 而 *on no account* 则必须用 on. ~ ***my word*** 一定,的确,决无虚言。~ ***this*** 于是。

up·per [ˈʌpə; ˋʌpɚ] I *a*. 1. (更)上面的,上方的,上部的;较高的;上级的;(议会)上院的;(衣服)穿在外面的。2. 上流的;高原地带的;内地的。3.【地】地表层的;〔常 U-〕后期的。*the* ~ *seats* [*circle*] (戏院的)楼座,花楼。*the* ~ *lip* 上唇。***get*** [***have***] ***the*** ~ ***hand of*** 胜过,占上风[优势]。II *n*. 1.〔常 *pl*.〕鞋面皮,鞋帮;〔*pl*.〕布绑腿;〔口〕(车船卧铺的)上铺。2.〔美俚〕兴奋剂,刺激性药物〔尤指安非他命〕。(***down***) ***on one's*** ~***s*** 鞋底完全磨平;非常贫穷。**U- Bench**【英史】高等法院。~ **Benjamin**〔美〕外套。~ **bound**【数】上界。**U- Cambrian**【地】后期寒武纪。~ **case**【印】大写字母(盘)。~-**case** 1. *a*. 大写字母(盘)的。2. *vt*. 用大写字母排印。~ **course** 上游。~ **crust**〔美俚〕上层阶级;头,脑袋。~ **cut**【机】二次割削。~ **dead center**【机】上静点。**U- Germany** 上德意志[德国南部]。**U- House** 上院,参议院。~ **keyboard**【乐】键盘的右方。~ **leather** 鞋面皮。~ **story** 二楼;〔俚〕头;头脑。~ **ten** (**thousand**) 上层阶级。~ **works**【船】水线以上的船体;〔口〕头,脑袋;智力。

up·per-class [ˈʌpəˈklɑːs; ˋʌpɚˋklæs] *a*. 上层阶级(特有)的。

up·per·class·man [ˈʌpəˈklɑːsmən; ˏʌpɚˋklæsmən] *n*. (*pl*. ***-men***)〔美〕(高等学校的)高班生〔三、四年级学生〕。

up·per-crust [ˈʌpəˈkrʌst; ˋʌpɚˏkrʌst] *n*., *a*. 1. (馅饼、面包等的)上外皮(的)。2.〔美口〕上层阶级(的)。3.〔俚〕头(的)。

up·per·cut [ˈʌpəkʌt; ˋʌpɚˏkʌt] *vt*., *vi*., *n*.【拳击】上击。

up·per·most [ˈʌpəməust; ˋʌpɚˏmost] I *a*. 1. 最上的,最高的。2. 最主要的,首先浮现在心头的。*one's* ~ *thoughts* 首先发生的念头。II *ad*. 1. 最上,最高。2. 首先,最初。

up·per·ten·dom [ˌʌpəˈtendəm; ˏʌpɚˋtɛndəm] *n*. 上流社会,贵族阶级。

Upper Volta [ˈʌpə ˈvɔltə; ˋʌpɚˋvɑltə] 上沃尔特(上塔)〔非洲〕。

up·pish [ˈʌpiʃ; ˋʌpɪʃ] *a*. 1.〔口〕骄傲的,傲慢的。2.〔主英〕稍微朝上的。**-ly** *ad*. **-ness** *n*.

up·pi·ty [ˈʌpiti; ˋʌpətɪ] *a*.〔口〕= uppish.

up·raise [ʌpˈreiz; ʌpˋrez] *vt*.〔常用被动语态〕举起,抬起;提高。*hands* ~*d in prayer* 高举双手祷告。

up·rear [ʌpˈriə; ʌpˋrɪr] *vt*. 1. 举起,竖起。2. 养育。3. 赞扬;支持。~ *a monument in marble* 建造大理石纪念碑。~ *children* 养儿育女。~ *one's head* 抬起头。

up·right [ˈʌpˈrait; ˋʌpˋraɪt] I *a*. 1. 笔直的,直立的,竖立的。2. [ˈʌprait; ˋʌpraɪt] 正直的。*set things* ~ 把东西竖直。*an* ~ *piano* 竖钢琴。*an* ~ *man* 正直的人。II *ad*. 笔直,竖立着。III [ˈʌprait; ˋʌpraɪt] *n*. 1. 笔直的东西,【建】柱。2.【乐】竖钢琴。3.〔*pl*.〕【足球】球门柱(= goal posts)。**bolt** ~ 笔直。**-ly** *ad*. **-ness** *n*.

up·rise [ʌpˈraiz; ʌpˋraɪz] I *vi*. (***up·rose*** [ʌpˈrəuz; ʌpˋroz]; ***up·ris·en*** [ʌpˈrizn; ʌpˋrɪzn]) 1. 上升,升起;立起,站起来。2. 起身,起床。3. 爬上;登上。4. 起坡,成坡;高起,高涨;起浪。5. 起义,暴动;行动起来。6. 出现。II *n*. = uprising.

up·ris·ing [ʌpˈraiziŋ; ʌpˋraɪzɪŋ] *n*. 1. 升起;立起;起床。2. 起义,暴动。3. (逐渐升高的)斜坡。*armed* ~ 武装起义。

up·riv·er [ˈʌpˈrivə; ˋʌpˏrɪvɚ] I *a*. 上游的,源头的。II *ad*. 向上游。

up·roar [ˈʌprɔː, -rɔə; ˋʌpˏror, -ˏrɔr] *n*. 喧闹,鼓噪,骚嚷,人声鼎沸,轰鸣[响]。

up·roar·i·ous [ʌpˈrɔːriəs; ʌpˋrɔrɪəs] *a*. 喧闹的。~ *laughter* 轰然大笑。**-ly** *ad*. **-ness** *n*.

up·root [ʌpˈruːt; ʌpˋrut] *vt*. 1. 连根拔[掘起];根绝,绝灭。2. 把(某人)赶出住所[家园等]。*the* ~*ed* 被逐出家乡的人们。~ *poverty* 彻底消除贫困。— *vi*. 1. 被连根拔起。2. 成为无家可归。

up·rose [ʌpˈrəuz; ʌpˋroz] uprise 的过去式。

up·rouse [ʌpˈrauz; ʌpˋraʊz] *vt*. 唤起,唤醒;激起。

up·sa·dai·sy [ˈʌpsəˈdeizi; ˋʌpsəˋdezɪ] *int*. = upsy-daisy.

up·scale [ˈʌpskeil; ˋʌpskel] *a*.〔美〕(收入、受教育程度、社会地位等)属于上层的,社会高层的。

up·set [ʌpˈset; ʌpˋsɛt] I *vt*. (***up·set***; ***-set·ting***) 1. 推翻,颠覆;弄翻,打翻。2. 搅乱,打破(计划);(体育比赛、政党竞选等中)意外地击败(被认为强悍的对手)。3. 使狼狈,使烦乱;使(胸口、肚子等)不舒服。4.【机】缩锻,顿锻;顿粗;压缩(车轮内径)。~ *a glass of wine* 弄翻一杯酒。*A boat was* ~. 一条船(被风)吹翻了。~ *sb.'s plan* 打乱某人的计划。~ *a room* 把房间弄乱。— *vi*. 翻倒,颠覆。~ ***sb.'s apple cart*** 打乱某人的计划。~ ***the dope***〔美俚〕(形势大变)使预测[打算]落空。II *n*. 1. 倾覆,翻倒;颠覆。2. 心乱,烦乱,混乱。3. 不和,吵架。4. 意外的失败。5.【机】缩锻;缩锻过的金属棒的粗大部分;缩锻用陷型模。III [ˈʌpset; ˋʌpsɛt] *a*. 1. 被推翻[弄翻]了的;混乱的;被挫败的。2. 心绪烦乱的。3. 固定的,一定的。~ **price** (拍卖开始时的)最低价格;开拍底价。

up·shift [ˈʌpʃift; ˋʌpˏʃɪft] *vi*. 1. (汽车驾驶)换高一档;加速。2. 工作升格[指做提级增薪的工作]。

up·shot [ˈʌpʃɔt; ˋʌpˏʃɑt] *n*. 1. 结果,结局;终点。2. 结论;要点。***be brought*** [***come***] ***to the*** ~ 得出结论。***in the*** ~ 最后,终于。***when it comes to the*** ~ 如果细细推究起来。

up·side [ˈʌpsaid; ˋʌpsaɪd] *n*. 1. 上边,上面,上部,上段。2.【铁路】上行线月台。3. 正面;有利的一面;优点。

up·side-down [ˈʌpsaidˈdaun; ˋʌpˏsaɪdˋdaʊn] I *ad*. 颠倒;混乱,乱七八糟。*He turned the room* ~ *to hunt for the lost key*. 他把屋子翻得乱七八糟,寻找遗失的钥匙。II *a*. 颠倒的,混乱的,乱七八糟的。~ **cake** 把水果放在下层烤的蛋糕〔食用时翻转来则水果在上〕。

up·sides [ʌpˈsaidz; ʌpˋsaɪdz] *ad*.〔Scot. 方〕各半,不相上下地。***be*** ~ ***with*** 与…不相上下。***get*** ~ ***with***〔方〕同样回敬;报复。

up·si·lon [juːpˈsailən; jupˋsaɪlən] *n*. 1. 希腊语字母表第二十字〔Υ, υ 相当于英语的 u〕。2.【物】υ子。

up·size [ˈʌpsaiz; ˋʌpsaɪz] *vi*., *vt*. 扩大(…的)规模。

up·siz·ing *n*.

up·skill [ʌpˈskil; ʌpˋskɪl] *vt*., *vi*. 对(职员、工人等)进行再培训以提高其技能(或知识等);提高(工作的)技术性。

up·spring [ʌpˈspriŋ; ʌpˋsprɪŋ] **I** *vi*. (*-sprang* [ʌpˈspræŋ; ʌpˋspræŋ], *-sprung* [ʌpˈsprʌŋ; ʌpˋsprʌŋ]; *-sprung*) 向上弹,跃起。**II** *n*. 向上弹(跳)。

up·stage [ˈʌpˈsteidʒ; ˋʌpˋstedʒ] **I** *a*. **1**. 在[向]舞台后方的。**2**. 〔口〕傲慢的,狂妄自大的。**II** *ad*. 在舞台后方;朝着舞台后方。**III** *vt*. **1**. (在演出中占据舞台后方)逼使(另一演员)背向观众,抢(别人的)戏。**2**. 傲慢地对待。**IV** *n*. **1**. 后台。**2**. 舞台上较后的位置。

up·stair [ˈʌpˈstɛə; ˋʌpˋstɛr] *a*. = upstairs (*a*.).

up·stairs [ˈʌpˈstɛəz; ˋʌpˋstɛrz] **I** *ad*. **1**. 在楼上;往楼上。**2**. 〔口〕在较高地位上;〔空军口〕在高空。**3**. 〔美俚〕在头脑里。*kick* ~ 〔口〕把…明升暗降。**II** *a*. **1**. 楼上的。**2**. 【空】在高空的。**3**. 上层的。**III** *n*. 楼上;楼上房间。

up·stand·ing [ʌpˈstændiŋ; ʌpˋstændɪŋ] *a*. **1**. 直立的,挺拔的。**2**. 正直的,诚实的。**-ness** *n*.

up·start [ˈʌpstɑːt; ˋʌpˏstɑrt] **I** *n*. **1**. 暴发户;新贵,突然获得地位的人。**2**. 傲慢无礼的人。**II** *a*. 暴发的,突然出现[显赫]的。*the ~s pushing into society* 这些正在挤进上流社会的新贵。**III** [ʌpˈstɑːt; ʌpˋstɑrt] *vt*., *vi*. (使)突然跳起[出];(使)暴发,(使)一步高升。

up·state [ˈʌpˈsteit; ˋʌpˋstet] **I** *a*. 〔美〕(一州内)远离大都市[海边]的,北边的。**II** *n*. 内地,(特指)纽约州北部地区。**-r** *n*. 〔美〕内地人;纽约州北部的人。

up·stream [ˈʌpˈstriːm; ˋʌpˋstrim] **I** *ad*. 向上游,溯流。**II** *a*. **1**. 溯流而上的。**2**. (石油工业等)上游的,和石油的勘探、开采及输送到起运港口有关的〔石油工业此后的提炼等过程则称为下游(downstream)产业〕。

up·stretched [ʌpˈstretʃt; ˋʌpˏstretʃt] *a*. 向上伸张,向上延伸的。

up·stroke [ˈʌpstrəuk; ˋʌpˏstrok] *n*. 向上的一笔[一击]。

up·surge [ʌpˈsəːdʒ; ʌpˋsɝdʒ] **I** *vi*. **1**. 高涨,上涌。**2**. 增长。**II** [ˈʌpˌsəːdʒ; ˋʌpˏsɝdʒ] *n*. 高涨;高潮 (*opp*. ebb)。*the tempestuous ~ of the national liberation movement* 风起云涌的民族解放运动。**up·sur·gence** [-əns; -əns] *n*.

up·sweep [ˈʌpswiːp; ˋʌpswip] **I** *n*. **1**. 向上倾斜,向上卷曲。**2**. 头发在头顶上卷起的发型。**II** [ʌpˈswiːp; ʌpˋswip] *vt*., *vi*. (*up·swept* [ˈʌpˌswept; ˋʌpˏswɛpt]) (使)向上斜,(使)向上弯曲。

up·swell [ʌpˈswel; ʌpˋswɛl] *vi*. (*-swelled*; *-swelled*, *-swol·len* [ʌpˈswəulən; ʌpˋswolən]) 膨胀,增加,壮大。

up·swept [ˈʌpˌswept; ˋʌpˏswɛpt] **I** upsweep 的过去式和过去分词。**II** *a*. 向上卷曲的,向上倾斜的;(一种发型)头发在头顶上卷起的。

up·swing [ˈʌpswiŋ; ˋʌpˏswɪŋ] **I** *n*. **1**. 向上的摆动;向上趋势;向上的运动;〔尤指〕(生意的)兴隆。**2**. 进步,改进。提高。**II** [ʌpˈswiŋ; ʌpˋswɪŋ] *vi*. (*up·swung* [ʌpˈswʌŋ; ʌpˋswʌŋ]) **1**. 向上摆动;上进。**2**. 提高;改进。

up·sy-dai·sy [ˈʌpsəˈdeizi, ˈʌpsi-; ˋʌpsɪˏdezɪ] *int*. 举高高儿〔举高小孩时的戏耍语〕。

up·take [ˈʌpteik; ˋʌpˏtek] *n*. **1**. 举起,拿起。**2**. 了解,领会。**3**. 【物,生】吸收;【机】(把烟尘等抽吸到屋外的)升烟道,上升通风管;扬水管;【矿】上风井,上风口。*quick* [*slow*] *in the* ~ 领会得快[慢]。

up·talk [ˈʌptɔːk; ʌpˋtɔk] *vi*. (在一句话快说完时忽然)用升调说话。

up-tem·po [ˈʌpˌtempəu; ˋʌpˏtɛmpo] *a*. 快节奏的;节奏愈来愈快的。

up·throw [ˈʌpˌθrəu; ˋʌpˏθro] *n*. **1**. 向上的一投。**2**. 【地】上投(地貌);隆起。

up·thrust [ˈʌpˌθrʌst; ˋʌpˏθrʌst] *n*. **1**. 向上的一推[一冲]。**2**. 【地】上冲断层。

up·tick [ˈʌptik; ˋʌptɪk] *n*. 〔美〕【商】(股票)报升〔比上一盘交易高的成交价格〕;(经济图表等上显示的)上升[回升]趋势。

up·time [ˈʌptaim; ˋʌptaɪm] *n*. (电子计算机等的)正常运行时间。

up-tight, up·tight [ˈʌpˈtait; ˋʌpˋtaɪt] *a*. 〔俚〕**1**. 非常紧张的,非常神经质的;非常焦急的。**2**. 极端保守的;过于严格的。**3**. (经济情况)很糟糕的 (= up tight)。

up·tilt [ʌpˈtilt; ʌpˋtɪlt] *vt*. **1**. 使倾斜。**2**. (拿枪)向上斜刺,上击。

up-to-date [ˈʌptəˈdeit; ˋʌptəˋdet] *a*. **1**. 直到最近的。**2**. 最新(式)的;现代化的,尖端的。**-ly** *ad*. **-ness** *n*.

Up·ton [ˈʌptən; ˋʌptən] *n*. 厄普顿〔姓氏〕。

up-to-the-min·ute [ˈʌptəðəˈminit; ˋʌptəðəˋmɪnɪt] *a*. 最近的,最新的。~ *news* 最新消息。

up·town [ˈʌpˈtaun; ˋʌpˋtaʊn] **I** *ad*. 〔美〕远离商业区;在[向]非商业区;在住宅区。**II** *n*., *a*. (住在)远离商业区的市区(的),住宅区(的)。

up·turn [ʌpˈtəːn; ʌpˋtɝn] **I** *vt*., *vi*. **1**. (使)朝上翻;翻起,掘翻。**2**. (使)向上,(使)好转。**II** [ˈʌptəːn; ˋʌpˏtɝn] *n*. **1**. 上升;升迁。**2**. 好转,改善。**-ed** [ˈʌpˈtəːnd; ˋʌpˋtɝnd] *a*. **1**. 朝上(翘)的。**2**. 翻转的。

UPU = Universal Postal Union 万国邮政联盟(联合国)。

up·ward [ˈʌpwəd; ˋʌpwɚd] **I** *a*. 向上的,朝上的;上涨的。*an ~ glance* 抬眼一看。*Prices show an ~ tendency*. 物价趋涨。**II** *ad*. = upwards. ~ **mobility** 社会地位和经济地位上升的流动性〔指努力提高自己经济与社会地位的能力和倾向〕。**-ly** *ad*. (*upwardly mobile* 在社会地位等方面努力向上的,向上升迁的)。

up·wards [ˈʌpwədz; ˋʌpwɚdz] *ad*. **1**. 在上面,向上头。**2**. 向水源[震源地]方面;向内地。**3**. 上涨,腾贵。**4**. 从…起以后;以上。*look* ~ 仰望。*Prices tend* ~. 物价趋涨。*from her school days* ~ 从她学生时代开始。*children of six years and* ~ 六岁及六岁以上的孩子。~ *of* …以上 (~ *of ten years* 十年以上)。

up·wind [ˈʌpˈwind; ˋʌpˋwɪnd] **I** *ad*., *a*. 迎风向地[的],逆风向地[的]。**II** *n*. 逆风。

ur [ʌ(ː), ə(ː); ʌ, ɚ] *int*. 呃,嗯〔表示踌躇〕。

UR 〔美空俚〕= unsatisfactory report.

ur-[1] *pref*. [G.] 原始的,原来的,最初的。

ur-[2] *pref*. uro- 的异体。

u·ra·cil [ˈjurəsil; ˋjʊrəsəl] *n*. 【化】尿嘧啶。

u·rae·mi·a [juəˈriːmiə; jʊˋrimɪə] *n*. 【医】尿毒症。**-mic** *a*. (患)尿毒症的。

u·rae·us [juˈriəs; jʊˋriəs] *n*. (*pl*. *u·rae·i* [juˈriai; jʊˋriaɪ]) (古埃及神像及帝王头饰上的)毒蛇形标记。

u·ra·gogue [ˈjuərəgɔg; ˋjʊrəgɑg] *n*. 【药】一种利尿剂。

U·ral [ˈjuərəl; ˋjurəl, ʊˋral] *n*. 乌拉尔〔俄罗斯一地区〕。

U·ral-Al·ta·ic [ˈjuərəlælˈteiik; ˋjurəlælˋteɪk] **I** *a*. 乌拉尔阿尔泰 (Ural-Altai) 地方(居民)的;乌拉尔阿尔泰语族的。**II** *n*. 乌拉尔阿尔泰语族〔芬兰语、土耳其语、蒙古语等〕。

U·ral·ic [juˈrælik; jʊˋrælɪk], **U·ra·li·an** [juˈreiliən; jʊˋrelɪən] **I** *a*. 乌拉尔语系的〔包括芬兰—乌戈尔语和萨摩耶德语族〕。**II** *n*. 乌拉尔语系。

u·ral·ite [ˈjuərəlait; ˋjʊrəlˏaɪt] *n*. 【地】纤闪石。**-ic** [juəˈrælik; jʊˋrælɪk] *a*.

u·ra·nal·y·sis, u·ri·nal·y·sis [ˌjuərəˈnælisis; ˏjʊrəˋnæləsɪs] *n*. 【医】尿分析。

U·ra·ni·a [juəˈreiniə; jʊˋrenɪə] *n*. **1**. 【希神】掌管天文的缪斯 (Muse) 女神。**2**. 爱情与美之女神 (Aphrodite) 的别名。

U·ra·ni·an[1] [juəˈreiniən; jʊˋrenɪən] *a*. 缪斯女神的。

U·ra·ni·an[2] [juəˈreiniən; jʊˋrenɪən] *a*. 【天】天王星的。

u·ran·ic[1] [juəˈrænik; jʊˋrænɪk] *a*. 天的,天文学的。

u·ran·ic[2] [juəˈrænik; jʊˋrænɪk] *a*. 【化】六价铀的,(正)

铀的,含铀的。～ *acid*【化】铀酸。

u·ra·nide [ˈjuərənaid; ˋjurənaɪd] ***n*.**【化】铀系;超铀元素。

u·ran·i·nite [juəˈræninait; juˋrænə,naɪt] ***n*.**【矿】晶质铀矿,沥青铀矿;天然氧化铀。

u·ra·nite [ˈjuərənait; ˋjurə,naɪt] ***n*.**【矿】铀矿类;云母铀。

u·ra·ni·um [juəˈreiniəm; juˋrenɪəm] ***n*.**【化】铀(U)。**fertile** ～ 铀238。～ **dioxide**【化】二氧化铀。～ **fission** 铀核裂变。～ **product** 铀变物。～ **trioxide**【化】三氧化铀。

urano- *pref*. 表示"天": *urano*metry.

u·ra·nog·ra·phy [ˌjuərəˈnɔgrəfi; ,jurəˋnɑgrəfɪ] ***n*.**【天】星图学。**-ra·pher** ***n*.** 星图学家。**-graph·ic** [ˌjuərənə*u*ˈgræfik; ,juronoˋgræfɪk], **-graph·i·cal** ***a*.**

u·ra·nol·o·gy [ˌjuərəˈnɔlədʒi; ,jurəˋnɑlədʒɪ] ***n*.** 天体学;天文学〔旧称〕。

u·ra·nom·e·try [ˌjuərəˈnɔmitri; ,jurəˋnɑmətrɪ] ***n*.** **1.** (古代)天体志[图];星座志。**2.** 天体测量(术)。

u·ra·nous [ˈjuərənəs, juəˈrei-; ˋjurənəs, juˋre-] ***a*.**【化】铀的,含铀的〔尤指含低价铀〕。

Ura·nus [ˈjuərənəs; ˋjurənəs] ***n*.** **1.**【希神】优拉纳斯神〔大地女神 Gaca 的儿子〕。**2.**【天】天王星。

u·ra·nyl [ˈjuərənil; ˋjurənɪl] ***n*.**【化】氧铀,铀酰。

u·rate [ˈjuəreit; ˋjuret] ***n*.**【化】脲酸盐[酯]。

ur·ban [ˈəːbən; ˋɝbən] ***a*.** **1.** 城市的,在城市里的,住在城市中的,城市居民的。**2.** 习惯于[喜爱]城市生活的。*the* ～ *population* 城市人口。～**-centered** ***a*.** 以城市为中心的。～ **critic** 城市问题评论家。～ **district**〔英〕准自治市。～ **guerrilla** 城市游击队(员)。～ **homesteading**〔美〕城市旧房改造与返迁计划。～ **ore** 城市矿藏〔指城市垃圾中的瓶罐及其他固体废物可再生利用的资源〕。～ **legend** 街头小道消息,街谈巷议。～ **renewal** 城市环境更新,城市改造。～ **sprawl** (无限制的)城市扩张。～ **town** [**township**]〔美〕城镇〔人口 25,000 以上或人口密度至少为 1500 人/平方英里〕。

ur·bane [əːˈbein; ɝˋben] ***a*.** **1.** 都[城]市气派的。**2.** 有礼貌的,文雅的(*opp*. rustic)。**-ly** ***ad*.** **-ness** ***n*.**

ur·ban·ism [ˈəːbənizəm; ˋɝbənɪzm] ***n*.** **1.** 城市生活的特点;城市生活(组织、问题等);对城市生活等的研究。**2.** 人口流入城市;人口集中于城市;城市化。**ur·ban·ist** ***n*.** 城市规划专家。**ur·ban·is·itic** ***a*.**

ur·ban·ist [ˈəːbənist; ˋɝbənɪst] ***n*.** 城市计划者。

ur·ban·ite [ˈəːbənait; ˋɝbənaɪt] ***n*.** 城市居民。

ur·ban·i·ty [əːˈbæniti; ɝˋbænətɪ] ***n*.** **1.** 有礼;文雅,优雅。**2.** 〔*pl*.〕文雅的举止。

ur·ban·i·za·tion [ˌəːbənaiˈzeiʃən; ,ɝbənaɪˋzeʃən] ***n*.** 城市化;使具有城市特点。

ur·ban·ize [ˈəːbənaiz; ˋɝbən,aɪz] ***vt*.** **1.** 使都[城]市化。**2.** 使文雅,使有礼貌,使优雅。

ur·ban·oid [ˈəːbənɔid; ˋɝbənɔɪd] ***a*.** 具有大城市特点的。

ur·ban·ol·o·gist [ˌəːbəˈnɔlədʒist; ,ɝbəˋnɑlədʒɪst] ***n*.** 都市学专家,城市问题学者[专家]。

ur·ba·nol·o·gy [ˌəːbəˈnɔlədʒi; ,ɝbəˋnɑlədʒɪ] ***n*.** 城市学,都市学。

ur·bi·a [ˈəːbiə; ˋɝbɪə] ***n*.** 〔集合词〕市区〔以区别于郊区(suburbia)和远郊(exurbia)〕。

ur·bi·ci·dal [ˌəːbiˈsaidl; ,ɝbɪˋsaɪdl] ***a*.** (因胡乱建设导致破坏城市景观与自然环境等因而)毁灭城市的,对城市起毁灭作用的。

ur·bi·cide [ˌəːbiˈsaid; ,ɝbɪˋsaɪd] ***n*.** 城市自杀〔因胡乱建设而破坏城市景观及自然环境,从而毁掉城市〕。

ur·bi·cul·ture [ˈəːbiˌkʌltʃə; ˋɝbɪ,kʌltʃɚ] ***n*.** 城市(生活)特有的习俗[社会问题等]。

ur·bi et or·bi [ˈuəbi et ˈɔːbiː; ˋurbɪ ɛt ˋɔrbi]〔L.〕(降福于)城市〔指罗马〕和世界〔教皇祝福用语〕。

URBM = ultimate range ballistic missile 最远程弹道导弹。

ur·ce·o·late [ˈəːsiəlit; ˋɝsɪəlɪt] ***a*.** 瓶形的,瓮形的,缸状的。

ur·chin [ˈəːtʃin; ˋɝtʃɪn] ***n*.** **1.** 顽童;儿童;少年。**2.**【动】海胆〔通常称 sea-urchin〕。**3.**〔方〕刺猬。

urd [əːd; ɝd] ***n*.**〔Hind.〕【植】黑绿豆(*Phaseolus mungo*)。

Ur·du [ˈuəduː, Hind. wrdu; ˋurdu, Hind. wrdu] ***n*.** 乌尔都语〔用阿拉伯字母写的一种印地语;巴基斯坦的正式语言〕。

-ure *suf*. 由动词构成名词的词尾,表示:动作(例: cens*ure*);结果(例: creat*ure*);集合体(例: legislat*ure*)等。

u·re·a [ˈjuəriə; ˋjurɪə] ***n*.**【化】尿素,脲。**-l**, **u·re·ic** [ˌjuəˈriːik; ,juˋriɪk] ***a*.**

u·re·a-form·al·de·hyde [juriəfɔːˈmældihaid; jurɪəfɔrˋmældɪhaɪd] **re·sins**【化】脲醛树脂,尿素甲醛树脂。

u·re·ase [ˈjuərieis, -eiz; ˋjurɪes, -ez] ***n*.**【化】尿素酶。

u·re·din·i·um, u·re·di·um [ˌjuəriˈdiniəm, -ˈdiəm; ,jurɪˋdɪnɪəm, -ˋdɪəm] ***n*.** (*pl*. ***-i·a*** [-ə; -ə])【植】夏孢子堆。**-din·i·al** ***a*.**

u·re·do [juˈriːdəu; juˋrido] ***n*.**【医】= urticaria.

u·re·do·spore, u·re·di·o·spore [juˈriːdəspɔː, -diəspɔː; juˋridəspɔr, -dɪəspɔr] ***n*.**【植】夏孢子。

u·re·do·stage [juˈriːdəsteidʒ; juˋridəstedʒ] ***n*.**【植】夏孢子期。

u·re·ide [ˈjuəriaid, -id; ˋjurɪaɪd, -ɪd] ***n*.**【化】醯脲。

u·remi·a [juˈriːmiə; juˋrimɪə] ***n*.** = uraemia. **u·remic** [juˈriːmik; juˋrimɪk] ***a*.** = uraemic.

u·re·ter [juəˈriːtə; juˋritɚ] ***n*.**【解】输尿管。**-al**, **-ic** [ˌjuəriˈterik; ,jurɪˋtɛrɪk] ***a*.**

u·re·ter·i·tis [juˌriːtəˈraitis; ju,ritəˋraɪtɪs] ***n*.**【医】输尿管炎。

u·re·ter·os·to·my [juˌriːtəˈrɔstəmi; ju,ritəˋrɑstəmɪ] ***n*.** (*pl*. ***-mies***)【医】输尿管造口术。

u·re·thane [ˈjuəriθein; ˋjurə,θen], **u·re·than** [ˈjuəriθæn; ˋjurɪθæn] ***n*.**【化】尿烷,氨基甲酸乙酯。

u·re·thra [juəˈriːθrə; juˋriθrə] ***n*.** (*pl*. ***-thrae*** [-θriː; -θri], ～***s***)【解】尿道。**-l** ***a*.**

u·re·thri·tis [ˌjuəriˈθraitis; ,jurɪˋθraɪtɪs] ***n*.**【医】尿道炎。

u·re·thro·scope [juˈriːθrəskəup; juˋriθrə,skop] ***n*.**【医】尿道镜。**-scop·ic** [juˌriːθrəˈskɔpik; ju,riθrəˋskɑpɪk] ***a*.**

u·ret·ic [juəˈretik; juˋrɛtɪk] **I** ***a*.**【医】尿的;利尿的。**II** ***n*.** 利尿剂。

U·rey [ˈjuəri; ˋjurɪ] ***n*.** 尤里〔姓氏〕。

urge [əːdʒ; ɝdʒ] **I** ***vt*.** **1.** 推进,驱策,赶(马等)。**2.** 催促,强迫;促进,奖励,鼓励,劝告,怂恿;号召。**3.** 权力主张,强调。**4.** 苦练,勤苦地使用。～ *a horse on* [*onward*] 赶马前跑。～ *sb. to take steps in the matter* 催人处理事件。～ *upon sb. the necessity of doing so* 向某人强调有这样做的必要。～ *a programme* 提出一个纲领。— ***vi*.** 极力主张;强烈要求。**II** ***n*.** **1.** 推动力。**2.** 〔常用 *sing*.〕刺激,冲动,迫切要求。*the sex* ～ 性的冲动。

ur·gen·cy [ˈəːdʒənsi; ˋɝdʒənsɪ] ***n*.** **1.** 迫切,紧急;【政】紧急决议。**2.** 催促,硬要,强调。*a matter of great* ～ 非常紧急的事。*an* ～ *signal* 紧急信号。

ur·gent [ˈəːdʒənt; ˋɝdʒənt] ***a*.** **1.** 紧急的,迫切的。**2.** 催促的,硬要的,极力主张的,纠缠不休的。*an* ～ *telegram* 急电。*be in* ～ *need of* (*help*) 急需(援助)。*on* ～ *business* 因急务。*an* ～ *motion* 紧急动议。*He was* ～ *with me for* [*to disclose*] *further particulars*. 他硬要我说得更详细点。**-ly** ***ad*.**

urg·er [ˈəːdʒə; ˋɝdʒɚ] ***n*.** 推进者,催促者,劝告者,极力

主张者。

ur·gi·cen·ter [ˈəːdʒiˌsentə; ˋɝdʒɪsɛntɚ] *n*. 〔口〕急诊中心。

-urgy *comb. f*. 构成名词,表示:制作技术;加工:chem*urgy*, metall*urgy*.

-uria *comb. f*. 表示:因含某种物质而使尿呈病态:glycos*uria*, albumin*uria*.

U·riah [juəˈraiə; juˋraɪə] *n*. 尤那依[姓氏]。~ **Heep** 尤那依·希普〔阴险虚伪的小职员典型,狄更斯小说《大卫·科柏菲尔》中的人物〕。

u·ric [ˈjuərik; ˋjʊrɪk] *a*. 【化】尿的。~ *acid* 尿酸。

u·ri·cos·u·ric [ˌjuərikəuˈsjuərik; ˏjʊrəkoˋsurɪk] *a*. 【医】增加[促进]尿酸排泄的。

u·ri·dine [ˈjuəridiːn; ˋjʊrədin] *n*. 【化】尿(嘧啶核)苷。

u·ri·dyl·ic [juəriˈdilik; jʊrɪˋdɪlɪk] *a*. ~ **acid** 【生化】尿(嘌呤核)苷酸。

u·ri·nal [ˈjuərinl; ˋjʊrənl] *n*. 尿壶;小便处[池]。

u·ri·nal·y·sis [ˌjuəriˈnælisis; ˏjʊrəˋnæləsɪs] *n*. (*pl*. *-ses* [-siːz; -siz]) 【医】尿分析(法)。

u·ri·na·ry [ˈjuərinəri; ˋjʊrəˏnɛrɪ] **I** *a*. 尿的,泌尿(器)的。**II** *n*. 〔*pl*.〕 **1**. 小便处。**2**. 尿池。~ **bladder** 膀胱。~ **calculus** 尿结石。~ **diseases** 泌尿系统疾病。~ **tubule** 尿细管。

u·ri·nate [ˈjuərineit; ˋjʊrəˏnet] *vt*., *vi*. (使)小便,(使)排尿。

u·ri·na·tion [ˌjuəriˈneiʃən; ˏjʊrəˋneʃən] *n*. 小便,排尿。

u·rine [ˈjuərin; ˋjʊrɪn] *n*. 尿。*pass* [*discharge*] (*one's*) ~ 小便,排尿。

u·ri·nif·er·ous [ˌjuəriˈnifərəs; ˏjʊrəˋnɪfərəs] *a*. 【医】导尿的。

u·ri·no·gen·i·tal [ˌjuərinəuˈdʒenitl; ˏjʊrənoˋdʒɛnətl̩] *a*. = urogenital.

u·ri·nom·e·ter [ˌjuəriˈnɔmitə; ˏjʊrəˋnɑmɪtɚ] *n*. 尿比重计,量尿器。

u·ri·nous [ˈjuərinəs; ˋjʊrənəs], **u·ri·nose** [-nəus; -nos] *a*. 尿(似)的,含尿的。

URL = uniform [universal] resource locator 【计】统一资源定位器。

urn [əːn; ɝn] **I** *n*. **1**. 瓮,缸,坛。**2**. 骨灰瓮;坟墓。**3**. 水壶;咖啡壶。**4**. 【植】蒴壶。**II** *vt*. 〔罕〕把(遗骨等)装进瓮里。**-ing** *n*. 〔卑〕(男子)同性恋。

uro- *pref*. **1**. 表示"尿":*uro*chrome. **2**. 表示"尾":*uro*dele.

u·ro·chrome [ˈjuərəukrəum; ˋjʊrəˏkrom] *n*. 【生化】尿色素,尿色肽。

u·ro·dele [ˈjuərəudiːl; ˋjʊrədil] *n*. 【动】有尾目(*Caudata*)动物。

u·ro·gen·i·tal [ˌjuərəuˈdʒenitl; ˏjʊrəˋdʒɛnətl̩] *a*. 尿(生)殖的,泄殖的。

u·rog·e·nous [juˈrɔdʒinəs; juˋrɑdʒənəs] *a*. **1**. 生尿的。**2**. 尿中含有的,出自尿中的。

u·ro·ki·nase [ˌjuərəuˈkaineis, -ˈkineis; ˏjʊroˋkaɪnes, -ˋkɪnes] *n*. 【生化】尿激酶,尿致活酶。

u·ro·lith [ˈjuərəliθ; ˋjʊrəlɪθ] *n*. 【医】= urinary calculus. **-ic** *a*.

u·ro·log·ic [ˌjuərəuˈlɔdʒik; jʊroˋlɑdʒɪk] *a*. 泌尿学的(= urological)。

u·rol·o·gy [juəˈrɔlədʒi; juˋrɑlədʒɪ] *n*. 【医】泌尿学。**-log·i·cal** [ˌjuərəuˈlɔdʒikəl; ˏjʊroˋlɑdʒɪkl̩] *a*.

u·ro·pod [ˈjuərəpɔd; ˋjʊrəˏpɑd] *n*. 【动】尾足;腹足。

u·ro·pyg·i·um [ˌjuərəuˈpidʒiəm; ˏjʊrəˋpaɪdʒɪəm] *n*. (*pl*. *-i·a* [-ə; -ə], ~*s*) (鸟的)尾臀。**-pyg·i·al** *a*.

u·ro·scop·ic [ˌjuərəuˈskɔpik; ˏjʊroˋskɑpɪk] *a*. 检尿(法)的。

u·ros·co·py [juəˈrɔskəpi; juˋrɑskəpɪ] *n*. 【医】尿检,尿检视法。

Ur·quhart [ˈəːkət; ˋɝkɚt] *n*. 厄克特[姓氏]。

Ur·sa [ˈəːsə; ˋɝsə] *n*. 〔L.〕= bear. ~ ***Major*** [***Minor***] 【天】大[小]熊座。

ur·si·form [ˈəːsifɔːm; ˋɝsəfɔrm] *a*. 熊状的。

ur·sine [ˈəːsain; ˋɝsaɪn] *a*. **1**. 熊的,熊类的;似熊的。**2**. (毛虫等)长满硬毛的。

Ur·spra·che [ˈuːəˌʃprɑːkhə; ˋurˏʃprækhə] *n*. 〔G.〕原始语〔一种由推论而重新构定的母语,如原始日耳曼语〕。

Ur·su·la [ˈəːsjulə; ˋɝsjulə] *n*. 厄休拉[女子名]。

Ur·ti·ca [ˈəːtikə, əːˈtaikə; ˋɝtɪkə, ɝˋtaɪkə] *n*. **1**. 【植】荨麻属。**2**. 〔u-〕荨麻属植物。**3**. 〔u-〕【医】荨麻疹团,风疹块。

Ur·ti·cant [ˈəːtikənt; ˋɝtɪkənt] *a*. 产生痒[痛]的;(毛虫)能刺人使生痒肿块的。

ur·ti·car·i·a [ˌəːtiˈkeəriə; ˏɝtiˋkɛrɪə] *n*. 【医】荨麻疹,风疹。**-al** *a*.

ur·ti·cate [ˈəːtikeit; ˋɝtəket] *vt*. **1**. 用荨麻拍打(麻痹的肢体等)使恢复感觉。**2**. 刺痛,用荨麻刺。— *vi*. 诱发荨麻症。

ur·ti·ca·tion [ˌəːtiˈkeiʃən; ˏɝtəˋkeʃən] *n*. 【医】**1**. 用荨麻拍打。**2**. 刺痒的感觉。**3**. 生风疹块,生荨麻疹。

Uru. = Uruguay.

Uru·guay [ˈurugwai; ˋʊrəgwe] *n*. 乌拉圭[南美洲]。

Uru·guay·an [ˌuruˈgwaiən, ˏʊrəˋgwaɪən] **I** *n*. 乌拉圭人。**II** *a*. 乌拉圭(人)的;乌拉圭文化的。

U·rum·chi, U·rum·tsi [uˈrumtʃi; uˋrumtʃɪ] *n*. 乌鲁木齐〔中国新疆维吾尔自治区首府〕。

u·rus [ˈjuərəs; ˋjʊrəs] *n*. 原牛(*Bos primigenius*)〔一种已绝种的野牛,过去在欧洲常见,被认为是现今家牛的祖先〕。

u·ru·shi·ol [ˈuːruːʃiˌɔːl, uˈruː-, -əul; ˋuruʃɪˏol, uˋru-; -ol] *n*. 【化】漆醇。

us [强 ʌs, 弱 əs; ʌs, əs] *pron*. **1**. 〔we 的宾格〕我们。**2**. 〔诗、古〕朕(= ourselves)。**3**. 〔口〕〔用作表语〕我们(= we)。**4**. 〔方、口〕我(= me, to me)。*Let* ~ [ˈletəs; ˋlɛtəs] *go*. = *Let's* [lets; lɛts] *go*. 我们走吧。*Let* ~ [let ʌs; lɛt ʌs] *go*. 让我们走吧,放我们走吧。*Who are you?* — *It's* ~. 谁呀?——是我们。*Give* ~ *a penny*. 〔口〕给我一个铜板吧。

U. S., US = **1**. the United States (of America) 美国,美利坚合众国。**2**. Uncle Sam 〔口〕山姆大叔〔美国、美国政府或美国人的绰号〕。

US **1**. = U. S. **2**. 如果后面附有一个阿拉伯数码,则意为"美国某号公路"如 US40,即美国第 40 号公路。

u. s. = 〔L.〕 **1**. *ubi supra* 〔书籍等中的参照用语〕在上面提及之处。**2**. *ut supra* 如上所述,如上所示。

U. S. A., USA = **1**. the United States of America 美利坚合众国。**2**. the United States Army 美国陆军。

us·a·bil·i·ty [ˌjuːzəˈbiliti; ˏjuzəˋbɪlətɪ] *n*. **1**. 可用;有用。**2**. 适用,便于使用(= usableness)。

us·a·ble [ˈjuːzəbl; ˋjuzəbl̩] *a*. **1**. 可用的,能使用的。**2**. 便于使用的。**-ness** *n*.

USAEC = United States Atomic Energy Commission 美国原子能委员会。

USAF = **1**. United States Air Force 美国空军。**2**. United States Army Forces 美国陆军部队。

USAFE = United States Air Force in Europe 美国驻欧空军。

USAFI = United States Armed Forces Institute 美国武装部队业余进修学院。

us·age [ˈjuːzidʒ; ˋjusɪdʒ] *n*. **1**. 使用;用法;对待。**2**. 习惯,惯例,习俗。**3**. 【语法】惯用法;【法】习惯(法)。**4**. 【机】用损,损蚀;使用度。*an old man who met with harsh* ~ 一个受到虐待的老人。*a car damaged by harsh* ~ 一辆因使用不经心而被损坏的汽车。*modern English* ~ 现代英语惯用法。*keep an old* ~ *alive* 保持旧习俗。***according to*** ~ 依照惯例。***by*** ~ 习惯上;视为惯例。

U

us·ance [ˈjuːzəns; ˋjuzns] ***n*.** 1.【商】支付汇票的习惯期限,支付期票的期限。2.【经】利得;(高利贷的)利息。3.〔古〕使用;惯例,习惯。***at*** ~ 在(习惯)期限内支付。

USAREUR = United States Army in Europe 美国驻欧陆军。

USB = universal serial bus【计】通用串行总线〔一种简化了插接多种附件的薄型插座〕。

U. S. C. = 1. United States of Colombia〔旧〕哥伦比亚合众国。2. United States Code《美国法典》。

USCG = United States Coast Guard 美国海岸警卫队。

use [juːs; jus] **I** ***n*.** 1. 使用,利用,应用;使用的机会[需要]。2. 使用的能力。3. 使用的自由,使用权。4. 使用法。5. 用途;效用,用处,利益。6. 习惯,惯例;惯常的作法[仪式]。7.【法】(托管土地等的)收益权。*Will there be any further ~ for big battleship in the future war?* 在未来的战争中还有使用大型战舰的必要[机会]吗? *He has lost the ~ of an arm*. 他的一只胳膊残废了。*What is the ~ of talking?* 说有什么用吗? *put the ~ of one's house at sb.'s disposal* 让某人自由使用自己的房子。*a computer with many ~s* 一种多用途的电子计算机。*according to an ancient ~* 按照一种古老的习俗。*Use is (a) second nature*. 习惯是第二天性。*Use makes perfect*. 熟能生巧。*Once a ~, forever a custom*. 习惯成自然。***be of (great)*** ~ (非常)有益。***be out of*** ~ 没有人用,不时行,现在不用,作废。***bring sth. into*** ~ 开始使用(某物)。***come into*** ~ (某物)开始被使用。***for the*** ~ ***of*** (*students*) 供(学生)使用。***get*** [***go, fall***] ***out of*** ~ 开始不用,渐废。***have no*** ~ ***for*** 1. 不需要,用不着。2.〔口〕不愿再与之打交道,不喜欢,厌腻。***in*** ~ 正在用;通行。***make*** ~ ***of*** 利用,使用。***no*** ~〔口〕没(有)用(处) (*It is no ~ talking* [*to talk*]. 说也没用)。***of no*** ~ = *no* ~. ***of*** ~ 有用 (*It is of great ~*. 这非常有用)。***put to*** ~ 用,利用 (*put to a good ~* 善用)。~ ***and wont*** 习惯;惯例。***with*** ~ 经常在用 (*The carpet has got worn with ~*. 这块地毯由于经常使用,已经磨坏了)。**II** [juːz; juz] ***vt*.** 1. 用,使用,利用,应用;服用,食用。2. 消费;耗费。3. 对待(人)。4. 行使,动用。5. 使习惯〔此义现在只将过去分词 used 用如形容词,参看 used[1]〕。~ *one's revolver upon sb*. 对某人使用手枪。~ *tobacco* 抽烟。~ *five tons of coal a week* 每周耗煤 5 吨。~ *sb. well* [*ill*] 待人好[不好]。~ *one's brains* 用脑筋,想。~ *care* 小心,注意。~ *diligence* 努力。~ *economy* 节省。~ *one's ears* [*eyes*] 听[看]。*U- your discretion*. 请考虑考虑吧。*U- your pleasure*. 请自便,请随意。*How is the world using you?*〔俚〕近来好吗? — ***vi*.** 常,惯常〔此义现在只用过去式,参看 used[2]〕。~ ***oneself*** 处身。***U- others as you would have them ~ you***. 你愿意别人怎样待你,你就应该怎样待人。~ ***up*** 1. 用完,用光。2.〔口〕使筋疲力尽。~**-by date** (食品包装上的)食用期限。~ **immunity**【法】使用证词豁免权〔指保护被迫作证的证人,使其证词不被用来对其自身提出起诉的一种豁免权〕。**-a·ble** ***a*.** = usable.

used[1] [juːst; just, 〔在 to 前〕juːsṭ; just] ***a*.** 1. 习惯于〔作表语用〕。2. [juːzd; juzd]〔美〕用过的,用旧了的,半旧的;精疲力尽的。~ *books*〔美〕旧书。~ *heat* 废热,余热。***be*** ~ ***to*** 惯于 (*be ~ to getting up early* 习惯早起。*be ~ to hard work* 惯于吃苦耐劳)。***get*** [***become***] ~ ***to*** 变得习惯于。~ ***up*** 1.〔美〕筋疲力尽的,疲劳不堪的。2. 用完了的;〔美〕被杀死了的,已阵亡的。

used[2] [〔带 to 时〕juːsṭ; jus, 〔不带 to 时〕juːst; just] ***vi*.** 〔用法同助动词,其后的不定式表示过去多次发生的动作〕常常,经常,往往。*I ~ to go there*. 我(以前)常到那里。*He does not come as often as he ~ (to)*. 他不像从前那样常来了。*What ~ he to say?* — *He ~ not to answer*. 他向来怎么讲?——他向来不回答。*It ~ to be said that ...* 过去(人家)常说…。*There ~ to be a house here*. 原来这里是有一幢房子的。*Used there to be swallows here?* 这里是否一向都有燕子? ★口语或美国用法说作 Did there use to ...

used-to-be [ˈjuːstəbi; ˋjustəbɪ] ***n*.**〔美口〕时代落伍者,过时人物。

used-up [ˈjuːzdˈʌp; ˋjuzdˋʌp] ***a*.** 1. 精疲力竭的。2. (因年龄、荒唐的生活而变得)无用的。*a ~ drunk* 一个无用的酒鬼。3. 用罄的,耗尽的。

use·ful [ˈjuːsfʊl; ˋjusfəl] ***a*.** 1. 有用的,有益的,有效的,有帮助的。2.〔俚〕值得称赞的,精通…的 (*at*)。***make oneself generally*** ~ 事事有用,事事帮得来忙 (*He must make himself generally ~*. 他可事事都干得来)。*a pretty ~ performance* 相当精彩的演出。*His wife is very ~ at cooking*. 他的妻子很会做菜。~ **area** 有效面积,可用面积。~ **life** 有效期限,使用寿命。~ **load**【空】实用负载。**-ly** ***ad*.** **-ness** ***n*.**

use·less [ˈjuːslis; ˋjuslɪs] ***a*.** 1. 没用的,无益的,无效的。2.〔俚〕身体不舒服的,没精神的。*I am feeling ~*. 我觉得精神不行了[不舒服]。**-ly** ***ad*.** **-ness** ***n*.**

Use·net [ˈjuːsnet; ˋjusnet] ***n*.**【计】Usenet 网〔因特网上美国多家兴趣专题网站组成的一个论坛〕。

us·er[1] [ˈjuːzə; ˋjuzɚ] ***n*.** 1. 使用者,用户。2. 吸毒成瘾者。*U- pays*. 使用者须付费〔指由政府出资提供公用设施,但使用者须付费〕。~**-friendly.** ***a*.** 方便使用的;【计】(质量好而且设计的操作程序简单)方便用户操作的。

user[2] [ˈjuːzə; ˋjuzɚ] ***n*.**【法】(财产等的)使用(权),行使(权),享受(权),享有(权)。

USES = United States Employment Service 美国就业局。

USEUCOM = United States European Command 美军驻欧司令部。

ush [ʌʃ; ʌʃ] ***n*., *vt*., *vi*.**〔俚〕= usher.

ush·er [ˈʌʃə; ˋʌʃɚ] **I** ***n*.** (*fem*. **-ette** [ˈʌʃəˈret; ˏʌʃɚˋet]) 1. 看门人,门房;传达;〔美〕(戏院的)引座员,领票(员),(婚礼中的)迎宾(员);〔英〕皇室礼宾官。2.〔英〕〔谑〕助理教员,助教。**II** ***vt*.** 1. 引导,领引,招待。2. 宣告,展示 (*in*)。*The waiter ~ed the guests into the dining room*. 服务员把客人领进宴会厅。*She ~ed me to my seat*. 她把我领到座位上。~ *in a new era of computer* 宣告一个电脑新世纪的到来。— ***vi*.** 作招待员;担任前导。~ ***in*** 迎接(来客);传报,预报,告诉(来临等)。~ ***out*** [***forth***] 送出。

USIA = United States Information Agency 美国新闻署。

USIB = United States Intelligence Board 美国情报局。

USIS = United States Information Service 美国新闻处。

USL = United States Legation 美国公使馆。

USM = 1. underwater-to-surface missile 水下对地导弹。2. United States Mail 美国邮政。3. United States Marine(s) 美国海军陆战队。4. United States Mint 美国造币厂。

USMA = United States Military Academy 美国陆军军官学校〔即西点军校〕。

USMC = United States Marine Corps 美国海军陆战队。

USN = United States Navy 美国海军。

USNA = 1. United States National Army 美国国民军。2. United States Naval Academy 美国海军军官学校。

USNG = United States National Guard 美国国民警卫队。

USNR = United States Naval Reserve 美国海军后备队。

USO = United Services Organizations〔英旧〕劳军联合组织,美军慰问协会。

USOC = United States Olympic Committee 美国奥(林匹克)委(员)会。

USOM = United States Operations Mission 美国援外使团。

USP, U. S. P. = **1.** United States Patent 美国专利。**2.** = U. S. Pharm.

U. S. Pharm. = United States Pharmacopoeia 美国药典(规格)。

USPO 1. = United States Patent Office 美国专利局。**2.** = United States Post Office 美国邮政局。

us·que·baugh [ˈʌskwibɔː; ˋʌskwɪbɔ] ***n.*** 〔Scot., Ir.〕 = whisky.

USS = **1.** United States Senate 美国参议院。**2.** United States Ship [Steamer, Steamship] 美国船。**3.** United States Standard 美国(工业)规格,美国(工业)标准。

USSC = United States Supreme Court 美国最高法院。

USSR, U. S. S. R. = the Union of Soviet Socialist Republics (前)苏维埃社会主义共和国联邦。

Us·su·ri [uˈsuːri; ʊˋsurɪ] ***n.*** 乌苏里江〔黑龙江支流〕(= Wusuli River)。

us·tu·late [ˈʌstjuleit, -lit; ˋʌstʃəlɪt, -ˏlet] ***a.*** (烧焦而)变色的,变黑的。

us·tu·la·tion [ˌʌstjuˈleiʃən; ˏʌstʃəˋleʃən] ***n.*** 燃烧,烧焦,烧灼。

usu. = usual; usually.

u·su·al [ˈjuːʒuəl; ˋjuʒʊəl] ***a.*** 通常的,常有的,常见的;平常的,普通的;平时的,平日的;一向的;老是那一套的。*He came earlier than* ~. 他比平时来得早。*She came early as was* ~ *with her*. 她像平日那样来得很早。*the* ~ (*thing*) 老一套,老调。*He said all the* ~ *things*. 他讲的全是老一套。***as per*** ~ 〔谑〕 = *as* ~. ***as*** ~ 照例,照常,仍然 (*He was late, as* ~. 他照例迟到了)。**-ly** ***ad.*** **-ness** ***n.***

u·su·ca·pion [juːzjuˈkeipiən; ˏjuzjʊˋkepɪən], **u·su·cap·tion** [ˌjuːzjuˈkæpʃən; ˏjuzjʊˋkæpʃən] ***n.*** 【法】时效所有权〔在法定时间内始终占有而取得的所有权〕。

u·su·fruct [ˈjuːsju(ː)frʌkt; ˋjusjʊˏfrʌkt] **I** ***n.*** 【法】收益享用,用益权。**II** ***vt.*** 根据用益权占有。

u·su·fruc·tu·ar·y [ˌjuːsjuˈfrʌktjuəri; ˏjuzjʊˋfrʌktʃʊˏɛrɪ] **I** ***n.*** 【法】有用益权者。**II** ***a.*** (有)用益权的。

u·su·rer [ˈjuːʒərə; ˋjuʒərɚ] ***n.*** 高利贷者,吃重利的人,重利盘剥者。

u·su·ri·ous [juːˈʒuəriəs; juˋʒʊrɪəs] ***a.*** 高利贷(者)的,高利的;重利盘剥的;掠夺性的。**-ly** ***ad.*** **-ness** ***n.***

u·surp [juːˈzəːp; jʊˋzɝp] ***vt.*** 篡夺,侵占,盗用;强夺。~ *state* (*government*) *power* 篡政。~ *the throne* 篡夺王位。~ *the name of*... 盗用…的名义。*a* ~*ed beard* 假胡须。— ***vi.*** 〔罕〕篡夺,篡位;侵占,侵犯;侵害(*up*; *upon*)。**-er** ***n.*** 篡夺者;篡位者,侵占者。

u·sur·pa·tion [ˌjuːzəːˈpeiʃən; ˏjuzɚˋpeʃən] ***n.*** 篡夺,侵占,强夺;【法】冒认。

u·sur·pa·to·ry [ju(ː)ˈzəːpətəri; juˋzɝpətorɪ] ***a.*** 篡夺的;侵占的;夺取的。

u·surp·ing·ly [ju(ː)ˈzəːpiŋli; juˋzɝpɪŋlɪ] ***ad.*** 篡夺地;侵占地;夺取地。

u·su·ry [ˈjuːʒuri, -ʒəri; ˋjuʒərɪ] ***n.*** **1.** 高利贷;高利。**2.** 〔喻〕利益。

usus loquendi [ˈjuːsəs ləuˈkwendai; ˋjusəs ləˋkwɛndaɪ] 〔L.〕习惯说法;语言习惯,文风。

USV = United States Volunteers 美国志愿兵。

U. S. W., u. s. w. = ultrashort wave 超短波。

u. s. w. = 〔G.〕 *und so weiter* (= and so forth) 诸如此类。

USWB = United States Weather Bureau 美国气象局。

UT, U. T., u. t. = universal time 世界时,格林威治时。

ut [ʌt; ʌt] ***conj.*** 〔L.〕 如。~ ***dictum*** [ˈdiktəm; ˋdɪktəm] 【处方】照(医生)所嘱,如医嘱,照指示。~ ***infra*** [ˈinfrə; ˋɪnfrə] 如下(所述)。~ ***supra*** [ˈsjuːprə; ˋsjuprə] 如上(所述)。

ut [ʌt, uːt; ʌt, ut] ***n.*** 【乐】音阶的第一音,七个唱名的第一个,Do 音。

ut. = utilities.

UTA = 〔F.〕 *Union Transports Aériens* 〔法〕联合航空运输公司。

U·tah [ˈjuːtɑː; 美 ˈjuːtɔː; ˋjutɔ, ˋjutɑ] ***n.*** 犹他〔美国州名〕。

U. T. C. = Uncle Tom's Cabin 〔美国作家斯陀夫人所作反蓄奴制小说《汤姆叔叔的小屋》〕。

ut dict. = 〔L.〕 *ut dictum* 〔见 *ut* 条〕。

Ute [juːt, ˈjuːti; jut, ˋjutɪ] ***n.*** **1.** (*pl.* ~(*s*)) 犹特人〔以游牧为生的肖松尼印第安人一个部落,曾居住在美国科罗拉多州,犹他州,后到新墨西哥州和亚利桑那州〕。**2.** 犹特语〔属肖松尼语〕。

u·ten·sil [ju(ː)ˈtensil; juˋtɛnsḷ] ***n.*** 器具,用具;家庭厨房用具。*farming* ~*s* 农具。*kitchen* ~*s* 厨房用具。~*s of war* 武器。*writing* ~*s* 文具。

u·ter·ec·to·my [ˌjuːtəˈrektəmi; ˏjutəˋrɛktəmɪ] ***n.*** 【医】子宫切除术。

u·ter·ine [ˈjuːtərain; ˋjutəraɪn] ***a.*** **1.** 【解】子宫的。**2.** 同母异父的。~ *diseases* 子宫病。~ *brothers* 异父兄弟。~ *descent* 母系。~ **cake** 胎盘。

u·ter·i·tis [ˌjuːtəˈraitis; ˏjutəˋraɪtɪs] ***n.*** 【医】子宫炎。

u·te·rus [ˈjuːtərəs; ˋjutərəs] ***n.*** (*pl.* **-ri** [-rai; -raɪ]) 【解】子宫。

u·ti·le dul·ci [ˈjuːtili ˈdʌlsi; ˋjutɪlɪ ˋdʌlsɪ] 〔L.〕 愉快而有益的东西。

u·ti·lise [ˈjuːtilaiz; ˋjutḷˏaɪz] ***vt.*** = utilize.

u·til·i·tar·ian [ˌjuːtiliˈtɛəriən; ˏjutɪləˋtɛrɪən] **I** ***a.*** **1.** 功利的;实利的。**2.** 功利主义的,实利主义的。**II** ***n.*** 功利主义者,实利主义者。**-ism** ***n.*** 【哲】功利主义,实利主义。

u·til·i·ty [juːˈtiliti; juˋtɪlətɪ] **I** ***n.*** **1.** 有用,有益;实用,【经】效用;功利;〔常 *pl.*〕有用的东西。**2.** 【哲】功利主义。**3.** 【剧】跑龙套的[演配角的]演员。**4.** 〔美〕公用事业(= public ~);〔*pl.*〕公用事业股票。*marginal* ~ 【经】边际效用,限界效用。***of no*** ~ 没用的,无益的。**II** ***a.*** **1.** 多用途的,各种工作都会做的,通用性的。**2.** 实用的,经济实惠的。**3.** (牲畜)为谋利而饲养的〔不是为了玩赏的〕。**4.** 公用事业的,公用事业公司股票价格的。~ **aircraft** 运输机。~ **factor** (设备)使用率。~ **man** 跑龙套的演员;打杂人员;【棒球】全能候补队员。~ **room** 家庭用具存放室。~ **service** 公用服务事业。~ **vehicle** 多用途运载工具。

u·ti·li·za·tion [ˌjuːtilaiˈzeiʃən; ˏjutḷaɪˋzeʃən] ***n.*** 利用;效用。

u·ti·lize [ˈjuːtilaiz; ˋjutḷˏaɪz] ***vt.*** 利用。**-liz·a·ble** ***a.*** 可利用的。

ut inf. = 〔L.〕 *ut infra* 〔见 *ut* 条〕。

u·ti pos·si·de·tis [ˈjuːti pɔsiˈdiːtis; ˋjutɪˏpɑsɪˋditɪs] 〔L.〕【国际法】占领地保有原则〔指交战国各方可在战后占有实际占领的地区〕;【罗马法】保护现在占有者权利的法律。

ut·most [ˈʌtməust; ˋʌtˏmost] **I** ***a.*** **1.** 极度的,极端的。**2.** 最远的,尽头处的。*a state of the* ~ *confusion* 极端的混乱状态。*the* ~ *limits* 极限。*to the* ~ *ends of the earth* 到世界的尽头,到天涯海角。**II** ***n.*** 极限,极度,极端,最大限度。***at the*** ~ 至多。***do one's*** ~ 尽所有力量,竭力。***make the*** ~ ***of*** ... 充分利用。***to the*** ~ 尽力,极力,极度(*enjoy oneself to the* ~ 尽情享受一番)。***to the*** ~ ***of one's power*** 竭力。

U·to-Az·tec·an [ˈjuːtəuˈæztekən; ˋjutoˋæztɛkən] **I** ***a.*** 犹特—阿兹特卡语系的〔美国西部、墨西哥和中美洲一个大的美洲印第安语系〕。**II** ***n.*** 犹特—阿兹特卡语〔包括肖松语、尤蒂—阿茨蒂克语、比马语、霍皮语、犹特语等〕。

U·to·pi·a [juːˈtəupjə, -piə; juˋtopɪə] ***n.*** 乌托邦;〔常 u-〕理想的国土[社会等];空想的社会改良计划〔源出英国空想社会主义者托·摩尔所作《乌托邦》一书〕。

U·to·pian [juːˈtəupjən; juˋtopɪən] **I** ***a.*** 〔有时作 u-〕乌托邦(似)的;理想的,空想的。**II** ***n.*** **1.** 乌托邦[理想国]

U

的居民。**2**. 空想社会主义者,理想家。～ **socialism** 空想社会主义。

u·to·pi·an·ism [juˈtəupiənizəm; juˋtopiənɪzm] ***n***. 乌托邦思想(理论);不切实际的社会改革方案。

UTP = 【化】Uridine triphosphate 尿苷三磷酸。

U·trecht [ˈjuːtrekt; ˋjutrɛkt] ***n***. 乌得勒支〔荷兰城市〕。

u·tri·cle [ˈjuːtrikl; ˋjutrɪkl] ***n***. **1**. 小囊,小胞。**2**.【植】胞果;胞囊。**3**.【解】椭圆囊;前列腺囊。

u·tric·u·lar [juːˈtrikjulə; juˋtrɪkjələ˞] ***a***. 小囊(状)的,(具)胞果的。

ut sup. =〔L.〕*ut supra*〔见 *ut* 条〕。

ut·ter^1 [ˈʌtə; ˋʌtə˞] ***a***. (*superl*. ～***most***) **1**. 完全的,十足的。**2**. 无条件的,绝对的,断然的。**3**. 外边的〔现在除 ～ bar (【法】外席)及 ～ barrister (【法】外席律师)二例外罕用〕。*an* ～ *stranger* 完全不认识的人。～ *darkness* 漆黑。*an* ～ *fool* 大傻瓜。*an* ～ *refusal* 断然的拒绝。***be at an*** ～ ***loss what to do*** 完全不晓得怎样才好。**-ly *ad***.

utter^2 [ˈʌtə; ˋʌtə˞] ***vt***. **1**. 发出(声音等);讲,说;说出,说明,表明,吐露(心事等);公开申言。**2**. 使用,行使,流通(伪钞等)。**3**. 发射;喷射。～ *a groan* 发出呻吟声。～ *the truth* [*a lie*] 说真话[谎话]。～ *false coin* 使用伪造的钱币。**-a·ble *a***.

ut·ter·ance^1 [ˈʌtərəns; ˋʌtərəns] ***n***. **1**. 发声;发言;发言能力。**2**. 〔仅用 *sing*.〕口才;语调,发音。**3**. (说出的)话;言辞。**4**. 〔罕〕表达,发表。**5**. 〔罕〕使用,行使;流通。*his public* ～*s* 他的公开言论。*a clear* ～ 清楚的语调[发音]。*a man of good* ～ 口才好的人。*a defective* ～ 有缺陷的发音。***give*** ～ ***to*** (*one's rage*) 说出,讲出,表明(愤怒)。

ut·ter·ance^2 [ˈʌtərəns; ˋʌtərəns] ***n***. 〔英、古〕最后,死〔现仅用于 ***to the*** ～ 到最后,到死〕。

ut·ter·ly [ˈʌtəli; ˋʌtə˞lɪ] ***ad***. 完全地,全然地;绝对地。*I fail* ～ *to see why*. 我完全不懂为什么如此。

utter·most [ˈʌtəməust, -məst; ˋʌtə˞ˏmost, -məst] **I *a***. 最远的;最大限度的。**II *n***. 最大限度。*to the* ～ *of one's power* [*capacity*] 竭力,尽(可能)。

U-turn [ˈjuːˈtəːn; ˋjuˏtə˞n] **I *n***. **1**. (车辆等的)作 U 形转弯〔尤指车辆在街道上作 180° 调头〕。**2**. 似 U 形转弯的东西;〔喻〕方向的大改变。*an* ～ *worker* 返回原地[原就业场所]工作的人。**II *vi***. 作 180 度大转弯。

UUM = underwater-to-underwater missile 水下对水下导弹。

UV = ultraviolet. ～ **A** 紫外线 A,长波紫外线。～ **B** 紫外线 B,短波紫外线。～ **index** = ultraviolet index.

U-value [ˈjuːˈvælju; ˋjuˋvæljʊ] ***n***.【物】U 值〔绝缘材料等阻挡热流通过墙壁、屋顶或地板等的阻力计量单位。U 值越低则绝缘有效级越高〕。

u·van·ite [ˈjuvænait; ˋjuvænaɪt] ***n***.【矿】钒铀矿。

u·va·rov·ite [uːˈvɑːrəvait; uˋvɑrəfaɪt] ***n***.【矿】钙铬榴石。

u·ve·a [ˈjuːviə; ˋjuvɪə] ***n***.【解】眼色素层;眼葡萄膜。

u·ve·i·tis [ˌjuːviˈaitis; ˏjuvɪˋaɪtɪs] ***n***.【医】眼色素层炎,眼葡萄膜炎。

u·vi·ol(glass) [ˈjuviəul(glɑːs); ˋjuvɪolˏ(glæs)] ***n***. 紫外玻璃。

u·vu·la [ˈjuːvjulə; ˋjuvjələ] ***n***. (*pl*. ～***s***, ***-lae*** [-liː; -lɪ])【解】**1**. 悬雍垂,小舌。**2**. 小脑悬壅垂,蚓垂。

u·vu·lar [ˈjuːvjulə; ˋjuvjələ˞] **I *a***. **1**.【解】悬雍垂[小舌]的。**2**.【语音】软腭的。**II *n***.【语言】软腭音。

UW = under water 水下。

U/w(s), U/WS = underwriters.

UX$_1$ = uranium X$_1$〔即 Th (钍)^{234}〕。

UX$_2$ = uranium X$_2$〔即 Po (钋)^{231}〕。

Ux. =〔L.〕*uxor* (= wife).

ux·or·i·cide [ʌkˈsɔːrisaid; ʌkˋsorɪˏsaɪd] ***n***. 杀妻(罪);杀妻者。

ux·o·ri·ous [ʌkˈsɔːriəs; ʌkˋsorɪəs] ***a***. 溺爱妻子的;怕老婆的。**-ly *ad***. **-ness *n***.

UY = uranium Y〔即 Th (钍)^{234}〕。

UZ = uranium Z〔即 Po (钋)^{231}〕。

Uz·beg, Uz·bek [ˈʌzbeg; ˋʌzbɛg] **I *n***. **1**. 乌兹别克人。**2**. 乌兹别克语。**II *a***. **1**. 乌兹别克的。**2**. 乌兹别克人[语]的。

Uz·bek·i·stan [ˌuzbekiˈstɑːn; ˏʊzbɛkɪˋstæn] ***n***. 乌兹别克斯坦〔亚洲国家名〕。

V

V

V, v [viː; vi] (*pl*. ***V's***, ***v's*** [viːz; viz]) **1**. 英语字母表第二十二字母。**2**. V 字形;V 形物。**3**. 〔V〕(罗马数码)五;〔美俚〕票面额为五元的钞票;五年徒刑;保险箱。**4**. 〔V〕【化】元素钒 (vanadium) 的符号。*a V-belt*【机】三角皮带。*a V sign* 胜利手势〔向上伸出食指和中指的手势〕(V = Victory)。*a V spot*〔美〕一张五元钞票。IV = 4。VI = 6。XV = 15。VL = 45。LV = 55。$\bar{V}$ = 5,000。

V., v. = **1**. Venerable. **2**. Vicar. **3**. Viscount. **4**. valve. **5**. verb. **6**. version. **7**. versus. **8**. very. **9**. vice. **10**. 〔L.〕*vide*. **11**. village. **12**. vise. **13**. vocative. **14**. voice. **15**. voltage. **16**. volume. **17**. 〔G.〕*von*. **18**. vowel.

V-1 [ˈvi(ː)ˈwʌn; ˋviˋwʌn] ***n***. "报复"武器第一号,V-1 火箭〔第二次世界大战末期德国的火箭,用以轰炸英国〕。

V-2 [ˈvi(ː)ˈtu(ː); ˋviˋtu] ***n***. "报复"武器第二号,V-2 火箭(*cf*. V-1 条)。

V-8 [viːˈeit; ˋviˋet] **I *a***.【机】〔美〕V 形八汽缸式的。**II *n***. **1**. V 形八汽缸式发动机。**2**. 装有 V 形八汽缸式发动机的汽车。

VA = **1**. Veterans' Administration〔美〕退伍军人管理局。**2**. vicar apostolic【天主】名誉主教。**3**. vice admiral 海军中将。**4**. volt-ampere【电】伏安,伏特安培。**5**. value analysis【社会学】价值分析。

Va. = Virginia 维吉尼亚〔美国州名〕。

va [vɑː; vɑ]〔It.〕【乐】继续下去,继续…〔指挥用语〕。～ ***piano*** 继续弱。

v.a. = **1**. verb active. **2**. verbal adjective.

vac. = **1**. vacant. **2**. 〔口〕vacation. **3**. vacuum.

va·can·cy [ˈveikənsi; ˋvekənsɪ] ***n***. **1**. 空虚,空;空间,空隙,空处;空地,空房(等)。**2**. 精神空虚,心不在焉,没精神,出神,茫然若失。**3**. 空位,空额。**4**. 闲暇;无所事事。

gaze into [*at*, *on*] ~凝视空中。*fill a ~ in one's knowledge* 填补知识空白。*fill* (*up*) *the* ~ (*by election*) (用选举办法)补充空额。*when a ~ occurs* 有空额的时候。

va·cant [ˈveikənt; ˋvekənt] *a*. **1**. 空无所有的,空虚的。**2**. (房子等)空着的,没人住的;(位置等)空缺的。**3**. 精神空虚的;茫然的,出神的,无精打采的;无意义的,无聊的;不感兴趣的。**4**. 空闲的;无所事事的;没职业的。**5**. 【法】无人利用的;无主的;遗弃的;无继承人的。*The house is still* ~. 这房子还空着。*a ~ lot* 一块空地。*a ~ possession* [出租广告用语]空房。*a ~ succession* 【法】继承人不明的遗产。*situation ~ columns* (报纸的)召聘(广告)栏。*a ~ look* 发呆的样子。~ *frivolities* 无聊的举动。~ *hours* 暇时,闲暇时光。**-ly** *ad*. **1**. 发呆地,茫然;无所事事地。**2**. 〔美俚〕离开,走掉。

va·cate [vəˈkeit, veiˈk-, Am. ˈveikeit; ˋvəket, veˋk-, ˋveket] *vt*. **1**. 使空无所有,使空虚;腾出,搬出,退出(房间、市镇等)。**2**. 解除[辞去](职位);空出(地位、席位)。**3**. 【军】使撤退;【法】使作废,取消(契约等)。—*vi*. **1**. 空出,退出,腾出。**2**. 〔美〕休假,度假;辞职。

va·ca·tion [vəˈkeiʃən; veˋkeʃən] **I** *n*. **1**. 假期;休假;(法庭等的)休庭期。**2**. 搬出,迁出,退出;辞职。**3**. (职位的)空缺(期间)。*the long* [*summer*] ~暑假;(法院的)暑期休庭。~ *subscriptions* 〔美〕(报纸)星期增刊的订阅。**be on** ~在度假,放假期间。**II** *vi*. 〔美〕放假,休假;度假。*go ~ing* 去休假旅行。~**land** 旅游胜地,休假地。~ **school** 暑期中的讲习会,暑期学校。**-er**, **-ist** *n*. 〔美〕度假者,放假休息的人,休假旅行的人。

vac·ci·nal [ˈvæksinl; ˋvæksɪnl] *a*. 【医】疫苗的;接种的,种痘的。

vac·ci·nate [ˈvæksineit; ˋvæksnˏet] *vt*., *vi*. **1**. (给…)接种(疫苗);(给…)种痘;(给…)打预防接种针。**2**. 给(电脑)安装免疫程序软件。

vac·ci·na·tion [ˌvæksiˈneiʃən; ˏvæksnˋeʃən] *n*. 【医】接种(疫苗);种痘;预防注射。**-ist** *n*. 主张(强迫)接种疫苗[种痘,预防注射]的人。

vac·ci·na·tor [ˈvæksineitə; ˋvæksnˏetɚ] *n*. **1**. 接种[种痘]员。**2**. 种痘刀[器],接种针。

vac·cine [ˈvæksiːn; ˋvæksin] **I** *a*. 牛痘的;预防疫苗的;种痘的。**II** *n*. **1**. 疫苗,牛痘苗;菌苗。**2**. 【计】免疫程序软件,抗病毒软件。~ **lymph** [**virus**] 痘苗。~ **farm** 疫苗培养所。~ **point** 接种针。

vac·cin·ee [ˌvæksiˈniː; ˏvæksɪˋni] *n*. 已接种牛痘[疫苗]者。

vac·cin·i·a [vækˈsiniə; vækˋsɪnɪə] *n*. 【医】牛痘。**-l** *a*.

vac·ci·no·ther·a·py [ˌvæksinəuˈθerəpi; ˏvæksɪnoˋθɛrəpɪ] *n*. 接种疫苗疗法。

vac·il·lant [ˈvæsilənt; ˋvæslənt] *a*. 游移的,踌躇的,摇摆不定的。

vac·il·late [ˈvæsileit; ˋvæslˏet] *vi*. **1**. 摆动,波动,振荡。**2**. 动摇不定,踌躇莫决。~ *between different opinions* 在种种不同意见间摇摆。*a vacillating person* 三心二意的人。

vac·il·lat·ing [ˈvæsileitiŋ; ˋvæslˏetɪŋ] *a*. **1**. 摇动的,摇摆的。**2**. 优柔寡断的,犹疑不决的。

vac·il·la·tion [ˌvæsiˈleiʃən; ˏvæsəˋleʃən] *n*. **1**. 摇摆,波动,振荡。**2**. 犹豫不决,踌躇,优柔寡断。

vac·u·a [ˈvækjuə; ˋvækjʊə] *n*. vacuum 的复数。

vac·u·i·ty [væˈkju(:)iti, və-; væˋkjuətɪ, və-] *n* 空,空虚;真空;空间,空处。**2**. 精神空虚,出神 失,发呆。**3**. 无聊,无所事事。**4**. 〔常 *pl*.〕无 话。*the ~ of expression* 没有表情。 *n*.

va·cu·o [ˈvækjuəu; ˋvækjʊˏo] *n*.

vac·u·o·late, **-lated** [ˈvækjuəleit -letɪd] *a*. 【生】有液泡[空泡]的

vac·u·o·la·tion [ˌvækju 【生】空泡[液泡]形成。

vac·u·ole [ˈvækjuəul; ˋvækjʊˏol] *n*. 【生】空泡;液泡。

vac·u·om·e·ter [ˌvækjuˈɔmitə; ˏvækjʊˋɑmətɚ] *n*. 真空计;低压计。

vac·u·ous [ˈvækjuəs; ˋvækjuəs] *a*. **1**. 空虚的;空洞的。**2**. 精神空虚的;发呆的,茫然若失的,出神的。**3**. 无所事事的。**4**. 无思考力的。**5**. (生活)没意义的。**-ly** *ad*. **-ness** *n*.

vac·u·um [ˈvækjuəm; ˋvækjuəm] **I** *n*. (*pl*. ~*s*, ***vac·u·a*** [ˈvækjuə; ˋvækjuə]) **1**. 真空;空处,空虚,空白。**2**. 〔美口〕吸尘器(= ~ cleaner)。*a low* [*partial*] ~低度[未尽]真空。***feel a ~ in the lower regions*** 〔谑〕觉得饿。**II** *vi*., *vt*. 〔美口〕**1**. 用吸尘器扫除。**2**. 用真空干燥机干燥。**III** *a*. **1**. 真空的。**2**. 用以产生真空的。**3**. 利用真空的。~ **aspiration** 【医】真空吸引术〔在妇女怀孕第10周至12周内施行的一种人工流产术,以一根管子吸出子宫内的受精卵〕。~ **bottle** 热水瓶。~ **brake** 真空制动器,低压煞车。~ **canning** 真空装罐(法)。~ **cleaner** 吸尘器。~ **flask** = ~ bottle. ~ **gauge** 真空计。~**-packed** *a*. 真空包装的〔包装前抽去大量空气的〕。~ **pump** 真空泵,真空抽气机。~ **tube** 〔美〕= ~ valve. ~ **valve** 〔主英〕【无】电子管,真空管。**-ize** *vt*. **1**. 在…内造成真空。**2**. 用真空装置打扫[干燥]。**3**. 真空包装。

vad [væd] *n*. 【计】增值与数据网络;附加数据服务通信网络〔系 value-added and data 缩略〕。

V.A.D. = Voluntary Aid Detachment 志愿辅助勤务队。

va·de me·cum [ˈveidi ˈmiːkəm; ˋvedɪ ˋmikəm] *n*. 〔L.〕手册,便览;随身物件。

V.-Adm. = Vice-Admiral.

va·dose [ˈveidəus; ˋvedos] *a*. 【地】渗流的。

Va·duz [vɑːˈduːts; vɑˋduts] *n*. 瓦杜兹〔列支敦士登首都〕。

vae vic·tis [viː ˈviktis; vi ˋvɪktɪs] 〔L.〕被征服者惨矣;战败者活该遭殃!

vag *n*. 〔美〕= vagrant.

vag·a·bond [ˈvægəbənd, -ˌbɔnd; ˋvægəˏbɑnd] **I** *n*. 流浪者,漂泊无定的人;〔口〕流氓,无赖,浪荡子。**II** *a*. 流浪(性)的,漂泊不定的;懒散的,无赖(一样)的。*a ~ life* 流浪生活。**III** *vi*. 〔口〕流浪,漂泊。**-age** [-idʒ; -ɪdʒ] *n*. 流浪(生活、习惯)(*live in* [*take to*] ~*age* 过[开始]流浪生活);〔集合词〕流浪者。**-ism** *n*. = vagabondage. **-ize** *vi*. 〔常作 ~ it〕过流浪生活 流浪。

va·gal [ˈveigl; ˋvegl] *a*. 【解】迷走神经的。

va·ga·ry [vəˈgɛəri, ˈveigəri; vəˋgɛrɪ, gerɪ] *n*. 狂妄古怪的行为,异想天开;怪想,妄想 想;变幻莫测。*a ~ of fashion* 古怪的时髦风气 装式样]。**-gar·i·ous** *a*.

vag·ile [ˈvædʒail, ˈvædʒil; ail, ˋvædʒəl] *a*. 漫游的。

va·gi·na [vəˈdʒain ʒaɪnə] *n*. (*pl*. ~*s*, **-nae** [-niː; -ni]) 【动 阴道;【植】鞘,叶鞘。**-l** *a*.

vag·i·nate ˋvædʒənɪt], **vag·i·nat·ed** ʒəˏnetɪd] *a*. 【动】**1**. 有鞘的。**2**. 鞘状

[ˈvædʒi- -dʒiˈnaitis; ˏvædʒəˋnaɪtɪs] *n*. 【医】阴道 vəˈdʒaitəs; vəˋdʒaɪtəs] *n*. 【医】婴儿哭声。

vag·pres·sor [ˌveigəudiˈpresə; ˏvegodɪˋprɛsɚ] **I** 【医】抑制迷走神经的。**II** *n*. 迷走神经抑制剂。

got·o·my [veiˈgɔtəmi; vəˋgɑtəmɪ] *n*. (*pl*. **-mies**) 【医】迷走神经切断术。

va·go·to·ni·a [ˌveigəuˈtəuniə; ˏvegoˋtonɪə] *n*. 【医】迷走神经过敏,副交感神经过敏。**-ton·ic** [-ˈtɔnik; -ˋtɑnɪk] *a*.

va·go·trop·ic [ˌveigəuˈtrɔpik; ˏvegoˋtrɑpɪk] *a*. 影响迷走神经[交感神经]的,作用于迷走神经[交感神经]的。

va·gran·cy [ˈveigrənsi; ˋvegrənsɪ] *n*. **1**. 漂泊,流浪(生活)。2. 变幻无常,游移不定。**3**.【法】流浪罪。**4**.〔集合词〕流浪者。

va·grant [ˈveigrənt; ˋvegrənt] **I** *a*. **1**. 流离失所的,漂流浪荡的;流浪(性)的。**2**. 多变的,不定的,见异思迁的,(心、思想等)变化无常的。~ *habits* 流浪习性。~ *clouds* 浮云。**II** *n*. 流浪者,漂流浪荡的人,无定居的人;游民;无赖,流氓。**-ly** *ad*. **-ness** *n*.

vague [veig; veg] **I** *a*. **1**. 含糊的,笼统的,暧昧的;不说明的。**2**. 无表情的;发呆的,出神的。*a* ~ *answer* 含糊的回答。*I haven't the vaguest notion what to do*. 我一点儿也不晓得怎样办才好。**II** *n*. 模糊不定状态。*My plans are still in the* ~. 我的计划还没有确定呢。**-ly** *ad*. **-ness** *n*.

va·gus [ˈveigəs; ˋvegəs] *n*. (*pl*. **va·gi** [-dʒai; -dʒaɪ])【解】迷走神经,交感神经(= ~ nerve)。

va·hi·ne [vɑːˈhiːnei; vɑˋhine] *n*. (大洋洲东部塔希提岛上的)波利尼西亚女人;妻〔当地居民的土语〕。

vail[1] [veil; vel] *vt*. 〔古〕脱(帽等表示投降或敬意);低下。— *vi*. 脱帽(等),低头。

vail[2] [veil; vel] **I** *vt*., *vi*. 〔古〕有用(于),有利(于),有助(于)。**II** *n*. 〔古〕〔常 *pl*.〕赠与,赏钱;贿赂。

vail[3] [veil; vel] *n*., *vt*. 〔古〕= veil.

vain [vein; ven] *a*. **1**. 徒然的,无益的,没效果的;愚蠢的;不足道的。**2**. 空的,空虚的;虚有其表的,表面好看的,虚饰的。**3**. 自夸的,自负的;爱虚荣的。~ *efforts* 徒劳。~ *titles* 空名,虚衔。*a* ~ *attempt* 妄想。*a* ~ *man* 虚荣心强的人。**be** ~ **of** 自夸,自以为…了不起(*She is* ~ *of her voice*. 她自以为她的嗓音了不起)。**in** ~ **1**. 无益地,徒然(*We protested in* ~. 我们白白抗议了。*pass one's life in* ~ 虚度一生)。**2**. 轻忽地,轻慢地,亵渎地(*take sb.'s name in* ~ 轻慢地提到某人的名字(尤指轻慢地谈到上帝))。

vain·glo·ri·ous [veinˈglɔːriəs; venˋglɔrɪəs] *a*. 过于自负的,狂妄自大的;虚荣心很强的。

vain·glo·ry [veinˈglɔːri; venˋglɔrɪ] *n*. 自负;虚荣心。

vain·ly [ˈveinli; ˋvenlɪ] *ad*. 虚妄地,无益地;自负地。**be** ~ **proud of** 以…而目空一切。~ **hope for** 妄想。

vain·ness [ˈveinnis; ˋvennɪs] *n*. 无益;〔罕〕自负,自夸,虚荣。

vair [vɛə; vɛr] *n*. 〔古〕(中世高级阶层作服饰的)灰鼠毛皮;【徽】毛皮纹。

Vaish·na·va [ˈvaiʃnəvə; ˋvaɪʃnəvə] *n*. 〔印度教〕信奉毗湿奴(Vishnu, 印度教三大神之一)的人。

Vais·ya [ˈvais... vaɪsjə] *n*. 〔Sansk.〕吠舍,毗舍〔印度四种姓的第三等级,...商人和农民〕。

va·keel, va·kil [və... kiː... vəˋkil] *n*. 〔英,印〕印度律师。

Val [væl; væl] *n*. 瓦尔〔男子名,Valentine 的昵称〕。

Val. = **1**. valentin... valuation. **3**. value.

val·ance [ˈvæləns; ...] *n*. **1**. (窗帘顶部的)挂布式框架。**2**. 床沿挂布;桌...

vale [veil; vel] *n*. 谷,峪... *the White Horse V-* 白马峪。*the earthly* ~ = ... ~ *of tears* 现世。*the* ~ *of years* 老年。

va·le [ˈveiliː, ˈwɑːlei; ˋveli, ... *t*. 〔L.〕再见!〔道别语,原意为"愿你健康"。〕**II** ...

val·e·dic·tion [ˌvæliˈdikʃən; ˌvælə... 别。别辞。

val·e·dic·to·ri·an [ˌvælidikˈtɔːriən; ... 告别;告 *n*. 〔美〕作告别演说者;(代表毕业生)致告...

val·e·dic·to·ry [ˌvæliˈdiktəri; ˌvæləˋdɪktərɪ... 〔美〕毕业生代表的。**II** *n*. 告别演说,告别辞;〔美〕毕业生代表辞。

va·lence[1] [ˈveiləns; ˋveləns] *n*. 【化】(化合)价;(... 价;【生】效价。~ **electrons**【物】价电子。

val·ence[2] [ˈvæləns; ˋvæləns] *n*. = valance.

Va·len·ci·a [vəˈlenʃiə; vəˋlɛnʃɪə] *n*. **1**. 巴伦西亚〔西班牙港市〕。**2**. 巴伦西亚〔委内瑞拉城市〕。

va·len·ci·a [vəˈlenʃiə; vəˋlɛnʃɪə] *n*. **1**. 〔常 *pl*.〕(英国)华冷西亚斜纹薄呢;凸纹背心料。**2**. 〔*pl*.〕(西班牙)(巴伦西亚出产的)巴旦杏〔干葡萄〕。

Va·len·ci·ennes [ˌvælənsiˈen; vəˏlɛnsɪˋɛnz] *n*. (法国)华冷西恩花边。

valen·cy [ˈveilənsi; ˋvelənsɪ] *n*. 【化】= valence[1].

-valent *comb*. *f*. 【化】原子〔化合〕价的,…价的〔常作复合词用〕: mono*valent*.

Val·en·tine [ˈvæləntain, ˈvæləntin; ˋvæləntaɪn, ˋvæləntɪn] *n*. **1**. [ˈvæləntin; ˋvæləntɪn] 瓦伦丁〔姓氏〕。**2**. [ˈvæləntain; ˋvæləntaɪn] **St**. ~ 圣瓦伦丁〔公元三世纪的基督教殉道者〕。~**'s day** 圣瓦伦丁节(2 月 14 日)。

val·en·tine [ˈvæləntain; ˋvæləntaɪn] *n*. **1**. 在圣瓦伦丁节寄给异性的卡片〔书信,礼物〕。**2**. (圣瓦伦丁节时作为自己选中对象而赠与礼品的)对象;情人。**3**. 〔喻〕任何表示想念的事物。*His essay is a* ~ *to London*. 他那篇散文是为怀念伦敦而写的。

val·en·tin·ite [ˈvæləntinait; ˋvæləntɪˏnaɪt] *n*. 【矿】锑华。

va·ler·ate [ˈvæləreit; ˋvæləret] *n*. 【化】戊酸盐;戊酸酯。

va·le·ri·an [vəˈliəriən; vəˋlɪrɪən] *n*. 【植】缬草属植物;拔地麻。

val·et [ˈvælit, ˈvæli, F. vaˈle; ˋvælɪt, ˋvælɪ, F. vaˋlɛ] **I** *n*. **1**. (专司看管衣物及替主人穿衣的)男仆,随从。**2**. (旅馆,客船中)照料旅客衣服烫洗等事的服务员。**3**. 衣架。**4**. 驯马用刺针。**II** *vt*. 做…的男仆;侍候。~ ***de pied*** 〔F.〕= footman. ~ ***de place*** 〔F.〕(尤指法国的)导游者。~ ***de chambre*** 〔F.〕= valet.

val·e·tu·di·nar·i·an [ˈvæliˌtjuːdiˈnɛəriən; ˏvæləˏtjudnˋɛrɪən] *a*., *n*. 多病[虚弱]的(人);过分关心个人健康的(人)。**-ism** *n*. 病弱。**-na·ry** [ˌvæliˈtjuːdinəri; ˏvæləˋtjudnˏɛrɪ] *a*., *n*. = valetudinarian.

val·gus [ˈvælgəs; ˋvælgəs] **I** *n*. 【医】**1**. 外翻足。**2**. 外偏手[膝、臀、拇趾等]。**II** *a*. **1**. 外翻的。**2**. 内翻的,膝内弯的。

Val·hal·la [vælˈhælə; vælˋhælə] *n*. 【北欧神】**1**. (Odin) 神招待阵亡英灵的殿堂。**2**. 烈士纪念堂,忠烈祠。

val·iant [ˈvæljənt; ˋvæljənt] **I** *a*. **1**. 勇敢的,英勇的,英雄的。**2**. 〔方〕(身体)强健的。*the* ~ *record* 英勇事迹。**II** *n*. 勇敢的人。**-ly** *ad*.

val·id [ˈvælid; ˋvælɪd] *a*. **1**. (理由、证据等)有确实根据的,确凿的;正确的;健全的,站得住的。**2**. 【法】(契约、选举等)经过正式手续的,有效的(*opp*. void)。**3**. 〔罕〕强健的;有力的。**4**. 【逻】含有暗示之结论的前提的。~ *ballot papers* 有效选票。**-ly** *ad*.

val·i·date [ˈvælideit; ˋvæləˏdet] *vt*. **1**. 证实,确证;证明正确。**2**. 使(在法律上)有效,使生效,使合法化(*opp*. invalidate);批准,确认。**-da·tion** [ˌvæliˈdeiʃən; ˏvælɪˋdeʃən] *n*.

va·lid·i·ty [vəˈliditi; vəˋlɪdətɪ] *n*. **1**. 正确,正当,妥当,确实性。**2**. 【法】有效,真确,合法性。**3**. 【哲】效准。*the term of* ~ 有效期间。

valin(e) [ˈvæliːn; ˋvælin] *n*. 【生化】缬胺酸。

va·lise [vəˈliːz, -liːs; vəˋlis] *n*. 〔主、美〕旅行手提包[箱];旅行袋;【军】背包。

val·la·tion [væˈleiʃən; vəˋleʃən] *n*. **1**. 壁垒,堡垒。**2**. 筑城术。

val·lec·u·la [vəˈlekjulə; vəˋlɛkjələ] *n*. (*pl*. **-lae** [-liː; ...li]) **1**. 【植】(线)沟。**2**. 【解】谷,窝,溪。**-r** *a*.

...t·ta [vəˈletə; vəˋlɛtə] *n*. 瓦莱塔〔马耳他首都〕。

... [ˈvæli; ˋvælɪ] *n*. **1**. 谷,峪,河谷;凹处。**2**. 流域。... 谷,屋面天沟。*the* ~ *of the shadow of* ... 幽谷〔源出《圣经》《诗篇》〕;临死的(痛苦)时

val·lum [ˈvæləm; ˋvæləm] *n*. (*pl*. **-la** [-lə; -lə]) 1. 【古罗马】壁垒,阵营。2.【解】眉毛,睫毛。

va·lo·ni·a [vəˈləuniə; vəˋlonɪə] *n*. (欧洲、亚洲的)大鳞栎〔含单柠酸的橡树果实壳,可作染料〕。

val·or [ˈvælə; ˋvælɚ] *n*. 〔美〕= valour.

val·o·rize [ˈvæləraiz; ˋvæləˏraɪz] *vt*. (政府)以给予各种补助的形式稳定[维持](商品)价格。**-ri·za·tion** [ˌvæləraiˈzeiʃən; ˏvæləraɪˋzeʃən] *n*.

val·or·ous [ˈvælərəs; ˋvælərəs] *a*. 勇敢的,英勇的,大胆的;气概豪迈的。**-ly** *ad*.

val·o(u)r [ˈvælə; ˋvælɚ] *n*. 1. 勇猛,英勇;豪迈气概。2. 〔罕〕勇士。

Val·pa·rai·so [ˌvælpəˈreizəu; ˏvælpəˋrezo], **Val·para·i·so** 〔Sp.〕[ˌbalparaˈiso; ˏbalparaˋɪso] *n*. 瓦尔帕莱索〔智利港市〕。

Val·sal·va [vælˈsælvə; vælˋsælvə] **maneuver** 佛萨瓦氏(Valsalva)压力均衡法〔在飞机升降时,紧紧地捏鼻,闭嘴,使劲鼓气〕。

valse [vɑːls; vɑls] *n*., *vi*. 〔F.〕= waltz.

val·u·a·ble [ˈvæljuəbl; ˋvæljuəbl] I *a*. 1. 有价值的。2. 贵重的,宝贵的。3. 可评价[估价]的。II *n*. 〔常 *pl*.〕贵重物品。~ *papers* 有价证券。~ **consideration** 与受益价值相等的报酬。**-a·bly** *ad*. **-ness** *n*.

val·u·ate [ˈvæljueit; ˋvæljʊˏet] *vt*. (**-at·ed**; **-at·ing**) 评价,估价;鉴定,品定。**-a·tor** *n*. 评价者,估价者;鉴定者。

val·u·a·tion [væljuˈeiʃən; ˏvæljʊˋeʃən] *n*. 估价,评价;估定价格;价值;【数】赋值。***be disposed of at a low*** ~ 廉价售出[处理]。***put*** [*set*] ***too high a*** ~ ***on*** ... 把…估计得[看得]太高。

val·u·a·tor [ˈvæljueitə; ˋvæljʊˏetɚ] *n*. 评价者;估价者;核价员;价格核定人。

val·ue [ˈvæljuː, -ju; ˋvælju] I *n*. 1. 价值;重要性;益处。2. 估价,评价。3. 价格,所值;交换力。4. (邮票的)面值。5. 等值;值得花的代价。6. (字等的)真义,意义。7. 【数】值;【语】音值;【生】(分类上的)等级;【乐】音的长短;【绘】明暗配合。8. 〔*pl*.〕生活的理想,道德价值;社会准则。*rated* ~ 额定值。*proper* ~ 【物】本征值。*commercial* [*economic*] ~ 经济价值。*exchange*(*able*) ~ (= ~ in exchange) 交换价值。~ *in use* 使用价值。*surplus* ~ 剩余价值。*face* ~ 票面价格。*market* ~ 市价。*pay full* ~ *for sth*. 对某物付足代价。*the* ~ *of the dollar* 美元的购买力。*the* ~ *of a symbol* 某符号的意义。***be of*** [***no***] ~有[无]价值。(***for***) ~ ***received*** 〔支票用语〕贷款…正。***of*** ~有价值的 (*news of* ~重要消息)。***out of*** ~(绘画等)明暗不调和。***place a*** ~ ***on*** 估价,评价。***put*** [***set***] ***a high*** [***much***] ~ (***up***)***on*** 高估;重视,看重。II *vt*. 1. 给…估价,定…的价。2. 对…作出评价;尊重,看重(*Troops are* ~*d for quality rather than for number*. 兵贵精不贵多)。~ ***oneself for*** (*what one does, etc*.) 夸耀(自己事业等)。~ ***oneself*** (***up***)***on*** 自夸 (*sth*.) (~ *up*(*on*) *one's knowledge* 夸耀自己的知识)。~**-added** *n*. (商品等的)增值,增值价值。~ **engineering** 价值工程学〔研究如何以最低成本提高产品价值的科学〕。~ **judg(e)ment** 评头品足;多管闲事的议论;对人[事物]的价值、善恶等所作的主观论断。

val·ued [ˈvæljud; ˋvæljud] *a*. 1. 贵重的;被尊重的,重要的。2. 估定了价格的;有(一定)价值的。~ ***favour*** 〔美〕1. 定货。2.【商】信;通信。

val·ue·less [ˈvæljulis; ˋvæljulɪs] *a*. 没有价值的,不足道的,没有用处的。

val·u·er [ˈvæljuə; ˋvæljuɚ] *n*. 估价者,评价者。

va·lu·ta [vəˈluːtə; vɑˋlutɑ] *n*. 1. 币值〔尤指欧洲某些国家的货币、汇率〕。2. 可使用的外汇总额。

val·val [ˈvælvəl; ˋvælvl] *a*. = valvular.

val·vate [ˈvælveit; ˋvælvet] *a*. 1. 具阀的,有阀门的。2. 【植】镊合状〔指花被卷叠式〕;瓣裂的〔指雄蕊,果实〕。

valve [vælv; vælv] *n*. 1. 【机】阀,活门,舌门;汽门。2. 【解、动】瓣,瓣膜;(贝)壳瓣;【植】荚片;(藻的)瓣;(果实的)裂片。3. 【建】门的一扇。4. 〔英〕【无】电子管,真空管。*a change* ~ 三通阀。*an exhaust* ~ 排气阀。*a pulmonary* ~【解】肺动脉瓣。*a safety* ~安全阀,保险阀。**-d** *a*. 有阀[瓣等]的。**-less** *a*. 无阀[瓣等]的。**-let** *n*. 小阀[瓣等]。

val·vu·la [ˈvælvjulə; ˋvælvjələ] *n*. (*pl*. **-lae** [-liː; -li]) = valvule.

val·vu·lar [ˈvælvjulə; ˋvælvjəlɚ] *a*. 1. 阀的,瓣的;活门的;瓣膜的。2.【植】由瓣形成的。~ *disease* (*of the heart*)【医】心脏瓣膜病。~ *insufficiency* 心瓣闭锁不全。

val·vule [ˈvælvjuːl; ˋvælvjul] *n*. 【解、植】小瓣,瓣膜;(昆虫的)产卵瓣。

val·vu·li·tis [ˌvælvjuˈlaitis; ˏvælvjʊˋlaɪtɪs] *n*. 【医】心脏瓣膜炎。

val·vu·lot·o·my [ˌvælvjuˈlɔtəmi; ˏvælvjʊˋlɑtəmɪ] *n*. 【医】心瓣切开(术)。

vam·brace [ˈvæmbreis; ˋvæmbres] *n*. 下臂护甲。

va·moos(e) [vəˈmuːs; væˋmus], **va·mos(e)** [vəˈməus; vəˋmos] *vi*., *vt*. 〔美俚〕(从某处)突然[匆匆]离开,跑掉,逃亡。★常用命令式。

vamp[1] [væmp; væmp] I *n*. 1. 鞋面,靴面;鞋面皮。2. 补块,补丁;旧物上蒙的新面;任何补缀物。3.【乐】即席伴奏。II *vt*. 1. 给(鞋、靴等)换面。2. 修补,翻新 (*up*)。3. 拼凑,拼拢来做 (*up*)。4. 捏造。5.【乐】为(独唱等)作即席伴奏。— *vi*. 【乐】即席伴奏。~ ***up*** 1. 把(旧物)翻新。2. 拼凑。3. 捏造(谣言等)。

vamp[2] [væmp; væmp] I *n*. 〔美俚〕(诱引男子的)妖妇。II *vt*., *vi*. 用媚术诱惑(男人)借以勒索金钱。

vamp·er [ˈvæmpə; ˋvæmpɚ] *n*. 补鞋工人;修补者;即席伴奏者。

vam·pire [ˈvæmpaiə; ˋvæmpaɪr] *n*. 1. 吸血鬼;吸人膏血的人。2. 〔美〕= vamp[2]. 3. 演妖妇角色的演员;勾引男子的女人。4.【动】吸血蝠,蝙蝠 (= ~ bat)。5.【剧】(舞台的)机关活门[活盖]。

vam·pir·ic [væmˈpirik; væmˋpɪrɪk] *a*. (像)吸血鬼的。

vam·pir·ism [ˈvæmpaiərizm; ˋvæmpaɪrɪzm] *n*. 1. 吸血鬼迷信。2. (民间传说中的)吸血鬼行为;〔尤指〕吸血。3. 吮人膏血;勒索钱财。

vam·plate [ˈvæmpleit; ˋvæmˏplet] *n*. 矛柄的护手金属板。

Van [væn, væn] *n*. 范〔男子名〕。

van[1] [væn; væn] I *n*. 1. (有盖的)载货大马车,搬运车;【铁路】行李车,有盖货车。2. (吉卜赛人所住的)大篷车;囚车。*a luggage* ~行李车。*a radio diffusion* ~广播车。*a television reporting* ~流动电视车。II *vt*. 用车搬运(货物)。~ **line** 〔美〕长途搬运公司。**-ner** *n*. 大棚车车主。~**pool** *vi*. 〔美〕合伙使用大篷车(上下班)。

van[2] [væn; væn] *n*. 1.【军】先锋,前锋部队[舰队]。2. 先驱,前驱;领袖,领导人(= vanguard)。***in the*** ~ ***of*** 在…的前列,作为先驱,领导着。***lead the*** ~ ***of*** 担任…的先驱。

van[3] [væn; væn] I *n*. 1. 〔古、方〕簸扬器[机]。2. 〔古、诗〕翼。3.【矿】洗矿铲。II *vt*. 选(矿)。

van[4] [væn; væn] *prep*. 〔D.〕= of, from〔出现于荷兰人姓名中,表示出生地,亦作 Van〕。

van·a·date [ˈvænədeit; ˋvænədet] *n*. 【化】钒酸盐,钒酸酯。

va·nad·ic [vəˈnædik; vəˋnædɪk] *a*. 【化】钒的〔指含有三价钒或五价钒的化合物的〕。~ **acid** 钒酸。

va·nad·i·nite [vəˈnædinait; vəˋnædəˏnaɪt] *n*. 【矿】钒铅矿。

va·na·di·um [vəˈneidiəm, -djəm; vəˋnedɪəm, -djəm] *n*. 【化】钒〔符号为 V〕。~ **steel** 【冶】钒钢。

V

van·a·dous [ˈvænədəs; ˋvænədəs] *a*. 【化】亚钒的〔指含有二价钒或三价钒的化合物〕。

Van Al·len [vænˈælin; vænˋælɪn] *n*. 范阿伦(姓氏)。

Van·brugh [ˈvænbrə; ˋvænbrə] *n*. 范布勒〔姓氏〕。

Van·bu·ren [vænˈbjuərən; vænˋbjurən] *n*. 范布伦〔姓氏〕。

Vance [væns; væns] *n*. 万斯〔姓氏,男子名〕。

van·co·my·cin [ˌvænkəˈmaisin; ˏvænkoˋmaɪsɪn] *n*. 【药】万古霉素。

Van·cou·ver [vænˈkuːvə; vænˋkuvɚ] *n*. **1.** 范库弗〔姓氏〕。**2.** 温哥华〔加拿大西南角一港口〕。

van·da [ˈvændə; ˋvændə] *n*. 【植】万带兰属 (*Vanda*) 植物。

Van·dal [ˈvændəl; ˋvændl] **I** *n*. **1.** 汪达尔人〔四、五世纪时侵入罗马帝国的日耳曼民族〕。**2.** 〔常 v-〕文化、艺术的摧残者。**II** *a*. 汪达尔人的;〔有时作 v-〕摧残文化艺术的,野蛮的。**-ic** [vænˈdælik; vænˋdælɪk] *a*.

Van·dal·ism [ˈvændəlizəm; ˋvændlˏɪzəm] *n*. **1.** 汪达尔人的行为。**2.** 〔v-〕(对公私财物,尤指文化、艺术品的)恶意破坏;野蛮行为。

van·dal·ize [ˈvændlaiz; ˋvændlˏaɪz] *vt*. (*-iz·ed*; *-iz·ing*) 破坏(公私财物,尤指文化艺术品)。

Van·de·grift [ˈvændəgrift; ˋvændəgrɪft] *n*. 范德格里夫特〔姓氏〕。

Van·den·berg [ˈvændənbəːg; ˋvændənˏbɝg] *n*. 范登堡〔姓氏〕。

Van·der·bilt [ˈvændəbilt; ˋvændəbɪlt] *n*. 范德比尔特〔姓氏〕。

V. and M. = Virgin and Martyr.

Van Do·ren [vænˈdɔːrən; vænˋdorən] *n*. 范多伦〔姓氏〕。

van·drag·ger [ˈvænˈdrægə; ˋvænˋdrægɚ] *n*. 〔英俚〕打劫货车的强盗。

Van·dyke[1] [vænˈdaik; vænˋdaɪk] *n*. **1.** 范戴克〔姓氏〕。**2. Sir Anthony** ~ 安·范戴克〔1599-1641,出生于英国的弗兰德斯画家〕。

Van·dyke[2] [vænˈdaik; vænˋdaɪk] **I** *n*. **1.** 范戴克(风格)的画。**2.** 锯齿饰边领(= ~ collar [cape])。**3.** 【纺】人字形穿综法;锯齿形饰边。**4.** (下巴上的)尖髯(= ~ beard)。**II** [ˈvændaik; ˋvændaɪk] *a*. **1.** 画家范戴克(创作、风格)的。**2.** 锯齿形饰边的。~ **brown** 深褐色(颜料);【化】铁棕。

Vane [vein; ven] *n*. 文恩〔姓氏〕。

vane [vein; ven] *n*. **1.** 【气】风向标,风信旗;〔喻〕随风倒的人。**2.** (风车、推进机等的)翼,(导向)叶片,叶轮。**3.** 【测】瞄准板;(罗盘等的)视准器。**4.** 【鸟】羽片;(翮上的)短毛,翈。*a guide* ~ 导流片。*an air* ~【火箭】空气舵。

Van Fleet [vænˈfliːt; vænˋflit] *n*. 范佛里特〔姓氏〕。

vang [væŋ; væŋ] *n*. 【海】斜桁支索。

van·guard [ˈvængɑːd; ˋvænˏgɑrd] *n*. **1.** 【军】先锋,前卫,(列成战斗队形的舰队的)先头舰只。**2.** 先进分子,先驱,前导者。

va·nil·la [vəˈnilə; vəˋnɪlə] *n*. **1.** 〔V-〕【植】香荚兰属。**2.** 【植】香荚兰;香草子;香草精。

va·nil·lic [vəˈnilik; vəˋnɪlɪk] *a*. 【化】香荚兰的;香草醛的。

van·il·lin [ˈvænilin, vəˈnilin; ˋvænəlɪn, vəˋnɪlɪn] *n*. 【化】香草醛[精],香兰精[醛]。

van·ish [ˈvæniʃ; ˋvænɪʃ] **I** *vi*. **1.** 消失不见;消灭,消散(*from*)。**2.** 【数】成零。~ *into smoke* 烟消云散。~ *into thin air* 消失。**II** *n*. 【语音】弱化音〔ei, ou 的 *i*, *u* 等〕。~**ing cream** 雪花膏。~**ing point** (透视画的)消灭点;没影点;〔口〕快消灭的最后一点。~**ing target** 【军】隐显目标。

van·i·ty [ˈvæniti; ˋvænətɪ] *n*. **1.** 空虚;无用,无益[无聊]的事物[行为等]。**2.** 虚荣,浮华;虚荣心,自负,自大,浮夸。**3.** (妇女装随身化妆品的)小手提包(= ~ bag [box, case])。**4.** 梳妆台。*the pomps and* ~ 浮华与虚荣。**V- Fair** **1.** (英国作家班扬在宗教小说《天路历程》中所写的)浮华市场。**2.** 《名利场》〔英国作家萨克雷所著小说名〕;浮华虚荣的社会。~ **plate** 〔美〕大款汽车牌照〔数字"吉利",需出高价购买,有时甚至拍卖〕。~ **press** [**publisher**] 专为著者自费印制书籍的出版社。~ **surgery** 整容外科。

van·load [ˈvænləud; ˋvænˏlod] *n*. 一货车的载运量。

van·quish [ˈvæŋkwiʃ; ˋvæŋkwɪʃ] *vt*. 征服,战胜,击败;克服,抑制(感情等)。*the ~ed* 被征服者。—*vi*. 得到胜利,成为胜利者。**-er** *n*. 征服者,胜利者。

Van·sit·tart [ˈvænsitət; ˋvænsɪtɚt] *n*. 范西塔特〔姓氏〕。

van·tage [ˈvɑːntidʒ; ˋvæntɪdʒ] *n*. **1.** 优势;优越的地位。**2.** 【网球】平分 (deuce) 后得到的一分〔发球手 (server) 得到的叫~-in, 接球手 (receiver) 得到的叫 ~-out〕。**3.** 〔罕〕= advantage. **4.** 〔古〕利益,获利。*a point of* ~ = *a coign*(*e*) *of* ~ = ~-ground. *for the* ~ 何况,加之。*have* [*take*] (*sb.*) *at* ~ 比(某人)处于有利的地位,占(某人)上风。*to the* ~ = *for the* ~. ~**-ground**, ~**-point** 有利的地位;上风。

van·ward [ˈvænwəd; ˋvænwɚd] **I** *a*. 在前的,先头的,(部队)先锋的。**II** *ad*. 向前。

vap·id [ˈvæpid; ˋvæpɪd] *a*. **1.** (食物等)没味道的,(啤酒等)走了味的。**2.** 无趣味的,没有生气的,没有趣味的。**3.** 不尖锐的,不痛快的。*run* ~ 走气。**-ly** *ad*. **-ness** *n*.

va·pid·i·ty [vəˈpiditi; vəˋpɪdətɪ] *n*. **1.** 无味,乏味;走味,走气。**2.** 没生气,没精神;没趣味。

va·por [ˈveipə; ˋvepɚ] *n*. 〔美〕= vapour.

va·po·rar·i·um [ˌveipəˈrɛəriəm; ˏvepəˋrɛrɪəm] *n*. (*pl*. ~*s*, *-rar·i·a*) 蒸汽浴室。

va·po·ret·to [ˌvɑːpɔːˈretəu, Eng. ˌvæpəˈretəu; vɑpoˋreto, ˏvæpəˋrɛto] *n*. (*pl*. ***-ret·ti*** [-tiː;-ti], ~*s*) 〔It.〕(威尼斯运河上的)公共汽艇。

va·por·if·ic [ˌveipəˈrifik; ˏvepəˋrɪfɪk] *a*. 发生蒸汽的。

va·por·im·e·ter [ˌveipəˈrimitə; ˏvepəˋrɪmətɚ] *n*. 【化】挥发度计。

va·por·i·sa·tion, -za·tion [ˌveipəraiˈzeiʃən; ˏvepərəˋzeʃən] *n*. 蒸发[挥发](作用),汽化。

va·por·ise, -ize [ˈveipəraiz; ˋvepəˏraɪz] *vt*., *vi*. (使)蒸发[挥发],(使)汽化。

va·por·is·er [ˈveipəraizə; ˋvepəraɪzɚ] *n*. 蒸发器,汽化器;喷雾器。

va·por·ous [ˈveipərəs; ˋvepərəs] *a*. **1.** 汽状的;蒸气状的,雾气弥漫的。**2.** 朦胧的。**3.** 无实质的,空幻的;幻想的。**4.** 夸夸其谈的,浮夸的。**5.** 〔古〕忧郁性的。

va·pour [ˈveipə; ˋvepɚ] **I** *n*. **1.** 汽,蒸气,水蒸气;烟雾,雾,霭;【物】汽化液体,汽化固体。**2.** 没有实质的东西;幻想,空想,妄想;〔古〕狂妄,自大。**3.** 〔*pl*.〕郁闷,忧郁病。**4.** 【医】吸入剂。**II** *vt*. **1.** 使蒸发,使汽化。**2.** 〔古〕使患忧郁症。—*vi*. **1.** 蒸发,挥发(*away*)。**2.** 自夸,吹牛。~ *forth high-flown fancies* 大吹牛皮。~ **bath** 蒸汽浴。~ **lock** 【机】汽塞现象。~ **trail** 【空】雾化尾迹(= contrail)。~**ware** 【计】空中楼阁件〔指已经广为宣传但实际上并未供应市场的所谓电脑新产品〕。

va·pour·ing [ˈveipəriŋ; ˋvepərɪŋ] **I** *a*. 自负的,傲慢的,自夸的,夸张的。**II** *n*. 夸口的言谈;放肆的言谈,傲慢的态度,无节制的举动。

va·pour·ish [ˈveipəriʃ; ˋvepərɪʃ] *a*. **1.** 蒸汽状的,多蒸汽的。**2.** 忧郁的。**-ness** *n*.

va·pour·y [ˈveipəri; ˋvepərɪ] *a*. = vaporous.

va·que·ro [væˈkɛərəu; væˋkɛro] *n*. 〔Sp.〕(*pl*. ~*s*) (墨西哥、美国西南部的)牧放牲畜者,牧童。

VAR = visual-aural (radio) range【无】可见可听式无线电航向信标,声影显示无线电航向信标。

var = volt-ampere reactive【电】乏,无功伏安。

var. = **1.** variable. **2.** variant. **3.** variation. **4.** variety. **5.** various.

va·ra [ˈvɑːrɑː; ˋvɑrɑ] *n.* **1.** 西班牙及拉丁美洲的尺度名,约合 31 至 33 英寸。**2.** 西班牙及拉丁美洲的面积单位,即 31 至 33 平方英寸。

va·rac·tor [vəˈræktə; vəˋræktə˞] *n.*【电子】变容二极管;可变电抗器。

var·ec(h) [ˈværek; ˋværɛk] *n.* **1.**【植】海草;巨藻,浮游海草。**2.** 海藻灰。

vari- *comb. f.* 表示"各种各样的","变异的"(= vario-)。

var·i·a [ˈvɛəriə; ˋvɛrɪə] *n.* 〔*pl.*〕**1.** 杂物。**2.** 杂录,杂文集。

var·i·a·bil·i·ty [ˌvɛəriəˈbiliti; ˏvɛrɪəˋbɪlətɪ] *n.* 易变,变化性;【生】变异性。

var·i·a·ble [ˈvɛəriəbl; ˋvɛrɪəbl] **I** *a.* **1.** 易变的,变化无常的,无定的(*opp.* constant, steady)。**2.** 可变的,能变的;变换的。**3.**【数】变量的;【天】变光的;【生】变异的。*Prices are ~ according to the exchanges.* 物价跟着汇率变动。*a man of ~ character* 反复无常的人。*a rod of ~ length* (伸缩)如意棒。*a word of ~ construction* 可以作种种解释的词。*~ capital* 可变资本。*a ~ budget* 临时预算。**II** *n.* **1.** 易变的东西。**2.**【数】变量,变数,变项,变元(*opp.* constant);【天】变星(= ~ star);【海】(方向不定的)变风,不定风(*opp.* trade wind);〔*pl.*〕(贸易风带中的)变风带。~ **rate mortgage** 可变利率抵押〔利率随金融市场情况而涨落的一种抵押法〕。**V- Zone**【地理】温带。**-a·bly** *ad.* **-ness** *n.*

va·ri·a lec·ti·o [ˈvɛəriə ˈlekʃiəu; ˋvɛrɪə ˋlɛkʃɪˏo] 〔L.〕(*pl.* ***vari·ae lec·tio·nes*** [ˈvɛərii ˈlekʃiəuniːs; ˋvɛrɪiˏlɛkʃɪˋoniz]) (不同版本间的)异文,异读。

va·ri·ance [ˈvɛəriəns; ˋvɛrɪəns] *n.* **1.** 变化,变动,变更;变度,变量;【统计】(平)方(偏)差。**2.** (意见等的)相异;不和,冲突,争论。**3.**【法】诉状和供词的不符。***at ~ with*** 和…不和;和…不符(*at ~ with the facts* 不符事实。*His conduct is at ~ with his words.* 他言行不符)。***set at ~*** 使不睦,离间。

va·ri·ant [ˈvɛəriənt; ˋvɛrɪənt] **I** *a.* **1.** 相异的,不同的,不一致的。**2.** 各种各样的。**3.** 易变的,不定的。*a ~ reading (in some MSS.)* (某抄本的)异文。*40 ~ types of pigeons* 鸽子的四十种变种。**II** *n.* **1.** 变体,变形;变量。**2.** (字音的)转讹;(字的)异体。**3.**【统】变式;【生】变种,变异体。

var·i·ate [ˈvɛəriit; ˋvɛrɪɪt] **I** *n.*【数】变量。**II** [ˈvɛərieit; ˋvɛrɪet] *vt.* 使变化,使变异。

var·i·a·tion [ˌvɛəriˈeiʃən; ˏvɛrɪˋeʃən] *n.* **1.** 变化,变动。**2.** 变量,变度,偏差。**3.**【语言】语尾变化;变体,异体;【数】变分,协变;顺列;【生】变异,演变,变种;【乐】变奏曲;【天】变差;(月的)二均差;【物】磁差。*a principle without ~* 不变的方针[原则]。*be capable of ~* 可能变化。*be liable to ~* 容易变化。*These prices are subject to ~.* 上列价格可能变更。**-al** *a.*

var·i·a·tor [ˈvɛərieitə; ˋvɛrɪetə˞] *n.* **1.**【机】(伸)胀缝,伸缩(接)缝。**2.**【机】变速器;变化器。**3.**【无】聚束栅。

varic- *comb. f.* = varico-.

var·i·cel·la [ˌværiˈselə; ˏværɪˋsɛlə] *n.*【医】水痘。

var·i·cel·late [ˌværiˈselit, -ait; ˏværɪˋsɛlɪt, -et] *a.* (某些贝壳)有细明脊纹的。

var·i·cel·loid [ˌværiˈselɔid; ˏværɪˋsɛlɔɪd] *a.*【医】水痘状的,水痘样的。

var·i·ces [ˈværiˌsiːz; ˋvɛrɪˏsiz, ˋvær-] *n.* varix 的复数。

varico- *comb. f.* 表示"静脉曲张": *varico*cele.

var·i·co·cele [ˈværikəusiːl; ˋværɪkoˏsil] *n.*【医】精索静脉曲张。

var·i·col·o(u)red [ˈvɛərikʌləd; ˋvɛrɪˏkʌlə˞d] *a.* 杂色的,多色的,五色缤纷的;各种各样的。

var·i·cose [ˈværikəus; ˋværɪˏkos] *a.* (治疗)静脉曲张的。

var·i·co·sis [ˌværiˈkəusis; ˏværɪˋkosɪs], **var·i·cos·i·ty** [-ˈkɔsəti; -ˋkɑsətɪ] *n.*【医】静脉曲张。

var·i·cot·o·my [ˌværiˈkɔtəmi; ˏværɪˋkɑtəmɪ] *n.* (*pl.* **-mies**)【医】曲张静脉切开术。

var·ied [ˈvɛərid; ˋvɛrɪd] *a.* **1.** 各种各样的。**2.** 改变了的,有变化的。**3.** 杂色的,斑驳的。*birds of the most ~ kinds* 变种最多的鸟。*a ~ life* 变动多的生活。**-ly** *ad.*

var·ie·gate [ˈvɛərigeit; ˋvɛrɪˏget] *vt.* **1.** 使成杂色,使斑驳。**2.** 使丰富多彩;使多样化。

va·r·ie·gat·ed [ˈvɛərigeitid; ˋvɛrɪˏgetɪd] *a.* **1.** 杂色的,斑驳的。**2.** (经验等)富于变化的,变化多端的;多样化的。*~ copper ore* 斑铜矿。

var·ie·ga·tion [ˌvɛəriˈgeiʃən; ˏvɛrɪˋgeʃən] *a.* 杂色,花斑,彩斑。

var·i·er [ˈvɛəriə, ˈvær-; ˋvɛrɪə, ˋvær-] *n.* **1.** 性喜变异的人。**2.** 串种的植物。

va·ri·e·tal [vəˈraiətl; vəˋraɪətl] *a.* **1.** 有变异的,变种的。**2.** (具有某种特性的)品种的。**-ly** *ad.*

va·ri·e·ty [vəˈraiəti; vəˋraɪətɪ] *n.* **1.** 变化,多样化(*opp.* monotony, uniformity)。**2.** (各种东西的)杂凑。**3.** 异种;种类;项目;【生】品种;变种;【语】异体。**4.**〔主英〕杂耍表演(= ~ show)。*an improved ~* 育成[改良]品种。***every ~ of form*** 各种形式。***for a ~ of reasons*** 因种种理由。***for ~'s sake*** 为了不单调起见。***full of ~*** 富于变化的,丰富多彩的。***have a great ~ to choose from*** 有很多种类可供选择。***in a ~ of ways*** 用种种方法。~ **entertainment** 杂耍演出。~ **house** [**theater**]〔英〕杂耍剧场。~ **shop** [〔美〕 **store**] 杂货铺,百货店。~ **show** 杂耍演出。

var·i·form [ˈvɛərifɔːm; ˋvɛrɪˏfɔrm] *a.* 有种种形态的。

var·i·o·coup·ler [ˌvɛəriəuˈkʌplə, ˌvær-; ˏvɛrɪoˋkʌplə˞, ˏvær-] *n.*【无】可变耦合器。

va·ri·o·la [vəˈraiələ; vəˋraɪələ] *n.*【医】天花,痘疮(= smallpox)。

va·ri·o·lar [vəˈraiələ; vəˋraɪələ˞] *a.* 天花的;有痘痕的,脸麻的。

var·i·ole [ˈvɛəriəul; ˋvɛrɪˏol] *n.* **1.**【动】小凹陷,痘斑。**2.**【地】(球颗玄武岩中的)球颗。

va·ri·o·mat·ic [ˌvɛəriəuˈmætik; ˏvɛrɪoˋmætɪk] *a.*【自】可变自动程序的。

var·i·o·lite [ˈvɛəriəlait; ˋvɛrɪəˏlaɪt] *n.*【地】球颗玄武岩。

var·i·o·loid [ˈvɛəriəlɔid; ˋvɛrɪəˏlɔɪd] **I** *a.* 类似[轻型]天花的,变形痘的。**II** *n.*【医】变形痘,轻型天花。

va·ri·o·lous [vəˈraiələs; vəˋraɪələs] *a.*【医】天花的,痘症的;有痘痕的,脸麻的。

var·i·om·e·ter [ˌvɛəriˈɔmitə; ˏvɛrɪˋɑmətə˞] *n.*【电】磁力比较器,磁偏计;【无】(可)变(电)感器,【空】气压测量器;变压表;升降速度表。

var·i·o·rum [ˌvɛəriˈɔːrəm; ˏvɛrɪˋorəm] **I** *a.* **1.** (古典作品)有诸家注解的,集注的。**2.** (例证等)引自不同来源[版本]的。**II** *n.* **1.** (古典作品的)集注版。**2.** 附有异文的校刊本。

va·ri·ous [ˈvɛəriəs; ˋvɛrɪəs] *a.* **1.** 不同的,各种各样的。**2.** 多样的,多方面的;富于变化的;〔古〕多才多艺的。**3.** 好几个的,许多的;许多种类的。**4.** 各个的,个别的。**5.**〔用作代词〕〔口〕好几个人,许多人。*~ opinions* 种种意见。*riots in ~ places* 各地的暴动。*too ~ to form a group* 种类杂多难成一类。*V- have assured me.* 许多人已向我保证。***for ~ reasons*** 因种种理由。**-ly** *ad.* **-ness** *n.*

var·is·cite [ˈværisait; ˋværɪˏsaɪt] *n.*【矿】磷酸铝石。

va·ri·sized [ˈvɛərisaizd; ˋvɛrɪsaɪzd] *a.* 各种大小的,不同尺寸的。

va·ris·tor [vəˈristə; vəˋrɪstə˞] *n.*【电子】变阻器,非线性

电阻,可变电阻。

var·i·tron [ˈvɛəritrən; ˋvɛrɪtrɑn] ***n.*** 【原】变换子。

var·ix [ˈvɛəriks; ˋvɛrɪks] ***n.*** (*pl.* ***var·i·ces*** [ˈværisiːz, ˈvɛər-; ˋværɪsiz, ˋvɛr-]) **1.** 【医】静脉曲张。**2.** 【动】(卷贝的)螺层。

var. lect. = *varia lectio*.

var·let [ˈvɑːlit; ˋvɑrlɪt] ***n.*** **1.** 【史】侍童,跟班;仆人。**2.** 〔古〕无赖,歹徒。

var·let·ry [ˈvɑːlitri; ˋvɑrlətrɪ] ***n.*** **1.** 〔古〕仆从,走卒。**2.** 〔蔑〕乱民;群氓,乌合之众。

var·mint [ˈvɑːmint; ˋvɑrmɪnt] ***n.*** **1.** 〔俚、方〕顽童,淘气鬼;歹徒。**2.** 有害动物。*the* ~ 〔猎俚〕狐〔vermin 的别字〕。

Var·na [ˈvɑːnə; ˋvɑrnə] ***n.*** 瓦尔纳〔保加利亚港市〕。

var·na [ˈvɑːnə; ˋvɑrnə] ***n.*** (印度的)种姓(= caste)。

var·nish [ˈvɑːniʃ; ˋvɑrnɪʃ] **I** ***n.*** **1.** 清漆,罩光漆,凡立水;釉子。**2.** (天然的)光泽面;表面光泽,外饰;(坏事等的)粉饰;掩饰。**3.** 〔英〕指甲油。**4.** 〔*pl.*〕〔美俚〕旅客列车。***put a ~ on*** …文饰,掩饰。**II** ***vt.*** **1.** 给…上清漆。**2.** 使表面光泽;美化,文饰;掩饰(*up*; *over*)。~ **paint** (清)漆。~ **tree** 清漆树。**-er** ***n.***

var·nish·ing-day [ˈvɑːniʃiŋdei; ˋvɑrnɪʃɪŋde] ***n.*** **1.** 画展之前作者修饰作品的一天。**2.** 艺术展览会开幕日。

va·room [vəˈruːm; vəˋrum] ***n.***, ***vi.*** = vroom.

vars·al [ˈvəːsəl; ˋvɜsl] ***a.*** 〔口、方〕= universal.

var·si·ty [ˈvɑːsiti; ˋvɑrsətɪ, ˋvɑrstɪ] **I** ***n.*** **1.** 〔英口〕= university. **2.** 〔美运〕大学代表队。**II** ***a.*** 大学代表队的。

Var·u·na [ˈvərunə, ˈvær-, ˈvɑːr-; ˋvərʊnə, ˋvær-, ˋvɑr-] 〔Sans.〕(印度教的)宇宙神。

var·us [ˈvɛərəs, ˈvær-; ˋvɛrəs, ˋvær-] **I** ***n.*** 【医】内翻,内偏〔尤指足向内翻的残疾〕。**II** ***a.*** 内翻的,内偏的〔指臀部、膝盖或足〕。

varve [vɑːv; vɑrv] ***n.*** 【地】纹泥,冲积层。

va·ry [ˈvɛəri; ˋvɛrɪ] ***vt.*** **1.** 改变,变更,修改。**2.** 使变化,使多样化。**3.** 【乐】变奏;使变调。~ *one's plans* 改变计划。— ***vi.*** **1.** 变化;多样化;不同,相异。**2.** 违背,逸出(*from*)。**3.** 【生】变异;【数】(随着另一个值的改变)变化。*Opinions* ~ *on this point.* 在这一点上意见各不相同。~ *from a rule* 违背规则。~ (***directly***) ***as*** 和…成正比例而变化。~ ***inversely as*** 和…成反比例而变化。~ ***with*** 照…变化,跟着…变化。

vas [væs; væs] ***n.*** (*pl.* ***va·sa*** [ˈveisə; ˋvesə]) 〔L.〕【解,生】管,血[脉]管;导管。~ ***deferens*** [ˈdefərenz; ˋdɛfə͵rɛnz] 输精管。**vas·al** ***a.***

VASCAR, Vascar [ˈvæskɑː; ˋvæskɑ] ***n.*** 〔商标〕目视平均车速电脑记录器(= Visual Average Speed Computer And Recorder)。

vas·cu·lar [ˈvæskjulə; ˋvæskjələ˞] ***a.*** 【解、生】脉管的,由脉管形成的;血管的。~ **bundle** 【植】维管束。~ **cylinder** 【植】维管柱(= stele)。~ **plant** 【植】维管植物(= tracheophyte)。~ **ray** 【植】髓线(= medullary ray)。~ **system** 导管[血管、淋巴管等]系统。~ **tissue** 【植】导管组织;【动】脉管组织。**-ly** ***ad.*** **-i·ty** ***n.***

vas·cu·lum [ˈvæskjuləm; ˋvæskjələm] ***n.*** (*pl.* ***-la*** [-lə; -lə], ~***s***) **1.** 植物标本采集箱。**2.** 【植】瓶状体。**3.** 【解】小(脉)管;阴茎。

vase [vɑːz; Am. veis; ves, vez, vɑz] ***n.*** **1.** (花)瓶,水瓮。**2.** 希腊瓶。**3.** 【建、家具】瓶饰。

vas·ec·to·my [væˈsektəmi; væsˋɛktəmɪ] ***n.*** 【医】输精管切除(术)。

vas·e·line [ˈvæziliːn; ˋvæsl͵in, -ɪn] ***n.*** **1.** 【化】凡士林,石油冻,矿脂。**2.** 〔美俚〕奶油。

vas·o·con·stric·tor [ˌvæsəukənˈstriktə, ˌveiz-; ͵væsokənˋstrɪktə˞, ͵vez-] **I** ***a.*** 【医】血管收缩的。**II** ***n.*** 血管收缩神经;血管收缩药。**-stric·tion** ***n.*** 血管收缩。

vas·o·di·la·tor [ˌvæsəuˈdaileitə, ˌveiz-; ͵væsodaɪˋletə˞, ͵vez-] **I** ***a.*** 【医】血管舒张的。**II** ***n.*** 血管舒张神经;血管舒张药。**-dil·a·ta·tion** [-ˌdiləˈteiʃən; -͵dɪləˋteʃən], **-di·la·tion** [-daiˈleiʃən; -daɪˋleʃən] ***n.***

vas·o·in·hib·i·tor [ˌvæsəuinˈhibitə, ˌveiz-; ͵væsoɪnˋhɪbɪtə˞, ͵vez-] ***n.*** 【医】血管抑制药,血管抑制剂。**-y** ***a.***

vas·o·li·gate [ˌvæsəuˈlaigeit; ͵væsoˋlaɪget] ***vt.*** 结扎(人或动物)的输精管,对(人或动物)作输精管结扎手术。

vas·o·li·ga·tion [ˌvæsəuliˈgeiʃən, ˌveiz-; ͵væsolɪˋgeʃən, ͵vez-] ***n.*** 【医】输精管结扎术。

vas·o·mo·tor [ˌvæsəuˈməutə, ˌveiz-; ͵væsəmotə˞, ͵vez-] ***a.*** 【生理】血管舒缩的。

vas·o·pres·sin [ˌvæsəuˈpresn, ˌveiz-; ͵væsoˋprɛsɪn, ͵vez-] ***n.*** 【生化、医】血管加压素,血压激素。

vas·o·pres·sor [ˌvæsəuˈpresə, ˌveiz-; ͵væsoˋprɛsə˞, ͵vez-] **I** ***a.*** 【医】血管加压的。**II** ***n.*** 血管加压神经,血管加压素。

vas·o·spasm [ˈvæsəuˌspæzm, ˈveiz-; ͵væsoˋspæzm, ˋvez-] ***n.*** 【医】血管痉挛。

vas·ot·o·my [væsˈɔtəmi, veiz-; væˋsɑtəmɪ, vez-] ***n.*** (*pl.* ***-mies***) 【医】输精管造口[切断]术。

vas·o·ton·ic [ˌvæsəuˈtɔnik; ͵væsoˋtɑnɪk] ***a.*** 【医】血管紧张的。

vas·o·tribe [ˈvæsətraib; ˋvæsə͵traɪb] ***n.*** 【医】血管压轧器。

vas·o·va·gal [ˌvæsəuˈveigl, ˈveiz-; ͵væsoˋvegl, ˋvez-] ***a.*** 【医】迷走神经作用于(血管)循环系统(引起)的〔如晕厥〕。

vas·sal [ˈvæsəl; ˋvæsl] **I** ***n.*** **1.** (封建时代的)诸侯,陪臣。**2.** 附庸;部属;奴隶。**II** ***a.*** **1.** 陪臣的,臣属的。**2.** 隶属的;效忠的;奴隶的。*a ~ state* 仆从国。*a ~ court* 陪臣的小朝廷。

vas·sal·age [ˈvæsəlidʒ; ˋvæslɪdʒ] ***n.*** **1.** 陪臣身分;附庸[臣属]地位。**2.** 效忠,臣属。**3.** 领地,采地。

vast [vɑːst; væst] **I** ***a.*** **1.** 广大的,辽阔的,(海、平原等)茫茫的,浩瀚的。**2.** 许许多多的,(数、量等)巨大的。**3.** 〔口〕非常的,很大的。*a ~ expanse of desert* [*ocean*] 茫茫沙漠[大海]。*a ~ scheme = a scheme of ~ scope* 庞大的计划。*a ~ calamity* 大灾祸。*a ~ difference* 〔口〕天渊之别。*a ~ sum of money* 一笔巨款。*a ~ multitude* 一大群人。*of ~ importance* 非常重要的。**II** ***n.*** 〔诗〕广大无边的空间;大海。*the* [*a*] ~ *of ocean* [*water*] 汪洋大海。**-ly** ***ad.*** **-ness** ***n.*** **-y** ***a.*** 〔诗〕= vast.

vas·ti·tude [ˈvɑːstitjuːd, ˈvæstituːd; ˋvɑstə͵tjud, ˋvæstə͵tud] ***n.*** **1.** 广度。**2.** 广阔境界[空间]。

vat [væt; væt] **I** ***n.*** **1.** (酿造、制革等用的)大桶,大缸。**2.** 比利时和荷兰的液量名。**3.** 【染】还原染缸[染剂]。**II** ***vt.*** (***-tt-***) 把…装入大桶;在大桶里处理。~ **dyes** 还原性染料,瓮染料。~**-dyed** ***a.*** 用还原染料染的。

VAT = Value-Added Tax 增值税。

Vat. = Vatican.

vat·ic [ˈvætik; ˋvætɪk] ***a.*** 预言的,先知的。

Vat·i·can [ˈvætikən; ˋvætɪkən] ***n.*** **1.** 梵蒂冈〔欧洲〕〔罗马教廷所在地〕。**2.** 〔the ~〕罗马教廷。**V- City** 梵蒂冈城。**-ism** ***n.*** 教皇绝对权主义。**-ist** ***n.*** 教皇绝对权主义的支持者。

vat·ic·i·nal [væˈtisinl; vəˋtɪsənl] ***a.*** 预言的。

vat·ic·i·nate [væˈtisineit; vəˋtɪsə͵net] ***vt.***, ***vi.*** 预言,预告。**-na·tor**, **-na·tion** ***n.***

vaude [ˈvəud; ˋvod] ***n.*** 〔美〕杂耍。

vau·de·ville [ˈvəudəvil, -viːl; ˋvodə͵vɪl, -vil] ***n.*** **1.** 〔英〕轻松歌舞剧,轻松喜剧。**2.** 〔美〕杂耍。**3.** (法国的)讽刺民歌。~ **house** 〔美〕杂耍场(=〔英〕music hall)。~ **performance** 〔美〕杂耍表演。

vaude·vil·lian [ˌvəudəˈviljən; ͵vodəˋvɪljən] **I** ***n.*** 轻歌舞演员;杂耍演员。**II** ***a.*** 杂耍的。

Vau·din [ˈvəudin; ˋvodɪn] ***n.*** 沃丁〔姓氏〕。

Vaughan [vɔːn; vɔn] *n*. 沃恩〔姓氏,男子名〕。

vault[1] [vɔːlt; vɔlt] I *n*. 1.【建】拱顶,穹窿。2. 穹窿状覆盖物;天空,苍穹。3. 圆顶房间[地下室];〔美〕地窖;地下保险库;安放骨灰的地下灵堂;地牢;洞窟。4.【解】腔拱,穹窿。*the blue ~ of heaven* 苍穹。II *vt*. 给…盖圆顶;使造成穹窿形。— *vi*. 成穹状。

vault[2] [vɔːlt; vɔlt] I *vi*. (用棒或手撑着)跳,跳跃,进行撑竿跳。— *vt*. (以手撑物或撑竿)跳过。~ *from* [*into*] *the saddle* 跳下[跳上]马鞍。~ *on* (*to*) [*upon*] *a horse* 跳上马。~ *over a ditch* 跳过沟。II *n*. 跳过,跳跃;撑竿跳〔又称 pole-~〕。

vault·ed [ˈvɔːltid; ˋvɔltɪd] *a*. 有拱顶的;圆顶的,穹窿形的,拱状的。

vault·ing[1] [ˈvɔːltiŋ; ˋvɔltɪŋ] *n*.【建】拱顶工程;〔集合词〕拱顶。

vault·ing[2] [ˈvɔːltiŋ; ˋvɔltɪŋ] I *n*. = vault[2]. II *a*. 1. 支撑着跳的;跳跃用的。2. 夸大的;过度的。~ *ambition* 狂妄的野心。*a* ~ *imagination* 大胆[腾空]的想像。~ **horse**【运】鞍马。

vaunt [vɔːnt; vɔnt] I *vi*., *vt*. 夸张,自夸;宣扬(优点);称扬。II *n*. 自夸,自负。***make a ~ of*** 夸扬。~-**courier** 1. 先遣者,先驱。2.〔古〕先锋队的一员(= avant-courier)。-**y** *a*.

vaunt·er [ˈvɔːntə; ˋvɔntɚ] *n*. 自负[自夸]的人,爱说大话的人。

vaunt·ing·ly [ˈvɔːntiŋli; ˋvɔntɪŋlɪ] *ad*. 自夸着,自负地,骄傲地。

Vaux [vɔːz, vɔks; vɔz, vɑks] *n*. 沃克斯〔姓氏〕。

v. aux. = verb auxiliary【语法】助动词。

vav [vɔv, vɔːv; vɑv, vɔv] *n*. 希伯来字母表的第六个字母。

vav·a·sor, vav·a·sour [ˈvævəˌsɔː, -ˌsuə; ˋvævəˏsor, -ˏsɔr] *n*. 中世纪低于男爵的小诸侯;陪臣。-**y** *n*. 小诸侯的土地[租地权]。

va·ward [ˈvɑːwɔːd; ˋvɑˏwɔrd] *n*.〔古〕= vanguard.

vb. = verb; verbal.

V-belt [ˈviːˈbelt; ˋviˋbɛlt] *n*.【机】三角皮带。

vb. n. = verbal noun【语法】动名词。

VC = 1. veterinary corps 陆军兽医队。2. vice-chairman 副主席,副议长。3. vice-chancellor 大学副校长,副大法官。4. vice-consul 副领事。5. Victoria Cross〔英〕维多利亚十字勋章。6. Vietcong. 7. volunteer corps 志愿军[队]。

V chip【计】滤除暴力镜头芯片,V 芯片〔装在电视机上的一种微型芯片,可滤除暴力或色情镜头〕。

VCR = 1. video cassette recording 盒式磁带录像。2. video cassette recorder 盒式磁带录像机。

VD = vapour density 蒸气密度。

V.D. = 1. venereal disease 性病,花柳病。2. Volunteer (Officer's) Decoration〔英〕志愿军官勋带。

Vd =【化】vanadium.

v. d. = various dates 不同日期。

V-Day [ˈviːdei; ˋvide] *n*. (第二次世界大战的)胜利日,胜利节。

v.dep. = verb deponent 字形被动词义主动的动词。

V.D.H. = valvular disease of the heart 心脏瓣膜病。

VDT = visual display terminal【计】可见显示终端设备〔有一个显示荧光屏和键盘的电脑终端设备〕。

VDU = visual display unit【计】可见显示器〔荧光屏上显示数据的装置〕。

VE = value engineering 价值工程学。

've [v; v] *v*.〔口〕= have. ★(1)英语仅用于 I, we, you, they 及 who 之后: I've = I have. (2)美俚语亦用于 would, might 等之后: might've been.

Ve·a·dar [ˌveiɑːˈdɑː, ˌviːɑːdɑː; ˏveəˋdɑ, ˋviədɑ] *n*. 犹太历的闰月。

veal [viːl; vil] *n*. 1. (食用)小牛肉。2. 小牛(= vealer)。

veal·er [ˈviːlə; ˋvilɚ] *n*. 小牛,犊。

veal·y [ˈviːli; ˋvilɪ] *a*. 〔口〕小牛一样的;幼稚的。

Veb·len [ˈveblən; ˋvɛblən] *n*. 维布伦〔姓氏〕。

vec·to·graph [ˈvektəgrɑːf; ˋvɛktəˏgræf, -ˏgrɑf] *n*. 1. (用偏光眼镜看的)立体电影[照片等]。2.【数】矢量图,向量图。-**ic** [ˌvektəˈgræfik; ˏvɛktəˋgræfɪk] *a*.

vec·tor [ˈvektə; ˋvɛktɚ] I *n*. 1.【数】向量,矢量,动径。2.【空】飞机航线;航向指示。3.【天】幅,矢径。4.【生】带菌者[体],传病媒介。II *vt*.【空】(对飞行中的飞机)指示航向。— *vi*.【空】电(磁)波导航。~ **analysis** 向量解析。~ **diagram** 向量图。~ **product**【数】矢积。~ **quantity** 有向量。~ **sum**【数】矢和。

Ve·da [ˈveidə, ˈviːdə; ˋvedə, ˋvidə] *n*. 〔Sans.〕吠陀〔印度婆罗门教四部古经的总称,或指其中之一〕。-**ic** *a*. = Vedic.

ve·da·li·a [viˈdeiliə, -ˈdeiljə; vɪˋdelɪə, -ˋdeljə] *n*.【动】澳洲瓢虫(*Rodolia cardinalis*)〔现已引进世界各地以治介壳虫〕。

Ve·dan·ta [viˈdɑːntə, -ˈdæn-; vɪˋdɑntə, -ˋdæn-] *n*.【哲】吠檀多〔以吠陀经最后一部分即《奥义书》为基础的印度哲学〕。**Ve·dan·tic** *a*. **Ve·dan·tism** *n*.

V-E Day [ˈviːˈiːdei; ˋviˋide]〔美〕(第二次世界大战中的)欧洲胜利日〔1945 年 5 月 8 日,即德国投降日〕。

Ved·da(h) [ˈvedə; ˋvɛdə] *n*. 维达人〔斯里兰卡的原住民〕。

ve·dette [viˈdet, vəˈd-; vəˋdɛt] *n*.【军】骑哨;舰载水雷艇,哨艇。

Ve·dic [ˈveidik, ˈviːdik; ˋvedɪk, ˋvidɪk] I *a*. 〔Sans.〕吠陀的。II *n*. 吠陀梵语,早期梵语。

vee [viː; vi] I *n*. 1. 英语字母 V, v. 2. V 形的东西。3.〔美口〕五元票面的钞票。II *a*. V 形的。

vee·no [ˈviːnəu; ˋvino] *n*. 〔美俚〕酒;葡萄酒。

Veep [viːp; vip] *n*. 〔美口〕1. (美国的)副总统(= vice-president)。2. [v-]〔*pl*.〕要人们。

veer [viə; vɪr] I *vi*. 1. (风)转变方向;【气】风向(按时针方向)顺转;【海】掉转船尾向着风;顺风换抢。2. (意见、感情等)转变,改变(*round*)。— *vt*. 1. 使转变方向;【海】把(船尾)转向风;使处顺风方位。2. 放松(锚、缆等)(*away*; *out*)。~ ***and haul*** (把绳等)一会儿放松一会儿拉紧;(风向)改变。II *n*. 方向的改变。-**ing·ly** *ad*.

vee·ry [ˈviəri; ˋvɪrɪ] *n*. (*pl*. ***veer·ies***)〔美〕【动】韦氏鸫〔产于美国〕。

vee·tol [ˈviːtɔːl; ˋvitol] *n*. (飞机的)垂直起落(= VTOL)。

veg [vedʒ; vɛdʒ] I *n*. 〔单复同〕〔口〕= vegetable. *a dinner with two* ~有两道蔬菜的正餐。II *vi*. 〔口〕= vegetate. ~ ***oat*** 吃长素,过素食生活。

Ve·ga [ˈviːgə; ˋvigə] *n*.【天】织女一,天琴座 α 星。

ve·ga [ˈveigə; ˋvegɑ] *n*. 〔Sp.〕(南美的)低显平原[草地];(古巴的)烟草种植地。

ve·gan [ˈvegən; ˋvegən] *n*. 严守素食主义的人。

veg·e·mite [ˈvedʒ*i*mait; ˋvɛdʒəmaɪt] *n*. (用酵母制成的)咸味酱〔可直接涂在食品上吃或用于调味〕。

veg·e·ta·ble [ˈvedʒ*i*təbl; ˋvɛdʒətəbl] I *n*. 1. 植物。2. 蔬菜〔俗指豆类、芜菁、青菜等,有时不指马铃薯〕。3. (生理上或精神上)像植物一样没有生气的人。*green ~s* 青菜;蔬菜。***become a mere*** ~变得像植物一样呆板;呆板单调地过日子。II *a*. 1. 植物(性)的;得自植物的;关于植物的。2. 蔬菜的。~ *fibers* 植物纤维。~ *oil* 植物油。~ *crops* 蔬菜。*a* ~ *dish* 一盘蔬菜。~ *soup* 蔬菜汤。~ **anatomy** 植物解剖学。~ **butter** 素奶油,(食用)植物脂。~ **charcoal** 木炭。~ **earth** [**mould**] 腐殖土。~ **ivory** 植物象牙。~ **down** 木棉。~ **kingdom** 植物界。~ **life** 植物。~ **marrow**〔主英〕菜瓜[南瓜之类],食用葫芦;菜瓜瓤。~ **medicine** 草药。~ **oyster**〔美〕【植】波罗门参(= salsify)。~ **parchment** 充羊皮纸。~ **silk** 植物丝。~ **sponge** 丝瓜筋,丝瓜瓤。~ **tallow**

V

植物脂。

veg·e·tal [ˈvedʒitl; ˋvedʒətl] **I** *a*. **1.** 植物(性)的。**2.** = vegetative. **II** *n*. 植物;青菜,蔬菜。

veg·e·tant [ˈvedʒitənt; ˋvedʒətənt] *a*. 使生长旺盛的,促进生长的,促使强壮的;植物性的。

veg·e·tar·i·an [ˌvedʒiˈtɛəriən; ˏvedʒəˋtɛrɪən] **I** *a*. **1.** 素食主义(者)的。**2.** 只有蔬菜的,素菜的。*a* ~ *diet* 素食。~ *principles* 素食主义。*a* ~ *restaurant* 素菜馆。**II** *n*. 素食主义者,吃素的人;〔美〕怕吃荤腥肉类的人。**-ism** *n*. 素食主义;素食。

veg·e·tate [ˈvedʒiteit; ˋvedʒəˏtet] *vi*. **1.** (植物)生长;像植物一样发育。**2.** 坐吃,过呆板的闲静生活,过单调的生活。**3.** 【医】(赘疣等)生长,长大;增殖。

veg·e·ta·tion [ˌvedʒiˈteiʃən; ˏvedʒəˋteʃən] *n*. **1.** 【植】营养体生长,发育;〔集合词〕植物,植被,植生,草木。**2.** 无所作为的生活,单调的生活。**3.** 【医】赘生物,增殖体。*natural* ~自然植被。*tropical* ~热带植物。*the luxuriant* ~ 茂盛的草木。**-al** *a*.

veg·e·ta·tive [ˈvedʒitətiv; ˋvedʒəˏtetɪv] *a*. **1.** 植物的;蔬菜的。**2.** 会生长的,有生长力的;发育生长的(*opp*. reproductive);无性繁殖的;能使植物生长的;植物生长和营养的,(土地)肥沃的。**3.** 植物似的;生活单调的,无所作为的,闲混日子的。**4.** 【医】生长性的,植物性的。*during the* ~ *stage* 在生长过程中。*a* ~ *hybrid* 营养杂种,无性杂种。~ *propagation* 营养繁殖,无性繁殖。*a* ~ *little* 营养性小菌落。~ *functions* 营养机能。~ *mass* 营养体。*a placid and* ~ *sort of character* 静如草木的性格。*the philosophy of mere* ~ *existence* 苟且偷生的哲学。**-ly** *ad*.

veg·e·tive [ˈvedʒitiv; ˋvedʒətɪv] **I** *a*. = vegetative. **II** *n*. **1.** 〔废〕植物。**2.** 食用植物。

veg·gies [ˈvedʒiz; ˋvedʒiz] *n*. 〔*pl*.〕〔口〕蔬菜(= vegetables)。

Veh Dep 〔英〕= Vehicle Depot 停车处。

ve·he·mence [ˈviːiməns; ˋviəməns] *n*. 激烈;猛烈;热烈。

ve·he·men·cy [ˈviːimənsi; ˋviəmənsɪ] *n*. 〔罕〕= vehemence.

ve·he·ment [ˈviːimənt; ˋviəmənt] *a*. **1.** 激烈的;猛烈的。**2.** 激情的,热烈的。**-ly** *ad*.

ve·hi·cle [ˈviːikl, ˈviəkl; ˋviɪkl, ˋviəkl] *n*. **1.** 车辆;载运工具;飞行器;运行工具。**2.** 媒介物,媒质。**3.** 【药】赋形剂。**4.** 【绘画、化】展色料,载色剂。*a space* ~太空船。*an escape* ~太空飞行器。*a rocket* ~火箭。*a staged* ~多级火箭。*a seeking* ~自动寻找目标的火箭。*an airborne* ~飞机载运导弹。*the greater* [*lesser*] ~【佛教】大[小]乘。*Language is the* ~ *of thought*. 语言是表达思想的工具。

ve·hic·u·lar, 〔罕〕**-lar·y** [viˈhikjulə, -ləri; viˋhɪkjələ˞; -lərɪ] *a*. **1.** 车辆的;车辆交通的;供车辆用的。*a* ~ *tunnel* 供车辆通行的隧道。**2.** 由车辆引起的。~ *death* 车祸造成的死亡。**3.** 车载的,车运的。~ *recording units* 车载录音装置。**4.** 作为媒介的。

ve·hic·u·lum [viˈhikjuləm; vɪˋhɪkjələm] *n*. (*pl*. **-la**) 【医】赋形药。

veil [veil; vel] **I** *n*. **1.** 面纱,面罩。**2.** (修女的)头巾;〔喻〕修女生活。**3.** 幔,帐,幕;遮布;遮蔽物。**4.** 口实,假托。**5.** 【解、动、植】= velum. **6.** 声音不响亮。***beyond the*** ~在来世,在死后的无知境界。***draw a*** [***the***] ~ ***over*** 遮掩,掩藏;避不说明。***drop a*** ~放下面罩。***pass the*** ~死去。***raise a*** ~揭开面罩。***take the*** ~(带上面纱)做修女。***under the*** ~ ***of*** 躲在…的背后,假托…。***within the*** ~在天国。**II** *vt*. 使盖上面纱;遮盖;隐匿。— *vi*. 蒙上面纱。*be ~ed in mystery* 隐藏在神秘中。*~ed threats* 暗示性的恫吓。*a ~ed voice* 不清楚的声音,微哑的声音。

veil·ing [ˈveiliŋ; ˋvelɪŋ] *n*. 用面纱遮掩;面纱(料);帐幔(料)。~ **luminance**【物】光度耗散。

vein [vein; ven] **I** *n*. **1.** 【解】静脉;〔口〕血管。**2.** 【植】叶脉;【动】翅脉;【地】矿脉,岩脉;水脉。**3.** 裂痕,裂缝,缺隙。**4.** 脉,筋;纹理。**5.** 气质,倾向;性情,性格,风格;心境,情绪。*systemic ~s* 大静脉。*a* ~ *of ore* 矿脉。*a* ~ *of humour* 幽默气质。*I am not in* (*the*) ~ *just now*. 我现在没有兴致。*in a humorous* ~ 带着诙谐的情绪。*in the giving* ~在慷慨的情绪下。***in the*** ~ ***for*** 想…,有心…。**II** *vt*. 〔常用被动语态〕使有筋脉[纹理],使显出静脉。*a piece of ~ed crape* 一块花纹绉绸。~ *print* (手背上的)静脉纹(每个人都不相同)。

vein·er [ˈveinə; ˋvenə˞] *n*. (木刻用的)V形小凿。

vein·let [ˈveinlit; ˋvenlɪt] *n*. 【解】小静脉;【动】小翅脉;【植】细叶脉,支叶脉。

vein·ous [ˈveinəs; ˋvenəs], **vein·y** [-i; -ɪ] *a*. (***-i·er***; ***-i·est***) 静脉[叶脉、翅脉、纹理]的;(手等)筋脉多的。

vein·stone [ˈveinstəun; ˋvenˏston] *n*. 脉石、矿石中杂质(= gangue)。

vein·ule [ˈveinjuːl; ˋvenjul] *n*. = venule.

vein·y [ˈveini; ˋvenɪ] *a*. (***-i·er***; ***-i·est***) **1.** 有静脉的。**2.** 多纹理的[大理石等]。**3.** 有叶脉的。

vel. = **1.** vellum. **2.** velocity.

ve·la [ˈviːlə; ˋvilə] *n*. velum 的复数。

Ve·la [ˈviːlə; ˋvilə] *n*. 【天】船帆座〔南天星座名〕。~-**Hotel** 〔美〕"船帆座旅馆"〔监视宇宙空间核爆炸的人造卫星系统〕。

ve·la·men [viˈleimən; vɪˋlemen] *n*. (*pl*. **-lam·i·na** [-ˈlæminə; -ˋlæmɪnə]) **1.** 【解】帆,膜,被膜。**2.** 【植】根被。

ve·lar [ˈviːlə; ˋvilə˞] **I** *a*. **1.** 【解】帆的,膜的。**2.** 【语音】(子音等)软腭音的。**II** *n*. 【语音】软腭音。

ve·lar·i·um [viˈlɛəriəm; vɪˋlɛrɪəm] *n*. (*pl*. **-ria** [-riə; -riɑ]) (古罗马)露天剧场的遮阳(帐篷),天幕。**2.** 【动】拟缘膜。

ve·lar·ize [ˈviːləraiz; ˋviləˏraɪz] *vt*. (***-iz·ed***; ***-iz·ing***) 【语音】使软腭化。**-i·za·tion** [ˌviːləraiˈzeiʃən; ˏviləraɪˋzeʃən] *n*.

ve·late [ˈviːleit, -lit; ˋvilet, -lɪt] *a*. 【解,生】有帆的,有软腭的;有膜的;有缘膜的;有菌幕的。

Vel·cro [ˈvelkrəu; ˋvelkro] *n*. 〔美〕尼龙拉带〔原商标名〕。~**lips** 紧闭嘴唇,守口如瓶。

veld(t) [velt; vɛlt] *n*. (南非)无林[疏林]草原。

vel·i·ta·tion [ˌveliˈteiʃən; ˏvɛləˋteʃən] *n*. 〔古〕小争斗,小争执,争论。

ve·li·tes [ˈviːlitiːz; ˋvilɪˏtiz] *n*. 〔*pl*.〕(古罗马的)轻步兵。

vel·le·i·ty [veˈliːiti; vɛˋliətɪ] *n*. 极微弱的意欲;无行动的单纯愿欲;【哲】不完全意欲。

vel·li·cate [ˈvelikeit; ˋvɛlɪˏket] *vt*., *vi*. 扯;(使)跳动,(使)抽动[痉挛];掐。

vel·li·ca·tion [ˌveliˈkeiʃən; ˏvɛlɪˋkeʃən] *n*. 痉挛;抽动。

vel·lum [ˈveləm; ˋvɛləm] *n*. **1.** 精制犊[羔]皮纸,上等皮纸。**2.** 皮纸文件[抄本]。~ **paper** 仿羔皮纸。**-y** *a*.

Vel·ma [ˈvelmə; ˋvɛlmə] *n*. 维尔玛〔女子名〕。

ve·lo·ce [viˈləutʃi; veˋlotʃe] *ad*. 〔It.〕【乐】快速地,敏捷地。

vel·o·cim·e·ter [ˌveləˈsimitə; ˏvɛləˋsɪmətə˞] *n*. 速度计;测速仪。

ve·loc·i·pede [viˈlɔsipiːd; vəˋlɑsəˏpid] *n*. **1.** 旧式自行车;〔谑〕自行车。**2.** 〔英俚〕儿童三轮脚踏车。**3.** 【铁路】轻便手压车(= handcar)。

ve·loc·i·ty [viˈlɔsiti; vəˋlɑsətɪ] *n*. **1.** 迅速;快速。**2.** 速度,速率。**3.** 周转率。*at a* ~ *of 100 miles per hour* 用每小时一百英里的速度。*dart off with the* ~ *of a bird* 像鸟一样迅速飞跑过去。*drag-free* ~无阻力飞速,真空飞速。*escape* ~(克服地球引力的)第二宇宙速度,逃逸速度。*final* ~ (发射物的)终速。*initial*

V

[*muzzle*] ~(发射物的)初速[腔口速度]。*uniform* [*variable*] ~匀[变]速。~ **microphone**【无】振速传声器。

ve·lo·drome [ˈviːləudrəum; ˋviləˏdrom] ***n.*** (自行车等的)倾斜赛车场。

ve·lom·e·ter [viˈlɔmitə; vɪˋlɑmətɚ] ***n.*** 速度计;【海】(轮船用)调速器;【空】升力系数指示器。

ve·lour, ve·lours [vəˈluə; vəˋlʊr] ***n.*** **1.** 丝绒;天鹅绒;棉绒。**2.** 绒皮帽 (= ~ hat)。**3.** (制皮帽用的兔、海狸等的)毛皮。

ve·lou·té [viluːˈtei; vəˏluˋte] ***n.*** 〔F.〕奶油,鲜肉[鱼]调味汁[肉汁或鱼汁中加面粉和奶油调浓而成] (= valouté sauce)。

ve·lou·tine [vəluˈtiːn; vəluˋtin] ***n.*** 〔F.〕绒面呢。

vel·skoen [ˈvelˌskjuːn, ˈfel-; ˋvelˏskjun, ˋfɛl-] ***n.*** 〔*pl.*〕南非粗皮鞋〔非洲南部人穿用的未经鞣制的皮鞋〕(= veldskoen)。

ve·lum [ˈviːləm; ˋviləm] ***n.*** (*pl.* ***ve·la*** [ˈviːlə; ˋvilə]) **1.**【解、动】帆;软腭;膜,缘膜;(水母类的)边膜,游泳盘;膜突。**2.**【植、生】(唇形花的)小唇;菌幕。

vel·ure [vəˈljuə; vəˋljʊr] **I** ***n.*** **1.** 天鹅绒;似天鹅绒的织物。**2.** 绒垫子。**II** ***vt.*** 用丝绒装饰[擦](帽子)。

ve·lu·ti·nous [vəˈljuːtinəs; vɪˋljutɪnəs] ***a.***【植、动】有短绒毛的;天鹅绒似的 (= velvety)。

vel·ver·et [ˈvelvərit; ˏvɛlvəˋrɛt] ***n.*** 粗天鹅绒。

vel·vet [ˈvelvit; ˋvɛlvɪt] **I** ***n.*** **1.** 丝绒,天鹅绒,天鹅绒一样的东西[表面];天鹅绒海绵 (= ~ sponge)。**2.** 鹿角上的绒毛状嫩皮,鹿茸的嫩皮。**3.**〔俚〕(赌博中)赢得的钱;盈利,赚头。**4.**〔口〕舒适愉悦的景况。*cotton* ~棉天鹅绒。*silk* ~(反面是棉的)丝(天鹅)绒。*cut* ~修剪过的天鹅绒。*pile* [*terry*] ~没有剪毛的天鹅绒。~ *pile* 天鹅绒一样的织品。***be on*** ~= ***stand on*** ~在有利地位上,(现在主指投机)在必赚地位上。***to the*** ~【商】给贷方。**II** ***a.*** 天鹅绒制的;天鹅绒似的,柔软的;(脚声等)轻软的。***a*** [***the***] ~ ***glove*** 丝绒手套 (*an iron hand in a* ~ *glove* 外柔内刚。*handle with a* ~ *glove* 用外柔内刚的手段处理)。***a*** ~ ***paw*** 猫脚;隐藏的[外貌和善的]残忍。~ **ant**【动】蚁蜂。~ **bean**【植】绒毛黧豆。**V- Divorce** 天鹅绒分裂[指 1993 年捷克和斯洛伐克和平地分裂为两个独立国家]。**V- Revolution**, ~ **revolution** 天鹅绒革命[指 1989 年秋季捷克斯洛伐克未经流血的政权易手]。

vel·vet·een [ˈvelviˈtiːn; ˏvɛlvəˋtin] ***n.*** **1.** 棉(天鹅)绒,假天鹅绒,平绒。**2.** 〔*pl.*〕棉(天鹅)绒裤。**3.** 〔*pl.*〕猎场看守(人)。

vel·vet·ing [ˈvelvitiŋ; ˋvɛlvɪtɪŋ] ***n.*** **1.** 天鹅绒的绒毛。**2.** 〔*pl.*〕〔集合词〕天鹅绒制品。

vel·ve·ty [ˈvelviti; ˋvɛlvɪtɪ] ***a.*** **1.** 天鹅绒似的;柔软的。**2.** (酒等)温和的,可口的。

Ven. = **1.** Venerable. **2.** Venice.

ve·na [ˈviːnə; ˋvinə] ***n.*** (*pl.* ***ve·nae*** [-niː; -ni]) 〔L.〕静脉。~ **cave**【解】大静脉,腔静脉。

ve·nal [ˈviːnl; ˋvinl] ***a.*** **1.** (地位、选票等)可用金钱得来的,能收买的。**2.** (人等)贪财的,贪污的,腐败的。**-ly** ***ad.***

ve·nal·i·ty [vi(ː)ˈnæliti; viˋnælətɪ] ***n.*** 贪财,见利忘义;贪污,受贿。

ve·nat·ic, -al [viˈnætik, -əl; viˋnætɪk, -l] ***a.*** 〔罕〕狩猎的,狩猎用的。

ve·na·tion [viːˈneiʃən; viˋneʃən] ***n.*** 脉络,纹理;【植】脉理,脉序;【昆】脉相;〔集合词〕叶脉,翅脉。

vend [vend; vɛnd] ***vt.***, ***vi.*** **1.** 卖,出售〔主要为法律用语〕。**2.** 贩卖,叫卖(小商品)。**3.** 发表(意见,言论)。

ven·dace [ˈvendeis, ˈvendis; ˋvɛndes, ˋvɛndɪs] ***n.*** (*pl.* ~, ***-dac·es***) 英白鲑 (*Coregonus vandesius*)〔产于英格兰和苏格兰的少数湖中〕。

Ven·dée [vɑːnˈdei; ˏvɑ̃ˋde] ***n.*** (法国西部的)旺代省;(1793—1796 年间的)旺代保皇党的叛乱。**Ven·de·an** [venˈdiːən; vɛnˋdiən] **1.** ***a.*** 旺代省(人)的。**2.** ***n.*** 旺代省人,旺代保皇党成员。

ven·dee [venˈdiː; vɛnˋdi] ***n.***【法】买主,买受人。

vend·er [ˈvendə; ˋvɛndɚ] ***n.***【法】出卖人;叫卖商,负贩。

ven·det·ta [venˈdetə; vɛnˋdɛtə] ***n.*** (特指意大利某些地区和 Corsica 岛的)族间世仇;族间仇杀;长期争斗。**-tist** ***n.***

vend·i·ble [ˈvendəbl; ˋvɛndəbl] **I** ***a.*** 可以出卖的;有销路的。**II** ***n.*** 〔主 *pl.*〕可卖物品。**-bil·i·ty** [ˌvædəˈbiliti; ˏvɛndəˋbɪlətɪ] ***n.*** **-bly** ***ad.***

ven·di·tion [venˈdiʃən; vɛnˋdɪʃən] ***n.*** 卖,出售。

ven·dor [ˈvendɔː; ˋvɛndɚ] ***n.*** **1.** = vender. **2.** 自动售货机 (= vending machine)。*street* ~*s* 摊贩。

ven·due [venˈdjuː; vɛnˋdju] ***n.*** 〔美〕公开拍卖。

ve·neer [vəˈniə; vəˋnɪr] **I** ***n.*** **1.** 镶面板;表层饰板;镶饰表面的东西,表面镶饰;饰面,护面。**2.** 外饰,虚饰。*a thin* ~ *of respectability* 薄薄的一层表面尊严。*barbarians with a* ~ *of culture* 披着文化外皮的野蛮人。**II** ***vt.*** 在…盖镶片,在…盖镶板,(用象牙、大理石、珍珠等)镶盖(木、石等);虚饰,粉饰。~ **sheet** 层板,胶合板。

ve·neer·ing [vəˈniəriŋ; vəˋnɪrɪŋ] ***n.*** **1.** 镶盖术,镶木术,镶面。**2.** 胶合薄片料,镶木,镶盖板。

ven·e·nate [ˈvenineit; ˋvɛnɪnet] **I** ***vt.*** 使中毒。— ***vi.*** (虫等在吮血时)放出毒液。**II** ***a.*** **1.** 中毒的。**2.** 有毒的。

ven·e·na·tion [ˌveniˈneiʃən; ˏvɛnɪˋneʃən] ***n.***【医】中毒。

ve·nene [vəˈniːn; vəˋnin] ***n.***【生化】蛇毒。

ven·en·ous [ˈveninəs; ˋvɛnɪnəs] ***a.*** 有毒的。

ven·e·punc·ture [ˈveniˌpʌŋktʃə, ˌviːni-; ˏvɛnəˋpʌŋktʃɚ] ***n.***【医】静脉穿刺术 (= venipuncture)。

ven·er·a·ble [ˈvenərəbl; ˋvɛnərəbl] ***a.*** **1.** 可尊敬的;〔特指〕年高而值得尊敬的,年高德劭的。**2.** 森严的,(神殿)神圣的,古老的;历史悠久的,有来历的。**3.** 基督教会一种尊称〔英国国教中对副主教;天主教对最低一级圣徒,略作 Ven.〕。*your* ~ *father* 令尊。~ *age* 高龄。~ *antiquity* 太古。*a* ~ *commander* 老司令官。*a* ~ *building* 古建筑物。~ *relics* 古代文物。*a* ~ *oak* 古槲。**-a·bil·i·ty** ***n.*** **-a·bly** ***ad.***

ven·er·ate [ˈvenəreit; ˋvɛnəˏret] ***vt.*** 尊敬;尊崇。

ven·er·a·tion [ˌvenəˈreiʃən; ˏvɛnəˋreʃən] ***n.*** 尊敬;尊崇。

ven·er·a·tor [ˈvenəreitə; ˋvɛnəretɚ] ***n.*** 尊敬者,崇拜者。

ve·ne·re·al [viˈniəriəl; vəˋnɪrɪəl] ***a.*** **1.** 性交的;因性交发生的。**2.** 性病的。**3.** (药)治性病的。**4.** 引起性欲的。~ *desire* 性欲。*a* ~ *disease* 性病〔略 V.D.〕。

ve·ne·re·ol·o·gy [viˌniəriˈɔlədʒi; vɪˏnɪrɪˋɑlədʒɪ] ***n.***【医】性病学。**-gist** ***n.*** 性病学专家。

ven·er·y¹ [ˈvenəri; ˋvɛnərɪ] ***n.*** 〔古〕性欲;性交;纵欲。

ven·er·y² [ˈvenəri; ˋvɛnərɪ] ***n.*** 〔古〕狩猎。

ven·e·sec·tion [ˌveniˈsekʃən; ˏvɛnɪˋsɛkʃən] ***n.***【医】静脉切开(放血)术。

Ve·ne·tian [viˈniːʃən; vəˋniʃən] **I** ***a.*** 威尼斯(式)的。**II** ***n.*** **1.** 威尼斯 (Venice) 人。**2.** 〔或作 v-〕= ~ blind. **3.** 〔v-〕直贡呢,威尼斯缩绒呢。~ **blind**【建】威尼斯式软百叶帘,板帘。~ **carpet** (铺走廊等的)威尼斯地毯。~ **chalk**【裁缝】(划线用的)滑石。~ **glass** 威尼斯玻璃器皿[料器]。~ **mast** (装饰街市的)彩色饰柱。~ **pearl** 人造珍珠。~ **red** 威尼斯红;褐红色。~ **school** (意大利文艺复兴时期的)威尼斯画派。~ **window**【建】三尊窗。

Ve·net·ic [viˈnetik; vɪˋnɛtɪk] ***n.*** 维尼提亚语〔一种灭绝了的意大利语言,留存于大约 200 篇短碑文中〕。

Ven·e·zue·la [ˌveneˈzweilə; ˏvɛnəˋzwilə] ***n.*** 委内瑞拉〔拉丁美洲〕。**-n** **1.** ***a.*** 委内瑞拉的;委内瑞拉人的;委内瑞拉文化的。**2.** ***n.*** 委内瑞拉人。

V

venge·ance [ˈvendʒəns; ˋvɛndʒəns] ***n*.** 报仇,复仇,报复。***exact a ~ from sb. for*** …对某人报…的仇。***inflict*** [***take***] ~ (***up***)***on*** 对…报仇[雪恨]。***with a ~*** 〔口〕猛烈地,厉害地;彻底地;过度地(*It rains with a ~*. 雨下得很凶)。***wreak ~ (up)on*** = *inflict ~ (up)on*.

venge·ful [ˈvendʒful; ˋvɛndʒfəl] ***a*.** 报仇心重的;报复性的;利于报复的。**-ly *ad*.**

V-en·gine [ˈviːˈendʒin; ˋviˋɛndʒɪn] ***n*.** (双汽缸排成 V 形的)内燃机,V 型发动机。

ve·ni·al [ˈviːniəl, -njəl; ˋvinɪəl, -njəl] ***a*.** 可原谅的;(罪过)不大的,轻微的(*opp*. deadly; mortal)。**-i·ty** [ˌviːniːˈæliti; ˏviniˋælətɪ] ***n*.** **-ly *ad*.** **-ness *n*.**

Ven·ice [ˈvenis; ˋvɛnɪs] ***n*.** 威尼斯〔意大利港市〕。*Gulf of ~* 威尼斯湾〔Adriatic Sea 的别名〕。~ **glass** = Venetian glass.

Ve·nik [ˈviːnik; ˋvinɪk] ***n*.** (前苏联的)金星探测器。

ven·in [ˈvenin; ˋvɛnɪn] ***n*.** 动物毒液中所含的毒素。

ven·i·punc·ture [ˌveniˈpʌŋktʃə, ˌvini-; ˏvɛnəˋpʌŋktʃɚ, ˏvinə-] ***n*.** 【医】静脉穿刺术。

ve·ni·re (fa·ci·as) [viˈnaiəri(ˈfeiʃiæs); vɪˋnaɪrɪ(ˋfeʃɪˏæs)] 〔L.〕【法】陪审员召集令。

ve·ni·re·man [viˈnaiərimən; vəˋnaɪrimən] ***n*.** (*pl*. ***-men***) 【法】候召陪审员。

ven·i·son [ˈvenizn; ˋvɛnəzn] ***n*.** **1.** 鹿肉。**2.** 野味。

ve·ni, vi·di, vi·ci [ˈveini ˈviːdiː ˈviːtʃiː, ˈweiniː ˈwiːdiː ˈwiːki, ˈviːnai ˈvaidai ˈvaisai; ˋvenɪ ˋvidi ˋvitʃi, ˋweni ˋwidi ˋwiki, ˋvinaɪ ˋvaɪdaɪ ˋvaɪsaɪ] 〔L.〕我来了,我见到了,我胜利了〔朱利乌斯·凯撒(Julius Caesar)向元老院报告胜利的文字〕。

ve·ni·te [viˈnaiti; vɪˋnaɪti] ***n*.** 【地】脉混合岩。

ven·om [ˈvenəm; ˋvɛnəm] **I *n*.** **1.** (毒蛇、蜘蛛等的)毒液;毒,毒物。**2.** 恶意,恶毒;怨恨;恶意行为;诽谤。*a ~ duct* [*fang*, *gland*] 毒管[牙,腺]。*a look of ~* 恶意的样子。**II *vt*.** 放毒。

ven·om·ous [ˈvenəməs; ˋvɛnəməs] ***a*.** **1.** 有毒的,分泌毒液的,有毒腺的。**2.** 恶意的,怀恨的。~ *snakes* 毒蛇。*a ~ attack* 恶毒的攻击。**-ly *ad*.** **-ness *n*.**

ve·nose [ˈviːnəus; ˋvinos] ***a*.** 【生】具脉的,翅脉的。

ve·nos·i·ty [viˈnɔsiti; vɪˋnɑsətɪ] ***n*.** 【生】具脉性,翅脉性。

ve·nous [ˈviːnəs; ˋvinəs] ***a*.** 静脉的;静脉中的。~ *blood* 静脉血。**-ly *ad*.**

vent [vent; vɛnt] **I *n*.** **1.** 孔,口,漏口,喷口,裂口;通风孔;(烟囱的)烟道;出气孔,喷气孔;排气孔[道]。**2.** (管乐器的)指孔。**3.** 炮眼,火门。**4.** 【动】(鸟、虫、鱼的)肛门。**5.** (感情等的)发泄,吐露。***find*** [***make***] ***a ~ in*** 在…上找到发泄处;出现在;发泄在。***find (a) ~ for*** 找到…的出气口。***give ~ to*** 发出,发泄,吐出(*give ~ to one's flames of anger* 发泄怒火,出气)。***take ~*** 泄漏于世;传播,被大家知道。**II *vt*.** **1.** 给…一个出口,在…上开孔。**2.** 放出,发出,发泄,吐露(感情)。*He ~ed himself in grief*. 他借发泄悲痛获得自慰。~ ***one's disgust on*** 向…发泄愤恨。~ ***itself*** 出来,出现;表现(*His anger ~ed itself in curses*. 他用咒骂来出气[发泄愤怒])。— ***vi*.** 〔英〕(水獭)露头呼吸。~ **gutter** 通风道。~ **hole** 通风孔;排气孔。~ **peg** (桶等的)气孔塞。~ **pipe** 排气[通风]管。~ **plug** **1.** 通气孔塞。**2.** (枪炮的)火门塞。

vent. = ventilation.

vent·age [ˈventidʒ; ˋvɛntɪdʒ] ***n*.** **1.** 小孔;出口;排气[排水(等)]口。**2.** (感情的)发泄。**3.** (笛的)指孔。*give ~ to anger* 发怒。

ven·tail [ˈventeil; ˋvɛntel] ***n*.** (可移动,用以通气的)盔弁,盔的护面。

ven·ter[1] [ˈventə; ˋvɛntɚ] ***n*.** **1.** 【解】腹部;(鸟的)下腹;【虫】腹部,腹面。**2.** 【法】母,胎。*a son by another ~* = *the son of another ~* 异母子。*brothers of same ~* 同母[同产]兄弟。

ven·ter[2] [ˈventə; ˋvɛntɚ] ***n*.** **1.** 打孔者;钻孔机。**2.** 发表错误或不正当言论者。

ven·ti·duct [ˈventidʌkt; ˋvɛntɪˏdʌkt] ***n*.** 【建】(地下)通风管[道]。

ven·ti·fact [ˈventifækt; ˋvɛntɪfækt] ***n*.** 【地】风棱石,风磨石。

ven·ti·late [ˈventileit; ˋvɛntḷˏet] ***vt*.** **1.** 使通风,使换气;给…装置通风设备;在…上开气孔;使通气。**2.** 【医】使(血液)吸取氧气;用新鲜空气净化(血液)。**3.** 发泄(感情),发表(意见);公开讨论;让舆论来决定(问题等)。~ *a room by opening windows* 开窗使室内透气。*The lungs ~ the blood*. 肺以新鲜空气使血液净化。**ventilating shaft** 【采】通气井。

ven·ti·la·tion [ˌventiˈleiʃən; ˏvɛntḷˋeʃən] ***n*.** **1.** 通风,换气(法);通风装置。**2.** 发泄,发表;(问题的)公开讨论;诉诸舆论。

ven·ti·la·tive [ˈventileitiv; ˋvɛntəˏletɪv] ***a*.** 通风的,换气的。

vent·i·la·tor [ˈventileitə; ˋvɛntḷˏetɚ] ***n*.** 通风设备,换气装置;通风机;风箱;通风孔,通风管,气窗;(帽子等的)气孔。

ven·ti·la·to·ry [ˈventilətəri; ˋvɛntḷəˏtorɪ] ***a*.** **1.** 通风的,有通风孔的;换气的,有换气孔的。**2.** 【医】(给血液)充氧的。

ven·tral [ˈventrəl; ˋvɛntrəl] **I *a*.** 【解、动】腹(部、面)的;【空】机身的;【植】腹面的,前面的,下面的。**II *n*.** 【鱼】腹鳍。~ *fin* 腹鳍。~ *massage* 腹部按摩。**-ly *ad*.**

ven·tre à terre [ˈvɑːtrɑːˈtɛə; ˋvɑ̃trɑˋtɛr] 〔F.〕用全速,全速地。

ven·tri- *pref*. 腹: *ventri*cose.

ven·tri·cle [ˈventrikl; ˋvɛntrɪkḷ] ***n*.** 【解】室;心室。

ven·tri·cose [ˈventrikəus; ˋvɛntrɪˏkos], **ven·tri·cous** [-kəs; -kəs] ***a*.** 【动、植】一面膨的,半边膨起的;大腹便便的。

ven·tric·u·lar [venˈtrikjulə; vɛnˋtrɪkjəlɚ] ***a*.** **1.** 【解】(心)室的。**2.** 膨胀的。

ven·tric·u·los·to·my [venˌtrikjuˈlɔstəmi; vɛnˏtrɪkjəˋlɑstəmɪ] ***n*.** 【医】脑室开孔术。

ven·tric·u·lus [venˈtrikjuləs; vɛnˋtrɪkjələs] ***n*.** (*pl*. ***-u·li*** [-kjulai; -kjəlaɪ]) **1.** = ventricle. **2.** (昆虫的)胃;(鸟类的)砂囊。

ven·tri·lo·qui·al [ˌventriˈləukwiəl; vɛnˋtrɪləkwəl] ***a*.** 口技的,腹语的。**-ly *ad*.**

ven·tril·o·quism, ven·tril·o·quy [venˈtriləkwizəm, -kwi; vɛnˋtrɪləˏkwɪzəm, -kwɪ] ***n*.** 口技;腹语;腹语术。

ven·tril·o·quist [venˈtriləkwist; vɛnˋtrɪləkwɪst] ***n*.** 口技表演者,腹语(术)者。

ven·tril·o·quize [venˈtriləkwaiz; vɛnˋtrɪləˏkwaɪz] ***vt*., *vi*.** 用口技发(声),用腹语术讲(话)。

ven·tro·dor·sal [ˌventrəˈdɔːsl; ˏvɛntrəˋdɔrsḷ] ***a*.** 腹背面的。

ven·tro·lat·er·al [ˌventrəˈlætərəl; ˏvɛntrəˋlætərəl] ***a*.** 腹侧的。

ven·trot·o·my [venˈtrɔtəmi; vɛnˋtrɑtəmɪ] ***n*.** 【医】剖腹术。

ven·ture [ˈventʃə; ˋvɛntʃɚ] **I *n*.** **1.** 冒险(行动),冒险事业;(商业)风险投资。**2.** 有风险物品〔船、船货、商品等〕;代销货;赌注。**3.** 〔古、罕〕幸运,偶然,侥幸。*joint ~* 合资经营。***at a ~*** 冒险,碰运气。***ready for any ~*** 不辞任何危险。**II *vi*.** 冒险,孤注一掷地试一试(*on*; *upon*),大胆…,胆敢…;冒着危险去;〔与不定式连用,缺乏自信时的谨慎说法〕奋勇,敢勇,十分冒昧。*I shall ~ on a mild protest*. 我要冒昧提一个温和的抗议。*Will you ~ on another glass of wine?* 再喝一杯葡萄酒怎么样? *I ~ to differ from you*. 对不起,我不同意你的

意见。*I hardly* ～ *to say it*, *but*....。我不敢跟你说,可是…。*May I* ～ *to ask your opinion*? 请问您的意见怎么样? *I* ～ *to say*. 我要大胆[冒昧]地说。— ***vt***. **1**. 冒险,敢…,大胆干,下决心干,(冒着危险把意见等)说说看,提出来看看。**2**. 拿(生命、财产等)冒险。*I won't* ～ *a step farther*. 我没勇气[不想]再上前一步了。～ *one's life for a cause* 为主义[事业]冒生命的危险。***Nothing*** ～, ***nothing have***. 不入虎穴,焉得虎子。～ **arbitrage** 冒险套汇[套利]。～ **buyout** 冒险收购。～ **capital** 〔美〕风险资本(投资)。**-r** [ˈventʃərə; ˋvεntʃərɚ] ***n***. 冒险者;投机者。

ven·ture·some [ˈventʃəsəm; ˋvεntʃɚsəm] ***a***. **1**. 冒险的,鲁莽的,大胆的,投机的。**2**. (有)危险的。**-ly** ***ad***. **-ness** ***n***.

ven·tu·ri [venˈtuəri; vεnˋturi] (**tube**) ***n***. 【物、机】文氏管,文土里流量计。

ven·tur·ous [ˈventʃərəs; ˋvεntʃərəs] ***a***. (爱)冒险的,大胆的,鲁莽的;危险性的。**-ly** ***ad***. **-ness** ***n***.

ven·ue [ˈvenjuː; ˋvεnju] ***n***. **1**. 【法】犯罪地点;现场;审判管辖区,审判地点;起诉书上对审判地点的指示。**2**. 〔俚〕(指定的)集合地点;立场,根据。*change the* ～变更审判地点。*lay* [*fix*, *place*] *a* ～指定审判地点。

ven·ule [ˈvenjuːl; ˋvεnjul] ***n***. **1**. 【解】小静脉。**2**. 【生】(叶的)细脉;(昆虫的)支脉。**ven·u·lar** [-julə; -jəlɚ] ***a***. **ven·u·lose** [-juˌləus; -jəˏlos] ***a***.

Ve·nus [ˈviːnəs; ˋvinəs] ***n***. **1**. 【罗神】维纳斯〔司爱和美的女神〕;维纳斯雕像[画像]。**2**. 美女,美人。**3**. 性爱,色情。**4**. 【天】金星,太白星。**5**. 【贝】帘介属。～**berg** 维纳斯山〔中世纪传说,维纳斯在此设有宫殿,引诱旅客〕。～**'s hair** 【植】掌叶铁线蕨。～**'s flower-basket** 【动】偕老同穴(海绵)。～**'s fly-trap** 【植】捕蝇草。～**'s-slipper** ***n***. = lady's-slipper.

Ve·nus·i·an [ˈviːnəsiən; vəˋnusɪən] **I** ***a***. 金星的。**II** ***n***. (科学幻想小说中的)金星人。

ver. = verse(s).

Ver·a[1] [ˈviərə; ˋvεrə] ***n***. 维拉〔女子名〕。

Ve·ra[2] [ˈviːrə; ˋvεrə] ***n***. 【无】(录放电视图像和声音的)电子录像机(= vision electronic recording apparatus)。

ve·ra·cious [vəˈreiʃəs; vəˋreʃəs] ***a***. **1**. 说真话的,诚实的,老实的。**2**. 真实的。**-ly** ***ad***.

ve·rac·i·ty [vəˈræsiti; vəˋræsətɪ] ***n***. **1**. 诚实。**2**. 确实;真实(性),正确(度),精确率。

Ver·a·cruz [ˈverəˈkruːz; ˋvεrəˋkruz] ***n***. **1**. 韦拉克鲁斯〔墨西哥港市〕。**2**. 韦拉克鲁斯〔墨西哥州名〕。

ve·ran·da(h) [vəˈrændə; vəˋrændə] ***n***. 游廊;走廊;阳台。

ve·rat·ri·dine [vəˈrætridiːn; vəˋrætrɪdin] ***n***. 【化】藜芦定。

... vεrəˏtrin, -tr... ***n***. ...atridine.

ver... ...trəm; vəˋretrəm] ***n***. **1**. 藜芦属植物 ...藜芦 (*V. album*) 和绿藜芦 (*V. virid*)]。**2**. 藜芦碱。

verb [vəːb; vɚb] ***n***. 【语法】动词。*strong* [*weak*] ～*s* 强[弱]变化动词。*substantive* [*copulative*] ～*s* 存在[连系]动词。

ver·bal [ˈvəːbəl; ˋvɚbl] **I** ***a***. **1**. 话的,言语(上)的;文字的;字句的,用字上的;口头的(*opp*. written)。**2**. (翻译等)逐字的。**3**. 【语法】(出自)动词的。*a* ～ *picture of a scene* 某一场面的文字描述。*a* ～ *note* 便条,字条;【外交】不署名备忘录,口头照会。*a purely* ～ *criticism* 纯言语上的批评。*a* ～ *agreement* [*contract*] 口头协议[约定]。*a* ～ *dispute* 口头争论,舌战。～ *evidence* 口头证据。*a* ～ *message* 口信。*a* ～ *translation* 逐字翻译,直译。**II** ***n***. 【语法】**1**. 非限定动词〔gerund, infinitive, participle〕。**2**. 〔罕〕= ～ noun. **3**. 〔美口〕口供。～ **nouns** 动名词〔infinitive 和 gerund 以及动词派生的名词〕。**-ism** ***n***. 言语表现,措词;咬文嚼字;赘语;措词啰嗦[冗长]。**-ist** ***n***. 善于措词用句的人;咬文嚼字的人;措词啰嗦的人。**-ize** **1**. ***vt***. 把…变成动词;用言语表现。**2**. ***vi***. 措词冗长。**-ly** ***ad***. **1**. 口头(上);用语言文字。**2**. 逐字地。**3**. 作为动词。

ver·bal·i·ty [vəˈbæliti; vɚˋbælətɪ] ***n***. (*pl*. ***-ties***) **1**. 冗词。**2**. 言语的表达。**3**. 动词的特性。

ver·ba·tim [vəːˈbeitim; vɚˋbetɪm] **I** ***ad***., ***a***. 逐字(的),一字不变地[的]。**II** ***n***. 逐字报告。

ver·ba·tim et lit·e·ra·tim [vəːˈbeitim et ˌlitəˈreitim; vɚˋbetɪm εt ˏlɪtəˋretɪm] 〔L.〕一字不改,完全照字面;逐字逐句。

ver·be·na [vəːˈbiːnə; vɚˋbinə] ***n***. 【植】美人樱,(戟叶)马鞭草。

ver·bi·age [ˈvəːbiidʒ; ˋvɚbɪɪdʒ] ***n***. **1**. (措词)啰嗦,冗长。**2**. 〔蔑〕风格,措辞。***to indulge in*** ～ 夸夸其谈。

ver·bid [ˈvəːbid; ˋvɚbɪd] ***n***. 【语法】动词性词,非限定动词〔指动名词、不定式和分词等非谓语形式〕。

verb·i·fy [ˈvəːbifai; ˋvɚbəˏfaɪ] ***vt***. 使动词化;把…用作动词。

verbi gratia [ˈvəːbi greiʃə; ˋvɚbɪ greʃə] 〔L.〕例如(= for example)〔略 v.g.〕。

ver·bose [vəːˈbəus; vɚˋbos] ***a***. (措词)啰嗦的,(说话)唠叨的;冗长的。**-ly** ***ad***.

ver·bos·i·ty [vəːˈbɔsiti; vɚˋbɑsətɪ] ***n***. 啰嗦,唠叨,冗长。

ver·bo·ten [fεəˈbəutən; fεrˋbotn̩] ***a***. 〔G.〕被禁止的。

verb. (***sat***) ***sap***. = ***verbum*** (***sat***) ***sapienti*** [ˈvəːbəm(ˈsæt)ˌsæpiˈentai; ˋvɚbəm(ˋsæt)ˏsæpɪˋεntaɪ] 〔L.〕对聪明人说一个字就够了(= A word is enough for the wise.);举一反三,不必多言。

ver·dan·cy [ˈvəːdənsi; ˋvɚdn̩sɪ] ***n***. **1**. 翠绿,新绿。**2**. 不成熟,无知,单纯,幼稚。

ver·dant [ˈvəːdənt; ˋvɚdn̩t] ***a***. **1**. 青葱的,绿叶繁茂的。**2**. 年轻不懂事的,没有经验的,幼稚的。～ **green** 浅绿,嫩绿(*Mr. V- green* 〔口〕幼稚的人)。**-ly** ***ad***.

verd an·tique [ˈvəːd ænˈtiːk; ˏvɚd ænˋtik] **1**. (古铜器上的)铜绿。**2**. (古罗马作室内装饰用的)绿斑蛇纹石。**3**. 【矿】古绿石,美斑石。

ver·der·er, ver·der·or [ˈvəːdərə; ˋvɚdərɚ] ***n***. 【英史】王室护林官。

ver·dict [ˈvəːdikt; ˋvɚdɪkt] ***n***. **1**. 【法】(陪审团的)评决,裁决。**2**. 判断,意见,决定。*the popular* ～ 公众的意见。*a* ～ *for the plaintiff* 原告胜诉的评决。*What is your* ～ *on the coffee*? 你觉得这咖啡怎么样? ***an open*** ～ 存疑裁决〔指判定某行为有罪而不确知犯人,或指死因未详的裁决〕。***a partial*** ～ 部分裁判〔只判定行为的一部分有罪〕。***a privy*** [***sealed***] ～ 密封裁决书〔陪审员在法官休庭后交给法院书吏的初步书面裁决〕。***a special*** ～ 特别裁决〔陪审团只提供已证明的事实,交由法庭进行判决〕。***bring in*** [***deliver***, ***give***, ***return***] ***a*** ～ ***of* 'not guilty'** (陪审团)评决无罪。***pass one's*** ～ ***upon*** 对…下判断。***to reverse the*** ～ 翻案。

ver·di·gris [ˈvəːdigris; ˋvɚdɪˏgris] ***n***. **1**. 铜绿。**2**. 【化】碱性碳[醋]酸铜。

ver·din [ˈvəːdin; ˋvɚdɪn] ***n***. 【动】黄头山雀(*Auriparus flaviceps*)〔产于美国西南部和墨西哥北部〕。

ver·di·ter [ˈvəːditə; ˋvɚdɪtɚ] ***n***. 铜盐颜料,碳酸铜。～ **blue** (蓝铜矿研制的)蓝色铜盐颜料。～ **green** (孔雀石研制的)绿色铜盐颜料。

ver·do·glo·bin [ˈvəːdəuˈgləubin; ˋvɚdoˋglobɪn] ***n***. 【化】绿球蛋白。

Ver·dum ***n***. **1**. [ˈveədʌn; vεrˋdʌn] 凡尔登〔法国城市〕。**2**. [vəːˈdʌn; vɚˋdʌn] 凡尔登〔加拿大城市〕。

ver·dure [ˈvəːdʒə, -djə; ˋvɚdʒɚ, -djɚ] ***n***. **1**. 青绿,新绿;青青的草木;新绿的嫩叶。**2**. 新鲜,生气;繁盛。**3**. 风景壁毯。

ver·dur·ous [ˈvəːdʒərəs; ˋvɚdʒərəs] ***a***. 〔诗〕青青的,翠

V

绿的;草木葱茏的。

Ver·ein [fəˈriːn, -ˈrain; fəˋraɪn, fɛrˋaɪn] ***n.*** 〔G.〕同盟,联盟,公会,协会,社,组。

verge[1] [vəːdʒ; vɝdʒ] **I** ***n.*** **1.** 边缘;(长草的)路边;(花坛的)镶边;界限,范围,境界。**2.** 权杖,节杖。**3.** 【建】饰柱;蝼羽〔凸出檐边的屋瓦〕。**4.** (钟表等的)轴。***bring sb. to the ~ of ...*** 使某人濒于…。***on the ~ of*** 将近(几岁);即将…,快要…(*He was on the ~ of betraying his secret.* 他险些儿[差点]泄露了秘密)。**II** ***vi.*** 接近,逼近,濒临。*~ on madness* 濒于疯狂。

verge[2] [vəːdʒ; vɝdʒ] ***vi.*** 向…倾斜,斜向;倾向,趋向。*~ to a close* 将近末了。*~ towards old age* 渐渐趋于老年。

ver·ger [ˈvəːdʒə; ˋvɝdʒɚ] ***n.*** **1.** 〔英〕(为主教、大学副校长等在举行仪式的行列中)执权标的人。**2.** 教堂管理人。

ver·glas [vɛəˈglɑː; vɛrˋglɑ] ***n.*** 地上薄冰,(薄)冰面。

ve·rid·ic, -i·cal [vəˈridik, -ikəl; vɪˋrɪdɪk, -ɪkəl] ***a.*** 〔常谑〕不骗人的;不说谎的,诚实的;真实的。**-ly** ***ad.***

ver·i·est [ˈveriist; ˋvɛrɪɪst] ***a.*** 〔very 的最高级〕极端的,彻底的,十足的。*the ~ rascal* 不可救药的恶棍。*The ~ baby could do it.* 最小的小孩也能做得到。***a ~ tyro*** 〔美运〕十足的生手。

ver·i·fi·a·ble [ˈverifaiəbl; ˋvɛrəˏfaɪəbl] ***a.*** 可证实的;可检验的;可考证的。**-bil·i·ty** [-ˈbiliti; -ˋbɪlətɪ] ***n.***

ver·i·fi·ca·tion [ˌverifiˈkeiʃən; ˏvɛrɪfɪˋkeʃən] ***n.*** **1.** 证实,证明,确定;核验,验证,核对;检验,校验。**2.** 【法】诉状[答辩书]结尾的举证说明。*~ of machines* 机器的校准[检定]。

ver·i·fi·er [ˈverifaiə; ˋvɛrəfaɪɚ] ***n.*** **1.** 证实者,确定者;核验者;证明者。**2.** 煤气计量器。**3.** 检验器;(计算数据的)核对器,核对员。

ver·i·fy [ˈverifai; ˋvɛrəˏfaɪ] ***vt.*** (***-fied***) **1.** 证实;证明,核验,核实,验证;校准。**2.** 【法】(用证据或宣誓)证实;在(诉状或答辩书结尾)提供举证说明。*verified statistics* 核实的(统计)数字。

ver·i·ly [ˈverili; ˋvɛrəlɪ] ***ad.*** 〔古〕真正地;肯定地;忠实地;真实地。

ver·i·sim·i·lar [ˌveriˈsimilə; ˏvɛrəˋsɪmələ] ***a.*** 好像真(实)的;可能的。**-ly** ***ad.***

ver·i·si·mil·i·tude [ˌverisiˈmilitjuːd; ˏvɛrəsəˋmɪləˏtjud] ***n.*** **1.** 貌似真实;逼真;可能性。**2.** 逼真的事物。

ver·ism [ˈviərizəm, ˈvɛərizəm; ˋvɪrɪzm, ˋvɛrɪzm] ***n.*** 写实主义〔尤指在歌剧艺术中优先采用日常生活题材的主张〕。**ver·ist** **1.** ***a.*** 写实主义的。**2.** ***n.*** 写实主义者。**ve·ris·tic** [viˈristik; vɪˋrɪstɪk] ***a.***

ver·is·mo [veiˈriːzməu; vɛrˋɪsmo] ***n.*** 〔It.〕= verism.

ver·it·a·ble [ˈveritəbl; ˋvɛrətəbl] ***a.*** 真实的,的的确确的,真正的。**-a·bly** ***ad.***

ve·ri·tas [ˈveritæs; ˋvɛrɪˏtæs] ***n.*** 〔L.〕**1.** 真理。**2.** = ***bureau ~*** 法国船舶协会。

ver·i·ty [ˈveriti; ˋvɛrətɪ] ***n.*** 真实(性);真实,真理。*the eternal verities* 永久不变的真理。***in all ~*** 确实〔发誓用〕。***in ~*** 真正,的确。***of a ~*** 〔古〕真正,的确。

ver·juice [ˈvəːdʒuːs; ˋvɝˏdʒus] ***n.*** **1.** 酸果汁。**2.** (脾气的)乖戾;(脸色的)阴沉;(情况的)别扭。

ver·meil [ˈvəːmeil; ˋvɝml, -mɪl] **I** ***n.*** **1.** 〔诗〕朱红色;【矿】朱砂。**2.** 镀金的银[青铜、铜]。**3.** 亮漆,清漆(= transparent varnish)。**II** ***a.*** 朱红色的,(嘴唇)鲜红的。

Ver·mes [ˈvəːmiːz; ˋvɝmiz] ***n.*** 〔***pl.***〕【动】蠕形动物,蠕虫类。

ver·mi- *comb. f.* 蠕虫: *vermi*an.

ver·mi·an [ˈvəːmiən; ˋvɝmɪən] ***a.*** 蠕虫类的,蠕虫一样的。

ver·mi·cel·li [ˌvəːmiˈseli, -ˈtʃeli; ˏvɝməˋsɛlɪ, -ˋtʃɛlɪ] ***n.*** 〔It.〕(用通心粉做的)细面条,挂面。

ver·mi·cide [ˈvəːmisaid; ˋvɝmɪˏsaɪd] ***n.*** 杀蠕虫剂;(特指)杀肠虫药;打虫药。**-ci·dal** ***a.***

ver·mic·u·lar [vəˈmikjulə; vɚˋmɪkjələ] ***a.*** **1.** 蠕虫(状)的;蠕动的。**2.** 虫蛀形的,虫迹形的。*~ motion* (肠子的)蠕动(作用)。*~* **appendix** [**process**]【解】阑尾。*~* **work** 虫迹形镶工,虫蛀形雕刻。

ver·mic·u·late [vəˈmikjulit; vɚˋmɪkjəˏlet] **I** ***a.*** **1.** 蠕虫状的;虫蛀(形)的,虫迹形的。**2.** 蠕虫多的。**3.** 〔罕〕转弯抹角的,婉转的,暗指的。**II** [-leit; -let] ***vt.*** 使成虫蛀状;给…作虫迹形装饰。— ***vi.*** 变成虫蛀形。

ver·mic·u·la·tion [vəˌmikjuˈleiʃən; vɚˏmɪkjəˋleʃən] ***n.*** **1.** 成蠕虫状,成虫迹状。**2.** 蛀迹,虫迹。**3.** 蠕动。

ver·mic·u·lite [vəˈmikjulait; vɚˋmɪkjəˏlaɪt] ***n.*** 【矿】蛭石。

ver·mi·cul·ture [ˌvəːmiˈkʌltʃə; ˏvɝmɪˋkʌltʃɚ] ***n.*** 蠕虫养殖业。

ver·mi·form [ˈvəːmifɔːm; ˋvɝməˏfɔrm] ***a.*** 蠕虫形状的。*~* **appendix**【解】阑尾。*~* **process**【解】**1.** 脑中叶。**2.** 阑尾。

ver·mi·fuge [ˈvəːmifjuːdʒ; ˋvɝməˏfjudʒ] ***n.*** 【医】驱虫药,打虫药。**-fu·gal** [-fjuːgəl; -fjugəl] ***a.***

ver·mi·grade [ˈvəːmigreid; ˋvɝmɪgred] ***a.*** 蠕动的,蜿蜒前进的。

ver·mil·(l)ion [vəˈmiljən; vɚˋmɪljən] **I** ***n.*** 银朱,朱砂;朱红色。**II** ***a.*** (涂)朱红色的。**III** ***vt.*** 染[涂]朱红色于。*~* **paint** 朱红涂料。

ver·min [ˈvəːmin; ˋvɝmɪn] ***n.*** 〔*sing.*, *pl.*〕**1.** 害虫;寄生虫;害兽,害鸟。**2.** (社会的)害人虫;歹徒,坏蛋。

ver·mi·nate [ˈvəːmineit; ˋvɝməˏnet] ***vi.*** 生(肠)虫;生害虫;生寄生虫。

ver·mi·na·tion [ˌvəːmiˈneiʃən; ˏvɝməˋneʃən] ***n.*** **1.** 生害虫。**2.** 寄生虫病,肠虫病。

ver·mi·no·sis [ˌvəːmiˈnəusis; ˏvɝmɪˋnosɪs] ***n.*** 蠕虫病;肠虫病;蠕虫[肠虫]病的蔓延。

ver·min·ous [ˈvəːminəs; ˋvɝmɪnəs] ***a.*** **1.** 生虫的;害虫丛生的;蚤[虱等]多的;因害虫而引起的。**2.** 虫一般的,卑劣的,讨厌的。

ver·mis [ˈvəːmis; ˋvɝmɪs] ***n.*** (***pl.*** ***-mes*** [-miːz; -miz])【解】小脑蚓部。

ver·miv·o·rous [vəːˈmivərəs; vɚˋmɪvərəs] ***a.*** (鸟等)吃虫的。

Ver·mont [vəːˈmɔnt; vɚˋmɑnt] ***n.*** 佛蒙特〔美国州名〕。**-er** ***n.*** 佛蒙特州人。**-ese** [-tiːz; -tiz] **1.** ***a.*** 佛蒙特州(人)的。**2.** ***n.*** 佛蒙特州人。

ver·m(o)uth [ˈvəːməθ, ˈvəːmuːθ; ˋvɝməθ, ˋvɝmuθ; 老式读法 ˈvəːmuːt; ˋvɝmut] ***n.*** 苦艾酒。

ver·nac·u·lar [vəˈnækjulə; vɚˋnækjələ] **I** ***n.*** **1.** 本国语,本地话,土话;口语,日常语;方言。**2.** 行话;俗话;下流话。**3.** [illegible] ... *forcibly in the ~.* 他用下流话[illegible] **II** ***a.*** **1.** (语言等)本乡的;日常语的;民间的。**2.** 用当地语(土话)写的,用土话的;民间的[illegible] *~ language = the ~ tongue* 土话,口语,俗话(*opp.* literary [learned] language)。*the ~ Chinese* 中国白话文。*~ papers* 当地语报纸。*a ~ disease*【医】地方病。**-ism** ***n.*** 当地语(表达法);俗话(表达法);方言(表达法);土腔,土调。**-ize** ***vt.*** **1.** 把…说成当地语。**2.** 使口语化。**3.** 用俗话说。**-ly** ***ad.***

ver·nal [ˈvəːnl; ˋvɝnl] ***a.*** **1.** 春的,春天似的;春天发生的;(花等)春天开的。**2.** 有生气的,朝气蓬勃的;青春的,青年的,妙龄的。*~ breezes* 春风。*~ flowers* 春天开的花。*the ~ spirits of youth* 青年人的朝气。*~* **equinox** [**point**] 春分(点)。**-ly** ***ad.***

ver·nal·ize [ˈvəːnəlaiz; ˋvɝnlˏaɪz] ***vt.*** 【植】催进发育;使春化,用春化处理。**ver·nal·i·za·tion** [ˌvəːnəlaiˈzeiʃən; ˏvɝnəlaɪˋzeʃən] ***n.*** 春化作用;春化处理。

ver·na·tion [vəːˈneiʃən; vɚˋneʃən] ***n.*** 【植】**1.** 芽型。**2.** 多叶卷叠式;幼叶卷叠式。

Vern(e) [vəːn; vɛrn] ***n.*** 弗恩〔男子名〕。

Ver·ner [ˈvəːnə; ˋvɛrnɚ] *n*. 弗纳〔姓氏〕。

ver·ni·cose [ˈvəːnikəus; ˋvɚnəkos] *a*. 【植】表面发光的。

ver·ni·er(scale) [ˈvəːniə; ˋvɚnɪɚ] *n*. 【机】游标(尺),微分尺,千分尺。~ **cal(l)iper** 游标卡尺。~ **condenser** 【电】微变电容器。~ **depth gauge** 【机】精密测深尺。~ **dial** 游标刻度盘。~ **rocket** 微调火箭发动机。

ver·nin [ˈvəːnin; ˋvɚnɪn] *n*. 【化】维尔宁,蚕豆嘌呤核苷。

ver·nis·sage [ˌvɛniˈsɑːʒ; ˏvɛrnɪˋsɑʒ] *n*. (*pl*. **-sages** [-ˈsɑːʒ; -ˋsɑʒ]) 美术展览会首日;预展〔正式开幕的前一日〕。

Ver·non [ˈvəːnən; ˋvɚnən] *n*. 弗农〔姓氏,男子名〕。

Ve·ro·na [vəˈrəunə, viˈrəunə; vəˋronə, veˋronɑ] *n*. 维罗纳〔意大利城市〕。

Ve·ro·nal [ˈverənl; ˋvɛrənl̩] *n*. 【药】佛罗拉〔巴比妥(barbital)的商品名,一种安眠药〕。

Ve·ro·ne·se [verəˈniːz; verəˋniz] **I** *n*. 〔*sing*., *pl*.〕意大利维罗纳(Verona)人。**II** *a*. 威洛纳的。

ve·ron·i·ca [vəˈrɔnikə; vəˋrɑnɪkə] *n*. **1**. 【植】婆婆纳(属);水苦荬(属)。**2**. = sudarium. **3**. 〔V-〕维罗妮卡〔女子名〕。

ver·ru·ca [veˈruːkə; vɛˋrukə] *n*. (*pl*. **-cae** [-siː; -si]) 【医】疣,瘊子;【动】肉赘;毛瘤。

ver·ru·ci·form [veˈruːsifɔːm; vɛˋrusɪˏfɔrm] *a*. 疣状的。

ver·ru·cose [veˈruːkəus; ˋvɛrʊˏkos] *a*. 多疣的。

ve·ru·cous [ˈverukəs; ˋvɛrukəs] *a*. 疣的;疣状的。

vers [vəːs; vɚs] *n*. 【数】= versed sine.

Ver·sailles [vɛəˈsai, vəːˈseilz; vɛrˋsaɪ, vɚˋselz] *n*. **1**. 凡尔赛〔法国城市〕。**2**. 凡尔赛宫。~ **Treaty** 凡尔赛和约〔1919 年 6 月签订,结束第一次世界大战〕。

ver·sant[1] [ˈvəːsənt; ˋvɚsənt] *a*. **1**. 熟悉…的,精通…的。**2**. 专心从事…的,关心…的。

ver·sant[2] [ˈvəːsənt; ˋvɚsənt] *n*. (山或山脉的)斜面;倾斜;山坡,山侧;坡度;(一个地区的)总倾斜度。

ver·sa·tile [ˈvəːsətail; ˋvɚsətaɪl] *a*. **1**. 多面手的,多才多艺的。**2**. 通用的,万能的。**3**. 〔罕〕易变的,多变的,反复无常的,三心两意的。**4**. 【动】(足趾等)可向前或向后转动的。**5**. 【植】丁字形的。*a* ~ *man* 多面手。*a* ~ *writer* 多才多艺的作家。**-ly** *ad*.

ver·sa·til·i·ty [ˌvəːsəˈtiliti; ˏvɚsəˋtɪlətɪ] *n*. **1**. 多面性;多才多艺。**2**. 易变性;反复无常。**3**. 可转性。

vers de so·cié·té [vɛr də sɔsjete; vɛr də sɑsjɛtɛ] 〔F.〕社交诗,诙谐俏皮的酬应诗(= society verse)。

verse [vəːs; vɚs] **I** *n*. **1**. 诗句,诗行。**2**. 诗篇;诗节。**3**. 韵文(*opp*. prose);诗,诗歌。**4**. (圣经的)节〔略 v.〕。**5**. 【宗】= versicle. **6**. 【乐】(赞美诗等的)独唱部。*blank* ~ 无韵诗。*elegiac* ~ 哀歌,挽歌。*free* ~ 自由诗。***give chapter and*** ~ ***for*** 注明(引用文句等的)章节[确切出处]。***in*** ~ 用诗写的,韵文的。***put*** [***turn***] ***into*** ~***s*** 把…写成诗。***set Greek*** [***Latin***] ~ 叫(学生)翻译希腊[拉丁]诗。**II** *vt*. **1**. 用诗表现。**2**. (把…)写成诗。— *vi*. 作诗。~**monger** 打油诗人,拙劣的诗人,作劣诗者。

versed[1] [vəːst; vɚst] *a*. 熟练的,精通的(*in*)。*be* (*well*) ~ *in* 通晓,精通,对…有造诣。

versed[2] [vəːst; vɚst] *a*. 【数】反,反转的。~ **cosine** 【数】余矢。~ **sine** 【数】正矢。

vers·et [ˈvəːset, ˈvəːsit; ˋvɚsɛt, ˋvɚsɪt] *n*. **1**. 短诗〔尤指宗教经典中的〕。**2**. (为管风琴谱写的)短插曲[序曲]。

ver·si·cle [ˈvəːsikl; ˋvɚsɪkl̩] *n*. 短诗;【宗】(牧师领唱或领读的)短句。

ver·si·co·lo(u)r [ˈvəːsikʌlə; ˋvɚsɪˏkʌlɚ] *a*. **1**. 杂色的,多色的。**2**. (因光的不同)颜色多变化的,变色的,虹色的。

ver·si·fi·ca·tion [ˌvəːsifiˈkeiʃən; ˏvɚsəfəˋkeʃən] *n*. **1**. 作诗(法);诗律。**2**. 韵文化。

ver·si·fi·er [ˈvəːsifaiə; ˋvɚsəˏfaɪɚ] *n*. **1**. 诗人;改写散文成诗的人。**2**. 打油诗人。

ver·si·fy [ˈvəːsifai; ˋvɚsəˏfaɪ] *vi*. (**-fied**) 作诗。— *vt*. **1**. 把(散文)改成韵文;改(散文)成诗。**2**. 用诗表达。

ver·sion [ˈvəːʃən; ˋvɚʃən] *n*. **1**. 翻译;译本,译文。**2**. (个人对某事的)说法,不同看法[意见]。**3**. 版本;形式,型;变形,变体。**4**. 改写本;经过改编的乐曲。**5**. 〔常 V-〕基督教《圣经》的译本。**6**. 表演。**7**. 【医】胎位倒转(术);子宫倾侧。*the Authorized V-* (詹姆斯王)钦定《圣经》英译本〔略 A.V.〕。*the Revised V-* 《圣经》英译修订本〔略 R.V.〕。*the dramatic* ~ *of a novel* 一部小说的戏剧改编本。*What is your* ~ *of the affair*? 你对于这件事的看法怎么样?

ver·si·tron [ˈvəːsitrən; ˋvɚsəˏtrɑn] *n*. 一种能测知远处温度轻微变动的仪器。

vers li·bre [vɛə ˈliːbr; ˏvɛr ˋlibr] *n*. 〔F.〕自由体诗。

vers li·brist(e) [vɛə ˈliːbrist; ˏvɛr ˋlibrɪst] *n*. 〔F.〕自由诗作者。

ver·so [ˈvəːsəu; ˋvɚso] *n*. (*pl*. ~**s**) **1**. (书的)左页,反页(*opp*. recto);封四,封底。**2**. (货币、金牌等的)反面,背面(*opp*. obverse)。

verst [vəːst; vɚst] *n*. 俄里〔=1.067 公里〕。

ver·sus [ˈvəːsəs; ˋvɚsəs] ***prep***. 〔L.〕**1**. (诉讼、运动等中的)对(= against)。**2**. 与…相对[相比]〔略作 v. 或 vs.〕。*Korea v. Japan* 【运】韩国对日本。*traveling by plane* ~ *traveling by train* 乘飞机与坐火车旅行的比较。

Vert. = Vertebrata.

vert[1] [vəːt; vɚt] *n*. **1**. 【英国山林法】林中草木(采伐权)。**2**. 【纹】绿色。

vert[2] [vəːt; vɚt] **I** *vi*. 〔英口〕改宗,改变信仰。**II** *n*. 改宗者;变节者;〔美〕改邪归正的人。

ver·te·bra [ˈvəːtibrə; ˋvɚtəbrə] *n*. (*pl*. **-brae** [-briː; -bri]) 【解】脊椎;椎骨。

ver·te·bral [ˈvəːtibrəl; ˋvɚtəbrəl] *a*. 脊椎的,椎骨的,由脊骨形成的。*the* ~ *column* 脊柱。

Ver·te·bra·ta [ˌvəːtiˈbreitə, -ˈbrɑː-; ˏvɚtəˋbretə, -ˋbrɑ-] *n*. 〔*pl*.〕【动】脊椎动物门。

ver·te·brate [ˈvəːtibrit; ˋvɚtəˏbret] **I** *n*. 【动】脊椎动物。**II** *a*. **1**. 有脊骨[脊椎]的;脊椎动物的。**2**. (作品等)结构严密的。**-d** *a*.

ver·te·bra·tion [ˌvəːtiˈbreiʃən; ˏvɚtəˋbreʃən] *n*. **1**. 脊椎形成,椎骨形成。**2**. 结构的严密性。

ver·te·bra·tus [ˌvəːtəˈbreitəs; ˏvɚtəˋbretəs] *a*. 【气】脊椎状云的。

ver·tex [ˈvəːteks; ˋvɚtɛks] *n*. (*pl*. ~**s**, **-ti·ces** [-tisiːz; -tɪsiz]) **1**. 顶(点),绝顶。**2**. 【解】颅顶,头顶;【天】天顶;【几】顶(点)。~ *of a cone* 锥点。~ *of an angle* 角的顶点。

ver·ti·cal [ˈvəːtikəl; ˋvɚtɪkl̩] **I** *a*. **1**. 垂直的,直立的,竖立的,纵的(*opp*. horizontal)。**2**. 顶上的,顶点的,绝顶的。**3**. 【解】头顶的。**4**. 【植】纵长的,直上的。*a* ~ *line* 垂直线,纵线。*a* ~ *section* 纵断面。*a* ~ *motion* 上下运动。*a* ~ *angle* 对顶角;顶角。~ *extent* 深度。~ *range* 纵度。**II** *n*. **1**. 垂直线;垂直面;垂直圈。**2**. 竖立位置。**3**. 【建】竖杆。~ **axis** 【数】(直)立轴。~ **circle** 【天】地平经圈。~ **combination** 【经】垂直统一管理〔指从生产一直到销售〕。~ **drill** 竖式钻床。~ **envelopment** 【军】(伞兵配合地上部队所成的)垂直包围。~ **erosion** 【地】向下浸蚀。~ **file** **1**. 直立式档案箱。**2**. 可供迅速查阅的资料。~ **fins** **1**. 【鱼】竖鳍。**2**. (飞机的)垂直尾翼。~ **fire** 【军】高角射击。~ **integration** = ~ combination. ~ **marketing** 垂直行销〔选定企业为其设计制造切合其需求之行销法〕。~ **plane** 垂直面,铅垂面。~ **rudder** 【空】纵舵,方向舵。~ **thinking** 按常识进行的思考。~ **turn** 【空】垂直旋转。~ **union** 同一工业部门内跨行业的工会(= industrial union)。**-ly** *ad*. **-i·ty** *n*.

V

ver·ti·ces [ˈvəːtisiːz; ˋvɝtɪˏsiz] ***n.*** vertex 的复数。

ver·ti·cil, -cel [ˈvəːtisil; ˋvɝtəsɪl] ***n.*** 【植、动】轮；环；轮生体；环生体；(昆虫的)触角毛轮。

ver·ti·cil·las·ter [ˌvəːtisiˈlæstə; ˏvɝtəsɪˋlæstɚ] ***n.*** 【植】1. 轮状聚伞花序。2. 轮伞。

ver·tic·il·late [vəˈtisilit, ˌvəːtiˈsileit; vɚˋtɪsəlɪt, ˏvɝtɪˋsɪlet] ***a.*** 【植】轮生的 (= verticillated)。**-la·tion *n.***

ver·tig·i·nes [vəːˈtidʒiniːz; vɚˋtɪdʒəˏniz] ***n.*** vertigo 的复数。

ver·tig·i·nous [vəːˈtidʒinəs; vɚˋtɪdʒənəs] ***a.*** 1. 滴溜溜转的，旋转的。2. 眩晕的，发晕的，眼花的；(高度等)使人眼花的。3. 迅速变动的；不稳定的。*a ~ wind* 旋风。**-ly *ad.***

ver·ti·go [ˈvəːtigəu; ˋvɝtɪˏgo] ***n.*** (*pl.* *~es*, ***-tig·i·nes*** [ˈvəːˈtidʒiniːz; vɚˋtɪdʒɪniz]) 【医】眩晕，眼花；【兽医】(马羊等的)晕倒症。

ver·tim·e·ter [vəːˈtimitə; vɝˋtɪmətɚ] ***n.*** 【空】升降速度表。

ver·ti·port [ˈvəːtipɔːt; ˋvɝtɪpɔrt] ***n.*** 垂直升降机机场。

ver·tu [vəːˈtuː; vɝˋtu] ***n.*** = virtu.

ver·vain [ˈvəːvein; ˋvɝven] ***n.*** 【植】马鞭草。

verve [vεəv, vəːv; vεrv, vɝv] ***n.*** 1. (艺术品等的)气韵，神韵。2. 活力，热情，生气。3. 〔古〕才能。

ver·vet [ˈvəːvit; ˋvɝvɪt] ***n.*** 【动】(非洲产)长尾黑颌猴。

ver·y [ˈveri; ˋvεrɪ] **I *ad.*** 1. 〔用于修饰形容词、副词或分词〕很，甚，颇，极，非常。2. 〔与否定词结合〕(不)怎样，(不)大。3. 〔在形容词最高级前以加强语气〕充分，完全，真，实在，正。*a ~ cold day* 很冷的一天。*I like it ~ much.* 我很喜欢它。*I am not ~ keen on going there.* 我不大想到那里去。*not of ~ much use* 不怎么有用。*It is the ~ last thing I expected.* 这完全出乎我意料之外。*my ~ own* 绝对是[完全是、实在是]我自己的(东西)。*Keep it for your ~ own.* 替你自己收下来吧。*I will do my ~ best.* 我要尽我的力量。*in the ~ same place* 就是在这同一个地方。*Very fine!* 〔常作反语用〕好极了！*Very good* [*well*]. 好的〔表示同意、承认，但 Very well 常作反语用，如：Oh, ~ well! if you insist. 你要是坚持，那就这样吧！(没有办法)〕。**II *a.*** (***ver·i·er***; ***-i·est***) 1. 真的，实在的，真正的；十足的。2. 〔加强语气，和 the, this, that 或 my, your, his 等连用〕那个，同一个，就是那个，正是那个；甚至于，连。3. 〔修饰作名词用的 many, few, little 等〕很，非常。*a ~ knave* 真正的恶棍。*A verier humbug would be hard to meet.* 比这个更坏的骗子恐怕没有了。*The veriest coward would fight.* 就是最懦弱的人也会起来反抗的。*He is the ~ man I saw yesterday.* 他就是我昨天看见的那个人。*He is the ~ picture of his father.* 他活像他父亲。*For ~ pity's sake have mercy.* 千万请饶了我吧。*That's the ~ thing!* 正是那个。*in the ~ act* 当场(被捕等)。*His ~ children despise him.* 连他的孩子也看不起他。*The ~ stones cry out.* 连石头也叫起来了。*V- few believe in it.* 很少人相信。~ **high frequency** 【讯】甚高频〔略 V.H.F., v.h.f.〕。~ **low frequency** 【讯】甚低频〔略 V.L.F., v.l.f.〕。

Ver·y [ˈveri; ˋvεrɪ] ***n.*** 维利〔姓氏〕。~ **light** 【海军】(用信号手枪射出的)维利式色光信号(弹)。~ **pistol** 【海军】维利式信号手枪。

ves·i·ca [veˈsaikə; vəˋsaɪkə] ***n.*** (*pl.* ***-cae*** [-siː; -si]) 【解】囊；膀胱；胆囊；(鱼的)鳔；【植】(孢粉的)气囊，小泡；泡囊。~ **piscis** (哥德式建筑、绘画的)双圆光轮。~ **urinaria** 【解】膀胱。

ves·i·cal [ˈvesikəl; ˋvεsɪkl̩] ***a.*** 【解】膀胱的。~ **calculus** 【医】膀胱(结)石。

ves·i·cant [ˈvesikənt; ˋvεsɪkənt] **I *n.*** 【医】发疱膏，糜烂剂。**II *a.*** 发疱的，(使)起疱的，糜烂性的。

ves·i·cate [ˈvesikeit; ˋvεsɪˏket] ***vt.***, ***vi.*** 【医】(使)起疱，(使)发疱，(使)糜烂。

ves·i·ca·tion [ˌvesiˈkeiʃən; ˏvεsɪˋkeʃən] ***n.*** 【医】发疱，糜烂。

ves·i·ca·to·ry [ˈvesikətəri; ˋvεsɪkəˏtorɪ] ***n.***, ***a.*** = vesicant.

ves·i·cle [ˈvesikl; ˋvεsɪkl] ***n.*** 囊，泡；【医】小水疱；【植、解】小泡；气泡囊；【地】气泡。*the seminal ~s* 精囊。

ve·sic·u·lar [viˈsikjulə; vəˋsɪkjulɚ], **ve·sic·u·late** [-leit; -let] ***a.*** (有)小泡的，多泡(状)的，起泡的；多孔(状)的，小囊(状)的。~ **emphysema** 【医】肺气肿。~ **lava** 多孔状熔岩。~ **murmur** 【医】肺泡呼吸音。~ **tissue** 泡沫组织。

ves·per [ˈvespə; ˋvεspɚ] **I *n.*** 1. 〔V-〕金星，太白星，长庚星；〔诗〕傍晚，黄昏。2. 【宗】晚祷钟 (= ~ bell)；〔*pl.*〕〔有时作 V-〕晚祷；晚祷时间；晚祷曲[词]。***Sicilian Vespers*** 西西里晚祷事件〔1282 年复活节翌日在西西里岛 Palermo 地方以晚祷钟声为信号驱杀法国人的事件〕。**II *a.*** 1. 夜晚的。2. 晚祷的。~ **sparrow** 【动】夜鸣鹀。~ **tide** 晚祷时间；晚上，黄昏。

ves·per·al [ˈvespərəl; ˋvεspərəl] **I *a.*** 〔罕〕傍晚的，黄昏的，晚祷的。**II *n.*** 【宗】1. 晚祷书。2. 祭坛罩布。

ves·per·tide [ˈvespətaid; ˋvεspɚˏtaɪd] ***n.*** 1. 晚祷时间。2. 黄昏；晚上。

ves·per·til·i·o·nid [ˌvespəˈtiliənid; ˏvεspɚˋtɪlɪənɪd] ***n.*** 【动】蝙蝠科 (*Vespertilionide*) 动物。

ves·per·tine [ˈvespətain; ˋvεspɚˋtaɪn], **ves·per·ti·nal** [ˌvespəˈtainəl; ˏvεspɚˋtaɪnəl] ***a.*** 1. 傍晚的，黄昏的。2. 【植】傍晚开花的；【动】傍晚出来(找吃)的。3. 【天】日没时没落的(星)。

ves·pi·a·ry [ˈvespiəri; ˋvεspɪˏεrɪ] ***n.*** 黄蜂窠[群]。

ves·pid [ˈvespid; ˋvεspɪd] **I *n.*** 【动】黄蜂科 (*Vespidoe*) 动物。**II *a.*** 黄蜂(科)的。

ves·pine [ˈvespain; ˋvεspaɪn] ***a.*** 黄蜂(似)的。

Ves·puc·ci [vesˈpuːtʃi; vεsˋputʃɪ], **Amerigo** (*Americus Vespucius*) 维斯普奇〔1451—1512，意大利商人、冒险家、航海家，一说 'America' 就是由他得名的〕。

ves·sel [ˈvesl; ˋvεsl] ***n.*** 1. 容器，器皿〔桶、钵、碗等〕。2. 船，舰；飞船。3. 〔喻、谑〕人。4. 【解、动】管，脉管，血管；【植】导管。*a coasting ~* 沿海商船。*a composite ~* 铁骨木船。*a sailing ~* 帆船。*a war ~* 战舰。*a ~ drawing twenty feet of water* 吃水二十英尺的船。*a ~ under way* 航行中的船。*a weak ~* 不牢靠的器皿；不能依靠的人。*the weaker ~* 女人，女性。*the lymphatic ~* 淋巴腺。***the ~s of wrath*** 遭天谴的人〔宗教说法，喻人为接受某种影响的容器〕。

vest [vest; vεst] **I *n.*** 1. 〔美〕背心；马甲。2. 〔英〕汗衫。3. 内衣、衬衣〔美国只指女人和孩子的〕。4. 女服胸前 V 形饰布。5. 〔古〕衣服；外衣，上衣；法衣；礼服。***play*** (***it***) ***close to the ~*** 把…保守秘密；避免不必要的危险。***pull down one's ~*** 〔美俚〕从容不迫；不乱说乱动(不多管闲事)；保持安静。**II *vt.*** 1. 授予，给与，赋与；【法】授与所有[行使]权。2. 使穿衣服，给穿上(法衣、祭服等)。3. 在(祭坛上)挂布。*be ~ed power to do sth.* 被授予做某事的权力。*~ sb. with authority* [*rights*] 授予某人权柄[权益]。— ***vi.*** 1. (权利、财产等)属于，归属 (*in*)。2. 穿衣服，穿祭服。*Upon the death of the father, the property ~ed in* [*upon*] *his son.* 父死后财产归属其子。~**-pocket *n.***, ***a.*** 背心口袋；袖珍的，小型的(照片，书等)。

Ves·ta [ˈvestə; ˋvεstə] ***n.*** 1. 【罗神】女灶神。2. 【天】四号小行星，灶神星。3. 【商】〔v-〕〔英〕一种涂蜡的短火柴，蜡火柴 (= wax ~)。

ves·tal [ˈvestl; ˋvεstl̩] **I *a.*** 1. 女灶神的；献身给女灶神的；修女的。2. 处女的，贞洁的。**II *n.*** 1. 灶神守护祭司〔四名守护女灶神神殿里永远点燃圣火的处女祭司之一，后减为一人，亦作 ~ virgin〕。2. 处女，贞洁的女子。3. 修女，尼姑。

vest·ed [ˈvestid; ˋvεstɪd] ***a.*** 1. 【法】既定的，既得的。2.

V

穿着祭服的。~ **interest** 1. 既得利益[权利]。2. 〔*pl*.〕既得利益集团。~ **rights** 既得权利〔尤指职工在达到退休年龄以前离职仍应获得的权利〕。

vest·ee [ves'tiː; vɛs'ti] *n*. 1. 女式小背心,假背心。2. 女服胸前 V 形饰布。

ves·ti·ar·y ['vestiεəri; 'vɛstɪ,ɛrɪ] I *a*. 衣服的,服装的;官服的;祭服的。II *n*. 1. 衣帽间。2. 教堂中放置法衣、圣物等的房间。

ves·ti·bule ['vestibjuːl; 'vɛstə,bjul] I *n*. 1. 门道,门厅。2. 〔美〕连廊,通廊〔客车车厢两头出入处〕。3.【解】前庭;(昆虫的)外生殖腔。II *vt*. 1. 给…设门廊。2. 用通廊连接(两节车厢等)。~ **car** = ~ train. ~ **door** 避风门。~ **school** (工厂训练新来工人的)工人训练所。~ **train** 〔美〕(各车相通的)连廊列车 (= 〔英〕 corridor train)。**ves·tib·u·lar** *a*.

ves·tige ['vestidʒ; 'vɛstɪdʒ] *n*. 1. 痕迹,遗迹;证据。2. 〔罕、诗〕足迹。3.【生】(退化器官的)残迹。4. 一点儿,丝毫〔通常带否定词〕。*without a ~ of clothing* 一丝不挂。*He has not a ~ of evidence for this assertion*. 他没有丝毫证据证明这个论断。**ves·tig·i·al** [ves'tidʒiəl; vɛs'tɪdʒɪəl] *a*. 1. 尚留有痕迹的。2. (器官)发育不全的,萎缩的,退化的。

ves·ti·ment ['vestimənt; 'vɛstəmənt] *n*. = vestment.

vest·ing ['vestiŋ; 'vɛstɪŋ] *n*. 1. 背心料子。2. (雇工)保留退休金的权利。

vest·ment ['vestmənt; 'vɛstmənt] *n*. 1. 衣服;外衣;制服。2. 礼服;法衣,弥撒祭服。3. 祭坛布。

ves·try ['vestri; 'vɛstrɪ] *n*. 1. 祭服室,祭具室。2. (教堂的)小礼拜室〔也用作事务室、星期学校教室等〕。3. 教区纳税人(代表);教区会(会议室)。~**man** 教区代表,教区委员。

ves·ture ['vestʃə; 'vɛstʃɚ] I *n*. 1. 罩衣;笼罩着的东西;〔诗〕衣服。2.【法】地面生长物〔树林除外〕。*a ~ of mist* 雾幕。*a ~ of verdure* 绿色的覆盖〔指原野上青翠的草木〕。II *vt*. 使穿衣服;(雾等)笼罩;覆盖。

Ve·su·vi·an [vi'suːviən, -vjən; və'suvɪən, -vjən] I *a*. 1. 维苏威 (Vesuvius) 火山的;火山(性)的。2. 突然暴发的。II *n*. 〔v-〕 1. (抽烟用的)耐风火柴。2.【矿】符山石〔又叫 vesuvianite〕。

vet[1] [vet; vɛt] I *n*. 〔口〕 = veterinarian. II *vt*. (*-tt-*) 〔口〕诊疗,治疗(马、狗等);〔口〕检查。— *vi*. 当兽医。

vet[2] [vet; vɛt] *n*. 〔美口〕 = veteran.

vet., veter. = veteran; veterinarian; veterinary surgeon.

vetch [vetʃ; vɛtʃ] *n*.【植】巢菜(属);箭筈豌豆,大巢菜,苕子。*common ~* 苕子。*hairy ~* 毛苕子。*Chinese milk ~* 紫云英。

vetch·ling ['vetʃliŋ; 'vɛtʃlɪŋ] *n*.【植】山黧豆(属);牧地香豌豆。

vet·er·an ['vetərən; 'vɛtərən] I *n*. 1. 老手,老练的人;老练的兵,老兵;有战斗经验的军人。2. 〔美〕复员军人,退役军人。3. 老树〔尤指胸径二英尺以上的〕。***put on the airs of ~s*** 摆老资格。***Veterans of Foreign Wars of the United States*** 美国海外退伍军人协会〔曾在海外作战的美国退伍军人组织,略作 V.F.W.〕。II *a*. 1. (尤指军事方面)老练的,经验丰富的;资格老的。2. 由老兵组织成的。~ *troops* 战斗经验丰富的军队。~ *skill* 熟练。~ *service* 多年的服务资历,老资格。*a ~ worker* 经验丰富的工人;老工人。**Veterans' Administration** 〔美〕退伍军人管理局。**Veterans' Day** 〔美〕退伍军人节 (11 月 11 日)。~**s' preference** 〔美〕对退伍军人的优待〔尤指文职官员选拔考试时的优先录取〕。

vet·er·i·nar·i·an [ˌvetəri'nεəriən; ˌvɛtərə'nɛrɪən] I *n*. 兽医。II *a*. = veterinary.

vet·er·i·na·ry ['vetərinəri; 'vɛtərə,nɛrɪ] I *a*. 兽医(学)的。II *n*. 兽医〔略 Vet., vet.〕(= ~ surgeon)。

vet·i·ver ['veitivə; 'vɛtəvɚ] *n*.【植】1. (东印度)香根草(岩兰草)(*Vetiveria zizanioides*)。2. 香根草根。

ve·to ['viːtəu; 'vito] I *n*. (*pl*. *~es*) 1. 否决;禁止。2. 否决权,禁止权。3. (行政机构反对立法机构所通过的法案时申述的)否决理由 (= ~ message)。*exercise one's ~* 行使否决权。*a pocket ~* 〔美〕(总统的)不签署议案,"口袋否决"。***put a*** [***one's***] ~ (***up***) ***on*** 否决,不批准。~ ***in detail***【法】部分否决(权)。II *vt*. 否决(议案等);不批准;禁止。**-er, -ist** *n*. 否决者。**-less** *a*. 无否决权的;不否决的。

vet·tu·ra [vet'tuːrɑː; vɛt'turɑ] *n*. (*pl*. ***-re*** [-rei; -re]) 〔It.〕(意大利式)四轮马车。

VEWS = very early warning system 极早期预警系统,超远程预警系统。

vex [veks; vɛks] *vt*. 1. 使烦恼,使苦恼;使焦急,使为难;使悲伤。2. 使恼怒,使生气〔主用被动语态〕。3. 〔诗〕使激荡,使汹涌。4. 纷纷议论;长期争论。*I shall be ~ed if you* ... 假若你…我就要生气了。*winds that ~ the sea* 使海洋澎湃汹涌湃的风。*a ~ed question* 为人长期争论的问题。***be ~ed at*** 对…生气;为…懊恼;因…为难。***be ~ed with sb. for*** 因某人…而发怒。***feel ~ed*** 生气;着急。***How ~ing!*** 真令人着急[生气]! ~ ***oneself*** 生气;不耐烦。

vex·a·tion [vek'seiʃən; vɛks'eʃən] *n*. 1. 苦恼,懊恼;烦恼;着急;生气。2. 苦恼[烦恼]的原因;使人生气的事情。*Much to my ~ I just missed a chance of visiting* .... 错过一个参观…的机会,真气人。

vex·a·tious [vek'seiʃəs; vɛks'eʃəs] *a*. 1. 令人烦恼[着急]的,气人的;令人恼火的。2. 混乱的,麻烦的。3.【法】(诉讼)无确实根据的,旨在使被告恼火的。*How ~ to miss one's train!* 没赶上火车真气人! ~ **suit**【法】缠讼〔旨在困扰对方的诉讼〕。**-ly** *ad*. **-ness** *n*.

vex·il·la [vek'silə; vɛk'sɪlə] vexillum 的复数。

vex·il·lar ['veksilə; 'vɛksələ] *a*. 1. (古罗马的)军旗的,旗帜的。2.【植】旗瓣的;【动】羽瓣的。

vex·il·la·ry ['veksiləri; 'vɛksə,lɛrɪ] I *a*. = vexillar. II *n*. 1.【古罗马】(编属某面军旗下的)旗兵。2. 持旗者;旗手。

vex·il·late ['veksilit; 'vɛksəlɪt] *a*. 1. 有(古罗马骑兵的)军旗的;(在同一面军旗下服役的)一队士兵的。2.【植】有旗瓣的;【动】有羽片的,有翈的。

vex·il·lum [vek'siləm; vɛk'sɪləm] *n*. (*pl*. ***-la*** [-lə; -lə]) 1.【古罗马】军旗;统属同一军旗下的部队。2.【宗】牧杖上的小旗;行列旒旗;行列十字架。3.【植】旗瓣;【动】翈,羽片;膨大附端。

VF = 1. very fair, very fine 很好〔作业批语〕。2. video frequency【无】(电视)视频。3. visual field 视野。4. fighter plane【美海军】战斗机。

VFR = visual flight rules【空】目视飞航规则。

VFR flight【空】目视飞航。

VFW, V.F.W. = Veterans of Foreign Wars 〔美〕参加过国外战争的退伍军人。

v.g. = 1. very good 很好。2. 〔L.〕 *verbi gratia* 例如 (= for example)。

VHF, vhf = very high frequency【无】甚高频。

VHS = video home system 录像家用系统,录像机的 VHS 制式。

VI = 1. viscosity index【油】黏度指数。2. volume indicator【无】音量计,音量指示器。3. Virgin Islands 维尔京群岛〔拉丁美洲〕。

Vi【化】元素 virginium (钫)的符号。

v.i. = 1. verb intransitive【语法】不及物动词。2. 〔L.〕 *vide infra* 见于,参看下文 (= see below)。

vi·a ['vaiə, 'viːə; 'vaɪə, 'viə] I *n*. 道路。II ***prep***. 1. 经过,经由,取道。2. 凭藉,以…为媒介,通过(某种手段)。~ *New York* 经由纽约。~ *airmail* 航空(邮递)。

vi·a ['vaiə; 'vaɪə] *n*. 〔L.〕 1. 道;路。2.【医】管道。~ **crucis** ['kruːsis; 'krusɪs] 十字架之路,苦难之路。**V-**

V

Lactea [ˈlæktiə; ˋlæktɪə] 银河。~ ***media*** [ˈmiːdiə; ˋmidɪə] 中间道路,中间路线。

vi·a·bil·i·ty [ˌvaiəˈbiliti; ˏvaɪəˋbɪlətɪ] ***n.*** (尤指胎儿或婴儿的)生存能力,生活力,成活力。

vi·a·ble [ˈvaiəbl; ˋvaɪəbl] ***a.*** **1.** 能养活的,能成活的;能生存的;有生活力的;能生长的。**2.** 可行的。~ **count** 活菌计数。

vi·a·duct [ˈvaiədʌkt; ˋvaɪəˏdʌkt] ***n.*** **1.** (山谷中的)高架桥,跨线桥,旱桥。**2.** 高架铁路[公路];栈道。**3.**【美拳】鼻。

Vi·ag·ra [vaiˈægrə; vaɪˋægrə] ***n.***【药】伟哥〔一种阳痿治疗药〕。

vi·a·graph [ˈvaiəgrɑːf, -græf; ˋvaɪəˏgræf, -ˏgrɑf] ***n.*** 道路阻力测定器〔测定道路的坡度、路面对车辆的阻力〕。

vi·al [ˈvaiəl; ˋvaɪəl] ***n.*** (小)玻璃瓶;药水瓶;管(状)瓶。***pour out the ~s of*** (***one's***) ***wrath*** (***up***) ***on*** 向…报仇;〔口〕找…发泄怒气。

vi·am·e·ter [vaiˈæmitə; vaɪˋæmətɚ] ***n.*** 路程计 (= hodometer)。

vi·and [ˈvaiənd; ˋvaɪənd] ***n.*** **1.** (一件)食品。**2.** 〔*pl.*〕菜肴,佳肴;食物。

vi·at·ic [vaiˈætik; vaɪˋætɪk] ***a.*** 道路的;旅行的,旅途的。

vi·at·i·cal [vaiˈætikəl; vaɪˋætəkl̩] **I** ***a.*** 道路的;旅行的。**II** ***n.*** 〔*pl.*〕旅行所必需之物〔尤指行军的辎重〕。~ **settlement** 临终保险安排〔指以现金支付人寿保险部份保险金,以换取死后的抚恤金〕。

vi·at·i·cum [vaiˈætikəm; vaɪˋætɪkəm] ***n.*** **1.**【古罗马】(官员出差的)旅费[供应品]。**2.** 旅行的用费[用品]。**3.** 〔常 V-〕【天主】临终的圣餐。**4.**【天主】活动祭坛〔常置于临终者床侧〕。

vi·a·tor [vaiˈeitə; vaɪˋetɚ] ***n.*** (*pl.* ***-tor·es*** [ˌvaiəˈtɔːriːz; ˏvaɪəˋtɔriz]) 旅行者,走路的人,徒步旅行者。

vibes [ˈvaibz; ˋvaɪbz] ***n.*** *pl.* **1.** 〔美口〕= vibraphone. **2.** 〔美俚〕= vibration.

vib·ist [ˈvaibist; ˋvaɪbɪst] ***n.*** = vibraphonist.

vi·brac·u·lum [vaiˈbrækjuləm; vaɪˋbrækjʊləm] ***n.*** (*pl.* ***-la*** [-lə; -lə])【动】振鞭体;鞭器。**-u·lar** ***a.***

vi·bra·harp [ˈvaibrəˈhɑːp; ˋvaɪbrəˋhɑrp] ***n.*** = vibraphone.

vi·brance, vi·bran·cy [ˈvaibrəns, -si; ˋvaɪbrəns, -sɪ] ***n.*** 振动;颤动;响亮;活跃。

vi·brant [ˈvaibrənt; ˋvaɪbrənt] **I** ***a.*** **1.** 振动的,颤动的。**2.** 振响的;响亮的。**3.** 精神振奋的,生气勃勃的。**4.**【语音】振动声带发出的,有声音的。*cities ~ with life and energy* 生气勃勃的城市。**II** ***n.***【语音】有声音 (*opp.* surd)。**-ly** ***ad.***

vi·bra·phone [ˈvaibrəfəun; ˋvaɪbrəfon] ***n.***【乐】电颤琴〔型似木琴,共鸣器有电动阀门产生颤音〕。**-phon·ist** ***n.*** 电颤琴演奏者。

vi·brate [vaiˈbreit, ˈvaib-; ˋvaɪbret] ***vi.*** **1.** 摇动,振动;颤动。**2.** 心中打颤,胸口噗噗地跳;精神振奋。**3.** 振响,反响。**4.** (像钟摆一样地)摆动;〔罕〕动摇,犹豫。— ***vt.*** **1.** 使摇动;使振动;使颤动;使摆动。**2.** 振动着发出(声音,光);摆动着表示。*a vibrating type regulator*【机】摆动式调节器。

vi·bra·tile [ˈvaibrətail; ˋvaɪbrətaɪl] ***a.*** 能振动的;颤动性的。~ *cilia* 颤动纤毛。**-til·i·ty** [ˌvaibrəˈtiliti; ˏvaɪbrəˋtɪlətɪ] ***n.*** 振动性,颤动性。

vi·bra·tion [vaiˈbreiʃən; vaɪˋbreʃən] ***n.*** **1.** 振动,颤动;摆动;【物】振动。**2.** (心的)震颤。**3.** (思想情绪的)激动。**4.** 犹豫。*the amplitude of ~*【物】振幅。*the ~ period = the period of ~* 振动周期。~**-proof** ***a.*** 耐振的,防振的。**-al** ***a.***

vi·bra·ti·un·cle [vaiˈbreiʃiˌʌŋkəl; vaɪˋbreʃɪˏʌŋkl̩] ***n.*** 轻微的震动。

vi·bra·tive [vaiˈbreitiv; ˋvaɪbrətɪv] ***a.*** = vibratory.

vi·bra·to [viˈbrɑːtəu; vɪˋbrɑto] ***n.*** (*pl.* ~***s***) 〔It.〕【乐】(演奏[演唱]时的)颤动效果;轻微颤音。

vi·bra·tor [vaiˈbreitə; ˋvaɪbretɚ] ***n.*** **1.** (使)振动的人[物]。**2.**【电】振子。**3.** 振动器[装置];【建】(混凝土)振捣器。**4.**【医】颤振按摩器。**5.**【印】振动滚筒。**6.**【乐】(风琴等的)簧。

vi·bra·to·ry [ˈvaibrətəri; ˋvaɪbrəˏtorɪ] ***a.*** (使)振动的;振动(性)的。~ *motion* 振动。

vib·ri·o [ˈvibriəu; ˋvɪbrɪˏo] ***n.*** (*pl.* ~***s***)【生】弧菌属细菌〔如霍乱弧菌 (*Vibrio comma*)〕。

vi·bris·sa [vaiˈbrisə; vaɪˋbrɪsə] ***n.*** (*pl.* ***-sae*** [-siː; -si]) **1.** 鼻毛。**2.** 触毛,触须。**3.** (鸟的)羽须。

vi·bro·graph [ˈvaibrəgrɑːf; ˋvaɪbrəˏgrɑf] ***n.***【物】示振器;震动计。

vi·broll [ˈvaibrəul; ˋvaɪbrol] ***n.*** 震动压路机。

vi·bron·ic [vaiˈbrɔnik; vaɪˋbrɑnɪk] ***a.*** 电子振动的。

vi·bro·pack [ˈvaibrəpæk; ˋvaɪbrəpæk] ***n.***【电】振动子整流器[换流器]。

vi·bro·scope [ˈvaibrəskəup; ˋvaɪbrəˏskop] ***n.*** 振动计,示振仪。

vi·bro·shock [ˈvaibrəʃɔk; ˋvaɪbrəʃɑk] ***n.*** 减振器,缓冲器。

vi·bro·tron [ˈvaibrətrɔn; ˋvaɪbrətrɑn] ***n.***【电】振敏管。

vi·bur·num [vaiˈbəːnəm; vaɪˋbɝnəm] ***n.***【植】荚蒾(属)。~ *sargenti*【药】鸡树条。

vic [vik; vɪk] ***n.*** **1.** 〔美俚〕犯人 (= convict)。**2.** 〔英空俚〕V 字队形〔因信号兵把 V 读作 vik〕。

Vic. = **1.** Vicar. **2.** Victor. **3.** Victoria(n).

vic·ar [ˈvikə; ˋvɪkɚ] ***n.*** **1.** 教区牧师;〔美〕教堂牧师。**2.**【天主】教皇。**3.** 教皇[主教]代理。**4.** 〔诗〕代理人。**5.**【生】代换种〔和其他同宗相传的物种分开培育而获得的变种〕。*a ~ of Bray* 随风转舵的人,两面派。*the V- of Christ*【天主】教皇。~ **apostolic**【天主】(在传教地区代表教皇的)名誉主教。~**-general** **1.** (英国国教在诉讼事务等方面协助大主教或主教的)代理监督。**2.**【天主】教区代理主教。

vic·a·rage [ˈvikəridʒ; ˋvɪkərɪdʒ] ***n.*** 教区牧师的薪俸[住宅、职位]。

vi·car·i·al [vaiˈkeəriəl, vi-; vaɪˋkɛrɪəl, vɪ-] ***a.*** **1.** 教区牧师的。**2.** 执行教区牧师职务的。**3.** 代理的。

vi·car·i·ate [vaiˈkeərit, -ˌeit; vaɪˋkɛrɪt, -ˏet] ***n.*** **1.** 教区牧师的职权。**2.** 教区牧师管辖的教区。

vi·car·i·ous [vaiˈkeəriəs; vaɪˋkɛrɪəs, vɪ-] ***a.*** **1.** 代理(人)的。**2.** 替代(别人)的;做替身的;(想像别人的苦乐而)产生同感[共鸣]的。**3.**【医】替代(性)的。~ *authority* 代理职权。~ *haemorrhage*【医】替代性出血。**-ly** ***ad.*** **-ness** ***n.***

vice[1] [vais; vaɪs] ***n.*** **1.** 罪恶,不道德;缺德行为;恶习,坏习惯;(马等的)恶癖。**2.** (人格、文体等的)缺点,瑕疵,毛病。**3.** (肉体的)缺陷,疾病。**4.** 〔the V-〕(英国劝善剧中)道德败坏的丑角。*virtue and ~* 善与恶,德行与邪恶。~ *of intemperance* 嗜酒。~ **squad** 〔美〕风化纠察队〔取缔卖淫、赌博的警察〕。**-less** ***a.***

vice[2] [vais; vaɪs] **I** ***n.***【机】老虎钳,轧钳。*a grip like a ~* 像老虎钳一般的紧握。**II** ***vt.*** 用老虎钳夹紧;钳制。

vice[3] [vais; vaɪs] ***n.*** 〔口〕= vice-chancellor, vice-president 等。

vi·ce[4] [ˈvaisi; ˋvaɪsɪ] ***prep.*** 代,代替。*He was gazetted as captain ~ Captain Jones promoted.* 公报上刊载他被任为上尉以代替迁升的琼斯上尉。

vice- [vais; vaɪs] ***pref.*** 〔用于表示职位的名词前〕副,代理,次。~**-admiral** 海军中将。~**-chairman** 副主席,副会长,副委员长,副议长。~**-chancellor** 大学副校长;副大法官。~**-consul** 副领事。~**-governor** 副州长,副总督。~**-king** = viceroy. ~**-minister** 副部长,次长。~**-president** 副总统;副会长;副社长;(大学)副校长。~**-principal** 副校长。~**-regent** ***n.***, ***a.*** 副摄政(的)。

vice·ge·ren·cy [ˌvaisˈdʒiərinsi; ˌvaɪsˋdʒɪrənsɪ] ***n***. (*pl*. *-cies*) 摄政,代理职,代理权。

vice·ger·ent [ˈvaisˈdʒerənt; vaɪsˋdʒɪrənt] **I** ***a***. 代理的。**II** ***n***. 代理人;摄政官;代理官。*God's* ～ 教皇。

vic·e·nar·y [ˈvisinəri; ˋvɪsəˌnɛrɪ] ***a***. **1**. 二十的。**2**. 以二十记数的。

vi·cen·ni·al [vaiˈsenjəl; vaɪˋsɛnɪəl] ***a***. 二十周年的;二十年(一次)的;连续二十年的。*a* ～ *celebration* 二十周年纪念。

Vice-Pres. = Vice-President.

vice·re·gal [ˈvaisˈriːgəl; vaɪsˋrigl] ***a***. **1**. 副王的;代表王权的。**2**. 总督的。

vice·reine [ˈvaisˈrein; ˋvaɪsren] ***n***. 总督夫人;女总督。

vice·roy [ˈvaisrɔi; ˋvaɪsrɔɪ] ***n***. **1**. 副王;总督。**2**. 【动】副王蝶(*Limenitis archippus*)〔美洲产一种红黑色蝴蝶〕。

vi·ce ver·sa [ˈvaisiˈvəːsə; ˋvaɪsɪˋvɝsə] 〔L.〕反过来;反过来也是一样,反之亦然。*He distrusts her, and vice versa* (= *She distrusts him*). 他不信任她,她也不信任他。

Vi·chy [ˈviːʃiː; ˋviʃi] ***n***. **1**. 维希〔法国城市〕。**2**. 维希矿泉水 (= ～ water)。**3**. 与维希矿泉水相似的人造[天然]水。

Vi·chy·ite [ˈviːʃiait; ˋviʃɪˌaɪt] ***n***. 维希分子〔第二次世界大战期间拥护设在维希的贝当傀儡政权的法国投降派〕。

vi·chys·soise [ˌviʃiˈswɔz; ˌviʃɪˋswɑz] ***n***. 维希奶油浓汤〔用马铃薯、洋葱配制的浓奶油汤,常供冷食〕。

vic·i·nage [ˈvisinidʒ; ˋvɪsn̩ɪdʒ] ***n***. **1**. 附近(地区),邻近。**2**. 邻近居民;邻舍。

vic·i·nal [ˈvisinəl; ˋvɪsnəl] ***a***. **1**. 附近的。**2**. 地方性的;本地区的。**3**.【矿】邻晶的;【化】连位的。*a* ～ *way* 本地的路;支路〔 *cf*. highway 〕。

vi·cin·i·ty [viˈsiniti; vəˋsɪnətɪ] ***n***. **1**. 附近(地区),邻近;近傍;近邻。**2**. 〔罕〕近亲。***in the*** ～ ***of*** **1**. 在…附近;靠近…的,…左近的。**2**. 在…上下;在…左右。*in the* ～ *of 50* 五十上下[左右]。

vi·cious [ˈviʃəs; ˋvɪʃəs] ***a***. **1**. 罪恶的,恶劣的;不道德的(*opp*. virtuous);品行坏的,习惯坏的。**2**. 有错误的,有缺陷的,不完全的。**3**. 脾气坏的;(马等)难骑的。**4**. 恶毒的;凶恶的;恶意的。**5**. 恶性的;(空气、水等)污浊的。～ *companions* 坏朋友。*a* ～ *headache* 剧烈的头痛。*a* ～ *pronunciation* 不正确的发音。*a* ～ *text* 错误百出的文本[课本]。*a* ～ *remark* 刻毒话。～ **circle** **1**. 恶性循环。**2**.【逻】循环论法。**-ly** ***ad***. **-ness** ***n***.

vi·cis·si·tude [viˈsisitjuːd; vəˋsɪsəˌtjud] ***n***. **1**. 变动,变迁。**2**. 荣枯,盛衰。**3**. (昼夜、四季的)推移。**4**. 〔古、诗〕代谢,交替。*a life marked by* ～*s* 多变的生活。*the* ～ *of day and night* 昼夜的推移。**-tu·di·nous** [viˌsisiˈtjuːdinəs; vəˌsɪsəˋtjudɪnəs], **-tu·di·na·ry** [-ˈtjuːdinəri; -ˋtjudɪnɛrɪ] ***a***.

Vick·i, Vick·y, Vick·ie [ˈviki; ˋvɪkɪ] ***n***. 维基〔女子名, Victoria 的昵称〕。

vi·comte [viˈkɔ̃t; viˋkɔ̃t] ***n***. 〔F.〕子爵。***vi·com·tesse*** [-tes; -tɛs] ***n***. 〔F.〕子爵夫人。

vi·con·ti·el [vaiˈkɔntiəl; vaɪˋkɑntɪəl] ***a***. 【英国早期法律】行政司法长官或子爵。

Vict. = Victoria(n).

vic·tim [ˈviktim; ˋvɪktɪm] ***n***. **1**. 牺牲(品)。**2**. 牺牲者,受害者,遭难者 (*of*); 受骗者。～*s of war* = *war* ～*s* 战争受害者。*a* ～ *of disease* 病人。***become the*** ～ ***of*** = ***fall a*** ～ ***to*** 成为…的牺牲品。**-ism** ***n***. 受迫害[受苦受难]意识。**-less** [-les; -lɛs] ***a***. (～*less crime* 无原告犯罪〔如卖淫、吸毒等〕)。

vic·tim·ize [ˈviktimaiz; ˋvɪktɪmˌaɪz] ***vt***. **1**. 屠杀(牲畜等)供作牺牲。**2**. 使牺牲[受损害];迫害。**3**. 欺骗。**-i·za·tion** [ˌviktimaiˈzeiʃən; ˌvɪktɪmaɪˋzeʃən], **-r** ***n***.

vic·tim·o·lo·gist [ˌviktiˈmɔlədʒist; ˌvɪktɪˋmɑlədʒɪst] ***n***. 受害者研究专家。

vic·tim·o·lo·gy [ˌviktiˈmɔlədʒi; ˌvɪktɪˋmɑlədʒɪ] ***n***. 受害者研究〔研究受害者在罪案中的作用〕。

Vic·tor [ˈviktə; ˋvɪktɚ] ***n***. **1**. 维克托〔男子名〕。**2**. 通讯中用以代表字母 v 的词。

vic·tor [ˈviktə; ˋvɪktɚ] **I** ***n***. 胜利者,战胜者。**II** ***a***. 胜利(者)的。

Vic·to·ri·a [vikˈtɔːriə; vɪkˋtorɪə] ***n***. **1**. 维多利亚〔塞舌耳首都〕。**2**. 维多利亚〔澳大利亚州名〕。**3**. 维多利亚〔加拿大港市〕。**4**. 维多利亚〔女子名〕。**5**. 胜利女神像。**6**. 维多利亚女王〔英国女王,1819—1901,在位期为 1837—1901〕。～ **Cross** (英国)维多利亚十字勋章〔最高军功章,略作 VC〕。

vic·tori·a [vikˈtɔːriə; vɪkˋtorɪə] ***n***. **1**. 双人四轮折篷马车;折篷汽车。**2**.【植】(南美)睡莲 (= ～ (water) lily)。

Vic·to·ri·an [vikˈtɔːriən; vɪkˋtorɪən] **I** ***a***. 维多利亚(Victoria) 女王(时代、式)的;旧式的。**II** ***n***. 维多利亚女王时代的人[文学家、名士、文物]。**-ism** ***n***. 维多利亚女王时代的风格[风气]。

vic·to·rine [ˌviktəˈriːn; ˌvɪktəˋrin] ***n***. (女用)毛皮围脖。

vic·to·ri·ous [vikˈtɔːriəs; vɪkˋtorɪəs] ***a***. 得胜的;胜利的,战胜的;象征胜利的。*the* ～ *team* 优胜队。**-ly** ***ad***.

vic·to·ry [ˈviktəri; ˋvɪktərɪ] ***n***. **1**. 胜利,战胜;征服,克服。**2**. 〔V-〕【罗神】胜利女神(像)。*a decisive* ～ 决定性的胜利。～ ***over oneself*** [***one's lower self***] 克制自己。***win a*** [***the***] ～ ***over*** 战胜,击败。***win*** ～ 得到胜利。～ **garden** 〔美〕(二次大战中为增加食物用庭园改作的)战时菜园。

vic·tress [ˈviktris; ˋvɪktrɪs] ***n***. 〔罕〕女胜利者。

vic·tro·la [vikˈtrəulə; vɪkˋtrolə] ***n***. (旧式的)胜利牌留声机;留声机的旧称。

vict·ual [ˈvitl; ˋvɪtl̩] **I** ***n***. 〔*pl*.〕〔主口、方〕食物,粮食;〔美〕剩饭。**II** ***vt***. (〔英〕 ***-ll-***)给…供应食物;给…储备粮食。— ***vi***. **1**. 〔罕〕吃饭;(牛、羊)吃草。**2**. (船等)装贮食物。

vict·ual(l)·er [ˈvitlə; ˋvɪtl̩ɚ] ***n***. **1**. 食物供应者。**2**. 〔英〕(有卖酒执照的)饮食店主,餐馆老板,旅馆老板 (= licensed ～)。**3**. 食物补给船。

vict·ual(l)·ing [ˈvitliŋ; ˋvɪtlɪŋ] ***n***. 储备[供给]粮食[食物]。～ **bill** 〔英〕船用食品装载申报单。～ **house** 餐馆。～ **note** 〔英海军〕(给新兵持交炊事管理员的)准餐通知书。～ **yard** 〔英海军〕后勤(给养)仓库。

vi·cu·gna, vi·cu·ña [viˈkjuːnjə; vɪˋkunjə] ***n***. 〔Sp.〕【动】**1**. (南美)骆马。**2**. 骆马绒(软呢)。

vid. = 〔L.〕 *vide*.

Vi·da [ˈviːdə; ˋvidɑ] ***n***. 维达〔女子名〕。

vi·de [ˈvaidi; ˋvaɪdɪ] ***v***. 〔L.〕见,参看〔略 *v*., *vid*.〕。***quod*** [kwɔd; kwɔd] ～参看该条,见该项。～ ***ante*** [ˈænti; ˋæntɪ] 见前。～ ***infra*** [ˈinfrə; ˋɪnfrə] 见下。～ ***p. 30*** = ***v. p. 30*** 见第 30 页。～ ***post*** 见后。～ ***supra*** [ˈsjuːprə; ˋsjuprə] 见上。～ ***the press passim*** [ˈpæsim; ˋpæsɪm] 见各报刊。～ ***ut supra*** 见上所述,见前所述,参见上述。

vi·de·li·cet [viˈdiːliset, vai-; vɪˋdɛləsɪt, vaɪ-] ***ad***. 〔L.〕即,就是说。★略作 viz, 通常读作 namely.

vid·e·o [ˈvidiəu; ˋvɪdɪˌo] **I** ***n***. 电视;视频;影像。**II** ***a***. 电视(用)的,视频的,录像的。～ **art** 电视艺术,视频艺术。～ **cam**〔口〕摄录机。～ **cartridge** [**cassette**] 录像带盒。～ **cast** 电视广播。～**disc** 录像盘,开卷式录像带。～ **junkie** 〔美俚〕不分片子优劣成天沉迷于看电影录像带的人,录像带迷。～ **frequency** 【视】视频(率)。～**-on-demand** 视频点播〔略作 VOD〕。～**phone** 电视电话。～**-player** 录像带放映机,放像电视机。～ **recording** 录像。～ **release** 新上市的电影录像带。～ **signal** 视频信号。～**tape** ***n***. 录像(磁)带。～**tape** ***vt***. 给…录像。～**-(tape) recorder** (磁带)录像机。

vi·dette [viˈdet; vɪˋdɛt] ***n***. = vedette.

V

vid·i·con [ˈvidikɔn; ˋvɪdɪkɑn] ***n.***【无】光导摄像管。

vi·di·mus [ˈvaidiməs; ˋvaɪdɪməs] ***n.*** (*pl.* ~*es*)〔L.〕 **1.** (账目等的)检查。**2.** (文件等的)摘要。

vie[1] [vai; vaɪ] ***vi.*** (~***d***; ***vying***) 竞争。~ *with another for sth.* [*in doing sth.*] 和人争夺某物[竞争某事]。— ***vt.*** **1.**〔罕〕下(赌注);冒…危险。**2.**〔古〕使竞争。

Vi·en·na [viˈenə; vɪˋɛnə] ***n.*** 维也纳〔奥地利首都〕。

Vi·en·nese [vieˈniːz; ˏviəˋniz] **I *a.*** **1.** 维也纳(式)的。**2.** 维也纳人的。**II *n.*** 〔 *sing.*, *pl.* 〕维也纳人。

Vien·tiane [ˌvjɛ̃ˈtjan; ˏvjɛ̃ˋtjan] ***n.*** 万象〔老挝首都〕。

Vi·et [vjet; vjɛt] ***n.***〔口〕**1.** = Viet Nam. **2.** ***n.***, ***a.*** = Vietnamese.

vi et ar·mis [ˈvaiet ˈɑːmis; ˋvaɪɛtˋɑrmɪs]〔L.〕【法】用武力,用暴力。

Vi·et·cong [ˈvjetˈkɔŋ; ˏviɛtˋkɑŋ] ***n.*** 〔 *sing.*, *pl.* 〕越共;越共成员〔西方报刊用语〕。

Vi·et·minh [ˈviətˈmin, ˈvjet-; ˋviətmɪn] **I *n.*** 〔 *sing.*, *pl.* 〕**1.** 越盟〔西方报刊用语〕。**2.** 越盟成员。**II *a.*** 越盟的。

Vi·et Nam, Vi·et·nam [ˈvjetˈnæm; ˋvjɛtˋnæm] ***n.*** 越南〔亚洲〕。

Vi·et·nam·ese [ˌvjetnəˈmiːz; ˏvjɛtnɑˋmiz] **I *a.*** 越南的;越南人的;越南语的。**II *n.*** 〔 *sing.*, *pl.* 〕**1.** 越南人。**2.** 越南语。

view [vjuː; vju] **I *n.*** **1.** 看,望;眺望,展望;观察,考察。**2.** 视力;视域,视野,眼界。**3.** 看见的东西,风景,情景,景色;风景画;风景照片;【工】(视)图。**4.** 看法,意见,见解。**5.** 目的,意向,意图;期待。**6.**【法】查验,检查;验尸。*a house with a ~ of the sea* 能望见海的房子。*a field of ~* 视界,视野。*a back* [*front*] *~* 背视[正视]图。*an end ~* 侧视图。*a difference of ~* 意见的不同。*a point of ~* 观点。*do some ~s of ...* 画…的风景。*be lost to ~* 看不见了。*be exposed to ~* 看得见,暴露。*fall in with sb.'s ~s* 和某人意见一致。*from a clear ~ of the situation* 根据对形势的清楚估量。***give a ~ of*** 大致说一说。***have ... in ~*** **1.** = *keep ... in ~*. **2.** 订(计划),筹划,企图。***have ~s upon*** (眼睛)盯牢,注视。***in my ~*** 照我看来。***in ~*** **1.** 看见,望见。**2.** 放在心里,作为目的;考虑中的 (*a project in ~* 考虑中的计划)。***in ~ of*** **1.** 在看得见…的地方,在…能看见的地方,…看得见了 (*come in ~ of* 来到看得见…的地方,…能看见了。*stand in full ~ of the crowd* 站在人群能清楚看见的地方)。**2.** 鉴于,由…看来 (*in ~ of the fact that ...* 由…这一事实看来,考虑到…这个事实)。**3.** 估计[预料]到才。**4.**〔俚〕认为。**5.** 为要,为了。***keep*** (*something*) ***in ~*** 眼睛盯牢;放在看得见的地方;记在心里,记住。***leave sth. out of ~*** 不加以考虑,不当做问题。***meet sb.'s ~*** 附和某人意见。***on*** (***the***) ***~ of*** 一见…就;观察着。***on ~*** 供人观看;陈列着。***take a ~ of*** 观察,视察,检查 (*take a dark ~ of* 对…抱悲观态度。*take a general ~ of* 综观,概观。*take a grave ~ of* 很重视)。***take long*** [***short***] ***~s*** 作[不作]长期打算;眼光远大[短浅];有[没有]先见之明。***to the ~*** 公开,公然。***upon the ~ of*** = *on* (*the*) *~ of*. ***with a ~ to*** **1.** 以…为目的;希望…而。**2.** 为…起见;抱着…的目的。**3.**〔俚〕= *in ~ of*. ***with no ~ of*** 无…的希望。***with the*** [〔俚〕***a***] ***~ of*** = *with a ~ to* 1. 2. ***with this*** [***that***] ***~*** 因为这个[那个]目的;因为这个[那个]。**II *vt.*** **1.** 看,望,眺望。**2.** 观察;视察。**3.**【法】查验,检查。**4.** 揣度,估料;看做,认为。**5.**〔口〕用电视机观看(演出节目等) (= teleview)。**6.** (猎狐时)见到(狐)。*an order to ~*【法】检查许可(证)。*~ the body* 验尸。*I ~ the matter in a different light.* 我的看法不同。*I ~ his conduct in the gravest light.* 我以极严重的态度看待他的行为。~ **data**【计】视传系统,视频信号传输系统〔把电视机和电脑数据库接通,让数据显示在电视机屏幕上〕。~ **finder**【摄】取景器;【物】探视器。~ **halloa** [**hallo(o)**] 狐狸出来啦!〔猎狐时看见猎物时的喊声〕。~**phone** 电视电话 (= videophone)。~**point** ***n.***〔口〕观点;看法,见解;【物】视点。**-er** ***n.*** **1.** 观看者,观众;电视观众。**2.** 观察者;检查者,【法】查验员,视察员。**3.**【物】视察器。**-less** ***a.***〔诗〕**1.** 看不见的;瞎的,盲的。**2.** 没有意见的。

view·a·ble [ˈvjuːəbəl; ˋvjuəbl̩] ***a.*** **1.** 看得见的。**2.** 值得一看的。*a ~ movie* 值得一看的电影。**-bil·i·ty** ***n.***

view·y [ˈvjuːi; ˋvjuɪ] ***a.***〔口〕**1.** 空想的,胡思乱想的;好奇的。**2.** 外表漂亮的,引人注目的,炫耀的。**-i·ness** ***n.***

vi·ga [ˈviːgə; ˋvigə] ***n.*** (西班牙老式房屋建筑中用的)椽,木角。

vi·ges·i·mal [vaiˈdʒesiməl; vaɪˋdʒɛsəml] ***a.*** **1.** (第)二十的;二十分之一的。**2.** 以二十为基础的;【数】二十进位(法)的。

vi·gi·a [viˈdʒiːə; vɪˋdʒiə] ***n.*** (*pl.* ***-gi·as*** [-ˈdʒiːəz; -dʒiəz]) **1.** 海图上的警戒记号。**2.** 海上的不明事物或现象。

vig·il [ˈvidʒil; ˋvɪdʒəl] ***n.*** **1.** 守夜;熬夜。**2.**〔常 *pl.*〕节日[斋戒]前夜的守夜[祝祷仪式]。*keep ~* 守夜;熬夜。*sick-room ~s* 病房的值夜。

vig·i·lance [ˈvidʒiləns; ˋvɪdʒələns] ***n.*** **1.** 守夜,警戒。**2.** 警惕(性)。**3.**【医】警醒(症);失眠症。*relax ~* 放松警惕。*sharpen one's ~* 提高警惕。~ **committee**〔美〕自警团〔市民不通过司法机关维持治安的自治组织〕。~**man** 自警团团员。

vig·i·lant [ˈvidʒilənt; ˋvɪdʒələnt] ***a.*** 不睡的,时时警惕着的,警戒着的;极留神的;警醒的。**-ly** ***ad.***

vig·i·lan·te [ˌvidʒiˈlænti; ˏvɪdʒəˋlæntɪ] ***n.***〔美〕自卫队员。~ **corps**〔美〕自卫队。

vig·i·lan·tism [ˌvidʒiˈlæntizəm; ˏvɪdʒəˋlæntɪzəm] ***n.***〔美〕自警团的政策[制度,做法]。

vi·gin·til·lion [ˌvaidʒinˈtiljən; ˏvaɪdʒɪnˋtɪljən] **I *n.*** (*pl.* ***-lions***, ***-lion***) **1.**【美、法】1 后加 63 个零之数 (10^{63})。**2.**【英、德】后加 120 个零之数 (10^{120})。**II *a.*** 上述之数的。**-lionth** ***a.***

vig·na [ˈvignə; ˋvɪgnə] ***n.***【植】豇豆。

vi·gnette [viˈnjet ; vɪnˋjɛt] **I *n.*** **1.**【建】(葡萄藤)蔓叶花样。**2.** 起头字母的蔓叶花饰;书籍章头章尾的小花饰[小插图]。**3.** (晕影)半身照片[画像]。**4.** (简短优美的)描述;简介;小品文。**II *vt.*** **1.** 用蔓草花样装饰。**2.** 使(画或照片的背景)晕映。**3.** 简洁地描述。*a vignetting effect* 晕影效应。

vig·or [ˈvigə; ˋvɪgɚ] ***n.***〔美〕= vigour.

vig·or·ish [ˈvigəriʃ; ˋvɪgərɪʃ] ***n.***〔美俚〕**1.** (赌博中的)抽头。**2.** (高利贷者索取的)超额利息。

vi·go·ro·so [ˌvigəˈrəusəu; ˏvigəˋrosə] ***a.***, ***ad.***〔It.〕【乐】有力的[地];精力充沛的[地]。

vig·or·ous [ˈvigərəs; ˋvɪgərəs] ***a.*** **1.** 精力旺盛的,强健的;精神饱满的,活泼的。**2.** 有力的,有魄力的。*a ~ mass movement* 轰轰烈烈的群众运动。*a ~ style* 富有活力的文体。~ *development of ...* …的蓬勃发展。~ *expansion of production* 大力发展生产。~ *in spirit* 精神振奋。**-ly** ***ad.***

vig·our [ˈvigə; ˋvɪgɚ] ***n.*** **1.** 精力,活力。**2.** 气力,精神;生气;体力;强壮;气魄,魄力。**3.** 有力行动;【生】优势。***be in full ~*** 精力旺盛。***in ~*** 仍然有效的。***with ~*** 有力地,精神饱满地。**-less** ***a.*** 没有精力的;没有精神的。

Vi·king [ˈvaikiŋ; ˋvaɪkɪŋ] ***n.*** **1.** (8—10 世纪的)北欧海盗。**2.**〔v-〕海盗。**3.**〔口〕斯堪的纳维亚人。

vil. = village.

vile [vail; vaɪl] ***a.*** **1.** 卑劣的,恶劣的;粗鄙的,恶俗的。**2.**〔口〕极坏的,讨厌的。**3.**〔罕、古〕不足道的,无价值的。*resort to ~ means* 采取卑劣手段。*What a ~ pen!* 这个笔尖坏透了。~ *weather* 恶劣的天气。**-ly** ***ad.***

vil·i·fi·ca·tion [ˌvilifiˈkeiʃən; ˏvɪləfəˋkeʃən] ***n.*** 诽谤。

vil·i·fier [ˈvilifaiə; ˋvɪləˏfaɪɚ] ***n.*** 诽谤者,诬蔑者,中伤

者。

vil·i·fy [ˈvilifai; ˋvɪlə͵faɪ] *vt*. (*-fied*) 1. 说…的坏话,诬蔑,诽谤;辱骂。2. 贬低。3. 〔罕〕使卑劣,使堕落。

vil·i·pend [ˈvilipend; ˋvɪlə͵pɛnd] *vt*. 1. 诬蔑,诋毁。2. 轻视;贬低。

vil·la [ˈvilə; ˋvɪlə] *n*. 1. 别墅。2. 〔英〕郊区住宅。

vil·la·dom [ˈvilədəm; ˋvɪlədəm] *n*. 〔英〕〔集合词〕1. 市郊住宅(区)。2. 居住市郊住宅区的人们〔常指有闲阶级〕。

Vil·la·fran·chi·an [ˌviləˈfræŋtʃiən; ͵vɪləˋfræntʃɪən] *a*. 【地】维拉夫兰的〔第一冰蚀期以前的下更新世的〕。~ *stage* 维拉夫兰期。

vil·lage [ˈvilidʒ; ˋvɪlɪdʒ] *n*. 1. 村庄,农村,乡村〔小于 town, 大于 hamlet〕。2. 〔集合词〕村民。3. (动物的)群落。~ *industry* 农村工业。~ **community**【经济史】农村社区;村社。

vil·lag·er [ˈvilidʒə; ˋvɪlɪdʒɚ] *n*. 村民;乡村居民,乡下人。

vil·lain [ˈvilən; ˋvɪlən] *n*. 1. 坏人,坏蛋;(戏剧等的)反派角色;〔口〕淘气孩子。2. 〔口〕村夫,庄稼汉。3.【英史】〔有时作 -lin〕隶农,半自由的农奴(= villein)。*play the* ~ 演反派角色。*You little* ~! 你这小淘气!

vil·la(i)n·age [ˈvilinidʒ; ˋvɪlənɪdʒ] *n*. = villeinage.

vil·lain·ous [ˈvilənəs; ˋvɪlənəs] *a*. 1. 坏人(似)的;极恶的,凶恶的;卑劣的;腐化堕落的。2. 〔口〕(旅馆、衣服、饭菜等)极坏的,讨厌的。*a* ~ *character* 反面人物。**-ly** *ad*. **-ness** *n*.

vil·lain·y [ˈviləni; ˋvɪlənɪ] *n*. 1. 卑劣,凶恶;腐化堕落。2. 〔*pl*.〕坏事,恶劣行为,罪恶。

vil·la·nel·la [ˌviləˈnelə; ͵vɪləˋnɛlə; It. ˌviːlaːˈnelaː; ͵vɪlaˋnɛla] *n*. (*pl*. **-le** [-iː; -i; It. -li; -lɪ])【乐】1. 农村舞曲,农村舞蹈;维拉涅拉歌舞〔意大利古代农村的一种歌舞〕。2. 那不勒斯民歌〔意大利十六世纪时的一种无伴奏的歌曲,如牧歌〕。

Vil·lard [viˈlɑːd; vɪˋlard] *n*. 维拉德〔姓氏〕。

vil·lat·ic [viˈlætik; vɪˋlætɪk] *a*. 别墅的;农场的;田园的,乡村的,农家的。~ *fowl* 家禽。

vil·lein [ˈvilin; ˋvɪlɪn] **I** *n*.【英史】隶农〔对于领主说是农奴,对于外人说是自由民〕。**II** *a*. 隶农的。

vil·le(i)n·age [ˈvilinidʒ; ˋvɪlənɪdʒ] *n*. 隶农制;隶农租地(条件);隶农身分;〔集合词〕隶农。

ville Lumière [vilˌlyˈmjɛir; vɪl͵lyˋmjɛr] *n*. 〔F.〕巴黎的别名〔意为光明的城市〕。

vil·li [ˈvilai; ˋvɪlaɪ] *n*. villus 的复数。

vil·li·form [ˈvilifɔːm; ˋvɪlə͵fɔrm] *a*. 1. 绒毛(或长柔毛)状的。2. 绒毛开的,绒毛齿的。

vil·lose [ˈviləus; ˋvɪlos], **vil·lous** [ˈviləs; ˋvɪləs] *a*.【解】(被覆)绒毛的;【植】有长柔软毛的。

vil·los·i·ty [viˈlɔsiti; vɪˋlɑsɪtɪ] *n*. 1. 长柔毛性,毛茸。2. 绒毛。3. 长柔毛覆盖。

vil·lus [ˈviləs; ˋvɪləs] *n*. (*pl*. *-li* [-lai; -laɪ])【解】绒毛;〔*pl*.〕【植】长柔毛。

Vil·na [ˈvilnə; ˋvɪlnə] *n*. = Vilnius.

Vil·ni·us, Vil·ny·us [ˈvilniəs; ˋvɪlnɪəs] *n*. 维尔纽斯〔立陶宛首都〕。

vim [vim; vɪm] *n*. 〔口〕力气,精力,活力。

vi·men [ˈvaimen; ˋvaɪmɛn] *n*. (*pl*. *vim·i·na* [ˈviminə; ˋvɪmənə])【植】枝条,柔韧枝条;苗。

vim·i·nal [ˈviminəl; ˋvɪmənl] *a*.【植】(发)小枝的。

vi·min·e·ous [vaiˈminiəs; vɪˋmɪnɪəs] *a*. 1. 枝条(编制)的。2.【植】(生有)柔韧的枝条的。

v.imp. = verb impersonal 非人称动词。

vin [vɛ̃; vɛ̃] *n*. 〔F.〕酒;葡萄酒。

vi·na [ˈviːnə; ˋvinɑ] *n*. (印度的)七弦琴。

vi·na·ceous [vaiˈneiʃəs; vaɪˋneʃəs] *a*. 葡萄(似)的;(红)葡萄酒色的。

vin·ai·grette [ˌvineiˈgret; ͵vɪnəˋgrɛt] *n*. 1. (提神的)香醋盒[瓶];嗅瓶。2. 调味酸酱油。

vi·nal[1] [ˈvainl; ˋvaɪnl] *a*. = vinous.

vi·nal[2] [ˈvainl; ˋvaɪnl] *n*.【纺】维纳尔,聚乙烯醇纤维。

vi·nasse [viˈnæs; vɪˋnæs] *n*. 酿酒蒸馏后的残渣,酒糟。

Vin·cent [ˈvinsənt; ˋvɪnsn̩t] *n*. 文森特〔男子名〕。

Vin·ci [ˈvintʃi(ː); ˋvɪntʃɪ], ***Leonardo da*** 达·芬奇〔1452—1519,意大利的画家、雕刻家、建筑家、科学家〕。

vin·ci·ble [ˈvinsibl; ˋvɪnsəbl̩] *a*. 〔罕〕可战胜的,可征服的。**-bil·i·ty** [ˌvinsiˈbiliti; ͵vɪnsəˋbɪlətɪ], **-ness** *n*.

vin·cris·tine [vinˈkristiːn, -tin; vɪnˋkrɪstin, -tɪn] *n*.【化】长春新碱〔治白血症的抗肿瘤药〕。

vin·cu·lum [ˈviŋkjuləm; ˋvɪŋkjʊləm] *n*. (*pl*. *-la* [-lə; -lə]) 1. 联结,纽带,结合(物)。2.【数】插线,线括号。3.【解】纽,系带。

vin·di·ca·ble [ˈvindikəbl; ˋvɪndəkəbl̩] *a*. 可辩护的;可维护的;可证明为正常的。**-bil·i·ty** [ˌvindikəˈbiliti; ͵vɪndəkəˋbɪlətɪ] *n*.

vin·di·cate [ˈvindikeit; ˋvɪndə͵ket] *vt*. 1. 维护。2. 为…辩护;为…辩明,剖白。3. 证明…为正当。4. 〔古〕为…报仇。~ *one's rights* 为权利申辩。~ *oneself* 维护自己权利;为自己辩护。~ *oneself a permanent place in history* 保持永久不变的历史地位。*Subsequent events* ~*d their policy*. 以后的结果证明他们的政策是正确的。

vin·di·ca·tion [ˌvindiˈkeiʃən; ͵vɪndəˋkeʃən] *n*. 维护;辩解,辩白,证明。

vin·dic·a·tive [ˈvindikətiv; vɪnˋdɪkətɪv] *a*. 1. 起维护[辩护]作用的。2. 〔古〕报复的;惩罚的。**-ly** *ad*. **-ness** *n*.

vin·di·ca·tor [ˈvindikeitə; ˋvɪndəketɚ] *n*. 1. 维护者。2. 辩白者;证明者。3. 〔古〕报仇者,复仇者。

vin·di·ca·to·ry [ˈvindikətəri; ˋvɪndəkə͵torɪ] *a*. 1. 维护的。2. 辩明的;证明的。3.【法】惩罚的;报复性的;复仇的。

vin·dic·tive [vinˈdiktiv; vɪnˋdɪktɪv] *a*. 1. 复仇的,报复的。2. 仇恨深的。3. 〔古〕惩罚的。~ [*exemplary*] *damages* 惩罚性赔偿损失。

vine [vain; vaɪn] *n*. 1. 葡萄树(=〔美〕grape-vine)。2. 有蔓植物,蔓草,藤。*love* ~【植】菟丝子。*rose* ~*s*〔美〕【植】蔓蔷薇。***a clinging*** ~ 依赖男子的孤苦妇女。***die on the*** ~ (计划)夭折。***dwell under one's*** ~ ***and fig tree*** 在自己家里过安闲日子。~**dresser** 修剪葡萄枝的人。~**yard** 1. 葡萄园。2. 工作场所,苦心经营的地方。

vin·e·gar [ˈvinigə; ˋvɪnɪgɚ] **I** *n*. 1. 醋。2. 乖戾;尖酸刻薄〔常作表语用〕。3. 〔口〕充沛的精力。*aromatic* ~ 香醋。*a* ~ *countenance* 乖戾[不快]的神色。**II** *vt*. 加醋于。~ **blink**〔美〕白葡萄酒。~ **eel** [**worm**]【动】醋线虫。**-ish** *a*. 不愉快的;乖戾的。

vin·e·gar·y [ˈvinigəri; ˋvɪnɪgərɪ] *a*. 1. 醋似的,有酸味的,酸的。2. (性情,情绪)乖戾的。*a* ~ *spinster* 乖张的老处女。*a* ~ *smile* 苦笑。

vin·er·y [ˈvainəri; ˋvaɪnərɪ] *n*. 1. 葡萄温室;葡萄园;藤本植物温室[园圃]。2. 〔集合词〕葡萄丛。

vingt-et-un [ˈvænteiˈəːŋ; ˋvænteˋəŋ] *n*. 〔F.〕二十一点〔牌戏〕。

vini- *comb. f*. 葡萄酒。

vi·nic [ˈvainik, ˈvinik; ˋvaɪnɪk, ˋvɪnɪk] *a*. 葡萄酒的,在葡萄酒中的,从葡萄酒(提取)的。

vin·i·cul·ture [ˈviniˌkʌltʃə; ˋvɪnɪ͵kʌltʃɚ] *n*. (酿酒)葡萄栽培。**-tur·al** *a*. **-tur·ist** *n*.

vi·nif·er·ous [vaiˈnifərəs; vaɪˋnɪfərəs] *a*. 生产[酿造]葡萄酒(用)的。

vin·i·fy [ˈvinifai; ˋvɪnɪfaɪ] *vt*. (*-fied*) 发酵(葡萄等的)果汁酿酒。

vi·no [ˈviːnəu; ˋvino] *n*. 〔It., Sp.〕葡萄酒;果酒。

vi·nom·e·ter [vaiˈnɔmitə; vaɪˋnɑmətɚ] *n*. 酒精比重

计。

vin or·di·naire [vɛ̃ɔrdiːˈnɛr; væ̃ɔrdiˋnɛr] 〔F.〕普通葡萄酒,廉价葡萄酒。

vi·nos·i·ty [vaiˈnɔsiti; vaiˋnɑsɪtɪ] ***n.*** **1.** 葡萄酒性,酒质。**2.** 嗜好葡萄酒。

vi·nous [ˈvainəs; ˋvaɪnəs] ***a.*** **1.** 葡萄酒的;具有葡萄酒性质的;有葡萄酒味的;葡萄酒色的。**2.** 用(葡萄)酒提神的;爱喝(葡萄)酒的;有酒意的。*in a somewhat* ~ *condition* 有点儿醉。

vin ro·sé [vɛ̃ rəuˈzei; vɛ̃ roˋze] 〔F.〕= rose 玫瑰色葡萄酒。

vins de liqueur [vɛ̃ də likɔːr; vɛ̃ də lɪkɔr] 〔F.〕甜葡萄酒。

Vin·son [ˈvinsn; ˋvɪnsn] ***n.*** 文森〔姓氏〕。

vint [vint; vɪnt] ***vt.*** (用水果)酿造(酒)。

vin·tage [ˈvintidʒ; ˋvɪntɪdʒ] **I** ***n.*** **1.** 葡萄收获;葡萄收获期。**2.** 葡萄收获量;(当年)葡萄酒产量。**3.** 酒;(特指某年某地所产的)佳酿酒,美酒(= vintage wine)。**4.** (同年代的)一批产品。**5.** 制造的时期。*a hat of last year's* ~ 去年制成的帽子。*He is of the Yale* ~. 他是耶鲁大学毕业生。**II** ***a.*** **1.** 酒的;酿造的。**2.** 属于某一时期制造的。**3.** 最佳的。**4.** 古老的;过时的。**III** ***vt.*** 为酿酒而收(葡萄)。— ***vi.*** 收葡萄。~ **wine** (陈年)佳酿。~ **year** 佳酿酒酿成的年分。

vin·tag·er [ˈvintidʒə; ˋvɪntɪdʒɚ] ***n.*** 葡萄采收人。

vint·ner [ˈvintnə; ˋvɪntnɚ] ***n.*** 〔主英〕(葡萄)酒商。

vin·y [ˈvaini; ˋvaɪnɪ] ***a.*** (像)葡萄树的;多葡萄树[蔓藤]的。

vi·nyl [ˈvainil, ˈvinil; ˋvaɪnɪl, ˋvɪnɪl] ***n.*** 【化】乙烯基。~ **alcohol** 乙烯醇。~ **chloride** 氯乙烯,氯化乙烯基。~ **idene** 亚乙烯基。~ **plastic** 乙烯基塑料。~ **resin** 乙烯基树脂。

vi·nyl·on [ˈvainilɔn; ˋvaɪnɪlɑn] ***n.*** 【织】维尼纶〔聚乙烯醇缩纤维的总称〕。

vi·ol [ˈvaiəl, vail, viəl; ˋvaɪəl, vaɪl] ***n.*** 中世纪六弦提琴。*a bass* ~ = violoncello.

Vi·o·la [ˈvaiələ, ˈviələ; ˋvaɪələ, ˋviələ] ***n.*** 怀奥拉〔女子名〕。

vi·o·la[1] [ˈvaiələ; ˋvaɪələ] ***n.*** 【植】堇菜(属)。

vi·o·la[2] [viˈəulə, ˈviələ; vɪˋolə, ˋvɪələ] ***n.*** 【乐】中提琴;【史】= viol. ~ **da braccio** (旧式)次中音提琴。~ **da gamba** (旧式)低音提琴,膝琴。~ **clef** 中音谱号(= alto clef)。~ **d'amore** 一种古提琴。

vi·o·la·ble [ˈvaiələbl; ˋvaɪələbl̩] ***a.*** 可违犯的,可破坏的;可亵渎的;易受侵犯的。

vi·o·la·ceous [ˌvaiəˈleiʃəs; ˏvaɪəˋleʃəs] ***a.*** 紫罗兰色的。

vi·o·late [ˈvaiəleit; ˋvaɪəˏlet] ***vt.*** **1.** 违犯,违反,破坏。**2.** 亵渎(神圣);污辱。**3.** 妨碍,妨害;侵犯,侵害,侵入。**4.** 强奸,蹂躏(妇女)。~ *the law* 犯法。~ *sleep* 妨碍睡眠。~ *sb.'s privacy* 侵扰某人(的安静);闯入私室。**vi·o·la·tor** ***n.*** 违犯者;侵扰者;亵渎者;强奸者。

vi·o·la·tion [ˌvaiəˈleiʃən; ˏvaɪəˋleʃən] ***n.*** **1.** 违犯,违背。**2.** 妨害;侵害,侵犯。**3.** 亵渎;污辱。**4.** 强奸。**5.** 【体】违例,犯规。***in*** ~ ***of*** 违反,违背。

vi·o·la·tive [ˈvaiəleitiv; ˋvaɪəˏletɪv] ***a.*** **1.** 违犯的,违反的。**2.** 妨害的,侵犯的;**3.** 亵渎的。**4.** 强奸的;蹂躏的。

vi·o·lence [ˈvaiələns; ˋvaɪələns] ***n.*** **1.** 猛烈,激烈;热烈;【炸药】烈度。**2.** 暴力,强暴,暴虐。**3.** 冒渎,不敬。**4.** 歪曲(事实),曲解(意义);窜改(语句)。**5.** 【法】强奸。***do*** ~ ***to*** 对…行凶;侵害,伤害;违犯;歪曲(事实等);亵渎。***offer*** ~ ***to*** 袭击。***resort to*** ~ 用暴力,动武。***use*** ~ 用暴力。

vi·o·lent [ˈvaiələnt; ˋvaɪələnt] ***a.*** **1.** (风、爆炸等)猛烈的,狂暴的。**2.** (话等)热烈的,激烈的。**3.** 厉害的,极端的;(病等)剧烈的。**4.** 强暴的,暴虐的。**5.** (死等)暴力(造成)的;非自然的。*a* ~ *wind* 暴风。*a* ~ *attack* 猛击,猛攻。~ *contrast* 极端的不同。~ *assumption* 瞎猜,乱推测。***lay*** ~ ***hands on*** 对…行凶,对…下毒手。***resort to*** ~ ***means*** 用强暴手段。~ **death** 横死。~ **presumption** 【法】根据几乎已具决定性的证据所作的推断。**-ly** ***ad.***

vi·o·les·cent [ˌvaiəˈlesnt; ˏvaɪəˋlɛsnt] ***a.*** (带)紫罗兰色的。

Vi·o·let [ˈvaiəlit; ˋvaɪəlɪt] ***n.*** 怀奥莱特〔女子名〕。

vi·o·let [ˈvaiəlit; ˋvaɪəlɪt] **I** ***n.*** 【植】堇菜(属);紫罗兰;紫罗兰色,兰光紫。**II** ***a.*** 紫罗兰色的。*the March* ~ = *the English* ~ = *the sweet* ~ 香堇菜(花)。~ **rays** 【物】**1.** 紫射线,紫光。**2.** 〔误用〕紫外线(= ultraviolet rays)。

vi·o·lin [ˌvaiəˈlin; ˏvaɪəˋlɪn] ***n.*** 【乐】小提琴;小提琴手。*the first* [*second*] ~ 第一[第二]小提琴(手)。***play first*** ~ 奏第一小提琴;担任主要职位,当第一把手。

vi·o·lin·ist [ˌvaiəˈlinist; ˏvaɪəˋlɪnɪst] ***n.*** 小提琴手,小提琴家。

vi·ol·ist [ˈvaiəlist; ˋvaɪəlɪst] ***n.*** 中提琴手。

vi·o·lon·cel·lo [ˌvaiələnˈtʃeləu; ˏviələnˋtʃɛlo] ***n.*** (*pl.* ~*s*)【乐】= 大提琴(cello)。**-cel·list** ***n.*** 大提琴手(= cellist)。

vi·o·lone [vjəuˈləunei; vjoˋlone] ***n.*** **1.** 低音提琴。**2.** (风琴的)低音提琴音音栓。

vi·o·my·cin [ˌvaiəˈmaisin; ˏvaɪəˋmaɪsɪn] ***n.*** 【药】紫霉素。

vi·os·ter·ol [vaiˈɔstərɔːl; vaɪˋɑstərˏɑl] ***n.*** 【化】= calciferol.

VIP, V.I.P. = very important person 要人;大人物。

vi·per [ˈvaipə; ˋvaɪpɚ] ***n.*** **1.** 【动】蝰蛇;毒蛇。**2.** 毒蛇般的坏人。**3.** 〔美俚〕毒品贩子。***cherish*** [***nourish***] ***a*** ~ ***in one's bosom*** 厚待忘恩负义的人,姑息养奸。~**'s bugloss** 【植】蓝蓟(= blue weed)。

vi·per·ine [ˈvaipərin; ˋvaɪpɚɪn] ***a.*** 毒蛇(般)的;有毒的。

vi·per·ish [ˈvaipəriʃ; ˋvaɪpɚɪʃ], **vi·per·ous** [-rəs; -rəs] ***a.*** 毒蛇般的,有毒的;阴险的,恶毒的。

VIPs ***n.*** VIP 的复数。

vi·ra·go [viˈreigəu; vəˋrego] ***n.*** (*pl.* ~(*e*)*s*) **1.** 泼妇,悍妇。**2.** 〔英古〕男子气的健壮女人。

vi·ral [ˈvairəl; ˋvaɪrəl] ***a.*** 病毒(的),含病毒的,病毒所致的。

vi·re·mi·a [vaiˈriːmiə; vaɪˋrimɪə] ***n.*** 【医】病毒血症,滤毒血症。

vir·e·o [ˈviriəu; ˋvɪrɪˏo] ***n.*** (*pl.* ~*s*)【动】(美洲)维丽俄鸟〔绿色小鸣禽,又称 greenlet〕。

vi·res [ˈvairiːz; ˋvaɪriz] ***n.*** 〔L.〕*vis* 的复数。

vi·res·cent [vaiˈresnt; vaɪˋrɛsnt] ***a.*** 淡绿[嫩绿]的,带绿的;开始转绿的;【植】变绿的,绿化的。**-cence** ***n.***

Virg. = Virginia 弗吉尼亚〔美国州名〕。

vir·ga [ˈvəːgə; ˋvɝgə] ***n.*** 【气】幡状(云),雨幡。

vir·gate[1] [ˈvəːgit, -geit; ˋvɝgɪt, -get] ***n.*** 威尔格〔英国旧地积单位,无一定算法,通常约合 30 英亩〕。

vir·gate[2] [ˈvəːgit; ˋvɝgɪt] ***a.*** 棒状的;【植】直细枝(多)的;帚状的。

Vir·gil [ˈvəːdʒil; ˋvɝdʒəl] ***n.*** **1.** 弗吉尔〔男子名〕。**2.** 维吉尔〔公元前 70—19 年,古罗马诗人,其主要作品为史诗《埃涅伊德》〕。

Vir·gil·i·an [vəːˈdʒiliən; vɚˋdʒɪlɪən] ***a.*** 诗人维吉尔(风格)的。

vir·gin [ˈvəːdʒin; ˋvɝdʒɪn] **I** ***n.*** **1.** 处女,未婚少女;【宗】童贞修女。**2.** 〔the V-〕圣母马利亚。**3.** 〔罕〕童贞男子。**4.** 【动】单性生殖雌虫;未交配雌虫。**5.** 【天】〔V-〕室女座,室女宫(= Virgo)。~ *paper* 白纸。~ *whiteness* 纯白。*a* ~ *forest* 处女林,原生林。*a* ~ *blade* 还没有用过的刀。**II** ***a.*** **1.** 处女的。**2.** 处女特有的,像处女的,易害羞的。**3.** 没有玷污的,纯洁的,新鲜的。**4.** 没有搅乱的,没有搀杂的;还没有用过的;没有耕过的;原来的;

【化】直馏的;(植物油)初榨的;【冶】由矿石直接提炼的。5. 首次的,创始的。~ **clay** (没有烧过的)生黏土。~ **birth** [**generation**]【生】单性生殖。~ **fortress** 从未陷落过的要塞。~ **gold** 纯金。~ **honey** 未产过卵的蜂箱中取出的蜂蜜;蜂房中自然流出的蜂蜜。**V- Islands** 维尔京群岛〔西印度群岛中一群小岛〕。~ **kerosene** 直馏煤油。**V- Mother**【宗】圣母马利亚。~ **queen** 还没有受孕的蜂王;〔**the V- Q-**〕伊丽莎白 Elizabeth 女王一世的别名。~**s-bower**【植】维吉利亚铁线莲。~ **soil** 处女地,生荒地。~ **stand** 原始林。

vir·gin·al [ˈvəːdʒinl; ˋvɚdʒɪnl] *a*. 处女的,像处女的,纯洁的;【动】未受精的。~ *bloom* 纯洁而美好的少女(时代)。~ **generation**【生】单性生殖。~ **membrane**【解】处女膜。

Vir·gin·i·a [və(ː)ˈdʒinjə; vɚˋdʒɪnjə] *n*. 1. 维吉尼亚〔女子名〕。2. (美国)维吉尼亚州。3. 美国维吉尼亚烟叶。~ **creeper**【植】五叶地锦。~ **cowslip** [**bluebell**]【植】维吉尼亚风铃草。~ (**rail**) **fence** 犬牙形篱笆。

vir·gin·i·bus pu·er·is·que [vəːˈdʒinibəs pjuəˈriskwiː; vɚˋdʒɪnɪbəs,pjuəˋrɪskwi]〔L.〕为少年男女(的),适合少年男女(的)。

vir·gin·i·ty [vəːˈdʒiniti; vɚˋdʒɪnətɪ] *n*. 童贞;纯洁;新鲜。

vir·gin·i·um [vəːˈdʒiniəm; vɚˋdʒɪnɪəm] *n*.【化】钫(Vi)。

Vir·go [ˈvəːgəu; ˋvɚgo] *n*.【天】室女座;室女宫。~ ***intacta***【法】未与人交接过的处女。

vir·gu·late [ˈvəːgjulit; ˋvɚgjulɪt] *a*. 细枝状的,小帚状的。

vir·gule [ˈvəːgjuːl; ˋvɚgjul] *n*.【印】斜线号(/)。*A* and/or *B*. 甲与乙或甲或乙。

vi·ri·cide [ˈvaiərisaid; ˋvaɪrə,saɪd] *n*. 杀病毒剂。**-ci·dal** *a*.

vir·i·des·cence [ˌviriˈdesns; ˏvɪrəˋdɛsns] *n*. 1. 嫩绿;淡绿。2. 新鲜,生气,活气。

vir·i·des·cent [ˌviriˈdesnt; ˏvɪrəˋdesnt] *a*. 淡绿色的,带绿色的;变成绿色的。

vi·rid·i·an [viˈridiən; vəˋrɪdɪən] *n*. 铬绿〔水合氧化铬的一种蓝绿色颜料〕。

vi·rid·i·ty [viˈriditi; vəˋrɪdətɪ] *n*. 1. 新绿,鲜绿。2. 新鲜,生气。3. 纯洁,天真,无经验。

vir·ile [ˈvirail, ˈvaiər-; ˋvɪrəl, ˋvaɪrəl] *a*. 1. 成年男子的,壮年的,年富力强的;有生殖力的。2. 男性的,有男子气概的,刚强有力的,强壮的。*a* ~ *government* 强有力的政府。

vir·i·les·cent [ˌviriˈlesnt; ˏvɪrɪˋlɛsnt] *a*. (年老的雌性动物的)雄性化;(女性的)男性化。**-cence** *n*.

vir·i·lism [ˈvirilizəm; ˋvɪrəl,ɪzəm] *n*.【医】(妇女的)男性现象,男性化;(妇女)发生男性第二性征。

vi·ril·i·ty [viˈriliti; vəˋrɪlətɪ] *n*. 1. (男子的)成人,成年;年富力强;生殖力。2. 男子气,丈夫气;气魄,雄劲,雄浑。

vir·i·lo·cal [ˌviriˈləukəl; ˏvɪrəˋlokl] *a*.【人类】与夫家住在一起的,以夫家为中心的。**-ly** *ad*.

vi·ri·on [ˈvairiˌɔn; ˋvaɪrɪ,ɑn] *n*.【医】病毒颗粒。

vi·ro·gene [ˈvaiəˌdʒiːn; ˋvaɪə,dʒin] *n*.【医】病毒基因〔尤指能在正常细胞中产生致癌病毒者〕。

vi·rol·o·gy [ˌvaiəˈrɔlədʒi; vaɪˋrɑlədʒɪ] *n*. 病毒学 (= virulogy)。**-gist** *n*. 病毒学家。

vi·ro·pause [ˈvairəpɔːz; ˋvaɪrəpɔz] *n*.【医】男性更年期。

vi·rose [ˈvaiərəus; ˋvaɪros], **vi·rous** [ˈvaiərəs; ˋvaɪrəs] *a*. 有(病)毒的;【植】有恶臭的。

vi·ro·sis [ˌvaiəˈrəusis; vaɪˋrosɪs] *n*.【医】病毒病[症]。

v·irr. = verb irregular 不规则动词。

vir·tu [vəːˈtuː; vɚˋtu] *n*. 1. 艺术品的嗜好;古玩癖。2. 〔集合词〕艺术品,古玩。*articles* [*objects*] *of* ~ 古玩,古董。*a piece of* ~ 一件古董。

vir·tu·al [ˈvəːtjuəl, -tʃuəl; ˋvɚtʃuəl] *a*. 1. 实际上的,实质上的,事实上的。2.【物】虚像的。3.【物】有效的;【计】(网上)虚拟的。4. 〔古〕具有可产生某种效果之内在力的。*a* ~ *ruler* 事实上的统治者。~ **ampere** [**value**]【电】有效安培[值]。~ **chat**【计】虚拟交谈〔上网者在电脑网络上的文字交谈,如聊天室等〕。~ **displacement** [**work**]【物】虚位移[功]。~ **height**【物】有效高度。~ **image**【物】虚像。~ **memory**【计】虚存,虚拟存储器〔重新组织硬盘后所获得的额外储存容量〕。~ **reality**【计】虚拟现实〔由电脑生成的对场景环境和图像的逼真模拟〕。~ **shopping** 网上购物。

vir·tu·al·ly [ˈvəːtjuəli; ˋvɚtʃuəlɪ] *ad*. 实际上,实质上,事实上。

vir·tue [ˈvəːtjuː; ˋvɚtʃu] *n*. 1. 德,品德;德行,善行 (*opp*. vice),美德;节操,贞操。2. 价值,长处,优点。3. 力,效能,效力,功效。4.【宗】〔*pl*.〕第七级天使。*paint sb. utterly without a single* ~ 把某人说得一无是处。*a man of* ~ 有品德的人。*a woman of* ~ 贞淑的女人。*a lady of easy* ~ 行为不检的女人。*drugs of great* ~ 效力大的药。***by*** ~ ***of*** = ***in*** ~ ***of*** 靠,因,靠…的力量(*He was promoted in* ~ *of his abilities*. 他是靠他的才能被提升的)。***make a*** ~ ***of necessity*** 见 necessity 条。

vir·tue·less [ˈvəːtjuːlis; ˋvɚtʃulɪs] *a*. 无道德的;无长处[优点]的;没有效力的。

vir·tu·o·sic [ˌvəːtjuˈɔsik, -əusik; ˏvɚtʃʊˋɑsɪk, -ˋosɪk] *a*. 艺术名家的,美术品收藏家的,专家的。

vir·tu·os·i·ty [ˌvəːtjuˈɔsiti; ˏvɚtʃʊˋɑsətɪ] *n*. 1. 艺术鉴别力。2. 艺术(尤其是音乐)上的熟练技巧。3. 〔集合词〕艺术鉴赏界。4. 〔罕〕(浅尝的)艺术趣味。

vir·tu·o·so [vəːtjuˈəuzəu, -səu; vɚtjʊˋozo, -so] *n*. (*pl*. ~**s**, **-si** [-siː; -si]) 1. 艺术鉴赏家[爱好者]。2. (艺术的)大师,名家;〔尤指〕音乐演奏名手。**-ship** *n*. = virtuosity.

vir·tu·ous [ˈvəːtjuəs; ˋvɚtʃuəs] *a*. 1. 有道德的,有德行的,善良的。2. 贞洁的。3. 〔古〕有效力的;勇敢的。**-ly** *ad*. **-ness** *n*.

vi·ru·cide [ˈvaiərəsaid; ˋvaɪrə,saɪd] *n*. = viricide. **-ci·dal** *a*.

vir·u·lence [ˈvirulәns; ˋvɪrulәns] *n*. 1. 有毒,毒力,毒性。2. 剧毒,恶毒,恶意。3.【医】病毒性;致病力。

vir·u·lent [ˈvirulənt; ˋvɪrulənt] *a*. 1. 有剧毒的,致死的,有毒害的。2. 病毒的,致病性强的;恶性的。3. 有恶意的,恶毒的。*a* ~ (*bacterio*) *phage* 病毒噬菌体。*a* ~ *poison* 剧毒。**-ly** *ad*.

vi·ruol·o·gy [ˌvaiəˈrɔlədʒi; vaɪˋrɑlədʒɪ] *n*. 病毒学。

vi·rus [ˈvaiərəs; ˋvaɪrəs] *n*. 1.【医】病毒;滤过性病原体。2. 毒素;毒害。3. 恶意,恶毒。4.【计】(电脑)病毒〔指扰乱或破坏电脑原有程序和所存文件的非法指令,多具潜伏性,常常在某个特定的时间发作,多为电脑黑客编制,口语中亦作 bug〕。~(-)**buster**【计】1. 病毒清除程序,杀毒软件。2. 电脑杀毒专家。~ **scan**【计】病毒(预防)扫描〔以杀毒软件对电脑磁盘和软件进行扫描以防感染病毒〕。

vis. = visual.

Vis. = Viscount(ess).

vis [vis; vɪs] *n*. (*pl*. ***vi·res*** [ˈvaiəriːz; ˋvaɪriz])〔L.〕力。~ ***a fronte*** [-əˈfrɔnte; -əˋfrɑnte] 前面来的力。~ ***a tergo*** [-əˈtəːgəu; -əˋtɚgo] 后面来的力。~ ***animi*** [ˈænimi; ˋænɪmɪ] 勇气。~ ***elastica*** [eˈlæstikə; ɛˋlæstɪkə] 弹力。~ ***inertiae*** [iˈnəːʃiiː; ɪˋnɚʃɪi] 惰性,惯性力。~***major*** [ˈmeidʒə; ˋmedʒɚ]【法】不可抗力。~ ***medicatrix naturae*** [mediˈkeitriks neiˈtjuːriː; mɛdɪˋketrɪks neˋtjuri]【医】自然治愈力,自愈力。~ ***mortua*** [ˈmɔːtjuə; ˋmɔtjuə]【物】死势,致动力。~ ***motiva*** [məuˈtaivə; moˋtaɪvə] 原动力。~ ***vitae*** [ˈvaiti; ˋvaɪtɪ] = ~ ***vitalis*** [ˈvaitəlis; vaɪˋtelɪs] 活力;生命力。~ ***viva*** [ˈvaivə; ˋvaɪvə]【物】活劲,活势;工作能力。

V

vi·sa [ˈviːzə; ˋvizə] ***n.***, ***vt.*** (***~ed***, ***~'d***; ***~ing***) = visé.

vis·age [ˈvizidʒ; ˋvɪzɪdʒ] ***n.*** 脸,面貌,容貌,外表。

vis·ard [ˈvizəd, ˈvaizəd; ˋvɪzɚd, ˋvaɪzɚd] ***n.*** = visor.

vis-à-vis [ˈviːzɑːviː; ˋvizəˋvi] **I *n.*** **1.** 相对[面对面]的人[物];对等人物;对方,对谈者,对舞者。**2.** 面对面的谈话;密谈。**3.** 两人[四人]对坐马车;两人对坐的 S 形长椅。**II *a.*** 相对[面对面]的,相向的。**III *ad.*** 相对着,面对面,对坐着 (*to*; *with*)。**IV *prep.*** 在…的对过,对着。

Vi·sa·yan [viˈsɑːjən; vɪˋsɑjən] **I *n.*** **1.** (菲律宾的)米沙鄢人。**2.** 米沙鄢语。**II *a.*** 米沙鄢人的;米沙鄢语的。

Vi·sa·yan Is·lands, Visayas [viːˈsɑːjɑːz; viˋsajɑz] ***n.*** (菲律宾的)米沙鄢群岛。

Visc. = Viscount(ess).

vis·ca·cha [visˈkɑːtʃə; vɪsˋkɑtʃə] ***n.*** 【动】鼩 (*Lagostomus trichodactylus*) 〔产于南美大草原〕。

vis·cer·a [ˈvisərə; ˋvɪsərə] ***n.*** [*pl.*] (*sing.* ***vis·cus***) **1.** 内脏,脏腑。**2.** 内容;内部的东西。

vis·cer·al [ˈvisərəl; ˋvɪsərəl] ***a.*** **1.** 内脏的。**2.** 内心的。**3.** 本能的;食欲的;粗鄙的。*the ~ cavity* 腹腔,体腔。~ **cleft** 【生】鳃裂。~ **learning** 【生】内脏熟习〔指内脏逐渐获得的控制不随意生理过程的能力〕。

vis·cer·ate [ˈvisəreit; ˋvɪsəˏret] ***vt.*** 挖出…的内脏。

vis·cer·o·gen·ic [ˌvisərəˈdʒenik; ˏvɪsərəˋdʒɛnɪk] ***a.*** 发自体内的。

vis·cer·o·ton·ic [ˌvisərəˈtɔnik; ˏvɪsərəˋtɑnɪk] **I *n.*** 爱享乐而外向的人。**II *a.*** 爱享乐而外向的。

vis·cid [ˈvisid; ˋvɪsɪd] ***a.*** **1.** 黏的,胶黏的,黏质的。**2.** 半流体的。**-ly *ad.*** **-i·ty** [viˈsiditi; vɪˋsɪdətɪ] ***n.*** 黏(着)性。

vis·co·e·las·tic [ˌviskəuiˈlæstik; ˏvɪskoɪˋlæstɪk] ***a.*** 黏弹性的。

vis·coid [ˈviskɔid; ˋvɪskɔɪd], **vis·coi·dal** [visˈkɔidəl; vɪsˋkɔɪdəl] ***a.*** 黏丝体的。

vis·com·e·ter [visˈkɔmitə; vɪsˋkɑmətɚ] ***n.*** = viscosimeter.

vis·cose [ˈviskəus; ˋvɪskos] **I *n.*** 【化】黏胶液,黏胶(纤维)。**II *a.*** **1.** 黏胶(制)的。**2.** 黏滞的;黏性的。

vis·co·sim·e·ter [ˌviskəuˈsimitə; ˏvɪskəˋsɪmətɚ] ***n.*** 【物】黏度计,黏滞计。

vis·cos·i·ty [visˈkɔsiti; vɪsˋkɑsətɪ] ***n.*** 黏性;黏(滞)度;【物】黏滞性。

vis·count [ˈvaikaunt; ˋvaɪkaʊnt] ***n.*** 子爵。**-cy, -y, -ship *n.*** 子爵的地位[头衔、身分]。**-ess *n.*** 子爵夫人;女子爵。

V

vis·cous [ˈviskəs; ˋvɪskəs] ***a.*** **1.** 黏的,胶黏的;【物】黏性的。**2.** 【植】具有黏质的。~ **fluid** 黏滞流体。**-ly *ad.***

Visc(t). = Viscount(ess).

vis·cus [ˈviskəs; ˋvɪskəs] ***n.*** 〔L.〕〔罕〕内脏。

vise [vais; vaɪs] ***n.***, ***vt.*** 〔美〕= vice[2].

vi·sé [ˈvizei; ˋvize] **I *n.*** (护照等的)背签,签证。*a tourist ~* 旅游签证。*an entry* [*exit*] *~* 入境[出境]签证。**II *vt.*** (***~ed***, ***~d***, ***~'d***; ***~ing***) 在…上背签,发给签证。

Vish·nu [ˈviʃnuː; ˋvɪʃnu] ***n.*** 【宗】毗湿奴〔印度教三大神之一,保持之神〕。

vis·i·bil·i·ty [ˌviziˈbiliti; ˏvɪzəˋbɪlətɪ] ***n.*** **1.** 能见性[度];可见物;可见度;可见性。**2.** 可见距离;视界。**3.** 显著,明显(度),明白。

vis·i·ble [ˈvizəbl; ˋvɪzəbl] **I *a.*** **1.** 可见的,看得见的,肉眼能见的。**2.** 显著的,显明的,明白的。**3.** 能会见的。**4.** (资料等)显露式的,露出部分内容以便易于查找的。*the ~ phenomena* 可视现象。*with ~ impatience* 带着显然不耐烦的样子。*When will he be ~?* 什么时候可以会见他呢? *Is he ~?* 能会见他吗? *~ distance* 可见距离。**II *n.*** **1.** 看得见的事物;直观教具。**2.** 〔the ~〕物质世界,现实世界 (*opp.* the invisible)。~ **exports** [**imports**] 【商】有形进[出]口,商品进[出]口。~ **horizon** 可见地平线。~ **means** 有形财产。~ **ray** 【物】可见光。~ **signal** 可见信号。~ **sound** (收音机的)示波器,电眼。~ **spectrum** 【物】可见光谱(段)。~ **speech** 【语】可见语言;视觉信号传话法;(教聋人说话用的)发音部位分解图。~ **supply** 有形供应量,商品粮总量 (*opp.* invisible supply)。

vis·i·bly [ˈvizəbli; ˋvɪzəblɪ] ***ad.*** 看得见地;显然,明明白白。

Vis·i·goth [ˈvizigɔθ, -gɔːθ; ˋvɪzɪˏgɑθ, -gɔθ] ***n.*** 西哥特人〔公元四世纪入侵罗马帝国并在法国和西班牙建立王国的条顿族人〕。**-ic** [ˌvisiˈgɔθik; ˏvɪsəˋgɑθɪk] ***a.***

vis in·er·ti·ae [ˌvisiˈnəːʃiiː; ˏvɪsɪnˋɝʃɪˏi] 〔L.〕惰性,惰力 (= force of inertia)。

vi·sion [ˈviʒən; ˋvɪʒən] **I *n.*** **1.** 视力,视觉。**2.** 〔不用冠词〕先见,洞察;想像力。**3.** 景象,光景;姿态;美景;极美的人〔尤指妇女〕;绝妙的东西。**4.** 幻影,幻象;【宗】显圣;【医】幻视。**5.** 【修】想像描述;【影】回忆场面;幻想场面。**6.** 电视〔与收听广播相对〕。*the field of ~* 视野。*a man of broad ~* 见识广的人。*The bride was a lovely ~.* 新娘子模样儿很可爱。*a poet's ~* 诗人的想像力。*~s of youth* 青春的梦想。***beyond one's ~*** 看不见的。**II *vt.*** 在梦(幻)中看见;想像,想见。~**-mix** 【影】溶合(镜头)。

vi·sion·al [ˈviʒənəl; ˋvɪʒənəl] ***a.*** 梦幻的,在梦幻中看见的,幻影的,幻象的;幻想的,梦想的,空想的。**-ly *ad.***

vi·sion·a·ry [ˈviʒənəri; ˋvɪʒənˏɛrɪ] **I *a.*** **1.** 幻影的;幻想的,梦想的,空想的,非现实的,(计划等)不能实行的。**2.** 专爱空想的。*a ~ image* 幻影。**II *n.*** 幻想家,梦想者,空想家。

vis·it [ˈvizit; ˋvɪzɪt] **I *vt.*** **1.** 拜访,访问,探望,问候;(作客)暂住;去…游览,参观;常常去,常常出入。**2.** 视察,调查,巡视;去(某处)检查;出诊。**3.** (疾病、灾害等)侵袭;降临。**4.** 惩罚(罪人);施加(报复,报应)。**5.** 〔古〕降福于。*~ a friend* 拜访朋友。*~ Rome* 去罗马游览。*~ public houses* 出入小酒馆。*The plague ~ed London in 1665.* 瘟疫在 1665 年侵袭过伦敦。— ***vi.*** **1.** 访问,拜访,拜望,探望;参观,游览;视察,巡视;逗留。**2.** 〔美〕叙谈,闲谈 (*with*)。*~ at strange houses* 客居在陌生人家。*~ with one's friend* 留住在朋友那里。*~ with a return in kind* 用同样东西报答。*We don't ~.* 我们互不往来。*~ a friend on the telephone* 在电话里与朋友交谈。**II *n.*** **1.** 访问;往来;参观,游览。**2.** (作客)逗留。**3.** 巡视,视察;出诊。*a farewell ~* 辞行。*a domiciliary ~* 【法】住所搜查。***give*** [***make***, ***pay***] ***sb.*** ***a ~*** 访问(某人)。***make*** [***pay***] ***a ~ to some place*** 参观(某地)。***on a ~ to ...*** **1.** 去看某人;住在…家里。**2.** 在访问…,在参观…。***pay ... a long ~*** 在…家住一个很长时期。***receive a ~ from sb.*** 受(某人)访问。***return a ~*** 回拜,答访。***the right of ~*** = *the right of visitation*. *~ of ceremony* 正式访问。*~ of civility* [*courtesy*, *respect*] 拜谒。

vis·it·a·ble [ˈvizitəbl; ˋvɪzɪtəbl] ***a.*** **1.** 可拜访的。**2.** 适于访问的,值得访问的。**3.** 会受到检查[访问,视察等]的。

vis·it·ant [ˈvizitənt; ˋvɪzətənt] **I *n.*** **1.** (特指身分高的)来访者;贵宾。**2.** (神话中所说)下凡的神仙。**3.** 【鸟】候鸟。**4.** 〔V-〕圣母访问会的修道女。**II *a.*** 访问的,来访的。

vis·it·a·tion [ˌviziˈteiʃən; ˏvɪzəˋteʃən] ***n.*** **1.** 访问,游览,参观。**2.** 巡视,视察,检查;船舶检查。**3.** 天罚,祸;天惠,福;(良心的)谴责,报应。**4.** 〔V-〕【宗】圣母访问节〔7月2日〕。**5.** 〔口〕久坐(不走)。**6.** (候鸟的)群集。*the right of ~* 【国际法】(船舶的)检查权。

vis·it·a·to·ri·al [ˌvizitəˈtɔːriəl; ˏvɪzətəˋtɔrɪəl] ***a.*** 访问的;巡视的,视察的;(有权)检查的。

vis·it·ing [ˈvizitiŋ; ˋvɪzɪtɪŋ] ***a.***, ***n.*** 访问(的);视察

(的)。a ~ *committee* 视察委员会。**be on ~ *terms with* = *have a ~ acquaintance with*** 和…常互相访问,和…关系密切。~ **book** 来宾留名簿。~ **card** 名片。~ **day** 会客日,接见来客日。~ **fireman** 〔美俚〕游客。

vis·i·tor [ˈvizitə; ˋvɪzɪtɚ] ***n.*** (*fem*. ***vis·i·tress*** [-tris; -trɪs]) **1.** 访问者,来客,来宾;留住客,住客;游客,来游者,参观者。**2.** 〔*pl.*〕【运】客队,来访队。**3.** 〔常 V-〕巡视员,视察员,检查员;(大学的)监察员。*Visitors not admitted*. 谢绝参观。~**'s book** (旅馆等的)旅客登记簿;来客留名簿。

vis·i·to·ri·al [ˌviziˈtɔːriəl; ˏvɪzəˋtorɪəl] ***a.*** = visitatorial.

vi·sor [ˈvaizə, ˈvi-; ˋvaɪzɚ, ˋvɪ-] ***n.*** **1.** 【史】(盔的)面罩,脸甲。**2.** 〔美〕帽舌,遮阳。**3.** 【机】护目镜,防眩罩;遮阳板。

VISTA [ˈvistə; ˋvɪstə] = Volunteers in Service to America 美国志愿服务队〔1964 年美国政府制定一项计划,派遣志愿队员去美国及其属地以及波多黎各等地的贫困区服务〕。

vis·ta [ˈvistə; ˋvɪstə] ***n.*** **1.** 展望;林荫路景,峡谷风光〔从两排树木或房屋之间一直望过去的景色〕。**2.** 瞻望前途;追溯往事。*look back through the ~ of the past* 追溯一件件往事。

vis·u·al [ˈvizjuəl; ˋvɪʒuəl] ***a.*** **1.** 视觉的,观看的;视力的。**2.** 看得见的。**3.** 光学的。**4.** 形象化的。~ **acuity** 【医】视敏度。~ **aids** 直观教具。~ **art** 观赏艺术〔如绘画、摄影、雕刻、建筑等〕。~ **binary** [**double**] 【天】幻视双星〔肉眼看为一单星,望远镜中看才能看出为双星〕。~ **display unit** 可视显示单位。~ **field** 视野。~ **instrument** 电子视觉琴。~ **literacy** 直观力;观赏能力。~ **nerve** 视神经。~ **organ** 视觉器官。~ **pollution** (市内广告牌等造成破坏自然景观的)视觉污染。~ **resolution** 视力分辨率。~ **sensations** 视觉。**-ly *ad.*** (*the ~ly impaired* 〔婉〕盲人;视力很差的人)。

vis·u·al·i·sa·tion, 〔美〕**-za·tion** [ˌvizjuəlaiˈzeiʃən; ˏvɪzjuəlaɪˋzeʃən] ***n.*** 显现;形象;想像;形象化。

vis·u·al·ize, -ise [ˈvizjuəlaiz; ˋvɪʒuəlˏaɪz] ***vt.***, ***vi.*** (使)显现;想像;(使)形象化,(使)具体化。

vis·u·o·spa·tial [ˈviʒuəuˈspeiʃəl; ˋvɪʒuəˋspeʃəl] ***a.*** 视觉空间的。

vi·ta [ˈvaitə, ˈviːtə, ˈwiːtə; ˋvaɪtə, ˋvitə, ˋwitə] ***n.*** (*pl*. *-tae* [ˈvaitiː; ˋvaɪti, ˋwi-]) 〔L.〕 **1.** 传记,自传〔通常指传略或小传〕。**2.** 履历书 (= curriculum vitae)。

Vi·ta·glass [ˈvaitəglɑːs; ˋvaɪtəglæs] ***n.*** (能透过紫外线的)维他玻璃〔商品名〕。

vi·tal [ˈvaitl; ˋvaɪtl] ***a.*** **1.** 生命的;维持生命所必需的;有生命的;充满活力的,生气勃勃的,生动的。**2.** 生死攸关的,致命的;重大的,紧要的;不可缺少的。~ *energies* [*power*] 生命力,活力。~ *functions* 生活机能。~ *phenomena* 生命现象。~ *warmth* 体温。*a ~ wound* 致命伤。~ *interests* 切身利益。*Perseverance is ~ to success*. 坚忍是成功的重要条件。*of ~ importance* 极重要的。~ **capacity** 肺活量。~ **centre** 【生理】生命中枢。~ **hardiness** 生活抵抗力,抗性。~ **measuring** 机能测量〔指体温,脉搏等〕。~ **part** (身体的)要害处,命门。~ **signs** 生命特征〔指脉搏、呼吸、体温和血压〕。~ **staining** 活体染色(法)。~ **statistics** **1.** 人口动态统计。**2.** 〔谑〕(女性的)身材尺寸〔指胸围、腰围和臀围〕。**-ly *ad.* -ness *n.***

vi·tal·ism [ˈvaitəlizəm; ˋvaɪtlˏɪzm] ***n.*** 【哲】活力论,生机说[论] (*opp*. mechanism)。

vi·tal·ist [ˈvaitəlist; ˋvaɪtlˏɪst] ***n.*** 活力论者;生机论者。

vi·tal·is·tic [ˌvaitəˈlistik; ˏvaɪtlˋɪstɪk] ***a.*** 活力论的;生机论的。

vi·tal·i·ty [vaiˈtæliti; vaɪˋtælətɪ] ***n.*** **1.** 生命力,(生)活力;生命强度,茂盛度;体力;(植物的)发芽力。**2.** 活气,生气;生动性。**3.** (文艺作品等的)持久力,持久性,(物件的)使用寿命。

vi·tal·ize, -ise [ˈvaitəlaiz; ˋvaɪtlˏaɪz] ***vt.*** 赋与…生命,给与…活力[生气];使生动活泼;激发,鼓舞。**-i·za·tion** [ˌvaitəlaiˈzeiʃən; ˏvaɪtəlaɪˋzeʃən] ***n.***

vi·tal·li·um [vaiˈtæliəm; vaɪˋtælɪəm] ***n.*** 维他良〔一种抗腐蚀的钴铬钼合金的商品名称,用于牙科、骨科、整形术、铸造等〕。

vi·tals [ˈvaitlz; ˋvaɪtlz] ***n.*** 〔*pl.*〕要害器官〔心、肺、脑〕;要害,紧要处,核心。*tear the ~ out of a subject* 抓住问题的要害。

vi·ta·min(e) [ˈvaitəmin, ˈvi-; ˋvaɪtəmɪn, ˋvɪ-] ***n.*** 维生素,维他命。**-ic** [ˌvaitəˈminik; ˏvaɪtəˋmɪnɪk] ***a.*** 维生素(性)的。

vi·ta·min·i·za·tion [ˌvaitəminaiˈzeiʃən; ˏvaɪtəmɪnaɪˋzeʃən] ***n.*** 加入维生素;增加生气。

vi·ta·phone [ˈvaitəfəun; ˋvaɪtəfon] ***n.*** 维太风〔蜡盘配音的有声电影〕。

vi·ta·scope [ˈvaitəskəup; ˋvaɪtəˏskop] ***n.*** 一种早期电影放映机。

vi·tel·lin [viˈtelin; vɪˋtɛlɪn] ***n.*** 【生化】卵黄磷朊[蛋白],卵黄素。

vi·tel·line [viˈtelin; vɪˋtɛlɪn] **I *a.*** 卵黄的。**II *n.*** 卵黄。

vi·tel·lus [viˈteləs; vɪˋtɛləs] ***n.*** 卵黄;【植】胚乳。

viti- *comb. f.* 葡萄: *viti*culture.

vi·ti·a·ble [ˈviʃiəbl; ˋvɪʃɪəbl] ***a.*** **1.** 可损害的,可弄坏的。**2.** 可腐蚀的;可使道德败坏的,堕落的。**3.** 可使(合同等)失去法律作用的;可使变无效的。

vi·ti·ate [ˈviʃieit; ˋvɪʃɪˏet] ***vt.*** **1.** 损害,弄坏;弄脏,弄污,使腐败。**2.** 使失效[无效]。**3.** 使道德败坏。~*d air* 污浊的空气。~ *a contract* 使契约失效。**-a·tion** [ˌviʃiˈeiʃən; ˏvɪʃɪˋeʃən], **-a·tor** [ˈviʃieitə; ˋvɪʃɪˏetɚ] ***n.***

vit·i·ce·tum [ˌvitiˈsiːtəm; vɪtɪˋsitəm] ***n.*** (*pl*. *-tums*, *-ta* [-tə; -tə]) 葡萄园。

vi·tic·o·lous [vaiˈtikələs; vaɪˋtɪkələs] ***a.*** (霉菌、昆虫等)寄生于葡萄藤的。

vit·i·cul·ture [ˈvitikʌltʃə, ˈvait-; ˋvɪtɪˏkʌltʃɚ, ˋvaɪ-] ***n.*** 葡萄栽培(学)。**-tur·al** [ˌvitiˈkʌltʃərəl; ˏvɪtɪˋkʌltʃɚəl] ***a.***

vit·i·li·go [ˌvitiˈlaigəu; ˏvɪtɪˋlaɪgo] ***n.*** 【医】白斑(病),白癜疯。

vit·rain [ˈvitrein; ˋvɪtren] ***n.*** 【矿】镜煤,闪炭。

vit·re·ous [ˈvitriəs; ˋvɪtrɪəs] ***a.*** 玻璃的;玻璃质[状]的;透明的。~ *china* 玻璃瓷。~ *luster* 玻璃光泽。~ **body** (眼睛的)玻璃体。~ **copper** 【矿】辉铜矿。~ **electricity** 玻璃电〔摩擦玻璃发生的阳电〕。~ **humour** (眼睛的)玻璃液。~ **layer** 角膜层。~ **silver** 【矿】熔凝[透明]石英 (= fused quartz)。**-ly *ad.* -ness *n.***

vi·tres·cence [viˈtresns; vɪˋtrɛsns] ***n.*** 玻(璃)态,玻(璃)状。

vi·tres·cent [viˈtresnt; vɪˋtrɛsnt] ***a.*** 会变成玻璃质的,能化为玻璃质的。

vitri- *comb. f.* 玻璃: *vitri*form.

vit·ric [ˈvitrik; ˋvɪtrɪk] ***a.*** 玻璃的;有玻璃特性的;玻璃状的。

vit·rics [ˈvitriks; ˋvɪtrɪks] ***n.*** 〔*pl.*〕 **1.** 〔动词用单数〕玻璃制品工艺学,玻璃器皿制作术。**2.** 玻璃制品,玻璃器皿。

vit·ri·fac·tion [ˌvitriˈfækʃən; ˏvɪtrəˋfækʃən] ***n.*** 玻璃化,透明化。

vit·ri·fi·a·ble [ˈvitrifaiəbl; ˋvɪtrəˏfaɪəbl] ***a.*** 能玻璃化的。

vit·ri·fi·ca·tion [ˌvitrifiˈkeiʃən; ˏvɪtrəfɪˋkeʃən] ***n.*** = vitrifaction.

vit·ri·form [ˈvitrifɔːm; ˋvɪtrəˏfɔrm] ***a.*** 玻璃状的。

vit·ri·fy [ˈvitrifai; ˋvɪtrəˏfaɪ] ***vt.***, ***vi.*** (*-fied*) (使)玻璃化。*a vitrified pipe* 陶管。

vit·rine [vi'tri:n; vɪ`trin] ***n*.** 玻璃柜〔置放艺术陈列品或古玩等用〕。

vit·ri·ol ['vitriəl; `vɪtrɪəl] **I *n*. 1.**【化】硫酸(盐);矾。**2.** 刻薄话;尖酸刻薄的讽刺。*black* ~ 粗制胆矾。*blue* [*copper*] ~ 胆矾,硫酸铜。*green* [*iron*] ~ 绿矾。*nickel* ~ = ~ *sulfate* 翠矾。*oil of* ~ 浓硫酸。*red* [*cobalt*] ~ 红矾,硫酸钴。*white* [*zinc*] ~ 皓矾,硫酸锌。***dip one's pen in*** ~ 写尖酸刻薄的文章。***throw*** ~ ***over*** [*at*] (*sb.'s face*) (在某人脸上)泼硫酸(以毁损其容貌)。**II *vt*.** (〔英〕*-ll-*) 用硫酸烧伤;浸在稀硫酸内,用硫酸处理。~**-throwing** 以硫酸泼人面部毁其容貌的行为。

vit·ri·ol·ic [ˌvitri'ɔlik; ˏvɪtrɪ`ɑlɪk] ***a*. 1.** 硫酸(盐)的,由硫酸制成的。**2.** (批评等)尖酸刻薄的,辛辣的。*a* ~ *plant* 硫酸厂。

vit·ri·ol·ize ['vitriəlaiz; `vɪtrɪəlˏaɪz] ***vt*.** 用硫酸烧;用硫酸(盐)处理。

vit·ta ['vitə; `vɪtə] ***n*.** (*pl*. ***vit·tae*** ['viti:; `vɪti]) **1.** (古罗马人的)头带。**2.**【植】(伞形科果实的)油道,油管。**3.**【动,植】色带,色条。

vit·tle ['vitl; `vɪtl] ***n*., *v*.** 〔发、方〕= victual.

vit·u·line ['vitjulain; `vɪtʃʊˏlaɪn] ***a*.** (像)小牛(肉)的。

vi·tu·per·ate [vi'tju:pəreit, vai't-; vɪ`tjupəret, vaɪ`t-] ***vt*.** 骂,责骂,辱骂。**-a·tion** [-'reiʃən; -`reʃən] ***n*.** **-a·tive** [-reitiv; -retɪv] ***a*.** **-a·tor** [-reitə; -ˏretɚ] ***n*.** 辱骂者。

vi·va ['vi:və; `vivə] **I *int*.** 〔It.〕万岁! **II *n*.** 万岁声;〔*pl*.〕欢声,欢呼声。

vi·va·ce [vi'vɑ:tʃi; vɪ`vɑtʃɪ] ***ad*.** 〔It.〕【乐】活泼地〔速度极快〕。

vi·va·cious [vi'veiʃəs, vai-; vaɪ`veʃəs, vɪ-] ***a*. 1.** 快活的,活泼的;生气勃勃的。**2.** 〔古〕长生的,长寿的;难杀死的。**3.**【植】多年生的。**-ly *ad*.**

vi·vac·i·ty [vi'væsiti, vai-; vaɪ`væsətɪ, vɪ-] ***n*.** 活泼;快活;愉快。

vi·van·dière [vivɑ̃:ndi'ɛə; vɪvɑ̃`djɛr] ***n*.** 〔F.〕(特指法国军队中卖烟酒等的)女随军商贩。

vi·var·i·um [vai'vɛəriəm; vaɪ`vɛrɪəm] ***n*.** (*pl*. ~***s***, ***-var·i·a*** [-riə; -rɪə]) (由人工造成环境与动植物所处自然条件相似的)生态动物园,生态饲养场[室、箱]。

vi·vat ['vaivæt; `vaɪvæt] **I *int*.** 〔L.〕万岁! *V- regina* 女王[王后]万岁! *V- rex* 国王万岁! **II *n*.** 万岁声,欢呼声。

vi·va vo·ce ['vaivə 'vəusi; `vaɪvə`vosɪ] ***ad*.** 〔L.〕**1.** 大声地;口头地。**2.** 口试。*be voted viva voce* 口头表决。**viva-voce *a*.** 口头的 (*a viva-voce vote* 口头的表决)。

vive [vi:v; viv] ***int*.** 〔F.〕万岁! *V- le roi*! 国王万岁!

vi·ver·rine [vai'verin; vaɪ`verɪn] **I *a*.**【动】灵猫科(*Viverridae*)的。**II *n*.** 灵猫科动物。

vi·vers ['vaivəz; `vivɚz] ***n*. *pl*.** 〔Scot.〕食物,粮食。

vives [vaivz; vaɪvz] ***n*.**【野医】(马的)颌下腺炎。

vivi- *comb*. *f*. 表示"活的": *vivi*fy.

Viv·i·an ['viviən; `vɪvɪən] ***n*.** 维维安〔男子名,女子名〕。

viv·i·an·ite ['viviənait; `vɪvɪənˏaɪt] ***n*.**【矿】蓝铁矿。

viv·id ['vivid; `vɪvɪd] ***a*. 1.** 活泼的,生气横溢的。**2.** (光、色)鲜明的,鲜艳的,闪亮的。**3.** 如在眼前的,生动的,栩栩如生的,逼真的,清楚的。*a* ~ *imagination* 活跃的想像力。*a* ~ *description* 生动的描写。~ *in one's memory* 记得清清楚楚。**-ly *ad*.** **-ness *n*.**

viv·i·fy ['vivifai; `vɪvəˏfaɪ] ***vt*.** (*-fied*) **1.** 给与生气;使活泼,使生动。**2.** 使复生。**-fi·ca·tion** [ˌvivifi'keiʃən; ˏvɪvɪfə`keʃən] ***n*.** **-fi·er** [-ə; -ə] ***n*.**

vi·vip·a·ra [vi'vipərə, vai-; vɪ`vɪpərə, vaɪ-] ***n*.** 〔*pl*.〕【动】胎生动物。

viv·i·par·i·ty [ˌvivi'pæriti; ˏvɪvɪ`pærətɪ] ***n*. 1.**【动】胎生。**2.**【植】(种子在母株上发芽的)胎萌,株上萌发。

vi·vip·a·rous [vi'vipərəs, vai-; vɪ`vɪpərəs, vaɪ-] ***a*. 1.**【动】胎生的。**2.**【植】(种子)在母株上发芽的,母体萌芽的。

viv·i·sect [ˌvivi'sekt, 'vivisekt; ˏvɪvə`sɛkt, `vɪvəˏsɛkt] ***vt*., *vi*.** 活体解剖(动物)。

viv·i·sec·tion [ˌvivi'sekʃən; ˏvɪvə`sɛkʃən] ***n*.** 活体解剖。**-al *a*.** **-ist *n*.** 活体解剖(论)者。

viv·i·sec·tor [ˌvivi'sektə; `vɪvəˏsɛktɚ] ***n*.** 活体解剖者。

vi·vo ['vi:vəu; `vivo] ***ad*.** 〔It.〕【乐】= vivace.

vix·en ['viksn; `vɪksn] ***n*. 1.** 雌狐。**2.** 泼妇,悍妇。

vix·en·ish ['viksəniʃ; `vɪksnɪʃ] ***a*.** 泼辣的;爱吵架〔骂人〕的;狠毒的。

Vi·yel·la [vai'jelə, vi-; vaɪ`jɛlə] ***n*.** 维也拉(法兰绒)〔一种英国制毛棉混纺物商品名称〕。

viz(.) = 〔L.〕*videlicet*. ★ viz. 通常都读作 namely.

viz·ard ['vizəd; `vɪzɚd] ***n*.** = visor.

vi·zi(e)r [vi'ziə, 'viziə; vɪ`zɪr, `vɪzjɚ] ***n*.** (伊斯兰教国家的)大臣。*the grand* ~ (土耳其等国的)内阁总理,首相。**-ate *n*.** 伊斯兰教国家大臣的职位[职权]。

vi·zor ['vaizə; `vaɪzɚ, `vɪzɚ] ***n*.** = visor.

VJ (Day) = Victory over Japan (Day) (第二次世界大战)对日作战[抗日战争]胜利(日)〔1945年8月15日〕。

VL = Vulgar Latin 通俗拉丁语。

v.l. = 〔L.〕*varia lectio* (稿本的)异文 (= variant reading)。

VLA = Very Large Array 极大阵列〔美国国家射电天文台的一组射电望远镜〕。

Vla·di·vos·tok [ˌvlædi'vɔstɔk; ˏvlædɪ`vɑstɑk] ***n*.** 符拉迪沃斯托克〔即海参崴〕〔俄罗斯港市〕。

v.l.c.c. = very large crude carrier 超级油轮〔载重超过三十万吨的原油运输船〕。

VLF, vlf = very low frequency【无】甚低频。

Vlo·ra, Vlo·rë ['vləurə; `vlorə] ***n*.** 发罗拉〔阿尔巴尼亚港市〕。

VLSIC = very large scale integrated circuit【计】超大规模集成电路。

v.m. = voltmeter.

v / m = volts per metre 每米的伏特数。

V-mail ['vi:meil; `viˏmel] ***n*.** 〔美〕(用微型胶片缩制的)缩印邮件〔寄达目的地后再放大〕。

VMD, V.M.D. = 〔L.〕*Veterinariae Medicinae Doctor* 兽医学博士 (= Doctor of Veterinary Medicine)。

vn, v.n. = verb neuter 不及物动词。

V-neck ['vi:nek; `vinɛk] ***n*.** V形领口。

V.O. = Victorian Order, Royal 〔英〕皇家维多利亚勋章。

vo. = verso.

vo = verbal orders 口头命令。

VOA = Voice of America 美国之音(电台)。

Voc. = **1.** vocational. **2.** vocative.

vocab. = vocabulary.

vo·ca·ble ['vəukəbl; `vokəbl] ***n*.** (特指不作为意义单位、只作为语音单位的)词,单词。

vo·cab·u·la·ry [və'kæbjuləri; və`kæbjəˏlɛrɪ] ***n*. 1.** 词汇,单词集。**2.** (某作家、某一阶层人们的)用词数,用词范围。*the* ~ *of a dictionary* 词典的词汇。*His* ~ *is limited*. 他的词汇很有限。*exhaust one's* ~ 用尽自己知道的词汇。~ **control** 词汇控制。~ **entry** (词典中的)词条,词目。

vo·cal ['vəukəl; `vokl] **I *a*. 1.** 声的,(关于)声音的。**2.** 发为声的;口头的;表现为言语的;(用言语)把意见表达出来的。**3.** 〔诗〕(流水等)响,鸣,作声。**4.**【语音】有声音的,母音(性)的;浊音的;【乐】声乐的,歌唱的。*a* ~ *communication* 口头传达。*a* ~ *performer* 歌手。*Public opinion has at last become* ~. 舆论终于喧嚷起来了。**II *n*. 1.**【语音】母音。**2.**【乐】声乐作品;声乐表演。**3.**【天主】有股票权的人。~ **bands** [**c(h)ords, ligaments**]【解】声带。~ **music**【乐】声乐。~ **print** 声纹

V

(= voice print)。~ **solo**【乐】独唱。**-ly** *ad*. 用声音,口头。

vo·cal·ic [vəu'kælik; vo'kælɪk] **I** *a*.【语音】母音的;由母音构成的;含母音的;多母音的。**II** *n*. (构成音节中最响亮部分的)母音[复合母音]。

vo·cal·ise [ˌvəukl'iːz; ˏvokə'liz] *n*.【乐】(不用歌词而用唱名或母音来练唱)练声;练声练习曲。

vo·cal·ism ['vəukəlizəm; 'vokəlɪzəm] *n*. **1.** 发声;母音发音;母音系统。**2.**【乐】声乐(技巧);歌唱。

vo·cal·ist ['vəukəlist; 'voklɪst] *n*.【乐】声乐家,歌唱家[者]。

vo·cal·i·za·tion [ˌvəukəlai'zeiʃən; ˏvokəlaɪ'zeʃən] *n*. **1.** 发声;有声化;发声法。**2.**【乐】练唱,练声[特指用母音的练唱法]。

vo·cal·ize ['vəukəlaiz; 'voklˏaɪz] *vt*. **1.** 发为声,清晰的发音;使成有声音,有声化。**2.** 在(字母)上加母音符号(如在希伯来字母上等)。**3.** 使发成母音[浊音]。— *vi*. **1.** (声音)被发成母音,母音化。**2.**【乐】母音练唱,练声。**3.**〔谑〕讲,谈,叫,喊,唱,哼。

vo·ca·tion [vəu'keiʃən; vo'keʃən] *n*. **1.** 天命;天职,使命。**2.** (对于某种职业的)适合性,才能。**3.** 职业,行业。*He felt no ~ for the ministry*. 他不以为做牧师是自己的天职。*He has little* [*no*] *~ to* [*for*] *literature*. 他不大[完全不]适合搞文学。*mistake one's ~* 选错职业。*take up the ~ of engineering* 选择工程技术作专业。

vo·ca·tion·al [vəu'keiʃənəl; vo'keʃənl] *a*. 职业(上)的;天职的;有助于职业的。~ *education* 职业教育。*a ~ school* 职业学校。~ *diseases* 职业病。~ *studies* 业务学习。*one's ~ level* 业务水准。**-ism** *n*. 强调职业教育的主张,职业教育论。**-ly** *ad*.

voc·a·tive ['vɔkətiv; 'vɑkətɪv] **I** *a*.【语法】呼格的;呼唤的。*the ~ case* 呼格。**II** *n*. 呼唤语;呼格。

vo·ces ['vəusiːz; 'vosiz] *n*. *vox* 的复数。

vo·cif·er·ance [vəu'sifərəns; vo'sɪfərəns] *n*. 大声叫嚷[吵闹]。

vo·cif·er·ant [vəu'sifərənt; vo'sɪfərənt] *a*., *n*. 大声叫嚷[吵闹]的(人)。

vo·cif·er·ate [vəu'sifəreit; vo'sɪfəˏret] *vt*. (大声)叫喊着说。*He ~d "Sit down!"* 他大声叫喊'坐下来!' — *vi*. 叫嚣,喧嚷,吵闹。**-ation** [-ˌsifə'reiʃən; ˏsɪfə'reʃən] *n*. **-ator** [-ə; -ɚ] *n*. 叫喊者。

vo·cif·er·ous [vəu'sifərəs; vo'sɪfərəs] *a*. 大声叫嚷的,喧嚷的,吵闹的,叫嚣的。**-ly** *ad*.

vo·cod·er ['vəuˌkəudə; 'voˏkodɚ] *n*.〔美〕语音编码机。

vo·coid ['vəukɔid; 'vokɔɪd]【语音】**I** *a*. 如元音的。**II** *n*. 如元音的声音。

VOD = video-on-demand.

Vo·da·phone, Vo·da·fone ['vɔdəfəun; 'vɑdəfon] *n*.〔商标〕音控数据电话系统,便携式移动电话〔系由 voice, data 和 phone 三个词拼缀而成〕。

vo·der ['vəudə; 'vodɚ] *n*. 语音合成器〔由 *vo*ice *o*peration *de*monstrato*r* 缩略而成〕。

vod·ka ['vɔdkə; 'vɑdkə] *n*.〔Russ.〕伏特加酒。

voe [vəu; vo] *n*. 小湾,小海湾。

Vogt [vəukt; vokt] *n*. 沃格特[姓氏]。

vogue [vəug; vog] **I** *n*. **1.** 时髦,时样,风气,时尚;流行。**2.** 时髦的事物[人物],流行物。*a mere passing ~* 仅仅是一时风尚。*It is now the ~*. 这是现在流行的东西[风气]。*His lectures had a great ~*. 他的演讲大受欢迎。**all the ~** 最新流行品。**be in (full) ~** (十分)流行。**be out of ~** 已不流行。**bring into ~** 使流行,使时兴。**come into ~** 开始流行。**give ~ to** 使流行。**have a great** [**short**] **~** 大[不很]流行。**II** *a*. 时髦的,流行的。*a ~ word* 时髦的词,流行字眼。**vogu(e)ing** *n*. (流行音乐伴奏下的)时装表演式舞蹈。

vogue la galère [vəug lɑ gɑlɛːr; vog lɑ gɑlɛr]〔F.〕划船呀!不管怎样坚持下去吧!(= Row the galley! Keep on, come what may!)。

vo·guey ['vəugi; 'vogɪ] *a*. 流行的,时髦的。

vo·guish ['vəugiʃ; 'vogɪʃ] *a*. **1.** 时髦的,漂亮的。**2.** 一度流行的,流行时期短暂的。

Vo·gul ['vəugul; 'vogʊl] *n*. **1.** (西伯利亚西部的)芬兰—乌戈尔人。**2.** 芬兰—乌戈尔语。

voice [vɔis; vɔɪs] **I** *n*. **1.** 语声;嗓音;鸣声;〔喻〕呼声。**2.** 发声力,语言(力);想说话的欲望。**3.** (学说、主义等的)代言人,表述者,喉舌。**4.** (尤指投票时的)愿望,意见,选择;发言权,投票权,参与权。**5.**【语法】语态。**6.**【语音】有声音;声带振动;浊音(特性)。**7.**【乐】声部;歌唱才能,歌喉,嗓子;歌声;歌手。**8.**【电】口声。*a chest ~* 胸音。*a head ~* 头音。*a deep ~* 深沉有力的嗓音。*a veiled ~* 嗄哑的语声。*the ~ of the tempter* 诱惑。*Indignation gave me ~*. 气得我开了口。*My ~ is against* [*for*]...我的意见是反对[赞成]…。*a chorus of 100 ~s* 一百人的大合唱。**at the top of one's ~** 用最大的嗓门。**be in ~** 嗓子好。**find one's ~** 开口说,发出声音。**find ~ in song** 借歌发泄[表露]。**give one's ~ for** 赞成。**give ~ to** 说出,吐露,表现(*The dog gave ~ to his joy*. 狗高兴得汪汪地叫)。**have a** [**no**] **~ in** 对…有[没有]发言权。**in a hushed ~** 低声私语地。**in a loud ~** 用高声,大声。**in bad ~** 嗓子不好。**in good ~** 用嘹亮的声音,嗓子好。**lift up one's ~** 提高嗓门说话,喧嚷;抗议,诉苦。**lose one's ~** 嗓子哑了,(尤指)倒了嗓子,说不出话来。**not in ~ = out of ~** 嗓子不好。**recover one's ~** 开口说起话来。**speak under one's ~** 低声说。**with one ~** 异口同声,全场一致(*He was chosen with one ~*. 全场一致选了他)。**II** *vt*. **1.** 把…发为声音,把…发为言语,用话把…说出来,讲出。**2.**【乐】调准(风琴管);【语音】把…发成声音,使发成浊音。~ *opinions* 发表意见。~ *one's discontent* 发牢骚,鸣不平。~**-over 1.** *n*. (电视等的)画面外的语声,画外音〔评论员的说明等〕。**2.** *vi*. 为(电视画面、广告等)配画外音。~**print**〔美〕(用特殊设备记录下来,像指纹一样因人而异的)声纹,语音特征波纹。~**printing** 声纹鉴别法。

voiced [vɔist; vɔɪst] *a*. **1.** 发为声音的,…声的〔用以构成复合词〕。**2.**【语音】有声的,浊音的。*rough-~* 粗声的。~ *consonants* 浊子音。

voice·less ['vɔislis; 'vɔɪslɪs] *a*. **1.** 无声的;沉默无言的,哑的。**2.** 无发言[投票]权的。**3.**【语音】清音的。~ *consonants* 清子音。**-ly** *ad*.

voic·er ['vɔisə; 'vɔɪsɚ] *n*. **1.** (风琴音栓的)调准者。**2.** 表示意见者;投票者。

V

void [vɔid; vɔɪd] **I** *a*. **1.** 空的,空虚的,没人住的;(职位)空缺着的。**2.** 没有的,缺乏的(*of*)。**3.**〔诗〕无益的;【法】无效的。*a ~ space* 空无所有的空间。*a ~ dwelling-house* 空房。*The office is ~* [*fell ~*]. 这个职位空着。*a proposal wholly ~ of sense* 一个完全缺乏考虑的建议。**null and ~**【法】无效(的)。~ **and voidable**【法】无效且可作废的。**II** *n*. **1.** 空虚;空处,空隙,空穴;空席,空位;真空。**2.** 空虚的感觉,寂寞的心情。**3.**【桥牌】缺门。*emerging out of the ~* 凭空出现。**III** *vt*. **1.** 排泄,放出。**2.** 使[宣告]无效,把…作废,取消。**3.**〔古〕退出,搬出(房子等),出空。~ **volume**【物】孔隙率。**-ness** *n*.

void·a·ble ['vɔidəbl; 'vɔɪdəbl] *a*. 可以宣告无效的,可以作废[取消]的。

void·ance ['vɔidəns; 'vɔɪdns] *n*. **1.** 排泄,放出;放弃,退出,脱出。**2.** (职位等)出缺。

void·ed ['vɔidid; 'vɔɪdɪd] *a*. **1.** 空的,成空的;成无用的,无效的;空虚的。**2.**【纹】中空的。

voi·là [vwa'la; vwa'la] *int*.〔F.〕那就是!瞧!可不是!

voile [vwɑːl, vɔil; vwɑrl, vɔɪl] *n*.〔F.〕【纺】巴里纱〔一种透明薄纱〕。

voir dire [ˌvwɑː ˈdiə; ˌvwar ˋdir] 〔F.〕 **1.** 【法】一切照实陈述〔见证人或陪审员在接受审核时的誓语〕。**2.** 对见证人、陪审员的审查。

voi·ture [ˈvwaˈtyr; ˌvwaˋtyr] ***n.*** 〔F.〕 轻便马车;轻便敞篷汽车。

voi·tur·ette [vwɑːtjuəˈret; ˌvwa ˌtyˋret] ***n.*** 〔F.〕 小型汽车。

voix cé·leste [vwɑː seiˈlest; vwa seˋlɛst] 〔F.〕 【乐】音质柔颤如弦的风琴音节栓。

vol. = **1.** volcano; volcanic. **2.** volume. **3.** volunteer.

vo·la [ˈvəulə; ˋvolə] ***n.*** 〔L.〕 手掌,脚掌。

vo·lant [ˈvəulənt; ˋvolənt] ***a.*** 〔F.〕 **1.** 【动】会飞的,能飞的,飞行的。**2.** 【纹】飞翔态的。**3.** 迅速的,敏捷的。

vo·lan·te [vəuˈlɑːntei; voˋlante] ***ad.***, ***a.*** 【乐】轻快地(的)。

Vol·a·pük, Vol·a·puk [ˈvɔləpuk; ˋvɑlə ˌpuk] ***n.*** 一种世界语〔德国人施莱尔(Johann Martin Schleyer)于1879年创制〕。

VOLAR = volunteer army 志愿军。

vo·lar [ˈvəulə; ˋvolɚ] ***a.*** 【解】手掌的;脚掌的。

vo·la·ry [ˈvəuləri, ˈvɔlə-; ˋvolərɪ, ˋvɑlə-] ***n.*** (***pl. -ries***) **1.** 〔罕〕大鸟笼。**2.** 大鸟笼内的鸟。**3.** 鸟群;飞翔中的鸟群。

vol·a·tile [ˈvɔlətail; ˋvɑlətḷ, -tɪl] ***a.*** **1.** 挥发(性)的,飞散(性)的。**2.** 快活的,轻快的。**3.** 易变的,反复无常的,轻浮的。~ *camphor oil* 白(樟脑)油。~ *matter* 挥发性物质。~ *oil* 挥发油,精油。

vol·a·til·i·ty [ˌvɔləˈtiliti; ˌvɑləˋtɪlətɪ] ***n.*** **1.** 挥发性;挥发度。**2.** 轻快,快活。**3.** 变动不止,反复无常;轻浮。

vol·at·il·i·za·tion [vɔˌlætilaiˈzeiʃən; ˌvɑlətɪlaɪˋzeʃən] ***n.*** 挥发(作用)。

vol·at·il·ize, -ise [vɔˈlætilaiz; ˋvɑlətḷ ˌaɪz] ***vt.***, ***vi.*** (使)挥发。

vol-au-vent [ˈvɔləuˈvɑ̃ːŋ; ˌvoloˋvɑ̃] ***n.*** 〔F.〕 肉馅油酥合。

vol·can·ic [vɔlˈkænik; vɑlˋkænɪk] ***a.*** **1.** 火山(性)的;火山作用形成的,火成的。**2.** 有火山的,火山多的。**3.** 暴发性的,猛烈的,激烈的。~ *ash(es)* 火山灰。*a* ~ *character* 暴烈的性格。~ **glass** 【矿】火山玻璃,黑耀石。~ **rocks** 【矿】火山岩。**-i·cal·ly** ***ad.***

vol·can·ic·i·ty [ˌvɔlkəˈnisiti; ˌvɑlkənˋɪsətɪ] ***n.*** 火山性;火山活动[作用、现象]。

vol·can·ism [ˈvɔlkənizəm; ˋvɑlkənɪzṃ] ***n.*** = volcanicity.

vol·can·ist [ˈvɔlkənist; ˋvɑlkənɪst] ***n.*** 火山学家;火成论者。

vol·can·ize [ˈvɔlkənaiz; ˋvɑlkən ˌaɪz] ***vt.*** (***-iz·ed, -iz·ing***) 【地】使受火山热,因火山热而变化,受火山影响。**-i·za·tion** [ˌvɔlkənaiˈzeiʃən; ˌvɑlkənaɪˋzeʃən] ***n.***

vol·ca·no [vɔlˈkeinəu; vɑlˋkeno] ***n.*** (***pl.*** ~***(e)s***) 火山。*an active* [*extinct*] ~ 活[死]火山。*a submarine* ~ 海底火山。

vol·ca·no·gen·ic [vɔlˌkeinəuˈdʒenik; vɑl ˌkenoˋdʒɛnɪk] ***a.*** 火山(生成)的;来源于火山的。

vol·can·ol·o·gist [ˌvɔlkəˈnɔlədʒist; ˌvɑlkəˋnɑlədʒɪst] ***n.*** 火山学家。

vol·can·ol·o·gy [ˌvɔlkəˈnɔlədʒi; ˌvɑlkənˋɑlədʒɪ] ***n.*** 火山学。

vole[1] [vəul; vol] ***n.*** 【动】鮃,田鼠。

vole[2] [vəul; vol] **I** ***n.*** 【牌戏】全赢。***go the*** ~ 孤注一掷。**II** ***vi.*** 【牌戏】全胜,大满贯。

Vol·ga [ˈvɔlgə; ˋvɑlgə] ***n.*** 伏尔加河〔俄罗斯〕。

Vol·go·grad [ˈvɔlgəgrɑːd; ˋvɑlgə ˌgræd] ***n.*** 伏尔加格勒〔俄罗斯一城市〕。

vol·i·tant [ˈvɔlitənt; ˋvɑlɪtənt] ***a.*** 【动】(能)飞翔的。

vol·i·ta·tion [ˌvɔliˈteiʃən; ˌvɑlɪˋteʃən] ***n.*** **1.** 飞行,飞翔。**2.** 飞行本领,飞翔能力。

vo·li·tion [vəuˈliʃən; voˋlɪʃən] ***n.*** 意志(力),决心,意志作用,愿欲。***of one's own*** ~ 出于本人自己的意志。

vo·li·tion·al, -a·ry [vəuˈliʃənl, -əri; voˋlɪʃənḷ, -ɛrɪ] ***a.*** 意志的。~ *power* 意志力。

vol·i·tive [ˈvɔlitiv; ˋvɑlətɪv] ***a.*** **1.** 意志的,愿欲的。**2.** 【语法】表示意愿的。~ *faculty* 意志力。

Volks·lied [ˈfəulksliːt; ˋfolks ˌlit] ***n.*** 〔G.〕 (***pl.*** ~***s***, ~***er*** [-ə; -ɚ]) 民歌,民谣。

vol·ley [ˈvɔli; ˋvɑlɪ] **I** ***n.*** **1.** (箭、子弹等的)齐射;排枪[排炮]发射。**2.** (质问、咒骂等的)迸发,连发。**3.** 【网球、足球】(不待球着地)挡击,飞击,飞踢。*a* ~ *of laughter* 一阵哄笑。*a* ~ *of oaths* 齐声咒骂。*a* ~ *of applause* 齐声喝采。***by*** ~***(s)*** 一齐。**II** ***vt.*** **1.** 齐射(子弹等);迸发(咒骂等)。**2.** 【网球、足球】飞击,飞踢。— ***vi.*** **1.** 一齐射击;(枪炮等)齐响。**2.** 【网球、足球】飞击,飞踢。~**ball** 【运】排球。~**baller** 排球运动员。

vol·om·e·ter [ˈvəulɔˌmiːtə; ˋvolɑ ˌmitɚ] ***n.*** 【电】伏安表;万能电表。

vo·lost [ˈvəulɔst; ˋvolɑst] ***n.*** 〔Russ.〕 (沙俄时代的)乡。

vol·plane [ˈvɔlˈplein; ˋvɑl ˌplen] ***n.***, ***vi.*** 【空】(向地面)滑翔。

vols. = volumes.

Vol·sci [ˈvɔlsai; ˋvɑlsaɪ] ***n.*** 〔*pl.*〕 〔L.〕 沃尔斯奇民族〔古代拉齐奥人,公元前四世纪被罗马人征服〕。

Vol·scian [ˈvɔlʃən; ˋvɑlʃən] **I** ***a.*** 沃尔斯奇人的,沃尔斯奇语的。**II** ***n.*** **1.** 沃尔斯奇人。**2.** 沃尔斯奇语。

Vol·stead Act [ˈvɔlsted-; ˋvɑlsted-] 〔美〕禁酒法〔由议员 Volstead 提出〕。

Vol·stead·ism [ˈvɔlstedizəm; ˋvɑlstedɪzṃ] ***n.*** 〔美〕禁酒主义。

volt[1] [vəult, vɔlt; volt, vɔlt] ***n.*** **1.** 【马术】环骑,环行成圈的步伐;环行的场地。**2.** 【剑术】闪避。

volt[2] [vəult; volt] ***n.*** 【电】伏(特)。*the heater* ~ 灯丝电压。*the legal* ~ 法定[国际]伏特。~**-ampere** 伏(特)安(培)。

Vol·ta [ˈvɔltə; ˋvoltɑ], **A.** 伏打(1745—1827),意大利物理学家。

vol·ta [ˈvɔltə; ˋvɑltə] ***n.*** (***pl. -te*** [-ti; -te]) 〔It.〕 【乐】次,回。*prima* [*seconda*] ~ 第一[二]回。*una* [*due*] ~ 一[二]次,一[二]回。

volt·age [ˈvəultidʒ, ˈvɔl-; ˋvoltɪdʒ, ˋvɑl-] ***n.*** 【电】电压,电压量,伏特数。*the working* ~ (电气的)耐压限度。~ **amplifier** 电压放大器。~ **divider** 分压器。~ **regulator** 电压调整器。~ **sensitivity** 电压灵敏度。

Vol·ta·ic [vɔlˈteiik; vɑlˋteɪk] **I** ***a.*** **1.** 上沃尔特的;上沃尔特人的;属于上沃尔特的;属于上沃尔特人的。**2.** 沃尔特语支的;属于沃尔特语支的。**II** ***n.*** 沃尔特语支〔属尼日尔—刚果语族〕。

vol·ta·ic [vɔlˈteiik; vɑlˋteɪk] ***a.*** 电流的;动电的;伏打(式)的。~ **battery** 伏打电池组。~ **cell** 伏打[一次]电池。~ **pile** 伏打电堆。~ **wire** 导线。

Vol·taire [ˈvɔlteə; vɑlˋtɛr], **F.M.A. de** 伏尔泰〔1694—1778,法国作家、哲学家、启蒙思想家〕。

vol·ta·ism [ˈvɔltəizəm; ˋvɑltəɪzṃ] ***n.*** 【电】流电,动电;流电学,动电学 (= galvanism)。

vol·tam·e·ter [vɔlˈtæmitə; vɑlˋtæmətɚ] ***n.*** 【电】库仑计[表],电量计。*a gas* [*water*] ~ 气解[水解]电量计。

volt·am·me·ter [ˈvəulˈtæmmiːtə; ˋvolˋtæmmitɚ] ***n.*** 【电】伏(特)安(培)计,电压电流两用表。

volt-am·pere [ˈvəultˈæmpiə; ˋvoltˋæmpɪr] ***n.*** 【电】伏安〔伏特安培〕。

vol·te [vɔlt; vɔlt] ***n.*** = volt[1].

vol·te [ˈvɔlti; ˋvolte] volta 的复数。

volte-face [ˈvɔltfɑːs; ˋvɑlt ˌfɑs, ˋvɑltə-] ***n.*** 〔F.〕 转向,(意见、议论等的)逆转,变卦,180度转变。

vol·ti [ˈvɔːltiː; ˋvolti] ***v.*** 【乐】〔祈使〕翻页,翻至下页。

volt·me·ter [ˈvɔltmiːtə; ˋvolt ˌmitɚ] ***n.*** 【电】电压表,伏

特计。

vol·to·lize [ˈvɔltəlaiz; ˋvɑltəlaɪz] *vt*. 对…作无声放电处理,对…作高电压处理。**-li·za·tion** [-laiˈzeiʃən; -laɪˋzeʃən] *n*. 无声放电处理(法);高电压处理(法)。

vol·u·bil·ate [vɔˈljuːbilit; vɑˋljubɪlɪt], **vol·u·bile** [ˈvɔljubil; ˋvɑljubɪl] *a*.【植】缠绕的。

vol·u·bil·i·ty [ˌvɔljuˈbiliti; ˏvɑljʊˋbɪlətɪ] *n*. 1. (口才、文章的)流畅,流利;有口才,善辩。2. 旋转性。*with* ~ 流利地,滔滔不绝地。

vol·u·ble [ˈvɔljubl; ˋvɑljəbl] *a*. 1. 流利的,流畅的,口若悬河的,善辩的。2. 易旋转的,旋转性的。3.【植】会缠绕的。~ *excuses* 流利的辩解。

vol·u·bly [ˈvɔljubli; ˋvɑljʊblɪ] *ad*. 流畅地,滔滔不绝地。

vol·ume [ˈvɔljum; ˋvɑljəm] *n*. 1. 卷,册;书籍;【史】书卷,卷轴。2.〔常 *pl*.〕大块,大量,许多。3. 体积;容积;分量,额;【物、乐】音量;强度,响度。*a novel in three* ~*s* 一部总共有三卷的小说。~*s of vapour* 大量的水蒸气,蒸汽弥漫。*atomic* ~ 原子体积。*the* ~ *of retail sales* 商品零售额。***express*** ~***s*** 说得意义很充实[很有内容]。***gather*** ~ (程度)增大(*Her anger was gathering* ~. 她越来越生气了)。***pour out*** ~***s of abuse*** 破口大骂。***speak*** ~***s*** = *express* ~*s*. ***speak*** ~***s for*** 足够证明,有力地说明。***tell*** ~***s*** = *express* ~*s*. ~ **expansion**【物】体积膨胀。~ **indicator** 容积指示器,体积指示器;强[响]度指示器。~ **level**【物】强[响]度级。~-**produce** *vt*. 1. 大量生产。2.【林】材积收获。~ **unit** 响度[音量]单位。

vol·umed [ˈvɔljumd, -jəmd; ˋvɑljʊmd, -jəmd] *a*. 1.〔现罕〕包括数卷的。2.【诗】大量的。

vol·u·me·nom·e·ter [ˌvɔljumiˈnɔmitə; ˏvɑljəmɪˋnɑmɪtɚ] *n*.【物】排水容积计,体积计;视密度计。

vo·lu·me·ter [vɔˈljuːmitə; vəˋlumətɚ] *n*.【物】体积计,容积计。

vol·u·met·ric [ˌvɔljuˈmetrik; ˏvɑljəˋmɛtrɪk] *a*. 测量容积[体积]的;容积的,容量的,体积的。~ *analysis* 容量[体积]分析(法)。*a* ~ *flask* 量瓶。

vo·lu·mi·nous [vəˈljuːminəs; vəˋljumənəs] *a*. 1. 卷数多的,大部头的;著作多的。2. 很多的;容积[体积]大的,广大的;(衣服)宽大的。*a* ~ *work* 大部头的著作。*a* ~ *writer* 多产作家。**-ly** *ad*. **-ness** *n*. **vo·lu·mi·nos·i·ty** [vəˌljuːmiˈnɔsiti; vəˏljumɪˋnɑsətɪ] *n*.

vol·un·tar·i·ly [ˈvɔləntərili; ˋvɑlənˏtɛrəlɪ] *ad*. 自愿地,志愿地,自动地。

vol·un·tar·i·ness [ˈvɔləntərinis; ˋvɑlənˏtɛrɪnɪs] *n*. 自愿,自动。

vol·un·tar·ism [ˈvɔləntərizəm; ˋvɑləntərɪzm̩] *n*.【哲】唯意志论 (= voluntaryism)。

vol·un·ta·ry [ˈvɔləntəri; ˋvɑlənˏtɛrɪ] **I** *a*. 1. 自愿的,自发的,自动的 (*opp*. compulsory);志愿的。2. 靠自愿捐助的。3. 故意的,有意的。4.【生理】随意的。5.【法】无偿的;自愿的。*a* ~ *confession* 自动供认。*a* ~ *army* 志愿[义勇]军。~ *murder* 蓄意谋杀。~ *conveyance* 无偿让与。*a* ~ *grantee* 无偿受让人。*a* ~ *escape* (得监视人同意的)同意逃走。**II** *n*. 1. 自愿捐助者;自动行为;自愿地做的工作。2.【乐】(教堂礼拜仪式中的)风琴独奏;即兴演奏,自选节目。~ **bankruptcy**【法】自动破产申请。~ **muscle**【解】随意肌。~ **school**〔英〕靠自由捐助维持的学校。~ **service** 志愿服役。~ **waste** (对他人不动产的)故意损害。

vol·un·ta·ry·ism [ˈvɔləntəriizəm; ˋvɑlənˏtɛrɪɪzm̩] *n*. 自愿捐助制度[办法,主义];募兵制。

vol·un·teer [ˌvɔlənˈtiə; ˏvɑlənˋtɪr] **I** *n*. 1. 自愿者,志愿者。2.【军】义勇军,志愿兵。3.【法】自愿行为者;自愿为他人还债者。4.【植】自生植物;【林】先锋树种。5.〔V-〕〔美〕田纳西州的别名;〔Volunteers〕田纳西州人的别名。**II** *a*. 1. 自愿的,志愿的;志愿兵的;自动的。2.【植】自生的。*a* ~ *corps* 义勇军团。**III** *vt*. 自愿去做,自动请求去做。~ *a difficult duty* 自愿担任困难任务。一 *vi*. 1. 志愿;当志愿兵[义勇军]。2.【植】自生自长。~ *for service* 自动参军,自愿入伍从军。~ **growth**【林】前生树。~ **plants**【植】自生植物。

vo·lup·tu·a·ry [vəˈlʌptjuəri; vəˋlʌptʃʊˏɛrɪ] *a*., *n*. 纵欲的(人),纵情官能享乐的(人),淫逸的(人),迷恋酒色的(人)。

vo·lup·tu·ous [vəˈlʌptjuəs; vəˋlʌptʃʊəs] *a*. 1. 淫逸的,贪恋酒色的。2. 肉欲的;色情的,妖娆的。~ *beauty* 妖艳。~ *music* 色情音乐。**-ly** *ad*. **-ness** *n*.

vo·lute [vəˈljuːt; vəˋlut] **I** *n*. 1. 涡旋形(物)。2.【建】(Ionic 和 Corinthian 式柱头的)盘蜗(饰)。3.【空】集气环;【化】涡囊。4.【贝】涡螺;(壳上的)螺环。**II** *a*. 涡旋形的,盘蜗形的,螺旋形的。*a* ~ *spring*【机】涡形螺簧。**-d** *a*. = volute (*a*.).

vol·u·tin [ˈvɔljutin; ˋvɑljʊtɪn] *n*.【微】异染粒。

vo·lu·tion [vəˈljuːʃən; vəˋljuʃən] *n*. 涡旋,(贝壳的)涡卷,螺环;【解】旋转。

vol·va [ˈvɔlvə; ˋvɑlvə] *n*.【植】菌托。**-te** [-ˌveit, -vit; -ˏvet, -vɪt] *a*.

vol·vox [ˈvɔlvɔks; ˋvɑlvɑks] *n*.【植】团藻属 (*Volvox*) 植物。

vol·vu·lus [ˈvɔlvjuləs; ˋvɑlvjələs] *n*.【医】肠扭转。

vo·mer [ˈvəumə; ˋvomɚ] *n*.【解】(鼻的)犁骨。**-ine** [-rin; -rɪn] *a*.

vom·it [ˈvɔmit; ˋvɑmɪt] **I** *vi*., *vt*. 呕吐;吐出,喷出(烟、脏话等)。**II** *n*. 吐出物;吐剂;脏话。*black* ~【医】= vomito (negro). **-er** *n*. 呕吐者。

vom·i·tive [ˈvɔmitiv; ˋvɑmɪtɪv] **I** *a*. 令人作呕的,催吐的。**II** *n*. 1. 催吐剂。2. (古罗马圆形剧场等的)大门。

vom·i·to (negro) [ˈvɔmitəu (ˈniːgrəu); ˋvɑmɪˏto (ˋnigro)] *n*.【医】(黄热病人的)黑色吐出物;黄热病。

vom·i·to·ri·um [ˌvɔmiˈtɔːriəm; ˏvɑməˋtorɪəm, -ˋtor-] *n*. (*pl*. *-to·ri·a*) (剧场或体育场的)大出入口。

vom·i·to·ry [ˈvɔmitəri; ˋvɑmɪˏtorɪ] *a*. = vomitive.

vom·i·tu·ri·tion [ˌvɔmitjuəˈriʃən; ˏvɑmɪtʃʊˋrɪʃən] *n*.【医】干呕;作呕。

vom·i·tus [ˈvɔmitəs; ˋvɑmətəs] *n*. 呕吐物。

von [fɔn; fɑn] *prep*.〔G.〕= of; from. ★ 在德国人人名中,最初用于地名前表示出生地,领地,后来也用于贵族的姓氏前: Fürst (= Prince) ~ Bismarck 俾斯麦公爵。

V-one, V-1 [ˈviːˈwʌn; ˋviˏwʌn] *n*. V-1 型火箭〔第二次大战末期德方的一种火箭炸弹,参见 V-1 条〕。

V

voo·doo [ˈvuːduː; ˋvudu] **I** *n*. 1.〔美〕伏都教〔西印度群岛和美国南部等地某些黑人中流行的巫术信仰〕。2. 伏都教徒;黑人巫师。**II** *a*. 伏都教的。**III** *vt*.〔美〕对…施行(伏都教)巫术。**-ism** *n*. = voodoo 1.

Vo·po [ˈvəupəu; ˋvopo] *n*.〔G.〕民警。

VOR【空】全向(无线电)导航系统〔very high frequency omnirange〕。

vo·ra·cious [vəˈreiʃəs; voˋreʃəs] *a*. 1. 狼吞虎咽的,贪吃的。2. 贪婪的,贪心的,难满足的。*a* ~ *reader* 饥不择食的读者。*a* ~ *whirlpool* 什么都要卷进去的旋涡。**-ly** *ad*. **-ness** *n*.

vor·spiel [ˈfəurʃpiːl, ˈfɔːr-; ˋforʃpil] *n*. (音乐的)前奏曲,序曲。

vo·rac·i·ty [vɔ(ː)ˈræsiti; vəˋræsətɪ] *n*. 贪食;暴食;贪婪。

-vorous *comb. f*. 吃…的: carni*vorous*, gramini*vorous*, omni*vorous*.

vor·tex [ˈvɔːteks; ˋvɔrtɛks] *n*. (*pl*. ~*es* [-iz; -ɪz], *-tices* [-tisiːz; -tɪsiz]) 1. 旋涡;旋风;旋卷行云。2.【物】涡旋;【空】涡流;【动】〔V-〕单肠涡虫的一属。*the* ~ *of war* 战乱。*the* ~ *of revolution* 革命的旋涡。***be drawn into the*** ~ ***of*** 被卷入…的旋涡中。~ **street**【物】涡列。~ **theory** 原子涡动说。~-**ring** (喷烟所成

的）涡环。

vor·ti·cal [ˈvɔːtikəl; ˋvɔrtɪkḷ] *a*. 旋涡（似）的；卷成旋涡的；旋转的。**-ly** *ad*.

vor·ti·cel·la [ˌvɔːtiˈselə; ˏvɔrtɪˋsɛlə] *n*. (*pl*. **-cel·lae** [-iː; -i])【动】钟虫（*Vorticella*）属动物。

vor·ti·ces [ˈvɔːtisiːz; ˋvɔrtɪˏsiz] vortex 的复数。

vor·tic·ism [ˈvɔːtisizəm; ˋvɔrtɪsɪzm] *n*.【绘画】旋涡画派〔未来派的一种〕。**-tic·ist** *n*. 旋涡派画家。

vor·ti·cose [ˈvɔːtikəus; ˋvɔrtɪˏkos] *a*. 旋涡的，回旋的。

vor·tig·i·nous [vɔːˈtidʒinəs; vɔrˋtɪdʒənəs] *a*.〔古〕1. 旋转的。2. 在旋涡中转动的；旋涡似的。

vot·a·ble [ˈvəutəbl; ˋvotəbḷ] *a*. 可提交表决的，可选举的；付诸表决的。

vo·ta·ry [ˈvəutəri; ˋvotərɪ], **vo·ta·rist** [-st; -st] *n*. (*fem*. **vo·ta·ress** [ˈvəutəris; ˋvotərɪs]) 1. 皈依者，信仰者，信徒。2. 热心者，崇拜者；爱好者；提倡者。*a* ~ *of science* 献身科学的人。*a* ~ *of sports* 运动爱好者。

vote [vəut; vot] **I** *n*. 1. 投票（过程，手续）；表决。2. 投票权，选举权；投票人，选举人；（属于同一派别的）一群投票者。3. 投票纸；（选）票；投票数，得票数。4. 议决，议决事项，议决（金）额。5.〔英〕〔V-〕下院会议记录。*an open* [*a secret*] ~ 记名[无记名]投票。*chosen by* ~ 投票选出的。~ *by rising* [*a show of hands*] 起立[举手]表决。*pass a* ~ 通过议案；议决。*The motion was carried by fourteen* ~*s*. 该项动议以十四票获得通过。*At what age should women have a* ~? 妇女要到几岁才有选举权？*a casting* ~（主席的）决定性投票。*The candidate polled two thousand* ~*s*. 这个候选人得了两千票。*a* ~ *of $ 1000 for a new building* 建筑费一千元的拨款决议。***cast a*** ~ ***for*** [***against***] 投票拥护[反对]。***come to the*** ~ = *go to the* ~. ***get out a*** [***the***] ~〔美〕获得预期的投票者[支持者]。***give*** [***record***] ***one's*** ~ ***to*** [***for***] 投…的票。***go back upon a*** ~ 重新表决。***go to the*** ~（议案等）被提交表决。***put to the*** ~ 付表决。***take a*** ~ ***on*** (*a question*)（对某问题）进行表决。~ ***of account***〔英〕（议会拨与政府使用的）预算金额。~(*s*) ***of credit***〔英〕（议会给予政府的）预算外可借用金额。**II** *vi*. 投票（*for*; *against*），选举；提议。— *vt*. 1. 投票给…，投…的票；投票决定，表决。2.〔口〕由舆论[公议]决定，（舆论）公认。3.〔口〕提议。*The measure was* ~*d a failure*. 大家都说这个办法是要失败的。*I* ~ *that we go to the theatre tonight*. 我提议今晚看戏去。***be*** ~***d***〔美〕被公认为。~ (***a measure***) ***through*** 使（议案）表决通过。~ ***a split ticket***〔美〕兼投两党候选人的票。~ ***by ballot*** 不记名投票。~ ***by* "*yes*" *and* "*no*"** 口头表决。~ ***down*** 否决。~ ***for*** 1. 投票赞成，赞成，选举（某人）。2.〔口〕建议，提议（*I* ~ *for stopping*. 我提议停止）。~ ... ***in*** 选出，选举。~ ... ***out*** [***out of***] 投票驱逐，对…投反对票；（公议）停止。~**-winner** 争取选票的手段。**-able** = votable.

vot·er [ˈvəutə; ˋvotɚ] *n*. 投票者；选举人。*a casting* ~ 决定性投票者[主席]。

vot·ing [ˈvəutiŋ; ˋvotɪŋ] *n*., *a*. 投票（的），选举（的）。~ **district** 选举区。~ **machine** 票数计算机。~ **paper**〔英〕投票纸；选票。

vo·tive [ˈvəutiv; ˋvotɪv] *a*. 奉献的，还愿的；诚心祈求的，许愿的。**-ly** *ad*.

vo·tress [ˈvəutris; ˋvotrɪs] *n*. = votaress.

vou. = voucher.

vouch [vautʃ; vautʃ] *vi*. 保证，担保，作证。~ *for sb.'s honesty* 保证某人诚实。— *vt*. 1. 担保，保证。2. 确定；断言。*I can't* ~ *that* ... 我不能断定…。

vouch·er [ˈvautʃə; ˋvautʃɚ] *n*. 1. 保证人，证明人。2. 证件；证书；收据，收条；（付款）凭单。3.〔美〕（给贫困线以下家庭发放的）教育补助金券〔可用来代替现金交私立学校学费等〕。

vouch·safe [vautʃˈseif; vautʃˋsef] *vt*. 给，赐；允诺（*to do*）。*V- me a visit*. 请赐予光临。*He did not* ~ *a reply*. 他一句回话也不给。

vous·soir [ˈvuːswɑː; ˏvuˋswar] *n*.【建】楔形拱石。

vow [vau; vau] **I** *n*. 1. 誓言，誓约；誓愿。2. 誓约内容，誓约行为（等）。***be bound by a*** ~ = ***be under a*** ~ (*to do*) 已立誓…；在誓言约束下（*I am under a* ~ *to drink no wine*. 我已立誓不喝酒）。***make*** [***take***] ***the*** ~***s*** 立誓，发誓。***take*** ~***s*** 立誓出家当修士[修女]。**II** *vt*. 1. 起誓，许愿；誓约；申言誓必…。2.〔古〕断言。~ *vengeance against the oppressor* 发誓要对压迫者复仇。— *vi*. 发誓；许愿。~ ***and declare***〔古、俚〕指天发誓地说。

vow·el [ˈvauəl; ˋvauəl] **I** *n*.【语音】母音（符号）(*opp*. consonant)。**II** *a*. 母音的。**III** *vt*. 加母音（符号）于。~ **mark**, ~ **point** 母音符号。~ **system** 母音系统。

vow·el·ize, -ise [ˈvauəlaiz; ˋvauəlˏaɪz] *vt*.【语音】加母音符号于（希伯来语、阿拉伯语等的字母）之上。**-i·zation** [ˌvauəlaiˈzeiʃən; ˏvauəlaɪˋzeʃən] *n*.

vox [vɔks; vɑks] *n*.〔L.〕(*pl*. **vo·ces** [ˈvəusiz; ˋvosɪz]) 语声，声音；语言，呼声。~ ***humana*** [hjuːˈmɑːnə; hjuˋmɑnə]（风琴的）仿人声音栓。~ ***pop***〔美〕1.〔英俚〕街头民意〔行人被临时采访时发表的政见等〕。2. =〔L.〕~ *populi*. ~ ***populi*** [ˈpɔpjulai; ˋpɑpjulaɪ] 大众的呼声，舆论（~ *populi*, ~ ***Dei*** [ˈdiːai; ˋdiaɪ]〔L.〕民声即天声）。~ ***angelica***【乐】= *voix celeste*.

voy·age [vɔidʒ, ˈvɔiidʒ; vɔɪdʒ, ˋvɔɪɪdʒ] **I** *n*. 航海，航行；旅行；航程。*a* ~ *round the world* 环球航行。*a rough* ~ 艰难的航程。***a broken*** ~【捕鲸】没有渔获的一次航行。***go on a*** ~ 航海去。***on the*** ~ 航行中。**II** *vi*. 航行，航海。— *vt*. 渡过；飞过。~ **charter**【海】航次租赁。~ **policy**【海】航次保险。

voy·age·a·ble [ˈvɔidʒəbl; ˋvɔɪ·ɪdʒəbḷ] *a*. 能[可]航行[航海]的。

voy·ag·er [ˈvɔiədʒə, ˈvɔiidʒə; ˋvɔɪdʒɚ, ˋvɔɪɪdʒɚ] *n*. 航行者，（特指冒险的）航海者；旅行者。

vo·ya·geur [vwɑːjɑːˈʒəː; vwajaˋʒœːr] *n*.〔F.〕（从前在加拿大水道上为毛皮公司运送货物人员的）包运船户；（僻远地区的）木材流放者，船夫。

vo·yeur [vwɑˈjəː; ˏvwɑˋjɚ] *n*.〔F.〕【医，心】窥淫狂者〔从观看性器官或性行为中得到变态的性满足〕。**-ism** *n*. 窥淫癖。**-is·tic** *a*.

V.P., VP = 1. vice-president 副总统，大学副校长。2. vapour pressure 蒸气压力。

VPA = Vietnam People's Army 越南人民军。

VPM, vpm = 1. vibrations per minute 每分钟的振动数。2. volts per mil 每密耳的伏特数。

VPOTUS = vice-president of the United States 美国副总统。

VR = virtual reality.

V.R. = 1.〔L.〕*Victoria Regina* (= Queen Victoria)〔英〕维多利亚女王。2. Volunteer Reserve〔英〕（皇家空军）志愿后备队。

v.r. = verb reflexive 反身动词。

vrai·sem·blance [vreisɑ̃ːmˈblɑ̃ːns; vrɛsɑ̃ˋblɑ̃ːs] *n*.〔F.〕逼真；神似；似真的情况。

V.R.C. = Volunteer Rifle Corps〔英〕志愿步枪队。

v.refl. = verb reflexive 反身动词。

V.Rev. = Very Reverend 最尊敬的〔对教长的尊称〕。

vrille [vriːj, vril; vrij, vrɪl] **I** *n*.〔F.〕【空】旋转下降的技术。**II** *vi*. 作旋转下降。

vroom [vruːm; vrum] **I** *n*.〔拟声〕弗鲁〔汽车加速时发出的声音〕。**II** *vi*.〔口〕发弗鲁声，弗鲁声中开动。

VS, V.S. = veterinary surgeon〔主英〕兽医。

vs. = 1. verse. 2. versus.

v.s. =〔L.〕*vide supra* 见上 (= see above)。

VSAT = very small-aperture terminal【电信】甚小(天线)孔径地面站〔一种小型卫星地面站〕。

V-shaped [ˈviːʃeipt; ˋviˏʃept] *a*. V 字形的。

V / STOL = vertical / short takeoff and landing 垂直短距离起落(飞机)。

VT, V.T. = **1**. vacuum tube 真空管,电子管。**2**. 〔L.〕*Vetus Testamentum*《旧约全书》。

Vt. = Vermont.

v.t. = verb transitive【语法】及物动词。

V.T.C. = Volunteer Training Corps 〔英〕志愿人员训练团。

Vte. = 〔F.〕*Vicomte* 子爵。

VT fuze = variable timing fuze 无线电引信,变时引信。

VTOL = vertical takeoff and landing 垂直起落(飞机)。

VTR = **1**. video tape recorder 视频信号磁带记录器,磁带录像器。**2**. = video tape recording (磁带)录像。

V-two, V-2 [ˈviːˈtuː; ˋviˋtu] *n*. V-2 型火箭〔第二次大战末期德方的一种火箭炸弹,参见 V-2 条〕。

vug, vugg, vugh [vʌg, vuːg; vʌg, vug] *n*.【地】晶簇。**vug·gy** *a*.

Vul·can [ˈvʌlkən; ˋvʌlkən] *n*. **1**.【罗神】火与锻冶之神。**2**.【天】祝融星。**3**. 〔v-〕锻冶者;铁匠。

Vul·ca·ni·an [vʌlˈkeiniən; vʌlˋkenɪən], **Vul·can·ic** [-ˈkænik; -ˋkænɪk] *a*. **1**. 火与锻冶之神的。**2**. 〔v-〕锻冶的,铁工的;【地】火山的,火山作用的;火成的。

vul·can·ism [ˈvʌlkənizəm; ˋvʌlkənɪzəm] *n*.【地】= volcanism.

vul·can·ist [ˈvʌlkənist; ˋvʌlkənɪst] *n*. **1**.【地】火成论者;火山学家。**2**. 热月学家〔认为月球内部有热能和火山活动的科学家,亦作 hot mooner〕。

vul·can·ite [ˈvʌlkənait; ˋvʌlkənˏaɪt] *n*. 硬橡皮。

vul·can·i·zate [ˈvʌlkənizeit; ˋvʌlkənəˏzet] *n*. 硫化物〔产品,橡胶〕;橡皮。

vul·can·i·za·tion [ˌvʌlkənaiˈzeiʃən; ˏvʌlkənaɪˋzeʃən] *n*. 硫化(作用);(橡胶)硬化(作用)。

vul·can·ize, -ise [ˈvʌlkənaiz; ˋvʌlkənˏaɪz] *vt*. 使硫化,在…中加硫,使硬化。— *vi*. (橡胶等)硫化;硬化。

vul·can·ol·o·gy [ˌvʌlkəˈnɔlədʒi; ˏvʌlkəˋnɑlədʒɪ] *n*. = volcanology. **-o·gist** *n*. = volcanologist.

Vulg. = Vulgate.

vulg. = **1**. vulgar. **2**. vulgarly.

vul·gar [ˈvʌlgə; ˋvʌlgɚ] *a*. **1**. 平民的,民众的。**2**. 庸俗的,俚俗的,粗俗的,下流的。**3**. 通俗的;世俗的;一般大众的,老百姓的。~ *manners* 粗俗的态度。~ *words* 粗俗话。~ *errors* 世俗谬见[误解]。~ *superstitions* 世俗[民间]迷信。***the*** ~ ***tongue*** (尤指从前对拉丁语说的)本国话。~ **fraction** 普通分数 (= common fraction)。**V- Latin**【语言】俗拉丁文,民间拉丁文。**-ly** *ad*.

vul·ga·ri·an [vʌlˈgeəriən; vʌlˋgɛrɪən] *n*. 粗俗的人,〔特指〕庸俗的暴发户。

vul·gar·ism [ˈvʌlgərizəm; ˋvʌlgəˏrɪzəm] *n*. **1**. 粗俗,庸俗,粗鄙。**2**.【语言】粗俗话[词语];词语的非规范用法。

vul·gar·i·ty [vʌlˈgæriti; vʌlˋgærətɪ] *n*. **1**. 粗俗,庸俗,下流。**2**. 粗俗语;粗俗行为。

vul·gar·i·za·tion [ˌvʌlgəraiˈzeiʃən; ˏvʌlgəraɪˋzeʃən] *n*. 庸俗化,粗俗化;〔罕〕世俗化;大众化。

vul·gar·ize, -ise [ˈvʌlgəˌraiz; ˋvʌlgəˏraɪz] *vt*. 使庸俗,使粗俗;〔罕〕使通俗化,使大众化。

Vul·gate [ˈvʌlgit; ˋvʌlgɪt] **I** *n*. **1**. 拉丁文圣经〔公元四世纪译出,为天主教所承认的唯一文本〕。**2**. 〔v-〕定本,通行本。**3**. 白话,口语,土话,俗话。**II** *a*. **1**. 拉丁文圣经的。**2**. 〔v-〕公认的,通行的。

vul·gus [ˈvʌlgəs; ˋvʌlgəs] *n*. **1**. 〔英学俚〕拉丁[希腊]文短诗翻译作业。**2**. 平民,老百姓。

vul·ner·a·ble [ˈvʌlnərəbl; ˋvʌlnərəbl] *a*. **1**. 易受伤的,脆弱的;易受责难[攻击、损坏]的,有弱点的。**2**.【桥牌】有局的。*a* ~ *point* (易受伤的)弱点。*be* ~ *to criticism* 易受抨击。**-bil·i·ty** [ˌvʌlnərəˈbiliti; ˏvʌlnərəˋbɪlətɪ] *n*. **-a·bly** *ad*.

vul·ner·a·ry [ˈvʌlnərəri; ˋvʌlnəˏrɛrɪ] **I** *a*. 医治创伤的,敷创伤的。**II** *n*. 创伤愈合剂。

Vul·pec·u·la [vʌlˈpekjulə; vʌlˋpɛkjulə] *n*.【天】狐狸座。

vul·pi·cide [ˈvʌlpisaid; ˋvʌlpɪˏsaɪd] *a*. **1**. (不用猎犬而用其他方法的)捕杀狐狸。**2**. (不用猎犬狩猎的)捕杀狐狸者。

vul·pine [ˈvʌlpain; ˋvʌlpaɪn] *a*. 狐(狸)的;狐狸似的;狡猾的。

vul·ture [ˈvʌltʃə; ˋvʌltʃɚ] *n*.【鸟】兀鹰;秃鹫;贪得无厌者,劫掠者。**-tur·ine** [-tʃurain; -tʃʊraɪn] *a*.

vul·tur·ish [ˈvʌltʃuriʃ; ˋvʌltʃʊrɪʃ], **vul·tur·ous** [-rəs; -rəs] *a*. 兀鹰似的;贪得无厌的,掠夺性的。

vul·va [ˈvʌlvə; ˋvʌlvə] *n*. (*pl*. **-vae** [-viː; -vi], ~s)【解】女阴,外阴,阴户,阴门;【动】孔。**-l, -r** *a*.

vul·vate [ˈvʌlveit; ˋvʌlvet] *a*. 阴门(状)的。

vul·vi·form [ˈvʌlviˌfɔːm; ˋvʌlvɪˏfɔrm] *a*.【解】似阴门(的)。

vul·vi·tis [vʌlˈvaitis; vʌlˋvaɪtɪs] *n*.【医】外阴炎。

vul·vo·vag·i·ni·tis [ˌvʌlvəuˌvædʒiˈnaitis; ˏvʌlvoˏvædʒɪˋnaɪtɪs] *n*.【医】外阴阴道炎。

vum [vʌm; vʌm] *vi*. 〔美方〕发誓,赌咒。

vv. = **1**. verses. **2**. violins.

v.v. = 〔L.〕vice versa.

vv.ll. = 〔L.〕*variae lectiones* (稿本的)异文 (= variant readings)。

vy = very.

vy·cor [ˈvaikə; ˋvaɪkɔr] *n*. 石英玻璃;硼硅酸耐热玻璃。

vy·ing [ˈvaiiŋ; ˋvaɪɪŋ] **I** *vt*., *vi*. vie 的现在分词。**II** *a*. 竞争的。

W

W

W, w [ˈdʌblju(ː); ˋdʌbljʊ] (*pl*. ***W's, w's*** [ˈdʌblju(ː)z; ˋdʌbljuz]) **1**. 英语字母表第二十三个字母。**2**. W 字形物。**3**. 〔W〕【化】元素钨 (wolfram) 的符号。**4**.【印】W 铅字。

W, w = **1**. warden. **2**. warehouse. **3**. watt(s). **4**. weight. **5**. west; western. **6**. width. **7**.【物】work. **8**. Wales; Welsh. **9**. Washington. **10**. week(s). **11**. wide. **12**. wife. **13**. with. **14**. won.

WA = **1**. West Africa 西非。**2**. Western Australia 西澳大利亚。**3**. with average【商】水渍险(承保单独海损)。

wa' [wɔː, wɑː; wɔ, wɑ] ***n.*** [Scot.] wall 的缩略词。

Waadt [vɑːt; vɑt] = Vaud 沃州[瑞士西部]。

WAAF [wæf; wæf] ***n.*** **1.** (英国或澳大利亚)空军妇女辅助队。**2.** (英国或澳大利亚)空军妇女辅助队队员。

wab·ble [ˈwɔbl; `wɑbl] **I** ***vi.*** (陀螺、人等)摇摆,摆动,摇晃;(声音)震颤;(政策、人心等)动摇。— ***vt.*** 使摇摆[颤动,动摇]。**II** ***n.*** 摇摆,摇晃;摆动;动摇 (= wobble)。**-r** ***n.*** **1.** 摇动者;摇摆者,迟疑不决的人。**2.**【机】(能旋转的)削截器。**3.** [英方]煮过的羊腿。**-bling** ***a.***

WAC = Women's Army Corps [美]陆军妇女队。

Wac [wæk; wæk] ***n.*** [美]陆军妇女队成员。

wack [wæk; wæk] ***a.*** [美俚]没用的;糟糕的;二流的。

wack·e [ˈwækə; `wækə] ***n.***【地】玄(武)土。

wack·y [ˈwæki; `wækɪ] ***a.*** [美俚]古怪的,反常的,疯癫的。

WACS, Wacs [wæks; wæks] ***n.*** [美] Wac 的复数。

wad[1] [wɔd; wɑd] **I** ***n.*** **1.** (棉絮等软物的)一团,一撮。**2.** [口](纸币的)一叠;(布的)一块;一捆。**3.** 填料,填絮;【军】炮塞,弹塞。**4.** [常 *pl.*] [俚]钞票,钱;一大笔(钱)。*plug one's ears with ~s of cotton* 用棉絮团塞住耳朵。*a ~ of bills* [美]一叠钞票。***shoot one's ~*** [美俚] **1.** 说出想说的话。**2.** 表示反对,诉怨。**3.** 用尽最后手段;把钱花完。**II** ***vt.*** (**-dd-**) **1.** 把…弄成一团;[美俚]把(纸)卷成一卷。**2.** 填塞;填棉花(入衣服);装填弹塞(入枪)。*be well wadded with conceit* 十分自负[自满];得意洋洋。

wad[2] [wɔd; wɑd] ***n.***【矿】锰土,沼锰矿。

wad·a·ble [ˈweidəbl; `wedəbl] ***a.*** 可涉水而过的。

wad·ding [ˈwɔdiŋ; `wɑdɪŋ] ***n.*** 填料,填絮;填弹塞原料;填塞物;填塞。

wad·dle [ˈwɔdl; `wɑdl] **I** ***vi.*** (鸭、矮胖子等)摇摇摆摆地走,蹒跚而行。**II** ***n.*** 摇摆的步子。**-dling·ly** ***ad.***

wad·dy[1] [ˈwɔdi; `wɑdɪ] **I** ***n.*** **1.** [澳](土著居民战斗用)棍棒。**2.** 手杖。**II** ***vt.*** 用棍棒打。

wad·dy[2] [ˈwɔdi; `wɑdɪ] ***n.*** [澳、美西部]牧童,骑马牧童,牛仔。

Wade [weid; wed] ***n.*** 韦德[姓氏,男子名]。

wade [weid; wed] **I** ***vi., vt.*** **1.** 蹚,蹚过。**2.** 费力前进,好容易通过。**II** ***n.*** 跋涉,蹚水;(可以蹚过的)浅水。*the wading bird*【动】涉水禽鸟。*a wading pool* (公园中的)儿童玩水池。*~ through a book* 很吃力地读完一本书。*~* ***in*** **1.** 入浅水;参加,干涉。**2.** 猛烈地攻击对方。**3.** [美口]精神抖擞地开始[动手]。*~* ***into*** 猛烈攻击;[美口]精神抖擞地开始。*~* ***through slaughter*** [***blood***] ***to*** (*a throne*) 踏着杀戮的鲜血取得(王位),用屠杀办法达到[取得]。**-able** ***a.*** = wadable.

wad·er [ˈweidə; `wedɚ] ***n.*** **1.** 蹚水的人,涉渡者;【鸟】涉水禽鸟。**2.** [*pl.*](钓鱼用)涉水长靴。

wad·i, wad·y [ˈwɔdi; `wɑdɪ] ***n.*** **1.** (仅雨季有水的)干涸河床,旱河;【地】干谷。**2.** 流经干涸河床的水流。**3.** (沙漠中的)绿洲 (= oasis)。

wad·na [ˈwɑːdnə; `wɑdnə] [Scot.] = would not.

wae [wei, we] ***n.*** [Scot.] 悲哀,苦恼,忧伤 (= woe)。

wae·sucks [ˈweisʌks; `wesʌks] ***int.*** [Scot.] 唉 (= alas)。

WAF = Women in the Air Force [美]空军妇女队。

Waf [wæf; wæf, wɑf] ***n.*** [美]空军妇女队成员。

w.a.f. = with all faults 一经售出,概不退换。

wa·fer [ˈweifə; `wefɚ] **I** ***n.*** **1.** 薄脆饼;薄饼一样的东西;【物、无】圆片;薄片;晶片;【医】糯米纸[包药用的干糊片]。**2.** (封信用的)胶纸。**3.**【宗】圣饼[一种供圣餐用的未发酵圆面包皮]。*thin as a ~* 非常薄的。**II** ***vt.*** 用胶纸封。**-er** ***n.*** 压片机,切片机。

wa·fer·y [ˈweifəri; `wefərɪ] ***a.*** 薄脆饼似的;极薄的。

waff[1] [wɑːf, wæf; wæf, wɑf] ***n.*** **1.** (作为信号的)挥动。**2.** 噗的一吹[喷];阵风。**3.** 一瞥。**4.** 鬼,幽灵。

waff[2] [wɑːf, wæf; wæf, wɑf] ***a.*** [Scot.] 没有价值的,不足取的,不足道的。

waf·fle [ˈwɔfl; `wɑfl] ***n.*** 奶蛋烘饼,华夫饼。~ **iron** 奶蛋烘饼烤模。

WAFS, Wafs [wæfs] ***n.*** [美] Waf 的复数。

waft [wɑːft, wɔft; wɑft, wæft] **I** ***vt.*** 吹送,飘送;使浮动,使漂荡。~ *a kiss* 丢吻。*a fragrance ~ed from the meadow* 牧场上吹来的香气。— ***vi.*** 浮动,漂荡。**II** ***n.*** **1.** 浮动,漂荡,飘浮。**2.** 一吹;一阵风。**3.** (鸟翅膀的)一扇。**4.** 飘香。**5.**【海】信号旗;(遇险)信号。*a ~ of bells* 风中传来的钟[铃]声。*a ~ of joy* 一阵短暂的欢乐。**-er** ***n.*** 转盘风扇。

waft·age [ˈwɑːftidʒ; `wæftɪdʒ] ***n.*** [古] **1.** 吹送;飘浮;飘荡。**2.** 运送;传达;传播。

waf·ture [ˈwɑːftʃə, ˈwæf-; `wæftʃɚ, `wɑf-] ***n.*** **1.** 浮动,飘荡,波动;飘送,浮运。**2.** 飘动物[如因微风飘动的东西]。

wag. = wagon.

wag[1] [wæg; wæg] **I** ***vt.*** 摇,摆动(特指尾巴等)。*A dog ~s its tail.* 狗摇尾巴。— ***vi.*** **1.** 摇动;摆动。**2.** (舌头)不停地动;喋喋不休。**3.** [古](时势等)推移,变迁。**4.** 摇摇摆摆地走。**5.** [俚]动身,出发,走掉。*How ~s the world* (*with you*)? (你)情形怎么样? *So the world ~s.* 人世变迁就是这样,这就是人生。*The beards* [*chins, jaws, tongues*] *are wagging.* 大家不停地谈着。*Your tongue ~s too freely.* 你的嘴太随便了。~ ***one's finger at*** 向…摇指头(表责难、轻视)。***The tail ~s the dog.*** 上下颠倒;小人物掌权。**II** ***n.*** 摇动,摆动。

wag[2] [wæg; wæg] **I** ***n.*** **1.** 滑稽角色,爱说笑的人。**2.** [英俚]逃学,偷懒。***play*** (***the***) ~ [英俚]逃学,偷懒。**II** ***vi.*** [英俚]逃学。~ ***it*** [英俚]赖学,逃学。

wage[1] [weidʒ; wedʒ] ***n.*** [常 *pl.*] **1.** 工资。**2.** 报应。★ *pl.* 常作 *sing.* 用。*time ~s* 计时工资。*~s by the piece* 计件工资。***at a ~*** [***at ~s***] ***of $ ... a month*** 每月工资…美元。***get good ~s*** 拿高薪。~ **day** 发工资日。~ **differential** 工资差额。~ **earner** 工资劳动者,工资生活者;雇佣劳动者。~ **freeze** [英]工资冻结。~ **hike** 工资的增加。~ **level** 工资水平。~ **packet** [英]工资袋。~ **pattern** 工资标准。~ **scale** 工资等级。~-**worker** [美] = wage earner.

wage[2] [weidʒ; wedʒ] ***vt.*** **1.** 实行,进行,作(战等) (*on; against*)。**2.** [方]雇佣。**3.** [古]打赌;抵押;担保。

wa·ger [ˈweidʒə; `wedʒɚ] **I** ***n.*** 赌金,赌注;打赌。**II** ***vt.*** 打赌;担保,保证。~ *five dollars on the white horse* 在那匹白马身上下五美元赌注。*I ~ that it shall be so.* 我保证(它)会这样。

wag·ger·y [ˈwægəri; `wægərɪ] ***n.*** 诙谐;恶作剧,开玩笑。

wag·gish [ˈwægiʃ; `wægɪʃ] ***a.*** 玩笑的;诙谐的;淘气的,恶作剧的。**-ly** ***ad.***

wag·gle [ˈwægl; `wægl] ***vi., vt., n.*** = wag[1].

wag·gly [ˈwægli; `wæglɪ] ***a.*** 摇摇晃晃的。

wag·(g)on [ˈwægən; `wægən] **I** ***n.*** **1.** (二马以上的四轮)运货马车。**2.** [英](铁路的)无盖货车。**3.** 手推车。**4.**【采】矿车。**5.** [美]面包车[小型多座汽车]。**6.** 巡逻警车。**7.** [美俚]婴孩车。**8.** [the ~] 囚车。**9.** [the W-]【天】北斗七星。**10.** [美俚]左轮(手枪)。***hitch one's ~ to a star*** 妄想登天;追求力所不及的东西。***on*** [***off***] ***the ~*** [美俚]在[不]戒酒。**II** ***vt.*** 用运货马车[货车、手推车等]运送。~ **boss** [美]运货马车队队长。~ **drift** 工资浮动。~ **box** 大篷马车[旅行车]的车厢。~**-headed** ***a.*** (建筑)拱形的。~**load** 一车货载。~ **stop** [英]工资限额法[规定失业津贴不得多于工作时的工资]。~**-stop** ***vt.*** 对(失业者)采取工资限额法。~ **top**【机】斜顶。~ **train** 车队;护送车队;辎重车队;【美史】向西部移民车队。

wag·(g)on·age [ˈwægənidʒ; `wægənɪdʒ] ***n.*** **1.** 运货马

车运输。2. 运货马车运费。3.〔集合词〕运货(马)车。

wag·(g)on·er [ˈwæɡənə; ˋwæɡənɚ] *n*. 1. (运货马车的)御者;【采】矿车工。2.〔the W-〕【天】御夫座。

wag·(g)on·ette [wæɡəˈnet; ˏwæɡənˋɛt] *n*. (坐六人或八人的)四轮游览轻便马车。

Wag·ner [ˈvɑːɡnə; ˋvɑɡnɚ] *n*. 1. 华格纳〔姓氏〕。2. **Richard** ~ 李·华格纳〔1813—1883,德国歌剧家〕。

Wag·ne·ri·an [vɑːɡˈniəriən; vɑɡˋnɪriən] **I** *a*. 1. (德国歌剧家)华格纳的;华格纳音乐的;华格纳音乐论的;华格纳音乐手法[风格]的。2. 华格纳歌剧专业歌唱家的。*a* ~ *soprano* 华格纳歌剧女高音。**II** *n*. 华格纳音乐的崇拜者[门徒];华格纳音乐论的崇拜者[门徒]。

wa-gon-lit [ˈvæɡɔːnliː, ˈwæɡ-; vɑɡõˋli, ˋwæɡ-] *n*. 〔F.〕铁路卧车。

wa·hi·ne [wɑːˈhiːnei; wɑˋhine] *n*. 〔美〕(大洋洲东部)玻里尼西亚 (Polynesian) 女人〔尤指夏威夷女人〕。

wa·hoo[1] [wɑːˈhuː, ˈwɑːhuː; wɑˋhu, ˋwɑhu] *n*. 〔美〕【植】火树 (*Euonymus* 属);翅榆 (*Ulmus alata*)。

wa·hoo[2] [wɑːˈhuː; wɑˋhu] *n*. (*pl*. **-hoo**, **-hoos**)【动】刺鲅鱼 (*Acanthocybium solanderi*)〔产于暖水海洋〕。

wa·hoo[3] [wɑːˈhuː, ˈwɑːhuː; wɑˋhu, ˋwɑhu] *int*. 啊哈!〔开心或兴奋时的喊叫声〕。

waif [weif; wef] *n*. 1. 流浪者,无家可归的人;〔特指〕流浪儿童;无主[迷途]动物。2. 无主物品,拾得物品;漂流物;盗贼丢弃的赃物。3.【海】信号(旗)。~***s and strays*** 1. 无家可归的人们,流浪儿童们。2. 零碎东西。

wail [weil; wel] **I** *vi*. 1. 痛哭,大哭。2. 悲叹;哀悼;(风)哀鸣,悲号。3.〔美俚〕(爵士乐)表演得特别好。4.〔美俚〕用音乐或语言表现情感。— *vt*. 1.〔古〕哀悼,为…恸哭。2. 哀号着说。**II** *n*. 痛哭,恸哭;(风的)哀鸣声。**Wailing Wall** 饮泣墙,哭墙〔耶路撒冷犹太会堂的残壁,犹太人作为祈祷的场所〕;〔喻〕安慰物;慰藉。**-er** *n*. 哀悼者,恸哭者。**-ful** *a*. **-ing·ly** *ad*.

wain [wein; wen] *n*. 1.〔主、诗〕= wagon, cart;〔古〕战车。2.〔the W-〕【天】= the Wagon.

wain·scot [ˈweinskət; ˋwenskət] **I** *n*.【建】护壁板;腰板;室内墙壁有装饰的下部;护壁材料。**II** *vt*. (〔英〕**-tt-**)【建】在…装护壁板。

wain·scot(t)·ing [ˈweinskətiŋ; ˋwenskətɪŋ] *n*. 1. 护壁材料。2.〔集合词〕装有护壁板的墙壁。

wain·wright [ˈweinrait; ˋwenˏraɪt] *n*. (四轮)运货马车制造人。

WAIS = wide area information service【计】广域信息服务系统。

waist [weist; west] *n*. 1. 腰;腰部;(衣服的)腰身。2.〔美〕(女人、小孩子的)背心。3.【海】中部上甲板;船腰;(帆船的)主桅与前桅之间部分;【空】机身中部[腰部]。4.【动】蜂腰。*She has no* ~. 她胖得腰身也看不出了。~**-band**, ~**belt** 腰带,裤带。~**cloth** 围腰布。~**coat**〔英〕背心。~**-deep** *ad*., *a*. 深到腰(的)。~**-down** *a*. 下半身的。~**-high** *ad*., *a*. 深[高]齐腰(的)。~**line**【裁缝】腰围。

waist·ing [ˈweistiŋ; ˋwestɪŋ] *n*. 〔美〕背心料子。

wait [weit; wet] **I** *vi*. 1. 等,等候,等待 (*for*)。2. 服侍,伺候。*This can* ~. 这个不急。— *vt*. 等待;〔口〕耽搁,拖延。*Don't* ~ *dinner for me*. 晚饭不要等我。*W- a moment*! 等一等。***be kept*** ~***ing*** 一直等着。***keep sb***. ~***ing*** = ***make sb***. ~ 叫人等着。~ ***at*** [〔美〕***on***] ***table*** 侍候(用膳)。~ ***for*** 等;等待。***W- for it***.〔英〕等一等,听着!〔要听者注意下面要讲的令人惊奇的事〕。~ (***up***) ***on*** 1. 服侍,侍奉;伺候。2. 拜访,进谒(上面的人)。3. 跟随[追随]着…而来 (*May good luck* ~ *upon you*. 祝你幸运)。4.〔古〕护卫,侍从。~ ***out*** 一直等到…完毕。~ (***the***) ***table***〔Scot.〕= ~ *at table*. **II** *n*. 1. 等,等待;等候(的时间);埋伏。2.〔the ~s〕(特别是圣诞节期晚上为募集慈善捐赠在街头或挨户演唱的)募捐合唱队。***lay*** [***lie in***] ~ ***for*** 埋伏着等候。~**-a-bit** 荆棘,有刺植物。~**-and-see** *a*. 观望的 (*adopt a* ~*-and-see attitude* 采取观望态度)。~**-list** *vt*. 把…登入申请人名单 (~*-list them for the afternoon flight* 把他们列入下午班机的等候名单中)。~**people**, ~**staff** (男或女)侍者〔亦作 waitron〕。

wait·er [ˈweitə; ˋwetɚ] *n*. 1. 侍者,服务员;盆,托盘。2. 等候(时机)的人。3. 轻便食品台;运送食物升降机 (= dumbwaiter)。

wait·ing [ˈweitiŋ; ˋwetɪŋ] *n*. 等,等候,等待;侍候,服侍。***in*** ~ 侍奉(王室)的 (*a lady-in-*~ 侍从女官。*a lord in* ~ 侍从)。~ **game** 待机而动的策略。~ **maid** 侍女,丫头。~ **list** 候补[申请]人名单。~ **room** 候车室,候诊室(等)。~ **woman** = ~ maid.

wait·ress [ˈweitris; ˋwetrɪs] *n*. 女侍者,女服务员。

waive [weiv; wev] *vt*. 1. 放弃(权利、要求等),丢弃(赃物等),撤回;停止,不继续(坚持等)。2. 暂时搁置,推延。3. 省免;撇开,不予考虑。~ *formalities* 省免正式手续。

waiv·er [ˈweivə; ˋwevɚ] *n*.【法】1. 放弃,弃权。2. 弃权声明书。

Wake [weik; wek] *n*. 威克岛〔北太平洋〕(= ~ Island)。

wake[1] [weik; wek] **I** *vi*. (***woke*** [wəuk; wok], ***waked***; ***waked***, ***woken*** [ˈwəukən; ˋwokən]) 1. 醒,醒来;醒着。2. 警觉,醒悟。3. 苏醒,复活,活过来。— *vt*. 1. 弄醒,叫醒 (*up*);使觉醒,使醒悟。2. 使振作,使发奋 (*up*);激发(感情等);引起(反响等)。3. 使苏醒,使复活。4.〔古、方〕为…守夜,为…守灵。***a waking dream*** 白日梦,空想。***in one's waking hours*** 在醒着的时候。***kept sb***. ***waking*** 使…一直睡不着。~ ***the echoes*** 引起回响。~ ***to*** 发觉,意识到 (~ *to the gravity of the situation* 意识到事态的严重性)。~ ***up*** 1. 叫醒。2. 醒来;振作起来。***waking or sleeping*** 无论睡着或醒着。**II** *n*. 1. 通宵礼拜[仪式];(葬礼前通宵)守灵;通宵宴会。2.〔常 *pl*.〕(Lancashire, Yorkshire 等英国北部工业都市工人的)一年一次的假日。~**-up call** 警钟〔譬喻用法〕。

wake[2] [weik; wek] *n*. (船航过时的)尾波,航迹;【空】尾流;余迹;踪迹;(气流中的)涡区,扰流。***in the*** ~ ***of*** 在…后接踵而来;在后追随,仿效。~**board** 尾流跳板。~**-boarding** 尾流跳板运动。~ **surfing** (尾流)滑水〔以机动船拖动的乘浪滑行运动〕。

Wake·field [ˈweikfiːld; ˋwekˏfild] *n*. 韦克菲尔德〔姓氏〕。

wake·ful [ˈweikful; ˋwekfəl] *a*. 睡不着的,醒着的;不眠的;警醒的,不睡地警戒着的,警惕性高的。**-ly** *ad*. **-ness** *n*.

wak·en [ˈweikən; ˋwekən] *vi*. 醒来;醒着。— *vt*. 弄醒,唤醒;使觉醒,振起,鼓励。

wake·rife [ˈweikraif; ˋwekˏraɪf] *a*. 〔Scot. 英方〕= wakeful.

wake-rob·in [ˈweikˌrɔbin; ˋwekˏrɑbɪn] *n*.【植】1.〔英〕海芋属植物 (= cuckoopint)。2.〔美〕延龄草属植物;天南星。

wake-up [ˈweikˌʌp; ˋwekˏʌp] *n*. 〔美口〕北美金翼啄木鸟 (= flicker)。

Waks·man [ˈwæksmən; ˋwæksmən] *n*. 瓦克斯曼〔姓氏〕。

Wal·ach [ˈwɔlək; ˋwɑlək] *n*. = Wallach.

Wa·la·chi·a [wɑˈleikiə; wɑˋlekɪə] *n*. = Wallachia.

Wa·la·chi·an [wɑˈleikiən; wɑˋlekɪən] *a*. = Wallachian.

Walds·ter·ben, **walds·ter·ben** [ˈwældʃtεəbən; ˋwældʃtεrbən] *n*. 〔G.〕环境灾难,生态灾难。

Wal·do [ˈwɔːldəu; ˋwɔldo] *n*. 沃尔多〔姓氏,男子名〕。

wale [weil; wel] **I** *n*. 1. (肿起的)鞭痕,血痕。2. (织物上隆起的)条纹,棱纹;(筐篮上编得特粗而隆起的)箍;(木船船舷上)加固的木条或腰板。**II** *vt*. 1. 把…抽出血痕,鞭打。2. 在…上织出隆起条纹,为…编上筐箍。

W

Wal·er [ˈweilə; ˋwelɚ] ***n*.** 新南威尔士(New South Wales)产的马;澳洲马。
Wales [weilz; welz] ***n*.** 威尔士[英国]。
Wa·ley [ˈweili; ˋwelɪ] ***n*.** 韦利[姓氏]。
Wal·hal·la [vælˈhælə; wælˋhælə] ***n*.** = Valhalla.
walk [wɔːk; wɔk] **I** ***vi*.** **1.** 走,步行;【篮球】带球走,走步;(马)用常步走。**2.** 走着去;散步。**3.** (鬼等)出来。**4.** 〔喻〕处世,处身,生活。**4.** 【宇】(宇宙飞船)环绕天体作慢速飞行。— ***vt*.** **1.** 在…走;踩,踏。**2.** 使行走;使(马)用常步走。**3.** 带着走,领着走。**4.** 〔口〕把(笨重箱子等)一步一步移走。**5.** 与…竞走。**6.** 步测;用步行执行。**7.** 跳(走步舞)。~ *the floor* 在屋子里走来走去。*I'll ~ you ten miles any day you like*. 随便哪一天我跟你竞走十英里吧。~ ***about*** 闲步;散步。~ ***after*** [***in***] ***the flesh*** 过(放纵的)肉欲生活。~ ***around*** 〔美俚〕跳舞。~ ***... away*** 带走。~ ***away from*** **1.** 从…走开;从…脱身。**2.** 毫不费力地就超过[胜过]。~ ***away with*** 拐逃,偷走,抢走,夺走。~ ***by faith*** 过宗教生活。~ ***chalk mark*** = ~ the chalk. ~ ***one's chalks*** 〔俚〕不告而去,不辞而行。~ ***in darkness*** 过罪孽生活。~ ***in sb.'s shoe*** 仿效(某人)。~ ***in the light*** 在光亮中行走,过光明正大的生活。~ ***into*** **1.** 走进。**2.** 〔俚〕打骂(仆人等)。**3.** 〔俚〕大吃。~ ***off*** **1.** 离开;用走路来消散。**2.** 带走,拉去(犯人等)。~ (***sb.***) ***off his legs*** 使某人走得脚软腿酸。~ ***off with*** 拐逃,偷走,抢走(奖品)。~ ***on air*** (因成功)高兴得飘飘然。~ ***out*** 出去,离开;〔美〕罢工;(丢开人)走掉(*on*)。~ ***out with*** 和(异性朋友)出去玩。~ ***over*** (无竞争者时)独自走完(跑场);轻易击败(对方)。~ ***one's round*** (***s***) 巡回。~ ***the boards*** 做演员。~ ***the chalk*** 顺着车道白线笔直地走[向警察证明自己没有喝醉]。~ ***the earth*** (鬼)出现。~ ***the hospitals*** [***wards***] 在医院里实习。~ ***the plank*** **1.** 被海盗强迫从跳板上坠海。**2.** 被迫辞职;被迫放弃。~ ***the streets*** **1.** 走马路。**2.** 卖淫。~ ***the*** ~ 〔口〕说干就干,采取实际行动。~ ***through*** 〔美影〕排练(= to rehearse)。~ ***through a part*** 【剧】毫无兴趣地扮演所担任的角色;走过场。~ ***through life*** [***the world***] 度日,涉世。~ ***up*** 使猎犬将(鸟等)惊飞。***W- up***! 请进来![戏院管门人的呼声]。~ ***up to*** 走近。
II ***n*.** **1.** 行走,步行;徒步;散步。**2.** 步法;步态;〔W-〕走步舞;(马的)慢步;【宇航】(宇宙飞船)环绕天体所作的慢速飞行。**3.** 步行距离,步程,走路时间;【运】竞走。**4.** 步道,人行道;散步场。**5.** 牧羊场;养禽场,鸡舍;(小狗等的)饲养所;(某种作物的)种植物。**6.** 〔英〕负责地区,管区;【林】巡视地区;〔古〕(商贩等)常去的地区。**7.** 制绳所(= ropewalk)。**8.** 生活态度,处世;行为。*a mile* ~ 一英里路程。*I know him by his* ~. 我从步态上就知道是他。***a cock of the*** ~ 自命不凡的人。***an upright*** ~ 老老实实的生活态度。***at a*** ~ 用常步,用普通步子。***fall into a*** ~ (跑着的马)改成常步行走。***go at a*** ~ (马)用慢步走;散步。***in a*** ~ 〔美〕容易地。~ ***in life*** = ~ ***of life*** 职业;身分;阶级,阶层。**-able** ***a*.** 适于步行的,可以步行的。
walk·away [ˈwɔːkəˌwei; ˋwɔkəˏwe] ***n*.** 〔美〕轻易得到的胜利;轻而易举的工作。
walk·down [ˈwɔːkdaun; ˋwɔkˏdaʊn] ***n*.** 地下室;地下商店。
walk·er [ˈwɔːkə; ˋwɔkɚ] ***n*.** **1.** 步行者;散步者。**2.** 〔美〕(供幼孩学步或病残者用)助步车。**3.** 【鸟】走禽。**4.** 〔*pl*.〕走路用的短裤[鞋]。**5.** 〔俚〕(女子的)男伴。***be much of a*** ~ 爱散步[步行]。
Walk·er[1] [ˈwɔːkə; ˋwɔkɚ] ***n*.** 沃克[姓氏]。
Walk·er[2] [ˈwɔːkə; ˋwɔkɚ] ***int*.** 〔俚〕(表示不相信)不会吧。
walk·ie-look·ie [ˈwɔːkiˈluki; ˋwɔkɪˋlʊkɪ] ***n*.** 手提式电视摄影机。
walk·ie-talk·ie [ˈwɔːkiˈtɔːki; ˋwɔkɪˏtɔkɪ] ***n*.** 〔美〕步话机。
walk-in [ˈwɔːkˌin; ˋwɔkˏɪn] **I** ***a*.** 〔美〕**1.** 宽敞得可在里面步行的。**2.** (不经门廊)直接进入的。**3.** 〔口〕(建筑物)空着且可立刻占用的。**II** ***n*.** **1.** (人进得去的)大壁橱;大房间。**2.** 容易取得的胜利。**3.** 简易门诊所。**4.** 未经预约而来的人,不请自来的人。
walk·ing [ˈwɔːkiŋ; ˋwɔkɪŋ] **I** ***n*.** **1.** 步行;步法,步态。**2.** 道路状态。**II** ***a*.** **1.** 步行(用)的。**2.** (能)行走的。**3.** 解雇的,被免职的。*a* ~ *plow* (牛马拉的)步犁。*The* ~ *is slippery*. 路滑。~**-around money** (随身携带的)零花钱。~ **chair** 婴儿学步用的有轮小车(= go cart)。~ **delegate** (工会的)工厂巡视员。~ **dictionary** 活字典。~ **dress** 散步服装,出去穿的衣服。~ **fern** 〔美〕【植】根叶过山蕨菜。~ **gentleman** [**lady**] 跑龙套的男[女]配角。~ **leaf** **1.** 【动】蝻。**2.** 【植】根叶过山蕨(= ~ fern)。~ **machine** 助走机[系在人身上助人攀登障碍物或携带重物的一种机械]。~ **papers** 〔*pl*.〕〔美口〕解雇(通知)。~ **shorts** 百慕大(齐膝)短裤。~ **stick** **1.** 〔英〕手杖。**2.** 【动】竹节虫(= stick-insect)。~ **through** 【计】(附有答案的)电脑历险游戏指导手册。~ **ticket** = ~ papers. ~**-tour** 徒步旅行。~ **tractor** 手扶拖拉机。~ **wounded** 受伤后仍能行走的。
Walk·ley [ˈwɔːkli; ˋwɔklɪ] ***n*.** 沃克利[姓氏]。
Walk·man [ˈwɔːkmən; ˋwɔkmən] ***n*.** 〔商标〕随身听(收录机)。
walk-on [ˈwɔːkˌɔn; ˋwɔkˏɑn] **I** ***n*.** 次要演员,跑龙套演员。**II** ***a*.** 出现于舞台上的。
walk·out [ˈwɔːkˈaut; ˋwɔkˏaut] ***n*.** **1.** 〔美〕罢工(者);罢课(者)。**2.** 退席(以示抗议)。**3.** 告别仪式。
walk·over [ˈwɔːkˈəuvə; ˋwɔkˏovɚ] ***n*.** 〔口〕【赛马】只有一匹马参加的比赛,单骑走完跑道;一帆风顺,轻易得胜,轻易得到。*have a* ~ 轻易得胜。
walk-through [ˈwɔːkθruː; ˋwɔkˏθru] ***n*.** **1.** (戏剧等的)初排;(电视)不拍摄的排练;草率的表演。**2.** 地下步行道。
walk-up [ˈwɔːkʌp; ˋwɔkˏʌp] **I** ***n*.** 〔美口〕**1.** 无电梯设备的公寓(房间)。**2.** 宣传攻势。**II** ***a*.** **1.** (公寓)无电梯设备的;(房间)在无电梯的楼上的。**2.** (服务设施等)临街的[不用走进房子就可得到服务]。
walk·way [ˈwɔːkˌwei; ˋwɔkˏwe] ***n*.** 走道,通道,人行道[尤指其上有遮蔽者]。
walk·y-talk·y [ˈwɔːkiˈtɔːki; ˋwɔkɪˏtɔkɪ] ***n*.** (*pl*. **-talkies**) 〔美〕= walkie-talkie.
wall[1] [wɔːl; wɔl] **I** ***n*.** **1.** 墙壁;(石、砖等的)围墙;城墙。**2.** (形状、用途)像墙壁的东西,障壁;土堤,堤防。**3.** (矿井、容器的)内壁,壁面。**4.** (路的)靠墙部分,沿墙。*a blank* ~ 没有装饰的墙壁;没有门、窗的墙壁。*the* ~ *of the chest* 【生理】胸壁。*the cell* ~ 【生】细胞壁。(***can***) ***see through*** [***into***] ***a brick*** ~ 怪有眼光,怪精明[常作反语用]。***drive*** [***push, thrust***] (***sb.***) ***to the*** ~ 把(某人)逼至绝境。***give sb. the*** ~ 把靠墙的路让给某人[表示好感等]。***go over the*** ~ 〔美俚〕越狱。***go to the*** ~ 陷入绝境;(事业)失败;被遗忘。***hang by the*** ~ 被遗忘。***jump over the*** ~ 舍弃教会[教职]。***run one's head against a*** ~ 拿头去撞墙;一心要蛮干。***take the*** ~ ***of sb.*** 不给某人让路;抢着出风头,抢先。***the Great W- of China*** 万里长城。***the W-*** **1.** (把东、西柏林分开的)柏林墙。**2.** = Wailing W-. ***with one's back to the*** ~ 陷入绝境;以寡敌众;负隅(顽抗)。***within four*** ~***s*** 在房屋内。**II** ***vt*.** 筑墙[城]围住,筑城防御;筑墙堵塞(孔、口等)(*up*)。*a* ~*ed-in garden* 有围墙的花园。*a* ~*ed city* 〔美俚〕监狱。~**board** 墙板;建筑纸板。~ **creeper** 【动】旋壁雀。~**eye** **1.** (马的)白星眼;(鱼等的)大而闪亮的眼睛。**2.** 大眼鱼。**3.** 【医】角膜白斑;分开性斜视。~**eyed** ***a*.** **1.** 白星眼的;眼睛大而闪亮的。**2.** 【医】患角膜白斑[分开性斜视]的。**3.** 〔美俚〕喝醉了的。~**eyed pike** 【动】大眼鰤鲈。~**eyed pollack** 【动】狭鳕,

W

明太鱼。~ **eye surfperch**【动】鼓眼鱼,鼓眼浪鲈。~ **fern**【植】水龙骨〔一种攀缘植物〕。~ **flower** 1.【植】桂竹香。2.〔口〕(舞会中没有舞伴的人,尤指女子)墙花。~ **knot** 绳端结。~ **lizard** 壁蜥蜴,壁虎。~ **painting** 壁画。~**paper** 1. *n*. 壁纸。2. *vt*. 在…上糊以壁纸。~-**piece** (旧时)装于墙边或船边的小炮。~ **plate**【建】承梁板。~ **rock**【地,矿】围岩,母岩。~ **rocket**【植】芸苔(属)。~ **rue**【植】墙生铁角蕨。~ (**telephone**) **set**【电话】墙机,挂机。~-**to**-~ *a*. 铺满地板的(地毯)。-**less** *a*. 没有围墙[城墙]的。

wall[2] [wɔl; wɔl] *vt*., *vi*. 演戏般转动(眼睛)。

wal·la [ˈwɑːlə; ˋwɑlɑ] *n*. = wallah.

wal·la·by [ˈwɔləbi; ˋwɑləbɪ] *n*. (*pl*. -*bies*) ★也作集合词用。1.【动】鷚;小(种)袋鼠;〔美俚〕(马戏团里的)袋鼠。2.〔俚〕澳洲人。*on the* ~ (*track*)〔澳俚〕流浪中;失业。

Wal·lace [ˈwɔlis; ˋwɑlɪs] *n*. 华莱士〔姓氏,男子名〕。

Wal·lach [ˈwɔlək; ˋwɑlək] *n*. 瓦拉几亚人。

Wal·la·chi·a [wɔˈleikiə; wɑˋlekɪə] *n*. 瓦拉几亚〔从前欧洲东南部一王国;1861 年与摩尔多瓦合并作罗马尼亚的一部分〕。

Wal·la·chi·an [wɔˈleikiən; wɑˋlekɪən] I *a*. 瓦拉几亚的;瓦拉几亚人[语]的。II *n*. 瓦拉几亚人[语]。

wal·lah [ˈwɑːlə; ˋwɑlə] *n*.〔印英〕1. 干某种事的人,执行某种任务的人〔作后缀用〕。2.〔口〕人。*a punka*-~ 拉布风扇的仆人。

wal·la·roo [wɔləˈruː; ˏwɑləˋru] *n*.【动】大袋鼠〔尤指岩大袋鼠(属)〕。

walled [wɔːld; wɔld] *a*. 1. 有墙的,有围墙的。2. 设(防御)工事的。3. (如墙似)围着的,用篱笆围着的,设了障碍的。

Wal·ler [ˈwɔlə; ˋwɑlɚ] *n*. 沃勒〔姓氏〕。

wal·let [ˈwɔlit; ˋwɑlɪt] *n*. 1. 钱包,皮夹子。2. (皮制)零星工具袋。3.〔古〕(旅行者等的)行囊。*X-ray the* ~〔口〕(医院)检查(患者的)钱包〔意为了解其医疗费支付能力〕。~ **curve**【数】钱囊线。~ **X-ray** 对患者钱包的检查〔患者支付医疗费用能力的检查〕。

Wal·lis [ˈwɔlis; ˋwɑlɪs] *n*. 沃利斯〔姓氏〕。

Wal·loon [wɔˈluːn; wɑˋlun] *n*. (比利时南部的)窝龙人;窝龙语〔法语的一种方言〕。

wal·lop [ˈwɔləp; ˋwɑləp] I *vt*.〔口〕猛击;击溃,打垮;【棒球】猛打。— *vi*.〔方、口〕1. 窜过去,冲过去;笨拙沉重地走,摇摇晃晃地走;(动物)在泥中打滚;(车等)颠簸。2. 沸腾作声。3.〔古、方〕= gallop. II *n*. 1.〔方、口〕笨拙的动作。2.〔口〕猛击,痛打;冲击力;〔喻〕作用力,效力。3.〔美口〕强烈快感。4.〔英俚〕啤酒。III *ad*.〔仅用于下列习语〕: *go* (*down*) ~ 唏哩哗啦地落下。

wal·lop·er [ˈwɔləpə; ˋwɑləpɚ] *n*. 1.〔口〕猛击者,痛殴者。2.〔英方〕特大物,异常的东西,怪物,怪事。

wal·lop·ing [ˈwɔləpiŋ; ˋwɑləpɪŋ]〔口〕I *n*. 猛打;溃败。II *a*. 巨大的;极好的。

wal·low [ˈwɔləu; ˋwɑlo] I *vi*. 1. (猪等在泥、水中)翻滚,打滚;〔喻〕沉迷(在酒、色等中)(*in*)。2. 起浪。3. (烟、水等)进出,涌出,喷出。~ *in money* 非常有钱。II *n*. (水牛等)打滚(的泥潭);动物打滚形成的凹坑。

wall·pa·per·ize [ˈwɔːlpeipəraiz; ˋwɔlpepəraɪz] *vt*. 使成废币,使(纸币)无价值。

Wall Street [ˈwɔːl striːt; ˋwɔlˏstrit] 华尔街〔美国纽约市的一条街道,是美国的金融机构的集中地〕。**Wall Streeter** 华尔街大老板。

wall·y [ˈweili; ˋwelɪ] I *a*.〔Scot.〕1. 好的,第一流的;漂亮的。2. 魁伟的,强大的,健壮的。3. 令人愉快的。II *n*. 装饰品,玩具;〔*pl*.〕漂亮的服饰。

wall·y·ball [ˈwɔːlibɔːl; ˋwɔlɪbɔl] *n*.【体】壁排球〔一种类似排球的运动,比赛场四面有墙壁,球可弹回而不会出界〕。

wal·ly·drag [ˈweilidræg; ˋwelɪˏdræg] *n*.〔Scot.〕1. 孱弱而发育不良的动物。2. 懒散的人;〔尤指〕懒婆娘(= wallydraigle)。

Walms·ley [ˈwɔːmzli; ˋwɔmzlɪ] *n*. 沃姆斯利〔姓氏〕。

wal·nut [ˈwɔːlnət; ˋwɔlnət] *n*.【植】胡桃;胡桃树;胡桃木。*an English* [*a Persian*] ~ 薄壳核桃。*over the* ~*s and the wine* 在饭后闲谈中,在餐后吃水果等的时候。

Wal·pole [ˈwɔːlpəul; ˋwɔlpol] *n*. 沃波尔〔姓氏〕。

Wal·pur·gis [vælˈpuəgis, vɑːl-; vɑlˋpʊrgɪs] **Night** 华尔普吉斯之夜〔四月三十日夜,民间传说是夜女巫在德国布罗肯山聚会,进行狂欢酒宴〕。

wal·rus [ˈwɔːlrəs; ˋwɔlrəs] *n*.【动】海象;〔美俚〕矮胖子。

Walsh [wɔːlʃ; wɔlʃ] *n*. 沃尔什〔姓氏〕。

Wal·ter [ˈwɔːltə; ˋwɔltɚ] *n*. 1. 沃尔特〔姓氏,男子名〕。2.〔w-〕飞机应急雷达发射机。

Wal·ton [ˈwɔːltən; ˋwɔltən] *n*. 沃尔顿〔姓氏,男子名〕。

waltz [wɔːls; wɔlts] I *n*. 华尔兹舞(曲),圆舞(曲);〔喻〕轻松愉快的工作。*a deux-temps* [*trois-temps*] ~ 二拍子[三拍子]华尔兹。II *vi*. 1. 跳华尔兹舞;〔口〕轻快顺利地走动;旋转。2. 轻易地进行(*through*)。~ *across the street* 蹦蹦跳跳[轻快地]走过街去。~ *off on the ear*〔美〕急匆匆做。~ *through an exam* 轻而易举地通过考试。— *vt*. 1. 与…跳华尔兹舞。2. (像跳华尔兹舞一样)轻快地引领(他人)。-**er** *n*. 跳华尔兹舞的人。

wam·ble [ˈwɑːmbl, ˈwæmbl; ˋwɑmbl, ˋwæmbl] I *vi*.〔主方〕1. 晕转。2. 摇摆,摇晃,眼花。3.〔废〕恶心;(胃产生)恶心感。II *n*.〔主方〕1. 晕,昏转;摇摆,摇晃。2. 恶心感。-**bly** *a*.

wame [weim; wem] *n*.〔Scot. 英方〕肚子,腹。

wam·pa·no·ag [ˌwɑːmpəˈnəuæg; ˏwɑmpəˋnoæg] *n*. (*pl*. ~(*s*)) 瓦帕浓人〔北美印第安人阿尔衮琴族一部落,后移居美国麻萨诸塞州东南部〕。

wam·pum [ˈwɔmpəm; ˋwɑmpəm] *n*. 1. (以前印第安人作货币或饰品的)贝壳串珠。2.〔美俚〕钱。

WAN = wide area network【计】(把许多小区域网络联接起来的)宽域网(络)。

wan[1] [wɔn; wɑn] *a*. 1. 苍白的;没有血色的。2. 病弱的,软弱无力的。3.〔古〕暗淡的,阴暗的。

wan[2] [wɑːn, wɔːn; wɑn, wɔn]〔废〕win 的过去式。

Wan·a·ma·ker [ˈwɔnəmeikə; ˋwɑnəˏmekɚ] *n*. 沃纳梅克〔姓氏〕。

wand [wɔnd; wɑnd] *n*. 1. (柳树等的)嫩枝,细枝。2. (魔术师的)短杖;权杖;【乐】指挥棒。3.〔英〕(做箭靶的)细枝条;〔美〕(做箭靶的)狭长木板。

Wan·da [ˈwɔndə; ˋwɑndə] *n*. 旺达〔女子名〕。

wan·der [ˈwɔndə; ˋwɑndɚ] I *vi*. 1. (无目的地)漫步;漫游;徘徊,彷徨;流浪,漂移。2. 迷路;走岔,离开。3. (河)曲曲折折地流;(山脉)蜿蜒错列。4. (思想等)离开正道;错乱;离题乱说。5.【医】游走。~ *from the subject* (谈话)离开本题。*His mind is* ~*ing*. 他心不在焉。*His wits are* ~*ing*. 他有点疯了。— *vt*.〔诗〕漫游。~ *about* 徘徊,彷徨,流浪。II *n*. 徘徊,彷徨,流浪。-**er** *n*. 1. 漫游者,流浪汉。2. 彷徨者;迷路的动物。

wan·der·ing [ˈwɔndəriŋ; ˋwɑndərɪŋ] I *a*. 1. 漫游的,徘徊的。2. 流离失所的;迷途的。3. (河流)曲折的。4. 错乱的;胡说乱讲的。5.【植】攀绕的;有卷须的。6.【医】游走的。II *n*.〔常 *pl*.〕1. 徘徊;流浪;漫游;漂移,偏移。2. 错乱,胡话。3.【地】迁[漂]移。*the* ~*s of a madman* 狂人的胡话。~ **albatross**【动】阿房鸟。~ **cell**【生】游走细胞。**W- Jew** 1.〔the W- J-〕流浪的犹太人〔中古传说中一个名叫 Joannes Buttadeus 的犹太人,因其嘲弄被钉上十字架的耶稣,遭天谴永远流浪〕;流浪者。2.〔w- Jew, W- jew〕【植】攀绕植物。~ **nursery** 移动苗圃。

Wan·der·jahr [ˈvɑːndəjɑː; ˋvɑndɚˏjɑr] *n*. (*pl*. -*jahre* [-jɑːrə; -jɑrə])〔G.〕漫游时代〔原为欧洲中世纪习俗,学徒满师后就业前到各地漫游一年〕。

Wan·der·lust [ˈvɑːndəlust; ˋwɑndɚˏlʌst] *n*.〔G.〕旅

W

行热;流浪癖。

wan·der·oo [ˌwɔndəˈruː; ˏwandəˋru] *n*. 【动】獅猴,大黑猴。

W and W = Wash and Wear 【织】洗了就可穿;免烫。

wane [wein; wen] **I** *vi*. (月)缺损,亏;(*opp*. wax);(光、势力等)衰落,衰微;减少。~ *to the close* 接近末了。*wax and* ~ 盈亏;盛衰。**II** *n*. **1**. 月亏(期)。**2**. 衰退(期)。**3**. (木材的)缺损。*on* [*in*] *the* ~ (月)正在亏缺中;衰落中,减少中。

wane·y [ˈweini; ˋwenɪ] *a*. (*wan·i·er*; *wan·i·est*) **1**. 衰落的;减少的;没落的。**2**. 常缺损的;不整齐的〔尤指锯解的木料还带树皮的〕。

wan·gle [ˈwæŋgl; ˋwæŋgl] **I** *vt*. 〔口〕**1**. 用计谋办到,巧妙地取得。**2**. (从人群中)扭身挤出;从(困境中)脱身。**3**. 哄骗;掩饰,捏造;伪造。~ *an extra week's holiday* 巧妙地弄到一周额外的休假。~ *business records* 伪造业务记录。~ *a book out of sb*. 从某人手上骗得一本书。— *vi*. **1**. 扭身挤出,脱身。**2**. 玩弄诡计;花言巧语。**II** *n*. **1**. 诡计;哄骗;骗得的东西。**2**. 虚饰,伪造。

wan·i·gan, wan·ni·gan [ˈwaːnigən; ˋwanɪgən] *n*. 〔美〕**1**. (伐木场的食物等)贮藏柜。**2**. 小寝室;炊事棚车。

wan·ion [ˈwaːnjən, ˈwɔːn-; ˋwanjən, ˋwɔn-] *n*. 〔古〕不幸,倒霉;灾祸;天灾,灾害。

wan·na [ˈwɔnə; ˋwanə] 〔美俚〕= want to. ~**bee 1**. *n*. 〔美口〕对名流的狂热仰慕者,疯狂崇拜…的人;想望成功[出名、发财]的人〔系 want to be之缩略〕**2**. *a*. 有抱负的。

wan·nish [ˈwɔniʃ; ˋwanɪʃ] *a*. 有点苍白的。

want [wɔnt; wɑnt] **I** *vt*. **1**. (想)要,想望;想得到。**2**. 需要,必要;必须。**3**. 征求;征聘;通缉。**4**. 缺少,没有;不够,差欠。*I* ~ *you to come*. (=〔俚〕*I* ~ *for you to come*. 或 *I* ~ (*that*) *you should come*). 我希望你来。*What do you* ~ *with me*? 你找我有什么事? *You're* ~*ed*. 有人找你。*You won't be* ~*ed this afternoon*. 今天下午没事需要你做。*the* ~*ed man* 被通缉的人。*You don't* ~ *to be rude*. 你不必粗暴。*a typist* ~*ed* 征聘打字员。*Situation* ~*ed by a typist*. 打字员求职。*It* ~*s 3 inches of 6 feet*. 六英尺差三英寸。*It* ~*s something of perfection*. 还有一点不完满的地方。— *vi*. **1**. 缺少,没有;不够,差 (*in*)。**2**. 生活困难,穷困。~ *in stature* 身长不够。*Let him* ~ *for nothing*. 不要让他短缺什么东西〔生活上有什么匮乏〕。~ *in* [*out, off*] 〔口、方〕想要进来[出去] (*The cat* ~*s in*. 那只猫想进来)。~ *to* 〔口〕应该 (*You* ~ *to eat a balanced diet*. 你应该吃营养均衡的食物)。**II** *n*. **1**. 缺乏,不足;需要。**2**. 匮乏,穷困,贫穷。**3**. 欲求;〔主 *pl*.〕想要的东西,必需品。*know the bitterness of* ~ 知道贫穷的苦处。*a man of few* ~*s* 欲求少的人。*for* ~ *of* 因缺少…。*in* ~ 贫穷。*in* ~ *of* 需要…(的),缺少…(的)。~ **ad**. (报刊上的)征聘[征求,求职]广告。~ **column** (报纸上的)征聘[求职]栏。~ **list** (收藏家或博物馆等向商人发出的)需购艺术品货单。**-able** *a*. 称心的,有吸引力的。**-age** *n*. 缺少(量)。**-er** *n*. **1**. 缺乏者;贫乏者。**2**. 〔方〕求偶者。**-less** *a*. 无欲求的。

want·ing [ˈwɔntiŋ; ˋwantɪŋ] **I** *a*. **1**. 短缺的,缺失的;不足的;不够的 (*in*)。**2**. 〔方〕智力不足的,低能的。*He is* ~ *in honesty*. 他不老实。*be a bit* ~ 有点笨。**II** *prep*. 缺,短少。*a year* ~ *three days* 一年差三天。*W- courage, victory is impossible*. 没有勇气就无法取得胜利。

wan·ton [ˈwɔntən; ˋwantən] **I** *a*. **1**. 放肆的,放纵的;任性的;反复不定的,变化无常的;卤莽的,粗暴的;荒唐的,没有理由的,胡作非为的。**2**. 行为不检的,淫荡的。**3**. 淘气的,顽皮的;嬉闹的。**4**. 〔诗〕(花草)繁茂的。*a* ~ *breeze* 变化无常的微风。~ *rivers* 奔流的江河。~ *profusion* 浪费。~ *mischief* 瞎胡闹。*a* ~ *woman* 荡妇。*a* ~ *child* 顽童。**II** *n*. 水性杨花的人,荡妇;〔罕〕任性的孩子。**III** *vi*. **1**. 任性,反复无常;放肆。**2**. 挥霍,胡闹,嬉戏。**3**. 繁茂。— *vt*. 挥霍;浪费。**-ly** *ad*. **-ness** *n*.

wan·y [ˈweini; ˋwenɪ] *a*. (*wan·i·er*; *wan·i·est*) = waney.

wap [wɔp; wæp] *vt*. (*-pp-*) **1**. 〔方〕打;打败,击败。**2**. 〔古〕= whop.

wap·en·take [ˈwɔpənteik; ˋwapənˏtek] *n*. 【英史】百户村 (= hundred)。

wap·i·ti [ˈwɔpiti; ˋwapətɪ] *n*. (*pl*. ~**s**, 〔集合词〕~) 【动】(北美)马鹿。

Wap·pen·s(c)haw [ˈwaːpənʃɔː; ˋwapənˏʃɔ] *n*. 〔Scot.〕**1**. 【史】武装检阅。**2**. 来福枪射击比赛。

wap·per-jawed [ˈwɔpədʒɔːd; ˋwapəˏdʒɔd] *a*. 〔英方〕歪下巴的;〔美口〕突下巴的。

war[1] [wɔː, wɔə; wɔr] **I** *n*. **1**. 战争,军事。**2**. 兵学,战术。**3**. 武器,兵器。**4**. 斗争;敌意,不和。*an aggressive* ~ 侵略战争。*a people's* ~ 人民战争。*the civil* ~ 国内战争。*conventional* ~ 常规战争。*guerrilla* ~ 游击战。*nuclear* ~ 核战争。*revolutionary* ~ 革命战争。*the W- of American Independence* 〔英〕= *the W- of Independence* 〔美〕(美国)独立战争。*the seat* [*theater*] of ~ 战场。*a* ~ *criminal* 战犯。*a prisoner of* ~ 战俘。*the* ~ *of the pen* 笔战。*a* ~ *of words* 舌战。*a* ~ *of annihilation* 歼灭战。*a* ~ *of attrition* 消耗战。*a* ~ *of propaganda* 宣传战。*art of* ~ 战术,兵法。*the Secretary* (*of State*) *for W-* = *the W- Secretary* 〔英〕陆军大臣。*the W- Department* 〔美〕陆军部〔国防部中的一部〕。*the W- Office* 〔英〕陆军部。~ *expenditure* 军费。~ *industries* 军事工业。*at* ~ *with* 和…交战;和…不和。*declare* ~ (*against*; *on, upon*) (对…)宣战。*drift into* ~ 逐渐卷入[陷入]战争。*go to the* ~(*s*) 去参军;〔古〕出征。*go to* ~ (*against*) (和…)进行战争。*have been in the* ~*s* 打过仗,受过伤;〔谑〕经历过忧患,吃过苦头。*levy* [*make, wage*] ~ (*on, upon, against*) (和…)开战,作战。**II** *a*. 战争的,军事的。**III** (*-rr-*) *vi*. 打仗,作战;斗争,竞争 (*with*; *against*)。— *vt*. 〔Scot.〕击败。~ **baby 1**. 战时诞生的孩子;士兵的私生子。**2**. 因战争需要而大为发展的工业。~**bird** 〔美俚〕作战飞机。~ **bonnet** (印第安人的)战帽。~ **chest** 战争基金;竞选基金。~ **cloud** 战云。~ **colour** 卡其色,保护色。~ **correspondent** 随军记者。~ **crime** 战争罪。~ **cry** 战斗呐喊;政党的(战斗)口号[标语]。~ **fatigue** 厌战(情绪)。~**fighting** 弹道导[飞]弹战〔指互射弹道导[飞]弹或以导弹拦截敌方导弹的战事〕。~ **footing** 战时编制;战时体制。~ **game** 摹拟演习 (= kriegspiel)。~**head** 弹头 (*a nuclear* ~*head* 核弹头)。~**-horse** 〔古、诗〕军马,战马;〔口语〕老兵;〔口〕老练的人;〔美俚〕男子气概的女人。~**lock** 〔古〕魔术师;骗子。~**lord** 军阀。~**-monger** 战争贩子。~ **paint** 印第安人打仗前身上涂抹的颜料;〔美俚〕盛装,正式宴会打扮;化妆(品)。~**party** 主战派。~**path** (美洲印第安人的)征途;〔转义〕敌对行动[情绪]。~**plane** 军用飞机。~ **scape** 战争[战场]景色(图片,画幅)。~**ship** 军舰。~**song** 军歌。~**-time** 战时。~ **vessel** 军舰。~**-weariness** 厌战情绪。~**-weary** *a*. 厌战的。~**worn** *a*. 久经战阵的;被战争弄得筋疲力尽的;被战火破坏的,饱经战祸的。

war[2] [waː; war] *a*., *ad*. 〔Scot.〕= worse.

War. = Warwickshire.

war·ble[1] [ˈwɔːbl; ˋwɔrbl] **I** *vi*., *vt*. **1**. (鸟)啼啭;(人)像鸟啭似地唱,用颤音唱。**2**. 〔美〕= yodel. **II** *n*. 啼啭;颤音;颤音歌唱(法);唱歌。

war·ble[2] [ˈwɔːbl; ˋwɔrbl] *n*. **1**. (马背的)鞍瘤;(马背的)虻肿。**2**. 牛蝇(的幼虫)。~ *fly* 【动】皮蝇。

war·bler [ˈwɔːblə; ˋwɔrblɚ] *n*. **1**. 鸣禽;(颤音)歌手。**2**.

【动】苔莺。3.【物】颤音器;【电】电抗管调制器;频率摆动器。

war·craft [ˈwɔːkrɑːft; ˋwɔrˏkræft] ***n***.〔*sing*., *pl*.〕 1. 军舰;军用飞机。2. 战略;战术;谋略。

Ward [wɔːd; wɔrd] ***n***. 沃德〔姓氏,男子名〕。

ward [wɔːd; wɔrd] **I** ***n***. 1. 监视,监督,监护,守护;监禁;防卫。2.【法】受监护人(*opp*. guardian)。3.(行政)区,选举区。4. 病房,病室;(监狱的)监房;(济贫院的)收容室;(城堡内的)旷场。5.〔古〕看守人;守卫队。6.(锁内的)齿凸;(钥匙的)齿凹。7.(剑术等的)防卫姿势。*an isolation* [*a maternity*] ~ 隔离[产科]病房。*a condemned* ~ 死刑犯监房。*a casual* ~ 临时收容室。***be in*** ~ ***to*** 在…的监护下(*To whom is this patient in* ~? 这病人由谁监护?)。***be under*** ~ 被监禁着。***keep watch and*** ~ 日夜监视。***put sb. in*** ~ 对某人加以保护;监禁(某人)。**II** ***vt***. 1.〔古〕保护,守护。2. 收容。3. 挡住,架住,击退,防止(*off*)。~ *off an attack* 挡开对手的攻击。~ **aide** 病房勤杂工。~ **boss**〔美〕选区政客。~ **damage** 战争破坏,战争损失。~ **heeler**〔美俚〕〔贬〕选区政客的走卒;为政党拉选票的小角色。

-ward(s) *suf*. 向…: south*wards*.

ward·ed [ˈwɔːdid; ˋwɔrdɪd] ***a***. 有看守的,有监护的,有防护的〔如用锁或钥匙锁上的〕。

Ward·en [ˈwɔːdn; ˋwɔrdn] ***n***.〔有时用 w-〕华登冬梨〔供煮食〕。

ward·en [ˈwɔːdn; ˋwɔrdn] ***n***. 1.〔古〕看门人,看守人;保管人;监察人;〔美〕典狱长;【史】摄政者。2.〔英〕校长;(同业公会)会长;院长;某些主管官员的称号;【史】州长,县长,区长(等);教区委员;〔美 Connecticut 州〕市长。3. 民间防空员[消防员]。**-cy**, **-ship** ***n***. 看守人[保管人等]的职位[职权]。

ward·er [ˈwɔːdə; ˋwɔrdɚ] ***n***. 1.(监狱)看守;保管员;守望员;卫兵。2.(王或司令官的)权杖。

Ward·our [ˈwɔːdə; ˋwɔrdɚ] **Street** 沃德街〔伦敦古董(店)街〕。***Wardour-street English*** 古腔古调的英语。

ward·ress [ˈwɔːdris; ˋwɔrdrɪs] ***n***.〔英〕监狱女看守员。

ward·robe [ˈwɔːdrəub; ˋwɔrdˏrob] ***n***. 1. 衣橱。2. 藏衣室。3.(个人、戏团的)全部服装。*a* ~ *dealer* 旧衣商。*a* ~ *trunk* 衣橱式衣箱。*a* ~ *mistress* 服装女保管员。**ward·rob·ing** ***n***. 选购和配置一系列服装,置办行头。

ward-room [ˈwɔːdrum; ˋwɔrdˏrum] ***n***.【海】1.(舰长以外军官休息及进餐用的)军官室。2.〔集合词〕(舰长以外)全部军官。

ward·ship [ˈwɔːdʃip; ˋwɔrdʃɪp] ***n***. 1. 监护。2.(封建主对佃户的子女和财产的)监护权。

ware[1] [wɛə; wɛr] ***n***. 1.〔用作复合词〕制品,成品,器皿,物件〔如 hardware, ironware 等〕;〔常冠以产地地名〕陶器。2.〔*pl*.〕商品,货品;(演员等的)看家本领。*glass* ~*s* 料器。*toilet* ~*s* 化妆品。*small* ~*s* 小百货〔带子、钮扣等〕。*praise one's own* ~*s* 自夸自赞。

ware[2] [wɛə; wɛr] ***a***. 1.〔古、诗〕谨慎的,小心的。2. 有知觉的,意识[注意]到的。

ware[3] [wɛə; wɛr] ***vt***. 1. 小心,留心,注意。2. 避免。*W- the dog*! 小心狗! *W- your money*. 不要浪费银钱。*W- the bottle*! 请节制喝酒。

ware·house [ˈwɛəhaus; ˋwɛrˏhaʊs] **I** ***n***. 1. 仓库,货栈。2. 批发庄;大零售店。3.〔美,贬〕"福利库"〔指收容精神病患者、老人、贫困者等的大型公共福利设施〕。**II** [-hauz; -haʊz] ***vt***. 把…存入仓库,使落栈;把…存入保税仓库。**-man** ***n***. 仓库业者;仓库管理员;批发商。~ **party** 迷幻狂欢舞会〔一面吸毒,一面跳舞,常在仓库等场所内非法举行〕。

ware·room [ˈwɛəruːm; ˋwɛrˏrum] ***n***. 商品贮藏室;商品陈列室。

warez [wɛəz; wɛrz] ***n***.〔*sing*., *pl*.〕【计】(通过因特网发送的)盗版软件。

war·fare [ˈwɔːfɛə; ˋwɔrˏfɛr] ***n***. 战争,战争状态[行为],斗争;冲突;军事行为。*the science of* ~ 战争科学,战术(学)。*chemical* ~ 化学战。*To learn* ~ *through* ~. 从战争学习战争。

war·fa·rin [ˈwɔːfərin; ˋwɔrfərɪn] ***n***. 1. 杀鼠灵,华法令。2.【医】华法令阻凝剂〔用华法令与氢氧化钠中和的一种阻凝剂〕。

war·fight·ing [ˈwɔːfaitiŋ; ˋwɔrfaɪtɪŋ] ***n***. 1. 作战。2.(导弹)弹头战。

war·gasm [ˈwɔːgæzəm; ˋwɔrgæzəm] ***n***.〔美〕全面战争突然爆发;全面战争危机。

war·i·bash [ˈwɛəribæʃ; ˋwɛrɪbæʃ] ***n***.〔Jap.〕一次性木筷〔用单块木片制成,用时扳开〕。

war·i·ly [ˈwɛərili; ˋwɛrəlɪ] ***ad***. 注意地,谨慎地,小心地。

war·i·ness [ˈwɛərinis; ˋwɛrɪnɪs] ***n***. 注意,谨慎,小心。

war·like [ˈwɔːlaik; ˋwɔrˏlaɪk] ***a***. 1. 战争的,军事的;好战的;尚武的。2. 有战争迹象的。~ *preparations* 备战。~ *spirit* 尚武精神。~ *times* 乱世。

warm [wɔːm; wɔrm] **I** ***a***. 1. 暖和的,温暖的;保暖的。2. 热情的,热心的,热烈的;多情的。3. 易怒的;兴奋的;激烈的,激昂的。4. 亲热的;亲密的。5.(颜色等)有温暖感觉的,暖色的;浓艳的;挑拨性的,色情的;【猎】(嗅迹等)新鲜的,强烈的。6.〔俚〕富裕的,宽裕的。7.〔口〕费力的,困难的;不愉快的,待不下去的。8.〔口〕差一点就要找到[猜中]的。9.(官员等)职位稳固的。*a* ~ *heart* 热情的心。*a* ~ *water port* 不冻港。*a* ~ *welcome* 热烈的欢迎。*a* ~ *temper* 急性子。*a* ~ *friend* 亲密的朋友。~ *descriptions* 色情描写。*The place became too* ~ *for him*. 那里他已经待不下去了。***be getting*** ~ (隐藏者、待猜事物)差一点就要被找到[猜中];〔喻〕接近真实。***get*** ~ 暖起来;激昂起来,兴奋起来。***grow*** ~ 激昂,热烈。***have*** ~ ***work in doing it*** 那件事做起来有困难。***in*** ~ ***blood*** 生气,激忿。***keep a place*** ~ (代表人)暂时占据某地。***keep it*** ~〔美〕继续讨论某一问题〔不使冷却〕。***make things*** ~ ***for sb***. 烦扰[攻击]某人,使某人不愉快。~ ***with*** 加开水和糖的白兰地酒〔*cf*. cold without〕。~ ***words***〔美俚〕骂上帝(的话)。~ ***work*** 吃力的[危险的]工作;激战,苦斗。**II** ***vt***. 1. 使暖,使加温;【体】使热身,使作比赛前的准备活动;使热心,激发,鼓励,使兴奋。2.〔口〕占(座位)。3.〔口〕鞭打,责打。~ *oneself at the fire* 烤火取暖。— ***vi***. 暖,变暖;热中;兴奋;同情(*to*; *towards*)。*a* ~*ing match* 热身赛。~ ***sb.'s jacket***〔口〕打某人。~ ***up*** 加热,热一热(汤);变暖;热中[热心]起来,兴奋起来;【运】作准备动作;(机件等)预热。**III** ***n***.〔口〕暖一暖。~ **blood** 温血〔指哺乳动物及禽类体温,在 98°—112°F. 之间〕。~**-blooded** ***a***. 温血的;热血的;热烈的;热情的。~ **corner**〔口〕激战地区;不愉快的处境。~ **front**【气】暖锋。~**-hearted** ***a***. 热情的,恳切的,亲切的。~**-heartedness** 热忱。~ **sector**【气】暖区。~ **spring** 水温低于 98°F. 的温泉。

warmed-over [ˈwɔːmdˈəuvə; ˋwɔrmdˋovɚ] ***a***. 1. 再热的,回锅的。2. 老一套的,"炒冷饭"的,旧事重提的。~ *ideas* 重弹的老调。~ *hash* 回锅肉丁,回锅肉丝。

warm·er [ˈwɔːmə; ˋwɔrmɚ] ***n***. 取暖器,加温器;使热的人[东西]。*a foot-* ~ 脚炉。

warm·ing-pan [ˈwɔːmiŋpæn; ˋwɔrmɪŋpæn] ***n***. 1. 暖床器;火盆;焊炉。2.(本人就职前的)代理人。

warm·ing-up [ˈwɔːmiŋˈʌp; ˋwɔrmɪŋˋʌp] ***a***.【运】(比赛前的)准备动作的;热身的。

warm·ly [ˈwɔːmli; ˋwɔrmlɪ] ***ad***. 暖和地,温暖地;热心地;亲热地。

warmth [wɔːmθ; wɔrmθ] ***n***. 1. 暖和,温暖。2. 热心,热情;兴奋;忿激;亲切,诚恳。

warm-up [ˈwɔːmˈʌp; ˋwɔrmˏʌp] ***n***. 1. 加温;使暖,变暖。2.【运】(比赛前的)准备动作,热身;(引擎,马达,收音机等)预热。

W

warn [wɔːn; wɔrn] *vt*. 1. 警戒,警告;训诫,告诫。2. 预先通知,预告。~ (*sb.*) ***against*** (*another*) 告诫(某人)提防(别人)。~ (*sb.*) ***of*** (*danger*) 警告(某人)有危险。

War·ner [ˈwɔːnə; ˋwɔrnɚ] *n*. 沃纳〔姓氏,男子名〕。

warn·er [ˈwɔːnə; ˋwɔrnɚ] *n*. 警告者;通知者,告知者。

warn·ing [ˈwɔːniŋ; ˋwɔrnɪŋ] *n*. 1. 警告,警报;警戒;训诫。2. 预告,通知。3. 号召,召唤。4. 殷鉴;前兆。*Don't blame the speaker but take his words as a* ~. 言者无罪,闻者足戒。*a beacon lighted as a* ~ 报警的烽火。*a* ~ *network* 警报网。*a* ~ *order* 准备命令。***at a minute's*** [***moment's***] ~ (不预先通知地)突然之间。***give*** (*sb. a month's* ~) 早一个月通知(解雇)。***give*** ~ 警告;告诫,预告。***take*** ~ ***by*** (*me*) 拿(我)做前车之鉴吧。~ **coloration**【动】警戒色。~ **track**【棒球】警告跑道〔用以警告接球的外场队员已接近看台等〕。

warp [wɔːp; wɔrp] **I** *vt*. 1. 使卷曲,翘曲,弯曲;挠曲,扭歪。2. 歪曲,使偏倾。3.【海】用绞船索牵曳。4. (为利用河泥等沉积物肥田而)引水淹没(土地)。5.【纺织】整经。*timber* ~*ed by heat* 因受热而翘曲的木材。*judgement* ~*ed by self-interest* 被私利所歪曲了的判断。— *vi*. 卷曲,翘曲;歪曲;歪,偏。**II** *n*. 1. 翘曲;歪曲,歪斜;偏倾;乖戾。2. (织物的)经 (*opp*. woof)。3.【海】绞船索。4.【农】沉泥。~ **beam**【纺】经轴。**-er** *n*.【纺】整经工;整经机。

war·rant [ˈwɔrənt; ˋwɔrənt] **I** *n*. 1. 正常理由;根据;(被授予的)权力。2. 保证;证明文件;许可证,执照;收据;认股证书;栈单;委任状;授权证书;【法】搜查证,拘票(等)。3.【商】付款通知单;(仓库给货主的)栈单。4.【军】准尉委任状。*Diligence is a sure* ~ *of success*. 勤勉是成功的可靠保证。***search*** ~ (住宅)搜查证。~ ***for*** [***of***] ***arrest*** 拘票。~ ***of attorney*** 诉讼代理委托状。***with the*** ~ ***of a good conscience*** 问心无愧地。***without a*** ~ 没有正当理由地。**II** *vt*. 1. 证明…正当,证明…具有充分根据。2. 授权,批准。3. 保证,保用(…年)。4. 〔口〕断定。*Coffee* ~*ed pure*. 咖啡保证纯净。*Nothing can* ~ *such rudeness*. 这样无礼是不行的。*This* ~*s our attention*. 这是值得我们注意的。***I*** [***I'll***] ~ (***you***) 〔插入句〕的确,真的。~**-officer** 〔英美陆海空军〕准尉(*a chief* ~*-officer* 〔美陆空军〕一级准尉。*a commissioned* ~*-officer* 〔美海军〕一级准尉)。

war·rant·a·ble [ˈwɔrəntəbl; ˋwɔrəntəbl] *a*. 1. 可保证的。2. 可承认[批准]的;可以认为是正当的。3. (公鹿)已达可猎年龄的〔五、六岁〕。**-a·bly** *ad*.

war·ran·tee [ˌwɔrənˈtiː; ˏwɔrənˋti] *n*.【法】被保证人。

war·rant·er [ˈwɔrəntə; ˋwɔrəntɚ], **war·ran·tor** [-tɔː; -tɔr] *n*. 保证人,担保人。

war·ran·ty [ˈwɔrənti; ˋwɔrəntɪ] *n*. 1. 保证(书)。2. 根据,理由。3. 授权(证)。4.【法】(商品等的)保单。~ **deed**【法】(房地产)担保契约。

War·ren [ˈwɔrin; ˋwɔrɪn] *n*. 沃伦〔姓氏,男子名〕。

war·ren [ˈwɔrin; ˋwɔrɪn] *n*. 1. 养兔场;〔英〕【法】野生鸟兽育猎特许地[特权]。2. 大杂院,住户拥挤的公寓[地区]。**-er** *n*. 养兔场主,养兔场看管人。

war·ring [ˈwɔːriŋ; ˋwɔrɪŋ] *a*. 进行战争的,交战的;斗争的;敌对的;势不两立的。

war·ri·or [ˈwɔriə; ˋwɑrɪɚ] *n*. 勇士,战士,武士,军人。*the Unknown W-* [*Soldier*] (遗体被选出代表阵亡将士接受国葬的)无名战士。*a* ~ *nation* 勇武的民族。

War·saw [ˈwɔːsɔː; ˋwɔrsɔ], **War·sza·wa** [vɑːˈʃɑːvə; vɑˋʃɑvə] *n*. 华沙〔波兰首都〕。

war·saw [ˈwɔːsɔː; ˋwɔrsɔ] *n*. 〔美〕【动】黑石斑鱼(*Epinephelus nigritus*)〔产于西印度洋和美国佛罗里达州的暖水海洋中〕。

wart [wɔːt; wɔrt] *n*. 1.【医】疣,肉赘,瘊子。2.【植】树瘤。3. 〔美俚〕讨厌的人,不重要的人。***paint*** (*sb.*) ***with his*** ~***s*** 把(某人)一切如实地描绘出来。~***s and all*** 如实描绘,对缺点不加掩饰〔出自英国历史人物奥列弗·克伦威尔对其肖像画作者说的话,意为"连脸上的疣子也都画出来"(*a* ~*s-and-all exposé* 缺点大曝光)〕。~ **hog**【动】(非洲野生)疣猪。

War·ton [ˈwɔːtn; ˋwɔrtn̩] *n*. 沃顿〔姓氏〕。

wart·y [ˈwɔːti; ˋwɔrtɪ] *a*. (**-i·er**; **-i·est**) 疣似的;有瘊子的;(有)树瘤的。

War·wick [ˈwɔrik; ˋwɔrɪk] *n*. 沃里克〔姓氏〕。

War·wick·shire [ˈwɔrikʃiə; ˋwɔrɪkˏʃɪr] *n*. 沃里克郡〔英格兰中南部〕。

war·y [ˈweəri; ˋwɛrɪ] *a*. (**-i·er**; **-i·est**) 小心的,留神的;谨慎的。**-i·ly** *ad*.

was [强 wɔz, 弱 wəz; wɑz, wəz] be 的过去式、第一人称及第三人称单数。

Wash [wɔʃ; wɑʃ], **the** 沃希湾〔英国东部 Norfolk 与 Lincolnshire 两郡之间的海湾〕。

Wash. = Washington 华盛顿〔美国州名〕。

wash [wɔʃ; wɑʃ] **I** *vt*. 1. 洗,洗涤。2. 洗掉,洗去 (*off*; *out*);洗净,洗清;【矿】洗(矿),冲洗,冲选。3. (雨露)滋润;(浪)冲击。4. 〔主用被动语态〕冲走,冲垮 (*away*; *off*, *along*; *up*; *down*);冲刷,冲蚀。5. 薄薄着色于;薄薄镀(金等)于。*The rose is* ~*ed with dew*. 蔷薇有露水滋润。*a district* ~*ed by the sea* 沿海地区。*The bridge was* ~*ed away*. 桥被冲走了。*the walls* ~*ed with blue* 淡淡地刷上蓝色的墙壁。*a gold* ~*ed cup* 镀金杯子。— *vi*. 1. 洗(脸、手等),洗身体,洗澡。2. 洗衣服(等)。3. 可洗,经洗。4. 〔口〕(话等)可靠,过硬,经得住考验。5. 冲洗,哗啦哗啦地冲击。*W- before dinner*. 吃饭前洗手。*This cloth* ~ *well* [*won't* ~]. 这布经洗[不经洗]。*That story won't* ~. 那段话靠不住。(***be***) ~***ed out*** 褪了色的;筋疲力尽的;失败了的;形容憔悴的;被冲蚀的。***be*** ~***ed up*** 〔美俚〕筋疲力竭的,失败了的;终止了的,断绝了的。***W- and Use*** [***Wear***] 〔商业用语〕洗后不烫即平,免烫 (= ~-wear)。~ ***against*** 洗,洗刷,冲洗。~ ***down*** 洗掉;冲进,冲下。~ ***for a living*** 做洗衣生意。~ ***one's dirty linen at home*** [***in public***] 〔美〕掩藏[暴露]家丑。~ ***one's hands*** 1. 洗手;〔婉〕上厕所。2. 洗手不干,断绝…的关系 (*of*)。~ ***oneself*** 洗澡。~ ***out*** 1. *vt*. 漱(口);〔美〕(洪水)冲走;〔美俚〕淘汰,剔除,排斥,丢掉。2. *vi*. 颜色被洗掉,洗去;(铁路等)被冲走。~ ***up*** 1. 洗(手、碗碟)。2. 〔美口〕洗手不干,不再过问。

II *n*. 1. 洗濯,洗涤;【矿】洗矿,冲选;〔the ~〕〔集合词〕洗濯物。2. 〔the ~〕奔流;(浪的)冲洗,冲击;波浪声;(船、飞机驶过后的)尾流;涡流;〔美〕浅水湾;(常受涝害的)低湿地;〔美西部〕干河床。3. 冲击物,冲积土,污泥。4. (厨房的)泔水〔猪的食料〕;稀薄的食物。5. 洗涤剂;化妆水;(涂墙面的)水泥浆。6. 淡彩,淡涂;金属涂覆,(金等的)薄镀。7. 无聊话,废话。*This soup is mere* ~. 这汤淡得没味儿。***come out in the*** ~ 〔俚〕暴露,真相大白。***get a*** ~ 洗。***hang out the*** ~ 〔美俚〕降落伞兵。***send to the*** ~ 送去洗。***stand*** ~ 经洗。~ **basin** 脸盆。~ **basket** 洗衣篓。~**board** 洗衣板;【建】壁脚板;【船】防波板。~**bowl** 〔美〕脸盆。~**cloth** 毛巾。~**day** 〔美〕洗衣日〔普通是星期一〕。~ **drawing** (透明色)水彩画;淡墨画。~ **goods** 耐洗纺物[衣服]。~**-hand basin** 脸盆。~**-hand stand** 脸盆架。~**house** 洗衣所;洗衣房。~**leather** 麂皮,软皮;充软皮。~**man** 男洗衣工。~**out** 〔美〕1. (道路、桥梁的)冲溃,冲溃的土地。2. 〔俚〕大失败。3. 失败者;无用的人,靠不住的人。~**pot** 1. 洗手盘。2.【冶】浸槽。~**rag** 〔美〕毛巾。~**room** 〔美〕厕所,盥洗室。~ **sale** [**trade**] 〔美〕(股票的)虚抛,虚卖。~**-stand** 脸盆架。~**-trade** *vt*. 虚假买卖(股票)〔交易结束后很快便予以冲销〕。~**tub** 洗衣盆;洗涤槽。~**up**【矿】1. 冲洗出来的矿沙量。2. 洗涤(处所)。3. 被潮水[风等]冲[刮]上岸的东西。~**woman** 〔美〕= washer-woman.

-able *a*. 经洗的。

W

wash·er [ˈwɔʃə; ˋwɑʃɚ] ***n*.** 1. 洗涤者。2. 洗衣机,洗涤器[机]。3.【矿】洗矿机;洗煤机。4.【机】垫圈。~**-drier** 附有脱水机的洗衣机。~**man** 洗衣工。~**woman** 1. 洗衣女工。2.【鸟】〔英方〕斑羽鹡鸰。

wash·ing [ˈwɔʃiŋ; ˋwɑʃɪŋ] **I *n*.** 1. 洗涤;〔集合词〕需要洗涤的衣物。2. 洗出物。3. 镀金。4. = washsale. 5.〔*pl*.〕洗涤剂。**II *a*.** 洗涤用的;经洗的。~ **machine** 洗涤机。~ **soda** 洗用碱,晶碱。~ **stand** 洗脸架,脸盆架。

Wash·ing·ton[1] [ˈwɔʃiŋtən; ˋwɑʃɪŋtən] ***n*.** 1. 华盛顿〔姓氏〕。2. **George** ~ 华盛顿〔1732—1799,美国第一任总统(1789—1797)〕。~**'s Birthday** (美国首任总统)华盛顿诞辰〔二月二十二日,美国大多数州的法定假日〕。

Wash·ing·ton[2] [ˈwɔʃiŋtən; ˋwɑʃɪŋtən] ***n*.** 1. 华盛顿(市)〔美国首都〕;美国政府。~, *D.C.* (或 ~, District of Columbia)哥伦比亚特区华盛顿〔即美国首都华盛顿〕。2. 华盛顿〔美国州名〕(=~ State)。~ **pie**〔美〕夹心(多层)蛋糕。

Wash·ing·to·ni·an [ˌwɔʃiŋˈtəunien; ˏwɑʃɪŋˋtonɪən] **I *a*.** 华盛顿市[州]的(人的)。**II *n*.** 华盛顿市[州]的人。

wash·y [ˈwɔʃi; ˋwɑʃɪ] ***a*.** (*-i·er*; *-i·est*) 1. 水分多的,淡的;(颜色等)浅的。2. (文章等)无力的,贫乏的。**-wash·i·ness *n*.**

wasn't [ˈwɔznt; ˋwɑznt]〔口〕= was not.

Wasp, WASP [wɔsp; wɑsp] ***n*.** 祖先是英国新教徒的美国人;美国社会中享有特权的白人(= White Anglo-Saxon Protestant)。**Waspy, Waspish *a*.**

wasp [wɔsp; wɑsp] ***n*.** 1. 黄蜂。2. 暴躁的人,脾气不好的人。~ **waist** (束紧的)细腰。**-y *a*.**

wasp·ish [ˈwɔspiʃ; ˋwɑspɪʃ] ***a*.** 1. 黄蜂似的;腰细的。2. 易怒的;刻毒的。**-ly *ad*. -ness *n*.**

was·sail [ˈwɔseil; ˋwɑsl] **I *n*.**〔古〕宴会,欢宴;宴会的祝酒。**II *vi*.** 干杯;祝酒;欢宴;痛饮。— ***vt*.** 为…干杯,向…祝酒。

Was·ser·mann [ˈvɑːsəmɑːn; ˋvɑsɚˏmɑn], **A·von** 瓦塞尔曼〔1866—1952,德国细菌学家〕。~ **test** [**reaction**] (梅毒的)瓦塞尔曼氏检查[反应]。

wast [强 wɔst, 弱 wəst; wɑst, wəst]〔古〕be 的过去式,第二人称单数〔主词为 thou 时〕。

wast·age [ˈweistidʒ; ˋwestɪdʒ] ***n*.** 浪费;损耗(量);废料。

waste [weist; west] **I *a*.** 1. 荒芜的,不毛的,荒废了的;未开垦的;荒凉的。2. 废弃的,无用的;多余的;身体内排泄的。~ *land(s)* 荒地。~ *water* 废水。~ *heat* 废热,余热。~ *products* (工厂出品中的)废品。~ *product* (身体组织中的)废料。***lay*** ~ 糟蹋,毁坏,蹂躏;劫掠。***lie*** ~ (土地)荒芜,未开垦。***the*** ~ ***periods of history*** 历史上单调平凡[荒芜]的时期。**II *vt*.** 1. 糟蹋,浪费。2. 毁坏,破坏,蹂躏,使荒芜。3. 消耗,使衰弱;【法】(因使用不当而)损坏(房屋等);【石工】把(石头)解成适当的大小。4.〔美俚〕毒打;消灭;凶杀。~ *an opportunity* 浪费机会。*Kind words are ~d (up) on him*. 跟他说好话是白说了。— ***vi*.** 1. 消耗;消瘦,衰弱。2. 浪费。3. (时间)过去,消逝。*Day* [*Night*] ~*s*. 太阳下山[天快亮]了。~ ***away*** 消瘦。***W- not, want not***. 不浪费,不愁穷。~ ***one's words*** [***breath***] 徒费口舌。**III *n*.** 1. 浪费。2.〔常 *pl*.〕荒地,荒野,未开垦地;沙漠;荒芜。3. 消耗(量),损耗;衰弱;渐损;【法】毁损,损坏。4. 废料,废品,废物;剩余物,废屑;破布。5.【机】碎纱,纱头〔机器工人擦手用〕。6.【地】风化物;(被水流冲蚀的)岩屑。7. 垃圾;污水;〔*pl*.〕粪便。~ *of time* 浪费时间。(*a*) ~ *of speech* 浪费唇舌。*a* ~ *of waters* 茫茫大海。***run*** [***go***] ***to*** ~ 糟蹋掉;(钱财等)被浪费掉。~ ***and repair*** 消耗和补充。~ ***recovering*** 废料回收。~**basket**〔美〕字纸篓。~ **book**【簿】流水账。~**bin** 废物箱,垃圾桶。~**-butt** 1. 客栈[酒馆]老板。2.〔谑〕小饭店。~**d work**【机】耗功。~**land** 荒地,荒野,荒漠。~**lot**〔加〕(长满野草或堆满垃圾的)荒地。~**paper** 废纸。~**paper basket** = ~ basket. ~ **pipe** 废水[污水]管。~ **stream** 泛滥成灾的废品。~**-to-energy *a*.** 以垃圾作为能源的;以焚烧垃圾产生电能的。**-plex *n*.** 废物再生利用联合企业。

waste·ful [ˈweistf*u*l; ˋwestfəl] ***a*.** 浪费的;糟蹋的,不经济的;破坏性的;〔诗〕荒芜的。*be* ~ *of resources* 浪费资源。*a* ~ *man* 挥霍无度的人。**-ly *ad*.**

wast·er [ˈweistə; ˋwestɚ] ***n*.** 1. 浪费者;挥霍者。2.〔口〕无用的人。3. 破坏者。4. 废物,废品。5.【医】瘦弱的婴儿。

wast·ing [ˈweistiŋ; ˋwestɪŋ] **I *a*.** 消耗性的,渐减的;使荒废的;破坏性的。**II *n*.** 浪费;糟蹋;消耗,【医】虚痨。*a* ~ *disease* 消耗性疾病〔如结核病〕;痨病。

wast·rel [ˈweistrəl; ˋwestrəl] ***n*.** 1. 流浪儿童。2. 无用的人,饭桶。3. 浪费者。4. 废物;废品。

wat [wɑːt; wæt] ***n*.** (泰国等的)佛寺,寺院。

watch [wɔtʃ; wɑtʃ] **I *n*.** 1. 表;船钟。2. 值夜,值班;守夜;看守人;哨兵。3. 看守,监视;注意;警戒。4.【海】(每4小时轮换的)值班(时间);〔集合词〕值班人员,一班。5.〔古〕更〔犹太人把一夜分作 *first* ~ 首更, *middle* ~ 中更, *morning* ~ 末更;罗马人分为 *first* [*evening*] ~ 头更, *second* [*midnight*] ~ 二更, *third* [*cock crowing*] ~ 三更, *fourth* [*morning*] ~ 四更〕。***be on*** [***off***] ~ 值班[不值班]。***be on the*** ~ ***for*** 看守着,监视着,提防着;守候着。***call the*** ~ 召集值班人。***in the night*** ~***es*** = ***in the*** ~***es of the night*** 在睡不着的夜里。***keep*** (***a***) ~ 看守;值班。***keep*** ~ ***over*** 守护;密切注意。***pass as*** [***like***] ***a*** ~ ***in the night*** 立刻被忘记掉。***through the silent*** ~***es of the night*** 更深夜静的时候。~ ***and ward*** 昼夜警戒。~ ***and*** ~【海】四小时轮流值班,半舷值班。**II *vt*.** 1. 注视;注意,留心观察。2. 看守,监视。3. 守候(机会等)(*for*)。— ***vi*.** 1. 注视,看着;密切注意。2. 警戒,守卫,监视。3. 守候,期待(*for*)。4.〔古〕守夜;通夜看护;【宗】守夜[作通宵祈祷]。~ *and say nothing* 静观不语。~ *all night at the bedside of a patient* 在病人床边通宵侍候。***A*** ~***ed pot never boils***. 见 pot 条。***be closely*** ~***ed*** 被严密监视。***if you don't*** ~ ***it***〔俚〕你要是不小心。~ ***one's time*** 等待时机。~ ***out*** 1.〔美俚〕监视,警戒。2. 密切注视(*for*)(*W- out for cars*. 当心车辆)。~ ***over*** 监视;留心,注视;看护,照顾。~**-and-wait policy** 观望政策。~**band** 表带。~ **cap** 水手冬帽。~**case** 表壳。~ **chain** 表链。**W- Committee**〔英〕市镇治安委员会。~**dog** 看门狗;监视者〔也指一个集体〕。~ **file** 钟表锉。~ **fire** 营火。~ **glass** 表玻璃。~ **guard** 表链,表带(等)。~ **gun** (水手于晚上八时值夜班时鸣放的)值班枪。~**house** 哨房,班房,岗房;拘留所。~**list**〔美〕注意事项一览表;监督项目明细表。~**maker** 钟表匠。~**man** 更夫;看守人;夜班警卫员。~ **meeting**【宗】除夕礼拜。~ **night**【宗】除夕(礼拜);圣诞节前夜礼拜。~ **oil** 机器油。~**out** 监视,警戒。~ **pocket** (背心上的)表袋。~ **spring** 表的发条。~**-tower** 望楼。~**word** 暗号;(回答步哨的)口令;标语,口号。~**work** 手表结构。**-able *a*.** 值得注意[注视]的。

watch·er [ˈwɔtʃə; ˋwɑtʃɚ] ***n*.** 注视者;看守人;值班员;守夜人;看护人;哨兵;〔美〕(投票所)监票员。

watch·ful [ˈwɔtʃf*u*l; ˋwɑtʃfəl] ***a*.** 1. 注意的,注视的,留心的,小心提防的,警戒的(*of*; *against*)。2.〔古〕不眠的。~ *waiting* 待机,观察,警戒。

wa·ter [ˈwɔːtə; ˋwɔtɚ] **I *n*.** 1. 水;雨水;露;〔常作 *pl*.〕矿泉,温泉;药水。2.〔常 *pl*.〕水体;水域;水道;海;湖;河;海域;领海。3. 水深,水位,水面。4. 分泌液,体液〔如尿、汗、口水、泪等〕;(船的)漏水。5. 水色〔宝石的光泽透明度〕,品质。6. (织品的)波纹,光泽。7.〔*pl*.〕积水;洪水。8.【商】(超过实际资产的)虚值;虚[清水]股。*fresh* [*sweet*] ~ 淡水。*piped* ~ 自来水。*brandy and* ~ 白兰地加水〔特别调制的饮料〕。*He is taking the ~s at Karlsbad*. 他正在卡斯巴托作矿泉疗养。~ *of hydration*【化】化合水。*the distant* [*near*] ~*s* 远[近]海。*the blue* ~ 苍海。*cross the* ~*s* 渡过大海。*an* *ornamental* ～（人工修造的）装饰用水池。*high* [*low*] ～ 高[低]潮。*high* ～ *season* 汛期。*dead* ～（静止的）死水；船尾涡流；（最低）小潮。*The boat is making* ～. 船漏水了。***above*** ～ 摆脱（经济）困难。***back*** ～ **1.** 倒划桨。**2.**〔美〕立场倒退，退缩。***bring the*** ～ ***to sb.'s mouth*** 使垂涎。***by*** ～ 经由水道，用船运。***cast one's bread upon the*** ～ 只做好事不求报酬；积阴德。***cast*** ～ ***into the Thames*** 白费气力。***draw*** ～ ***to one's mill*** 牟取私利。***draw*** ～ ***with a sieve*** 竹篮打水一场空。***drink the*** ～***s*** 喝矿泉；作矿泉疗养。***fish in troubled*** ～ 浑水摸鱼。***get into hot*** ～ 陷入困境。***go over the*** ～ 越过河流[湖海]；流亡；被流放。***hold*** ～ **1.** 不漏水；无漏洞，无疵蜱，（理由）站得住；完好。**2.**（用桨）别住，制住。***in deep*** ～（***s***）遭遇艰难，在水深火热中，陷入困境。***in hot*** ～ 处于困境。***in low*** ～〔俚〕不如意，经济不宽裕。***in smooth*** ～（***s***）平稳地，顺利地。***in rough*** [***troubled***] ～ 处境很困难。***keep one's head above*** ～ 避免破产，设法保住地位[应付困境]。***like*** ～（用钱）如水；（流血）如注。***make*** ～ **1.** 小便。**2.**【海】（船只）漏水。***Much*** ～ ***runs by the mill that the miller knows not of.*** 世上有许多事是我们所不知道的。***of the first*** ～ 品质最好的；第一流的（*a diamond of the first* ～ 第一等的钻石。*a blunder of the first* ～ 无比的疏忽）。***on the*** ～ **1.** 漂在水上。**2.** 在船上。***pass*** ～ = *make* ～. ***pour oil on the*** ～***s*** 调停[平息]纠纷。***take*** (***the***) ～（船）下水；举行下水礼；下水游泳；乘船。***take the*** ～***s*** = *drink the* ～*s*. ***take*** (***to***) ***the*** ～【空】在水上降落。***take the*** ～***s*** 作矿泉疗养。***take*** ～〔美俚〕沮丧，退却；投降。***throw cold*** ～ ***on*** [***over***] 泼冷水[打击别人的热情]。***tread*** ～ 踩水，立游。***turn on*** [***off***] ***the*** ～ 扭开[关上]水龙头。***under*** ～ 在水中；浸水。～ ***and soil conservation*** 水土保持。～ ***bewitched*** 淡茶；搀水的酒。～ ***of life*** 生命之水；起死回生[长生不老]的神水；白兰地酒。***Still*** ～***s run deep.*** 静水流深；大智若愚。***strong*** ～***s***〔古〕烈酒。***written in*** ～ 昙花一现的，转眼即逝的。

II *vt*. **1.** 注水于，灌水于；把…浸在水中；给浇水；灌溉。**2.** 给…水喝，给水。**3.** 在（织物上）加波纹。**4.** 在…中搀水，冲淡。**5.**【商】名义增（资），发行（虚股）；不增加资本而虚增（股额等）。～ *the milk* 在牛奶中搀水。～ *cattle* 给家畜饮水。— *vi*. **1.**（动物）饮水；被供给水，加水。**2.** 淌眼泪；垂涎；渴望。***make sb.'s eyes*** ～ 使淌眼泪。***make sb.'s mouth*** ～ 使垂涎，使渴望。～ ***down*** 冲淡，打折扣。～**age**〔英〕水道运输（运费）。～**-ash** *n*.【植】加罗林梣。～ **back** 炉后热水箱。～ **bag** 水袋；（胎儿的）衣胞。～ **bailiff** 船舶检查员。～ **barrow** 洒水车。～ **bed** 电热温水褥〔病人用装水橡皮褥〕。～ **beetle**【虫】（龙虱等）水虫。～ **biscuit** 薄脆饼干。～ **blister**【医】水疱。～ **boatman** 水虫（科）。～**-borne** *a*. **1.** 水道运输的；漂流着的。**2.** 水传播的，饮水传染的。～ **brash**【医】反酸；胃灼热。～**brain**（羊的）回旋病（= gid）。～**buck**【动】（南非）大羚羊。～ **buffalo 1.**【动】水牛。**2.**〔军俚〕登陆牵引车。～ **bug**【动】**1.** 水生蝽。**2.** 茶婆虫。～**-butt**（盛雨水的）水桶。～ **can** 浇水壶。～ **cannon** 水炮。～ **capacity** 持水量。～ **carriage** 水上运输[交通]（工具）；〔英方〕排水道。～ **carrier 1.** 从事水上运输的人；运水的人，卖水的人。**2.**〔W-〕【天】宝瓶宫。～ **cart** 运水车；洒水车。～ **chestnut**【植】**1.** 荸荠。**2.** 欧菱。～ **chinquapin**【植】美洲黄花莲；黄花莲果。～ **chute**（乘小船从高斜处滑入水中的）滑水运动（滑槽）。～ **circulation**【机】冷水环流。～ **circulator**【机】环流器。～ **clock** 水钟，滴漏。～ **closet**（有卫生设备的）厕所，抽水马桶。～ **cock 1.** 自来水龙头。**2.**【动】鸟翁。～**colo(u)r**【绘画】水彩（画）；水彩颜料。～**colo(u)rist** 水彩画家。～ **content** 含水量。～ **control** 治水。～**-convolvulus**【植】蕹菜。～**-cool** *vt*. 以水冷却。～**-cooled** *a*.【机】水冷式的。～ **cooler**【机】水冷器。～**-cooling**【机】水冷法。～**course** 水流，河，运河；水道；河床。～**craft 1.** 驾船技艺；水上运动技艺。**2.** 船只。～ **crane**【机】水鹤；水压起重机。～ **cress**【植】水田芹。～ **croop** 吸水管。～ **cure**【医】水疗法；（热）水处治；（热）水熟化；（热）水硫化；〔美俚〕灌水逼供的刑罚。～ **cushion**【机】水垫。～ **cycle** 踏行船。～ **dog 1.** 会游水的狗；〔俚〕老练的水手；熟习水性的人。**2.**【动】（美洲）大蝾螈。～ **diviner** = ～ finder. ～**-drinker** 喜喝矿泉水的人；绝对戒酒者。～ **electrode**【电】水（成）电极。～ **equivalent**【化】水当量。～**fall** 瀑布；〔美俚〕（披垂的）波型长发。～ **faucet** 水龙头。～**feed(er)**【机】给水器。～**-finder** 找地下水脉的人；试水器。～ **flea**【动】水蚤。～**-flood** *vt*. 注水入（油井）。～**front 1.** 水边，滨湖[河等]地，湖滨[沿河]马路。**2.** 装在火炉前部的热水缸。～ **gap**〔美〕水峡。～ **gas**【化】水煤气。～ **gate** 水门，水闸。～ **gauge** 水位尺，测水表。～**glass 1.** 计时玻璃水漏。**2.**【化】水玻璃；硅酸钠。**3.**（玻璃）水标尺；水底观察镜；水杯。～ **gruel** 薄粥，米汤。～**guard** 水上警察；海关水上巡察员。～**-hardening**【冶】水淬硬化。～**head 1.** 水源；水位差。**2.**【医】脑积水。～ **hemlock**【植】毒芹（属）。～ **hen**【鸟】鷭。～ **hole**（干河床上的）水坑。～ **hyacinth**【植】凤眼莲。～ **ice** 水冰，人造冰；〔英〕= sherbet. ～**-inch** 在最小压力下口径一英寸管子 24 小时放水量〔约 500 立方英尺〕。～**ing call**【军】饮马号。～**ing can** 喷壶，浇水器。～**ing cart** = water cart. ～**ing place**（牛马的）饮水处；温泉地，水疗场；海水浴场。～**ing pot 1.** = ～ing can. **2.**【贝】喷壶介。～ **inlet**【机】入水口。～ **jacket**【机】水套；（机枪的）冷水套筒。～ **jet** 水注。～ **joint**【机】水密接头，防水接头。～ **jump**（越野赛马中的）水沟。～**leaf**【植】田茎麻科植物。～ **lettuce**【植】大藻。～ **level** 水平面；【地】汗水面，地下水位；水准器；（船的）吃水线。～ **lily**【植】睡莲。～**line**（吃）水线；（纸张上的）水印。～**-locks** 水闸。～ **locust**【植】水生皂荚。～**logged** *a*.（船）因进水而航行困难的；（木材等）浸饱水的；水涝的（～*logged farmland* 水涝地）。～ **main** 自来水总管。～**manship** 桨手本领；划船术，水上职业；熟习水性。～**mark 1.** *n*.（压印在纸里的）水印。**2.** *vt*. 印水印（在纸上）。～ **mass**【海洋】（同温度、同化学成分的）水团。～**melon**【植】西瓜。～ **meter** 水量计，水表。～ **milfoil**【植】狐尾藻（属）。～ **mill** 水车；水磨。～ **moccassin**（北美）水栖蝮蛇；水蛇。～ **monkey**（冷开水用的）长颈水缸。～ **motor** 水力发动机。～ **nymph** 水精。～ **oak**【植】黑栎。～ **outlet**【机】出水口。～ **ouzel**【动】河鸟。～ **paint** 水粉涂料。～ **parting**【地】分水岭。～ **pepper**【植】蓼；美洲线叶萍。～ **pimpernel**【植】**1.** 水茴草。**2.** 水绿。～ **pipe** 水管，给水管，自来水管；水烟筒。～**plane 1.**【海】（船的）水线平面。**2.**【空】水上飞机。～ **plant** 水生植物。～ **plantain**【植】泽泻（属）。～ **polo**【运】水球。～**power** 水力。～ **press**【机】水压机。～ **privilege** 用水权，水力使用权。～**proof 1.** *a*. 不透水的，防水的。**2.** *n*. 防水物，防水材料；防水布，油布；防水服，雨衣。**3.** *vt*. 使（布等）作防水处理，给（布）上胶。～ **pump** 水泵。～**-quenching**【冶】水淬火。～ **race**（工业用）水道。～ **ram** 水力夯锤。～**-raising engine**【机】扬水机。～ **rat**【动】河鼠；〔美〕麝香鼠；〔美俚〕徘徊江边的小偷[无业游民]。～ **rate** 自来水费；【机】耗汽率，耗水率。～**-repellent** *a*. 拒水的。～**-resistant** *a*. 抗水的。～ **right**【法】取水权，用水权。～ **sapphire**【矿】蓝堇青石。～**scape** 水上[海洋]风景（画）。～ **scorpion**【动】红娘华科昆虫。～ **seal**【机】水封闭。～ **seasoning** 树液抽出干燥法。～**shed**〔英〕分水岭；〔口〕流域。～ **shield**【植】莼菜。～**shoot** 排水管（= ～ chute）。～**side** 水边。～ **ski**【运】（用汽艇拖的）滑水橇。～**skin** 运水用皮袋。～ **snake**【动】水蛇；游蛇（属）。～ **softener**【化】软水剂；软水槽。～ **soldier**【植】水兵草。～**-soluble** *a*.【化】水溶性的，可溶于水的。～**-souchet**, ～**-souchy** 原汁炆鱼。～**spout** 水落管；水龙卷；暴雨。～ **sprout**【植】速发枝条。～**-strainer**【机】滤水器。～ **supply** 供水（设备）；给

水(量)。~ **system** 水系;供水(系统)。~ **table** 1.【建】承雨线脚;泻水台。2.【地】潜水面,地下水位。~ **tank** 水箱。~ **thrush**【动】鹩鸲。~**-tight** *a*. 不漏水的,不透水的,防水的;(讨论等)无懈可击的。~ **toothpick** 水柱洁齿器〔利用压力水柱清洁牙齿或牙缝的设备〕。~ **tower** 水塔;灭火用喷水塔。~ **trade** 休闲餐饮业〔主要为各界人士提供社交场合,如酒吧间等〕。~ **vapor** 水蒸气,水汽。~**-vascular system** (棘皮动物的)水管系统。~ **vole** = water rat. ~ **wag(g)on** 洒水车,运水车 (*on the* ~ *waggon* 戒酒)。~**-wave** 水烫卷发。~**-waving**【理发】水烫。~**way** 水路,航路;【船】水口,排水沟。~ **weed**【植】菲藻(属);加拿大菲藻。~ **wheel** 水车;扬水车。~**-white** *a*. 无色的;清澈的。~ **wings** (学游泳的)浮袋。~**works** 水道设备;给水装置;自来水厂;喷水装置;〔俚〕眼泪 (*turn on the ~works* 〔俚〕哭起来)。~**worn** *a*. 水蚀的。**-ing** *n*.【纺】波纹,云纹。**-less** *a*. 无水的,干的;不用水的。

wa·tered [ˈwɔːtəd; ˋwɔtɚd] *a*. 1. 搀水的。2. 灌溉过的。3. 有波纹的;有波光的。4.【经】虚增的,空头发行的。~ *silk* 波纹绸。~ *capital* 虚增资本。*a* ~ *stock*【商】虚股。

Wa·ter·gate [ˈwɔːtəgeit; ˋwɔtɚˏget] I *n*. 1. 水门事件〔美国政治丑闻,共和党总统竞选连任委员会于 1972 年 6 月 17 日派人潜入水门大厦民主党总部安装窃听器,此事暴露后导致尼克松总统辞职〕。2. (类似水门事件的)政治丑闻。II *vt*. 使卷入丑闻。

wa·ter·i·ness [ˈwɔːtərinis; ˋwɔtərɪnɪs] *n*. 1. 多水,像有雨的光景。2. 清淡;稀薄;(食物)淡薄,无味。

Wa·ter·loo [ˌwɔːtəˈluː; ˏwɔtɚˋlu] *n*. 1. 滑铁卢〔比利时城镇〕(1815 年拿破仑军队战败处)。2. [喻]惨败。***meet one's*** ~ 遭遇惨败。

Wa·ter·man [ˈwɔːtəmən; ˋwɔtɚmən] *n*. 沃特曼〔姓氏〕。

Wa·ters [ˈwɔːtəz; ˋwɔtɚz] *n*. 沃特斯〔姓氏〕。

wa·ter·y [ˈwɔːtəri; ˋwɔtərɪ] *a*. 1. 水的;水汪汪的,水分多的。2. 含泪的。3. 水一般的,搀水(过多)的;无味的;淡,浅(色等)。4. 软弱无力的,(文章等)缺乏内容的。5. 潮湿的,像要下雨的。*a* ~ *grave* 水葬。~ *clouds* 雨云。~ *sky* 像要下雨的天空。

Wat·son [ˈwɔtsn; ˋwɑtsn] *n*. 沃森〔姓氏〕。

Watt [wɔt; wɑt] *n*. 1. 瓦特〔姓氏〕。2. **James** ~ 詹·瓦特〔1736—1819,苏格兰发明家,蒸气机发明人〕。

watt [wɔt; wɑt] *n*.【电】瓦特〔电力单位〕。~**-hour** *n*. 瓦(特)小时。~**-hour meter** 瓦时计,电(度)表〔俗名 wattmeter〕。

watt·age [ˈwɔtidʒ; ˋwɑtɪdʒ] *n*.【电】瓦(特)数。

Wat·teau [vaˈtəu, F. waːˈtəu; vɑˋto, wɑˋto] *a*. 华托式的〔一种女服式样,因常见于法国画家让·安东尼·华托 (Jean Antoine Watteau) 的绘画中而得名〕。

Wat·ter·son [ˈwɔːtəsn; ˋwɑtɚsn] *n*. 沃特森〔姓氏〕。

watt-hr. = watt-hour.

wat·tle [ˈwɔtl; ˋwɑtl] I *n*. 1. 枝条,篱巴条,篱笆。2. (火鸡等的)垂肉。3. (鱼的)触须。4.【植】金合欢属。~ *and daub*【建】夹条墙,泥笆墙。II *vt*. 用枝条编制(篱笆、篮等)。~**bird**【动】(澳洲的)食蜜鸟。

wat·tled [ˈwɔtld; ˋwɑtld] *a*. 1. 用枝条编[做]的。2. 有垂肉的。

watt·me·ter [ˈwɔtmiːtə; ˋwɑtˏmitɚ] *n*. 瓦特计,电表。

Watts [wɔts; wɑts] *n*. 瓦茨〔姓氏〕。

Wa·tu·si [waːˈtuːsi; wɑˋtusɪ] *n*. (*pl*. ~(*s*)) 瓦图西〔非洲布隆迪和卢旺达的隆迪人中的牧主阶级〕(= Watutsi)。

Waugh [wɔː; wɔ] *n*. 沃〔姓氏〕。

waul [wɔːl ; wɔl] *vi*. 像猫一样叫唤;哇哇地哭。

WAVE, Wave [weiv; wev] *n*. 〔美海军〕女志愿军人〔见 WAVES 条〕。

wave [weiv; wev] I *n*. 1. 波浪;碎浪;〔the ~(s)〕〔诗〕海。2. 波动;波状起伏;波浪形;【军】(攻击)波;批;(绸缎的)波纹;波线。3. 波动,风潮;高潮。4. (用手等的)挥动(信号);【火箭】振动,射流;【物】波;【气象】浪。*attack in ~s*【军】波状进攻。*They defy difficulties and advance ~ upon ~*. 他们不怕困难,前扑后继。*a ~ of prosperity* [*depression*] 一阵子的繁荣[萧条]。*permanent ~s* 电烫(头发)。*a ~ of buying* 一阵子的抢购浪潮。*a ~ of revolution* 革命高潮。*a tidal ~* 海啸。*long* [*short*] *~s* 长[短]波。*ultra-short ~s* 超短波。*a cold ~* 寒潮。*a heat ~* 热浪。***attack in ~s***【军】作波状攻击。***make ~s*** 兴风作浪;打乱正常的进程[惯例等]。II *vi*. 1. 起波,波动;摇摆;招展,飘扬。2. (头发等)作波浪形,起伏。3. 挥手[招手]示意。*Her hair ~s*. 她的头发呈波浪形。— *vt*. 1. 摇;挥;使招展。2. 摇[挥]动表示。3. 使起浪;将(头发)弄成波浪形;加波纹。~ *a farewell* = ~ *sb. adieu* 挥手告别。~ *sb. nearer* 招手叫某人走近一点。~ ***aside*** 挥手使站开;挥手拒绝[排斥]。~ ***away*** [***off***] 挥手使去;拒绝。~ ***the bloody shirt*** 〔美〕唤起复仇心,挑拨敌对情绪。~**band**【无】波段。~ **base** 波底〔指波浪作用的限界深度〕。~ **cloud**【气】波状云。~ **detector**【无】检波器。~ **equation**【数】波动方程式。~ **front**【物】波阵面,波前。~ **function**【数】波函数。~**guide**【电】波导(管)。~**-hopping**【空】掠水飞行。~**length**【无】波长。~**let** 小浪;【物】子波,弱波,小波,基元波,成分波。~ **mechanics**【物】波动力学。~**meter**【电】波频计,波长计。~ **motion** 波状运动。~ **power** 波浪动力〔指利用波浪的运动作为能源〕。~ **propagation**【物】波的传播。~**-sailing** 风帆滑浪〔驾驭风帆滑水板的水上运动〕。~ **train**【物】波列。~ **velocity**【无】波速。**-d** *a*. 1. 波浪形的,起伏的;(织物等)有波纹的。2. 飘动的。**-less** *a*. 没有浪的,不起浪的,平静的。

wa·vell·ite [ˈweivəlait; ˋwevəˏlaɪt] *n*.【地】银星石。

wa·ver[1] [ˈweivə; ˋwevɚ] *n*. 1. 挥动者,摇动者;波动的东西。2. 做卷发的理发师[美容师];卷发器。3.【无】波段开关;波形转换器。

wa·ver[2] [ˈweivə; ˋwevɚ] I *vi*. 1. 摇摆;(火焰等)颤动。2. (军队等)动摇;(声音等)震颤。3. 犹豫不决,拿不定主意。~ *in determination* 犹豫不定,踌躇不决。II *n*. 犹豫。*be upon* ~ 犹豫不决。**-er** *n*. 动摇[摇摆]者,犹豫不决的人。**-ing** *a*. 摇摆的,动摇的,犹豫不决的。

WAVES = Women Accepted for Volunteer Emergency Service 〔美旧〕(海军)妇女预备队。

wav·y [ˈweivi; ˋwevɪ] *a*. (*-i·er*; *-i·est*) 1. 波状的,起伏的。2. 动摇的,摇摆的。3. 波涛汹涌的。*a ~ terrain* 起伏不平的地形。**-i·ly** *ad*. **-i·ness** *n*.

wawl [wɔːl; wɔl] *vi*. = waul.

wax[1] [wæks; wæks] I *n*. 1. (蜂)蜡;蜡状物。2. 耳垢。3. (鞋匠用的)擦线蜡 (= cobbler's ~);石蜡;树蜡;火漆,封蜡。4. 〔美〕(糖枫制的)糖蜜。5. 〔美俚〕蓄音蜡盘,唱片。*vegetable* [*Japan*] ~ 植物蜡。*a ~ candle* 蜡烛。***be mo(u)lded like*** ~ (像蜡一样柔软)任人摆布;毫无抵抗能力。II *a*. 蜡制的。III *vt*. 涂蜡于,上蜡于,用蜡擦;灌(唱片)。— *vi*. 录音在唱片上,灌唱片。~ **bean**【植】扁豆。~**berry**【植】1. = snowberry. 2. = bayberry. ~**bill**【动】梅花雀。~ **cloth** 蜡布。~ **doll** 蜡人;美貌而没表情的女人,蜡美人。~ **end** (鞋匠上过蜡的)底线。~ **insect**【动】水蜡虫。~ **myrtle**【植】(= bayberry) 南部杨梅。~ **palm**【植】蜡棕榈;巴西蜡棕。~ **paper** 蜡纸。~ **tree** 野漆树。

wax[2] [wæks; wæks] *vi*. 1. 大起来,变大,增大;(月)渐渐变大,变圆 (*opp*. wane)。2. 渐渐变化。~ *and wane* (月)盈亏,盈虚;盛衰。~ *old* 渐渐变老。~ *angry* 生起气来。~ *facetious* 变得好笑。~ *indignant* 变忿慨。~ *fat* 胖起来。

wax[3] [wæks; wæks] *n*. 〔英口〕生气,发怒。***get into*** ~ 发怒,动气。***in a*** ~ 气忿;生气。***put*** (*sb.*) ***in a*** ~ 使(人)发怒。

W

wax[4][wæks; wæks] *vt*.〔美俚〕击败。

wax·en[1][ˈwæksən; ˋwæksn] *a*. 1. 蜡制的；上过蜡的。2. 像蜡的，蜡质的；苍白的；蜡黄的。3. 柔软的；柔顺的。

wax·en[2][ˈwæksn; ˋwæksn]〔古〕wax 的过去分词。

wax·i·ness[ˈwæksinis; ˋwæksɪnɪs] *n*. 蜡质，柔软；柔顺。

wax·wing[ˈwækswiŋ; ˋwæks͵wɪŋ] *n*.【鸟】连雀。

wax·work[ˈwækswəːk; ˋwæks͵wɝk] *n*. 1. 蜡制品。2.〔*pl*. 作单数用〕蜡像(馆)；蜡制品展览馆。

wax·y[1][ˈwæksi; ˋwæksɪ] *a*. (*-i·er*; *-i·est*) 1. 蜡(似)的，蜡制的，上过蜡的；蜡质的。2. 柔顺的。3.【医】蜡样变性的。～ *crude*【油】含蜡[多蜡]原油。

wax·y[2][ˈwæksi; ˋwæksɪ] *a*.〔俚〕生气的，动气的，忿怒的。

way[1][wei; we] *n*. 1. 路，道路，通路。2. 路程；距离。3. (要走的)路线；途中，路上；进行，前进；【法】通行权。4. 方向，方面。5. 方法，手段。6. 方式，式样，样子。7. 习惯，风气；〔常 *pl*.〕一贯作风。8. 方针，决心；自己的意向。9. (某)点，事项。10. (职业、行动等的)范围；规模；〔口〕行业，专业。11.〔口〕状况，情况；〔英口〕激动状况。12.【海】航行；〔*pl*.〕(新船的)下水台；【机】(车床等的)导轨。13.〔口〕近邻，附近；地区。14.〔the W-〕【宗】(基督教的)教义。*ask the* ～ 问路。*the* ～ *to the station* 到车站去的路。*The furthest* [*longest*] ～ *about is the nearest* [*shortest*] ～ *home*. 按部就班反而先到；欲速则不达。*The plan is making good* ～. 计划正在顺利进行中。*Look this* ～. 看这边。*That was always her* ～. 那是她的一贯作风。～ *of production* 生产方式。*a statement false in two* ～*s* 有两点错误的声明。*He is in a grocery* ～. 他在做杂货生意。*live somewhere London* ～ 住在伦敦附近的一个地方。**a little** [**long**] ～ 在…的不远处[很远处]；不长一段[老远一段]路。**a little** [**great**, **long**] ～ **off** 在不远处[很远处]；离得近[远]。**affect foreign** ～**s** 模仿外国方式。**all the** ～ 1. 一路上，路上一直；远远，老远。2.〔美〕(从…到…)逐一，逐步（*It is estimated all the* ～ *from 50 to 100 dollars*. 据估计为50元到100元)。**all the** ～ **up to** 直至。**be in a bad** ～ 情况不好。**be in a** (**great**) ～ 正在(非常)生气[激动]。**both** ～**s** = this ～ and that. **by the** ～ 1. 在路旁；在路上。2.〔插入语〕顺便说；附带说说。**by** ～ **of** 1. 当做，作为；作出…的样子。2. 经由。3.〔英〕正逐步，在…中。4. 以便，为了（*a stick by* ～ *of weapon* 当做武器的棍子。*by* ～ *of apology* 作为辩解，作为道歉。*She is by* ～ *of becoming a fine pianist*. 她正在逐步成长为一个优秀钢琴家)。**come one's** ～ 1. 临头，发生于某人身上。2. 到…处。3.〔俚〕进行；(事情)进行顺利。**cut both** ～**s** 模棱两可。**each** ～ 单程。**face two** ～**s** 碰到叉路站住。**find one's** ～ **into** 进入…；进入…的境遇（*It found its* ～ *into the papers*. 这事上了报了)。**find one's** [**the**] ～ **to** 到达(目的地)。**find one's** ～ **out of** 设法走出，脱出。**force one's** ～ (**out**) 挤(出去)，冲(出去)。**gather** ～ 加大速度，快起来。**get in the** ～ 妨碍。**get out of the** ～ 1. *vi*. 避开，让开。2. *vt*. 除去；处分。**get under** ～ 开始进行，开始；开船。**give** ～ 1. 崩溃，倒塌；失败，屈服，让步（*to*）；支持不住，忍不住…了出来[起来]。2. 划起来，用力划。3. (价格)跌落。**go a good** [**long**] ～ **with** 非常有用，非常有效。**go a little** ～ 有一点点用处[效果]。**go little** ～ 不怎么有用[有效]，不够。**go one's** ～**s** 动身，出发，走掉。**go out of one's** ～ 1. 绕弯儿走；不怕麻烦。2. 特地；故意（*go out of the* [*one's*] ～ *to be rude* 故意蛮干)。**go some** ～ = *go a little* ～. **go the** ～ **of all the earth** [**of all flesh**, **of nature**] 死。**have a** ～ **with** 善于处理。**have** (**everything**) **one's own** ～ 为所欲为，一意孤行。**have** ～ **on** (船)正在开行。**hold one** ～ = *keep one's* ～. **in a bad** ～ 情形不见好；(病人)情形不好。**in a big** [**great**] ～ 大规模地；豪华地（*go in for industry in a big* ～ 大办工业)。**in a hundred and one** ～**s** 千方百计地。**in a small** ～ 小，小规模地，简朴地（*an author in a small* ～ 一个小小的作家。*live in a small* ～ 生活简朴)。**in a** [**one**] ～ 在某一点上，在某种程度上。**in an all-round** ～ 全面。**in no** ～ 决不，无论如何不。**in one's** (**own**) ～ 本来，原来；有特色的（*He is a poet in his own* ～. 他是一个有特色的诗人)。(**in**) **one's own** ～ 照…自己的办法[想法]（*Do it your own* ～. 照你自己的办法去做吧)。(**in**) **one** ～ **or another** [**the other**] (好歹)设法。**in the family** ～ 怀孕。**in the** ～ 1. 在路上，在途中。2. 妨碍。**in the** ～ **of** 1. 妨碍。2. 在…方面，关于。3. 使能于，使能遇见…，在便于做[得到]…的地位。**keep one's** ～ 继续前进。**keep out of the** ～ 避开。**lose the** [**one's**] ～ 迷路。**lose** ～ 慢起来。**make much** [**little**] ～ 走得快[慢]；进步[不进步]。**make one's** (**own**) ～ 1. 走向，前往。2. 繁荣，兴隆，发迹（*make one's* ～ *home* 回家去。*make one's* ～ *in the world* 发迹，成功)。**make the best of one's** ～ 尽量快去。**make** ～ 开路，让路（*for*）；前进，进步（*cannot make any* ～ 一点也不能前进)。**mend one's** ～ 改变习惯。**no** ～〔美方〕无论如何不，决不，一点也不（*no* ～ *inferior* 一点也不次)。**nothing out of the** ～ 没有什么特别的地方，平凡。**on one's** ～ **to** 到…去的途中。**on the** ～ 在路上；在旅行中。**once in a** ～ 时或，偶然。**one** ～ **or another** [**the other**] 以某种方式；想方设法。**out of the** ～ 1. 向旁边，使不妨碍；让开，离开，避开。2. 迷失；误；异常。3. 特意，不顾困难地。**pay one's** ～ 不借债过日子（*pay one's* ～ *through college* 刻苦自持地上完大学)。**put sb. in the** ～ **of doing** 给(某人)…的机会。**see one's** ～ (**clear**) **to** (*do* or *doing*) (清楚)知道怎么做；能做到。**stand in the** ～ **of** 妨碍，阻住…的路。**take one's own** ～ = *go one's own* ～. **take one's** ～ **to** [**towards**] 上…去，向…出发。**that** ～〔美俚〕在恋爱中。**that** ～ **about** 爱着。**the easy** [**hard**] ～ 用巧[笨]法。**that good old** ～**s** 自古以来的习惯。**the other** [**wrong**] ～ **about** [**round**, **around**] 相反(地)，以相反方式[方向]。**the parting of the** ～**s** 岔路；必须抉择其一的重要关头。**the right of** ～ 通行权；得到通行权的地带；〔美〕铁路路线。**the right** ～ 1. 正道。2. 最正确的方法。3. 方向正确地[作修饰语]。**the specific** ～**s and means of ...** 的具体方式和方法。**the** ～ 1. (做…)的方式[办法]。2.〔美口〕= as. **the** ～ **I see it ...** 照我看来。**the** ～ **of the world** (世上的)一般习惯，常情。**this** ～ **and that** 忽左忽右；下不了决心。**to sb.'s** ～ **of thinking** 据某人的想法。**to put it** (**in**) **another** ～ 换言之。**under** ～ 进行着；【海】航行中。**W- enough!**【海】停划！～ **in** [**out**] 入[出]口。～**s and means** 方式方法；财源（*the Committee on* [〔英〕*of*] *Ways and Means* 岁入调查委员会)。～ **car** 1. (铁路)守车。2. 沿途零担货车。～**port** 中转航空港。～ **station**〔美〕(快车不停的)小站。～ **train**【美、铁路】逢站必停的普通客车。

way[2], **'way**[wei; we] *ad*. 1. = away. 2.〔美口〕…得多，远为。★与 above, ahead, behind, below, down, off, out, over, up 等副词、介词连用，以加强语气。～ *back* 老早以前。～ *down upon the river Thames* 在老远老远的泰晤士河边。～ *up* 还在上面；好得多。～ *out of balance* 逆差很大很大。

way·bill[ˈweibil; ˋwe͵bɪl] *n*. 乘客单；(铁路等的)运货单。

way·board[ˈweibɔːd; ˋwe͵bɔrd] *n*. (两厚层之间的)薄隔板。

way·far·er[ˈweifεərə; ˋwe͵fεrɚ] *n*. 赶路的人，旅客，徒步旅行者。

way·far·ing[ˈweifεəriŋ; ˋwe͵fεrɪŋ] I *a*. (徒步)旅行的，旅行中的。II *n*. (徒步)旅行。～**tree** *n*.【植】棉毛荚蒾。

W